Headquarters USA

A Directory of Contact Information for Headquarters and Other Central Offices of Major Businesses & Organizations in the United States and in Canada

2021

43rd EDITION

Volume 1:
Alphabetical by Organization Name

Mailing Addresses, Telephone Numbers, Toll-Free Phone Numbers, Fax Numbers, and World Wide Web Addresses for:

- Associations, Foundations, and Similar Organizations
- Businesses, Industries, and Professions of All Types
- Colleges, Universities, Vocational & Technical Schools, and Other Educational Institutions
- Electronic Resources, including Internet Companies, Organizations, and Websites
- Embassies, Consulates, and UN Missions & Agencies
- Government Agencies & Offices at All Levels — City, County, State, and Federal
- Libraries, Museums & Galleries, Zoos & Botanical Gardens, Performing Arts Organizations & Facilities, and Other Cultural Institutions
- Media Newspapers, Magazines, Newsletters; and Radio & Television Companies, Networks, Stations and Syndicators
- Research Centers & Organizations, including Scientific, Public Policy, and Market Research
- Professional Sports Teams, Other Sports Organizations, and Sports Facilities

and also including an Area/Zip Code Guide Covering more than 12,000 U.S. Cities and Towns, as well as Area Code Tables in State & Numerical Order; and a detailed Index to Classified Headings under which listings are organized in the Directory's Classified Section.

OMNIGRAPHICS

Omnigraphics

Pearline Jaikumar, *Editor*

* * *

ISBN 978-0-7808-1830-9

ISSN 1531-2909

Printed in the United States of America

Omnigraphics
615 Griswold St., Ste. 520, Detroit, MI 48226
Phone Orders: 800-234-1340 • Fax Orders: 800-875-1340
Mail Orders: P.O. Box 8002 • Aston, PA 19014-8002
www.omnigraphics.com

Table of Contents

Volume 1:
Alphabetical by Organization Name

Volume 2:
Classified by Subject

How To Use This Directory

Headquarters USA lists headquarters and other central offices for the largest and most important businesses, organizations, agencies, and institutions in the United States. Listings also are included for top Canadian businesses and organizations.

The 2021 edition of *Headquarters USA* contains 130,096 listings, presented by name and by subject. Individual listings in both the Alphabetical and Classified sections present each company or organization name along with its full address and telephone number. Most listings also include fax numbers (57,898) and websites (128,426), and 44,789 listings include toll-free telephone numbers. Trading symbols and corresponding stock exchanges are provided for 2,111 publicly traded companies.

Research and Verification a Year-Round Effort

Headquarters USA is compiled by a team of experienced editorial personnel who research the information to be published in the directory on a year-round basis. Data are verified as accurate by direct contact with the companies and organizations listed, and this effort is also carried out continuously.

Preparation of *Headquarters USA* includes not only the addition of completely new types of information but also the re-evaluation of listing criteria for some of the existing categories of information. This may result in changes in the number of listings published for certain categories—for instance, some very large subject categories may be reduced in size to allow for the introduction of completely new categories of information; a relatively small subject category may be expanded to provide more significant companies in that area; or, in some cases, new, more specific categories may be developed from larger, existing categories that are more general in nature.

What's Included in *Headquarters USA?*

Headquarters USA provides detailed, accurate contact information for a wide range of US and Canadian **businesses, professions, and organizations,** including:

- agricultural establishments
- associations & organizations
- Better Business Bureaus
- building & construction industries
- colleges & universities
- consulates & embassies
- chambers of commerce
- convention centers
- cultural organizations
- financial institutions
- foundations
- government offices
- internet resources
- libraries
- manufacturing companies
- media & communications
- military bases
- mining companies
- political organizations
- research centers
- retail sales
- service industries
- sports teams
- transportation and utilities
- United Nations missions
- wholesalers & distributors
- world trade centers

Criteria for Listing

For the most part, criteria employed in selecting listings for *Headquarters USA* parallel the ranking systems used by the industries represented. A variety of resources are used in gathering rankings data, including "top lists" compiled by associations as well as those found in business magazines and other published sources.

Most ranking schemes are based on annual sales, and this is reflected in the selection of data for *Headquarters USA*. However, other criteria are employed as well. For example, hospitals are selected on the basis of the number of beds available, law firms are selected according to the number of attorneys in the firm, newspapers are chosen by circulation, and so on.

It should be noted that some companies are listed even if they don't meet the listing criterion established for that particular type of business. Examples of this include some companies that are involved in new technologies, companies that are publicly traded on major U.S. stock exchanges, and subsidiaries or divisions of certain large companies, provided that the parent company meets the criterion.

Special Features

- a U.S. map denoting **time zones**;
- **area code** tables that provide up-to-date lists of all valid U.S. telephone area codes in state and area code order;
- tables of **abbreviations** — one that lists the standard abbreviations used throughout *Headquarters USA* and another providing two-letter state and Canadian province abbreviations;

- a **Classified Headings Table** that lists all of the subject categories under which listings appear in the Classified Section;
- an **Area Code and Zip Code Guide** listing area codes and zip codes for the more than 12,000 U.S. cities in which the companies and organizations listed in *Headquarters USA* are located. Information is presented in alphabetical order by city name, with the area code(s) and zip code(s) provided for each city; and
- an **Index to Classified Headings** that identifies all of the subject headings under which listings are organized in the Classified Section of *Headquarters USA*. The index also includes "See" and "See also" references to help guide users to appropriate subject categories. The number given with each index citation refers to the page on which a particular subject category begins.

How Do I Find What I'm Looking For?

The overall arrangement of *Headquarters USA* is much like that found in a local telephone directory and is just as easy to use. Listings are organized in two main sections: an **Alphabetical Section** and a **Classified Section**. As the names suggest, the Alphabetical Section presents listings alphabetically, by company or organization name, and the Classified Section presents the same information in a classified subject arrangement according to business or organization type. For the most part, listings appear at least once in both sections of the directory.

Listings in the Classified Section are organized according to organization type or, for businesses, a company's primary business activity. At least one classified listing is provided for each company or organization included in *Headquarters USA*, but very large companies that conduct business in a variety of areas may be listed more than once so that the company is represented in all appropriate subject categories.

Some of the subject headings in the Classified Section also include information about listing criteria, other explanatory comments, or notes regarding a special arrangement of listings (i.e., while listings generally appear in alphabetical order within each classified subject category, some information is grouped by state or city name within a particular subject, with listings then alphabetized within this framework).

- **Alphabetizing *in Headquarters USA***

Alphabetizing throughout *Headquarters USA* is on a word-by-word, rather than letter-by-letter, basis. No distinction is made between upper and lower case letters, and articles, conjunctions, and most prepositions are ignored for sorting purposes. Names that begin with symbols or numerals rather than letters file first. Symbols that may accompany numerals (e.g., a pound sign [#] or dollar sign [$]) are ignored for alphabetical sorting.

The following example illustrates these alphabetizing rules:

1 on 1 Computing
$1 Sunglasses Ltd
3M Co
All Weather Vacuuming
C & S Inc
Calido Hotels
Cambridge Fire Insurance
Damon Corp
DAS Co
Data Generation Inc
La Quinta Motor Inns
Laacke Co

- **Classification Codes**

The subject headings under which listings appear in the Classified Section are numbered sequentially, and these numbered headings are duplicated in the Classified Headings Table that precedes the Classified Section. The numbers are also used as "classification codes" that appear in the "Class" column to the right of listings in the Alphabetical Section. Users of the Alphabetical Section can quickly determine a company's principal business activity by simply matching the "Class" number for a particular listing to the corresponding subject heading number. (This "linking" mechanism is illustrated in the sample pages and accompanying explanatory comments presented just inside the back cover of this directory.)

Some listings in the Classified Section are organized under a second level of subheadings within a broader category named in a heading. In situations where there are two levels of headings, two levels of classification codes are given as well. For instance, if a heading numbered as 200 is followed by a series of subheadings, the first subheading would be numbered 200-1, the second would be 200-2, and so on. Headings that have been created *only* to provide a reference to another heading category (i.e., "See" references) are not numbered.

Content of Individual Listings

Each listing in *Headquarters USA* consists of the formal name of the company, organization, institution, or government office; street or other mailing address; city, state, and zip code; and telephone number (with area code). Fax numbers also are provided for most listings, and, where available, toll-free numbers are given as well. Most listings also include websites. Trading symbols and corresponding stock exchanges are provided for Public companies.

- **Company and Organization Names**

  As a general rule, complete official names are given for companies and organizations listed in *Headquarters USA*. In the case of listings for companies that are clearly named after individuals, information usually is presented both by the person's first name *and* by the last name. For example, Matthew Bender & Co Inc would be listed that way and as Bender Matthew & Co Inc; LL Bean Inc would also be listed as Bean LL Inc; and so on. However, listings in the people categories (such as U.S. Senators, Representatives, Delegates) are always presented with the last name first—e.g., Leahy, Patrick, but not Patrick Leahy. Companies that are well known by an acronym or initialism—for example, IBM—usually are listed both by acronym and by full name (i.e., "IBM" and "International Business Machines Corp").

- **Addresses**

  Addresses provided in this directory usually are street addresses, unless mail cannot be accepted at a particular location, in which case a post office box or other mailing address is provided. All listings also include the city, state (or province, if Canadian), and zip code (five-digit for U.S. listings, six-digit for Canadian listings).

- **Telephone Numbers**

  Phone numbers listed in *Headquarters USA* are for the main switchboard of a company or organization. Area codes are included with all telephone numbers listed.

- **Fax Numbers**

  Most fax listings provided in *Headquarters USA* represent a company's direct facsimile number. In instances where this is not the case, an asterisk appears next to the fax number and a brief explanatory note is inserted below the name/address data (example: **Fax:* Cust Svc indicates that the fax number given is for the company's Customer Service department).

  Since fax area codes are almost always the same as the telephone area code, the area code given with the phone number is not repeated with the fax number. However, if the area code for the fax number is *different* from the telephone area code, an asterisk appears to the right of the fax number, indicating that the correct area code is provided below the company name and address.

- **Toll-Free Telephone Numbers**

  Toll-free numbers are listed below the company or organization's name and address. If the number given is intended for a specific use (e.g., for orders, technical support, customer service, sales, etc.), a notation is included to that effect.

- **Websites**

  Websites are provided for 128,426 listings in this edition. The "http://" that begins most website addresses is ***not*** included with that information here.

- **Stock Exchange Information**

  Trading symbols and corresponding stock exchanges are given as bulleted items under the individual listings for publicly traded companies in both the Alphabetical and Classified sections of the book.

Comments Welcome

The editors and staff of *Headquarters USA* are committed to maintaining the highest degree of accuracy possible, and our efforts to provide the most up to date information available are ongoing. Comments from readers concerning this publication, including suggestions for additions and improvements, are welcome. Please send to:

Editor — *Headquarters USA*
Omnigraphics
615 Griswold St., Ste. 520
Detroit, MI 48226
editorial@omnigraphics.com

TIME ZONES MAP

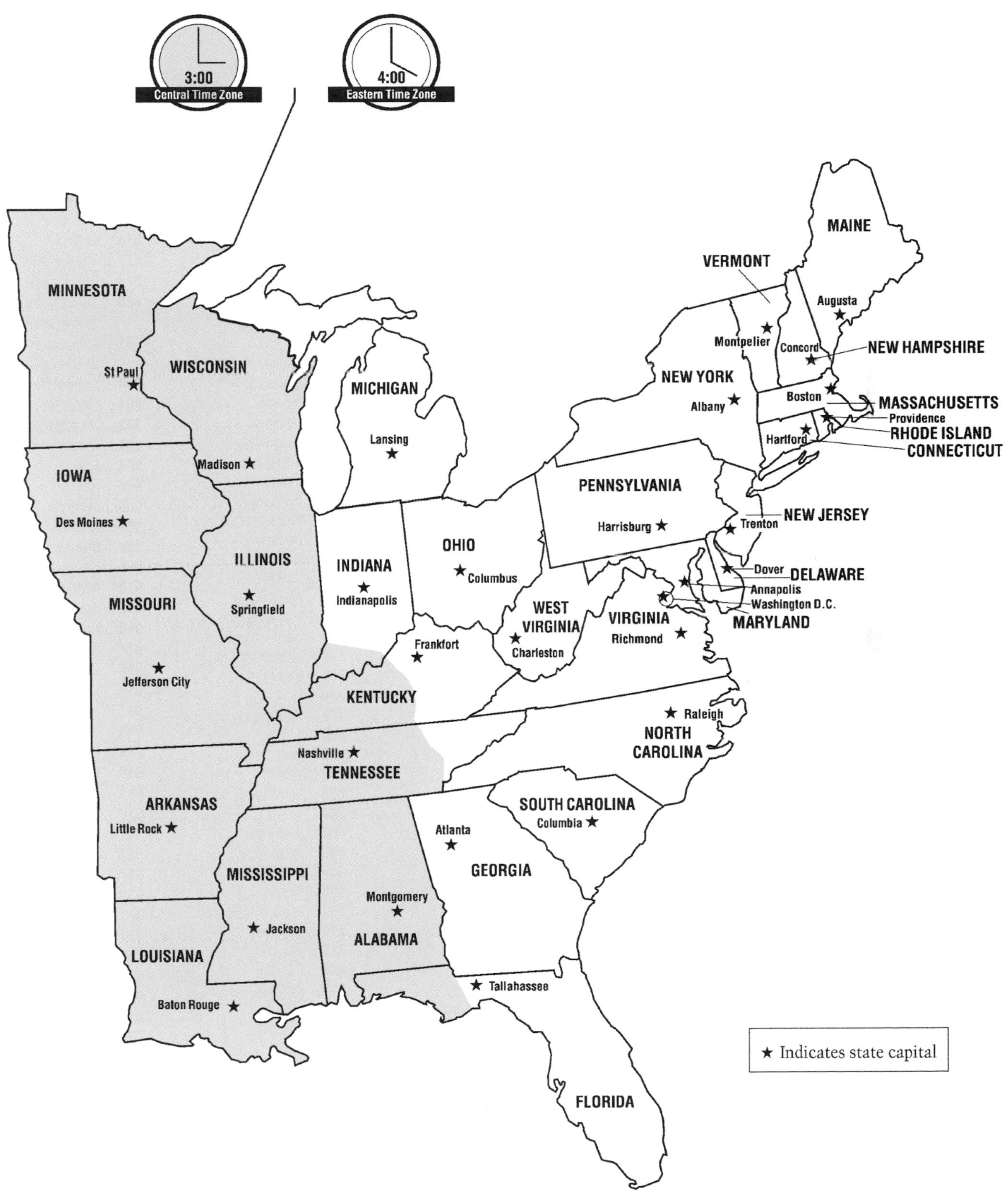
3:00
Central Time Zone
4:00
Eastern Time Zone
MINNESOTA
St Paul
WISCONSIN
Madison
IOWA
Des Moines
ILLINOIS
Springfield
MISSOURI
Jefferson City
MICHIGAN
Lansing
INDIANA
Indianapolis
OHIO
Columbus
KENTUCKY
Frankfort
WEST VIRGINIA
Charleston
VIRGINIA
Richmond
TENNESSEE
Nashville
ARKANSAS
Little Rock
MISSISSIPPI
Jackson
ALABAMA
Montgomery
LOUISIANA
Baton Rouge
GEORGIA
Atlanta
SOUTH CAROLINA
Columbia
NORTH CAROLINA
Raleigh
FLORIDA
Tallahassee
PENNSYLVANIA
Harrisburg
NEW YORK
Albany
VERMONT
Montpelier
MAINE
Augusta
NEW HAMPSHIRE
Concord
MASSACHUSETTS
Boston
RHODE ISLAND
Providence
CONNECTICUT
Hartford
NEW JERSEY
Trenton
DELAWARE
Dover
MARYLAND
Annapolis
Washington D.C.
★ Indicates state capital

Area Codes in Numerical Order

201 ... New Jersey
202 ... District of Columbia
203 ... Connecticut
204 ... Manitoba
205 ... Alabama
206 ... Washington
207 ... Maine
208 ... Idaho
209 ... California
210 ... Texas
212 ... New York
213 ... California
214 ... Texas
215 ... Pennsylvania
216 ... Ohio
217 ... Illinois
218 ... Minnesota
219 ... Indiana
224 ... Illinois
225 ... Louisiana
226 ... Ontario
228 ... Mississippi
229 ... Georgia
231 ... Michigan
234 ... Ohio
239 ... Florida
240 ... Maryland
242 ... Bahamas
246 ... Barbados
248 ... Michigan
250 ... British Columbia
251 ... Alabama
252 ... North Carolina
253 ... Washington
254 ... Texas
256 ... Alabama
260 ... Indiana
262 ... Wisconsin
264 ... Anguilla
267 ... Pennsylvania
268 ... Antigua and Barbuda
269 ... Michigan
270 ... Kentucky
276 ... Virginia
281 ... Texas
284 ... British Virgin Islands
289 ... Ontario
301 ... Maryland
302 ... Delaware
303 ... Colorado
304 ... West Virginia
305 ... Florida
306 ... Saskatchewan
307 ... Wyoming
308 ... Nebraska
309 ... Illinois
310 ... California
312 ... Illinois
313 ... Michigan
314 ... Missouri
315 ... New York
316 ... Kansas
317 ... Indiana
318 ... Louisiana
319 ... Iowa
320 ... Minnesota
321 ... Florida
323 ... California
325 ... Texas
330 ... Ohio
331 ... Illinois
334 ... Alabama
336 ... North Carolina
337 ... Louisiana
339 ... Massachusetts
340 ... US Virgin Islands
345 ... Cayman Islands
347 ... New York
351 ... Massachusetts
352 ... Florida
360 ... Washington
361 ... Texas
385 ... Utah
386 ... Florida
401 ... Rhode Island
402 ... Nebraska
403 ... Alberta
404 ... Georgia
405 ... Oklahoma
406 ... Montana
407 ... Florida
408 ... California
409 ... Texas
410 ... Maryland
412 ... Pennsylvania
413 ... Massachusetts
414 ... Wisconsin
415 ... California
416 ... Ontario
417 ... Missouri
418 ... Quebec
419 ... Ohio
423 ... Tennessee
424 ... California
425 ... Washington
430 ... Texas
432 ... Texas
434 ... Virginia
435 ... Utah
438 ... Quebec
440 ... Ohio
441 ... Bermuda
442 ... California
443 ... Maryland
450 ... Quebec
458 ... Oregon
469 ... Texas
470 ... Georgia
473 ... Grenada
475 ... Connecticut
478 ... Georgia
479 ... Arkansas
480 ... Arizona
484 ... Pennyslvania
501 ... Arkansas
502 ... Kentucky
503 ... Oregon
504 ... Louisiana
505 ... New Mexico
506 ... New Brunswick
507 ... Minnesota
508 ... Massachusetts
509 ... Washington
510 ... California
512 ... Texas
513 ... Ohio
514 ... Quebec
515 ... Iowa
516 ... New York
517 ... Michigan
518 ... New York
519 ... Ontario
520 ... Arizona
530 ... California
534 ... Wisconsin
540 ... Virginia
541 ... Oregon
551 ... New Jersey
559 ... California
561 ... Florida
562 ... California
563 ... Iowa
567 ... Ohio
570 ... Pennsylvania
571 ... Virginia
573 ... Missouri
574 ... Indiana
575 ... New Mexico
580 ... Oklahoma
581 ... Quebec
585 ... New York
586 ... Michigan
587 ... Alberta
601 ... Mississippi
602 ... Arizona
603 ... New Hampshire
604 ... British Columbia
605 ... South Dakota
606 ... Kentucky
607 ... New York
608 ... Wisconsin
609 ... New Jersey
610 ... Pennsylvania
612 ... Minnesota
613 ... Ontario
614 ... Ohio
615 ... Tennessee
616 ... Michigan
617 ... Massachusetts
618 ... Illinois
619 ... California
620 ... Kansas
623 ... Arizona
626 ... California
630 ... Illinois
631 ... New York
636 ... Missouri
641 ... Iowa
646 ... New York
647 ... Ontario
649 ... Turks and Caicos
650 ... California
651 ... Minnesota
657 ... California
660 ... Missouri
661 ... California
662 ... Mississippi
664 ... Montserrat
671 ... Guam
678 ... Georgia
681 ... West Virginia
682 ... Texas
684 ... American Samoa
689 ... Florida
701 ... North Dakota
702 ... Nevada
703 ... Virginia
704 ... North Carolina
705 ... Ontario
706 ... Georgia
707 ... California
708 ... Illinois
709 ... Newfoundland
712 ... Iowa
713 ... Texas
714 ... California
715 ... Wisconsin
716 ... New York
717 ... Pennsylvania
718 ... New York
719 ... Colorado
720 ... Colorado
724 ... Pennsylvania
727 ... Florida
731 ... Tennessee
732 ... New Jersey
734 ... Michigan
740 ... Ohio
747 ... California
754 ... Florida
757 ... Virginia
758 ... Saint Lucia
760 ... California
762 ... Georgia
763 ... Minnesota
765 ... Indiana
767 ... Dominica
769 ... Mississippi
770 ... Georgia
772 ... Florida
773 ... Illinois
774 ... Massachusetts
775 ... Nevada
778 ... British Columbia
779 ... Illinois
780 ... Alberta
781 ... Massachusetts
784 ... Saint Vincent & the Grenadines
785 ... Kansas
786 ... Florida
787 ... Puerto Rico
800 ... Toll-free; all states
801 ... Utah
802 ... Vermont
803 ... South Carolina
804 ... Virginia
805 ... California
806 ... Texas
807 ... Ontario
808 ... Hawaii
809 ... Dominican Republic
810 ... Michigan
812 ... Indiana
813 ... Florida
814 ... Pennsylvania
815 ... Illinois
816 ... Missouri
817 ... Texas
818 ... California
819 ... Quebec
828 ... North Carolina
829 ... Dominican Republic
830 ... Texas
831 ... California
832 ... Texas
843 ... South Carolina
845 ... New York
847 ... Illinois
848 ... New Jersey
850 ... Florida
855 ... Toll-free; all states
856 ... New Jersey
857 ... Massachusetts
858 ... California
859 ... Kentucky
860 ... Connecticut
862 ... New Jersey
863 ... Florida
864 ... South Carolina
865 ... Tennessee
866 ... Toll-free; all states
867 ... NorthWest Territories
868 ... Trinidad and Tobago
869 ... Saint Kitts and Nevis
870 ... Arkansas
876 ... Jamaica
877 ... Toll-free; all states
878 ... Pennsylvania
880 ... Toll Calls: From Canada & The Caribbean
881 ... Toll Calls: From Canada & The Caribbean
888 ... Toll-free; all states
901 ... Tennessee
902 ... Nova Scotia
903 ... Texas
904 ... Florida
905 ... Ontario
906 ... Michigan
907 ... Alaska
908 ... New Jersey
909 ... California
910 ... North Carolina
912 ... Georgia
913 ... Kansas
914 ... New York
915 ... Texas
916 ... California
917 ... New York
918 ... Oklahoma
919 ... North Carolina
920 ... Wisconsin
925 ... California
928 ... Arizona
931 ... Tennessee
936 ... Texas
937 ... Ohio
939 ... Puerto Rico
940 ... Texas
941 ... Florida
947 ... Michigan
949 ... California
951 ... California
952 ... Minnesota
954 ... Florida
956 ... Texas
959 ... Connecticut
970 ... Colorado
971 ... Oregon
972 ... Texas
973 ... New Jersey
978 ... Massachusetts
979 ... Texas
980 ... North Carolina
985 ... Louisiana
989 ... Michigan

Area Codes in State Order

Alabama
205 Birmingham & Tuscaloosa
251 Southwest
256 North & East Central
334 South
Alaska
907 All locations
American Samoa
684 All locations
Arizona
480 East of Phoenix including Tempe & Scottsdale
520 Southeast
602 Phoenix
623 West of Phoenix including Glendale
928 Most of State except South Central & Southeast areas
Arkansas
479 West Central & Northwest
501 Little Rock & surrounding areas
870 East & South
California
209 Central
213 Los Angeles
310 Long Beach/West
323 Los Angeles
408 West Central
415 San Francisco
424 Long Beach/West
442 Southeast except San Diego Area
510 Oakland
530 North
559 Central
562 Long Beach
619 San Diego & surrounding area (except North)
626 Pasadena/East
650 South of San Francisco
657 Northern Orange County
661 Bakersfield & Northern La County
707 Northwest
714 Northern Orange County
747 Burbank & Glendale Area
760 Southeast except San Diego Area
805 South
818 Burbank & Glendale Area
831 West Central
858 San Diego/North
909 San Bernardino & surrounding area
916 Sacramento & surrounding area
925 East of Oakland
949 Southern Orange County
951 Riverside & surrounding area (except North)
Canada
204 All locations in Manitoba
226 Southern Ontario
250 Outside Vancouver Area including Vancouver Island
289 North of Toronto
306 All locations in Saskatchewan
403 Southern Alberta
416 Toronto
418 Eastern Quebec
438 Montreal Metro Area
450 Outside Montreal Metro Area
506 All locations in New Brunswick
514 Montreal Metro Area
519 Southern Ontario
581 Eastern Quebec
587 All locations in Alberta
604 Vancouver Area
613 Northeast of Toronto
647 Toronto
705 Eastern Ontario
709 All locations in Newfoundland
778 Vancouver Area
780 Central & Northern Alberta
807 Western Ontario
819 Western Quebec
867 All locations in Yukon & Northwest Territories
902 All locations in Nova Scotia & Prince Edward Island
905 North of Toronto
Caribbean, Bahamas & Bermuda
242 Bahamas
246 Barbados
264 Anguilla
268 Antigua & Barbuda
284 British Virgin Islands
340 US Virgin Islands
345 Cayman Islands
441 Bermuda
473 Grenada
649 Turks & Caicos
664 Montserrat
758 Saint Lucia
767 Dominica
784 Saint Vincent & Grenadines
787 Puerto Rico
809 Dominican Republic
829 Dominican Republic
868 Trinidad & Tobago
869 Saint Kitts & Nevis
876 Jamaica
939 Puerto Rico
Colorado
303 Denver
719 South & East
720 Denver
970 West & North
Connecticut
203 Southwest
475 Southwest
860 Except Southwest
959 Except Southwest
Delaware
302 All locations
District of Columbia
202 All locations
Florida
239 Southwest (Lee, Collier & part of Monroe Counties)
305 Southeast
321 Central & East Central
352 Gainesville, Ocala & surrounding areas
386 Northeast except Jacksonville, St. Augustine & surrounding areas
407 Central
561 Palm Beach County
689 Central & East Central
727 Saint Petersburg/Clearwater
754 Fort Lauderdale & surrounding area
772 Martin, St. Lucie, Indian River & part of Brevard Counties
786 Southeast
813 Tampa
850 Northwest
863 South Central
904 Jacksonville, St. Augustine & surrounding areas
941 Southwest (Sarasota, Char Lotte & Manatee Counties)
954 Fort Lauderdale & surrounding area
Georgia
229 Southwest
404 Atlanta
470 Atlanta & surrounding area
478 Central
678 Atlanta Area
706 North except Atlanta Area
762 North except Atlanta Area
770 Atlanta suburbs
912 Southeast
Guam
671 All locations
Hawaii
808 All locations
Idaho
208 All locations
Illinois
217 Central
224 Suburban Chicago
309 West
312 Chicago
331 Northeast
618 South
630 Northeast
708 Northeast
773 Chicago (outside central commercial area)
779 North
815 North
847 Suburban Chicago
Indiana
219 North West
260 Northeast
317 Indianapolis Metro Area
574 North Central
765 Central except Indianapolis Metro Area
812 South
Iowa
319 East Central
515 Central including Des Moines & Ames
563 East
641 South central & East Central
712 West
Kansas
316 Wichita & surrounding area
620 South except Wichita & surrounding area
785 North except Kansas City
913 Kansas City
Kentucky
270 West & Central
502 North including Louisville
606 East
859 North Central
Louisiana
225 East Central
318 North & West
337 West Central & Southwest
504 New Orleans Area
985 Southeast except New Orleans Area
Maine
207 All locations
Maryland
240 West
301 West
410 East
443 East
Massachusetts
339 Outside Metro Boston
351 North
413 West
508 Southeast
617 Boston Metro Area
774 Southeast
781 Outside Metro Boston
857 Boston Metro Area
978 North
Michigan
231 Northwest
248 East (Oakland County)
269 Southwest
313 Detroit & inner suburbs
517 South Central
586 East (Macomb County)
616 West/Southwest
734 West of Detroit
810 East (except Oakland & Macomb Counties)
906 North
947 East (Oakland County)
989 Central
Minnesota
218 North
320 Central except Minneapolis/Saint Paul Metro Area
507 South
612 Minneapolis
651 Saint Paul & East Central
763 Suburbs North & Northwest of Minneapolis
952 Suburbs South & Southwest of Minneapolis
Mississippi
228 Gulfport/Biloxi & surrounding area
601 South except Gulfport/Biloxi & surrounding area
662 North
769 South except Gulfport/Biloxi & surrounding area
Missouri
314 Saint Louis
417 Southwest
573 East except Saint Louis Metro Area
636 East (outside Saint Louis)
660 North except Kansas City & Saint Joseph
816 Kansas City & Saint Joseph
Montana
406 All locations
Nebraska
308 West
402 East
Nevada
702 Las Vegas Area
775 All locations except Las Vegas
New Hampshire
603 All locations
New Jersey
201 Northeast
551 Northeast
609 Southeast
732 East Central
848 East Central
856 Southwest
862 Northwest
908 West Central
973 Northwest

Area Codes in State Order (continued)

New Mexico
505 Northwest
575 Entire State except Northwest

New York
212 New York City
315 North Central
347 New York City
516 Nassau County
518 Northeast
585 West-Central
607 South Central
631 Suffolk County
646 New York City
716 West
718 New York City
845 North & West of Westchester County
914 Westchester County
917 New York City

North Carolina
252 East
336 Greensboro & Winston-Salem areas
704 Southwest
828 West
910 South Central
919 North Central
980 Southwest

North Dakota
701 All locations

Ohio
216 Cleveland Metro Area
234 Northeast except Cleveland
330 Northeast except Cleveland
419 Northwest
440 North Central except Cleveland Metro Area
513 Southwest
567 Northwest
614 Columbus Area
740 East & Central except Columbus Area
937 Southwest except Cincinnati Area

Oklahoma
405 Central
580 South & West
918 Northeast

Oregon
458 Outside Portland Area
503 Portland Area
541 Outside Portland Area
971 Portland Area

Pennsylvania
215 Philadelphia
267 Philadelphia
412 Pittsburgh Metro Area
484 Southeast
570 Northeast
610 Southeast
717 Southeast
724 Outside Pittsburgh Metro Area
814 West
878 Pittsburgh & surrounding area

Rhode Island
401 All locations

South Carolina
803 Central
843 East
864 Northwest

South Dakota
605 All locations

Tennessee
423 Northeast & Southeast
615 North Central
731 West except Shelby, Fayette & Tipton Counties
865 Knoxville & surrounding area
901 Southwest (Shelby, Fayette & Tipton Counties)
931 Nashville & North Central

Texas
210 San Antonio Metro Area
214 Dallas
254 North Central
281 Houston
325 Central
361 Corpus Christi & surrounding Area
409 East of Houston Area
430 Northeast
432 West Central
469 Dallas
512 Austin & surrounding area
682 Fort Worth Metro Area & Arlington
713 Houston
806 Northwest
817 Fort Worth Metro Area & Arlington
830 South Central
832 Houston
903 Northeast
915 West (including El Paso)
936 North of Houston Area
940 North
956 South
972 Dallas
979 West of Houston Area

Toll Calls: From Canada & The Caribbean
880
881

Toll-Free; All States
800
833
844
855
866
877
888

Utah
385 Salt Lake City, Ogden & Provo Metro areas
435 All locations except Salt Lake City/Ogden/Provo Metro areas
801 Salt Lake City, Ogden & Provo Metro areas

Vermont
802 All locations

Virginia
276 Southwest
434 South & Central
540 North
571 Northeast
703 Northeast
757 Norfolk & surrounding area
804 East

Washington
206 Seattle Area
253 Tacoma Area
360 West except Seattle, Tacoma & Everett areas
425 East of Seattle between Everett & Kent
509 East

West Virginia
304 All locations
681 All locations

Wisconsin
262 Southeast except Milwaukee
414 Milwaukee
534 North
608 Southwest
715 North
920 Southeast except Milwaukee & surrounding area (South)

Wyoming
307 All locations

Alphabetical Section

Listings in this section are presented in alphabetical order by company or organization name. Alphabetizing is on a word-by-word rather than letter-by-letter basis.

For a detailed explanation of the scope and arrangement of listings, please refer to "How to Use This Directory" at the beginning of this book.Page elements and listing formats are illustrated on the sample pages with accompanying explanatory notes found just inside the back cover.

SYMBOLS & NUMERALS

				Phone	Fax	Class
1 & 1 Internet Inc 701 Lee Rd Ste 300 *Fax Area Code: 610 ■ TF: 877-461-2631 ■ Web: www.ionos.com	Chesterbrook	PA	19087	877-461-2631	560-1501*	690
1 Beyond Inc 529 Main St Ste 109 Web: 1beyond.com	Boston	MA	02129	617-591-2200		180
1 Diamond Source (1DS) 36 W 47th St TF: 877-968-7342 ■ Web: www.1diamondsource.com	New York	NY	10036	877-968-7342		411
1 Digital 2430 106th St Web: www.1digital.com	Urbandale	IA	50322	515-771-8282		514
1 EDI Source Inc 31875 Solon Rd TF: 877-334-9650 ■ Web: www.1edisource.com	Solon	OH	44139	877-334-9650		179
1 Stop Design Shop Inc 30 BB Sixth Rd Web: www.1stopdesign.com	Woburn	MA	01801	781-938-3866	932-5996	344
1 to 1 Printers LLC 15031 Woodham Dr Ste 370 Web: www.1to1printers.com	Houston	TX	77073	281-821-4400		627
10 Degrees South 4183 Roswell Rd NE Web: 10degreessouth.com	Atlanta	GA	30342	404-705-8870		671
10 X Rock 2118 AZ-95 Ste A Web: 10xrock.com	Bullhead City	AZ	86442	928-855-9336		647
100 Fountain Spa at the Pillar & Post Inn 48 John St PO Box 48 TF: 888-669-5566 ■ Web: www.vintage-hotels.com	Niagara-on-the-Lake	ON	L0S1J0	905-468-2123	468-3551	707
100.3 The Q! (CKKQ-FM) 2750 Quadra St Top Fl TF: 800-717-1003 ■ Web: www.theq.fm	Victoria	BC	V8T4E8	250-475-0100	475-3299	643
100.3 WHEB 815 Lafayette Rd Web: wheb.iheart.com	Portsmouth	NH	03801	603-436-7300		647
100.7 BIG FM 6160 Cornerstone Ct E Ste 150 TF: 888-570-1007 ■ Web: bigfmsd.com	San Diego	CA	92121	888-570-1007		645-141
100.7 Star 2158 Ave C Ste 100 Web: starpittsburgh.radio.com	Bethlehem	PA	18017	610-720-1007		645
100.7 The Bay 11350 McCormick Rd Executive Plz III Ste 701 Web: www.thebayonline.com	Hunt Valley	MD	21031	410-771-8484	771-1616	645
1000 Cranes LLC 1425 K St NW Ste 350 TF: 877-378-4430 ■ Web: 1000cranes.com	Washington	DC	20005	202-587-2737	434-5610	194
101 Livestock Market Inc 4400 Hwy 101 Web: www.101livestock.com	Aromas	CA	95004	831-726-3303		446
101 Pipe & Casing Inc 30300 Agoura Rd Ste 240 *Fax Area Code: 818 ■ TF: 800-332-9101 ■ Web: www.101pipe.com	Agoura Hills	CA	91301	800-332-9101	707-9126*	492
101 Things To Do 2383 Myrtle Ave TF: 800-640-8439 ■ Web: www.101things.com	Eureka	CA	95501	707-443-1234		637-9
101.1 Big FM 1125 Bayfield St N PO Box 101 Web: www.b101fm.com	Barrie	ON	L4M4Y6	705-726-1011		647
101.1 FM The Answer 415 N McKinley St Ste 700 Web: 1011fmtheanswer.com	Little Rock	AR	72205	501-492-0253		647
101.5 Lite FM 20450 NW 2nd Ave *Fax Area Code: 305 ■ TF: 877-790-1015 ■ Web: litemiami.radio.com	Miami	FL	33169	877-790-1015	521-1414*	645-96
101.5 The Eagle 50 W Broadway Ste 200 TF: 866-551-1015 ■ Web: 1055theeagle.com	Salt Lake City	UT	84101	801-524-2600		645-139
101.7 The Beach 60 Garden Ct Ste 300 Web: www.1017thebeach.com	Monterey	CA	93940	831-658-5200		645-101
101.9 Jack FM - KRWK 1020 25th St S Web: www.jackfmfargo.com	Fargo	ND	58103	701-237-5346	235-4042	645-56
1010data Inc 750 Third Ave 4th Fl Web: www.1010data.com	New York	NY	10017	212-405-1010		180
1013 Integrated 1013 Kawaiahao St Web: www.1013integrated.com	Honolulu	HI	96814	808-593-8848		514
102.1 KLVJ 5700 W Oaks Blvd Ste 200 Web: ww2.klove.com	Rocklin	CA	95765	800-434-8400		645-141
102.5 The Game 1824 Murfreesboro Pk Web: www.thegamenashville.com	Nashville	TN	37217	615-737-1025	361-9873	645-106
102.7 WXBM 6565 N W St Web: www.nashpensacola.com	Pensacola	FL	32505	850-310-9102	478-3971	645
102.9 The Wolf 625 2nd Ave S Web: 1029thewolf.radio.com	Minneapolis	MN	55402	612-370-0611		645-99
103.1 Max FM 234 Airport Plz Ste 5 Web: www.1031maxfm.com	Farmingdale	NY	11735	631-955-1031	770-0101	645
103.3 The Eagle 7136 S Yale Ave Ste 500 Web: www.1033theeagle.com	Tulsa	OK	74136	918-493-3434	493-2376	645-166
103.5 WGRR 4805 Montgomery Rd Ste 300 Web: www.wgrr.com	Cincinnati	OH	45212	513-241-9898	241-6689	645-35
103.5 WIMZ 1100 Sharps Ridge Memorial Pk Dr Web: www.wimz.com	Knoxville	TN	37917	865-656-7625		645-82
103.7 KSON 9665 Granite Ridge Dr Ste 600 TF: 833-287-1037 ■ Web: www.kson.com	San Diego	CA	92123	619-291-9797		645-141
103.7 The Beat 83 E Shaw Ave Ste 150 TF: 844-289-7234 ■ Web: thebeat1037.iheart.com	Fresno	CA	93710	559-230-4300		645-61
103.9 The Bear WRBR 237 W Edison Rd TF: 888-835-5322 ■ Web: www.1039thebear.com	Mishawaka	IN	46545	574-258-5483		645
104.1 KRBE 9801 Westheimer Rd Ste 700 TF: 888-955-2993 ■ Web: www.krbe.com	Houston	TX	77042	713-954-2344		645-72
104.5 SNX 77 Monroe Ctr 10th Fl Web: 1045snx.iheart.com	Grand Rapids	MI	49503	616-459-1919		645-63
104.7 FM Praize Power 1350 WLOU 2001 W Broadway Web: www.wlouonline.com	Louisville	KY	40203	502-776-1240		645-89
104.7 KISS FM 150 Nichols Ave Web: kisscasper.com	Casper	WY	82601	307-266-5252		645-27
104.7 WTUE 101 Pine St Web: wtue.iheart.com	Dayton	OH	45402	937-224-1137		645-44
1040+ Quality Tax & Financial Services 5625 Cypress Creek Pkwy Ste 321 Web: www.tenfortyplus.com	Houston	TX	77069	281-397-7777		2
105.1 The Bounce 1 Radio Plaza St Web: 1051thebounce.com	Ferndale	MI	48220	248-414-5600	542-8800	645
105.3 The Buzz 9111 E Douglas Ste 130 Web: 1053thebuzz.radio.com	Wichita	KS	67207	316-869-1053		645-173
105.5 The Beat 13320 Metro Pkwy Ste 1 TF: 866-843-2328 ■ Web: 1055thebeat.iheart.com	Fort Myers	FL	33966	239-225-4300		645
105.7 KOKZ 514 Jefferson St Web: www.1057kokz.com	Waterloo	IA	50701	319-234-2200		645
105.7 Now FM (KZBD) 1601 E 57th Ave	Spokane	WA	99223	509-448-1000		645-151
105.9 The Monkey 9471 Three Rivers Rd Ste A Web: 1059themonkey.com	Gulfport	MS	39503	228-388-1071		645-66
106.1 KISS FM 14001 N Dallas Pkwy Ste 300 Web: 1061kissfm.iheart.com	Dallas	TX	75240	214-866-8000	866-8008	645-43
106.1 Kiss FM Seattle 645 Elliott Ave W Ste 400 TF: 888-343-1061 ■ Web: kissfmseattle.iheart.com	Seattle	WA	98119	866-311-9806		645-147
106.5 The Beat 3245 Basie Rd Web: www.1065thebeat.com	Richmond	VA	23228	804-474-0000		645-132
106.5 The End 5345 Madison Ave Web: endonline.radio.com	Sacramento	CA	95841	916-334-7777	334-1092	645-137
107.3 The Fox Rocks 100 W Central Texas Expwy Ste 300 Web: 1073rocks.iheart.com	Killeen	TX	76348	254-699-5000		647
107.5 Kiss FM 2141 Grand Ave Web: 1075kissfm.iheart.com	Des Moines	IA	50312	515-245-8900		645-47
107.5 KOLT County 2409 N Fourth St Ste 101 Web: www.koltcountry.com	Flagstaff	AZ	86004	928-779-1177	774-5179	645-57
107.5 WGCI FM 233 N Michigan Ave Ste 2800 Web: wgci.iheart.com	Chicago	IL	60601	312-591-1075		645-34
107.9 The Link 1 Julian Price Pl Web: www.1079thelink.com	Charlotte	NC	28208	704-570-1079		645-32
10C Technologies Inc 130 E John Carpenter Fwy Web: www.10ctech.com	Irving	TX	75062	972-385-2486		253
10x Business Consultants Inc 8181 E Tufts Ave Ste 500 Web: www.dbs-cpas.com	Denver	CO	80237	303-689-0844	689-0074	2
11 X 17 Inc 2034 N Jackson St Web: www.11x17.com	Jacksonville	TX	75766	903-541-0100		627
1105 Media Inc 9201 Oakdale Ave Ste 101 Web: www.1105media.com	Chatsworth	CA	91311	818-814-5200	734-1522	637-9
111 Chop House 111 Shrewsbury St Web: www.111chophouse.com	Worcester	MA	01604	508-799-4111		671
11400 Inc 2207 Old Philadelphia Pke Web: www.11400inc.com	Lancaster	PA	17602	717-392-7429	509-6111	189-11
1185 Design Inc 941Emerson St Web: www.1185design.com	Palo Alto	CA	94301	650-325-4804		344
1199 Seiu Federal Credit Union 310 W 43rd St 2nd Fl Web: www.1199federalcu.org	New York	NY	10036	212-957-1055	767-1732	219
12 Tribes Colville Casinos 28968 Hwy 97 TF: 844-526-8600 ■ Web: colvillecasinos.com	Omak	WA	98841	509-422-4646		452
12 WBOY 904 W Pike St Web: www.wboy.com	Clarksburg	WV	26301	304-623-3311	624-6152	116
1-2-1 Marketing Services Group Inc 20195 S Diamond Lake Rd Ste 700 Web: www.121msg.com	Rogers	MN	55374	763-428-8123		195

	Phone	Fax	Class
1-2-3 Payroll & HR Services Inc PO Box 96 .... Holtsville NY 11742 *Web:* www.1-2-3payroll.com	631-654-1811		734
123Greetingscom Inc 1674 Broadway Ste 403 .... New York NY 10019 *Web:* www.123greetings.com	212-246-0044	202-4738	130
12th Armored Div Memorial Museum 1289 N Second St .... Abilene TX 79601 *Web:* www.12tharmoredmuseum.com	325-677-6515		520
12Volt-Travel 1863 Ross Ln .... Linesville PA 16424 **Fax Area Code:* 724 ■ *TF:* 888-412-8058 ■ *Web:* www.12volt-travel.com	888-412-8058	927-2552*	54
13 Coins 125 Boren Ave N .... Seattle WA 98109 *Web:* www.13coins.com	206-682-2513		671
1310 News 2001 Thurston Dr .... Ottawa ON K1G6C9 *Web:* www.1310news.com	613-736-2001		645-115
1360 KHNC PO Box 104 .... Johnstown CO 80534 *TF:* 800-205-6245 ■ *Web:* 1360khnc.com	970-587-5003		647
1394 Trade Assn 23117 39th Ave SE .... Bothell WA 98021 *Web:* 1394ta.org	425-870-6574	320-3897	48-9
13D Research (USVI) LLC 6115 Estate Smith Bay Ste 333 PO Box 2 .... Saint Thomas VI 00802 *Web:* www.13d.com	340-775-3330		401
14 Carrot Whole Foods Inc 5300 Sunset Blvd .... Lexington SC 29072 *Web:* 14carrot.net	803-359-2920		345
1440 KEYS 2117 Leopard St .... Corpus Christi TX 78408 *Web:* keys1440.com	361-883-3516	882-9767	645-41
1450 WDAD 840 Philadelphia St .... Indiana PA 15701 *Web:* www.wdadradio.com	724-465-4700	471-1040	647
1500 KSTP-AM LLC 3415 University Ave .... Minneapolis MN 55414 *TF:* 877-615-1500 ■ *Web:* www.skornorth.com	651-646-8255		645-99
15Five 12 Gallagher Ln .... San Francisco CA 94103 *Web:* www.15five.com	415-967-3483		178-8
160 Over 90 510 Wallnut St 19th Fl .... Philadelphia PA 19106 *Web:* 160over90.com	215-732-3200		4
17 Hundred 90 Restaurant 307 E President St .... Savannah GA 31401 *Web:* 1790restaurant.com	912-236-7122		671
1703 Restaurant 1703 Robin Hood Rd .... Winston-Salem NC 27104 *TF:* 800-388-8255 ■ *Web:* localedge.com	336-725-5767		671
1789 Restaurant 1226 36th St NW .... Washington DC 20007 *Web:* www.1789restaurant.com	202-965-1789	337-1541	671
17th Street Photo Supply Inc 181 E Merrick Rd .... Valley Stream NY 11580 *TF:* 800-664-1971 ■ *Web:* www.17photo.com	516-500-3605		628
180 Medical Inc 5324 W Reno Ste A .... Oklahoma City OK 73127 *TF:* 877-688-2729 ■ *Web:* www.180medical.com	405-702-7700		475
1-800 Postcards Inc 121 Varick St .... New York NY 10013 *TF:* 800-767-8227 ■ *Web:* www.1800postcards.com	800-767-8227		627
1-800-Flowerscom Inc 1 Old Country Rd Ste 110 .... Carle Place NY 11514 *NASDAQ: FLWS* ■ *TF:* 800-356-9377 ■ *Web:* www.1800flowerscarleplace.com	888-609-0796		292
1-800-Got-Junk 887 Great Northern Way .... Vancouver BC V5T4T5 *TF:* 800-468-5865 ■ *Web:* www.1800gotjunk.com	800-468-5865		310
1800PetSupplies.com 395 Oakhill Rd Ste 210 .... Mountain Top PA 18707 *TF:* 800-738-7877 ■ *Web:* www.petsupplies.com	800-738-7877		791
1-800-Radiator 4401 Park Rd .... Benicia CA 94510 *TF:* 866-780-9392 ■ *Web:* 1800radiator.com	707-747-7400	747-7401	61
1-800-Water Damage 12600 Interurban Ave S Ste 130 .... Seattle WA 98168 *TF:* 800-928-3732 ■ *Web:* www.1800waterdamage.com	206-381-3041		310
1859 Historic Hotels Ltd PO Box 59 .... Galveston TX 77553 *Web:* www.1859historichotels.com	409-763-8536		379
1859 Jail Marshal's Home & Museum 217 N Main St .... Independence MO 64050 *Web:* www.jchs.org	816-252-1892		50-3
1880 Bank 304 High St .... Cambridge MD 21613 *TF:* 844-301-1880 ■ *Web:* 1880bank.com	410-228-5600		70
1881 Custer County Courthouse Museum 411 Mt Rushmore Rd PO Box 826 .... Custer SD 57730 *Web:* www.1881courthousemuseum.com	605-673-2443		520
1886 Crescent Hotel & Spa 75 Prospect Ave .... Eureka Springs AR 72632 *TF:* 877-342-9766 ■ *Web:* www.crescent-hotel.com	855-725-5720		379
1888 Mills LLC 375 Airport Rd .... Griffin GA 30224 *TF:* 800-346-3660 ■ *Web:* www.1888mills.com	800-346-3660		746
18th Street Deli Inc 8800 Conant .... Hamtramck MI 48211 *TF:* 800-498-3354 ■ *Web:* nuvuefoods.com	313-921-7710		366
1901 Inc 2801 Syene Rd .... Madison WI 53713 *Web:* www.1901inc.com	608-308-1901	273-9654	189-10
1920's Radio Network, The 5200 Hampton Blvd .... Norfolk VA 23508 *Web:* www.the1920snetwork.com	757-889-9400	489-0007	647
1928 Jewelry Co 3000 W Empire Blvd .... Burbank CA 91504 *TF:* 800-227-1928 ■ *Web:* www.1928.com	800-227-1928		408
1938 Media 1 Astor Pl PH J Ste J .... New York NY 10003 *Web:* 1938media.com	917-407-7600		7
1access.net LLC 221 Tremont St .... Carver MA 02330 *Web:* www.1access.net	508-866-7266		224
1Biotechnology PO Box 758 .... Oneco FL 34264 **Fax Area Code:* 941 ■ *TF:* 800-951-4246 ■ *Web:* 1biotechnology.com	800-951-4246	351-0026*	415
1Cloud 4 Bedford Farms Dr Ste 210 .... Manchester NH 03101 *TF:* 855-256-8300 ■ *Web:* 1cloudbusiness.com	855-256-8300		225
1DS (1 Diamond Source) 36 W 47th St .... New York NY 10036 *TF:* 877-968-7342 ■ *Web:* www.1diamondsource.com	877-968-7342		411
1MAGE Software Inc 7200 S Alton Way .... Centennial CO 80112 **Fax Area Code:* 303 ■ *TF:* 800-844-1468 ■ *Web:* www.1mage.com	800-844-1468	796-0587*	178-1
1secureaudit LLC 400 Continental Blvd 6th Fl .... El Segundo CA 90245 *Web:* 1secureaudit.com	424-220-8940		194

	Phone	Fax	Class
1st Advantage Federal Credit Union 110 Cybernetics Way .... Yorktown VA 23693 *Web:* www.1stadvantage.org	757-877-2444		219
1st Bank 201 N Wilbur PO Box 347 .... Broadus MT 59317 *Web:* www.our1stbank.com	406-436-2611		70
1st Bank & Trust of Broken Bow 710 S Park Dr .... Broken Bow OK 74728 *Web:* www.firstbank-ok.com	580-584-9123		70
1st Colonial Bancorp Inc 1040 Haddon Ave .... Collingswood NJ 08108 *OTC: FCOB* ■ *TF:* 800-500-1044 ■ *Web:* www.1stcolonial.com	856-858-1100	858-9255	70
1st Constitution Bancorp 2650 Rt 130 & Dey Rd .... Cranbury NJ 08512 *NASDAQ: FCCY* ■ *Web:* www.1stconstitution.com	609-655-4500	655-5653	360-2
1st Discount Brokerage Inc 8927 Hypoluxo Rd Ste A-5 .... Lake Worth FL 33467 *TF:* 888-642-2811 ■ *Web:* www.1db.com	561-515-3200	515-3201	690
1st Express Inc 227 Matzinger Rd .... Toledo OH 43612 *TF:* 800-521-8989 ■ *Web:* www.1stexpressinc.com	800-521-8989		780
1st Gateway Credit Union Hwy 67 N .... Camanche IA 52730 *Web:* 1stgateway.org	563-243-4121		219
1st Mechanical Services Inc 303 Curie Dr .... Alpharetta GA 30005 **Fax Area Code:* 678 ■ *TF:* 888-346-0792 ■ *Web:* www.1stmech.com	770-346-0792	205-0554*	610
1st Midamerica Credit Union 731 E Bethalto Dr .... Bethalto IL 62010 *TF:* 800-345-4216 ■ *Web:* www.1stmidamerica.org	618-258-3168		219
1st Movement LLC, The 177 E Colorado Blvd Ste 200 .... Pasadena CA 91105 *Web:* www.the1stmovement.com	626-733-8863		7
1st Security Bank of Washington (FSB) 19002 33rd Ave W .... Lynnwood WA 98036 *TF:* 800-683-0973 ■ *Web:* www.fsbwa.com	425-774-5536		70
1st Source Bank 100 N Michigan St .... South Bend IN 46601 *TF:* 800-513-2360 ■ *Web:* www.1stsource.com	574-235-2260	239-4388	70
1st Street Graphics Inc 1205 S 11th St .... Saint Joseph MO 64503 *TF:* 800-530-5909 ■ *Web:* 1ststreet.com	816-233-4567	233-0489	627
1st Summit Bancorp 125 Donald Ln PO Box 5480 .... Johnstown PA 15904 *TF:* 888-262-4010 ■ *Web:* 1stsummit.bank	814-262-4000		70
1st United Door Technologies Inc 1016 W Geneva Dr .... Tempe AZ 85282 *TF:* 866-366-7636 ■ *Web:* firstudt.com	480-705-6632	705-8497	236
1st West Background Due Diligence LLC 1536 Cole Blvd Ste 335 .... Lakewood CO 80401 *TF:* 866-670-3443 ■ *Web:* www.1stwest.com	866-670-3443		466
1-Stop Translation USA LLC 3700 Wilshire Blvd Ste 630 .... Los Angeles CA 90010 *Web:* www.1stopasia.com	213-480-0011		317
2 Checkoutcom Inc 1785 O'Brien Rd .... Columbus OH 43228 *TF:* 877-294-0273 ■ *Web:* www.2checkout.com	614-921-2450		459
2 Places At 1 Time Inc 1000 NW 57th Crt Ste 590 .... Miami FL 33126 *TF:* 877-275-2237 ■ *Web:* www.2placesat1time.com	877-275-2237		463
20/20 Engineering 1032 E South Boulder Rd Ste 208 .... Louisville CO 80027 *Web:* 2020engineer.com	303-926-0020		261
20/20 Eyecare Plan Inc 2900 W Cypress Creek Rd Ste 4 .... Fort Lauderdale FL 33309 *TF:* 800-525-9778 ■ *Web:* www.2020eyecareplan.com	800-525-9778		543
2020 Cos 3575 Lone Star Cir Ste 200 .... Fort Worth TX 76177 *Web:* www.2020companies.com	817-490-0100		195
2020 Exhibits Inc 10550 S Sam Huston Pkwy W .... Houston TX 77071 *TF:* 800-856-6659 ■ *Web:* www.2020exhibits.com	713-354-0900		196
2030 Inc 607 Cerrillos Rd .... Santa Fe NM 87505 *Web:* architecture2030.org	505-988-5309	983-9526	463
2101 Cooperative Inc 118 S 21st St .... Philadelphia PA 19103 *Web:* 2101cooperative.com	215-567-1780		652
211 Clover Lane 211 Clover Ln .... Louisville KY 40207 *Web:* 211clover.com	502-896-9570		671
212 Market Restaurant 212 Market St .... Chattanooga TN 37402 *Web:* www.212market.com	423-265-1212	267-6757	671
215 Holding Co 215 S 11th St .... Minneapolis MN 55403 *Web:* ffmbank.com	612-332-4732		360-2
215 McCann 215 Leidesdorff St .... San Francisco CA 94111 *Web:* www.215mccann.com	415-820-8700		7
216Digital Inc 2208 E Enterprise Pkwy .... Twinsburg OH 44087 *Web:* 216digital.com	216-505-4400		396
219 Design 67 E Evelyn Ave Ste 1 .... Mountain View CA 94041 *Web:* www.219design.com	650-969-4219		261
219 Restaurant 219 King St .... Alexandria VA 22314 *Web:* www.219restaurant.com	703-549-1141	549-0035	671
21C Museum Hotel 700 W Main St .... Louisville KY 40202 **Fax Area Code:* 513 ■ *Web:* www.21cmuseumhotels.com	502-217-6300	578-6601*	379
21st Amendment Inc 1158 W 86th St .... Indianapolis IN 46260 *Web:* www.21stamendment.com	317-846-1678		443
21st Century Christian Inc PO Box 40526 .... Nashville TN 37204 *TF:* 800-251-2477 ■ *Web:* www.21stcc.com	615-383-3842		96
21st Century Parks Inc 471 W Main St Ste 202 .... Louisville KY 40202 *Web:* 21cparks.org	502-584-0350		302
22 Bowen's 22 Bowen's Wharf .... Newport RI 02840 *Web:* www.22bowens.com	401-841-8884		671
22 Squared Inc 1170 Peachtree St NE 14th Fl .... Atlanta GA 30309 *Web:* www.22squared.com	404-347-8700		4
220 Group LLC, The 3405 Kenyon St Ste 301 .... San Diego CA 92110 **Fax Area Code:* 866 ■ *TF:* 877-220-6584 ■ *Web:* www.220marketing.com	619-758-9696	726-5114*	195
220 Laboratories Inc 2321 3rd St .... Riverside CA 92507 *Web:* www.220labs.com	951-683-2912	683-0952	214

				Phone	Fax	Class
230 Fifth Avenue Newmark Knight Frank 230 Fifth Ave Ste 1018 *TF:* 800-698-5617 ■ *Web:* www.230fifthave.com	New York	NY	10001	212-689-4721	545-0435	393
24 Asset Management Corp 13155 SW 42nd St Ste 200 *TF:* 855-414-2424 ■ *Web:* www.24asset.com	Miami	FL	33175	855-414-2424		393
24 Hour Co 6521 Arlington Blvd *Web:* www.24hrco.com	Falls Church	VA	22042	703-533-7209		344
24/7 Express Logistics Inc 1851 N S Rd *Web:* www.247expresslogistics.com	Kansas City	MO	64120	913-730-9445		311
240 Union 240 Union Blvd *Web:* 240union.com	Lakewood	CO	80228	303-989-3562	989-3565	671
247Sports 12 Cadillac Dr Ste 230 *TF:* 888-508-3055 ■ *Web:* 247sports.com	Brentwood	TN	37027	888-508-3055		387
24hourtek LLC 268 Bush St *TF:* 855-378-0787 ■ *Web:* www.24hourtek.com	San Francisco	CA	94104	415-294-4449		175
24HourWristbands.com 14550 Beechnut St *TF:* 855-712-4467 ■ *Web:* 24hourwristbands.com	Houston	TX	77083	281-786-3764		594
2600 Magazine PO Box 752 *Web:* www.2600.com	Middle Island	NY	11953	631-751-2600	474-2677	457-7
284 Partners LLC 215 E Washington St Ste 201	Ann Arbor	MI	48104	734-369-8723	369-8772	463
2B Technologies Inc 2100 Central Ave Ste 104 *Web:* www.twobtech.com	Boulder	CO	80301	303-273-0559	277-1812	743
2H Offshore Inc 15990 N Barkers Landing Ste 200 *Web:* 2hoffshore.com	Houston	TX	77079	281-258-2000		256
2Is Inc 75 West St *Web:* www.2is-inc.com	Walpole	MA	02081	508-850-7520	850-7521	256
2KDirect Inc 3000 Broad St Ste 115 *Web:* www.ipromote.com	San Luis Obispo	CA	93401	805-597-5000		387
2Leaf Press PO Box 4378 *Web:* www.2leafpress.org	New York	NY	10163	646-801-4227	998-1318	637-2
2nd Chance Home Furnishings 12226 Beach Blvd Ste 1 *Web:* www.2ndchancehomefurnishings.com	Jacksonville	FL	32246	904-580-2947		361
2nd Edison Inc 11 El Gavilan Rd *Web:* www.2ndedison.com	Orinda	CA	94563	925-253-1002		196
2nd Swing Inc 13031 Ridgedale Dr *Web:* www.2ndswing.com	Minnetonka	MN	55305	952-546-1906		711
2nd.MD 1300 Post Oak Blvd Ste 725 *TF:* 866-841-2575 ■ *Web:* www.2nd.md	Houston	TX	77056	866-841-2575		177
2plus2 Partners Inc 6711 Hollis St *Web:* www.2plus2.com	Emeryville	CA	94608	510-652-7700		177
2V Industries Inc 48553 West Rd *Web:* 2vindustries.com	Wixom	MI	48393	248-624-7943	624-1824	350
3 Amigos 1657 St Catherine W *Web:* www.3amigosrestaurant.com	Montreal	QC	H3H1L7	514-939-3329		671
3 Arts Entertainment Inc 9460 Wilshire Blvd *Web:* 3arts.com	Beverly Hills	CA	90212	310-888-3200		708
3 Axis Engineering 5929 Knight Ave *Web:* 3axisllc.com	Tuscaloosa	AL	35405	205-758-4488		261
3 Ball Entertainment 3650 Redondo Beach Ave *Web:* 3ballentertainment.com	Redondo Beach	CA	90278	424-236-7500		514
3 Doors Down Cafe 1429 SE 37th St *Web:* www.3doorsdowncafe.com	Portland	OR	97214	503-236-6886		671
3 Kings Environmental Inc 15001 NE Tenth Ave *Web:* 3kingsenvironmental.com	Vancouver	WA	98685	360-666-5464	666-8202	192
3 KMTV News Now 10714 Mockingbird Dr *Web:* www.3newsnow.com	Omaha	NE	68127	402-592-3333	592-9434	741-94
3 Mark Financial Inc 1600 Hwy 6 Ste 400 *TF:* 888-533-6275 ■ *Web:* 3mark.com	Sugar Land	TX	77478	281-269-2300		390
3 Media Web Solutions Inc 7 Felton St *Web:* www.3mediaweb.com	Hudson	MA	01749	508-845-8900	484-4101	195
3 Rivers Telephone Cooperative Inc 202 5th St S *Web:* www.3rivers.net	Fairfield	MT	59436	406-467-3490		224
3 Sixty Manufacturing 158 Martinvale Ln *Web:* www.3sixtymfg.com	San Jose	CA	95119	408-365-0360		767
3 Strikes Inc 1905 Elizabeth Ave *Web:* www.3strikes.com	Rahway	NJ	07065	732-382-3820		344
3 U Technologies 11681 Leonidas Horton Rd *Web:* www.3utech.com	Conroe	TX	77304	936-441-3043		256
30 Dps 118 N Tejon St 304 *Web:* www.30dps.com	Colorado Springs	CO	80903	719-380-9996		180
300 Feet Out 1035 Folsom St *Web:* www.300feetout.com	San Francisco	CA	94103	415-551-2377		344
3030 Ocean 3030 Holiday Dr *Web:* www.3030ocean.com	Fort Lauderdale	FL	33316	954-765-3030		671
305 Fitness 33 E 33rd St *Web:* 305fitness.com	New York	NY	10016	212-603-9932		354
31 Inc 100 Enterprise Dr *Web:* www.31inc.com	Newcomerstown	OH	43832	740-498-8324		754
313 Presents 2525 Woodward Ave *Web:* www.313presents.com	Detroit	MI	48201	313-471-3200		720
32 Automotive 610 W Main St	Batavia	OH	45103	513-732-2124		57
32 Degrees Capital 635 Eighth Ave SW *Web:* www.32degrees.ca	Calgary	AB	T2P3M3	403-695-1069	233-8040	528
320 Guest Ranch Inc 205 Buffalo Horn Creek Rd *TF:* 800-243-0320 ■ *Web:* www.320ranch.com	Gallatin Gateway	MT	59730	406-995-4283		239
321Launch 2 W 45th St 9th Fl *Web:* www.321launch.com	New York	NY	10036	212-845-5800	845-5899	195
33Across Inc 229 W 28th St 12th Fl *TF:* 888-297-4094 ■ *Web:* 33across.com	New York	NY	10001	888-297-4094		387
33rd Company Inc 1800 Wooddale Dr Ste 100 *Web:* www.33rdcompany.com	Woodbury	MN	55125	651-777-5500	777-5501	652
33rd Street Bistro 3301 Folsom Blvd *Web:* www.33rdstreetbistro.com	Sacramento	CA	95816	916-455-2233	346-4520	671
352 Inc 133 SW 130th Way Ste D *Web:* www.threefivetwo.com	Newberry	FL	32669	352-374-9657		196
360 Advanced Inc 200 Central Ave Ste 2105 *TF:* 866-418-1708 ■ *Web:* 360advanced.com	Saint Petersburg	FL	33701	866-418-1708		2
360 Business Consulting 1576 N Batavia Ave *TF:* 877-360-2492 ■ *Web:* www.360-biz.com	Orange	CA	92867	949-916-9120	608-3663	195
360 Cloud Solutions LLC 1475 N Scottsdale Rd *TF:* 800-360-8150 ■ *Web:* www.360cloudsolutions.com	Scottsdale	AZ	85257	888-360-8150		196
360 Electrical LLC 1935 E Vine St Ste 360 *Web:* 360electrical.com	Salt Lake City	UT	84121	801-364-4900		815
360 Imaging Inc 2 Concourse Pkwy Ste 140 *TF:* 866-360-6622 ■ *Web:* www.360imaging.com	Atlanta	GA	30328	404-236-7700		92
360 Media Ventures 30 Danforth St *Web:* 360mediaventures.com	Portland	ME	04101	207-699-2360		195
360 Press Solutions 2009 Windy Terr *Web:* 360presssolutions.com	Cedar Park	TX	78613	512-381-2360		194
360 Solutions LLC 2114 Austin Ave *Web:* www.360solutions.com	Waco	TX	76701	254-755-7000		194
360 Systems Inc 3281 Grande Vista Dr *Web:* 360systems.com	Newbury Park	CA	91320	818-991-0360	991-1360	246
360 Trading Networks Inc 521 Fifth Ave 38th Fl *Web:* www.360t.com	New York	NY	10175	212-776-2900	776-2902	690
3660 on the Rise 3660 Waialae Ave *Web:* 3660ontherise.com	Honolulu	HI	96816	808-737-1177	735-6105	671
39 Rue De Jean 39 John St *Web:* www.holycityhospitality.com	Charleston	SC	29403	843-722-8881	722-8835	671
390th Memorial Museum 6000 E Valencia Rd *Web:* 390th.org	Tucson	AZ	85730	520-574-0287	574-3030	520
3balls LLC PO Box 90083 *TF:* 888-289-0300 ■ *Web:* www.3balls.com	Raleigh	NC	27675	919-987-3222		711
3C Consultants 850 W Jackson Blvd Ste 730 *Web:* www.3ccomp.com	Chicago	IL	60607	312-226-8118		194
3CLogic Inc 9201 Corporate Blvd Ste 470 *TF:* 800-350-8656 ■ *Web:* www.3clogic.com	Rockville	MD	20850	800-350-8656		177
3D Exhibits Inc 2900 Lively Blvd *Web:* www.3dexhibits.com	Elk Grove Village	IL	60007	847-250-9000	860-8165	232
3D Internet 633 W Fifth St US Bank Twr 28th Fl *TF:* 800-442-5299 ■ *Web:* www.3dinternet.com	Los Angeles	CA	90071	800-442-5299		243
3D Intl 1825 Smelter Ave	Black Eagle	MT	59414	406-453-6561		671
3D Lacrosse LLC 1301 S Jason St Unit K *TF:* 800-941-9193 ■ *Web:* www.3dlacrosse.com	Denver	CO	80223	800-941-9193		713
3D Medical Manufacturing Inc 1006 W 15th St	Riviera Beach	FL	33404	561-842-7175		228
3D Systems Inc 333 Three D Systems Cir *TF:* 800-793-3669 ■ *Web:* www.3dsystems.com	Rock Hill	SC	29730	803-326-3900		178-8
3D2B Inc 80-02 Kew Gardens Rd Ste 903 *Web:* www.3d2b.com	Kew Gardens Hills	NY	11415	718-709-0900		5
3Degrees 407 Sansome St 4th Fl *TF:* 866-476-9378 ■ *Web:* www.3degreesinc.com	San Francisco	CA	94111	866-476-9378		463
3Dlabs Incorporated Ltd 1901 McCarthy Blvd *TF:* 800-464-3348 ■ *Web:* www.3dlabs.com	Milpitas	CA	95035	408-530-4700		625
3E Consulting Services 126 Commons Ct *Web:* 3econsultingservices.com	Chadds Ford	PA	19317	610-358-5950		196
3G Capital 600 3rd Ave 37th Fl *Web:* www.3g-capital.com	New York	NY	10016	212-893-6727		792
3Gtms 4 Armstrong Rd Ste 210 *Web:* www.3gtms.com	Shelton	CT	06484	203-567-4610		180
3H Group Inc 505 Riverfront Pkwy *Web:* www.3h.group	Chattanooga	TN	37402	423-499-0497	499-0476	463
3i Law Group PC 3900 E Mexico Ave Ste 530	Denver	CO	80210	303-481-6360		41
3i People Inc 5755 N Point Pkwy Ste 9 *Web:* www.3ipeople.com	Alpharetta	GA	30022	404-636-2397		624
3K Technologies LLC 1114 Cadillac Ct *Web:* 3ktechnologies.com	Milpitas	CA	95035	408-716-5900		177
3LK Construction LLC 1401 Howard St *Web:* www.3lkconstruction.com	Detroit	MI	48216	313-962-8700	962-8701	186
3M ESPE Dental Products 3M Ctr Bldg 275-2SE-03 *TF:* 800-634-2249 ■ *Web:* www.3m.com	Saint Paul	MN	55133	800-634-2249		228
3M Littmann Stethoscopes 3M Healthcare Bldg 502 Ste 200 *TF:* 800-228-3957 ■ *Web:* www.littmann.com	Oakdale	MN	55128	800-228-3957		475
3M Visual Systems Div 6801 River Place Blvd *TF:* 800-328-1371 ■ *Web:* www.mmm.com	Austin	TX	78726	800-328-1371		628
3Marketeers Advertising Inc 785 The Almeda *Web:* www.3marketeers.com	San Jose	CA	95126	408-293-3233	293-2433	4
3Play Media 34 Farnsworth St 4th Fl *Web:* www.3playmedia.com	Boston	MA	02210	617-764-5189	245-0510	514
3Plus Logistics Co 20250 S Alameda St *Web:* e3pl.com	Compton	CA	90221	310-667-5160	667-5166	194
3Q Digital Inc 155 Bovet Rd Ste 480 *Web:* 3qdigital.com	San Mateo	CA	94402	650-539-4124		5
3rd Alternative Inc 380 Main St Ste 304 *Web:* 3rdalternative.com	Farmingdale	NY	11735	516-753-1515		396

	Phone	Fax	Class
3rd Home Ltd 5200 Maryland Way Ste 260 .... Brentwood TN 37027 *Web:* www.thirdhome.com	615-454-2329		653
3S Global Business Solutions 21900 Burbank Blvd Ste 300 .... Woodland Hills CA 91367 *Web:* www.3sgbs.com	818-584-6183		180
3S Services LLC 2535 Loop 517 .... Carrizo Springs TX 78834 *Web:* 3sservices.com	830-876-4155	876-4125	538
3Sharp 18300 Redmond Way Ste 130 .... Redmond WA 98052 *Web:* 3sharp.com	425-882-1032	558-5710	180
3Tech Corp 2828 W Parker Rd Ste B101 .... Plano TX 75075 *Web:* www.3tech.com	972-490-4443		180
4 Bells Restaurant 1610 Harmon Pl .... Minneapolis MN 55403	612-904-1163		671
4 Consulting Inc 10440 N Central Express Way Ste 643 .... Dallas TX 75231 *Web:* 4ci-usa.com	214-698-8633		177
4 County Electric Power Assn 5265 S Frontage Rd .... Columbus MS 39701 **Fax Area Code:* 662 ■ *TF:* 800-431-1544 ■ *Web:* www.4county.org	800-431-1544	327-8790*	245
4 D Designs LLC 5940 Bertcliff Dr .... Columbus GA 31909 *Web:* www.patrickspress.com	706-221-7410	221-9964	459
4 Guys Inc 230 Industrial Park Rd .... Meyersdale PA 15552 *Web:* www.4guysfire.com	814-634-8373	634-0076	59
4 Sight Inc 135 Fifth Ave .... New York NY 10010 *Web:* www.4sightinc.com	212-253-0525		186
4 Star Contracting Inc 276 Newtown Rd .... Plainview NY 11803 *Web:* 4starcontracting.com	516-756-0700	756-0773	653
4 Wheel Parts 20315 96 Ave .... Langley BC V1M0E4 **Fax Area Code:* 604 ■ *TF:* 855-554-2402 ■ *Web:* www.4wheelparts.com	778-726-2787	882-0680*	755
40 Steak & Seafood 1401 Interchange Ave .... Bismarck ND 58501 *Web:* www.40steakandseafood.com	701-255-4040		671
401 K Advisors LLC 1000 Skokie Blvd Ste 370 .... Wilmette IL 60091 *Web:* www.401kadvisorschicago.com	847-256-4300	256-4311	251
40-Up Tackle Co 16 Union Ave .... Westfield MA 01085 *Web:* www.40uptackleco.com	413-562-0385		208
411 Local Search Corp 1500 Don Mills Rd Ste 600 N York .... Toronto ON M3B3K4 *TF:* 866-411-4411 ■ *Web:* www.411.ca	647-723-9929	722-3583	387
419 West 3865 Electric Rd .... Roanoke VA 24018 *Web:* 419-west.com	540-776-0419		671
42 Inc David Brower Ctr 2150 Allston Way Ste 300 .... Berkeley CA 94704 *Web:* www.42inc.com	510-548-7948		180
42Connect Inc 1100 Superior Ave Ste 1260 .... Cleveland OH 44114 *Web:* 42connect.com	216-279-9567		180
45 Allen Plaza Development LLC 45 Ivan Allen Jr Blvd .... Atlanta GA 30308 *Web:* www.watlantadowntown.com	404-582-5800		378
45 Bistro 123 E Broughton St .... Savannah GA 31401 *TF:* 800-589-6304 ■ *Web:* www.marshallhouse.com	912-234-3111		671
456 Fish 456 Granby St .... Norfolk VA 23510 *Web:* www.456fish.com	757-625-4444		671
45th Infantry Div Museum 2145 NE 36th St .... Oklahoma City OK 73111 *Web:* www.45thdivisionmuseum.com	405-424-5313		520
48 Degrees North 6327 Seaview Ave NW .... Seattle WA 98107 *Web:* 48north.com	206-789-7350	789-6392	457-4
480 Biomedical Inc 480 Arsenal St .... Watertown MA 02472	617-393-4600		475
495 Productions Holdings LLC 9560 Wilshire Blvd 5th Fl .... Beverly Hills CA 90212 *Web:* 495productions.com	818-840-2750		514
4aBetterBusiness Inc 1417 Main St .... Evanston IL 60202 *Web:* www.4abetterbusiness.com	847-606-2605		196
4C Foods Corp 580 Fountain Ave .... Brooklyn NY 11208 *Web:* www.4c.com	718-272-4242	272-2899	296-40
4Ctechnologies Inc 1500 Ardmore Blvd Ste 100 .... Pittsburgh PA 15221 *TF:* 855-873-4233 ■ *Web:* cccctech.com	412-871-7100		180
4D Inc 95 S Market St Ste 240 .... San Jose CA 95113 *Web:* us.4d.com	408-557-4600		178-1
4D Molecular Therapeutics 5858 Horton St Ste 455 .... Emeryville CA 94608 *Web:* www.4dmoleculartherapeutics.com	510-505-2680		85
4-D Properties LLP 2870 N Swan Rd Ste 100 .... Tucson AZ 85712	520-325-9600		652
4D Technology Corp 3280 E Hemisphere Loop Ste 146 .... Tucson AZ 85706 *Web:* www.4dtechnology.com	520-294-5600		544
4G Clinical LLC 370 Washington St .... Wellesley MA 02481 *Web:* 4gclinical.com	781-694-1400		180
4G Unwired Inc 1751 Sarno Rd Ste 1 .... Melbourne FL 32935 *Web:* www.4gunwired.com	321-726-4183	726-4185	256
4L Communications Inc 1555 Regent Ave W .... Winnipeg MB R2C4J2 *Web:* www.4lcommunications.com	204-336-0606		736
4Life Research 9850 S 300 W .... Sandy UT 84070 *TF:* 888-454-3374 ■ *Web:* www.4life.com	801-256-3102	562-3611	366
4M Building Solutions 2827 Clark Ave .... Saint Louis MO 63103 *TF:* 800-535-8285 ■ *Web:* www.4-m.com	314-535-2100	535-2218	152
4-M Precision Stamping Inc 4000 Technology Park Blvd .... Auburn NY 13021 *Web:* 4mprecision.com	315-252-8415	253-9611	488
4Over Inc 5900 San Fernando Rd .... Glendale CA 91202 *TF:* 877-782-2737 ■ *Web:* 4over.com	877-782-2737		627
4P Therapeutics LLC 680 Engineering Dr Ste 150 .... Peachtree Corners GA 30092 **Fax Area Code:* 866 ■ *Web:* 4ptherapeutics.com	770-263-1900	381-2103*	743
4PatientCare 100 Oceangate Ste 1200 .... Long Beach CA 90802 *Web:* 4patientcare.com	562-861-1800		196
4Refuel Canada LP 9440 - 202 St Ste 215 .... Langley BC V1M4A6 **Fax Area Code:* 604 ■ *TF:* 888-473-3835 ■ *Web:* 4refuel.com	888-473-3835	881-4446*	539
4Rivers Equipment 3763 Monarch St .... Frederick CO 80516 *TF:* 800-490-6162 ■ *Web:* www.4riversequipment.com	800-490-6162		358
4SGM (Four Seasons General Merchandise) 2801 E Vernon .... Los Angeles CA 90058 *Web:* www.4sgm.com	323-582-4444	582-9630	812
4Sight Group LLC 4023 Kennett Pk Ste 233 .... Wilmington DE 19807 *TF:* 800-490-2131 ■ *Web:* www.4sightgroup.com	800-490-2131		180
4-Star Trailers Inc 10 000 NW Tenth St .... Oklahoma City OK 73127 *TF:* 800-848-3095 ■ *Web:* www.4startrailers.com	405-324-7827		779
5 Alarm Fire & Safety Equipment LLC 350 Austin Cir .... Delafield WI 53018 *TF:* 800-615-6789 ■ *Web:* www.5alarm.com	262-646-5911		693
5 Metacom Inc 10401 N Meridian St Ste 100 .... Indianapolis IN 46290 *Web:* 5metacom.com	317-580-7540	580-7550	7
5 Star Equine Products Inc 4589 Hwy 71 S .... Hatfield AR 71945 *Web:* www.5starequineproducts.com	870-389-6328		711
500 Festival Inc 500 Festival Bldg 21 Virginia Ave Ste 500 .... Indianapolis IN 46204 *Web:* www.500festival.com	317-927-3378		720
50000 Feet Inc 1700 W Irving Park Rd Ste 110 .... Chicago IL 60613 *Web:* www.50000feet.com	773-529-6760		226
501creative Inc 303 Union Blvd Ste 200 .... Saint Louis MO 63108 *TF:* 888-501-0501 ■ *Web:* www.501creative.com	314-863-0501	863-0508	344
511 Inc 3201 N Airport Way .... Manteca CA 95337 *TF:* 866-451-1726 ■ *Web:* www.511tactical.com	866-451-1726		157-5
518 Prints LLC 1548 Burden Lake Rd Ste 4 .... Averill Park NY 12018 *Web:* www.fiveoneeightprints.com	518-674-5346		627
5280 Publishing Inc 1515 Wazee St Ste 400 .... Denver CO 80202 *TF:* 866-271-5280 ■ *Web:* www.5280.com	303-832-5280	832-0470	637-9
529 Wellington 529 Wellington Crescent .... Winnipeg MB R3M0B9 *Web:* 529wellington.ca	204-487-8325		671
530Medialab 11235 Knott Ave .... Cypress CA 90630 *Web:* www.530medialab.com	562-624-5888		344
540 ESPN 720 E Capitol Dr Ste 100 .... Milwaukee WI 53212 *TF:* 800-990-3776 ■ *Web:* www.espn.in	414-273-3776	291-3776	645-98
54th Street Grill 18700 E 38th Terr .... Independence MO 64057 *TF:* 866-402-5454 ■ *Web:* www.54thstreetgrill.com	866-402-5454		671
555 East 555 E Ocean Blvd .... Long Beach CA 90802 *Web:* www.555east.com	562-437-0626		671
55KRC 8044 Montgomery Rd Ste 650 .... Cincinnati OH 45236 *Web:* 55krc.iheart.com	513-686-8314		645-35
57th Street Antique and Design Ctr 855 - 891 57th St .... Sacramento CA 95819 *Web:* 57thstreetantiquerow.com	916-451-3110		460
5J Oilfield Services LLC 4090 N Hwy 79 .... Palestine TX 75801 *Web:* www.5joilfield.net	903-723-0253	729-2051	536
5th & Main Furniture 430 Main St .... Rapid City SD 57702 *Web:* 5thandmainfurniture.com	605-342-3822	343-3662	321
5th Avenue Theatre Assn 1308 Fifth Ave .... Seattle WA 98101 *Web:* www.5thavenue.org	206-625-1900		749
5th Business 5100 Orbitor Dr Ste 100 .... Mississauga ON L4W4Z4 *Web:* www.5thbusiness.com	905-275-2220		195
5th Wheel Training Institute 536 Brazeau Blvd .... New Liskeard ON P0J1P0 *Web:* 5thwheeltraining.com	705-647-7202		507
5W Public Relations LLC 230 Park Ave 32nd Fl .... New York NY 10169 *Web:* www.5wpr.com	212-999-5585		636
600 ESPN El Paso 4180 N Mesa St .... El Paso TX 79902 *Web:* krod.com	915-880-5763		645-52
610 Magnolia 610 Magnolia Ave .... Louisville KY 40208 *Web:* 610magnolia.com	502-636-0783		671
614 Media Group Inc 458 E Main St .... Columbus OH 43215 *Web:* 614mediagroup.com	614-488-4400		5
62ABOVE 444 W Beech St .... San Diego CA 92101 *Web:* 62above.com	619-295-8232		636
63 Ranch PO Box 979 .... Livingston MT 59047 *TF:* 888-395-5151 ■ *Web:* 63ranch.com	888-395-5151		239
66 Diner 1405 Central Ave NE .... Albuquerque NM 87106 *Web:* 66diner.com	505-247-1421		671
680 Partners LLC 600 Madison Ave 11th Fl .... New York NY 10022 *Web:* www.680partners.com	212-931-5311	931-5310	260
6D Global Technologies Inc 1500 Broadway Ste 505 .... New York NY 10036 *TF:* 800-787-3006 ■ *Web:* www.6dglobal.com	800-787-3006		787
6E Technologies LLC 6795 E Tennessee Ave .... Denver CO 80224 *Web:* 6etech.com	303-417-6332		177
6K Systems Inc 11710 Plz America Dr Ste 810 .... Reston VA 20190 *Web:* 6ksystems.com	703-724-1320	724-0433	177
6th Street Consulting 250 N Harbor Dr Ste 321 .... Redondo Beach CA 90277 *Web:* 6sc.com	310-694-3844		196
7 Cedars Casino 270756 Hwy 101 .... Sequim WA 98382 *Web:* 7cedars.com	360-683-7777		452
7 D Ranch 7D Ranch PO Box 100 .... Cody WY 82414 *TF:* 888-587-9885 ■ *Web:* www.7dranch.com	307-587-9885		239
7 Layers Inc 15 Musick .... Irvine CA 92618 *Web:* www.7layers.com	949-716-6512	716-6521	261
7 Medical Systems LLC 651 Nicollet Mall Ste 501 .... Minneapolis MN 55402 *TF:* 800-440-7119 ■ *Web:* 7medical.com	612-230-7700		177

Name / Address	City	State	ZIP	Phone	Fax	Class
7 Stars Test Only 7905 Balboa Ave Ste D *Web:* 7starstestonly.com	San Diego	CA	92111	858-278-8737		62
700 WLW 8044 Montgomery Rd Ste 650 *Web:* 700wlw.iheart.com	Cincinnati	OH	45236	513-686-8300		645-35
71 Sainte Peter 71 N San Pedro St *Web:* www.71saintpeter.com	San Jose	CA	95110	408-971-8523	938-3440	671
710 WOR 32 Avenue of the Americas *Web:* 710wor.iheart.com	New York	NY	10013	212-377-7900		645-108
717 Parking Services Inc 1523 N Franklin St *TF:* 800-310-7275 ■ *Web:* 717parking.com	Tampa	FL	33602	813-228-7722		562
74th Street Productions 350 N 74th St *Web:* 74thstreet.com	Seattle	WA	98103	206-781-1447		637-2
75 Chestnut 75 Chestnut St *Web:* 75chestnut.com	Boston	MA	02108	617-227-2175	227-3675	671
757 Makerspace 421 W 22nd St *Web:* www.757makerspace.com	Norfolk	VA	23517	757-301-1118		393
7clans Paradise Casino 7500 Hwy 177 *TF:* 866-723-4005 ■ *Web:* sevenclans.com	Red Rock	OK	74651	866-723-4005		132
7-Eleven Inc 1722 Routh Ste 100 *TF:* 800-255-0711 ■ *Web:* www.7-eleven.com	Dallas	TX	75221	800-255-0711		204
7-Sigma Inc 2843 26th Ave S *TF:* 888-722-8396 ■ *Web:* www.7-sigma.com	Minneapolis	MN	55406	612-722-5358		608
7SM (Seven Simple Machines) 5429 Russell Ave NW No 201 *Web:* www.7simplemachines.com	Seattle	WA	98107	206-545-4850		177
7Strategy LLC 117 N Cooper St **Fax Area Code:* 801 ■ *TF:* 888-231-3062 ■ *Web:* 7strategy.com	Olathe	KS	66061	888-231-3062	751-4688*	180
7Summits LLC 1110 Old World Third St Ste 500 *TF:* 866-705-6372 ■ *Web:* www.7summitsinc.com	Milwaukee	WI	53203	877-803-9286		195
7th Online Inc 24 W 40th St 11th Fl *Web:* www.7thonline.com	New York	NY	10018	212-997-1717		224
802 Creative Partners Inc 42 Gulch Rd PO Box 1075 *Web:* www.802creative.com	Stowe	VT	05672	802-779-5369		7
804 Technology LLC 5381 Hwy N Ste 201 *Web:* 804technology.com	Cottleville	MO	63304	636-928-0330		261
810 WHB Sports Radio 6721 W 121st St *Web:* www.810whb.com	Overland Park	KS	66209	913-344-1500	344-1599	645
82 Queen 82 Queen St *Web:* www.82queen.com	Charleston	SC	29401	843-723-7591		671
84 Lumber Co 1019 Rt 519 *TF:* 800-664-1984 ■ *Web:* www.84lumber.com	Eighty Four	PA	15330	724-228-8820		191-3
840 CFCW 2394 W Edmonton Mall (Entrance 55) 8882-170 St *TF:* 800-424-1344 ■ *Web:* www.cfcw.com	Edmonton	AB	T5T4M2	780-490-2479	435-0844	647
866UNP 866 UN Plz Ste 222 *Web:* 866unp.com	New York	NY	10017	212-355-2100	759-6156	784
889 Global Solutions 2501 Brookwood Rd *Web:* www.889globalsolutions.com	Columbus	OH	43209	614-235-8889		787
89 North Inc 20 Winter Sport Ln Ste 135 *Web:* www.chroma.com	Williston	VT	05495	802-881-0302		382
89.1 KANW-FM 2020 Coal Ave SE *Web:* www.kanw.com	Albuquerque	NM	87106	505-242-7163		645-4
89.1 WBOI 3204 Clairmont Ct *TF:* 800-471-9264 ■ *Web:* wboi.org	Fort Wayne	IN	46808	260-452-1189		645-60
89.7 FM KXGR 18900 E Hampden Ave *Web:* gracefm.com	Aurora	CO	80013	303-628-7200		647
89.9 The Wave 90 Lovett Lake Ct *Web:* 899thewave.fm	Halifax	NS	B3S0H6	902-422-1651		645-67
8th Air Force Museum 88 Shreveport Rd *Web:* www.barksdaleglobalpowermuseum.com	Bossier City	LA	71112	318-752-0055		520
8x8 Inc 810 W Maude Ave *NASDAQ: EGHT* ■ *TF:* 888-898-8733 ■ *Web:* www.8x8.com	Sunnyvale	CA	94085	408-727-1885	980-0432	696
9 Bangkok Restaurant 571 Central Ave *Web:* www.9bangkok.info	Saint Petersburg	FL	33701	727-894-5990	826-6164	671
9 Story Entertainment Inc 23 Fraser Ave *Web:* 9story.com	Toronto	ON	M6K1Y7	416-530-9900		514
911 Restoration Enterprises Inc 7721 Densmore Ave *Web:* www.911restoration.com	Van Nuys	CA	91406	818-373-4880		667
919 Marketing Company Inc 102 Avent Ferry Rd *Web:* 919marketing.com	Holly Springs	NC	27540	919-557-7890		195
92 KQRS 2000 SE Elm St	Minneapolis	MN	55414	612-617-4000		645-99
92 Moose 56 W Ave Ste 1 *Web:* 92moose.fm	Augusta	ME	04330	207-623-4735	626-5948	645-12
92.1 The Beat 1003 Norfolk Sq *Web:* thebeatva.iheart.com	Norfolk	VA	23502	757-466-0009		645-110
92.1 WROU 717 E David Rd *Web:* www.921wrou.com	Dayton	OH	45429	937-294-5858		645-44
92.3 FM KGON 0700 SW Bancroft St *TF:* 800-222-9236 ■ *Web:* kgon.radio.com	Portland	OR	97239	503-223-1441	223-6909	645-126
92.5 FM WVNN 1717 Hwy 72 E *TF:* 866-494-9866 ■ *Web:* www.wvnn.com	Athens	AL	35611	256-830-8300	232-6842	645
92.5 KOMA 400 E Britton Rd *Web:* komaradio.com	Oklahoma City	OK	73114	405-616-5500		645-112
92.5 The Wolf-KWOF 720 S Colorado Blvd *Web:* www.925thewolf.com	Denver	CO	80246	303-832-5665		645-46
92.5 WESC-FM 101 N Main St Ste 1000 Tenth Fl *TF:* 800-248-0863 ■ *Web:* wescfm.iheart.com	Greenville	SC	29601	800-248-0863		645-65
92.9 The Bull Studios 366 3rd Ave S *Web:* www.thebull.ca	Saskatoon	SK	S7K1M5	306-938-2855		647
92nd St Young Men's & Young Women's Hebrew Assn 1395 Lexington Ave *TF:* 800-385-1689 ■ *Web:* www.92y.org	New York	NY	10128	212-415-5500	415-5788	48-20
93.1 FM WZAK 6555 Carnegie Ave *TF:* 866-781-0931 ■ *Web:* wzakcleveland.com	Cleveland	OH	44103	216-578-0931	771-4164	645-36
93.1 KISS FM 4180 N Mesa St *Web:* kisselpaso.com	El Paso	TX	79902	915-544-9300		645-52
93.1 The Mountain 2880 Meade Ave Ste B-250 *Web:* 931themountain.iheart.com	Las Vegas	NV	89102	702-238-7300	732-4890	645-85
93.3 ALT AZ 1100 N 52nd St *Web:* altaz933.com	Phoenix	AZ	85008	480-712-9393		645
93.9 KSOU 128 20th St SE PO Box 298 *Web:* siouxcountyradio.com	Sioux Center	IA	51250	712-722-1090	722-1102	647
93.9 LITE FM 233 N Michigan Ave No 2800 *Web:* 939litefm.iheart.com	Chicago	IL	60601	312-540-2000		647
93.9 The Mountain 1117 W Rt 66 *Web:* 939themountain.gcmaz.com	Flagstaff	AZ	86001	928-773-1000	779-2988	645-57
930 AM The Answer 9601 McAllister Fwy Ste 1200 *TF:* 866-308-8867 ■ *Web:* 930amtheanswer.com	San Antonio	TX	78216	210-344-8481		645-140
94 HJY 75 Oxford St Ste 301 *Web:* 94hjy.iheart.com	Providence	RI	02905	401-224-1994		645-127
94.1 The Beat 245 Alfred St *Web:* 941thebeat.iheart.com	Savannah	GA	31408	912-964-7794		645-145
94.5 WARO FM 2824 Palm Beach Blvd *Web:* 945thearrow.com	Fort Myers	FL	33916	239-479-5506		645
94.7 WCSX 1 Radio Plz *Web:* wcsx.com	Ferndale	MI	48220	248-398-9470		645
94th Aero Squadron Restaurants 16320 Raymer St *Web:* www.94thvannuys.com	Van Nuys	CA	91406	818-994-7437		670
95.3 KRTY 750 Story Rd *Web:* www.krty.com	San Jose	CA	95122	408-293-8030		645-143
95.7 Hallelujah FM 2650 Thousand Oaks Blvd Ste 4100 *TF:* 844-885-9425 ■ *Web:* hallelujahfm.iheart.com	Memphis	TN	38118	901-259-1300		645-95
96.1 KISS 200 Fleet St *Web:* 961kiss.iheart.com	Pittsburgh	PA	15220	412-937-1441		645-123
96.1 KISS FM 4270 Byrd Dr *TF:* 877-498-9600 ■ *Web:* kissfmcolorado.iheart.com	Loveland	CO	80538	970-461-2560		645
96.1 The Fox 505 University Ave *Web:* 961thefox.iheart.com	Grand Forks	ND	58203	701-775-0575		645-62
96.3 BIG FM 170 Queen St *Web:* www.963bigfm.com	Kingston	ON	K7K1B2	613-544-2340	544-5508	647
96.5 FM KISS Country 600 Old Marion Rd NE *TF:* 800-258-0096 ■ *Web:* 965kisscountry.iheart.com	Cedar Rapids	IA	52402	319-395-0530		645-28
96.5 The Mill FM 500 Commercial St *Web:* 965themill.com	Manchester	NH	03101	603-669-5777	669-4641	645-93
97.1 Kiss FM 27 N 27th St Crowne Plz 23rd Fl *Web:* 971kissfm.com	Billings	MT	59101	406-245-9700		645-18
97.1 The Fan (WBNS-FM) 605 S Front St Ste 300 *Web:* www.971thefan.com	Columbus	OH	43215	614-460-3850		645-40
97.1 The Wave 1666 Blairs Pond Rd **Fax Area Code:* 302 ■ *Web:* www.971thewave.com	Milford	DE	19963	410-912-9710	422-3069*	645
97.1 ZHT 2801 S Decker Lake Dr *Web:* 971zht.iheart.com	Salt Lake City	UT	84119	801-908-1300		645-139
97.3 The Game 12100 W Howard Ave *Web:* 973thegame.iheart.com	Greenfield	WI	53228	414-545-8900		645
97.9 CPR Rock 9471 Three Rivers Rd Ste A *Web:* www.979cprrocks.com	Gulfport	MS	39503	228-388-2001		645-66
97.9 WIBB 7080 Industrial Hwy *Web:* wibb.iheart.com	Macon	GA	31210	478-781-1063		645-91
98 Rock 59 Windermere Blvd *Web:* www.my98rock.com	Charleston	SC	29407	843-769-4799		645-30
98 TXT 3900 11th Ave S *Web:* 98txt.iheart.com	Tuscaloosa	AL	35401	205-344-4589		645-168
98.1 Charlotte FM 112 Milltown Blvd *Web:* www.charlottefm.ca	Saint Stephen	NB	E3L1G6	506-466-4500		647
98.1 KDD 7755 Freedom Ave *Web:* wkdd.iheart.com	North Canton	OH	44720	330-836-4700		645
98.1 KHAK 425 Second St SE 4th Fl *Web:* www.khak.com	Cedar Rapids	IA	52401	319-365-9431		645-28
98.1 The Bull 2601 Nicholasville Rd *Web:* wbul.iheart.com	Lexington	KY	40503	859-422-1000		645-86
98.5 KFOX 2001 Junipero Serra Blvd Ste 350 *TF:* 877-410-5369 ■ *Web:* www.kfox.com	Daly City	CA	94014	415-546-8300		645-143
98.7 The Gater 3071 Continental Dr *Web:* gaterrocks.iheart.com	West Palm Beach	FL	33407	561-616-6600		645-23
98.7 WNNS 1510 N Third St *Web:* www.wnns.com	Riverton	IL	62561	217-629-5483	629-7952	645-152
98.9 The Vibe (WKIM-FM) 5629 Murray Rd	Memphis	TN	38119	901-682-1106		645-95
98.9 XFM c/o Atlantic Broadcasters Ltd 5663 Hwy Unit 7 PO Box 5800 *TF:* 800-350-2539 ■ *Web:* www.989xfm.ca	Antigonish	NS	B2G2L9	902-863-4000	863-6300	647
98point6 Inc 701 5th Ave Ste 2300 *TF:* 866-657-7991 ■ *Web:* 98point6.com	Seattle	WA	98104	866-657-7991		39
99 Cents Only Stores 4000 Union Pacific Ave *TF:* 888-582-5999 ■ *Web:* 99only.com	Commerce	CA	90023	323-980-8145		791
99.3/105.7 Kiss FM 2809 Emerywood Pkwy Ste 300 *Web:* kissrichmond.com	Richmond	VA	23294	804-672-9299		645-132
99.5 Magic FM 500 4th St NW 5th Fl *Web:* www.995magicfm.com	Albuquerque	NM	87102	505-767-6700		645-4
99.5 QYK 9721 Executive Center Dr N No 200 *TF:* 800-992-1099 ■ *Web:* www.995qyk.com	Saint Petersburg	FL	33702	727-579-1925	563-8202	645-160

				Phone	Fax	Class
99.5 The River 1203 Troy-Schenectady Rd *Fax Area Code: 210 ■ Web: 995theriver.iheart.com	Latham	NY	12110	518-452-4800	832-3149*	645
99.5 WMAG 2-B PAI Pk TF: 800-876-0995 ■ Web: 995wmag.iheart.com	Greensboro	NC	27409	336-822-2000		645
99.7 Blitz, The 1458 Dublin Rd TF: 800-821-9970 ■ Web: www.theblitz.com	Columbus	OH	43215	614-481-7800		645-40
99.9 KEZ 4686 E Van Buren St Web: kez999.iheart.com	Phoenix	AZ	85008	602-374-6000		645-121
99.9 KISS Country 13 Summerlin Rd Web: 99kisscountry.iheart.com	Asheville	NC	28806	828-257-2700		645-10
9Dots Management Corp 1100 E Hector St Ste 245 Web: www.ixdots.com	Conshohocken	PA	19428	610-684-6220		178-10
9Marks 525 A St NE TF: 888-543-1030 ■ Web: 9marks.org	Washington	DC	20002	202-543-1224	543-6113	48-20
@Comm Corp 150 Dow St TF: 800-641-5400 ■ Web: www.atcomm.com	Manchester	NH	03101	603-624-4424	624-8269	178-7
&Barr 600 E Washington St Web: andbarr.co	Orlando	FL	32801	407-849-0100		4
#1 Cochran 4520 William Penn Hwy Web: www.cochran.com	Monroeville	PA	15146	412-373-3333		57

A

				Phone	Fax	Class
A & A Consulting Engineers PC 125-10 Queens Blvd Silver Twr Ste 318 Web: www.anaconsultingengineers.com	Kew Gardens	NY	11415	718-544-7878		196
A & A Express Inc PO Box 707 TF: 800-658-3549 ■ Web: www.aaexpressinc.com	Brandon	SD	57005	605-582-2402	582-7300	780
A & A Global Industries Inc 17 Stenersen Ln TF: 800-638-6000 ■ Web: aaglobal.com	Cockeysville	MD	21030	410-252-1020		483
A & A Home Health Services Inc 9610 Long Point Rd Ste 250	Houston	TX	77055	713-783-8803		363
A & A Industrial Piping Inc 6 Gardner Rd Web: www.a-agroup.com	Fairfield	NJ	07004	973-882-2622		610
A & A Industries Inc 320 Jubilee Dr Web: www.aandaindustries.com	Peabody	MA	01960	978-977-9660		91
A & A Machine & Development Company Inc 16625 Gramercy Pl Web: www.aamach.com	Gardena	CA	90247	310-532-7706	532-7626	621
A & A Machine & Fabrication LLC 3101 Texas Ave Web: www.aagroup.com	La Marque	TX	77568	409-938-4274		454
A & A Maintenance Enterprise Inc 965 Midland Ave TF: 800-280-0601 ■ Web: aamaintenance.com	Yonkers	NY	10704	800-280-0601		192
A & A Merchandising Ltd 3250 Lakeshore Blvd W Web: aamerch.com	Toronto	ON	M8V1M1	416-503-3343		636
A & A Pharmachem Inc 4-77 Auriga Dr Web: www.aapharmachem.com	Ottawa	ON	K2E7Z7	613-224-1234		231
A & A Safety Inc 1126 Ferris Rd Web: www.aasafetyinc.com	Amelia	OH	45102	513-943-6100		8
A & A Stepping Stone Manufacturing Inc 10291 Ophir Rd Web: www.aasteppingstone.com	Newcastle	CA	95658	530-885-7481	885-3431	183
A & A Transfer & Storage Inc 113 Hollywood Blvd NW Web: www.anatransfer.com	Fort Walton Beach	FL	32549	850-244-7661		780
A & B Aerospace Inc 612 Ayon Ave Web: abaerospace.com	Azusa	CA	91702	626-334-2976	334-6539	21
A & B Aluminum & Brass Foundry 11165 Denton Dr TF: 800-743-4995 ■ Web: www.abfoundryonline.com	Dallas	TX	75229	972-247-3579	247-4981	492
A & B Brush Manufacturing Corp 1150 Three Ranch Rd Web: abbrush.com	Duarte	CA	91010	626-303-8856	303-1207	103
A & B Freight Line Inc 4805 Sandy Hollow Rd TF: 800-231-2235 ■ Web: www.aandbfreight.com	Rockford	IL	61109	815-874-4700	874-5656	314
A & B Homecare Solutions LLC 446a Blake St 3rd Fl Web: www.abhomecare.com	New Haven	CT	06515	203-495-1900	495-1933	363
A & B Lobster House 700 Front St Web: aandblobsterhouse.com	Key West	FL	33040	305-294-5880		671
A & B Mechanical Contractors Inc 272 W 3620 S Web: www.abmechanicalcontractors.com	Salt Lake City	UT	84115	801-263-1700		189-10
A & B Pipe & Supply Inc 6500 NW 37th Ave Web: www.abpipe.com	Miami	FL	33147	305-691-5000		612
A & B Precision Metals Inc 13715 Mt Anderson St Web: www.abprecisionmetals.com	Reno	NV	89506	775-323-2546		567
A & B Printing & Mailing 2908 S Highland Dr Ste B Web: www.abprint.com	Las Vegas	NV	89109	702-731-5888		627
A & B Tube Benders Inc 13465 E 9 Mile Rd Web: abtubebenders.com	Warren	MI	48089	586-773-0440	773-1104	350
A & B Wiper Supply Inc 11350 Norcom Rd Web: www.bestrags.com	Philadelphia	PA	19143	215-482-6100	482-6190	508
A & C Welding Inc 80 Cuyhoga Fls Indus Pky Web: acweld.com	Peninsula	OH	44264	330-762-4777	762-8562	697
A & D Constructors Inc 1449 Kimber Ln Ste 103 Web: adconstructors.com	Evansville	IN	47712	812-428-3708		492
A & D Environmental Services Inc PO Box 484 *Fax Area Code: 336 ■ TF: 800-434-7750 ■ Web: www.adenviro.com	High Point	NC	27261	800-434-7750	434-7752*	192
A & D Home Health Solutions 27 Garfield St Web: www.adhomehealthsolutions.com	Newington	CT	06111	860-667-2275		363
A & D Technical Supply Company Inc 4320 S 89th St TF: 800-228-2753 ■ Web: adtechsupply.com	Omaha	NE	68127	402-592-4950		113
A & D Technology Inc 4622 Runway Blvd Web: www.aanddtech.com	Ann Arbor	MI	48108	734-973-1111	973-1103	407
A & E Arts & Entertainment Network 235 E 45th St Web: www.aetv.com	New York	NY	10017	212-850-9317		42
A & E Construction Co 152 Garrett Rd Web: www.aeconstruction.com	Upper Darby	PA	19082	610-449-3152	449-6325	186
A & E Designs 1283 Commons Ct Web: buycoolshirts.com	Clermont	FL	34711	352-708-6727		327
A & E Machine Shop Inc 920 Industrial Blvd Web: www.aemach.com	Lone Star	TX	75668	903-656-3485	656-3489	454
A & E Manufacturing Company Inc 2110 Hartel St Web: www.ae-mfg.com	Levittown	PA	19057	215-943-9460		697
A & E Testing 1514 Rochester St Web: www.shawndra.com	Lima	NY	14485	585-624-4500	624-5300	743
A & F Machine Products Co 454 Geiger St Web: www.helwigpumps.com	Berea	OH	44017	440-243-0040	243-3009	641
A & G Management Inc 7779 New York Ln TF: 888-820-4681 ■ Web: aandgmanagement.com	Glen Burnie	MD	21061	410-766-8900	766-6557	655
A & J Automation Inc 21356 Carlo Dr Web: ajautomation.com	Clinton Township	MI	48038	586-468-7555	468-7111	386
A & J Capital Investment Inc 1609 W Valley Blvd Ste 328 Web: www.ajcap.com	Alhambra	CA	91803	626-289-8887	289-8848	401
A & J Manufacturing Co 70 Icon Web: www.aj-racks.com	Foothill Ranch	CA	92610	714-544-9570	544-4215	254
A & J Printing Inc PO Box 518 Hwy 160 N Web: aandjprinting.com	Nixa	MO	65714	417-725-2674	725-2682	627
A & J Washroom Accessories Inc 509 Temple Hill Rd Web: www.ajwashroom.com	New Windsor	NY	12553	845-562-3332		361
A & K Development Company Inc 410 Chambers St Web: www.akdco.net	Eugene	OR	97402	541-686-0012	485-2892	298
A & K Railroad Materials Inc 1505 S Redwood Rd TF: 800-453-8812 ■ Web: www.akrailroad.com	Salt Lake City	UT	84104	801-974-5484	972-2041	770
A & L Great Lakes Laboratories Inc 3505 Conestoga Dr Web: algreatlakes.com	Fort Wayne	IN	46808	260-483-4759		743
A & L Handles Inc 244 Shoemaker Rd Web: www.alhandles.com	Pottstown	PA	19464	610-323-1516		499
A & L Metal Processing 1920 George St	Sandusky	OH	44870	419-627-0022		481
A & M Aviation Inc 130 S Clow International Pkwy Ste B Web: www.aandmaviation.com	Bolingbrook	IL	60490	630-759-1555		63
A & M Business Interior Services 1300 Washington Ave N Web: www.ambis.com	Minneapolis	MN	55411	612-627-1600		320
A & M Dental Laboratories Inc 425 S Santa Fe St TF: 800-487-8051 ■ Web: www.aandmdental.com	Santa Ana	CA	92705	714-547-8051		415
A & M Printing 3589 Nevada St Web: www.anmprinting.com	Pleasanton	CA	94566	925-484-3690		627
A & M Supply Corp 6701 90th Ave N TF: 800-877-8551	Pinellas Park	FL	33782	727-541-6631	546-3617	820
A & M Tool & Die Company Inc 64 Mill St Web: www.am-tool.com	Southbridge	MA	01550	508-764-3241		757
A & N Trailer Parts 6028 S 118th E Ave TF: 800-272-1898 ■ Web: www.antrailerparts.com	Tulsa	OK	74146	918-461-8404		120
A & R Mechanical Contractors Inc 11244 E 55th Pl Web: aandrmechanical.com	Tulsa	OK	74146	918-250-6500		610
A & S Building Systems LP 1880 Hwy 116 Web: www.a-s.com	Caryville	TN	37714	865-426-2141		106
A & S Engineers Inc 10377 Stella Link Rd Web: as-engineers.com	Houston	TX	77025	713-942-2700		261
A & S Mold & Die Corp 9705 Eton Ave Web: www.aandsmold.com	Chatsworth	CA	91311	818-341-5393		596
A & S Services Group LLC 310 N Zarfoss Dr Web: askinard.com	York	PA	17404	717-759-3017		311
A & S Suppliers 1970 W 84 St TF: 800-454-6368 ■ Web: www.hotelitems.com	Hialeah	FL	33014	305-557-1688	557-1067	361
A & S Wholesale 14643 Lull St Web: www.aswhsl.com	Van Nuys	CA	91405	818-989-3345		297-2
A & T Chevrolet Inc 801 Bethlehem Pk Web: www.atchevrolet.com	Sellersville	PA	18960	215-253-5836		57
A & W Products Company Inc 14 Gardner St Web: www.awproducts.com	Port Jervis	NY	12771	845-856-5156		534
A & W Sheet Metal Inc 602 Blazier St	West Monroe	LA	71292	318-387-9489		697
A & Z Pharmaceutical Inc 350 Wireless Blvd Web: azpharmaceutical.com	Hauppauge	NY	11788	631-952-3802	952-3900	231

Company	City	State	ZIP	Phone	Fax	Class
A 1 Auto Recyclers 7804 S Hwy 79 *TF:* 800-456-0715 ■ *Web:* www.a1autorecyclers.com	Rapid City	SD	57702	605-348-8442		54
A 1 Nethosting 211 Casper Ln *Web:* a1nethosting.com	Vista	CA	92084	760-758-4007		396
A 1 Termite & Pest Control Inc 2686 Morganton Blvd SW *TF:* 800-532-7378 ■ *Web:* www.a-1pc.com	Lenoir	NC	28645	828-758-4312		577
A 2000 Network Solutions 550 Fairway Dr Ste 102 *Web:* a2000ns.com	Deerfield Beach	FL	33442	954-363-8008		180
A A Blueprint Company Inc 2757 Gilchrist Rd *TF:* 800-821-3700 ■ *Web:* www.aablueprint.com	Akron	OH	44305	330-794-8803		781
A B C Awning & Venetian Blind Corp 858 St Andrews Blvd *Web:* abcawning.com	Charleston	SC	29407	843-766-6311		362
A B C Doors 5100 S Willow *Web:* www.abcdoors.com	Houston	TX	77035	713-729-9700		236
A B Salon Interiors Inc 14220 66th St N Ste E *Web:* www.absalonequipment.com	Clearwater	FL	33764	727-531-5405		77
A Bales Security Agency Inc 625 E Twiggs St Ste 101 *TF:* 800-255-7328 ■ *Web:* www.balessecurity.com	Tampa	FL	33602	800-255-7328		693
A Better Chance Inc 253 W 35th St 6th Fl. *TF:* 800-562-7865 ■ *Web:* abetterchance.org	New York	NY	10001	646-346-1310	346-1311	48-11
A Better Image Printing 4310 Garrett Rd *Web:* www.abetterimageprinting.com	Durham	NC	27707	919-402-0318		627
A Better Solution Inc 4303 Cedar Lake Cv *Web:* www.abs-consulting.com	Conley	GA	30288	770-252-1500		693
A Betterway Rent-a-car Inc 1092 Roswell Rd. *TF:* 800-527-0700 ■ *Web:* www.budgetatl.com	Marietta	GA	30067	770-240-3305		126
A Ble Advocates for Basic Legal Equality Inc 525 Jefferson Ave **Fax Area Code:* 937 ■ *TF:* 800-837-0814 ■ *Web:* www.lawolaw.org	Toledo	OH	43604	419-255-0814	535-4600*	428
A Bommarito Wines Inc 2827 S Brentwood Blvd *Web:* abommaritowines.com	Saint Louis	MO	63144	314-961-8996		80-3
A Bright Idea LLC 210 Archer St *Web:* www.abrightideaonline.com	Bel Air	MD	21014	410-836-7180		4
A C I Media 2485 S Marion Ave	Lake City	FL	32025	386-758-2266		809
A C Nelson Rv World 11818 L St *TF:* 888-655-2332 ■ *Web:* www.acnrv.com	Omaha	NE	68137	402-333-1122	333-1054	57
A C Tool Supply 5456 E Mcdowell Rd Ste 123 *Web:* www.aikencolon.com	Mesa	AZ	85215	480-968-6698		544
A Camino Real Driving & Traffic School 3976 W 6th St. *Web:* www.acaminorealschool.com	Los Angeles	CA	90020	213-382-4806		685
A Caring Experience Nursing Services 815 Reservoir Ave. *Web:* www.acaringexperience.com	Cranston	RI	02910	401-453-4545		393
A Carlisle & Company of Nevada Inc 1080 Bible Way. *Web:* www.acarlisleprinting.com	Reno	NV	89502	775-323-5163		627
A Colonial Moving & Storage Co 17 Mercer St. *TF:* 877-549-7783 ■ *Web:* www.colonialmoving.com	Hackensack	NJ	07601	201-343-5777	343-1934	519
A Contemporary Theatre (ACT) Kreielsheimer Pl 700 Union St *Web:* www.acttheatre.org	Seattle	WA	98101	206-292-7660	292-7670	572
A Cut Above Lawn Service Inc 370 Commerce Parkway West Dr *Web:* acutabovelawnserviceinc.com	Greenwood	IN	46143	317-885-1500		422
A D Morgan Corp, The 716 N Renellie Dr *Web:* www.admorgan.com	Tampa	FL	33609	813-832-3033	831-9860	186
A Daigger & Company Inc 620 Lakeview Pkwy. **Fax Area Code:* 800 ■ *TF:* 800-621-7193 ■ *Web:* www.daigger.com	Vernon Hills	IL	60061	847-816-5060	320-7200*	603
A Dr. Jot LLC 2601 W Cary St *Web:* acaciarestaurant.com	Richmond	VA	23220	804-562-0138		671
A Duchini Inc 2550 McKinley Ave *TF:* 800-937-7317 ■ *Web:* www.duchini.com	Erie	PA	16503	814-456-7027		183
A Duda & Sons Inc 1200 Duda Trl *Web:* www.duda.com	Oviedo	FL	32765	407-365-2111	365-2147	10-11
A Epstein & Sons International Inc 600 W Fulton St *Web:* www.epsteinglobal.com	Chicago	IL	60661	312-454-9100		261
A F A Industries 140 E Pond Dr *Web:* www.afaindustries.com	Romeo	MI	48065	586-752-2900		326
A F K Corp 300 Pacific St *Web:* www.afkfoundry.com	Ripon	WI	54971	920-748-2265		492
A Few of My Favorite Things Flower & Gift Shop 110 S 7th St *Web:* www.afewofmyfavoritethingswyoming.com	Wyoming	IL	61491	309-695-9966		292
A Finkl & Sons Co 1355 E 93rd St *Web:* www.finkl.com	Chicago	IL	60614	773-975-2510	348-5347	723
A Fish Called Avalon 700 Ocean Dr *Web:* www.afishcalledavalon.com	Miami Beach	FL	33139	305-532-1727		671
A G Adjustments Ltd 740 Walt Whitman Rd *Web:* www.agaltd.com	Melville	NY	11747	631-425-8800		160
A G Equipment Company Inc 3401 W Albany *Web:* www.agequipmentcompany.com	Broken Arrow	OK	74012	918-250-7386		172
A G H Industries Inc 1103 Stanley Dr *Web:* www.aghindustries.com	Euless	TX	76040	817-284-1742	284-1745	22
A G Miller Company Inc 53 Batavia St *Web:* www.agmiller.com	Springfield	MA	01109	413-732-9297	734-1236	192
A G Wassenaar Inc 2180 S Ivanhoe St Ste 5 *Web:* agwco.com	Denver	CO	80222	303-759-8100		196
A Glimmer of Hope 3600 N Capital of Texas Hwy Bldg B Ste 330 *Web:* glimmer.org	Austin	TX	78746	512-328-9944	328-8872	305
A Grooming Place 255 SW Pacific Blvd *Web:* www.agroomingplace.com	Albany	OR	97321	541-926-0698		167-3
A H Belo Corp 1954 Commerce St PO Box 224866 *NYSE:* AHC ■ *TF:* 800-230-1074 ■ *Web:* www.ahbelo.com	Dallas	TX	75201	214-977-8200	977-8201	580
A H Lundberg Associates Inc 13201 Bel Red Rd *Web:* lundbergllc.com	Bellevue	WA	98005	425-283-5070		261
A H Stock Manufacturing Corp 8402 Center Rd *Web:* www.ahstockmfg.com	Newton	WI	53063	920-726-4211	726-4214	567
A J Blosenski Inc 1600 Chestnut Tree Rd *Web:* www.ajblosenski.com	Honey Brook	PA	19344	610-942-2707		638
A J Johns Inc 3225 Anniston Rd *Web:* www.ajjohns.com	Jacksonville	FL	32246	904-641-2055	641-2102	189-11
A J Sackett & Sons Co, The 1701 S Highland Ave *Web:* www.sackettwaconia.com	Baltimore	MD	21224	410-276-4466		480
A L Schutzman Company Inc N21 W23560 Ridge View Pkwy W *TF:* 800-284-6887 ■ *Web:* www.alschutzman.com	Waukesha	WI	53188	800-284-6887		805
A La Cart Inc 1480 Old Deerfield Rd *Web:* www.alacarteinc.com	Highland Park	IL	60035	847-256-4102	256-0387	806
A La Lucia 315 Madison St *Web:* www.alalucia.com	Alexandria	VA	22314	703-836-5123		671
A La Lucie 159 N Limestone St *Web:* www.alalucie.com	Lexington	KY	40507	859-252-5277		671
A Larry Ross Communications Inc 4300 Marsh Ridge Rd Ste 114 *Web:* alarryross.com	Carrollton	TX	75010	972-267-1111		636
A Lava & Son Co 4800 S Kilbourn Ave *TF:* 800-777-5282 ■ *Web:* www.alavason.com	Chicago	IL	60632	773-254-2800		320
A M C Colorgrafix Inc 2085 Peck Rd *Web:* www.amc-color.com	El Monte	CA	91733	626-575-1788	575-1688	502
A M Solutions 100 Interstate Blvd *TF:* 800-410-6245 ■ *Web:* www.amsolutionswi.com	Edgerton	WI	53534	800-410-6245		5
A Matter of Fax 105 Harrison Ave. *TF:* 800-433-3329 ■ *Web:* www.amatteroffax.com	Harrison	NJ	07029	973-482-3700		179
A Media Web & Graphic Design 2200 Adeline St Ste 320 *Web:* www.amedianysf.com	Oakland	CA	94607	510-763-5442		344
A Meyers & Sons Corp 221 Arleigh Rd	New York	NY	11363	212-279-6632		594
A Morton Thomas & Associates Inc 800 King Farm Blvd 4th Fl *Web:* amtengineering.com	Rockville	MD	20850	301-881-2545		186
A N Culbertson & Company Inc 1 Boars Head Pointe Ste 101 *Web:* anculbertson.com	Charlottesville	VA	22903	434-972-7766		401
A New Concept Optical & Eyecare Inc 2528 Dell Range Blvd *Web:* anceyecare.com	Cheyenne	WY	82009	307-634-2503	634-4878	543
A New Path 2527 Doubletree Rd *Web:* www.anewpath.org	Spring Valley	CA	91978	619-670-1184		787
A Noble Grille 380 Knollwood St *Web:* roosterskitchen.com	Winston-Salem	NC	27103	336-777-8477		671
A Nonini Winery Inc 2640 N Dickenson Ave *Web:* noniniwines.com	Fresno	CA	93723	559-275-1936		50-7
A One Staffing LLC 3639 New Getwell Rd Ste 1 *Web:* www.aonestaffing.com	Memphis	TN	38118	901-367-5757	367-7577	260
A Partner in Technology 105 Dresden Ave. *TF:* 877-582-0888 ■ *Web:* www.apitechnology.com	Gardiner	ME	04345	207-582-0888		180
A Pineywoods Hospice Inc 103 B Carriage Dr *TF:* 888-729-1831 ■ *Web:* apineywoods.com	Lufkin	TX	75904	936-634-1617		450
A Plus Benefits Inc 395 W 600 N *TF:* 800-748-5102 ■ *Web:* www.helpside.com	Lindon	UT	84042	801-443-1090		390
A Plus Designs Incorporated & Outfitters Plus Outlet Store 56988 635th St *Web:* www.aplusdesignsinc.com	Atlantic	IA	50022	712-243-4379		687
A Plus Family Care LLC 9514 Console Dr Ste 200	San Antonio	TX	78229	210-342-2819		363
A Plus International Inc 5138 Eucalyptus Ave. *TF:* 800-762-1123 ■ *Web:* www.aplusgroup.net	Chino	CA	91710	909-591-5168	591-0359	475
A Plus Letter Service Inc 200 Syracuse Ct *Web:* www.aplusletter.com	Lakewood	NJ	08701	732-905-2010		5
A R Mays Construction Inc 6900 E Indian School Rd Ste 200 *Web:* www.armays.com	Scottsdale	AZ	85251	480-850-6900		186
A Rifkin Co 1400 Sans Souci Pkwy *TF:* 800-458-7300 ■ *Web:* arifkin.com	Wilkes-Barre	PA	18706	570-825-9551	825-5282	67
A Ruiz Construction Company & Associates Inc 1601 Cortland Ave *Web:* aruizconstruction.com	San Francisco	CA	94110	415-647-4010	285-9243	186
A S E Industries Inc 23850 Pinewood *Web:* www.aseind.com	Warren	MI	48091	586-754-7480	758-7460	207
A Schulman Inc 3550 W Market St *NASDAQ:* SHLM ■ *Web:* shlm-elianprofile.com	Akron	OH	44333	330-666-3751		605-2
A Smith & Company Productions 4130 Cahuenga Blvd Ste 315 *Web:* www.asmithco.com	Toluca Lake	CA	91602	818-432-2900	432-8216	738
A Smith Bowman Distillery 1 Bowman Dr *Web:* www.asmithbowman.com	Fredericksburg	VA	22408	540-373-4555		80-1
A Star Electric Co 200 Seegers Ave *Web:* www.astareg.com	Elk Grove Village	IL	60007	847-439-4122		625
A Stucki Co 2600 Neville Rd *TF:* 888-266-6630 ■ *Web:* www.stucki.com	Pittsburgh	PA	15225	412-771-7300	771-7308	650

	Phone	Fax	Class
A T Klemens (ATK) 814 12th St N, Great Falls MT 59401 *Web:* www.atklemens.com	406-452-9541		610
A T R Sales Inc 41 Talbot Rd, Northborough MA 01532 *Web:* www.atrsales.com	508-393-8529		814
A T Secure Net 2001 Columbus St, Bakersfield CA 93305 *Web:* atsecure.net	661-872-4807	872-3316	225
A Taste of New York Inc 10 Roberta Ln, Syosset NY 11791 *Web:* www.tasteofny.com	516-677-0239		742
A Tavola 2148 W Chicago Ave, Chicago IL 60622 *Web:* www.atavolachi.com	773-276-7567		671
A Teichert & Son Inc 3500 American River Dr, Sacramento CA 95864 *Web:* www.teichert.com	916-484-3011		182
A to B Realty 1975 Hamilton Ave Ste 9, San Jose CA 95125 *Web:* www.atobrealty.com	408-626-4800	626-9384	652
A to Z Logos 3947 Catamarca Dr, San Diego CA 92124 *Web:* a2zlogos.espwebsite.com	858-715-4775		475
A to Z Vet Supply 9876 Hwy 22, Dresden TN 38225 *TF:* 800-979-2869 ■ *Web:* www.atozvetsupply.com	800-979-2869	979-2870	45
A Very Private Eye Inc 3936 S Semoran Blvd Ste 487, Orlando FL 32822 **Fax Area Code:* 866 ■ *Web:* www.averyprivateeye.com	407-273-6646	687-8880*	400
A W North Carolina Inc 4112 Old Oxford Hwy, Durham NC 27712 *Web:* www.aw-nc.com	919-479-6400		247
A William Roberts Jr & Associates Inc 234 Seven Farms Dr Ste 210, Charleston SC 29492 *TF:* 800-743-3376	843-722-8414		768
A Word with You Press 310 E A St Ste B, Moscow ID 83843 *Web:* awordwithyoupress.com	760-500-5409		49-19
A Y R Consulting Group 3708 Rodale Way Ste 200, Dallas TX 75287 *Web:* ayrconsulting.com	972-820-8400		194
A Yankee Line 370 W First St, Boston MA 02127 *TF:* 800-942-8890 ■ *Web:* yankeeline.us	617-268-8890	268-6960	107
A Zahner Sheet Metal Company Inc 1400 E Ninth St, Kansas City MO 64106 *Web:* www.azahner.com	816-474-8882	474-7994	189-12
A Zerega's Sons Inc PO Box 241, Fair Lawn NJ 07410 *Web:* www.zerega.com	201-797-1400	797-0148	296-31
A'Gaci LLC 12460 Network Blvd Ste 106, San Antonio TX 78249 *TF:* 866-265-3036 ■ *Web:* www.agacistore.com	210-694-8889		157-6
A'viands LLC 767 Eustis St Ste 145, Saint Paul MN 55114 *Web:* aviands.com	651-631-0940	631-0941	299
A+ Arts Academies 270 S Napoleon Ave, Columbus OH 43213 *Web:* www.phalenacademies.org	614-338-0767		463
A+ Micro Inc PO Box 94746, Pasadena CA 91109 *Web:* www.aplusmicro.com	626-353-7216		178-1
A+ Pet Grooming Academy 49 Maine St PO Box 1330, New Gloucester ME 04260 *Web:* www.apluspetgroomingacademy.com	207-657-3399		167-3
A+ School Apparel 401 Knoss Ave, Star City AR 71667 **Fax Area Code:* 888 ■ *TF:* 800-227-3215 ■ *Web:* www.schoolapparel.com	800-227-3215	628-9020*	155-19
A. B. Data Ltd 600 A B Data Dr, Milwaukee WI 53217 *Web:* abdata.com	414-961-6400		260
A. C. Coy Co 395 Valley Brook Rd, Canonsburg PA 15317 *TF:* 800-784-5773 ■ *Web:* www.accoy.com	724-820-1820		194
A. C. Schultes of Maryland Inc 8221 Cloverleaf Dr, Millersville MD 21108 *Web:* www.acschultes.com	410-841-6710	841-6711	393
A. D. D. Marketing Inc 6600 Lexington Ave, Los Angeles CA 90038 *Web:* www.addmarketing.com	323-790-0500		195
A. D. Marble 2200 Renaissance Blvd Ste 260, King of Prussia PA 19406 *Web:* admarble.com	484-533-2500	533-2599	463
A. D. Susman & Associates Inc 3033 Chimney Rock Rd Ste 690, Houston TX 77056 *Web:* www.adsusman.com	713-668-7998		260
A. Dicesare Associates PC 690 Clinton Ave, Bridgeport CT 06604 *Web:* adicesarepc.com	203-696-0444		261
A. E. Litho Offset Printers Inc 450 Broad St, Beverly NJ 08010 *Web:* aelitho.com	609-239-0700		627
A. F. Lorts Company Inc 15836 W Eddie Albert Way, Goodyear AZ 85338 *Web:* www.lorts.com	623-936-1437	936-8839	319-2
A. George Diack Inc 1250 S Johnson Dr, City of Industry CA 91745 *Web:* www.showcasesbydiack.com	626-961-2491	968-0377	286
A. J. Edmond Co 1530 W 16th St, Long Beach CA 90813 *Web:* ajedmondco.com	562-437-1802		108
A. M. Ortega Construction Inc 10125 Ch Rd, Lakeside CA 92040 *Web:* www.amortega.com	619-390-1988	390-1941	189-4
A. Paolino & Co 401 Broadway, Providence RI 02909 *Web:* apaolinotax.com	401-272-7217		2
A. Perri Farms Inc 865 Marconi Ave, Ronkonkoma NY 11779 *Web:* www.perrifarms.com	631-471-3060		293
A. R. M. Solutions Inc PO Box 2929, Camarillo CA 93011 *TF:* 888-772-6468 ■ *Web:* www.armsolutions.com	888-772-6468		160
A. W. G. Dewar Inc 4 Batterymarch Pk, Quincy MA 02169 *Web:* www.tuitionrefundplan.com	617-774-1555	774-1715	390
A. W. Lookup Corp 500 Fayette St Ste 100, Conshohocken PA 19428 *Web:* awlookup.com	610-825-2600		261
A.C. Graphics Inc 1056 E 24th St NW 78th St, Hialeah FL 33013 *Web:* www.acgraphics.com	305-691-3778		627
A.C. Supply PO Box 1523, Saint Charles MO 63302 *TF:* 800-842-7859 ■ *Web:* www.acsupplyco.com	800-842-7859	466-4354	459
A.C. White Relocations 1775 Founders Pkwy, Alpharetta GA 30009 *Web:* atlantamovingcorp.com	770-325-9025		685

	Phone	Fax	Class
A.C.T. Home Care Inc 1075 Gaines School Rd, Athens GA 30605 *Web:* acthomecare.com	706-559-4432		363
A.C.T. Home Health Inc 4401 N I-35 Ste 208, Denton TX 76207 *Web:* healthcare4ppl.com	940-566-3700		363
A.E. Moore Janitorial Inc 262 W State St, Millsboro DE 19966 *TF:* 800-787-7448 ■ *Web:* www.aemoorejanitorial.com	302-934-7055	934-6661	146
A.E.R. Supply Inc 2301 Nasa Pky, Seabrook TX 77586 *TF:* 800-767-7606 ■ *Web:* www.aersupply.com	281-474-3276	474-2714	770
A.E.S.O.P.S. Inc 301 Dayton St, Dalton GA 30720 *TF:* 800-235-8817 ■ *Web:* www.aesops.com	706-226-0628	278-6562	202
A.F. Macedo Insurance Agency Inc 646 Broadway, Raynham MA 02767 *Web:* afmacedoins.com	508-977-0000		390
A.G. Ferrari Foods 2000 N Loop Rd, Alameda CA 94502 *TF:* 877-878-2783 ■ *Web:* agferrari.com	510-351-5520	351-2672	345
A.G. Scientific Inc 6450 Lusk Blvd Ste E102, San Diego CA 92121 *TF:* 877-452-9925 ■ *Web:* www.agscientific.com	858-452-9925	452-9926	146
A.I. solutions Inc 4500 Forbes Blvd Ste 300, Lanham MD 20706 *Web:* ai-solutions.com	301-306-1756		194
A.I.R. Gallery 155 Plymouth St, Brooklyn NY 11201 *Web:* www.airgallery.org	212-255-6651		590
A.J. Antunes & Co 180 Kehoe Blvd, Carol Stream IL 60188 *Web:* antunes.com	630-784-1000		253
A.J. Billig & Company LLC 6500 Falls Rd, Baltimore MD 21209 *Web:* ajbillig.com	410-296-8440		366
A.J. Catagnus Inc 1299 W James St, Norristown PA 19401 *Web:* ajcatagnus.com	610-277-2727		660
A.J. Cornell Publications 18-74 Corporal Kennedy St, Bayside NY 11360 *Web:* www.vocabularybuilders.com	718-423-4082		637-2
A.J. Leblanc Heating Inc 45 S River Rd, Bedford NH 03110 *Web:* leblanchvac.com	603-623-0412	624-1981	316
A.J. Rod Company Ltd 5011 Navigation Blvd, Houston TX 77011 *TF:* 800-392-3714 ■ *Web:* www.ajrodco.com	713-921-6111	926-4704	385
A.J. Tuck Co 32 Tucks Rd, Brookfield CT 06804 *Web:* www.ajtuckco.com	203-775-1234		454
A.Johnson & Sons Florists 1738 Grand Ave, Saint Paul MN 55105 *TF:* 800-959-8010 ■ *Web:* www.jflorist.com	651-698-6000		292
A.K. Industries Inc 2055 Pidco Dr, Plymouth IN 46563 *Web:* www.akindustries.com	574-936-6022	936-5811	604
A.M. Express Inc 3000 29th Ave N, Escanaba MI 49829 *TF:* 800-548-9783 ■ *Web:* amexpressinc.com	800-548-9783		780
A.N. Nunes Agency Inc 549 Hope St PO Box 627, Bristol RI 02809 *Web:* nunesagency.com	401-253-5300	253-9485	390
A.N. Webber Inc 2150 US-45, Kankakee IL 60901 *Web:* www.anwebber.com	815-939-2235	935-6544	780
A.O.W. Associates Inc 30 Essex St, Albany NY 12206 *Web:* aowassoc.com	518-482-3400		186
A.P. Lee & Company Ltd PO Box 340292, Columbus OH 43234 *Web:* www.apleeco.com	614-798-1998		637-2
A.R. Harding Publishing Co 2878 E Main St, Columbus OH 43209 *Web:* www.furfishgame.com	614-231-9585		637-2
A.R. Sandri Inc 400 Chapman St, Greenfield MA 01301 *TF:* 800-628-1900 ■ *Web:* sandri.com	800-628-1900		579
A.R. Schmeidler and Company Inc 500 5th Ave 14th Fl, New York NY 10110 *Web:* www.arschmeidler.com	212-687-9800	687-1392	401
A.R. Young Company Inc 520 Dorman St, Indianapolis IN 46202 *TF:* 800-843-5312 ■ *Web:* www.aryoung.com	317-263-3800	263-3806	385
A.R.E. Manufacturing Inc 518 S Springbrook Rd, Newberg OR 97132 *Web:* www.aremanufacturing.com	503-538-0350	538-5148	454
A.S.G. Staffing Inc 508 W Boughton Rd, Bolingbrook IL 60440 *Web:* www.asgstaffing.com	630-378-9719	378-9729	193
A.S.P. Security Services 1450 Appleby Line Ste 200, Burlington ON L7L6V1 **Fax Area Code:* 416 ■ *TF:* 877-552-5535 ■ *Web:* www.security-asp.com	905-333-4242	481-1966*	693
A.T. Information Products Inc 575 Corporate Dr, Mahwah NJ 07430 *Web:* www.atip-usa.com	201-529-0202	529-5603	629
A.T. Still University of Health Sciences 800 W Jefferson St, Kirksville MO 63501 *TF:* 866-626-2878 ■ *Web:* www.atsu.edu	660-626-2121		162
A/E Graphics Inc 4075 N 124th St Ste A, Brookfield WI 53005 *Web:* aegraphics.com	262-781-7744		113
A/G (Assemblies of God) 1445 N Boonville Ave, Springfield MO 65802 *TF:* 800-641-4310 ■ *Web:* ag.org	417-862-2781		48-20
A-1 Action Nursing Care Inc 3508 Greencastle Rd, Burtonsville MD 20866 *Web:* a1actionnursingcare.com	301-890-7575		363
A-1 Concrete Leveling Inc 388 S Main St Ste 402, Akron OH 44311 *TF:* 888-675-3835 ■ *Web:* www.a1concrete.com	888-675-3835		189-3
A-1 Contract Staffing Inc 3829 Coconut Palm Dr, Tampa FL 33619 *Web:* www.a1hr.com	813-620-1661		631
A-1 Creative Packaging Corp 400 Industrial Blvd, Palmyra WI 53156 *Web:* www.a1creativepackaging.com	262-495-2151		88
A-1 Energy Audits 16047 Stoneham, Pflugerville TX 78660 *Web:* www.a1energyaudits.com	512-636-9728		652
A-1 Freeman Moving Group 2242 Manana Dr, Dallas TX 75220 *Web:* www.a-1freeman.com	972-885-6567		803-1

Name	Address	City	State	ZIP	Phone	Fax	Class	Notes
A-1 Healthcare Ctr	1205 N Melrose Dr Ste N	Vista	CA	92083	760-945-4700	945-0382	475	*Web:* www.a-1healthcarecenter.com
A-1 Healthcare Management	5011 Argosy Ave Ste 4	Huntington Beach	CA	92649	714-650-8519	650-8520	363	*Web:* a-1hm.com
A-1 Hospitality LLC	7809 W Quinault Ave	Kennewick	WA	99336	509-783-2164		377	*Web:* a1hospitalitygroup.com
A-1 Jays Machinery	2228 Oakland Rd	San Jose	CA	95131	408-262-1845	262-4561	454	*Web:* www.a1jays.com
A-1 Machine Inc	799 Sandstone Ave	Farmington	NM	87401	505-327-9572	326-2386	454	*Web:* www.a-1machineinc.com
A-1 Outdoor Power Inc	7630 Commerce St	Corcoran	MN	55340	763-420-2748	420-2448	351	*Web:* a1outdoorpower.com
A-1 Pioneer Moving and Storage	2001 Warm Springs Rd	Salt Lake City	UT	84116	801-997-9976		519	*TF:* 800-825-9664 ■ *Web:* www.a1pioneer.com
A-1 Production Inc	5809 E Leighty Rd	Kendallville	IN	46755	260-347-0960	347-4727	621	*Web:* www.a1production.com
A-1 Quilting Machine Inc	3232 Evans Rd Hwy 65 & Evans Rd	Springfield	MO	65804	417-883-6883	883-2883	36	*TF:* 800-566-4276 ■ *Web:* a1quiltingmachines.com
A1 Roof Trusses Limited Co	4451 St Lucie Blvd	Fort Pierce	FL	34946	772-409-1010		194	*Web:* www.a1truss.com
A1 Staffing & Recruiting Agency Inc	3000 United Founder Blvd Ste 230	Oklahoma City	OK	73112	405-787-7600		260	*TF:* 800-233-1261 ■ *Web:* www.a1staffingok.com
A-1 Telecom Inc	3030 S 11th St	Niles	MI	49120	269-683-3870	683-0937	38	*TF:* 800-238-1786 ■ *Web:* www.a1telecom.com
A-1 Tool Corp	1425 Armitage Ave	Melrose Park	IL	60160	708-345-5000	345-2089	697	*Web:* www.a1toolco.com
A123 Systems Inc	200 W St	Waltham	MA	02451	617-778-5700	924-8910	74	*Web:* www.a123systems.com
A2 Global Electronics + Solutions	2600 118th Ave N	Saint Petersburg	FL	33716	727-573-0000	573-0606	240	*TF:* 800-767-2637 ■ *Web:* www.a2globalelectronics.com
A2 Hosting Inc	PO Box 2998	Ann Arbor	MI	48106	734-222-4678	527-6565	225	*TF:* 888-546-8946 ■ *Web:* www.a2hosting.com
A2 Inc	245 W 29th St Ste 1601	New York	NY	10001	212-807-8772		187	*Web:* www.a2inc.com
A2F-Consulting LLC	7220 Wisconsin Ave Ste 210	Bethesda	MD	20814	301-907-9400	907-9477	463	*Web:* www.a2f-c.com
A2LA (American Association for Laboratory Accreditation)	5202 Presidents Ct Ste 220	Frederick	MD	21703	301-644-3248	454-9449*	49-19	**Fax Area Code:* 240 ■ *Web:* www.a2la.org
A2Z Field Services LLC	7450 Industrial Pkwy Ste 105	Plain City	OH	43064	614-873-0211		365	*TF:* 800-713-2001 ■ *Web:* www.a2zfieldservices.com
A2Z Global LLC	7905 Browning Rd Ste 112B	Pennsauken Township	NJ	08109	856-910-0300		768	*Web:* a2zglobal.com
A2Z Science & Nature Store	57 King St	Northampton	MA	01060	413-586-1611		761	*Web:* a2zscience.com
A3 Artists Agency	750 N San Vicente Blvd E Twr 11th Fl	Los Angeles	CA	90069	310-859-0625		708	*Web:* www.a3artistsagency.com
A3 Communications Inc	1038 Kinley Rd Bldg B	Irmo	SC	29063	888-809-1473		196	*TF:* 888-809-1473 ■ *Web:* www.a3communications.com
A-588 & A-572 Steel Co, The	133 Sebago Lake Dr	Sewickley	PA	15143	412-366-1980		492	*Web:* www.a588a572steel.com
AA (Alcoholics Anonymous)	475 Riverside Dr 11th Fl	New York	NY	10115	212-870-3400	870-3003	48-21	*TF:* 800-437-3584 ■ *Web:* www.aa.org
A&A (Anderson & Anderson)	2300 Westridge Rd	Los Angeles	CA	90049	310-476-0908	476-6789	194	*Web:* www.andersonservices.com
AA Consulting Inc	9 Locust St	Douglas	MA	01516	774-280-9036		463	*Web:* www.aa-consulting-inc.com
AA Importing Company Inc	7700 Hall St	Saint Louis	MO	63147	314-383-8800		361	*TF:* 800-325-0602 ■ *Web:* www.aaimporting.com
AA Office Equipment Company Inc	1278 W Winton Ave	Hayward	CA	94545	510-782-6110	351-9078	321	*Web:* www.aaoffice.com
AA Precisioneering Inc	247 Race St	Meadville	PA	16335	814-724-6668	337-5961	757	*Web:* www.aaprecisioneering.com
AA Temps Inc	7002 Little River Tpke	Annandale	VA	22003	703-642-9050		194	*TF:* 800-901-8367 ■ *Web:* www.ardelle.com
AA Wheel & Truck Supply Inc	717 E 16th Ave	Kansas City	MO	64116	816-221-9556		61	*TF:* 800-688-2953 ■ *Web:* aawheel.com
AAA (American Academy of Audiology)	11730 Plaza America Dr Ste 300	Reston	VA	20190	703-226-1032	790-8631	49-8	*TF:* 800-222-2336 ■ *Web:* audiology.org
AAA (American Automobile Association Inc)	321 Whittington Pkwy	Louisville	KY	40222	502-425-7885		53	*Web:* www.aaa.com
AAA (American Angus Assn)	3201 Frederick Ave	Saint Joseph	MO	64506	816-383-5100	233-9703	48-2	*TF:* 800-821-5478 ■ *Web:* www.angus.org
AAA (American Anthropological Assn)	2300 Clarendon Blvd Ste 1301	Arlington	VA	22201	703-528-1902	528-3546	49-5	*Web:* www.americananthro.org
AAA (American Arbitration Association Inc)	1633 Broadway 10th Fl	New York	NY	10019	212-716-5800		41	*TF:* 800-778-7879 ■ *Web:* www.adr.org
AAA (Appraisers Association of America)	386 Park Ave S Ste 2000	New York	NY	10016	212-889-5404	889-5503	49-12	*Web:* www.appraisersassociation.org
AAA Carolinas	6600 AAA Dr	Charlotte	NC	28212	877-282-3682		53	*TF:* 877-282-3682 ■ *Web:* locator.carolinas.aaa.com
AAA Chicago Motor Club	975 Meridian Lake Dr	Aurora	IL	60504	866-968-7222	499-8200*	53	**Fax Area Code:* 630 ■ *TF:* 866-968-7222 ■ *Web:* chicago.aaa.com
AAA Collections Inc	3500 S First Ave Cir	Sioux Falls	SD	57105	605-339-1333	335-3832	160	*TF:* 877-215-3456 ■ *Web:* www.aaa-coll.com
AAA Colorado	4100 E Arkansas Ave	Denver	CO	80222	303-753-8800		53	*TF:* 866-625-3601 ■ *Web:* www.colorado.aaa.com
AAA Concrete Products	1224 E Broad Ave PO Box 737	Albany	GA	31705	229-436-4626	436-5460	182	*Web:* www.aaaconcrete.biz
AAA Cooper Transportation	1751 Kinsey Rd	Dothan	AL	36303	334-793-2284		780	*TF:* 800-633-7571 ■ *Web:* www.aaacooper.com
AAA Digital Reprographics	5706 New Peachtree Rd	Chamblee	GA	30341	770-451-7861		174	*Web:* www.aaadi.com
AAA Environmental Inc	2036 Chesnee Hwy	Spartanburg	SC	29303	864-582-1222		667	*TF:* 888-296-3803 ■ *Web:* www.aaaenvironmental.com
AAA Financial Corp	8811 Miralago Way Ste 1647	Parkland	FL	33076	954-344-2530		509	*Web:* aaafinancial.com
AAA Flag & Banner Manufacturing Co	8937 National Blvd	Los Angeles	CA	90034	310-836-3200	280-1061	287	*TF:* 855-836-3200 ■ *Web:* www.aaaflag.com
AAA Glass	7500 Jack Newell Blvd S	Fort Worth	TX	76118	817-924-4444		362	*Web:* www.aaa-glass.com
AAA Hawaii	1130 N Nimitz Hwy Ste A-170	Honolulu	HI	96817	877-440-6943		53	*TF:* 800-736-2886 ■ *Web:* www.hawaii.aaa.com
AAA Hudson Valley	618 Delaware Ave	Albany	NY	12209	518-426-1000	426-1595	53	*Web:* www.hudsonvalley.aaa.com
AAA Life Insurance Co	17900 N Laurel Park Dr	Livonia	MI	48152	800-624-1662	591-6602*	796	**Fax Area Code:* 734 ■ *TF:* 800-624-1662 ■ *Web:* www.aaalife.com
AAA Manufacturing Inc	5055 Convair Dr	Carson City	NV	89706	775-883-6901		757	*Web:* irdjigs.com
AAA Michigan	1 Auto Club Dr	Dearborn	MI	48126	800-222-6424		53	*TF:* 800-222-6424 ■ *Web:* www.michigan.aaa.com
AAA Minneapolis	7151 France Ave S	Minneapolis	MN	55416	952-927-2600	927-2559	53	*Web:* www.minneapolis.aaa.com
AAA MountainWest	2100 11th Ave	Helena	MT	59601	406-447-8100	442-5671	53	*TF:* 800-332-6119 ■ *Web:* www.mountainwest.aaa.com
AAA Moving & Storage Inc	747 E Ship Creek Ave	Anchorage	AK	99501	888-927-3330		780	*TF:* 888-995-3331 ■ *Web:* www.alliedalaska.com
AAA Northampton County	3914 Hecktown Rd	Easton	PA	18045	610-258-2371		53	*Web:* www.northampton.aaa.com
AAA Northeast	110 Royal Little Dr	Providence	RI	02904	800-222-8252		53	*TF:* 800-222-8252 ■ *Web:* northeast.aaa.com
AAA Northern New England	68 Marginal Way	Portland	ME	04104	207-780-6950		53	*Web:* www.northernnewengland.aaa.com
AAA of Minnesota & Iowa	600 W Travelers Trl	Burnsville	MN	55337	800-222-1333		78	*TF:* 800-222-1333 ■ *Web:* mn-ia.aaa.com
AAA Ohio Auto Club	90 E Wilson Bridge Rd	Worthington	OH	43085	614-431-7901		53	*TF:* 888-222-6446 ■ *Web:* ohio.aaa.com
AAA Oklahoma	2121 E 15th St	Tulsa	OK	74104	918-748-1000		53	*TF:* 800-222-2582 ■ *Web:* www.ok.aaa.com
AAA Pallet & Lumber Co	3401 W Harrison St	Phoenix	AZ	85009	602-278-1450	278-3358	191-3	*TF:* 800-289-4840 ■ *Web:* www.aaapalletco.com
AAA Properties	330 W 5th St PO Box 4724	Chico	CA	95928	530-895-3500		379	*Web:* aaapropertieschico.com
AAA Refrigeration Service Inc	1804 Nereid Ave	Bronx	NY	10466	718-324-2231	994-6867	610	*Web:* www.aaarefrig.com
AAA Security	180 Nature Pkwy	Winnipeg	MB	R3P0X7	204-949-0078		693	*TF:* 866-949-0078 ■ *Web:* www.aaasecure.ca
AAA Southern Pennsylvania	2840 E Blvd	York	PA	17402	800-222-1469		53	*TF:* 800-222-1469 ■ *Web:* www.southpa.aaa.com
AAA Standard Services Inc	4117 S Ave	Toledo	OH	43615	419-535-0274		104	*Web:* aaastandardservices.com
AAA Western & Central New York	100 International Dr	Williamsville	NY	14221	716-630-3799	633-4439	53	*TF:* 800-836-2582 ■ *Web:* westerncentralny.aaa.com
AAA Wisconsin	8401 Excelsior Dr	Madison	WI	53717	608-836-6555		53	*Web:* newsroom.aaa.com
AAAA (American Association of Adv Agencies)	1065 Avenue of the Americas 16th Fl	New York	NY	10018	212-682-2500	682-8391	49-18	*Web:* www.aaaa.org
AAAA (Army Aviation Association of America)	593 Main St	Monroe	CT	06468	203-268-2450	268-5870	48-19	*Web:* www.quad-a.org
AAAA Benefits	11020 David Taylor Dr Ste 305	Charlotte	NC	28262	704-594-6270	594-6290	138	*Web:* www.aaaabenefits.com
AAAAI (American Academy of Allergy Asthma & Immunology)	555 E Wells St Ste 1100	Milwaukee	WI	53202	414-272-6071		49-8	*Web:* www.aaaai.org
AAAASF (American Association for Accreditation of Ambulatory Surgery Facilities Inc)	5101 Washington St Ste 2F PO Box 9500	Gurnee	IL	60031	847-775-1985		48-1	*TF:* 888-545-5222 ■ *Web:* www.aaaasf.org
AAACCVB (Annapolis & Anne Arundel County Conference & Visitors Bureau)	26 West St	Annapolis	MD	21401	410-280-0445	263-9591	206	*TF:* 888-302-2852 ■ *Web:* www.visitannapolis.org
AAACE (American Association for Adult & Continuing Education)	1827 Powers Ferry Rd Bldg 14 Ste 100	Atlanta	GA	30339	678-271-4319	393-9506*	49-5	**Fax Area Code:* 404 ■ *Web:* www.aaace.org
AAAE (American Association of Airport Executives)	601 Madison St	Alexandria	VA	22314	703-824-0500	820-1395	49-21	*Web:* www.aaae.org

Phone | Fax | Class

AAAHC (Accreditation Association for Ambulatory Health Care)
5250 Old Orchard Rd Ste 200 ... Skokie IL 60077 847-853-6060 853-9028 48-1
Web: www.aaahc.org

AAAI (Association for the Advancement of Artificial Intelligence)
445 Burgess Dr Ste 100 ... Menlo Park CA 94025 650-328-3123 321-4457 48-9
TF: 800-548-4664 ■ *Web:* www.aaai.org

AAAOM (American Association of Acupunture & Oriental Medicine)
PO Box 162340 ... Sacramento CA 95816 916-443-4770 48-17
TF: 866-455-7999 ■ *Web:* www.aaaomonline.org

AAAP (American Academy of Addiction Psychiatry)
400 Massasoit Ave 2nd Fl Ste 307 ... East Providence RI 02914 401-524-3076 272-0922 49-15
TF: 800-263-6317 ■ *Web:* www.aaap.org

AAAS (American Association for the Advancement of Science)
1200 New York Ave NW ... Washington DC 20005 202-326-6400 49-19
Web: www.aaas.org

AAASPD (Pacific Division of the American Association for the Advancement of Science)
Dept. of Biology
Southern Oregon University 1250 Siskiyou Blvd ... Ashland OR 97520 541-552-6869 552-8457 49-19
Web: associations.sou.edu

AAB (American Association of Bioanalysts)
906 Olive St Ste 1200 ... Saint Louis MO 63101 314-241-1445 241-1449 49-8
TF: 800-457-3332 ■ *Web:* www.aab.org

AAB Style Inc
6851 W Sunrise Blvd Ste 170 ... Plantation FL 33313 954-327-4262 327-4266 411
Web: www.aabstyle.com

Aabaco Plastics Inc
9520 Midwest Ave ... Garfield Heights OH 44125 216-663-9494 663-9475 66
Web: www.aabacoplastics.com

AABBA (Anchorage Alaska Bed & Breakfast Assn)
PO Box 242623 ... Anchorage AK 99524 907-272-5909 376
Web: www.anchorage-bnb.com

Aabbitt Adhesives Inc 2403 N Oakley ... Chicago IL 60647 800-222-2488 3
TF: 800-222-2488 ■ *Web:* www.aabbitt.com

AABBN (Alexandria & Arlington Bed & Breakfast Networks)
4938 Hampden Ln Ste 164 ... Bethesda MD 20814 703-549-3415 517-9179* 376
**Fax Area Code:* 202 ■ *TF:* 888-549-3415 ■ *Web:* www.aabbn.com

AABC (American Amateur Baseball Congress)
100 W Broadway ... Farmington NM 87401 505-327-3120 48-22
Web: www.aabc.us

AABC (Association for Biblical Higher Education)
5850 T G Lee Blvd Ste 130 ... Orlando FL 32822 407-207-0808 48-1
TF: 800-525-1611 ■ *Web:* www.abhe.org

AABP (American Association of Bovine Practitioners)
1130 E Main St Ste 302 ... Ashland OH 44805 419-496-0685 496-0697 48-2
Web: www.aabp.org

AABR (Association for the Advancement of the Blind & Retarded)
1508 College Pt Blvd ... College Point NY 11356 718-321-3800 48-17
Web: www.aabr.org

AAC (Arlington Arts Ctr)
3550 Wilson Blvd ... Arlington VA 22201 703-248-6800 248-6849 50-2
Web: arlingtonartscenter.org

AAC (American Adoption Congress)
PO Box 42730 ... Washington DC 20015 202-483-3399 48-6
Web: americanadoptioncongress.org

AAC Contracting Inc 175 Humboldt St ... Rochester NY 14610 585-527-8000 667
Web: www.aac-contracting.com

AACA (Antique Automobile Club of America)
501 W Governor Rd PO Box 417 ... Hershey PA 17033 717-534-1910 534-9101 48-18
TF: 800-452-9910 ■ *Web:* aaca.org

AACA Parts & Supplies
3227 Military Pkwy Ste 244 ... Mesquite TX 75149 972-285-0263 289-0760 35
Web: www.aacapartsandsupplies.com

AACAP (American Academy of Child & Adolescent Psychiatry)
3615 Wisconsin Ave NW ... Washington DC 20016 202-966-7300 966-2891 49-15
TF: 800-333-7636 ■ *Web:* www.aacap.org

AACC (Australian American Chamber of Commerce)
PO Box 218219 ... Houston TX 77218 713-527-9688 600-2050* 138
**Fax Area Code:* 978 ■ *Web:* www.aacc-texas.org

AACC (American Association for Clinical Chemistry Inc)
1850 K St NW Ste 625 ... Washington DC 20006 202-857-0717 887-5093 49-19
TF: 800-892-1400 ■ *Web:* www.aacc.org

AACC (American Association of Cereal Chemists Inc)
3340 Pilot Knob Rd ... Saint Paul MN 55121 651-454-7250 454-0766 49-6
Web: www.aaccnet.org

AACC (American Association of Community Colleges)
1 Dupont Cir NW Ste 410 ... Washington DC 20036 202-728-0200 833-2467 49-5
Web: www.aacc.nche.edu

AACC (Atchison Area Chamber of Commerce)
200 S 10th St ... Atchison KS 66002 913-367-2427 367-2485 139
TF: 800-234-1854 ■ *Web:* www.atchisonkansas.net

AACC (Athens Area Chamber of Commerce)
246 W Hancock Ave ... Athens GA 30601 706-549-6800 549-5636 139
Web: www.athenschamber.net

A-Account Plumbing & Drain Cleaning LLC
5128 S E Ave ... Oklahoma City OK 73129 405-672-5754 610

AACD (American Academy of Cosmetic Dentistry)
402 W Wilson St ... Madison WI 53703 608-222-8583 222-9540 49-8
TF: 800-543-9220 ■ *Web:* www.aacd.com

AACE (American Association of Clinical Endocrinologists)
245 Riverside Ave Ste 200 ... Jacksonville FL 32202 904-353-7878 353-8185 49-8
TF: 800-393-2223 ■ *Web:* www.aace.com

AACE (Association for the Advancement of Computing in Education)
PO Box 1545 ... Chesapeake VA 23327 757-366-5606 997-8760* 49-5
**Fax Area Code:* 703 ■ *Web:* www.aace.org

AACE International - Association for the Advancement of Cost Engineering
1265 Suncrest Towne Centre Dr ... Morgantown WV 26505 304-296-8444 291-5728 49-1
Web: web.aacei.org

AACI (American Association of Crop Insurers)
1201 Pennsylvania Ave NW Ste 800 ... Washington DC 20004 202-659-8201 49-9
Web: www.aacinsurers.com

AACN (American Association of Critical-Care Nurses)
101 Columbia ... Aliso Viejo CA 92656 949-362-2000 362-2020 49-8
TF: 800-809-2273 ■ *Web:* www.aacn.org

AACOM (American Association of Colleges of Osteopathic Medicine)
7700 Old Georgetown Rd Ste 250 ... Bethesda MD 20814 301-968-4100 968-4101 49-8
TF: 800-356-7836 ■ *Web:* www.aacom.org

Aacom Inc 201 Stuyvesant Ave ... Lyndhurst NJ 07071 201-438-2244 196
TF: 800-273-3719 ■ *Web:* www.aacomnj.com

AACP (Asian American Curriculum Project)
529 E 3rd Ave ... San Mateo CA 94401 650-375-8286 375-8797 48-6
Web: www.asianamericanbooks.com

AACPDM (American Academy for Cerebral Palsy & Developmental Medicine)
555 E Wells St Ste 1100 ... Milwaukee WI 53202 414-918-3014 276-2146 48-17
Web: www.aacpdm.org

AACPM (American Association of Colleges of Podiatric Medicine)
15850 Crabbs Branch Way Ste 320 ... Rockville MD 20855 301-948-9760 948-1928 49-8
Web: www.aacpm.org

AACR (American Association for Cancer Research)
615 Chestnut St 17th Fl ... Philadelphia PA 19106 215-440-9300 49-8
TF: 866-423-3965 ■ *Web:* www.aacr.org

AACRAO (American Association of Collegiate Registrars & Admissions Officers)
1108 16th St NW Ste 400 ... Washington DC 20036 202-293-9161 872-8857 49-5
TF: 800-222-4922 ■ *Web:* www.aacrao.org

AACS (American Academy of Cosmetic Surgery)
225 W Wacker Dr Ste 650 ... Chicago IL 60606 312-981-6760 265-2908 49-8
Web: www.cosmeticsurgery.org

AACSB Intl
777 S Harbour Island Blvd Ste 750 ... Tampa FL 33602 813-769-6500 769-6559 48-11
Web: www.aacsb.edu

AACSC (Apartment Association, California Southern Cities)
333 W Broadway St Ste 101 ... Long Beach CA 90802 562-426-8341 414
Web: aacsc.org

AACTE (American Association of Colleges for Teacher Education)
1307 New York Ave NW Ste 300 ... Washington DC 20005 202-293-2450 457-8095 49-5
Web: www.aacte.org

AAC&U (Association of American Colleges & Universities)
1818 R St NW ... Washington DC 20009 202-387-3760 265-9532 49-5
Web: www.aacu.org

AAD (American Academy of Dermatology)
9500 W Bryn Mawr Ave Ste 500 ... Rosemont IL 60018 888-462-3376 240-1859* 49-8
**Fax Area Code:* 847 ■ *TF:* 888-462-3376 ■ *Web:* www.aad.org

AADEP (American Academy of Disability Evaluating Physicians)
PO Box 1537 ... Elk Grove Village IL 60009 312-663-1171 663-1175 49-8
Web: www.iaime.org

AADFW Inc 1350 Westpark Way ... Euless TX 76040 817-540-0153 192
Web: www.aadfwinc.com

AADGP (American Academy of Dental Group Practice)
27W525 High Lake Rd Unit 539 ... Winfield IL 60190 602-381-1185 49-8
Web: www.aadgp.org

AADL (Ann Arbor District Library)
343 S Fifth Ave ... Ann Arbor MI 48104 734-327-4200 327-8309 434-3
Web: aadl.org

AADMM (American Association of Daily Money Managers)
174 Crestview Dr ... Bellefonte PA 16823 877-326-5991 355-2452* 49-2
**Fax Area Code:* 814 ■ *TF:* 877-326-5991 ■ *Web:* secure.aadmm.com

AADP (American Association of Drugless Practitioners)
2200 Market St Ste 803 ... Galveston TX 77550 409-621-2600 48-17
TF: 888-764-2237 ■ *Web:* www.aadp.net

Aaduna Inc 144 Genesee St Ste 102-259 ... Auburn NY 13021 315-283-8074 637-9
Web: www.aaduna.org

AAE (American Association of Endodontists)
211 E Chicago Ave Ste 1100 ... Chicago IL 60611 312-266-7255 266-9867 49-8
TF: 800-872-3636 ■ *Web:* www.aae.org

AAE Systems Inc
5150 El Camino Real Ste B-31 ... Los Altos CA 94022 408-732-1710 180
Web: www.aaesys.com

AAEA (American Agricultural Economics Assn)
555 E Wells St Ste 1100 ... Milwaukee WI 53202 414-918-3190 48-2
Web: www.aaea.org

AAEC Credit Union
115 S Wilke Rd Ste 106 ... Arlington Heights IL 60005 847-392-1922 219
Web: aaeccu.com

AAEI (American Association of Exporters & Importers)
1050 17th St NW Ste 810 ... Washington DC 20036 202-857-8009 857-7843 49-18
Web: aaei.org

AAEP (American Association of Equine Practitioners)
4075 Iron Works Pkwy ... Lexington KY 40511 859-233-0147 233-1968 48-3
TF: 800-443-0177 ■ *Web:* aaep.org

AAES (American Association of Engineering Societies)
1801 Alexander Bell Dr ... Reston VA 20191 202-296-2237 296-1151 49-19
TF: 888-400-2237 ■ *Web:* www.aaes.org

AAF (American Adv Federation)
1101 Vermont Ave NW 5th Fl ... Washington DC 20005 202-898-0089 898-0159 49-18
Web: www.aaf.org

AAF International Corp
10300 Ormsby Pk Pl Ste 600 ... Louisville KY 40223 502-637-0011 223-6500* 18
**Fax Area Code:* 888 ■ *TF:* 888-223-2003 ■ *Web:* www.aafintl.com

AAFA (American Apparel & Footwear Assn)
740 Sixth St NW 3rd & Fourth Fl ... Washington DC 20001 202-853-9080 49-4
TF: 800-520-2262 ■ *Web:* www.aafaglobal.org

AAFA (Asthma & Allergy Foundation of America)
8201 Corporate Dr Ste 1000 ... Landover Hills MD 20785 202-466-7643 466-8940 48-17
TF: 800-727-8462 ■ *Web:* www.aafa.org

AAFCS (American Association of Family & Consumer Sciences)
400 N Columbus St Ste 202 ... Alexandria VA 22314 703-706-4600 706-4663 49-5
TF: 800-424-8080 ■ *Web:* www.aafcs.org

AAFD (American Association of Franchisees & Dealers)
PO Box 10158 ... Palm Desert CA 92255 619-209-3775 855-1988* 49-18
**Fax Area Code:* 866 ■ *TF:* 800-733-9858 ■ *Web:* www.aafd.org

AAFEDT, Forde, Gray, Monson & Hager PA
920 Second Ave S ... Minneapolis MN 55402 612-339-8965 349-6839 428
Web: www.aafedt.com

AAFP (American Academy of Family Physicians)
11400 Tomahawk Creek Pkwy ... Leawood KS 66211 913-906-6000 906-6075 49-8
Web: www.aafp.org

AAFPRS (American Academy of Facial Plastic & Reconstructive Surgery)
310 S Henry St ... Alexandria VA 22314 703-299-9291 299-8898 49-8
Web: www.aafprs.org

AAG (Association of American Geographers)
1710 16th St NW ... Washington DC 20009 202-234-1450 234-2744 49-19
TF: 800-696-7353 ■ *Web:* www.aag.org

AAGL (American Association of Gynecological Laparoscopists)
6757 Katella Ave ... Cypress CA 90630 714-503-6200 503-6201 49-8
TF: 800-554-2245 ■ *Web:* www.aagl.org

AAGP (American Association for Geriatric Psychiatry)
7910 Woodmont Ave Ste 1050 ... Bethesda MD 20814 301-654-7850 654-4137 49-15
Web: www.aagponline.org

	Phone	Fax	Class
AAHA (American Animal Hospital Assn) 12575 W Bayaud Ave . . . Lakewood CO 80228 *TF:* 800-252-2242 ■ *Web:* www.aaha.org	303-986-2800	986-1700	48-3
AAH-PERD (American Alliance for Health Physical Education Recreation & Dance) 1900 Association Dr . . . Reston VA 20191 *Web:* www.shapeamerica.org	703-476-3400	476-9527	48-22
AAHPM (American Academy of Hospice & Palliative Medicine) 4700 W Lake Ave Ste 300 . . . Glenview IL 60025 *Web:* www.aahpm.org	847-375-4712	375-6475	49-8
AAI (Africa-America Institute) 420 Lexington Ave Ste 1706 . . . New York NY 10170 *Web:* www.aaionline.org	212-949-5666	682-6174	48-14
AAI (American Athletic Inc) 200 American Ave . . . Jefferson IA 50129 *TF:* 800-247-3978 ■ *Web:* www.americanathletic.com	800-247-3978		346
AAI (Arab American Institute) 1600 K St NW Ste 601 . . . Washington DC 20006 *Web:* www.aaiusa.org	202-429-9210	429-9214	48-8
AAI (African American Images) PO Box 1799 . . . Chicago IL 60601 *TF:* 800-552-1991 ■ *Web:* www.africanamericanimages.com	708-672-4909	672-0466	637-2
AAI (Advertising Associates Intl) 65 Sprague St . . . Boston MA 02136 *TF:* 877-866-8500 ■ *Web:* www.aai-agency.com	877-866-8500		4
AAI Corp 124 Industry Ln . . . Hunt Valley MD 21030 *TF:* 800-655-2616 ■ *Web:* www.textronsystems.com	410-666-1400		529
AAIA (Association on American Indian Affairs) 966 Hungerford Dr Ste 12-B . . . Rockville MD 20850 *Web:* www.indian-affairs.org	240-314-7155	314-7159	457-17
AAIA (Automotive Aftermarket Industry Assn) 7101 Wisconsin Ave . . . Bethesda MD 20814 *Web:* www.autocare.org	301-654-6664	654-3299	49-21
AAIDD (American Association on Intellectual & Developmental Disabilities) 8403 Colesville Rd Ste 900 . . . Silver Spring MD 20910 *TF:* 800-424-3688 ■ *Web:* aaidd.org	202-387-1968	387-2193	48-17
AAIHDS (American Association of Integrated Healthcare Delivery Systems Inc) 4435 Waterfront Dr Ste 101 . . . Glen Allen VA 23060 *Web:* www.aaihds.org	804-747-5823	747-5316	49-8
AAII (American Association of Individual Investors) 625 N Michigan Ave Ste 1900 . . . Chicago IL 60611 *TF:* 800-428-2244 ■ *Web:* www.aaii.com	312-280-0170	280-9883	49-2
AAIM Employers' Association LLC 1600 S Brentwood Ste 400 . . . Saint Louis MO 63144 *TF:* 800-948-5700 ■ *Web:* aaimea.org	314-968-3600		764
AAIP (Association of American Indian Physicians) 1225 Sovereign Row Ste 103 . . . Oklahoma City OK 73108 *Web:* www.aaip.org	405-946-7072	946-7651	49-8
Aaipharma Services Corp 2320 Scientific Park Dr . . . Wilmington NC 28405 *TF:* 800-575-4224 ■ *Web:* www.alcaminow.com	910-254-7000		238
AAIS (American Association of Insurance Services Inc) 701 Warrenville Rd Ste 100 . . . Lisle IL 60532 *TF:* 800-564-2247 ■ *Web:* www.aaisonline.com	630-681-8347	681-8356	49-9
AAJ (American Association for Justice) 777 Sixth St NW Ste 200 . . . Washington DC 20001 *TF:* 800-424-2725 ■ *Web:* www.justice.org	202-965-3500		49-10
AAK USA Inc 131 Marsh St . . . Newark NJ 07114 *Web:* aak.com	973-344-1300		296-30
AAKP (All About Kids Publishing) PO Box 159 . . . Gilroy CA 95021 *Web:* www.allaboutkidspub.com	408-337-1152		637-2
Aakron Rule Corp 8 Indianola Ave . . . Akron NY 14001 *Web:* www.aakronline.com	716-542-5483		534
Aaladin Industries Inc 32584 477th Ave . . . Elk Point SD 57025 *Web:* www.aaladin.com	605-356-3325		454
AALAS (American Association for Laboratory Animal Science) 9190 Crestwyn Hills Dr . . . Memphis TN 38125 *Web:* www.aalas.org	901-754-8620	753-0046	49-19
Aalborg Instruments & Controls Inc 20 Corporate Dr . . . Orangeburg NY 10962 *TF:* 800-866-3837 ■ *Web:* www.aalborg.com	845-770-3000	770-3010	201
AALDEF (Asian American Legal Defense & Education Fund) 99 Hudson St 12th Fl . . . New York NY 10013 *TF:* 800-966-5946 ■ *Web:* www.aaldef.org	212-966-5932	966-4303	48-8
Aalfs Manufacturing Co 1005 Fourth St . . . Sioux City IA 51101 *Web:* aalfs.com	712-252-1877	252-5205	155-11
AALL (American Association of Law Libraries) 219 S Dearborn St . . . Chicago IL 60604 *Web:* www.aallnet.org	312-939-4764	431-1097	49-11
AALS (Association of American Law Schools) 1201 Connecticut Ave NW Ste 800 . . . Washington DC 20036 *Web:* www.aals.org	202-296-8851	296-8869	49-5
AALU (Association for Advanced Life Underwriting) 11921 Freedom Dr Ste 1100 . . . Reston VA 20190 *TF:* 888-275-0092 ■ *Web:* www.aalu.org	703-641-9400	641-9885	49-9
AAM (Aspen Art Museum) 637 E Hyman Ave . . . Aspen CO 81611 *Web:* aspenartmuseum.org	970-925-8050	925-8054	520
AAM (American Association of Museums) 1575 Eye St NW Ste 400 . . . Washington DC 20005 *TF:* 866-226-2150 ■ *Web:* www.aam-us.org	202-289-1818	289-6578	48-4
AAMA (American Amusement Machine Assn) 450 E Higgins Rd Ste 201 . . . Elk Grove Village IL 60007 *Web:* coin-op.org	847-290-9171	290-9121	48-23
AAMA (Asia America MultiTechnology Assn) 555 Bryant St Ste 332 . . . Palo Alto CA 94301 *Web:* www.aamasv.com	408-736-2554		49-13
AAMA (American Academy of Medical Acupuncture) 1970 E Grand Ave Ste 330 . . . El Segundo CA 90245 *Web:* www.medicalacupuncture.org	310-379-8261		48-17
AAMA (American Architectural Manufacturers Assn) 1827 Walden Office Sq Ste 550 . . . Schaumburg IL 60173 *Web:* aamanet.org	847-303-5664	303-5774	49-3
AAMA (American Association of Medical Assistants) 20 N Wacker Dr Ste 1575 . . . Chicago IL 60606 *TF:* 800-228-2262 ■ *Web:* www.aama-ntl.org	312-899-1500	899-1259	49-8
AAMC (Association of American Medical Colleges) 2450 N St NW . . . Washington DC 20037 *Web:* www.aamc.org	202-828-0400	828-1125	49-5
A-American Self Storage Management Company Inc 11560 Tennessee Ave . . . Los Angeles CA 90064 **Fax Area Code: 310* ■ *TF:* 800-499-3524 ■ *Web:* www.aamericanselfstorage.com	800-499-3524	914-4042*	803-3
AAMFT (American Association for Marriage & Family Therapy) 112 S Alfred St . . . Alexandria VA 22314 *Web:* www.aamft.org	703-838-9808	838-9805	48-6
AAMI (Association for the Advancement of Medical Instrumentation) 4301 N Fairfax Dr Ste 301 . . . Arlington VA 22203 *TF:* 800-332-2264 ■ *Web:* www.aami.org	703-525-4890	276-0793	49-8
AAMRO (American Association of Medical Review Officers) PO Box 12873 . . . Research Triangle Park NC 27709 *TF:* 800-489-1839 ■ *Web:* www.aamro.com	919-489-5407	490-1010	49-8
AAMSE (American Association of Medical Society Executives) 1000 Westgate Dr Ste 252 . . . Saint Paul MN 55114 *Web:* www.aamse.org	651-288-3432	290-2266	49-8
AAMVA (American Association of Motor Vehicle Administrators) 4301 Wilson Blvd Ste 400 . . . Arlington VA 22203 *TF:* 800-221-9253 ■ *Web:* www.aamva.org	703-522-4200	522-1553	49-7
AAN (Association of Alternative Newsweeklies) 115615th St NW . . . Washington DC 20005 *Web:* archive.altweeklies.com	202-289-8484		49-14
AAN (American Academy of Neurology) 1080 Montreal Ave . . . Saint Paul MN 55116 *TF:* 800-879-1960 ■ *Web:* www.aan.com	651-695-1940	695-2791	49-8
AANA (Arthroscopy Association of North America) 9400 W Higgins Rd Ste 200 . . . Rosemont IL 60018 *TF:* 877-924-0305 ■ *Web:* www.aana.org	847-292-2262	292-2268	49-8
AANA (American Association of Nurse Anesthetists) 222 S Prospect Ave . . . Park Ridge IL 60068 *TF:* 855-526-2262 ■ *Web:* www.aana.com	847-692-7050	692-6968	49-8
AANEM (American Association of Neuromuscular & Electrodiagnostic Medicine) 2621 Superior Dr NW . . . Rochester MN 55901 *TF:* 844-347-3277 ■ *Web:* www.aanem.org	507-288-0100	288-1225	49-8
Aaniiih Nakoda College 269 Blackfeet Ave . . . Harlem MT 59526 *Web:* www.ancollege.edu	406-353-2607		165
AANN (American Association of Neuroscience Nurses) 4700 W Lake Ave . . . Glenview IL 60025 *TF:* 888-557-2266 ■ *Web:* www.aann.org	847-375-4733	375-6430	49-8
AANP (American Academy of Nurse Practitioners) PO Box 12846 . . . Austin TX 78711 *TF:* 800-981-2491 ■ *Web:* www.aanp.org	512-442-4262	442-6469	49-8
AANP (American Association of Naturopathic Physicians) 818 18th St Ste 250 . . . Washington DC 20006 *TF:* 866-538-2267 ■ *Web:* www.naturopathic.org	202-237-8150	237-8152	48-17
AANS (American Association of Neurological Surgeons) 5550 Meadowbrook Dr . . . Rolling Meadows IL 60008 *TF:* 888-566-2267 ■ *Web:* www.aans.org	847-378-0500	378-0600	49-8
AAO (American Academy of Optometry) 6110 Executive Blvd Ste 506 . . . Rockville MD 20852 *TF:* 844-323-3937 ■ *Web:* www.aaopt.org	301-984-1441	984-4737	49-8
AAO (American Association of Orthodontists) 401 N Lindbergh Blvd . . . Saint Louis MO 63141 *TF:* 800-424-2841 ■ *Web:* www.aaoinfo.org	314-993-1700		49-8
AAO-HNS (American Academy of Otolaryngology-Head & Neck Surgery) 1650 Diagonal Rd . . . Alexandria VA 22314 *TF:* 877-722-6467 ■ *Web:* www.entnet.org	703-836-4444	683-5100	49-8
AAOMS (American Association of Oral & Maxillofacial Surgeons) 9700 W Bryn Mawr Ave . . . Rosemont IL 60018 *TF:* 800-822-6637 ■ *Web:* www.aaoms.org	847-678-6200	678-6286	49-8
AAON Inc 2425 S Yukon Ave . . . Tulsa OK 74107 *NASDAQ: AAON* ■ *Web:* www.aaon.com	918-583-2266	583-6094	14
AAOS (American Academy of Orthopaedic Surgeons) 6300 N River Rd . . . Rosemont IL 60018 *TF:* 800-346-2267 ■ *Web:* www.aaos.org	847-823-7186	823-8125	49-8
AAP (American Academy of Pediatrics) 141 NW Pt Blvd . . . Elk Grove Village IL 60007 *TF:* 800-433-9016 ■ *Web:* www.aap.org	847-434-4000	434-8000	49-8
AAP (American Academy of Periodontology) 737 N Michigan Ave Ste 800 . . . Chicago IL 60611 *TF:* 800-282-4867 ■ *Web:* www.perio.org	312-787-5518	787-3670	49-8
AAP (Association of American Publishers) 71 Fifth Ave . . . New York NY 10003 *Web:* www.publishers.org	212-255-0200	255-7007	49-16
AAP (Action Auto Parts) 795 N Main St . . . Providence RI 02904 *Web:* www.actionautoparts.com	401-273-0330	751-5393	61
AAP St Marys Corp 1100 McKinley Rd . . . Saint Marys OH 45885 *Web:* www.aapstmarys.com	419-394-7840	394-4776	61
AAPA (American Academy of Pas) 2318 Mill Rd Ste 1300 . . . Alexandria VA 22314 *Web:* www.aapa.org	703-836-2272	684-1924	615
AAPA (American Association of Port Authorities) 1010 Duke St . . . Alexandria VA 22314 *Web:* www.aapa-ports.org	703-684-5700	684-6321	49-21
AAPB (Association for Applied Psychophysiology & Biofeedback) 10200 W 44th Ave Ste 304 . . . Wheat Ridge CO 80033 *TF:* 800-477-8892 ■ *Web:* www.aapb.org	303-422-8436		49-8
AAPCC (American Association of Poison Control Centers) 3201 New Mexico Ave Ste 310 . . . Washington DC 20016 *TF:* 800-222-1222 ■ *Web:* www.aapcc.org	800-222-1222		49-8
AAPCO Southeast Inc 506 Webb Rd . . . Concord NC 28025 *TF:* 800-728-2690 ■ *Web:* www.aapcogroup.com	704-784-2690	784-4995	186
AAPD (American Academy of Pediatric Dentistry) 211 E Chicago Ave Ste 1600 . . . Chicago IL 60611 *Web:* www.aapd.org	312-337-2169	337-6329	49-8
AAPG (American Association of Petroleum Geologists) 1444 S Boulder Ave PO Box 979 . . . Tulsa OK 74119 *TF:* 800-364-2274 ■ *Web:* www.aapg.org	918-584-2555	560-2665	48-12
AAPL (American Academy of Psychiatry & the Law) 1 Regency Dr PO Box 30 . . . Bloomfield CT 06002 *TF:* 800-331-1389 ■ *Web:* www.aapl.org	860-242-5450		49-15
AAPL (American Association of Professional Landmen) 4100 Fossil Creek Blvd . . . Fort Worth TX 76137 *Web:* www.landman.org	817-847-7700	847-7704	48-12

	Phone	Fax	Class
AAPM&R (American Academy of Physical Medicine & Rehabilitation) 9700 W Bryn Mawr Ave Ste 200 .... Rosemont IL 60018 *TF:* 877-227-6799 ■ *Web:* www.aapmr.org	847-737-6000	754-4368	49-8
AAPPO (American Association of Preferred Provider Organizations) 222 S 1st St Ste 303 .... Louisville KY 40202 *Web:* nasho.org	502-403-1122	403-1128	49-8
AAPS (American Association of Pharmaceutical Scientists) 2107 Wilson Blvd Ste 700 .... Arlington VA 22201 *TF:* 877-998-2277 ■ *Web:* www.aaps.org	703-243-2800	243-9650	49-19
AAPS (American Association of Physician Specialists Inc) 5550 W Executive Dr Ste 400 .... Tampa FL 33609 *Web:* www.aapsus.org	813-433-2277	830-6599	49-8
AAPT (American Association of Physics Teachers) 1 Physics Ellipse .... College Park MD 20740 *TF:* 800-446-8923 ■ *Web:* www.aapt.org	301-209-3311	209-0845	49-5
AAR (American Academy of Religion) 825 Houston Mill Rd NE Ste 300 .... Atlanta GA 30329 *Web:* www.aarweb.org	404-727-3049	727-7959	48-20
AAR (Alliance for Aging Research) 750 17th St NW Ste 1100 .... Washington DC 20006 **Fax Area Code:* 770 ■ *Web:* www.agingresearch.org	202-293-2856	234-5030*	48-17
AAR (Association of American Railroads) 425 Third St SW .... Washington DC 20024 *TF:* 800-533-6644 ■ *Web:* www.aar.org	202-639-2100	639-2286	49-21
AAR Corp 1100 N Wood Dale Rd .... Wood Dale IL 60191 *NYSE:* AIR ■ *TF:* 800-422-2213 ■ *Web:* www.aarcorp.com	630-227-2000	227-2039	21
AARC (American Association for Respiratory Care) 9425 N MacArthur Blvd Ste 100 .... Irving TX 75063 *Web:* aarc.org	972-243-2272	484-2720	49-8
Aarch Caster & Equipment 314 Axminister Dr .... Fenton MO 63026 *TF:* 888-349-0220 ■ *Web:* www.aarchcaster.net	866-206-8792		351
Aarcher 910 Commerce Rd .... Annapolis MD 21401 *Web:* www.aarcherinc.com	410-897-9100	897-9104	192
AARDA (American Autoimmune Related Disease Assn) 22100 Gratiot Ave .... Eastpointe MI 48021 *TF:* 800-598-4668 ■ *Web:* www.aarda.org	586-776-3900	776-3903	48-17
Aardvark 1935 Puddingstone Dr .... La Verne CA 91750 *Web:* aardvarktactical.com	909-451-6100		366
Aardvark Record Mastering 4485 Utica St .... Denver CO 80212 *Web:* www.aardvarkmastering.com	303-455-1908		658
Aardwolf Publishing 179-15 Rte 46 W Ste 252 .... Rockaway NJ 07866 *Web:* aardwolfpublishing.com	862-245-2273		637-2
Aareas Interactive 1120 Finch Ave W .... North York ON M3J3H7 *TF:* 888-613-2677 ■ *Web:* aareas.com	416-661-2244		809
AArete LLC 200 East Randolph St Ste 2100 .... Chicago IL 60601 *Web:* www.aarete.com	312-585-0800		463
A&ARF (Antiques & Art Around Florida) PO Box 980 .... Keystone Heights FL 32656 *TF:* 800-847-1740 ■ *Web:* www.aarf.com	352-475-1336	475-5326	637-9
Aargus Plastics Inc 540 Allendale Dr .... Wheeling IL 60090 *Web:* aargusplastics.com	847-325-4444	325-4260	66
Aaris LLC 7953 Washington Woods Dr .... Dayton OH 45459 **Fax Area Code:* 702 ■ *Web:* www.aaris-llc.com	937-573-4675	926-4128*	723
Aaron & Company Inc PO Box 8310 .... Piscataway NJ 08855 *TF:* 800-734-4822 ■ *Web:* www.aaronco.com	732-752-8200		612
Aaron Bell International Inc 9101 E Kenyon Ave Ste 2300 .... Denver CO 80237 *Web:* www.aaron-bell.com	720-200-0470		401
Aaron Brothers Inc 8001 Ridgepoint Dr .... Irving TX 75063 *TF:* 877-372-6370 ■ *Web:* www.michaelscustomframing.com	877-372-6370		45
Aaron Diamond AIDS Research Ctr 701 W 168th St HHSC 1102 .... New York NY 10032 *Web:* www.infectiousdiseases.cumc.columbia.edu	212-448-5000	725-1126	668
Aaron M. Priest Literary Agency 200 W 41st St 21st Fl .... New York NY 10036 *Web:* aaronpriest.com	212-818-0344	573-9417	444
Aaron Riechert Carpol & Riffle APC 900 Veterans Blvd Ste 600 .... Redwood City CA 94063 *Web:* www.arcr.com	650-368-4662		41
Aaron Thomas Company Inc 7421 Chapman Ave .... Garden Grove CA 92841 *TF:* 800-394-4776 ■ *Web:* www.packaging.com	714-894-4468		88
Aaron's Creek Farm Inc 380 Greenhouse Dr .... Buffalo Junction VA 24529 *Web:* www.acfplugs.com	434-374-2174	374-2055	293
AaronEquipment Company Inc 735 E Green St .... Bensenville IL 60106 *TF:* 800-492-2766 ■ *Web:* www.aaronequipment.com	630-350-2200	350-9047	385
Aarons Grant & Habif LLC (AGH) 3500 Piedmont Rd Ste 600 .... Atlanta GA 30305 *Web:* aghllc.com	404-233-5486	237-8325	2
Aaronson, Dickerson, Cohn & Lanzone APC 1001 Laurel St Ste A .... San Carlos CA 94070 *Web:* adcl.com	650-593-3117		41
AARP Services 601 East St NW .... Washington DC 20049 *TF:* 888-687-2277 ■ *Web:* www.aarp.org	888-687-2277		353
Aarrowcast Inc 2900 E Richmond St .... Shawano WI 54166 *Web:* www.aarrowcast.com	715-526-3600	526-9758	307
AAS (American Association of Suicidology) 5221 Wisconsin Ave NW .... Washington DC 20015 *Web:* www.suicidology.org	202-237-2280	237-2282	48-17
AAS (Association for Asian Studies, The) 825 Victors Way Ste 310 .... Ann Arbor MI 48108 *Web:* www.asianstudies.org	734-665-2490	665-3801	48-11
AAS (American Antiquarian Society) 185 Salisbury St .... Worcester MA 01609 *Web:* www.americanantiquarian.org	508-755-5221	754-9069	48-4
AAS (American Astronomical Society) 1667 K St NW Ste 800 .... Washington DC 20006 *Web:* aas.org	202-328-2010	234-2560	49-19
AASA (American Association of School Administrators) 801 N Quincy St Ste 700 .... Arlington VA 22203 *TF:* 800-771-1162 ■ *Web:* www.aasa.org	703-528-0700	841-1543	49-5
AASC (Applied Aerospace Structures Corp) 3437 S Airport Way PO Box 6189 .... Stockton CA 95206 *Web:* www.aascworld.com	209-982-0160	983-3375	504
AASCU (American Association of State Colleges & Universities) 1307 New York Ave NW 5th Fl .... Washington DC 20005 *TF:* 800-558-3417 ■ *Web:* www.aascu.org	202-293-7070	296-5819	49-5
Aasgard Summit Management Services Inc 4017 13th Ave W .... Seattle WA 98119 *Web:* www.aasgardsummit.net	206-284-0475	284-0095	193
AASHTO (American Association of State Highway & Transportation Officials) 555 12th Street NW Ste 1000 .... Washington DC 20001 *Web:* www.transportation.org	202-624-5800	624-5806	49-7
AASLD (American Association for the Study of Liver Diseases) 1001 N Fairfax St 4th Fl .... Alexandria VA 22314 *Web:* www.aasld.org	703-299-9766	299-9622	49-8
AASLH (American Association for State & Local History) 2021 21st Ave S Ste 320 .... Nashville TN 37212 *Web:* aaslh.org	615-320-3203	327-9013	48-4
AASM (American Academy of Sleep Medicine) 2510 N Frontage Rd .... Darien IL 60561 *Web:* aasm.org	630-737-9700	737-9790	48-17
Aasys Group 11301 N US Hwy 301 Ste 106 .... Thonotosassa FL 33592 *TF:* 800-852-7091 ■ *Web:* www.aasysgroup.com	813-246-4757	246-4576	180
AATB (American Association of Tissue Banks) 8200 Greensboro Dr Ste 320 .... McLean VA 22102 *Web:* www.aatb.org	703-827-9582	992-0504	49-8
AATBS (Association for Advanced Training in the Behavioral Sciences) 5126 Ralston St .... Ventura CA 93003 *TF:* 800-472-1931 ■ *Web:* www.aatbs.com	805-676-3030	676-3033	49-5
AATCC (American Association of Textile Chemists & Colorists) 1 Davis Dr PO Box 12215 .... Research Triangle Park NC 27709 *Web:* www.aatcc.org	919-549-8141	549-8933	49-13
AATF (American Association of Teachers of French) 302 N Granite St .... Marion IL 62959 **Fax Area Code:* 815 ■ *Web:* www.frenchteachers.org	618-453-5731	310-5754*	49-5
AATG (American Association of Teachers of German) 112 Haddontowne Ct Ste 104 .... Cherry Hill NJ 08034 *TF:* 800-835-6770 ■ *Web:* www.aatg.org	856-795-5553	795-9398	49-5
AATH (Association for Applied & Therapeutic Humor) 220 E State St FL G .... Rockford IL 61104 **Fax Area Code:* 949 ■ *Web:* www.aath.org	815-708-6587	715-6931*	48-17
AATS (American Association for Thoracic Surgery) 800 Cummings Ctr Ste 350-V .... Beverly MA 01915 *TF:* 800-424-5249 ■ *Web:* aats.org	978-252-2200	522-8469	49-8
AATSP (American Association of Teachers of Spanish & Portuguese) 900 Ladd Rd .... Walled Lake MI 48390 *Web:* www.aatsp.org	248-960-2180	960-9570	49-5
AAU (Amateur Athletic Union of the US) 1910 Hotel Plaza Blvd .... Lake Buena Vista FL 32830 *TF:* 800-228-4872 ■ *Web:* aausports.org	407-934-7200	934-7242	48-22
AAU (Association of American Universities) 1200 New York Ave NW Ste 550 .... Washington DC 20005 *Web:* www.aau.edu	202-408-7500	408-8184	49-5
Aaudio Imports 4871 Raintree Dru .... Parker CO 80134 **Fax Area Code:* 720 ■ *Web:* www.aaudioimports.com	303-264-8831	851-7575*	35
AAUP (American Association of University Professors) 1133 Nineteenth St NW Ste 200 .... Washington DC 20036 *TF:* 800-424-2973 ■ *Web:* www.aaup.org	202-737-5900	737-5526	49-5
AAUW (American Association of University Women) 1310 L St NW Ste 1000 .... Washington DC 20036 *TF:* 800-326-2289 ■ *Web:* www.aauw.org	202-785-7700	872-1425	49-5
Aava Whistler Hotel Ltd 4005 Whistler Way .... Whistler BC V0N1B4 *TF:* 800-663-5644 ■ *Web:* www.aavawhistlerhotel.com	604-932-2522		378
AAVIN Private Equity 1245 First Ave SE .... Cedar Rapids IA 52402 *Web:* www.aavin.com	319-247-1072		792
Aavispro LLC 113 Amberwood Ct .... Bethel Park PA 15102 *Web:* www.aavispro.com	412-833-5444	203-1271	194
AAVSO (American Association of Variable Star Observers) 49 Bay State Rd .... Cambridge MA 02138 *Web:* www.aavso.org	617-354-0484	354-0665	49-19
Aaxon Laundry Systems 6100 N Powerline Rd .... Fort Lauderdale FL 33309 *TF:* 800-826-1012 ■ *Web:* www.aaxon.com	954-772-7100	772-4125	111
AAyuja Inc 35453B Dumbarton Ct .... Newark CA 94560 *Web:* www.aayuja.com	980-222-9852		5
AB (AllianceBernstein Holding LP) 1345 Avenue of the Americas .... New York NY 10105 *NYSE:* AB ■ *TF:* 800-221-5672 ■ *Web:* www.alliancebernstein.com	212-486-5800	969-2293	401
AB Carter Inc 4801 York Hwy .... Gastonia NC 28052 *Web:* www.abcarter.com	704-865-1201	864-8870	744
AB Controls Inc 15530 Rockfield Blvd Ste B2 .... Irvine CA 92618 *Web:* www.abcontrols.com	949-341-0977	341-0988	177
AB Staffing Solutions LLC 3451 Mercy Rd .... Gilbert AZ 85297 *TF:* 888-515-3900 ■ *Web:* www.abstaffing.com	480-345-6668		631
AB Watley Direct Inc 50 Broad St Ste 1614 .... New York NY 10004 **Fax Area Code:* 212	646-753-9301	202-5204*	690
AB Young Co 14701 Cumberland Rd Ste 190 .... Noblesville IN 46060 *TF:* 800-886-7001 ■ *Web:* www.abyoung.com	317-565-5000	565-5010	612
ABA (American Bicycle Assn) 1645 W Sunrise Blvd .... Gilbert AZ 85233 *TF:* 866-650-4867 ■ *Web:* www.usabmx.com	480-961-1903	961-1842	48-22
ABA (American Burn Assn) 311 S Wacker Dr Ste 4150 .... Chicago IL 60606 *Web:* ameriburn.org	312-642-9260	642-9130	49-8
ABA (American Bar Assn) 321 N Clark St .... Chicago IL 60654 *TF:* 800-285-2221 ■ *Web:* www.americanbar.org	312-988-5000		49-10
ABA (American Booksellers Assn) 333 Westchester Ave Ste S202 .... White Plains NY 10604 **Fax Area Code:* 914 ■ *TF:* 800-637-0037 ■ *Web:* www.bookweb.org	800-637-0037	417-4013*	49-18
ABA Commission on Law & Aging (COLA) 1050 Connecticut Ave NW Ste 400 .... Washington DC 20036 *Web:* www.americanbar.org	202-662-1000	662-8698	49-10

Phone | Fax | Class

ABA Marketing Network
1120 Connecticut Ave NW . . . Washington DC 20036 202-663-5000 828-5053 49-2
TF: 800-226-5377 ■ *Web:* www.aba.com

Ababa Bolt 1466-1 Pioneer Way . . . El Cajon CA 92020 619-440-1781 440-5394 350
Web: abababolt.com

Abacus 4511 McKinney Ave . . . Dallas TX 75205 214-559-3111 559-3113 671
Web: abacusjaspers.com

Abacus Automation Inc
264 Shields Dr . . . Bennington VT 05201 802-442-3662 442-8759 194
Web: www.abacusautomation.com

Abacus Corp 610 Gusryan St . . . Baltimore MD 21224 410-633-1900 631
TF: 800-230-0043 ■ *Web:* www.abacuscorporation.com

Abacus Group LLC 14 Penn Plz . . . New York NY 10122 212-812-8444 812-8448 193
Web: www.abacusgrpllc.com

Abacus Planning Group Inc
2500 Devine St . . . Columbia SC 29205 803-933-0054 194
Web: www.abacusplanninggroup.com

Abacus Project Management Inc
3030 N Central Ave Ste 803 . . . Phoenix AZ 85012 602-265-6870 265-9360 194
Web: www.abacuspm.com

Abacus Technology Corp
5404 Wisconsin Ave Ste 1100 . . . Chevy Chase MD 20815 800-225-2135 180
TF: 800-225-2135 ■ *Web:* www.abacustech.com

Abad Foam Inc 6560 Caballero Blvd . . . Buena Park CA 90620 714-994-2223 601

Abalon Precision Manufacturing Corp
1 Landing Way . . . Bronx NY 10464 718-589-5682 589-0300 697

Abalonetti Seafood Trattoria
57 Fisherman's Wharf . . . Monterey CA 93940 831-373-1851 373-2058 671
Web: www.abalonetti.com

Abanaki Corp 17387 Munn Rd . . . Chagrin Falls OH 44023 440-543-7400 543-7404 537
Web: www.abanaki.com

ABA-PGT Inc 10 Gear Dr . . . Manchester CT 06042 860-649-4591 643-7619 757
Web: www.abapgt.com

Abarca Health LLC
650 Ave Munoz Rivera . . . San Juan PR 00918 305-697-7525 363
Web: abarcahealth.com

Abaris Training Resources Inc
5401 Longley Ln Ste 49 . . . Reno NV 89511 775-827-6568 507
TF: 800-638-8441 ■ *Web:* www.abaris.com

ABARTA Oil & Gas Company Inc
200 Alpha Dr . . . Pittsburgh PA 15238 412-963-6443 536
Web: www.abartaenergy.com

Abatech Inc PO Box 356 . . . Blooming Glen PA 18911 215-258-3640 679-2464* 261
**Fax Area Code:* 772 ■ *Web:* www.abatech.com

Abatement Technologies
605 Satellite Blvd Ste 300 . . . Suwanee GA 30024 678-889-4200 37
TF: 800-634-9091 ■ *Web:* www.abatement.com

Abatix Corp 2400 Skyline Dr Ste 400 . . . Mesquite TX 75149 214-381-0322 388-0443 385
TF: 800-426-3983 ■ *Web:* www.abatix.com

ABB Enterprise Inc 1010 E 18th St . . . Los Angeles CA 90021 213-748-7480 627
Web: www.abblabels.com

ABB Inc 843 N Jefferson St . . . Lewisburg WV 24901 304-647-4358 419
Web: www.abb.com

ABB Ovo Inc 2320 Walsh Ave Ste H . . . Santa Clara CA 95051 408-567-9088 549-0782* 196
**Fax Area Code:* 866 ■ *Web:* www.abovoinc.com

Abba Restaurant 89 Old Colony Way . . . Orleans MA 02653 508-255-8144 671
Web: www.abbarestaurant.com

Abba Staffing & Consulting Services
2350 Airport Fwy Ste 130 . . . Bedford TX 76022 817-354-2800 354-2801 260
Web: www.abbastaffing.com

Abba Technologies
5301 Beverly Hills Ave NE . . . Albuquerque NM 87113 505-889-3337 889-3338 194
TF: 888-222-2832 ■ *Web:* www.abbatech.com

AbbaDox
3511 W Commercial Blvd . . . Fort Lauderdale FL 33309 954-484-0969 177
TF: 866-437-4572 ■ *Web:* www.idssite.com

Abbco Inc 304 Meyer Rd . . . Bensenville IL 60106 630-595-7115 595-0431 455
TF: 866-986-6546 ■ *Web:* www.abbcoinc.net

Abbe Museum 26 Mt Desert St . . . Bar Harbor ME 04609 207-288-3519 288-8979 520
Web: www.abbemuseum.org

Abbeville Community Federal Credit Union
603 E Greenwood St . . . Abbeville SC 29620 864-366-5615 366-2983 219
TF: 866-546-8273 ■ *Web:* youracfcu.com

Abbeville County
21 Old Calhoun Falls Rd . . . Abbeville SC 29620 864-446-6000 446-6050 338
Web: www.abbevillecountysc.com

Abbeville County School District 60
400 Greenville St . . . Abbeville SC 29620 864-366-5427 685
Web: www.acsd.k12.sc.us

Abbey Capital (Us) LLC
350 Park Ave Ste 1315 . . . New York NY 10022 646-453-7850 691
Web: abbeycapital.com

Abbey Credit Union Inc
800 Falls Creek Dr . . . Vandalia OH 45377 937-898-7800 898-7803 219
TF: 800-546-8882 ■ *Web:* abbeycu.com

Abbey Group Ltd
2121 Kinnickinnic Ave Ste 111 . . . Milwaukee WI 53207 414-803-8086 194
Web: www.abbeygroupltd.com

Abbey Hospice 215 Azalea Ct . . . Social Circle GA 30025 770-464-5858 464-5870 450
Web: www.abbeyhospice.com

Abbey Party Rents 411 Allan St . . . Daly City CA 94014 415-715-6900 292
Web: www.abbeyrentssf.com

Abbey Resort & Fontana Spa
269 Fontana Blvd . . . Fontana WI 53125 262-275-9000 669
TF: 800-709-1323 ■ *Web:* www.theabbeyresort.com

Abbey Travel Ltd
522 N Washington St . . . Naperville IL 60563 630-420-0400 420-6799 772
TF: 800-338-0900

Abbey's Restaurant & Lounge
145 Zane St . . . Wheeling WV 26003 304-233-0729 671

Abbey, Weitzenberg, Warren & Emery PC
100 Stony Point Rd Ste 200 . . . Santa Rosa CA 95401 707-542-5050 428
Web: www.abbeylaw.com

Abbi Agency Inc, The 1385 Haskell St . . . Reno NV 89509 775-323-2977 636
Web: theabbiagency.com

Abbington Distinctive Banquets
3S002 IL Rt 53 . . . Glen Ellyn IL 60137 630-942-8600 671
Web: www.abbingtonbanquets.com

Phone | Fax | Class

Abbit Management Corp
16986 Robbins Rd Ste 100 . . . Grand Haven MI 49417 616-842-0280 690
Web: abbit.biz

Abbot & Abbot Box Corp
37-11 Tenth St . . . Long Island City NY 11101 888-525-7186 392-8439* 200
**Fax Area Code:* 718 ■ *TF:* 888-525-7186 ■ *Web:* www.abbotbox.com

Abbot Construction 3408 First Ave S . . . Seattle WA 98134 206-467-8500 447-1885 186
Web: www.abbottconstruction.com

Abbotsford Chamber of Commerce
207-32900 S Fraser Way . . . Abbotsford BC V2S5A1 604-859-9651 850-6880 137
Web: www.abbotsfordchamber.com

Abbotsford Virtual School
33952 Pine St . . . Abbotsford BC V2S2P3 604-859-9803 685
Web: avs.abbyschools.ca

Abbott 100 Abbott Park Rd . . . Abbott Park IL 60064 224-667-6100 296-10
Web: www.abbott.com

Abbott Associates Inc
500 Providence Sq . . . Greenville SC 29615 864-297-9598 194
Web: effectivecallcenters.com

Abbott Ball Company Inc
PO Box 330100 . . . West Hartford CT 06133 860-236-5901 233-1069 492
Web: www.abbottball.com

Abbott Communications Group
110 Atlantic Dr . . . Maitland FL 32751 407-831-2999 627
Web: www.abbottcg.com

Abbott Company Ltd 345 E Flower St . . . Phoenix AZ 85012 602-224-9092 2
Web: acoabbott.com

Abbott Enterprises Inc
901 W 4th Ave . . . Pine Bluff AR 71601 870-535-4973 535-4970 495
TF: 800-643-5973 ■ *Web:* www.atrol.com

Abbott Interfast Corp 190 Abbott Dr . . . Wheeling IL 60090 800-422-2688 459-4076* 621
**Fax Area Code:* 847 ■ *TF:* 800-877-0789 ■ *Web:* www.aicfast.com

Abbott Nicholson PC
300 River Pl Ste 3000 . . . Detroit MI 48207 313-566-2500 466
Web: www.abbottnicholson.com

Abbott Point of Care Inc
400 College Rd E . . . Princeton NJ 08540 800-827-7828 250
TF: 800-827-7828 ■ *Web:* pointofcare.abbott

Abbott Stringham & Lynch
1530 Meridian Ave 2nd Fl . . . San Jose CA 95125 408-377-8700 377-0821 2
Web: www.aslcpa.com

Abbott's Meat Inc 3623 Blackington Ave . . . Flint MI 48532 810-232-7128 473
Web: www.abbottsmeat.com

Abbottstown Industries Inc
420 W Fleet St . . . Abbottstown PA 17301 717-259-8715 259-8393 757
TF: 800-661-0976 ■ *Web:* abbind.com

Abbozzo Gallery
401 Richmond Stt W Ste 128 . . . Toronto ON M5V3A8 416-260-2220 42
Web: abbozzogallery.com

ABBTECH Professional Resources Inc
45625 Willow Pond Plz . . . Sterling VA 20164 703-450-5252 344
TF: 877-936-7569 ■ *Web:* abbtech.com

AbbVie Pharmaceutical Contract Manufacturing
1401 Sheridan Rd . . . North Chicago IL 60064 847-938-8524 938-0659 584
TF: 888-299-7416 ■ *Web:* www.abbviecontractmfg.com

Abby Manufacturing Company Inc
501 Pulliam Rd . . . Walnut MS 38683 888-794-4004 223-5340* 454
**Fax Area Code:* 662 ■ *TF:* 888-794-4004 ■ *Web:* abby-usa.com

Abbyland Foods Inc
502 E Linden St PO Box 69 . . . Abbotsford WI 54405 715-223-6386 223-6388 473
TF: 800-732-5483 ■ *Web:* www.abbyland.com

ABBYY Language Services
890 Hillview Ct Ste 300 . . . Milpitas CA 95035 408-457-9777 457-9778 393
Web: www.abbyy.com

ABC (America's Blood Centers)
725 15th St NW Ste 700 . . . Washington DC 20005 202-393-5725 393-1282 49-8
TF: 888-872-5663 ■ *Web:* www.americasblood.org

ABC (American Business Conference)
1828 L St NW Ste 280 . . . Washington DC 20036 202-822-9300 467-4070 49-12
Web: www.americanbusinessconference.org

ABC (ArcBest) 3801 Old Greenwood Rd . . . Fort Smith AR 72903 800-610-5544 785-6124* 780
NASDAQ: ARCB ■ **Fax Area Code:* 479 ■ *TF:* 800-610-5544 ■ *Web:* arcb.com

ABC (Associated Builders & Contractors Inc)
4250 Fairfax Dr . . . Arlington VA 22203 202-595-1505 49-3
TF: 877-889-5627 ■ *Web:* www.abc.org

ABC (Audit Bureau of Circulations)
48 W Seegers Rd . . . Arlington Heights IL 60005 224-366-6939 49-18
Web: www.auditedmedia.com

ABC 33 40
800 Concourse Pkwy Ste 200 . . . Birmingham AL 35244 205-403-3340 741-15
TF: 800-784-8669 ■ *Web:* abc3340.com

ABC Appliance Inc
1 Silverdome Industrial Pk . . . Pontiac MI 48343 800-981-3866 35
TF: 800-981-3866 ■ *Web:* www.abcwarehouse.com

ABC Barber College 103 Brenda St . . . Hot Springs AR 71913 501-624-0885 167-3
Web: www.abcbarbercollege.com

ABC Bartending School 7329 W Flagler St . . . Miami FL 33144 305-267-1446 685
Web: www.abcbartending.com

ABC Bartending School
2359 Windy Hill Rd Ste 330 . . . Marietta GA 30067 770-952-6271 685
Web: www.bartendingschoolsabc.com

ABC Billing Solutions
13200 Strickland Rd Ste 114 . . . Raleigh NC 27613 919-870-5939 393

ABC Coffee Service
24691 Telegraph Rd . . . Southfield MI 48033 248-352-1222 352-4869 393
Web: www.abccoffeeservice.com

ABC Columbia 5807 Shakespeare Rd . . . Columbia SC 29223 803-754-7525 741-33
Web: www.abccolumbia.com

ABC Compounding Company Incorporated & Acme Wholesale
6970 Jonesboro Rd . . . Morrow GA 30260 770-968-9222 968-7281 151
TF: 800-795-9222 ■ *Web:* www.abccompounding.com

ABC Electric Corp 2425 46th St . . . Astoria NY 11103 718-956-0000 112
Web: abcec.com

ABC Fence Systems Inc
963 Industrial Dr . . . Chipley FL 32428 850-638-8876 200
Web: www.abcfencesystems.com

ABC Fine Wines & Spirits
8989 S Orange Ave . . . Orlando FL 32824 407-851-0000 443
Web: www.abcfws.com

Company / Address	City	State	ZIP	Phone	Fax	Class
ABC Global Services 6001 Broken Sound Pkwy NW Ste 340 *TF:* 800-722-5179 ■ *Web:* abcglobalservices.com	Boca Raton	FL	33487	800-722-5179		771
ABC Home & Commercial Services 9475 Hwy 290 E *Web:* www.abchomeandcommercial.com	Austin	TX	78724	512-837-9500		577
ABC Home Medical Supply Inc 397 Eagleview Blvd *TF:* 866-897-8588 ■ *Web:* www.abc-med.com	Exton	PA	19341	866-897-8588		475
ABC Hospice PO Box 1486 *TF:* 866-847-8660 ■ *Web:* www.abchospice.com	Rainsville	AL	35986	866-847-8660		450
ABC Industrie PO Box 77 *TF:* 800-426-0921 ■ *Web:* www.abc-industries.net	Warsaw	IN	46581	574-267-5166	267-2045	370
ABC Internet 3350 W Kathy Loop *TF:* 866-663-8845 ■ *Web:* www.abcinet.net	Coeur d'Alene	ID	83815	208-676-0742		175
ABC Metals Inc 500 W Clinton St *Fax Area Code: 574 ■ *TF:* 800-238-8470 ■ *Web:* www.abcmetals.com	Logansport	IN	46947	800-238-8470	753-6110*	492
ABC NewsOne 47 W 66th St *Web:* abcnews.go.com	New York	NY	10023	212-456-2700	456-2795	742
ABC Office Equipment Company Inc 1404 E Estates Rd	Spokane	WA	99224	509-922-4600		535
ABC Packaging Machine Corp 811 Live Oak St *TF:* 800-237-5975 ■ *Web:* www.abcpackaging.com	Tarpon Springs	FL	34689	727-937-5144	938-1239	547
ABC Professional Tree Services Inc 201 Flint Ridge Rd *Web:* www.abctree.com	Webster	TX	77598	281-280-1100	282-9086	776
ABC Quality Consulting Services 1115 Grand Cyn *Web:* www.abcquality.com	Brea	CA	92821	714-256-0223		196
ABC Seamless 3001 Fiechtner Dr *TF:* 800-732-6577 ■ *Web:* abcseamless.com	Fargo	ND	58103	701-293-5952		191-4
ABC Security Service Inc 1840 Embarcadero *Fax Area Code: 510 ■ *Web:* abcsecurityservice.us	Oakland	CA	94606	800-872-1666	436-0826*	693
ABC Supply Company Inc 1 ABC Pkwy *TF:* 888-492-1047 ■ *Web:* www.abcsupply.com	Beloit	WI	53511	608-362-7777		191-4
ABC Testing Inc 95 First St PO Box 868 *Web:* www.abcndt.com	Bridgewater	MA	02324	508-697-6068	697-6154	418
ABC Tutors In Home Tutoring 7234 W 151st St *TF:* 888-222-3935 ■ *Web:* www.abctutors.com	Overland Park	KS	66223	913-961-7800	685-0533	423
ABC21 WPTA 3401 Butler Rd *Web:* www.wpta21.com	Fort Wayne	IN	46808	260-483-0584	483-2568	741-51
ABC4 Utah 2175 W 1700 S *Web:* www.good4utah.com	Salt Lake City	UT	84104	801-975-4526	924-8099	741-115
ABCA (American Baseball Coaches Assn) 4101 Piedmont Pkwy *Web:* www.abca.org	Greensboro	NC	27410	989-775-3300		48-22
ABC-Amega Inc 1100 Main St *TF:* 844-937-3268 ■ *Web:* www.abc-amega.com	Buffalo	NY	14209	716-885-4444	878-2872	160
ABC-CLIO Inc 130 Cremona Dr *TF:* 800-368-6868 ■ *Web:* abc-clio.com	Goleta	CA	93117	805-968-1911	685-9685	637-2
Abcm Corp 1320 Fourth St NE PO Box 436 *Web:* www.abcmcorp.com	Hampton	IA	50441	641-456-5636	456-2320	450
Abco Automation Inc 6202 Technology Dr *TF:* 800-965-8259 ■ *Web:* goabco.com	Browns Summit	NC	27214	336-375-6400		201
Abco Cleaning Products 6800 NW 36th Ave *TF:* 888-694-2226 ■ *Web:* www.abcoproducts.com	Miami	FL	33147	305-694-2226	694-0451	508
ABCO Inc 1621 Wall St *TF:* 800-969-2226 ■ *Web:* abcodigital.com	Dallas	TX	75215	214-565-1191	428-8996	86
ABCO Laboratories Inc 2450 S Watney Way *TF:* 800-678-2226 ■ *Web:* www.abcolabs.com	Fairfield	CA	94533	707-432-2200	432-2240	296-37
ABCO Printing 512 Trade Rd *TF:* 800-821-9435 ■ *Web:* printingbyabco.com	Columbus	OH	43204	800-821-9435		628
ABCO Refrigeration Supply Corp 49-70 31st St *Fax Area Code: 718 ■ *TF:* 800-786-2075 ■ *Web:* abcohvacr.com	Long Island City	NY	11101	800-786-2075	392-1296*	665
ABCO Technology 6733 Sepulveda Blvd Ste 106 *Web:* abcotechnology.edu	Los Angeles	CA	90045	310-216-3067	216-4311	167-3
ABCT (Association for Behavioral & Cognitive Therapies) 305 Seventh Ave 16th Fl *TF:* 800-685-2228 ■ *Web:* www.abct.org	New York	NY	10001	212-647-1890	647-1865	49-15
Abdill Career College 843 E Main St Ste 203 *TF:* 800-866-9017 ■ *Web:* www.abdill.com	Medford	OR	97504	541-779-8384	779-7645	167-3
ABDO Eick & Meyers LLP 5201 Eden Ave *Web:* www.aemcpas.com	Edina	MN	55436	952-835-9090	835-3261	734
Abe & Louie's 793 Boylston St *Web:* abeandlouies.com	Boston	MA	02116	617-536-6300		671
ABeam Consulting (USA) Ltd 8445 Freeport Pkwy Ste 400	Irving	TX	75063	972-929-3130	929-3131	194
Abec Inc 3998 Schelden Cir *Web:* www.abec.com	Bethlehem	PA	18017	610-861-4666	861-2636	298
Abe-El Produce 42143 Rd 120 *Web:* abe-el.com	Orosi	CA	93647	559-528-3030		10-11
Abel Automatics Inc 165 N Aviador St *Web:* abelreels.com	Camarillo	CA	93010	805-484-8789		710
Abeln, Magy, Underberg & Assoc 1907 E Wayzata Blvd Ste 120 *Web:* www.abelnmagy.com	Wayzata	MN	55391	952-404-5085		260
ABELSoft Inc 3310 S Service Rd *TF:* 800-267-2235 ■ *Web:* www.abelsoft.com	Burlington	ON	L7M4K8	905-333-3200		463
Abelson-Taylor Inc 33 W Monroe St *Web:* www.abelsontaylor.com	Chicago	IL	60603	312-894-5500		4
Abendroth Berns & Warner LLC 40 Grove St Ste 320 *Web:* abwllc.com	Wellesley	MA	02482	781-237-9188		41
Abercrombie & Fitch Co 6301 Fitch Pass *NASDAQ: ANF* ■ *TF:* 866-681-3115 ■ *Web:* www.abercrombie.com	New Albany	OH	43054	866-681-3115		157-4
Abercrombie Oil Company Inc PO Box 1422 *Web:* abercrombieoilcom.websitecreatorpropreview2421.com	Danville	VA	24543	434-792-8022		579
Aberdare Ventures 235 Montgomery St Ste 1230 *Web:* www.aberdare.com	San Francisco	CA	94104	415-392-7442	392-4264	792
Aberdeen 123 S Lincoln St *Web:* www.aberdeen.sd.us	Aberdeen	SD	57401	605-626-7025		21
Aberdeen & Rockfish Railroad Co 101 E Main St *TF:* 800-849-8985 ■ *Web:* www.aberdeen-rockfish.com	Aberdeen	NC	28315	910-944-2341	944-9738	648
Aberdeen Alliance Church of The Christian & Missionary Alliance, The 1106 S Roosevelt St *Web:* www.aberdeenalliance.org	Aberdeen	SD	57401	605-225-9724		48-20
Aberdeen American News 124 S 2nd St *TF:* 800-925-4100 ■ *Web:* www.aberdeennews.com	Aberdeen	SD	57402	605-229-5555		532-2
Aberdeen Area Chamber of Commerce 516 S Main St *TF:* 800-874-9038 ■ *Web:* www.aberdeen-chamber.com	Aberdeen	SD	57401	605-225-2860	225-2437	139
Aberdeen Asset Management Inc 1735 Market St 32nd Fl *Web:* www.aberdeenstandard.com	Philadelphia	PA	19103	215-405-5700		401
Aberdeen Barn 1601 Richmond Rd *Web:* www.aberdeen-barn.com	Williamsburg	VA	23185	757-229-6661		671
Aberdeen Barn Steakhouse 5805 Northampton Blvd *Web:* aberdeenbarn.net	Virginia Beach	VA	23455	757-464-1580		671
Aberdeen Chrysler Center Inc 901 Auto Plaza Dr *Web:* www.aberdeenchrysler.com	Aberdeen	SD	57401	605-225-1656		57
Aberdeen Convention & Visitors Bureau 10 Railroad Ave SW PO Box 78 *TF:* 800-645-3851 ■ *Web:* www.visitaberdeensd.com	Aberdeen	SD	57401	605-225-2414	225-3573	206
Aberdeen Dynamics Inc 17717 E Admiral Pl *Web:* www.aberdeendynamics.com	Tulsa	OK	74158	918-437-8420		385
Aberdeen Flying Service Municipal Airport 4430 East Hwy 12 *TF:* 800-273-8987 ■ *Web:* www.aberdeenflyingservice.com	Aberdeen	SD	57401	605-225-1384	225-1570	167-3
Aberdeen Group Inc 60 Hickory Dr 5th Fl *TF:* 800-577-7891 ■ *Web:* www.aberdeen.com	Waltham	MA	02451	617-854-5200		466
Aberdeen Hospital 835 E River Rd *Web:* aberdeenhealthfoundation.ca	New Glasgow	NS	B2H3S6	902-752-7600	755-2356	374-2
Aberdeen LLC 9130 Norwalk Blvd *TF:* 800-500-9526 ■ *Web:* www.aberdeeninc.com	Santa Fe Springs	CA	90670	562-699-6998	695-5570	173-2
Aberdeen School District 5 216 N G St *Web:* www.asd5.org	Aberdeen	WA	98520	360-538-2000		685
Aberfoyle Metal Treaters Ltd 18 Kerr Cres *Web:* www.aberfoyle-mt.com	Puslinch	ON	N0B2J0	519-763-1120	763-1121	484
Aberhart Ctr 11402 University Ave *TF:* 866-407-1970 ■ *Web:* albertahealthservices.ca	Edmonton	AB	T6G2J3	780-407-3796		545
ABET Inc 415 N Charles St *Web:* www.abet.org	Baltimore	MD	21201	410-347-7700		48-1
ABG (Atlanta Botanical Garden) 1345 Piedmont Ave NE *Web:* www.atlantabotanicalgarden.org	Atlanta	GA	30309	404-876-5859		823
ABG Sundal Collier Inc 850 3rd Ave Ste 9-C *Web:* abgsc.com	New York	NY	10022	212-605-3800		360-2
Abha Architects Inc 1621 N Lincoln St *Web:* abha.com	Wilmington	DE	19806	302-658-6426		261
Abhasa Waikiki Spa at the Royal Hawaiian 2259 Kalakaua Ave Luxury Collection Resort 1st Fl Ste 1-A *Web:* en.abhasa.com	Honolulu	HI	96815	808-922-8200		707
Abhe & Svoboda Inc 18100 Dairy Ln *Web:* www.abheonline.com	Jordan	MN	55352	952-447-6025	447-1000	186
ABHES (Accrediting Bureau of Health Education Schools) 7777 Leesburg Pk Ste 314 N *Web:* www.abhes.org	Falls Church	VA	22043	703-917-9503	917-4109	48-1
ABI (Advanced Biotechnologies Inc) 1545 Progress Way *Fax Area Code: 301 ■ *TF:* 800-426-0764 ■ *Web:* abionline.com	Eldersburg	MD	21784	410-792-9779	497-9773*	231
ABI (Atkinson-Baker Inc) 500 N Brand Blvd 3rd Fl *TF:* 800-288-3376 ■ *Web:* www.depo.com	Glendale	CA	91203	818-551-7300		445
ABI (ABI Tape) 105 Whittendale Dr *Fax Area Code: 888 ■ *Web:* www.abitape.com	Moorestown	NJ	08057	856-778-0700	224-6325*	732
ABI (American Bankruptcy Institute) 66 Canal Center Plz Ste 600 *Web:* www.abi.org	Alexandria	VA	22314	703-739-0800	739-1060	49-10
ABI Professional Publications PO Box 149 *TF:* 800-551-7776 ■ *Web:* www.abipropub.com	Saint Petersburg	FL	33731	727-556-0950	556-2560	637-2
ABI Tape (ABI) 105 Whittendale Dr *Fax Area Code: 888 ■ *Web:* www.abitape.com	Moorestown	NJ	08057	856-778-0700	224-6325*	732
ABIA (Austin-Bergstrom International Airport) 3600 Presidential Blvd *Web:* www.ci.austin.tx.us	Austin	TX	78719	512-530-2242		27
Abide International Inc 561 First St W *Web:* www.abideinternational.com	Sonoma	CA	95476	707-935-1577		186
Abiding Faith Free Lutheran Church 433 Crestview Ave *Fax Area Code: 763 ■ *Web:* www.aflc.org	Ortonville	MN	56278	320-839-3949	545-0079*	48-20
Abigal Press Inc 9735 133rd Ave *Web:* abigal.com	Ozone Park	NY	11417	718-641-5350		627
Abila Inc 7901 Jones Branch Dr *Web:* www.abila.com	McLean	VA	22102	703-506-7000		177
Abilene Aero 2850 Airport Blvd *Web:* www.abileneaero.com	Abilene	TX	79602	325-677-2601		63
Abilene Ag Service & Supply Inc 303 S 14th St *Web:* abileneag.com	Abilene	TX	79602	325-677-4371		276

Name / Address	City	State	Zip	Phone	Fax	Class
Abilene Ballet Theatre 1265 N Second St *Web:* www.abileneballettheatre.org	Abilene	TX	79601	325-675-0303		573-1
Abilene Chamber of Commerce 174 Cypress St Ste 200 *Web:* www.abilenechamber.com	Abilene	TX	79601	325-677-7241		139
Abilene Christian University Brown Library (ACU) 221 Brown Library *TF:* 800-460-6228 ■ *Web:* www.acu.edu	Abilene	TX	79699	325-674-2316		434-6
Abilene City Hall 555 Walnut St PO Box 60 *Web:* abilenetx.gov	Abilene	TX	79601	325-676-6200		337
Abilene Civic Ctr 1100 N Sixth St *Web:* abilenetx.gov	Abilene	TX	79601	325-676-6211	676-6343	572
Abilene Community Theatre (ACT) 809 Barrow *Web:* www.abilenecommunitytheatre.org	Abilene	TX	79605	325-673-6271		572
Abilene Convention & Visitors Bureau 1101 N First St *TF:* 800-727-7704 ■ *Web:* www.abilenevisitors.com	Abilene	TX	79601	325-676-2556	676-1630	206
Abilene Machine Inc PO Box 129 *TF:* 800-255-0337 ■ *Web:* www.abilenemachine.com	Abilene	KS	67410	785-655-9455	655-3838	274
Abilene Motor Express 1700 Willis Rd *Web:* www.abilenemotor.com	North Chesterfield	VA	23237	804-275-0224	275-1533	780
Abilene Philharmonic Orchestra 1102 N 3rd St Ste C *Web:* www.abilenephilharmonic.org	Abilene	TX	79601	325-677-6710		573-3
Abilene Public Library 202 Cedar St *Web:* abilenetx.gov	Abilene	TX	79601	325-677-2474	676-6024	434-3
Abilene Regional Airport 2933 Airport Blvd *Web:* abilenetx.gov	Abilene	TX	79602	325-676-6367	676-6317	27
Abilene Regional Medical Ctr 6250 S Hwy 83-84 *TF:* 800-888-2504 ■ *Web:* www.abileneregional.com	Abilene	TX	79606	325-428-1000	795-2113	374-3
Abilene Reporter-News 101 Cypress St *TF:* 866-604-2020 ■ *Web:* www.reporternews.com	Abilene	TX	79601	325-671-8318	670-5242	532-2
Abilene State Park 150 Park Rd 32 *Web:* tpwd.texas.gov	Tuscola	TX	79562	325-572-3204		565
Abilene Zoological Gardens 2070 Zoo Ln Nelson Pk *TF:* 800-899-9841 ■ *Web:* abilenetx.gov	Abilene	TX	79602	325-676-6085	676-6084	823
Ability Building Center Inc 1911 14th St NW *Web:* abcinc.org	Rochester	MN	55903	507-281-6262		627
Ability Center of Greater Toledo Inc 5605 Monroe St *TF:* 866-885-5733 ■ *Web:* www.abilitycenter.org	Sylvania	OH	43560	419-885-5733	882-4813	672
Ability Engineering Technology inc 16140 S Vincennes Ave *Web:* www.abilityengineering.com	South Holland	IL	60473	708-331-0025		454
Ability Metal Co 1355 Greenleaf Ave *Web:* abilitymetal.com	Elk Grove Village	IL	60007	847-437-7040	437-1089	492
ABIM (American Board of Internal Medicine) 510 Walnut St Ste 1700 *TF:* 800-441-2246 ■ *Web:* www.abim.org	Philadelphia	PA	19106	215-446-3590		48-1
AbiMar Foods Inc 5425 N 1st *Web:* www.abimarfoods.com	Abilene	TX	79603	325-691-5425		296-9
Abingdon Convention & Visitors Bureau 335 Cummings St *TF:* 800-435-3440 ■ *Web:* visitabingdonvirginia.com	Abingdon	VA	24210	276-676-2282		206
Abington Memorial Hospital 1200 Old York Rd *Web:* www.abingtonhealth.org	Abington	PA	19001	215-481-2000		374-3
ABIOMED Inc 22 Cherry Hill Dr *NASDAQ: ABMD* ■ *TF:* 800-422-8666 ■ *Web:* www.abiomed.com	Danvers	MA	01923	978-646-1400	777-8411	250
Abipa Canada Inc 3700 Ave des Grandes Tourelles *TF:* 877-963-6888 ■ *Web:* www.abipa.com	Boisbriand	QC	J7H0A1	450-963-6888		21
Abita Brewing Co 21084 Hwy 36 *TF:* 800-737-2311 ■ *Web:* abita.com	Covington	LA	70433	985-893-3143	898-3546	102
Abita Trace Animal Clinic 69142 Hwy 59 Ste E *TF:* 800-640-3274 ■ *Web:* www.medi-vet.com	Mandeville	LA	70471	985-892-5656		794
Abitec Corporation Inc 501 W 1st Ave *TF:* 800-555-1255 ■ *Web:* www.abiteccorp.com	Columbus	OH	43215	614-429-6464		296-29
Abitibi Geophysique Ltd 1740 ch Sullivan 1400 *Web:* www.ageophysics.com	Val-d'Or	QC	J9P7H1	819-874-8800		192
ABKCO Music & Records Inc 85 5th Ave *Web:* www.abkco.com	New York	NY	10003	212-399-0300		657
ABL (American Beverage Licensees) 5101 River Rd Ste 108 *Web:* www.ablusa.org	Bethesda	MD	20816	301-656-1494	656-7539	49-6
ABL Employment 777 Guelph Line Ste 212 *Web:* www.ablemployment.com	Burlington	ON	L7R3N2	905-631-7050		260
Able 2 Products Co 804 E Highway 248 PO Box 543 *TF:* 800-641-4098 ■ *Web:* www.able2products.com	Cassville	MO	65625	417-847-4791	847-2222	438
Able Aerospace Services Inc 7706 E Velocity Way *Web:* www.ableengineering.com	Mesa	AZ	85212	602-304-1227		21
Able Care Health Equipment 5911 NW Barry Rd Ste 100 *Web:* ablecarehealth.com	Kansas City	MO	64154	816-587-4640	587-5320	475
Able Die Casting Corp 3907 Wesley Terr *Web:* www.ablediecasting.com	Schiller Park	IL	60176	847-678-1991		358
Able Distributing Co 2727 W Growers Ave *Web:* abledistributing.com	Phoenix	AZ	85053	602-993-0957	942-3491	612
Able Durable Medical Equipment 3562 Forest Ln *Web:* www.ablemedical.net	Dallas	TX	75234	214-350-2760		475

Name / Address	City	State	Zip	Phone	Fax	Class
Able Electric Service Inc 2626 Electronic Ln *Web:* ableelectricservice.com	Dallas	TX	75220	214-350-5721		362
Able Global Partners LLC 830 3rd Ave 14th Fl *Web:* www.ableglobalps.com	New York	NY	10022	212-581-7011		691
Able Health Products 2070 Springdale Rd Ste 300 *TF:* 888-834-4325 ■ *Web:* www.ablehealthproducts.com	Cherry Hill	NJ	08003	856-751-9222	751-3374	475
Able Infosat Communications Inc 5906 Broadway St *Web:* www.able-usa.com	Pearland	TX	77581	281-485-8800	485-8230	45
Able Management Solutions Inc 470 Olde Worthington Rd Ste 200 *Web:* www.ablemgt.com	Westerville	OH	43082	614-868-1144	868-1177	47
Able Manufacturing & Assembly LLC 1000 Schifferdecker *Web:* www.ablemfg.com	Joplin	MO	64801	417-623-3060		480
Able Plumbing Inc 2336 Bob Boozer Dr	Omaha	NE	68130	402-334-8887		610
Able Service Contractors Inc 13505 Dulles Technology Dr Ste 2 *Web:* ableservice.com	Herndon	VA	20171	571-323-2990		104
Able Services 868 Folsom St *TF:* 800-461-9577 ■ *Web:* ableserve.com	San Francisco	CA	94107	415-546-6534		256
Able Steel Fabricators Inc 4150 E Quartz Cir *Web:* www.ablesteel.com	Mesa	AZ	85215	480-830-2253		480
Able Wire Edm Inc 440 W Atlas St *Web:* www.ableedm.com	Brea	CA	92821	714-255-1967		757
Ables & Craig PA 551 S Commerce Ave *Web:* heartlandfloridalaw.com	Sebring	FL	33870	863-385-0112		41
AbleSys Corp 20954 Corsair Blvd *Web:* www.ablesys.com	Hayward	CA	94545	510-265-1883		177
ABM One Liberty Plaza 7th Fl *TF:* 866-624-1520 ■ *Web:* www.locations.abm.com	New York	NY	10006	212-297-0200		27
ABM Equipment & Supply LLC 333 Second St NE *TF:* 800-229-5451 ■ *Web:* www.abm-highway.com	Hopkins	MN	55343	952-938-5451	938-0159	61
ABM Industries 600 Harrison St Ste 600 *Web:* www.abm.com	San Francisco	CA	94107	415-351-4386		152
ABM International Inc PO Box 1820 **Fax Area Code:* 281 ■ *Web:* abminternational.com	Montgomery	TX	77356	936-597-4410	443-4404*	55
ABMA (American Boiler Manufacturers Assn) 8221 Old Courthouse Rd Ste 380 *TF:* 800-227-1966 ■ *Web:* www.abma.com	Vienna	VA	22182	703-356-7172		49-13
ABMC (American Bio Medica Corp) 122 Smith Rd *OTC: ABMC* ■ *TF:* 800-227-1243 ■ *Web:* www.abmc.com	Kinderhook	NY	12106	518-758-8158	758-8172	85
ABMECH Acquisitions LLC 976 Forest Ave *TF:* 800-686-3626 ■ *Web:* abmechllc.com	West Homestead	PA	15120	412-462-7440		667
ABMP (Associated Bodywork & Massage Professionals) 25188 Genesee Trl Rd Ste 200 **Fax Area Code:* 800 ■ *TF:* 800-458-2267 ■ *Web:* www.abmp.com	Golden	CO	80401	303-674-8478	667-8260*	48-17
ABMS (American Board of Medical Specialties) 353 N Clark St Ste 1400 *Web:* www.abms.org	Chicago	IL	60654	312-436-2600		48-1
ABNA Engineering Inc 4140 Lindell Blvd *Web:* abnacorp.com	Saint Louis	MO	63108	314-454-0222		256
Abone Agency 7763 Turin Rd *Web:* allprorealtyabone.com	Rome	NY	13440	315-339-2222		652
Abonmarche Consultants Inc 361 First St *Web:* www.abonmarche.com	Manistee	MI	49660	231-723-1198		256
Aboriginal People's Television Network Inc 339 Portage Ave *TF:* 888-330-2786 ■ *Web:* aptn.ca	Winnipeg	MB	R3B2C3	204-947-9331		116
Abound Credit Union PO Box 900 *TF:* 800-756-3678 ■ *Web:* www.aboundcu.com	Radcliff	KY	40159	502-942-0254		219
About Face Productions Inc 900 Ogden Ave Ste 371 *Web:* www.afpevents.com	Downers Grove	IL	60515	630-974-6310		260
About Faces Models & Talent 3399 Peachtree Rd NE Ste 400 *Web:* www.aboutfacesmt.com	Atlanta	GA	30326	404-233-2006		214
Above & Beyond Home Health Care 417 E 1st St *TF:* 877-233-1533 ■ *Web:* www.abovebeyondhc.com	Monticello	IA	52310	319-465-4637	465-4070	363
Above All Advertising Inc 6980 Corte Sante Fe Ste A *TF:* 866-552-2683 ■ *Web:* abovealladvertising.net	San Diego	CA	92126	858-549-2226	777-3537	8
ABRA (ABRA Inc) PO Box 33098 *TF:* 800-458-4283 ■ *Web:* www.americanbuckskin.com	Tulsa	OK	74135	918-936-4707		48-3
ABRA Inc (ABRA) PO Box 33098 *TF:* 800-458-4283 ■ *Web:* www.americanbuckskin.com	Tulsa	OK	74135	918-936-4707		48-3
Abraham Baldwin Agricultural College 2802 Moore Hwy *TF:* 800-733-3653 ■ *Web:* www.abac.edu	Tifton	GA	31793	229-391-5001	391-4931	162
Abraham Lincoln Birthplace National Historic Site 2995 Lincoln Farm Rd *Web:* www.nps.gov	Hodgenville	KY	42748	270-358-3137	358-3874	564
Abraham Lincoln Capital Airport 1200 Capital Airport Dr *Web:* www.flyspi.com	Springfield	IL	62707	217-788-1060	788-8056	27
Abraham Lincoln Presidential Library & Museum 212 N 6th St *Web:* www2.illinois.gov	Springfield	IL	62701	217-558-8844		50-3
Abraham Ralph (Rep R - LA) 417 Cannon House Office Bldg *Web:* abraham.house.gov	Washington	DC	20515	202-225-8490	225-5639	342-2
Abraham Watkins Nichols Sorrels Agosto & Friend 800 Commerce St *TF:* 800-580-9121 ■ *Web:* www.abrahamwatkins.com	Houston	TX	77002	713-222-7211	225-0827	428
Abrahamson Uiterwyk & Barnes 2639 Mccormick Dr *Web:* www.theinjurylawyers.com	Clearwater	FL	33759	727-725-9411		428

Phone | Fax | Class

Abrakadoodle Inc
46030 Manekin Pl Ste 110 . . . Sterling VA 20166 703-860-6570 310
Web: www.abrakadoodle.com

Abram Friedman Occupational Ctr
1646 S Olive St. . . . Los Angeles CA 90015 213-765-2400 167-3
Web: www.abramfriedmanoc.org

Abrams & Jossel Consulting Inc
100 Tri - State International Ste 215 . . . Lincolnshire IL 60069 847-607-8120 607-8640 463
Web: www.ajworkout.com

Abrams Airborne Manufacturing Inc
3735 N Romero Rd. . . . Tucson AZ 85705 520-887-1727 293-8807 697
Web: www.abrams.com

Abrams Consulting Group Inc
3020 Westchester Ave. . . . Purchase NY 10577 914-696-5100 194
Web: www.abramsconsulting.com

Abrams Foster Nole & Williams PA
W Quadrangle 2 Hamill Rd Ste 241 . . . Baltimore MD 21210 410-433-6830 433-6871 2
Web: afnw.com

Abrams Hebrew Academy
31 W College Ave. . . . Yardley PA 19067 215-493-1800 685
Web: abramsonline.org

Abrams Planetarium
Michigan State University. . . . East Lansing MI 48824 517-355-4676 598
Web: www.web.pa.msu.edu

Abrams Properties LLC
123 St Paul St. . . . Brookline MA 02446 617-821-4005 186
Web: www.abrams-properties.com

Abramson, Brown & Dugan
1819 Elm St . . . Manchester NH 03104 603-627-1819 41
Web: arbd.com

Abrasive Blast Systems Inc
418 NE 14th St . . . Abilene KS 67410 785-263-3786 386
Web: www.abs-airblast.com

Abrasive Specialists Inc (ASI)
15825 Central Ave NE. . . . Ham Lake MN 55304 763-571-4111 571-5026 385
Web: www.asimn.com

Abrasive Technology Inc
8400 Green Meadows Dr . . . Lewis Center OH 43035 740-548-4100 1
Web: www.abrasive-tech.com

Abrasive-Form Inc 454 Scott Dr. . . . Bloomingdale IL 60108 630-893-7800 893-6313 757
Web: www.abrasive-form.com

Abraxas Energy Consulting LLC
811 Palm St . . . San Luis Obispo CA 93401 805-547-2050 261
Web: www.abraxasenergy.com

Abraxas Petroleum Corp
18803 Meisner Dr. . . . San Antonio TX 78258 210-490-4788 490-8816 536
NASDAQ: AXAS ■ *Web:* www.abraxaspetroleum.com

Abrazo Community Health Network
10020 N 25th Ave. . . . Phoenix AZ 85021 602-674-6758 353
Web: www.abrazohealth.com

Abreo 515 E State St . . . Rockford IL 61104 815-968-9463 671
Web: www.abreorockford.com

Abrisa Industrial Glass Inc
200 S Hallock Dr . . . Santa Paula CA 93060 805-525-4902 329
Web: abrisatechnologies.com

Abrisa Technologies
200 S Hallock Dr . . . Santa Paula CA 93060 877-622-7472 525-8604* 332
**Fax Area Code:* 805 ■ *TF:* 877-622-7472 ■ *Web:* www.abrisatechnologies.com

A-Brite Plating Company Inc
3000 W 121st St. . . . Cleveland OH 44111 800-252-2995 481
TF: 800-252-2995 ■ *Web:* www.abriteplating.com

ABRY Partners LLC 888 Boylston Ste 1600 . . . Boston MA 02199 617-859-2959 405
Web: www.abry.com

ABS (American Bureau of Shipping)
16855 Northchase Dr . . . Houston TX 77060 281-877-6000 877-5803 49-21
Web: ww2.eagle.org

ABS (American Bonanza Society)
3595 N Webb Rd Ste 200 . . . Wichita KS 67226 316-945-1700 945-1710 48-18
Web: www.bonanza.org

ABS Alaskan Inc 2130 Van Horn Rd . . . Fairbanks AK 99701 907-452-2002 451-1949 45
Web: www.absak.com

ABS Capital Partners
400 E Pratt St Ste 910. . . . Baltimore MD 21202 410-246-5600 246-5606 792
Web: www.abscapital.com

ABS Corp 7031 N 16th St . . . Omaha NE 68112 402-453-6970 584
Web: www.abs-corporation.com

ABS Direct Inc 4724 Enterprise Ave . . . Modesto CA 95356 209-545-6090 317
Web: www.absdirectinc.com

ABS Global Inc 1525 River Rd. . . . De Forest WI 53532 608-846-3721 846-6442 11-2
Web: www.absglobal.com

ABS Graphics Inc 900 N Rohlwing Rd . . . Itasca IL 60143 630-495-2400 627
Web: www.absgraphics.com

ABS Group of Companies Inc
Abs Plz 16855 Northchase Dr. . . . Houston TX 77060 281-673-2800 194
Web: www.abs-group.com

ABS Telecom
2607 S Decker Lake Blvd Ste 102. . . . Salt Lake City UT 84107 801-327-9400 327-9390 224
TF: 877-227-8353 ■ *Web:* www.abstelecom.com

ABS Ventures 950 Winter St Ste 2600. . . . Waltham MA 02451 781-250-0400 792
Web: www.absventures.com

Absaroka Ranch PO Box 929 . . . Dubois WY 82513 307-455-2275 239
Web: www.absarokaranch.com

Abscope Environmental Inc
7086 Commercial Dr . . . Canastota NY 13032 315-697-8437 667
TF: 800-273-5318 ■ *Web:* www.abscope.com

Absecon Lighthouse
31 S Rhode Island Ave . . . Atlantic City NJ 08401 609-449-1360 50-3
Web: www.abseconlighthouse.org

Absentee Shawnee Tribe of Indians of Oklahoma
2025 Gordon Cooper Dr. . . . Shawnee OK 74801 405-275-4030 186
Web: www.astribe.com

Absher Construction Company Inc
1001 Shaw Rd . . . Puyallup WA 98372 253-845-9544 841-0925 186
Web: absherco.com

Absinthe Brasserie & Bar
398 Hayes St . . . San Francisco CA 94102 415-551-1590 671
Web: absinthe.com

ABSMC (Alta Bates Summit Medical Ctr)
2450 Ashby Ave . . . Berkeley CA 94705 510-204-4444 374-3
Web: www.altabatessummit.org

Absocold PO Box 1545. . . . Richmond IN 47374 800-843-3714 935-3450* 35
**Fax Area Code:* 765 ■ *TF:* 800-843-3714 ■ *Web:* absocold.com

ABSOFT Corp
2111 Cass Lake Rd Ste 102 . . . Keego Harbor MI 48320 248-220-1190 220-1194 177
TF: 888-414-5846 ■ *Web:* absoft.com

Absolut Aire Inc
5496 N Riverview Dr. . . . Kalamazoo MI 49004 269-382-1875 382-5291 14
TF: 800-804-4000 ■ *Web:* www.absolutaire.com

Absolut Manufacturing LLC
68150 Front St . . . Iron River WI 54847 715-372-8988 372-8977 454
Web: www.absolutmfg.com

AbsolutData Technologies Inc
1320 Harbor Bay Pkwy Ste 170 . . . Alameda CA 94502 510-748-9922 466
Web: www.absolutdata.com

Absolute Consulting Engineers
3839 Birch St . . . Newport Beach CA 92660 949-852-8700 261
Web: absoluteco.com

Absolute Electronics Inc
W137 N8589 Landover Ct . . . Menomonee Falls WI 53051 262-250-1151 203
Web: www.absoluteelectronics.net

Absolute Energy LLC
1372 State Line Rd . . . Saint Ansgar IA 50472 641-326-2220 539
Web: www.absenergy.org

Absolute Exhibits Inc
1382 Valencia Ave Ste H. . . . Tustin CA 92780 714-685-2800 184
TF: 888-760-6555 ■ *Web:* www.absoluteexhibits.com

Absolute Investment Advisers
4 North St. . . . Hingham MA 02043 781-740-1904 401
Web: www.absoluteadvisers.com

Absolute Machine Tools Inc
7420 Industrial Pkwy . . . Lorain OH 44053 440-960-6911 358
TF: 800-852-7825 ■ *Web:* www.absolutemachine.com

Absolute Magic Computers/Internet
PO Box 672 . . . San Juan Capistrano CA 92693 714-899-8154 196
Web: www.absolutemagic.com

Absolute Media Inc 1150 Summer St . . . Stamford CT 06905 203-327-9090 7
Web: www.absolutemediainc.com

Absolute Mfg 24 Lomar Park Dr Ste 6F. . . . Pepperell MA 01463 978-433-0760 454
Web: www.absolutemanufacturing.com

Absolute Software Inc
430-11401 Century Oaks Ter . . . Austin TX 78758 512-600-7455 178-1
TF: 800-220-0733 ■ *Web:* www.absolute.com

Absolute Standards Inc 44 Rossotto Dr . . . Hamden CT 06514 203-281-2917 743
Web: www.absolutestandards.com

Absolute Technologies Inc
4890 E La Palma Ave . . . Anaheim CA 92807 714-692-6570 463
Web: www.absolutetechnologies.com

Absolute Total Care Inc (ATC)
1441 Main St No 900. . . . Columbia SC 29201 866-433-6041 912-3610 391-3
TF: 866-433-6041 ■ *Web:* www.absolutetotalcare.com

Absopure Water Co 8845 General Dr . . . Plymouth MI 48170 800-422-7678 805
TF: 800-422-7678 ■ *Web:* www.absopure.com

ABT (American Ballet Theatre)
890 Broadway 3rd Fl. . . . New York NY 10003 212-477-3030 573-1
Web: www.abt.org

ABT Associates Inc 55 Wheeler St. . . . Cambridge MA 02138 617-492-7100 492-5219 466
Web: www.abtassociates.com

ABT Inc 259 Murdock Rd . . . Troutman NC 28166 800-438-6057 492
TF: 800-438-6057 ■ *Web:* www.abtdrains.com

ABTA (American Brain Tumor Assn)
8550 W Bryn Mawr Ave Ste 550. . . . Chicago IL 60631 847-827-9910 827-9918 48-17
TF: 800-886-2282 ■ *Web:* www.abta.org

Abtech Technologies
2042 Corte Del Nogal . . . Carlsbad CA 92009 760-827-5100 180
TF: 800-474-7397 ■ *Web:* abtechtechnologies.com

Abtex Corp 89 Main St PO Box 188. . . . Dresden NY 14441 315-536-7403 586
Web: www.abtex.com

Abuelo's | Food Concepts Intl
4401 82nd St . . . Lubbock TX 79424 806-794-1762 671
Web: www.abuelos.com

Abundant Health Resources Inc
112 Douglas Blvd. . . . Roseville CA 95678 916-242-0045 880-1673* 810
**Fax Area Code:* 888 ■ *Web:* www.abundanthealth.com

Abundant Life Christian Academy
1494 Banks Rd . . . Margate FL 33063 954-979-2665 148
TF: 800-948-6291 ■ *Web:* www.alcaeagles.com

Abundant Life Tabernacle
389 Broadway. . . . Kingston NY 12401 845-338-9883 48-20

Abundant Love Church Inc
2615 New Haven Ave . . . Fort Wayne IN 46803 260-420-5683 48-20
Web: abundantlove.faithweb.com

ABWA (American Business Women's Assn)
11050 Roe Ave Ste 200 . . . Overland Park KS 66211 800-228-0007 660-0101* 49-12
**Fax Area Code:* 913 ■ *TF:* 800-228-0007 ■ *Web:* www.abwa.org

ABX Air Inc 145 Hunter Dr. . . . Wilmington OH 45177 937-382-5591 366-3116 12
Web: www.abxair.com

ABX Engineering 880 Hinckley Rd . . . Burlingame CA 94010 650-552-2322 256
TF: 800-366-4588 ■ *Web:* www.abxengineering.com

ABYC (American Boat & Yacht Council Inc)
613 Third St Ste 10. . . . Annapolis MD 21403 410-990-4460 990-4466 49-21
Web: www.abycinc.org

AC & T Company Inc
11535 Hopewell Rd . . . Hagerstown MD 21740 301-582-2700 316
TF: 800-458-3835 ■ *Web:* www.acandt.com

AC Central Reservations Inc
201 Tilton Rd London Sq Mall Ste 17B . . . Northfield NJ 08225 609-383-8880 383-8616 376
TF: 888-227-6667 ■ *Web:* www.acrooms.com

AC Corp 301 Creek Ridge Rd. . . . Greensboro NC 27406 336-273-4472 765-0416 189-10
TF: 800-422-7378 ■ *Web:* accorporation.com

AC Dellovade Inc 108 Cavasina Dr. . . . Canonsburg PA 15317 724-873-8190 189-12
Web: www.acdellovade.com

AC Doctor LLC
2151 W Hillsboro Blvd Ste 400 . . . Deerfield Beach FL 33442 866-264-1479 791
TF: 866-264-1479 ■ *Web:* www.acdoctor.com

Name	Address	City	State	ZIP	Phone	Fax	Class	Notes
AC Electric Co	2921 Hangar Way PO Box 81977	Bakersfield	CA	93308	661-410-0000	410-0400	189-4	*TF:* 855-550-8324 ■ *Web:* www.a-celectric.com
AC Gentrol Inc	100 S 4th St	Chillicothe	IL	61523	309-274-5486	274-9001	729	*Web:* acgentrol.com
AC Gilbert's Discovery Village	116 Marion St NE	Salem	OR	97301	503-371-3631	316-3485	521	*Web:* www.acgilbert.org
AC Group Inc	118 Lyndsey Dr	Montgomery	TX	77316	281-413-5572		194	*Web:* www.acgroup.org
AC Horn & Co	1269 Majesty Dr	Dallas	TX	75247	214-630-3311		697	*TF:* 800-657-6155 ■ *Web:* www.achornmfg.com
AC Inc	1085 Jordan Rd	Huntsville	AL	35810	256-851-9020	851-9025	91	*Web:* www.acincorp.com
AC Lordi Corp	75 Valley Stream Pkwy Ste 201	Malvern	PA	19355	610-738-0100		194	*Web:* www.bdo.com
AC Miller Concrete Products Inc	31 E Bridge St	Spring City	PA	19475	610-948-4600	948-9750	183	*Web:* www.acmiller.com
AC Nutrition	158 N Main St	Winters	TX	79567	325-754-4546		447	*TF:* 800-588-3333 ■ *Web:* www.acnutrition.com
AC Systems Inc	3990 S Lipan St	Englewood	CO	80110	303-953-3113	789-1111	174	*Web:* www.acsystems.com
AC/C Tech	4415 Forest Manor Ave	Indianapolis	IN	46226	317-545-7071	545-6377	167-3	*Web:* www.acctech.us
ACA (Agriculture Council of America)	11020 King St Ste 205	Overland Park	KS	66210	913-491-1895		48-2	*Web:* www.agday.org
ACA (Auto Club of America Corp)	9411 N Georgia St	Oklahoma City	OK	73120	405-751-4430	751-4462	53	*TF:* 800-411-2007 ■ *Web:* www.autoclubofamerica.com
ACA (American Camp Assn)	5000 State Rd 67 N	Martinsville	IN	46151	765-342-8456	342-2065	48-23	*TF:* 800-428-2267 ■ *Web:* www.acacamps.org
ACA (American Canoe Assn)	503 Sophia St Ste 100	Fredericksburg	VA	22401	540-907-4460	229-3792*	48-22	**Fax Area Code:* 888 ■ *Web:* www.americancanoe.org
ACA (American Chiropractic Assn)	1701 Clarendon Blvd Ste 200	Arlington	VA	22209	703-276-8800	243-2593	49-8	*TF:* 800-986-4636 ■ *Web:* www.acatoday.org
ACA (American Composers Alliance Inc)	802 W 190th St Ste 1B	New York	NY	10040	212-925-0458		48-4	*Web:* composers.com
ACA (American Correctional Assn)	206 N Washington St Ste 200	Alexandria	VA	22314	703-224-0000		49-7	*TF:* 800-222-5646 ■ *Web:* www.aca.org
ACA (American Counseling Assn)	5999 Stevenson Ave	Alexandria	VA	22304	703-823-9800	823-0252	49-15	*TF:* 800-347-6647 ■ *Web:* www.counseling.org
ACA (American AgCredit)	PO Box 1120	Santa Rosa	CA	95402	707-545-1200		216	*TF:* 800-800-4865 ■ *Web:* www.agloan.com
ACA (Arizona Commerce Authority)	333 N Central Ave Ste 1900	Phoenix	AZ	85004	602-845-1200	845-1201	637-10	*Web:* www.azcommerce.com
ACA Associates Inc	545 5th Ave Ste 640	New York	NY	10017	212-808-4420	808-4428	463	*Web:* www.aca-assoc.com
ACA Galleries	529 W 20th St 5th Fl	New York	NY	10011	212-206-8080		42	*Web:* www.acagalleries.com
ACA Group of Cos	3585 Laird Rd Unit 15 & 16	Mississauga	ON	L5L5Z8	905-890-2010	890-1959	246	*Web:* www.aca.ca
ACA International - Association of Credit & Collection Professionals	4040 W 70th St PO Box 390106	Minneapolis	MN	55439	952-926-6547	926-1624	49-2	*Web:* www.acainternational.org
ACAA (American Coal Ash Assn)	15200 E Girard Ave Ste 3050	Aurora	CO	80014	720-870-7897	870-7889	48-12	*Web:* www.acaa-usa.org
ACAAI (American College of Allergy Asthma & Immunology)	85 W Algonquin Rd Ste 550	Arlington Heights	IL	60005	847-427-1200	427-1294	49-8	*Web:* acaai.org
Acacia	2637 Lawrenceville Rd	Lawrenceville	NJ	08648	609-895-9885		671	*Web:* www.acacianj.com
Acacia Capital Corp	101 S Ellsworth Ave Ste 300	San Mateo	CA	94401	650-372-6400		217	*Web:* www.acacia-capital.com
Acacia Home & Garden Inc	101 McLin Creek Rd N PO Box 426	Conover	NC	28613	828-465-1700	465-4205	319-2	*Web:* www.acaciahomeandgarden.com
Acacia Research Corp	520 Newport Center Dr 12th Fl	Newport Beach	CA	92660	949-480-8300	480-8301	405	*NASDAQ: ACTG* ■ *Web:* www.acaciaresearch.com
Academi	PO Box 1029	Moyock	NC	27958	252-435-2488	435-6388	693	*Web:* www.academi.com
Academic Apparel	20644 Superior St	Chatsworth	CA	91311	818-886-8697	886-8743	155-14	*TF:* 800-626-5000 ■ *Web:* www.academicapparel.com
Academic Approach LLC, The	342 W Armitage Ave	Chicago	IL	60614	773-348-8914		242	*Web:* www.academicapproach.com
Academic Keys LLC	1066 Storrs Rd Ste D	Storrs	CT	06268	860-429-0218		194	*Web:* www.academickeys.com
Academic Software Inc	3504 Tates Creek Rd	Lexington	KY	40517	859-552-1020		178-1	*Web:* www.acsw.com
Academic Studies Press (ASP)	28 Montfern Ave	Brighton	MA	02135	617-782-6290	241-3149*	637-10	**Fax Area Code:* 857 ■ *Web:* www.academicstudiespress.com
Academic Therapy Publications (ATP)	20 Commercial Blvd	Novato	CA	94949	415-883-3314	287-9975*	637-2	**Fax Area Code:* 888 ■ *TF:* 800-422-7249 ■ *Web:* www.academictherapy.com
Academica	6340 Sunset Dr	Miami	FL	33143	305-669-2906	669-4390	623	*Web:* www.academica.org
Academie Ste Cecile International School (ASCIS)	925 Cousineau Rd	Windsor	ON	N9G1V8	519-969-1291	969-7953	622	*Web:* academiestececile.ca
Academy Bus LLC	111 Paterson Ave	Hoboken	NJ	07030	201-420-7000	420-8087	760	*TF:* 800-442-7272 ■ *Web:* www.academybus.com
Academy Capital Management	500 N Vly Mills Dr Ste 200	Waco	TX	76710	254-751-0555		528	*Web:* www.academycapitalmgmt.com
Academy Di Capelli	950 Yale Ave Unit 20	Wallingford	CT	06492	203-294-9496	294-9068	167-3	*Web:* www.academydicapelli.com
Academy Fire Protection Inc	42 Broadway 2nd Fl	Lynbrook	NY	11563	800-773-4736		393	*TF:* 800-773-4736 ■ *Web:* www.academyfire.com
Academy for Guided Imagery Inc	30765 Pacific Coast Hwy Ste 355	Malibu	CA	90265	424-242-6369	474-2777*	766	**Fax Area Code:* 310 ■ *Web:* www.acadgi.com
Academy Graphic Communication Inc	1000 Brookpark Rd	Cleveland	OH	44109	216-661-2550	661-8899	627	*TF:* 800-201-2327 ■ *Web:* www.agcinc.org
Academy Hotel Colorado Springs, The	8110 N Academy Blvd	Colorado Springs	CO	80920	719-598-5770	598-5965	379	*TF:* 800-766-8524 ■ *Web:* www.theacademyhotel.com
Academy Leadership LLC	10120 Vly Forge Cir	King of Prussia	PA	19406	610-783-0630		194	*Web:* www.academyleadership.com
Academy of Art University	79 New Montgomery St	San Francisco	CA	94105	415-274-2200	618-6287	166	*TF:* 800-544-2787 ■ *Web:* www.academyart.edu
Academy of General Dentistry (AGD)	211 E Chicago Ave Ste 900	Chicago	IL	60611	312-440-4300	440-0559	49-8	*TF:* 888-243-3368 ■ *Web:* www.agd.org
Academy of Managed Care Pharmacy (AMCP)	100 N Pitt St Ste 400	Alexandria	VA	22314	703-683-8416	683-8417	49-8	*TF:* 800-827-2627 ■ *Web:* www.amcp.org
Academy of Management (AOM)	235 Elm Rd PO Box 3020	Briarcliff Manor	NY	10510	914-923-2607	923-2615	49-12	*TF:* 800-633-4931 ■ *Web:* aom.org
Academy of Model Aeronautics (AMA)	5161 E Memorial Dr	Muncie	IN	47302	800-435-9262	289-4248*	48-18	**Fax Area Code:* 765 ■ *TF:* 800-435-9262 ■ *Web:* www.modelaircraft.org
Academy of Motion Picture Arts & Sciences	8949 Wilshire Blvd	Beverly Hills	CA	90211	310-247-3000	859-9619	48-4	*Web:* www.oscars.org
Academy of Natural Sciences of Drexel University, The	1900 Benjamin Franklin Pkwy	Philadelphia	PA	19103	215-299-1000	299-1028	520	*Web:* www.ansp.org
Academy of Notre Dame De Namur	560 Sproul Rd	Villanova	PA	19085	610-687-0650		685	*Web:* www.ndapa.org
Academy of Osseointegration	85 W Algonquin Rd Ste 550	Arlington Heights	IL	60005	847-439-1919	439-1569	49-8	*TF:* 800-656-7736 ■ *Web:* osseo.org
Academy of Political Science	475 Riverside Dr Ste 1274	New York	NY	10115	212-870-2500	870-2202	48-11	*Web:* www.psqonline.org
Academy of Vocal Arts (AVA)	1920 Spruce St	Philadelphia	PA	19103	215-735-1685	732-2189	573-2	*Web:* www.avaopera.org
Academy Packing Company Inc	2881 Wyoming St	Dearborn	MI	48120	313-841-4900		473	
Academy Solutions Group LLC	6700 Alexander Bell Dr Ste 195	Columbia	MD	21046	410-290-0871		261	*Web:* www.asg-llc.com
Academy Sports & Outdoors	1800 N Mason Rd	Katy	TX	77449	281-646-5200		711	*TF:* 888-922-2336 ■ *Web:* www.academy.com
Academy Systems Inc (ASI)	1343 E 10 St	Brooklyn	NY	11230	718-645-2330	645-2415	178-1	*TF:* 800-446-6619 ■ *Web:* www.academysystems.com
AcademyHealth	1801 K St NW Ste 701	Washington	DC	20006	202-292-6700	292-6800	49-8	*Web:* www.academyhealth.org
AcademyOne Inc	101 Lindenwood Dr Ste 220	Malvern	PA	19355	888-434-2150		177	*TF:* 888-434-2150 ■ *Web:* www.academyone.com
Acadia	1303 NE Fremont St	Portland	OR	97212	503-249-5001		671	*Web:* www.acadiapdx.com
Acadia Broadcasting Ltd	58 King St 3rd Fl	Saint John	NB	E2L1G4	506-648-2100		647	*Web:* www.acadiabroadcastinglimited.ca
Acadia Divinity College	38 Highland Ave	Wolfville	NS	B4P2R6	902-585-2210		167-3	*TF:* 866-875-8975 ■ *Web:* acadiadiv.ca
Acadia Federal Credit Union	9 E Main St	Fort Kent	ME	04743	207-834-6167		219	*TF:* 855-692-2234 ■ *Web:* acadiafcu.org
Acadia Inn	98 Eden St	Bar Harbor	ME	04609	207-288-3500		379	*TF:* 800-638-3636 ■ *Web:* acadiainn.com
Acadia National Park	20 McFarland Hill Dr	Bar Harbor	ME	04609	207-288-3338	288-8813	564	*Web:* www.nps.gov
Acadia National Park Tours	53 Main St	Bar Harbor	ME	04609	207-288-0300		760	*Web:* www.acadiatours.com
Acadia Parish Library	1125 N Parkerson Ave	Crowley	LA	70526	337-788-1880	788-3759	434-3	*Web:* www.acadia.lib.la.us
ACADIA Pharmaceuticals Inc	3911 Sorrento Valley Blvd	San Diego	CA	92121	858-558-2871	558-2872	85	*NASDAQ: ACAD* ■ *TF:* 800-901-5231 ■ *Web:* www.acadia-pharm.com
Acadia Realty Trust	1311 Mamaroneck Ave Ste 260	White Plains	NY	10605	914-288-8100		655	*NYSE: AKR* ■ *Web:* www.acadiarealty.com
Acadia University	15 University Ave	Wolfville	NS	B4P2R6	902-542-2001		785	*TF:* 877-585-1121 ■ *Web:* www2.acadiau.ca
Acadian Ambulance Service Inc	PO Box 98000	LaFayette	LA	70509	800-259-3333		30	*TF:* 800-259-3333 ■ *Web:* acadian.com
Acadian Asset Management Inc	260 Franklin St	Boston	MA	02110	617-850-3500		401	*Web:* www.acadian-asset.com
Acadian Contractors Inc	17102 W La Hwy 330	Abbeville	LA	70510	337-893-6397		538	*Web:* www.acadiancontractors.com

				Phone	Fax	Class
Acadiana Center for the Arts 101 W Vermilion St. *Web:* www.acadianacenterforthearts.org	LaFayette	LA	70501	337-233-7060	233-7062	50-2
Acadiana Computer Systems Inc 324 Dulles Dr *Web:* www.acsmd.com	LaFayette	LA	70506	337-981-2494		180
Acadiana Legal Service Corp 1020 Surrey St *TF:* 800-256-1175 ■ *Web:* www.la-law.org	LaFayette	LA	70501	337-237-4320		428
Acadiana Symphony Orchestra 412 Travis St. *Web:* www.acadianasymphony.org	LaFayette	LA	70503	337-232-4277	237-4712	573-3
ACAI Solutions LLC 1285 Avenue of Americas 35th Fl *Web:* www.acaisolutions.com	New York	NY	10019	212-554-4460		194
Acalanes Union High School Dist 1212 Pleasant Hill Rd *Web:* www.acalanes.k12.ca.us	LaFayette	CA	94549	925-280-3900	280-3903	685
ACAOM (Accreditation Commission for Acupuncture & Oriental Medicine) 8941 Aztec Dr *Web:* acaom.org	Eden Prairie	MN	55347	952-212-2434	657-7068	48-1
Acappella Co, The 900 N Dixieland Rd *Web:* acappella.org	Rogers	AR	72756	615-855-1770		657
Acara Solutions Inc 500 Pearl St Ste 800 *TF:* 800-568-8310 ■ *Web:* acarasolutions.com	Buffalo	NY	14202	716-929-1400	633-2026	360-3
Acaria Inc 963 S Kipling Pkwy *Web:* acariainc.com	Lakewood	CO	80226	303-403-8888	424-3333	363
AcariaHealth Pharmacy Inc 6923 Lee Vista Blvd Ste 200 **Fax Area Code:* 407 ■ *TF:* 855-422-2742 ■ *Web:* acariahealth.envolvehealth.com	Orlando	FL	32822	855-422-2742	380-9153*	391-3
ACAWSO (Adult Children of Alcoholics World Service Organization Inc) PO Box 3216 *Web:* www.adultchildren.org	Torrance	CA	90510	562-595-7831		48-21
ACB (American Council of the Blind) 2200 Wilson Blvd Ste 650 **Fax Area Code:* 703 ■ *TF:* 800-424-8666 ■ *Web:* www.acb.org	Arlington	VA	22201	202-467-5081	465-5085*	48-11
ACB Insurance Inc 7715 Loma Ct Ste E *Web:* www.acb-insurance.com	Fishers	IN	46038	317-915-8601		390
ACB Solutions 551 W Dimond Blvd *TF:* 888-238-4225 ■ *Web:* www.acbsolutions.net	Anchorage	AK	99515	888-238-4225		180
Acbel Polytech Inc 251 Dominion Dr Ste 103 *Web:* www.acbel.com	Morrisville	NC	27560	919-388-4316		396
ACBL (American Contract Bridge League) 6575 Windchase Blvd *TF:* 800-264-2743 ■ *Web:* www.acbl.org	Horn Lake	MS	38637	662-253-3100	253-3187	48-18
ACBSP (Association of Collegiate Business Schools & Programs) 11520 W 119th St *Web:* www.acbsp.org	Overland Park	KS	66213	913-339-9356	339-6226	48-1
ACC (Alice Chamber of Commerce) 612 E Main St PO Box 1609 *TF:* 800-379-4222 ■ *Web:* www.alicetxchamber.org	Alice	TX	78333	361-664-3454	664-2291	139
ACC (Alpena Community College) 665 Johnson St *TF:* 888-468-6222 ■ *Web:* discover.alpenacc.edu	Alpena	MI	49707	989-356-9021		162
ACC (American College of Cardiology) 2400 N St NW *TF:* 800-253-4636 ■ *Web:* www.acc.org	Washington	DC	20037	202-375-6000	375-7000	49-8
ACC (Association of Corporate Counsel) 1025 Connecticut Ave NW Ste 200 *TF:* 877-647-3411 ■ *Web:* www.acc.com	Washington	DC	20036	202-293-4103	293-4701	49-10
ACC Environmental Consultants Inc 7977 Capwell Dr Ste 100 *Web:* www.accenv.com	Oakland	CA	94621	510-638-8400		194
Acc Technical Services Inc 106 Dwight Park Cir *TF:* 855-484-4500 ■ *Web:* www.acctek.com	Syracuse	NY	13209	315-484-4500		463
ACCA (Air Conditioning Contractors of America) 2800 S Shirlington Rd Ste 300 *TF:* 888-290-2220 ■ *Web:* www.acca.org	Arlington	VA	22206	703-575-4477	575-8107	49-3
ACCCE (American Coalition for Clean Coal Electricity) 1152 15th St NW Ste 400 *Web:* americaspower.org	Washington	DC	20005	202-459-4833		48-12
ACC&CE (Association of Consulting Chemists & Chemical Engineers) 514 Corrigan Way *Web:* chemconsult.org	Cary	NC	27519	908-500-9333		49-19
ACCCI (American Coke & Coal Chemicals Institute) 25 Massachusetts Ave NW Ste 800 *Web:* www.accci.org	Washington	DC	20001	202-452-7198		48-12
ACCE (American Chamber of Commerce Executives) 1330 Braddock Pl Ste 300 *TF:* 800-394-2223 ■ *Web:* www.acce.org	Alexandria	VA	22314	703-998-0072	212-9512	49-12
ACCE (American Council for Construction Education) 1717 N Loop 1604 E Ste 320 *Web:* www.acce-hq.org	San Antonio	TX	78232	210-495-6161	495-6168	48-1
Accede Mold & Tool Company Inc 1125 Lexington Ave *Web:* www.accedemold.com	Rochester	NY	14606	585-254-6490		697
Accel Aviation Accessories LLC 11900 Lacy Ln *TF:* 888-686-4880 ■ *Web:* accelaviation.com	Fort Myers	FL	33966	239-275-8202	275-7311	359
Accel Law Group PC 65 LaSalle Rd Ste 400 *TF:* 855-243-8698 ■ *Web:* accellawgroup.com	West Hartford	CT	06107	860-761-8551		41
Accel Partners 428 University Ave *Web:* www.accel.com	Palo Alto	CA	94301	650-614-4800		792
Accel Plastics 4146 B Pl NW *Web:* www.accelplastics.com	Auburn	WA	98001	253-854-0034		596
Accelerant Sales Group LLC 39 E Hanover Ave Ste C3 *Web:* accelerantsales.com	Morris Plains	NJ	07950	973-331-0600		195
Accelerated Genetics E 10890 Penny Ln *TF:* 800-451-9275 ■ *Web:* www.accelgen.com	Baraboo	WI	53913	608-356-8357	356-4387	11-2
Accelerated Technology Laboratories Inc 496 Holly Grove School Rd *Web:* www.atlab.com	West End	NC	27376	910-673-8165		177
Accelero Health Partners LLC 117 VIP Dr Ste 320 *Web:* accelerohealth.com	Wexford	PA	15090	724-799-8210		194
Acceleron Pharma Inc 128 Sidney St *Web:* acceleronpharma.com	Cambridge	MA	02139	617-649-9200		231
Acceleros 11900 Metric Blvd Ste J-163 *Web:* www.acceleros.com	Austin	TX	78758	512-736-8385		41
Acceles Inc 13771 N Fountain Hills Blvd Ste 114-115 *TF:* 877-260-6725 ■ *Web:* www.acceles.com	Fountain Hills	AZ	85268	877-260-6725		196
Acceleware Ltd 435 10 Ave SE *Web:* www.acceleware.com	Calgary	AB	T2G0W3	403-249-9099		177
Accelian LLC 1222 Earnestine St *TF:* 888-543-0051 ■ *Web:* www.accelianllc.com	McLean	VA	22101	703-543-1616		809
Accent 7171 Mercy Rd Ste 100 *TF:* 800-397-7243 ■ *Web:* www.onlineaccent.com	Omaha	NE	68106	402-390-2667		393
Accent Communication Services Inc 585 Sunbury Rd *TF:* 800-589-7379 ■ *Web:* www.accentvoice.com	Delaware	OH	43015	740-548-7378		196
Accent Computer Solutions Inc 8438 Red Oak St *TF:* 800-481-4369 ■ *Web:* www.accentonit.com	Rancho Cucamonga	CA	91730	909-204-4801		463
Accent Controls Inc 1601 Burlington St *Web:* www.accentcontrols.com	North Kansas City	MO	64116	816-483-6330	483-6360	256
Accent Imaging Inc 8121 Brownleigh Dr *TF:* 800-280-0755 ■ *Web:* www.accentimaging.com	Raleigh	NC	27617	919-782-3332	783-0702	344
Accent Inns Ltd 3233 Maple St *TF:* 800-663-0298 ■ *Web:* www.accentinns.com	Victoria	BC	V8X4Y9	250-475-7500		707
Accent Marble & Granite Inc 21609 N 12th Ave Ste 800 *Web:* accentmarblegranite.com	Phoenix	AZ	85027	623-582-1501		191-1
Accent Office Interiors Inc 2108-3 Gilliam Ln *TF:* 866-953-9958 ■ *Web:* www.accentoffice.com	Tallahassee	FL	32308	850-386-5201	386-1615	393
Accent on Arrangements Inc 615 Baronne St Ste 303 *Web:* accent-dmc.com	New Orleans	LA	70113	504-524-1227		149
Accent on Cincinnati Inc 225 E 5th St Ste 2400 *Web:* www.accentcinti.com	Cincinnati	OH	45202	513-721-8687		184
Accent on Music 19363 Willamette Dr *TF:* 800-313-4406 ■ *Web:* www.accentonmusic.com	West Linn	OR	97068	503-699-1814		637-2
Accent Packaging Inc 10131 FM 2920 Rd *TF:* 800-383-8047 ■ *Web:* www.accentwiretie.com	Tomball	TX	77375	281-251-3700	255-0710	492
Accent Plastics Inc 1925 Elise Cir *Web:* www.accentplastics.com	Corona	CA	92879	951-273-7777		608
Accent Plumbing Inc 21101 Fm 685 Ste A	Pflugerville	TX	78660	512-251-2819		189-10
Accentuate Staffing 3200 Fairhill Dr Ste 100 *Web:* www.accentuatestaffing.com	Raleigh	NC	27612	919-844-2900		631
Accenture Inc 5450 Explorer Dr Ste 400 *Web:* www.accenture.com	Mississauga	ON	L4W5M1	416-641-5000		194
ACCEO Retail-1 7075 Pl Robert-Joncas *TF:* 888-474-2001 ■ *Web:* retail-1.acceo.com	Montreal	QC	H4M2Z2	514-631-3336		178-1
Access Alpha Worldwide LLC 444 W Lake St Ste 1700 *Web:* www.accessalpha.com	Chicago	IL	60606	312-585-6000		428
Access America 673 Emory Valley Rd *TF:* 800-860-2140 ■ *Web:* www.accessam.com	Oak Ridge	TN	37830	865-482-2140	482-2306	736
Access Bio Inc 65 Clyde Rd Ste A *Web:* www.accessbio.net	Somerset	NJ	08873	732-873-4040		415
Access Broadband 106 S 5th Ave *Web:* www.accessmn.com	Virginia	MN	55792	218-741-4650		224
Access Business Group 5600 Beach Blvd *Web:* www.accessbusinessgroup.com	Buena Park	CA	90621	714-562-6250		799
Access Cable Television Inc 302 Enterprise Dr *TF:* 877-821-2288 ■ *Web:* www.accesshsd.com	Somerset	KY	42501	606-677-2444	677-2443	116
Access College Foundation 7300 Newport Ave Ste 500 *Web:* www.accesscollege.org	Norfolk	VA	23505	757-962-6113		242
Access Communications Co-operative Ltd 2250 Park St *Web:* www.myaccess.ca	Regina	SK	S4N7K7	306-569-2225		116
Access Communications Inc 976 Rincon Cir **Fax Area Code:* 408 ■ *TF:* 800-342-4439 ■ *Web:* www.access-comm.net	San Jose	CA	95131	800-342-4439	970-0941*	224
Access Community Credit Union 6401 S Bell St *TF:* 800-687-2990 ■ *Web:* accesscreditunion.com	Amarillo	TX	79109	806-353-9999		219
Access Computers Inc 538 W Main St *Web:* www.accesscomputersus.com	Lebanon	OH	45036	513-932-5454		175
Access Credit Management Inc 11225 Huron Ln Ste 222 *Web:* arcollectors.com	Little Rock	AR	72211	501-664-2922		160
Access Credit Union 1807 W Cermak Rd *Web:* access-cu.com	Broadview	IL	60155	708-343-0228		219
Access Direct Systems Inc 91 Executive Blvd *Web:* www.accessdirect.com	Farmingdale	NY	11735	631-420-0770	420-1647	5
Access Energy Co-op 1800 W Washington St *TF:* 866-242-4232 ■ *Web:* accessenergycoop.com	Mount Pleasant	IA	52641	319-385-1577	385-6873	245
Access ESP LLC 13215 N Promenade Blvd *Web:* accessesp.com	Stafford	TX	77477	713-589-2599		539
Access Financial Resources Inc 3621 NW 63rd Ste A1 *Web:* www.afradvice.com	Oklahoma City	OK	73116	405-848-9826		690
Access Industries Inc 730 Fifth Ave *Web:* www.accessindustries.com	New York	NY	10019	212-247-6400		360-3

Phone | Fax | Class

Access Innovations Inc
4725 Indian School Rd NE Ste 100 Albuquerque NM 87110 505-265-3591 256-1080 177
TF: 800-926-8328 ■ *Web:* www.accessinn.com

Access Intelligence LLC
4 Choke Cherry Rd 2nd Fl Rockville MD 20850 301-354-2000 637-9
TF: 800-777-5006 ■ *Web:* www.accessintel.com

Access International Inc
5959 W Century Blvd Ste 562 Los Angeles CA 90045 310-258-9480 258-9483 194
Web: www.access-int.com

Access Management Group
1100 Northmeadow Pkwy Ste 114 Roswell GA 30076 770-777-6890 391-4
Web: www.accessmgt.com

Access Optics LLC
2201 N Maple Ave Broken Arrow OK 74012 918-294-1234 544
Web: www.accessoptics.com

Access Products Inc
4192 Ctr Pk Dr Colorado Springs CO 80916 719-591-9660 573-0899 361
TF: 800-779-7799 ■ *Web:* www.accessproductsinc.com

Access Property Management
4 Walter E Foran Blvd Ste 311 Flemington NJ 08822 908-806-2600 652
Web: www.accesspm.com

Access Securities Inc
30 Buxton Farm Rd Stamford CT 06905 203-322-3377 690
Web: www.accesssecurities.com

Access Softek Inc
727 Allston Way Ste C Berkeley CA 94710 510-898-7606 177
Web: www.accesssoftek.com

Access Specialties International LLC
15230 Carrousel Way Rosemount MN 55068 651-453-1283 174
TF: 800-332-1013 ■ *Web:* www.access-specialties.com

Access Systems America
1188 E Arques Ave Sunnyvale CA 94085 408-400-3000 400-1500 178-12
Web: www.access-company.com

Access to Care LLC
3645 N Briarwood Ln Ste D Muncie IN 47304 765-282-4766 282-4588 363
Web: www.infusionpharmacy.com

Access To Home Care Services Inc
69 South St Auburn NY 13021 315-258-2842 363
Web: accesshomecareny.com

Access To Media 432 Front St Chicopee MA 01013 866-612-0034 7
TF: 866-612-0034 ■ *Web:* www.accesstomedia.com

Access US 712 N Second St Ste 300 Saint Louis MO 63102 314-655-7700 655-7701 398
TF: 800-638-6373 ■ *Web:* accessus.net

Access Venture Partners
8787 Turnpike Dr Ste 260 Westminster CO 80031 303-426-8899 792
Web: www.accessvp.com

Access Worldwide 76 Southwoods Pkwy Atlanta GA 30354 404-675-0633 5
TF: 877-564-8581 ■ *Web:* www.accessworldwide.net

AccessCom Inc
1340 Poydras St Ste 350 New Orleans LA 70112 504-962-2000 962-2001 180
Web: www.accesscom.net

AccessiG PO Box 245 East Hanover NJ 07936 973-360-0750 178-10
Web: www.accessig.com

AccessIT Group Inc
2000 Valley Forge Cir Ste 106 King of Prussia PA 19406 610-783-5200 783-5151 180
TF: 866-748-2484 ■ *Web:* www.accessitgroup.com

Accesso LLC
1025 Greenwood Blvd Ste 500 Lake Mary FL 32746 407-333-7311 387
Web: accesso.com

Accesso Partners LLC
1140 E Hallandale Beach Blvd Hallandale Beach FL 33009 954-454-4665 205
TF: 844-330-1818 ■ *Web:* accessopartners.com

Accessorie Air Compressor Systems Inc
1858 N Case St Orange CA 92865 714-634-2292 172
Web: accessorieair.com

Accessories Etc. Inc
9696 Bonita Beach Rd Ste 102 Bonita Springs FL 34135 239-444-1400 362
Web: accetc.net

Accessories Palace Inc
585 105th Ave N Ste 11 Royal Palm Beach FL 33411 561-793-5565 793-5562 328
TF: 866-725-2234 ■ *Web:* shop.accessoriespalace.com

Accessory Export LLC 4105 Indus Way Riverside CA 92503 951-687-1140 48-21

Accessory Place Inc
12850 Memorial Dr Ste 1500 Houston TX 77024 713-467-2106 362
Web: accplace.net

AccessPoint LLC
28800 Orchard Lake Rd Farmington Hills MI 48334 866-513-3861 734
TF: 866-513-3861 ■ *Web:* www.apteam.com

ACCET (Accrediting Council for Continuing Education & Training)
1722 N St NW Washington DC 20036 202-955-1113 955-1118 48-1
Web: accet.org

ACCF (American Council for Capital Formation)
1001 Connecticut Ave NW Ste 620 Washington DC 20036 202-293-5811 785-8165 49-2
Web: accf.org

Accident Fund Co
232 S Capitol Ave PO Box 40790 Lansing MI 48901 517-342-4200 391-4
TF: 888-276-0327 ■ *Web:* www.accidentfund.com

Accion Intl 1101 15th St NW Ste 400 Washington DC 20005 202-393-5113 545-0361 217
Web: www.accion.org

Accion Labs Inc
DDI Plz 1 1225 Washington Pk Ste 401 Bridgeville PA 15017 724-260-5139 631
Web: www.accionlabs.com

Accion Texas Inc 2007 W Martin St San Antonio TX 78207 210-226-3664 217
TF: 888-215-2373 ■ *Web:* liftfund.com

Accipiter Radar Technologies Inc
576 Hwy 20 W Fonthill ON L0S1C0 905-228-6888 256
Web: www.accipiterradar.com

Acclaim Group LLC, The
108 N Union Ave Cranford NJ 07016 908-653-0880 652
Web: acclaim-group.com

Acclaim Home Health Services Inc
7566 Central Parke Blvd Mason OH 45040 513-336-6133 363
Web: www.ahhsi.com

Acclaim Marketing & Sales 549 Mercury Ln Brea CA 92821 714-256-9388 256-9387 466
Web: acclaimmktg.net

Acclaim Print & Copy Centers Inc
6345 Scarlett Ct Dublin CA 94568 925-829-7750 113
Web: www.acclaimprint.com

Phone | Fax | Class

Acclaim Software
1907 Chesapeake Trl SW Decatur AL 35603 866-531-6562 296-4765* 178-1
**Fax Area Code:* 877 ■ *TF:* 866-531-6562 ■ *Web:* www.acclaim-software.com

Acclaim Systems Inc
110 E Pennsylvania Blvd Feasterville-Trevose PA 19053 215-354-1420 177
Web: www.acclaimsystems.com

Acclaim Telecom Services Inc
PO Box 515772 Dallas TX 75251 972-331-1777 331-1701 177
TF: 866-324-6416 ■ *Web:* www.acclaimtelecom.com

Acclinet Corp 490 S Stark Hwy Weare NH 03281 603-529-4220 396
Web: acclinet.com

Acclivus Corp 14520 Midway Rd Dallas TX 75244 972-628-2500 194
Web: www.acclivus.com

Acco Material Handling Solutions
76 Acco Dr York PA 17402 800-243-5432 190
TF: 800-243-5432 ■ *Web:* www.accomhs.com

Accokeek Foundation 3400 Bryan Pt Rd Accokeek MD 20607 301-283-2113 520
TF: 800-217-4273 ■ *Web:* www.accokeekfoundation.org

Accomack County
23296 Courthouse Ave Ste 203 PO Box 388 Accomac VA 23301 757-787-5700 787-2468 338
Web: www.co.accomack.va.us

Accomack County Public Schools
PO Box 330 Accomac VA 23301 757-787-5754 787-2951 449
Web: www.accomack.k12.va.us

Accommodations Plus Inc
265 Broadhollow Rd Melville NY 11747 516-798-4444 376
Web: www.apiglobalsolutions.com

Accord Carton 6155 W 115th St Alsip IL 60803 800-648-6780 45
TF: 800-648-6780 ■ *Web:* accordcarton.com

Accord Creditor Services LLC
PO Box 10005 Newnan GA 30271 800-373-0760 393
TF: 800-373-0760 ■ *Web:* www.accordcreditorservices.com

Accord Financial Corp
40 Eglinton Ave E Ste 602 Toronto ON M4P3A2 416-961-0007 403
Web: www.accordfinancial.com

Accordant Company LLC
365 S St Ste 100 Morristown NJ 07960 973-887-8900 179
TF: 800-303-1002 ■ *Web:* www.accordantco.com

Account Control Systems Inc
85 Chestnut Ridge Rd Ste 113 Montvale NJ 07645 800-482-8026 160
TF: 800-482-8026 ■ *Web:* www.accountcontrolsystems.com

Accountability Services PLLC
10564 Fifth Ave NE Ste 201 Seattle WA 98125 206-522-0110 734
TF: 888-513-9280 ■ *Web:* accountabilityservices.com

Accountants in Transition Inc
10509 Vista Sorrento Pkwy Ste 300 San Diego CA 92121 858-404-9900 2
Web: calltsg.com

Accounting Career Consultants
12747 Olive Blvd Ste 210 Saint Louis MO 63141 314-569-9898 2
Web: careeradvancers.com

Accounting Principals
10151 Deerwood Park Blvd
Bldg 400 Third Fl Jacksonville FL 32256 904-360-2400 721
Web: www.accountingprincipals.com

Accounting Professionals LLC
16841 N 31st Ave Ste 102 Phoenix AZ 85053 602-482-9101 2
Web: atlascpas.com

Accountix Inc 875 S Orem Blvd Ste 2 Orem UT 84058 801-224-2900 177
TF: 888-235-2700 ■ *Web:* www.accountix.com

Accounts Management Center Inc
1976 E Grand Ave Hot Springs AR 71901 501-623-5594 160

ACCP (American College of Clinical Pharmacy)
13000 W 87th St Pkwy Lenexa KS 66215 913-492-3311 492-0088 49-8
Web: www.accp.com

ACCP (American College of Chest Physicians)
3300 Dundee Rd Northbrook IL 60062 847-498-1400 498-5460 49-8
TF: 800-343-2227 ■ *Web:* www.chestnet.org

Accraline Inc 1420 W Bike St Bremen IN 46506 574-546-3484 546-5094 454
Web: www.accraline.com

Accram Inc 2901 W Clarendon Ave Phoenix AZ 85017 602-285-4110 175
TF: 800-220-0547 ■ *Web:* accram.com

Accratronics Seals Corp
2211 Kenmere Ave Burbank CA 91504 818-843-1500 841-2117 326
Web: www.accratronics.com

Accreditation Association for Ambulatory Health Care (AAAHC)
5250 Old Orchard Rd Ste 200 Skokie IL 60077 847-853-6060 853-9028 48-1
Web: www.aaahc.org

Accreditation Commission for Acupuncture & Oriental Medicine (ACAOM)
8941 Aztec Dr Eden Prairie MN 55347 952-212-2434 657-7068 48-1
Web: acaom.org

Accreditation Council for Graduate Medical Education (ACGME)
401 N Michigan Ave Ste 2000 Chicago IL 60611 312-755-5000 755-7498 48-1
Web: www.acgme.org

Accreditation Council for Pharmacy Education
135 S LaSalle St Ste 4100 Chicago IL 60603 312-664-3575 228-2631* 48-1
**Fax Area Code:* 866 ■ *Web:* www.acpe-accredit.org

Accreditation Review Commission on Education for the Physician Assistant Inc (ARC-PA)
12000 Findley Rd Ste 275 Johns Creek GA 30097 770-476-1224 476-1738 48-1
Web: www.arc-pa.org

Accredited Home Care Inc
27733 Schoenherr Rd Warren MI 48088 586-427-6640 427-6642 363
TF: 888-813-6244 ■ *Web:* www.accreditedhomecare.com

Accredited Surety & Casualty Company Inc
4798 New Broad St Ste 200 Orlando FL 32814 407-629-2131 629-4571 390
TF: 800-432-2799 ■ *Web:* www.accredited-inc.com

Accrediting Bureau of Health Education Schools (ABHES)
7777 Leesburg Pk Ste 314 N Falls Church VA 22043 703-917-9503 917-4109 48-1
Web: www.abhes.org

Accrediting Commission of Career Schools & Colleges of Technology (ACCSCT)
2101 Wilson Blvd Ste 302 Arlington VA 22201 703-247-4212 247-4533 48-1
TF: 800-842-0229 ■ *Web:* www.accsc.org

Accrediting Council for Continuing Education & Training (ACCET)
1722 N St NW Washington DC 20036 202-955-1113 955-1118 48-1
Web: accet.org

Accrediting Council for Independent Colleges & Schools (ACICS)
750 First St NE Ste 980 Washington DC 20002 202-336-6780 842-2593 48-1
TF: 800-258-3826 ■ *Web:* www.acics.org

Company / Address	Phone	Fax	Class
Accredo Health Group Inc 1640 Century Center Pkwy, Memphis TN 38134 *TF:* 877-222-7336 ■ *Web:* www.accredo.com	877-381-8243		587
Accrete Construction LLC 801 Valley Ave NW Ste A, Puyallup WA 98371 *Web:* accrete.build	253-286-3900	286-3901	186
Accretech USA Inc 1778 N Piano Rd Ste 212, Richardson TX 75081 *Web:* www.accretech.jp	214-459-1688	459-1696	696
Accretive Technologies Inc 4032 Wild Ginger Path, Norcross GA 30092 *Web:* www.accretive.com	770-313-7644	246-9186	225
Accro Tool Inc 401 Hunt Valley Dr, New Kensington PA 15068 *Web:* www.accrotool.com	724-339-3560	339-9852	567
ACCS Enterprises Inc 587 Sawgrass Corporate Pkwy, Sunrise FL 33325 *Web:* www.headsuponline.com	954-472-3300		608
ACCSCT (Accrediting Commission of Career Schools & Colleges of Technology) 2101 Wilson Blvd Ste 302, Arlington VA 22201 *TF:* 800-842-0229 ■ *Web:* www.accsc.org	703-247-4212	247-4533	48-1
Accsense Inc 8437 Mayfield Rd, Chesterland OH 44026 *TF:* 800-956-4437 ■ *Web:* accsense.com	440-729-2570	729-2586	693
Accsys Inc 4010 W Boy Scout Blvd Ste 300, Tampa FL 33607 *TF:* 800-933-4711 ■ *Web:* restaurantmagic.com	813-288-2633	315-6489	177
Accsys Technology Inc 1177 A Quarry Ln, Pleasanton CA 94566 *Web:* www.accsys.com	925-462-6949	462-6993	425
ACCT (Association of Community College Trustees) 1101 17th St NW Ste 300, Washington DC 20036 *TF:* 866-895-2228 ■ *Web:* www.acct.org	202-775-4667	223-1297	49-5
Accton Technology Corp 1200 Crossman Ave Ste 130, Sunnyvale CA 94089 *Web:* www.accton.com	408-747-0994	747-0982	176
Accu Fire Fabrication Inc 8 Progress Dr, Morrisville PA 19067 *TF:* 800-641-0005 ■ *Web:* www.accu-fire.com	215-428-2400		595
Accu Personnel Inc 911 Kings Hwy N, Cherry Hill NJ 08034 *TF:* 800-437-2228 ■ *Web:* accustaffing.com	856-482-2222	482-9036	260
Accu Reference Medical Lab 1901 E Linden Ave Unit 4, Linden NJ 07036 *TF:* 877-733-4522 ■ *Web:* www.accureference.com	877-733-4522		415
Accu Rx Inc 100 Federal Way, Johnston RI 02919 *TF:* 800-234-2369 ■ *Web:* www.accurxinc.com	800-234-2369	234-2371	542
Accu Solution Services Ltd 3 Mays Cres, Waterdown ON L0R2H4 *TF:* 800-668-0831 ■ *Web:* www.accusolutionservices.com	800-668-0831		317
Accu Therm Inc PO Box 249, Monroe City MO 63456 *TF:* 888-925-4332 ■ *Web:* accutherm.com	573-735-1060	735-1066	386
ACCU-BREAK Pharmaceuticals Inc 1000 S Pine Island Rd Ste 230, Plantation FL 33324 *Web:* accubreakpharmaceuticals.com	954-236-7351		231
AccuCode Inc 6886 S Yosemite St Ste 100, Centennial CO 80112 *TF:* 866-705-9879 ■ *Web:* accucode.com	303-639-6111		177
Accucom Consulting Inc 250 Post Rd E, Westport CT 06880 *Web:* www.accucomci.com	203-221-1212	221-1946	194
ACCUCOM Technical Services Inc 900 N Bower Ste 840, Richardson TX 75080 *Web:* www.accucom.com	972-238-7502		179
AccuData Holdings Inc 5220 Summerlin Commons Blvd Ste 200, Fort Myers FL 33907 *Web:* www.accudata.com	239-425-4400		387
Accuduct Manufacturing Inc 316 Ellingson Rd, Algona WA 98001 *Web:* www.accuduct.com	253-939-7741		697
Accudyn Products Inc 2400 Yoder Dr, Erie PA 16506 *Web:* www.accudyn.com	814-833-7615		608
Accudynamics LLC 240 Kenneth Welch Dr, Lakeville MA 02347 *Web:* www.accudynamics.com	508-946-4545		454
AccuFab 232 Cherry St, Ithaca NY 14850 *Web:* www.accufabinc.com	607-273-3706	277-8295	480
Accu-Fab Inc 801 Beacon Lake Dr, Raleigh NC 27610 *Web:* www.accufabnc.com	919-212-6400	882-0115	697
Accufax PO Box 35563, Tulsa OK 74153 **Fax Area Code:* 866 ■ *TF:* 800-256-8898 ■ *Web:* www.accufax-us.com	800-256-8898	936-3027*	635
Accu-Form Polymers Inc 170 Water Tank Rd, Warsaw NC 28398 *Web:* www.accuform-polymers.com	910-293-6961	293-2962	604
Accuimage LLC 2807 Biloxi Ave, Nashville TN 37204 *Web:* accuimagellc.com	615-242-7226		317
Accuity Delivery Systems 810 7th Ave Ste 1110, New York NY 10019 *Web:* accds.com	646-568-2801		177
Accu-Label Inc 2021 Research Dr, Fort Wayne IN 46808 *TF:* 888-482-5223 ■ *Web:* acculabel.com	260-482-5223		627
Acculease Construction Equipment Inc 63 Clifton St, Farmingdale NY 11735 *TF:* 844-481-7733 ■ *Web:* www.acculease.com	844-481-7733		690
Acculink 1055 Greenville Blvd SW, Greenville NC 27834 *TF:* 800-948-4110 ■ *Web:* acculink.com	252-321-5805		627
Acculynk Inc 3225 Cumberland Blvd SE Ste 550, Atlanta GA 30339 *Web:* acculynk.com	678-894-7010		387
Accuma Corp 133 Fanjoy Rd, Statesville NC 28625 *Web:* www.accuma.com	704-873-1488		596
Accumedic Computer Systems Inc 11 Grace Ave Ste 401, Great Neck NY 11021 *TF:* 800-765-9300 ■ *Web:* www.accumedic.com	516-466-6800		177
Accumulators Inc 15102 Sommermeyer St Ste 125, Houston TX 77043 *Web:* www.accumulators.com	713-465-0202		537
Accumyn LLC Po Box 541190, Houston TX 77254	713-800-2550		194
Accupac Inc 1501 Industrial Blvd, Mainland PA 19451 *Web:* www.accupac.com	215-256-7000		583
AccuPay Payroll Inc 50 S Penn St Ste A5, Hatboro PA 19040 *Web:* www.accupay.net	267-803-1213		2
Accuplace 1800 NW 69th Ave, Plantation FL 33313 *TF:* 866-820-0434 ■ *Web:* accuplace.com	954-791-1500	791-1501	547
Accuplan Benefits Services 515 East 4500 South Ste G200, Salt Lake City UT 84107 **Fax Area Code:* 877 ■ *TF:* 800-454-2649 ■ *Web:* www.accuplan.net	801-266-9900	890-0929*	49-2
Accuprint Inc 2414 Palumbo Dr, Lexington KY 40509 *Web:* www.accuprint.us	859-268-8844		627
Accupro Trademark Services LLP 401 W Georgia St Ste 702, Vancouver BC V6B5A1 *Web:* accuprotm.com	604-661-9292		196
Accuprobe Corp 35 Congress St, Salem MA 01970 *Web:* www.accuprobe.com	978-745-7878	745-7922	248
Accura Engineering 3200 Presidential Dr, Atlanta GA 30340 *Web:* www.accuraengineering.com	404-241-8722	241-4577	225
Accuracy in Media Inc (AIM) 4350 E West Hwy Ste 555, Bethesda MD 20814 *TF:* 800-787-4567 ■ *Web:* www.aim.org	202-364-4401	364-4098	49-14
Accurate Air Engineering Inc 16207 Carmennita Rd, Cerritos CA 90703 *Web:* www.accurateair.com	562-484-6370	484-6371	385
Accurate Alloys Inc 5455 Irwindale Ave, Irwindale CA 91706 *TF:* 800-842-2222 ■ *Web:* www.accuratealloys.com	626-338-4012	337-8393	492
Accurate Biometrics Inc 4849 N Milwaukee Ave Ste 101, Chicago IL 60630 *TF:* 866-361-9944 ■ *Web:* accuratebiometrics.com	773-685-5699		400
Accurate Boring Co 17420 Malyn Blvd, Fraser MI 48026 *Web:* www.accurateboring.com	586-294-7555	294-2530	455
Accurate Box Company Inc 86 Fifth Ave, Paterson NJ 07524 *Web:* www.accuratebox.com	973-345-2000		100
Accurate Bushing Company Inc 443 N Ave, Garwood NJ 07027 *TF:* 800-932-0076 ■ *Web:* www.smithbearing.com	908-789-1121	789-9429	75
Accurate Chemical & Scientific Corp 300 Shames Dr, Westbury NY 11590 *TF:* 800-645-6264 ■ *Web:* www.accuratechemical.com	516-333-2221	997-4948	231
Accurate Circuit Engineering Inc 3019 Kilson Dr, Santa Ana CA 92707 *Web:* www.ace-pcb.com	714-546-2162		625
Accurate Color & Compounding Inc 1666 Dearborn Ave, Aurora IL 60505 *Web:* www.accurate-color.com	630-978-1227		596
Accurate Computer Technology Inc 30 Corporate Pk Ste 307, Irvine CA 92606 *Web:* www.act-mail.com	949-261-6677		177
Accurate Controls 326 Blackburn St, Ripon WI 54971 *Web:* www.accuratecontrols.com	920-748-6603		693
Accurate Diagnostic Labs Inc 3000 Hadley Rd, South Plainfield NJ 07080 *Web:* accuratediagnosticlabs.com	732-839-3300		415
Accurate Dial & Nameplate Inc 329 Mira Loma Ave, Glendale CA 91204 **Fax Area Code:* 818 ■ *TF:* 800-400-4455 ■ *Web:* www.accuratedial.com	323-245-9181	243-6793*	413
Accurate Elastomer Products Inc 1112 Swenson Blvd, Elgin TX 78621 *Web:* www.accurateelastomer.com	512-285-4585		596
Accurate Energetics Systems LLC 5891 Hwy 230 W, McEwen TN 37101 *Web:* www.aesys.biz	931-729-4207		268
Accurate Engineering & Manufacturing LLC 13569 New Holland St, Holland MI 49424 *Web:* accurateengmfg.com	616-738-1261		261
Accurate Expediting Inc 28950 Goddard Rd, Romulus MI 48174 *Web:* www.accuratedtw.com	734-722-0514		311
Accurate Graphics Inc 2650 Pleasantdale Rd Ste 1, Doraville GA 30340 *Web:* Www.agprepress.com	770-448-9408	840-0489	629
Accurate Heating & Cooling 3001 River Rd, Chillicothe OH 45601 *Web:* www.accuratehvac.com	740-775-5005		610
Accurate Imaging Resources 22532 Avenida Empresa, Rancho Santa Margarita CA 92688 *TF:* 800-700-7377 ■ *Web:* www.accurate-imaging.com	949-888-3880	888-3883	535
Accurate Industrial Machining Inc 1711 Church St, Holbrook NY 11741 *Web:* www.accurateindustrialmachining.com	631-242-0566	242-6469	454
Accurate Insurance Inc 508 S Locust St, Glenwood IA 51534 *Web:* www.accurateinsinc.com	712-527-9106	527-9388	390
Accurate Mailings Inc 215 O'Neill Ave, Belmont CA 94002 *TF:* 800-732-3290 ■ *Web:* www.accuratemailings.com	650-508-8885		5
Accurate Metal Fabricating 1657 N Kostner Ave, Chicago IL 60639 *Web:* www.accuratemetalfab.com	773-235-0400	235-3633	295
Accurate Metal Machining Inc 882 Callendar Blvd, Painesville OH 44077 *Web:* www.accuratemetalmachining.com	440-350-8225	350-8190	454
Accurate Partitions Corp 160 Tower Dr PO Box 287, Burr Ridge IL 60527 *TF:* 800-933-4525 ■ *Web:* accuratepartitions.com	708-442-6800	442-7439	609
Accurate Perforating Co 3636 S Kedzie Ave, Chicago IL 60632 *TF:* 800-621-0273 ■ *Web:* accurateperforating.com	773-254-3232	254-9453	488
Accurate Plumbing 7595 Fishel Dr S, Dublin OH 43016 *Web:* www.accurateplumbinginc.com	614-526-0131		610
Accurate Printing Inc 2380 Research Ct Ste 100, Woodbridge VA 22192 *Web:* www.accurateprinting.com	703-494-0707		113
Accurate Staffing Consultants Inc 804 First Ave S, Conover NC 28613 *Web:* www.accuratestaffing.com	828-466-1018		260

	Phone	Fax	Class
Accurate Surgical & Scientific Instruments Corp 300 Shames Dr. . . . . Westbury NY 11590 *TF:* 800-645-3569 ■ *Web:* www.accuratesurgical.com	516-333-2570	997-4948	476
Accurate Technologies Inc 47199 Cartier Dr. . . . . Wixom MI 48393 *Web:* www.accuratetechnologies.com	248-848-9200		153
Accuray Inc 1310 Chesapeake Terr . . . . . Sunnyvale CA 94089 *NASDAQ: ARAY* ■ *TF:* 888-522-3740 ■ *Web:* www.accuray.com	408-716-4600	716-4601	476
Accu-Read Inc PO Box 18277. . . . . Spokane WA 99228 *Web:* accureadinc.com	509-670-5894		463
Accurecord Inc 200 Broadhollow Rd Ste 308 . . . . . Melville NY 11747 *Web:* www.accurecord-direct.com	631-243-6400	271-1939	2
Accuride Corp 7140 Office Cir. . . . . Evansville IN 47715 *NYSE: ACW* ■ *TF:* 800-823-8332 ■ *Web:* www.accuridecorp.com	812-962-5000		60
Accuride International Inc 12311 Shoemaker Ave . . . . . Santa Fe Springs CA 90670 *Web:* www.accuride.com	562-903-0200	903-0208	487
Accuristix 2844 Bristol Cir. . . . . Oakville ON L6H6G4 *TF:* 866-356-6830 ■ *Web:* www.accuristix.com	905-829-9927		360-2
Accuromm USA Inc 101 W Hampton Dr . . . . . Lexington KY 40511 *Web:* www.accuromm.com	859-254-4334	231-8347	493
Accu-Router Inc 634 Mt View Industrial Dr. . . . . Morrison TN 37357 *Web:* accu-router.com	931-668-7127	668-9187	821
Accurus Aerospace Tulsa LLC 12716 E Pine St . . . . . Tulsa OK 74116 *Web:* www.precisemachining.com	918-438-3121	438-1188	22
Accuscreen Systems 1038 Main St. . . . . Baton Rouge LA 70802 *Web:* www.accuscreensystems.com	225-343-8378		196
Accusemble Electronics Inc 5 Esquire Rd. . . . . Billerica MA 01821 *Web:* www.accusemble.com	978-392-0211	392-0012	625
Accu-Sembly Inc 1835 Huntington Dr . . . . . Duarte CA 91010 *Web:* www.accu-sembly.com	626-357-3447	357-0778	625
Accushim Inc 4601 Lawndale Ave. . . . . Lyons IL 60534 *Web:* www.accushim.com	708-442-6448	442-6918	482
Accusource Inc 1240 E Ontario Ave Ste 102-140 . . . . . Corona CA 92881 *TF:* 888-649-6272 ■ *Web:* accusource-online.com	951-734-0082		743
AccuSpec Electronics LLC 8140 Hawthorne Dr. . . . . Erie PA 16509 *Web:* 4frontsolutions.com	814-464-2000		253
AccuSport Inc 4310 Enterprise Dr Ste C . . . . . Winston-Salem NC 27106 *Web:* www.accusport.com	336-759-3300		639
Accutax Inc 953 N Plum Grove Rd Unit B . . . . . Schaumburg IL 60173 *Web:* accutaxpro.com	847-278-7200		2
Accu-Tec Inc 1735 W Burnett St . . . . . Louisville KY 40210 *Web:* accu-tec.com	502-339-7511	339-7571	88
Accutemp Engineering Inc 100 Maple St Bldg B. . . . . Watertown MA 02472 *Web:* www.accutemp-eng.com	617-926-1221		256
Accutemp Products Inc 8415 N Clinton Pk . . . . . Fort Wayne IN 46825 *TF:* 800-210-5907 ■ *Web:* www.accutemp.net	260-493-0415	493-0318	406
Accu-time Systems Inc 420 Somers Rd . . . . . Ellington CT 06029 *TF:* 800-355-4648 ■ *Web:* www.accu-time.com	860-870-5000	872-1511	56
Accutrack Medical Billing 15703 Freeman Ave . . . . . Lawndale CA 90260	310-679-2141		2
Accutrans Inc 2740 Indiana Ave . . . . . Kenner LA 70062 *Web:* www.accutransinc.com	504-469-0500		610
AccuTrex Products Inc 112 Southpointe Blvd. . . . . Canonsburg PA 15317 *Web:* www.accutrex.com	724-746-4300		599
Accutron Inc 1733 Parkside Ln. . . . . Phoenix AZ 85027 *TF:* 800-531-2221 ■ *Web:* www.accutron-inc.com	623-780-2020		228
Accuturn Corp 7189 Old 215 Frontage Rd Ste 101. . . . . Moreno Valley CA 92553 *Web:* accuturninc.com	951-656-6621	656-2086	454
Accuvoice Inc 343 Wainwright Dr. . . . . Northbrook IL 60062 *Web:* www.accuvoice.com	847-559-7272		194
AccuWeather Inc 385 Science Park Rd. . . . . State College PA 16803 *TF:* 800-566-6606 ■ *Web:* www.accuweather.com	814-235-8500	238-1339	530
Accuzip 3216 El Camino Real. . . . . Atascadero CA 93422 *TF:* 800-233-0555 ■ *Web:* www.accuzip.com	805-461-7300		177
ACD (American College of Dentists) 839 Quince Orchard Blvd Ste J. . . . . Gaithersburg MD 20878 *Web:* www.acd.org	301-977-3223	977-3330	49-8
ACD Systems International Inc 129-1335 Bear Mtn Pkwy. . . . . Victoria BC V9B6T9 *TF:* 888-767-9888 ■ *Web:* www.acdsee.com	778-817-1168	402-8305	178-8
ACDA (American Choral Directors Assn) 545 Couch Dr. . . . . Oklahoma City OK 73102 *Web:* acda.org	405-232-8161	232-8162	48-4
ACDI (American Computer & Digital Components) 7435 New Technology Way Ste A . . . . . Frederick MD 21703 *Web:* www.acdi.com	301-363-4182	694-5152	696
ACDI/VOCA 50 F St NW Ste 1000. . . . . Washington DC 20001 *TF:* 800-929-8622 ■ *Web:* www.acdivoca.org	202-469-6208		48-5
ACDS (Association for Children with Down Syndrome Inc) 4 Fern Pl. . . . . Plainview NY 11803 *Web:* www.acds.org	516-933-4700	933-9524	48-17
ACE (American Council on Exercise) 4851 Paramount Dr . . . . . San Diego CA 92123 *TF:* 800-825-3636 ■ *Web:* www.acefitness.org	858-576-6500	576-6564	48-17
ACE (Altamont Corridor Express) 949 E Ch St . . . . . Stockton CA 95202 *TF:* 800-411-7245 ■ *Web:* www.acerail.com	800-411-7245		468
ACE (Auto Credit Express) 3252 University Dr Ste 250. . . . . Auburn Hills MI 48326 *TF:* 888-535-2277 ■ *Web:* www.goacegroup.com	888-535-2277		57
ACE Alternator & Starter Exchange 5770 E Midland Ave. . . . . Wichita KS 67216 *TF:* 800-843-2211 ■ *Web:* www.acealternatorstarter.com	316-529-8854		62-5
ACE Bakery 1 Hafis Rd. . . . . Toronto ON M6M2V6 **Fax Area Code:* 905 ■ *TF:* 800-443-7929 ■ *Web:* www.acebakery.com	416-241-8433	565-7098*	297-8
ACE Battery Inc 2166 Bluff Rd . . . . . Indianapolis IN 46225 *Web:* www.acebatteryinc.com	317-786-2717	783-4844	686
ACE Billing Group Inc 450 Blackbrook Rd. . . . . Painesville OH 44077 *Web:* www.acebillinggroup.com	440-856-7000		160
ACE Branded Products 12801 W Silver Spring Rd . . . . . Butler WI 53007 *TF:* 800-294-9007 ■ *Web:* www.brandedproducts.com	262-754-8490	754-8494	463
ACE Business Machines Inc 1545 N Verdugo Rd Ste 16. . . . . Glendale CA 91208 *TF:* 800-910-4223 ■ *Web:* www.acebminc.com	818-548-7870	548-7621	112
ACE Cash Express 1231 Greenway Dr Ste 600. . . . . Irving TX 75038 *TF:* 800-224-4338	972-550-5000		141
ACE Casino Equipment PO Box 32582 . . . . . Tucson AZ 85719 *Web:* www.acecasinoequipment.com	520-529-7488		23
ACE Charter High School 1929 N Stone Ave. . . . . Tucson AZ 85705 *Web:* www.acehs.org	520-628-8316		138
ACE Clearwater Enterprises 19815 Magellan Dr. . . . . Torrance CA 90502 *Web:* aceclearwater.com	310-538-5380		22
ACE Composites Inc 1394 Sky Harbor Dr . . . . . Olivehurst CA 95961 *Web:* acecomposites.net	530-743-1885		604
ACE Doran Hauling & Rigging Company Inc 1601 Blue Rock St . . . . . Cincinnati OH 45223 *TF:* 800-829-0929 ■ *Web:* www.acedoran.com	513-681-7900		780
ACE DuraFlo Systems LLC 3122 W Alpine St . . . . . Santa Ana CA 92704 **Fax Area Code:* 949 ■ *TF:* 888-775-0220 ■ *Web:* www.aceduraflo.com	888-775-0220	263-8771*	189-10
ACE Endico Corp 80 International Blvd. . . . . Brewster NY 10509 *Web:* www.aceendico.com	845-230-8811		68
ACE Glass Inc 1430 NW Blvd PO Box 688. . . . . Vineland NJ 08360 **Fax Area Code:* 800 ■ *TF:* 800-223-4524 ■ *Web:* www.aceglass.com	856-692-3333	543-6752*	333
ACE Golf Inc 820 S Kings Ave . . . . . Brandon FL 33511 *Web:* ace-golf.com	813-651-4653		354
ACE Group Inc, The 11 Wall St 14th Fl. . . . . New York NY 10005	212-255-7846		626
ACE Handyman Services 12567 W Cedar Dr Ste 150. . . . . Lakewood CO 80228 *Web:* www.acehandymanservices.com	866-349-6946		310
ACE Hardware Corp 2200 Kensington Ct . . . . . Oak Brook IL 60523 *TF:* 866-290-5334 ■ *Web:* www.acehardware.com	866-290-5334		364
ACE Hotel & Swim Club 701 E Palm Canyon Dr . . . . . Palm Springs CA 92264 *Web:* www.acehotel.com	760-325-9900		377
ACE ImageWear 4120 Truman Rd . . . . . Kansas City MO 64127 *TF:* 800-366-0564 ■ *Web:* www.aceimagewear.com	816-231-5737	231-3550	442
ACE Industries Inc 738 Design Ct Ste 302 . . . . . Chula Vista CA 91911 *Web:* www.aceindustriesinc.com	619-482-2700	482-8643	454
ACE International Company Inc 85 Independence Dr . . . . . Taunton MA 02780 *TF:* 800-223-4685 ■ *Web:* www.arc1weldsafe.com	800-223-4685		194
ACE Irrigation & Manufacturing Co 4740 E 39th St . . . . . Kearney NE 68847 *Web:* www.acenebraska.com	308-237-5173		697
ACE Machine Shop Inc 11200 Wright Rd . . . . . Lynwood CA 90262 *Web:* www.aceconstructions.com	310-608-2277	608-6011	454
ACE Mailing Corp 2757 16th St . . . . . San Francisco CA 94103 *Web:* www.acemailingsf.com	415-863-4223		225
ACE Mart Restaurant Supply 2653 Austin Hwy . . . . . San Antonio TX 78218 *TF:* 888-898-8079 ■ *Web:* acemart.com	210-224-0082	224-1629	114
ACE Medical Inc 94-910 Moloalo St Ste B . . . . . Waipahu HI 96797 *TF:* 866-678-3601 ■ *Web:* www.acemedicalinc.com	808-678-3600	678-3604	475
ACE Paper Co 2835 E Washington Blvd. . . . . Los Angeles CA 90023 *Web:* www.acepaper.com	323-268-1900	262-5144	559
ACE Parking Management Inc 645 Ash St . . . . . San Diego CA 92101 *TF:* 855-223-7275 ■ *Web:* www.aceparking.com	619-233-6624	233-0741	562
ACE Payroll Services Inc 1860 Walt Whitman Rd. . . . . Melville NY 11747 *TF:* 800-856-0700	516-420-9500	420-9615	2
ACE Personnel (AP) 5909 Woodson Rd . . . . . Mission KS 66202 *Web:* www.acepersonnel.com	913-384-1100		721
ACE Precision Machining Corp 977 Blue Ribbon Cir N . . . . . Oconomowoc WI 53066 *Web:* www.aceprecision.com	262-252-4003		454
ACE Printing Company Inc 1748 Mill St. . . . . Wailuku HI 96793 *Web:* www.aceprintingmaui.com	808-244-9033	244-7302	627
ACE Pump & Supply 6013 Johnson St . . . . . Hollywood FL 33024 *Web:* www.acepumpandsupply.com	954-981-7424		641
ACE Pump Corp PO Box 13187 . . . . . Memphis TN 38113 *Web:* www.acepumps.com	901-948-8514	774-6147	641
ACE Ranking 211 Sutter St Ste 400 . . . . . San Francisco CA 94108 *Web:* acerankings.com	415-536-3929	433-4304	195
ACE Relocation Systems Inc 5608 Eastgate Dr . . . . . San Diego CA 92121 *TF:* 877-217-9661 ■ *Web:* www.acerelocation.com	858-677-5500	677-5587	780
ACE Rent A Car 8639 W Washington St. . . . . Indianapolis IN 46241 *TF:* 877-822-3872 ■ *Web:* www.acerentacar.com	317-399-5247		126
ACE Reprographic Service Inc 74 E 30th St . . . . . Paterson NJ 07514 *TF:* 888-245-6328 ■ *Web:* www.acereprographics.com	973-684-5945		627
ACE Sign Systems Inc 3621 W Royerton Rd. . . . . Muncie IN 47304 *TF:* 800-607-6010 ■ *Web:* www.acesign.com	765-288-1000		701
ACE Speedway 3401 Altamahaw Race Track Rd . . . . . Elon NC 27244 *Web:* acespeedway.net	336-266-5653	585-1209	515
ACE Tech Copier 4689 Convoy St. . . . . San Diego CA 92111 *Web:* www.acetechcopier.com	619-316-4182		112

Company / Address	Phone	Fax	Class
ACE Technologies 2375 Zanker Rd Ste 250 ..... San Jose CA 95131 *Web:* www.acetechnologies.com	408-442-3662	324-1367	177
ACE Tool Co 7337 Bryan Dairy Rd ..... Largo FL 33777 *TF:* 800-777-5910 ■ *Web:* www.acetoolco.com	727-544-6652	544-7760	61
ACE Transfer Co 1017 Hometown St ..... Springfield OH 45504 *Web:* www.acetransco.com	937-398-1109		687
ACE Truck Body Inc 1600 Thrailkill Rd ..... Grove City OH 43123 *Web:* www.acetruck.com	614-871-3100		61
ACE Tube Bending 14 Journey ..... Aliso Viejo CA 92656 *Web:* www.acetubebending.com	949-362-2220		595
ACE Weekly 118 Constitution St ..... Lexington KY 40507 *Web:* www.aceweekly.com	859-225-4889		532-5
ACE Wire & Cable Company Inc 7201 51st Ave ..... Woodside NY 11377 *TF:* 800-225-2354 ■ *Web:* www.acewireco.com	718-458-9200	335-6340	813
ACE World Wide Moving 1900 E College Ave ..... Cudahy WI 53110 *TF:* 800-558-3980 ■ *Web:* www.aceworldwide.com	414-764-1000	764-1650	519
ACE-Atlas Corp 5214 Flushing Ave ..... Maspeth NY 11378 *Web:* www.ace-atlas.com	718-497-3003		610
ACEC (Allamakee-Clayton Electric Co-op) 229 Hwy 51 PO Box 715 ..... Postville IA 52162 *TF:* 888-788-1551 ■ *Web:* www.acrec.com	563-864-7611		245
ACEC (American Council of Engineering Cos) 1015 15th St NW 8th Fl ..... Washington DC 20005 *TF:* 800-338-1391 ■ *Web:* www.acec.org	202-347-7474	898-0068	49-19
Aceco 4419 Federal Way ..... Boise ID 83716 *TF:* 800-359-7012 ■ *Web:* www.aceco.com	208-343-7712		350
ACEEE (American Council for an Energy-Efficient Economy) 529 14th St NW Ste 600 ..... Washington DC 20045 *Web:* www.aceee.org	202-507-4000	429-2248	48-7
ACEI (Association for Childhood Education Intl) 1875 Connecticut Ave NW 10th Fl ..... Washington DC 20009 **Fax Area Code:* 301 ■ *TF:* 800-423-3563 ■ *Web:* ceinternational1892.org	202-372-9986	570-2212*	49-5
Acelero Learning Inc 63 W 125th St 6th Fl ..... New York NY 10027 *TF:* 877-223-5376 ■ *Web:* www.acelero.net	212-289-2402	214-0411	196
Acentech Inc 33 Moulton St ..... Cambridge MA 02138 *Web:* www.acentech.com	617-499-8000		463
Acento Advertising Inc 2001 Whilshire Blvd Ste 600 ..... Santa Monica CA 90403 *Web:* acento.com	310-943-8300		4
ACEP (American College of Emergency Physicians) 1125 Executive Cir PO Box 619911 ..... Dallas TX 75261 *TF:* 800-798-1822 ■ *Web:* www.acep.org	972-550-0911	580-2816	49-8
Acer America Corp 333 W San Carlos St Ste 1500 ..... San Jose CA 95110 *TF:* 866-695-2237 ■ *Web:* www.acer.com	408-533-7700	533-4574	173-2
Acer Group 2320 E Valencia Dr ..... Fullerton CA 92831 *Web:* acergroup.com	714-632-9701		358
ACERS (American Ceramic Society) 600 N Cleveland Ave Ste 210 ..... Westerville OH 43082 *TF:* 866-721-3322 ■ *Web:* ceramics.org	614-890-4700	899-6109	48-4
ACES (American College of Eye Surgeons/American Board of Eye Surgery) 334 E Lake Rd Ste 135 ..... Palm Harbor FL 34685 *TF:* 800-223-2233 ■ *Web:* www.aces-abes.org	727-366-1487	836-9783	49-8
ACES 4140 W 99th St ..... Carmel IN 46032 *Web:* www.acespower.com	317-344-7000		463
ACES Systems 10737 Lexington Dr ..... Knoxville TN 37932 *Web:* www.acessystems.com	865-671-2003		256
Ace-Tex Enterprises 7601 Central St ..... Detroit MI 48210 *TF:* 800-444-3800 ■ *Web:* www.ace-tex.com	313-834-4000	834-0260	442
AceWeb PO Box 2160 ..... North Hills CA 91393 *TF:* 866-477-9378 ■ *Web:* www.aceweb.com	818-891-5941		681
ACF (Association of Consulting Forester) 312 Montgomery St Ste 208 ..... Alexandria VA 22314 *TF:* 800-438-5800 ■ *Web:* www.acf-foresters.org	703-548-0990	548-6395	48-2
ACF (American Culinary Federation Inc) 180 Center Pl Way ..... Saint Augustine FL 32095 *TF:* 800-624-9458 ■ *Web:* www.acfchefs.org	904-824-4468	825-4758	49-6
ACF (Alaska Conservation Foundation) 1227 W 9th Ave Ste 300 ..... Anchorage AK 99501 *Web:* alaskaconservation.org	907-276-1917		48-6
ACF (Administration for Children & Families) 370 L'Enfant Promenade SW ..... Washington DC 20447 *Web:* www.acf.hhs.gov	202-401-9200	401-5450	340-10
ACF Components & Fasteners Inc 31012 Huntwood Ave ..... Hayward CA 94544 *TF:* 800-227-2901 ■ *Web:* www.acfcom.com	510-487-2100	471-7018	246
ACF Industries LLC 101 Clark St ..... Saint Charles MO 63301 *Web:* www.acfindustries.com	636-949-2399	949-2825	650
ACFA (Alameda County Fair Assn) 4501 Pleasanton Ave ..... Pleasanton CA 94566 *TF:* 800-874-9253 ■ *Web:* www.alamedacountyfair.com	925-426-7600	426-7599	642
ACFAS (American College of Foot & Ankle Surgeons) 8725 W Higgins Rd Ste 555 ..... Chicago IL 60631 *TF:* 800-421-2237 ■ *Web:* www.acfas.org	773-693-9300	693-9304	49-8
ACFC (American Coalition for Fathers & Children) 1718 M St NW Ste 1187 ..... Washington DC 20036 *TF:* 800-978-3237 ■ *Web:* www.acfc.org	800-978-3237		48-6
ACFE (Association of Certified Fraud Examiners) 716 W Ave ..... Austin TX 78701 *TF:* 800-245-3321 ■ *Web:* www.acfe.com	512-478-9000	478-9297	49-1
ACG (American College of Gastroenterology) 6400 Goldsboro Rd Ste 200 ..... Bethesda MD 20817 *Web:* gi.org	301-263-9000	263-9025	49-8
ACG (Association for Corporate Growth) 125 S Wacker Dr Ste 3100 ..... Chicago IL 60606 *TF:* 877-358-2220 ■ *Web:* www.acg.org	312-957-4260		49-12
ACG Advisory Services Inc 1640 Huguenot Rd ..... Midlothian VA 23113 *TF:* 800-231-6409 ■ *Web:* www.acgworldwide.com	804-323-1886		528
ACG Inc 77 W Elmwood Dr Ste 200 ..... Dayton OH 45459	937-433-8122		180
ACG Research 1780 E Tradewind Ct ..... Gilbert AZ 85234 *Web:* www.acgcc.com	408-200-0967		466
ACG Systems Inc 133 Defense Hwy Ste 206 ..... Annapolis MD 21401 *Web:* www.acgsys.com	410-224-0224		647
ACG Tech Systems Inc 6 Rock Is ..... Ardmore OK 73401 *Web:* www.acgsystem.com	580-222-4467		396
ACGIH (American Conference of Governmental Industrial Hygienists) 1330 Kemper Meadows Dr ..... Cincinnati OH 45240 *Web:* www.acgih.org	513-742-2020	742-3355	49-7
ACGME (Accreditation Council for Graduate Medical Education) 401 N Michigan Ave Ste 2000 ..... Chicago IL 60611 *Web:* www.acgme.org	312-755-5000	755-7498	48-1
ACH (Alliance Community Hospital) 200 E State St ..... Alliance OH 44601 *Web:* aultmanalliance.org	330-596-6000		374-3
ACH Foam Technologies LLC 5250 Sherman St ..... Denver CO 80216 *TF:* 800-525-8697 ■ *Web:* www.achfoam.com	303-297-3844		601
ACH Food Companies Inc 7171 Goodlet Farms Pkwy ..... Cordova TN 38016 *Web:* www.achfood.com	901-381-3000		296-30
ACH Payment Solutions Inc 6919 Treymore Ct ..... Sarasota FL 34243 *Web:* www.achpaymentsolutions.com	941-360-8859		225
ACHA (American College Health Assn) 8455 Colesville Rd Ste 740 ..... Silver Spring MD 20910 *Web:* www.acha.org	410-859-1500	859-1510	49-8
ACHE (Association for Continuing Higher Education) 1700 Asp Ave ..... Norman OK 73072 *TF:* 800-807-2243 ■ *Web:* www.acheinc.org	800-807-2243		49-5
ACHE (American College of Healthcare Executives) 1 N Franklin St Ste 1700 ..... Chicago IL 60606 *Web:* www.ache.org	312-424-2800	424-0023	49-8
A-Check America Inc 1501 Research Park Dr ..... Riverside CA 92507 *TF:* 877-345-2021 ■ *Web:* www.acheckglobal.com	951-750-1501		260
Achieve IT Solutions 640 Belle Terre Rd Bldg B ..... Port Jefferson NY 11777 *Web:* www.achieveits.com	631-543-3200		177
Achieve LLC 2000 Palm Beach Lakes Blvd Ste 901 ..... West Palm Beach FL 33409 *Web:* www.achieveagency.com	561-962-1962	833-4141	195
Achievement Gallery 4421 Mcleod Rd NE Ste D ..... Albuquerque NM 87109 *Web:* achievementgallery.com	505-881-4625		327
Achievement Incentives & Meetings 64 River Rd ..... East Hanover NJ 07936 *TF:* 800-454-1424 ■ *Web:* www.aimtrav.com	973-386-9500		194
Achilles USA Inc 1407 80th St SW ..... Everett WA 98203 *Web:* www.achillesusa.com	425-353-7000		600
achoo! Allergy & AIR Products Inc 1960 Will Ross Ct Ste 100 ..... Atlanta GA 30341 *TF:* 800-339-7123 ■ *Web:* www.achooallergy.com	800-339-7123		690
ACHS (Adams County Historical Society) PO Box 102 ..... Hastings NE 68902 *Web:* www.adamshistory.org	402-463-5838		49-19
ACI (Arkansas Correctional Industries) 6841 W 13th St ..... Pine Bluff AR 71602 *TF:* 877-635-7213 ■ *Web:* www.acicatalog.com	877-635-7213		630
ACI (Axis Communications Inc) 100 Apollo Dr ..... Chelmsford MA 01824 *TF:* 800-444-2947 ■ *Web:* www.axis.com	978-614-2000	614-2100	176
ACI (Atlantic Corporate Interiors Inc) 7001 Muirkirk Meadows Dr Ste A ..... Beltsville MD 20705 *Web:* www.aciinc.com	301-931-3600	931-3601	321
ACI (American Concrete Institute Intl) 38800 Country Club Dr PO Box 9094 ..... Farmington Hills MI 48331 *Web:* www.concrete.org	248-848-3700	848-3701	49-3
ACI 500 W 57th St ..... New York NY 10018 **Fax Area Code:* 646 ■ *TF:* 800-724-4444 ■ *Web:* www.acirehab.org	212-293-3000	565-3404*	726
ACI (New Mexico Association of Commerce & Industry) 2201 Buena Vista Dr SE Ste 410 ..... Albuquerque NM 87106 *Web:* www.nmaci.org	505-842-0644		140
ACI Capital 299 Park Ave 34th Fl ..... New York NY 10171 *Web:* www.acicapital.com	212-634-3333	634-3330	792
ACI Communications 5115 Douglas Fir Rd Ste A ..... Calabasas CA 91302 *Web:* www.acicommunications.com	818-223-3600	223-3609	225
ACI Consulting Corp 155 N Riverview Dr ..... Anaheim Hills CA 92808 *Web:* aciconsulting.com	714-282-0378		180
ACI Controls Inc 295 Main St ..... West Seneca NY 14224 *TF:* 800-333-7519 ■ *Web:* www.aci-controls.com	716-675-9450	675-1906	358
ACI Event Group 652 Hayes St ..... San Francisco CA 94102 *Web:* www.acieventgroup.com	415-553-7880		195
ACI Plastics Inc 2945 Davison Rd ..... Flint MI 48506 *Web:* www.aciplastics.com	810-767-3800	767-3883	604
ACI Worldwide Inc 3520 Kraft Rd Ste 300 ..... Naples FL 34105 *Web:* www.aciworldwide.com	402-390-7600		178-1
ACIC Pharmaceuticals Inc 81 St Claire Blvd ..... Brantford ON N3S7X6 *TF:* 800-265-6727 ■ *Web:* acic.com	519-751-3668	751-1378	479
ACICS (Accrediting Council for Independent Colleges & Schools) 750 First St NE Ste 980 ..... Washington DC 20002 *TF:* 800-258-3826 ■ *Web:* www.acics.org	202-336-6780	842-2593	48-1
Acid Piping Technology Inc 2890 Arnold Tenbrook Rd ..... Arnold MO 63010 *Web:* acidpiping.com	636-296-4668	296-1824	492
Acier Picard Inc 3000 Rue De L' Etchemin ..... Levis QC G6W7X6 *TF:* 888-834-0646 ■ *Web:* groupepicard.ca	418-834-8300		492
ACIL (American Council of Independent Laboratories) 1875 I St NW Ste 500 ..... Washington DC 20006 *TF:* 800-368-1131 ■ *Web:* www.acil.org	202-887-5872	887-0021	49-19
ACI-NA (Airports Council International of North America) 1615 L St NW Ste 300 ..... Washington DC 20006 *Web:* airportscouncil.org	202-293-8500	331-1362	49-21
ACIPCO (American Cast Iron Pipe Co) 1501 31st Ave N ..... Birmingham AL 35207 *TF:* 800-442-2347 ■ *Web:* www.american-usa.com	205-325-7701		307

Name / Address	City	State	Zip	Phone	Fax	Class
ACIST Medical Systems Inc 7905 Fuller Rd *TF:* 888-667-6648 ■ *Web:* acist.com	Eden Prairie	MN	55344	952-941-3507		476
ACK Controls Inc 2600 Happy Valley Rd *Web:* www.chuosna.com	Glasgow	KY	42141	270-678-6200		57
ACK Electronics 554 Deering Rd NW *TF:* 800-282-7954 ■ *Web:* www.acksupply.com	Atlanta	GA	30309	404-351-6340	351-1879	246
ACK Engineering Services Ltd 203 N Lasalle St Ste 2100 *Web:* ackstructural.com	Chicago	IL	60601	312-827-7997		261
Acker & Sons Inc 10516 Summit Ave	Kensington	MD	20895	301-897-0700		610
Acker Merrall & Condit Company Inc 160 W 72nd St *Web:* www.ackerwines.com	New York	NY	10023	212-787-1700	799-1984	443
Ackerman McQueen (AM) 1133 N Robinson Ave	Oklahoma City	OK	73103	405-843-7777	848-8034	4
Ackerman Oil Company Inc 2060 S Lube Way *TF:* 800-880-6666 ■ *Web:* www.ackoil.com	Jasper	IN	47546	812-482-6666	482-6676	541
Ackermann Public Relations & Marketing 1111 Northshore Dr Ste N-400 *TF:* 877-325-9453 ■ *Web:* thinkackermann.com	Knoxville	TN	37919	865-584-0550	588-3009	636
Ackerman-practicon Inc 801 E Charleston Rd *Web:* www.apcts.com	Palo Alto	CA	94303	650-965-1000	494-9312	256
Ackley Lake State Park 989 Ackley Lake Rd *Web:* stateparks.mt.gov	Hobson	MT	59452	406-727-1212		565
Ackley, Kopecky & Kingery LLP 4056 Glass Rd NE *Web:* akklaw.com	Cedar Rapids	IA	52402	319-393-9090		41
Ackman-Ziff Real estate Group LLC 711 Third Ave 11th Fl *Web:* www.ackmanziff.com	New York	NY	10017	212-697-3333		652
Ackroo Canada Inc 1250 S Service Rd Unit A3-1 3rd Fl *TF:* 888-405-0066 ■ *Web:* www.ackroo.com	Hamilton	ON	L8E5R9	613-599-2396		317
ACL (Atlantic Container Line) 50 Cardinal Dr *Web:* www.aclcargo.com	Woctfiold	NJ	07000	900-510-5300	518-7321	313
ACL Distribution Inc 4722 Danvers Dr *Web:* www.aclperformance.com.au	Grand Rapids	MI	49512	616-956-1300		75
ACLI (American Council of Life Insurers) 101 Constitution Ave NW Ste 700 W *TF:* 877-674-4659 ■ *Web:* www.acli.com	Washington	DC	20001	202-624-2000		49-9
ACLU (American Civil Liberties Union) 125 Broad St 18th Fl *TF:* 877-867-1025 ■ *Web:* www.aclu.org	New York	NY	10004	212-549-2500	549-2580	48-8
ACM (Association of Children's Museums) 2711 Jefferson Davis Hwy Ste 600 *Web:* www.childrensmuseums.org	Arlington	VA	22202	703-224-3100	224-3099	48-4
ACM (Association for Computing Machinery) 2 Penn Plz Ste 701 *TF:* 800-342-6626 ■ *Web:* www.acm.org	New York	NY	10121	212-626-0500	944-1318	48-9
ACM Capital Partners 2103 Coral Way Ste 604 *Web:* www.acmcapitalpartners.com	Miami	FL	33145	305-960-8851	960-9188	194
ACM Chemistries Inc 3190 Reps Miller Rd Ste 100 *Web:* acmchem.com	Norcross	GA	30071	770-417-3490		183
ACM Medical Laboratory Inc 160 Elmgrove Pk *Web:* www.acmgloballab.com	Rochester	NY	14624	585-247-3500		415
ACMA (American Composites Manufacturers Assn) 3033 Wilson Blvd Ste 420 *Web:* acmanet.org	Arlington	VA	22201	703-525-0743		49-13
ACMAT Corp 30 South Rd *OTC:* ACMT ■ *Web:* www.acmatcorp.com	Farmington	CT	06032	860-946-4800		391-5
ACMC (Ashtabula County Medical Ctr) 2420 Lake Ave *TF:* 800-722-3330 ■ *Web:* www.acmchealth.org	Ashtabula	OH	44004	440-997-2262	997-6644	374-3
ACME (Association for Couples in Marriage Enrichment) PO Box 21374 *TF:* 800-634-8325 ■ *Web:* www.bettermarriages.org	Winston-Salem	NC	27120	800-634-8325		48-6
Acme Aerospace Inc 528 W 21st St *Web:* www.acme-aero.com	Tempe	AZ	85282	480-894-6864		21
Acme Architectural Products Inc 251 Lombardy St *Web:* www.acmesalesgroup.com	Brooklyn	NY	11222	718-384-7800		480
Acme Auto Electric Inc 508 Baxter Ave *Web:* www.acmeae.com	Louisville	KY	40204	502-584-6200		61
Acme Block & Brick Inc 248 Dayton Spur Rd *Web:* www.acmeblockandbrick.com	Crossville	TN	38555	931-484-8435	484-8436	183
Acme Brick 3024 Acme Brick Plz *Web:* brick.com	Fort Worth	TX	76109	817-332-4101	390-2404	150
Acme Communications Inc 4790 Irvine Blvd Ste 105-319 *OTCPK:* ACME ■ *Web:* www.acmecommunications.com	Santa Ana	CA	92620	714-245-9499		738
Acme Construction Company Inc 7695 Bond St *TF:* 800-686-5077 ■ *Web:* www.acmerrinc.com	Cleveland	OH	44139	440-232-7474	232-7477	188-8
Acme Construction Company Inc 1565 Cummins Dr *Web:* www.acmeconstruction.com	Modesto	CA	95358	209-523-2674	523-0213	186
Acme Corrugated Box Company Inc 2700 Turnpike Dr *Web:* www.acmebox.com	Hatboro	PA	19040	215-444-8000		100
Acme Cosmetic Components 80 Seaview Dr *Web:* www.acmecomponents.com	Secaucus	NJ	07094	718-335-3000		488
Acme Cryogenics Inc 2801 Mitchell Ave *TF:* 800-422-2790 ■ *Web:* www.acmecryo.com	Allentown	PA	18103	610-966-4488		454
Acme Design Company Inc 1327 Palmetto St *Web:* www.acmecompany.com	Los Angeles	CA	90013	213-624-8756		344
Acme Distribution Centers Inc 18101 E Colfax Ave *TF:* 800-444-3614 ■ *Web:* www.acmedistribution.com	Aurora	CO	80011	303-340-2100	340-2424	803-1
Acme Electric Co 1060 Capital Dr SW *Web:* www.acmeelectric.com	Cedar Rapids	IA	52404	319-365-8677		189-4
Acme Engineering & Manufacturing Corp PO Box 978 *TF:* 800-382-2263 ■ *Web:* www.acmefan.com	Muskogee	OK	74402	918-682-7791	682-0134	18
Acme Federal Credit Union 34799 Curtis Blvd Ste B *TF:* 800-325-3678 ■ *Web:* acmefcu.org	Eastlake	OH	44095	440-946-1980	946-0560	219
Acme Food Sales Inc 5940 First Ave S *TF:* 800-777-2263 ■ *Web:* www.acmefood.com	Seattle	WA	98108	206-762-5150		297-8
Acme Gear Company Inc 130 W Forest Ave *Web:* www.acmegear.com	Englewood	NJ	07631	201-568-2245		709
Acme Grinding & Manufacturing Inc 6871 Belford Indus Dr *Web:* acmegrinding.com	Belvidere	IL	61008	815-323-1380	323-1381	454
Acme Holding Co 24200 Marmon Ave *Web:* www.acmeabrasive.com	Warren	MI	48089	586-759-3332	759-3334	1
Acme Industrial Co 441 Maple Ave *TF:* 800-323-5582 ■ *Web:* www.acmeindustrial.com	Carpentersville	IL	60110	847-428-3911	428-1820	493
Acme Industries Inc 1325 Pratt Blvd *Web:* www.acmeind.com	Elk Grove Village	IL	60007	847-296-3346	296-8622	454
Acme Machell 2000 Airport Rd *Web:* www.acmemachell.com	Waukesha	WI	53187	262-521-2870	521-2894	677
Acme Manufacturing Co 4240 N Atlantic Blvd *Web:* www.acmemfg.com	Auburn Hills	MI	48326	248-393-7300		455
Acme Markets Inc 75 Valley Stream Pkwy *TF:* 877-932-7948 ■ *Web:* www.acmemarkets.com	Malvern	PA	19355	610-889-4000		345
Acme Masking Company Inc 240 S Production Dr *Web:* acmemasking.com	Avon	IN	46123	317-272-6202	272-5314	676
Acme Merchandise & Apparel 46 Blackburn Ctr *Web:* www.acmeapparel.com	Gloucester	MA	01930	978-282-4800	282-7300	195
Acme Metals & Steel Supply Inc 14930 S San Pedro St *TF:* 800-978-2263 ■ *Web:* www.acmemetalsonline.com	Gardena	CA	90248	310-329-2263	329-4429	492
Acme Mills Co 33 Bloomfield Hills Pky Ste 120 *TF:* 888-894-7110 ■ *Web:* www.acmemills.com	Bloomfield Hills	MI	48304	888-894-7110		594
Acme Oyster House 724 Iberville St *Web:* www.acmeoyster.com	New Orleans	LA	70130	225-906-2372		671
Acme Paper & Supply Company Inc 8229 Sandy Ct PO Box 422 *TF:* 800-462-5812 ■ *Web:* www.acmepaper.com	Savage	MD	20763	410-792-2333	792-2137	548
Acme Pizza & Bakery Equipment Inc 7039 E Slauson Blvd *TF:* 800-428-2263 ■ *Web:* www.acmepbe.com	Commerce	CA	90040	323-722-7900	726-4700	298
Acme Portable Machines Inc 1330 Mtn View Cir *Web:* www.acmeportable.com	Azusa	CA	91702	626-610-1888	610-1881	173-2
Acme Press Inc 2312 Stanwell Dr *Web:* calitho.com	Concord	CA	94520	925-682-1111	682-9911	41
Acme Rolling Steel Door Corp 1099 Linden Ave *TF:* 800-281-5680 ■ *Web:* www.acmedoor.com	Ridgefield	NJ	07657	201-943-7070	943-1206	234
Acme Sample Books Inc 2410 Schirra Pl *Web:* www.acmesample.com	High Point	NC	27263	336-883-4107	883-4505	80
Acme School - Locksmith Div 11350 S Harlem Ave *Web:* www.acmelocksmithschool.net	Worth	IL	60482	708-361-3750	448-9306	685
Acme Screw Co 1201 W Union Ave *Web:* www.acmecompanies.com	Wheaton	IL	60187	630-665-2200	665-9630	278
Acme Smoked Fish Corp 30 Gem St *Web:* www.acmesmokedfish.com	Brooklyn	NY	11222	718-383-8585		296-13
Acme Spirally Wound Paper Products Inc 4810 W 139th St PO Box 35320 *TF:* 800-274-2797 ■ *Web:* www.acmespiral.com	Cleveland	OH	44135	216-267-2950	267-0239	125
Acme Truck Line Inc 200 Westbank Expy PO Box 183 *Fax Area Code: 888 ■ *TF:* 800-825-6246 ■ *Web:* www.acmetruck.com	Gretna	LA	70053	504-368-2510	345-2263*	780
Acme United Corp 55 Walls Dr Ste 201 *NYSE:* ACU ■ *TF:* 800-835-2263 ■ *Web:* www.acmeunited.com	Fairfield	CT	06824	800-835-2263		476
Acme Vial and Glass Company Inc 1601 Commerce Way *TF:* 800-394-2745 ■ *Web:* www.acmevial.com	Paso Robles	CA	93446	805-239-2666	239-9406	331
Acme Wire Products Co 7 Broadway Ave *TF:* 800-723-7015 ■ *Web:* www.acmewire.com	Mystic	CT	06355	860-572-0511		449
Acme Worldwide Enterprises Inc 1710 Randolph Ct SE *Web:* www.acme-worldwide.com	Albuquerque	NM	87106	505-243-0400	243-0500	256
Acme-McCrary Corp 159 N St PO Box 1287 *Web:* www.acme-mccrary.com	Asheboro	NC	27204	336-625-2161	629-2263	155-10
Acme-Monaco Corp 75 Winchell Rd *Web:* www.acmemonaco.com	New Britain	CT	06052	860-224-1349		492
ACMH (Armstrong County Memorial Hospital) One Nolte Dr *Web:* www.acmh.org	Kittanning	PA	16201	724-543-8500	543-8704	374-3
ACMI (Art & Creative Materials Institute Inc, The) 99 Derby St Ste 200 *Web:* www.acmiart.org	Hingham	MA	02043	781-556-1044	207-5550	48-18
Acmp Foundation 1133 Broadway Ste 810 *Web:* acmp.net	New York	NY	10010	212-645-7424		526
ACMRS (Arizona Center for Medieval and Renaissance Studies) PO Box 874402 *Web:* www.acmrs.org	Tempe	AZ	85287	480-727-6503	965-1681	637-2
ACMT Inc 369 Progress Dr *Web:* www.acmtct.com	Manchester	CT	06042	860-645-0592		370

Name / Address	City	State	ZIP	Phone	Fax	Class
ACN 1100 Ave des Canadiens-de-Montreal Ste 450 *Web:* acncanada.ca	Montreal	QC	H3B2S2	514-390-8666		224
ACN Group of California Inc PO Box 880009 **Fax Area Code: 619 ■ TF: 800-428-6337 ■ Web:* www.myoptumhealthphysicalhealthofca.com	San Diego	CA	92168	800-428-6337	641-7185*	391-3
ACNM (American College of Nurse-Midwives) 8403 Colesville Rd Ste 1550 *TF:* 800-468-3571 ■ *Web:* www.midwife.org	Silver Spring	MD	20910	240-485-1800	485-1818	49-8
ACO Polymer Products Inc 9470 Pinecore Dr *TF:* 800-543-4764 ■ *Web:* acousa.com	Mentor	OH	44060	440-639-7230	639-7235	608
ACOEM (American College of Occupational & Environmental Medicine) 25 NW Pt Blvd Ste 700 *Web:* www.acoem.org	Elk Grove Village	IL	60007	847-818-1800	818-9266	49-8
ACOFP (American College of Osteopathic Family Physicians) 330 E Algonquin Rd Ste 1 *TF:* 800-323-0794 ■ *Web:* www.acofp.org	Arlington Heights	IL	60005	847-952-5100	228-9755	49-8
ACOG (American College of Obstetricians & Gynecologists) 409 12th St SW PO Box 96920 *TF:* 800-673-8444 ■ *Web:* www.acog.org	Washington	DC	20090	202-863-1648		49-8
ACOM Publishing Inc PO Box 115 *Web:* www.acenturyofmotorcycling.com	Monson	MA	01057	413-267-4999		637-2
ACOM Solutions Inc 2850 E 29th St *TF:* 800-347-3638 ■ *Web:* acom.com	Long Beach	CA	90806	562-424-7899	424-8662	178-1
Acoma Business Enterprise PO Box 310 **Fax Area Code: 505 ■ TF: 888-759-2489 ■ Web:* www.skycity.com	Acoma	NM	87034	888-759-2489	552-7804*	377
Acon Inc 22 Bristol Dr *Web:* www.aconinc.com	South Easton	MA	02375	508-230-8022	230-2371	253
Acon Investments LLC 1133 Connecticut Ave NW Ste 700 *Web:* aconinvestments.com	Washington	DC	20036	202-454-1100	454-1101	169
Acopian Technical Co 131 Loomis St *Web:* www.acopian.com	Easton	PA	18045	610-258-5441	258-2842	253
Acor Orthopaedic Inc 18530 S Miles Pkwy *Web:* www.acor.com	Cleveland	OH	44128	216-662-4500	662-4547	301
ACORD (Association for Co-opeartive Operations Research & Development) 1 Blue Hill Plz 15th Fl PO Box 1529 *TF:* 800-444-3341 ■ *Web:* www.acord.org	Pearl River	NY	10965	845-620-1700	620-3600	49-9
Acorda Therapeutics Inc 420 Saw Mill River RD *NASDAQ: ACOR ■ Web:* www.acorda.com	Ardsley	NY	10502	914-347-4300	347-4560	85
Acorio 230 Congress St *Web:* www.acorio.com	Boston	MA	02110	617-933-7588		39
Acorn Deck House Co 852 Main St *TF:* 800-727-3325 ■ *Web:* www.deckhouse.com	Acton	MA	01720	800-727-3325		106
Acorn Energy Inc 1000 N W St Ste 1200 *Web:* www.acornenergy.com	Wilmington	DE	19801	302-656-1708		787
Acorn Environmental Consultants Inc 8040 Stevens Ave S *Web:* acornenvironmental.com	Minneapolis	MN	55420	952-240-6227	888-4901	196
Acorn Gencon Plastics Inc 15125 Proctor Ave *TF:* 800-782-7706 ■ *Web:* www.whitehallmfg.com	City of Industry	CA	91746	626-968-6681	855-4860	386
Acorn Industrial LLC 7311 Acc Blvd	Raleigh	NC	27617	919-256-6500		610
Acorn Manufacturing Company Inc 457 School St *TF:* 800-835-0121 ■ *Web:* www.acornmfg.com	Mansfield	MA	02048	508-339-2977		350
Acorn Petroleum Inc 529 Sahwatch St *Web:* www.acornpetroleuminc.com	Colorado Springs	CO	80903	719-634-8874		581
Acorn Technology 23103 Miles Rd *Web:* www.acorntechnology.com	Cleveland	OH	44128	216-663-1244	663-1005	729
Acorn Ventures Inc PO Box 6847 *Web:* www.acornventures.net	Bellevue	WA	98008	425-462-6144	999-4853	792
Acorn Wire & Iron Works LLC 2035 S Racine Ave *TF:* 800-552-2676 ■ *Web:* www.acornwire.com	Chicago	IL	60608	773-585-0600	585-2403	279
Acorns 5300 California Ave *TF:* 855-739-2859 ■ *Web:* www.acorns.com	Irvine	CA	92617	855-739-2859		113
A-Corp 268 Rangeway Rd *TF:* 800-700-8062 ■ *Web:* www.acorpsystems.com	North Billerica	MA	01862	978-667-1144	663-0061	189-10
Acosta Inc 6600 Corporate Center Pky *Web:* www.acosta.com	Jacksonville	FL	32216	904-281-9800		297-8
Acousti Engineering Company of Florida Inc 4656 34th St SW *TF:* 800-434-3467 ■ *Web:* www.acousti.com	Orlando	FL	32811	407-425-3467	425-5108	189-9
Acoustic Neuroma Assn (ANA) 600 Peachtree Pkwy Ste 108 *TF:* 877-200-8211 ■ *Web:* www.anausa.org	Cumming	GA	30041	770-205-8211	205-0239	48-17
Acoustic Sounds Inc 605 W North St *TF:* 888-926-2564 ■ *Web:* store.acousticsounds.com	Salina	KS	67401	785-825-8609	825-0156	463
Acoustic Technology Inc 30 Jeffries St *TF:* 800-653-1494 ■ *Web:* www.atisystem.com	Boston	MA	02128	617-567-4969	569-2964	261
Acoustical Society of America (ASA) 1305 Walt Whitman Rd Ste 300 *Web:* acousticalsociety.org	Melville	NY	11747	516-576-2360	576-2377	49-19
Acoustilog Inc 19 Mercer St *Web:* www.acoustilog.com	New York	NY	10013	212-925-1365		393
ACP (American College of Physicians) 190 N Independence Mall W *TF:* 800-523-1546 ■ *Web:* www.acponline.org	Philadelphia	PA	19106	215-351-2400	351-2594	49-8
ACP (Associated Collegiate Press) 2221 University Ave SE Ste 121 *Web:* www.studentpress.org	Minneapolis	MN	55414	612-625-8335	626-0720	48-11
ACP (Associated Church Press, The) 109 State St **Fax Area Code: 407 ■ Web:* www.theacp.org	Louisville	KY	40206	503-583-8655	386-3236*	49-16
ACP CreativIT 851 Commerce Ct *TF:* 800-548-5105 ■ *Web:* www.acpcreativit.com	Buffalo Grove	IL	60089	847-541-6333		180
ACPA (American College Personnel Assn) 1 Dupont Cir NW Ste 300 *Web:* www.myacpa.org	Washington	DC	20036	202-835-2272	296-3286	49-5
ACPA (American Concrete Pavement Assn) 9450 W Bryn Mawr Ave Ste 150 *TF:* 800-281-7899 ■ *Web:* www.acpa.org	Rosemont	IL	60018	847-966-2272	966-9970	49-3
ACPA (American Chronic Pain Assn) PO Box 850 **Fax Area Code: 916 ■ TF: 800-533-3231 ■ Web:* www.theacpa.org	Rocklin	CA	95677	800-533-3231	652-8190*	48-17
ACPE (American College of Physician Executives) 400 N Ashley Dr Ste 400 **Fax Area Code: 813 ■ TF: 800-562-8088 ■ Web:* www.physicianleaders.org	Tampa	FL	33602	800-562-8088	287-8993*	49-8
ACPE (Association for Clinical Pastoral Education) 1549 Clairmont Rd Ste 103 *Web:* www.acpe.edu	Decatur	GA	30033	404-320-1472		48-1
ACPHS (Albany College of Pharmacy) 106 New Scotland Ave *TF:* 888-203-8010 ■ *Web:* www.acphs.edu	Albany	NY	12208	518-694-7221		166
ACPM (American College of Preventive Medicine) 455 Massachusetts Ave NW *Web:* www.acpm.org	Washington	DC	20001	202-466-2044	466-2662	49-8
Acqua Fine Foods 671 The Queensway *Web:* www.acqua.ca	Toronto	ON	M8Y1K8	416-368-7171		671
Acqua Hotel 555 Redwood Hwy *TF:* 888-662-9555 ■ *Web:* www.marinhotels.com	Mill Valley	CA	94941	415-380-0400	380-9696	379
Acqualina 17875 Collins Ave *TF:* 877-312-9742 ■ *Web:* www.acqualinaresort.com	Sunny Isles Beach	FL	33160	305-918-8000	918-8100	379
Acquavella Galleries Inc 18 E 79th St *Web:* www.acquavellagalleries.com	New York	NY	10075	212-734-6300	794-9394	42
Acquerello 1722 Sacramento St *Web:* www.acquerello.com	San Francisco	CA	94109	415-567-5432	567-6432	671
Acquest International LP 909 3rd Ave 27th Fl *Web:* acquestinternational.com	New York	NY	10022	212-719-1500		194
Acquidata Inc 4222 22nd Ave S PO Box 531691 *Web:* acquidata.com	Saint Petersburg	FL	33747	860-910-4747		177
Acquire Media Corp 3 Becker Farm Rd Ste 401 *Web:* www.acquiremedia.com	Roseland	NJ	07068	973-422-0800		387
Acquireo.com 14584 Baseline Ave Ste 300142 *TF:* 800-362-7203 ■ *Web:* www.acquireo.com	Fontana	CA	92336	909-266-0840		366
Acquisitions Northwest Inc 2929 NW Mcchesney Ct Ste 600 *Web:* www.acquisitionsnw.com	Portland	OR	97204	503-225-0479		401
Acquizition.biz 1100 Rene-Levesque Blvd W 24th Fl *TF:* 866-499-0334 ■ *Web:* www.acquizition.biz	Montreal	QC	H3B4X9	514-499-0334		387
ACR (American College of Radiology) 1891 Preston White Dr *TF:* 800-227-5463 ■ *Web:* www.acr.org	Reston	VA	20191	703-648-8900		49-8
ACR (American College of Rheumatology) 2200 Lake Blvd NE *Web:* www.rheumatology.org	Atlanta	GA	30319	404-633-3777	633-1870	49-8
ACR Aircraft Component Repair Inc 25058 Anza Dr *Web:* www.acr.aero	Valencia	CA	91355	661-295-6677	295-6679	20
ACR Electronics Inc 5757 Ravenswood Rd *TF:* 800-432-0227 ■ *Web:* www.acrartex.com	Fort Lauderdale	FL	33312	954-981-3333	983-5087	678
ACR Group Inc 3200 Wilcrest Dr Ste 440	Houston	TX	77042	713-780-8532	780-4067	612
ACR Publications 1298 Elm St SW *Web:* acrp.com	Albany	OR	97321	541-928-6199	926-3478	637-2
ACR Supply Company Inc 4040 S Alston Ave *TF:* 800-442-4044 ■ *Web:* www.acrsupply.com	Durham	NC	27713	919-765-8081		111
ACRA Machinery Inc 13173 Arrow Rte *TF:* 800-225-4631 ■ *Web:* www.acramachinery.com	Rancho Cucamonga	CA	91739	909-899-3000	899-8188	385
Acraloc Corp 113 Flint Rd *Web:* www.acraloc.com	Oak Ridge	TN	37830	865-483-1368	483-3500	547
Acranet 521 W Maxwell Ave *TF:* 800-304-1249 ■ *Web:* www.acranet.com	Spokane	WA	99201	800-304-1249		463
Acres Enterprises Inc 610 W Liberty St *Web:* www.acresgroup.com	Wauconda	IL	60084	815-609-2420		776
Acrilex Inc 230 Culver Ave *TF:* 800-222-4680 ■ *Web:* www.acrilex.com	Jersey City	NJ	07305	800-222-4680		596
Acro Automation Systems Inc 2900 W Green Tree Rd *Web:* www.acro.com	Milwaukee	WI	53209	414-352-4540	352-1609	811
Acro Industries Inc 554 Colfax St *Web:* www.acroind.com	Rochester	NY	14606	585-254-3661	254-0415	454
Acro Labels Inc 2530 Wyandotte Rd *TF:* 800-355-2235 ■ *Web:* www.acrolabels.com	Willow Grove	PA	19090	215-657-5366	657-3325	413
Acro Machining Inc 15303 39th Ave Ne *Web:* www.acromachining.com	Marysville	WA	98271	360-653-1492		454
Acro Media Inc 2303 Leckie Rd Ste 103 *TF:* 877-763-8844 ■ *Web:* www.acromedia.com	Kelowna	BC	V1X6Y5	250-763-8884	763-6936	809
AcrobatAnt LLC 1336 E 15th St *TF:* 800-984-7239 ■ *Web:* www.acrobatant.com	Tulsa	OK	74120	918-938-7901		195
Acromag Inc 30765 S Wixom Rd **Fax Area Code: 248 ■ TF: 877-295-7092 ■ Web:* www.acromag.com	Wixom	MI	48393	800-882-2055	624-9234*	625
Acromil Corp 18421 Railroad St *Web:* www.acromil.com	City of Industry	CA	91748	626-964-2522	810-6100	22
Acropolis Family Restaurant 708 Elmwood Ave *Web:* acropolisopa.com	Buffalo	NY	14222	716-886-2977		671
Acropolis Restaurant, The 416 N Eugene St *Web:* www.acropolisrestaurantgreensboro.com	Greensboro	NC	27401	336-273-3306		671
Acropolis Technology Group 300 Hunter Ave Ste 103 *TF:* 800-742-6316 ■ *Web:* www.acropolistech.com	Clayton	MO	63124	314-890-2208	721-8788	175
Acropolis, The 2213 Hamilton Pl Blvd *Web:* www.acropolisgrill.com	Chattanooga	TN	37421	423-899-5341		671
Acroprint Time Recorder Co 5640 Departure Dr *TF:* 800-334-7190 ■ *Web:* www.acroprint.com	Raleigh	NC	27616	919-872-5800	850-0720	534

	Phone	Fax	Class
Acrow Corporation of America 181 New Rd Ste 202 ...... Parsippany NJ 07054 *Web:* www.acrow.com	973-244-0080		480
Acrowood Corp 4425 S Third Ave ...... Everett WA 98203 *Web:* acrowood.com	425-258-3555	252-7622	821
ACRP (Association of Clinical Research Professionals) 999 Canal Center Plz Ste 800 ...... Alexandria VA 22314 *Web:* www.acrpnet.org	703-254-8100	254-8101	49-8
ACRS (Associated Communications & Research Services Inc) 2601 NW Expy Ste 405W ...... Oklahoma City OK 73112 *Web:* acrsokc.com	405-843-9966	843-9852	196
ACRT Inc 1333 Home Ave ...... Akron OH 44310 *TF:* 800-622-2562 ■ *Web:* acrt.com	800-622-2562		193
Acrylic Concepts Inc 17932 NE 65th St ...... Redmond WA 98052 *Web:* customacrylicfabricationplastic.com	425-881-3603	881-5398	599
Acrylic Design Assoc 6050 Nathan Ln N ...... Plymouth MN 55442 *TF:* 800-445-2167 ■ *Web:* www.acrylicdesign.com	763-559-8395	559-2589	233
Acrylic Designs Inc 2948 N 30th Ave ...... Phoenix AZ 85017 *TF:* 800-209-4204 ■ *Web:* www.acrylic-designs.com	602-272-9683	272-9353	603
Acrylic Plastic Products Company Inc 4815 Hwy 80 W ...... Jackson MS 39209 *TF:* 800-331-8819 ■ *Web:* www.acrylic1plasticproducts.com	601-922-2651		608
Acrylicore Inc 15902 S Broadway St ...... Gardena CA 90248 *TF:* 888-406-4846 ■ *Web:* www.shahrooz-art.com	888-406-4846		603
Acryline USA Inc 2015 Becancour ...... Lyster QC G0S1V0 *TF:* 800-567-0920 ■ *Web:* www.acryline.ca	800-567-0920		350
ACS (American Cancer Society) 250 William St NW ...... Atlanta GA 30303 *TF:* 800-227-2345 ■ *Web:* www.cancer.org	404-816-7800		48-17
ACS (American Chemical Society) 1155 16th St NW ...... Washington DC 20036 *TF:* 800-227-5558 ■ *Web:* www.acs.org	202-872-4600	872-4615	49-19
ACS (American College of Surgeons) 633 N St Clair St ...... Chicago IL 60611 *TF:* 800-621-4111 ■ *Web:* www.facs.org	312-202-5000	202-5001	49-8
ACS (American Cetacean Society) PO Box 51691 ...... Pacific Grove CA 93950 *Web:* www.acsonline.org	310-548-6279		48-3
ACS (American Cybersystems Inc) 2400 Meadowbrook Pkwy ...... Duluth GA 30096 **Fax Area Code:* 877 ■ *TF:* 800-800-5044 ■ *Web:* www.acsicorp.com	770-493-5588	270-6248*	194
ACS (Archaeological Consulting Services Ltd) 424 W Broadway Rd ...... Tempe AZ 85282 *Web:* www.acstempe.com	480-894-5477	894-5478	727
ACS Associates USA Inc 2145 Edge Hill Rd ...... Huntingdon Valley PA 19006	215-784-0661		194
ACS Division of Environmental Chemistry 210 Cypress Ct ...... Woodway TX 76712 **Fax Area Code:* 254 ■ *Web:* acsenvr.com	806-781-1513	751-9138*	637-2
ACS Group, The 2900 S 160th St ...... New Berlin WI 53151 *TF:* 800-423-3183 ■ *Web:* www.acscorporate.com	262-641-8600		14
ACS Industries Inc 1 New England Way ...... Lincoln RI 02865 *TF:* 866-783-4838 ■ *Web:* www.acsindustries.com	401-769-4700	333-6088	688
ACS Manufacturing Inc 1601 Commerce Blvd ...... Denison TX 75020 *Web:* www.acsmanufacturing.com	903-462-2001	462-2000	192
ACS of Texas 16622 Sperry Gardens Dr ...... Houston TX 77095 *Web:* www.acsoftexas.com	832-593-9989		35
ACS Software Inc 2463 208th St Ste 202 ...... Torrance CA 90501 *Web:* www.acssoftware.com	310-755-6040	755-6050	178-1
ACSA (Association of Collegiate Schools of Architecture) 1735 New York Ave NW 3rd Fl ...... Washington DC 20006 *Web:* www.acsa-arch.org	202-785-2324	628-0448	49-5
Acsel Corp 2876 Guardian Ln ...... Virginia Beach VA 23452 *TF:* 800-336-3038 ■ *Web:* acsel.org	757-463-5240	216-1638	2
ACSH (American Council on Science & Health) 110 E 42nd St Ste 1300 ...... New York NY 10017 *TF:* 866-905-2694 ■ *Web:* www.acsh.org	212-362-7044	362-4919	49-19
ACSI (Association of Christian Schools Intl) 731 Chapel Hills Dr ...... Colorado Springs CO 80920 *TF:* 800-367-0798 ■ *Web:* www.acsi.org	719-528-6906		49-5
ACSI (Automated Conveyor Systems Inc) 3850 Southland Dr ...... West Memphis AR 72301 *Web:* www.automatedconveyors.com	870-732-5050	732-5191	207
ACSI (Architectural Cladding Services Inc) 5570 Fireleaf Dr ...... Saint Louis MO 63129 *Web:* www.curtainwall.com	314-842-9555		194
Acsia Partners LLC 5110 Carillon Pt ...... Kirkland WA 98033 *TF:* 866-471-4072 ■ *Web:* acsiapartners.com	425-284-2148	284-2145	390
Acsion Industries Inc 24-24 Aberdeen Ave PO Box 429 ...... Pinawa MB R0E1L0 *Web:* www.acsion.com	204-753-2255	753-8466	317
Acsis Inc 9 E Stow Rd ...... Marlton NJ 08053 *Web:* www.acsisinc.com	856-673-3000		180
ACSM (American College of Sports Medicine) 401 W Michigan St PO Box 1440 ...... Indianapolis IN 46202 *Web:* www.acsm.org	317-637-9200	634-7817	49-8
ACSN (Aspartame Consumer Safety Network) PO Box 2001 ...... Frisco TX 75034 *TF:* 800-969-6050 ■ *Web:* www.aspartamesafety.com	800-969-6050		192
Acstar Insurance Co 30 South Rd ...... Farmington CT 06032 *Web:* www.acstarins.com	860-415-8400	404-5394	391-5
ACT (Association of Civilian Technicians) 12620 Lake Ridge Dr ...... Woodbridge VA 22192 *Web:* actnat.com	703-494-4845	494-0961	48-19
ACT (A Contemporary Theatre) Kreielsheimer Pl 700 Union St ...... Seattle WA 98101 *Web:* www.acttheatre.org	206-292-7660	292-7670	572
ACT (Abilene Community Theatre) 809 Barrow ...... Abilene TX 79605 *Web:* www.abilenecommunitytheatre.org	325-673-6271		572
ACT (American Conservatory Theater) 30 Grant Ave 7th Fl ...... San Francisco CA 94108 *Web:* www.act-sf.org	415-834-3200	749-2291	573-4
ACT (Action Communication Technology Inc) 27417 Hanna Rd ...... Conroe TX 77385 *Web:* www.actioncti.com	281-364-3710		681
ACT 1 Systems Inc 21031 Ventura Blvd Ste 1020 ...... Woodland Hills CA 91364 *Web:* site.act1systems.com	818-347-6400	346-2023	225
ACT Home Health Services Inc 1121 S 11th St ...... Philadelphia PA 19147 *Web:* www.acthomehealthservices.com	215-389-1800	389-1899	363
ACT Inc 500 Act Dr PO Box 168 ...... Iowa City IA 52243 *Web:* www.act.org	319-337-1000	337-1735	244
ACT Too Consulting Inc 917 W Inyokern Rd Ste C ...... Ridgecrest CA 93555 *Web:* www.acttooconsulting.com	760-301-5566		463
ACT UP 12 Wooster St ...... New York NY 10013 *Web:* www.actupny.org	212-966-4873		48-8
ACT Video Productions Inc 8319 Cirque Dr W Ste 3 ...... University Place WA 98467 *Web:* www.actvp.com	253-926-2440	926-1130	514
Act2 Retirement Consulting LLC 100 Painters Mill Rd ...... Owings Mills MD 21117 *TF:* 866-992-9256 ■ *Web:* www.act2retirement.com	443-379-0375		463
Acta Inc 2790 Skypark Dr Ste 310 ...... Torrance CA 90505 *Web:* www.actainc.com	310-530-1008		261
Actco Tool & Manufacturing Co 14421 Baldwin St Ext ...... Meadville PA 16335 *Web:* www.actcotool.com	814-336-4235	337-0101	757
ACTE (Association for Career & Technical Education) 1410 King St ...... Alexandria VA 22314 *TF:* 800-826-9972 ■ *Web:* www.acteonline.org	703-683-3111	683-7424	49-5
ACTE (Association of Corporate Travel Executives) 526 King St Ste 215 ...... Alexandria VA 22314 *TF:* 800-228-3669 ■ *Web:* www.acte.org	703-683-5322		48-23
ACTEC (American College of Trust & Estate Counsel) 901 15th St NW Ste 525 ...... Washington DC 20005 *Web:* www.actec.org	202-684-8460	684-8459	49-10
Actelis Networks Inc 47800 Westinghouse Dr ...... Fremont CA 94538 *TF:* 866-228-3547 ■ *Web:* actelis.com	510-545-1045	657-8006	729
ACTEON North America Inc 124 Gaither Dr Ste 140 ...... Mount Laurel NJ 08054 *TF:* 800-289-6367 ■ *Web:* www.acteongroup.com	856-222-9988		228
Acterra Environmental Library & Resource Ctr 3921 E Bayshore Rd ...... Palo Alto CA 94303 *Web:* www.acterra.org	650-962-9876		434-3
Acterra Group Inc Corporate Centre 200 200 35th St ...... Marion IA 52302 *TF:* 800-289-7371 ■ *Web:* www.acterragroup.com	319-377-6357	377-0075	61
ACTFL (American Council on the Teaching of Foreign Languages) 1001 N Fairfax St Ste 200 ...... Alexandria VA 22314 *Web:* www.actfl.org	703-894-2900	894-2905	49-5
ActForex Inc 110 Wall St 7th Fl ...... New York NY 10005 *Web:* www.actforex.com	212-425-7111		225
Actico Corp 200 S Wacker Dr Ste 3100 ...... Chicago IL 60606 *Web:* actico.com	312-471-5530		180
ActiFi Inc 3030 Harbor Ln ...... Plymouth MN 55447 *Web:* www.actifi.com	763-746-1280		225
Actify LLC 7635 Interactive Way Ste 200 ...... Indianapolis IN 46278 *TF:* 800-467-0830 ■ *Web:* www.actifywireless.com	800-467-0830		246
Actinix Inc 1800 Green Hills Rd Ste 105 ...... Scotts Valley CA 95066 *Web:* www.actinix.com	831-440-9388		419
Actinobac Biomed Inc 15 Pelham Rd ...... Kendall Park NJ 08824 *Web:* www.actinobac.com	732-371-2694		231
Actinver Securities Inc 5075 Wheimer Rd Galleria Financial Tower Ste 650 ...... Houston TX 77056 *Web:* actinversecurities.com	713-885-9843		690
Action Against Hunger 247 W 37th St 10th Fl ...... New York NY 10018 *TF:* 877-777-1420 ■ *Web:* www.actionagainsthunger.org	212-967-7800	967-5480	48-5
Action Aircraft 10570 Olympic Dr ...... Dallas TX 75220 *TF:* 800-909-7616 ■ *Web:* www.actionaircraft.com	214-351-1284	351-1286	21
Action Auto Parts (AAP) 795 N Main St ...... Providence RI 02904 *Web:* www.actionautoparts.com	401-273-0330	751-5393	61
Action Capital Corp 230 Peachtree St Ste 1910 ...... Atlanta GA 30303 *TF:* 800-525-7767 ■ *Web:* www.actioncapital.com	404-524-3181	577-4880	272
Action Career Training 598 Westwood Dr Ste 204 ...... Abilene TX 79603 *TF:* 800-725-6465	800-725-6465		167-3
Action Co 1425 N Tennessee St ...... McKinney TX 75069 *TF:* 800-937-3700 ■ *Web:* www.actioncompany.com	972-542-8700	562-7300	431
Action Coach 5781 S Ft Apache Rd ...... Las Vegas NV 89148 *TF:* 888-483-2828 ■ *Web:* www.actioncoach.com	702-795-3188	795-3183	765
Action Communication Technology Inc (ACT) 27417 Hanna Rd ...... Conroe TX 77385 *Web:* www.actioncti.com	281-364-3710		681
Action Craft 830 NE 24th Ln ...... Cape Coral FL 33909 *Web:* www.actioncraft.com	239-574-7800	574-7805	90
Action Equipment Sales Company Inc 5801 S Harding St ...... Indianapolis IN 46217 *TF:* 800-333-0368 ■ *Web:* actionequipmentsales.com	317-788-9781		366
Action Fabricating Inc 1244 Hawk St ...... Detroit Lakes MN 56501 *Web:* www.actionfabricating.com	218-847-4034		697
Action Fabrication & Truck Equipment Inc 1476 L&R Industrial Blvd ...... Tarpon Springs FL 34689 *TF:* 800-330-1229 ■ *Web:* www.actionfabrication.com	727-943-8911	938-0114	59
Action Facilities Management Inc 115 Malone Dr ...... Morgantown WV 26501 *Web:* actionfacilities.com	304-599-6850		256
Action Fasteners 265 Edinburgh Dr ...... Moncton NB E1E2K9 *Web:* www.actionfasteners.com	506-857-8950		351
Action Floor Systems LLC 4781 N US Hwy 51 ...... Mercer WI 54547 *TF:* 800-746-3512 ■ *Web:* www.actionfloors.com	715-476-3512		290
Action Inc 1308 Church St ...... Barling AR 72923 *TF:* 888-753-3401 ■ *Web:* www.action-mechanical.com	479-452-5723	452-5931	189-10

Phone | Fax | Class

Action Kit for Hospital Law
4614 5th Ave. Pittsburgh PA 15213 800-245-1205 687-7692* 637-10
Fax Area Code: 412 ■ *TF:* 800-245-1205 ■ *Web:* www.hortyspringer.com

Action Lead Solutions
2299 N Clybourn Ave Chicago IL 60614 773-661-1570 195
Web: actionleadsolutions.com

Action Lift Inc 1 Memco Dr. Pittston PA 18640 570-655-2100 358
TF: 800-294-5438 ■ *Web:* www.actionliftinc.com

Action Machined Products Inc
1355 Bangor St. Copiague NY 11726 631-842-2333 842-5902 488
Web: www.actionmachined.com

Action Mailing Corp
3165 W Heartland Dr Liberty MO 64068 816-415-9000 5
TF: 866-990-9001 ■ *Web:* www.action-mailing.com

Action Maintenance Systems Inc
251 E Empire St PO Box 90236 San Jose CA 95112 408-287-8000 104

Action Manufacturing Co
190 Rittenhouse Cir Bristol PA 19007 267-540-4041 268
Web: www.action-mfg.com

Action Moving and Storage Inc
359 Jasper Mine Rd Colchester VT 05446 802-893-1234 780
TF: 800-639-6683 ■ *Web:* actionmovingvt.com

Action On-Line Inc
4 S Central Ave Ste 1 Saint Louis MO 63105 314-726-4994 637-9
Web: actionol.com

Action Packaging Automation Inc
15 Oscar Dr Roosevelt NJ 08555 609-448-9210 448-8116 547
TF: 800-241-2724 ■ *Web:* www.apaiusa.com

Action Pact Inc 7709 W Lisbon Ave Milwaukee WI 53222 414-258-3649 463
Web: www.actionpact.com

Action Pest Control Inc
2301 S Green River Rd Evansville IN 47715 812-477-5546 577
TF: 800-467-5530 ■ *Web:* www.actionpest.com

Action Plastics Inc 14720 Main St Rogers MN 55374 763-428-4900 604
Web: www.actionplastics.com

Action Plumbing Supply Co
5411 NW 15th St Margate FL 33063 954-971-7782 612

Action Precision Products Inc
100 E North Ave Pioneer OH 43554 419-737-2348 737-3039 454
Web: actionprecision.com

Action Printers 300 E Harrison Coeur d'Alene ID 83814 208-667-2488 627
TF: 800-848-9688 ■ *Web:* www.actionprinters.net

Action Sales & Metal Company Inc
1625 E Pacific Coast Hwy Wilmington CA 90744 310-549-5666 723
Web: www.actionsalesmetal.com

Action Screen Print Inc
30w260 Butterfield Rd Unit 203 Warrenville IL 60555 630-393-1990 687
TF: 800-661-5892 ■ *Web:* actionscreen.com

Action Security Inc
2375 E 63rd Ave Ste 2 Anchorage AK 99501 907-279-7050 693
Web: actionsecurity.com

Action Shopper 249 W Washington St Marquette MI 49855 906-228-8920 228-5777 532-2

Action Stainless & Alloys Inc
1505 Halsey Way Carrollton TX 75007 972-466-1500 492
Web: www.actionstainless.com

Action Super Abrasive Products Inc
945 Greenbriar Pkwy Kent OH 44240 330-673-7333 295
Web: www.actionsuper.com

Action Supply Inc
1413 Old Stagecoach Rd Ocean View NJ 08230 609-390-0663 390-2491 182
Web: actionsupplynj.com

Action Team Realty Inc
6265 Lehman Dr Ste 100 Colorado Springs CO 80918 719-559-8400 652
Web: actionteamcolorado.com

Action Tire 2405 Weaver Way Doraville GA 30340 770-263-9695 57
Web: actiontireco.com

Action Title Services LLC
3733 Tamiami Trl N. Naples FL 34103 239-262-2200 652
Web: actiontitlenaples.com

Action Tool Service Inc
2202 Mingee Dr Hampton VA 23661 757-838-4555 825-0619 455
Web: www.actiontoolservice.com

Action Travel Center Inc 5900 Harper Rd Solon OH 44139 440-248-4949 775
Web: www.actiontravelnow.com

Action Water Sports 4155 32nd Ave Hudsonville MI 49426 616-896-3100 711
Web: actionwater.com

ActioNet Inc
2600 Park Tower Dr Ste 1000 Vienna VA 22180 703-204-0090 204-4782 624
Web: www.actionet.com

Actionlink LLC 2213 Romig Rd Akron OH 44333 888-737-8757 196
TF: 888-737-8757 ■ *Web:* www.actionlink.com

Action-Pak Inc 2550 Pearl Buck Rd Bristol PA 19007 215-785-4548 788-1760 549
Web: www.actionpakinc.com

ActionTec Electronics Inc
760 N Mary Ave Sunnyvale CA 94085 408-752-7700 541-9003 173-3
TF: 888-436-0657 ■ *Web:* www.actiontec.com

Activar Inc 9700 Newton Ave S Bloomington MN 55431 952-944-3533 881-3307 360-2
Web: www.activar.com

Activation Laboratories Ltd
1336 Sandhill Dr Ancaster ON L9G4V5 905-648-9611 743
TF: 888-228-5227 ■ *Web:* www.actlabs.com

Active Captive Management
16485 Laguna Canyon Rd Ste 250 Irvine CA 92618 949-727-0155 391-6
Web: www.activecaptive.com

Active Concepts LLC
107 Technology Dr Lincolnton NC 28092 704-276-7100 276-7101 317
Web: activeconceptsllc.com

Active Day/Senior Care Inc
6 Neshaminy Interplex Ste 401 Trevose PA 19053 888-338-6898 642-6610* 451
Fax Area Code: 215 ■ *TF:* 877-435-3372 ■ *Web:* www.activeday.com

Active Environmental Technologies Inc
203 Pine St. Mount Holly NJ 08060 609-702-1500 194
Web: www.activeenv.com

Active Grinding Inc (AGI) 871 S Rose Pl Anaheim CA 92805 714-772-7610 772-2163 481
Web: www.activegrind.com

Active Imagination Inc 2507 N Blvd Houston TX 77098 713-528-6100 344

Active Intl 1 Blue Hill Plz Pearl River NY 10965 845-735-1700 735-0717 393
TF: 800-448-7233 ■ *Web:* www.activeinternational.com

Active Learning Corp PO Box 254 New Paltz NY 12561 845-255-0844 637-2
Web: activelearningcorp.com

Active Network
10182 Telesis Ct Ste 100 San Diego CA 92121 858-964-3800 551-7619 7
TF: 888-543-7223 ■ *Web:* www.activenetwork.com

Active Parenting Publishers
1220 Kennestone Cir Ste 110 Marietta GA 30066 770-429-0565 429-0334 513
TF: 800-825-0060 ■ *Web:* www.activeparenting.com

Active PDF Inc
27405 Puerta Real Ste 100 Mission Viejo CA 92691 949-582-9002 582-9004 178-12
TF: 866-468-6733 ■ *Web:* www.activepdf.com

Active Plumbing Supply Co
216 Richmond St Painesville OH 44077 440-352-4411 612
Web: www.activeplumbing.com

Active Power Inc 2128 W Breaker Ln Bk12 Austin TX 78758 512-836-6464 767
NASDAQ: ACPW ■ *Web:* www.activepower.com

Active Recycling Company Inc
2000 W Slauson Ave. Los Angeles CA 90047 323-295-7774 660
Web: www.activelosangeles.com

Active Screw & Fastener
5422 Dansher Rd Countryside IL 60525 847-967-0800 482-7795* 351
Fax Area Code: 708 ■ *Web:* www.activescrew.com

Active Staffing Services
41 W 33rd St New York NY 10001 212-244-6444 244-1015 260
Web: www.activestaffing.com

Active Strategy Inc
620 W Germantown Pk Plymouth Meeting PA 19462 484-690-0711 225

Active Transport Messenger Service
285 5th Ave. Brooklyn NY 11215 718-965-1300 546
Web: www.activetransport.net

Active Transportation Alliance
35 E Wacker Dr Ste 1782 Chicago IL 60601 312-427-3325 711
Web: www.activetrans.org

Active USA LLC
10801 Corporate Dr Pleasant Prairie WI 53158 262-564-7401 780
TF: 800-237-4441 ■ *Web:* www.activetransport.com

ActiveForever 10799 N 90th St Scottsdale AZ 85260 800-377-8033 321
TF: 800-377-8033 ■ *Web:* www.activeforever.com

Activeworlds Inc 95 Parker St Newburyport MA 01950 978-499-0222 499-0221 178-7
Web: www.activeworlds.com

Activision Inc
3100 Ocean Pk Blvd Santa Monica CA 90405 310-255-2000 178-6
Web: www.activision.com

Activities for Learning Inc
321 Hill St Hazelton ND 58544 701-782-2000 782-2007 637-10
TF: 888-272-3291 ■ *Web:* www.alabacus.com

Activo Inc 161 Alden Rd Unit 6 Markham ON L3R3W7 905-752-1900 180
Web: www.activo.ca

Acton Institute 98 E Fulton St Grand Rapids MI 49503 616-454-3080 454-9454 634
TF: 800-345-2286 ■ *Web:* acton.org

Acton Technologies Inc
100 Thompson St Pittston PA 18640 570-654-0612 605-2
Web: www.actontech.com

Actor's Theatre of Charlotte
1900 Selwyn Ave Ste 1252 Charlotte NC 28274 704-342-2251 572
Web: www.atcharlotte.org

Actors Theatre of Louisville
316 W Main St Louisville KY 40202 502-584-1205 561-3300 749
TF: 800-428-5849 ■ *Web:* actorstheatre.org

Actors' Equity Assn 165 W 46th St New York NY 10036 212-869-8530 719-9815 414
TF: 866-270-4232 ■ *Web:* www.actorsequity.org

Actron Manufacturing Inc
1841 Railroad St Corona CA 92880 951-371-0885 22
Web: www.actronmfginc.com

Actron Steel Inc 2866 Cass Rd Traverse City MI 49685 231-947-3981 198
Web: actronsteel.com

ACTS Communications PO Box 73545 San Clemente CA 92673 949-481-4262 481-3686 637-2
Web: www.actscom.com

ACTS Retirement-Life Communities Inc
375 Morris Rd PO Box 90 West Point PA 19486 215-661-8330 672
Web: www.actsretirement.org

Actsoft Inc
10006 N Dale Mabry Hwy Ste 100 Tampa FL 33618 813-936-2331 936-7541 177
TF: 888-732-6638 ■ *Web:* actsoft.com

Actuarial Management Resources Inc
4964 University Pkwy Winston-Salem NC 27106 336-759-0008 463
Web: www.actmanre.com

Actuarial Research Corp
6928 Little River Tpke Ste E Annandale VA 22003 703-941-7400 196
Web: www.aresearch.com

Actuarial Systems Corp
15840 Monte St Ste 108 Sylmar CA 91342 800-950-2082 390
TF: 800-950-2082 ■ *Web:* www.asc-net.com

Actus Manufacturing Inc
240 Arlington Ave E Saint Paul MN 55117 651-487-8716 487-4173 203
Web: actusinc.com

ACU (Abilene Christian University Brown Library)
221 Brown Library Abilene TX 79699 325-674-2316 434-6
TF: 800-460-6228 ■ *Web:* www.acu.edu

ACU Serve Corp
2020 Front St Ste 205 Cuyahoga Falls OH 44221 800-887-8965 2
TF: 800-887-8965 ■ *Web:* acuservecorp.com

Acucote Inc 910 E Elm St Graham NC 27253 800-228-2683 807-0795 552-1
TF: 800-228-2683 ■ *Web:* www.acucote.com

ACUGEN Software Inc
379 Amherst St Ste 222 Nashua NH 03063 603-261-2468 178-1
Web: www.acugen.com

ACUHO-I (Association of College & University Housing Officers Intl)
1445 Summit St Columbus OH 43201 614-292-0099 292-3205 49-5
Web: www.acuho-i.org

ACUI (Association of College Unions Intl)
1 City Ctr Ste 200 Bloomington IN 47404 812-245-2284 245-6710 49-5
Web: www.acui.org

Acuity Audio Visual
11301 Industrial Rd Manassas VA 20109 703-361-6080 361-6463 196
Web: acuityav.com

Acuity Brands Inc
1170 Peachtree St NE Ste 2400 Atlanta GA 30309 404-853-1400 360-3
NYSE: AYI ■ *Web:* www.acuitybrands.com

Name / Address	City	State	Zip	Phone	Fax	Class
Acuity Inc 11710 Plaza America Dr Ste 700 *Web:* www.myacuity.com	Reston	VA	20190	703-766-0977		196
Acuity Insurance 2800 S Taylor Dr **Fax Area Code:* 888 ■ *TF:* 800-242-7666 ■ *Web:* www.acuity.com	Sheboygan	WI	53081	800-242-7666	880-9588*	391-4
Acuity Solutions LLC 2451 S Buffalo No 112 *Web:* www.acuitynv.com	Las Vegas	NV	89117	702-966-2000		194
Aculabs Inc 2 Kennedy Blvd *Web:* www.aculabs.com	East Brunswick	NJ	08816	732-777-2588		415
Acumen Capital Finance Partners Ltd 500 4th Ave SW Ste 800 *TF:* 888-422-8636 ■ *Web:* www.acumencapital.com	Calgary	AB	T2P2V6	403-571-0300		401
Acumen Connections Inc 6840 W Central Ave *TF:* 800-864-4644 ■ *Web:* www.acumenconnections.com	Wichita	KS	67212	800-864-4644		251
Acumen Data Systems Inc 2223 Westfield St No 101 *TF:* 888-816-0933 ■ *Web:* acumendatasystems.com	West Springfield	MA	01089	413-737-4800	737-5544	177
Acumen Enterprises Inc 1504 Falcon *Web:* acumen-enterprises.com	DeSoto	TX	75115	972-572-0701		261
Acumen Fiscal Agent 4542 E Inverness Ave Ste 210 **Fax Area Code:* 888 ■ *TF:* 877-211-3738 ■ *Web:* www.acumenfiscalagent.com	Mesa	AZ	85206	877-211-3738	249-7023*	734
Acumen Industrial Hygiene Inc 1032 Irving St Ste 922 *Web:* www.acumen-ih.com	San Francisco	CA	94122	415-242-6060	242-6006	196
Acumen Learning LLC 226 N Orem Blvd *Web:* acumenlearning.com	Orem	UT	84057	801-224-5444		765
Acumen Solutions Inc 8280 Greensboro Dr Ste 400 *Web:* www.acumensolutions.com	McLean	VA	22102	703-600-4000		180
Acumenex Com 2201 Brant St *TF:* 877-788-5028 ■ *Web:* www.acumenex.com	Burlington	ON	L7P3N8	905-319-2468		396
Acumentra Health Inc 2020 SW 4th Ave Ste 520	Portland	OR	97201	503-382-3929		194
Acumera Inc 3307 Northland Dr Ste 170 *Web:* www.acumera.net	Austin	TX	78731	512-687-7410		624
Acumeter Laboratories 2021 County Rd C2 W *Web:* acumeter.com	Saint Paul	MN	55113	651-765-9686		821
Acupay System LLC 30 Broad St 46th Fl *Web:* www.acupay.com	New York	NY	10004	212-422-1222		401
Acupressure Therapy Institute 44 Pearl St *Web:* www.blanchardbarbara.wordpress.com	Cambridge	MA	02139	617-492-3798		167-3
Acupuncture & Massage College 10506 N Kendall Dr *Web:* www.amcollege.edu	Miami	FL	33176	305-595-9500	595-2622	800
Acura Hunt Valley 10400 York Rd *Web:* www.acurahuntvalley.com	Cockeysville	MD	21030	443-720-7378		57
Acura Medical Systems Inc 8990 Cotter St *Web:* acuramed.com	Lewis Center	OH	43035	614-781-0600		57
Acura Neon 1801 N Willow Ave *Web:* anisigns.com	Broken Arrow	OK	74012	918-252-2258		57
Acura of Bellevue 13424 NE 20th St *TF:* 833-264-5723 ■ *Web:* www.acuraofbellevue.com	Bellevue	WA	98005	833-264-5723		57
Acuren Group Inc 7450 - 18th St *TF:* 800-663-9729 ■ *Web:* www.acuren.com	Edmonton	AB	T6P1N8	780-440-2131		787
Acushnet holdings Corp 333 Bridge St *TF:* 800-225-8500 ■ *Web:* www.acushnetholdingscorp.com	Fairhaven	MA	02719	508-979-2000	979-3927	710
Acusis LLC 4 Smithfield St *Web:* www.acusis.com	Pittsburgh	PA	15222	412-209-1300	209-1299	478
Acutec Precision Machining Inc 16891 State Hwy 198 *Web:* acutecprecision.com	Saegertown	PA	16433	814-763-3214		454
AcuTech Group Inc 1919 Gallows Rd Ste 900 *Web:* acutech-consulting.com	Vienna	VA	22182	703-676-3180	842-8854	194
Acutrack Inc 350 Sonic Ave *TF:* 888-234-3472 ■ *Web:* www.acutrack.com	Livermore	CA	94551	925-579-5000	579-5001	514
Acutronic USA Inc 700 Waterfront Dr *Web:* www.acutronic.com	Pittsburgh	PA	15222	412-926-1200	697-8111	529
Acutus Medical Inc 2210 Faraday Ave Ste 100 *Web:* www.acutusmedical.com	Carlsbad	CA	92008	442-232-6080		743
ACW Management Corp 2527 Echester Dr *Web:* www.acleanerworld.com	High Point	NC	27265	336-841-4188	841-4117	426
ACWM (American Clock & Watch Museum) 100 Maple St *Web:* www.clockandwatchmuseum.org	Bristol	CT	06010	860-583-6070		520
Acxiom 301 E Dave Ward Dr *NASDAQ: ACXM* ■ *TF:* 888-322-9466 ■ *Web:* www.acxiom.com	Conway	AR	72032	888-322-9466		5
Acxius Strategic Consulting LLC 500 Campus Dr Ste 300 *Web:* www.acxius.com	Morganville	NJ	07751	732-972-7970		180
ACY (Atlantic City International Airport) 101 Atlantic City International Airport Ste 106 *Web:* sjta.com	Egg Harbor Township	NJ	08234	609-645-7895		27
AD Art Co 3260 E 26th St *TF:* 800-266-7522 ■ *Web:* www.adartco.com	Los Angeles	CA	90058	323-981-8941	980-0515	701
AD Astra Information Systems LLC 6900 W 80th St *Web:* www.aais.com	Overland Park	KS	66204	913-652-4100		177
AD Cetera Inc 15570 Quorum Dr *Web:* adceterainc.com	Addison	TX	75001	972-387-5577		7
AD Display Sign Systems Inc 27255 Katy Fwy *Web:* addisplaysigns.com	Katy	TX	77494	281-392-2828	392-7446	701
AD Graphics 1050 Larrabee Ave Ste 104-365 *TF:* 800-830-1212 ■ *Web:* www.adgraphics.com	Bellingham	WA	98225	800-830-1212		344
AD Makepeace Company Inc 158 Tihonet Rd *Web:* www.admakepeace.com	Wareham	MA	02571	508-295-1000		315-1
AD Partners Inc 5020 W Linebaugh Ave Ste 240 *Web:* adpartnersagency.com	Tampa	FL	33624	813-542-4095		4
AD Potts & Associates Inc 11524 Jefferson Ave	Newport News	VA	23601	757-595-4610		727
AD Results Media LLC 320 Westcott St Ste 101	Houston	TX	77007	713-783-1800		7
AD Singleton & Company CPA Inc 16870 W Bernardo Dr Ste 400 *Web:* www.adscpa.com	San Diego	CA	92127	760-747-4605		2
AD Solutions Group Inc 1200 Harger Rd Ste 203 *Web:* www.adsgroup.net	Oak Brook	IL	60523	630-574-4545		177
AD Sutton & Sons Inc 20 W 33rd St *Web:* adsutton.com	New York	NY	10001	212-695-7070	947-6253	430
AD Systems Inc 212 S White St *Web:* www.adsys.com	Wake Forest	NC	27587	919-562-4248		178-1
AD Ventures in Texas Inc 900 RR620 S Ste C101 *Web:* www.adventuresintexas.com	Austin	TX	78734	512-413-2748		194
ADA (American Dental Assn) 211 E Chicago Ave *TF:* 800-621-8099 ■ *Web:* www.ada.org	Chicago	IL	60611	312-440-2500		49-8
ADA (American Diabetes Assn) 1701 N Beauregard St *TF:* 800-232-3472 ■ *Web:* www.diabetes.org	Alexandria	VA	22311	703-549-1500		48-17
ADA (Americans for Democratic Action) 1629 K St NW Ste 300 *Web:* adaction.org	Washington	DC	20006	202-600-7762	204-8637	48-7
ADA Area Chamber of Commerce 209 W Main St *Web:* adachamber.com	Ada	OK	74820	580-332-2506		139
ADA Business Computers 1003 N Mississippi Ave *Web:* www.adacomp.com	Ada	OK	74820	580-436-2803	436-2318	177
ADA Coca Cola Bottling Co 1205 Cradduck Rd *Web:* www.adacocacola.com	Ada	OK	74820	580-427-2000	332-1838	805
ADA Community Library 10664 W Victory Rd *Web:* www.adalib.org	Boise	ID	83709	208-362-0181	229-2666	31
ADA Evening News Corp PO Box 489 *Web:* www.theadanews.com	Ada	OK	74821	580-332-8810	332-8734	637-8
ADA Metal Products Inc 7120 Capitol Dr *Web:* www.adametal.com	Lincolnwood	IL	60712	847-673-1190	673-4860	489
ADA Station Communication Inc 1079 Livingston Rd *Web:* www.adastation.com	Crossville	TN	38555	931-707-5389		179
ADA Technologies Inc 11149 Bradford Rd *Web:* www.adatech.com	Littleton	CO	80127	303-792-5615	792-5633	668
ADAA (Art Dealers Association of America) 205 Lexington Ave Ste 901 **Fax Area Code:* 646 ■ *Web:* artdealers.org	New York	NY	10016	212-488-5550	688-6809*	48-4
ADAA (Anxiety Disorders Association of America) 8701 Georgia Ave Ste 412 *TF:* 800-922-8947 ■ *Web:* adaa.org	Silver Spring	MD	20910	240-485-1001	485-1035	48-17
ADAA (American Dental Assistants Assn) 140 N Bloomingdale Rd *TF:* 877-874-3785 ■ *Web:* www.adaausa.org	Bloomingdale	IL	60108	312-541-1550		49-8
Adacel Technologies Ltd 9677 Tradeport Dr *Web:* www.adacel.com	Orlando	FL	32827	407-581-1560	581-1581	178-10
ADA-ES Inc 640 Plz Dr Ste 270 *NASDAQ: ADES* ■ *TF:* 888-822-8617 ■ *Web:* www.adaes.com	Highlands Ranch	CO	80129	720-598-3500	598-3501	145
Adair County 424 Public Sq *Web:* columbia-adaircounty.com	Columbia	KY	42728	270-384-4703		338
Adair County 400 Public Sq *Web:* www.adaircountyiowa.org	Greenfield	IA	50849	641-743-2546	743-2565	338
Adair County 106 W Washington St *Web:* adaircountymissouri.com	Kirksville	MO	63501	660-665-3350	785-3212	338
Adair County PO Box 88 *Web:* ltap.okstate.edu	Stilwell	OK	74960	918-696-5310	696-6829	338
Adair County Board of Education 1204 Greensburg St *Web:* www.adair.k12.ky.us	Columbia	KY	42728	270-384-2476		685
Adair Printing Technologies 7850 Second St *TF:* 800-637-5025 ■ *Web:* adairgraphic.com	Dexter	MI	48130	734-426-2822	426-4360	626
Adair State Park Hwy 51 & Hwy 59 *Web:* www.oklahomacampers.com	Stilwell	OK	74960	918-696-6613		565
Adalet 4801 W 150th St *Web:* www.adalet.com	Cleveland	OH	44135	216-267-9000	267-1681	816
Adam and Gillian's Sensual Whips and Toys 40 Grant Ave *Web:* www.aswgt.com	Copiague	NY	11726	631-842-1711		322
Adam Barlow Law PC 4704 E Southern Ave *Web:* adambarlowlaw.com	Mesa	AZ	85206	602-688-4529		41
Adam Broderick Salon & Spa 89 Danbury Rd *TF:* 800-438-3834 ■ *Web:* www.adambroderick.com	Ridgefield	CT	06877	203-431-3994		77
Adam Matthews Inc 2104 Plantside Dr *Web:* www.adammatthews.com	Louisville	KY	40299	502-499-2253		345
Adam Moore Law Firm, The 3773 Cherry Creek N Dr Ste 575 *Web:* www.adammoorelaw.com	Denver	CO	80209	303-228-2171		428
Adam Ross Cut Stone Company Inc 1003 Broadway	Albany	NY	12204	518-463-6674		724
Adam's European Contracting Inc 589 Johnson Ave *Web:* www.adamseuro.com	Brooklyn	NY	11237	718-417-9000		251
Adam's Rib 1210 State St *Web:* adams-rib-smoke-house.com	Salem	OR	97301	503-362-2194		671

Name / Address	City	State	ZIP	Phone	Fax	Class
Adamo Construction Inc 11980 Woodside Ave Ste 5 *TF:* 800-554-6364 ■ *Web:* www.adamosecurity.com	Lakeside	CA	92040	619-390-6706		186
Adams & Associates of Nevada Inc 10395 Double R Blvd *Web:* www.adamsaai.com	Reno	NV	89521	775-348-0900		195
Adams & Brooks Inc 1915 S Hoover St *Web:* www.adams-brooks.com	Los Angeles	CA	90007	909-880-2305	475-4930	296-8
Adams & Clark Inc 1720 W Fourth Ave *Web:* www.adamsandclark.com	Spokane	WA	99201	509-747-4600	747-8913	727
Adams & Knight Inc 80 Avon Meadow Ln *Web:* www.adamsknight.com	Avon	CT	06001	860-676-2300		4
Adams & Longino Advertising Inc 605 Lynndale Ct Ste F *Web:* www.adamsadv.com	Greenville	NC	27858	252-355-5566		7
Adams & Smith Inc 1380 W Center St *Web:* www.adamsandsmith.com	Lindon	UT	84042	801-785-6900	785-6400	189-14
Adams & Westlake Ltd 940 N Michigan St *Web:* www.adlake.com	Elkhart	IN	46514	574-264-1141		650
Adams & Wilson Development Inc 835 Lowcountry Blvd *Web:* adamswilsondevelopment.com	Mount Pleasant	SC	29464	843-216-9990		652
Adams Air & Hydraulics Inc 904 S 20th St *TF:* 800-282-4165 ■ *Web:* adamscorp.com	Tampa	FL	33605	813-626-4128		358
Adams Alma (Rep D - NC) 2436 Rayburn House Office Bldg *Web:* www.adams.house.gov	Washington	DC	20515	202-225-1510	225-1512	342-2
Adams Arms 21228 Powell Rd *Web:* www.adamsarms.net	Brooksville	FL	34604	727-853-0550		807
Adams Auto Corp 501 NE Colbern Rd	Lee's Summit	MO	64086	816-358-7600		57
Adams Avenue Business Assn 4649 Hawley Blvd *Web:* www.adamsavenuebusiness.com	San Diego	CA	92116	619-282-7329		460
Adams Benefit Corp 600 Corporate Dr Ste 305 *Web:* adamsbenefit.com	Fort Lauderdale	FL	33334	954-772-9320		390
Adams Capital Management Inc 500 Blackburn Ave *Web:* www.acm.com	Sewickley	PA	15143	412-749-9454	749-9459	792
Adams Cattle LLC 327 S First Ave *Web:* www.adamslandandcattle.com	Broken Bow	NE	68822	308-872-6494		446
Adams Co 8040 Chavenelle Rd *Web:* www.theadamscompany.com	Dubuque	IA	52002	563-583-3591	583-8048	620
Adams Communication & Engineering Technology Inc 11637 Terr Dr Ste 201 *Web:* www.adamscomm.com	Waldorf	MD	20602	301-861-5000		256
Adams Construction Co 523 Rutherford Ave NE *Web:* www.adamspaving.com	Roanoke	VA	24016	540-982-2366	982-2942	188-4
Adams County 500 Ninth St *Web:* www.adamscountyia.com	Corning	IA	50841	641-322-3240	322-4647	338
Adams County 201 Industrial Ave *Web:* www.co.adams.id.us	Council	ID	83612	208-253-6125	253-6127	338
Adams County 313 W Jefferson St *Web:* www.co.adams.in.us	Decatur	IN	46733	260-724-5300	724-5313	338
Adams County PO Box 95 *Web:* www.adamscounty.org	Hastings	NE	68901	402-461-7107	461-7185	338
Adams County 314 State St *Web:* www.adamscountyms.net	Natchez	MS	39120	601-442-2431		338
Adams County 507 Vermont St *Web:* www.co.adams.il.us	Quincy	IL	62301	217-277-2150	277-2155	338
Adams County 210 W Broadway *Web:* www.co.adams.wa.us	Ritzville	WA	99169	509-659-3257	659-0118	338
Adams County 110 W Main St *TF:* 800-840-5711 ■ *Web:* adamscountyoh.gov	West Union	OH	45693	937-544-2364		338
Adams County Historical Society (ACHS) PO Box 102 *Web:* www.adamshistory.org	Hastings	NE	68902	402-463-5838		49-19
Adams County Public Library 140 Baltimore St *TF:* 800-548-3240 ■ *Web:* www.adamslibrary.org	Gettysburg	PA	17325	717-334-5716	334-7992	434-3
Adams County Travel & Visitors Bureau 509 E Main St *TF:* 877-232-6764 ■ *Web:* www.adamscountytravel.org	West Union	OH	45693	937-544-5639		139
Adams County Winery 251 Peach Tree Rd *TF:* 877-601-7936 ■ *Web:* www.adamscountywinery.com	Orrtanna	PA	17353	717-334-4631		50-7
Adams Dairy Bank 651 NE Coronado Dr *Web:* equitybank.com	Blue Springs	MO	64014	816-655-3333		70
Adams Direct & Media Services 39 Faranella Dr *TF:* 800-631-6245 ■ *Web:* adamsdms.com	East Hanover	NJ	07936	800-631-6245		195
Adams Electric Co-op PO Box 247 *TF:* 800-232-4797 ■ *Web:* www.adamselectric.coop	Camp Point	IL	62320	217-593-7701	593-7120	245
Adams Electric Co-opeartive Inc 1338 Biglerville Rd PO Box 1055 *TF:* 888-232-6732 ■ *Web:* www.adamsec.coop	Gettysburg	PA	17325	717-334-2171		245
Adams Elevator Equipment Co 6310 W Howard St **Fax Area Code:* 847 ■ *TF:* 800-929-9247 ■ *Web:* www.adamselevator.com	Niles	IL	60714	800-929-9247	581-2949*	678
Adams Extract & Spice LLC 3217 Johnson Rd *Web:* www.adamsextract.com	Gonzales	TX	78629	512-359-3050		297-8
Adams Foam Rubber Co 4737 S Christiana Ave *Web:* www.adamsfoam.com	Chicago	IL	60632	773-523-5252		328
Adams Funds 500 E Pratt St Ste 1300 *NYSE:* ADX ■ *TF:* 800-638-2479 ■ *Web:* www.adamsfunds.com	Baltimore	MD	21202	410-752-5900		405
Adams Globalization 10801 N Mopace Expwy/Loop 1 Bldg 3 Ste 720 *TF:* 800-880-0667 ■ *Web:* www.adamsglobalization.com	Austin	TX	78759	512-821-1818	821-1888	393
Adams Group Inc, The 925 Gervais St *TF:* 888-765-1223 ■ *Web:* adamsgroup.com	Columbia	SC	29201	803-765-1223		195
Adams Hemingway Wilson Rutledge LLC 544 Mulberry St Ste 1000 *Web:* www.adamshemingway.com	Macon	GA	31201	478-201-9941		41
Adams Homestead & Nature Preserve 272 Westshore Dr *Web:* gfp.sd.gov	McCook Lake	SD	57049	605-232-0873		565
Adams Insurance Service Inc 427 W 20th St Ste 500 *TF:* 800-438-8346 ■ *Web:* adamsinsurance.com	Houston	TX	77008	713-869-8346	869-9144	390
Adams Investment Co 2500 Industrial Pkwy PO Box 9 **Fax Area Code:* 918 ■ *TF:* 800-331-0920	Dewey	OK	74029	800-331-0920	534-3470*	110
Adams Jhonson & Duncan 3128 Colby Ave *Web:* www.adamslawyers.com	Everett	WA	98201	425-339-8556		428
Adams Keegan Inc 6750 Poplar Ave Ste 400 *TF:* 800-621-1308 ■ *Web:* www.adamskeegan.com	Memphis	TN	38138	800-621-1308		631
Adams Manufacturing Company Inc 9790 Midwest Ave *Web:* www.adamsmanufacturing.com	Cleveland	OH	44125	216-587-6801	587-6807	37
Adams Manufacturing Corp 109 W Park Rd *Web:* www.adamsmfg.com	Portersville	PA	16051	724-368-8837		596
Adams McClure LP 1245 S Inca St *TF:* 888-777-1984 ■ *Web:* www.adamsmcclure.com	Denver	CO	80223	303-777-1984		627
Adams Museum 54 Sherman St *TF:* 800-335-0275 ■ *Web:* www.deadwoodhistory.com	Deadwood	SD	57732	605-578-1714		520
Adams National Historical Park 135 Adams St *Web:* www.nps.gov	Quincy	MA	02169	617-773-1177		564
Adams Oceanfront Resort 4 Read St *TF:* 800-448-8080 ■ *Web:* adamsoceanfront.com	Dewey Beach	DE	19971	302-227-3030		379
Adams Outdoor Adv 500 Colonial Center Pkwy Ste 120 *Web:* www.adamsoutdoor.com	Roswell	GA	30076	770-333-0399	333-0599	8
Adams Physical Therapy Services Inc 111 W North St *Web:* Www.adamsptservices.com	Portland	IN	47371	260-726-6828	726-2257	352
Adams Products Co 5701 McCrimmon Pkwy *TF:* 800-672-3131 ■ *Web:* www.adamsproducts.com	Morrisville	NC	27560	919-467-2218		183
Adams Radio Group Inc 16233 Kenyon Ave S Ste 220 **Fax Area Code:* 612 ■ *Web:* www.adamsradiogroup.com	Lakeville	MN	55044	952-232-0588	437-4520*	643
Adams Rehmann & Heggan Assn 215 Bellevue Ave *Web:* www.civilsolutions.biz	Hammonton	NJ	08037	609-561-0482	567-8909	261
Adams Remco Inc 2612 Foundation Dr *TF:* 800-627-2113 ■ *Web:* adamsremco.com	South Bend	IN	46628	574-288-2113		112
Adams Resources & Energy Inc 17 S Briar Hollow Ln Ste 100 *NYSE:* AE ■ *TF:* 800-577-8853 ■ *Web:* www.adamsresources.com	Houston	TX	77027	713-881-3600		536
Adams Rite Aerospace 4141 N Palm St *Web:* www.ar-aero.com	Fullerton	CA	92835	714-278-6500	278-6510	22
Adams Rite Manufacturing Co 10027 S 51st St Ste 102 *Web:* www.adamsrite.com	Phoenix	AZ	85044	909-632-2300		350
Adams Rural Electric Co-opeartive Inc 4800 SR 125 *TF:* 800-283-1846 ■ *Web:* www.adamsrec.com	West Union	OH	45693	937-544-2305		245
Adams State Bank 649 Main *Web:* adamsstate.com	Adams	NE	68301	402-988-2255		70
Adams State College 208 Edgemont Blvd *TF:* 800-824-6494 ■ *Web:* www.adams.edu	Alamosa	CO	81102	719-587-7712	587-7522	166
Adams Street Partners LLC 1 N Wacker Dr Ste 2200 *Web:* www.adamsstreetpartners.com	Chicago	IL	60606	312-553-7890	553-7891	792
Adams Wholesale Company Inc 1020 Benvenue Rd *Web:* www.fredsfoodclub.com	Rocky Mount	NC	27804	252-977-2421		297-8
Adamsahern Sign Solutions Inc 30 Arbor St *Web:* adamsahern.com	Hartford	CT	06106	860-523-8835	523-7701	701
Adams-Burch Inc 1901 Stanford Ct *TF:* 800-347-8093 ■ *Web:* www.adams-burch.com	Landover Hills	MD	20785	301-276-2000		300
Adams-Columbia Electric Co-op 401 E Lake St **Fax Area Code:* 608 ■ *TF:* 800-831-8629 ■ *Web:* www.acecwi.com	Friendship	WI	53934	800-831-8629	339-7756*	245
AdamsGabbert 9200 Indian Creek Pkwy Ste 205 *Web:* adamsgabbert.com	Overland Park	KS	66210	913-735-4390		463
Adamson Analytical Laboratories Inc 200 Crouse Dr *Web:* adamsonlab.com	Corona	CA	92879	951-549-9657	549-9659	743
Adamson Associates Architects 401 Wellington St W 3rd Fl *Web:* www.adamson-associates.com	Toronto	ON	M5V1E7	416-967-1500		123
Adamson Global Technology Corp 13101 N Eron Church Rd *TF:* 800-525-7703 ■ *Web:* www.adamsontank.com	Chester	VA	23836	804-748-6453		91
Adamson Industries Corp 45 Research Dr *Web:* www.adamsonindustries.com	Haverhill	MA	01832	978-681-0370		295
Adamson Motors Inc 4800 Hwy 52 N *Web:* www.adamsonmotors.com	Rochester	MN	55901	507-289-4004		57
Adamy Valuation Advisors 50 Louis St NW Ste 405 *Web:* adamyvaluation.com	Grand Rapids	MI	49503	616-284-3700		734
Adapt Corp 1733 Woodside Rd Ste 220 *Web:* adapt.risa.com	Redwood City	CA	94061	650-306-2400		261
Adapt Inc 5610 Rowland Rd Ste 160 *TF:* 888-522-3278 ■ *Web:* adaptdata.com	Minnetonka	MN	55343	952-939-0538		225
Adapt Plastics Inc 7949 Forest Hills Rd *Web:* www.adaptplastics.com	Loves Park	IL	61111	815-633-9263	654-2817	608
Adaptek Systems Inc 14224 Plank St *Web:* www.adapteksystems.com	Fort Wayne	IN	46818	260-637-8660	637-8597	194

Name / Address	City	State	ZIP	Phone	Fax	Class
Adaptiva 4010 Lake Washington Blvd NE Ste 200 *Web:* adaptiva.com	Kirkland	WA	98033	425-823-4500		196
Adaptive Driving Access Inc 3430 E Sam Houston Pkwy S *Web:* www.adaptivedriving.com	Pasadena	TX	77505	281-487-1969		62
Adaptive Equipment Inc 2512 NE 1st Blvd Ste 100 *Web:* www.adaptivequipment.com	Gainesville	FL	32609	352-372-7821		180
Adaptive Flight Inc 5555 Oakbrook Pkwy Ste 345	Norcross	GA	30093	770-951-8755		256
Adaptive Micro Systems Inc 7840 N 86th St *TF:* 800-558-4187 ■ *Web:* www.adaptivedisplays.com	Milwaukee	WI	53224	414-357-2020	357-2029	178-7
Adaptive Networks Inc 123 Highland Ave *Web:* www.adaptivenetworks.com	Needham	MA	02494	781-444-4170		387
Adaptive Sports USA PO Box 621023 *Fax Area Code: 866 ■ *Web:* www.wasusa.org	Littleton	CO	80162	720-412-7979	204-8918*	48-22
Adaptive Switch Laboratories Inc 125 Spur 191 Ste C *TF:* 800-626-8698 ■ *Web:* www.asl-inc.com	Spicewood	TX	78669	830-798-0005	798-6221	250
Adaptive Systems Inc 9785 Crosspoint Blvd Rm 118 *Web:* www.adaptivesys.com	Indianapolis	IN	46256	317-806-6421		177
adaQuest 14450 NE 29th Pl Ste 120 *Web:* www.adaquest.com	Bellevue	WA	98007	425-284-7800	671-0827	194
Adastra Pharmaceuticals Inc 12481 High Bluff Dr Ste 150 *Web:* www.tragarapharma.com	San Diego	CA	92130	760-208-6900		231
ADB (American Drill Bushings Co) 5740 Hunt Rd *TF:* 800-423-4425 ■ *Web:* americandrillbushing.com	Valdosta	GA	31606	229-253-8928	253-8929	493
ADB Consulting & CRO Inc 8569 Pines Blvd Ste 215 *Web:* www.adbccro.com	Pembroke Pines	FL	33024	954-517-1970		196
ADC (American-Arab Anti Discrimination Committee) 1990 M St NW Ste 610 *TF:* 800-253-3931 ■ *Web:* www.adc.org	Washington	DC	20036	202-244-2990		48-8
ADC Engineering Inc 1226 Yeamans Hall Rd *Web:* adcengineering.com	Hanahan	SC	29410	843-566-0161		261
ADC Information Technologies Inc 950 Michigan Ave *Web:* www.ibswebsite.com	Columbus	OH	43215	614-240-5999		180
AdCare Hospital of Worcester 107 Lincoln St *TF:* 800-252-6465 ■ *Web:* www.adcare.com	Worcester	MA	01605	508-799-9000		726
Adcetera Design Studio Inc 3000 Louisiana St *Web:* www.adcetera.com	Houston	TX	77006	713-522-8006		344
Adchem Corp 1852 County Rd 58 *Web:* www.adchem.com	Riverhead	NY	11901	631-208-4440	727-6010	732
ADCO Advertising Agency Inc 1302 W Pioneer Pkwy *Web:* www.adcoagency.com	Peoria	IL	61615	309-692-7880	692-9925	7
ADCO Circuits 2868 Bond St *Web:* www.adcocircuits.com	Rochester Hills	MI	48309	248-853-6620	853-6698	253
ADCO Companies LTD 3657 Pine Ln *TF:* 800-222-7815 ■ *Web:* adcoboiler.com	Bessemer	AL	35022	205-428-2326	428-2395	612
ADCO Inc 1909 W Oakridge *TF:* 800-821-7556 ■ *Web:* www.adco-inc.com	Albany	GA	31707	800-821-7556		151
ADCO Industries 11333 Pagemill Rd *TF:* 800-527-4609 ■ *Web:* www.adcoindustries.com	Dallas	TX	75243	214-217-7800	217-7810	43
ADCO Landscaping 1532 W Olympic Blvd *Web:* www.adcoservices.org	Montebello	CA	90640	323-725-2581		776
ADCO Manufacturing Inc 2170 Academy Ave *TF:* 888-608-5946 ■ *Web:* www.adcomfg.com	Sanger	CA	93657	559-875-5563	875-7665	385
Adcole Corp 669 Forest St *Web:* www.adcole.com	Marlborough	MA	01752	508-485-9100	481-6142	472
Adcom 1370 W 6th St Ste 300 *Web:* www.theadcomgroup.com	Cleveland	OH	44113	216-574-9100		4
Adcomm Inc 89 Leuning St *Web:* adcomminc.com	South Hackensack	NJ	07606	201-342-6349		767
Adcor Industries Inc 234 S Haven St *Web:* adcorindustries.com	Baltimore	MD	21224	410-327-3083		454
Adcotron EMS Inc Marine Industrial Pk 12 Ch St *Web:* www.adcotron.com	Boston	MA	02210	617-598-3000	598-3001	695
Adcraft Products Company Inc 1230 S Sherman St *TF:* 800-892-1051 ■ *Web:* adcraftlabels.com	Anaheim	CA	92805	714-776-1230	999-5577	627
Add On Systems Inc 100 NW 63rd St Ste 215 *Web:* addonsystems.com	Oklahoma City	OK	73116	405-843-8142		177
Add Staff Inc 2118 Hollow Brook Dr *Web:* addstaffinc.com	Colorado Springs	CO	80918	719-528-8888		260
Add3 Marketing Agency 500 E Pike St Fl 2 Ste 200A *Web:* www.add3.com	Seattle	WA	98122	206-568-3772	374-3091	195
ADDA (American Design Drafting Assn) 105 E Main St *Web:* www.adda.org	Newbern	TN	38059	731-627-0802	627-9321	48-4
ADDCO LLC 240 Arlington Ave E *TF:* 800-616-4408 ■ *Web:* www.addco.com	Saint Paul	MN	55117	651-488-8600		700
AdDent Inc 43 Miry Brook Rd *TF:* 855-211-3413 ■ *Web:* www.addent.com	Danbury	CT	06810	203-778-0200	792-2275	228
Addessi Jewelers Inc 387 Main St *Web:* addessijewelers.com	Ridgefield	CT	06877	203-438-6549		410
Addictive Mobility Inc 72 Fraser Ave Ste 201 *Web:* addictivemobility.com	Toronto	ON	M6K3J7	416-535-0706		224
Addicus Books Inc PO Box 45327 *TF:* 800-888-4741 ■ *Web:* www.addicusbooks.com	Omaha	NE	68145	402-330-7493	330-1707	637-2
Addington Oil Corp 2154 US Hwy 23 N Ste 102 *TF:* 866-643-4352 ■ *Web:* www.addingtonoil.com	Weber City	VA	24290	276-386-3961		324
Addis Red Sea 544 Tremont St *Web:* www.addisredsea.com	Boston	MA	02116	617-426-8727		671
Addison Biological Laboratory Inc 507 N Cleveland Ave *TF:* 800-331-2530 ■ *Web:* addisonlabs.com	Fayette	MO	65248	660-248-2215	248-2554	584
Addison Capital Partners 319 Clematis St Ste 211 *Web:* www.addisoncapitalpartners.com	West Palm Beach	FL	33401	561-835-4041		401
Addison Chamber of Commerce & Industry 777 W Army Trial Blvd Ste D *Web:* addisonchamber.org	Addison	IL	60101	630-543-4300	543-4355	139
Addison County Chamber of Commerce 93 Court St *Web:* www.addisoncounty.com	Middlebury	VT	05753	802-388-7951	388-8066	139
Addison House 5201 NW 77th Ave Ste 400 *TF:* 800-426-2988 ■ *Web:* addisonhouse.com	Doral	FL	33166	305-640-2400		321
Addison Precision Manufacturing 500 Avis St *Web:* addisonprec.com	Rochester	NY	14615	585-254-1386	254-5342	454
Addison Public Library 4 Friendship Plz *Web:* www.addisonlibrary.org	Addison	IL	60101	630-543-3617		434-3
Addison The Grand Del Mar 5200 Grand Del Mar Way *Web:* www.addisondelmar.com	San Diego	CA	92130	858-314-1900		671
Addison Whitney 11525 N Community House Rd Ste 400 *Web:* www.addisonwhitney.com	Charlotte	NC	28277	704-347-5700		463
Addison's An American Grill 709 Cherry St *Web:* www.addisonsgrill.com	Columbia	MO	65201	573-256-1995		671
Addison, The 2 E Camino Real *Web:* www.theaddison.com	Boca Raton	FL	33432	561-372-0568		671
Addmaster Corp 225 E Huntington Dr *Web:* www.addmaster.com	Monrovia	CA	91016	626-358-2395	358-2784	173-6
Addonics Technologies Inc 1918 Junction Ave *Web:* www.addonics.com	San Jose	CA	95131	408-573-8580		174
Addus HealthCare Inc 6801 Gaylord Pkwy Ste 110 *NASDAQ:* ADUS	Frisco	TX	75034	469-535-8200		353
Addvantage Group LLC, The 20 N Clark St Ste 3300 *Web:* www.theaddvantagegroup.com	Chicago	IL	60602	312-626-1848		463
ADDvantage Technologies Group Inc 1221 E Houston *NASDAQ:* AEY ■ *Web:* www.addvantagetechnologies.com	Broken Arrow	OK	74012	918-251-9121		246
Addx Corp 4900 Seminary Rd Ste 570 *Web:* www.addxcorp.com	Alexandria	VA	22311	703-933-7637	933-7638	194
Addy's Dutch Cafe & Restaurant 17 E Coffee St *Web:* www.addysdutchcafe.com	Greenville	SC	29601	864-232-2339		671
ADEA (American Dental Education Assn) 1400 K St NW Ste 1100 *TF:* 800-353-2237 ■ *Web:* www.adea.org	Washington	DC	20005	202-289-7201	289-7204	49-5
Ad-Ease Communications Inc 823 Overhill Dr *Web:* www.adeaseinc.com	Penn	PA	15675	412-678-6266		4
ADEC (Association for Death Education & Counseling) 111 Deer Lake Rd Ste 100 *Web:* www.adec.org	Deerfield	IL	60015	847-509-0403	480-9282	49-8
A-Dec Inc 2601 Crestview Dr *TF:* 800-547-1883 ■ *Web:* www.a-dec.com	Newberg	OR	97132	503-538-7478	538-0276	228
Adec Industries 2700 Industrial Pkwy *TF:* 866-730-3111 ■ *Web:* adecinc.com	Elkhart	IN	46516	574-295-3167		88
ADEC Solutions USA 10 Monument St *Web:* www.adecsolutions-usa.com	Deposit	NY	13754	800-768-2070		225
Adecco USA Inc 175 Broad Hollow Rd *Web:* www.adeccousa.com	Melville	NY	11747	631-844-7650	844-7614	721
Adega 33 Elm St *Web:* www.adegarestaurante.ca	Toronto	ON	M5G1H1	416-977-4338		671
Adega Grill 130 Ferry St *Web:* www.adegagrill.com	Newark	NJ	07105	973-589-8830		671
Adelaide Environmental Health Associates Inc 1511 Rt 22 Ste C24 *Web:* www.adelaidellc.com	Brewster	NY	10509	845-278-7710		463
Adelberg Rudow 7 St Paul St Ste 600 *Web:* adelberg.com	Baltimore	MD	21202	410-539-5195		428
Adelis Development Systems (ADS) 3863 Ridge Crest Dr *Fax Area Code: 910 ■ *Web:* www.adelisdevelopment.com	Southport	NC	28461	908-510-6810	253-4222*	194
Adell Plastics Inc 4530 Annapolis Rd *TF:* 800-638-5218 ■ *Web:* www.adellplas.com	Baltimore	MD	21227	410-789-7780		745-2
Adelman Broadcasting 42010 50th St W *Web:* www.adelmanbroadcasting.com	Quartz Hill	CA	93536	661-718-1552	718-1553	647
Adelman Sand & Gravel Inc 34 Bozrah St *Web:* www.adelmaninc.com	Bozrah	CT	06334	860-889-3394		191-1
Adelman Travel Group 6980 N Port Washington Rd *TF:* 800-248-5562 ■ *Web:* www.adelmantravel.com	Milwaukee	WI	53217	414-352-7600	352-3900	771
Adelphi Consulting Group Inc 7783 SW Cirrus Dr *TF:* 800-698-1942 ■ *Web:* adelphigroup.net	Beaverton	OR	97008	800-698-1942		196
Adelphi University 1 South Ave PO Box 701 *TF:* 800-233-5744 ■ *Web:* www.adelphi.edu	Garden City	NY	11530	516-877-3050	877-3039	166
Adelphia Steel Equipment Company Inc 7372 State Rd	Philadelphia	PA	19136	215-333-6300		319-1
Adelphoi Village Inc 1119 Village Way *Web:* www.adelphoi.org	Latrobe	PA	15650	724-520-1111	520-1878	303
Adelsberger Donna & Assn 2782 Jenkintown Rd *Web:* dlalawyers.com	Glenside	PA	19038	215-576-8690		428

Name / Address	City	State	ZIP	Phone	Fax	Class
AdelWiggins Group 5000 Triggs St. *TF:* 800-624-3576 ■ *Web:* www.adelwiggins.com	Los Angeles	CA	90022	323-269-9181	269-3759	567
Adena Regional Medical Ctr 272 Hospital Rd *Web:* www.adena.org	Chillicothe	OH	45601	740-779-7500		374-3
Adept Consulting Services Inc 410 W Main St Ste 201 *Web:* www.adeptusa.com	Lansdale	PA	19446	215-855-3610		196
Adept Corp 4601 N Susquehanna Trial *TF:* 800-451-2254 ■ *Web:* www.adeptcorp.com	York	PA	17406	717-266-3606		358
Adept Fasteners Inc 28709 Industry Dr *Web:* www.adeptfasteners.com	Valencia	CA	91355	661-257-6600		621
Adept Technologies LLC 2865 Wall Triana Hwy *Web:* www.adept-technologies.com	Huntsville	AL	35824	256-851-2932		21
Adera Development Corp 1055 Dunsmuir St Ste 2200 Four Bentall Centre PO Box 49214 *Web:* adera.com	Vancouver	BC	V7X1K8	604-684-8277		627
Aderans Hair Goods Inc 9135 Independence Ave *TF:* 877-413-5225 ■ *Web:* reneofparis.com	Chatsworth	CA	91311	877-413-5225		348
Aderholt Robert (Rep R - AL) 1203 Longworth House Office Bldg *Web:* aderholt.house.gov	Washington	DC	20515	202-225-4876	225-5587	342-2
ADESA Inc 13085 Hamilton Crossing Blvd **Fax Area Code:* 317 ■ *TF:* 800-923-3725 ■ *Web:* www.adesa.com	Carmel	IN	46032	800-923-3725	249-4600*	51
Adex Corp 1035 Windward Ridge Pkwy Ste 500 *TF:* 800-451-9899 ■ *Web:* www.adextelecom.com	Alpharetta	GA	30005	678-393-7900		224
AD-EX International Inc 1301 Glendale-Milford Rd *Web:* adex-intl.com	Cincinnati	OH	45215	513-771-2339		195
Adex Media Inc 883 N Shoreline Blvd Ste A200 *Web:* www.adex.com	Mountain View	CA	94043	650-967-3040	967-3185	195
Adex Medical Inc 6101 Quail Valley Ct *TF:* 800-873-4776 ■ *Web:* www.adexmed.com	Riverside	CA	92507	951-653-9122	653-9133	477
Adexa Inc 5777 W Century Blvd Ste 1100 *Web:* www.adexa.com	Los Angeles	CA	90045	310-642-2100	338-9878	178-1
ADF Engineering Inc 228 Byers Rd Ste 202 *Web:* www.adfengineering.com	Miamisburg	OH	45342	937-847-2700	847-0777	256
ADF Systems Ltd 1302 19th St N **Fax Area Code:* 800 ■ *TF:* 800-959-1191 ■ *Web:* www.adfsystems.com	Humboldt	IA	50548	515-332-5400	798-5100*	806
Adflex Corp 300 Ormond St *Web:* www.adflexcorp.com	Rochester	NY	14605	585-454-2950		781
ADFLOW Networks Inc 3170 Harvester Rd Ste 102 *Web:* www.adflownetworks.com	Burlington	ON	L7N3W8	905-333-0200		7
ADG (Art Directors Guild) 11969 Ventura Blvd 2nd Fl *Web:* www.adg.org	Studio City	CA	91604	818-762-9995	762-9997	48-4
ADG Promotional Products 2300 Main St *TF:* 800-852-5208 ■ *Web:* www.adgpromo.com	Hugo	MN	55038	800-852-5208	886-6790	9
ADGA (American Dairy Goat Assn) 161 W Main St PO Box 865 *Web:* adga.org	Spindale	NC	28160	828-286-3801	287-0476	48-2
Adgo Inc 3988 Mcmann Rd *Web:* www.adgoinc.com	Cincinnati	OH	45245	513-752-6880	752-5723	729
ADH Health Products Inc 215 N Rt 303 *Web:* www.adhhealth.com	Congers	NY	10920	845-268-0027	268-2988	231
ADH Liquidating Corp 506 15th St Ste 600 *Web:* www.adhuesing.com	Moline	IL	61265	309-788-5652		805
ADHA (American Dental Hygienists Assn) 444 N Michigan Ave Ste 3400 *TF:* 800-243-2342 ■ *Web:* www.adha.org	Chicago	IL	60611	312-440-8900	467-1806	49-8
Higher Education Dept 423 Main St Ste 400 *Web:* www.adhe.edu	Little Rock	AR	72201	501-371-2000		339-4
Adherent Technologies Inc 11208 Cochiti SE *Web:* www.adherent-tech.com	Albuquerque	NM	87123	505-346-1688		668
Adhesive & Sealant Council Inc (ASC) 7101 Wisconsin Ave Ste 990 *Web:* www.ascouncil.org	Bethesda	MD	20814	301-986-9700	986-9795	49-13
Adhesive Applications Inc 41 O'Neill St *Web:* adhesiveapps.com	Easthampton	MA	01027	413-527-7120	527-7249	732
Adhesive Packaging Specialties Inc 103 Foster St *TF:* 800-222-1117 ■ *Web:* www.adhesivepackaging.com	Peabody	MA	01960	978-531-3300	532-8901	548
Adhesives Research Inc 400 Seaks Run Rd PO Box 100 *TF:* 800-445-6240 ■ *Web:* www.adhesivesresearch.com	Glen Rock	PA	17327	717-235-7979	235-8320	3
AdHub LLC, The 146 Alexander St *TF:* 866-712-2986 ■ *Web:* www.adhub.com	Rochester	NY	14607	585-442-2585		393
ADI American Distributors Inc 2 Emery Ave *TF:* 800-877-0510 ■ *Web:* americandistr.com	Randolph	NJ	07869	973-328-1181	328-2302	246
ADI Medical 1565 S Shields Dr **Fax Area Code:* 847 ■ *TF:* 877-647-7699 ■ *Web:* www.adimedical.com	Waukegan	IL	60085	877-647-7699	688-9768*	477
ADI Meetings & Events 4801 S Lakeshore Dr Ste 108 *Web:* www.adimeetings.com	Tempe	AZ	85282	480-350-9090		384
ADI Services 210 Commerce Cir *Web:* www.adiservices.com	Kearneysville	WV	25430	304-870-4384	870-4394	770
ADI Technologies Inc 4501 Daly Dr Ste 103 *Web:* aditechnologies.com	Chantilly	VA	20151	703-734-9626	448-8591	463
Adial Pharmaceuticals 204 E High St *Web:* www.adialpharma.com	Charlottesville	VA	22902	434-422-9800		668

Name / Address	City	State	ZIP	Phone	Fax	Class
Adicio Inc 5993 Avenida Encinas Ste 100 *TF:* 800-276-1332 ■ *Web:* www.adicio.com	Carlsbad	CA	92008	760-602-9502		177
Adidas Printing Inc 264 Salem St *Web:* adidasprinting.com	Medford	MA	02155	781-391-8850	393-0776	627
Adiligy LLC 321 W 29th St Ste 5B	New York	NY	10001	646-290-5288		194
Adino Inc 360 W Alden Ct *Web:* www.adinoinc.com	Chicago Heights	IL	60411	708-481-1000		177
Adirondack Beverages Inc 701 Corporations Pk *Web:* www.adirondackbeverages.com	Scotia	NY	12302	518-370-3621		80-2
Adirondack Community College 640 Bay Rd *TF:* 888-786-9235 ■ *Web:* www.sunyacc.edu	Queensbury	NY	12804	518-743-2200	745-1433	162
Adirondack Correctional Facility 196 Ray Brook Rd PO Box 110 *Web:* www.doccs.ny.gov	Ray Brook	NY	12977	518-891-1343		213
Adirondack Council 103 Hand Ave Ste 3 *TF:* 877-873-2240 ■ *Web:* www.adirondackcouncil.org	Elizabethtown	NY	12932	518-873-2240	873-6675	48-13
Adirondack Mountain Club 814 Goggins Rd *TF:* 800-395-8080 ■ *Web:* www.adk.org	Lake George	NY	12845	518-668-4447		48-23
Adirondack Natural Stone LLC 8986 State Rte 4 *Web:* www.adirondacknaturalstone.com	Whitehall	NY	12887	518-499-0602	499-2670	191-1
Adirondack Regional Chambers of Commerce 136 Glen St Ste 3 *TF:* 888-516-7247 ■ *Web:* www.adirondackchamber.org	Glens Falls	NY	12801	518-798-1761	792-4147	139
Adirondack Regional Federal Credit Union 280 Park St *Web:* adkcreditunion.com	Tupper Lake	NY	12986	518-359-2921		219
Adirondack Rock Press LLC 2795 Henneberry Rd *Web:* www.adirondackrock.com	Pompey	NY	13138	315-677-5272		637-2
Adirondack Trailways 499 Hurley Ave *TF:* 800-858-8555 ■ *Web:* trailways.com	Hurley	NY	12443	845-339-4230		108
Adistec 7620 NW 25 St Unit 7 *Web:* www.adistec.com	Miami	FL	33122	786-221-2300		196
Adizes 6404 Via Real *Web:* adizes.com	Carpinteria	CA	93013	805-565-2901		194
Adjacent Technologies Inc 10415 Morado Cir Bldg 1 Ste 350 *Web:* www.adjacent-tech.com	Austin	TX	78759	512-388-1338	388-0836	180
Adjeleian Allen Rubeli Ltd 75 Albert St Ste 1005 *Web:* aar.ca	Ottawa	ON	K1P5E7	613-232-5786	230-8916	261
Adjustable Clamp Co 404 N Armour St *Web:* adjustableclamp.com	Chicago	IL	60642	312-666-0640		758
Adjustable Forms Inc 1 E Progress Rd *Web:* www.adjustableconcrete.com	Lombard	IL	60148	630-953-8700		135
Adjust-A-Brush 10445 49th St N *Web:* www.adjust-a-brush.com	Clearwater	FL	33762	727-571-1234		361
Adjuvancy LLC, The PO Box 25766 **Fax Area Code:* 202 ■ *Web:* www.adjuvancy.com	Alexandria	VA	22313	703-548-1343	239-1124*	393
AdKarma 3806 Buttonwood Dr Ste 101 *Web:* www.adkarma.com	Columbia	MO	65201	573-446-7366		5
Adkins & Kimbrough Mechanical 4415 Turin Dr *Web:* www.jadkinsmechanical.com	Bessemer	AL	35020	205-432-4000		189-10
Adkins Arboretum 12610 Eveland Rd PO Box 100 *Web:* www.adkinsarboretum.org	Ridgely	MD	21660	410-634-2847	634-2878	97
Adko Engineering 2267 Lava Ridge Ct Ste 100 *Web:* adkoengineering.com	Roseville	CA	95661	916-788-0100		261
ADL (Anti-Defamation League) 605 Third Ave *TF:* 866-386-3235 ■ *Web:* www.adl.org	New York	NY	10158	212-885-7700	867-0779	48-8
ADL (Amalgamated Dairies Ltd) 79 Water St *Web:* adl.ca	Summerside	PE	C1N1A6	902-888-5088		578
Adler & Manson LC 9233 Ward Pkwy Ste 240 *Web:* adlerandmanson.com	Kansas City	MO	64114	816-333-0400		41
Adler Display 7140 Windsor Blvd **Fax Area Code:* 410 ■ *TF:* 855-552-3537 ■ *Web:* www.adlerdisplay.com	Baltimore	MD	21244	855-552-3537	281-2187*	7
Adler Group Inc 1400 NW 107 Ave *Web:* adlergroup.com	Miami	FL	33172	305-392-4100		186
Adler Planetarium & Astronomy Museum 1300 S Lake Shore Dr *Web:* www.adlerplanetarium.org	Chicago	IL	60605	312-922-7827		598
Adler School of Professional Psychology 17 N Dearborn St *Web:* www.adler.edu	Chicago	IL	60602	312-662-4000		166
Adler Tank Rentals LLC 260 Mack Pl *TF:* 877-471-3336 ■ *Web:* www.adlertankrentals.com	South Plainfield	NJ	07080	908-462-9800	561-6474	23
Adleta Co 1645 Diplomat Dr *TF:* 800-423-5382 ■ *Web:* www.adleta.com	Carrollton	TX	75006	972-620-5600	620-5666	361
Adlhoch & Associates Inc 19515 Mack Ave *Web:* adlhoch.com	Grosse Pointe Woods	MI	48236	313-882-5200		652
ADM (Asphalt Drum Mixers Inc) 1 ADM Pkwy *Web:* www.admasphaltplants.com	Huntertown	IN	46748	260-637-5729	637-3164	190
ADM Corp 100 Lincoln Blvd *TF:* 800-327-0718 ■ *Web:* www.admcorporation.com	Middlesex	NJ	08846	732-469-0900	469-0785	263
ADM Productions Inc 40 Seaview Blvd *Web:* www.admpro.com	Port Washington	NY	11050	516-484-6900		514
AdMail Express Inc 31640 Hayman St **Fax Area Code:* 510 ■ *TF:* 800-273-6245 ■ *Web:* www.admail.com	Hayward	CA	94544	800-273-6245	489-4522*	627
Ad-mail Inc 5000 N Basin Ave *Web:* www.admailinc.com	Portland	OR	97217	503-223-1101		5
Admar Supply Company Inc 1950 Brighton Henriett *TF:* 800-836-2367 ■ *Web:* www.admarsupply.com	Rochester	NY	14623	585-272-9390	272-9165	358

Name / Address	City	State	ZIP	Phone	Fax	Class
ADMARC 10 Desta Dr Ste 170LL *Web:* www.admarc.com	Midland	TX	79705	432-687-1127		636
Admark Graphic Systems Inc 9700 Metromont Indus Blvd *Web:* www.admarkgraphics.com	Charlotte	NC	28269	704-596-5180	598-1681	34
ADME (Association of Destination Management Executives) PO Box 2464 **Fax Area Code:* 937 ■ *Web:* www.admei.org	Wimberley	TX	78676	512-345-8833	586-3699*	48-23
Admerasia Inc 159 W 25th St 6th Fl *Web:* www.admerasia.com	New York	NY	10001	212-686-3333		7
Administration for Children & Families (ACF) 370 L'Enfant Promenade SW *Web:* www.acf.hhs.gov	Washington	DC	20447	202-401-9200	401-5450	340-10
Administration for Children & Families Regional Offices						
Atlanta 61 Forsyth St Ste 4M60 *Web:* www.acf.hhs.gov	Atlanta	GA	30303	404-562-2800	562-2981	340-10
Boston JFK Federal Bldg Rm 2000 *Web:* www.acf.hhs.gov	Boston	MA	02203	617-565-1020	565-2493	340-10
Dallas 1301 Young St Ste 914 *Web:* www.acf.hhs.gov	Dallas	TX	75202	214-767-9648	767-3743	340-10
Philadelphia Public Ledger Bldg Ste 864 *Web:* www.acf.hhs.gov	Philadelphia	PA	19106	215-861-4000	861-4070	340-10
San Francisco 90 Seventh St 9th Fl *Web:* www.acf.hhs.gov	San Francisco	CA	94103	415-437-8400	437-8444	340-10
Administration on Aging (AOA) 330 C St SW *Web:* acl.gov	Washington	DC	20201	202-401-4634		340-10
Administration on Aging Regional Offices *Region V* 233 N Michigan Ave Ste 790 *Web:* www.acl.gov	Chicago	IL	60601	312-938-9858	886-8533	340-10
Administrative Controls Management Inc 525 Avis Dr Ste 2 *Web:* www.acmpm.com	Ann Arbor	MI	48108	734-995-9640	995-9638	194
Administrative Office of the Courts 244 Washington St SW Ste 300 *Web:* www.georgiacourts.org	Atlanta	GA	30334	404-656-5171		339-11
Administrative Office of the United States Courts 1 Columbus Cir NE *Web:* www.uscourts.gov	Washington	DC	20544	202-502-2600		341
Administrative Resource Options Inc 200 W Adams St Ste 2000 *Web:* www.aroptions.com	Chicago	IL	60606	312-634-0300	648-6410	193
Administrative-Maximum US Penitentiary *Florence* 5880 Hwy 67 S *Web:* www.bop.gov	Florence	CO	81226	719-784-9464	784-5290	212
ADMINS Inc 219 Lewis Wharf *Web:* www.admins.com	Boston	MA	02110	617-494-5100		177
Admiral at the Lake 929 W Foster *Web:* admiral.kendal.org	Chicago	IL	60640	610-335-1223		672
Admiral Beverage Corp 721 Pulliam Ave PO Box 58 *Web:* www.admiralbeverage.com	Worland	WY	82401	307-278-6414	347-3571	81-2
Admiral Craft Equipment Corp 940 S Oyster Bay Rd **Fax Area Code:* 800 ■ *TF:* 800-223-7750 ■ *Web:* www.admiralcraft.com	Hicksville	NY	11801	516-433-3535	447-7751*	488
Admiral Farragut Academy 501 Park St N *Web:* farragut.org	Saint Petersburg	FL	33710	727-384-5500	347-5160	622
Admiral Fell Inn 888 S Broadway *TF:* 866-583-4162 ■ *Web:* www.harbormagic.com	Baltimore	MD	21231	410-522-7377	522-0707	379
Admiral Inc 10 Taylor Ave *TF:* 800-864-4429 ■ *Web:* www.admiralcleaners.com	Annapolis	MD	21401	410-267-8381		426
Admiral Linen Service Inc 2030 Kipling St *TF:* 800-321-1948 ■ *Web:* www.alsco.com	Houston	TX	77098	713-529-2608		442
Admiral on Baltimore 2 Baltimore Ave *TF:* 888-882-4188 ■ *Web:* www.admiralonbaltimore.com	Rehoboth Beach	DE	19971	302-227-1300		379
Admiral Packaging Inc 10 Admiral St *TF:* 800-556-6454 ■ *Web:* www.admiralpkg.com	Providence	RI	02908	401-274-7000	331-1910	548
Admiral Security Services Inc 5550 W Touhy Ave Ste 101 *Web:* admiralsecuritychicago.com	Skokie	IL	60077	847-588-0888		693
Admiral-Merchants Motor Freight Inc 215 S 11th St *TF:* 866-880-3567 ■ *Web:* www.ammf.com	Minneapolis	MN	55403	612-332-4819		780
AdMobilize LLC 1680 Michigan Ave Ste 910 *TF:* 888-628-7494 ■ *Web:* www.admobilize.com	Miami Beach	FL	33139	888-628-7494		387
ADMS (American Donkey & Mule Society) PO Box 1210 *Web:* www.lovelongears.com	Lewisville	TX	75067	972-219-0781	420-9980	48-3
Adnet Adv Agency Inc 111 John St Ste 701 *Web:* www.adnet-nyc.com	New York	NY	10038	212-587-3164		4
Adnet Technologies LLC 312 Farmington Ave *Web:* thinkadnet.com	Farmington	CT	06032	860-409-1700		180
Adobe Associates Inc 1220 N Dutton Ave *Web:* www.adobeinc.com	Santa Rosa	CA	95401	707-541-2300	541-2301	261
Adobe Systems Inc 345 Park Ave *NASDAQ:* ADBE ■ *TF:* 800-833-6687 ■ *Web:* www.adobe.com	San Jose	CA	95110	408-536-6000	537-6000	178-8
Adobe Theater Inc 9813 Fourth St NW *Web:* adobetheater.org	Albuquerque	NM	87114	505-898-9222		572
ADOI (Arizona) *Department of Insurance* 100 N 15th Ave Ste 102 *TF:* 800-325-2548 ■ *Web:* insurance.az.gov	Phoenix	AZ	85007	602-364-2499	364-2505	339-3
Adolf Meller Co 120 Corliss St **Fax Area Code:* 401 ■ *TF:* 800-821-0180 ■ *Web:* www.melleroptics.com	Providence	RI	02904	800-821-0180	331-0519*	544
Adolfson & Peterson Construction Inc 6701 W 23rd St *Web:* www.a-p.com	Minneapolis	MN	55426	952-544-1561	525-2333	186
Adolph Coors Foundation 215 St Paul St Ste 300 *Web:* www.coorsfoundation.org	Denver	CO	80206	303-388-1636		305
Adolphus, The 1321 Commerce St *Web:* www.adolphus.com	Dallas	TX	75202	214-742-8200	651-3588	379
Adoption ARC Inc 4247 Locust St Apt 16 *TF:* 888-558-6561 ■ *Web:* www.adoptionarc.com	Philadelphia	PA	19104	215-748-1441	842-9881	48-6
Adoption Associates LLC 368 Thornbrook Ave **Fax Area Code:* 610 ■ *TF:* 888-505-2367 ■ *Web:* ababystepadoption.com	Bryn Mawr	PA	19010	888-505-2367	376-6783*	41
Adoptive Families Magazine 108 W 39th St Ste 805 *TF:* 800-372-3300 ■ *Web:* www.adoptivefamilies.com	New York	NY	10018	646-366-0830	366-0842	457-10
Adorama Camera Inc 42 W 18th St *TF:* 800-223-2500 ■ *Web:* www.adorama.com	New York	NY	10011	212-741-0052	463-7223	119
Adorno-Denker Associates Inc 45-02 Broadway *Web:* www.adorno-denker.com	Long Island City	NY	11103	718-278-5030		390
ADP (Association of Directory Publishers) PO Box 209 *TF:* 800-267-9002 ■ *Web:* www.adp.org	Traverse City	MI	49685	231-486-2182		49-16
ADP (Automatic Data Processing Inc) 1 ADP Blvd *NASDAQ:* ADP ■ *TF:* 800-225-5237 ■ *Web:* www.adp.com	Roseland	NJ	07068	800-225-5237		225
ADP (Amcom Data Processing) 2 Annabel Ln *Web:* www.amcomtech.net	San Ramon	CA	94583	925-355-1580	355-1582	180
ADP Media Group LLC 7700 Camp Bowie W Blvd Ste B *TF:* 800-925-5700 ■ *Web:* www.adpmediagroup.com	Fort Worth	TX	76116	817-244-2740		627
ADP Screening & Selection Services Inc 301 Remington St *TF:* 888-606-7868 ■ *Web:* www.adpselect.com	Fort Collins	CO	80524	970-484-7722		260
ADP Surfaces Inc 841 Drive Buick Ave *Web:* www.adpsurfaces.com	Orlando	FL	32808	407-299-9394	299-8602	319-2
Adpay Inc 391 Inverness Pkwy Ste 100 *Web:* www.adpay.com	Englewood	CO	80112	720-863-3808		387
ADPEN Laboratories Inc 11757 Central Pkwy *Web:* www.adpen.com	Jacksonville	FL	32224	904-645-9169	641-8423	743
ADPI (American Dairy Products Institute) 116 N York St Ste 200 *Web:* www.adpi.org	Elmhurst	IL	60126	630-530-8700	530-8707	49-6
Adprint International Inc 6500 Greenbriar Dr *Web:* www.adprint.com	Houston	TX	77030	713-665-4578		7
AdPro-Ads LLC 2106 E 16th St *Web:* www.adpro-ads.com	Russellville	AR	72802	479-280-1990	567-5602	4
AdQuadrant Inc 3200 Bristol St Ste 550 **Fax Area Code:* 949 ■ *Web:* www.adquadrant.com	Costa Mesa	CA	92626	714-596-9000	333-2275*	4
ADR & Associates Ltd 88 W Church St *Web:* adrinnovation.com	Newark	OH	43055	740-345-1921		261
ADRA (Adventist Development & Relief Agency) 12501 Old Columbia Pk *TF:* 800-424-2372 ■ *Web:* adra.org	Silver Spring	MD	20904	800-424-2372		48-5
Adrenalin Inc 54 W 11th Ave *TF:* 888-757-5646 ■ *Web:* www.goadrenalin.com	Denver	CO	80204	303-454-8888		344
Adrian Bank 130 E Main St *Web:* adrianbank.com	Adrian	MO	64720	816-297-2194		70
Adrian College 110 S Madison St *TF:* 800-877-2246 ■ *Web:* www.adrian.edu	Adrian	MI	49221	517-265-5161	264-3331	166
Adrian Dominican Sisters 1257 E Siena Heights Dr *Web:* www.adriandominicans.org	Adrian	MI	49221	517-266-3400		48-20
Adrian Fabricators Inc 545 Industrial Dr *Web:* www.cylex.us.com	Adrian	MI	49221	517-266-5700		73
Adrian L. Merton Inc 9011 E Hampton Dr *Web:* almertoninc.com	Capitol Heights	MD	20743	301-336-2700		189-10
Adrian Miller Sales Training 43 Park Ave *Web:* adriansnetwork.com	Port Washington	NY	11050	516-767-9288		195
Adrian's Beauty College of Turlock 1340 W Main St *Web:* www.adrians.edu	Turlock	CA	95380	209-632-2233		167-3
Adriana's 771 Grand Ave *Web:* adrianasnewhaven.com	New Haven	CT	06511	203-865-6474		671
Adriance Memorial Library 93 Market St *TF:* 800-804-0092 ■ *Web:* poklib.org	Poughkeepsie	NY	12601	845-485-3445		435
Adrianna Papell 500 Seventh Ave 10th Fl *TF:* 800-325-9450 ■ *Web:* www.adriannapapell.com	New York	NY	10018	800-325-9450		155-21
Adrienne Arsht Center for the Performing Arts of Miami-Dade County Inc 1300 Biscayne Blvd *Web:* www.arshtcenter.org	Miami	FL	33132	786-468-2000	468-2001	572
Adrienne Electronics Corp 7225 Bermuda Rd Unit G *Web:* www.adrielec.com	Las Vegas	NV	89119	702-896-1858		647
Adroit Medical Systems Inc 1146 Carding Machine Rd *TF:* 800-267-6077 ■ *Web:* adroitmedical.com	Loudon	TN	37774	865-458-8600	458-0880	477
Adroit Software Inc 23 Faulkner Rd *Web:* www.adroitgroup.com	Shrewsbury	MA	01545	508-755-5252		180
ADS (Adelis Development Systems) 3863 Ridge Crest Dr **Fax Area Code:* 910 ■ *Web:* www.adelisdevelopment.com	Southport	NC	28461	908-510-6810	253-4222*	194
ADS Data Direct PO Box 607 *TF:* 888-963-7824 ■ *Web:* adsdatadirect.com	Durham	NH	03824	603-343-1315		194
ADS Engineers 45 Broadway Ste 1220 *Web:* www.adsce.com	New York	NY	10006	212-645-6060		261
ADS Environmental Services 4940 Research Dr *TF:* 800-633-7246 ■ *Web:* www.adsenv.com	Huntsville	AL	35805	256-430-3366	430-6633	201
ADS Group 2155 Niagra Ln N *TF:* 800-759-0992 ■ *Web:* theadsgroup.com	Plymouth	MN	55447	763-449-5500	449-5555	657

Phone | Fax | Class

ADS Machinery Corp 1201 Vine Ave NE, Warren OH 44483 — 330-399-3601 399-1190 494
Web: adsmachinery.com

ADS Media Group 1100 N Main St Ste 205, Boerne TX 78006 — 210-655-6613 5
Web: www.adsmediagroup.com

ADS Programming Services Inc
429 Green Springs Hwy Ste 161-234, Homewood AL 35209 — 205-222-1661 439-5642* 177
**Fax Area Code:* 866 ■ *Web:* www.adsprogramming.com

ADS Security LP
3001 Armory Dr Ste 100, Nashville TN 37204 — 615-269-4448 692
TF: 800-448-5852 ■ *Web:* adssecurity.com

ADS Tactical Inc
621 Lynnhaven Pkwy Ste 160, Virginia Beach VA 23452 — 757-481-7758 449
TF: 866-845-3012 ■ *Web:* adsinc.com

ADS/Transicoil 9 Iron Bridge Dr, Collegeville PA 19426 — 484-902-1100 902-1150 518
TF: 800-323-7115 ■ *Web:* www.avtechtyee.com

ADSA (American Dairy Science Assn)
1800 S Oak St Ste 100, Champaign IL 61820 — 217-356-5146 398-4119 48-2
TF: 888-670-2250 ■ *Web:* www.adsa.org

ADS-B Technologies LLC 819 Orca St, Anchorage AK 99501 — 907-258-2372 647
Web: www.ads-b.com

Ad-Sell Co 5001 SW Ave, Saint Louis MO 63110 — 314-773-0500 773-0555 627
Web: adsell.com

Adserts Inc 14750 W Capitol Dr, Brookfield WI 53005 — 800-346-6919 2
TF: 800-346-6919 ■ *Web:* www.adserts.com

ADSII (Advanced Digital Solutions International Inc)
4255 Business Center Dr, Fremont CA 94538 — 510-490-6667 490-6665 174
TF: 800-877-9642 ■ *Web:* www.adsii.com

Adsoft Direct Inc 740 Tunbridge Rd, Danville CA 94526 — 925-407-3101 463
Web: www.adsoftdirect.com

Adsport Inc 389 E Palm Ln, Phoenix AZ 85004 — 602-262-0500 7
Web: www.adsport.com

Adstrategies Inc 101 Bay St Ste 201, Easton MD 21601 — 888-456-2450 7
TF: 888-456-2450 ■ *Web:* adstrategies.com

ADT Security Services Inc
14200 E Exposition Ave, Aurora CO 80012 — 800-521-1734 692
TF: 800-246-9147 ■ *Web:* www.adt.com

Adtec Digital 408 Russell St, Nashville TN 37206 — 615-256-6619 351
Web: www.adtecdigital.com

Adtech IT Solutions 1571 E Whitmore Ave, Ceres CA 95307 — 209-541-1111 541-1401 174
TF: 877-455-7777 ■ *Web:* adtech-it.com

Ad-tech Medical Instrument Corp
400 W Oakview Pky, Oak Creek WI 53154 — 262-634-1555 634-5668 476
TF: 800-776-1555 ■ *Web:* www.adtechmedical.com

Adtegrity 408 Broadway NW, Grand Rapids MI 49504 — 616-285-5429 5
Web: www.adtegrity.com

ADTRAN Inc 901 Explorer Blvd, Huntsville AL 35806 — 256-963-8000 735
NASDAQ: ADTN ■ *TF:* 800-923-8726 ■ *Web:* www.adtran.com

ADTRAV Travel Management
4555 S Lake Pkwy, Birmingham AL 35244 — 205-444-4800 771
TF: 800-476-2952 ■ *Web:* www.adtrav.com

Adult Children of Alcoholics World Service Organization Inc (ACAWSO)
PO Box 3216, Torrance CA 90510 — 562-595-7831 48-21
Web: www.adultchildren.org

AdvaCare Home Services Inc
405 Freeport Rd, Pittsburgh PA 15215 — 412-249-9000 363
Web: www.advacare-home.com

Advacare Systems 2939 N Pulaski Rd, Chicago IL 60641 — 773-725-8858 725-1970 475
TF: 888-233-7677 ■ *Web:* www.advacaresystems.com

Advaita Press 927-B 6th St, Hermosa Beach CA 90254 — 310-376-9636 637-2
Web: www.advaita.org

Advance America Cash Advance Centers Inc
135 N Church St, Spartanburg SC 29306 — 864-342-5600 141
NYSE: AEA ■ *Web:* www.advanceamerica.net

Advance Auto Parts Inc
5008 Airport Rd, Roanoke VA 24012 — 877-238-2623 54
NYSE: AAP ■ *TF:* 877-238-2623 ■ *Web:* www.shop.advanceautoparts.com

Advance Automation Company Inc
3526 N Elston Ave, Chicago IL 60618 — 773-539-7633 539-7299 223
Web: www.advanceautomationco.com

Advance Bag & Packaging Technologies
5720 Williams Lake Rd, Waterford MI 48329 — 248-674-3126 674-2630 600
TF: 800-475-2247 ■ *Web:* www.advancepac.com

Advance Beauty College - Garden Grove
10121 Westminster Ave, Garden Grove CA 92843 — 714-530-2131 167-3
Web: www.advancebeautycollege.com

Advance Business Systems
10755 York Rd, Cockeysville MD 21030 — 410-252-4800 683-6691 112
Web: www.advancestuff.com

Advance Carbon Products Inc
2036 National Ave, Hayward CA 94545 — 510-293-5930 293-5939 127
TF: 800-283-1249 ■ *Web:* store.advancecarbon.com

Advance Care Home Health Agency Inc
1510 Hancock Bridge Pky Ste 3, Cape Coral FL 33909 — 239-443-5300 443-5950 363
Web: www.advancecarehha.com

Advance Case Loans LLC
205 W Wacker Dr Ste 901, Chicago IL 60606 — 312-332-4100 41
TF: 877-305-5600 ■ *Web:* www.advancecaseloans.com

Advance Communications & Consulting Inc
8803 Swigert Ct Unit A, Bakersfield CA 93311 — 661-664-0177 664-0277 196
TF: 800-510-2148 ■ *Web:* advancecomm.net

Advance Corp
Braille-Tac Div 8200 97th St S, Cottage Grove MN 55016 — 651-771-9297 771-2121 701
TF: 800-328-9451 ■ *Web:* www.advancecorp.com

Advance Design Inc
7100 E Vly Green Rd, Fort Washington PA 19034 — 215-774-1000 233-9932 5
TF: 800-523-5990 ■ *Web:* www.advancewebdesign.com

Advance Electrical Supply Co
263 N Oakley Blvd, Chicago IL 60612 — 312-421-2300 246
Web: www.advanceelectrical.com

Advance Energy Technologies Inc
1 Solar Dr, Clifton Park NY 12065 — 518-371-2140 371-0737 664
TF: 800-724-0198 ■ *Web:* www.advanceet.com

Advance Engineering Co 7505 Baron Dr, Canton MI 48187 — 313-537-3500 489
TF: 800-497-6388 ■ *Web:* www.adveng.net

Advance Fire Protection Company Inc
1451 W Lambert Rd, La Habra CA 90631 — 562-691-0918 189-13
Web: www.firesprinkleradvisoryboard.org

Advance Food Company Inc
9987 Carver Rd Ste 500, Cincinnati OH 45242 — 800-969-2747 299
TF: 800-969-2747 ■ *Web:* www.advancepierre.com

Advance Graphic Systems Inc
1806 Rochester Indl Dr, Rochester Hills MI 48309 — 248-656-8000 656-8181 9
Web: www.advancegraphic.net

Advance Group, The 185 Price Pkwy, Farmingdale NY 11735 — 877-273-6481 393
TF: 877-273-6481 ■ *Web:* www.theadvancegrp.com

Advance Industrial Machine LLP
W6335 Design Dr, Greenville WI 54942 — 920-757-6786 757
Web: www.aim-msm.com

Advance Insurance Company of Kansas
1133 SW Topeka Blvd, Topeka KS 66629 — 785-273-9804 391-2
TF: 800-530-5989 ■ *Web:* www.advanceinsurance.com

Advance Lifts Inc 701 Kirk Rd, Saint Charles IL 60174 — 630-584-9881 584-9405 470
TF: 800-843-3625 ■ *Web:* www.advancelifts.com

Advance Local Media LLC
1801 Superior Ave Ste 100, Cleveland OH 44114 — 216-999-3900 658
Web: www.advance-ohio.com

Ad-vance Magnetics Inc
625 Monroe St, Rochester IN 46975 — 574-223-3158 583-8719 295
Web: www.advancemag.com

Advance Manufacturing Company Inc
Turnpike Industrial Rd, Westfield MA 01086 — 413-568-2411 568-6011 454
Web: www.advancemfg.com

Advance Mcs Electronics Inc
67928 Us Hwy 33, Goshen IN 46526 — 877-349-5891 459
TF: 877-349-5891 ■ *Web:* www.advancemcs.com

Advance Mechanical Contractors
1301 E Burnett St, Signal Hill CA 90755 — 562-268-5559 189-10
Web: www.advancemechanicalcontractors.com

Advance Mechanical Systems Inc
425 E Algonquin Rd, Arlington Heights IL 60005 — 847-593-2510 189-10
Web: www.advmech.com

Advance Notice Inc PO Box 593, Peabody MA 01960 — 978-531-6722 7
TF: 800-992-0313 ■ *Web:* www.advancenotice.com

Advance Packaging Corp
4459 40th St SE PO Box 888311, Grand Rapids MI 49588 — 616-949-6610 100
Web: www.advancepkg.com

Advance Paper and Maintenance Supply Inc
240 E Coury Ave Ste 141, Mesa AZ 85210 — 480-964-6108 559
Web: www.advancepaper.com

Advance Paper Box Co
6100 S Gramercy Pl, Los Angeles CA 90047 — 323-750-2550 752-8133 101
Web: www.advancepaperbox.com

Advance Petroleum Distributing Company Inc
2451 Great SW Pkwy, Fort Worth TX 76106 — 817-626-5458 579
Web: www.advancefuel.com

Advance Print & Graphics Inc
4553 Concourse Dr, Ann Arbor MI 48108 — 734-663-6816 627
TF: 800-696-9627 ■ *Web:* advprint.net

Advance Printers Machine Shop Inc
4271 N Elston Ave, Chicago IL 60618 — 773-588-3169 588-2608 454
Web: www.advanceprintersmachine.com

Advance Printing & Graphics
1349 Delashmut Ave, Columbus OH 43212 — 614-299-9770 299-9786 627
Web: www.advancecolumbus.com

Advance Refrigeration Co
1177 Industrial Dr, Bensenville IL 60106 — 630-766-2000 766-2147 38
Web: www.advancerefrigeration.com

Advance Reproductions Corp
100 Flagship Dr, North Andover MA 01845 — 978-685-2911 685-1771 591
Web: advancerepro.com

Advance Research Chemicals Inc
1110 Keystone Ave, Catoosa OK 74015 — 918-266-6789 266-6796 143
Web: www.fluoridearc.com

Advance Scale of MD LLC
2400 Egg Harbor Rd, Lindenwold NJ 08021 — 856-627-0700 684
TF: 888-447-2253 ■ *Web:* advancescale.com

Advance Search Technical Staffing
540 Lake Cook Rd Ste 140, Deerfield IL 60015 — 847-706-9400 260
Web: www.advancesearch.com

Advance Tabco 200 Heartland Blvd, Edgewood NY 11717 — 631-242-6900 300
TF: 800-645-3166 ■ *Web:* advancetabco.com

Ad-VANCE Talent Solutions Inc
3911 Golf Park Loop Ste 103, Bradenton FL 34203 — 941-739-8883 260
Web: ad-vance.com

Advance Tank & Construction Co
3700 E County Rd 64 PO Box 219, Wellington CO 80549 — 970-568-3444 568-3435 189-14
TF: 800-422-3488 ■ *Web:* www.advancetank.com

Advance Transportation Systems Inc
10558 Taconic Ter, Cincinnati OH 45215 — 513-771-4848 771-4877 311
TF: 800-878-4849 ■ *Web:* atslogistics.com

Advanced Adhesive Technologies Inc
424 S Spencer St, Dalton GA 30721 — 706-226-0610 278-6207 3
TF: 800-228-4583 ■ *Web:* aatglue.com

Advanced Alarm Systems Inc
101 Lindsey St, Fall River MA 02720 — 508-675-1937 693
TF: 800-442-5276

Advanced Analytical Consulting Group Inc
211 Congress St, Boston MA 02110 — 617-338-2224 194
Web: aacg.com

Advanced Animations PO Box 34, Stockbridge VT 05772 — 802-746-8974 746-8971 33
Web: www.advancedanimations.com

Advanced Auto Trends 3485 Metamora Rd, Oxford MI 48371 — 248-628-4850 596
Web: www.advancedautotrends.com

Advanced Benefit Strategies Inc
30 Mill St, Unionville CT 06085 — 860-675-2261 390
Web: abs125.com

Advanced Bionics LLC
28515 Westinghouse Pl, Valencia CA 91355 — 661-362-1400 362-1503 253
TF: 877-829-0026 ■ *Web:* advancedbionics.com

Advanced BioNutrition Corp
7155 Columbia Gateway Dr, Columbia MD 21046 — 410-730-8600 730-9311 447
Web: www.advancedbionutrition.com

Advanced Biotechnologies Inc (ABI)
1545 Progress Way, Eldersburg MD 21784 — 410-792-9779 497-9773* 231
**Fax Area Code:* 301 ■ *TF:* 800-426-0764 ■ *Web:* abionline.com

	City	State	Zip	Phone	Fax	Class
Advanced Business Systems Inc						
5630 Silverado Way Ste A4	Anchorage	AK	99518	907-562-5505		175
Web: www.abs-ak.com						
Advanced C4 Solutions Inc						
4017 W Dr Martin Luther King Junior Blvd.	Tampa	FL	33614	813-282-3031		224
Web: www.ac4s.com						
Advanced Cable Ties Inc						
245 Suffolk Ln	Gardner	MA	01440	800-861-7228		814
TF: 800-861-7228 ■ *Web:* www.advancedcableties.com						
Advanced Call Center Technologies LLC						
1235 Westlakes Dr Ste 160	Berwyn	PA	19312	866-704-5580		393
TF: 866-704-5580 ■ *Web:* www.acttoday.com						
Advanced Career Institute - Visalia Campus						
1728 N Kelsey St	Visalia	CA	93291	877-649-9614		167-3
TF: 877-649-9614 ■ *Web:* www.advanced.edu						
Advanced Cell Diagnostics Inc						
3960 Point Eden Way	Hayward	CA	94545	510-576-8800		668
TF: 877-576-3636 ■ *Web:* acdbio.com						
Advanced Ceramics Mfg						
7800 A S Nogales Hwy	Tucson	AZ	85706	520-547-0850		22
Web: www.acmtucson.com						
Advanced Chemical Sensors Inc						
101 Glades Rd	Boca Raton	FL	33432	561-417-0303	338-5737	196
TF: 888-338-4230 ■ *Web:* acsbadge.com						
Advanced Chemistry Development Inc						
110 Yonge St 14th Fl	Toronto	ON	M5C1T4	416-368-3435		177
TF: 800-304-3988 ■ *Web:* www.acdlabs.com						
Advanced Circuits Inc						
21101 E 32nd Pkwy	Aurora	CO	80011	303-576-6610	224-3291*	625
**Fax Area Code:* 888 ■ *TF:* 800-979-4722 ■ *Web:* www.4pcb.com						
Advanced Clinical Services LLC						
10 Pkwy N Ste 350	Deerfield	IL	60015	847-267-1176		174
Web: www.advancedclinical.com						
Advanced Composites Inc						
2575 S 3270 W	West Valley City	UT	84119	801-467-1204		261
Web: advancedcomposites.com						
Advanced Computer Technologies LLC						
101 Market Pl	Montgomery	AL	36117	334-262-6002		177
Web: www.actinnovations.com						
Advanced Computing Solutions Group Inc						
19125 Northcreek Pkwy	Bothell	WA	98011	425-609-3165		177
TF: 800-550-8007 ■ *Web:* www.acsgrp.com						
Advanced Concrete Systems						
55 Advanced Ln	Middleburg	PA	17842	800-521-3788	837-1182*	183
**Fax Area Code:* 570 ■ *TF:* 800-521-3788 ■ *Web:* www.yourbasement.com						
Advanced Containment Systems Inc						
8720 Lambright Rd	Houston	TX	77075	713-987-0336	987-0355	806
Web: www.acsi-us.com						
Advanced Control Systems Inc						
2755 Northwoods Pky	Norcross	GA	30071	770-446-8854	448-0957	201
Web: acspower.com						
Advanced Conversion Technology Inc						
2001 Fulling Mill Rd	Middletown	PA	17057	717-939-2300		767
Web: www.actpower.com						
Advanced Counseling Services PC						
5958 Canton Center Rd Ste 900	Canton	MI	48187	734-737-1200	737-1205	374-5
Web: advancedcounseling.info						
Advanced Data Systems Corp						
15 Prospect St	Paramus	NJ	07652	201-368-2001		180
Web: www.adsc.com						
Advanced Decorative Systems Inc						
4705 Industrial Dr	Millington	MI	48746	989-871-4550		247
Web: advanceddecorative.com						
Advanced Design & Manufacturing Inc						
350 Heritage Ave	Portsmouth	NH	03801	603-430-7573	427-1624	253
Web: www.advanceddesign.com						
Advanced Design Corp						
9447B Lorton Market St	Lorton	VA	22079	703-550-5510		261
Web: www.advdesign.com						
Advanced Diagnostics Inc						
2440 Cinnabar Loop	Anchorage	AK	99507	907-344-3456		475
TF: 800-399-5368 ■ *Web:* www.adialaska.com						
Advanced Digital Data Inc						
6 Laurel Dr	Flanders	NJ	07836	973-584-4026	584-3205	177
TF: 800-922-0972 ■ *Web:* www.addsys.com						
Advanced Digital Research Inc						
1813 E Dyer Rd Ste 410	Santa Ana	CA	92705	949-252-1055		56
Web: www.adrco.com						
Advanced Digital Solutions International Inc (ADSII)						
4255 Business Center Dr	Fremont	CA	94538	510-490-6667	490-6665	174
TF: 800-877-9642 ■ *Web:* www.adsii.com						
Advanced Disposal Services Inc						
90 Fort Wade Rd	Ponte Vedra Beach	FL	32081	904-737-7900		360-3
Web: www.advanceddisposal.com						
Advanced Distribution Systems Inc						
105-107 Stonehurst Ct	Northvale	NJ	07647	201-767-7350		231
Web: www.ads-outsource.com						
Advanced Distributor Products LLC						
2175 West Park Place Blvd	Stone Mountain	GA	30087	770-465-5560		5
Web: www.adpnow.com						
Advanced Drainage Systems Inc						
4640 Trueman Blvd	Hilliard	OH	43026	800-821-6710		596
TF: 800-821-6710 ■ *Web:* www.ads-pipe.com						
Advanced Dynamics Corporation Ltd						
1700 Marie Victorin	Saint-Bruno	QC	J3V6B9	450-653-7220		256
Web: www.advanceddynamics.com						
Advanced Electronics Inc						
721 Winston St	West Chicago	IL	60185	630-293-3300		625
Web: www.advel.com						
Advanced E-Media Inc						
81 Columbia Ste 200	Aliso Viejo	CA	92656	949-600-8868		180
Web: webjaguar.com						
Advanced Energy Corp						
909 Capability Dr Ste 2100	Raleigh	NC	27606	919-857-9000		194
TF: 800-869-8001 ■ *Web:* www.advancedenergy.org						
Advanced Energy Industries Inc						
1625 Sharp Pt Dr	Fort Collins	CO	80525	800-446-9167	221-5583*	695
NASDAQ: AEIS ■ **Fax Area Code:* 970 ■ *TF:* 800-446-9167 ■ *Web:* www.advancedenergy.com						

	City	State	Zip	Phone	Fax	Class
Advanced Engineering & Environmental Services Inc (AE2S)						
4050 Garden View Dr Ste 200	Grand Forks	ND	58201	701-746-8087		261
Web: www.ae2s.com						
Advanced Engineering Associates International Inc						
185 Alewife Brook Pkwy Ste 400	Cambridge	MA	02138	617-868-0018		261
Web: aeaiinc.com						
Advanced Equipment Corp						
2401 W Commonwealth Ave	Fullerton	CA	92833	714-635-5350	525-6083	286
Web: www.advancedequipment.com						
Advanced Equities Financial Corp						
311 S Wacker Dr Ste 6100	Chicago	IL	60606	312-377-5278		691
Web: www.advancedequities.com						
Advanced Filtration Systems Inc						
3206 Farber Dr	Champaign	IL	61822	217-351-3073		454
Web: www.afsifilters.com						
Advanced Focus 44 E 32nd St 4th Fl	New York	NY	10016	212-217-2000		668
Web: www.advancedfocus.com						
Advanced Forming Technology Inc						
7040 Weld County Rd 20	Longmont	CO	80504	303-833-6000		483
Web: www.aftmim.com						
Advanced Fuller School of Massage Therapy						
195 S Rosemont Rd Ste 105	Virginia Beach	VA	23452	757-340-7132		685
Web: www.advancedfullerschool.com						
Advanced Generation Telecom Group Inc						
752 Walker Rd Ste H	Great Falls	VA	22066	703-757-6757		463
Web: www.adgentelecom.com						
Advanced Glazings Ltd 870 King's Rd	Sydney	NS	B1P6R7	902-794-2899		330
TF: 888-452-9464 ■ *Web:* www.advancedglazings.com						
Advanced Government Solutions Inc						
2138 Priest Bridge Ct Ste 4	Crofton	MD	21114	240-260-4040	260-4039	261
Web: agswebhosting.com						
Advanced Green Components LLC						
4005 Corporate Dr	Winchester	KY	40391	859-737-6000	737-4666	75
Web: www.advgreen.com						
Advanced HealthCare Services						
3900 Pintail Dr Ste A	Springfield	IL	62711	217-726-6956	726-7082	363
Web: www.advancedhealthcareservices.org						
Advanced Heat Treat Corp						
2825 MidPort Blvd	Waterloo	IA	50703	319-232-5221		484
Web: www.ahtcorp.com						
Advanced Home Care 580 Kirts Blvd Ste 309	Troy	MI	48084	866-605-0069	284-1101*	363
**Fax Area Code:* 248 ■ *TF:* 866-605-0069 ■ *Web:* www.advancedhomecare.net						
Advanced Home Medical Inc						
312 Paseo Tesoro	Walnut	CA	91789	909-444-2991	444-5503*	475
**Fax Area Code:* 919 ■ *TF:* 800-230-4761 ■ *Web:* www.advancedhomemed.com						
Advanced Hydraulics Inc						
13568 Vintage Pl	Chino	CA	91710	909-590-7644	590-7049	456
TF: 888-581-8079 ■ *Web:* www.advancedhydraulicsinc.com						
Advanced Image Direct						
1415 S Acacia Ave	Fullerton	CA	92831	714-502-3900	502-3901	459
TF: 800-540-3848 ■ *Web:* www.advancedimagedirect.com						
Advanced Imaging Research Inc						
4700 Lakeside Ave Ste 400	Cleveland	OH	44114	216-426-1461		475
Web: www.advimg.com						
Advanced Industrial Services Inc						
3250 Susquehanna Trial	York	PA	17406	717-764-9811		186
TF: 800-544-5080 ■ *Web:* www.ais-york.com						
Advanced Information Systems Group Inc						
11315 Corporate Blvd Ste 210	Orlando	FL	32817	407-581-2929	581-2935	180
TF: 800-593-8359 ■ *Web:* www.aisg.com						
Advanced Innovative Technologies LLC (AIT)						
530 Wilbanks Dr	Ball Ground	GA	30107	770-479-1900	479-4179	744
Web: www.aitequipment.com						
Advanced Insulation Concepts Inc						
8055 Production Dr	Florence	KY	41042	859-342-8550		14
Web: www.advancedinsulationconcepts.com						
Advanced Integration Group Inc						
1 Mccormick Rd Ste A	McKees Rocks	PA	15136	412-722-0065	722-0066	261
Web: aigcontrols.com						
Advanced Integration LLC						
4601 Hilton Corporate Dr	Columbus	OH	43232	614-863-2433		350
Web: www.advint.com						
Advanced Integration Technologies (AIT)						
481 N Dean Ave	Chandler	AZ	85226	480-568-8300		454
Web: www.uct.com						
Advanced Interactive Media Group LLC						
402 Spring Valley Rd	Altamonte Springs	FL	32714	407-788-2780		194
Web: www.aimgroup.com						
Advanced Laser Machining Inc						
600 Cashman Dr	Chippewa Falls	WI	54729	715-720-8093		492
Web: www.laser27.com						
Advanced Laser Materials LLC						
3115 Lucius Mccelvey	Temple	TX	76504	254-773-3080		605-2
Web: alm-llc.com						
Advanced Laser Solutions						
735 8th Ave N	Kirkland	WA	98033	425-822-4400	999-9999	179
Web: www.adlaso.com						
Advanced Lease Systems Inc						
7658 Avianca Dr	Redding	CA	96002	530-378-6868		311
Web: advancedlease.com						
Advanced Legal Software						
PO Box 347	Carolina Beach	NC	28428	910-458-2731		178-1
Web: www.advlegal.com						
Advanced Lifeline Services Pharmacy Inc						
618 Hatherleigh Ln	Louisville	KY	40222	502-494-8325	425-4934	237
Web: alspharmacy.com						
Advanced Logistics						
11190 NW 25th St Bldg 5 Ste	Miami	FL	33172	305-718-4160	718-6661	601
Web: advanced-logistics.net						
Advanced Logistics Support Corp						
609 Broadway Blvd NE Ste 221	Albuquerque	NM	87102	575-524-3542	524-3544	261
Web: alscorporation.net						
Advanced Looseleaf Technologies Inc						
1424 Somerset Ave	Dighton	MA	02715	508-669-6354	669-6143	86
TF: 800-339-6354 ■ *Web:* www.binder.com						
Advanced Machine & Engineering Co						
2500 Latham St	Rockford	IL	61103	815-962-6076	962-6483	493
TF: 800-225-4263 ■ *Web:* www.ame.com						

Phone | Fax | Class

Advanced Machine & Tool Corp
3706 Transportation Dr.... Fort Wayne IN 46818 260-489-3572 489-6720 454
Web: www.amt-corp.com

Advanced Machine Design Company Inc
45 Roberts Ave.... Buffalo NY 14206 716-826-2000 826-2394 455
Web: www.amd-co.com

Advanced Management Concepts
110 N Main St Ste 1000.... Dayton OH 45402 937-222-1024 47

Advanced Management Solutions Inc (AMS)
PO Box 9445.... Yucaipa CA 92399 909-790-4680 790-4682 178-1
TF: 800-397-6829 ■ *Web:* www.amsrealtime.com

Advanced Manufacturing Technologies Inc
1090 Falls Rd.... Grafton WI 53024 262-375-4414 454
Web: www.amt-wi.com

Advanced Massage Therapeutics
2932 Breckenridge Ln.... Louisville KY 40220 502-895-3500 167-3
Web: www.advancedmassagetherapeutics.com

Advanced Mechanical Technology Inc
176 Waltham St.... Watertown MA 02472 617-926-6700 926-5045 407
Web: www.amti.biz

Advanced Media Technologies Inc
3150 SW 15th St.... Deerfield Beach FL 33442 954-427-5711 427-9688 647
TF: 888-293-5856 ■ *Web:* www.goamt.com

Advanced Medical Equipment Inc
2655 S Dixie Dr.... Kettering OH 45409 937-534-1080 534-1081 475
TF: 800-543-1249 ■ *Web:* www.advancedmedequipment.com

Advanced Medical Solutions Inc
106 W Grand River Ave.... Howell MI 48843 517-548-1443 548-1588 475
TF: 800-248-2229 ■ *Web:* www.amsdme.com

Advanced Medical Technology Assn
701 Pennsylvania Ave NW Ste 800.... Washington DC 20004 202-783-8700 783-8750 49-4
Web: www.advamed.org

Advanced Metal Components Inc
720 Empire Expy.... Swainsboro GA 30401 478-237-8994 483
Web: www.advancedmetalcomponents.com

Advanced Metals Machining LLC
1159 Midvalley Dr.... Olyphant PA 18447 570-487-2830 487-2289 567
Web: www.advancedmetalsmachining.com

Advanced Micro Devices Inc
2485 Augustine Dr.... Santa Clara CA 95054 408-749-4000 344
Web: www.amd.com

Advanced Micro Robotics LLC
43676 Trade Center Pl Unit 135.... Sterling VA 20166 703-661-4141 661-4041 386
Web: www.advancedmicrorobotics.com

Advanced Microsensors Inc
333 S St Bldg 2.... Shrewsbury MA 01545 508-770-6600 696
Web: www.advancedmicrosensors.com

Advanced Microtechnology Inc
480 Vista Way.... Milpitas CA 95035 408-945-9191 945-3548 248
Web: www.advancedmicrotech.com

Advanced Modern Technologies Corp
19800 Nordhoff Pl.... Chatsworth CA 91311 818-883-2682 883-2620 612
TF: 800-874-7822 ■ *Web:* www.amtcorporation.com

Advanced Network Solutions LLC
43720 Trade Center Pl Ste 260.... Dulles VA 20166 703-444-9700 177
Web: ansnetworks.com

Advanced Networking Technology
5007 Wrightsville Ave.... Wilmington NC 28403 910-395-2597 799-5378 189-4
Web: alternatephonesystems.com

Advanced Office Systems Inc
296 E Main St.... Branford CT 06405 203-481-5349 225
Web: aosinc.com

Advanced Orthomolecular Research Inc
3900 - 12 St NE.... Calgary AB T2E8H9 403-250-9997 345
TF: 800-387-0177 ■ *Web:* aor.ca

Advanced Orthopro Inc
1820 N Illinois St.... Indianapolis IN 46202 317-924-4444 924-6319 477
Web: advancedorthopro.com

Advanced Ozone Engineering Inc
6038 Oakwood Ave.... Cincinnati OH 45224 513-681-3871 83
Web: www.advancedozone.com

Advanced Paper Forming 541 W Rincon St.... Corona CA 92878 951-738-1800 548
Web: www.advancedpaper.com

Advanced Personnel Systems Inc
4167 Avenida De La Plata Ste 126.... Oceanside CA 92056 760-941-2800 941-3287 225
Web: aps2k.com

Advanced Photographic Solutions
1525 Hardeman Ln.... Cleveland TN 37312 423-479-5481 588
TF: 800-241-9234 ■ *Web:* www.advancedphoto.com

Advanced Plastiform Inc
535 Mack Todd Rd.... Zebulon NC 27597 919-404-2080 596
Web: advancedplastiform.com

Advanced Poly Packaging Inc
1331 Emmitt Rd.... Akron OH 44306 330-785-4000 557
TF: 800-754-4403 ■ *Web:* ecom.advancedpoly.com

Advanced Polymer Technology Corp
109 Conica Ln.... Harmony PA 16037 724-452-1330 452-1703 601
Web: advpolytech.com

Advanced Polymers Inc
400 Paterson Plank Rd.... Carlstadt NJ 07072 201-933-0600 146
Web: www.advpolymer.com

Advanced Power & Controls LLC
605 E Alton Ave Ste A.... Santa Ana CA 92705 714-540-9010 540-5313 518
Web: www.advancedpowercontrols.com

Advanced Pressure Systems
701 S Persimmon St Ste J.... Tomball TX 77375 281-290-9950 290-9952 641
TF: 877-290-4277 ■ *Web:* advancedpressuresystems.com

Advanced Probing Systems Inc
2300 Central Ave.... Boulder CO 80301 303-939-9384 594
TF: 800-631-0005 ■ *Web:* www.advancedprobing.com

Advanced Process Technologies Inc
150 Swendra Blvd.... Cokato MN 55321 320-286-5060 286-3055 298
TF: 877-230-5060 ■ *Web:* apt-inc.com

Advanced Radiology PA
7253 Ambassador Rd.... Baltimore MD 21244 443-436-1100 415
Web: www.advancedradiology.com

Advanced Receiver Research
535 Burlington Rd.... Harwinton CT 06791 860-485-0310 485-0311 647
Web: www.advancedreceiver.com

Advanced Recovery Service
5434 King Ave Ste 200.... Pennsauken Township NJ 08109 856-488-8860 488-8863 194
Web: www.advancedrecoveryservice.com

Advanced Resource Technologies Inc
1555 King St Ste 400.... Alexandria VA 22314 703-682-4740 682-4820 180
Web: www.team-arti.com

Advanced Resources & Construction Enterprises Inc
27 Commercial Rd.... Kingfield ME 04947 207-265-2646 480
Web: www.arcenterprisesinc.com

Advanced Risk Managers LLC
298 Fourth Ave Ste 398.... San Francisco CA 94118 415-854-0800 177
Web: advanrm.com

Advanced Rotorcraft Technology Inc
635 Vaqueros Ave.... Sunnyvale CA 94085 408-523-5100 732-1206 256
Web: www.flightlab.com

Advanced Sciences & Technologies LLC
20 E Taunton.... Berlin NJ 08009 856-719-9001 261
Web: adv-sci-tech.com

Advanced Scientific Concepts Inc
135 E Ortega St.... Santa Barbara CA 93101 805-966-3331 466
Web: www.advancedscientificconcepts.com

Advanced Sealing Inc
15500 Blackburn Ave.... Norwalk CA 90650 562-802-7782 802-7742 326
Web: advseal.com

Advanced Server Management Group Inc
800 Superior Ave E Ste 1050.... Cleveland OH 44114 216-255-3040 274-9647 177
Web: asmgi.com

Advanced Sign Co 2024 Fifth St NW.... Albuquerque NM 87102 505-246-8458 243-3575 8
TF: 800-444-7407 ■ *Web:* www.advancedsignco.com

Advanced Software Products Group Inc
3185 Horseshoe Dr.... Naples FL 34104 239-649-1548 178-1
TF: 800-662-6090 ■ *Web:* www.aspg.com

Advanced Software Talent LLC
308 Lang Rd.... Burlingame CA 94010 650-596-2800 596-2900 631
Web: www.advancedtalent.com

Advanced Solar Products Inc
270 S Main St Ste 203.... Flemington NJ 08822 908-751-5818 612
Web: www.advancedsolarproducts.com

Advanced Solutions Inc
7815 Shaffer Pkwy.... Littleton CO 80127 303-979-2417 261
Web: go-asi.com

Advanced Solutions International Inc
901 N Pitt St Ste 200.... Alexandria VA 22314 703-739-3100 739-3218 177
TF: 800-727-8682 ■ *Web:* www.advsol.com

Advanced Sterilization Products (ASP)
33 Technology Dr.... Irvine CA 92618 888-783-7723 477
TF: 888-783-7723 ■ *Web:* www.asp.com

Advanced Support Products Inc
20820 FM 2854 Rd.... Montgomery TX 77316 936-597-4731 597-2483 492
TF: 800-941-5737 ■ *Web:* www.aspbase.com

Advanced Surface Microscopy Inc (ASM)
3250 N Post Rd Ste 120.... Indianapolis IN 46226 317-895-5630 895-5652 743
TF: 800-374-8557 ■ *Web:* www.asmicro.com

Advanced Systems and Controls Inc
15773 Leone Dr.... Macomb MI 48042 586-816-4450 816-4458 472
Web: www.advancedsyst.com

Advanced Systems Concepts Inc (ASCI)
1180 Headquarters Plz West Twr 4th Fl.... Morristown NJ 07960 973-539-2660 539-3390 178-1
TF: 800-229-2724 ■ *Web:* www.advsyscon.com

Advanced Systems Consultants Inc (ASC)
4074 E Patterson Rd.... Dayton OH 45430 937-429-1428 177

Advanced Systems For Power Engineering Inc
49 N San Mateo Dr.... San Mateo CA 94401 650-347-3997 261
Web: aspeninc.com

Advanced Systems Group LLC (ASG)
1226 Powell St.... Emeryville CA 94608 510-654-8300 654-8370 174
Web: www.asgllc.com

Advanced Systems Integrators LLC
717 Northampton St.... Holyoke MA 01040 413-230-5010 498-4525 201
TF: 800-456-3355 ■ *Web:* www.asiopen.com

Advanced Technologies Consultants Inc
5755 Oberlin Dr Ste 112.... San Diego CA 92121 858-658-0304 261
Web: atconsultants.net

Advanced Technology & Research Corp
6650 Eli Whitney Dr.... Columbia MD 21046 443-766-7888 261
Web: www.atrcorp.com

Advanced Technology Co
2858 E Walnut St.... Pasadena CA 91107 626-449-2696 22
TF: 800-447-2442 ■ *Web:* www.at-co.com

Advanced Technology for Large Structural Systems Ctr (ATLSS)
117 ATLSS Dr.... Bethlehem PA 18015 610-758-3525 758-5902 668
Web: www.atlss.lehigh.edu

Advanced Technology Investigations LLC
8 Dundas Cir Ste H.... Greensboro NC 27404 336-298-1556 492
TF: 888-274-5701 ■ *Web:* detectiveati.com

Advanced Technology Products Inc
12740 SR-4.... Milford Center OH 43045 937-349-4055 349-4155 370
Web: www.atp4pneumatics.com

Advanced Technology Ventures
500 Boylston St Ste 1380.... Boston MA 02116 617-850-9700 850-9750 792
Web: www.atvcapital.com

Advanced Telecom Services Inc
1150 First Ave Ste 105.... King of Prussia PA 19406 610-688-6000 736
Web: advancedtele.com

Advanced Testing Technologies Inc
110 Ricefield Ln.... Hauppauge NY 11788 631-231-8777 231-7174 256
Web: attinet.com

Advanced Textile Composites
700 E Parker St.... Scranton PA 18509 570-207-7000 207-7070 745-7
Web: www.advtextile.com

Advanced Therapy Institute Inc
3250 Wilshire Blvd Ste 1505.... Los Angeles CA 90010 213-384-2330 384-2320 637-2
Web: www.advtherapy.net

Advanced Thermal Sciences Corp
3355 E La Palma Ave.... Anaheim CA 92806 714-688-4200 688-4153 504
Web: www.atschiller.com

Advanced Training Assoc
1810 Gillespie Way Ste 104.... El Cajon CA 92020 619-596-2766 596-4526 167-3
TF: 800-720-2125 ■ *Web:* www.advancedtraining.edu

Company / Address	City	State	ZIP	Phone	Fax	Class
Advanced Trim & Kitchens (ATK) 4966 Lincoln Hwy E *Web:* www.advancedtrimandkitchens.com	Kinzers	PA	17535	717-442-8098	442-0307	499
Advanced Vacuum Company Inc 1215 Business Pkwy N *TF:* 800-272-2525 ■ *Web:* www.advaco.com	Westminster	MD	21157	410-876-8200		406
Advanced Vehicle Technologies Inc 1509 Manor View Rd *Web:* www.avt-hq.com	Davidsonville	MD	21035	410-798-4038		419
Advanced Vessel & Alloy Inc 5420 Perimeter Rd *Web:* advancedvessel.com	Valdosta	GA	31601	229-249-9370		480
Advanced Veterinary Care Inc 1021 East 3300 South *Web:* avcslc.net	Salt Lake City	UT	84106	801-942-3951		794
Advanced Veterinary Care LLC 1500 - 125th Ave NE *Web:* avetcare.com	Blaine	MN	55449	763-310-3500		794
Advanced Vision Science Inc 5743 Thornwood Dr *Web:* www.advancedvisionscience.com	Goleta	CA	93117	805-683-3851	964-3065	542
Advanced Visual Systems Inc (AVS) 2 Burlington Woods Dr Ste 100 *OTC:* AVSC ■ *Web:* www.avs.com	Burlington	MA	01803	781-890-4300	890-8287	178-5
Advanced Web Offset Inc 2260 Oak Ridge Way	Vista	CA	92081	760-727-1700		174
Advanced World Products 44106 Old Warm Springs Blvd *Web:* www.awp1.com	Fremont	CA	94538	510-226-9062	226-9144	179
Advancedware Corp 13844 Alton Pkwy Ste 136 *Web:* advancedware.com	Irvine	CA	92618	949-609-1240	609-0799	177
Advansoft International Inc 415 W Golf Rd Ste 55 *Web:* www.adso.com	Arlington Heights	IL	60005	847-952-0000		225
Advanta Ira 13191 Starkey Rd Ste 9 *TF:* 800-425-0653 ■ *Web:* advantaira.com	Largo	FL	33773	800-425-0653		2
Advanta Medical Solutions LLC 10830 Guilford Rd Ste 312 *Web:* www.advantamedicalsolutions.com	Annapolis Junction	MD	20701	240-554-1200		215
Advantage Capital Partners 190 Carondelet Plz Ste 1500 *Web:* www.advantagecap.com	Saint Louis	MO	63105	314-725-0800		792
Advantage Community Bank 101 W Business County Rd PO Box 200 *Web:* www.advantagecommunity.com	Dorchester	WI	54425	715-352-7161	352-7282	70
Advantage Container & Trailer 931 Metro Media Pl *Web:* www.advantagerents.com	Dallas	TX	75247	214-637-4506		778
Advantage Controls LLC 4700 Harold Abitz Dr *Web:* www.advantagecontrols.com	Muskogee	OK	74403	918-686-6211	686-6212	385
Advantage Credit Inc 32065 Castle Ct Ste 300 *TF:* 800-670-7993 ■ *Web:* www.advcredit.com	Evergreen	CO	80439	800-670-7993		218
Advantage Credit Union PO Box 822 *Web:* acuiowa.org	Newton	IA	50208	641-792-5660		219
Advantage Dental Plan Inc 442 SW Umatilla Ave Ste 200 **Fax Area Code:* 541 ■ *TF:* 866-268-9616 ■ *Web:* www.secure.advantagedental.com	Redmond	OR	97756	866-268-9616	504-3907*	391-3
Advantage Electronic Product Development 34 Garden Ctr *TF:* 866-841-5581 ■ *Web:* advantage-dev.com	Broomfield	CO	80020	303-410-0292		696
Advantage Electronics Inc 525 E Stop 18 Rd *Web:* www.advantageelectronics.com	Greenwood	IN	46143	317-888-1946		203
Advantage Engineering LLC 435 Independence Ave Ste C *Web:* www.advantageengineers.com	Mechanicsburg	PA	17055	717-458-0800	458-0801	256
Advantage Fayetteville LLC 3800 Raeford Rd *Web:* homescba.com	Fayetteville	NC	28304	910-483-5353	483-7586	652
Advantage Funding Corp 1000 Parkwood Cir SE *TF:* 800-241-2274 ■ *Web:* www.advantagefunding.com	Atlanta	GA	30339	770-955-2274		272
Advantage Futures LLC 231 S LaSalle St Ste 1400 *Web:* www.advantagefutures.com	Chicago	IL	60604	312-800-7000		169
Advantage Group Ga LLC 510 Alderson St *Web:* advantagegroupga.com	Schofield	WI	54476	715-241-5372	241-5375	390
Advantage Health Systems 9663 Tierra Grande St Ste 101 *Web:* www.advhealthsystems.com	San Diego	CA	92126	858-433-0469	433-0479	363
Advantage Home Care 1404 Eureka Rd *TF:* 877-783-4955 ■ *Web:* www.advantagehomecareinc.us	Wyandotte	MI	48192	734-282-2627	282-2639	363
Advantage Home Care LLC 550 Forest Ave Ste 206 *Web:* advantagehomecaremaine.com	Portland	ME	04101	207-699-2570		363
Advantage Home Health Care Inc 4008 N Wheeling Ave *TF:* 800-884-5088 ■ *Web:* advantagehhc.com	Muncie	IN	47304	765-284-1211		363
Advantage Home Health Care Services 1778 Washington St Ste 7B *Web:* www.ahhcs.com	Stoughton	MA	02072	781-436-5071	436-3192	363
Advantage Learning Solutions Inc 160-9521 Franklin Ave *Web:* advantagels.ca	Fort McMurray	AB	T9H3Z7	780-743-5001		449
Advantage Limousine Services Inc 8310 Castleford St Ste 200 *Web:* www.advantagelimos.com	Houston	TX	77040	713-983-9991		441
Advantage Machining Inc 601 W New York St *Web:* www.advantage-machining.com	Aurora	IL	60506	630-897-7344	897-7336	358
Advantage Manufacturing Inc 616 S Santa Fe St *TF:* 800-636-8866 ■ *Web:* www.advantageman.com	Santa Ana	CA	92705	800-636-8866		518
Advantage Marketing Inc 14 W Main St *TF:* 800-670-7479 ■ *Web:* www.advantagemkt.com	Ashland	OH	44805	419-281-4762		96
Advantage Metals Recycling LLC (AMR) 510 Walnut St Ste 300 *TF:* 866-527-4733 ■ *Web:* www.advantagerecycling.com	Kansas City	MO	64106	816-861-2700	922-1795	686
Advantage Mortgage Group Inc, The 5343 N 16th St Ste 135 *Web:* tamg.biz	Phoenix	AZ	85016	602-953-6500		509
Advantage Office Solutions 573 Charcot Ave *Web:* advantageofficeinc.com	San Jose	CA	95131	408-577-0708		321
Advantage One Tax Consulting Inc 20610 Quarterpath Trace Cir *TF:* 888-692-6829 ■ *Web:* www.aotax.com	Sterling	VA	20165	703-584-5533		734
Advantage Payroll Services Inc 126 Merrow Rd PO Box 1330 *Web:* www.advantagepayroll.com	Auburn	ME	04211	207-784-0178	786-0490	570
Advantage Performance Group Inc 700 Larkspur Landing Cir *TF:* 800-494-6646 ■ *Web:* www.advantageperformance.com	Larkspur	CA	94939	415-925-6832	925-9512	194
Advantage Plastics & Engineering Inc 4524 Bishop Ln *Web:* www.advantageplastics.net	Louisville	KY	40218	502-473-7331		256
Advantage Rent-A-Car 1030 W Manchester Blvd *TF:* 800-777-5500 ■ *Web:* www.advantage.com	Inglewood	CA	90301	800-777-5500		126
Advantage Resource Inc 1750 Alexandria Dr Ste 100 *Web:* advantageresource.com	Lexington	KY	40544	859-313-5472		225
Advantage Resourcing 220 Norwood Pk S *Web:* www.advantageresourcing.com	Norwood	MA	02062	781-251-8000		721
Advantage RN LLC 9021 Meridian Way *TF:* 866-301-4045 ■ *Web:* www.advantagern.com	West Chester	OH	45069	866-301-4045		260
Advantage Sci 222 N Sepulveda Blvd Ste 1780 *Web:* advantagesci.com	El Segundo	CA	90245	310-536-9876	943-2351	693
Advantage Software Inc 925 Central Pkwy *TF:* 800 800 1760 ■ *Web:* eclipsecat.com	Stuart	FL	34994	772-288-3266	288-1737	177
Advantage Title Agency Inc 201 Old Country Rd Ste 200 *Web:* www.advantagegroupny.com	Melville	NY	11747	631-424-6100		391-6
Advantage Truck Accessories Inc 5400 S State Rd **Fax Area Code:* 877 ■ *TF:* 800-773-3110 ■ *Web:* www.advantagetruckaccessories.com	Ann Arbor	MI	48108	800-773-3110	227-8899*	61
Advantagene Inc 440 Lexington St *Web:* www.advantagene.com	Auburndale	MA	02466	617-916-5445		668
AdvantageWare Inc PO Box 230308 *Web:* www.advantageware.com	New York	NY	10023	212-319-1903		809
Advantec Engineering LLC 219 Stagecoach Rd *Web:* www.advantec-eng.com	Avon	CT	06001	860-977-3099		261
Advantec Information Systems LLC 2007 Yanceyville St Ste 205 *Web:* www.advantecis.com	Greensboro	NC	27405	336-275-2832	272-6939	194
Advantec MFS Inc 6723 Sierra Ct Ste A *TF:* 800-334-7132 ■ *Web:* www.advantecmfs.com	Dublin	CA	94568	925-479-0625	479-0630	18
Advantech Corp 380 Fairview Way *TF:* 888-576-9668 ■ *Web:* www.advantech.com	Milpitas	CA	95035	408-519-3898	519-3899	175
AdvanTech Inc 2661 Riva Rd Ste 1050 *TF:* 888-266-2841 ■ *Web:* advantech-inc.com	Annapolis	MD	21401	410-266-8000	266-8842	177
Advantech Manufacturing Inc 2450 S Commerce Dr *TF:* 800-511-2096 ■ *Web:* www.advantechmfg.com	New Berlin	WI	53151	262-786-1600		463
Advantest America Inc 3061 Zanker Rd *Web:* www.advantest.com	San Jose	CA	95134	408-456-3600		696
AdVantis Hospitality Alliance LLC 615 N Highland Ste 2A *TF:* 866-218-4782 ■ *Web:* www.vistarez.com	Murfreesboro	TN	37130	615-904-6133		707
Advantix Solutions Group 1202 Richardson Dr Ste 200 *TF:* 866-238-2684 ■ *Web:* www.advantixsolutions.com	Richardson	TX	75080	866-238-2684		387
Advantor Systems Corp 12612 Challenger Pkwy Ste 300 *TF:* 800-238-2686 ■ *Web:* www.advantor.com	Orlando	FL	32826	800-238-2686	523-1921	692
Advatech Pacific Inc 10230 S 50th Pl Ste 150 *Web:* www.advatechpacific.com	Phoenix	AZ	85044	480-598-4005	598-6767	647
Advenir Real Estate 17501 Biscayne Blvd *Web:* advenir.net	Aventura	FL	33160	305-948-3535		652
Advent Capital Management LLC 888 Seventh Ave 31st Fl *TF:* 888-523-8368 ■ *Web:* www.adventcap.com	New York	NY	10019	212-482-1600	480-9655	401
Advent Communication Systems Inc 250 Meadowlands Blvd *Web:* www.adventcom.com	Washington	PA	15301	724-916-2500	916-2539	194
Advent Design Corp Canal St & Jefferson Ave *Web:* adventdesign.com	Bristol	PA	19007	215-781-0500	781-0508	386
Advent Electric Inc 301 E Fourth St *Web:* adventelect.com	Bridgeport	PA	19405	610-277-6610		358
Advent Global Solutions Inc 12777 Jones Rd Ste 445 *Web:* www.adventglobal.com	Houston	TX	77070	832-678-3889		180
Advent Home Health Services Inc 1S450 Summit Ave Ste 350 *Web:* advent-homehealth.com	Oakbrook Terrace	IL	60181	630-705-9030		363
Advent Home Medical 291 Collier Rd *TF:* 877-944-9800 ■ *Web:* adventhomemedical.com	Auburn Hills	MI	48326	877-944-9800		363
Advent Industries LLC 17901 Mt Savage Rd NW *Web:* www.firebricks.com	Frostburg	MD	21532	301-689-1788	689-1798	751
Advent International Corp 800 Boylston St *Web:* www.adventinternational.com	Boston	MA	02199	617-951-9400		792
Advent Security Corp 101 Roesch Ave *Web:* www.adventsecurity.com	Oreland	PA	19075	215-576-7111		693

Name / Address	City	State	Zip	Phone	Fax	Class
Advent Software Inc						
600 Townsend St 5th Fl Ste 500	San Francisco	CA	94103	415-543-7696	543-5070	178-1
NASDAQ: ADVS ■ *TF:* 800-727-0605 ■ *Web:* www.advent.com						
Advent Telecom						
2510 Southwell Rd Ste 102	Dallas	TX	75229	888-484-6766		681
TF: 888-484-6766 ■ *Web:* www.adventtelecom.com						
Adventace LLC 2166 Chardonnay Cir	Gibsonia	PA	15044	724-443-2383		196
Web: adventacesms.com						
AdventGX Inc						
216 W 26th St 1700 Research Pky Ste 165	Bryan	TX	77803	979-216-0548		771
Web: www.adventgx.com						
AdventHealth						
601 E Altamonte Dr	Altamonte Springs	FL	32701	407-303-2200		353
Web: www.adventhealth.com						
Adventist Development & Relief Agency (ADRA)						
12501 Old Columbia Pk	Silver Spring	MD	20904	800-424-2372		48-5
TF: 800-424-2372 ■ *Web:* adra.org						
Adventist Health 2100 Douglas Blvd	Roseville	CA	95661	888-366-3833		353
TF: 877-336-3566 ■ *Web:* www.adventisthealth.org						
Adventist HealthCare						
820 W Diamond Ave Ste 600	Gaithersburg	MD	20878	301-315-3030		353
Web: www.adventisthealthcare.com						
Adventium LLC 320 E 35th St Ste 5B	New York	NY	10016	212-481-9576		193
Web: www.adventium.net						
Adventure Alaska Tours Inc PO Box 64	Hope	AK	99605	907-782-3730	782-3725	760
TF: 800-365-7057 ■ *Web:* adventurealaskatours.com						
Adventure Aquarium 1 Riverside Dr	Camden	NJ	08103	844-474-3474	365-3311*	40
**Fax Area Code:* 856 ■ *TF:* 844-474-3474 ■ *Web:* www.adventureaquarium.com						
Adventure Connection PO Box 475	Coloma	CA	95613	530-626-7385		760
TF: 800-556-6060 ■ *Web:* raftcalifornia.com						
Adventure Cycling Assn						
150 E Pine St PO Box 8308	Missoula	MT	59807	406-721-1776	721-8754	48-22
TF: 800-755-2453 ■ *Web:* www.adventurecycling.org						
Adventure Guild L L C, The						
888 Highpoint Dr	Dunlap	TN	37327	423-266-5709		148
Web: theadventureguild.com						
Adventure House 914 Laredo Rd	Silver Spring	MD	20901	301-754-1589		637-2
Web: www.adventurehouse.com						
Adventure in Food Trading Company Inc						
381 Broadway Bldg 7	Menands	NY	12204	518-436-7603	436-9035	297-8
Web: www.adventureinfood.com						
Adventure Landing 3311 Capital Blvd	Raleigh	NC	27604	919-872-1688	872-3408	32
Web: www.adventurelanding.com						
Adventure Life South America						
712 W Spruce St Ste 1	Missoula	MT	59802	406-541-2677	541-2676	760
TF: 800-344-6118 ■ *Web:* www.adventure-life.com						
Adventure Medical Kits PO Box 43309	Oakland	CA	94624	800-324-3517	261-7419*	475
**Fax Area Code:* 510 ■ *TF:* 800-324-3517 ■ *Web:* www.adventuremedicalkits.com						
Ad-venture Promotions LLC						
2625 Regency Rd	Lexington	KY	40503	859-263-4299		129
TF: 800-218-5488 ■ *Web:* www.ad-venturepromotions.com						
Adventure Quest Laser Tag						
1200 S Clearview Pkwy Ste 1106	New Orleans	LA	70123	504-207-4444		226
Web: www.lasertagnola.com						
Adventure Science Ctr						
800 Ft Negley Blvd	Nashville	TN	37203	615-862-5160	862-5178	520
Web: www.adventuresci.org						
Adventuredome 2880 Las Vegas Blvd S	Las Vegas	NV	89109	702-691-5861	794-3906	32
TF: 800-634-3450 ■ *Web:* www.circuscircus.com						
Adventureland Inn 305 34th Ave NW	Altoona	IA	50009	515-265-7321	265-3506	379
TF: 800-910-5382 ■ *Web:* www.adventurelandresort.com						
Adventureland Park						
3200 Adventureland Dr	Altoona	IA	50009	515-266-2121	266-9831	32
TF: 800-532-1286 ■ *Web:* adventurelandpark.com						
AdventureLink Inc 2400 Lincoln Ave	Altadena	CA	91001	626-539-7506	296-6301	771
TF: 877-691-4488 ■ *Web:* www.adventurelink.com						
Adventures Out West						
1680 S 21st St	Colorado Springs	CO	80904	800-755-0935		760
TF: 800-755-0935 ■ *Web:* advoutwest.com						
Adventures Unlimited Press						
1 Adventure Pl	Kempton	IL	60946	815-253-6390		690
Web: www.adventuresunlimitedpress.com						
Advertical Media LLC						
14 Palm Harbor Village Way	Palm Coast	FL	32137	386-986-1600		5
Web: www.adverticalmedia.com						
Advertiser-Tribune 320 Nelson St	Tiffin	OH	44883	419-448-3200	447-3274	532-2
TF: 800-448-3235 ■ *Web:* www.advertiser-tribune.com						
Advertising Age 685 Third Ave	New York	NY	10017	212-210-0100		532-3
Web: adage.com						
Advertising Associates Intl (AAI)						
65 Sprague St	Boston	MA	02136	877-866-8500		4
TF: 877-866-8500 ■ *Web:* www.aai-agency.com						
Advertising Council Inc						
815 Second Ave 9th Fl	New York	NY	10016	212-922-1500	922-1676	49-18
TF: 888-200-4005 ■ *Web:* www.adcouncil.org						
Advertising Premium Sales Inc						
11675 Lilburn Park Rd	Saint Louis	MO	63146	314-872-7000		4
Web: apspromos.com						
Advertising Research Foundation (ARF)						
432 Park Ave S	New York	NY	10016	212-751-5656	689-1859	49-18
Web: thearf.org						
Advertising Specialties Institute						
4800 St Rd	Trevose	PA	19053	215-942-8600	953-3045	637-9
TF: 800-546-1350 ■ *Web:* www.asicentral.com						
Advex Corp 41 Research Dr	Hampton	VA	23666	757-865-0920		295
Web: www.advex.net						
Advice Media LLC PO Box 982064	Park City	UT	84098	800-260-9497		631
TF: 800-260-9497 ■ *Web:* advicemedia.com						
Advics Manufacturing Ohio Inc						
1650 Kingsview Dr	Lebanon	OH	45036	513-932-7878		247
Web: www.advics-ohio.com						
Advion BioSciences Inc 19 Brown Rd	Ithaca	NY	14850	607-266-0665	266-0749	668
Web: advion.com						
Adviso 4388 Rue Saint-Denis Ste 300	Montreal	QC	H2J2L1	514-598-1881		5
TF: 888-598-1881 ■ *Web:* www.adviso.ca						
Advisor Software Inc						
2175 N California Blvd Ste 400	Walnut Creek	CA	94596	925-299-7782	962-0658	178-1
TF: 844-257-9255 ■ *Web:* www.advisorsoftware.com						
Advisor Today 2901 Telestar Ct	Falls Church	VA	22042	703-770-8267		457-5
TF: 877-866-2432 ■ *Web:* www.advisortoday.com						
Advisornet Financial Inc						
701 Fourth Ave S Ste 1500	Minneapolis	MN	55415	612-347-8600		390
Web: www.advisornet.com						
AdvisorNet financial Partners						
7373 Kirkwood Ct Ste 300	Maple Grove	MN	55369	763-315-8000		401
TF: 800-278-5988 ■ *Web:* www.advisornetfinancialpartners.com						
Advisors Excel LLC 2950 SW McClure Rd	Topeka	KS	66614	866-363-9595		195
TF: 866-363-9595 ■ *Web:* www.advisorsexcel.com						
Advisors Resource						
7900 Excelsior Blvd Ste 80	Hopkins	MN	55343	763-287-0219		390
Web: advisorsres.com						
Advisory Board Co, The						
2445 M St NW	Washington	DC	20037	202-266-5600		194
NASDAQ: ABCO ■ *Web:* www.advisory.com						
Advisory Council Inc, The						
1 Stiles Rd Ste 105	Salem	NH	03079	781-791-9582		463
Web: tacadvisory.com						
Advisory Council on Historic Preservation						
401 F St NW Ste 308	Washington	DC	20001	202-606-8503	606-8647	340-20
Web: www.achp.gov						
Advisory Research Inc						
2 Prudential Plz 180 N Stetson Ave Ste 5500	Chicago	IL	60601	312-565-1414	565-2002	401
Web: www.advisoryresearch.com						
Advocacy Center for Persons With Disabilities						
2728 Centerview Dr Ste 102	Tallahassee	FL	32301	850-488-9071		48-6
TF: 800-342-0823 ■ *Web:* www.disabilityrightsflorida.org						
Advocacy Solutions LLC						
4 Richmond Sq Ste 300	Providence	RI	02906	401-831-3700		636
Web: advocacysolutionsllc.com						
Advocado Press Inc PO Box 406781	Louisville	KY	40201	888-713-3211		637-2
TF: 888-713-3211 ■ *Web:* www.advocadopress.org						
AdvoCare International LLC						
2800 Telecom Pkwy	Richardson	TX	75082	972-665-5900		366
TF: 800-542-4800 ■ *Web:* www.advocare.com						
Advocate 330 N 4th St	Clifton	IL	60927	815-694-2649		532-2
Web: cliftonadvocate.com						
Advocate Brokerage Corp						
820 Scarsdale Ave	Scarsdale	NY	10583	914-723-7100		390
Web: advocatebrokerage.com						
Advocate Health Care Inc						
836 W Wellington Ave	Chicago	IL	60657	773-975-1600		374-3
Web: www.advocatehealth.com						
Advocate Media Inc						
181 Brown's Point Rd	Pictou	NS	B0K1H0	902-485-1990		539
Web: advocatemediainc.com						
Advocate, The 22 N First St	Newark	OH	43055	740-345-4053	328-8581	532-2
TF: 877-424-0208 ■ *Web:* www.newarkadvocate.com						
Advocates for Highway & Auto Safety						
750 First St NE Ste 1130	Washington	DC	20002	202-408-1711	408-1699	48-10
Web: saferoads.org						
ADW Acosta 1180 NW Maple St Ste 330	Issaquah	WA	98027	425-507-3100		708
Web: www.adww.com						
Adwerks Inc 512 N Main Ave	Sioux Falls	SD	57104	605-357-3690		7
Web: www.adwerks.com						
Adwerx Inc 324 Blackwell St Ste 510	Durham	NC	27701	888-746-5678		5
TF: 888-746-5678 ■ *Web:* www.adwerx.com						
AdWriter Inc 520 Warren St	Sandusky	OH	44870	800-646-7323		178-1
TF: 800-646-7323 ■ *Web:* www.adwriter.com						
ADX Computer Services Inc						
655 N Central Ave Ste 1700	Glendale	CA	91203	818-244-1121	330-7312	175
Web: www.adxusa.com						
Adynxx Inc 100 Pine St Ste 500	San Francisco	CA	94111	415-512-7740		231
Web: www.adynxx.com						
ADZ Etc Inc N88w16749 Main St	Menomonee Falls	WI	53051	262-502-0507	502-0508	7
Web: www.adzetc.com						
Adzzup 2600 N Central Ave Ste 1700	Phoenix	AZ	85004	888-723-9987		5
TF: 888-723-9987 ■ *Web:* www.adzzup.com						
AE Global Media Inc						
2540 Beltway Blvd	Charlotte	NC	28266	704-323-5201	394-7883	35
TF: 800-467-3709 ■ *Web:* www.aeglobalmedia.com						
AE Petsche Company Inc						
1501 Nolan Ryan Expy	Arlington	TX	76011	844-237-7600		246
TF: 844-237-7600 ■ *Web:* www.aepetsche.com						
AE Stone Inc						
1435 Doughty Rd	Egg Harbor Township	NJ	08234	609-641-2781		46
Web: www.aestone.com						
AE Wholesale Inc 9 Huegel Ct	Madison	WI	53719	608-218-4124		459
Web: www.aewholesale.com						
AE Works Ltd 209 Sandusky St	Pittsburgh	PA	15212	412-287-7333		256
Web: ae-works.com						
AE2S (Advanced Engineering & Environmental Services Inc)						
4050 Garden View Dr Ste 200	Grand Forks	ND	58201	701-746-8087		261
Web: www.ae2s.com						
AEA (American Economic Assn)						
2014 Broadway Ste 305	Nashville	TN	37203	615-322-2595	343-7590	49-2
Web: www.aeaweb.org						
AEA Advocate Magazine 345 E Palm Ln	Phoenix	AZ	85004	602-264-1774	240-6887	457-8
TF: 800-352-5411 ■ *Web:* www.arizonaea.org						
AEA Investors Inc						
666 Fifth Ave 36th Fl	New York	NY	10103	212-644-5900	888-1459	405
Web: www.aeainvestors.com						
Aearo Technologies LLC						
5457 W 79th St	Indianapolis	IN	46268	877-327-4332		576
TF: 877-327-4332 ■ *Web:* www.earglobal.com						
AEB (American Egg Board)						
8755 W Higgins Rd Ste 300	Chicago	IL	60631	847-296-7043	296-7007	48-2
TF: 888-549-2140 ■ *Web:* www.aeb.org						
AEB (American Exchange Bank)						
510 W Main St PO Box 818	Henryetta	OK	74437	918-652-3321	652-7057	70
TF: 888-652-3321 ■ *Web:* www.americanexchange.bank						
AEB International Inc						
654 Madison Ave Ste 1809	New York	NY	10065	212-752-4647		492
Web: aebint.com						
AEC (Applied Energy Company Inc)						
1205 Venture Ct Ste 100	Carrollton	TX	75006	214-355-4200	355-4201	640
TF: 800 580-1171 ■ *Web:* www.appliedenergyco.com						

Name / Address	City	State	ZIP	Phone	Fax	Class
AEC (Allen Engineering Corp) 819 S Fifth St PO Box 819 *TF:* 800-643-0095 ■ *Web:* www.alleneng.com	Paragould	AR	72450	870-236-7751	236-3934	190
AEC Engineering 172 Lower Main St *Web:* www.aecmaine.com	Freeport	ME	04032	207-865-4190	865-4199	201
AEC Group Inc 3000 Montour Church Rd *Web:* www.aecgroup.com	Oakdale	PA	15071	412-838-0100	446-4770	189-4
AEC Repro 44 W 39th St *Web:* www.buildflow.com	New York	NY	10018	212-624-9474		344
AECOM Technology Corp 1999 Avenue of the Stars Ste 2600 *Web:* www.aecom.com	Los Angeles	CA	90067	213-593-8100	593-8178	261
Aecometric Corp 15 Sims Crescent Unit 7 *Web:* www.aecometric.com	Richmond Hill	ON	L4B1C9	905-883-9555		261
Aecon Group Inc 20 Carlson Ct Ste 800 *Web:* www.aecon.com	Toronto	ON	M9W7K6	416-293-7004		186
AED (Alpha Epsilon Delta) 2955 S University Dr Winton-Scott Ste 213 *Web:* aednational.com	Fort Worth	TX	76129	817-257-4550		48-16
AED (Associated Equipment Distributors) 650 E Algonquin Rd Ste 305 *Web:* www.aednet.org	Schaumburg	IL	60173	630-574-0650	574-0132	49-18
AED Inc 6525 Belcrest Rd Ste 426 **Fax Area Code:* 240 ■ *Web:* www.aedworld.com	Hyattsville	MD	20782	301-683-2112	465-0653*	463
AEDC Public Affairs 100 Kindel Dr Ste A-242 *Web:* www.arnold.af.mil	Arnold AFB	TN	37389	931-454-5655	454-6720	743
Aedes De Venustas 16A Orchard St *TF:* 888-233-3715 ■ *Web:* www.aedes.com	New York	NY	10002	212-206-8674		77
AEE (Association of Energy Engineers) 3168 Mercer University Dr *Web:* www.aeecenter.org	Atlanta	GA	30341	770-447-5083	446-3969	48-12
Aeec LLC 11710 Plaza America Dr Ste 125 *Web:* americanconsultants.com	Reston	VA	20190	703-766-4300		177
AEFK (Athletes & Entertainers for Kids) 14340 Bolsa Chica Rd Ste C *TF:* 800-933-5437 ■ *Web:* www.911golfclassic.com	Westminster	CA	92683	714-894-5450	894-8424	48-6
Aegean Publishing Co PO Box 6790 *Web:* www.aegeanpublishing.com	Santa Barbara	CA	93160	805-964-6669	683-4798	637-2
Aegion 17988 Edison Ave *TF:* 800-325-1159 ■ *Web:* www.aegion.com	Saint Louis	MO	63005	636-530-8000		261
Aegir Systems 2140 Eastman Ave Ste 106 *Web:* www.aegir.com	Ventura	CA	93003	805-765-4146	765-4148	256
Aegis Assisted Living 4585 W Lake Sammamish Pkwy NE *TF:* 888-252-3447 ■ *Web:* www.aegisliving.com	Redmond	WA	98052	866-688-5829		451
Aegis Credit Union 1200 N Second St *Web:* aegiscu.com	Clinton	IA	52732	563-242-0531		219
Aegis Film Group Inc 7510 Sunset Blvd Ste 275 *Web:* aegisfilmgroup.com	Los Angeles	CA	90046	323-848-7977		116
Aegis Insurance Group LLC 2575 Ulmerton Rd Ste 250 *Web:* aegisinsurance-group.com	Clearwater	FL	33762	727-216-4088	608-5930	390
Aegis Power Systems Inc 805 Greenlawn Rd *Web:* www.aegispower.com	Murphy	NC	28906	828-837-4029		729
Aegis Realty Inc 2100 Main St Ste 205 *Web:* aegisfunding.com	Huntington Beach	CA	92648	714-465-4611		652
Aegis Sales & Engineering Inc 5411 Industrial Rd *Web:* www.aegisparts.com	Fort Wayne	IN	46825	260-483-4160		757
Aegis Sciences Corp 515 Great Cir Rd *TF:* 800-533-7052 ■ *Web:* www.aegislabs.com	Nashville	TN	37228	800-533-7052		256
Aegis Security Insurance Co 4507 N Front St Ste 200 **Fax Area Code:* 717 ■ *TF:* 800-233-2160 ■ *Web:* www.aegisinsurance.com	Harrisburg	PA	17110	800-233-2160	657-0340*	391-4
AEGIS Systems Engineering & Technology Partners Corp 5520 Research Park Dr Ste 100 **Fax Area Code:* 703 ■ *Web:* www.asetpartners.com	Baltimore	MD	21228	571-297-1916	995-0462*	463
Aegis Technologies Group Inc, The 410 Jan Davis Dr *Web:* aegistg.com	Huntsville	AL	35806	256-922-0802		261
Aegis Technology Inc 12630 G Westminster Ave *Web:* www.aegistech.net	Santa Ana	CA	92706	714-265-1238		261
AEHI Inc 14586 Central Ave *Web:* www.aehiinc.com	Chino	CA	91710	909-606-6998	606-6885	350
Aehr Test Systems 400 Kato Terr *NASDAQ:* AEHR ■ *Web:* aehr.com	Fremont	CA	94539	510-623-9400	623-9450	695
AEI (Affiliated Engineers Inc) 5802 Research Pk Blvd *Web:* www.aeieng.com	Madison	WI	53719	608-238-2616		261
AEI (American Enterprise Institute for Public Policy Research) 1789 Massachusetts Ave NW *TF:* 800-862-5801 ■ *Web:* www.aei.org	Washington	DC	20036	202-862-5800	862-7177	634
AEI Engineering Inc 11450 Compaq Center Dr Ste 660 *Web:* www.aeiengineering.com	Houston	TX	77070	281-350-7027	350-7035	194
AEI Speakers Bureau 300 Western Ave Ste 2 *TF:* 800-447-7325 ■ *Web:* aeispeakers.com	Allston	MA	02134	617-782-3111		708
AEL Financial LLC 600 N Buffalo Grove Rd *Web:* www.aelfinancial.com	Buffalo Grove	IL	60089	847-465-2009		401
AELE (Americans for Effective Law Enforcement) 841 W Touhy Ave *TF:* 800-763-2802 ■ *Web:* www.aele.org	Park Ridge	IL	60068	847-685-0700	685-9700	48-8
AELI (Agape English Language Institute) 1600 Park Cir Unit 116 *Web:* aeliusa.com	Columbia	SC	29201	803-445-1998		423
AEM (Association of Equipment Manufacturers) 6737 W Washington St Ste 2400 *TF:* 866-236-0442 ■ *Web:* www.aem.org	Milwaukee	WI	53214	414-272-0943	272-1170	49-13
AEM Inc 6610 Cobra Way *Web:* www.aem-usa.com	San Diego	CA	92121	858-481-0210		253
Aeneas Communications LLC 300 N Cumberland St Ste 200 *TF:* 800-470-7288 ■ *Web:* www.aeneas.com	Jackson	TN	38301	731-554-9200		387
Aeon Global Health 300 Connell Dr Ste 5100 *Web:* www.aeonglobalhealth.com	Berkeley Heights	NJ	07922	908-787-1700		787
Aeon Group PO Box 396 *Web:* www.aeongroup.com	Accord	NY	12404	845-658-3068		637-10
Aeon Nexus Corp 174 Glen St *TF:* 866-252-1251 ■ *Web:* aeonnexus.com	Glens Falls	NY	12801	518-338-1551		177
AEP Industries Inc 125 Phillips Ave *NASDAQ:* AEPI ■ *TF:* 800-999-2374 ■ *Web:* www.aepinc.com	South Hackensack	NJ	07606	201-641-6600		600
AEPHI (Alpha Epsilon Phi Sorority) 11 Lake Ave Ext Ste 1A *TF:* 888-668-4293 ■ *Web:* www.aephi.org	Danbury	CT	06811	203-748-0029	748-0039	48-16
Aequor Technologies Inc 377 Hoes Ln *TF:* 877-366-2580 ■ *Web:* www.aequor.com	Piscataway	NJ	08854	732-494-4999		177
Aer Lingus 300 Jericho Quad Ste 130 *Web:* www.aerlingus.com	Jericho	NY	11753	516-622-4226		26
Aer Manufacturing Inc PO Box 979 *TF:* 800-753-5237 ■ *Web:* www.aermanufacturing.com	Carrollton	TX	75011	972-417-2582		60
Aer Travel Inc 7701 Herschel Ave *TF:* 855-877-7127 ■ *Web:* www.aertravel.com	La Jolla	CA	92037	858-455-5773		771
AERA (American Educational Research Assn) 1430 K St NW Ste 1200 *TF:* 800-893-7950 ■ *Web:* www.aera.net	Washington	DC	20005	202-238-3200	238-3250	49-5
AERA (Automotive Engine Rebuilders Assn) 500 Coventry Ln Ste 180 *TF:* 888-326-2372 ■ *Web:* www.aera.org	Crystal Lake	IL	60014	847-541-6550	541-5808	49-21
Aera Energy LLC 10000 Ming Ave *Web:* www.aeraenergy.com	Bakersfield	CA	93311	661-665-5000		540
Aera Technology Inc 707 California St *Web:* www.aeratechnology.com	Mountain View	CA	94041	408 524 2222		390
Aeration Industries International Inc 4100 Peavey Rd *Web:* www.aireo2.com	Chaska	MN	55318	952-448-6789		427
Aerco International Inc 159 Paris Ave *TF:* 800-526-0288 ■ *Web:* www.aerco.com	Northvale	NJ	07647	201-768-2400	784-8073	357
Aereon Corp 16310 Bratton Ln Bldg 3 Ste 350 *TF:* 800-475-9473 ■ *Web:* www.aereon.com	Austin	TX	78728	512-836-9473	836-3025	22
Aerex Industries Inc 3504 Industrial 27th St *Web:* www.aerexglobal.com	Fort Pierce	FL	34946	772-461-0004		492
Aerial BioPharma LLC 9001 Aerial Center Pkwy Aerial Ctr Executive Pk Ste 110 *Web:* aerialbio.com	Morrisville	NC	27560	919-460-9500		231
Aerial Innovations Inc 3703 W Azeele St *TF:* 800-223-1701 ■ *Web:* www.flythis.com	Tampa	FL	33609	813-254-7339		196
Aerial Photography Services Inc (APS) 2511 S Tryon St *Web:* www.aps-1.com	Charlotte	NC	28203	704-333-5143	333-4911	328
Aerial Rigging & Leasing Inc 2940 Drane Field Rd *Web:* www.aerialrigging.com	Lakeland	FL	33811	863-607-9100		358
Aeris 2350 Mission College Blvd Ste 600 *Web:* www.aeris.com	Santa Clara	CA	95054	408-557-1993		387
Aero Air LLC 2050 NE 25th Ave *TF:* 800-448-2376 ■ *Web:* www.aeroair.com	Hillsboro	OR	97124	503-640-3711	681-6514	13
Aero ALL-GAS Company Inc, The 3150 Main St *Web:* www.allgas.com	Hartford	CT	06120	860-278-2376		316
Aero Automatic Sprinkler Co 21605 N Central Ave *Web:* www.aerofire.com	Phoenix	AZ	85024	623-580-7800		610
Aero Aviation Flight School L L C 4225-A Donald Douglas Dr *Web:* www.flyaeroaviation.com	Long Beach	CA	90808	562-425-6774		685
Aero Business Group 151 S Whittier *Web:* theaerogroup.com	Wichita	KS	67207	316-689-4272		454
Aero Chip Inc 13563 Freeway Dr *Web:* www.aerochip.com	Santa Fe Springs	CA	90670	562-404-6300	404-6322	454
Aero CNC Inc 960 S Burleson Blvd *Web:* www.aerocnc.com	Burleson	TX	76028	817-295-0184		22
Aero Components Inc 5124 Kaltenbrun Rd *Web:* foreaero.com	Fort Worth	TX	76119	817-572-3003		350
Aero Controls Inc 1610 20th St NW *Web:* aerocontrols.com	Auburn	WA	98001	253-269-3000		22
Aero Energy 230 Lincoln Way E *TF:* 855-779-6899 ■ *Web:* www.aeroenergy.com	New Oxford	PA	17350	717-624-4311	624-5850	610
Aero Engineering & Manufacturing Co 28217 Ave Crocker *Web:* aeroeng.com	Valencia	CA	91355	661-295-0875	295-5886	22
Aero Fulfillment Services Corp 3900 Aero Dr *Web:* www.aerofulfillment.com	Mason	OH	45040	513-459-3900		88
Aero Gear Inc 1050 Day Hill Rd *Web:* www.aerogear.com	Windsor	CT	06095	860-688-0888	285-8514	22
Aero Graphics Inc 40 W Oakland Ave *Web:* www.aero-graphics.com	Salt Lake City	UT	84115	801-487-3273		592
Aero Grinding Inc 28300 Groesbeck Hwy *Web:* aerogrinding.com	Roseville	MI	48066	586-774-6450		358
Aero Hardware & Parts Company Inc 130 Business Pk Dr *Web:* www.aerohardwareparts.com	Armonk	NY	10504	914-273-8550	273-8612	770

	Phone	Fax	Class
Aero Industries Richmond International Airport 5745 Huntsman Rd ... Richmond VA 23250 *TF:* 800-845-1308 ■ *Web:* www.aeroind.com	804-226-7200	236-1670	63
Aero Industries Inc 4243 W Bradbury Ave ... Indianapolis IN 46241 *TF:* 800-535-9545 ■ *Web:* www.aeroindustries.com	317-244-2433	244-1311	733
Aero Instruments & Avionics Inc 7290 Nash Rd ... North Tonawanda NY 14120 *Web:* www.aeroinst.com	716-694-7060		22
Aero Kool Corp 1495 SE Tenth Ave ... Hialeah FL 33010 *TF:* 888-560-6153 ■ *Web:* www.aerokool.com	305-887-6912		790
Aero Manufacturing Company Inc 310 Allwood Rd ... Clifton NJ 07012 *TF:* 800-631-8378 ■ *Web:* www.aeromfg.com	973-473-5300	473-3794	427
Aero Manufacturing Corp 100 Sam Fonzo Dr ... Beverly MA 01915 *Web:* aeromanufacturing.com	978-720-1000		21
Aero Metals Inc 1201 E Lincoln Way ... La Porte IN 46350 *Web:* www.aerometals.com	219-326-1976	326-1972	306
Aero Mobility Inc 1001 N Weir Canyon Rd ... Anaheim CA 92807 *TF:* 877-325-4000 ■ *Web:* www.aeromobility.com	877-325-4000		60
Aero Pacific Corp 588 Porter Way ... Placentia CA 92870 *Web:* www.aeropacificcorp.com	714-961-9200	961-9206	22
Aero Parts Manufacturing & Repair Inc 431 Rio Rancho Blvd NE ... Rio Rancho NM 87124 *Web:* www.aeroparts.aero	505-891-6600	891-6650	22
Aero Plastics Inc 91 Citation Dr ... Concord ON L4K2Y8 *Web:* www.aeroplastics.ca	905-738-9010	738-9175	601
Aero Precision Products Inc 14000 Nw 19th Ave ... Opa Locka FL 33054 *Web:* www.appiusa.com	305-688-2565	953-3504	454
Aero Products Component Services Inc 551 N 40th St ... Show Low AZ 85901 *Web:* www.aeroproducts.com	928-537-1000		770
Aero Rubber Company Inc 8100 W 185th St ... Tinley Park IL 60487 *TF:* 800-662-1009 ■ *Web:* www.aerorubber.com	800-662-1009	662-4400	370
Aero Seating Technologies LLC 5795 Martin Rd ... Irwindale CA 91706 *Web:* aeroseating.com	626-969-1130	969-1140	22
Aero Tec Labs Inc 45 Spear Rd Industrial Pk ... Ramsey NJ 07446 *TF:* 800-526-5330 ■ *Web:* www.atlinc.com	201-825-1400	825-1962	676
Aero Tech Designs Cycling Apparel 1132 Fourth Ave ... Coraopolis PA 15108 *TF:* 800-783-8326 ■ *Web:* www.aerotechdesigns.com	412-262-3255		711
Aero Tech Manufacturing Inc 395 W 1100 N ... North Salt Lake UT 84054 *Web:* www.aerotechmfg.com	801-292-0493		697
Aero Thermic Shields 8560 Roland St Unit E ... Buena Park CA 90621 *TF:* 800-698-2402 ■ *Web:* www.vandalshields.com	714-523-0572	523-3328	439
Aero Trades Manufacturing Corp 65 Jericho Tpke ... Mineola NY 11501 *Web:* www.aerotrades.com	516-746-3360	746-3417	697
Aero Twin Inc 2403 Merrill Field Dr ... Anchorage AK 99501 *Web:* www.aerotwin.com	907-274-6166	274-4285	24
Aerobics & Fitness Association of America (AFAA) 1750 E Northrop Blvd Ste 200 ... Chandler AZ 85286 *TF:* 800-446-2322 ■ *Web:* www.afaa.com	800-446-2322		48-22
Aerobiology Laboratory Associates Inc 43760 Trade Center Pl Ste 100 ... Dulles VA 20166 *TF:* 877-648-9150 ■ *Web:* www.aerobiology.net	703-648-9150		416
AeroCare Holdings Inc 3325 Bartlett Blvd ... Orlando FL 32811 *TF:* 866-456-0040 ■ *Web:* www.aerocareusa.com	407-206-0040		360-3
AeroCentury Corp 1440 Chapin Ave Ste 310 ... Burlingame CA 94010 *NYSE: ACY* ■ *Web:* www.aerocentury.com	650-340-1888		23
Aerocon Engineering Co 7716 Kester Ave ... Van Nuys CA 91405 *Web:* www.aeroconengineering.com	818-785-2743		256
AeroControlex Group 313 Gillett St ... Painesville OH 44077 *Web:* www.aerocontrolex.com	440-352-6182	354-2912	201
Aerocraft Heat Treating Company Inc 15701 Minnesota Ave ... Paramount CA 90723 *Web:* www.aerocraft-ht.com	562-674-2400	633-0364	484
Aero-craft Hydraulics Inc 392 N Smith Ave ... Corona CA 92880 *Web:* www.aero-craft.com	951-736-4690		790
Aerodirect Inc 860 Chaddick Dr Bldg A ... Wheeling IL 60090 *Web:* www.aerodirect.com	224-588-4100		770
Aerodynamic Engineering Inc 15495 Graham St ... Huntington Beach CA 92649 *Web:* www.aerodynamic.net	714-891-2651	892-5146	454
Aerodynamics Inc 114 Townpark Dr Ste 500 ... Kennesaw GA 30144	404-410-7612		63
Aerodyne Research Inc 45 Manning Rd ... Billerica MA 01821 *Web:* www.aerodyne.com	978-663-9500	663-4918	668
Aerofil Technology Inc 225 Industrial Park Dr ... Sullivan MO 63080 *Web:* www.aerofil.com	573-468-5551	468-5557	393
Aerofin Corp 4621 Murray Pl PO Box 10819 ... Lynchburg VA 24506 *TF:* 800-237-6346 ■ *Web:* www.aerofin.com	434-845-7081	528-6242	91
Aeroflex Holding Corp 35 S Service Rd ... Plainview NY 11803 *TF:* 800-843-1553 ■ *Web:* www.aeroflex.com	516-694-6700		360-3
Aeroflex RAD Inc 5030 Centennial Blvd ... Colorado Springs CO 80919 *Web:* www.radiationassureddevices.com	719-531-0800	531-0805	180
Aeroflex USA Inc 282 Industrial Park Dr ... Sweetwater TN 37874 *Web:* www.aeroflexusa.com	423-337-2493		370
Aero-Flite Inc 8520 W Electric Ave ... Spokane WA 99224 *Web:* www.aerofliteinc.com	509-747-6001	838-9154	167-3
Aeroflot Russian International Airlines 10 Rockefeller Plaza Ste 1015 ... New York NY 10001 *TF:* 866-879-7647 ■ *Web:* www.aeroflot.com	866-879-7647		25
Aeroflow Inc 3165 Sweeten Creek Rd ... Asheville NC 28803 *TF:* 888-345-1780 ■ *Web:* aeroflowinc.com	888-345-1780		475
AeroGo Inc 1170 Andover Park W ... Seattle WA 98188 *TF:* 866-537-0153 ■ *Web:* www.aerogo.com	206-575-3344	575-3505	22
Aerojet PO Box 13222 ... Sacramento CA 95813 *TF:* 800-637-7200 ■ *Web:* www.rocket.com	916-355-4000	351-8667	504
Aerojet Rocketdyne Holdings Inc 222 N Sepulveda Blvd ... El Segundo CA 90245 *NYSE: AJRD* ■ *TF:* 877-889-2023 ■ *Web:* www.aerojetrocketdyne.com	310-252-8100		185
Aero-K Inc 10764 Lower Azusa Rd ... El Monte CA 91731 *Web:* www.aero-k.com	626-350-5125	350-1545	454
Aero-mach Laboratories Inc 7707 E Funston St ... Wichita KS 67207 *Web:* www.aeromach.com	316-682-7707		22
Aeroman Inc 139 SW 51st Terr ... Cape Coral FL 33914 *Web:* www.aeromanaircraftparts.com	239-540-0040	540-0041	57
Aeromedevac Inc 1860 Joe Crosson Drive Hanger 1 ... El Cajon CA 92020 *Web:* www.aeromedevac.com	619-284-7910	284-7918	463
AeroMedical Training Institute 125 James Way ... Southampton PA 18966 *TF:* 866-482-0933 ■ *Web:* www.etcaeromedicaltraining.com	866-482-0933		167-3
Aeromedixcom LLC PO Box 14730 ... Jackson WY 83002 *TF:* 888-362-7123 ■ *Web:* www.aeromedix.com	307-732-2642		459
Aeromet Industries Inc 739 S Arbogast St ... Griffith IN 46319 *TF:* 800-899-7442 ■ *Web:* www.aerometindustries.com	219-924-7442		757
Aeromix Systems Inc 7135 Madison Ave W ... Golden Valley MN 55427 *Web:* www.estormwater.com	763-746-8400	746-8408	640
Aeromotive Inc 7805 Barton St ... Lenexa KS 66214 *Web:* www.aeromotiveinc.com	913-647-7300		54
Aeronautical Accessories Inc 423 Century Ct ... Piney Flats TN 37686 *Web:* www.aero-access.com	423-538-5151		20
Aeronautical Systems Inc 43671 Trade Center Pl Ste 100 ... Sterling VA 20166 *Web:* www.aeronautical.com	703-996-8090	996-8095	770
Aeronavdata Inc 1839 Ghent Rd Ste 230 ... Columbia IL 62236 *Web:* aeronavdata.com	618-281-8986		177
Aeronet Worldwide 42 Corporate Pk ... Irvine CA 92606 *TF:* 800-552-3869 ■ *Web:* www.aeronet.com	949-474-3000		12
Aero-News Network 6001 Argyle Forest Blvd Ste 21-252 ... Jacksonville FL 32244 *Web:* www.aero-news.net	863-299-8680		530
Aeronix Inc 1775 W Hibiscus Blvd Ste 200 ... Melbourne FL 32901 *Web:* www.aeronix.com	321-984-1671	984-0366	668
Aeropost International Services Inc 6703 NW Seventh St ... Miami FL 33126 *Web:* www.aeropost.com	305-592-5534		311
Aeroprobe 200 Technology Dr ... Christiansburg VA 24073 *Web:* www.aeroprobe.com	540-443-9215	443-6525	529
Aerosmith Aviation 321 Corporate Rd ... Longview TX 75603 *Web:* www.aerosmithaviation.com	903-643-0898		63
Aerosoles Inc 201 Meadow Rd ... Edison NJ 08817 *TF:* 800-798-9478 ■ *Web:* www.aerosoles.com	732-985-6900		301
AeroSolutions Group Inc 10681 Frank Marshall Ln ... Manassas VA 20110 *Web:* www.aerosolutions.com	703-257-7008		770
Aerospace & Commercial Technologies Inc 970 Fm 2871 ... Fort Worth TX 76126 *Web:* aero-com-tech.com	817-560-6600		21
Aerospace Alloys Inc 11 Britton Dr ... Bloomfield CT 06002 *TF:* 800-214-0475 ■ *Web:* www.aalloys.com	860-882-0019		492
Aerospace America Inc 900 Harry S Truman Pkwy ... Bay City MI 48706 **Fax Area Code: 989* ■ *TF:* 800-237-6414 ■ *Web:* www.aerospaceamerica.com	800-237-6414	684-4486*	480
Aerospace Coatings International Inc 370 Knight Dr ... Oxford AL 36203 *TF:* 866-506-0249 ■ *Web:* www.aerocoatings.com	256-241-2750	241-2760	22
Aerospace Corp, The 2310 E El Segundo Blvd PO Box 92957 ... Los Angeles CA 90009 *Web:* www.aerospace.org	310-336-5000	336-7055	668
Aerospace Engineering & Support Inc 1307 W 2550 S ... Ogden UT 84401 *Web:* aesut.com	801-394-9565		120
Aerospace Fabrications of Georgia Inc 305 Butler Industrial Dr ... Dallas GA 30132 *Web:* www.afog.com	770-505-8801	505-8804	697
Aerospace Industries Assn (AIA) 1000 Wilson Blvd Ste 1700 ... Arlington VA 22209 *Web:* www.aia-aerospace.org	703-358-1000		49-21
Aerospace Maintenance Solutions LLC 8759 Mayfield Rd ... Chesterland OH 44026 *Web:* aerospacellc.com	440-729-7703		359
Aerospace Medical Assn (AMA) 320 S Henry St ... Alexandria VA 22314 *Web:* www.asma.org	703-739-2240	739-9652	49-8
Aerospace Museum of California 3200 Freedom Pk Dr ... McClellan CA 95652 *Web:* aerospaceca.org	916-643-3192		520
Aerospace Semiconductor Inc 439 S Union St ... Lawrence MA 01843 *Web:* www.aerospacesemi.com	978-688-1299		696
Aero-Space Southwest Inc 21450 N Third Ave ... Phoenix AZ 85027 *TF:* 800-289-2779 ■ *Web:* www.aerospacesw.com	623-582-2779		351
Aerospace Techniques Inc 1100 Country Club Rd ... Middletown CT 06457 *Web:* www.aerospacetechniques.com	860-347-1200		454
Aerospace Technologies Group Inc 620 NW 35th St ... Boca Raton FL 33431 *Web:* atgshades.com	561-244-7400		20
Aerospec Inc 505 E Alamo Dr ... Chandler AZ 85225 *TF:* 888-854-2376 ■ *Web:* aerospecinc.com	480-892-7195		256

	Phone	Fax	Class
Aerospike Inc 2525 E Charleston Rd Ste 201 ....Mountain View CA 94043 *Web:* www.aerospike.com	408-462-2376		387
Aerostar Aerospace Manufacturing Inc 2688 E Rose Garden Ln ....Phoenix AZ 85050 *Web:* www.aerostaraerospace.com	602-861-1145		757
Aerotec International Inc 3007 E Chambers St.........................Phoenix AZ 85040 *Web:* www.aerotecinternational.com	602-253-4540	252-0395	21
Aerotech Inc 101 Zeta Dr.................... Pittsburgh PA 15238 *Web:* www.aerotech.com	412-963-7470	967-6870	518
Aerotech Laboratories Inc 1501 W Knudsen Dr.........................Phoenix AZ 85027 *TF:* 888-836-5227 ■ *Web:* www.emlab.com	888-836-5227		743
Aerotech Mapping Inc 2580 Montessouri St .... Las Vegas NV 89117 *Web:* www.atmlv.com	702-228-6277		727
Aerotek Inc 7301 Pkwy Dr.....................Hanover MD 21076 *Web:* www.aerotek.com	410-694-5100		721
Aerotron AirPower Inc 456 Aerotron Pkwy ....LaGrange GA 30240 *Web:* www.aerotron.com	706-812-1700		21
Aerotronics Marketing Inc 5331 Derry Ave Ste O.....................Agoura Hills CA 91301 *Web:* www.aerotronics.net	818-735-6633		195
Aerovent Inc 5959 Trenton Ln..............Minneapolis MN 55442 *TF:* 888-444-4831 ■ *Web:* www.aerovent.com	763-551-7500	551-7501	18
AeroVironment Inc 181 W Huntington Dr Ste 202................Monrovia CA 91016 *NASDAQ: AVAV* ■ *TF:* 888-833-2148 ■ *Web:* www.avinc.com	626-357-9983	359-9628	20
Aerpio Therapeutics Inc 9987 Carver Rd Ste 420.................... Cincinnati OH 45242 *Web:* aerpio.com	513-985-1920		231
AerSale Component Solutions 4901 Rockaway Blvd...................... Rio Rancho NM 87124 *Web:* www.aersale.com	505-896-2644		22
Aervoe Industries Inc 1100 Mark Cir ....Gardnerville NV 89410 *TF:* 800-227-0196 ■ *Web:* aervoe.com	775-783-3100	782-6687	550
AES (American Epilepsy Society) 342 N Main St ....West Hartford CT 06117 *TF:* 888-233-2334 ■ *Web:* www.aesnet.org	860-586-7505	586-7550	48-17
AES (Anesthesia Equipment Supply Inc) 24301 Roberts Dr..................... Black Diamond WA 98010 *Web:* www.aesol.com	253-631-8008		475
AES an Employment Source Inc 1335 N Main St .... Meridian ID 83642 *Web:* www.anemploymentsource.com	208-887-7740		260
AES Corp 4300 Wilson Blvd 11th Fl .... Arlington VA 22203 *NYSE: AES* ■ *TF:* 800-824-7175 ■ *Web:* www.aes.com	703-522-1315		787
AES Electrophoresis Society 1202 Ann St .... Madison WI 53713 *Web:* www.aesociety.org	608-258-1565	258-1569	49-19
AESC (Association of Energy Service Cos) 14531 Fm 529 Ste 250......................Houston TX 77095 *TF:* 800-692-0771 ■ *Web:* www.aesc.net	713-781-0758	781-7542	48-12
AESCULAP Inc 3773 Corporate Pkwy....................Center Valley PA 18034 **Fax Area Code:* 610 ■ *TF:* 800-282-9000 ■ *Web:* www.aesculapusa.com	800-282-9000	791-6886*	476
AESP Inc 999 NW 159 Dr...................... Miami FL 33169	305-944-7710	949-4483	253
Aesseal Inc 355 Dunavant Dr................. Rockford TN 37853 *Web:* www.aesseal.com	865-531-0192		326
Aesthetic Green Power Inc 410 Manchester Rd.................... Poughkeepsie NY 12603 *Web:* aestheticgreenpower.com	916-897-6876		357
AESU Travel Inc 3922 Hickory Ave ....Baltimore MD 21211 *TF:* 800-638-7840 ■ *Web:* www.aesu.com	410-366-5494	366-6900	771
AESYS Technologies LLC 693 N Hills Rd ....York PA 17402 *Web:* www.york-shipleyglobal.com	717-755-1081		91
AETA (American Embryo Transfer Assn) 1800 S Oak St Ste 100.................... Champaign IL 61820 *Web:* www.aeta.org	217-398-2217	398-4119	49-8
AETC (Air Education & Training Command) 100 H St Ste 4 ....Randolph AFB TX 78150 *Web:* www.aetc.af.mil	210-652-6564	652-2027	340-4
AETEA Information Technology Inc 1445 Research Blvd Ste 210.................. Rockville MD 20850 *TF:* 888-772-3832 ■ *Web:* www.aetea.com	301-721-4200	721-1730	180
Aeterna Zentaris Inc 315 Sigma Dr...........Charleston SC 29486 *NASDAQ: AEZS* ■ *TF:* 833-475-8247 ■ *Web:* www.zentaris.com	833-475-8247		85
Aether Investment Partners LLC 1900 Sixteenth St Ste 825 ....Denver CO 80202 *Web:* aetherip.com	720-961-4190		528
Aethercomm Inc 3205 Lionshead Ave .... Carlsbad CA 92010 *Web:* www.aethercomm.com	760-208-6002	208-6059	647
Aethon Inc 200 Business Center Dr............ Pittsburgh PA 15205 *TF:* 888-201-9522 ■ *Web:* aethon.com	412-322-2975		475
AETN (Arkansas Educational Television Network) 350 S Donaghey Ave.........................Conway AR 72034 *TF:* 800-662-2386 ■ *Web:* www.myarkansaspbs.org	501-682-2386	682-4122	632
Aetna Bearing Co 1081 Sesame St.......... Franklin Park IL 60131 *Web:* www.aetnabearing.com	630-694-0024		75
Aetna Felt Corp 2401 W Emaus Ave...........Allentown PA 18103 *TF:* 800-526-4451 ■ *Web:* www.aetnafelt.com	610-791-0900	791-5791	745-6
Aetna Foundation Inc 151 Farmington Ave ....Hartford CT 06156 *Web:* www.aetna.com	860-273-6382		304
Aetna Integrated Services 646 Parsons Ave.......................... Columbus OH 43206 *TF:* 866-238-6201 ■ *Web:* www.aetnais.com	866-238-6201		393
Aetna Plastics Corp 1702 St Clair Ave ....Cleveland OH 44114 *TF:* 800-634-3074 ■ *Web:* www.aetnaplastics.com	216-781-4421	781-4474	603
Aetna Plywood 1401 St Charles Rd............Maywood IL 60153 *Web:* www.aetnaplywood.com	708-343-1515	343-1616	613
Aetna Properties Inc PO Box 69181 ....Portland OR 97239 *Web:* aetnaproperties.com	503-699-4732		391-3
AEW (AEW Capital Management LP) 2 Seaport Ln................................Boston MA 02210 *Web:* www.aew.com	617-261-9000	261-9555	401
AEW Capital Management LP (AEW) 2 Seaport Ln................................Boston MA 02210 *Web:* www.aew.com	617-261-9000	261-9555	401
Aexcel Corp 7373 Production Dr.................Mentor OH 44060 *TF:* 800-854-0782 ■ *Web:* www.aexcelcorp.com	440-974-3800	974-3808	550
AF & L Insurance Co 580 Virginia Dr Ste 330 .... Fort Washington PA 19034 *TF:* 800-659-9206 ■ *Web:* www.aflltc.com	215-918-0515	918-0565	391-3
AFA (American Fence Assn) 6404 Internationa Pkwy Ste 2250-A...............Plano TX 75093 **Fax Area Code:* 314 ■ *TF:* 800-822-4342 ■ *Web:* www.americanfenceassociation.com	800-822-4342	480-7118*	49-3
AFA (American Federation of Astrologers) 6535 S Rural Rd .... Tempe AZ 85283 *TF:* 888-301-7630 ■ *Web:* www.astrologers.com	480-838-1751	838-8293	48-18
AFA (Air Force Assn) 1501 Lee Hwy........... Arlington VA 22209 *TF:* 800-727-3337 ■ *Web:* www.afa.org	703-247-5800	247-5853	48-19
AFA (American Federation of Arts) 305 E 47th St 10th Fl ....New York NY 10017 *TF:* 800-232-0270 ■ *Web:* www.amfedarts.org	212-988-7700	861-2487	48-4
AFA Protective Systems Inc 155 Michael Dr............................. Syosset NY 11791 *OTC: AFAP* ■ *Web:* www.afap.com	516-496-2322	496-2848	692
AFA Systems Inc 8 Tilbury Ct.................Brampton ON L6T3T4 *Web:* www.afasystemsinc.com	905-456-8700		757
AFAA (Aerobics & Fitness Association of America) 1750 E Northrop Blvd Ste 200 .... Chandler AZ 85286 *TF:* 800-446-2322 ■ *Web:* www.afaa.com	800-446-2322		48-22
AFAF Vicky Farah 201 E Liberty St............ Ann Arbor MI 48104 *Web:* vickyfarah.com	734-663-9813	663-2920	428
AFAR (American Federation for Aging Research) 55 W 39th St 16th Fl.........................New York NY 10018 *TF:* 888-582-2327 ■ *Web:* www.afar.org	212-703-9977	997-0330	49-8
Afareast Inc 380 Brogdon Rd .... Suwanee GA 30024 **Fax Area Code:* 888 ■ *TF:* 866-408-2825 ■ *Web:* www.buckwholesale.com	770-904-2052	855-7068*	156
AFB (American Foundation for the Blind) 1401 S Clark St Ste 730.................... Arlington VA 22202 *TF:* 800-232-5463 ■ *Web:* www.afb.org	212-502-7600	502-7777	48-17
AFC (AMPAC Fine Chemicals) MS 1007 PO Box 1718................ Rancho Cordova CA 95741 *TF:* 800-311-9668 ■ *Web:* ampacfinechemicals.com	916-357-6880	353-3523	145
AFC (Automotive Finance Corp) 13085 Hamilton Crossing Blvd..................Carmel IN 46032 *TF:* 888-335-6675 ■ *Web:* www.afcdealer.com	865-384-8250		216
AFC Cable Systems Inc 960 Flaherty Dr......................... New Bedford MA 02745 *TF:* 800-757-6996 ■ *Web:* www.afcweb.com	508-998-1131		813
AFC Finishing Systems Inc 250 Airport Pkwy .... Oroville CA 95965 *TF:* 800-331-7744 ■ *Web:* afc-ca.com	800-331-7744		295
AFC Holcroft LLC 49630 Pontiac Trl ....Wixom MI 48393 *Web:* www.afc-holcroft.com	248-624-8191	624-3710	318
AFC Industries Inc 13-16 133rd Pl.........................College Point NY 11356 *TF:* 800-663-3412 ■ *Web:* www.afcindustries.com	718-747-0237		194
AFC Tool Company Inc 4900 Webster St..........Dayton OH 45414 *Web:* www.afctool.com	937-275-8700		454
AFCA (American Football Coaches Assn) 100 Legends Ln ....Waco TX 76706 *TF:* 877-557-5338 ■ *Web:* www.afca.com	254-754-9900		48-22
AFCEA (Armed Forces Communications & Electronics Assn) 4114 Legato Rd Ste 1000...................... Fairfax VA 22033 *TF:* 800-336-4583 ■ *Web:* www.afcea.org	703-631-6100	631-4693	48-19
AFCI (Association of Film Commissioners Intl) 8606 Wilshire Blvd Ste 900 .... Beverly Hills CA 90212 **Fax Area Code:* 413 ■ *TF:* 888-765-5777 ■ *Web:* afci.org	323-461-2324	375-2903*	48-4
AFCO (Alex C. Fergusson LLC) 5000 Letterkenny Rd....................Chambersburg PA 17201 **Fax Area Code:* 717 ■ *TF:* 800-345-1329 ■ *Web:* www.afcocare.us	800-345-1329	264-9182*	145
AFCO Credit Corp 14 Wall St ....New York NY 10005 *TF:* 800-288-6901 ■ *Web:* www.afco.com	212-401-4400	401-4436	216
AFCO Industries Inc 3400 Roy St............ Alexandria LA 71302 *TF:* 800-551-6576 ■ *Web:* www.afco-ind.com	800-551-6576		482
AFCO Manufacturing Corp 428 Cogshall St PO Box 230 .... Holly MI 48442 *Web:* www.afcomfg.com	248-634-4415	634-6301	480
AFCO Products Inc 1030 Commerce Dr .... Lake Zurich IL 60047 *Web:* www.afco-products.com	847-299-1055	299-8455	621
AFCO Steel Inc 1423 E Sixth St............... Little Rock AR 72202 *Web:* www.afcosteel.com	501-340-6233	340-6260	480
Afcon Products Incorporated Elec Equip 35 Sargent Dr..............................Bethany CT 06524 *Web:* www.afconproducts.com	203-393-9301		14
AFCU (Andrews Federal Credit Union) 5711 Allentown Rd..........................Suitland MD 20746 *TF:* 800-487-5500 ■ *Web:* www.andrewsfcu.org	301-702-5500	702-5330	219
AFD Contract Furniture Inc 810 Seventh Ave Ste 2 ....New York NY 10019 *Web:* www.afd-inc.com	212-721-7100		320
AFE (Association for Facilities Engineering) 1901 N Fort Myer Dr Ste 500 .... Arlington VA 22209 *Web:* afe.clubexpress.com	571-814-8296	766-2142	49-13
AFE (Artesia Fire Equipment Inc) 1014 S First St............................. Artesia NM 88210 *TF:* 800-748-2076 ■ *Web:* www.artesiafire.com	575-746-2426	748-1128	76
Afena Federal Credit Union 424 N Bradner Ave ....Marion IN 46952 *TF:* 888-296-4328 ■ *Web:* afenafcu.org	765-664-8089		219
AFF (American Forest Foundation) 2000 M St NW Ste 550...................Washington DC 20036 *TF:* 800-325-2954 ■ *Web:* forestfoundation.org	202-765-3660	827-7924	48-2
Affant Communication 2900 Bristol St D 204.................... Costa Mesa CA 92626 *Web:* affant.com	714-338-7100		387
Affect NY 1350 Broadway Ste 2303 ....New York NY 10018 *Web:* www.affect.com	212-398-9680	504-8211	194

				Phone	Fax	Class
Affeldt Law Offices SC 8741 W National Ave *Web:* affeldtlaw.com	West Allis	WI	53227	414-321-4560		41
AFFI (American Frozen Food Institute) 2000 Corporate Ridge Blvd Ste 1000 *Web:* www.affi.org	McLean	VA	22102	703-821-0770	821-1350	615
Affiliated Car Rental 105 Hwy 36 *TF:* 800-367-5159 ■ *Web:* www.affiliatedcarrental.com	Eatontown	NJ	07724	732-380-0888	380-0404	126
Affiliated Control Equipment Inc 640 Wheat Ln *TF:* 800-942-8753 ■ *Web:* www.affiliatedcontrol.com	Wood Dale	IL	60191	630-595-4680	595-6151	55
Affiliated Engineering Laboratories Inc 777 New Durham Rd *Web:* aelgroup.net	Edison	NJ	08817	732-429-1200		261
Affiliated Engineers Inc (AEI) 5802 Research Pk Blvd *Web:* www.aeieng.com	Madison	WI	53719	608-238-2616		261
Affiliated Foods Inc 1401 W Farmers Ave *TF:* 800-234-3661 ■ *Web:* www.afiama.com	Amarillo	TX	79118	806-372-3851		297-8
Affiliated Laboratory Inc 417 State St Ste 240 *Web:* affiliatedlab.com	Portland	ME	04101	207-973-6900	973-6999	415
Affiliated Managers Group Inc (AMG) 600 Hale St *NYSE:* AMG ■ *Web:* www.amg.com	Prides Crossing	MA	01965	617-747-3300		360-3
Affiliated Medical Services Laboratory Inc 2916 E Central Ave *TF:* 800-876-0243 ■ *Web:* www.amsreferencelab.com	Wichita	KS	67214	316-265-4533		415
Affiliated Products Inc 207 River Knoll Dr *Web:* www.affprod.com	Mayville	WI	53050	920-387-7400	387-7404	253
Affinia Hotels & Suite 551 Fifth Ave *Web:* www.affinia.com	New York	NY	10176	646-424-2600		379
Affinigent Inc 4 Kent Rd Ste 200 *TF:* 800-932-3380 ■ *Web:* www.affinigent.com	York	PA	17402	717-600-0033		225
Affinimark PO Box 122 *Web:* affinimark.com	Guilford	CT	06437	203-350-2211		743
Affinitas Corp 1015 N 98th St Ste 100 *TF:* 800-369-6495 ■ *Web:* www.affinitas.net	Omaha	NE	68114	402-505-5000		194
Affinitive LLC 11 E 26th St 12th Fl	New York	NY	10010	212-684-9100		7
Affinity Circles Inc 701 B St Ste 520 *Web:* www.affinitycircles.com	San Diego	CA	92113	619-618-4200		387
Affinity Consultants Inc 222 N Canal St *Web:* affinityconsultants.com	Canal Fulton	OH	44614	330-854-9066	854-9067	194
Affinity Custom Molding Inc 21198 M 60 *Web:* www.affinitycustommolding.com	Mendon	MI	49072	269-496-8423		604
Affinity Federal Credit Union 73 Mountain View Blvd PO Box 621 *TF:* 800-325-0808 ■ *Web:* www.affinityfcu.com	Basking Ridge	NJ	07920	800-325-0808		219
Affinity First Federal Credit Union 811 S Broadway Ste A *Web:* affinityfcund.com	Minot	ND	58701	701-857-5541		219
Affinity Gaming 3755 Breakthrough Way Ste 300 *Web:* www.affinitygaming.com	Las Vegas	NV	89135	702-341-2400		132
Affinity Home Care Agency Inc 2569 Union Lake Rd *Web:* www.affinityhomecareagency.com	Commerce Charter Township	MI	48382	248-363-8650	363-8652	363
Affinity Home Health Care Inc 121 Sandwich St *Web:* www.affinityhomehealthcare.com	Plymouth	MA	02360	508-732-8988		363
Affinity Inc 10850 W Park Pl Ste 470 **Fax Area Code:* 414 ■ *TF:* 877-399-2220 ■ *Web:* www.affinityit.com	Milwaukee	WI	53224	877-399-2220	258-2630*	196
Affinity Management Group LLC 10205 Westheimer Rd Ste 460 *Web:* www.affinity-mgt.com	Houston	TX	77042	713-452-3100		194
Affinity Medical Ctr 875 Eigth St NE *Web:* www.affinitymedicalcenter.com	Massillon	OH	44646	330-832-8761		374-3
Affinity One Federal Credit Union 545 E Second St *Web:* affinityonefcu.org	Jamestown	NY	14701	716-483-2798	483-2266	219
Affinity Wealth Management Inc 1702 Lovering Ave *TF:* 800-825-8399 ■ *Web:* www.affinitywealth.com	Wilmington	DE	19806	302-652-6767		194
Affirm Inc 650 California St *TF:* 855-423-3729 ■ *Web:* affirm.com	San Francisco	CA	94108	855-423-3729		668
Affirmative Insurance Holdings Inc 4450 Sojourn Dr Ste 500 *OTC:* AFFM ■ *Web:* www.affirmative.com	Addison	TX	75001	630-560-7000		360-4
Affordable Concepts Inc 2975 W Lake Mead *Web:* www.affordableconcepts.com	North Las Vegas	NV	89032	702-399-3330		186
Affordable Optical Inc 6170 W Grand Ave Ste 451 *Web:* affordableoptical.com	Gurnee	IL	60031	847-855-9009		543
AffordableTours.com 11150 Cash Rd **Fax Area Code:* 281 ■ *TF:* 800-935-2620 ■ *Web:* www.affordabletours.com	Stafford	TX	77477	800-935-2620	269-2690*	772
Affton Chamber of Commerce 9815 Mackenzie Rd *TF:* 800-877-1234 ■ *Web:* www.afftonchamber.com	Affton	MO	63123	314-631-3100		139
Affton Fabricating & Welding Company Inc 1635 Sauget Business Blvd *Web:* www.afwc.com	Sauget	IL	62206	618-337-5450	337-5470	480
Affymax Inc 600 5th Ave 2nd Fl *OTC:* AFFY ■ *TF:* 800-962-4284 ■ *Web:* www.affymax.com	New York	NY	10020	650-812-8700		85
AFG (Avrett Free Ginsberg) 71 5th Ave *Web:* avrettfreeginsberg.com	New York	NY	10003	212-832-3800		4
Afghan Horseman 1833 Anderson St *Web:* afghanhorsemen.com	Vancouver	BC	V6H4E5	604-873-5923		671
Afghanistan Embassy 2341 Wyoming Ave NW *Web:* www.afghanembassy.us	Washington	DC	20008	202-483-6410	483-6488	257
AFGlobal 19450 State Hwy 249 Ste 500 *Web:* afgholdings.com	Houston	TX	77070	713-393-4200		483

				Phone	Fax	Class
AFGM Enterprises Federal Credit Union 132 Cayuga Rd *Web:* afgmentfcu.com	Cheektowaga	NY	14225	716-634-3636		219
AFI (American Film Institute) 2021 N Western Ave *TF:* 866-234-3378 ■ *Web:* www.afi.com	Los Angeles	CA	90027	323-856-7600	467-4578	48-4
AFI (Armed Forces Insurance Exchange) 550 Eisenhower Rd *TF:* 800-255-6792 ■ *Web:* www.afi.org	Leavenworth	KS	66048	800-255-6792	828-7731	391-4
AFI (Association of Food Industries Inc) 3301 Rt 66 Bldg C Ste 205 *Web:* afius.org	Neptune City	NJ	07753	732-922-3008	922-3590	49-6
AFIA (American Feed Industry Assn) 2101 Wilson Blvd Ste 916 *Web:* www.afia.org	Arlington	VA	22201	703-524-0810	524-1921	48-2
AFIMAC Inc 8160 Parkhill Dr *TF:* 800-554-4622 ■ *Web:* afimacglobal.com	Milton	ON	L9T5V7	800-554-4622		194
AFJ (Alliance for Justice) 11 Dupont Cir NW Ste 500 *Web:* www.afj.org	Washington	DC	20036	202-822-6070	822-6068	48-7
AFL Network Services Inc 170 Ridgeview Center Dr *Web:* www.aflglobal.com	Duncan	SC	29334	864-433-0333		41
AFLAC Inc 1932 Wynnton Rd *NYSE:* AFL ■ *TF:* 800-992-3522 ■ *Web:* www.aflac.com	Columbus	GA	31999	800-992-3522		360-4
AFL-CIO (American Federation of Labor & Congress of Industrial Organizations) 815 16th St NW *Web:* www.aflcio.org	Washington	DC	20006	202-637-5215		414
AFL-CIO Committee on Political Education 815 16th St NW *TF:* 855-712-8441 ■ *Web:* aflcio.org	Washington	DC	20006	855-712-8441		615
AFM (American Federation of Musicians of the US & Canada) 1501 Broadway Ste 600 *TF:* 800-762-3444 ■ *Web:* www.afm.org	New York	NY	10036	212-869-1330	764-6134	414
AFNI Inc 404 Brock Dr *TF:* 866-377-8844 ■ *Web:* afnicareers.com	Bloomington	IL	61701	866-377-8844		160
AFOP (Association of Farmworker Opportunity Programs) 1120 20th St NW Ste 300 *Web:* afop.org	Washington	DC	20036	202-828-6006	828-6005	48-2
AFOSR (Air Force Office of Scientific Research) 875 N Randolph St Ste 325 *Web:* www.wpafb.af.mil	Arlington	VA	22203	703-696-7797		668
AFP (Agence France-Presse) 1500 K St NW Ste 600 *Web:* www.afp.com	Washington	DC	20005	202-414-0600		530
AFP (Association of Fundraising Professionals) 4300 Wilson Blvd Ste 300 *TF:* 800-666-3863 ■ *Web:* afpglobal.org	Arlington	VA	22203	703-684-0410	684-1950	49-12
AFP (Association for Financial Professionals) 4520 E W Hwy Ste 800 *Web:* www.afponline.org	Bethesda	MD	20814	301-907-2862	907-2864	49-2
AFP Advanced Food Products LLC 402 S Custer Ave *Web:* www.afpllc.com	New Holland	PA	17557	717-355-8500		296-36
AFP Transformers Inc 206 Talmedge Rd *TF:* 800-843-1215 ■ *Web:* www.afp-transformers.com	Edison	NJ	08817	732-248-0305	248-0542	767
AF&PA (American Forest & Paper Assn) 1101 K St NW Ste 700 *TF:* 800-878-8878 ■ *Web:* www.afandpa.org	Washington	DC	20036	202-463-2700		48-2
AFPM (American Fuel & Petrochemical Manufacturers) 1667 K St NW Ste 700 *Web:* www.afpm.org	Washington	DC	20006	202-457-0480	457-0486	48-12
AFR Labs 22981 Triton Way Ste E *Web:* www.afrlabs.com	Laguna Hills	CA	92653	949-462-9822	462-9929	415
Africa Adventure Co, The 2601 E Oakland Park Blvd Ste 600 *TF:* 800-882-9453 ■ *Web:* www.africa-adventure.com	Fort Lauderdale	FL	33308	954-491-8877	491-9060	760
Africa Fortesa Corp 7880 San Felipe St Ste 105 *Web:* fortesa.com	Houston	TX	77063	713-278-2727		536
Africa Imports 240 S Main St Unit A *TF:* 800-500-6120 ■ *Web:* africaimports.com	South Hackensack	NJ	07606	201-457-1995		820
Africa Oil Corp 885 W Georgia St Ste 2000 *Web:* www.africaoilcorp.com	Vancouver	BC	V6C3E8	604-689-7842		536
Africa-America Institute (AAI) 420 Lexington Ave Ste 1706 *Web:* www.aaionline.org	New York	NY	10170	212-949-5666	682-6174	48-14
Africair Inc 13551 SW 132nd Ave Ste 1 *Web:* www.africair.com	Miami	FL	33186	305-255-6973		770
African American Art & Culture Complex 762 Fulton St *Web:* aaacc.org	San Francisco	CA	94102	415-922-2049	922-5130	50-2
African American Cultural Center of Buffalo Inc 350 Masten Ave *Web:* www.aaccbuffalo.org	Buffalo	NY	14209	716-884-2013		50-2
African American Hall of Fame Museum 309 Du Sable St *Web:* aahfmpeoria.org	Peoria	IL	61605	309-673-2206		520
African American Historical & Cultural Museum of San Joaquin Valley 1857 Fulton St *Web:* aahcmsjv.org	Fresno	CA	93721	559-544-1857		520
African American Images (AAI) PO Box 1799 *TF:* 800-552-1991 ■ *Web:* www.africanamericanimages.com	Chicago	IL	60601	708-672-4909	672-0466	637-2
African American Museum 3536 Grand Ave *Web:* www.aamdallas.org	Dallas	TX	75210	214-565-9026	421-8204	520
African American Museum & Library in Oakland 659 14th St *Web:* oaklandlibrary.org	Oakland	CA	94612	510-637-0200		520
African American Museum of Iowa 55 12th Ave SE *Web:* blackiowa.org	Cedar Rapids	IA	52401	319-862-2101		520
African American Museum of the Arts 325 S Clara Ave *Web:* africanmuseumdeland.org	DeLand	FL	32721	386-736-4004	736-4088	520

Phone | Fax | Class

African Burial Ground National Monument
c/o Federal Hall National Memorial 26 Wall St
New York NY 10005 212-637-2019 227-2026 564
Web: www.nps.gov

African Heritage Press
PO Box 1433 New Rochelle NY 10802 855-247-7737 481-8489* 637-2
Fax Area Code: 914 ■ TF: 855-247-7737 ■ Web: www.africanheritagepress.com

African Lion Safari & Game Farm
RR 1 Ste 1 Cambridge ON N1R5S2 519-623-2620 623-9542 823
Web: lionsafari.com

African Safari Wildlife Park
267 S Lightner Rd Port Clinton OH 43452 419-732-3606 734-1919 823
TF: 800-521-2660 ■ *Web:* www.africansafariwildlifepark.com

African Travel Inc
330 N Brand Blvd Ste 225 Glendale CA 91203 818-507-7893 507-5802 760
TF: 800-421-8907 ■ *Web:* www.africantravelinc.com

African Wildlife Foundation (AWF)
1100 New Jersey Ave SE Ste 900 Washington DC 20003 202-939-3333 939-3332 48-3
TF: 888-494-5354 ■ *Web:* www.awf.org

African-American Civil War Memorial & Museum
1925 Vermont Ave NW Washington DC 20001 202-667-2667 667-6771 520
TF: 800-753-9222 ■ *Web:* www.afroamcivilwar.org

African-American Museum in Philadelphia
701 Arch St Philadelphia PA 19106 215-574-0380 574-3110 520
Web: www.aampmuseum.org

African-American Panoramic Experience Museum
135 Auburn Ave NE Atlanta GA 30303 404-523-2739 520
Web: www.apexmuseum.org

Africare Inc 440 R St NW Washington DC 20001 202-462-3614 387-1034 48-5
TF: 800-429-9493 ■ *Web:* www.africare.org

Afro World Hair Goods Inc
7276 Natural Bridge Rd Normandy MO 63121 314-474-0151 348
Web: www.afroworld.com

Afro-American Cultural Ctr
551 S Tryon St Charlotte NC 28202 704-547-3700 50-2
Web: www.ganttcenter.org

Afro-American Historical Society Museum
1841 Kennedy Blvd Jersey City NJ 07305 201-547-5262 547-5302 520
Web: www.cityofjerseycity.org

Afro-American Newspapers Co
2519 N Charles St Baltimore MD 21218 410-554-8200 570-9297* 637-8
Fax Area Code: 877 ■ TF: 800-237-6892 ■ Web: www.afro.com

AFS (American Folklore Society)
800 E Third St Bloomington IN 47405 812-856-2379 856-2483 48-14
TF: 866-315-9403 ■ *Web:* www.afsnet.org

AFS (American Fisheries Society)
5410 Grosvenor Ln Ste 110 Bethesda MD 20814 301-897-8616 897-8096 48-2
Web: fisheries.org

AFS (American Foundry Society)
1695 N Penny Ln Schaumburg IL 60173 847-824-0181 49-13
TF: 800-537-4237 ■ *Web:* www.afsinc.org

AFS (Automated Financial Systems Inc)
123 Summit Dr Exton PA 19341 610-524-9300 178-11
Web: www.afsvision.com

AFS Energy Systems 420 Oak St Lemoyne PA 17043 717-763-0286 490
Web: www.afsenergy.com

AFS International Inc
71 W 23rd St 6th Fl New York NY 10010 212-807-8686 807-1001 48-11
Web: afs.org

AFS Technologies Inc
2141 E Highland Ave Ste 100 Phoenix AZ 85016 602-522-8282 178-1
TF: 877-821-3007 ■ *Web:* www.afsi.com

AFSA (American Federation of School Administrators)
1101 17th St NW Ste 408 Washington DC 20036 202-986-4209 49-5
Web: www.theschoolleader.org

AFSA (American Fire Sprinkler Assn)
12750 Merit Dr Ste 350 Dallas TX 75251 214-349-5965 343-8898 49-3
Web: www.firesprinkler.org

AFSA (American Foreign Service Assn)
2101 E St NW Washington DC 20037 202-338-4045 338-6820 49-7
TF: 800-704-2372 ■ *Web:* www.afsa.org

AFSC (Alaska Fisheries Science Ctr)
7600 Sand Point Way NE Bldg 4 Seattle WA 98115 206-526-4000 526-4004 668
Web: www.fisheries.noaa.gov

AFSC (American Friends Service Committee)
1501 Cherry St Philadelphia PA 19102 215-241-7000 48-5
TF: 800-621-4000 ■ *Web:* www.afsc.org

AFSP (American Foundation for Suicide Prevention)
120 Wall St 29th Fl New York NY 10005 212-363-3500 363-6237 48-17
TF: 888-333-2377 ■ *Web:* afsp.org

AFT (American Farmland Trust)
1200 18th St Washington DC 20036 202-331-7300 659-8339 48-2
TF: 800-431-1499 ■ *Web:* www.farmland.org

AFT (American Federation of Teachers)
555 New Jersey Ave NW Washington DC 20001 202-879-4400 457-8
Web: www.aft.org

AFT Michigan 2661 E Jefferson Detroit MI 48207 313-393-2200 393-2236 414
Web: aftmichigan.org

Afterburner Inc
3525 Piedmont Rd NE Ste 5-435 Atlanta GA 30305 404-835-3500 193
TF: 877-765-5607 ■ *Web:* www.afterburner.com

Afton Alps Inc 6600 Peller Ave S Hastings MN 55033 651-436-1320 378
TF: 866-709-1026 ■ *Web:* www.aftonalps.com

Afton Chemical Corp 500 Spring St Richmond VA 23219 804-788-5800 788-5184 145
TF: 800-424-9300 ■ *Web:* www.aftonchemical.com

Afton State Park 6959 Peller Ave S Hastings MN 55033 651-436-5391 436-6912 565
Web: www.dnr.state.mn.us

AFTRA (American Federation of Television & Radio Artists)
260 Madison Ave 7th Fl New York NY 10016 212-532-0800 532-2242 414
TF: 800-638-6796 ■ *Web:* www.sagaftra.org

AFX Inc 2345 Ernie Krueger Cir Waukegan IL 60087 847-249-5970 249-2618 439
TF: 800-873-2326 ■ *Web:* www.afxinc.com

AFX Industries 1411 Third St Ste G Port Huron MI 48060 810-966-4650 966-9522 61
Web: www.afxindustries.com

AFYA Inc 8101 Sandy Spring Rd 3rd Fl Laurel MD 20707 301-957-3040 497-9902 194
Web: www.afyainc.com

AG (Augusta Grill) 1818 Augusta St Greenville SC 29605 864-242-0316 671
Web: www.augustagrill.com

Phone | Fax | Class

AG (Alhambra-Grantfork Telephone Co)
305e Main St Alhambra IL 62001 618-488-2165 488-2121 224
Web: www.agtelco.com

AG Body Inc 565 South 600 West Salt Lake City UT 84101 801-355-8053 247
Web: agbody.com

AG Communications LLC PO Box 1604 Fairfield CT 06825 203-373-0599 373-0535 463
Web: www.agcomm.com

AG Computer Center Inc PO Box 872 Westwood NJ 07675 201-666-6290 666-0530 179
Web: www.agcomputer.com

AG Connections Inc 1576 Killdeer Trl Murray KY 42071 270-435-4369 180
Web: www.agconnections.com

AG Davis Gage & Engineering Co
6533 Sims Dr Sterling Heights MI 48313 586-977-9000 977-9190 493
Web: www.agdavis-aagage.com

AG Editions Inc PO Box 545 New York NY 14851 800-727-9593 393
TF: 800-727-9593 ■ *Web:* www.agpix.com

AG Georgia Farm Credit PO Box 1820 Perry GA 31069 478-987-8300 216
Web: www.aggeorgia.com

AG Industries Inc
75 Chestnut St North Attleboro MA 02760 508-695-4219 697
Web: www.agindustriesmass.com

AG Informaton Systems
306 Primrose Ln Mountville PA 17554 717-285-7105 177
Web: www.ag-is.com

AG Insurance Services 1790 32nd Ave S Fargo ND 58104 701-232-4574 390
Web: aginsinc.com

AG Leader Technology Inc
2202 S Riverside Dr Ames IA 50010 515-735-7000 407
Web: www.agleader.com

AG Machining & Industries Inc
4607 S Windermere St Englewood CO 80110 303-783-0081 697
Web: www.agmachining.com

AG Partners Inc
512 S Eigth St PO Box 467 Lake City MN 55041 651-345-3328 447
TF: 800-772-2990 ■ *Web:* agpartners.net

AG Plus Inc
401 N Main St PO Box 306 South Whitley IN 46787 260-723-5141 11-1
Web: www.agplucino.oom

AG Press Inc 1531 Yuma Manhattan KS 66505 785-539-7558 539-2679 532-2
Web: www.grassandgrain.com

AG Processing Inc
12700 W Dodge Rd PO Box 2047 Omaha NE 68103 402-496-7809 296-29
TF: 800-247-1345 ■ *Web:* agp.com

AG Russell Knives Inc 2900 S 26th St Rogers AR 72758 479-631-0130 631-8493 361
TF: 800-255-9034 ■ *Web:* agrussell.com

AG RX 751 S Rose Ave Oxnard CA 93030 805-487-0696 483-6146 144
Web: www.agrx.com

AG Source Inc
4910 Corporate Centre Dr Ste 110 Lawrence KS 66047 785-841-1315 169
Web: ag-source.com

AG Spanos Cos
10100 Trinity Pkwy 5th Fl Stockton CA 95219 209-478-7954 473-3703 653
Web: www.agspanos.com

AG Spray Equipment Inc
1000 Fimco Ln North Sioux City SD 57049 605-232-6800 273
Web: www.agspray.com

AG Trucking Inc 2430 Lincolnway E Goshen IN 46526 800-336-1216 642-4387* 780
Fax Area Code: 574 ■ TF: 800-336-1216 ■ Web: www.agtrucking.com

AG West Supply Inc
9055 Rickreall Rd Rickreall OR 97371 503-363-2332 363-5662 274
TF: 800-842-2224 ■ *Web:* www.agwestsupply.com

AGA (American Gastroenterological Assn)
4930 Del Ray Ave Bethesda MD 20814 301-654-2055 654-5920 49-8
TF: 800-227-7888 ■ *Web:* www.gastro.org

AGA (American Gaming Assn)
1299 Pennsylvania Ave NW Ste 1175 Washington DC 20004 202-552-2675 552-2676 48-23
Web: www.americangaming.org

AGA (American Galvanizers Assn)
6881 S Holly Cir Ste 108 Centennial CO 80112 720-554-0900 554-0909 49-13
TF: 800-468-7732 ■ *Web:* galvanizeit.org

AGA (Association of Government Accountants)
2208 Mt Vernon Ave Alexandria VA 22301 703-684-6931 548-9367 49-1
TF: 800-242-7211 ■ *Web:* www.agacgfm.org

AGA Khan Foundation USA (AKF)
1825 K St NW Ste 901 Washington DC 20006 202-293-2537 785-1752 48-5
Web: www.akfusa.org

AGA Service Co PO Box 71533 Richmond VA 23255 800-284-8300 391-7
TF: 866-884-3556 ■ *Web:* www.allianztravelinsurance.com

Against the Grain Brewery
401 E Main St Louisville KY 40202 502-515-0174 671
Web: www.atgbrewery.com

AgaMatrix Inc 7C Raymond Ave Salem NH 03079 603-328-6000 743
Web: agamatrix.com

Agape English Language Institute (AELI)
1600 Park Cir Unit 116 Columbia SC 29201 803-445-1998 423
Web: aeliusa.com

Agape Home Healthcare
18770 Lyndon B Johnson Fwy Mesquite TX 75150 972-681-8420 363
Web: www.agapehomehealth.com

Agape Plastics Inc
11474 First Ave NW Grand Rapids MI 49534 616-735-4091 735-4392 608
Web: www.agapeplastics.com

Agar Corporation Inc 5150 Tacoma Dr Houston TX 77041 832-476-5100 476-5299 358
Web: www.agarcorp.com

Agate Fossil Beds National Monument
301 River Rd Harrison NE 69346 308-668-2211 668-2318 564
Web: www.nps.gov

Agati Inc 1219 W Lake St Chicago IL 60607 312-829-1977 321
Web: www.agati.com

Agatina's 2967 Buffalo Rd Rochester NY 14624 585-426-0510 426-0208 671
Web: agatinas.com

Agatucci's 2607 N University St Peoria IL 61604 309-688-8200 671
Web: agatuccis.com

Agave 242 Blvd SE Atlanta GA 30312 404-588-0006 671
Web: www.agaverestaurant.com

Agave Tequila Bar 211 N Main St Ann Arbor MI 48104 734-214-7775 671
Web: www.agaveannarbor.com

Agawam Public Library 750 Cooper St Agawam MA 01001 413-789-1550 434-3
Web: agawamlibrary.org

	Phone	Fax	Class
AGB (Association of Governing Boards of Universities & Colleges) 1133 20th St NW Ste 300 .... Washington DC 20036 *TF:* 800-356-6317 ■ *Web:* www.agb.org	202-296-8400	223-7053	49-5
AGB Investigative Services Inc 2033 W 95th St .... Chicago IL 60643 *Web:* agbinvestigative.com	773-445-4300		177
Agbayani Construction Corp 88 Dixon Ct .... Daly City CA 94014 *Web:* www.agbayani.com	415-221-2065		187
AgBest 2101 N Granville Ave .... Muncie IN 47308 *TF:* 800-368-7372 ■ *Web:* www.agbest.com	765-288-5001	282-4006	276
AGBU (Armenian General Benevolent Union) 55 E 59th St .... New York NY 10022 *Web:* agbu.org	212-319-6383	319-6507	48-14
AGC (Armstrong Garden Centers Inc) 2200 E Rt 66 Ste 200 .... Glendora CA 91740 *Web:* www.armstronggarden.com	626-914-1091		323
AGC (Associated General Contractors of America) 2300 Wilson Blvd Ste 300 .... Arlington VA 22201 *TF:* 800-242-1766 ■ *Web:* www.agc.org	703-548-3118	548-3119	49-3
AGC Biologics 22021 20th Ave SE .... Bothell WA 98021 *TF:* 800-845-6973 ■ *Web:* www.agcbio.com	425-485-1900	486-0300	85
AGC Chemicals Americas Inc 55 E Uwchlan Ave Ste 201 .... Exton PA 19341 *Web:* www.agcchem.com	610-423-4300		601
AGC Inc 106 Evansville Ave .... Meriden CT 06451 *Web:* www.agcincorporated.com	203-639-7125	235-6543	677
AGC Manufacturing Services Inc 20701 E 81st St .... Broken Arrow OK 74014 *TF:* 800-752-0604 ■ *Web:* www.agcmfg.com	918-251-0490	251-1048	518
Agcall Inc 251 Midpark Blvd SE .... Calgary AB T2X1S3 *TF:* 877-273-4333 ■ *Web:* www.agcall.com	403-256-1229		194
AGCO (AGCO Corp) 4205 River Green Pkwy .... Duluth GA 30096 *NYSE: AGCO* ■ *TF:* 877-525-4384 ■ *Web:* www.agcocorp.com	770-813-9200		273
AGCO (Carter Agri-System) 45 W 1st N .... Lund NV 89317 *Web:* www.carterag.com	775-238-5295	238-5410	274
AGCO Corp (AGCO) 4205 River Green Pkwy .... Duluth GA 30096 *NYSE: AGCO* ■ *TF:* 877-525-4384 ■ *Web:* www.agcocorp.com	770-813-9200		273
AGCO Inc 2782 Simpson Cir .... Norcross GA 30071 *Web:* agcomarble.com	770-447-6990		610
A-GCS (Avant-Garde Consulting Services Inc) 10993 N Harrells Ferry Rd .... Baton Rouge LA 70816 *TF:* 866-839-7230 ■ *Web:* agcs.imiscloud.com	225-272-5432		194
AGD (Academy of General Dentistry) 211 E Chicago Ave Ste 900 .... Chicago IL 60611 *TF:* 888-243-3368 ■ *Web:* www.agd.org	312-440-4300	440-0559	49-8
Age Consulting Inc 575 Market St Ste 2150 .... San Francisco CA 94105 *Web:* agesfhost.com	415-979-1502		261
Age Industries Ltd 3601 County Rd 316C .... Cleburne TX 76031 *Web:* www.ageindustries.com	817-641-8178	641-2509	100
Ageatia Global Soultions (AGS) 949 N Plum Grove Rd .... Schaumburg IL 60173 *Web:* www.ageatia.com	847-517-8415	517-7796	194
AgeCare 19655 Walden Blvd SE .... Calgary AB T2X0N7 *Web:* www.agecare.ca	403-873-3200	873-3225	371
Agecroft Hall 4305 Sulgrave Rd .... Richmond VA 23221 *Web:* www.agecrofthall.org	804-353-4241		520
Ageless Living Home Health LLC 431 Wolfe Rd Ste 102 .... San Antonio TX 78216 *Web:* agelesslivinghh.com	210-582-5840		363
Agellan Capital Partners Inc 156 Front St W Ste 303 .... Toronto ON M5J2L6 *Web:* agellancommercialreit.com	416-593-6800		655
Agemark Corp 25 Avenida De Orinda .... Orinda CA 94563 *Web:* www.agemark.com	510-548-6600		371
Agence France-Presse (AFP) 1500 K St NW Ste 600 .... Washington DC 20005 *Web:* www.afp.com	202-414-0600		530
Agency for Health Care Administration 2727 Mahan Dr .... Tallahassee FL 32308 *TF:* 888-419-3456 ■ *Web:* ahca.myflorida.com	888-419-3456		363
Agency for Healthcare Research & Quality 540 Gaither Rd .... Rockville MD 20850 *TF:* 800-358-9295 ■ *Web:* www.ahrq.gov	301-427-1364		340-10
Agency For the Performing Arts Inc 405 S Beverly Dr .... Beverly Hills CA 90212 *Web:* apa-agency.com	310-888-4200		708
Agency for Toxic Substances & Disease Registry 4770 Buford Hwy NE .... Atlanta GA 30341 *Web:* www.atsdr.cdc.gov	770-488-0736		340-10
Agency Insurance Brokers Inc 41 Broad St .... Plattsburgh NY 12901 *TF:* 800-562-0228 ■ *Web:* agencyins.net	518-561-1000	563-4327	390
Agency Mabu 1003 Gateway Ave .... Bismarck ND 58503 *TF:* 800-568-9346 ■ *Web:* www.agencymabu.com	701-250-0728		7
Agency Revolution 2783 NW Lolo Dr Ste 120 .... Bend OR 97701 *TF:* 800-606-0477 ■ *Web:* www.agencyrevolution.com	800-606-0477		5
Agency Software Inc 215 W Commerce Dr .... Hayden Lake ID 83835 *TF:* 800-342-7327 ■ *Web:* www.agencysoftware.com	208-762-7188	762-1265	390
agencyQ 1825 K St NW Ste 500 .... Washington DC 20006 *TF:* 866-734-7932 ■ *Web:* www.agencyq.com	202-776-9090		177
Agenda Global 400 Gold Ave SW Ste 1200 .... Albuquerque NM 87102 *TF:* 877-398-8763 ■ *Web:* agenda-global.com	505-888-5877		636
Agent 16 228 E 45th St .... New York NY 10017	212-367-3800		4
Agentis 29 N Wacker Dr Ste 200 .... Chicago IL 60606 *Web:* www.agentisenergy.com	630-359-6210		387
Agentours Inc 126 W Portal Ave .... San Francisco CA 94127 *Web:* www.agentours.com	415-661-5200		760
Aget Manufacturing Co 1408 E Church St .... Adrian MI 49221 *TF:* 800-832-2438 ■ *Web:* www.agetmfg.com	517-263-5781	263-7154	18
AgeVenture News Service 19432 Preserve Dr .... Boca Raton FL 33428 *Web:* www.demko.com	904-629-6020		530
AGF Burner Inc 814 Asbury Ave .... Asbury Park NJ 07712 *Web:* www.agfburner.com	732-730-8090	730-8060	318

	Phone	Fax	Class
AGF Management Ltd 66 Wellington St W 31st Fl .... Toronto ON M5K1E9 *TF:* 800-268-8583 ■ *Web:* www.agf.com	905-214-8203	214-8243	401
AGFA Corp 611 River Dr .... Elmwood Park NJ 07407 *TF:* 888-274-8626 ■ *Web:* www.agfa.com	201-373-4025		591
AGFA HealthCare Corp 10 S Academy St .... Greenville SC 29601 *Web:* global.agfahealthcare.com	864-421-1600		178-10
Agfinity 260 Factory Rd .... Eaton CO 80615 *TF:* 800-433-4688 ■ *Web:* www.agfinityinc.com	970-454-4000		276
Aggreko 15600 John F Kennedy Blvd Ste 600 .... Houston TX 77032 *TF:* 833-507-6491 ■ *Web:* www.aggreko.com	844-550-3618		264-3
AGH (Aarons Grant & Habif LLC) 3500 Piedmont Rd Ste 600 .... Atlanta GA 30305 *Web:* aghllc.com	404-233-5486	237-8325	2
AGI (American Geosciences Institute) 4220 King St .... Alexandria VA 22302 *Web:* www.americangeosciences.org	703-379-2480	379-7563	49-19
AGI (Audio General Inc) 1680 Republic Rd .... Huntingdon Valley PA 19006 *TF:* 866-866-2600 ■ *Web:* www.audiogeneral.com	267-288-0300	288-0301	514
AGI (Alexander Group Inc, The) 8155 E Indian Bend Rd Ste 111 .... Scottsdale AZ 85250 *Web:* www.alexandergroup.com	480-998-9644		194
AGI (Guttmacher Institute) 125 Maiden Ln 7th Fl .... New York NY 10038 *TF:* 800-355-0244 ■ *Web:* www.guttmacher.org	212-248-1111	248-1951	48-5
AGI (Active Grinding Inc) 871 S Rose Pl .... Anaheim CA 92805 *Web:* www.activegrind.com	714-772-7610	772-2163	481
AGI Goldratt Institute 440 Wheelers Farms Rd Ste 304 .... Milford CT 06461 *Web:* www.goldratt.com	203-624-9026		261
AGI Industries Inc 2110 S W Evangeline Thwy .... LaFayette LA 70508 *TF:* 800-256-8101 ■ *Web:* www.agiindustries.com	337-233-0626	233-0828	539
Agile Frameworks 10900 Hampshire Ave S Ste 110 .... Bloomington MN 55438 *TF:* 800-779-1196 ■ *Web:* www.agileframeworks.com	800-779-1196		631
Agile Sourcing Partners Inc 2385 Railroad St .... Corona CA 92880 *TF:* 888-718-1988 ■ *Web:* agilesourcingpartners.com	888-718-1988		612
Agile Ticketing Solutions 3810 Central Pk Ste 301 .... Hermitage TN 37076 *Web:* agiletix.com	615-360-6700		376
AgileAssets Inc 3001 Bee Caves Rd Ste 200 .... Austin TX 78746 *TF:* 800-877-8734 ■ *Web:* www.agileassets.com	512-327-4200		177
AgileCat 1818 Market St Ste 220 .... Philadelphia PA 19103 *Web:* agilecat.com	215-508-2082		195
Agilence Inc 1020 Briggs Rd Ste 110 .... Mount Laurel NJ 08054 *Web:* www.agilenceinc.com	856-366-1200		177
Agilent Technologies 5301 Stevens Creek Blvd .... Santa Clara CA 95051 *NYSE: A* ■ *TF:* 800-227-9770 ■ *Web:* www.agilent.com	800-227-9770		419
Agilepath Corp 4 Middle St Ste 208 .... Newburyport MA 01950 *Web:* agile-path.com	978-462-5737		177
Agilis Engineering Inc 3930 Rca Blvd Ste 3000 .... Palm Beach Gardens FL 33410 *Web:* www.agilis.com	561-626-8900		21
Agilis Software LLC 548 Market St Ste 95777 .... San Francisco CA 94104 *Web:* www.agilis-sw.com	415-458-2614		178-1
Agilith Capital Inc 20 Queen St W Ste 3311 PO Box 30 .... Toronto ON M5H3R3 *TF:* 866-345-1231 ■ *Web:* agilith.com	416-915-0284		528
Agility 480 Production Ave .... Madison AL 35758 *Web:* www.agility.com	256-772-7743		770
Agility Manufacturing Inc 279 Locust St .... Dover NH 03820 *Web:* www.agilitymfg.com	603-742-7339		625
AgilQuest Corp 9407 Hull St Rd .... Richmond VA 23236 *TF:* 888-745-7455 ■ *Web:* agilquest.com	804-745-0467	745-6243	178-1
Agiltron Inc 15 Presidential Way .... Woburn MA 01801 *Web:* www.agiltron.com	781-935-1200	935-2040	392
Agilysys NV LLC 1000 Windward Concourse Ste 250 .... Alpharetta GA 30005 *TF:* 800-241-8768 ■ *Web:* www.agilysys.com	770-810-7800		177
Aging Aircraft Consulting LLC 64 Green St .... Warner Robins GA 31093 *Web:* www.agingaircraftconsulting.com	478-923-8786		261
Aging At Home Ltd 142 Mineola Blvd .... Mineola NY 11501 *Web:* aahny.com	516-746-6451		363
Aging Life Care Assn 3275 W Ina Rd Ste 130 .... Tucson AZ 85741 *Web:* www.aginglifecare.org	520-881-8008	325-7925	49-8
Aging News Alert 8204 Fenton St .... Silver Spring MD 20910 *TF:* 800-666-6380 ■ *Web:* www.cdpublications.com	301-588-6385		531-8
AGIS LLC 16 Poplar St .... Ambler PA 19002 *Web:* www.agismfg.com	215-646-8010	646-8013	326
Agissar Corp 526 Benton St .... Stratford CT 06615 *Web:* www.agissar.com	203-375-8662		111
Agj Systems & Networks Inc 14257 Dedeaux Rd .... Gulfport MS 39503 *Web:* www.agjsystems.com	228-392-7133	392-7601	180
Agland Coop 300 US Hwy 2 .... Wolf Point MT 59201 *Web:* www.agland-coop.com	406-653-1510		579
Agland Coop 115 S First St .... Parkston SD 57366 *TF:* 800-201-3381 ■ *Web:* www.aglandsd.net	605-928-3381	928-3653	276
AG-Land FS Inc 1505 Valle Vista Blvd .... Pekin IL 61554 *Web:* www.aglandfs.com	309-346-4145		276
AG-Land Implement Inc 1819 McCloud Ave PO Box 31 .... New Hampton IA 50659 *Web:* www.aglandimp.com	641-394-4226	394-3936	274
Agler & Gaeddert, Chartered 1225 W Sixth Ave .... Emporia KS 66801 *Web:* agc-cpas.com	620-342-7641		2

				Phone	Fax	Class
AGM (Associated Grant Makers Inc) 133 Federal St Ste 802 *Web:* www.agmconnect.org	Boston	MA	02110	617-426-2606	426-2849	634
AGM Container Controls Inc 3526 E Ft Lowell Rd *TF:* 800-995-5590 ■ *Web:* www.agmcontainer.com	Tucson	AZ	85716	520-881-2130	881-4983	350
AGM Industries Inc 16 Jonathan Dr *TF:* 800-225-9990 ■ *Web:* www.agmind.com	Brockton	MA	02301	508-587-3900		811
AGMA (American Guild of Musical Artists) 1430 Broadway 14th Fl *TF:* 800-543-2462 ■ *Web:* www.musicalartists.org	New York	NY	10018	212-265-3687	262-9088	48-4
AGMA (American Gear Manufacturers Assn) 500 Montgomery St Ste 350 *Web:* www.agma.org	Alexandria	VA	22314	703-684-0211	684-0242	49-13
Agmet LLC 7800 Medusa Rd *Web:* agmet-us.com	Oakwood Village	OH	44146	440-439-7400	439-7446	686
AGN International-North America 2851 S Parker Rd Ste 850 *TF:* 800-782-2272 ■ *Web:* www.agn.org	Aurora	CO	80014	303-743-7880	743-7660	49-1
Agnes Scott College 141 E College Ave *TF:* 800-868-8602 ■ *Web:* agnesscott.edu	Decatur	GA	30030	404-471-6000	471-6414	166
Agnew Associates Inc 13033 Quaker Ave Ste A *Web:* www.agnewassociates.com	Lubbock	TX	79423	806-799-0753	799-2014	261
Agnew Multilingual 741 Lakefield Rd Ste C *Web:* www.agnew.com	Thousand Oaks	CA	91361	805-494-3999		768
Agnico-Eagle Mines Ltd 145 King St E Ste 500 *NYSE:* AEM ■ *TF:* 888-822-6714 ■ *Web:* www.agnicoeagle.com	Toronto	ON	M5C2Y7	416-947-1212	367-4681	502
Agnik LLC 8840 Stanford Blvd Ste 1300 *Web:* www.agnik.com	Columbia	MD	21045	410-290-0864		177
AgniTEK LLC 424 Tarrow *Web:* www.agnitek.com	College Station	TX	77840	979-260-8324		180
AGO (American Guild of Organists) 475 Riverside Dr Ste 1260 *TF:* 855-631-0759 ■ *Web:* www.agohq.org	New York	NY	10115	212-870-2310	870-2163	48-4
AGO Industries Inc 500 Sovereign Rd PO Box 7132 *Web:* www.ago1.com	London	ON	N6M1A4	519-452-3780	452-3053	576
Agora 2101 28th St N *Web:* www.agoraedge.com	Saint Petersburg	FL	33713	727-321-0707		432
Agora Inc 2804 Mission College Blvd Ste 110 *Web:* www.agora.io	Santa Clara	CA	95054	408-879-5885		178-1
AGPA (American Group Psychotherapy Assn) 25 E 21st St 6th Fl *TF:* 877-668-2472 ■ *Web:* www.agpa.org	New York	NY	10010	212-477-2677	979-6627	49-15
AgPark 822 15th St *Web:* www.agpark.com	Columbus	NE	68601	402-564-0133		642
AG-Pro Cos 4281 US-84 *Web:* agprocompanies.com	Dixie	GA	31629	229-263-4133		274
AGR Group Nevada LLC 6275 S Pearl St Ste 100-300 **Fax Area Code:* 702 ■ *TF:* 877-860-5780 ■ *Web:* agrgroupinc.com	Las Vegas	NV	89120	877-860-5780	410-5785*	737
AGR International Inc 615 Whitestown Rd *Web:* www.agrintl.com	Butler	PA	16001	724-482-2163	482-2767	472
AGRA Industries Inc 1211 W Water St *TF:* 800-842-8033 ■ *Web:* www.agraind.com	Merrill	WI	54452	715-536-9584		261
Agrace HospiceCare 5395 E Cheryl Pkwy *TF:* 800-553-4289 ■ *Web:* www.agrace.org	Madison	WI	53711	608-276-4660	276-4672	371
Agracel Inc 2201 Willenborg Ave *Web:* agracel.com	Effingham	IL	62401	217-342-4443		271
Agralite Electric Co-op 320 Hwy 12 SE *TF:* 800-950-8375 ■ *Web:* www.agralite.coop	Benson	MN	56215	320-843-4150	843-3738	245
Agrecolor Inc 400 Sagamore Ave *TF:* 866-506-1781 ■ *Web:* www.agrecolor.com	Mineola	NY	11501	516-741-8700		627
Agree Realty Corp 70 E Long Lake Rd *NYSE:* ADC ■ *Web:* www.agreerealty.com	Bloomfield Hills	MI	48304	248-737-4190		655
AgreeYa Solutions Inc 605 Coolidge Dr **Fax Area Code:* 925 ■ *Web:* www.agreeya.com	Folsom	CA	95630	916-294-0075	369-7135*	463
Agren Appliance Service Corp 40 Minot Ave *TF:* 800-335-0235 ■ *Web:* agrenappliance.com	Auburn	ME	04210	800-335-0235		35
Agrex Inc 10975 Grandview Dr St Ste 200 *TF:* 800-523-8181 ■ *Web:* www.agrexinc.com	Overland Park	KS	66210	913-851-6300		10-4
Agri Beef Co 1555 Shoreline Dr Ste 320 *TF:* 800-657-6305 ■ *Web:* www.agribeef.com	Boise	ID	83702	208-338-2500	338-2605	10-1
Agri Bolt & Cabinet Co 18134 Hwy 71 *Web:* agribolt.com	Carroll	IA	51401	712-792-3376	792-2427	321
Agri Drain Corp 1462 340th St *TF:* 800-232-4742 ■ *Web:* www.agridrain.com	Adair	IA	50002	800-232-4742	282-3353	605-2
Agri Feed Pet Supply 5716 Middlebrooke Pke *Web:* www.agrifeedpetsupply.com	Knoxville	TN	37921	865-584-3959		276
Agri Ventilation Systems LLC 3101 John Wayland Hwy *Web:* www.agrivent.com	Dayton	VA	22821	540-879-9864	879-9948	18
agriCAREERS Inc 613 Main St *TF:* 800-633-8387 ■ *Web:* www.agricareersinc.com	Massena	IA	50853	712-779-3300		260
Agricenter International Inc 7777 Walnut Grove Rd Ste 9 *Web:* www.agricenter.org	Memphis	TN	38120	901-757-7777		232
Agricor Inc 1626 S Joaquin Dr *Web:* agricor.org	Marion	IN	46953	765-662-0606		11-1
Agricultural Commodities Inc 2224 Oxford Rd *TF:* 800-359-8899 ■ *Web:* www.agcominc.com	New Oxford	PA	17350	717-624-8249	624-3216	280
Agricultural Retailers Assn (ARA) 1156 15th St NW Ste 500 *TF:* 800-535-6272 ■ *Web:* www.aradc.org	Washington	DC	20005	202-457-0825	457-0864	48-2
Agricultural Workers Mutual Auto Insurance Co PO Box 88 *TF:* 800-772-7424 ■ *Web:* agworkers.com	Fort Worth	TX	76101	817-831-9900	831-7565	391-4
Agriculture Council of America (ACA) 11020 King St Ste 205 *Web:* www.agday.org	Overland Park	KS	66210	913-491-1895		48-2
Agri-Education Inc 801 Shakespeare Ave *Web:* www.agri-ed.com	Stratford	IA	50249	515-838-3000	838-2788	393
Agri-Empire Corp 630 W 7th St PO Box 490	San Jacinto	CA	92583	951-654-7311		10-11
Agri-Fab Inc 809 S Hamilton St *TF:* 800-448-9282 ■ *Web:* www.agri-fab.com	Sullivan	IL	61951	800-448-9282		360-3
AgriGold Hybrids 5381 Akin Rd **Fax Area Code:* 618 ■ *TF:* 800-262-7333 ■ *Web:* www.agrigold.com	Saint Francisville	IL	62460	800-262-7333	943-7333*	694
Agri-Industrial Plastics Co 301 N 22nd St *Web:* www.agriindustrialplastics.com	Fairfield	IA	52556	641-472-4188	472-7120	604
Agri-King Inc 18246 Waller Rd *TF:* 800-435-9560 ■ *Web:* www.agriking.com	Fulton	IL	61252	800-435-9560		447
Agrilectric Power Inc 3063 Hwy 397 *Web:* agrilectric.com	Lake Charles	LA	70615	337-430-0006	421-6344	477
Agri-Mark Inc PO Box 5800 *TF:* 800-225-0532 ■ *Web:* www.agrimark.coop	Lawrence	MA	01842	978-689-4442	794-8304	296-27
AgriNorthwest 6716 W Rio Grande *Web:* www.agrinorthwest.com	Kennewick	WA	99336	509-734-1195		10-5
Agri-Sales Associates Inc 209 Louise Ave *TF:* 800-251-1141 ■ *Web:* www.agri-sales.com	Nashville	TN	37203	615-329-1141	329-2770	274
Agri-Service 300 Agri-Service Way *TF:* 800-388-3599 ■ *Web:* www.agri-service.com	Kimberly	ID	83341	208-734-7772	734-7775	274
Agron Inc 2440 S Sepulveda Blvd Ste 201 *TF:* 800-966-7697 ■ *Web:* www.agron.com	Los Angeles	CA	90064	800-966-7697		34
AGS (American Gem Society) 8881 W Sahara Ave **Fax Area Code:* 702 ■ *TF:* 866-805-6500 ■ *Web:* www.americangemsociety.org	Las Vegas	NV	89117	866-805-6500	255-7420*	49-4
AGS (Ageatia Global Soultions) 949 N Plum Grove Rd *Web:* www.ageatia.com	Schaumburg	IL	60173	847 517 0415	517-7790	194
AGS (American Gaming Supply Inc) 729 Kohler St *TF:* 866-765-3731 ■ *Web:* www.americangamingsupply.com	Los Angeles	CA	90021	213-228-2447	402-5250	320
AGS (Augusta Regional Airport - Bush Field) 1501 Aviation Way *Web:* www.flyags.com	Augusta	GA	30906	706-798-3236	798-1551	27
AGS BookWorks PO Box 460313 *Web:* www.agsbookworks.com	San Francisco	CA	94146	415-285-8799		94
AGS Custom Graphics Inc 8107 Bavaria Rd *Web:* www.agscustomgraphics.com	Macedonia	OH	44056	330-963-7770		627
AgScience Inc 206 W Bridgers Ave *Web:* www.agsciencebookstore.com	Auburndale	FL	33823	863-967-8898		637-2
Agsco Corp 160 W Hintz Rd *Web:* www.agsco.com	Wheeling	IL	60090	847-520-4455		1
AGSI 800 Battery Ave SE Ste 100 *TF:* 800-768-2474 ■ *Web:* www.agsi.com	Atlanta	GA	30339	404-816-7577		180
AGSI (Alliance Group Services Inc) 1221 Post Rd E **Fax Area Code:* 203 ■ *TF:* 800-756-2236 ■ *Web:* www.alliancegrp.com	Westport	CT	06880	800-756-2236	221-8705*	224
AgSource Cooperative Services 106 N Cecil St *Web:* laboratories.agsource.com	Bonduel	WI	54107	608-845-1900		368
AGTA (American Gem Trade Assn) 3030 LBJ Fwy Ste 840 *TF:* 800-972-1162 ■ *Web:* agta.org	Dallas	TX	75234	214-742-4367	742-7334	49-4
AGU (American Geophysical Union) 2000 Florida Ave NW *TF:* 800-966-2481 ■ *Web:* www.agu.org	Washington	DC	20009	202-462-6900	328-0566	49-19
Agua Caliente Casino Resort Spa 32-250 Bob Hope Dr *TF:* 866-923-7244 ■ *Web:* www.hotwatercasino.com	Rancho Mirage	CA	92270	866-923-7244		133
Agua Caliente Cultural Museum 219 S Palm Canyon Dr *Web:* www.accmuseum.org	Palm Springs	CA	92262	760-778-1079		520
Agua Verde Cafe 1303 NE Boat St *Web:* aguaverde.com	Seattle	WA	98105	206-545-8570		671
Agudath Israel of America 42 Broadway 14th Fl **Fax Area Code:* 646 ■ *Web:* ourlli.org	New York	NY	10004	212-797-9000	254-1600*	48-20
Aguilar Pete (Rep D - CA) 109 Cannon House Office Bldg *Web:* aguilar.house.gov	Washington	DC	20515	202-225-3201	226-6962	342-2
Aguirre Roden Inc 10670 N Central Expwy 6th Fl *Web:* aguirreroden.com	Dallas	TX	75231	972-788-1508	788-1583	261
AgustaWestland Philadelphia Corp 3020 Red Lion Rd *Web:* www.agustawestland.com	Philadelphia	PA	19114	215-281-1400		21
AGVA (American Guild of Variety Artists) 363 Seventh Ave 17th Fl *TF:* 800-331-0890 ■ *Web:* agvausa.com	New York	NY	10001	212-675-1003	633-0097	48-4
AgVantage FS Inc 1600 Eigth St SW **Fax Area Code:* 319 ■ *TF:* 800-346-0058 ■ *Web:* www.agvantagefs.com	Waverly	IA	50677	800-346-0058	483-4992*	276
AgVenture McKillip Seeds 565 N 500 W *Web:* www.mckillipseeds.com	Wabash	IN	46992	260-563-3833	563-4141	276
Agview FS Inc Walton Plant 902 IL Rt 26 *Web:* www.agviewfs.com	Amboy	IL	61310	815-456-4522		276
AH Computer Services Inc 7221 Aloma Ave Ste 300 *Web:* ahcomputers.net	Winter Park	FL	32792	407-671-3557		175
AH Stephens State Historic Park 456 Alexander St NW *Web:* gastateparks.org	Crawfordville	GA	30631	706-456-2602		565
AHA (American Hydrogen Assn) 2350 W Shangri La *Web:* www.clean-air.org	Phoenix	AZ	85029	602-328-4238		48-12
AHA (American Heart Assn) 7272 Greenville Ave *TF:* 800-242-8721 ■ *Web:* www.heart.org	Dallas	TX	75231	214-373-6300		48-17

Name / Address	Phone	Fax	Class
AHA (American Historical Assn) 400 A St SE .... Washington DC 20003 *Web:* www.historians.org	202-544-2422	544-8307	49-5
AHA (American Hospital Assn) 155 N Wacker Dr. .... Chicago IL 60606 *TF:* 800-424-4301 ■ *Web:* www.aha.org	312-422-3000		49-8
AHA (American Humane Assn) 63 Inverness Dr E .... Englewood CO 80112 *Fax Area Code: 303 ■ *TF:* 800-227-4645 ■ *Web:* www.americanhumane.org	800-227-4645	792-5333*	48-6
AHA (Arabian Horse Assn) 10805 E Bethany Dr .... Aurora CO 80014 *Web:* www.arabianhorses.org	303-696-4500	696-4599	48-3
AHA (American Homeowners Assn) 3001 Summer St. .... Stamford CT 06905 *TF:* 800-470-2242 ■ *Web:* www.ahahome.com	203-323-7715		226
AHA (Anne Holmes & Associates) 9672 US Hwy 20 W .... Galena IL 61036 *Fax Area Code: 888 ■ *TF:* 800-465-6373 ■ *Web:* www.anneholmes.com	815-777-2523	465-6378*	196
AHA Consulting Engineers Inc 24 Hartwell Ave 3rd Fl .... Lexington MA 02421 *Web:* www.aha-engineers.com	781-372-3000		261
AHA Labs Inc 20 Gloria Cir .... Menlo Park CA 94025 *TF:* 888-926-2240 ■ *Web:* www.aha.io	888-926-2240		39
AHAM (Association of Home Appliance Manufacturers) 1111 19th St NW Ste 402 .... Washington DC 20036 *TF:* 800-829-5034 ■ *Web:* www.aham.org	202-872-5955	872-9354	49-4
AHAUS 200 Industrial Pkwy .... Richmond IN 47374 *Web:* www.ahaus.com	765-962-3571	962-3426	757
AHAVA North America 330 Seventh Ave. .... New York NY 10001 *TF:* 800-366-7254 ■ *Web:* www.ahava.com	800-366-7254		214
AHBL Inc 2215 N 30th St Ste 300 .... Tacoma WA 98403 *Web:* www.ahbl.com	253-383-2422	383-2572	261
AHC (Association of Academic Health Centers) 1400 16th St NW Ste 720 .... Washington DC 20036 *Web:* www.aahcdc.org	202-265-9600	265-7514	49-8
AHC (American Horse Council) 1616 H St NW 7th Fl. .... Washington DC 20006 *Web:* www.horsecouncil.org	202-296-4031	296-1970	48-3
AHC Inc 2230 N Fairfax Dr Ste 100 .... Arlington VA 22201 *Web:* www.ahcinc.org	703-486-0626		196
AHCA (American Health Care Assn) 1201 L St NW .... Washington DC 20005 *TF:* 800-321-0343 ■ *Web:* www.ahcancal.org	202-842-4444	842-3860	49-8
AHDI (Association for Healthcare Documentation Integrity) 4230 Kiernan Ave Ste 130 .... Modesto CA 95356 *TF:* 800-982-2182 ■ *Web:* www.ahdionline.org	209-527-9620	527-9633	49-8
Ahead Hum Resources 2209 Heather Ln .... Louisville KY 40218 *TF:* 888-749-1000 ■ *Web:* aheadhr.com	502-485-1000		177
Ahead LLC 270 Samuel Barnet Blvd .... New Bedford MA 02745 *TF:* 800-282-2246 ■ *Web:* www.aheadweb.com	508-985-9898	985-2371	155-9
AheadTek Inc 6410 Via Del Oro .... San Jose CA 95119 *TF:* 800-971-9191 ■ *Web:* www.aheadtek.com	408-226-9991	226-9195	647
Ahearn & Soper Inc 100 Woodbine Downs Blvd. .... Toronto ON M9W5S6 *TF:* 800-263-4258 ■ *Web:* www.ahearn.com	416-675-3999	675-3457	174
AHEPA (American Hellenic Educational Progressive Assn) 1909 Q St NW Ste 500 .... Washington DC 20009 *TF:* 855-473-3512 ■ *Web:* ahepa.org	202-232-6300	232-2140	48-14
Ahern Rentals Inc 4241 Arville St .... Las Vegas NV 89103 *TF:* 800-589-6797 ■ *Web:* www.ahern.com	702-362-0623		264-3
Ahern, Adcock, Devlin LLP 1650 Iowa Ave Ste 200 .... Riverside CA 92507	951-683-0672		2
AHF (American Homeowners Foundation) 6776 Little Falls Rd .... Arlington VA 22213 *TF:* 800-489-7776 ■ *Web:* www.americanhomeowners.org	800-489-7776		49-17
AHHA (American Holistic Health Assn) PO Box 17400 .... Anaheim CA 92817 *Web:* ahha.org	714-779-6152		48-17
AHI (Animal Health Institute) 1325 G St NW Ste 700 .... Washington DC 20005 *Web:* www.ahi.org	202-637-2440		48-3
AHI (AHI Facility Services Inc) 1253 Round Table Dr .... Dallas TX 75247 *TF:* 800-472-5749 ■ *Web:* www.ahifs.com	214-741-3714		104
AHI Facility Services Inc (AHI) 1253 Round Table Dr .... Dallas TX 75247 *TF:* 800-472-5749 ■ *Web:* www.ahifs.com	214-741-3714		104
AHI International Corp 8550 W Bryn Mawr Ave Ste 600 .... Chicago IL 60631 *TF:* 800-323-7373 ■ *Web:* www.ahitravel.com	800-323-7373		760
AHI Supply 2800 N Gordon PO Box 2789 .... Alvin TX 77512 *TF:* 800-873-5794 ■ *Web:* www.ahi-supply.com	281-331-0088		191-1
AHIA (Association of Healthcare Internal Auditors) 10200 W 44th Ave Ste 304 .... Wheat Ridge CO 80033 *TF:* 888-275-2442 ■ *Web:* www.ahia.org	303-327-7546	422-8894	49-1
AHIMA (American Health Information Management Assn) 233 N Michigan Ave 21st Fl .... Chicago IL 60601 *TF:* 800-335-5535 ■ *Web:* www.ahima.org	312-233-1100	233-1090	49-8
AHIP (America's Health Insurance Plans) 601 Pennsylvania Ave NW Ste 500 .... Washington DC 20004 *TF:* 800-509-4422 ■ *Web:* www.ahip.org	202-778-3200	331-7487	49-9
AHJ Engineers PC 5418 N Eagle Rd Ste 140 .... Boise ID 83713 *Web:* www.ahjengineers.com	208-323-0199		261
Ahjumawi Lava Springs State Park c/o Northern Buttes District Ofc 400 Glen Dr .... Oroville CA 95966 *Web:* www.parks.ca.gov	530-538-2200		565
AHLA (Alberta Hotel & Lodging Assn) 2707 Ellwood Dr .... Edmonton AB T6X0P7 *TF:* 888-436-6112 ■ *Web:* www.ahla.ca	780-436-6112	436-5404	48-23
AH&LA (American Hotel & Lodging Assn) 1201 New York Ave NW Ste 600 .... Washington DC 20005 *Web:* www.ahla.com	202-289-3100		48-23
AHLA (American Health Lawyers Assn) 1620 Eye St NW 6th Fl .... Washington DC 20006 *Web:* www.americanhealthlaw.org	202-833-1100	833-1105	49-10
Ahlstrom-Munksjo 122 W Butler St Mt Holly Springs Plant .... Mount Holly Springs PA 17065 *Web:* www.ahlstrom-munksjo.com	717-486-3438		557
Ahlum & Arbor Tree Preservation 1740 Walcutt Rd .... Columbus OH 43228 *Web:* ahlumarbor.com	614-876-5622		422
Ahmad's Persian Cuisine 4646 Dodge St .... Omaha NE 68132 *Web:* www.ahmadspersiancuisine.com	402-341-9616		671
Ahmad, Zavitsanos, Anaipakos, Alavi & Mensing PC 1 Houston Ctr 1221 McKinney St Ste 3460 .... Houston TX 77010 *TF:* 800-856-8153 ■ *Web:* azalaw.com	713-655-1101		428
Ahmanson Foundation 9215 Wilshire Blvd .... Beverly Hills CA 90210 *Web:* www.theahmansonfoundation.org	310-278-0770		305
Ahmuty, Demers & McManus 200 IU Willets Rd .... Albertson NY 11507 *Web:* www.admlaw.com	516-294-5433		428
AHNA (American Holistic Nurses Assn) 2900 SW Plass Ct. .... Topeka KS 66611 *TF:* 800-278-2462 ■ *Web:* www.ahna.org	785-234-1712	234-1713	48-17
Ahni Health Services Inc 119 SW Main .... Keota OK 74941 *TF:* 855-524-4125 ■ *Web:* ahnihealthservices.com	918-966-3322	966-3319	363
Ahola Corp, The 6820 W Snowville Rd .... Brecksville OH 44141 *TF:* 800-727-2849 ■ *Web:* www.ahola.com	800-727-2849		2
Ahoskie Chamber of Commerce 310 S Catherine Creek Rd PO Box 7 .... Ahoskie NC 27910 *Web:* www.ahoskiechamber.net	252-332-2042	332-8617	139
AHP (Association for Healthcare Philanthropy) 313 Park Ave Ste 400 .... Falls Church VA 22046 *Web:* www.ahp.org	703-532-6243	532-7170	49-8
AHP (American History Press) 404 Locust St .... Staunton VA 24401 *TF:* 888-521-1789 ■ *Web:* americanhistorypress.com	888-521-1789		637-2
AHPA (American Herbal Products Assn) 8630 Fenton St Ste 918 .... Silver Spring MD 20910 *TF:* 800-358-2104 ■ *Web:* www.ahpa.org	301-588-1171	588-1174	49-8
AHR Metals Inc 20 Division St .... Bessemer AL 35020 *Web:* ahrmetals.com	205-428-8888		697
AHRA (American Healthcare Radiology Administrators) 490-B Boston Post Rd Ste 200 .... Sudbury MA 01776 *TF:* 800-334-2472 ■ *Web:* www.ahra.org	978-443-7591	443-8046	49-8
Ahrberg Milling Co 200 S Depot PO Box 968 .... Cushing OK 74023 *TF:* 800-324-0267 ■ *Web:* ahrbergmilling.com	918-225-0267		447
Ahrens, Fuller, St John & Vincent Inc 1699 King St Ste 209 .... Enfield CT 06082 *Web:* afsvinsurance.com	860-668-3960		390
Ahresty Wilmington Corp 2627 S South St .... Wilmington OH 45177 *Web:* www.ahresty.com	937-382-6112	382-5871	308
AHRI - Air-Conditioning Heating & Refrigeration Institute 4100 N Fairfax Dr Ste 200 .... Arlington VA 22203 *Web:* www.ahrinet.org	703-524-8800	528-3816	49-4
AHS (American Headache Society) 19 Mantua Rd .... Mount Royal NJ 08061 *Web:* americanheadachesociety.org	856-423-0043	423-0082	49-8
AHS (American Hiking Society) 8605 Second Ave .... Silver Spring MD 20910 *TF:* 800-972-8608 ■ *Web:* americanhiking.org	301-565-6704		48-23
AHS (American Horticultural Society) 7931 E Blvd Dr .... Alexandria VA 22308 *TF:* 800-777-7931 ■ *Web:* ahsgardening.org	703-768-5700	768-8700	48-18
AHS (Ames Historical Society) 416 Douglas Ave Ste 101 .... Ames IA 50010 *Web:* www.ameshistory.org	515-232-2148		49-19
Ahsahta Press 1910 University Dr Education Bldg Ste 726 .... Boise ID 83725 *Web:* www.ahsahtapress.org	208-866-8017		637-2
Ah-So 1919 S Gilbert Rd .... Mesa AZ 85204 *Web:* ahsomesa.com	480-497-1114		671
Ahtna Engineering Services LLC 110 W 38th Ave Ste 100 .... Anchorage AK 99503 *Web:* www.ahtnaes.com	907-646-2969		261
Ahwatukee Foothills News 10631 S 51st St Ste 1 .... Phoenix AZ 85044 *Web:* www.ahwatukee.com	480-898-7900		532-4
AI Control Systems 90 Water St .... Muhlenberg PA 19605 *Web:* aicontrols.com	610-921-9670		463
AI Signal Research Inc 2001 Nichols Dr SW Ste 300 .... Huntsville AL 35802 *Web:* www.aisignal.com	256-551-0008	551-0099	261
AI Software Inc 250 E Fifth St Ste 1500 .... Cincinnati OH 45202 *TF:* 866-987-8889 ■ *Web:* aisoftware.us	866-987-8889		177
AI Squared 130 Taconic Business Park Rd .... Manchester Center VT 05255 *TF:* 800-859-0270 ■ *Web:* www.aisquared.com	802-362-3612	362-1670	178-1
AI Technology Inc (AIT) 70 Washington Rd .... Princeton Junction NJ 08550 *TF:* 800-735-5040 ■ *Web:* www.aitechnology.com	609-799-9388	799-9308	801
AIA (AIA Corp) 800 Winneconne Ave .... Neenah WI 54956 *Web:* aiacommunity.com	920-886-3734		9
AIA (Aerospace Industries Assn) 1000 Wilson Blvd Ste 1700 .... Arlington VA 22209 *Web:* www.aia-aerospace.org	703-358-1000		49-21
AIA (American Institute of Architects) 1735 New York Ave NW .... Washington DC 20006 *TF:* 800-242-3837 ■ *Web:* www.aia.org	202-626-7300	626-7547	48-4
AIA (Archaeological Institute of America) 44 Beacon St .... Boston MA 02108 *TF:* 877-524-6300 ■ *Web:* www.archaeological.org	617-353-9361	353-6550	48-11
AIA Benefit Advisors Inc 13747 Montfort Dr Ste 260 .... Dallas TX 75240 *Web:* aiabenefits.com	972-519-0721		390
AIA Corp (AIA) 800 Winneconne Ave .... Neenah WI 54956 *Web:* aiacommunity.com	920-886-3734		9

Name / Address	City	State	Zip	Phone	Fax	Class
AIA Engineers Ltd 15310 Park Row	Houston	TX	77084	281-493-4140		261
Web: www.aiaengineering.com						
AIAA (American Institute of Aeronautics & Astronautics Inc)						
12700 Sunrise Valley Dr Ste 200	Reston	VA	20191	703-264-7500	264-7551	49-19
TF: 800-639-2422 ■ *Web:* www.aiaa.org						
AIADA (American International Automobile Dealers Assn)						
500 Montgomery St Ste 800	Alexandria	VA	22314	800-462-4232	519-7810*	49-18
**Fax Area Code:* 703 ■ *TF:* 800-462-4232 ■ *Web:* www.aiada.org						
AIAG (Automotive Industry Action Group)						
26200 Lahser Rd Ste 200	Southfield	MI	48033	248-358-3570	358-3253	49-21
TF: 877-275-2424 ■ *Web:* www.aiag.org						
AIB International Inc						
1213 Bakers Way PO Box 3999	Manhattan	KS	66505	785-537-4750	537-1493	463
TF: 800-633-5137 ■ *Web:* www.aibinternational.com						
AIBS (American Institute of Biological Sciences)						
1313 Dolley Madison Blvd Ste 402	McLean	VA	22101	703-674-2500	674-2509	49-19
Web: www.aibs.org						
AIC (American Institute of Chemists)						
315 Chestnut St	Philadelphia	PA	19106	215-873-8224	925-1954	49-19
Web: www.theaic.org						
AIC (American Institute of Constructors)						
700 N Fairfax St Ste 510	Alexandria	VA	22314	703-683-4999	527-3105*	49-3
**Fax Area Code:* 571 ■ *Web:* www.professionalconstructor.org						
AIC (American Institute for Conservation of Historic & Artistic Works)						
725 15th St NW Ste 500	Washington	DC	20005	202-452-9545	452-9328	48-4
Web: www.culturalheritage.org						
AIC (Alaska Instrument Company Inc)						
907 E Dowling Rd Ste 5	Anchorage	AK	99518	907-561-7511	561-0762	201
Web: www.alaskainstrument.com						
AIC (Association of Idaho Cities)						
3100 S Vista Ave Ste 310	Boise	ID	83705	208-344-8594		637-10
Web: www.idahocities.org						
AIC College of Design						
1171 E Kemper Rd	Cincinnati	OH	45246	513-751-1206		167-3
Web: www.aic-arts.edu						
AIC International Inc PO Box DR	Hagatna	GU	96932	671-565-9142		186
Web: www.aicconstruction.com						
AIC Ventures LP						
4131 N Central Expy Ste 020	Dallas	TX	75204	214-363-5620		653
Web: aicventures.com						
AICA (American-International Charolais Assn)						
11700 NW Plaza Cir	Kansas City	MO	64153	816-464-5977	464-5759	48-2
TF: 800-270-7711 ■ *Web:* charolaisusa.com						
AICC (American-Israel Chamber of Commerce Southeast Region)						
400 Northridge Rd Ste 250	Atlanta	GA	30350	404-843-9426	843-1416	138
Web: www.conexx.org						
AICHE (American Institute of Chemical Engineers)						
120 Wall St 2nd Fl	New York	NY	10005	203-702-7660	775-5177	49-19
TF: 800-242-4363 ■ *Web:* www.aiche.org						
Aichi Forge USA Inc 596 Triport Rd	Georgetown	KY	40324	502-863-7575	863-4928	483
Web: www.aichiforge.com						
AICPA (American Institute of CPAS)						
1211 Avenue of the Americas	New York	NY	10036	212-596-6200	596-6213	49-1
Web: www.aicpa.org						
AICPCU/IIA (American Institute for CPCU & Insurance Institute of America)						
720 Providence Rd Ste 100	Malvern	PA	19355	610-644-2100	640-9576	49-9
TF: 800-644-2101 ■ *Web:* www.theinstitutes.org						
AICR (American Institute for Cancer Research)						
1759 R St NW	Washington	DC	20009	202-328-7744	328-7226	668
TF: 800-843-8114 ■ *Web:* www.aicr.org						
Aid Mailing & Fulfillment						
1988 Leghorn St	Mountain View	CA	94043	650-919-1999	919-1990	5
Web: www.aidmail.com						
AID Maintenance Co						
300 Roosevelt Ave	Pawtucket	RI	02860	401-722-6627	723-6860	104
TF: 800-886-6627 ■ *Web:* www.aidmaintenance.com						
Aida's Bistro 2208 4th St SW	Calgary	AB	T2S1W9	403-541-1189		671
Web: www.aidasbistro.ca						
Aida-America Corp						
7660 Center Point 70 Blvd	Dayton	OH	45424	937-237-2382		455
Web: www.aida-global.com						
Aidells Sausage Company Inc						
1625 Alvarado St	San Leandro	CA	94577	877-243-3557		296-26
TF: 855-600-7697 ■ *Web:* www.aidells.com						
AIDS Foundation of Chicago						
200 W Jackson Blvd Ste 2200	Chicago	IL	60606	312-922-2322		305
Web: www.aidschicago.org						
AIDS Healthcare Foundation						
6255 W Sunset Blvd 21st Fl	Los Angeles	CA	90028	323-860-5200		305
Web: www.aidshealth.org						
AIDS Library						
1233 Locust St 2nd Fl	Philadelphia	PA	19107	215-985-4851	985-4492	434-4
TF: 877-613-4533 ■ *Web:* critpath.org						
AIDS United 1424 K St NW Ste 200	Washington	DC	20005	202-408-4848	408-1818	48-7
Web: www.aidsunited.org						
AIDSinfo PO Box 6303	Rockville	MD	20849	301-315-2816	519-6616	340-10
TF: 800-448-0440 ■ *Web:* aidsinfo.nih.gov						
AIE Pharmaceuticals Inc						
1845 S Vineyard Ave Ste 5	Ontario	CA	91761	909-947-9898	947-9813	582
Web: www.naturalvigor.com						
Aiello Home Services Inc						
600 Old County Cir	Windsor Locks	CT	06096	860-292-2600		610
Web: www.aiellohomeservices.com						
Aiesec Canada Inc						
164 Eglinton Ave E Ste 208	Toronto	ON	M4P1G4	416-978-3335	978-5433	242
Web: www.aiesec.ca						
AIFD (American Institute of Floral Designers)						
9 Newport Dr Ste 200	Forest Hill	MD	21050	443-966-3850	640-1031	49-4
Web: aifd.org						
AIFP (American International Forest Products LLC)						
5560 SW 107th Ave	Beaverton	OR	97005	503-641-1611	641-2800	191-3
TF: 800-366-1611 ■ *Web:* www.lumber.com						
AIG SunAmerica Inc						
21650 Oxnard St	Woodland Hills	CA	91367	800-445-7862		360-4
TF: 800-445-7862 ■ *Web:* www.aig.com						
AIG Technologies Inc						
5001 NW 13th Ave Ste B	Deerfield Beach	FL	33064	954-433-0618		196
Web: www.aigtechnologies.net						
AIGA (American Institute of Graphic Arts)						
164 Fifth Ave	New York	NY	10010	212-807-1990	807-1799	48-4
TF: 800-548-1634 ■ *Web:* www.aiga.org						
Aigner Index Inc						
23 Mac Arthur Ave	New Windsor	NY	12553	845-562-4510	562-2638	608
TF: 800-242-3919 ■ *Web:* www.aignerlabelholder.com						
AIHA (American Industrial Hygiene Assn)						
2700 Prosperity Ave Ste 250	Fairfax	VA	22031	703-849-8888	207-3561	49-13
Web: www.aiha.org						
Aiken and Scoptur						
2600 N Mayfair Rd Ste 1030	Wauwatosa	WI	53226	414-225-0260	225-9666	41
TF: 855-783-3786 ■ *Web:* www.plaintiffslaw.com						
Aiken County 420 Hampton Ave NE	Aiken	SC	29801	803-642-2012		338
TF: 866-876-7074 ■ *Web:* www.aikencountysc.gov						
Aiken Electric Co-opeartive Inc						
2790 Wagener Rd	Aiken	SC	29802	803-649-6245	641-8310	245
TF: 877-264-5368 ■ *Web:* www.aikenco-op.org						
Aiken Regional Medical Centers						
302 University Pkwy	Aiken	SC	29801	803-641-5000		374-3
TF: 800-245-3679 ■ *Web:* www.aikenregional.com						
Aiken State Natural Area						
1145 State Park Rd	Windsor	SC	29856	803-649-2857		565
TF: 866-345-7275 ■ *Web:* southcarolinaparks.com						
Aiken Technical College						
2276 J Davis Hwy	Graniteville	SC	29829	803-593-9231	593-6526	162
TF: 800-246-6198 ■ *Web:* www.atc.edu						
Aiken-Bamberg-Barnwell-Edgefield Regional Library System						
314 Chesterfield St	Aiken	SC	29801	803-642-7575		434-3
Web: www.abbe-lib.org						
Aiken-Rhett House 48 Elizabeth St	Charleston	SC	29401	843-723-1159		50-3
Web: www.historiccharleston.org						
AIL (American Income Life Insurance Co)						
1200 Wooded Acres	Waco	TX	76710	254-761-6400		391-2
TF: 800-433-3405 ■ *Web:* www.ailife.com						
AILA (American Immigration Lawyers Assn)						
918 F St NW	Washington	DC	20004	202-216-2400	783-7853	49-10
TF: 800-982-2839 ■ *Web:* www.aila.org						
Ailey School, The 405 W 55th St	New York	NY	10019	212-405-9000	405-9001	685
Web: www.theaileyschool.edu						
Aillet/Fenner/Jolly/Mcclelland Inc						
3003 Knight St Ste 120	Shreveport	LA	71105	318-425-7452		261
Web: afjmc.com						
AIM (Accuracy in Media Inc)						
4350 E West Hwy Ste 555	Bethesda	MD	20814	202-364-4401	364-4098	49-14
TF: 800-787-4567 ■ *Web:* www.aim.org						
Aim Aerospace Inc 705 SW 7th St	Renton	WA	98057	425-235-2750		22
Web: www.aim-aerospace.com						
AIM Engineering & Surveying Inc						
2161 Fowler St	Fort Myers	FL	33901	239-332-4569		261
Web: www.aimengr.com						
AIM ImmunoTech Inc						
2117 SW Hwy 484 Ste 500	Ocala	FL	34473	352-448-7797		85
NYSE: HEB ■ *Web:* aimimmuno.com						
AIM Inc						
20399 Rte 19 Ste 203	Cranberry Township	PA	16066	724-742-4470	742-4476	49-19
Web: www.aimglobal.org						
AIM Meetings and Events						
212 S Henry St	Alexandria	VA	22314	703-549-9500		184
Web: www.aimmeetings.com						
AIM Mro LLC						
8500 Glendale Milford Rd	Camp Dennison	OH	45111	513-831-2938	831-3859	770
Web: aimmro.com						
AIM Personnel Service 183 Whiting St	Hingham	MA	02043	781-740-8808		260
Web: www.aimpersonnel.com						
AIM Screen Printing Supply LLC						
PO Box 9645	Naperville	IL	60567	630-357-1103		007
TF: 800-515-5841 ■ *Web:* aimsupply.net						
AIM Systems 350 Speedvale Ave W Unit 12	Guelph	ON	N1H7M7	519-837-1072		180
Web: www.aimsystems.ca						
AIMCAL (Association of Industrial Metallizers Coaters & Laminators)						
201 Springs St	Fort Mill	SC	29715	803-802-7820	802-7821	49-13
Web: www.aimcal.org						
Aimclear 9 W Superior St Ste 200	Duluth	MN	55802	218-310-7539		195
Web: www.aimclear.com						
Aimco 10000 SE Pine St	Portland	OR	97216	800-852-1368	582-9015	385
TF: 800-852-1368 ■ *Web:* www.aimco-global.com						
AIME (Association for Information Media & Equipment)						
PO Box 378	West Milton	PA	17866	570-701-4202		48-4
Web: www.aime.org						
AIME (American Institute of Mining Metallurgical & Petroleum Engineers)						
12999 E Adam Aircraft Cir	Englewood	CO	80112	303-325-5185	702-0049*	48-12
**Fax Area Code:* 888 ■ *Web:* www.aimehq.org						
Aimpoint Inc 7309 Gateway Ct	Manassas	VA	20109	703-263-9795	263-9463	21
TF: 877-246-7646 ■ *Web:* aimpoint.us						
Aims Community College 5401 W 20th St	Greeley	CO	80634	970-330-8008	506-6958	162
TF: 800-301-5388 ■ *Web:* www.aims.edu						
AIMS Education Foundation						
1595 S Chestnut Ave	Fresno	CA	93702	559-255-4094	255-6396	196
TF: 888-733-2467 ■ *Web:* www.aimsedu.org						
AIMS Inc 235 Desiard St	Monroe	LA	71201	318-323-2467	322-3472	178-10
TF: 800-729-2467 ■ *Web:* www.aims1.com						
Aimtron Corp 555 S Vermont St	Palatine	IL	60067	630-372-7500	372-7505	625
Web: www.aimtron.com						
AIMU (American Institute of Marine Underwriters)						
14 Wall St Ste 820	New York	NY	10005	212-233-0550	227-5102	49-9
Web: www.aimu.org						
Ain & Gruda Associates PA						
20764 W Dixie Hwy	Aventura	FL	33180	305-931-9844	931-9312	2
TF: 877-931-9844 ■ *Web:* aingruda.com						
Aina Haina Pet Hospital Inc						
3405 Waialae Ave	Honolulu	HI	96816	808-732-9111		794
Web: ainahainapethospital.com						
Ainley & Associates Ltd						
280 Pretty River Pkwy	Collingwood	ON	L9Y4J5	705-445-3451	445-0968	261
Web: www.ainleygroup.com						
Ainsworth Pet Nutrition						
18746 Mill St	Meadville	PA	16335	814-724-7710	337-2743	578
TF: 800-323-7738 ■ *Web:* www.ainsworthpets.com						

	Phone	Fax	Class
Ainsworth Rock Sales Inc 5600 N Washington St . . . . Denver CO 80216 *Web:* www.ainsworthrocksales.com	303-295-2990		191-1
Aioli Bodega Espanola 1800 L St . . . . Sacramento CA 95811 *Web:* www.aiolilabodega.com	916-447-9440		671
AIP (American Institute of Philanthropy) 3450 N Lake Shore Dr . . . . Chicago IL 60657 *Web:* www.charitywatch.org	773-529-2300	529-0024	48-5
AIPAC (American Israel Public Affairs Committee) 251 H St . . . . Washington DC 20001 *Web:* www.aipac.org	202-639-5200		48-7
AIPB (American Institute of Professional Bookkeepers) 6001 Montrose Rd Ste 500 . . . . Rockville MD 20852 *TF:* 800-622-0121 ■ *Web:* www.aipb.org	800-622-0121	541-0066	49-1
AIPG (American Institute of Professional Geologists) 1400 W 122nd Ave Ste 250 . . . . Westminster CO 80234 *TF:* 800-337-3140 ■ *Web:* www.aipg.org	303-412-6205	253-9220	49-19
Aiphone Corp 1700 130th Ave NE . . . . Bellevue WA 98005 *Web:* www.aiphone.com	425-455-0510		693
AIPLA (American Intellectual Property Law Assn) 1400 Crystal Dr Ste 600 . . . . Arlington VA 22202 *Web:* www.aipla.org	703-415-0780	415-0786	49-10
AIR (Association of Independents in Radio) PO Box 220400 . . . . Boston MA 02122 *Web:* airmedia.org	617-825-4400	825-4422	632
Air & Waste Management Assn (A&WMA) 436 Seventh Ave Ste 2100 . . . . Pittsburgh PA 15219 *TF:* 800-270-3444 ■ *Web:* www.awma.org	412-232-3444	232-3450	48-12
Air 1 Radio Network PO Box 2118 . . . . Omaha NE 68103 *TF:* 888-937-2471 ■ *Web:* www.air1.com	888-937-2471		647
Air Age Media 88 Danbury Rd . . . . Wilton CT 06897 *Web:* www.airagestore.com	203-431-9000		457-14
Air Center Inc 1201 E Whitcomb Ave . . . . Madison Heights MI 48071 **Fax Area Code:* 248 ■ *TF:* 800-247-2959 ■ *Web:* www.teamaircenter.com	800-247-2959	268-2651*	358
Air Center Inc, The 270 Monroe Ave . . . . Kenilworth NJ 07033 *Web:* www.aircenternj.com	908-858-5788		358
Air Chair Inc 2175 N Kiowa Blvd Ste 101 . . . . Lake Havasu City AZ 86403 *Web:* www.airchair.com	928-505-2226	505-2229	710
Air Charter Team 4151 N Mulberry Dr Ste 250 . . . . Kansas City MO 64116 *TF:* 800-205-6610 ■ *Web:* www.aircharterteam.com	816-283-3280	283-3185	13
Air Chek Inc 1936 Butler Bridge Rd . . . . Mills River NC 28759 *TF:* 800-247-2435 ■ *Web:* www.radon.com	800-247-2435		196
Air Cleaning Technologies Inc 1300 W Detroit . . . . Broken Arrow OK 74012 *TF:* 800-351-1858 ■ *Web:* www.aircleaningtech.com	918-251-8000		35
Air Combat Command 205 Dodd Blvd Ste 101 . . . . Langley AFB VA 23665 *Web:* www.acc.af.mil	757-764-8346		340-4
Air Comfort Corp 2550 Braga Dr . . . . Broadview IL 60155 *TF:* 800-466-3779 ■ *Web:* www.aircomfort.com	708-345-1900	345-2730	189-10
Air Compressor Products Inc 2362 Emerson St . . . . Jacksonville FL 32207 *TF:* 800-394-5575 ■ *Web:* www.air-compressor.com	904-396-5575		172
Air Compressor Solutions 3001 Kermit Hwy . . . . Odessa TX 79764 *Web:* acsir.com	432-335-5900		317
Air Compressor Supply Inc 3916 S I-35 Service Rd . . . . Oklahoma City OK 73129 *Web:* www.aircompressorsupplyinc.com	405-672-0382	672-5580	172
Air Con Refrigeration & Heating Inc 123 Lake St . . . . Waukegan IL 60085	847-336-4128		189-10
Air Conditioning by Luquire Inc 1155 NE Blvd . . . . Montgomery AL 36117 *Web:* www.acbyluquire.com	334-230-5870		189-10
Air Conditioning Contractors of America (ACCA) 2800 S Shirlington Rd Ste 300 . . . . Arlington VA 22206 *TF:* 888-290-2220 ■ *Web:* www.acca.org	703-575-4477	575-8107	49-3
Air Conditioning Products Co 30350 Ecorse Rd . . . . Romulus MI 48174 *Web:* www.acpshutters.com	734-326-0050	326-9632	697
Air Consulting & Engineering Solutions Ltd 5615 NW Central Dr Ste C109 . . . . Houston TX 77092 *Web:* www.aces-llc.com	713-690-2237		192
Air Contact Transport Inc PO Box 570 . . . . Budd Lake NJ 07828 **Fax Area Code:* 973 ■ *TF:* 800-765-2769 ■ *Web:* actovernight.com	800-765-2769	691-0127*	187
Air Controls Bozeman Inc 7510 Shedhorn Dr . . . . Bozeman MT 59718 *Web:* www.hvacbozeman.com	406-587-6292		189-10
Air Courier Dispatch 12333 S Van Ness Ave . . . . Hawthorne CA 90250 *Web:* www.aics.com	323-777-7072		311
Air Craftsmen Inc 617 N Greensboro St . . . . Lexington NC 27292 *Web:* www.aircraftsmen.com	336-248-5777	248-2460	18
Air Creebec Inc 101 Fecteau St . . . . Val-d'Or QC J9P0G4 *TF:* 800-567-6567 ■ *Web:* www.aircreebec.ca	819-825-8375		12
Air Cruisers Co 1747 New Jersey 34 . . . . Wall Township NJ 07727 *Web:* www.zodiacaerospace.com	732-681-3527		678
Air Cycle Corp 2200 Ogden Ave Ste 100 . . . . Lisle IL 60532 *TF:* 800-909-9709 ■ *Web:* www.aircycle.com	800-909-9709		295
Air Diffusion Systems 3964 Grove Ave . . . . Gurnee IL 60031 *Web:* airdiffusion.com	847-782-0044	782-0055	261
Air Distribution Technologies Inc 605 Shiloh Rd . . . . Plano TX 75074 *Web:* www.airdistribution.com	972-943-6100		18
Air Education & Training Command (AETC) 100 H St Ste 4 . . . . Randolph AFB TX 78150 *Web:* www.aetc.af.mil	210-652-6564	652-2027	340-4
Air Fixtures Inc 1108 N Sycamore St . . . . North Manchester IN 46962 *Web:* www.air-fixtures.com	260-982-2169	982-7839	172
Air Force Assn (AFA) 1501 Lee Hwy . . . . Arlington VA 22209 *TF:* 800-727-3337 ■ *Web:* www.afa.org	703-247-5800	247-5853	48-19
Air Force Federal Credit Union 1560 Cable Ranch Rd Ste 200 . . . . San Antonio TX 78245 *TF:* 800-227-5328 ■ *Web:* goaffcu.com	210-673-5610	673-5102	219
Air Force Materiel Command 4375 Chidlaw Rd Rm N-B225 . . . . Wright-Patterson AFB OH 45433 *Web:* www.afmc.af.mil	937-257-7648		340-4
Air Force medical service 307 Boatner Rd . . . . Eglin AFB FL 32542 *Web:* www.airforcemedicine.af.mil	850-883-9042	883-8112	374-4
Air Force Office of Scientific Research (AFOSR) 875 N Randolph St Ste 325 . . . . Arlington VA 22203 *Web:* www.wpafb.af.mil	703-696-7797		668
Air Force Reserve Command 155 Richard Ray Blvd . . . . Robins Air Force Base GA 31098 *TF:* 800-257-1212 ■ *Web:* www.afrc.af.mil	478-327-1748	327-0625	340-4
Air Force Space Command 150 Vandenberg St . . . . Peterson Air Force Base CO 80914 *TF:* 800-525-0102 ■ *Web:* www.afspc.af.mil	719-554-3731	554-6013	340-4
Air Force Special Operations Command 229 Cody Ave Ste 103 . . . . Hurlburt Field FL 32544 *Web:* www.afsoc.af.mil	850-884-5515		340-4
Air Georgian Ltd 2450 Derry Rd E Shell Aerocentre . . . . Mississauga ON L5S1B2 *Web:* www.airgeorgian.ca	905-676-1221		21
Air Hollywood 13240 Weidner St . . . . Pacoima CA 91331 *Web:* www.airhollywood.com	818-890-0444	890-7041	344
Air India 570 Lexington Ave 15th Fl . . . . New York NY 10022 *TF:* 800-223-7776 ■ *Web:* www.airindia.in	800-223-7776		25
Air Industries Co 12570 Knott St . . . . Garden Grove CA 92841 *Web:* www.air-industries.com	714-892-5571	892-7904	278
Air Industries Group 1460 5th Ave . . . . Bay shore NY 11706 *Web:* www.airindustriesgroup.com	631-328-7083		21
Air Ivanhoe Ltd George & Jeanne Theriault PO Box 99 . . . . Foleyet ON P0M1T0 *TF:* 800-955-2951 ■ *Web:* www.airivanhoe.com	705-899-2155		239
Air Land & Sea Travel Wedding Crdn 126 N Orlando Ave . . . . Cocoa Beach FL 32931 *TF:* 800-799-1094 ■ *Web:* www.als-travel.com	321-783-4900		775
Air Lift Co 2727 Snow Rd . . . . Lansing MI 48917 *TF:* 800-248-0892 ■ *Web:* www.airliftcompany.com	517-322-2144		54
Air Line Pilots Assn 535 Herndon Pkwy . . . . Herndon VA 20170 **Fax Area Code:* 202 ■ *TF:* 877-331-1223 ■ *Web:* www.alpa.org	703-689-2270	232-0438*	414
Air Liquide USA LLC 9811 Katy Fwy Ste 100 . . . . Houston TX 77024 *TF:* 877-855-9533 ■ *Web:* www.airliquide.com	713-624-8000		143
Air Logic Power Systems LLC 1745 S 38th St Ste 100 . . . . Milwaukee WI 53215 *Web:* www.alpsleak.com	414-671-3332		201
Air Logistics Inc 4605 Industrial Dr . . . . New Iberia LA 70560 *TF:* 800-365-6771 ■ *Web:* www.bristowgroup.com	337-365-6771	364-8222	359
Air Mobility Command 402 Scott Dr Unit 1M8 . . . . Scott Air Force Base IL 62225 *Web:* www.amc.af.mil	618-229-7839		340-4
Air Monitor Corp 1050 Hopper Ave . . . . Santa Rosa CA 95403 *TF:* 800-247-3569 ■ *Web:* www.airmonitor.com	707-544-2706	526-9970	612
Air Movement & Control Association International Inc (AMCA) 30 W University Dr . . . . Arlington Heights IL 60004 *Web:* www.amca.org	847-394-0150	253-0088	49-3
Air North Charter & Training Ltd 150 Condor Rd . . . . Whitehorse YT Y1A0M7 *TF:* 800-661-0407 ■ *Web:* www.flyairnorth.com	867-668-2228		12
Air Palm Springs 145 N Gene Autry Trl Ste 14 . . . . Palm Springs CA 92262 *TF:* 800-760-7774 ■ *Web:* www.airps.com	800-760-7774		13
Air Power Inc 1430 Trinity Ave . . . . High Point NC 27262 *TF:* 800-334-1001 ■ *Web:* www.airpower-usa.com	336-886-5081	889-2745	21
Air Products & Chemicals Inc 7201 Hamilton Blvd . . . . Allentown PA 18195 *NYSE: APD* ■ *TF:* 800-345-3148 ■ *Web:* www.airproducts.com	610-481-4911		143
Air Professionals Inc 705 Jennings St . . . . Bethlehem PA 18017 *Web:* www.airprofessionalsinc.com	610-865-0749	865-9412	385
Air Purchases Inc 24 Blanchard Rd . . . . Burlington MA 01803 *Web:* www.airpurchases.com	781-273-2050		612
Air Quality Engineering Inc 7140 Northland Dr N . . . . Brooklyn Park MN 55428 *TF:* 888-883-3273 ■ *Web:* www.air-quality-eng.com	763-531-9823	531-9900	18
Air Resources Laboratory 5830 University Research Ct Rm 4204 . . . . College Park MD 20740 *Web:* www.arl.noaa.gov	301-683-1365	713-0119	668
Air Serv Intl 410 Rosedale Ct Ste 190 . . . . Warrenton VA 20186 *Web:* www.airserv.org	540-428-2323	428-2326	48-5
Air Specialists Inc 1675 Larkin Williams . . . . Fenton MO 63026 *Web:* airspec.com	636-326-5900		54
Air Structures American Technologies Inc 211 S Ridge St . . . . Rye Brook NY 10573 *Web:* www.asati.com	914-937-4500	937-6331	733
Air Sunshine PO Box 37698 . . . . San Juan PR 00937 *TF:* 800-435-8900 ■ *Web:* www.airsunshine.com	954-434-8900		25
Air Systems International Inc 829 Juniper Crescent . . . . Chesapeake VA 23320 *TF:* 800-866-8100 ■ *Web:* www.airsystems.com	757-424-3967		641
Air Systems of Sacramento Inc 10381 Old Placerville Rd Ste 100 . . . . Sacramento CA 95827 *Web:* www.airsystems1.com	916-368-0336		35
Air T Inc 5930 Balsom Ridge Rd . . . . Denver NC 28037 *NASDAQ: AIRT* ■ **Fax Area Code:* 828 ■ *Web:* www.airt.net	612-843-4302	465-5281*	546
Air Technical Industries 7501 Clover Ave . . . . Mentor OH 44060 *TF:* 800-321-9680 ■ *Web:* www.airtechnical.com	440-951-5191	953-9237	470
Air Techniques Inc 1295 Walt Whitman Rd . . . . Melville NY 11747 *TF:* 888-247-8481 ■ *Web:* www.airtechniques.com	516-433-7676		228
Air Tractor Inc 1524 Lelind Snow Way . . . . Olney TX 76374 *Web:* airtractor.com	940-564-5616	564-5612	20

Name / Address	City	State	ZIP	Phone	Fax	Class
Air Traffic Control Assn (ATCA) 1101 King St Ste 300 *Web:* www.atca.org	Alexandria	VA	22314	703-299-2430	299-2437	49-21
Air Transport World Magazine 8380 Colesville Rd Ste 500 *Web:* atwonline.com	Silver Spring	MD	20910	301-755-0165		457-21
Air Trek Inc 28000 A-5 Airport Rd **Fax Area Code:* 888 ■ *TF:* 800-247-8735 ■ *Web:* www.medjets.com	Punta Gorda	FL	33982	941-639-7855	519-1006*	30
Air Van 2340 130th Ave NE Ste 201 *TF:* 800-989-8905 ■ *Web:* www.airvanmoving.com	Bellevue	WA	98005	425-629-4101	629-4120	519
Air Vent Inc 4117 Pinnacle Pnt Dr Ste 400 *TF:* 800-247-8368 ■ *Web:* www.airvent.com	Dallas	TX	75211	800-247-8368		697
Air Waves Inc 7750 Green Meadows Dr N *TF:* 844-543-8339 ■ *Web:* airwavesinc.com	Lewis Center	OH	43035	740-548-1200		627
Air Way Automation 2268 Industrial St *Web:* www.airwayautomation.com	Grayling	MI	49738	989-348-5176		494
Air Wisconsin Airlines Corp W6390 Challenger Dr Ste 203 *Web:* www.airwis.com	Appleton	WI	54914	920-739-5123		25
Air Zoo, The 6151 Portage Rd *TF:* 866-524-7966 ■ *Web:* www.airzoo.org	Portage	MI	49002	269-382-6555		520
Airbiquity Inc 1011 Western Ave Ste 600 *TF:* 888-334-7741 ■ *Web:* www.airbiquity.com	Seattle	WA	98104	206-219-2700	842-9259	647
Airborn Electronics Inc 2230 Picton Pky *Web:* www.airborn.com	Akron	OH	44312	330-245-2630	245-2631	246
Airborne Systems 5800 N Magnolia Ave *Web:* airborne-sys.com	Pennsauken	NJ	08109	856-663-1275	663-8146	576
AirBoss of America Corp 16441 Yonge St *TSE: BOS* ■ *Web:* www.airbossofamerica.com	Newmarket	ON	L3X2G8	905-751-1188	751-1101	677
Airbrush Action Inc PO Box 438 *TF:* 800-876-2472 ■ *Web:* www.airbrushaction.com	Allenwood	NJ	08720	732-223-7878		457-2
Airbus Group Inc 2550 Wasser Terr Ste 9000 *Web:* www.airbus.com	Herndon	VA	20171	703-466-5600		21
Airbus Helicopters Canada 1100 Gilmore Rd PO Box 250 *TF:* 800-267-4999 ■ *Web:* www.airbushelicopters.ca	Fort Erie	ON	L2A5M9	905-871-7772		13
Airbus Helicopters Inc 2701 Forum Dr *TF:* 800-873-0001 ■ *Web:* www.airbus.com	Grand Prairie	TX	75052	972-641-0000		20
Aircastle 300 First Stamford Pl 5th Fl *NYSE: AYR* ■ *Web:* www.aircastle.com	Stamford	CT	06902	203-504-1020	504-1021	23
Aircel LLC 323 Crisp Cir *TF:* 800-767-4599 ■ *Web:* airceldryers.com	Maryville	TN	37801	865-681-7066		172
AirClean Systems Inc 2179 E Lyon Station Rd *TF:* 800-849-0472 ■ *Web:* www.aircleansystems.com	Raleigh	NC	27604	919-255-3220		476
Airco Group 1853 S Eisenhower Ct *Web:* www.airco-ict.com	Wichita	KS	67209	316-945-0445	945-8014	770
Airco Mechanical Inc 8210 Demetre Ave *Web:* www.aircomech.com	Sacramento	CA	95828	916-381-4523	386-0350	14
Aircoastal Helicopters 2615 Lantana Rd Ste J *Web:* www.aircoastal.com	Lantana	FL	33462	561-642-6840		359
Aircon Corp 2873 Chelsea Ave *Web:* aircon-corporation.com	Memphis	TN	38108	901-452-0230	452-0750	480
Aircon Engineering Inc 7 Williams St *TF:* 800-638-6270 ■ *Web:* www.airconeng.com	Cumberland	MD	21502	301-722-7269		261
Aircraft Belts Inc 1176 Telecom Dr *TF:* 800-847-5651 ■ *Web:* aircraftbelts.com	Creedmoor	NC	27522	919-956-4395	956-4216	22
Aircraft Hinge Inc 24930 Ave Tibbitts *Web:* www.aircrafthinge.com	Valencia	CA	91355	661-257-3434	257-3287	22
Aircraft Owners & Pilots Assn (AOPA) 421 Aviation Way *TF:* 800-872-2672 ■ *Web:* www.aopa.org	Frederick	MD	21701	301-695-2000	695-2375	49-21
Aircraft Performance Group Inc 4348 Woodlands Blvd Ste 200 *Web:* flyapg.com	Castle Rock	CO	80104	303-539-0410	539-0415	177
Aircraft Precision Products 185 Industrial Pkwy *Web:* www.aircraftprecision.net	Ithaca	MI	48847	989-875-4186		21
Aircraft Specialists Inc 6005 Propeller Ln **Fax Area Code:* 812 ■ *TF:* 800-776-5387 ■ *Web:* chooseasi.com	Sellersburg	IN	47172	800-776-5387	246-4365*	63
Aircraft Technical Book Company LLC 72413 US Hwy 40 *Web:* www.actechbooks.com	Tabernash	CO	80478	970-726-5111	726-5115	637-10
Aircraft Technical Publishers 101 S Hill Dr *TF:* 800-227-4610 ■ *Web:* www.atp.com	Brisbane	CA	94005	415-330-9500	468-1596	637-11
Aircraft X-Ray Labs Inc 5216 Pacific Blvd *Web:* aircraftxray.com	Huntington Park	CA	90255	323-587-4141		743
Air-Cure Inc 8501 Evergreen Blvd *Web:* www.aircure.com	Minneapolis	MN	55433	763-717-0707	717-0394	723
Airdex Intl 4675 MacArthur Crt Ste 1470 *Web:* airdex.com	Newport Beach	CA	92660	702-575-0625	270-9178	601
Airdrie Stud Inc 2641 Old Frankfort Pk PO Box 487 *Web:* www.airdriestud.com	Midway	KY	40347	859-873-7270	873-6140	368
Airdrome Precision Components 3251 E Airport Way *Web:* www.airdrome.com	Long Beach	CA	90806	562-426-9411	492-6909	595
AIRE Inc 2021 E Wilson Ln *Web:* www.outcastboats.com	Meridian	ID	83642	208-991-5771		711
Airecon Manufacturing Corp 5271 Brotherton Ct *Web:* www.airecon.com	Cincinnati	OH	45227	513-561-5522	561-0166	697
Airefco Inc 18755 SW Teton Ave PO Box 1349 *TF:* 800-869-1349 ■ *Web:* www.airefco.com	Tualatin	OR	97062	503-692-3210	691-2392	15
Aire-Master of America Inc 1821 N State Hwy CC *TF:* 800-525-0957 ■ *Web:* www.airemaster.com	Nixa	MO	65714	417-725-2691	725-5737	310
Aires Jewelers Co 3 Harrison Ave *Web:* www.airesjewelers.com	Morris Plains	NJ	07950	973-292-0950	292-2719	410
Airespring Inc 6060 Sepulveda Blvd Ste 220 *TF:* 888-389-2899 ■ *Web:* www.airespring.com	Van Nuys	CA	91411	818-786-8990		387
Airetel Staffing Inc 415 Montgomery Rd Ste 125 **Fax Area Code:* 866 ■ *Web:* airetel.com	Altamonte Springs	FL	32714	407-788-2015	712-7295*	260
Airex Corp 15 Lilac Ln *Web:* airex.com	Somersworth	NH	03878	603-841-2040		767
Airfasco Industries Inc 2655 Harrison Ave SW *Web:* airfasco.com	Canton	OH	44706	330-430-6190		454
Airflex Industrial Inc 965 Conklin St *Web:* www.airflexind.com	Farmingdale	NY	11735	631-752-1234	752-1309	491
Airfloat LLC 2230 Brush College Rd *TF:* 800-888-0018 ■ *Web:* www.airfloat.com	Decatur	IL	62526	217-423-6001	422-1049	207
Airflow Sciences Corp 12190 Hubbard St *Web:* www.airflowsciences.com	Livonia	MI	48150	734-525-0300		261
Airflow Systems Inc 11221 Pagemill Rd *TF:* 800-818-6185 ■ *Web:* www.airflowsystems.com	Dallas	TX	75243	214-503-8008	503-9596	18
Airfoil Impellers Corp PO Box 9966 *Web:* www.airfoil.com	College Station	TX	77842	979-822-6418	775-5588	18
AirG Inc 1133 Melville St Ste 710 *TF:* 866-874-8136 ■ *Web:* corp.airg.com	Vancouver	BC	V6E4E5	604-408-2228		387
Airgas Inc 259 N Radnor-Chester Rd Ste 100 *NYSE: ARG* ■ *TF:* 800-255-2165 ■ *Web:* www.airgas.com	Radnor	PA	19087	610-687-5253	687-1052	146
Airgas Specialty Products 2530 Sever Rd Ste 300 **Fax Area Code:* 770 ■ *TF:* 800-295-2225 ■ *Web:* www.airgasspecialtyproducts.com	Lawrenceville	GA	30043	800-295-2225	717-2222*	280
Air-Hydraulics Inc 545 Hupp Ave *Web:* www.airhydraulics.com	Jackson	MI	49203	517-787-9444	787-7585	456
AirIQ Inc 1845 Sandstone Manor Unit 10 *TF:* 888-606-6444 ■ *Web:* airiq.com	Pickering	ON	L1W3X9	905-831-6444	581-3121	736
Airista LLC 913 Ridgebrook Rd *Web:* www.airistaflow.com	Sparks Glencoe	MD	21152	410-878-2700		21
AIRK (AmeriCandy Retail Interactive Kiosk) 3618 St Germaine Ct *Web:* americandybar.com	Louisville	KY	40207	502-583-1776		123
Air-Land Transport Service 1020 Birchwood St *Web:* www.air-land.com	Morton	IL	61550	309-263-7084	263-7572	780
Airlie Conference Ctr 6809 Airlie Rd *TF:* 800-288-9573 ■ *Web:* www.airlie.com	Warrenton	VA	20187	540-347-1300		377
Airlie Gardens 300 Airlie Rd *Web:* airliegardens.org	Wilmington	NC	28403	910-798-7700		97
Airline History Museum 201 NW Lou Holland Dr *Web:* www.airlinehistory.org	Kansas City	MO	64116	816-421-3401	421-3421	520
Airline Hydraulics Corp 3557 Progress Dr *TF:* 800-999-7378 ■ *Web:* www.airlinehyd.com	Bensalem	PA	19020	215-638-4700	638-1707	22
Airline Services International Inc 5160 Explorer Dr Ste 4 *Web:* www.airlineservices.com	Mississauga	ON	L4W4T7	905-629-4522		63
Airline Spares America Inc (ASA) 1022 E Newport Center Dr *Web:* www.asaspares.com	Deerfield Beach	FL	33442	954-429-8258	429-8388	770
Airline Tariff Publishing Co (ATPCO) 45005 Aviation Dr *Web:* www.atpco.net	Dulles	VA	20166	703-471-7510	661-8061	16
Airline Transport Professionals PO Box 1784 *TF:* 800-255-2877 ■ *Web:* www.atpflightschool.com	Ponte Vedra Beach	FL	32004	904-273-3018	273-2164	167-3
Airlines for America 1301 Pennsylvania Ave NW Ste 1100 *Web:* airlines.org	Washington	DC	20004	202-626-4000		49-21
Airlite Plastics Co 6110 Abbott Dr *Web:* www.airliteplastics.com	Omaha	NE	68110	402-341-7300		596
Air-Lock Inc 108 Gulf St *Web:* www.airlockinc.com	Milford	CT	06460	203-301-6060	876-7436	22
Airmall Pittsburgh International Airport Landslide Bldg - Mezzanine Level *TF:* 800-487-3247 ■ *Web:* www.fraport-usa.com	Pittsburgh	PA	15231	412-472-5180	472-5190	45
Airmaster Fan Co 9229 S Meridian Rd *TF:* 800-410-3267 ■ *Web:* www.airmasterfan.com	Clarklake	MI	49234	517-764-2300	764-5876	18
Airmate Company Inc 16280 County Rd D *TF:* 800-544-3614 ■ *Web:* www.airmateplasticfabrication.com	Bryan	OH	43506	419-636-3184	636-4210	9
Airmatic Inc 284 Three Tun Rd **Fax Area Code:* 888 ■ *TF:* 800-332-9770 ■ *Web:* www.airmatic.com	Malvern	PA	19355	215-333-5600	964-3866*	385
Airmax International Inc PO Box 5206 *TF:* 800-247-6291 ■ *Web:* www.airmax.net	Manchester	NH	03108	603-471-1000		18
Airmotive Enterprises 16384 Airport Rd Ste 8 *TF:* 877-273-3266 ■ *Web:* www.airmotive.net	Brainerd	MN	56401	218-829-3398		167-3
AirNet Communications Corp 295 N Dr Ste G *TF:* 800-984-1990 ■ *Web:* www.aircom.com	Melbourne	FL	32934	321-984-1990	676-9914	735
AirNet II 3041 George Page Jr *TF:* 877-293-8463 ■ *Web:* www.airnet.com	Columbus	OH	43217	614-409-4900		546
Airolite Company LLC PO Box 410 *Web:* www.airolite.com	Schofield	WI	54476	715-841-8757	841-8773	491
Airosol Company Inc 1206 Illinois St *TF:* 800-633-9576 ■ *Web:* www.airosol.com	Neodesha	KS	66757	620-325-2666	325-2602	145

Company / Address	City	State	Zip	Phone	Fax	Class
Airparts Company Inc 2310 NW 55th Ct *TF:* 800-392-4999 ■ *Web:* www.airpartsco.com	Fort Lauderdale	FL	33309	954-739-3575	739-9514	770
Airphrame Inc 25 Taylor St *Web:* www.airphrame.com	San Francisco	CA	94102	415-857-5387		387
AirPol Inc 1000A Lake St *Web:* www.airpol.com	Ramsey	NJ	07446	973-599-4400		261
Airport Community Schools 11270 Grafton Rd *Web:* www.airportschools.com	Carleton	MI	48117	734-869-7000	654-4014	685
Airport Design Consultants Inc 6031 University Blvd Ste 330 *Web:* adci-corp.com	Ellicott City	MD	21043	410-465-9600		261
Airports Council International of North America (ACI-NA) 1615 L St NW Ste 300 *Web:* airportscouncil.org	Washington	DC	20006	202-293-8500	331-1362	49-21
Airput Inc 3819 Germantown Pk Ste D *Web:* www.airput.com	Collegeville	PA	19426	610-454-5100		177
AirRoamer Inc Adelaide St W Ste 354 - 157 *Web:* www.airroamer.com	Toronto	ON	M5H4E7	647-258-6589		224
AirSage Inc 1330 Spring St NW Ste 475 *Web:* airsage.com	Atlanta	GA	30309	404-809-2499		180
AirScan Inc 3505 Murrell Rd *Web:* www.airscan.com	Rockledge	FL	32955	321-631-0005		693
Air-Sea Forwarders Inc PO Box 90637 *Web:* airseainc.com	Los Angeles	CA	90009	310-216-1616	216-2625	12
Air-Serv Group LLC 1370 Mendota Heights Rd *TF:* 800-247-8363 ■ *Web:* www.air-serv.com	Mendota Heights	MN	55120	800-247-8363		55
Airspace Technologies 5909 Sea Otter Pl Ste 200 *TF:* 855-524-7772 ■ *Web:* www.airspacetechnologies.com	Carlsbad	CA	92010	855-524-7772		311
Airspan Networks Inc 777 Yamato Rd *OTC: AIRO* ■ *Web:* www.airspan.com	Boca Raton	FL	33431	561-893-8670	893-8671	735
AirStar Intl 13006 E Vista Park Dr *Web:* airstarintl.com	Moorpark	CA	93021	805-553-9996		194
AirStream Books 15608 S New Century Dr *TF:* 800-729-6423 ■ *Web:* www.airstreambooks.net	Gardena	CA	90248	310-532-9400	532-7001	637-10
Airtable 155 5th St 6th Fl *Web:* airtable.com	San Francisco	CA	94103	781-797-0878		39
Airtech International Inc 5700 Skylab Rd *Web:* www.airtechintl.com	Huntington Beach	CA	92647	714-899-8100	899-8179	386
Airtek Inc PO Box 466 *Web:* airtek-inc.com	Irwin	PA	15642	724-863-1350	864-7853	172
AirTek Indoor Air Solutions Inc 1241 Johnson Ave Ste 209 *TF:* 877-858-6213 ■ *Web:* www.air-tek.net	San Luis Obispo	CA	93401	877-858-6213		192
Airtel Plaza Hotel 7277 Valjean Ave *TF:* 877-939-9268 ■ *Web:* www.airtelplaza.com	Van Nuys	CA	91406	818-997-7676		379
Airtex 259 Lower Morrisville Rd *Web:* www.airtexinteriors.com	Fallsington	PA	19054	215-295-4115		22
Airtex Consumer Products a Div of Federal Foam Technologies 150 Industrial Pk Blvd **Fax Area Code:* 320 ■ *TF:* 800-851-8887 ■ *Web:* www.airtex.com	Cokato	MN	55321	800-851-8887	286-2428*	745-6
Airtex Manufacturing Inc 32050 W 83rd St *Web:* www.engineeredair.com	De Soto	KS	66018	913-583-3181	583-1406	14
Airtex Products 407 W Main St *Web:* airtexproducts.com	Fairfield	IL	62837	618-842-2111		60
Air-Transport IT Services Inc 5950 Hazeltine National Dr Ste 210	Orlando	FL	32822	407-370-4664		196
AirTrav Inc 181 Bay St PO Box 30025 *Web:* airtrav.com	Toronto	ON	M5J0A5	289-346-0071		463
Airtreks International LLC 237 NE Chkalov Dr Ste 210 *TF:* 877-247-8735 ■ *Web:* www.airtreks.com	Vancouver	WA	98684	415-977-7100		772
Airtrim Inc 1940 S Yellow Springs St *TF:* 888-247-8746 ■ *Web:* www.airtrim.com	Springfield	OH	45506	937-324-2272	324-3999	393
Airtrol Components Inc 17400 W Liberty Ln *Web:* airtrolinc.com	New Berlin	WI	53146	262-786-1711	786-0211	201
Airtrol Mechanical 3960 N St *Web:* airtrolmechanical.com	Baton Rouge	LA	70806	225-383-2617	343-7986	189-10
Airtronics Inc 1822 S Research Loop *Web:* www.airtronicsinc.com	Tucson	AZ	85710	520-881-3982		350
Airtronics Metal Products Inc 140 San Pedro Ave *Web:* airtronics.com	Morgan Hill	CA	95037	408-977-7800	977-7810	697
Air-Vac Engineering Company Inc 30 Progress Ave *Web:* air-vac-eng.com	Seymour	CT	06483	203-888-9900	888-1145	811
Airvoice Wireless LLC 2425 Franklin Rd *TF:* 888-944-2355 ■ *Web:* www.airvoicewireless.com	Bloomfield Hills	MI	48302	888-944-2355		736
Airway Heights Corrections Ctr 11919 W Sprague Ave PO Box 1899 *Web:* www.doc.wa.gov	Airway Heights	WA	99001	509-244-6700	244-6710	213
Air-Way Manufacturing Co 586 N Main St *TF:* 800-253-1036 ■ *Web:* www.air-way.com	Olivet	MI	49076	269-749-2161	749-3161	790
Airway Surgical Appliances Ltd 189 Colonnade Rd *TF:* 800-267-3476 ■ *Web:* www.airwaysurgical.ca	Nepean	ON	K2E7J4	613-723-4790		42
Airways Freight Corp 3849 W Wedington Dr PO Box 1888 *TF:* 800-643-3525 ■ *Web:* www.airwaysfreight.com	Fayetteville	AR	72704	479-442-6301	442-6522	311
Airwest Aviation Academy 24017 N 55th Ave *Web:* www.aaaheli.com	Glendale	AZ	85310	623-516-2790	581-5592	167-3
AIS (American Institute of Stress, The) 124 Park Ave *Web:* www.stress.org	Yonkers	NY	10703	682-239-6823		48-17
AIS (Alaska Insulation Supply Inc) 261 E 56th Ave Bldg B *Web:* www.alaskainsulation.com	Anchorage	AK	99518	907-563-4125		191-4
AIS (American Integrated Services Inc) 1502 E Opp St *TF:* 888-423-6060 ■ *Web:* www.americanintegrated.com	Wilmington	CA	90744	310-522-1168	522-0474	194
AIS RealTime 4440 Bowen Blvd SE *TF:* 877-314-1100 ■ *Web:* aisservice.com	Grand Rapids	MI	49508	877-314-1100		195
AISC (American Institute of Steel Construction) 130 E Randolph Ste 2000 *Web:* www.aisc.org	Chicago	IL	60601	312-670-2400		49-3
AISD (Amarillo Independent School District) 7200 I- 40 W *Web:* www.amaisd.org	Amarillo	TX	79106	806-326-1000	354-4378	685
Aisen Shiatsu School 1314 S King St Ste 601 *Web:* www.aisenshiatsu.com	Honolulu	HI	96814	808-596-4633		685
AISES (American Indian Science & Engineering Society) 2305 Renard SE Ste 200 *Web:* www.aises.org	Albuquerque	NM	87106	505-765-1052	765-5608	49-19
AISG LLC 1036 E Iron Eagle Dr Ste 105 *Web:* americanisg.com	Eagle	ID	83616	208-489-3131		690
Aisin Automotive Casting LLC 4870 E Hwy 552 *TF:* 888-888-8888 ■ *Web:* www.aisinauto.com	London	KY	40744	606-878-6523		455
Aisin Holdings of America Inc 1665 E Fourth St *Web:* www.aisinworld.com	Seymour	IN	47274	812-524-8144	524-8146	60
Aisin USA Manufacturing Inc 1700 E Fourth St *Web:* www.aisinusa.com	Seymour	IN	47274	812-523-1969		60
Aisle 7 215 NW Park Ave *TF:* 877-659-7630 ■ *Web:* www.healthnotes.com	Portland	OR	97209	503-234-4092	234-4052	393
AIST (Association for Iron & Steel Technology) 186 Thorn Hill Rd *TF:* 800-759-4867 ■ *Web:* www.aist.org	Warrendale	PA	15086	724-814-3000	814-3001	49-13
AIT (AI Technology Inc) 70 Washington Rd *TF:* 800-735-5040 ■ *Web:* www.aitechnology.com	Princeton Junction	NJ	08550	609-799-9388	799-9308	801
AIT (Advanced Integration Technologies) 481 N Dean Ave *Web:* www.uct.com	Chandler	AZ	85226	480-568-8300		454
AIT (Advanced Innovative Technologies LLC) 530 Wilbanks Dr *Web:* www.aitequipment.com	Ball Ground	GA	30107	770-479-1900	479-4179	744
AIT (Avery Island Technologies LLC) 601 Poydras St Ste 1815 *Web:* www.averytech.com	New Orleans	LA	70130	504-200-4248	895-5344	196
AIT Inc 421 Maiden Ln **Fax Area Code:* 910 ■ *TF:* 877-549-2881 ■ *Web:* www.ait.com	Fayetteville	NC	28301	877-549-2881	321-1390*	396
AIT Worldwide Logistics 701 N Rohlwing Rd *TF:* 800-323-6649 ■ *Web:* www.aitworldwide.com	Itasca	IL	60143	630-766-8300	766-0205	311
AITC (American Institute of Timber Construction) 7012 S Revere Pkwy Ste 140 *Web:* www.aitc-glulam.org	Centennial	CO	80112	303-792-9559	792-0669	49-3
Aitken Products Inc 566 N Eagle St PO Box 151 *Web:* www.aitkenproducts.com	Geneva	OH	44041	440-466-5711	466-5716	14
Aitkin Iron Works Inc 301 Bunker Hill Dr *Web:* www.aiw.com	Aitkin	MN	56431	218-927-2400		454
Aitoro Appliance Co 401 Westport Ave *Web:* aitoro.com	Norwalk	CT	06851	203-847-2471		35
AIUM (American Institute of Ultrasound in Medicine) 14750 Sweitzer Ln Ste 100 *TF:* 800-638-5352 ■ *Web:* www.aium.org	Laurel	MD	20707	301-498-4100	498-4450	49-8
AIUSA (Amnesty International USA) 5 Penn Plz 16th Fl **Fax Area Code:* 212 ■ *TF:* 866-273-4466 ■ *Web:* www.amnestyusa.org	New York	NY	10001	800-266-3789	627-1451*	48-5
AIV LP 7140 W Sam Houston Pkwy N Ste 100 *TF:* 800-447-4230 ■ *Web:* www.aivinc.com	Houston	TX	77040	713-462-4181		385
Aiwohi Bros Inc 91-1600 Wahane St *Web:* aiwohibros.com	Kapolei	HI	96707	808-668-4285	674-2376	311
Aixtek 890 Cowan Rd Ste C *TF:* 800-342-4525 ■ *Web:* www.eatonassoc.com	Burlingame	CA	94010	415-282-1188	282-1108	175
AJ Demor & Sons Inc 2150 Eldo Rd *Web:* www.ajdemor.com	Monroeville	PA	15146	412-242-6125	372-5818	610
AJ Desmond & Sons Funeral Directors 2600 Crooks Rd *TF:* 800-210-7135 ■ *Web:* www.desmondfuneralhome.com	Troy	MI	48084	248-362-2500	362-0190	510
AJ Funk & Co 1471 Timber Dr *Web:* sparkle-glasscleaner.com	Elgin	IL	60123	847-741-6760	741-6767	151
AJ Images Inc 259 E First Ave *Web:* ajimages.com	Roselle	NJ	07203	908-241-6900		627
AJ Jersey Inc 125 St Nicholas Ave *Web:* www.ajjersey.net	South Plainfield	NJ	07080	908-754-7333		358
AJ Manufacturing Inc 1217 Oak St *Web:* ajdoor.com	Bloomer	WI	54724	715-568-2204		480
AJ Perri Inc 1162 Pine Brook Rd *Web:* www.ajperri.com	Tinton Falls	NJ	07724	732-733-2548		189-10
AJ Rose Manufacturing Co 38000 Chester Rd *Web:* www.ajrose.com	Avon	OH	44011	440-934-7700	934-2806	489
AJ Ross Creative Media 62 Wood Rd *Web:* www.ajross.com	Sugar Loaf	NY	10981	845-783-5770		4
AJ Squared Security 110-20 Jamaica Ave Ste G2 *Web:* aj2security.com	Richmond Hill	NY	11418	718-849-2725		693
AJA (American Jail Assn) 1135 Professional Ct *TF:* 800-211-2754 ■ *Web:* www.americanjail.org	Hagerstown	MD	21740	301-790-3930	790-2941	49-7
Ajacs Die Sales Corp 4625 Clay Ave SW *TF:* 800-968-6868 ■ *Web:* www.ajacs.com	Grand Rapids	MI	49548	616-452-1469		358
Ajamie LLP 711 Louisiana Ste 2150 *Web:* ajamie.com	Houston	TX	77002	713-860-1600		41

Company / Address	City	State	Zip	Phone	Fax	Class
Ajanta 12215 N Pennsylvania Ave	Oklahoma City	OK	73120	405-752-5283		671
Web: www.ajantacuisineofindia.com						
Ajanta Pharma USA Inc						
440 US Hwy 22 E Ste 150	Bridgewater	NJ	08807	908-252-1165	393-5505	582
Web: www.ajantapharma.com						
Ajax Building Company LLC						
1080 Commerce Blvd	Midway	FL	32343	850-224-9571		186
Web: www.ajaxbuilding.com						
Ajax Company Inc						
1500 E Eighth St	Jacksonville	FL	32206	904-353-4783		350
Web: www.ajaxco.com						
Ajax Electric Co						
60 Tomlinson Rd	Huntingdon Valley	PA	19006	215-947-8500	947-6757	318
TF: 800-516-9916 ■ *Web:* www.ajaxelectric.com						
Ajax Metal Processing Inc						
4651 Bellevue St	Detroit	MI	48207	313-267-2100		484
Web: www.ajaxmetal.com						
Ajax Paving Industries Inc						
1957 Crooks Rd Ste A	Troy	MI	48084	248-244-3300		188-4
Web: www.ajaxpaving.com						
Ajax Pickering Hospital						
580 Harwood Ave S	Ajax	ON	L1S2J4	905-683-2320		374-2
TF: 866-752-6989 ■ *Web:* www.rougevalley.ca						
Ajax Santa Barbara Refrigeration & Heating						
401 E Montecito St	Santa Barbara	CA	93101	805-963-1322		610
Web: ajaxrefrigerationandac.com						
Ajax Tocco Magnethermic Corp						
1745 Overland Ave NE	Warren	OH	44483	330-372-8511	372-8608	318
TF: 800-547-1527 ■ *Web:* www.ajaxtocco.com						
AJB (Alice James Books)						
114 Prescott St	Farmington	ME	04938	207-778-7071	778-7766	637-2
Web: www.alicejamesbooks.org						
AJC (American Jewish Committee)						
165 E 56th St	New York	NY	10022	212-751-4000	750-0326	48-8
Web: www.ajc.org						
AJC (American Jury Centers) PO Box 3677	Hailey	ID	83333	561-542-8590		261
Web: www.americanjurycenters.com						
AJC Intl 1000 Abernathy Rd NE Ste 600	Atlanta	GA	30328	404-252-6750	252-9340	297-8
Web: www.ajcfood.com						
AJCU (Association of Jesuit Colleges & Universities)						
1 Dupont Cir NW Ste 405	Washington	DC	20036	202-862-9893		48-11
Web: www.ajcunet.edu						
Ajel Technologies Inc						
347 Plainfield Ave	Edison	NJ	08817	732-777-1800		809
Web: www.ajel.com						
AJH (Anna Jaques Hospital)						
25 Highland Ave	Newburyport	MA	01950	978-463-1000		374-3
Web: www.ajh.org						
Ajilitee 2 Pierce Pl Ste 1900	Itasca	IL	60143	224-265-4570	265-0401	196
TF: 866-781-0723 ■ *Web:* www.ajilitee.com						
Ajinomoto Health & Nutrition North America Inc						
1300 N Arlington Heights Rd Ste 110	Itasca	IL	60143	630-931-6800		296-37
TF: 888-425-8432 ■ *Web:* www.ajinorthamerica.com						
AJL Manufacturing Corp						
100 Holleder Pkwy	Rochester	NY	14615	585-254-1128	458-6400	454
Web: www.ajlmfg.com						
AJLI (Association of Junior Leagues International Inc)						
80 Maiden Ln Ste 305	New York	NY	10038	212-951-8300	481-7196	48-15
TF: 800-955-3248 ■ *Web:* www.ajli.org						
AJM Packaging Corp						
E-4111 Andover Rd	Bloomfield Hills	MI	48302	248-901-0040	901-0062	65
Web: www.ajmpack.com						
AJO Al's						
Arrowhead 7458 W Bell Rd	Glendale	AZ	85308	623-334-9899		671
Web: www.ajoals.com						
AJR Industries Inc						
117 Gordon St	Elk Grove Village	IL	60007	847-439-0380	439-0230	454
Web: www.ajrindustries.com						
Ajubita, Leftwich & Salzer LLC						
1100 Poydras Ste 1500	New Orleans	LA	70163	504-582-2300	582-2310	41
Web: alsfirm.com						
AJWS (American Jewish World Service)						
45 W 36th St	New York	NY	10018	212-792-2900	792-2930	48-5
TF: 800-889-7146 ■ *Web:* ajws.org						
AK Capital LLC 445 Park Ave 9th Fl	New York	NY	10022	212-333-8600	307-3282	194
Web: www.akcapital.com						
AK Draft Seal Ltd 7470 Buller Ave	Burnaby	BC	V5J4S5	604-451-1080		234
TF: 888-520-9009 ■ *Web:* www.draftseal.com						
AK Press 674-A 23rd St	Oakland	CA	94612	510-208-1700	208-1701	637-2
Web: www.akpress.org						
AK Smiley Public Library						
125 W Vine St	Redlands	CA	92373	909-798-7565	798-7566	434-3
Web: www.akspl.org						
AK Stamping Company Inc						
1159 US Rt 22	Mountainside	NJ	07092	908-232-7300	232-5202	488
Web: www.akstamping.com						
AK Steel Corp 9227 Centre Pt Dr	West Chester	OH	45069	513-425-5000	601-4332*	723
NYSE: AKS ■ **Fax Area Code:* 312 ■ *TF:* 800-331-5050 ■ *Web:* www.aksteel.com						
AK Tube LLC 30400 E Broadway	Walbridge	OH	43465	419-661-4150	661-4380	490
TF: 800-955-8031 ■ *Web:* www.aktube.com						
AKA Direct 2415 N Ross Ave	Portland	OR	97227	800-647-8587		5
TF: 800-647-8587 ■ *Web:* www.akadirect.com						
AKA Energy Group LLC 65 Mercado St	Durango	CO	81301	970-382-0828		325
Web: www.akaenergy.com						
AKA Enterprise Solutions						
875 Sixth Ave 20th Fl	New York	NY	10001	212-502-3900		393
Web: www.akaes.com						
Akal Global Inc 7 Infinity Loop	Espanola	NM	87532	505-692-6600	753-8689	692
TF: 888-325-2527 ■ *Web:* www.akalglobal.com						
Akamai Technologies Inc						
150 Broadway	Cambridge	MA	02142	617-444-3000	444-3001	178-7
NASDAQ: AKAM ■ *TF:* 877-425-2624 ■ *Web:* www.akamai.com						
Akanthos Capital Management LLC						
21600 Oxnard St Ste 1758	Woodland Hills	CA	91367	818-883-8270		401
Web: akanthoscapital.com						
Akar Capital Management						
8551 W Sunrise Blvd Ste 102A	Plantation	FL	33322	954-476-7011		690
Web: akarcapital.com						
Akashi Sushi Bar 2020 Harshman Rd	Dayton	OH	45424	937-233-8005		671
Web: www.akashirestaurant.com						
Akashic Books 232 3rd St Ste A115	Brooklyn	NY	11215	718-643-9193	643-9195	95
Web: www.akashicbooks.com						
Akbar 823 N Charles St	Baltimore	MD	21201	410-539-0944		671
Web: www.akbar-restaurant.com						
AKC (American Kennel Club)						
260 Madison Ave	New York	NY	10016	212-696-8200	696-8299	48-18
Web: www.akc.org						
Ak-Chin Indian Community						
42507 W Peters & Nall Rd	Maricopa	AZ	85138	520-568-1000		393
Web: www.ak-chin.nsn.us						
Akdo Intertrade Inc 1435 State St	Bridgeport	CT	06605	203-336-5199		724
TF: 800-811-2536 ■ *Web:* akdo.com						
Akebia Therapeutics Inc						
245 St 1 Ste 1100	Cambridge	MA	02142	617-871-2098	871-2099	668
Web: akebia.com						
Akebono Brake Corp 300 Ring Rd	Elizabethtown	KY	42701	270-234-5500		247
Web: www.akebonobrakes.com						
Akehurst Landscaping Service Inc						
712 Philadelphia Rd	Joppa	MD	21085	410-538-4018		776
Web: www.akehurst.com						
Akerman Senterfitt						
Three Brickell City Ctr 98 SE Seventh St						
Ste 1100	Miami	FL	33131	305-374-5600	374-5095	428
Web: www.akerman.com						
Akers Biosciences Inc 201 Grove Rd	Thorofare	NJ	08086	856-848-8698		231
Web: www.akersbio.com						
Akers Packaging Service Inc						
2820 Lefferson Rd	Middletown	OH	45044	513-422-6312	422-2829	100
TF: 800-327-7308 ■ *Web:* www.akers-pkg.com						
AKF (American Kidney Fund)						
6110 Executive Blvd Ste 1010	Rockville	MD	20852	800-638-8299	881-0898*	48-17
**Fax Area Code:* 301 ■ *TF:* 800-638-8299 ■ *Web:* www.kidneyfund.org						
AKF (AKF Group LLC)						
1 Liberty Plz 22nd Fl 165 Broadway	New York	NY	10006	212-354-5656		196
TF: 800-945-1497 ■ *Web:* akfgroup.com						
AKF (AGA Khan Foundation USA)						
1825 K St NW Ste 901	Washington	DC	20006	202-293-2537	785-1752	48-5
Web: www.akfusa.org						
AKF Group LLC (AKF)						
1 Liberty Plz 22nd Fl 165 Broadway	New York	NY	10006	212-354-5656		196
TF: 800-945-1497 ■ *Web:* akfgroup.com						
AKG of America Inc 7315 Oakwood St Ext	Mebane	NC	27302	919-563-4286		358
Web: www.akg-america.com						
Akhurst Machinery Ltd						
1669 Foster's Way (Annacis Is)	Delta	BC	V3M6S7	604-540-1430		358
TF: 888-265-4826 ■ *Web:* www.akhurst.com						
Akin Doherty Klein & Feuge PC						
8610 N New Braunfels Ste 101	San Antonio	TX	78217	210-829-1300		2
Web: www.adkf.com						
Akin Gump Strauss Hauer & Feld LLP						
1333 New Hampshire Ave NW	Washington	DC	20036	202-887-4000	887-4288	428
Web: www.akingump.com						
Akins Fresh Market 106 F St SW	Quincy	WA	98848	509-292-6790	559-6048	345
Web: www.akinsfoods.com						
AKITA Drilling Ltd						
1000 333 Seventh Ave SW	Calgary	AB	T2P2Z1	403-292-7979		540
Web: www.akita-drilling.com						
AkitaBox 212 E Washington Ave 4th Fl	Madison	WI	53703	628-400-1778		178-8
Web: home.akitabox.com						
Akiva Goldman PC						
3150 Livernois Rd Ste 335	Troy	MI	48083	586-268-2400		41
TF: 877-737-8800 ■ *Web:* akivagoldman.com						
Akkerman Inc 58256 - 266th St	Brownsdale	MN	55918	800-533-0386		190
TF: 800-533-0386 ■ *Web:* akkerman.com						
Akm Consulting Engineers Inc 553 Wald	Irvine	CA	92618	949-753-7333		261
Web: akmce.com						
AKM Semiconductor Inc						
1731 Technology Dr Ste 500	San Jose	CA	95110	408-436-8580		696
Web: www.akm.com						
Akorn Inc 1925 W Field Ct	Lake Forest	IL	60045	847-279-6100	279-6123	231
NASDAQ: AKRX ■ *TF:* 800-932-5676 ■ *Web:* www.akorn.com						
Akoya 2325 E Carson St	Pittsburgh	PA	15203	412-481-9800		344
Web: www.akoyaonline.com						
AKPIRG (Alaska Public Interest Research Group)						
PO Box 201416 Ste 206	Anchorage	AK	99520	907-278-3661		633
Web: www.akpirg.org						
AKPSI (Alpha Kappa Psi)						
7801 E 88th St	Indianapolis	IN	46256	317-872-1553	872-1567	48-16
Web: akpsi.org						
AKQA Inc 360 Third St 5th Fl	San Francisco	CA	94107	415-645-9400		4
Web: www.akqa.com						
Akra Plastic Products Inc						
1504 E Cedar St	Ontario	CA	91761	909-930-1999	930-1948	602
Web: akraplastics.com						
AKRF Inc 440 Park Ave S	New York	NY	10016	212-696-0670		261
TF: 800-899-2573 ■ *Web:* www.akrf.com						
Akrochem Corp 255 Fountain St	Akron	OH	44304	330-535-2100	535-8947	605-3
TF: 800-321-2260 ■ *Web:* www.akrochem.com						
Akro-Mils Inc 1293 S Main St	Akron	OH	44301	800-253-2467	761-6348*	199
**Fax Area Code:* 330 ■ *TF:* 800-253-2467 ■ *Web:* www.akro-mils.com						
Akron Art Museum 1 S High St	Akron	OH	44308	330-376-9185	376-1180	520
Web: akronartmuseum.org						
Akron Auto Auction Inc 2471 Ley Dr	Akron	OH	44319	330-773-8245	773-1641	51
TF: 800-773-0033 ■ *Web:* www.akronautoauction.com						
Akron Brass Co 1615 Old Mansfeild Rd	Wooster	OH	44691	330-264-5678	264-2944	350
TF: 800-228-1161 ■ *Web:* www.akronbrass.com						
Akron City Hall 146 S High St Rm 211	Akron	OH	44308	330-375-2554	375-2308	337
Web: www.akronohio.gov						
Akron Civic Theatre 182 S Main St	Akron	OH	44308	330-535-3179	535-9828	572
Web: www.akroncivic.com						
Akron Community Foundation						
345 W Cedar St	Akron	OH	44307	330-376-8522		305
Web: www.akroncf.org						
Akron Dispersions Inc 3291 Sawmill Rd	Akron	OH	44321	330-666-0045	666-7842	143
TF: 800-664-1455 ■ *Web:* akrondispersions.com						

Name / Address	Phone	Fax	Class
Akron Foundry Co 2728 Wingate Ave . . . Akron OH 44314 *Web:* www.akronfoundry.com	330-745-3101	745-7999	308
Akron Gasket & Packing Enterprises Inc 445 NE Ave . . . Tallmadge OH 44278 *Web:* akron-gasket.com	330-633-3742	633-3462	326
Akron Gear & Engineering Inc 501 Morgan Ave . . . Akron OH 44311 *TF:* 800-258-6608 ■ *Web:* akrongear.com	330-773-6608	773-9005	709
Akron Hardware LLC 170 Main Ave . . . Akron CO 80720	970-345-6600		350
Akron Law Library (ALL) Summit County Court House 209 S High St Rm 4 . . . Akron OH 44308 *Web:* akronlawlib.summitoh.net	330-643-2804	643-7457	434-3
Akron Police - Community Relations 217 S High St Rm 403A . . . Akron OH 44308 *Web:* akronohio.gov	330-375-2390	375-2412	520
Akron Porcelain & Plastics Co 2739 Cory Ave PO Box 15157 . . . Akron OH 44314 *TF:* 800-737-9664 ■ *Web:* www.akronporcelain.com	330-745-2159	745-6688	604
Akron Public Schools 10 N Main St . . . Akron OH 44308 *Web:* akronschools.com	330-761-1661	761-3225	685
Akron Rubber Development Laboratory Inc 2887 Gilchrist Rd . . . Akron OH 44305 *TF:* 866-778-2735 ■ *Web:* www.ardl.com	330-794-6600	434-0004	743
Akron Special Machinery Inc 2740 Cory Ave . . . Akron OH 44314 *Web:* www.polinggroup.com	330-753-1077		757
Akron Steel Treating Co 336 Morgan Ave . . . Akron OH 44311 *TF:* 800-364-2782 ■ *Web:* www.akronsteeltreating.com	330-773-8211		484
Akron Testing Laboratory & Welding School Ltd 1171 Wooster Rd N . . . Barberton OH 44203 *TF:* 888-859-0664 ■ *Web:* www.akronweldingschool.com	330-753-2268	753-2269	685
Akron Zoological Park 500 Edgewood Ave . . . Akron OH 44307 *Web:* www.akronzoo.org	330-375-2550	375-2575	823
Akron-Canton Airport 5400 Lauby Rd NW . . . North Canton OH 44720 *TF:* 888-434-2359 ■ *Web:* www.akroncantonairport.com	330-499-4221	499-5176	27
Akron-Summit County Public Library 60 S High St . . . Akron OH 44326 *Web:* www.akronlibrary.org	330-643-9000		434-3
Akros Pharma Inc 302 Carnegie Ctr Ste 300 . . . Princeton NJ 08540 *Web:* www.akrospharma.com	609-919-9570	919-9575	743
AKS Infotech 2088 US 130 N Ste 203 . . . Monmouth Junction NJ 08852 *TF:* 800-771-7000 ■ *Web:* www.aksinfotech.net	609-301-4607		463
AKS Technologies Inc 1416 N Sam Houston Pkwy E Ste 140 . . . Houston TX 77032	281-987-2244		539
Aksia LLC 599 Lexington Ave 37th Fl . . . New York NY 10022 *Web:* www.aksia.com	212-710-5710		401
AKSM (American Kidney Stone Management Ltd) 100 W Third Ave Ste 150 . . . Columbus OH 43214 *TF:* 800-637-5188 ■ *Web:* www.aksm.com	614-447-0281		353
AKT Enterprises 6424 Forest City Rd . . . Orlando FL 32810 *TF:* 877-306-3651 ■ *Web:* www.aktenterprises.com	877-306-3651		5
Aktina Medical Physics Corp 360 N Rt 9W . . . Congers NY 10920 *TF:* 888-433-3380 ■ *Web:* www.aktina.com	845-268-0101		475
Aktion Associates Inc 1687 Woodlands Dr . . . Maumee OH 43537 *TF:* 800-425-8466 ■ *Web:* www.aktion.com	419-893-7001	893-2840	179
Akumina Inc 30 Temple St Ste 301 . . . Nashua NH 03060 *Web:* akumina.com	603-943-7109		177
AKVMA (Alaska State Veterinary Medical Assn) 1731 Bragaw St . . . Anchorage AK 99508 *Web:* www.akvma.org	907-205-4272		795
AKWEL Cadillac USA Inc 603 W 7th St . . . Cadillac MI 49601 *Web:* akwel-automotive.com	231-775-6571		677
Akzo Nobel Chemicals Inc 10 Finderne Ave . . . Bridgewater NJ 08807 **Fax Area Code:* 908 ■ *TF:* 888-331-6212 ■ *Web:* www.akzonobel.com	888-331-6212	707-3664*	145
Al Basha Restaurant 1076 Main St . . . Paterson NJ 07503 *Web:* www.albashanj.com	973-345-3700		671
AL Betz & Associates Inc PO Box 665 . . . Westminster MD 21158 **Fax Area Code:* 410 ■ *TF:* 877-402-3376 ■ *Web:* www.albetzreporting.com	877-402-3376	875-2857*	445
AL Biernat's 4217 Oak Lawn Ave . . . Dallas TX 75219 *Web:* www.albiernats.com	214-219-2201	219-2093	671
AL C. Rinaldi Inc 1718 Chestnut St . . . Philadelphia PA 19103 *Web:* www.jacobsmusic.com	215-568-0021		526
AL Copeland Investments Inc 1001 Harimaw Ct S . . . Metairie LA 70001 *TF:* 800-401-0401 ■ *Web:* www.alcopeland.com	504-830-1000		670
AL Dente Pasta 491 N Palm Canyon Dr . . . Palm Springs CA 92262 *Web:* www.aldentepalmsprings.com	760-325-1160	325-2199	671
AL Forno Restaurant 577 S Water St . . . Providence RI 02903 *Web:* alforno.com	401-273-9760		671
Al Fresco 11710 Jefferson Ave . . . Newport News VA 23606 *Web:* www.alfrescoitalianrestaurant.com	757-873-0644		671
AL Gilbert Co 304 N Yosemite Ave . . . Oakdale CA 95361 *TF:* 800-400-6377 ■ *Web:* farmerswarehouse.com	209-847-1721		447
AL Gordon Plumbing & Heating LC 3855 W Airline Hwy . . . Waterloo IA 50703 *Web:* algordonplumbing.com	319-233-3991		189-10
AL Hansen Manufacturing Co 701 Pershing Rd . . . Waukegan IL 60085 *Web:* www.alhansen.com	847-244-8900	244-7222	350
AL Hirschfeld Theatre 246 West 44th St . . . New York NY 10036 *Web:* www.telecharge.com	212-239-6262		747
AL Knoch Interiors Inc 9010 N Desert Blvd . . . Canutillo TX 79835 *Web:* www.alknochinteriors.com	915-886-5800	886-4767	131
AL Larson Boat Shop Inc 1046 S Seaside Ave . . . Terminal Island CA 90731 *Web:* larsonboat.com	310-514-4100	831-4912	698
AL Neyer Inc 302 W Third St Ste 800 . . . Cincinnati OH 45202 *TF:* 877-271-6400 ■ *Web:* www.neyer.com	513-271-6400	271-1350	653
AL Phillips the Cleaner 3250 W Ali Baba Ln Ste C-F . . . Las Vegas NV 89118 *Web:* alphillipslv.com	702-798-7333	798-1731	426
AL Tiramisu 2014 P St NW . . . Washington DC 20036 *Web:* www.altiramisu.com	202-467-4466		671
AL Xander Company Inc 36 E South St . . . Corry PA 16407 *TF:* 800-541-5467 ■ *Web:* www.alxander.com	814-665-8268	664-7343	789
Al's Garden Art Inc 19930 Jolora Ave . . . Corona CA 92881 **Fax Area Code:* 951 ■ *Web:* www.alsgardenart.com	909-424-0221	582-0420*	364
Al's Restaurant 1200 N First St . . . Saint Louis MO 63102 *Web:* www.alsrestaurant.net	314-421-6399		671
ALA (American Library Assn) 50 E Huron St . . . Chicago IL 60611 *TF:* 800-545-2433 ■ *Web:* www.ala.org	312-944-6780	944-2641	49-11
ALA (American Logistics Assn) 1101 Vermont Ave NW Ste 1002 . . . Washington DC 20005 *TF:* 800-791-7146 ■ *Web:* www.ala-national.org	202-466-2520	296-4419	48-19
ALA (Association of Legal Administrators) 75 Tri-State International Ste 222 . . . Lincolnshire IL 60069 *Web:* www.alanet.org	847-267-1252	267-1329	49-10
ALA (American Lighting Assn) 2050 Stemmons Fwy Ste 10046 . . . Dallas TX 75207 *TF:* 800-605-4448 ■ *Web:* alalighting.com	214-698-9898	698-9899	49-4
ALA Moana Shopping Ctr 1450 Ala Moana Blvd . . . Honolulu HI 96814 *Web:* www.alamoanacenter.com	808-955-9517	955-2193	460
Alaark Tooling & Automation Inc 4336 Gateway Dr . . . Sheboygan WI 53081 *Web:* www.alaark.com	920-452-8231		757
Alabama			
Administrative Office of Alabama Courts 300 Dexter Ave . . . Montgomery AL 36104 *TF:* 866-954-9411 ■ *Web:* www.alacourt.gov	334-954-5000		339-1
Agriculture & Industries Dept 1445 Federal Dr PO Box 3336 . . . Montgomery AL 36109 *Web:* agi.alabama.gov	334-240-7171	240-7190	339-1
Arts Council 201 Monroe St Ste 110 . . . Montgomery AL 36130 *Web:* www.arts.alabama.gov	334-242-4076	240-3269	339-1
Child Support Enforcement Div 50 N Ripley St Gordon Persons Bldg Ste 2104 . . . Montgomery AL 36130 *TF:* 800-458-7214 ■ *Web:* dhr.alabama.gov	334-242-1350	353-1115	339-1
Conservation & Natural Resources Dept 64 N Union St . . . Montgomery AL 36130 *Web:* www.outdooralabama.com	334-242-3486		339-1
Consumer Affairs Office 11 S Union St . . . Montgomery AL 36130 *Web:* www.aldoi.gov	334-242-7334		339-1
Corrections Dept 301 S Ripley St PO Box 301501 . . . Montgomery AL 36130 *Web:* www.doc.state.al.us	334-353-3883		339-1
Crime Victims Compensation Commission 5845 Carmichael Rd . . . Montgomery AL 36117 *TF:* 800-541-9388 ■ *Web:* acvcc.alabama.gov	334-290-4420	290-4455	339-1
Department of Finance Alabama State Capitol 600 Dexter Ave Ste N-200 . . . Montgomery AL 36130 *Web:* finance.alabama.gov	334-242-7160	353-3300	339-1
Department of Homeland Security PO Box 304115 . . . Montgomery AL 36130 *Web:* www.ready.gov	334-956-7250		339-1
Economic & Community Affairs Dept PO Box 5690 . . . Montgomery AL 36103 *Web:* www.adeca.alabama.gov	334-242-5100	242-5099	339-1
Emergency Management Agency 5898 County Rd 41 PO Box 2160 . . . Clanton AL 35046 *Web:* ema.alabama.gov	205-280-2312		339-1
Ethics Commission 100 N Union St Ste 104 . . . Montgomery AL 36104 *Web:* www.ethics.alabama.gov	334-242-2997	242-0248	339-1
Forensic Sciences Dept 1051 Wire Rd . . . Auburn AL 36849 *Web:* www.adfs.alabama.gov	334-844-4648	887-7531	339-1
Highway Patrol Div 301 S Ripley St . . . Montgomery AL 36104 *TF:* 800-272-7930 ■ *Web:* www.alea.gov	334-517-2950		339-1
Historical Commission 468 S Perry St PO Box 300900 . . . Montgomery AL 36130 *Web:* ahc.alabama.gov	334-242-3184		339-1
Human Resources Dept 50 N Ripley St Ste 2104 Gordon Persons Bldg . . . Montgomery AL 36130 *Web:* dhr.alabama.gov	334-242-1310	353-1115	339-1
Information Services Div 64 N Union St Ste 200 . . . Montgomery AL 36130 *Web:* oit.alabama.gov	334-242-3800		339-1
Insurance Dept 201 Monroe St Ste 502 . . . Montgomery AL 36104 *Web:* www.aldoi.gov	334-269-3550	241-4192	339-1
Kay Ivey Governor 600 Dexter Ave . . . Montgomery AL 36130 *Web:* www.governor.alabama.gov	334-242-7100	353-0004	339-1
Labor Dept 649 Monroe St . . . Montgomery AL 36131 *Web:* labor.alabama.gov	334-954-4701	956-7494	339-1
Lieutenant Governor 11 S Union St . . . Montgomery AL 36130 *Web:* ltgov.alabama.gov	334-261-9590	353-4418	339-1
Mental Health & Mental Retardation Dept 100 N Union St PO Box 301410 . . . Montgomery AL 36130 *TF:* 800-367-0955 ■ *Web:* mh.alabama.gov	334-242-3454	242-0725	339-1
Motor Vehicle Div 50 N Ripley St . . . Montgomery AL 36104 *Web:* revenue.alabama.gov	334-242-9000		339-1
National Guard 853 Lagoon Commercial Blvd PO Box 3711 Montgomery AL 36109 *TF:* 800-464-8273 ■ *Web:* www.state.nationalguard.com	334-271-7200		339-1
Pardons & Paroles Board 100 Capitol Commerce Blvd PO Box 302405Montgomery AL 36130 *Web:* paroles.alabama.gov	334-242-8700	306-3188	339-1
Prepaid Affordable College Tuition (PACT) 100 N Union St Ste 660 . . . Montgomery AL 36104 *TF:* 800-252-7228 ■ *Web:* treasury.alabama.gov	800-252-7228		725

Name / Address	City	State	Zip	Phone	Fax	Class
Public Health Dept 201 Monroe St Ste 1200 *TF:* 800-252-1818 ■ *Web:* www.alabamapublichealth.gov	Montgomery	AL	36104	334-206-5300		339-1
Public Safety Dept PO Box 1511 **Fax Area Code:* 256 ■ *TF:* 800-392-8011 ■ *Web:* www.alea.gov	Montgomery	AL	36102	334-517-2800	268-9663*	339-1
Public Service Commission 100 N Union St RSA Union PO Box 304260 *TF:* 800-392-8050 ■ *Web:* www.psc.state.al.us	Montgomery	AL	36130	334-242-5218		339-1
Rehabilitation Services Dept 602 S Lawrence St *TF:* 800-441-7607 ■ *Web:* www.rehab.alabama.gov	Montgomery	AL	36104	334-293-7500	293-7383	339-1
Revenue Dept 2545 Taylor Rd *Web:* revenue.alabama.gov	Montgomery	AL	36117	334-242-1170		339-1
Secretary of State PO Box 5616 *Web:* sos.alabama.gov	Montgomery	AL	36103	334-242-7200	242-4993	339-1
Securities Commission RSA Dexter Avenue Bldg 445 Dexter Ave Ste 12000 *TF:* 800-222-1253 ■ *Web:* asc.alabama.gov	Montgomery	AL	36104	334-242-2984	242-0240	339-1
Senior Services Dept 201 Monroe Ste 350 *TF:* 877-425-2243 ■ *Web:* alabamaageline.gov	Montgomery	AL	36104	334-242-5743	242-5594	339-1
State Banking Dept 401 Adams Ave Ste 680 *TF:* 866-465-2279 ■ *Web:* www.banking.alabama.gov	Montgomery	AL	36104	334-242-3452	242-3500	339-1
State Port Authority 250 N Water St *Web:* www.asdd.com	Mobile	AL	36602	251-441-7234	441-7216	339-1
Tourism Department 401 Adams Ave PO Box 4927 *TF:* 800-252-2262 ■ *Web:* www.tourism.alabama.gov	Montgomery	AL	36104	334-242-4169	242-4554	339-1
Treasury Dept 600 Dexter Ave Ste S-106 *Web:* treasury.alabama.gov	Montgomery	AL	36104	334-242-7500		339-1
Veterans Affairs Dept 2209 Alabama Ave S E *Web:* va.alabama.gov	Washington	DC	20420	334-242-5077	242-5102	339-1
Vital Records PO Box 5625 *Web:* www.alabamapublichealth.gov	Montgomery	AL	36103	334-206-5418	262-9563	339-1
Weights & Measures Div 1445 Federal Dr *Web:* agi.alabama.gov	Montgomery	AL	36107	334-240-7133	240-7175	339-1
Alabama Agricultural & Mechanical University 4900 Meridian St N PO Box 908 *TF:* 800-553-0816 ■ *Web:* www.aamu.edu	Normal	AL	35762	256-372-5000	372-5906	166
Alabama Aircraft Industries 1943 50th St N	Birmingham	AL	35212	205-592-0011		24
Alabama Art Supply Inc 1006 23rd St S *TF:* 800-749-4741 ■ *Web:* www.alabamaart.com	Birmingham	AL	35205	205-322-4741	254-3116	45
Alabama Association of Realtors 522 Washington Ave PO Box 4070 *TF:* 800-446-3808 ■ *Web:* www.alabamarealtors.com	Montgomery	AL	36104	334-262-3808	263-9650	656
Alabama Ballet 2726 First Ave S *Web:* alabamaballet.org	Birmingham	AL	35233	205-322-4300		573-1
Alabama Bolt & Supply Inc 630 Air Base Blvd *Web:* www.albolt.com	Montgomery	AL	36108	334-269-9560	269-6969	351
Alabama Brick Delivery Inc 2201 24th Ave N *Web:* www.alabamabrick.com	Birmingham	AL	35234	815-323-1560		191-1
Alabama Christian Academy 4700 Wares Ferry Rd *Web:* www.alabamachristian.org	Montgomery	AL	36109	334-277-1985		148
Alabama Commission on Higher Education 100 N Union St Ste 782 PO Box 302000 *Web:* ache.edu	Montgomery	AL	36104	334-242-1998	242-0268	339-1
Alabama Correctional Industries 1400 Lloyd St PO Box 70084 *Web:* www.aci-al.org	Montgomery	AL	36107	334-261-3600	240-3162	630
Alabama Credit Union 220 Paul Bryant Dr E *TF:* 888-817-2002 ■ *Web:* www.alabamacu.com	Tuscaloosa	AL	35401	205-348-5944	348-9205	219
Alabama Crown Distributing 1330 Corporate Woods Dr *TF:* 800-548-1869 ■ *Web:* www.alabamacrown.com	Alabaster	AL	35007	205-941-1155		81-3
Alabama Cullman Yutaka Technologies LLC 460 Alabama Hwy 157 *Web:* www.yutakagiken.co.jp	Cullman	AL	35058	256-739-3533	739-3476	60
Alabama Dance Theatre 1018 Madison Ave *Web:* www.alabamadancetheatre.com	Montgomery	AL	36104	334-241-2590		573-1
Alabama Democratic Party 501 Adams Ave *Web:* www.aldemocrats.org	Montgomery	AL	36104	334-262-2221		616-1
Alabama Dental Assn 836 Washington Ave *TF:* 800-489-2532 ■ *Web:* www.aldaonline.org	Montgomery	AL	36104	334-265-1684	262-6218	227
Alabama Department of Archives & History 624 Washington Ave PO Box 300100 *Web:* archives.alabama.gov	Montgomery	AL	36104	334-242-4435	240-3433	520
Alabama Department of Corrections 301 South Ripley St PO Box 301501 *TF:* 855-937-2362 ■ *Web:* www.doc.alabama.gov	Montgomery	AL	36130	855-937-2362		339-1
Alabama Electric Company Inc 1728 Headland Ave *Web:* www.alaelectric.com	Dothan	AL	36304	334-792-5164		518
Alabama Eye Bank 500 Robert Jemison Rd *TF:* 800-423-7811 ■ *Web:* alabamaeyebank.org	Birmingham	AL	35209	800-423-7811		269
Alabama Farmers Co-opeartive Inc PO Box 2227 *TF:* 800-589-3206 ■ *Web:* www.alafarm.com	Decatur	AL	35609	256-353-6843	350-1770	280
Alabama Goodwill Industries Inc 2350 Green Springs Hwy S *Web:* www.alabamagoodwill.org	Birmingham	AL	35205	205-323-6331		256
Alabama Graphics & Engineering Supply Inc 2801 Fifth Ave S *TF:* 800-292-3806 ■ *Web:* www.algraphics.com	Birmingham	AL	35233	205-252-8505		256
Alabama Gulf Coast Zoo, The 1204 Gulf Shores Pkwy *Web:* www.alabamagulfcoastzoo.com	Gulf Shores	AL	36542	251-968-5732	967-3358	823
Alabama Housing Finance Authority 7460 Halcyon Pointe Dr Ste 200 *TF:* 800-325-2432 ■ *Web:* www.ahfa.com	Montgomery	AL	36117	334-244-9200	244-9214	339-1
Alabama Jazz Hall of Fame 1701B 4th Ave N *Web:* www.jazzhall.com	Birmingham	AL	35203	205-254-2731	254-2785	520
Alabama Livestock Auction Inc Hwy 80 E PO Box 279 *Web:* www.allivestock.com	Uniontown	AL	36786	334-628-2371	628-6268	446
Alabama Media Group 200 Westside Sq Ste 100 *TF:* 800-239-5271 ■ *Web:* www.alabamamediagroup.com	Huntsville	AL	35801	256-532-4000		532-2
Alabama Medical Assn 19 S Jackson St *TF:* 800-239-6272 ■ *Web:* www.alamedical.org	Montgomery	AL	36104	334-954-2500	269-5200	474
Alabama Metal Industries Corp (AMICO) 3245 Fayette Ave *TF:* 800-366-2642 ■ *Web:* amicoglobal.com	Birmingham	AL	35208	205-787-2611		491
Alabama Motor Express Inc 10720 E US Hwy 84 E *TF:* 800-633-7590 ■ *Web:* www.amxtrucking.com	Ashford	AL	36312	800-633-7590		780
Alabama Museum of Natural History PO Box 870340 *Web:* almnh.museums.ua.edu	Tuscaloosa	AL	35487	205-348-7550	348-9292	520
Alabama Newsnet 3251 Harrison Rd *TF:* 800-467-0401 ■ *Web:* www.alabamanews.net	Montgomery	AL	36109	334-270-9252	272-6444	741-86
Alabama One Credit Union 1215 Veterans Memorial Pkwy *TF:* 800-225-0110 ■ *Web:* www.alabamaone.org	Tuscaloosa	AL	35404	205-759-1595		219
Alabama Outdoors Inc 3054 Independence Dr *Web:* alabamaoutdoors.com	Birmingham	AL	35209	205-870-1919		711
Alabama Paper Products LLC 1300 Industrial Park Dr *Web:* www.marylandpaper.com	Tuscaloosa	AL	35401	205-339-9660		557
Alabama Pharmacy Assn 1211 Carmichael Way *TF:* 877-877-3962 ■ *Web:* www.aparx.org	Montgomery	AL	36106	334-271-4222	271-5423	585
Alabama Public Library Service 6030 Monticello Dr *Web:* aplsws1.apls.state.al.us	Montgomery	AL	36117	334-213-3900	213-3993	434-5
Alabama Public Radio 920 Paul W Bryant Dr PO Box 870370 *TF:* 800-654-4262 ■ *Web:* www.apr.org	Tuscaloosa	AL	35487	800-654-4262		645-168
Alabama Public Television (APT) 2112 11th Ave S Ste 400 *TF:* 800-239-5233 ■ *Web:* www.aptv.org	Birmingham	AL	35205	205-328-8756	251-2192	632
Alabama Republican Party 3505 Lorna Rd *Web:* www.algop.org	Birmingham	AL	35216	205-212-5900	212-5910	616-2
Alabama Rivers Alliance 2014 6th Ave N Ste 200 *TF:* 877-862-5260 ■ *Web:* alabamarivers.org	Birmingham	AL	35203	205-322-6395		532-5
Alabama Roll Products 5350 Laurendine Rd *Web:* alabamarollproducts.com	Theodore	AL	36582	251-973-0120	973-0130	492
Alabama School Journal 422 Dexter Ave *TF:* 800-392-5839 ■ *Web:* myaea.org	Montgomery	AL	36104	334-834-9790	262-8377	457-8
Alabama Shakespeare Festival 1 Festival Dr **Fax Area Code:* 334 ■ *TF:* 800-841-4273 ■ *Web:* www.asf.net	Montgomery	AL	36117	800-841-4273	271-5348*	749
Alabama Small Business Development Ctr 1500 1st Ave N *Web:* www.asbdc.org	Birmingham	AL	35203	205-348-1582	324-5234	627
Alabama Specialty Products Inc 152 Metal Samples Rd PO Box 8 *TF:* 888-388-1006 ■ *Web:* www.alspi.com	Munford	AL	36268	256-358-5200	358-4515	318
Alabama Sports Hall of Fame 2150 Richard Arrington Junior Blvd *Web:* www.ashof.org	Birmingham	AL	35203	205-323-6665	252-2212	522
Alabama State Bar 415 Dexter Ave *TF:* 800-392-5660 ■ *Web:* www.alabar.org	Montgomery	AL	36104	334-269-1515	261-6310	72
Alabama State Department of Education 50 N Ripley St PO Box 302101 *Web:* www.alsde.edu	Montgomery	AL	36104	334-694-4900		339-1
Alabama State Nurses Assn (ASNA) 360 N Hull St *TF:* 800-270-2762 ■ *Web:* alabamanurses.org	Montgomery	AL	36104	334-262-8321		533
Alabama State University 915 S Jackson St *TF:* 800-253-5037 ■ *Web:* www.alasu.edu	Montgomery	AL	36104	334-229-4100	229-4984	166
Alabama Symphony Orchestra 3621 Sixth Ave S *Web:* alabamasymphony.org	Birmingham	AL	35222	205-251-6929	251-6840	573-3
Alabama Theatre 1817 Third Ave N *TF:* 800-745-3000 ■ *Web:* alabamatheatre.com	Birmingham	AL	35203	205-252-2262		572
Alabama Theatre 4750 Hwy 17 S *TF:* 800-342-2262 ■ *Web:* www.alabama-theatre.com	North Myrtle Beach	SC	29582	843-272-1111		572
Alabama Veterinary Medical Assn PO Box 803 *Web:* www.alvma.com	Fayetteville	TN	37334	334-395-0086	270-3399	795
Alabama WMU Camp 1404 Fairview Ave Po Box 681970 *Web:* alabamawmu.org	Prattville	AL	36066	334-613-2226		239
Alabaster Caverns State Park 217036 SH 50A *Web:* www.travelok.com	Freedom	OK	73842	580-621-3381	621-3572	565
AlaBev 211 Citation Ct *Web:* www.alabev.com	Birmingham	AL	35209	205-942-9403		81-1
Alacare Home Health & Hospice 2400 John Hawkins Pkwy *TF:* 800-852-4724 ■ *Web:* www.alacare.com	Birmingham	AL	35244	205-981-8000	981-8743	363
Alachua County 12 SE 1st St 4th Fl *TF:* 855-984-1187 ■ *Web:* www.alachuacounty.us	Gainesville	FL	32601	352-374-5204	338-7363	338

	Phone	Fax	Class
Alachua County Library District 401 E University Ave... Gainesville FL 32601 *TF:* 866-341-2730 ■ *Web:* www.aclib.us	352-334-3900	334-3918	434-3
Alachua County Visitors & Convention Bureau 30 E University Ave... Gainesville FL 32601 *TF:* 866-778-5002 ■ *Web:* www.visitgainesville.com	352-374-5260	338-3213	206
ALACO Ladder Co 5167 G St... Chino CA 91710 *TF:* 888-310-7040 ■ *Web:* www.alacoladder.com	909-591-7561	591-7565	421
Alacrinet Inc 530 Lytton Ave 2nd Fl... Palo Alto CA 94301 *TF:* 866-321-2638 ■ *Web:* www.alacrinet.com	650-646-2670		196
Alacrity House Publishing LLC 695 Main St... Sanford CO 81151 *Web:* www.alacrityhousepublishing.com	719-580-4114		637-2
Alacrity Solutions 9725 Windermere Blvd... Fishers IN 46037 *Web:* www.alacritysolutions.com	800-968-4456		390
Alacron Inc 71 Spit Brook Rd Ste 200... Nashua NH 03060 *Web:* www.alacron.com	603-891-2750		253
Aladco LLC 1100B S Prairie Ave... Waukesha WI 53186 *TF:* 800-383-6994 ■ *Web:* www.aladco.com	262-544-5994	544-0116	789
Aladdin 651 Union Blvd... Allentown PA 18109 *Web:* aladdinlv.com	610-437-4023		671
Aladdin Bakers Inc 240 25th St... Brooklyn NY 11232 *Web:* www.aladdinbakersinc.com	718-499-1818		297-8
Aladdin Steel Inc PO Box 89... Gillespie IL 62033 *TF:* 800-637-4455 ■ *Web:* www.aladdinsteel.com	217-839-2121	839-3823	492
Aladdin Temp-Rite LLC 250 E Main St... Hendersonville TN 37075 *TF:* 800-888-8018 ■ *Web:* aladdintemprite.com	615-537-3600		427
Aladdin's Eatery 2931 N High St... Columbus OH 43202 *Web:* aladdins.com	614-262-2414		671
Aladdin's Natural Eatery 646 Monroe Ave... Rochester NY 14607 *Web:* www.myaladdins.com	585-442-5000		671
Alafia River State Park 14326 S County Rd 39... Lithia FL 33547 *Web:* www.floridastateparks.org	813-672-5320		565
Alaglass Swimming Pools 165 Sweet Bay Rd... Saint Matthews SC 29135 *TF:* 877-655-7179 ■ *Web:* www.alaglaspools.com	877-655-7179		375
Alain Pinel Realtors Inc 12772 Saratoga-Sunnyvale Rd Ste 1000... Saratoga CA 95070	408-741-1111		652
Alaka'i Mechanical Corp 2655 Waiwai Loop... Honolulu HI 96819 *TF:* 800-600-1085 ■ *Web:* www.alakaimechanical.com	808-834-1085	834-1800	189-10
Alamance Community College PO Box 8000... Graham NC 27253 *TF:* 877-667-7533 ■ *Web:* www.alamancecc.edu	336-578-2002	578-3964	162
Alamance County 124 W Elm St... Graham NC 27253 *Web:* www.alamance-nc.com	336-228-1312	570-6788	338
Alamance County Area Chamber of Commerce 610 S Lexington Ave... Burlington NC 27215 *Web:* www.alamancechamber.com	336-228-1338		139
Alamance Crossing 1080 Piper Ln... Burlington NC 27215 *Web:* www.alamancecrossing.com	336-584-8157		655
Alamance-Burlington School District 1712 Vaughn Rd... Burlington NC 27217 *Web:* www.abss.k12.nc.us	336-570-6060	570-6218	685
Alamar Marina Restaurant and Bar 5999 Garden Hwy... Sacramento CA 95837 *Web:* www.alamarmarina.net	916-922-0200		671
Alamar Resort Inn 311 16th St... Virginia Beach VA 23451 *TF:* 800-346-5681 ■ *Web:* www.alamarresortinn.net	757-428-7582		669
Alameda Animal Hospital 431 12th Ave NE... Norman OK 73071 *Web:* alamedaanimalhospital.com	405-360-0045		794
Alameda Associates Insurance Agency Inc 2515 Santa Clara Ave Ste 200... Alameda CA 94501 *Web:* alamedaassociates.com	510-522-2090		390
Alameda Bible Church Home of Victory Christian School 220 El Pueblo Rd NW... Albuquerque NM 87114 *Web:* www.alamedabiblechurch.com	505-898-2311		685
Alameda Chamber of Commerce 2210D S Shore Ctr... Alameda CA 94501 *Web:* alamedachamber.com	510-522-0414	522-7677	139
Alameda County 1221 Oak St Ste 555... Oakland CA 94612 *TF:* 800-878-1313 ■ *Web:* www.acgov.org	510-272-6984	272-3784	338
Alameda County Fair Assn (ACFA) 4501 Pleasanton Ave... Pleasanton CA 94566 *TF:* 800-874-9253 ■ *Web:* www.alamedacountyfair.com	925-426-7600	426-7599	642
Alameda County Library 2450 Stevenson Blvd... Fremont CA 94538 *TF:* 888-663-0660 ■ *Web:* aclibrary.org	510-745-1500		434-3
Alameda County Water District 43885 S Grimmer Blvd... Fremont CA 94538 *Web:* acwd.org	510-668-4200		787
Alameda Free Library 1550 Oak St... Alameda CA 94501 *Web:* alamedaca.gov	510-747-7777	337-1471	434-3
Alameda Health System 2070 Clinton Ave... Alameda CA 94501 *Web:* www.alamedahealthsystem.org	510-522-3700		353
Alameda Natural Grocery 1650 Park St... Alameda CA 94501 *Web:* www.alamedanaturalgrocery.com	510-865-1500		345
Alameda Sun 3215 Encinal Ave Ste J... Alameda CA 94501 *Web:* www.alamedasun.com	510-263-1470		532-3
Alameda Times-Star 7677 Oakport St... Oakland CA 94621 *TF:* 866-225-5277 ■ *Web:* alamedaca.gov	510-208-6300		637-8
Alameda-Contra Costa Transit District 1600 Franklin St 10th Fl... Oakland CA 94612 *Web:* www.actransit.org	510-891-4777	891-4705	468
Alamo Aircraft Ltd 2538 SW 36th St PO Box 37343... San Antonio TX 78237 *Web:* alamoaircraft.com	210-434-5577	434-1030	770
Alamo Analytical Laboratories Ltd 10526 Gulfdale... San Antonio TX 78216 *Web:* www.alamoanalytical.com	210-340-8121	340-8123	743
Alamo Biologics 5844 Rocky Point Dr... San Antonio TX 78249 *TF:* 800-226-9091 ■ *Web:* alamobiologics.com	210-738-2663	732-4263	545
Alamo Cafe 10060 W IH-10... San Antonio TX 78230 *Web:* alamocafe.com	210-691-8827		671
Alamo Capital Financial Services 201 N Civic Dr Ste 360... Walnut Creek CA 94596 *Web:* www.alamocapital.com	925-472-5700		690
Alamo Concrete Pavers 1008 Hoefgen... San Antonio TX 78261 *Web:* alamopavers.net	210-534-8821	534-8997	182
Alamo Group Inc 1627 E Walnut... Seguin TX 78155 *NYSE: ALG* ■ *TF:* 800-788-6066 ■ *Web:* alamo-group.com	830-379-1480	372-9683	273
Alamo Industrial Inc 1502 E Walnut St... Seguin TX 78155 **Fax Area Code: 830* ■ *TF:* 800-356-6286 ■ *Web:* www.alamo-industrial.com	800-356-6286	379-0864*	295
Alamo Inn 2203 E Commerce St... San Antonio TX 78203 *Web:* alamoinnmotel.com	210-227-2203	222-2860	379
Alamo Iron Works Inc 943 AT&T Center Pkwy... San Antonio TX 78219 *TF:* 800-292-7817 ■ *Web:* www.aiwdirect.com	210-223-6161	704-8351	385
Alamo Lumber Co 10800 Sentinel St... San Antonio TX 78217 *TF:* 855-828-9792 ■ *Web:* alamo.doitbest.com	210-352-1300		191-3
Alamo Music Ctr 425 N Main Ave... San Antonio TX 78205 *TF:* 800-822-5010 ■ *Web:* www.alamomusic.com	844-251-1922		526
Alamo Public Telecommunications Council 501 Broadway PO Box 9... San Antonio TX 78215 *TF:* 800-627-8193 ■ *Web:* www.klrn.org	210-270-9000	270-9078	647
Alamo Tee's & Advertising 12814 Cogburn... San Antonio TX 78249 *TF:* 888-562-3800 ■ *Web:* alamotees.com	210-699-3800		7
Alamo Travel Group 8930 Wurzbach Rd... San Antonio TX 78240 *TF:* 800-692-5266 ■ *Web:* www.alamotravel.com	210-593-3997	614-2448	771
Alamo, The 300 Alamo Plz... San Antonio TX 78205 *Web:* www.thealamo.org	210-225-1391		520
Alamodome 100 Montana St... San Antonio TX 78203 *TF:* 800-884-3663 ■ *Web:* www.alamodome.com	210-207-3663	207-3646	720
Alamogordo Chamber of Commerce 1301 N White Sands Blvd... Alamogordo NM 88310 *TF:* 800-826-0294 ■ *Web:* www.alamogordo.com	575-437-6120	437-6334	139
Alamon Telephone Training Ctr 315 W Idaho St... Kalispell MT 59901 **Fax Area Code: 800* ■ *Web:* www.alamon.com	406-752-8838	752-2074*	167-3
Alamos Gold Inc 181 Bay St Ste 3910... Toronto ON M5J2T3 *NYSE: AGI* ■ *TF:* 866-788-8801 ■ *Web:* www.auricogold.com	416-368-9932	368-2934	502
Alamosa County 8900 Independence Way... Alamosa CO 81101 *Web:* alamosacounty.colorado.gov	719-589-4848	587-5207	338
Alan B. Harris Attorney at Law 409 N Texas Ave... Odessa TX 79761 *TF:* 800-887-1676 ■ *Web:* alanbharris.com	432-580-3118		428
Alan B. Lancz & Associates Inc 2400 N Reynolds Rd... Toledo OH 43615 *Web:* www.ablonline.com	419-536-5200	536-5401	463
Alan C. Chen PC 801 E Campbell Rd Ste 130... Richardson TX 75081 *Web:* immigrationwork.net	972-235-5772	235-3710	41
Alan Ferguson Assn 1212 N Main St... High Point NC 27262 *Web:* alanferguson.com	336-889-3866		393
Alan Gordon Enterprises Inc 5625 Melrose Ave... Hollywood CA 90038 *TF:* 800-825-6684 ■ *Web:* www.alangordon.com	323-466-3561	871-2193	591
Alan McIlvain Co (AMC) 501 Market St... Marcus Hook PA 19061 *TF:* 800-523-4231 ■ *Web:* www.alanmcilvain.com	610-485-6600	485-0471	191-3
Alan Plummer & Associates Inc 1320 S University Dr... Fort Worth TX 76107 *Web:* www.apaienv.com	817-806-1700	870-2536	261
Alan Ritchey Inc 740 S I-35 E Frontage Rd... Valley View TX 76272 *TF:* 800-877-0273 ■ *Web:* alanritchey.com	940-726-3276		780
Alan Shintani Inc 94-409 Akoki St... Waipahu HI 96797 *Web:* www.alan-shintani.com	808-841-7631	841-0014	186
Alan Utz & Associates Inc (AU&A) PO Box 131857... Tyler TX 75713 *Web:* auainc.com	903-566-9797		186
Alan Weber & Associates Inc 4131 Spicewood Springs Rd Ste L4... Austin TX 78759 *Web:* www.alanweberassociates.com	512-777-2608		809
Alan White Factory 111 S St... Shannon MS 38868 *Web:* www.alanwhiteco.com	870-533-4471		319-2
Alan Wong's 1857 S King St... Honolulu HI 96826 *Web:* www.alanwongs.com	808-949-2526	951-9520	671
Alana's Food & Wine 2333 N High St... Columbus OH 43202 *Web:* alanas.com	614-294-6783		671
Alandale Industries Inc 208 Burnette St... Troy NC 27371 *Web:* www.alandale.net	910-576-1291	576-1997	744
Al-Anon Family Group Inc 1600 Corporate Landing Pkwy... Virginia Beach VA 23454 *TF:* 888-425-2666 ■ *Web:* al-anon.org	757-563-1600	563-1655	48-21
Alaric Compliance Services LLC 150 Broadway Ste 302... New York NY 10038 *TF:* 888-243-2448 ■ *Web:* www.alariccompliance.com	212-243-5241	679-3570	192
Alarm Lock Systems Inc 345 Bayview Ave... Amityville NY 11701 *Web:* www.alarmlock.com	631-789-4871	789-3383	692
Alarm Security Group LLC 12301 Kiln Ct Ste A... Beltsville MD 20705 *Web:* www.asgsecurity.com	301-623-4000	937-3229	693
Alaska			
Arts Council 161 Klevin St Ste 102... Anchorage AK 99508 *TF:* 888-278-7424 ■ *Web:* education.alaska.gov	907-269-6610	269-6601	339-2
Banking Securities & Corporations Div 333 Willoughby Ave 9th Fl PO Box 110800... Juneau AK 99801 *TF:* 888-925-2521 ■ *Web:* www.commerce.alaska.gov	907-465-2521	465-1230	339-2
Behavioural Health Div 3601 C St... Juneau AK 99811 *Web:* www.hss.state.ak.us	907-269-3600	269-3623	339-2
Child Support Enforcement Div 550 W Seventh Ave Ste 310... Anchorage AK 99501 *TF:* 800-478-3300 ■ *Web:* www.csed.state.ak.us	907-269-6900	787-3220	339-2
Children's Services Office 130 Seward St Ste 512 PO Box 110602... Juneau AK 99811 *Web:* www.dhss.alaska.gov	907-465-3120	465-5149	339-2

Listing	City	State	ZIP	Phone	Fax	Class
Commission on Postsecondary Education						
PO Box 110510	Juneau	AK	99811	907-465-6671		725
TF: 800-770-8973 ■ *Web:* acpe.alaska.gov						
Court System 303 K St	Anchorage	AK	99501	907-264-0612		339-2
Web: www.courts.alaska.gov						
Department of Administration, Division of Personnel & Labor Relations						
10th Fl State Office Bldg PO Box 110201	Juneau	AK	99811	907-465-4430		339-2
Web: doa.alaska.gov						
Department of Fish & Game						
1255 W Eigth St PO Box 25526	Juneau	AK	99811	907-465-4100	465-2332	339-2
Web: www.adfg.alaska.gov						
Division of State Troopers						
5700 E Tudor Rd	Anchorage	AK	99507	907-269-5511	337-2059	339-2
Web: dps.alaska.gov						
Education & Early Development Dept						
801 W Tenth St Ste 200 PO Box 110500	Juneau	AK	99811	907-465-2800	465-4156	339-2
Web: education.alaska.gov						
Employment Security Div PO Box 115509	Juneau	AK	99811	907-465-2757	465-2374	259
TF: 888-448-3527 ■ *Web:* www.labor.alaska.gov						
Enterprise Technology Services Div						
State Office Bldg 333 Willoughby Ave 5th Fl	Juneau	AK	99801	888-565-8680	465-3450*	339-2
**Fax Area Code:* 907 ■ *TF:* 888-565-8680 ■ *Web:* alaska.gov						
Environmental Conservation Dept						
410 Willoughby Ave Ste 303	Juneau	AK	99811	907-465-5066	465-5070	339-2
Web: www.alaska.gov						
Health & Social Services Dept						
PO Box 110601	Juneau	AK	99811	907-465-3030	465-3068	339-2
Web: www.hss.state.ak.us						
Housing Finance Corp						
4300 Boniface Pkwy 99504	Anchorage	AK	99504	907-338-6100		339-2
TF: 800-478-2432 ■ *Web:* www.ahfc.us						
Insurance Div PO Box 110805	Juneau	AK	99811	907-465-2515	465-3422	339-2
Web: www.commerce.alaska.gov						
Labor & Workforce Development Dept						
1111 W Eighth St	Juneau	AK	99801	907-465-2700	465-2784	339-2
Web: www.labor.state.ak.us						
Legislative Ethics Committee						
1500 W Benson Blvd Ste 230	Anchorage	AK	99503	907-269-0111	269-0229	265
Web: anchorage.akleg.gov						
Lieutenant Governor 240 Main St Ste 301	Juneau	AK	99811	907-465-3520	465-3532	339-2
Web: gov.alaska.gov						
Military & Veterans Affairs Dept (DMVA)						
PO Box 5800	Fort Richardson	AK	99505	907-428-6031	428-6019	339-2
Web: dmva.alaska.gov						
Motor Vehicles Div						
1300 W Benson Blvd	Anchorage	AK	99503	907-269-3755		339-2
Web: www.doa.alaska.gov						
Natural Resources Dept						
550 W Seventh Ave Ste 1260	Anchorage	AK	99501	907-269-8400	269-8917	339-2
Web: www.dnr.alaska.gov						
Parole Board 550 W 7th Ave Ste 1800	Anchorage	AK	99501	907-269-4642	269-4697	339-2
Web: www.correct.state.ak.us						
Permanent Fund Dividend Div						
333 Willoughby Ave 11th Fl	Juneau	AK	99811	907-465-2326	465-3470	339-2
Web: pfd.alaska.gov						
Postsecondary Education Commission						
3030 Vintage Blvd PO Box 110510	Juneau	AK	99811	907-465-2962	465-5316	339-2
TF: 800-441-2962 ■ *Web:* acpe.alaska.gov						
Public Assistance Div						
350 Main St Rm 304 PO Box 110640	Juneau	AK	99811	907-465-1216	465-5154	339-2
Web: www.dhss.alaska.gov						
Real Estate Commission						
550 W Seventh Ave Ste 1535	Anchorage	AK	99501	907-269-8100	269-8125	339-2
Web: www.commerce.alaska.gov						
Regulatory Commission						
701 W Eigth Ave Ste 300	Anchorage	AK	99501	907-276-6222	276-0160	339-2
Web: rca.alaska.gov						
Revenue Dept						
550 W Seventh Ave Ste 500	Anchorage	AK	99501	907-269-0080	276-3338	339-2
Web: tax.alaska.gov						
Secretary of State						
State Capitol PO Box 110001 3rd Fl	Juneau	AK	99811	907-465-3500		339-2
Web: www.gov.alaska.gov						
State Legislature						
State Capitol Terry Miller Bldg Ste 111	Juneau	AK	99801	907-465-4648	465-2864	339-2
Web: akleg.gov						
State Libraries Archives & Museums Div						
395 Whittier St PO Box 110571	Juneau	AK	99801	907-465-2910	465-2151	339-2
Web: education.alaska.gov						
State Medical Examiner						
5455 Dr Martin Luther King Jr Ave	Anchorage	AK	99507	907-334-2200	334-2216	339-2
Web: www.hss.state.ak.us						
Supreme Court 303 K St	Anchorage	AK	99501	907-264-0608	264-0878	339-2
Web: www.courts.alaska.gov						
Tourism Development Office						
State Office Bldg 333 Willoughby Ave 9th Fl						
PO Box 110804	Juneau	AK	99801	907-465-2510	465-2103	339-2
Web: www.commerce.alaska.gov						
Transportation & Public Facilities Dept						
3132 Channel Dr	Juneau	AK	99811	907-465-3900		339-2
Web: www.dot.state.ak.us						
Violent Crimes Compensation Board						
240 Main St	Juneau	AK	99801	907-465-3040	465-2379	339-2
Web: doa.alaska.gov						
Vital Statistics Bureau						
5441 Commercial Blvd PO Box 110675	Juneau	AK	99801	907-465-3391	465-3618	339-2
Web: www.dhss.alaska.gov						
Workers' Compensation Div						
1111 W Eighth St Rm 305	Juneau	AK	99801	907-465-2790	465-2797	339-2
Web: www.labor.state.ak.us						
Alaska Aerofuel Inc PO Box 60669	Fairbanks	AK	99706	907-474-0062	474-0085	316
Web: www.alaskaaerofuel.com						
Alaska Air Group Inc						
19300 International Blvd	Seattle	WA	98188	206-433-3200		360-1
NYSE: ALK ■ *TF:* 800-654-5669 ■ *Web:* www.alaskaair.com						
Alaska Airlines Magazine						
2701 First Ave Ste 250	Seattle	WA	98121	206-441-5871	448-6939	457-22
Web: www.alaskaairlinesmagazine.com						
Alaska Angler Publications						
PO Box 1205	Talkeetna	AK	99676	907-455-8000		637-2
Web: www.alaskaangler.com						
Alaska Association of Realtors						
4205 Minnesota Dr	Anchorage	AK	99503	907-563-7133	561-1779	656
TF: 800-478-3763 ■ *Web:* www.alaskarealtors.com						
Alaska Aviation Heritage Museum						
4721 Aircraft Dr	Anchorage	AK	99502	907-248-5325		520
Web: www.alaskaairmuseum.org						
Alaska Bar Assn						
840 K St Ste 100 PO Box 100279	Anchorage	AK	99501	907-272-7469	272-2932	72
Web: alaskabar.org						
Alaska Bible College 248 E Elmwood Ave	Palmer	AK	99645	907-745-3201		161
TF: 800-478-7884 ■ *Web:* www.akbible.edu						
Alaska Botanical Garden						
4601 Campbell Airstrip Rd	Anchorage	AK	99507	907-770-3692	770-0555	97
Web: alaskabg.org						
Alaska Business Monthly						
501 W Northern Lights Blvd Ste 100	Anchorage	AK	99503	907-276-4373	279-2900	457-5
TF: 800-770-4373 ■ *Web:* www.akbizmag.com						
Alaska Career College						
1415 E Tudor Rd	Anchorage	AK	99507	907-563-7575		167-3
TF: 800-770-7575 ■ *Web:* www.alaskacareercollege.edu						
Alaska Center for the Performing Arts						
621 W Sixth Ave	Anchorage	AK	99501	907-263-2900	263-2927	572
Web: www.alaskapac.org						
Alaska Clean Seas Inc						
3300 C St Ste 200	Anchorage	AK	99503	907-659-2405		539
Web: www.alaskacleanseas.org						
Alaska Club Inc, The						
5201 E Tudor Rd	Anchorage	AK	99507	907-205-9773		354
Web: www.thealaskaclub.com						
Alaska Collection 509 W Fourth Ave	Anchorage	AK	99501	907-777-2800	777-2888	760
TF: 800-808-8068 ■ *Web:* www.alaskacollection.com						
Alaska Commercial Co 125 Main St	Aniak	AK	99557	800-563-0002		345
TF: 800-563-0002 ■ *Web:* www.alaskacommercial.com						
Alaska Communications Systems Group Inc						
600 Telephone Ave	Anchorage	AK	99503	907-563-8000		736
NASDAQ: ALSK ■ *TF:* 800-808-8083 ■ *Web:* www.alaskacommunications.com						
Alaska Conservation Foundation (ACF)						
1227 W 9th Ave Ste 300	Anchorage	AK	99501	907-276-1917		48-6
Web: alaskaconservation.org						
Alaska Construction Academy						
8005 Schoon St	Anchorage	AK	99518	907-222-0999	562-6118	167-3
Web: labor.alaska.gov						
Alaska Democratic Party						
2602 Fairbanks St	Anchorage	AK	99503	907-258-3050		616-1
Web: www.alaskademocrats.org						
Alaska Denali Winery						
11901 Industry Way Bldg A Ste 1	Anchorage	AK	99515	907-563-9434		50-7
Web: www.alaskadenaliwinery.com						
Alaska Dental Society						
1407 W 31st Ave Ste 304	Anchorage	AK	99503	907-563-3003	563-3009	227
TF: 800-478-4675 ■ *Web:* www.akdental.org						
Alaska Department of Corrections						
550 W 7th Ave Ste 1800	Anchorage	AK	99501	907-334-2381	465-3390	339-2
TF: 844-934-2381 ■ *Web:* doc.alaska.gov						
Alaska Department of Law						
Civil Division PO Box 110300	Juneau	AK	99811	907-269-5100	269-5110	339-2
Web: www.law.state.ak.us						
Alaska Division of Homeland Security & Emergency Management						
PO Box 5750	Fort Richardson	AK	99505	907-428-7000	428-7009	339-2
TF: 800-478-2337 ■ *Web:* www.ready.gov						
Alaska Executive Search Inc						
821 N St Ste 201	Anchorage	AK	99501	907-276-5707	276-5708	260
Web: akexec.com						
Alaska Fisheries Science Ctr (AFSC)						
7600 Sand Point Way NE Bldg 4	Seattle	WA	98115	206-526-4000	526-4004	668
Web: www.fisheries.noaa.gov						
Alaska Glacier Seafoods Inc						
13555 Glacier Hwy	Juneau	AK	99803	907-790-3590	790-4286	297-5
Web: www.alaskaglacierseafoods.com						
Alaska Humanities Forum						
421 W 1st Ave Ste 200	Anchorage	AK	99501	907-272-3979		533
Web: www.akhf.org						
Alaska Industrial Hardware Inc						
2192 Viking Dr	Anchorage	AK	99501	907-276-7201	258-3054	364
TF: 800-478-7201 ■ *Web:* www.aih.com						
Alaska Instrument Company Inc (AIC)						
907 E Dowling Rd Ste 5	Anchorage	AK	99518	907-561-7511	561-0762	201
Web: www.alaskainstrument.com						
Alaska Insulation Supply Inc (AIS)						
261 E 56th Ave Bldg B	Anchorage	AK	99518	907-563-4125		191-4
Web: www.alaskainsulation.com						
Alaska Interstate Construction LLC						
2525 C St Ste 305	Anchorage	AK	99503	907-562-2792		539
Web: www.aicllc.com						
Alaska Junior Theater						
430 W Seventh Ave Ste 30	Anchorage	AK	99501	907-272-7546	272-3035	573-4
Web: www.akjt.org						
Alaska Laser Printing & Mailing Services						
165 E 56th Ave	Anchorage	AK	99518	907-561-8000		5
Web: www.alaskalaserprint.com						
Alaska Magazine						
301 Arctic Slope Ave Ste 300	Anchorage	AK	99518	386-246-0444		457-22
TF: 800-288-5892 ■ *Web:* www.alaskamagazine.com						
Alaska Marine Highway System						
6858 Glacier Hwy PO Box 112505	Juneau	AK	99811	907-465-3941	465-8824	468
TF: 800-642-0066 ■ *Web:* www.dot.state.ak.us						
Alaska Mining & Diving Supply Inc						
3222 Commercial Dr	Anchorage	AK	99501	907-277-1741	279-6398	711
TF: 800-478-3444 ■ *Web:* www.akmining.com						
Alaska Municipal League Joint Insurance Association Inc						
807 G St Ste 356	Anchorage	AK	99501	907-258-2625		533
TF: 800-337-3682 ■ *Web:* www.amljia.org						
Alaska Native Heritage Ctr						
8800 Heritage Center Dr	Anchorage	AK	99504	907-330-8000	330-8030	520
TF: 800-315-6608 ■ *Web:* www.alaskanative.net						

				Phone	Fax	Class
Alaska Native Medical Ctr (ANMC) 4315 Diplomacy Dr. *TF:* 800-478-6661 ■ *Web:* www.anmc.org	Anchorage	AK	99508	907-563-2662		374-3
Alaska Native Tribal Health Consortium Inc 4000 Ambassador Dr *TF:* 800-655-4837 ■ *Web:* anthc.org	Anchorage	AK	99508	907-729-1900		363
Alaska Nurses Assn (ANA) 3701 E Tudor Rd Ste 208 *Web:* www.aknurse.org	Anchorage	AK	99507	907-274-0827	272-0292	533
Alaska Operating Engineers/Employers Training Trust 5400 Cunningham Rd. *TF:* 800-478-5338 ■ *Web:* www.aoeett.org	Palmer	AK	99645	907-746-3117	563-4571	167-3
Alaska Pacific University 4101 University Dr *TF:* 800-252-7528 ■ *Web:* www.alaskapacific.edu	Anchorage	AK	99508	907-564-8248		166
Alaska Permanent Capital Management Co 900 W Fifth Ave Ste 601 *Web:* www.apcm.net	Anchorage	AK	99501	907-272-7575		194
Alaska Pharmacist's Assn 203 W 15th Ave Ste 100 *Web:* alaskapharmacy.org	Anchorage	AK	99501	907-563-8880	563-7880	585
Alaska Power & Telephone Co 193 Otto St PO Box 3222 *OTC:* APTL ■ *TF:* 800-982-0136 ■ *Web:* www.aptalaska.com	Port Townsend	WA	98368	360-385-1733	385-5177	787
Alaska Primary Care Association Inc 1231 Gambell St Ste 200 *TF:* 800-478-2221 ■ *Web:* www.alaskapca.org	Anchorage	AK	99501	907-929-2722	929-2734	138
Alaska Psychiatric Institute 3700 Piper St *Web:* www.dhss.alaska.gov	Anchorage	AK	99508	907-269-7100		374-5
Alaska Public Broadcasting Inc (APBI) 135 Cordova St. *Web:* www.akpb.org	Anchorage	AK	99501	907-277-6300		632
Alaska Public Interest Research Group (AKPIRG) PO Box 201416 Ste 206 *Web:* www.akpirg.org	Anchorage	AK	99520	907-278-3661		633
Alaska Public Media 3877 University Dr *Web:* www.alaskapublic.org	Anchorage	AK	99508	907-550-8400		647
Alaska Railroad Corp 327 W Ship Creek Ave *TF:* 800-544-0552 ■ *Web:* www.alaskarailroad.com	Anchorage	AK	99501	907-265-2494		651
Alaska Republican Party PO Box 201049 *Web:* www.alaskagop.net	Anchorage	AK	99520	907-276-4467		616-2
Alaska Salmon Bake In Alaskaland 2300 Airport Way *Web:* www.akvisit.com	Fairbanks	AK	99701	907-452-7274		671
Alaska Snow Removal PO Box 243002 *Web:* www.akplow.com	Anchorage	AK	99507	907-349-5000	349-5008	776
Alaska State Chamber of Commerce 471 W 36th Ave *Web:* www.alaskachamber.com	Anchorage	AK	99503	907-278-2722		140
Alaska State Library PO Box 110571 *Web:* library.alaska.gov	Juneau	AK	99811	907-465-2920	465-2665	434-5
Alaska State Medical Assn 4107 Laurel St *Web:* asmadocs.org	Anchorage	AK	99508	907-562-0304	561-2063	474
Alaska State Museum 395 Whittier St. *Web:* museums.alaska.gov	Juneau	AK	99801	907-465-2901	465-2976	520
Alaska State Veterinary Medical Assn (AKVMA) 1731 Bragaw St *Web:* www.akvma.org	Anchorage	AK	99508	907-205-4272		795
Alaska Stock Images 2505 Fairbanks St. *TF:* 800-487-4285 ■ *Web:* www.alaskastock.com	Anchorage	AK	99503	907-276-1343	258-7848	593
Alaska Tanker Company LLC 15400 NW Greenbrier Pkwy Parkside Bldg Ste A400 *Web:* www.aktanker.com	Beaverton	OR	97006	503-207-0046		311
Alaska Technical Ctr 834 4th St PO Box 51 *TF:* 800-478-3733 ■ *Web:* www.nwarctic.org	Kotzebue	AK	99752	907-442-1500	442-2764	167-3
Alaska Textiles Inc 620 W Fireweed Ln *Web:* www.alaskatextiles.com	Anchorage	AK	99503	907-265-4880		791
Alaska Tour & Travel 3900 Arctic Blvd Ste 304 PO Box 221011 *TF:* 800-208-0200 ■ *Web:* www.alaskatravel.com	Anchorage	AK	99503	907-245-0200	245-0400	771
Alaska Travel Adventures Inc 9085 Glacier Hwy Ste 301 *TF:* 800-323-5757 ■ *Web:* www.alaskatraveladventures.com	Juneau	AK	99801	907-789-0052		771
Alaska USA Federal Credit Union 4000 Credit Union Dr PO Box 196613 *TF:* 800-525-9094 ■ *Web:* www.alaskausa.org	Anchorage	AK	99503	907-563-4567		219
Alaska Village Electric Co-opeartive Inc 4831 Eagle St *TF:* 800-478-1818 ■ *Web:* avec.org	Anchorage	AK	99503	907-561-1818		245
Alaska Waterpark Company Inc 1520 O'Malley Rd *Web:* www.h2oasiswaterpark.com	Anchorage	AK	99507	907-522-4420		186
Alaska Wilderness League 122 C St NW Ste 240 *Web:* www.alaskawild.org	Washington	DC	20001	202-544-5205	544-5197	48-13
Alaska Wildlife Alliance PO Box 202022 *Web:* akwildlife.org	Anchorage	AK	99520	907-277-0897		48-3
Alaska Wildlife Conservation Ctr Mile 79 Seward Hwy PO Box 949 *Web:* www.alaskawildlife.org	Girdwood	AK	99587	907-783-2025	783-2370	823
Alaska Zoo 4731 O'Malley Rd *Web:* www.alaskazoo.org	Anchorage	AK	99507	907-346-2133	346-2673	823
Alaskan Brewing Co 5429 Shaune Dr *Web:* alaskanbeer.com	Juneau	AK	99801	907-780-5866	780-4514	102
Alaskan Campers Inc 801 NW Kerron Ave. *Web:* alaskancampers.com	Winlock	WA	98596	360-748-6494		120
Alaskan Copper & Brass Co 27402 72nd Ave S *TF:* 800-552-7661 ■ *Web:* www.alaskancopper.com	Kent	WA	98032	206-623-5800	382-7335	492

				Phone	Fax	Class
Alastin Skincare 3129 Tiger Run Ct *TF:* 844-858-7546 ■ *Web:* www.alastin.com	Carlsbad	CA	92010	844-858-7546		574
ALBA Editorial Inc 19706-B One Norman Blvd Ste 221 *Web:* www.albaedit.com	Cornelius	NC	28031	704-894-0639	894-0642	178-1
ALBA Enterprises Inc 10260 Indiana Ct *Web:* albaent.com	Rancho Cucamonga	CA	91730	909-941-0600		358
ALBA Manufacturing Inc 8950 Seward Rd *TF:* 866-252-2634 ■ *Web:* www.albamfg.com	Fairfield	OH	45011	513-874-0551	874-9476	207
ALBA Spectrum Technologies 1715 W Wabansia Ave *Web:* www.albaspectrum.com	Chicago	IL	60622	773-384-9264		194
ALBA Wheels Up 1 E Lincoln Ave *Web:* albawheelsup.com	Valley Stream	NY	11580	718-276-3000	712-1222	311
Albach Company Inc 301 E Prosper St *Web:* www.albachco.com	Chalmette	LA	70043	504-271-1113		189-14
Albano Systems Inc 1 Hartfield Blvd Ste 304 *Web:* www.albanosystems.com	Windsor	CT	06095	860-627-9555	627-9999	809
Albany Area Chamber of Commerce 225 W Broad Ave *TF:* 800-475-8700 ■ *Web:* albanyga.com	Albany	GA	31701	229-434-8700	434-8716	139
Albany Area Chamber of Commerce 435 W First Ave *Web:* www.albanychamber.com	Albany	OR	97321	541-926-1517	926-7064	139
Albany Bank & Trust Company NA 3400 W Lawrence Ave. *Web:* www.albanybank.com	Chicago	IL	60625	773-267-7300	267-7337	70
Albany City Hall 24 Eagle St *Web:* www.albanyny.gov	Albany	NY	12207	518-434-5100	434-5013	337
Albany College of Pharmacy (ACPHS) 106 New Scotland Ave *TF:* 888-203-8010 ■ *Web:* www.acphs.edu	Albany	NY	12208	518-694-7221		166
Albany County 112 State St Rm 1200 *Web:* www.albanycounty.com	Albany	NY	12207	518-447-7040	447-5589	338
Albany County Convention & Visitors Bureau 25 Quackenbush Sq *TF:* 800-258-3582 ■ *Web:* www.albany.org	Albany	NY	12207	518-434-1217	434-0887	206
Albany County Public Library 310 S Eigth St. *Web:* www.acplwy.org	Laramie	WY	82070	307-721-2580	721-2584	434-3
Albany County School 1948 Grand Ave. *Web:* www.acsd1.org	Laramie	WY	82070	307-721-4400		685
Albany Democrat-Herald 600 Lyons St SW PO Box 130 *Web:* www.democratherald.com	Albany	OR	97321	541-926-2211	926-4799	532-2
Albany Herald Publishing Company Inc 126 N Washington St *Web:* www.albanyherald.com	Albany	GA	31702	229-888-9300	888-9357	637-8
Albany Industries Inc 504 N Glenfield Rd *Web:* albanyindustries.com	New Albany	MS	38652	662-534-9800	534-9805	319-2
Albany Institute of History & Art 125 Washington Ave. *Web:* www.albanyinstitute.org	Albany	NY	12210	518-463-4478	462-1522	520
Albany International Corp 216 Airport Dr. *NYSE:* AIN ■ *TF:* 877-327-5378 ■ *Web:* www.albint.com	Rochester	NH	03867	518-445-2200	445-2250	745-3
Albany Law School of Union University (ALS) 80 New Scotland Ave *TF:* 800-448-3500 ■ *Web:* www.albanylaw.edu	Albany	NY	12208	518-445-2311		167-1
Albany Medical Ctr 43 New Scotland Ave *TF:* 866-262-7476 ■ *Web:* www.amc.edu	Albany	NY	12208	518-262-3125		374-3
Albany Memorial Hospital 600 N Blvd *Web:* www.sphp.com	Albany	NY	12204	518-471-3606		374-3
Albany Park Chamber of Commerce 3403 W Lauren Ave Ste 201 *TF:* 800-662-1875 ■ *Web:* www.northrivercommission.org	Chicago	IL	60625	773-478-0202	478-0282	139
Albany Public Library (APL) 161 Washington Ave. *Web:* www.albanypubliclibrary.org	Albany	NY	12210	518-427-4300	449-3386	434-3
Albany State University (ASU) 504 College Dr *Web:* www.asurams.edu	Albany	GA	31705	229-430-4600		166
Albany Steel Inc 566 Broadway *TF:* 800-342-9317 ■ *Web:* www.albanysteel.net	Albany	NY	12204	518-436-4851	436-1458	189-14
Albany Symphony Orchestra 19 Clinton Ave *Web:* www.albanysymphony.com	Albany	NY	12207	229-430-8933		573-3
Albany Visitors Assn 110 Third Ave SE PO Box 965 *TF:* 800-526-2256 ■ *Web:* albanyvisitors.com	Albany	OR	97321	541-928-0911	926-1500	206
Albany Weld-Trade School 91120-B Cape Arago Hwy PO Box 5771. *Web:* www.weldschool.com	Charleston	OR	97420	541-928-9353		685
Albany-Colonie Regional Chamber of Commerce 5 Computer Dr S. *Web:* capitalregionchamber.com	Albany	NY	12205	518-431-1400	431-1402	139
Albar Industries Inc 780 Whitney Dr *Web:* www.albar.com	Lapeer	MI	48446	810-667-0150		608
Albarella Design Inc 100 Bridgepoint Dr. *Web:* www.albarella.com	South Saint Paul	MN	55075	651-552-8966	552-9042	344
Albasha Greek Lebanese Restaurant 5454 Bluebonnet Rd Ste G *Web:* www.albashabr.com	Baton Rouge	LA	70809	225-292-7988		671
Albemarle 140 Midway Dr *TF:* 866-539-8430 ■ *Web:* www.albemarleboats.com	Edenton	NC	27932	252-482-7423	482-4099	90
Albemarle County 401 McIntire Rd *Web:* www.albemarle.org	Charlottesville	VA	22902	434-296-5841	296-5800	338
Albemarle Electric Membership Corp PO Box 69 *TF:* 800-215-9915 ■ *Web:* www.aemc.coop	Hertford	NC	27944	252-426-5735		245
Alberic Colon Auto Sales 551 Marginal JF Kennedy *TF:* 888-510-0718 ■ *Web:* www.albericgm.com	San Juan	PR	00920	877-292-4610		57

Name / Address	City	State	Zip	Phone	Fax	Class
Alberni Valley Chamber of Commerce 2533 Port Alberni Hwy *Web:* albernichamber.ca	Port Alberni	BC	V9Y8P2	250-724-6535	724-6560	137
Albert & Goodman CPAS PC 100 Lexington Dr Ste 150 *Web:* ag-cpas.com	Buffalo Grove	IL	60089	847-947-4411		2
Albert & Mackenzie LLP 28216 Dorothy Dr Ste 105 *Web:* albmac.com	Agoura Hills	CA	91301	818-575-9876	575-9006	428
Albert A. List College of Jewish Studies 3080 Broadway *Web:* www.jtsa.edu	New York	NY	10027	212-678-8832		166
Albert A. Webb Assoc 3788 Mccray St *Web:* www.webbassociates.com	Riverside	CA	92506	951-686-1070		256
Albert Arno Inc 5000 Claxton Ave *Web:* albertarnostl.com	Saint Louis	MO	63120	314-383-2700	383-7193	189-10
Albert at Bay Suite Hotel 435 Albert St *TF:* 800-267-6644 ■ *Web:* www.albertatbay.com	Ottawa	ON	K1R7X4	613-238-8858	238-1433	379
Albert C. Kobayashi Inc 94-535 Ukee St *Web:* www.ack-inc.com	Waipahu	HI	96797	808-671-6460		186
Albert College 160 Dundas St W *TF:* 800-952-5237 ■ *Web:* www.albertcollege.ca	Belleville	ON	K8P1A6	613-968-5726	968-9651	622
Albert E Erickson Co 1111 Honeyspot Rd *Web:* ericksonae.com	Stratford	CT	06615	203-386-8931	375-9455	454
Albert E. Brumley and Sons PO Box 27 *TF:* 800-435-3725 ■ *Web:* www.brumleymusic.com	Powell	MO	65730	417-435-2225	435-2227	637-10
Albert E. Sleeper State Park 6573 State Park Rd *TF:* 888-784-7328 ■ *Web:* www.michigan.org	Caseville	MI	48725	888-784-7328		565
Albert G's Bar-BQ 2748 S Harvard Ave *Web:* www.albertgs.com	Tulsa	OK	74114	918-747-4799		671
Albert Guarnieri & Co 151 E Market St *TF:* 800-686-2639 ■ *Web:* www.albertguarnieri.com	Warren	OH	44481	330-394-5636	394-4982	297-8
Albert J. Marchionne Insurance Agency Inc 11 Independence Ave *Web:* marchionneinsurance.com	Quincy	MA	02169	617-471-5010	471-1386	390
Albert Kahn Associates Inc 3011 W Grand Blvd Ste 1800 *TF:* 800-833-0062 ■ *Web:* albertkahn.com	Detroit	MI	48202	313-202-7000	202-7001	261
Albert Lea City Arena 701 Lake Chapeau Dr *Web:* cityofalbertlea.org	Albert Lea	MN	56007	507-377-4374		720
Albert Lea Public Library 211 E Clark St *Web:* alplonline.org	Albert Lea	MN	56007	507-377-4350		434-3
Albert Lea Seed House 1414 W Main St *TF:* 800-352-5247 ■ *Web:* www.alseed.com	Albert Lea	MN	56007	507-373-3161	373-7032	694
Albert Lea Tribune, The 808 W Front St *Web:* www.albertleatribune.com	Albert Lea	MN	56007	507-373-1411	373-0333	637-8
Albert Lea-Freeborn County Chamber of Commerce 2580 Bridge Ave *Web:* www.albertlea.org	Albert Lea	MN	56007	507-373-3938	373-0344	139
Albert M. Higley Co 2926 Chester Ave *Web:* www.amhigley.com	Cleveland	OH	44114	216-861-2050	861-0038	186
Albert Moving 4401 Barnett Rd *TF:* 800-460-9333 ■ *Web:* albertmoving.com	Wichita Falls	TX	76310	940-696-7020	696-7030	194
Albert Paper Co (AP) 1225 N Union St *Web:* albertpaperco.com	Stockton	CA	95205	209-466-7931		559
Albert R. Maccani CPA 1537 S Delsea Dr *Web:* www.maccani albert-r-cpa.business.site	Vineland	NJ	08360	856-691-3279		2
Albert Risk Management Consultants 72 River Park St *Web:* www.albertrisk.com	Needham	MA	02494	781-449-2866		195
Albert Screen Print Inc 3704 Summit Rd *Web:* www.albertinc.com	Norton	OH	44203	330-753-7559		745-7
Albert Wisner Public Library (AWPL) 1 McFarland Dr *Web:* www.albertwisnerlibrary.org	Warwick	NY	10990	845-986-1047	987-1228	434-3
Albert's Organics Inc 3268 E Vernon Ave *TF:* 800-899-5944 ■ *Web:* albertsorganics.com	Vernon	CA	90058	800-899-5944		297-7
Alberta Agriculture Food & Rural Development Food Processing Development Ctr 6309 45 St *Web:* www.alberta.ca	Leduc	AB	T9E7C5	780-986-4793	986-5138	299
Alberta Association of Municipal Districts & Counties 2510 Sparrow Dr *Web:* www.aamdc.com	Nisku	AB	T9E8N5	780-955-3639		138
Alberta Aviation Museum 11410 Kingsway Ave *Web:* www.albertaaviationmuseum.com	Edmonton	AB	T5G0X4	780-451-1175		520
Alberta Bair Theater for the Performing Arts 2722 Third Ave N Ste 200 PO Box 1556 *TF:* 877-321-2074 ■ *Web:* www.albertabairtheater.org	Billings	MT	59103	406-256-8915	256-5060	572
Alberta Blue Cross 10009 108th St NW *TF:* 800-661-6995 ■ *Web:* www.ab.bluecross.ca	Edmonton	AB	T5J3C5	780-498-8000	425-4627	391-3
Alberta Boilers Safety Assn 9410 20 Av NW *Web:* www.absa.ca	Edmonton	AB	T6N0A4	780-437-9100		261
Alberta Cancer Foundation 1331 29 St NW *Web:* albertacancer.ca	Calgary	AB	T2N4N2	403-521-3433		305
Alberta Chambers of Commerce 10025 - 102A Ave Ste 1808 *TF:* 800-272-8854 ■ *Web:* abchamber.ca	Edmonton	AB	T5J2Z2	780-425-4180	429-1061	137
Alberta Enterprise Corp 10088 102 Ave *TF:* 877-336-3474 ■ *Web:* www.alberta-enterprise.ca	Edmonton	AB	T5J2Z2	587-402-6601	402-6612	528
Alberta Hotel & Lodging Assn (AHLA) 2707 Ellwood Dr *TF:* 888-436-6112 ■ *Web:* www.ahla.ca	Edmonton	AB	T6X0P7	780-436-6112	436-5404	48-23
Alberta Newsprint Company Ltd Whitecourt Plant Postal Bag 9000 10km W Hwy 43 *Web:* www.albertanewsprint.com	Whitecourt	AB	T7S1P9	780-778-7000		532-3
Alberta Oil Tool 9530 60th Ave *TF:* 877-432-3404 ■ *Web:* www.albertaoiltool.com	Edmonton	AB	T6E0C1	780-434-8566	436-4329	537
Alberta Oilsands Inc 815-8th Ave SW Ste 600 *Fax Area Code: 416 ■ *Web:* www.aboilsands.ca	Calgary	AB	T2P3P2	403-263-6700	907-1788*	536
Alberta Senior Citizens Housing Assn 9711 47 Ave NW *Web:* www.ascha.com	Edmonton	AB	T6E5M7	780-439-6473		138
Alberta Soccer 9023 111 Ave NW *TF:* 866-250-2200 ■ *Web:* albertasoccer.com	Edmonton	AB	T5B0C3	780-474-2200		138
Alberta Sports Hall of Fame & Museum 4200 Hwy 2 Ste 102 *Web:* www.albertasportshall.ca	Red Deer	AB	T4N1E3	403-341-8614	341-8619	522
Alberta Union of Prov Employees 10451 170 St NW *TF:* 800-232-7284 ■ *Web:* www.aupe.org	Edmonton	AB	T5P4S7	780-930-3300		414
Alberta University of the Arts 1407 14th Ave NW *TF:* 800-251-8290 ■ *Web:* www.auarts.ca	Calgary	AB	T2N4R3	403-284-7600	289-6682	785
Alberta Workers' Compensation Board 9912-107 St *Web:* www.wcb.ab.ca	Edmonton	AB	T5K1G5	780-498-3999		393
Alberta-Pacific Forest Industries Inc PO Box 8000 *TF:* 800-661-5210 ■ *Web:* alpac.ca	Boyle	AB	T0A0M0	780-525-8000		638
Albertsons LLC 250 E Parkcenter Blvd *Web:* www.albertsons.com	Boise	ID	83706	208-395-6200		297-8
Albertus Magnus College 700 Prospect St *TF:* 800-578-9160 ■ *Web:* www.albertus.edu	New Haven	CT	06511	203-773-8550	773-5248	166
Albest Metal Stamping Corp 1 Kent Ave *Web:* www.albest.com	Brooklyn	NY	11211	718-388-6000	388-0404	488
Albin Engineering Services Inc 3350 Scott Blvd Ste 27 *Web:* aesi.com	Santa Clara	CA	95054	408-733-2374		177
Albion College 611 E Porter St *TF:* 800-858-6770 ■ *Web:* www.albion.edu	Albion	MI	49224	517-629-0354	629-0569	166
Albion Correctional Facility 3595 State School Rd *TF:* 800-995-6423 ■ *Web:* nicic.gov	Albion	NY	14411	585-589-5511		213
Albion Creative 622 SW St *Web:* albioncreative.com	High Point	NC	27260	336-883-8028		592
Albion Hotel 1650 James Ave *TF:* 877-782-3557 ■ *Web:* www.rubellhotels.com	Miami Beach	FL	33139	305-913-1000	674-0507	379
Albion Industries Inc 800 N Clark St *TF:* 800-835-8911 ■ *Web:* www.albioncasters.com	Albion	MI	49224	517-629-9441		350
Albion Investors LLC 501 Madison Ave 27th Fl *Web:* albioninvestors.com	New York	NY	10022	212-277-7520		690
Albion Laboratories Inc 67 S Main St Ste 100 *TF:* 800-453-2406 ■ *Web:* www.albionminerals.com	Layton	UT	84041	801-773-4631	773-4633	447
Albion Staffing Solutions Inc 2520 NW 97th Ave Ste 110 *Web:* jobs.albionstaffing.com	Miami	FL	33172	305-406-1000	406-1010	195
Albion Telephone Company Inc 225 W N St *Web:* www.atcnet.net	Albion	ID	83311	208-673-5335		387
Albion-Holley Pennysaver Inc 170 N Main St *Web:* www.lakecountrypennysaver.com	Albion	NY	14411	585-589-5641	589-1239	532-2
Albrecht- Viggiano- Zureck & Co 25 Suffolk Ct *Web:* www.avz.com	Hauppauge	NY	11788	631-434-9500	434-9518	2
Albrektson & Shumate LLP 1801 Orange Tree Ln Ste 230 *Web:* albshulaw.com	Redlands	CA	92374	909-335-9658	335-9489	41
Albright Capital Management 601 13th St NW Ste 1000 *Web:* www.albrightcapital.com	Washington	DC	20005	202-370-3500		528
Albright College 1621 N 13th St *TF:* 800-252-1856 ■ *Web:* www.albright.edu	Reading	PA	19604	610-921-2381	921-7294	166
Albright Memorial Library 500 Vine St *Web:* www.lclshome.org	Scranton	PA	18509	570-348-3000		434-3
Albright Stonebridge Group 601 13th St NW 10th Fl *Web:* www.albrightstonebridge.com	Washington	DC	20005	202-759-5100	759-5101	194
Albright, Stoddard, Warnick & Albright, A Professional Corp 801 So Rancho Dr Ste D-4 *Web:* albrightstoddard.com	Las Vegas	NV	89106	702-384-7111		41
Albright-Knox Art Gallery 1285 Elmwood Ave *TF:* 877-817-1319 ■ *Web:* www.albrightknox.org	Buffalo	NY	14222	716-882-8700		520
Albu & Associates Inc 2711 W Fairbanks Ave *Web:* albu.biz	Winter Park	FL	32789	407-788-1450	788-1463	186
Albuquerque Academy 6400 Wyoming Blvd NE *Web:* www.aa.edu	Albuquerque	NM	87109	505-828-3200		623
Albuquerque Barber College 601 San Pedro Dr NE *Web:* www.abqbarbercollege.com	Albuquerque	NM	87108	505-266-4900		167-3
Albuquerque Convention & Visitors Bureau 20 First Plz Ste 601 *TF:* 800-733-9918 ■ *Web:* www.visitalbuquerque.org	Albuquerque	NM	87102	505-842-9918	247-9101	206
Albuquerque Convention Ctr 401 Second St NW *Web:* www.albuquerquecc.com	Albuquerque	NM	87102	505-768-4575	768-3239	205
Albuquerque Equine Clinic PC 6901 Second St NW *Web:* albuquerqueequineclinic.com	Albuquerque	NM	87107	505-344-1131		794

				Phone	Fax	Class
Albuquerque International Sunport 2200 Sunport Blvd *Web:* www.cabq.gov	Albuquerque	NM	87106	505-244-7700	842-4278	27
Albuquerque Journal 7777 Jefferson St NE *Web:* www.abqjournal.com	Albuquerque	NM	87109	505-823-7777	823-3994	532-2
Albuquerque Little Theatre 224 San Pasquale SW *Web:* albuquerquelittletheatre.org	Albuquerque	NM	87104	505-242-4750		572
Albuquerque Public Schools (APS) 6400 Uptown Blvd NE *TF:* 866-563-9297 ■ *Web:* www.aps.edu	Albuquerque	NM	87110	505-880-3700	889-4883	685
Albuquerque Winnelson 3545 Princeton Dr NE PO Box 25726 *Web:* www.albuquerquewinsupply.com	Albuquerque	NM	87107	505-884-1553		791
Alburg Dunes State Park 151 Coon Pt Rd *TF:* 800-262-5226 ■ *Web:* www.vtstateparks.com	Alburg	VT	05440	802-796-4170		565
Albury Bros Boats 1401 Broadway *Web:* www.alburybrothers.com	Riviera Beach	FL	33404	561-863-7006	863-7746	90
ALC (Anderson Lumber Co) 780 Louisville Rd *Web:* www.andersonlumbercompany.com	Alcoa	TN	37701	865-983-3060		191-3
ALC Group, The 219 W 18th St *Web:* thealcgroup.com	Kansas City	MO	64108	816-421-8335		628
Alcalde & Fay 2111 Wilson Blvd 8th Fl *Web:* www.alcalde-fay.com	Arlington	VA	22201	703-841-0626		636
Alcam Metal Distributors Inc 12951 W 43rd Dr *Web:* www.alcammetals.com	Golden	CO	80403	303-463-5879	463-5908	492
Alcamo Supply Corp 1152 Jericho Tpke *Web:* alcamopools.com	Commack	NY	11725	631-543-8820		186
Alcan Electrical & Engineering Inc 6670 Arctic Spur Rd *Web:* www.alcanelectric.com	Anchorage	AK	99518	907-563-3787	562-6286	186
Alcast Foundry Inc 2910 Fisk Ln *Web:* www.alcast-foundry.com	Redondo Beach	CA	90278	310-542-3581	542-9927	492
Alcazar Networks Inc 419 State Ave Ste 3 *TF:* 800-349-6192 ■ *Web:* www.alcazarnetworks.com	Emmaus	PA	18049	484-664-2800		463
Alchemy 575 Double Eagle Ct *Web:* alchemy.us	Reno	NV	89521	775-372-9050		408
Alchemy of England 3516 Roberts Cut Off Rd *TF:* 800-578-1065 ■ *Web:* www.alchemyofengland.com	Fort Worth	TX	76114	817-236-3141		361
Alchemy Systems LP 5301 Riata Park Ct Bldg F *TF:* 888-988-8832 ■ *Web:* www.alchemysystems.com	Austin	TX	78727	512-637-5100	637-5168	423
ALCO (Alico Inc) 10070 Daniels Interstate Ct Ste 100 *NASDAQ: ALCO* ■ *Web:* www.alicoinc.com	Fort Myers	FL	33913	239-226-2000		315-2
Alco Gas & Oil Production Equipment Ltd 5203-75th St NW *Web:* www.alcoenergy.ca	Edmonton	AB	T6E5S5	780-465-9061		539
Alco Iron & Metal Co 2140 Davis St *Web:* www.alcometals.com	San Leandro	CA	94577	510-562-1107	562-1354	686
Alco Manufacturing Corporation LLC 10584 Middle Ave *Web:* alco.com	Elyria	OH	44035	440-458-5165	458-6821	621
Alco Parking Corp 501 Martindale St *Web:* alcoparking.com	Pittsburgh	PA	15212	412-323-4455	323-4492	562
Alco Pharmaceuticals Inc 11435 Cronhill Dr Ste A *Web:* alcopharmacy.com	Owings Mills	MD	21117	443-394-7300		237
Alco Plastics Inc 160 E Pond Dr *Web:* www.alcoplastics.com	Romeo	MI	48065	586-752-4527		608
Alco Sales & Service Co 6851 High Grove Blvd *TF:* 800-323-4282 ■ *Web:* www.alcosales.com	Burr Ridge	IL	60527	630-655-1900		194
Alco Tool Supply Inc (ATS) 54847 County Rd 17 *TF:* 800-437-2911 ■ *Web:* www.alcotoolsupply.com	Elkhart	IN	46516	574-295-5535	293-2254	351
Alcoa Corp 201 Isabella St Ste 500 *Web:* www.alcoa.com	Pittsburgh	PA	15212	412-315-2900		485
Alcock Law Group Pc 19751 E MainSt Ste 210 *Web:* alcocklawgroup.com	Parker	CO	80138	303-993-5400		41
Alcohol & Tobacco Tax & Trade Bureau 1310 G St NW PO Box 12 *TF:* 877-882-3277 ■ *Web:* www.ttb.gov	Washington	DC	20005	202-453-2180	453-2912	340-18
Alcoholic Beverage Control PO Box 27491 *TF:* 800-552-3200 ■ *Web:* www.abc.virginia.gov	Richmond	VA	23261	804-213-4565	213-4574	531-7
Alcoholics Anonymous (AA) 475 Riverside Dr 11th Fl *TF:* 800-437-3584 ■ *Web:* www.aa.org	New York	NY	10115	212-870-3400	870-3003	48-21
Alcom Printing Group Inc 140 Christopher Ln *Web:* www.alcomprinting.com	Harleysville	PA	19438	215-513-1600		627
Alcon Canada Inc 2665 Meadowpine Blvd *TF:* 800-268-4574 ■ *Web:* www.alcon.ca	Mississauga	ON	L5N8C7	905-826-6700		544
Alcon Entertainment LLC 10390 Santa Monica Blvd Ste 250 *Web:* www.alconent.com	Los Angeles	CA	90025	310-789-3040		514
Alcon Laboratories Inc 6201 S Fwy *TF:* 800-862-5266 ■ *Web:* www.alcon.com	Fort Worth	TX	76134	817-293-0450		269
Alcon Tool Co 565 Lafollete St *Web:* www.alcontool.com	Akron	OH	44311	330-773-9171	773-8042	493
Alcona Tool & Machine Inc PO Box 340 *Web:* www.alconatool.com	Lincoln	MI	48742	989-736-8151	736-6717	757
Alconex Specialty Products Inc 4204 W Ferguson Rd *Web:* www.alconex.com	Fort Wayne	IN	46809	260-744-3446		362
Alcop Adhesive Label Co 826 Perkins Ln *TF:* 888-313-3017 ■ *Web:* www.alcoplabels.com	Beverly	NJ	08010	609-871-4400	871-3017	413
Alcopro Inc 2547 Sutherland Ave *TF:* 800-227-9890 ■ *Web:* www.alcopro.com	Knoxville	TN	37919	865-525-4900		415
Alcorn Career & Technology Ctr 2101 Norman Rd *Web:* www.alcornschools.org	Corinth	MS	38834	662-286-7727	286-5674	242
Alcorn County 600 Waldron St PO Box 179 *Web:* www.alcorncounty.org	Corinth	MS	38834	662-286-7733	286-2548	338
Alcorn County Electric Power Assn 1909 S Tate St *TF:* 844-741-7071 ■ *Web:* www.ace-power.com	Corinth	MS	38834	662-287-4402		245
Alcorn Fence Co 9901 Glenoaks Blvd **Fax Area Code:* 818 ■ *Web:* www.alcorn-fence.com	Sun Valley	CA	91352	323-875-1342	768-9719*	189-11
Alcose Credit Union 3001 Jacks Run Rd Ste 101 *TF:* 866-842-5208 ■ *Web:* alcosecu.com	White Oak	PA	15131	412-673-2450		219
Alcott Group 71 Executive Blvd *Web:* www.alcottgroup.com	Farmingdale	NY	11735	631-420-0100	420-1894	631
Aldag Honold Mechanical Inc 3509 Business Dr PO Box 1265 *Web:* aldaghonold.com	Sheboygan	WI	53082	920-458-5558	458-3750	189-10
Aldagen Inc 2810 Meridian Pkwy Ste 148 *Web:* www.aldagen.com	Durham	NC	27713	919-484-2571		2
Aldan International Inc 242 E 137th St *Web:* aldan.com	Bronx	NY	10451	718-665-8699	473-7003	76
Aldea Solutions Inc 8550 Cote de Liesse Blvd Ste 200 *TF:* 866-344-5432 ■ *Web:* aldea.tv	Saint-Laurent	QC	H4T1H2	514-461-4136	344-5439	224
Aldebaran Capital LLC 10293 N Meridian St Ste 100 *Web:* www.aldebarancapital.com	Indianapolis	IN	46290	317-818-7827	818-7830	401
Aldelo LP 6800 Koll Center Pkwy Ste 310 *TF:* 800-801-6036 ■ *Web:* www.aldelo.com	Pleasanton	CA	94566	925-621-2410		253
Alden & Ott Printing Inks LP 616 E Brook Dr *Web:* www.aldenottink.com	Arlington Heights	IL	60005	847-956-6830	956-6509	388
Alden Buick Gmc Truck Inc 6 Whalers Way *Web:* www.aldengmc.com	Fairhaven	MA	02719	774-473-8915		57
Alden Films PO Box 449 *Web:* www.aldenfilms.com	Clarksburg	NJ	08510	732-462-3522	294-0330	45
Alden Hauk Inc 215 Salem St Ste G *Web:* www.aldenhauk.com	Everett	MA	02149	617-394-0302		627
Alden Hebron High School 9604 Illinois St *Web:* www.alden-hebron.org	Hebron	IL	60034	815-648-2442		685
Alden Research Laboratory Inc 30 Shrewsbury St *Web:* www.aldenlab.com	Holden	MA	01520	508-829-6000	829-5939	419
Alden Tool Company Inc 199 New Park Dr *Web:* www.aldentool.com	Berlin	CT	06037	860-828-3556	828-8872	757
Alderbrook Resort & Spa 7101 E SR-106 *TF:* 800-622-9370 ■ *Web:* www.alderbrookresort.com	Union	WA	98592	360-898-2200	898-4610	669
Alderman & Company Capital LLC 35 Warrington Round *Web:* www.aldermancapital.com	Danbury	CT	06810	203-917-4672		401
Alderman Studios 325 Model Farm Rd *Web:* www.aldermancompany.com	High Point	NC	27263	336-889-6121	889-7717	590
Alderney Advisors LLC 1 Towne Sq Ste 1870 *Web:* www.alderneyadvisors.com	Southfield	MI	48076	248-504-0690	918-2009	463
Aldersgate United Methodist Church 460 Aldersgate Dr *Web:* aldersgatechurch.com	Nixa	MO	65714	417-725-4949	725-4317	48-20
Aldersgate Village 7220 SW Asbury Dr *Web:* www.aldersgatevillage.org	Topeka	KS	66614	785-478-9440	478-9104	672
Alderson Reporting Co 1111 14th St NW Ste 1050 *Web:* www.aldersonreporting.com	Washington	DC	20005	202-289-2260		445
Alderson-Broaddus College 101 College Hill Rd *TF:* 800-263-1549 ■ *Web:* www.ab.edu	Philippi	WV	26416	304-457-1700	457-6239	166
ALDI Inc 1200 N Kirk Rd *Web:* www.aldi.us	Batavia	IL	60510	630-879-8100		345
Aldila Inc 14145 Danielson St Ste B *OTC: ALDA* ■ *TF:* 800-854-2786 ■ *Web:* www.aldila.com	Poway	CA	92064	858-513-1801	513-1870	710
Aldine Metal Products Corp 566 Danbury Rd *Web:* www.aldinemetal.com	New Milford	CT	06776	860-350-2552	350-1061	482
Aldinger Company Inc 1440 Prudential Dr *TF:* 888-822-1299 ■ *Web:* www.aldingerco.com	Dallas	TX	75235	214-638-1808		393
Aldo Shoes 2300 Emile Belanger *TF:* 888-818-2536 ■ *Web:* www.aldoshoes.com	Montreal	QC	H4R3J4	514-747-2536		301
Aldo Ventures Inc 7370 Viewpoint Rd *Web:* www.aldo.com	Aptos	CA	95003	831-662-2536		463
Aldo's 306 S High St *Web:* www.aldositaly.com	Baltimore	MD	21202	410-727-0700		671
Aldo's Ristorante 1860 Laskin Rd *Web:* www.aldosvb.com	Virginia Beach	VA	23454	757-491-1111		671
Aldrich Group 5665 SW Meadows Rd Ste 200 *Web:* aldrichadvisors.com	Lake Oswego	OR	97035	503-620-4489	624-0817	2
Aldrich-Thomas Group Inc 18 N 3rd St *Web:* aldrich-thomas.com	Temple	TX	76501	254-773-4901		652
Aldridge Botanical Gardens 3530 Lorna Rd *Web:* aldridgegardens.com	Hoover	AL	35216	205-682-8019	776-7833	97
Aldridge Electric Inc 844 E Rockland Rd *Web:* www.aldridgegroup.com	Libertyville	IL	60048	847-680-5200		189-4
Ale House LLC 623 E Main St *Web:* capitalalehouse.com	Richmond	VA	23219	804-780-2537		671
Ale Solutions Inc 1 W Illinois St Ste 300 **Fax Area Code:* 866 ■ *TF:* 866-885-9785 ■ *Web:* www.alesolutions.com	Saint Charles	IL	60174	630-513-6434	814-6832*	652

				Phone	Fax	Class
Ale-8-one Bottling Co 25 Carol Rd *Web:* ale8one.com	Winchester	KY	40391	859-744-3484		297-8
Alebra Technologies Inc 3810 Pheasant Ridge Dr NE Ste 100 *TF:* 888-340-2727 ■ *Web:* alebra.com	Minneapolis	MN	55449	651-366-6140		177
ALEC (American Legislative Exchange Council) 2900 Crystal Dr 6th Fl *Web:* www.alec.org	Arlington	VA	22202	703-373-0933	373-0927	48-7
Alecia's Specialty Foods Inc 2332 Montevallo Rd SW *Web:* aleciaschutney.com	Leeds	AL	35094	205-352-4900		297-2
Aledo BroadBand PO Box 364 *Web:* www.aledobroadband.com	Aledo	TX	76008	817-441-8541		225
Alegria Cocina Latina Restaurant 115 Pine Ave. *Web:* www.alegriacocinalatina.com	Long Beach	CA	90802	562-436-3388		671
Alejandra Hair Salon 20170 Pines Blvd Ste 107 *Web:* www.alejandrahair.com	Pembroke Pines	FL	33029	954-447-9561	342-9340	77
Alembic Global Advisors 140 E 45th St 5th Fl *Web:* www.alembicglobal.com	New York	NY	10017	212-907-5350	207-4296	401
Alembic Inc 3005 Wiljan Ct. *TF:* 800-322-5893 ■ *Web:* www.alembic.com	Santa Rosa	CA	95407	707-523-2611	523-2935	527
Alemite LLC 1057-521 Corporate Center Dr Ste 100 *TF:* 800-267-8022 ■ *Web:* www.skf.com	Fort Mill	SC	29715	803-802-0001		386
Alenco Inc 16201 W 110th St *Web:* www.alenconline.com	Lenexa	KS	66219	913-686-6166		106
Alene Candles LLC 51 Scarborough Ln *Web:* alene.com	Milford	NH	03055	603-673-5050		364
Alent Technologies LLC 8201 Bondage Dr *Web:* www.alent.net	Gaithersburg	MD	20882	301-520-3080		138
Alere Toxicology Services Inc 1111 Newton St *Web:* www.aleretoxicology.com	Gretna	LA	70053	504-361-8989		743
Alerion Capital Group 7702 E Doubletree Ranch Blvd *Web:* alerion.com	Scottsdale	AZ	85258	480-367-0900		792
Alerion Partners 23 Old Kings Hwy S. *Web:* www.alerionpartners.com	Darien	CT	06820	203-202-9900		792
Aleris International Inc 25825 Science Pk Dr Ste 400 *TF:* 866-266-2586 ■ *Web:* www.aleris.com	Beachwood	OH	44122	216-910-3400	910-3650	723
Alert Media 901 S MoPac Expy Ste 500 *TF:* 800-826-0777 ■ *Web:* www.alertmedia.com	Austin	TX	78746	800-826-0777		39
Alerton 6670 185th Ave NE *Web:* www.alerton.com	Redmond	WA	98052	425-869-8400	869-8445	202
AlertOne Services Inc 1000 Commerce Park Dr Ste 300 *TF:* 866-581-4540 ■ *Web:* www.alert-1.com	Williamsport	PA	17701	866-581-4540		575
Alerus Ctr 1200 42nd St S *Web:* www.aleruscenter.com	Grand Forks	ND	58201	701-792-1200	746-6511	205
Alerus Financial 2300 S Columbia Rd *Web:* alerus.com	Grand Forks	ND	58201	701-795-2684		70
Alerus Retirement & Benefits 2 Pine Tree Dr Ste 400 *TF:* 800-433-1685 ■ *Web:* www.alerusrb.com	Arden Hills	MN	55112	800-795-2697		528
Alesco Data Group LLC 5276 Summerlin Commons Way *TF:* 800-701-6531 ■ *Web:* www.alescodata.com	Fort Myers	FL	33907	239-275-5006		4
Alessi Bakeries 2909 W Cypress St *Web:* www.alessibakery.com	Tampa	FL	33609	813-879-4544		296-1
Aletheia House 201 Finley Ave W *Web:* specialkindofcaring.org	Birmingham	AL	35204	205-324-6502		726
Aleut Management Services LLC 5540 Tech Center Dr Ste 100 *TF:* 800-377-7765 ■ *Web:* www.aleutmgt.com	Colorado Springs	CO	80919	719-531-9090		194
Aleutian Peninsula Broadcasting Inc 100 Main St *Web:* apradio.org	Sand Point	AK	99661	907-383-5737	383-5271	645-141
Aleutians East Borough 3380 C St Ste 205 *TF:* 888-383-2699 ■ *Web:* www.aleutianseast.org	Anchorage	AK	99503	907-274-7555	276-7569	338
Alevistar Group 101 W Elm St Ste 360 *Web:* www.alevistar.com	Conshohocken	PA	19428	610-617-7800		196
Alex Alonzo Accountancy Corp 650 N 1st St	San Jose	CA	95112	408-295-3214		2
Alex C. Fergusson LLC (AFCO) 5000 Letterkenny Rd *Fax Area Code: 717 ■ *TF:* 800-345-1329 ■ *Web:* www.afcocare.us	Chambersburg	PA	17201	800-345-1329	264-9182*	145
Alex E. Paris Contracting Co 1595 Smith Township State *Web:* www.alexparis.com	Atlasburg	PA	15004	724-947-2235	947-3820	189-3
Alex Lee Inc PO Box 800 *Web:* www.alexlee.com	Hickory	NC	28603	828-725-4424		360-3
Alex Lyon & Son Sales Managers & Auctioneers Inc 7697 Rt 31 *Web:* www.lyonauction.com	Bridgeport	NY	13030	315-633-2944		41
Alex M. Greenberg, DDS PC 18 E 48th St Rm 1702 *Web:* www.dralexgreenberg.com	New York	NY	10017	212-319-9700	319-9778	428
Alex Mccoy Plumbing 1-718 Fortune Crescent *Web:* amph.ca	Kingston	ON	K7P2T3	613-546-6846		610
Alex Nichols Agency PO Box 20146 *Web:* www.anaht.com	Floral Park	NY	11002	516-678-9100	678-1344	12
Alex Orthopedic Inc 510 Fountain Pky *Web:* www.alexorthopedic.com	Grand Prairie	TX	75050	972-641-9680	641-9681	477
Alex Theatre 216 N Brand Blvd *Web:* www.alextheatre.org	Glendale	CA	91203	818-243-7700	241-2089	572
Alexa Internet Inc Presidio Bldg 37 *Web:* www.alexa.com	San Francisco	CA	94129	415-561-6900	561-6795	178-7
Alexa's Angels Inc 621 Innovation Cir *Web:* www.roman.com	Bloomingdale	IL	60108	970-686-7247		411
Alexandar School of Natural Therapeutics 4026 Pacific Ave *TF:* 877-472-1142 ■ *Web:* www.alexandarmassageschool.com	Tacoma	WA	98418	253-473-1142		685
Alexander & Baldwin Inc 822 Bishop St *NYSE:* ALEX ■ *TF:* 866-442-6551 ■ *Web:* www.alexanderbaldwin.com	Honolulu	HI	96813	808-525-6611	525-6652	185
Alexander & Bonin LLC 132 Tenth Ave *Web:* www.alexanderandbonin.com	New York	NY	10011	212-367-7474	367-7337	42
Alexander & Tom Inc 3500 Boston St *Web:* www.alextom.com	Baltimore	MD	21224	410-327-7400		180
Alexander Chemical Corp 7593 S First Rd Kingbury Industrial Pk. *Fax Area Code: 219 ■ *TF:* 800-445-9458 ■ *Web:* www.alexanderchemical.com	Kingsbury	IN	46345	800-445-9458	393-5364*	146
Alexander City Chamber of Commerce 120 Tallapoosa St *Web:* www.alexandercity.org	Alexander City	AL	35010	256-234-3461	234-0094	139
Alexander City Outlook 548 Cherokee Rd *Web:* www.alexcityoutlook.com	Alexander City	AL	35010	256-234-4281		96
Alexander Clark Inc 10801 Emerald St *Web:* www.alexanderclark.com	Boise	ID	83713	208-322-0611	323-7258	627
Alexander Co, The 345 W Washington Ave Ste 301 *Web:* www.alexandercompany.com	Madison	WI	53703	608-258-5580	258-5599	187
Alexander Communications Group Inc 712 Main St Ste 187B *Web:* ddc.downtowndevelopment.com	Boonton	NJ	07005	973-265-2300	402-6056	531-2
Alexander County 2000 Washington Ave *Web:* www.alexandercountyil.com	Cairo	IL	62914	618-734-7000		338
Alexander County Economic Development Corp 621 Liledoun Rd *Web:* alexanderedc.org	Taylorsville	NC	28681	828-632-9332	632-0059	338
Alexander County Library 77 First Ave SW *Web:* alexanderlibrary.org	Taylorsville	NC	28681	828-632-4058		434-3
Alexander Group Inc, The (AGI) 8155 E Indian Bend Rd Ste 111 *Web:* www.alexandergroup.com	Scottsdale	AZ	85250	480-998-9644		194
Alexander Hay Greenhouses Inc 75 Oakwood Ave *Web:* www.alexanderhaygreenhouses.com	North Haledon	NJ	07508	973-427-1193	427-6856	293
Alexander Hutton Venture Partners 1301 Fifth Ave Ste 3405 *Web:* alexanderhutton.com	Seattle	WA	98101	206-341-9800		792
Alexander L. Palenzuela PA 1200 Brickell Ave Ste 1440 *Web:* alp-law.com	Miami	FL	33131	305-375-9510	375-9511	41
Alexander Lamar (Sen R - TN) 455 Dirksen Senate Office Bldg *Web:* www.alexander.senate.gov	Washington	DC	20510	202-224-4944	228-3398	342-2
Alexander Lumber Co 515 Redwood Dr *Web:* www.alexlbr.com	Aurora	IL	60506	630-844-5123	844-6594	191-3
Alexander Macnab and Co 900 N Franklin St Ste 604 *TF:* 800-708-2060 ■ *Web:* www.alexandermacnab.com	Chicago	IL	60610	800-708-2060		194
Alexander Majors Historic House & Museum 8201 State Line Rd *Web:* www.wornallmajors.org	Kansas City	MO	64114	816-333-5556		520
Alexander Manufacturing Co 12978 Tesson Ferry Rd *TF:* 800-258-2743 ■ *Web:* alexandermc.com	Sappington	MO	63128	800-467-5343		9
Alexander Oil Company Inc Intersection of 1-10 & 123 N Bypass PO Box 469 *Web:* alexander-oil.com	Seguin	TX	78155	830-379-1736		316
Alexander Smith Academy Inc 10255 Richmond Ave Ste 100 *Web:* www.alexandersmith.com	Houston	TX	77042	713-266-0920	266-8857	685
Alexander Street Press LLC 3212 Duke St *Web:* alexanderstreet.com	Alexandria	VA	22314	703-212-8520		194
Alexander Summer LLC 205 Robin Rd Ste 120 *Web:* alexandersummer.com	Paramus	NJ	07652	201-712-1000	712-1274	655
Alexander X. Kuhn & Co 123 W Front St Ste 200 *Web:* www.axk.com	Wheaton	IL	60187	630-681-8100	681-8120	2
Alexander's 105 S Jefferson St *Web:* alexandersva.com	Roanoke	VA	24011	540-982-6983		671
Alexander's Inc 210 Rt 4 E *NYSE:* ALX ■ *Web:* www.alx-inc.com	Paramus	NJ	07652	201-587-8541	708-6214	655
Alexander's Print Advantage Co 245 S 1060 W *Web:* alexanders.com	Lindon	UT	84042	801-224-8666		174
Alexander's Seafood Restaurant & Wine Bar 76 Queens Folly Rd *TF:* 855-706-4319 ■ *Web:* www.alexandersrestaurant.com	Hilton Head Island	SC	29928	855-706-4319		671
Alexandra Hotel 77 Ryerson Ave. *TF:* 800-567-1893 ■ *Web:* alexandrahotel.com	Toronto	ON	M5T2V4	416-504-2121	504-9195	377
Alexandra Park Neighbourhood Learning Ctr 707 Dundas St W *Web:* www.apnlc.org	Toronto	ON	M5T2W6	416-591-7384		148
Alexandre de Paris Inc 12751 Federal Systems Park Dr *Web:* www.alexandredeparis.com	Fairfax	VA	22033	703-222-7661		77
Alexandre Mouton House/Lafayette Museum 1122 Lafayette St *Web:* www.lafayettemuseum.com	LaFayette	LA	70501	337-234-2208		520
Alexandria & Arlington Bed & Breakfast Networks (AABBN) 4938 Hampden Ln Ste 164 *Fax Area Code: 202 ■ *TF:* 888-549-3415 ■ *Web:* www.aabbn.com	Bethesda	MD	20814	703-549-3415	517-9179*	376
Alexandria Archaeology Museum 301 King St. *Web:* www.alexandriava.gov	Alexandria	VA	22314	703-746-4399	838-6491	520

	Phone	Fax	Class
Alexandria Black History Museum 301 King St. . . . . Alexandria VA 22314 *Web:* www.alexandriava.gov	703-746-4356	706-3999	520
Alexandria Center for Life Science 430 E 29th St Ste 100. . . . . New York NY 10016 *Web:* www.alexandrianyc.com	646-223-3882		393
Alexandria Chamber of Commerce 333 N Fairfax St Ste 302. . . . . Alexandria VA 22314 *Web:* www.thechamberalx.com	703-549-1000	549-1001	139
Alexandria City Hall 301 King St. . . . . Alexandria VA 22314 *TF:* 800-543-8911 ■ *Web:* www.alexandriava.gov	703-746-4357	838-6433	337
Alexandria Convention & Visitors Assn 221 King St. . . . . Alexandria VA 22314 *TF:* 800-388-9119 ■ *Web:* www.visitalexandriava.com	703-746-3301		206
Alexandria Daily Town Talk PO Box 7558 . . . . Alexandria LA 71306 *TF:* 800-523-8391 ■ *Web:* www.thetowntalk.com	318-487-6397	487-6488	532-2
Alexandria (Independent City) 301 King St. . . . . Alexandria VA 22314 *Web:* www.alexandriava.gov	703-838-4500		338
Alexandria Industries 401 County Rd 22 NW . . . . Alexandria MN 56308 *TF:* 800-568-6601 ■ *Web:* www.alexandriaindustries.com	320-763-6537	763-9250	492
Alexandria Lakes Area Chamber of Commerce 206 Broadway. . . . . Alexandria MN 56308 *TF:* 800-235-9441 ■ *Web:* www.alexandriamn.org	320-763-3161		139
Alexandria Law Library 520 King St Ste LL34 . . . . Alexandria VA 22314 *Web:* alexlibraryva.org	703-746-4077		434-3
Alexandria Moulding 20352 Powerdam Rd . . . . Alexandria ON K0C1A0 **Fax Area Code:* 800 ■ *TF:* 866-377-2539 ■ *Web:* www.alexmo.com	613-525-2784	265-8746*	309
Alexandria National Cemetery 209 E Shamrock St. . . . . Pineville LA 71360 *Web:* www.cem.va.gov	318-449-1793	449-9327	136
Alexandria Real Estate Equities Inc 385 E Colorado Blvd Ste 299 . . . . Pasadena CA 91101 *NYSE: ARE* ■ *Web:* www.are.com	626-578-0777	578-0896	655
Alexandria School of Scientific Therapeutics 809 S Harrison St. . . . . Alexandria IN 46001 *TF:* 800-622-8756 ■ *Web:* www.assti.com	765-724-9152		685
Alexandria Symphony Orchestra 700 N Fairfax St Ste 501. . . . . Alexandria VA 22314 *Web:* www.alexsym.org	703-548-0885	548-0985	573-3
Alexandria Technical & Community College 1601 Jefferson St . . . . Alexandria MN 56308 *TF:* 888-234-1222 ■ *Web:* www.alextech.edu	320-762-0221	762-4501	162
Alexandria Veterans Affairs Medical Ctr 2495 Shreveport Hwy 71 N. . . . . Pineville LA 71360 *TF:* 800-375-8387 ■ *Web:* www.alexandria.va.gov	318-473-0010		374-8
Alexandria Zoological Park 3016 Masonic Dr . . . . Alexandria LA 71301 *Web:* www.thealexandriazoo.com	318-441-6810	473-1149	823
Alexandria/Pineville Area Convention & Visitors Bureau (APACVB) 707 2nd St . . . . Alexandria LA 71301 **Fax Area Code:* 318 ■ *TF:* 800-551-9546 ■ *Web:* alexandriapinevillela.com	800-551-9546	443-1617*	206
Alexandro's 2125 Missouri Blvd . . . . Jefferson City MO 65109 *Web:* alexandrosandtgs.com	573-634-7740		671
Alexi's Grill 3550 N Central Ave Ste 120 . . . . Phoenix AZ 85012 *Web:* alexisgrill.com	602-279-0982		671
Alexim Trading Corp 7800 NW 46th St . . . . Miami FL 33166 *Web:* alexim.com	305-513-0808		311
Alexion Pharmaceuticals Inc 352 Knotter Dr . . . . Cheshire CT 06410 *NASDAQ: ALXN* ■ **Fax Area Code:* 203 ■ *Web:* alexion.com	475-230-2596	271-8198*	85
Alexis Hotel 1007 First Ave. . . . . Seattle WA 98104 *TF:* 866-356-8894 ■ *Web:* www.alexishotel.com	206-624-4844	621-9009	379
Alexis Park Resort 375 E Harmon Ave. . . . . Las Vegas NV 89169 *TF:* 800-582-2228 ■ *Web:* www.alexispark.com	702-796-3300	796-4334	669
Alexsys Corp 14 Pebble Pl. . . . . Stoneham MA 02180 *Web:* alexsys.team	781-279-0170		396
Alexza Pharmaceuticals Inc 2091 Stierlin Ct . . . . Mountain View CA 94043 *NASDAQ: ALXA* ■ *Web:* www.alexza.com	650-944-7000	944-7999	85
ALF (American Liver Foundation) 39 Broadway. . . . . New York NY 10006 *TF:* 800-465-4837 ■ *Web:* liverfoundation.org	212-668-1000	483-8179	48-17
Alfa Aesar Co 26 Parkridge Rd . . . . Ward Hill MA 01835 **Fax Area Code:* 800 ■ *TF:* 800-343-0660 ■ *Web:* www.alfa.com	978-521-6300	322-4757*	145
Alfa Corp 2108 E S Blvd. . . . . Montgomery AL 36116 *TF:* 800-964-2532 ■ *Web:* www.alfainsurance.com	800-964-2532		457-1
Alfa Intl 2400 Pershing Rd Ste 500 . . . . Kansas City MO 64108 *Web:* www.alfainternational.com	816-471-2121		434-3
Alfa Laval Inc 1201 S 9th St. . . . . Broken Arrow OK 74012 *Web:* www.alfalaval.com	918-251-7477		567
Alfa Laval Tank Equipment Inc 604 Jeffers Cir . . . . Exton PA 19341 *TF:* 877-426-2538 ■ *Web:* www.gamajet.com	610-408-9940		76
Alfa Medical Equipment Specialists Inc 59 Madison Ave. . . . . Hempstead NY 11550 *TF:* 800-762-1586 ■ *Web:* sterilizers.com	516-489-3855	489-9364	228
Alfa Scientific Designs Inc 13200 Gregg St . . . . Poway CA 92064 *TF:* 877-204-5071 ■ *Web:* www.alfascientific.com	858-513-3888	513-8388	476
Alfa Wassermann Inc 4 Henderson Dr . . . . West Caldwell NJ 07006 *TF:* 800-220-4488 ■ *Web:* www.alfawassermannus.com	973-882-8630		476
Alfab Inc 220 Boll Weevil Cir E . . . . Enterprise AL 36330 *TF:* 800-239-9451 ■ *Web:* www.alfabinc.com	334-347-9516		499
Alfalfa County Sheriff 300 S Grand Ave. . . . . Cherokee OK 73728 *Web:* www.oklahomasheriffs.org	580-596-3269		338
Alfalfa Electric Co-opeartive Inc 121 E Main St. . . . . Cherokee OK 73728 *TF:* 888-736-3837 ■ *Web:* www.aec.coop	580-596-3333	596-2464	245
Alfe Heat Treating Inc 6920 Pointe Inverness Way Ste 140 . . . . Fort Wayne IN 46804 *TF:* 888-747-2533 ■ *Web:* www.al-fe.com	888-747-2533		484
Alfiniti Inc 1152 Rue Manic. . . . . Chicoutimi QC G7K1A2 *TF:* 800-334-8731 ■ *Web:* www.spectube.com	418-696-2545		492
Alford Motors Inc US Hwy 171 S. . . . . Leesville LA 71446 *Web:* www.alfordmotors.com	337-397-4144		57
Alforex Seeds 38001 County Rd 27. . . . . Woodland CA 95695 *TF:* 877-560-5181 ■ *Web:* www.alforexseeds.com	530-666-3331	666-5317	276
Alfred B. Maclay State Gardens 3540 Thomasville Rd . . . . Tallahassee FL 32309 *Web:* www.floridastateparks.org	850-487-4556	487-8808	97
Alfred I. duPont Hospital for Children 1600 Rockland Rd . . . . Wilmington DE 19803 *TF:* 800-416-4441 ■ *Web:* www.nemours.org	302-651-4000		374-1
Alfred M. Shiver PA 260 E Court St. . . . . Marion NC 28752 *Web:* shivercpa.com	828-652-7319		2
Alfred Mann Foundation, The 25134 Rye Canyon Loop . . . . Valencia CA 91355 *Web:* aemf.org	661-702-6700		415
Alfred Manufacturing Co 4398 Elati St. . . . . Denver CO 80216 *Web:* www.alfredmfg.com	303-433-6385	433-4156	608
Alfred Nickles Bakery Inc 26 N Main St . . . . Navarre OH 44662 *Web:* www.nicklesbakery.com	330-879-5635		296-1
Alfred P. Sloan Foundation 630 Fifth Ave Ste 2550. . . . . New York NY 10111 *TF:* 800-401-8004 ■ *Web:* sloan.org	212-649-1649	757-5117	305
Alfred Williams & Co 410 S Salisbury St . . . . Raleigh NC 27601 *Web:* alfredwilliams.com	919-832-9570		52
Alfredo's Mexican Food 2849 S 14th St. . . . . Abilene TX 79605	325-698-0104		671
Alfredo's Pizza & Pasta 251 W Baseline St . . . . San Bernardino CA 92410 *Web:* alfredospizzaandpasta.com	909-885-0218		671
Alfresco 1085 Bixby Dr . . . . Hacienda Heights CA 91745 **Fax Area Code:* 323 ■ *TF:* 888-383-8800 ■ *Web:* alfrescogrills.com	888-383-8800	726-4700*	106
Al-Gar Federal Credit Union 316 Paca St . . . . Cumberland MD 21502 *TF:* 800-750-1070 ■ *Web:* algarfcu.org	301-722-5446		219
Alger Correctional Facility N 6141 Industrial Pk Dr . . . . Munising MI 49862 *Web:* www.michigan.gov	906-387-5000		213
Alger County 101 Court St. . . . . Munising MI 49862 *Web:* algercourthouse.com	906-387-2076	387-2156	338
Alger Family of Funds PO Box 8480 . . . . Boston MA 02266 *TF:* 800-992-3863 ■ *Web:* www.alger.com	800-992-3863		528
Alger Farms Inc 950 NW Eigth St . . . . Homestead FL 33030 *Web:* www.algerfarms.com	305-247-4334		10-5
Alger Precision Machining LLC 724 S Bon View Ave . . . . Ontario CA 91761 **Fax Area Code:* 909 ■ *TF:* 800-854-9833 ■ *Web:* www.alger1.com	800-854-9833	983-3351*	621
Algeria Embassy 2118 Kalorama Rd NW . . . . Washington DC 20008 *Web:* www.algerianembassy.org	202-265-2800	986-5906	257
Algo Communication Products Ltd 4500 Beedie St. . . . . Burnaby BC V5J5L2 *TF:* 800-226-7722 ■ *Web:* www.algo.ca	604-438-3333	437-5726	246
Algo Design Inc 6455 Doris Lussier Ste 300 . . . . Boisbriand QC J7H0E8 *TF:* 800-267-2584 ■ *Web:* www.algodesign.com	450-681-2584		180
Algoa Correctional Ctr 8501 Fenceline Rd . . . . Jefferson City MO 65102 *Web:* www.mo.gov	573-751-3911	526-1385	213
Algolia 301 Howard St Ste 300. . . . . San Francisco CA 94105 *Web:* www.algolia.com	415-366-9672		788
Algoma Central Corp 63 Church St Ste 600 . . . . Saint Catharines ON L2R3C4 *Web:* www.algonet.com	905-687-7888		312
Algoma Net Co 1525 Mueller St . . . . Algoma WI 54201 *Web:* www.algomanet.com	920-487-5577	487-2852	208
Algoma University 1520 Queen St E. . . . . Sault Sainte Marie ON P6A2G4 *TF:* 888-254-6628 ■ *Web:* algomau.ca	705-949-2301	949-6583	167
Algonac State Park 8732 River Rd. . . . . Marine City MI 48039 *Web:* www.michigan.org	810-765-5605		565
Algonquin Area Public Library District 2600 Harnish . . . . Algonquin IL 60102 *Web:* www.aapld.org	847-658-4343		434-3
Algonquin College of Applied Arts & Technology 1385 Woodroffe Ave . . . . Ottawa ON K2G1V8 *Web:* www.algonquincollege.com	613-727-4723		162
Algonquin Hotel 59 W 44th St. . . . . New York NY 10036 *Web:* www.thealgonquin.net	212-840-6800		379
Algonquin Industries Inc 139 Farm St . . . . Bellingham MA 02019 *Web:* www.algonquinindustries.com	508-966-4600	966-3276	454
Algonquin Power 2845 Bristol Cir . . . . Oakville ON L6H7H7 *Web:* algonquinpower.com	905-465-4500		767
Algonquin/Lake in the Hills Chamber of Commerce 2114 W Algonquin Rd . . . . Lake in the Hills IL 60156 *Web:* www.alchamber.com	847-658-5300	658-6546	139
Algood Food Company Inc 7401 Trade Port Dr . . . . Louisville KY 40258 *Web:* www.algoodfood.com	502-637-3631	637-1502	296-32
Algy Team Collection 440 NE First Ave. . . . . Hallandale Beach FL 33009 **Fax Area Code:* 888 ■ *TF:* 800-458-2549 ■ *Web:* www.algyteam.com	954-457-8100	928-2282*	155-19
Alhambra 8 Governor Wentworth Hwy . . . . Wolfeboro NH 03894 *TF:* 800-329-9099 ■ *Web:* us.alhambrait.com	603-569-0600	569-0609	178-7
Alhambra Beauty College 200 W Main St . . . . Alhambra CA 91801 *Web:* www.alhambrabeauty.edu	626-282-7765	282-1626	167-3
Alhambra Chamber of Commerce 104 S First St . . . . Alhambra CA 91801 *Web:* www.alhambrachamber.org	626-282-8481	282-5596	139
Alhambra Civic Center Library 101 S First St . . . . Alhambra CA 91801 *Web:* www.alhambralibrary.org	626-570-5008	457-1104	434-3
Alhambra Foundry Company Ltd 1147 Meridian Ave. . . . . Alhambra CA 91803 *Web:* www.alhambrafoundry.com	626-289-4294		751

Name / Address	Phone	Fax	Class
Alhambra Hospital 100 S Raymond Ave. . . . . Alhambra CA 91801 *Web:* www.alhambrahospital.com	626-570-1606		374-3
Alhambra-Grantfork Telephone Co (AG) 305e Main St . . . . Alhambra IL 62001 *Web:* www.agtelco.com	618-488-2165	488-2121	224
ALI (American Laboratories Inc) 4410 S 102nd St. . . . . Omaha NE 68127 *Web:* americanlaboratories.com	402-339-2494		479
ALI (American Law Institute) 4025 Chestnut St . . . . Philadelphia PA 19104 *TF:* 800-253-6397 ■ *Web:* www.ali.org	215-243-1600	243-1636	49-10
Ali Akbar College of Music 215 W End Ave. . . . . San Rafael CA 94901 *Web:* www.aacm.org	415-454-6372	454-9396	167-3
Ali Baba 404 S Craig St . . . . Pittsburgh PA 15213 *Web:* www.alibabapittsburgh.com	412-682-2829		671
Ali Baba Restaurant 110 Hartfield Rd . . . . Morgantown WV 26505 *Web:* www.alibabaexpress.com	304-777-4120		671
ALI's Database Consultants 1151 Williams Dr . . . . Aiken SC 29803 *TF:* 866-257-8970 ■ *Web:* www.aliconsultants.com	803-648-5931		180
Alia Conseil Inc Place Iberville III 2960 Laurier Blvd Ste 214 . . . . Quebec City QC G1V4S1 *TF:* 800-567-8906 ■ *Web:* www.aliaconseil.com	418-652-1737		194
Aliante Gaming LLC 7300 Aliante Pkwy . . . . North Las Vegas NV 89084 *Web:* www.aliantegaming.com	702-495-3695		707
Alibates Flint Quarries National Monument PO Box 1460 . . . . Fritch TX 79036 *Web:* www.nps.gov	806-857-6680	857-2319	564
Alibris Inc 1250 45th St Ste 100 . . . . Emeryville CA 94608 *Web:* www.alibris.com	510-594-4500		95
Alice 95.5 1856 S Glenstone Ave. . . . . Springfield MO 65804 *Web:* alice955.iheart.com	417-890-5555		645-153
Alice Arts Ctr 1428 Alice St. . . . . Oakland CA 94612 *Web:* mccatheater.com	510-238-7526		520
Alice Austen House 2 Hylan Blvd. . . . . Staten Island NY 10305 *Web:* aliceausten.org	718-816-4506		520
Alice Chamber of Commerce (ACC) 612 E Main St PO Box 1609. . . . . Alice TX 78333 *TF:* 800-379-4222 ■ *Web:* www.alicetxchamber.org	361-664-3454	664-2291	139
Alice G. Gosfield & Associates PC 2309 Delancey Pl . . . . Philadelphia PA 19103 *Web:* gosfield.com	215-735-2384	735-4778	41
Alice Hyde Medical Ctr 133 Park St . . . . Malone NY 12953 *Web:* www.alicehyde.com	518-483-3000	481-2320	374-3
Alice James Books (AJB) 114 Prescott St. . . . . Farmington ME 04938 *Web:* www.alicejamesbooks.org	207-778-7071	778-7766	637-2
Alice Lloyd College 100 Purpose Rd . . . . Pippa Passes KY 41844 *TF:* 888-280-4252 ■ *Web:* www.alc.edu	606-368-6000		166
Alice Public Library 401 E Third St . . . . Alice TX 78332 *Web:* www.cityofalice.org	361-664-9506	668-4353	434-3
Alice Travel Luxury Cruises & Tour 277 Fairfield Rd Ste 218. . . . . Fairfield NJ 07004 *TF:* 800-229-2542 ■ *Web:* www.alicetravel.com	973-439-1700		772
Aliceville Manor Nursing Home 703 17th St NW . . . . Aliceville AL 35442 *Web:* alicevillemanornursinghome.com	205-373-6307		371
Aliceville Public Library (APL) 416 Third Ave NE . . . . Aliceville AL 35442 *Web:* pickenslibrary.com	205-373-6691	373-3731	434-3
Alico Inc (ALCO) 10070 Daniels Interstate Ct Ste 100 . . . . Fort Myers FL 33913 *NASDAQ: ALCO* ■ *Web:* www.alicoinc.com	239-226-2000		315-2
Alidade Technology Inc 111 Knoll Dr. . . . . Collegeville PA 19426 *TF:* 877-265-1581 ■ *Web:* www.alidadetech.com	877-265-1581		196
Alien Technology LLC 845 Embedded Way . . . . San Jose CA 95138 *Web:* www.alientechnology.com	408-782-3900	782-3908	647
Alight 430 Oak Grove St Ste 204. . . . . Minneapolis MN 55403 *TF:* 800-875-7060 ■ *Web:* www.wearealight.org	612-872-7060	607-6499	48-5
Align Aerospace 21123 Nordhoff St. . . . . Chatsworth CA 91311 *TF:* 800-554-4449 ■ *Web:* www.alignaero.com	818-727-7800	727-8037	351
Align Technology Inc 2560 Orchard Pkwy . . . . San Jose CA 95131 *NASDAQ: ALGN* ■ *TF:* 800-577-8767 ■ *Web:* www.aligntech.com	408-470-1000	470-1010	228
Alignment Health Plan 1100 W Town & Country Rd Ste 1600 . . . . Orange CA 92868 *TF:* 866-327-2247 ■ *Web:* www.alignmenthealthplan.com	323-728-7232		391-3
Alignment Nashville Inc 21 White Bridge Rd Ste 201 . . . . Nashville TN 37205 *TF:* 866-243-7495 ■ *Web:* www.alignmentnashville.org	615-585-8497		396
Alimak Hek Inc 12552 Galveston Rd Ste A 160. . . . . Webster TX 77598 *Web:* www.alimakhek.us	713-640-8500	640-8519	385
Aliments Asta Inc 767 Rte 289 . . . . Saint-Alexandre-de-Kamouraska QC G0L2G0 *TF:* 800-463-1355 ■ *Web:* alimentsasta.com	418-495-2728	495-2879	296-26
Aliments Ouimet-Cordon Bleu Inc 8383 Rue J-Ren Ouimet . . . . Anjou QC H1J2P8 *Web:* www.cordonbleu.ca	514-352-3000		296-37
Alin Party Supplies Co 4139 Woodruff Ave. . . . . Lakewood CA 90713 *Web:* www.alinpartysupply.com	562-420-2489		566
Alinabal Inc 28 Woodmont Rd. . . . . Milford CT 06460 *Web:* www.alinabal.com	203-877-3241	874-5063	75
Aline Components Inc 1830 Tomlinson Rd PO Box 263. . . . . Kulpsville PA 19443 *Web:* alinecomponents.com	215-368-0300	361-1400	604
ALine Inc 2206 E Gladwick St. . . . . Rancho Dominguez CA 90220 *TF:* 877-707-8575 ■ *Web:* alineinc.com	877-707-8575		743
ALine Systems Corp 13844 Struikman Rd. . . . . Cerritos CA 90703 *Web:* www.alinesys.com	562-229-9727		547

Name / Address	Phone	Fax	Class
Alinea 1723 N Halsted St . . . . Chicago IL 60614 *Web:* www.alinearestaurant.com	312-867-0110		671
A-Lined Handling Systems Inc 92 Burnside Ave . . . . East Hartford CT 06108 *Web:* a-lined.com	860-289-1571		261
Alion Inc 870 Harbour Way S . . . . Richmond CA 94804 *Web:* www.alionenergy.com	510-965-0868		253
Alion Science & Technology 1750 Tysons Blvd Ste 1300 . . . . McLean VA 22102 *Web:* www.alionscience.com	703-918-4480		261
Alipes CME Inc 28 Atlantic Ave Ste 131 . . . . Boston MA 02110 *Web:* www.alipes.com	617-303-1045		195
Aliquot Associates Inc 1390 S Main St Ste 310 . . . . Walnut Creek CA 94596 *Web:* aliquot.com	925-476-2300	476-2350	261
Alisa Na CPA PC 8319 238th St SW . . . . Edmonds WA 98026 *Web:* alisanacpa.com	425-744-2742	744-2378	2
Alisal Guest Ranch & Resort 1054 Alisal Rd . . . . Solvang CA 93463 *TF:* 800-425-4725 ■ *Web:* www.alisal.com	805-693-4208	688-2510	669
Alisal Union Elementary School District 1205 E Market St . . . . Salinas CA 93905 *Web:* www.alisal.org	831-753-5700	753-5709	685
ALISE (Association for Library & Information Science Education) 2150 N 107th St Ste 205 . . . . Seattle WA 98133 *TF:* 877-275-7547 ■ *Web:* www.alise.org	206-209-5267	367-8777	49-11
Alishaev Bros Inc 20 W 47th St Ste 203 . . . . New York NY 10036 *TF:* 877-859-6020 ■ *Web:* www.alishaevbros.com	877-859-6020		411
Alison Group Inc, The 2090 Northeast 163rd St. . . . . North Miami Beach FL 33162 *Web:* www.alisongroup.com	305-354-3300		4
Alison's Pantry 580 W State St . . . . Pleasant Grove UT 84062 *Web:* www.alisonspantry.com	801-796-6411	796-9309	297-6
Alisto Engineering Group Inc 2737 N Main St Ste 200 . . . . Walnut Creek CA 94597 *Web:* www.alisto.com	925-279-5000		261
Alithya Group Inc 2875 Laurier Blvd Ste 1250 . . . . Quebec City QC G1V2M2 *TF:* 800-233-7924 ■ *Web:* www.alithya.com	418-650-2866		631
Alive Hospice Inc 1718 Patterson St . . . . Nashville TN 37203 *TF:* 800-327-1085 ■ *Web:* www.alivehospice.org	615-327-1085	321-8902	371
Alive Radio Network 30 Park Ave . . . . Cohoes NY 12047 *Web:* www.aliveradionetwork.com	518-237-1330	235-4468	647
Aljex Software Inc 50 Division St Ste 204 . . . . Somerville NJ 08876 **Fax Area Code:* 732 ■ *TF:* 833-262-2314 ■ *Web:* www.aljex.com	833-262-2314	357-8777*	179
Aljon Graphics 1721 E Lambert Rd C . . . . La Habra CA 90631 *Web:* www.aljongraphics.com	562-694-3144	691-0453	344
ALK 35-151 Brunel Rd . . . . Mississauga ON L4Z2H6 *TF:* 800-663-0972 ■ *Web:* www.alk.net	905-290-9952		231
Alkaloid USA LLC 6535 W Campus Oval Ste 130 . . . . New Albany OH 43054 *Web:* www.alkaloid.com.mk	614-939-9488	939-9498	582
Alken Inc 40 Hercules Dr . . . . Colchester VT 05446 *TF:* 800-357-4777 ■ *Web:* polhemus.com	802-655-3159		692
Alken Industries Inc 2175 Fifth Ave. . . . . Ronkonkoma NY 11779 *Web:* alkenind.com	631-467-2000		22
Alken-Ziegler Tool Company LLC 25575 Brest Rd. . . . . Taylor MI 48180 *Web:* www.cofs.lara.state.mi.us	734-946-4444		483
Alkermes Inc 852 Winter St. Waltham MA 02451 *NASDAQ: ALKS* ■ *TF:* 800-848-4876 ■ *Web:* www.alkermes.com	781-609-6000		85
Alkinco PO Box 278 . . . . New York NY 10116 *TF:* 800-424-7110 ■ *Web:* www.alkincohair.com	212-719-3070	764-7804	348
Alkon & Levine PC 29 Crafts St . . . . Newton MA 02458 *Web:* alkon-levine.com	617-969-6630	969-1223	2
Alkon Corp 728 Graham Dr . . . . Fremont OH 43420 *Web:* www.alkoncorp.com	419-333-7000		789
ALL (Akron Law Library) Summit County Court House 209 S High St Rm 4 . . . . Akron OH 44308 *Web:* akronlawlib.summitoh.net	330-643-2804	643-7457	434-3
All - Fill Inc 418 Creamery Way. Exton PA 19341 *TF:* 866-255-3455 ■ *Web:* www.all-fill.com	866-255-3455		547
All 4 Paws Veterinary Services 274 Sunset Ave Ste I. . . . . Suisun City CA 94585 *Web:* all4pawsvet.com	707-207-4242		41
All Aboard Benefits 6162 E Mockingird Ln Ste 104. . . . . Dallas TX 75214 *TF:* 800-462-2322 ■ *Web:* www.allaboardbenefits.com	214-821-6677	821-6676	391-7
All Aboard Cruises Inc 11114 S W 127th Ct. . . . . Miami FL 33186 **Fax Area Code:* 786 ■ *TF:* 800-883-8657 ■ *Web:* www.allaboardcruises.com	305-385-8657	419-4873*	771
All About Kids Home Health 2102 W Teege Ave . . . . Harlingen TX 78550 *TF:* 877-412-3337 ■ *Web:* allaboutkidshomehealth.com	956-412-3337	412-3338	363
All About Kids Publishing (AAKP) PO Box 159 . . . . Gilroy CA 95021 *Web:* www.allaboutkidspub.com	408-337-1152		637-2
All About Packaging Inc 2200 W Everett St. . . . . Appleton WI 54912 *TF:* 800-446-1552 ■ *Web:* www.aapack.com	920-830-2700		627
All About Wisconsin Inc 816 State St . . . . Madison WI 53706 *Web:* www.wisconline.com	608-264-6500		339-50
All America Bank 444 W State Hwy 152. . . . . Mustang OK 73064 *TF:* 888-210-2028 ■ *Web:* allamerica.bank	405-376-2265		70
All American Containers Inc 9330 NW 110th Ave . . . . Miami FL 33178 *TF:* 844-295-4656 ■ *Web:* allamericancontainers.com	305-887-0797	888-4133	603
All American Ford Inc 520 River St . . . . Hackensack NJ 07601 *Web:* www.allamericanfordofhackensack.com	201-487-6700		57
All American Grating Inc 3001 Grand Ave . . . . Pittsburgh PA 15225 *TF:* 800-962-9692 ■ *Web:* www.aagrating.com	412-771-6970		492
All American Moving Group LLC 4340 US Hwy 51 N . . . . Memphis TN 38127	901-353-3900	353-4113	780

Company / Address	City	State	Zip	Phone	Fax	Class
All American Poly 135 Industrial Park Cir *Web:* allamericanpoly.com	Lawrenceville	GA	30045	770-338-8505		600
All American Pool-N-Patio Inc 2021 Curry Ford Rd *Web:* www.orlandopool.com	Orlando	FL	32806	407-898-8722		45
All American Private Security Inc 421 S Glendora Ave Ste 200 *Web:* allamericansecurity.com	West Covina	CA	91790	626-962-9620		693
All American Racers Inc 2334 S Brdwy *Web:* allamericanracers.com	Santa Ana	CA	92707	714-540-1771	540-3749	82
All American Recycling Corp 2 Hope St *Web:* allamericanrecyclingcorp.com	Jersey City	NJ	07307	201-656-3363		660
All American Scales Inc 12943 Lisbon St Ne *TF:* 800-397-0481 ■ *Web:* www.aacalibration.com	Paris	OH	44669	330-862-8100		300
All American Seasonings 10600 E 54th Ave *Web:* www.allamericanseasonings.com	Denver	CO	80239	303-623-2320	623-1920	296-37
All American Ticket Service 2616 Philadelphia Pk Ste E **Fax Area Code:* 302 ■ *TF:* 800-669-0571 ■ *Web:* www.allamericantickets.com	Claymont	DE	19703	800-669-0571	798-6552*	750
All American Title Company Inc 2407 109th Ave NE Ste 250 *Web:* allamericantitleco.com	Blaine	MN	55449	763-235-1800		653
All Bay Animal Hospital 1739 Willow Pass Rd *Web:* allbayanimalhospital.com	Concord	CA	94520	925-687-7346		794
All Book Covers Inc 1445 S Mcclintock Dr *Web:* allbookcovers.business.site	Tempe	AZ	85281	480-966-6283		552-2
All Brands 8079 W Broad St *Web:* allbrandssewvac.com	Richmond	VA	23294	804-270-1882		35
All by Grace Home Health Care Inc 1910 Pacific Ave Ste 10300 *Web:* www.allbygracehomehealthcare.com	Dallas	TX	75201	214-550-0215	550-0885	363
All Campus LLC 500 W Madison St Ste 2900 *Web:* www.allcampus.com	Chicago	IL	60661	312-525-3100		4
All City Metal inc 54-35 46th St *TF:* 888-682-5757 ■ *Web:* www.allcitymetal.com	Maspeth	NY	11378	718-472-5700	472-5813	697
All Classical Portland 211 SE Caruthers St Ste 200 *TF:* 888-306-5277 ■ *Web:* www.allclassical.org	Portland	OR	97214	503-943-5828	802-9456	645-126
All Copy Products LLC 4141 Colorado Blvd *TF:* 800-332-2352 ■ *Web:* www.allcopyproducts.com	Denver	CO	80216	303-295-0741		45
All Creatures Animal Hospital 1894 SR-125 *Web:* all-creatures.com	Amelia	OH	45102	513-797-7387		794
All Creatures Veterinary Hospital 20 Commercial St *Web:* creaturehealth.com	Salem	MA	01970	978-740-0290		794
All Cruise Travel 1723 Hamilton Ave *TF:* 800-227-8473 ■ *Web:* www.allcruise.com	San Jose	CA	95125	408-295-1200	295-2254	771
All Custom Gasket & Materials 355 Watline Ave *Web:* www.allcustomgasket.com	Mississauga	ON	L4Z1P3	905-507-4580	507-4589	326
All Direct Travel Services Inc 19772 MacArthur Blvd Ste 150 *TF:* 800-862-1516 ■ *Web:* alldirecttravel.com	Irvine	CA	92612	949-474-8100	266-8146	772
All Dressed Up 901 N Batavia Ave *Web:* www.alldressedupcostumes.com	Batavia	IL	60510	630-879-5130	879-6783	810
All Flex Flexible Circuits & Heaters 1705 Cannon Ln **Fax Area Code:* 507 ■ *TF:* 800-959-0865 ■ *Web:* www.allflexinc.com	Northfield	MN	55057	800-959-0865	663-1070*	625
All Foils Inc 16100 Imperial Pkwy *TF:* 800-521-0054 ■ *Web:* www.allfoils.com	Strongsville	OH	44149	440-572-3645	378-0161	492
All Graphic Supplies 6691 Edwards Blvd *TF:* 800-501-4451 ■ *Web:* www.allgraphicsupplies.com	Mississauga	ON	L5T2H8	800-501-4451		791
All Hvac Service Company Inc 9030 Ft Hamilton Pkwy *Web:* www.allhvac.com	Brooklyn	NY	11209	718-833-0148	921-6236	189-10
All in One Poster Co 8521 Whitaker St *TF:* 800-273-0307 ■ *Web:* www.allinoneposters.com	Buena Park	CA	90621	714-521-7720		45
All Inc 185 Plato Blvd W *Web:* www.allinc.com	Saint Paul	MN	55107	651-227-6331	292-0541	38
All Languages Ltd 306-421 Bloor St E *TF:* 800-567-8100 ■ *Web:* www.alllanguages.com	Toronto	ON	M4W3T1	416-975-5000	975-0505	423
All Line Inc 16851 E Parkview Ave Unit 2 *Web:* www.alllinerope.com	Fountain Hills	AZ	85268	480-306-6001	306-6112	208
All Makes Office Equipment Co 2558 Farnam St *TF:* 800-341-2413 ■ *Web:* allmakes.com	Omaha	NE	68131	402-341-2413		321
All Market Inc 250 Park Ave S 7th Fl *TF:* 877-848-2262 ■ *Web:* www.vitacoco.com	New York	NY	10003	212-206-0763		80
All Media Art Supply 417 E Main St *Web:* allmediaartsupply.com	Kent	OH	44240	330-678-8078		45
All Media Ventures 1 Quincy Ln **Fax Area Code:* 914 ■ *Web:* www.allmediaventures.com	White Plains	NY	10605	917-806-6373	683-5090*	466
All Metals Fabricating Inc 200 Allentown Pkwy *Web:* www.ametals.com	Allen	TX	75002	972-747-1234		697
All Metals Industries Inc 4 Higgins Dr *TF:* 800-654-6043 ■ *Web:* www.allmetalsindustries.com	Belmont	NH	03220	603-267-7023	267-7025	492
All Metals Processing of Orange County LLC 8401 Standustrial St *Web:* www.allmetalsprocessing.com	Stanton	CA	90680	714-828-8238	828-4552	481
All Metals Service & Warehousing Inc 100 All Metals Dr *Web:* www.allmetals.com	Cartersville	GA	30120	770-427-7379		480
All Motorists Insurance Agency 5230 Las Virgenes Rd Ste 100 *Web:* westerngeneral.com	Calabasas	CA	91302	818-880-9070		390
All Native Solutions 503 Ho-Chunk Plz **Fax Area Code:* 402 ■ *TF:* 866-224-7208 ■ *Web:* www.allnativesolutions.com	Winnebago	NE	68071	866-224-7208	878-2771*	180
All Native Systems LLC 1 Mission Dr *TF:* 866-323-7636 ■ *Web:* www.allnativesystems.com	Winnebago	NE	68071	866-323-7636		180
All Natural Landscape Inc 6149 S Rainbow Blvd *Web:* allnaturallandscape.net	Las Vegas	NV	89118	702-938-2245		422
All Needs Computer & Mailing Services Inc 8100 S 13th St *Web:* www.ancms.com	Lincoln	NE	68512	402-421-1083		5
All New Stamping Co 10801 Lower Azusa Rd *TF:* 800-877-7775 ■ *Web:* www.allnewstamping.com	El Monte	CA	91731	800-877-7775	877-8121	488
All Nippon Airways Company Ltd 2050 W 190th St Ste 100 *TF:* 800-235-9262 ■ *Web:* www.ana.co.jp	Torrance	CA	90504	800-235-9262		25
All Ny Title Agency Inc 222 Bloomingdale Rd Ste 306 *Web:* allnyt.com	White Plains	NY	10605	914-686-5600		653
All of E Solutions 2510 W Sixth St *Web:* www.allofe.com	Lawrence	KS	66049	785-832-2900		177
All Plastics & Fiberglass 8201 Zeigler Blvd *Web:* www.allplastics-fiberglass.com	Mobile	AL	36608	251-633-2130	633-2178	596
All Plastics Molding Inc 15700 Midway Rd *Web:* www.all-plastics.com	Addison	TX	75001	972-239-2686	239-2256	608
All Pool & Spa Inc 905 Kalanianaole Hwy *Web:* www.allpoolandspa.com	Kailua	HI	96734	808-261-8991		186
All Power Brokers Real Estate Inc 847 N Hwy 49/88 Ste 1 *Web:* www.allpower.com	Jackson	CA	95642	209-223-0237	223-3188	652
All Products Automotive Inc 4701 W Cortland St *Web:* allprodauto.com	Chicago	IL	60639	773-889-4500		61
All Property Management 104 Riverside Ave Ste 325 *TF:* 877-234-9723 ■ *Web:* www.allpropertymanagement.com	Winthrop	WA	98862	877-234-9723		387
All Purpose Manufacturing Inc 614 Airport Rd *Web:* www.apmfg.net	Oceanside	CA	92058	760-967-8464		320
All Rite Industries Inc 470 Oakwood Rd *Web:* www.allriteindustries.com	Lake Zurich	IL	60047	847-540-0300		488
All Saints Health Care 11810 Saticoy St *Web:* www.allsaints-subacute.com	North Hollywood	CA	91605	818-982-4600	982-6905	371
All Seas Wholesale Inc 2390 Jerrold Ave *Web:* www.allseaswholesale.com	San Francisco	CA	94124	415-206-7327	206-7733	297-5
All Seasons Resort Lodging 1794 Olympic Pkwy Ste 200 **Fax Area Code:* 435 ■ *TF:* 888-667-2775 ■ *Web:* www.allseasonsresortlodging.com	Park City	UT	84098	800-395-8639	645-9602*	669
All Seniors Care Living Centres Ltd 175 Bloor St E Ste 601 *Web:* www.allseniorscare.com	Toronto	ON	M4W3R8	416-323-3773		371
All Source Security Container Manufacturing Corp 40 Mills Rd *TF:* 866-526-4579 ■ *Web:* www.allsourcemfg.com	Barrie	ON	L4N6H4	705-726-6460	726-5017	803-1
All Squared Web Design LLC 284 Susquehanna Trl *Web:* allsquared.com	Allentown	PA	18104	610-351-5416		177
All Star Adventures 1010 N Webb Rd *Web:* www.allstarwichita.com	Wichita	KS	67206	316-682-3700	683-0409	31
All Star Awards & Ad Specialties Inc 835 W 39th St *Web:* allstaryeswecan.com	Kansas City	MO	64111	816-531-3635	531-7376	45
All Star Flooring Inc 10742 Tucker St *Web:* www.allstarflooring.com	Beltsville	MD	20705	301-595-9300		290
All Star Glass Company Inc 1845 Morena Blvd **Fax Area Code:* 619 ■ *TF:* 800-225-4184 ■ *Web:* www.allstarglass.net	San Diego	CA	92110	800-225-4184	275-6367*	62-2
All Star Metals LLC 101 Box Car Rd *Web:* www.allstarmetals.wixsite.com	Brownsville	TX	78521	956-838-2110		492
All Star Moving and Storage Inc 2525 Tilden Ave *Web:* allstarnewyork.com	Brooklyn	NY	11226	718-643-9080		780
All Star Software Systems LLC 440 Smith St *Web:* www.allstarss.com	Middletown	CT	06457	860-613-1500		180
All Star Wine & Spirits 579 Troy Schenectady Rd *Web:* www.allstarwine.com	Latham	NY	12110	518-220-9463		443
All State Beverage Co 130 Sixth St *Web:* www.allstatebeverage.com	Montgomery	AL	36104	334-265-0507		81-1
All State Fastener Corp 15460 E 12 Mile Rd *TF:* 800-755-8959 ■ *Web:* www.allstatefastener.com	Roseville	MI	48066	586-773-5400		351
All States Inc 602 N 12th St *TF:* 800-621-5837 ■ *Web:* cable-ties.com	Saint Charles	IL	60174	773-728-0525		608
All Steel Fabricating Company Inc 84 Creeper Hill Rd *Web:* allsteelfab.com	North Grafton	MA	01536	508-839-4471		480
All Systems Inc 3241 N 7th St Trfwy *TF:* 888-677-5333 ■ *Web:* allsystemsonline.com	Kansas City	KS	66115	913-281-5100	281-5511	180
All Tech Engineering 1030 58th St SW *Web:* www.alltech-eng.com	Wyoming	MI	49509	616-406-0681		454
All Terrain 2675 W Grand Ave *Web:* allterrain.net	Chicago	IL	60612	312-588-3700		195
All Tile Inc 1201 Chase Ave *Web:* www.alltile.com	Elk Grove Village	IL	60007	847-979-2500		191-1

Phone | Fax | Class

All Tune & Lube International Inc
ATL International Inc
8334 Veterans Hwy ..... Millersville MD 21108 877-978-1758 62-5
TF: 877-978-1758 ■ *Web:* alltuneandlube.com

All Waste Inc 143 Murphy Rd ..... Hartford CT 06114 860-724-4575 192
Web: www.allwaste.com

All Weather Inc 1165 National Dr ..... Sacramento CA 95834 916-928-1000 928-1165 472
TF: 800-824-5873 ■ *Web:* www.allweatherinc.com

All Web Leads Inc
7300 FM 2222 Bldg 2 Ste 100 ..... Austin TX 78730 888-522-7355 349-7910* 387
**Fax Area Code:* 512 ■ *TF:* 888-522-7355 ■ *Web:* www.allwebleads.com

All West Communications Inc 50 W 100 N ..... Kamas UT 84036 435-783-4361 116
Web: www.allwest.com

All West Select Sires PO Box 507 ..... Burlington WA 98233 800-426-2697 757-7808* 446
**Fax Area Code:* 360 ■ *TF:* 800-426-2697 ■ *Web:* www.allwestselectsires.com

All World Travel Inc
314 Gilmer St ..... Sulphur Springs TX 75482 903-885-0896 775
TF: 866-298-6067 ■ *Web:* www.allworldtravel.com

All4 Inc
2393 Kimberton Rd PO Box 299 ..... Kimberton PA 19442 610-933-5246 933-5127 194
Web: www.all4inc.com

AllAfrica 920 M St SE ..... Washington DC 20003 202-546-0777 530
Web: allafrica.com

Allagash Wilderness Waterway
106 Hogan Rd Ste 7 ..... Bangor ME 04401 207-941-4014 565
TF: 800-332-1501 ■ *Web:* www.maine.gov

Allaire Elder Law LLC
271 Farmington Ave ..... Bristol CT 06010 860-259-1500 41
Web: allaireelderlaw.com

Allaire State Park PO Box 220 ..... Farmingdale NJ 07727 732-938-2371 565
Web: www.njparksandforests.org

Allamakee County 110 Allamakee St ..... Waukon IA 52172 563-864-7454 338
TF: 800-728-0131 ■ *Web:* www.allamakeecounty.com

Allamakee-Clayton Electric Co-op (ACEC)
229 Hwy 51 PO Box 715 ..... Postville IA 52162 563-864-7611 245
TF: 888-788-1551 ■ *Web:* www.acrec.com

All-American Co-op PO Box 125 ..... Stewartville MN 55976 507-533-4222 280-0066 273
TF: 888-354-4058 ■ *Web:* www.allamericancoop.com

All-American Engineering & Manufacturing Inc
4099 White Bear Pky ..... White Bear Lake MN 55110 651-483-4140 483-9221 454
Web: www.aae-mfg.com

All-American Farms Inc
2400 High Ridge Rd 101 ..... Boynton Beach FL 33426 561-479-0205 360-3
Web: allamericanfarms.com

Allamon Tool Company Inc
18935 Freeport Dr ..... Montgomery TX 77356 877-449-5433 539
TF: 877-449-5433 ■ *Web:* allamontool.com

Allan A. Myers Inc
1805 Berks Rd PO Box 1340 ..... Worcester PA 19490 610-560-7900 188-4
TF: 800-596-6118 ■ *Web:* www.allanmyers.com

Allan Briteway Electrical Contractors Inc
228 E 45th St 9th Fl ..... New York NY 10017 646-694-8900 568-7720 189-4
Web: www.allanbriteway.com

Allan Hackel Organization
1330 Center St ..... Newton Center MA 02459 617-965-4400 527-6005 6
TF: 800-970-2499 ■ *Web:* hackelbarter.com

Allan Hancock College
800 S College Dr ..... Santa Maria CA 93454 805-922-6966 922-3477 162
TF: 866-342-5242 ■ *Web:* hancockcollege.edu

Allan Industries 131 Allan Rd ..... Wilkes-Barre PA 18703 570-826-0123 829-4099 686
Web: allanrecyclers.com

Allan N. Karlin 174 Chancery Row ..... Morgantown WV 26505 304-296-8266 41
Web: wvjustice.com

Allan R. Nelson Consulting Engineers
17510-102 Ave 2nd Fl ..... Edmonton AB T5S1K2 780-483-3436 466
Web: arneng.ab.ca

Allan Stone Projects
535 W 22nd St 3rd Fl ..... New York NY 10011 212-987-4997 421-9895* 42
**Fax Area Code:* 917 ■ *Web:* www.allanstoneprojects.com

Allan Tool & Machine Company Inc
1822 E Maple Rd ..... Troy MI 48083 248-585-2910 585-7728 621
Web: allantool.com

Allan Wiser Insurance Services Inc
4809 Sparks Ave ..... San Diego CA 92110 800-371-6200 390
TF: 800-371-6200 ■ *Web:* wiser-insurance.com

Allan's Coffee 1852 Fescue St SE ..... Albany OR 97322 541-812-8000 297-8
TF: 800-926-6886 ■ *Web:* www.allanscoffee.com

Allana Buick & Bers Inc
990 Commercial St ..... Palo Alto CA 94303 650-543-5600 256
TF: 800-378-3405 ■ *Web:* abbae.com

Allant Group Inc, The
2655 Warrenville Rd Ste 200 ..... Downers Grove IL 60515 800-367-7311 194
TF: 800-367-7311 ■ *Web:* www.allantgroup.com

Allard & Company PA 107 N 37th St ..... Rogers AR 72756 479-636-3731 2
Web: allard-cpa.com

Allard Engineering Inc
16866 Seville Ave ..... Fontana CA 92335 909-356-1815 261
Web: allardeng.com

Allbirds 57 Hotaling Pl ..... San Francisco CA 94111 415-469-1455 301
Web: allbirds.com

Allbridge
10200 Innovation Dr Ste 300 ..... Milwaukee WI 53226 877-838-2089 387
TF: 877-838-2089 ■ *Web:* allbridge.com

Allcan Distributors Inc
12612 - 124 St ..... Edmonton AB T5L0N7 780-451-2357 480
Web: www.allcan.com

AllCare Health 740 SE Seventh St ..... Grants Pass OR 97526 541-471-4106 363
TF: 888-460-0185 ■ *Web:* www.allcarehealth.com

All-Clad Metalcrafters LLC
424 Morganza Rd ..... Canonsburg PA 15317 724-745-8300 746-5035 486
TF: 800-255-2523 ■ *Web:* www.all-clad.com

Allclasses Inc 109 Kingston St 5th Fl ..... Boston MA 02111 617-379-0245 387
Web: allclasses.com

Allco Fullerton Insurance Agencies
830 S Euclik Ave ..... Fullerton CA 92832 714-992-2390 390
Web: allcoinsurance.com

Allcraft Printing Inc 4802 Memphis St ..... Dallas TX 75207 214-742-6994 748-8571 627
Web: www.allcraftprinting.com

Alle Processing Corp 56-20 59th St ..... Maspeth NY 11378 718-894-2000 296-11
Web: alleprocessing.com

Allegacy Federal Credit Union
1691 Westbrook Plaza Dr ..... Winston-Salem NC 27103 336-774-3400 219
TF: 800-782-4670 ■ *Web:* www.allegacy.org

Allegan County Tourist Council
3255 122nd Ave Ste 102 ..... Allegan MI 49010 269-686-9088 206
TF: 888-425-5342 ■ *Web:* www.visitallegancounty.org

Allegan General Hospital 555 Linn St ..... Allegan MI 49010 269-673-8424 686-4239 374-3
Web: www.aghosp.org

Allegan Metal Finishing Co
1274 Lincoln Rd ..... Allegan MI 49010 269-673-6604 673-7291 481
Web: www.amfco.biz

Allegan Tubular Products Inc
1276 Lincoln Rd ..... Allegan MI 49010 269-673-6636 673-2477 595
Web: www.allegantube.com

Allegany College of Maryland
12401 Willowbrook Rd SE ..... Cumberland MD 21502 301-784-5000 784-5027 162
Web: allegany.edu

Allegany County 7 Court St ..... Belmont NY 14813 585-268-7612 338
Web: www.alleganyco.com

Allegany County Chamber of Commerce
24 Frederick St ..... Cumberland MD 21502 301-722-2820 722-5995 139
Web: www.alleganycountychamber.com

Allegany County Public Library System
31 Washington St ..... Cumberland MD 21502 301-777-1200 777-7299 434-3
Web: www.alleganycountylibrary.info

Allegany State Park
2373 ASP Rt 1 Ste 3 ..... Salamanca NY 14779 716-354-9121 565
Web: parks.ny.gov

Allegent Community Federal Credit Union
1001 Liberty Ave Ste 100 ..... Pittsburgh PA 15222 412-642-2875 219
Web: allegentfcu.org

Alleghany Corp 1411 Broadway 34th Fl ..... New York NY 10018 212-752-1356 185
NYSE: Y ■ *Web:* www.alleghany.com

Allegheny Bradford Corp
1522 South Ave ..... Lewis Run PA 16738 814-362-2590 595
Web: www.alleghenybradford.com

Allegheny College 520 N Main St ..... Meadville PA 16335 814-332-4351 166
TF: 800-521-5293 ■ *Web:* allegheny.edu

Allegheny Design Management Inc
1154 Parks Industrial Dr ..... Vandergrift PA 15690 724-845-7336 780
Web: www.alleghenydesignmgmt.com

Allegheny Health Network
1301 Carlisle St ..... Natrona Heights PA 15065 724-224-5100 226-7385 374-3
Web: www.ahn.org

Allegheny Institute for Public Policy
305 Mt Lebanon Blvd Ste 208 ..... Pittsburgh PA 15234 412-440-0079 440-0085 634
Web: www.alleghenyinstitute.org

Allegheny Investments Ltd
Stone Quarry Crossing 811 Camp Horne Rd
Ste 100 ..... Pittsburgh PA 15237 412-367-3880 401
TF: 800-899-3880 ■ *Web:* www.alleghenyfinancial.com

Allegheny Iron & Metal Company Inc
2200 Adams Ave ..... Philadelphia PA 19124 215-743-7759 686
Web: alleghenyiron.com

Allegheny Kiski Postal Federal Credit Union
501 11th St Rm 206 ..... New Kensington PA 15068 724-337-3717 337-9346 219
Web: akpostalfcu.org

Allegheny Metal Federal Credit Union
260 Pershing Ave ..... Leechburg PA 15656 724-845-8923 219
Web: www.alleghenymetalfcu.com

Allegheny Millwork PBT
104 Commerce Blvd ..... Lawrence PA 15055 724-873-8700 499
Web: www.alleghenymillwork.com

Allegheny Petroleum Products Co
999 Airbrake Ave ..... Wilmerding PA 15148 412-829-1990 580
TF: 800-600-2900 ■ *Web:* www.oils.com

Allegheny Portage Railroad National Historic Site
110 Federal Park Rd ..... Gallitzin PA 16641 814-886-6150 564
Web: www.nps.gov

Allegheny Technologies Inc
1000 Six PPG Pl ..... Pittsburgh PA 15222 412-394-2800 723
NYSE: ATI ■ *TF:* 800-258-3586 ■ *Web:* www.atimetals.com

Allegheny Tool & Manufacturing Company Inc
19320 Cochranton Rd ..... Meadville PA 16335 814-337-2795 337-3263 757
Web: www.algtool.com

Allegheny Valley School District
300 Pearl Ave ..... Cheswick PA 15024 724-274-5300 685
Web: www.avsdweb.org

Allegheny Wesleyan College
2161 Woodsdale Rd ..... Salem OH 44460 330-337-6403 161
TF: 800-292-3153 ■ *Web:* www.awc.edu

Allegheny West Conference of Seventh Day Adventists
1339 E Broad St ..... Columbus OH 43205 614-252-5271 48-20
Web: www.awconf.org

Allegiance Abstract Services Inc
111 Conklin St ..... Farmingdale NY 11735 516-249-1200 653
Web: allegianceabstract.com

Allegiance Capital Corp
16400 Dallas Pkwy Ste 300 ..... Dallas TX 75248 214-217-7750 217-7751 70
Web: allcapcorp.com

Allegiance Consultinginc
10822 W Toller Dr Ste 250 ..... Littleton CO 80127 720-947-9201 379-6412* 225
**Fax Area Code:* 303 ■ *Web:* www.acinow.net

Allegiance Financial Group LLC
374 Maple Ave E Ste 204 ..... Vienna VA 22180 703-242-7900 242-5718 401
Web: www.afgllc.net

Allegiance Retail Services LLC
485D Rt 1 S Ste 420 ..... Iselin NJ 08830 732-596-6000 345
Web: allegianceretailservices.com

Allegiant Air 8360 S Durango Dr ..... Las Vegas NV 89113 702-851-7300 851-7301 25
NASDAQ: ALGT ■ *Web:* www.allegiantair.com

Allegis Group Inc 7301 Pkwy Dr ..... Hanover MD 21076 800-927-8090 721
TF: 800-927-8090 ■ *Web:* www.allegisgroup.com

AllegisCyber Capital
200 Page Mill Rd Ste 100 ..... Palo Alto CA 94306 650-687-0500 687-0234 792
Web: allegiscyber.com

Name / Address	City	State	Zip	Phone	Fax	Class
Allegra Network LLC 47585 Galleon Dr *Web:* www.allegramarketingprint.com	Plymouth	MI	48170	248-697-2435		113
Allegro Coffee Co 12799 Claude Ct *TF:* 800-530-3995 ■ *Web:* www.allegrocoffee.com	Thornton	CO	80241	303-444-4844	920-5468	296-7
Allegro Consultants Ltd 9800 JEB Stuart Pkwy Ste 106 *Web:* www.allegroconsultants.com	Glen Allen	VA	23059	804-553-1130		196
Allegro Industries 1360 Shiloh Church Rd *TF:* 800-622-3530 ■ *Web:* www.allegrosafety.com	Piedmont	SC	29673	864-846-8740		475
Allegro Italian Kitchen 10011-109 St *Web:* www.allegroitaliankitchen.ca	Edmonton	AB	T5J3S8	780-424-6644		671
Allegro Microsystems Inc 115 NE Cutoff *Web:* www.allegromicro.com	Worcester	MA	01606	508-853-5000		696
Allegro Ophthalmics LLC 31473 Rancho Viejo Rd Ste 204 *Web:* www.allegroeye.com	San Juan Capistrano	CA	92675	949-940-8130	940-8121	743
Allen 525 Burbank St *TF:* 800-876-8600 ■ *Web:* byallen.com	Broomfield	CO	80020	303-469-1857	466-7437	188-4
Allen & Allen Company Inc 202 Culebra Ave *Web:* www.lumberhardware.com	San Antonio	TX	78201	210-733-9191		362
Allen & Company of Florida Inc 1401 S Florida Ave *TF:* 800-950-2526 ■ *Web:* alleninvestments.com	Lakeland	FL	33803	863-688-9000	616-6354	690
Allen & Gerritsen 2 Seaport Ln *Web:* www.a-g.com	Boston	MA	02210	857-300-2000		4
Allen & Hoshall Inc 1661 International Dr Ste 100 *Web:* www.allenhoshall.com	Memphis	TN	38120	901-820-0820	683-1001	261
Allen & Kimbell LLP 317 E Carrillo St *Web:* www.aklaw.net	Santa Barbara	CA	93101	805-963-8611		445
Allen & Major Associates Inc 100 Commerce Way *Web:* www.allenmajor.com	Woburn	MA	01801	781-935-6889		727
Allen & O'Hara Development Company LLC PO Box 771889 *Web:* www.allenoharadev.com	Memphis	TN	38117	901-471-2080		653
Allen & Shariff Corp 7061 Deepage Dr *Web:* www.allenshariff.com	Columbia	MD	21045	410-381-7100		188
Allen Agency 34-36 Elm St PO Box 578 *TF:* 800-439-4311 ■ *Web:* www.andovercompanies.com	Camden	ME	04843	800-439-4311		390
Allen Aircraft Products Inc 6168 Woodbine Ave *Web:* www.allenaircraft.com	Ravenna	OH	44266	330-296-9621		529
Allen Avionics Inc 255 E 2nd St *Web:* www.allenavionics.com	Mineola	NY	11501	516-248-8080	747-6724	246
Allen Blasting & Coating Inc 1668 Old Hwy 61 *TF:* 800-760-9186 ■ *Web:* www.allenblastingandcoating.com	Wever	IA	52658	319-367-5500		186
Allen Bros Inc 3737 S Halsted St *TF:* 800-548-7777 ■ *Web:* www.allenbrothers.com	Chicago	IL	60609	773-890-5100		473
Allen C. Ewing & Co 50 N Laura St Ste 3625 *Web:* www.allenewing.com	Jacksonville	FL	32202	904-354-5573		690
Allen Care Inc 6201 Bonhomme Ste 308N **Fax Area Code:* 713 ■ *Web:* www.allencarehhs.com	Houston	TX	77036	281-933-8463	583-3808*	363
Allen Chamber of Commerce 210 W McDermott Dr *Web:* www.allenfairviewchamber.com	Allen	TX	75013	972-727-5585	727-9000	139
Allen Commercial Industries Inc 11301 Mosier Valley Rd *Web:* www.allen-commercial.com	Euless	TX	76040	817-267-4919		393
Allen Communication Learning Services 55 West 900 South *Web:* www.allencomm.com	Salt Lake City	UT	84101	801-537-7800		178-3
Allen Correctional Ctr 3751 Lauderdale Woodyard Rd *Web:* doc.louisiana.gov	Kinder	LA	70648	337-639-2942		213
Allen Correctional Institution 770 W Broad St *Web:* www.drc.ohio.gov	Columbus	OH	43222	419-224-8000	224-5828	213
Allen County 715 S Calhoun St Rm 101 *TF:* 888-604-7888 ■ *Web:* www.allencounty.us	Fort Wayne	IN	46802	260-449-7245	449-7658	338
Allen County 513 N State St *TF:* 866-444-1407 ■ *Web:* www.allencounty.org	Iola	KS	66749	620-365-1407	365-1441	338
Allen County 301 N Main St Ste 203 PO Box 123 *Web:* allencountyohtreasurer.com	Lima	OH	45801	419-223-8515	222-7852	338
Allen County PO Box 115 *Web:* allencountykentucky.com	Scottsville	KY	42164	270-237-4782		338
Allen County Community College 1801 N Cottonwood St *TF:* 800-444-0535 ■ *Web:* www.allencc.edu	Iola	KS	66749	620-365-5116	365-7406	162
Allen County Law Library 204 N Main St *Web:* userpages.bright.net	Lima	OH	45801	419-223-1426		434-3
Allen County Museum and Historical Society 620 W Market St *Web:* allencountymuseum.org	Lima	OH	45801	419-222-9426		49-19
Allen County Public Library 900 Library Plz *Web:* acpl-cms.wise.oclc.org	Fort Wayne	IN	46802	260-421-1200	421-1386	434-3
Allen County War Memorial Coliseum 4000 Parnell Ave *Web:* www.memorialcoliseum.com	Fort Wayne	IN	46805	260-482-9502	484-1637	720
Allen Dell PA 202 S Rome Ave Ste 100 *Web:* www.allendell.com	Tampa	FL	33606	813-223-5351	229-6682	428
Allen Engineering Corp (AEC) 819 S Fifth St PO Box 819 *TF:* 800-643-0095 ■ *Web:* www.alleneng.com	Paragould	AR	72450	870-236-7751	236-3934	190
Allen Evans Klein Intl 305 Madison Ave *Web:* www.allenevans.com	New York	NY	10165	212-983-9300	983-9272	463
Allen Family Foods Inc 126 N Shipley St *Web:* www.allenharimllc.com	Seaford	DE	19973	302-629-9163	629-0514	619
Allen Flavors Inc 23 Progress St *Web:* www.allenflavors.com	Edison	NJ	08820	908-561-5995		297-8
Allen Furniture City Inc 7808 L St *Web:* allenshome.com	Omaha	NE	68127	402-331-8480		321
Allen Gibbs & Houlik LC 301 N Main Ste 1700 *Web:* www.aghlc.com	Wichita	KS	67202	316-267-7231		2
Allen Group, The 50 Washington St *Web:* www.theallengroup.com	Norwalk	CT	06854	203-855-5777		462
Allen Industries Inc 6434 Burnt Poplar Rd *TF:* 800-967-2553 ■ *Web:* www.allenindustries.com	Greensboro	NC	27409	336-668-2791	668-7875	701
Allen Interactions Inc 1120 Centre Pointe Dr Ste 800 *Web:* www.alleninteractions.com	Mendota Heights	MN	55120	651-203-3700		765
Allen Lumber Company Inc 502 N Main St *Web:* www.allenlumbercompany.com	Barre	VT	05641	802-476-4156		115
Allen Lund Company Inc 4529 Angeles Crest Hwy *TF:* 800-811-0083 ■ *Web:* www.allenlund.com	La Canada Flintridge	CA	91011	800-777-6142	434-5863	311
Allen Machine Products Inc 120 Ricefield Ln *Web:* www.allenmachine.com	Hauppauge	NY	11788	631-630-8800	630-8801	488
Allen Morgan Health Ctr 177 N Highland Ave *Web:* www.trezevantmanor.org	Memphis	TN	38111	901-325-4003		450
Allen Morris Co 121 Alhambra Plz Ste 1600 *Web:* www.allenmorris.com	Coral Gables	FL	33134	305-443-1000	443-1462	652
Allen Norton & Blue P A 121 Majorca Ave Ste 300 *Web:* www.anblaw.com	Coral Gables	FL	33134	305-445-7801	442-1578	445
Allen Oil Co 1215 Old Birmingham Hwy *Web:* www.allenoil.com	Sylacauga	AL	35150	256-245-5478		579
Allen Organ Co 150 Locust St *TF:* 800-582-4466 ■ *Web:* www.allenorgan.com	Macungie	PA	18062	610-966-2202		527
Allen Packaging Co 1150 Valencia Ave *Web:* allenpkg.com	Tustin	CA	92780	714-259-0100		557
Allen Paint 2498 W Hampden *Web:* denverautopaint.com	Sheridan	CO	80110	303-744-1755		802
Allen Parish 8904 Hwy 165 *TF:* 888-639-4868 ■ *Web:* www.allenparish.com	Oberlin	LA	70655	337-639-4868	639-4884	338
Allen Park Chamber of Commerce 6543 Allen Rd *Web:* www.allenparkchamber.org	Allen Park	MI	48101	313-382-7303	382-4409	139
Allen Partners Inc 20519 SE 198th St *Web:* allenpartners.com	Renton	WA	98058	206-812-1440		260
Allen Press Inc 810 E Tenth St PO Box 1897 *TF:* 800-627-0932 ■ *Web:* www.allenpress.com	Lawrence	KS	66044	785-843-1234	843-1274	47
Allen Printing Inc 415-A Spence Ln *Web:* www.allenprinting.com	Nashville	TN	37210	615-255-2078		627
Allen Refractories Co 131 Shackelford Rd *Web:* www.allenrefractories.net	Pataskala	OH	43062	740-927-8000	927-9404	191-1
Allen Rick (Rep R - GA) 2400 Rayburn House Office Bldg *Web:* allen.house.gov	Washington	DC	20515	202-225-2823	225-3377	342-2
Allen School of Health Sciences 163-18 Jamaica Ave *TF:* 888-620-6745 ■ *Web:* www.allenschool.edu	Jamaica	NY	11432	888-620-6745		685
Allen Schwartz 1231 Long Beach Ave *Web:* allenschwartz.com	Los Angeles	CA	90021	213-895-4400		157-6
Allen Systems Group Inc (ASG) 1333 Third Ave S **Fax Area Code:* 800 ■ *TF:* 800-932-5536 ■ *Web:* www.asg.com	Naples	FL	34102	239-435-2200	325-2555*	178-12
Allen Tel Products Inc 30 TV5 Dr *TF:* 855-347-2839 ■ *Web:* www.allentel.com	Henderson	NV	89014	702-855-5700		791
Allen Tool Phoenix Inc 6821 Ellicott Dr *Web:* www.allentoolphoenix.com	East Syracuse	NY	13057	315-463-7533	463-0303	454
Allen Turner Hyundai Inc 6000 Pensacola Blvd *Web:* www.allenturnerhyundai.com	Pensacola	FL	32505	850-479-9667		57
Allen University 1530 Harden St *TF:* 877-625-5368 ■ *Web:* www.allenuniversity.edu	Columbia	SC	29204	803-376-5700	376-5733	166
Allen Ventures Inc 517 State Farm Rd *TF:* 877-423-9800 ■ *Web:* www.allenventures.com	Deerfield	WI	53531	608-423-9800		661
Allen Village School 706 W 42nd St *Web:* www.allenvillageschool.com	Kansas City	MO	64111	816-931-0177		685
Allen's Crosley Lanes 2400 E Evergreen Blvd *Web:* crosleylanes.com	Vancouver	WA	98661	360-693-4789		99
Allen's of Hastings Inc 1115 W Second St *Web:* www.allensfoodmart.com	Hastings	NE	68901	402-463-5633	463-5730	345
Allen'S Tri-State Mechanical 404 S Hayden St *Web:* www.allenstristate.com	Amarillo	TX	79101	806-376-8345		189-10
Allen's TV Cable Service Inc 800 Victor II Blvd *Web:* www.atvc.net	Morgan City	LA	70380	985-384-8335		116
Allen, Summers, Simpson, Lillie & Gresham PLLC 80 Monroe Ave Ste 650 *Web:* www.allensummers.com	Memphis	TN	38103	901-763-4200		428
Allen-Bailey Tag & Label Inc 3177 Lehigh St *Web:* www.abtl.com	Caledonia	NY	14423	585-538-2324		548
Allenberry Resort 1559 Boiling Springs Rd *Web:* allenberry.com	Boiling Springs	PA	17007	717-258-3211		669
Allenbrand-Drews & Associates Inc 122 N Water St *Web:* allenbrand-drews.com	Olathe	KS	66061	913-764-1076		261

Phone | Fax | Class

Allendale Correctional Institution
1057 Revolutionary Trl PO Box 1151 Fairfax SC 29827 803-734-0653 213
Web: doc.sc.gov

Allendale County
526 Memorial Ave PO Box 190 Allendale SC 29810 803-584-3438 584-7042 338
Web: www.allendalecounty.com

Allendale Machinery Systems Inc
16 Park Way Upper Saddle River NJ 07458 201-327-5215 697
Web: hfoallendale.com

Allendorph Specialties Inc
201 Stanton St Broussard LA 70518 337-232-0503 358
Web: www.allendorph.com

Allen-Edmonds Shoe Corp
201 E Seven Hills Rd Port Washington WI 53074 262-235-9261 301
TF: 800-235-2348 ■ *Web:* www.allenedmonds.com

Allensville Planing Mill Inc
108 E Main St Allensville PA 17002 717-483-6386 106
Web: www.apm-inc.net

Allentown Art Museum 31 N Fifth St Allentown PA 18101 610-432-4333 434-7409 520
Web: www.allentownartmuseum.org

Allentown Bartender School Inc
1541 Alta Dr Ste 201 Whitehall PA 18052 610-821-9450 821-0594 685
Web: www.bartenderschool.com

Allentown City Hall 435 Hamilton St Allentown PA 18101 610-439-5999 437-7554 337
Web: www.allentownpa.gov

Allentown Inc 165 Rte 526 Allentown NJ 08501 609-259-7951 386
Web: www.allentowninc.com

Allentown Police Academy
2110 Park Dr Allentown PA 18103 610-437-7744 167-3
Web: www.allentownpa.gov

Allentown Public Library
1210 Hamilton St Allentown PA 18102 610-820-2400 820-0640 434-3
Web: www.allentownpl.org

Allentown School District (ASD)
31 S Penn St PO Box 328 Allentown PA 18105 484-765-4000 765-4140 685
Web: www.allentownsd.org

Allentown Symphony Orchestra
23 N Sixth St Allentown PA 18101 610-432-7961 432-6735 573-3
Web: www.millcrsymphonyhall.org

Allen-Vanguard Corp
2400 St Laurent Blvd Ottawa ON K1G5B4 613-739-9646 576
TF: 800-644-9078 ■ *Web:* www.allenvanguard.com

Allergan Inc 2525 Dupont Dr Irvine CA 92612 714-246-4500 582
NYSE: AGN ■ *TF:* 800-347-4500 ■ *Web:* www.allergan.com

Allergy Partners PA 14 McDowell St Asheville NC 28801 828-277-1300 463
Web: www.allergypartners.com

Allergy Research Group LLC
2300 N Loop Rd Alameda CA 94502 510-263-2000 583
Web: www.allergyresearchgroup.com

Allergychoices Inc 2731 National Dr Onalaska WI 54650 608-793-1580 237
TF: 866-793-1680 ■ *Web:* www.allergychoices.com

ALLETE Inc 30 W Superior St Duluth MN 55802 218-279-5000 360-5
NYSE: ALE ■ *Web:* www.allete.com

Allevant Solutions LLC
4714 Gettysburg Rd Mechanicsburg PA 17055 717-972-3803 194
Web: www.allevant.com

Allevity HR & Payroll
870 Manzanita Ct Ste A Chico CA 95926 530-345-2406 345-0400 631
TF: 800-447-8233 ■ *Web:* www.allevityhr.com

Alley Theatre 615 Texas Ave Houston TX 77002 713-220-5700 222-6542 572
Web: www.alleytheatre.org

Alley-Cassetty Companies Inc
2 Oldham St Nashville TN 37213 615-244-0440 191-1
Web: www.alley-cassetty.com

Alleyway Theatre 1 Curtain Up Alley Buffalo NY 14202 716-852-2600 572
Web: www.alleyway.com

All-Fab Building Components Inc
1755 Dugald Rd Winnipeg MB R2J0H3 204-661-8880 45
TF: 800-665-0335 ■ *Web:* www.all-fab.com

Allfab Engineering Company Inc
3015 S 40th St Phoenix AZ 85040 602-437-0497 261
Web: allfabeng.com

Allfast Fastening Systems Inc
15200 Don Julian Rd City of Industry CA 91745 626-968-9388 968-9393 278
Web: trsaero.com

Allflex Packaging 100 Race St Ambler PA 19002 215-789-4441 643-3339 554
TF: 800-448-2467 ■ *Web:* www.allflex.com

Allgeier Auto Parts Inc
7650 Harrison Ave Cincinnati OH 45247 513-353-3377 57
Web: allgeierautoparts.com

Alliance Abroad Group
1645 E 6th St Ste 100 Austin TX 78702 512-457-8062 41
TF: 866-622-7623 ■ *Web:* www.allianceabroad.com

Alliance Abstract LLC
2 Mott St Ste 605 New York NY 10013 212-962-2228 390
Web: allianceabstract.com

Alliance Advisory & Securities Inc
3390 Auto Mall Dr Westlake Village CA 91362 805-371-8020 371-8008 690
TF: 888-234-7526 ■ *Web:* www.allianceadvisory.com

Alliance Area Chamber of Commerce
210 E Main St Alliance OH 44601 330-823-6260 139
Web: www.allianceohiochamber.org

Alliance Brokerage Corp 990 Wbury Rd Westbury NY 11590 516-465-1100 390
Web: www.alliancebrokeragecorp.com

Alliance Communications Management
2610-B Dauphin St Ste 103 Mobile AL 36606 251-433-6566 192
TF: 888-277-4490 ■ *Web:* www.alliancemanaged.com

Alliance Community Bank
6530 N SR-29 Springfield IL 62707 217-487-7766 70
TF: 800-367-7576 ■ *Web:* www.bankacb.com

Alliance Community Hospital (ACH)
200 E State St Alliance OH 44601 330-596-6000 374-3
Web: aultmanalliance.org

Alliance Construction Solutions
12789 Emerson St Thornton CO 80241 303-813-0035 228-7434 187
Web: www.allianceconstruction.com

Alliance Corp
2395 Meadowpine Blvd Mississauga ON L5N7W6 888-821-4797 492
TF: 888-821-4797 ■ *Web:* www.alliancecorporation.ca

Alliance Credit Counseling
10720 Sikes Pl Ste 100 Charlotte NC 28277 704-341-1010 41
TF: 888-995-7856 ■ *Web:* www.knowdebt.org

Alliance Data Systems Corp
7500 Dallas Pkwy Plano TX 75024 214-494-3000 255
NYSE: ADS ■ *Web:* www.alliancedata.com

Alliance Energy Services LLC
318 Armour Rd Kansas City MO 64116 816-421-5192 466
Web: www.alliancec3.com

Alliance Financial Services Inc
200 Great Rd Ste 222 Bedford MA 01730 781-275-4243 390
Web: alliancefinancialservices.com

Alliance Fire Protection Co
2114 E Cedar St Tempe AZ 85281 480-966-9178 406

Alliance Foods Inc 605 W Chicago Rd Coldwater MI 49036 517-278-2396 345
Web: www.alliance-foods.com

Alliance for Aging Research (AAR)
750 17th St NW Ste 1100 Washington DC 20006 202-293-2856 234-5030* 48-17
**Fax Area Code:* 770 ■ *Web:* www.agingresearch.org

Alliance for Children & Families Inc
11700 W Lake Park Dr Milwaukee WI 53224 800-221-3726 359-1074* 48-6
**Fax Area Code:* 414 ■ *TF:* 800-221-3726 ■ *Web:* www.alliance1.org

Alliance For Employee Growth & Development Inc, The
80 Cottontail Ln Ste 220 Somerset NJ 08873 800-323-3436 193
TF: 800-323-3436 ■ *Web:* www.employeegrowth.com

Alliance for Excellent Education
1201 Connecticut Ave Ste 901 Washington DC 20036 202-828-0828 828-0821 48-11
Web: www.all4ed.org

Alliance for International Exchange
1828 L St NW Ste 1150 Washington DC 20036 202-293-6141 293-6144 48-11
Web: www.alliance-exchange.org

Alliance for Justice (AFJ)
11 Dupont Cir NW Ste 500 Washington DC 20036 202-822-6070 822-6068 48-7
Web: www.afj.org

Alliance for Pharmacy Compounding
100 Daingerfield Rd Ste 1 401 Alexandria VA 22314 281-933-8400 495-0602 49-8
TF: 800-927-4227 ■ *Web:* www.iacp.site-ym.com

Alliance for Responsible Atmospheric Policy
2111 Wilson Blvd 8th Fl Arlington VA 22201 703-243-0344 243-2874 48-13
Web: www.alliancepolicy.org

Alliance for Retired Americans
815 16th St NW 4th Fl Washington DC 20006 202-637-5399 48-6
TF: 888-373-6497 ■ *Web:* retiredamericans.org

Alliance for Telecommunications Industry Solutions (ATIS)
1200 G St NW Ste 500 Washington DC 20005 202-628-6380 393-5453 49-20
Web: www.atis.org

Alliance Geotechnical Group Inc
3228 Halifax St Dallas TX 75247 972-444-8889 444-8893 194
Web: www.aggengr.com

Alliance Grain Co 1306 W Eigth St Gibson City IL 60936 217-784-4284 784-8949 275
TF: 800-222-2451 ■ *Web:* www.alliance-grain.com

Alliance Group Services Inc (AGSI)
1221 Post Rd E Westport CT 06880 800-756-2236 221-8705* 224
**Fax Area Code:* 203 ■ *TF:* 800-756-2236 ■ *Web:* www.alliancegrp.com

Alliance Health Networks
9 Exchange Pl Salt Lake City UT 84111 801-355-6002 463
Web: www.alliancehealth.com

Alliance Holdings Inc
1021 Old York Rd 3rd Fl Abington PA 19001 215-706-0877 360-3
Web: www.allianceholdings.com

Alliance Home Health Care
9607 N College Ave Indianapolis IN 46280 317-581-1100 816-3131 693
Web: alliancehomehealthcare.net

Alliance Home Health Services Inc
3408 Miller Rd Ste 201 Kalamazoo MI 49001 269-349-1726 337-9461* 363
**Fax Area Code:* 866 ■ *TF:* 800-316-0332 ■ *Web:* www.alliancehhs.com

Alliance Hospitality Hotel Management
215 N Boylan Ave Raleigh NC 27603 919-791-1801 378
Web: alliancehospitality.com

Alliance Imaging Inc
100 Bayview Cir Ste 400 Newport Beach CA 92660 949-242-5300 383
TF: 800-544-3215 ■ *Web:* www.alliancehealthcareservices-us.com

Alliance Insurance Agency of Mankato
895 E Madison Ave Mankato MN 56001 507-720-6466 390
Web: aiamankato.com

Alliance International Forwarders Inc
7155 Old Katy Rd Ste 100 Houston TX 77024 713-428-3100 311

Alliance Investigations LLC
125 E Gurley St PO Box 11990 Prescott AZ 86303 928-717-1196 400
Web: alliance-investigations-llc.business.site

Alliance Land Co 19550 Michael Ave Hastings MN 55033 651-438-9333 438-2913 652
Web: www.allianceland.com

Alliance Landscaping & Excavation LLC
140 Rockingham Rd Auburn NH 03032 603-622-1111 422
Web: alliancelandscaping.com

Alliance Laundry Systems LLC PO Box 990 Ripon WI 54971 920-748-3121 748-4564 427
Web: www.alliancelaundry.com

Alliance Legal Staffing Solutions
2909 Cole Ave Ste 230 Dallas TX 75204 214-954-1250 260
Web: www.alliancelegal.com

Alliance Limousine
14553 Delano St Ste 210 Van Nuys CA 91411 800-954-5466 786-8810* 441
**Fax Area Code:* 818 ■ *TF:* 800-954-5466 ■ *Web:* www.alliancelimo.net

Alliance Management Group LLC
2651 Whispering Creek Cir Fargo ND 58104 701-356-6688 47
Web: www.alliancemgmtgroup.com

Alliance Material Handling Inc
8320 Sherwick Ct Jessup MD 20794 301-497-2600 497-2690 695
TF: 866-264-5438 ■ *Web:* www.alliancemat.com

Alliance Mep Engineers Inc
12355 Sunrise Valley Dr Ste 220 Reston VA 20191 703-749-7941 261
Web: allianceengineers.com

Alliance Nursing
14615 NE N Woodinville Way Ste 108 Woodinville WA 98072 425-483-3303 483-3309 363
TF: 800-473-3303 ■ *Web:* alliancenursing.com

Alliance of Motion Picture & Television Producers (AMPTP)
15301 Ventura Blvd Bldg E Sherman Oaks CA 91403 818-995-3600 48-4
Web: amptp.org

Company / Address	City	State	Zip	Phone	Fax	Class
Alliance of Nonprofit Mailers (ANM) 1211 Connecticut Ave NW Ste 610 *Web:* www.nonprofitmailers.org	Washington	DC	20036	202-462-5132		48-7
Alliance of Professionals & Consultants Inc 8200 Brownleigh Dr *Web:* www.apcinc.com	Raleigh	NC	27617	919-510-9696		463
Alliance of Transylvanian Saxons 5393 Pearl Rd *Web:* www.atsaxons.com	Cleveland	OH	44129	440-842-8442		390
Alliance One International Inc 8001 Aerial Center Pkwy PO Box 2009 *NYSE: AOI* ■ *Web:* www.aointl.com	Morrisville	NC	27560	919-379-4300	379-4346	756
Alliance Packaging LLC 1000 SW 43rd St *Web:* www.alliancepackaging.net	Renton	WA	98057	425-291-3500		100
Alliance Paper & Food Service Inc 11058 W Addison St *Web:* alliancepfs.com	Franklin Park	IL	60131	847-349-1500		96
Alliance Pipeline Limited Partnership 6385 Old Shady Oak Rd Ste 150 *Web:* www.alliancepipeline.com	Eden Prairie	MN	55344	952-944-3183		325
Alliance Precision Plastics 1220 Lee Rd *Web:* www.allianceppc.com	Rochester	NY	14606	585-426-5310	426-5081	757
Alliance Publishing Company Inc 40 S Linden Ave *TF:* 800-778-0098 ■ *Web:* www.the-review.com	Alliance	OH	44601	330-821-1200		532-3
Alliance Recycling Group 115 31st Ave N *Web:* www.alliancesteelco.com	Minneapolis	MN	55411	612-588-2721	588-2724	686
Alliance Resource Partners LP 1717 S Boulder Ave Ste 400 *NASDAQ: ARLP* ■ *TF:* 800-485-6875 ■ *Web:* www.arlp.com	Tulsa	OK	74119	918-295-7600	295-7358	501
Alliance Rubber Co 210 Carpenter Dam Rd *TF:* 800-626-5940 ■ *Web:* www.rubberband.com	Hot Springs	AR	71901	501-262-2700	262-3948	676
Alliance Scale Inc 1020 Turnpike St *Web:* www.alliancescale.com	Canton	MA	02021	781-828-8386		362
Alliance Shippers Inc 516 Sylvan Ave *Web:* www.alliance.com	Englewood Cliffs	NJ	07632	201-227-0400		311
Alliance Solutions Group Inc 11818 Rock Landing Dr Ste 105 *Web:* www.asg-inc.org	Newport News	VA	23606	757-223-7233		194
Alliance Source Testing LLC 214 Central Cir SW *Web:* stacktest.com	Decatur	AL	35603	256-351-0121		743
Alliance Support Partners Inc 5036 Commercial Cir Unit C *Web:* asp-support.com	Concord	CA	94520	925-363-5382	363-7882	261
Alliance Theatre Co Woodruff Arts Ctr 1280 Peachtree St NE *Web:* alliancetheatre.org	Atlanta	GA	30309	404-733-4650	733-4625	749
Alliance Tickets Inc 333 W Hampden Ave Ste 410	Englewood	CO	80110	303-781-2220		514
Alliance to Save Energy (ASE) 1850 M St NW Ste 600 *TF:* 800-862-2086 ■ *Web:* www.ase.org	Washington	DC	20036	202-857-0666	331-9588	48-12
Alliance Tractor Trailer Training Center Inc PO Box 883 *TF:* 800-334-1203 ■ *Web:* www.alliancetractortrailer.com	Arden	NC	28704	828-684-4454		167-3
Alliance Water Resources Inc 206 S Keene St *Web:* alliancewater.com	Columbia	MO	65201	573-874-8080		806
Alliance Winding Equipment Inc 3939 Vanguard Dr *Web:* www.alliance-winding.com	Fort Wayne	IN	46809	260-478-2200		518
Alliance Worldwide Investigative Group Inc 23 Executive Park Dr *TF:* 800-579-2911 ■ *Web:* www.allianceriskgroup.com	Clifton Park	NY	12065	518-514-2944		390
Alliance, The 502 Wick St *Web:* www.corinthalliance.com	Corinth	MS	38834	662-287-5269		139
AllianceBernstein Holding LP (AB) 1345 Avenue of the Americas *NYSE: AB* ■ *TF:* 800-221-5672 ■ *Web:* www.alliancebernstein.com	New York	NY	10105	212-486-5800	969-2293	401
AllianceOne Inc 4850 E St Rd Ste 300 *TF:* 877-876-7886 ■ *Web:* www.allianceoneinc.com	Trevose	PA	19053	877-876-7886		160
Alliant Consulting Inc 2815 Camino del Rio S Ste 126 **Fax Area Code:* 909 ■ *Web:* alliantconsulting.net	San Diego	CA	92108	619-831-0704	747-0404*	463
Alliant Coopeartive Data Solutions 301 Fields Ln N Ctr *Web:* info.alliantinsight.com	Brewster	NY	10509	845-617-5500		194
Alliant Credit Union 1200 Associates Dr Ste 102 *Web:* alliantcu.com	Dubuque	IA	52002	563-585-3737		219
Alliant Energy Center of Dane County 1919 Alliant Energy Ctr Way *Web:* www.alliantenergycenter.com	Madison	WI	53713	608-267-3976	267-0146	205
Alliant Energy Corp 4902 N Biltmore Ln Ste 1000 *NYSE: LNT* ■ **Fax Area Code:* 608 ■ *TF:* 800-255-4268 ■ *Web:* www.alliantenergy.com	Madison	WI	53718	800-255-4268	458-0100*	787
Alliant Insurance Services Inc 1301 Dove St *TF:* 844-764-9200 ■ *Web:* www.alliant.com	Newport Beach	CA	92660	949-756-0271		391-2
Alliant International University 10455 Pomerado Rd *TF:* 866-825-5426 ■ *Web:* www.alliant.edu	San Diego	CA	92131	858-635-4772	635-4555	166
Allianz Global Investors 1633 Broadway *TF:* 877-716-9787 ■ *Web:* us.allianzgi.com	New York	NY	10019	877-716-9787		690
Allianz Global Investors of America LP 600 West Broadway *TF:* 800-656-6226 ■ *Web:* www.allianzgi.com	San Diego	CA	92101	800-656-6226		401
Allianz Life Insurance Company of North America PO Box 1344 *TF:* 800-950-5872 ■ *Web:* www.allianzlife.com	Minneapolis	MN	55416	800-950-5872		391-2
Allianz Real Estate of America 60 E 42nd St Ste 3710 *Web:* allianz-realestate.com	New York	NY	10165	212-938-0670		401
Allied 100 LLC 1800 US Hwy 51 N *TF:* 800-544-0048 ■ *Web:* www.aedsuperstore.com	Woodruff	WI	54560	715-358-2329		475
Allied Air Enterprises 215 Metropolitan Dr *TF:* 800-448-5872 ■ *Web:* www.alliedair.com	West Columbia	SC	29170	800-448-5872		15
Allied Automation Inc 5220 E 64th St *TF:* 800-214-0322 ■ *Web:* www.allied-automation.com	Indianapolis	IN	46220	317-253-5900		385
Allied Bindery LLC 32501 Dequindre Rd *TF:* 800-833-0151 ■ *Web:* www.alliedbindery.com	Madison Heights	MI	48071	248-588-5990		781
Allied Blending & Ingredients 121 Royal Rd *TF:* 800-758-4080 ■ *Web:* www.alliedblending.com	Keokuk	IA	52632	800-758-4080		123
Allied Blower & Sheet Metal 1350 Polson Dr *Web:* www.alliedblower.com	Vernon	BC	V1T8H2	250-503-2533		610
Allied Body Works Inc 625 S 96th St *TF:* 800-733-7450 ■ *Web:* www.alliedbody.com	Seattle	WA	98108	206-763-7811	763-8836	516
Allied Box Co 1015 Chesley Ave *Web:* www.alliedbox.com	Richmond	CA	94801	510-253-1030	412-0520	559
Allied Building Products Corp 15 E Union Ave *TF:* 800-541-2198 ■ *Web:* www.alliedbuilding.com	East Rutherford	NJ	07073	201-507-8400		191-3
Allied Building Service Company of Detroit Inc 1801 Howard St *Web:* www.teamallied.com	Detroit	MI	48216	313-230-0800		104
Allied Business Consulting 295 Durham Ave Ste 212 *Web:* www.abcinc-us.com	South Plainfield	NJ	07080	908-222-7015	834-0930	194
Allied Business Intelligence Inc 249 S St *Web:* www.abiresearch.com	Oyster Bay	NY	11771	516-624-2500		668
Allied Business Systems Inc 18627 Brookhurst St Ste 374 *Web:* www.alliedhr.com	Fountain Valley	CA	92708	714-963-5554	964-0061	177
Allied Chucker & Engineering Co 3529 Scheele Dr *Web:* alliedchucker.com	Jackson	MI	49202	517-787-1370	787-2878	595
Allied Computer Graphics Inc PO Box 541449 *TF:* 800-330-4488 ■ *Web:* www.allcompu.com	Lake Worth	FL	33454	561-649-6300		344
Allied Concrete Co 1000 Harris St *Web:* alliedconcrete.com	Charlottesville	VA	22903	434-296-7181	220-4846	182
Allied Construction Products LLC 3900 Kelley Ave *TF:* 800-321-1046 ■ *Web:* www.alliedcp.com	Cleveland	OH	44114	216-431-2600	431-2601	190
Allied Construction Services & Color Inc 2122 Fleur Dr PO Box 937 *TF:* 800-365-4855 ■ *Web:* www.alliedconst.com	Des Moines	IA	50304	515-288-4855	288-2069	189-9
Allied Consultants Inc 1304 W Ave *Web:* www.alliedconsultants.com	Austin	TX	78701	512-236-8535		196
Allied Container Systems Inc PO Box 10573 *TF:* 800-943-6510 ■ *Web:* www.alliedcontainer.com	San Rafael	CA	94912	925-944-7600	944-7601	549
Allied Contractors Inc 204 E Preston St *Web:* www.alliedcontractor.com	Baltimore	MD	21202	410-539-6727	332-4594	189-3
Allied Controls Inc 150 E Aurora St *TF:* 800-788-0955 ■ *Web:* alliedcontrols.com	Waterbury	CT	06708	203-757-4200		203
Allied Converters Inc 64 Drake Ave *Web:* www.alliedconverters.com	New Rochelle	NY	10805	914-235-1585	235-7123	66
Allied Corrosion Industries Inc 1550 Cobb Industrial Dr *TF:* 800-241-0809 ■ *Web:* www.alliedcorrosion.com	Marietta	GA	30066	770-425-1355		256
Allied Court Reporters 115 Phenix Ave *Web:* alliedcourtreporters.com	Cranston	RI	02920	401-946-5500	946-9228	445
Allied Electric Motor Co 924 3rd Ave S *Web:* www.alliedelectricmotorcompany.com	Nashville	TN	37210	615-259-3896		518
Allied Electronics Inc 7151 Jack Newell Blvd S *TF:* 866-433-5722 ■ *Web:* www.alliedelec.com	Fort Worth	TX	76118	817-595-3500		246
Allied Electronics Trading Inc 2730 NW 31st Ave *Web:* www.aetrecycler.com	Lauderdale Lakes	FL	33311	954-358-8200	358-8201	660
Allied Employer Group 4400 Buffalo Gap Rd Ste 4500 *TF:* 800-495-3836 ■ *Web:* coemployer.com	Abilene	TX	79606	325-695-5822	692-9660	631
Allied Energy Company LLC 2700 Ishkooda Wenonah Rd *Web:* www.alliedenergycorp.com	Birmingham	AL	35211	205-925-6600	925-3555	581
Allied Entertainment Inc 9595 Wilshire Blvd Ste 900 *Web:* www.alliedentertainment.com	Beverly Hills	CA	90212	310-271-0703	271-0706	512
Allied Envelope Company Inc 33 Commerce Rd *TF:* 800-842-5951 ■ *Web:* alliedprintingresources.com	Carlstadt	NJ	07072	201-440-2000	507-8812	534
Allied Erecting & Dismantling Company Inc 2100 Poland Ave *Web:* www.aed.cc	Youngstown	OH	44502	330-744-0808	744-3218	189-16
Allied Fastener & Tool Inc 1130 Ng St *TF:* 877-353-3731 ■ *Web:* www.alliedfastener.com	Lake Worth	FL	33460	561-585-2113		350
Allied Fire & Security Inc 425 W Second Ave *TF:* 888-333-2632 ■ *Web:* www.alliedfireandsecurity.com	Spokane	WA	99201	509-321-8778	321-8767	692
Allied Fire Protection LP PO Box 2842 *TF:* 800-604-2600 ■ *Web:* www.alliedfireprotection.com	Pearland	TX	77588	281-485-6803	412-9668	189-10
Allied Foam Fabricators LLC 216 Kelsey Ln *TF:* 800-338-9140 ■ *Web:* alliedfoamfab.com	Tampa	FL	33619	813-626-0090	569-0629	601
Allied Group Inc, The 25 Amflex Dr *TF:* 800-556-6310 ■ *Web:* www.thealliedgrp.com	Cranston	RI	02921	401-946-6100		174

Company / Address	Phone	Fax	Class
Allied Healthcare Products Inc 1720 Sublette Ave. . . . . Saint Louis MO 63110 *NASDAQ: AHPI* ■ **Fax Area Code:* 800 ■ *TF:* 800-444-3954 ■ *Web:* www.alliedhpi.com	314-771-2400	477-7701*	477
Allied Home Health 2421 W Holcombe Blvd Ste 300. . . . . Houston TX 77030 *Web:* www.alliedhomehealthhouston.com	713-522-5773	522-0796	363
Allied Hotel Properties Inc 515 W Pender St Ste 300 . . . . Vancouver BC V6B6H5 *Web:* alliedhotels.com	604-669-5335		655
Allied Insurance & Financial Services 9301 SW Fwy Ste 250-B6. . . . . Houston TX 77074 *Web:* alliedinsuranceandfinancial.com	713-432-9944		390
Allied International Corp 7 Hill St . . . . Bedford Hills NY 10507 *Web:* www.alliedinter.com	914-241-6900	241-6985	770
Allied International Credit Corp 6800 Paragon Pl Ste 26 . . . . Richmond VA 23230 *TF:* 877-451-2594 ■ *Web:* www.aiccorp.com	877-451-2594		160
Allied International NA Inc 700 Oakmont Ln. . . . . Westmont IL 60559 *TF:* 800-444-6787 ■ *Web:* www.allied.com	630-570-3500		519
Allied Intl 13207 Bradley Ave. . . . . Sylmar CA 91342 *Web:* www.alliedtools.com	818-364-2333		351
Allied Irish Banks 1166 Avenue of the Americas 18th Fl . . . . New York NY 10036 *Web:* www.aib.ie	212-339-8080		70
Allied Litho Inc 2199 E 9th St. . . . . Kansas City MO 64124 *Web:* www.alliedlitho.net	816-842-5770		627
Allied Machine & Engineering Corp 120 Deeds Dr . . . . Dover OH 44622 *TF:* 800-321-5537 ■ *Web:* www.alliedmachine.com	330-343-4283		493
Allied Marine & Industrial Inc 1 Lake Rd . . . . Port Colborne ON L3K1A2 *Web:* www.allmind.com	905-834-8275	834-5645	698
Allied Marketing Group Inc 15455 Dallas Pkwy Ste 600 . . . . Dallas TX 75001 *Web:* www.alliedmarketinggroup.com	214-915-7000		459
Allied Mechanical Services Inc 5688 E ML Dr. . . . . Kalamazoo MI 49048 *TF:* 888-237-3017 ■ *Web:* www.alliedmechanical.com	203-294-8880		189-10
Allied Metals Corp 1750 Stephenson Hwy. . . . . Troy MI 48083 *Web:* www.alliedmet.com	248-680-2400		492
Allied Mineral Products Inc 2700 Scioto Pkwy. . . . . Columbus OH 43221 *Web:* alliedmineral.com	614-876-0244	876-0981	663
Allied Motion Technologies Inc 495 Commerce Dr Ste 3. . . . . Amherst NY 14228 *NASDAQ: AMOT* ■ *Web:* www.alliedmotion.com	716-242-7535		248
Allied Moulded Products Inc 222 N Union St. . . . . Bryan OH 43506 *TF:* 800-722-2679 ■ *Web:* www.alliedmoulded.com	419-636-4217	636-2450	816
Allied Oil & Supply Inc 2209 S 24th St. . . . . Omaha NE 68108 *TF:* 800-333-3717 ■ *Web:* alliedoil.com	402-267-1375	344-4360	579
Allied Oil LLC 25 Old Camplain Rd . . . . Hillsborough NJ 08844 *Web:* www.alliedoilco.com	908-575-7577		579
Allied Oilfield Machine & Pump LLC 202 Hulon Moreland Rd . . . . Levelland TX 79336 *TF:* 855-378-4787 ■ *Web:* www.alliedoilfield.com	806-894-7263	894-2311	538
Allied Old English Inc 100 Markley St. . . . . Port Reading NJ 07064 *Web:* alliedoldenglish.com	732-636-2060	636-2538	123
Allied Pallet Co 7151 Poindexter Rd. . . . . New Kent VA 23124 *TF:* 800-366-5597 ■ *Web:* alliedpalletco.com	804-966-5597	966-7231	551
Allied Paper Company LLC 5700 Plauche Ct. . . . . Harahan LA 70123 *Web:* www.alliedpapercompany.com	504-733-5700	733-4949	638
Allied Personnel Services Inc 118-21 Queens Blvd Ste 610 . . . . Forest Hills NY 11375 *Web:* www.alliedpersonnel.com	718-261-7979		260
Allied Pilots Assn 14600 Trinity Blvd O'Connell Bldg Ste 500. . . . . . Fort Worth TX 76155 *TF:* 800-272-7456 ■ *Web:* www.alliedpilots.org	817-302-2272		414
Allied Plastic Supply LLC 10828 Shady Trl . . . . Dallas TX 75220 *TF:* 800-350-7672 ■ *Web:* www.alliedplastic.org	800-350-7672		608
Allied Plastics Company Inc 2001 Walnut St. . . . . Jacksonville FL 32206 **Fax Area Code:* 904 ■ *TF:* 800-999-0386 ■ *Web:* www.alliedplasticsco.com	800-999-0386	353-4746*	319-1
Allied Plastics Inc 150 Holy Hill Rd. . . . . Twin Lakes WI 53181 *Web:* alliedplastics.com	262-877-4700	877-4701	489
Allied Power Group LLC 10131 Mills Rd. . . . . Houston TX 77070 *TF:* 888-830-3535 ■ *Web:* alliedpg.com	281-444-3535		262
Allied Printing Services Inc 1 Allied Way . . . . Manchester CT 06042 *Web:* www.alliedprinting.com	860-643-1101		627
Allied Propane Service 5000 Seaport Ave . . . . Richmond CA 94804 *Web:* www.alliedpropaneservice.com	510-237-7077		579
Allied Property Services LLC 2524 Ford Rd . . . . Bristol PA 19007	215-785-5900		290
Allied Residential 1601 E Valley Rd Ste 180 . . . . Renton WA 98057 *Web:* www.alliedresidential.com	425-226-5150		652
Allied Schools 22952 Alcalde Dr. . . . . Laguna Hills CA 92653 *TF:* 888-501-7686 ■ *Web:* www.alliedschools.com	949-707-5082	707-5579	685
Allied Scrap Processors Inc 3330 E Main St. . . . . Lakeland FL 33801 *Web:* www.alliedscrap.com	863-665-7157	667-1926	686
Allied Screw Products Inc 815 E Lowell Ave . . . . Mishawaka IN 46546 *Web:* www.aspi-nc.com	574-255-4718	255-4173	621
Allied Seed LLC 9311 Hwy 45. . . . . Nampa ID 83686 *Web:* www.alliedseed.com	208-989-1551		276
Allied services 710 W Broadway . . . . Ardmore OK 73401 *Web:* www.alliedservicesardmore.com	580-223-5434		390
Allied Services Integrated Health System 100 Abington Executive Pk. . . . . Clarks Summit PA 18411 *TF:* 888-734-2272 ■ *Web:* www.allied-services.org	888-734-2272		374-6
Allied Shipyard Inc 310 Ledet Ln. . . . . Larose LA 70373	985-693-3323		698
Allied Sinterings Inc 29 Briar Ridge Rd . . . . Danbury CT 06810 *Web:* www.alliedsinterings.com	203-743-7502		492
Allied Solutions LLC 350 Veterans Way . . . . Carmel IN 46032 **Fax Area Code:* 317 ■ *TF:* 800-826-9384 ■ *Web:* alliedsolutions.net	800-826-9384	706-7606*	390
Allied Staffing Inc 556 N Diamond Bar Blvd . . . . Diamond Bar CA 91765 *Web:* www.alliedstaffinginc.com	909-861-5200	861-2777	260
Allied Steel Construction Company Inc 2211 NW First Terr . . . . Oklahoma City OK 73107 *TF:* 800-522-4658 ■ *Web:* www.alliedsteelerectors.com	405-232-7531	236-3705	264-3
Allied Steel Fabricators Inc 4604 148th Ave NE. . . . . Redmond WA 98052 *Web:* www.alliedsteelfab.com	425-861-9558		480
Allied Steel Rule Dies Inc 5811 W Minnesota St. . . . . Indianapolis IN 46241 *Web:* www.allieddies.com	317-634-9835	634-8835	757
Allied Supply Company Inc 1100 E Monument Ave . . . . Dayton OH 45402 *TF:* 800-589-5690 ■ *Web:* www.alliedsupply.com	937-224-9833	224-5648	665
Allied Systems Co 21433 SW Oregon St . . . . . . Sherwood OR 97140 *TF:* 800-285-7000 ■ *Web:* www.alliedsystems.com	503-625-2560	625-7269	273
Allied T Pro Inc 501 7th Ave Ste 1610 . . . . New York NY 10036 *Web:* www.alliedtpro.com	212-596-1000		772
Allied Telesyn International Corp 19800 N Creek Pkwy Ste 100. . . . . Bothell WA 98011 *TF:* 800-424-4284 ■ *Web:* www.alliedtelesis.com	408-519-8700		176
Allied Tool & Die Co 3807 S 7th St . . . . Phoenix AZ 85040 *Web:* www.alliedtool.com	602-276-2439		697
Allied Tool Products 9334 N 107th St. . . . . Milwaukee WI 53224 *TF:* 800-558-5147 ■ *Web:* www.atptools.com	414-355-8280	355-8297	455
Allied Toyotalift 1640 Island Home Ave . . . . Knoxville TN 37920 *TF:* 866-538-0667 ■ *Web:* www.alliedtoyotalift.com	865-573-0995		247
Allied Transmission Inc 26 Commerce Dr . . . . Farmingdale NY 11735 *Web:* www.richardscompany.com	631-845-1212	845-1346	385
Allied Uniking Corporation Inc 4750 Cromwell Ave. . . . . Memphis TN 38118 *Web:* www.allieduniking.com	901-365-7240		207
Allied Vaughn 7600 Parklawn Ste 300. . . . . Minneapolis MN 55435 *TF:* 800-323-0281 ■ *Web:* www.alliedvaughn.com	952-832-3100	832-3179	658
Allied Welding Inc 1820 N Santa Fe Ave. . . . . Chillicothe IL 61523 *Web:* www.alliedwelding.net	309-274-6227	274-5448	454
Allied Wheel Components 12300 Edison Way . . . . Garden Grove CA 92841 *TF:* 800-529-4335 ■ *Web:* www.alliedwheel.com	714-893-4160	893-4190	247
AlliedCook Construction Corp 8 US Rt 1 . . . . Scarborough ME 04074 *Web:* www.alliedcook.com	207-772-2888		186
Allied-Horizontal Wireline Services 3200 Wilcrest Dr Ste 170 . . . . Houston TX 77042 *TF:* 888-494-9580 ■ *Web:* alliedhorizontal.com	713-343-7280		536
Allied-Locke Industries 1088 Corregidor Rd . . . . Dixon IL 61021 *TF:* 800-435-7752 ■ *Web:* www.alliedlocke.com	815-288-1471	288-7945	620
Allies for Freedom 1222 Fulton St. . . . . Palo Alto CA 94301 *Web:* www.alliesforfreedom.org	415-505-5131		637-10
Alligato Inc 1450-1055 W Hastings St . . . . Vancouver BC V6E2E9 *TF:* 866-355-0187 ■ *Web:* alligatomobile.com	866-355-0187		224
Alligator Adventure Barefoot Landing Hwy 17 . . . . North Myrtle Beach SC 29582 *Web:* www.alligatoradventure.com	843-361-0789		823
Alligator Records & Artist Management Inc PO Box 60234 . . . . Chicago IL 60660 *TF:* 800-344-5609 ■ *Web:* www.alligator.com	773-973-7736	973-2088	657
Alligator Soul 114 Barnard St . . . . Savannah GA 31401 *Web:* alligatorsoul.com	912-232-7899		671
Allina Health 2925 Chicago Ave . . . . Minneapolis MN 55407 *TF:* 888-425-5462 ■ *Web:* www.allinahealth.org	888-425-5462		353
All-Inclusive Vacations Inc 1595 Iris St. . . . . Denver CO 80215 *TF:* 866-980-6483 ■ *Web:* all-inclusivevacations.com	303-980-6483		771
Allingham & Readyoff LLC 54 Bridge St . . . . New Milford CT 06776 *Web:* allinghamlaw.com	860-350-5454		41
Allis Information Management Inc 4300 W Sugnet Rd . . . . Midland MI 48640 *Web:* allisinfo.com	989-835-5811		466
Allis Roller LLC 5801 W Franklin Dr . . . . Franklin WI 53132 *Web:* www.allis-roller.com	414-423-9000	423-9216	190
Allis State Park 284 Allis State Park Rd. . . . . Randolph VT 05060 *Web:* www.vtstateparks.com	802-276-3175		565
Allis Tool & Machine Corp 647 S 94th Pl . . . . Milwaukee WI 53214 *Web:* www.allistool.com	414-453-5500		494
Allison Abrasives Inc 141 Industry Rd . . . . Lancaster KY 40444 *Web:* www.allisonabrasives.com	859-792-3033		1
Allison Companies 9828 Hwy 182 E. . . . . Amelia LA 70340 *Web:* allison.industries	985-631-2000	631-2008	698
Allison Partners LLC 1716-2 Allied St . . . . Charlottesville VA 22903 *Web:* www.allisonpartners.com	434-270-8861	270-8885	194
Allison Payment Systems LLC 2200 Production Dr . . . . Indianapolis IN 46241 **Fax Area Code:* 317 ■ *TF:* 800-755-2440 ■ *Web:* www.apsllc.com	800-755-2440	808-2477*	110
Allison Royce & Associates Inc PO Box 790010 Ste 760 . . . . San Antonio TX 78279 *Web:* www.allisonroyce.com	210-564-7000	564-7001	225

Name / Address	City	State	ZIP	Phone	Fax	Class
Allison Systems Inc						
245 Regency Ct Ste 210	Brookfield	WI	53045	262-522-9800	522-9600	425
TF: 800-536-9077 ■ *Web:* www.allisonsystems.com						
Allison-Ide Structural Engineers LLC						
900 Fort Street Mall Ste 1670	Honolulu	HI	96813	808-536-2108	521-3000	261
Web: www.allisonide.com						
Allison-Smith Co						
1869 S Cobb Industrial Blvd	Smyrna	GA	30082	404-351-6430	350-1065	189-4
Web: www.allisonsmith.com						
All-League Sports Photos & Lab Inc						
27062 Burbank	Foothill Ranch	CA	92610	949-598-9297		590
Web: www.allleaguesportsphotos.com						
Allman Spry Davis Leggett & Crumpler						
380 Knollwood St Ste 700	Winston-Salem	NC	27103	336-722-2300	722-2382	445
Web: allmanspry.com						
Allmar Inc 287 Riverton Ave	Winnipeg	MB	R2L0N2	204-668-1000	668-3029	236
TF: 800-230-5516 ■ *Web:* www.allmar.com						
AllMed Healthcare Management Inc						
111 SW Fifth Ave Ste 1400	Portland	OR	97204	800-400-9916	223-6244*	463
**Fax Area Code:* 503 ■ *TF:* 800-400-9916 ■ *Web:* www.allmedmd.com						
All-Med Medical Supply LLC						
6321 Commerce Dr	Westland	MI	48185	800-434-2909		475
TF: 800-434-2909 ■ *Web:* www.amms.net						
AllMeds Inc 151 Lafayette Dr Ste 401	Oak Ridge	TN	37830	865-482-1999	481-0921	39
TF: 888-343-6337 ■ *Web:* www.allmeds.com						
Allmetal Inc 1 Pierce Pl Ste 295W	Itasca	IL	60143	630-250-8090	250-8387	234
TF: 800-638-2599 ■ *Web:* www.allmetalinc.com						
Allmetal Screw Products Corp						
94A E Jefryn Blvd	Deer Park	NY	11729	631-243-5200	243-5307	621
Web: allmetalcorp.com						
Allnorth Consultants Ltd						
2011 Prince George Pulpmill Rd PO Box 968	Prince George	BC	V2L4V1	250-614-7291		261
Web: www.allnorth.com						
Allomatic Products Co						
609 E Chaney St	Sullivan	IN	47882	516-775-0330		61
TF: 800-568-0330 ■ *Web:* www.allomatic.com						
Allor Manufacturing Inc						
12534 Emerson Dr	Brighton	MI	48116	248-486-4500		207
TF: 888-382-6300 ■ *Web:* allorpleshinc.com						
AlloSource 6278 S Troy Cir	Centennial	CO	80111	720-873-0213	873-0212	545
TF: 800-557-3587 ■ *Web:* www.allosource.org						
Allot Communications						
300 Tradecenter Dr Ste 4680	Woburn	MA	01801	781-939-9300	939-9393	178-10
TF: 877-255-6826 ■ *Web:* www.allot.com						
Allout Marketing Inc						
1769 Lexington Ave N PO Box 347	Roseville	MN	55113	952-404-0800		195
Web: alloutsuccess.com						
Alloy Bellows & Precision Welding						
653 Miner Rd	Cleveland	OH	44143	440-684-3000		454
Web: alloybellows.com						
Alloy Carbide Co 7827 Ave H	Houston	TX	77012	713-923-2700	923-4652	537
Web: www.alloycarbide.com						
Alloy Cast Products Inc						
700 Swenson Dr	Kenilworth	NJ	07033	908-245-2255		308
Web: alloycastproducts.com						
Alloy Die Casting Co						
6550 Caballero Blvd	Buena Park	CA	90620	714-521-9800	521-5510	308
Web: www.alloydie.com						
Alloy Engineering & Casting Co						
1700 W Washington St	Champaign	IL	61821	217-398-3200		307
TF: 800-348-2880 ■ *Web:* www.wirco.com						
Alloy Engineering Co, The						
844 Thacker St	Berea	OH	44017	440-243-6800	243-6489	480
Web: alloyengineering.com						
Alloy Gutter Company Inc						
13400 Huron Dr	Taylor	MI	48180	734-374-2100	374-2218	189-11
Web: www.alloygutter.com						
Alloy Hardfacing & Engineering Company Inc						
20425 Johnson Memorial Dr	Jordan	MN	55352	952-492-5569	492-3100	256
TF: 800-328-8408 ■ *Web:* alloyhardfacing.com						
Alloy Product Development						
944 Folsom St	San Francisco	CA	94107	415-992-5512		261
Web: alloypd.com						
Alloy Products Corp 1045 Perkins Ave	Waukesha	WI	53186	262-542-6603		298
Web: www.alloyproductscorp.com						
Alloy Silverstein Financial Services						
900 Kings Hwy N	Cherry Hill	NJ	08034	856-667-4100		401
Web: alloysilverstein.com						
Alloy Stainless Products Co						
611 Union Blvd	Totowa	NJ	07512	973-256-1616	256-5256	595
TF: 800-631-8372 ■ *Web:* www.alloystainless.com						
Alloy Surfaces Company Inc						
121 N Commerce Dr	Aston	PA	19014	610-497-7979		492
Web: www.alloysurfaces.com						
Alloy Tool Steel Inc (ATSI)						
13525 E Freeway Dr	Santa Fe Springs	CA	90670	562-921-8605	802-1728	492
TF: 800-288-9800 ■ *Web:* www.alloytoolsteel.com						
Alloy Ventures						
400 Hamilton Ave 4th Fl	Palo Alto	CA	94301	650-687-5000	687-5010	792
Web: www.alloyventures.com						
Allpak Co 715 S Kenilworth Ave	Oak Park	IL	60304	708-383-7200		603
Allparts Music Corp						
13027 Brittmoore Park Dr	Houston	TX	77041	713-466-6414	466-5803	527
Web: www.allparts.com						
Allplus Computer Systems Corp						
3075 NW 107th Ave	Doral	FL	33172	305-436-3993	436-3994	179
Web: www.allplus.com						
Allpoint Home Health Inc						
11340 Olympic Blvd Ste 220	Los Angeles	CA	90064	310-441-2009		363
Web: allpointhomehealth.com						
All-Points Inc 909 Lunt Ave	Schaumburg	IL	60193	847-585-0160		189-10
Web: allpointsinc.net						
All-Points Technology Corporation PC						
3 Saddlebrook Dr	Killingworth	CT	06419	860-663-1697		256
Web: www.allpointstech.com						
All-Power Inc (API) 2228 Murray	Sioux City	IA	51111	712-258-0681	258-6561	385
Web: www.allpowerinc.com						
All-Pro Fasteners Inc						
1916 Peyco Dr N	Arlington	TX	76001	817-467-5700	467-5365	351
TF: 800-361-6627 ■ *Web:* apf.com						
Allpro Parking LLC						
465 Main St Lafayette Court Bldg Ste 105	Buffalo	NY	14203	716-849-7275	849-2715	562
TF: 877-849-7275 ■ *Web:* www.allproparking.com						
Allrecipes 413 Pine St Ste 500	Seattle	WA	98101	206-436-7419	292-1793	637-10
Web: www.allrecipes.com						
Allred Bacon Halfhill & Young PC						
11350 Random Hills Rd Ste 700	Fairfax	VA	22030	703-352-1300		41
Web: dufflawfirm.com						
Allred Colin (Rep D - TX)						
328 Cannon House Office Bldg	Washington	DC	20515	202-225-2231		342-2
Web: www.allred.house.gov						
Allright Tool Company Inc						
1428 18th St S	Birmingham	AL	35205	205-591-1468		567
Web: www.allrighttool.com						
Allsafe Technologies Inc						
290 Creekside Dr	Amherst	NY	14228	716-691-0400	691-0404	596
TF: 800-828-7162 ■ *Web:* www.allsafe.com						
ALLSCO 70 Rideout St	Moncton	NB	E1E2C2	506-853-8080		499
Web: www.allsco.com						
Allscripts Healthcare Solutions						
222 Merchandise Mart Plz Ste 2024	Chicago	IL	60654	800-654-0889		178-10
NASDAQ: MDRX ■ *TF:* 800-654-0889 ■ *Web:* www.allscripts.com						
All-Search & Inspection Inc						
1108 E South Union Ave	Midvale	UT	84047	800-227-3152	984-8170*	635
**Fax Area Code:* 801 ■ *TF:* 800-227-3152 ■ *Web:* www.all-search.com						
Allset 12130 Millennium Dr	Los Angeles	CA	90094	510-210-1052		39
Web: allsetnow.com						
Allsopp Design Inc 587 Bay Rd	South Hamilton	MA	01982	978-468-1556		344
Web: allsoppdesign.com						
AllSource Analysis Inc						
350 Terry St Ste 300	Longmont	CO	80503	303-219-1720		466
Web: allsourceanalysis.com						
All-South Subcontractors Inc						
2678 Queenstown Rd	Birmingham	AL	35210	205-836-8111	836-4227	189-12
Web: www.allsouthsub.com						
All-Spec Industries Inc						
5228 US Hwy 421 N	Wilmington	NC	28401	800-537-0351		246
TF: 800-537-0351 ■ *Web:* www.all-spec.com						
Allstar Fasteners Inc						
1550 Arthur Ave	Elk Grove Village	IL	60007	847-640-7827		487
Web: www.allstarfasteners.com						
Allstar Fire Equipment Inc						
12328 Lower Azusa Rd	Arcadia	CA	91006	626-652-0900	652-0920	679
TF: 800-425-5787 ■ *Web:* allstarfire.com						
Allstar Magnetics LLC						
6205 NE 63rd St	Vancouver	WA	98661	360-693-0213	693-0639	246
Web: allstarmagnetics.com						
Allstar Microelectronics Inc						
30191A Avenida de las Banderas	Rancho Santa Margarita	CA	92688	949-546-0888	546-0898	174
TF: 888-728-7203 ■ *Web:* www.allstarshop.com						
All-Star Recruiting LLC						
6119 Lyons Rd	Coconut Creek	FL	33073	800-928-0229		260
TF: 800-928-0229 ■ *Web:* www.allstarrecruiting.com						
All-Star Team Realtors, The						
4 Willow Bend Dr Ste 2A	Hattiesburg	MS	39402	601-545-3900		652
Web: www.allstarteam.com						
Allstar Tech 1856 Angus St	Regina	SK	S4T1Z4	306-522-7827		180
Web: allstartech.com						
Allstate 2775 Sanders Rd	Northbrook	IL	60062	877-525-5727		390
TF: 800-255-7828 ■ *Web:* agents.allstate.com						
Allstate Can Corp 1 Wood Hollow Rd	Parsippany	NJ	07054	973-560-9030		124
Web: www.allstatecan.com						
Allstate Commercial Driver Training						
249 Pearl St	Seymour	CT	06483	800-246-9567	888-8977*	167-3
**Fax Area Code:* 203 ■ *TF:* 800-246-9567 ■ *Web:* www.allstatetraining.com						
Allstate Construction Inc						
5718 Tower Rd	Tallahassee	FL	32303	850-514-1004	514-1206	186
Web: www.allstateconstruction.com						
Allstate Floral & Craft Inc						
14038 Park Pl	Cerritos	CA	90703	562-926-2302	926-8613	293
TF: 800-433-4056 ■ *Web:* allstatefloral.com						
Allstate Hairstyling & Barber College						
2546 Lorain Ave	Cleveland	OH	44113	216-241-6684	241-1048	348
Web: www.allstatehairstyling.com						
All-State Industries Inc						
1400 Lakeway Dr	Lewisville	TX	75057	972-434-4222	434-0250	4
TF: 800-441-1562 ■ *Web:* www.all-stateind.com						
Allstate Insurance Co						
2775 Sanders Rd	Northbrook	IL	60062	847-402-5000		304
NYSE: ALL ■ *Web:* www.allstate.com						
Allstate Leasing Inc 1 Olympic Pl	Towson	MD	21204	877-711-4211		289
TF: 800-223-4885 ■ *Web:* www.allstateleasing.com						
Allstate Steel Company Inc						
130 S Jackson Ave	Jacksonville	FL	32220	904-781-6040		189-14
TF: 888-781-6040 ■ *Web:* www.allstatesteel.com						
Allstate Sugar Bowl						
1500 Sugar Bowl Dr	New Orleans	LA	70112	504-828-2440		181
Web: allstatesugarbowl.org						
Allstates Textile Machinery Inc						
547 Mill St	Williamston	SC	29697	864-847-7757	847-7513	385
Web: www.allstatestextile.com						
Allsteel Inc 2210 Second Ave	Muscatine	IA	52761	563-272-4800	272-4887	319-1
TF: 888-255-7833 ■ *Web:* www.allsteeloffice.com						
Allstream Corp 200 Wellington St W	Toronto	ON	M5V3G2	416-345-2000		736
TF: 888-288-2273 ■ *Web:* allstream.com						
Allstyle Coil Company LP						
7037 Brittmore Dr	Houston	TX	77041	713-466-6333		187
Web: www.allstyle.com						
Allsup Inc 300 Allsup Pl	Belleville	IL	62223	800-854-1418	236-5778*	194
**Fax Area Code:* 618 ■ *TF:* 800-854-1418 ■ *Web:* www.allsup.com						
All-system Aerospace Int'l Inc						
75 Beacon Dr	Holbrook	NY	11741	631-582-9200	582-9353	770
Web: allsystem.com						

Company	City	State	ZIP	Phone	Fax	Class
Alltech Consulting Services Inc 258 Wall St *Web:* www.alltechconsultinginc.com	Princeton	NJ	08540	609-945-2590		196
Alltech Inc 3031 Catnip Hill Pk *TF:* 800-289-8324 ■ *Web:* www.alltech.com	Nicholasville	KY	40356	859-885-9613	887-3256	584
Alltech International Inc 8298-B Old Courthouse Rd Centennial Plz - Tysons *Web:* www.alltech.net	Vienna	VA	22182	703-506-1222	506-1223	177
Alltek Energy Systems 58 Hudson River Rd *Web:* www.alltekenergy.com	Waterford	NY	12188	518-238-2600		612
Alltek Services 4755 Drane Field Rd *Web:* www.alltekservices.com	Lakeland	FL	33811	863-709-0709		396
AllTek Staffing & Resource Group Inc 600 Davidson Rd *Web:* www.alltekstaffing.com	Pittsburgh	PA	15239	412-573-0077		194
All-Temp Refrigeration Services Inc 271 Hwy 1085 *TF:* 888-626-1277 ■ *Web:* alltempinc.com	Madisonville	LA	70447	888-626-1277		610
All-Test Pro LLC 123 Spencer Plain Rd *TF:* 800-952-8776 ■ *Web:* www.alltestpro.com	Old Saybrook	CT	06475	860-399-4222		201
All-Tex Pipe & Supply Inc 9743 Brockbank **Fax Area Code:* 512 ■ *TF:* 866-738-7501 ■ *Web:* www.alltexsupply.com	Dallas	TX	75220	214-350-5886	833-6269*	610
AllTranstek LLC 1101 W 31st St Ste 200 *Web:* www.alltranstek.com	Downers Grove	IL	60515	630-325-9977		463
Alltrax Inc 1111 Cheney Creek Rd *Web:* alltraxinc.com	Grants Pass	OR	97527	541-476-3565		518
Alltronics LLC 2761 Scott Blvd *Web:* www.alltronics.com	Santa Clara	CA	95050	408-778-3868	778-2558	246
All-Type Welding and Fabrication Inc 7690 Bond St *Web:* atwf-inc.com	Cleveland	OH	44139	440-439-3990	439-2165	454
AllU.S. Credit Union 1410 N Main St *Web:* alluscu.com	Salinas	CA	93906	831-540-4627		219
Allure Travel 2343 Honolulu Ave *TF:* 800-666-8767 ■ *Web:* www.montrosetravel.com	Montrose	CA	91020	818-553-3200		771
Alluvion Staffing Inc 4190 Belfort Rd Ste 160 *Web:* alluvion.com	Jacksonville	FL	32216	904-296-0626		260
Allvend Management Corp 800 W Airport Fwy Ste 705 *Web:* allvend.com	Irving	TX	75062	972-607-2517		463
Allview Services Inc 2215 S Castle Way *Web:* www.allview.com	Lynnwood	WA	98036	425-483-6103	402-8334	173-2
Allway Tools Inc 1255 Seabury Ave *TF:* 800-422-5592 ■ *Web:* allwaytools.com	Bronx	NY	10462	718-792-3636	823-9640	758
All-Ways Adv Co 1442 Broad St *TF:* 800-255-9291 ■ *Web:* www.awadv.com	Bloomfield	NJ	07003	973-338-0700	338-1410	4
All-Ways Home Care 9159 SW 87th Ave *Web:* www.allwayshomecare.net	Miami	FL	33176	305-446-6120	446-6121	363
Allways Precision Inc 14001 Van Dyke Rd *Web:* www.allwaysprecision.com	Plainfield	IL	60544	815-577-1600		757
Allwire Inc 16395 Ave 24 1/2 *Web:* www.allwire.com	Chowchilla	CA	93610	559-665-4893		813
Allwrite Advertising and Publishing PO Box 1071 *Web:* www.allwritepublishing.com	Atlanta	GA	30301	530-691-9005		637-2
Ally Parker Brown Title 2691 SW Port St Lucie Blvd *Web:* apbtitle.com	Port Saint Lucie	FL	34953	772-323-2777		390
Ally Press Ctr 524 Orleans St *TF:* 800-729-3002 ■ *Web:* www.allypress.com	Saint Paul	MN	55107	651-291-2652		637-2
Allyn & Betty Taylor Library Natural Sciences Ctr 1151 Richmond St *Web:* www.lib.uwo.ca	London	ON	N6A3K7	519-661-3168	661-3435	434-1
ALM Media Properties LLC 150 East 42nd St *Web:* www.alm.com	New York	NY	10017	877-256-2472		658
Alma College 614 W Superior St *TF:* 800-321-2562 ■ *Web:* www.alma.edu	Alma	MI	48801	989-463-7111	463-7057	166
Alma Container Corp 1000 Charles Ave *Web:* almacontainer.com	Alma	MI	48801	989-463-2106		100
Alma de Cuba 1623 Walnut St *Web:* almadecubarestaurant.com	Philadelphia	PA	19103	215-988-1799		671
Alma Lasers Inc 485 Half Day Rd Ste 100 *TF:* 866-414-2562 ■ *Web:* www.almalasers.com	Buffalo Grove	IL	60089	866-414-2562		475
Alma Products Co 2000 Michigan Ave **Fax Area Code:* 800 ■ *TF:* 877-427-2624 ■ *Web:* www.almaproducts.com	Alma	MI	48801	989-463-1151	457-2719*	60
Alma Telephone Co 102 3rd St *TF:* 888-371-6821 ■ *Web:* www.almanet.net	Alma	MO	64001	660-674-2297	674-2613	224
Alma Telephone Company Inc (ATC) 405 W 11th St *TF:* 877-217-2842 ■ *Web:* www.atcbroadband.com	Alma	GA	31510	912-632-8603	634-4519	224
Alma: Cafe, Hotel & Restaurant 528 University Ave SE *Web:* www.almampls.com	Minneapolis	MN	55414	612-379-4909		671
Almaco 99 M Ave *Web:* www.almaco.com	Nevada	IA	50201	515-382-3506	382-2973	194
Almaco Group Inc 7900 Glades Rd Ste 630 *Web:* www.almaco.cc	Boca Raton	FL	33434	877-831-6156		106
Almanac, The 122 S Main St *Web:* thealmanac.net	Washington	PA	15301	724-941-7725	941-8685	532-4
Almanac, The 3525 Alameda De Las Pulgas *TF:* 800-799-4811 ■ *Web:* www.almanacnews.com	Menlo Park	CA	94025	650-854-2626		532-4
Almatis Inc 501 W Park Rd *TF:* 800-643-8771 ■ *Web:* www.almatis.com	Leetsdale	PA	15056	412-630-2903	630-2900	143
Almco Inc 507 W Front St *TF:* 800-521-2740 ■ *Web:* almco.com	Albert Lea	MN	56007	507-377-2102	377-0451	494
Almeda Mall 555 Almeda Mall *Web:* www.almedamall.com	Houston	TX	77075	713-944-1010		460
Almet Inc 300 Hartzell Rd *Web:* www.almetinc.com	New Haven	IN	46774	260-493-1556	493-1299	492
Almetals Inc 51035 Grand River Ave *TF:* 800-968-7730 ■ *Web:* www.almetals.com	Wixom	MI	48393	248-348-7722		492
Almich & Associates 26463 Rancho Pkwy S *Web:* almichcpa.com	Lake Forest	CA	92630	949-600-7550		2
Almo Corp 2709 Commerce Way *TF:* 800-345-2566 ■ *Web:* www.almo.com	Philadelphia	PA	19154	215-698-4000		38
Almond Brothers Lumber Co 403 Ringgold Ave *Web:* www.almondlumber.com	Coushatta	LA	71019	318-932-4041	932-4086	683
Almond Products Inc 17150 148th Ave *Web:* www.almondproducts.com	Spring Lake	MI	49456	616-844-1813		481
Almont:MediaLAB 5 Grapevine Way *Web:* www.touchman.com	Medway	MA	02053	508-533-0333		392
Almost Home Restaurant & Steakhouse 3310 Market St NE *Web:* almosthomesalem.com	Salem	OR	97301	503-378-0100		671
Almquist, Maltzahn, Galloway & Luth PC 1203 W Second St *Web:* gicpas.com	Grand Island	NE	68802	308-381-1810	381-4824	2
Alnylam Pharmaceuticals Inc 300 Third St 3rd Fl *NASDAQ:* ALNY ■ *TF:* 866-330-0326 ■ *Web:* www.alnylam.com	Cambridge	MA	02142	617-551-8200	551-8101	85
ALOA (Associated Locksmiths of America) 3500 Easy St *TF:* 800-532-2562 ■ *Web:* www.aloa.org	Dallas	TX	75247	214-819-9733	819-9736	49-3
Aloe Up Suncare 9700 W 76th St Ste 112 *Web:* www.aloeup.com	Eden Prairie	MN	55344	952-933-7724		77
Aloesoftware Group LLC 1102 N William St *TF:* 800-561-2563 ■ *Web:* aloesoft.com	Victoria	TX	77901	361-485-0004	485-0330	225
Aloft Broomfield Denver 8300 Arista Pl *TF:* 866-716-8143 ■ *Web:* www.aloftbroomfielddenver.com	Broomfield	CO	80021	303-635-2000		707
Alogic US LLC 1845 Ferguson Rd *Web:* www.alogic-us.com	Allison Park	PA	15101	412-635-2500		178-1
Aloha Animal Hospital Inc 7341 S Torrey Pines *Web:* alohavegasvets.com	Las Vegas	NV	89139	702-567-5222		794
Aloha Freight Forwarders Inc 1800 S Anderson Ave *Web:* www.alohafreight.com	Compton	CA	90220	310-631-6116	639-6973	311
Aloha Hotels and Resorts PO Box 15341 *Web:* www.alohahotels.com	Honolulu	HI	96830	808-826-6244		379
Aloha Kitchen 2950 S Alma School Rd Ste 12 *Web:* www.alohakitchen.com	Mesa	AZ	85210	480-897-2451		671
Aloha Medicinals Inc 2300 Arrowhead Dr *TF:* 877-835-6091 ■ *Web:* www.alohamedicinals.com	Carson City	NV	89706	775-886-6300		231
Aloha Petroleum Ltd 1132 Bishop St Ste 1700 *TF:* 800-621-4654 ■ *Web:* www.alohagas.com	Honolulu	HI	96813	808-522-9700	522-9707	113
Aloha Restaurants Inc 204 Main St Ste 960 *Web:* aloharestaurants.com	Newport Beach	CA	92661	949-250-0331	673-5085	670
Aloha School of Massage Therapy 70 Kapi Ln Apt 202 *Web:* www.alohamassageschool.com	Wailuku	HI	96793	808-871-9966		685
Aloha Shoyu Company Ltd 91-544 Awakumoku St *Web:* alohashoyu.com	Kapolei	HI	96707	808-456-5929	456-8999	123
Aloha Stadium 99-500 Salt Lake Blvd *Web:* alohastadium.hawaii.gov	Honolulu	HI	96818	808-483-2500	483-2823	720
Aloha Surf Hotel, The 1146 Fort St Mall Ste 205	Honolulu	HI	96815	808-923-0222		377
Aloha United Way Inc 200 N Vineyard Blvd Ste 700 *Web:* www.auw.org	Honolulu	HI	96817	808-536-1951		226
Alohilani Resort 2490 Kalakaua Ave *TF:* 800-367-6060 ■ *Web:* www.alohilaniresort.com	Honolulu	HI	96815	808-922-1233	922-0129	379
Aloia, Roland, Lubell & Morgan PLLC 2222 2nd St *TF:* 800-724-7902 ■ *Web:* lawdefined.com	Fort Myers	FL	33901	239-791-7950	791-7951	652
Alomere Health 111 17th Ave E *Web:* alomerehealth.com	Alexandria	MN	56308	320-762-1511	762-6120	374-3
Alon USA Energy Inc 7616 LBJ Fwy Ste 300 *NYSE:* ALJ ■ *Web:* www.alonusa.com	Dallas	TX	75251	972-367-3600		580
Alonso Consulting 204 Passaic Ave Ste 1 *Web:* www.alonso.com	Fairfield	NJ	07004	973-575-1414		196
Alonzo King LINES Ballet 26 7th St *Web:* linesballet.org	San Francisco	CA	94103	415-863-3040	863-1180	573-1
Alorica Inc 5 Park Plz Ste 1100 *TF:* 866-256-7422 ■ *Web:* www.alorica.com	Irvine	CA	92614	866-256-7422		178-11
Alostar Bank 3595 Grandview Pkwy Ste 425 **Fax Area Code:* 866 ■ *TF:* 877-738-6391 ■ *Web:* www.alostarbank.com	Birmingham	AL	35243	205-298-6391	715-6601*	70
ALOT Inc 6441 Dysinger *Web:* www.alot.com	New York	NY	10013	212-231-2000		387
Alouette Cheese USA LLC 400 S Custer Ave *TF:* 800-322-2743 ■ *Web:* www.alouettecheese.com	New Holland	PA	17557	800-322-2743		296-5
ALP Lighting Components Inc 6333 Gross Point Rd *Web:* alpadvantage.com	Niles	IL	60714	773-774-9550	774-9331	608
Alpac Inc 5752 Cedar Ridge Dr *Web:* www.alpacinc.com	Ann Arbor	MI	48103	734-623-2866		180
Alpak Display Group 575 N Midland Ave *Web:* www.alpak.com	Saddle Brook	NJ	07663	201-797-1411		8

Name / Address	City	State	ZIP	Phone	Fax	Class
Alpena Agency Inc 102 S Third Ave *TF:* 800-864-3252 ■ *Web:* www.alpenaagency.com	Alpena	MI	49707	989-354-2175		390
Alpena Area Chamber of Commerce 235 W Chisholm St *Web:* alpenachamber.com	Alpena	MI	49707	989-354-4181	356-3999	139
Alpena Beverage Company Inc 1313 Kline Rd *Web:* mbwwa.org	Alpena	MI	49707	989-356-3511		81-1
Alpena Community College (ACC) 665 Johnson St *TF:* 888-468-6222 ■ *Web:* discover.alpenacc.edu	Alpena	MI	49707	989-356-9021		162
Alpena County 720 W Chisholm St *TF:* 800-999-4487 ■ *Web:* www.alpenacounty.org	Alpena	MI	49707	989-354-9500	354-9648	338
Alpena County George N Fletcher Public Library 211 N First Ave *TF:* 877-737-4106 ■ *Web:* alpenalibrary.org	Alpena	MI	49707	989-356-6188	356-2765	434-3
Alpena County Regional Airport 1617 Airport Rd *Web:* www.alpenaairport.com	Alpena	MI	49707	989-354-2907	358-9988	27
Alpena Oil Company Inc 235 Water St *TF:* 800-968-1098 ■ *Web:* www.alpenaoil.net	Alpena	MI	49707	989-356-1098	356-9486	324
Alpena Public Schools (Inc) 3303 S Third Ave *Web:* www.alpenaschools.com	Alpena	MI	49707	989-358-5040	358-5041	685
Alpenhof Lodge 3255 W Village Dr *TF:* 800-732-3244 ■ *Web:* alpenhoflodgereservations.com	Teton Village	WY	83025	307-733-3242		379
Alper Strategies 17000 Kercheval Ave Ste 211 *Web:* www.alperstrategies.com	Grosse Pointe	MI	48230	313-886-4850		194
Alperin Law PLLC 500 Viking Dr Ste 202 *Web:* alperinlaw.com	Virginia Beach	VA	23452	757-490-3500		41
Alpern Myers Stuart LLC 14 N Sierra Madre St Ste A *Web:* www.coloradolawyers.net	Colorado Springs	CO	80903	719-471-7955		428
Alpha & Omega Financial Management Consultants Inc 8580 La Mesa Blvd Ste 100 *TF:* 800-755-5060 ■ *Web:* www.alpha-omega-inc.com	La Mesa	CA	91942	619-462-7812	462-1766	194
Alpha 1 Induction Service Center Inc 1525 Old Alum Creek Dr *TF:* 800-991-2599 ■ *Web:* www.alpha1induction.com	Columbus	OH	43209	614-253-8900	253-8981	318
Alpha Analytical Inc 255 Glendale Ave Ste 21 *Web:* www.alpha-analytical.com	Sparks	NV	89431	775-355-1044		794
Alpha Associates Inc 145 Lehigh Ave *TF:* 800-631-5399 ■ *Web:* www.alphainc.com	Lakewood	NJ	08701	732-634-5700	634-1430	745-2
Alpha Beta Gamma International Business Honor Society 75 Grasslands Rd *Web:* www.abg.org	Valhalla	NY	10595	914-606-6877		48-16
Alpha Building Corp 24850 Blanco Rd *Web:* alphabuilding.com	San Antonio	TX	78260	210-491-9925		186
Alpha Capital Partners Ltd 150 N Michigan Ave Ste 800 *Web:* www.alphacapital.com	Chicago	IL	60603	312-322-9800		792
Alpha Chemical Services Inc 46 Morton St *TF:* 800-464-9872 ■ *Web:* www.alphachemical.com	Stoughton	MA	02072	781-344-8688		151
Alpha Chi Honor Society 124 W Capitol Ave *TF:* 800-477-4225 ■ *Web:* www.alphachihonor.org	Searcy	AR	72201	800-477-4225		48-16
Alpha Chi Omega 5939 Castle Creek Pkwy N Dr *Web:* www.alphachiomega.org	Indianapolis	IN	46250	317-579-5050	579-5051	48-16
Alpha Chi Rho Fraternity Inc 109 Oxford Way *Web:* www.alphachirho.org	Neptune City	NJ	07753	732-869-1895	988-5357	48-16
Alpha Chi Sigma 2141 N Franklin Rd *Web:* www.alphachisigma.org	Indianapolis	IN	46219	317-357-5944	351-9702	48-16
Alpha Coatings Inc 622 S Corporate Dr *Web:* www.alpha-coatings.com	Fostoria	OH	44830	419-436-1255	436-1245	481
Alpha Consulting Engineers Inc 115 Limekiln Rd *Web:* www.alphacei.com	New Cumberland	PA	17070	717-770-2500		256
Alpha Corp 21351 Ridgetop Cir Ste 200 *Web:* www.alphacorporation.com	Dulles	VA	20166	703-450-0800	450-0043	194
Alpha Delta Phi International Fraternity 60 S Sixth St Ste 2800 *Web:* www.alphadeltaphi.org	Minneapolis	MN	55402	508-226-1832		48-16
Alpha Delta Pi 1386 Ponce de Leon Ave NE *Web:* www.alphadeltapi.org	Atlanta	GA	30306	404-378-3164	373-0084	48-16
Alpha Distribution Solutions 350 Rt 61 S *Web:* alphadistsol.com	Schuylkill Haven	PA	17972	570-385-8420		155-18
Alpha Distributors Inc 4700 N Ronald St *Web:* www.alphadist.com	Harwood Heights	IL	60706	708-867-5200		665
Alpha Engineering Associates Inc 716 Giddings Ave Ste 32 *Web:* alphaengr.com	Annapolis	MD	21401	410-295-9500		180
Alpha Epsilon Delta (AED) 2955 S University Dr Winton-Scott Ste 213 *Web:* aednational.com	Fort Worth	TX	76129	817-257-4550		48-16
Alpha Epsilon Phi Sorority (AEPHI) 11 Lake Ave Ext Ste 1A *TF:* 888-668-4293 ■ *Web:* www.aephi.org	Danbury	CT	06811	203-748-0029	748-0039	48-16
Alpha Epsilon Pi Fraternity Inc 8815 Wesleyan Rd *Web:* www.aepi.org	Indianapolis	IN	46268	317-876-1913	876-1057	48-16
Alpha Gallery 460C Harrison Ave *Web:* www.alphagallery.com	Boston	MA	02118	617-536-4465	536-5695	42
Alpha Gamma Delta 8710 N Meridian St *Web:* alphagammadelta.org	Indianapolis	IN	46260	317-663-4200		48-16
Alpha Gamma Rho 10101 NW Ambassador Dr *Web:* www.alphagammarho.org	Kansas City	MO	64153	816-891-9200	891-9401	48-16
Alpha Grainger Manufacturing Inc 20 Discovery Way *Web:* agmi.com	Franklin	MA	02038	508-520-4005	520-4185	621
Alpha Group, The 61 E Main St *Web:* www.thealphagroup.com	Norton	MA	02766	508-285-8500		631
Alpha Home Healthcare 2735 N Holland Sylvania Rd Ste A1 *TF:* 800-705-4799 ■ *Web:* www.alphahomehealthcareinc.com	Toledo	OH	43615	419-720-0028		363
Alpha I Marketing Corp 65 W Red Oak Ln *Web:* www.alpha1marketing.com	White Plains	NY	10604	914-697-5300		196
Alpha Imaging Inc 4455 Glenbrook Rd *TF:* 800-331-7327 ■ *Web:* www.alpha-imaging.com	Willoughby	OH	44094	440-953-3800	953-1455	475
Alpha Industries Inc 14200 Park Meadow Dr Ste 110 S Tower **Fax Area Code:* 703 ■ *TF:* 866-631-0719 ■ *Web:* www.alphaindustries.com	Chantilly	VA	20151	866-631-0719	378-4910*	155-5
Alpha Investment Consulting Group LLC 111 E Kilbourn Ave Ste 1600 *Web:* www.alpha-investment.com	Milwaukee	WI	53202	414-319-4100		194
Alpha Kappa Alpha Sorority Inc 5656 S Stony Island Ave *Web:* www.aka1908.com	Chicago	IL	60637	773-684-1282		48-16
Alpha Kappa Psi (AKPSI) 7801 E 88th St *Web:* akpsi.org	Indianapolis	IN	46256	317-872-1553	872-1567	48-16
Alpha Lambda Delta 6800 Pittsford-Palmyra Rd Ste 340 *TF:* 800-925-7421 ■ *Web:* www.nationalald.org	Fairport	NY	14450	800-925-7421		48-16
Alpha Lehigh Tool & Machine Co 41 Industrial Rd *Web:* www.alphalehigh.com	Alpha	NJ	08865	908-454-6481		454
Alpha Lex Systems Integration 11100 Bradner Pl *Web:* alphalex.com	Porter Ranch	CA	91326	818-407-9200		177
Alpha Manufacturing Company Inc 100 Old Barnwell Rd *Web:* www.alphamfg.com	West Columbia	SC	29170	803-739-4500	739-0517	493
Alpha Mechanical Inc 4885 Greencraig Ln *Web:* www.alphamechanical.com	San Diego	CA	92123	858-278-3500		610
Alpha Mechanical Service Inc 7200 Distribution Dr **Fax Area Code:* 866 ■ *TF:* 888-212-6324 ■ *Web:* alphamechanicalservice.com	Louisville	KY	40258	888-212-6324	296-8035*	610
Alpha Media 1321 N Gene Autry Trl *Web:* www.mix1005.fm	Palm Springs	CA	92262	760-323-1005		645-117
Alpha Media USA LLC 1211 SW 5th Ave Ste 750 *Web:* www.alphamediausa.com	Portland	OR	97204	503-517-6200		645-126
Alpha Net Consulting LLC 3080 Olcott St Ste 235C *Web:* www.anetcorp.com	Santa Clara	CA	95054	408-343-4070	762-2638	177
Alpha Omega International Dental Fraternity 50 W Edmonston Dr *TF:* 877-368-6326 ■ *Web:* www.ao.org	Rockville	MD	20852	301-738-6400	738-6403	48-16
Alpha Omega Tours & Charters PO Box 6484 *Web:* aocharters.com	Spokane	WA	99217	509-299-5594		760
Alpha Omicron Pi Intl 5390 Virginia Way *TF:* 855-230-1183 ■ *Web:* www.alphaomicronpi.org	Brentwood	TN	37027	615-370-0920	371-9736	48-16
Alpha Packaging 1555 Page Industrial Blvd *Web:* www.alphap.com	Saint Louis	MO	63132	314-427-4300	427-5445	98
Alpha Phi Alpha Fraternity Inc 2313 St Paul St *Web:* www.apa1906.net	Baltimore	MD	21218	410-554-0040	554-0054	48-16
Alpha Phi Delta Fraternity PO Box 80466 *Web:* www.apd.org	Staten Island	NY	10308	718-874-0219		48-16
Alpha Phi International Fraternity 1930 Sherman Ave *Web:* alphaphi.org	Evanston	IL	60201	847-475-0663	475-6820	48-16
Alpha Phi Omega (APO) 14901 E 42nd St *Web:* apo.org	Independence	MO	64055	816-373-8667	373-5975	48-16
Alpha Plastics Co 9315 Evergreen Blvd NW *Web:* www.alphaplasticscorp.com	Coon Rapids	MN	55433	763-786-6940	786-4287	604
Alpha Plastics Solutions Inc S82 W19362 Apollo Dr *Web:* www.myapsi.com	Muskego	WI	53150	262-971-2774	971-2775	596
Alpha Precision Machining Inc 19652 70th Ave S *Web:* alphapre.com	Kent	WA	98032	253-395-7381	395-7476	757
Alpha Pro Tech Ltd 60 Centurian Dr *TF:* 800-749-1363 ■ *Web:* www.alphaprotech.com	Markham	ON	L3R9R2	905-479-0654		228
Alpha Products Inc 5570 W 70th Pl *Web:* www.alphaproductsinc.com	Bedford Park	IL	60638	708-594-3883		488
Alpha Q Inc 87 Upton Rd *Web:* alphaqinc.com	Colchester	CT	06415	860-537-4681	537-4332	21
Alpha Rae Personnel Inc 347 W Berry St 7th Fl *TF:* 800-837-8940 ■ *Web:* www.alpha-rae.com	Fort Wayne	IN	46802	260-426-8227	426-1152	260
Alpha School of Massage Inc 4642 San Juan Ave *Web:* www.alphaschoolofmassage.com	Jacksonville	FL	32210	904-389-9117		685
Alpha Search Advisory Partners 240 Plandome Rd Ste 200 *Web:* alphasearchadvisory.com	Manhasset	NY	11030	516-626-7896		260
Alpha Sigma Alpha (ASA) 9002 Vincennes Cir *Web:* www.alphasigmaalpha.org	Indianapolis	IN	46268	317-871-2920	871-2924	48-16

Company / Address	City	State	Zip	Phone	Fax	Class
Alpha Sigma Phi National Fraternity 710 Adams St *Web:* alphasigmaphi.org	Carmel	IN	46032	317-843-1911	843-2966	48-16
Alpha Software Inc 70 Blanchard Rd *Web:* www.alphasoftware.com	Burlington	MA	01803	781-229-4500	272-4876	178-1
Alpha Source Inc 6619 W Calumet Rd *TF:* 800-654-9845 ■ *Web:* www.alphasource.com	Milwaukee	WI	53223	414-760-2222		475
Alpha Tau Omega Fraternity (ATO) 1 N Pennsylvania St 12th Fl *TF:* 800-798-9286 ■ *Web:* www.ato.org	Indianapolis	IN	46204	317-684-1865	684-1862	48-16
Alpha Tech Inc 388 Cane Creek Rd PO Box 519 *Web:* atimfg.com	Fletcher	NC	28732	828-684-9709		491
Alpha Tech Pet Inc 119 Russell St Ste 21 *Web:* www.alphatechpet.com	Littleton	MA	01460	978-486-3690		237
Alpha Technologies Inc 3767 Alpha Way *TF:* 800-322-5742 ■ *Web:* www.alpha.com	Bellingham	WA	98226	360-647-2360	671-4936	253
Alpha Technologies Services LLC 3030 Gilchrist Rd *TF:* 800-356-9886 ■ *Web:* www.alpha-technologies.com	Akron	OH	44305	330-745-1641	848-7326	201
Alpha Technology Corp 1450 McPherson Park Dr Ste 200 *Web:* www.altec-us.com	Howell	MI	48844	517-546-9700	546-5926	60
Alpha Ten Technologies Inc 2720 Loker Ave W Ste K *Web:* www.alphaten.com	Carlsbad	CA	92010	760-438-9144	438-0968	187
Alpha Testing Inc 2209 Wisconsin St Ste 100 *Web:* www.alphatesting.com	Dallas	TX	75229	972-620-8911	620-1302	256
Alpha Windward LLC 200 Lowder Brook Dr Ste 2400 *Web:* www.alphawindward.com	Westwood	MA	02090	781-326-8880		401
Alpha Wire Co 711 Lidgerwood Ave *TF:* 800-522-5742 ■ *Web:* alphawire.com	Elizabeth	NJ	07207	908-925-8000	925-5411	814
Alpha Xi Delta Women's Fraternity 8702 Founders Rd *Web:* www.alphaxidelta.org	Indianapolis	IN	46268	317-872-3500	872-2947	48-16
Alphabet 1600 Amphitheatre Pkwy *NASDAQ: GOOG* ■ *Web:* abc.xyz	Mountain View	CA	94043	650-253-0000		360-3
AlphaGraphics Inc 215 S State St Ste 320 *TF:* 800-955-6246 ■ *Web:* www.alphagraphics.com	Salt Lake City	UT	84111	801-595-7270	595-7271	627
AlphaKOR Group Inc 7800 Twin Oaks Dr *TF:* 877-944-6009 ■ *Web:* www.alphakor.com	Windsor	ON	N8N5B6	519-944-6009		180
Alphamark Advisors LLC 810 Wright's Summit Pkwy Ste 100 *Web:* www.alphamarkadvisors.com	Fort Wright	KY	41011	859-957-1803		401
Alphamicron Inc 1950 SR-59 *Web:* www.alphamicron.com	Kent	OH	44240	330-676-0648	676-0649	194
Alphanumeric Systems Inc 3801 Wake Forest Rd *TF:* 800-638-6556 ■ *Web:* www.alphanumeric.com	Raleigh	NC	27609	919-781-7575	872-1440	113
Alphaport Inc 18013 Cleveland Pkwy Ste 170 *Web:* www.alpha-port.com	Cleveland	OH	44135	216-619-2400		194
Alpharetta Historical Society Mansell House 1835 Old Milton Pkwy *Web:* www.n-georgia.com	Alpharetta	GA	30009	770-475-4663		49-19
Alphaserve Technologies 104 W 40th St 9th Fl *Web:* www.alphaserveit.com	New York	NY	10018	212-763-5500		180
AlphaStaff Inc 800 Corporate Dr Ste 600 *TF:* 888-335-9545 ■ *Web:* www.alphastaff.com	Fort Lauderdale	FL	33334	954-267-1760		631
Alphavax Inc 2 Triangle Dr *Web:* www.alphavax.com	Research Triangle Park	NC	27709	919-595-0400		363
Alphinat Inc 2000 Peel Ste 680 *TF:* 877-773-9799 ■ *Web:* www.alphinat.com	Montreal	QC	H3A2W5	514-398-9799		177
Alphion Corp 196 Princeton Hightstown Rd Bldg 1A *Web:* www.alphion.com	Princeton Junction	NJ	08550	609-936-9001		256
Alphora Research Inc 2395 Speakman Dr Ste 2001 *Web:* www.alphoraresearch.com	Mississauga	ON	L5K1B3	905-403-0477		231
Alpin Haus Ski Shop 1863 State Hwy 5S *TF:* 888-454-3691 ■ *Web:* www.alpinhaus.com	Amsterdam	NY	12010	518-843-4400		90
Alpina Manufacturing LLC 6460 W Cortland St **Fax Area Code: 800* ■ *TF:* 800-915-2828 ■ *Web:* www.fastchangeframes.com	Chicago	IL	60707	773-202-8887	217-9431*	45
Alpina Sports Corp 93 Etna Rd *Web:* www.alpinasports.com	Lebanon	NH	03766	603-448-3101		711
Alpine Accessories Inc - Ski Snowboard Paddleboard 9219 S SR-31 *Web:* www.alpineaccessories.com	Lake In The Hills	IL	60156	847-854-4754		711
Alpine Adventure Trails Tours Inc 7495 Lower Thomaston Rd *TF:* 888-478-4004 ■ *Web:* swisshiking.com	Macon	GA	31220	478-477-4702	477-4117	760
Alpine Air 1177 Alpine Air Way *Web:* alpine-air.com	Provo	UT	84601	801-373-1508		12
Alpine Animal Hospital 5120 NW Highland Dr *Web:* alpineanimalhosp.net	Corvallis	OR	97330	541-752-7747	752-7749	794
Alpine Archery 3101 N S Hwy PO Box 319 *Web:* www.alpinearchery.com	Lewiston	ID	83501	208-746-4717		710
Alpine Bank of Colorado 2200 Grand Ave PO Box 10000 *TF:* 888-425-7463 ■ *Web:* www.alpinebank.com	Glenwood Springs	CO	81601	970-945-2424	947-1242	360-2
Alpine Building Maintenance & Supply 2920 SE Loop 820 *Web:* alpinemaintenance.com	Fort Worth	TX	76140	817-795-6470	795-9833	256
Alpine Business Systems Inc 1661 Rt 22 W Ste 104 *Web:* alpinebiz.com	Bound Brook	NJ	08805	908-707-9696		225
Alpine Capital Bank 680 Fifth Ave *Web:* www.alpinecapitalbank.com	New York	NY	10019	212-328-2555		70
Alpine Castle Lake Insurance 3385 S Holmes Ave *Web:* alpineinsagency.com	Idaho Falls	ID	83404	208-522-7778		390
Alpine Communications LC 923 Humphrey St *TF:* 800-635-1059 ■ *Web:* www.alpinecom.net	Elkader	IA	52043	563-245-4000		116
Alpine Consulting Inc 12600 Hill Country Blvd Ste R-275 *Web:* alpineinc.com	Austin	TX	78738	512-277-3177		180
Alpine Datasystems Inc 11660 SW Terrace Trls Ste 35 *Web:* www.alpinesw.com	Tigard	OR	97223	503-805-9888		178-1
Alpine Electronics of America 19145 Gramercy Pl *TF:* 800-257-4631 ■ *Web:* alpine-usa.com	Torrance	CA	90501	310-326-8000		52
Alpine Engineering & Design Inc 111 W Canyon Crest Rd *Web:* alpineeng.com	Alpine	UT	84004	801-763-8484		261
Alpine Fresh Inc 9300 NW 58th St Ste 201 *TF:* 800-292-8777 ■ *Web:* www.alpinefresh.com	Miami	FL	33178	305-594-9117	594-8506	297-7
Alpine Group Inc 1 Meadowlands Plz Ste 801	East Rutherford	NJ	07073	201-549-4400		360-3
Alpine Helen/White County Convention & Visitors Bureau 726 Bruckenstrasse PO Box 730 *TF:* 800-858-8027 ■ *Web:* www.helenga.org	Helen	GA	30545	706-878-2181		206
Alpine Helicopters Ltd 1295 Industrial Rd *Web:* www.alpinehelicopter.com	Kelowna	BC	V1Z1G4	250-769-4111		13
Alpine Innovations 275 N 950 E *Web:* www.alpineproducts.com	Lehi	UT	84043	801-766-4994		194
Alpine Investors 2 Embarcadero Ctr Ste 2320 *Web:* alpine-investors.com	San Francisco	CA	94111	415-392-9100		690
Alpine Lodge 434 Indian Creek Cir *TF:* 888-563-4388 ■ *Web:* alpinelodgeresort.com	Branson	MO	65616	417-338-2514		707
Alpine Lumber Co 10170 Church Ranch Way Ste 350 *TF:* 800-499-1634 ■ *Web:* alpinelumber.com	Westminster	CO	80021	303-451-8001	451-5232	191-3
Alpine Meats 9850 Lowr Sacramento Rd *TF:* 800-399-6328 ■ *Web:* www.alpinemeats.com	Stockton	CA	95210	209-477-2691	477-1994	473
Alpine Overhead Doors Inc 8 Hulse Rd *TF:* 800-257-4634 ■ *Web:* www.alpinedoors.com	East Setauket	NY	11733	631-473-9300	642-0800	234
Alpine Packaging Inc 4000 Crooked Run Rd *TF:* 844-682-2361 ■ *Web:* www.alpinepackaging.com	North Versailles	PA	15137	412-664-4000		627
Alpine Plumbing Inc 14580 W Greenfield Ave *Web:* www.alpineplumbinginc.com	Brookfield	WI	53005	262-797-4130		610
Alpine Power Systems 24355 Capitol *TF:* 877-993-8855 ■ *Web:* alpinepowersystems.com	Redford	MI	48239	877-993-8855	993-8865	759
Alpine Precision LLC 152 Rangeway Rd *Web:* www.alpineprecisionllc.com	North Billerica	MA	01862	978-600-0035	667-4805	454
Alpine Propane LLC 2121 Dickerson Rd PO Box 1693 *Web:* alpine-propane.com	Gaylord	MI	49734	989-732-9800	448-2807	316
Alpine Publications Inc 38262 Linman Rd *Web:* www.alpinepub.com	Crawford	CO	81415	970-921-5081		637-2
Alpine Resort 7715 Alpine Rd PO Box 200 *TF:* 888-281-8128 ■ *Web:* www.alpineresort.com	Egg Harbor	WI	54209	920-868-3000		669
Alpine Securities Corp 39 Exchange Pl *Web:* www.alpine-securities.com	Salt Lake City	UT	84111	801-355-5588		690
Alpine Solutions Inc 3222 Corte Malpaso Ste 203-206 *TF:* 855-388-1883 ■ *Web:* www.alpinesolutionsinc.com	Camarillo	CA	93012	805-388-1699		382
Alpine Sun 2144 Alpine Blvd *Web:* www.thealpinesun.com	Alpine	CA	91901	619-445-3288	445-6776	532-2
Alpine Testing Inc 51 W Center St Ste 514 *TF:* 844-625-7463 ■ *Web:* www.alpinetesting.com	Orem	UT	84057	844-625-7463		244
Alpine Tracks Inc 1184 Williston Rd *Web:* alpineshopvt.com	South Burlington	VT	05403	802-862-2714		711
Alpine Valley Ski Area 6775 E Highland Rd *Web:* www.skialpinevalley.com	White Lake	MI	48383	248-887-2180		360-3
Alpine Valley Water Company Inc 10341 Julian Dr *Web:* www.alpinevalleyps.com	Cincinnati	OH	45215	513-672-3400	672-3408	366
Alpine Woodworking Inc 9118 Davenport St NE *Web:* www.alpinewoodworking.com	Blaine	MN	55449	763-784-0333		115
Alpine Wurst & Meathouse Inc 1106 Texas Palmyra Hwy *Web:* www.thealpineonline.com	Honesdale	PA	18431	570-253-5899		296-26
AlpineWeb Design PO Box 506 *Web:* www.alpineweb.com	Bartlett	NH	03812	603-356-8797		177
Alpla Inc 289 Hwy 155 S *Web:* www.alpla.com	Mcdonough	GA	30253	770-914-1407		601
Alps Construction Inc 15745 Annico Dr *Web:* alps.construction	Homer Glen	IL	60491	708-301-3366		187
Alqimi 2101 Gaither Rd Ste 510 *Web:* www.alqimi.com	Rockville	MD	20850	301-337-0100	977-0260	317
Alr Systems & Software Inc 11707 M Cir *Web:* www.alrsys.com	Omaha	NE	68137	402-891-1500		177
ALR Technologies Inc 7400 Beaufont Springs Dr Ste 300 *Web:* www.alrt.com	Richmond	VA	23225	804-554-3500		250
ALRA (American Land Rights Assn) 30218 NE 82nd Ave PO Box 400 *Web:* www.landrights.org	Battle Ground	WA	98604	360-687-3087	687-2973	48-2

Name / Address	City	State	Zip	Phone	Fax	Class
Alretta Truck Parts Inc (ATP) 1 Watson Pl Bldg 5B 2nd Fl *Web:* www.alretta.com	Framingham	MA	01701	508-788-9409	788-9499	61
Alro Steel Corp 3100 E High St *TF:* 800-877-2576 ■ *Web:* www.alro.com	Jackson	MI	49204	517-787-5500	787-6390	492
ALS (Albany Law School of Union University) 80 New Scotland Ave *TF:* 800-448-3500 ■ *Web:* www.albanylaw.edu	Albany	NY	12208	518-445-2311		167-1
ALS (American Littoral Society) 18 Hartshorne Dr Ste 1 *Web:* www.littoralsociety.org	Highlands	NJ	07732	732-291-0055	291-3551	48-13
ALS Group, The 379 Thronall St 9th Fl **Fax Area Code:* 201 ■ *Web:* www.thealsgroup.com	Edison	NJ	08837	732-395-4250	221-7534*	194
Als Quality Oil Company Inc 329 Tremont St *Web:* alsqualityoil.net	Rehoboth	MA	02769	508-339-3353		316
ALSAC (American Lebanese Syrian Associated Charities) 262 Danny Thomas Pl *TF:* 800-822-6344 ■ *Web:* www.stjude.org	Memphis	TN	38105	901-595-3306	578-2805	48-5
Alsay Inc 6615 Gant St *Web:* www.alsaywater.com	Houston	TX	77066	281-444-6960	444-7081	189-15
Alsco Inc 3370 W 1820 S *TF:* 800-408-0208 ■ *Web:* alsco.com	Salt Lake City	UT	84104	801-973-7771	973-7894	787
Alstate Steel Inc 203 Murry Rd SE *Web:* www.alstatesteel.com	Albuquerque	NM	87105	505-877-5454		492
Alster Communications 3062 North Cir *Web:* www.alster.com	Anchorage	AK	99507	907-344-9674		194
Alstom 641 Lexington Ave 28th Fl *Web:* www.alstom.com	New York	NY	10022	212-692-5353		648
Alston, Courtnage & Bassetti LLP 1420 Fifth Ave Ste 3650 *Web:* alcourt.com	Seattle	WA	98101	206-623-7600		41
ALT & Witzig Engineering Inc 4105 W 99th St *Web:* www.altwitzig.com	Carmel	IN	46032	317-875-7000		256
ALT 104.5 111 Presidential Blvd Ste 100 *Web:* alt1045philly.iheart.com	Bala Cynwyd	PA	19004	610-784-3333		643
ALTA (American Land Title Assn) 1800 M St NW Ste 300S *TF:* 800-787-2582 ■ *Web:* www.alta.org	Washington	DC	20036	202-296-3671	223-5843	49-10
Alta Associates Inc 8 Bartles Corner Rd *Web:* www.altaassociates.com	Flemington	NJ	08822	908-806-8442		624
Alta Bates Summit Medical Ctr (ABSMC) 2450 Ashby Ave *Web:* www.altabatessummit.org	Berkeley	CA	94705	510-204-4444		374-3
Alta Capital Management LLC 6440 S Wasatch Blvd Ste 260 *Web:* www.altacapital.com	Salt Lake City	UT	84121	801-274-6010		528
Alta Communications c/o 1000 Winter St S Entrance Ste 3500	Waltham	MA	02451	617-262-7770		792
Alta Consulting Services Inc 11000 NE 33rd Pl Ste 300 *Web:* www.altaconsulting.com	Bellevue	WA	98004	425-576-1202	576-0522	631
Alta Devices Inc 545 Oakmead Pkwy *TF:* 833-425-3932 ■ *Web:* www.altadevices.com	Sunnyvale	CA	94085	408-988-8600		696
Alta Equipment Co 28775 Beck Rd *TF:* 800-261-9642 ■ *Web:* www.altaequipment.com	Wixom	MI	48393	800-261-9642		358
Alta Lodge PO Box 8040 *TF:* 800-707-2582 ■ *Web:* www.altalodge.com	Alta	UT	84092	801-742-3500	742-3504	669
Alta Loma School District 9390 Base Line Rd *Web:* www.alsd.k12.ca.us	Alta Loma	CA	91701	909-484-5151		685
Alta Manufacturing Inc 47650 Westinghouse Dr *Web:* www.altamfg.com	Fremont	CA	94539	510-668-1870	668-1877	477
Alta Mira Recovery Programs LLC 125 Bulkley Ave *Web:* www.altamirarecovery.com	Sausalito	CA	94965	415-332-1350		378
Alta Partners 1 Embarcadero Ctr 37th Fl *Web:* www.altapartners.com	San Francisco	CA	94111	415-362-4022	362-6178	792
Alta Resources 120 N Commercial St **Fax Area Code:* 920 ■ *TF:* 877-464-2582 ■ *Web:* www.altaresources.com	Neenah	WI	54956	877-464-2582	727-9954*	737
Alta Ski Lifts Co Alta Ski Area Hwy 210 Little Cottonwood Canyon *TF:* 800-453-8488 ■ *Web:* www.alta.com	Alta	UT	84092	801-359-1078		452
ALTA Systems Inc 6825 NW 18th Dr *Web:* altainc.com	Gainesville	FL	32653	352-372-2534		627
Alta Via Consulting LLC 525 Tanasi Cir *TF:* 877-258-2842 ■ *Web:* altavia.com	Loudon	TN	37774	877-258-2842		177
Alta Vista Gardens 829 N Alta Vista Blvd *Web:* www.altavistagardens.org	Vista	CA	92084	760-945-3954		97
AltaCorp Capital Inc 585-8 Ave SW Ste 410 *Web:* www.atbcapitalmarkets.com	Calgary	AB	T2P1G1	403-539-8600	539-8575	70
Altadena Chamber of Commerce 730 E Altadena Dr *Web:* www.altadenachamber.org	Altadena	CA	91001	626-794-3988		139
Alta-Fab Structures Ltd 1205-5th St *TF:* 800-252-7990 ■ *Web:* www.altafab.com	Nisku	AB	T9E7L6	780-955-7733	955-7851	188
Altair 8481 Jefferson Hwy *Web:* www.altair-usa.net	Osseo	MN	55369	763-488-3700	488-3704	390
Altair Advisers LLC 303 W Madison St Ste 600 *Web:* altairadvisers.com	Chicago	IL	60606	312-429-3000		401
Altair Engineering Inc 1820 E Big Beaver Rd *TF:* 888-222-7822 ■ *Web:* www.altair.com	Troy	MI	48083	248-614-2400	614-2411	194
Altair Nanotechnologies Inc 204 Edison Way *NASDAQ: ALTI* ■ *Web:* www.altairnano.com	Reno	NV	89502	775-856-2500		144
Altair Technology Inc 1116 W Blanco Rd *Web:* www.altairtech.com	San Antonio	TX	78232	210-764-9900		177
Altamaha Electric Membership Corp 611 W Liberty Ave PO Box 346 *TF:* 800-822-4563 ■ *Web:* www.altamahaemc.com	Lyons	GA	30436	912-526-8181		245
Altamed Health Services Corp 4650 W Sunset Blvd M/S 76 *TF:* 877-462-2582 ■ *Web:* www.altamed.org	Los Angeles	CA	90027	323-669-2113		363
Altametrics 3191 Red Hill Ave Ste 100 *TF:* 800-676-1281 ■ *Web:* altametrics.com	Costa Mesa	CA	92626	800-676-1281		174
Altamira Instruments Inc 149 Delta Dr Ste 200 *Web:* www.altamirainstruments.com	Pittsburgh	PA	15238	412-963-6385		419
Altamont Capital Partners 400 Hamilton Ave Ste 230 *Web:* www.altamontcapital.com	Palo Alto	CA	94301	650-264-7750		196
Altamont Corridor Express (ACE) 949 E Ch St *TF:* 800-411-7245 ■ *Web:* www.acerail.com	Stockton	CA	95202	800-411-7245		468
Altamont Pharmacy Inc 12 N Third St *Web:* www.altamontpharmacy.com	Altamont	IL	62411	618-483-5614		238
Altamonte Mall 451 E Altamonte Dr *Web:* www.altamontemall.com	Altamonte Springs	FL	32701	321-280-1901		460
Altapacific Inc 1525 E Shaw Ave Ste 201 *TF:* 800-659-3655 ■ *Web:* altapacific.com	Fresno	CA	93710	559-439-5700		225
AltaPaints & Coatings 136 W 3300 S *Web:* www.altapaints.com	Salt Lake City	UT	84115	801-466-9625		385
AltaRock Energy Inc 4010 Stone Way N Ste 400 *Web:* altarockenergy.com	Seattle	WA	98103	415-331-0130		196
Altarum Institute 3520 Green Ct Ste 300 *TF:* 800-879-6505 ■ *Web:* altarum.org	Ann Arbor	MI	48105	734-302-4600	302-4991	544
AltaVista Research LLC 243 Fifth Ave Ste 235 *Web:* www.altavista-research.com	New York	NY	10016	646-435-0569		401
Altavista Wealth Management Inc 4 Vanderbilt Park Dr Ste 310 *TF:* 866-684-2600 ■ *Web:* altavistawealth.com	Asheville	NC	28803	866-684-2600		528
Altec Aluminum Technologies Bldg 242 America Pl *TF:* 800-922-9692 ■ *Web:* www.altecextrusions.com	Jeffersonville	IN	47130	812-282-8256		485
Altec Engineering Inc 2401 W Mishawaka Rd *Web:* www.altecengineering.com	Elkhart	IN	46517	574-293-1965		604
Altec Industries Inc 210 Inverness Center Dr *Web:* www.altec.com	Birmingham	AL	35242	205-991-7733	408-8601	190
Altech Environment USA Corp 2623 Kaneville Ct *Web:* www.altechusa.com	Geneva	IL	60134	630-262-4400		201
Altech Services Inc 695 US Rt 46W Ste 301B *TF:* 888-725-8324 ■ *Web:* altechts.com	Fairfield	NJ	07004	888-725-8324	925-8725	177
Altek Systems Inc 7776 US Hwy 50 *Web:* www.alteksystemsinc.com	Lamar	CO	81052	719-336-3403	336-3946	815
Altemp Alloys Inc 330 W Taft Ave *TF:* 800-227-8103 ■ *Web:* www.altempalloys.com	Orange	CA	92865	714-279-0249	279-3991	492
Alten Construction 1141 Marina Way S *TF:* 800-360-6397 ■ *Web:* www.altenconstruction.com	Richmond	CA	94804	510-234-4200	234-4402	186
Altendorf Express Inc 105 7th St *TF:* 800-437-0167 ■ *Web:* www.altendorfinc.com	Minto	ND	58261	701-248-3204	248-3318	780
AltEnergy LLC 137 Rowayton Ave *Web:* altenergyllc.com	Rowayton	CT	06853	203-299-1400		194
Alter Group 5500 W Howard St *Web:* www.altergroup.com	Skokie	IL	60077	847-676-4300	676-4302	653
Alter Logistics Co 2117 State St Ste 300 *Web:* www.alterlogistics.com	Bettendorf	IA	52722	563-344-5114	344-5102	313
Alter Trading Corp 700 Office Pkwy *TF:* 888-337-2727 ■ *Web:* www.altertrading.com	Saint Louis	MO	63141	314-872-2400	872-2420	686
Altera Corp 101 Innovation Dr *NASDAQ: ALTR* ■ *TF:* 800-767-3753	San Jose	CA	95134	408-544-7000	544-6403	696
Altera Payroll Inc 2400 Northside Crossing *TF:* 877-474-6060 ■ *Web:* www.alterapayroll.com	Macon	GA	31210	478-477-6060		2
Alte-Rego Corp 36 Tidemore Ave *Web:* www.alte-rego.com	Toronto	ON	M9W5H4	416-740-3397		600
Alterian Inc 35 E Wacker Dr Ste 200 *Web:* www.sdl.com	Chicago	IL	60601	312-704-1700		178-1
Alteris Group 26600 Telegraph Rd Ste 101 *Web:* www.alterisgroup.com	Southfield	MI	48033	248-477-5560		466
Alterity Inc 600 6 Flags Dr Ste 642 *TF:* 866-877-1311 ■ *Web:* www.acctivate.com	Arlington	TX	76011	817-870-1311	546-0667	178-1
Alterman & Boop LLP 99 Hudson St 8th Fl *Web:* www.altermanandboop.com	New York	NY	10013	212-226-2800	431-3614	445
Altermann Galleries Inc 7172 E Main St *Web:* altermann.com	Scottsdale	AZ	85251	505-983-1590		42
Alterna-Care 319 E Madison St Ste 3n *Web:* alterna-care.com	Springfield	IL	62701	217-525-3733		363
Alternative Apparel Inc 1650 Indian Brook Way Bldg 200 *TF:* 877-747-2915 ■ *Web:* www.alternativeapparel.com	Norcross	GA	30093	678-380-1890		156
Alternative Comics 21607B Stevens Creek Blvd *Web:* indyworld.com	Cupertino	CA	95014	408-921-5164		637-2
Alternative Engineering Inc 5670 W River Dr NE *Web:* alternative-engineering.com	Belmont	MI	49306	616-785-7200		261
Alternative Home Health Inc 280 E Main St *TF:* 800-266-4524 ■ *Web:* alternativehh.com	Saint Clairsville	OH	43950	740-699-7000		363

	Phone	Fax	Class
Alternative Hospice 1749 Gilsinn Ln Fenton MO 63026 *TF:* 866-266-3421 ■ *Web:* www.alternativehospice.com	636-343-3839	343-6367	363
Alternative Solutions Inc W3131 County Hwy C Sheboygan Falls WI 53085 *Web:* asiwi.com	920-467-1200		177
Alternative Strategy Advisers LLC 601 Carlson Pkwy Ste 1125 Minnetonka MN 55305 *Web:* www.asallc.com	952-847-2450		401
Alternatives for Industry Inc 2251 Whitfield Park Ave Sarasota FL 34243 *TF:* 800-739-6566 ■ *Web:* www.afi-tools.com	800-739-6566		237
Alterra Group PO Box 201355 Cleveland OH 44120 *Web:* alterra-group.com	216-539-9710		7
Alterra Real Estate Advisors 300 Spruce St Ste 110 Columbus OH 43215 *Web:* alterrare.com	614-365-9000	280-0244	652
Altest Corp 898 Faulstich Ct San Jose CA 95112 *Web:* www.altestcorp.com	408-436-9900		757
Altfest Personal Wealth Management 445 Park Ave 6th Fl New York NY 10022 *TF:* 888-525-8337 ■ *Web:* www.altfest.com	212-406-0850		194
Althea Ctr 1400 Williams St Denver CO 80218 *Web:* www.altheacenter.org	303-322-7738		48-20
Althoff Industries Inc 8001 S Rt 31 Crystal Lake IL 60014 *TF:* 800-225-2443 ■ *Web:* www.althoffind.com	815-455-7000		189-10
Altia Inc 7222 Commerce Center Dr Ste 240 Colorado Springs CO 80919 *Web:* www.altia.com	719-598-4299		177
Altierus Career College 14555 Potomac Mills Rd Woodbridge VA 22192 **Fax Area Code:* 703 ■ *TF:* 833-692-4264 ■ *Web:* www.altierus.edu	571-408-2100	494-3242*	800
Altify 2500 Northwinds Pky Ste 350 Alpharetta GA 30009 *TF:* 866-570-3836 ■ *Web:* www.altify.com	770-667-5352		177
AltiGen Communications Inc 410 E Plumeria Dr San Jose CA 95134 *OTC:* ATGN ■ *TF:* 888-258-4436 ■ *Web:* www.altigen.com	408-597-9000	597-9020	735
Altima Technologies Inc 2300 Cabot Dr Ste 535 Lisle IL 60532 *Web:* www.altimatech.com	630-281-6464		764
Altimate Medical Inc 262 W First St Morton MN 56270 *TF:* 800-342-8968 ■ *Web:* easystand.com	507-697-6393		476
Altimus Distributing Inc 21 8th St W Billings MT 59101 *TF:* 800-999-9816 ■ *Web:* www.altimusdistributing.com	406-259-9816	259-7632	76
Altira Group LLC 1675 Broadway Ste 2400 Denver CO 80202 *Web:* www.altiragroup.com	303-592-5500	592-5519	792
Altira Inc 3225 NW 112th St Miami FL 33167 *Web:* www.altira.com	305-687-8074	688-8029	333
Altitude Marketing 417 State Rd 2nd Fl Emmaus PA 18049 *Web:* altitudemarketing.com	610-421-8601		195
Altium Inc 4225 Executive Sq Level 7 La Jolla CA 92037 *TF:* 800-544-4186 ■ *Web:* www.altium.com	858-864-1500	864-1710	178-5
Altium Packaging 2500 Windy Ridge Parkway SE Ste 1400 Atlanta GA 30339 *TF:* 888-831-2184 ■ *Web:* altiumpkg.com	678-742-4600	742-4750	548
Altius Broadband Inc 3314 Papermill Rd Ste 100 Phoenix MD 21131 *TF:* 800-864-6546 ■ *Web:* www.altiuscomm.com	410-667-1638		224
ALTL Inc 3000 Corporate Grove Hudsonville MI 49426 *TF:* 800-290-2585 ■ *Web:* www.altl.com	616-669-6060	669-3559	780
Altland House 1 Center Sq Ste 100 Abbottstown PA 17301 *Web:* altlandhouse.com	717-259-9535		671
Altman & Associates PC 11300 Rockville Pk Ste 708 Rockville MD 20852 *Web:* altmanassociates.net	301-468-3220	468-3255	41
Altman Lighting Inc 57 Alexander St Yonkers NY 10701 *Web:* www.altmanlighting.com	914-476-7987		439
Altman Specialty Plants Inc 3742 Blue Bird Canyon Rd Vista CA 92084 *Web:* altmanplants.com	760-744-8191	744-8835	369
Altman Vilandrie & Co 101 Federal St 28th Fl Boston MA 02110 *Web:* www.altvil.com	617-753-7200		463
Altman Weil Inc PO Box 625 Newtown Square PA 19073 *TF:* 866-886-3600 ■ *Web:* www.altmanweil.com	610-359-9900	359-0467	194
Altmeyer Home Stores Inc 6515 Rt 22 Delmont PA 15626 *TF:* 800-394-6628 ■ *Web:* www.bedbathhome.com	724-468-3434	468-3233	362
Alt-N Technologies Ltd 4550 State Hwy 360 Ste 100 Grapevine TX 76051 *Web:* www.altn.com	817-601-3222		180
Alto Cinco 526 Westcott St Syracuse NY 13210 *Web:* www.altocinco.net	315-422-6399		671
Alto Consulting & Training 7210 Metro Blvd Minneapolis MN 55439 *Web:* www.altoconsulting.com	952-831-6604	893-8080	196
Alto Development Corp 5206 Asbury Rd PO Box 758 Farmingdale NJ 07727 **Fax Area Code:* 732 ■ *Web:* aemedical.com	919-361-9191	938-2399*	476
Alto Products Corp 1 Alto Way Atmore AL 36502 *Web:* www.altousa.com	251-368-7777	368-7774	61
Alton Baker Park 1820 Roosevelt Blvd Eugene OR 97402 *Web:* www.eugene-or.gov	541-682-4800		564
Alton E. Woodford Inc 10 N Main St West Hartford CT 06107 *TF:* 866-227-0431 ■ *Web:* aewoodford.com	860-236-5861		390
Alton Memorial Hospital 1 Memorial Dr Alton IL 62002 *Web:* www.altonmemorialhospital.org	618-463-7311		374-3
Alton Mental Health Ctr 4500 College Ave Alton IL 62002 *Web:* www.dhs.state.il.us	618-474-3800	474-3807	374-5
Alton National Cemetery 600 Pearl St Alton IL 62002 *TF:* 800-535-1117 ■ *Web:* www.cem.va.gov	314-845-8320		136
Alton Regional Convention & Visitors Bureau (ARCVB) 200 Piasa St Alton IL 62002 *TF:* 800-258-6645 ■ *Web:* www.riversandroutes.com	618-465-6676	465-6151	206
Alton Steel Inc 5 Cut St Alton IL 62002 *Web:* www.altonsteel.com	618-463-4490		492
Altona Correctional Facility 555 Devil Den Rd Altona NY 12910 *Web:* www.doccs.ny.gov	518-236-7841		213
Altoona Area Public Library 1600 Fifth Ave Altoona PA 16602 *Web:* www.altoonalibrary.org	814-946-0417	946-3230	434-3
Altoona Beauty School Inc 1554 Valley View Blvd Altoona PA 16602 *Web:* www.altoonabeautyschool.com	814-942-3141	943-5188	685
Altoona Ctr 1020 Green Ave Altoona PA 16601 *Web:* www.myaltoonacenterfornursingcare.com	814-946-2700		230
Altoona Mirror 301 Cayuga Ave Altoona PA 16602 *TF:* 800-222-1962 ■ *Web:* www.altoonamirror.com	814-946-7411		532-2
Altoona VA Medical Ctr 2907 Pleasant Vly Blvd Altoona PA 16602 **Fax Area Code:* 814 ■ *TF:* 877-626-2500 ■ *Web:* www.altoona.va.gov	877-626-2500	940-7898*	374-8
Altoona-Blair County Chamber of Commerce 3900 Industrial Park Dr Ste 12 Altoona PA 16602 *Web:* www.blairchamber.com	814-943-8151	943-5239	139
Altoros Systems 830 Stewart Dr Ste 119 Sunnyvale CA 94085 *Web:* www.altoros.com	650-395-7002		194
Altos Express Inc 2301 Garry Rd Cinnaminson NJ 08077 *Web:* safer.fmcsa.dot.gov	856-829-6900		311
Altos Ventures Management Inc 2882 Sand Hill Rd Ste 100 Menlo Park CA 94025 *Web:* altos.vc	650-234-9771		792
Alto-Shaam Inc W 164 N 9221 Water St PO Box 450 Menomonee Falls WI 53052 *TF:* 800-329-8744 ■ *Web:* www.alto-shaam.com	262-251-3800	251-7067	298
Altour International Inc 80 Pine St Ste 17 New York NY 10005 *Web:* www.altour.com	212-509-2375		772
ALTRES Inc 967 Kapiolani Blvd Honolulu HI 96814 *Web:* www.altres.com	808-591-4940		721
Altria Group Inc 6601 W Broad St Richmond VA 23230 *NYSE:* MO ■ *TF:* 800-627-5200 ■ *Web:* www.altria.com	804-274-2200		185
Altrius Capital Management Inc 1323 Commerce Dr New Bern NC 28562 *Web:* www.altrius-capital.com	252-638-7598	635-6739	796
Altron Inc 6700 Bunker Lake Blvd NW Minneapolis MN 55303 *Web:* www.altronmfg.com	763-427-7735		625
Altronic Inc 712 Trumbull Ave Girard OH 44420 *Web:* www.altronicinc.com	330-545-9768	545-9005	247
Altru Apparel 718 Gladys Ave Ste 2 Los Angeles CA 90021 *Web:* www.altruapparel.com	213-622-0588		157-6
Altruent Systems 1017 Passport Way Cary NC 27513 *TF:* 888-843-9392 ■ *Web:* altruent.com	919-828-4419		174
Altschul & Altschul Inc 18 E 12th St Frnt 1 New York NY 10003 *Web:* www.altschul.biz	212-924-1505		428
Altsource 1120 SE Madison St Portland OR 97214 *Web:* altsrc.net	971-373-8449		177
Altura Bistro 4240 Old Seward Hwy Ste 20 Anchorage AK 99503 *Web:* www.aladdinsak.com	907-561-2373		671
Altura Communication Solutions LLC 1335 S Acacia Ave Fullerton CA 92831 *Web:* www.alturacs.com	714-948-8727		246
Alturas Analytics Inc 1324 Alturas Dr Moscow ID 83843 *Web:* www.alturasanalytics.com	208-883-3400		743
Alturdyne Inc 660 Steele St El Cajon CA 92020 *Web:* www.alturdyne.com	619-440-5531		262
Altus Alliance LLC 800 5th Ave Ste 4100 Seattle WA 98104 *Web:* www.altusalliance.com	206-438-1890		194
Altus Capital Partners Inc 10 Westport Rd Ste C204 Wilton CT 06897 *Web:* www.altuscapitalpartners.com	203-429-2007	429-2010	792
Altus Consulting Corp 1401 Greystone Rd Upperville VA 20184 *Web:* altuscc.com	703-929-4000		463
Alu-Bra Foundry Inc 630 E Green St Bensenville IL 60106 *Web:* alubra.com	630-766-3112	766-3307	492
Aluchem Inc 1 Landy Ln Cincinnati OH 45215 *TF:* 800-336-8519 ■ *Web:* aluchem.com	513-733-8519		487
ALULA 500 Cherrington Pkwy Ste 350 Moon Township PA 15108 *Web:* alula.clg.com	412-269-7240		463
Alum Creek State Park 3615 S Old State Rd Delaware OH 43015 *Web:* alum-creek-state-park.org	740-548-4631		565
Aluma Tower Company Inc 1639 Old Dixie Hwy Vero Beach FL 32960 *Web:* www.alumatower.com	772-567-3423	567-3432	647
Alumacraft Boat Co 315 St Julien St Saint Peter MN 56082 *Web:* www.alumacraft.com	507-931-1050		90
Aluma-Form Inc 3625 Old Getwell Rd Memphis TN 38118 *Web:* www.alumaform.com	901-362-0100	794-9515	816
Alum-A-Lift Inc 7909 US Hwy 78 Winston GA 30187 *Web:* alum-a-lift.com	770-489-0328		256
Alum-alloy Company Inc 603 S Hope Ave Ontario CA 91761 *Web:* www.alumalloy.com	909-986-0410	986-6537	492
Alumawall Inc 1701 S Seventh St Ste 9 San Jose CA 95112 *Web:* www.alumawall.com	408-292-6353	275-6225	492
Alumaweld Boats Inc 1601 Ave F White City OR 97503 *TF:* 800-401-2628 ■ *Web:* www.alumaweldboats.com	541-826-7171	830-6907	90
Alumet Supply 150 Lackawanna Ave Parsippany NJ 07054 *TF:* 888-925-8638 ■ *Web:* www.alumetsupply.com	973-675-8400	334-0002	492
Alumicor Ltd 290 Humberline Dr Toronto ON M9W5S2 *TF:* 877-258-6426 ■ *Web:* www.alumicor.com	416-745-4222		481
Alumi-Guard Inc 2401 Corporate Blvd Brooksville FL 34604 *Web:* alumi-guard.com	352-754-8555		567
AluminArt 1 Summerlea Rd Brampton ON L6T4V2 *Web:* aluminartwindows.ca	905-791-7521		350

Name / Address	City	State	ZIP	Phone	Fax	Class
Aluminum & Stainless Inc PO Box 3484 *TF:* 800-252-9074 ■ *Web:* www.aluminumandstainless.com	LaFayette	LA	70502	337-837-4381		492
Aluminum Association Inc 1525 Wilson Blvd Ste 600 *Web:* www.aluminum.org	Arlington	VA	22209	703-358-2960	358-2961	49-13
Aluminum Coil Anodizing Corp 501 E Lake St *Web:* acacorp.com	Streamwood	IL	60107	630-837-4000	837-0814	481
Aluminum Distributing 2930 SW Second Ave *TF:* 866-825-9271 ■ *Web:* www.adimetal.com	Fort Lauderdale	FL	33315	954-523-6474		492
Aluminum Extruded Shapes Inc 10549 Reading Rd *Web:* alum-ext.com	Cincinnati	OH	45241	513-563-2205		492
Aluminum Extrusions Inc 140 Matthews Dr *Web:* www.aeialuminum.com	Senatobia	MS	38668	662-562-6663	562-4190	492
Aluminum Ladder Co 1430 W Darlington St *TF:* 800-752-2526 ■ *Web:* www.fireladder.com	Florence	SC	29501	843-662-2595	661-0972	487
Aluminum Line Products Co 24460 Sperry Cir *TF:* 800-321-3154 ■ *Web:* aluminumline.com	Westlake	OH	44145	440-835-8880	835-8879	697
Aluminum Precision Products Inc 3333 W Warner St *TF:* 800-411-8983 ■ *Web:* www.aluminumprecision.com	Santa Ana	CA	92704	714-546-8125	540-8662	483
Aluminum Resources Inc 789 Swan Dr *Web:* www.aluminumresources.com	Smyrna	TN	37167	615-355-6500	355-6567	492
ALung Technologies Inc 2500 Jane St Ste 1 *Web:* www.alung.com	Pittsburgh	PA	15203	412-697-3370		250
Aluprof USA LLC 355 Lexington Ave *Web:* www.aluprofusa.com	New York	NY	10017	212-687-0300		45
Alutiiq LLC 3909 Arctic Blvd Ste 500 *TF:* 800-829-8547 ■ *Web:* www.alutiiq.com	Anchorage	AK	99503	907-222-9500	222-9501	360-3
Alva-Amco Pharmacal Companies Inc 7711 Merrimac Ave *TF:* 800-792-2582 ■ *Web:* www.alva-amco.com	Niles	IL	60714	847-663-0700		582
Alvah Bushnell Co 519 E Chelten Ave **Fax Area Code:* 215 ■ *TF:* 800-255-7434 ■ *Web:* www.bushnellco.com	Philadelphia	PA	19144	800-814-7296	843-7725*	560
Alvarado Construction Inc 924 W Colfax Ave Ste 301 *Web:* www.alvaradoconstruction.com	Denver	CO	80204	303-629-0783	595-4354	186
Alvarado Hospital Medical Ctr 6655 Alvarado Rd *TF:* 800-258-2723 ■ *Web:* www.alvaradohospital.com	San Diego	CA	92120	619-287-3270		374-3
Alvarado Manufacturing Company Inc 12660 Colony St *TF:* 800-423-4143 ■ *Web:* www.alvaradomfg.com	Chino	CA	91710	909-591-8431	628-1403	491
Alvarado Street Bakery 2225 S Mcdowell Blvd Ext *Web:* www.alvaradostreetbakery.com	Petaluma	CA	94954	707-283-0300	789-6720	68
Alvarado's Mexican Restaurant 11641 S Western Ave *Web:* www.alvaradosmexican.com	Oklahoma City	OK	73170	405-692-2007		671
Alvarez & Marsal Holdings LLC 600 Lexington Ave 8th Fl *Web:* www.alvarezandmarsal.com	New York	NY	10022	212-759-4433	759-5532	194
Alvarez and Bremer Travel 9336 Transit Rd *TF:* 800-259-0244 ■ *Web:* www.aandbtravel.com	East Amherst	NY	14051	716-688-4567	688-6135	771
Alvarez Technology Group Inc 209 Pajaro St Ste A *Web:* www.alvareztg.com	Salinas	CA	93901	831-753-7677		177
Alvarez, Sambol, Winthrop & Madson PA 390 N Orange Ave *Web:* www.awtspa.com	Orlando	FL	32801	407-210-2796		428
Alva-Tech Inc 1208 Columbus Rd Ste G *Web:* www.alva-tech.com	Burlington Township	NJ	08016	609-747-1133	747-1136	604
Alvernia College 400 Saint Bernardine St *TF:* 888-258-3764 ■ *Web:* www.alvernia.edu	Reading	PA	19611	610-796-8200	790-2873	166
Alverno College PO Box 343922 *TF:* 800-933-3401 ■ *Web:* www.alverno.edu	Milwaukee	WI	53234	414-382-6100		166
Alverson, Taylor, Mortensen & Sanders 7401 W Charleston Blvd *Web:* alversontaylor.com	Las Vegas	NV	89117	702-384-7000	385-7000	428
Alvin & Company Inc 1335 Blue Hills Ave **Fax Area Code:* 800 ■ *TF:* 800-444-2584 ■ *Web:* www.alvinco.com	Bloomfield	CT	06002	860-243-8991	777-2896*	43
Alvin C. York Campus 3400 Lebanon Pk *Web:* www.va.gov	Murfreesboro	TN	37129	615-867-6000	225-4901	374-8
Alvin Community College 3110 Mustang Rd *Web:* www.alvincollege.edu	Alvin	TX	77511	281-756-3500	756-3952	162
Alvin Goldfarb Jeweler of Seattle Inc 305 Bellevue Way NE *Web:* agjeweler.com	Bellevue	WA	98004	425-454-9393		410
Alvin H. Butz Inc 840 W Hamilton St Ste 600 *Web:* www.butz.com	Allentown	PA	18101	610-395-6871	395-3363	186
Alvin Hollis & Co 1 Hollis St *TF:* 800-649-5090 ■ *Web:* www.alvinhollis.com	South Weymouth	MA	02190	781-335-2100	335-6134	316
Alvin's Island - Tropical Department Stores 216 Lincon Rd Miami Beach *Web:* www.alvinsisland.com	Miami	FL	33139	305-531-9766		157-5
Alvine Engineering Inc 1102 Douglas On The Mall *Web:* www.alvine.com	Omaha	NE	68102	402-346-7007		256
Alvin-Manvel Area Chamber of Commerce 105 W Willis St *Web:* www.alvinmanvelchamber.org	Alvin	TX	77511	281-331-3944		139
Alvopetro Energy Ltd 525 - Eighth Ave SW Ste 1700 *Web:* alvopetro.com	Calgary	AB	T2P1G1	587-794-4224		536
Alwan Printing 7825 S Roberts Rd *Web:* alwanprinting.com	Bridgeview	IL	60455	708-598-9600		627
Always A Good Sign 407 Bloomfield Dr Ste 3 *Web:* alwaysagoodsign.com	West Berlin	NJ	08091	856-753-7800		701
Always Compassionate Veterinary Care Pc 4701 Clairton Blvd *Web:* acvetcare.com	Pittsburgh	PA	15236	412-882-3070	882-1805	794
Alweather Windows & Doors Ltd 27 Troop Ave *Web:* www.awwd.ca	Dartmouth	NS	B3B2A7	902-468-2605		234
Alwin Manufacturing Company Inc PO Box 10887 *Web:* alwin.com	Green Bay	WI	54307	920-499-1424		488
Alyce 75 Federal St 7th Fl *TF:* 888-861-6608 ■ *Web:* www.alyce.com	Boston	MA	02110	888-861-6608		657
Alyeska Pipeline Service Co 3700 Centerpoint Dr PO Box 196660 *Web:* www.alyeska-pipe.com	Anchorage	AK	99503	907-787-8700	787-8448	597
Alyeska Prince Hotel & Resort 1000 Arlberg Ave PO Box 249 *TF:* 800-880-3880 ■ *Web:* www.alyeskaresort.com	Girdwood	AK	99587	907-754-1111		669
Alyeska Resort 1000 Arlberg Ave PO Box 249 *Web:* www.alyeskaresort.com	Girdwood	AK	99587	907-754-2111		669
Alzheimer's Assn 225 N Michigan Ave 1st Fl **Fax Area Code:* 866 ■ *TF:* 800-272-3900 ■ *Web:* alz.org	Chicago	IL	60601	312-335-8700	699-1246*	48-17
AM (Ackerman McQueen) 1133 N Robinson Ave	Oklahoma City	OK	73103	405-843-7777	848-8034	4
AM 1150 WTMP Pan Am Circle *Web:* www.am1150wtmp.com	Tampa	FL	33607	813-620-1300	628-0713	647
AM 1300 The Zone 3601 S Congress Ave Bldg F *Web:* am1300thezone.iheart.com	Austin	TX	78704	512-390-5483		645-13
AM 570 LA Sports 3400 W Olive Ave Ste 550 *TF:* 866-987-2570 ■ *Web:* am570lasports.iheart.com	Burbank	CA	91505	818-559-2252		645
AM 740 KTRH Newsradio 2000 W Loop S Ste 300 *Web:* ktrh.iheart.com	Houston	TX	77027	713-212-5740		645-72
AM 880 KIXI 3650 131st Ave SE Ste 550 *TF:* 866-880-5494 ■ *Web:* www.kixi.com	Bellevue	WA	98006	425-562-8964	653-1088	645
AM Best Company Inc Ambest Rd *Web:* www.ambest.com	Oldwick	NJ	08858	908-439-2200		531-1
AM Facility Services 6886 Hillsdale Ct *TF:* 800-956-3862 ■ *Web:* amincorporated.com	Indianapolis	IN	46250	317-578-2290		104
AM General LLC 105 N Niles Ave PO Box 7025 *Web:* www.amgeneral.com	South Bend	IN	46617	574-237-6222		59
AM Kinney 150 E 4th St *Web:* www.amkinney.com	Cincinnati	OH	45202	513-421-2265		261
AM New York 240 W 35th St 9th Fl **Fax Area Code:* 212 ■ *Web:* www.amny.com	New York	NY	10001	646-293-9499	239-2828*	532-2
AM Private Enterprises Inc 59 Grove St *Web:* www.aminet.com	New Canaan	CT	06840	203-972-5095		401
AM Resorts LLC 7 Campus Blvd *Web:* www.amresorts.com	Newtown Square	PA	19073	610-359-6500		707
AM Skier Insurance 209 Main Ave *Web:* www.amskier.com	Hawley	PA	18428	570-226-4571	226-1105	390
AM Systems Inc 131 Business Park Loop *TF:* 800-426-1306 ■ *Web:* www.a-msystems.com	Sequim	WA	98382	360-683-8300		477
AM Technical Solutions Inc 2213 RR 620 N Ste 105 *TF:* 888-729-1548 ■ *Web:* www.amts.com	Austin	TX	78734	888-729-1548		393
AM Todd Co 1717 Douglas Ave **Fax Area Code:* 222 ■ *Web:* www.wildflavors.com	Kalamazoo	MI	49007	269-343-2603	681-4141*	479
AM860 The Answer 5211 W Laurel St Ste 101 *Web:* theanswertampa.com	Tampa	FL	33607	813-425-8625		645-160
AMA (Aerospace Medical Assn) 320 S Henry St *Web:* www.asma.org	Alexandria	VA	22314	703-739-2240	739-9652	49-8
AMA (American Motorcyclist Assn) 13515 Yarmouth Dr *TF:* 800-262-5646 ■ *Web:* www.americanmotorcyclist.com	Pickerington	OH	43147	614-856-1900	856-1920	48-22
AMA (Academy of Model Aeronautics) 5161 E Memorial Dr **Fax Area Code:* 765 ■ *TF:* 800-435-9262 ■ *Web:* www.modelaircraft.org	Muncie	IN	47302	800-435-9262	289-4248*	48-18
AMA Capital Partners 405 Lexington Ave 67th Fl *Web:* www.amausa.com	New York	NY	10174	212-682-3344	682-3464	216
AMA Plastics Inc 1100 Citrus St *Web:* amaplastics.com	Riverside	CA	92507	951-734-5600		604
Amac Enterprises 5909 W 130th St *Web:* www.amacent.com	Cleveland	OH	44130	216-362-1880	362-0812	484
AMACO (American Art Clay Co) 6060 Guion Rd *TF:* 800-374-1600 ■ *Web:* www.amaco.com	Indianapolis	IN	46254	317-244-6871	248-9300	43
Amada America Inc 7025 Firestone Blvd *TF:* 800-626-6612 ■ *Web:* www.amada.com	Buena Park	CA	90621	714-739-2111	739-4099	456
Amada Machine Tools America Inc 2324 Palmer Dr *TF:* 800-877-4729 ■ *Web:* amadamt.com	Schaumburg	IL	60173	847-285-4800	519-2127	455
Amadas Industries Inc 1100 Holland Rd *Web:* www.amadas.com	Suffolk	VA	23434	757-539-0231	934-3264	273
Amadeus 122 E Washington St *Web:* www.amadeusrestaurant.com	Ann Arbor	MI	48104	734-665-8767		671
Amadeus North America Inc 3470 NW 82nd Ave Ste 1000 *TF:* 888-262-3387 ■ *Web:* www.amadeus.com	Miami	FL	33122	305-499-6000	499-6889	335
Amador County 810 Ct St *TF:* 800-775-9772 ■ *Web:* www.amadorgov.org	Jackson	CA	95642	209-223-6470	257-0619	338
Amador County Archives 12200-A Airport Rd *Web:* www.co.amador.ca.us	Jackson	CA	95642	209-223-6389		520

Name / Address	City	State	Zip	Phone	Fax	Class
Amador County Chamber of Commerce 1 Prosperity Ct *Web:* amadorchamber.com	Sutter Creek	CA	95685	209-223-0350		139
Amador County Unified School District 217 Rex Ave *Web:* www.amadorcoe.org	Jackson	CA	95642	209-223-1750		685
Amador Publishers LLC 611 Delamar NW *Web:* www.amadorbooks.com	Albuquerque	NM	87107	505-344-6102		637-2
AMAG Pharmaceuticals 1100 Winter St Ste 3000 *Web:* www.amagpharma.com	Waltham	MA	02451	617-498-3300	649-1654	231
AMAG Technology Inc 20701 Manhattan Pl *TF:* 800-889-9138 ■ *Web:* www.amag.com	Torrance	CA	90501	310-518-2380	834-0685	692
Amal Law Group LLC 225 W Washington St Ste 2200 *Web:* www.amallaw.com	Chicago	IL	60606	708-361-3600		428
AMALCO (American Aluminum Co) 230 Sheffield St *Web:* www.amalco.com	Mountainside	NJ	07092	908-233-3500	233-3241	482
Amalfi's 4703 NE Fremont St *Web:* www.amalfisrestaurant.com	Portland	OR	97213	503-284-6747		671
Amalgamated Bank of Chicago 30 N LaSalle *Web:* www.aboc.com	Chicago	IL	60602	312-822-3000	267-8767	70
Amalgamated Bank of New York 275 Seventh Ave *TF:* 800-662-0860 ■ *Web:* www.amalgamatedbank.com	New York	NY	10001	800-662-0860		70
Amalgamated Dairies Ltd (ADL) 79 Water St *Web:* adl.ca	Summerside	PE	C1N1A6	902-888-5088		578
Amalgamated Life 333 Westchester Ave *TF:* 866-975-4089 ■ *Web:* www.amalgamatedbenefits.com	White Plains	NY	10604	914-367-5000		391-2
Amalgamated Sugar Company LLC 1951 S Saturn Way Ste 100 *Web:* amalgamatedsugar.com	Boise	ID	83709	208-383-6500	383-6688	296-38
Amalgamated Transit Union (ATU) 10000 New Hampshire Ave *TF:* 888-240-1196 ■ *Web:* www.atu.org	Silver Spring	MD	20903	202-537-1645	244-7824	414
Amana Colonies 622 46th Ave *TF:* 800-579-2294 ■ *Web:* www.amanacolonies.com	Amana	IA	52203	319-622-7622		10-4
Amana Society Inc 506 39th Ave *Web:* www.amanasociety.com	West Amana	IA	52203	319-622-7500		594
Amanda Manufacturing 1120 CIC Dr *Web:* amandamanufacturing.com	Logan	OH	43138	740-385-9380	385-5445	73
Amanda's Fonda 3625 W Colorado Ave *Web:* www.amandascantina.com	Colorado Springs	CO	80904	719-227-1975		671
Amangani Resort 1535 NE Butte Rd *TF:* 877-734-7333 ■ *Web:* www.aman.com	Jackson	WY	83001	307-734-7333	734-7332	669
Amano Cincinnati Inc 140 Harrison Ave *TF:* 800-526-2559 ■ *Web:* www.amano.com	Roseland	NJ	07068	973-403-1900	364-1086	111
Amano Enzyme USA Company Ltd 1415 Madeline Ln *Web:* www.amano-enzyme.com	Elgin	IL	60124	847-649-0101		390
Amara Resort LLC 100 Amara Ln *Web:* www.amararesort.com	Sedona	AZ	86336	928-282-4828		378
Amaram Technology Corp 8230 Boone Blvd Ste 445 *Web:* amaram.com	Vienna	VA	22182	703-288-4113	879-7555	177
Amare Global 17872 Gillette Ave Ste 100 *TF:* 888-898-8551 ■ *Web:* www.amare.com	Irvine	CA	92614	888-898-8551		49-15
Amarillo Biosciences Inc 4134 Business Pk Dr *Web:* amarbio.com	Amarillo	TX	79110	806-376-1741	376-9301	85
Amarillo Botanical Gardens 1400 Streit Dr *Web:* www.amarillobotanicalgardens.org	Amarillo	TX	79106	806-352-6513		97
Amarillo Chamber of Commerce 1000 S Polk St *Web:* www.amarillo-chamber.org	Amarillo	TX	79101	806-373-7800	373-3909	139
Amarillo Civic Ctr 401 S Buchanan St *Web:* amarillociviccenter.com	Amarillo	TX	79101	806-378-4297	378-4234	205
Amarillo Club 600 S Tyler St *Web:* amarilloclub.com	Amarillo	TX	79101	806-373-4361	373-4334	671
Amarillo College 2201 S Washington St *TF:* 800-227-8784 ■ *Web:* www.actx.edu	Amarillo	TX	79109	806-371-5000	371-5066	162
Amarillo Convention & Visitor Council 1000 S Polk St *TF:* 800-692-1338 ■ *Web:* www.visitamarillo.com	Amarillo	TX	79101	800-692-1338		206
Amarillo Economic Development Corp 801 S Fillmore Ste 205 *TF:* 800-333-7892 ■ *Web:* www.amarilloedc.com	Amarillo	TX	79101	806-379-6411		463
Amarillo Gear Co 2401 W Sundown Ln *Web:* www.amarillogear.com	Amarillo	TX	79118	806-622-1273	622-3258	709
Amarillo Globe News PO Box 2091 *TF:* 800-692-4052 ■ *Web:* www.amarillo.com	Amarillo	TX	79166	806-376-4488	373-0810	532-2
Amarillo Independent School District (AISD) 7200 I- 40 W *Web:* www.amaisd.org	Amarillo	TX	79106	806-326-1000	354-4378	685
Amarillo Museum of Art 2200 S Van Buren St *Web:* www.amarilloart.org	Amarillo	TX	79109	806-371-5050		520
Amarillo National Bank 410 S Taylor St *TF:* 800-253-1031 ■ *Web:* www.anb.com	Amarillo	TX	79101	806-378-8000	378-8066	70
Amarillo Opera 2223 S Van Buren St *Web:* www.amarilloopera.org	Amarillo	TX	79109	806-372-7464		573-2
Amarillo Public Library 413 E Fourth *Web:* www.amarillolibrary.org	Amarillo	TX	79101	806-378-3054		434-3
Amarillo Wind Machine Co 20513 Ave 256 *TF:* 800-311-4498 ■ *Web:* www.amarillowind.com	Exeter	CA	93221	559-592-4256	592-4194	273
Amarillo Zoo 700 Comanchero Trl *Web:* zoo.amarillo.gov	Amarillo	TX	79107	806-381-7911	381-7901	823
A-Mark Precious Metals Inc 429 Santa Monica Blvd Ste 230 *Web:* www.amark.com	Santa Monica	CA	90401	310-587-1485	319-0317	360-3
Amash Justin (Rep R - MI) 106 Cannon House Office Bldg *Web:* amash.house.gov	Washington	DC	20515	202-225-3831	225-5144	342-2
Amason & Associates Inc PO Box 1729 *Web:* www.amason-associates.com	Tuscaloosa	AL	35403	205-345-9626	345-9686	610
Amatech Inc 1460 Grimm Dr *TF:* 800-403-6920 ■ *Web:* www.amatechinc.com	Erie	PA	16501	800-403-6920		601
Amateur Athletic Union of the US (AAU) 1910 Hotel Plaza Blvd *TF:* 800-228-4872 ■ *Web:* aausports.org	Lake Buena Vista	FL	32830	407-934-7200	934-7242	48-22
Amateur Trapshooting Assn (ATA) 601 W National Rd *Web:* www.shootata.com	Vandalia	OH	45377	937-898-4638		48-22
Amatex Corp 1032 Stambridge St *TF:* 800-441-9680 ■ *Web:* www.amatex.com	Norristown	PA	19404	610-277-6100	277-6106	745-3
Amato Industries Inc 9120 Talbot Ave *TF:* 800-992-6286 ■ *Web:* www.amatoind.com	Silver Spring	MD	20910	301-565-3220	565-9227	146
Amato Legal Search Inc 2321 Old Maple Ct *Web:* www.amatolegalsearch.com	Ellicott City	MD	21042	410-750-7550		428
AmaWaterways 26010 Mureau Rd *TF:* 800-626-0126 ■ *Web:* www.amawaterways.com	Calabasas	CA	91302	800-626-0126		760
Amax Engineering Corp 1565 Reliance Way *TF:* 800-889-2629 ■ *Web:* www.amax.com	Fremont	CA	94539	510-651-8886	651-4119	173-2
Amazing Mail-print Ctr 2130 S Seventh Ave Ste 170 *TF:* 888-681-1214 ■ *Web:* www.amazingmail.com	Phoenix	AZ	85007	888-681-1214		5
Amazing Recycled Products Inc PO Box 312 **Fax Area Code:* 303 ■ *TF:* 800-241-2174 ■ *Web:* amazingrecycled.blogspot.com	Denver	CO	80201	800-241-2174	699-2102*	661
Amazon.com Inc 410 Terry Ave N *NASDAQ: AMZN* ■ *Web:* www.amazon.com	Seattle	WA	98109	206-266-4064	266-7010	459
AMB Financial Corp 8230 Hohman Ave *OTC: AMFC* ■ *TF:* 800-436-5113 ■ *Web:* www.acbanker.com	Munster	IN	46321	219-836-5870	836-5883	360-2
AMBA (American Malting Barley Assn) 740 N Plankinton Ave Ste 830 *Web:* www.ambainc.org	Milwaukee	WI	53203	414-272-4640		49-6
AMBAC Financial Group Inc One World Trade Ct 41st Fl *NASDAQ: AMBC* ■ *TF:* 800-221-1854 ■ *Web:* www.ambac.com	New York	NY	10007	212-658-7470	208-3414	360-4
AMBAC International Inc 910 Spears Creek Ct **Fax Area Code:* 803 ■ *TF:* 800-628-6894 ■ *Web:* www.ambacinternational.com	Elgin	SC	29045	800-628-6894	735-2163*	60
Ambarella Inc 3101 Jay St *Web:* www.ambarella.com	Santa Clara	CA	95054	408-734-8888	734-0788	696
Ambassador Dining Room 3811 Canterbury Rd *Web:* ambassadordining.com	Baltimore	MD	21218	443-386-7049		671
Ambassador Duty Free Store 707 Patricia St *Web:* www.ambassadordutyfree.com	Windsor	ON	N9B0B5	519-977-9100	977-7811	241
Ambassador Hotel 2308 W Wisconsin Ave *TF:* 877-935-2189 ■ *Web:* www.ambassadormilwaukee.com	Milwaukee	WI	53233	414-345-5000		379
Ambassador Hotel Inc 2040 Kuhio Ave *Web:* ambassadorwaikiki.com	Honolulu	HI	96815	808-941-7777		378
Ambassador Speakers Bureau PO Box 50358 *Web:* www.ambassadorspeakers.com	Nashville	TN	37205	615-370-4700	661-4344	708
Ambassador Travel 5236 Vogel Rd Ste B *TF:* 800-937-8688 ■ *Web:* www.myambassadortravel.com	Evansville	IN	47715	812-479-8687	474-3270	167-3
Ambeck Mortgage Assoc 4265 Spyres Way Ste A *TF:* 800-678-4480 ■ *Web:* ambeckmortgage.com	Modesto	CA	95356	209-521-4480		653
Ambella Home Collection Corporate Office 4910 Lakawana St *Web:* www.ambellahome.com	Dallas	TX	75247	214-631-8901		321
Amber Association Partners LLC 801 N Fairfax St Ste 211 *Web:* www.amberllc.com	Alexandria	VA	22314	703-299-0000	299-9233	47
Amber Diagnostics Inc 2180 Premier Row *Web:* www.amberusa.com	Orlando	FL	32809	407-867-3965		475
Amber India Restaurant 377 Santana Row *Web:* www.amber-india.com	San Jose	CA	95128	408-248-5400		671
Amber Lotus Publishing PO Box 11329 *TF:* 800-326-2375 ■ *Web:* www.amberlotus.com	Portland	OR	97211	503-284-6400	284-6417	130
Amber Network PO Box 1125 *Web:* www.avivconsulting.com	Woodinville	WA	98072	425-415-6155		271
Amber Precision Instruments Inc 746 San Aleso Ave *Web:* www.amberpi.com	Sunnyvale	CA	94085	408-752-0199		407
Amber Resources LLC 1543 W 16th St *Web:* amberresources.com	Long Beach	CA	90813	562-432-3946		579
Amber Rose 1400 Valley St *Web:* www.theamberrose.com	Dayton	OH	45404	937-228-2511		671
Amber Science Inc 277 Blair Blvd *Web:* www.conductivity-meters.com	Eugene	OR	97402	541-345-6877	345-6277	419
Amber Waves Inc 11 S Ave W *Web:* amberwavesinc.com	Richardton	ND	58652	701-974-4230		77
Amber-Allen Publishing Inc PO Box 6657 *TF:* 800-624-8855 ■ *Web:* www.amberallen.com	San Rafael	CA	94903	415-499-4657	499-3174	637-2
Amberton University 1700 Eastgate Dr *Web:* www.amberton.edu	Garland	TX	75041	972-279-6511	279-9773	166
AmberWave Inc 45 NW Dr Ste 1 *Web:* www.amberwave.com	Salem	NH	03079	603-324-0358		180
AMBEST Inc 5115 Maryland Way *TF:* 800-910-7220 ■ *Web:* am-best.com	Brentwood	TN	37027	615-371-5187		324

Phone | Fax | Class

Ambiance Day Spa & Salon
1777 Monte Vista Ave . . . Claremont CA 91711 — 909-625-5535 — 77
Web: www.claremontclub.com

Ambiance Models & Talent Inc
6918 Shallowford Rd Ste 300 . . . Chattanooga TN 37421 — 423-265-2121 — 507
Web: ambiancemodels.com

Ambient Consulting
10900 Wayzata Blvd Ste 850 . . . Minnetonka MN 55305 — 763-582-9000 — 582-7901 — 225
Web: ambientconsulting.com

Ambient Group Inc 470 7th Ave 12th Fl . . . New York NY 10018 — 212-944-4615 — 944-4618 — 194
Web: www.ambientgroup.com

Ambiente Wine Importing Company Inc
2314 Rutland Dr Ste 205 . . . Austin TX 78758 — 512-835-2299 — 80-3
Web: www.ambientewine.com

AmbioPharm Inc (API)
1024 Dittman Ct . . . North Augusta SC 29842 — 803-442-7590 — 41
Web: www.ambiopharm.com

Ambis Home Health Care LLC
7552 S 84th St . . . La Vista NE 68128 — 402-934-3441 — 991-0674 — 363
Web: www.ambishomehealthcare.com

Ambit Consulting Inc
1200 W 73rd Ave Ste 1220 . . . Vancouver BC V6P6G5 — 604-662-3130 — 194
Web: www.ambit-consulting.com

Ambit Energy LP 1801 N Lamar St Ste 200 . . . Dallas TX 75202 — 877-282-6248 — 787
TF: 877-282-6248 ■ *Web:* www.ambitenergy.com

Ambit Pacific Recycling Inc
16228 S Figueroa St . . . Gardena CA 90248 — 310-538-3798 — 660
Web: www.ambitpacific.com

Ambius Plants 485 E Half Day Rd . . . Buffalo Grove IL 60089 — 800-581-9946 — 104
TF: 800-581-9946 ■ *Web:* ambius.com

Ambix Manufacturing Inc
71 Hobbs St Ste 104 . . . Conway NH 03818 — 603-452-5247 — 393
Web: ambixllc.com

Amboy National Bank
3590 US Hwy 9 S . . . Old Bridge NJ 08857 — 732-591-8700 — 591-0705 — 70
TF: 800-942-6269 ■ *Web:* www.amboybank.com

Ambra Italian Kitchen + Bar
3799 Las Vegas Blvd S . . . Las Vegas NV 89109 — 702-891-7600 — 671
Web: www.mgmgrand.com

Ambric Technology Corp 100 Pine St . . . Darby PA 19023 — 215-928-8930 — 261
Web: ambrictech.com

Ambrico & Company PA
425 W Colonial Dr Ste 305 . . . Orlando FL 32804 — 407-316-8900 — 2

Ambriola Company Inc
7 Patton Dr . . . West Caldwell NJ 07006 — 800-962-8224 — 297-4
TF: 800-962-8224 ■ *Web:* www.ambriola.com

Ambrogi Law Office 722 Pine St . . . Manchester NH 03104 — 603-782-3021 — 41
Web: ambrogilawoffice.com

Ambrose & Grant Insurance Agency
1500 Providence Hwy Ste 24B . . . Norwood MA 02062 — 781-762-2300 — 762-5844 — 390
Web: ambrosegrant.com

Ambrose Engineering Inc
W66n215 Commerce Ct . . . Cedarburg WI 53012 — 262-377-7602 — 261
Web: www.ambroseengineering.com

Ambrose Printing Co
210 Cumberland Bend . . . Nashville TN 37228 — 615-256-1151 — 627
TF: 800-334-6524 ■ *Web:* www.ambroseprint.com

Ambrosia House Tropical Lodging
622 Fleming St . . . Key West FL 33040 — 305-296-9838 — 296-2425 — 379
TF: 800-535-9838 ■ *Web:* www.ambrosiakeywest.com

Ambrosia Restaurant 174 E Broadway . . . Eugene OR 97401 — 541-342-4141 — 671
Web: www.ambrosiarestaurant.com

Ambrx Inc 10975 N Torrey Pines Rd . . . La Jolla CA 92037 — 858-875-2400 — 238
Web: ambrx.com

Ambry 3016 E Commercial Blvd . . . Fort Lauderdale FL 33308 — 954-771-7342 — 671
Web: www.ambryrestaurant.net

AMBS 3003 Benham Ave . . . Elkhart IN 46517 — 574-295-3726 — 167-3
TF: 800-964-2627 ■ *Web:* www.ambs.edu

Ambulatory Infusion Care Inc
121 E Broadway St Ste C . . . Alma MI 48801 — 989-772-7770 — 772-7490 — 363
TF: 800-367-4879 ■ *Web:* www.ambulatoryinfusioncare.com

Ambush Boarding Co
1690 Roberts Blvd NW Ste 105 . . . Kennesaw GA 30144 — 770-420-9111 — 711
TF: 800-408-9945 ■ *Web:* www.ambushboardco.com

AMC (Augusta Medical Ctr)
78 Medical Center Dr PO Box 1000 . . . Fishersville VA 22939 — 540-932-4000 — 374-3
TF: 800-932-0262 ■ *Web:* www.augustahealth.com

AMC (Appalachian Mountain Club) 5 Joy St . . . Boston MA 02108 — 617-523-0655 — 523-0722 — 48-13
TF: 800-262-4455 ■ *Web:* www.outdoors.org

AMC (AMC Global) 721 Arbor Way Ste 190 . . . Blue Bell PA 19422 — 610-238-9200 — 466
Web: amcglobal.com

AMC (Alan McIlvain Co) 501 Market St . . . Marcus Hook PA 19061 — 610-485-6600 — 485-0471 — 191-3
TF: 800-523-4231 ■ *Web:* www.alanmcilvain.com

AMC Global (AMC) 721 Arbor Way Ste 190 . . . Blue Bell PA 19422 — 610-238-9200 — 466
Web: amcglobal.com

AMC Institute 1940 Duke St Ste 200 . . . Alexandria VA 22314 — 571-527-3108 — 49-12
Web: amcinstitute.org

AMC Management Group Inc
34 Abby Rd . . . Farmingdale NJ 07727 — 732-938-5457 — 463
Web: www.amcinc.biz

AMC Network LLC
6366 Commerce Blvd Ste 334 . . . Rohnert Park CA 94928 — 707-829-9484 — 184
Web: www.amcnetwork.com

AMC Networks Inc 11 Penn Plz . . . New York NY 10001 — 212-324-8500 — 740
NASDAQ: AMCX ■ *Web:* www.amcnetworks.com

AMC Theatres 11500 Ash St . . . Leawood KS 66211 — 913-213-2000 — 573-4
TF: 877-262-4450 ■ *Web:* www.amctheatres.com

AMCA (Air Movement & Control Association International Inc)
30 W University Dr . . . Arlington Heights IL 60004 — 847-394-0150 — 253-0088 — 49-3
Web: www.amca.org

Amcep Metals 4484 E Tennessee St . . . Tucson AZ 85714 — 520-748-1900 — 748-2752 — 686
Web: www.amcepmetals.com

Amcest Nationwide Monitoring
1017 Walnut St . . . Roselle NJ 07203 — 800-631-7370 — 196
TF: 800-631-7370 ■ *Web:* www.amcest.com

AmChel Communications Inc
1703 Martinez Ln . . . Wylie TX 75098 — 972-442-1030 — 429-7985 — 480
TF: 866-388-6959 ■ *Web:* www.amchel.com

AMCHP (Association of Maternal & Child Health Programs)
2030 M St NW Ste 350 . . . Washington DC 20036 — 202-775-0436 — 478-5120 — 49-7
Web: www.amchp.org

AMCI 5353 Grosvenor Blvd . . . Los Angeles CA 90066 — 855-486-5527 — 7
TF: 855-486-5527 ■ *Web:* amciglobal.com

Amco Manufacturing Inc
800 S Indl Pky . . . Yazoo City MS 39194 — 662-746-4464 — 746-6825 — 273
TF: 800-748-9022 ■ *Web:* www.amcomfg.com

Amco Precision Tools Inc
921 Farmington Ave . . . Kensington CT 06037 — 860-828-5640 — 828-7727 — 250
Web: www.amcoprecision.com

Amcom Data Processing (ADP)
2 Annabel Ln . . . San Ramon CA 94583 — 925-355-1580 — 355-1582 — 180
Web: www.amcomtech.net

Amcom Software Inc
10400 Yellow Cir Dr . . . Eden Prairie MN 55343 — 952-230-5200 — 230-5510 — 178-7
TF: 800-852-8935 ■ *Web:* www.spok.com

AMCON Distributing Co 7405 Irvington Rd . . . Omaha NE 68122 — 402-331-3727 — 331-4834 — 756
NYSE: DIT ■ *TF:* 888-201-5997 ■ *Web:* www.amcon.com

Amcor Ltd 935 Technology Dr Ste 100 . . . Ann Arbor MI 48108 — 734-428-9741 — 546
Web: www.amcor.com

AMCP (Academy of Managed Care Pharmacy)
100 N Pitt St Ste 400 . . . Alexandria VA 22314 — 703-683-8416 — 683-8417 — 49-8
TF: 800-827-2627 ■ *Web:* www.amcp.org

AMCS Corp 135 US Hwy 202-206 Ste 12 . . . Bedminster NJ 07921 — 908-719-6560 — 719-6565 — 261
Web: www.amcscorp.com

AMD Industries Inc 4620 W 19th St . . . Cicero IL 60804 — 708-863-8900 — 233
TF: 800-367-9999 ■ *Web:* www.amdpop.com

AMDA (American Medical Directors Assn)
10500 Little Patuxent Pkwy Ste 210 . . . Columbia MD 21044 — 410-740-9743 — 740-4572 — 49-8
TF: 800-876-2632 ■ *Web:* paltc.org

Amdocs Ltd
1390 Timberlake Manor Pkwy . . . Chesterfield MO 63017 — 314-212-7000 — 212-7500 — 178-10
NYSE: DOX ■ *Web:* www.amdocs.com

AME (Applied Molecular Evolution Inc)
10300 Campus Point Dr Ste 200 . . . San Diego CA 92121 — 858-597-4990 — 85

AME (Association for Manufacturing Excellence)
3701 W Algonquin Rd Ste 225 . . . Rolling Meadows IL 60008 — 224-232-5980 — 232-5981 — 49-12
Web: www.ame.org

AME Inc 2467 Coltharp Rd PO Box 909 . . . Fort Mill SC 29716 — 803-548-7766 — 548-7448 — 188-6
TF: 800-849-7766 ■ *Web:* www.ameonline.com

AME Label Corp 25155 W Ave Stanford . . . Valencia CA 91355 — 661-257-2200 — 257-7981 — 413
TF: 866-278-9268 ■ *Web:* www.amelabel.com

AME Software Products Inc
205 W 5th Ave Ste 101 . . . Escondido CA 92025 — 760-738-3720 — 738-0834 — 178-1
TF: 800-263-9455 ■ *Web:* amesoftware.com

Amec Foster Wheeler
1002 Walnut St Ste 200 . . . Boulder CO 80302 — 303-443-7839 — 225
Web: www.amecfw.com

AMECO (American Equipment Co)
4775 Technology Way Ste 208 . . . Boca Raton FL 33431 — 561-997-2080 — 997-2110 — 770
Web: www.ameco.net

Amedisys Inc
3854 American Way Ste A . . . Baton Rouge LA 70816 — 225-292-2031 — 352
NASDAQ: AMED ■ *TF:* 800-464-0020 ■ *Web:* www.amedisys.com

Ameduri, Galante & Friscia LLP
471 Bement Ave . . . Staten Island NY 10310 — 347-682-2351 — 273-5219* — 41
**Fax Area Code:* 718 ■ *Web:* sipersonalinjury.com

Amegy Bancorp Inc
4203 Yoakum Blvd Ste 310 . . . Houston TX 77027 — 713-235-8810 — 360-2
Web: amegybank.com

Amegy Bank of Texas
4400 Post Oak Pkwy . . . Houston TX 77027 — 713-235-8800 — 70
TF: 800-287-0301 ■ *Web:* www.amegybank.com

Amel's Restaurant 435 McNeilly Rd . . . Pittsburgh PA 15226 — 412-563-3466 — 671
Web: www.amelsrestaurantpgh.com

Amelia County
16360 Dunn St Ste 101 . . . Amelia Court House VA 23002 — 804-561-3039 — 561-6039 — 338
Web: www.ameliacova.com

Amelia Island Book Festival
PO Box 15286 . . . Fernandina Beach FL 32035 — 904-624-1665 — 281
Web: www.ameliaislandbookfestival.org

Amelia Island Museum of History
233 S Third St . . . Fernandina Beach FL 32034 — 904-261-7378 — 261-9701 — 520
Web: ameliamuseum.org

Amelia Island Plantation
39 Beach Lagoon Rd . . . Amelia Island FL 32034 — 904-261-6161 — 669
TF: 800-834-4900 ■ *Web:* www.villasofameliaisland.com

Amelia Island State Park
12157 Heckscher Dr . . . Jacksonville FL 32226 — 904-251-2320 — 565
Web: www.floridastateparks.org

Amelia Island-Fernandina Beach-Yulee Chamber of Commerce
961687 Gateway Blvd Ste 101-G . . . Fernandina Beach FL 32034 — 904-261-3248 — 261-6997 — 139
Web: islandchamber.com

Amelia's 235 S Main St Ste 107 . . . Gainesville FL 32601 — 352-373-1919 — 671
Web: www.ameliasgainesville.com

Amelia's Bistro 187 Warren St . . . Jersey City NJ 07302 — 201-332-2200 — 671
Web: ameliasbistro.com

Amelicor 1525 W 820 N . . . Provo UT 84601 — 800-992-1344 — 374-5316* — 178-11
**Fax Area Code:* 801 ■ *TF:* 800-992-1344 ■ *Web:* www.amelicor.com

Amer Technology Inc
5717 Northwest Pkwy . . . San Antonio TX 78249 — 210-256-7070 — 177
Web: www.amersolutions.com

Amerant Bank NA PO Box 226555 . . . Miami FL 33222 — 305-629-1212 — 460-4010 — 360-2
TF: 888-629-0810 ■ *Web:* www.amerantbank.com

AmerCable Inc 350 Bailey Rd . . . El Dorado AR 71730 — 870-862-4919 — 862-9613 — 813
TF: 800-643-1516 ■ *Web:* www.amercable.com

Amerco 5555 Kietzke Ln Ste 100 . . . Reno NV 89502 — 602-263-6601 — 185
NASDAQ: UHAL ■ *Web:* www.amerco.com

Amerco Real Estate Co
2727 N Central Ave Ste 500 . . . Phoenix AZ 85004 — 602-263-6555 — 653
Web: www.amercorealestate.com

Ameren Corp 1901 Chouteau Ave . . . Saint Louis MO 63103 — 314-621-3222 — 360-5
NYSE: AEE ■ *Web:* www.ameren.com

Amerequip Corp 1015 Calumet Ave . . . Kiel WI 53042 — 920-894-2000 — 894-3799 — 273
Web: www.amerequip.com

Ameresco Inc 111 Speen St Ste 410 . . . Framingham MA 01701 — 508-661-2200 — 661-2201 — 192
TF: 866-263-7372 ■ *Web:* www.ameresco.com

Phone | Fax | Class

Amerex Corp 7595 Gadsden Hwy .... Trussville AL 35173 205-655-3271 678
TF: 800-654-5980 ■ *Web:* www.amerex-fire.com

Amerex Energy Services LLC
1 Sugar Creek Center Blvd Ste 700 .... Sugar Land TX 77478 281-340-5200 340-5266 194
Web: www.amerexenergy.com

Amerge Corp PO Box 161033 .... Cleveland OH 44116 216-574-2602 928-6008 41

Amergraph Corp 520 Lafeyette Rd Rte 15 .... Sparta NJ 07871 973-383-8700 383-9225 628
Web: amergraph.com

Americ Machinery Corp 820 Walnut Ave .... Vallejo CA 94592 253-236-8555 111
Web: www.americmachinery.com

America Chung Nam Inc
1163 Fairway Dr .... City of Industry CA 91789 909-839-8383 553
Web: www.acni.net

America First Credit Union
1344 W 4675 S .... Ogden UT 84405 801-627-0900 778-8079 219
TF: 800-999-3961 ■ *Web:* www.americafirst.com

America Hears Inc 806 Beaver St .... Bristol PA 19007 215-788-0330 281-7230* 477
**Fax Area Code:* 888 ■ *TF:* 888-573-3237 ■ *Web:* www.americahears.com

America Law Group
2800 N Parham Rd Ste 100 .... Henrico VA 23294 804-308-0051 41
Web: americalawgroup.com

America Online Inc (AOL) 22000 AOL Way .... Dulles VA 20166 703-265-2100 398
Web: www.aol.com

America Outdoors 5816 Kingston Pk .... Knoxville TN 37919 800-524-4814 558-3598* 48-23
**Fax Area Code:* 865 ■ *TF:* 800-524-4814 ■ *Web:* www.americaoutdoors.org

America The Beautiful Dreamer Inc
9700 NE 126th Ave .... Vancouver WA 98682 360-816-0167 321
Web: www.atbd.com

America's ATM
5846 S Flamingo Rd Ste 256 .... Cooper City FL 33330 954-414-0341 717-5156 569
TF: 877-478-1104 ■ *Web:* americanatm.com

America's Blood Centers (ABC)
725 15th St NW Ste 700 .... Washington DC 20005 202-393-5725 393-1282 49-8
TF: 888-872-5663 ■ *Web:* www.americasblood.org

America's Business Software
PO Box 505 .... Carmichael CA 95609 916-483-7266 483-7453 177
Web: www.abs-mist.com

America's Call Center Inc
7901 Baymeadows Way Ste 14 .... Jacksonville FL 32256 904-224-2000 737
TF: 800-598-2580 ■ *Web:* webcallusa.com

America's Car-Mart Inc
802 Southeast Plaza Ave Ste 200 .... Bentonville AR 72712 866-819-9944 273-7556* 57
NASDAQ: CRMT ■ **Fax Area Code:* 479 ■ *TF:* 866-819-9944 ■ *Web:* www.car-mart.com

America's Choice Home Loans LP
8584 Katy Fwy Ste 200 .... Houston TX 77024 713-821-9700 652
Web: www.wechooseamerica.com

America's Ctr Convention Ctr
701 Convention Plz Ste 300 .... Saint Louis MO 63101 314-342-5036 342-5040 205
TF: 800-325-7962 ■ *Web:* explorestlouis.com

America's Essential Hospitals
401 Ninth St NW Ste 900 .... Washington DC 20004 202-585-0100 585-0101 49-8
Web: essentialhospitals.org

America's Health Insurance Plans (AHIP)
601 Pennsylvania Ave NW Ste 500 .... Washington DC 20004 202-778-3200 331-7487 49-9
TF: 800-509-4422 ■ *Web:* www.ahip.org

America's HealthCare at Home Inc
1510 Caton Center Dr .... Baltimore MD 21227 410-737-9200 737-9292 363
TF: 800-545-6026 ■ *Web:* www.ahcah.com

America's Packard Museum
420 S Ludlow St .... Dayton OH 45402 937-226-1710 520
Web: www.americaspackardmuseum.org

America's PPO 7201 W 78 St Ste 100 .... Minneapolis MN 55439 952-896-1200 390
TF: 800-948-9451 ■ *Web:* www.americasppo.com

America's Promise - the Alliance for Youth
1110 Vermont Ave Ste 900 .... Washington DC 20005 202-657-0600 657-0601 48-6
Web: www.americaspromise.org

America's Public Television Stations (APTS)
2100 Crystal Dr Ste 700 .... Arlington VA 22202 202-654-4200 654-4236 49-14
Web: apts.org

America's Second Harvest
35 E Wacker Dr Ste 2000 .... Chicago IL 60601 800-771-2303 263-5626* 48-5
**Fax Area Code:* 312 ■ *TF:* 800-771-2303 ■ *Web:* www.feedingamerica.org

America's Training Ctr
919 Reserve Dr .... Roseville CA 95678 916-927-7299 834-3577* 167-3
**Fax Area Code:* 773 ■ *TF:* 800-669-4799 ■ *Web:* learning.americastrainingcenteronline.com

Americad Technology Corp
700 Pleasant St .... Norwood MA 02062 781-551-8220 551-8222 604
Web: www.americadtech.com

America-Israel Chamber of Commerce - Chicago
222 W Merchandise Mart Plz Ste 1212 c/o 1871 ... Chicago IL 60654 312-858-7174 138
Web: americaisrael.org

Americall 1502 Tacoma Ave S .... Tacoma WA 98402 360-252-1111 41
TF: 800-964-3556 ■ *Web:* www.americall.com

American Academy for Cerebral Palsy & Developmental Medicine (AACPDM)
555 E Wells St Ste 1100 .... Milwaukee WI 53202 414-918-3014 276-2146 48-17
Web: www.aacpdm.org

American Academy McAllister Institute of Funeral Service
619 W 54th St 2nd Fl .... New York NY 10019 212-757-1190 765-5923 800
TF: 866-932-2264 ■ *Web:* www.funeraleducation.org

American Academy of Actuaries
1850 M St NW Ste 300 .... Washington DC 20036 202-223-8196 872-1948 49-9
Web: www.actuary.org

American Academy of Addiction Psychiatry (AAAP)
400 Massasoit Ave 2nd Fl Ste 307 .... East Providence RI 02914 401-524-3076 272-0922 49-15
TF: 800-263-6317 ■ *Web:* www.aaap.org

American Academy of Allergy Asthma & Immunology (AAAAI)
555 E Wells St Ste 1100 .... Milwaukee WI 53202 414-272-6071 49-8
Web: www.aaaai.org

American Academy of Art
332 S Michigan Ave .... Chicago IL 60604 312-461-0600 294-9570 164
TF: 888-461-0600 ■ *Web:* www.aaart.edu

American Academy of Arts & Letters
633 W 155th St .... New York NY 10032 212-368-5900 48-4
Web: artsandletters.org

American Academy of Arts & Sciences
136 Irving St .... Cambridge MA 02138 617-576-5000 576-5050 48-4
Web: www.amacad.org

Phone | Fax | Class

American Academy of Audiology (AAA)
11730 Plaza America Dr Ste 300 .... Reston VA 20190 703-226-1032 790-8631 49-8
TF: 800-222-2336 ■ *Web:* audiology.org

American Academy of Child & Adolescent Psychiatry (AACAP)
3615 Wisconsin Ave NW .... Washington DC 20016 202-966-7300 966-2891 49-15
TF: 800-333-7636 ■ *Web:* www.aacap.org

American Academy of Cosmetic Dentistry (AACD)
402 W Wilson St .... Madison WI 53703 608-222-8583 222-9540 49-8
TF: 800-543-9220 ■ *Web:* www.aacd.com

American Academy of Cosmetic Surgery (AACS)
225 W Wacker Dr Ste 650 .... Chicago IL 60606 312-981-6760 265-2908 49-8
Web: www.cosmeticsurgery.org

American Academy of Dental Group Practice (AADGP)
27W525 High Lake Rd Unit 539 .... Winfield IL 60190 602-381-1185 49-8
Web: www.aadgp.org

American Academy of Dermatology (AAD)
9500 W Bryn Mawr Ave Ste 500 .... Rosemont IL 60018 888-462-3376 240-1859* 49-8
**Fax Area Code:* 847 ■ *TF:* 888-462-3376 ■ *Web:* www.aad.org

American Academy of Disability Evaluating Physicians (AADEP)
PO Box 1537 .... Elk Grove Village IL 60009 312-663-1171 663-1175 49-8
Web: www.iaime.org

American Academy of Dramatic Arts
120 Madison Ave .... New York NY 10016 800-463-8990 164
TF: 800-463-8990 ■ *Web:* www.aada.edu

American Academy of English
530 Golden Gate Ave .... San Francisco CA 94102 415-567-0189 567-1475 423
Web: www.aae.edu

American Academy of Environmental Engineers & Scientists
147 Old Solomons Island Rd Ste 303 .... Annapolis MD 21401 410-266-3311 266-7653 48-12
Web: www.aaees.org

American Academy of Facial Plastic & Reconstructive Surgery (AAFPRS)
310 S Henry St .... Alexandria VA 22314 703-299-9291 299-8898 49-8
Web: www.aafprs.org

American Academy of Family Physicians (AAFP)
11400 Tomahawk Creek Pkwy .... Leawood KS 66211 913-906-6000 906-6075 49-8
Web: www.aafp.org

American Academy of Hospice & Palliative Medicine (AAHPM)
4700 W Lake Ave Ste 300 .... Glenview IL 60025 847-375-4712 375-6475 49-8
Web: www.aahpm.org

American Academy of Medical Acupuncture (AAMA)
1970 E Grand Ave Ste 330 .... El Segundo CA 90245 310-379-8261 48-17
Web: www.medicalacupuncture.org

American Academy of Neurology (AAN)
1080 Montreal Ave .... Saint Paul MN 55116 651-695-1940 695-2791 49-8
TF: 800-879-1960 ■ *Web:* www.aan.com

American Academy of Nurse Practitioners (AANP)
PO Box 12846 .... Austin TX 78711 512-442-4262 442-6469 49-8
TF: 800-981-2491 ■ *Web:* www.aanp.org

American Academy of Ophthalmology
655 Beach St .... San Francisco CA 94109 415-561-8500 561-8575 49-8
TF: 866-561-8558 ■ *Web:* www.aao.org

American Academy of Optometry (AAO)
6110 Executive Blvd Ste 506 .... Rockville MD 20852 301-984-1441 984-4737 49-8
TF: 844-323-3937 ■ *Web:* www.aaopt.org

American Academy of Orthopaedic Surgeons (AAOS)
6300 N River Rd .... Rosemont IL 60018 847-823-7186 823-8125 49-8
TF: 800-346-2267 ■ *Web:* www.aaos.org

American Academy of Otolaryngology-Head & Neck Surgery (AAO-HNS)
1650 Diagonal Rd .... Alexandria VA 22314 703-836-4444 683-5100 49-8
TF: 877-722-6467 ■ *Web:* www.entnet.org

American Academy of Pas (AAPA)
2318 Mill Rd Ste 1300 .... Alexandria VA 22314 703-836-2272 684-1924 615
Web: www.aapa.org

American Academy of Pediatric Dentistry (AAPD)
211 E Chicago Ave Ste 1600 .... Chicago IL 60611 312-337-2169 337-6329 49-8
Web: www.aapd.org

American Academy of Pediatrics (AAP)
141 NW Pt Blvd .... Elk Grove Village IL 60007 847-434-4000 434-8000 49-8
TF: 800-433-9016 ■ *Web:* www.aap.org

American Academy of Periodontology (AAP)
737 N Michigan Ave Ste 800 .... Chicago IL 60611 312-787-5518 787-3670 49-8
TF: 800-282-4867 ■ *Web:* www.perio.org

American Academy of Physical Medicine & Rehabilitation (AAPM&R)
9700 W Bryn Mawr Ave Ste 200 .... Rosemont IL 60018 847-737-6000 754-4368 49-8
TF: 877-227-6799 ■ *Web:* www.aapmr.org

American Academy of Psychiatry & the Law (AAPL)
1 Regency Dr PO Box 30 .... Bloomfield CT 06002 860-242-5450 49-15
TF: 800-331-1389 ■ *Web:* www.aapl.org

American Academy of Religion (AAR)
825 Houston Mill Rd NE Ste 300 .... Atlanta GA 30329 404-727-3049 727-7959 48-20
Web: www.aarweb.org

American Academy of Sleep Medicine (AASM)
2510 N Frontage Rd .... Darien IL 60561 630-737-9700 737-9790 48-17
Web: aasm.org

American Acceptance Corp
26050 Mureau Rd .... Calabasas CA 91302 818-591-8715 390
Web: www.aacloans.com

American Accessories International Inc
550 W Main St Ste 825 .... Knoxville TN 37902 865-525-9100 361
Web: americanaccessoriesintl.com

American Accounts & Advisers
PO Box 250 .... Cottage Grove MN 55016 651-287-6100 287-6190 160
TF: 866-714-0489 ■ *Web:* amaccts.com

American Acctg Assn 5717 Bessie Dr .... Sarasota FL 34233 941-921-7747 923-4093 49-1
Web: aaahq.org

American Achievement Corp
7211 Cir S Rd .... Austin TX 78745 512-444-0571 409
TF: 800-531-5055 ■ *Web:* www.artcarved.com

American Acrylic Corp
400 Sheffield Ave .... West Babylon NY 11704 631-422-2200 422-2811 596
Web: www.americanacrylic.com

American Adoption Congress (AAC)
PO Box 42730 .... Washington DC 20015 202-483-3399 48-6
Web: americanadoptioncongress.org

American Adv Federation (AAF)
1101 Vermont Ave NW 5th Fl .... Washington DC 20005 202-898-0089 898-0159 49-18
Web: www.aaf.org

Name / Address	City	State	ZIP	Phone	Fax	Class
American Advisors Group 3800 W Chapman Ave 3rd Fl TF: 866-948-0003 ■ Web: www.americanadvisorsgroup.com	Orange	CA	92868	866-948-0003		215
American Aerogel 460 Buffalo Rd Ste 200 Web: www.aerosafeglobal.com	Rochester	NY	14611	585-328-2140	785-8624	480
American Aerospace Controls Inc 570 Smith St. TF: 888-873-8559 ■ Web: a-a-c.com	Farmingdale	NY	11735	631-694-5100		256
American Aerospace Technical Castings Inc 2950 W Catalina Dr *Fax Area Code: 866 ■ Web: www.aatcinc.com	Phoenix	AZ	85017	602-268-1467	792-2814*	306
American Aerospace Technologies INC 14 Union Hill Rd. Web: americanaerospace.com	Conshohocken	PA	19428	610-225-2604		256
American AgCredit (ACA) PO Box 1120 TF: 800-800-4865 ■ Web: www.agloan.com	Santa Rosa	CA	95402	707-545-1200		216
American Agencies Inc 21 E Ogden Ave Ste 201	Westmont	IL	60559	630-493-1776		391
American Agricultural Economics Assn (AAEA) 555 E Wells St Ste 1100 Web: www.aaea.org	Milwaukee	WI	53202	414-918-3190		48-2
American Agricultural Insurance Co 1501 E Woodfield Rd Ste 300 W. Web: www.aaic.com	Schaumburg	IL	60173	847-969-2900	969-2752	391-4
American Agriculturist 5227-B Baltimore Pk TF: 800-441-1410 ■ Web: www.americanagriculturist.com	Littlestown	PA	17340	717-359-0150	359-0250	457-1
American Air Charter Inc 577 Bell Ave TF: 888-532-2710 ■ Web: www.americanaircharter.com	Chesterfield	MO	63005	636-532-2707	532-1486	13
American Aircraft Products Inc 15411 S Broadway Web: www.americanaircraft.com	Gardena	CA	90248	310-532-7434	532-0758	697
American Airlines Arena 601 Biscayne Blvd TF: 877-432-8246 ■ Web: www.aaarena.com	Miami	FL	33132	786-777-1132	777-1600	720
American Airlines CR Smith Museum 4601 Hwy 360 at FAA Rd Web: www.crsmithmuseum.org	Fort Worth	TX	76155	817-967-1560	967-5737	520
American Airlines Ctr 2500 Victory Ave Web: www.americanairlinescenter.com	Dallas	TX	75219	214-222-3687		720
American Airlines Employees Federal Credit Union 4151 Amon Carter Blvd TF: 800-533-0035 ■ Web: www.aacreditunion.org	Fort Worth	TX	76155	817-952-4500		219
American Airlines Inc 4333 Amon Carter Blvd TF: 800-433-7300 ■ Web: www.americanairlines.in	Fort Worth	TX	76155	817-963-1234		25
American Alliance for Health Physical Education Recreation & Dance (AAH-PERD) 1900 Association Dr. Web: www.shapeamerica.org	Reston	VA	20191	703-476-3400	476-9527	48-22
American Alloy Fabrication Inc 2842 Jordan Ln NW Web: americanalloy.com	Huntsville	AL	35816	256-837-6369	837-6090	295
American Alpine Club 710 Tenth St Ste 15 Web: americanalpineclub.org	Golden	CO	80401	303-384-0112		434-3
American Aluminum Co (AMALCO) 230 Sheffield St Web: www.amalco.com	Mountainside	NJ	07092	908-233-3500	233-3241	482
American Aluminum Extrusion Company LLC 5253 McCurry Rd. TF: 877-896-2236 ■ Web: www.americanaluminum.com	Roscoe	IL	61073	815-525-3100	525-3101	492
American Amateur Baseball Congress (AABC) 100 W Broadway. Web: www.aabc.us	Farmington	NM	87401	505-327-3120		48-22
American Ambulance Service Inc 1 American Way TF: 888-489-4273 ■ Web: americanamb.com	Norwich	CT	06360	860-886-1463		30
American Amicable Life Insurance Co 425 Austin Ave PO Box 2549 Web: www.americanamicable.com	Waco	TX	76702	254-297-2777		391-2
American Amusement Machine Assn (AAMA) 450 E Higgins Rd Ste 201. Web: coin-op.org	Elk Grove Village	IL	60007	847-290-9171	290-9121	48-23
American Angler Sportfishing 1403 Scott St Web: www.americananglersportfishing.com	San Diego	CA	92106	619-223-5414		90
American Angus Assn (AAA) 3201 Frederick Ave. TF: 800-821-5478 ■ Web: www.angus.org	Saint Joseph	MO	64506	816-383-5100	233-9703	48-2
American Animal Hospital Assn (AAHA) 12575 W Bayaud Ave TF: 800-252-2242 ■ Web: www.aaha.org	Lakewood	CO	80228	303-986-2800	986-1700	48-3
American Animal Hospital PC 1202 Sussex Tpke Web: americananimalhospital.com	Randolph	NJ	07869	973-895-4999		794
American Anthropological Assn (AAA) 2300 Clarendon Blvd Ste 1301. Web: www.americananthro.org	Arlington	VA	22201	703-528-1902	528-3546	49-5
American Antiquarian Society (AAS) 185 Salisbury St. Web: www.americanantiquarian.org	Worcester	MA	01609	508-755-5221	754-9069	48-4
American Antique Mall 3130 E Grant Rd Web: www.americanantiquemall.com	Tucson	AZ	85716	520-326-3070		460
American Anti-Slavery Group, The 198 Tremont St. *Fax Area Code: 270 ■ TF: 800-884-0719 ■ Web: www.iabolish.org	Boston	MA	02116	617-426-8161	964-2716*	48-5
American Apparel & Footwear Assn (AAFA) 740 Sixth St NW 3rd & Fourth Fl TF: 800-520-2262 ■ Web: www.aafaglobal.org	Washington	DC	20001	202-853-9080		49-4
American Apparel LLC 747 Warehouse St. TF: 888-747-0070 ■ Web: www.americanapparel.com	Los Angeles	CA	90021	213-488-0226		155-12
American Arbitration Association Inc (AAA) 1633 Broadway 10th Fl. TF: 800-778-7879 ■ Web: www.adr.org	New York	NY	10019	212-716-5800		41
American Architectural Manufacturers Assn (AAMA) 1827 Walden Office Sq Ste 550 Web: aamanet.org	Schaumburg	IL	60173	847-303-5664	303-5774	49-3
American Art Clay Co (AMACO) 6060 Guion Rd TF: 800-374-1600 ■ Web: www.amaco.com	Indianapolis	IN	46254	317-244-6871	248-9300	43
American Artists Group Inc PO Box 49313 *Fax Area Code: 270 ■ Web: www.americanartistsgroup.com	Athens	GA	30604	706-227-0708	637-3105*	130
American Arts Alliance *Performing Arts Alliance* 1800 M St NW PO Box 33001 Web: www.theperformingartsalliance.org	Washington	DC	20033	202-207-3850		48-4
American Artstone Co 2025 N Broadway St TF: 800-967-2076 ■ Web: www.american-artstone.com	New Ulm	MN	56073	507-233-3700		183
American Asphalt Paving Co 500 Chase Rd Web: www.amerasphalt.com	Shavertown	PA	18708	570-696-1181	696-3486	46
American Assembly 475 Riverside Dr Ste 456 Web: americanassembly.org	New York	NY	10115	212-870-3500	870-3555	634
American Assets Inc 11455 El Camino Real Web: www.americanassetstrust.com	San Diego	CA	92130	858-350-2600	350-2620	655
American Association for Accreditation of Ambulatory Surgery Facilities Inc (AAAASF) 5101 Washington St Ste 2F PO Box 9500 TF: 888-545-5222 ■ Web: www.aaaasf.org	Gurnee	IL	60031	847-775-1985		48-1
American Association for Adult & Continuing Education (AAACE) 1827 Powers Ferry Rd Bldg 14 Ste 100 *Fax Area Code: 404 ■ Web: www.aaace.org	Atlanta	GA	30339	678-271-4319	393-9506*	49-5
American Association for Cancer Research (AACR) 615 Chestnut St 17th Fl TF: 866-423-3965 ■ Web: www.aacr.org	Philadelphia	PA	19106	215-440-9300		49-8
American Association for Clinical Chemistry Inc (AACC) 1850 K St NW Ste 625 TF: 800-892-1400 ■ Web: www.aacc.org	Washington	DC	20006	202-857-0717	887-5093	49-19
American Association for Geriatric Psychiatry (AAGP) 7910 Woodmont Ave Ste 1050. Web: www.aagponline.org	Bethesda	MD	20814	301-654-7850	654-4137	49-15
American Association for Homecare 241 18th St S Ste 500. TF: 866-289-0492 ■ Web: www.aahomecare.org	Arlington	VA	22202	202-372-0107	835-8306	49-8
American Association for Justice (AAJ) 777 Sixth St NW Ste 200 TF: 800-424-2725 ■ Web: www.justice.org	Washington	DC	20001	202-965-3500		49-10
American Association for Laboratory Accreditation (A2LA) 5202 Presidents Ct Ste 220 *Fax Area Code: 240 ■ Web: www.a2la.org	Frederick	MD	21703	301-644-3248	454-9449*	49-19
American Association for Laboratory Animal Science (AALAS) 9190 Crestwyn Hills Dr. Web: www.aalas.org	Memphis	TN	38125	901-754-8620	753-0046	49-19
American Association for Marriage & Family Therapy (AAMFT) 112 S Alfred St Web: www.aamft.org	Alexandria	VA	22314	703-838-9808	838-9805	48-6
American Association for Respiratory Care (AARC) 9425 N MacArthur Blvd Ste 100. Web: aarc.org	Irving	TX	75063	972-243-2272	484-2720	49-8
American Association for State & Local History (AASLH) 2021 21st Ave S Ste 320 Web: aaslh.org	Nashville	TN	37212	615-320-3203	327-9013	48-4
American Association for the Advancement of Science (AAAS) 1200 New York Ave NW Web: www.aaas.org	Washington	DC	20005	202-326-6400		49-19
American Association for the Study of Liver Diseases (AASLD) 1001 N Fairfax St 4th Fl Web: www.aasld.org	Alexandria	VA	22314	703-299-9766	299-9622	49-8
American Association for Thoracic Surgery (AATS) 800 Cummings Ctr Ste 350-V TF: 800-424-5249 ■ Web: aats.org	Beverly	MA	01915	978-252-2200	522-8469	49-8
American Association of Acupunture & Oriental Medicine (AAAOM) PO Box 162340 TF: 866-455-7999 ■ Web: www.aaaomonline.org	Sacramento	CA	95816	916-443-4770		48-17
American Association of Adv Agencies (AAAA) 1065 Avenue of the Americas 16th Fl Web: www.aaaa.org	New York	NY	10018	212-682-2500	682-8391	49-18
American Association of Airport Executives (AAAE) 601 Madison St Web: www.aaae.org	Alexandria	VA	22314	703-824-0500	820-1395	49-21
American Association of Bioanalysts (AAB) 906 Olive St Ste 1200. TF: 800-457-3332 ■ Web: www.aab.org	Saint Louis	MO	63101	314-241-1445	241-1449	49-8
American Association of Bovine Practitioners (AABP) 1130 E Main St Ste 302 Web: www.aabp.org	Ashland	OH	44805	419-496-0685	496-0697	48-2
American Association of Cereal Chemists Inc (AACC) 3340 Pilot Knob Rd Web: www.aaccnet.org	Saint Paul	MN	55121	651-454-7250	454-0766	49-6
American Association of Clinical Endocrinologists (AACE) 245 Riverside Ave Ste 200 TF: 800-393-2223 ■ Web: www.aace.com	Jacksonville	FL	32202	904-353-7878	353-8185	49-8
American Association of Colleges for Teacher Education (AACTE) 1307 New York Ave NW Ste 300. Web: www.aacte.org	Washington	DC	20005	202-293-2450	457-8095	49-5
American Association of Colleges of Nursing 655 K St Ste 750. Web: www.aacnnursing.org	Washington	DC	20036	202-887-6791	887-8476	48-1
American Association of Colleges of Osteopathic Medicine (AACOM) 7700 Old Georgetown Rd Ste 250. TF: 800-356-7836 ■ Web: www.aacom.org	Bethesda	MD	20814	301-968-4100	968-4101	49-8
American Association of Colleges of Podiatric Medicine (AACPM) 15850 Crabbs Branch Way Ste 320 Web: www.aacpm.org	Rockville	MD	20855	301-948-9760	948-1928	49-8
American Association of Collegiate Registrars & Admissions Officers (AACRAO) 1108 16th St NW Ste 400. TF: 800-222-4922 ■ Web: www.aacrao.org	Washington	DC	20036	202-293-9161	872-8857	49-5
American Association of Community Colleges (AACC) 1 Dupont Cir NW Ste 410. Web: www.aacc.nche.edu	Washington	DC	20036	202-728-0200	833-2467	49-5

	Phone	Fax	Class
American Association of Critical-Care Nurses (AACN) 101 Columbia............................Aliso Viejo CA 92656 *TF:* 800-809-2273 ■ *Web:* www.aacn.org	949-362-2000	362-2020	49-8
American Association of Crop Insurers (AACI) 1201 Pennsylvania Ave NW Ste 800..........Washington DC 20004 *Web:* www.aacinsurers.com	202-659-8201		49-9
American Association of Daily Money Managers (AADMM) 174 Crestview Dr ....Bellefonte PA 16823 **Fax Area Code:* 814 ■ *TF:* 877-326-5991 ■ *Web:* secure.aadmm.com	877-326-5991	355-2452*	49-2
American Association of Drugless Practitioners (AADP) 2200 Market St Ste 803 ....Galveston TX 77550 *TF:* 888-764-2237 ■ *Web:* www.aadp.net	409-621-2600		48-17
American Association of Endodontists (AAE) 211 E Chicago Ave Ste 1100 ....Chicago IL 60611 *TF:* 800-872-3636 ■ *Web:* www.aae.org	312-266-7255	266-9867	49-8
American Association of Engineering Societies (AAES) 1801 Alexander Bell Dr.........................Reston VA 20191 *TF:* 888-400-2237 ■ *Web:* www.aaes.org	202-296-2237	296-1151	49-19
American Association of Equine Practitioners (AAEP) 4075 Iron Works Pkwy ....Lexington KY 40511 *TF:* 800-443-0177 ■ *Web:* aaep.org	859-233-0147	233-1968	48-3
American Association of Exporters & Importers (AAEI) 1050 17th St NW Ste 810..................Washington DC 20036 *Web:* aaei.org	202-857-8009	857-7843	49-18
American Association of Family & Consumer Sciences (AAFCS) 400 N Columbus St Ste 202.................Alexandria VA 22314 *TF:* 800-424-8080 ■ *Web:* www.aafcs.org	703-706-4600	706-4663	49-5
American Association of Franchisees & Dealers (AAFD) PO Box 10158 ....Palm Desert CA 92255 **Fax Area Code:* 866 ■ *TF:* 800-733-9858 ■ *Web:* www.aafd.org	619-209-3775	855-1988*	49-18
American Association of Gynecological Laparoscopists (AAGL) 6757 Katella Ave.............................Cypress CA 90630 *TF:* 800-554-2245 ■ *Web:* www.aagl.org	714-503-6200	503-6201	49-8
American Association of Individual Investors (AAII) 625 N Michigan Ave Ste 1900 ....Chicago IL 60611 *TF:* 800-428-2244 ■ *Web:* www.aaii.com	312-280-0170	280-9883	49-2
American Association of Insurance Services Inc (AAIS) 701 Warrenville Rd Ste 100 ....Lisle IL 60532 *TF:* 800-564-2247 ■ *Web:* www.aaisonline.com	630-681-8347	681-8356	49-9
American Association of Integrated Healthcare Delivery Systems Inc (AAIHDS) 4435 Waterfront Dr Ste 101 .... Glen Allen VA 23060 *Web:* www.aaihds.org	804-747-5823	747-5316	49-8
American Association of Law Libraries (AALL) 219 S Dearborn St ....Chicago IL 60604 *Web:* www.aallnet.org	312-939-4764	431-1097	49-11
American Association of Medical Assistants (AAMA) 20 N Wacker Dr Ste 1575.....................Chicago IL 60606 *TF:* 800-228-2262 ■ *Web:* www.aama-ntl.org	312-899-1500	899-1259	49-8
American Association of Medical Review Officers (AAMRO) PO Box 12873 .... Research Triangle Park NC 27709 *TF:* 800-489-1839 ■ *Web:* www.aamro.com	919-489-5407	490-1010	49-8
American Association of Medical Society Executives (AAMSE) 1000 Westgate Dr Ste 252 .... Saint Paul MN 55114 *Web:* www.aamse.org	651-288-3432	290-2266	49-8
American Association of Motor Vehicle Administrators (AAMVA) 4301 Wilson Blvd Ste 400 ....Arlington VA 22203 *TF:* 800-221-9253 ■ *Web:* www.aamva.org	703-522-4200	522-1553	49-7
American Association of Museums (AAM) 1575 Eye St NW Ste 400...................Washington DC 20005 *TF:* 866-226-2150 ■ *Web:* www.aam-us.org	202-289-1818	289-6578	48-4
American Association of Naturopathic Physicians (AANP) 818 18th St Ste 250 ....Washington DC 20006 *TF:* 866-538-2267 ■ *Web:* www.naturopathic.org	202-237-8150	237-8152	48-17
American Association of Neurological Surgeons (AANS) 5550 Meadowbrook Dr................Rolling Meadows IL 60008 *TF:* 888-566-2267 ■ *Web:* www.aans.org	847-378-0500	378-0600	49-8
American Association of Neuromuscular & Electrodiagnostic Medicine (AANEM) 2621 Superior Dr NW.......................Rochester MN 55901 *TF:* 844-347-3277 ■ *Web:* www.aanem.org	507-288-0100	288-1225	49-8
American Association of Neuroscience Nurses (AANN) 4700 W Lake Ave ....Glenview IL 60025 *TF:* 888-557-2266 ■ *Web:* www.aann.org	847-375-4733	375-6430	49-8
American Association of Nurse Anesthetists (AANA) 222 S Prospect Ave........................Park Ridge IL 60068 *TF:* 855-526-2262 ■ *Web:* www.aana.com	847-692-7050	692-6968	49-8
American Association of Oral & Maxillofacial Surgeons (AAOMS) 9700 W Bryn Mawr Ave .... Rosemont IL 60018 *TF:* 800-822-6637 ■ *Web:* www.aaoms.org	847-678-6200	678-6286	49-8
American Association of Orthodontists (AAO) 401 N Lindbergh Blvd..................... Saint Louis MO 63141 *TF:* 800-424-2841 ■ *Web:* www.aaoinfo.org	314-993-1700		49-8
American Association of Petroleum Geologists (AAPG) 1444 S Boulder Ave PO Box 979 .... Tulsa OK 74119 *TF:* 800-364-2274 ■ *Web:* www.aapg.org	918-584-2555	560-2665	48-12
American Association of Pharmaceutical Scientists (AAPS) 2107 Wilson Blvd Ste 700 ....Arlington VA 22201 *TF:* 877-998-2277 ■ *Web:* www.aaps.org	703-243-2800	243-9650	49-19
American Association of Physician Specialists Inc (AAPS) 5550 W Executive Dr Ste 400................... Tampa FL 33609 *Web:* www.aapsus.org	813-433-2277	830-6599	49-8
American Association of Physics Teachers (AAPT) 1 Physics Ellipse .... College Park MD 20740 *TF:* 800-446-8923 ■ *Web:* www.aapt.org	301-209-3311	209-0845	49-5
American Association of Poison Control Centers (AAPCC) 3201 New Mexico Ave Ste 310.............Washington DC 20016 *TF:* 800-222-1222 ■ *Web:* www.aapcc.org	800-222-1222		49-8
American Association of Port Authorities (AAPA) 1010 Duke St ....Alexandria VA 22314 *Web:* www.aapa-ports.org	703-684-5700	684-6321	49-21
American Association of Preferred Provider Organizations (AAPPO) 222 S 1st St Ste 303........................Louisville KY 40202 *Web:* nasho.org	502-403-1122	403-1128	49-8
American Association of Professional Landmen (AAPL) 4100 Fossil Creek Blvd.....................Fort Worth TX 76137 *Web:* www.landman.org	817-847-7700	847-7704	48-12
American Association of School Administrators (AASA) 801 N Quincy St Ste 700 ....Arlington VA 22203 *TF:* 800-771-1162 ■ *Web:* www.aasa.org	703-528-0700	841-1543	49-5
American Association of State Colleges & Universities (AASCU) 1307 New York Ave NW 5th Fl ....Washington DC 20005 *TF:* 800-558-3417 ■ *Web:* www.aascu.org	202-293-7070	296-5819	49-5
American Association of State Highway & Transportation Officials (AASHTO) 555 12th Street NW Ste 1000...............Washington DC 20001 *Web:* www.transportation.org	202-624-5800	624-5806	49-7
American Association of Suicidology (AAS) 5221 Wisconsin Ave NW ....Washington DC 20015 *Web:* www.suicidology.org	202-237-2280	237-2282	48-17
American Association of Teachers of French (AATF) 302 N Granite St.............................Marion IL 62959 **Fax Area Code:* 815 ■ *Web:* www.frenchteachers.org	618-453-5731	310-5754*	49-5
American Association of Teachers of German (AATG) 112 Haddontowne Ct Ste 104.................Cherry Hill NJ 08034 *TF:* 800-835-6770 ■ *Web:* www.aatg.org	856-795-5553	795-9398	49-5
American Association of Teachers of Spanish & Portuguese (AATSP) 900 Ladd Rd.............................Walled Lake MI 48390 *Web:* www.aatsp.org	248-960-2180	960-9570	49-5
American Association of Textile Chemists & Colorists (AATCC) 1 Davis Dr PO Box 12215.......... Research Triangle Park NC 27709 *Web:* www.aatcc.org	919-549-8141	549-8933	49-13
American Association of Tissue Banks (AATB) 8200 Greensboro Dr Ste 320 .... McLean VA 22102 *Web:* www.aatb.org	703-827-9582	992-0504	49-8
American Association of University Professors (AAUP) 1133 Nineteenth St NW Ste 200............Washington DC 20036 *TF:* 800-424-2973 ■ *Web:* www.aaup.org	202-737-5900	737-5526	49-5
American Association of University Women (AAUW) 1310 L St NW Ste 1000 ....Washington DC 20036 *TF:* 800-326-2289 ■ *Web:* www.aauw.org	202-785-7700	872-1425	49-5
American Association of Variable Star Observers (AAVSO) 49 Bay State Rd ....Cambridge MA 02138 *Web:* www.aavso.org	617-354-0484	354-0665	49-19
American Association on Intellectual & Developmental Disabilities (AAIDD) 8403 Colesville Rd Ste 900 .... Silver Spring MD 20910 *TF:* 800-424-3688 ■ *Web:* aaidd.org	202-387-1968	387-2193	48-17
American Astronomical Society (AAS) 1667 K St NW Ste 800...................Washington DC 20006 *Web:* aas.org	202-328-2010	234-2560	49-19
American Athletic Inc (AAI) 200 American Ave..........................Jefferson IA 50129 *TF:* 800-247-3978 ■ *Web:* www.americanathletic.com	800-247-3978		346
American Augers Inc 135 US Rt 42.......... West Salem OH 44287 *TF:* 800-324-4930 ■ *Web:* www.americanaugers.com	419-869-7107	869-7727	57
American Autoimmune Related Disease Assn (AARDA) 22100 Gratiot Ave......................... Eastpointe MI 48021 *TF:* 800-598-4668 ■ *Web:* www.aarda.org	586-776-3900	776-3903	48-17
American Automated Engineering Inc 5382 Argosy Ave.................... Huntington Beach CA 92649 *Web:* www.aaeaerospace.com	714-898-9951		504
American Automatrix Inc 1 Technology Ln............................. Export PA 15632 *TF:* 877-226-7767 ■ *Web:* www.aamatrix.com	724-733-2000	327-6124	407
American Automobile Association Inc (AAA) 321 Whittington Pkwy.......................Louisville KY 40222 *Web:* www.aaa.com	502-425-7885		53
American Aviation 2495 Broad St ....Brooksville FL 34604 *Web:* www.americanaviation.com	352-796-5173	799-4681	63
American Baby Magazine 375 Lexington Ave ....New York NY 10017 *Web:* www.parents.com	212-499-2000		457-11
American Backflow Specialties 3940 Home Ave .... San Diego CA 92105 *TF:* 800-662-5356 ■ *Web:* americanbackflow.com	619-527-2525		612
American Bakers Association PAC 601 Pennsylvania Ave NW Ste 230...........Washington DC 20004 *Web:* www.americanbakers.org	202-789-0300	898-1164	615
American Baler Co 800 E Center St.............Bellevue OH 44811 *TF:* 800-843-7512 ■ *Web:* americanbaler.com	419-483-5790	483-3815	386
American Ballet Theatre (ABT) 890 Broadway 3rd Fl........................New York NY 10003 *Web:* www.abt.org	212-477-3030		573-1
American Bank 4029 W Tilghman St ....Allentown PA 18104	610-366-1800		70
American Bank & Trust Company Inc 1819 N Columbia St....................... Covington LA 70433 *Web:* americanbankandtrust.com	985-898-0206	809-9296	70
American Bank Ctr 1901 N Shoreline Blvd ....Corpus Christi TX 78401 *Web:* www.americanbankcenter.com	361-826-4700	826-4905	205
American Bank of Commerce 610 W 5th St....... Austin TX 78701 *Web:* www.theabcbank.com	512-391-5500		70
American Bankruptcy Institute (ABI) 66 Canal Center Plz Ste 600................. Alexandria VA 22314 *Web:* www.abi.org	703-739-0800	739-1060	49-10
American Baptist Churches USA PO Box 851 ....Valley Forge PA 19482 *TF:* 800-222-3872 ■ *Web:* www.abc-usa.org	610-768-2000	768-2275	48-20
American Baptist College 1800 Baptist World Center Dr................. Nashville TN 37207 *Web:* www.abcnash.edu	615-256-1463		161
American Baptist Seminary of the West 2606 Dwight Way ....Berkeley CA 94704 *Web:* www.absw.edu	510-841-1905	841-2446	167-3
American Bar Assn (ABA) 321 N Clark St........Chicago IL 60654 *TF:* 800-285-2221 ■ *Web:* www.americanbar.org	312-988-5000		49-10
American Bartending School 3310 W Cypress St Ste 203 .... Tampa FL 33607 *Web:* www.americanbartending.com	813-876-1616		685
American Baseball Coaches Assn (ABCA) 4101 Piedmont Pkwy .... Greensboro NC 27410 *Web:* www.abca.org	989-775-3300		48-22
American Battery 2800 SW 4th Ave Ste 20................Fort Lauderdale FL 33315 *Web:* www.americanbattery-deka.com	954-583-2470	583-6898	74
American Battle Monuments Commission Courthouse Plz II 2300 Clarendon Blvd Ste 500.................................Arlington VA 22201 *Web:* www.abmc.gov	703-696-6900	696-6666	340-20

Name	Address	City	State	ZIP	Phone	Fax	Class	Details
American Battlefield Trust *Civil War Trust, The*	1156 15th St NW Ste 900	Washington	DC	20005	202-367-1861	367-1865	48-5	*TF:* 888-606-1400 ■ *Web:* www.battlefields.org
American Behavioral Benefits Managers	2204 Lakeshore Dr Ste 135	Birmingham	AL	35209	205-871-7814	868-9600	462	*TF:* 800-925-5327 ■ *Web:* www.americanbehavioral.com
American Benefits Council	1501 M St NW Ste 600	Washington	DC	20005	202-289-6700	289-4582	49-2	*TF:* 877-829-5500 ■ *Web:* www.americanbenefitscouncil.org
American Beverage Assn	1275 Pennsylvania Ave NW Ste 1100	Washington	DC	20004	202-463-6732		49-6	*Web:* www.ameribev.org
American Beverage Licensees (ABL)	5101 River Rd Ste 108	Bethesda	MD	20816	301-656-1494	656-7539	49-6	*Web:* www.ablusa.org
American Bible Sales	900 S Euclid St	La Habra	CA	90631	800-535-5131		95	*TF:* 800-535-5131 ■ *Web:* www.americanbiblesales.com
American Bible Society	111 Eighth Ave	New York	NY	10023	212-408-1200	408-1512	637-3	*Web:* www.americanbible.org
American Bicycle Assn (ABA)	1645 W Sunrise Blvd	Gilbert	AZ	85233	480-961-1903	961-1842	48-22	*TF:* 866-650-4867 ■ *Web:* www.usabmx.com
American Biltrite Inc	57 River St	Wellesley	MA	02481	781-237-6655	237-6880	291	*OTC:* ABLT ■ *Web:* www.ambilt.com
American Bin & Conveyor Inc	221 Front St	Burlington	WI	53105	262-763-0123		492	*TF:* 800-763-0125 ■ *Web:* www.americanconveyor.com
American Bio Medica Corp (ABMC)	122 Smith Rd	Kinderhook	NY	12106	518-758-8158	758-8172	85	*OTC:* ABMC ■ *TF:* 800-227-1243 ■ *Web:* www.abmc.com
American Bio-Clinical Laboratories	2730 N Main St	Los Angeles	CA	90031	323-222-6688	222-3388	418	*TF:* 800-262-1688 ■ *Web:* www.abclab.com
American Biodiesel Inc	PO Box 23-4249	Encinitas	CA	92023	760-942-9306		579	*Web:* www.communityfuels.com
American Biosurgical	1850-B Beaver Ridge Cir	Norcross	GA	30071	781-799-3613		476	*Web:* www.americanbiosurgical.com
American Blues Network	PO Box 6216	Gulfport	MS	39506	228-896-5307	896-5703	647	*TF:* 800-896-5307 ■ *Web:* www.americanbluesnetwork.com
American BOA Inc	1420 Redi Rd	Cumming	GA	30040	770-889-9400		480	*Web:* www.americanboa.com
American Board of Internal Medicine (ABIM)	510 Walnut St Ste 1700	Philadelphia	PA	19106	215-446-3590		48-1	*TF:* 800-441-2246 ■ *Web:* www.abim.org
American Board of Medical Specialties (ABMS)	353 N Clark St Ste 1400	Chicago	IL	60654	312-436-2600		48-1	*Web:* www.abms.org
American Boat & Yacht Council Inc (ABYC)	613 Third St Ste 10	Annapolis	MD	21403	410-990-4460	990-4466	49-21	*Web:* www.abycinc.org
American Boiler Manufacturers Assn (ABMA)	8221 Old Courthouse Rd Ste 380	Vienna	VA	22182	703-356-7172		49-13	*TF:* 800-227-1966 ■ *Web:* www.abma.com
American Bolt & Screw Manufacturing Corp	14650 Miller Ave Ste 200	Fontana	CA	92336	909-390-0522		350	*TF:* 800-325-0844 ■ *Web:* www.absfasteners.com
American Bonanza Society (ABS)	3595 N Webb Rd Ste 200	Wichita	KS	67226	316-945-1700	945-1710	48-18	*Web:* www.bonanza.org
American Booksellers Assn (ABA)	333 Westchester Ave Ste S202	White Plains	NY	10604	800-637-0037	417-4013*	49-18	*Fax Area Code: 914 ■ *TF:* 800-637-0037 ■ *Web:* www.bookweb.org
American Borate Corp	5700 Cleveland St Ste 350	Virginia Beach	VA	23462	757-490-2242	490-1548	503-1	*TF:* 800-486-1072 ■ *Web:* www.americanborate.com
American Botanical Council	6200 Manor Rd	Austin	TX	78723	512-926-4900	926-2345	48-17	*TF:* 800-373-7105 ■ *Web:* www.abc.herbalgram.org
American Brain Tumor Assn (ABTA)	8550 W Bryn Mawr Ave Ste 550	Chicago	IL	60631	847-827-9910	827-9918	48-17	*TF:* 800-886-2282 ■ *Web:* www.abta.org
American Brass Manufacturing Co	5000 Superior Ave	Cleveland	OH	44103	216-431-6565	431-9420	609	*TF:* 800-431-6440 ■ *Web:* www.rvfaucets.com
American Bridge Co	1000 American Bridge Way	Coraopolis	PA	15108	412-631-1000	631-2000	188-4	*Web:* www.americanbridge.net
American Bright Optoelectronics Corp	13815-C Magnolia Ave	Chino	CA	91710	909-628-5050		253	*Web:* www.americanbrightled.com
American Broach & Machine Co	575 S Mansfield	Ypsilanti	MI	48197	734-961-0300	961-9999	493	*Web:* www.americanbroach.com
American Broadband	1605 Washington St	Blair	NE	68008	402-426-6200	426-6300	224	*TF:* 888-262-2661 ■ *Web:* www.abbnebraska.com
American Broadband Communications LLC	153 W Dave Dugas Rd	Sulphur	LA	70665	337-583-2111		387	*Web:* www.americanbroadband.com
American Broadcasting School - Oklahoma City Campus	4511 SE 29th St	Oklahoma City	OK	73115	405-672-6511		685	*Web:* www.radioschool.com
American Brokerage Services Inc	803 E Willow Grove Ave	Wyndmoor	PA	19038	215-233-9410	420-1034*	390	*Fax Area Code: 267 ■ *TF:* 866-233-2854 ■ *Web:* absgo.com
American Brush Company Inc	300 Industrial Blvd	Claremont	NH	03743	603-542-9951		103	*Web:* www.americanbrush.com
American Building Supply Inc	8360 Elder Creek Rd	Sacramento	CA	95828	916-503-4100		499	*Web:* www.abs-abs.com
American Buildings Co	1150 State Docks Rd	Eufaula	AL	36027	334-687-2032	688-2261	105	*TF:* 888 307 4338 ■ *Web:* www.americanbuildings.com
American Bullion Inc	12301 Wilshire Blvd Ste 650	Los Angeles	CA	90025	800-465-3472		792	*TF:* 800-326-9598 ■ *Web:* www.americanbullion.com
American Bureau of Shipping (ABS)	16855 Northchase Dr	Houston	TX	77060	281-877-6000	877-5803	49-21	*Web:* ww2.eagle.org
American Burn Assn (ABA)	311 S Wacker Dr Ste 4150	Chicago	IL	60606	312-642-9260	642-9130	49-8	*Web:* ameriburn.org
American Bus Assn	111 K St NE 9th Fl	Washington	DC	20002	202-842-1645	842-0850	615	*TF:* 800-283-2877 ■ *Web:* www.buses.org
American Business	45 W 45th St 15th Fl	New York	NY	10036	212-359-4400	944-1281	796	*Web:* www.americanbusiness.com
American Business Conference (ABC)	1828 L St NW Ste 280	Washington	DC	20036	202-822-9300	467-4070	49-12	*Web:* www.americanbusinessconference.org
American Business Systems Inc	315 Littleton Rd	Chelmsford	MA	01824	800-356-4034	250-8027*	178-1	*Fax Area Code: 978 ■ *TF:* 800-356-4034 ■ *Web:* www.abs-software.com
American Business Women's Assn (ABWA)	11050 Roe Ave Ste 200	Overland Park	KS	66211	800-228-0007	660-0101*	49-12	*Fax Area Code: 913 ■ *TF:* 800-228-0007 ■ *Web:* www.abwa.org
American Cabaret Theatre	924 N Pennsylvania St Ste B	Indianapolis	IN	46204	317-275-1169		572	*Web:* www.thecabaret.org
American Cable Company Inc	231 E Luzerne St	Philadelphia	PA	19124	215-456-0700	456-1330	116	*Web:* www.americancableco.com
American Camp Assn (ACA)	5000 State Rd 67 N	Martinsville	IN	46151	765-342-8456	342-2065	48-23	*TF:* 800-428-2267 ■ *Web:* www.acacamps.org
American Campus Communities Inc	12700 Hill Country Blvd Ste T-200	Austin	TX	78738	512-732-1000	732-2450	654	*NYSE:* ACC ■ *Web:* www.americancampus.com
American Cancer Society (ACS)	250 William St NW	Atlanta	GA	30303	404-816-7800		48-17	*TF:* 800-227-2345 ■ *Web:* www.cancer.org
American Canoe Assn (ACA)	503 Sophia St Ste 100	Fredericksburg	VA	22401	540-907-4460	229-3792*	48-22	*Fax Area Code: 888 ■ *Web:* www.americancanoe.org
American Capital Group Inc	23382 Mill Creek Dr Ste 115	Laguna Hills	CA	92653	949-271-5800		792	*TF:* 877-814-6871 ■ *Web:* www.acgcapital.com
American Capital Partners LLC	205 Oser Ave	Hauppauge	NY	11788	631-851-0918		401	*TF:* 800-393-0493 ■ *Web:* www.americancapitalpartners.com
American Career College Inc	151 Innovation Dr	Irvine	CA	92617	877-832-0790		166	*TF:* 877-832-0790 ■ *Web:* americancareercollege.edu
American Cargo Express Inc	2345 Vauxhall Rd	Union	NJ	07083	908-351-3400	289-2490*	449	*Fax Area Code: 980 ■ *Web:* www.americancargoexpress.com
American Carrier Equipment Trailer Sales LLC	2285 E Date Ave	Fresno	CA	93706	559-442-1500		779	*TF:* 800-344-2174 ■ *Web:* www.americancarrierequipment.com
American Cast Iron Pipe Co (ACIPCO)	1501 31st Ave N	Birmingham	AL	35207	205-325-7701		307	*TF:* 800-442-2347 ■ *Web:* www.american-usa.com
American Casting & Manufacturing Corp	51 Commercial St	Plainview	NY	11803	516-349-7010	349-8389	326	*TF:* 800-342-0333 ■ *Web:* seals.com
American Catholic Press	16565 S State St	South Holland	IL	60473	708-331-5485	331-5484	637-2	*Web:* www.americancatholicpress.org
American Cause, The	501 Church St Ste 315	Vienna	VA	22180	703-255-2632	255-2219	48-7	*Web:* www.theamericancause.org
American Cave Conservation Assn	119 E Main St	Horse Cave	KY	42749	270-786-1466		48-13	*Web:* www.hiddenrivercave.com
American Center for Mongolian Studies	c/o Ctr for East Asian Studies 642 Williams Hall	Philadelphia	PA	19104	360-356-1020		167-3	*Web:* www.mongoliacenter.org
American Central Transport Inc	8731 NE Parvin Rd	Kansas City	MO	64161	816-781-9600	781-9641	780	*TF:* 888-428-5228 ■ *Web:* www.americancentral.com
American Century Life Insurance Co	4785 E 91st St Ste 200	Tulsa	OK	74137	918-712-7770	712-7773	796	*TF:* 888-712-7770 ■ *Web:* www.acl-ok.com
American Century Life Insurance Company of Texas	1333 W McDermott Dr Ste 150	Allen	TX	75013	855-966-1111		796	*TF:* 855-966-1111 ■ *Web:* acl-tx.com
American Ceramic Society (ACERS)	600 N Cleveland Ave Ste 210	Westerville	OH	43082	614-890-4700	899-6109	48-4	*TF:* 866-721-3322 ■ *Web:* ceramics.org
American Certified Equipment Inc	1650 Swan Lake Rd	Bossier City	LA	71111	318-425-0266	425-0934	789	*TF:* 888-425-0266 ■ *Web:* www.valveworksusa.com
American Cetacean Society (ACS)	PO Box 51691	Pacific Grove	CA	93950	310-548-6279		48-3	*Web:* www.acsonline.org
American Chamber of Commerce Executives (ACCE)	1330 Braddock Pl Ste 300	Alexandria	VA	22314	703-998-0072	212-9512	49-12	*TF:* 800-394-2223 ■ *Web:* www.acce.org
American Chemet Corp	740 Waukegan Rd Ste 202	Deerfield	IL	60015	847-948-0800		143	*Web:* www.chemet.com
American Chemical Society (ACS)	1155 16th St NW	Washington	DC	20036	202-872-4600	872-4615	49-19	*TF:* 800-227-5558 ■ *Web:* www.acs.org
American Chiropractic Assn (ACA)	1701 Clarendon Blvd Ste 200	Arlington	VA	22209	703-276-8800	243-2593	49-8	*TF:* 800-986-4636 ■ *Web:* www.acatoday.org
American Chiropractor, The	8619 NW 68th St	Miami	FL	33166	888-369-1396		530	*TF:* 888-369-1396 ■ *Web:* theamericanchiropractor.com

Name / Address	City	State	ZIP	Phone	Fax	Class
American Choral Directors Assn (ACDA) 545 Couch Dr *Web:* acda.org	Oklahoma City	OK	73102	405-232-8161	232-8162	48-4
American Chrome Co 518 W Crossroads Pkwy *TF:* 800-562-4488 ■ *Web:* www.americanchrome.com	Bolingbrook	IL	60440	630-685-2200		492
American Chronic Pain Assn (ACPA) PO Box 850 **Fax Area Code:* 916 ■ *TF:* 800-533-3231 ■ *Web:* www.theacpa.org	Rocklin	CA	95677	800-533-3231	652-8190*	48-17
American City Business Journals Inc 120 W Morehead St Ste 400 *Web:* www.bizjournals.com	Charlotte	NC	28202	704-973-1500		637-9
American Civil Constructors Inc 4901 S Windemere St *Web:* www.accbuilt.com	Littleton	CO	80120	303-795-2582	347-1844	188-4
American Civil Liberties Union (ACLU) 125 Broad St 18th Fl *TF:* 877-867-1025 ■ *Web:* www.aclu.org	New York	NY	10004	212-549-2500	549-2580	48-8
American Classic Agency 201 Atp Tour Blvd *Web:* www.aclassic.com	Ponte Vedra Beach	FL	32082	904-285-4030		390
American Clay Enterprises LLC 2418 Second St SW *TF:* 866-404-1634 ■ *Web:* www.americanclay.com	Albuquerque	NM	87102	505-243-5300		503-6
American Cleaning Solutions 39-30 Review Ave PO Box 1943 *TF:* 888-929-7587 ■ *Web:* www.cleaning-solutions.com	Long Island City	NY	11101	718-392-8080	482-9366	151
American Clock & Watch Museum (ACWM) 100 Maple St *Web:* www.clockandwatchmuseum.org	Bristol	CT	06010	860-583-6070		520
American Club, The 419 Highland Dr *TF:* 800-344-2838 ■ *Web:* www.americanclubresort.com	Kohler	WI	53044	920-457-8000	457-0299	669
American Coach Limousine 1100 Jorie Blvd Ste 314 *TF:* 888-709-5466 ■ *Web:* www.americancoachlimousine.com	Oak Brook	IL	60523	630-629-0001		441
American Coal Ash Assn (ACAA) 15200 E Girard Ave Ste 3050 *Web:* www.acaa-usa.org	Aurora	CO	80014	720-870-7897	870-7889	48-12
American Coalition for Clean Coal Electricity (ACCCE) 1152 15th St NW Ste 400 *Web:* americaspower.org	Washington	DC	20005	202-459-4833		48-12
American Coalition for Fathers & Children (ACFC) 1718 M St NW Ste 1187 *TF:* 800-978-3237 ■ *Web:* www.acfc.org	Washington	DC	20036	800-978-3237		48-6
American Coke & Coal Chemicals Institute (ACCCI) 25 Massachusetts Ave NW Ste 800 *Web:* www.accci.org	Washington	DC	20001	202-452-7198		48-12
American College 270 S Bryn Mawr Ave *TF:* 888-263-7265 ■ *Web:* www.theamericancollege.edu	Bryn Mawr	PA	19010	610-526-1000	526-1300	800
American College Health Assn (ACHA) 8455 Colesville Rd Ste 740 *Web:* www.acha.org	Silver Spring	MD	20910	410-859-1500	859-1510	49-8
American College of Allergy Asthma & Immunology (ACAAI) 85 W Algonquin Rd Ste 550 *Web:* acaai.org	Arlington Heights	IL	60005	847-427-1200	427-1294	49-8
American College of Cardiology (ACC) 2400 N St NW *TF:* 800-253-4636 ■ *Web:* www.acc.org	Washington	DC	20037	202-375-6000	375-7000	49-8
American College of Chest Physicians (ACCP) 3300 Dundee Rd *TF:* 800-343-2227 ■ *Web:* www.chestnet.org	Northbrook	IL	60062	847-498-1400	498-5460	49-8
American College of Clinical Pharmacy (ACCP) 13000 W 87th St Pkwy *Web:* www.accp.com	Lenexa	KS	66215	913-492-3311	492-0088	49-8
American College of Dentists (ACD) 839 Quince Orchard Blvd Ste J *Web:* www.acd.org	Gaithersburg	MD	20878	301-977-3223	977-3330	49-8
American College of Emergency Physicians (ACEP) 1125 Executive Cir PO Box 619911 *TF:* 800-798-1822 ■ *Web:* www.acep.org	Dallas	TX	75261	972-550-0911	580-2816	49-8
American College of Eye Surgeons/American Board of Eye Surgery (ACES) 334 E Lake Rd Ste 135 *TF:* 800-223-2233 ■ *Web:* www.aces-abes.org	Palm Harbor	FL	34685	727-366-1487	836-9783	49-8
American College of Foot & Ankle Surgeons (ACFAS) 8725 W Higgins Rd Ste 555 *TF:* 800-421-2237 ■ *Web:* www.acfas.org	Chicago	IL	60631	773-693-9300	693-9304	49-8
American College of Gastroenterology (ACG) 6400 Goldsboro Rd Ste 200 *Web:* gi.org	Bethesda	MD	20817	301-263-9000	263-9025	49-8
American College of Healthcare Executives (ACHE) 1 N Franklin St Ste 1700 *Web:* www.ache.org	Chicago	IL	60606	312-424-2800	424-0023	49-8
American College of Musicians 808 Rio Grande St *Web:* www.pianoguild.com	Austin	TX	78701	512-478-5775		48-4
American College of Nurse-Midwives (ACNM) 8403 Colesville Rd Ste 1550 *TF:* 800-468-3571 ■ *Web:* www.midwife.org	Silver Spring	MD	20910	240-485-1800	485-1818	49-8
American College of Obstetricians & Gynecologists (ACOG) 409 12th St SW PO Box 96920 *TF:* 800-673-8444 ■ *Web:* www.acog.org	Washington	DC	20090	202-863-1648		49-8
American College of Occupational & Environmental Medicine (ACOEM) 25 NW Pt Blvd Ste 700 *Web:* www.acoem.org	Elk Grove Village	IL	60007	847-818-1800	818-9266	49-8
American College of Orgonomy 4419 Rt 27 *Web:* www.orgonomy.org	Princeton	NJ	08540	732-821-1144	821-0174	766
American College of Osteopathic Family Physicians (ACOFP) 330 E Algonquin Rd Ste 1 *TF:* 800-323-0794 ■ *Web:* www.acofp.org	Arlington Heights	IL	60005	847-952-5100	228-9755	49-8
American College of Physician Executives (ACPE) 400 N Ashley Dr Ste 400 **Fax Area Code:* 813 ■ *TF:* 800-562-8088 ■ *Web:* www.physicianleaders.org	Tampa	FL	33602	800-562-8088	287-8993*	49-8
American College of Physicians (ACP) 190 N Independence Mall W *TF:* 800-523-1546 ■ *Web:* www.acponline.org	Philadelphia	PA	19106	215-351-2400	351-2594	49-8
American College of Preventive Medicine (ACPM) 455 Massachusetts Ave NW *Web:* www.acpm.org	Washington	DC	20001	202-466-2044	466-2662	49-8
American College of Psychiatrists 111 E Wacker Dr Ste 1440 *Web:* www.acpsych.org	Chicago	IL	60601	312-938-8840	938-8845	49-15
American College of Radiology (ACR) 1891 Preston White Dr *TF:* 800-227-5463 ■ *Web:* www.acr.org	Reston	VA	20191	703-648-8900		49-8
American College of Real Estate Lawyers 11300 Rockville Pk Ste 903 *Web:* acrel.org	Rockville	MD	20852	301-816-9811	816-9786	653
American College of Rheumatology (ACR) 2200 Lake Blvd NE *Web:* www.rheumatology.org	Atlanta	GA	30319	404-633-3777	633-1870	49-8
American College of Sports Medicine (ACSM) 401 W Michigan St PO Box 1440 *Web:* www.acsm.org	Indianapolis	IN	46202	317-637-9200	634-7817	49-8
American College of Surgeons (ACS) 633 N St Clair St *TF:* 800-621-4111 ■ *Web:* www.facs.org	Chicago	IL	60611	312-202-5000	202-5001	49-8
American College of Trust & Estate Counsel (ACTEC) 901 15th St NW Ste 525 *Web:* www.actec.org	Washington	DC	20005	202-684-8460	684-8459	49-10
American College Personnel Assn (ACPA) 1 Dupont Cir NW Ste 300 *Web:* www.myacpa.org	Washington	DC	20036	202-835-2272	296-3286	49-5
American Combustion Industries Inc 7100 Holladay Tyler Rd Ste 233 *Web:* www.aciindustries.com	Glenn Dale	MD	20769	301-779-3400	779-0425	256
American Commerce Insurance Co 3590 Twin Creeks Dr *TF:* 800-848-2945 ■ *Web:* www.mapfreinsurance.com	Columbus	OH	43204	614-308-3366	308-3365	391-4
American Commercial Barge Lines Inc 1701 E Market St *TF:* 800-457-6377 ■ *Web:* www.bargeacbl.com	Jeffersonville	IN	47130	800-457-6377		314
American Compliance Technologies Inc 1875 W Main St *TF:* 800-226-0911 ■ *Web:* a-c-t.com	Bartow	FL	33830	863-533-2000	533-1991	261
American Composers Alliance Inc (ACA) 802 W 190th St Ste 1B *Web:* composers.com	New York	NY	10040	212-925-0458		48-4
American Composers Orchestra 494 Eighth Ave *Web:* www.americancomposers.org	New York	NY	10001	212-977-8495	977-8995	573-3
American Composites 20751 NE Hwy 27 **Fax Area Code:* 773 ■ *Web:* www.qualityfrp.com	Williston	FL	32696	352-281-0473	913-6144*	22
American Composites Manufacturers Assn (ACMA) 3033 Wilson Blvd Ste 420 *Web:* acmanet.org	Arlington	VA	22201	703-525-0743		49-13
American Computer & Digital Components (ACDI) 7435 New Technology Way Ste A *Web:* www.acdi.com	Frederick	MD	21703	301-363-4182	694-5152	696
American Concrete Institute Intl (ACI) 38800 Country Club Dr PO Box 9094 *Web:* www.concrete.org	Farmington Hills	MI	48331	248-848-3700	848-3701	49-3
American Concrete Pavement Assn (ACPA) 9450 W Bryn Mawr Ave Ste 150 *TF:* 800-281-7899 ■ *Web:* www.acpa.org	Rosemont	IL	60018	847-966-2272	966-9970	49-3
American Concrete Pipe Assn 8445 Freeport Pkwy Ste 350 *Web:* www.concretepipe.org	Irving	TX	75063	972-506-7216	506-7682	49-3
American Conference of Governmental Industrial Hygienists (ACGIH) 1330 Kemper Meadows Dr *Web:* www.acgih.org	Cincinnati	OH	45240	513-742-2020	742-3355	49-7
American Conservatory of Music 252 Wildwood Rd *Web:* www.americanconservatory.edu	Hammond	IN	46324	219-931-6000		166
American Conservatory Theater (ACT) 30 Grant Ave 7th Fl *Web:* www.act-sf.org	San Francisco	CA	94108	415-834-3200	749-2291	573-4
American Consolidated Transportation Companies Inc 2513 E Higgins Rd *TF:* 800-323-0312 ■ *Web:* www.bus-charter.com	Elk Grove Village	IL	60007	800-323-0312		49-21
American Consulting Inc 7260 Shadeland Stn *Web:* www.structurepoint.com	Indianapolis	IN	46256	317-547-5580	543-0270	261
American Consumer News LLC 1401 S Discovery Ave *TF:* 844-978-6257 ■ *Web:* marketbeat.com	Sioux Falls	SD	57106	844-978-6257		180
American Contract Bridge League (ACBL) 6575 Windchase Blvd *TF:* 800-264-2743 ■ *Web:* www.acbl.org	Horn Lake	MS	38637	662-253-3100	253-3187	48-18
American Converters Inc 5360 Main St NE *Web:* www.amconfoam.com	Fridley	MN	55421	763-574-1044		601
American Coolair Corp PO Box 2300 *Web:* www.coolair.com	Jacksonville	FL	32203	904-389-3646	387-3449	14
American Cooling Technology Inc 715 Willow Springs Ln *Web:* actusa.us.com	York	PA	17406	717-767-2775		14
American Cord & Webbing Co 88 Century Dr *Web:* acw1.com	Woonsocket	RI	02895	401-762-5500		745-5
American Correctional Assn (ACA) 206 N Washington St Ste 200 *TF:* 800-222-5646 ■ *Web:* www.aca.org	Alexandria	VA	22314	703-224-0000		49-7
American Council for an Energy-Efficient Economy (ACEEE) 529 14th St NW Ste 600 *Web:* www.aceee.org	Washington	DC	20045	202-507-4000	429-2248	48-7
American Council for Capital Formation (ACCF) 1001 Connecticut Ave NW Ste 620 *Web:* accf.org	Washington	DC	20036	202-293-5811	785-8165	49-2
American Council for Construction Education (ACCE) 1717 N Loop 1604 E Ste 320 *Web:* www.acce-hq.org	San Antonio	TX	78232	210-495-6161	495-6168	48-1

	Phone	Fax	Class
American Council of Engineering Companies of New York (Acecny) 6 Airline Dr . . . Albany NY 12205 *Web:* acecny.org	518-452-8611		261
American Council of Engineering Cos (ACEC) 1015 15th St NW 8th Fl . . . Washington DC 20005 *TF:* 800-338-1391 ■ *Web:* www.acec.org	202-347-7474	898-0068	49-19
American Council of Hypnotist Examiners 3435 Camino del Rio S Ste 316 . . . San Diego CA 92108 **Fax Area Code:* 818 ■ *Web:* www.hypnotistexaminers.org	619-280-7200	247-9379*	49-15
American Council of Independent Laboratories (ACIL) 1875 I St NW Ste 500 . . . Washington DC 20006 *TF:* 800-368-1131 ■ *Web:* www.acil.org	202-887-5872	887-0021	49-19
American Council of Life Insurers (ACLI) 101 Constitution Ave NW Ste 700 W . . . Washington DC 20001 *TF:* 877-674-4659 ■ *Web:* www.acli.com	202-624-2000		49-9
American Council of the Blind (ACB) 2200 Wilson Blvd Ste 650 . . . Arlington VA 22201 **Fax Area Code:* 703 ■ *TF:* 800-424-8666 ■ *Web:* www.acb.org	202-467-5081	465-5085*	48-11
American Council on Exercise (ACE) 4851 Paramount Dr . . . San Diego CA 92123 *TF:* 800-825-3636 ■ *Web:* www.acefitness.org	858-576-6500	576-6564	48-17
American Council on Science & Health (ACSH) 110 E 42nd St Ste 1300 . . . New York NY 10017 *TF:* 866-905-2694 ■ *Web:* www.acsh.org	212-362-7044	362-4919	49-19
American Council on the Teaching of Foreign Languages (ACTFL) 1001 N Fairfax St Ste 200 . . . Alexandria VA 22314 *Web:* www.actfl.org	703-894-2900	894-2905	49-5
American Councils for International Education 1828 L St NW Ste 1200 . . . Washington DC 20036 *Web:* www.americancouncils.org	202-833-7522	833-7523	49-5
American Counseling Assn (ACA) 5999 Stevenson Ave . . . Alexandria VA 22304 *TF:* 800-347-6647 ■ *Web:* www.counseling.org	703-823-9800	823-0252	49-15
American Country Insurance Co 150 NW Point Blvd 3rd Fl . . . Elk Grove Village IL 60007 *TF:* 800-897-2551 ■ *Web:* www.atlas-fin.com	847-472-6700		391-4
American Craft Beer LLC 3817 Legation St NW . . . Washington DC 20015 *Web:* americancraftbeer.com	202-364-2421		637-10
American Craft Council 1224 Marshall St Ste 200 . . . Minneapolis MN 55413 *TF:* 800-836-3470 ■ *Web:* craftcouncil.org	612-206-3100	355-2330	48-4
American Crane & Equipment Corp 531 Old Swede Rd . . . Douglassville PA 19518 *TF:* 877-877-6778 ■ *Web:* www.americancrane.com	610-385-6061	385-3191	470
American Crane & Tractor Parts Inc 2200 State Line Rd . . . Kansas City KS 66103 *Web:* www.actparts.com	913-371-8585		54
American Critical Care Services 221 Ruthers Rd Ste 103 . . . North Chesterfield VA 23235 *TF:* 800-245-4011 ■ *Web:* www.accsnurses.com	804-320-1113	330-9460	260
American Cruise Lines 741 Boston Post Rd Ste 200 . . . Guilford CT 06437 *TF:* 800-814-6880 ■ *Web:* www.americancruiselines.com	203-453-6800	453-0417	221
American Crystal Sugar Co 101 N Third St . . . Moorhead MN 56560 *Web:* www.crystalsugar.com	218-236-4400	236-4494	296-38
American Culinary Federation Inc (ACF) 180 Center Pl Way . . . Saint Augustine FL 32095 *TF:* 800-624-9458 ■ *Web:* www.acfchefs.org	904-824-4468	825-4758	49-6
American Custom Drying 109 Elbow Ln . . . Burlington NJ 08016 *Web:* www.acdprocessing.com	609-326-6000		172
American Cybersystems Inc (ACS) 2400 Meadowbrook Pkwy . . . Duluth GA 30096 **Fax Area Code:* 877 ■ *TF:* 800-800-5044 ■ *Web:* www.acsicorp.com	770-493-5588	270-6248*	194
American Cylinder Company Inc 481 S Governors Hwy . . . Peotone IL 60468 *Web:* www.americancylinder.com	708-258-3935	258-3980	223
American Dairy Goat Assn (ADGA) 161 W Main St PO Box 865 . . . Spindale NC 28160 *Web:* adga.org	828-286-3801	287-0476	48-2
American Dairy Products Institute (ADPI) 116 N York St Ste 200 . . . Elmhurst IL 60126 *Web:* www.adpi.org	630-530-8700	530-8707	49-6
American Dairy Science Assn (ADSA) 1800 S Oak St Ste 100 . . . Champaign IL 61820 *TF:* 888-670-2250 ■ *Web:* www.adsa.org	217-356-5146	398-4119	48-2
American Dehydrated Foods Inc 3801 E Sunshine . . . Springfield MO 65809 *TF:* 800-456-3447 ■ *Web:* www.adf.com	417-881-7755		619
American Dental Assistants Assn (ADAA) 140 N Bloomingdale Rd . . . Bloomingdale IL 60108 *TF:* 877-874-3785 ■ *Web:* www.adaausa.org	312-541-1550		49-8
American Dental Assn (ADA) 211 E Chicago Ave . . . Chicago IL 60611 *TF:* 800-621-8099 ■ *Web:* www.ada.org	312-440-2500		49-8
American Dental Education Assn (ADEA) 1400 K St NW Ste 1100 . . . Washington DC 20005 *TF:* 800-353-2237 ■ *Web:* www.adea.org	202-289-7201	289-7204	49-5
American Dental Hygienists Assn (ADHA) 444 N Michigan Ave Ste 3400 . . . Chicago IL 60611 *TF:* 800-243-2342 ■ *Web:* www.adha.org	312-440-8900	467-1806	49-8
American Dental Partners Inc 401 Edgewater Pl Ste 430 . . . Wakefield MA 01880 *TF:* 800-838-6563 ■ *Web:* www.amdpi.com	781-213-6500	224-4216	463
American Derringer Corp 127 N Lacy Dr . . . Waco TX 76705 *Web:* www.amderringer.com	254-799-9111	799-7935	284
American Design Drafting Assn (ADDA) 105 E Main St . . . Newbern TN 38059 *Web:* www.adda.org	731-627-0802	627-9321	48-4
American Diabetes Assn (ADA) 1701 N Beauregard St . . . Alexandria VA 22311 *TF:* 800-232-3472 ■ *Web:* www.diabetes.org	703-549-1500		48-17
American Diabetes Association Inc 2451 Crystal Dr Ste 900 . . . Arlington VA 22202 *TF:* 800-342-2383 ■ *Web:* www.diabetesforecast.org	800-806-7801		457-16
American Direct Mail Company Inc 350 Hudson St . . . New York NY 10014	212-924-5400		629

	Phone	Fax	Class
American Direct Procurement Inc 11000 Lakeview Ave . . . Lenexa KS 66219 *Web:* www.americandirectco.com	913-677-5588		191-3
American Distillation Inc 1690 Royster Rd NE . . . Leland NC 28451 *Web:* www.americandistillation.net	910-371-0993	371-2485	146
American Distilling & Manufacturing Company Inc 31 E High St . . . East Hampton CT 06424 *Web:* www.americandistilling.com	860-267-4444		583
American Donkey & Mule Society (ADMS) PO Box 1210 . . . Lewisville TX 75067 *Web:* www.lovelongears.com	972-219-0781	420-9980	48-3
American Douglas Metals Inc 783 Thorpe Rd . . . Orlando FL 32824 *TF:* 800-428-0023 ■ *Web:* www.americandouglasmetals.com	407-855-6590	857-3290	492
American Drill Bushings Co (ADB) 5740 Hunt Rd . . . Valdosta GA 31606 *TF:* 800-423-4425 ■ *Web:* americandrillbushing.com	229-253-8928	253-8929	493
American Dryer Corp 88 Currant Rd . . . Fall River MA 02720 *Web:* www.adclaundry.com	508-678-9000	678-9447	427
American Eagle Federal Credit Union 417 Main St . . . East Hartford CT 06118 *TF:* 800-842-0145 ■ *Web:* www.americaneagle.org	860-568-2020		219
American Eagle Outfitters Inc 77 Hot Metal St . . . Pittsburgh PA 15203 *NYSE:* AEO ■ *TF:* 888-232-4535 ■ *Web:* www.ae.com	412-432-3300		157-4
American Eagle Steel Corp 716 Giddings Ave . . . Annapolis MD 21401 *Web:* www.americaneaglesteel.com	410-573-0335		791
American Economic Assn (AEA) 2014 Broadway Ste 305 . . . Nashville TN 37203 *Web:* www.aeaweb.org	615-322-2595	343-7590	49-2
American Economics Group Inc 2100 M St NW Ste 810 . . . Washington DC 20037 *Web:* www.americaneconomics.com	202-328-1545	462-0594	466
American Ecotech LLC 100 Elm St Factory D . . . Warren RI 02885 *TF:* 877-247-0403 ■ *Web:* www.americanecotech.com	877-247-0403		196
American Educational Music Publications Inc 1200 E Burlington Ave . . . Fairfield IA 52556 *Web:* www.perfectpitch.com	641-472-2700		637-10
American Educational Products LLC 401 Hickory St PO Box 2121 . . . Fort Collins CO 80522 *TF:* 800-289-9299 ■ *Web:* amep.business.site	970-484-7445	484-1198	243
American Educational Research Assn (AERA) 1430 K St NW Ste 1200 . . . Washington DC 20005 *TF:* 800-893-7950 ■ *Web:* www.aera.net	202-238-3200	238-3250	49-5
American Egg Board (AEB) 8755 W Higgins Rd Ste 300 . . . Chicago IL 60631 *TF:* 888-549-2140 ■ *Web:* www.aeb.org	847-296-7043	296-7007	48-2
American Electric Power Company Inc 1 Riverside Plz . . . Columbus OH 43215 *NYSE:* AEP ■ *Web:* www.aep.com	614-716-1000		360-5
American Electric Supply Inc 361 Maple St . . . Corona CA 92880 *Web:* www.amelect.com	951-734-7910	737-9906	246
American Electronic Components 1101 Lafayette St . . . Elkhart IN 46516 *TF:* 888-847-6552 ■ *Web:* www.aecsensors.com	574-295-6330	293-8013	247
American Embryo Transfer Assn (AETA) 1800 S Oak St Ste 100 . . . Champaign IL 61820 *Web:* www.aeta.org	217-398-2217	398-4119	49-8
American Emergency Vehicles 165 American Way . . . Jefferson NC 28640 *TF:* 800-374-9749 ■ *Web:* www.aev.com	336-982-9824		59
American Emo Trans Inc 2600 Hutchison McDonald Rd . . . Charlotte NC 28269 *Web:* americanemotrans.com	704-359-0045		787
American Endodontic Society 265 N Main St . . . Glen Ellyn IL 60137 **Fax Area Code:* 630 ■ *Web:* www.aesoc.com	773-519-4879	858-0525*	49-8
American Engineering Testing Inc 550 Cleveland Ave N . . . Saint Paul MN 55114 *TF:* 800-972-6364 ■ *Web:* www.amengtest.com	651-659-9001		261
American Engineers Group LLC 1220 Valley Forge Rd Ste 4 . . . Phoenixville PA 19460 *Web:* aegroup-llc.com	484-920-8018		261
American Enterprise Institute for Public Policy Research (AEI) 1789 Massachusetts Ave NW . . . Washington DC 20036 *TF:* 800-862-5801 ■ *Web:* www.aei.org	202-862-5800	862-7177	634
American Epilepsy Society (AES) 342 N Main St . . . West Hartford CT 06117 *TF:* 888-233-2334 ■ *Web:* www.aesnet.org	860-586-7505	586-7550	48-17
American Equipment Co (AMECO) 4775 Technology Way Ste 208 . . . Boca Raton FL 33431 *Web:* www.ameco.net	561-997-2080	997-2110	770
American Equipment Company Inc 2106 Anderson Rd . . . Greenville SC 29611 *Web:* www.ameco.com	864-295-7800		264-3
American Equity Investment Life Insurance Co 6000 Westown Pkwy . . . West Des Moines IA 50266 *TF:* 888-221-1234 ■ *Web:* www.american-equity.com	515-221-0002		391-2
American Esoteric Laboratories Inc 1701 Century Ctr Cove . . . Memphis TN 38134 **Fax Area Code:* 423 ■ *TF:* 800-423-0504 ■ *Web:* www.ael.com	901-405-8200	581-0229*	415
American Excelsior Co 850 Ave H E . . . Arlington TX 76011 **Fax Area Code:* 817 ■ *TF:* 800-777-7645 ■ *Web:* americanexcelsior.com	800-777-7645	649-7816*	601
American Exchange Bank (AEB) 510 W Main St PO Box 818 . . . Henryetta OK 74437 *TF:* 888-652-3321 ■ *Web:* www.americanexchange.bank	918-652-3321	652-7057	70
American Exchanger Services Inc 1950 Innovation Way . . . Hartford WI 53027 *Web:* www.amexservices.com	262-670-6625		268
American Executive Management Inc 30 Federal St . . . Salem MA 01970 *Web:* americanexecutive.us	978-744-5923		194
American Express Company Inc World Financial Ctr 200 Vesey St . . . New York NY 10285 *NYSE:* AXP ■ *TF:* 800-528-4800 ■ *Web:* www.americanexpress.com	212-640-2000	640-0404	215

Phone | Fax | Class

American Fabricators Inc
570 Metroplex Dr .... Nashville TN 37211 — 615-834-8700 — 697
Web: www.americanfabricators.com

American Factory Direct Furniture Outlets Inc
210 New Camellia Blvd. .... Covington LA 70433 — 985-845-2465 — 321
Web: www.afd-furniture.com

American Family Assn 107 Parkgate Dr .... Tupelo MS 38801 — 662-844-5036 — 644
TF: 800-326-4543 ■ *Web:* www.afa.net

American Family Care
3700 Cahaba Beach Rd. .... Birmingham AL 35242 — 833-361-4643 — 352
TF: 833-361-4643 ■ *Web:* www.afcurgentcare.com

American Family Insurance
6000 American Pkwy .... Madison WI 53783 — 800-692-6326 — 391-2
TF: 800-692-6326 ■ *Web:* www.amfam.com

American Family Radio PO Box 3206 .... Tupelo MS 38803 — 662-844-8888 — 647
Web: www.afr.net

American Fan Company Inc
2933 Symmes Rd .... Fairfield OH 45014 — 513-874-2400 — 870-6249 — 18
TF: 866-771-6266 ■ *Web:* www.americanfan.com

American Farm Bureau Federation
600 Maryland Ave SW Ste 1000-W .... Washington DC 20024 — 202-406-3600 — 48-2
TF: 800-327-6287 ■ *Web:* www.fb.org

American Farm Publications Inc
PO Box 2026 .... Easton MD 21601 — 410-822-3965 — 822-5068 — 532-2
TF: 800-634-5021 ■ *Web:* www.americanfarm.com

American Farmland Trust (AFT)
1200 18th St. .... Washington DC 20036 — 202-331-7300 — 659-8339 — 48-2
TF: 800-431-1499 ■ *Web:* www.farmland.org

American Faucet & Coating Corp
3280 Corporate Vw. .... Vista CA 92081 — 760-598-5895 — 612
TF: 800-621-8383 ■ *Web:* www.sigmafaucet.com

American Federation for Aging Research (AFAR)
55 W 39th St 16th Fl. .... New York NY 10018 — 212-703-9977 — 997-0330 — 49-8
TF: 888-582-2327 ■ *Web:* www.afar.org

American Federation of Arts (AFA)
305 E 47th St 10th Fl .... New York NY 10017 — 212-988-7700 — 861-2487 — 48-4
TF: 800-232-0270 ■ *Web:* www.amfedarts.org

American Federation of Astrologers (AFA)
6535 S Rural Rd .... Tempe AZ 85283 — 480-838-1751 — 838-8293 — 48-18
TF: 888-301-7630 ■ *Web:* www.astrologers.com

American Federation of Government Employees
80 F St NW .... Washington DC 20001 — 202-737-8700 — 639-6441 — 414
TF: 888-844-2343 ■ *Web:* www.afge.org

American Federation of Labor & Congress of Industrial Organizations (AFL-CIO)
815 16th St NW .... Washington DC 20006 — 202-637-5215 — 414
Web: www.aflcio.org

American Federation of Musicians of the US & Canada (AFM)
1501 Broadway Ste 600 .... New York NY 10036 — 212-869-1330 — 764-6134 — 414
TF: 800-762-3444 ■ *Web:* www.afm.org

American Federation of School Administrators (AFSA)
1101 17th St NW Ste 408 .... Washington DC 20036 — 202-986-4209 — 49-5
Web: www.theschoolleader.org

American Federation of State County & Municipal Employees
1625 L St NW .... Washington DC 20036 — 202-429-1000 — 429-1293 — 414
Web: www.afscme.org

American Federation of Teachers (AFT)
555 New Jersey Ave NW .... Washington DC 20001 — 202-879-4400 — 457-8
Web: www.aft.org

American Federation of Television & Radio Artists (AFTRA)
260 Madison Ave 7th Fl .... New York NY 10016 — 212-532-0800 — 532-2242 — 414
TF: 800-638-6796 ■ *Web:* www.sagaftra.org

American Feed Industry Assn (AFIA)
2101 Wilson Blvd Ste 916 .... Arlington VA 22201 — 703-524-0810 — 524-1921 — 48-2
Web: www.afia.org

American Felt & Filter Co
361 Walsh Ave .... New Windsor NY 12553 — 845-561-3560 — 563-4422 — 745-6
Web: www.abbfco.com

American Fence Assn (AFA)
6404 Internationa Pkwy Ste 2250-A .... Plano TX 75093 — 800-822-4342 — 480-7118* — 49-3
**Fax Area Code:* 314 ■ *TF:* 800-822-4342 ■ *Web:* www.americanfenceassociation.com

American Fence Inc 2502 N 27th Ave .... Phoenix AZ 85009 — 602-272-2333 — 191-2
TF: 888-691-4565 ■ *Web:* www.americanfence.com

American Fiber & Finishing Inc
225 N Depot St. .... Albemarle NC 28001 — 704-983-6102 — 983-1943 — 745-1
Web: affinc.com

American Fidelity Life Insurance Co
500 S Palafox Ste 200 .... Pensacola FL 32502 — 850-456-7401 — 453-5440 — 391-2
Web: www.amfilife.com

American Film Institute (AFI)
2021 N Western Ave .... Los Angeles CA 90027 — 323-856-7600 — 467-4578 — 48-4
TF: 866-234-3378 ■ *Web:* www.afi.com

American Financial Group Inc
301 E Fourth St. .... Cincinnati OH 45202 — 513-579-2121 — 579-2580 — 360-4
NYSE: AFG ■ *Web:* www.afginc.com

American Financial Printing Inc
404 Industrial Blvd .... Minneapolis MN 55413 — 612-378-0711 — 781
Web: www.afpi.com

American Fire Journal
9072 E Artesia Blvd Ste 7 .... Bellflower CA 90706 — 562-866-1664 — 637-9
Web: www.interfire.org

American Fire Sprinkler Assn (AFSA)
12750 Merit Dr Ste 350 .... Dallas TX 75251 — 214-349-5965 — 343-8898 — 49-3
Web: www.firesprinkler.org

American First National Bank
9999 Bellaire Blvd .... Houston TX 77036 — 713-596-2888 — 70
Web: afnb.com

American Fisheries Society (AFS)
5410 Grosvenor Ln Ste 110 .... Bethesda MD 20814 — 301-897-8616 — 897-8096 — 48-2
Web: fisheries.org

American Fitness
8630 SW Scholls Ferry Rd Ste 323 .... Beaverton OR 97008 — 800-895-4181 — 354
TF: 800-895-4181 ■ *Web:* www.americanfitness.net

American Floor Products Company Inc
7977 Cessna Ave .... Gaithersburg MD 20879 — 800-342-0424 — 987-0422* — 291
**Fax Area Code:* 301 ■ *TF:* 800-342-0424 ■ *Web:* www.afco-usa.com

American Floor Systems Inc
707 Moore Station Industrial Pk .... Prospect Park PA 19076 — 610-534-1770 — 290
Web: americanfloorsystems.com

American Flyers Flight School
2501 Airport Ave. .... Santa Monica CA 90405 — 310-390-2099 — 685
TF: 800-233-0808 ■ *Web:* www.americanflyers.com

American Foam Products Inc
753 Liberty St .... Painesville OH 44077 — 440-352-3434 — 352-0134 — 601
Web: www.americanfoamproducts.com

American Folk Art Museum
2 Lincoln Sq. .... New York NY 10023 — 212-595-9533 — 520
Web: folkartmuseum.org

American Folklore Society (AFS)
800 E Third St. .... Bloomington IN 47405 — 812-856-2379 — 856-2483 — 48-14
TF: 866-315-9403 ■ *Web:* www.afsnet.org

American Food & Vending Corp
124 Metropolitan Park Dr .... Liverpool NY 13088 — 800-466-9261 — 299
TF: 800-466-9261 ■ *Web:* www.afvusa.com

American Foods Group Inc
500 S Washington St .... Green Bay WI 54302 — 920-437-6330 — 473
TF: 800-345-0293 ■ *Web:* www.americanfoodsgroup.com

American Football Coaches Assn (AFCA)
100 Legends Ln .... Waco TX 76706 — 254-754-9900 — 48-22
TF: 877-557-5338 ■ *Web:* www.afca.com

American Foreign Service Assn (AFSA)
2101 E St NW .... Washington DC 20037 — 202-338-4045 — 338-6820 — 49-7
TF: 800-704-2372 ■ *Web:* www.afsa.org

American Foreign Service Protective Assn
1620 L St NW Ste 800 .... Washington DC 20036 — 202-833-4910 — 49-7
Web: www.afspa.org

American Forest & Paper Assn (AF&PA)
1101 K St NW Ste 700 .... Washington DC 20036 — 202-463-2700 — 48-2
TF: 800-878-8878 ■ *Web:* www.afandpa.org

American Forest Foundation (AFF)
2000 M St NW Ste 550 .... Washington DC 20036 — 202-765-3660 — 827-7924 — 48-2
TF: 800-325-2954 ■ *Web:* forestfoundation.org

American Forest Management Inc
407 N Pike Rd E PO Box 1919 .... Sumter SC 29151 — 803-773-5461 — 302
Web: americanforestmanagement.com

American Forests
1220 L St NW Ste 750 .... Washington DC 20005 — 202-737-1944 — 737-2457 — 48-13
Web: www.americanforests.org

American Foundation for AIDS Research (AMFAR)
120 Wall St 13th Fl .... New York NY 10005 — 212-806-1600 — 806-1601 — 48-17
Web: amfar.org

American Foundation for Suicide Prevention (AFSP)
120 Wall St 29th Fl .... New York NY 10005 — 212-363-3500 — 363-6237 — 48-17
TF: 888-333-2377 ■ *Web:* afsp.org

American Foundation for the Blind (AFB)
1401 S Clark St Ste 730 .... Arlington VA 22202 — 212-502-7600 — 502-7777 — 48-17
TF: 800-232-5463 ■ *Web:* www.afb.org

American Foundry Group Inc
14602 S Grant .... Bixby OK 74008 — 918-366-4401 — 492
Web: www.americanfoundry.com

American Foundry Society (AFS)
1695 N Penny Ln .... Schaumburg IL 60173 — 847-824-0181 — 49-13
TF: 800-537-4237 ■ *Web:* www.afsinc.org

American Freight Inc
2770 Lexington Ave .... Mansfield OH 44904 — 419-884-2224 — 321
TF: 800-420-2337 ■ *Web:* www.americanfreight.com

American Friends Service Committee (AFSC)
1501 Cherry St .... Philadelphia PA 19102 — 215-241-7000 — 48-5
TF: 800-621-4000 ■ *Web:* www.afsc.org

American Frozen Food Institute (AFFI)
2000 Corporate Ridge Blvd Ste 1000 .... McLean VA 22102 — 703-821-0770 — 821-1350 — 615
Web: www.affi.org

American Fuel & Petrochemical Manufacturers (AFPM)
1667 K St NW Ste 700 .... Washington DC 20006 — 202-457-0480 — 457-0486 — 48-12
Web: www.afpm.org

American Fuel Cell & Coated Fabrics Co
601 Firestone Dr. .... Magnolia AR 71753 — 870-234-3381 — 22
Web: amfuel.com

American Fuji Seal Inc
1051 Bloomfield Rd .... Bardstown KY 40004 — 502-348-9211 — 348-9558 — 596
TF: 866-291-2387 ■ *Web:* www.fujiseal.com

American Funeral Financial LLC
3515 Pelham Rd Ste 200 .... Greenville SC 29615 — 864-232-4233 — 676-2280 — 390
TF: 877-213-4233 ■ *Web:* www.americanfuneralfinancial.com

American Furniture Warehouse Co
8501 Grant St. .... Thornton CO 80229 — 303-289-3300 — 321
TF: 888-615-9415 ■ *Web:* www.afw.com

American Furukawa Inc
47677 Galleon Dr .... Plymouth MI 48170 — 734-446-2200 — 54
Web: www.americanfurukawa.com

American Galvanizers Assn (AGA)
6881 S Holly Cir Ste 108 .... Centennial CO 80112 — 720-554-0900 — 554-0909 — 49-13
TF: 800-468-7732 ■ *Web:* galvanizeit.org

American Gaming & Electronics Inc
223 Pratt St. .... Hammonton NJ 08037 — 609-704-3000 — 322
TF: 800-727-6807 ■ *Web:* www.agegaming.com

American Gaming Assn (AGA)
1299 Pennsylvania Ave NW Ste 1175 .... Washington DC 20004 — 202-552-2675 — 552-2676 — 48-23
Web: www.americangaming.org

American Gaming Supply Inc (AGS)
729 Kohler St .... Los Angeles CA 90021 — 213-228-2447 — 402-5250 — 320
TF: 866-765-3731 ■ *Web:* www.americangamingsupply.com

American Gas Assn
400 N Capitol St NW .... Washington DC 20001 — 202-824-7000 — 615
Web: www.aga.org

American Gastroenterological Assn (AGA)
4930 Del Ray Ave .... Bethesda MD 20814 — 301-654-2055 — 654-5920 — 49-8
TF: 800-227-7888 ■ *Web:* www.gastro.org

American Gear Manufacturers Assn (AGMA)
500 Montgomery St Ste 350 .... Alexandria VA 22314 — 703-684-0211 — 684-0242 — 49-13
Web: www.agma.org

American Gelbvieh Assn
10900 Dover St. .... Westminster CO 80021 — 303-465-2333 — 465-2339 — 48-2
Web: www.gelbvieh.org

American Gem Society (AGS)
8881 W Sahara Ave. .... Las Vegas NV 89117 — 866-805-6500 — 255-7420* — 49-4
**Fax Area Code:* 702 ■ *TF:* 866-805-6500 ■ *Web:* www.americangemsociety.org

Name / Address	City	State	ZIP	Phone	Fax	Class
American Gem Trade Assn (AGTA) 3030 LBJ Fwy Ste 840 TF: 800-972-1162 ■ Web: agta.org	Dallas	TX	75234	214-742-4367	742-7334	49-4
American General Media Corp 1400 Easton Dr Ste 144 Web: www.americangeneralmedia.com	Bakersfield	CA	93309	661-328-1410	328-0873	645-11
American General Supplies Inc 7840 Airpark Rd Web: www.agsusa.com	Gaithersburg	MD	20879	301-590-9200	590-3069	770
American Geophysical Union (AGU) 2000 Florida Ave NW TF: 800-966-2481 ■ Web: www.agu.org	Washington	DC	20009	202-462-6900	328-0566	49-19
American Geosciences Institute (AGI) 4220 King St Web: www.americangeosciences.org	Alexandria	VA	22302	703-379-2480	379-7563	49-19
American Geothermal Systems Inc 8650 Spicewood Springs Rd Web: www.amgeosystems.com	Austin	TX	78759	512-219-1465		194
American GFM Corp 1200 Cavalier Blvd Web: www.agfm.com	Chesapeake	VA	23323	757-487-2442		455
American Gilsonite Co 29950 S Bonanza Hwy Web: www.americangilsonite.com	Bonanza	UT	84008	435-789-1921		601
American Girl Inc 8400 Fairway Pl TF: 800-845-0005 ■ Web: www.americangirl.com	Middleton	WI	53562	800-845-0005		762
American Glass Distributors 3901 Airline Dr Web: allamericanglass.com	Houston	TX	77022	713-692-8522		54
American GNC Corp 888 E Easy St Web: www.americangnc.com	Simi Valley	CA	93065	805-582-0582		237
American Golf Corp 2951 28th St TF: 800-238-7267 ■ Web: www.americangolf.com	Santa Monica	CA	90405	310-664-4000		655
American Governor Co 27 Richard Rd Web: americangovernor.com	Ivyland	PA	18974	215-354-1144		261
American Gramaphone LLC 9130 Mormon Bridge Rd	Omaha	NE	68152	402-457-4341	457-4332	657
American Granby Inc 7652 Morgan Rd TF: 800-776-2266 ■ Web: www.americangranby.com	Liverpool	NY	13090	315-451-1100	451-1876	612
American Greetings Corp 1 American Rd NYSE: AM ■ TF: 800-777-4891 ■ Web: www.corporate.americangreetings.com	Cleveland	OH	44144	216-252-7300	252-6778	130
American Grinding & Machine Co 2000 N Mango Ave TF: 877-988-4343 ■ Web: www.americangrinding.com	Chicago	IL	60639	773-889-4343	889-3781	454
American Group Psychotherapy Assn (AGPA) 25 E 21st St 6th Fl TF: 877-668-2472 ■ Web: www.agpa.org	New York	NY	10010	212-477-2677	979-6627	49-15
American Growth Fund Inc 1636 Logan st TF: 800-525-2406 ■ Web: www.americangrowthfund.com	Denver	CO	80203	303-626-0600	626-0614	401
American Guard Services Inc 1299 E Artesia Blvd TF: 800-662-7372 ■ Web: www.americanguardservices.com	Carson	CA	90746	310-645-6200		400
American Guild of Musical Artists (AGMA) 1430 Broadway 14th Fl TF: 800-543-2462 ■ Web: www.musicalartists.org	New York	NY	10018	212-265-3687	262-9088	48-4
American Guild of Organists (AGO) 475 Riverside Dr Ste 1260 TF: 855-631-0759 ■ Web: www.agohq.org	New York	NY	10115	212-870-2310	870-2163	48-4
American Guild of Variety Artists (AGVA) 363 Seventh Ave 17th Fl TF: 800-331-0890 ■ Web: agvausa.com	New York	NY	10001	212-675-1003	633-0097	48-4
American Gypsum 3811 Turtle Creek Blvd Ste 1200 TF: 866-439-5800 ■ Web: www.americangypsum.com	Dallas	TX	75219	214-530-5500		347
American Hardware Manufacturing Inc 79 Stewart Ave TF: 800-258-2800 ■ Web: www.americanhardwaremfg.com	Washington	PA	15301	724-225-7200	225-3290	505
American Headache Society (AHS) 19 Mantua Rd Web: americanheadachesociety.org	Mount Royal	NJ	08061	856-423-0043	423-0082	49-8
American Health Assoc 671 Ohio Pk Ste K TF: 800-522-7556 ■ Web: www.themedlab.com	Cincinnati	OH	45245	800-522-7556		415
American Health Care Assn (AHCA) 1201 L St NW TF: 800-321-0343 ■ Web: www.ahcancal.org	Washington	DC	20005	202-842-4444	842-3860	49-8
American Health Information Management Assn (AHIMA) 233 N Michigan Ave 21st Fl TF: 800-335-5535 ■ Web: www.ahima.org	Chicago	IL	60601	312-233-1100	233-1090	49-8
American Health Lawyers Assn (AHLA) 1620 Eye St NW 6th Fl Web: www.americanhealthlaw.org	Washington	DC	20006	202-833-1100	833-1105	49-10
American Healthcare Alliance 9229 Ward Pky Ste 300 TF: 800-870-6252 ■ Web: www.americanhealthcareallianceonline.com	Kansas City	MO	64114	816-523-7799		391-3
American HealthCare Group LLC 1910 Cochran Rd Manor Oak One Ste 405 Web: www.american-healthcare.net	Pittsburgh	PA	15220	412-563-8800	563-8319	352
American Healthcare Radiology Administrators (AHRA) 490-B Boston Post Rd Ste 200 TF: 800-334-2472 ■ Web: www.ahra.org	Sudbury	MA	01776	978-443-7591	443-8046	49-8
American Hearing Research Foundation 275 N York St Ste 401 Web: www.american-hearing.org	Elmhurst	IL	60126	630-617-5079		48-17
American Heart Assn (AHA) 7272 Greenville Ave TF: 800-242-8721 ■ Web: www.heart.org	Dallas	TX	75231	214-373-6300		48-17
American Heat Treating Inc 16 Commerce Dr Web: americanheattreating.com	Monroe	CT	06468	203-268-1750		484
American Helicopter Museum & Education Ctr 1220 American Blvd W Web: americanhelicopter.museum	West Chester	PA	19380	610-436-9600		520
American Hellenic Educational Progressive Assn (AHEPA) 1909 Q St NW Ste 500 TF: 855-473-3512 ■ Web: ahepa.org	Washington	DC	20009	202-232-6300	232-2140	48-14

Name / Address	City	State	ZIP	Phone	Fax	Class
American Herbal Products Assn (AHPA) 8630 Fenton St Ste 918 TF: 800-358-2104 ■ Web: www.ahpa.org	Silver Spring	MD	20910	301-588-1171	588-1174	49-8
American Hereford Assn 1501 Wyandotte St Web: hereford.org	Kansas City	MO	64108	816-842-3757	842-6931	48-2
American Heritage Bank 2 S Main PO Box 1408 Web: www.ahb.bank	Sapulpa	OK	74067	918-224-3210	224-7689	70
American Heritage Securities Inc 655 W Market St TF: 800-968-2437 ■ Web: www.egifinancial.com	Akron	OH	44303	330-535-0881	535-0884	690
American Hermetics Inc 2935 E Ponce de Leon Ave Web: www.americanhermetics.net	Decatur	GA	30030	404-373-8782	378-0232	14
American Highway Users Alliance 1920 L St NW Ste 525 TF: 800-388-0650 ■ Web: www.highways.org	Washington	DC	20036	202-857-1200	857-1220	49-21
American Hiking Society (AHS) 8605 Second Ave TF: 800-972-8608 ■ Web: americanhiking.org	Silver Spring	MD	20910	301-565-6704		48-23
American Historical Assn (AHA) 400 A St SE Web: www.historians.org	Washington	DC	20003	202-544-2422	544-8307	49-5
American Historical Society of Germans from Russia 631 D St Web: www.ahsgr.org	Lincoln	NE	68502	402-474-3363	474-7229	48-14
American History Press (AHP) 404 Locust St TF: 888-521-1789 ■ Web: americanhistorypress.com	Staunton	VA	24401	888-521-1789		637-2
American Holistic Health Assn (AHHA) PO Box 17400 Web: ahha.org	Anaheim	CA	92817	714-779-6152		48-17
American Holistic Nurses Assn (AHNA) 2900 SW Plass Ct TF: 800-278-2462 ■ Web: www.ahna.org	Topeka	KS	66611	785-234-1712	234-1713	48-17
American Home Base Inc 428 Childers St TF: 800-549-0595 ■ Web: amhomebase.com	Pensacola	FL	32513	850-857-0860	484-8661	737
American Home Furnishings 3535 Menaul Blvd NE TF: 800-854-6755 ■ Web: www.americanhome.com	Albuquerque	NM	87107	505-883-2211		321
American Home Shield 150 Peabody Pl TF: 888-682-1043 ■ Web: www.ahs.com	Memphis	TN	38103	901-537-8000		367
American Homeowners Assn (AHA) 3001 Summer St TF: 800-470-2242 ■ Web: www.ahahome.com	Stamford	CT	06905	203-323-7715		226
American Homeowners Foundation (AHF) 6776 Little Falls Rd TF: 800-489-7776 ■ Web: www.americanhomeowners.org	Arlington	VA	22213	800-489-7776		49-17
American HomePatient Inc 5200 Maryland Way Ste 400 TF: 800-890-7271 ■ Web: www.ahom.com	Brentwood	TN	37027	615-221-8884		363
American Homestar Corp 2450 S Shore Blvd Ste 300 Web: americanhomestar.com	League City	TX	77573	281-334-9700	334-9737	505
American Hometown Media Inc 782 Melrose Ave Web: americanhometownmedia.com	Nashville	TN	37211	615-599-8751		532-3
American Honda Motor Company Inc 1919 Torrance Blvd TF: 800-999-1009 ■ Web: www.honda.com	Torrance	CA	90501	310-783-2000		59
American Horse Council (AHC) 1616 H St NW 7th Fl Web: www.horsecouncil.org	Washington	DC	20006	202-296-4031	296-1970	48-3
American Horticultural Society (AHS) 7931 E Blvd Dr TF: 800-777-7931 ■ Web: ahsgardening.org	Alexandria	VA	22308	703-768-5700	768-8700	48-18
American Hose & Rubber Company Inc 3645 E 44th St Web: amhose.com	Tucson	AZ	85713	520-514-1666		370
American Hospital Assn (AHA) 155 N Wacker Dr TF: 800-424-4301 ■ Web: www.aha.org	Chicago	IL	60606	312-422-3000		49-8
American Hotel & Lodging Assn (AH&LA) 1201 New York Ave NW Ste 600 Web: www.ahla.com	Washington	DC	20005	202-289-3100		48-23
American Hotel Register Co 100 S Milwaukee Ave TF: 800-323-5686 ■ Web: www.americanhotel.com	Vernon Hills	IL	60061	800-323-5686	688-9108	559
American Humane Assn (AHA) 63 Inverness Dr E *Fax Area Code: 303 ■ TF: 800-227-4645 ■ Web: www.americanhumane.org	Englewood	CO	80112	800-227-4645	792-5333*	48-6
American Hydrogen Assn (AHA) 2350 W Shangri La Web: www.clean-air.org	Phoenix	AZ	85029	602-328-4238		48-12
American Immigration Lawyers Assn (AILA) 918 F St NW TF: 800-982-2839 ■ Web: www.aila.org	Washington	DC	20004	202-216-2400	783-7853	49-10
American Income Life Insurance Co (AIL) 1200 Wooded Acres TF: 800-433-3405 ■ Web: www.ailife.com	Waco	TX	76710	254-761-6400		391-2
American Independence Museum 1 Governors Ln Web: www.independencemuseum.org	Exeter	NH	03833	603-772-2622	772-2662	520
American Indian College 10020 N 15th Ave	Phoenix	AZ	85021	602-944-3335		166
American Indian College Fund 8333 Greenwood Blvd TF: 800-776-3863 ■ Web: collegefund.org	Denver	CO	80221	303-426-8900	426-1200	48-11
American Indian Science & Engineering Society (AISES) 2305 Renard SE Ste 200 Web: www.aises.org	Albuquerque	NM	87106	505-765-1052	765-5608	49-19
American Industrial Hygiene Assn (AIHA) 2700 Prosperity Ave Ste 250 Web: www.aiha.org	Fairfax	VA	22031	703-849-8888	207-3561	49-13
American Instants Inc 117 Bartley Flanders Rd Web: www.americaninstants.com	Flanders	NJ	07836	973-584-8811	584-0444	805

Phone | Fax | Class

American Institute 99 South St ... West Hartford CT 06110 | 888-387-5260 | | 167-3
TF: 888-387-5260 ■ *Web:* www.americaninstitute.edu

American Institute for Cancer Research (AICR)
1759 R St NW ... Washington DC 20009 | 202-328-7744 | 328-7226 | 668
TF: 800-843-8114 ■ *Web:* www.aicr.org

American Institute for Conservation of Historic & Artistic Works (AIC)
725 15th St NW Ste 500 ... Washington DC 20005 | 202-452-9545 | 452-9328 | 48-4
Web: www.culturalheritage.org

American Institute for CPCU & Insurance Institute of America (AICPCU/IIA)
720 Providence Rd Ste 100 ... Malvern PA 19355 | 610-644-2100 | 640-9576 | 49-9
TF: 800-644-2101 ■ *Web:* www.theinstitutes.org

American Institute of Aeronautics & Astronautics Inc (AIAA)
12700 Sunrise Valley Dr Ste 200 ... Reston VA 20191 | 703-264-7500 | 264-7551 | 49-19
TF: 800-639-2422 ■ *Web:* www.aiaa.org

American Institute of Architects (AIA)
1735 New York Ave NW ... Washington DC 20006 | 202-626-7300 | 626-7547 | 48-4
TF: 800-242-3837 ■ *Web:* www.aia.org

American Institute of Biological Sciences (AIBS)
1313 Dolley Madison Blvd Ste 402 ... McLean VA 22101 | 703-674-2500 | 674-2509 | 49-19
Web: www.aibs.org

American Institute of Chemical Engineers (AICHE)
120 Wall St 2nd Fl ... New York NY 10005 | 203-702-7660 | 775-5177 | 49-19
TF: 800-242-4363 ■ *Web:* www.aiche.org

American Institute of Chemists (AIC)
315 Chestnut St ... Philadelphia PA 19106 | 215-873-8224 | 925-1954 | 49-19
Web: www.theaic.org

American Institute of Constructors (AIC)
700 N Fairfax St Ste 510 ... Alexandria VA 22314 | 703-683-4999 | 527-3105* | 49-3
**Fax Area Code:* 571 ■ *Web:* www.professionalconstructor.org

American Institute of CPAS (AICPA)
1211 Avenue of the Americas ... New York NY 10036 | 212-596-6200 | 596-6213 | 49-1
Web: www.aicpa.org

American Institute of Floral Designers (AIFD)
9 Newport Dr Ste 200 ... Forest Hill MD 21050 | 443-966-3850 | 640-1031 | 49-4
Web: aifd.org

American Institute of Food Distribution
10 Mountainview Rd Ste S125 ... Upper Saddle River NJ 07450 | 201-701-6670 | 701-5222 | 49-6
Web: foodinstitute.com

American Institute of Graphic Arts (AIGA)
164 Fifth Ave ... New York NY 10010 | 212-807-1990 | 807-1799 | 48-4
TF: 800-548-1634 ■ *Web:* www.aiga.org

American Institute of Marine Underwriters (AIMU)
14 Wall St Ste 820 ... New York NY 10005 | 212-233-0550 | 227-5102 | 49-9
Web: www.aimu.org

American Institute of Mining Metallurgical & Petroleum Engineers (AIME)
12999 E Adam Aircraft Cir ... Englewood CO 80112 | 303-325-5185 | 702-0049* | 48-12
**Fax Area Code:* 888 ■ *Web:* www.aimehq.org

American Institute of Philanthropy (AIP)
3450 N Lake Shore Dr ... Chicago IL 60657 | 773-529-2300 | 529-0024 | 48-5
Web: www.charitywatch.org

American Institute of Physics
1 Physics Ellipse ... College Park MD 20740 | 301-209-3100 | 209-0843 | 49-19
TF: 800-892-8259 ■ *Web:* www.aip.org

American Institute of Professional Bookkeepers (AIPB)
6001 Montrose Rd Ste 500 ... Rockville MD 20852 | 800-622-0121 | 541-0066 | 49-1
TF: 800-622-0121 ■ *Web:* www.aipb.org

American Institute of Professional Geologists (AIPG)
1400 W 122nd Ave Ste 250 ... Westminster CO 80234 | 303-412-6205 | 253-9220 | 49-19
TF: 800-337-3140 ■ *Web:* www.aipg.org

American Institute of Steel Construction (AISC)
130 E Randolph Ste 2000 ... Chicago IL 60601 | 312-670-2400 | | 49-3
Web: www.aisc.org

American Institute of Stress, The (AIS)
124 Park Ave ... Yonkers NY 10703 | 682-239-6823 | | 48-17
Web: www.stress.org

American Institute of Timber Construction (AITC)
7012 S Revere Pkwy Ste 140 ... Centennial CO 80112 | 303-792-9559 | 792-0669 | 49-3
Web: www.aitc-glulam.org

American Institute of Ultrasound in Medicine (AIUM)
14750 Sweitzer Ln Ste 100 ... Laurel MD 20707 | 301-498-4100 | 498-4450 | 49-8
TF: 800-638-5352 ■ *Web:* www.aium.org

American Institutes for Research
1000 Thomas Jefferson St NW ... Washington DC 20007 | 202-403-5000 | 403-5454 | 668
TF: 877-334-3499 ■ *Web:* www.air.org

American Insurance Professionals
4545 E Shea Blvd Ste 130 ... Phoenix AZ 85028 | 602-424-3351 | | 390
Web: aminspro.com

American Insurance Services Group Inc
545 Washington Blvd ... Jersey City NJ 07310 | 201-469-2000 | 748-1472 | 391-4
TF: 800-888-4476 ■ *Web:* www.iso.com

American Integrated Services Inc (AIS)
1502 E Opp St ... Wilmington CA 90744 | 310-522-1168 | 522-0474 | 194
TF: 888-423-6060 ■ *Web:* www.americanintegrated.com

American Intellectual Property Law Assn (AIPLA)
1400 Crystal Dr Ste 600 ... Arlington VA 22202 | 703-415-0780 | 415-0786 | 49-10
Web: www.aipla.org

American Intercontinental University
231 N Martingale Rd 6th Fl ... Schaumburg IL 60173 | 877-701-3800 | 695-4538* | 166
**Fax Area Code:* 866 ■ *TF:* 877-221-5800 ■ *Web:* www.aiuniv.edu

American Interiors 302 S Byrne Rd ... Toledo OH 43615 | 419-535-1808 | | 320
Web: www.aminteriors.com

American International Automobile Dealers Assn (AIADA)
500 Montgomery St Ste 800 ... Alexandria VA 22314 | 800-462-4232 | 519-7810* | 49-18
**Fax Area Code:* 703 ■ *TF:* 800-462-4232 ■ *Web:* www.aiada.org

American International College
1000 State St ... Springfield MA 01109 | 413-205-3201 | 205-3051 | 166
TF: 800-242-3142 ■ *Web:* www.aic.edu

American International Forest Products LLC (AIFP)
5560 SW 107th Ave ... Beaverton OR 97005 | 503-641-1611 | 641-2800 | 191-3
TF: 800-366-1611 ■ *Web:* www.lumber.com

American International Inc
1040 Avendia Acaso ... Camarillo CA 93012 | 805-388-6800 | 388-7950 | 253
TF: 800-336-6500 ■ *Web:* www.aius.net

American International Manufacturing Co
1230 Fortna Ave ... Woodland CA 95776 | 530-666-2446 | 666-7325 | 273
Web: www.aimfab.com

American International Radio Inc
3601 E Algonquin Rd Ste800 ... Rolling Meadows IL 60008 | 847-818-9999 | | 681
Web: www.airadio.com

American International Rattlesnake Museum
202 San Felipe NW Ste A ... Albuquerque NM 87104 | 505-242-6569 | | 520
Web: www.rattlesnakes.com

American Iron & Steel Institute PAC
25 Massachusetts Ave NW Ste 800 ... Washington DC 20001 | 202-452-7100 | 463-6573 | 615
Web: www.steel.org

American Iron Magazine
1010 Summer St ... Stamford CT 06905 | 203-425-8777 | | 457-3
TF: 877-693-3572 ■ *Web:* www.aimag.com

American Islamic College
640 W Irving Park Rd ... Chicago IL 60613 | 773-281-4700 | 281-8552 | 166
Web: www.aicusa.edu

American Israel Public Affairs Committee (AIPAC)
251 H St ... Washington DC 20001 | 202-639-5200 | | 48-7
Web: www.aipac.org

American Jail Assn (AJA)
1135 Professional Ct ... Hagerstown MD 21740 | 301-790-3930 | 790-2941 | 49-7
TF: 800-211-2754 ■ *Web:* www.americanjail.org

American Jazz Museum
1616 E 18th St ... Kansas City MO 64108 | 816-474-6262 | | 572
Web: www.americanjazzmuseum.com

American Jersey Cattle Assn
6486 E Main St ... Reynoldsburg OH 43068 | 614-861-3636 | 861-8040 | 48-2
Web: www.usjersey.com

American Jewish Committee (AJC)
165 E 56th St ... New York NY 10022 | 212-751-4000 | 750-0326 | 48-8
Web: www.ajc.org

American Jewish Congress
745 Fifth Ave 30th Fl ... New York NY 10151 | 212-879-4500 | 758-1633 | 48-7
Web: ajcongress.org

American Jewish Historical Society
101 Newbury St ... Boston MA 02116 | 617-226-1245 | 226-1248 | 520
Web: www.ajhs.org

American Jewish Joint Distribution Committee (JDC)
711 Third Ave ... New York NY 10017 | 212-687-6200 | 370-5467 | 48-5
Web: www.jdc.org

American Jewish World Service (AJWS)
45 W 36th St ... New York NY 10018 | 212-792-2900 | 792-2930 | 48-5
TF: 800-889-7146 ■ *Web:* ajws.org

American Journalism Review
University of Maryland
Knight Hall ... College Park MD 20742 | 301-405-8805 | | 457-5
Web: ajr.org

American Jury Centers (AJC) PO Box 3677 ... Hailey ID 83333 | 561-542-8590 | | 261
Web: www.americanjurycenters.com

American Kennel Club (AKC)
260 Madison Ave ... New York NY 10016 | 212-696-8200 | 696-8299 | 48-18
Web: www.akc.org

American Kennel Club Museum of the Dog
101 Park Ave ... New York NY 10178 | 212-696-8360 | | 520
Web: museumofthedog.org

American Key Products Inc 1 Reuten Dr ... Closter NJ 07624 | 201-767-8022 | | 791
Web: akfponline.com

American Kidney Fund (AKF)
6110 Executive Blvd Ste 1010 ... Rockville MD 20852 | 800-638-8299 | 881-0898* | 48-17
**Fax Area Code:* 301 ■ *TF:* 800-638-8299 ■ *Web:* www.kidneyfund.org

American Kidney Stone Management Ltd (AKSM)
100 W Third Ave Ste 150 ... Columbus OH 43214 | 614-447-0281 | | 353
TF: 800-637-5188 ■ *Web:* www.aksm.com

American Labor Museum/Botto House National Landmark
83 Norwood St ... Haledon NJ 07508 | 973-595-7953 | 595-7291 | 520
Web: www.labormuseum.net

American Laboratories Inc (ALI)
4410 S 102nd St ... Omaha NE 68127 | 402-339-2494 | | 479
Web: americanlaboratories.com

American Laboratory
395 Oyster Pt Blvd Ste 321 ... South San Francisco CA 94080 | 650-243-5600 | | 457-19
Web: americanlaboratory.com

American Ladders & Scaffolds Inc
129 Kreiger Ln ... Glastonbury CT 06033 | 860-657-9252 | | 385
Web: www.americanladders.com

American Laminates
3142 Talbot Ave Bldg D ... Riverbank CA 95367 | 209-869-2536 | | 200
Web: americanlaminates.com

American Laminators
600 Applegate St PO Box 297 ... Drain OR 97435 | 541-836-2000 | | 817
Web: www.americanlaminators.com

American Land Rights Assn (ALRA)
30218 NE 82nd Ave PO Box 400 ... Battle Ground WA 98604 | 360-687-3087 | 687-2973 | 48-2
Web: www.landrights.org

American Land Title Assn (ALTA)
1800 M St NW Ste 300S ... Washington DC 20036 | 202-296-3671 | 223-5843 | 49-10
TF: 800-787-2582 ■ *Web:* www.alta.org

American Land Ventures LLC
800 Brickell Ave Ph 1 ... Miami FL 33131 | 305-350-1901 | 350-1977 | 652
Web: americanlandventures.com

American Landmark Properties
8114 Lawndale Ave ... Skokie IL 60076 | 847-568-0808 | 568-1717 | 652
Web: www.americanlandmark.com

American Language Communication Ctr
229 W 36th St ... New York NY 10018 | 212-736-2373 | 947-6403 | 423
Web: www.learnenglish.com

American Latvian Association Inc
400 Hurley Ave ... Rockville MD 20850 | 301-340-1914 | 340-8732 | 48-14
Web: www.alausa.org

American Law Institute (ALI)
4025 Chestnut St ... Philadelphia PA 19104 | 215-243-1600 | 243-1636 | 49-10
TF: 800-253-6397 ■ *Web:* www.ali.org

American Law Label Inc
1677 S Research Loop ... Tucson AZ 85710 | 888-529-5223 | 546-6203* | 413
**Fax Area Code:* 520 ■ *TF:* 888-529-5223 ■ *Web:* americanlawlabel.com

American Lawn Mower Co
7444 Shadeland Sta Way ... Indianapolis IN 46256 | 317-392-3615 | | 429
Web: www.americanlawnmower.com

American Lawyers Co, The
853 Westpoint Pky Ste 710 ... Cleveland OH 44145 | 440-871-8700 | 871-9997 | 637-10
TF: 800-843-4000 ■ *Web:* www.alqlist.com

Phone | Fax | Class

American Lebanese Syrian Associated Charities (ALSAC)
262 Danny Thomas Pl ... Memphis TN 38105 901-595-3306 578-2805 48-5
TF: 800-822-6344 ■ *Web:* www.stjude.org

American Lecithin Company Inc
115 Hurley Rd Unit 2B ... Oxford CT 06478 203-262-7100 262-7101 296-29
TF: 800-364-4416 ■ *Web:* www.americanlecithin.com

American Legacy Media
1544 W 1620 N Ste 1a ... Clearfield UT 84015 866-233-8165 774-5472* 637-2
**Fax Area Code:* 801 ■ *TF:* 866-233-8165 ■ *Web:* www.americanlegacymedia.com

American LegalNet Inc
16501 Ventura Blvd Ste 615 ... Encino CA 91436 818-817-9225 428
TF: 800-293-2771 ■ *Web:* www.alncorp.com

American Legion, The
700 N Pennsylvania St ... Indianapolis IN 46204 317-630-1200 630-1223 48-19
TF: 800-433-3318 ■ *Web:* www.legion.org

American Legislative Exchange Council (ALEC)
2900 Crystal Dr 6th Fl ... Arlington VA 22202 703-373-0933 373-0927 48-7
Web: www.alec.org

American Liberty Hospitality Inc
2901 Wilcrest Dr Ste 120 ... Houston TX 77042 713-977-5556 975-6025 379
Web: amliberty.com

American Library Assn (ALA)
50 E Huron St ... Chicago IL 60611 312-944-6780 944-2641 49-11
TF: 800-545-2433 ■ *Web:* www.ala.org

American Lighting Assn (ALA)
2050 Stemmons Fwy Ste 10046 ... Dallas TX 75207 214-698-9898 698-9899 49-4
TF: 800-605-4448 ■ *Web:* alalighting.com

American Limousines Inc
4401 E Fairmount Ave ... Baltimore MD 21224 410-522-0400 441
TF: 800-787-1690 ■ *Web:* www.amerlimo.com

American Littoral Society (ALS)
18 Hartshorne Dr Ste 1 ... Highlands NJ 07732 732-291-0055 291-3551 48-13
Web: www.littoralsociety.org

American Liver Foundation (ALF)
39 Broadway ... New York NY 10006 212-668-1000 483-8179 48-17
TF: 800-465-4837 ■ *Web:* liverfoundation.org

American Locker Group Inc
4170-103 Distribution Cir ... North Las Vegas NV 89030 817-329-1600 481-3993 692
OTC: ALGI ■ *TF:* 800-828-9118 ■ *Web:* www.americanlocker.com

American Logistics Assn (ALA)
1101 Vermont Ave NW Ste 1002 ... Washington DC 20005 202-466-2520 296-4419 48-19
TF: 800-791-7146 ■ *Web:* www.ala-national.org

American Louver Co 7700 N Austin Ave ... Skokie IL 60077 800-772-0355 966-8074* 439
**Fax Area Code:* 847 ■ *TF:* 800-772-0355 ■ *Web:* americanlouver.com

American Lubrication Equipment Corp
11212A McCormick Rd PO Box 1350 ... Hunt Valley MD 21030 410-252-9300 759-2637* 541
**Fax Area Code:* 800 ■ *TF:* 888-252-9300 ■ *Web:* www.americanlube.com

American Lumber Distributors & Brokers Inc
2405 Republic Blvd ... Birmingham AL 35201 205-791-0155 752
TF: 800-433-8578

American Machine Works Inc
803 S 20th St ... Omaha NE 68108 402-342-4881 454
Web: www.americanmachineworks.com

American Made Cutlery
905 Industrial Rd ... Waverly IA 50677 319-352-2080 362
Web: americanmadecutlery.com

American Malting Barley Assn (AMBA)
740 N Plankinton Ave Ste 830 ... Milwaukee WI 53203 414-272-4640 49-6
Web: www.ambainc.org

American Manufacturing Company Inc
22011 Greenhouse Rd ... Elkwood VA 22718 800-345-3132 825-1785* 640
**Fax Area Code:* 540 ■ *TF:* 800-345-3132 ■ *Web:* www.americanonsite.com

American Marazzi Tile Inc
359 Clay Rd ... Sunnyvale TX 75182 972-232-3801 226-5629 751
Web: www.marazziusa.com

American Marketing Services & Consultant
939 Tower Rd ... Mundelein IL 60060 847-566-4545 194
Web: amscinc.com

American Marking Systems Inc
1015 Paulison Ave PO Box 1677 ... Clifton NJ 07011 973-478-5600 478-0039 467
TF: 800-782-6766 ■ *Web:* www.ams-stamps.com

American Massage Therapy Assn (AMTA)
500 Davis St Ste 900 ... Evanston IL 60201 847-864-0123 864-1178 48-17
TF: 877-905-2700 ■ *Web:* www.amtamassage.org

American Master Products Inc
PO Box 930006 ... Wixom MI 48393 248-437-3000 45
TF: 800-690-0099

American Mathematical Society (AMS)
201 Charles St ... Providence RI 02904 401-455-4000 331-3842 49-19
TF: 800-321-4267 ■ *Web:* www.ams.org

American Mechanical Services
13300 Mid Atlantic Blvd ... Laurel MD 20708 301-206-5070 206-2520 189-10
Web: www.amsofusa.com

American Media Inc 4 New York Plz ... New York NY 10004 212-545-4800 637-9
Web: www.americanmediainc.com

American Medical Assn
AMA Plaza 330 N Wabash Ave Ste 39300 ... Chicago IL 60611 312-464-4782 48-5
Web: www.ama-assn.org

American Medical Directors Assn (AMDA)
10500 Little Patuxent Pkwy Ste 210 ... Columbia MD 21044 410-740-9743 740-4572 49-8
TF: 800-876-2632 ■ *Web:* paltc.org

American Medical Group Assn (AMGA)
1422 Duke St ... Alexandria VA 22314 703-838-0033 548-1890 49-8
Web: www.amga.org

American Medical ID
949 Wakefield Ste 100 ... Houston TX 77018 800-363-5985 475
TF: 800-363-5985 ■ *Web:* www.americanmedical-id.com

American Medical Informatics Assn (AMIA)
4720 Montgomery Ln Ste 500 ... Bethesda MD 20814 301-657-1291 657-1296 49-8
Web: www.amia.org

American Medical News 515 N State St ... Chicago IL 60654 312-464-4429 457-16
Web: www.amednews.com

American Medical Rehabilitation Providers Assn (AMRPA)
529 14th St, NW Ste 1280 ... Washington DC 20045 202-223-1920 223-1925 49-8
TF: 888-346-4624 ■ *Web:* www.amrpa.org

American Medical Response (AMR)
6200 S Syracuse Way Ste 200 ... Greenwood Village CO 80111 303-495-1200 30
TF: 877-244-4890 ■ *Web:* www.amr.net

American Medical Student Assn (AMSA)
1902 Assn Dr ... Reston VA 20191 703-620-6600 620-5873 49-5
TF: 800-767-2266 ■ *Web:* www.amsa.org

American Medical Technologists (AMT)
10700 W Higgins Rd Ste 150 ... Rosemont IL 60018 847-823-5169 823-0458 49-8
TF: 800-275-1268 ■ *Web:* www.americanmedtech.org

American Medical Writers Assn (AMWA)
30 W Gude Dr Ste 525 ... Rockville MD 20850 240-238-0940 294-9006* 49-14
**Fax Area Code:* 301 ■ *Web:* www.amwa.org

American Megatrends Inc (AMI)
5555 Oakbrook Pkwy Bldg 200 ... Norcross GA 30093 770-246-8600 246-8790 176
TF: 800-828-9264 ■ *Web:* www.ami.com

American Memorial Park
PO Box 5198-CHRB ... Saipan MP 96950 670-234-7207 234-6698 564
Web: www.nps.gov

American Mensa Ltd
1229 Corporate Dr W ... Arlington TX 76006 817-607-0060 649-5232 48-15
TF: 800-666-3672 ■ *Web:* www.us.mensa.org

American Mental Health Counselors Assn (AMHCA)
107 S W St Ste 779 ... Alexandria VA 22314 703-548-6002 548-5233 49-15
TF: 800-326-2642 ■ *Web:* www.amhca.org

American Metal & Plastics Inc
450 32nd St SW ... Grand Rapids MI 49548 616-452-6061 452-3835 489
Web: www.ampi-gr.com

American Metal Bearing Co
7191 Acacia Ave ... Garden Grove CA 92841 714-892-5527 898-3217 620
TF: 800-888-3048 ■ *Web:* www.ambco.net

American Metal Crafters LLC
695 High St ... Middletown CT 06457 860-343-1960 198
TF: 800-840-9243 ■ *Web:* www.americanmetalcraftersllc.com

American Metal Fab Inc
55515 Franklin Dr ... Three Rivers MI 49093 269-279-5108 689
Web: americanmetalfab.com

American Metal Fibers Inc
13420 Rockland Rd ... Lake Bluff IL 60044 847-362-2634 362-7494 485
Web: www.amfi-usa.com

American Metal Market LLC
225 Park Ave S 6th Fl ... New York NY 10003 212-213-6202 345
Web: www.amm.com

American Metal Technologies LLC
8213 Durand Ave ... Sturtevant WI 53177 262-633-1756 454
Web: amermetals.com

American Metalcraft Inc
3708 N River Rd Ste 800 ... Franklin Park IL 60131 708-345-1177 333-6046* 488
**Fax Area Code:* 800 ■ *TF:* 800-333-9133 ■ *Web:* www.amnow.com

American Metals Company Inc
740 W Broadway Rd ... Mesa AZ 85210 480-834-1923 686
Web: www.amcrecycling.com

American Metals Corp
1499 Pkwy Blvd ... West Sacramento CA 95691 916-371-7700 492
TF: 800-547-9032 ■ *Web:* american-metals.com

American Meteorological Society (AMS)
45 Beacon St ... Boston MA 02108 617-227-2425 742-8718 49-19
TF: 800-824-0405 ■ *Web:* www.ametsoc.org

American Metro Bank 4878 N Broadway ... Chicago IL 60640 773-769-6868 70
Web: www.americanmetrobank.com

American Micro Products Inc
4288 Armstrong Blvd ... Batavia OH 45103 800-479-2193 567
TF: 800-479-2193 ■ *Web:* www.american-micro.com

American Microsemiconductor Inc
133 Kings Rd ... Madison NJ 07940 973-377-9566 377-3078 246
Web: www.americanmicrosemi.com

American Millwork Corp 4840 Beck Dr ... Elkhart IN 46516 574-295-4158 293-5378 499
Web: www.americanmillwork.com

American Miniature Horse Assn (AMHA)
5601 S IH-35 W ... Alvarado TX 76009 817-783-5600 783-6403 48-3
Web: www.amha.org

American Modern Home Insurance Co
PO Box 5323 ... Cincinnati OH 45201 513-943-7200 391-4
TF: 800-543-2644 ■ *Web:* www.amig.com

American Modular Systems Inc
787 Spreckels Ave ... Manteca CA 95336 209-825-1921 186
Web: www.americanmodular.com

American Modular Technologies (AMT)
6306 Old 421 Rd PO Box 1069 ... Liberty NC 27298 336-622-6200 622-6473 105
Web: www.americanmodulartechnologies.com

American Moistening Company Inc
10402 Rodney St ... Pineville NC 28134 704-889-7281 610
TF: 800-948-5540 ■ *Web:* www.amco.com

American Montessori Society (AMS)
281 Park Ave S 6th Fl ... New York NY 10010 212-358-1250 358-1256 48-11
Web: www.amshq.org

American Morgan Horse Assn (AMHA)
4066 Shelburne Rd Ste 5 ... Shelburne VT 05482 802-985-4944 985-8897 48-3
TF: 888-436-3700 ■ *Web:* www.morganhorse.com

American Motel Hotel Brokers Inc
5151 N 16th St Ste 224 ... Phoenix AZ 85016 602-230-2110 652
Web: www.amhbnetwork.com

American Motel Management
1872 Montreal Rd Ste A ... Tucker GA 30084 770-939-1801 939-1419 655
TF: 800-580-8258 ■ *Web:* www.americanmotelonline.com

American Motive Power Inc
9431 Foster Wheeler Rd ... Dansville NY 14437 585-335-3131 335-2063 650
Web: www.americanmotivepower.com

American Motorcyclist Assn (AMA)
13515 Yarmouth Dr ... Pickerington OH 43147 614-856-1900 856-1920 48-22
TF: 800-262-5646 ■ *Web:* www.americanmotorcyclist.com

American Moving & Storage Assn (AMSA)
1611 Duke St ... Alexandria VA 22314 703-683-7410 683-7527 49-21
TF: 888-849-2672 ■ *Web:* www.moving.org

American MSC Inc 2401 Elliott Dr ... Troy MI 48083 248-589-7770 589-7777 718
Web: www.americanmsc.com

American Municipal Power Inc
1111 Schrock Rd Ste 100 ... Columbus OH 43229 614-540-1111 540-1113 787
Web: www.amppartners.org

American Muscle 7 Lee Blvd ... Malvern PA 19355 610-251-2397 791
TF: 888-332-7930 ■ *Web:* www.americanmuscle.com

	Phone	Fax	Class
American Museum of Fly Fishing 4104 Main Rd. . . . Manchester VT 05254 *TF:* 800-333-1550 ■ *Web:* www.amff.org	802-362-3300	362-3308	522
American Museum of Science & Energy (AMSE) 300 S Tulane Ave . . . . Oak Ridge TN 37830 *Web:* amse.org	865-576-3200	576-6024	520
American Music Therapy Association Inc (AMTA) 8455 Colesville Rd Ste 1000 . . . . Silver Spring MD 20910 *Web:* www.musictherapy.org	301-589-3300	589-5175	48-17
American Musical Supply PO Box 152. . . . Spicer MN 56288 *TF:* 800-458-4076 ■ *Web:* www.americanmusical.com	320-796-2088		526
American Musicological Society (AMS) 6010 College Stn . . . . Brunswick ME 04011 **Fax Area Code:* 207 ■ *Web:* www.ams-net.org	212-992-6340	798-4254*	48-4
American Mutual Share Insurance Corp 5656 Frantz Rd . . . . Dublin OH 43017 *Web:* www.excessshare.com	614-764-1900		390
American National Bank 628 Main St. . . . Danville VA 24541 *NASDAQ:* AMNB ■ *TF:* 800-240-8190 ■ *Web:* www.amnb.com	434-792-5111		360-2
American National CattleWomen Inc (ANCW) 200 NW 66th St . . . . Oklahoma City OK 73116 *Web:* ancw.org	303-850-3441		48-2
American National Insurance Co 1 Moody Plz . . . . Galveston TX 77550 *NASDAQ:* ANAT ■ *Web:* www.americannational.com	409-763-4661		391-2
American National Logistics Inc 4856 Interstate 30 W. . . . Rockwall TX 75087 *Web:* www.anlinc.com	972-772-3132		194
American National Property and Casualty Co (ANPAC) 1949 E Sunshine . . . . Springfield MO 65899 *Web:* www.anpac.com	417-887-0220	887-1801	391-4
American National Red Cross *Portland Platelet Donation Ctr* 3131 N Vancouver Ave. . . . Portland OR 97227 *TF:* 800-733-2767 ■ *Web:* www.redcrossblood.org	800-733-2767		417
American National Rubber Co Main & High St. . . . Ceredo WV 25507 *TF:* 800-624-3410 ■ *Web:* www.anr-co.com	304-453-1311	453-2347	677
American National Standards Institute (ANSI) 25 W 43rd St 4th Fl . . . . New York NY 10036 *TF:* 800-374-3818 ■ *Web:* www.ansi.org	212-642-4900	398-0023	48-1
American National University (ANU) 1328 Hwy 11 W . . . . Bristol TN 37620 *TF:* 888-956-2732 ■ *Web:* www.an.edu	423-878-4440		800
American Natural Soda Ash Corp 15 Riverside Ave. . . . Westport CT 06880 *Web:* www.ansac.com	203-226-9056	227-1484	144
American Naturopathic Medical Assn (ANMA) PO Box 96273 . . . . Las Vegas NV 89193 *Web:* www.anma.org	702-450-3477		48-17
American Needle Inc 1275 Busch Pkwy. . . . Buffalo Grove IL 60089 *Web:* americanneedle.com	847-215-0011		155-9
American Nephrology Nurses Assn (ANNA) 200 E Holly Ave . . . . Sewell NJ 08080 *TF:* 888-600-2662 ■ *Web:* www.annanurse.org	856-256-2320	589-7463	49-8
American NetLink PO Box 205. . . . Good Hope GA 30641 *Web:* www.americannetlink.com	770-266-7682		180
American Neurological Assn (ANA) 1120 Rte 73 Ste 200. . . . Mount Laurel NJ 08054 *Web:* myana.org	856-638-0423		49-8
American Nickeloid Co 2900 Main St. . . . Peru IL 61354 *TF:* 800-645-5643 ■ *Web:* www.nickeloid.com	815-223-0373	223-5344	481
American Nonwovens Inc 9141 Arrow Rte. . . . Rancho Cucamonga CA 91730 *Web:* www.americannonwoven.com	909-466-8897	466-9302	745-6
American Nuclear Insurers (ANI) 95 Glastonbury Blvd Ste 300 . . . . Glastonbury CT 06033 *Web:* www.amnucins.com	860-682-1301		49-9
American Nuclear Society (ANS) 555 N Kensington Ave . . . . LaGrange IL 60526 *TF:* 800-323-3044 ■ *Web:* www.ans.org	708-352-6611	352-0499	49-19
American Numismatic Society 75 Varick St 11th Fl . . . . New York NY 10013 *Web:* numismatics.org	212-571-4470	571-4479	520
American Nurses Assn (ANA) 8515 Georgia Ave Ste 400 . . . . Silver Spring MD 20910 *TF:* 800-274-4262 ■ *Web:* www.nursingworld.org	301-628-5000	628-5001	49-8
American Nurses Association California (ANA\C) 1121 L St Ste 406. . . . Sacramento CA 95814 *Web:* www.anacalifornia.org	916-346-4590	400-3599	533
American Nutrition Inc PO Box 1405 . . . . Ogden UT 84401 *Web:* www.anibrands.com	801-394-3477		578
American Occupational Therapy Association Inc (AOTA) 6116 Executive Blvd Ste 200 . . . . Bethesda MD 20852 *TF:* 800-877-1383 ■ *Web:* www.aota.org	301-652-2682	652-7711	49-8
American Office Equipment Company Inc 309 N Calvert St. . . . Baltimore MD 21202 *Web:* americanoffice.com	410-539-7529		321
American Oil Chemists Society (AOCS) 2710 S Boulder PO Box 17190. . . . Urbana IL 61802 *TF:* 866-535-2730 ■ *Web:* www.aocs.org	217-359-2344	351-8091	48-12
American Organization for Bodywork Therapies of Asia (AOBTA) 391 Wilmington Pk Ste 3 PO Box 260 . . . . Glen Mills PA 19342 *Web:* www.aobta.org	484-841-6023		48-17
American Organization of Nurse Executives (AONE) 155 N Wacker Dr Ste 400 . . . . Chicago IL 60606 *Web:* www.aonl.org	312-422-2800	422-4503	49-8
American Orthodontics Corp 1714 Cambridge Ave . . . . Sheboygan WI 53081 *TF:* 800-558-7687 ■ *Web:* www.americanortho.com	920-457-5051	457-1485	228
American Orthopaedic Society for Sports Medicine (AOSSM) 9400 W Higgins Rd Ste 300 . . . . Rosemont IL 60018 *TF:* 877-321-3500 ■ *Web:* www.sportsmed.org	847-292-4900	292-4905	49-8
American Orthotic & Prosthetic Assn (AOPA) 330 John Carlyle St Ste 200. . . . Alexandria VA 22314 *Web:* www.aopanet.org	571-431-0876	431-0899	48-17
American Osteopathic Assn (AOA) 142 E Ontario St . . . . Chicago IL 60611 **Fax Area Code:* 312 ■ *TF:* 800-621-1773 ■ *Web:* www.osteopathic.org	888-626-9262	202-8200*	49-8
American Outdoor Products Inc 6350 Gunpark Dr . . . . Boulder CO 80301 *TF:* 800-641-0500 ■ *Web:* www.backpackerspantry.com	800-641-0500		296-37
American Outfitters Ltd 3700 Sunset Ave. . . . Waukegan IL 60087 *TF:* 800-397-6081 ■ *Web:* www.americanoutfitters.com	847-623-3959		711
American Overseas Marine Corp 100 Newport Ave Ext. . . . Quincy MA 02171	617-786-8300	472-4925	313
American Packaging Corp 777 Driving Park Ave . . . . Rochester NY 14613 *TF:* 800-551-8801 ■ *Web:* www.americanpackaging.com	585-254-9500	254-5801	548
American Packaging Machinery Inc 2550 S Eastwood Dr. . . . Woodstock IL 60098 *Web:* www.americanpackagingmachinery.com	815-337-8580	337-8583	547
American Packing & Gasket Co (APG) 6039 Armour Dr PO Box 213 . . . . Houston TX 77020 *TF:* 800-888-5223 ■ *Web:* callapg.com	713-675-5271	675-2730	326
American Paint Horse Assn (APHA) 2800 Meacham Blvd. . . . Fort Worth TX 76137 *Web:* apha.com	817-834-2742	834-3152	48-3
American Pallet Inc 1001 Knox Rd . . . . Oakdale CA 95361 *Web:* www.americanpallet.com	209-847-6122	847-6154	551
American Panel Corp 5800 SE 78th St . . . . Ocala FL 34472 *TF:* 800-327-3015 ■ *Web:* www.americanpanel.com	352-245-7055	245-0726	664
American Paper & Twine Co 7400 Cockrill Bend Blvd. . . . Nashville TN 37209 **Fax Area Code:* 877 ■ *TF:* 800-251-2437 ■ *Web:* shopapt.com	615-350-9000	413-5055*	559
American Parkinson Disease Assn (APDA) 135 Parkinson Ave . . . . Staten Island NY 10305 *TF:* 800-223-2732 ■ *Web:* www.apdaparkinson.org	718-981-8001	981-4399	48-17
American Pavilion 1706 Warrington Ave . . . . Danville IL 61832 *TF:* 800-424-9699 ■ *Web:* americanpavilion.com	217-443-0800	443-9619	733
American Paving Company Inc PO Box 4348 . . . . Fresno CA 93706 *Web:* www.americanpavingco.com	559-268-9886		188-4
American Payroll Assn (APA) 660 N Main Ave Ste 100. . . . San Antonio TX 78205 *Web:* www.americanpayroll.org	210-226-4600	226-4027	49-12
American Peanut Shellers Assn 2336 Lake Pk Dr. . . . Albany GA 31707 *Web:* www.peanut-shellers.org	229-888-2508	888-5150	49-6
American Pet Products Manufacturers Assn (APPMA) 255 Glenville Rd . . . . Greenwich CT 06831 *TF:* 800-452-1225 ■ *Web:* www.americanpetproducts.org	203-532-0000	532-0551	49-4
American Petroleum Institute (API) 1220 L St NW. . . . Washington DC 20005 *Web:* www.api.org	202-682-8000		48-12
American Pharmacists Association PAC 2215 Constitution Ave NW . . . . Washington DC 20037 *TF:* 800-237-2742 ■ *Web:* www.pharmacist.com	202-628-4410	783-2351	615
American Pharmacy Services Corp (APSC) 102 Enterprise Dr . . . . Frankfort KY 40601 *TF:* 800-928-2228 ■ *Web:* www.apscnet.com	502-695-8899		238
American Philatelic Society (APS) 100 Match Factory Pl . . . . Bellefonte PA 16823 *Web:* www.stamps.org	814-933-3803	933-6128	48-18
American Philosophical Society (APS) 104 S Fifth St . . . . Philadelphia PA 19106 *Web:* www.amphilsoc.org	215-440-3400		48-11
American Physical Security Group LLC 1030 Goodworth Dr . . . . Apex NC 27539 *Web:* www.americanpsg.com	919-363-1894		234
American Physical Society (APS) 1 Physics Ellipse . . . . College Park MD 20740 *TF:* 866-918-1164 ■ *Web:* www.aps.org	301-209-3200	209-0865	49-19
American Physical Therapy Assn (APTA) 1111 N Fairfax St . . . . Alexandria VA 22314 *TF:* 800-999-2782 ■ *Web:* www.apta.org	703-684-2782	706-8536	49-8
American Pilots' Assn 499 S Capitol St SW Ste 409 . . . . Washington DC 20003 *Web:* www.americanpilots.org	202-484-0700	484-9320	49-21
American Pipe & Supply Company Inc 4100 Eastlake Blvd . . . . Birmingham AL 35217 *TF:* 800-476-9460 ■ *Web:* www.americanpipe.com	205-252-9460	252-9457	612
American Planning Assn (APA) 1030 15th St NW Ste 750 W. . . . Washington DC 20005 *Web:* www.planning.org	202-872-0611	872-0643	49-17
American Plastic Molding Corp 965 S Elm St. . . . Scottsburg IN 47170 *TF:* 877-527-8427 ■ *Web:* www.apmc.com	812-752-7000	752-5155	604
American Plastic Profiles Inc 2121 S Economy Rd. . . . Morristown TN 37813 *Web:* www.americanplasticprofiles.com	423-586-3718		605-2
American Plastic Toys Inc 799 Ladd Rd. . . . Walled Lake MI 48390 *TF:* 800-521-7080 ■ *Web:* www.americanplastictoys.com	248-624-4881		762
American Players Theater 5950 Golf Course Rd PO Box 819 . . . . Spring Green WI 53588 *Web:* americanplayers.org	608-588-2361		572
American Pneumatic Tool Inc 1000 S Grand Ave. . . . Santa Ana CA 92705 *TF:* 800-532-7402 ■ *Web:* www.apt-tools.com	562-204-1555	204-1773	759
American Podiatric Medical Assn (APMA) 9312 Old Georgetown Rd . . . . Bethesda MD 20814 *TF:* 800-275-2762 ■ *Web:* www.apma.org	301-581-9200	530-2752	49-8
American Polarity Therapy Assn (APTA) PO Box 10942 . . . . Parkville MD 21234 *Web:* polaritytherapy.org	336-574-1121	574-1151	48-17
American Polarizers Inc 141 S Seventh St . . . . Reading PA 19602 *TF:* 800-736-9031 ■ *Web:* www.apioptics.com	610-373-5177	373-2229	544
American Police Hall of Fame & Museum 6350 Horizon Dr. . . . Titusville FL 32780 *Web:* www.aphf.org	321-264-0911	264-0033	520

Name / Address	City	State	Zip	Phone	Fax	Class
American Political Science Assn (APSA) 1527 New Hampshire Ave NW *Web:* www.apsanet.org	Washington	DC	20036	202-483-2512	483-2657	49-5
American Polywater Corp 11222 60th St N *TF:* 800-328-9384 ■ *Web:* www.polywater.com	Stillwater	MN	55082	651-430-2270	430-3634	145
American Pool Enterprises Inc 11515 Cronridge Dr Ste Q *Web:* americanpool.com	Owings Mills	MD	21117	443-471-1190		271
American Poolplayers Association Inc (APA) 1000 Lake St Louis Blvd Ste 325 *Web:* poolplayers.com	Lake Saint Louis	MO	63367	636-625-8611	625-2975	48-22
American Portfolios Holdings Inc 4250 Veterans Memorial Hwy Ste 420E *Web:* www.americanportfolios.com	Holbrook	NY	11741	631-439-4600		401
American Portwell Technology Inc 44200 Christy St *Web:* www.portwell.com	Fremont	CA	94538	510-403-3399		174
American Postal Workers Union PAC 1300 L St NW *Web:* www.apwu.org	Washington	DC	20005	202-842-4200		615
American Power Connection Systems Inc 2460 Midland Rd *TF:* 800-759-7833 ■ *Web:* www.american-power.com	Bay City	MI	48706	989-686-6302	686-8720	815
American Power Conversion Corp (APC) 132 Fairgrounds Rd *TF:* 800-788-2208 ■ *Web:* www.apc.com	West Kingston	RI	02892	401-789-5735	789-3710	253
American Power Pull Corp 550 W Linfoot St PO Box 109 *TF:* 800-808-5922 ■ *Web:* www.americanpowerpull.com	Wauseon	OH	43567	419-335-7050	335-7070	470
American Presence Inc 134 Fifth Ave Ste 206 *TF:* 800-429-8983 ■ *Web:* www.international-presence.com	Indialantic	FL	32903	321-726-9941	726-6210	178-1
American Press 4900 Hwy 90 E *Web:* www.americanpress.com	Lake Charles	LA	70615	337-433-3000		532-2
American Printing House for the Blind 1839 Frankfort Ave PO Box 6085 *TF:* 800-223-1839 ■ *Web:* www.aph.org	Louisville	KY	40206	502-895-2405	899-2274	637-10
American Product Distributors Inc (APD) 8350 Arrowridge Blvd *TF:* 800-849-5842 ■ *Web:* www.americanproduct.com	Charlotte	NC	28273	704-522-9411		534
American Products Company Inc 610 Rahway Ave *Web:* www.amerprod.com	Union	NJ	07083	908-687-4100	687-0037	621
American Products Inc (API) 13909 Lynmar Blvd *Web:* www.americanproducts.com	Tampa	FL	33626	813-925-0144		295
American Products LLC 597 Evergreen Rd *TF:* 855-736-2135 ■ *Web:* amprod.us	Strafford	MO	65757	417-736-2135	736-2662	488
American Professional Services Inc 111 Harrison Ave *Web:* www.americanpi.net	Oklahoma City	OK	73104	405-636-4222	632-7667	400
American Profol Inc 4333 C St SW *Web:* www.americanprofol.com	Cedar Rapids	IA	52404	319-365-0599		600
American Prospect 1710 Rhode Island Ave NW 12th Fl *Web:* prospect.org	Washington	DC	20036	202-776-0730		457-17
American Psychiatric Assn (APA) 1000 Wilson Blvd Ste 1825 *TF:* 888-357-7924 ■ *Web:* www.psychiatry.org	Arlington	VA	22209	703-907-7300	907-1085	49-15
American Psychiatric Nurses Assn (APNA) 1555 Wilson Blvd Ste 530 *TF:* 866-243-2443 ■ *Web:* www.apna.org	Arlington	VA	22209	703-243-2443	243-3390	49-8
American Psychiatric Publishing Inc 1000 Wilson Blvd Ste 1825 *TF:* 800-368-5777 ■ *Web:* www.appi.org	Arlington	VA	22209	703-907-7322	907-1091	637-9
American Psychoanalytic Assn (APSAA) 309 E 49th St *Web:* www.apsa.org	New York	NY	10017	212-752-0450	593-0571	49-15
American Psychological Assn (APA) 750 First St NE *TF:* 800-374-2721 ■ *Web:* www.apa.org	Washington	DC	20002	202-336-5500	336-5962	49-15
American Public Communications Council Inc (APCC) 625 Slaters Ln Ste 104 *Web:* www.apccsideas.com	Alexandria	VA	22314	703-739-1322	739-1324	49-20
American Public Gas Assn (APGA) 201 Massachusetts Ave NE Ste C-4 *TF:* 800-927-4204 ■ *Web:* www.apga.org	Washington	DC	20002	202-464-2742	464-0246	48-12
American Public Health Assn (APHA) 800 'I' St NW *Web:* www.apha.org	Washington	DC	20001	202-777-2742	777-2533	49-8
American Public Human Services Assn (APHSA) 1133 19th St NW Ste 400 *Web:* www.aphsa.org	Washington	DC	20036	202-682-0100	289-6555	49-7
American Public Land Exchange Company Inc 125 Bank St Ste 610 *Web:* american-lands.com	Missoula	MT	59802	406-728-4176		653
American Public Life Insurance Co 2305 Lakeland Dr PO Box 925 *TF:* 800-256-8606 ■ *Web:* www.ampublic.com	Jackson	MS	39205	601-936-6600		391-5
American Public Power Assn (APPA) 1875 Connecticut Ave NW Ste 1200 *Web:* www.publicpower.org	Washington	DC	20009	202-467-2900	467-2910	48-12
American Public Television (APT) 55 Summer St 4th Fl *Web:* www.aptonline.org	Boston	MA	02110	617-338-4455	338-5369	632
American Public Transportation Assn (APTA) 1666 K St NW Ste 1100 *Web:* www.apta.com	Washington	DC	20006	202-496-4800	496-4321	49-21
American Public University System (AMU) 111 W Congress St *TF:* 877-755-2787 ■ *Web:* www.amu.apus.edu	Charles Town	WV	25414	877-755-2787		167
American Public Works Assn (APWA) 2345 Grand Blvd Ste 700 *TF:* 800-848-2792 ■ *Web:* www.apwa.net	Kansas City	MO	64108	816-472-6100	472-1610	49-7
American Qualex Scientific Products (AQSP) 920-A Calle Negocio *Web:* www.aqsp.com	San Clemente	CA	92673	949-492-8298		231

Name / Address	City	State	Zip	Phone	Fax	Class
American Quality Schools Corp 910 W Van Buren St *Web:* www.aqs.org	Chicago	IL	60607	312-226-3355		685
American Quarter Horse Assn (AQHA) 1600 Quarter Horse Dr *TF:* 800-291-7323 ■ *Web:* www.aqha.com	Amarillo	TX	79104	806-376-4811	349-6411	48-3
American Rabbit Breeders Assn (ARBA) PO Box 5667 *TF:* 800-753-9448 ■ *Web:* arba.net	Bloomington	IL	61702	309-664-7500	664-0941	48-3
American Radio Relay League (ARRL) 225 Main St *TF:* 888-277-5289 ■ *Web:* www.arrl.org	Newington	CT	06111	860-594-0200	594-0259	49-14
American Radiolabeled Chemicals Inc (ARC) 101 ARC Dr *TF:* 800-331-6661 ■ *Web:* www.arcincusa.com	Saint Louis	MO	63146	314-991-4545	991-4692	145
American Railcar Industries 100 Clark St *NASDAQ: ARII* ■ *TF:* 800-489-9888 ■ *Web:* www.americanrailcar.com	Saint Charles	MO	63301	636-940-6000	940-6030	650
American Railway Engineering & Maintenance-of-Way Assn (AREMA) 4501 Forbes Blvd Ste 130 *Web:* www.arema.org	Lanham	MD	20706	301-459-3200		49-21
American Raisin Packers Inc 2335 Chandler PO Box 30 *Web:* www.americanraisinpacking.com	Selma	CA	93662	559-896-4760	896-8942	11-1
American Ramp Sales Co 601 S Mckinley Ave *TF:* 800-949-2024 ■ *Web:* americanrampcompany.com	Joplin	MO	64801	417-206-6816		295
American Real Estate Institute 211 Catoma St *TF:* 800-489-2701	Montgomery	AL	36104	334-262-2701	262-2799	167-3
American Realty Investors Inc 1603 Lyndon B Johnson Fwy Ste 800 One Hickory Ctr *NYSE: ARL* ■ *Web:* www.americanrealtyinvest.com	Dallas	TX	75234	469-522-4200	522-4299	655
American Recycled Plastic Inc 773 N Union Grove Rd *Web:* itsrecycled.com	Friendsville	TN	37737	865-738-3439	738-3731	661
American Red Ball Transit Company Inc PO Box 1127 *TF:* 800-733-8139 ■ *Web:* www.redball.com	Indianapolis	IN	46206	800-733-8139		519
American Red Cross 2025 E St NW *TF:* 800-257-7575 ■ *Web:* www.redcross.org	Washington	DC	20006	202-303-4498	303-0044	48-5
American Reeling Devices Inc 15 Airpark Vista Blvd *TF:* 800-354-7335 ■ *Web:* www.americanreeling.net	Dayton	NV	89403	800-354-7335		117
American Refining Group Inc 77 N Kendall Ave *Web:* www.amref.com	Bradford	PA	16701	814-368-1200		580
American Refrigeration Supplies 2632 E Chambers St *Web:* arsnet.com	Phoenix	AZ	85040	602-243-2792	243-2893	665
American Registry for Internet Numbers (ARIN) 3635 Concorde Pkwy Ste 200 *Web:* www.arin.net	Chantilly	VA	20151	703-227-9840		48-9
American Registry of Diagnostic Medical Sonographers (ARDMS) 1401 Rockville Pk Ste 600 *TF:* 800-541-9754 ■ *Web:* www.ardms.org	Rockville	MD	20852	301-738-8401	738-0312	49-8
American Relays Inc 15537 S Blackburn Ave *Web:* www.americanrelays.com	Norwalk	CA	90650	562-926-2837	944-0590	203
American Reliance Inc (AMREL) 3445 Fletcher Ave *TF:* 800-882-6735 ■ *Web:* amrel.com	El Monte	CA	91731	626-443-6818		529
American Religious Town Hall Meeting Inc PO Box 180118 *TF:* 800-783-9828 ■ *Web:* www.americanreligious.org	Dallas	TX	75218	214-328-9828	328-3042	451
American Renal Associates Inc 500 Cummings Ctr Ste 6550 *TF:* 877-997-3625 ■ *Web:* www.americanrenal.com	Beverly	MA	01915	978-922-3080		353
American Renolit Corp 1207 E Lincolnway *Web:* laminatefinder.com	La Porte	IN	46350	219-324-6886	324-5332	599
American Rental Assn (ARA) 1900 19th St *TF:* 800-334-2177 ■ *Web:* www.ararental.org	Moline	IL	61265	309-764-2475	764-1533	49-4
American Repertory Ballet 7 Livingston Ave *Web:* www.arballet.org	New Brunswick	NJ	08901	732-249-1254	249-8475	573-1
American Repertory Theatre (ART) 64 Brattle St *Web:* americanrepertorytheater.org	Cambridge	MA	02138	617-547-8300		749
American Republic Insurance Co 601 6th Ave	Des Moines	IA	50309	515-245-2000		391-2
American Research & Management Co 145 Front St *Web:* www.arm-co.com	Marion	MA	02738	508-748-1665		401
American Residential Services LLC 9010 Maier Rd Ste 105 *TF:* 866-399-2885 ■ *Web:* www.ars.com	Laurel	MD	20723	901-271-9700		189-10
American Resort Development Assn (ARDA) 1201 15th St NW Ste 400 *Web:* www.arda.org	Washington	DC	20005	202-371-6700	289-8544	49-17
American Rifleman Magazine 11250 Waples Mill Rd *TF:* 800-672-3888 ■ *Web:* www.americanrifleman.org	Fairfax	VA	22030	800-672-3888		457-20
American River Bankshares 3100 Zinfandel Dr Ste 450 *NASDAQ: AMRB* ■ *TF:* 800-544-0545 ■ *Web:* www.americanriverbank.com	Rancho Cordova	CA	95670	800-544-0545		360-2
American River College 4700 College Oak Dr *Web:* www.arc.losrios.edu	Sacramento	CA	95841	916-484-8011	484-8864	162
American River Messenger 7144 Fair Oaks Blvd Ste 5 *Web:* www.AmericanRiverMessenger.com	Carmichael	CA	95608	916-773-1111	773-2999	532-2
American River Ventures 2270 Douglas Blvd Ste 212 *Web:* www.arventures.com	Roseville	CA	95661	916-780-2828	780-5443	792
American Rivers 1101 14th St NW Ste 1400 *TF:* 877-347-7550 ■ *Web:* www.americanrivers.org	Washington	DC	20005	202-347-7550		48-13

Name / Address	City	State	ZIP	Phone	Fax	Class
American Road & Transportation Builders Assn (ARTBA) 1219 28th St NW *Web:* www.artba.org	Washington	DC	20007	202-289-4434	289-4435	49-3
American Road Machinery Inc 3026 Saratoga Ave *TF:* 844-294-5862 ■ *Web:* www.toughequipment.com	Canton	OH	44706	844-294-5862		190
American Rock Mechanics Assn (ARMA) 600 Woodland Terr *Web:* www.armarocks.org	Alexandria	VA	22302	703-683-1808	683-1815	49-19
American Rock Salt Company LLC 5520 Rte 63 *TF:* 888-762-7258 ■ *Web:* www.americanrocksalt.com	Mount Morris	NY	14510	585-991-6827	991-6927	503-1
American Roentgen Ray Society (ARRS) 44211 Slatestone Ct *TF:* 800-438-2777 ■ *Web:* www.arrs.org	Leesburg	VA	20176	703-729-3353	729-4839	49-8
American Roller Bearing Co 400 Second Ave NW *Web:* www.amroll.com	Hickory	NC	28601	828-624-1460		75
American Roller Co 1440 13th Ave *Web:* americanroller.com	Union Grove	WI	53182	262-878-8665		677
American Roofing Supply Inc 4550 E 52nd Ave *Web:* www.amroofing.com	Commerce City	CO	80022	303-333-3700		191-4
American Rose Society (ARS) 8877 Jefferson Paige Rd *TF:* 800-637-6534 ■ *Web:* www.rose.org	Shreveport	LA	71119	800-637-6534		48-18
American Royal Assn 1701 American Royal Ct *Web:* www.americanroyal.com	Kansas City	MO	64102	816-221-9800	221-8189	48-2
American Saddlebred Horse Assn (ASHA) 4083 Iron Works Pkwy *Web:* www.asha.net	Lexington	KY	40511	859-259-2742	259-1628	48-3
American Saddlebred Museum 4083 Iron Works Pkwy *TF:* 800-829-4438 ■ *Web:* asbmuseum.org	Lexington	KY	40511	859-259-2746	255-4909	520
American Safety Clothing Inc 30 E Park Ave *Web:* americansafetyclothingmfg.com	Sellersville	PA	18960	215-257-7667		477
American Safety Technologies Inc 565 Eagle Rock Ave **Fax Area Code:* 973 ■ *TF:* 800-631-7841 ■ *Web:* itwast.com	Roseland	NJ	07068	800-631-7841	403-1108*	550
American Sanitary Partition Corp 300 Enterprise St PO Box 99 *Web:* www.am-sanitary-partition.com	Ocoee	FL	34761	407-656-0611	656-8189	286
American Savings Bank 312 S Main St PO Box 909 *Web:* asbtripoli.com	Tripoli	IA	50676	319-882-4279		70
American Savings Bank FSB 1001 Bishop St *TF:* 800-272-2566 ■ *Web:* www.asbhawaii.com	Honolulu	HI	96813	808-627-6900		70
American Savings Life Insurance Co 935 E Main St Ste 100 *TF:* 800-880-2112 ■ *Web:* www.americansavingslife.com	Mesa	AZ	85203	480-835-5000	835-5355	390
American Scale Service & Supply Co 8590 W 14th Ave *Web:* ameriscale.com	Lakewood	CO	80215	303-232-5656		362
American Scholar 1606 New Hampshire Ave NW *TF:* 800-821-4567 ■ *Web:* theamericanscholar.org	Washington	DC	20009	202-265-3808	265-0083	457-10
American School Counselor Assn (ASCA) 1101 King St Ste 625 *TF:* 800-306-4722 ■ *Web:* www.schoolcounselor.org	Alexandria	VA	22314	703-683-2722	683-1619	49-5
American School Health Assn (ASHA) 7918 Jones Branch Dr Ste 300 *Web:* www.ashaweb.org	McLean	VA	22102	703-506-7675	506-3266	49-5
American School of Classical Studies at Athens (ASCSA) 6-8 Charlton St *Web:* www.ascsa.edu.gr	Princeton	NJ	[illegible]	[illegible]	924-0578	[illegible]
American Science & Engineering Inc 829 Middlesex Tpke *NASDAQ: ASEI* ■ *Web:* www.as-e.com	Billerica	MA	01821	978-262-8700		692
American Seafoods Holdings LLC 2025 First Ave Ste 900 *Web:* www.americanseafoods.com	Seattle	WA	98121	206-374-1515	374-1516	285
American Seal & Engineering Company Inc 295 Indian River Rd *TF:* 800-719-1869 ■ *Web:* www.ameriseal.com	Orange	CT	06477	203-789-8819		529
American Seating Co 401 American Seating Ctr NW *TF:* 800-748-0268 ■ *Web:* www.americanseating.com	Grand Rapids	MI	49504	616-732-6600	732-6401	319-3
American Security Products Inc 11925 Pacific Ave *Web:* www.amsecusa.com	Fontana	CA	92337	951-685-9680	685-9685	692
American Seed Trade Assn (ASTA) 1701 Duke St Ste 275 *TF:* 888-890-7333 ■ *Web:* www.betterseed.org	Alexandria	VA	22304	703-837-8140	837-9365	48-2
American Seminar Leaders Assn (ASLA) 2405 E Washington Blvd *Web:* www.asla.com	Pasadena	CA	91104	626-791-1211	791-0701	49-12
American Seniors Housing Assn (ASHA) 5225 Wisconsin Ave NW Ste 502 *Web:* www.seniorshousing.org	Washington	DC	20015	202-237-0900	237-1616	48-6
American SensoRx Inc 31 N Monroe St *Web:* www.americansensorx.com	Ridgewood	NJ	07450	201-447-8999	447-8998	256
American Sentinel University 2260 S Xanadu Way Ste 310 **Fax Area Code:* 866 ■ *TF:* 800-729-2427 ■ *Web:* www.americansentinel.edu	Aurora	CO	80014	800-729-2427	505-2450*	786
American Services Inc 1300 Rutherford Rd *TF:* 800-338-7217 ■ *Web:* www.american-services-inc.com	Greenville	SC	29609	864-292-7450		693
American Services Technology Inc (ASTI) 1028 Harvin Way Ste 120 *Web:* www.americanservicestech.com	Rockledge	FL	32955	321-631-8771	631-7291	194
American Shared Hospital Services 4 Embarcadero Ctr Ste 3700 *NYSE: AMS* ■ *TF:* 800-735-0641 ■ *Web:* www.ashs.com	San Francisco	CA	94111	415-788-5300	788-5660	264-4
American Sheep Industry Assn (ASI) 9785 Maroon Cir Ste 360 *Web:* www.sheepusa.org	Englewood	CO	80112	303-771-3500	771-8200	48-2
American Shetland Pony Club (ASPC) 81B E Queenwood Rd *Web:* www.shetlandminiature.com	Morton	IL	61550	309-263-4044	263-5113	48-3
American Shore & Beach Preservation Assn (ASBPA) 5460 Beaujolais Ln *TF:* 800-331-1600 ■ *Web:* asbpa.org	Fort Myers	FL	33919	239-489-2616	489-9917	48-13
American Short Line & Regional Railroad Assn (ASLRRA) 50 F St NW Ste 7020 *Web:* www.aslrra.org	Washington	DC	20001	202-628-4500	628-6430	49-21
American Shorthorn Assn 7607 NW Prairie View Rd *Web:* shorthorn.org	Kansas City	MO	64151	816-599-7777	599-7782	48-3
American Showa Inc 707 W Cherry St *Web:* www.amshowa.com	Sunbury	OH	43074	740-965-1133		247
American SIDS Institute 528 Raven Way *Web:* sids.org	Naples	FL	34110	239-431-5425	431-5536	48-6
American Silk Mills Corp 75 Stark St *Web:* www.americansilk.com	Hudson	PA	18705	570-822-7147	829-7044	745-1
American Simmental Assn (ASA) 1 Genetics Way *Web:* www.simmental.org	Bozeman	MT	59718	406-587-4531	587-9301	48-2
American Slate Co 1900 Olympic Blvd *TF:* 888-259-4249 ■ *Web:* www.americanslate.com	Walnut Creek	CA	94596	888-259-4249		724
American Sleep Apnea Assn (ASAA) 6856 Eastern Ave NW Ste 203 *TF:* 888-293-3650 ■ *Web:* www.sleepapnea.org	Washington	DC	20012	202-293-3650	293-3656	48-17
American Society for Adolescent Psychiatry (ASAP) PO Box 3948 *TF:* 866-672-9060 ■ *Web:* www.adolescent-psychiatry.org	Parker	CO	80134	866-672-9060		49-15
American Society for Aesthetic Plastic Surgery, The (ASAPS) 11262 Monarch St *TF:* 800-364-2147 ■ *Web:* www.surgery.org	Garden Grove	CA	92841	562-799-2356	799-1098	49-8
American Society for Biochemistry & Molecular Biology Inc (ASBMB) 11200 Rockville Pk **Fax Area Code:* 301 ■ *Web:* www.asbmb.org	Rockville	MD	20852	240-283-6600	881-2080*	49-19
American Society for Bone & Mineral Research (ASBMR) 2025 M St NW Ste 800 *Web:* www.asbmr.org	Washington	DC	20036	202-367-1161	367-2161	49-8
American Society for Cell Biology (ASCB) 8120 Woodmont Ave Ste 750 *Web:* www.ascb.org	Bethesda	MD	20814	301-347-9300	347-9310	49-19
American Society for Clinical Pathology (ASCP) 33 W Monroe St Ste 1600 *TF:* 800-621-4142 ■ *Web:* ascp.org	Chicago	IL	60603	312-541-4999	541-4998	49-8
American Society for Colposcopy and Cervical Pathology (ASCCP) 131 Rollins Ave Ste 2 *TF:* 800-787-7227 ■ *Web:* www.asccp.org	Rockville	MD	21740	301-857-7877		49-8
American Society for Dermatologic Surgery (ASDS) 5550 Meadowbrook Dr Ste 120 *TF:* 800-714-1374 ■ *Web:* asds.net	Rolling Meadows	IL	60008	847-956-0900	956-0999	49-8
American Society for Engineering Education (ASEE) 1818 N St NW Ste 600 *Web:* www.asee.org	Washington	DC	20036	202-331-3500	265-8504	49-19
American Society for Gastrointestinal Endoscopy (ASGE) 1520 Kensington Rd Ste 202 *TF:* 866-353-2743 ■ *Web:* www.asge.org	Oak Brook	IL	60523	630-573-0600	573-0691	49-8
American Society for Histocompatibility & Immunogenetics (ASHI) 15000 Commerce Pkwy Ste C *Web:* www.ashi-hla.org	Mount Laurel	NJ	08054	856-638-0428		49-8
American Society for Horticultural Science (ASHS) 1018 Duke St *Web:* www.ashs.org	Alexandria	VA	22314	703-836-4606	836-2024	48-2
American Society for Laser Medicine & Surgery Inc (ASLMS) 2100 Stewart Ave Ste 240 *TF:* [illegible] ■ *Web:* www.aslms.org	Wausau	WI	54401	715-845-9283	848-2493	49-8
American Society for Microbiology (ASM) 1752 North St NW *TF:* 800-546-2416 ■ *Web:* www.asm.org	Washington	DC	20036	202-737-3600		49-8
American Society for Nondestructive Testing Inc (ASNT) 1711 Arlingate Ln PO Box 28518 *TF:* 800-222-2768 ■ *Web:* www.asnt.org	Columbus	OH	43228	614-274-6003	274-6899	49-19
American Society for Nutrition (ASNS) 9211 Corporate Blvd Ste 300 **Fax Area Code:* 301 ■ *TF:* 800-627-8723 ■ *Web:* nutrition.org	Rockville	MD	20850	240-428-3650	634-7894*	49-6
American Society for Pharmacology & Experimental Therapeutics (ASPET) 1801 Rockville Pk Ste 210 *Web:* www.aspet.org	Rockville	MD	20852	301-634-7060	634-7061	49-8
American Society for Photogrammetry & Remote Sensing, The (ASPRS) 5410 Grosvenor Ln Ste 210 *Web:* www.asprs.org	Bethesda	MD	20814	301-493-0290	493-0208	49-19
American Society for Public Administration (ASPA) 1730 Rhode Island Ave NW Ste 500 *Web:* www.aspanet.org	Washington	DC	20036	202-393-7878	638-4952	49-7
American Society for Quality (ASQ) 600 N Plankinton Ave *TF:* 800-248-1946 ■ *Web:* asq.org	Milwaukee	WI	53203	414-272-8575	272-1734	49-13
American Society for Reproductive Medicine (ASRM) 1209 Montgomery Hwy *Web:* www.asrm.org	Birmingham	AL	35216	205-978-5000	978-5005	49-8
American Society for Surgery of the Hand (ASSH) 822 W Washington Blvd **Fax Area Code:* 847 ■ *Web:* assh.org	Chicago	IL	60607	312-880-1900	384-1435*	49-8
American Society for the Prevention of Cruelty to Animals (ASPCA) 424 E 92nd St *TF:* 800-582-5979 ■ *Web:* www.aspca.org	New York	NY	10128	212-876-7700		48-3
American Society for Therapeutic Radiology & Oncology (ASTRO) 8280 Willow Oaks Corporate Dr Ste 500 *TF:* 800-962-7876 ■ *Web:* www.astro.org	Fairfax	VA	22031	703-502-1550	502-7852	49-8
American Society of Access Professionals (ASAP) 1444 'I' St NW Ste 700 *Web:* www.accesspro.org	Washington	DC	20005	202-712-9054	216-9646	48-8
American Society of Addiction Medicine (ASAM) 11400 Rockville Pk Ste 200 *Web:* www.asam.org	Rockville	MD	20852	301-656-3920	656-3815	49-8
American Society of Agricultural Consultants (ASAC) 605 Columbus Ave *Web:* www.agconsultants.org	New Prague	MN	56071	952-758-5811		48-2

Phone | Fax | Class

American Society of Agronomy (ASA)
5585 Guilford Rd ... Madison WI 53711 608-273-8080 273-2021 48-2
TF: 866-359-9161 ■ *Web:* www.agronomy.org

American Society of Andrology (ASA)
1061 E Main St Ste 300 ... East Dundee IL 60173 847-752-5355 49-8
Web: www.andrologysociety.org

American Society of Anesthesiologists (ASA)
520 N NW Hwy ... Park Ridge IL 60068 847-825-5586 825-1692 49-8
Web: www.asahq.org

American Society of Appraisers (ASA)
11107 Sunset Hills Rd Ste 310 ... Reston VA 20170 800-272-8258 742-8471* 49-17
**Fax Area Code:* 703 ■ *TF:* 800-272-8258 ■ *Web:* www.appraisers.org

American Society of Artists
PO Box 1326 ... Palatine IL 60078 312-751-2500 48-4
Web: www.americansocietyofartists.info

American Society of Association Executives (ASAE)
1575 'I' St NW ... Washington DC 20005 202-626-2723 49-12
TF: 888-950-2723 ■ *Web:* www.asaecenter.org

American Society of Business Publication Editors (ASBPE)
214 N Hale St ... Wheaton IL 60187 727-553-4214 510-4501* 49-16
**Fax Area Code:* 630 ■ *Web:* www.asbpe.org

American Society of Cataract & Refractive Surgery (ASCRS)
4000 Legato Rd Ste 700 ... Fairfax VA 22033 703-591-2220 591-0614 49-8
TF: 877-996-4464 ■ *Web:* www.ascrs.org

American Society of Cinematographers (ASC)
1782 N Orange Dr ... Hollywood CA 90028 323-969-4333 882-6391 48-4
TF: 800-448-0145 ■ *Web:* theasc.com

American Society of Civil Engineers (ASCE)
1801 Alexander Bell Dr ... Reston VA 20191 703-295-6300 295-6211 457-21
TF: 800-548-2723 ■ *Web:* www.asce.org

American Society of Clinical Hypnosis (ASCH)
140 N Bloomingdale Rd ... Bloomingdale IL 60108 630-980-4740 351-8490 49-8
TF: 800-227-6963 ■ *Web:* www.asch.net

American Society of Clinical Oncology (ASCO)
2318 Mill Rd Ste 800 ... Alexandria VA 22314 571-483-1300 299-0255* 49-8
**Fax Area Code:* 703 ■ *TF:* 888-282-2552 ■ *Web:* www.asco.org

American Society of Consultant Pharmacists (ASCP)
1321 Duke St ... Alexandria VA 22314 703-739-1300 739-1321 49-8
TF: 800-355-2727 ■ *Web:* www.ascp.com

American Society of Dermatopathology, The
1 Parkview Plz Ste 800 ... Oakbrook Terrace IL 60181 847-686-2231 686-2251 49-8
Web: www.asdp.org

American Society of Echocardiography (ASE)
2100 Gateway Centre Blvd Ste 310 ... Morrisville NC 27560 919-861-5574 882-9900 49-8
Web: www.asecho.org

American Society of Farm Managers & Rural Appraisers Inc (ASFMRA)
720 S Colordo Blvd Ste 360-S ... Glendale CO 80246 303-758-3513 758-0190 48-2
Web: www.asfmra.org

American Society of Golf Course Architects (ASGCA)
125 N Executive Dr Ste 106 ... Brookfield WI 53005 262-786-5960 786-5919 48-22
Web: asgca.org

American Society of Health-System Pharmacists (ASHP)
7272 Wisconsin Ave ... Bethesda MD 20814 301-664-8700 664-8877 49-8
TF: 866-279-0681 ■ *Web:* www.ashp.org

American Society of Heating Refrigerating & Air-Conditioning Engineers Inc (ASHRAE)
1791 Tullie Cir NE ... Atlanta GA 30329 404-636-8400 321-5478 49-3
TF: 800-527-4723 ■ *Web:* www.ashrae.org

American Society of Hematology (ASH)
2021 L St NW Ste 900 ... Washington DC 20036 202-776-0544 776-0545 49-8
Web: www.hematology.org

American Society of Home Inspectors (ASHI)
932 Lee St Ste 101 ... Des Plaines IL 60016 847-759-2820 759-1620 49-3
TF: 800-743-2744 ■ *Web:* www.homeinspector.org

American Society of Human Genetics (ASHG)
6120 Executive Blvd Ste 500 ... Rockville MD 20852 301-634-7300 634-7079 49-19
Web: www.ashg.org

American Society of Ichthyologists & Herpetologists
PO Box 1897 ... Lawrence KS 66044 785-843-1235 843-1274 49-19
Web: www.asih.org

American Society of Indexers (ASI)
1628 E Southern Ave Ste 9-223 ... Tempe AZ 85282 480-245-6750 49-16
Web: www.asindexing.org

American Society of Interior Designers (ASID)
608 Massachusetts Ave ... Washington DC 20002 202-546-3480 546-3240 48-4
Web: www.asid.org

American Society of International Law, The (ASIL)
2223 Massachusetts Ave NW ... Washington DC 20008 202-939-6000 797-7133 49-10
Web: www.asil.org

American Society of Landscape Architects (ASLA)
636 'I' St NW ... Washington DC 20001 202-898-2444 898-1185 48-2
TF: 888-999-2752 ■ *Web:* www.asla.org

American Society of Limnology & Oceanography (ASLO)
5400 Bosque Blvd Ste 680 ... Waco TX 76710 254-399-9635 49-19
TF: 800-929-2756 ■ *Web:* aslo.org

American Society of Media Photographers (ASMP)
150 N Second St ... Philadelphia PA 19106 215-451-2767 451-0880 49-14
Web: www.asmp.org

American Society of Military Comptrollers (ASMC)
415 N Alfred St ... Alexandria VA 22314 703-549-0360 549-3181 48-19
TF: 800-462-5637 ■ *Web:* www.asmconline.org

American Society of Naval Engineers (ASNE)
1452 Duke St ... Alexandria VA 22314 703-836-6727 836-7491 49-21
Web: www.navalengineers.org

American Society of Neuroradiology (ASNR)
800 Enterprise Dr Ste 205 ... Oak Brook IL 60523 630-574-0220 574-0661 49-8
Web: www.asnr.org

American Society of News Editors (ASNE)
11690-B Sunrise Vly Dr ... Reston VA 20191 703-453-1122 453-1133 49-14
Web: www.asne.org

American Society of Notaries (ASN)
PO Box 5707 ... Tallahassee FL 32314 850-671-5164 671-5165 49-12
Web: www.notaries.org

American Society of Nuclear Cardiology (ASNC)
4550 Montgomery Ave Ste 780-N ... Bethesda MD 20814 301-215-7575 215-7113 49-8
Web: www.asnc.org

American Society of Pension Professionals & Actuaries (ASPPA)
4245 N Fairfax Dr Ste 750 ... Arlington VA 22203 703-516-9300 516-9308 49-12
Web: www.asppa.org

American Society of PeriAnesthesia Nurses (ASPAN)
90 Frontage Rd ... Cherry Hill NJ 08034 856-616-9601 49-8
TF: 877-737-9696 ■ *Web:* www.aspan.org

American Society of Plant Biologists (ASPB)
15501 Monona Dr ... Rockville MD 20855 301-251-0560 279-2996 49-19
Web: aspb.org

American Society of Plastic Surgeons (ASPS)
444 E Algonquin Rd ... Arlington Heights IL 60005 847-228-9900 228-9131 49-8
Web: www.plasticsurgery.org

American Society of Professional Estimators (ASPE)
PO Box 140710 ... Nashville TN 37214 615-316-9200 316-9800 49-3
TF: 888-378-6283 ■ *Web:* www.aspenational.org

American Society of Radiologic Technologists (ASRT)
15000 Central Ave SE ... Albuquerque NM 87123 505-298-4500 298-5063 49-8
TF: 800-444-2778 ■ *Web:* www.asrt.org

American Society of Regional Anesthesia & Pain Medicine (ASRA)
4 Penn Ctr W Ste 401 ... Pittsburgh PA 15276 412-471-2718 471-7503 49-8
TF: 855-795-2772 ■ *Web:* www.asra.com

American Society of Safety Professionals (ASSE)
1800 E Oakton St ... Des Plaines IL 60018 847-699-2929 768-3434 49-19
Web: www.assp.org

American Society of Travel Agents (ASTA)
675 N Washington St Ste 490 ... Alexandria VA 22314 703-739-2782 684-8319 48-23
TF: 800-275-2782 ■ *Web:* www.asta.org

American Society of Tropical Medicine & Hygiene
111 Deer Lake Rd Ste 100 ... Deerfield IL 60015 847-480-9592 49-8
Web: www.astmh.org

American Society on Aging (ASA)
575 Market St Ste 2100 ... San Francisco CA 94105 415-974-9600 974-0300 48-6
TF: 800-537-9728 ■ *Web:* www.asaging.org

American Sociological Assn (ASA)
1307 New York Ave ... Washington DC 20005 202-383-9005 638-0882 49-5
Web: www.asanet.org

American Software Inc
470 E Paces Ferry Rd ... Atlanta GA 30305 404-261-4381 178-1
NASDAQ: AMSWA ■ *TF:* 800-726-2946 ■ *Web:* www.amsoftware.com

American Solar Energy Society (ASES)
2525 Arapahoe Ave Ste E4 253 ... Boulder CO 80302 303-443-3130 48-12
Web: www.ases.org

American Solutions for Business
31 E Minnesota Ave E ... Glenwood MN 56334 800-862-3690 534
TF: 800-862-3690 ■ *Web:* home.americanbus.com

American Southern Insurance Co
3715 Northside Pkwy NW Bldg 400 Ste 800 ... Atlanta GA 30327 404-266-9599 266-8327 391-4
TF: 800-241-1172 ■ *Web:* www.amsou.com

American Soybean Assn (ASA)
12125 Woodcrest Executive Dr Ste 100 ... Saint Louis MO 63141 314-576-1770 576-2786 48-2
TF: 800-688-7692 ■ *Web:* soygrowers.com

American Special Metals Corp
11890 SW 8th St Penthouse VII ... Miami FL 33184 305-551-4215 551-3436 492
Web: www.americanspecialmetals.com

American Specialties Inc (ASI)
441 Saw Mill River Rd ... Yonkers NY 10701 914-476-9000 476-0688 609
Web: americanspecialties.com

American Specialty Health Plans
10221 Wateridge Cir ... San Diego CA 92121 800-848-3555 391-3
TF: 800-848-3555 ■ *Web:* www.ashcompanies.com

American Spectator Magazine
933 N Kenmore St Ste 405 ... Arlington VA 22201 703-807-2011 457-17
TF: 800-524-3469 ■ *Web:* spectator.org

American Speech-Language-Hearing Assn (ASHA)
2200 Research Blvd ... Rockville MD 20850 301-296-5700 296-8580 49-8
TF: 800-498-2071 ■ *Web:* www.asha.org

American Spice Trade Assn (ASTA)
1101 17th St NW Ste 700 ... Washington DC 20036 202-331-2460 49-6
Web: www.astaspice.org

American Spirit Corp
801 SE Ninth St ... Minneapolis MN 55414 612-623-3333 623-9314 627
Web: americanspiritcorp.com

American Spirit Federal Credit Union
1110 Elkton Rd ... Newark DE 19711 302-738-4515 219
Web: americanspirit.org

American Spool & Packaging Inc
1832 N 5th St ... Hartsville SC 29550 843-332-3314 332-7237 125
TF: 800-762-1800 ■ *Web:* amspak.com

American Spoon Foods Inc
1668 Clarion Ave ... Petoskey MI 49770 888-735-6700 296-20
TF: 800-222-5886 ■ *Web:* www.spoon.com

American Sport Art Museum & Archives (ASAMA)
1 Academy Dr ... Daphne AL 36526 251-626-3303 626-3874 520
Web: www.asama.org

American Sportfishing Assn (ASA)
1001 N Fairfax St Ste 501 ... Alexandria VA 22314 703-519-9691 519-1872 49-4
Web: asafishing.org

American Sports 74 Albe Dr Ste 1 ... Newark DE 19702 866-207-3179 250-4024* 710
**Fax Area Code:* 302 ■ *TF:* 866-207-3179 ■ *Web:* www.americansports.com

American Sports Institute (ASI)
116 E Blithedale Ave ... Mill Valley CA 94941 415-383-5750 48-22
Web: americansportsinstitute.org

American Spring Wire Corp
26300 Miles Rd ... Cleveland OH 44128 216-292-4620 718
Web: www.americanspringwire.com

American Staffing Assn (ASA)
277 S Washington St Ste 200 ... Alexandria VA 22314 703-253-2020 253-2053 49-12
Web: americanstaffing.net

American Stage
163 Third St N ... Saint Petersburg FL 33701 727-823-1600 821-2444 572
Web: www.americanstage.org

American Stainless & Supply LLC
815 State Rd ... Cheraw SC 29520 843-537-5231 537-6885 605-2
TF: 800-845-5511 ■ *Web:* americanstainlessandsupply.com

American Stair Corp 3510 Calumet Ave ... Hammond IN 46320 800-872-7824 491
TF: 800-872-7824 ■ *Web:* www.americanstair.com

American State Bank
1000 Jeffreys Dr PO Box 463 ... Osceola IA 50213 641-342-2175 70
Web: americanstatebank.com

American States Water Co
630 E Foothill Blvd ... San Dimas CA 91773 909-394-3600 360-5
NYSE: AWR ■ *TF:* 800-999-4033 ■ *Web:* www.americanstateswatercompany.com

Name / Address	City	State	ZIP	Phone	Fax	Class
American Statistical Assn (ASA) 732 N Washington St *TF:* 888-231-3473 ■ *Web:* www.amstat.org	Alexandria	VA	22314	703-684-1221	684-2037	49-19
American Steamship Co Centerpointe Corporate Pk 500 Essjay Rd *Web:* www.americansteamship.com	Williamsville	NY	14221	716-635-0222	635-0220	314
American Steel & Aluminum Company Inc 3545 E Main St *Web:* www.asafab.com	Grand Prairie	TX	75050	972-264-1533		492
American Steel Corp 4884 S Desert View Dr *Web:* www.americansteelcorporation.com	Apache Junction	AZ	85220	480-474-0100	474-0109	492
American Stitchco Inc 4662 Hwy 62 W *TF:* 888-903-0049 ■ *Web:* www.stitchco.com	Mountain Home	AR	72653	870-425-7777	425-4900	34
American Stone Virginia LLC 8179 Arba Ave *Web:* asiprecast.com	Ruther Glen	VA	22546	804-448-9460		183
American String Teachers Assn (ASTA) 4155 Chain Bridge Rd *Web:* www.astastrings.org	Fairfax	VA	22030	703-279-2113	279-2114	49-5
American Strip Steel Inc 901 Coopertown Rd **Fax Area Code:* 908 ■ *TF:* 800-526-1216 ■ *Web:* www.americanstrip.com	Delanco	NJ	08075	800-526-1216	412-1442*	492
American Structural Metals Inc 777 Lehmann Way PO Box 40 *Web:* www.asm-mmf.com	Somerset	WI	54025	715-247-5950		480
American Student Assistance 33 Arch St Ste 2100 *TF:* 800-999-9080 ■ *Web:* www.asa.org	Boston	MA	02110	800-999-9080		423
American Studies Assn (ASA) 1120 19th St NW Ste 301 *Web:* theasa.net	Washington	DC	20036	202-467-4783	467-4786	49-5
American Subcontractors Association Inc (ASA) 1004 Duke St *Web:* www.asaonline.com	Alexandria	VA	22314	703-684-3450	836-3482	49-3
American Sugar Cane League P O Drawer 938 206 E Bayou Rd *Web:* www.amscl.org	Thibodaux	LA	70301	985-448-3707	448-3722	10-9
American Superconductor Corp 64 Jackson Rd *Web:* www.amsc.com	Devens	MA	01434	978-842-3000		815
American Supply Association PAC 1200 N Arlington Heights Rd Ste 150 *Web:* www.asa.net	Itasca	IL	60143	630-467-0000		615
American Surplus Inc 1 Noyes Ave Bldg B *Web:* www.americansurplus.com	Rumford	RI	02916	401-434-4355		321
American Suzuki Motor Corp 3251 Imperial Hwy *Web:* www.suzuki.com	Brea	CA	92821	714-996-7040		517
American Swedish Historical Museum 1900 Pattison Ave *Web:* www.americanswedish.org	Philadelphia	PA	19145	215-389-1776	389-7701	520
American Swedish Institute, The (ASI) 2600 Park Ave *Web:* www.asimn.org	Minneapolis	MN	55407	612-871-4907	871-8682	520
American Symphony Orchestra 263 W 38 St 10th Fl *Web:* americansymphony.org	New York	NY	10018	212-868-9276	868-9277	573-3
American Synthetic Fiber LLC 312 S Holland Dr *Web:* asfiber.com	Pendergrass	GA	30567	706-693-2422		683
American Systems Corp 14151 Pk Meadow Dr Ste 500 *TF:* 800-733-2721 ■ *Web:* www.americansystems.com	Chantilly	VA	20151	703-968-6300	968-5151	180
American Systems of the Southeast Inc 999 Harbor Rd **Fax Area Code:* 800 ■ *TF:* 800-845-9895 ■ *Web:* www.americansystems.net	West Columbia	SC	29169	803-796-9790	328-6890*	534
American Tank & Fabricating Co (AT&F) 12314 Elmwood Ave *TF:* 800-544-5316 ■ *Web:* www.atfco.com	Cleveland	OH	44111	216-252-1500	251-4963	723
American Target Advertising Inc 9625 Surveyor Ct Ste 400 *Web:* americantarget.com	Manassas	VA	20110	703-392-7676	392-7654	5
American Taximeters & Communications Inc 2146 44th Dr *Web:* www.at-c.com	Long Island City	NY	11101	718-937-4600	937-4805	54
American Tcb 7560 Lindbergh Dr *Web:* www.wll.com	Gaithersburg	MD	20879	301-216-1500		193
American Technical Ceramics Corp 1 Norden Ln *Web:* www.atceramics.com	Huntington Station	NY	11746	631-622-4700	622-4748	249
American Technology Network Corp 1341 San Mateo Ave *TF:* 800-910-2862 ■ *Web:* www.atncorp.com	South San Francisco	CA	94080	650-989-5100		544
American Technology Services Inc 2751 Prosperity Ave 6th Fl *Web:* networkats.com	Fairfax	VA	22031	703-876-0300		177
American Telecast Corp 835 Springdale Dr Ste 206 **Fax Area Code:* 484 ■ *Web:* americantelecast.com	Exton	PA	19341	610-430-7800	879-4046*	4
American Tennis Courts Inc 1272 Bolton's Bridge Dr *TF:* 800-854-1921 ■ *Web:* www.americantenniscourts.net	Mobile	AL	36606	251-476-4714	476-4723	188-3
American Textile Co 10 N Linden St *TF:* 800-289-2826 ■ *Web:* www.americantextile.com	Duquesne	PA	15110	412-948-1020	948-1002	746
American Textile History Museum 491 Dutton St *Web:* www.athm.org	Lowell	MA	01854	978-441-0400	441-1412	520
American Textile Machinery Assn (ATMA) 201 Park Washington Ct *Web:* www.atmanet.org	Falls Church	VA	22046	703-538-1789		49-13
American Theological Library Assn (ATLA) 300 S Wacker Dr Ste 2100 *TF:* 888-665-2852 ■ *Web:* www.atla.com	Chicago	IL	60606	312-454-5100	454-5505	48-20
American Therapeutic Recreation Assn (ATRA) 11130 Sunrise Valley Dr Ste 350 *Web:* www.atra-online.com	Reston	VA	20191	703-234-4140	435-4390	48-17
American Thermoplastic Extrusion Co 4851 NW 128th St Rd	Opa Locka	FL	33054	305-769-9566	769-1998	599
American Thoracic Society (ATS) 61 Broadway 4th Fl *Web:* www.thoracic.org	New York	NY	10006	212-315-8600	315-6498	49-8
American Tile & Sales Company Inc 2142 Wabash Ave *Web:* americantile.net	Terre Haute	IN	47807	812-232-6923	232-7367	290
American Time & Signal Co 140 Third St *Web:* www.american-time.com	Dassel	MN	55325	320-275-2101		411
American Tinnitus Assn (ATA) 522 SW Fifth Ave Ste 825 *TF:* 800-634-8978 ■ *Web:* www.ata.org	Portland	OR	97204	503-248-9985	248-0024	48-17
American Tire Depot 14407 Alondra Blvd *TF:* 855-899-3764 ■ *Web:* www.americantiredepot.com	La Mirada	CA	90638	562-677-3950	677-3956	755
American Tool & Engineering Inc 102 Industrial Pky *Web:* www.atemold.com	Greene	IA	50636	641-816-4921	823-4923	723
American Tool & Mold Inc 1700 Sunshine Dr *Web:* a-t-m.com	Clearwater	FL	33765	727-447-7377	447-0125	757
American Tool and Machining Inc 1910 S Benton St *Web:* www.amtsearcy.com	Searcy	AR	72143	501-268-7011	268-5923	757
American Tool Co 623 George Washington Hwy *Web:* www.americantoolcompany.com	Lincoln	RI	02865	401-333-0111	334-3577	454
American Torch Tip Co 6212 29th St E *TF:* 800-342-8477 ■ *Web:* americantorchtip.com	Bradenton	FL	34203	800-342-8477		811
American Tort Reform Assn (ATRA) 1101 Connecticut Ave NW Ste 400 *Web:* www.atra.org	Washington	DC	20036	202-682-1163	682-1022	49-10
American Tower Corp 116 Huntington Ave 11th Fl *NYSE:* AMT ■ *TF:* 877-282-7483 ■ *Web:* www.americantower.com	Boston	MA	02116	617-375-7500	375-7575	170
American Trademark Construction Services Inc 200 Lau Pkwy *Web:* www.atcs-inc.com	Englewood	OH	45315	937-832-8885		186
American Traffic Safety Services Assn (ATSSA) 15 Riverside Pkwy Ste 100 *TF:* 800-272-8772 ■ *Web:* www.atssa.com	Fredericksburg	VA	22406	540-368-1701	368-1717	49-21
American Traffic Solutions Inc 450 Veterans Memorial Parkway E Ste 7A *OTC:* NEST	Providence	RI	02914	401-274-5658		178-10
American Trails PO Box 491797 *TF:* 866-363-7226 ■ *Web:* www.americantrails.org	Redding	CA	96049	530-605-4395	867-9014	48-23
American Trails West (ATW) 92 Middle Neck Rd *TF:* 800-645-6260 ■ *Web:* www.atwteentours.com	Great Neck	NY	11021	516-487-2800	487-2855	760
American Train Dispatchers Assn 4239 W 150th St	Cleveland	OH	44135	216-251-7984		414
American Translators Assn (ATA) 225 Reinekers Ln Ste 590 *Web:* www.atanet.org	Alexandria	VA	22314	703-683-6100	683-6122	49-5
American Transport Group LLC (ATG) 1900 W Kinzie **Fax Area Code:* 773 ■ *TF:* 888-284-5623 ■ *Web:* www.atgfreight.com	Chicago	IL	60622	888-284-5623	235-9600*	311
American Trim 1005 W Grand Ave *Web:* www.amtrim.com	Lima	OH	45801	419-228-1145	996-4850	488
American Trucking Assn (ATA) 950 N Glebe Rd Ste 210 *TF:* 800-282-5463 ■ *Web:* www.trucking.org	Arlington	VA	22203	703-838-1700		49-21
American Trust Administrators Inc 7223 W 95th St Ste 301 *TF:* 800-842-4121 ■ *Web:* www.ataamerica.com	Overland Park	KS	66212	913-378-9938	378-9936	391-2
American Trust Publications (ATP) 721 Enterprise Dr *Web:* islamicbookservice.org	Oak Brook	IL	60523	630-789-9191	789-9455	637-2
American Tubing Inc 2191 Ford Ave *Web:* www.americantubing.com	Springdale	AR	72764	479-756-1291		567
American Turned Products Inc 7626 Klier Dr *Web:* www.atpteam.com	Fairview	PA	16415	814-474-4200	474-4718	621
American Twisting Co 1675 Stieve Dr *TF:* 800-253-3230 ■ *Web:* americantwisting.com	South Haven	MI	49090	269-637-8581		548
American Type Culture Collection (ATCC) 10801 University Blvd PO Box 1549 *TF:* 800-638-6597 ■ *Web:* www.atcc.org	Manassas	VA	20108	703-365-2700	365-2701	668
American Ultraviolet Co 40 Morristown Rd *TF:* 800-288-9288 ■ *Web:* www.americanultraviolet.com	Bernardsville	NJ	07924	908-696-1130	696-1131	811
American Underwriters Insurance Agencies Inc 6429 S Tacoma Way *Web:* auiagency.com	Tacoma	WA	98409	253-473-1415		390
American Uniform Co 114 Stuart Rd NE Ste 205	Cleveland	TN	37312	423-476-6561		155-19
American Unit Inc Pky Ctr I 2901 N Dallas Pky Ste 333 *Web:* www.americanunit.com	Plano	TX	75093	972-398-3333		180
American University 4400 Massachusetts Ave NW *Web:* www.american.edu	Washington	DC	20016	202-885-1000	885-2558	166
American University Washington College of Law 4801 Massachusetts Ave NW *Web:* www.wcl.american.edu	Washington	DC	20016	202-274-4101	274-4107	167-1
American Urban Radio Networks 938 Penn Ave Ste 701 *TF:* 800-456-4211 ■ *Web:* www.aurn.com	Pittsburgh	PA	15222	412-456-4099	456-4077	646
American Urethane Inc 1905 Betson Ct *TF:* 800-394-7883 ■ *Web:* americanurethane.com	Odenton	MD	21113	410-672-2100	672-2191	604
American Urological Assn (AUA) 1000 Corporate Blvd *TF:* 866-746-4282 ■ *Web:* www.auanet.org	Linthicum Heights	MD	21090	410-689-3700	689-3800	49-8

	Phone	Fax	Class
American Valve & Hydrant Manufacturing Company LP 3525 Hollywood St .... Beaumont TX 77701 *Web:* www.avhmc.com	409-832-7721		789
American Vanguard Corp 4695 MacArthur Ct .... Newport Beach CA 92660 *NYSE:* AVD ■ *Web:* www.american-vanguard.com	949-260-1200		145
American Veterinary Medical Assn (AVMA) 1931 N Meacham Rd Ste 100 .... Schaumburg IL 60173 *TF:* 800-248-2862 ■ *Web:* www.avma.org	847-925-8070	925-1329	49-8
American Veterinary Supply Inc (AVS) 3555 NW 33rd St .... Miami FL 33142 *Web:* www.americanvet.com	305-637-8616	637-9398	238
American Visionary Art Museum 800 Key Hwy .... Baltimore MD 21230 *Web:* www.avam.org	410-244-1900	244-5858	520
American Volkssport Assn (AVA) 1001 Pat Booker Rd Ste 101 .... Universal City TX 78148 *Web:* www.ava.org	210-659-2112	659-1212	48-22
American Warehouse Equipment Inc 1371 Kuehner Dr .... Simi Valley CA 93063 *Web:* www.aweonline.com	805-526-5501	526-5509	803-1
American Warehouses Ltd 1918 Collingsworth St .... Houston TX 77009 *Web:* www.americanwarehouses.com	713-228-6381	228-5913	803-1
American Warmblood Registry (AWR) PO Box 1332 .... De Leon Springs FL 32130 **Fax Area Code:* 775 ■ *Web:* www.americanwarmblood.com	406-734-5499	667-0516*	48-3
American Warming & Ventilating Inc 7301 International Dr .... Holland OH 43528 *Web:* www.awv.com	419-865-5000	865-1375	697
American Watchmakers-Clockmakers Institute (AWI) 701 Enterprise Dr .... Harrison OH 45030 *TF:* 866-367-2924 ■ *Web:* www.awci.com	513-367-9800	367-1414	49-4
American Water 1 Water St .... Camden NJ 08102 *Web:* www.amwater.com	856-955-4001		787
American Water Ski Hall of Fame & Museum 1251 Holy Cow Rd .... Polk City FL 33868 *TF:* 800-533-2972 ■ *Web:* www.usa-wwf.org	863-324-2472	324-3996	522
American Water Works Assn (AWWA) 6666 W Quincy Ave .... Denver CO 80235 *TF:* 800-926-7337 ■ *Web:* www.awwa.org	303-794-7711	347-0804	48-12
American Water Works Company Inc 1025 Laurel Oak Rd .... Voorhees NJ 08043 *NYSE:* AWK ■ *TF:* 888-282-6816 ■ *Web:* amwater.com	856-346-8200	346-8360	360-5
American Waterways Operators (AWO) 801 N Quincy St Ste 200 .... Arlington VA 22203 *Web:* www.americanwaterways.com	703-841-9300	841-0389	49-21
American Welding Society (AWS) 550 NW 42nd Ave .... Miami FL 33126 *TF:* 800-443-9353 ■ *Web:* www.aws.org	305-443-9353	443-7559	49-3
American West Homes 250 Pilot Rd Ste 140 .... Las Vegas NV 89119 *Web:* www.americanwesthomes.com	702-736-6434		653
American Whitewater (AW) PO Box 1540 .... Cullowhee NC 28723 *TF:* 866-262-8429 ■ *Web:* www.americanwhitewater.org	828-586-1930	586-2840	48-23
American Wind Energy Assn (AWEA) 1501 M St NW Ste 1000 .... Washington DC 20005 *Web:* www.awea.org	202-383-2500	383-2505	48-12
American Wind Power Ctr 1701 Canyon Lake Dr .... Lubbock TX 79403 *Web:* windmill.com	806-747-8734		520
American Window & Glass Inc 2715 Lynch Rd .... Evansville IN 47711 *TF:* 877-671-6943 ■ *Web:* www.americanwindowandglass.com	812-464-9400	464-3131	608
American Wire Producers Assn (AWPA) PO Box 151387 .... Alexandria VA 22315 *Web:* www.awpa.org	703-299-4434		49-13
American Wire Rope & Sling 3122 Engle Rd .... Fort Wayne IN 46809 **Fax Area Code:* 260 ■ *TF:* 800-466-7520 ■ *Web:* www.awrsling.com	866-578-4700	478-8184*	492
American Wire Tie Inc PO Box 696 .... North Collins NY 14111 *TF:* 800-448-1222 ■ *Web:* americanwiretie.com	716-337-2412	337-3728	454
American Wood Dryers LLC 15495 SE Formor Ct .... Clackamas OR 97015 *Web:* www.drykilns.com	503-655-1955		454
American Wood Fibers Inc 9841 Broken Land Pkwy Ste 302 .... Columbia MD 21046 *TF:* 800-624-9663 ■ *Web:* awf.com	410-290-8700	290-6660	820
American Woodmark Corp 561 Shady Elm Rd PO Box 1980 .... Winchester VA 22602 *NASDAQ:* AMWD ■ *Web:* www.americanwoodmark.com	540-665-9100	665-9176	115
American Woodworking Academy Inc 1304 W Lark Industrial Pk .... Fenton MO 63026 *Web:* www.awacademy.com	636-343-3750	326-0871	167-3
American Yacht Institute Inc 1684 SE 10th Ave .... Fort Lauderdale FL 33315 *Web:* www.americanyachtinstitute.com	954-522-1044		167-3
American Youth Soccer Organization (AYSO) 19750 S Vermont Ave Ste 200 .... Torrance CA 90502 **Fax Area Code:* 310 ■ *TF:* 800-872-2976 ■ *Web:* www.ayso.org	800-872-2976	525-1155*	48-22
American Zettler Inc 75 Columbia .... Aliso Viejo CA 92656 *Web:* www.azettler.com	949-831-5000	831-8642	203
American Zinc Recycling Corp 3000 GSK Dr Ste 201 .... Moon Township PA 15108 *TF:* 800-648-8897 ■ *Web:* azr.com	724-774-1020		143
American Zoetrope 916 Kearny St .... San Francisco CA 94133 *Web:* www.zoetrope.com	415-788-7500		514
Americana Coin Exchange Inc 217 Paterson Ave .... East Rutherford NJ 07073 *Web:* americanacoinexchange.com	201-933-2000		411
American-Arab Anti Discrimination Committee (ADC) 1990 M St NW Ste 610 .... Washington DC 20036 *TF:* 800-253-3931 ■ *Web:* www.adc.org	202-244-2990		48-8
AmericanChurch Inc 100 Noll Plz .... Huntington IN 46750 **Fax Area Code:* 877 ■ *TF:* 800-446-3035 ■ *Web:* www.americanchurch.com	800-446-3035	275-5771*	263
AmeriCandy Retail Interactive Kiosk (AIRK) 3618 St Germaine Ct .... Louisville KY 40207 *Web:* americandybar.com	502-583-1776		123
American-Indonesian Chamber of Commerce 521 5th Ave Ste 1700 .... New York NY 10175 *Web:* www.aiccusa.org	212-687-4505	687-5844	138
American-International Charolais Assn (AICA) 11700 NW Plaza Cir .... Kansas City MO 64153 *TF:* 800-270-7711 ■ *Web:* charolaisusa.com	816-464-5977	464-5759	48-2
American-Iowa Manufacturing Inc 117 Nixon St SE .... Cascade IA 52033 *Web:* www.american-iowa.com	563-852-7397	852-7539	273
American-Israel Chamber of Commerce & Industry of Minnesota PO Box 5644 .... Hopkins MN 55343 **Fax Area Code:* 612 ■ *Web:* www.aiccmn.org	952-593-8666	455-2215*	138
American-Israel Chamber of Commerce Southeast Region (AICC) 400 Northridge Rd Ste 250 .... Atlanta GA 30350 *Web:* www.conexx.org	404-843-9426	843-1416	138
Americanna Co 101 Charles Eldridge Dr .... Lakeville MA 02347 *TF:* 888-747-5550 ■ *Web:* americanna.com	508-747-5550		9
American-Russian Chamber of Commerce & Industry 1101 Pennsylvania Ave 6th Fl .... Washington DC 20004 *Web:* www.arcci.org	202-756-4943	362-4634	138
Americans for Democratic Action (ADA) 1629 K St NW Ste 300 .... Washington DC 20006 *Web:* adaction.org	202-600-7762	204-8637	48-7
Americans for Effective Law Enforcement (AELE) 841 W Touhy Ave .... Park Ridge IL 60068 *TF:* 800-763-2802 ■ *Web:* www.aele.org	847-685-0700	685-9700	48-8
Americans for Fair Taxation PO Box 4929 .... Clearwater FL 33758 *TF:* 800-324-7829 ■ *Web:* www.fairtax.org	800-324-7829		48-7
Americans for Nonsmokers' Rights (ANR) 2530 San Pablo Ave Ste J .... Berkeley CA 94702 *Web:* no-smoke.org	510-841-3032	841-3071	48-17
Americans for Peace Now (APN) 1101 14th St NW 6th Fl .... Washington DC 20005 *TF:* 877-429-0678 ■ *Web:* peacenow.org	202-728-1893	728-1895	48-7
Americans for Tax Reform (ATR) 722 12th St NW Ste 4 .... Washington DC 20005 *Web:* atr.org	202-785-0266	785-0261	48-8
Americans for the Arts 1000 Vermont Ave NW 6th Fl .... Washington DC 20005 *Web:* www.americansforthearts.org	202-371-2830	371-0424	48-4
Americans United for Separation of Church & State 518 C St NE .... Washington DC 20002 *TF:* 800-875-3707 ■ *Web:* www.au.org	202-466-3234	466-2587	48-7
AmericanTours International LLC (ATI) 6053 W Century Blvd .... Los Angeles CA 90045 *Web:* www.americantours.com	310-641-9953	216-5807	760
Americarb Inc 1025 Faultless Dr .... Ashland OH 44805 *Web:* www.americarb.com	419-281-5800		127
Americare Certified Special Services Inc 5923 Strickland Ave .... Brooklyn NY 11234 *TF:* 800-704-4341 ■ *Web:* www.americareny.com	718-535-3100	872-2450	363
AmeriCare Medical Inc 1938 Woodslee Dr .... Troy MI 48083 *TF:* 800-782-3394 ■ *Web:* www.americaremedical.com	248-280-2020	288-5713	363
AmeriCares Foundation 88 Hamilton Ave .... Stamford CT 06902 *TF:* 800-486-4357 ■ *Web:* www.americares.org	203-658-9500		48-5
Americas electric cooperatives 4301 Wilson Blvd .... Arlington VA 22203 *TF:* 866-751-1238 ■ *Web:* www.electric.coop	703-907-5939		48-12
Americas First Financial Corp 2046 Queensbrooke Blvd Ste 200 .... Saint Peters MO 63376 *Web:* 4affc.com	636-940-0068		390
Americas Floor Source 3442 Millennium Ct .... Columbus OH 43219 *Web:* www.americasfloorsource.com	614-237-3181		131
Americas Office Source Inc 706 Turnbull Ave Ste 305 .... Altamonte Springs FL 32701 *Web:* americasofficesource.com	407-478-0637		366
Americas Styrenics LLC 24 Waterway Ave Ste 1200 .... The Woodlands TX 77380 *TF:* 844-512-1212 ■ *Web:* www.amsty.com	832-616-7800		146
Americas Trade & Supply Co 7630 NW 63rd St .... Miami FL 33166 *Web:* www.atsmia.com	305-594-0797	592-8210	61
AmericasMart Alanta 240 Peachtree St NW Ste 2200 .... Atlanta GA 30303 *TF:* 800-285-6278 ■ *Web:* www.americasmart.com	800-285-6278		205
Americh Corp 13212 Saticoy St .... North Hollywood CA 91605 *TF:* 800-453-1463 ■ *Web:* www.americh.com	818-982-1711		610
Americhem Inc 2000 Americhem Way .... Cuyahoga Falls OH 44221 *TF:* 800-228-3476 ■ *Web:* www.americhem.com	330-929-4213	929-4144	143
Americhip Inc 19032 S Vermont Ave .... Gardena CA 90248 *Web:* www.americhip.com	310-323-3697		195
Americo Federal Credit Union 4101 Main St .... Erie PA 16511 *Web:* www.americofcu.com	814-899-6608		219
Americo Financial Life & Annuity Insurance Co PO Box 410288 .... Kansas City MO 64141 *TF:* 800-231-0801 ■ *Web:* www.americo.com	800-231-0801		391-2
Americo Manufacturing Company Inc 6224 N Main St .... Acworth GA 30101 *TF:* 800-241-9902 ■ *Web:* americomfg.com	770-974-7000		1
AmeriCom Inc PO Box 2146 .... Sandy UT 84091 **Fax Area Code:* 775 ■ *TF:* 800-820-6296 ■ *Web:* www.americom.com	801-571-2446	257-6643*	736
Americor Electronics Ltd 675 S Lively Blvd .... Elk Grove Village IL 60007 *TF:* 800-830-5337 ■ *Web:* www.americor-usa.com	847-956-6200	956-0300	253
Americorp Financial LLC 877 S Adams Rd .... Birmingham MI 48009 *Web:* www.americorpusa.com	248-723-4500		194
Americrown Service Corp 1 Daytona Blvd .... Daytona Beach FL 32114 *Web:* www.americrown.com	386-681-3850		670
Americtraining Inc 4315 Brook Rd NW .... Lancaster OH 43130 *Web:* www.ameritraining.com	740-756-7461		196

	Phone	Fax	Class
Americu Credit Union 1916 Black River Blvd. .... Rome NY 13440 *TF:* 866-210-3876 ■ *Web:* americu.org	800-388-2000		219
Ameridial Inc 4535 Strausser St NW .... North Canton OH 44720 **Fax Area Code:* 330 ■ *TF:* 800-445-7128 ■ *Web:* www.ameridial.com	800-445-7128	497-5500*	737
Ameridrives 1802 Pittsburgh Ave .... Erie PA 16502 *TF:* 800-352-0141 ■ *Web:* www.ameridrives.com	814-480-5000	453-5891	620
AmeriFab Inc 3501 E 9th St. .... Indianapolis IN 46201 *Web:* www.amerifabinc.com	317-231-0100		492
AmeriFactors Financial Group LLC 215 Celebration Pl Ste 340. .... Celebration FL 34747 **Fax Area Code:* 407 ■ *TF:* 800-884-3863 ■ *Web:* amerifactors.com	800-884-3863	566-1250*	272
Ameri-Fax Corp 6520 W 20th Ave Unit 2 .... Hialeah FL 33016 *TF:* 800-262-8214 ■ *Web:* www.posconcepts.com	305-828-1701	824-1606	554
Ameriflex Inc 2390 Railroad St .... Corona CA 92880 *Web:* www.ameriflex.net	951-737-5557		492
Ameriflight Inc 1515 W 20th St PO Box 612763. .... DFW Airport TX 75261 **Fax Area Code:* 818 ■ *TF:* 800-800-4538 ■ *Web:* w3.ameriflight.com	800-800-4538	846-3950*	12
Ameri-Force Inc 9485 Regency Sq Blvd Ste 300. .... Jacksonville FL 32225 *TF:* 800-522-8998 ■ *Web:* www.ameriforce.com	904-633-9918		721
Ameriglobe Imports Inc 2227 Troy Ave. .... South El Monte CA 91733 *Web:* www.ameriglobe.net	626-388-9618	452-0798	410
Amerigo Nashville 1920 W End Ave. .... Nashville TN 37203 *Web:* amerigo.net	615-320-1740		671
AMERIgreen Energy Inc 1650 Manheim Pk Ste 201. .... Lancaster PA 17601 *TF:* 888-423-8357 ■ *Web:* www.amerigreen.com	717-945-1392	665-1403	536
AMERIGROUP Corp 4425 Corporation Ln .... Virginia Beach VA 23462 *NYSE: AGP* ■ *TF:* 800-600-4441 ■ *Web:* www.amerigroup.com	757-490-6900		391-3
Ameriguard Security Services Inc 5470 W Spruce Ave Ste 102. .... Fresno CA 93722 *Web:* ameriguardsecurity.com	559-271-5984	271-5987	693
AmeriHealth Casualty 1700 Market St Ste 700 .... Philadelphia PA 19103 *TF:* 800-297-2726 ■ *Web:* www.amerihealthcasualty.com	215-587-1901	587-1826	353
AmeriHealth Mercy Health Plan 8040 Carlson Rd Ste 500 .... Harrisburg PA 17112 *TF:* 888-991-7200 ■ *Web:* www.amerihealthcaritaspa.com	717-651-3540		352
Ameril-Co Carriers Inc 1702 E Overland. .... Scottsbluff NE 69361 *TF:* 800-445-5400 ■ *Web:* www.americo-carriers.com	308-635-3157		780
Amerijet International Inc 2800 S Andrews Ave. .... Fort Lauderdale FL 33316 *TF:* 800-927-6059 ■ *Web:* amerijet.com	954-320-5300		12
Ameri-Kart Corp 17196 State Rd 120 .... Bristol IN 46507 *Web:* www.ameri-kart.com	574-848-7462		596
Amerikohl Mining Inc 202 Sunset Dr .... Butler PA 16001 *Web:* amerikohl.com	724-282-2339		501
Amerilab Technologies Inc 2765 Niagara Ln N .... Minneapolis MN 55447 *TF:* 866-445-6468 ■ *Web:* www.amerilabtech.com	763-525-1262		583
Amerilist Inc 978 Rt 45 Ste L2 .... Pomona NY 10970 *TF:* 800-457-2899 ■ *Web:* www.amerilist.com	845-362-6737		317
Amerilodge 1040 W Hamlin Rd .... Rochester Hills MI 48309 *Web:* www.amerilodgegroup.com	248-601-2500		377
Amerimac Cal-West Financial Inc 743 S Winchester Blvd Ste 210 .... San Jose CA 95128 *Web:* www.amerimac.com	408-559-4444	559-9538	509
Amerimade Technology Inc 449 Mtn Vista Pkwy .... Livermore CA 94551 *TF:* 800-938-3824 ■ *Web:* amerimade.com	925-243-9090	243-9266	608
Amerimax Home Products Inc 450 Richardson Dr .... Lancaster PA 17603 *TF:* 800-347-2586 ■ *Web:* www.amerimax.com	800-347-2586		480
Amerine Systems Inc 10866 Cleveland Ave .... Oakdale CA 95361 *Web:* www.amerinesystems.com	209-847-5968	847-9082	274
Amerinst Professional Services 4200 Commerce Court St 102 .... Lisle IL 60532 *TF:* 888-803-9898 ■ *Web:* protexure.com	630-799-2000	799-1796	390
Ameripack Inc 107 N Gold Dr. .... Robbinsville NJ 08691 *TF:* 800-456-7963 ■ *Web:* www.ameripack.com	609-259-7004		453
AmeriPark 3200 Cobb Galleria Pkwy Ste 299 .... Atlanta GA 30339 *TF:* 866-426-7275 ■ *Web:* www.ameripark.com	866-426-7275		192
AmeriPoint Title Inc 2823 E Southcross Blvd .... San Antonio TX 78223	210-531-9491		391-6
AmeriPride Linen & Uniform Services 1050 W Whitesbridge Ave. .... Fresno CA 93706 *TF:* 800-750-4628 ■ *Web:* www.ameripride.com	559-825-5501		442
Ameriprise Brokerage 70400 Ameriprise Financial Ctr .... Minneapolis MN 55474 *TF:* 800-535-2001 ■ *Web:* www.ameriprise.com	800-535-2001		690
Ameriqual Group LLC 18200 Hwy 41 N .... Evansville IN 47725 *Web:* ameriqualgroup.com	812-867-1444		296-36
Ameris Bank 24 Second Ave SE PO Box 3668. .... Moultrie GA 31768 *TF:* 866-616-6020 ■ *Web:* www.amerisbank.com	866-616-6020		186
AMERISAFE Inc 2301 Hwy 190 W .... DeRidder LA 70634 *NASDAQ: AMSF* ■ *TF:* 800-256-9052 ■ *Web:* www.amerisafe.com	337-463-9052		391-4
Ameriserv Financial 216 Franklin St PO Box 520 .... Johnstown PA 15907 *NASDAQ: ASRV* ■ *TF:* 800-837-2265 ■ *Web:* www.ameriserv.com	800-837-2265		70
Amerisource Funding Inc 7225 Langtry St .... Houston TX 77040 *TF:* 800-876-6639 ■ *Web:* amerisource.us.com	713-863-8300	460-1364	216
Amerispa 100 Boul From the Navy Ste 2A .... Varennes QC J3X2B1 *TF:* 866-263-7477 ■ *Web:* www.amerispa.ca	866-263-7477		706
AmeriSpan 1500 Walnut St. .... Philadelphia PA 19102 *TF:* 800-879-6640 ■ *Web:* www.amerispan.com	215-751-1100	751-1986	423
AmeriSpec Inc 3839 Forest Hill Irene Rd .... Memphis TN 38125 *TF:* 877-769-5217 ■ *Web:* www.amerispec.com	877-769-5217		365
Ameristar Casino & Hotel 3200 N Ameristar Dr. .... Kansas City MO 64161 *Web:* www.ameristar.com	816-414-7000		379
Ameristar Fence Products Inc 1555 N Mingo Rd .... Tulsa OK 74116 *TF:* 888-333-3422 ■ *Web:* www.ameristarfence.com	918-835-0898		491
Ameristat Pharmaceuticals Inc Northdale Shopping Ctr .... Coon Rapids MN 55448 *Web:* www.aipharma.com	763-754-8181	754-2824	237
Amerisure Insurance Co 26777 Halsted Rd .... Farmington Hills MI 48331 *TF:* 800-257-1900 ■ *Web:* www.amerisure.com	248-615-9000		391-4
Amerit Fleet Solutions 1331 N California Blvd Ste 150 .... Walnut Creek CA 94596 *TF:* 877-512-6374 ■ *Web:* www.ameritfleetsolutions.com	877-512-6374		289
Amerita Inc 7307 S Revere Pky Ste 200. .... Centennial CO 80112 *TF:* 800-360-4755 ■ *Web:* ameritaiv.com	303-355-4745	322-7022	363
Ameritas Direct 5900 'O' St .... Lincoln NE 68510 *TF:* 800-555-4655 ■ *Web:* www.ameritasdirect.com	800-555-4655		391-2
Ameritech College of Healthcare 12257 Business Park Dr Ste 108 .... Draper UT 84020 *TF:* 800-652-0907 ■ *Web:* www.ameritech.edu	801-816-1444	816-1456	167-3
Ameri-Tech Reality Inc 24701 Us 19 N Ste 102 .... Clearwater FL 33763 *Web:* ameritechcompanies.com	727-726-8000		652
Ameritek USA 125 130th St SE Ste 200. .... Everett WA 98208 *Web:* www.ameritek.org	425-379-2580	379-2624	476
AmeriTel Inc 8910 Quartz Ave .... Northridge CA 91324 *TF:* 800-974-6637 ■ *Web:* www.ameritelinc.com	818-734-7400	734-7444	224
Ameri-Tool Industries Inc 2420 Three Lakes Rd SE. .... Albany OR 97322 *Web:* www.ameri-tool.com	541-926-8647		604
AmeriTrust Group Inc 26255 American Dr. .... Southfield MI 48034 *NYSE: MIG* ■ *TF:* 800-482-2726 ■ *Web:* ameritrustgroup.com	248-358-1100	358-1614	360-4
Ameritube LLC 1000 N State Hwy 77. .... Hillsboro TX 76645 *Web:* ameritube.net	254-580-9888		492
Amerivon Holdings LLC 2815 Townsgate Rd Ste 225 .... Westlake Village CA 91361 *Web:* www.amerivon.com	805-719-4800		195
AmeriWater Inc 1303 Stanley Ave. .... Dayton OH 45404 *TF:* 800-535-5585 ■ *Web:* www.ameriwater.com	937-461-8833		45
Ameriwood Home 410 E S First St .... Wright City MO 63390 *TF:* 800-489-3351 ■ *Web:* www.ameriwoodhome.com	636-745-3351		319-2
Amernet 315 Montgomery St .... San Francisco CA 94104 *TF:* 877-616-5100 ■ *Web:* www.amer.net	877-616-5100		387
Amerril Energy LLC 3536 Hwy 6. .... Sugar Land TX 77478	713-660-1620		536
AmerTac 250 Boulder Dr. .... Breinigsville PA 18031 *Web:* www.amertac.com	610-336-1330	336-1336	350
Amery Hospital & Clinic 265 Griffin St E .... Amery WI 54001 *TF:* 800-424-5273 ■ *Web:* amerymedicalcenter.org	715-268-8000	268-0311	353
Ames Chamber of Commerce 1601 Golden Aspen Dr Ste 110 .... Ames IA 50010 *TF:* 800-288-7470 ■ *Web:* www.ameschamber.com	515-232-2310	232-6716	139
Ames Community School District 2005 24th St. .... Ames IA 50010 *Web:* www.ames.k12.ia.us	515-268-6600	268-6633	685
Ames Computer Forms Inc 2810 E Lincoln Way .... Ames IA 50010 **Fax Area Code:* 800 ■ *TF:* 800-475-2234 ■ *Web:* www.amescomputerforms.com	515-232-3947	728-7179*	110
Ames Corp 19 Ames Blvd. .... Hamburg NJ 07419 *Web:* amescorp.com	973-827-9101	827-8893	677
Ames Historical Society (AHS) 416 Douglas Ave Ste 101 .... Ames IA 50010 *Web:* www.ameshistory.org	515-232-2148		49-19
Ames Laboratory 111 TASF .... Ames IA 50011 *Web:* www.ameslab.gov	515-294-9557	294-3226	668
Ames National Corp 405 Fifth St PO Box 846. .... Ames IA 50010 *NASDAQ: ATLO* ■ *Web:* www.amesnational.com	515-232-6251	663-3033	360-2
Ames Nowell State Park Linwood St. .... Abington MA 02351 *Web:* www.mass.gov	781-857-1336		565
Ames Public Library 515 Douglas Ave. .... Ames IA 50010 *Web:* www.amespubliclibrary.org	515-239-5646	232-4571	434-3
Ames Rubber Manufacturing Company Inc 4516 Brazil St. .... Los Angeles CA 90039 *TF:* 800-275-9006 ■ *Web:* www.amesrubberonline.com	818-240-9313	240-0256	677
Ames Taping Tools 1327 Northbrook Pkwy Ste 400 .... Suwanee GA 30024 *TF:* 800-303-1827 ■ *Web:* amestools.com	800-303-1827		758
Ames True Temper Inc 465 Railroad Ave. .... Camp Hill PA 17011 *TF:* 800-393-1846 ■ *Web:* www.ames.com	800-393-1846		758
Amesbury Group 700 West Bridge St .... Owatonna MN 55060 *TF:* 800-866-7884 ■ *Web:* www.amesburytruth.com	800-866-7884		385
Ametco Manufacturing Corp 4326 Hamann Industrial Pky. .... Willoughby OH 44094 *TF:* 800-321-7042 ■ *Web:* www.ametco.com	800-321-7042		488
AMETEK Inc 1100 Cassatt Rd PO Box 1764. .... Berwyn PA 19312 *NYSE: AME* ■ **Fax Area Code:* 215 ■ *Web:* www.ametek.com	610-647-2121	323-9337*	360-3
Ameublements Tanguay Inc 7200 Armand-Viau St .... Quebec City QC G2C2A7 *TF:* 800-826-4829 ■ *Web:* www.tanguay.ca	418-847-4411		321
Amex Inc 256 Marginal St .... East Boston MA 02128 *Web:* www.amexinc.net	617-569-5630	569-4110	463
Amex International Inc 1615 L St NW Ste 340 .... Washington DC 20036 *Web:* www.amexdc.com	202-429-0222		770
Amex World Trade Corp 19151 SW 108th Ave Unit 26 .... Miami FL 33157 *Web:* amexworldtrade.com	305-274-5055	274-5934	54
AMF Bakery Systems 2115 W Laburnum Ave .... Richmond VA 23227 *TF:* 800-225-3771 ■ *Web:* www.amfbakery.com	804-355-7961	355-1074	207
AMF Bowling Worldwide Inc 7313 Bell Creek Rd. .... Mechanicsville VA 23111 *TF:* 800-342-5263 ■ *Web:* www.amf.com	800-342-5263		99

	Phone	Fax	Class
AMFAR (American Foundation for AIDS Research) 120 Wall St 13th Fl.......... New York NY 10005 *Web:* amfar.org	212-806-1600	806-1601	48-17
Amfed Companies LLC 576 Highland Colony Pkwy .... Ridgeland MS 39157 *Web:* www.amfed.com	601-853-4949	853-2727	390
Amfine Chemical Corp 777 Terrace Ave Ste 602B.......... Hasbrouck Heights NJ 07604 *Web:* www.amfine.com	201-818-0159	818-0259	146
AMFM Inc 240 Capitol St Ste 500 .... Charleston WV 25301 *TF:* 800-348-1623 ■ *Web:* www.amfmwv.com	304-344-1623		463
AMG (Affiliated Managers Group Inc) 600 Hale St.......... Prides Crossing MA 01965 *NYSE:* AMG ■ *Web:* www.amg.com	617-747-3300		360-3
AMG Inc 301 Jefferson Ridge Pkwy Lynchpin Industrial Ctr .... Lynchburg VA 24501 *TF:* 800-800-0358 ■ *Web:* www.amg-inc.net	434-385-7525	385-8345	454
AMG Industries Inc 200 Commerce Dr .... Mount Vernon OH 43050 *Web:* www.amgindustries.com	740-397-4044	397-3092	489
AMG Medical Inc 8505 Dalton.......... Montreal QC H4T1V5 *TF:* 800-363-2381 ■ *Web:* www.amgmedical.com	514-737-5251		477
AMG Publishers 6815 Shallowford Rd .... Chattanooga TN 37421 *TF:* 800-266-4977 ■ *Web:* www.amgpublishers.com	423-894-6060	894-9511	637-2
AMG Resources Corp 2 Robinson Plz Ste 350 .... Pittsburgh PA 15205 *TF:* 877-395-8338 ■ *Web:* www.amgresources.com	412-777-7300	331-0972	686
AMGA (American Medical Group Assn) 1422 Duke St.......... Alexandria VA 22314 *Web:* www.amga.org	703-838-0033	548-1890	49-8
AM-Gard Security Inc 600 Main St.......... Pittsburgh PA 15215 *TF:* 800-554-0412 ■ *Web:* am-gard.com	800-554-0412		693
Amgen Canada Inc 6775 Financial Dr Ste 100 .... Mississauga ON L5N0A4 *TF:* 800-665-4273 ■ *Web:* www.amgen.ca	905-285-3000	285-3100	85
Amgen Inc 1 Amgen Center Dr.......... Thousand Oaks CA 91320 *TF:* 800-563-9798 ■ *Web:* www.amgen.com	805-447-1000		85
Amglo Kemlight Laboratories Inc 215 Gateway Rd .... Bensenville IL 60106 *Web:* www.amglo.com	630-350-9470	350-9474	437
Amgraf Inc 1501 Oak St.......... Kansas City MO 64108 *TF:* 800-304-4797 ■ *Web:* amgraf.com	816-474-4797		180
AmGraph Group, The 2091 Del Rio Way .... Ontario CA 91761 *TF:* 877-321-8421 ■ *Web:* theamgraphgroup.com	877-321-8421		344
AMHA (American Miniature Horse Assn) 5601 S IH-35 W .... Alvarado TX 76009 *Web:* www.amha.org	817-783-5600	783-6403	48-3
AMHA (American Morgan Horse Assn) 4066 Shelburne Rd Ste 5 .... Shelburne VT 05482 *TF:* 888-436-3700 ■ *Web:* www.morganhorse.com	802-985-4944	985-8897	48-3
AMHCA (American Mental Health Counselors Assn) 107 S W St Ste 779 .... Alexandria VA 22314 *TF:* 800-326-2642 ■ *Web:* www.amhca.org	703-548-6002	548-5233	49-15
Amherst Alarm Inc 2361 Wehrle Dr .... Amherst NY 14221 *Web:* amherstalarm.com	716-632-4600		693
Amherst Area Chamber of Commerce 28 Amity St.......... Amherst MA 01002 *TF:* 800-593-4052 ■ *Web:* www.amherstarea.com	413-253-0700	256-0771	139
Amherst Capital Partners LLC 255 E Brown St Ste 120 .... Birmingham MI 48009 *Web:* amherstpartners.com	248-642-5660	642-9247	194
Amherst Chamber of Commerce 400 Essjay Rd Ste 150 .... Williamsville NY 14221 *Web:* amherst.org	716-632-6905	632-0548	139
Amherst College 220 S Pleasant St .... Amherst MA 01002 *TF:* 866-542-4438 ■ *Web:* www.amherst.edu	413-542-2000	542-2040	166
Amherst County 153 Washington St.......... Amherst VA 24521 *Web:* www.countyofamherst.com	434-946-9400	946-9370	338
Amherst County Chamber of Commerce 154 S Main St.......... Amherst VA 24521 *Web:* www.amherstvachamber.com	434-946-0990	946-0879	139
Amherst Federal Credit Union 6470 Main St Ste 5.......... Amherst NY 14221 *Web:* amherstcu.org	716-634-3881		219
Amherst Museum 3755 Tonawanda Creek Rd .... Amherst NY 14228 *Web:* www.bnhv.org	716-689-1440	689-1409	520
Amherst Telephone Co 120 Mill St.......... Amherst WI 54406 *Web:* wi-net.com	715-824-5529	824-2050	224
Amherst Town Library 14 Main St.......... Amherst NH 03031 *Web:* www.amherstlibrary.org	603-673-2288	672-6063	434-3
Amherst Veterinary Hospital 311 Willow St.......... Amherst NS B4H3Y3 *Web:* amherstvethospital.ca	902-667-8405		794
Amhof Trucking Inc 651 N 6th Ave.......... Eldridge IA 52748 *Web:* www.amhof.com	563-285-9887		780
AMI (American Megatrends Inc) 5555 Oakbrook Pkwy Bldg 200.......... Norcross GA 30093 *TF:* 800-828-9264 ■ *Web:* www.ami.com	770-246-8600	246-8790	176
AMI (Associated Materials Inc) 3773 State Rd .... Cuyahoga Falls OH 44223 *TF:* 800-922-6009 ■ *Web:* www.associatedmaterials.com	800-922-6009		697
Ami Adini Environmental Services Inc 100 N Brand Blvd Ste 264 .... Glendale CA 91203 *Web:* www.amiadini.com	323-913-4073		194
AMI Asset Management Corp 10866 Wilshire Blvd Ste 770 .... Los Angeles CA 90024 *Web:* www.amiassetmanagement.com	424-320-4000		401
AMI Bearings Inc 570 N Wheeling Rd.......... Mount Prospect IL 60056 *TF:* 800-882-8642 ■ *Web:* www.amibearings.com	847-759-0620	759-0630	385
AMI Environmental 8802 S 135th St Ste 100.......... Omaha NE 68138 *TF:* 800-828-8487 ■ *Web:* amienvironmental.com	402-397-5001		463
AMI Imaging Systems Inc 7815 Telegraph Rd .... Bloomington MN 55438 *Web:* www.ami-imaging.com	952-828-0080		415

	Phone	Fax	Class
AMI Mechanical Inc 12141 Pennsylvania St.......... Thornton CO 80241 *Web:* www.amimechanical.com	303-280-1401		610
AMI Metals Inc 1738 General George Patton Dr .... Brentwood TN 37027 *TF:* 800-727-1903 ■ *Web:* www.amimetals.com	615-377-0400		492
AMI Strategies 17187 N Laurel Park Dr Ste 125.......... Livonia MI 48152 *TF:* 866-264-8870 ■ *Web:* www.amistrategies.com	866-264-8870		177
AMIA (American Medical Informatics Assn) 4720 Montgomery Ln Ste 500 .... Bethesda MD 20814 *Web:* www.amia.org	301-657-1291	657-1296	49-8
Amica at City Ctr 380 Princess Royal Dr .... Mississauga ON L5B4M9 *Web:* www.amica.ca	905-803-8100		371
Amica Mutual Insurance Co 100 Amica Way.......... Lincoln RI 02865 *TF:* 800-652-6422 ■ *Web:* www.amica.com	800-652-6422		391-4
Amicalola Electric Membership Corp 544 Hwy 515 S.......... Jasper GA 30143 *TF:* 800-282-7411 ■ *Web:* www.amicalolaemc.com	706-253-5200		245
Amicalola Falls State Park & Lodge 418 Amicalola Falls State Park Rd .... Dawsonville GA 30534 *Web:* gastateparks.org	706-265-4703		565
Amicci's of Little Italy 231 S High St.......... Baltimore MD 21202 *Web:* amiccis.com	410-528-1096		671
Amick Farms Inc 2079 Batesburg Hwy.......... Batesburg SC 29006 *TF:* 800-926-4257 ■ *Web:* www.amickfarms.com	803-532-1400		10-8
AMICO (Alabama Metal Industries Corp) 3245 Fayette Ave.......... Birmingham AL 35208 *TF:* 800-366-2642 ■ *Web:* amicoglobal.com	205-787-2611		491
Amico Corp 85 Fulton Way.......... Richmond Hill ON L4B2N4 *TF:* 877-462-6426 ■ *Web:* www.amico.com	905-764-0800		641
Amico Group 2199 Blackacre Dr RR 1 .... Oldcastle ON N0R1L0 *Web:* www.amico.build	519-737-1577		261
Amicus Technology 2118 Wilshire Blvd Ste 430 .... Santa Monica CA 90403 *Web:* www.amicustech.com	310-670-4962		179
Amida Technology Solutions Inc 1640 Rhode Island Ave NW Ste 650.......... Washington DC 20036 *Web:* amida.com	202-735-1790		177
Amidon Graphics 1966 Benson Ave .... Saint Paul MN 55116 *TF:* 800-328-6502 ■ *Web:* amidongraphics.com	651-690-2401	690-4009	627
Amidus LLC 1450 S Rolling Rd Ste 2-5 .... Baltimore MD 21227 *Web:* amidus.com	410-926-0520	455-5901	463
Amigo Farms Inc 4245 E Hwy 80 .... Yuma AZ 85365 *Web:* www.amigofarms.com	928-726-3738	726-3744	10-11
Amigos de las Americas 1800 W Loop S Ste 1325 .... Houston TX 77027 *TF:* 800-231-7796 ■ *Web:* amigosinternational.org	800-231-7796		48-5
Amigos Foods 4669 Hwy 90 W .... San Antonio TX 78237 *Web:* www.amigosfoods.com	210-798-5360	798-5365	296-36
Amigos Library Services 14400 Midway Rd.......... Dallas TX 75244 *TF:* 800-843-8482 ■ *Web:* www.amigos.org	972-851-8000	991-6061	387
Amigos Meat Distributors 611 Crosstimbers St.......... Houston TX 77022	713-928-3111	699-4721	297-9
Amika Mobile Corp 700 March Rd Ste 203 .... Ottawa ON K2K2V9 *Web:* www.amikamobile.com	613-599-4445		179
Aminex Therapeutics Inc 11335 NE 122nd Way Ste 105 .... Kirkland WA 98034 *Web:* aminextx.com	425-286-4222		582
Amini Innovation Corp 8725 Rex Rd .... Pico Rivera CA 90660 *Web:* www.amini.com	562-222-2500	222-2525	320
Aminian Business Services Inc 50 Tesla.......... Irvine CA 92618 *TF:* 888-800-5207 ■ *Web:* www.aminian.com	949-724-1155		113
Amino Transport Inc 223 NE Loop 820 Ste 101.......... Hurst TX 76053 *TF:* 800-304-3360 ■ *Web:* www.shipamino.com	800-304-3360		194
Amira Intl PO Box 461028 .... Aurora CO 80046 *Web:* amira.global	303-400-3982		501
Amira Resort & Spa 1999 W Canyon View Dr.......... Saint George UT 84770 *Web:* amiraresort.com	435-669-5880		706
Amirit Technologies Inc 271 Rte 46 W Ste C103 .... Fairfield NJ 07004	973-575-7557	828-0205	194
Amirsys Inc 2180 S 1300 E Ste 405.......... Salt Lake City UT 84106 *Web:* www.amirsys.com	801-485-6500		41
Amistad National Recreation Area 4121 Hwy 90 W .... Del Rio TX 78840 *Web:* www.nps.gov	830-775-7491		564
Amistad Research Ctr 6823 Saint Charles Ave.......... New Orleans LA 70118 *Web:* www.amistadresearchcenter.org	504-862-3222		466
Amistar Automation Inc 1269 Linda Vista.......... San Marcos CA 92078 *Web:* www.amistarautomation.com	760-471-1700	471-9065	695
AMITA Corp 2650 Queensview Dr Ste 250.......... Ottawa ON K2B8H6 *Web:* www.worldreach.com	613-742-6482		196
AMITA Health 2601 Navistar Dr.......... Lisle IL 60532 *Web:* www.amitahealth.org	224-273-2387		352
Amitron Inc 2001 Landmeier Rd .... Elk Grove Village IL 60007 *Web:* www.amitroncorp.com	847-290-9800		625
Amity Die and Stamping Co 13870 W Polo Trail Dr .... Lake Forest IL 60045 *Web:* amitydie.com	847-680-6600	680-6677	488
Amity Home Health Inc 17042 Devonshire Ste 220.......... Northridge CA 91325 *Web:* www.amityhomehealth.com	818-831-8270	831-8272	363
Amity Machine of Alburtis 3750 Chestnut Rd.......... Alburtis PA 18011 *Web:* www.amityindustries.com	610-966-3115		454
Amivest Capital Management 703 Market St 18th Fl.......... San Francisco CA 94103 **Fax Area Code:* 415 ■ *TF:* 800-541-7774 ■ *Web:* www.wrapmanager.com	800-541-7774	541-9760*	401

Name	Address	City	State	ZIP	Phone	Fax	Class	Other
Amiya	101 Hudson St	Jersey City	NJ	07302	201-433-8000	433-8866	671	*Web:* www.amiyarestaurant.com
AMJ Campbell Intl	1445 Courtneypark Dr E	Mississauga	ON	L5T2E3	905-670-6683		314	*TF:* 800-363-6683 ■ *Web:* www.amj-international.com
AMK Drives & Controls Inc	5631 S Laburnum Ave	Richmond	VA	23231	804-222-0323	222-0339	518	*Web:* www.amk-group.com
Amkor Technology Inc	1900 S Price Rd	Chandler	AZ	85248	480-821-5000		696	*NASDAQ: AMKR* ■ *Web:* amkor.com
AML Partners LLC	347 Village St	Concord	NH	03303	201-484-8835		466	*Web:* www.amlpartners.com
AMLI Residential	200 W Monroe St Ste 2200	Chicago	IL	60606	312-283-4700		654	*Web:* www.amli.com
Ammann & Whitney Inc	96 Morton St	New York	NY	10014	212-462-8500	929-5356	261	*Web:* www.louisberger.com
Ammar's Inc	710 S College Ave	Bluefield	VA	24605	276-322-4686	326-1060	229	*Web:* www.magicmartstores.com
Ammeraal Beltech USA	7501 N St Louis Ave	Skokie	IL	60076	847-673-6720	673-6373	370	*TF:* 800-323-4170 ■ *Web:* www.ammeraalbeltech.com
Ammo Alley LLC	11562 County Rd 395	Hartsburg	MO	65039	573-634-6196		711	*Web:* ammoalley.com
Ammunition	1500 Sansome St Roundhouse 1	San Francisco	CA	94111	415-632-1170		194	*Web:* ammunitiongroup.com
AMN Healthcare Services Inc	12400 High Bluff Dr	San Diego	CA	92130	866-871-8519		721	*NYSE: AMN* ■ *TF:* 866-871-8519 ■ *Web:* www.amnhealthcare.com
AMNAV Maritime Services	201 Burma Rd	Oakland	CA	94607	510-834-8847	834-8873	313	*Web:* www.amnav.com
Amneal Pharmaceuticals LLC	75 Adams Ave	Hauppauge	NY	11788	631-952-0214	656-1009	582	*NYSE: AMRX* ■ *Web:* www.amneal.com
Amnesty International USA (AIUSA)	5 Penn Plz 16th Fl	New York	NY	10001	800-266-3789	627-1451*	48-5	**Fax Area Code:* 212 ■ *TF:* 866-273-4466 ■ *Web:* www.amnestyusa.org
Amnet Inc	219 W Colorado Ave Ste 200	Colorado Springs	CO	80903	719-442-6683		174	*TF:* 800-343-9019 ■ *Web:* www.amnet.net
Amnet Technology Solutions	26 Fahey St	Stamford	CT	06907	203-355-2400		180	*TF:* 888-652-6638 ■ *Web:* www.amnetsystems.com
Amnicon Falls State Park	4279 County Hwy U	South Range	WI	54874	715-398-3000		565	*Web:* dnr.wi.gov
AmniSure International LLC	24 School St 6th Fl	Boston	MA	02108	617-234-4441		85	*Web:* www.amnisure.com
AMOA (Amusement & Music Operators Assn)	380 Terra Cotta Rd Ste F	Crystal Lake	IL	60012	815-893-6010	893-6248	48-23	*TF:* 800-937-2662 ■ *Web:* amoa.memberclicks.net
AMOA-National Dart Assn (NDA)	10070 W 190th Pl	Mokena	IL	60448	800-808-9884	226-1310*	48-22	**Fax Area Code:* 708 ■ *TF:* 800-808-9884 ■ *Web:* www.ndadarts.com
Amoco Federal Credit Union	PO Box 889	Texas City	TX	77592	409-948-8541		219	*TF:* 800-231-6053 ■ *Web:* www.amocofcu.org
Amodei Mark (Rep R - NV)	104 Cannon House Office Bldg	Washington	DC	20515	202-225-6155	225-5679	342-2	*Web:* www.amodei.house.gov
Amog Consulting Inc	770 S Post Oak Ln Ste 310	Houston	TX	77056	713-255-0020		261	*Web:* amog.consulting
Amols' Specialty Inc	710 S Flores St	San Antonio	TX	78204	210-227-1457	229-1915	601	*TF:* 800-683-2665 ■ *Web:* www.amols.com
Amon Carter Museum	3501 Camp Bowie Blvd	Fort Worth	TX	76107	817-738-1933		520	*TF:* 800-573-1933 ■ *Web:* www.cartermuseum.org
Amon G. Carter Foundation	201 Main St Ste 1945	Fort Worth	TX	76102	817-332-2783	332-2787	305	*Web:* www.agcf.org
Amoray Dive Resort Inc	104250 Overseas Hwy	Key Largo	FL	33037	305-451-3595		707	*TF:* 800-426-6729 ■ *Web:* www.amoray.com
Amore	6931 Snider Plz	Dallas	TX	75205	214-739-0502		671	*Web:* amoreitalian.net
Amorim Cork Composites	26112 110th St	Trevor	WI	53179	262-862-2311		209	*Web:* amorimcorkcomposites.com
Amory Engineers PC	25 Depot St PO Box 1768	Duxbury	MA	02332	781-934-0178	934-6499	261	*Web:* www.amoryengineers.com
Amos Media Co	911 S Vandemark Rd	Sidney	OH	45365	937-498-2111		457-14	*TF:* 800-253-4555 ■ *Web:* www.amosmedia.com
Amos-Hill Associates Inc	112 Shelby Ave	Edinburgh	IN	46124	812-526-2671	526-5865	613	*TF:* 800-745-1778 ■ *Web:* www.koppensteiner.com
Amot Controls Corp	8824 Fallbrook Dr	Houston	TX	77064	281-940-1800	559-9419*	201	**Fax Area Code:* 713 ■ *Web:* www.amotusa.com
Amotec Inc	1701 E 12th St Ste 103	Cleveland	OH	44114	440-250-4600	583-0218*	194	**Fax Area Code:* 216 ■ *Web:* www.amotecinc.com
AMP (Applied Measurement Professionals Inc)	18000 W 105th St	Olathe	KS	66061	913-895-4600	895-4650	47	*TF:* 800-345-6559 ■ *Web:* www.goamp.com
AMP (Automatic Machine Products Co)	400 Constitution Dr	Taunton	MA	02780	508-822-4226	822-4476	621	*Web:* ampcomp.com
AMP Agency	77 N Washington St	Boston	MA	02114	617-723-8929		4	*Web:* www.ampagency.com
Amp Machinery Systems Inc	1098 Chetwood Dr	Carol Stream	IL	60188	630-213-8970		358	*Web:* www.ampmachinery.com
AMPAC Fine Chemicals (AFC)	MS 1007 PO Box 1718	Rancho Cordova	CA	95741	916-357-6880	353-3523	145	*TF:* 800-311-9668 ■ *Web:* ampacfinechemicals.com
Ampac Machinery LLC	319 Hwy 70 E Bypass	Durham	NC	27703	919-596-5320	596-0073	190	*TF:* 800-647-2629 ■ *Web:* www.ampacmachinery.com
Ampac Packaging LLC	12025 Tricon Rd	Cincinnati	OH	45246	513-671-1777	671-2920	66	*TF:* 800-543-7030 ■ *Web:* www.proampac.com
Ampac Seed Co	32727 Hwy 99 E	Tangent	OR	97389	541-928-1651	928-2430	694	*TF:* 800-547-3230 ■ *Web:* www.ampacseed.com
Ampacet Corp	660 White Plains Rd	Tarrytown	NY	10591	914-631-6600	631-7197	143	*TF:* 800-888-4267 ■ *Web:* www.ampacet.com
Ampco Manufacturers Inc	9 Burbidge St Ste 101	Coquitlam	BC	V3K7B2	604-472-3800		627	*TF:* 800-663-5482 ■ *Web:* www.ampcomanufacturers.com
Ampco Metal Inc	1117 E Algonquin Rd	Arlington Heights	IL	60005	847-437-6000	437-6008	485	*TF:* 800-844-6008 ■ *Web:* www.ampcometal.com
Ampco Products Inc	11400 NW 36th Ave	Miami	FL	33167	305-821-5700	642-5300*	286	**Fax Area Code:* 866 ■ *Web:* www.ampco.com
Ampco Pumps Company Inc	2045 W Mill Rd	Glendale	WI	53209	414-643-1852		641	*TF:* 800-737-8671 ■ *Web:* www.ampcopumps.com
Ampco-Pittsburgh Corp	600 Grant St Ste 4600	Pittsburgh	PA	15219	412-456-4400		674	*NYSE: AP* ■ *Web:* ampcopgh.com
Ampcus	14900 Conference Center Dr Ste 203	Chantilly	VA	20151	703-637-7299	991-3241	180	*Web:* www.ampcus.com
AMPERAGE Marketing	6711 Chancellor Dr	Cedar Falls	IA	50613	319-268-9151		195	*Web:* www.amperagemarketing.com
Amperity Inc	1000 1st Ave S 6th Fl	Seattle	WA	98134	206-432-8302		39	*Web:* amperity.com
Ampersand Art Supply	1235 S Loop 4 Ste 400	Buda	TX	78610	512-322-0278	322-9928	43	*TF:* 800-822-1939 ■ *Web:* ampersandart.com
Ampersand Capital Partners	55 William St Ste 240	Wellesley	MA	02481	781-239-0700	239-0824	792	*Web:* ampersandcapital.com
Ampersand Inc	1050 N State St	Chicago	IL	60610	312-280-8905	944-1582	637-2	*Web:* www.ampersandworks.com
Ampex Casting Corp	23 W 47th St 4th Fl	New York	NY	10036	212-719-1318		407	
Ampex Corp	26460 Corporate Ave	Hayward	CA	94545	415-706-2353		658	*Web:* www.ampex.com
Amphastar Pharmaceuticals Inc	11570 Sixth St	Rancho Cucamonga	CA	91730	909-980-9484		582	*TF:* 800-423-4136 ■ *Web:* www.amphastar.com
Amphenol Aerospace	40-60 Delaware Ave	Sidney	NY	13838	607-563-5011	563-5157	253	*TF:* 800-678-0141 ■ *Web:* www.amphenol-aerospace.com
Amphenol Automotive NA	25865 Meadowbrook	Novi	MI	48187	734-451-6400		253	*Web:* amphenol-automotive.de
Amphenol Corp	358 Hall Ave	Wallingford	CT	06492	203-265-8900	265-8516	815	*NYSE: APH* ■ *Web:* www.amphenol.com
Amphenol Optimize Manufacturing Co	482 N Mariposa Rd Bldg A	Nogales	AZ	85621	520-397-7015	397-7014	466	*Web:* www.amphenol-optimize.com
Amphenol PCD	72 Cherry Hill Dr	Beverly	MA	01915	978-624-3400	927-1513	253	*Web:* www.amphenolpcd.com
Amphenol RF	4 Old Newtown Rd	Danbury	CT	06810	203-743-9272	796-2032	253	*TF:* 800-627-7100 ■ *Web:* www.amphenolrf.com
Amphenol Sine Systems	44724 Morley Dr	Clinton Township	MI	48036	800-394-7732		253	*TF:* 800-394-7732 ■ *Web:* www.amphenol-sine.com
Amphenol Spectra-Strip	720 Sherman Ave	Hamden	CT	06514	203-281-3200	281-5872	253	*TF:* 800-846-6400
AMPI	315 N Broadway	New Ulm	MN	56073	507-354-8295		297-4	*TF:* 800-533-3580 ■ *Web:* www.ampi.com
Amplicon Express Inc	2345 NE Hopkins Ct	Pullman	WA	99163	509-332-8080		743	*TF:* 877-332-8080 ■ *Web:* ampliconexpress.com
Amplifi Commerce	15851 Dallas Pky Ste 500	Dallas	TX	75201	888-963-9309		194	*TF:* 888-963-9309 ■ *Web:* www.goamplifi.com
Amplified Geochemical Imaging LLC	210 Executive Dr Ste 1	Newark	DE	19702	302-266-2428		539	*Web:* www.agisurveys.net
Amplifier Technologies Inc (ATI)	1749 Chapin Rd	Montebello	CA	90640	323-278-0001	278-0083	52	*Web:* www.bgw.com
Amplify Clearwater	600 Cleveland St Ste 200	Clearwater	FL	33755	727-461-0011	449-2889	139	*Web:* www.clearwaterflorida.org
Amplify Education Inc	55 Washington St Ste 800	Brooklyn	NY	11201	212-213-8177	796-2311	196	*TF:* 800-823-1969 ■ *Web:* www.amplify.com
Amplion Clinical Communications	632 Melrose Ave	Nashville	TN	37211	615-843-9000	843-9001	177	*TF:* 877-938-6439 ■ *Web:* www.amplionalert.com
Amplitude Inc	631 Howard St 5th Fl	San Francisco	CA	94105	415-231-2353		39	*Web:* amplitude.com
AmpliVox Sound Systems LLC	3995 Commercial Ave	Northbrook	IL	60062	847-498-9000	498-6691	52	*TF:* 800-267-5486 ■ *Web:* www.ampli.com
AMPLS Mailing Service	1164 N Kraemer Pl	Anaheim	CA	92806	714-630-1313		463	*Web:* ampls.com
Amplyx Pharmaceuticals Inc	12730 High Bluff Dr Ste 160	San Diego	CA	92130	858-345-1755		582	*Web:* amplyx.com
AMPORTS	2901 Childs St	Baltimore	MD	21226	410-350-0400	354-8812	465	*TF:* 833-260-1147 ■ *Web:* www.amports.com
Ampro	30 Bunting Ln	Primos	PA	19018	610-623-9000		594	*Web:* www.store.amprogo.com
Ampronix Inc	15 Whatney	Irvine	CA	92618	949-273-8000		475	*TF:* 800-400-7972 ■ *Web:* www.ampronix.com
Amptech Inc	201 Glocheski Dr	Manistee	MI	49660	231-299-1230		179	*Web:* amptechinc.com
AMPTP (Alliance of Motion Picture & Television Producers)	15301 Ventura Blvd Bldg E	Sherman Oaks	CA	91403	818-995-3600		48-4	*Web:* amptp.org

				Phone	Fax	Class
Amqui Hospital 135 Ave Ga,tan-Archambault Web: www.cisss-bsl.gouv.qc.ca	Amqui	QC	G5J2K5	418-629-2211	629-4498	374-2
AMR (American Medical Response) 6200 S Syracuse Way Ste 200 TF: 877-244-4890 ■ Web: www.amr.net	Greenwood Village	CO	80111	303-495-1200		30
AMR (Advantage Metals Recycling LLC) 510 Walnut St Ste 300 TF: 866-527-4733 ■ Web: www.advantagerecycling.com	Kansas City	MO	64106	816-861-2700	922-1795	686
AMR Care Group Inc 375 N Broadway Ste 209 Web: amrcaregroup.com	Jericho	NY	11753	516-605-0434		363
AMR Insurance LLC 3815 100th St SW Web: amrinsurance.com	Lakewood	WA	98496	253-581-1500		390
AMR Management Services 201 E Main St Ste 1405 Web: www.amrms.com	Lexington	KY	40507	859-514-9150	514-9207	47
AmRad Engineering Inc 32 Hargrove Grade TF: 800-445-6033 ■ Web: www.americanradionic.com	Palm Coast	FL	32137	386-445-6000	445-6871	253
AMREL (American Reliance Inc) 3445 Fletcher Ave TF: 800-882-6735 ■ Web: amrel.com	El Monte	CA	91731	626-443-6818		529
AmRent 250 E Broad St TF: 800-324-3681 ■ Web: www.amrent.com	Columbus	OH	43215	800-324-3681		635
AMREP Corp 620 W Germantown Pk Ste 175 NYSE: AXR ■ Web: www.amrepcorp.com	Plymouth Meeting	PA	19462	610-487-0905	487-0713	653
AMREP Southwest Inc 333 Rio Rancho Blvd NE Ste 202 Web: amrepsw.com	Rio Rancho	NM	87124	505-896-9000		653
AMRESCO Commercial Finance LLC 412 E Parkcenter Blvd Web: www.amresco.com	Boise	ID	83706	208-333-2000	333-2050	216
Amrex Electro-Therapy Equipment 7034 Jackson St *Fax Area Code: 310 ■ TF: 800-221-9069 ■ Web: www.amrexusa.com	Paramount	CA	90723	800-221-9069	366-7343*	250
Amridge University 1200 Taylor Rd TF: 888-790-8080 ■ Web: www.amridgeuniversity.edu	Montgomery	AL	36117	334-387-3877	387-3878	166
Amro Fabrication Corp 1430 Adelia Ave Web: amrofab.com	South El Monte	CA	91733	626-579-2200		529
Amro Music Stores 2918 Poplar Ave TF: 800-626-2676 ■ Web: www.amromusic.com	Memphis	TN	38111	901-323-8888		526
AmRod Corp 305 A Craneway St Web: www.amrod.com	Newark	NJ	07114	973-344-3806	344-0365	492
AMRPA (American Medical Rehabilitation Providers Assn) 529 14th St, NW Ste 1280 TF: 888-346-4624 ■ Web: www.amrpa.org	Washington	DC	20045	202-223-1920	223-1925	49-8
AMS (American Montessori Society) 281 Park Ave S 6th Fl Web: www.amshq.org	New York	NY	10010	212-358-1250	358-1256	48-11
AMS (American Musicological Society) 6010 College Stn *Fax Area Code: 207 ■ Web: www.ams-net.org	Brunswick	ME	04011	212-992-6340	798-4254*	48-4
AMS (Association Management Solutions LLC) 5177 Brandin Ct Web: www.amsl.com	Fremont	CA	94538	510-492-4000	492-4001	47
AMS (American Mathematical Society) 201 Charles St TF: 800-321-4267 ■ Web: www.ams.org	Providence	RI	02904	401-455-4000	331-3842	49-19
AMS (American Meteorological Society) 45 Beacon St TF: 800-824-0405 ■ Web: www.ametsoc.org	Boston	MA	02108	617-227-2425	742-8718	49-19
AMS (Advanced Management Solutions Inc) PO Box 9445 TF: 800-397-6829 ■ Web: www.amsrealtime.com	Yucaipa	CA	92399	909-790-4680	790-4682	178-1
AMS Controls Inc 12180 Prichard Farm Rd Web: www.amscontrols.com	Maryland Heights	MO	63043	314-344-3144		358
AMS Entertainment 1221 State St Ste 12 Web: www.ams-events.com	Santa Barbara	CA	93101	805-899-4000		181
AMS Filling Systems 2500 Chestnut Tree Rd TF: 800-647-5390 ■ Web: www.amsfilling.com	Honey Brook	PA	19344	610-942-4200		547
AMS Genetics International LLC 1515 Livingstone Rd Ste B Web: www.amsgenetics.com	Hudson	WI	54016	240-329-0169	469-4231	11-2
AMS Mechanical Systems Inc 9341 Adam Don Pkwy TF: 800-794-5033 ■ Web: amsmechanicalsystems.com	Woodridge	IL	60517	630-887-7700	887-0770	261
AMS Plastics Inc 1530 Hilton Head Rd Ste 205 Web: amsplastics.com	El Cajon	CA	92019	619-713-2000	713-2975	604
AMS Production Machining Inc 800 Andico Rd PO Box 376 Web: www.amsmachining.com	Plainfield	IN	46168	317-838-9273	838-0949	757
AMSA (American Medical Student Assn) 1902 Assn Dr TF: 800-767-2266 ■ Web: www.amsa.org	Reston	VA	20191	703-620-6600	620-5873	49-5
AMSA (American Moving & Storage Assn) 1611 Duke St TF: 888-849-2672 ■ Web: www.moving.org	Alexandria	VA	22314	703-683-7410	683-7527	49-21
AmSafe Inc 1043 N 47th Ave Web: www.amsafe.com	Phoenix	AZ	85043	602-850-2850	850-2812	678
Amscan Inc 80 Grasslands Rd TF: 800-444-8887 ■ Web: www.amscan.com	Elmsford	NY	10523	914-345-2020	345-3884	566
AMSCO (Automotive Manufacturing & Supply Co) 90 Plant Ave TF: 800-645-5604 ■ Web: www.amscovf.com	Hauppauge	NY	11788	631-435-1400	435-1475	61
Amsco Windows Inc 1880 S 1045 W TF: 800-748-4661 ■ Web: www.amscowindows.com	Salt Lake City	UT	84104	801-972-6441	974-0498	234
AMSE (American Museum of Science & Energy) 300 S Tulane Ave Web: amse.org	Oak Ridge	TN	37830	865-576-3200	576-6024	520
Amset Technical Consulting Inc 1864 S Elmhurst Rd TF: 888-982-6783 ■ Web: amsetusa.com	Mount Prospect	IL	60056	847-229-1155	229-1166	261
Amsher 4524 Southlake Pkwy Ste 15 TF: 844-227-4627 ■ Web: www.amsher.com	Birmingham	AL	35244	205-322-4110		160
AMSNET Inc 502 Commerce Way *Fax Area Code: 925 ■ TF: 800-893-3660 ■ Web: www.ams.net	Livermore	CA	94551	800-893-3660	245-6150*	177
Amsoil Inc 925 Tower Ave TF: 800-777-7094 ■ Web: www.amsoil.com	Superior	WI	54880	715-392-7101	392-5225	541
AMSplus Inc 400 Washington St TF: 888-239-9575 ■ Web: www.amsplus.com	Braintree	MA	02184	888-239-9575		225
Amstan Logistics Inc 7570 Bales St Ste 310 TF: 855-301-7599 ■ Web: amstan.com	Hamilton	OH	45011	513-817-0937	448-0547	780
AMSTED Industries Inc 180 N Stetson St Ste 1800 Web: www.amsted.com	Chicago	IL	60601	312-645-1700		307
Amsted Rail Company Inc 311 S Wacker Dr Ste 5300 TF: 800-621-8442 ■ Web: www.amstedrail.com	Chicago	IL	60606	312-922-4501	922-4502	770
Amstek Metal LLC 2408 W Mcdonough TF: 800-551-9473 ■ Web: www.amstekmetal.com	Joliet	IL	60436	815-725-2520	725-2663	492
Amstel House 30 Market St Web: www.newcastlehistory.org	New Castle	DE	19720	302-322-2794	322-8923	50-3
Amsterdam Hospitality 888 7th Ave 20th Fl Web: www.amsterdamhospitality.com	New York	NY	10019	212-247-9700		379
Amsterdam Nursing Home Corp 1060 Amsterdam Ave Web: www.amsterdamcares.com	New York	NY	10025	212-316-7700		371
Amsterdam Printing & Litho Corp 166 Wallins Corners Rd TF: 800-833-6231 ■ Web: www.amsterdamprinting.com	Amsterdam	NY	12010	800-833-6231		9
Amster-Kirtz Co 2830 Cleveland Ave NW TF: 800-257-9338 ■ Web: www.amsterkirtz.com	Canton	OH	44709	330-535-6021		297-8
AMSUS (Association of Military Surgeons of the United States) 9320 Old Georgetown Rd TF: 800-761-9320 ■ Web: www.amsus.org	Bethesda	MD	20814	301-897-8800	530-5446	49-8
AMT (American Medical Technologists) 10700 W Higgins Rd Ste 150 TF: 800-275-1268 ■ Web: www.americanmedtech.org	Rosemont	IL	60018	847-823-5169	823-0458	49-8
AMT (Association for Manufacturing Technology) 7901 Westpark Dr TF: 800-524-0475 ■ Web: www.amtonline.org	McLean	VA	22102	703-893-2900	893-1151	49-12
AMT (American Modular Technologies) 6306 Old 421 Rd PO Box 1069 Web: www.americanmodulartechnologies.com	Liberty	NC	27298	336-622-6200	622-6473	105
AMT Datasouth Corp 803 Camarillo Springs Rd Ste D TF: 800-215-9192 ■ Web: www.amtdatasouth.com	Camarillo	CA	93012	805-388-5799	484-5282	173-6
AMT Pump Co 400 Spring St *Fax Area Code: 610 ■ TF: 888-268-7867 ■ Web: www.amtpump.com	Royersford	PA	19468	888-268-7867	948-5300*	641
AMTA (American Music Therapy Association Inc) 8455 Colesville Rd Ste 1000 Web: www.musictherapy.org	Silver Spring	MD	20910	301-589-3300	589-5175	48-17
AMTA (American Massage Therapy Assn) 500 Davis St Ste 900 TF: 877-905-2700 ■ Web: www.amtamassage.org	Evanston	IL	60201	847-864-0123	864-1178	48-17
Amtec Precision Products Inc 1875 Holmes Rd Web: www.amtecprecision.com	Elgin	IL	60123	847-695-8030		621
Amtech Microelectronics Inc 485 Cochrane Cir Web: www.amtechmicro.com	Morgan Hill	CA	95037	408-612-8888		253
Amtech Systems Inc 131 S Clark Dr NASDAQ: ASYS ■ Web: www.amtechsystems.com	Tempe	AZ	85281	480-967-5146	968-3763	695
AMTEK Information Service Inc 4001 Sherwood Web: www.amtekusa.com	Houston	TX	77092	713-956-0100		463
AMTEL 9707 Key West Ave Ste 202 TF: 800-989-5566 ■ Web: www.amtelnet.com	Rockville	MD	20850	301-721-3010		196
Amtelco 4800 Curtin Dr TF: 800-356-9148 ■ Web: www.amtelco.com	McFarland	WI	53558	608-838-4194	838-8367	735
Amtex Corp 832 East Walnut St Web: www.amtexcorp.com	Garland	TX	75040	972-276-7626		360-3
Amtex Enterprises Inc 4699 Old Ironsides Dr Ste 270 Web: amtexenterprises.com	Santa Clara	CA	95054	408-734-4050		177
AmTex Machine Products Inc 4517 Brittmoore Rd Web: amtexmachine.com	Houston	TX	77041	713-896-4488	896-6363	358
Amtex Precision Fabrication 3920 Bahler Ave Web: amtexprecision.com	Manvel	TX	77578	281-489-7042		697
Amtex Systems Inc 28 Liberty St 6th Fl Web: www.amtexsystems.com	New York	NY	10005	212-269-6448	269-6458	180
AMTIS Inc 12124 High Tech Ave Ste 150 Web: www.amtisinc.com	Orlando	FL	32817	407-513-9490	513-9495	463
Amtote International Inc 11200 Pepper Rd TF: 800-345-1566 ■ Web: www.amtote.com	Hunt Valley	MD	21031	410-771-8700		322
Am-Touch Dental 28703 Industry Dr TF: 800-350-4568 ■ Web: www.amtouch.com	Valencia	CA	91355	800-350-4568		228
Amtrol Inc 1400 Div Rd Web: www.amtrol.com	West Warwick	RI	02893	401-884-6300	885-2567	91
Amtrust Realty Corp 250 Broadway Ste 3001	New York	NY	10007	212-732-4776		652
AMU (American Public University System) 111 W Congress St TF: 877-755-2787 ■ Web: www.amu.apus.edu	Charles Town	WV	25414	877-755-2787		167
Amundsen Educational Ctr 995 E Roald Ave Web: www.aecak.org	Soldotna	AK	99669	907-260-8041	262-7144	167-3
Amundson Appliance 124 Bridge St Web: amundsonsappliance.com	Rice Lake	WI	54868	715-234-8904		35
Amuneal Manufacturing Corp 4737 Darrah St TF: 800-755-9843 ■ Web: www.amuneal.com	Philadelphia	PA	19124	215-535-3000		697

Name / Address	City	State	ZIP	Phone	Fax	Class
Amunix Operating Inc 500 Ellis St *Web:* www.amunix.com	Mountain View	CA	94043	650-428-1800		668
Amusement & Music Operators Assn (AMOA) 380 Terra Cotta Rd Ste F *TF:* 800-937-2662 ■ *Web:* amoa.memberclicks.net	Crystal Lake	IL	60012	815-893-6010	893-6248	48-23
Amusement Park 217 N Main St Ste 200 *Web:* www.amusementparkinc.com	Santa Ana	CA	92701	714-881-2300		4
Amvac Chemical Corp 4100 E Washington Blvd *Web:* www.amvac-chemical.com	Los Angeles	CA	90023	323-264-3910	268-1028	280
AMVC Management Services LLC 508 Market St *Web:* www.amvcms.com	Audubon	IA	50025	712-563-2080		194
AMVETS 4647 Forbes Blvd *TF:* 877-726-8387 ■ *Web:* www.amvets.org	Lanham	MD	20706	301-459-9600	459-7924	48-19
Amvic Inc 501 McNicoll Ave *TF:* 877-470-9991 ■ *Web:* www.amvicsystem.com	Toronto	ON	M2H2E2	416-410-5674		183
AMWA (American Medical Writers Assn) 30 W Gude Dr Ste 525 **Fax Area Code:* 301 ■ *Web:* www.amwa.org	Rockville	MD	20850	240-238-0940	294-9006*	49-14
Amway Grand Plaza Hotel 187 Monroe Ave NW *TF:* 800-253-3590 ■ *Web:* amwaygrand.com	Grand Rapids	MI	49503	616-774-2000	776-6489	379
Amy Hereford 6400 Minnesota Ave **Fax Area Code:* 815 ■ *Web:* www.ahereford.org	Saint Louis	MO	63111	314-467-8038	550-1329*	192
Amy's Ice Creams 3500 Guadalupe St *Web:* amysicecreams.com	Austin	TX	78705	512-458-6895		381
Amy's Kitchen Inc PO Box 449 *Web:* www.amys.com	Petaluma	CA	94953	707-781-6600	578-7995	296-36
AMZ Financial Insurance Services LLC 1107 Investment Blvd Ste 150	El Dorado Hills	CA	95762	916-939-3765		463
Amzak Corp 980 N Federal Hwy Ste 400 *Web:* amzak.com	Boca Raton	FL	33432	561-953-4164	338-7677	188-10
Amzi! inc 83 Vance Crescent Ext *Web:* www.amzi.com	Asheville	NC	28806	828-350-0350		178-2
Amzur Technologies Inc 405 N Reo St Ste 110 *Web:* amzur.com	Tampa	FL	33609	813-600-4060		177
AN Deringer Inc 64 N Main St *TF:* 800-448-8108 ■ *Web:* www.anderinger.com	Saint Albans	VT	05478	802-524-8110		449
ANA (American Neurological Assn) 1120 Rte 73 Ste 200 *Web:* myana.org	Mount Laurel	NJ	08054	856-638-0423		49-8
ANA (Acoustic Neuroma Assn) 600 Peachtree Pkwy Ste 108 *TF:* 877-200-8211 ■ *Web:* www.anausa.org	Cumming	GA	30041	770-205-8211	205-0239	48-17
ANA (Alaska Nurses Assn) 3701 E Tudor Rd Ste 208 *Web:* www.aknurse.org	Anchorage	AK	99507	907-274-0827	272-0292	533
ANA (American Nurses Assn) 8515 Georgia Ave Ste 400 *TF:* 800-274-4262 ■ *Web:* www.nursingworld.org	Silver Spring	MD	20910	301-628-5000	628-5001	49-8
ANA Business Marketing 155 E 44th St *Web:* www.marketing.org	New York	NY	10017	212-697-5950	687-7310	49-18
ANA Consultants LLC 5000 Thompson Terr Ste 100	Colleyville	TX	76034	817-335-9900		261
ANA Idaho 6126 W State St Ste 306 **Fax Area Code:* 404 ■ *TF:* 888-721-8904 ■ *Web:* idahonurses.nursingnetwork.com	Boise	ID	83703	208-367-1171	240-0998*	533
ANAC (American Nurses Association California) 1121 L St Ste 406 *Web:* www.anacalifornia.org	Sacramento	CA	95814	916-346-4590	400-3599	533
AnaBios San Diego Science Ctr 3030 Bunker Hill St Ste 312 *Web:* www.anabios.com	San Diego	CA	92109	858-224-7360		743
Anabliss 1023 Walnut St *Web:* anabliss.com	Boulder	CO	80302	303-825-4441		344
ANAC (Association of Nurses in AIDS Care) 3538 Ridgewood Rd *TF:* 800-260-6780 ■ *Web:* www.nursesinaidscare.org	Akron	OH	44333	330-670-0101	670-0109	49-8
Anacom General Corp 1240 S Claudina St *TF:* 800-955-9540 ■ *Web:* www.anacom-medtek.com	Anaheim	CA	92805	714-774-8484	774-7388	392
Anacom Inc 3000 Tasman Dr *Web:* www.anacominc.com	Santa Clara	CA	95054	408-519-2062		196
Anaconda-Deer Lodge County 800 S Main *Web:* adlc.us	Anaconda	MT	59711	406-563-4000	563-4001	338
Anacortes Public Library PO Box 547 *Web:* www.anacorteswa.gov	Anacortes	WA	98221	360-293-1910		434-3
Anacostia Rail Holdings Co 224 S Michigan Ave Ste 330 *Web:* www.anacostia.com	Chicago	IL	60604	312-341-1026		648
Anadarko Bank & Trust Co 110 W Oklahoma Ave *Web:* www.bocokonline.com	Anadarko	OK	73005	405-247-3311		70
Anadigm Inc 2036 N Gilbert Rd Ste 2-417 *Web:* www.anadigm.com	Mesa	AZ	85203	480-422-0191	659-3511	246
Anadyne Inc 1729 Seabright Ave Ste C *Web:* www.anadyneinc.com	Santa Cruz	CA	95061	831-438-4898	438-3569	253
Anagram International Inc 7700 Anagram Dr *Web:* anagramballoons.com	Eden Prairie	MN	55344	952-949-5600		600
Anaheim Automation 910 E Orangefair Ln *TF:* 800-345-9401 ■ *Web:* www.anaheimautomation.com	Anaheim	CA	92801	714-992-6990	992-0471	203
Anaheim Chamber of Commerce 2400 E Katella Ave Ste 725 *Web:* www.anaheimchamber.org	Anaheim	CA	92806	714-758-0222	758-0468	139
Anaheim City Hall 200 S Anaheim Blvd *Web:* www.anaheim.net	Anaheim	CA	92805	714-765-4311	765-5164	337
Anaheim Custom Extruders 4640 E La Palma Ave *TF:* 800-229-2760 ■ *Web:* acextrusions.com	Anaheim	CA	92807	714-693-8508	693-9531	600
Anaheim Elementary School District 1001 SE St *Web:* anaheimelementary.org	Anaheim	CA	92805	714-517-7500		685
Anaheim Extrusion Company Inc 1330 N Kraemer Blvd PO Box 6380 *TF:* 800-660-3318 ■ *Web:* anaheimextrude.com	Anaheim	CA	92806	714-630-3111	630-0443	485
Anaheim Hotel, The 1700 S Harbor Blvd *TF:* 800-631-4144 ■ *Web:* www.theanaheimhotel.com	Anaheim	CA	92802	714-772-5900	772-8386	379
Anaheim Indoor Marketplace 1440 S Anaheim Blvd *Web:* anaheimmarketplace.com	Anaheim	CA	92805	714-999-0888	999-0885	460
Anaheim Union High School District (AUHSB) 501 N Crescent Way *Web:* www.auhsd.us	Anaheim	CA	92801	714-999-3511		685
Anaheim University 1240 S State College Blvd Rm 110 *TF:* 800-955-6040 ■ *Web:* www.anaheim.edu	Anaheim	CA	92806	714-772-3330		165
Anaheim White House 887 S Anaheim Blvd *Web:* www.anaheimwhitehouse.com	Anaheim	CA	92805	714-772-1381	772-7062	671
Anaheim/Orange County Visitor & Convention Bureau 800 W Katella Ave *Web:* visitanaheim.org	Anaheim	CA	92802	714-765-8888	991-8963	206
AnaJet LLC 3050 Redhill Ave *Web:* anajet.com	Costa Mesa	CA	92626	714-662-3200		194
Anakena Solutions Inc 18345 Ventura Blvd *Web:* www.anakenasolutions.com	Tarzana	CA	91356	310-929-7869		180
Ana-Lab Corp PO Box 9000 *Web:* www.ana-lab-work.com	Kilgore	TX	75663	903-984-0551	984-5914	743
Analog Devices Inc 3 Technology Way *NASDAQ: ADI* ■ *TF:* 800-262-5643 ■ *Web:* www.analog.com	Norwood	MA	02062	781-329-4700	461-3113	696
Analogix Semiconductor Inc 3211 Scott Blvd Ste 103 *Web:* www.analogix.com	Santa Clara	CA	95054	408-988-8848		696
Analynk Wireless LLC 790 Cross Pointe Rd *Web:* www.analynk.com	Columbus	OH	43230	614-755-5091		179
Analysis Group Inc 111 Huntington Ave 10th Fl *Web:* www.analysisgroup.com	Boston	MA	02199	617-425-8000	425-8001	194
Analystik 1430 Rue Belanger *TF:* 855-514-2727 ■ *Web:* www.analystik.ca	Montreal	QC	H2G1A4	514-278-2727		180
Analytica Group-environmental Laboratories 4307 Arctic Blvd *Web:* www.analyticagroup.com	Anchorage	AK	99503	907-258-2155		743
Analytical Design Service Corp 540 Avis Dr Ste E *Web:* www.adsc-usa.com	Ann Arbor	MI	48108	734-761-2626		256
Analytical Graphics Inc 220 Vly Creek Blvd *TF:* 800-220-4785 ■ *Web:* www.agi.com	Exton	PA	19341	610-981-8000	981-8001	177
Analytical Group Inc, The 16638 N 90th St *TF:* 800-946-2767 ■ *Web:* www.analyticalgroup.com	Scottsdale	AZ	85260	480-483-7505	905-1416	195
Analytical Industries Inc 2855 Metropolitan Pl *Web:* www.aii1.com	Pomona	CA	91767	909-392-6900		295
Analytical Lab Group 2341 Stanwell Dr *Web:* www.microqa.com	Concord	CA	94520	925-270-3800	270-3806	463
Analytical Mechanics Associates Inc 21 Enterprise Pkwy Ste 300 *Web:* www.ama-inc.com	Hampton	VA	23666	757-865-0000	865-1881	177
Analytical Sensors & Instruments Ltd 12800 Pk One Dr *Web:* www.asi-sensors.com	Sugar Land	TX	77478	281-565-8818	565-8811	419
Analytical Spectral Devices Inc 2555 55th St Ste 100 *Web:* www.malvernpanalytical.com	Boulder	CO	80301	303-444-6522		419
Analytics Corp 10329 Stony Run Ln *TF:* 800-888-8061 ■ *Web:* analyticscorp.com	Ashland	VA	23005	804-365-3000		743
Analytics Press PO Box 1545 *Web:* www.numbersintoknowledge.com	Burlingame	CA	94011	510-550-2844		637-2
Anamet Inc 26102 Eden Landing Rd *TF:* 800-377-7768 ■ *Web:* anametinc.com	Hayward	CA	94545	510-887-8811		261
Ananke IT Solutions 20 Main St *TF:* 877-626-2653 ■ *Web:* www.ananke.com	East Greenwich	RI	02818	401-331-2780	331-2790	196
Anaqua 31 St James Ave Ste 1100 *Web:* www.anaqua.com	Boston	MA	02116	617-375-5808		177
Anara Spa at the Hyatt Regency Kauai 1571 Poipu Rd *Web:* www.anaraspa.com	Koloa	HI	96756	808-742-1234		707
Anaren Microwave Inc 6635 Kirkville Rd *NASDAQ: ANEN* ■ *TF:* 800-544-2414 ■ *Web:* www.anaren.com	East Syracuse	NY	13057	315-432-8909	432-9121	253
Anasazi State Park Museum 1594 WN Temple Ste 116 *Web:* stateparks.utah.gov	Salt Lake City	UT	84116	435-335-7308	335-7352	565
Anaseal Impregnation Inc 185 Bluegrass Valley Pky *Web:* www.anaseal.com	Alpharetta	GA	30005	770-664-6624	664-6620	143
AnaSpec Inc 34801 Campus Dr *TF:* 800-452-5530 ■ *Web:* www.anaspec.com	Fremont	CA	94555	510-791-9560	791-9572	231
Anastasi Trucking & Paving Inc 4430 Walden St *Web:* www.anastasitrucking.com	Lancaster	NY	14086	716-683-5003	683-5045	189-5
Anasteel & Supply Company LLC 2272 Mabros Industrial Pkwy *Web:* www.anasteel.com	Ellenwood	GA	30294	404-675-9501	675-7032	480
Anatech Electronics Inc 70 Outwater Ln *Web:* www.anatechelectronics.com	Garfield	NJ	07026	973-772-4242		262
Anatech Ltd 1020 Harts Lake Rd *TF:* 800-262-8324 ■ *Web:* www.anatechltdusa.com	Battle Creek	MI	49037	269-964-6450	964-8084	420
Anatek Labs Inc 1282 Alturas Dr *Web:* www.anateklabs.com	Moscow	ID	83843	208-883-2839		743
Anatolia 48 White Bridge Rd *Web:* www.anatolia-restaurant.com	Nashville	TN	37205	615-356-1556	356-1551	671

Name / Address	City	State	ZIP	Phone	Fax	Class
Anatolia's 992 Willamette St *Web:* www.poppisanatolia.com	Eugene	OR	97401	541-343-9661		671
Anatom-e Information Systems Ltd 7505 Fannin St Ste 422 *TF:* 800-561-0874 ■ *Web:* anatom-e.com	Houston	TX	77054	800-561-0874		743
Anatometal Inc 165 DuBois St *Web:* anatometal.com	Santa Cruz	CA	95060	831-454-9880		411
Anbakam Metals Inc 1200 Tices Ln Ste 201 *Web:* www.anbakam.com	East Brunswick	NJ	08816	732-710-4360		686
Ancero LLC 1001 Briggs Rd Ste 220 *Web:* ancero.com	Mount Laurel	NJ	08054	856-210-5800		387
Anchin Block & Anchin LLP 1375 Broadway *Web:* www.anchin.com	New York	NY	10018	212-840-3456	840-7066	2
Anchor Animal Hospital Inc 750 State Rd *Web:* anchoranimalhospital.com	North Dartmouth	MA	02747	508-996-3731	996-3750	794
Anchor Bar 651 Delaware Ave *TF:* 866-248-9623 ■ *Web:* www.anchorbar.com	Buffalo	NY	14202	716-883-1134		671
Anchor Bay Packaging Corp 30905 23 Mile Rd *Web:* www.anchorbaypackaging.com	New Baltimore	MI	48047	586-949-4040	949-9998	100
Anchor Bay School District 5201 County Line Rd *Web:* www.anchorbay.misd.net	Casco Township	MI	48064	586-725-2861		685
Anchor Bay Veterinary Ctr 36755 Green St *Web:* www.anchorbayvc.com	New Baltimore	MI	48047	586-725-7700	725-7777	794
Anchor Benefit Consulting Inc 2400 Maitland Center Pkwy Ste 111 *TF:* 800-845-7629 ■ *Web:* www.anchorbenefit.com	Maitland	FL	32751	407-667-8766		194
Anchor Brake Shoe Co 1920 Downs Dr *Web:* www.nyab.com	West Chicago	IL	60185	630-293-1110	293-7188	650
Anchor Brewing Co 1705 Mariposa St *Web:* www.anchorbrewing.com	San Francisco	CA	94107	415-863-8350	552-7094	102
Anchor Brokerage Company Inc 8232 18th Ave *Web:* anchorbrokerage.com	Brooklyn	NY	11214	718-234-9800		390
Anchor Capital Advisors LLC 1 Post Office Sq Ste 3850 *Web:* anchorcapital.com	Boston	MA	02109	617-338-3800		401
Anchor Commercial Bank 13951 US Hwy One *Web:* www.anchorcommercialbank.com	Juno Beach	FL	33408	561-383-3150		70
Anchor Computer Inc 1900 New Hwy *TF:* 800-728-6262 ■ *Web:* www.anchorcomputer.com	Farmingdale	NY	11735	631-293-6100	293-0891	178-10
Anchor Construction Corp 2254 25th Pl NE *Web:* anchorconst.com	Washington	DC	20018	202-269-6694		186
Anchor Conveyor Products Inc 6830 Kingsley St *TF:* 800-959-1347 ■ *Web:* www.anchorconveyor.com	Dearborn	MI	48126	313-846-6000	846-6004	207
Anchor Coupling Inc 5520 13th St *Web:* anchorcoupling.com	Menominee	MI	49858	906-863-2671	863-3242	621
Anchor Fabrication 1200 Lawson Rd *TF:* 800-635-0386 ■ *Web:* www.anchorfabrication.com	Fort Worth	TX	76131	800-635-0386		480
Anchor Financial Group 415 Fallowfield Rd Ste 300 *Web:* www.jfswa.com	Camp Hill	PA	17011	717-975-0509		390
Anchor Glass Container Corp 401 E Jackson St Ste 1100 *Web:* www.anchorglass.com	Tampa	FL	33602	813-884-0000		330
Anchor Hocking Co 519 Pierce Ave *TF:* 800-562-7511 ■ *Web:* theoneidagroup.com	Lancaster	OH	43130	740-681-6900		334
Anchor Hospital 5454 Yorktowne Dr *Web:* anchorhospital.com	Atlanta	GA	30349	770-991-6044		726
Anchor Industries Inc 7701 Hwy 41 N *TF:* 800-544-4445 ■ *Web:* www.anchorinc.com	Evansville	IN	47725	812-867-2421	867-1429	733
Anchor Manufacturing Group inc 12200 Brookpark Rd *TF:* 888-341-8910 ■ *Web:* www.anchor-mfg.com	Cleveland	OH	44130	216-362-1850	265-7833	757
Anchor Marketing Inc 2726 17th Ave S *Web:* www.anchorwebsite.com	Grand Forks	ND	58208	701-787-8230		195
Anchor Packaging Inc 13515 Barrett Pkwy Dr *Web:* www.anchorpackaging.com	Ballwin	MO	63021	314-822-7800		601
Anchor Paper Company Inc 480 Broadway St *TF:* 800-652-9755 ■ *Web:* www.anchorpaper.com	Saint Paul	MN	55101	651-298-1311	298-0060	553
Anchor Products Company Inc 52 Official Rd *Web:* www.anchorsurgical.com	Addison	IL	60101	630-543-9124		476
Anchor Publishing PO Box 2630 *TF:* 800-448-6280 ■ *Web:* www.antion.com	Landover Hills	MD	20784	301-459-0738	552-0225	637-2
Anchor QEA LLC 720 Olive Way Ste 1900 *Web:* www.anchorqea.com	Seattle	WA	98101	206-287-9130	287-9131	194
Anchor Realty Associates Inc 1113 W Baker Rd Ste D *Web:* www.har.com	Baytown	TX	77521	281-427-4747		652
Anchor Seaport Escrow 5602 E 2nd St *Web:* anchorseaportescrow.com	Long Beach	CA	90803	562-434-4437		652
Anchor Subaru LLC 949 Eddie Dowling Hwy *Web:* www.anchorsubaru.com	North Smithfield	RI	02896	401-769-1199		57
Anchor Tampa Inc 3907 W Osborne Ave *TF:* 800-879-8685 ■ *Web:* www.anchortampa.com	Tampa	FL	33614	813-879-8685	874-9589	186
Anchorage Alaska Bed & Breakfast Assn (AABBA) PO Box 242623 *Web:* www.anchorage-bnb.com	Anchorage	AK	99524	907-272-5909		376
Anchorage Chamber of Commerce 1016 W Sixth Ave Ste 303 *Web:* www.anchoragechamber.org	Anchorage	AK	99501	907-272-2401	272-4117	139
Anchorage City Hall 632 W Sixth Ave *Web:* www.muni.org	Anchorage	AK	99501	907-343-6543		337
Anchorage Convention & Visitors Bureau 524 W Fourth Ave *TF:* 800-478-6657 ■ *Web:* www.anchorage.net	Anchorage	AK	99501	907-276-4118		206
Anchorage Correctional Complex 1400 E 4th Ave *Web:* doc.alaska.gov	Anchorage	AK	99501	907-269-4100	269-4208	213
Anchorage Daily News 240 Muldoon Rd *TF:* 800-478-4200 ■ *Web:* www.adn.com	Anchorage	AK	99508	907-257-4200		532-2
Anchorage Museum of History & Art 625 C St *Web:* www.anchoragemuseum.org	Anchorage	AK	99501	907-929-9200	929-9290	520
Anchorage Opera 1507 Spar Ave *Web:* anchorageopera.org	Anchorage	AK	99501	907-279-2557	279-7798	573-2
Anchorage Press 540 E Fifth Ave *Web:* www.anchoragepress.com	Anchorage	AK	99501	907-561-7737	561-7777	532-4
Anchorage School District (ASD) 5530 E Northern Lights Blvd *Web:* www.asdk12.org	Anchorage	AK	99504	907-742-4000	742-4176	685
Anchorage Symphony Orchestra 400 D St Ste 230 *Web:* www.anchoragesymphony.org	Anchorage	AK	99501	907-274-8668	272-7916	573-3
Anchorage Uptown Suites 235 E Second Ct *Web:* www.anchorageuptownsuites.com	Anchorage	AK	99501	907-279-4232		379
Anchor-Harvey Components LLC 600 W Lamm Rd *Web:* anchorharvey.com	Freeport	IL	61032	815-233-3833		483
Anchor-In 1 South St *Web:* www.anchorin.com	Hyannis	MA	02601	508-775-0357	775-1313	379
Anchorspace 337 Main St *Web:* anchorspace.com	Bar Harbor	ME	04609	207-613-5344		393
Ancilla College 9601 Union Rd PO Box 1 *TF:* 866-262-4552 ■ *Web:* www.ancilla.edu	Donaldson	IN	46513	574-936-8898	935-1773	167-3
Ancilla Systems Inc 1419 S Lake Park Ave *Web:* ancilla.org	Hobart	IN	46342	219-947-8500	947-4037	353
Ancillary Benefit Consulting Inc 3370C Annapolis Ln *Web:* eabcinc.com	Plymouth	MN	55447	763-201-6990	201-6991	192
Ancillary Care Services Inc 5429 Lyndon B Johnson Fwy *NASDAQ: ANCI* ■ **Fax Area Code:* 806	Dallas	TX	75240	972-308-6830	473-3228*	353
Ancira Winton Chevrolet 6111 Bandera Rd *TF:* 800-299-5286 ■ *Web:* www.ancirachev.com	San Antonio	TX	78238	210-681-4900		57
ANCO Insurance 1111 Briarcrest Dr PO Box 3889 *TF:* 800-749-1733 ■ *Web:* www.anco.com	Bryan	TX	77802	979-776-2626	774-5372	390
Anco Products Inc (API) 1100 Old Hwy 8 NW	New Brighton	MN	55112	574-293-5574		389
Ancora Psychiatric Hospital 301 Spring Garden Rd *Web:* nj.gov	Hammonton	NJ	08037	609-561-1700		374-5
Ancora Waterfront Dining & Patio 1600 Howe St *Web:* www.ancoradining.com	Vancouver	BC	V6Z2L9	604-681-1164		671
ANCW (American National CattleWomen Inc) 200 NW 66th St *Web:* ancw.org	Oklahoma City	OK	73116	303-850-3441		48-2
Andaloro, Smith & Krueger LLP N19W24400 Riverwood Dr Ste 200 *Web:* www.askcpas.com	Waukesha	WI	53188	262-544-2000		2
Andaluca 407 Olive Way *Web:* www.andaluca.com	Seattle	WA	98101	206-382-6999	382-6997	671
Andalusia Health 849 S Three Notch St PO Box 760 *TF:* 855-426-0151 ■ *Web:* www.andalusiahealth.com	Andalusia	AL	36420	334-222-8466	222-6983	374-3
Andaluz 125 Second St NW *Web:* www.hotelandaluz.com	Albuquerque	NM	87102	505-242-9090		379
ANDalyze Inc 2109 S Oak St Ste 102 *Web:* andalyze.com	Champaign	IL	61820	217-328-0045		407
Andantex USA Inc 1705 Valley Rd *Web:* andantex.com	Wanamassa	NJ	07712	732-493-2812		770
Andavo Meetings and Incentives Inc 6430 S Fiddler's Green Cir Ste 220 **Fax Area Code:* 303 ■ *Web:* andavomeetings.com	Greenwood Village	CO	80111	720-398-5500	721-1762*	771
Andco Inc 170 Amaral St *Web:* www.andersonmotors.com	Riverside	RI	02915	401-487-5415	431-2623	62-7
Andcor Companies Inc 825 Wayzata Blvd E *Web:* www.andcor.com	Wayzata	MN	55391	952-404-8060		260
Andeen-Hagerling Inc 31200 Bainbridge Rd *Web:* andeen-hagerling.com	Cleveland	OH	44139	440-349-0370	349-0359	248
Andersen Bakery Inc 30703 San Clemente St *TF:* 800-464-4450 ■ *Web:* www.andersenbakery.com	Hayward	CA	94544	800-464-4450		345
Andersen Construction Company Inc 6712 N Cutter Cir *Web:* www.andersen-const.com	Portland	OR	97217	503-283-6712		186
Andersen Corp 100 Fourth Ave N *TF:* 888-888-7020 ■ *Web:* www.andersenwindows.com	Bayport	MN	55003	651-264-5150		236
Andersen Manufacturing Inc 3125 N Yellowstone Hwy *TF:* 800-635-6106 ■ *Web:* andersenhitches.com	Idaho Falls	ID	83401	208-523-6460		647
Andersen Products Inc 3202 Caroline Dr *Web:* www.sterility.com	Haw River	NC	27258	336-376-3000		475
Anderson & Anderson (A&A) 2300 Westridge Rd *Web:* www.andersonservices.com	Los Angeles	CA	90049	310-476-0908	476-6789	194
Anderson Accounting & Tax Services Inc 1706 York St Ste 1 *Web:* anderson-accounting.com	Bloomer	WI	54724	715-568-4423		2

	Phone	Fax	Class
Anderson America Anderson Group 10620 S Loop Blvd .... Pineville NC 28134 *TF:* 888-999-9386 ■ *Web:* andersonamerica.com	704-522-1823		807
Anderson and Murison Inc 800 W Colorado Blvd .... Los Angeles CA 90041 **Fax Area Code:* 323 ■ *TF:* 800-234-6977 ■ *Web:* www.andersonmurison.com	800-234-6977	255-0957*	390
Anderson Area Chamber of Commerce 907 N Main St Ste 200 .... Anderson SC 29621 *Web:* www.andersonscchamber.com	864-226-3454	226-3300	139
Anderson Area Chamber of Commerce 7850 Five Mile Rd .... Cincinnati OH 45230 *TF:* 888-227-6446 ■ *Web:* www.andersonareachamber.org	513-474-4802	474-4857	139
Anderson Automatics Inc 6401 Welcome Ave N Brooklyn Pk .... Minneapolis MN 55429 *Web:* andersonautomatics.com	763-533-2206	533-0320	621
Anderson Brass Co 1629 W Bobo Newsome Hwy .... Hartsville SC 29550 *TF:* 800-476-9876 ■ *Web:* www.andersonbrass.com	843-332-4111	332-3752	789
Anderson Bros Construction Company Inc 11325 State Hwy 210 .... Brainerd MN 56401 *Web:* www.andersonbrothers.com	218-829-1768	829-7607	188-4
Anderson Bros Town & Country Pharmacy Inc 2900 Fulton Ave .... Sacramento CA 95821 *Web:* andersonbrospharmacy.com	916-489-3638		237
Anderson Brothers Storage and Moving Corp 2701 SW Ave .... Chicago IL 60608 *Web:* www.andersonmovers.com	773-935-0013	847-7772	803-1
Anderson Brule Architects Inc 325 S First St 4th Fl .... San Jose CA 95113 *Web:* aba-arch.com	408-298-1885	298-1887	41
Anderson Center For Autism Inc 4885 Rt 9 PO Box 367 .... Staatsburg NY 12580 *Web:* www.andersoncenterforautism.org	845-889-4034		371
Anderson Chemical Co 325 S Davis .... Litchfield MN 55355 *TF:* 800-366-2477 ■ *Web:* www.accomn.com	320-693-2477	693-8238	145
Anderson Coach & Travel 1 Anderson Plz .... Greenville PA 16125 *TF:* 800-345-3435 ■ *Web:* www.goanderson.com	724-588-8310	588-0257	760
Anderson Columbia Company Inc 871 NW Guerdon St .... Lake City FL 32055 *Web:* www.andersoncolumbia.com	386-752-7585		188-4
Anderson Compounding Pharmacy Inc 310 Bluff City Hwy .... Bristol TN 37620 *TF:* 800-263-8890 ■ *Web:* andersoncompounding.com	423-764-4136	764-5167	237
Anderson Concrete Corp 400 Frank Rd .... Columbus OH 43207 *Web:* www.andersonconcrete.com	614-443-0123	443-4001	182
Anderson Cook Inc 17650 15-Mile Rd .... Fraser MI 48026 *Web:* www.andersoncook.com	586-293-0800		456
Anderson Copper & Brass Co 255 Industry Ave .... Frankfort IL 60423 *TF:* 800-323-5284 ■ *Web:* andersonfittings.com	708-535-9030		609
Anderson Corporate Solutions Inc 1735 N Brown Rd Ste 220 .... Lawrenceville GA 30043 *Web:* andersoncsi.com	678-965-8700		390
Anderson County 100 N Main St .... Clinton TN 37716 *Web:* www.anderson-county.com	865-457-5400		338
Anderson County 100 E Fourth Ave .... Garnett KS 66032 *Web:* andersoncountyks.org	785-448-6841	448-3205	338
Anderson County 1090 Glensboro Rd Ste 6A .... Lawrenceburg KY 40342 *Web:* www.andersoncountyclerk.ky.gov	502-839-3471	839-3043	338
Anderson County 500 N Church St .... Palestine TX 75801 *Web:* www.co.anderson.tx.us	903-723-7403	723-4625	338
Anderson County Chamber of Commerce 245 N Main St Ste 200 .... Clinton TN 37716 *Web:* www.andersoncountychamber.org	865-457-2559	463-7480	139
Anderson County Library 300 S McDuffie St .... Anderson SC 29621 *Web:* www.andersonlibrary.org	864-260-4500		434-3
Anderson County Public Library 114 N Main St .... Lawrenceburg KY 40342 *Web:* aplkentucky.org	502-839-6420		434-3
Anderson Dairy Inc 801 Searles Ave .... Las Vegas NV 89101 *Web:* www.andersondairy.com	702-642-7507	642-3480	296-27
Anderson DDB Health & Lifestyle 33 Bloor St E .... Toronto ON M4W3H1 *Web:* www.andersonddb.com	416-934-7498		5
Anderson Development Co 1415 E Michigan St .... Adrian MI 49221 *Web:* www.andersondevelopment.com	517-263-2121	263-1000	145
Anderson Districts I & II Career & Technology Ctr 702 Belton Hwy .... Williamston SC 29697 *Web:* www.andersonctc.org	864-847-4121	847-3539	800
Anderson Economic Group LLC 1555 Watertower Pl Ste 100 .... East Lansing MI 48823 *Web:* www.andersoneconomicgroup.com	517-333-6984	333-7058	256
Anderson Electric Controls Inc 8639 S 212th St .... Kent WA 98031 *Web:* www.aecontrols.com	253-395-3003	395-4446	203
Anderson Electric Inc 3501 6th Street Frontage Rd W .... Springfield IL 62703 *Web:* www.anderson-electric.com	217-529-5471	529-0412	189-4
Anderson Engineering of New Prague Inc 20526 330th St .... New Prague MN 56071 *TF:* 800-893-4047 ■ *Web:* aenpi.com	507-364-7373		261
Anderson Equipment Co 1000 Washington Pk .... Bridgeville PA 15017 *TF:* 800-414-4554 ■ *Web:* www.andersonequip.com	412-343-2300		358
Anderson Erickson Dairy Co 2420 E University Ave .... Des Moines IA 50317 *TF:* 800-234-6455 ■ *Web:* www.aedairy.com	515-265-2521		296-27
Anderson Fabrics Inc 348 Summit Ave W .... Blackduck MN 56630 **Fax Area Code:* 800 ■ *TF:* 800-328-1791 ■ *Web:* orders.andersonfabrics.com	218-835-6677	419-3979*	746
Anderson Financial Services Inc 4840 N River Blvd Ste 200 .... Cedar Rapids IA 52411 *TF:* 800-971-2374 ■ *Web:* andersonfinancialsvcs.com	319-378-7498	393-5931	390

	Phone	Fax	Class
Anderson Forest Products Inc 1267 Old Edmonton Rd .... Tompkinsville KY 42167 **Fax Area Code:* 270 ■ *TF:* 800-489-6778 ■ *Web:* www.afp-usa.com	800-489-6778	487-8953*	551
Anderson Gallery 325 N Harrison St .... Richmond VA 23284 *TF:* 866-534-3201 ■ *Web:* www.arts.vcu.edu	804-828-1709	828-6469	520
Anderson Global Inc 500 W Sherman Blvd .... Muskegon Heights MI 49444 *Web:* www.andersonglobal.com	231-733-2164	733-1288	567
Anderson H. Thomas 6160 St Andrews Rd Ste 2 .... Columbia SC 29212 *Web:* hthomasanderson.com	803-798-9586	798-4102	428
Anderson Home Health Supplies 4063 Henderson Blvd .... Tampa FL 33629 *Web:* www.andersonhhs.com	813-289-3811	282-1723	475
Anderson Hospital 6800 SR 162 .... Maryville IL 62062 *Web:* andersonhospital.org	618-288-5711		374-3
Anderson Independent-Mail 1000 Williamston Rd .... Anderson SC 29621 *Web:* www.independentmail.com	864-224-4321	260-1276	532-2
Anderson International Corp 4545 Boyce Pkwy .... Stow OH 44224 **Fax Area Code:* 330 ■ *TF:* 800-336-4730 ■ *Web:* www.andersonintl.net	216-641-1112	688-0117*	298
Anderson Japanese Gardens 318 Spring Creek Rd .... Rockford IL 61107 *Web:* andersongardens.org	815-229-9390		97
Anderson LeNeave & Co 6000 Fairview Rd Ste 625 .... Charlotte NC 28210 *Web:* www.andersonleneave.com	704-552-9212		194
Anderson Lumber Co (ALC) 780 Louisville Rd .... Alcoa TN 37701 *Web:* www.andersonlumbercompany.com	865-983-3060		191-3
Anderson Machinery Company Inc 6535 Leopard St .... Corpus Christi TX 78409 *Web:* www.andersonmachinerytexas.com	361-289-6043	289-6047	358
Anderson Machining Service Inc 211 Collins Rd .... Jefferson WI 53549 *Web:* www.basinprecision.com	920-674-6003		454
Anderson Manufacturing Company Inc 2885 Country Dr Ste 190 .... Saint Paul MN 55117 *TF:* 800-348-1316 ■ *Web:* www.leaktools.com	651-484-1316	484-0930	326
Anderson Marketing Group 7420 Blanco Rd Ste 200 .... San Antonio TX 78216 *Web:* www.andadv.com	210-223-6233		7
Anderson Merchandisers LP 5601 Granite Pkwy Ste 1400 .... Plano TX 75024 *Web:* www.amerch.com	855-894-2780		530
Anderson Pacific Engineering Construction Inc 1390 Norman Ave .... Santa Clara CA 95054 *Web:* andpac.com	408-970-9900	970-9975	256
Anderson Partners Advertising 444 Regency Pkwy Dr Ste 311 .... Omaha NE 68114 *TF:* 800-551-9737 ■ *Web:* www.andersonpartners.com	402-341-4807	341-2846	4
Anderson Perry & Associates Inc 1901 N Fir St .... La Grande OR 97850 *Web:* www.andersonperry.com	541-963-8309		256
Anderson Power Products 13 Pratts Junction Rd .... Sterling MA 01564 *Web:* www.andersonpower.com	978-422-3600		596
Anderson Precision Inc 20 Livingston Ave .... Jamestown NY 14701 *Web:* www.andersonprecision.com	716-484-6516		621
Anderson Public Library 111 E 12th St .... Anderson IN 46016 *Web:* www.and.lib.in.us	765-641-2456		434-3
Anderson Ranch Arts Ctr 5263 Owl Creek Rd PO Box 5598 .... Snowmass Village CO 81615 *TF:* 800-525-6363 ■ *Web:* www.andersonranch.org	970-923-3181	923-3871	50-2
Anderson Rowe & Buckley Inc 2833 Third St .... San Francisco CA 94107 *Web:* arbmechanical.com	415-282-1625		189-10
Anderson Satuloff Machado 20700 Ventura Blvd Ste 205 .... Woodland Hills CA 91364 *Web:* asmmcpa.com	818-710-0622		2
Anderson Security Agency Ltd 2555 W Morningside Dr .... Phoenix AZ 85023 *Web:* andersonsecurity.com	602-331-7000		693
Anderson Shumaker Co 824 S Central Ave .... Chicago IL 60644 *TF:* 800-932-0357 ■ *Web:* www.andersonshumaker.com	773-287-0874		390
Anderson Symphony Orchestra (ASO) 1124 Meridian Plz .... Anderson IN 46016 *Web:* andersonsymphony.org	765-644-2111		573-3
Anderson Technologies Inc 14000 172nd St .... Grand Haven MI 49417 *Web:* www.andtec.com	616-844-2505		596
Anderson Tile Sales Inc (ATS) 1703 S Midkiff Rd .... Midland TX 79701 *Web:* www.andersontile.net	432-683-5116		191-1
Anderson Trucking Service Inc 725 Opportunity St .... Saint Cloud MN 56301 *TF:* 800-328-2316 ■ *Web:* www.atsinc.com	320-255-7400	255-7494	780
Anderson Tube Company Inc 1400 Fairgrounds Rd .... Hatfield PA 19440 *TF:* 800-523-2258 ■ *Web:* www.atube.com	215-855-0118		612
Anderson University 1100 E Fifth St .... Anderson IN 46012 **Fax Area Code:* 765 ■ *TF:* 800-428-6414 ■ *Web:* www.anderson.edu	800-428-6414	641-4091*	166
Anderson Wood Products Co 1381 Beech St .... Louisville KY 40211 *Web:* www.andersonwood.com	502-778-5591	778-5599	499
Anderson ZurMuehlen & Co 828 Great N Blvd .... Helena MT 59624 *Web:* azworld.com	406-442-1040	442-1100	2
Anderson's BBQ House 5410 Harry Hines Blvd .... Dallas TX 75235 *Web:* www.mikeandersonsbbq.com	214-630-0735		671
Anderson, Eckstein & Westrick Inc 51301 Schoenherr Rd .... Shelby Township MI 48315 *Web:* aewinc.com	586-726-1234	726-8780	261

Name / Address	Phone	Fax	Class
Anderson, Julian & Hull LLP 250 S Fifth St Ste 700 .... Boise ID 83702 *Web:* www.ajhlaw.com	208-344-5800	344-5510	428
Anderson, O'Brien, Bertz, Skrenes & Golla 1257 Main St .... Stevens Point WI 54481 *TF:* 800-281-3643 ■ *Web:* www.andlaw.com	715-344-0890	344-1012	428
Anderson, Zeigler, Disharoon, Gallagher & Gray PC 50 Old Courthouse Sq 5th Fl .... Santa Rosa CA 95404 *Web:* andersonzeigler.com	707-545-4910	544-0260	428
Anderson/Madison County Visitors & Convention Bureau 6335 S Scatterfield Rd .... Anderson IN 46013 *TF:* 800-533-6569 ■ *Web:* visitandersonmadisoncounty.com	765-643-5633		206
Anderson-Bogert Engineers & Surveyors Inc 4001 River Ridge Dr NE .... Cedar Rapids IA 52402 *Web:* anderson-bogert.com	319-377-4629		261
Anderson-DuBose Co 5300 Tod Ave SW .... Lordstown OH 44481 **Fax Area Code:* 330 ■ *Web:* www.a-d.us	440-248-8800	824-2256*	300
Anderson-Krause Insurance 238 E Main St PO Box 110 .... Branford CT 06405 *Web:* andersonkrause.com	203-488-6386		390
Andersons Inc 1947 Briarfield Blvd PO Box 119 .... Maumee OH 43537 *NASDAQ:* ANDE ■ *TF:* 800-537-3370 ■ *Web:* andersonsinc.com	419-893-5050		185
Andersonville National Historic Site 496 Cemetery Rd .... Andersonville GA 31711 *Web:* www.nps.gov	229-924-0343	924-1086	564
Andes Candies Inc 1400 E Wisconsin St .... Delavan WI 53115 *Web:* www.tootsie.com	262-728-9121		296-8
Andex Industries Inc 1911 Fourth Ave N .... Escanaba MI 49829 **Fax Area Code:* 906 ■ *TF:* 800-338-9882 ■ *Web:* www.andex.net	800-338-9882	786-3133*	88
Andiamo 322 Garfield St .... Santa Fe NM 87501 *Web:* www.andiamosantafe.com	505-995-9595		671
Andiamo 400 Renaissance Ctr Ste A403 .... Detroit MI 48243 *Web:* andiamoitalia.com	313-567-6700	567-6701	671
Andiamo Partners 17 State St 8th Fl .... New York NY 10004 *Web:* www.andiamogo.com	212-488-1595		260
Andiamo Ristorante-Bar 5950 Santo Rd .... San Diego CA 92124	858-277-3501		671
Andina 1314 NW Glisan St .... Portland OR 97209 *Web:* www.andinarestaurant.com	503-228-9535		671
Andis Co 1800 Renaissance Blvd .... Sturtevant WI 53177 **Fax Area Code:* 262 ■ *TF:* 800-558-9441 ■ *Web:* andis.com	800-558-9441	884-1100*	37
Andor Technology Plc 425 Sullivan Ave Ste No3 .... South Windsor CT 06074 *Web:* www.andor.oxinst.com	860-290-9211		419
Andover Animal Hospital 233 Lowell St .... Andover MA 01810 *Web:* andoveranimal.com	978-475-3600	475-7510	794
Andover Corp 4 Commercial Dr .... Salem NH 03079 *Web:* www.andcorp.com	603-893-6888		544
Andover Townsman, The 33 Chestnut St .... Andover MA 01810 *Web:* www.andovertownsman.com	978-475-7000		532-2
Andpak Inc 400 Jarvis Dr .... Morgan Hill CA 95037 *Web:* www.andpak.com	408-782-2500	782-6304	88
AndPlus LLC 257 Turnpike Rd Ste 200 .... Southborough MA 01772 *Web:* www.andplus.com	508-425-7533		196
Andra Partners LLC 2550 Meridian Blvd Ste 200 .... Franklin TN 37067 *Web:* www.andrapartners.com	615-567-8090		463
Andraski Law Offices LLC 610 Jackson St .... Wausau WI 54403 *Web:* andraskilaw.com	715-842-1647		41
Andre Bollier Ltd 5018 Main St .... Kansas City MO 64112 *Web:* www.andreschocolates.com	816-561-3440	561-2922	670
Andrea Blain Public Relations Inc 9750 Crawford Ave .... Skokie IL 60076 *Web:* www.andreablainpr.com	847-933-9884	673-5836	317
Andrea Obston Marketing Communications LLC 3 Regency Dr .... Bloomfield CT 06002 *Web:* aomc.com	860-243-1447		636
Andreas 268 Thayer St .... Providence RI 02906 *Web:* www.andreasri.com	401-331-7879	331-7300	671
Andreas Furniture Company Inc 114 Dover Rd NE .... Sugarcreek OH 44681 *TF:* 800-846-7448 ■ *Web:* www.andreasfurniture.com	330-852-2494		321
Andreini & Co 220 W 20th Ave .... San Mateo CA 94403 *TF:* 800-969-2522 ■ *Web:* www.andreini.com	650-573-1111	378-4361	390
Andreou & Casson Ltd 661 W Lake St Ste 2n .... Chicago IL 60661 *Web:* www.andreou-casson.com	312-935-2001		428
Andres Restaurant 1235 Morena Blvd .... San Diego CA 92110 *Web:* www.andresrestaurantsd.com	619-275-4114	276-4245	671
Andretti Green Racing 7615 Zionsville Rd .... Indianapolis IN 46268 *Web:* www.andrettiautosport.com	317-872-2700		787
Andrew Associates Inc 6 Pearson Way .... Enfield CT 06082 *Web:* www.andrewdm.com	860-253-0000	253-0007	5
Andrew College 501 College St .... Cuthbert GA 39840 *TF:* 800-664-9250 ■ *Web:* www.andrewcollege.edu	800-664-9250		162
Andrew County PO Box 206 .... Savannah MO 64485 *Web:* www.andrewcounty.org	816-324-3624	324-6154	338
Andrew Edson & Associates Inc 61 E 77th S .... New York NY 10075 *Web:* www.edsonpr.com	516-850-3195		636
Andrew G. Gordon Inc 306 Washington St .... Norwell MA 02061 *TF:* 866-243-2259 ■ *Web:* www.agordon.com	781-659-2262		390
Andrew Garrett Inc 52 Vanderbilt Ave Ste 510 .... New York NY 10017 *TF:* 800-899-1883 ■ *Web:* www.andrewgarrett.com	800-899-1883		690
Andrew H. Meyer PC 5605 Glenridge Dr NE Ste 800 .... Atlanta GA 30342 *Web:* www.mfllaw.com	404-257-0330		41
Andrew Jackson State Park 196 Andrew Jackson Park Rd .... Lancaster SC 29720 *Web:* southcarolinaparks.com	803-285-3344		565
Andrew Low House, The 329 Abercorn St .... Savannah GA 31401 *Web:* www.andrewlowhouse.com	912-233-6854	233-9239	50-3
Andrew Moore & Assoc 1132 Old York Rd .... Abington PA 19001 *TF:* 866-485-9400 ■ *Web:* www.moore4law.com	215-885-3500		428
Andrew R. Mancini Associates Inc 129 Odell Ave .... Endicott NY 13760 *Web:* andrewmancini.com	607-754-7070	786-0410	360-2
Andrew Seybold Inc 16402 N 40th Pl .... Phoenix AZ 85032 *Web:* andrewseybold.com	602-788-1530	992-0814	466
Andrew Shubin Attorney At Law PC 333 S Allen St .... State College PA 16801 *Web:* statecollegelaw.com	814-867-3115		41
Andrew Smith Gallery Inc 122 Grant Ave .... Santa Fe NM 87501 *Web:* www.andrewsmithgallery.com	505-984-1234	983-2428	637-2
Andrew T. Johnson Company Inc 15 Tremont Pl .... Boston MA 02108 *Web:* www.andrewtjohnson.com	617-742-1610	523-0719	240
Andrew Technologies LLC 1421 Edinger Ave Ste D .... Tustin CA 92780 *TF:* 888-959-7674 ■ *Web:* www.hydrasolve.com	888-959-7674		475
Andrew Tool & Machining Inc 15300 28th Ave N .... Plymouth MN 55447 *Web:* andrewtool.com	763-559-0402		454
Andrew Toyota 1620 W Silver Spring Dr .... Milwaukee WI 53209 *TF:* 877-308-0883 ■ *Web:* www.andrewtoyota.com	414-228-1450		57
Andrew W. Mellon Foundation 140 E 62nd St .... New York NY 10065 *Web:* mellon.org	212-838-8400	888-4172	305
Andrew's Downtown 228 S Adams St .... Tallahassee FL 32301 *Web:* andrewsdowntown.com	850-222-3444		671
Andrews & Arbenz PLLC 2200 N 30th St Ste 202 .... Tacoma WA 98403 *Web:* www.thenarrowslawgroup.com	253-302-4849		41
Andrews & Hamilton Company Inc 3829 S Miami Blvd .... Durham NC 27703 *TF:* 800-443-6866 ■ *Web:* www.storageequip.com	919-787-4100		358
Andrews & Manno PA 701 Harbour Post Dr .... Tampa FL 33602 *Web:* andrewsmanno.com	813-463-9800		41
Andrews County 215 NW First St PO Box 727 .... Andrews TX 79714 *Web:* www.co.andrews.tx.us	432-524-1426		338
Andrews Excavating Inc 5 W Willow Rd PO Box 249 .... Willow Street PA 17584 *TF:* 800-730-6822 ■ *Web:* andrewsexcavating.com	717-464-3329	464-4963	189-5
Andrews Federal Credit Union (AFCU) 5711 Allentown Rd .... Suitland MD 20746 *TF:* 800-487-5500 ■ *Web:* www.andrewsfcu.org	301-702-5500	702-5330	219
Andrews Hammock Powell Inc 250 Charter Ln .... Macon GA 31210 *Web:* www.ahpengr.com	478-405-8301		256
Andrews Hooper Pavlik Plc 5300 Gratiot Rd .... Saginaw MI 48638 *TF:* 888-754-8478 ■ *Web:* ahpplc.com	989-497-5300		2
Andrews Hotel 624 Post St .... San Francisco CA 94109 *TF:* 800-926-3739 ■ *Web:* www.andrewshotel.info	415-563-6877	928-6919	379
Andrews Industrial Controls 108 Rosslyn Rd .... Carnegie PA 15106 *Web:* andrewsic.com	412-279-5335		407
Andrews Kurth LLP 600 Travis Ste 4200 .... Houston TX 77002 *Web:* www.andrewskurth.com	713-220-4200	220-4285	428
Andrews Logistics Inc 2445 E Southlake Blvd .... Southlake TX 76092 *TF:* 866-536-1234 ■ *Web:* www.andrewslogistics.com	817-527-2770		194
Andrews McMeel Universal 1130 Walnut .... Kansas City MO 64106 *Web:* www.andrewsmcmeel.com	816-581-7500	932-6684	530
Andrews Myers PC 1885 St James Pl 15th Fl .... Houston TX 77027 *TF:* 866-535-2329 ■ *Web:* andrewsmyers.com	713-850-4200	850-4211	41
Andrews Osborne Academy 38588 Mentor Ave .... Willoughby OH 44094 *Web:* www.andrewsosborne.org	440-942-3600		622
Andrews Produce Inc 717 E Industrial Blvd .... Pueblo West CO 81007 *Web:* www.andrewsfoodservice.com	719-543-3846		297-8
Andrews Products Inc 431 Kingston Ct .... Mount Prospect IL 60056 *Web:* www.andrewsproducts.com	847-759-0190	759-0848	517
Andrews University 4355 International Ct .... Berrien Springs MI 49104 *TF:* 800-253-2874 ■ *Web:* www.andrews.edu	269-471-7771	471-2670	166
Andrie Inc 561 E Western Ave .... Muskegon MI 49442 *TF:* 800-722-2421 ■ *Web:* www.andrietg.com	231-728-2226	726-6747	314
Andritz Inc 35 Sherman St .... Muncy PA 17756 *Web:* www.andritz.com	570-546-8211		454
Android Industries 2155 Executive Hills Dr .... Auburn Hills MI 48326 *Web:* www.android-ind.com	248-732-0000	454-0501	247
Androscoggin Title Co 95 Main St .... Auburn ME 04210 *Web:* androtitle.com	207-784-6413		653
Androscoggin Wayside Park 1607 Berlin Rd .... Errol NH 03579 *Web:* www.nhstateparks.org	603-538-6707		565
Andrus on Hudson 185 Old Broadway .... Hastings-on-Hudson NY 10706 *Web:* www.andrusonhudson.org	914-478-3700	478-3541	672
Andrus Transportation Services LLC 3185 E Deseret Dr N .... Saint George UT 84790 *TF:* 800-888-5838 ■ *Web:* andrustrans.com	435-673-1566		360-2
Andy & Bax 324 SE Grand Ave .... Portland OR 97214 *Web:* www.andyandbax.com	503-234-7538	239-8817	711
Andy Frain Services Inc 761 Shoreline Dr .... Aurora IL 60504 *TF:* 877 707 4771 ■ *Web:* www.andyfrain.com	630-820-3820		693

Name / Address	City	State	ZIP	Phone	Fax	Class
Andy Gump Inc 26410 Summit Cir *TF:* 800-992-7755 ■ *Web:* www.andygump.com	Santa Clarita	CA	91350	661-251-7721	251-7729	23
Andy J. Egan Company Inc 2001 Waldorf NW *Web:* www.andyegan.com	Grand Rapids	MI	49544	616-791-9952		595
Andy Rice Photography 7226 Rue De Roark *Web:* www.andyricephoto.com	La Jolla	CA	92037	858-459-8458		590
Andy Sterns Office Furniture Inc 10523A Ewing Rd *Web:* andysterns.com	Beltsville	MD	20705	301-614-0500		321
Andy Warhol Foundation For The Visual Arts Inc 65 Bleecker St 7th Fl *Web:* warholfoundation.org	New York	NY	10012	212-387-7555		305
Andy Warhol Museum 117 Sandusky St *Web:* www.warhol.org	Pittsburgh	PA	15212	412-237-8300	237-8340	520
Andy Williams Moon River Theatre 2500 Hwy 76 *Web:* www.andywilliamspac.com	Branson	MO	65616	417-334-1800	337-9627	572
Andy's Assurance Agency Inc 1441 W Flagler St *Web:* andysassurance.net	Miami	FL	33135	305-642-8407	643-5969	390
Andy's Mediterranean Grille 906 Nassau St *Web:* andyskabob.com	Cincinnati	OH	45206	513-281-9791		671
ANE Resources Inc 111 Deer Lake Rd Ste 111 *Web:* www.keypak.com	Deerfield	IL	60015	403-235-5939	235-5886	178-1
Anel Corp 3244 Hwy 51 *Web:* www.anelcorp.com	Winona	MS	38967	662-283-1540	283-2949	492
Anemostat 1220 Watsoncenter Rd PO Box 4938 *TF:* 877-423-7426 ■ *Web:* www.anemostat.com	Carson	CA	90745	310-835-7500	835-0448	234
ANERA 1111 14th St NW Ste 400 *Web:* www.anera.org	Washington	DC	20005	202-266-9700	266-9701	48-5
Anest Iwata USA Inc 5325 Muhlhauser Rd *TF:* 800-440-0282 ■ *Web:* www.anestiwata.com	Hamilton	OH	45011	513-755-3100	755-0888	385
Anest Iwata-Medea Inc 1336 N Mason St *Web:* www.iwata-medea.com	Portland	OR	97217	503-253-7308	253-0721	385
Anesthesia Equipment Supply Inc (AES) 24301 Roberts Dr *Web:* www.aesol.com	Black Diamond	WA	98010	253-631-8008		475
Anesthesia Service Inc 1821 N Classen Blvd *TF:* 800-336-3356 ■ *Web:* www.anesthesiaservice.com	Oklahoma City	OK	73106	405-525-3588		475
Anfield Inc 2501 Blue Ridge Rd Ste 210 *Web:* www.anfield-information.com	Raleigh	NC	27607	919-851-8681		344
Anfinson Thompson & Company PA 1604 1st St S Ste 230 *Web:* www.anfinsonthompson.com	Willmar	MN	56201	320-235-7491		2
ANG Federal Credit Union PO Box 170204 *TF:* 800-237-6211 ■ *Web:* www.angfcu.org	Birmingham	AL	35217	205-841-4525	841-4545	219
Angarai International Inc 9111 Edmonston Rd Ste 305 *Web:* www.angarai-intl.com	Greenbelt	MD	20770	410-472-5000		196
Angel Baby Brokerage 26 Red Ball Trl *Web:* www.angelbabybrokerage.com	Coffeen	IL	62017	217-534-2557		796
Angel City Press 2118 Wilshire Blvd Ste 880 *Web:* www.angelcitypress.com	Santa Monica	CA	90403	310-395-9982		637-2
Angel Commercial LLC 2425 Post Rd Ste 303 *Web:* angelcommercial.com	Southport	CT	06890	203-335-6600		652
Angel Connection Inc 4401 Atlantic Ave Ste 405 *Web:* myangelconnect.com	Long Beach	CA	90803	562-984-2714		363
Angel Fire Resort PO Box 130 *TF:* 800-633-7463 ■ *Web:* www.angelfireresort.com	Angel Fire	NM	87710	575-377-6401		669
Angel Medical Systems Inc 788 Shrewsbury Ave Ste 2144 *Web:* www.angel-med.com	Tinton Falls	NJ	07724	732-542-5551		363
Angel Mounds State Historic Site 8215 Pollack Ave *Web:* www.indianamuseum.org	Evansville	IN	47715	812-853-3956	858-7686	637-2
Angel of The Winds Casino 3438 Stoluckquamish Ln *TF:* 800-547-6133 ■ *Web:* www.angelofthewinds.com	Arlington	WA	98223	360-474-9740		132
Angel Plants Inc 560 W Deer Park Ave *Web:* www.angelplants.com	Dix Hills	NY	11746	631-242-7788		292
Angel Printing & Reproduction Inc 1400 W 57th St *Web:* www.angelprinting.com	Cleveland	OH	44102	216-631-5225	631-8266	627
Angel Reyes & Associates PC 8222 Douglas Ave Ste 400 *Web:* www.reyeslaw.com	Dallas	TX	75225	214-935-2580	526-7910	41
Angel Sales Inc 4147 N Ravenswood Ave *Web:* www.angelsales.com	Chicago	IL	60613	773-883-8858	883-8889	328
Angela Hospice Home Care 14100 Newburgh Rd *TF:* 866-464-7810 ■ *Web:* www.angelahospice.org	Livonia	MI	48154	734-464-7810	464-6930	371
Angelas Marble & Tile Inc 4375 Enterprise Ave *Web:* angelasmarbleandtile.com	Naples	FL	34104	239-403-4445		290
Angeles Contractor Inc 783 Phillips Dr *Web:* angelescontractor.com	City of Industry	CA	91748	626-923-3800	923-3801	186
Angeles Investment Advisors LLC 429 Santa Monica Blvd Ste 650 *Web:* www.angelesinvestments.com	Santa Monica	CA	90401	310-393-6300		401
Angelina County Junior College District Texas 3500 S First St *Web:* www.angelina.edu	Lufkin	TX	75904	936-639-1301		166
Angelina Federal Employees Credit Union 900 Pershing Ave *Web:* afecu.net	Lufkin	TX	75904	936-632-7691		219
Angelina's 1563 E Fremont St *Web:* www.angelinas.com	Stockton	CA	95205	209-948-6609		671
Angelina's Ristorante 399 Ellis St *Web:* angelinasristorante.com	Staten Island	NY	10307	718-227-2900	227-3329	671
Angelina's Ristorante Italiano 11 Depot St *Web:* www.angelinasrestaurant.com	Concord	NH	03301	603-228-3313		671
Angelini Osteria 7313 Beverly Blvd *Web:* www.angelinirestaurantgroup.com	Los Angeles	CA	90036	323-297-0070		671
Angell & Company PLLC 5700 Crooks Rd Ste 102 *Web:* www.angellcompany.com	Troy	MI	48098	248-649-8720	649-8727	2
Angell & Giroux Inc 2727 Alcazar St *Web:* www.angellandgiroux.com	Los Angeles	CA	90033	323-269-8596		482
Angell & Phelps Chocolate Factory 154 S Beach St *TF:* 800-969-2634 ■ *Web:* www.angellandphelps.com	Daytona Beach	FL	32114	386-252-6531		671
Angelo Gordon & Co 245 Park Ave Ste 26 *Web:* www.angelogordon.com	New York	NY	10167	212-692-2000		41
Angelo Iafrate Construction Co 26300 Sherwood Ave *Web:* www.iafrate.com	Warren	MI	48091	586-756-1070	756-0467	188-4
Angelo State University 2601 W Ave N ASU Stn 11014 *TF:* 800-946-8627 ■ *Web:* www.angelo.edu	San Angelo	TX	76909	325-942-2041	942-2078	166
Angelo's 4107 S Providence Rd *Web:* angelospizzaandsteak.com	Columbia	MO	65203	573-443-6100		671
Angelo's Fairmount Tavern 2300 Fairmount Ave *Web:* www.angelosfairmounttavern.com	Atlantic City	NJ	08401	609-344-2439	348-1043	671
Angelo's Italian Restaurant Inc 305 Main St *Web:* angelosevansville.com	Evansville	IN	47708	812-428-6666	428-6699	671
Angelo Unaware Inc 4010 W Linebaugh Ave *Web:* www.angelsunaware.com	Tampa	FL	33624	813-961-1159	265-1656	371
Angelus Block Company Inc 11374 Tuxford St *Web:* angelusblock.com	Sun Valley	CA	91352	818-767-8576	768-3124	183
Angie Brewer & Associates LC 9104 58th Dr E *Web:* www.angiebrewer.com	Bradenton	FL	34202	941-756-5800		195
Angie's Cantina 11 E Buchanan St *TF:* 800-706-7672 ■ *Web:* www.grandmasrestaurants.com	Duluth	MN	55802	218-727-6117		671
Anglebrook Golf Club 100 Rte 202 *Web:* www.anglebrookgc.com	Lincolndale	NY	10540	914-245-5588		48-22
Angler Restaurant 312 Talbot St *Web:* www.angleroc.net	Ocean City	MD	21842	410-289-7424		671
Anglin Flewelling Rasmussen Campbell & Trytten LLP 301 N Lake Ave Ste 1100 *Web:* www.afrct.com	Pasadena	CA	91101	626-535-1900		428
Angola Embassy 2108 16th St NW *Web:* www.angola.org	Washington	DC	20009	202-785-1156	822-9049	257
Angola Wire Products Inc 803 Wohlert St *TF:* 800-800-7225 ■ *Web:* www.angolawire.com	Angola	IN	46703	260-665-9447	665-6182	286
Angotti's Family Restaurant Inc 725 Burnet Ave	Syracuse	NY	13203	315-472-8403		671
Angstrom Graphics Print 4437 E 49th St *Web:* www.angstromgraphics.com	Cleveland	OH	44125	216-271-5300		627
Angstrom Lighting 12224 Montague St *Web:* www.angstromlighting.com	Pacoima	CA	91331	323-462-4246		722
Angstrom Sciences Inc 40 S Linden St *Web:* www.angstromsciences.com	Duquesne	PA	15110	412-469-8466	469-8511	492
Angstrom Technologies Inc 7880 Foundation Dr *TF:* 800-543-7358 ■ *Web:* www.angstromtechnologies.com	Florence	KY	41042	859-282-0020	282-8577	145
Anguil Environmental Systems Inc 8855 N 55th St *TF:* 800-488-0230 ■ *Web:* www.anguil.com	Milwaukee	WI	53223	414-365-6400	365-6410	18
Angus Barn 9401 Glenwood Ave *Web:* www.angusbarn.com	Raleigh	NC	27617	919-781-2444	783-5568	671
Angus Systems Group Ltd 1125 Leslie St *TF:* 877-442-6487 ■ *Web:* www.angus-systems.com	Toronto	ON	M3C2J6	416-385-8550	385-8551	393
Angy's Food Products Inc 77 Servistar Industrial Way *Web:* angyslandolfifoodgroup.com	Westfield	MA	01085	413-572-1010	572-4785	297-6
Anheuser-Busch Companies Inc 1 Busch Pl *TF:* 800-342-5283 ■ *Web:* www.anheuser-busch.com	Saint Louis	MO	63118	800-342-5283		80-1
Anheuser-Busch InBev 250 Park Ave *Web:* www.ab-inbev.com	New York	NY	10177	212-573-8800		102
Anholt Technologies Inc 440 Church Rd *Web:* anholt.com	Avondale	PA	19311	610-268-2758		273
ANI (American Nuclear Insurers) 95 Glastonbury Blvd Ste 300 *Web:* www.amnucins.com	Glastonbury	CT	06033	860-682-1301		49-9
ANI Networks Inc 250 Pilot Rd Ste 300 *TF:* 888-886-5775 ■ *Web:* www.aninetworks.com	Las Vegas	NV	89119	888-886-5775		224
ANI Pharmaceuticals Inc 210 Main St W *Web:* www.anipharmaceuticals.com	Baudette	MN	56623	218-634-3500	634-3540	418
Anika Therapeutics Inc 32 Wiggins Ave *NASDAQ:* ANIK ■ *TF:* 800-299-7089 ■ *Web:* www.anikatherapeutics.com	Bedford	MA	01730	781-457-9000	305-9720	479
Animal & Plant Health Inspection Service (APHIS) *National Veterinary Services Laboratories* 4700 River Rd *TF:* 844-820-2234 ■ *Web:* www.aphis.usda.gov	Riverdale	MD	20737	844-820-2234		743
Animal Alliance of Canada 221 Broadview Ave *Web:* www.animalalliance.ca	Toronto	ON	M4M2G3	416-462-9541	462-9647	48-3

Name / Address	City	State	Zip	Phone	Fax	Class
Animal Ark Wildlife Sanctuary & Nature Ctr 1265 Deerlodge Rd	Reno	NV	89508	775-970-3111	366-5771*	823
*Fax Area Code: 866 ■ Web: www.animalark.org						
Animal Arts Academy of Pet Grooming 1744 E 116th St	Carmel	IN	46032	317-575-1122		167-3
Web: www.animalartsacademy.com						
Animal Care Unlimited 2665 Billingsley Rd	Columbus	OH	43235	614-766-2317		794
Web: animalcareunlimited.com						
Animal Center West Omaha 15811 W Dodge Rd	Omaha	NE	68118	402-758-0123	758-0377	794
Web: animalcenterwestomaha.com						
Animal Emergency Clinic 37 Strawberry Ave	Lewiston	ME	04240	207-777-1110		794
Web: aec-midmaine.com						
Animal Eye Care 1612 Washington Blvd	Fremont	CA	94539	510-623-0444	657-6855	794
Web: animaleyecare.com						
Animal Eye Specialty Clinic 3421 Forest Hill Blvd W	West Palm Beach	FL	33406	561-967-5966		794
Web: www.animaleyespecialtyclinic.com						
Animal Health Institute (AHI) 1325 G St NW Ste 700	Washington	DC	20005	202-637-2440		48-3
Web: www.ahi.org						
Animal Hospital Inc 5001 N 12th Ave	Pensacola	FL	32504	850-479-2900		794
Web: petcarehospital.com						
Animal Hospital of East Cobb 3770 Lower Roswell Rd	Marietta	GA	30068	770-578-8522		794
Web: ahecobb.com						
Animal Hospital of Havasu PC 1990 Mesquite Ave	Lake Havasu City	AZ	86403	928-855-8122		794
Web: animalhospitalofhavasu.com						
Animal Hospital of Pittsford 2816 Monroe Ave	Rochester	NY	14618	585-271-7700	244-7287	794
Web: www.pittsfordvet.com						
Animal Hospital of Valley Ranch Inc 8600 N Macarthur Blvd Ste 132	Irving	TX	75063	972-409-0186		794
Web: ahofvr.com						
Animal Hospital Pc 904 Second Ave E	Oneonta	AL	35121	205-625-3291		794
Web: oneontaanimalhospital.com						
Animal Medical Center Inc 1556 Mill Dam Rd	Virginia Beach	VA	23454	757-481-5213		794
Web: animalmedicalcenterinc.com						
Animal Medical Center of Chicago 1618 W Diversey Pkwy	Chicago	IL	60614	773-525-3353	525-3280	794
Web: animalmedicalcenterofchicago.com						
Animal Medical Center of Somerset County Inc 1911 N Center Ave	Somerset	PA	15501	814-443-6979		794
Web: amcdocs.com						
Animal Medical Clinic Ltd 4113 Morsay Dr	Rockford	IL	61107	815-398-4410		794
Web: rockfordvetclinics.com						
Animal Medical Ctr, The 510 E 62nd St	New York	NY	10065	212-838-8100	752-2592	794
Web: www.amcny.org						
Animal Medical Surgical Center PC 487 SR-18	New Wilmington	PA	16142	724-946-8787		794
Web: animalmedicalsurgical.com						
Animal Planet 1 Discovery Pl	Silver Spring	MD	20910	240-662-2000		647
Web: www.animalplanet.com						
Animal Protection of New Mexico Incorporated Foundation PO Box 11395	Albuquerque	NM	87192	505-265-2322		305
Web: apnm.org						
Animal Science Products Inc 3418 Rayburn Dr	Nacogdoches	TX	75961	936-560-0003	560-0157*	328
*Fax Area Code: 409 ■ Web: www.asp-inc.com						
Animal Supply Company LLC 32001 32nd Ave S Ste 420	Federal Way	WA	98001	800-323-2963		297-8
TF: 800-323-2963 ■ Web: animalsupply.com						
Animal Surgical Center of Michigan 5045 Miller Rd	Flint	MI	48507	810-671-0088		794
Web: animalsurgicalcenter.com						
Animal Welfare Assn 509 Centennial Blvd	Voorhees	NJ	08043	856-424-2288		794
Web: www.awanj.org						
Animas Credit Union 2101 E 20th St	Farmington	NM	87401	505-326-7701		219
Web: animascu.com						
Animated Story Boards (ASB) 1001 Avenue of the Americas 24th Fl	New York	NY	10018	212-595-0400		514
Web: animatedstoryboards.com						
Animation Magazine Inc 26500 W Agoura Rd Ste 102-651	Calabasas	CA	91302	818-883-2884	883-3773	637-9
Web: www.animationmagazine.net						
Animation Mentor 1400 65th St Ste 250	Emeryville	CA	94608	877-326-4628		764
TF: 877-326-4628 ■ Web: www.animationmentor.com						
Anis Cafe & Bistro 2974 Grandview Ave	Atlanta	GA	30305	404-233-9889		671
Web: www.anisbistro.com						
Anita Borg Institute for Women & Technology (IWT) 1501 Page Mill Rd MS 1105	Palo Alto	CA	94304	650-352-7500	852-8172	48-9
Web: anitab.org						
Anita Purves Nature Ctr 1401 N Broadway	Urbana	IL	61801	217-384-4062	384-1052	50-5
Web: www.urbanaparks.org						
Anita's Biscotti 3001 Shillington Rd	Sinking Spring	PA	19608	610-678-7178		297-3
Web: anitas-biscottis.com						
Anitox Corp 1055 Progress Cir	Lawrenceville	GA	30043	678-376-1055		146
Web: www.anitox.com						
Anixa Biosciences Inc 12100 Wilshire Blvd Ste 1275	Los Angeles	CA	90025	310-484-5200		735
NASDAQ: ITUS ■ Web: www.anixa.com						
Anixter Inc 2301 Patriot Blvd	Glenview	IL	60026	224-521-8000	521-8100	189-4
TF: 800-492-1212 ■ Web: www.anixter.com						
ANJEC (Association of New Jersey Environmental Commissions) PO Box 157	Mendham	NJ	07945	973-539-7547	539-7713	48-13
Web: www.anjec.org						
Anka Behavioral Health Inc 1850 Gateway Blvd Ste 900	Concord	CA	94520	925-825-4700		104
Anklesaria Group Inc 1172 Cuchara Dr	Del Mar	CA	92014	858-755-7119		244
Web: www.anklesaria.com						
Ankom Technology 2052 Oneil Rd	Macedon	NY	14502	315-986-8090	986-8091	419
Web: www.ankom.com						
ANL (Argonne National Laboratory) 9700 S Cass Ave	Lemont	IL	60439	630-252-2000		668
TF: 800-632-8990 ■ Web: www.anl.gov						
Anlin Industries 1665 Tollhouse Rd	Clovis	CA	93611	559-322-1531		499
TF: 800-287-7996						
ANM (Alliance of Nonprofit Mailers) 1211 Connecticut Ave NW Ste 610	Washington	DC	20036	202-462-5132		48-7
Web: www.nonprofitmailers.org						
ANMA (American Naturopathic Medical Assn) PO Box 96273	Las Vegas	NV	89193	702-450-3477		48-17
Web: www.anma.org						
Anmar Metrology Inc 7726 Arjons Dr	San Diego	CA	92126	858-621-2630	621-6019	743
Web: www.anmar.com						
ANMC (Alaska Native Medical Ctr) 4315 Diplomacy Dr	Anchorage	AK	99508	907-563-2662		374-3
TF: 800-478-6661 ■ Web: www.anmc.org						
AnMed Health 800 N Fant St	Anderson	SC	29621	864-512-1000		374-3
TF: 866-735-2963 ■ Web: www.anmedhealth.org						
Ann Arbor Area Board of Realtors 1919 W Stadium Blvd	Ann Arbor	MI	48103	734-822-2267		653
Web: aaabor.com						
Ann Arbor Area Convention & Visitors Bureau 315 W Huron St Ste 340	Ann Arbor	MI	48103	734-995-7281	995-7283	206
Web: www.annarbor.org						
Ann Arbor Art Ctr 117 W Liberty St	Ann Arbor	MI	48104	734-994-8004	994-3610	50-2
Web: www.annarborartcenter.org						
Ann Arbor City Hall 301 E Huron St	Ann Arbor	MI	48104	734-794-6000	994-1765	337
Web: www.a2gov.org						
Ann Arbor Civic Theatre 322 W Ann St	Ann Arbor	MI	48104	734-971-2228	971-2769	572
Web: www.a2ct.org						
Ann Arbor Distribution 1942 Mcgregor Rd	Ypsilanti	MI	48198	734-484-0100		463
Web: annarbordist.com						
Ann Arbor District Library (AADL) 343 S Fifth Ave	Ann Arbor	MI	48104	734-327-4200	327-8309	434-3
Web: aadl.org						
Ann Arbor Film Festival 230 Collingwood Dr Ste 160B	Ann Arbor	MI	48103	734-995-5356	995-5396	282
Web: www.aafilmfest.org						
Ann Arbor Symphony Orchestra 35 Research Dr Ste 100	Ann Arbor	MI	48103	734-994-4801	994-3949	573-3
Web: www.a2so.com						
Ann Arbor Transportation Authority 2700 S Industrial Hwy	Ann Arbor	MI	48104	734-973-6500	973-6338	468
TF: 800-835-4603 ■ Web: www.theride.org						
Ann Arbor T-Shirt Company LLC 2275 S Industrial Hwy	Ann Arbor	MI	48104	734-274-2659		157-5
Web: annarbortees.com						
Ann Arbor/Ypsilanti Regional Chamber 2010 Hogback Rd Ste 4	Ann Arbor	MI	48104	734-665-4433	665-4191	139
Web: www.a2ychamber.org						
Ann Clark Ltd 453 Quality Ln	Rutland	VT	05701	802-773-7886		362
Web: www.annclarkcookiecutters.com						
Ann Coppel Productions LLC 8306 17th Ave NW	Seattle	WA	98117	206-282-7720		514
Web: anncoppelproductions.com						
Ann Mcgee-cooper & Associates Inc 4236 Hockaday Dr	Dallas	TX	75229	214-357-8550		194
Web: amca.com						
Ann Norton Sculpture Gardens 253 Barcelona Rd	West Palm Beach	FL	33401	561-832-5328	835-9305	50-3
Web: www.ansg.org						
Ann Sacks Tile & Stone Inc 8120 NE 33rd Dr	Portland	OR	97211	800-278-8453		751
TF: 800-278-8453 ■ Web: www.annsacks.com						
ANNA (American Nephrology Nurses Assn) 200 E Holly Ave	Sewell	NJ	08080	856-256-2320	589-7463	49-8
TF: 888-600-2662 ■ Web: www.annanurse.org						
Anna Griffin Inc 99 Armour Dr	Atlanta	GA	30324	404-817-8170		552-2
TF: 888-817-8170 ■ Web: annagriffin.com						
Anna Jaques Hospital (AJH) 25 Highland Ave	Newburyport	MA	01950	978-463-1000		374-3
Web: www.ajh.org						
Anna Maria College 50 Sunset Ln	Paxton	MA	01612	800-344-4586		166
TF: 800-344-4586 ■ Web: www.annamaria.edu						
Anna Maria of Aurora Inc 889 N Aurora Rd	Aurora	OH	44202	330-562-6171		371
Web: www.annamariaofaurora.com						
Anna Quarries Inc 1000 Quarry Rd	Anna	IL	62906	618-833-5121	833-4584	503-6
Web: www.annaquarries.com						
Anna's Greek Cuisine 7370 Sawmill Rd	Columbus	OH	43235	614-799-2207		671
Web: annasgreekcuisine.com						
Anna's Trattoria Italian Cuisine 304 Seabreeze Blvd	Daytona Beach	FL	32118	386-239-9624		671
Web: www.annastrattoria.com						
Annabelle Candy Co 27211 Industrial Blvd	Hayward	CA	94545	510-783-2900	785-7675	297-3
Web: annabellecandy.com						
Annals of Family Medicine Inc 11400 Tomahawk Creek Pky	Leawood	KS	66211	800-274-2237		637-9
TF: 800-274-2237 ■ Web: www.annfammed.org						
Annan & Bird Lithographers Ltd 1060 Tristar Dr	Mississauga	ON	L5T1H9	905-670-0604		627
TF: 800-565-5618 ■ Web: www.annan-bird.com						
Annandale Chamber of Commerce 7263 Maple Pl Ste 207	Annandale	VA	22003	703-256-7232	256-7233	139
TF: 800-357-2110 ■ Web: www.annandalechamber.com						
Annandale Millwork Allied Systems 220 Arbor Ct	Winchester	VA	22602	540-665-9600		499
Web: www.amcasc.com						
Annapolis & Anne Arundel County Chamber of Commerce 134 Holiday Ct Ste 316	Annapolis	MD	21401	410-266-3960	266-8270	139
TF: 800-624-8887 ■ Web: annearundelchamber.org						

	Phone	Fax	Class
Annapolis & Anne Arundel County Conference & Visitors Bureau (AAACCVB) 26 West St . . . Annapolis MD 21401 *TF:* 888-302-2852 ■ *Web:* www.visitannapolis.org	410-280-0445	263-9591	206
Annapolis Bancorp Inc 1000 Bestgate Rd . . . Annapolis MD 21401 *NASDAQ: ANNB* ■ **Fax Area Code:* 800 ■ *TF:* 800-555-5455 ■ *Web:* www.fnb-online.com	410-224-4455	278-6265*	360-2
Annapolis Capital Ltd 9 Ave SW . . . Calgary AB T2P0T1 *Web:* www.annapoliscapital.ca	403-231-4430		528
Annapolis City Hall 160 Duke of Gloucester St . . . Annapolis MD 21401 *TF:* 833-940-0008 ■ *Web:* www.annapolis.gov	410-263-7997	216-9284	337
Annapolis Harbour Shopping Ctr 2512A Solomon'S Island Rd . . . Annapolis MD 21401 *Web:* www.annapolisharbourcenter.com	410-267-3437		460
Annapolis Maritime Museum 723 Second St PO Box 3088 . . . Annapolis MD 21403 *Web:* amaritime.org	410-295-0104		520
Annapolis Micro Systems Inc 190 Admiral Cochrane Dr . . . Annapolis MD 21401 *Web:* www.annapmicro.com	410-841-2514	841-2518	668
Annapolis Summer Garden Theatre 143 Compromise St . . . Annapolis MD 21401 *Web:* summergarden.com	410-268-9212		572
Annapolis Symphony Orchestra Maryland Hall 801 Chase St . . . Annapolis MD 21401 *Web:* www.annapolissymphony.org	410-269-1132	263-0616	573-3
Annapurna Chai House 1620 St Michaels . . . Santa Fe NM 87505 *Web:* www.chaishoppe.com	505-988-9688		671
Anne Arundel County 44 Calvert St . . . Annapolis MD 21401 *Web:* www.aacounty.org	410-222-7000		338
Anne Arundel County Public Library 5 Harry S Truman Pkwy . . . Annapolis MD 21401 *Web:* www.aacpl.net	410-222-7371	222-7188	434-3
Anne Arundel Medical Ctr 2001 Medical Pkwy . . . Annapolis MD 21401 *Web:* www.aahs.org	443-481-1000		374-3
Anne Holmes & Associates (AHA) 9672 US Hwy 20 W . . . Galena IL 61036 **Fax Area Code:* 888 ■ *TF:* 800-465-6373 ■ *Web:* www.anneholmes.com	815-777-2523	465-6378*	196
Anne Klein & Associates Inc 1000 Atrium Way Ste 102 . . . Mount Laurel NJ 08054 *Web:* www.akcgfirm.com	856-866-0411		636
Anne Kolb Nature Ctr 751 Sheridan St . . . Hollywood FL 33019 *Web:* www.floridanaturepictures.com	954-357-5161		50-5
Anne Koplik Designs Inc 173 Main St . . . Brewster NY 10509 *TF:* 800-542-3134 ■ *Web:* annekoplik.com	845-279-8244		411
Anne Murray Ctr 36 Main St . . . Springhill NS B0M1X0 *Web:* www.annemurraycentre.com	902-597-8614	597-2001	520
Anneken, Huey, & Moser PLLC 909 Wright Summit Pkwy Ste 120 . . . Fort Wright KY 41011 *Web:* www.ahm-cpa.com	859-331-5622		2
Annenberg Center for the Performing Arts 3680 Walnut St . . . Philadelphia PA 19104 *Web:* www.annenbergcenter.org	215-898-3900		572
Annenberg Foundation 101 W Elm St Ste 640 . . . Conshohocken PA 19428 **Fax Area Code:* 610 ■ *Web:* annenberg.org	310-209-4560	964-8688*	305
Annenberg Media 1301 Pennsylvania Ave NW Ste 302 . . . Washington DC 20004 **Fax Area Code:* 202 ■ *TF:* 800-532-7637 ■ *Web:* www.learner.org	800-532-7637	783-0333*	632
Annenberg Theater Palm Springs Art Museum 101 Museum Dr . . . Palm Springs CA 92262 *Web:* www.psmuseum.org	760-325-4490		572
Annette Willis Insurance Agency Inc 18401 NW 27th Ave . . . Miami Gardens FL 33056 *Web:* www.annettewillisinsurance.com	305-625-2403		390
Annex Brands Inc 7580 Metropolitan Dr Ste 200 . . . San Diego CA 92108 *TF:* 877-722-5236 ■ *Web:* www.gopackagingstore.com	619-563-4800		113
Annex Cloud 5301 Beethoven St Ste 260 . . . Los Angeles CA 90066 *TF:* 866-802-8806 ■ *Web:* www.annexcloud.com	866-802-8806		387
Annex Pro Inc 49 Dunlevy Ave Ste 220 . . . Vancouver BC V6A3A3 *TF:* 800-682-6639 ■ *Web:* www.annexpro.com	604-682-6639		526
Annex Wealth Management LLC 12700 W Bluemound Rd Ste 200 . . . Elm Grove WI 53122 *Web:* annexwealth.com	262-786-6363	792-8930	463
Annie E. Casey Foundation 701 St Paul St . . . Baltimore MD 21202 *TF:* 800-222-1099 ■ *Web:* www.aecf.org	410-547-6600	547-6624	305
Annie Wright School 827 N Tacoma Ave . . . Tacoma WA 98403 *Web:* www.aw.org	253-272-2216	572-3616	622
Annie's Thai Castle 3195 Roswell Rd NE . . . Atlanta GA 30305 *Web:* anniesthai.com	404-264-9546		671
Annin Flagmakers 105 Eisenhower Pkwy Ste 203 . . . Roseland NJ 07068 *Web:* www.annin.com	973-228-9400		287
Anning Johnson Co 1959 Anson Dr . . . Melrose Park IL 60160 *Web:* anningjohnson.com	708-681-1300	681-1310	189-9
Annmarie Garden 13480 Dowell Rd PO Box 99 . . . Dowell MD 20629 *Web:* www.annmariegarden.org	410-326-4640	326-4887	97
Annodyne Inc 751 Arbor Way Ste 100 . . . Blue Bell PA 19422 *Web:* www.annodyne.com	215-540-9110		7
AnnTaylor Inc 7 Times Sq . . . New York NY 10036 *TF:* 800-342-5266 ■ *Web:* www.anntaylor.com	212-541-3300		157-6
Annual Reviews 4139 El Camino Way . . . Palo Alto CA 94306 *Web:* www.annualreviews.org	650-493-4400	855-9815	637-9
Annuity Investors Life Insurance Co c/o:Great American Insurance Group 301 E 4th St . . . Cincinnati OH 45202 *TF:* 800-789-6771 ■ *Web:* www.greatamericaninsurancegroup.com	800-789-6771		796
Annuvia Inc 1725 Clay St Ste 100 . . . San Francisco CA 94109 *TF:* 866-364-7940 ■ *Web:* annuvia.com	866-364-7940	331-6442	41
Anoka Area Chamber of Commerce 12 Bridge Sq . . . Anoka MN 55303 *Web:* www.anokaareachamber.com	763-421-7130	421-0577	139
Anoka County 325 E Main St . . . Anoka MN 55303 *Web:* www.anokacounty.us	763-422-7350	422-6919	338
Anoka Technical College 1355 W Hwy 10 . . . Anoka MN 55303 *TF:* 800-627-3529 ■ *Web:* www.anokatech.edu	763-433-1100	576-7701	800
Anoka-Hennepin School District 2727 N Ferry St . . . Anoka MN 55303 *TF:* 800-729-6164 ■ *Web:* www.ahschools.us	763-506-1000	506-1003	685
Anoka-Ramsey Community College 11200 Mississippi Blvd NW . . . Coon Rapids MN 55433 *Web:* www.anokaramsey.edu	763-433-1230	433-1521	162
Anomatic Corp 1650 Tamarack Rd . . . Newark OH 43055 *Web:* www.anomatic.com	740-522-2203	522-3339	481
Anonymous Content LLC 3532 Hayden Ave . . . Culver City CA 90232 *Web:* www.anonymouscontent.com	310-558-6000	558-2724	514
Anoplate Inc 459 Pulaski St 475 . . . Syracuse NY 13204 *Web:* www.anoplate.com	315-471-6143	471-7132	621
Anotek Inc 2349 Hill St . . . Santa Monica CA 90405 *Web:* www.anotek.com	310-450-5027	450-0867	178-1
Another Printer Inc 10 Bush River Ct . . . Columbia SC 29210 *TF:* 888-689-6399 ■ *Web:* anotherprinterinc.com	803-798-1380		627
Anova Home Health Care Services Inc 1229 Silver Ln Ste 201 . . . McKees Rocks PA 15136 *Web:* www.anovahomehealth.com	412-859-8801		363
ANPAC (American National Property and Casualty Co) 1949 E Sunshine . . . Springfield MO 65899 *Web:* www.anpac.com	417-887-0220	887-1801	391-4
Anpec Industries Inc 216 Main St . . . Pecatonica IL 61063 *Web:* www.anpecindustries.com	815-239-2303		621
ANR (Americans for Nonsmokers' Rights) 2530 San Pablo Ave Ste J . . . Berkeley CA 94702 *Web:* no-smoke.org	510-841-3032	841-3071	48-17
ANR Pipeline Co 717 Texas St . . . Houston TX 77002 *TF:* 800-827-5267 ■ *Web:* www.anrpl.com	888-427-2875		325
Anresco Inc 1375 Van Dyke Ave . . . San Francisco CA 94124 *TF:* 800-359-0920 ■ *Web:* anresco.com	415-822-1100		41
Anritsu Co 490 Jarvis Dr . . . Morgan Hill CA 95037 *TF:* 800-267-4878 ■ *Web:* www.anritsu.com	408-778-2000	776-1744	248
ANRO Inc 931 S Matlack St . . . West Chester PA 19382 *TF:* 800-355-2676 ■ *Web:* www.anro.com	610-687-1200		627
Anron Air Systems Inc 440 Wyandanch Ave . . . West Babylon NY 11704 *TF:* 800-421-0389 ■ *Web:* anronac.com	631-643-3433	491-6983	189-10
ANS (American Nuclear Society) 555 N Kensington Ave . . . LaGrange IL 60526 *TF:* 800-323-3044 ■ *Web:* www.ans.org	708-352-6611	352-0499	49-19
ANS (Audubon Naturalist Society) 8940 Jones Mill Rd . . . Chevy Chase MD 20815 *Web:* www.audubonnaturalist.org	301-652-9188		637-2
ANSA McAL (US) Inc 11403 NW 39th St . . . Doral FL 33178 *Web:* ansamcal.com	305-599-8766	599-3376	360-3
ANSAR Medical Technologies Inc PO Box 424 . . . Media PA 19063 **Fax Area Code:* 215 ■ *TF:* 888-883-7804 ■ *Web:* www.ans-hrv.com	877-228-6863	922-6463*	475
Ansata Publications 240 Polk 712 . . . Mena AR 71953 *Web:* www.ansata.com	479-394-5288		637-2
Ansatel Communications Inc 940 Kingsway . . . Vancouver BC V5V3C4 *TF:* 866-872-6500 ■ *Web:* ansatel.com	604-872-6500		224
Ansay Consulting LLC 417 W Michigan St . . . Port Washington WI 53074 *TF:* 800-451-2260 ■ *Web:* www.wiscomp.com	262-544-5504	544-5933	180
Anschutz Family foundation, The 555 Seventeenth St Ste 2400 . . . Denver CO 80202 *Web:* anschutzfamilyfoundation.org	303-293-2338		305
Ansco Machine Co 60 Cuyhoga Fls Indus Pky . . . Cuyahoga Falls OH 44221 *Web:* www.ansco-machine.com	330-929-8181	929-7474	454
Ansel & Miller LLC 1939 Tyler St . . . Hollywood FL 33020 *Web:* anselmiller.com	954-922-9100		41
Ansel Adams Gallery, The 9031 Village Dr . . . Yosemite National Park CA 95389 *Web:* anseladams.com	209-372-4413		522
Ansell & Anderson PA 40 S River Rd Bedford Pl Unit 32 . . . Bedford NH 03110 *Web:* ansellpa.com	603-644-8211		41
Ansell Healthcare Inc 111 S Wood Ave Ste 210 . . . Iselin NJ 08830 *Web:* www.ansell.com	732-345-5400	219-5114	576
Ansell Sandel Medical Solutions LLC 19736 Dearborn St . . . Chatsworth CA 91311 *Web:* www.sandelmedical.com	818-534-2500		475
Ansen Corp 100 Chimney Pt Dr . . . Ogdensburg NY 13669 *Web:* www.ansencorp.com	315-393-3573	393-7638	625
Ansett Aircraft Spares & Services Inc 12675 Encinitas Ave . . . Sylmar CA 91342 *Web:* www.ansettspares.com	818-362-1100		246
ANSI (American National Standards Institute) 25 W 43rd St 4th Fl . . . New York NY 10036 *TF:* 800-374-3818 ■ *Web:* www.ansi.org	212-642-4900	398-0023	48-1
Ansira Inc 2300 Locust St . . . Saint Louis MO 63103 *Web:* ansira.com	314-783-2300		5
Ansol Inc 4250 Pacific Hwy Ste 118 PO Box 82044 . . . San Diego CA 92110 *Web:* www.ansolinc.com	619-523-2040		393
Anson County 101 S Greene St . . . Wadesboro NC 28170 *Web:* www.co.anson.nc.us	704-994-3201	994-3238	338
Anson County School District 320 Camden Rd . . . Wadesboro NC 28170 *Web:* www.ansonschools.org	704-694-4417	694-7479	780
Anson Machine Works Inc PO Box 269 . . . Peachland NC 28133 *Web:* ansonmachine.com	704-272-7657	272-8916	493
Ansonia Nature & Recreation Ctr 10 Deerfield Ln . . . Ansonia CT 06401 *Web:* www.ansonianaturecenter.org	203-736-1053		50-5

Name	Address	City	State	Zip	Phone	Fax	Class
Anson-Stoner Inc	111 E Fairbanks Ave *Web:* www.anson-stoner.com	Winter Park	FL	32789	407-629-9484		7
Anstiss & Company PC	1115 Westford St *Web:* anstisscpa.com	Lowell	MA	01851	978-452-2500		2
Answer Co, The	502-233 Nelson's Crescent *Web:* www.theanswerco.com	New Westminster	BC	V3L0E4	604-473-9166	473-9155	179
Answer Heating & Cooling Inc	8490 Midland Rd *Web:* www.answersos.com	Freeland	MI	48623	989-695-9461		610
AnswerLive LLC	1034 X-Ray Dr *TF:* 800-472-4495 ■ *Web:* www.answerlive.com	Gastonia	NC	28054	704-481-1280		393
AnswerOn Inc	1707 Main St Ste 500 *Fax Area Code: 303 ■ *Web:* answeron.com	Longmont	CO	80501	720-684-4900	651-2089*	177
Answerport Inc	10200 N Port Washington Rd Ste 101 *Web:* www.answerport.com	Mequon	WI	53092	414-289-9100		194
Answers Corp	237 W 35th St Ste 1101 *Web:* www.answers.com	New York	NY	10001	646-502-4778		178-7
Answers in Genesis Ky Inc	2800 Bullittsburg Church Rd *Web:* answersingenesis.org	Petersburg	KY	41080	859-727-2222		48-20
AnswersMedia Inc	30 N Racine Ave Ste 300 *Web:* www.answersmediainc.com	Chicago	IL	60607	312-421-0113		5
ANSYS Inc	275 Technology Dr *NASDAQ: ANSS* ■ *TF:* 800-937-3321 ■ *Web:* www.ansys.com	Canonsburg	PA	15317	724-820-4367	514-9494	178-5
Antaean Solutions LLC	11700 Preston Rd Ste 600-213 *Web:* www.antaeans.com	Dallas	TX	75230	214-987-3439		194
Antaeus Capital Inc	1100 Glendon Ave Ste 9	Los Angeles	CA	90024	310-443-9000		690
Antaeus Fashions Group Inc	2411 Loma Ave *Web:* www.atfusa.com	South El Monte	CA	91733	626-452-0797	452-0984	155-3
Antarctica Asset Management Ltd	1177 Avenue of the Americas Fl 5 Ste 1111 *Web:* www.antarcticaam.com	New York	NY	10036	212-925-1419	219-8266	194
Antares Pharma Inc	3905 Annapolis Ln N Ste 105 *NASDAQ: ATRS* ■ *Web:* www.antarespharma.com	Minneapolis	MN	55447	763-475-7700		476
Antares Technology Solutions	8282 Goodwood Blvd Ste W-2 *TF:* 800-366-8807 ■ *Web:* www.antaresnet.com	Baton Rouge	LA	70806	225-922-7748	922-7749	180
Antaya Technologies Corp	333 Strawberry Field Rd *Web:* antaya.com	Warwick	RI	02886	401-921-3197		261
Antcom Corp	367 Van Ness Way Ste 602 *Web:* www.antcom.com	Torrance	CA	90501	310-782-1076	782-1086	261
Antea Group	5910 Rice Creek Pkwy Ste 100 *TF:* 800-477-7411 ■ *Web:* www.anteagroup.com	Saint Paul	MN	55126	651-639-9449	639-9473	667
Antec Inc	47900 Fremont Blvd *TF:* 800-222-6832 ■ *Web:* www.antec.com	Fremont	CA	94538	510-770-1200	770-1288	253
Antedo Inc	21952 Lindy Ln	Cupertino	CA	95014	408-253-1870		647
Antelope County	501 Main St *Web:* antelopecounty.nebraska.gov	Neligh	NE	68756	402-887-4410	887-4719	338
Antelope Island State Park	4528 W 1700 S *Web:* stateparks.utah.gov	Syracuse	UT	84075	801-773-2941		565
Antelope Valley Board of Trade (AVBOT)	41319 W 12th St Ste 104 *Web:* www.avbot.org	Palmdale	CA	93551	661-947-9033		139
Antelope Valley Chambers of Commerce	554 W Lancaster Blvd *Web:* lancasterchamber.org	Lancaster	CA	93534	661-948-4518	949-1212	139
Antelope Valley College	3041 W Ave K *Web:* www.avc.edu	Lancaster	CA	93536	661-722-6300	722-6531	162
Antelope Valley Hospital	1600 W Ave J *Web:* www.avhospital.org	Lancaster	CA	93534	661-949-5000		374-3
Antelope Valley Indian Museum State Historic Park	Antelope Vly Fwy Avenue M *Web:* www.avim.parks.ca.gov	Perris	CA	92571	661-946-3055		565
Antelope Valley Press	37404 Sierra Hwy *TF:* 888-874-2527 ■ *Web:* www.avpress.com	Palmdale	CA	93550	661-273-2700	947-4870	532-2
Antenen Robotics	9910 Charter Park Dr *TF:* 800-323-9555 ■ *Web:* www.antenen.com	West Chester	OH	45069	513-860-8800	860-8807	668
Antenna House Inc	3844 Kennett Pk Ste 200 *Web:* www.rainbowpdf.com	Greenville	DE	19807	302-427-2456	691-4647	809
Antenna Products Corp	101 SE 25th Ave *Web:* www.antennaproducts.com	Mineral Wells	TX	76067	940-325-3301	325-0716	647
Antenna Technology Communications Inc	450 N McKemy Ave *Web:* www.atci.com	Chandler	AZ	85226	480-844-8501		647
Antennas for Communications	2499 SW 60 Ave *Web:* www.afcsat.com	Ocala	FL	34474	352-687-4121	687-1203	647
Antex Electronics Corp	19160 Van Ness Ave *Web:* www.antex.com	Torrance	CA	90501	310-532-3092		625
Anthem	537 E Pete Rose Way Ste 100 *Web:* www.anthemww.com	Cincinnati	OH	45202	513-784-0066		344
Anthem Heatlh Services Inc	57 Karner Rd Ste B *Web:* www.lincare.com	Albany	NY	12205	518-690-1060	862-1400	363
Anthem Inc	220 Virginia Ave *TF:* 800-331-1476 ■ *Web:* www.anthemcorporateresponsibility.com	Indianapolis	IN	46204	800-331-1476		391-3
Anthem Life Insurance Co	6740 N High St Ste 200 *TF:* 800-551-7265 ■ *Web:* www.anthem.com	Worthington	OH	43085	614-436-0688		391-2
Anthony & Sylvan Pools	3739 Easton Rd Rt 611 *TF:* 877-729-7946 ■ *Web:* www.anthonysylvan.com	Doylestown	PA	18901	215-489-5605		728
Anthony Business Forms Inc	3160 Plainfield Rd *Web:* www.anthonybusinessforms.com	Dayton	OH	45432	937-253-0072	253-8107	534
Anthony Forest Products Co	PO Box 1877 *TF:* 800-221-2326 ■ *Web:* www.anthonyforest.com	El Dorado	AR	71730	870-862-3414		683
Anthony Intl	12391 Montera Ave *TF:* 800-772-0900 ■ *Web:* www.anthonyintl.com	Sylmar	CA	91342	818-365-9451	361-9611	329
Anthony J. Bilotti & Associates LLC	1400 N Providence Rd Ste 4035 *Web:* bilottilaw.com	Media	PA	19063	484-444-4400	444-0774	41
Anthony Liftgates Inc	1037 W Howard St *TF:* 800-482-0003 ■ *Web:* www.anthonyliftgates.com	Pontiac	IL	61764	815-842-3383	844-3612	54
Anthony Louis Ctr	115 Forestview Ln *Web:* www.anthonylouiscenter.com	Plymouth	MN	55441	763-757-2906	542-9248	726
Anthony Marano Company Inc	3000 S Ashland Ave *Web:* www.anthonymarano.com	Chicago	IL	60608	773-321-7500		297-7
Anthony Ostlund Baer & Louwagie PA	3600 Wells Fargo Bldg 90 S Seventh St *Web:* www.anthonyostlund.com	Minneapolis	MN	55402	612-349-6969		428
Anthony Publishing Company Inc	206 Gleasondale Rd *Web:* www.ichingoracle.com	Stow	MA	01775	978-897-7191		637-2
Anthony Timberlands Inc	111 S Plum St PO Box 137 *Web:* www.anthonytimberlands.com	Bearden	AR	71720	870-687-3611	687-2283	683
Anthony Underwood Inc	4006 Bessemer Hwy *Web:* www.anthonyunderwood.com	Bessemer	AL	35020	205-424-4033		57
Anthony Wayne Board of Education	9565 Bucher Rd PO Box 2487 *Web:* www.anthonywayneschools.org	Whitehouse	OH	43571	419-877-5377	877-9352	685
Anthony Wayne Business Exchange	3508 Stellhorn Rd *Web:* www.anthonywayne.com	Fort Wayne	IN	46815	260-485-1990		196
Anthony's	7220 F St *Web:* www.anthonyssteakhouse.com	Omaha	NE	68127	402-331-7575		671
Anthony's Fish Grotto	1360 N Harbor Dr *Web:* www.anthonysfishgrotto.com	San Diego	CA	92101	619-232-5103		671
Anthony's Restaurant Group	PO Box 3805 *Web:* www.anthonys.com	Bellevue	WA	98009	425-455-0732		670
Anthony-Thomas Candy Co	1777 Arlingate Ln *TF:* 877-226-3921 ■ *Web:* www.anthony-thomas.com	Columbus	OH	43228	614-274-8405		296-8
Anthracite Power and Light	10 Gilberton Rd *Web:* www.anthracitepower.com	Gilberton	PA	17934	570-874-1602		787
Antibodies Inc	PO Box 1560 *Fax Area Code: 530 ■ *TF:* 800-824-8540 ■ *Web:* www.antibodiesinc.com	Davis	CA	95617	800-824-8540	758-6307*	85
Antica Posta	519 E Paces Ferry Rd *Web:* www.anticaposta.com	Atlanta	GA	30305	404-262-7112	262-7335	671
AntiCancer Inc	7917 Ostrow St *TF:* 800-511-2555 ■ *Web:* www.anticancer.com	San Diego	CA	92111	858-654-2555	268-4175	231
Antico Forno	93 Salem St *Web:* www.anticofornoboston.com	Boston	MA	02113	617-723-6733		671
Anti-Defamation League (ADL)	605 Third Ave *TF:* 866-386-3235 ■ *Web:* www.adl.org	New York	NY	10158	212-885-7700	867-0779	48-8
Antietam Cable Television Inc	1000 Willow Cir *Web:* www.antietambroadband.com	Hagerstown	MD	21740	301-797-5000		116
Antietam National Battlefield	5831 Dunker Church Rd PO Box 158 *Web:* www.nps.gov	Sharpsburg	MD	21782	301-432-5124	432-4590	564
Antigone Books	411 N Fourth Ave *Web:* www.antigonebooks.com	Tucson	AZ	85705	520-792-3715	882-8802	95
Antigua & Barbuda	305 E 47th St - 6A *TF:* 888-268-4227 ■ *Web:* www.antigua-barbuda.org	New York	NY	10017	212-541-4117	541-4789	784
Antigua Group Inc, The	16651 N 84 Ave *TF:* 800-528-3133 ■ *Web:* www.antigua.com	Peoria	AZ	85382	623-523-6000		155-12
Antillean Marine Shipping Corp	3038 NW N River Dr *TF:* 888-633-6361 ■ *Web:* www.antillean.com	Miami	FL	33142	305-633-6361		313
Antimicrobial Therapy Inc	11771 Lee Hwy *Web:* www.sanfordguide.com	Sperryville	VA	22740	540-987-9480	987-9486	180
Antimite Associates Inc	5867 Pine Ave *TF:* 800-974-2847 ■ *Web:* www.antimitepestcontrol.com	Chino Hills	CA	91709	909-606-2300		577
Antioch Chamber of Commerce	101 H St Unit 4 *Web:* antiochchamber.com	Antioch	CA	94509	925-757-1800	757-5286	139
Antioch International Inc	410 Winding View *Web:* www.antioch-intl.com	New Braunfels	TX	78132	402-289-2217		256
Antioch Speedway	1201 W Tenth St *Web:* www.antiochspeedway.com	Antioch	CA	94509	925-779-9220	779-9213	515
Antioch University	900 Dayton St *Web:* www.antioch.edu	Yellow Springs	OH	45387	937-769-1340		166
Antiochian Orthodox Christian Archdiocese of North America	358 Mountain Rd *TF:* 888-421-1442 ■ *Web:* www.antiochian.org	Englewood	NJ	07631	201-871-1355	871-7954	48-20
Antiok Holdings Inc	34 Shining Willow Way Ste 132 *Web:* www.antiok.com	La Plata	MD	20646	301-743-2100	743-5318	624
Antiquarian Book Store, The	1070 Lafayette Rd *Web:* www.antiquarianbookstore.com	Portsmouth	NH	03801	603-436-7250		95
Antique Automobile Club of America (AACA)	501 W Governor Rd PO Box 417 *TF:* 800-452-9910 ■ *Web:* aaca.org	Hershey	PA	17033	717-534-1910	534-9101	48-18

Name / Address	City	State	ZIP	Phone	Fax	Class
Antique Automobile Radio Inc 700 Tampa Rd *TF:* 800-933-4926 ■ *Web:* www.radiosforoldcars.com	Palm Harbor	FL	34683	727-785-8733		647
Antique Car Museum, The 111 Grovewood Rd *Web:* www.grovewood.com	Asheville	NC	28804	828-253-7651		520
Antique Collectors Club 116 Pleasant St *TF:* 800-254-4100 ■ *Web:* businessfinder.masslive.com	Easthampton	MA	01027	413-529-0861		637-2
Antique Mall 1251 S Virginia St *TF:* 888-316-6255 ■ *Web:* www.antiquemalls.com	Reno	NV	89502	775-324-4141		460
Antique Powerland Museum 3995 Brooklake Rd NE *Web:* www.antiquepowerland.com	Salem	OR	97303	503-393-2424		520
Antique Trader 700 E State St **Fax Area Code:* 715 ■ *TF:* 800-258-0929 ■ *Web:* www.antiquetrader.com	Iola	WI	54990	503-319-0799	445-4087*	457-14
Antique Village 10203 Chamberlayne Rd *Web:* www.antiquevillageva.com	Mechanicsville	VA	23116	804-746-8914		460
Antique World 11111 Main St *Web:* www.antiqueworldmarket.com	Clarence	NY	14031	716-759-8483	759-0437	460
Antiques & Art Around Florida (A&ARF) PO Box 980 *TF:* 800-847-1740 ■ *Web:* www.aarf.com	Keystone Heights	FL	32656	352-475-1336	475-5326	637-9
Antiques Mall of Madison 4748 Cottage Grove Rd *Web:* www.antiquesmadison.com	Madison	WI	53716	608-222-2049		460
Antiquity 112 Romero St NW *Web:* antiquityrestaurant.com	Albuquerque	NM	87104	505-247-3545		671
Antler Inn 43 W Pearl St PO Box 575 *TF:* 800-483-8667 ■ *Web:* www.townsquareinns.com	Jackson	WY	83001	307-733-2535		379
Antoine du Chez 2700 E Second Ave *Web:* antoineduchez.com	Denver	CO	80206	303-320-6012	996-1061	707
Antoine's 713 St Louis St *Web:* www.antoines.com	New Orleans	LA	70130	504-581-4422		671
Anton & Michel PO Box 4917 *Web:* www.antonandmichel.com	Carmel By The Sea	CA	93921	831-624-2406		671
Anton Cabinetry 2002 W Pioneer Pkwy *Web:* www.antoncabinetry.com	Pantego	TX	76013	817-460-8601		115
Anton Collins Mitchell LLP 303 E 17th Ave Ste 600 *Web:* www.acmllp.com	Denver	CO	80203	303-830-1120	830-8130	2
Anton's Cleaners Inc 500 Clark Rd *TF:* 877-861-9750 ■ *Web:* www.antons.com	Tewksbury	MA	01876	978-851-3721		426
Anton/Bauer Inc 14 Progress Dr *TF:* 800-422-3473 ■ *Web:* www.antonbauer.com	Shelton	CT	06484	203-929-1100		591
Antonelli Brothers Meat Fish 3585 California St *Web:* antonellibros.com	San Francisco	CA	94118	415-752-7413		345
Antonelli Institute 300 Montgomery Ave *TF:* 800-722-7871 ■ *Web:* www.antonelli.edu	Erdenheim	PA	19038	215-836-2222	836-2794	164
Antonello Ristorante 3800 S Plaza Dr *Web:* www.antonello.com	Santa Ana	CA	92704	714-751-7153		671
AntonGear Music 7644 E Keller Ln *Web:* www.antongear.com	South Range	WI	54874	218-393-5790		526
Antoni's Italian Cafe 1118 Coolidge Blvd Ste A *Web:* www.antonisitaliancafe.com	LaFayette	LA	70503	337-232-8384		671
Antonia Canero Pa 1101 Brickell Ave South Tower Ste 700 *Web:* acanero.com	Miami	FL	33131	305-579-9218		41
Antonini Enterprises LLC 701 D'Arcy Pky *TF:* 800-548-7825 ■ *Web:* www.antoniniusa.com	Lathrop	CA	95330	209-466-9041	466-1411	393
Antonio's Mexican Restaurant 840 Paredes Line Rd *Web:* www.antoniomexicanrestaurant.com	Brownsville	TX	78521	956-542-6504		671
Antonios' of Nashville 7097 Old Harding Pk *Web:* antoniosofnashville.com	Nashville	TN	37221	615-646-9166		671
Antonucci & Associates Arch & Engrs 50 Fifth Ave *Web:* www.aa-ae.com	Pelham	NY	10803	914-636-4000		261
Antrim County 203 E Cayuga St *Web:* www.antrimcounty.org	Bellaire	MI	49615	231-533-6353	533-6935	338
Antrim Energy Inc 610-301 8 Ave SW *Web:* www.antrimenergy.com	Calgary	AB	T2P1C5	403-264-5111	264-5113	536
Antrim House 21 Goodrich Rd *Web:* www.antrimhousebooks.com	Simsbury	CT	06070	860-217-0023		637-2
Antron Engineering & Machine Company Inc 170 Mechanic St *TF:* 877-225-2362 ■ *Web:* www.antroneng.com	Bellingham	MA	02019	877-225-2362		261
Antronix Inc 440 Forsgate Dr *TF:* 888-644-6075 ■ *Web:* www.antronix.com	Cranbury	NJ	08512	609-860-0160		647
Antwerp Diamond Distributors Inc 581 5th Ave Ste 560 *TF:* 800-223-0444 ■ *Web:* www.antwerpdistributors.com	New York	NY	10017	800-223-0444		411
Antwerp Insurance Agency Inc 312 S Main St *Web:* antwerpinsuranceagency.com	Antwerp	OH	45813	419-258-5511		390
ANU (American National University) 1328 Hwy 11 W *TF:* 888-956-2732 ■ *Web:* www.an.edu	Bristol	TN	37620	423-878-4440		800
Anvasion Inc 53 Taylor Rd *Web:* anvasion.com	Bethel	CT	06801	203-770-3415		463
Anvil Corp 1675 W Bakerview Rd *Web:* www.anvilcorp.com	Bellingham	WA	98226	360-671-1450		261
Anvil Media Inc 310 NE Failing St *Web:* www.anvilmediainc.com	Portland	OR	97212	503-595-6050		6
Anvil Mountain Correctional Ctr 1810 Ctr Creek Rd PO Box 730 *Web:* www.doc.alaska.gov	Nome	AK	99762	907-443-2241	443-5195	213
Anworth Mortgage Asset Corp 1299 Ocean Ave 2nd Fl *NYSE:* ANH ■ *Web:* www.anworth.com	Santa Monica	CA	90401	310-255-4493	434-0070	654
ANX Home Healthcare 455 Hickey Blvd Ste 415 *Web:* www.anxlife.com	Daly City	CA	94015	650-991-5177	991-5178	363
Anxiety & Stress Management Institute, The 1640 Powers Ferry Rd SE Bldg 9 Ste 100 *Web:* www.stressmgt.net	Marietta	GA	30067	770-953-0080	953-0031	352
Anxiety Disorders Association of America (ADAA) 8701 Georgia Ave Ste 412 *TF:* 800-922-8947 ■ *Web:* adaa.org	Silver Spring	MD	20910	240-485-1001	485-1035	48-17
Any Budget Printing & Mailing 8170 Ronson Rd Ste L *Web:* www.anybudget.com	San Diego	CA	92111	858-278-3151		627
Any Lab Test Now 235 Bloomfield Dr 110 Bldg *Web:* www.anylabtestnow.com	Lititz	PA	17543	717-823-6787		415
AnyDoc Software Inc 5404 Cypress Center Dr Ste 140 **Fax Area Code:* 813 ■ *TF:* 888-495-2638 ■ *Web:* www.onbase.com	Tampa	FL	33609	888-495-2638	222-0018*	178-7
Anytime Fitness Inc 12181 Margo Ave S *TF:* 888-827-9262 ■ *Web:* www.anytimefitness.com	Hastings	MN	55033	888-827-9262		354
Any-Time Home Care Inc 127 S Broadway PO Box 995 *Web:* anytimehomecare.com	Nyack	NY	10960	845-353-8280	353-8275	363
ANZ 1177 Avenue of the Americas *Web:* www.anz.com	New York	NY	10036	212-801-9800	801-9163	70
Anza Electric Co-opeartive Inc 58470 Hwy 371 PO Box 391909 *TF:* 844-311-7201 ■ *Web:* www.anzaelectric.org	Anza	CA	92539	951-763-4333	763-5297	245
Anza Inc 312 Ninth Ave SE Ste B *Web:* www.anza.com	Watertown	SD	57201	605-886-3889		701
Anza-Borrego Desert State Park 200 Palm Canyon Dr *Web:* www.parks.ca.gov	Borrego Springs	CA	92004	760-767-4205	767-3427	565
Anzellotti, Sperling, Pazol & Small Company LPA 21 N Wickliffe Cir *Web:* aspands.com	Youngstown	OH	44515	330-792-6033		41
AO Precision Manufacturing LLC 1870 Mason Ave *Web:* www.aopmfg.com	Daytona Beach	FL	32117	386-274-5882		350
AO Reed & Co 4777 Ruffner St *Web:* www.aoreed.com	San Diego	CA	92111	858-565-4131	292-6958	189-10
AO Smith 11270 W Pk Pl Ste 170 PO Box 245008 *NYSE:* AOS ■ *Web:* aosmith.com	Milwaukee	WI	53224	414-359-4000		518
AO Smith Electrical Products Co 531 N Fourth St *TF:* 800-543-9450 ■ *Web:* www.centuryelectricmotor.com	Tipp City	OH	45371	937-667-2431	667-5030	518
AO Smith Water Products Co 500 Tennessee Waltz Pkwy **Fax Area Code:* 615 ■ *TF:* 800-527-1953 ■ *Web:* www.hotwater.com	Ashland City	TN	37015	800-527-1953	792-2163*	36
AOA (American Osteopathic Assn) 142 E Ontario St **Fax Area Code:* 312 ■ *TF:* 800-621-1773 ■ *Web:* www.osteopathic.org	Chicago	IL	60611	888-626-9262	202-8200*	49-8
AOA (Administration on Aging) 330 C St SW *Web:* acl.gov	Washington	DC	20201	202-401-4634		340-10
AOA Products LLC 3618 King Rd Unit D *Web:* www.aoaproductsllc.com	Toledo	OH	43617	419-350-1244		358
AOAC Intl 481 N Frederick Ave Ste 500 *TF:* 800-379-2622 ■ *Web:* www.aoac.org	Gaithersburg	MD	20877	301-924-7077	924-7089	49-19
AOAExcel Inc 243 N Lindbergh Blvd 1st Fl *TF:* 800-365-2219 ■ *Web:* www.aoa.org	Saint Louis	MO	63141	800-365-2219		387
AOBTA (American Organization for Bodywork Therapies of Asia) 391 Wilmington Pk Ste 3 PO Box 260 *Web:* www.aobta.org	Glen Mills	PA	19342	484-841-6023		48-17
AOC (Association of Old Crows) 1555 King St Ste 500 *Web:* www.crows.org	Alexandria	VA	22314	703-549-1600	549-2589	48-19
AOC LLC 955 Tennessee 57 *Web:* www.aoc-resins.com	Collierville	TN	38017	901-854-2800	854-1183	605-2
AOC Wine Bar & Restaurant 8700 W Third St *Web:* www.aocwinebar.com	Los Angeles	CA	90048	310-859-9859		671
AOCA (Automotive Oil Change Assn) 330 N Wabash Ave Ste 2000 *TF:* 800-230-0702 ■ *Web:* www.aoca.org	Chicago	IL	60611	312-321-5132	673-6832	49-21
AOCS (American Oil Chemists Society) 2710 S Boulder PO Box 17190 *TF:* 866-535-2730 ■ *Web:* www.aocs.org	Urbana	IL	61802	217-359-2344	351-8091	48-12
Aok Networking LLC 820 Clark St *Web:* www.aoknetworking.com	Oviedo	FL	32765	407-249-1989		196
AOL (America Online Inc) 22000 AOL Way *Web:* www.aol.com	Dulles	VA	20166	703-265-2100		398
AOM (Academy of Management) 235 Elm Rd PO Box 3020 *TF:* 800-633-4931 ■ *Web:* aom.org	Briarcliff Manor	NY	10510	914-923-2607	923-2615	49-12
AOML (Atlantic Oceanographic & Meteorological Laboratory) 4301 Rickenbacker Cswy *Web:* www.aoml.noaa.gov	Miami	FL	33149	305-361-4300	361-4449	668
Aon plc Aon Ctr 200 East Randolph St *Web:* www.aon.com	Chicago	IL	60601	312-381-1000		363
AONE (American Organization of Nurse Executives) 155 N Wacker Dr Ste 400 *Web:* www.aonl.org	Chicago	IL	60606	312-422-2800	422-4503	49-8
AOPA (Aircraft Owners & Pilots Assn) 421 Aviation Way *TF:* 800-872-2672 ■ *Web:* www.aopa.org	Frederick	MD	21701	301-695-2000	695-2375	49-21
AOPA (American Orthotic & Prosthetic Assn) 330 John Carlyle St Ste 200 *Web:* www.aopanet.org	Alexandria	VA	22314	571-431-0876	431-0899	48-17
AORN Inc 2170 S Parker Rd Ste 400 *TF:* 800-755-2676 ■ *Web:* www.aorn.org	Denver	CO	80231	303-755-6300	750-3212	49-8
AOS Thermal Compounds LLC 22 Meridian Rd Ste 6 *TF:* 888-662-7337 ■ *Web:* www.aosco.com	Eatontown	NJ	07724	732-389-5514		579

				Phone	Fax	Class
AOSS Medical Supply LLC 4971 Central Ave *Web:* aossmedicalsupply.com	Monroe	LA	71203	318-325-8290		475
AOSSM (American Orthopaedic Society for Sports Medicine) 9400 W Higgins Rd Ste 300 *TF:* 877-321-3500 ■ *Web:* www.sportsmed.org	Rosemont	IL	60018	847-292-4900	292-4905	49-8
AOTA (American Occupational Therapy Association Inc) 6116 Executive Blvd Ste 200 *TF:* 800-877-1383 ■ *Web:* www.aota.org	Bethesda	MD	20852	301-652-2682	652-7711	49-8
AP (ACE Personnel) 5909 Woodson Rd *Web:* www.acepersonnel.com	Mission	KS	66202	913-384-1100		721
AP (Atlantic Pacific Industries) 4223 W Jefferson Blvd *Web:* www.atlanticpacificind.com	Los Angeles	CA	90016	323-766-9075	766-8866	351
AP (Albert Paper Co) 1225 N Union St *Web:* albertpaperco.com	Stockton	CA	95205	209-466-7931		559
AP (Atlantic Promotions) 1405 Eastbrooke Way 1st Fl *TF:* 877-442-4828 ■ *Web:* www.atlanticpromotions.com	Marietta	GA	30066	770-565-9906	321-4738	328
AP Chexs Inc 6327 Bowness Rd NW *TF:* 888-437-0624 ■ *Web:* www.apchexs.com	Calgary	AB	T3B0E4	403-247-8913		2
AP Exhaust Technologies Inc 300 Dixie Trl *TF:* 800-277-2787 ■ *Web:* www.sales.apexhaust.com	Goldsboro	NC	27530	919-580-2000		60
AP Machine & Tool Inc 1301 Elm St	Terre Haute	IN	47807	812-232-4939		697
AP Nonweiler 3321 County Rd A PO Box 1007 *Web:* apnonweiler.com	Oshkosh	WI	54903	920-231-0850		550
APA (American Poolplayers Association Inc) 1000 Lake St Louis Blvd Ste 325 *Web:* poolplayers.com	Lake Saint Louis	MO	63367	636-625-8611	625-2975	48-22
APA (At-Sea Processors Assn) 4039 21st Ave W Ste 400 *Web:* www.atsea.org	Seattle	WA	98199	206-285-5139	285-1841	49-6
APA (Architectural Precast Assn) 6710 Winkler Rd Ste 8 *Web:* archprecast.org	Fort Myers	FL	33919	239-454-6989		49-3
APA (American Planning Assn) 1030 15th St NW Ste 750 W *Web:* www.planning.org	Washington	DC	20005	202-872-0611	872-0643	49-17
APA (American Psychiatric Assn) 1000 Wilson Blvd Ste 1825 *TF:* 888-357-7924 ■ *Web:* www.psychiatry.org	Arlington	VA	22209	703-907-7300	907-1085	49-15
APA (American Psychological Assn) 750 First St NE *TF:* 800-374-2721 ■ *Web:* www.apa.org	Washington	DC	20002	202-336-5500	336-5962	49-15
APA (American Payroll Assn) 660 N Main Ave Ste 100 *Web:* www.americanpayroll.org	San Antonio	TX	78205	210-226-4600	226-4027	49-12
APA - Engineered Wood Assn 7011 S 19th St *Web:* www.apawood.org	Tacoma	WA	98466	253-565-6600	565-7265	49-3
APA Search Inc 24 E Ave Ste 1366 *Web:* www.apasearch.com	New Canaan	CT	06840	914-273-6000	273-8025	260
APA Services 4150 International Plaza Tower I Ste 510 *TF:* 877-425-5023 ■ *Web:* www.apaservices.net	Fort Worth	TX	76109	877-425-5023		734
A-Pac Manufacturing Company Inc 2719 Courier NW *TF:* 800-272-2634 ■ *Web:* www.polybags.com	Grand Rapids	MI	49534	800-272-2634		345
Apache Capital Management LLC 230 Park Ave Ste 1518 *Web:* www.apachecapital.com	New York	NY	10169	212-972-0991		401
Apache Corp 2000 Post Oak Blvd Ste 100 *NYSE:* APA ■ *TF:* 800-272-2434 ■ *Web:* www.apachecorp.com	Houston	TX	77056	713-296-6000		536
Apache County 75 W Cleveland St *Web:* www.co.apache.az.us	Saint John	AZ	85936	928-337-4364		338
Apache Farmers Co-op 230 W Floyd PO Box 332 *Web:* www.apachecoop.com	Apache	OK	73006	580-588-3110	588-9277	275
Apache Hose & Belting Company Inc 4805 Bowling St SW *TF:* 800-553-5455 ■ *Web:* apache-inc.com	Cedar Rapids	IA	52404	319-365-0471	365-2522	370
Apache Junction & Gold Canyon News, The 1075 S Idaho Rd Ste 102 *Web:* ajnews.com	Apache Junction	AZ	85119	480-982-6397	982-3707	532-4
Apache Junction Chamber of Commerce, The 567 W Apache Trl PO Box 1747 *Web:* www.ajchamber.com	Apache Junction	AZ	85120	480-982-3141	982-3234	139
Apache Junction Public Library 1177 N Idaho Rd *Web:* ajpl.org	Apache Junction	AZ	85119	480-474-8555		434-3
Apache Mills Inc 197 Royal Dr *TF:* 800-456-7791 ■ *Web:* www.apachemills.com	Calhoun	GA	30701	706-629-7791		131
Apache Software Foundation (ASF) 1901 Munsey Dr *Web:* www.apache.org	Forest Hill	MD	21050	410-803-2258		48-9
Apache Stainless Equipment Corp 200 W Industrial Dr PO Box 538 *TF:* 800-444-0398 ■ *Web:* www.apachestainless.com	Beaver Dam	WI	53916	920-356-9900	887-0206	386
Apacheta Corp 53 W Baltimore Pk Ste 200 *Web:* www.apacheta.com	Media	PA	19063	610-558-5852		809
APAC-Tennessee Inc 1210 Harbor Ave *Web:* www.apactn.com	Memphis	TN	38113	901-947-5600	947-5699	503-5
APACVB (Alexandria/Pineville Area Convention & Visitors Bureau) 707 2nd St **Fax Area Code:* 318 ■ *TF:* 800-551-9546 ■ *Web:* alexandriapinevillela.com	Alexandria	LA	71301	800-551-9546	443-1617*	206
Apahouser Inc 40 Hayes Memorial Dr *Web:* www.apahouser.com	Marlborough	MA	01752	508-786-0309	786-0310	697
Apalachee Correctional Institution 35 Apalachee Dr *Web:* dc.state.fl.us	Sneads	FL	32460	850-718-0688	593-6445	213
Apalachicola Bay Chamber of Commerce 122 Commerce St *Web:* www.apalachicolabay.org	Apalachicola	FL	32320	850-653-9419		139
Apantec LLC 805 W Fifth St Ste 13 *Web:* www.apantec.com	Lansdale	PA	19446	267-638-0362	263-4577	639
Aparaa Corp 7104 Barbican Dr *Web:* www.aparaa.com	Plano	TX	75025	214-683-5120		177
Apartment Association, California Southern Cities (AACSC) 333 W Broadway St Ste 101 *Web:* aacsc.org	Long Beach	CA	90802	562-426-8341		414
Apartment Hunters 11425 N Dale Mabry *TF:* 800-370-4868 ■ *Web:* www.apartmenthunters.com	Tampa	FL	33618	813-961-1419	969-3651	652
Apartment Investment & Management Co 4582 S Ulster St Ste 1100 *NYSE:* AIV ■ *TF:* 888-789-8600 ■ *Web:* www.aimco.com	Denver	CO	80237	303-757-8101	759-3226	655
Apartment Magz 4425 E 31st St Ste 210 *Web:* apartmentmagz.com	Tulsa	OK	74135	918-728-8118		637-9
APB (Automotive Profit Builders Inc) PO Box 2011 *Web:* www.apb.cc	Natick	MA	01760	508-626-9200		393
APBI (Alaska Public Broadcasting Inc) 135 Cordova St *Web:* www.akpb.org	Anchorage	AK	99501	907-277-6300		632
APBPA (Association of Professional Ball Players of America) 23623 N Scottsdale Rd Ste 290 *Web:* apbpa.org	Scottsdale	AZ	85255	480-404-9339		48-22
APC (American Power Conversion Corp) 132 Fairgrounds Rd *TF:* 800-788-2208 ■ *Web:* www.apc.com	West Kingston	RI	02892	401-789-5735	789-3710	253
APC Hegeman 8-12 Dietz St Ste 201 *Web:* www.eap-counseling.com	Oneonta	NY	13820	607-432-9039		462
APC Integrated Services Inc 770 Spirit of St Louis Blvd *TF:* 888-294-7886 ■ *Web:* www.apcisg.com	Chesterfield	MO	63005	888-294-7886		317
APC International Ltd 213 Duck Run Rd *Web:* www.americanpiezo.com	Mackeyville	PA	17750	570-726-6961	726-7466	253
APC Paper Company Inc 130 Sullivan St *Web:* www.apcpapergroup.com	Claremont	NH	03743	603-542-0411		557
APCC (American Public Communications Council Inc) 625 Slaters Ln Ste 104 *Web:* www.apccsideas.com	Alexandria	VA	22314	703-739-1322	739-1324	49-20
APCO Employees Credit Union 750 17th St N *TF:* 800-249-2726 ■ *Web:* www.apcocu.org	Birmingham	AL	35203	205-257-3601		219
APCO Extruders Inc 180 National Rd *TF:* 800-942-8725 ■ *Web:* www.apcoext.com	Edison	NJ	08817	732-287-3000	287-1421	548
APCO Graphics Inc 388 Grant St SE *TF:* 877-988-2726 ■ *Web:* www.apcosigns.com	Atlanta	GA	30312	404-688-9000		701
APCO Worldwide 1299 Pennsylvania Ave NW Ste 300 *Web:* www.apcoworldwide.com	Washington	DC	20004	202-778-1000		636
APCOM 125 SE Pkwy *Web:* www.apcom-inc.com	Franklin	TN	37064	615-794-5574	791-0660	202
APCON Inc 9255 SW Pioneer Ct *TF:* 800-624-6808 ■ *Web:* www.apcon.com	Wilsonville	OR	97070	503-682-4050		174
APD (American Product Distributors Inc) 8350 Arrowridge Blvd *TF:* 800-849-5842 ■ *Web:* www.americanproduct.com	Charlotte	NC	28273	704-522-9411		534
APDA (American Parkinson Disease Assn) 135 Parkinson Ave *TF:* 800-223-2732 ■ *Web:* www.apdaparkinson.org	Staten Island	NY	10305	718-981-8001	981-4399	48-17
Apeel Sciences 71 S Los Carneros Rd *TF:* 877-926-5184 ■ *Web:* apeelsciences.com	Goleta	CA	93117	877-926-5184		634
Apel Steel Corp 2345 Second Ave NW *Web:* www.apelsteel.net	Cullman	AL	35058	256-739-6280	739-6304	492
Apelan Hobbies & Collectibles LLC 6225 W 87th St Ste 103 *Web:* apelan.com	Los Angeles	CA	90045	310-417-9910	417-9912	761
Apelles LLC 3700 Corporate Dr Ste 240 *TF:* 800-825-4425 ■ *Web:* www.apellesnow.com	Columbus	OH	43231	614-899-7322		317
Apelon Inc 750 Main St Ste 1500 *Web:* www.apelon.com	Hartford	CT	06103	203-431-2530	431-2523	475
Apergy 2445 Technology Forest Rd Bldg 4 Ste 1200 *Web:* www.apergyals.com	The Woodlands	TX	77381	281-403-5742		538
Aperia Technologies Inc 1616 Rollins Rd *Web:* www.aperiatech.com	Burlingame	CA	94010	415-494-9624	524-2449	755
Aperio Group LLC Three Harbor Dr Ste 204 *Web:* www.aperiogroup.com	Sausalito	CA	94965	415-339-4300		401
Aperion Information Technologies Inc 90 S Washington St *Web:* www.aperion.com	Oxford	MI	48371	248-969-9791		196
Aperto Networks Inc 598 Gibraltar Dr *Web:* www.apertonet.com	Milpitas	CA	95035	408-719-9977	719-9970	736
Aperture Venture Partners 645 Madison Ave 20th Fl *Web:* www.aperturevp.com	New York	NY	10022	212-758-7325	319-8779	792
Apetito Canada Ltd 12 Indell Ln *TF:* 800-268-8199 ■ *Web:* apetito.ca	Brampton	ON	L6T3Y3	905-799-1022		297-8
Apex Advertising Inc 2959 Old Tree Dr *TF:* 800-666-5556 ■ *Web:* www.apexadv.com	Lancaster	PA	17603	717-396-7100		7
Apex Airtronics Inc 2465 Atlantic Ave	Brooklyn	NY	11207	718-485-8560		647
Apex Anodizing Nev Inc 280 Coney Island Dr Ste B *Web:* apexanodizing.com	Sparks	NV	89431	775-355-8121		481
Apex Asset Management LLC 2501 Oregon Pk Ste 201 *TF:* 888-592-2149 ■ *Web:* apexasset.com	Lancaster	PA	17601	888-592-2149		195
Apex Behavioral Health Western Wayne PLLC 1547 S Wayne Rd *Web:* www.apexwesternwayne.com	Westland	MI	48186	734-729-3133	729-3130	726
Apex Broach & Machine Co 22862 Hoover Rd *Web:* www.apbsi.com	Warren	MI	48089	586-758-2626	758-2627	493
Apex Co 100 Main St *TF:* 800-450-2739 ■ *Web:* www.theapexcompanies.com	Pawtucket	RI	02860	401-729-7200		229

Phone | Fax | Class

Apex Color 200 N Lee St ... Jacksonville FL 32204 | 800-367-6790 | | 110
TF: 800-367-6790 ■ *Web:* www.apexcolor.net

Apex Companies LLC
15850 Crabbs Branch Way Ste 200 ... Rockville MD 20855 | 301-417-0200 | 975-0169 | 261
TF: 800-733-2739 ■ *Web:* www.apexcos.com

Apex Computer Systems Inc
13875 Cerritos Corp Dr Ste A ... Cerritos CA 90703 | 562-926-6820 | 926-0825 | 196
Web: www.acsi2000.com

Apex CoVantage LLC
198 Van Buren St 200 Presidents Plz ... Herndon VA 20170 | 703-709-3000 | | 178-12
Web: apexcovantage.com

Apex Digital Imaging Inc
16057 Tampa Palms Blvd W ... Tampa FL 33647 | 813-973-3034 | | 701
TF: 866-973-3034 ■ *Web:* www.apexdigitalimaging.com

Apex Engineering PLLC
2601 S 35th St No 200 ... Tacoma WA 98409 | 253-473-4494 | | 261

Apex Fa 4221 Forbes Blvd ... Lanham MD 20706 | 888-323-4555 | | 207
TF: 888-323-4555 ■ *Web:* www.apexfa.com

Apex Facility Resources Inc
2323 1st Ave ... Seattle WA 98121 | 206-686-3357 | 932-1198 | 320
Web: www.apexfacility.com

Apex Financial Services Inc
11800 Singletree Ln Ste 314 ... Eden Prairie MN 55344 | 952-238-1315 | | 41
Web: www.apexfsi.com

Apex Group, The 1201 K St Ste 750 ... Sacramento CA 95814 | 916-444-3116 | 415-8020 | 636
Web: theapexgroup.net

Apex Homes Inc 7172 Rt 522 ... Middleburg PA 17842 | 570-837-2333 | 837-2346 | 186
TF: 800-326-9524 ■ *Web:* www.apexhomesofpa.com

Apex Industries Inc
100 Millennium Blvd ... Moncton NB E1E2G8 | 506-857-1620 | | 480
TF: 800-268-3331 ■ *Web:* www.apexindustries.com

Apex Innovations Inc 19951 W 162nd St ... Olathe KS 66062 | 913-254-0250 | 254-0320 | 177
Web: www.apex-innovations.com

Apex Insurance Group of WI LLC
1400 Main St ... Bloomer WI 54724 | 715-568-5050 | | 390
Web: aigwi.com

Apex Machine Co
3000 NE 12th Terr ... Fort Lauderdale FL 33334 | 954-566-1572 | 563-2844 | 629
Web: www.apexmachine.com

Apex Maritime Company (ORD) Inc
1900 E Golf Rd ... Schaumburg IL 60173 | 630-227-9818 | | 311
Web: www.apexshipping.com

Apex Marketing Strategy
3504 Country Club Dr NW ... Olympia WA 98502 | 360-402-6487 | | 194
Web: www.apexstrategy.com

Apex Medical Technologies Inc
10064 Mesa Ridge Ct Ste 202 ... San Diego CA 92121 | 858-535-0012 | 535-9715 | 476
Web: www.apexmedtech.com

Apex Mills Corp 168 Doughty Blvd ... Inwood NY 11096 | 516-239-4400 | 239-4951 | 745-4
TF: 800-989-2739 ■ *Web:* www.apexmills.com

Apex Oil Company Inc
8235 Forsyth Blvd Ste 400 ... Clayton MO 63105 | 314-889-9600 | 854-8539 | 579
Web: www.apexoil.com

Apex Piping Systems Inc
302 Falco Dr ... Wilmington DE 19804 | 888-995-2739 | | 610
TF: 888-995-2739 ■ *Web:* apexpiping.com

Apex Resources Inc 549 Stonegate Dr ... Katy TX 77494 | 832-786-7492 | | 539
Web: apexr.com

Apex Software Solutions LLC
5039 Beckwith Blvd Ste 109 ... San Antonio TX 78249 | 210-699-6666 | | 525
Web: www.apexwin.com

Apex Spring & Stamping Corp
11420 First Ave NW ... Grand Rapids MI 49534 | 616-453-5463 | | 492
Web: www.apexspring.com

Apex Systems Inc
4400 Cox Rd Ste 100 ... Glen Allen VA 23060 | 804-254-2600 | 254-7290 | 721
TF: 844-463-6178 ■ *Web:* www.apexsystems.com

Apex Technical School
24-02 Queens Plz S ... Long Island City NY 11101 | 212-645-3300 | | 685
Web: www.apextechnical.com

Apex Tool Works Inc
3200 Tollview Dr ... Rolling Meadows IL 60008 | 847-394-5810 | 394-2739 | 757
Web: www.apextool.com

Apex-Information Management Consultants I LLC
4515 Culver Rd Ste 310 ... Rochester NY 14622 | 585-225-8430 | | 177

Apex-Petroleum Corp
9500 Arena Dr Ste 360 ... Upper Marlboro MD 20774 | 301-773-9009 | 773-9030 | 579
Web: www.apexpetroleum.com

APF Travel Inc
1721 W Garvey Ave 2nd Fl ... Alhambra CA 91803 | 626-282-9988 | 282-9889 | 775
TF: 800-888-9168

APG (Automation Products Group Inc)
1025 W 1700 N ... Logan UT 84321 | 435-753-7300 | 753-7490 | 201
TF: 888-525-7300 ■ *Web:* www.apgsensors.com

APG (American Packing & Gasket Co)
6039 Armour Dr PO Box 213 ... Houston TX 77020 | 713-675-5271 | 675-2730 | 326
TF: 800-888-5223 ■ *Web:* callapg.com

APG Cash Drawer LLC
5250 Industrial Blvd NE ... Minneapolis MN 55421 | 763-571-5000 | 571-5771 | 488
Web: www.cashdrawer.com

APG Office Furnishings Inc
12075 Northwest Blvd Ste 100 ... Cincinnati OH 45246 | 513-621-9111 | | 321
Web: apgof.com

APGA (American Public Gas Assn)
201 Massachusetts Ave NE Ste C-4 ... Washington DC 20002 | 202-464-2742 | 464-0246 | 48-12
TF: 800-927-4204 ■ *Web:* www.apga.org

APHA (American Paint Horse Assn)
2800 Meacham Blvd ... Fort Worth TX 76137 | 817-834-2742 | 834-3152 | 48-3
Web: apha.com

APHA (American Public Health Assn)
800 'I' St NW ... Washington DC 20001 | 202-777-2742 | 777-2533 | 49-8
Web: www.apha.org

APHC (Appaloosa Horse Club)
2720 W Pullman Rd ... Moscow ID 83843 | 208-882-5578 | 882-8150 | 48-3
TF: 888-304-7768 ■ *Web:* www.appaloosa.com

APHIS (Animal & Plant Health Inspection Service)
National Veterinary Services Laboratories
4700 River Rd ... Riverdale MD 20737 | 844-820-2234 | | 743
TF: 844-820-2234 ■ *Web:* www.aphis.usda.gov

Phone | Fax | Class

APHL (Association of Public Health Laboratories)
8515 Georgia Ave Ste 700 ... Silver Spring MD 20910 | 240-485-2745 | 485-2700 | 49-7
Web: www.aphl.org

APHSA (American Public Human Services Assn)
1133 19th St NW Ste 400 ... Washington DC 20036 | 202-682-0100 | 289-6555 | 49-7
Web: www.aphsa.org

API (Anco Products Inc)
1100 Old Hwy 8 NW ... New Brighton MN 55112 | 574-293-5574 | | 389

API (American Petroleum Institute)
1220 L St NW ... Washington DC 20005 | 202-682-8000 | | 48-12
Web: www.api.org

API (AmbioPharm Inc)
1024 Dittman Ct ... North Augusta SC 29842 | 803-442-7590 | | 41
Web: www.ambiopharm.com

API (Associated Pharmacies Inc)
211 Lonnie E Crawford Blvd ... Scottsboro AL 35769 | 256-574-6819 | | 238
TF: 877-797-9227 ■ *Web:* www.rxaap.com

API (All-Power Inc) 2228 Murray ... Sioux City IA 51111 | 712-258-0681 | 258-6561 | 385
Web: www.allpowerinc.com

API Construction Co
1100 Old Hwy 8 NW ... New Brighton MN 55112 | 651-636-4320 | 636-0312 | 189-9
Web: www.apiconst.com

API Delevan 270 Quaker Rd ... East Aurora NY 14052 | 716-652-3600 | 652-4814 | 253
Web: www.delevan.com

API Group Inc 1100 Old Hwy 8 NW ... New Brighton MN 55112 | 800-223-4922 | | 185
TF: 800-223-4922 ■ *Web:* www.apigroupinc.com

API Heat Transfer Inc 2777 Walden Ave ... Buffalo NY 14225 | 716-684-6700 | 684-2129 | 91
TF: 877-274-4328 ■ *Web:* www.apiheattransfer.com

API Security Services & Investigations Inc
867 High St Ste D ... Worthington OH 43085 | 614-310-1980 | 310-1960 | 693
Web: apisecurity.us

API Supply Inc 624 Arthur St NE ... Minneapolis MN 55413 | 612-379-8000 | 379-8038 | 264-3
Web: www.apisupplyinc.com

API Systems Group Inc
10575 Vista Park Rd ... Dallas TX 75238 | 214-349-2221 | 349-2281 | 692
TF: 800-566-0845 ■ *Web:* www.afpgusa.com

API Technologies 400 Nickerson Rd ... Marlborough MA 01752 | 855-294-3800 | | 261
TF: 855-294-3800 ■ *Web:* www.apitech.com

APIC (Association for Professionals in Infection Control & Epidemiology Inc)
1275 K St NW Ste 1000 ... Washington DC 20005 | 202-789-1890 | 789-1899 | 49-8
TF: 800-650-9883 ■ *Web:* apic.org

Apicius - The Culinary Institute of Florence
7160 Keating Ave ... Sebastopol CA 95472 | 800-655-8965 | 824-0198* | 167-3
**Fax Area Code:* 707 ■ *TF:* 800-655-8965 ■ *Web:* www.tuscancooking.com

Apio Inc 2811 Air Park Dr ... Santa Maria CA 93455 | 800-454-1355 | | 296-21
TF: 800-454-1355 ■ *Web:* www.apioinc.com

Apiture 1805 Tiburon Dr ... Wilmington NC 28403 | 910-499-0077 | | 178-8
Web: www.apiture.com

Apkudo LLC 3500 Boston St Ste 333 ... Baltimore MD 21224 | 410-777-8612 | | 387
Web: apkudo.com

APL (Aliceville Public Library)
416 Third Ave NE ... Aliceville AL 35442 | 205-373-6691 | 373-3731 | 434-3
Web: pickenslibrary.com

APL (Albany Public Library)
161 Washington Ave ... Albany NY 12210 | 518-427-4300 | 449-3386 | 434-3
Web: www.albanypubliclibrary.org

APL (Atchison Public Library)
401 Kansas Ave ... Atchison KS 66002 | 913-367-1902 | 367-2717 | 434-3
Web: www.atchisonlibrary.org

APL Access & Security Inc
115 S William Dillard Dr ... Gilbert AZ 85233 | 480-497-9471 | | 693
TF: 866-873-2288 ■ *Web:* www.aplsecurity.com

APL Federal Credit Union
11050 Johns Hopkins Rd ... Laurel MD 20723 | 443-778-5250 | | 219
Web: aplfcu.org

APL Logistics Inc
17600 N Perimeter Dr Ste 150 ... Scottsdale AZ 85255 | 602-457-4297 | 473-1815* | 449
**Fax Area Code:* 480 ■ *TF:* 844-479-9620 ■ *Web:* www.apllogistics.com

Aplifi Inc
500 W Cypress Creek Rd Ste 700 ... Pompano Beach FL 33309 | 954-788-0700 | | 177

Aplix Inc 12300 Steele Creek Rd ... Charlotte NC 28273 | 704-588-1920 | 588-1941 | 594
Web: www.aplix.com

APLU (Association of Public & Land-Grant Universities)
1307 New York Ave NW Ste 400 ... Washington DC 20005 | 202-478-6040 | 478-6046 | 49-5
Web: www.aplu.org

Aplus 3680 Victoria St N ... Shoreview MN 55126 | 651-481-4598 | 532-0132* | 398
**Fax Area Code:* 877 ■ *Web:* www.aplus.net

Aplus Corp 14752 Yorba Ave ... Chino CA 91710 | 909-597-8818 | 597-2883 | 238
Web: www.apluspharmaceuticals.com

A-Plus Marine Supply Inc
212 McClure Dr ... Gulf Breeze FL 32561 | 850-934-3890 | | 710
TF: 800-352-2360 ■ *Web:* www.aplusmarine.com

A-Plus Printing & Graphic Center Inc
6561 NW 18th Ct ... Plantation FL 33313 | 954-327-7315 | | 627
Web: www.a-plusprinting.com

APlus Technologies Inc
10015 Old Columbia Rd ... Columbia MD 21046 | 410-290-6233 | 290-6234 | 177
Web: www.aplustechnologies.com

APM Hexseal Corp 44 Honeck St ... Englewood NJ 07631 | 201-569-5700 | | 326
TF: 800-498-9034 ■ *Web:* apmhexseal.com

APM Systems
1313 S Pennsylvania Ave ... Morrisville PA 19067 | 215-295-1097 | | 311
Web: www.apmit.com

APM Vocational Institute
6507 Columbia Pke ... Annandale VA 22003 | 703-980-0863 | | 800
Web: www.apmvocational.com

APMA (American Podiatric Medical Assn)
9312 Old Georgetown Rd ... Bethesda MD 20814 | 301-581-9200 | 530-2752 | 49-8
TF: 800-275-2762 ■ *Web:* www.apma.org

APMP (Association of Proposal Management Professionals)
PO Box 668 ... Dana Point CA 92629 | 949-493-9398 | | 49-12
Web: www.apmp.org

APN (Americans for Peace Now)
1101 14th St NW 6th Fl ... Washington DC 20005 | 202-728-1893 | 728-1895 | 48-7
TF: 877-429-0678 ■ *Web:* peacenow.org

APN Consulting Inc 475 Wall St ... Princeton NJ 08540 | 609-924-3400 | | 194
Web: apnconsultinginc.com

Company / Address	City	State	ZIP	Phone	Fax	Class
APN Healthcare Inc 320 W Hefner Rd *Web:* www.apnhealthcare.com	Oklahoma City	OK	73114	405-418-8500		361
APN Media LLC PO Box 20113 *TF:* 800-470-7599 ■ *Web:* www.ohranger.com	New York	NY	10023	212-581-3380	245-4226	637-9
APNA (American Psychiatric Nurses Assn) 1555 Wilson Blvd Ste 530 *TF:* 866-243-2443 ■ *Web:* www.apna.org	Arlington	VA	22209	703-243-2443	243-3390	49-8
APO (Alpha Phi Omega) 14901 E 42nd St *Web:* apo.org	Independence	MO	64055	816-373-8667	373-5975	48-16
Apogee Consulting Group PA 1151 Kildaire Farm Rd Ste 120 *Web:* www.acg-pa.com	Cary	NC	27511	919-858-7420		256
Apogee Designs Ltd 101 S Kane St *Web:* www.apogeedesigns.com	Baltimore	MD	21224	410-633-6336		596
Apogee Enterprises Inc 4400 W 78th St Ste 520 *NASDAQ: APOG* ■ *TF:* 877-752-3432 ■ *Web:* www.apog.com	Minneapolis	MN	55435	952-835-1874		329
Apogee Software Inc 1999 S Bascom Ave Ste 250 *Web:* www.apogee.com	Campbell	CA	95008	408-369-9001	369-9018	178-6
Apogee Technology Inc 129 Morgan Dr *OTC: ATCS* ■ *Web:* www.apogeebio.com	Norwood	MA	02062	781-551-9450	769-9107	696
Apollo Athletics Inc 1428 S Central Park Ave *Web:* www.apolloathletics.com	Anaheim	CA	92802	714-533-8118		360-3
Apollo Cafe 1310 E Brady St *Web:* apollocafe.com	Milwaukee	WI	53202	414-272-2233		671
Apollo Career Ctr 3325 Shawnee Rd *TF:* 866-998-2824 ■ *Web:* www.apollocareercenter.com	Lima	OH	45806	419-998-2908		167-3
Apollo Chemical Company LLC 2001 Willow Springs Ln *TF:* 800-374-3827 ■ *Web:* www.apollochemical.com	Burlington	NC	27215	336-226-1161	226-7494	145
Apollo Coating Technologies Inc 2953 Ladybird Ln *Web:* www.apollocoatings.com	Dallas	TX	75220	214-351-2774	351-0019	550
Apollo Design Technology Inc 4130 Fourier Dr *Web:* www.apollodesign.net	Fort Wayne	IN	46818	260-497-9191	497-9192	722
Apollo Distributing Co 128 Passaic Ave *Web:* www.apollodist.com	Fairfield	NJ	07004	973-228-5000		361
Apollo Education Group Inc 4025 S Riverpoint Pkwy *TF:* 800-990-2765 ■ *Web:* www.apollo.edu	Phoenix	AZ	85040	800-990-2765		242
Apollo Home Care Inc 3030 Finley Rd Ste 140 *Web:* apollohomehealth.com	Downers Grove	IL	60515	630-541-8238	541-8790	363
Apollo Oil LLC 1175 Early Dr *TF:* 800-473-5823 ■ *Web:* www.apollooil.com	Winchester	KY	40391	859-744-5444	745-5823	316
Apollo PACS Inc 7700 Leesburg Pk Ste 419 *Web:* www.apolloei.com	Falls Church	VA	22043	703-288-1474		177
Apollo Plastics Corp 5333 N Elston Ave *Web:* spcmfg.com	Chicago	IL	60630	773-282-9222	282-2763	604
Apollo Professional Svc 29 Stiles Rd Ste 302 *TF:* 866-277-3343 ■ *Web:* apollopros.com	Salem	NH	03079	866-277-3343		194
Apollo Retail Specialists LLC 4450 E Adamo Dr *TF:* 866-872-0666 ■ *Web:* www.apolloretail.com	Tampa	FL	33605	813-712-2525	712-2526	393
Apollo Theater 2540 N Lincoln Ave *Web:* www.apollochicago.com	Chicago	IL	60614	773-935-6100		572
Apollo Theatre 253 W 125th St *Web:* www.apollotheater.org	New York	NY	10027	212-531-5300	749-2743	572
Apollo Wood Products 7225 Edison Ave *Web:* apollowoodproducts.com	Ontario	CA	91762	909-371-9510		660
ApolloMD 5665 New Northside Dr Ste 200 *TF:* 866-827-6556 ■ *Web:* www.apollomd.com	Atlanta	GA	30328	770-874-5400	874-5433	353
Apollo-Ridge School District PO Box 219 *Web:* www.apolloridge.com	Spring Church	PA	15686	724-478-6000	478-1149	685
Apologetics Press Inc 230 Landmark Dr *TF:* 800-234-8558 ■ *Web:* www.apologeticspress.org	Montgomery	AL	36117	334-272-8558	270-2002	532-3
APOS Systems Inc 100 Conestoga College Blvd Ste 1118 *Web:* www.apos.com	Kitchener	ON	N2P2N6	519-894-2767		177
Apostolic Assembly of The Faith In Christ Jesus 10807 Laurel St *Web:* www.apostolicassembly.org	Rancho Cucamonga	CA	91730	909-987-3013		48-20
Apostolic Bible Institute Inc 6944 Hudson Blvd N *Web:* www.apostolic.org	Oakdale	MN	55128	651-739-7686	730-8669	166
Apostolic Christian Restmor Inc 1500 Parkside Ave *Web:* www.acrestmor.org	Morton	IL	61550	309-284-1400	266-7877	450
Apostolic Press 547 NW Coast St *Web:* www.apostolicbible.com	Newport	OR	97365	541-264-0452		637-9
Apotex Corp 2400 N Commerce Pkwy Ste 400 **Fax Area Code:* 800 ■ *TF:* 877-427-6839 ■ *Web:* www1.apotex.com	Weston	FL	33326	954-384-8007	706-5576*	583
Apotex Pharmachem Inc 34 Spalding Dr *Web:* www.apotexpharmachem.com	Brantford	ON	N3T6B8	519-756-8942	753-3051	479
Apothecary Products 11750 12th Ave S *TF:* 800-328-2742 ■ *Web:* www.apothecaryproducts.com	Burnsville	MN	55337	800-328-2742	328-1584	214
App Lovin 849 High St *Web:* www.applovin.com	Palo Alto	CA	94301	650-838-9153		39
APPA (American Public Power Assn) 1875 Connecticut Ave NW Ste 1200 *Web:* www.publicpower.org	Washington	DC	20009	202-467-2900	467-2910	48-12
Appalachian Brewing Co 50 N Cameron St *Web:* www.abcbrew.com	Harrisburg	PA	17101	717-221-1080	221-1083	671

Company / Address	City	State	ZIP	Phone	Fax	Class
Appalachian Electric Co-op 1109 Hill Dr *Web:* aecoop.org	New Market	TN	37820	865-475-2032		245
Appalachian Electronic Instruments Inc 428 AEI Dr *Web:* www.aei-wv.com	Ronceverte	WV	24970	304-647-5855		201
Appalachian Freight Carriers 12919 Old Valley Pke *Web:* www.appalachianfreight.com	Edinburg	VA	22824	540-984-8514	984-4572	780
Appalachian Mountain Club (AMC) 5 Joy St *TF:* 800-262-4455 ■ *Web:* www.outdoors.org	Boston	MA	02108	617-523-0655	523-0722	48-13
Appalachian National Scenic Trail PO Box 807 *Web:* www.nps.gov	Harpers Ferry	WV	25425	304-535-6278	535-2667	564
Appalachian Regional Healthcare Service (ARH) 80 Hospital Dr PO Box 8086 *TF:* 888-654-0015 ■ *Web:* www.arh.org	Barbourville	KY	40906	859-226-2440		353
Appalachian Regional Healthcare System 336 Deerfield Rd PO Box 2600 *TF:* 800-443-7385 ■ *Web:* www.apprhs.org	Boone	NC	28607	828-262-4100		374-3
Appalachian School of Law 1169 Edgewater Dr *TF:* 800-895-7411 ■ *Web:* www.asl.edu	Grundy	VA	24614	276-935-4349		167-1
Appalachian State University *Belk Library* 218 College St PO Box 32026 *TF:* 877-423-0086 ■ *Web:* library.appstate.edu	Boone	NC	28608	828-262-2300	262-3001	434-6
Appalachian Stove & Fabricators Inc 329 Emma Rd *Web:* www.appalachianstove.com	Asheville	NC	28806	828-253-0164		357
Appalachian Timber Services LLC 393 Edgar Givens Pkwy *Web:* www.atstimber.com	Sutton	WV	26601	304-765-7393		818
Appalachian Trail Conservancy (ATC) 799 Washington St PO Box 807 *TF:* 888-287-8673 ■ *Web:* appalachiantrail.org	Harpers Ferry	WV	25425	304-535-6331	535-2667	48-23
Appalachian Wood Products Inc 171 Loop Rd *Web:* www.appwood.com	Clearfield	PA	16830	814-765-2003	765-4751	499
Appalachia-Science in the Public Interest (ASPI) 50 Lair St *Web:* www.appalachia-spi.org	Mount Vernon	KY	40456	606-256-0077		48-13
Appaloosa Horse Club (APHC) 2720 W Pullman Rd *TF:* 888-304-7768 ■ *Web:* www.appaloosa.com	Moscow	ID	83843	208-882-5578	882-8150	48-3
Appaloosa Management LP 51 John F Kennedy Pkwy *Web:* www.amlp.com	Short Hills	NJ	07078	973-701-7000		403
Apparel Group, The 250 Belmont Ave *Web:* apparelgroup.org	Haledon	NJ	07508	973-942-6800		426
Apparel Machinery & Supply Co 1836 E Ontario St *Web:* apparelmachinery.com	Philadelphia	PA	19134	215-634-2626	426-8060	385
ApparelMaster 123 Harrison Ave *TF:* 877-543-1678 ■ *Web:* www.tryapparelmaster.com	Harrison	OH	45030	513-202-1600		442
Apparent Technologies Inc 11202 Georgian Dr Unit A *Web:* apparenttech.com	Austin	TX	78753	512-873-0023		454
Appcues 54 Canal St 6th Fl *Web:* www.appcues.com	Boston	MA	02114	857-991-1676		788
AppDetex 609 W Main St Ste 202 *TF:* 855-693-3839 ■ *Web:* www.appdetex.com	Boise	ID	83702	855-693-3839	780-8991	196
Appeal-Democrat 1530 Ellis Lake Dr PO Box 431 *Web:* www.appeal-democrat.com	Marysville	CA	95901	530-749-4700		532-2
Appelrouth Farah & Company PA 999 Ponce De Leon Blvd Ste 625 *Web:* appelrouth.com	Coral Gables	FL	33134	305-444-0999	443-5171	2
Apperson Inc 17315 Studebaker Rd Ste 211 **Fax Area Code:* 800 ■ *TF:* 800-473-6761 ■ *Web:* apperson.com	Cerritos	CA	90703	562-356-3333	321-8558*	110
APPI Energy 2013 Northwood Dr Ste 1 *TF:* 800-520-6685 ■ *Web:* www.appienergy.com	Salisbury	MD	21804	800-520-6685		194
Appian Corp 11955 Democracy Dr Ste 1700 *Web:* www.appian.com	Reston	VA	20190	703-442-8844		178-1
Appian Digital 3102 Church St *Web:* appiandigital.com	Burlington	NC	27215	336-538-4747		180
Applanix Corp 85 Leek Cresent *Web:* www.applanix.com	Richmond Hill	ON	L4B3B3	905-709-4600		387
Apple & Assoc PO Box 996 *TF:* 800-326-8490 ■ *Web:* www.appleassoc.com	Chapin	SC	29036	803-932-2000		260
Apple & Eve Inc 2 Seaview Blvd *TF:* 800-969-8018 ■ *Web:* www.appleandeve.com	Port Washington	NY	11050	516-621-1122		296-20
Apple Bank for Savings 122 E 42nd St *TF:* 800-824-0710 ■ *Web:* www.applebank.com	New York	NY	10168	914-902-2775		70
Apple Creek Banc Corp 3 W Main St PO Box 237 *Web:* applecreekbank.com	Apple Creek	OH	44606	330-698-2631		70
Apple Discount Drugs 404 N Fruitland Blvd *TF:* 800-424-8401 ■ *Web:* www.appledrugs.com	Salisbury	MD	21801	410-749-8401		23
Apple Farm Bakery 2015 Monterey St *TF:* 800-255-2040 ■ *Web:* www.applefarm.com	San Luis Obispo	CA	93401	805-544-2040		378
Apple Farm Service Inc 10120 W Versailles Rd *Web:* www.applefarmservice.com	Covington	OH	45318	937-526-4851		274
Apple Growth Partners 1540 W Market St *Web:* www.applegrowth.com	Akron	OH	44313	330-867-7350	867-8866	2
Apple Home Healthcare 123 W Madison St Ste 300 *Web:* applehomehealthcare.com	Chicago	IL	60602	773-871-8700		363
Apple Inc One Apple Park Way *NASDAQ: AAPL* ■ *TF:* 800-854-3680 ■ *Web:* www.apple.com	Cupertino	CA	95014	408-996-1010		173-2
Apple Jade 300 N Clippert St *Web:* www.applejadelansing.com	Lansing	MI	48912	517-332-1111		671
Apple Lane Animal Hospital PA 2909 Apple Ln *Web:* applelaneanimalhospital.com	Hutchinson	KS	67502	620-662-0515		794

	Phone	Fax	Class

Apple Machine & Supply Co
5900 Orange Ave ... Fort Pierce FL 34947 772-466-9353 466-4025 454
TF: 800-942-7640 ■ *Web:* applemachineandsupply.com

Apple Press Ltd 307 Commerce Dr ... Exton PA 19341 610-363-1776 627
Web: applepress.net

Apple Printing & Advertising Specialties Inc
5055 NW Tenth Terr ... Fort Lauderdale FL 33309 954-776-5691 7
Web: appleprinting.com

Apple Rehab 21 Waterville Rd ... Avon CT 06001 860-927-5368 450
Web: www.apple-rehab.com

Apple River Canyon State Park
8763 E Canyon Rd ... Apple River IL 61001 815-745-3302 565
Web: www2.illinois.gov

Apple Rock Adv & Promotion
7602 Business Park Dr ... Greensboro NC 27409 336-232-4800 4
Web: www.applerock.com

Apple Rubber Products Inc
310 Erie St ... Lancaster NY 14086 716-684-6560 684-8302 326
TF: 800-828-7745 ■ *Web:* www.applerubber.com

Apple Saddlery 1875 Innes Rd ... Ottawa ON K1B4C6 613-744-4040 711
TF: 800-867-8225 ■ *Web:* www.applesaddlery.com

Apple Spice 2235 S 1300 W ... Salt Lake City UT 84119 801-359-8821 363-2323 194
Web: www.applespice.com

Apple Tree Inn 9508 N Div St ... Spokane WA 99218 509-466-3020 379
TF: 800-323-5796 ■ *Web:* www.appletreeinnmotel.com

Apple Vacations Inc
101 NW Pt Blvd ... Elk Grove Village IL 60007 800-517-2000 640-1950* 771
**Fax Area Code:* 847 ■ *TF:* 800-517-2000 ■ *Web:* www.applevacations.com

Apple Valley Chamber of Commerce
16010 Apple Valley Rd ... Apple Valley CA 92307 760-242-2753 242-0303 139
Web: avchamber.org

Apple Valley Chamber of Commerce
14800 Galaxie Ave Ste 101 ... Apple Valley MN 55124 952-432-8422 139
TF: 800-301-9435 ■ *Web:* applevalleychamber.com

Apple Valley Medical Clinic Ltd
14655 Galaxie Ave ... Apple Valley MN 55124 952-432-6161 237
TF: 800-233-8504 ■ *Web:* www.applevalleymedicalcenter.com

Apple Valley Unified School District (AVUSD)
12555 Navajo Rd ... Apple Valley CA 92308 760-247-8001 247-8907 685
Web: www.avusd.org

Appleby & Wyman Insurance Agency Inc
152 Conant St ... Beverly MA 01915 800-928-2289 692-0728* 390
**Fax Area Code:* 978 ■ *TF:* 800-928-2289 ■ *Web:* applebywyman.com

Appleby College 540 Lakeshore Rd W ... Oakville ON L6K3P1 905-845-4681 845-9828 622
TF: 888-438-6646 ■ *Web:* www.appleby.on.ca

Appledore Marine Engineering LLC
600 State St Ste E ... Portsmouth NH 03801 603-766-1870 509-3820 261
Web: appledoremarine.com

Applegate Insulation Manufacturing Inc
1000 Highview Dr ... Webberville MI 48892 517-521-3545 521-3597 389
TF: 800-627-7536 ■ *Web:* www.applegateinsulation.com

AppleOne 327 W Broadway PO Box 29048 ... Glendale CA 91209 800-872-2677 265-5514* 721
**Fax Area Code:* 818 ■ *TF:* 800-872-2677 ■ *Web:* www.appleone.com

AppleOne Inc
170 University Ave Ste 401 ... Toronto ON M5H3B3 416-363-1663 193
Web: www.appleone.ca

Apples of Gold Center for Learning
604 Liberty St Ste 233 ... Pella IA 50219 641-620-1160 194
Web: www.applesofgold.biz

Appleseed 80 Broad St Room 611 ... New York NY 10004 212-964-9711 194
Web: www.appleseedinc.com

Appleton Group LLC, The
100 W Lawrence St Ste 306 ... Appleton WI 54911 920-993-7727 993-7779 401
TF: 866-993-7727 ■ *Web:* www.appletongrouponline.com

Appleton Manufacturing
1025 Breezewood Ln ... Neenah WI 54956 920-751-1555 751-1525 493
TF: 800-531-2002 ■ *Web:* www.appletonmfg.com

Appleton Medical Ctr 1818 N Meade St ... Appleton WI 54911 920-731-4101 738-6319 374-3
TF: 800-236-4101 ■ *Web:* www.thedacare.org

Appleton Papers Inc
825 E Wisconsin Ave PO Box 359 ... Appleton WI 54912 920-734-9841 552-1
Web: www.appvion.com

Appleton Partners Inc
1 Post Office Sq 6th Fl ... Boston MA 02109 617-338-0700 401
TF: 800-338-0745 ■ *Web:* www.appletonpartners.com

Appletree Press Inc
151 Good Counsel Dr Ste 125 ... Mankato MN 56001 507-345-4848 345-3002 637-2
Web: www.appletreepress.com

Applewood Books Inc 1 River Rd ... Carlisle MA 01741 800-277-5312 637-2
TF: 800 277 5312 ■ *Web:* www.applewoodbooks.com

Applewood Centers Inc
2525 E 22nd St ... Cleveland OH 44115 216-696-5800 696-6592 726
Web: www.applewoodcenters.org

Applewood Manor Inn
62 Cumberland Cir ... Asheville NC 28801 828-254-2244 254-0899 379
TF: 800-442-2197 ■ *Web:* www.applewoodmanor.com

Applewood Seed Co 5380 Vivian St ... Arvada CO 80002 303-431-7333 467-7886 694
Web: www.applewoodseed.com

Applewood the CS Mott Estate
1400 E Kearsley St ... Flint MI 48503 810-233-0170 233-7022 50-3
Web: www.ruthmottfoundation.org

Appliance Distributors of Louisiana
6721 Pecue Ln ... Baton Rouge LA 70817 225-344-6793 35
Web: www.adlferguson.com

Appliance Parts Center Inc
501 NE Ave ... Las Vegas NV 89101 702-384-8888 38
Web: www.appliancepartscenter.us

Appliance Parts Co 2001 SW Ave ... Las Vegas NV 89102 702-382-6532 246
TF: 800-293-2726 ■ *Web:* www.appliancepartscompany.com

Appliance Recycling Centers of America Inc
7400 Excelsior Blvd ... Minneapolis MN 55426 952-930-9000 660
NASDAQ: ARCI ■ *TF:* 800-452-8680 ■ *Web:* www.arcainc.com

Applicad Inc 5029 Industrial Rd ... Farmingdale NJ 07727 732-751-2555 625
Web: www.aci-applicad.com

Applicant Insight Ltd
5652 Meadowlane St ... New Port Richey FL 34652 800-771-7703 890-6454 635
TF: 800-771-7703 ■ *Web:* www.applicantinsight.com

ApplicantPro
3688 Campus Dr Ste 150 ... Eagle Mountain UT 84005 801-766-0174 225
Web: www.applicantpro.com

Application Consulting Group
1639 NJ-10 Ste 107 ... Parsippany NJ 07054 973-898-0012 898-6647 39
Web: www.acgi.com

Applied Aerodynamics Inc
2265 Valley Branch Cir ... Farmers Branch TX 75234 972-620-2100 22
Web: applied-aero.com

Applied Aerospace Concepts PLLC
10800 Lyndale Ave S Ste 275 ... Bloomington MN 55437 888-290-5878 261
TF: 888-290-5878 ■ *Web:* aacengineering.com

Applied Aerospace Structures Corp (AASC)
3437 S Airport Way PO Box 6189 ... Stockton CA 95206 209-982-0160 983-3375 504
Web: www.aascworld.com

Applied Analysis Inc
515 Groton Rd Ste 1101 ... Westford MA 01886 978-392-4500 261
Web: www.discover-aai.com

Applied Art and Technology
2430 106th St ... Des Moines IA 50322 515-331-7401 514
Web: www.appliedart.com

Applied Broadband Inc
2741 Mapleton Ave ... Boulder CO 80304 303-449-2033 196
TF: 866-993-0781 ■ *Web:* www.appliedbroadband.com

Applied Business Software Inc
2847 Gundry Ave ... Long Beach CA 90755 800-833-3343 426-5535* 177
**Fax Area Code:* 562 ■ *TF:* 800-833-3343 ■ *Web:* www.themortgageoffice.com

Applied Cad Knowledge Inc
18 Westech Dr ... Tyngsboro MA 01879 978-649-9800 649-3282 177
Web: www.appliedcad.com

Applied Capital Inc
3700 Rio Grande Blvd NW Ste 4 ... Albuquerque NM 87107 505-342-1840 342-2246 272
Web: www.appliedcapital.net

Applied Card Systems
50 Applied Card Way ... Glen Mills PA 19342 866-227-5627 840-2758* 215
**Fax Area Code:* 484 ■ *TF:* 866-227-5627 ■ *Web:* www.appliedcard.com

Applied Ceramics Inc 48630 Milmont Dr ... Fremont CA 94538 510-249-9700 249-9797 174
Web: www.appliedceramics.net

Applied Clinical Intelligence LLC
251 St Asaphs Rd 3 Bala Plaza W Ste 402 ... Bala Cynwyd PA 19004 484-429-7200 193
Web: www.aciclinical.com

Applied Control Engineering Inc
700 Creek View Rd ... Newark DE 19711 302-738-8800 261
Web: ace-net.com

Applied Cos 28020 Ave Stanford ... Valencia CA 91355 661-257-0090 257-3770 14
Web: www.appliedcompanies.net

Applied Cryogenics Inc 25 Adams St ... Burlington MA 01803 781-270-1180 695
Web: ctpcryogenics.com

Applied Data Resources Inc
1303 N Glenville Dr ... Richardson TX 75081 972-238-8111 658

Applied Diagnostics Inc
1140 Business Center Dr Ste 370 ... Houston TX 77043 713-271-4133 271-6885 415
TF: 855-239-8378 ■ *Web:* www.applieddiagnostics.com

Applied Dynamics International Inc
3800 Stone School Rd ... Ann Arbor MI 48108 734-973-1300 668-0012 178-2
Web: www.adi.com

Applied Educational Systems Inc
208 Bucky Dr ... Lititz PA 17543 800-220-2175 194
TF: 800-220-2175 ■ *Web:* www.aeseducation.com

Applied Energy Company Inc (AEC)
1205 Venture Ct Ste 100 ... Carrollton TX 75006 214-355-4200 355-4201 640
TF: 800-580-1171 ■ *Web:* www.appliedenergyco.com

Applied Energy Group Inc
1377 Motor Pkwy Ste 401 ... Islandia NY 11749 631-434-1414 434-1212 194
Web: appliedenergygroup.com

Applied Energy Solutions LLC
1 Technology Pl ... Caledonia NY 14423 585-538-4421 538-6345 74
TF: 800-836-2132 ■ *Web:* www.appliedenergysol.com

Applied Engineering Inc 2008 E Hwy 50 ... Yankton SD 57078 605-665-4425 665-1479 482
Web: www.appliedeng.com

Applied Fiber Inc PO Box 1339 ... Leesburg GA 31763 229-759-8301 544
TF: 800-226-5394 ■ *Web:* appliedfiber.com

Applied Financial Concepts Inc
4603 W Streetsboro Rd ... Richfield OH 44286 330-659-2234 390
Web: appliedfin.com

Applied Flow Technology Corp
2955 Professional Pl Ste 301 ... Colorado Springs CO 80904 719-686-1000 178-5
TF: 800-589-4943 ■ *Web:* www.aft.com

Applied Fusion Inc
1915 Republic Ave ... San Leandro CA 94577 510-351-8314 351-0692 811
TF: 800-704-1078 ■ *Web:* www.appliedfusioninc.com

Applied Graphics Inc 61 S Hunt Rd ... Amesbury MA 01913 978-241-5300 388-6259 481
Web: www.appliedgraphics.com

Applied Imaging Inc
5555 Glenwood Hills Pkwy SE ... Grand Rapids MI 49512 616-554-5200 554-6200 225
TF: 800-521-0983 ■ *Web:* www.appliedimaging.com

Applied Industrial Technologies Inc
1 Applied Plz Eulid Ave ... Cleveland OH 44115 216-267-2400 385
NYSE: AIT ■ *Web:* www.applied.com

Applied Innovations Corp
1001 Yamato Rd Ste 300W ... Boca Raton FL 33431 561-981-8196 423-0390 225
TF: 866-706-8691 ■ *Web:* www.appliedi.net

Applied Integrated Technologies Inc
7120 Samuel Morse Dr Ste 150 ... Columbia MD 21046 410-872-0022 872-0044 177
Web: www.ait-i.com

Applied Laboratories Inc
3240 N Indianapolis Rd PO Box 2127 ... Columbus IN 47202 812-372-2607 372-2631 418
Web: www.appliedlabs.com

Applied Laser Technologies
8404 Venture Cir ... Schofield WI 54476 715-359-3002 492
TF: 888-359-3002 ■ *Web:* www.aplaser.com

Applied Laser Technology Inc
14155 SW Brigadoon Ct ... Beaverton OR 97005 503-641-4400 641-6696 425
Web: www.altinc.com

Applied LNG
5716 Corsa Ave Ste 200 ... Westlake Village CA 91362 818-450-3650 536
TF: 800-609-1702 ■ *Web:* www.appliedlng.com

Name / Address	City	State	ZIP	Phone	Fax	Class
Applied Manufacturing Technologies 219 Kay Industrial Dr *Web:* www.appliedmfg.com	Orion	MI	48359	248-409-2100		256
Applied Marketing Research Inc 2040 W 31st St Ste 111 *TF:* 800-381-5599 ■ *Web:* www.appliedmr.com	Lawrence	KS	66046	800-381-5599		195
Applied Materials Inc 3050 Bowers Ave PO Box 58039 *NASDAQ: AMAT* ■ *Web:* www.appliedmaterials.com	Santa Clara	CA	95054	408-727-5555		695
Applied Math Modeling Inc 75 S Main St Ste 7 PMB144 **Fax Area Code:* 866 ■ *Web:* www.coolsimsoftware.com	Concord	NH	03301	603-369-3793	594-8864*	261
Applied Measurement Professionals Inc (AMP) 18000 W 105th St *TF:* 800-345-6559 ■ *Web:* www.goamp.com	Olathe	KS	66061	913-895-4600	895-4650	47
Applied Mechanical Systems Inc 5598 Wolf Creek Pk *Web:* www.appliedmechanicalsys.com	Dayton	OH	45426	937-854-3073		610
Applied Medical Technology Inc 8006 Katherine Blvd *TF:* 800-869-7382 ■ *Web:* www.appliedmedical.net	Brecksville	OH	44141	440-717-4000		475
Applied Membranes Inc 2450 Business Park Dr *TF:* 800-321-9321 ■ *Web:* www.appliedmembranes.com	Vista	CA	92081	760-727-3711	727-4427	612
Applied Merchandising Concepts LLC 15 Beechwood Ave *TF:* 800-378-7124 ■ *Web:* www.appliedmerchandising.com	New Rochelle	NY	10801	800-378-7124		393
Applied Minds LLC 2937 N Ontario St *Web:* appliedminds.com	Burbank	CA	91504	818-545-1400		180
Applied Molecular Evolution Inc (AME) 10300 Campus Point Dr Ste 200	San Diego	CA	92121	858-597-4990		85
Applied OLAP Inc 120 Holmes Ave NE Ste 405 *Web:* www.appliedolap.com	Huntsville	AL	35801	256-885-4371	885-4372	177
Applied Pavement Technology Inc 115 W Main St Ste 400 *Web:* appliedpavement.com	Urbana	IL	61801	217-398-3977		261
Applied Physics Laboratory University of Washington 1013 NE 40th St PO Box 355640 *Web:* www.apl.washington.edu	Seattle	WA	98105	206-543-1300	543-6785	668
Applied Physics Systems Inc 281 E Java Dr *Web:* www.appliedphysics.com	Sunnyvale	CA	94089	650-965-0500		256
Applied Plastics Company Inc 7320 S Sixth St *Web:* www.appliedplasticsinc.com	Oak Creek	WI	53154	414-764-2900		599
Applied Polymer Systems Inc 519 Industrial Dr **Fax Area Code:* 800 ■ *Web:* www.siltstop.com	Woodstock	GA	30189	678-200-9868	494-5298*	605-2
Applied Process Cooling Corp 555 Price Ave **Fax Area Code:* 707 ■ *TF:* 877-231-6406 ■ *Web:* www.apcco.net	Redwood City	CA	94063	650-595-0665	433-1310*	664
Applied Process Inc 12238 Newburgh Rd *Web:* www.appliedprocess.com	Livonia	MI	48150	734-464-2030	464-6314	484
Applied Research & Technology (ART) 215 Tremont St *Web:* artproaudio.com	Rochester	NY	14608	716-436-2720		52
Applied Research Associates Inc 8537 6 Forks Rd Ste 600 *Web:* www.ara.com	Raleigh	NC	27615	919-582-3300	582-3301	261
Applied Research Co, The 53 W Jackson Blvd Ste 240 *Web:* www.appliedresearch.com	Chicago	IL	60604	312-922-7882	922-7893	169
Applied Research Laboratory University Pk *Web:* www.arl.psu.edu	State College	PA	16802	814-865-6531		668
Applied Resources Inc 205 S Mckemy Ave *Web:* www.morschmachine.com	Chandler	AZ	85226	480-961-7673	961-7642	393
Applied Roller Technology Inc 8800 Statesville Rd *Web:* www.appliedroller.com	Charlotte	NC	28269	704-598-9500	597-5656	472
Applied Sciences Group Inc 2495 Main St Ste 407 *TF:* 877-274-9811 ■ *Web:* www.asgrp.com	Buffalo	NY	14214	716-626-5100	626-0629	180
Applied Sciences Laboratory Inc 13111 Brooks Dr Ste A *Web:* asl-ca.com	Baldwin Park	CA	91706	626-960-8800		261
Applied Separations Inc 930 Hamilton St *Web:* appliedseparations.com	Allentown	PA	18101	610-770-0900	740-5520	419
Applied Services & Information Systems Inc 209 Business Park Dr Ste 200	Virginia Beach	VA	23462	757-498-0100		225
Applied Skills & Knowledge PO Box 776 *Web:* www.appliedskills.com	Montville	NJ	07045	973-265-4086		195
Applied Software Inc 3915 National Dr Ste 200 *TF:* 888-624-8439 ■ *Web:* www.magview.com	Burtonsville	MD	20866	888-624-8439		177
Applied Statistics & Management Inc 32848 Wolf Store Rd Ste A *Web:* www.mdstaff.com	Temecula	CA	92592	951-699-4600	699-0374	809
Applied Systems Engineering Inc 1480 Hickory St Ste 106 *Web:* aseifl.com	Niceville	FL	32578	850-729-7550	729-3039	256
Applied Systems Inc 200 Applied Pkwy *TF:* 800-786-1362 ■ *Web:* www1.appliedsystems.com	University Park	IL	60484	708-534-5575	534-8016	178-11
Applied Technical Services Inc 6300 Merrill Creek Pkwy Ste A100 *Web:* www.atscorp.net	Everett	WA	98203	425-249-5555		625
Applied Technology & Management Inc 2201 NW 40th Ter **Fax Area Code:* 904 ■ *TF:* 800-275-6488 ■ *Web:* www.appliedtm.com	Gainesville	FL	32605	386-256-1477	249-8007*	261
Applied Textiles Inc 555 76th St SW *TF:* 866-891-6266 ■ *Web:* www.applied-textiles.com	Byron Center	MI	49315	866-891-6266		393

Name / Address	City	State	ZIP	Phone	Fax	Class
Applied Thermal Engineering Inc 7400 Brown Rd Ste 200 *Web:* www.ate-inc.com	Ostrander	OH	43061	740-666-4872	666-1145	261
Applied Thermal Systems 8401 73rd Ave N Ste 74 *TF:* 800-479-4783 ■ *Web:* www.apptherm.com	Brooklyn Park	MN	55428	763-535-5545		612
Applied Thin-Film Products Inc 3439 Edison Way *Web:* www.thinfilm.com	Fremont	CA	94538	510-661-4287		481
Applied Video Systems Inc 5816-D Shakespeare Rd *TF:* 800-325-2281 ■ *Web:* www.appliedvideosystems.com	Columbia	SC	29223	803-735-1120	735-1121	38
Applied Voice & Speech Technologies Inc 27042 Towne Centre Dr Ste 200 *TF:* 844-466-1668 ■ *Web:* www.avst.com	Foothill Ranch	CA	92610	949-699-2300		179
Appling County 69 Tippins St *Web:* www.baxley.org	Baxley	GA	31513	912-367-8100		338
Appling County School District 249 Blackshear Hwy *Web:* www.appling.k12.ga.us	Baxley	GA	31513	912-367-8600	367-1011	685
Applus Technologies Inc 120 S LaSalle Ste 1450 *Web:* www.applustech.com	Chicago	IL	60603	312-661-1100	661-0070	393
APPMA (American Pet Products Manufacturers Assn) 255 Glenville Rd *TF:* 800-452-1225 ■ *Web:* www.americanpetproducts.org	Greenwich	CT	06831	203-532-0000	532-0551	49-4
AppNeta Inc 285 Summer St 4th Fl *TF:* 800-664-4401 ■ *Web:* www.appneta.com	Boston	MA	02210	800-508-5233		809
Appomattox Court House National Historical Park Hwy 24 PO Box 218 *Web:* www.nps.gov	Appomattox	VA	24522	434-352-8987	352-8330	564
Appomattox Regional Library 209 E Cawson St *Web:* www.arls.org	Hopewell	VA	23860	804-458-6329		434-3
Appperfect Corp 20065 Stevens Creek Blvd Ste 2A *Web:* www.appperfect.com	Cupertino	CA	95014	408-252-4100		225
Appraisal Institute 200 W Madison Ste 1500 *TF:* 888-756-4624 ■ *Web:* www.appraisalinstitute.org	Chicago	IL	60606	888-756-4624		653
Appraisers Association of America (AAA) 386 Park Ave S Ste 2000 *Web:* www.appraisersassociation.org	New York	NY	10016	212-889-5404	889-5503	49-12
Apprentice School 3101 Washington Ave 1st Fl *Web:* www.as.edu	Newport News	VA	23607	757-380-3809		685
Apprimus Inc 291 Rt 22 E Ste 20 *Web:* www.apprimus.biz	Lebanon	NJ	08833	908-534-4669		809
Apprio Inc 425 Third St SW *Web:* www.apprioinc.com	Washington	DC	20024	202-684-8266	863-0396	180
Apprise Software Inc 3101 Emrick Blvd *Web:* www.apprise.com	Bethlehem	PA	18020	610-991-3900	991-3901	177
AppRiver LLC 1101 Gulf Breeze Pky Ste 200 *TF:* 866-223-4645 ■ *Web:* www.appriver.com	Gulf Breeze	FL	32561	850-932-5338	932-5339	178-1
Apprize Technology 10405 Sixth Ave N Ste 100 *Web:* apprizetechnology.com	Plymouth	MN	55441	952-746-3725		390
Approach Information Technology Inc 2027 Blue Heron Dr *Web:* www.approachit.com	Melbourne	FL	32940	321-223-1040	242-6760	196
Approved Color LLC 101 Adams Hill Rd *Web:* www.approvedcolor.com	Greenville	NH	03048	603-878-1470		802
AppsFlyer 100 1st St 25th Fl *Web:* www.appsflyer.com	San Francisco	CA	94105	415-636-9430		194
AppsHosting Inc 13772 Goldenwest St Ste 321 *TF:* 877-625-6610	Westminster	CA	92683	877-625-6610		387
AppTech Corp 2011 Palomar Airport Rd Ste 102 *TF:* 877-720-0022 ■ *Web:* www.apptechcorp.com	Carlsbad	CA	92011	760-707-5959		177
App-Techs Corp 505-B Willow Ln *Web:* www.app-techs.com	Lancaster	PA	17601	717-735-0848		174
Apptegy 425 W Capitol Ave Ste 800 *Web:* www.apptegy.com	Little Rock	AR	72201	501-613-0370		193
Apptio Inc 11100 NE 8th St Ste 600 *TF:* 866-470-0320 ■ *Web:* www.apptio.com	Bellevue	WA	98004	866-470-0320		178-1
Apptix Inc 13461 Sunrise Valley Dr Ste 300 *TF:* 800-962-9329 ■ *Web:* www.apptix.com	Herndon	VA	20171	703-890-2800	890-2801	177
Apptopia Inc 132 Lincoln St 3rd Fl *TF:* 855-277-8674 ■ *Web:* apptopia.com	Boston	MA	02111	855-277-8674		387
Apptricity Corp 5605 N Macarthur Blvd Ste 900 *Web:* www.apptricity.com	Irving	TX	75038	214-596-0601		177
Apptunix 11200 Manchaca Ste 304 *Web:* www.apptunix.com	Austin	TX	78748	415-670-9326		180
APPX Software Inc 11363 San Jose Blvd Ste 301 *TF:* 800-879-2779 ■ *Web:* www.appx.com	Jacksonville	FL	32223	904-880-5560	880-6635	178-1
AppZen Inc 6201 America Center Dr Ste 300 *Web:* www.appzen.com	San Jose	CA	95002	408-647-5253		178-1
APQC 123 N Post Oak Ln Ste 300 *TF:* 800-776-9676 ■ *Web:* www.apqc.org	Houston	TX	77024	713-681-4020	681-8578	49-12
APR Plastic Fabricating Inc 3685 Lima Rd *Web:* aprtanks.com	Fort Wayne	IN	46805	260-482-8523	483-5616	604
APRA (Automotive Parts Remanufacturers Assn) 4215 Lafayette Center Dr Ste 3 *TF:* 877-734-4827 ■ *Web:* www.apra.org	Chantilly	VA	20151	703-968-2772	968-2878	49-21
Apria Healthcare Group Inc 26220 Enterprise Ct *TF:* 800-277-4288 ■ *Web:* www.apria.com	Lake Forest	CA	92630	949-639-2000		363
Apricorn Inc 12191 Kirkham Rd *TF:* 800-458-5448 ■ *Web:* www.apricorn.com	Poway	CA	92064	858-513-2000	513-2020	173-8

Company	Address	City	State	ZIP	Phone	Fax	Class
Apricus Biosciences	11975 El Camino Real Ste 300 *NASDAQ: APRI* ■ *Web:* www.apricusbio.com	San Diego	CA	92130	858-222-8041	866-0482	85
Apriva Inc	8501 N Scottsdale Rd Ste 110 *TF:* 877-277-0728 ■ *Web:* www.apriva.com	Scottsdale	AZ	85253	480-421-1210		177
APRO (Association of Progressive Rental Organizations)	1504 Robin Hood Trl *TF:* 800-204-2776 ■ *Web:* www.rtohq.org	Austin	TX	78703	512-794-0095	794-0097	49-18
APS (Aerial Photography Services Inc)	2511 S Tryon St *Web:* www.aps-1.com	Charlotte	NC	28203	704-333-5143	333-4911	328
APS (Albuquerque Public Schools)	6400 Uptown Blvd NE *TF:* 866-563-9297 ■ *Web:* www.aps.edu	Albuquerque	NM	87110	505-880-3700	889-4883	685
APS (American Philatelic Society)	100 Match Factory Pl *Web:* www.stamps.org	Bellefonte	PA	16823	814-933-3803	933-6128	48-18
APS (American Philosophical Society)	104 S Fifth St *Web:* www.amphilsoc.org	Philadelphia	PA	19106	215-440-3400		48-11
APS (American Physical Society)	1 Physics Ellipse *TF:* 866-918-1164 ■ *Web:* www.aps.org	College Park	MD	20740	301-209-3200	209-0865	49-19
APS (Arizona Public Service Co)	400 N Fifth St PO Box 53999 *TF:* 800-253-9405 ■ *Web:* www.aps.com	Phoenix	AZ	85004	602-371-7171		787
APS Materials Inc	4011 Riverside Dr *Web:* apsmaterials.com	Dayton	OH	45405	937-278-6547	278-4352	481
APS Technology Inc	7 Laser Ln **Fax Area Code:* 203 ■ *Web:* www.aps-tech.com	Wallingford	CT	06492	860-613-4450	284-7428*	261
APSA (American Political Science Assn)	1527 New Hampshire Ave NW *Web:* www.apsanet.org	Washington	DC	20036	202-483-2512	483-2657	49-5
APSAA (American Psychoanalytic Assn)	309 E 49th St *Web:* www.apsa.org	New York	NY	10017	212-752-0450	593-0571	49-15
Apsara	71 Rue D'Auteuil *Web:* restaurantapsara.com	Quebec City	QC	G1R4C3	418-694-0232		671
APSC (American Pharmacy Services Corp)	102 Enterprise Dr *TF:* 800-928-2228 ■ *Web:* www.apscnet.com	Frankfort	KY	40601	502-695-8899		238
Apscreen Inc	PO Box 80639 **Fax Area Code:* 888 ■ *TF:* 800-277-2733 ■ *Web:* apscreen.com	Rancho Santa Margarita	CA	92688	949-646-4003	277-2733*	635
APSP (Association of Pool & Spa Professionals)	2111 Eisenhower Ave Ste 500 *TF:* 800-323-3996 ■ *Web:* www.apsp.org	Alexandria	VA	22314	703-838-0083	549-0493	49-4
APT (Association for Play Therapy)	401 Clovis Ave Ste 107 *Web:* www.a4pt.org	Clovis	CA	93612	559-298-3400	294-2129	49-15
APT (Alabama Public Television)	2112 11th Ave S Ste 400 *TF:* 800-239-5233 ■ *Web:* www.aptv.org	Birmingham	AL	35205	205-328-8756	251-2192	632
APT (American Public Television)	55 Summer St 4th Fl *Web:* www.aptonline.org	Boston	MA	02110	617-338-4455	338-5369	632
Apt Electronics Inc	241 N Crescent Way *Web:* www.aptelectronics.com	Anaheim	CA	92801	714-687-6760	687-6900	253
APT Foundation	1 Long Wharf Dr Ste 321 *TF:* 888-527-5646 ■ *Web:* aptfoundation.org	New Haven	CT	06511	203-781-4600		726
APT Research Inc	4950 Research Dr NW *Web:* www.apt-research.com	Huntsville	AL	35805	256-327-3373		256
APTA (American Polarity Therapy Assn)	PO Box 10942 *Web:* polaritytherapy.org	Parkville	MD	21234	336-574-1121	574-1151	48-17
APTA (American Physical Therapy Assn)	1111 N Fairfax St *TF:* 800-999-2782 ■ *Web:* www.apta.org	Alexandria	VA	22314	703-684-2782	706-8536	49-8
APTA (American Public Transportation Assn)	1666 K St NW Ste 1100 *Web:* www.apta.com	Washington	DC	20006	202-496-4800	496-4321	49-21
Aptara Inc	2901 Telestar Ct Ste 522 *Web:* www.aptaracorp.com	Falls Church	VA	22042	703-352-0001		781
AptarGroup Inc	475 W Terra Cotta Ave Ste E *NYSE: ATR* ■ *TF:* 800-401-1957 ■ *Web:* www.aptar.com	Crystal Lake	IL	60014	815-477-0424	477-0481	154
Aptech Computer Systems Inc	135 Delta Dr *TF:* 800-245-0720 ■ *Web:* www.aptech-inc.com	Pittsburgh	PA	15238	412-963-7440		178-11
Aptech Systems Inc	PO Box 618 *Web:* www.aptech.com	Higley	AZ	85236	360-886-7100		809
Apteryx Imaging Inc	313 S High St Ste 200 *Web:* apteryx.com	Akron	OH	44308	877-899-9036		582
APTI (Association for Psychological Type Intl)	PO Box 4538 *Web:* www.aptinternational.org	Itasca	IL	60143	518-320-7416		49-15
Aptify Corp	7900 Westpark Dr 5th Fl *TF:* 800-355-6738 ■ *Web:* www.aptify.com	Washington	DC	20006	202-223-2600		178-1
Aptima Inc	12 Gill St Ste 1400 *Web:* www.aptima.com	Woburn	MA	01801	781-935-3966		668
Aptium Oncology	4607 Lakeview Canyon Rd Ste 260 *Web:* www.aptiumoncology.com	Westlake Village	CA	91361	818-851-9455		352
Apto Solutions Inc	1910 MacArthur Blvd *Web:* www.aptosolutions.com	Atlanta	GA	30318	404-605-0992	605-0998	463
Aptos Chamber of Commerce	7605-A Old Dominion Ct *Web:* www.aptoschamber.com	Aptos	CA	95003	831-688-1467	688-6961	139
APTS (America's Public Television Stations)	2100 Crystal Dr Ste 700 *Web:* apts.org	Arlington	VA	22202	202-654-4200	654-4236	49-14
Apure Distribution LLC	5555 Biscayne Blvd 3rd Fl *Web:* apure-system.com	Miami	FL	33137	305-351-1025		362
APVA Preservation Virginia	204 W Franklin St *Web:* preservationvirginia.org	Richmond	VA	23220	804-648-1889	775-0802	48-13
APW Knoxseeman Warehouse Inc	1073 E Artesia Blvd *Web:* apwks.com	Carson	CA	90746	310-884-5000	604-5088	61
APWA (American Public Works Assn)	2345 Grand Blvd Ste 700 *TF:* 800-848-2792 ■ *Web:* www.apwa.net	Kansas City	MO	64108	816-472-6100	472-1610	49-7
APX Enclosures Inc	200 Oregon St *Web:* www.apx-enclosures.com	Mercersburg	PA	17236	717-328-9399		697
Apx Power Markets Inc	224 Airport Pkwy Ste 600 *Web:* apx.com	San Jose	CA	95110	408-517-2100		225
AQ Pharmaceuticals Inc	11555 Monarch St *Web:* www.aqpharmaceuticals.com	Garden Grove	CA	92841	714-903-1000		479
AQ Technologies	60 E Van Buren *Web:* www.aqtechnologies.com	Chicago	IL	60605	312-867-5400		317
AQHA (American Quarter Horse Assn)	1600 Quarter Horse Dr *TF:* 800-291-7323 ■ *Web:* www.aqha.com	Amarillo	TX	79104	806-376-4811	349-6411	48-3
AQL Decorating Company Inc	215 Bergen Blvd *Web:* www.aqldecorating.com	Fairview	NJ	07022	201-941-1610		88
AQSP (American Qualex Scientific Products)	920-A Calle Negocio *Web:* www.aqsp.com	San Clemente	CA	92673	949-492-8298		231
AQT Solutions Inc	860 Napa Valley Corporate Way Ste R *Web:* www.aqtsolutions.com	Napa	CA	94558	916-248-5720		809
Aqtis	1001 De Maisonneuve East Blvd Ste 900 *TF:* 888-647-0681 ■ *Web:* www.aqtis.qc.ca	Montreal	QC	H2L4P9	514-844-2113	844-3540	414
Aqua Air Industries Inc	639 Manhattan Blvd *Web:* www.aquaairind.com	Harvey	LA	70058	504-362-8124	362-3600	711
Aqua America Inc	762 W Lancaster Ave *NYSE: WTR* ■ *TF:* 877-987-2782 ■ *Web:* www.aquaamerica.com	Bryn Mawr	PA	19010	877-987-2782		787
Aqua Bamboo Waikiki	2425 Kuhio Ave *TF:* 855-747-0754 ■ *Web:* www.aquaaston.com	Honolulu	HI	96815	808-922-7777	943-8555	379
Aqua Bath Company Inc	921 Cherokee Ave *TF:* 800-232-2284 ■ *Web:* www.aquabath.com	Nashville	TN	37207	615-227-0017		610
Aqua Cal Inc	2737 24th St N *TF:* 800-786-7751 ■ *Web:* www.aquacal.com	Saint Petersburg	FL	33713	727-823-5642		14
Aqua Data Inc	95 5th Ave *TF:* 800-567-9003 ■ *Web:* www.aquadata.com	Pincourt	QC	J7W5K8	514-425-1010	425-3506	242
Aqua Finance Inc	1 Corporate Dr Ste 300 *TF:* 800-234-3663 ■ *Web:* www.aquafinance.com	Wausau	WI	54401	800-234-3663		194
Aqua Hotel	1530 Collins Ave *TF:* 800-227-1842 ■ *Web:* aquamiami.com	Miami Beach	FL	33139	305-538-4361		379
Aqua Pharmaceuticals LLC	707 Eagleview Blvd Ste 200 *Web:* www.aquapharm.com	Exton	PA	19341	610-644-7000	644-1985	238
Aqua Quest Publications Inc	486 Bayville Rd *TF:* 800-933-8989 ■ *Web:* www.aquaquest.com	Locust Valley	NY	11560	516-759-0476		637-2
Aqua Rehab Inc	2145 Rue Michelin *TF:* 800-661-3472 ■ *Web:* www.aquarehab.com	Laval	QC	H7L5B8	450-687-3472		242
Aqua Solutions Inc	6913 Hwy 225 **Fax Area Code:* 281 ■ *Web:* www.aquasolutions.org	Deer Park	TX	77536	800-256-2586	479-2790*	145
AQUA TERRA Consultants Inc	2685 Marine Way Ste 1314 *Web:* www.aquaterra.com	Mountain View	CA	94043	650-962-1864		256
Aqua Test Inc	28620 Maple Valley Black Diamond Rd SE **Fax Area Code:* 425 ■ *TF:* 800-221-3159 ■ *Web:* www.aquatestinc.com	Maple Valley	WA	98038	800-221-3159	413-9431*	743
Aqua-Aerobic Systems Inc	6306 N Alpine Rd *TF:* 800-940-5008 ■ *Web:* www.aqua-aerobic.com	Loves Park	IL	61111	815-654-2501	654-2508	806
Aquablast Inc	6339 E Greenway Rd Ste 102-180 *Web:* www.id-inside.com	Scottsdale	AZ	85254	602-690-9264	971-4474	762
Aqua-Chem Inc	3001 E Governor John Sevier Hwy *Web:* www.aqua-chem.com	Knoxville	TN	37914	865-544-2065		610
Aqua-Dyne Inc	701 S Persimmon St Ste 85 *TF:* 888-997-1483 ■ *Web:* www.aqua-dyne.com	Tomball	TX	77375	888-997-1483		641
Aquafine Corp	29010 Ave Paine *Web:* www.aquafineuv.com	Valencia	CA	91355	661-257-4770		427
Aquafor Beech Ltd	2600 Skymark Ave Bldg 6 Ste 202 *Web:* www.aquaforbeech.com	Mississauga	ON	L4W5B2	905-629-0099		261
Aquagrill Inc	210 Spring St *Web:* www.aquagrill.com	New York	NY	10012	212-274-0505	274-0587	671
Aqualaw Plc	6 S Fifth St *Web:* aqualaw.com	Richmond	VA	23219	804-716-9021		41
Aqua-Leisure Industries Inc	525 Bodwell Street Ext *TF:* 866-807-3998 ■ *Web:* www.aqualeisure.com	Avon	MA	02322	866-807-3998		710
Aqualogic Inc	30 Devine St *Web:* www.aqualogic.com	North Haven	CT	06473	203-248-8959	288-4308	806
Aqualung America Inc	2340 Cousteau Ct *TF:* 800-446-2671 ■ *Web:* www.aqualung.com	Vista	CA	92083	760-597-5000	597-4900	710
Aquarian Capital LLC	5345 Annabel Ln *Web:* aquariancapital.com	Plano	TX	75093	469-361-2177	361-6918	668
Aquarion Co	835 Main St *TF:* 800-732-9678 ■ *Web:* www.aquarionwater.com	Bridgeport	CT	06604	203-336-7662		787
Aquarium du Quebec	1675 des Hotels Ave *TF:* 866-659-5264 ■ *Web:* www.sepaq.com	Quebec City	QC	G1W4S3	418-659-5264	646-9238	40

	Phone	Fax	Class
Aquarium of the Bay The Embarcadero at Beach St Pier 39....... San Francisco CA 94133 *Web:* www.bayecotarium.org	415-623-5300	623-5324	40
Aquarium of the Pacific 100 Aquarium Way....................... Long Beach CA 90802 *Web:* www.aquariumofpacific.org	562-590-3100		40
Aquarius Casino Resort 1900 S Casino Dr.......................... Laughlin NV 89029 *TF:* 888-662-5825 ■ *Web:* www.aquariuscasinoresort.com	702-298-5111		133
Aquarius Imaging LLC 4846 N University Dr Ste 271................ Lauderhill FL 33351 *Web:* aquariusimaging.com	954-777-2729		177
Aquascape Environmental 605 Mauldin Dr .... Woodstock GA 30188 *Web:* aquascape.net	678-445-0077	445-0078	196
Aquatec Inc 1235 Shappert Dr.......... Machesney Park IL 61115 *Web:* www.aquatecinc.com	815-654-1500	654-0038	358
Aquatech Consultancy Inc 1 Commercial Blvd Ste 201 .... Novato CA 94949 *Web:* noleak.com	415-884-2121		194
Aquaterra Technologies Inc PO Box 774 .... West Chester PA 19381 *Web:* aquaterra-tech.com	610-431-5733	431-5734	196
Aquatherm Industries Inc 1940 Rutgers University Blvd................ Lakewood NJ 08701 **Fax Area Code:* 732 ■ *TF:* 800-535-6307 ■ *Web:* www.warmwater.com	800-535-6307	905-9899*	357
Aquatic Development Group Inc 13 Green Mountain Dr .... Cohoes NY 12047 *Web:* www.aquaticgroup.com	518-783-0038		697
Aquatic Informatics Inc 1111 W Georgia St Ste 2400 .... Vancouver BC V6E4M3 *TF:* 877-870-2782 ■ *Web:* aquaticinformatics.com	604-873-2782		192
Aquatrol Inc 600 E North St PO Box 8012.......... Elburn IL 60119 *TF:* 800-323-0688 ■ *Web:* www.aquatrol.com	630-365-5400	365-5434	237
Aquaveo LLC 3210 N Canyon Rd Ste 300 .... Provo UT 84604 *Web:* www.aquaveo.com	801-691-5528		256
Aquavit 65 E 55th St......................... New York NY 10022 *Web:* www.aquavit.org	212-307-7311		671
Aquent LLC 711 Boylston St..................... Boston MA 02116 *TF:* 855-767-6333 ■ *Web:* aquent.com	617-535-5000		721
Aqueos Corp 101 Millstone Rd .... Broussard LA 70518 *Web:* www.aqueossubsea.com	337-714-0033		539
Aquestive Therapeutics 30 Technology Dr............................ Warren NJ 07059 *Web:* www.aquestive.com	908-941-1900		231
Aqui Cal-Mex Grill 1145 Lincoln Ave........... San Jose CA 95125 *Web:* www.aquicalmex.com	408-995-0381		671
Aquila Commercial LLC 1717 W Sixth St .... Austin TX 78703 *Web:* aquilacommercial.com	512-684-3800		652
Aquila Group of Funds 120 W 45th St Ste 3600..................... New York NY 10036 *TF:* 800-437-1020 ■ *Web:* aquilafunds.com	212-697-6666		528
Aquila Sedco Drilling Company Lp 2525 Kell Blvd Ste 405.................. Wichita Falls TX 76308 *Web:* aquilasedcodrilling.com	940-761-3153	761-4827	540
Aquinas & More Catholic Goods Inc 4727 N Academy Blvd Ste A........... Colorado Springs CO 80918 *TF:* 866-428-2820 ■ *Web:* www.aquinasandmore.com	719-495-7493	495-7505	45
Aquinas College 4210 Harding Rd .... Nashville TN 37205 *TF:* 800-649-9956 ■ *Web:* www.aquinascollege.edu	615-297-7545		166
Aquinas Institute of Theology 23 S Spring Ave .... Saint Louis MO 63108 *TF:* 800-977-3869 ■ *Web:* www.ai.edu	314-256-8800	256-8888	167-3
Aquion Inc 101 S Gary Ave...................... Roselle IL 60172 *Web:* aquion.com	847-725-3000		806
Aquionics Inc 21 Kenton Lands Rd .... Erlanger KY 41018 *Web:* www.aquionics.com	859-341-0710		427
Aquitaine 569 Tremont St....................... Boston MA 02118 *Web:* www.aquitaineboston.com	617-424-8577		671
Aqumin LLC 1415 S Voss Ste 110 .... Houston TX 77057 *Web:* www.aquminmedical.com	713-781-2121		809
Aqwest 8276 Eagle Rd .... Larkspur CO 80118 *Web:* www.aqwest.com	303-681-0456		261
AR Editions Inc 1600 Aspen Cmns Ste 100.................. Middleton WI 53562 *TF:* 800-736-0070 ■ *Web:* www.areditions.com	608-836-9000		523
AR Medicom Inc 1200 55th Ave .... Lachine QC H8T3J8 *Web:* www.medicom.com	514-636-6262		475
AR RF/Microwave Instumentation 160 Schoolhouse Rd .... Souderton PA 18964 **Fax Area Code:* 866 ■ *TF:* 800-933-8181 ■ *Web:* www.arworld.us	215-723-8181	859-0582*	647
AR Systems 297 E Harrison St.................. Corona CA 92879 *Web:* www.automatedretailingsystems.com	951-465-7700		180
AR Thomson Group 3420 189 St................. Surrey BC V3Z1A7 *Web:* arthomson.com	604-507-6050	507-6098	326
AR Wilfley & Sons Inc 5870 E 56th Ave...................... Commerce City CO 80022 *TF:* 800-525-9930 ■ *Web:* www.wilfley.com	303-779-1777	779-1277	641
ARA (American Rental Assn) 1900 19th St........ Moline IL 61265 *TF:* 800-334-2177 ■ *Web:* www.ararental.org	309-764-2475	764-1533	49-4
ARA (Agricultural Retailers Assn) 1156 15th St NW Ste 500.................. Washington DC 20005 *TF:* 800-535-6272 ■ *Web:* www.aradc.org	202-457-0825	457-0864	48-2
ARA (Awards & Personalization Assn) 8735 W Higgins Rd Ste 300.................. Chicago IL 60631 *TF:* 800-344-2148 ■ *Web:* www.awardspersonalization.org	847-375-4800	375-6480	49-4
ARA (Automotive Recyclers Assn) 9113 Church St .... Manassas VA 20110 *TF:* 888-385-1005 ■ *Web:* www.a-r-a.org	571-208-0428	208-0430	49-21
Arab American Institute (AAI) 1600 K St NW Ste 601 .... Washington DC 20006 *Web:* www.aaiusa.org	202-429-9210	429-9214	48-8
Arabel Inc 16301 NW 49th Ave .... Hialeah FL 33014 *TF:* 800-759-5959 ■ *Web:* www.arabel.com	305-623-8302	624-0714	191-2
Arabia Steamboat Museum 400 Grand Blvd.......................... Kansas City MO 64106 *Web:* www.1856.com	816-471-1856		520
Arabian Horse Assn (AHA) 10805 E Bethany Dr .... Aurora CO 80014 *Web:* www.arabianhorses.org	303-696-4500	696-4599	48-3
Arabian Horse World 1316 Tamson Dr Ste 101 .... Cambria CA 93428 *TF:* 800-955-9423 ■ *Web:* arabianhorseworld.com	805-771-2300		457-14
ArabMedicare.com PO Box 12547 .... Research Triangle Park NC 27709 *Web:* www.arabmedicare.com	919-781-5838	781-3166	393
Arachnid Inc 6212 Material Ave.............. Loves Park IL 61111 *TF:* 800-435-8319 ■ *Web:* www.bullshooter.com	815-654-0212	654-0447	322
Aragon Elastomers LLC 740 S Pierce Ave............................ Louisville CO 80027 *Web:* www.aragonelastomers.com	303-666-9519		601
Aram a Kaz Co, The 365 Silas Deane Hwy .... Wethersfield CT 06109 *TF:* 800-969-2251 ■ *Web:* aramkaz.com	860-529-6900		393
Aramaic Broadcasting Network PO Box 724 .... Walled Lake MI 48390 *Web:* www.abnsat.com	248-416-1300	416-1301	647
ARAMARK Corp 1101 Market St .... Philadelphia PA 19107 *TF:* 800-388-3300 ■ *Web:* www.aramark.com	215-238-3000		185
ARAMARK Uniform & Career Apparel LLC 2860 Rudder Rd .... Memphis TN 38118 *TF:* 800-272-6275 ■ *Web:* www.aramarkuniform.com	800-272-6275		271
Aramsco Inc 1480 Grandview Ave............. Paulsboro NJ 08066 *TF:* 800-767-6933 ■ *Web:* www.aramsco.com	856-686-7700		146
Aranda Tooling Inc 13950 Yorba Ave.............. Chino CA 91710 *Web:* www.arandatooling.com	714-379-6565	379-6570	488
Arandell Inc N82 W13118 Leon Rd .... Menomonee Falls WI 53051 *TF:* 800-558-8724 ■ *Web:* www.arandell.com	800-558-8724		627
Aransas County 301 N Live Oak St............. Rockport TX 78382 *Web:* www.aransascounty.org	361-790-0122	790-0119	338
Arant & Broesder LLC 312 S Ivy St .... Medford OR 97501 *Web:* broesderlaw.com	541-773-1222		41
Arapahoe Community College 5900 S Santa Fe Dr........................... Littleton CO 80160 *Web:* www.arapahoe.edu	303-797-0100	797-5970	162
Arapahoe Philharmonic 5601 S Broadway Ste 345..................... Littleton CO 80121 *Web:* www.arapahoe-phil.org	303-781-1892		573-3
Ararat Rock Products Co 525 Quarry Rd .... Mount Airy NC 27030 *Web:* www.surrybusiness.com	336-786-4693		503-5
Arata Expositions Inc 15928 Tournament Dr.................... Gaithersburg MD 20877 *Web:* www.arataexpo.com	301-921-0800	990-1717	184
Arazoza Brothers Corp 15901 SW 242nd St....................... Homestead FL 33031 *TF:* 800-238-1510 ■ *Web:* www.arazozabrothers.com	305-246-3223		293
ARB Inc 26000 Commercentre Dr............. Lake Forest CA 92630 *Web:* www.primoriscorp.com	949-598-9242		188-9
ARBA (American Rabbit Breeders Assn) PO Box 5667 .... Bloomington IL 61702 *TF:* 800-753-9448 ■ *Web:* arba.net	309-664-7500	664-0941	48-3
Arbco Industries Inc 2040 Borland Rd............ Export PA 15632 *Web:* www.arbcowheels.com	724-327-6300		596
Arbec Forest Products Inc 8000 Langelier Blvd Ste 210.............. Saint-Leonard QC H1P3K2 *Web:* www.arbec.ca	514-327-3350		683
Arbee Associates Inc 1531 S Washington Ave.................... Piscataway NJ 08854 *Web:* www.arbee.net	732-424-3900	752-6034	320
Arbella Insuranc 1100 Crown Colony Dr PO Box 699103........... Quincy MA 02269 *TF:* 800-972-5348 ■ *Web:* www.arbella.com	617-328-2800	328-2970	391-4
Arben Group LLC 175 Marble Ave........... Pleasantville NY 10570 *Web:* arbengroup.com	914-741-5459	741-2923	189-14
Arbill PO Box 820542 .... Philadelphia PA 19154 *TF:* 800-523-5367 ■ *Web:* www.arbill.com	800-523-5367	426-5808	679
Arbitech LLC 15330 Barranca Pkwy................ Irvine CA 92618 *Web:* www.arbitech.com	949-376-6650		174
Arbitron Inc 9705 Patuxent Woods Dr........... Columbia MD 21046 *NYSE: ARB* ■ *TF:* 800-543-7300 ■ *Web:* www.arbitron.com	410-312-8000		466
Arbon Steel & Service Company Inc 2355 Bond St .... University Park IL 60466	708-534-6800	534-6826	492
Arbonne Intl 9400 Jeronimo Rd.................. Irvine CA 92618 *TF:* 800-886-5974 ■ *Web:* www.arbonne.com	800-886-5974		76
Arbor Acres 1240 Arbor Rd .... Winston-Salem NC 27104 *TF:* 866-658-2724 ■ *Web:* www.arboracres.org	336-724-7921		672
Arbor Associates Inc 6 Pleasant St Ste 409 .... Malden MA 02148 *TF:* 888-272-6767 ■ *Web:* arborstaffing.com	617-227-8829		260
Arbor Brewing Co 114 E Washington St .... Ann Arbor MI 48104 *Web:* arborbrewing.com	734-213-1393		671
Arbor Capital Management Inc 1400 W Benson Blvd Ste 575................ Anchorage AK 99503 *Web:* www.acminc.com	907-222-7581		401
Arbor Care Piekarski & Sons Inc 17900 Harper Ave........................... Lansing IL 60438 *Web:* piekarskitree.com	708-895-8891		422
Arbor Centers for Eyecare 2640 W 183rd St .... Homewood IL 60430 *TF:* 866-798-6633 ■ *Web:* www.arboreyecare.com	708-798-6633		237
Arbor Crest Wine Cellars 4705 N Fruithill Rd.......................... Spokane WA 99217 *Web:* www.arborcrest.com	509-927-9463	927-0574	50-7
Arbor Hospice & Home Care 2366 Oak Vly Dr.......................... Ann Arbor MI 48103 *TF:* 888-992-2273 ■ *Web:* www.arborhospice.org	734-662-5999		371
Arbor House Publishing 47 Steinwehr Ave .... Gettysburg PA 17325 *Web:* arborhousepublishing.com	717-338-0664		637-2
Arbor Lodge State Historical Park 2600 Arbor Ave......................... Nebraska City NE 68410 *TF:* 800-546-5433 ■ *Web:* www.arbordayfarm.org	402-873-7222		565

Name	Address	City	State	ZIP	Phone	Fax	Class	Additional
Arbor Masters Tree & Landscape Inc	8250 Cole Pkwy	Shawnee	KS	66227	913-441-8888		776	*Web:* arbormasters.com
Arbor Material Handling Inc	2465 Maryland Rd	Willow Grove	PA	19090	215-657-2700	657-5188	385	*TF:* 800-934-6568 ■ *Web:* www.arbor-inc.com
Arbor Partners LLC	130 S First St	Ann Arbor	MI	48104	734-668-9000	669-4195	792	*Web:* www.arborpartners.com
Arbor Realty Trust Inc	333 Earle Ovington Blvd Ste 900	Uniondale	NY	11553	800-272-6710		654	*NYSE: ABR* ■ *TF:* 800-272-6710 ■ *Web:* arbor.com
Arbor Research & Trading LLC	1000 Hart Rd Ste 260	Barrington	IL	60010	800-606-1872		668	*TF:* 800-606-1872 ■ *Web:* www.arborresearch.com
Arbor Rose Senior Care	6063 E Arbor Ave	Mesa	AZ	85206	480-630-3647		793	*Web:* www.milestoneretirement.com
Arbor Solutions Inc	1345 Monroe Ave NW Ste 309	Grand Rapids	MI	49505	616-451-2500		196	*Web:* arbsol.com
Arbor Tree Surgery Inc	802 Paso Robles St	Paso Robles	CA	93446	805-239-1239		776	*TF:* 800-247-8733 ■ *Web:* www.arbortree.com
Arborcare/Arborscape Inc	772 West 1355 South	Salt Lake City	UT	84104	801-972-8733		302	*Web:* arborcare-arborscape.com
Arborcrest Gardens Inc	205 Evergreen Ln	Boone	NC	28607	828-265-4873		40	*Web:* www.arborcrestgardens.org
Arboretum & Botanic Garden	1156 High St	Santa Cruz	CA	95064	831-502-2998	427-1524	97	*Web:* arboretum.ucsc.edu
Arboretum at California State University Fresno	2351 E Barstow Ave	Fresno	CA	93740	559-278-7422	278-7698	97	*Web:* www.fresnostate.edu
Arboretum at Flagstaff	4001 S Woody Mtn Rd	Flagstaff	AZ	86001	928-774-1442		97	*Web:* www.thearb.org
Arboretum at Penn State	336 Forest Resources Bldg	University Park	PA	16802	814-865-9118	865-3725	97	*Web:* arboretum.psu.edu
Arboretum of the Barnes Foundation	50 Lapsley Ln	Merion Station	PA	19066	215-278-7350		97	*Web:* www.barnesfoundation.org
Arboretum Ventures	303 Detroit St	Ann Arbor	MI	48104	734-998-3688		792	*Web:* www.arboretumvc.com
ArborOakland Group	4303 Normandy Ct	Royal Oak	MI	48073	248-549-0150	549-5270	627	*TF:* 800-886-5661 ■ *Web:* www.arboroakland.com
Arbors of Hop Brook	403 W Center St	Manchester	CT	06040	860-647-9343		672	*Web:* www.arborsct.com
Arborwell Inc	2337 American Ave	Hayward	CA	94545	888-969-8733	881-5208*	776	**Fax Area Code:* 510 ■ *TF:* 888-969-8733 ■ *Web:* arborwell.com
Arbour Counseling Services	116 Summer St	Haverhill	MA	01830	978-373-7010		48-17	*Web:* www.arbourhealth.com
Arbutus Park Retirement Community	207 Ottawa St	Johnstown	PA	15904	814-266-8621		672	*Web:* arbutusparkmanor.com
Arbutus Software Inc	6450 Roberts St	Burnaby	BC	V5G4E1	604-437-7873		179	*TF:* 877-333-6336 ■ *Web:* www.arbutussoftware.com
Arby's Restaurant Group Inc	1155 Perimeter Ctr W 12th Fl	Atlanta	GA	30338	678-514-4100	514-5346	670	*Web:* arbys.com
ARC (Association Resource Ctr)	950 Glenn Dr Ste 150	Folsom	CA	95630	916-932-2200	932-2209	47	*Web:* 4arc.aaiden.com
ARC (American Radiolabeled Chemicals Inc)	101 ARC Dr	Saint Louis	MO	63146	314-991-4545	991-4692	145	*TF:* 800-331-6661 ■ *Web:* www.arcincusa.com
ARC (ARC Document Solutions)	ARC 1981 N Broadway Ste 385	Walnut Creek	CA	94596	925-405-0420		781	*NYSE: ARC* ■ *Web:* www.e-arc.com
ARC Aspicio LLC	1725 I St NW Ste 300	Washington	DC	20006	703-465-2060		196	*Web:* www.arcaspicio.com
ARC Automotive Inc	1729 Midpark Rd Ste 100	Knoxville	TN	37921	865-544-8426		60	*Web:* www.arcautomotive.com
ARC Baltimore, The	7215 York Rd	Baltimore	MD	21212	410-296-2272		49-15	*Web:* www.thearcbaltimore.org
ARC Document Solutions (ARC)	ARC 1981 N Broadway Ste 385	Walnut Creek	CA	94596	925-405-0420		781	*NYSE: ARC* ■ *Web:* www.e-arc.com
ARC Equipment Inc	139 S Weber Dr	Chandler	AZ	85226	480-961-0051	961-0551	676	*Web:* www.arcequip.com
ARC Human Services Inc	470 Johnson Rd Meadow Pointe Bldg Ste 200	Washington	PA	15301	724-745-3010	206-9584	793	*Web:* www.archumanservices.org
ARC Industries Inc	2780 Airport Dr	Columbus	OH	43219	614-479-2500	479-2501	721	*TF:* 800-734-7007 ■ *Web:* arcind.com
ARC Informatique Inc	1776 Rue Mitis	Chicoutimi	QC	G7K1H4	418-545-9224		180	*TF:* 877-880-9224 ■ *Web:* www.arcinformatique.com
ARC Machines Inc	10500 Orbital Way	Pacoima	CA	91331	818-896-9556	890-3724	811	*Web:* www.arcmachines.com
ARC Medical Devices Inc	8-3071 No 5 Rd	Richmond	BC	V6X2T4	604-222-9577		794	*Web:* www.arcmedicaldevices.com
ARC New York, The	29 British American Blvd 2nd Fl	Latham	NY	12110	518-439-8311		428	*Web:* www.nysarc.org
ARC of Essex County	123 Naylon Ave	Livingston	NJ	07039	973-535-1181		49-19	*Web:* www.arcessex.org
ARC of Stanly County, The	350 Pee Dee Ave Ste A	Albemarle	NC	28001	704-986-1500		49-15	*TF:* 800-230-7525 ■ *Web:* www.monarchnc.org
ARC of the US	1010 Wayne Ave Ste 650	Silver Spring	MD	20910	301-565-3842	565-3843	48-17	*TF:* 800-433-5255 ■ *Web:* www.thearc.org
ARC Pressure Data Inc	3718 Warschun Rd	Aubrey	TX	76227	940-565-8090	565-9180	539	*Web:* www.arcpressure.com
ARC Resources Ltd	308 Fourth Ave SW Ste 1200	Calgary	AB	T2P0H7	403-503-8600		675	*TSX: ARX* ■ *TF:* 888-272-4900 ■ *Web:* www.arcresources.com
ARC San Joaquin Inc	41 W Yokuts Ave	Stockton	CA	95207	209-955-1625		260	*TF:* 800-847-3030 ■ *Web:* www.thearcsj.org
ARC Tech Inc	14100 Park Meadow Dr	Chantilly	VA	20151	703-222-0820		268	*Web:* www.arctech.com
ARC Technologies	185 Vallecitos De Oro	San Marcos	CA	92069	760-744-7400		454	*Web:* arc-tech.com
ARC Technology Solutions LLC	165 Ledge St	Nashua	NH	03060	603-883-3027	883-3239	295	*Web:* www.arcserv.com
ARC the Hotel	824 New Hampshire Ave NW	Washington	DC	20037	202-337-6620		379	*Web:* arcthehoteldc.com
ARC Trust	1401 Broad St	Clifton	NJ	07013	973-249-1000	249-1001	655	*Web:* arctrust.com
ARC Worldwide	35 W Wacker Dr	Chicago	IL	60601	312-220-5959	220-6212	7	*Web:* arcww.com
Arca Biopharma	11080 CirPoint Rd Ste 140	Westminster	CO	80020	720-940-2200		668	*NASDAQ: ABIO* ■ *Web:* arcabio.com
Arcade Partners LLC	62 La Salle Rd Ste 304	West Hartford	CT	06107	860-236-6320		401	*Web:* www.arcadepartners.com
Arcade Printing Co	8489 Delport Dr	Saint Louis	MO	63114	314-427-4301	427-2233	627	*Web:* arcadestl.com
Arcade Publishing Inc	307 W 36th St 11th Fl	New York	NY	10018	212-643-6816	643-6819	637-2	*Web:* www.arcadepub.com
Arcadia	100 W San Carlos St	San Jose	CA	95113	408-278-4555		671	*Web:* www.michaelmina.net
Arcadia Academy of Music	205 Marycroft Ave Unit 6	Woodbridge	ON	L4L5X8	905-851-8631		167-3	*Web:* www.arcadiamusicacademy.com
Arcadia Association of Realtors Inc	601 S First Ave	Arcadia	CA	91006	626-446-2115		652	*Web:* theaar.com
Arcadia Biosciences	202 Cousteau Pl Ste 105	Davis	CA	95618	530-756-7077	756-7027	743	*Web:* arcadiabio.com
Arcadia Chamber of Commerce	388 W Huntington Dr	Arcadia	CA	91007	626-447-2159	445-0273	139	*Web:* arcadiacachamber.org
Arcadia Content	6454 Quinpool Rd	Halifax	NS	B3L1A9	902-446-3414		514	*Web:* arcadiacontent.com
Arcadia Convalescent Hospital Inc	1601 S Baldwin Ave	Arcadia	CA	91007	626-445-2170		371	
Arcadia Data Inc	999 Baker Way Ste 120	San Mateo	CA	94404	415-680-3535		396	*Web:* www.arcadiadata.com
Arcadia Farms Cafe	7014 E First Ave	Scottsdale	AZ	85251	480-941-5665		671	*Web:* www.arcadiafarmscafe.com
Arcadia Manufacturing Group Inc	80 Cohoes Ave	Green Island	NY	12183	518-434-6213		480	*Web:* arcadiamfg.com
Arcadia Retirement Residence	1434 Punahou St	Honolulu	HI	96822	808-941-0941	949-4965	672	*Web:* www.arcadia.org
Arcadia Solutions LLC	20 Blanchard Rd Unit 10	Burlington	MA	01803	781-202-3600		196	*Web:* www.arcadia.io
Arcadia University	450 S Easton Rd	Glenside	PA	19038	215-572-2900	881-8767	166	*TF:* 877-272-2342 ■ *Web:* www.arcadia.edu
Arcadis	630 Plaza Dr Ste 100	Highlands Ranch	CO	80129	720-344-3500		192	*Web:* www.arcadis.com
Arcady Bay Partners LLC	40417 Aldie Springs Dr	Aldie	VA	20105	703-359-4773		691	*Web:* www.arcadybay.com
ArcaMax Publishing Inc	729 Thimble Shoals Blvd Ste 1-B	Newport News	VA	23606	757-596-9730	596-9731	637-10	*Web:* www.arcamax.com
Arcamed Inc	5101 Decatur Blvd Ste A	Indianapolis	IN	46241	317-910-1822	375-7717	475	*TF:* 877-545-6622 ■ *Web:* arcamed.com
Arcane Technologies Inc	918 Monticello Ave	Charlottesville	VA	22902	434-979-7979		180	*Web:* www.arcanetech.com
ARCAT Inc	173 Sherman St	Fairfield	CT	06824	203-335-3700	335-1075	197	*Web:* www.arcat.com
Arcata Associates Inc	2588 Fire Mesa St	Las Vegas	NV	89128	702-642-9500	968-2237	261	*Web:* www.arcataassoc.com
ArcBest (ABC)	3801 Old Greenwood Rd	Fort Smith	AR	72903	800-610-5544	785-6124*	780	*NASDAQ: ARCB* ■ **Fax Area Code:* 479 ■ *TF:* 800-610-5544 ■ *Web:* arcb.com
Arcca Inc	2288 Second St Pk	Penns Park	PA	18943	215-598-9750		256	*Web:* arcca.com
Arccon Construction Inc	543 W Rich St	Columbus	OH	43215	614-298-0430		261	*Web:* arcconconstruction.com
ArcelorMittal Burns Harbor LLC	250 W US Hwy 12	Burns Harbor	IN	46304	219-787-2120		492	*Web:* corporate.arcelormittal.com
ArcelorMittal Dofasco Library Resource Ctr	1330 Burlington St E PO Box 2460	Hamilton	ON	L8N3J5	905-548-7200		434-3	*TF:* 800-363-2726 ■ *Web:* www.dofasco.arcelormittal.com
Arcet Equipment Company Inc	1700 Chamberlayne Ave	Richmond	VA	23222	800-388-0302		201	*TF:* 800-388-0302 ■ *Web:* arc3gases.com
Arch Chemicals Inc	1200 Old Lower River Rd PO Box 800	Charleston	TN	37310	423-780-2724	780-2330	145	*NYSE: ARJ* ■ *TF:* 800-638-8174 ■ *Web:* www.lonza.com

Name / Address	City	State	ZIP	Phone	Fax	Class
Arch Communications Inc 1327 Hampton Ave *Web:* archcom.net	Saint Louis	MO	63139	314-645-8000		393
Arch Crown Tags Inc 460 Hillside Ave *TF:* 800-526-8353 ■ *Web:* www.archcrown.com	Hillside	NJ	07205	973-731-6300	731-2228	413
ARCH Cutting Tools - KEO (Plant I) 25040 Easy St *TF:* 888-390-2050 ■ *Web:* www.archcuttingtools.com	Warren	MI	48090	586-771-2050	771-2062	493
ARCH Design, Artwork & Framing Inc 1188 Walters Way Ln *Web:* arch-design.com	Saint Louis	MO	63132	314-447-3300		45
Arch Insurance Group Inc 1 Liberty Plz 53rd Fl *TF:* 866-993-9978 ■ *Web:* www.archcapgroup.com	New York	NY	10006	212-651-6500	651-6499	391-2
Arch Language Network Inc 125 Little Canada Rd W Ste 200 *Web:* www.archlanguage.com	Little Canada	MN	55117	651-789-7897	789-7898	768
ARCH Medical and Aerospace 2600 S Telegraph Rd Ste 180 *Web:* archglobalprecision.com	Bloomfield Hills	MI	48302	763-533-2261	533-1735	454
ARCH Street Meeting House 320 Arch St *Web:* www.historicasmh.org	Philadelphia	PA	19106	215-625-0627		50-1
ARCH Venture Partners 8755 W Higgins Rd Ste 1025 *Web:* www.archventure.com	Chicago	IL	60631	773-380-6600	380-6606	792
Archadeck 2924 Emerywood Pkwy Ste 101 **Fax Area Code:* 804 ■ *TF:* 888-687-3325 ■ *Web:* www.archadeck.com	Richmond	VA	23294	888-687-3325	358-1878*	189-2
Archaeological Consulting Services Ltd (ACS) 424 W Broadway Rd *Web:* www.acstempe.com	Tempe	AZ	85282	480-894-5477	894-5478	727
Archaeological Institute of America (AIA) 44 Beacon St *TF:* 877-524-6300 ■ *Web:* www.archaeological.org	Boston	MA	02108	617-353-9361	353-6550	48-11
Archaeology Magazine 36-36 33rd St *TF:* 877-275-9782 ■ *Web:* www.archaeology.org	Long Island City	NY	11106	718-472-3050	472-3051	457-19
Archangel Systems Inc 1635 Pumphrey Ave *Web:* www.archangel.com	Auburn	AL	36832	334-826-8008	826-8038	529
Archbold Medical Ctr Gordon Ave at Mimosa Dr *TF:* 800-341-1009 ■ *Web:* www.archbold.org	Thomasville	GA	31792	229-228-2000		250
Arch-Con Corp 1335 W Gray Ste 210 *Web:* arch-con.com	Houston	TX	77019	713-533-1900		186
Archdale-Trinity Chamber of Commerce 213 Balfour Dr *TF:* 800-626-2672 ■ *Web:* www.archdaletrinitychamber.com	Archdale	NC	27263	336-434-2073	431-5845	139
Archdiocese of Louisville 1200 S Shelby St *Web:* www.archlou.org	Louisville	KY	40203	502-585-3291		48-20
Archdiocese of Newark 171 Clifton Ave *Web:* www.rcan.org	Newark	NJ	07104	973-497-4126		48-20
Archdiocese of Philadelphia 222 N 17th St *Web:* archphila.org	Philadelphia	PA	19103	215-587-3500		48-20
Archdiocese of Portland in Oregon 2838 E Burnside St *Web:* www.archdpdx.org	Portland	OR	97214	503-234-5334		48-20
Archdiocese of Saint Paul & Minneapolis 226 Summit Ave *TF:* 877-290-1605 ■ *Web:* www.archspm.org	Saint Paul	MN	55102	651-291-4411		48-20
Archdiocese of San Francisco 1 Peter Yorke Way *Web:* www.sfarchdiocese.org	San Francisco	CA	94109	415-614-5500		48-20
Archdiocese of St Boniface Resource Library 622 Tache Ave Catholic Centre Main Fl *Web:* www.archsaintboniface.ca	Winnipeg	MB	R2H2B4	204-237-9851		434-3
Archer Advanced Rubber Components Inc 2860 Lowery St *Web:* www.archerseal.com	Winston-Salem	NC	27101	336-996-7776	996-4449	326
Archer Books PO Box 1254 *Web:* www.archer-books.com	Santa Maria	CA	93456	805-878-8279		637-2
Archer Communications Inc 252 Alexander St *Web:* www.archercom.com	Rochester	NY	14607	585-461-1570		7
Archer Daniels Midland Co 77 W Wacker Dr *TF:* 800-637-5843 ■ *Web:* www.adm.com	Chicago	IL	60601	312-634-8100		296-8
Archer Heights Credit Union 6554 W Archer Ave *TF:* 877-874-9811 ■ *Web:* archerheights.com	Chicago	IL	60638	773-229-1500	229-1824	219
Archer Screw Products Inc 11341 Melrose Ave *TF:* 800-952-7897 ■ *Web:* www.archerscrew.com	Franklin Park	IL	60131	800-952-7897		454
Archer Wire International Corp 7300 S Narragansett Ave *Web:* www.archerwire.com	Bedford Park	IL	60638	708-563-1700	563-1740	73
Archer/Malmo Adv Inc 65 Union Ave Ste 500 *Web:* www.archermalmo.com	Memphis	TN	38103	901-523-2000		4
Archetype Agency Ltd 100 Montgomery St Ste 1101 *Web:* www.archetype.co	San Francisco	CA	94104	415-365-0222		636
Archi's Thai Kitchen 9310 S E Ave Ste 101 *Web:* www.archisthai.com	Las Vegas	NV	89123	702-916-3949	916-1965	671
Archibald Bush Foundation 332 Minnesota St Ste E-900 *Web:* www.bushfoundation.org	Saint Paul	MN	55101	651-227-0891	297-6485	305
Archibald Gray & McKay Ltd 3514 White Oak Rd *TF:* 800-336-9708 ■ *Web:* agm.on.ca	London	ON	N6E2Z9	519-685-5300		256
Archibus Inc 18 Tremont St *Web:* archibus.com	Boston	MA	02108	617-227-2508	227-2509	177
Archie Comic Publications Inc 325 Fayette Ave *Web:* www.archiecomics.com	Mamaroneck	NY	10543	914-381-5155	381-4015	637-5
Archie McPhee & Co 10915 47th Ave W *Web:* mcphee.com	Mukilteo	WA	98275	425-349-3009		195
Archie Moore's Bar & Restaurant 188 1/2 Willow St *Web:* www.archiemoores.com	New Haven	CT	06511	203-773-9870		671
Archimede Gruden USA Inc 51 Newark St Ste 302 *Web:* www.archimedegruden.us	Hoboken	NJ	07030	201-798-0222		194
Arch-I-Tech Doors Inc 799 Allgood Rd *Web:* www.architechdoors.com	Marietta	GA	30062	770-426-0773		191-3
Archi-Tech Systems Inc 238 W Delaware Ave *Web:* www.archi-tech.com	Pennington	NJ	08534	609-882-2447		224
Architectual Engineering Consultants Inc 40801 Hwy 6 24 Ste 214 *Web:* aec-vail.com	Avon	CO	81620	970-748-8520		256
Architectural & Transportation Barriers Compliance Board 1331 F St NW Ste 1000 *TF:* 800-872-2253 ■ *Web:* www.access-board.gov	Washington	DC	20004	202-272-0080	272-0081	340-20
Architectural Brass Co 1130 Donald Lee Hollowell Pkwy NW *TF:* 800-752-6837 ■ *Web:* www.architecturalbrass.com	Atlanta	GA	30318	404-351-0594	351-5721	295
Architectural Bronze Aluminum Corp 655 Deerfield Rd Ste 100 **Fax Area Code:* 847 ■ *TF:* 800-339-6581 ■ *Web:* architecturalbronze.com	Deerfield	IL	60015	800-339-6581	266-7301*	777
Architectural Builders Hardware Manufacturing 1222 Ardmore Ave Apt W *TF:* 800-932-9224 ■ *Web:* www.abhmfg.com	Itasca	IL	60143	630-875-9900		350
Architectural Building Supply Co 2965 S Main St *Web:* www.cookandboardman.com	Salt Lake City	UT	84115	801-486-3481	484-6817	350
Architectural Ceramics Inc 800 E Gude Dr Ste F *TF:* 800-287-1742 ■ *Web:* www.architecturalceramics.com	Rockville	MD	20850	301-762-4140	542-0132	191-1
Architectural Cladding Services Inc (ACSI) 5570 Fireleaf Dr *Web:* www.curtainwall.com	Saint Louis	MO	63129	314-842-9555		194
Architectural Digest 1 World Trade Ctr *TF:* 800-365-8032 ■ *Web:* www.architecturaldigest.com	New York	NY	10007	800-365-8032		457-2
Architectural Engineers Inc 63 Franklin St 5th Fl *Web:* www.arcengrs.com	Boston	MA	02110	617-542-0810		261
Architectural Polymers 1220 Little Gap Rd *Web:* www.apformliner.com	Palmerton	PA	18071	610-824-3322		596
Architectural Precast Assn (APA) 6710 Winkler Rd Ste 8 *Web:* archprecast.org	Fort Myers	FL	33919	239-454-6989		49-3
Architectural Surfaces Inc 5801 Midway Pk NE *Web:* asitileandstone.com	Albuquerque	NM	87109	505-273-2883	888-5012	290
Architectural Woodwork Institute (AWI) 46179 Westlake Dr Ste 120 *Web:* www.awinet.org	Potomac Falls	VA	20165	571-323-3636	323-3630	49-3
Architecture Plus Information 16 W 22nd St 11th Fl *Web:* www.architectureplusinformation.com	New York	NY	10010	212-460-9500		2
Architecture Technology Corp (ATC) 9971 Vly View Rd *Web:* www.atcorp.com	Eden Prairie	MN	55344	952-829-5864	944-1859	178-1
Architelos Inc 43622 Merchant Mill Terr	Leesburg	VA	20176	310-418-7162		387
Architex Intl 3333 Commercial Ave **Fax Area Code:* 847 ■ *TF:* 800-621-0827 ■ *Web:* www.architex-ljh.com	Northbrook	IL	60062	800-621-0827	205-1510*	361
Architrave Interiors 1337 Ocean Ave Ste D *Web:* architraveinteriors.com	Santa Monica	CA	90401	310-310-4500		393
Archive of Contemporary Music 54 White St *Web:* arcmusic.org	New York	NY	10013	212-226-6967		434-3
Archive-cd LLC 910 Beverly Way *TF:* 800-323-1868 ■ *Web:* www.archive-cd.com	Jacksonville	OR	97530	541-899-5704		177
Archives & Museum Informatics 5501 Walnut St Ste 203 *Web:* www.archimuse.com	Pittsburgh	PA	15232	412-683-7366		196
Archives of American Art 750 Ninth St NW Ste 2200 *Web:* www.aaa.si.edu	Washington	DC	20001	202-633-7940		48-4
Archmill House Inc 1276 Osprey Dr *Web:* archmillhouse.com	Ancaster	ON	L9G4V5	905-648-7330		499
Archon Information Systems LLC 935 Gravier St Ste 1700 *Web:* civicsource.com	New Orleans	LA	70112	504-267-0065		177
Archrival Inc 720 O St *Web:* www.archrival.com	Lincoln	NE	68508	402-435-2525		7
Archway Marketing Services Inc 19850 S Diamond Lake Rd *TF:* 866-779-9855 ■ *Web:* www.archway.com	Rogers	MN	55374	763-428-3300		463
Archway Programs Inc PO Box 668 *Web:* www.archwayprograms.org	Atco	NJ	08004	856-767-5757		685
Archway Systems Inc 2134 Main St Ste 160 *Web:* www.archwaysystems.com	Huntington Beach	CA	92648	714-374-0440	374-0301	177
ARCI (Association of Racing Commissioners Intl) 1510 Newtown Pike Ste 210 *Web:* www.arci.com	Lexington	KY	40511	859-224-7070		49-7
Arclyte Technologies Inc 953 S Meridian *Web:* arclyte.com	Alhambra	CA	91803	626-281-2220	281-2223	196
ARCO Coffee Co 2206 Winter St *TF:* 800-283-2726 ■ *Web:* www.arcocoffee.com	Superior	WI	54880	715-392-4771	392-4776	296-7
ARCO Electric Products Corp 2325 E Michigan Rd *TF:* 800-428-4370 ■ *Web:* www.arco-electric.com	Shelbyville	IN	46176	317-398-9713	398-2655	518
ARCO Ideas & Design Inc 212 N Tennessee St *Web:* www.arcoideas.com	Cartersville	GA	30120	770-386-2799		711

	Phone	Fax	Class
Arcobasso Foods Inc 8850 Pershall Rd .... Hazelwood MO 63042 *Web:* www.arcobasso.com	314-381-8083	381-4522	297-8
Arcola First Bank 127 S Oak St PO Box 100 .... Arcola IL 61910 *Web:* arcolafb.com	217-268-4911		70
Arcomm Communications Corp 462 W Main St 3 .... Hillsboro NH 03244 *Web:* www.arcomm1.com	603-464-4600		175
ARCON Corp 260 Bear Hill Rd Ste 200 .... Waltham MA 02451 *Web:* www.arcon.com	781-890-3330	890-5189	225
Arcos Industries 1 Arcos Dr .... Mount Carmel PA 17851 *TF:* 800-233-8460 ■ *Web:* www.arcos.us	570-339-5200	339-5206	811
ARC-PA (Accreditation Review Commission on Education for the Physician Assistant Inc) 12000 Findley Rd Ste 275 .... Johns Creek GA 30097 *Web:* www.arc-pa.org	770-476-1224	476-1738	48-1
ArcPro Inc 6738 Bayou Isle Ln .... Theodore AL 36582 *Web:* www.arcpromobile.com	251-272-1580		167-3
Arcsine Engineering 950 Executive Way .... Redding CA 96002 *Web:* www.arc-sine.com	530-222-7204	222-7210	261
Arcsoft Inc 46601 Fremont Blvd .... Fremont CA 94538 *Web:* arcsoft.com	510-440-9901	979-5592	180
Arctern Inc 50 Charles Lindbergh Blvd Ste 206 .... Uniondale NY 11553 *TF:* 800-231-4973 ■ *Web:* www.arctern.com	800-231-4973		260
Arctic Cat Inc 601 Brooks Ave S .... Thief River Falls MN 56701 *NASDAQ: ACAT* ■ *TF:* 877-412-7467 ■ *Web:* www.arcticcat.com	218-681-8558		705
Arctic Cir Restaurants Inc PO Box 339 .... Midvale UT 84047 *Web:* www.acburger.com	801-561-3620		670
Arctic Engineering Company Inc 8410 Minnesota St .... Merrillville IN 46410 *Web:* arcticengineering.com	219-947-4999		261
Arctic Glacier Holdings Inc 625 Henry Ave .... Winnipeg MB R3A0V1 *Web:* arcticglacier.com	204-772-2473		578
Arctic Hunter Energy Inc 1610 675 W Hastings St .... Vancouver BC V6B1N2 *Web:* www.arctichunter.com	604-681-3131		536
Arctic Industries Inc 9731 NW 114th Way .... Miami FL 33178 **Fax Area Code:* 305 ■ *TF:* 800-325-0123 ■ *Web:* www.arcticwalkins.com	800-325-0123	883-4651*	14
Arctic Information Technology Inc 375 W 36th Ave Ste 300 .... Anchorage AK 99503 *TF:* 844-461-9500 ■ *Web:* arcticit.com	907-261-9500	261-9591	317
Arctic Research Consortium of the US (ARCUS) 3535 College Rd Ste 101 .... Fairbanks AK 99709 *Web:* www.arcus.org	907-474-1600	474-1604	668
Arctic Slope Regional Corp 1230 Agvik St PO Box 129 .... Barrow AK 99723 *TF:* 800-770-2772 ■ *Web:* www.asrc.com	907-852-8633	852-5733	538
Arctic Star Refrigeration Manufacturing Company Inc 3540 W Pioneer Pkwy .... Arlington TX 76013 *TF:* 800-229-6562 ■ *Web:* www.arcticstar.com	817-274-1396	277-4828	664
Arctic Storm Management Group LLC 2727 Alaskan Way Pier 69 .... Seattle WA 98121 *TF:* 800-929-0908 ■ *Web:* www.arcticstorm.com	206-547-6557	547-3165	285
Arctic Wolf Networks Inc 111 W Evelyn Ave Ste 115 .... Sunnyvale CA 94086 *TF:* 888-272-8429 ■ *Web:* arcticwolf.com	888-272-8429		196
ArcticDx Inc Mars Ctr 661 University Ave Ste 455 .... Toronto ON M5G1M1 *TF:* 866-964-5182 ■ *Web:* www.arcticdx.com	866-964-5182		416
Arc-Tronics Inc 1150 Pagni Dr .... Elk Grove Village IL 60007 *Web:* www.arc-tronics.com	847-437-0211		625
ARCUS (Arctic Research Consortium of the US) 3535 College Rd Ste 101 .... Fairbanks AK 99709 *Web:* www.arcus.org	907-474-1600	474-1604	668
Arcus Capital Partners LLC 3060 Peachtree Rd NW Ste 1880 .... Atlanta GA 30305 *Web:* www.arcuscp.com	404-949-2111		251
Arcus Foundation 44 W 28th St 17th Fl .... New York NY 10001 *Web:* www.arcusfoundation.org	212-488-3000	488-3010	303
ARCVB (Alton Regional Convention & Visitors Bureau) 200 Piasa St .... Alton IL 62002 *TF:* 800-258-6645 ■ *Web:* www.riversandroutes.com	618-465-6676	465-6151	206
Arcways Inc 1076 Ehlers Rd .... Neenah WI 54956 *TF:* 800-558-5096 ■ *Web:* www.arcways.com	800-558-5096		499
Arcweb Technologies LLC 234 Market St 5th Fl .... Philadelphia PA 19106 *TF:* 800-846-7980 ■ *Web:* arcweb.co	800-846-7980		463
ARD Group, The 11 Hanover Sq Ste 501 .... New York NY 10005 *Web:* www.ardcareers.com	212-571-1111		193
ARD Trucking Company Inc 1702 N Governor Williams Hwy .... Darlington SC 29540 *Web:* www.ardtrucking.com	843-393-5101		780
ARDA (American Resort Development Assn) 1201 15th St NW Ste 400 .... Washington DC 20005 *Web:* www.arda.org	202-371-6700	289-8544	49-17
Ardaman and Associates Inc 8008 S Orange Ave .... Orlando FL 32809 *Web:* www.ardaman.com	407-855-3860	859-8121	261
Ardelyx Inc 34175 Ardenwood Blvd .... Fremont CA 94555 *Web:* www.ardelyx.com	510-745-1700		231
Arden Cos 30400 Telegraph Rd Ste 200 .... Bingham Farms MI 48025 **Fax Area Code:* 248 ■ *TF:* 800-876-7336 ■ *Web:* www.ardencompanies.com	800-876-7336	415-8520*	746
Arden Engineering Constructors LLC 505 Narragansett Pk Dr .... Pawtucket RI 02861 *TF:* 800-992-3603 ■ *Web:* www.ardeneng.com	401-727-3500	727-3540	189-10
Arden Engineering Inc 1878 N Main St .... Orange CA 92865 *Web:* www.cadenceaerospace.com	714-998-6410		22
Arden Group Inc 1600 Market St Ste 2600 .... Philadelphia PA 19103 *Web:* ardengroup.com	215-735-1313	735-1123	360-3
Arden Jewelry Manufacturing Co 10 Industrial Ln .... Johnston RI 02919 *Web:* www.ardenjewelry.com	401-274-9800		408
Arden Theatre Co 40 N Second St .... Philadelphia PA 19106 *Web:* www.ardentheatre.org	215-922-8900	922-7011	749
Ardent Health Services 1 Burton Hills Blvd Ste 250 .... Nashville TN 37215 *Web:* ardenthealth.com	615-296-3000		353
Ardent Media Inc 151 W 25th 2nd Fl .... New York NY 10001	212-861-1501		94
Ardent Sound Inc 3370 N Hayden Rd Ste 123-979 .... Scottsdale AZ 85251 *Web:* www.ardentsound.com	480-649-1806		194
Ardenwood Historic Farm 34600 Ardenwood Blvd .... Fremont CA 94555 *TF:* 888-327-2757 ■ *Web:* www.ebparks.org	510-544-2797	796-0231	520
ARDEX Inc 400 Ardex Park Dr .... Aliquippa PA 15001 *TF:* 888-512-7339 ■ *Web:* www.ardexamericas.com	724-203-5000	203-5001	183
Ardham Technologies Inc 5411 Jefferson St NE Ste 200 .... Albuquerque NM 87109 *Web:* ardham.com	505-872-9040		180
Ardica Technologies Inc 2325 Third St Ste 424 .... San Francisco CA 94107 *Web:* ardica.com	415-568-9270	520-5422	253
ARDL Inc 400 Aviation Dr PO Box 1566 .... Mount Vernon IL 62864 *Web:* www.ardlinc.com	618-244-3235	244-1149	192
Ardmore Associates LLC 33 N Dearborn St Ste 1720 .... Chicago IL 60602 *Web:* ardmoreassociates.com	312-795-1400	795-1228	261
Ardmore Banking Advisors 44 E Lancaster Ave 2nd Fl PO Box 533 .... Ardmore PA 19003 *Web:* www.ardmoreadvisors.com	610-649-4643		194
Ardmore Telephone Company Inc 30190 Ardmore Ave .... Ardmore AL 35739 *TF:* 800-830-9946 ■ *Web:* ardmore.net	256-423-2131	423-2208	387
ARDMS (American Registry of Diagnostic Medical Sonographers) 1401 Rockville Pk Ste 600 .... Rockville MD 20852 *TF:* 800-541-9754 ■ *Web:* www.ardms.org	301-738-8401	738-0312	49-8
Ardour Capital Investments LLC 26 Broadway Ste 1107 .... New York NY 10004 *Web:* www.ardourcapital.com	212-375-2950		690
Ardsley Musical Instrument Service Ltd 219 Sprain Rd .... Scarsdale NY 10583 *Web:* ardsleymusic.com	914-693-6639		526
Ardus Medical Inc 11297 Grooms Rd .... Cincinnati OH 45242 *Web:* www.ardusmedical.com	513-469-7867	469-2329	475
ARE (Association for Research & Enlightenment) 215 67th St .... Virginia Beach VA 23451 *TF:* 800-333-4499 ■ *Web:* www.edgarcayce.org	757-428-3588	422-6921	48-17
Area 51 Esg Inc 51 Post .... Irvine CA 92618 *Web:* www.area51esg.com	949-387-0051	748-7051	246
Area Access Inc 7131 Gateway Ct .... Manassas VA 20109 *TF:* 800-333-2732 ■ *Web:* www.areaaccess.com	703-396-4949		385
Area Agency On Aging 9549 Koger Blvd Gadsden Bldg Ste 100 .... Saint Petersburg FL 33702 *TF:* 800-963-5337 ■ *Web:* agingcarefl.org	727-570-9696		450
Area Agency On Aging 10b Inc 1550 Corporate Woods Pkwy .... Uniontown OH 44685 *TF:* 800-421-7277 ■ *Web:* www.dhad.org	330-896-9172	896-6644	450
Area Community Credit Union 2800 S Washington St .... Grand Forks ND 58201 *Web:* gfaccu.com	701-772-2690		219
Area Development Magazine 400 Post Ave .... Westbury NY 11590 *TF:* 800-735-2732 ■ *Web:* www.areadevelopment.com	516-338-0900	338-0100	457-5
Area Development Partnership 1 Convention Center Plz .... Hattiesburg MS 39401 *Web:* www.theadp.com	601-296-7500	296-7505	139
Area Diesel Service Inc 1300 University St .... Carlinville IL 62626 **Fax Area Code:* 217 ■ *TF:* 800-637-2658 ■ *Web:* areadieselservice.com	800-637-2658	854-8972*	54
Area Erectors Inc 2323 Harrison Ave .... Rockford IL 61104 *TF:* 800-270-2732 ■ *Web:* www.areaerectors.com	815-398-6700	398-6787	189-14
Area Iron & Steel Works Inc 4605 Osborne Dr .... El Paso TX 79922 *Web:* www.areaironandsteel.com	915-833-9494	833-1510	492
Area Mental Health Ctr 531 Campusview .... Garden City KS 67846 *Web:* compassbh.org	620-276-7689		726
Area Metropolitan Ambulance Authority 551 E Berry St .... Fort Worth TX 76110 *Web:* www.medstar911.org	817-632-0535		30
Area Temps Inc 1228 Euclid Ave .... Cleveland OH 44115 *TF:* 866-995-5627 ■ *Web:* www.areatemps.com	440-646-1333		721
Area Wide Communication 260 Hwy 45E N ...... Medina TN 38355 *Web:* areawidecomm.com	731-783-5380	783-3317	196
Area Wide Technologies 2110 Clearlake Blvd Ste 100 .... Champaign IL 61822 *Web:* ww2.areawidetech.com	217-359-8041	359-8113	180
Areias Systems Inc 5900 Butler Ln Ste 280 .... Scotts Valley CA 95066 *Web:* areiasys.com	831-440-9800		256
Arelia James Island 10880 Angelfish Way .... Jacksonville FL 32256 *TF:* 888-537-3778 ■ *Web:* www.areliajamesisland.com	888-537-3778		78
Arellano Construction Co 9675 NW 117th Ave Ste 108 .... Miami FL 33178	786-418-3740		360-3
AREMA (American Railway Engineering & Maintenance-of-Way Assn) 4501 Forbes Blvd Ste 130 .... Lanham MD 20706 *Web:* www.arema.org	301-459-3200		49-21
Arena Energy 4200 RES Forest Dr Ste 500 .... The Woodlands TX 77381 *Web:* www.arenaenergy.com	281-681-9500	681-9503	538
Arena Hotel 817 The Alameda .... San Jose CA 95126 *Web:* www.pacifichotels.com	408-294-6500	294-6585	379
Arena Pharmaceuticals Inc 6166 Nancy Ridge Dr .... San Diego CA 92121 *NASDAQ: ARNA* ■ *Web:* www.arenapharm.com	858-453-7200		85
Arena Stage 1101 Sixth St SW .... Washington DC 20024 *Web:* www.arenastage.org	202-554-9066	488-4056	572

Name / Address	City	State	Zip	Phone	Fax	Class
Arenac County						
120 N Grove St PO Box 747	Standish	MI	48658	989-846-4626		338
TF: 800-232-5216 ■ *Web:* www.arenaccountymi.gov						
Arend Laukhuf & Stoller Inc						
117 N Main St	Paulding	OH	45879	419-399-3686		2
Web: www.brsw-cpa.com						
Arenson Office Furnishings Inc						
1115 Broadway 6th Fl	New York	NY	10010	646-395-3563		321
Web: www.aof.com						
Arenson Office Furniture						
8185 Camino Santa Fe	San Diego	CA	92121	858-453-2411		321
Web: www.arensonof.com						
Ares Corp 1440 Chapin Ave Ste 390	Burlingame	CA	94010	650-401-7100	401-7101	113
Web: www.arescorporation.com						
Ares Insurance Brokerage Service						
14140 Magnolia Blvd	Sherman Oaks	CA	91423	818-986-4207		390
Web: aresins.com						
Ares Management LLC						
2000 Avenue of the Stars 12th Fl	Los Angeles	CA	90067	310-201-4100		463
Web: www.aresmgmt.com						
Ares Printing & Packaging Corp						
63 Flushing Ave Bldg 5	Brooklyn	NY	11205	718-858-8760	260-8692	627
Web: www.aresny.com						
Ares Sportswear Ltd 3704 Lacon Rd	Hilliard	OH	43026	614-767-1950		687
TF: 800-439-8614 ■ *Web:* www.areswear.com						
Arete Corp PO Box 1299	Center Harbor	NH	03226	603-253-9797	253-9799	792
Web: www.arete-microgen.com						
Arete Inc 65 S Main St Bldg E	Pennington	NJ	08534	609-737-1212		174
Web: www.areteinc.com						
Arete Industries Inc						
7260 Osceola St	Westminster	CO	80030	303-427-8688		536
Web: www.areteindustries.com						
Aretech LLC 21720 Red Rum Dr Ste 187	Ashburn	VA	20147	571-292-8889		350
Web: www.aretechllc.com						
Arett Sales 9285 Commerce Hwy	Pennsauken	NJ	08110	856-751-1224		276
TF: 800-257-8220 ■ *Web:* www.arett.com						
AREVA Transnuclear Inc						
7135 Minstrel Way Ste 300	Columbia	MD	21045	410-910-6900		261
Web: www.us.areva.com						
ARF (Advertising Research Foundation)						
432 Park Ave S	New York	NY	10016	212-751-5656	689-1859	49-18
Web: thearf.org						
Arfstrom Pharmacies Inc						
415 Ashmun St	Sault Sainte Marie	MI	49783	906-632-9661		237
Web: arfstrompharmacy.com						
ARG Recovery LLC						
3308 Preston Rd Ste 350-215	Plano	TX	75093	972-335-2090		194
Web: www.argrecovery.com						
ARG Trucking Corp 369 Bostwick Rd	Phelps	NY	14532	315-789-8871	789-8879	780
TF: 800-334-1314 ■ *Web:* www.wadhams.com						
Arganteal Corp 211 E 7th St Ste 620	Austin	TX	78759	512-801-6729		196
Argen Corp, The 8515 Miralani Dr	San Diego	CA	92126	858-455-7900		228
TF: 800-255-5524 ■ *Web:* www.argen.com						
Argenia LLC 11524 Fairview Rd	Little Rock	AR	72212	501-227-9670		390
TF: 800-482-5968 ■ *Web:* argenia.com						
Argent Associates Inc						
140 Fieldcrest Ave	Edison	NJ	08837	732-512-9009		224
Web: www.argentassociates.com						
Argent International Inc						
41016 Concept Dr	Plymouth	MI	48170	734-582-9800	473-1526*	393
**Fax Area Code:* 248 ■ *TF:* 800-223-9890 ■ *Web:* argent-international.com						
Argent Wealth Management						
404 Wyman St Ste 375	Waltham	MA	02451	781-290-4900		194
Web: argentwm.com						
Argentech Solutions Inc 201 Kent Pl	Newmarket	NH	03857	888-848-8019		261
TF: 888-848-8019 ■ *Web:* argentechsolutions.com						
Argentina						
Consulate General						
2200 W Loop S Ste 1025	Houston	TX	77027	713-871-8935	871-0639	257
Web: www.chous.mrecic.gov.ar						
Consulate General						
5055 Wilshire Blvd Ste 210	Los Angeles	CA	90036	323-954-9155		257
Web: clang.cancilleria.gob.ar						
Consulate General						
245 Peachtree Center Ave NE Ste 2450	Atlanta	GA	30303	404-880-0805	880-0806	257
Web: www.catla.cancilleria.gov.ar						
Embassy 1600 New Hampshire Ave NW	Washington	DC	20009	202-238-6400	332-3171	257
Web: www.embassyofargentina.us						
Argentine Santa Fe Industries Credit Union						
4150 Kansas Ave	Kansas City	KS	66106	913-342-9039		219
NYSE: BCV						
Argentum Group, The						
60 Madison Ave Ste 701	New York	NY	10010	212-949-6262	949-8294	402
Web: www.argentumgroup.com						
ARGI (ARGI Investment Services LLC)						
2110 High Wickham Pl	Louisville	KY	40223	502-753-0609		401
TF: 866-568-9719 ■ *Web:* argifinancialgroup.com						
ARGI Investment Services LLC (ARGI)						
2110 High Wickham Pl	Louisville	KY	40223	502-753-0609		401
TF: 866-568-9719 ■ *Web:* argifinancialgroup.com						
Argie Cooper Public Library						
220 S Jefferson St	Shelbyville	TN	37160	931-684-7323	685-4848	434-3
Argo & Lehne Jewelers Inc						
3100 Tremont Rd	Columbus	OH	43221	614-457-6261		410
Web: argolehne.com						
Argo AI 2545 Railroad St	Pittsburgh	PA	15222	412-525-3483		39
Web: www.argo.ai						
Argo Connections Inc						
1880 Swantown Rd	Oak Harbor	WA	98277	404-702-1954		681
Web: www.argoconnections.com						
Argo Consulting						
455 N Cityfront Plz Dr Ste 2750	Chicago	IL	60611	312-988-9220		463
Web: www.argoconsulting.com						
Argo Data Resource Corp						
1500 N Greenville Ave	Richardson	TX	75081	972-866-3300		177
Web: argodata.com						
Argo International Corp						
71 Veronica Ave Unit 1	Somerset	NJ	08873	732-979-2996	246-3160	246
TF: 866-289-2746 ■ *Web:* www.argointl.com						
Argo Marketing Group 64 Lisbon St	Lewiston	ME	04240	207-514-0744		195
Web: www.argocontact.com						
Argo Products Co						
3500 Goodfellow Blvd	Saint Louis	MO	63120	314-385-1803	385-1808	488
Web: www.argoproducts.com						
Argo Sales 717-7th Ave SW Ste 650	Calgary	AB	T2P3H6	403-265-6633	266-2770	358
TF: 866-930-6633 ■ *Web:* www.argosales.com						
Argo Strategies						
1631 15th Ave W Ste 301	Seattle	WA	98119	206-486-0085		194
Web: argostrategies.com						
Argo Systems LLC						
1362 Mellon Rd Ste 100	Hanover	MD	21076	410-768-2444		261
Web: www.argo-sys.com						
Argo Translation Inc 1884 Johns Dr	Glenview	IL	60025	847-901-4075		768
TF: 888-961-9291 ■ *Web:* www.argotrans.com						
Argon ST Inc						
12701 Fair Lakes Cir Ste 800	Fairfax	VA	22033	703-322-0881		735
Web: www.argonst.com						
Argon Technologies Inc						
4612 Wesley St	Greenville	TX	75401	903-455-5036		224
TF: 888-651-1010 ■ *Web:* www.argontech.com						
Argonaut 1268 Sutter St	San Francisco	CA	94109	415-633-8200		5
Web: www.argonautinc.com						
Argonaut Constructors Inc						
360 Sutton Pl	Santa Rosa	CA	95407	707-542-4862	542-3210	188-10
Web: www.argonautconstructors.com						
Argonaut Hotel 495 Jefferson St	San Francisco	CA	94109	415-563-0800		379
TF: 866-415-0704 ■ *Web:* www.argonauthotel.com						
Argonaut, The PO Box 11209	Marina	CA	90295	310-822-2089		532-4
Web: argonautnews.com						
Argonaut, The 709 Deakin Ave	Moscow	ID	83844	208-885-7825		532-2
Web: www.uiargonaut.com						
Argonne National Laboratory (ANL)						
9700 S Cass Ave	Lemont	IL	60439	630-252-2000		668
TF: 800-632-8990 ■ *Web:* www.anl.gov						
Argos Computer Systems Inc						
110 W 32nd St	New York	NY	10001	212-594-5400	967-1195	180
Web: argosnyc.com						
Argos Systems Inc 30 Temple St Ste 303	Nashua	NH	03060	781-271-9111		225
Web: www.argos.com						
Argosy Casino Alton 1 Piasa St	Alton	IL	62002	800-711-4263		133
TF: 800-711-4263 ■ *Web:* www.argosyalton.com						
Argosy Publishing Inc						
109 Oak St Ste 102	Newton	MA	02464	617-527-9999	527-3335	627
Web: www.argosymedical.com						
Argosy University						
3601 West Sunflower Ave	Santa Ana	CA	92704	714-620-0900		167-3
Web: www.argosy.edu						
Arguedas Cassman & Headley						
803 Hearst Ave	Berkeley	CA	94710	510-845-3000	845-3003	428
Web: achlaw.com						
Arguindegui Oil Cos						
4506 State 359 & Loop 20	Laredo	TX	78042	956-286-8330		316
TF: 800-722-5251 ■ *Web:* argpetro.com						
Argus Communications Inc 280 Summer St	Boston	MA	02210	617-261-7676		4
Argus Industrial Co 16 W Huron	Pontiac	MI	48342	248-745-5828	745-5825	190
TF: 866-745-5828 ■ *Web:* www.ez-screen.com						
Argus Leader 200 S Minnesota Ave	Sioux Falls	SD	57104	605-331-2200		532-2
Web: www.argusleader.com						
Argus Machine Company Ltd						
5820 97th St NW	Edmonton	AB	T6E3J1	780-434-9451		539
TF: 888-434-9451 ■ *Web:* www.argusmachine.com						
Argus Research Co						
61 Broadway Ste 1910	New York	NY	10006	212-425-7500		218
Web: www.argusresearch.com						
Argyle Lake State Park						
640 Argyle Park Rd	Colchester	IL	62326	309-776-3422		565
Web: www.dnr.illinois.gov						
ARH (Appalachian Regional Healthcare Service)						
80 Hospital Dr PO Box 8086	Barbourville	KY	40906	859-226-2440		353
TF: 888-654-0015 ■ *Web:* www.arh.org						
ARHMF (Avila Rodriguez Hernandez Mena & Ferri LLP)						
2525 Ponce De Leon Blvd PH 1225	Coral Gables	FL	33134	305-779-3560		445
Web: arhmf.com						
ARHP (Association of Reproductive Health Professionals)						
1300 19th St NW Ste 200	Washington	DC	20036	202-466-3825	466-3826	49-8
TF: 877-311-8972 ■ *Web:* www.arhp.org						
ARI (Autism Research Institute)						
4182 Adams Ave	San Diego	CA	92116	833-281-7165	563-6840*	48-17
**Fax Area Code:* 619 ■ *TF:* 866-366-3361 ■ *Web:* www.autism.org						
ARI Industries Inc 381 Ari Ct	Addison	IL	60101	630-953-9100		201
TF: 800-237-6725 ■ *Web:* www.ariindustries.biz						
ARI Network Services Inc						
10850 W Park Pl Ste 1200	Milwaukee	WI	53224	414-973-4300	283-4357	178-10
TF: 877-805-0803 ■ *Web:* arinet.com						
ARI Products 102 Gaither Dr Ste 3	Mount Laurel	NJ	08054	856-234-0757	234-6465	291
Web: ariproducts.com						
Aria - Jefferson Health						
10800 Knights Rd	Philadelphia	PA	19114	215-612-4000		374-3
Web: northeast.jeffersonhealth.org						
Aria Communications						
717 W St Germain St	Saint Cloud	MN	56301	800-955-9924		737
TF: 800-955-9924 ■ *Web:* ariacallsandcards.com						
Aria Group Inc 17395 Daimler St	Irvine	CA	92614	949-475-2915		516
Web: www.aria-group.com						
Aria Health Bucks County Campus						
380 N Oxford Valley Rd	Langhorne	PA	19047	877-808-2742		374-3
TF: 877-808-2742 ■ *Web:* www.ariahealth.org						
Aria Restaurant						
490 E Paces Ferry Rd NE	Atlanta	GA	30305	404-233-7673		671
Web: www.aria-atl.com						
Aria Solutions Inc						
110 - 12th Ave SW Ste 600	Calgary	AB	T2R0G7	403-235-0227		624
TF: 866-235-1181 ■ *Web:* www.ariasolutions.com						
Aria Tuscan Grill 100 N Tryon St	Charlotte	NC	28202	704-376-8880		671
Web: www.sonomarestaurants.net						
Arial Software LLC						
1201 Puerta Del Sol Ste 309	San Clemente	CA	92673	949-218-3852		178
Web: www.arialsoftware.com						

Company / Address	City	State	Zip	Phone	Fax	Class
Arias & Associates Inc 142 Chula Vista Dr *Web:* www.ariasinc.com	San Antonio	TX	78232	210-308-5884		192
Ariat International Inc 3242 Whipple Rd *Web:* www.ariat.com	Union City	CA	94587	510-477-7000		301
Ariba Inc 910 Hermosa Ct *TF:* 866-772-7422 ■ *Web:* www.ariba.com	Sunnyvale	CA	94089	866-772-7422		39
Aridis Pharmaceuticals LLC 5941 Optical Ct *Web:* aridispharma.com	San Jose	CA	95138	408-385-1742	960-3822	85
Ariel Corp 35 Blackjack Rd Ext *TF:* 888-397-7766 ■ *Web:* www.arielcorp.com	Mount Vernon	OH	43050	740-397-0311	397-3856	172
Ariel Group Inc, The 1050 Waltham St Ste 600 *Web:* www.arielgroup.com	Lexington	MA	02421	781-761-9000		194
Ariel Partners LLC 1501 Broadway 12th Fl *Web:* www.arielpartners.com	New York	NY	10036	646-467-7394		177
Ariel Technologies 1980 E Lohman Ave *TF:* 877-524-6860 ■ *Web:* www.arielusa.com	Las Cruces	NM	88001	877-524-6860		175
Ariel Ventures LLC 1163 E 40th St Ste 201 *Web:* www.arielventures.com	Cleveland	OH	44114	216-344-9441	373-7356	196
Ariens Co 655 W Ryan St *TF:* 800-678-5443 ■ *Web:* www.ariens.com	Brillion	WI	54110	920-756-2141	756-2407	429
Aries Computer Solutions Inc 2211 Sheridan Dr Ste 203 *Web:* www.customswebclearance.com	Buffalo	NY	14223	716-876-4004		809
Aries Electronics Inc 2609 Bartram Rd *Fax Area Code: 908 ■ *Web:* www.arieselec.com	Bristol	PA	19007	215-781-9956	996-3891*	253
Aries Engineering Company Inc 130 Aries Dr PO Box 110 *Web:* hypercyl.com	Dundee	MI	48131	734-529-8855		261
Aries Engineering Inc 104 Pleasant St *Web:* aries-eng.com	Concord	NH	03301	603-228-0008		261
Aries Industries Inc 550 Elizabeth St *Web:* www.ariesindustries.com	Waukesha	WI	53186	262-896-7205		647
Aries Technology Inc 1445 W 12th Pl *TF:* 800-497-5452 ■ *Web:* www.aries.net	Tempe	AZ	85281	480-784-4818	967-8422	177
Arima Boats 7510 Bree Dr *Web:* arimaboats.com	Bremerton	WA	98312	360-813-3600	813-3613	90
Arimed Orthotics & Prosthetics Inc 302 Livingston St *Web:* www.arimed.com	Brooklyn	NY	11217	718-875-8754		477
Arimon Technologies Inc 251 E 5th St *TF:* 800-825-7565 ■ *Web:* www.arimon.com	Montello	WI	53949	608-297-9244	297-9037	253
ARIN (American Registry for Internet Numbers) 3635 Concorde Pkwy Ste 200 *Web:* www.arin.net	Chantilly	VA	20151	703-227-9840		48-9
Aring Equipment Company Inc 13001 W Silver Spring Dr *Web:* www.aringequipment.com	Butler	WI	53007	262-781-3770		358
Arion Systems Inc (ASI) 15040 Conference Center Dr Ste 200 *Web:* www.arionsys.com	Chantilly	VA	20151	703-815-1130	815-1135	261
Aris Horticulture Inc 115 Third St SE *Fax Area Code: 330 ■ *TF:* 800-232-9557 ■ *Web:* www.arishort.com	Barberton	OH	44203	800-232-9557	745-3098*	369
Arise Health Plan PO Box 11625 *TF:* 888-332-0144 ■ *Web:* www.wecareforwisconsin.com	Green Bay	WI	54307	920-490-6928		391-3
Arista Industries Inc 557 Danbury Rd *Web:* aristaindustries.com	Wilton	CT	06897	203-761-1009		296-25
Arista Information Systems 2220 Northmont Pkwy Ste 100 *Web:* www.aristainfo.com	Duluth	GA	30096	678-473-1885	473-1051	5
Aristatek Inc 710 E Garfield St Ste 220 *TF:* 877-912-2200 ■ *Web:* www.aristatek.com	Laramie	WY	82070	307-721-2126		177
Aristech Acrylics LLC 7350 Empire Dr *Web:* www.aristechacrylics.com	Florence	KY	41042	859-283-1501		600
Aristo Cast Inc 7400 Research Dr *Web:* www.aristo-cast.com	Almont	MI	48003	810-798-2900		492
Aristocrat Technologies 7230 Amigo St *TF:* 800-748-4156 ■ *Web:* www.aristocrat.com	Las Vegas	NV	89119	702-270-1000	270-1001	322
Aristotle Capital Management LLC 11100 Santa Monica Blvd Ste 1700 *TF:* 877-478-4722 ■ *Web:* www.aristotlecap.com	Los Angeles	CA	90025	310-478-4005	478-8496	401
Aristotle Inc 205 Pennsylvania Ave SE *TF:* 800-296-2747 ■ *Web:* www.aristotle.com	Washington	DC	20003	202-543-8345	543-6407	178-11
Arizon Cos 11880 Dorsett Rd *TF:* 800-325-1303 ■ *Web:* arizoncompanies.com	Maryland Heights	MO	63043	314-739-0037	739-1556	256
Arizona						
Agriculture Dept 1688 W Adams St *TF:* 800-294-0308 ■ *Web:* agriculture.az.gov	Phoenix	AZ	85007	602-542-4373	542-5420	339-3
Arts Commission 417 W Roosevelt St *Web:* azarts.gov	Phoenix	AZ	85003	602-771-6501	256-0282	339-3
Attorney General 1275 W Washington St *Web:* www.azag.gov	Phoenix	AZ	85007	602-542-5025	542-4085	339-3
Boxing Commission 1110 W Washington St Ste 450 *Web:* www.gaming.az.gov	Phoenix	AZ	85007	602-364-1700	364-1703	339-3
Children Youth & Families Div 2428 W Lone Cactus Dr Ste 306 *Web:* www.azdes.gov	Phoenix	AZ	85015	602-542-0419		339-3
Corrections Dept 1601 W Jefferson St *Web:* corrections.az.gov	Phoenix	AZ	85007	602-542-5497	542-2859	339-3
Criminal Justice Commission 1110 W Washington St Ste 230 *Web:* www.azcjc.gov	Phoenix	AZ	85007	602-364-1146	364-1175	339-3
Department of Economic Security Statewide Locations *Web:* www.facebook.com	Phoenix	AZ	85007	602-542-4791		339-3
Department of Emergency & Military Affairs, The 5636 E McDowell Rd *Web:* dema.az.gov	Phoenix	AZ	85008	602-267-2700		339-3
Department of Insurance 100 N 15th Ave Ste 102 *TF:* 800-325-2548 ■ *Web:* insurance.az.gov	Phoenix	AZ	85007	602-364-2499	364-2505	339-3
Education Dept 1535 W Jefferson St *TF:* 800-352-4558 ■ *Web:* www.azed.gov	Phoenix	AZ	85007	602-542-5393	542-5010	339-3
Employment Administration PO Box 6123 *Web:* des.az.gov	Phoenix	AZ	85005	602-542-3957	542-2491	259
Executive Clemency Board 1645 W Jefferson Ste 101 *Web:* boec.az.gov	Phoenix	AZ	85007	602-542-5656	542-5680	339-3
Game & Fish Dept 5000 W Carefree Hwy *Web:* www.azgfd.com	Phoenix	AZ	85086	602-942-3000		339-3
Government Information Technology Agency 100 N 15th Ave Ste 440 *Web:* www.azdfi.gov	Phoenix	AZ	85007	602-771-2800	364-4799	339-3
Health Services Dept 150 N 18th Ave *TF:* 888-816-5907 ■ *Web:* www.azdhs.gov	Phoenix	AZ	85007	602-542-1025	542-0883	339-3
Highway Patrol Div 2222 W Encanto Blvd *Web:* www.azdps.gov	Phoenix	AZ	85005	602-223-2000	223-2938	339-3
Historic Preservation Office 1100 W Washington St *Web:* azstateparks.com	Phoenix	AZ	85007	602-542-4009		339-3
Housing Dept 1110 W Washington St Ste 310 *Web:* housing.az.gov	Phoenix	AZ	85007	602-771-1000	771-1002	339-3
Industrial Commission 800 W Washington St *Web:* www.azica.gov	Phoenix	AZ	85007	602-542-4661	542-7889	339-3
Land Dept 1616 W Adams St *Web:* land.az.gov	Phoenix	AZ	85007	602-542-4631		339-3
Legislature Arizona State Capitol Complex 1700 W Washington St *TF:* 800-352-8404 ■ *Web:* www.azleg.gov	Phoenix	AZ	85007	602-926-3559		339-3
Lottery 4740 E University Dr *TF:* 800-639-8783 ■ *Web:* www.arizonalottery.com	Phoenix	AZ	85034	480-921-4400		452
Medical Board 9545 Doubletree Ranch Rd *TF:* 877-255-2212 ■ *Web:* www.azmd.gov	Scottsdale	AZ	85258	480-551-2700	551-2828	339-3
Motor Vehicle Div PO Box 2100 MD 555M *Web:* azdot.gov	Phoenix	AZ	85001	602-255-0072		339-3
Nursing Board 4747 N Seventh St Ste 200 *Web:* www.azbn.gov	Phoenix	AZ	85014	602-771-7800	771-7888	339-3
Postsecondary Education Commission 2020 N Central Ave Ste 650 *Web:* highered.az.gov	Phoenix	AZ	85004	602-258-2435	258-2483	339-3
Real Estate Dept 2910 N 44th St Ste 100 *Web:* www.re.state.az.us	Phoenix	AZ	85018	602-771-7799	468-0562	339-3
Rehabilitation Services Admin 3321 N 16th St Ste 200 *TF:* 800-563-1221 ■ *Web:* des.az.gov	Phoenix	AZ	85016	602-266-9206	250-8576	339-3
Revenue Dept 1600 W Monroe St *Web:* azdor.gov	Phoenix	AZ	85007	602-255-3381		339-3
Secretary of State 1700 W Washington St 7th Fl *TF:* 800-458-5842 ■ *Web:* azsos.gov	Phoenix	AZ	85007	602-542-4285	542-1575	339-3
Securities Div 1300 W Washington St 3rd Fl *TF:* 866-837-4399 ■ *Web:* www.azinvestor.gov	Phoenix	AZ	85007	602-542-4242		339-3
State Boards Office 1400 W Washington St *TF:* 877-820-7831 ■ *Web:* ppse.az.gov	Phoenix	AZ	85007	602-542-5709	542-1253	339-3
State Parks 1300 W Washington St *Web:* azstateparks.com	Phoenix	AZ	85007	602-542-4174		339-3
Supreme Court 1501 W Washington St *Web:* www.azcourts.gov	Phoenix	AZ	85007	602-452-6700	452-3226	339-3
Tourism Office 1950 E Watkins St Ste 140 *Web:* tourism.az.gov	Phoenix	AZ	85007	602-364-3700	364-3702	339-3
Treasurer 1700 W Washington St Ste 102 *TF:* 877-365-8310 ■ *Web:* aztreasury.gov	Phoenix	AZ	85007	602-542-7800	542-7176	339-3
Veterans Service Dept 3839 N Third St Ste 200 *Web:* dvs.az.gov	Phoenix	AZ	85012	602-255-3373		339-3
Vital Records Office 1818 W Adams St *Web:* www.azdhs.gov	Phoenix	AZ	85007	602-364-1300		339-3
Weights & Measures Services Div 4425 W Olive Ave Ste 134 *Web:* www.agriculture.az.gov	Glendale	AZ	85302	602-771-4938		339-3
Arizona Academy of Beauty - East 5631 E Speedway Blvd *Web:* www.arizonaacademy.com	Tucson	AZ	85712	520-885-4120		167-3
Arizona Art Supply 4025 N 16th St *TF:* 877-264-9514 ■ *Web:* www.arizonaartsupply.com	Phoenix	AZ	85016	602-264-9514		45
Arizona Association of Realtors 255 E Osborne Rd Ste 200 *TF:* 800-426-7274 ■ *Web:* www.aaronline.com	Phoenix	AZ	85012	602-248-7787	351-2474	656
Arizona Automobile Dealers Assn 3419 E University Dr *TF:* 800-678-3875 ■ *Web:* www.aada.com	Phoenix	AZ	85034	602-468-0888		138
Arizona Automotive Institute 6829 N 46th Ave *TF:* 888-419-9440 ■ *Web:* www.aai.edu	Glendale	AZ	85301	888-419-9440		167-3
Arizona Bag Company LLC 2530 W Buckeye Rd *TF:* 800-270-2247 ■ *Web:* www.arizonabag.com	Phoenix	AZ	85009	602-272-1333	278-7871	351
Arizona Bankers Assn 111 W Monroe St Ste 440 *Web:* azbankers.org	Phoenix	AZ	85003	602-258-1200		138
Arizona Biltmore Resort & Spa 2400 E Missouri *TF:* 800-950-0086 ■ *Web:* www.arizonabiltmore.com	Phoenix	AZ	85016	602-955-6600	381-7600	669

Name / Address	City	State	Zip	Phone	Fax	Class
Arizona Bridge To Independent Living						
5025 E Washington St Ste 200	Phoenix	AZ	85034	602-256-2245	254-6407	363
TF: 800-280-2245 ■ *Web:* ability360.org						
Arizona Cardinals 8701 S Hardy Dr	Tempe	AZ	85284	602-379-0101		715-3
TF: 800-999-1402 ■ *Web:* www.azcardinals.com						
Arizona Center for Medieval and Renaissance Studies (ACMRS)						
PO Box 874402	Tempe	AZ	85287	480-727-6503	965-1681	637-2
Web: www.acmrs.org						
Arizona Chamber of Commerce & Industry						
3200 N Central Ave Ste 1125	Phoenix	AZ	85012	602-248-9172	265-1262	140
TF: 866-275-5816 ■ *Web:* azchamber.com						
Arizona Charlie's Boulder Casino & Hotel						
4575 Boulder Hwy	Las Vegas	NV	89121	702-951-5800		379
TF: 888-236-9066 ■ *Web:* www.arizonacharliesboulder.com						
Arizona Charlie's Decatur Casino & Hotel						
740 S Decatur Blvd	Las Vegas	NV	89107	702-258-5200		133
TF: 800-342-2695 ■ *Web:* arizonacharliesdecatur.com						
Arizona Commerce Authority (ACA)						
333 N Central Ave Ste 1900	Phoenix	AZ	85004	602-845-1200	845-1201	637-10
Web: www.azcommerce.com						
Arizona Community Foundation						
2201 E Camelback Rd Ste 405B	Phoenix	AZ	85016	602-381-1400	381-1575	303
TF: 800-222-8221 ■ *Web:* www.azfoundation.org						
Arizona Components Company Inc						
2901 W McDowell Rd	Phoenix	AZ	85009	602-269-5655	278-6375	246
TF: 800-255-5420 ■ *Web:* www.azcompco.com						
Arizona Correctional Industries						
3701 W Cambridge Ave	Phoenix	AZ	85009	602-272-7600	255-3108	630
TF: 800-992-1738 ■ *Web:* aci.az.gov						
Arizona Culinary Institute						
10585 N 114th St Ste 401	Scottsdale	AZ	85259	480-603-1066		163
TF: 866-294-2433 ■ *Web:* azculinary.edu						
Arizona Daily Star 4850 S Park Ave	Tucson	AZ	85714	520-573-4343	573-4107	532-2
TF: 800-695-4492 ■ *Web:* tucson.com						
Arizona Daily Sun						
1751 S Thompson St	Flagstaff	AZ	86001	928-774-4545	774-4790	532-2
Web: azdailysun.com						
Arizona Dental Assn						
3193 N Drinkwater Blvd	Scottsdale	AZ	85251	480-344-5777	344-1442	227
TF: 800-866-2732 ■ *Web:* www.azda.org						
Arizona Electric Power Cooperative Inc						
1000 S Hwy 80	Benson	AZ	85602	520-586-3631		787
Web: www.azgt.coop						
Arizona Energy Masters						
219 W Lone Cactus	Phoenix	AZ	85027	602-427-0007		192
Web: www.arizonaenergymasters.com						
Arizona Farm Bureau Federation						
325 S Higley Rd	Gilbert	AZ	85296	480-635-3600		391-4
Web: www.azfb.org						
Arizona Federal Credit Union						
PO Box 60070	Phoenix	AZ	85082	602-683-1000		219
TF: 800-523-4603 ■ *Web:* www.arizonafederal.org						
Arizona Federal Theatre						
400 W Washington St	Phoenix	AZ	85003	602-379-2800		572
Web: www.arizonafederaltheatre.com						
Arizona Golf Resort & Conference Ctr						
425 S Power Rd	Mesa	AZ	85206	480-832-3202	981-0151	669
TF: 800-528-8282 ■ *Web:* www.arizonagolfresort.com						
Arizona Grand Resort						
Grand Pkwy 8000 S Arizona	Phoenix	AZ	85044	602-438-9000	431-6535	669
TF: 866-267-1321 ■ *Web:* www.arizonagrandresort.com						
Arizona Highways Magazine						
2039 W Lewis Ave	Phoenix	AZ	85009	800-543-5432	254-4505*	457-22
**Fax Area Code:* 602 ■ *TF:* 800-543-5432 ■ *Web:* www.arizonahighways.com						
Arizona Historical Society Museum						
1300 N College Ave	Tempe	AZ	85281	480-929-0292	967-5450	520
Web: www.arizonahistoricalsociety.org						
Arizona Home Care LLC 1626 S Edward Dr	Tempe	AZ	85281	602-252-5000	323-5070	237
Web: www.azhomecare.com						
Arizona Inn 2200 E Elm St	Tucson	AZ	85719	520-325-1541	881-5830	379
TF: 800-933-1093 ■ *Web:* www.arizonainn.com						
Arizona Jewish Post						
3822 E River Rd Ste 300	Tucson	AZ	85718	520-319-1112	577-0734	532-3
Web: www.jewishtucson.org						
Arizona Leather Company Inc						
4235 Schaefer Ave	Chino	CA	91710	909-993-5101		321
TF: 888-669-5328 ■ *Web:* www.arizonaleather.com						
Arizona Library Assn (AZLA)						
6101 S Rural Rd Ste 106	Tempe	AZ	85283	480-609-3999		435
Web: www.azla.org						
Arizona Limousines Inc						
8900 N Central Ave Ste 101	Phoenix	AZ	85020	602-267-7097	870-3388	441
TF: 800-678-0033 ■ *Web:* www.arizonalimos.com						
Arizona Materials LLC 3636 S 43rd Ave	Phoenix	AZ	85009	602-278-4444		182
Web: arizonamaterials.net						
Arizona Medical Assn, The						
810 W Bethany Home Rd	Phoenix	AZ	85013	602-246-8901	242-6283	474
TF: 800-482-3480 ■ *Web:* www.azmed.org						
Arizona Microtek Inc						
4515 S Mcclintock Dr Ste 211	Tempe	AZ	85282	480-962-5881	505-2414*	253
**Fax Area Code:* 623 ■ *Web:* www.azmicrotek.com						
Arizona Natural Resources						
2525 E Beardsley Rd	Phoenix	AZ	85050	602-569-6900	569-9697	214
Web: arizonanaturalresources.com						
Arizona Nurses Assn 1850 E S Ave Ste 1	Tempe	AZ	85282	480-831-0404	839-4780	533
Web: aznurse.site-ym.com						
Arizona Osteopathic Medical Assn						
5150 N 16th St Ste A122	Phoenix	AZ	85016	602-266-6699		533
TF: 888-266-6699 ■ *Web:* www.az-osteo.org						
Arizona Partsmaster 7125 W Sherman St	Phoenix	AZ	85043	602-233-3580	233-3607	612
TF: 888-924-7278 ■ *Web:* www.azpartsmaster.com						
Arizona Pharmacy Assn						
1845 E Southern Ave	Tempe	AZ	85282	480-838-3385	838-3557	585
Web: azpharmacy.org						
Arizona Precision Sheet Metal Inc						
2140 W Pinnacle Peak Rd	Phoenix	AZ	85027	623-516-3700	516-3701	697
TF: 800-443-7039 ■ *Web:* www.apsmsystems.com						
Arizona Public Service Co (APS)						
400 N Fifth St PO Box 53999	Phoenix	AZ	85004	602-371-7171		787
TF: 800-253-9405 ■ *Web:* www.aps.com						
Arizona Rattlers 201 E Jefferson St	Phoenix	AZ	85004	602-514-8383		715-1
Web: www.azrattlers.com						
Arizona Republic 200 E Van Buren St	Phoenix	AZ	85004	602-444-8000	444-8044	532-2
TF: 800-331-9303 ■ *Web:* www.azcentral.com						
Arizona Republican Party						
3501 N 24th St	Phoenix	AZ	85016	602-957-7770		616-2
Web: www.azgop.com						
Arizona School of Acupuncture & Oriental Medicine						
2856 E Fort Lowell Rd	Tucson	AZ	85716	520-795-0787	222-4606*	685
**Fax Area Code:* 877 ■ *Web:* www.asaom.edu						
Arizona School of Integrative Studies						
639 N 6th Ave	Tucson	AZ	85705	928-639-3455		685
Web: www.asismassage.com						
Arizona Science Ctr						
600 E Washington St	Phoenix	AZ	85004	602-716-2000	716-2099	520
Web: www.azscience.org						
Arizona Sealing Devices Inc						
150 E Alamo Dr Ste 4	Chandler	AZ	85225	480-892-7325	892-7388	385
Web: azseal.com						
Arizona Sport Shirts Inc						
100 Gasoline Alley	Indianapolis	IN	46222	800-922-9918	247-4392*	157-3
**Fax Area Code:* 317 ■ *TF:* 800-922-9918 ■ *Web:* www.arizonasportshirts.com						
Arizona Sports & Tourism Authority						
1 Cardinals Dr	Glendale	AZ	85305	623-433-7500		772
Web: www.az-sta.com						
Arizona State Capitol Museum						
1700 W Washington St	Phoenix	AZ	85007	602-542-4675	256-7985	520
TF: 800-228-4710 ■ *Web:* www.azlibrary.gov						
Arizona State Hospital						
2500 E Van Buren St	Phoenix	AZ	85008	602-244-1331	220-6355	374-5
TF: 877-588-5163 ■ *Web:* www.azdhs.gov						
Arizona State Library						
1700 W Washington St 7th Fl	Phoenix	AZ	85007	602-926-3815		434-5
Web: azlibrary.gov						
Arizona State Museum						
University of Arizona 1013 E University Blvd	Tucson	AZ	85721	520-621-6302		520
Web: www.statemuseum.arizona.edu						
Lyman Lake State Park PO Box 1428	Saint John	AZ	85936	928-337-4441		565
TF: 877-697-2757 ■ *Web:* azstateparks.com						
Arizona State Prison Complex-Douglas						
6911 N BDI Blvd PO Box 3867	Douglas	AZ	85607	520-364-7521	364-7445	213
Web: corrections.az.gov						
Arizona State Prison Complex-Eyman						
4374 E Butte Ave	Florence	AZ	85132	520-868-0201	868-0276	213
TF: 866-333-2039 ■ *Web:* corrections.az.gov						
Arizona State Prison Complex-Florence						
1305 E Butte Ave PO Box 629	Florence	AZ	85132	520-868-4011	868-5333	213
Web: corrections.az.gov						
Arizona State Prison Complex-Lewis						
26700 S Hwy 85 PO Box 70	Buckeye	AZ	85326	623-386-6160		213
Web: corrections.az.gov						
Arizona State Prison Complex-Perryville						
2105 N Citrus Rd PO Box 3000	Goodyear	AZ	85395	623-853-0304		213
Web: corrections.az.gov						
Arizona State Prison Complex-Phoenix						
2500 E Van Buren St PO Box 52109	Phoenix	AZ	85008	602-685-3100		213
Web: corrections.az.gov						
Arizona State Prison Complex-Safford						
896 S Crook Rd	Safford	AZ	85546	928-428-4698	428-3235	213
Web: corrections.az.gov						
Arizona State Prison Complex-Winslow						
2100 S Hwy 87	Winslow	AZ	86047	928-289-9551	289-2951	213
Web: az.gov						
Arizona State Prison Complex-Yuma						
7125 E Juan Sanchez Blvd	San Luis	AZ	85349	928-627-8871	627-6703	213
Web: corrections.az.gov						
Arizona State Retirement System						
3300 N Central Ave	Phoenix	AZ	85012	602-240-2000		528
TF: 800-621-3778 ■ *Web:* www.azasrs.gov						
Arizona State University						
1151 S Forest Ave PO Box 870312	Tempe	AZ	85281	480-965-9011	727-6453	166
Web: www.asu.edu						
Arizona State Veterans Home						
4141 N Third St	Phoenix	AZ	85012	602-248-1550		793
Web: dvs.az.gov						
Arizona Technology Council						
2800 N Central Ave Ste 1920	Phoenix	AZ	85004	602-343-8324		78
Web: www.aztechcouncil.org						
Arizona Ultralight Aviation Inc						
4901 N Axtell Ave	Marana	AZ	85653	520-682-7504		20
Web: www.azsportflying.com						
Arizona Veterinary Medical Assn						
100 W Coolidge St	Phoenix	AZ	85013	602-242-7936	249-3828	795
Web: azvma.org						
Arizona Western College 2020 S Ave 8 E	Yuma	AZ	85366	928-317-6000	344-7543	162
TF: 888-293-0392 ■ *Web:* www.azwestern.edu						
Arizona Wholesale Supply						
2020 E University Dr	Phoenix	AZ	85034	602-258-7901	258-8335	612
Web: www.arizonawholesalesupply.com						
Arizona Wing Commemorative Air Force Museum						
2017 N Greenfield Rd	Mesa	AZ	85215	480-924-1940		520
Web: azcaf.org						
Arizona-Sonora Desert Museum Inc						
2021 N Kinney Rd	Tucson	AZ	85743	520-883-1380		522
Web: www.desertmuseum.org						
ARJ Infusion Services Inc						
10049 Lakeview Ave	Lenexa	KS	66219	866-451-8804		237
TF: 866-451-8804 ■ *Web:* www.arjinfusion.com						
ARJ Software Inc PO Box 249	Norwood	MA	02062	508-339-1070		178-1
Web: www.arjsoftware.com						
Arjobex America Inc						
10901 Westlake Dr	Charlotte	NC	28273	800-765-9278	587-1174*	557
**Fax Area Code:* 704 ■ *TF:* 800-765-9278 ■ *Web:* www.polyart.com						
ArjoHuntleigh Inc						
2349 W Lake St Ste 250	Addison	IL	60101	800-323-1245	594-2756*	477
**Fax Area Code:* 888 ■ *TF:* 800-323-1245 ■ *Web:* www.arjohuntleigh.com						

	Phone	Fax	Class
ARK Animal Hospital LLC 6718 Goshen Rd ... Edwardsville IL 62025 *Web:* arkpetvet.net	618-207-4000		794
ARK Diagnostics Inc 48089 Fremont Blvd ... Fremont CA 94538 **Fax Area Code:* 510 ■ *TF:* 877-869-2320 ■ *Web:* www.ark-tdm.com	877-869-2320	270-6298*	363
ARK Restaurants Corp 85 Fifth Ave 14th Fl ... New York NY 10003 *NASDAQ: ARKR* ■ *Web:* arkrestaurants.com	212-206-8800	206-8814	670
ARK Solutions 1939 Roland Clarks Pl Ste 300 ... Reston VA 20191 *Web:* www.arksolutionsinc.com	703-502-6999	657-0670	463
ARK Technologies Inc 3655 Ohio Ave ... Saint Charles IL 60174 *Web:* www.arktechno.com	630-377-8855	377-0300	492
ARK TeleServices 2 E Merrick Rd ... Valley Stream NY 11580 **Fax Area Code:* 516 ■ *TF:* 800-898-5367 ■ *Web:* www.arktele.com	800-898-5367	561-8822*	393
ARK Valley Electric Cooperative Assn 10 E 10th St PO Box 1246 ... Hutchinson KS 67505 *TF:* 888-297-9212 ■ *Web:* arkvalley.com	620-662-6661		245
ARK Veterinary Clinic 5613 S US Hwy 377 ... Stephenville TX 76401 *Web:* arkveterinary.com	254-968-7916		794
ARK Veterinary Hospital 5070 Shelburne Rd ... Shelburne VT 05482 *Web:* arkvet.vet	802-985-5233		794
Arkadin Inc 5 Concourse Pkwy Ste 1600 ... Atlanta GA 30328 *TF:* 866-551-1432 ■ *Web:* www.arkadin.com	866-551-1432		387
Arkansas			
Administrative Office of the Courts 625 Marshall St ... Little Rock AR 72201 *TF:* 800-950-8221 ■ *Web:* www.courts.arkansas.gov	501-682-9400	682-9410	339-4
Arts Council 1100 N St ... Little Rock AR 72201 *Web:* www.arkansasarts.org	501-324-9150	324-9207	339-4
Attorney General 323 Center St Ste 200 ... Little Rock AR 72201 *TF:* 800-482-8982 ■ *Web:* arkansasag.gov	501-682-2007	682-8084	339-4
Bank Dept 400 Hardin Rd Ste 100 ... Little Rock AR 72211 *Web:* banking.arkansas.gov	501-324-9019	324-9028	339-4
Bureau of Standards 4608 W 61st St ... Little Rock AR 72209 *Web:* www.agriculture.arkansas.gov	501-225-1598		339-4
Child Support Enforcement Office 1509 W Seventh St ... Little Rock AR 72201 *Web:* dfa.arkansas.gov	501-682-8398		339-4
Children & Family Services Div Slot S560 PO Box 1437 ... Little Rock AR 72203 *Web:* humanservices.arkansas.gov	501-682-8008	682-6968	339-4
Contractors Licensing Board PO Box 1651 ... North Little Rock AR 72117 *Web:* aclb.arkansas.gov	501-372-4661	372-2247	339-4
Cosmetology Board 4815 W Markham St Slot 8 ... Little Rock AR 72201 *Web:* www.accessarkansas.org	501-682-2168	682-5640	339-4
Dept of Corrections Maximum Security Unit 10 Ballobar Trce ... Tucker AR 72168 *TF:* 866-801-3435 ■ *Web:* portal.arkansas.gov	501-842-3800	842-1977	213
Development Finance Authority 900 W Capitol Ste 310 ... Little Rock AR 72201 *Web:* portal.arkansas.gov	501-682-5900	682-5859	339-4
Education Dept 4 Capitol Mall ... Little Rock AR 72201 *Web:* www.dese.ade.arkansas.gov	501-682-4475		339-4
Environmental Quality Dept 5301 Northshore Dr ... North Little Rock AR 72118 *TF:* 888-233-0326 ■ *Web:* www.adeq.state.ar.us	501-682-0744	682-0880	339-4
Ethics Commission 501 Woodlane St Ste 301N ... Little Rock AR 72203 *TF:* 800-422-7773 ■ *Web:* www.arkansasethics.com	501-324-9600	324-9606	265
Financial Aid Office 114 Silas Hunt Hall ... Fayetteville AR 72701 *Web:* finaid.uark.edu	479-575-3806	575-7790	725
Game & Fish Commission 2 Natural Resource Dr ... Little Rock AR 72205 *TF:* 800-364-4263 ■ *Web:* www.agfc.com	501-223-6300		339-4
General Assembly State Capitol Bldg ... Little Rock AR 72201 *Web:* www.arkleg.state.ar.us	501-682-6107	682-2917	339-4
Governor State Capitol Rm 250 ... Little Rock AR 72201 *Web:* www.sos.arkansas.gov	501-682-2345	682-1382	339-4
Higher Education Dept 423 Main St Ste 400 ... Little Rock AR 72201 *Web:* www.adhe.edu	501-371-2000		339-4
Highway & Transportation Dept 10324 I-30 ... Little Rock AR 72209 *TF:* 800-245-1672 ■ *Web:* www.arkansashighways.com	501-569-2000	569-2400	339-4
Human Services Dept PO Box 1437 ... Little Rock AR 72203 *Web:* humanservices.arkansas.gov	501-682-8590	682-2317	339-4
Insurance Dept 1200 W Third St ... Little Rock AR 72201 *TF:* 800-282-9134 ■ *Web:* insurance.arkansas.gov	501-371-2600	371-2618	339-4
Labor Dept 900 W Capitol Ave ... Little Rock AR 72201 *Web:* www.labor.arkansas.gov	501-682-4500	682-4535	339-4
Lieutenant Governor State Capitol 800 S Gaines St ... Little Rock AR 72201 *Web:* www.ltgovernor.arkansas.gov	501-682-2144	682-2894	339-4
Natural Resources Commission 101 E Capitol Ste 350 ... Little Rock AR 72201 *Web:* www.anrc.arkansas.gov	501-682-1611	682-3991	339-4
Parks & Tourism Dept 1 Capitol Mall Ste 4A-900 ... Little Rock AR 72201 *TF:* 800-628-8725 ■ *Web:* www.arkansas.com	501-682-7777	324-1525	339-4
Public Accountancy Board 900 W Capitol Ave Ste 400 ... Little Rock AR 72201 *Web:* www.asbpa.arkansas.gov	501-682-1520	682-5538	339-4
Rehabilitation Services 525 W Capitol Ave ... Little Rock AR 72201 *TF:* 800-330-0632 ■ *Web:* www.arcareereducation.org	501-296-1600	296-1655	339-4
Revenue Div 1816 W Seventh St ... Little Rock AR 72201 *Web:* www.dfa.arkansas.gov	501-682-7751	682-7599	339-4
Secretary of State 500 Woodlane Ave Ste 256 ... Little Rock AR 72201 *Web:* www.sos.arkansas.gov	501-682-1010	682-3510	339-4
Securities Dept 201 E Markham St Ste 300 ... Little Rock AR 72201 *TF:* 800-981-4429 ■ *Web:* securities.arkansas.gov	501-324-9260	324-9268	339-4
State Medical Board 1401 W Capitol Ave Ste 340 ... Little Rock AR 72201 *TF:* 888-228-1233 ■ *Web:* www.armedicalboard.org	501-296-1802	296-1805	339-4
State Police 1 State Police Plaza Dr ... Little Rock AR 72209 *Web:* www.dps.arkansas.gov	501-618-8000		339-4
Treasurer 500 Woodlane State Capitol Ste 220 ... Little Rock AR 72201 *Web:* www.artreasury.gov	501-682-5888	682-9692	339-4
Veterans Affairs Dept 501 Woodlane Dr Ste 401N ... Little Rock AR 72201 *Web:* www.veterans.arkansas.gov	501-683-2382		339-4
Vital Records Div 4815 W Markham St Slot 44 ... Little Rock AR 72205 *Web:* www.healthy.arkansas.gov	501-661-2000		339-4
Arkansas Alligator Farm & Petting Zoo 847 Whittington Ave ... Hot Springs AR 71901 *Web:* www.alligatorfarmzoo.com	501-623-6172		823
Arkansas Arts Ctr 2510 Cantrell Rd PO Box 2137 ... Little Rock AR 72203 *Web:* www.arkansasartscenter.org	501-372-4000	375-8053	520
Arkansas Baptist Foundation 10 Remington Dr ... Little Rock AR 72204 *TF:* 800-838-2272 ■ *Web:* www.abf.org	501-376-4791		48-20
Arkansas Bar Assn 2224 Cottondale Ln ... Little Rock AR 72202 *TF:* 800-609-5668 ■ *Web:* www.arkbar.com	501-375-4606	375-4901	72
Arkansas Blue Cross Blue Shield PO Box 2181 ... Little Rock AR 72203 *TF:* 800-238-8379 ■ *Web:* www.arkansasbluecross.com	800-238-8379		391-3
Arkansas Business LP 114 Scott St ... Little Rock AR 72201 *TF:* 888-322-6397 ■ *Web:* www.arkansasbusiness.com	501-372-1443	375-7933	457-5
Arkansas Capital Corporation Group 200 River Market Ave Ste 400 ... Little Rock AR 72201 *TF:* 800-216-7237 ■ *Web:* arcapital.com	501-374-9247	374-9425	216
Arkansas Children's Hospital 1 Children's Way ... Little Rock AR 72202 *Web:* www.archildrens.org	501-364-1100		374-1
Arkansas City Area Chamber of Commerce PO Box 795 ... Arkansas City KS 67005 *TF:* 800-794-4780 ■ *Web:* www.arkcity.org	620-442-0236		139
Arkansas College of Barbering & Hair Design 200 Washington Ave ... North Little Rock AR 72114 *Web:* www.acbhd.edu	501-376-9696		162
Arkansas Correctional Industries (ACI) 6841 W 13th St ... Pine Bluff AR 71602 *TF:* 877-635-7213 ■ *Web:* www.acicatalog.com	877-635-7213		630
Arkansas Craft School 101 N Peabody Ave ... Mountain View AR 72560 *Web:* www.arkansascraftschool.org	870-269-8397		685
Arkansas Data Services 27 Macarthur Dr ... Conway AR 72032 *Web:* www.ark-data-services.com	501-327-8000		177
Arkansas Democrat-Gazette 121 E Capital St ... Little Rock AR 72203 *TF:* 800-482-1121 ■ *Web:* www.arkansasonline.com	501-378-3400	372-4765	532-2
Arkansas Department of Correction 6814 Princeton Pke ... Pine Bluff AR 71602 *Web:* www.adc.arkansas.gov	870-523-2639		213
Arkansas Department of Corrections East Arkansas Regional Unit PO Box 970 ... Marianna AR 72360 *Web:* adc.arkansas.gov	870-295-4700	295-6564	213
Arkansas Department of Corrections Varner Unit PO Box 600 ... Grady AR 71644 *Web:* adc.arkansas.gov	870-575-1800	479-3803	213
Arkansas Department of Corrections Wrightsville Unit PO Box 1000 ... Wrightsville AR 72183 *Web:* adc.arkansas.gov	501-897-5806	897-5716	213
Arkansas Educational Television Network (AETN) 350 S Donaghey Ave ... Conway AR 72034 *TF:* 800-662-2386 ■ *Web:* www.myarkansaspbs.org	501-682-2386	682-4122	632
Arkansas Educator Magazine 1500 W Fourth St ... Little Rock AR 72201 *TF:* 800-632-0624 ■ *Web:* www.aeaonline.org	501-375-4611	375-4620	457-8
Arkansas Federal Credit Union 2424 Marshall Rd ... Jacksonville AR 72076 *Web:* www.afcu.org	501-982-1000		219
Arkansas Graphics Inc 800 S Gaines St ... Little Rock AR 72201 *TF:* 877-918-4847 ■ *Web:* arkansasgraphics.com	501-376-8436		627
Arkansas Headwaters Recreation Area 307 W Sackett Ave ... Salida CO 81201 *Web:* www.colorado.com	719-539-7289		565
Arkansas Hospice 14 Parkstone Cir ... North Little Rock AR 72116 *TF:* 877-257-3400 ■ *Web:* www.arkansashospice.org	501-748-3333		371
Arkansas Lions Eye Bank & Laboratory 4301 W Markham St Ste 523 ... Little Rock AR 72205 *Web:* eye.uams.edu	501-686-5822	686-7037	269
Arkansas Methodist Medical Ctr 900 W KingsFwy ... Paragould AR 72451 *Web:* www.myammc.org	870-239-7000	239-7202	374-3
Arkansas Municipal League 301 W 2nd St ... North Little Rock AR 72114 *Web:* www.arml.org	501-374-3484	374-0541	474
Arkansas Museum of Natural Resources 3853 Smackover Hwy ... Smackover AR 71762 *Web:* www.arkansasstateparks.com	870-725-2877		565
Arkansas Museum of Science & History			
Museum of Discovery 500 President Clinton Ave Ste 150 ... Little Rock AR 72201 *Web:* museumofdiscovery.org	501-396-7050	396-7054	520

Name / Address	City	State	ZIP	Phone	Fax	Class
Arkansas Northeastern College 2501 S Div St PO Box 1109 *Web:* www.anc.edu	Blytheville	AR	72315	870-762-1020	763-1654	162
Arkansas Nurses Assn (ARNA) 1123 S University Ste 1015 *Web:* arna.org	Little Rock	AR	72204	501-244-2363	244-9903	533
Arkansas Pharmacists Assn 417 S Victory St *Web:* www.arpharmacists.org	Little Rock	AR	72201	501-372-5250		585
Arkansas Poly Inc 1248 S 28th St *TF:* 800-364-5036 ■ *Web:* arkpoly.com	Van Buren	AR	72956	479-474-5036		345
Arkansas Post Museum 5530 Hwy 165 S *Web:* www.arkansasstateparks.com	Gillett	AR	72055	870-548-2634		565
Arkansas Post National Memorial 1741 Old Post Rd *Web:* www.nps.gov	Gillett	AR	72055	870-548-2207		564
Arkansas Power Steering & Hydraulics Inc 900 Fiber Optic Dr *TF:* 800-734-9411 ■ *Web:* apshyd.com	North Little Rock	AR	72117	501-372-4828		112
Arkansas Realtors Assn 11224 Executive Center Dr *TF:* 888-333-2206 ■ *Web:* www.arkansasrealtors.com	Little Rock	AR	72211	501-225-2020	225-7131	656
Arkansas Repertory Theatre 601 Main St PO Box 110 *TF:* 866-684-3737 ■ *Web:* www.therep.org	Little Rock	AR	72203	501-378-0405		573-4
Arkansas Research Inc PO Box 303 *Web:* www.arkansasresearch.com	Conway	AR	72033	646-470-1120		466
Arkansas River Valley Regional Library 501 N Front St *Web:* www.arvrls.com	Dardanelle	AR	72834	479-229-4418	229-2595	434-3
Arkansas State Dental Assn 7480 Hwy 107 *TF:* 800-501-2732 ■ *Web:* arkansasdentistry.org	Sherwood	AR	72120	501-834-7650	834-7657	227
Arkansas State Hospital 4313 W Markham St *Web:* portal.arkansas.gov	Little Rock	AR	72205	501-686-9000	682-1197	374-5
Arkansas State Library 900 W Capitol Ste 100 *Web:* www.library.arkansas.gov	Little Rock	AR	72201	501-682-2053	682-1529	434-5
Arkansas State University 2105 Aggie Rd *TF:* 800-382-3030 ■ *Web:* www.astate.edu	Jonesboro	AR	72401	870-972-2100	972-3406	166
Arkansas Steel Associates LLC 2803 Van Dyke Rd *Web:* sumitomocorp.com	Newport	AR	72112	870-523-3693	523-4619	723
Arkansas Symphony Orchestra 2417 N Tyler St PO Box 7328 *Web:* www.arkansassymphony.org	Little Rock	AR	72217	501-666-1761	666-3193	573-3
Arkansas Tech University Administration Bldg Ste 210 *Web:* www.atu.edu	Russellville	AR	72801	479-968-0389	890-6493	786
Arkansas Times 201 E Markham Ste 200 *Web:* www.arktimes.com	Little Rock	AR	72201	501-375-2985	375-3623	532-5
Arkansas Tool & Die Inc 1317 Orange St *Web:* www.arktool.com	North Little Rock	AR	72114	501-374-6972	374-9439	757
Arkansas Trailer Manufacturing Co 3200 S Elm St *Web:* arkansastrailer.com	Little Rock	AR	72204	501-666-5417	666-1787	779
Arkansas Valley Communications 1201 E Eigth St *Web:* avc-wireless.com	Russellville	AR	72801	479-968-1502		647
Arkansas Valley Correctional Facility (AVCF) 12750 Hwy 96 Ln 13 *Web:* www.colorado.gov	Crowley	CO	81033	719-267-3520	267-5024	213
Arkansas Valley Electric Co-opeartive Corp 1811 W Commercial St PO Box 47 *TF:* 800-468-2176 ■ *Web:* www.avecc.com	Ozark	AR	72949	479-667-2176	667-5238	245
Arkansas Valley Petroleum Inc 8336 E 73rd St Ste 100 *Web:* arkvalprop.com	Tulsa	OK	74133	918-252-0508	250-4921	579
Arkansas Valley Regional Medical Ctr (AVRMC) 1100 Carson Ave *Web:* www.avrmc.org	La Junta	CO	81050	719-384-5412	383-6005	374-3
Arkansas Veterinary Medical Assn PO Box 17687 *Web:* www.arkvetmed.org	Little Rock	AR	72222	501-868-3036	868-3034	795
Arkay Packaging 350 E Pk Dr *Web:* www.arkay.com	Roanoke	VA	24019	540-977-3031	977-2503	101
Arkel International Inc 1055 Convention St *Web:* www.arkel.com	Baton Rouge	LA	70802	225-343-0525		261
Arkos Field Services LP 1010 Lamar St Ste 1700 *Web:* www.arkos.com	Houston	TX	77002	832-783-5400		538
Arkose Tax & Consulting 2440 Junction Pl Ste 100 *Web:* arkosetax.com	Boulder	CO	80301	303-545-5755		2
Arkwin Industries Inc 686 Main St *TF:* 800-284-2551 ■ *Web:* arkwin.com	Westbury	NY	11590	516-333-2640	334-6786	790
ARL (U.S. Army Research Laboratory) Attn: AMSRD-ARL-O-PA 2800 Powder Mill Rd	Adelphi	MD	20783	301-394-2500		668
ARL (Association of Research Libraries) 21 Dupont Cir NW Ste 800 *Web:* www.arl.org	Washington	DC	20036	202-296-2296		49-5
Arland Tool & Manufacturing Inc PO Box 207 *Web:* www.arland.com	Sturbridge	MA	01566	508-347-3368		487
Arlans Market Inc 6500 Fm 2100 *Web:* www.arlansmarket.com	Crosbyton	TX	77532	281-328-4868		345
Arledge & Associates Inc 309 N Bryant Ave *Web:* www.jmacpas.com	Edmond	OK	73034	405-348-0615	348-0931	2
Arley Wholesale 700 N South Rd *Fax Area Code: 800 ■ *TF:* 800-233-4107 ■ *Web:* www.arleywholesale.com	Scranton	PA	18504	570-344-9874	652-7539*	191-1
Arlington 1616 Lakeside Dr *TF:* 800-323-4147 ■ *Web:* www.arli.com	Waukegan	IL	60085	847-689-2754	689-1616	534
Arlington Arts Ctr (AAC) 3550 Wilson Blvd *Web:* arlingtonartscenter.org	Arlington	VA	22201	703-248-6800	248-6849	50-2
Arlington Baptist University 3001 W Div St *TF:* 800-899-0012 ■ *Web:* www.abu.edu	Arlington	TX	76012	817-461-8741	274-1138	166
Arlington Capital Management Inc 21 S Evergreen Ave Ste 210 *Web:* www.arlington-capital.com	Arlington Heights	IL	60005	847-670-4030		194
Arlington Capital Partners 5425 Wisconsin Ave Ste 200 *Web:* arlingtoncap.com	Chevy Chase	MD	20815	202-337-7500	337-7525	403
Arlington Career Institute 901 Avenue K *TF:* 800-394-5445 ■ *Web:* www.arlingtoncareerinstitute.edu	Grand Prairie	TX	75050	972-647-1607	647-4044	167-3
Arlington Central School District 144 Todd Hill Rd *Web:* www.arlingtonschools.org	LaGrangeville	NY	12540	845-486-4460	486-4457	685
Arlington Chamber of Commerce 2009 14th St N Ste 111 *Web:* www.arlingtonchamber.org	Arlington	VA	22201	703-525-2400		139
Arlington Chamber of Commerce 505 E Border St *Web:* www.arlingtontx.com	Arlington	TX	76010	817-275-2613	701-0893	139
Arlington Chamber of Commerce 611 Massachusetts Ave *Web:* arlcc.org	Arlington	MA	02474	781-643-4600	646-5581	139
Arlington Coal & Lumber Company Inc 41 Park Ave *TF:* 800-649-8101 ■ *Web:* www.arlcoal.com	Arlington	MA	02476	781-643-8100	643-7414	364
Arlington Connection 1606 King St *Web:* www.connectionnewspapers.com	Alexandria	VA	22314	703-778-9431		532-4
Arlington Convention & Visitors Bureau 1905 E Randol Mill Rd *TF:* 800-433-5374 ■ *Web:* www.arlington.org	Arlington	TX	76011	800-433-5374		206
Arlington County 2100 Clarendon Blvd Rm 300 *Web:* www.arlingtonva.us	Arlington	VA	22201	703-228-3130	228-7430	338
Arlington County Central Library 1015 N Quincy St *Web:* www.arlingtonva.us	Arlington	VA	22201	703-228-5990		434-3
Arlington Hat Company Inc 47-25 34th St	Long Island City	NY	11101	718-361-3000		155-9
Arlington Heights Chamber of Commerce 3400 W Stonegate Blvd Ste 2133 *Web:* arlingtonhcc.com	Arlington Heights	IL	60005	847-253-1703	253-9133	139
Arlington Heights Memorial Library 500 N Dunton Ave *Web:* www.ahml.info	Arlington Heights	IL	60004	847-392-0100	506-2650	434-3
Arlington Historical Museum 1805 S Arlington Ridge Rd *Web:* arlingtonhistoricalsociety.org	Arlington	VA	22202	703-892-4204		520
Arlington House-Robert E Lee Memorial Turkey Run Pk George Washington Memorial Pkwy *Web:* www.nps.gov	McLean	VA	22101	703-235-1530	235-1546	564
Arlington Industries Inc 1 Stauffer Industrial Pk *TF:* 800-233-4717 ■ *Web:* www.aifittings.com	Scranton	PA	18517	570-562-0270	562-0646	815
Arlington Iron Works 9127 Euclid Ave *TF:* 800-637-6829 ■ *Web:* www.arlingtonironworks.com	Manassas	VA	20110	703-368-3193		480
Arlington Machine & Tool Co 90 New Dutch Ln *Web:* www.arlingtonmachine.com	Fairfield	NJ	07004	973-276-1377		757
Arlington Metals Corp 11355 Franklin Ave *Web:* www.arlingtonmetals.com	Franklin Park	IL	60131	847-451-9100	451-9676	482
Arlington Museum of Art 201 W Main St *Web:* www.arlingtonmuseum.org	Arlington	TX	76010	817-275-4600		520
Arlington Park 2200 W Euclid Ave PO Box 7 *Web:* www.arlingtonpark.com	Arlington Heights	IL	60005	847-385-7500	385-7251	642
Arlington Plating Co 600 S Vermont St PO Box 974 *Web:* arlingtonplating.com	Palatine	IL	60067	847-359-1490	359-1499	481
Arlington Residence Court Hotel 1200 N Courthouse Rd *Web:* www.arlingtoncourthotel.com	Arlington	VA	22201	703-524-4000		707
Arlington Resort Hotel & Spa 239 Central Ave *TF:* 800-643-1502 ■ *Web:* www.arlingtonhotel.com	Hot Springs	AR	71901	501-623-7771		669
Arlington School District 315 N French Ave *TF:* 877-766-4753 ■ *Web:* www.asd.wednet.edu	Arlington	WA	98223	360-618-6200	618-6221	685
Arlington Times 1085 Cedar Ave *Web:* www.arlingtontimes.com	Marysville	WA	98270	360-659-1300		532-2
Arlington Toyota Inc 10939 Atlantic Blvd *Web:* arlingtontoyota.com	Jacksonville	FL	32225	904-302-9611		57
Arlington (TX) City Hall 101 W Abram St PO Box 90231 *Web:* www.arlingtontx.gov	Arlington	TX	76010	817-459-6777	459-6116	337
Arlo G Lott Trucking Inc 257 S 100 E *TF:* 800-443-5688 ■ *Web:* arloglotttrucking.com	Jerome	ID	83338	208-324-5053	324-8668	780
Arlon Graphics 200 Boysenberry Ln *Fax Area Code: 800 ■ *TF:* 800-232-7161 ■ *Web:* www.arlon.com	Santa Ana	CA	92704	714-540-2811	329-2756*	3
ARM (Associated Risk Managers International Inc) 6611 W N Ave *TF:* 800-735-5441 ■ *Web:* www.armiweb.com	Oak Park	IL	60302	630-285-4324	285-3590	49-9
ARM (Association of Rotational Molders Intl) 800 Roosevelt Rd Ste C-312 *Web:* www.rotomolding.org	Glen Ellyn	IL	60137	630-942-6589	790-3095	49-13
ARMA (American Rock Mechanics Assn) 600 Woodland Terr *Web:* www.armarocks.org	Alexandria	VA	22302	703-683-1808	683-1815	49-19
ARMA (Asphalt Roofing Manufacturers Assn) 529 14th St NW Ste 750 *TF:* 800-247-6637 ■ *Web:* asphaltroofing.org	Washington	DC	20045	202-207-0917	223-9741	49-3

Name / Address	City	State	ZIP	Phone	Fax	Class
ARMA Intl 11880 College Blvd Ste 450 *TF:* 800-422-2762 ■ *Web:* www.arma.org	Overland Park	KS	66210	913-341-3808	341-3742	49-12
Armacell LLC 7600 Oakwood St Ext *Web:* www.armacell.us	Mebane	NC	27302	919-304-3846		601
Armada Group, The 325 Soquel Ave *TF:* 800-408-2120 ■ *Web:* www.thearmadagroup.com	Santa Cruz	CA	95062	800-408-2120		344
Armada Hoffler 222 Central Park Ave Ste 2100 *Web:* www.armadahoffler.com	Virginia Beach	VA	23462	757-366-4000		186
Armada Oil & Gas Company Inc 3335 Greenfield Rd *Web:* armadaoil.com	Melvindale	MI	48122	313-582-1777		579
Armada Rubber Manufacturing Co 24586 Armada Ridge Rd PO Box 579 *Web:* www.armadarubber.com	Armada	MI	48005	586-784-9135	784-5023	677
Armadillo Enterprises Inc 4924 W Waters Ave *Web:* www.armadilloent.com	Tampa	FL	33634	813-600-3920		526
ArmaLite Inc 745 S Hanford St *TF:* 800-336-0184 ■ *Web:* www.armalite.com	Geneseo	IL	61254	309-944-6939		807
Armand Manufacturing Inc 2399 Silver Wolf Dr *TF:* 800-669-9811 ■ *Web:* armandmfg.com	Henderson	NV	89011	702-565-7500	565-3838	66
Armando's Mexican Restaurant 4242 W Vernor Hwy *Web:* www.mexicantown.com	Detroit	MI	48209	313-554-0666		671
Armandos 2630 Westheimer *Web:* armandosrestaurant.com	Houston	TX	77098	713-520-1738		671
Armanino Foods of Distinction Inc 30588 San Antonio St *OTC:* AMNF ■ *TF:* 800-255-5855 ■ *Web:* www.armaninofoods.com	Hayward	CA	94544	510-441-9300	441-0101	296-36
Armanino LLP 12657 Alcosta Blvd Ste 500 **Fax Area Code:* 925 ■ *TF:* 844-582-8883 ■ *Web:* www.armaninollp.com	San Ramon	CA	94583	844-582-8883	790-2601*	2
Armatron International Inc 15 Highland Ave *TF:* 800-343-3280 ■ *Web:* www.flowtron.com	Malden	MA	02148	781-321-2300		429
Armature Dns 2000 Inc 11001 Jean Meunier *Web:* www.dns-2000.com	Montreal	QC	H1G4S7	514-324-1141		791
Armbrae Academy 1400 Oxford St *Web:* www.armbrae.ns.ca	Halifax	NS	B3H3Y8	902-423-7920		685
Armbrecht Jackson LLP 63 S Royal St Riverview Plz 13th Fl *Web:* www.ajlaw.com	Mobile	AL	36602	251-405-1300	432-6843	428
Armbrust International Ltd 735 Allens Ave *Web:* www.armbrustintl.com	Providence	RI	02905	401-781-3300		409
Armbrust Paper Tubes Inc 6255 S Harlem Ave *Web:* www.tubesrus.com	Chicago	IL	60638	773-586-3232		125
Armec Corp 8113 Beaver Ridge Rd	Knoxville	TN	37931	865-483-9969		454
Armed Forces Communications & Electronics Assn (AFCEA) 4114 Legato Rd Ste 1000 *TF:* 800-336-4583 ■ *Web:* www.afcea.org	Fairfax	VA	22033	703-631-6100	631-4693	48-19
Armed Forces Financial Network LLC 11601 Roosevelt Blvd TA-94 *Web:* www.affn.org	Saint Petersburg	FL	33716	727-227-2880	227-5773	225
Armed Forces Insurance Exchange (AFI) 550 Eisenhower Rd *TF:* 800-255-6792 ■ *Web:* www.afi.org	Leavenworth	KS	66048	800-255-6792	828-7731	391-4
Armed Forces Retirement Home - Washington 3700 N Capitol St NW **Fax Area Code:* 202 ■ *TF:* 800-422-9988 ■ *Web:* www.afrh.gov	Washington	DC	20011	800-422-9988	541-7519*	450
Armed Services Mutual Benefit Assn (ASMBA) 1000 NorthChase Dr Ste 220 *TF:* 800-251-8434 ■ *Web:* asmba.com	Goodlettsville	TN	37072	615-851-0800	851-9484	48-19
Armellini Express Lines Inc 3446 SW Armellini Ave *TF:* 800-327-7887 ■ *Web:* www.armellini.com	Palm City	FL	34990	772-287-0575	221-3284	780
Armenian Assembly of America 734 15th St NW Ste 500 *Web:* armenian-assembly.org	Washington	DC	20005	202-393-3434	638-4904	48-14
Armenian Church of America 630 2nd Ave *Web:* armenianchurch.us	New York	NY	10016	212-686-0710		48-20
Armenian General Benevolent Union (AGBU) 55 E 59th St *Web:* agbu.org	New York	NY	10022	212-319-6383	319-6507	48-14
Armentor Glenn Law Corp 300 Stewart St *TF:* 800-960-5551 ■ *Web:* www.glennarmentor.com	LaFayette	LA	70501	337-233-1471		428
Armijo High School 824 Washington St *Web:* www.fsusd.org	Fairfield	CA	94533	707-399-5000	421-4234	685
Armil/Cfs Inc 15660 La Salle St *Web:* www.armilcfs.com	South Holland	IL	60473	708-339-6810		318
Armin Tool & Manufacturing Company Inc 1500 N La Fox St *TF:* 800-427-3607 ■ *Web:* armin-ind.com	South Elgin	IL	60177	847-742-1864	742-0253	757
Armistead Mechanical Inc 168 Hopper Ave *TF:* 800-587-5267 ■ *Web:* www.armisteadmechanical.com	Waldwick	NJ	07463	201-447-6740	447-6744	189-10
Armite Laboratories Inc 1560 Superior Ave Ste A4 *Web:* armitelabs.com	Costa Mesa	CA	92627	949-646-9035	646-8319	541
Armm Inc 17744 Sampson Ln *Web:* www.armminc.com	Huntington Beach	CA	92647	714-848-8190	848-6141	476
Armor Group Inc, The 4600 N Mason-Montgomery Rd *TF:* 800-255-0393 ■ *Web:* www.thearmorgroup.com	Mason	OH	45040	800-255-0393		318
Armor Protective Packaging 951 Jones St *TF:* 800-365-1117 ■ *Web:* www.armorvci.com	Howell	MI	48843	517-546-1117		557
Armor Security Inc 2601 Stevens Ave S *Web:* www.armorsecurity.com	Minneapolis	MN	55408	612-870-4142		45

Name / Address	City	State	ZIP	Phone	Fax	Class
Armorstruxx Inc 850 Thurman St *Web:* www.armorstruxx.com	Lodi	CA	95240	209-365-9400	224-0959	59
Armortex Inc 5926 Corridor Pkwy *Web:* www.armortex.com	Schertz	TX	78154	210-661-8306	661-8308	194
Armory Art Ctr 1700 Parker Ave *Web:* www.armoryart.org	West Palm Beach	FL	33401	561-832-1776	832-0191	50-2
Armour Risk Management Inc 1880 JFK Blvad Ste 801 *Web:* www.armourholdings.com	Philadelphia	PA	19103	215-665-5000		391-4
Armour Transportation Systems Inc 689 Edinburgh Dr *TF:* 800-561-7987 ■ *Web:* armour.ca	Moncton	NB	E1E2L4	506-857-0205		23
Arms Acres 75 Seminary Hill Rd *TF:* 800-989-2676 ■ *Web:* www.armsacres.com	Carmel	NY	10512	845-225-3400		726
Arms Communications Inc 1517 Maurice Dr *Web:* www.armscomm.com	Woodbridge	VA	22191	703-690-3338	490-3810	590
Arms Control Assn 1313 L St NW Ste 130 *Web:* www.armscontrol.org	Washington	DC	20005	202-463-8270	463-8273	48-5
Arms Family Museum of Local History 648 Wick Ave *Web:* mahoninghistory.org	Youngstown	OH	44502	330-743-2589	743-7210	520
Armstrong Ambulance Service Inc 87 Mystic St *Web:* armstrongambulance.com	Arlington	MA	02474	781-648-0612		30
Armstrong Consultants Inc 861 Rood Ave *Web:* www.armstrongconsultants.com	Grand Junction	CO	81501	970-242-0101		256
Armstrong County 100 Trice St PO Box 189 *Web:* www.co.armstrong.tx.us	Claude	TX	79019	806-553-2860		338
Armstrong County 450 E Market St *TF:* 800-368-1066 ■ *Web:* www.co.armstrong.pa.us	Kittanning	PA	16201	724-543-2500		338
Armstrong County Chamber of Commerce 124 Market St *Web:* allekiskistrong.com	Kittanning	PA	16201	724-543-1305		139
Armstrong County Memorial Hospital (ACMH) One Nolte Dr *Web:* www.acmh.org	Kittanning	PA	16201	724-543-8500	543-8704	374-3
Armstrong County Tourist Bureau 125 Market St *TF:* 888-265-9954 ■ *Web:* armstrongcounty.com	Kittanning	PA	16201	724-543-4003	545-3119	206
Armstrong Donohue & Ceppos 204 Monroe St Ste 101 *Web:* www.adclawfirm.com	Rockville	MD	20850	301-251-0440	279-5929	428
Armstrong Engineering Associates Inc 1101 W Strasburg *Web:* www.rmarmstrong.com	West Chester	PA	19382	610-436-6080		91
Armstrong Garden Centers Inc (AGC) 2200 E Rt 66 Ste 200 *Web:* www.armstronggarden.com	Glendora	CA	91740	626-914-1091		323
Armstrong Group of Cos 1 Armstrong Pl *Web:* agoc.com	Butler	PA	16001	724-283-0925		116
Armstrong International Inc 2081 SE Ocean Blvd 4th Fl *TF:* 866-738-5125 ■ *Web:* www.armstronginternational.com	Stuart	FL	34996	772-286-7175	286-1001	789
Armstrong Kelly (Rep R - ND) 1004 Longworth House Office Bldg *Web:* www.armstrong.house.gov	Washington	DC	20515	202-225-2611		342-2
Armstrong Law Firm 75 E Santa Clara St Ste 1200 *Web:* armlawfirm.com	San Jose	CA	95113	408-279-6400		41
Armstrong Law Offices PC 257 East 200 South Ste 410 *Web:* armstronglaw.com	Salt Lake City	UT	84111	801-359-5511	359-5570	41
Armstrong Law PC 27 Central St *Web:* ncalaw.com	Lowell	MA	01852	978-453-1044	453-1055	41
Armstrong Lumber Company Inc 2709 Auburn Way N *TF:* 800-868-9066 ■ *Web:* www.armstrong-homes.com	Auburn	WA	98002	253-833-6666		817
Armstrong Manufacturing Co 2700 SE Tacoma St *TF:* 800-426-6226 ■ *Web:* www.armstrongblue.com	Portland	OR	97202	503-228-8381	228-8384	494
Armstrong Medical Industries Inc 575 Knightsbridge Pkwy *TF:* 800-323-4220 ■ *Web:* www.armstrongmedical.com	Lincolnshire	IL	60069	847-913-0101	913-0138	477
Armstrong Mold Corp 6910 Manlius Center Rd *Web:* www.armstrongrm.com	East Syracuse	NY	13057	315-437-1517	437-9198	757
Armstrong Oil & Gas Inc 1421 BLk St *Web:* armstrongoilandgas.com	Denver	CO	80202	303-623-1821		538
Armstrong Partnership LP 23 Prince Andrew Pl *Web:* www.armstrongpartnership.com	Toronto	ON	M3C2H2	416-444-3050		195
Armstrong Pumps Inc 93 E Ave *Web:* armstrongfluidtechnology.com	North Tonawanda	NY	14120	716-693-8813		641
Armstrong School District 181 Heritage Park Dr Ste 2 *Web:* www.asd.k12.pa.us	Kittanning	PA	16201	724-548-7200		685
Armstrong Shaw Associates Inc 237 Elm St *Web:* www.armstrongshaw.com	New Canaan	CT	06840	203-972-9600		401
Armstrong Systems & Consulting 5101 Tremont Ave Ste A *Web:* www.armstrongsystems.com	Davenport	IA	52807	563-386-9090		608
Armstrong Wealth Management 308 Market St *TF:* 888-545-1919 ■ *Web:* armstrongwm.com	Kittanning	PA	16201	724-545-1919	543-1515	390
Armstrong World Industries Inc 2500 Columbia Ave *NYSE:* AWI ■ *TF:* 800-233-3823 ■ *Web:* www.armstrong.com	Lancaster	PA	17603	717-397-0611		291
Army & Navy Academy 2605 Carlsbad Blvd *TF:* 888-762-2338 ■ *Web:* armyandnavyacademy.org	Carlsbad	CA	92008	760-729-2385	434-5948	622
Army & Navy Club, The 901 Seventeenth St NW *Web:* armynavyclub.org	Washington	DC	20006	202-628-8400	785-2481	48-19

Name / Address	City	State	Zip	Phone	Fax	Class
Army Aviation Association of America (AAAA) 593 Main St. *Web:* www.quad-a.org	Monroe	CT	06468	203-268-2450	268-5870	48-19
Army Distaff Foundation 6200 Oregon Ave NW. *Web:* www.armydistaff.org	Washington	DC	20015	202-541-0492		48-19
Army Logistics University Library 562 Quarters Rd Bldg 12420. *Web:* www.almc.army.mil	Fort Lee	VA	23801	804-765-8170		434-3
Army Residence Community 7400 Crestway. *TF:* 800-725-0083 ■ *Web:* www.armyresidence.com	San Antonio	TX	78239	210-646-5316		672
Arn Mullins Unruh Kuhn & Wilson LLP 300 W Douglas Ste 330. *Web:* arnmullins.com	Wichita	KS	67202	316-267-5267		41
ARNA (Arkansas Nurses Assn) 1123 S University Ste 1015. *Web:* arna.org	Little Rock	AR	72204	501-244-2363	244-9903	533
Arnan Services Inc PO Box 4067. *TF:* 866-607-2111 ■ *Web:* www.arnan.com	Saint Paul	MN	55104	612-720-0350	670-0385	194
Arnaud's 813 Bienville St. *TF:* 866-230-8895 ■ *Web:* www.arnaudsrestaurant.com	New Orleans	LA	70112	504-523-5433		671
Arndt's Fudgery LLC 106 W Washington St. *Fax Area Code: 618 ■ *TF:* 800-753-8343 ■ *Web:* www.fudgery.biz	Newton	IL	62448	800-753-8343	783-2183*	297-3
Arne Fogel Productions 8401 Wayzata Blvd Ste 202. *Web:* www.arnefogel.com	Golden Valley	MN	55426	952-546-3822		514
Arneg Canada Inc 18 Rue Richelieu. *TF:* 800-363-3439 ■ *Web:* www.arneg.ca	Lacolle	QC	J0J1J0	450-246-3837	246-2368	610
Arneg LLC 750 Old Hargrave Rd. *Web:* www.arnegusa.com	Lexington	NC	27295	336-956-5300		610
Arnellwest Inc 3441 South 2200 West Ste 103. *Web:* arnell-west.com	Salt Lake City	UT	84119	801-975-9966	975-9967	186
Arnerich Massena & Associates Inc 2045 NE Martin Luther King Jr Blvd. *Web:* arnerichmassena.com	Portland	OR	97212	503-239-0475		401
Arneson River Theatre 418 Villita St. *Web:* www.getcreativesanantonio.com	San Antonio	TX	78205	210-207-8614		572
Arney Computer Systems PO Box 382511. *Fax Area Code: 972 ■ *Web:* www.arneycomputer.com	Duncanville	TX	75138	214-306-0754	890-9899*	177
Arnie's 722 Leonard St NW. *Web:* www.arniesrestaurants.com	Grand Rapids	MI	49503	616-454-3098		296-1
Arnima Design Inc 518 N Tampa St Ste 320. *Web:* www.arnimadesign.com	Tampa	FL	33602	813-341-3500		177
Arnoff Moving & Storage Inc 1282 Dutchess Tpke. *Fax Area Code: 845 ■ *TF:* 800-633-6683 ■ *Web:* www.arnoff.com	Poughkeepsie	NY	12603	888-430-9542	452-3606*	519
Arnold & Assn 14275 Midway Rd Ste 170. *TF:* 800-535-6329 ■ *Web:* elarnoldandassociates.com	Addison	TX	75001	972-991-1144		256
Arnold & Itkin LLP 6009 Memorial Dr. *TF:* 888-493-1629 ■ *Web:* www.arnolditkin.com	Houston	TX	77007	713-222-3800		428
Arnold & Mabel Beckman Foundation 100 Academy Dr. *Web:* www.beckman-foundation.org	Irvine	CA	92617	949-721-2222		305
Arnold & Placek PC 203 E Main St Ste 201. *Web:* arnoldplacek.com	Round Rock	TX	78664	512-341-7044		41
Arnold & Porter Kaye Scholer LLP 601 Massachusetts Ave NW. *Web:* www.arnoldporter.com	Washington	DC	20001	202-942-5000	942-5999	428
Arnold Arboretum of Harvard University 125 Arborway. *Web:* www.arboretum.harvard.edu	Jamaica Plain	MA	02130	617-524-1718	524-1418	97
Arnold Companies 700 Gervais St. *Web:* www.arnoldfamilycorp.com	Columbia	SC	29201	803-731-4321		186
Arnold Insurance Agency Inc 1400 Haft Dr. *Web:* arnoldinsuranceagency.com	Reynoldsburg	OH	43068	614-863-0455		390
Arnold Lumber Company Inc 251 Fairgrounds Rd. *TF:* 800-339-0116 ■ *Web:* www.arnoldlumber.com	West Kingston	RI	02892	401-783-2266		191-3
Arnold Motor Supply & The Merrill Co 601 1st Ave S W. *Web:* arnoldmotorsupply.com	Spencer	IA	51301	712-262-1141		61
Arnold Printing 630 Lunken Park Dr. *Web:* madebyarnold.com	Cincinnati	OH	45226	513-533-6900		627
Arnold Refrigeration Inc 1122 N Cherry. *Web:* www.arnoldrefrigeration.com	San Antonio	TX	78202	210-225-5493	225-2605	189-10
Arnold Sanders Consulting Engineers Inc 12651 Mcgregor Blvd Ste 103. *Web:* arnoldsanders.com	Fort Myers	FL	33919	239-267-3666		261
Arnold State Recreation Area PO Box 117 Hc 69. *TF:* 800-746-8420 ■ *Web:* nrrs.ne.gov	Anselmo	NE	68813	308-749-2235		565
Arnold Steel Company Inc 79 Randolph Rd. *Web:* www.arnoldsteel.com	Howell Township	NJ	07731	732-363-1079		492
Arnold Supply Inc 2409 Pasadena Blvd. *Web:* arnoldsupply.com	Pasadena	TX	77502	713-477-3333		358
Arnold Transportation Services Inc 9523 Florida Mining Blvd. *Web:* www.arnoldtrans.com	Jacksonville	FL	32257	904-262-4285		780
Arnold Walker & Arnold & Company PC 915 N Jefferson Ave. *Web:* www.awacpa.com	Mount Pleasant	TX	75455	903-572-6606	572-3751	2
Arnold's Beauty School 1179 S 2nd St. *Web:* www.arnoldsbeautyschool.com	Milan	TN	38358	731-686-7351		685
Arnot Ogden Medical Ctr 600 Roe Ave. *TF:* 800-952-2662 ■ *Web:* www.arnothealth.org	Elmira	NY	14905	607-737-4100		374-3
Arnprior Aerospace Inc 107 Baskin Dr E. *Web:* www.arnprioraerospace.com	Arnprior	ON	K7S3M1	613-623-4267		21
ARNS Law Firm, The 515 Folsom St 3rd Fl. *Web:* www.arnslaw.com	San Francisco	CA	94105	415-495-7800		428
Arnstein & Lehr LLP 120 S Riverside Plz Ste 1200. *Web:* www.saul.com	Chicago	IL	60606	847-843-2900		445
ARO Welding 48500 Structural Dr. *Web:* www.arotechnologies.com	Chesterfield	MI	48051	586-949-9353	949-4493	811
Arobella Medical LLC 5929 Baker Rd Ste 470. *Web:* www.arobella.com	Minnetonka	MN	55345	952-345-6841		250
Arobotech Systems Inc 1524 E Avis Dr. *Web:* www.arobotech.com	Madison Heights	MI	48071	248-588-9080		757
AROG Pharmaceuticals Inc 12400 Coit Rd. *Web:* www.arogpharma.com	Dallas	TX	75251	214-593-0500		582
Aromaland Inc 1326 Rufina Cir. *TF:* 800-933-5267 ■ *Web:* www.aromaland.com	Santa Fe	NM	87507	800-933-5267		77
Aronoff Center for the Arts 650 Walnut St. *Web:* www.cincinnatiarts.org	Cincinnati	OH	45202	513-721-3344	977-4150	572
Aronov Realty 3500 Eastern Blvd. *Web:* www.aronov.com	Montgomery	AL	36116	334-277-1000	272-0747	655
Aronson & Co 805 King Farm Blvd Ste 300. *Web:* aronsonllc.com	Rockville	MD	20850	301-231-6200	231-7630	2
Aronson + Johnson + Ortiz LP 230 S Broad St 20th Fl. *Web:* www.ajopartners.com	Philadelphia	PA	19102	215-546-7500		690
Aronson Security Group Inc 600 Oakesdale Ave SW Ste 100. *TF:* 800-547-9988 ■ *Web:* www.aronsonsecurity.com	Renton	WA	98057	206-284-3553		692
Aroostook Home Health Services 658 Main St Ste 2. *TF:* 877-688-9977 ■ *Web:* aroostookhomehealthservices.com	Caribou	ME	04736	207-492-8290	492-8245	363
Aroostook Medical Ctr, The (TAMC) 140 Academy St. *Web:* www.northernlighthealth.org	Presque Isle	ME	04769	207-768-4000		374-3
Arora & Associates PC 1200 Lenox Dr Ste 200. *Web:* www.arorapc.com	Lawrence Township	NJ	08648	609-844-1111	844-9799	256
Around The Clock Care 5251 Office Park Dr Ste 400. *TF:* 800-828-3232 ■ *Web:* bakersfieldcare.com	Bakersfield	CA	93309	661-395-5800		363
Arowana Consulting Inc 1550 Park Ave Ste 202. *Web:* www.arowanaconsulting.com	South Plainfield	NJ	07080	732-412-3567		177
Arpa International Film Festival 2919 Maxwell St. *Web:* affma.org	Los Angeles	CA	90027	323-663-1882		282
ARPAC LLC 9511 W Irving Park Rd. *Web:* www.arpac.com	Schiller Park	IL	60176	847-678-9034	671-7006	547
Arpin International Group Inc 4372 Post Rd. *Web:* www.arpinintl.com	East Greenwich	RI	02818	401-885-4600		360-3
Arque Capital Ltd 7001 N Scottsdale Rd Ste 1005. *Web:* arquecapital.com	Scottsdale	AZ	85258	602-971-9000		690
Arquitectonica International Corp 2900 Oak Ave. *Web:* arquitectonica.com	Miami	FL	33133	305-372-1812	372-1175	261
ArQule Inc 19 Presidential Way. *NASDAQ: ARQL* ■ *TF:* 800-373-7827 ■ *Web:* www.arqule.com	Woburn	MA	01801	781-994-0300	376-6019	85
Arradiance Inc 142 N Rd Ste F-150. *TF:* 800-659-2970 ■ *Web:* www.arradiance.com	Sudbury	MA	01776	800-659-2970		253
Array Healthcare Facilities Solutions 2520 Renaissance Blvd Ste 110. *Web:* www.array-architects.com	King of Prussia	PA	19406	610-270-0599	270-0995	261
Array Marketing 45 Progress Ave. *TF:* 800-295-4120 ■ *Web:* arraymarketing.com	Toronto	ON	M1P2Y6	416-299-4865	292-9759	233
ArrayComm LLC 701 DeMers Ave. *Fax Area Code: 866 ■ *Web:* www.arraycomm.com	Grand Forks	ND	58201	701-317-7586	739-0355*	178-1
Arrayworks Inc 200 Chauncy St Ste 101. *Fax Area Code: 407 ■ *Web:* arrayworks.com	Mansfield	MA	02048	781-849-9797	637-2053*	177
Arrel Enterprises Inc 2800-H Bob Wallace Ave. *Web:* arrelenterprises.com	Huntsville	AL	35805	256-534-5853	534-5856	189-4
Arrendale Associates Inc 20484 Chartwell Center Dr Ste G. *Web:* aaita.com	Cornelius	NC	28031	704-895-8025		177
Arrhythmia Technologies Institute 400 Executive Center Dr Ste 116. *Web:* www.atischool.org	Greenville	SC	29615	864-297-9232	297-9250	167-3
Arribas Bros Inc 1500 Live Oak Ln. *Web:* www.arribas.com	Orlando	FL	32830	407-828-4840		327
Arrietty Solutions 2707 Keystone Ln 101. *Web:* arriettysolutions.com	Vienna	VA	22180	610-718-0666		177
Arrington Jodey (Rep R - TX) 1029 Longworth House Office Bldg. *TF:* 888-217-0281 ■ *Web:* arrington.house.gov	Washington	DC	20515	202-225-4005	225-9615	342-2
Arrington Manufacturing LLC 67 Motorsport Dr. *Web:* www.shophemi.com	Martinsville	VA	24112	276-666-6767		247
Arris Builders Inc 27261 Las Ramblas Ste 320. *Web:* www.arrisbuilders.com	Mission Viejo	CA	92691	949-261-3113	261-3119	186
Arris Group Inc 3871 Lakefield Dr. *NASDAQ: ARRS* ■ *TF:* 866-362-7747 ■ *Web:* www.arris.com	Suwanee	GA	30024	678-473-2000	473-8470	647
ARRL (American Radio Relay League) 225 Main St. *TF:* 888-277-5289 ■ *Web:* www.arrl.org	Newington	CT	06111	860-594-0200	594-0259	49-14
Arro Consulting Inc 108 W Airport Rd. *Web:* www.arroconsulting.com	Lititz	PA	17543	717-569-7021		261
Arro Tool & Die Inc 4687 Gleason Rd. *Web:* www.arrotool.com	Lakewood	NY	14750	716-763-6203	763-8511	757

Name / Address	City	State	ZIP	Phone	Fax	Class
Arrojo Cosmetology School 200 Hudson St *Web:* www.arrojocosmetology.com	New York	NY	10013	212-242-7786		685
Arrow Bicycle Inc 5108 Baltimore Ave *Web:* arrowbicycle.com	Hyattsville	MD	20781	301-531-9250		711
Arrow Diversified Tooling Inc 17 Pinney St *Web:* www.arrowdiversified.com	Ellington	CT	06029	860-872-9072		757
Arrow Electric Company Inc 317 Wabasso Ave *TF:* 888-999-5591 ■ *Web:* www.arrowelectric.com	Louisville	KY	40209	502-367-0141	361-8613	189-4
Arrow Electronics Corp 7459 S Lima St *NYSE: ARW* ■ *Web:* www.arrow.com	Englewood	CO	80112	303-824-4000		174
Arrow Energy Services 3001 W Big Beaver Rd Ste 525 *Web:* www.arrowenergyservices.com	Troy	MI	48084	248-283-7100		540
Arrow Engine Co 2301 E Independence St *TF:* 800-331-3662 ■ *Web:* www.arrowengines.com	Tulsa	OK	74110	918-583-5711		262
Arrow Environmental Services Inc 6225 Tower Ln *TF:* 888-424-2324 ■ *Web:* www.arrowservices.com	Sarasota	FL	34240	888-420-9457		577
Arrow Fastener Company Inc 271 Mayhill St *TF:* 800-776-2228 ■ *Web:* www.arrowfastener.com	Saddle Brook	NJ	07663	201-843-6900	843-3911	758
Arrow Financial Corp 250 Glen St *NASDAQ: AROW* ■ *TF:* 888-444-0058 ■ *Web:* www.arrowfinancial.com	Glens Falls	NY	12801	518-415-4307		360-2
Arrow Freight Management Inc 1001 Berryville St *TF:* 888-598-9891 ■ *Web:* www.arrowelp.com	El Paso	TX	79928	888-598-9891		311
Arrow Gear Company Inc 2301 Curtiss St *Web:* www.arrowgear.com	Downers Grove	IL	60515	630-969-7640	969-0253	22
Arrow J Landscape & Design Inc 909 E 68th Ave *Web:* ajifence.com	Denver	CO	80229	303-289-4388		422
Arrow Lock Co 100 Arrow Dr *TF:* 800-839-3157 ■ *Web:* www.arrowlock.com	New Haven	CT	06511	800-839-3157	421-6615	350
Arrow Machining Company Inc 7224 44th Ave NE *Web:* www.arrowmachining.com	Marysville	WA	98270	360-659-0342	653-8945	454
Arrow Pneumatics Inc 2111 W 21st St *Web:* www.arrowpneumatics.com	Broadview	IL	60155	708-343-9595		18
Arrow Printing Company Inc 115 W Woodland Ave *Web:* www.arrowprintco.com	Salina	KS	67402	785-825-8124	825-0784	627
Arrow Road Construction 3401 S Busse Rd *TF:* 800-523-4417 ■ *Web:* arrowroad.com	Mount Prospect	IL	60056	847-437-0700	437-0779	188-4
Arrow Rock State Historic Site PO Box 1 *Web:* mostateparks.com	Arrow Rock	MO	65320	660-837-3330		565
Arrow Security Patrols 60 Knickerbocker Ave *Web:* www.arrowsecurity.net	Bohemia	NY	11716	631-675-2430		693
Arrow Staffing Services 499 W State St *Web:* www.arrowstaffing.com	Redlands	CA	92373	909-792-1252		260
Arrow Stage Lines 720 E Norfolk Ave *TF:* 800-672-8302 ■ *Web:* www.arrowstagelines.com	Norfolk	NE	68701	402-371-3850		107
Arrow Storage Products 1101 N 4th St *TF:* 800-851-1085 ■ *Web:* arrowsheds.com	Breese	IL	62230	618-526-4546	526-4617	105
Arrow Strategies LLC 27777 Franklin Rd Ste 1200 *Web:* arrowstrategies.com	Southfield	MI	48034	248-502-2500		180
Arrow Surfboards 1115 Thompson Ave Ste 7 *Web:* www.arrowsurfshop.com	Santa Cruz	CA	95062	831-462-2791		710
Arrow Tank & Engineering Co 650 N Emerson St *TF:* 888-892-7769 ■ *Web:* www.arrowtank.com	Cambridge	MN	55008	763-689-3360	689-1263	91
Arrow Tool & Stamping Company Inc 4548 W Mitchell St *Web:* www.arrowtool.com	Milwaukee	WI	53214	414-383-5710	383-6910	697
Arrow Trading Inc 5290 NW 20th Ter Hangar 57-101 *Web:* www.arrowtrading.com	Fort Lauderdale	FL	33309	954-771-9366	771-8966	770
Arrow Truck Sales Inc 3200 Manchester Trfy *TF:* 800-311-7144 ■ *Web:* www.arrowtruck.com	Kansas City	MO	64129	888-468-9626		57
Arrow Tru-Line Inc 2211 S Defiance St *TF:* 800-446-6433 ■ *Web:* www.arrowtruline.com	Archbold	OH	43502	419-446-2785		488
Arrow Uniform Rental Inc 6400 Monroe Blvd *TF:* 888-332-7769 ■ *Web:* www.arrowuniform.com	Taylor	MI	48180	313-299-5000		442
Arrow United Industries 450 Riverside Dr *Web:* www.arrowunited.com	Wyalusing	PA	18853	570-746-1888	746-9286	697
Arrowcopter Inc PO Box 1807 *Web:* www.arrowcopter.com	Hollister	CA	95024	831-634-0145	634-0167	44
Arrowhead Animal Hospital PC 11490 Sheridan Blvd *Web:* arrowheadvets.com	Westminster	CO	80020	303-469-1616	438-6693	794
Arrowhead Containers Inc 4330 Clary Blvd *TF:* 888-861-9225 ■ *Web:* www.smcpackaging.com	Kansas City	MO	64130	816-861-8050		100
Arrowhead Electric Co-opeartive Inc 5401 West Hwy 61 PO Box 39 *TF:* 800-864-3744 ■ *Web:* www.aecimn.com	Lutsen	MN	55612	218-663-7239	663-7850	245
Arrowhead Library System 430 E High St Ste 200 *Web:* www.als.lib.wi.us	Milton	WI	53563	608-868-2872	868-2875	434-3
Arrowhead Plastic Engineering Inc 2909 S Hoyt Ave *Web:* www.arrowheadinc.com	Muncie	IN	47302	765-286-0533	286-1681	604
Arrowhead Press Inc 220 W Maple Ave *TF:* 800-821-5629 ■ *Web:* www.arrowheadpress.com	Monrovia	CA	91016	626-358-1168	303-3205	627

Name / Address	City	State	ZIP	Phone	Fax	Class
Arrowhead Products Corp 4411 Katella Ave *Web:* www.arrowheadproducts.net	Los Alamitos	CA	90720	714-828-7770	220-6488	22
Arrowhead Promotion & Fulfillment Company Inc 1105 SE Eighth St *Web:* www.apfco.com	Grand Rapids	MN	55744	218-327-1165		195
Arrowhead Regional Medical Ctr 400 N Pepper Ave *TF:* 855-422-8029 ■ *Web:* www.arrowheadmedcenter.org	Colton	CA	92324	909-580-1000		374-3
Arrowhead State Park 3995 Main Park Rd *Web:* www.travelok.com	Canadian	OK	74425	918-339-2204	339-7236	565
Arrowhead Systems Inc 3255 Medalist Dr **Fax Area Code: 866* ■ *Web:* www.arrowheadsystems.com	Oshkosh	WI	54902	920-235-5562	580-3212*	470
Arrowhead Towne Ctr 7700 W Arrowhead Towne Ctr *Web:* www.arrowheadtownecenter.com	Glendale	AZ	85308	623-412-7991		460
Arrow-Magnolia Intl 2646 Rodney Ln *TF:* 800-527-2101 ■ *Web:* www.arrowmagnolia.com	Dallas	TX	75229	972-247-7111	484-2896	151
Arrowmont School of Arts & Crafts 556 Pky PO Box 556 *Web:* www.arrowmont.org	Gatlinburg	TN	37738	865-436-5860		685
ArroWorthy 248 Wyandanch Ave *TF:* 888-444-4949 ■ *Web:* www.arroworthy.com	West Babylon	NY	11704	631-643-0436	253-9428	802
Arrowpoint Capital 3600 Arco Corporate Dr Ste 100 *TF:* 866-236-7750 ■ *Web:* www.arrowpointcap.com	Charlotte	NC	28273	704-522-2000		391-4
Arrowsight Inc 2875 Rte 35 6N Ste 200 *TF:* 866-261-5656 ■ *Web:* arrowsight.com	Katonah	NY	10536	866-261-5656		366
Arrowwood Resort & Conference Ctr 2100 Arrowwood Ln NW *TF:* 866-386-5263 ■ *Web:* arrowwoodresort.com	Alexandria	MN	56308	320-762-1124	762-0133	669
Arroyo Animal Clinic 1211 Sycamore Ter *Web:* arroyoanimalclinic.com	Sunnyvale	CA	94086	408-241-4450		794
Arroyo Chop House 536 S Arroyo Pkwy *Web:* www.arroyochophouse.com	Pasadena	CA	91105	626-577-7463		671
ARRS (American Roentgen Ray Society) 44211 Slatestone Ct *TF:* 800-438-2777 ■ *Web:* www.arrs.org	Leesburg	VA	20176	703-729-3353	729-4839	49-8
ARS (American Rose Society) 8877 Jefferson Paige Rd *TF:* 800-637-6534 ■ *Web:* www.rose.org	Shreveport	LA	71119	800-637-6534		48-18
ARS Adv LLC 4100 Mountain View Ave *Web:* aislerocket.com	Chattanooga	TN	37415	423-875-3743		6
ARS Antiqua Inc 3052 Ramble Rd W *Web:* www.arsantiqua.com	Bloomington	IN	47408	812-322-2250	333-5454	637-10
ARS National Services Inc 201 W Grand Ave *TF:* 800-456-5053 ■ *Web:* www.arsnational.com	Escondido	CA	92025	800-456-5053		393
ARS Recycling Systems LLC 4000 Mccartney Rd *Web:* www.arsrecycling.com	Lowellville	OH	44436	330-536-8210	536-8211	806
ARSC (Association for Recorded Sound Collections) PO Box 543 *Web:* www.arsc-audio.org	Annapolis	MD	21404	410-757-0488		48-4
Arsee Engineers Inc 9715 Kincaid Dr *Web:* arsee-engineers.com	Fishers	IN	46037	317-594-5152		261
Arsenal Capital Partners 100 Park Ave 31st Fl *Web:* www.arsenalcapital.com	New York	NY	10017	212-771-1717		696
ART (American Repertory Theatre) 64 Brattle St *Web:* americanrepertorytheater.org	Cambridge	MA	02138	617-547-8300		749
ART (Applied Research & Technology) 215 Tremont St *Web:* artproaudio.com	Rochester	NY	14608	716-436-2720		52
Art & Creative Materials Institute Inc, The (ACMI) 99 Derby St Ste 200 *Web:* www.acmiart.org	Hingham	MA	02043	781-556-1044	207-5550	48-18
Art & Logic Inc 87 N Raymond Ave Ste 531 *Web:* artandlogic.com	Pasadena	CA	91103	626-427-7184		180
Art Academy of Cincinnati 1212 Jackson St *TF:* 800-323-5692 ■ *Web:* www.artacademy.edu	Cincinnati	OH	45202	513-562-6262	562-8778	164
Art Anderson Associates Inc 202 Pacific Ave *Web:* www.artanderson.com	Bremerton	WA	98337	360-479-5600		256
Art Brands LLC 225 Business Center Dr *TF:* 877-755-4278 ■ *Web:* www.artbrands.com	Blacklick	OH	43004	614-755-4278		687
Art Calendar 1500 Park Center Dr *Web:* professionalartistmag.com	Orlando	FL	32835	407-563-7000	563-7099	457-2
Art Center of Corpus Christi 100 N Shoreline Blvd *Web:* www.artcentercc.org	Corpus Christi	TX	78401	361-884-6406		50-2
Art Cir Public Library 3 East St *Web:* www.artcirclelibrary.info	Crossville	TN	38555	931-484-6790	484-2350	434-3
Art Communication Systems Inc 1340 N 17th St *TF:* 800-336-2522 ■ *Web:* www.artcomsys.com	Harrisburg	PA	17103	717-232-0144	232-2283	627
Art Concepts 1555 Botelho Dr Ste 318 *Web:* www.artconcepts.com	Walnut Creek	CA	94596	925-930-0157		344
Art Connection Inc 2860 Ctr Port Cir *Web:* www.artconnectionusa.com	Pompano Beach	FL	33064	954-977-8177		820
Art Corner, The 264 Washington St *Web:* artcornersalem.com	Salem	MA	01970	978-745-9524		45
Art Craft Display Inc 500 Business Centre Dr *TF:* 800-878-0710 ■ *Web:* artcraftdisplay.com	Lansing	MI	48917	517-485-2221		226
Art Ctr 1700 Lida St *Web:* www.artcenter.edu	Pasadena	CA	91103	626-396-2200		164

Name / Address	City	State	Zip	Phone	Fax	Class
Art Dealers Association of America (ADAA) 205 Lexington Ave Ste 901 *Fax Area Code: 646 ■ Web: artdealers.org	New York	NY	10016	212-488-5550	688-6809*	48-4
Art Directors Guild (ADG) 11969 Ventura Blvd 2nd Fl Web: www.adg.org	Studio City	CA	91604	818-762-9995	762-9997	48-4
Art Display Company Inc 401 Hampton Park Blvd Web: www.artdisplayco.com	Capitol Heights	MD	20743	240-765-1400		344
Art Emporium 2928 Granville St Web: www.southgranville.org	Vancouver	BC	V6H3J7	604-738-3510		42
Art Enables 2204 Rhode Island Ave NE Web: art-enables.org	Washington	DC	20018	202-554-9455		42
Art Essentials 32 E Victoria St	Santa Barbara	CA	93101	805-965-5456		45
Art for Everyday Inc 420 Canarctic Dr TF: 866-850-2680 ■ Web: artforeveryday.com	Toronto	ON	M3J2V3	416-645-5120	645-5121	820
Art Furniture Inc 1165 Auto Center Dr Web: www.arthomefurnishings.com	Ontario	CA	91761	909-390-1039		321
Art Gallery of Ontario 317 Dundas St W TF: 877-225-4246 ■ Web: ago.ca	Toronto	ON	M5T1G4	416-979-6660		305
Art Guild Inc 300 Wolf Dr Web: www.artguildinc.com	West Deptford	NJ	08086	856-853-7500		701
Art Hardware 119 E Costilla Web: www.art-hardware.com	Colorado Springs	CO	80903	719-635-2348		45
Art Image Publications PO Box 160 TF: 800-361-2598 ■ Web: www.artimagepublications.com	Derby Line	VT	05830	800-361-2598	559-2598	637-10
Art Inc, The 2470 Fox Hill Rd TF: 800-458-3401 ■ Web: www.resistor.com	State College	PA	16803	800-458-3401		203
Art Institute of Chicago 111 S Michigan Ave Web: www.artic.edu	Chicago	IL	60603	312-443-3600		520
Art Institutes, The 1400 Penn Ave TF: 800-275-2470 ■ Web: www.artinstitutes.edu	Pittsburgh	PA	15222	800-275-2470		164
Art Iron Inc 860 Curtis St TF: 800-472-1113 ■ Web: www.artiron.com	Toledo	OH	43609	419-241-1261		492
Art Laboe 7120 Sunset Blvd Hollywood Web: artlaboe.com	Los Angeles	CA	90046	323-851-2500	851-8162	192
Art Material Services Inc 625 Joyce Kilmer Ave TF: 888-522-5526 ■ Web: www.artmaterialsservice.com	New Brunswick	NJ	08901	732-545-8888		362
Art Media Resources Inc 1965 W Pershing Rd Web: www.artmediaresources.com	Chicago	IL	60609	312-663-5351	663-5177	637-2
Art Metals Group Inc 3795 Symmes Rd Web: artmetalsgroup.com	Fairfield Township	OH	45015	513-942-8800	942-3200	620
Art Moehn 2200 Seymour Rd Web: www.artmoehn.com	Jackson	MI	49201	517-455-7721		516
Art Morrison Enterprises Inc 5301 Eighth St E TF: 888-640-0516 ■ Web: www.artmorrison.com	Fife	WA	98424	253-922-7188		57
Art of The Knot Inc 5893 Sunset Dr	South Miami	FL	33143	305-667-2000		131
Art Optical Contact Lens Inc 3175 3 Mile Rd NW PO Box 1848 TF: 800-253-9364 ■ Web: www.artoptical.com	Grand Rapids	MI	49501	616-453-1888	453-8702	542
Art Placement Inc 228 Third Ave S Web: www.artplacement.com	Saskatoon	SK	S7K1L9	306-664-3385	933-2521	42
Art Resource Inc 65 Bleecker St 12th Fl TF: 888-505-8666 ■ Web: www.artres.com	New York	NY	10012	212-505-8700		624
Art Salt Lake 50 W 200 S Web: www.saltlakecountyarts.org	Salt Lake City	UT	84101	801-355-2787		572
Art Supply Warehouse 6672 Westminster Blvd TF: 800-854-6467 ■ Web: www.artsupplywarehouse.com	Westminster	CA	92683	714-891-3626		45
Art/Life Limited Editions PO Box 23020 Web: art-life.com	Ventura	CA	93002	805-648-4331		637-9
ARTA Travel 5700 W Plano Pkwy Ste 1400 Web: www.artatravel.com	Plano	TX	75093	972-422-4000		772
Artafact LLC 43165 Sabercat TF: 800-618-3228 ■ Web: www.artafact.com	Fremont	CA	94539	510-651-9178		466
ARTBA (American Road & Transportation Builders Assn) 1219 28th St NW Web: www.artba.org	Washington	DC	20007	202-289-4434	289-4435	49-3
Artbeats Software Inc 1405 N Myrtle Rd Web: www.artbeats.com	Myrtle Creek	OR	97457	541-391-0301		225
ArtCentre of Plano, The 901 18th St Web: www.artcentreofplano.org	Plano	TX	75074	972-423-7809		50-2
Artco-Bell Corp 1302 Industrial Blvd TF: 877-778-1811 ■ Web: www.artcobell.com	Temple	TX	76504	254-778-1811		319-3
Artcraft Company Inc, The 200 John L Dietsch Blvd TF: 800-659-4042 ■ Web: www.artcraft.com	North Attleboro	MA	02763	800-659-4042		429
Art-Craft Optical Company Inc 57 Goodway Dr S TF: 800-828-8288 ■ Web: www.artcraftoptical.com	Rochester	NY	14623	585-546-6640	546-5133	542
Artcraft Signs Co 1717 S Acoma St Web: www.artcraftsign.com	Denver	CO	80223	303-777-7771	778-7175	701
Artech Industries Inc 1966 Keats Dr TF: 800-654-8181 ■ Web: www.artechloadcell.com	Riverside	CA	92501	951-276-3331	276-4556	253
Artech Information Systems LLC 360 Mt Kemble Ave Ste 2000 TF: 888-436-4339 ■ Web: www.artech.com	Morristown	NJ	07960	973-998-2500	998-2599	721
Artel 25 Bradley Dr TF: 888-406-3463 ■ Web: www.artel.com	Westbrook	ME	04092	207-854-0860		250
Artel LLC 13665 Dulles Technology Dr Ste 300 Web: www.artelllc.com	Herndon	VA	20171	703-620-1700	620-4262	224
Artemis Financial Advisors LLC 54 Chandler St Web: www.artemisadvisors.net	Boston	MA	02116	617-542-2420		401
Artemus Group 317 Office Square Ln Ste 202B *Fax Area Code: 757 ■ TF: 866-744-7101 ■ Web: www.artemusgroupusa.com	Virginia Beach	VA	23462	866-744-7101	257-0668*	313
Artesia Fire Equipment Inc (AFE) 1014 S First St TF: 800-748-2076 ■ Web: www.artesiafire.com	Artesia	NM	88210	575-746-2426	748-1128	76
Artesian Resources Corp 664 Churchmans Rd NASDAQ: ARTNA ■ TF: 800-332-5114 ■ Web: www.artesianwater.com	Newark	DE	19702	302-453-6900	453-6957	360-5
Artex Knitting Mills Inc 300 Harvard Ave Web: www.artexknit.com	Westville	NJ	08093	856-456-2800	456-4111	155-16
Artex Risk Solutions Inc 2 Pierce Pl Web: www.artexrisk.com	Itasca	IL	60143	630-694-5050		317
Artforum International Magazine 350 Seventh Ave TF: 800-966-2783 ■ Web: www.artforum.com	New York	NY	10001	212-475-4000	529-1257	457-2
Arthaus 3840 Ridgewood Ave Web: www.arthaus.org	Port Orange	FL	32129	386-767-0076	761-3888	522
Arthouse Hotel 2178 Broadway 77th St TF: 800-509-7598 ■ Web: www.arthousehotelnyc.com	New York	NY	10024	212-362-1100		378
Arthrex Inc 1370 Creekside Blvd TF: 800-934-4404 ■ Web: www.arthrex.com	Naples	FL	34108	239-643-5553	598-5534	477
Arthritis Foundation 1330 W Peachtree St Ste 100 TF: 800-283-7800 ■ Web: www.arthritis.org	Atlanta	GA	30309	404-872-7100		48-17
Arthroscopy Association of North America (AANA) 9400 W Higgins Rd Ste 200 TF: 877-924-0305 ■ Web: www.aana.org	Rosemont	IL	60018	847-292-2262	292-2268	49-8
Arthur Agency Inc 104 E Jackson St Web: www.arthuragency.com	Carbondale	IL	62901	618-351-1599		463
Arthur Bryant's Barbeque 1727 Brooklyn Ave Web: www.arthurbryantsbbq.com	Kansas City	MO	64127	816-231-1123		671
Arthur County 205 Fir St Web: arthurcounty.nebraska.gov	Arthur	NE	69121	308-764-2201		338
Arthur D. Little Inc 1 Federal St Ste 2810 Web: www.adlittle.com	Boston	MA	02110	617-532-9503	261-6630	194
Arthur Dyson Architects 1295 N Wishon Ave Web: www.arthurdyson.com	Fresno	CA	93728	559-486-3582	486-4909	261
Arthur Edwards Inc 1 Dewolf Rd Web: arthuredwardsinc.com	Old Tappan	NJ	07675	201-722-9600		653
Arthur F. Schultz Co 939 W 26th St Web: www.arthurfschultz.com	Erie	PA	16508	814-454-8171	454-3052	35
Arthur Financial Services LLC 1516 E Palm Valley Blvd Bldg B Ste 1 Web: www.arthurfinancial.com	Round Rock	TX	78664	512-218-6948		251
Arthur Groom & Company Inc 262 E Ridgewood Ave Web: www.arthurgroom.com	Ridgewood	NJ	07450	201-670-0300		410
Arthur J. Gallagher & Co 2 Pierce Pl NYSE: AJG ■ TF: 888-285-5106 ■ Web: www.ajg.com	Itasca	IL	60143	630-773-3800	285-4000	390
Arthur J. Glatfelter Agency Inc PO Box 2726 TF: 800-233-1957 ■ Web: www.glatfelters.com	York	PA	17405	717-741-0911	741-4160	390
Arthur K. Williams Microbusiness Enterprise Center 230 S Jackson St Web: www.albanymbec.biz	Albany	GA	31701	229-420-4600		393
Arthur Langhus Layne LLC 1718 S Cheyenne Web: www.all-llc.com	Tulsa	OK	74119	918-382-7581		194
Arthur Louis Steel Co 505 W 51st St Web: www.arthurlouissteel.com	Ashtabula	OH	44004	440-997-5545	992-9726	492
Arthur P. Jones & Associates Inc 98 Cottage St Web: www.apjones.com	Easthampton	MA	01027	413-527-2388		160
Arthur P. Ohara Inc 2801 Centre Cir Web: arthurpohara.com	Downers Grove	IL	60515	630-786-5454		321
Arthur Rutenberg Homes Inc 13922 58th St N Web: www.arthurrutenberghomes.com	Clearwater	FL	33760	727-536-5900		187
Arthur S. Reinherz Charitable Foundation Inc 11 Dartmouth St Ste 202	Malden	MA	02148	781-321-6300		363
Arthur Shuster Inc (ASI) 2229 Uinversity Ave Web: shusterinteriors.net	Saint Paul	MN	55114	651-319-5569		393
Arthur State Bank 100 E Main St PO Box 769 TF: 888-825-2265 ■ Web: www.arthurstatebank.com	Union	SC	29379	864-427-1213	429-8537	70
Arthur Strand Insurance Inc 205 Bolstad Ave E Ste 1 TF: 800-700-8281 ■ Web: strandinsurance.com	Long Beach	WA	98631	360-642-2345		390
Arthur Vining Davis Foundations 225 Water St Web: www.avdf.org	Jacksonville	FL	32202	904-359-0670	359-0675	305
Arthur W. Boyce PA 308 W Patrick St TF: 800-778-1640 ■ Web: fredericklegal.com	Frederick	MD	21701	301-663-4025	696-1528	41
Arthur W. Wood Company Inc 50 Congress St Ste 700 Web: www.arthurwood.com	Boston	MA	02109	617-542-0500		194
Arthur Weiler Inc 12247 W Russell Rd Web: weilernursery.com	Zion	IL	60099	847-746-2393		422
Arthur's Beauty College 2600 John Harden Dr TF: 800-288-2527 ■ Web: www.arthursbeautycollege.com	Jacksonville	AR	72076	501-982-8987	982-1133	214
Arthur, Chapman, Kettering, Smetak & Pikala PA 500 Young Quinlan Bldg 81 S Ninth St TF: 800-916-9262 ■ Web: www.arthurchapman.com	Minneapolis	MN	55402	612-339-3500		428
Artichoke Cafe 424 Central SE Web: www.artichokecafe.com	Albuquerque	NM	87102	505-243-0200	243-3365	671
Articulon 8480 Honeycutt Rd Ste 200 Web: www.articulon.com	Raleigh	NC	27612	919-232-5008		636
Artifex Software Inc 7 Mt Lassen Dr Ste A-134 Web: www.artifex.com	San Rafael	CA	94903	415-492-9861	492-9862	178-1

Company	City	State	ZIP	Phone	Fax	Class
Artifice Inc 1342 High St TF: 800-203-8324 ■ Web: www.artifice.com	Eugene	OR	97401	541-345-7421	345-7438	178-1
Artificial Intelligence In Medicine Inc 2 Berkeley St Ste 403 TF: 866-645-2224 ■ Web: www.aim.ca	Toronto	ON	M5A4J5	416-594-9393		179
Artillery Company of Newport Military Museum 23 Clark St Web: www.newportartillery.org	Newport	RI	02840	401-846-8488		520
Artime Group 65 N Raymond Ave Ste 205 Web: www.artimegroup.com	Pasadena	CA	91103	626-583-1855		4
Artisan Books & Bindery 111 Derby Rd Web: www.artisanbooksandbindery.com	Islesboro	ME	04848	207-734-6852		95
Artisan Cinema & Sound LLC 15876 N 76th St Ste 100 Web: www.artisanaz.com	Scottsdale	AZ	85260	480-538-1071	538-1072	748
Artisan Colour Inc 8970 E Bahia Dr TF: 800-274-2422 ■ Web: www.artisancolour.com	Scottsdale	AZ	85260	480-948-0009		781
Artisan Communications Inc 12400 St Hwy 71 W Ste 350-407 TF: 888-988-8647 ■ Web: www.artisan.tv	Austin	TX	78738	512-600-4200		387
Artisan Controls Corp 111 Canfield Ave Bldg B15-18 TF: 800-457-4950 ■ Web: www.artisancontrols.com	Randolph	NJ	07869	973-598-9400		203
Artisan Funds PO Box 8412 TF: 800-344-1770 ■ Web: www.artisanpartners.com	Boston	MA	02266	800-344-1770		528
Artisan Hotel Boutique 1501 W Sahara Ave Web: www.artisanhotel.com	Las Vegas	NV	89102	702-214-4000		378
Artisan Industries Inc 44 Campanelli Pkwy Web: artisanind.com	Stoughton	MA	02072	781-893-6800	647-0143	256
Artisan Laboratories Inc 2532 SE Hawthorne Blvd TF: 800-222-6721 ■ Web: artisandental.com	Portland	OR	97214	503-238-6006		476
Artisan of Grand Haven 1322 Washington St Web: www.artisanofgrandhaven.com	Grand Haven	MI	49417	616-296-9200		167-3
Artisan Publishers 1409 W Shawnee Web: www.artisanpublishers.com	Muskogee	OK	74401	918-682-8341		45
Artisan Salon LLC 1228 S El Camino Real Web: artisan-salon.com	San Mateo	CA	94402	650-350-1313		77
Artisan's Bank 2961 Centerville Rd TF: 800-282-8255 ■ Web: www.artisansbank.com	Wilmington	DE	19808	302-658-6881	654-0559	70
Artisans Inc PO Box 1059 TF: 800-311-8756 ■ Web: www.artisanscarpet.com	Calhoun	GA	30703	800-311-8756		131
Artist Brand Canvas 2448 Loma Ave TF: 888-579-2704 ■ Web: artistbrandcanvas.com	South El Monte	CA	91733	626-579-2740		43
Artist's Magazine, The 4700 E Galbraith Rd TF: 800-422-2550 ■ Web: www.artistsnetwork.com	Cincinnati	OH	45236	513-531-2222	891-7153	457-2
Artistic Carton Co 1975 Big Timber Rd TF: 800-735-7225 ■ Web: www.artisticcarton.com	Elgin	IL	60123	847-741-0247	741-8529	100
Artistic Checks PO Box 40003 TF: 800-824-3255 ■ Web: www.artisticchecks.com	Colorado Springs	CO	80935	800-824-3255		142
Artistic Frame Corp 979 Third Ave 17th Fl Web: www.artisticframe.com	New York	NY	10022	212-289-2100	289-2101	319-1
Artistic Maintenance Inc 15510-C Rockfield Blvd Web: www.artisticmaintenance.com	Irvine	CA	92618	949-581-9817		422
Artistic Media Partners Inc 5520 E 75th St Web: www.artisticradio.com	Indianapolis	IN	46250	317-594-0600	594-9567	643
Artistic Nails & Beauty Academy 4951-A Adamo Dr No 120 Web: www.artistic.edu	Tampa	FL	33605	813-654-4529		166
Artistic Stone Kitchen & Bath Inc 2973 Teagarden St Web: www.artisticstoneinc.com	San Leandro	CA	94577	510-483-1298	483-6389	361
Artistica Metal Designs Inc 3200 Golf Course Dr Ste A Web: artisticahome.com	Ventura	CA	93003	805-483-1195		492
Artistry in Motion Inc 19411 Londelius St Web: www.artistryinmotion.com	Northridge	CA	91324	818-994-7388	994-7688	554
Artists Club, The 13118 NE Fourth St TF: 800-574-1323 ■ Web: www.knitpicks.com	Vancouver	WA	98684	800-574-1323		761
Artists for Humanity Inc 100 W Second St Web: afhboston.org	Boston	MA	02127	617-268-7620		260
Artists International Management Inc 2901 Clint Moore Rd Ste 420 Web: www.aimrocks.com	Boca Raton	FL	33496	561-498-1300	498-2004	226
Artists Repertory Theatre 1516 SW Alder St Web: www.artistsrep.org	Portland	OR	97205	503-241-9807	241-8268	573-4
Artizen Inc 5635 San Diego St Web: www.artizen.com	Redwood City	CA	94063	650-261-9400		260
Artkraft Strauss LLC 1776 Broadway Ste 1810 Web: www.artkraft.com	New York	NY	10019	212-265-5155	265-5159	233
Artman Lutheran Home 250 N Bethlehem Pk Web: www.artmanhome.org	Ambler	PA	19002	215-643-6335		48-20
Artmart 2355 S Hanley Rd Web: www.artmartstl.com	Saint Louis	MO	63144	314-781-9999		45
Artnet Worldwide Corp 233 Broadway 26th Fl *Fax Area Code: 212 ■ TF: 800-427-8638 ■ Web: www.artnet.com	New York	NY	10279	800-427-8638	497-9707*	7
ARTnews Magazine 110 Greene St 2nd Fl TF: 800-284-4625 ■ Web: www.artnews.com	New York	NY	10012	212-398-1690	819-0394	457-2
Artone LLC 1089 Allen St Web: www.artonemfg.com	Jamestown	NY	14701	716-664-2232	664-1511	319-1
Artonomy 544 W Liberty St Web: www.artonomyinc.com	Cincinnati	OH	45214	513-651-2787		522

Company	City	State	ZIP	Phone	Fax	Class
Artos Engineering Co 21605 Gateway Ct Web: www.artosengineering.com	Brookfield	WI	53045	262-252-4545	252-4544	494
Artoy Trading LLC 3528 Garfield Ave TF: 877-742-7869 ■ Web: www.artoytrading.com	Commerce	CA	90040	323-266-8881		44
Artpark 450 S Fourth St TF: 800-715-6722 ■ Web: www.artpark.net	Lewiston	NY	14092	716-754-9000	754-2741	572
ARTS Anonymous PO Box 230175 Web: www.artsanonymous.org	New York	NY	10023	718-251-3828		48-21
Arts Center of Cannon County Inc, The 1424 John Bragg Hwy Web: www.artscenterofcc.com	Woodbury	TN	37190	615-563-2787		522
Arts Center of Coastal Carolina 14 Shelter Cove Ln TF: 888-860-2787 ■ Web: www.artshhi.com	Hilton Head Island	SC	29928	843-686-3945	842-7877	572
Arts Club of Chicago, The 201 E Ontario St Web: www.artsclubchicago.org	Chicago	IL	60611	312-787-3997		522
Arts Foundation of Cape Cod, The 396 Main St Ste 10 Web: artsfoundation.org	Hyannis	MA	02601	508-362-0066		305
Arts Mexican Products Inc 615 Kansas Ave Web: www.artsmexicanfoodproducts.com	Kansas City	KS	66105	913-371-2163		296-37
Arts Midwest 2908 Hennepin Ave Ste 200 Web: www.artsmidwest.org	Minneapolis	MN	55408	612-341-0755		720
ArtSouth 5825 SW 68th St Ste 2 Office 202 Web: www.artsouthmiami.org	South Miami	FL	33143	305-662-1423	247-7308	50-2
ARTspace 165 King St W Web: www.artspacechathamkent.com	Chatham-Kent	ON	N7M1E4	519-352-1064		520
Artspace Inc 201 E Davie St Web: artspacenc.org	Raleigh	NC	27601	919-821-2787	821-0383	520
Arts-Way Manufacturing Company Inc 5556 Hwy 9 PO Box 288 NASDAQ: ARTW ■ TF: 800-535-4517 ■ Web: www.artsway-mfg.com	Armstrong	IA	50514	712-864-3131	864-3154	273
Artus Corp PO Box 511 Web: www.artuscorp.com	Englewood	NJ	07631	201-568-1000	568-8865	326
ArtVoice 810 Main St Web: artvoice.com	Buffalo	NY	14202	716-881-6604	881-6682	532-5
ArtWax 31 Intervale St TF: 877-427-8929 ■ Web: www.artwax.com	Lynn	MA	01904	781-477-1984	645-1319	328
Artwork Conversion Software Inc 417 Ingalls St Web: www.artwork.com	Santa Cruz	CA	95060	831-426-6163		177
Artworks Around Town Gallery & Art Ctr 2200 Market St Web: www.artworksaroundtown.com	Wheeling	WV	26003	304-233-7540		50-2
Aruba Networks Inc 1344 Crossman Ave TF: 800-943-4526 ■ Web: www.arubanetworks.com	Sunnyvale	CA	94089	408-227-4500	752-0626	177
Aruba Petroleum Inc 555 Republic Dr Ste 505 Web: www.arubapetroleum.com	Plano	TX	75074	972-312-9366	312-1474	536
Aruba Tourism Authority 1750 Powder Springs St Ste 190 TF: 800-862-7822 ■ Web: www.aruba.com	Marietta	GA	30064	404-892-7822		775
Arugula 953 Farmington Ave Web: www.arugula-bistro.com	West Hartford	CT	06107	860-561-4888		671
Arun's 4156 N Kedzie Ave Web: www.arunsthai.com	Chicago	IL	60618	773-539-1909		671
Arundel FSB 333 E Patapsco Ave Web: www.arundelfederal.com	Baltimore	MD	21225	410-355-9300	355-0335	70
Arup 560 Mission St Ste 700 Web: www.arup.com	San Francisco	CA	94105	415-957-9445		256
Arup Laboratories 500 Chipeta Way TF: 800-242-2787 ■ Web: www.aruplab.com	Salt Lake City	UT	84108	801-583-2787		418
Aruze Gaming America Inc 955 Grier Dr Ste A TF: 877-268-4119 ■ Web: aruzegaming.com	Las Vegas	NV	89119	702-361-3166	361-3403	761
Arvada Center for the Arts & Humanities 6901 Wadsworth Blvd Web: www.arvadacenter.org	Arvada	CO	80003	720-898-7200	898-7204	572
Arvada Chamber of Commerce 7305 Grandview Ave Web: arvadachamber.org	Arvada	CO	80002	303-424-0313		139
Arvan Inc 14083 S Normandie Ave Web: www.arvaninc.com	Gardena	CA	90249	310-327-1818	324-6634	22
Arvco Container Corp 845 Gibson St TF: 800-968-9127 ■ Web: www.arvco.com	Kalamazoo	MI	49001	269-381-0900	381-2919	100
Arvest Bank PO Box 799 TF: 888-271-1253 ■ Web: www.arvest.com	Lowell	AR	72745	479-271-1253		360-2
Arvin Sango Inc 2905 Wilson Ave Web: www.arvinsango.com	Madison	IN	47250	812-265-2888	273-8339	488
ArvinMeritor Inc 2135 W Maple Rd NYSE: MTOR ■ TF: 800-535-5560 ■ Web: www.meritor.com	Troy	MI	48084	248-435-1000	435-1393	60
Arvinyl Metal Laminates Corp 233 N Sherman Ave *Fax Area Code: 951 ■ TF: 800-278-4695 ■ Web: www.arvinyl.com	Corona	CA	92882	800-278-4695	371-7118*	485
Arvizu Advertising & Promotions Inc 2224 W N Ave Ste D101 Web: www.arvizu.com	Phoenix	AZ	85021	602-279-4669		4
ARVO (Association for Research in Vision & Ophthalmology) 12300 Twinbrook Pkwy Ste 250 TF: 888-503-1050 ■ Web: www.arvo.org	Rockville	MD	20852	240-221-2900	221-0370	49-8
Arvon Inc 5544 Greenwich Rd Ste 102 Web: arvon.com	Virginia Beach	VA	23462	757-499-9900		260
Arw Engineers 1594 Park Cir Web: www.arwengineers.com	Ogden	UT	84404	801-782-6008	782-4656	261
ARW Optical Corp 2021 Capital Dr Web: arwoptical.com	Wilmington	NC	28405	910-452-7373		237
Arwood Machine Corp 95 Parker St Web: www.arwoodmachine.com	Newburyport	MA	01950	978-463-3777	463-0666	454
ARX Networks Corp 37100 Central Cy Web: www.arxnetworks.com	Newark	CA	94560	650-403-4000		180

Company / Address	City	State	ZIP	Phone	Fax	Class
ARX Publishing LLC PO Box 1333 *Web:* www.arxpub.com	Merchantville	NJ	08109	856-486-1310	665-0170	637-10
Arylessence Inc 1091 Lake Dr *TF:* 800-553-2440 ■ *Web:* www.arylessence.com	Marietta	GA	30066	770-924-3775	928-6571	144
Arzel Zoning Technology Inc 4801 Commerce Pkwy *TF:* 800-611-8312 ■ *Web:* www.arzelzoning.com	Cleveland	OH	44128	800-611-8312		201
A-S Hospitality 3493 Lamar Ave *TF:* 877-511-8488 ■ *Web:* www.ashospitality.com	Memphis	TN	38118	877-511-8488		393
AS220 115 Empire St *Web:* as220.org	Providence	RI	02903	401-831-9327	454-7445	572
ASA (Autism Society of America) 4340 E West Hwy Ste 350 *TF:* 800-328-8476 ■ *Web:* www.autism-society.org	Bethesda	MD	20814	301-657-0881	657-0869	48-17
ASA (Acoustical Society of America) 1305 Walt Whitman Rd Ste 300 *Web:* acousticalsociety.org	Melville	NY	11747	516-576-2360	576-2377	49-19
ASA (American Studies Assn) 1120 19th St NW Ste 301 *Web:* theasa.net	Washington	DC	20036	202-467-4783	467-4786	49-5
ASA (American Society of Andrology) 1061 E Main St Ste 300 *Web:* www.andrologysociety.org	East Dundee	IL	60173	847-752-5355		49-8
ASA (Airline Spares America Inc) 1022 E Newport Center Dr *Web:* www.asaspares.com	Deerfield Beach	FL	33442	954-429-8258	429-8388	770
ASA (Alpha Sigma Alpha) 9002 Vincennes Cir *Web:* www.alphasigmaalpha.org	Indianapolis	IN	46268	317-871-2920	871-2924	48-16
ASA (American Sportfishing Assn) 1001 N Fairfax St Ste 501 *Web:* asafishing.org	Alexandria	VA	22314	703-519-9691	519-1872	49-4
ASA (American Simmental Assn) 1 Genetics Way *Web:* www.simmental.org	Bozeman	MT	59718	406-587-4531	587-9301	48-2
ASA (American Society of Agronomy) 5585 Guilford Rd *TF:* 866-359-9161 ■ *Web:* www.agronomy.org	Madison	WI	53711	608-273-8080	273-2021	48-2
ASA (American Society of Anesthesiologists) 520 N NW Hwy *Web:* www.asahq.org	Park Ridge	IL	60068	847-825-5586	825-1692	49-8
ASA (American Society of Appraisers) 11107 Sunset Hills Rd Ste 310 **Fax Area Code:* 703 ■ *TF:* 800-272-8258 ■ *Web:* www.appraisers.org	Reston	VA	20170	800-272-8258	742-8471*	49-17
ASA (American Society on Aging) 575 Market St Ste 2100 *TF:* 800-537-9728 ■ *Web:* www.asaging.org	San Francisco	CA	94105	415-974-9600	974-0300	48-6
ASA (American Sociological Assn) 1307 New York Ave *Web:* www.asanet.org	Washington	DC	20005	202-383-9005	638-0882	49-5
ASA (American Soybean Assn) 12125 Woodcrest Executive Dr Ste 100 *TF:* 800-688-7692 ■ *Web:* soygrowers.com	Saint Louis	MO	63141	314-576-1770	576-2786	48-2
ASA (American Statistical Assn) 732 N Washington St *TF:* 888-231-3473 ■ *Web:* www.amstat.org	Alexandria	VA	22314	703-684-1221	684-2037	49-19
ASA (American Subcontractors Association Inc) 1004 Duke St *Web:* www.asaonline.com	Alexandria	VA	22314	703-684-3450	836-3482	49-3
ASA (Automotive Service Assn) 1901 Airport Fwy **Fax Area Code:* 817 ■ *TF:* 800-272-7467 ■ *Web:* asashop.org	Bedford	TX	76021	800-272-7467	685-0225*	49-21
ASA (American Staffing Assn) 277 S Washington St Ste 200 *Web:* americanstaffing.net	Alexandria	VA	22314	703-253-2020	253-2053	49-12
ASA Alloys Inc 81 Steinway Blvd *TF:* 800-387-9166 ■ *Web:* www.asaalloys.com	Etobicoke	ON	M9W6H6	416-213-0000		492
ASA Computers Inc 645 National Ave *TF:* 800-732-5727 ■ *Web:* www.asacomputers.com	Mountain View	CA	94043	650-230-8000		176
ASA Controls Inc 10051 Simonson Rd Ste 8 *Web:* asacontrols.com	Harrison	OH	45030	513-353-3101		189-10
ASA Entertainment LLC 201 N Riverside Dr Ste C *Web:* www.asaentertainment.com	Indialantic	FL	32903	321-722-9300		226
ASA Inc 2200 S State St *Web:* asainsure.com	Salt Lake City	UT	84115	801-486-7463		390
ASA Solutions Inc 2155 W Pinnacle Peak Rd Ste 201 *Web:* asasolutions.com	Phoenix	AZ	85027	480-922-9532		177
ASAA (American Sleep Apnea Assn) 6856 Eastern Ave NW Ste 203 *TF:* 888-293-3650 ■ *Web:* www.sleepapnea.org	Washington	DC	20012	202-293-3650	293-3656	48-17
ASAC (American Society of Agricultural Consultants) 605 Columbus Ave *Web:* www.agconsultants.org	New Prague	MN	56071	952-758-5811		48-2
ASAE (American Society of Association Executives) 1575 'I' St NW *TF:* 888-950-2723 ■ *Web:* www.asaecenter.org	Washington	DC	20005	202-626-2723		49-12
ASAH 2125 Rte 33 Lexington Sq *TF:* 800-955-2321 ■ *Web:* asah.org	Hamilton Square	NJ	08690	609-890-1400	890-8860	474
Asahi Beer USA Inc 3625 Del Amo Blvd Ste 250 *Web:* www.asahisuperdry.com	Torrance	CA	90503	310-214-9051	542-5108	102
Asahi Kasei America Inc 800 Third Ave 30th Fl *Web:* www.ak-america.com	New York	NY	10022	212-371-9900	371-9050	605-2
Asahi Kasei Pharma America 200 Fifth Ave 6th Fl *Web:* www.akpamerica.com	Waltham	MA	02451	781-419-1919	890-0660	668
Asahi Kasei Plastics North America Inc 900 E Van Riper Rd *TF:* 800-993-5382 ■ *Web:* www.akplastics.com	Fowlerville	MI	48836	517-223-5100	223-2002	605-2
ASAHP (Association of Schools of Allied Health Professions) 122 C St NW Ste 650 *Web:* www.asahp.org	Washington	DC	20001	202-237-6481	237-6485	49-8
ASAM (American Society of Addiction Medicine) 11400 Rockville Pk Ste 200 *Web:* www.asam.org	Rockville	MD	20852	301-656-3920	656-3815	49-8
ASAMA (American Sport Art Museum & Archives) 1 Academy Dr *Web:* www.asama.org	Daphne	AL	36526	251-626-3303	626-3874	520
Asana Studio 5701 Yukon St *Web:* asanastudio.com	Arvada	CO	80002	303-431-6311		148
ASAP (American Society of Access Professionals) 1444 'I' St NW Ste 700 *Web:* www.accesspro.org	Washington	DC	20005	202-712-9054	216-9646	48-8
ASAP (American Society for Adolescent Psychiatry) PO Box 3948 *TF:* 866-672-9060 ■ *Web:* www.adolescent-psychiatry.org	Parker	CO	80134	866-672-9060		49-15
ASAP Inc 1750 W 96th St *Web:* www.asap.net	Bloomington	MN	55431	952-564-2727		781
ASAP Industries LLC 908 Blimp Rd *Web:* www.asapind.net	Houma	LA	70363	985-851-7272		358
ASAP Personnel Services Inc 10301 N Rodney Parham Rd *Web:* asapworksforme.com	Little Rock	AR	72227	501-537-2727		260
Asap Printing Corp 643 Billinis Rd **Fax Area Code:* 801 ■ *TF:* 888-727-2863 ■ *Web:* www.asapprintingcorp.com	Salt Lake City	UT	84119	888-727-2863	606-7055*	627
ASAP Solutions Group LLC 3885 Holcomb Bridge Rd *Web:* www.myasap.com	Norcross	GA	30092	770-246-1718		179
ASAP Ventures LLC 132 King St Ste 200 *Web:* www.asapventures.com	Alexandria	VA	22314	703-837-5150	548-6210	463
ASAPP Inc World Trade Center One 80th Fl *Web:* asapp.com	New York	NY	10007	212-658-0990		657
ASAPS (American Society for Aesthetic Plastic Surgery, The) 11262 Monarch St *TF:* 800-364-2147 ■ *Web:* www.surgery.org	Garden Grove	CA	92841	562-799-2356	799-1098	49-8
ASB (Animated Story Boards) 1001 Avenue of the Americas 24th Fl *Web:* animatedstoryboards.com	New York	NY	10018	212-595-0400		514
Asbarez 1203 N Vermont Ave **Fax Area Code:* 323 ■ *Web:* asbarez.com	Los Angeles	CA	90029	818-500-9363	284-0080*	532-2
Asbestos Removal Technologies Inc 21421 Hilltop St *Web:* www.healthyhomesinc.com	Southfield	MI	48033	248-358-3311	358-5678	189-11
ASBMB (American Society for Biochemistry & Molecular Biology Inc) 11200 Rockville Pk **Fax Area Code:* 301 ■ *Web:* www.asbmb.org	Rockville	MD	20852	240-283-6600	881-2080*	49-19
ASBMR (American Society for Bone & Mineral Research) 2025 M St NW Ste 800 *Web:* www.asbmr.org	Washington	DC	20036	202-367-1161	367-2161	49-8
ASBO (Association of School Business Officials Intl) 11401 N Shore Dr **Fax Area Code:* 703 ■ *TF:* 866-682-2729 ■ *Web:* asbointl.org	Reston	VA	20190	866-682-2729	478-0205*	49-5
ASBPA (American Shore & Beach Preservation Assn) 5460 Beaujolais Ln *TF:* 800-331-1600 ■ *Web:* asbpa.org	Fort Myers	FL	33919	239-489-2616	489-9917	48-13
ASBPE (American Society of Business Publication Editors) 214 N Hale St **Fax Area Code:* 630 ■ *Web:* www.asbpe.org	Wheaton	IL	60187	727-553-4214	510-4501*	49-16
Asbury Automotive Group Inc 2905 Premiere Pkwy Ste 300 *NYSE:* ABG ■ *Web:* www.asburyauto.com	Duluth	GA	30097	770-418-8200		57
Asbury Graphite Mills Inc 405 Old Main St *Web:* asbury.com	Asbury Park	NJ	08802	908-537-2155	537-2908	500
Asbury Methodist Village 201 Russell Ave *TF:* 800-327-2879 ■ *Web:* www.asbury.org	Gaithersburg	MD	20877	301-216-4001		672
Asbury Park Chamber of Commerce 1201 Springwood Ave *Web:* www.asburyparkchamber.com	Asbury Park	NJ	07712	732-775-7676	775-7675	139
Asbury Park Press 3601 Hwy 66 PO Box 1550 *TF:* 800-822-9770 ■ *Web:* www.app.com	Neptune City	NJ	07754	732-922-6000		532-2
Asbury Theological Seminary 204 N Lexington Ave *TF:* 800-227-2879 ■ *Web:* asburyseminary.edu	Wilmore	KY	40390	859-858-3581		167-3
Asbury University 1 Macklem Dr *TF:* 800-888-1818 ■ *Web:* www.asburyeagles.com	Wilmore	KY	40390	859-858-3511	858-3921	166
ASC (American Society of Cinematographers) 1782 N Orange Dr *TF:* 800-448-0145 ■ *Web:* theasc.com	Hollywood	CA	90028	323-969-4333	882-6391	48-4
ASC (Advanced Systems Consultants Inc) 4074 E Patterson Rd	Dayton	OH	45430	937-429-1428		177
ASC (Adhesive & Sealant Council Inc) 7101 Wisconsin Ave Ste 990 *Web:* www.ascouncil.org	Bethesda	MD	20814	301-986-9700	986-9795	49-13
ASC Capacitors 301 W O St *Web:* www.ascapacitor.com	Ogallala	NE	69153	308-284-3611	284-8324	253
ASC Industries Inc 1227 Corporate Dr W *Web:* www.ascintl.com	Arlington	TX	76006	817-640-1300	649-2685	770
ASC Profiles LLC 2110 Enterprise Blvd *TF:* 800-360-2477 ■ *Web:* www.ascprofiles.com	West Sacramento	CA	95691	916-372-0933		697
ASCA (American School Counselor Assn) 1101 King St Ste 625 *TF:* 800-306-4722 ■ *Web:* www.schoolcounselor.org	Alexandria	VA	22314	703-683-2722	683-1619	49-5
ASCB (American Society for Cell Biology) 8120 Woodmont Ave Ste 750 *Web:* www.ascb.org	Bethesda	MD	20814	301-347-9300	347-9310	49-19
ASCC Inc 15 Ogle View Rd *TF:* 800-772-0797 ■ *Web:* www.asccinc.com	Cranberry Township	PA	16066	800-772-0797		196
ASCCP (American Society for Colposcopy and Cervical Pathology) 131 Rollins Ave Ste 2 *TF:* 800-787-7227 ■ *Web:* www.asccp.org	Rockville	MD	21740	301-857-7877		49-8
ASCD (Association for Supervision & Curriculum Development) 1703 N Beauregard St *TF:* 800-933-2723 ■ *Web:* www.ascd.org	Alexandria	VA	22311	703-578-9600	575-5400	49-5

	Phone	Fax	Class
ASCDI (Association of Service & Computer Dealers Intl) 131 NW First Ave . . . Delray Beach FL 33444 *TF:* 800-393-2505 ■ *Web:* www.ascdi.com	561-266-9016	431-6302	48-9
ASCE (American Society of Civil Engineers) 1801 Alexander Bell Dr . . . Reston VA 20191 *TF:* 800-548-2723 ■ *Web:* www.asce.org	703-295-6300	295-6211	457-21
Ascedia Inc 161 S First St . . . Milwaukee WI 53204 *Web:* www.ascedia.com	414-292-3200		224
Ascend Advisory Group LLC 6760 Perimeter Dr . . . Dublin OH 43016 *Web:* www.ascendadvisory.com	614-784-6000		194
Ascend Analytics LLC 1877 Broadway Ste 706 . . . Boulder CO 80302 *Web:* www.ascendanalytics.com	303-415-1400		463
Ascend Federal Credit Union 520 Airpark Dr PO Box 1210 . . . Tullahoma TN 37388 *TF:* 800-342-3086 ■ *Web:* www.ascend.org	931-455-5441		219
Ascend Laboratories LLC 339 Jefferson Rd Ste 101 . . . Parsippany NJ 07054 *Web:* www.ascendlaboratories.com	201-476-1977		231
Ascend Marketing LLC 2301 Ira E Woods Ave . . . Fort Worth TX 76107 *Web:* www.ascend.marketing	817-886-0014		636
Ascend Therapeutics Inc 607 Herndon Pkwy Ste 110 . . . Herndon VA 20170 *TF:* 888-412-5751 ■ *Web:* www.ascendtherapeutics.com	703-471-4744		231
Ascendant Engineering Solutions 12303 Technology Blvd Ste 925 . . . Austin TX 78727 *TF:* 866-234-6465 ■ *Web:* www.aesaustin.com	512-371-5704	744-1807	256
Ascendant Pictures 406 Wilshire Blvd . . . Santa Monica CA 90401 *Web:* www.ascendantpictures.com	310-288-4600	288-4601	514
Ascendiant Capital Group LLC 18881 Von Karman Ave 16th Fl . . . Irvine CA 92612 *Web:* www.ascendiant.com	949-259-4900		463
Ascendum Solutions LLC 10290 Alliance Rd . . . Cincinnati OH 45242 *Web:* ascendum.com	513-792-5100		196
Ascension Chamber of Commerce 1006 W Hwy 30 . . . Gonzales LA 70737 *Web:* ascensionchamber.com	225-647-7487	647-5124	139
Ascension Crittenton Hospital 1101 W University Dr . . . Rochester Hills MI 48307 *Web:* healthcare.ascension.org	248-652-5000		374-3
Ascension Industries 1254 Erie Ave . . . North Tonawanda NY 14120 *Web:* www.asmfab.com	716-693-9381	693-9882	482
Ascension Parish 208 E Railroad St . . . Gonzales LA 70737 *Web:* www.ascensionparish.net	225-621-5709	621-5704	338
Ascension Press PO Box 1990 . . . West Chester PA 19380 *TF:* 800-376-0520 ■ *Web:* ascensionpress.com	484-875-4550		637-2
Ascension Sacred Heart Rehabilitation Institute 2301 N Lake Dr . . . Milwaukee WI 53211 *Web:* www.columbia-stmarys.org	414-298-6750		374-6
Ascension Saint Elizabeth Hospital 1506 S Oneida St Ste100 . . . Appleton WI 54915 *TF:* 800-223-7332 ■ *Web:* www.affinityhealth.org	920-738-2000		374-3
Ascension Seton 1345 Philomena St . . . Austin TX 78723 *Web:* www.seton.net	512-324-9999		354
Ascension Ventures 101 S Hanley Rd Ste 200 . . . Clayton MO 63105 *Web:* ascensionventures.org	314-733-8000		792
Ascent Aviation Group 1 Mill St . . . Parish NY 13131 *TF:* 800-272-3681 ■ *Web:* www.ascent1.com	800-272-3681		579
Ascent Biomedical Ventures 142 W 57th St Ste 4A . . . New York NY 10019 *Web:* www.abvlp.com	212-303-1680	752-3633	476
Ascent Capital Group Inc 5251 DTC Pkwy Ste 1000 . . . Greenwood Village CO 80111 *Web:* www.ascentcapitalgroupinc.com	303-628-5600		692
Ascent Capital Management LLC 2796 NW Clearwater Dr . . . Bend OR 97701 *Web:* www.ascentbend.com	541-382-4847	388-1124	194
Ascent Hospitality 3616 S Bogan Rd Ste 201 . . . Buford GA 30519 *Web:* ascent-hospitality.com	770-904-0765	904-6302	378
Ascent LLC 2350 Ball Dr . . . Saint Louis MO 63146 *TF:* 877-427-2368 ■ *Web:* www.ascent-corp.com	314-989-1011		463
Ascent Services Group, The 1001 Galaxy Way Ste 405 . . . Concord CA 94520 *Web:* www.ascentsg.com	925-627-4900		180
Ascent Solar Technologies Inc 12300 Grant St . . . Thornton CO 80241 *Web:* www.ascentsolar.com	720-872-5000		696
Ascent Venture Partners 255 State St 5th Fl . . . Boston MA 02109 *Web:* www.ascentvp.com	617-720-9400		792
Ascenta Therapeutics Inc 101 Lindenwood Dr Ste 405 . . . Malvern PA 19355	610-408-0301		231
Ascentek Inc 12 Betnr Industrial Dr . . . Pittsfield MA 01201 *Web:* www.ascentek.com	413-496-9900		396
Ascentium Capital LLC 23970 Hwy 59 N . . . Kingwood TX 77339 *TF:* 866-722-8500 ■ *Web:* ascentiumcapital.com	866-722-8500		509
Ascentive LLC 50 S 16th St Ste 3575 . . . Philadelphia PA 19102 *Web:* www.ascentive.com	215-320-6000		177
Ascentra Credit Union 1710 Grant St . . . Bettendorf IA 52722 *TF:* 800-426-5241 ■ *Web:* www.ascentra.org	563-355-0152		219
ASCH (American Society of Clinical Hypnosis) 140 N Bloomingdale Rd . . . Bloomingdale IL 60108 *TF:* 800-227-6963 ■ *Web:* www.asch.net	630-980-4740	351-8490	49-8
Ascher Bros Company Inc 3033 W Fletcher St . . . Chicago IL 60618 *Web:* www.ascherbrothers.com	773-588-0001		189-8
Aschinger Electric Co 877 Horan Dr . . . Fenton MO 63026 *Web:* www.aschinger.com	636-343-1211		189-4
ASCI (Advanced Systems Concepts Inc) 1180 Headquarters Plz West Twr 4th Fl . . . Morristown NJ 07960 *TF:* 800-229-2724 ■ *Web:* www.advsyscon.com	973-539-2660	539-3390	178-1
Ascinc.com 22 Haverhill Rd PO Box 128 . . . Windham NH 03087 *Web:* www.ascinc.com	603-437-2234		178-10
ASCIS (Academie Ste Cecile International School) 925 Cousineau Rd . . . Windsor ON N9G1V8 *Web:* academiestececile.ca	519-969-1291	969-7953	622
ASCO (Association of Schools & Colleges of Optometry) 6110 Executive Blvd Ste 420 . . . Rockville MD 20852 *Web:* optometriceducation.org	301-231-5944	770-1828	49-8
ASCO (American Society of Clinical Oncology) 2318 Mill Rd Ste 800 . . . Alexandria VA 22314 **Fax Area Code:* 703 ■ *TF:* 888-282-2552 ■ *Web:* www.asco.org	571-483-1300	299-0255*	49-8
ASCO Sintering Co 2750 Garfield Ave . . . Commerce CA 90040 *Web:* www.ascosintering.com	323-725-3550	888-9968	350
ASCO Valve Inc 50-60 Hanover Rd . . . Florham Park NJ 07932 *Web:* www.asco.com	973-966-2000		201
Ascom North America 300 Perimeter Park Dr . . . Morrisville NC 27560 *TF:* 877-712-7266 ■ *Web:* www.ascom.com	877-712-7266		647
Ascot Enterprises Inc 503 S Main St . . . Nappanee IN 46550 *Web:* www.ascotent.com	574-773-7751	773-2894	746
Ascot Staffing 1939 Harrison St Ste 150 . . . Oakland CA 94612 *Web:* www.ascotstaffing.com	510-839-9520		260
ASCP (American Society of Consultant Pharmacists) 1321 Duke St . . . Alexandria VA 22314 *TF:* 800-355-2727 ■ *Web:* www.ascp.com	703-739-1300	739-1321	49-8
ASCP (American Society for Clinical Pathology) 33 W Monroe St Ste 1600 . . . Chicago IL 60603 *TF:* 800-621-4142 ■ *Web:* ascp.org	312-541-4999	541-4998	49-8
ASCRS (American Society of Cataract & Refractive Surgery) 4000 Legato Rd Ste 700 . . . Fairfax VA 22033 *TF:* 877-996-4464 ■ *Web:* www.ascrs.org	703-591-2220	591-0614	49-8
ASCSA (American School of Classical Studies at Athens) 6-8 Charlton St . . . Princeton NJ 08540 *Web:* www.ascsa.edu.gr	609-683-0800	924-0578	037-2
Ascutney State Park 1826 Black Mtn Rd . . . Windsor VT 05089 *Web:* www.vtstateparks.com	802-674-2060		565
ASD (Allentown School District) 31 S Penn St PO Box 328 . . . Allentown PA 18105 *Web:* www.allentownsd.org	484-765-4000	765-4140	685
ASD (Anchorage School District) 5530 E Northern Lights Blvd . . . Anchorage AK 99504 *Web:* www.asdk12.org	907-742-4000	742-4176	685
ASD Data Services LLC PO Box 1184 . . . Manchester TN 37349 *TF:* 877-742-7297 ■ *Web:* asddataservices.com	877-742-7297		637-6
ASD MarketWeek 600 Corporate Pointe Ste 1000 10th Fl . . . Culver City CA 90230 *TF:* 800-421-4511 ■ *Web:* www.asdonline.com	323-817-2200	957-1131	184
ASDS (American Society for Dermatologic Surgery) 5550 Meadowbrook Dr Ste 120 . . . Rolling Meadows IL 60008 *TF:* 800-714-1374 ■ *Web:* asds.net	847-956-0900	956-0999	49-8
ASE (American Society of Echocardiography) 2100 Gateway Centre Blvd Ste 310 . . . Morrisville NC 27560 *Web:* www.asecho.org	919-861-5574	882-9900	49-8
ASE (Alliance to Save Energy) 1850 M St NW Ste 600 . . . Washington DC 20036 *TF:* 800-862-2086 ■ *Web:* www.ase.org	202-857-0666	331-9588	48-12
ASE Inc 1255 E Arques Ave . . . Sunnyvale CA 94085 *Web:* www.aseglobal.com	408-636-9500		246
ASEE (American Society for Engineering Education) 1818 N St NW Ste 600 . . . Washington DC 20036 *Web:* www.asee.org	202-331-3500	265-8504	49-19
Asel Art Supply 2701 Cedar Springs . . . Dallas TX 75201 *Web:* www.aselart.com	214-871-2425	871-0007	45
Asen Computer Associates Inc 900 N National Pky Ste 155 . . . Schaumburg IL 60173 *Web:* www.asen.com	847-995-1300		180
Asen Marketing 18 Emory Pl Ste 100 . . . Knoxville TN 37917 *Web:* asenmarketing.com	865-769-0006		195
Aseptico Inc 8333 216th St SE . . . Woodinville WA 98072 **Fax Area Code:* 360 ■ *TF:* 866-244-2954 ■ *Web:* aseptico.com	425-487-3157	668-8722*	475
AseraCare Hospice 1000 Fianna Way . . . Fort Smith AR 72919 *TF:* 888-868-1957 ■ *Web:* www.aseracare.com	888-868-1957		371
Asereth Medical Services Inc 257 Fair Oaks Ave Ste 100 . . . Pasadena CA 91105 *Web:* www.asereth.com	626-449-0099		260
Asero Insurance Services Inc 200 Nalmaden Blvd Ste 100 . . . San Jose CA 95110 *TF:* 866-966-8928 ■ *Web:* aseroins.com	408-271-2300		390
ASES (American Solar Energy Society) 2525 Arapahoe Ave Ste E4 253 . . . Boulder CO 80302 *Web:* www.ases.org	303-443-3130		48-12
ASF (Apache Software Foundation) 1901 Munsey Dr . . . Forest Hill MD 21050 *Web:* www.apache.org	410-803-2258		48-9
ASF (Atlantic Salmon Federation) PO Box 5200 . . . Saint Andrews NB E5B3S8 *TF:* 800-565-5666 ■ *Web:* www.asf.ca	506-529-1033		48-3
ASF Foundation 2530 E South Blvd . . . Montgomery AL 36116 *Web:* www.asffoundation.org	334-280-0065		713
ASFMRA (American Society of Farm Managers & Rural Appraisers Inc) 720 S Colordo Blvd Ste 360-S . . . Glendale CO 80246 *Web:* www.asfmra.org	303-758-3513	758-0190	48-2
ASG (Allen Systems Group Inc) 1333 Third Ave S . . . Naples FL 34102 **Fax Area Code:* 800 ■ *TF:* 800-932-5536 ■ *Web:* www.asg.com	239-435-2200	325-2555*	178-12
ASG (Advanced Systems Group LLC) 1226 Powell St . . . Emeryville CA 94608 *Web:* www.asgllc.com	510-654-8300	654-8370	174
ASG Renaissance 22226 Garrison St . . . Dearborn MI 48124 *TF:* 800-238-0890 ■ *Web:* asgren.com	313-565-4700	565-4701	261
ASGCA (American Society of Golf Course Architects) 125 N Executive Dr Ste 106 . . . Brookfield WI 53005 *Web:* asgca.org	262-786-5960	786-5919	48-22

Name / Address	City	State	Zip	Phone	Fax	Class
ASGE (American Society for Gastrointestinal Endoscopy) 1520 Kensington Rd Ste 202 *TF:* 866-353-2743 ■ *Web:* www.asge.org	Oak Brook	IL	60523	630-573-0600	573-0691	49-8
ASH (American Society of Hematology) 2021 L St NW Ste 900 *Web:* www.hematology.org	Washington	DC	20036	202-776-0544	776-0545	49-8
Ash Brokerage Corp 7609 W Jefferson Blvd *Web:* www.ashbrokerage.com	Fort Wayne	IN	46804	260-478-0600		390
Ash Creek Enterprises Inc 1110 Broadbridge Ave *TF:* 866-866-2487 ■ *Web:* www.ashcreek.com	Stratford	CT	06615	203-290-1395		387
Ash Grove Press Inc, The PO Box 8564 *Web:* www.ashgrovepress.com	Prairie Village	KS	66208	913-530-4308		49-19
Ash Hollow State Historical Park PO Box 70 *Web:* www.outdoornebraska.gov	Lewellen	NE	69147	308-778-5651		565
Ash Law Firm PLLC 4915 I-55 N Ste 203-B *Web:* ashlaw.ms	Jackson	MS	39206	601-981-5600		41
Ash Tree Publishing PO Box 64 *TF:* 800-667-3399 ■ *Web:* www.ashtreepublishing.com	Woodstock	NY	12498	845-246-8081		637-2
ASHA (American School Health Assn) 7918 Jones Branch Dr Ste 300 *Web:* www.ashaweb.org	McLean	VA	22102	703-506-7675	506-3266	49-5
ASHA (American Seniors Housing Assn) 5225 Wisconsin Ave NW Ste 502 *Web:* www.seniorshousing.org	Washington	DC	20015	202-237-0900	237-1616	48-6
ASHA (American Speech-Language-Hearing Assn) 2200 Research Blvd *TF:* 800-498-2071 ■ *Web:* www.asha.org	Rockville	MD	20850	301-296-5700	296-8580	49-8
ASHA (American Saddlebred Horse Assn) 4083 Iron Works Pkwy *Web:* www.asha.net	Lexington	KY	40511	859-259-2742	259-1628	48-3
Ashaway Line & Twine Manufacturing Co 24 Laurel St *TF:* 800-556-7260 ■ *Web:* www.ashawayusa.com	Ashaway	RI	02804	401-377-2221	377-9091	208
Ashbaugh Beal LLP 4400 Columbia Ctr 701 Fifth Ave *Web:* ashbaughbeal.com	Seattle	WA	98104	206-386-5900		428
Ashbrook Ctr Ashland University 401 College Ave *TF:* 877-289-5411 ■ *Web:* ashbrook.org	Ashland	OH	44805	419-289-5411		634
Ashburn Consulting LLC 43848 Goshen Farm Ct *TF:* 866-576-9382 ■ *Web:* www.ashburnconsulting.com	Leesburg	VA	20176	703-652-9120		180
Ashbury College 362 Mariposa Ave *Web:* www.ashbury.ca	Rockcliffe	ON	K1M0T3	613-749-5954		685
Ashcroft Inc 250 E Main St *TF:* 800-328-8258 ■ *Web:* www.ashcroftinc.com	Stratford	CT	06614	203-378-8281		407
Ashe County Chamber of Commerce 1 N Jefferson Ave Ste C PO Box 31 *TF:* 888-343-2743 ■ *Web:* ashechamber.com	West Jefferson	NC	28694	336-846-9550		338
Asheboro Elastics Corp 150 N Park St *Web:* www.aecnarrowfabrics.com	Asheboro	NC	27203	336-629-2626	629-3782	745-4
Asher Agency Inc 535 W Wayne St *Web:* asheragency.com	Fort Wayne	IN	46802	260-424-3373		636
Asher's Chocolates 80 Wambold Rd *TF:* 800-223-4420 ■ *Web:* www.ashers.com	Souderton	PA	18964	215-721-3000	721-3265	296-8
Asheville Area Chamber of Commerce 36 Montford Ave *TF:* 888-314-1041 ■ *Web:* www.ashevillechamber.org	Asheville	NC	28802	828-258-6101	251-0926	139
Asheville Art Museum 175 Biltmore Ave *Web:* www.ashevilleart.org	Asheville	NC	28801	828-253-3227		520
Asheville Catholic School 12 Culvern St *Web:* www.ashevillecatholic.org	Asheville	NC	28804	828-252-7896	252-5708	685
Asheville Chevrolet Inc 205 Smokey Park Hwy *TF:* 866-921-1073 ■ *Web:* www.ashevillechevrolet.com	Asheville	NC	28806	828-348-7326		57
Asheville Citizen Times 14 O'Henry Ave *TF:* 800-672-2472 ■ *Web:* www.citizen-times.com	Asheville	NC	28801	828-252-5611		532-2
Asheville City Hall 70 Ct Plz PO Box 7148 *Web:* www.ashevillenc.gov	Asheville	NC	28802	828-259-5600	259-5499	337
Asheville Community Theatre 35 E Walnut St *Web:* ashevilletheatre.org	Asheville	NC	28801	828-254-1320	252-4723	572
Asheville Mall 3 S Tunnel Rd *Web:* www.asheville-mall.com	Asheville	NC	28805	828-298-0012		655
Asheville Racquet Club Inc 200 Racquet Club Rd *Web:* ashevilleracquetclub.com	Asheville	NC	28803	828-274-3361		354
Asheville Regional Airport 61 Terminal Dr Ste 1 *TF:* 866-719-3910 ■ *Web:* flyavl.com	Fletcher	NC	28732	828-684-2226	684-3404	27
Asheville Savings Bank S S B PO Box 652 *TF:* 800-222-3230 ■ *Web:* www.localfirstbank.com	Asheville	NC	28802	828-254-7411	252-1512	70
Asheville School 360 Asheville School Rd *Web:* www.ashevilleschool.org	Asheville	NC	28806	828-254-6345		622
Asheville Specialty Hospital (ASH) 428 Biltmore Ave *Web:* www.mission-health.org	Asheville	NC	28801	828-213-5400		374-3
Asheville Symphony Orchestra PO Box 2852 *Web:* ashevillesymphony.org	Asheville	NC	28802	828-254-7046	254-1761	573-3
Asheville-Buncombe Technical Community College 340 Victoria Rd *Web:* www.abtech.edu	Asheville	NC	28801	828-254-1921	251-6718	162
Ashfall Fossil Beds State Historical Park 86930 517th Ave *Web:* ashfall.unl.edu	Royal	NE	68773	402-893-2000		565
Ashfield Capital Partners LLC 801 Montgomery St Ste 200 *TF:* 877-391-4747 ■ *Web:* www.ashfield.com	San Francisco	CA	94133	415-391-4747	391-1234	401
Ashford Hospitality Trust Inc 14185 Dallas Pkwy Ste 1100 *NYSE: AHT* ■ *Web:* www.ahtreit.com	Dallas	TX	75254	972-490-9600	980-2705	654
Ashford University 400 N Bluff Blvd *TF:* 800-242-4153 ■ *Web:* www.ashford.edu	Clinton	IA	52732	563-242-4023		166
ASHG (American Society of Human Genetics) 6120 Executive Blvd Ste 500 *Web:* www.ashg.org	Rockville	MD	20852	301-634-7300	634-7079	49-19
ASHI (American Society for Histocompatibility & Immunogenetics) 15000 Commerce Pkwy Ste C *Web:* www.ashi-hla.org	Mount Laurel	NJ	08054	856-638-0428		49-8
ASHI (American Society of Home Inspectors) 932 Lee St Ste 101 *TF:* 800-743-2744 ■ *Web:* www.homeinspector.org	Des Plaines	IL	60016	847-759-2820	759-1620	49-3
Ashiana Indian Restaurant 12610 Briar Forest Rd *Web:* ashianarestaurant.net	Houston	TX	77077	281-679-5555		671
Ashkenazy Acquisition Corp 150 E 58th St 39th Fl *Web:* www.aacrealty.com	New York	NY	10155	212-213-4444	213-5713	528
Ashland Addison Florist Co 1640 W Fulton St *TF:* 800-348-1157 ■ *Web:* www.ashaddflorist.com	Chicago	IL	60612	312-432-1800		292
Ashland Alliance Chamber of Commerce 1733 Winchester Ave *Web:* www.ashlandalliance.com	Ashland	KY	41101	606-324-5111	325-4607	139
Ashland Community & Technical College 1400 College Dr *TF:* 800-928-4256 ■ *Web:* ashland.kctcs.edu	Ashland	KY	41101	606-326-2000	326-2192	162
Ashland Construction Co 4601 Atlantic Ave *Web:* www.ashlandconstruction.com	Raleigh	NC	27604	919-872-7500		186
Ashland County 1205 E Main St *Web:* ashlandcounty.org	Ashland	OH	44805	419-282-4242		338
Ashland County 201 W Main St Rm 202 *Web:* co.ashland.wi.us	Ashland	WI	54806	715-682-7015	682-7078	338
Ashland County West Holmes Career Ctr 1783 St Rt 60 *Web:* www.acwhcc.org	Ashland	OH	44805	419-289-3313		165
Ashland Creek Press 2305 Ashland St Ste C417 *Web:* www.ashlandcreekpress.com	Ashland	OR	97520	760-300-3620		637-2
Ashland Hardware Systems 545 E John Carpenter Fwy Ste 610 *Web:* www.ashlandhardware.com	Irving	TX	75062	469-621-9830		608
Ashland Inc 50 E River Center Blvd PO Box 391 *NYSE: ASH* ■ *TF:* 877-546-2782 ■ *Web:* www.ashland.com	Covington	KY	41012	859-815-3333		185
Ashland Independent School District 1820 Hickman St *Web:* www.ashland.kyschools.us	Ashland	KY	41105	606-327-2706	327-2705	685
Ashland Industries Inc 1115 Rail Dr *TF:* 877-634-4622 ■ *Web:* ashlandind.com	Ashland	WI	54806	877-634-4622		190
Ashland Institute of Massage 280 E Hersey St A-8 PO Box 1233 *Web:* www.aimashland.com	Ashland	OR	97520	541-482-5134	488-2383	167-3
Ashland Lumber Co 134 Front St *Web:* www.ashlandlumber.com	Ashland	MA	01721	508-881-2660		364
Ashland Partners 4400 Livingston Rd *Web:* www.ashlandpartners.com	Central Point	OR	97502	541-857-8800		393
Ashland Springs Hotel 212 E Main St *TF:* 888-795-4545 ■ *Web:* www.ashlandspringshotel.com	Ashland	OR	97520	541-488-1700	488-0240	379
Ashland University 401 College Ave *TF:* 800-882-1548 ■ *Web:* www.ashland.edu	Ashland	OH	44805	419-289-4142	289-5999	166
Ashland-The Henry Clay Estate 120 Sycamore Rd *Web:* www.henryclay.org	Lexington	KY	40502	859-266-8581	268-7266	50-3
Ashlar Inc 9600 Great Hills Trl Ste 150W-1625 *TF:* 800-877-2745 ■ *Web:* www.ashlar.com	Austin	TX	78759	512-250-2186	250-5811	178-5
Ashley County 215 E Jefferson St *Web:* local.arkansas.gov	Hamburg	AR	71646	870-853-2000		338
Ashley Furniture Industries Inc 1 Ashley Way *TF:* 800-477-2222 ■ *Web:* www.ashleyfurniture.com	Arcadia	WI	54612	608-323-3377		319-2
Ashley Hall School 172 Rutledge Ave *Web:* www.ashleyhall.org	Charleston	SC	29403	843-722-4088		685
Ashley Home Stores Ltd 9536 Airline Hwy *Web:* stores.ashleyfurniture.com	Baton Rouge	LA	70815	225-926-3380		321
Ashley Lighting Inc 405 Industrial Dr *Web:* ashleylighting.com	Trumann	AR	72472	870-483-6181	483-7140	439
Ashley Madison Agency, The 2300 Yonge St *TF:* 866-742-2218 ■ *Web:* www.ashleymadison.com	Toronto	ON	M4P1E4	866-742-2218		226
Ashley Ward Inc 7490 Easy St *Web:* www.ashleyward.com	Mason	OH	45040	513-398-1414	398-1125	621
Ashley-Chicot Electric Co-opeartive Inc 307 E Jefferson St *TF:* 800-281-5212 ■ *Web:* www.ashley-chicot.com	Hamburg	AR	71646	870-853-5212		245
Ashmore Inn & Suites 4019 S Loop 289 *Web:* www.ashmoreinn.com	Lubbock	TX	79423	806-785-0060		379
Ashoka the Great 9474 Black Mountain Rd *Web:* ashokasd.com	San Diego	CA	92126	858-695-9749		671
ASHP (American Society of Health-System Pharmacists) 7272 Wisconsin Ave *TF:* 866-279-0681 ■ *Web:* www.ashp.org	Bethesda	MD	20814	301-664-8700	664-8877	49-8
ASHRAE (American Society of Heating Refrigerating & Air-Conditioning Engineers Inc) 1791 Tullie Cir NE *TF:* 800-527-4723 ■ *Web:* www.ashrae.org	Atlanta	GA	30329	404-636-8400	321-5478	49-3
Ashram, The PO Box 8009 *Web:* www.theashram.com	Calabasas	CA	91372	818-222-6900		673

				Phone	Fax	Class
ASHS (American Society for Horticultural Science) 1018 Duke St *Web:* www.ashs.org	Alexandria	VA	22314	703-836-4606	836-2024	48-2
Ashta Chemicals Inc 3509 Middle Rd *TF:* 800-492-5082 ■ *Web:* www.ashtachemicals.com	Ashtabula	OH	44004	440-997-5221	992-0151	143
Ashtabula Area Chamber of Commerce 4536 Main Ave *Web:* www.ashtabulachamber.net	Ashtabula	OH	44004	440-998-6998	992-8216	139
Ashtabula Area City School District 2630 W 13th St *Web:* www.aacs.net	Ashtabula	OH	44004	440-992-1200	992-1209	685
Ashtabula County District Library 4335 Park Ave *Web:* www.acdl.info	Ashtabula	OH	44004	440-997-9341	992-7714	434-3
Ashtabula County Medical Ctr (ACMC) 2420 Lake Ave *TF:* 800-722-3330 ■ *Web:* www.acmchealth.org	Ashtabula	OH	44004	440-997-2262	997-6644	374-3
Ashtabula Rubber Co 2751 W Ave *Web:* www.ashtabularubber.com	Ashtabula	OH	44004	440-992-2195	992-7829	677
Ashtead Technology Inc 3311 Preston Ave Ste 170 *TF:* 800-242-3910 ■ *Web:* www.ashtead-technology.com	Houston	TX	77084	281-398-9533		193
Ashton Benefits Corp 600 Sylvan Ave Ste 301 *TF:* 877-640-2813 ■ *Web:* ashtonbenefits.com	Englewood Cliffs	NJ	07632	877-640-2813		390
Ashton College 1190 Melville St *Web:* www.ashtoncollege.ca	Vancouver	BC	V6E3W1	604-899-0803		162
Ashton Company Inc, The 2727 S Country Club Rd PO Box 26927 *Web:* www.ashtoncoinc.com	Tucson	AZ	85713	520-624-5500	791-9059	186
Ashton Gardens Houston 21919 Inverness Forest Blvd *Web:* www.ashtongardens.com	Houston	TX	77073	281-362-0011		184
Ashton Hotel 610 Main St *Web:* www.theashtonhotel.com	Fort Worth	TX	76102	817-332-0100		379
Ashton Metzler & Assoc PO Box 1640 *Web:* www.ashtonmetzler.com	Sanibel	FL	33957	239-395-3152		41
Ashton Staffing 4255 Wade Green NW Rd Ste 515 *Web:* www.q-staffing.com	Kennesaw	GA	30144	770-419-1776	405-0069	260
Ashton Technologies Inc 2100 Centerwood Dr *Web:* ashton-tech.com	Warren	MI	48091	586-756-6500		261
Ashton-Potter (USA) Ltd 10 Curtwright Dr *Web:* www.ashtonpotter.com	Williamsville	NY	14221	716-633-2000		627
Ashwaubenon School District 1055 Griffiths Ln *Web:* www.ashwaubenon.k12.wi.us	Green Bay	WI	54304	920-492-2900	492-2911	685
Ashwood Computer Company Inc 10671 Techwoods Cir Ste B *TF:* 800-219-8613 ■ *Web:* ashwoodcomputer.com	Cincinnati	OH	45242	513-563-2800	554-6412	225
ASI (American Swedish Institute, The) 2600 Park Ave *Web:* www.asimn.org	Minneapolis	MN	55407	612-871-4907	871-8682	520
ASI (American Sports Institute) 116 E Blithedale Ave *Web:* americansportsinstitute.org	Mill Valley	CA	94941	415-383-5750		48-22
ASI (American Society of Indexers) 1628 E Southern Ave Ste 9-223 *Web:* www.asindexing.org	Tempe	AZ	85282	480-245-6750		49-16
ASI (American Sheep Industry Assn) 9785 Maroon Cir Ste 360 *Web:* www.sheepusa.org	Englewood	CO	80112	303-771-3500	771-8200	48-2
ASI (American Specialties Inc) 441 Saw Mill River Rd *Web:* americanspecialties.com	Yonkers	NY	10701	914-476-9000	476-0688	609
ASI (Arion Systems Inc) 15040 Conference Center Dr Ste 200 *Web:* www.arionsys.com	Chantilly	VA	20151	703-815-1130	815-1135	261
ASI (Abrasive Specialists Inc) 15825 Central Ave NE *Web:* www.asimn.com	Ham Lake	MN	55304	763-571-4111	571-5026	385
ASI (Arthur Shuster Inc) 2229 University Ave *Web:* shusterinteriors.net	Saint Paul	MN	55114	651-319-5569		393
ASI (Academy Systems Inc) 1343 E 10 St *TF:* 800-446-6619 ■ *Web:* www.academysystems.com	Brooklyn	NY	11230	718-645-2330	645-2415	178-1
ASI Automation LLC 11005 Long Lake Dr	Sparta	MI	49345	616-887-8201		261
ASI Computer Systems Inc 5250 Nordic Dr *TF:* 800-544-1274 ■ *Web:* sales.asicomp.com	Cedar Falls	IA	50613	319-266-7688	235-5543	180
ASI Constructors Inc 1850 E Platteville Blvd *Web:* www.asiconstructors.com	Pueblo	CO	81007	719-647-2821	647-2890	186
ASI Corp 48289 Fremont Blvd *TF:* 800-200-0274 ■ *Web:* www.asipartner.com	Fremont	CA	94538	510-226-8000	445-4157	174
ASI DataMyte Inc 2800 Campus Dr Ste 60 **Fax Area Code:* 844 ■ *TF:* 800-455-4359 ■ *Web:* www.asidatamyte.com	Plymouth	MN	55441	763-553-1040	760-7232*	178-10
ASI Global Partitions 2171 Liberty Hill Rd *Web:* globalpartitions.com	Eastanollee	GA	30538	706-827-2700	827-2710	609
ASI Health Services 4950 Keller Springs Rd Ste 190 *TF:* 800-766-5167 ■ *Web:* www.asihealthservices.com	Addison	TX	75001	972-458-0202	458-0234	196
ASI Industrial 1300 Minnesota Ave *Web:* www.asi-industrial.com	Billings	MT	59101	406-245-6231	245-6236	186
ASI Networks Inc 19331 E Walnut Dr N *TF:* 800-251-1336 ■ *Web:* www.asi-networks.com	City of Industry	CA	91748	800-251-1336		180
ASI Technologies 209 Progress Dr *Web:* www.asidrives.com	Montgomeryville	PA	18936	215-661-1002	661-1009	350
ASI Technologies Inc 5848 N 95th Ct *TF:* 800-558-7068 ■ *Web:* www.asidoors.com	Milwaukee	WI	53225	414-464-6200	464-9863	234
Asia America MultiTechnology Assn (AAMA) 555 Bryant St Ste 332 *Web:* www.aamasv.com	Palo Alto	CA	94301	408-736-2554		49-13
Asia Center Publications CGIS S 1st Fl 1730 Cambridge St *Web:* fas.harvard.edu	Cambridge	MA	02138	617-496-6273		637-2
Asia Pacific Capital 515 S Figueroa St Ste 1850 *Web:* apccusa.com	Los Angeles	CA	90071	213-680-8811		528
Asia Pacific Center for Security 2058 Maluhia Rd *Web:* apcss.org	Honolulu	HI	96815	808-971-8900		693
Asian American Business Development Center Inc 132 Nassau St Ste 719 *Web:* www.aabdc.com	New York	NY	10038	212-966-0100		194
Asian American Civic Association Inc 87 Tyler St 5th Fl *Web:* aaca-boston.org	Boston	MA	02111	617-426-9492	482-2316	554
Asian American Curriculum Project (AACP) 529 E 3rd Ave *Web:* www.asianamericanbooks.com	San Mateo	CA	94401	650-375-8286	375-8797	48-6
Asian American Legal Defense & Education Fund (AALDEF) 99 Hudson St 12th Fl *TF:* 800-966-5946 ■ *Web:* www.aaldef.org	New York	NY	10013	212-966-5932	966-4303	48-8
Asian Art Museum 200 Larkin St *Web:* www.asianart.org	San Francisco	CA	94102	415-581-3500	581-4700	520
Asian Inc 1167 Mission St 4th Fl *Web:* www.asianinc.org	San Francisco	CA	94103	415-928-5910		194
Asian Mint 11617 N Central Expy Ste 135 *Web:* asianmint.com	Dallas	TX	75243	214-363-6655		671
Asian Network Hospice 212 9th St Ste 205 *Web:* www.anphc.com	Oakland	CA	94607	510-268-1118	268-9905	363
Asian Pacific American Legal Center of Southern California 1145 Wilshire Blvd 2nd Fl *TF:* 800-520-2356 ■ *Web:* advancingjustice-la.org	Los Angeles	CA	90017	213-977-7500		428
Asian Television Network (ATN) 330 Cochrane Dr *Web:* www.asiantelevision.com	Markham	ON	L3R8E4	905-948-8199	948-8108	740
Asian University for Women 1100 Massachusetts Ave Ste 3 *Web:* asian-university.org	Cambridge	MA	02138	617-914-0500		166
Asiana Cafe 130 E Putnam Ave *Web:* www.asianacafe.com	Greenwich	CT	06830	203-622-6833	861-2680	671
Asiana Cuisine Enterprises Inc 22771 S W Ave *Web:* acesushi.com	Torrance	CA	90501	310-327-2233	327-9193	297-8
AsiaSF 201 Ninth St *Web:* asiasf.com	San Francisco	CA	94103	415-255-2742		671
Asiatico & Associates PLLC 5850 Granite Pkwy Ste 900 *Web:* www.baalegal.com	Plano	TX	75024	214-570-0700		428
Asico LLC 26 Plaza Dr *TF:* 800-628-2879 ■ *Web:* www.asico.com	Westmont	IL	60559	630-986-8032	986-0065	475
Asics America Corp 29 Parker Ste 100 *TF:* 800-333-8404 ■ *Web:* www.asics.com	Irvine	CA	92618	949-453-8888	453-0292	301
ASID (American Society of Interior Designers) 608 Massachusetts Ave *Web:* www.asid.org	Washington	DC	20002	202-546-3480	546-3240	48-4
ASIL (American Society of International Law, The) 2223 Massachusetts Ave NW *Web:* www.asil.org	Washington	DC	20008	202-939-6000	797-7133	49-10
Asilomar State Beach & Conference Grounds 804 Crocker Ave *Web:* www.parks.ca.gov	Pacific Grove	CA	93950	831-646-6440		565
ASIS Intl 1625 Prince St *Web:* www.asisonline.org	Alexandria	VA	22314	703-519-6200	519-6299	49-12
Asist Translation Services 4891 Sawmill Rd Ste 200 *Web:* www.asisttranslations.com	Columbus	OH	43235	614-451-6744	451-1349	768
ASIWPCA (Association of State & Interstate Water Pollution Control Administrators) 1221 Connecticut Ave NW 2nd Fl *Web:* www.acwa-us.org	Washington	DC	20036	202-756-0600		49-7
ASK Associates Inc 1201 Wakarusa Ste C-1 *TF:* 800-315-4333 ■ *Web:* www.askusa.com	Lawrence	KS	66049	785-841-8194		738
ASK Foods Inc 77 N Hetrick Ave *TF:* 800-879-4275 ■ *Web:* askfoods.com	Palmyra	PA	17078	717-838-6356	838-7458	296-36
ASK LLP 2600 Eagan Woods Dr Ste 400 *Web:* askllp.com	Eagan	MN	55121	651-406-9665		41
ASK Services Inc 42180 Ford Rd Ste 101 *TF:* 888-416-1313 ■ *Web:* www.ask-services.com	Canton	MI	48187	734-983-9040	983-9041	400
ASK Telemarketing Inc 5665 Carmichael Rd *Web:* www.asktelemarketing.com	Montgomery	AL	36117	334-387-2758		737
Askcom 555 12th St Ste 500 *Web:* www.ask.com	Oakland	CA	94607	510-985-7400		397
Askey Hughey Inc 25 E 13th St Ste 9 *Web:* ahieng.com	Saint Cloud	FL	34769	407-957-3308		261
Aski Capital Inc 419 Notre Dame Ave *TF:* 866-987-7180 ■ *Web:* www.askifinancial.ca	Winnipeg	MB	R3B1R3	204-987-7180		138
Askins Family LTP 208 S Blanding St *OTC:* BRRE ■ **Fax Area Code:* 570	Lake City	SC	29560	843-394-8555	443-8412*	189-8
AskMencom Solutions Canada Inc 4200 St Laurent Ste 801 *Web:* in.askmen.com	Montreal	QC	H2W2R2	514-908-2552		4
ASKO Appliances Inc PO Box 44848 *TF:* 800-898-1879 ■ *Web:* www.askona.com	Madison	WI	53744	800-898-1879		36
ASKO Inc 501 W Seventh Ave *TF:* 800-321-1310 ■ *Web:* www.askoinc.com	Homestead	PA	15120	412-461-4110	461-5400	493
ASL Distribution Services Ltd 2160 Buckingham Rd *TF:* 800-387-7995 ■ *Web:* asldistribution.com	Oakville	ON	L6H6M7	905-829-5141		478
ASL Marketing 2 Dubon Ct *Web:* www.aslmarketing.com	Farmingdale	NY	11735	516-248-6100	248-6364	195
ASL Services 3700 Commerce Blvd Ste 216 *TF:* 888-744-6275 ■ *Web:* aslservices.com	Kissimmee	FL	34741	407-518-7900		701
ASLA (American Seminar Leaders Assn) 2405 E Washington Blvd *Web:* www.asla.com	Pasadena	CA	91104	626-791-1211	791-0701	49-12

	Phone	Fax	Class
ASLA (American Society of Landscape Architects)			
636 'I' St NW .... Washington DC 20001	202-898-2444	898-1185	48-2
TF: 888-999-2752 ■ *Web:* www.asla.org			
ASLMS (American Society for Laser Medicine & Surgery Inc)			
2100 Stewart Ave Ste 240.................... Wausau WI 54401	715-845-9283	848-2493	49-8
TF: 877-258-6028 ■ *Web:* www.aslms.org			
ASLO (American Society of Limnology & Oceanography)			
5400 Bosque Blvd Ste 680...................... Waco TX 76710	254-399-9635		49-19
TF: 800-929-2756 ■ *Web:* aslo.org			
ASLRRA (American Short Line & Regional Railroad Assn)			
50 F St NW Ste 7020 .... Washington DC 20001	202-628-4500	628-6430	49-21
Web: www.aslrra.org			
ASLU LLC 12178 Fourth St Rancho .... Cucamonga CA 91730	951-934-4200	727-9520	711
TF: 800-588-3911 ■ *Web:* www.activerideshop.com			
ASM (American Society for Microbiology)			
1752 North St NW .... Washington DC 20036	202-737-3600		49-8
TF: 800-546-2416 ■ *Web:* www.asm.org			
ASM (Advanced Surface Microscopy Inc)			
3250 N Post Rd Ste 120..................Indianapolis IN 46226	317-895-5630	895-5652	743
TF: 800-374-8557 ■ *Web:* www.asmicro.com			
ASM Aerospace Specification Metals Inc			
2501 NW 34th Pl Ste B28..............Pompano Beach FL 33069	954-977-0666	977-3858	492
TF: 800-398-4345 ■ *Web:* www.aerospacemetals.com			
ASM America Inc 3440 E University Dr .... Phoenix AZ 85034	602-470-5700		695
Web: www.asm.com			
ASM Auto Supply 5617 W 63rd St ....Chicago IL 60638	773-735-1140		61
Web: www.asmautoparts.com			
ASM Beauty World Academy			
6423 Stirling Rd.............................. Davie FL 33314	954-321-8411	321-8683	167-3
TF: 877-678-9532 ■ *Web:* www.asmbeautyworld.org			
ASM Consulting Services			
2301 Roscomare Rd Unit 104...............Los Angeles CA 90077	650-780-9321		196
ASM Engineering Consultants LLC			
202 E Rhondda Ste C PO Box 452 .... Andover KS 67002	316-260-5895	260-5954	261
Web: asm4.com			
ASM Industries Inc			
Pacer Pumps Div 41 Industrial Cir.............Lancaster PA 17601	717-656-2161	656-0477	641
TF: 800-233-3861 ■ *Web:* www.pacerpumps.com			
ASM Intl 9639 Kinsman Rd............... Materials Park OH 44073	440-338-5151	338-4634	49-13
TF: 800-336-5152 ■ *Web:* www.asminternational.org			
Asmara Inc 108 Clematis Ave Ste C..............Waltham MA 02453	617-261-0222	894-1914*	131
**Fax Area Code:* 781 ■ *TF:* 800-451-7240 ■ *Web:* www.asmarainc.com			
ASMBA (Armed Services Mutual Benefit Assn)			
1000 NorthChase Dr Ste 220 ....Goodlettsville TN 37072	615-851-0800	851-9484	48-19
TF: 800-251-8434 ■ *Web:* asmba.com			
ASMC (American Society of Military Comptrollers)			
415 N Alfred St............................. Alexandria VA 22314	703-549-0360	549-3181	48-19
TF: 800-462-5637 ■ *Web:* www.asmconline.org			
ASMC Foundation			
5225 Wisconsin Ave NW Ste 316............ Washington DC 20015	202-293-1414	293-1702	637-9
Web: www.asmcfoundation.org			
ASME International Gas Turbine Institute (IGTI)			
6525 the Corners Pkwy...................... Norcross GA 30092	404-847-0072	847-0151	49-19
Web: www.asme.org			
ASML US Inc 8555 S River Pkwy .... Tempe AZ 85284	480-383-4422		695
Web: www.asml.com			
ASMO North America LLC			
470 Crawford Rd.......................... Statesville NC 28625	704-878-6663		518
ASMP (American Society of Media Photographers)			
150 N Second St.........................Philadelphia PA 19106	215-451-2767	451-0880	49-14
Web: www.asmp.org			
ASN (American Society of Notaries)			
PO Box 5707 .... Tallahassee FL 32314	850-671-5164	671-5165	49-12
Web: www.notaries.org			
ASNA (Alabama State Nurses Assn)			
360 N Hull St .... Montgomery AL 36104	334-262-8321		533
TF: 800-270-2762 ■ *Web:* alabamanurses.org			
ASNC (American Society of Nuclear Cardiology)			
4550 Montgomery Ave Ste 780-N .... Bethesda MD 20814	301-215-7575	215-7113	49-8
Web: www.asnc.org			
ASNE (American Society of News Editors)			
11690-B Sunrise Vly Dr .... Reston VA 20191	703-453-1122	453-1133	49-14
Web: www.asne.org			
ASNE (American Society of Naval Engineers)			
1452 Duke St .... Alexandria VA 22314	703-836-6727	836-7491	49-21
Web: www.navalengineers.org			
ASNR (American Society of Neuroradiology)			
800 Enterprise Dr Ste 205................... Oak Brook IL 60523	630-574-0220	574-0661	49-8
Web: www.asnr.org			
ASNS (American Society for Nutrition)			
9211 Corporate Blvd Ste 300................. Rockville MD 20850	240-428-3650	634-7894*	49-6
**Fax Area Code:* 301 ■ *TF:* 800-627-8723 ■ *Web:* nutrition.org			
ASNT (American Society for Nondestructive Testing Inc)			
1711 Arlingate Ln PO Box 28518............. Columbus OH 43228	614-274-6003	274-6899	49-19
TF: 800-222-2768 ■ *Web:* www.asnt.org			
Asnuntuck Community College			
170 Elm St .... Enfield CT 06082	860-253-3000	253-3014	162
TF: 800-501-3967 ■ *Web:* asnuntuck.edu			
ASO (Anderson Symphony Orchestra)			
1124 Meridian Plz .... Anderson IN 46016	765-644-2111		573-3
Web: andersonsymphony.org			
ASO LLC 300 Sarasota Center Blvd ....Sarasota FL 34240	941-379-0300	378-9040	477
Web: www.asocorp.com			
Asolo Repertory Theatre			
5555 N Tamiami Tr ....Sarasota FL 34243	941-351-9010	351-5796	749
TF: 800-361-8388 ■ *Web:* www.asolorep.org			
Asotin County 135 Second St .... Asotin WA 99402	509-243-2016	243-2099	338
Web: www.co.asotin.wa.us			
ASP (Advanced Sterilization Products)			
33 Technology Dr............................. Irvine CA 92618	888-783-7723		477
TF: 888-783-7723 ■ *Web:* www.asp.com			
ASP (Academic Studies Press)			
28 Montfern Ave........................... Brighton MA 02135	617-782-6290	241-3149*	637-10
**Fax Area Code:* 857 ■ *Web:* www.academicstudiespress.com			
ASP (Association of Shareware Professionals)			
PO Box 1522 .... Martinsville IN 46151	765-349-4740	301-3756*	48-9
**Fax Area Code:* 815 ■ *Web:* www.asp-software.org			

	Phone	Fax	Class
ASP Global			
3450 Atlanta Industrial Pkwy .... Atlanta GA 30331	404-696-6999	699-6080	475
Web: www.aspglobal.com			
ASPA (Association of Specialized & Professional Accreditors)			
3304 N Broadway St Ste 214 ....Chicago IL 60657	773-857-7900		48-1
Web: www.aspa-usa.org			
ASPA (American Society for Public Administration)			
1730 Rhode Island Ave NW Ste 500.......... Washington DC 20036	202-393-7878	638-4952	49-7
Web: www.aspanet.org			
ASPAN (American Society of PeriAnesthesia Nurses)			
90 Frontage Rd...........................Cherry Hill NJ 08034	856-616-9601		49-8
TF: 877-737-9696 ■ *Web:* www.aspan.org			
Aspartame Consumer Safety Network (ACSN)			
PO Box 2001 .... Frisco TX 75034	800-969-6050		192
TF: 800-969-6050 ■ *Web:* www.aspartamesafety.com			
Aspasie Inc			
221 Saint-Georges ....Saint-Barnabe-Nord QC G0X2K0	819-264-2116		195
Web: www.aspasie.com			
ASPB (American Society of Plant Biologists)			
15501 Monona Dr .... Rockville MD 20855	301-251-0560	279-2996	49-19
Web: aspb.org			
ASPC (American Shetland Pony Club)			
81B E Queenwood Rd.........................Morton IL 61550	309-263-4044	263-5113	48-3
Web: www.shetlandminiature.com			
ASPCA (American Society for the Prevention of Cruelty to Animals)			
424 E 92nd St.............................New York NY 10128	212-876-7700		48-3
TF: 800-582-5979 ■ *Web:* www.aspca.org			
ASPE (American Society of Professional Estimators)			
PO Box 140710 .... Nashville TN 37214	615-316-9200	316-9800	49-3
TF: 888-378-6283 ■ *Web:* www.aspenational.org			
ASPE Inc 114 Edinburgh S Dr Ste 200 ....Cary NC 27511	877-800-5221		764
TF: 877-800-5221 ■ *Web:* aspetraining.com			
Aspect Automation LLC			
1185 Willow Lake Blvd..................... Saint Paul MN 55110	651-643-3700		407
Web: www.aspectautomation.com			
Aspect Consulting Inc			
20140 Vly Forge Cir .... King of Prussia PA 19406	610-783-0600	783-5155	177
Web: www.aspect-consulting.com			
Aspen Art Museum (AAM) 637 E Hyman Ave ...... Aspen CO 81611	970-925-8050	925-8054	520
Web: aspenartmuseum.org			
Aspen Beauty Academy of Laurel			
3535 Ft Meade Rd .... Laurel MD 20724	301-490-8580		167-3
Web: www.aspenbeautyacademylaurel.com			
Aspen Chamber Resort Assn 590 N Mill St....... Aspen CO 81611	970-925-1940	920-1173	139
TF: 800-670-0792 ■ *Web:* www.aspenchamber.org			
Aspen Electronics Inc 7288 NW 54th St.......... Miami FL 33166	305-863-2151		253
Web: www.aspenelectronics.us			
Aspen Environmental Group			
5020 Chesebro Rd Ste 200................Agoura Hills CA 91301	818-597-3407	597-8001	194
Web: www.aspeneg.com			
Aspen Equipment Co			
9150 Pillsbury Ave S ....Minneapolis MN 55420	952-888-2525		59
Web: www.aspenequipment.com			
Aspen Grove			
7301 S Santa Fe Dr Ste 550 ....Littleton CO 80120	303-794-0640		460
Web: aspengrovecenter.com			
Aspen Hill Club			
14501 Homecrest Rd .... Silver Spring MD 20906	301-598-5200		42
Web: aspenhillclub.com			
Aspen Institute			
1 DuPont Cir NW Ste 700..................Washington DC 20036	202-736-5823	467-0790	634
Web: www.aspeninstitute.org			
Aspen Marketing Services			
1240 N Ave........................... West Chicago IL 60185	630-293-9600		4
TF: 800-848-0212 ■ *Web:* www.aspenms.com			
Aspen Meadows Resort 845 Meadows Rd .... Aspen CO 81611	970-925-4240		669
TF: 800-452-4240 ■ *Web:* www.aspenmeadows.com			
Aspen Medical Products 6481 Oak Cyn........... Irvine CA 92618	800-295-2776		476
TF: 800-295-2776 ■ *Web:* www.aspenmp.com			
Aspen Music Festival & School			
225 Music School Rd.......................... Aspen CO 81611	970-925-3254	920-1643	685
Web: www.aspenmusicfestival.com			
Aspen Networks Inc			
3777 Stevens Creek Blvd .... Santa Clara CA 95051	408-246-4059	246-7264	180
Web: www.aspen-networks.com			
Aspen Products Inc			
4231 Clary Blvd ....Kansas City MO 64130	816-921-0234		558
Web: www.aspenpro.com			
Aspen Real Estate Inc 727 Mechem Dr..........Ruidoso NM 88345	575-257-9057		652
Web: c21aspenruidoso.com			
Aspen Santa Fe Ballet 0245 Sage Way........... Aspen CO 81611	970-925-7175	925-1127	573-1
Web: www.aspensantafeballet.com			
Aspen Ski & Board Co			
1170 E Powell Rd .... Lewis Center OH 43035	614-848-6600		711
TF: 877-861-0777 ■ *Web:* www.aspenskiandboard.com			
Aspen Skiing Co			
117 Aspen Airport Business Ctr................. Aspen CO 81611	970-925-1220		669
TF: 800-525-6200 ■ *Web:* www.aspensnowmass.com			
Aspen Square Condominium Association Inc			
617 E Cooper Ave .... Aspen CO 81611	970-925-1000		378
Web: aspensquarehotel.com			
Aspen Square Management Inc			
380 Union St .... West Springfield MA 01089	413-781-0712		177
Web: www.aspensquare.com			
Aspen Surgical 6945 Southbelt Dr SE.......... Caledonia MI 49316	616-698-7100		477
TF: 888-364-7004 ■ *Web:* www.aspensurgical.com			
Aspen Technology Inc			
200 Wheeler Rd .... Burlington MA 01803	855-882-7736		178-5
NASDAQ: AZPN ■ *TF:* 888-996-7100 ■ *Web:* www.aspentech.com			
Aspen Times, The 314 E Hyman Ave .... Aspen CO 81611	970-925-3414	925-5647	532-2
Web: www.aspentimes.com			
Aspen Waste Systems Inc			
2951 Weeks Ave SE ....Minneapolis MN 55414	612-884-8000		804
Web: www.aspenwaste.com			
ASPET (American Society for Pharmacology & Experimental Therapeutics)			
1801 Rockville Pk Ste 210.................. Rockville MD 20852	301-634-7060	634-7061	49-8
Web: www.aspet.org			

	Phone	Fax	Class
ASPH (Association of Schools of Public Health) 1900 M St NW Ste 710 .... Washington DC 20036 *Web:* www.aspph.org	202-296-1099	296-1252	49-5
Asphalt Drum Mixers Inc (ADM) 1 ADM Pkwy .... Huntertown IN 46748 *Web:* www.admasphaltplants.com	260-637-5729	637-3164	190
Asphalt Equipment & Service Co 1531 20th St NW .... Auburn WA 98001 *Web:* www.asphaltequipment.com	253-939-4150	939-1689	190
Asphalt Equipment Company Inc 13333 Hwy 24 W .... Fort Wayne IN 46804 *Web:* almix.com	260-672-3004	399-2444	190
Asphalt Green 555 E 90th St .... New York NY 10128 *Web:* www.asphaltgreen.org	212-369-8890		354
Asphalt Institute 2696 Research Park Dr .... Lexington KY 40511 *Web:* www.asphaltinstitute.org	859-288-4960	288-4999	49-3
Asphalt Materials Inc PO Box 5 .... West Jordan UT 84084 *Web:* asphaltmaterials.net	801-561-4231	561-7795	46
Asphalt Roofing Manufacturers Assn (ARMA) 529 14th St NW Ste 750 .... Washington DC 20045 *TF:* 800-247-6637 ■ *Web:* asphaltroofing.org	202-207-0917	223-9741	49-3
Asphalt Specialists Inc 1780 Highwood E .... Pontiac MI 48340 *Web:* www.asipaving.com	248-745-5785	334-4135	189-3
ASPI (Appalachia-Science in the Public Interest) 50 Lair St .... Mount Vernon KY 40456 *Web:* www.appalachia-spi.org	606-256-0077		48-13
Aspira 717 North Harwood St Ste 2400 .... Dallas TX 75201 *Web:* www.reserveamerica.com	214-885-6741		760
ASPIRA Association Inc 1444 'I' St NW Ste 800 .... Washington DC 20005 *Web:* www.aspira.org	202-835-3600		48-14
Aspire Economic Development + Chamber Alliance 65 Airport Pkwy .... Greenwood IN 46143 *TF:* 800-462-7585 ■ *Web:* www.aspirejohnsoncounty.com	317-888-4856	865-2609	139
Aspirus Wausau Hospital 333 Pine Ridge Blvd .... Wausau WI 54401 *TF:* 800-283-2881 ■ *Web:* www.aspirus.org	715-847-2121		374-3
Asplundh Tree Expert Co 708 Blair Mill Rd .... Willow Grove PA 19090 *TF:* 800-248-8733 ■ *Web:* www.asplundh.com	800-248-8733		776
Asponte Technology Inc 11523 Palmbrush Trl Ste 137 .... Lakewood Ranch FL 34202 *TF:* 888-926-9434 ■ *Web:* www.asponte.com	888-926-9434		180
ASPPA (American Society of Pension Professionals & Actuaries) 4245 N Fairfax Dr Ste 750 .... Arlington VA 22203 *Web:* www.asppa.org	703-516-9300	516-9308	49-12
ASPRS (American Society for Photogrammetry & Remote Sensing, The) 5410 Grosvenor Ln Ste 210 .... Bethesda MD 20814 *Web:* www.asprs.org	301-493-0290	493-0208	49-19
ASPS (American Society of Plastic Surgeons) 444 E Algonquin Rd .... Arlington Heights IL 60005 *Web:* www.plasticsurgery.org	847-228-9900	228-9131	49-8
aspStation Inc 4736 Penn Ave .... Pittsburgh PA 15224 *Web:* www.aspstation.net	412-661-6001		514
Aspyr Media Inc 1250 S Capital of Texas Hwy Ste 650 .... Austin TX 78746 *Web:* www.aspyr.com	512-708-8100	708-9595	179
Aspyra LLC 7400 Baymeadows Way Ste 101 .... Jacksonville FL 32256 *OTC:* APYI ■ **Fax Area Code:* 818 ■ *TF:* 800-437-9000 ■ *Web:* www.aspyra.com	800-437-9000	880-4398*	178-10
ASQ (American Society for Quality) 600 N Plankinton Ave .... Milwaukee WI 53203 *TF:* 800-248-1946 ■ *Web:* asq.org	414-272-8575	272-1734	49-13
Asquith & Mahoney PC 155 S Main St Ste 202 .... Providence RI 02903 *Web:* am-lawoffice.com	401-331-6363	331-7373	41
ASR Analytics LLC 1389 Canterbury Way .... Potomac MD 20854 *Web:* www.asranalytics.com	301-738-9502		194
ASR International Corp 580 Old Willets Path .... Hauppauge NY 11788 *Web:* www.asrintl.com	631-231-1086	231-1087	463
ASRA (American Society of Regional Anesthesia & Pain Medicine) 4 Penn Ctr W Ste 401 .... Pittsburgh PA 15276 *TF:* 855-795-2772 ■ *Web:* www.asra.com	412-471-2718	471-7503	49-8
ASRC Energy Services Inc 3900 C St .... Anchorage AK 99503 *Web:* www.asrcenergy.com	907-339-6200		539
ASRM (American Society for Reproductive Medicine) 1209 Montgomery Hwy .... Birmingham AL 35216 *Web:* www.asrm.org	205-978-5000	978-5005	49-8
ASRT (American Society of Radiologic Technologists) 15000 Central Ave SE .... Albuquerque NM 87123 *TF:* 800-444-2778 ■ *Web:* www.asrt.org	505-298-4500	298-5063	49-8
Assa Abloy 110 Sargent Dr .... New Haven CT 06511 **Fax Area Code:* 203 ■ *TF:* 800-377-3948 ■ *Web:* www.assaabloydss.com	800-377-3948	777-9042*	234
ASSA ABLOY Accessories & Door Controls Group Inc 300 Main St PO Box 79 .... Rockwood PA 15557 **Fax Area Code:* 800 ■ *TF:* 800-458-2424 ■ *Web:* www.assaabloydooraccessories.us	814-926-2026	922-9212*	350
Assa Abloy of Canada Ltd 160 Four Vly Dr .... Vaughan ON L4K4T9 *TF:* 800-461-3007 ■ *Web:* www.assaabloy.ca	905-738-2466		350
ASSA Inc 110 Sargent Dr .... New Haven CT 06511 **Fax Area Code:* 800 ■ *TF:* 800-235-7482 ■ *Web:* www.assalock.com	203-562-2151	892-3256*	350
Assabet Valley Chamber of Commerce 18 Church St PO Box 578 .... Hudson MA 01749 *Web:* www.assabetvalleychamber.org	978-568-0360	562-4118	139
Assaggio 95-1249 Meheula Pkwy .... Mililani HI 96789 *Web:* assaggiohawaii.com	808-623-5115		671
Assaggio 29 Prince St .... Boston MA 02113 *Web:* www.assaggioboston.com	617-227-7380		671
Assaggio Ristorante 2010 Fourth Ave .... Seattle WA 98121 *Web:* www.assaggioseattle.com	206-441-1399		671
Assante Financial Management Ltd 199 Bay St Ste 2700 .... Toronto ON M5L1E2 *TF:* 888-348-9994 ■ *Web:* www.assante.com	416-348-9994		401
Assateague Island National Seashore 7206 National Seashore Ln PO Box 38 .... Berlin MD 21811 *Web:* www.nps.gov	410-641-1441		564
Assateague State Park 7307 Stephen Decatur Hwy .... Berlin MD 21811 *TF:* 888-432-2267 ■ *Web:* www.dnr.maryland.gov	410-641-2120	260-8595	565
Assay Technology Inc 1382 Stealth St .... Livermore CA 94551 *Web:* www.assaytech.com	925-461-8880		639
ASSE (American Society of Safety Professionals) 1800 E Oakton St .... Des Plaines IL 60018 *Web:* www.assp.org	847-699-2929	768-3434	49-19
Assemblies of God (A/G) 1445 N Boonville Ave .... Springfield MO 65802 *TF:* 800-641-4310 ■ *Web:* ag.org	417-862-2781		48-20
Assemblies of God Theological Seminary 1435 N Glenstone Ave .... Springfield MO 65802 *TF:* 800-467-2487 ■ *Web:* agts.edu	417-268-1000	268-1001	167-3
Assemblies Unlimited Inc 141 Covington Dr .... Bloomingdale IL 60108 *Web:* www.assemblies.com	630-980-0200		41
Assembly & Design Inc 425 Southlake Blvd Ste 1b .... North Chesterfield VA 23236 *Web:* www.assemblyanddesign.com	804-379-5432	379-6312	625
Assembly Automation Industries 1849 Business Centre Dr .... Duarte CA 91010 *Web:* www.assemblyauto.com	626-303-2777	303-8874	494
Assembly Line Inc 231 Wharf St .... Brookings OR 97415 *Web:* www.assembly-line.com	541-469-0696	412-1005	253
Assembly of Turkish American Assn (ATAA) 1526 18th St NW .... Washington DC 20036 *Web:* www.ataa.org	202-483-9090	483-9092	48-14
Assembly Technologies Inc 6716 Orr Rd .... Charlotte NC 28213 *Web:* www.assemblytechinc.com	704-596-3903	596-2345	625
Assessment Technology Inc 6700 E Speedway Blvd .... Tucson AZ 85710 *TF:* 800-367-4762 ■ *Web:* www.ati-online.com	800-367-4762		225
Asset 15050 Avenue of Science .... San Diego CA 92128 *TF:* 888-303-8755 ■ *Web:* www.assetfmo.com	888-303-8755		367
Asset Allocation & Management Co 30 W Monroe St 3rd Fl .... Chicago IL 60603 *Web:* www.aamcompany.com	312-263-2900		401
Asset Appraisal Services Inc 10216 F St .... Omaha NE 68154 *Web:* www.assetappraisalservices.com	402-390-0505		41
Asset Based Lending Consultant 1641 NW 71st Terr .... Hollywood FL 33024 *Web:* www.ablc.net	954-962-0099		194
Asset Communications Inc 1764 Prospector Ave .... Park City UT 84060 *Web:* assetcommunications.com	435-645-9108		463
Asset Consulting Group LLC 231 S Bemiston Ave 14th Fl .... Saint Louis MO 63105 *Web:* acgnet.com	314-862-4848		401
ASSET InterTech 2201 N Central Expy Ste 105 .... Richardson TX 75080 *TF:* 888-694-6250 ■ *Web:* www.asset-intertech.com	972-437-2800		178-1
Asset Management Ventures 2100 Geng Rd Ste 200 .... Palo Alto CA 94303 *Web:* www.assetman.com	650-621-8808		792
Asset Plus Co 950 Corbindale Rd Ste 300 .... Houston TX 77024 *Web:* www.assetpluscorp.com	713-782-5800	268-5111	653
Asset Preservation Advisors Inc 3344 Peachtree Rd Ste 2050 .... Atlanta GA 30326 *TF:* 800-833-8985 ■ *Web:* www.assetpreservationadvisors.com	404-261-1333		528
Asset Protection Associates Inc 205 Braeden Way .... Alpharetta GA 30009	678-566-0222		693
Asset Recovery Specialists Inc 9707 Aero Dr .... San Diego CA 92123 *TF:* 888-253-3869 ■ *Web:* www.equipmentrecovery.com	858-277-7555	277-9807	792
Asset Sales Inc 301 Post Office Dr Ste C .... Indian Trail NC 28079 *Web:* asset-sales.com	704-821-4315		41
Asset Staffing of South Florida 1415 Diplomat Pkwy .... Hollywood FL 33019 *Web:* assetstaffing.com	305-371-5969	371-5979	260
Asset Strategy Consultants LLC 6 N Park Dr Ste 208 .... Hunt Valley MD 21030 *TF:* 866-344-8282 ■ *Web:* www.assetstrategyconsultants.com	410-528-8282		401
Assetbuilder Inc 1255 W 15th St Ste 1000 .... Plano TX 75075 *Web:* assetbuilder.com	972-535-4040		401
AssetMark Inc 1655 Grant St 10th Fl .... Concord CA 94520 *TF:* 800-664-5345 ■ *Web:* www.assetmark.com	800-664-5345		401
AssetPoint LLC 770 Pelham Rd .... Greenville SC 29615 *Web:* www.assetpoint.com	864-679-3500		809
ASSETT Inc 11220 Assett Loop Ste 204 .... Manassas VA 20109 *TF:* 888-980-1197 ■ *Web:* assett.net	888-980-1197		180
Assette LLC 1 Faneuil Hall 4th Fl .... Boston MA 02109 *Web:* www.assette.com	617-723-6161		177
AssetWorks Inc 998 Old Eagle School Rd Ste 1215 .... Wayne PA 19087 *Web:* www.assetworks.com	610-687-9202		178-1
ASSH (American Society for Surgery of the Hand) 822 W Washington Blvd .... Chicago IL 60607 **Fax Area Code:* 847 ■ *Web:* assh.org	312-880-1900	384-1435*	49-8
ASSI Security Inc 1370 Reynolds Ave Ste 201 .... Irvine CA 92614 *Web:* www.assisecurity.com	949-955-0244		693
Assicurazioni Generali US Branch 250 Greenwich St 33rd Fl .... New York NY 10007 *Web:* www.generaliusa.com	212-602-7600		360-4
Assiniboine Gordon Inn on the Park 1975 Portage Ave .... Winnipeg MB R3J0J9 *Web:* gordonhotels.com	204-888-4806	897-9870	379
Assiniboine Park Zoo 55 Pavilion Crescent .... Winnipeg MB R3P2N6 *TF:* 877-927-6006 ■ *Web:* assiniboinepark.ca	204-927-8080		823
Assist Cornerstone Technologies Inc 150 W Civic Center Dr Ste 601 .... Sandy UT 84070 *TF:* 800-732-0136 ■ *Web:* www.assistcornerstone.com	800-732-0136		177

					Phone	Fax	Class	
ASSIST Information Services	1077 E Pacific Coast Hwy Ste 197	Seal Beach	CA	90740	562-598-7785		387	*Web:* www.travelassist.com
Assist-2-Sell Inc	1610 Meadow Wood Ln	Reno	NV	89502	775-688-6060	823-8823	652	*TF:* 800-528-7816 ■ *Web:* assist2sell.com
Assisted Daily Living Inc	2809 Post Rd	Warwick	RI	02886	401-738-5470	738-2366	363	*Web:* www.assisteddailyliving.com
Associated Administrators LLC	911 Ridgebrook Rd	Sparks	MD	21152	410-683-6500		390	*TF:* 800-638-2972 ■ *Web:* www.associated-admin.com
Associated Agencies Inc	1701 Golf Rd Tower 3 Seventh Fl	Rolling Meadows	IL	60008	847-427-8400	427-3559	390	*Web:* www.assocagencies.com
Associated Aircraft Manufacturing & Sales Inc	2735 NW 63rd Ct	Fort Lauderdale	FL	33309	954-772-6606		21	*Web:* www.aamsi.com
Associated Appliance	2318 NW 12th St	Oklahoma City	OK	73107	405-525-2003	521-9679	246	*Web:* www.associatedapplianceparts.com
Associated Appliance Sales	10924 W Bell Rd Ste 2	Sun City	AZ	85351	623-815-7561		38	*Web:* www.associatedappliancesales.com
Associated Bag Co	400 W Boden St	Milwaukee	WI	53207	414-769-1000	926-4610*	66	**Fax Area Code:* 800 ■ *TF:* 800-926-6100 ■ *Web:* www.associatedbag.com
Associated Bank	1305 Main St MS 7722	Stevens Point	WI	54481	800-236-8866		70	*TF:* 800-236-8866 ■ *Web:* www.associatedbank.com
Associated Behavioral Health	4700 42nd Ave SW Ste 470	Seattle	WA	98116	206-935-1282	671-6496*	462	**Fax Area Code:* 425 ■ *TF:* 800-858-6702 ■ *Web:* www.abhc.com
Associated Beth Rivkah Schools	310 Crown St	Brooklyn	NY	11225	718-735-0400	735-0422	685	*Web:* www.bethrivkah.edu
Associated Bodywork & Massage Professionals (ABMP)	25188 Genesee Trl Rd Ste 200	Golden	CO	80401	303-674-8478	667-8260*	48-17	**Fax Area Code:* 800 ■ *TF:* 800-458-2267 ■ *Web:* www.abmp.com
Associated Builders & Contractors Inc (ABC)	4250 Fairfax Dr	Arlington	VA	22203	202-595-1505		49-3	*TF:* 877-889-5627 ■ *Web:* www.abc.org
Associated Building Maintenance Company Inc	2140 Priest Bridge Ct Ste 3	Crofton	MD	21114	410-721-1818	721-8616	104	*TF:* 800-721-9068 ■ *Web:* www.abmcoinc.com
Associated Ceramics & Technology Inc	400 N Pike Rd	Sarver	PA	16055	724-353-1585	353-1050	249	*Web:* www.associatedceramics.com
Associated Church Press, The (ACP)	109 State St	Louisville	KY	40206	503-583-8655	386-3236*	49-16	**Fax Area Code:* 407 ■ *Web:* www.theacp.org
Associated Clinical Laboratories	1526 Peach St	Erie	PA	16501	814-461-2420		415	*TF:* 800-937-8028 ■ *Web:* www.associatedclinicallabs.com
Associated Collegiate Press (ACP)	2221 University Ave SE Ste 121	Minneapolis	MN	55414	612-625-8335	626-0720	48-11	*Web:* www.studentpress.org
Associated Communications & Research Services Inc (ACRS)	2601 NW Expy Ste 405W	Oklahoma City	OK	73112	405-843-9966	843-9852	196	*Web:* acrsokc.com
Associated Electric Co-opeartive Inc	2814 S Golden PO Box 754	Springfield	MO	65801	417-881-1204		245	*Web:* www.aeci.org
Associated Electrics Inc	21062 Bake Pkwy	Lake Forest	CA	92630	949-544-7500		711	*Web:* www.teamassociated.com
Associated Electro-Mechanics Inc	185 Rowland St	Springfield	MA	01107	413-781-4276	788-4471	385	*Web:* www.aemservices.com
Associated Energy Systems	8621 S 180th St	Kent	WA	98032	425-251-9190	251-6230	362	*TF:* 800-682-9722 ■ *Web:* www.aes4home.com
Associated Engineering Group Ltd	9888 Jasper Ave Ste 500	Edmonton	AB	T5J5C6	780-451-7666	454-7698	256	*Web:* www.ae.ca
Associated Engineering Inc	11410 N Cave Creek Rd	Phoenix	AZ	85020	602-274-8988		261	*Web:* aeiphx.com
Associated Environmental Systems Inc	8 Post Office Sq	Acton	MA	01720	978-772-0022	772-0088	419	*Web:* www.associatedenvironmentalsystems.com
Associated Equipment Corp	5043 Farlan Ave	Saint Louis	MO	63115	314-385-5178	385-3254	248	*TF:* 800-949-1472 ■ *Web:* associatedequip.com
Associated Equipment Distributors (AED)	650 E Algonquin Rd Ste 305	Schaumburg	IL	60173	630-574-0650	574-0132	49-18	*Web:* www.aednet.org
Associated Fabrics Corp	15-01 Pollitt Dr Unit 7	Fair Lawn	NJ	07410	800-232-4077	710-3850*	594	**Fax Area Code:* 866 ■ *TF:* 800-232-4077 ■ *Web:* www.afcfabrics.com
Associated Floors	32 Morris Ave	Springfield	NJ	07081	800-800-4320		189-2	*TF:* 800-800-4320 ■ *Web:* www.assocint.com
Associated Food Stores Inc	1850 West 2100 South	Salt Lake City	UT	84119	801-973-4400		297-8	*TF:* 888-574-7100 ■ *Web:* www.afstores.com
Associated General Contractors of America (AGC)	2300 Wilson Blvd Ste 300	Arlington	VA	22201	703-548-3118	548-3119	49-3	*TF:* 800-242-1766 ■ *Web:* www.agc.org
Associated Global Systems Inc	3333 New Hyde Park Rd	New Hyde Park	NY	11042	516-627-8910	627-6051	449	*TF:* 800-645-8300 ■ *Web:* www.agsystems.com
Associated Grant Makers Inc (AGM)	133 Federal St Ste 802	Boston	MA	02110	617-426-2606	426-2849	634	*Web:* www.agmconnect.org
Associated Grocers Inc	8600 Anselmo Ln	Baton Rouge	LA	70810	225-444-1000	763-6194	297-8	*TF:* 800-637-2021 ■ *Web:* www.agbr.com
Associated Grocers of Florida Inc	1141 SW 12th Ave	Pompano Beach	FL	33069	954-876-3000		297-8	*Web:* www.agfla.com
Associated Grocers of New England Inc	11 Co-op Way	Pembroke	NH	03275	603-223-6710		297-8	*TF:* 800-242-2248 ■ *Web:* www.agne.com
Associated Grocers of the South	3600 Vanderbilt Rd	Birmingham	AL	35217	205-841-6781		297-8	*TF:* 800-695-6051 ■ *Web:* www.agsouth.com
Associated Healthcare Credit Union	360 Sherman St Ste B-10	Saint Paul	MN	55102	651-383-4000		219	*Web:* ahcu.org
Associated Industries	11347 Vanowen St	North Hollywood	CA	91605	818-760-1000	760-2142	647	*Web:* www.associated-ind.com
Associated Industries	1206 N Lincoln Ste 200	Spokane	WA	99201	509-326-6885		194	*TF:* 800-720-4291 ■ *Web:* www.aiin.com
Associated Industries of Massachusetts Mutual Insurance Com	PO Box 4070	Burlington	MA	01803	781-221-1600	270-5599	391-4	*TF:* 866-270-3354 ■ *Web:* www.aimmutual.com
Associated Insurance Agency of Westchester Inc	200 Business Park Dr Ste 206	Armonk	NY	10504	914-273-8511		390	*Web:* avantiassociates.com
Associated Locksmiths of America (ALOA)	3500 Easy St	Dallas	TX	75247	214-819-9733	819-9736	49-3	*TF:* 800-532-2562 ■ *Web:* www.aloa.org
Associated Material Handling Industries Inc	133 N Swift Rd	Addison	IL	60101	630-588-8800	588-8815	385	*TF:* 877-638-8002 ■ *Web:* www.associated-solutions.com
Associated Materials Inc (AMI)	3773 State Rd	Cuyahoga Falls	OH	44223	800-922-6009		697	*TF:* 800-922-6009 ■ *Web:* www.associatedmaterials.com
Associated Media Companies Ltd	PO Box 489	Gleneden Beach	OR	97388	800-258-0615	764-4233*	393	**Fax Area Code:* 541 ■ *TF:* 800-258-0615 ■ *Web:* www.vipaddress.com
Associated Mortgage Bankers Inc	2395 Ocean Ave	Ronkonkoma	NY	11779	800-684-1045		217	*TF:* 800-684-1045 ■ *Web:* ambmortgage.com
Associated Packaging Inc	435 Calvert Dr	Gallatin	TN	37066	615-452-2131	452-7890	385	*Web:* www.associatedpackaging.com
Associated Pallets Inc	71 Premium Dr	South Carrollton	KY	42374	270-754-4087		200	*Web:* www.associatedpallet.com
Associated Petroleum Carriers Inc	PO Box 2808	Spartanburg	SC	29304	864-573-9301		780	*TF:* 800-573-9301 ■ *Web:* www.apccorporate.com
Associated Petroleum Products Inc	2320 Milwaukee Way PO Box 1397	Tacoma	WA	98401	253-627-6179		579	*Web:* world-kinect.com
Associated Pharmacies Inc (API)	211 Lonnie E Crawford Blvd	Scottsboro	AL	35769	256-574-6819		238	*TF:* 877-797-9227 ■ *Web:* www.rxaap.com
Associated Press Inc, The	121 SW Salmon St Ste 1450	Portland	OR	97204	503-228-2169		530	*Web:* www.ap.org
Associated Production Services Inc	325 Andrews Rd	Trevose	PA	19053	215-364-0211	364-2865	393	*Web:* www.apspackage.com
Associated Resources Inc	15 E 5th St Ste 200	Tulsa	OK	74103	918-584-2111	584-3111	539	*Web:* www.associated-resources.com
Associated Risk Managers International Inc (ARM)	6611 W N Ave	Oak Park	IL	60302	630-285-4324	285-3590	49-9	*TF:* 800-735-5441 ■ *Web:* www.armiweb.com
Associated Rubber Inc	115 S 6th St	Quakertown	PA	18951	215-536-2800	536-7852	677	*Web:* associatedrubber.com
Associated School Employee Credit Union	1690 S Canfield - Niles Rd	Austintown	OH	44515	330-792-4000		219	*Web:* asecu.com
Associated Sign Co	3335 W Vernon Ave	Phoenix	AZ	85009	602-278-8464	278-8933	9	*Web:* www.associatedsign.net
Associated Southwest Investors Inc	1650 University Blvd NE Ste 200	Albuquerque	NM	87102	505-247-4050	666-2050*	403	**Fax Area Code:* 510
Associated Steel Corp	18200 Miles Rd	Cleveland	OH	44128	800-321-9300	475-6067*	351	**Fax Area Code:* 216 ■ *TF:* 800-321-9300 ■ *Web:* www.associatedsteel.com
Associated Steel Workers Ltd	1714 Silva St	Honolulu	HI	96819	808-841-8323		482	*Web:* www.aswcranes.com
Associated Students UCLA	308 Westwood Plz	Los Angeles	CA	90095	310-825-7711	267-2034	95	*Web:* asucla.ucla.edu
Associated Technical College	1670 Wilshire Blvd	Los Angeles	CA	90017	213-353-1845	413-6938	167-3	*Web:* www.atcla.edu
Associated Television Intl	4401 Wilshire Blvd	Los Angeles	CA	90010	323-556-5600		514	*Web:* www.associatedtelevision.com
Associated Thermoforming Inc	765 N 2nd St	Berthoud	CO	80513	970-532-2000	532-2942	604	*Web:* www.ati-forms.com
Associated Welding & Machine Works Inc	19555 SW 129th Ave	Tualatin	OR	97062	503-691-1818		454	*Web:* awmachineworks.com
Associated Wholesale Grocers Inc	5000 Kansas Ave	Kansas City	KS	66106	913-288-1000		297-8	*Web:* www.awginc.com
Associated Wholesalers Inc	PO Box 67	Robesonia	PA	19551	610-693-3161	693-3171	297-8	*TF:* 800-927-7771 ■ *Web:* www.awiweb.com
Associates of Glens Falls Inc	228 Glen St PO Box 190	Glens Falls	NY	12801	518-793-3444		390	*Web:* aogf.com
Association & Society Management International Inc	201 Pk Washington Ct	Falls Church	VA	22046	703-533-0251		47	*Web:* www.asmii.com

Name / Address	City	State	Zip	Phone	Fax	Class
Association Associates Inc 1255 Whitehorse-Mercerville Rd Bldg B - Ste 514 *Web:* www.hq4u.com	Trenton	NJ	08619	609-890-9207		47
Association Computer Services Inc 8932 Spicewood Ct *TF:* 888-227-9411 ■ *Web:* www.acsplus.com	Indianapolis	IN	46260	888-227-9411		177
Association for Advanced Life Underwriting (AALU) 11921 Freedom Dr Ste 1100 *TF:* 888-275-0092 ■ *Web:* www.aalu.org	Reston	VA	20190	703-641-9400	641-9885	49-9
Association for Advanced Training in the Behavioral Sciences (AATBS) 5126 Ralston St *TF:* 800-472-1931 ■ *Web:* www.aatbs.com	Ventura	CA	93003	805-676-3030	676-3033	49-5
Association for Advancing Physician and Provider Recruitment (AAPPR) 1000 Westgate Dr Ste 252 *TF:* 800-830-2777 ■ *Web:* member.aappr.org	Saint Paul	MN	55114	800-830-2777		49-8
Association for Applied & Therapeutic Humor (AATH) 220 E State St FL G **Fax Area Code:* 949 ■ *Web:* www.aath.org	Rockford	IL	61104	815-708-6587	715-6931*	48-17
Association for Applied Psychophysiology & Biofeedback (AAPB) 10200 W 44th Ave Ste 304 *TF:* 800-477-8892 ■ *Web:* www.aapb.org	Wheat Ridge	CO	80033	303-422-8436		49-8
Association for Asian Studies, The (AAS) 825 Victors Way Ste 310 *Web:* www.asianstudies.org	Ann Arbor	MI	48108	734-665-2490	665-3801	48-11
Association for Assessment & Accreditation of Laboratory Animal Care Intl 5283 Corporate Dr Ste 203 *TF:* 800-926-0066 ■ *Web:* www.aaalac.org	Frederick	MD	21703	301-696-9626	696-9627	48-1
Association for Behavioral & Cognitive Therapies (ABCT) 305 Seventh Ave 16th Fl *TF:* 800-685-2228 ■ *Web:* www.abct.org	New York	NY	10001	212-647-1890	647-1865	49-15
Association for Biblical Higher Education (AABC) 5850 T G Lee Blvd Ste 130 *TF:* 800-525-1611 ■ *Web:* www.abhe.org	Orlando	FL	32822	407-207-0808		48-1
Association for Business Communication 181 Turner St NW *Web:* www.businesscommunication.org	Blacksburg	VA	24061	540-231-1939		49-12
Association for Career & Technical Education (ACTE) 1410 King St *TF:* 800-826-9972 ■ *Web:* www.acteonline.org	Alexandria	VA	22314	703-683-3111	683-7424	49-5
Association for Childhood Education Intl (ACEI) 1875 Connecticut Ave NW 10th Fl **Fax Area Code:* 301 ■ *TF:* 800-423-3563 ■ *Web:* ceinternational1892.org	Washington	DC	20009	202-372-9986	570-2212*	49-5
Association for Children with Down Syndrome Inc (ACDS) 4 Fern Pl *Web:* www.acds.org	Plainview	NY	11803	516-933-4700	933-9524	48-17
Association for Clinical Pastoral Education (ACPE) 1549 Clairmont Rd Ste 103 *Web:* www.acpe.edu	Decatur	GA	30033	404-320-1472		48-1
Association for Computing Machinery (ACM) 2 Penn Plz Ste 701 *TF:* 800-342-6626 ■ *Web:* www.acm.org	New York	NY	10121	212-626-0500	944-1318	48-9
Association for Continuing Higher Education (ACHE) 1700 Asp Ave *TF:* 800-807-2243 ■ *Web:* www.acheinc.org	Norman	OK	73072	800-807-2243		49-5
Association for Co-opeartive Operations Research & Development (ACORD) 1 Blue Hill Plz 15th Fl PO Box 1529 *TF:* 800-444-3341 ■ *Web:* www.acord.org	Pearl River	NY	10965	845-620-1700	620-3600	49-9
Association for Corporate Growth (ACG) 125 S Wacker Dr Ste 3100 *TF:* 877-358-2220 ■ *Web:* www.acg.org	Chicago	IL	60606	312-957-4260		49-12
Association for Couples in Marriage Enrichment (ACME) PO Box 21374 *TF:* 800-634-8325 ■ *Web:* www.bettermarriages.org	Winston-Salem	NC	27120	800-634-8325		48-6
Association for Death Education & Counseling (ADEC) 111 Deer Lake Rd Ste 100 *Web:* www.adec.org	Deerfield	IL	60015	847-509-0403	480-9282	49-8
Association for Facilities Engineering (AFE) 1901 N Fort Myer Dr Ste 500 *Web:* afe.clubexpress.com	Arlington	VA	22209	571-814-8296	766-2142	49-13
Association for Financial Professionals (AFP) 4520 E W Hwy Ste 800 *Web:* www.afponline.org	Bethesda	MD	20814	301-907-2862	907-2864	49-2
Association for Healthcare Documentation Integrity (AHDI) 4230 Kiernan Ave Ste 130 *TF:* 800-982-2182 ■ *Web:* www.ahdionline.org	Modesto	CA	95356	209-527-9620	527-9633	49-8
Association for Healthcare Philanthropy (AHP) 313 Park Ave Ste 400 *Web:* www.ahp.org	Falls Church	VA	22046	703-532-6243	532-7170	49-8
Association for Information Media & Equipment (AIME) PO Box 378 *Web:* www.aime.org	West Milton	PA	17866	570-701-4202		48-4
Association for Iron & Steel Technology (AIST) 186 Thorn Hill Rd *TF:* 800-759-4867 ■ *Web:* www.aist.org	Warrendale	PA	15086	724-814-3000	814-3001	49-13
Association for Library & Information Science Education (ALISE) 2150 N 107th St Ste 205 *TF:* 877-275-7547 ■ *Web:* www.alise.org	Seattle	WA	98133	206-209-5267	367-8777	49-11
Association for Linen Management 138 N Keeneland Dr Ste D *TF:* 800-669-0863 ■ *Web:* www.almnet.org	Richmond	KY	40475	859-624-0177	624-3580	49-4
Association for Manufacturing Excellence (AME) 3701 W Algonquin Rd Ste 225 *Web:* www.ame.org	Rolling Meadows	IL	60008	224-232-5980	232-5981	49-12
Association for Manufacturing Technology (AMT) 7901 Westpark Dr *TF:* 800-524-0475 ■ *Web:* www.amtonline.org	McLean	VA	22102	703-893-2900	893-1151	49-12
Association for Play Therapy (APT) 401 Clovis Ave Ste 107 *Web:* www.a4pt.org	Clovis	CA	93612	559-298-3400	294-2129	49-15
Association for Postal Commerce 1800 Diagonal Rd Ste 600 *Web:* www.postcom.org	Alexandria	VA	22314	703-524-0096		49-18
Association for Professionals in Infection Control & Epidemiology Inc (APIC) 1275 K St NW Ste 1000 *TF:* 800-650-9883 ■ *Web:* apic.org	Washington	DC	20005	202-789-1890	789-1899	49-8
Association for Psychological Type Intl (APTI) PO Box 4538 *Web:* www.aptinternational.org	Itasca	IL	60143	518-320-7416		49-15
Association for Recorded Sound Collections (ARSC) PO Box 543 *Web:* www.arsc-audio.org	Annapolis	MD	21404	410-757-0488		48-4
Association for Research & Enlightenment (ARE) 215 67th St *TF:* 800-333-4499 ■ *Web:* www.edgarcayce.org	Virginia Beach	VA	23451	757-428-3588	422-6921	48-17
Association for Research in Vision & Ophthalmology (ARVO) 12300 Twinbrook Pkwy Ste 250 *TF:* 888-503-1050 ■ *Web:* www.arvo.org	Rockville	MD	20852	240-221-2900	221-0370	49-8
Association for Supervision & Curriculum Development (ASCD) 1703 N Beauregard St *TF:* 800-933-2723 ■ *Web:* www.ascd.org	Alexandria	VA	22311	703-578-9600	575-5400	49-5
Association for the Advancement of Artificial Intelligence (AAAI) 445 Burgess Dr Ste 100 *TF:* 800-548-4664 ■ *Web:* www.aaai.org	Menlo Park	CA	94025	650-328-3123	321-4457	48-9
Association for the Advancement of Computing in Education (AACE) PO Box 1545 **Fax Area Code:* 703 ■ *Web:* www.aace.org	Chesapeake	VA	23327	757-366-5606	997-8760*	49-5
Association for the Advancement of Medical Instrumentation (AAMI) 4301 N Fairfax Dr Ste 301 *TF:* 800-332-2264 ■ *Web:* www.aami.org	Arlington	VA	22203	703-525-4890	276-0793	49-8
Association for the Advancement of the Blind & Retarded (AABR) 1508 College Pt Blvd *Web:* www.aabr.org	College Point	NY	11356	718-321-3800		48-17
Association for Vascular Access (AVA) 5526 W 13400 S Ste 229 *TF:* 877-924-2821 ■ *Web:* www.avainfo.org	Herriman	UT	84096	801-792-9079	601-8012	49-8
Association for Women in Communications (AWC) 1717 E Republic Rd Ste A *Web:* www.womcom.org	Springfield	MO	65804	417-886-8606		49-14
Association for Women in Science Inc (AWIS) 1667 K St NW Ste 800 *Web:* www.awis.org	Washington	DC	20006	202-588-8175		49-19
Association for Women's Rights in Development (AWID) 215 Spadina Ave Ste 150 *Web:* www.awid.org	Toronto	ON	M5T2C7	416-594-3773	594-0330	48-8
Association Headquarters 1120 Rte 73 Ste 200 *TF:* 877-777-6753 ■ *Web:* associationheadquarters.com	Mount Laurel	NJ	08054	856-439-0500	439-0525	47
Association Management Ctr 8735 W Higgins Rd Ste 300 *Web:* connect2amc.com	Chicago	IL	60631	847-375-4700	375-6401	47
Association Management Resources 2123 University Park Dr Ste 100 *Web:* www.managedbyamr.com	Okemos	MI	48864	734-677-2270		47
Association Management Solutions LLC (AMS) 5177 Brandin Ct *Web:* www.amsl.com	Fremont	CA	94538	510-492-4000	492-4001	47
Association Management Systems 401 W St Charles Rd *Web:* www.association-mgmt.com	Lombard	IL	60148	630-510-4500	510-4501	47
Association of Academic Health Centers (AHC) 1400 16th St NW Ste 720 *Web:* www.aahcdc.org	Washington	DC	20036	202-265-9600	265-7514	49-8
Association of Alternative Newsweeklies (AAN) 115615th St NW *Web:* archive.altweeklies.com	Washington	DC	20005	202-289-8484		49-14
Association of American Chambers of Commerce in Latin America 1615 H St NW *TF:* 800-638-6582 ■ *Web:* www.aaccla.org	Washington	DC	20062	202-463-5485	463-3126	138
Association of American Colleges & Universities (AAC&U) 1818 R St NW *Web:* www.aacu.org	Washington	DC	20009	202-387-3760	265-9532	49-5
Association of American Geographers (AAG) 1710 16th St NW *TF:* [illegible] ■ *Web:* www.aag.org	Washington	DC	20009	202-234-1450	234-2744	49-19
Association of American Indian Physicians (AAIP) 1225 Sovereign Row Ste 103 *Web:* www.aaip.org	Oklahoma City	OK	73108	405-946-7072	946-7651	49-8
Association of American Law Schools (AALS) 1201 Connecticut Ave NW Ste 800 *Web:* www.aals.org	Washington	DC	20036	202-296-8851	296-8869	49-5
Association of American Medical Colleges (AAMC) 2450 N St NW *Web:* www.aamc.org	Washington	DC	20037	202-828-0400	828-1125	49-5
Association of American Publishers (AAP) 71 Fifth Ave *Web:* www.publishers.org	New York	NY	10003	212-255-0200	255-7007	49-16
Association of American Railroads (AAR) 425 Third St SW *TF:* 800-533-6644 ■ *Web:* www.aar.org	Washington	DC	20024	202-639-2100	639-2286	49-21
Association of American Universities (AAU) 1200 New York Ave NW Ste 550 *Web:* www.aau.edu	Washington	DC	20005	202-408-7500	408-8184	49-5
Association of Certified Fraud Examiners (ACFE) 716 W Ave *TF:* 800-245-3321 ■ *Web:* www.acfe.com	Austin	TX	78701	512-478-9000	478-9297	49-1
Association of Children's Museums (ACM) 2711 Jefferson Davis Hwy Ste 600 *Web:* www.childrensmuseums.org	Arlington	VA	22202	703-224-3100	224-3099	48-4
Association of Christian Schools Intl (ACSI) 731 Chapel Hills Dr *TF:* 800-367-0798 ■ *Web:* www.acsi.org	Colorado Springs	CO	80920	719-528-6906		49-5
Association of Civilian Technicians (ACT) 12620 Lake Ridge Dr *Web:* actnat.com	Woodbridge	VA	22192	703-494-4845	494-0961	48-19
Association of Clinical Research Professionals (ACRP) 999 Canal Center Plz Ste 800 *Web:* www.acrpnet.org	Alexandria	VA	22314	703-254-8100	254-8101	49-8
Association of College & University Housing Officers Intl (ACUHO-I) 1445 Summit St *Web:* www.acuho-i.org	Columbus	OH	43201	614-292-0099	292-3205	49-5
Association of College Unions Intl (ACUI) 1 City Ctr Ste 200 *Web:* www.acui.org	Bloomington	IN	47404	812-245-2284	245-6710	49-5
Association of Collegiate Business Schools & Programs (ACBSP) 11520 W 119th St *Web:* www.acbsp.org	Overland Park	KS	66213	913-339-9356	339-6226	48-1

Phone | Fax | Class

Association of Collegiate Schools of Architecture (ACSA)
1735 New York Ave NW 3rd Fl ... Washington DC 20006 | 202-785-2324 | 628-0448 | 49-5
Web: www.acsa-arch.org

Association of Community College Trustees (ACCT)
1101 17th St NW Ste 300 ... Washington DC 20036 | 202-775-4667 | 223-1297 | 49-5
TF: 866-895-2228 ■ *Web:* www.acct.org

Association of Consulting Chemists & Chemical Engineers (ACC&CE)
514 Corrigan Way ... Cary NC 27519 | 908-500-9333 | | 49-19
Web: chemconsult.org

Association of Consulting Forester (ACF)
312 Montgomery St Ste 208 ... Alexandria VA 22314 | 703-548-0990 | 548-6395 | 48-2
TF: 800-438-5800 ■ *Web:* www.acf-foresters.org

Association of Corporate Counsel (ACC)
1025 Connecticut Ave NW Ste 200 ... Washington DC 20036 | 202-293-4103 | 293-4701 | 49-10
TF: 877-647-3411 ■ *Web:* www.acc.com

Association of Corporate Travel Executives (ACTE)
526 King St Ste 215 ... Alexandria VA 22314 | 703-683-5322 | | 48-23
TF: 800-228-3669 ■ *Web:* www.acte.org

Association of Destination Management Executives (ADME)
PO Box 2464 ... Wimberley TX 78676 | 512-345-8833 | 586-3699* | 48-23
**Fax Area Code:* 937 ■ *Web:* www.admei.org

Association of Directory Publishers (ADP)
PO Box 209 ... Traverse City MI 49685 | 231-486-2182 | | 49-16
TF: 800-267-9002 ■ *Web:* www.adp.org

Association of Emergency Physicians
911 Whitewater Dr ... Mars PA 16046 | 724-772-1818 | | 49-8

Association of Energy Engineers (AEE)
3168 Mercer University Dr ... Atlanta GA 30341 | 770-447-5083 | 446-3969 | 48-12
Web: www.aeecenter.org

Association of Energy Service Cos (AESC)
14531 Fm 529 Ste 250 ... Houston TX 77095 | 713-781-0758 | 781-7542 | 48-12
TF: 800-692-0771 ■ *Web:* www.aesc.net

Association of Equipment Manufacturers (AEM)
6737 W Washington St Ste 2400 ... Milwaukee WI 53214 | 414-272-0943 | 272-1170 | 49-13
TF: 866-236-0442 ■ *Web:* www.aem.org

Association of Farmworker Opportunity Programs (AFOP)
1120 20th St NW Ste 300 ... Washington DC 20036 | 202-828-6006 | 828-6005 | 48-2
Web: afop.org

Association of Film Commissioners Intl (AFCI)
9595 Wilshire Blvd Ste 900 ... Beverly Hills CA 90212 | 323-461-2324 | 375-2903* | 48-4
**Fax Area Code:* 413 ■ *TF:* 888-765-5777 ■ *Web:* afci.org

Association of Flight Attendants
501 Third St NW ... Washington DC 20001 | 202-434-1300 | | 414
TF: 800-424-2401 ■ *Web:* www.afacwa.org

Association of Food Industries Inc (AFI)
3301 Rt 66 Bldg C Ste 205 ... Neptune City NJ 07753 | 732-922-3008 | 922-3590 | 49-6
Web: afius.org

Association of Fundraising Professionals (AFP)
4300 Wilson Blvd Ste 300 ... Arlington VA 22203 | 703-684-0410 | 684-1950 | 49-12
TF: 800-666-3863 ■ *Web:* afpglobal.org

Association of Governing Boards of Universities & Colleges (AGB)
1133 20th St NW Ste 300 ... Washington DC 20036 | 202-296-8400 | 223-7053 | 49-5
TF: 800-356-6317 ■ *Web:* www.agb.org

Association of Government Accountants (AGA)
2208 Mt Vernon Ave ... Alexandria VA 22301 | 703-684-6931 | 548-9367 | 49-1
TF: 800-242-7211 ■ *Web:* www.agacgfm.org

Association of Healthcare Internal Auditors (AHIA)
10200 W 44th Ave Ste 304 ... Wheat Ridge CO 80033 | 303-327-7546 | 422-8894 | 49-1
TF: 888-275-2442 ■ *Web:* www.ahia.org

Association of Higher Education Facilities Officers
1643 Prince St ... Alexandria VA 22314 | 703-684-1446 | 549-2772 | 49-5
Web: www.appa.org

Association of Home Appliance Manufacturers (AHAM)
1111 19th St NW Ste 402 ... Washington DC 20036 | 202-872-5955 | 872-9354 | 49-4
TF: 800-829-5034 ■ *Web:* www.aham.org

Association of Idaho Cities (AIC)
3100 S Vista Ave Ste 310 ... Boise ID 83705 | 208-344-8594 | | 637-10
Web: www.idahocities.org

Association of Independents in Radio (AIR)
PO Box 220400 ... Boston MA 02122 | 617-825-4400 | 825-4422 | 632
Web: airmedia.org

Association of Industrial Metallizers Coaters & Laminators (AIMCAL)
201 Springs St ... Fort Mill SC 29715 | 803-802-7820 | 802-7821 | 49-13
Web: www.aimcal.org

Association of Jesuit Colleges & Universities (AJCU)
1 Dupont Cir NW Ste 405 ... Washington DC 20036 | 202-862-9893 | | 48-11
Web: www.ajcunet.edu

Association of Jewish Libraries
PO Box 1118 ... Teaneck NJ 07666 | 201-371-3255 | | 49-11
Web: www.jewishlibraries.org

Association of Junior Leagues International Inc (AJLI)
80 Maiden Ln Ste 305 ... New York NY 10038 | 212-951-8300 | 481-7196 | 48-15
TF: 800-955-3248 ■ *Web:* www.ajli.org

Association of Legal Administrators (ALA)
75 Tri-State International Ste 222 ... Lincolnshire IL 60069 | 847-267-1252 | 267-1329 | 49-10
Web: www.alanet.org

Association of Magazine Media, The (MPA)
757 Third Ave 11th Fl ... New York NY 10017 | 212-872-3700 | 888-4217 | 49-16
TF: 800-234-3368 ■ *Web:* www.magazine.org

Association of Maternal & Child Health Programs (AMCHP)
2030 M St NW Ste 350 ... Washington DC 20036 | 202-775-0436 | 478-5120 | 49-7
Web: www.amchp.org

Association of Military Surgeons of the United States (AMSUS)
9320 Old Georgetown Rd ... Bethesda MD 20814 | 301-897-8800 | 530-5446 | 49-8
TF: 800-761-9320 ■ *Web:* www.amsus.org

Association of Minnesota Counties
125 Charles Ave ... Saint Paul MN 55103 | 651-224-3344 | | 338
Web: www.mncounties.org

Association of New Jersey Environmental Commissions (ANJEC)
PO Box 157 ... Mendham NJ 07945 | 973-539-7547 | 539-7713 | 48-13
Web: www.anjec.org

Association of Nurses in AIDS Care (ANAC)
3538 Ridgewood Rd ... Akron OH 44333 | 330-670-0101 | 670-0109 | 49-8
TF: 800-260-6780 ■ *Web:* www.nursesinaidscare.org

Association of Old Crows (AOC)
1555 King St Ste 500 ... Alexandria VA 22314 | 703-549-1600 | 549-2589 | 48-19
Web: www.crows.org

Association of Performing Arts Presenters
1211 Connecticut Ave NW Ste 200 ... Washington DC 20036 | 202-833-2787 | 833-1543 | 48-4
TF: 888-820-2787 ■ *Web:* www.apap365.org

Association of Pool & Spa Professionals (APSP)
2111 Eisenhower Ave Ste 500 ... Alexandria VA 22314 | 703-838-0083 | 549-0493 | 49-4
TF: 800-323-3996 ■ *Web:* www.apsp.org

Association of Professional Ball Players of America (APBPA)
23623 N Scottsdale Rd Ste 290 ... Scottsdale AZ 85255 | 480-404-9339 | | 48-22
Web: apbpa.org

Association of Professional Flight Attendants
1004 W Euless Blvd ... Euless TX 76040 | 817-540-0108 | 540-2077 | 414
Web: www.apfa.org

Association of Progressive Rental Organizations (APRO)
1504 Robin Hood Trl ... Austin TX 78703 | 512-794-0095 | 794-0097 | 49-18
TF: 800-204-2776 ■ *Web:* www.rtohq.org

Association of Proposal Management Professionals (APMP)
PO Box 668 ... Dana Point CA 92629 | 949-493-9398 | | 49-12
Web: www.apmp.org

Association of Public & Land-Grant Universities (APLU)
1307 New York Ave NW Ste 400 ... Washington DC 20005 | 202-478-6040 | 478-6046 | 49-5
Web: www.aplu.org

Association of Public Health Laboratories (APHL)
8515 Georgia Ave Ste 700 ... Silver Spring MD 20910 | 240-485-2745 | 485-2700 | 49-7
Web: www.aphl.org

Association of Public-Safety Communications Officials International Inc
351 N Williamson Blvd ... Daytona Beach FL 32114 | 386-322-2500 | 322-2501 | 49-7
TF: 888-272-6911 ■ *Web:* www.apcointl.org

Association of Racing Commissioners Intl (ARCI)
1510 Newtown Pike Ste 210 ... Lexington KY 40511 | 859-224-7070 | | 49-7
Web: www.arci.com

Association of Reproductive Health Professionals (ARHP)
1300 19th St NW Ste 200 ... Washington DC 20036 | 202-466-3825 | 466-3826 | 49-8
TF: 877-311-8972 ■ *Web:* www.arhp.org

Association of Research Libraries (ARL)
21 Dupont Cir NW Ste 800 ... Washington DC 20036 | 202-296-2296 | | 49-5
Web: www.arl.org

Association of Rotational Molders Intl (ARM)
800 Roosevelt Rd Ste C-312 ... Glen Ellyn IL 60137 | 630-942-6589 | 790-3095 | 49-13
Web: www.rotomolding.org

Association of School Business Officials Intl (ASBO)
11401 N Shore Dr ... Reston VA 20190 | 866-682-2729 | 478-0205* | 49-5
**Fax Area Code:* 703 ■ *TF:* 866-682-2729 ■ *Web:* asbointl.org

Association of Schools & Colleges of Optometry (ASCO)
6110 Executive Blvd Ste 420 ... Rockville MD 20852 | 301-231-5944 | 770-1828 | 49-8
Web: optometriceducation.org

Association of Schools of Allied Health Professions (ASAHP)
122 C St NW Ste 650 ... Washington DC 20001 | 202-237-6481 | 237-6485 | 49-8
Web: www.asahp.org

Association of Schools of Public Health (ASPH)
1900 M St NW Ste 710 ... Washington DC 20036 | 202-296-1099 | 296-1252 | 49-5
Web: www.aspph.org

Association of Science-Technology Centers Inc (ASTC)
1025 Vermont Ave NW Ste 500 ... Washington DC 20005 | 202-783-7200 | 783-7207 | 49-19
Web: www.astc.org

Association of Service & Computer Dealers Intl (ASCDI)
131 NW First Ave ... Delray Beach FL 33444 | 561-266-9016 | 431-6302 | 48-9
TF: 800-393-2505 ■ *Web:* www.ascdi.com

Association of Shareware Professionals (ASP)
PO Box 1522 ... Martinsville IN 46151 | 765-349-4740 | 301-3756* | 48-9
**Fax Area Code:* 815 ■ *Web:* www.asp-software.org

Association of Social Work Boards (ASWB)
400 S Ridge Pkwy Ste B ... Culpeper VA 22701 | 540-829-6880 | | 49-7
TF: 800-225-6880 ■ *Web:* www.aswb.org

Association of Specialized & Professional Accreditors (ASPA)
3304 N Broadway St Ste 214 ... Chicago IL 60657 | 773-857-7900 | | 48-1
Web: www.aspa-usa.org

Association of State & Interstate Water Pollution Control Administrators (ASIWPCA)
1221 Connecticut Ave NW 2nd Fl ... Washington DC 20036 | 202-756-0600 | | 49-7
Web: www.acwa-us.org

Association of State & Territorial Health Officials (ASTHO)
2231 Crystal Dr Ste 450 ... Arlington VA 22202 | 202-371-9090 | 527-3189* | 49-7
**Fax Area Code:* 571 ■ *Web:* www.astho.org

Association of State & Territorial Solid Waste Management Officials (ASTSWMO)
444 N Capitol St NW Ste 315 ... Washington DC 20001 | 202-624-5828 | 624-7875 | 49-7
Web: www.astswmo.org

Association of State Wetland Managers
32 Tandberg Trl Ste 2A ... Windham ME 04062 | 207-892-3399 | 892-3089 | 49-7
TF: 800-451-6027 ■ *Web:* www.aswm.org

Association of Support Professionals
500 Rincon De Romos SE ... Rio Rancho NM 87124 | 505-209-2426 | | 48-9
Web: www.asponline.com

Association of Surgical Technologists (AST)
6 W Dry Creek Cir Ste 200 ... Littleton CO 80120 | 303-694-9130 | 694-9169 | 49-8
TF: 800-637-7433 ■ *Web:* www.ast.org

Association of Talent Agents
9255 Sunset Blvd Ste 930 ... Los Angeles CA 90069 | 310-274-0628 | 274-5063 | 48-4
Web: www.agentassociation.com

Association of Test Publishers
601 Pennsylvania Ave NW Ste 900 ... Washington DC 20004 | 866-240-7909 | | 49-5
TF: 866-240-7909 ■ *Web:* www.testpublishers.org

Association of the US Army (AUSA)
2425 Wilson Blvd ... Arlington VA 22201 | 703-841-4300 | 525-9039 | 48-19
TF: 800-336-4570 ■ *Web:* www.ausa.org

Association of the Wall & Ceiling Industries Intl (AWCI)
513 W Broad St Ste 210 ... Falls Church VA 22046 | 703-538-1600 | 534-8307 | 49-3
TF: 800-233-8990 ■ *Web:* www.awci.org

Association of Theological Schools in the US & Canada (ATS)
10 Summit Pk Dr ... Pittsburgh PA 15275 | 412-788-6505 | 788-6510 | 49-5
Web: www.ats.edu

Association of Universities for Research in Astronomy (AURA)
1331 Pennsylvania Ave NW Ste 1475 ... Washington DC 20005 | 202-483-2101 | 483-2106 | 49-5
Web: www.aura-astronomy.org

Association of University Centers on Disabilities (AUCD)
1100 Wayne Ave Ste 1000 ... Silver Spring MD 20910 | 301-588-8252 | 588-2842 | 49-5
TF: 888-572-2249 ■ *Web:* www.aucd.org

Association of University Presses
28 W 36th St Ste 602 ... New York NY 10018 | 212-989-1010 | 989-0975 | 49-16
TF: 800-678 2120 ■ *Web:* www.aupresses.org

Name / Address	City	State	Zip	Phone	Fax	Class
Association of University Programs in Health Administration (AUPHA) 2000 N 14th St Ste 780 *TF:* 877-275-6462 ■ *Web:* www.aupha.org	Arlington	VA	22201	703-894-0941		49-8
Association of University Technology Managers (AUTM) 111 Deer Lake Rd Ste 100 *Web:* www.autm.net	Deerfield	IL	60015	847-559-0846		49-19
Association of Vacuum Equipment Manufacturers (AVEM) 201 Pk Washington Ct *Web:* avem.org	Falls Church	VA	22046	703-538-3543	241-5603	49-13
Association of Vineyard Churches 5115 Grove W Blvd. *Web:* vineyardusa.org	Stafford	TX	77477	281-313-8463	313-8464	48-20
Association of Washington Business PO Box 658 *TF:* 800-521-9325 ■ *Web:* www.awb.org	Olympia	WA	98507	360-943-1600	943-5811	140
Association of Water Technologies (AWT) 9707 Key West Ave Ste 100 *Web:* www.awt.org	Rockville	MD	20850	301-740-1421		48-2
Association of Western Pulp & Paper Workers 1430 SW Clay St PO Box 4566 *TF:* 877-992-9779 ■ *Web:* www.awppw.org	Portland	OR	97208	503-228-7486	972-7684	414
Association of Women's Health Obstetric & Neonatal Nurses (AWHONN) 2000 L St NW Ste 740 *TF:* 800-673-8499 ■ *Web:* www.awhonn.org	Washington	DC	20036	202-261-2400	728-0575	49-8
Association of Zoos & Aquariums (AZA) 8403 Colesville Rd Ste 710 *Web:* www.aza.org	Silver Spring	MD	20910	301-562-0777	562-0888	48-3
Association on American Indian Affairs (AAIA) 966 Hungerford Dr Ste 12-B *Web:* www.indian-affairs.org	Rockville	MD	20850	240-314-7155	314-7159	457-17
Association Resource Ctr (ARC) 950 Glenn Dr Ste 150 *Web:* 4arc.aaiden.com	Folsom	CA	95630	916-932-2200	932-2209	47
Association Resource Group 7926 Jones Branch Dr Ste 1150 *Web:* www.myarg.com	McLean	VA	22102	703-770-2400		387
Assumption College 500 Salisbury St *TF:* 888-882-7786 ■ *Web:* www.assumption.edu	Worcester	MA	01609	508-767-7000	799-4412	166
Assumption College for Sisters 350 Bernardsville Rd *Web:* acs350.org	Mendham	NJ	07945	973-543-6528	543-1738	162
Assumption Parish Police Jury 4813 Hwy 1 PO Box 520 *Web:* www.assumptionla.com	Napoleonville	LA	70390	985-369-7435	369-2972	338
Assurance Group 25 E Spring Valley Ave *Web:* www.theassurancegroup.com	Maywood	NJ	07607	201-845-6444	845-4156	631
Assurance Investment Management LLC 59 Brandywine Dr *Web:* www.assureim.com	Hudson	OH	44236	330-650-1750		463
Assurance Manufacturing Co 9010 Evergreen Blvd. *Web:* www.assurancemfg.com	Minneapolis	MN	55433	763-780-4252		488
Assurance Systems Inc 5855 Jimmy Carter Blvd Ste 200 *TF:* 800-229-2009 ■ *Web:* www.accuagency.com	Norcross	GA	30071	770-242-6832	840-7558	178-1
Assurant Employee Benefits 2323 Grand Blvd. *TF:* 800-733-7879 ■ *Web:* www.slfserviceresources.com	Kansas City	MO	64108	816-474-2345	881-8996	391-2
Assurant Group 11222 Quail Roost Dr *TF:* 800-852-2244 ■ *Web:* www.assurant.com	Miami	FL	33157	770-763-1000		360-4
Assured & Associates Personal Care of Georgia 8687 Hospital Dr **Fax Area Code:* 877 ■ *Web:* www.assuredandassociates.com	Douglasville	GA	30134	678-391-0140	797-3730*	363
Assured Document Destruction Inc 8050 Arville St Ste 105 *Web:* www.shreddinglv.com	Las Vegas	NV	89139	702-614-0001		317
Assured Guaranty Corp 1633 Broadway *Web:* assuredguaranty.com	New York	NY	10019	212-974-0100	581-3268	391-5
Assured Information Security 153 Brooks Rd *Web:* www.ainfosec.com	Rome	NY	13441	315-336-3306		177
Assured Information Technology Engineering 12001 Research Pkwy Ste 128 *Web:* aitengineering.com	Orlando	FL	32826	407-601-7148		261
Assured Mortgage Inc 12660 W Capitol Dr Ste 100 *Web:* 3668101880.mortgage-application.net	Brookfield	WI	53005	262-780-6500		217
Assured Packaging Inc 6080 Vipond Dr *Web:* www.assuredpackaging.com	Mississauga	ON	L5T2V4	905-565-1410		393
AssuredPartners Inc 4244 Mt Pleasant St NW Ste 200 *TF:* 800-451-1904 ■ *Web:* www.assuredpartners.com	North Canton	OH	44720	330-266-1904	498-9946	390
AssuredPartners NL 2305 River Rd *TF:* 888-499-8092 ■ *Web:* www.assuredpartners.com	Louisville	KY	40206	502-894-2100	894-8602	194
AssureImmune LLC 1095 Broken Sound Pky NW Ste 100 *TF:* 888-346-6863 ■ *Web:* www.assureimmune.com	Boca Raton	FL	33487	561-221-7522		352
Assurity Life Insurance Co 2000 Q St *TF:* 800-869-0355 ■ *Web:* assurity.com	Lincoln	NE	68503	402-476-6500	437-4395	390
AST (Association of Surgical Technologists) 6 W Dry Creek Cir Ste 200 *TF:* 800-637-7433 ■ *Web:* www.ast.org	Littleton	CO	80120	303-694-9130	694-9169	49-8
AST Bearings 115 Main Rd *TF:* 800-526-1250 ■ *Web:* www.astbearings.com	Montville	NJ	07045	973-335-2230	335-6987	75
AST Products Inc 9 Linnell Cir *Web:* www.astp.com	Billerica	MA	01821	978-667-4500	667-9778	481
AST Sports Science Inc 120 Capitol Dr. *TF:* 800-627-2788 ■ *Web:* ast-ss.com	Golden	CO	80401	303-278-1420	278-1417	799
ASTA (American Seed Trade Assn) 1701 Duke St Ste 275 *TF:* 888-890-7333 ■ *Web:* www.betterseed.org	Alexandria	VA	22304	703-837-8140	837-9365	48-2
ASTA (American String Teachers Assn) 4155 Chain Bridge Rd *Web:* www.astastrings.org	Fairfax	VA	22030	703-279-2113	279-2114	49-5
ASTA (American Society of Travel Agents) 675 N Washington St Ste 490 *TF:* 800-275-2782 ■ *Web:* www.asta.org	Alexandria	VA	22314	703-739-2782	684-8319	48-23
ASTA (American Spice Trade Assn) 1101 17th St NW Ste 700 *Web:* www.astaspice.org	Washington	DC	20036	202-331-2460		49-6
Asta Funding Inc 210 Sylvan Ave *NASDAQ: ASFI* ■ *TF:* 866-389-7627 ■ *Web:* www.astafunding.com	Englewood Cliffs	NJ	07632	201-567-5648		272
Astar Inc 645 Wilber St *Web:* www.astarinc.net	South Bend	IN	46628	574-234-2137		604
A-Star Staffing Inc 2835 Camino Del Rio S Ste 220 *Web:* www.astarstaffing.com	San Diego	CA	92108	619-574-7600	574-6700	260
Astara 10700 Jersey Blvd Ste 500 *Web:* www.astara.org	Rancho Cucamonga	CA	91730	909-948-7412		637-2
Astatech Inc 2525 Pearl Buck Rd *TF:* 800-387-2269 ■ *Web:* www.astatechinc.com	Bristol	PA	19007	215-785-3197		196
ASTC (Association of Science-Technology Centers Inc) 1025 Vermont Ave NW Ste 500 *Web:* www.astc.org	Washington	DC	20005	202-783-7200	783-7207	49-19
Astec Inc 4101 Jerome Ave *Web:* www.astecinc.com	Chattanooga	TN	37407	423-867-4210	867-7609	190
Astec Industries Inc 1725 Shepherd Rd *NASDAQ: ASTE* ■ *Web:* www.astecindustries.com	Chattanooga	TN	37421	423-899-5898	899-4456	190
As-Tech Industries 24296 Gibson *Web:* as-techindustries.com	Warren	MI	48089	586-754-6100		697
Astek Corp 5055 Corporate Plaza Dr. *Web:* www.astekcorp.com	Colorado Springs	CO	80919	719-260-1625		194
Astellas Pharma US Inc 1 Astellas Way *TF:* 800-695-4321 ■ *Web:* www.astellas.com	Northbrook	IL	60062	800-727-7003		85
AstenJohnson Inc 4399 Corporate Rd *TF:* 800-529-7990 ■ *Web:* www.astenjohnson.com	Charleston	SC	29405	843-747-7800	747-3856	745-3
Astex Pharmaceuticals 4420 Rosewood Dr Ste 200 *Web:* astx.com	Pleasanton	CA	94588	925-560-0100	560-0101	85
Asthma & Allergy Foundation of America (AAFA) 8201 Corporate Dr Ste 1000 *TF:* 800-727-8462 ■ *Web:* www.aafa.org	Landover Hills	MD	20785	202-466-7643	466-8940	48-17
ASTHO (Association of State & Territorial Health Officials) 2231 Crystal Dr Ste 450 **Fax Area Code:* 571 ■ *Web:* www.astho.org	Arlington	VA	22202	202-371-9090	527-3189*	49-7
ASTI (American Services Technology Inc) 1028 Harvin Way Ste 120 *Web:* www.americanservicestech.com	Rockledge	FL	32955	321-631-8771	631-7291	194
Asti Trattoria 408C E 43rd St *Web:* astiaustin.com	Austin	TX	78751	512-451-1218		671
Asticou Inn 15 Peabody Dr *TF:* 800-258-3373 ■ *Web:* www.asticou.com	Northeast Harbor	ME	04662	207-276-3344		379
Astley Gilbert Ltd 42 Carnforth Rd *TF:* 877-873-0788 ■ *Web:* astleygilbert.com	Toronto	ON	M4A2K7	416-288-8666		627
ASTM Intl 100 Barr Harbor Dr PO Box C700 *TF:* 800-814-1017 ■ *Web:* www.astm.org	West Conshohocken	PA	19428	610-832-9500	832-9555	49-19
Aston Home Health Inc 1021 Gilpin Ave Ste 100 *Web:* www.astonhomehealth.com	Wilmington	DE	19806	302-421-3687	421-3688	363
Aston Veterinarian Hospital 5200 Pennell Rd *Web:* www.astonvet.com	Media	PA	19063	610-494-5800		794
ASTONE Properties LLC 1466 Van Ness Ave Ste 210 **Fax Area Code:* 610	Fresno	CA	93721	559-375-7100	725-1515*	195
Astor & Sanders Corp 9900 Belward Campus Dr Ste 200 *Web:* www.astor-sanders.com	Rockville	MD	20850	301-838-3420	838-3421	387
Astor Crowne Plaza 739 Canal St *TF:* 877-408-9661 ■ *Web:* www.astorneworleans.com	New Orleans	LA	70130	504-962-0500	962-0503	379
Astor Home For Children, The 6339 Mill St PO Box 5005 *Web:* www.astorservices.org	Rhinebeck	NY	12572	845-871-1000		48-15
Astor Hotel, The 924 E Juneau Ave *TF:* 800-558-0200 ■ *Web:* www.theastorhotel.com	Milwaukee	WI	53202	414-271-4220	271-6370	379
Astor, Weiss, Kaplan & Mandel LLP 200 S Broad St The Bellevue, Ste 600 *Web:* www.astorweiss.com	Philadelphia	PA	19102	215-790-0100	790-0509	41
Astoria Ford 710 W Marine Dr. *TF:* 888-760-9303 ■ *Web:* www.astoriaford.net	Astoria	OR	97103	503-325-6411		57
Astoria-Pacific Inc 15130 SE 82nd Dr *TF:* 800-536-3111 ■ *Web:* www.astoria-pacific.com	Clackamas	OR	97015	503-657-3010		292
Astra Associates Inc 6500 Dobry Dr *Web:* www.midwestinstrument.com	Sterling Heights	MI	48314	248-254-6500		201
Astra Foods Inc 6430 Market St *Web:* www.astrafoods.com	Upper Darby	PA	19082	610-352-4400		297-8
Astral Diagnostics Inc 1224 Forest Pky *TF:* 800-441-0366 ■ *Web:* www.astraldiagnostics.com	West Deptford	NJ	08066	800-441-0366		85
Astralloy Steel Products Inc 1550 Red Hollow Rd *Web:* www.astralloy.com	Birmingham	AL	35215	205-853-0300		492
AstraZeneca Canada Inc 1004 Middlegate Rd *TF:* 800-565-5877 ■ *Web:* www.astrazeneca.ca	Mississauga	ON	L4Y1M4	905-277-7111	270-3248	582
AstraZeneca Pharmaceuticals LP 1800 Concord Pk PO Box 15437 *TF:* 800-236-9933 ■ *Web:* www.astrazeneca-us.com	Wilmington	DE	19850	800-236-9933		582
Astrix Technology Group 125 Half Mile Rd Ste 200 *Web:* astrixinc.com	Red Bank	NJ	07701	732-661-0400		396
ASTRO (American Society for Therapeutic Radiology & Oncology) 8280 Willow Oaks Corporate Dr Ste 500 *TF:* 800-962-7876 ■ *Web:* www.astro.org	Fairfax	VA	22031	703-502-1550	502-7852	49-8
Astro Apparel Inc 300 Brook St *Web:* astroapparel.com	Scranton	PA	18505	570-346-1700	343-6565	155-11

Company	Address	City	State	ZIP	Phone	Fax	Class	Details
Astro Chemical Company Inc	3 Mill Rd	Ballston Lake	NY	12019	518-399-5338	399-8859	605-2	*Web:* www.astrochemical.com
Astro Chemicals Inc	126 Memorial Dr	Springfield	MA	01104	413-781-7240		146	*Web:* astrochemicals.com
Astro Craft Inc	7509 Spring Grove Rd	Spring Grove	IL	60081	815-675-1500	675-1600	358	*Web:* www.astrocraft.com
Astro Industries Inc	4403 Dayton-Xenia Rd	Dayton	OH	45432	937-429-5900	429-4054	813	*TF:* 800-543-5810 ■ *Web:* www.astro-ind.com
Astro Machine Works Inc	470 Wenger Dr	Ephrata	PA	17522	717-738-4281		454	*Web:* astromachineworks.com
Astro Manufacturing & Design Corp	34459 Curtis Blvd	Eastlake	OH	44095	888-215-1746		295	*TF:* 888-215-1746 ■ *Web:* www.astromfg.com
Astro Mechanical Contractors Inc	603 S Marshall Ave	El Cajon	CA	92020	619-442-9686		610	*Web:* astro-mech.com
Astro Met Inc	9974 Springfield Pk	Cincinnati	OH	45215	513-772-1242	772-9080	500	*Web:* www.astromet.com
Astro Pak Corp	270 E Baker St Ste 100	Costa Mesa	CA	92626	888-278-7672	434-1376*	743	**Fax Area Code:* 714 ■ *TF:* 888-278-7672 ■ *Web:* astropak.com
Astro Shapes Inc	65 Main St	Struthers	OH	44471	330-755-1414		492	*Web:* www.astroshapes.com
Astro Studios Inc	348 Sixth St	San Francisco	CA	94103	415-487-6787		463	*Web:* www.astrostudios.com
Astro Tool & Die Company Inc	5201 S Whitnall Ave	Cudahy	WI	53110	414-483-0343	483-6965	488	*Web:* www.astrotool.net
Astro Tool & Machine Company Inc	810 Martin St	Rahway	NJ	07065	732-382-2450	382-6394	757	*Web:* www.astrotoolco.com
Astrocom Electronics Inc	115 Dk Lifgren Dr	Oneonta	NY	13820	607-432-1930	432-1286	735	*Web:* www.astrocom-electronics.com
Astrodyne Corp	375 Forbes Blvd	Mansfield	MA	02048	508-964-6300		256	*TF:* 800-823-8082 ■ *Web:* www.astrodynetdi.com
Astrofoam Molding Company Inc	4117 Calle Tesoro	Camarillo	CA	93012	805-482-7276	482-6599	601	*Web:* www.astrofoam.com
Astro-Geo-Marine Inc	2186 Knoll Dr Ste B	Ventura	CA	93003	805-654-8300	654-8314	668	*TF:* 800-200-0246 ■ *Web:* www.astrogeomarine.com
Astronautics Corporation of America	4115 N Teutonia Ave PO Box 523	Milwaukee	WI	53209	414-449-4000	447-8231	529	*Web:* www.astronautics.com
Astronic	2 Orion	Aliso Viejo	CA	92656	949-900-6060		625	*TF:* 877-724-4000 ■ *Web:* www.astronic-ems.com
Astronics Corp	130 Commerce Way	East Aurora	NY	14052	716-805-1599	655-0309	438	*NASDAQ: ATRO* ■ *Web:* www.astronics.com
Astronomical Society of the Pacific	390 Ashton Ave	San Francisco	CA	94112	415-337-1100	337-5205	48-11	*TF:* 800-335-2624 ■ *Web:* www.astrosociety.org
Astrophysics Inc	21481 Ferrero Pkwy	City of Industry	CA	91789	909-598-5488		692	*Web:* www.astrophysicsinc.com
Astrotech Corp	401 Congress Ave Ste 1650	Austin	TX	78701	512-485-9530	485-9531	504	*NASDAQ: ASTC* ■ *Web:* www.astrotechcorp.com
ASTSWMO (Association of State & Territorial Solid Waste Management Officials)	444 N Capitol St NW Ste 315	Washington	DC	20001	202-624-5828	624-7875	49-7	*Web:* www.astswmo.org
Astyra Corp	411 E Franklin St Ste 105	Richmond	VA	23219	804-433-1100		260	*Web:* astyra.com
ASU (Albany State University)	504 College Dr	Albany	GA	31705	229-430-4600		166	*Web:* www.asurams.edu
ASU Group, The	2120 University Park Dr PO Box 77	Okemos	MI	48805	517-349-2212	349-9053	194	*TF:* 800-968-0278 ■ *Web:* www.asugroup.com
ASU Keer cultural Ctr	6110 N Scottsdale Rd	Scottsdale	AZ	85253	480-596-2660		572	*Web:* www.asukerr.com
ASU Three Rivers	1 College Cir	Malvern	AR	72104	501-337-5000	337-9382	162	*TF:* 800-337-0266 ■ *Web:* asutr.edu
Asuragen Inc	2150 Woodward St Ste 100	Austin	TX	78744	512-681-5200	681-5201	476	*TF:* 877-777-1874 ■ *Web:* asuragen.com
Asure Software	110 Wild Basin Rd	Austin	TX	78746	512-437-2700	437-2365	178-7	*NASDAQ: ASUR* ■ *TF:* 888-323-8835 ■ *Web:* www.asuresoftware.com
Asuris Northwest Health	528 E Spokane Falls Blvd No 301	Spokane	WA	99202	509-922-8072	496-1543*	390	**Fax Area Code:* 888 ■ *TF:* 888-344-5593 ■ *Web:* www.asuris.com
ASUSTeK Computer Intl	800 Corporate Way	Fremont	CA	94539	510-739-3777	608-4555	625	*Web:* www.asus.com
ASW Global LLC	3375 Gilchrist Rd	Mogadore	OH	44260	330-798-5172		803-1	*TF:* 888-826-5087 ■ *Web:* www.aswglobal.com
ASWB (Association of Social Work Boards)	400 S Ridge Pkwy Ste B	Culpeper	VA	22701	540-829-6880		49-7	*TF:* 800-225-6880 ■ *Web:* www.aswb.org
Asylum Research Corp	6310 Hollister Ave	Santa Barbara	CA	93117	805-696-6466		419	*TF:* 888-472-2795 ■ *Web:* afm.oxinst.com
Asylum, The	440 W Los Feliz Rd	Glendale	CA	91204	323-850-1214	260-9811*	514	**Fax Area Code:* 818 ■ *Web:* www.theasylum.cc
AT & T Ctr	1 AT&T Center Pkwy	San Antonio	TX	78219	210-444-5140		720	*Web:* www.attcenter.com
AT & T Inc	175 E Houston St PO Box 2933	San Antonio	TX	78299	210-821-4105		736	*NYSE: AT&T* ■ *TF:* 800-351-7221 ■ *Web:* www.att.com
At Health LLC	2733 E Battlefield Ste 266	Springfield	MO	65804	888-284-3258		356	*TF:* 888-284-3258 ■ *Web:* athealth.com
At Home Health Equipment	4309 W 96th St	Indianapolis	IN	46268	317-872-9702	872-9704	363	*TF:* 800-848-4670 ■ *Web:* ahhe.com
At Home Realty	124 N Main St	Ashland City	TN	37015	615-792-6100		652	*Web:* athomerealtyteam.com
At Homehealth Inc	3344 W Peterson Ave Ste 104	Chicago	IL	60659	773-279-9244	279-9255	363	*Web:* ahhchicago.com
AT Kearney Inc	227 W Monroe St	Chicago	IL	60606	312-648-0111	223-6200	194	*Web:* www.kearney.com
At Last Naturals Inc	PO Box 8305	Sleepy Hollow	NY	10591	914-747-3599	747-3791	214	*TF:* 800-527-8123 ■ *Web:* atlastnaturals.com
At Rosewood	284 Troy Rd	Rensselaer	NY	12144	518-286-1621	286-1691	450	*Web:* rosewoodrehabilitation.com
AT/SCAN Ltd	PO Box 152	Portsmouth	RI	02871	888-837-8373	732-5659*	178-1	**Fax Area Code:* 401 ■ *TF:* 888-837-8373 ■ *Web:* www.vertere.com
ATA (American Tinnitus Assn)	522 SW Fifth Ave Ste 825	Portland	OR	97204	503-248-9985	248-0024	48-17	*TF:* 800-634-8978 ■ *Web:* www.ata.org
ATA (Amateur Trapshooting Assn)	601 W National Rd	Vandalia	OH	45377	937-898-4638		48-22	*Web:* www.shootata.com
ATA (American Trucking Assn)	950 N Glebe Rd Ste 210	Arlington	VA	22203	703-838-1700		49-21	*TF:* 800-282-5463 ■ *Web:* www.trucking.org
ATA (American Translators Assn)	225 Reinekers Ln Ste 590	Alexandria	VA	22314	703-683-6100	683-6122	49-5	*Web:* www.atanet.org
ATA College	10200 Linn Station Rd Ste 125	Louisville	KY	40223	502-371-8383		162	*Web:* www.ata.edu
ATA Engineering Inc	13290 Evening Creek Dr S	San Diego	CA	92128	858-480-2000		261	*Web:* www.ata-e.com
ATA Ventures	4300 El Camino Real Ste 205	Los Altos	CA	94022	650-594-0189	594-0257	792	*Web:* ataventures.com
ATAA (Assembly of Turkish American Assn)	1526 18th St NW	Washington	DC	20036	202-483-9090	483-9092	48-14	*Web:* www.ataa.org
ATAC Corp	2770 De La Cruz Blvd	Santa Clara	CA	95050	408-736-2822	727-8447	809	*Web:* www.atac.com
Ataco Steel Products Corp	PO Box 270	Cedarburg	WI	53012	262-377-3000	377-3452	488	*TF:* 800-536-4822 ■ *Web:* www.atacosteel.com
Atacs Products Inc	850 S Cambridge St	Seattle	WA	98108	206-433-9000	433-6200	22	*Web:* atacs.com
Atalanta Corp	1 Atalanta Plz	Elizabeth	NJ	07206	908-351-8000	555-8000	297-8	*Web:* www.atalantacorp.com
Atalanta Investment Company Inc	601 Fairview Blvd	Incline Village	NV	89451	775-833-1836		402	
Atalanta Sosnoff Capital LLC	505 Fifth Ave 17th Fl	New York	NY	10017	212-867-5000	922-1820	401	*Web:* www.atalantasosnoff.com
Atalasoft Inc	116 Pleasant St Ste 321	Easthampton	MA	01027	413-572-4443		177	*Web:* www.atalasoft.com
Atalian Global Service	417 Fifth Ave 9th Fl	New York	NY	10016	212-889-6353		104	*TF:* 888-750-7774 ■ *Web:* atalian.us
Atamian Manufacturing Corp	910 Plainfield St	Providence	RI	02909	401-944-9614	946-1210	488	*Web:* www.atamianmfg.com
ATANE Consulting	40 Wall St	New York	NY	10005	212-747-1997		261	*Web:* ataneconsulting.com
ATAP Inc	130 Industry Way	Eastaboga	AL	36260	256-362-2221		470	*TF:* 800-362-2827 ■ *Web:* www.atap.com
Atari Inc	475 Park Ave S	New York	NY	10016	212-726-6500		178-3	*Web:* atari.com
ATAS International Inc	6612 Snowdrift Rd	Allentown	PA	18106	610-395-8445	395-9342	491	*TF:* 800-468-1441 ■ *Web:* www.atas.com
Atascadero Chamber of Commerce	6904 El Camino Real	Atascadero	CA	93422	805-466-2044	466-9218	139	*TF:* 877-204-9830 ■ *Web:* www.atascaderochamber.org
Atascadero State Hospital	10333 S Camino Real	Atascadero	CA	93422	805-468-2000	468-3386	374-5	*TF:* 844-210-6207 ■ *Web:* dsh.ca.gov
Atascosa County Courthouse	1 Courthouse Circle Dr	Jourdanton	TX	78026	830-769-3434	787-6221*	338	**Fax Area Code:* 866 ■ *TF:* 888-773-8888 ■ *Web:* www.atascosacounty.texas.gov
ATC (Athens Technical College)	800 US Hwy 29 N	Athens	GA	30601	706-355-5000	369-5756	800	*Web:* athenstech.edu
ATC (Appalachian Trail Conservancy)	799 Washington St PO Box 807	Harpers Ferry	WV	25425	304-535-6331	535-2667	48-23	*TF:* 888-287-8673 ■ *Web:* appalachiantrail.org
ATC (Architecture Technology Corp)	9971 Vly View Rd	Eden Prairie	MN	55344	952-829-5864	944-1859	178-1	*Web:* www.atcorp.com
ATC (Absolute Total Care Inc)	1441 Main St No 900	Columbia	SC	29201	866-433-6041	912-3610	391-3	*TF:* 866-433-6041 ■ *Web:* www.absolutetotalcare.com
ATC (Alma Telephone Company Inc)	405 W 11th St	Alma	GA	31510	912-632-8603	634-4519	224	*TF:* 877-217-2842 ■ *Web:* www.atcbroadband.com
Atc Home Health LLC	20345 River Ridge Dr	Porter	TX	77365	281-354-7112	354-7116	363	*Web:* atchomehealth.com
ATC Inc	4037 Guion Ln	Indianapolis	IN	46268	317-328-8492	328-2686	639	*TF:* 866-282-4621 ■ *Web:* atcinc.net
ATC Lighting & Plastics Inc	101 Parker Dr	Andover	OH	44003	440-293-4064	293-4591	438	*Web:* www.atc-lighting-plastics.com
Atc Power Systems Inc	45 Depot St	Merrimack	NH	03054	603-429-0391	429-0795	253	*Web:* www.atcpowersystems-products.com
ATC Transportation LLC	10801 Corporate Dr	Pleasant Prairie	WI	53158	262-564-7954		652	*TF:* 800-558-3271 ■ *Web:* www.atctransportation.com

Name / Address	City	State	Zip	Phone	Fax	Class
ATCA (Air Traffic Control Assn)						
1101 King St Ste 300	Alexandria	VA	22314	703-299-2430	299-2437	49-21
Web: www.atca.org						
ATCC (American Type Culture Collection)						
10801 University Blvd PO Box 1549	Manassas	VA	20108	703-365-2700	365-2701	668
TF: 800-638-6597 ■ *Web:* www.atcc.org						
Atchison Area Chamber of Commerce (AACC)						
200 S 10th St	Atchison	KS	66002	913-367-2427	367-2485	139
TF: 800-234-1854 ■ *Web:* www.atchisonkansas.net						
Atchison County 423 N Fifth St	Atchison	KS	66002	913-367-1653	367-0227	338
Web: www.atchisoncountyks.org						
Atchison County						
405 S Main St PO Box 243	Rock Port	MO	64482	660-744-6562	744-6564	338
TF: 800-989-4115 ■ *Web:* www.atchisoncounty.org						
Atchison Public Library (APL)						
401 Kansas Ave	Atchison	KS	66002	913-367-1902	367-2717	434-3
Web: www.atchisonlibrary.org						
Atchison-Holt Electric Co-op						
18585 Industrial Rd PO Box 160	Rock Port	MO	64482	660-744-5344		245
TF: 888-744-5366 ■ *Web:* www.ahec.coop						
ATCO Industries Inc						
7300 Fifteen Mile Rd	Sterling Heights	MI	48312	586-795-9595		803-1
Web: www.mis.atcoindustries.com						
Atco Ltd 11721 170th St NW	Edmonton	AB	T5M3W7	780-962-3111		787
Web: www.atco.com						
Atco Manufacturing Co						
1401 Barclay Cir SE	Marietta	GA	30060	770-424-7550	422-1822	151
TF: 800-723-2826 ■ *Web:* www.atcointernational.com						
ATCO Products Inc						
189-V Frelinghuysen Ave	Newark	NJ	07114	973-242-5757	242-0131	350
Web: www.atcoproducts.com						
ATCO Properties & Management LLC						
555 Fifth Ave 16th Fl	New York	NY	10017	212-687-5154		463
Web: www.atco555.com						
Atco Raceway 1000 Jackson Rd	Atco	NJ	08004	856-768-2167		515
Web: atcodragway.rocks						
Atco Rubber Products Inc						
7101 Atco Dr	Fort Worth	TX	76118	817-595-2801		370
TF: 800-877-3828 ■ *Web:* www.atcoflex.com						
Atcoflex Inc 14261 172nd Ave	Grand Haven	MI	49417	616-842-4661	842-4623	370
Web: www.atcoflexinc.com						
ATD (Atlantic Tool & Die Co)						
19963 Progress Dr	Strongsville	OH	44149	440-238-6931		488
Web: atlantictool.com						
ATD Engineering & Machine LLC						
533 N Ct St	Au Gres	MI	48703	989-876-7161	876-7162	494
Web: www.atdemllc.com						
ATD-American Co 135 Greenwood Ave	Wyncote	PA	19095	215-576-1000	523-2300*	320
**Fax Area Code:* 800 ■ *TF:* 866-283-9327 ■ *Web:* www.atd.com						
ATDS 124 Truckers Ln	Elm Mott	TX	76640	254-829-1694	829-1955	167-3
Web: www.truckingschool.com						
ATEC 501 Bay Ave Ste 202	Somers Point	NJ	08244	609-904-5790		261
Web: atec-co.com						
ATEC Group 1762 Central Ave Ste 300	Albany	NY	12205	518-452-3700		174
Web: atecgroup.com						
ATEC Inc 12600 Executive Dr	Stafford	TX	77477	281-276-2700	240-2682	621
Web: atec.com						
A-tech Security Inc						
4616 Hawkins St NE	Albuquerque	NM	87109	505-821-5777	821-9357	77
Web: atechsecurity.com						
ATEK Access Technologies LLC						
10025 Valley View Rd Ste 190	Eden Prairie	MN	55344	763-553-7700		693
TF: 800-523-6996 ■ *Web:* atekcompanies.com						
ATEL Capital Group						
600 California St 9th Fl	San Francisco	CA	94111	800-543-2835	989-3796*	216
**Fax Area Code:* 415 ■ *TF:* 800-543-2835 ■ *Web:* www.atel.com						
Atelier Esthetique Institute of Esthetics						
226 W 26th St 7th Fl	New York	NY	10001	212-725-6130		167-3
TF: 800-626-1242 ■ *Web:* aeinstitute.net						
Ateliers Lesage Inc (les)						
1330 Rue Soucy	Saint-Hubert	QC	J4T1A3	450-445-5088		757
Web: www.ateliersleage.com						
ATEN 23 Hubble	Irvine	CA	92618	949-428-1111	428-1100	173-1
Web: www.aten.com						
Ater Wynne LLP						
1331 NW Lovejoy St Lovejoy Bldg Ste 900	Portland	OR	97209	503-226-1191		428
Web: www.aterwynne.com						
Atessa Inc 5000 Hopyard Rd Ste 400	Pleasanton	CA	94588	925-469-0063	469-0073	180
Web: atessainc.com						
ATF (Bureau of Alcohol Tobacco Firearms & Explosives)						
650 Massachusetts Ave NW	Washington	DC	20226	202-927-8210		340-14
Web: www.atf.gov						
AT&F (American Tank & Fabricating Co)						
12314 Elmwood Ave	Cleveland	OH	44111	216-252-1500	251-4963	723
TF: 800-544-5316 ■ *Web:* www.atfco.com						
Boston Field Div 10 Causeway St Ste 791	Boston	MA	02222	617-557-1200	557-1201	340-14
Web: www.atf.gov						
Atfocus 394 Old Orchard Grove	Toronto	ON	M5M2E9	416-485-4220		193
TF: 866-349-2661 ■ *Web:* atfocus.ca						
ATG (American Transport Group LLC)						
1900 W Kinzie	Chicago	IL	60622	888-284-5623	235-9600*	311
**Fax Area Code:* 773 ■ *TF:* 888-284-5623 ■ *Web:* www.atgfreight.com						
ATG LegalServe Inc						
105 W Adams St Ste 1350	Chicago	IL	60603	312-855-0303	855-0306	41
Web: www.atglegalserve.com						
ATG Technologies Inc						
2639 N Monroe St Cedars Bldg B Ste 200	Tallahassee	FL	32303	800-775-7790		393
TF: 800-775-7790 ■ *Web:* www.patlive.com						
ATG Trust Co 1 S Wacker Dr 24th Fl	Chicago	IL	60606	312-338-7878	338-1594	70
Web: www.atgtrust.com						
Ath Power Consulting Corp						
9 Bartlet St	Andover	MA	01810	978-474-6464		463
Web: www.athpower.com						
Athabasca University						
1 University Dr	Athabasca	AB	T9S3A3	780-675-6111	675-6174	785
TF: 800-788-9041 ■ *Web:* www.athabascau.ca						
Athana International Inc						
602 Faye	Redondo Beach	CA	90277	310-539-7280	539-6596	658
TF: 800-421-1591 ■ *Web:* www.athana.com						
Athavale Lystad & Associates Inc						
6720-B Rockledge Dr Ste 160	Bethesda	MD	20817	301-816-3237		256
Web: alaengr.com						
Athea Laboratories Inc						
1900 W Cornell St	Milwaukee	WI	53209	800-743-6417	354-9219*	145
**Fax Area Code:* 414 ■ *TF:* 800-743-6417 ■ *Web:* www.athea.com						
Athena Controls Inc						
5145 Campus Dr	Plymouth Meeting	PA	19462	610-828-2490	828-7084	201
TF: 800-782-6776 ■ *Web:* www.athenacontrols.com						
Athena Diagnostics Inc						
377 Plantation St 2nd Fl	Worcester	MA	01605	508-756-2886		231
TF: 800-394-4493 ■ *Web:* www.athenadiagnostics.com						
Athena Engineering Inc						
456 E Foothill Blvd	San Dimas	CA	91773	909-599-0947	599-5018	189-4
Web: athenaengineering.com						
Athena Pallas 556 22nd St S	Arlington	VA	22202	703-521-3870		671
Web: www.athenapallasrestaurant.net						
Athena Scientific PO Box 805	Nashua	NH	03061	617-489-3097	882-6621*	637-2
**Fax Area Code:* 603 ■ *Web:* www.athenasc.com						
Athenaeum of Ohio, The						
6616 Beechmont Ave	Cincinnati	OH	45230	513-231-2223	231-3254	167-3
Web: athenaeum.edu						
Athenaeum of Philadelphia						
219 S Sixth St	Philadelphia	PA	19106	215-925-2688	925-3755	434-4
Web: www.philaathenaeum.org						
Athenaeum, The 201 Prince St	Alexandria	VA	22314	703-548-0035		50-3
Web: www.nvfaa.org						
Athenahealth 311 Arsenal St	Watertown	MA	02472	617-402-1000	402-1099	178-1
NASDAQ: ATHN ■ *TF:* 800-981-5084 ■ *Web:* www.athenahealth.com						
Atheneum Suite Hotel & Conference Ctr						
1000 Brush Ave	Detroit	MI	48226	313-962-2323	962-2424	379
TF: 800-772-2323 ■ *Web:* www.atheneumsuites.com						
Athenian Garden						
6940 22nd Ave N	Saint Petersburg	FL	33710	727-345-7040		671
Web: www.atheniangardens.com						
Athenian School, The						
2100 Mt Diablo Scenic Blvd	Danville	CA	94506	925-837-5375		622
Web: www.athenian.org						
Athens 13600 Snow Rd	Brook Park	OH	44142	216-676-8500		296-2
Web: www.athensfoods.com						
Athens Area Chamber of Commerce						
449 E State St Ste 1	Athens	OH	45701	740-594-2251	594-2252	139
TF: 877-360-3608 ■ *Web:* athenschamber.com						
Athens Area Chamber of Commerce (AACC)						
246 W Hancock Ave	Athens	GA	30601	706-549-6800	549-5636	139
Web: www.athenschamber.net						
Athens Banner-Herald 1 Press Pl	Athens	GA	30601	706-549-0123	208-2246	532-2
TF: 800-533-4252 ■ *Web:* www.onlineathens.com						
Athens City School District						
25 S Plains Rd	The Plains	OH	45780	740-797-4544	797-2486	685
Web: www.athenscsd.org						
Athens Convention & Visitors Bureau						
300 N Thomas St	Athens	GA	30601	706-357-4430	546-8040	206
TF: 800-653-0603 ■ *Web:* www.visitathensga.com						
Athens County Board of Developmental Disabilities						
801 W Union St	Athens	OH	45701	740-594-3539		338
Web: athenscbdd.org						
Athens County Convention & Visitors Bureau						
667 E State St	Athens	OH	45701	740-592-1819	593-7365	206
TF: 800-878-9767 ■ *Web:* athensohio.com						
Athens Material Handling Inc						
316 Commerce Blvd	Athens	GA	30604	706-548-6023		385
Web: www.athensmaterialhandling.com						
Athens Messenger, The 9300 Johnson Rd	Athens	OH	45701	740-592-6612		637-8
Web: www.athensmessenger.com						
Athens on Fourth Avenue						
500 N Fourth Ave	Tucson	AZ	85705	520-624-6886		671
Web: athenson4thave.com						
Athens Regional Medical Ctr						
1114 W Madison Ave	Athens	TN	37303	423-745-1411		374-3
TF: 800-855-2880 ■ *Web:* starrregional.com						
Athens Services 14048 Valley Blvd	La Puente	CA	91746	626-336-3636		804
TF: 888-336-6100 ■ *Web:* www.athensservices.com						
Athens Technical College (ATC)						
800 US Hwy 29 N	Athens	GA	30601	706-355-5000	369-5756	800
Web: athenstech.edu						
Athens/Clarke County Library						
2025 Baxter St	Athens	GA	30606	706-613-3650	613-3660	434-3
Web: athenslibrary.org						
Athens-Clarke County						
325 E Washington St Rm 200 PO Box 1868	Athens	GA	30601	706-613-3031	613-3033	338
Web: www.accgov.com						
Athens-Limestone Hospital						
700 W Market St	Athens	AL	35611	256-233-9292	233-9278	374-3
Web: www.athenslimestonehospital.com						
Atherton Baptist Homes						
214 S Atlantic Blvd	Alhambra	CA	91801	626-289-4178		672
Web: www.abh.org						
Atherton Construction LLC						
50 N Gibson Rd Rm 115	Henderson	NV	89014	702-889-3600	222-1976	186
Web: athertonconstruction.com						
Athey & Company PA 1015 N Pearl St	Bridgeton	NJ	08302	856-451-8277	451-7750	2
Web: www.atheycocpa.com						
Athletes & Entertainers for Kids (AEFK)						
14340 Bolsa Chica Rd Ste C	Westminster	CA	92683	714-894-5450	894-8424	48-6
TF: 800-933-5437 ■ *Web:* www.911golfclassic.com						
Athletes in Action 651 Taylor Dr	Xenia	OH	45385	937-352-1000	352-1001	48-15
Web: athletesinaction.org						
Athletic Media Co, The						
332 Pine St 9th Fl	San Francisco	CA	94104	415-891-7354		6
Web: www.theathletic.com						
Athletic Supply Inc 1107 N Grant Ave	Odessa	TX	79761	432-332-1568		711
TF: 800-272-8555 ■ *Web:* athleticsupplytx.com						
Athletic Training Equipment Company Inc						
655 Spice Island Dr	Sparks	NV	89431	800-800-9931		711
TF: 800-800-9931 ■ *Web:* www.atecsports.com						
AtHomeNet Inc PO Box 1405	Suwanee	GA	30024	770-904-7930		225
Web: www.athomenet.com						

	Phone	Fax	Class
Athreya Inc 100 Jersey Ave Ste A 103 . . . New Brunswick NJ 08901 *Web:* athreyainc.com	732-246-2700		180
ATI (AmericanTours International LLC) 6053 W Century Blvd . . . Los Angeles CA 90045 *Web:* www.americantours.com	310-641-9953	216-5807	760
ATI (Amplifier Technologies Inc) 1749 Chapin Rd . . . Montebello CA 90640 *Web:* www.bgw.com	323-278-0001	278-0083	52
ATI (Atlantic Teleconnect Inc) 2529 Commerce Pky . . . North Port FL 34289 *TF:* 800-327-4642 ■ *Web:* www.aticonnect.com	941-429-8484		253
ATI Ambulance 8400 W 183rd Pl . . . Tinley Park IL 60487 *Web:* www.traceambulance.com	708-532-0088		30
ATI Industrial Automation Export Co 1031 Goodworth Dr . . . Apex NC 27539 *Web:* www.ati-ia.com	919-772-0115	772-8259	201
ATIS (Alliance for Telecommunications Industry Solutions) 1200 G St NW Ste 500 . . . Washington DC 20005 *Web:* www.atis.org	202-628-6380	393-5453	49-20
ATIS Elevator Inspections LLC 1976 Innerbelt Business Ctr . . . Saint Louis MO 63114 *TF:* 855-755-2847 ■ *Web:* atis.com	855-755-2847		393
Atiwa Computer Leasing Exchange 6950 Portwest Dr Ste 100 . . . Houston TX 77024 *TF:* 800-428-2532 ■ *Web:* www.atiwa.com	713-467-9390		179
ATK (A T Klemens) 814 12th St N . . . Great Falls MT 59401 *Web:* www.atklemens.com	406-452-9541		610
ATK (Advanced Trim & Kitchens) 4966 Lincoln Hwy E . . . Kinzers PA 17535 *Web:* www.advancedtrimandkitchens.com	717-442-8098	442-0307	499
ATK Foods Inc 1143 W Lake St . . . Chicago IL 60607 *TF:* 800-233-9629 ■ *Web:* www.atkfoods.com	800-233-9629		296-26
Atkins & Pearce Inc 1 Braid Way . . . Covington KY 41017 *TF:* 800-837-7477 ■ *Web:* www.atkinsandpearce.com	859-356-2001	356-2395	208
Atkins David LLC 229 Peachtree St International Twr Ste 950 . . . Atlanta GA 30303 *Web:* www.atkinsdavid.com	404-446-4488		41
Atkins Engineers Inc 2555 Ponce De Leon Blvd Ste 220 . . . Coral Gables FL 33134 *Web:* ae-fl.com	305-444-6260		261
Atkins Nutritionals Inc 1225 17th St Ste 1000 . . . Denver CO 80202 *TF:* 800-628-5467 ■ *Web:* www.atkins.com	800-628-5467		799
Atkins Savings Bank & Trust 97 Main Ave . . . Atkins IA 52206 *Web:* atkinssavingsbank.com	319-446-7700		70
Atkinson & Associates Insurance Inc 1537 Brantley Rd Bldg C . . . Fort Myers FL 33907 *Web:* www.atkinsoninsurance.com	239-437-5555		390
Atkinson Andelson Loya Ruud & Romo A Professional Law Corp 12800 Towne Center Dr . . . Cerritos CA 90703 *Web:* www.aalrr.com	562-653-3200		428
Atkinson Candy Co 1608 W Frank Ave . . . Lufkin TX 75904 *Web:* atkinsoncandy.com	936-639-2333	639-2337	296-8
Atkinson Conway & Gagnon Inc 420 L St Ste 500 . . . Anchorage AK 99501 *TF:* 800-478-1900 ■ *Web:* www.acglaw.com	907-276-1700		428
Atkinson County 86 Main St S PO Box 518 . . . Pearson GA 31642 *Web:* www.atkinsoncounty.org	912-422-3391	422-3429	338
Atkinson County School System 98 Roberts Ave E . . . Pearson GA 31642 *TF:* 800-639-0850 ■ *Web:* www.atkinson.k12.ga.us	912-422-7373	422-7369	685
Atkinson Electronics Inc 14 W Vine St . . . Salt Lake City UT 84107 *TF:* 800-261-3602 ■ *Web:* www.atkinsonelectronics.com	801-261-3600	261-3796	385
Atkinson Freight Lines Co 2950 State Rd . . . Bensalem PA 19020 **Fax Area Code:* 212	215-639-2678	705-2805*	780
Atkinson Industries Inc (AZZ) 1801 E 27th Ter . . . Pittsburg KS 66762 *Web:* www.azz.com	620-231-6900	231-7154	729
Atkinson Trading Company Inc 3911 W Saragosa St . . . Chandler AZ 85226 *TF:* 844-692-7729	480-899-9597		327
Atkinson's Mirror & Glass 909 N Orchard St . . . Boise ID 83706 *Web:* www.atkinsonsmirrorandglass.com	208-375-3762	375-3774	234
Atkinson-Baker Inc (ABI) 500 N Brand Blvd 3rd Fl . . . Glendale CA 91203 *TF:* 800-288-3376 ■ *Web:* www.depo.com	818-551-7300		445
ATL Inc W140 N9504 Fountain Blvd . . . Menomonee Falls WI 53051 *Web:* www.atlco.com	262-255-6150		393
ATLA (American Theological Library Assn) 300 S Wacker Dr Ste 2100 . . . Chicago IL 60606 *TF:* 888-665-2852 ■ *Web:* www.atla.com	312-454-5100	454-5505	48-20
Atlanta Airlines Terminal Corp Hartsfield-Jackson Atlanta International Airport PO Box 45170 . . . Atlanta GA 30320 *Web:* www.aatc.org	404-530-2100		25
Atlanta Area Chamber of Commerce 101 N East St . . . Atlanta TX 75551 *Web:* www.atlantatexas.org	903-796-3296		139
Atlanta Athletic Club 1930 Bobby Jones Dr . . . Johns Creek GA 30097 *Web:* www.atlantaathleticclub.org	770-448-2166		354
Atlanta Attachment Company Inc 362 Industrial Pk Dr . . . Lawrenceville GA 30045 *TF:* 877-206-5116 ■ *Web:* www.atlatt.com	770-963-7369	963-7641	36
Atlanta Ballet 1695 Marietta Blvd NW . . . Atlanta GA 30318 *Web:* www.atlantaballet.com	404-873-5811	874-7905	573-1
Atlanta Belting Co 560 Edgewood Ave SE . . . Atlanta GA 30312 **Fax Area Code:* 404 ■ *TF:* 800-241-5780 ■ *Web:* www.tennesseebelting.com	800-241-5780	688-3618*	370
Atlanta Beverage Co 5000 Fulton Industrial Blvd SW . . . Atlanta GA 30336 *Web:* www.atlantabev.com	404-699-6700		81-1
Atlanta Botanical Garden (ABG) 1345 Piedmont Ave NE . . . Atlanta GA 30309 *Web:* www.atlantabotanicalgarden.org	404-876-5859		823
Atlanta Bread Co 1200 Wilson Way Ste 100 . . . Smyrna GA 30082 *Web:* atlantabread.com	770-432-0933		68
Atlanta Capital Management Company LLC 1075 Peachtree St NW Ste 2100 . . . Atlanta GA 30309 *TF:* 800-836-2414 ■ *Web:* www.atlcap.com	404-876-9411	872-1672	401
Atlanta Carrier Hotel 56 Marietta St . . . Atlanta GA 30303 *Web:* 55mariettast.com	770-390-9378		377
Atlanta Casework Systems Inc 3815 Evans Rd . . . Cumming GA 30040 *Web:* www.atlcasework.com	770-887-4766		200
Atlanta City Hall 55 Trinity Ave SW . . . Atlanta GA 30303 *TF:* 800-897-1910 ■ *Web:* www.atlantaga.gov	404-330-6004	658-6893	337
Atlanta Civic Ctr 395 Piedmont Ave NE . . . Atlanta GA 30308 *TF:* 877-430-7596 ■ *Web:* www.atlantaga.gov	404-523-6275		572
Atlanta Commercial Tire Inc 5067 Kennedy Rd . . . Forest Park GA 30297 *TF:* 800-333-3292 ■ *Web:* www.actire.com	404-351-8016	352-8261	54
Atlanta Contemporary Art Ctr 535 Means St NW . . . Atlanta GA 30318 *Web:* atlantacontemporary.org	404-688-1970		50-2
Atlanta Convention & Visitors Bureau 233 Peachtree St NE Ste 1400 . . . Atlanta GA 30303 *Web:* www.atlanta.net	404-521-6600		206
Atlanta Cutlery Corp 2147 Gees Mill Rd . . . Conyers GA 30013 **Fax Area Code:* 770 ■ *TF:* 800-883-0300 ■ *Web:* www.atlantacutlery.com	800-883-8838	760-8993*	222
Atlanta Daily World Inc c/o Atlanta Daily World 1372 Peachtree St NE . . . Atlanta GA 30309 *Web:* atlantadailyworld.com	313-963-8100		532-3
Atlanta Dragway 500 E Ridgeway Rd . . . Commerce GA 30529 *Web:* www.atlantadragway.com	706-335-2301		515
Atlanta Falcons 4400 Falcon Pkwy . . . Flowery Branch GA 30542 *Web:* www.atlantafalcons.com	770-965-3115	965-3185	715-3
Atlanta Fixture & Sales Co 3185 NE Expy . . . Atlanta GA 30341 *TF:* 800-282-1977 ■ *Web:* www.atlantafixture.com	770-455-8844	986-9202	300
Atlanta Fuel Co 2324 Donald Lee Hollowell Pkwy . . . Atlanta GA 30318 *Web:* atlantafuel.com	404-792-9888		316
Atlanta Hardwood Corp 5596 Riverview Rd SE . . . Mableton GA 30126 *TF:* 800-476-5393 ■ *Web:* www.hardwoodweb.com	404-792-2290		364
Atlanta History Ctr 130 W Paces Ferry Rd . . . Atlanta GA 30305 *Web:* www.atlantahistorycenter.com	404-814-4000		520
Atlanta Hospital Hospitality House 1815 S Ponce De Leon Ave NE . . . Atlanta GA 30307 *Web:* www.atlhhh.org	404-377-6333		372
Atlanta Inquirer, The PO Box 92367 . . . Atlanta GA 30314 *Web:* www.atlinq.com	404-523-6086	523-6088	532-2
Atlanta International Consulting Group (aicg) 1401 Peachtree St NE Ste 500 . . . Atlanta GA 30309 *Web:* www.aicginc.com	404-872-4884	870-0440	194
Atlanta Intown Real Estate Services 181 Tenth St NE . . . Atlanta GA 30309 *Web:* www.atlantaintown.com	404-881-1810		652
Atlanta Journal-Constitution 223 Perimeter Center Pkwy NE . . . Atlanta GA 30346 *TF:* 800-933-9771 ■ *Web:* www.ajc.com	404-514-6162	526-5746	532-2
Atlanta Magazine 260 Peachtree St Ste 300 . . . Atlanta GA 30303 *TF:* 800-930-3019 ■ *Web:* www.atlantamagazine.com	404-527-5500	527-5575	457-22
Atlanta Metropolitan College 1630 Metropolitan Pkwy SW . . . Atlanta GA 30310 *Web:* www.atlm.edu	404-756-4000	756-4407	162
Atlanta Motor Speedway PO Box 500 . . . Hampton GA 30228 *TF:* 877-926-7849 ■ *Web:* www.atlantamotorspeedway.com	770-946-4211	946-3928	515
Atlanta Petroleum Equipment Co 4732 N Royal Atlanta Dr . . . Tucker GA 30084 *TF:* 800-562-4060 ■ *Web:* atlantapetroleum.com	770-491-6644		539
Atlanta Pops Orchestra PO Box 49493 . . . Atlanta GA 30359 *Web:* atlantapops.com	404-636-0020		573-3
Atlanta Postal Credit Union 515 Mulberry St Ste 100 . . . Atlanta GA 30312 *TF:* 800-849-8431 ■ *Web:* www.apcu.com	404-768-4126	768-0815	219
Atlanta Public Schools 130 Trinity Ave SW . . . Atlanta GA 30303 *Web:* www.atlantapublicschools.us	404-802-3500	802-1803	685
Atlanta School of Massage 2 Dunwoody Pk Ste 101 . . . Atlanta GA 30338 *TF:* 866-212-0367 ■ *Web:* www.atlantaschoolofmassage.com	770-677-0300		685
Atlanta State Park 927 Park Rd 42 . . . Atlanta TX 75551 *Web:* tpwd.texas.gov	903-796-6476		565
Atlanta Symphony Orchestra 1280 Peachtree St NE Ste 4074 . . . Atlanta GA 30309 *Web:* www.atlantasymphony.org	404-733-4900	733-4901	573-3
Atlanta Technical College 1560 Metropolitan Pky SW . . . Atlanta GA 30310 *Web:* www.atlantatech.edu	404-225-4400		167-3
Atlanta Toyota Inc 2345 Pleasant Hill Rd . . . Duluth GA 30096 *Web:* www.atlantatoyota.com	770-476-8282		57
Atlanta Voice 633 Pryor St Sw . . . Atlanta GA 30312 *Web:* www.theatlantavoice.com	404-524-6426	523-7853	532-2
Atlanta-Fulton Public Library 1 Margaret Mitchell Sq . . . Atlanta GA 30303 *Web:* www.afpls.org	404-730-1700		434-3
Atlantec Engineers PA 3221 Blue Ridge Rd Ste 113 . . . Raleigh NC 27612 *Web:* atlantecengineers.com	919-571-1111		261
Atlantech Online Inc 1010 Wayne Ave Ste 630 . . . Silver Spring MD 20910 *TF:* 800-256-1612 ■ *Web:* www.atlantech.net	301-589-3060		225

Name / Address	City	State	ZIP	Phone	Fax	Class
Atlantic & Pacific Management 11075 Carmel Mountain Rd Ste 200 *Web:* aphoamgmt.com	San Diego	CA	92129	858-672-3100		652
Atlantic Air Enterprises Inc 856 Elston St *Web:* www.atlanticairent.com	Rahway	NJ	07065	732-381-4000		697
Atlantic American Corp 4370 Peachtree Rd NE *NASDAQ: AAME* ■ *Web:* www.atlam.com	Atlanta	GA	30319	404-266-5500		360-4
Atlantic Aviation 17725 John F Kennedy Blvd *Web:* www.atlanticaviation.com	Houston	TX	77032	281-443-3434	821-9149	63
Atlantic Battery Company Inc 309 Main St *Web:* www.atlanticbatterycompany.com	Watertown	MA	02472	617-924-2868		74
Atlantic Bay Mortgage Group 596 Lynnhaven Pkwy Ste 102 *Web:* atlanticbay.com	Virginia Beach	VA	23452	757-213-1697		217
Atlantic Beverage Co 3775 Park Ave *Web:* atlanticbeverageco.com	Edison	NJ	08820	732-548-5800		805
Atlantic Blueberry Co 7201 Weymouth Rd *Web:* www.atlanticblueberry.com	Hammonton	NJ	08037	609-561-8600	561-5033	315-1
Atlantic Bridge & Engineering Inc 150 High St *Web:* atlanticbr.com	Hampton	NH	03842	603-601-7487		261
Atlantic British Ltd Halfmoon Light Industrial Pk 6 Enterprise Ave *TF:* 800-533-2210 ■ *Web:* www.roverparts.com	Clifton Park	NY	12065	518-664-6169		57
Atlantic Bulk Carrier Corp PO Box 112 *TF:* 800-966-0030 ■ *Web:* www.atlanticbulk.com	Providence Forge	VA	23140	804-966-5459	966-5081	449
Atlantic Carriers Inc 501 Ash St *TF:* 800-831-5740 ■ *Web:* www.atlanticcarriers.com	Atlantic	IA	50022	800-831-5740		780
Atlantic Center For The Arts Inc 1414 Art Center Ave *TF:* 800-393-6975 ■ *Web:* atlanticcenterforthearts.org	New Smyrna Beach	FL	32168	386-427-6975		327
Atlantic City - City Hall 1301 Bacharach Blvd *Web:* www.cityofatlanticcity.org	Atlantic City	NJ	08401	609-347-5300		337
Atlantic City Aquarium 800 N New Hampshire Ave *Web:* www.acaquarium.com	Atlantic City	NJ	08401	609-348-2880		40
Atlantic City Bar & Grill 1219 Pacific Ave *Web:* www.acbarandgrill.com	Atlantic City	NJ	08401	609-348-8080		671
Atlantic City Convention & Visitors Authority 2314 Pacific Ave *TF:* 888-228-4748 ■ *Web:* www.atlanticcitynj.com	Atlantic City	NJ	08401	609-348-7100		206
Atlantic City Federal Credit Union 1005 11th St *TF:* 800-870-5159 ■ *Web:* atlanticcity.coop	Lander	WY	82520	307-332-5151		219
Atlantic City Free Public Library 1 N Tennessee Ave *Web:* acfpl.org	Atlantic City	NJ	08401	609-345-2269	345-5570	434-3
Atlantic City International Airport (ACY) 101 Atlantic City International Airport Ste 106 *Web:* sjta.com	Egg Harbor Township	NJ	08234	609-645-7895		27
Atlantic Club, The 1904 Atlantic Ave *Web:* www.theatlanticclub.com	Manasquan	NJ	08736	732-223-2100		354
Atlantic Coast Seafood Inc 42-44 Boston Fish Pier *Web:* www.atlanticcoastsfd.com	Boston	MA	02110	617-482-0040	482-5643	297-5
Atlantic Concrete Products Inc 8900 Old Rt 13 PO Box 129 *Web:* www.atlanticconcrete.com	Tullytown	PA	19007	215-945-5600	946-3102	183
Atlantic Construction Fabrics Inc 2831 Cardwell Rd **Fax Area Code:* 804 ■ *TF:* 800-448-3636 ■ *Web:* www.acfenvironmental.com	Richmond	VA	23234	800-448-3636	743-7779*	190
Atlantic Constructors Inc 1401 Battery Brooke Pkwy *Web:* acibuilds.com	Richmond	VA	23237	804-222-3400	222-6638	189-10
Atlantic Container Line (ACL) 50 Cardinal Dr *Web:* www.aclcargo.com	Westfield	NJ	07090	908-518-5300	518-7321	313
Atlantic Cordage Corp 35 Mileed Way *Web:* atlantic-group.com	Avenel	NJ	07001	732-574-0700		492
Atlantic Corporate Interiors Inc (ACI) 7001 Muirkirk Meadows Dr Ste A *Web:* www.aciinc.com	Beltsville	MD	20705	301-931-3600	931-3601	321
Atlantic Council 1030 15th St NW *Web:* www.atlanticcouncil.org	Washington	DC	20005	202-463-7226	463-7241	634
Atlantic County 5901 E Main St *Web:* www.atlantic-county.org	Mays Landing	NJ	08330	609-641-7867	625-4738	338
Atlantic County Historical Society Museum 907 Shore Rd *Web:* www.atlanticcountyhistoricalsocietynj.org	Somers Point	NJ	08244	609-927-5218		520
Atlantic County Library-Mays Landing 40 Farragut Ave *TF:* 800-852-7899 ■ *Web:* atlanticlibrary.org	Mays Landing	NJ	08330	609-625-2776	625-8143	434-3
Atlantic Credit & Finance Inc 3353 Orange Ave **Fax Area Code:* 540 ■ *TF:* 800-888-9419 ■ *Web:* www.atlanticcreditfinance.com	Roanoke	VA	24012	800-888-9419	772-7895*	160
Atlantic Design Engineers Inc 39 Pleasant St PO Box 1051 *Web:* atlanticcompanies.com	Sandwich	MA	02563	508-888-9282		261
Atlantic Dodge Chrysler Jeep 2330-40 US 1 S *TF:* 877-343-8775 ■ *Web:* atlanticdodgechryslerjeep.com	Saint Augustine	FL	32086	877-343-8775		57
Atlantic Escrow Corp 2111 Huntingtion Dr *Web:* atlanticescrow.com	San Marino	CA	91108	626-685-9688		653
Atlantic Eyrie Lodge 6 Norman Rd **Fax Area Code:* 207 ■ *TF:* 800-422-2883 ■ *Web:* www.atlanticeyrielodge.com	Bar Harbor	ME	04609	800-422-2883	288-8500*	379
Atlantic Fasteners Inc 106 Longale Rd *Web:* afast.com	Greensboro	NC	27409	336-852-0700		350
Atlantic Federal Credit Union 37 Market St *Web:* atlfedcu.com	Kenilworth	NJ	07033	908-245-1750		219
Atlantic Financial Federal Credit U Nion 40 Schilling Rd *TF:* 800-505-7476 ■ *Web:* affcu.org	Hunt Valley	MD	21031	410-584-7474		219
Atlantic Firearms LLC 10337 Bunting Rd *Web:* www.atlanticfirearms.com	Bishopville	MD	21813	410-352-5183	352-3374	711
Atlantic Forest Products LLC 7000 Forest Dr *TF:* 800-551-2374 ■ *Web:* www.atlanticforest.com	Sparrows Point	MD	21219	410-752-8092	625-1889	191-2
Atlantic Gasket Corp 3908 Frankford Ave *TF:* 800-229-8881 ■ *Web:* www.atlanticgasket.com	Philadelphia	PA	19124	215-533-6400	533-4130	326
Atlantic India Rubber Co 1437 Kentucky Rt 1428 **Fax Area Code:* 606 ■ *TF:* 800-476-6638 ■ *Web:* www.atlanticindia.com	Hagerhill	KY	41222	800-476-6638	789-9098*	677
Atlantic Information Services Inc 1100 17th St NW Ste 300 *TF:* 800-521-4323 ■ *Web:* aishealth.com	Washington	DC	20036	202-775-9008	331-9542	637-9
Atlantic Institute of Oriental Medicine Inc 100 E Broward Blvd Ste 100 *Web:* www.atom.edu	Fort Lauderdale	FL	33301	954-763-9840		167-3
Atlantic International University 900 Ft St Mall *TF:* 800-993-0066 ■ *Web:* www.aiu.edu	Honolulu	HI	96813	808-924-9567		166
Atlantic Lift Truck Inc 2945 Whittington Ave *TF:* 800-638-4566 ■ *Web:* www.atlanticlift.com	Baltimore	MD	21230	410-644-7777		385
Atlantic Lottery Corporation Information & Research Ctr 922 Main St PO Box 5500 *TF:* 800-561-3942 ■ *Web:* www.alc.ca	Moncton	NB	E1C8W6	506-867-5450	867-5616	434-3
Atlantic Medical Supply Inc 261 Suburban Ave Ste A *Web:* www.atlanticmedsupply.com	Deer Park	NY	11729	516-249-0191	249-1386	475
Atlantic Monthly Magazine 600 New Hampshire Ave NW *TF:* 800-234-2411 ■ *Web:* www.theatlantic.com	Washington	DC	20037	202-266-6000		457-11
Atlantic Oceanographic & Meteorological Laboratory (AOML) 4301 Rickenbacker Cswy *Web:* www.aoml.noaa.gov	Miami	FL	33149	305-361-4300	361-4449	668
Atlantic Oceanside Hotel & Event Ctr 119 Eden St Rte 3 *TF:* 800-336-2463 ■ *Web:* barharbormainehotel.com	Bar Harbor	ME	04609	207-288-5801	288-8402	669
Atlantic Pacific Industries (AP) 4223 W Jefferson Blvd *Web:* www.atlanticpacificind.com	Los Angeles	CA	90016	323-766-9075	766-8866	351
Atlantic Packaging Co 806 N 23rd St *TF:* 800-722-5841 ■ *Web:* www.atlanticpkg.com	Wilmington	NC	28405	910-343-0624		553
Atlantic Palace Suites Hotel 1507 Boardwalk *Web:* www.atlanticpalacesuites.com	Atlantic City	NJ	08401	609-344-1200	345-0733	379
Atlantic Paper & Twine Company Inc 85 York Ave *TF:* 800-613-0950 ■ *Web:* www.atlanticpaper.com	Pawtucket	RI	02860	401-725-0950		559
Atlantic Personnel Search Inc 9624 Pennsylvania Ave *TF:* 877-229-5254 ■ *Web:* www.atlanticpersonnel.com	Upper Marlboro	MD	20772	301-599-2108		193
Atlantic Pharmaceuticals Inc 1 Glenlake Pkwy Ste 700 *Web:* www.atlanticpharma.com	Atlanta	GA	30328	404-994-5190		743
Atlantic Premium Shutters 29797 Beck Rd *TF:* 866-288-2726 ■ *Web:* www.atlanticpremiumshutters.com	Wixom	MI	48393	800-521-8486		699
Atlantic Promotions (AP) 1405 Eastbrooke Way 1st Fl *TF:* 877-442-4828 ■ *Web:* www.atlanticpromotions.com	Marietta	GA	30066	770-565-9906	321-4738	328
Atlantic Prsnnel Tnant Scrning Inc 8895 N Military Trl Ste 301C *TF:* 877-747-2104 ■ *Web:* www.atlanticscreening.com	Palm Beach Gardens	FL	33410	561-776-1804	776-1565	196
Atlantic Publishing Co 315 E Washington St **Fax Area Code:* 352 ■ *TF:* 800-814-1132 ■ *Web:* www.atlantic-pub.com	Starke	FL	32091	800-814-1132	622-1875*	637-2
Atlantic Realty Consultants Inc 8150 Leesburg Pk Ste 1100 *Web:* arcrealty.com	Vienna	VA	22182	703-760-9500		652
Atlantic Realty Partners Inc 3500 Lenox Rd One Alliance Ctr Ste 1250 *Web:* www.goarp.com	Atlanta	GA	30326	404-591-2900	591-2901	652
Atlantic Relocation Systems Inc 1314 Chattahoochee Ave NW *TF:* 800-241-1140 ■ *Web:* www.atlanticrelocation.com	Atlanta	GA	30318	404-351-5311	350-6530	519
Atlantic Ridge Telecasters Inc 4206 Bridges St Ext Ste B *Web:* wtkf107.com	Morehead City	NC	28557	252-247-6343		741-99
Atlantic Salmon Federation (ASF) PO Box 5200 *TF:* 800-565-5666 ■ *Web:* www.asf.ca	Saint Andrews	NB	E5B3S8	506-529-1033		48-3
Atlantic Sands Hotel 1 Baltimore Ave *TF:* 800-422-0600 ■ *Web:* www.atlanticsandshotel.com	Rehoboth Beach	DE	19971	302-227-2511		379
Atlantic Scale Company Inc 136 Washington Ave *Web:* atlanticscale.com	Nutley	NJ	07110	973-661-7090	661-3651	361
Atlantic School of Theology 660 Francklyn St *Web:* www.astheology.ns.ca	Halifax	NS	B3H3B5	902-423-6939	492-4048	167-3
Atlantic Services Group Inc 4200 Wisconsin Ave NW Ste 500 *Web:* www.asgpark.com	Washington	DC	20016	202-466-5050		441
Atlantic Sign Media Inc 111 Trail One Ste 101 *Web:* www.atlanticsignmedia.com	Burlington	NC	27215	336-584-1375	584-3848	701

				Phone	Fax	Class
Atlantic Software Technologies Inc						
340 Madison Ave 19th Fl	New York	NY	10173	212-682-4160		177
TF: 800-381-8576 ■ *Web:* www.astworld.com						
Atlantic Spas & Billiards						
8721 Glenwood Ave	Raleigh	NC	27617	919-783-7447	783-0146	375
TF: 800-849-8827 ■ *Web:* www.atlanticspasandbilliards.com						
Atlantic Speakers Bureau						
980 Rt 730	Scotch Ridge	NB	E3L5L2	506-465-0990		708
Web: atlanticspeakersbureau.com						
Atlantic Sportswear Inc						
36 Waldron Way	Portland	ME	04103	207-797-5028		687
Web: atlanticsportswear.com						
Atlantic Street Veterinary Hospitals						
1100 Atlantic St	Roseville	CA	95678	916-783-4655		794
Web: www.atlanticstreet.ethosvet.com						
Atlantic Surplus USA						
8209 Market St Ste A256	Wilmington	NC	28411	910-367-5899		812
Web: www.atlanticsurplus.com						
Atlantic Tape & Packaging						
100 Gardner Pk Ste 200	Peachtree City	GA	30269	770-461-3557	461-1378	557
Web: www.atlantictape.com						
Atlantic Technical Ctr						
4700 Coconut Creek Pkwy	Coconut Creek	FL	33063	754-321-5166	321-5380	167-3
Web: www.atlantictechnicalcollege.edu						
Atlantic Teleconnect Inc (ATI)						
2529 Commerce Pky	North Port	FL	34289	941-429-8484		253
TF: 800-327-4642 ■ *Web:* www.aticonnect.com						
Atlantic Testing Laboratories Ltd						
6431 US Hwy 11	Canton	NY	13617	315-386-4578	386-1012	261
Web: www.atlantictesting.com						
Atlantic Tire 7307 Pulaski Hwy	Baltimore	MD	21237	410-866-6400		755
Web: www.atlantictire.net						
Atlantic Tire & Supply Company Inc						
1430 St Georges Ave	Avenel	NJ	07001	732-381-0100		57
Web: www.atlantictirenj.com						
Atlantic Tool & Die Co (ATD)						
19963 Progress Dr	Strongsville	OH	44149	440-238-6931		488
Web: atlantictool.com						
Atlantic Tower Group of Companies Inc						
6260 Pine Slash Rd	Mechanicsville	VA	23116	804-559-6004	559-6041	170
Web: www.atlantic-tower.com						
Atlantic Track & Turnout Co						
270 N Broad St	Bloomfield	NJ	07003	973-748-5885	748-4520	770
TF: 800-631-1274 ■ *Web:* www.atlantictrack.com						
Atlantic Union College						
338 Main St	South Lancaster	MA	01561	978-368-2000	368-2517	166
TF: 800-282-2030 ■ *Web:* www.auc.edu						
Atlantic Valuation Consultants LLC						
25 Country Club Rd Unit 704	Gilford	NH	03249	603-279-9001	279-7085	196
Web: www.atlanticvaluation.com						
Atlantic Veal & Lamb Inc						
275 Morgan Ave	Brooklyn	NY	11211	718-599-6400		473
Web: www.atlanticvealandlamb.com						
Atlantic Ventilating & Equipment Co						
125 Sebethe Dr	Cromwell	CT	06416	860-635-1300		697
Web: atlanticventilating.com						
Atlantic Webworks & Consulting Inc						
331 S Swing Rd	Greensboro	NC	27409	336-855-8572		180
Web: www.atlanticwebworks.com						
Atlantic Wildfowl Heritage Museum						
1113 Atlantic Ave	Virginia Beach	VA	23451	757-437-8432	437-9950	520
Web: www.awhm.org						
Atlantic Zeiser Inc						
15 Patton Dr	West Caldwell	NJ	07006	973-228-0800	228-9064	111
Web: www.atlanticzeiser.com						
Atlantic, The						
601 N Ft Lauderdale Beach Blvd	Fort Lauderdale	FL	33304	954-567-8020	567-8040	379
Web: www.atlantichotelfl.com						
Atlanticare Regional Medical Ctr						
1925 Pacific Ave	Atlantic City	NJ	08401	609-344-4081		374-3
Web: atlanticare.org						
Atlantic-Pacific Capital Inc						
102 Greenwich Ave 2nd Fl	Greenwich	CT	06830	203-862-9182		401
Web: www.apcap.com						
Atlantis Adventures LLC						
Atlantis Submarines Waikiki - 252 Paoa Pl	Honolulu	HI	96815	808-973-9800		760
TF: 800-548-6262 ■ *Web:* www.atlantisadventures.com						
Atlantis Casino Resort						
3800 S Virginia St	Reno	NV	89502	775-825-4700		669
TF: 800-723-6500 ■ *Web:* www.atlantiscasino.com						
Atlantis Restaurant 3648 King St	Alexandria	VA	22302	703-671-0250		671
Web: alexandriaitalianfood.com						
Atlantis Software Inc						
34740 Blackstone Way	Fremont	CA	94555	510-796-2180		179
Web: www.atlantissoftware.com						
Atlantix Global Systems 1 Sun Ct	Norcross	GA	30092	770-248-7700	448-7726	174
TF: 888-400-6994 ■ *Web:* www.atlantixglobal.com						
Atlas Advertising LLC 1128 Grant St	Denver	CO	80203	303-292-3300		7
TF: 800-543-4402 ■ *Web:* www.atlas-integrated.com						
Atlas Advisors LLC						
140 E 45th St 18th Fl	New York	NY	10017	212-471-4100		690
Web: www.atlasadvisors.com						
Atlas Air Worldwide Holdings Inc						
2000 Westchester Ave	Purchase	NY	10577	914-701-8000	701-8001	12
NASDAQ: AAWW ■ *TF:* 866-434-1617 ■ *Web:* www.atlasair.com						
Atlas Aircraft Ctr						
115 Flight Line Ave	Portsmouth	NH	03801	603-501-7700		23
TF: 866-214-1212 ■ *Web:* www.planesense.com						
Atlas Automation Inc						
2450 W Ridge Rd Ste 300	Rochester	NY	14626	585-227-1110		177
Web: atlas-automation.com						
Atlas Aviation Tampa						
Peter O Knight Airport 825 Severn Ave	Tampa	FL	33606	813-251-1752	251-0731	167-3
Web: atlasaviation.com						
Atlas Bistro						
2515 N Scottsdale Rd Ste 18	Scottsdale	AZ	85257	480-990-2433		671
Web: www.azeats.com						
Atlas Bolt & Screw Co 1628 Troy Rd	Ashland	OH	44805	419-289-6171	289-2564	278
TF: 800-321-6977 ■ *Web:* www.atlasfasteners.com						
Atlas Bronze 445 Bunting Ave	Trenton	NJ	08611	800-478-0887		492
TF: 800-478-0887 ■ *Web:* www.atlasbronze.com						
Atlas Brown Investment Advisors Inc						
333 E Main St - 400	Louisville	KY	40202	502-271-2900		194
TF: 866-871-0334 ■ *Web:* www.atlasbrown.com						
Atlas Butler Heating & Cooling						
4849 Evanswood Dr	Columbus	OH	43229	614-294-8600		610
TF: 800-387-6223 ■ *Web:* atlasbutler.com						
Atlas Carpet Mills Inc						
2200 Saybrook Ave	Los Angeles	CA	90040	323-724-9000	724-4526	131
TF: 800-272-8527 ■ *Web:* www.atlascarpetmills.com						
Atlas Concrete Products						
65 Burritt St	New Britain	CT	06053	860-224-2244	224-2255	360-3
TF: 800-774-1112 ■ *Web:* atlasconcrete.com						
Atlas Construction Supply Inc						
4640 Brinnell St	San Diego	CA	92111	858-277-2100	277-0585	191-1
TF: 877-588-2100 ■ *Web:* www.atlasform.com						
Atlas Container Corp 8140 Telegraph Rd	Severn	MD	21144	410-551-6300	551-2703	100
TF: 800-394-4894 ■ *Web:* www.atlascontainer.com						
Atlas Copco North America LLC						
7 Campus Dr Ste 200	Parsippany	NJ	07054	973-397-3400		360-3
TF: 800-732-6762 ■ *Web:* www.atlascopco.com						
Atlas Design & Engineering Inc						
12800 University Dr Ste 402	Fort Myers	FL	33907	239-267-7432		261
Web: atlasdesignengineering.com						
Atlas Distributing Corp						
44 Southbridge St	Auburn	MA	01501	508-791-6221		81-1
TF: 800-649-6221 ■ *Web:* www.atlasdistributing.com						
Atlas Environmental Services Inc						
9032 Olive Dr	Spring Valley	CA	91977	619-463-1707		776
Web: www.atlastree.com						
Atlas Flooring 2971 India St	San Diego	CA	92103	619-299-9695	299-8488	361
Web: www.atlasflooring.com						
Atlas Foundry Company Inc						
601 N Henderson Ave	Marion	IN	46952	765-662-2525	662-2902	307
Web: www.atlasfdry.com						
Atlas Heating & Ventilating Co						
407 Cabot St	South San Francisco	CA	94080	650-873-7000		612
Web: atlasheat.com						
Atlas Industrial Holdings LLC						
5275 Sinclair Rd	Columbus	OH	43229	614-841-4500		207
Web: www.atlascos.com						
Atlas Legal Research Lp						
14241 Dallas Pkwy Ste 650	Dallas	TX	75254	214-526-8811		428
Web: www.atlaslegal.com						
Atlas Machine & Supply Inc						
7000 Global Dr	Louisville	KY	40258	502-584-7262		454
TF: 855-462-8527 ■ *Web:* atlasmachine.com						
Atlas Machining & Welding Inc						
777 Smith Ln	Northampton	PA	18067	610-262-1374		757
Web: www.atlasmw.com						
Atlas Match LLC 1801 S Airport Cir	Euless	TX	76040	817-354-7474		9
TF: 800-628-2426 ■ *Web:* atlasmatch.com						
Atlas Metal Industries 1135 NW 159th Dr	Miami	FL	33169	305-625-2451	623-0475	298
TF: 800-762-7565 ■ *Web:* atlasfoodserv.com						
Atlas Minerals & Chemicals Inc						
1227 Valley Rd	Mertztown	PA	19539	610-682-7171	682-9200	3
TF: 800-523-8269 ■ *Web:* www.atlasmin.com						
Atlas Model Railroad Company Inc						
378 Florence Ave	Hillside	NJ	07205	908-687-0880	687-8857	762
TF: 800-872-2521 ■ *Web:* shop.atlasrr.com						
Atlas Molded Products						
8240 Byron Center Rd SW	Byron Center	MI	49315	800-917-9138	878-9942*	600
**Fax Area Code:* 616 ■ *TF:* 800-917-9138 ■ *Web:* www.atlasmoldedproducts.com						
Atlas Oil Co 24501 Ecorse Rd	Taylor	MI	48180	313-292-5500	731-0264	579
TF: 800-878-2000 ■ *Web:* www.atlasoil.com						
Atlas Pacific Engineering Co						
1 Atlas Ave	Pueblo	CO	81001	719-948-3040		298
TF: 800-588-5438 ■ *Web:* www.atlaspacific.com						
Atlas Performing Arts Ctr						
1333 H St NE	Washington	DC	20002	202-399-7993		708
Web: www.atlasarts.org						
Atlas Precision Sheetmetal Solutions						
2950 Weeks Ave SE	Minneapolis	MN	55414	612-331-2566	331-1295	697
Web: www.atlasmfg.com						
Atlas Premium Finance Co						
1110 W Commercial Blvd Ste 300	Fort Lauderdale	FL	33309	800-425-9113		216
TF: 800-425-9113 ■ *Web:* www.atlaspfc.com						
Atlas Railroad Construction LLC						
1370 Washington Pk Ste 202	Bridgeville	PA	15017	412-677-2020		188-8
Atlas Refinery Inc 142 Lockwood St	Newark	NJ	07105	973-589-2002	589-7377	145
Web: www.atlasrefinery.com						
Atlas Roofing Corp 2322 Valley Rd	Meridian	MS	39307	601-483-7111	483-7344	46
TF: 800-478-0258 ■ *Web:* www.atlasroofing.com						
Atlas Scientific Technologies Inc						
2430 University Blvd W	Jacksonville	FL	32217	904-731-0241		194
Web: www.atlasscitech.com						
Atlas Sheet Metal Inc 19 Musick	Irvine	CA	92618	949-600-8787		610
Web: atlassheetmetal.com						
Atlas Sound 1601 Jack McKay Blvd	Ennis	TX	75119	800-876-3333	765-3435	52
TF: 800-876-3333 ■ *Web:* www.atlasied.com						
Atlas Spring Service 3535 E 7th St	Austin	TX	78702	512-385-3661	385-6863	62-5
Web: www.atlasspringservice.com						
Atlas Steel Products Co						
7990 Bavaria Rd	Twinsburg	OH	44087	330-425-1600	425-1611	492
TF: 800-444-1682 ■ *Web:* www.atlassteel.com						
Atlas Systems Inc						
5712 Cleveland St Ste 200	Virginia Beach	VA	23462	757-467-7872		177
TF: 800-567-7401 ■ *Web:* www.atlas-sys.com						
Atlas Technologies Inc 3100 Cotter Ave	Fenton	MI	48430	810-629-6663	629-8145	456
Web: www.atlastechnologies.com						
Atlas Testing Laboratories Inc						
9820 Sixth St	Rancho Cucamonga	CA	91730	909-373-4130	373-4132	743
Web: www.atlastesting.com						
Atlas Tool & Die Works Inc						
4633 Lawndale Ave	Lyons	IL	60534	708-442-1661	442-0016	488
Web: atlas-tool.com						
Atlas Tool Inc 29880 Groesbeck Hwy	Roseville	MI	48066	586-778-3570	778-3931	757
Web: www.atlastool.com						

Name / Address	City	State	ZIP	Phone	Fax	Class
Atlas Transfer and Storage Co 13026 Stowe Dr Ste A *TF:* 800-854-2938 ■ *Web:* www.atlasallied.com	Poway	CA	92064	858-513-3800	513-3900	519
Atlas Travel & Technology Group Inc 200 Donald Lynch Blvd Ste 323 *TF:* 800-362-8626 ■ *Web:* www.atlastravel.com	Marlborough	MA	01752	508-488-1100		775
Atlas Tube 1855 E 122nd St *TF:* 800-733-5683 ■ *Web:* www.atlastube.com	Chicago	IL	60633	773-646-4500	646-6128	490
Atlas Tubular LP 1710 S Hwy 77 *Web:* www.atlastubular.com	Robstown	TX	78380	361-387-7505	387-4613	490
Atlas Van Lines Inc 1212 St George Rd *TF:* 800-638-9797 ■ *Web:* www.atlasvanlines.com	Evansville	IN	47711	812-424-2222	421-7129	519
Atlas Wall Cl Board 2000 RiverEdge Pky Ste 800 *Web:* wall.atlasrwi.com	Atlanta	GA	30328	678-640-1580		189-9
AtlasPower Inc 10 Futurity Pl *Web:* www.atlaspower.com	Tijeras	NM	87059	505-286-9625		261
Atlatl Inc 3000 Croasdaile Dr 2nd Fl	Durham	NC	27701	919-384-0514		177
Atlee Hall LLP 415 N Duke St *TF:* 800-924-2309 ■ *Web:* atleehall.com	Lancaster	PA	17602	717-740-8629		41
ATLSS (Advanced Technology for Large Structural Systems Ctr) 117 ATLSS Dr *Web:* www.atlss.lehigh.edu	Bethlehem	PA	18015	610-758-3525	758-5902	668
Atlus USA Inc 6400 Oak Canyon Ste 100 *Web:* www.atlus.com	Irvine	CA	92618	949-788-0455	788-0433	553
Atm Merchant Systems 1667 Helm Dr *TF:* 888-878-8166 ■ *Web:* atmms.com	Las Vegas	NV	89119	702-837-8787		69
ATMA (American Textile Machinery Assn) 201 Park Washington Ct *Web:* www.atmanet.org	Falls Church	VA	22046	703-538-1789		49-13
Atmac Mechanical Services LP 1201 Summit Ave *Web:* www.atmac.com	Plano	TX	75074	214-428-1544		189-10
Atma-Sphere Music Systems 1742 Selby Ave *Web:* www.atma-sphere.com	Saint Paul	MN	55104	651-690-2246		52
Atmos Energy Corp PO Box 650205 *NYSE:* ATO ■ *TF:* 888-286-6700 ■ *Web:* www.atmosenergy.com	Dallas	TX	75265	972-934-9227		360-5
Atmos Tech Industries LLC 1108 Pollack Ave *Web:* www.atmostech.com	Ocean City	NJ	07712	732-493-8400		186
Atmosphere 1620 Piedmont Ave *Web:* www.atmospherebistro.com	Atlanta	GA	30324	678-702-1620		671
ATN (Asian Television Network) 330 Cochrane Dr *Web:* www.asiantelevision.com	Markham	ON	L3R8E4	905-948-8199	948-8108	740
AT-NET Services Inc 3401 St Vardell Ln Ste D *TF:* 866-708-0886 ■ *Web:* www.expertip.net	Charlotte	NC	28217	704-831-2500		396
AtNetPlus Inc 1000 Campus Dr Ste 700 *Web:* atnetplus.com	Stow	OH	44224	330-945-5685		225
ATO (Alpha Tau Omega Fraternity) 1 N Pennsylvania St 12th Fl *TF:* 800-798-9286 ■ *Web:* www.ato.org	Indianapolis	IN	46204	317-684-1865	684-1862	48-16
Atoka County PO Box 900 *Web:* atokaok.org	Atoka	OK	74525	580-889-3341	889-7584	338
Atom Group, The 33 Jewell Ct *Web:* www.theatomgroup.com	Portsmouth	NH	03801	603-501-0003		226
Atom Precision of America Inc 5410 Newport Dr Ste 27 *TF:* 844-468-2866 ■ *Web:* atomprecision.com	Rolling Meadows	IL	60008	844-468-2866		261
Atomic Aquatics Inc 3585 Cadillac Ave B *Web:* atomicaquatics.com	Costa Mesa	CA	92647	714-375-1433		711
Atomic Cartoons Inc 112 W Sixth Sve *Web:* atomiccartoons.com	Vancouver	BC	V5Y1K6	604-734-2866		33
Atomic Design 277 Alexander St Ste 208 *Web:* www.atomicdesign.net	Rochester	NY	14607	585-271-8661		195
Atomic Imaging Inc 1501 N Magnolia Ave *Web:* www.atomicimaging.com	Chicago	IL	60642	312-649-1800	642-7441	225
Atomic Loudspeakers 2311 Sturgis Rd *Web:* www.atomicspeakers.com	Oxnard	CA	93030	805-278-4087	278-4089	52
Atomic Object LLC 941 Wealthy St SE *Web:* atomicobject.com	Grand Rapids	MI	49506	616-776-6020		177
Atomic Testing Museum 755 E Flamingo Rd *Web:* www.nationalatomictestingmuseum.org	Las Vegas	NV	89119	702-794-5151		520
Atomic USA 2030 Lincoln Ave **Fax Area Code:* 801 ■ *TF:* 800-258-5020 ■ *Web:* www.atomic.com	Ogden	UT	84401	800-258-5020	334-4503*	710
AtomicLeads.com 4926 Windy Hill Dr *Web:* www.atomicleads.com	Raleigh	NC	27609	919-439-4900		195
Atom-Jet Industries Ltd 2110 Park Ave *TF:* 800-573-5048 ■ *Web:* www.atomjet.com	Brandon	MB	R7B0R9	800-573-5048		273
Atos Syntel Inc 525 E Big Beaver Rd Ste 300 *Web:* www.atos-syntel.net	Troy	MI	48083	248-619-2800	619-2888	180
Atossa Therapeutics 107 Spring St *Web:* atossatherapeutics.com	Seattle	WA	98104	206-588-0256		582
Atotech USA Inc 1750 Overview Dr *Web:* www.atotech.com	Rock Hill	SC	29730	803-817-3500	817-3602	253
AtoZdatabases com PO Box 27757 *TF:* 877-428-0101 ■ *Web:* www.atozdatabases.com	Omaha	NE	68127	877-428-0101		393
ATP (Academic Therapy Publications) 20 Commercial Blvd **Fax Area Code:* 888 ■ *TF:* 800-422-7249 ■ *Web:* www.academictherapy.com	Novato	CA	94949	415-883-3314	287-9975*	637-2
ATP (American Trust Publications) 721 Enterprise Dr *Web:* islamicbookservice.org	Oak Brook	IL	60523	630-789-9191	789-9455	637-2
ATP (Alretta Truck Parts Inc) 1 Watson Pl Bldg 5B 2nd Fl *Web:* www.alretta.com	Framingham	MA	01701	508-788-9409	788-9499	61
ATP Americas 201 ATP Tour Blvd *Web:* www.atptour.com	Ponte Vedra Beach	FL	32082	904-285-8000	285-5966	48-22
ATP Electronics Inc 2590 N First St Ste 150 *Web:* www.atpinc.com	San Jose	CA	95131	408-732-5000	732-5055	173-8
ATP Manufacturing LLC 761 Great Rd	North Smithfield	RI	02896	401-767-3100		301
ATP Oil & Gas Corp 4600 Post Oak Pl Ste 200	Houston	TX	77027	713-622-3311		536
ATPCO (Airline Tariff Publishing Co) 45005 Aviation Dr *Web:* www.atpco.net	Dulles	VA	20166	703-471-7510	661-8061	16
ATR (Americans for Tax Reform) 722 12th St NW Ste 4 *Web:* atr.org	Washington	DC	20005	202-785-0266	785-0261	48-8
ATR Inc 6405 Cypresswood Dr Ste 250 *Web:* www.atrco.com	Spring	TX	77379	281-370-9540		809
ATRA (Automatic Transmission Rebuilders Assn) 2400 Latigo Ave *TF:* 866-464-2872 ■ *Web:* www.atra.com	Oxnard	CA	93030	805-604-2000	604-2003	49-21
ATRA (American Therapeutic Recreation Assn) 11130 Sunrise Valley Dr Ste 350 *Web:* www.atra-online.com	Reston	VA	20191	703-234-4140	435-4390	48-17
ATRA (American Tort Reform Assn) 1101 Connecticut Ave NW Ste 400 *Web:* www.atra.org	Washington	DC	20036	202-682-1163	682-1022	49-10
ATRAHAN Transformation Inc 860 Chemin Des Acadiens *Web:* www.atrahan.com	Yamachiche	QC	G0X3L0	819-296-3791		473
Atrex Inc 1633 Farm Way Ste 505 *TF:* 800-874-4505 ■ *Web:* www.atrexinc.com	Middleburg	FL	32068	904-264-9086		647
Atria 137 Main St PO Box 561 *Web:* www.atriamv.com	Edgartown	MA	02539	508-627-5850		671
Atria Senior Living Inc 801 Cypress Way *Web:* www.atriaseniorliving.com	San Dimas	CA	91773	626-275-4376		672
AtriCure Inc 6217 Centre Pk Dr *NASDAQ:* ATRC ■ *TF:* 888-347-6403 ■ *Web:* www.atricure.com	West Chester	OH	45069	513-755-4100	755-4567	85
Atrilogy Solutions Group Inc 23422 Mill Creek Dr Ste C 105 **Fax Area Code:* 888 ■ *Web:* www.atrilogy.com	Laguna Hills	CA	92653	949-777-4700	716-5759*	463
ATRIO Health Plans 2270 NW Aviation Dr Ste 3 *TF:* 800-735-2900 ■ *Web:* www.atriohp.com	Roseburg	OR	97470	541-672-8620	672-8670	391-3
Atrion Corp 1 Allentown Pkwy *NASDAQ:* ATRI ■ *Web:* www.atrioncorp.com	Allen	TX	75002	972-390-9800	396-7581	476
Atrion Medical Products Inc 1426 Curt Francis Rd *Web:* www.atrionmedical.com	Arab	AL	35016	256-317-2123		596
Atris Inc 1151 S Trooper Rd Ste E *TF:* 800-724-3384 ■ *Web:* www.atris.biz	Norristown	PA	19403	800-724-3384		735
Atrium Health University City 8800 N Tryon St *TF:* 800-821-1535 ■ *Web:* atriumhealth.org	Charlotte	NC	28262	704-863-6000	863-6236	374-3
Atrium Hotel 18700 MacArthur Blvd *TF:* 800-854-3012 ■ *Web:* atriumhotel.com	Irvine	CA	92612	949-833-2770		379
Atrium Medical Corp 5 Wentworth Dr *TF:* 800-528-7486 ■ *Web:* www.atriummed.com	Hudson	NH	03051	603-880-1433	880-6718	476
Atrium Medical Ctr 1 Medical Center Dr *TF:* 866-608-3463 ■ *Web:* www.premierhealth.com	Middletown	OH	45005	513-424-2111		374-3
Atrium Staffing Services Ltd 71 Fifth Ave 3rd Fl *Web:* www.atriumstaff.com	New York	NY	10003	212-292-0550		260
Atrium Windows & Doors 3890 W NW Hwy Ste 500 *TF:* 800-938-1000 ■ *Web:* www.atrium.com	Dallas	TX	75220	214-630-5757		234
Atrixware LLC 141 S Black Horse Pk Ste 1 *TF:* 866-696-8709 ■ *Web:* atrixware.com	Blackwood	NJ	08012	866-696-8709		177
ATS (American Thoracic Society) 61 Broadway 4th Fl *Web:* www.thoracic.org	New York	NY	10006	212-315-8600	315-6498	49-8
ATS (Association of Theological Schools in the US & Canada) 10 Summit Pk Dr *Web:* www.ats.edu	Pittsburgh	PA	15275	412-788-6505	788-6510	49-5
ATS (Anderson Tile Sales Inc) 1703 S Midkiff Rd *Web:* www.andersontile.net	Midland	TX	79701	432-683-5116		191-1
ATS (Aviation Technical Services) 3121 109th St SW *TF:* 888-347-2341 ■ *Web:* atsmro.com	Everett	WA	98204	425-347-3030		24
ATS (Alco Tool Supply Inc) 54847 County Rd 17 *TF:* 800-437-2911 ■ *Web:* www.alcotoolsupply.com	Elkhart	IN	46516	574-295-5535	293-2254	351
ATS All Tire Supply Co 6600 Long Point Rd Ste 101 *TF:* 888-339-6665 ■ *Web:* www.alltiresupply.com	Houston	TX	77055	888-339-6665		54
ATS Group LLC 1200 Atwater Dr Ste 170 *TF:* 855-465-6858 ■ *Web:* theatsgroup.com	Malvern	PA	19355	855-465-6858		196
ATS Inc 7620 Penn Belt Dr *Web:* www.atsinconline.com	Forestville	MD	20747	301-735-3001	735-6829	351
ATS Systems Inc 30222 Esperanza *TF:* 800-321-1833 ■ *Web:* www.ats-s.com	Rancho Santa Margarita	CA	92688	949-888-1744		697
ATS Systems Oregon Inc 2121 NE Jack London St *Web:* www.atsautomation.com	Corvallis	OR	97330	541-758-3329		386
ATS Tech Solutions Inc 2550 Limestone Pky Ste F *Web:* www.atstech.net	Gainesville	GA	30501	770-538-2900		175
Atscott Manufacturing Company Inc 1150 Holstein Dr NE *Web:* www.atscott.com	Pine City	MN	55063	320-629-2501		757
At-Sea Processors Assn (APA) 4039 21st Ave W Ste 400 *Web:* www.atsea.org	Seattle	WA	98199	206-285-5139	285-1841	49-6
Atser LP 1150 Richcrest Dr *TF:* 888-241-8702 ■ *Web:* atser-eng.com	Houston	TX	77060	281-999-9961		261

Name / Address	City	State	Zip	Phone	Fax	Class
ATSI (Alloy Tool Steel Inc) 13525 E Freeway Dr *TF:* 800-288-9800 ■ *Web:* www.alloytoolsteel.com	Santa Fe Springs	CA	90670	562-921-8605	802-1728	492
ATSI Inc 415 Commerce Dr. *Web:* atsi.com	Amherst	NY	14228	716-691-9200		261
Atsim Inc 1825 George Ave Ste 1F	Annapolis	MD	21401	410-990-1711		261
ATSSA (American Traffic Safety Services Assn) 15 Riverside Pkwy Ste 100 *TF:* 800-272-8772 ■ *Web:* www.atssa.com	Fredericksburg	VA	22406	540-368-1701	368-1717	49-21
ATT Metrology Services Inc 30210 SE 79th St Ste 100 *TF:* 888-320-7011 ■ *Web:* www.attinc.com	Issaquah	WA	98027	425-867-5356		23
Attac Consulting Group 301 E Liberty St Ste 605 *Web:* www.attacconsulting.com	Ann Arbor	MI	48104	734-214-2990		196
Attachments International Inc 9 Industrial Park Dr. *Web:* www.attachments.com	Pelican Rapids	MN	56572	218-863-6444		190
Attala County 230 W Washington St *Web:* www.attalacounty.net	Kosciusko	MS	39090	662-289-2921	289-7662	338
Attaway Inc 1700 W Whitner St. *TF:* 800-868-4807 ■ *Web:* www.attawayprinting.com	Anderson	SC	29622	864-225-1286	224-8483	535
Attc Manufacturing Inc 10455 State Rd 37 *Web:* attcmfg.com	Tell City	IN	47586	812-547-5060	547-8390	247
Attema Sales Inc 117 E 13th St *Web:* attemasales.com	Pella	IA	50219	641-628-1787		195
Attendee Management Inc 15572 Ranch Rd 12 Ste 1 *TF:* 877-947-5174 ■ *Web:* attendeenet.com	Wimberley	TX	78676	512-847-5174		624
Attention Plus Care 1580 Makaloa St Ste 1060 *Web:* www.attentionplus.com	Honolulu	HI	96814	808-739-2811	739-0169	363
Attention Software Inc 1925 Dominion Way Ste 200 *Web:* www.attentionsoftware.com	Colorado Springs	CO	80909	719-591-9110		180
Attentive 156 Fifth Ave Ste 303 *Web:* attentivemobile.com	New York	NY	10010	610-308-6468		39
Attic, The 3441 E Broadway *Web:* www.theatticonbroadway.com	Long Beach	CA	90803	562-433-0153		671
Attica Correctional Facility 639 Exchange St. *Web:* www.doccs.ny.gov	Attica	NY	14011	585-591-2000		213
Attica Hydraulic Exchange Inc 48175 Gratiot Ave *TF:* 800-422-4279 ■ *Web:* www.ahx1.com	Chesterfield	MI	48051	586-949-4240		358
Attleboro Municipal Efcu 138 S Main St. *Web:* attleborofcu.com	Attleboro	MA	02703	508-226-0140		219
Attleboro Public Library 74 N Main St *Web:* www.sailsinc.org	Attleboro	MA	02703	508-222-0157	226-3326	434-3
Attlesey Storm LLP 2552 Walnut Ave Ste 100 *Web:* attleseystorm.com	Tustin	CA	92780	714-508-4949	508-0015	41
ATTO Technology Inc 155 CrossPoint Pky *Web:* attotech.com	Amherst	NY	14221	716-691-1999	691-9353	173-1
Attorney Aid Divorce & Bankruptcy Center Inc 3605 Long Beach Blvd Ste 300 *TF:* 877-905-5297 ■ *Web:* www.attorneyaid.com	Long Beach	CA	90807	562-988-0885		428
Attorney Dean Boyd PLLC 4423 SW 45th Ave *TF:* 844-332-6269 ■ *Web:* deanboyd.com	Amarillo	TX	79109	806-242-3333		41
Attorney Resource 1919 McKinney Ave Ste 100 *Web:* www.attorneyresource.com	Dallas	TX	75201	214-922-8050	871-3041	721
Attorney's Title Insurance Fund Inc 6545 Corporate Center Blvd *TF:* 800-336-3863 ■ *Web:* www.thefund.com	Orlando	FL	32822	407-240-3863		391-6
Attraction Inc 672 Rue du Parc *TF:* 800-567-6095 ■ *Web:* www.attraction.com	Lac-Drolet	QC	G0Y1C0	819-549-2477	549-2734	155-3
Attraction Media Inc 5455 de Gaspe Ave Ste 805 *Web:* www.attraction.ca	Montreal	QC	H2T3B3	514-846-1222		514
Attronica Computers Inc 15867 Gaither Dr **Fax Area Code: 240* ■ *Web:* www.attronica.com	Gaithersburg	MD	20877	301-417-0070	454-6494*	180
Attune Foods Inc 2600 Prairie Rd. *Web:* www.attunefoods.com	Eugene	OR	97402	415-486-2101		296-25
Attune Insurance 40 Exchange Pl Ste 410 *TF:* 888-530-4650 ■ *Web:* www.attuneinsurance.com	New York	NY	10005	888-530-4650		360-4
Attwood Corp 1016 N Monroe St. *TF:* 844-808-5704 ■ *Web:* www.attwoodmarine.com	Lowell	MI	49331	616-897-9241	897-8358	350
ATU (Amalgamated Transit Union) 10000 New Hampshire Ave. *TF:* 888-240-1196 ■ *Web:* www.atu.org	Silver Spring	MD	20903	202-537-1645	244-7824	414
Atul USA Inc 6917 Shannon Willow Rd Ste 400 *Web:* www.atul.co.in	Charlotte	NC	28226	704-540-8460		146
A-Tune Software Inc 19621 Fm 1431 Ste 402 *Web:* a-tune.de	Jonestown	TX	78645	512-243-8539		177
ATV Bakery Inc 36 S 3rd St. *TF:* 800-422-8364 ■ *Web:* atvbakery.com	Reading	PA	19602	610-374-5577	374-5930	296-1
ATW (American Trails West) 92 Middle Neck Rd *TF:* 800-645-6260 ■ *Web:* www.atwteentours.com	Great Neck	NY	11021	516-487-2800	487-2855	760
ATW Companies Inc 55 Service Ave. *Web:* www.atwcompanies.com	Warwick	RI	02886	401-739-0740		492
Atwater Brewing Co 237 Joseph Campau Ave *Web:* www.atwaterbeer.com	Detroit	MI	48207	313-877-9205		671
Atwater Chamber of Commerce 1181 Third St *TF:* 844-269-9688 ■ *Web:* atwaterchamberofcommerce.com	Atwater	CA	95301	209-358-4251		139
Atwater Kent Museum 15 S Seventh St *Web:* www.philadelphiahistory.org	Philadelphia	PA	19106	215-685-4830	685-4837	520
Atwill, Troxell & Leigh PC 50 Catoctin Cir NE Ste 303 *Web:* atandlpc.com	Leesburg	VA	20176	703-777-4000	777-4001	41
Atwood & Cherny PC 101 Huntington Ave 25th Fl *Web:* www.atwoodcherny.com	Boston	MA	02199	617-262-6400		41
Atwood Adhesives Inc 945 S Doris St. *Web:* atwoodadhesives.com	Seattle	WA	98108	206-762-7455	762-9852	3
Atwood Cafe 1 W Washington St. *Web:* atwoodrestaurant.com	Chicago	IL	60602	312-368-1900		671
AtWork Personnel Services 7212 Kingston Pke Ste 108 *Web:* www.lstaff.com	Knoxville	TN	37919	865-212-3853	212-3858	631
ATX Networks Corp 8-1602 Tricont Ave *TF:* 866-968-7289 ■ *Web:* atx.com	Whitby	ON	L1N7C3	289-204-7800		647
At-your-service Software Inc RPO Eglinton Sq PO Box 51141 *Web:* ayssoftware.com	Scarborough	ON	M1L4T2	416-749-3546	285-5525	177
aTyr Pharma 3545 General Atomics Ct Ste 250 *Web:* www.atyrpharma.com	San Diego	CA	92121	858-731-8389		668
Atzl, Nasher & Zigler, PC 234 N Main St *Web:* www.anzny.com	New City	NY	10956	845-634-4694		727
Au Authum Ki Inc 4645 S Ash Ave Ste I-1 *Web:* authumki.com	Tempe	AZ	85282	480-497-1997		685
Au Bon Pain 19 Fid Kennedy Ave *TF:* 800-825-5227 ■ *Web:* www.aubonpain.com	Boston	MA	02210	617-423-2100	423-7879	68
Au Naturel Wellness & Medical Spa at the Brookstreet Hotel 525 Legget Dr *TF:* 888-826-2220 ■ *Web:* www.brookstreethotel.com	Ottawa	ON	K2K2W2	613-271-1800		707
Au Petit Coin Breton 1029 Rue Saint-Jean *Web:* aupetitcoinbreton.ca	Quebec City	QC	G1R1R9	418-694-0758		671
AUA (American Urological Assn) 1000 Corporate Blvd. *TF:* 866-746-4282 ■ *Web:* www.auanet.org	Linthicum Heights	MD	21090	410-689-3700	689-3800	49-8
AU&A (Alan Utz & Associates Inc) PO Box 131857 *Web:* auainc.com	Tyler	TX	75713	903-566-9797		186
Auberge De La Fontaine b & b Inn 1301 Rue Rachel E *TF:* 800-597-0597 ■ *Web:* www.aubergedelafontaine.com	Montreal	QC	H2J2K1	514-597-0166		707
Auberge du Tresor 20 Rue Sainte-Anne *TF:* 800-566-1876 ■ *Web:* www.aubergedutresor.com	Quebec City	QC	G1R3X2	418-694-1876	694-0563	671
Auberge du Vieux-Port 97 Rue de la Commune E *TF:* 888-660-7678 ■ *Web:* www.aubergeduvieuxport.com	Montreal	QC	H2Y1J1	514-876-0081	876-8923	379
Auberge et spa Le Nordik Inc 16 Ch Nordik *TF:* 866-575-3700 ■ *Web:* chelsea.lenordik.com	Old Chelsea	QC	J9B2P7	819-827-1111		354
Auberge Resorts LLC 33 Reed Blvd *TF:* 866-311-2226 ■ *Web:* aubergeresorts.com	Mill Valley	CA	94941	624-145-6400		378
Auberge Saint-Antoine 8 Rue Saint-Antoine *TF:* 888-692-2211 ■ *Web:* www.saint-antoine.com	Quebec City	QC	G1K4C9	418-692-2211		379
Aubrey Silvey Enterprises Inc 371 Hamp Jones Rd *Web:* www.silvey.com	Carrollton	GA	30117	770-834-0738	834-1055	188-10
Auburn Area Chamber of Commerce 1103 High St *Web:* www.auburnchamber.net	Auburn	CA	95603	530-885-5616	885-5854	139
Auburn Area Chamber of Commerce 420 E Main St. *TF:* 800-395-0144 ■ *Web:* www.auburnareawa.org	Auburn	WA	98001	253-833-0700	735-4091	139
Auburn Banking Co 218 W Main St *TF:* 888-542-4186 ■ *Web:* auburnbankingcompany.com	Auburn	KY	42206	270-542-4185		70
Auburn Career Ctr 8140 Auburn Rd *Web:* www.auburncc.org	Concord Township	OH	44077	440-357-7542	358-8012	507
Auburn Citizen 110 N Fifth St	Auburn	IL	62615	217-438-6155	438-6156	532-2
Auburn Cord Duesenberg Museum 1600 S Wayne St *Web:* www.automobilemuseum.org	Auburn	IN	46706	260-925-1444	925-6266	520
Auburn Corp 10490 W 164th Pl *TF:* 800-393-1826 ■ *Web:* auburncorp.com	Orland Park	IL	60467	800-393-1826		191-3
Auburn Correctional Facility 135 State St PO Box 618 *Web:* www.doccs.ny.gov	Auburn	NY	13021	315-253-8401		213
Auburn Gear Inc 400 E Auburn Dr. *Web:* www.auburngear.com	Auburn	IN	46706	260-925-3200	925-4725	709
Auburn Journal Inc 1030 High St. *Web:* goldcountrymedia.com	Auburn	CA	95603	530-885-5656		532-3
Auburn Manor 501 Oak St N *Web:* www.auburnhomes.org	Chaska	MN	55318	952-448-9303		371
Auburn Manufacturing Co 29 Stack St *TF:* 800-427-5387 ■ *Web:* www.auburn-mfg.com	Middletown	CT	06457	860-346-6677	346-1334	326
Auburn Memorial Hospital 17 Lansing St. *Web:* www.auburnhospital.org	Auburn	NY	13021	315-255-7011	255-7382	374-3
Auburn Network PO Box 950 *Web:* www.aunetwork.com	Auburn	AL	36831	334-826-2929		645-141
Auburn Public Library 49 Spring St. *Web:* www.auburnpubliclibrary.org	Auburn	ME	04210	207-333-6640	333-6644	434-3
Auburn Publishers Inc 25 Dill St. *TF:* 800-878-5311 ■ *Web:* auburnpub.com	Auburn	NY	13021	315-253-5311		637-8
Auburn State Recreation Area 501 El Dorado St *Web:* www.parks.ca.gov	Auburn	CA	95603	530-885-4527		565
Auburn Supply Co 3850 W 167th St *Web:* www.auburnsupply.com	Markham	IL	60428	708-596-9800	596-0981	612
Auburn Systems LLC 8 Electronics Ave *TF:* 000-255 5008 ■ *Web:* www.auburnsys.com	Danvers	MA	01923	978-777-2460		201

Name / Address	City	State	ZIP	Phone	Fax	Class
Auburn Union School District 255 Epperle Ln *Web:* www.auburn.k12.ca.us	Auburn	CA	95603	530-885-7242	885-5170	685
Auburn University 104 Dudley Hall *TF:* 866-389-6770 ■ *Web:* www.auburn.edu	Auburn	AL	36849	334-844-6425	844-6436	166
Auburn Vacuum Forming Company Inc 40 York St *Web:* www.avfco.com	Auburn	NY	13021	315-253-2440		596
Auburn-Opelika Tourism Bureau 714 E Glenn Ave *TF:* 866-880-8747 ■ *Web:* www.aotourism.com	Auburn	AL	36830	334-501-3281	821-5500	206
AUCD (Association of University Centers on Disabilities) 1100 Wayne Ave Ste 1000 *TF:* 888-572-2249 ■ *Web:* www.aucd.org	Silver Spring	MD	20910	301-588-8252	588-2842	49-5
Aucoin & Associates Inc 433 N C C Duson St *Web:* www.aucoinandassoc.com	Eunice	LA	70535	337-457-7366		256
Aucoin-Hart 1525 Metairie Rd *TF:* 800-992-8743 ■ *Web:* www.aucoinhart.com	Metairie	LA	70005	504-834-9999		410
Audax Labs 101 Huntington Ave *Web:* www.audaxgroup.com	Boston	MA	02199	617-859-1500		194
Audcomp Computer Systems 611 Tradewind Dr Ste 100 *Web:* www.audcomp.com	Ancaster	ON	L9G4V5	905-304-1775		179
Audi of America 3800 Hamlin Rd *TF:* 888-237-2834 ■ *Web:* www.audiusa.com	Auburn Hills	MI	48326	888-237-2834		59
Audibel 6700 Washington Ave S *TF:* 800-769-2590 ■ *Web:* www.audibel.com	Eden Prairie	MN	55344	800-769-2590		352
Audible Inc 1 Washington Pk *TF:* 888-283-5051 ■ *Web:* www.audible.com	Newark	NJ	07102	888-283-5051		395
Audience Inc 326 Adelaide St W Ste 400 *Web:* www.audienceinc.ca	Toronto	ON	M5V1R3	416-703-3737		224
Audience Partners 630 W Germantown Pk Ste 250 *Web:* www.audiencepartners.com	Plymouth Meeting	PA	19462	484-928-1010		366
AudienceScience Inc 1120 112th Ave NE Ste 400 *Web:* www.audiencescience.com	Bellevue	WA	98004	425-201-3900		171
Audio Accessories Inc 25 Mill St *Web:* www.patchbays.com	Marlow	NH	03456	603-446-3335	446-7543	647
Audio Acoustics Inc 800 N Cedarbrook Ave *TF:* 800-240-0770 ■ *Web:* www.aaius.com	Springfield	MO	65802	800-240-0770		246
Audio Advisor 3427 Kraft Ave SE **Fax Area Code:* 616 ■ *TF:* 800-942-0220 ■ *Web:* www.audioadvisor.com	Grand Rapids	MI	49512	800-942-0220	254-8875*	194
Audio America 15132 Park of Commerce Blvd *TF:* 800-432-8532 ■ *Web:* audioamerica.com	Jupiter	FL	33478	561-863-7704		52
Audio Authority Corp 2048 Mercer Rd *TF:* 800-322-8346 ■ *Web:* www.audioauthority.com	Lexington	KY	40511	859-233-4599		387
Audio Book Co 235 Bellefontaine St *TF:* 800-423-8273 ■ *Web:* www.audiobookco.com	Pasadena	CA	91105	626-441-2024	441-2694	657
Audio Command Systems 694 Main St *TF:* 800-382-2939 ■ *Web:* audiocommand.com	Westbury	NY	11590	516-997-5800	997-2195	52
Audio Direct 2004 E Irvington Rd Ste 264 *TF:* 888-628-3467 ■ *Web:* www.audio-direct.com	Tucson	AZ	85714	888-628-3467		35
Audio Engineering Society 60 E 42nd St Rm 2520 *TF:* 800-541-7299 ■ *Web:* www.aes.org	New York	NY	10165	212-661-8528	682-0477	49-19
Audio General Inc (AGI) 1680 Republic Rd *TF:* 866-866-2600 ■ *Web:* www.audiogeneral.com	Huntingdon Valley	PA	19006	267-288-0300	288-0301	514
Audio Precision Inc 5750 SW Arctic Dr *Web:* www.ap.com	Beaverton	OR	97005	503-627-0832	641-8906	248
Audio Research Corp 3900 Annapolis Ln N *Web:* www.audioresearch.com	Plymouth	MN	55447	763-577-9700	577-0323	52
Audio Vision 50 Crooked Trail Rd **Fax Area Code:* 203 ■ *TF:* 800-367-1604 ■ *Web:* www.stressstop.com	Norwalk	CT	06854	800-367-1604	866-3421*	514
Audio Visual Dynamics 424 Sand Shore Rd *Web:* avdusa.com	Hackettstown	NJ	07840	973-993-8500		194
Audio Visual Mart Inc (AVM) 2016 5th ST *Web:* www.av-mart.com	Kenner	LA	70062	504-454-5945		23
AudioCodes Inc 200 Cottontail Ln Ste A101E *Web:* www.audiocodes.com	Somerset	NJ	08873	732-469-0880	469-2298	729
Audio-Digest Foundation 450 N Brand Blvd Ste 900 *TF:* 800-423-2308 ■ *Web:* www.audio-digest.org	Glendale	CA	91206	818-240-7500	240-7379	766
Audiokinetic Inc 409 St-Nicolas St Ste 300 *Web:* www.audiokinetic.com	Montreal	QC	H2Y2P4	514-499-9100		225
AudioQuest Inc 2621 White Rd *TF:* 800-747-2770 ■ *Web:* www.audioquest.com	Irvine	CA	92614	949-585-0111		253
Audiosears Corp 2 South St *TF:* 800-533-7863 ■ *Web:* www.audiosears.com	Stamford	NY	12167	607-652-7305	652-3653	52
Audio-technica US Inc 1221 Commerce Dr *TF:* 800-667-3745 ■ *Web:* www.audio-technica.com	Stow	OH	44224	330-686-2600	688-3752	246
Audio-Video Corp 213 Broadway *Web:* www.audiovideocorp.com	Albany	NY	12204	518-449-7213	449-1205	52
Audiovisual & Integrated Experience Assn 11242 Waples Mill Rd Ste 200 *TF:* 800-659-7469 ■ *Web:* www.avixa.org	Fairfax	VA	22030	703-273-7200	278-8082	49-20
Audiovox Corp 180 Marcus Blvd *NASDAQ: VOXX* ■ *TF:* 800-645-4994 ■ *Web:* www.voxxintl.com	Hauppauge	NY	11788	631-231-7750		52
Audit & Adjustment Company Inc 20700 44th Ave W Ste 100 *TF:* 800-526-1074 ■ *Web:* www.audit-adjustment.com	Lynnwood	WA	98036	425-776-9797		535
Audit Bureau of Circulations (ABC) 48 W Seegers Rd *Web:* www.auditedmedia.com	Arlington Heights	IL	60005	224-366-6939		49-18
Audit Group Inc, The 16141 Swingley Ridge Rd Ste 310 *TF:* 800-383-7963 ■ *Web:* www.theauditgroup.com	Chesterfield	MO	63017	636-536-6333		463
Audit Logistics LLC 1172 W Century Dr Ste 245 *Web:* www.auditlogistics.com	Louisville	CO	80027	303-951-9000		2
Audit Technology Group 1850 W Winchester Rd *Web:* www.atgaudits.com	Libertyville	IL	60048	847-281-8703		734
Auditorium Theatre 50 E Congress Pkwy *Web:* www.auditoriumtheatre.org	Chicago	IL	60605	312-341-2310		572
Audrain County 101 N Jefferson St *Web:* audraincounty.org	Mexico	MO	65265	573-473-5840	581-2380	338
Audrey Kitchen + Bar, The 9 E Wilson St *Web:* www.theaudreykitchenandbar.com	Madison	WI	53703	608-255-0165		671
Audubon County 318 Leroy St Ste 6 *Web:* www.iowacourts.gov	Audubon	IA	50025	712-563-4275		338
Audubon House & Tropical Garden 205 Whitehead St *Web:* www.audubonhouse.com	Key West	FL	33040	305-294-2116		520
Audubon Metals LLC 3055 Ohio Dr *Web:* www.audubonmetals.com	Henderson	KY	42420	270-830-1148		485
Audubon Naturalist Society (ANS) 8940 Jones Mill Rd *Web:* www.audubonnaturalist.org	Chevy Chase	MD	20815	301-652-9188		637-2
Audubon Nature Institute 6500 Magazine St *TF:* 800-774-7394 ■ *Web:* audubonnatureinstitute.org	New Orleans	LA	70118	504-581-4629		823
Audubon Society of Portland 5151 NW Cornell Rd *Web:* www.audubonportland.org	Portland	OR	97210	503-292-6855		48-13
Auer Precision Inc 1050 W Birchwood Ave *Web:* www.auerprecision.com	Mesa	AZ	85210	480-834-4637		621
Auer Steel & Heating Supply Co 2935 W Silver Spring Dr *TF:* 800-242-0406 ■ *Web:* www.auersteel.com	Milwaukee	WI	53209	414-463-1234		14
Auerbach Grayson & Company LLC 25 W 45th St *Web:* agco.com	New York	NY	10036	212-557-4444		690
Auerr Zajac & Associates LLP 29 Dean Ave *Web:* www.auerr-zajaccpa.com	Franklin	MA	02038	508-528-1305	528-8231	2
Augenblick & Company PC 4 Market Pl *Web:* augenblickpc.com	New Hope	PA	18938	215-862-9153		528
Augeo Affinity Marketing Inc 2561 Territorial Rd *Web:* augeomarketing.com	Saint Paul	MN	55114	651-917-9143		195
Augie Leopold Adv Specialties Inc 3214 Roman St *Web:* augieleopold.com	Metairie	LA	70001	504-836-0525		4
Auglaize & Mercer Counties Convention & Visitors Bureau 900 Edgewater Dr *TF:* 800-860-4726 ■ *Web:* seemore.org	Saint Marys	OH	45885	419-394-1294		206
Auglaize County 209 S Blackhoof St Ste 201 *Web:* www.auglaizecounty.org	Wapakoneta	OH	45895	419-739-6710		338
Augmentum Inc 1065 E Hillsdale Blvd Ste 413 *Web:* www.augmentum.com	Foster City	CA	94404	650-578-9221		225
Augsburg College 2211 Riverside Ave *TF:* 800-788-5678 ■ *Web:* www.augsburg.edu	Minneapolis	MN	55454	612-330-1000	330-1590	166
Augsburg Fortress PO Box 1209 **Fax Area Code:* 800 ■ *TF:* 800-328-4648 ■ *Web:* www.augsburgfortress.org	Minneapolis	MN	55440	612-330-3300	722-7766*	637-3
August 301 Tchoupitoulas St *Web:* www.restaurantaugust.com	New Orleans	LA	70130	504-299-9777		671
August Capital 2480 Sand Hill Rd Ste 101 *Web:* www.augustcap.com	Menlo Park	CA	94025	650-234-9900	234-9910	702
August Lang & Husak 2 Wisconsin Cir 7th Fl *Web:* www.alhadv.com	Chevy Chase	MD	20815	301-657-2772		7
August Law Group PC 19200 Von Karman Ste 900 *Web:* augustlawgroup.com	Irvine	CA	92612	949-752-7772		41
August Mack Environmental Inc 1302 N Meridian St Ste 300 *TF:* 800-579-0770 ■ *Web:* www.augustmack.com	Indianapolis	IN	46202	317-916-8000		194
August Moon 2269 Lexington Rd *Web:* www.augustmoonbistro.com	Louisville	KY	40206	502-456-6569		671
August Schell Brewing Co 1860 Schell Rd *Web:* schellsbrewery.com	New Ulm	MN	56073	507-354-5528		298
August Winter & Sons Inc 2323 N Roemer Rd *TF:* 800-236-8882 ■ *Web:* www.augustwinter.com	Appleton	WI	54911	920-739-8881	739-2230	189-13
Augusta Aviation Daniel Field Airport 1775 Highland Ave *Web:* www.augustaaviation.com	Augusta	GA	30904	706-733-8970	738-9746	167-3
Augusta Ballet Inc 1301 Greene St *Web:* www.augustaballet.org	Augusta	GA	30901	706-261-0555		573-1
Augusta Cooperative Farm Bureau Inc 1205 B Richmond Rd *Web:* www.augustacoop.com	Staunton	VA	24401	540-885-5582		45
Augusta Correctional Ctr 1821 Estaline Valley Rd *Web:* vadoc.virginia.gov	Craigsville	VA	24430	540-997-7000		213
Augusta County 18 Government Center Ln *Web:* www.co.augusta.va.us	Verona	VA	24482	540-245-5600	245-5621	338
Augusta County Library 1759 Jefferson Hwy *Web:* www.augustacountylibrary.org	Fishersville	VA	22939	540-885-3961		434-3
Augusta Fiberglass Coatings Inc 86 Lake Cynthia Rd *TF:* 800-995-8265 ■ *Web:* www.augustafiberglass.com	Blackville	SC	29817	803-671-4742	284-2309	596
Augusta Flooring 202 Bobby Jones Expy *Web:* www.augustaflooring.com	Augusta	GA	30907	706-251-9135		290
Augusta Grill (AG) 1818 Augusta St *Web:* www.augustagrill.com	Greenville	SC	29605	864-242-0316		671
Augusta Mall 3450 Wrightsboro Rd *Web:* www.augustamall.com	Augusta	GA	30909	706-731-8850		460

Name / Address	City	State	ZIP	Phone	Fax	Class
Augusta Medical Ctr (AMC) 78 Medical Center Dr PO Box 1000 *TF:* 800-932-0262 ■ *Web:* www.augustahealth.com	Fishersville	VA	22939	540-932-4000		374-3
Augusta Metro Chamber of Commerce 1 Tenth St Ste 120 *TF:* 888-639-8188 ■ *Web:* www.augustametrochamber.com	Augusta	GA	30901	706-821-1300	821-1330	139
Augusta Metropolitan Convention & Visitors Bureau 1450 Greene St *TF:* 800-726-0243 ■ *Web:* www.visitaugusta.com	Augusta	GA	30901	706-823-6600	823-6609	206
Augusta National Inc 2604 Washington Rd *Web:* www.masters.com	Augusta	GA	30904	706-667-6000		360-3
Augusta Regional Airport - Bush Field (AGS) 1501 Aviation Way *Web:* www.flyags.com	Augusta	GA	30906	706-798-3236	798-1551	27
Augusta School of Massage 608 Ponder Place Dr *Web:* www.augustamassage.com	Evans	GA	30809	706-863-4799	863-4779	685
Augusta State University 2500 Walton Way *Web:* www.augusta.edu	Augusta	GA	30904	706-737-1632	667-4355	166
Augusta Technical College 3200 Augusta Tech Dr *Web:* www.augustatech.edu	Augusta	GA	30906	706-771-4000	771-4034	800
Augusta Transportation Inc 940 Molly Pond Rd *TF:* 800-677-6670 ■ *Web:* www.augustatransportation.com	Augusta	GA	30901	706-722-0226		780
Augustana College 639 38th St *TF:* 800-798-8100 ■ *Web:* www.augustana.edu	Rock Island	IL	61201	309-794-7000	794-7174	166
Augustana University 2001 S Summit Ave *TF:* 800-727-2844 ■ *Web:* www.augie.edu	Sioux Falls	SD	57197	605-274-0770		167-3
Augusta-Richmond County 535 Telfair St *Web:* www.augustaga.gov	Augusta	GA	30901	706-821-2300	826-4790	338
Augusta-Richmond County Historical Society Reese Library GRU 2500 Walton Way *Web:* www.thearchs.org	Augusta	GA	30904	706-737-1532		49-19
Augusta-Richmond County Library 823 Telfair St *Web:* arcpls.org	Augusta	GA	30901	706-821-2600	724-6762	434-3
Auguste Escoffier School of Culinary Arts - Boulder 637 S Broadway Ste H *TF:* 877-149-0305 ■ *Web:* www.escoffier.edu	Boulder	CO	80305	303-494-7988		685
Augustin Egelsee LLP 8141 E Kaiser Blvd Ste 315 *TF:* 866-781-7723 ■ *Web:* ockidslaw.com	Anaheim Hills	CA	92808	866-781-7723		41
Augustine 532 Gibson Dr Ste 250 *Web:* augustineagency.com	Roseville	CA	95678	916-774-9600		7
Augustine Casino 84-001 Ave 54 *Web:* www.augustinecasino.com	Coachella	CA	92236	760-391-9500		133
Augusto Insurance Agency 32 N Front St *Web:* augusto-insurance.com	Rio Vista	CA	94571	707-374-6309	374-6804	390
Augustus C. Long Health Sciences Library Columbia University Medical Ctr 701 W 168th St *Web:* library.cumc.columbia.edu	New York	NY	10032	212-305-3605		434-1
AUHSB (Anaheim Union High School District) 501 N Crescent Way *Web:* www.auhsd.us	Anaheim	CA	92801	714-999-3511		685
Aui Contractors LLC 4775 N Fwy *Web:* www.auipartners.com	Fort Worth	TX	76106	817-926-4377		187
Auld & Associates Investigations Inc 4673 W Chester Pk *Web:* auldpi.com	Newtown Square	PA	19073	610-353-3830	353-3191	691
Auld & White Constructors LLC 4168 Southpoint Pkwy Ste 101 *Web:* www.auld-white.com	Jacksonville	FL	32216	904-296-2555		186
Aulick Leasing Corp 305 Ninth Ave PO Box 1369 *Web:* aulickleasing.com	Scottsbluff	NE	69361	308-220-4000		126
Aultman Hospital 2600 Sixth St SW *Web:* aultman.org	Canton	OH	44710	330-452-9911		374-3
Auman Machine Company Inc 1525 Joel Dr *Web:* www.aumanmachine.com	Lebanon	PA	17046	717-273-6748	273-5580	454
Aumkaara Inc 4340 Stevens Creek Blvd Ste 286 *Web:* aumkaarainc.com	San Jose	CA	95129	408-255-0099		177
Aumtech Inc 710 Old Bridge Tpke *Web:* www.aumtech.com	East Brunswick	NJ	08816	732-254-1875		180
Aunt Chilada's Easy Street Cafe 69 Pope Ave *Web:* www.auntchiladashhi.com	Hilton Head Island	SC	29928	843-785-7700		671
Aunt Emma's 700 E St *Web:* www.auntemmaspancakes.com	Chula Vista	CA	91910	619-427-2722		671
Aunt Lute Books PO Box 410687 *Web:* auntlute.com	San Francisco	CA	94141	415-826-1300	826-8300	637-2
Auntie Pasto's Restaurant Kunia Shopping Ctr 94-673 Kupuohi St Ste b-109 *Web:* www.auntiepastosrestaurant.com	Waipahu	HI	96797	808-680-0005	680-0009	671
AUPHA (Association of University Programs in Health Administration) 2000 N 14th St Ste 780 *TF:* 877-275-6462 ■ *Web:* www.aupha.org	Arlington	VA	22201	703-894-0941		49-8
AURA (Association of Universities for Research in Astronomy) 1331 Pennsylvania Ave NW Ste 1475 *Web:* www.aura-astronomy.org	Washington	DC	20005	202-483-2101	483-2106	49-5
Aura Advance Technologies Inc 1742 Tenth Ave SW *Web:* www.auraadvanced.com	Calgary	AB	T3C0J8	403-269-6123		175
Aura Engineering LLC 4801 W Orange St *Web:* aura-engineering.com	Pearland	TX	77581	281-485-1105		261
Aura Systems Inc 10541 Ashdale St *OTC: AUSI* ■ *TF:* 800-909-2872 ■ *Web:* aurasystems.com	Stanton	CA	90680	310-643-5300	643-7457	518
Auraria Higher Education Ctr 1068 Ninth St Pk *Web:* www.ahec.edu	Denver	CO	80204	303-556-2400		166
Aurea Planning Solutions 401 Congress Ave Ste 2650 *Web:* www.aurea.com	Austin	TX	78701	512-201-8222		178-1
Aurelia Osborn Fox Memorial Hospital 1 Norton Ave *Web:* www.bassett.org	Oneonta	NY	13820	607-432-2000		374-3
Aurelio's Pizza 18162 Harwood Ave *Web:* www.aureliospizza.com	Homewood	IL	60430	708-798-8050		670
Aurelius Capital Management LP 535 Madison Ave 22nd Fl *Web:* www.aurelius-capital.com	New York	NY	10022	646-445-6500		528
Aureole 135 W 42nd St *Web:* www.charliepalmer.com	New York	NY	10036	212-319-1660		671
Aureon 7760 Office Plaza Dr *Web:* www.internetsolver.com	West Des Moines	IA	50266	515-224-9229		631
Auric Systems Intl 85 Grove St *Web:* www.auricsystems.com	Peterborough	NH	03458	603-924-6079		253
Auriq Systems Inc 199 S Los Robles Ave Ste 440 *Web:* auriq.com	Pasadena	CA	91101	626-564-2781		180
Auritt Communications Group 555 Eigth Ave Ste 709 *Web:* auritt.com	New York	NY	10018	212-302-6230		514
Auromere Inc 2621 W Hwy 12 *TF:* 800-735-4691 ■ *Web:* www.auromere.com	Lodi	CA	95242	800-735-4691		238
Aurora Area Convention & Visitors Bureau 43 W Galena Blvd *TF:* 800-477-4369 ■ *Web:* www.enjoyaurora.com	Aurora	IL	60506	630-256-3190		206
Aurora Aviation 22785 Airport Rd NE *Web:* www.auroraaviation.com	Aurora	OR	97002	503-678-1217	678-1219	63
Aurora Bearing Co 901 Aucutt Rd *Web:* www.aurorabearing.com	Montgomery	IL	60538	630-859-2030	859-0971	75
Aurora Biomed Inc 1001 E Pender St *TF:* 800-883-2918 ■ *Web:* aurorabiomed.com	Vancouver	BC	V6A1W2	604-215-8700	215-9700	111
Aurora Chamber of Commerce 14305 E Alameda Ave Ste 300 *Web:* www.aurorachamber.org	Aurora	CO	80012	303-344-1500	344-1564	139
Aurora Chamber of Commerce 43 W Galena Blvd *TF:* 866-947-8081 ■ *Web:* www.aurora-chamber.com	Aurora	IL	60506	630-256-3180	256-3189	139
Aurora Charter Oak Hospital 1161 E Covina Blvd *Web:* charteroak.aurorabehavioral.com	Covina	CA	91724	626-654-2673		374-5
Aurora City Hall 15151 E Alameda Pkwy *TF:* 800-895-4999 ■ *Web:* auroragov.org	Aurora	CO	80012	303-739-7000	739-7594	337
Aurora Computer Technology Inc 6 Schubert St *Web:* www.auroracomputer.com	Staten Island	NY	10305	718-981-2363		180
Aurora Contractors Inc 100 Raynor Ave *TF:* 866-423-2197 ■ *Web:* www.auroracontractors.com	Ronkonkoma	NY	11779	631-981-3785		610
Aurora Cooperative Inc 605 12th St PO Box 209 *TF:* 800-642-6795 ■ *Web:* auroracoop.com	Aurora	NE	68818	402-694-2106	694-6943	275
Aurora Cord & Cable Co 325 S Union St *Web:* www.auroradefensegroup.com	Aurora	IL	60505	630-851-1616	851-1626	438
Aurora Corporation of America 3500 Challenger St *TF:* 800-327-8508 ■ *Web:* www.auroracorp.com	Torrance	CA	90503	310-793-5650		534
Aurora County 401 N Main St PO Box 366 *Web:* ujs.sd.gov	Plankinton	SD	57368	605-942-7165	942-7170	338
Aurora Credit Union 3355 W Forest Home Ave *Web:* auroracreditunion.org	Milwaukee	WI	53215	414-649-7949		219
Aurora Diagnostics LLC 11025 RCA Center Dr Ste 300 *TF:* 866-420-5512 ■ *Web:* www.auroradx.com	Palm Beach Gardens	FL	33410	866-420-5512		415
Aurora Federal Credit Union 610 S Abilene St *TF:* 877-755-2572 ■ *Web:* auroracu.com	Aurora	CO	80012	303-755-2572		219
Aurora Flight Sciences Corp 9950 Wakeman Dr *Web:* www.aurora.aero	Manassas	VA	20110	703-369-3633		22
Aurora Fox Arts Ctr 9900 E Colfax Ave *Web:* www.aurorafoxartscenter.org	Aurora	CO	80010	303-739-1970		572
Aurora Funds 3100 Tower Blvd *Web:* www.aurorafunds.com	Durham	NC	27707	919-484-0400		792
Aurora Health Care Inc 750 W Virginia St PO Box 341880 *Web:* www.aurorahealthcare.org	Milwaukee	WI	53234	414-647-3000	649-7982	353
Aurora Innovation 1880 Embarcadero Rd *Web:* aurora.tech	Palo Alto	CA	94303	412-983-6681		178-8
Aurora Investment Management LLC 1 Lincoln Ctr 18W140 Butterfield Rd Ste 1200 *Web:* www.aurorallc.com	Oakbrook Terrace	IL	60181	312-762-6700		401
Aurora Las Encinas Hospital 2900 E Del Mar Blvd *TF:* 800-792-2345 ■ *Web:* www.lasencinashospital.com	Pasadena	CA	91107	626-795-9901	792-2919	374-5
Aurora Metals Divison LLC 1995 Greenfield Ave *Web:* www.aurorametals.com	Montgomery	IL	60538	630-844-4900	844-6839	308
Aurora National Life Assurance Co PO Box 4490 *TF:* 800-265-2652 ■ *Web:* www.auroralife.com	Hartford	CT	06147	800-265-2652		391-2
Aurora Optics Inc 7 E Skippack Pke Ste 202 *Web:* aurora-optics.com	Ambler	PA	19002	215-646-0690	646-4721	668
Aurora Organic Dairy Corp 1919 14th St Ste 300 *Web:* www.auroraorganic.com	Boulder	CO	80302	720-564-6296		296-25
Aurora Pictures Inc 5249 Chicago Ave *TF:* 800-346-9487 ■ *Web:* www.aurorapictures.com	Minneapolis	MN	55417	612-821-6490		514

Name / Address	City	State	Zip	Phone	Fax	Class
Aurora Press Inc PO Box 573 *TF:* 888-894-8621 ■ *Web:* www.aurorapress.com	Santa Fe	NM	87504	505-989-9804	982-8321	637-2
Aurora Public Library 101 S River St *Web:* www.aurorapubliclibrary.org	Aurora	IL	60506	630-264-4117	892-5603	434-3
Aurora Public Library 14949 E Alameda Pkwy *Web:* www.odyssey.aurora.lib.co.us	Aurora	CO	80012	303-739-6600		434-3
Aurora Reservoir 5800 S Powhaton Rd *Web:* www.auroragov.org	Aurora	CO	80016	303-326-8425		50-5
Aurora Specialty Chemistries Inc 1520 Lake Lansing Rd *Web:* auroraspecialtychemistries.com	Lansing	MI	48912	517-372-9121	372-1956	261
Aurora Specialty Textiles Group Inc 2705 N Bridge St **Fax Area Code:* 630 ■ *TF:* 800-864-0303 ■ *Web:* www.auroratextile.com	Yorkville	IL	60560	800-864-0303	708-5208*	745-7
Aurora Symphony Orchestra PO Box 441481 *Web:* www.aurorasymphony.org	Aurora	CO	80044	303-873-6622		573-3
Aurora Systems Consulting Inc 2510 W 237th St Ste 202 *TF:* 888-282-0696 ■ *Web:* www.aurorait.com	Torrance	CA	90505	888-282-0696		463
Aurora University 347 S Gladstone Ave *TF:* 800-742-5281 ■ *Web:* aurora.edu	Aurora	IL	60506	630-844-5533		166
Aurora Worldwide Development Corp 2810 Crossroads Dr Ste 3100 *TF:* 800-924-4249 ■ *Web:* aurorawdc.com	Madison	WI	53718	608-268-3470		463
Auroros Inc 8420 Honeycutt Rd Ste 200 *Web:* www.aurorosinc.com	Raleigh	NC	27615	919-841-0553	841-0299	194
Aurotech Inc 6909 Timber Creek Ct *Web:* www.aurotechcorp.com	Clarksville	MD	21029	301-854-1326		194
Aurum Assembly Plus Inc 8827 Production Ave *Web:* www.aurumassembly.com	San Diego	CA	92121	858-578-8710	578-5071	625
Aurum Ceramic Dental Laboratories Ltd 115 17 Ave SW *TF:* 800-665-8815 ■ *Web:* www.aurumgroup.com	Calgary	AB	T2S0A1	403-228-5120		418
AUS Inc 155 Gaither Dr *Web:* ausinc.com	Mount Laurel	NJ	08054	856-234-9200		360-3
AUSA (Association of the US Army) 2425 Wilson Blvd *TF:* 800-336-4570 ■ *Web:* www.ausa.org	Arlington	VA	22201	703-841-4300	525-9039	48-19
Ausco Products Inc 2245 Pipestone Rd *Web:* www.auscoproducts.com	Benton Harbor	MI	49022	269-926-0700		247
Ausdal Financial Partners 220 N Main St Ste 400 *TF:* 800-722-8732 ■ *Web:* www.ausdal.com	Davenport	IA	52801	563-326-2064		690
Ausland Builders Inc 3935 Highland Ave *Web:* auslandgroup.com	Grants Pass	OR	97526	541-476-3788		186
Ausley McMullen 123 S Calhoun St *Web:* ausley.com	Tallahassee	FL	32302	850-224-9115	222-7560	428
Austad's Golf 2801 E Tenth St *TF:* 800-444-1234 ■ *Web:* austads.com	Sioux Falls	SD	57103	605-331-4653		711
Austal USA LLC 100 Addsco Rd *Web:* www.austal.com	Mobile	AL	36602	251-434-8000		698
AustarPharma LLC 18 Mayfield Ave *Web:* www.austarpharma.com	Edison	NJ	08837	732-225-2930	225-6334	582
Aus-Tex Printing & Mailing 2431 Forbes Dr *TF:* 800-472-7581 ■ *Web:* austex.com	Austin	TX	78754	512-476-7581		627
Austin Aerotech Repair Services Inc 2005 Windy Terr *Web:* austinaerotech.com	Cedar Park	TX	78613	512-335-6000		246
Austin American-Statesman 305 S Congress Ave *TF:* 800-445-9898 ■ *Web:* www.statesman.com	Austin	TX	78704	512-445-4040	445-3670	632-2
Austin Bridge & Road Inc 6330 Commerce Dr Ste 150 *Web:* www.austin-ind.com	Irving	TX	75063	214-596-7300		188-4
Austin Chamber Music Ctr 7600 Burnet Rd Ste 190 *Web:* www.austinchambermusic.org	Austin	TX	78757	512-454-0026	308-3429	573-3
Austin Chamber of Commerce 535 E Fifth St *Web:* www.austinchamber.com	Austin	TX	78701	512-478-9383	478-9615	139
Austin Chemical Company Inc 1565 Barclay Blvd *Web:* austinchemical.com	Buffalo Grove	IL	60089	847-520-9600	520-9160	146
Austin Chronicle PO Box 4189 *Web:* www.austinchronicle.com	Austin	TX	78765	512-454-5766	458-6910	532-5
Austin City Hall 301 W 2nd 3rd Fl *Web:* www.austintexas.gov	Austin	TX	78701	512-974-2000	974-2833	337
Austin City Limits Radio 8309 N IH-35 *Web:* www.acl-radio.com	Austin	TX	78753	512-832-4000	832-4071	645-13
Austin Civic Orchestra PO Box 27132 *Web:* www.austincivicorchestra.org	Austin	TX	78755	512-200-2261		573-3
Austin Co 6095 Parkland Blvd *Web:* www.theaustin.com	Cleveland	OH	44124	440-544-2600		186
Austin College 900 N Grand Ave *TF:* 800-526-4276 ■ *Web:* www.austincollege.edu	Sherman	TX	75090	903-813-3000	813-3197	166
Austin Community College 5930 Middle Fiskville Rd *TF:* 888-626-1697 ■ *Web:* www.austincc.edu	Austin	TX	78752	512-223-7000	223-2048	162
Austin Convention Ctr 500 E Cesar Chavez St PO Box 1088 *Web:* www.austinconventioncenter.com	Austin	TX	78701	512-404-4000	404-4416	205
Austin County 1 E Main St *Web:* www.austincounty.com	Bellville	TX	77418	979-865-5911	865-8786	338
Austin Creek State Recreation Area 17000 Armstrong Woods Rd *Web:* www.parks.ca.gov	Guerneville	CA	95446	707-869-2015		565
Austin Daily Herald Inc 310 NE Second St *Web:* www.austindailyherald.com	Austin	MN	55912	507-433-8851	437-8644	637-8
Austin Davis & Mitchell Attorneys at Law 109 Cherry St *Web:* www.austindavismitchell.com	Dunlap	TN	37327	423-949-4159		428
Austin Domsch Insurance Agency 400 S Colorado Blvd Ste 890 *Web:* austindomsch.com	Denver	CO	80246	303-321-0895		390
Austin Elementary School 1900 Duncan St *Web:* www.pampaisd.net	Pampa	TX	79065	806-669-4760		685
Austin Exploration Inc 10333 Westoffice Dr *Web:* austinex.com	Houston	TX	77042	713-780-7141	780-3118	727
Austin Film Festival 1801 Salina St *TF:* 800-310-3378 ■ *Web:* www.austinfilmfestival.com	Austin	TX	78702	512-478-4795	478-6205	282
Austin Graduate School of Theology 7640 Guadalupe St *TF:* 866-287-4723 ■ *Web:* www.austingrad.edu	Austin	TX	78752	512-476-2772	476-3919	166
Austin Graphics Inc 1198 2nd Ave E *TF:* 800-265-6964 ■ *Web:* austingraphics.ca	Owen Sound	ON	N4K2J1	519-376-2116		344
Austin Jewish Academy 7300 Hart Ln *Web:* www.austinjewishacademy.org	Austin	TX	78731	512-735-8350		685
Austin Land & Cattle Co 1205 N Lamar Blvd *Web:* alcsteaks.com	Austin	TX	78703	512-472-1813		671
Austin Museum of Art Downtown 700 Congress Ave *Web:* www.thecontemporaryaustin.org	Austin	TX	78701	512-453-5312		520
Austin N.C. Inc 505 E Huntland Dr Ste 370 *Web:* austinnc.com	Austin	TX	78752	512-458-1112		177
Austin Opera 3009 Industrial Terr Ste 100 *Web:* austinopera.org	Austin	TX	78758	512-472-5992		573-2
Austin Organs Inc 156 Woodland St *Web:* www.austinorgans.com	Hartford	CT	06105	860-522-8293	524-9828	527
Austin Peay State University 601 College St *TF:* 800-844-2778 ■ *Web:* www.apsu.edu	Clarksville	TN	37044	931-221-7661	221-6168	166
Austin Powder Co 25800 Science Pk Dr *TF:* 800-321-0752 ■ *Web:* www.austinpowder.com	Cleveland	OH	44122	216-464-2400	464-4418	268
Austin Presbyterian Theological Seminary 100 E 27th St *Web:* www.austinseminary.edu	Austin	TX	78705	512-472-6736		167-3
Austin Public Library 800 Guadalupe St *Web:* library.austintexas.gov	Austin	TX	78701	512-974-7400		434-3
Austin Pump & Supply Co PO Box 17037 *TF:* 800-252-9692 ■ *Web:* www.austinpump.com	Austin	TX	78760	512-442-2348	442-2932	385
Austin State Hospital 4110 Guadalupe St *TF:* 866-407-3773 ■ *Web:* www.dshs.texas.gov	Austin	TX	78751	512-452-0381	419-2163	374-5
Austin Symphony Orchestra 1101 Red River St *TF:* 888-462-3787 ■ *Web:* www.austinsymphony.org	Austin	TX	78701	512-476-6064	476-6242	573-3
Austin Tape & Label Inc 3350 Cavalier Trl *Web:* www.austintape.com	Stow	OH	44224	330-928-7999		787
Austin Trust Co 336 S Congress Ave Ste 100 *Web:* www.austintrust.com	Austin	TX	78704	512-478-2121	478-2616	69
Austin Ventures 300 W Sixth St Ste 2300 *Web:* www.austinventures.com	Austin	TX	78701	512-485-1900		792
Austin White Lime Company Ltd 14001 McNeil Round Rock Rd *TF:* 800-553-5463 ■ *Web:* www.austinwhitelime.com	Austin	TX	78728	800-553-5463		440
Austin Williams 80 Arkay Dr Ste 220 *TF:* 877-386-6035 ■ *Web:* www.austinwilliams.com	Hauppauge	NY	11788	631-498-5756		7
Austin Zoo 10807 Rawhide Trl *Web:* austinzoo.org	Austin	TX	78736	512-288-1490	288-3972	823
Austin's School of Spa Technology 855 Central Ave *Web:* www.austin.edu	Albany	NY	12206	518-438-7879	438-7946	685
Austin, Katzman & Thom PC 320 S Nevada Ave *Web:* libertylawcenter.com	Colorado Springs	CO	80903	719-578-1183		41
Austin-Bergstrom International Airport (ABIA) 3600 Presidential Blvd *Web:* www.ci.austin.tx.us	Austin	TX	78719	512-530-2242		27
AustinMohawk & Company Inc 2175 Beechgrove Pl *TF:* 800-765-3110 ■ *Web:* www.austinmohawk.com	Utica	NY	13501	315-793-9390	793-9370	91
Austins Entertainment Center LP 16231 N Ih-35 *Web:* austinspark.com	Pflugerville	TX	78660	512-670-9600		31
Austin-Westran LLC 602 E Blackhawk Dr *Web:* www.hyperams.com	Byron	IL	61010	815-234-2811	234-3009	779
Australia						
Consulate General 1000 Bishop St *Web:* www.usa.embassy.gov.au	Honolulu	HI	96813	808-529-8100	529-8142	257
Consulate General 2029 Century Pk E Ste 3150 *Web:* www.losangeles.consulate.gov.au	Los Angeles	CA	90067	310-229-2300		257
Embassy 2005 Massachusetts Ave NW *TF:* 800-345-6541 ■ *Web:* www.visahq.com	Washington	DC	20036	202-558-2216	318-0771	257
Australian American Chamber of Commerce (AACC) PO Box 218219 **Fax Area Code:* 978 ■ *Web:* www.aacc-texas.org	Houston	TX	77218	713-527-9688	600-2050*	138
Australian Government						
Australian Consulate-General in Chicago, United States of America 123 N Wacker Dr Ste 1330 *Web:* dfat.gov.au	Chicago	IL	60606	312-419-1480	419-1499	257
Australian-American Chamber of Commerce - San Francisco PO Box 471285 *TF:* 800-662-4455 ■ *Web:* sfaussies.com	San Francisco	CA	94147	415-485-6718		138
Austria						
Consulate General 11859 Wilshire Blvd Ste 501 *TF:* 800-255-2414 ■ *Web:* www.austria.org	Los Angeles	CA	90025	310-444-9310	477-9897	257
Consulate General 31 E 69th St *Web:* www.bmeia.gv.at	New York	NY	10021	212-933-5140	585-1992	257
Austrian & Associates Inc 5371 Chickadee Ln	Lyndhurst	OH	44124	216-621-6631		261

				Phone	Fax	Class
Austrian Tourist Office PO Box 1142 *Web:* www.austria.info	New York	NY	10108	212-944-6880	730-4568	775
Austro Mold Inc 3 Rutter St. *Web:* www.austromold.com	Rochester	NY	14606	585-458-1410	458-0963	757
Autco Inc 10900 Midwest Industrial Blvd *TF:* 800-777-6524 ■ *Web:* www.autco.com	Saint Louis	MO	63132	314-426-6524	426-7378	38
Autec Inc 2500 W Front St **Fax Area Code:* 724 ■ *TF:* 800-438-3028 ■ *Web:* www.autec-carwash.com	Statesville	NC	28677	704-871-9141	871-9101*	427
Auth0 Inc 10800 NE 8th St Ste 700 *TF:* 888-235-2699 ■ *Web:* auth0.com	Bellevue	WA	98004	888-235-2699		178-1
Authenex Inc 1413 Grant Rd *TF:* 877-288-4363 ■ *Web:* www.authenex.com	Mountain View	CA	94040	650-641-1198		224
Authentech Software Developers Inc 11285 Palmer Ln *Web:* authentech.com	Twinsburg	OH	44087	330-425-4528		177
Authentic Pine Floors Inc 4042 Hwy 42 *TF:* 800-283-6038 ■ *Web:* www.authenticpinefloors.com	Locust Grove	GA	30248	800-283-6038		752
Authenticity Consulting Inc 4008 Lake Dr Ave N *TF:* 800-971-2250 ■ *Web:* authenticityconsulting.com	Minneapolis	MN	55422	763-971-8890		463
Authentix Inc 4355 Excel Pkwy Ste 100 *Web:* authentix.com	Addison	TX	75001	469-737-4400	737-4409	692
Author House 1663 Liberty Dr *TF:* 888-519-5121 ■ *Web:* www.authorhouse.com	Bloomington	IN	47403	812-339-6000	339-6554	637-2
Author Services Inc 7051 Hollywood Blvd *TF:* 800-624-6504 ■ *Web:* authorservicesinc.com	Hollywood	CA	90028	323-466-3310	466-6474	463
AuthoraCare 914 Chapel Hill Rd *TF:* 800-588-8879 ■ *Web:* www.authoracare.org	Burlington	NC	27215	336-532-0100	532-0516	371
Authority Brands 7230 Lee Deforest Dr Ste 200 *TF:* 800-845-0428 ■ *Web:* www.theauthoritybrands.com	Columbia	MD	21046	800-845-0428		152
AuthorizeNet Corp PO Box 8999 *TF:* 877-447-3938 ■ *Web:* www.authorize.net	San Francisco	CA	94128	801-492-6450	492-6489	178-7
Authors Guild Bulletin 31 E 32nd St 7th Fl *Web:* www.authorsguild.org	New York	NY	10016	212-563-5904	564-5363	531-2
Autism Research Institute (ARI) 4182 Adams Ave **Fax Area Code:* 619 ■ *TF:* 866-366-3361 ■ *Web:* www.autism.org	San Diego	CA	92116	833-281-7165	563-6840*	48-17
Autism Society of America (ASA) 4340 E West Hwy Ste 350 *TF:* 800-328-8476 ■ *Web:* www.autism-society.org	Bethesda	MD	20814	301-657-0881	657-0869	48-17
Autistic Treatment Center Inc 10503 Metric Dr *TF:* 877-666-2747 ■ *Web:* www.atcoftexas.org	Dallas	TX	75243	972-644-2076		148
AUTM (Association of University Technology Managers) 111 Deer Lake Rd Ste 100 *Web:* www.autm.net	Deerfield	IL	60015	847-559-0846		49-19
Auto Barn 13 Harbor Pk Dr *Web:* www.autobarn.net	Port Washington	NY	11050	516-484-9500		54
Auto Builders 5715 Corporate Way *TF:* 800-378-5946 ■ *Web:* autobuilders.com	West Palm Beach	FL	33407	561-622-3515		186
Auto Cast Inc 4565 Spartan Industrial Dr SW *Web:* autocastinc.com	Grandville	MI	49418	616-534-4941		308
Auto Channel 332 W Broadway Ste 1604 *Web:* www.theautochannel.com	Louisville	KY	40202	502-992-0200	992-0201	740
Auto Chlor System 450 Ferguson Dr *Web:* www.autochlor.com	Mountain View	CA	94043	650-967-3085		386
Auto Clerk Inc 1981 North Bdwy Ste 430 *Web:* www.autoclerk.com	Walnut Creek	CA	94596	925-284-1005		177
Auto Club of America Corp (ACA) 9411 N Georgia St *TF:* 800-411-2007 ■ *Web:* www.autoclubofamerica.com	Oklahoma City	OK	73120	405-751-4430	751-4462	53
Auto Club Speedway 9300 Cherry Ave *TF:* 800-944-7223 ■ *Web:* www.autoclubspeedway.com	Fontana	CA	92335	909-429-5000	429-5500	515
Auto Crane Co PO Box 580697 **Fax Area Code:* 918 ■ *Web:* autocrane.us	Tulsa	OK	74158	800-777-2760	234-2177*	516
Auto Credit Express (ACE) 3252 University Dr Ste 250 *TF:* 888-535-2277 ■ *Web:* www.goacegroup.com	Auburn Hills	MI	48326	888-535-2277		57
Auto Data Direct Inc 1379 Cross Creek Cir *TF:* 866-923-3123 ■ *Web:* www.add123.com	Tallahassee	FL	32301	850-877-8804		224
Auto Europe 39 Commercial St *TF:* 800-223-5555 ■ *Web:* www.autoeurope.com	Portland	ME	04101	207-842-2000	842-2222	126
Auto Export Shipping Inc 187 Mill Ln Ste 103 *Web:* www.aesshipping.com	Mountainside	NJ	07092	908-436-2150		96
Auto FX Software 130 Inverness Plaz Ste 510 *TF:* 800-839-2008 ■ *Web:* www.autofx.com	Birmingham	AL	35242	205-980-0056	980-1121	178-8
Auto Industrial Marine Chemicals Inc 4595 Commerce Pky NE *Web:* www.aimchemicalsinc.com	Sugar Hill	GA	30518	770-945-2303		151
Auto Lenders Liquidation Ctr 104 Rt 73 *TF:* 888-305-5968 ■ *Web:* www.autolenders.com	Voorhees	NJ	08043	856-768-0053		57
Auto Mall, The 800 Pytney Rd *Web:* www.brattautomall.com	Brattleboro	VT	05301	802-275-4510		57
Auto Metal Craft Inc 12741 Capital St *Web:* www.autometal.com	Oak Park	MI	48237	248-398-2240	398-3411	489
Auto Meter Products Inc 413 W Elm St *TF:* 866-248-6356 ■ *Web:* www.autometer.com	Sycamore	IL	60178	815-895-8141	895-6786	495
Auto Pallets - Boxes Inc 28000 Southfield Rd *Web:* apallets.com	Lathrup Village	MI	48076	248-559-7744		104
Auto Parts Warehouse 16941 Keegan Ave *TF:* 800-913-6119 ■ *Web:* www.autopartswarehouse.com	Carson	CA	90746	801-214-2997		61

				Phone	Fax	Class
Auto Profit Masters 250 E Dry Creek Rd *TF:* 866-826-7911 ■ *Web:* autoprofitmasters.com	Littleton	CO	80122	303-795-5838		463
Auto Truck Inc 1420 Brewster Creek Blvd *TF:* 877-284-4440 ■ *Web:* www.autotruck.com	Bartlett	IL	60103	630-860-5600	860-5631	516
Auto Wheel Service Inc 1400 NW Raleigh St *TF:* 800-452-7270 ■ *Web:* autowheelservice.weebly.com	Portland	OR	97209	503-228-9346	273-2887	61
Autobahn Freight Lines Ltd 27 Automatic Rd *TF:* 877-989-9994 ■ *Web:* www.autobahnfreight.net	Brampton	ON	L6S5N8	416-741-5454	741-0155	311
Autobell Car Wash Inc 1521 E Third St *TF:* 800-582-8096 ■ *Web:* www.autobell.com	Charlotte	NC	28204	704-527-9274	333-0526	62-1
Autocar LLC 551 S Washington St *TF:* 888-218-3611 ■ *Web:* www.autocartruck.com	Hagerstown	IN	47346	765-489-5499		247
AutoCom Associates 100 W Long Lake Rd Ste 122 *Web:* www.usautocom.com	Bloomfield Hills	MI	48304	248-647-8621		636
Autodesk Inc 111 McInnis Pkwy *NASDAQ: ADSK* ■ *TF:* 800-964-6432 ■ *Web:* www.autodesk.com	San Rafael	CA	94903	415-507-5000	507-5100	178-5
Autodessys Inc 3518 Riverside Dr *Web:* www.formz.com	Columbus	OH	43221	614-488-8838	488-0848	178-8
Autodie LLC 44 Coldbrook St NW *Web:* www.autodie-llc.com	Grand Rapids	MI	49503	616-454-9361		757
Autodraft Inc 2815 Baird Rd *Web:* www.adraft.com	Fairport	NY	14450	585-389-1900		180
AutoFair Automotive Group 200 Keller St *Web:* www.autofair.com	Manchester	NH	03103	603-634-1000		57
Autofusion Corp 6215 Ferris Sq Ste 200 *TF:* 800-410-7354 ■ *Web:* www.autofusion.com	San Diego	CA	92121	800-410-7354		58
autoGraph Inc 999 N Northlake Way *Web:* www.autograph.me	Seattle	WA	98103	571-354-7273		195
Auto-Graphics Inc 10535 Foothill Blvd Ste 200 *TF:* 800-776-6939 ■ *Web:* www.auto-graphics.com	Rancho Cucamonga	CA	91730	909-595-7004	595-3506	781
AutoImmune Inc 1199 Madia St *OTC: AIMM* ■ *Web:* www.autoimmuneinc.com	Pasadena	CA	91103	626-792-1235	792-1236	582
Autoimmune Technologies LLC 1010 Common St Ste 1705 *Web:* www.autoimmune.com	New Orleans	LA	70112	504-529-9944	529-8982	85
Auto(in)Correct PO Box 201610 *Web:* www.auto-incorrect.com	Shaker Heights	OH	44120	216-647-0888	803-1165	637-10
Autoland 170 Rt 22 E *TF:* 877-813-7239 ■ *Web:* www.1800autoland.com	Springfield	NJ	07081	973-467-2900		57
Autoliv Inc 3350 Airport Rd *NYSE: ALV* ■ *Web:* www.autoliv.com	Ogden	UT	84405	801-625-8200		678
Autologic LLC 569B Southlake Blvd *Web:* autologicllc.com	North Chesterfield	VA	23236	804-675-3070		261
Autologue Computer Systems Inc 8452 Commonwealth Ave *Web:* www.autologue.com	Buena Park	CA	90621	714-522-3551		177
AutoManager Inc 7301 Topanga Canyon Blvd Ste 200 *TF:* 800-300-2808 ■ *Web:* www.automanager.com	Canoga Park	CA	91303	310-207-2202		809
Automann USA Inc 850 Randolph Rd *TF:* 888-288-6626 ■ *Web:* www.automann.com	Somerset	NJ	08873	201-529-4996		57
Automark Marking Systems 13475 Lakefront Dr	Earth City	MO	63045	314-739-0430		467
Automaster, The 3328 Shelburne Rd *TF:* 800-639-8033 ■ *Web:* www.theautomaster.com	Shelburne	VT	05482	802-985-8411	985-3730	57
Automatan 2911 Apache Dr *Web:* www.automatan.com	Plover	WI	54467	715-341-6501	345-1004	261
Automated Assembly Corp 20777 Kensington Blvd *TF:* 800-775-1699 ■ *Web:* www.autoassembly.com	Lakeville	MN	55044	952-469-6556		48-20
Automated Benefit Services Inc 8220 Irving Rd *TF:* 800-225-9369 ■ *Web:* www.abs-tpa.com	Sterling Heights	MI	48312	586-693-4300		390
Automated Building Components Inc 2359 Grant Rd *TF:* 800-837-2152 ■ *Web:* www.abctruss.com	North Baltimore	OH	45872	419-257-2152	257-2779	817
Automated Case Management Systems Inc 803 N Wilcox Ave Ste 7 *Web:* www.acmsinc.com	Hollywood	CA	90038	323-460-7700	460-7704	178-1
Automated Control Concepts Inc 3535 State Rte *Web:* automated-control.com	Neptune City	NJ	07753	732-922-6611	922-9611	173-1
Automated Conveyor Systems Inc (ACSI) 3850 Southland Dr *Web:* www.automatedconveyors.com	West Memphis	AR	72301	870-732-5050	732-5191	207
Automated Dispatch Systems LLC PO Box 490 *Web:* www.iasforensics.com	Parker	CO	80134	303-805-5301	841-7386	393
Automated Equipment 5140 Moundview Dr *Web:* www.autoequipllc.com	Red Wing	MN	55066	651-385-2271		298
Automated Equipment Co 10847 E Marginal Way S *TF:* 800-338-7649 ■ *Web:* www.aegates.com	Seattle	WA	98168	206-767-9080	767-9077	491
Automated Financial Systems Inc (AFS) 123 Summit Dr *Web:* www.afsvision.com	Exton	PA	19341	610-524-9300		178-11
Automated Installment Systems Inc 955 Executive Pky Ste 216 *TF:* 800-624-6308 ■ *Web:* www.automatedinstallment.com	Saint Louis	MO	63141	314-576-0007	878-7843	216
Automated Logic Corp 1150 Roberts Rd N *TF:* 877-866-1226 ■ *Web:* www.automatedlogic.com	Kennesaw	GA	30144	770-429-3000	429-3001	202
Automated Mailing Inc 4407 Wheeler Ave *Web:* www.amidirect.com	Alexandria	VA	22304	703-370-4606		5
Automated Medical Systems 2310 N Patterson St Bldg H *TF:* 800 256-3240 ■ *Web:* www.automedical.com	Valdosta	GA	31602	229-253-9526		179

	Phone	Fax	Class
Automated Office Systems 341 W Fallbrook Ave .... Fresno CA 93711 *Web:* aoscopy.com	559-431-3288		535
Automated Ophthalmics Inc 6671 Santa Barbara Rd Ste F .... Elkridge MD 21075 *TF:* 800-242-5602 ■ *Web:* www.auto-oph.com	410-772-1316	772-1388	542
Automated Packaging Systems Inc 10175 Phillip Pkwy .... Streetsboro OH 44241 *TF:* 800-527-0733 ■ *Web:* www.autobag.com	330-342-2000	342-2400	547
Automated Precision Inc 15000 Johns Hopkins Dr .... Rockville MD 20850 *TF:* 800-537-2720 ■ *Web:* www.apisensor.com	800-537-2720		295
Automated Production Machining Inc PO Box 1687 .... Gordonsville VA 22942 *Web:* apmmfg.com	540-832-0835	832-5842	454
Automated Products Inc 1812 Karau Dr .... Marshfield WI 54449 *Web:* apiebs.com	715-387-3426	387-6588	817
Automated Quality Technologies Inc 563 Shoreview Park Rd .... Saint Paul MN 55126 *TF:* 800-250-9297 ■ *Web:* www.lionprecision.com	651-484-6544		697
Automated Solutions Inc 1415 Fulton Rd Ste 205 .... Santa Rosa CA 95403 *TF:* 800-410-4632 ■ *Web:* www.automatedsolutions.com	707-578-5882	579-5756	178-1
Automated Systems Engineering Inc 2519 E Saint Vrain St .... Colorado Springs CO 80909 *Web:* www.goase.com	719-599-7477		202
Automated Systems Inc 2400 Commercial Dr .... Auburn Hills MI 48326 *Web:* www.automatedsystemsinc.org	248-373-5600		386
Automatic Data Processing Inc (ADP) 1 ADP Blvd .... Roseland NJ 07068 *NASDAQ: ADP* ■ *TF:* 800-225-5237 ■ *Web:* www.adp.com	800-225-5237		225
Automatic Feed Co 476 E Riverview Ave .... Napoleon OH 43545 *Web:* automaticfeed.com	419-592-0050	592-8590	494
Automatic Fire Protection Inc 4582 Old Christoval Rd .... San Angelo TX 76904 *Web:* www.automaticfireprotection.com	325-651-0000		610
Automatic Fire Sprinkler Inc 7272 Mars Dr .... Huntington Beach CA 92647 *TF:* 800-436-2066 ■ *Web:* www.afsfire.com	800-436-2066		610
Automatic Funds Transfer Services 151 S Landers St Ste C .... Seattle WA 98134 *TF:* 800-275-2033 ■ *Web:* www.afts.com	206-254-0975	254-0968	69
Automatic Ice & Beverage Inc 1400 Tuscaloosa Ave SW .... Birmingham AL 35211 *Web:* www.aibnow.com	205-787-9640		665
Automatic Machine Products Co (AMP) 400 Constitution Dr .... Taunton MA 02780 *Web:* ampcomp.com	508-822-4226	822-4476	621
Automatic Power Inc 10810 W Little York Rd Ste 130 .... Houston TX 77041 *Web:* www.automaticpower.com	713-228-5208	228-3717	439
Automatic Products Corp 2735 Forest Ln .... Garland TX 75042 *Web:* www.ap-corp.com	972-272-6422	494-0533	621
Automatic Slim's 83 S Second St .... Memphis TN 38103 *Web:* www.automaticslimsmemphis.com	901-525-7948		671
Automatic Spring Products Corp 803 Taylor Ave .... Grand Haven MI 49417 *Web:* www.automaticspring.com	616-842-7800	842-4380	718
Automatic Sprinkler of Texas Inc 1147 S Cedar Ridge Dr .... Duncanville TX 75137 *Web:* www.autosprinkleroftx.com	972-298-2772		610
Automatic Supply 4877 SR- 261 .... Newburgh IN 47630 *Web:* www.askautomatic.com	812-858-1809		420
Automatic Systems Inc 9230 E 47th St .... Kansas City MO 64133 *TF:* 800-366-3488 ■ *Web:* www.asi.com	816-356-0660	356-5730	207
Automatic Transmission Rebuilders Assn (ATRA) 2400 Latigo Ave .... Oxnard CA 93030 *TF:* 866-464-2872 ■ *Web:* www.atra.com	805-604-2000	604-2003	49-21
Automation & Control Technology Inc 6141 Avery Rd .... Dublin OH 43016 *Web:* advanzgauge.com	614-495-1120	495-1121	194
Automation & Modular Components Inc 10301 Enterprise Dr .... Davisburg MI 48350 *Web:* www.amcautomation.com	248-922-4740	625-3730	207
Automation Displays Inc 3533 White Ave .... Eau Claire WI 54703 *Web:* www.adipanel.com	715-834-9595	834-9596	392
Automation Engineering LLC 1100 W Grand Ave .... Salina KS 67401 **Fax Area Code:* 913 ■ *Web:* bcd.com	785-309-0505	677-0170*	190
Automation Graphics Inc 460 W 34th St .... New York NY 10001 *Web:* www.automationgraphics.com	212-290-8400		534
Automation Image Inc 2650 Vly View Ln Ste 100 .... Dallas TX 75234 *Web:* www.automationimage.com	972-247-8816		180
Automation International Inc 1020 Bahls St .... Danville IL 61832 *Web:* www.automation-intl.com	217-446-9500	446-6855	811
Automation Nth 491 Waldron Rd .... La Vergne TN 37086 *Web:* www.automationnth.com	615-793-7704		201
Automation Plastics Corp 150 Lena Dr .... Aurora OH 44202 *Web:* www.automationplastics.com	330-562-5148		608
Automation Products Group Inc (APG) 1025 W 1700 N .... Logan UT 84321 *TF:* 888-525-7300 ■ *Web:* www.apgsensors.com	435-753-7300	753-7490	201
Automation Service 13871 Parks Steed Dr .... Earth City MO 63045 *TF:* 800-325-4808 ■ *Web:* www.automationservice.com	314-785-6600	785-6610	201
Automation Services & Controls Inc 16765 Park Circle Dr .... Chagrin Falls OH 44023 *Web:* www.ascdrives.com	440-543-8146		261

	Phone	Fax	Class
Automation Specialists Inc 12555 Superior Ct .... Holland MI 49424 *Web:* www.automationspecialistsinc.com	616-738-8288	738-8285	494
Automation Systems Interconnect Inc 4700 Westport Dr Ste 500 .... Mechanicsburg PA 17055 *TF:* 877-650-5160 ■ *Web:* www.asi-ez.com	717-249-5581		201
Automation Technologies Inc 310 Roma Jean Pkwy .... Streamwood IL 60107 **Fax Area Code:* 703 ■ *Web:* www.automationtechnologiesinc.com	847-984-0882	883-1435*	180
Automation Tool Co 101 Mill Dr .... Cookeville TN 38501 *Web:* atcautomation.com	931-528-5417		207
Automec Inc 82 Calvary St .... Waltham MA 02453 *Web:* www.automec.com	781-893-3403	899-5708	493
Autometrix Precision Cutting Systems Inc 12098 Charles Dr .... Grass Valley CA 95945 *TF:* 800-635-3080 ■ *Web:* www.autometrix.com	530-477-5065		111
Automobile Consumer Services Inc 6249 Stewart Rd .... Cincinnati OH 45227 *TF:* 800-223-4882 ■ *Web:* www.acscorp.com	513-527-7700	527-7705	58
Automobile Magazine 831 S Douglas St .... El Segundo CA 90245 *Web:* www.automobilemag.com	310-531-9900		457-3
Automobile Racing Club of America 8117 Lewis Ave .... Temperance MI 48182 *Web:* www.arcaracing.com	734-847-6726		57
Automotive Aftermarket Industry Assn (AAIA) 7101 Wisconsin Ave .... Bethesda MD 20814 *Web:* www.autocare.org	301-654-6664	654-3299	49-21
Automotive Dealership Institute 6613 N Scottsdale Rd Ste 100 .... Scottsdale AZ 85250 *TF:* 877-998-7200 ■ *Web:* www.autodealerinstitute.com	480-998-7200	998-7220	167-3
Automotive Diagnostic Training 1205 N Red Gum St Ste L .... Anaheim CA 92806 *Web:* www.automotivediagnostictraining.com	714-634-3855	634-3985	167-3
Automotive Distribution Network 3085 Fountainside Dr Ste 210 .... Germantown TN 38138 *TF:* 800-616-7587 ■ *Web:* www.networkhq.org	800-616-7587		49-18
Automotive Distributors Company Inc 2981 Morse Rd .... Columbus OH 43231 **Fax Area Code:* 614 ■ *TF:* 800-421-5556 ■ *Web:* www.adw1.com	800-421-5556	476-9469*	61
Automotive Engine Rebuilders Assn (AERA) 500 Coventry Ln Ste 180 .... Crystal Lake IL 60014 *TF:* 888-326-2372 ■ *Web:* www.aera.org	847-541-6550	541-5808	49-21
Automotive Finance Corp (AFC) 13085 Hamilton Crossing Blvd .... Carmel IN 46032 *TF:* 888-335-6675 ■ *Web:* www.afcdealer.com	865-384-8250		216
Automotive Hall of Fame 21400 Oakwood Blvd .... Dearborn MI 48124 *Web:* www.automotivehalloffame.org	313-240-4000		520
Automotive Industry Action Group (AIAG) 26200 Lahser Rd Ste 200 .... Southfield MI 48033 *TF:* 877-275-2424 ■ *Web:* www.aiag.org	248-358-3570	358-3253	49-21
Automotive Management Institute 8209 Mid Cities Blvd .... North Richland Hills TX 76182 *Web:* www.amionline.org	817-514-2929		167-3
Automotive Manufacturing & Supply Co (AMSCO) 90 Plant Ave .... Hauppauge NY 11788 *TF:* 800-645-5604 ■ *Web:* www.amscovf.com	631-435-1400	435-1475	61
Automotive News Magazine 1155 Gratiot Ave .... Detroit MI 48207 *TF:* 877-812-1584 ■ *Web:* www.autonews.com	313-446-0450	446-0383	457-21
Automotive Oil Change Assn (AOCA) 330 N Wabash Ave Ste 2000 .... Chicago IL 60611 *TF:* 800-230-0702 ■ *Web:* www.aoca.org	312-321-5132	673-6832	49-21
Automotive Parts Headquarters 2959 Clearwater Rd .... Saint Cloud MN 56301 *TF:* 800-247-0339 ■ *Web:* www.autopartshq.com	320-252-5411	252-4256	61
Automotive Parts Remanufacturers Assn (APRA) 4215 Lafayette Center Dr Ste 3 .... Chantilly VA 20151 *TF:* 877-734-4827 ■ *Web:* www.apra.org	703-968-2772	968-2878	49-21
Automotive Profit Builders Inc (APB) PO Box 2011 .... Natick MA 01760 *Web:* www.apb.cc	508-626-9200		393
Automotive Quality & Logistics Inc 14744 Jib St .... Plymouth MI 48170 *Web:* www.aql-inc.com	734-459-1670		194
Automotive Racing Products Inc 1863 Eastman Ave .... Ventura CA 93003 *TF:* 800-826-3045 ■ *Web:* www.arp-bolts.com	805-339-2200	650-0742	350
Automotive Radiator Exchange Inc 10801 W 8 Mile Rd .... Detroit MI 48221 *TF:* 800-321-1532 ■ *Web:* www.radiatorexchange.com	800-321-1532		61
Automotive Recyclers Assn (ARA) 9113 Church St .... Manassas VA 20110 *TF:* 888-385-1005 ■ *Web:* www.a-r-a.org	571-208-0428	208-0430	49-21
Automotive Resources Inc 4119 Binion Way .... Lebanon OH 45036 *TF:* 800-562-3250 ■ *Web:* www.ari-hetra.com	800-562-3250		295
Automotive Resources Intl 4001 Leadenhall Rd .... Mount Laurel NJ 08054 *Web:* www.arifleet.com	856-778-1500	231-9106	289
Automotive Service Assn (ASA) 1901 Airport Fwy .... Bedford TX 76021 **Fax Area Code:* 817 ■ *TF:* 800-272-7467 ■ *Web:* asashop.org	800-272-7467	685-0225*	49-21
Automotive Service Inc 910 Mtn Home Rd PO Box 2157 .... Sinking Spring PA 19608 *Web:* reladyne.com	610-678-3421	678-3515	316
Automotive Training Center-Exton Campus 114 Pickering Way .... Exton PA 19341 *TF:* 888-321-8992 ■ *Web:* www.autotraining.edu	888-321-8992		166
AutoNation Ford Westlake 23775 Ctr Ridge Rd .... Westlake OH 44145 *Web:* autonationfordwestlake.com	440-296-3019		57
AutoNation Inc 200 SW 1st Ave Ste 1600 .... Fort Lauderdale FL 33301 *NYSE: AN* ■ *Web:* www.autonation.com	954-769-7000		57
Autonet Mobile Inc 3636 N Laughlin Dr Ste 150 .... Santa Rosa CA 95403 *TF:* 800-977-2107 ■ *Web:* www.autonetmobile.com	415-223-0316		645-11

Company	City	State	ZIP	Phone	Fax	Class
Auto-Owners Insurance Co 6101 Anacapri Blvd TF: 800-346-0346 ■ Web: www.auto-owners.com	Lansing	MI	48917	517-323-1200	323-8796	391-4
Autopacific Inc 2991 Dow Ave Web: www.autopacific.com	Tustin	CA	92780	714-838-4234		195
Autoquip Corp 1058 W Industrial Rd TF: 888-811-9876 ■ Web: www.autoquip.com	Guthrie	OK	73044	405-282-5200	282-8105	470
Autoquip Inc N57 W 13430 Reichert Ave Web: www.aqautomation.com	Menomonee Falls	WI	53051	262-781-6133	781-6188	189-11
AutoQuotes LLC 8800 W Baymeadows Way Ste 500 Web: aq-fes.com	Jacksonville	FL	32256	904-384-2279		57
Autorama Inc 3498 Jackson Ave Web: www.mbofmemphis.com	Memphis	TN	38119	901-345-6211		57
AutoRevo LTD 3820 American Dr Ste 110 TF: 888-311-7386 ■ Web: www.autorevo.com	Plano	TX	75075	888-311-7386		57
Autoscan Inc 4040 23rd Ave W Web: www.autoscaninc.com	Seattle	WA	98199	206-282-1616	352-6667	196
Autosplice Inc 10431 Wtridge Cir Ste 110 TF: 800-535-5538 ■ Web: autosplice.com	San Diego	CA	92121	858-535-0077	535-0130	815
Autotask Corp 26 Tech Valley Dr Ste 2 Web: www.autotask.com	East Greenbush	NY	12061	518-720-3500	720-3407	178-1
Autotest Co 5347 Dietrich Rd Web: www.autotest.com	San Antonio	TX	78219	210-661-8661	661-3624	248
Autotool 7875 Corporate Blvd Web: www.autotoolinc.com	Plain City	OH	43064	614-733-0222		454
Autotrol Corp 365 E Prairie St TF: 800-228-6207 ■ Web: www.autotrol.com	Crystal Lake	IL	60014	815-459-3080	459-3227	518
Autotruck Federal Credit Union 3611 Newburg Rd TF: 800-459-2328 ■ Web: www.autotruckfcu.org	Louisville	KY	40218	502-459-8981	458-0371	219
Auto-Turn Manufacturing Inc 9800 S 219th E Ave Web: www.auto-turn.com	Broken Arrow	OK	74014	918-451-4511	451-4404	454
AutoVIN Inc 13085 Hamilton Crossing Blvd TF: 866-585-8080 ■ Web: autovin.ca	Carmel	IN	46032	866-585-8080		58
AutoWeb Inc 18872 MacArthur Blvd Ste 200 NASDAQ: AUTO ■ TF: 888-422-8999 ■ Web: www.autobytel.com	Irvine	CA	92612	949-225-4500		58
AutoZone Inc 123 S Front St NYSE: AZO ■ TF: 800-288-6966 ■ Web: www.autozone.com	Memphis	TN	38103	901-495-6500		54
Autry Greer & Sons Inc 2850 W Main St TF: 800-999-7750 ■ Web: www.greers.com	Mobile	AL	36612	251-457-8655	456-3744	345
Autry National Center Museum of the American West 4700 Western Heritage Way Web: theautry.org	Los Angeles	CA	90027	323-667-2000	660-5721	520
Autry Technology Ctr 1201 W Willow Web: www.autrytech.edu	Enid	OK	73703	580-242-2750	233-8262	167-3
Autumn Harp Inc 26 Thompson Dr Web: www.autumnharp.com	Essex Junction	VT	05452	802-857-4600	857-4601	214
Autumn Leaves Publishing 8201 Golf Course Rd NW D3-334 TF: 800-247-6553 ■ Web: www.autumnleavespublishing.com	Albuquerque	NM	87120	505-899-1044	890-8385	637-2
Autumn Press Inc 945 Camelia St Web: www.autumnpress.com	Berkeley	CA	94710	510-654-4545		627
Auven Therapeutics Management LLP 6501 Redhook Plz Ste 201 Web: www.auventx.com	Saint Thomas	VI	00802	340-779-6908		528
Auvil Fruit Company Inc 21902 SR 97 Web: www.auvilfruit.com	Orondo	WA	98843	509-784-1711		315-3
AUX Anciens Canadiens 34 Rue Saint-Louis CP 175 Succursale Haute-Ville Web: www.auxancienscanadiens.qc.ca	Quebec City	QC	G1R4P3	418-692-1627	692-5419	671
Auxilius Heavy Industries LLC 301 S Adeway TF: 800-892-0118 ■ Web: auxheavyindustries.com	Fowler	IN	47944	800-892-0118		261
Auyuittuq National Park PO Box 353 Web: www.pc.gc.ca	Pangnirtung	NU	X0A0R0	867-473-2500	473-8612	563
AV & R 269 Prince St Web: avr-global.com	Montreal	QC	H3C2N4	514-788-1420		21
AV Homes Inc 4900 N Scottsdale Rd Ste 2000 NASDAQ: AVHI ■ TF: 800-284-6637 ■ Web: www.avhomesinc.com	Scottsdale	AZ	85253	480-214-7400		653
AV Nackawic Inc 103 Pinder Rd Web: av-group.ca	Nackawic	NB	E6G1W4	506-575-3200		638
AVA (Academy of Vocal Arts) 1920 Spruce St Web: www.avaopera.org	Philadelphia	PA	19103	215-735-1685	732-2189	573-2
AVA (Association for Vascular Access) 5526 W 13400 S Ste 229 TF: 877-924-2821 ■ Web: www.avainfo.org	Herriman	UT	84096	801-792-9079	601-8012	49-8
AVA (American Volkssport Assn) 1001 Pat Booker Rd Ste 101 Web: www.ava.org	Universal City	TX	78148	210-659-2112	659-1212	48-22
AVA Pork Products Inc 383 W John St PO Box 805 Web: www.avapork.com	Hicksville	NY	11802	516-750-1500	750-1501	297-9
AVAD Canada Ltd 5655 Kennedy Rd Unit 4 TF: 866-523-2823 ■ Web: avad.com	Mississauga	ON	L4Z3E1	866-523-2823		174
Avail Technologies Inc 1960 Old Gatesburg Rd Web: www.availtec.com	State College	PA	16803	814-234-3394		261
Avail Technology 415 N Prince St Ste 200 TF: 800-360-5000 ■ Web: www.availtechsolutions.com	Lancaster	PA	17603	888-342-8245		196
Availink Inc 20201 Century Blvd Ste 160 Web: www.availink.com	Germantown	MD	20874	301-515-6716	916-6199	256
Avalanche Creative Svcs Inc 135 W 29th St Web: avalanchecreative.tv	New York	NY	10001	212-206-9335		514
Avaleris Inc 1400-45 O'Connor St Web: www.avaleris.com	Ottawa	ON	K1P1A4	613-237-9695		196
Avalex Technologies Corp 2665 Gulf Breeze Pkwy Web: avalex.com	Gulf Breeze	FL	32563	850-470-8464		21
Avalign Technologies Inc 2275 Half Day R Ste 126 TF: 855-282-5446 ■ Web: www.advantismedical.com	Bannockburn	IL	60015	855-282-5446		225
Avalon Building Concepts 5017 Division Ave S Web: www.avalonbuildingconcepts.net	Grand Rapids	MI	49548	616-871-2507	261-9776	189-12
Avalon Capital Management 495 Seaport Ct Ste 106 Web: www.avaloncapital.com	Redwood City	CA	94063	650-306-1500		401
Avalon Consulting LLC 6850 TPC Dr Ste 202 Web: www.avalonconsult.com	McKinney	TX	75071	469-424-3449		196
Avalon Copy Centers of America Inc 901 N State St Web: www.teamavalon.com	Syracuse	NY	13208	315-471-3333		113
Avalon Corporate Furnished Apartments 1553 Empire Blvd TF: 800-934-9763 ■ Web: rochesterfurnished.com	Webster	NY	14580	585-671-4421	671-9771	379
Avalon Development Corp PO Box 80268 Web: avalonalaska.com	Fairbanks	AK	99708	907-457-5159	455-8069	393
Avalon Holdings Corp 1 American Way NYSE: AWX ■ Web: www.avalonholdings.com	Warren	OH	44484	330-856-8800	856-8480	804
Avalon Hotel Palm Springs 415 S Belardo Rd Web: www.avalon-hotel.com	Palm Springs	CA	92262	760-318-3012	318-3024	379
Avalon Hotel, The 16 E 32 St Web: www.avalonhotelnyc.com	New York	NY	10016	212-299-7000		378
Avalon Log Homes 1801 S Camas St Web: www.avalonloghomes.com	Nampa	ID	83686	208-467-6098		187
Avalon Motel Corp 1529 Broadway Web: avalon-motel.com	Saugus	MA	01906	781-233-4200		379
Avalon Net Worth 1001 Ave of the Americas 10th Fl Web: www.avalonnetworth.com	New York	NY	10018	212-764-5610		690
Avalon Pontoon Boats 903 Michigan Ave TF: 800-334-2913 ■ Web: www.avalonpontoons.com	Alma	MI	48801	800-334-2913		90
Avalon School of Cosmetology 410 E Bell Rd Ste G100 Web: www.avalon.edu	Phoenix	AZ	85022	602-443-0076	443-0087	685
Avalon School of Massage 2990 Richmond Ave Ste 200 TF: 866-994-8028 ■ Web: www.avalonmassageschool.com	Houston	TX	77098	713-333-5250	333-5255	685
Avalon Shutters Inc 725 S Lugo Ave Web: avalonshutters.com	San Bernardino	CA	92408	909-888-8227		499
Avalon Trust Co 125 Lincoln Ave Ste 301 Web: avalontrust.com	Santa Fe	NM	87501	505-983-1111		401
Avalon Ventures 1134 Kline St Web: www.avalon-ventures.com	La Jolla	CA	92037	858-348-2180		690
Avalon Vision Solutions LLC 422 Thornton Rd Ste 104 Web: www.avalonvisionsolutions.com	Lithia Springs	GA	30122	770-944-8445		407
Avalotis Co 400 Jones St Web: www.avalotis.com	Verona	PA	15147	412-828-9666	828-6599	189-8
Avanade Inc 818 Stewart St TF: 844-282-6233 ■ Web: www.avanade.com	Seattle	WA	98101	206-239-5600		39
Avancen MOD Corp 1156 Bowman Rd Ste 200 TF: 800-607-1230 ■ Web: www.avancen.com	Mount Pleasant	SC	29464	800-607-1230		250
Avancent Consulting Corp 1896 Kentucky Ave Web: www.avancent.com	Winter Park	FL	32789	407-897-8664		196
Avani Media LLC 315 Montgomery St Ste 900 Web: avanimedia.com	San Francisco	CA	94104	415-331-2150	331-2151	196
AVANIR Pharmaceuticals 30 Enterprise Ste 400 NASDAQ: AVNR ■ TF: 855-572-2722 ■ Web: www.avanir.com	Aliso Viejo	CA	92656	949-389-6700	643-6800	85
Avansis Ventures LLC 12710 Popes Head Rd Web: www.avansis.com	Clifton	VA	20124	703-796-0222		792
Avant Business Services Inc 60 E 42nd St Lowr Level Web: www.avantservices.com	New York	NY	10165	212-687-5145		41
Avant Ministries 10000 N Oak Trafficway TF: 800-468-1892 ■ Web: avantministries.org	Kansas City	MO	64155	816-734-8500		48-20
Avant Solution, The 22511 Telegraph Rd Ste 115 Web: avantsolution.com	Southfield	MI	48033	248-423-0052		177
Avant Strategies LLC 81 Pondfield Rd Ste 156 Web: avantstrategies.net	Bronxville	NY	10708	914-861-3131		195
Avant Systems Group 815-1661 Portage Ave Web: avant.ca	Winnipeg	MB	R3J3T7	204-789-9596		180
Avantax Wealth Management 3200 Olympus Blvd Ste 100 TF: 866-218-8206 ■ Web: www.avantaxwealthmanagement.com	Dallas	TX	75019	972-870-6000	870-6128	401
Avante Behavioral Health Plan 1111 E Herndon Ave Ste 308 TF: 800-498-9055 ■ Web: www.avantehealth.com	Fresno	CA	93720	559-261-9060	261-9073	194
Avante Group Inc 4601 Sheridan St 5th Fl Web: www.avantecenters.com	Hollywood	FL	33021	954-987-7180		371
Avante Security Inc 1959 Leslie St Web: www.avantesecurity.com	Toronto	ON	M3B2M3	416-923-6984		693
Avante Solutions Inc 728 W Jackson Ste 105 Web: www.avantesolutions.com	Chicago	IL	60661	312-715-1080		445

Company / Address	City	State	ZIP	Phone	Fax	Class
Avantec Vascular Corp 605 W California Ave *Web:* www.avantecvascular.com	Sunnyvale	CA	94086	408-329-5400		476
Avantech Inc 95-A Sunbelt Blvd *Web:* www.avantechinc.com	Columbia	SC	29203	803-407-7171		358
Avant-Garde Consulting Services Inc (A-GCS) 10993 N Harrells Ferry Rd *TF:* 866-839-7230 ■ *Web:* agcs.imiscloud.com	Baton Rouge	LA	70816	225-272-5432		194
Avanti 4620 Grandview Ave *Web:* avanticheyenne.com	Cheyenne	WY	82009	307-634-3432		671
Avanti Corp 6621 Richmond Hgwy Ste 200 *Web:* www.avanticorporation.com	Alexandria	VA	22306	703-765-0060	765-0694	194
Avanti Destinations Inc 111 SW Columbia St Ste 1200 **Fax Area Code:* 800 ■ *TF:* 800-422-5053 ■ *Web:* www.avantidestinations.com	Portland	OR	97201	503-295-1100	422-9505*	771
Avanti Engineering Inc 200 W Lake Dr *Web:* www.avantiengineering.com	Glendale Heights	IL	60139	630-260-1333	260-1762	621
Avanti Foods 109 Depot St *TF:* 800-243-3739 ■ *Web:* www.avantifoods.com	Walnut	IL	61376	815-379-2155		296-36
Avanti Home Health Care 31215 Novi Rd *Web:* www.avantihhc.com	Novi	MI	48377	248-863-4650	863-4655	363
Avanti Polar Lipids Inc 700 Industrial Pk Dr *TF:* 800-227-0651 ■ *Web:* avantilipids.com	Alabaster	AL	35007	205-663-2494	663-0756	479
Avanti Press Inc 155 W Congress St Ste 200 **Fax Area Code:* 800 ■ *TF:* 800-228-2684 ■ *Web:* www.avantipress.com	Detroit	MI	48226	313-961-0022	875-9690*	130
Avanti Restaurant 2728 E Thomas Rd *Web:* www.avanti-az.com	Phoenix	AZ	85016	602-956-0900		671
Avantia Inc 9655 Sweet Vly Dr *Web:* www.avantia-inc.com	Valley View	OH	44125	216-901-9366		196
Avantica Technologies 2680 Bayshore Pkwy Ste 416 *TF:* 877-372-1955 ■ *Web:* www.avantica.net	Mountain View	CA	94043	650-248-9678		196
Avantpage 1138 Villaverde Ln Ste 370 *Web:* www.avantpage.com	Davis	CA	95616	530-750-2040	750-2024	317
Avanzado LLC 25330 Interchange Ct *TF:* 800-913-1058 ■ *Web:* www.avanzadollc.com	Farmington Hills	MI	48335	800-913-1058		459
Avara's Academy of Hair Design 16 N Dundalk Ave *Web:* www.avarahairacademy.com	Baltimore	MD	21222	410-285-7820	288-5212	167-3
Avascent Group, The 1615 L St NW Ste 1200 *Web:* www.avascent.com	Washington	DC	20036	202-452-6990		463
Avatar Engineering Inc 14360 W 96th Terr *Web:* avatarpivot.com	Lenexa	KS	66215	913-897-6757		256
Avatar Management Services Inc 8157 Bavaria Dr E *TF:* 800-728-2827 ■ *Web:* avatarms.com	Macedonia	OH	44056	330-963-3900		463
Avatar Studios Inc 2675 Scott Ave Ste G *Web:* avatar-studios.com	Saint Louis	MO	63103	314-533-2242		514
Avatier Corp 2603 Camino Ramon Ste 110 *TF:* 800-609-8610 ■ *Web:* www.avatier.com	San Ramon	CA	94583	925-217-5170	275-0853	178-12
Avaya Government Solutions Inc 12730 Fair Lakes Cir *TF:* 800-492-6769 ■ *Web:* www.avaya.com	Fairfax	VA	22033	703-653-8000		178-10
Avaya Inc 211 Mt Airy Rd *TF:* 866-462-8292 ■ *Web:* www.avaya.com	Basking Ridge	NJ	07920	908-953-6000		176
AVBOT (Antelope Valley Board of Trade) 41319 W 12th St Ste 104 *Web:* www.avbot.org	Palmdale	CA	93551	661-947-9033		139
AVCF (Arkansas Valley Correctional Facility) 12750 Hwy 96 Ln 13 *Web:* www.colorado.gov	Crowley	CO	81033	719-267-3520	267-5024	213
Avchem Inc 5757 Phantom Dr Ste 300 *Web:* www.avchem.com	Hazelwood	MO	63042	314-880-2700	880-2701	146
Avcom Inc 22372 Lorain Rd *Web:* www.avcomcle.com	Cleveland	OH	44126	440-777-2442	777-9282	246
Avcom SMT Inc 213 E Broadway *Web:* avcomsmt.com	Westerville	OH	43081	614-882-8176		668
Avcon Industries Hangar M City County Airport *Web:* www.avconindustries.com	Newton	KS	67114	316-284-2842	284-2844	20
Avcorp Industries Inc 10025 River Way *Web:* www.avcorp.com	Delta	BC	V4G1M7	604-582-1137		22
Ave Intervision LLC 1840 W State St *TF:* 800-448-9126 ■ *Web:* www.amvonet.com	Alliance	OH	44601	800-448-9126		685
Ave Maria University 5050 Ave Maria Blvd *TF:* 877-283-8648 ■ *Web:* www.avemaria.edu	Naples	FL	34119	239-280-2500	280-2556	166
Ave Maria University School of Law 1025 Commons Cir *Web:* www.avemarialaw.edu	Naples	FL	34119	239-687-5300		167-1
Aveanna Healthcare 400 Interstate N Pkwy SE Ste 1600 *TF:* 800-408-4442 ■ *Web:* www.aveanna.com	Atlanta	GA	30339	770-441-1580		363
Avec Restaurant 615 W Randolph St *Web:* www.avecrestaurant.com	Chicago	IL	60661	312-377-2002		671
AV-ED Flight School Inc Winchester Regional Airport 615 Airport Rd Ste 101 *Web:* www.av-ed.com	Winchester	VA	22602	540-542-1123	542-1124	685
Aveda Arts & Sciences Institute Atlanta 1745 Peachtree St NE Ste A *Web:* avedaarts.edu	Atlanta	GA	30309	404-649-7119		167-3
Aveda Corp 4000 Pheasant Ridge Dr *TF:* 800-644-4831 ■ *Web:* www.aveda.com	Blaine	MN	55449	800-644-4831		214
Aveda Fredric's Institute 7664 Voice of America Centre Dr *Web:* www.avedafi.edu	West Chester	OH	45069	513-533-0700		167-3
Aveda Institute 210 N University Ave *Web:* www.aveda.edu	Provo	UT	84601	801-375-1501		167-3
Aveda Institute Chapel Hill 201 S Estes Dr University Pl 200-B *Web:* www.nurturavedainstitutes.com	Chapel Hill	NC	27516	919-629-2817	969-8390	167-3
Aveda Institute Charlotte 1520 S Blvd Ste 150 *Web:* www.avedainstitutessouth.edu	Charlotte	NC	28203	704-333-9940		167-3
Aveda Institute Denver 700 16th St *Web:* avedainspiregreatness.com	Denver	CO	80202	303-567-7500		167-3
Aveda Institute Las Vegas 4856 S Eastern Ave *Web:* www.avedalasvegas.com	Las Vegas	NV	89119	702-459-2900		167-3
Aveda Institute Tallahassee 2020 W Pensacola St *Web:* www.beaveda.com	Tallahassee	FL	32304	850-222-4299		167-3
Avedis Zildjian Co 22 Longwater Dr *TF:* 800-229-8672 ■ *Web:* zildjian.com	Norwell	MA	02061	781-871-2200		527
AVEM (Association of Vacuum Equipment Manufacturers) 201 Pk Washington Ct *Web:* avem.org	Falls Church	VA	22046	703-538-3543	241-5603	49-13
Avemco Insurance Co 8490 Progress Dr Ste 100 *TF:* 888-241-7891 ■ *Web:* www.avemco.com	Frederick	MD	21701	888-241-7891		391-4
Avenal State Prison 1 Kings Hwy PO Box 8 *Web:* cdcr.ca.gov	Avenal	CA	93204	559-386-0587		213
Avendra LLC 540 Gaither Rd Ste 200 *TF:* 866-283-6372 ■ *Web:* www.avendra.com	Rockville	MD	20850	301-825-0500	825-0497	379
Avenger Aircraft & Services LLC 125 Byrdland Dr *Web:* www.avengeraerospace.com	Greenville	SC	29607	864-232-8073	232-8074	194
Aventa Credit Union 2735 Dublin Blvd *Web:* aventa.com	Colorado Springs	CO	80918	719-482-7600		219
Aventura Mall 19501 Biscayne Blvd *Web:* aventuramall.com	Aventura	FL	33180	305-935-1110		460
Aventure International Aviation Services 108 International Dr *Web:* www.aventureaviation.com	Peachtree City	GA	30269	770-632-7930	632-7931	21
Avenue 365 W Passaic St *TF:* 888-843-2836 ■ *Web:* www.avenue.com	Rochelle Park	NJ	07662	201-845-0880		157-6
Avenue 954 W Washington Blvd *Web:* www.avenue-inc.com	Chicago	IL	60657	312-787-8300		5
Avenue Capital Group LLC 399 Park Ave 6th Fl *Web:* www.avenuecapital.com	New York	NY	10022	212-878-3500		401
Avenue Inn & Spa 33 Wilmington Ave *TF:* 800-433-5870 ■ *Web:* avenueinn.com	Rehoboth Beach	DE	19971	800-433-5870		379
Avenue Plaza Resort 2111 St Charles Ave *TF:* 800-614-8685 ■ *Web:* www.avenueplazaresort.com	New Orleans	LA	70130	504-566-1212		379
Avenue Staffing 7000 57th Ave N Ste 120 *Web:* www.avenuestaffing.com	Crystal	MN	55428	763-537-6104	537-7514	260
Aveo Pharmaceuticals Inc 75 Sidney St *NASDAQ: AVEO* ■ *Web:* www.aveooncology.com	Cambridge	MA	02139	617-588-1960	995-4995	668
Aveox Inc 2265A Ward Ave *Web:* www.aveox.com	Simi Valley	CA	93065	805-915-0200		518
Avera Health 3900 W Avera Dr *Web:* www.avera.org	Sioux Falls	SD	57108	605-322-4700	322-4799	353
Avera Health Plans Inc 3816 S Elmwood Ave Ste 100 *Web:* www.averahealthplans.com	Sioux Falls	SD	57105	605-322-4500		391-3
Avere Systems 910 River Ave *TF:* 888-882-8373 ■ *Web:* www.microsoft.com	Pittsburgh	PA	15212	412-894-2570	894-2589	173-8
Averitt Express Inc 1415 Neal St *TF:* 800-283-7488 ■ *Web:* www.averittexpress.com	Cookeville	TN	38501	800-283-7488		780
Avery Abrasives Inc 2225 Reservoir Ave *Web:* www.averyabrasives.com	Trumbull	CT	06611	203-372-3513		1
Avery Color Studios 511 D Ave *TF:* 800-722-9925 ■ *Web:* www.averycolorstudios.com	Gwinn	MI	49841	906-346-3908	346-3015	637-2
Avery County 4501 Tynecastle Hwy Unit 2 Intersection of NC 105 & NC 184 *TF:* 800-972-2183 ■ *Web:* averycounty.com	Banner Elk	NC	28604	828-898-5605	898-8287	338
Avery Dennison *Fastener Div* 224 Industrial Rd *TF:* 800-225-5913 ■ *Web:* fastener.averydennison.com	Fitchburg	MA	01420	800-225-5913	848-2169	608
Avery Dennison Corp 207 Goode Ave Bldg 8 *NYSE: AVY* ■ *TF:* 888-567-4387 ■ *Web:* www.averydennison.com	Glendale	CA	91203	626-304-2000		732
Avery Dennison Specialty Tapes 250 Chester St **Fax Area Code:* 888 ■ *TF:* 866-462-8379 ■ *Web:* www.tapes.averydennison.com	Painesville	OH	44077	866-462-8379	358-4469*	732
Avery Island Technologies LLC (AIT) 601 Poydras St Ste 1815 *Web:* www.averytech.com	New Orleans	LA	70130	504-200-4248	895-5344	196
Avery Point Marketing Solutions LLC 19 Ashley Ln	Colchester	CT	06415	860-537-2440		391
Avery Weigh-Tronix Inc 1000 Armstrong Dr *TF:* 800-458-7062 ■ *Web:* www.averyweigh-tronix.com	Fairmont	MN	56031	507-238-4461	238-8258	684
Aves Audio Visual Systems Inc PO Box 500 *TF:* 800-365-2837 ■ *Web:* www.avesav.com	Sugar Land	TX	77487	281-295-1300	295-1310	38
AVESTA 1 Executive Dr Ste 120 *Web:* avestacs.com	Somerset	NJ	08873	201-369-9400		196
Avfinity LLC 11782 Jollyville Rd *Web:* www.avfinity.com	Austin	TX	78759	512-535-3416		387
AVG Automation 4140 Utica St *TF:* 877-774-3279 ■ *Web:* www.ezautomation.net	Bettendorf	IA	52722	877-774-3279		253
AVI Career Training 10130 Colvin Run Rd Ste A & B *Web:* www.avicareertraining.com	Great Falls	VA	22066	703-759-2200		167-3
AVI Casino Enterprise Inc 10000 Aha Macav Pkwy *TF:* 800-522-4700 ■ *Web:* www.avicasino.com	Laughlin	NV	89029	702-535-5555		452

Phone | Fax | Class

AVI Systems Inc
9675 W 76th St Ste 200 . . . . Eden Prairie MN 55344 952-949-3700 949-6000 647
TF: 800-488-4954 ■ *Web:* www.avisystems.com
Avia Dental Plan 1025 Main St Ste 916 . . . . Wheeling WV 26003 304-233-2253 214-1257 391-3
TF: 888-431-2273 ■ *Web:* www.aviadental.com
Aviagen Group 5015 Bradford Dr. . . . . Huntsville AL 35805 256-890-3800 890-3919 10-8
Web: www.en.aviagen.com
Avian Veterinary Services of Georgia
3761 N Druid Hills Rd . . . . Decatur GA 30033 404-248-8977 794
Web: forpetssake.com
Aviat Aircraft Inc 672 S Washington . . . . Afton WY 83110 307-885-3151 529
Web: aviataircraft.com
Aviation Adventures
10600 Harry J Parrish Blvd. . . . . Manassas VA 20110 703-530-7737 530-8474 167-3
Web: www.aviationadventures.com
Aviation Brake Services Inc
7274 NW 34th St . . . . Miami FL 33122 305-594-4677 22
Web: www.aviationbrake.com
Aviation Capital Group Corp
840 Newport Center Dr Ste 300 . . . . Newport Beach CA 92660 949-219-4600 759-5675 23
Web: www.aviationcapitalgroup.com
Aviation Devices & Electronic Components LLC
1810 Mony St. . . . . Fort Worth TX 76102 817-738-9161 57
Web: www.avdec.com
Aviation Ground Equipment Corp
53 Hanse Ave . . . . Freeport NY 11520 516-546-0003 22
TF: 800-758-0044 ■ *Web:* aviationgroundequip.com
Aviation Institute of Maintenance
4455 South Blvd. . . . . Virginia Beach VA 23452 888-349-5387 20
TF: 888-349-5387 ■ *Web:* www.aviationmaintenance.edu
Aviation Insurance Managers Inc
11650 Cleveland Ave NW . . . . Uniontown OH 44685 330-494-1500 390
TF: 800-827-4554 ■ *Web:* aimofohio.com
Aviation Legal Group PA
5525 NW 15 Ave Ste 301A . . . . Fort Lauderdale FL 33309 954-763-5565 41
Web: aviationlegalgroup.com
Aviation Management Systems Inc
155 Fleet St . . . . Portsmouth NH 03801 603-431-3362 463
Web: amsinc.aero
Aviation Materials Management Inc
2581 Rulon White Blvd. . . . . Ogden UT 84404 801-782-8450 529
Web: www.avmat.com
Aviation Partners Inc
7299 Perimeter Rd S. . . . . Seattle WA 98108 206-762-1171 529
Web: www.aviationpartners.com
Aviation Spares & Services I
8920 152nd Ave NE . . . . Redmond WA 98052 425-869-7799 770
Web: www.assic.com
Aviation Supplies & Academics Inc
7005 132nd Pl SE. . . . . Newcastle WA 98059 425-235-1500 637-2
TF: 800-272-2359 ■ *Web:* www.asa2fly.com
Aviation Technical Services (ATS)
3121 109th St SW . . . . Everett WA 98204 425-347-3030 24
TF: 888-347-2341 ■ *Web:* atsmro.com
Aviation Week & Space Technology Magazine
2121 K St NW Ste 210 . . . . Washington DC 20037 202-383-2300 457-19
Web: www.aviationweek.com
Aviation Week Network
1200 G St NW Ste 900 . . . . Washington DC 20005 800-525-5003 383-2438* 531-13
**Fax Area Code:* 202 ■ *TF:* 800-525-5003 ■ *Web:* www.aviationweek.com
Aviator College of Aeronautical Science & Technology
3800 St Lucie Blvd . . . . Fort Pierce FL 34946 772-672-8222 466-4886 167-3
TF: 800-635-9032 ■ *Web:* www.aviator.edu
Avibank Manufacturing Inc
11500 Sherman Way. . . . . North Hollywood CA 91605 818-392-2100 255-2094 278
Web: www.avibank.com
Avid Identification Systems Inc
3185 Hamner Ave. . . . . Norco CA 92860 951-371-7505 10-3
TF: 800-336-2843 ■ *Web:* avidid.com
Avid Inc 29 West St. . . . . East Hartford CT 06108 860-528-1988 344
Web: www.avidinc.com
Avid Payment Solutions
950 S Old Woodward Ste 220. . . . . Birmingham MI 48009 248-723-5760 671-9773* 255
**Fax Area Code:* 866 ■ *TF:* 888-855-8644 ■ *Web:* www.avidpays.com
Avid Radiopharmaceuticals Inc
3711 Market St 7th Fl. . . . . Philadelphia PA 19104 215-298-0700 231
Web: www.avidrp.com
Avid Technology Inc
65-75 Network Dri . . . . Burlington MA 01803 978-640-6789 640-3366 178-8
NASDAQ: AVID ■ *TF:* 800-949-2843 ■ *Web:* www.avid.com
Avideon Corp PO Box 4830 . . . . Baltimore MD 21211 888-368-1237 195
TF: 888-368-1237 ■ *Web:* www.avideon.com
Avidex Industries LLC
13555 Bel-Red Rd Ste 226 . . . . Bellevue WA 98005 425-643-0330 52
TF: 800-798-0330 ■ *Web:* www.avidex.com
Avidian Technologies Inc
2053 152nd Ave NE . . . . Redmond WA 98052 800-399-8980 177
TF: 800-860-5534 ■ *Web:* www.avidian.com
Avidity LLC
10740 Nall Ave Ste 201 . . . . Overland Park KS 66211 913-890-2050 390
Web: avidityinsurance.com
Avidity Science 819 Bakke Ave. . . . . Waterford WI 53185 262-534-5181 534-5184 420
TF: 800-558-5913 ■ *Web:* www.avidityscience.com
Avidyne 710 North Dr . . . . Melbourne FL 32934 321-751-8520 22
Web: www.avidyne.com
Avila Retail Development & Management LLC
5001 Ellison St NE . . . . Albuquerque NM 87109 505-341-3753 292
Web: www.avilaretail.com
Avila Rodriguez Hernandez Mena & Ferri LLP (ARHMF)
2525 Ponce De Leon Blvd PH 1225 . . . . Coral Gables FL 33134 305-779-3560 445
Web: arhmf.com
Avila University 11901 Wornall Rd. . . . . Kansas City MO 64145 816-501-2400 501-2453 166
TF: 866-943-5787 ■ *Web:* www.avila.edu
Avila's Construction
1403 Janann Ave . . . . Arlington TX 76014 214-520-2700 671
Web: avilasconstructioncompany.com
Avilar Technologies Inc
6760 Alexander Bell Dr Ste 105 . . . . Columbia MD 21046 410-290-0008 177
Web: www.avilar.com

Aviles Engineering Corp
5790 Windfern Rd. . . . . Houston TX 77041 713-895-7645 895-7943 256
Web: www.avilesengineering.com
Avineon Inc 1430 Spring Hill Rd Ste 300 . . . . McLean VA 22102 703-671-1900 671-1901 177
Web: www.avineon.com
Aviojet Corp
76 Brookside Dr . . . . Upper Saddle River NJ 07458 201-825-3111 825-6950 770
Web: www.aviojet.com
Avion Solutions Inc
4905 Research Dr NW . . . . Huntsville AL 35805 256-721-7006 261
Web: www.avionsolutions.com
Avion Technologies Inc
1203 Lorimar Dr. . . . . Mississauga ON L5S1M9 905-670-1570 670-1568 709
Web: www.avion-tech.com
Avionic Instruments Inc
1414 Randolph Ave. . . . . Avenel NJ 07001 732-388-3500 382-4996 253
Web: avionicinstruments.com
Avionics Test & Analysis Corp
4540 E Hwy 20 Ste 6 . . . . Niceville FL 32578 850-897-4553 897-4331 261
Web: www.avtest.com
Avior Integrated Products Inc
1001 Autoroute 440 Ouest . . . . Laval QC H7L3W3 450-629-6200 21
Web: www.avior.ca
Aviotrade 10850 NW 21st St . . . . Miami FL 33172 305-717-5000 717-5001 492
Web: www.aviotradegroup.com
Avis Furniture Co 1410 Union Ave . . . . Kansas City MO 64101 816-421-5939 321
Web: www.avisfurniture.com
Avis Industrial Corp 1909 S Main St . . . . Upland IN 46989 765-998-8100 998-8111 60
Web: www.avisindustrial.com
Avis Rent A Car System Inc
6 Sylvan Way . . . . Parsippany NJ 07054 973-496-3500 496-3444 126
Web: www.avis.com
Avisen Securities Inc
3620 American River Dr Ste 145. . . . . Sacramento CA 95864 916-480-2747 690
TF: 800-230-7704 ■ *Web:* www.avisensecurities.com
Avista Capital Partners LLP
65 E 55th St 18th Fl . . . . New York NY 10022 212-593-6900 593-6901 690
Web: avistacapitalpartners.de
Avista Corp PO Box 3727 MSC-19 . . . . Spokane WA 99220 509-495-4203 787
NYSE: AVA ■ *TF:* 800-222-4931 ■ *Web:* www.avistacorp.com
Avista Resort
300 N Ocean Blvd. . . . . North Myrtle Beach SC 29582 843-249-2521 377
Web: www.avistaresort.com
Avista.com 5353 Conroy Rd Ste 200. . . . . Orlando FL 32811 407-581-9000 581-7777 377
Web: www.avista.com
Avistar Communications Corp
1855 S Grant St 4th Fl . . . . San Mateo CA 94402 650-525-3300 525-1360 178-7
OTC: AVSR ■ *TF:* 800-803-0153 ■ *Web:* www.avistar.com
Avitus Group 175 N 27th St. . . . . Billings MT 59101 800-454-2446 734
TF: 800-454-2446 ■ *Web:* avitusgroup.com
Aviva Metals 2929 W 12th St . . . . Houston TX 77008 800-231-0771 492
TF: 800-231-0771 ■ *Web:* www.avivametals.com
Avivo 1900 Chicago Ave S. . . . . Minneapolis MN 55404 612-752-8000 752-8001 48-5
Web: www.resource-mn.org
Avjobs Inc
9609 S University Blvd Unit 630830. . . . . Littleton CO 80163 303-683-2322 624-8691* 260
**Fax Area Code:* 888 ■ *Web:* www.avjobs.com
AVL Powertrain Engineering Inc
47519 Halyard Dr . . . . Plymouth MI 48170 734-414-9600 153
Web: www.avl.com
AVL Systems Design LLC
14901 Bristol Park Blvd . . . . Edmond OK 73013 405-749-1866 180
Web: www.avl1.com
AVM (Audio Visual Mart Inc) 2016 5th ST. . . . . Kenner LA 70062 504-454-5945 23
Web: www.av-mart.com
AVM Inc 3108 Hwy 76 E . . . . Mullins SC 29574 800-790-5438 60
TF: 800-790-5438 ■ *Web:* www.avmind.com
AVM LP 777 Yamato Rd. . . . . Boca Raton FL 33431 561-544-4600 690
Web: www.avmlp.com
AVMA (American Veterinary Medical Assn)
1931 N Meacham Rd Ste 100. . . . . Schaumburg IL 60173 847-925-8070 925-1329 49-8
TF: 800-248-2862 ■ *Web:* www.avma.org
AvMed 4300 NW 89th Blvd . . . . Gainesville FL 32606 352-372-8400 391-3
TF: 800-346-0231 ■ *Web:* www.avmed.org
AVMetrics LLC
90 W Cochran St Ste C. Simi Valley CA 93065 805-421-5056 466
TF: 800-240-1049 ■ *Web:* www.avmetrics.net
AVN Media Network Inc
9400 Penfield Ave Ste 100 . . . . Chatsworth CA 91311 818-718-5788 637-9
Web: avn.com
Avnet Inc 2211 S 47th St . . . . Phoenix AZ 85034 480-643-2000 246
NASDAQ: AVT ■ *TF:* 888-822-8638 ■ *Web:* www.avnet.com
Avnik Defense Solutions Inc
7262 Governors W Dr Ste 120 . . . . Huntsville AL 35806 256-513-5292 325-7499 463
Web: www.avnikdefense.com
Avoca Group 179 Nassau St Ste 3a . . . . Princeton NJ 08542 609-252-9020 252-9022 194
Web: theavocagroup.com
Avocet Environmental Inc
1 Technology Dr Ste C 515. . . . . Irvine CA 92618 949-296-0977 261
Web: avocetenv.com
Avocet Hospitality Group
38 Center St . . . . Folly Beach SC 29439 843-577-2525 377
Web: www.avocethospitality.com
Avocet Sales & Marketing Inc
737 2nd St Apt Ste 305. . . . . Oakland CA 94607 510-891-0093 366
Web: avocetsales.com
Avon Free Public Library
281 Country Club Rd . . . . Avon CT 06001 860-673-9712 675-6364 434-3
Web: avonctlibrary.info
Avon Health Center Inc 652 W Avon Rd . . . . Avon CT 06001 860-673-2521 450
Web: www.avonhealthcenter.com
Avon Lake Animal Clinic Inc
124 Miller Rd . . . . Avon Lake OH 44012 440-933-5297 794
Web: avonlakeanimalclinic.com
Avon Old Farms School 500 Old Farms Rd . . . . Avon CT 06001 860-404-4100 675-6051 622
TF: 800-464-2866 ■ *Web:* www.avonoldfarms.com
Avon Park Correctional Institution
8100 County Rd 64 E . . . . Avon Park FL 33825 863-453-3174 453-1511 213
Web: dc.state.fl.us

	Phone	Fax	Class
Avondale House 3611 Cummins St. Houston TX 77027 *Web:* avondalehouse.org	713-993-9544		685
Avondale Partners LLC 2 American Ctr 3102 W End Ave Ste 1100 Nashville TN 37203 *TF:* 866-775-2305 ■ *Web:* www.avondalepartnersllc.com	615-467-3500	312-7175	792
Avonworth School District 258 Josephs Ln Pittsburgh PA 15237 *Web:* www.avonworth.k12.pa.us	412-369-8738	369-8746	685
Avotaynu Inc 155 N Washington Ave Bergenfield NJ 07621 *TF:* 800-286-8296 ■ *Web:* www.avotaynu.com	800-286-8296		637-2
Avotus Corp 409 Matheson Blvd E Mississauga ON L4Z2H2 *TF:* 800-840-2580 ■ *Web:* www.avotus.com	905-890-9199		224
Avow Hospice Inc 1095 Whippoorwill Ln Naples FL 34105 *Web:* avowcares.org	239-261-4404		371
Avox Systems Inc 225 Erie St Lancaster NY 14086 *Web:* www.avoxsys.com	716-683-5100		22
Avoyelles Correctional Ctr 504 Mayflower St PO Box 94304 Baton Rouge LA 70802 *Web:* doc.la.gov	318-876-2891		213
Avoyelles Journal 105 N Main St Marksville LA 71351 *Web:* www.avoyellestoday.com	318-253-5413	253-7223	532-4
Avoyelles Parish Library System 660 N Main St Marksville LA 71351 *Web:* www.avoyelles.lib.la.us	318-253-7559		434-3
AVR Inc 14698 Galaxy Ave Apple Valley MN 55124 *Web:* www.avrconcrete.com	952-997-9100		182
Avrett Free Ginsberg (AFG) 71 5th Ave New York NY 10003 *Web:* avrettfreeginsberg.com	212-832-3800		4
Avrick Direct Inc 7120 185th Ave NE Ste 150 Redmond WA 98052 *Web:* avrickdirect.com	805-683-6551	683-6553	463
AVRMC (Arkansas Valley Regional Medical Ctr) 1100 Carson Ave La Junta CO 81050 *Web:* www.avrmc.org	719-384-5412	383-6005	374-3
Avrutine & Associates PLLC 575 Underhill Blvd Ste 140 Syosset NY 11791 *Web:* avrutinelaw.com	516-677-9400	677-9405	41
AVS (Advanced Visual Systems Inc) 2 Burlington Woods Dr Ste 100 Burlington MA 01803 *OTC:* AVSC ■ *Web:* www.avs.com	781-890-4300	890-8287	178-5
AVS (American Veterinary Supply Inc) 3555 NW 33rd St Miami FL 33142 *Web:* www.americanvet.com	305-637-8616	637-9398	238
AVS Cos 750 Morse Ave Elk Grove Village IL 60007 *TF:* 800-441-0009 ■ *Web:* avscompanies.com	847-439-9400	439-9405	55
AVS Group 3120 South Ave Ste 133 La Crosse WI 54601 *Web:* www.avsgroup.com	608-787-1010		194
AVS Inc 60 Fitchburg Rd Ayer MA 01432 *TF:* 800-772-0710 ■ *Web:* www.avsinc.com	978-772-0710	772-6462	318
AVS Installations LLC 400 Raritan Center Pkwy Ste D Edison NJ 08837 *TF:* 800-218-9177 ■ *Web:* www.avsillc.com	732-634-7903		180
AVS Science & Technology Society 120 Wall St 32nd Fl New York NY 10005 *Web:* www.avs.org	212-248-0200	248-0245	49-19
AVSI Group 4464 W 12th St Houston TX 77055 *Web:* www.avsigroup.com	713-290-8300		23
Avstar Aviation Ltd 12 N Haven Ln East Northport NY 11731 *TF:* 800-575-2359 ■ *Web:* avstarexec.com	631-499-0048		13
AVT Simulation Inc 2603 Challenger Tech Ct Ste 180 Orlando FL 32826 *Web:* avtsim.com	407-381-5311		256
AVTEC - Alaska's Institute of Technology 809 2nd Ave PO Box 889 Seward AK 99664 *TF:* 800-478-5389 ■ *Web:* www.avtec.edu	907-224-3322	224-4400	167-3
Avtec Inc 6 Industrial Pk Cahokia IL 62206 *TF:* 800-552-8832 ■ *Web:* www.avteclighting.com	618-337-7800	337-7976	438
Avtech Software Inc 16 Cutler St Cutler Mill Warren RI 02885 *TF:* 888-220-6700 ■ *Web:* avtech.com	888-220-6700		177
Avtone Management Consulting PO Box 104 Magalia CA 95954 *Web:* www.avtone.com	530-873-3056		194
Avue Technologies Corp 3560 Bridgeport Way W Ste 3B University Place WA 98466 *Web:* www.avuetech.com	253-573-1877	572-1192	178-1
AVUSD (Apple Valley Unified School District) 12555 Navajo Rd Apple Valley CA 92308 *Web:* www.avusd.org	760-247-8001	247-8907	685
Avval Inc 1235 Windham Pkwy Romeoville IL 60446 *Web:* www.avval.com	630-343-6860		177
Avvo Inc 705 5th Ave S Ste 600 Seattle WA 98104 *Web:* www.avvo.com	206-217-7457		387
AVX Corp 801 17th Ave S Myrtle Beach SC 29577 *NYSE:* AVX ■ *Web:* www.avx.com	843-448-9411		253
AW (American Whitewater) PO Box 1540 Cullowhee NC 28723 *TF:* 866-262-8429 ■ *Web:* www.americanwhitewater.org	828-586-1930	586-2840	48-23
AW Chesterton Co 860 Salem St Groveland MA 01834 *Web:* www.chesterton.com	781-438-7000	438-8971	326
AW Die Engraving Inc 8550 Roland St Buena Park CA 90621 *Web:* www.awdie.com	714-521-0842	521-2709	757
AW Mercer Inc 104 Industrial Dr PO Box 508 Boyertown PA 19512 *Web:* www.awmercer.com	610-367-8460	367-7491	697
AW Shucks 3601 Greenville Ave Dallas TX 75206 *Web:* www.awshucksdallas.com	214-821-9449		671
AW Solutions Inc 300 Crown Oak Centre Dr Longwood FL 32750 *Web:* awsolutionsinc.com	407-260-0231	260-0749	261
AW Technical Center USA Inc 1203 Woodridge Ave Ann Arbor MI 48105 *Web:* www.aisin.com	734-741-9900		668
AW Transmission Engineering USA Inc 14920 Keel St Plymouth MI 48170 *Web:* www.awtec.com	734-454-1710	454-1091	60
AW Zengeler Cleaners 550 Dundee Rd Northbrook IL 60062 *Web:* zengelercleaners.com	847-272-6550		426
Award Beauty School Inc 26 E Antietam St Hagerstown MD 21740 *Web:* www.awardbeautyschool.com	301-733-4520		685
Award Products Inc 4830 N Front St Philadelphia PA 19120	215-324-0414		777
Award Solutions Inc 2100 Lakeside Blvd Richardson TX 75082 *Web:* www.awardsolutions.com	972-664-0727		194
Award Winner Group 202 W Third St Mount Vernon NY 10550 *Web:* www.awardwinnercorp.com	914-664-7134	668-2858	453
Awards & Personalization Assn (ARA) 8735 W Higgins Rd Ste 300 Chicago IL 60631 *TF:* 800-344-2148 ■ *Web:* www.awardspersonalization.org	847-375-4800	375-6480	49-4
Aware Inc 40 Middlesex Tpke Bedford MA 01730 *NASDAQ:* AWRE ■ *Web:* www.aware.com	781-276-4000	276-4001	696
Awareness Technology Inc PO Box 1679 Palm City FL 34991 *Web:* www.awaretech.com	772-283-6540	283-8020	544
Awbury Arboretum & Historic Estate Francis Cope House 1 Awbury Rd Philadelphia PA 19138 *Web:* awbury.org	215-849-2855		97
AWC (Association for Women in Communications) 1717 E Republic Rd Ste A Springfield MO 65804 *Web:* www.womcom.org	417-886-8606		49-14
AWC Commercial Window Coverings Inc 825 Williamson Ave Fullerton CA 92832 *Web:* www.awc-cwc.com	714-879-3880	879-8419	189-1
AWC Inc 6655 Exchequer Dr Baton Rouge LA 70809 *Web:* www.awc-inc.com	225-752-1100		463
AWCI (Association of the Wall & Ceiling Industries Intl) 513 W Broad St Ste 210 Falls Church VA 22046 *TF:* 800-233-8990 ■ *Web:* www.awci.org	703-538-1600	534-8307	49-3
AWEA (American Wind Energy Assn) 1501 M St NW Ste 1000 Washington DC 20005 *Web:* www.awea.org	202-383-2500	383-2505	48-12
Awecomm Technologies L L C 165 Kirts Blvd Ste 400 Troy MI 48084 *Web:* www.awecomm.com	248-404-9910		224
Awerkamp Machine Co 237 N 7th St Quincy IL 62301 *Web:* awerkamp.com	217-222-3480	222-9408	454
AWF (African Wildlife Foundation) 1100 New Jersey Ave SE Ste 900 Washington DC 20003 *TF:* 888-494-5354 ■ *Web:* www.awf.org	202-939-3333	939-3332	48-3
AWHONN (Association of Women's Health Obstetric & Neonatal Nurses) 2000 L St NW Ste 740 Washington DC 20036 *TF:* 800-673-8499 ■ *Web:* www.awhonn.org	202-261-2400	728-0575	49-8
AWI (American Watchmakers-Clockmakers Institute) 701 Enterprise Dr Harrison OH 45030 *TF:* 866-367-2924 ■ *Web:* www.awci.com	513-367-9800	367-1414	49-4
AWI (Architectural Woodwork Institute) 46179 Westlake Dr Ste 120 Potomac Falls VA 20165 *Web:* www.awinet.org	571-323-3636	323-3630	49-3
AWID (Association for Women's Rights in Development) 215 Spadina Ave Ste 150 Toronto ON M5T2C7 *Web:* www.awid.org	416-594-3773	594-0330	48-8
AWIS (Association for Women in Science Inc) 1667 K St NW Ste 800 Washington DC 20006 *Web:* www.awis.org	202-588-8175		49-19
A&WMA (Air & Waste Management Assn) 436 Seventh Ave Ste 2100 Pittsburgh PA 15219 *TF:* 800-270-3444 ■ *Web:* www.awma.org	412-232-3444	232-3450	48-12
AWNEX Inc 260 Valley St Ste 100 Ball Ground GA 30107 *Web:* www.awnexinc.com	770-704-7140		350
Awningtec USA Inc 3265 Hwy 62 NW Corydon IN 47112 *Web:* www.awningtecusa.com	812-734-0423	734-0344	697
AWO (American Waterways Operators) 801 N Quincy St Ste 200 Arlington VA 22203 *Web:* www.americanwaterways.com	703-841-9300	841-0389	49-21
AWP University of Maryland 5245 Greenbelt Rd Ste 246 College Park MD 20740 *Web:* www.awpwriter.org	301-226-9710	226-9797	48-11
AWP Inc 826 Overholt Rd Kent OH 44240 *TF:* 800-343-2650 ■ *Web:* www.awptrafficsafety.com	800-343-2650		693
AWPA (American Wire Producers Assn) PO Box 151387 Alexandria VA 22315 *Web:* www.awpa.org	703-299-4434		49-13
AWPL (Albert Wisner Public Library) 1 McFarland Dr. Warwick NY 10990 *Web:* www.albertwisnerlibrary.org	845-986-1047	987-1228	434-3
AWR (American Warmblood Registry) PO Box 1332 De Leon Springs FL 32130 **Fax Area Code: 775* ■ *Web:* www.americanwarmblood.com	406-734-5499	667-0516*	48-3
AWR Corp 1960 E Grand Ave Ste 430 El Segundo CA 90245 *Web:* www.awrcorp.com	310-726-3000	726-3005	178-1
Awrey Bakeries LLC 12301 Farmington Rd Livonia MI 48150 *Web:* www.awreybakery.com	734-943-1301		68
AWS (American Welding Society) 550 NW 42nd Ave Miami FL 33126 *TF:* 800-443-9353 ■ *Web:* www.aws.org	305-443-9353	443-7559	49-3
AWS Industries Inc 2600 Henkle Dr Lebanon OH 45036 *Web:* www.tomak.com	513-932-7941	932-8791	22
AWT (Association of Water Technologies) 9707 Key West Ave Ste 100 Rockville MD 20850 *Web:* www.awt.org	301-740-1421		48-2
AWT World Trade Inc 4321 N Knox Ave Chicago IL 60641 *Web:* www.awt-gpi.com	773-777-7100	777-0909	629
AWWA (American Water Works Assn) 6666 W Quincy Ave Denver CO 80235 *TF:* 800-926-7337 ■ *Web:* www.awwa.org	303-794-7711	347-0804	48-12
AXA Equitable Life Insurance Co 1290 Avenue of the Americas New York NY 10104 *Web:* equitableholdings.com	212-554-1234		391-2
AXA Rosenberg Investment Management LLC 4 Orinda Way Bldg E Orinda CA 94563 *Web:* www.axa-im.com	925-254-6464		401

Company / Address	City	State	ZIP	Phone	Fax	Class
Axalta Powder Coatings 9800 Genard Rd *TF:* 800-247-3886 ■ *Web:* www.axaltacs.com	Houston	TX	77041	800-247-3886		550
Axcelis Technologies Inc 108 Cherry Hill Dr *NASDAQ: ACLS* ■ *Web:* www.axcelis.com	Beverly	MA	01915	978-787-4000	787-4200	695
Axcept Media LLC 1650 W End Blvd Ste 100 *Web:* axceptmedia.com	Saint Louis Park	MN	55416	612-279-1310	279-1311	195
Axcera Corp 103 Freedom Dr *TF:* 800-215-2614 ■ *Web:* www.axcera.com	Lawrence	PA	15055	724-873-8100	873-8105	647
Axcesor Inc 2260 Dakota Dr *TF:* 888-717-1471 ■ *Web:* www.axcesor.com	Grafton	WI	53024	262-375-7530	375-7539	246
Axcet HR Solutions 8325 Lenexa Dr Ste 410 *TF:* 800-801-7557 ■ *Web:* www.axcethr.com	Lenexa	KS	66214	913-383-2999		631
Axcient Inc 1161 San Antonio Rd *TF:* 800-715-2339 ■ *Web:* axcient.com	Mountain View	CA	94043	800-715-2339		177
Axel Plastics Research Laboratories Inc 5820 Broadway *Web:* axelplastics.com	Woodside	NY	11377	718-672-8300	565-7447	541
Axens North America Inc 650 College Rd E Ste 1200 *Web:* www.axens.net	Princeton	NJ	08540	609-243-8700		256
Axeon Specialty Products LLC 750 Washington Blvd Ste 600 *TF:* 855-378-4958 ■ *Web:* axeonsp.com	Stamford	CT	06901	855-378-4958		579
AXH air-coolers LLC 2230 E 49th St *TF:* 800-722-4116 ■ *Web:* www.axh.com	Tulsa	OK	74105	918-712-8268	283-9229	539
AXIA Consulting LLC 1391 W Fifth Ave Ste 320 *TF:* 866-937-5550 ■ *Web:* www.axiaconsulting.net	Columbus	OH	43212	614-675-4050		196
Axia Public Relations 222 E Forsyth St *Web:* www.axiapr.com	Jacksonville	FL	32202	904-416-1500		636
Axia Strategies Inc 8688 Eagle Creek Cir *Web:* www.axiastrategies.com	Savage	MN	55378	952-945-3535		463
Axial Networks Inc 443 Park Ave S 8th Fl *TF:* 800-860-4519 ■ *Web:* www.axial.net	New York	NY	10016	800-860-4519		691
axialHealthcare Cummins Station 209 10th Ave S Ste 332 *Web:* axialhealthcare.com	Nashville	TN	37203	615-345-3555		352
Axiam Inc 58 Blackburn Ctr *Web:* www.axiam.com	Gloucester	MA	01930	978-281-3550		20
Axian Inc 9600 SW Nimbus Ave *Web:* www.axian.com	Beaverton	OR	97008	503-644-6106		196
Axian Technology 21622 N 14th Ave *Web:* www.axiantech.com	Phoenix	AZ	85027	623-580-0800		454
Axim Systems Inc 15 Diamond Rd *Web:* www.axim.com	Lexington	MA	02420	781-430-0429		196
AxioBionics LLC 6111 Jackson Rd Ste 200 *TF:* 800-552-3539 ■ *Web:* axiobionics.com	Ann Arbor	MI	48103	734-327-2946		250
Axiom Design Inc 5117 Johnson Dr *Web:* www.axiomdesign.com	Pleasanton	CA	94588	925-416-2000	416-2002	35
Axiom Marketing Inc 624 E Park Ave *Web:* www.axmarketing.com	Libertyville	IL	60048	847-362-5656		195
Axiom Memory Solutions LLC 15 Chrysler *TF:* 888-658-3326 ■ *Web:* www.axiomupgrades.com	Irvine	CA	92618	949-581-1450		174
Axiom Mentor LLC 4 Research Dr Ste 402 *TF:* 888-801-8183 ■ *Web:* www.axiom-mentor.com	Shelton	CT	06484	888-801-8183		387
Axiom Resource Management Inc 2941 Fairview Pk Dr Ste 850 *Web:* www.axiom-rm.com	Falls Church	VA	22041	703-208-3000		194
Axiom Software Ltd 115 Stevens Ave Ste 320 *TF:* 800-588-8805 ■ *Web:* www.axiomsw.com	Valhalla	NY	10595	914-769-8800		177
Axiom Systems Inc 241 E Fourth St Ste 200 *TF:* 866-506-5059 ■ *Web:* www.axiom-systems.com	Frederick	MD	21701	301-815-5220	815-5221	177
Axiom Technology Group 900 Oakmont Ln Ste 350 *Web:* axiomtechgroup.com	Westmont	IL	60559	630-861-1000		196
Axiom Xcell Inc 13230 Evening Creek Dr Ste 217 *Web:* www.axiomxcell.com	San Diego	CA	92128	858-683-6100		656
Axioma Inc 17 State St Ste 2700 *TF:* 800-558-7983 ■ *Web:* www.axioma.com	New York	NY	10004	212-991-4500	991-4539	177
Axion BioSystems Inc 1819 Peachtree Rd NE Ste 350 *Web:* www.axionbiosystems.com	Atlanta	GA	30309	404-477-2557		261
Axion Corp 317 Nick Fitcheard Rd NW *Web:* axion-corp.com	Huntsville	AL	35806	256-851-9770		454
Axios HR 528 Fourth St NW **Fax Area Code:* 616 ■ *TF:* 844-442-9467 ■ *Web:* axioshr.com	Grand Rapids	MI	49504	844-442-9467	954-2824*	194
Axios Media 3100 Clarendon Blvd Ste 1300 *Web:* axios.com	Arlington	VA	22201	703-291-3600		568
Axios Press 94 Landfill Rd *TF:* 888-542-9467 ■ *Web:* www.axiosinstitute.org	Edinburg	VA	22824	540-984-3829	984-3843	637-2
Axis Communications Inc (ACI) 100 Apollo Dr *TF:* 800-444-2947 ■ *Web:* www.axis.com	Chelmsford	MA	01824	978-614-2000	614-2100	176
Axis Construction Corp 125 Laser Ct *Web:* www.theaxisgroup.com	Hauppauge	NY	11788	631-243-5970	243-5973	685
Axis Dance Co 1428 Alice St Ste 200 *Web:* www.axisdance.org	Oakland	CA	94612	510-625-0110	625-0321	573-1
Axis Financial Services Inc 2774 Gateway Rd *Web:* www.axisservicing.com	Carlsbad	CA	92009	760-929-6680		401
Axis Health Systems LLC 1711 W 38 Pl Unit 1107-A *Web:* www.axishealthsystems.com	Hialeah	FL	33012	305-824-3777	826-5075	363
Axis Jet 6133 Freeport Blvd *Web:* www.axisjet.com	Sacramento	CA	95822	916-391-5000	391-5001	23
Axis Personal Trainers Inc 550 Ravenswood Ave *Web:* www.axispt.com	Menlo Park	CA	94025	650-463-1920		354
Axis Technical Group Inc 300 S Ahrbor Blvd Ste 910 *TF:* 888-491-2636 ■ *Web:* www.axistechnical.com	Anaheim	CA	92805	888-491-2636		225
Axiscades 3008 W Willow Knolls Dr *Web:* www.axiscades.com	Peoria	IL	61614	309-691-3988	691-4172	261
Axle Logistics 520 W Summit Hill Dr SW Ste 1005 *TF:* 888-440-1888 ■ *Web:* www.axlelogistics.com	Knoxville	TN	37902	888-440-1888		780
AxleTech International Inc 1400 Rochester Rd *TF:* 877-877-9717 ■ *Web:* www.axletech.com	Troy	MI	48083	248-658-7200	435-1120	60
Axletree Solutions Inc 2 King Arthur Ct Lakeside W Ste A-1 *Web:* axletrees.com	North Brunswick	NJ	08902	732-296-0001		177
Axley 2 E Mifflin St Ste 200 *TF:* 800-368-5661 ■ *Web:* www.axley.com	Madison	WI	53703	608-257-5661	257-5444	445
Axley & Rode LLP 203 N Houston Ave *Web:* www.axleyrode.com	Lufkin	TX	75901	936-634-6621	634-8183	2
Axmen 7655 US Hwy 10 W *Web:* www.axmen.com	Missoula	MT	59808	406-728-7020		316
Axne Cynthia (Rep D - IA) 330 Cannon House Office Bldg *Web:* www.axne.house.gov	Washington	DC	20515	202-225-5476		342-2
Axon Circuit Inc 424 S Ware Blvd *Web:* www.axoncircuit.com	Tampa	FL	33619	813-623-5200	623-1019	625
Axon Inc 21 Walmsley Rd *Web:* www.axoninc.com	Darien	CT	06820	203-655-5175	202-9098	194
Axon Pressure Products Inc 8909 Jackrabbit Rd *Web:* www.axonep.com	Houston	TX	77095	281-855-3200	260-0118	539
Axon Sports 2100 Stewart Ave Ste 201 *TF:* 877-399-2966 ■ *Web:* www.axonsports.com	Wausau	WI	54401	877-399-2966		387
Axonify Inc 450 Phillip St Ste 300 *TF:* 855-296-6439 ■ *Web:* axonify.com	Waterloo	ON	N2L5J2	519-585-1200		242
Axsess Energy Group LLC 235 W Main St Ste 535 *Web:* www.axsessgroup.com	Northborough	MA	01532	508-351-9050		196
Axson Technologies US Inc 1611 Hults Dr *Web:* www.axson-technologies.com	Eaton Rapids	MI	48827	248-588-2270	588-5909	3
Axsun Group 4900 Armand Frappier *TF:* 888-992-9786 ■ *Web:* axsungroup.com	Saint-Hubert	QC	J3Z1G5	450-445-3003	445-3427	311
AXT Inc 4281 Technology Dr *NASDAQ: AXTI* ■ *Web:* www.axt.com	Fremont	CA	94538	510-438-4700		696
Axton Inc 441 Derwent Pl Annacis Business Pk *Web:* www.axton.ca	Delta	BC	V3M5Y9	604-522-2731		295
Axxess Intl 1804 Alstep Dr *Web:* www.axxessintl.com	Mississauga	ON	L5S1W1	905-672-0270		449
Axxiem Web Solutions 276 Fifth Ave Ste 704 *TF:* 877-429-9436 ■ *Web:* axxiem.com	New York	NY	10001	914-478-7600		177
Axxis Inc 1295 Bandana Blvd Ste 120 **Fax Area Code:* 866 ■ *Web:* www.axxispetro.com	Saint Paul	MN	55108	651-644-8280	329-6747*	177
AXYS Technologies Inc 2045 Mills Rd *TF:* 877-792-7878 ■ *Web:* axystechnologies.com	Sidney	BC	V8L5X2	250-655-5850		608
Axyz Automation Inc 2844 E Kemper Rd *TF:* 800-527-9670 ■ *Web:* www.axyz.com	Cincinnati	OH	45241	800-361-3408		180
AY McDonald Manufacturing Co 4800 Chavenelle Rd **Fax Area Code:* 563 ■ *TF:* 800-292-2737 ■ *Web:* www.aymcdonald.com	Dubuque	IA	52002	800-292-2737	588-0720*	595
AyA Kitchens & Baths Ltd 1551 Caterpillar Rd *TF:* 866-292-4968 ■ *Web:* www.ayakitchens.com	Mississauga	ON	L4X2Z6	905-848-1999	848-5127	819
Ayalogic Inc 530 S Main St Ste 1732 *Web:* www.ayalogic.com	Akron	OH	44311	330-253-2700		225
Ayanna Plastics & Engineering 4701 110th Ave N *Web:* www.ayannaplastics.com	Clearwater	FL	33762	727-561-4329		607
Aycan Medical Systems LLC 693 E Ave *Web:* aycan.com	Rochester	NY	14607	585-473-1350		475
Ayco Company LP 321 Broadway *TF:* 866-325-2215 ■ *Web:* www.ayco.com	Saratoga Springs	NY	12866	866-325-2215		401
Ayers Career College 8820 Jewella Ave *TF:* 800-317-0131 ■ *Web:* www.ayers.edu	Shreveport	LA	71108	800-317-0131		167-3
Ayers Meetings & Events Inc 19727 Whitewind Dr *Web:* www.ayersme.com	Houston	TX	77094	281-492-7272		184
Aylus Networks Inc 6 Technology Park Dr *Web:* www.aylus.com	Westford	MA	01886	978-392-4730		681
Aylward Enterprises Inc 401 Industrial Dr *Web:* aylward-usa.com	New Bern	NC	28562	252-633-5757		231
Ayn Rand Institute, Endowment 2121 Alton Pkwy Ste 250 *Web:* www.aynrand.org	Irvine	CA	92606	949-222-6550		305
Ayoka LLC 2313 Brookhollow Plz *Web:* www.ayokasystems.com	Arlington	TX	76006	817-210-4042		180
Ayothaya Thai Cuisine 7555 W Sand Lk *Web:* www.ayothayathai.com	Orlando	FL	32819	407-345-0040		671
Ayre Acoustics Inc 2300-B Central Ave *Web:* www.ayre.com	Boulder	CO	80301	303-442-7300	442-7301	52
Ayres Associates Inc 3433 Oakwood Hills Pkwy *Web:* www.ayresassociates.com	Eau Claire	WI	54701	715-834-3161		261
Ayres Hotel Anaheim 2550 E Katella Ave *TF:* 800-595-5692 ■ *Web:* www.ayreshotels.com	Anaheim	CA	92806	714-634-2106		379
Ayrshire Communications 1405 Silver Lake Ave *TF:* 888-795-2800 ■ *Web:* www.ayrshireia.com	Ayrshire	IA	50515	712-426-2800	426-2008	224

Name / Address	City	State	Zip	Phone	Fax	Class
AYSO (American Youth Soccer Organization) 19750 S Vermont Ave Ste 200 *Fax Area Code: 310 ■ TF: 800-872-2976 ■ Web: www.ayso.org	Torrance	CA	90502	800-872-2976	525-1155*	48-22
Ayzenberg Group Inc 49 E Walnut St Web: www.ayzenberg.com	Pasadena	CA	91103	626-584-4070		7
A-Z Sponge & Foam Products Ltd 811 Cundy Ave Annacis Is TF: 800-665-3990 ■ Web: www.a-zfoam.com	Delta	BC	V3M5P6	604-525-1665	525-1081	601
AZA (Association of Zoos & Aquariums) 8403 Colesville Rd Ste 710 Web: www.aza.org	Silver Spring	MD	20910	301-562-0777	562-0888	48-3
Azalea Moving & Storage Inc 7131 Bryhawke Cir TF: 866-642-6674 ■ Web: azaleamoving.com	North Charleston	SC	29418	843-419-8888		311
Azalea Software Inc PO Box 16660 Web: www.azaleabarcodes.com	Seattle	WA	98116	206-341-9500		396
Azalea State Reserve 15336 Hwy 101 PO Box 2006 Web: www.parks.ca.gov	Trinidad	CA	95570	707-677-3132		565
Azar Computer Software Services Inc 1200 Regal Row TF: 800-525-7844 ■ Web: azarinc.com	Austin	TX	78748	800-525-7844		179
Azar Nut Co 1800 NW Dr TF: 800-351-8178 ■ Web: www.azarnutco.com	El Paso	TX	79912	915-877-4079		296-28
Azar's Restaurant Inc 2501 N Monroe St	Spokane	WA	99205	509-844-2596		671
Azara Healthcare LLC 70 Blanchard Rd Ste 100 Web: azarahealthcare.com	Burlington	MA	01803	781-365-2208		177
Azavar Technologies 55 E Jackson Ste 2100 TF: 800-683-0800 ■ Web: www.azavar.com	Chicago	IL	60604	312-583-0100		194
Azco Inc PO Box 567 Web: www.azco-inc.com	Appleton	WI	54912	920-734-5791	734-7432	189-10
Azcon Metals 820 W Jackson Blvd Web: www.azcon.net	Chicago	IL	60607	312-559-3100	559-1543	686
Azenphony Press PO Box 130884 Web: www.azenphonypress.com	Ann Arbor	MI	48113	734-635-0577		637-10
Azerbaijan 515 W 20th St Ste 6W Web: un.mfa.gov.az	New York	NY	10017	212-371-2559	371-2784	784
Azevan Pharmaceuticals Inc 116 Research Dr Web: azevan.com	Bethlehem	PA	18015	610-419-1057		231
Azimuth Inc 3741 Morgantown Industrial Pk Web: www.azimuthinc.com	Morgantown	WV	26501	304-292-3700	292-0873	261
Azimuth Systems Inc 35 Nagog Pk Web: www.azimuthsystems.com	Acton	MA	01720	978-263-6610	263-5352	224
Azimuth Three Communications 127 Delta Park Blvd Web: www.az3.com	Brampton	ON	L6T5M8	905-793-7793		480
Aziza 5800 Geary Blvd Web: www.aziza-sf.com	San Francisco	CA	94121	415-752-2222		671
AZLA (Arizona Library Assn) 6101 S Rural Rd Ste 106 Web: www.azla.org	Tempe	AZ	85283	480-609-3999		435
Aznar Financial Advisors 21 Lakeview Dr Web: www.aznaradvisors.com	Morris Plains	NJ	07950	973-540-8850		401
Azon USA Inc 643 W Crosstown Pkwy TF: 800-788-5942 ■ Web: azonintl.com	Kalamazoo	MI	49008	269-385-5942	373-9295	386
Aztalan Engineering Inc 100 S Industrial Dr Web: aztalan.com	Lake Mills	WI	53551	920-648-3411	648-8066	757
Aztalan State Park N6200 County Rd Q Web: dnr.wi.gov	Jefferson	WI	53549	920-648-8774	648-5166	565
Aztec Building Systems Inc 3361 Deskin Dr Web: www.aztecbuildingsystems.com	Norman	OK	73069	405-329-0255		186
Aztec Communications Ltd 6830 Barney Rd Web: www.azteccom.com	Houston	TX	77092	713-462-6707	462-2533	256
Aztec Engineering Group Inc 4561 E Mcdowell Rd Web: www.aztec.us	Phoenix	AZ	85008	602-454-0402		261
Aztec International Inc 3010 Henson Rd *Fax Area Code: 615 ■ TF: 800-369-5357 ■ Web: www.candlemaking.com	Knoxville	TN	37921	865-588-5357	538-2062*	151
Aztec Landscaping Inc 7980 Lemon Grove Way TF: 800-281-9909 ■ Web: www.azteclandscaping.com	Lemon Grove	CA	91945	619-464-3303	460-1106	104
Aztec Mechanical Inc 2509 Comanche Rd NE Web: www.aztecmechanical.com	Albuquerque	NM	87107	505-884-2770	881-0252	189-10
Aztec Ruins National Monument 725 Ruins Rd Web: www.nps.gov	Aztec	NM	87410	505-334-6174	334-6372	564
Aztec Supply 954 N Batavia St TF: 800-836-3210 ■ Web: www.mezzaninesandmore.com	Orange	CA	92867	714-771-6580	771-3013	603
Aztec Well Servicing Company Inc 300 Legion Rd PO Box 100 Web: www.aztecwell.com	Aztec	NM	87410	505-334-6194		540
Azteca 4801 Tacoma Mall Blvd Web: www.aztecamex.com	Tacoma	WA	98409	253-472-0246		671
Azteca America 1139 Grand Central Ave Web: aztecaamerica.com	Glendale	CA	91201	818-241-5400	247-0190	116
Azteca Foods Inc 5005 S Nagle Ave Web: www.aztecafoods.com	Chicago	IL	60638	708-563-6600		296-35
Azteca Restaurant & Lounge 12911 Main St Web: www.theazteca.com	Garden Grove	CA	92840	714-638-3790		671
Aztech Associates Inc 805 Bayridge Dr *Fax Area Code: 940 ■ TF: 877-239-4878 ■ Web: www.myaztech.ca	Kingston	ON	K7P1T5	613-384-9400	322-8194*	261
Aztech Labs Inc 4005 Clipper Ct Web: www.aztech.com	Fremont	CA	94538	510-683-9800	683-9803	173-3
Az-Tech Software Inc 201 E Franklin St Ste 11 Web: www.az-tech.com	Richmond	MO	64085	816-533-7206	533-7218	178-1
Aztech Technologies Inc 5 McCrea Hill Rd Web: www.aztechtech.com	Ballston	NY	12020	518-885-5383		196
AZ-TV 4343 E Camelback Rd Ste 130 Web: www.aztv.com	Phoenix	AZ	85018	602-977-7700	224-2214	647
AzTx Cattle Co 311 E Park Ave TF: 800-999-5065 ■ Web: aztx.com	Hereford	TX	79045	806-364-8871	364-3842	10-1
Azul 7 Inc 1310 Quincy St NE Ste 102 Web: azulseven.com	Minneapolis	MN	55413	612-767-4335		4
Azul Partners 625 N Michigan Ave Ste 1220 Web: azulpartners.com	Chicago	IL	60611	773-525-7406		195
Azul Systems Inc 1600 Plymouth St Web: www.azul.com	Mountain View	CA	94043	650-230-6500		173-2
Azulstar Inc 1051 Jackson St Ste D Web: www.azulstar.com	Grand Haven	MI	49417	616-842-2763		387
Azur Global Imports 10576 W Alameda Ave Ste 1 *Fax Area Code: 303 ■ TF: 800-447-4583 ■ Web: www.azur1.com	Lakewood	CO	80226	800-447-4583	980-1407*	411
Azure Green Consultants LLC 409 E Pioneer Web: www.azuregreenconsultants.com	Puyallup	WA	98372	253-770-3144		256
Azure Horizons Inc 7115 W North Ave Ste 185 *Fax Area Code: 708 ■ TF: 877-494-6070 ■ Web: www.azure-horizons.com	Oak Park	IL	60302	877-494-6070	851-0456*	180
Azure Standard 79709 Dufur Valley Rd *Fax Area Code: 541 ■ Web: www.azurestandard.com	Dufur	OR	97021	971-200-8350	467-2210*	297-2
Azurea Inc 365 Gus Hipp Blvd Web: www.dragonpoint.com	Rockledge	FL	32955	321-631-0657		196
Azusa Chamber of Commerce 240 W Foothill Blvd Web: www.azusachamber.org	Azusa	CA	91702	626-334-1507	334-5217	139
Azusa City Library 729 N Dalton Ave Web: www.ci.azusa.ca.us	Azusa	CA	91702	626-812-5232	334-4868	434-3
Azusa Pacific University 901 E Alosta Ave PO Box 7000 TF: 800-825-5278 ■ Web: www.apu.edu	Azusa	CA	91702	626-969-3434	812-3096	166
AZZ (Atkinson Industries Inc) 1801 E 27th Ter Web: www.azz.com	Pittsburg	KS	66762	620-231-6900	231-7154	729
Azzur Group LLC 330 S Warminster Rd Ste 341 *Fax Area Code: 610 ■ Web: www.azzur.com	Hatboro	PA	19040	215-322-8322	363-0428*	393

B

Name / Address	City	State	Zip	Phone	Fax	Class
B & A Bolton Hill Bistro 1501 Bolton St Web: www.b-bistro.com	Baltimore	MD	21217	410-383-8600		671
B & A Manufacturing Co 3665 E Industrial Way TF: 800-327-8611 ■ Web: bamanufacturing.com	West Palm Beach	FL	33404	561-848-8648	848-8621	493
B & B Agency of Boston 47 Commercial Wharf Apt 3 TF: 800-248-9262 ■ Web: www.boston-bbagency.com	Boston	MA	02110	617-720-3540		376
B & B Automotive Inc 301 W Market St Web: www.bbauto.org	Aberdeen	WA	98520	360-533-4113		57
B & B Boats Inc 3568 Old Winter Garden Rd	Orlando	FL	32805	407-299-2190		90
B & B Contractors & Developers Inc 4531 Belmont Ave Ste A Web: bbcdonline.com	Youngstown	OH	44505	330-270-5020	270-5035	186
B & B Electronics Manufacturing Co PO Box 1040 TF: 800-346-3119 ■ Web: www.bb-elec.com	Ottawa	IL	61350	815-433-5100	433-5109	696
B & B Express Printing Inc 7519 W Kennewick Ave A Web: www.bbprinting.com	Kennewick	WA	99336	509-783-7383		627
B & B Lingerie Company Inc PO Box 5731 TF: 800-262-2789 ■ Web: www.bosombuddy.com	Boise	ID	83705	208-343-9696	343-9266	477
B & B Manufacturing Company Inc 27940 Beale Ct Web: www.bbmfg.com	Valencia	CA	91355	661-257-2161		454
B & B Molders LLC 58471 Fir Rd S Web: www.bandbmolders.com	Mishawaka	IN	46544	574-259-7838		596
B & B Paper Converters Inc 12500 Elmwood Ave Web: bbpaper.com	Cleveland	OH	44111	216-941-8100		554
B & B Petroleum LLC 42723 Merchant Ct Web: www.bbpetroleum.com	Ponchatoula	LA	70454	985-345-8160	345-8159	538
B & B Pipe and Tool Co 3035 Walnut Ave Web: www.bbpipe.com	Long Beach	CA	90807	562-424-0704	490-0682	152
B & B Precision Manufacturing Inc 310 W Main St Web: www.bbprecision.com	Avon	NY	14414	585-226-6226	226-3793	454
B & B Printing 521 Research Rd TF: 888-224-2656 ■ Web: www.bbsmartsolutions.com	Richmond	VA	23236	804-794-8273	379-4961	627
B & B Selectcom Inc 1109 S Fremont Ave TF: 877-882-0911 ■ Web: bbselectcom.com	Tucson	AZ	85719	520-882-0911	623-6606	54
B & B Trade Distribution Ctr 1950 Oxford St E TF: 800-265-0382 ■ Web: www.johnstonesupply.com	London	ON	N5V2Z8	519-679-1770		610
B & B Water-Waste Water Consultants Inc 4402 S Division TF: 800-968-4196 ■ Web: bbwater-wastewater.com	Wayland	MI	49348	616-877-4196	877-4220	660

Company	Address	City	State	ZIP	Phone	Fax	Class	Other
B & B Wrecking & Excavating Inc	4510 E 71st St	Cleveland	OH	44105	216-429-1700	429-1717	189-5	Web: www.bbwrecking.net
B & C Transportation Inc	427 Continental Dr	Maryville	TN	37804	865-983-4653		107	TF: 877-812-2287 ■ Web: bctransportation.net
B & D Industries Inc	9720 Bell Ave SE	Albuquerque	NM	87123	505-299-4464		246	TF: 866-315-8349 ■ Web: banddindustries.com
B & D Litho of Arizona	3820 N 38th Ave	Phoenix	AZ	85019	602-269-2526		627	TF: 800-735-0375 ■ Web: www.bndlithoaz.com
B & D Precision Tools Inc	2367 W 8th Ln	Hialeah	FL	33010	305-885-1583	883-8753	757	TF: 800-323-0915 ■ Web: bndplastic.com
B & D Publishing LLC	c/o Dietrich Maerz PO Box 652	Richmond	MI	48062	586-651-3623		637-2	Web: bdpublish.com
B & E Engineers	20 E Foothill Blvd Ste 230	Arcadia	CA	91006	626-446-4449		261	Web: beeng.com
B & F System Inc	3920 S Walton Walker	Dallas	TX	75236	214-333-2111	333-1511	361	Web: www.maxam.com
B & G Beauty Supply Inc	2440 Enterprise Rd	Reno	NV	89521	775-829-2704		76	Web: bandgbeautysupply.com
B & G Equipment Company Inc	135 Region S Dr	Jackson	GA	30233	678-688-5601		295	TF: 800-544-8811 ■ Web: bgequip.com
B & G Foods Inc	4 Gatehall Dr Ste 110	Parsippany	NJ	07054	800-811-8975		296-20	NYSE: BGS ■ TF: 800-811-8975 ■ Web: www.bgfoods.com
B & G House of Printing	1825-A W 169th St	Gardena	CA	90247	310-532-1533	532-2428	627	TF: 800-882-1844 ■ Web: bgprinting.com
B & G Manufacturing Company Inc	3067 Unionville Pk	Hatfield	PA	19440	215-822-1921	822-1006	278	TF: 800-366-3067 ■ Web: www.bgmfg.com
B & G Oysters	550 Tremont St	Boston	MA	02116	617-423-0550		671	Web: bandgoysters.com
B & G Security Intl	6631 Hwy 42	Rex	GA	30273	770-507-6409	507-6415	692	Web: www.bgsecurity.com
B & G Supply Co	800 Railroad Ave PO Box 748	Albertville	AL	35950	256-878-2928		311	TF: 800-624-6951 ■ Web: bngsupply.com
B & H Machine Sales Inc	9339 W Fort St	Detroit	MI	48209	313-843-6720	841-5553	385	Web: www.bhmachine.com
B & H Manufacturing Co	3461 Roeding Rd	Ceres	CA	95307	209-537-5785	537-6854	547	TF: 888-643-0444 ■ Web: www.bhlabeling.com
B & H Manufacturing Inc	141 County Rd 34 E	Jackson	MN	56143	800-240-3288		273	TF: 800-240-3288 ■ Web: bhmfg.com
B & H Pattern Inc	3240 W Highview Dr	Appleton	WI	54914	920-731-3861	731-6024	567	Web: www.bh-pattern.com
B & H Photo-Video-Pro Audio Corp	420 Ninth Ave	New York	NY	10001	212-444-6615	239-7770	119	TF: 800-947-9954 ■ Web: www.bhphotovideo.com
B & H Toolworks Inc	1785 Lancaster Rd	Richmond	KY	40475	859-624-2458	624-2511	757	Web: bhtoolworks.com
B & I Contractors Inc	2701 Prince St	Fort Myers	FL	33916	239-332-4646		189-10	Web: www.bandiflorida.com
B & J Machinery Company Inc	122 York St	Dalton	GA	30721	706-259-4841	259-4960	744	Web: www.bandjmachinery.com
B & J Parking Lot Maintenance	12207 Inkster Rd	Taylor	MI	48180	734-941-7570		562	Web: www.bandjmaint.com
B & J Specialty Inc	7919 N 100 E	Wawaka	IN	46794	260-761-5011	347-9480	385	Web: bjspecialtyinc.com
B & K Electric Wholesale	1225 S Johnson Dr	City of Industry	CA	91745	626-965-5040	964-1293	253	TF: 888-635-3111 ■ Web: www.bk-electric.com
B & K Installations Inc	246 SW 4th Ave	Homestead	FL	33030	305-245-6968	245-8119	480	TF: 800-624-7612 ■ Web: bkinstall.com
B & K Machine Products Inc	100 Aylworth Ave	South Haven	MI	49090	269-637-3001	637-3779	454	Web: www.bandkmachineproducts.com
B & L Associates Inc	13 Tech Cir	Natick	MA	01760	508-651-1404		177	Web: www.bandl.com
B & L Engineering Inc	319 Glenn St	Crawfordsville	IN	47933	765-362-3013		261	Web: bandlengineering.com
B & L Pipeco Services	20465 SH 249 Ste 200	Houston	TX	77070	281-955-3500		492	TF: 800-927-4732 ■ Web: www.blpipeco.com
B & L Wholesale Supply Inc	70 Hartford St	Rochester	NY	14605	585-546-6616	546-7326	191-4	Web: www.blwholesale.com
B & M Roofing of Colorado Inc	3768 Eureka Way	Frederick	CO	80516	303-443-5843	938-9642	189-12	Web: bmroofing.com
B & O Railroad Museum	901 W Pratt St	Baltimore	MD	21223	410-752-2490	752-2499	520	Web: www.borail.org
B & O Saws Inc	825 Reed St	Belding	MI	48809	616-794-7297	794-7468	455	Web: www.bosaws.com
B & P Littleford	1000 Hess Ave	Saginaw	MI	48601	989-757-1300		146	Web: www.bplittleford.com
B & R Eckel's Transport Ltd	5514B - 50 Ave	Bonnyville	AB	T9N2K8	780-826-3889		539	TF: 800-661-3290 ■ Web: www.breckels.com
B & R Equipment Company Inc	3100 Keller Hicks Rd	Keller	TX	76248	817-379-9922		264-3	Web: www.brequipmentco.com
B & R Plastics Inc	4550 Kingston St	Denver	CO	80239	303-373-0710	371-0221	604	TF: 800-624-4945 ■ Web: www.brplastics.com
B & R Stores Inc	4554 W St	Lincoln	NE	68503	402-464-6297		345	Web: www.russmarket.com
B & S Aircraft Alloys Inc	10 Aerial Way	Syosset	NY	11791	516-681-2400	681-2439	492	TF: 800-645-2401 ■ Web: www.bsaa.com
B & S Logging Inc	4411 NW Elliott Ln	Prineville	OR	97754	541-447-3175		448	
B & S Machine Tool Inc	158 Old Wagener Rd	Aiken	SC	29801	803-648-1826	642-5415	454	Web: www.bsmachinetool.com
B & T Service Station Contractors	630 S Frontage Rd	Nipomo	CA	93444	805-929-8944		324	TF: 888-862-2552 ■ Web: btssc.com
B & T Tool & Engineering Inc	2618 E Washington St	Phoenix	AZ	85034	602-267-1481	225-9582	493	Web: www.bnttool.us
B & W Energy Services	4440 Hwy 225 Ste 150	Deer Park	TX	77536	281-534-9300	826-4125*	256	*Fax Area Code: 603 ■ Web: bwenergyservices.com
B & W Engineering Corp	3303 Harbor Blvd	Costa Mesa	CA	92626	714-540-9975	540-2662	261	Web: www.b-w-engineering.com
B & W Manufacturing LLC	42-604 Aegean St Ste B	Indio	CA	92203	760-347-3200	347-9559	207	TF: 800-225-0057 ■ Web: www.liftconveyor.com
B & W Press Inc	401 E Main St Rte 133	Georgetown	MA	01833	978-352-6100		263	
B & W Tek Inc	19 Shea Way Ste 301	Newark	DE	19713	302-368-7824		407	Web: bwtek.com
B & W Tile Manufacturing Company Inc	14600 S Western Ave	Gardena	CA	90249	310-538-9579		751	Web: www.bwtile.com
B and B Metals	195 Thomason Ct	Shepherdsville	KY	40165	502-921-1991	921-9470	650	Web: www.bandbmetalsinc.com
B B C Security & Communication Inc	401 Mclean Ave	Yonkers	NY	10705	914-969-4000		693	Web: bbcsecurity.com
B Braun Medical Inc	824 12th Ave	Bethlehem	PA	18018	610-691-5400	997-5510	476	TF: 800-523-9676 ■ Web: www.bbraunusa.com
B C & G Weithman Construction Company Inc	1521 Lakewood Dr	Bucyrus	OH	44820	419-562-8027		186	
B C L of Texas	2212 S Congress Ave	Austin	TX	78704	512-912-9884		196	Web: bcloftexas.org
B C Szerlip Insurance Agency Inc	34 Sycamore Ave	Little Silver	NJ	07739	732-842-2020		390	Web: bcszerlip.com
B C Teachers Federation	100 - 550 W Sixth Ave	Vancouver	BC	V5Z4P2	604-871-2283		414	Web: www.bctf.ca
B D N Industrial Hygiene Consultants Inc	8105 Valleywood Ln	Portage	MI	49024	269-329-1237		196	Web: bdnihc.com
B E Meyers & Company Inc	9461 Willows Rd NE	Redmond	WA	98052	425-881-6648		544	TF: 800-327-5648 ■ Web: bemeyers.com
B E Peterson Inc	40 Murphy Dr Avon Industrial Pk	Avon	MA	02322	508-436-7900		492	Web: www.bepeterson.com
B Frank Joy LLC	5355 Kilmer Pl	Hyattsville	MD	20781	301-779-9400		188-10	Web: www.bfjoy.com
B G Consultants Inc	4806 Vue Du Lac Pl	Manhattan	KS	66503	785-537-7448	537-8793	261	Web: www.bgcons.com
B Green & Co	1300 S Monroe St	Baltimore	MD	21230	410-539-6134		345	Web: www.bgreenco.com
B H G Inc	PO Box 309	Garrison	ND	58540	701-463-2201		627	TF: 800-658-3485 ■ Web: www.bhgnews.com
B H Suhr & Company Inc	840 Custer	Evanston	IL	60202	847-864-6315		727	Web: www.bhsuhr.com
B J Bindery	833 S Grand Ave	Santa Ana	CA	92705	714-835-7342	835-1663	535	Web: www.bjbindery.com
B Line Express Inc	10440 Little Patuxent Pkwy Stes 300 & 900	Columbia	MD	21044	866-625-4639		809	TF: 866-625-4639 ■ Web: www.blinex.com
B M C Bil Mac Corp	2995 44th St SW	Grandville	MI	49418	616-538-1930		454	Web: www.bmcbil-mac.com
B M Ross & Associates Ltd	62 North St	Goderich	ON	N7A2T4	519-524-2641		256	TF: 888-524-2641 ■ Web: www.bmross.net
B Ma Media Group	4091 Erie St	Willoughby	OH	44094	440-975-4262		194	Web: www.bmamedia.com
B Oma Suburban Chicago	1515 E Woodfield Rd Ste 110	Schaumburg	IL	60173	847-995-0970	995-0971	533	Web: www.bomasuburbanchicago.com
B Resort & Spa	1905 Hotel Plaza Blvd	Lake Buena Vista	FL	32830	407-828-2828		378	Web: www.bhotelsandresorts.com
B Riley & Company LLC	11100 Santa Monica Blvd Ste 800	Los Angeles	CA	90025	310-966-1444		690	Web: brileyfbr.com
B Schoenberg & Company Inc	345 Kear St	Yorktown	NY	10598	914-962-1200		603	Web: www.bschoenberg.info
B Squared Inc	104 W 29th St 7th Fl	New York	NY	10001	212-777-2044		626	Web: www.bsqu.com
B Street Theatre	2711 B St	Sacramento	CA	95816	916-443-5300		572	Web: bstreettheatre.org
B Swing Inc	700 Washington Ave N Ste 102	Minneapolis	MN	55401	612-752-1160		177	Web: www.bswing.com
B Z Plumbing Company Inc	1901 Aviation Blvd	Lincoln	CA	95648	916-645-1600		610	Web: www.bzplumbing.com
B'Nai B'Rith Intl	2020 K St NW 7th Fl	Washington	DC	20006	202-857-6600	857-6609	48-20	TF: 888-388-4224 ■ Web: www.bnaibrith.org

Name / Address	City	State	ZIP	Phone	Fax	Class
B. Diaferia CPA PC 307 7th Ave Ste 910	New York	NY	10001	212-741-4255		2
B. E. Smith Inc 8801 Renner Ave *TF:* 855-296-6318 ■ *Web:* www.besmith.com	Lenexa	KS	66219	855-296-6318		193
B. Foschino & Son Landscape Inc 27 Brook St *Web:* foschinolandscape.com	Norwood	NJ	07648	201-768-0296	768-3221	422
B. J. Kirby Insurance Agency Inc 83 S Ave *Web:* www.bjkirbyinsurance.com	Whitman	MA	02382	781-447-5511	447-7297	390
B. P. Lesky Distributing Company Inc 120 W Maryland Pkwy	Hagerstown	MD	21740	301-733-0787		443
B. Radtke and Sons Inc 101 W Main St *Web:* www.radtkeandsons.com	Round Lake Park	IL	60073	847-546-3999	546-4008	454
B. Rugged Books 11 S Adelaide Ave *Web:* www.brugged.com	Highland Park	NJ	08904	732-828-6098		637-2
B. United International Inc PO Box 661 *Web:* www.bunitedint.com	Redding	CT	06896	203-938-0713	938-1124	81-1
B. W. B. Controls Inc 107 W Woodlawn Ranch Rd *Web:* www.bwbcontrols.com	Houma	LA	70363	985-876-4117	876-0718	790
B.A. Harris LLP 960 Broadway Ste 314 *Web:* harriscpa.com	Boise	ID	83706	208-424-5177		2
B.B. Italia Kitchen and B.B. Pizza 14795 Memorial Dr *Web:* www.bbitaliakitchen.com	Houston	TX	77079	281-531-0696		671
B.C.D. Software Services Inc 2450 Mission St Ste 6 *Web:* www.ondisplayapparel.com	San Marino	CA	91108	626-441-1203	441-8373	178-1
B.L. Duke Inc 6470 W Canal Bank Rd Forest View *Web:* www.blduke.com	Chicago	IL	60636	773-778-3000		686
B102.7 5100 S Tennis Ln *Web:* www.b1027.com	Sioux Falls	SD	57108	605-361-0300		645-149
B103.9 20125 S Tamiami Trl *Web:* www.b1039.com	Estero	FL	33928	239-765-1039		645
B105.7 40 Monument Cir Ste 600 *Web:* www.b1057.com	Indianapolis	IN	46204	317-681-1057		645-74
B2 Environmental Inc 4503 S 90th St *Web:* www.b2environmental.com	Omaha	NE	68127	402-330-0763	330-0792	196
B2 Gold Corp 595 Burrard St Ste 3100 PO Box 49143 *TF:* 800-316-8855 ■ *Web:* www.b2gold.com	Vancouver	BC	V7X1J1	604-681-8371	681-6209	502
B-21 Liquors Inc 43380 US Hwy 19 N *Web:* www.b-21.com	Tarpon Springs	FL	34689	727-937-5049		443
B27 Resources PO Box 1697	Houston	TX	77251	214-473-8580		194
B2B Staffing Services Inc 4501 Cerritos Ave Ste 200 *Web:* www.b2bstaffingservices.com	Cypress	CA	90630	714-243-8496		260
B2B Workforce Inc 60 Harvard Mill Sq	Wakefield	MA	01880	770-667-7200		113
B2B2C Inc 2700 Rue Michelin *TF:* 800-965-9065 ■ *Web:* www.b2b2c.ca	Laval	QC	H7L5Y1	514-908-5420	380-8512	224
B2E Data Marketing Inc 307 E Court Ave Unit 103 *TF:* 877-275-2360 ■ *Web:* b2edata.com	Des Moines	IA	50309	515-282-4933		225
B2i Technologies Inc 3100 Independence Pkwy Ste 311-165 *Web:* www.b2itech.com	Plano	TX	75074	972-234-9200		809
B3 Solutions LLC 901 N Pitt St Ste 300 *TF:* 877-872-9839 ■ *Web:* www.b3solutions.com	Alexandria	VA	22314	571-384-1400	384-1438	463
B93.9 New County 3100 Smokotree Ct Ste 700 *Web:* b939country.iheart.com	Raleigh	NC	27604	919-874-9800		645-128
B96.5 FM 520 S Fourth Ave *Web:* www.hiphopb965.com	Louisville	KY	40202	502-625-1220		645-89
B97.5 1100 Sharps Ridge Rd *Web:* b975.com	Knoxville	TN	37917	865-525-6000	525-2000	645-82
BA Consulting Group Ltd 45 St Clair Ave W Ste 300 *Web:* www.bagroup.com	Toronto	ON	M4V1K9	416-961-7110		261
BA Robinson Company Ltd 619 Berry St *TF:* 866-903-6275 ■ *Web:* www.barobinson.com	Winnipeg	MB	R3H0S2	204-784-0150		612
Baader-Johnson 2955 Fairfax Trafficway *TF:* 800-288-3434 ■ *Web:* www.baader.com	Kansas City	KS	66115	913-621-3366		298
Baan Sawan 2135 Devine St *Web:* www.baansawanthaibistro.com	Columbia	SC	29205	803-252-8992		671
Baan Thai 3235 N Anthony Blvd *Web:* baanthaiin.com	Fort Wayne	IN	46805	260-471-2929		671
BAASS Business Solutions BC Inc 305-9600 Cameron St *Web:* www.baass.com	Burnaby	BC	V3J7N3	604-420-1099		179
Baasten, Mckinley & Company LPA 4150 Belden Village St NW Ste 604 *Web:* baastenmckinleyatty.com	Canton	OH	44718	330-492-0550		41
BAB Inc 500 Lake Cook Rd Ste 475 *OTC:* BABB ■ **Fax Area Code:* 847 ■ *TF:* 800-251-6101 ■ *Web:* www.babcorp.com	Deerfield	IL	60015	800-251-6101	405-8140*	670
Babanikas Ziedman & King Pc 1247 Belmont St *Web:* bzklaw.com	Brockton	MA	02301	508-588-7000		41
Babb Inc 850 Ridge Ave *TF:* 800-207-4222 ■ *Web:* babbins.com	Pittsburgh	PA	15212	412-237-2020	322-1756	390
Babb Lumber Company Inc 6652 Hwy 41 *Web:* www.babb.com	Ringgold	GA	30736	706-935-2411		818
Babbitt Bearing Company Inc 1170 N 5th St *Web:* bbcmachine.com	San Jose	CA	95112	408-298-1101	998-4134	454
Babbitt Bearings Inc 734 Burnet Ave *TF:* 800-435-4445 ■ *Web:* www.babbitt-inc.com	Syracuse	NY	13203	315-479-6603		454
Babbitt International Inc 5155 April Ln *TF:* 800-835-8012 ■ *Web:* www.babbittinc.com	Houston	TX	77092	713-467-4438	467-8736	201
Babbo 110 Waverly Pl *Web:* www.babbonyc.com	New York	NY	10011	212-777-0303		671
Babbo Italian Eatery 20211 N 67th Ave *Web:* babboitalian.com	Glendale	AZ	85308	623-566-9898	566-5561	671
BABC (British-American Business Council) 52 Vanderbilt Ave 20th Fl *Web:* www.babc.org	New York	NY	10017	212-661-4060	661-4074	138
Babco International Inc 1931 W Grant Rd Ste320 *TF:* 888-332-2226 ■ *Web:* www.babcotucson.com	Tucson	AZ	85745	520-628-7596	628-9622	300
Babcock & Wilcox Co 13024 Ballantyne Corporate Pl Ste 700 **Fax Area Code:* 330 ■ *TF:* 800-222-2625 ■ *Web:* www.babcock.com	Charlotte	NC	28277	704-625-4900	860-1886*	91
Babcock Partners LLC 10101 Siegen Ln Ste 3C *Web:* stephenbabcock.com	Baton Rouge	LA	70810	225-222-2625		428
Babcock Power Inc 6 Kimball Ln Ste 210 *TF:* 800-523-0480 ■ *Web:* www.babcockpower.com	Lynnfield	MA	01940	978-646-3300	646-3301	91
Babcock State Park 486 Babcock Rd *Web:* wvstateparks.com	Clifftop	WV	25831	304-438-3004		565
Babcock-Davis 9300 73rd Ave N **Fax Area Code:* 763 ■ *TF:* 888-412-3726 ■ *Web:* www.babcockdavis.com	Brooklyn Park	MN	55428	888-412-3726	488-9248*	234
Babe Ruth Birthplace Museum 216 Emory St *Web:* baberuthmuseum.org	Baltimore	MD	21230	410-727-1539	727-1652	522
Babe Ruth League Inc 1770 Brunswick Pk PO Box 5000 *TF:* 800-880-3142 ■ *Web:* www.baberuthleague.org	Trenton	NJ	08638	609-695-1434	695-2505	48-22
Babe Winkelman Productions PO Box 407 *TF:* 800-333-0471 ■ *Web:* winkelman.com	Brainerd	MN	56401	800-333-0471		742
Babeco Inc 1101 Crlos Parker Blvd NW *Web:* www.babecoinc.com	Taylor	TX	76574	512-352-5355	352-8384	454
Babette's Cafe 573 N Highland Ave *Web:* www.babettescafe.com	Atlanta	GA	30307	404-523-9121		671
Babich & Assoc 6030 E Mockingbird Ln *Web:* www.babich.com	Dallas	TX	75206	214-823-9999		260
Babin Brian (Rep R - TX) 2236 Rayburn House Office Bldg *Web:* babin.house.gov	Washington	DC	20515	202-225-1555	226-0396	342-2
Babin Machine Works Inc 2510 N 9th St PO Box 2007	Beaumont	TX	77703	409-892-1231		455
Babin's Seafood House 17485 Tomball Pkwy *Web:* www.babinsseafood.com	Houston	TX	77064	281-477-9300		671
Babson College 231 Forest St *TF:* 800-488-3696 ■ *Web:* www.babson.edu	Babson Park	MA	02457	781-235-1200	239-4006	166
Baby Jogger Co 8575 Magellan Pkwy Ste 1000 **Fax Area Code:* 804 ■ *TF:* 800-241-1848 ■ *Web:* www.babyjogger.com	Richmond	VA	23227	800-241-1848	262-6277*	64
Baby Kay's Cajun Kitchen 2051 S Dobson Rd *Web:* www.babykayscajunkitchen.com	Mesa	AZ	85202	480-800-4811		671
Baby Trend Inc 1567 S Campus Ave **Fax Area Code:* 909 ■ *TF:* 800-328-7363 ■ *Web:* www.babytrend.com	Ontario	CA	91761	800-328-7363	773-0108*	64
BabyCenter LLC 163 Freelon St *TF:* 866-732-8243 ■ *Web:* www.babycenter.com	San Francisco	CA	94107	415-537-0900	537-0909	356
Babylist Inc 1625 Clay St *TF:* 888-827-7856 ■ *Web:* www.babylist.com	Oakland	CA	94612	888-827-7856		459
BAC (Big Apple Circus) 321 W 44th St Ste 400 *TF:* 888-541-3750 ■ *Web:* bigapplecircus.com	New York	NY	10036	212-257-2330		149
BAC (International Union of Bricklayers & Allied Craftworkers) 620 F St NW *TF:* 888-880-8222 ■ *Web:* www.bacweb.org	Washington	DC	20004	202-783-3788		414
Bac Sales Inc 1871 Rt 9H *Web:* www.bacsales.com	Hudson	NY	12534	518-828-6363		612
Baca & Howard PC 2155 Louisiana Blvd NE Ste 7000 *Web:* bacahoward.com	Albuquerque	NM	87110	505-200-3800		2
Baca County 741 Main St *Web:* www.springfieldcolorado.com	Springfield	CO	81073	719-523-6532		338
Bacall's Cafe 6118 Hamilton Ave *Web:* bacallscafe.com	Cincinnati	OH	45224	513-541-8804		671
Bacardi 2701 S Le Jeune Rd *TF:* 800-222-2734 ■ *Web:* www.bacardi.com	Coral Gables	FL	33134	800-222-2734		80-1
Bacardi Ltd 12200 N Main St *Web:* www.bacardilimited.com	Jacksonville	FL	32218	904-757-1290		81-3
Bacarella Transportation Service 375 Bridgeport Ave Ste 2 *Web:* www.btxair.com	Stratford	CT	06615	203-375-1180		366
BACC (British-American Chamber of Commerce Great Lakes Region) PO Box 360707 *Web:* www.baccohio.org	Strongsville	OH	44136	216-621-0222		138
BACC (Belgian-American Chamber of Commerce in the US) 1177 Avenue of the Americas 7th Fl *Web:* www.belcham.org	New York	NY	10036	212-541-0771		138
Baccala Concrete Corp 100 Armento St *Web:* baccalaconcrete.com	Johnston	RI	02919	401-231-8300	232-3965	182
Baccarat Hotel New York 28 W 53rd St *TF:* 866-957-5139 ■ *Web:* www.baccarathotels.com	New York	NY	10019	212-790-8800		707
Bacchanalia 1198 Howell Mill Rd *Web:* www.starprovisions.com	Atlanta	GA	30318	404-365-0410	365-8020	671
Bacchanalia Ristorante 2413 S Oakley Ave *Web:* www.bacchanaliainchicago.com	Chicago	IL	60608	773-254-6555		671
BACCHUS Network, The 111 K St NE 10th Fl *Web:* www.naspa.org	Washington	DC	20002	202-265-7500		48-17
Bacchus Press Inc 1287 66th St *Web:* www.bacchuspress.com	Emeryville	CA	94608	510-420-5800	420-0881	627
Bacchus Restaurant 925 E Wells St *Web:* www.bartolottas.com	Milwaukee	WI	53202	414-765-1166		671
Bacco Construction Co N3676 N Us-2 *Web:* www.baccoconstruction.com	Iron Mountain	MI	49801	906-774-2616	774-1160	188-4

Name / Address	City	State	ZIP	Phone	Fax	Class
Bacco's 263 Park Ave *Web:* baccosristorante.com	Rochester	NY	14607	585-442-5090		671
Bach James Mansour & Co 3885 Crestwood Pkwy NW Ste 590 *Web:* bjmco.com	Duluth	GA	30096	678-521-2900		2
Bach Medical Supply 1711 E Sunshine *Web:* bachmedicalsupply.com	Springfield	MO	65804	417-883-1400		475
Bach Pharma Inc 800 Turnpike St Ste 300 *Web:* www.bachpharma.com	North Andover	MA	01845	978-794-5510		238
Bachand & Bachand PA 959 N Cocoa Blvd Ste 1 *Web:* bachandfamilylaw.com	Cocoa	FL	32922	321-634-5256		41
Bacharach Inc 621 Hunt Vly Cir *TF:* 800-736-4666 ■ *Web:* www.mybacharach.com	New Kensington	PA	15068	724-334-5000	334-5001	201
Bacharach Institute for Rehabilitation 61 W Jimmie Leads Rd *Web:* www.bacharach.org	Pomona	NJ	08240	609-652-7000	652-7487	374-6
Bachecki, Crom & Company LLP 400 Oyster Point Blvd Ste 106 *Web:* bachcrom.com	South San Francisco	CA	94080	415-398-3534	788-0855	2
Bachelor Controls Inc 123 N Washington Ave *Web:* www.bachelorcontrols.com	Sabetha	KS	66534	785-284-3482		49-6
Bachem Bioscience Inc 3132 Kashiwa St *TF:* 888-422-2436 ■ *Web:* www.bachem.com	Torrance	CA	90505	310-539-4171		479
Bachman Machine Company Inc 4321 N Broadway *Web:* www.bachmanmachine.com	Saint Louis	MO	63147	314-231-4221		483
Bachman's Inc 6010 Lyndale Ave S *TF:* 888-222-4626 ■ *Web:* www.bachmans.com	Minneapolis	MN	55419	612-861-7600	861-7748	292
Bachmann Construction Company Inc 1201 S Stoughton Rd *Web:* www.bachmannconstruction.net	Madison	WI	53716	608-222-8869		186
Bachmann Industries Inc 1400 E Erie Ave *TF:* 800-356-3910 ■ *Web:* www.bachmanntrains.com	Philadelphia	PA	19124	215-533-1600	744-4699	762
Bachmann Software 270 Sparta Ave Ste 104 *Web:* www.bachmannsoftware.com	Sparta	NJ	07871	973-729-9427		177
Bachus & Schanker LLC 123 N College Ave Ste 211 *TF:* 877-653-9800 ■ *Web:* www.coloradolaw.net	Fort Collins	CO	80524	970-223-9802	221-9808	445
Baci Restaurant 18748 Beach Blvd *Web:* www.bacirestaurant.com	Huntington Beach	CA	92648	714-965-1194		671
Back Bay Grill 65 Portland St *Web:* backbaygrill.com	Portland	ME	04101	207-772-8833		671
Back Country Horsemen of America (BCHA) 59 Rainbow Rd *TF:* 888-893-5161 ■ *Web:* www.bcha.org	East Granby	CT	06026	860-586-7540	653-1702	48-23
Back Porch Grill, The 4810 Central Ave *Web:* www.backporchgrill.com	Hot Springs	AR	71913	501-525-0885		671
Back to Basics Learning Dynamics Inc 6 Stone Hill Rd *Web:* www.backtobasicslearning.com	Wilmington	DE	19803	302-594-0754		768
Back Yard Burgers Inc 500 Church St Ste 200 *Web:* www.backyardburgers.com	Nashville	TN	37219	615-620-2300	620-2301	670
BackBay Communications Inc 20 Park Plz Ste 801 *Web:* www.backbaycommunications.com	Boston	MA	02116	617-556-9982		636
Backblaze Inc 500 Ben Franklin Ct *Web:* www.backblaze.com	San Mateo	CA	94401	650-352-3738		45
Backbone Media Inc 69 Milk St Ste 306 *Web:* www.backbonemedia.com	Westborough	MA	01581	508-366-2100		636
Backbone State Park 1347 129th St *Web:* iowadnr.gov	Dundee	IA	52038	563-924-2527		565
Backchannelmedia Inc 107 S St Ste 2C **Fax Area Code:* 617 ■ *TF:* 800-676-0823 ■ *Web:* www.backchannelmedia.com	Boston	MA	02111	800-676-0823	517-7777*	6
Backcountry Gear LLC 1855 W Second Ave *TF:* 800-953-5499 ■ *Web:* www.backcountrygear.com	Eugene	OR	97402	541-485-4007		711
Backcountry Publishing (BP) 3303 Dick George Rd *TF:* 888-443-3826 ■ *Web:* www.braintan.com	Cave Junction	OR	97523	541-592-3778		637-2
Backcountry.com 2607 S 3200 W Ste A *TF:* 800-409-4502 ■ *Web:* www.backcountry.com	West Valley City	UT	84119	800-409-4502		459
Backer Springfield Inc 4700 John Bragg Hwy *Web:* www.backerspringfield.com	Murfreesboro	TN	37127	615-907-6900		815
Background Bureau Inc 2019 Alexandria Pk *TF:* 800-854-3990 ■ *Web:* backgroundbureau.com	Highland Heights	KY	41076	859-781-3400	781-9540	635
Background Information Services Inc 1800 30th St Ste 204 *TF:* 800-433-6010 ■ *Web:* www.bisi.com	Boulder	CO	80301	303-442-3960	442-1004	635
Backing Up Classics Auto Museum 4545 Concord Pkwy S *Web:* www.backingupclassics.com	Concord	NC	28027	704-788-9500		520
Backlot Cars 1100 Main St Ste 1500 *TF:* 855-925-2252 ■ *Web:* backlotcars.com	Kansas City	MO	64105	855-925-2252		58
BackOffice Associates LLC 75 Perseverance Way *Web:* www.boaweb.com	Hyannis	MA	02601	508-430-7100		177
Backpacker Magazine 2520 55th St Ste 210 *Web:* www.backpacker.com	Boulder	CO	80301	610-967-8296		457-14
Backroads 801 Cedar St *TF:* 800-462-2848 ■ *Web:* www.backroads.com	Berkeley	CA	94710	510-527-1555	527-1444	760
Backroads Magazine 160 Co Rd 521 *Web:* www.backroadsusa.com	Newton	NJ	07860	973-948-4176	948-0823	457-3
Backstage LLC 45 Main St Ste 416 *Web:* www.backstage.com	Brooklyn	NY	11201	212-493-4243		457-9

Name / Address	City	State	ZIP	Phone	Fax	Class
Backstreet Cafe 1103 S Shepherd Dr *Web:* www.backstreetcafe.net	Houston	TX	77019	713-521-2239		671
Backstrom McCarley Berry & Company LLC 115 Sansome St Mezzanine A *TF:* 866-878-2622 ■ *Web:* www.bmcbco.com	San Francisco	CA	94104	415-392-5505	392-5276	401
Backupify 50 Milk St *TF:* 800-571-4984 ■ *Web:* www.backupify.com	Boston	MA	02109	800-571-4984		809
Backus Meyer & Branch LLP 116 Lowell St *Web:* www.backusmeyer.com	Manchester	NH	03104	603-668-7272		428
Backus Turner Intl 3116 N Federal Hwy *Web:* www.backusturner.com	Lighthouse Point	FL	33064	305-573-9996		195
Backwoods 609 Castle Ridge Rd Ste 400 *Web:* www.backwoods.com	Austin	TX	78746	512-583-1700		711
Backyard brewery 1211 S Mammoth Rd *Web:* backyardbrewerynh.com	Manchester	NH	03109	603-623-3545	625-8420	671
Bacompt Systems Inc 12742 Hamilton Crossing Blvd *Web:* www.bacompt.com	Carmel	IN	46032	317-574-7474		781
Bacon Don (Rep R - NE) 1024 Longworth House Office Bldg *TF:* 888-221-7452 ■ *Web:* www.bacon.house.gov	Washington	DC	20515	202-225-4155		342-2
Bacon Free Library 58 Eliot St *Web:* baconfreelibrary.org	Natick	MA	01760	508-653-6730		434-3
Bacone College 2299 Old Bacone Rd *TF:* 888-682-5514 ■ *Web:* www.bacone.edu	Muskogee	OK	74403	918-683-4581	781-7416	166
Bacon-Universal Company Inc 918 Ahua St *TF:* 800-352-3508 ■ *Web:* www.baconuniversal.com	Honolulu	HI	96819	808-839-7202	834-8110	358
Bacova Guild Ltd 1000 Commerce Center Dr *Web:* www.bacova.com	Covington	VA	24426	540-863-2600		131
Bactolac Pharmaceutical Inc 7 Oser Ave *Web:* bactolac.com	Hauppauge	NY	11788	631-951-4908		583
BACVA (Baltimore Area Convention & Visitors Assn) 100 Light St 12th Fl *TF:* 877-225-8466 ■ *Web:* baltimore.org	Baltimore	MD	21202	410-659-7300	727-2308	206
Bad Animals 2212 4th Ave *TF:* 800-236-5544 ■ *Web:* www.badanimals.com	Seattle	WA	98121	206-443-1500	441-2910	658
Bad Ass Coffee Company of Hawaii Inc 3900 S Wadsworth Blvd Ste 650 *Web:* badasscoffeestore.com	Lakewood	CO	80235	801-463-1966		310
Bad Boy Furniture Warehouse Ltd 500 Fenmar Dr *Web:* www.badboy.ca	Weston	ON	M9L2V5	416-667-7546		321
Bad Boy Inc 102 Industrial Dr *TF:* 866-622-3269 ■ *Web:* www.badboymowers.com	Batesville	AR	72501	870-698-0090	698-2123	194
Bad Dog Tools 24 Broadcommon Rd *TF:* 800-252-1330 ■ *Web:* baddogtools.com	Bristol	RI	02809	800-252-1330		350
Bad Wolf Press 216 Mt Hermon Rd Ste E372 **Fax Area Code:* 650 ■ *TF:* 888-827-8661 ■ *Web:* www.badwolfpress.com	Scotts Valley	CA	95066	888-827-8661	285-6291*	637-10
Badawest Restaurant 4018 Corunna Rd	Flint	MI	48532	810-232-2479		671
Badcock's Economy Furniture Store Inc 3931 RCA Blvd *Web:* badcocksfl.com	Palm Beach Gardens	FL	33410	561-694-8588		321
Baden Gage & Schroeder LLC 6920 Pointe Inverness Way Ste 300 *TF:* 800-830-2551 ■ *Web:* www.badencpa.com	Fort Wayne	IN	46804	260-422-2551	422-7862	2
Baden Steelbar & Bolt Corp 852 Big Sewickly Crk Rd R *Web:* www.badensteel.com	Sewickley	PA	15143	724-266-3003		350
Bader Group, The 5090 Shoreham Pl Ste 108 *Web:* www.badergroup.com	San Diego	CA	92122	858-717-0601		193
Bader Martin PS 1000 2nd Ave 34th Fl *Web:* badermartin.com	Seattle	WA	98104	206-621-1900	682-1874	2
Bader Rutter 1433 N Water St Ste 100 *Web:* baderrutter.com	Milwaukee	WI	53202	262-784-7200	938-5595	4
Badge-A-Minit Ltd 345 N Lewis Ave **Fax Area Code:* 815 ■ *TF:* 800-223-4103 ■ *Web:* www.badgeaminit.com	Oglesby	IL	61348	800-223-4103	883-9696*	456
Badger Air Brush Co 9128 Belmont Ave *TF:* 800-247-2787 ■ *Web:* www.badgerairbrush.com	Franklin Park	IL	60131	847-678-3104	671-4352	43
Badger Books PO Box 2404 *Web:* www.knife-expert.com	Eugene	OR	97402	541-484-0294		637-2
Badger Coaches Inc 5501 Femrite Dr *Web:* www.badgerbus.com	Madison	WI	53718	608-255-1511		760
Badger Daylighting Corp 919 11th Ave SW 4th Fl *TF:* 877-322-3437 ■ *Web:* badgerinc.com	Calgary	AB	T2R1P3	403-264-8500	228-9773	539
Badger Express LLC 181 Quality Ct *TF:* 800-972-0084 ■ *Web:* www.badgerexpress.com	Fall River	WI	53932	920-484-5808		192
Badger Federal Services Inc 2701 S Oakwood Rd *TF:* 800-726-5553 ■ *Web:* www.badgerfederal.com	Oshkosh	WI	54904	920-233-3000	426-6404	780
Badger Foundry Co 1058 E Mark St PO Box 1306 *Web:* www.badgerfoundry.com	Winona	MN	55987	507-452-5760	452-6469	307
Badger Herald Inc 152 W Johnson St Ste 202 *Web:* www.badgerherald.com	Madison	WI	53703	608-257-4712	258-3029	532-2
Badger Land Car Wash Equipment & Supplies LLC 300A E Oak St *TF:* 800-472-9274 ■ *Web:* badgerlandcwe.com	Oak Creek	WI	53154	800-472-9274		406
Badger Liquor Company Inc 850 S Morris St *TF:* 800-242-9708 ■ *Web:* www.badgerliquor.com	Fond du Lac	WI	54936	920-923-8160	923-8169	81-3
Badger Meter Inc 4545 W Brown Deer Rd *NYSE: BMI* ■ *TF:* 800-876-3837 ■ *Web:* www.badgermeter.com	Milwaukee	WI	53224	414-355-0400		495
Badger Mining Corp CA Chier Resource Ctr 409 S Church St *TF:* 800-932-7263 ■ *Web:* badgerminingcorp.com	Berlin	WI	54923	920-361-2388	361-2826	502
Badger Mutual Insurance Co 1635 W National Ave *Web:* www.badgermutual.com	Milwaukee	WI	53204	414-383-1234		390

Name	Address	City	State	Zip	Phone	Fax	Class	Other
Badger Plug Company Inc	N1045 Technical Dr PO Box 199	Greenville	WI	54942	920-757-7300		612	*Web:* badgerplug.com
Badger Press Inc	100 E Blackhawk Dr	Fort Atkinson	WI	53538	920-563-5144		627	*Web:* badgergroup.com
Badger Sporting Goods Company Inc	2814 Bryant Rd	Madison	WI	53713	608-274-1353	274-5322	711	*TF:* 800-627-6699 ■ *Web:* bsgsports.com
Badger State Ethanol LLC	820 W 17th St PO Box 317	Monroe	WI	53566	608-329-3900	329-6909	144	*Web:* www.badgerstateethanol.com
Badger State Industries (BSI)	3099 E Washington Ave PO Box 8990	Madison	WI	53708	608-240-5200	240-3320	630	*TF:* 800-862-1086 ■ *Web:* buybsi.com
Badger Truck Center Inc	2326 W St Paul Ave	Milwaukee	WI	53233	414-344-9500		57	*Web:* www.badgertruck.com
Badgley Phelps & Bell Inc	1420 Fifth Ave Ste 3200	Seattle	WA	98101	206-623-6172		401	*TF:* 800-869-7173 ■ *Web:* www.badgley.com
Badia Spices Inc	PO Box 226497	Doral	FL	33172	305-629-8000		123	*Web:* www.badiaspices.com
Badiyan Inc	720 W 94th St	Minneapolis	MN	55420	952-888-5507		514	*Web:* www.badiyan.com
Badlands National Park	25216 Ben Reifel Rd PO Box 6	Interior	SD	57750	605-433-5361	433-5404	564	*Web:* www.nps.gov
Badorf Shoe Company Inc	1958 Auction Rd	Manheim	PA	17545	800-325-1545		301	*TF:* 800-325-1545 ■ *Web:* www.badorfshoe.com
BAE (Bay Area Economics)	2600 Tenth St Ste 300	Berkeley	CA	94710	510-547-9380		194	*Web:* www.bae1.com
BAE Industries Inc	26020 Sherwood Ave	Warren	MI	48091	586-754-3000	754-3007	489	*Web:* baeind.com
BAE Systems Aerospace & Defense Group Inc	7822 S 46th St	Phoenix	AZ	85044	602-643-7233		21	*Web:* www.baesystems.com
BAE Systems Platforms & Services	2000 North 15th St 11th Fl	Arlington	VA	22201	703-907-8225		516	*Web:* www.baesystems.com
Baer Supply Co	909 Forest Edge Dr	Vernon Hills	IL	60061	800-289-2237	913-2230*	351	**Fax Area Code:* 847 ■ *TF:* 800-944-2237 ■ *Web:* www.baersupply.com
Baer's Furniture	1589 Northwest 12th Ave	Pompano Beach	FL	33069	954-582-4200		321	*Web:* baers.com
Baerlocher production USA LLC	5890 Highland Ridge Dr	Cincinnati	OH	45232	513-482-6300		143	*Web:* www.baerlocher.com
Baesman Group Inc	274 Marconi Blvd	Columbus	OH	43215	614-771-2300		195	*Web:* www.baesman.com
BAF Industries Inc	1451 Edinger Ave	Tustin	CA	92780	714-258-8055		151	*TF:* 800-437-9893 ■ *Web:* www.prowax.com
Bag Makers Inc	6606 S Union Rd	Union	IL	60180	800-458-9031		66	*TF:* 800-458-9031 ■ *Web:* www.bagmakersinc.com
Bag to Earth Inc	201 Richmond Blvd	Napanee	ON	K7R3Z9	613-354-1330		557	*Web:* bagtoearth.com
Bagatelle	115 Duval St	Key West	FL	33040	305-296-6609		671	*Web:* bagatellekw.com
Bagby Elevator Company Inc	3608 Messer Airport Hwy	Birmingham	AL	35222	800-228-7544		256	*TF:* 800-228-7544 ■ *Web:* www.bagbyelevator.com
Bagcraft	3900 W 43rd St	Chicago	IL	60632	773-254-8000	254-8204	554	*TF:* 800-621-8468 ■ *Web:* www.bagcraft.com
Bagdad Roller Mills Inc	5740 Elmburg Rd	Bagdad	KY	40003	502-747-8968		447	*TF:* 800-928-3333 ■ *Web:* www.bagdadrollermillsfeed.com
Bagel Boy Inc	485 S Union St	Lawrence	MA	01843	978-682-8646		296-1	*Web:* www.bagelboy.net
Baggett Transportation Co	5 49th St N	Birmingham	AL	35233	888-224-4388		780	*TF:* 888-224-4388 ■ *Web:* www.baggetttransport.com
Baghouse & Industrial Sheet Metal Services Inc	1731 Pomona Rd	Corona	CA	92880	951-272-6610		18	*Web:* 1888baghouse.com
Bagley & Rhody PC	2661 Riva Rd Ste 1001	Annapolis	MD	21401	410-573-1626		41	*Web:* bagleyrhody.com
Bag-PackInc	9486 Sutton Pl	Hamilton	OH	45011	513-346-3900		596	*Web:* www.bagpackinc.com
Bagwell Marketting	13211 Deer Run Trl	Dallas	TX	75243	972-480-8192		7	*Web:* bagwell.com
Bahama Breeze	8849 International Dr	Orlando	FL	32819	407-248-2499		671	*TF:* 877-500-9715 ■ *Web:* www.bahamabreeze.com
Bahama Buck's Franchise Corp	5741 50th St	Lubbock	TX	79424	806-771-2189	771-2190	381	*Web:* www.bahamabucks.com
BAHAMA Consulting Corp	4651 Nicols Rd Ste 200	Eagan	MN	55122	651-994-7900		177	*Web:* www.bahama-consulting.com
Bahama House	2001 S Atlantic Ave	Daytona Beach	FL	32118	800-571-2001	248-0991*	379	**Fax Area Code:* 386 ■ *TF:* 800-571-2001 ■ *Web:* daytonabahamahouse.com
Bahamas								
Consulate General	25 SE Second Ave	Miami	FL	33131	800-224-2627	373-6312*	257	**Fax Area Code:* 305 ■ *TF:* 800-224-2627 ■ *Web:* www.bahamas.com
Embassy	2220 Massachusetts Ave NW	Washington	DC	20008	202-319-2660	319-2668	257	*Web:* www.bahamasembdc.org
Bahia Honda State Park	36850 Overseas Hwy	Big Pine Key	FL	33043	305-872-2353		565	*Web:* www.floridastateparks.org
Bahia Mar Beach Resort & Yachting Ctr	801 Seabreeze Blvd	Fort Lauderdale	FL	33316	954-627-6309		669	*TF:* 800-755-9558 ■ *Web:* bahiamaryachtingcenter.com
Bahia Mar Resort & Conference Ctr	3100 Padre Blvd	South Padre Island	TX	78597	800-926-6926		669	*TF:* 800-926-6926 ■ *Web:* www.pirentals.com
Bahia Resort Hotel	998 W Mission Bay Dr	San Diego	CA	92109	858-488-0551	488-7055	669	*TF:* 800-576-4229 ■ *Web:* www.bahiahotel.com
Bahl & Gaynor Investment Counsel	255 E 5th St Ste 2700	Cincinnati	OH	45202	513-287-6100	287-6110	401	*TF:* 800-341-1810 ■ *Web:* www.bahl-gaynor.com
Bahn Thai Restaurant	1319 S Monroe St	Tallahassee	FL	32301	850-224-4765		671	*Web:* www.bahnthaioftallahassee.com
Bahwan CyberTek Inc	209 W Central St 312	Natick	MA	01760	508-652-0001		177	*Web:* www.bahwancybertek.com
BAI (Bank Administration Institute)	115 S LaSalle St Ste 3300	Chicago	IL	60603	312-683-2464	683-2373	49-2	*TF:* 800-224-9889 ■ *Web:* www.bai.org
BAI Distributors Inc	2312 NE 29 Ave	Ocala	FL	34470	352-732-7009	732-1616	246	*TF:* 888-224-3446 ■ *Web:* www.baionline.com
BAI Inc	21 Airport Blvd Ste B	San Francisco	CA	94107	650-872-1700	872-1955	770	*Web:* www.bai-inc.eu
Baier Marine Company Inc	2920 Airway Ave	Costa Mesa	CA	92626	800-455-3917		350	*TF:* 800-455-3917 ■ *Web:* www.baiermarine.com
Bailard	950 Tower Ln Ste 1900	Foster City	CA	94404	650-571-5800	573-7128	401	*TF:* 800-224-5273 ■ *Web:* www.bailard.com
Bailey & Galyen	1901 W Airport Fwy	Bedford	TX	76021	817-288-1101	545-3677	428	*TF:* 844-402-3900 ■ *Web:* www.galyen.com
Bailey & Glasser LLP	209 Capitol St	Charleston	WV	25301	304-345-6555		428	*Web:* www.baileyglasser.com
Bailey Brand Consulting	200 W Germantown Pke	Plymouth Meeting	PA	19462	610-940-9030		4	*Web:* www.baileygp.com
Bailey Bridges Inc	119 40th St NE	Fort Payne	AL	35967	800-477-7320		480	*TF:* 800-477-7320 ■ *Web:* www.baileybridge.com
Bailey Carr CPAS PC	2565 Brighton Henrietta Tl Rd	Rochester	NY	14623	585-272-9870	272-0041	2	*Web:* baileycarrcpa.com
Bailey Cavalieri LLC	10 W Broad St Ste 2100	Columbus	OH	43215	614-221-3155		428	*Web:* baileycav.com
Bailey Company Inc, The	501 Cowan St	Nashville	TN	37207	800-342-1665		358	*TF:* 800-342-1665 ■ *Web:* www.baileycompany.com
Bailey County	300 S 1st St Ste 130	Muleshoe	TX	79347	806-272-3044	272-3538	338	*Web:* www.co.bailey.tx.us
Bailey House Inc	180 Christopher St	New York	NY	10014	212-337-3000		195	*Web:* baileyhouse.org
Bailey Lauerman & Associates Inc	1299 Farnam St Ste 920	Omaha	NE	68102	402-514-9400		4	*Web:* www.baileylauerman.com
Bailey Manufacturing	PO Box 130	Lodi	OH	44254	330-948-1080	948-4439	476	*TF:* 800-321-8372 ■ *Web:* baileymfg.com
Bailey Matthews Shell Museum	3075 Sanibel-Captiva Rd PO Box 1580	Sanibel	FL	33957	239-395-2233	395-6706	520	*TF:* 888-679-6450 ■ *Web:* www.shellmuseum.org
Bailey Metal Products Ltd	1 Caldari Rd	Concord	ON	L4K3Z9	905-738-9267		307	*TF:* 800-668-2154 ■ *Web:* www.bmp-group.com
Bailey Properties	106 Aptos Beach Dr	Aptos	CA	95003	831-688-7009		652	*TF:* 800-347-6830 ■ *Web:* www.baileyproperties.com
Bailey Seed Company Inc	4570 Ridge Dr NE	Salem	OR	97301	503-362-9700	362-1705	270	*TF:* 800-407-7713 ■ *Web:* www.baileyseed.com
Bailey's	185 Lombard Ave	Winnipeg	MB	R3B0W4	204-944-1180		671	*Web:* www.baileysprimedining.com
Bailey's Express Inc	61 Industrial Park Rd	Middletown	CT	06457	860-632-0388		780	*Web:* www.baileysxpress.com
Bailey's Seafood & Grill	5520-A Johnston St	LaFayette	LA	70503	337-988-6464		671	*Web:* baileyslafayette.com
Bailey, Javins & Carter Lc	213 Hale St	Charleston	WV	25301	304-345-0346	345-0375	428	*TF:* 800-497-0234 ■ *Web:* www.baileyjavinscarter.com
Bailey, Stultz, Oldaker & Greene PLLC	122 Court St	Weston	WV	26452	304-269-1311		41	*Web:* baileystultz.com
Bailey44	4700 S Boyle Ave	Vernon	CA	90058	844-894-8100		157-6	*TF:* 844-894-8100 ■ *Web:* www.bailey44.com
Bailey-Parks Urethane Inc	184 Gilbert Ave	Memphis	TN	38106	901-774-7930		610	*Web:* www.baileyparks.com
Baileys Furniture Outlet Inc	350 W Intl Airport Rd Ste 100	Anchorage	AK	99518	907-646-4900		321	*TF:* 888-563-4083 ■ *Web:* www.baileysfurniture.com
Bailiwick Services LLC	4260 Norex Dr	Chaska	MN	55318	800-935-8840		180	*TF:* 800-935-8840 ■ *Web:* bailiwick.com
Baille Lumber Co	4002 Legion Dr PO Box 6	Hamburg	NY	14075	716-649-2850	649-2811	191-3	*TF:* 800-950-2850 ■ *Web:* www.baillie.com
Baillio's Inc	5301 Menaul Blvd NE	Albuquerque	NM	87110	505-273-9795	338-3375	39	*TF:* 800-540-7511 ■ *Web:* www.baillios.com
Baily International Inc	1122 SR-3	National Stock Yards	IL	62071	618-271-1122		123	*Web:* www.bailyfoods.com
Bain & Co	131 Dartmouth St	Boston	MA	02116	617-572-2000	572-2427	194	*Web:* www.bain.com
Bain & Holden Tire Company Inc	100 N Amhurst Pl PO Box 168	Englewood	TN	37329	423-887-7932		57	
Bain Capital Inc	200 Clarendon St	Boston	MA	02116	617-516-2000	516-2010	792	*Web:* www.baincapital.com
Bain Freibaum & Company LLC	3515 N Arnoult Rd	Metairie	LA	70002	504-568-0086	568-0102	2	*Web:* www.bainfreibaumcpa.com
Bain Medina Bain Inc	7073 San Pedro	San Antonio	TX	78216	210-494-7223		261	*Web:* bmbi.com

	Phone	Fax	Class
Bain Pest Control Service Inc 1320 Middlesex St Lowell MA 01851 *TF:* 800-272-3661 ■ *Web:* bainpestcontrol.com	978-452-9621		577
Bainbridge Lending Group LLC 345 Knechtel Way NE Ste 200 Bainbridge Island WA 98110 *Web:* blgloans.com	206-842-7176		217
Bainbridge, Mims, Rogers & Smith LLP 600 Luckie Dr Ste 415 Birmingham AL 35223 *Web:* bainbridgemims.com	205-879-1100		41
Bainbridge-Decatur County Chamber of Commerce PO Box 755 Bainbridge GA 39818 *Web:* www.bainbridgegachamber.com	229-726-5126	243-7633	139
Bair Legal 405 Grand Ave Ste 204 South San Francisco CA 94080 *Web:* bairlegal.com	510-434-1400		41
Bair Rugs 5430 Pirrone Rd Salida CA 95368 *Web:* bairrugs.com	209-571-2327		290
Baird & Warner Inc 120 S LaSalle St 20th Fl Chicago IL 60603 *TF:* 888-661-1176 ■ *Web:* www.bairdwarner.com	312-368-1855	368-1490	652
Baird & Wilson Sheet Metal Inc 2703 Bond St Knoxville TN 37917 *Web:* bairdandwilson.com	865-523-9982	523-4531	697
Baird Associates Inc 11 Davis Ln Georgetown MA 01833 **Fax Area Code:* 617 ■ *TF:* 888-412-2473 ■ *Web:* www.bairdassociates.com	781-433-7128	484-1782*	180
Baird Hampton & Brown Inc 6300 Ridglea Pl Ste 700 Fort Worth TX 76116 *Web:* bhbinc.com	817-338-1277		256
Baird James (Rep R - IN) 532 Cannon House Office Bldg Washington DC 20515 *Web:* www.baird.house.gov	202-225-5037		342-2
Baird Patrick & Company Inc 305 Plz 10 Jersey City NJ 07311 *TF:* 800-221-7747 ■ *Web:* www.bairdpatrick.com	201-680-7300	680-7301	690
Baird, Crews, Schiller & Whitaker PC 15 N Main St Temple TX 76501 *Web:* bcswlaw.com	254-774-8333	774-9353	41
Baird, Williams & Greer LLP 6225 N 24th St Ste 125 Phoenix AZ 85016 *Web:* bwglaw.net	602-256-9400		41
Baird-Neece Packing Corp 60 S E St Porterville CA 93257	559-784-3393		11-1
BairesDev 1999 S Bascom Ave Ste 700 Campbell CA 95008 *Web:* www.bairesdev.com	408-915-4135		196
Baisch & Skinner Inc 2721 Lasalle St Saint Louis MO 63104 *TF:* 800-523-0013 ■ *Web:* www.baischandskinner.com	314-664-1212		292
Baisch Engineering Inc 809 Hyland Ave Kaukauna WI 54130 *Web:* www.baisch.com	920-766-3521		256
Baja Cafe 1310 S Federal Hwy Deerfield Beach FL 33441 *Web:* www.bajacafefl.com	954-596-1304		671
Baja Expeditions Inc 3096 Palm St San Diego CA 92104 *TF:* 800-843-6967 ■ *Web:* bajaex.com	858-581-3311		220
Baja Foods LLC 636 W Root St Chicago IL 60609 *Web:* www.bajafoodsllc.com	773-376-9030		297-6
Baja Fresh 9311 E Via De Ventura Scottsdale AZ 85258 *TF:* 866-452-4252 ■ *Web:* www.bajafresh.com	866-452-4252		671
Baja Marine Corp 1653 Whichards Beach Rd Washington NC 27889 *Web:* bajamarine.com	252-975-2000		90
Baja Mexican Cuisine 104 14th St Hoboken NJ 07030 *Web:* www.bajahoboken.com	201-653-0610		671
Baja Source 1945 Dehesa Rd El Cajon CA 92019 *TF:* 888-773-3131 ■ *Web:* www.bajaexpo.com	888-773-3131		637-2
BAJobs com 46 W Julian St Ste 229 San Jose CA 95110 *Web:* www.bajobs.com	408-596-5991		260
Baka Communications Inc 630 The East Mall Etobicoke ON M9B4B1 *TF:* 866-884-3329 ■ *Web:* www.baka.ca	416-641-2800		196
Bake'n Joy Foods Inc 351 Willow St S North Andover MA 01845 **Fax Area Code:* 978 ■ *TF:* 800-666-4937 ■ *Web:* www.bakenjoy.com	800-666-4937	683-1713*	296-16
Baker & Gilchrist 7388 Business Center Dr Avon IN 46123 *Web:* bakerandgilchrist.com	317-272-0008		41
Baker & McKenzie LLP 300 E Randolph St Ste 5000 Chicago IL 60601 *Web:* www.bakermckenzie.com	312-861-8800	861-2899	428
Baker & Sons Equipment Co 45381 SR- 145 Lewisville OH 43754 *Web:* www.bakerandsons.com	740-567-3317		273
Baker & Taylor Inc 2550 W Tyvola Rd Ste 300 Charlotte NC 28217 **Fax Area Code:* 704 ■ *TF:* 800-775-1800 ■ *Web:* www.baker-taylor.com	800-775-1800	998-3316*	96
Baker & Wick LLC 400 S Fifth St 2nd Fl Columbus OH 43215 *Web:* bakerandwick.com	614-362-3266		41
Baker - Wotring LLP (BW) 700 JPMorgan Chase Tower 600 Travis St Houston TX 77002 *Web:* www.bakerwotring.com	713-980-1700	980-1701	428
Baker Book House Company Inc *Revell Div* 6030 E Fulton St Ada MI 49301 *TF:* 800-877-2665 ■ *Web:* bakerpublishinggroup.com	616-676-9185	676-9573	637-3
Baker Botts LLP 910 Louisiana St Houston TX 77002 *Web:* www.bakerbotts.com	713-229-1234	229-1522	428
Baker Boy Bake Shop Inc 170 Gta Dr Dickinson ND 58601 *Web:* www.bakerboy.com	701-225-4444		578
Baker College 1020 S Washington St Owosso MI 48867 *TF:* 800-879-3797 ■ *Web:* www.baker.edu	989-729-3350	729-3359	166
Baker Commodities Inc 4020 Bandini Blvd Vernon CA 90058 *Web:* www.bakercommodities.com	323-268-2801		296-12
Baker Communications Inc 10101 SW Fwy Ste 630 Houston TX 77074 *TF:* 877-253-8506 ■ *Web:* www.bakercommunications.com	713-627-7700	587-2051	765
Baker Company Inc 175 Gatehouse Rd Sanford ME 04073 *TF:* 800-992-2537 ■ *Web:* bakerco.com	207-324-8773	324-3869	420
Baker Concrete Construction Inc 900 N Garver Rd Monroe OH 45050 *TF:* 800-539-2224 ■ *Web:* www.bakerconcrete.com	513-539-4000	539-4380	189-3
Baker Correctional Institution 20706 US Hwy 90 Sanderson FL 32087 *Web:* www.myflorida.com	386-719-4500	758-5759	213
Baker County 1995 Third St Ste 150 Baker City OR 97814 *Web:* www.bakercounty.org	541-523-8207	523-8240	338
Baker County 7790 S SR 228 Macclenny FL 32063 *Web:* www.bakercountyfl.org	904-259-8113		338
Baker County Visitors & Convention Bureau 490 Campbell St Baker City OR 97814 *Web:* www.visitbaker.com	541-523-5855	523-9187	206
Baker Creek State Park 863 Baker Creek Rd McCormick SC 29835 *Web:* southcarolinaparks.com	864-443-2457		565
Baker Distributing Co 14610 Breakers Dr Ste 100 Jacksonville FL 32258 *TF:* 844-289-0033 ■ *Web:* www.bakerdist.com	800-217-4698		612
Baker Donelson Bearman Caldwell & Berkowitz PC 165 Madison Ave 1st Tennessee Bldg Ste 2000 Memphis TN 38103 *TF:* 800-973-1177 ■ *Web:* www.bakerdonelson.com	901-526-2000	577-2303	428
Baker Electric Inc 111 Jackson Ave Des Moines IA 50315 *Web:* www.bakerelectric.com	515-288-6774	288-2226	189-4
Baker Foodservice Design Inc 2220 E Paris Ave SE Grand Rapids MI 49546 *TF:* 800-968-4011 ■ *Web:* bakergroup.com	616-942-4011		463
Baker Group 4224 Hubbell Ave Des Moines IA 50317 *TF:* 855-262-4000 ■ *Web:* www.thebakergroup.com	515-262-4000	266-1025	189-10
Baker Hostetler LLP Key Tower 127 Public Sq Ste 2000 Cleveland OH 44114 *Web:* www.bakerlaw.com	216-861-7535	696-0740	428
Baker Hughes INTEQ 3901 Fanucchi Way E Shafter CA 93263 *Web:* www.bakerhughes.com	661-831-7686		538
Baker Implement Co 421 E Main St Portageville MO 63873 *Web:* www.bakerimplement.com	573-379-5455	379-5313	274
Baker Institute for Animal Health Cornell University College of Veterinary Medicine 235 Hungerford Hill Rd Ithaca NY 14853 *Web:* www.vet.cornell.edu	607-256-5600	256-5608	668
Baker Krizner Financial Planning 2230 N Limestone St Springfield OH 45503 *TF:* 888-390-8753 ■ *Web:* www.bakerkrizner.com	937-390-8750		463
Baker Manock & Jensen 5260 N Palm Ste 421 Fresno CA 93704 *Web:* www.bakermanock.com	559-432-5400	432-5620	428
Baker Materials LLC 819 Hickory Ave Harahan LA 70123 *Web:* www.bakermaterials.com	504-353-1535		182
Baker McMillen Co 3688 Wyoga Lake Rd Stow OH 44224 *TF:* 800-845-8111 ■ *Web:* www.baker-mcmillen.com	330-923-8300		820
Baker Metal Products Inc 11140 Zodiac Ln Dallas TX 75229 *Web:* www.bakermetal.com	972-241-3553		480
Baker Motor Company Inc 1511 Savannah Hwy Charleston SC 29407 *Web:* www.bakermotorcompany.com	843-852-4000		57
Baker Perkins Inc 3223 Kraft Ave SE Grand Rapids MI 49512 *Web:* www.bakerperkins.com	616-784-3111	784-0973	298
Baker Printing Company Inc 1618 Main St Baker LA 70714 *Web:* www.bplink.com	225-775-0137	775-0174	627
Baker Products 55480 Hwy 21 N PO Box 128 Ellington MO 63638 *TF:* 800-548-6914 ■ *Web:* www.baker-online.com	573-663-7711		821
Baker Rock Resources 21880 SW Farmington Rd Beaverton OR 97007 *TF:* 800-340-7625 ■ *Web:* www.baker-rock.com	503-642-2531		46
Baker Roofing Co 517 Mercury St Raleigh NC 27603 *TF:* 800-849-4096 ■ *Web:* www.bakerroofing.com	919-828-2975	828-9352	189-12
Baker Septic Installations 7740 S George Blvd Sebring FL 33875 *Web:* bakersepticstanks.com	863-385-0917		610
Baker Sheet Metal Corp 3541 Argonne Ave Norfolk VA 23509 *TF:* 800-909-4325 ■ *Web:* bakersheetmetal.com	757-853-4325	855-6252	697
Baker Storey McDonald Properties Inc 3011 Armory Dr Ste 120 Nashville TN 37204 *Web:* www.bsmproperties.com	615-373-9511		505
Baker Tankhead Inc 10405 North Fwy Fort Worth TX 76177 *TF:* 866-232-8030 ■ *Web:* www.bakertankhead.com	866-232-8030		480
Baker Tilly 8219 Leesburg Pk Ste 800 Tysons VA 22182 *Web:* bakertilly.com	703-923-8300		2
Baker Triangle 341 Hwy 80 E Mesquite TX 75150 *TF:* 800-458-3480 ■ *Web:* bakertriangle.com	972-289-5534	289-4580	189-9
Baker University 618 E Eighth St Baldwin City KS 66006 *TF:* 800-873-4282 ■ *Web:* www.bakeru.edu	785-594-6451		165
Baker's Cay Resort Key Largo, Curio Collection by Hilton 97000 Overseas Hwy Key Largo FL 33037 *TF:* 888-871-3437 ■ *Web:* curiocollection3.hilton.com	305-852-5553	852-8669	669
Baker's Ribs 2223 S Voss Rd Houston TX 77057 *Web:* www.bakersribs.com	713-977-8725		671
Baker's School of Aeronautics 100 Glidepath Way Lebanon TN 37090 *TF:* 800-264-1787 ■ *Web:* www.bakersschool.com	615-784-4212		685
Baker, Keener & Nahra LLP 633 W Fifth St Ste 5500 Los Angeles CA 90071 *Web:* bknlawyers.com	213-241-0900	241-0990	428
Bakercorp 3020 Old Ranch Pkwy Ste 220 Seal Beach CA 90740 *TF:* 800-635-7349 ■ *Web:* www.bakercorp.com	562-430-6262	430-4865	264-2
Bakers Pride Inc 325 Paul Ave Saint Louis MO 63135 *Web:* www.bakerspridestl.com	314-524-6314		297-2
Bakers Pride Oven Company Inc 30 Pine St New Rochelle NY 10801 *Web:* www.bakerspride.com	914-576-0200		427
Bakersfield Barber College Inc 2844 Niles St Bakersfield CA 93306 *Web:* www.bakersfieldbarbercollegeinc.com	661-873-0512		167-3

Phone | Fax | Class

Bakersfield Californian Inc
1707 Eye St ... Bakersfield CA 93301 661-395-7500 532-4
Web: www.bakersfield.com

Bakersfield City Employees Federal Credit Union
2817 16th St ... Bakersfield CA 93301 661-861-6151 323-8709 219
TF: 800-808-7230 ■ *Web:* bakcityefcu.org

Bakersfield City School District
1300 Baker St ... Bakersfield CA 93305 661-631-4600 326-1485 685
Web: www.bcsd.com

Bakersfield College
1801 Panorama Dr ... Bakersfield CA 93305 661-395-4011 395-4500 162
Web: www.bakersfieldcollege.edu

Bakersfield Museum of Art
1930 R St ... Bakersfield CA 93301 661-323-7219 520
Web: www.bmoa.org

Bakersfield News Observer
1219 20th St ... Bakersfield CA 93301 661-324-9466 532-4
Web: bakersfield-news-observer.business.site

Bakersfield Pipe & Supply Inc
3301 Zachary Ave ... Shafter CA 93263 661-589-9141 589-3739 596
TF: 888-294-0933 ■ *Web:* www.bpssg.com

Bakersfield Symphony Orchestra
1328 34th St Ste A ... Bakersfield CA 93301 661-323-7928 323-7331 573-3
Web: www.bsonow.org

Bakerwell Inc
6295 Maxtown Rd PO Box 1678 ... Westerville OH 43086 614-898-7590 536
Web: bakerwell.com

Bakery Barn LLC 111 Terence Dr ... Pittsburgh PA 15236 412-655-1113 297-8
Web: www.bakery-barn.com

Bakery Confectionery Tobacco Workers & Grain Millers International Union
10401 Connecticut Ave ... Kensington MD 20895 301-933-8600 946-8452 414
Web: www.bctgm.org

Bakewise Brands Inc
1688 N Wayneport Rd ... Macedon NY 14502 315-986-9999 296-1
Web: bakewisebrands.com

Bakke Norman 1200 Heritage Dr ... New Richmond WI 54017 715-246-3800 445
Web: www.bakkenorman.com

Bakken, The 3537 Zenith Ave S ... Minneapolis MN 55416 612-926-3878 927-7265 520
Web: thebakken.org

Bal Seal Engineering Company Inc
19650 Pauling ... Foothill Ranch CA 92610 949-460-2100 460-2300 326
TF: 800-366-1006 ■ *Web:* www.balseal.com

Bala Consulting Engineers Inc
443 S Gulph Rd ... King of Prussia PA 19406 610-649-8000 649-8475 256
Web: www.bala.com

Balance Day Spa LLC
3111 Battleground Ave ... Greensboro NC 27408 336-574-2556 77
Web: balancedayspa.com

Balance Innovations LLC
11011 Eicher Dr ... Lenexa KS 66219 913-599-1177 628
Web: www.balanceinnovations.com

Balance Living A Home Health Agency Inc
49 E Huntington Dr ... Arcadia CA 91006 626-821-0822 363
Web: balancedlivinghomehealth.com

Balance Point
9201 Ward Pkwy Ste 200 ... Kansas City MO 64114 816-268-1400 196
Web: www.balancepointhcm.com

Balance Rock Inn 21 Albert Meadow ... Bar Harbor ME 04609 207-288-2610 288-5534 379
TF: 800-753-0494 ■ *Web:* www.balancerockinn.com

Balance Technology Inc
7035 Jomar Dr ... Whitmore Lake MI 48189 734-769-2100 769-2542 494
Web: www.balancetechnology.com

Balancing Company Inc, The
898 Center Dr ... Vandalia OH 45377 937-898-9111 898-6145 454
Web: balco.com

Balancing Pool
2350 330 - Fifth Ave SW ... Calgary AB T2P0L4 403-539-5050 539-5366 706
Web: www.balancingpool.ca

Balasa Dinverno Foltz LLC
500 Park Blvd Ste 1400 ... Itasca IL 60143 630-875-4900 41
TF: 800-840-4740 ■ *Web:* bdfllc.com

Balax Inc PO Box 96 ... North Lake WI 53064 262-966-2355 966-1028 493
TF: 800-886-1398 ■ *Web:* www.balax.com

Balboa City Schools 525 Hawthorn St ... San Diego CA 92101 619-298-2990 685
Web: balboaschool.com

Balboa Instruments Inc 1382 Bell Ave ... Tustin CA 92780 714-384-0382 203
Web: www.balboawatergroup.com

Balboa Park 1549 El Prado ... San Diego CA 92101 619-239-0512 50-5
Web: www.balboapark.org

Balboa Park Inn 3402 Pk Blvd ... San Diego CA 92103 619-298-0823 379
Web: www.balboaparkinnapartments.com

Balboa Software PO Box 3751 ... Scottsdale AZ 85271 480-632-1901 632-6097 178-1
TF: 800-763-8542 ■ *Web:* www.balboa-software.com

Balboa Travel Management Inc
5414 Oberlin Dr Ste 300 ... San Diego CA 92121 858-678-3300 678-3399 771
TF: 800-359-8773 ■ *Web:* www.balboa.com

Balcan Plastics Ltd
9340 Meaux St ... Saint-Leonard QC H1R3H2 514-326-0200 326-4565 601
TF: 877-422-5226 ■ *Web:* www.balcan.com

Balch & Bingham LLP
1901 Sixth Ave N Ste 1500 ... Birmingham AL 35203 205-251-8100 428
Web: www.balch.com

Balch Petroleum Contractors & Builders Inc
930 Ames Ave ... Milpitas CA 95035 408-942-8686 580
Web: www.balchpetroleum.com

Balchem Corp
52 Sunrise Park Rd PO Box 600 ... New Hampton NY 10958 845-326-5613 326-5742 479
NASDAQ: BCPC ■ *TF:* 877-407-8289 ■ *Web:* www.balchem.com

Balcom Agency 1413 Rio Grande Ave ... Fort Worth TX 76102 817-877-9933 4
Web: www.balcomagency.com

Balcones Dermatology Associates PA
7800 N Mopac Expy Ste 315 ... Austin TX 78759 512-459-4869 237
Web: www.balconesdermatology.com

Balcones Resources Inc
9301 Johnny Morris Rd ... Austin TX 78724 512-472-3355 660
Web: www.balconesresources.com

Balcony Publishing Inc PO Box 2175 ... Georgetown TX 78627 512-868-8803 637-2
Web: www.balconypublishing.com

Phone | Fax | Class

Bald Head Island Rentals LLC
21 Keelson Row ... Bald Head Island NC 28461 910-457-1702 652
Web: www.baldheadislandrentals.com

Bald Mountain Recreation Area
1330 E Greenshield Rd ... Lake Orion MI 48360 248-693-6767 565
Web: www.michigan.org

Bald Point State Park
146 PO Box Cut ... Alligator Point FL 32346 850-349-9146 565
Web: www.floridastateparks.org

Balderson Troy (Rep R - OH)
1221 Longworth House Office Bldg ... Washington DC 20515 202-225-5355 342-2
Web: www.balderson.house.gov

Baldknobbers Restaurant 645 MO-165 ... Branson MO 65616 417-231-4999 671
Web: baldknobbers.com

Baldomero Lopez State Veterans' Nursing Home
6919 Pkwy Blvd ... Land O' Lakes FL 34639 813-558-5000 793
Web: floridavets.org

Baldor Electric Co
5711 RS Boreham Jr St PO Box 2400 ... Fort Smith AR 72901 479-646-4711 648-5792 518
Web: www.baldor.com

Balduzzi Group, The
2020 Pennsylvania Ave NW Ste 335 ... Washington DC 20006 202-604-0017 194
Web: www.balduzzigroup.com

Baldwin & Clarke Corporate Finance Inc
Coldstream Park 116B S River Rd ... Bedford NH 03110 603-668-4353 70
Web: baldwinclarke.com

Baldwin & Lyons Inc
111 Congressional Blvd Ste 500 ... Carmel IN 46032 317-636-9800 632-9444 391-4
NASDAQ: BWINB ■ *Web:* www.baldwinlyons.com

Baldwin & Shell Construction Company Inc
1000 W Capitol PO Box 1750 ... Little Rock AR 72201 501-374-8677 375-7649 186
Web: www.baldwinshell.com

Baldwin Aviation Safety & Compliance
11 Palmetto Pkwy ... Hilton Head Island SC 29926 843-342-5434 302
Web: www.baldwinaviation.com

Baldwin Beauty School 8440 Burnet Rd ... Austin TX 78757 512-458-4127 685
Web: www.baldwinbeautyschools.com

Baldwin C. Mark Atty
112 Old Bridge St ... Jacksonville NC 28540 910-446-3080 428
Web: www.kinglawfirm.com

Baldwin Cooke PO Box 312 ... Gloversville NY 12078 800-762-5000 870-2966* 241
**Fax Area Code: 888* ■ *TF:* 800-762-5000 ■ *Web:* www.baldwincooke.com

Baldwin County 322 Courthouse Sq ... Bay Minette AL 36507 251-937-9561 580-2500 338
TF: 800-403-4872 ■ *Web:* baldwincountyal.gov

Baldwin County
121 N Wilkinson St Ste 314 ... Milledgeville GA 31061 478-445-4791 445-6320 338
Web: www.baldwincountyga.com

Baldwin EMC
19600 State Hwy 59 PO Box 220 ... Summerdale AL 36580 251-989-6247 989-0133 245
TF: 800-837-3374 ■ *Web:* www.baldwinemc.com

Baldwin Filters 4400 Hwy 30 ... Kearney NE 68847 800-822-5394 828-4453 60
TF: 800-822-5394 ■ *Web:* www.baldwinfilters.com

Baldwin Hackett & Meeks Inc
11602 W Center Rd ... Omaha NE 68144 402-333-3300 177
TF: 800-610-2464 ■ *Web:* www.bhmi.com

Baldwin Hardware Corp
841 E Wyomissing Blvd ... Reading PA 19611 610-777-7811 350
TF: 800-566-1986 ■ *Web:* www.baldwinhardware.com

Baldwin Haspel Burke & Mayer LLC
1100 Poydras St Energy Ctr 36th Fl ... New Orleans LA 70163 504-569-2900 569-2099 428
Web: bhbmlaw.com

Baldwin Intl
30403 Bruce Industrial Pkwy ... Solon OH 44139 440-248-9500 492
Web: www.russelmetals.com

Baldwin Metals Company Inc
1901 W Commerce St ... Dallas TX 75208 214-747-6722 607
Web: baldwinmetals.com

Baldwin Public Library
300 W Merrill St ... Birmingham MI 48009 248-647-1700 434-3
Web: www.baldwinlib.org

Baldwin Richardson Foods Co
1 Tower Ln Ste 2390 ... Oakbrook Terrace IL 60181 630-607-1780 296-25
TF: 866-644-2732 ■ *Web:* brfoods.com

Baldwin State Prison
140 Laying Farm Rd ... Hardwick GA 31034 478-445-5218 445-6507 213
Web: dcor.state.ga.us

Baldwin Tammy (Sen D - WI)
709 Hart Senate Office Bldg ... Washington DC 20510 202-224-5653 342-2
Web: www.baldwin.senate.gov

Baldwin Technology Company Inc
8040 Forsyth Blvd ... Saint Louis MO 63105 314-863-6640 726-2132 629
Web: www.baldwintech.com

Baldwinsville Public Library
33 E Genesee St ... Baldwinsville NY 13027 315-635-5631 635-6760 434-3
TF: 800-388-2000 ■ *Web:* www.bville.lib.ny.us

Baldwin-Wallace College 275 Eastland Rd ... Berea OH 44017 440-826-2222 826-3830 166
TF: 877-292-7759 ■ *Web:* www.bw.edu

Bale Chevrolet Co
13101 Chenal Pkwy ... Little Rock AR 72211 501-221-9191 57
Web: www.balechevrolet.com

Balfor Industries Inc 327 Riggs St ... Oxford CT 06478 203-828-6473 463-8796 604
Web: www.balfor.com

Balfour 7211 Cir S Rd ... Austin TX 78745 512-440-2203 409
TF: 800-225-3687 ■ *Web:* www.balfour.com

Balfour Beatty Construction (BBC)
3100 McKinnon St ... Dallas TX 75201 214-451-1177 186
Web: balfourbeattyus.com

Balfour Beatty Inc
600 Galleria Pkwy Ste 1500 ... Atlanta GA 30309 404-875-0356 188-4
Web: www.balfourbeattyus.com

Balfour Investors Inc
1 Rockefeller Ctr 14th Fl ... New York NY 10020 212-489-7077 307-5781 401
Web: www.balfourinvestors.com

Bali Cafe Miami 109 NE 2nd Ave ... Miami FL 33132 305-358-5751 671
Web: balicafemiami.com

Bali Steak & Seafood 2005 Kalia Rd ... Honolulu HI 96815 808-949-4321 671
Web: www.hiltonhawaiianvillage.com

Balihoo 404 S Eighth St Ste 300 ... Boise ID 83702 866-446-9914 179
TF: 866-446-9914 ■ *Web:* balihoo.com

Name / Address	City	State	Zip	Phone	Fax	Class
Balise Motor Sales Co 1399 Riverdale St *Web:* www.baliseauto.com	West Springfield	MA	01089	413-306-3037		57
Balkamp Inc 2601 Stout Heritage Pkwy	Plainfield	IN	46168	317-244-7241		61
Balkema Excavating Inc 1500 River St *Web:* www.balkemaexc.com	Kalamazoo	MI	49048	269-345-5289	345-1137	188-10
Ball Auto Group 2135 National City Blvd *Web:* www.ballauto.com	National City	CA	91950	619-474-6431		57
Ball Beauty Supplies 416 N Fairfax Ave *TF:* 800-588-0244 ■ *Web:* www.ballbeauty.com	Los Angeles	CA	90036	800-588-0244		77
Ball Chain Manufacturing Company Inc 741 S Fulton Ave *Web:* www.ballchain.com	Mount Vernon	NY	10550	914-664-7500	664-7460	483
Ball Corp 10 Longs Peak Dr *NYSE: BLL* ■ *Web:* www.ball.com	Broomfield	CO	80021	303-469-3131		185
Ball Heating & Air 8332 W Oaklawn Rd *Web:* www.callballthatsall.com	Biloxi	MS	39532	228-392-5432		610
Ball Homes LLC 3609 Walden Dr *TF:* 888-268-1101 ■ *Web:* ballhomes.com	Lexington	KY	40517	865-556-0574		187
Ball Horticultural Co 622 Town Rd *TF:* 800-879-2255 ■ *Web:* www.ballhort.com	West Chicago	IL	60185	630-231-3600	231-3605	293
Ball Janik LLP 101 SW Main St Ste 1100 *Web:* www.balljanik.com	Portland	OR	97204	503-228-2525	295-1058	428
Ball Kirk & Holm Pc 3324 Kimball Ave *Web:* www.ballkirkholm.com	Waterloo	IA	50704	319-234-2638	234-2237	428
Ball Metalpack 300 W Greger St *Web:* ballmetalpack.com	Oakdale	CA	95361	209-848-6500		124
Ball State University 2000 W University Ave *TF:* 800-382-8540 ■ *Web:* www.bsu.edu	Muncie	IN	47306	765-289-1241	285-1632	166
Ball Tire & Gas Inc 620 S Ripley Blvd *Web:* www.balltire.net	Alpena	MI	49707	989-354-4186	356-2080	755
Ball Watch USA 1920 Martin Luther King Jr St N Ste D *Web:* www.ballwatchusa.com	Saint Petersburg	FL	33704	727-896-4278		411
Ballad Health 1905 American Way *TF:* 800-535-9057 ■ *Web:* www.balladhealth.org	Kingsport	TN	37660	423-230-8200		353
Ballantine & Company Inc 268 Fiske St PO Box 705 **Fax Area Code:* 412	Carlisle	MA	01741	978-369-1772	777-3899*	195
Ballantine Corp 55 Lane Rd *TF:* 800-669-6801 ■ *Web:* ballantine.com	Fairfield	NJ	07004	973-305-1500		5
Ballantine Laboratories Inc 312 Old Allerton Rd *Web:* www.ballantinelabs.com	Annandale	NJ	08801	908-713-7742	713-7743	743
Ballantyne Resort Hotel 10000 Ballantyne Commons Pkwy *TF:* 866-248-4824 ■ *Web:* www.theballantynehotel.com	Charlotte	NC	28277	704-248-4000	248-4005	669
Ballantyne Strong Inc 13710 FNB Pkwy *NYSE: BTN* ■ *TF:* 800-424-1215 ■ *Web:* ballantynestrong.com	Omaha	NE	68154	800-424-1215		591
Ballard & Littlefield LLP 3700 Buffalo Speedway Ste 250 *Web:* ballardlittlefield.com	Houston	TX	77098	713-403-6400		41
Ballard Alliance 5306 Ballard Ave NW Ste 216 *Web:* www.visitballard.com	Seattle	WA	98107	206-784-9705		139
Ballard Care & Rehabilitation Ctr 820 NW 95th St *Web:* genesishcc.com	Seattle	WA	98117	206-782-0100		450
Ballard Direct 7000 W Palmetto Park Rd Ste 210 *Web:* www.ballarddirect.com	Boca Raton	FL	33433	914-262-6951		195
Ballard Group Inc, The 2525 S Wadsworth Blvd Ste 200 *Web:* www.theballardgroup.com	Lakewood	CO	80227	303-988-4514		261
Ballard Petroleum LLC 845 12th St W *Web:* www.ballardpetroleum.com	Billings	MT	59102	406-259-8790		536
Ballard Power Systems Inc 9000 Glenlyon Pkwy *NASDAQ: BLDP* ■ *Web:* www.ballard.com	Burnaby	BC	V5J5J8	604-454-0900	412-4700	253
Ballard Spahr Andrews & Ingersoll LLP 1735 Market St 51st Fl *Web:* ballardspahr.com	Philadelphia	PA	19103	215-665-8500	864-8999	428
Ballard's Farm Sausage Inc 7275 Right Fork Wilson Creek *TF:* 800-346-7675 ■ *Web:* www.ballardsfarm.com	Wayne	WV	25570	304-272-5147	272-5336	296-26
Ballay, Braud & Colon PLC 8114 Hwy 23 Ste 101 *Web:* bbc-law.net	Belle Chasse	LA	70037	504-394-9841		41
Ballco Manufacturing Inc 2375 E Liberty Rd *TF:* 800-848-8854 ■ *Web:* ballcomfg.com	Aurora	IL	60502	800-848-8854		790
Ballentine Associates PA 221 Providence Rd *Web:* bapa.eng.pro	Chapel Hill	NC	27514	919-929-0481		261
Baller Stokes & Lide PC 2014 P St NW Ste 200 *Web:* baller.com	Washington	DC	20036	202-833-5300		41
Ballet Arizona 2835 E Washington St *Web:* www.balletaz.org	Phoenix	AZ	85034	602-381-0184	381-0189	573-1
Ballet Arkansas 520 Main St *Web:* www.balletarkansas.org	Little Rock	AR	72201	501-223-5150		573-1
Ballet Austin 501 W Third St *Web:* balletaustin.org	Austin	TX	78701	512-476-9151		573-1
Ballet British Columbia 677 Davie St *TF:* 855-985-2787 ■ *Web:* balletbc.com	Vancouver	BC	V6B2G6	604-732-5003	732-4417	573-1
Ballet Chicago 17 N State St Ste 1900 *Web:* www.balletchicago.org	Chicago	IL	60602	312-251-8838	251-8840	573-1
Ballet Hispanico of New York 167 W 89th St *Web:* www.ballethispanico.org	New York	NY	10024	212-362-6710	362-7809	573-1
Ballet Idaho 501 S Eigth St *Web:* www.balletidaho.org	Boise	ID	83702	208-343-0556	424-3129	573-1
Ballet Lubbock 5702 Genoa Ave *Web:* balletlubbock.org	Lubbock	TX	79424	806-785-3090	785-3309	573-1
Ballet Magnificat 5406 I-55 N *Web:* www.balletmagnificat.com	Jackson	MS	39211	601-977-1001	977-8948	573-1
Ballet Mississippi 201 E Pascagoula St Ste 106 *Web:* balletms.com	Jackson	MS	39201	601-960-1560	960-2135	573-1
Ballet Quad Cities 613 17th St *Web:* balletquadcities.com	Rock Island	IL	61201	309-786-3779	786-2677	573-1
Ballet Repertory Theatre of New Mexico 6913 Natalie NE *Web:* www.brtnm.com	Albuquerque	NM	87110	505-888-1054		573-1
Ballet Tech 890 Broadway **Fax Area Code:* 646 ■ *Web:* ballettech.org	New York	NY	10003	212-777-7710	537-2629*	573-1
Ballet Tennessee 3202 Kelly's Ferry Rd *Web:* www.ballettennessee.org	Chattanooga	TN	37419	423-821-2055		573-1
Ballet Theatre of Maryland Maryland Hall 801 Chase St *Web:* www.balletmaryland.org	Annapolis	MD	21401	410-224-5644	626-1835	573-1
Ballet West 50 West 200 South *Web:* balletwest.org	Salt Lake City	UT	84101	801-869-6912	359-3504	573-1
Ballet Western Reserve 218 W Boardman St PO Box 1684 *Web:* www.balletwesternreserve.org	Youngstown	OH	44501	330-744-1934		573-1
BalletMet Columbus 322 Mt Vernon Ave *Web:* www.balletmet.org	Columbus	OH	43215	614-229-4860		573-1
Ballew's Aluminum Products Inc 2 Shelter Dr *TF:* 800-231-6666 ■ *Web:* www.ballews.com	Greer	SC	29650	864-272-4453		697
Ballinger 833 Chestnut St Ste 1400 *Web:* www.ballinger.com	Philadelphia	PA	19107	215-446-0900		261
Ballistic Recovery Systems Inc 380 Airport Rd *Web:* brsaerospace.com	South Saint Paul	MN	55075	651-457-7491		20
Ball-Martin Insurance Agency Inc 589 Southlake Blvd *Web:* ballmartin.com	Richmond	VA	23235	804-379-4600		390
Ballon Stoll Bader & Nadler PC 729 Seventh Ave 17th Fl *Web:* www.ballonstoll.com	New York	NY	10019	212-575-7900	764-5060	428
Balloons Everywhere Inc 16474 Greeno Rd **Fax Area Code:* 251 ■ *TF:* 800-239-2000 ■ *Web:* www.balloons.com	Fairhope	AL	36532	800-239-2000	210-2105*	566
Balls Bluff National Cemetery Ball's Bluff Battlefield Regional Park *Web:* www.cem.va.gov	Leesburg	VA	20176	540-825-0027		136
Balls Food Stores Inc 5300 Speaker Rd *Web:* www.henhouse.com	Kansas City	KS	66106	913-432-2992		345
Bally Refrigerated Boxes Inc 135 Little Nine Rd *Web:* www.ballyrefboxes.com	Morehead City	NC	28557	252-240-2829	240-0384	14
Bally Ribbon Mills 23 N Seventh St *Web:* www.ballyribbon.com	Bally	PA	19503	610-845-2211	845-8013	745-5
Ballymore Co 501 Gunnard Carlson Dr *TF:* 800-762-8327 ■ *Web:* www.ballymore.com	Coatesville	PA	19320	610-593-5062	593-8615	421
Balmoral Hall School 630 Westminster Ave *Web:* www.balmoralhall.com	Winnipeg	MB	R3C3S1	204-784-1600	774-5534	622
Balmoral Park 26435 S Dixie Hwy *Web:* www.balmoralpark.com	Crete	IL	60417	708-672-1414		642
Balmorhea State Park PO Box 15 *Web:* tpwd.texas.gov	Toyahvale	TX	79786	432-375-2370		565
Balnea Spa 319 Chemin du Lac Gale *TF:* 866-734-2110 ■ *Web:* www.balnea.ca	Bromont	QC	J2L2S5	450-534-0604		226
Balon Corp 3245 S Hattie Ave *Web:* www.balon.com	Oklahoma City	OK	73129	405-677-3321		789
Balsams Resort, The 1000 Cold Spring Rd *Web:* thebalsamsresort.com	Dixville Notch	NH	03576	603-255-2500		377
BalTec Corp 121 Hillpointe Dr Ste 900 *Web:* baltecorporation.com	Canonsburg	PA	15317	724-873-5757		358
Balthazar 80 Spring St *Web:* www.balthazarny.com	New York	NY	10012	212-965-1414		671
Baltimore Alarm & Security 5314 Reistertown Rd *Web:* www.baltimoresalarmandsecurity.com	Baltimore	MD	21215	410-358-8600		692
Baltimore Area Convention & Visitors Assn (BACVA) 100 Light St 12th Fl *TF:* 877-225-8466 ■ *Web:* baltimore.org	Baltimore	MD	21202	410-659-7300	727-2308	206
Baltimore Bar Library 100 N Calvert St Rm 618 *Web:* www.barlib.org	Baltimore	MD	21202	410-727-0280	685-4791	434-3
Baltimore Behavioral Health (BBH) 1101 W Pratt St *TF:* 800-789-2647 ■ *Web:* baltimorecity.md.networkofcare.org	Baltimore	MD	21223	410-962-7180	962-7194	726
Baltimore Book Festival 10 E Baltimore St 10th Fl *Web:* promotionandarts.org	Baltimore	MD	21202	410-752-8632	385-0361	281
Baltimore City Community College 2901 Liberty Heights Ave *TF:* 888-203-1261 ■ *Web:* www.bccc.edu	Baltimore	MD	21215	410-462-8300	462-8345	162
Baltimore City Public Schools 200 E N Ave **Fax Area Code:* 410 ■ *TF:* 800-422-0009 ■ *Web:* www.baltimorecityschools.org	Baltimore	MD	21202	443-984-2000	545-0897*	685
Baltimore Convention Ctr 1 W Pratt St *TF:* 800-327-4414 ■ *Web:* www.bccenter.org	Baltimore	MD	21201	410-649-7000	649-7008	205
Baltimore County 401 Bosley Ave *TF:* 800-332-6347 ■ *Web:* www.baltimorecountymd.gov	Towson	MD	21204	410-887-2139		338
Baltimore County Chamber of Commerce 102 W Pennsylvania Ave Ste 101 *Web:* www.baltcountychamber.com	Towson	MD	21204	410-825-6200	821-9901	139

Company	Phone	Fax	Class
Baltimore County Employees Federal Credit Union 23 W Susquehanna Ave .... Towson MD 21204 *Web:* bcefcu.com	410-828-4730		219
Baltimore County Public Library 320 York Rd .... Towson MD 21204 *Web:* www.bcpl.info	410-887-6100	887-6103	434-3
Baltimore County Revenue Authority 115 Towsontown Blvd E ....Baltimore MD 21286 *TF:* 888-246-5384 ■ *Web:* www.baltimoregolfing.com	410-887-8216	296-7459	562
Baltimore Credit & Collection Services Inc 6400 Baltimore National Pk Ste 469............Baltimore MD 21228 *Web:* www.bccs2.com	410-549-6444	549-3366	218
Baltimore Development Corp 36 S Charles St Ste 2100 ....Baltimore MD 21201 *Web:* baltimoredevelopment.com	410-837-9305		393
Baltimore Gas & Electric Co 110 W Fayette St...........................Baltimore MD 21201 *TF:* 800-685-0123 ■ *Web:* www.bge.com	800-685-0123		787
Baltimore Life Cos 10075 Red Run Blvd.....................Owings Mills MD 21117 *TF:* 800-628-5433 ■ *Web:* www.baltlife.com	410-581-6600		391-2
Baltimore Magazine 1000 Lancaster St Ste 400 ....Baltimore MD 21202 **Fax Area Code:* 410 ■ *TF:* 800-935-0838 ■ *Web:* www.baltimoremagazine.com	443-873-3900	625-0280*	457-22
Baltimore Museum of Art 10 Art Museum Dr ....Baltimore MD 21218 *Web:* artbma.org	443-573-1700	573-1582	520
Baltimore Museum of Industry 1415 Key Hwy.............................Baltimore MD 21230 *Web:* www.thebmi.org	410-727-4808	727-4869	520
Baltimore National Cemetery 5501 Frederick Ave.........................Baltimore MD 21228 *Web:* www.cem.va.gov	410-644-9696	644-1563	136
Baltimore Polytechnic Institute 1400 W Cold Spring Ln ....Baltimore MD 21209 *Web:* www.bpi.edu	410-396-7026	235-5027	685
Baltimore Ravens 1101 Russell St.............Baltimore MD 21230 *Web:* www.baltimoreravens.com	410-701-4000		715-3
Baltimore Rigging Company Inc, The 6601 Tributary St ....Baltimore MD 21224 *TF:* 800-626-2150 ■ *Web:* www.baltimorerigging.com	443-696-4001	696-4006	189-1
Baltimore Streetcar Museum 1901 Falls Rd.............................Baltimore MD 21211 *Web:* www.baltimoremd.com	410-547-0264		520
Baltimore Studio of Hair Design 318 N Howard St ....Baltimore MD 21201 *Web:* www.baltimorestudio.com	443-503-8630	503-8633	167-3
Baltimore Sun 501 N Calvert St................Baltimore MD 21278 *TF:* 800-829-8000 ■ *Web:* www.baltimoresun.com	410-332-6000	332 6455	532-2
Baltimore Symphony Orchestra 1212 Cathedral St..........................Baltimore MD 21201 *TF:* 877-276-1444 ■ *Web:* www.bsomusic.org	410-783-8100		573-3
Baltimore Teachers Union Seton Business Pk 5800 Metro Dr 2nd Fl........Baltimore MD 21215 *Web:* www.baltimoreteachers.org	410-358-6600	358-2894	260
Baltimore Times 2513 N Charles St ....Baltimore MD 21218 *Web:* baltimoretimes-online.com	410-366-3900	243-1627	532-4
Baltimore/Washington International Thurgood Marshall Airport (BWI) PO Box 8766 ....Baltimore MD 21240 *TF:* 800-435-9294 ■ *Web:* www.bwiairport.com	410-859-7111		27
Baltz & Co 49 W 23rd St 9th Fl ....New York NY 10010 *Web:* www.baltzco.com	212-982-8300		636
Balzekas Museum of Lithuanian Culture 6500 S Pulaski Rd ....Chicago IL 60629 *Web:* balzekasmuseum.org	773-582-6500	582-5133	520
Balzer & Leary PLLC 275 1/2 Lark St.............Albany NY 12210 *Web:* balzerleary.com	518-432-9700		41
Balzer Pacific 10830 SW Clutter Rd ....Portland OR 97214 *TF:* 800-442-0966 ■ *Web:* www.balzerpacific.com	503-232-5141	232-9556	358
BAM (Brooklyn Academy of Music) 30 Lafayette Ave ....Brooklyn NY 11217 *Web:* www.bam.org	718-636-4100		572
BAM Advisor Services 8182 Maryland Ave Ste 500 .... Saint Louis MO 63105 *TF:* 800-711-2027 ■ *Web:* www.bamadvisorservices.com	800-711-2027		401
Bama Pie Ltd 5377 E 66th St N................... Tulsa OK 74117 *Web:* www.bama.com	918-592-0778		296-1
Bama Theatre 600 Greensboro Ave............Tuscaloosa AL 35401 *Web:* www.tuscarts.org	205-758-5195	345-2787	572
Bamar Plastics Inc 1702 S Robinson St .... South Bend IN 46613 *Web:* bamarplastics.com	574-234-4066	234-1849	604
Bambara Restaurant 202 S Main St..........................Salt Lake City UT 84101 *Web:* www.bambara-slc.com	801-363-5454		671
Bambeck Systems Inc 1921 E Carnegie Ave....................... Santa Ana CA 92705 *TF:* 800-334-3101 ■ *Web:* www.bambecksystems.com	949-250-3100	757-1610	201
Bambee 304 S Broadway Ste 330.............Los Angeles CA 90013 *TF:* 844-398-9400 ■ *Web:* www.bambee.com	844-398-9400		194
Bamberg County 2340 Main Hwy .... Bamberg SC 29003 *Web:* www.bambergsc.com	803-245-5128	245-5156	338
Bamberger Polymers Inc 2 Jericho Plz...........Jericho NY 11753 *TF:* 800-888-8959 ■ *Web:* www.bambergerpolymers.com	516-622-3600	622-3610	603
Bamboo Court 4935 Centennial Blvd .... Colorado Springs CO 80919 *Web:* www.bamboocourtcoloradosprings.com	719-599-7383		671
Bamboo Restaurant 10835 Venice Blvd ....Los Angeles CA 90034 *Web:* www.bamboorestaurantmenu.com	310-287-0668		671
Bamboo Rose Inc 17 Rogers St ....Gloucester MA 01930 *Web:* www.bamboorose.com	978-281-3723	281-0673	178-1
Bamboo Solutions 11417 Sunset Hills Rd Ste 105.................. Reston VA 20190 *Web:* bamboosolutions.com	703-964-2002		177
Bamboo Worldwide Inc 2545 W Diversey Ave Ste 207..................Chicago IL 60647 *Web:* www.bambooworldwide.com	773-227-4848		463
BambooInk 807 Oliver Hill Way .... Richmond VA 23219 *Web:* bambooink.com	804-230-4515		627
Bambu Global 116 John St .... Lowell MA 01852 *Web:* bambuglobal.com	978-459-4500		194
BAMC (Brooke Army Medical Ctr) 3551 Roger Brooke Dr .... Fort Sam Houston TX 78234 *TF:* 800-443-2262 ■ *Web:* www.bamc.health.mil	210-916-9900		374-4
Bamco Inc 30 Baekeland Ave .... Middlesex NJ 08846 *TF:* 800-245-0210 ■ *Web:* www.gobamco.com	800-245-0210		480
Ban Thai Restaurant 792 Eastgate S Dr Ste 300 .... Cincinnati OH 45245 *Web:* www.banthaicincinnati.com	513-752-3200		671
Banana Banner Signs 3148 Duke St .... Alexandria VA 22314 *Web:* www.bananabanner.com	703-522-6262	823-5631	701
Banana Blossom Thai 4228 Pk Blvd .... Oakland CA 94602 *Web:* bananablossomcuisine.com	510-336-0990		671
Banana Leaf 820 W Broadway................ Vancouver BC V5Z1J9 *Web:* www.bananaleaf-vancouver.com	604-731-6333		671
Banana Patch Press 3865 Hanapepe Rd Kauai ....Hanapepe HI 96716 *TF:* 800-914-5944 ■ *Web:* www.bananapatchpress.com	808-335-5944	335-3830	637-2
Bananas at Large 1504 Fourth St.............. San Rafael CA 94901 *TF:* 888-900-1959 ■ *Web:* www.bananas.com	415-457-7600		526
Banc Statements Inc 4700 Birmingham St.......................Birmingham AL 35217 *Web:* www.bsisite.com	205-956-5004		70
Banca IMI Securities Corp 1 William St ....New York NY 10004 *Web:* www.bancaimi.com	212-326-1100		690
BancFirst Agency Inc 101 N Broadway Ave....................Oklahoma City OK 73102 *Web:* www.bancfirst.bank	405-272-8862		70
Bancker Construction Corp 218 Blydenburgh Rd......................... Islandia NY 11749 *TF:* 800-767-7565 ■ *Web:* www.bancker.com	631-582-8880	582-3698	188-10
Banco De Credito Del Peru 121 Alhambra Plz Ste 1200 .... Coral Gables FL 33134 *Web:* bcpmiami.com	305-448-0971		70
Bancography Inc 2301 First Ave N Ste 103 ....Birmingham AL 35203 *Web:* www.bancography.com	205-251-3227		256
Bancorp Bank 409 Silverside Rd Ste 105 .... Wilmington DE 19809 *NASDAQ: TBBK* ■ *TF:* 866-255-9831 ■ *Web:* thebancorp.com	302-385-5000		70
BancorpSouth Inc 2910 W Jackson St .... Tupelo MS 38801 *NYSE: BXS* ■ *TF:* 888-797-7711 ■ *Web:* www.bancorpsouth.com	662-680-2000	678-7263	360-2
Bancroft & Sons Transportation Inc 3390 High Prairie Rd ....Grand Prairie TX 75050 *Web:* bancroftandsons.com	972-790-3777		5
Bancroft Bag Inc 425 Bancroft Blvd.......................West Monroe LA 71292 *TF:* 800-551-4950 ■ *Web:* www.bancroftbag.com	318-387-2550		65
Bancroft Construction Co 1300 N Grant Ave Ste 101 .... Wilmington DE 19806 *Web:* www.bancroftconstruction.com	302-655-3434	655-4599	188-7
Bancroft Fund Ltd 65 Madison Ave .... Morristown NJ 07960	973-631-1177		405
Bancroft School of Massage Therapy 333 Shrewsbury St........................ Worcester MA 01604 *Web:* www.bancroftsmt.com	508-757-7923		685
Banda Group International LLC 1799 E Queen Creek Rd Ste 1................ Chandler AZ 85286 *Web:* www.bandagroupintl.com	480-636-8734	718-7890	194
Bandana's Bar-B-Q 11750 Gravois Rd........................ Saint Louis MO 63127 *Web:* www.bandanasbbq.com	314-849-1162		671
Bandar 845 Fourth Ave .... San Diego CA 92101 *Web:* www.bandarrestaurant.com	619-238-0101		671
Bandera Bulletin 1110 Main St .... Bandera TX 78003 *Web:* www.banderabulletin.com	830-796-3718	796-4885	532-2
Bandera County Convention & Visitors Bureau 126 State Hwy 16 S PO Box 171................ Bandera TX 78003 *TF:* 800-364-3833 ■ *Web:* www.banderacowboycapital.com	830-796-3045		206
Bandera Electric Co-opeartive Inc 3172 State Hwy 16 N .... Bandera TX 78003 **Fax Area Code:* 830 ■ *TF:* 866-226-3372 ■ *Web:* www.banderaelectric.com	866-226-3372	460-3030*	245
Bandido's Inc 6060 E State Blvd ....Fort Wayne IN 46815 *Web:* bandidos.com	260-493-0607		671
Bandimere Speedway 3051 S Rooney Rd .... Morrison CO 80465 *TF:* 800-664-8946 ■ *Web:* www.bandimere.com	303-697-6001	697-0815	515
Bandit Industries Inc 6750 W Millbrook Rd......................... Remus MI 49340 *TF:* 800-952-0178 ■ *Web:* www.banditchippers.com	989-561-2270	561-2273	190
Bandit Lites Inc 2233 Sycamore Dr .... Knoxville TN 37921 *Web:* www.banditlites.com	865-971-3071	971-3072	41
Band-It-IDEX Inc 4799 Dahlia St................ Denver CO 80216 **Fax Area Code:* 303 ■ *TF:* 800-525-0758 ■ *Web:* www.band-it-idex.com	800-525-0758	333-6549*	350
BandMerch LLC 3120 W Empire Ave............ Burbank CA 91504 *Web:* www.bandmerch.com	818-736-4800		5
Bandung Indonesian Restaurant 600 Williamson St Ste M .... Madison WI 53703 *Web:* www.bandungindorestaurant.com	608-255-6910		671
Bandy Carroll Hellige Advertising Inc 307 W Muhammad Ali Blvd ....Louisville KY 40202 *TF:* 800-607-7711 ■ *Web:* www.bch.com	502-589-7711		7
Bandy Inc 201 S International Rd............... Garland TX 75042 *Web:* www.bandyco.com	972-272-5455		697
Bandy Manufacturing 3420 N San Fernando Blvd.................... Burbank CA 91504 *Web:* www.glansteinllp.com	818-846-9020		22
Bane Machinery Inc PO Box 541355............. Dallas TX 75354 *Web:* www.banemachinery.com	214-352-2468	352-2460	358
Banetti Inc 55 NE 94th St .... Miami FL 33138 *TF:* 855-855-7800 ■ *Web:* banetti.com	855-855-7800		180
Banff Adventures Unlimited Bison Courtyard 211 Bear St .... Banff AB T1L1A8 *TF:* 800-644-8888 ■ *Web:* www.banffadventures.com	403-762-4554		760
Banff Centre for Arts & Creativity 107 Tunnel Mtn Dr PO Box 1020 .... Banff AB T1L1H5 *TF:* 800-884-7574 ■ *Web:* www.banffcentre.ca	403-762-6100		377

				Phone	Fax	Class
Banff Jasper Collection 100 Gopher St PO Box 1140 TF: 866-606-6700 ■ Web: www.banffjaspercollection.com	Banff	AB	T1L1J3	403-762-6700	762-6750	760
Banff National Park PO Box 900 TF: 877-737-3783 ■ Web: www.pc.gc.ca	Banff	AB	T1L1K2	403-762-1550	762-1551	563
Banfield the Pet Hospital 18101 SE Sixth Way TF: 866-894-7927 ■ Web: www.banfield.com	Vancouver	WA	98683	866-894-7927		794
Bang Printing Inc 3323 Oak St TF: 800-328-0450 ■ Web: www.bangprinting.com	Brainerd	MN	56401	218-829-2877	829-7145	626
Bangerter Law PA 810 W Frontview Web: blawpa.com	Dodge City	KS	67801	620-339-4103		41
Bangkok 54 2919 Columbia Pk Web: bangkok54restaurant.com	Arlington	VA	22204	703-521-4070		671
Bangkok Bistro 715 N Glebe Rd Web: bangkokbistrova.com	Arlington	VA	22203	703-243-9669		671
Bangkok Cafe 1203-C S Holden Rd	Greensboro	NC	27407	336-855-9370		671
Bangkok City 1129 E Walnut St Web: wordpress.com	Springfield	MO	65806	417-799-1221		671
Bangkok Cuisine 32166 Woodward Ave Web: www.bangkokcuisineroyaloak.com	Royal Oak	MI	48073	248-439-0529		671
Bangkok Garden 18 Elm St Web: bangkokgarden.ca	Toronto	ON	M5G1G7	416-977-6748		671
Bangkok Gardens 811 Cherry St Web: www.bangkokgardens.com	Columbia	MO	65201	573-874-3284		671
Bangkok House 1303 Ashley River Rd	Charleston	SC	29407	843-626-5384		671
Bangkok Restaurant 1492 Piedmont Ave Ste A Web: bangkokthaiatl.com	Atlanta	GA	30309	404-874-2514		671
Bangkok Thai Cuisine 3426 E Fourth St Web: bangkokthaicuisinelbc.com	Long Beach	CA	90814	562-433-0093		671
Bangladesh Consulate General 4201 Wilshire Blvd Ste 605 Web: www.bangladeshconsulatela.com	Los Angeles	CA	90010	323-932-0100	932-9703	257
Bangladesh Mission to the United Nations 820 Second Ave Diplomat Ctr Fourth Fl Web: www.un.int	New York	NY	10017	212-867-3434	972-4038	784
Bangor City Hall 73 Harlow St Web: www.bangormaine.gov	Bangor	ME	04401	207-992-4200	945-4449	337
Bangor Daily News 491 Main St PO Box 1329 TF: 800-432-7964 ■ Web: bangordailynews.com	Bangor	ME	04402	207-990-8000		532-2
Bangor Hydro Electric Co PO Box 932 TF: 800-499-6600 ■ Web: www.emeramaine.com	Bangor	ME	04401	207-945-5621		787
Bangor International Airport 287 Godfrey Blvd TF: 866-359-2264 ■ Web: www.flybangor.com	Bangor	ME	04401	207-992-4600	945-3607	27
Bangor Museum & History Ctr 159 Union St Web: www.bangorhistoricalsociety.org	Bangor	ME	04401	207-942-1900		520
Bangor Public Library 145 Harlow St Web: www.bangorpubliclibrary.org	Bangor	ME	04401	207-947-8336		434-3
Bangor Region Chamber of Commerce 208 Maine Ave Web: www.bangorregion.com	Bangor	ME	04401	207-947-0307	990-1427	139
Bangor Savings Bank 99 Franklin St TF: 877-226-4671 ■ Web: www.bangor.com	Bangor	ME	04401	207-942-5211		70
Bangor Symphony Orchestra PO Box 1441 TF: 800-639-3221 ■ Web: www.bangorsymphony.org	Bangor	ME	04402	207-942-5555	990-1272	573-3
Bangor Theological Seminary 97 India St TF: 800-287-6781 ■ Web: www.thebtscenter.org	Portland	ME	04101	207-774-5212		166
Bangs Ambulance Service Inc 205 W Green St Web: www.bangsambulance.com	Ithaca	NY	14850	607-273-1161		30
Banik Communications Inc 18 Sixth St N Ste 201 Web: banik.com	Great Falls	MT	59401	406-454-3422		7
Banjo Corp 150 Banjo Dr TF: 888-705-7020 ■ Web: www.banjocorp.com	Crawfordsville	IN	47933	765-362-7367	362-0744	641
Bank Administration Institute (BAI) 115 S LaSalle St Ste 3300 TF: 800-224-9889 ■ Web: www.bai.org	Chicago	IL	60603	312-683-2464	683-2373	49-2
Bank Advisory Group LLC, The 15100 Gebron Dr Web: www.bankadvisory.com	Austin	TX	78734	512-263-8800		196
Bank and Corporate Governance Law Reporter 1601 Connecticut Ave NW No 701 Web: www.lawreporters.com	Washington	DC	20009	202-462-5755	328-2430	637-9
Bank Financial 6415 W 95th St TF: 800-894-6900 ■ Web: bankfinancial.com	Chicago Ridge	IL	60415	800-894-6900		70
Bank First PO Box 10 TF: 800-468-9716 ■ Web: bankfirstwi.bank	Manitowoc	WI	54221	920-684-6611		70
Bank Five Nine 155 W Wisconsin Ave PO Box 1004 TF: 888-569-9909 ■ Web: www.bankfivenine.com	Oconomowoc	WI	53066	262-569-9900		70
Bank Independent 710 S Montgomery Ave TF: 877-865-5050 ■ Web: www.bibank.com	Sheffield	AL	35660	256-386-5000		360-2
Bank Leumi USA 350 Madison Ave TF: 800-892-5430 ■ Web: www.leumiusa.com	New York	NY	10017	917-542-2343		70
Bank Midwest NA 1111 Main St Web: www.bankmw.com	Kansas City	MO	64105	816-298-2100		70
Bank of Alapaha 201 W Marion Ave Web: bankofalapaha.com	Nashville	GA	31639	229-686-7491	686-7161	70
Bank of Albuquerque 400 S Tijeras Ave North W Ste 150 TF: 800-583-0709 ■ Web: www.bankofalbuquerque.com	Albuquerque	NM	87102	505-855-0855		70
Bank of America Corporate Center 100 N Tryon St Ste 170 NYSE: BAC ■ Web: www.bankofamerica.com	Charlotte	NC	28202	980-335-3561		528
Bank of America Pavilion 290 Northern Ave Web: www.bostonpavilion.net	Boston	MA	02210	617-728-1600		572
Bank of Bartlett Inc 6281 Stage Rd Web: www.bankofbartlett.com	Bartlett	TN	38134	901-382-6600		70
Bank of Bennington (Bennington NE) 12212 N 156th St Web: bankbenn.com	Bennington	NE	68007	402-238-2245		70
Bank of Bennington, The 155 North St Web: thebankofbennington.com	Bennington	VT	05201	802-442-8121	442-1641	70
Bank of Blue Valley PO Box 26128 Web: www.bankbv.com	Overland Park	KS	66225	913-338-1000		70
Bank of Bozeman 875 Harmon Stream Blvd Web: bankofbozeman.com	Bozeman	MT	59718	406-587-5626		70
Bank of Brodhead 806 E Exchange St Web: bankofbrodhead.com	Brodhead	WI	53520	608-897-2121		70
Bank of Brookfield - Purdin NA 939 Park Circle Dr Web: bankbp.com	Brookfield	MO	64628	660-258-3394	258-5755	70
Bank of Burlington, The 410 14th St PO Box 427 Web: thebankofburlington.com	Burlington	CO	80807	719-346-5376		70
Bank of Calhoun County 204 Main St Web: bankofcalhouncounty.com	Hardin	IL	62047	618-576-2211		70
Bank of Cashton 723 Main St PO Box 70 TF: 800-205-7203 ■ Web: www.bankofcashton.bank	Cashton	WI	54619	608-654-5121	654-5297	70
Bank of Castile 50 N Main St Web: bankofcastile.com	Castile	NY	14427	585-493-2576		70
Bank of Deerfield 15 S Main St Web: bankofdeerfield.com	Deerfield	WI	53531	608-764-5411		70
Bank of Delmar Inc 2245 Northwood Dr Web: www.bankofdelmarvahb.com	Salisbury	MD	21801	410-548-1100		70
Bank of Denver 810 E 17th Ave Web: www.thebankofdenver.com	Denver	CO	80218	303-572-3600	623-0624	70
Bank of Eastern Oregon 250 NW Gale St Web: www.beobank.com	Heppner	OR	97836	541-676-0201		70
Bank of Elgin 101 N Second St Web: bankofelgin.com	Elgin	NE	68636	402-843-2228		70
Bank of Erath 105 W Edwards Web: www.bankoferath.com	Erath	LA	70533	337-937-5816		70
Bank of Florence Museum 8502 N 30th St Web: www.historicflorence.org	Omaha	NE	68112	402-496-9923		520
Bank of Gleason 203 Main St PO Box 231 Web: www.gleasononline.com	Gleason	TN	38229	731-648-5506		70
Bank of Glen Burnie, The 101 Crain Hwy SE TF: 800-264-5578 ■ Web: thebankofglenburnie.com	Glen Burnie	MD	21061	410-766-3300		70
Bank of Gravett 211 SE Main St Web: www.bankofgravett.net	Gravette	AR	72736	479-787-5251		70
Bank of Greene County, The PO Box 470 NASDAQ: GCBC ■ TF: 888-439-4272 ■ Web: thebankofgreenecounty.com	Catskill	NY	12414	518-943-2600	943-3756	360-2
Bank of Hartington 229 N Broadway Ave Web: bankofhartington.com	Hartington	NE	68739	402-254-3994		70
Bank of Hawaii Corp 130 Merchant St 16th Fl NYSE: BOH ■ TF: 888-643-3888 ■ Web: www.boh.com	Honolulu	HI	96813	888-643-3888		360-2
Bank of Hazlehurst PO Box 628 Web: www.bankofhazlehurst.com	Hazlehurst	GA	31539	912-375-4228	375-3545	70
Bank of Hemet, The 3715 Sunnyside Dr Web: www.bankofhemet.com	Riverside	CA	92506	951-766-4100		70
Bank of Herrin, The 101 S Park Ave Web: www.bankofherrin.com	Herrin	IL	62948	618-942-6666	942-3618	70
Bank of Hillsboro 230 S Main St Web: www.bankhillsboro.com	Hillsboro	IL	62049	636-797-3337		70
Bank of Hindman 1362 Hindman Bypass PO Box 786 Web: bankofhindman.com	Hindman	KY	41822	606-785-3158		70
Bank of Holland 12 S Main St Web: bankofhollandny.com	Holland	NY	14080	716-537-2264		70
Bank of Holly Springs PO Box 250 Web: www.bankofhollysprings.com	Holly Springs	MS	38635	662-252-2511	252-1816	70
Bank of Internet USA 4350 La Jolla Village Dr Ste 140 TF: 877-541-2634 ■ Web: www.bankofinternet.com	San Diego	CA	92122	858-350-6200		70
Bank of Kirksville 214 S Franklin Web: bankofkirksville.com	Kirksville	MO	63501	660-665-7766		70
Bank of Landisburg, The 100 N Carlisle St PO Box 179 Web: www.bankoflandisburg.com	Landisburg	PA	17040	717-789-3213		70
Bank of Louisiana 300 St Charles Ave TF: 866-392-9952 ■ Web: www.bankoflouisiana.com	New Orleans	LA	70130	504-592-0600	592-0606	70
Bank of Luxemburg 630 Main St Web: bankofluxemburg.com	Luxemburg	WI	54217	920-845-2345		70
Bank of Maple Plain 4980 Hwy 12 PO Box 279 Web: bankofmapleplain.com	Maple Plain	MN	55359	763-479-1931		70
Bank of Marin 504 Tamalpais Dr NASDAQ: BMRC ■ TF: 800-654-5111 ■ Web: www.bankofmarin.com	Corte Madera	CA	94925	415-927-2265		70
Bank of Mauston, The 503 Gateway Ave TF: 877-438-4338 ■ Web: www.bankofmauston.com	Mauston	WI	53948	608-847-6200		70
Bank of Milan, The 2011 E Van Hook St PO Box 410 Web: bankofmilan.net	Milan	TN	38358	731-686-2255		70
Bank of Montgomery 814 Washington St TF: 800-264-4274 ■ Web: bofm.com	Natchitoches	LA	71457	318-238-8000		70
Bank of Montreal (BMO) 100 King St W 1 First Canadian Pl 21st Fl NYSE: BMO ■ TF: 800-340-5021 ■ Web: www.bmo.com	Toronto	ON	M5X1A1	416-867-6785	867-6793	70
Bank of Montreal 3 Times Sq 29th Fl TF: 877-225-5266 ■ Web: capitalmarkets.bmo.com	New York	NY	10036	877-225-5266		70
Bank of Morton 366 S Fourth St PO Box 229 TF: 800-523-4175 ■ Web: www.bankofmorton.com	Morton	MS	39117	601-732-8944	732-8599	70

Name / Address	Phone	Fax	Class
Bank of Nevada 2700 W Sahara Ave........... Las Vegas NV 89102 *Fax Area Code: 773* ■ *Web:* www.westernalliancebancorporation.com	702-248-4200	380-7028*	70
Bank of New Glarus 501 First St .... New Glarus WI 53574 *Web:* www.thebankofnewglarus.bank	608-527-5205		70
Bank of North Dakota 1200 Memorial Hwy........................ Bismarck ND 58504 *TF:* 800-472-2166 ■ *Web:* bnd.nd.gov	701-328-5600	328-5632	70
Bank of Oak Ridge 2211 Oak Ridge Rd .... Oak Ridge NC 27310 *OTC: BKOR* ■ *Web:* www.bankofoakridge.com	336-644-9944		70
Bank of Oklahoma NA PO Box 2300 .... Tulsa OK 74192 *TF:* 800-234-6181 ■ *Web:* www.bankofoklahoma.com	918-588-6010		70
Bank of Prairie Village 3515 W 75th St........................ Prairie Village KS 66208 *Web:* bankofprairievillage.com	913-713-0300		70
Bank of Rantoul 201 E Champaign Ave .... Rantoul IL 61866 *Web:* bankofrantoul.bank	217-892-2143		70
Bank of San Francisco 575 Market St Ste 900 .... San Francisco CA 94105 *TF:* 800-535-8440 ■ *Web:* www.bankofsf.com	415-744-6717	744-6718	196
Bank of South Carolina Corp 256 Meeting St........................... Charleston SC 29401 *NASDAQ: BKSC* ■ *Web:* www.banksc.com	843-724-1500		360-2
Bank of Springfield 2600 Adlai Stevenson Dr .... Springfield IL 62703 *TF:* 877-698-3278 ■ *Web:* www.bankwithbos.com	217-529-5555		70
Bank of Star Valley, The 384 Washington .... Afton WY 83110 *Web:* bosv.com	307-885-0000		70
Bank of Steinauer, The 215 Main St........... Steinauer NE 68441 *Web:* bankofsteinauer.com	402-869-2211	869-2212	70
Bank of Stockton PO Box 1110 .... Stockton CA 95201 *TF:* 800-941-1494 ■ *Web:* www.bankofstockton.com	209-929-1600		70
Bank of Sunset & Trust Co 863 Napoleon Ave............................ Sunset LA 70584 *Web:* www.bankofsunset.com	337-662-5222	662-5705	70
Bank of Tampa, The 601 Bayshore Blvd .... Tampa FL 33606 *Web:* www.bankoftampa.com	813-872-1216		70
Bank of Tescott, The 600 S Santa Fe .... Salina KS 67401 *Web:* www.bankoftescott.com	785-825-1621		70
Bank of the Lowcountry 1100 N Jeffries Blvd .... Walterboro SC 29488 *Web:* www.banklowcountry.com	843-549-2265	542-2752	70
Bank of the Orient 233 Sansome St........................ San Francisco CA 94104 *TF:* 800-881-2686 ■ *Web:* www.bankorient.com	415-338-0843	338-0619	186
Bank of Tokyo-Mitsubishi Ltd 1251 Avenue of the Americas .... New York NY 10020 *Web:* www.bk.mufg.jp	212-782-4000		70
Bank of Utica 222 Genesee St.................... Utica NY 13502 *OTC: BKUT* ■ *TF:* 800-442-1028 ■ *Web:* www.bankofutica.com	315-797-2700	797-2707	70
Bank of Washington 200 W Main St .... Washington MO 63090 *Web:* www.bankofwashington.com	636-239-7831	239-0452	70
Bank of Whittier 15141 E Whittier Blvd....................... Whittier CA 90603 *TF:* 855-269-1122 ■ *Web:* bankofwhittier.com	562-945-7553	945-5031	70
Bank of Yokohama Ltd, The 780 Third Ave 32nd Fl .... New York NY 10017 *Web:* boy.co.jp	212-750-0022		70
Bank OZK PO Box 8811 .... Little Rock AR 72231 *NASDAQ: OZK* ■ *TF:* 800-274-4482 ■ *Web:* www.ozk.com	501-978-2265		360-2
Bank Policy Institute 600 13th St NW Ste 400.................. Washington DC 20005 *Web:* bpi.com	202-289-4322		49-2
Bank Rhode Island 1 Turks Head Pl........... Providence RI 02903 *NASDAQ: BARI* ■ *Web:* www.bankri.com	401-456-5000		360-2
Bank Street College Library 610 W 112th St............................ New York NY 10025 *Web:* www.bankstreet.edu	212-875-4400		162
Bank Street Group LLC, The 4 Landmark Sq 3rd Fl....................... Stamford CT 06901 *Web:* www.bankstreet.com	203-252-2800		70
Bank's Seafood Kitchen 101 S Market St .... Wilmington DE 19801 *Web:* www.banksseafoodkitchen.com	302-777-1500	777-2406	671
Bank-A-Count Corp 1666 Main St PO Box 167 .... Rudolph WI 54475 *Web:* www.bank-a-count.com	715-435-3131		781
BankAtlantic Bancorp Inc 401 E Las Olas Blvd Ste 800............. Fort Lauderdale FL 33301 *Web:* www.bbxcapital.com	954-940-4000		360-2
Bankcard Central LLC PO Box 12317 .... Kansas City MO 64116 *TF:* 800-331-8882 ■ *Web:* www.bankcardcentral.com	816-221-1133		225
BankCard Services 21281 S Western Ave......................... Torrance CA 90501 *TF:* 888-339-0100 ■ *Web:* www.navyzebra.com	213-365-1122		395
Bankers Advertising Co 2800 Hwy 6 E .... Iowa City IA 52240 *Web:* www.bankersadvertising.com	319-354-1020		627
Bankers Business Management Services Inc 8121 Georgia Ave Ste 950 .... Silver Spring MD 20910 *Web:* www.bankersbms.com	301-565-0601	589-6419	194
Bankers Data Services Inc 521 W 11th St......... Alma GA 31510 *TF:* 888-458-8652 ■ *Web:* www.bdsalma.com	912-632-2060		396
Bankers Fidelity Life Insurance Co 4370 Peachtree Rd NE .... Atlanta GA 30319 *TF:* 866-458-7504 ■ *Web:* bankersfidelity.com	800-241-1439		391-2
Bankers Financial Products Corp 201 N Main St Ste 4..................... Fort Atkinson WI 53538 *TF:* 800-348-1831 ■ *Web:* www.rate-watch.com	800-348-1831	622-8741	401
Bankers Insurance LLC 4490 Cox Rd .... Glen Allen VA 23060 *TF:* 800-541-1419 ■ *Web:* www.bankersinsurance.net	804-497-3634		391-2
Bankers Life & Casualty Co 111 E Wacker Dr Ste 2100 .... Chicago IL 60601 *Fax Area Code: 312* ■ *TF:* 844-553-9083 ■ *Web:* www.bankerslife.com	844-553-9083	396-5975*	391-2
Bankers Life Fieldhouse 125 S Pennsylvania St .... Indianapolis IN 46204 *Web:* www.bankerslifefieldhouse.com	317-917-2500		720
Bankers Life Insurance Co 11101 Roosevelt Blvd N Ste 301 .... Saint Petersburg FL 33716 *TF:* 800-839-2731 ■ *Web:* www.bankerslifeinsurance.com	800-839-2731		390
Bankers Life Insurance Company of America PO Box 600337 .... Dallas TX 75360 *TF:* 800-825-9652 ■ *Web:* bankerslifeofamerica.com	214-521-7100	521-7122	796
Bankers Trust Co 453 Seventh St............ Des Moines IA 50304 *TF:* 800-362-1688 ■ *Web:* www.bankerstrust.com	515-245-2863		70
Bankers' Bank 7700 Mineral Point Rd .... Madison WI 53717 *TF:* 800-388-5550 ■ *Web:* www.bankersbank.com	608-833-5550		70
Bankers' Bank of Kansas 555 N Woodlawn Bldg 5...................... Wichita KS 67208 *TF:* 800-999-5725 ■ *Web:* bbok.com	316-681-2265		70
Bankers' Bank of The West 1099 18th St Ste 2700 .... Denver CO 80202 *Web:* bbwest.com	303-291-3700		70
Bank-Fund Staff Federal Credit Union PO Box 27755 .... Washington DC 20038 *TF:* 800-923-7328 ■ *Web:* bfsfcu.org	202-458-4300	522-1528	219
Banko Beverage Co 5001 Crackersport Rd....................... Allentown PA 18104 *Web:* www.bankobeverage.com	610-434-0147	391-1276	81-1
Bankrate Inc 10850 Gold Center Dr Ste 250 .... Gold River CA 95670	916-853-3300		114
Banks County Schools 1989 Historic Homer Hwy................... Commerce GA 30529 *Web:* www.banks.k12.ga.us	706-677-2224	677-2223	685
Banks Hardwoods Inc 69937 M-103........ White Pigeon MI 49099 *TF:* 800-221-7776 ■ *Web:* www.bankshardwoods.com	269-483-2323		820
Banks Jim (Rep R - IN) 1713 Longworth House Office Bldg .... Washington DC 20515 *Web:* banks.house.gov	202-225-4436		342-2
Banks of Colorado 55 S Elm Ave .... Eaton CO 80615 *Web:* www.bankofcolorado.com	970-454-1800	454-1802	70
Bankshot Sports Organization 330-U N Stonestreet Ave Ste 504.............. Rockville MD 20852 *TF:* 800-933-0140 ■ *Web:* www.bankshot.com	301-309-0260	309-0263	710
Banksys Management Inc 2000 Park Glenn Dr .... Alpharetta GA 30005	678-957-1234		180
BankTEL Systems LLC 310 Park Creek Dr .... Columbus MS 39705 *Web:* banktel.com	662-245-1007		809
BANKW Staffing LLC 5 Bedford Farms Dr Ste 304................... Bedford NH 03110 *Web:* www.bankwstaffing.com	603-792-2345		260
Bankwest 420 S Pierre St......................... Pierre SD 57501 *TF:* 800-253-0362 ■ *Web:* www.bankwest-sd.bank	605-224-7391	224-7393	70
Bankwest Corp 1530 N California Blvd .... Walnut Creek CA 94596 *Web:* www.bankofthewest.com	925-933-7810		70
Bannack State Park 4200 Bannack Rd .... Dillon MT 59725 *Web:* www.bannack.org	406-834-3413	834-3548	565
Banneker-Douglas Museum 84 Franklin St.............................. Annapolis MD 21401 *Web:* bdmuseum.maryland.gov	410-216-6180	974-2553	520
Banner - University Medical Center Phoenix 1111 E McDowell Rd .... Phoenix AZ 85006 *Web:* www.bannerhealth.com	602-839-2000		374-3
Banner & Witcoff Ltd 10 S Wacker Dr Ste 3000 .... Chicago IL 60606 *Web:* bannerwitcoff.com	312-463-5000		428
Banner Bank 10 S First Ave PO Box 907................. Walla Walla WA 99362 *TF:* 800-272-9933 ■ *Web:* www.bannerbank.com	509-527-3636		70
Banner County PO Box 67.................. Harrisburg NE 69345 *TF:* 800-788-9451 ■ *Web:* www.bannercountynegov.org	308-436-5265	436-4180	338
Banner Day Camp 1225 Riverwoods Rd...................... Lake Forest IL 60045 *Web:* www.bannerdaycamp.com	847-295-4900		121
Banner Engineering Corp 9714 Tenth Ave N........................ Minneapolis MN 55441 *TF:* 888-373-6767 ■ *Web:* www.bannerengineering.com	763-544-3164	544-3213	253
Banner Equipment Company Inc 1370 Bungalow Rd .... Morris IL 60450 *TF:* 800-621-4625 ■ *Web:* www.bannerbeer.com	800-621-4625		57
Banner Life Sciences 4125 Premier Dr.......................... High Point NC 27265 *Web:* www.patheon.com	336-812-3442	816-7030	582
Banner Marketing 16201 E Indiana Ave Ste 3240 .... Spokane Valley WA 99216 *TF:* 800-843-9271 ■ *Web:* bannermktg.com	800-843-9271		7
Banner Marsh State Fish & Wildlife Area 19721 N US 24.............................. Canton IL 61520 *Web:* www2.illinois.gov	309-647-9184		565
Banner Metals Group Inc 1308 Holly Ave........................... Columbus OH 43212 *Web:* www.bannermetalsgroup.com	614-291-3105	297-8262	488
Banner of Truth PO Box 621................... Carlisle PA 17013 *TF:* 800-263-8085 ■ *Web:* banneroftruth.org	717-249-5747	249-0604	96
Banner Personnel Service Inc 53 W Jackson Blvd Ste 1219 .... Chicago IL 60604 *Web:* www.bannerpersonnel.com	312-922-5400	347-1206	260
Banner Welder Inc N 117 W 18200 Fulton Dr................. Germantown WI 53022 *Web:* www.bannerweld.com	262-253-2900	253-2919	811
Banner Wholesale Grocers Inc 3000 S Ashland .... Chicago IL 60608 *TF:* 844-421-2650 ■ *Web:* www.bannerwholesale.com	312-421-2650		345
Banner-Press PO Box 585................... Brenham TX 77834 *Web:* www.brenhambanner.com	979-836-7956		532-2
Banning Museum, The 401 E 'M' St .... Wilmington CA 90744 *Web:* banningmuseum.org	310-548-7777		520
Banning State Park PO Box 643 .... Sandstone MN 55072 *Web:* www.dnr.state.mn.us	320-216-3910	245-0251	565
Bannister & Associates Inc 34 N High St............................ New Albany OH 43054 *Web:* www.bannister.com	614-895-1208	895-3466	47
Bannister's Wharf 1 Bannister's Wharf........... Newport RI 02840 *Web:* www.bannistersnewport.com	401-846-4500	849-8750	50-6
Bannock County PO Box 4016 .... Pocatello ID 83205 *Web:* www.bannockcounty.us	208-236-7211	236-7363	338

Name / Address	City	State	Zip	Phone	Fax	Class
Bannockburn Church 7100 Brodie Ln *Web:* bannockburnchurch.com	Austin	TX	78745	512-892-2703		48-20
Banorte Securities International Ltd 140 E 45th St 32nd Fl *Web:* www.banortesecurities.com	New York	NY	10017	212-484-5200	484-5290	401
Banque, The 1849 E Little Creek Rd *Web:* thebanque.com	Norfolk	VA	23518	757-480-3600		671
Bansley & Kiener LLP 8745 W Higgins Rd Ste 200 *Web:* www.bk-cpa.com	Chicago	IL	60631	312-263-2700		2
Bantam Group Inc 50 Bay Colony Dr *Web:* bantamgroup.com	Westwood	MA	02090	781-329-2020		449
Banterra Corp 1404 US Rt 45 S *TF:* 877-541-2265 ■ *Web:* www.banterra.com	Eldorado	IL	62930	618-273-9346		70
Bantrel Inc 1201 Glenmore Trail SW Ste 600 *Web:* www.bantrel.com	Calgary	AB	T2V4Y8	403-290-5000	290-5050	261
Banyan Air Service 5360 NW 20th Terr *TF:* 800-200-2031 ■ *Web:* www.banyanair.com	Fort Lauderdale	FL	33309	954-491-3170	771-0281	63
Banyan Medical Systems Inc 8701 F St *Web:* banyanmed.com	Omaha	NE	68127	402-403-4400		180
Banyan Resort 323 Whitehead St *TF:* 866-371-9222 ■ *Web:* www.thebanyanresort.com	Key West	FL	33040	305-296-7786	294-1107	669
Banyan Water Inc 11002-B Metric Blvd *TF:* 800-276-1507 ■ *Web:* banyanwater.com	Austin	TX	78758	800-276-1507		463
Banyon Data Systems Inc 350 W Burnsville Pky **Fax Area Code:* 952 ■ *TF:* 800-229-1130 ■ *Web:* www.banyon.com	Burnsville	MN	55337	800-229-1130	882-7734*	174
Baoding 4722 Sharon Rd 4722-F Sharon Rd *Web:* www.baodingsouthpark.com	Charlotte	NC	28210	704-552-8899	552-8828	671
Bap-Geon Import Auto Parts 3403 Gulf Fwy *TF:* 888-868-2281 ■ *Web:* www.bap-geon.com	Houston	TX	77003	713-227-1544	225-2333	54
Bapko Metal Fabricators Inc 1091 N Batavia St *Web:* bapko.com	Orange	CA	92867	714-639-9380	639-8278	492
Baptist Bible College 628 E Kearney St **Fax Area Code:* 417 ■ *TF:* 800-228-5754 ■ *Web:* gobbc.edu	Springfield	MO	65803	800-228-5754	268-6694*	161
Baptist Bible Fellowship Intl (BBFI) 720 E Kearney St *Web:* www.bbfi.org	Springfield	MO	65803	417-862-5001	865-0794	48-20
Baptist College of Florida 5400 College Dr *TF:* 800-328-2660 ■ *Web:* www.baptistcollege.edu	Graceville	FL	32440	850-263-3261	263-7506	166
Baptist Credit Union 5815 W Ih 10 *Web:* baptistcu.org	San Antonio	TX	78201	210-525-0100		219
Baptist Easley Hospital 200 Fleetwood Dr *Web:* www.ghs.org	Easley	SC	29640	864-442-7200		374-3
Baptist General Convention of Texas 7557 Rambler Rd Ste 1200 *TF:* 888-244-9400 ■ *Web:* texasbaptists.org	Dallas	TX	75231	888-244-9400		48-20
Baptist Health 2701 Eastpoint Pkwy *Web:* www.baptisthealth.com	Louisville	KY	40223	502-896-5000		353
Baptist Health South Florida Inc 5000 University Dr *Web:* www.baptisthealth.net	Coral Gables	FL	33146	786-662-7000		353
Baptist Hospital 1000 W Moreno St *Web:* ebaptisthealthcare.org	Pensacola	FL	32501	850-434-4011		374-3
Baptist Hospitals of Southeast Texas School of Radiologic Technology 3080 College St PO Box 1591 *Web:* www.bhset.net	Beaumont	TX	77701	409-212-5000		685
Baptist Housing 6165 Hwy 17 Ste 125 *Web:* www.baptisthousing.org	Delta	BC	V4K5B8	604-940-1960		371
Baptist Medical Center South 2105 E S Blvd *TF:* 800-356-9596 ■ *Web:* www.baptistfirst.org	Montgomery	AL	36116	334-288-2100		374-3
Baptist Medical Ctr 1225 N State St *TF:* 800-948-6262 ■ *Web:* www.mbhs.org	Jackson	MS	39202	601-968-1000		374-3
Baptist Medical Ctr 800 Prudential Dr *Web:* www.baptistjax.com	Jacksonville	FL	32207	904-202-2000		374-3
Baptist Medical Ctr 111 Dallas St *TF:* 866-309-2873 ■ *Web:* www.baptisthealthsystem.com	San Antonio	TX	78205	210-297-7000		374-3
Baptist Memorial Health Care Corp 350 N Humphreys Blvd *TF:* 800-422-7847 ■ *Web:* www.baptistonline.org	Memphis	TN	38120	901-227-5920		353
Baptist Mid-Missions 7749 Webster Rd *Web:* www.bmm.org	Cleveland	OH	44130	440-826-3930	826-4457	48-20
Baptist Missionary Association of America (BMA) 611 Locust Ave PO Box 878 *TF:* 800-333-1442 ■ *Web:* bmamissions.org	Conway	AR	72034	501-455-4977		48-20
Baptist Missionary Association Theological Seminary 1530 E Pine St *TF:* 800-259-5673 ■ *Web:* www.bmats.edu	Jacksonville	TX	75766	903-586-2501	586-0378	167-3
Baptist Progress 632 Farley St *Web:* baptistprogress.org	Waxahachie	TX	75165	972-923-0756		532-2
Baptist Spanish Publishing House 7000 Alabama St *TF:* 800-755-5958 ■ *Web:* www.editorialmh.org	El Paso	TX	79904	800-755-5958		637-2
Baptist Theological Seminary at Richmond 8040 Villa Park Dr Ste 250 *Web:* www.btsr.edu	Richmond	VA	23228	804-355-8135		167-3
Baptist University of the Americas 7838 Barlite Blvd *TF:* 800-721-1396 ■ *Web:* www.bua.edu	San Antonio	TX	78224	210-924-4338	924-2701	161
Baptist Village of Hugo 1200 W Finley St *TF:* 866-887-2872 ■ *Web:* www.baptistvillage.org	Hugo	OK	74743	580-326-8383		48-20
Baptist World Alliance 405 N Washington St *Web:* www.bwanet.org	Falls Church	VA	22046	703-790-8980	893-5160	48-20
Bar Engineering Company Ltd 5237 70th Ave *Web:* www.bareng.ca	Lloydminster	AB	T9V3N6	780-875-1683		261
Bar G. Feed Yard PO Box 1797 *TF:* 800-569-3736 ■ *Web:* www.bar-g.com	Hereford	TX	79045	806-357-2241		10-1
Bar Green Inc 4125 Yancey Rd *Web:* www.bargreeninc.com	Charlotte	NC	28273	704-552-6483	552-1403	194
Bar Harbor Bankshares 82 Main St PO Box 400 *NYSE:* BHB ■ *TF:* 888-853-7100 ■ *Web:* www.barharbor.bank	Bar Harbor	ME	04609	207-288-3314		360-2
Bar Harbor Chamber of Commerce 2 Cottage St *TF:* 888-540-9990 ■ *Web:* www.visitbarharbor.com	Bar Harbor	ME	04609	207-244-5388	667-9080	139
Bar Harbor Hotel-Bluenose Inn 90 Eden St *TF:* 800-445-4077 ■ *Web:* barharborhotel.com	Bar Harbor	ME	04609	207-288-3348	288-2183	379
Bar Harbor Inn Oceanfront Resort Newport Dr *TF:* 800-248-3351 ■ *Web:* barharborinn.com	Bar Harbor	ME	04609	207-288-3351		669
Bar Harbor Lobster Bakes 10 State Hwy 3 PO Box 152 *Web:* www.barharborlobsterbakes.com	Hulls Cove	ME	04644	207-288-4055	288-5767	671
Bar Harbor Lobster Co 2000 Premier Row *Web:* www.barharborseafood.com	Orlando	FL	32809	407-447-6455	857-1314	297-5
Bar Harbor Town Hall 93 Cottage St *TF:* 800-232-4733 ■ *Web:* www.barharbormaine.gov	Bar Harbor	ME	04609	207-288-4098	288-4461	337
Bar Italian Ristorante-Caffe 13 Maryland Plz *Web:* baritaliastl.com	Saint Louis	MO	63108	314-361-7010		671
Bar Lazy J Guest Ranch 447 County Rd 3 PO Box N *TF:* 800-396-6279 ■ *Web:* barlazyj.com	Parshall	CO	80468	970-725-3437	725-0121	239
Bar Method, The 3333 Fillmore St *Web:* barmethod.com	San Francisco	CA	94123	415-441-6333		354
Bar None Auction Inc 4751 Power Inn Rd **Fax Area Code:* 916 ■ *TF:* 866-372-1700 ■ *Web:* www.barnoneauction.com	Sacramento	CA	95826	866-372-1700	383-6865*	187
Bar Productscom Inc 1990 Lake Ave SE *TF:* 800-256-6396 ■ *Web:* www.barproducts.com	Largo	FL	33771	727-584-2093		321
Bar S Machine Inc 2575 N Hwy 89 *Web:* www.bar-smachine.com	Chino Valley	AZ	86323	928-636-2115	636-1155	454
Bar XH Air Inc 575 Palmer Rd NE (Esso Avitat) *Web:* www.barxh.com	Calgary	AB	T2E7G4	403-291-3227		23
Baraboo BanCorp Inc, The 101 Third Ave *Web:* www.baraboobank.com	Baraboo	WI	53913	608-356-7703		70
Baraboo Public Library 230 4th Ave *Web:* www.baraboopubliclibrary.org	Baraboo	WI	53913	608-356-6166	355-2779	434-3
Baracci Solutions Inc 24 Boul De La Concorde E *Web:* www.baracci.com	Laval	QC	H7G4X2	450-662-8700		225
Barada Associates Inc 130 E Second St *TF:* 800-616-5917 ■ *Web:* baradainc.com	Rushville	IN	46173	765-932-5917		463
Baraga Correctional Facility 13924 Wadaga Rd *TF:* 800-326-4537 ■ *Web:* www.michigan.gov	Baraga	MI	49908	906-353-7070		213
Baraga County 755 E Broad St *TF:* 800-743-4908 ■ *Web:* www.baragacounty.org	L'Anse	MI	49946	906-524-6183		338
Baraga State Park 1300 US Hwy 41 S *Web:* www.michigan.org	Baraga	MI	49908	906-353-6558		565
Baraga Telephone Co 204 State Ave *TF:* 866-353-6644 ■ *Web:* www.baragatelephone.com	Baraga	MI	49908	906-353-6644		224
Baranov Museum, The 101 E Marine Way *Web:* www.baranovmuseum.org	Kodiak	AK	99615	907-486-5920		520
Barantec Inc 777 Passaic Ave *Web:* www.barantec.com	Clifton	NJ	07012	917-732-7450		203
Baraonda 710 Peachtree St *Web:* www.baraondaatlanta.com	Atlanta	GA	30308	404-879-9962		671
Barash, Friedman, Friedberg & Adasko CPAS PC 1430 Broadway Ste 1208 *Web:* bffa.com	New York	NY	10018	212-696-4600	696-1324	2
Barattas 2320 S Union St *Web:* barattas.com	Des Moines	IA	50315	515-243-4516		671
Barbacoa Grill 276 W Bobwhite Ct *Web:* barbacoa-boise.com	Boise	ID	83706	208-338-5000		671
Barbados *Consulate General* 2121 Poncedaleon Blvd Ste 1300 *Web:* www.foreign.gov.bb	Coral Gables	FL	33134	305-442-1994	455-7975	257
Barbara A. Bowden, P.S. Inc 5611 76th St W *Web:* trafficticketsgone.com	Lakewood	WA	98499	253-473-4262		41
Barbara Ann Karmanos Cancer Institute 4100 John R St *TF:* 800-527-6266 ■ *Web:* www.karmanos.org	Detroit	MI	48201	800-527-6266		668
Barbara B. Mann Performing Arts Hall 13350 FSW Pkwy *TF:* 800-440-7469 ■ *Web:* www.bbmannpah.com	Fort Myers	FL	33919	239-481-4849	481-4620	572
Barbara Gladstone Gallery 515 W 24th St *Web:* gladstonegallery.com	New York	NY	10011	212-206-9300	206-9301	42
Barbara Katz Sportswear Co 2240 NW 19th St Ste 601 *Web:* www.barbarakatz.com	Boca Raton	FL	33431	561-391-1066	391-5284	157-6
Barbara Marshall Insurance Agency Inc 1045 Foothill Blvd *Web:* barbaraamarshall.com	La Canada Flintridge	CA	91011	818-790-1034		390
Barbara Mathes Gallery 22 E 80th St *Web:* www.barbaramathesgallery.com	New York	NY	10075	212-570-4190	570-4191	42
Barbaricum LLC 1714 N St NW *Web:* barbaricum.com	Washington	DC	20036	202-393-0873	999-4490	196
Barbaron Inc PO Box 2338 *Web:* barbaron.com	Crystal River	FL	34423	352-795-9010		188-3
Barbato Nursery Corp 1600 Railroad Ave *Web:* louisbarbatolandscaping.com	Holbrook	NY	11741	631-285-6767	285-6748	302
Barbato's Restaurant 7472 New Perry Hwy *Web:* www.barbatos.com	Erie	PA	16509	814-864-9999		670

Company	City	State	ZIP	Phone	Fax	Class
Barbee's Freeway Ford Inc 4471 E Evans Ave *Web:* www.freewayforddenver.com	Denver	CO	80222	303-584-6600		57
Barber & Associates 1308 Sumac Dr *Web:* barberandassociates.com	Knoxville	TN	37919	865-388-5296		708
Barber Bros Contracting Company LLC 2636 Dougherty Dr *Web:* www.barber-brothers.com	Baton Rouge	LA	70805	225-355-5611	355-5615	188-4
Barber Emerson Lc 1211 Massachusetts St *Web:* barberemerson.com	Lawrence	KS	66044	785-843-6600		41
Barber Martin & Assoc 7400 Beaufont Springs Dr *Web:* www.barbermartin.com	Richmond	VA	23225	804-320-3232		7
Barber Mfg 1824 Brown St *Web:* www.barbermfg.com	Anderson	IN	46016	765-643-6905		718
Barber Packaging Co 300 Industrial Park Rd *TF:* 800-554-9213 ■ *Web:* www.barberpackaging.com	Bangor	MI	49013	269-427-7995	427-5454	601
Barber School, The 1309 Jackson Ave *Web:* www.thebarberschool.edu	Memphis	TN	38107	901-726-4247	726-4663	685
Barber Styling Institute 3433 Simpson Ferry Rd *Web:* www.barberstylinginstitute.com	Camp Hill	PA	17011	717-763-4787		167-3
Barber Vintage Motorsports Museum 6030 Barber Motorsports Pkwy *Web:* www.barbermuseum.org	Leeds	AL	35094	205-699-7275		520
Barber's Poultry Inc 810 E 50th Ave *Web:* www.barberspoultry.com	Denver	CO	80216	303-466-7338	466-6960	619
Barber/Styling College of Lansing 2101 N E St *Web:* www.lansingbarbercollege.com	Lansing	MI	48906	517-482-8083		167-3
Barberian's Steak House 7 Elm St *Web:* www.barberians.com	Toronto	ON	M5G1H1	416-597-0335	597-1407	671
Barber-Nichols Inc 6325 W 55th Ave *Web:* www.barber-nichols.com	Arvada	CO	80002	303-421-8111	420-4679	621
Barbers Hill ISD (BHISD) 9600 Eagle Dr PO Box 1108 *Web:* www.bhisd.net	Mont Belvieu	TX	77580	281-576-2221		685
Barbers Point Coast Guard Air Station 1 Coral Sea Rd *Web:* www.uscg.mil	Kapolei	HI	96707	808-682-2771		158
Barbershop Harmony Society 110 Seventh Ave N *TF:* 800-876-7464 ■ *Web:* www.barbershop.org	Nashville	TN	37203	615-823-3993	313-7619	48-18
Barberton South Summitt Chamber of Commerce 211 Second St NW *Web:* www.southsummitchamber.org	Barberton	OH	44203	330-745-3141		139
Barbette 1600 W Lake St *Web:* www.barbette.com	Minneapolis	MN	55408	612-827-5710		671
Barbizon International LLC 4950 W Kennedy Blvd Ste 200 **Fax Area Code:* 813 ■ *TF:* 800-330-8361 ■ *Web:* www.barbizonmodeling.com	Tampa	FL	33615	800-330-8361	282-3530*	507
Barbizon Modeling of Pittsburgh 500 Mansfield Ave *TF:* 888-245-7718 ■ *Web:* www.barbizonpa.com	Pittsburgh	PA	15205	717-234-3277	234-4369	167-3
Barbour County 26 N Main St *Web:* barbourcountywv.org	Philippi	WV	26416	304-457-2232	457-5983	338
Barbour Publishing Inc 1810 Barbour Dr PO Box 719 *Web:* www.barbourbooks.com	Uhrichsville	OH	44683	740-922-6045		95
Barbour Welting Company Div Barbour Corp 1001 N Montello St *TF:* 800-955-9649 ■ *Web:* www.barbourcorp.com	Brockton	MA	02301	508-583-8200	583-4113	301
Barboursville Veterans Home 512 Water St *Web:* www.veterans.wv.gov	Barboursville	WV	25504	304-736-1027	736-1093	793
Bar-B-Q Shop, The 1782 Madison Ave *TF:* 888-372-8237 ■ *Web:* thebar-b-qshop.com	Memphis	TN	38104	901-272-1277	853-9298	671
Barbuto 775 Washington St *Web:* www.barbutonyc.com	New York	NY	10014	212-924-9700	924-9300	671
BARC Electric Co-op 84 High St PO Box 264 *TF:* 800-846-2272 ■ *Web:* www.barcelectric.com	Millboro	VA	24460	800-846-2272		245
Barcalounger Corp 2829 W Andrew Johnson Hwy *Web:* barcalounger.com	Morristown	TN	37814	423-353-1288	353-1291	361
Barcelona 263 E Whittier St *Web:* www.barcelonacolumbus.com	Columbus	OH	43206	614-443-3699	444-0539	671
Barcelona Restaurant & Wine Bar 4180 Black Rock Tpke *Web:* www.barcelonawinebar.com	Fairfield	CT	06824	203-255-0800		671
Barchartcom Inc 209 W Jackson 2nd Fl *TF:* 800-238-5814 ■ *Web:* www.barchart.com	Chicago	IL	60606	312-554-8122		317
Barclay College 607 N Kingman St *TF:* 800-862-0226 ■ *Web:* www.barclaycollege.edu	Haviland	KS	67059	620-862-5252	862-5403	161
Barclay Damon LLP 200 Delaware Ave Ste 1200 *Web:* barclaydamon.com	Buffalo	NY	14202	716-856-5500	856-5510	445
Barclay Hedge Ltd 2094 185th St Ste 1B *Web:* www.barclayhedge.com	Fairfield	IA	52556	641-472-3456	472-9514	194
Barclay Hotel 1348 Robson St *Web:* barclay-hotel.vancouver-hotels-bc.com	Vancouver	BC	V6E1C5	604-688-8850		379
Barclay Mechanical Services Inc 490 W 100 S *TF:* 800-438-7441 ■ *Web:* barclaymech.com	Paul	ID	83347	208-438-8108	438-5932	189-1
Barclay Prime 237 S 18th St *Web:* barclayprime.com	Philadelphia	PA	19103	215-732-7560		671
Barclay Products 4000 Porett Dr *TF:* 800-446-9700 ■ *Web:* barclayproducts.com	Gurnee	IL	60031	847-244-1234	244-1259	609
Barclay Water Management Inc 55 Chapel St *Web:* www.barclaywm.com	Newton	MA	02458	617-926-3400		145
Barclays 745 Seventh Ave *TF:* 888-227-2275 ■ *Web:* www.investmentbank.barclays.com	New York	NY	10019	212-526-7000		690
Barco Electronic Systems Pvt Ltd 11101 Trade Center Dr *TF:* 888-414-7226 ■ *Web:* www.barco.com	Rancho Cordova	CA	95670	916-859-2500	859-2515	173-4
Barco Products 24 N Washington Ave *TF:* 800-338-2697 ■ *Web:* www.barcoproducts.com	Batavia	IL	60510	800-338-2697		385
Barco Rent a Truck 717 South 5600 West *TF:* 800-453-4761 ■ *Web:* www.barcorentatruck.com	Salt Lake City	UT	84104	801-532-7777		778
Barco Uniforms 350 W Rosecrans Ave *TF:* 800-262-1559 ■ *Web:* www.barcouniforms.com	Gardena	CA	90248	310-323-7315		155-19
BarcodeDiscounters.com 3610 Dodge St Ste 200 *Web:* www.barcodediscounters.com	Omaha	NE	68131	402-345-9200	345-9945	459
Barcoding Inc 2220 Boston St *TF:* 888-412-7226 ■ *Web:* www.barcoding.com	Baltimore	MD	21231	888-860-7226		179
Barcom Inc 400B Chickamauga Rd *Web:* www.barcominc.com	Chattanooga	TN	37421	423-855-1822		180
Bar-Cons Federal Credit Union 1142 N Marr Rd *TF:* 855-510-0947 ■ *Web:* barcons.org	Columbus	IN	47201	812-372-8776	372-8186	219
Barcontrol Systems & Services Inc 105 Wall St Ste 3 *TF:* 800-947-4362 ■ *Web:* barcontrol.com	Clemson	SC	29631	864-421-0050		177
Bard Access Systems Inc 605 North 5600 West *TF:* 800-545-0890 ■ *Web:* www.bardaccess.com	Salt Lake City	UT	84116	801-522-5000	522-4948	476
Bard Advertising Inc 4900 Lincoln Dr *Web:* www.bardadvertising.com	Edina	MN	55436	952-345-8000		7
Bard College PO Box 5000 *TF:* 800-872-7423 ■ *Web:* www.bard.edu	Annandale-on-Hudson	NY	12504	845-758-7472	758-5208	166
Bard Consulting LLC 555 Montgomery St Ste 1288 *Web:* www.bardconsulting.com	San Francisco	CA	94111	415-421-2822		196
Bard Manufacturing Company Inc 1914 Randolph Dr *Web:* www.bardhvac.com	Bryan	OH	43506	419-636-1194	636-2640	15
Bard Materials 2021 325th Ave PO Box 246 *Web:* bardmaterials.com	Dyersville	IA	52040	563-875-7145	875-7860	182
Bard Peripheral Vascular Inc 1025 W 3rd St *TF:* 800-321-4254 ■ *Web:* www.crbard.com	Tempe	AZ	85281	480-894-9515	966-7062	476
Bard Rao + Athanas Consulting Engineers Inc 10 Guest St 4th Fl *Web:* www.brplusa.com	Boston	MA	02135	617-254-0016		261
Bardane Manufacturing Co 317 Delaware St PO Box 70 *Web:* www.bardane.com	Jermyn	PA	18433	570-876-4844	876-1938	308
Bardavon Health Innovations 6803 W 64th St Bldg 6 Ste 200 *Web:* www.bardavon.com	Overland Park	KS	66202	913-236-1020		48-17
Bardel Entertainment Inc 1523 Third Ave W *Web:* bardel.ca	Vancouver	BC	V6J1J8	604-669-5589	669-9079	514
Barden & Robeson Corp 103 Kelly Ave **Fax Area Code:* 716 ■ *TF:* 800-724-0141 ■ *Web:* www.bardenbp.com	Middleport	NY	14105	800-945-9400	735-3752*	106
Barden Corp 200 Park Ave *TF:* 800-243-1060 ■ *Web:* www.schaeffler.us	Danbury	CT	06810	203-744-2211	744-3756	620
Bardes Plastics Inc 5225 W Clinton Ave **Fax Area Code:* 414 ■ *TF:* 800-558-5161 ■ *Web:* www.bardesplastics.com	Milwaukee	WI	53223	800-558-5161	354-6331*	602
Bardex Corp 6338 Lindmar Dr *Web:* www.bardex.com	Goleta	CA	93117	805-964-7747		537
Bardin Palomo Ltd 432 W 19th St *Web:* bardinpalomo.com	New York	NY	10011	212-989-6113		292
Bardon Supplies Ltd 405 College St E PO Box 1023 *TF:* 800-267-2135 ■ *Web:* www.bardonsupplies.com	Belleville	ON	K8N4Z6	613-966-5643	966-2026	612
Bardons & Oliver Inc 5800 Harper Rd *Web:* www.bardonsoliver.com	Solon	OH	44139	440-498-5800	498-2001	455
Bardsong Press PO Box 775396 *Web:* www.bardsongpress.com	Steamboat Springs	CO	80477	970-819-9728	879-2657	637-2
Bare Bones Software Inc 73 Princeton St Ste 206 *Web:* www.barebones.com	North Chelmsford	MA	01863	978-251-0500		177
Bare Facts PO Box 3255 *Web:* www.barefacts.com	Santa Clara	CA	95055	408-249-2021		637-10
Bare Hill Correctional Facility 181 Brand Rd PO Box 20 *Web:* doccs.ny.gov	Malone	NY	12953	518-483-8411		213
Bare Woods and Home Furnishings 14150-B Willard Rd *Web:* www.barewoodsfurniture.com	Chantilly	VA	20151	703-378-1888	378-1917	321
Barefoot Landing 4898 Hwy 17 S *Web:* www.bflanding.com	North Myrtle Beach	SC	29582	843-272-8349		50-6
Barefoot Resort & Golf 4980 Barefoot Resort Bridge Rd *TF:* 866-638-4818 ■ *Web:* barefootgolf.com	North Myrtle Beach	SC	29582	843-390-3200	390-3213	669
Barenbrug USA Inc PO Box 239 *Web:* www.barenbrug.com	Tangent	OR	97389	541-926-5801	926-9435	694
Barfield Inc 4101 NW 29th St *TF:* 800-321-1039 ■ *Web:* www.barfieldinc.com	Miami	FL	33142	305-894-5300	894-5301	24
Barfield Murphy Shank & Smith PC 1121 Riverchase Office Rd *Web:* www.bmss.com	Birmingham	AL	35244	205-982-5500		2
Barg Coffin Lewis & Trapp LLP 350 California St 22nd Fl *Web:* www.bargcoffin.com	San Francisco	CA	94104	415-228-5400		428
Bargain Bob'S Carpets Inc 3954 Byron Dr *Web:* bargainbobsflooring.com	Riviera Beach	FL	33404	561-848-0808		290
Bargain Books Wholesale 3030 29th St SE *Web:* www.bargainbookswholesale.com	Grand Rapids	MI	49512	717-227-9576	227-9295	96
Bargain Supply Co 844 E Jefferson St *TF:* 800-322-5226 ■ *Web:* www.bargainsupply.com	Louisville	KY	40206	502-562-5000	562-5051	351

				Phone	Fax	Class
Barge Cauthen & Associates Inc 6606 Charlotte Pk Ste 210 *Web:* bargecauthen.com	Nashville	TN	37209	615-356-9911		256
Barge Design Solutions Inc 615 3rd Ave S Ste 700 *Web:* www.bargedesign.com	Nashville	TN	37210	615-254-1500	255-6572	261
Bargreen Coffee Co 2821 Rucker Ave *Web:* bargreenscoffee.com	Everett	WA	98201	425-252-3161		296-7
Bargreen Ellingson Inc 2925 70th Ave E **Fax Area Code:* 253 ■ *TF:* 866-722-2665 ■ *Web:* www.bargreen.com	Fife	WA	98424	866-722-2665	896-3620*	300
Bari-Jay Fashions Inc 1277 Bridge St Unit 1B *TF:* 800-735-5808 ■ *Web:* barijay.com	New Dundee	ON	N0B2E0	800-735-5808		155-21
Baring Asset Management Company Inc 470 Atlantic Ave Independence Wharf *Web:* www.barings.com	Boston	MA	02210	617-946-5200		401
Barington Capital Group LP 888 7th Ave *Web:* barington.com	New York	NY	10106	212-974-5710		690
Baritz & Colman LLP 1075 Broken Sound Pkwy NW Ste 102 *Web:* www.baritzcolman.com	Boca Raton	FL	33487	561-864-5100		428
Barix Clinics 135 S Prospect St *Web:* www.barixclinics.com	Ypsilanti	MI	48198	734-547-4700		810
Barkan & Barkan Company LPA 81 S 4th 4th St Ste 300 *Web:* www.barkanlaw.com	Columbus	OH	43215	614-221-9550	635-1334	428
Barkcamp State Park 65330 Barkcamp Rd *Web:* ohiodnr.gov	Belmont	OH	43718	740-484-4064		565
Barker & Williamson 603 Cidco Rd *Web:* www.bwantennas.com	Cocoa	FL	32926	321-639-1510	445-6031	647
Barker Air & Hydraulics Inc 1308 Miller Rd *TF:* 800-922-3324 ■ *Web:* www.barkerair.com	Greenville	SC	29607	864-288-3537		641
Barker Blue Digital Imaging Inc 363 N Amphlett Blvd *Web:* barkerblue.com	San Mateo	CA	94401	650-696-2100		627
Barker Brothers Inc 1666 Summerfield St	Ridgewood	NY	11385	718-456-6400		1
Barker Business Systems Inc 650 S Rock Blvd Ste 17 *Web:* www.e-totalprint.com	Reno	NV	89502	775-856-1771		535
Barker Contracting 2127 E Speedway Ste 101 *Web:* barkerone.com	Tucson	AZ	85719	520-323-3831	323-3834	186
Barker Martin PS 701 Pike St Ste 1150 *TF:* 888-381-9806 ■ *Web:* www.barkermartin.com	Seattle	WA	98104	360-756-9806		428
Barker Specialty Products LLC 27 Realty Dr *Web:* www.barkerspecialty.com	Cheshire	CT	06410	203-272-2222		296-5
BarkerGilmore LLC 1387 Fairport Rd Ste 845 *TF:* 877-571-5047 ■ *Web:* www.barkergilmore.com	Fairport	NY	14450	877-571-5047	571-5048	721
Barkley Co PO Box 5540 *Web:* www.barkleycompany.com	Yuma	AZ	85365	928-782-2571	782-4656	10-11
Barkley Inc 1740 Main St *Web:* barkleyus.com	Kansas City	MO	64108	816-842-1500		4
Barkman Honey 120 Santa Fe St *TF:* 800-364-6623 ■ *Web:* www.barkmanhoney.com	Hillsboro	KS	67063	800-364-6623		296-24
Barksdale Air Force Base 555 Davis Ave W *Web:* www.barksdale.af.mil	Barksdale AFB	LA	71110	318-456-1015		497-1
Barksdale Inc 3211 Fruitland Ave *TF:* 800-835-1060 ■ *Web:* www.barksdale.com	Los Angeles	CA	90058	323-589-6181	589-3463	201
Barletta & Associates Inc 1313 Campbell Rd Ste C *Web:* www.barlettainc.com	Houston	TX	77055	713-464-7700	464-3696	652
Barley House 132 N Main St *Web:* www.thebarleyhouse.com	Concord	NH	03301	603-228-6363		671
Barley, Snyder, Senft & Cohen LLC 126 E King St *Web:* www.barley.com	Lancaster	PA	17602	717-299-5201		428
Bar-Lo Carbon Products Inc 31 Daniel Rd *Web:* www.barlocarbon.com	Fairfield	NJ	07004	973-227-2717	575-7164	493
Barlo Signs International Inc 158 Greeley St *TF:* 800-227-5674 ■ *Web:* www.barlosigns.com	Hudson	NH	03051	603-882-2638	882-7680	9
Barlovento LLC 431 Technology Dr *Web:* barloventollc.com	Dothan	AL	36303	334-983-9979	983-9983	186
Barlow Garsek & Simon LLP 920 Foch St *Web:* www.bgsfirm.com	Fort Worth	TX	76107	817-731-4500	731-6200	428
Barlow Truck Lines inc 1305 SE Grand Dd Hwy *TF:* 800-688-1202 ■ *Web:* www.barlowtruckline.com	Faucett	MO	64448	816-396-1430		780
Barlow, Josephs & Holmes Ltd 101 Dyer St 5th Fl *Web:* barjos.com	Providence	RI	02903	401-273-4446		428
Barmache & Alford LLP 4035 E Thousand Oaks Blvd Ste 232 *Web:* westlaketax.com	Westlake Village	CA	91362	805-371-7898	371-7865	2
Barn Furniture Mart Inc 6206 N Sepulveda Blvd *TF:* 888-302-2276 ■ *Web:* www.barnfurnituremart.com	Van Nuys	CA	91411	818-780-4070		321
Barna, Guzy & Steffen Ltd 400 Northtown Financial Plz 200 Coon Rapids Blvd *Web:* www.bgs.com	Coon Rapids	MN	55433	763-780-8500		428
Barnacle Historic State Park, The 3485 Main Hwy *Web:* www.floridastateparks.org	Coconut Grove	FL	33133	305-442-6866	442-6872	565
Barnard & Sons Construction LLC 3054 Simpson Hwy 13 PO Box 517 *Web:* www.barnardandsons.com	Mendenhall	MS	39114	601-847-2420	847-0110	685
Barnard College Columbia University 3009 Broadway *Web:* www.barnard.edu	New York	NY	10027	212-854-2014	854-6220	166
Barnard Construction Company Inc PO Box 99 *Web:* www.barnard-inc.com	Bozeman	MT	59771	406-586-1995	586-3530	188-10
Barnegat Lighthouse State Park PO Box 167 *Web:* www.njparksandforests.org	Barnegat Light	NJ	08006	609-494-2016		565
Barnes & Conti Associates Inc 940 Dwight Way Ste 15 *Web:* www.barnesconti.com	Berkeley	CA	94710	510-644-0911		194
Barnes & Jones Corp 91 Pacella Pk Dr *Web:* www.barnesandjones.com	Randolph	MA	02368	781-963-8000	963-3322	357
Barnes & Noble College Bookstores Inc 120 Mtn View Blvd *Web:* www.bncollege.com	Basking Ridge	NJ	07920	908-991-2665		95
Barnes & Noble Inc 122 Fifth Ave *NYSE: BKS* ■ *Web:* www.barnesandnoble.com	New York	NY	10011	212-633-3300		95
Barnes & Thornburg LLP 11 S Meridian St *TF:* 800-236-1352 ■ *Web:* www.btlaw.com	Indianapolis	IN	46204	317-236-1313	231-7433	428
Barnes Advertising Corp 1580 Fairview Rd *TF:* 800-458-1410 ■ *Web:* barnesadvertisingcorp.com	Zanesville	OH	43701	740-453-6836		7
Barnes Aerospace 169 Kennedy Rd *Web:* www.barnesaerospace.com	Windsor	CT	06095	860-298-7740	298-7738	21
Barnes Alarm Systems Inc 3201 Flagler Ave Ste 503 *Web:* www.barnesalarmsystems.net	Key West	FL	33040	305-294-6753		693
Barnes Bullets LLC 38 N Frontage Rd *TF:* 800-574-9200 ■ *Web:* www.barnesbullets.com	Mona	UT	84645	435-856-1000	856-1040	711
Barnes County 230 Fourth St NW Rm 202 *Web:* www.co.barnes.nd.us	Valley City	ND	58072	701-845-8500		338
Barnes Farming Corp 7840 Old Bailey Hwy **Fax Area Code:* 252 ■ *TF:* 800-367-2799 ■ *Web:* www.farmpak.com	Spring Hope	NC	27882	800-367-2799	459-9020*	10-11
Barnes Foundation 50 Lapsley Ln *Web:* barnesfoundation.org	Merion Station	PA	19066	610-667-0290		520
Barnes Group Inc 123 Main St *NYSE: B* ■ *Web:* barnesgroupinc.com	Bristol	CT	06011	860-583-7070		718
Barnes Industries Inc 1161 E 11 Mile Rd *Web:* www.barnesballscrew.com	Madison Heights	MI	48071	248-541-2333		620
Barnes International Inc 814 Chestnut St PO Box 1203 *TF:* 800-435-4877 ■ *Web:* barnesintl.com	Rockford	IL	61105	815-964-8661	964-5074	455
Barnes Lodge 4520 Clayton Ave *Web:* www.barnesjewish.org	Saint Louis	MO	63110	314-652-4319		372
Barnes Nursery Inc 3511 W Cleveland Rd *TF:* 800-421-8722 ■ *Web:* www.barnesnursery.com	Huron	OH	44839	419-433-5525	433-3555	323
Barnes Transportation Services Inc 2309 Whitley Rd **Fax Area Code:* 252 ■ *TF:* 800-898-5897 ■ *Web:* www.barnestransport.com	Wilson	NC	27895	800-898-5897	291-2787*	360-2
Barnes Wendling CPA Inc 1350 Euclid Ave Ste 1400 *TF:* 800-369-6375 ■ *Web:* www.barneswendling.com	Cleveland	OH	44115	216-566-9000	566-9321	2
Barnes, Alford, Stork & Johnson LLP 1613 Main St PO Box 8448 *Web:* www.basjlaw.com	Columbia	SC	29201	803-799-1111		41
Barnes, Brock, Cornwell & Painter PLC 908 Eden Way N Ste 201 *Web:* bbchcpa.com	Chesapeake	VA	23320	757-961-5017		2
Barnes, Richardson & Colburn LLP 100 William St Ste 305 *Web:* barnesrichardson.com	New York	NY	10038	212-725-0200	889-4135	41
Barnes-Jewish Saint Peters Hospital 4901 Forest Park Ave *Web:* www.bjc.org	Saint Louis	MO	63108	314-747-9322		374-3
Barnesyard Books 444 Rt 604 *Web:* www.barnesyardbooks.com	Stockton	NJ	08559	609-397-6600	397-3262	637-2
Barnet Associates LLC 2 Round Lake Rd *TF:* 888-827-7070 ■ *Web:* www.barnetassociates.com	Ridgefield	CT	06877	888-827-7070		317
Barnet-Dulaney Eye Ctr 4800 N 22nd St *TF:* 866-742-6581 ■ *Web:* www.goodeyes.com	Phoenix	AZ	85016	602-955-1000		798
Barnett & Moro PC 495 E Main *Web:* barnettandmoro.com	Hermiston	OR	97838	541-567-5215		2
Barnett & Murphy Inc 1323 Brookhaven Dr *Web:* bmdm.com	Orlando	FL	32803	407-650-0264		7
Barnett & Ramel Optical Co 7154 N 16th St *Web:* www.secure.broptical.com	Omaha	NE	68112	402-453-4900		543
Barnett & Rubin, A Professional Corp 5450 Trabuco Rd *Web:* barnettrubin.com	Irvine	CA	92620	949-261-9700		41
Barnett Contracting Inc 7703 Bagby Ave *Web:* www.barnettcontracting.com	Waco	TX	76712	254-666-7117	666-7119	256
Barnett Engineering Ltd 550 71 St SE Ste 200 *TF:* 800-268-2646 ■ *Web:* www.barnettprotalk.com	Calgary	AB	T2H0S6	403-255-9544		261
Barnett Inc 4601-100 Bulls Bay Hwy *Web:* www.ebarnett.com	Jacksonville	FL	32219	904-899-0156		612
Barnett Millworks Inc 4915 Hamilton Blvd *Web:* barnettmillworks.com	Theodore	AL	36582	251-443-7710		499
Barnett Tool & Engineering 2238 Palma Dr *Web:* www.barnettclutches.com	Ventura	CA	93003	805-642-9435		256
Barney Trucking Inc 235 SR-24 *TF:* 800-524-7930 ■ *Web:* www.barneytrucking.com	Salina	UT	84654	800-524-7930		685
Barney's Bakery Inc 460 Park Dr *Web:* www.barneyspepperonirolls.com	Weirton	WV	26062	304-748-4370		296-9
Barney's Pumps Inc 2965 Barney's Pumps Pl *Web:* www.barneyspumps.com	Lakeland	FL	33812	863-665-8500	666-3858	641
Barneys New York Inc 575 5th Ave *Web:* www.saksfifthavenue.com	New York	NY	10017	212-450-8700		157-4

Name / Address	City	State	ZIP	Phone	Fax	Class
Barnhardt Manufacturing Co 1100 Hawthorne Ln *Fax Area Code: 704 ■ TF: 800-277-0377 ■ Web: www.barnhardt.net	Charlotte	NC	28205	800-277-0377	342-1892*	228
Barnhart 1641 California St *Web:* barnhartusa.com	Denver	CO	80202	303-626-7200		4
Barnhart Crane & Rigging Co 1701 Dunn Ave *Web:* www.barnhartcrane.com	Memphis	TN	38106	901-775-3000		190
Barnhart Display Inc 1170 Charming St	Maitland	FL	32751	407-637-2060		464
Barnhill Bolt Company Inc 2500 Princeton Dr NE *TF:* 800-472-3900 ■ *Web:* www.barnhillbolt.com	Albuquerque	NM	87107	505-884-1808		350
Barnhill Contracting Co 4325 Pleasant Valley Rd *Web:* www.barnhillcontracting.com	Raleigh	NC	27612	252-823-1021		188-4
Barnsco Inc 2609 Willowbrook *Web:* www.barnsco.com	Dallas	TX	75220	214-352-9091		480
Barnsider Management Corp 15 A Newbury St Rte 1 *Web:* www.barnsiderrestaurants.com	Danvers	MA	01923	978-777-3885	777-5038	463
Barnsley Resort 597 Barnsley Gardens Rd *TF:* 877-773-2447 ■ *Web:* www.barnsleyresort.com	Adairsville	GA	30103	770-773-7480	773-1779	669
Barnstead Inn 349 Bonnet St *TF:* 800-331-1619 ■ *Web:* www.barnsteadinn.com	Manchester Center	VT	05255	802-362-1619		379
Barnstormer Books PO Box 6893 *Web:* www.wecanfly.com	Reno	NV	89513	808-561-1439		637-2
Barnum Financial Group 6 Corporate Dr *Web:* barnumfinancialgroup.com	Shelton	CT	06484	203-513-6000		401
Barnum Museum 820 Main St *Web:* barnum-museum.org	Bridgeport	CT	06604	203-331-1104		520
Barnwell County 57 Wall St *Web:* www.barnwellcountysc.us	Barnwell	SC	29812	803-541-1047		338
Barnwell Industries Inc 1100 Alakea St Ste 2900 *NYSE: BRN* ■ *Web:* www.brninc.com	Honolulu	HI	96813	808-531-8400	531-7181	536
Barnwell State Park 223 State Park Rd *Web:* southcarolinaparks.com	Blackville	SC	29817	803-284-2212		565
Barnwell Whaley Patterson & Helms LLC 288 Meeting St *Web:* barnwell-whaley.com	Charleston	SC	29401	843-577-7700	577-7708	428
Baroan Technologies 385 Falmouth Ave *Web:* www.baroan.com	Elmwood Park	NJ	07407	201-796-0404		180
Barokas Public Relations 1012 First Ave 6th Fl *Web:* barokas.com	Seattle	WA	98104	206-264-8220		636
Barolo Grill 3030 E Sixth Ave *Web:* www.barologrilldenver.com	Denver	CO	80206	303-393-1040		671
Barometer Capital Management Inc 1 University Ave Ste 1800 *Web:* www.barometercapital.ca	Toronto	ON	M5J2P1	416-601-6888	601-9744	401
Baron & Associates Inc 6327 Chickaloon Dr *Web:* baronandassociatesinc.com	Mchenry	IL	60050	815-363-3366		390
Baron & Shelkin PC 291 Broadway Ste 1007 *Web:* baronandshelkinpc.com	New York	NY	10007	212-264-7500		41
Baron Barclay Bridge Supplies Inc 3600 Chamberlain Ln Ste 206 *TF:* 800-274-2221 ■ *Web:* www.baronbarclay.com	Louisville	KY	40241	502-426-0410	426-2044	95
Baron Brothers Nursery Inc 7568 Santa Rosa Rd *Web:* baronbrothers.com	Camarillo	CA	93012	805-484-0085		323
Baron Funds 767 Fifth Ave 49th Fl *TF:* 800-992-2766 ■ *Web:* www.baronfunds.com	New York	NY	10153	212-583-2000		528
Baron Manufacturing Company LLC 730 Baker St *TF:* 800-368-8585 ■ *Web:* www.baronsnaps.com	Itasca	IL	60143	630-628-9110		350
Baron Metal Industries Inc 101 Ashbridge Cir *Web:* www.baronmetal.com	Woodbridge	ON	L4L3R5	416-749-2111		480
Baron Oilfield Supply Ltd 9515-108 St *TF:* 888-532-5661 ■ *Web:* baronoilfield.ca	Grande Prairie	AB	T8V5R7	780-532-5661		358
Baron Services Inc 4930 Research Dr *Web:* www.baronservices.com	Huntsville	AL	35805	256-881-8811	881-8283	178-1
Baron Sign Manufacturing 900 W 13th St *Fax Area Code: 561 ■ TF: 800-531-9558 ■ Web: baronsign.com	Riviera Beach	FL	33404	800-531-9558	848-2270*	186
Baron Spices Inc 1440 Kentucky Ave *Web:* www.baronspices.com	Saint Louis	MO	63110	314-535-9020		297-8
Baron Telecommunications 1204 Rail Rd Ave Ste 101 *Web:* www.barontele.com	Bellingham	WA	98225	360-734-5082	734-1160	224
Barona Resort & Casino 1932 Wildcat Canyon Rd *TF:* 888-722-7662 ■ *Web:* www.barona.com	Lakeside	CA	92040	619-443-2300		133
Barone Galasso & Associates Inc 710 W Ivy *Web:* www.baronegalasso.com	San Diego	CA	92101	619-232-2100		653
Baronne Plaza Hotel 201 Baronne St *Web:* www.baronneplaza.com	New Orleans	LA	70112	504-522-0083		379
Baros and Company PC 1314 E Santara Blvd Ste 401 *Web:* www.barosandco.com	San Antonio	TX	78258	210-366-9444	340-9081	2
Barr & Barr 462 7th Ave 9th Fl *Web:* barrandbarr.com	New York	NY	10018	212-563-2330	967-2297	186
Barr Andy (Rep R - KY) 2430 Rayburn House Office Bldg *Web:* barr.house.gov	Washington	DC	20515	202-225-4706		342-2
Barr Engineering Co 4700 W 77th St *TF:* 800-632-2277 ■ *Web:* barr.com	Minneapolis	MN	55435	952-832-2600	832-2601	261
Barr Lake State Park 13401 Picadilly Rd *Web:* cpw.state.co.us	Brighton	CO	80603	303-659-6005		565
Barr Systems LLC 4500 NW 27th Ave *Web:* www.barrsystems.com	Gainesville	FL	32606	352-491-3100		174
Barrad & Shilling Accountancy Corp 6200 E Spring St Ste C *Web:* bsacpa.com	Long Beach	CA	90815	562-421-6950		2
Barragan Nanette (Rep D - CA) 1030 Longworth House Office Bldg *Web:* www.barragan.house.gov	Washington	DC	20515	202-225-8220		342-2
Barragan's 814 S Central Ave *Web:* barragansrestaurants.com	Glendale	CA	91204	818-243-1103		671
Barran Liebman LLP 601 SW Second Ave Ste 2300 *Web:* www.barran.com	Portland	OR	97204	503-228-0500		428
Barrancas National Cemetery Naval Air Stn 1 Cemetery Rd *Web:* www.cem.va.gov	Pensacola	FL	32508	850-453-4108	453-4635	136
Barrango 391 Forbes Blvd *Web:* www.barrango.com	South San Francisco	CA	94080	650-871-1931	872-3107	454
Barrantagh Investment Management Inc 100 Yonge St Ste 1700 *TF:* 833-246-8468 ■ *Web:* www.barrantagh.com	Toronto	ON	M5C2W1	416-868-6295		528
Barrasso John (Sen R - WY) 307 Dirksen Senate Office Bldg *TF:* 866-235-9553 ■ *Web:* www.barrasso.senate.gov	Washington	DC	20510	202-224-6441	224-1724	342-2
Barratt's Chapel & Museum 6362 Bay Rd *Web:* www.barrattschapel.org	Frederica	DE	19946	302-335-5544		520
Barre Opera House 6 N Main St PO Box 583 *Web:* barreoperahouse.org	Barre	VT	05641	802-476-8188	476-5648	572
Barre Y. Lane LLC 7231 Cold Harbor Rd PO Box 1856 *Web:* barreylane.com	Mechanicsville	VA	23111	804-723-4035		116
Barrel Service Co 105 S Pacific St *TF:* 800-437-9079 ■ *Web:* www.barrelservice.com	San Marcos	CA	92078	760-744-2122	744-5167	482
Barren County 117 N Public Sq Ste 3A *Web:* barrencounty.ky.gov	Glasgow	KY	42141	270-651-3338	651-2844	338
Barrent Group, The 3056 104th St *TF:* 866-318-4448 ■ *Web:* www.barrentgroup.com	Urbandale	IA	50322	866-318-4448		317
Barresi Financial 34 North St Ste 1 *Web:* barresifinancial.com	Presque Isle	ME	04769	207-764-5639		390
Barrett PO Box 1077 *Web:* www.barrett.net	Murfreesboro	TN	37133	615-896-2938	896-7313	401
Barrett & Co 42 Weybosset St Ste 2 *Web:* barrettandcompany.com	Providence	RI	02903	401-351-1000		690
Barrett & Company PLLC 4910 NW Camas Meadows Dr *Web:* www.barrett-cpa.com	Camas	WA	98607	360-210-5100		2
Barrett & McNagny LLP 215 E Berry St *Web:* www.barrettlaw.com	Fort Wayne	IN	46802	260-423-9551		428
Barrett Business Services Inc 8100 NE Pkwy Dr Ste 200 *NASDAQ: BBSI* ■ *TF:* 800-494-5669 ■ *Web:* mybbsi.com	Vancouver	WA	98662	360-828-0700	828-0701	631
Barrett Distribution Centers Inc 15 Freedom Way *TF:* 800-633-5800 ■ *Web:* www.barrettdistribution.com	Franklin	MA	02038	508-553-8800		803-1
Barrett Engineered Pumps Inc 1695 National Ave *Web:* www.barrettpump.com	San Diego	CA	92113	619-232-7867		641
Barrett Group LLC, The 100 Jefferson Blvd Ste 310 *TF:* 800-304-4473 ■ *Web:* www.careerchange.com	Warwick	RI	02888	800-304-4473		260
Barrett Industries Corp 3 Becker Farm Rd Ste 307 *Web:* www.barrettpaving.com	Roseland	NJ	07068	973-533-1001	533-1020	188-4
Barrett Oil Inc 2126 W Bay St *Web:* www.barrettoilsavannah.com	Savannah	GA	31415	912-234-7231	233-5609	316
Barrett Outdoor Communications Inc 381 Highland St *Web:* barrettoutdoor.com	West Haven	CT	06516	203-932-4601		8
Barrett Trailers Inc 1831 Hardcastle Blvd *Web:* www.barrett-trailers.com	Purcell	OK	73080	405-527-5050	527-3206	779
Barrett, Herman, Ragland & Schartz PA 10990 Quivira Rd Ste 160 *Web:* abbb.com	Overland Park	KS	66210	913-491-5080		2
Barrette Outdoor Living Inc 740 N Main St *Web:* www.barretteoutdoorliving.com	Bulls Gap	TN	37711	440-891-0790		596
Barrette-Chapais Ltee CP 248 Km 346 Rt 113 *Web:* www.barrette-chapais.qc.ca	Chapais	QC	G0W1H0	418-745-2545	745-3079	683
Barricade Books Inc 2037 Lemoine Ave Ste 362 *Web:* www.barricadebooks.com	Fort Lee	NJ	07024	201-944-7600		637-2
Barrick Gold Corp 161 Bay St Ste 3700 *TF:* 800-720-7415 ■ *Web:* www.barrick.com	Toronto	ON	M5J2S1	416-861-9911	861-2492	502
Barrie *Chamber of Commerce* 121 Commerce Park Dr Unit A *TF:* 888-220-2221 ■ *Web:* www.barriechamber.com	Barrie	ON	L4N8X1	705-721-5000	726-0973	137
Barrie Connolly & Associates 2188 Bluestem Ln *Web:* www.interiordesignbybca.com	Boise	ID	83706	208-345-6225	345-6233	393
Barrie House Coffee Co 4 Warehouse Ln *TF:* 800-876-2233 ■ *Web:* www.barriehousestore.com	Elmsford	NY	10523	800-876-2233		297-2
Barrie Public Library 60 Worsley St *TF:* 800-222-8477 ■ *Web:* www.barrielibrary.ca	Barrie	ON	L4M1L6	705-728-1010		435
Barriere Construction Company LLC 1 Galleria Blvd Ste 1650 *TF:* 800-234-5376 ■ *Web:* www.barriere.com	Metairie	LA	70001	504-581-7283	581-2270	188-4
Barrington Animal Hospital 216 S Northwest Hwy *Web:* barringtonanimalhospital.com	Barrington	IL	60010	847-381-4100		794

Name / Address	City	State	ZIP	Phone	Fax	Class
Barrington Area Chamber of Commerce 190 E James St *Web:* www.barringtonchamber.com	Barrington	IL	60010	847-381-2525	381-2540	139
Barrington Bank & Trust Company Na 201 S Hough St *Web:* www.barringtonbank.com	Barrington	IL	60010	847-842-4500	304-6697	70
Barrington Hotel & Suites 263 Shepherd of the Hills Expy *TF:* 800-760-8866 ■ *Web:* www.barringtonhotel.com	Branson	MO	65616	417-334-8866		379
Barrington Management Company Inc 10401 N Meridian St Ste 210 *Web:* www.barringtonmanagement.com	Indianapolis	IN	46290	317-581-0300	581-0900	652
Barrington Research Associates Inc 161 N Clark St Ste 2950 *TF:* 800-233-6205 ■ *Web:* brai.com	Chicago	IL	60601	312-634-6000	634-6350	401
Barrington's 7822 Fairview Rd *Web:* barringtonsrestaurant.com	Charlotte	NC	28226	704-364-5755		671
Barrio Cafe 2814 N 16th St *Web:* www.barriocafe.com	Phoenix	AZ	85006	602-636-0240		671
Barrio Logan College Institute 1625 Newton Ave Ste 200 *Web:* www.blci.org	San Diego	CA	92113	619-232-4686		196
Barrios Technology Inc 16441 Space Center Blvd Ste B-100 *Web:* www.barrios.com	Houston	TX	77058	281-280-1900	280-1901	668
Barris, Sott, Denn & Driker PLLC 333 W Fort St Ste 1200 *TF:* 877-529-8750 ■ *Web:* www.bsdd.com	Detroit	MI	48226	313-965-9725		428
Barrister Digital Solutions 1700 K St NW Ste B100 *Web:* barristerdigital.com	Washington	DC	20006	202-289-7279	289-6443	113
Barrister Executive Suites Inc 475 Washington Blvd *Web:* www.barrister-suites.com	Marina del Rey	CA	90292	800-576-0744		5
BarristerBooks Inc 615 Florida St *TF:* 866-808-5635 ■ *Web:* www.barristerbooks.com	Lawrence	KS	66044	866-808-5635		95
Barron & Newburger PC 7320 N Mopac Expy Ste 400 *TF:* 866-476-9103 ■ *Web:* bn-lawyers.com	Austin	TX	78731	512-476-9103	279-0310	428
Barron & Redding PA 220 Mckenzie Ave *Web:* barronredding.com	Panama City	FL	32401	850-785-7454	785-2999	41
Barron County Register Deeds 335 E Monroe Ave *Web:* www.barroncountywi.gov	Barron	WI	54812	715-537-6210	537-6817	338
Barron Electric Co-op 1434 State Hwy 25 N *TF:* 800-322-1008 ■ *Web:* www.barronelectric.com	Barron	WI	54812	715-537-3171		245
Barron Motor Supply Inc 1850 McCloud Pl NE *Web:* barronmotor.com	Cedar Rapids	IA	52402	319-393-6220		61
Barron Smith Daugert PLLC 300 N Commercial St *Web:* barronsmithlaw.com	Bellingham	WA	98225	360-733-0212		41
Barron's Educational Series Inc 250 Wireless Blvd *TF:* 800-645-3476 ■ *Web:* www.barronseduc.com	Hauppauge	NY	11788	631-434-3311	434-3723	637-2
Barron's Wholesale Tire Inc 1302 Eastport Rd *Web:* www.barrontire.com	Jacksonville	FL	32218	904-696-1200		755
Barrow & Grimm PC 110 W Seventh St Ste 900 *Web:* barrowgrimm.com	Tulsa	OK	74119	918-584-1600	585-2444	41
Barrow County 30 N Broad St *Web:* www.barrowga.org	Winder	GA	30680	770-307-3000	307-3141	338
Barrow County Chamber of Commerce PO Box 456 *Web:* barrowchamber.com	Winder	GA	30680	770-867-9444	867-6366	139
Barrow Hanley Mewhinney & Strauss LLC 2200 Ross Ave 31st Fl *TF:* 800-543-0407 ■ *Web:* www.barrowhanley.com	Dallas	TX	75201	214-665-1900		401
Barrow Industries Inc 3 Edgewater Dr **Fax Area Code:* 781 ■ *TF:* 800-496-8367 ■ *Web:* www.barrowindustries.com	Norwood	MA	02062	800-496-8367	440-2683*	594
Barrow News-Journal 122 W Athens St *Web:* www.mainstreetnews.com	Winder	GA	30680	770-867-7557		532-4
Barrow Utilities & Electric Co-opeartive Inc (BUECI) 1295 Agvik St PO Box 449 *Web:* www.bueci.org	Barrow	AK	99723	907-852-6166		245
Barry Associates Inc 17 Halls Mill Rd **Fax Area Code:* 978	Preston	CT	06365	860-889-8943	352-5955*	189-10
Barry Better Menswear 125 John W Morrow Pkwy Ste 242B *Web:* www.barrysmenswear.com	Gainesville	GA	30501	770-534-7685		155-12
Barry Bunker Chevrolet Inc 1307 N Wabash Ave *TF:* 866-603-8625 ■ *Web:* www.barrybunker.com	Marion	IN	46952	866-726-5519		57
Barry Callebaut USA LLC 400 Industrial Park Rd *TF:* 866-443-0460 ■ *Web:* www.barry-callebaut.com	Saint Albans	VT	05478	802-524-9711	524-5148	296-8
Barry County 220 W State St *TF:* 888-876-0993 ■ *Web:* barrycounty.org	Hastings	MI	49058	269-945-1290	945-0209	338
Barry County Advertiser 904 W St *Web:* www.4bcaonline.com	Cassville	MO	65625	417-847-4475	847-4523	627
Barry County Clerk 700 Main St Ste 3 *Web:* barrycountycollector.com	Cassville	MO	65625	417-847-2113		338
Barry Electric Co-op 4015 Main St PO Box 307 *TF:* 866-847-2333 ■ *Web:* barryelectric.com	Cassville	MO	65625	866-847-2333		245
Barry Financial Group Inc, The 102 NE 2nd St Ste 168 **Fax Area Code:* 816	Boca Raton	FL	33432	561-368-9120	931-8200*	401
Barry I. Finkel PA 12 Se Seventh St Ste 602 *Web:* bfinkelpa.com	Fort Lauderdale	FL	33301	954-776-1414	776-3833	41
Barry Industries Inc 60 Walton St *Web:* www.barryind.com	Attleboro	MA	02703	508-226-3350		253
Barry Road Animal Hospital Inc 3911 Northwest Barry Rd *Web:* barryroadanimalhospital.com	Kansas City	MO	64154	816-436-6700		794
Barry S. Franklin & Associates PA 3590 Mystic Pointe Dr *Web:* barrysfranklin.com	Aventura	FL	33180	305-940-4000	940-0940	41
Barry S. Silver PC 302 Saunders Rd Ste 200 *Web:* barrysilverlaw.com	Riverwoods	IL	60015	847-480-2070	480-2074	41
Barry Trucking Inc 400 W Marquette Ave *Web:* www.barrytrucking.com	Oak Creek	WI	53154	414-274-6150		780
Barry University 11300 NE Second Ave *TF:* 800-756-6000 ■ *Web:* www.barry.edu	Miami Shores	FL	33161	305-899-3000	899-2971	166
Barry W. James & Associates LLP 721 E Texas Ave *Web:* www.bwjames.com	Baytown	TX	77520	281-420-1040	420-2040	734
Barry's Bootcamp 1106 N La Cienega Blvd *Web:* www.barrys.com	West Hollywood	CA	90069	310-360-6262		354
Barrymore Theatre 2090 Atwood Ave *Web:* barrymorelive.com	Madison	WI	53704	608-241-8633		572
Barry-owen Company Inc 5625 Smithway St *TF:* 800-682-6682 ■ *Web:* www.barryowen.com	Los Angeles	CA	90040	323-724-4800	724-4996	292
Barry-Wehmiller Companies Inc *Accraply Div* 3580 Holly Ln N *TF:* 800-328-3997 ■ *Web:* accraply.com	Plymouth	MN	55447	763-557-1313	519-9656	547
Barry-Wehmiller Group Inc 8020 Forsyth Blvd *Web:* www.barrywehmiller.com	Saint Louis	MO	63105	314-862-8000	862-8858	547
Barse Jewelery 501 Main St *Web:* www.barse.com	Fort Worth	TX	76102	817-820-0404		411
Barshay Software Inc 900 Lenora St Ste 805 *Web:* barshaysoftware.com	Seattle	WA	98121	206-826-4231		177
Barshop & Oles Company Inc 901 S Mopac Expwy Barton Oaks Plz II Ste 550 *Web:* www.barshop-oles.com	Austin	TX	78701	512-477-1212		652
BARSKA Optics 1721 Wright Ave *TF:* 888-666-6769 ■ *Web:* www.barska.com	La Verne	CA	91750	888-666-6769		543
Barson Group PA 60 E Main St PO Box 8018 *Web:* barsongroup.com	Somerville	NJ	08876	908-203-9800		2
Barstow Community College 2700 Barstow Rd *Web:* barstow.edu	Barstow	CA	92311	760-252-2411	252-1875	162
Barstow School, The 11511 State Line Rd *Web:* www.barstowschool.org	Kansas City	MO	64114	816-942-3255		685
Bart Morrill CPA PC 24 S 200 E PO Box 356 *Web:* www.morrillcpa.com	Roosevelt	UT	84066	435-725-1900		2
Bar-T-5 Covered Wagon Cook Out & Wild West Show 812 Cache Creek Dr *Web:* www.bart5.com	Jackson	WY	83001	307-733-5386	739-9183	671
Barta - Schoenewald Inc 3805 Calle Tecate *Web:* www.a-m-c.com	Camarillo	CA	93012	805-389-1935	389-1165	518
Bartech Group 17199 N Laurel Park Dr Ste 224 *TF:* 800-828-4410 ■ *Web:* www.bartechgroup.com	Livonia	MI	48152	734-953-5050		721
Bartell & Bartell Ltd 432 Rolling Rdg Dr *Web:* bartellbartell.com	State College	PA	16801	814-861-6606		463
Bartell Hotels 4875 N Harbor Dr *TF:* 800-345-9995 ■ *Web:* www.bartellhotels.com	San Diego	CA	92106	619-224-1556		707
Bartell Machinery Systems LLC 6321 Elmer Hill Rd *TF:* 800-537-8473 ■ *Web:* bartellmachinery.com	Rome	NY	13440	315-336-7600	336-0947	494
Bartells, Parman & Pease Ltd 613 Forest St *TF:* 800-368-1801 ■ *Web:* bartellslaw.com	Wausau	WI	54403	715-848-1801	848-3013	41
Bartels, Sherman & Wallace 316 S Church St *Web:* bartelslawfirm.com	Jonesboro	AR	72401	870-972-5000		41
Bartelson Trucking LLC 8705 Canyon Rd E Ste B *Web:* bartelsontransport.com	Puyallup	WA	98371	253-845-6962	845-6908	311
Bartender Magazine PO Box 158 *Web:* bartender.com	Liberty Corner	NJ	07938	908-766-6006	766-6607	457-21
Bartending Academy 1250 E Apache Blvd Ste 108 *Web:* www.phoenixbartendingschool.com	Tempe	AZ	85281	480-921-9925		167-3
Bartending Academy of Tacoma 1036 S Sprague Ave *Web:* www.tacomabaracademy.com	Tacoma	WA	98405	253-474-0330		167-3
Bartending Schools of America Inc 321 E St Charles Rd *Web:* www.bartending.org	Villa Park	IL	60181	630-833-3233		242
Barter Depot 1107 W Veterans Hwy *Web:* barterdepot.com	Jackson	NJ	08527	732-833-2273		750
Barter Theatre 127 W Main St *Web:* bartertheatre.com	Abingdon	VA	24210	276-628-3991	619-3335	749
Barth Ballenger & Lewis LLP 205 N Irby St PO Box 107 *Web:* bbllawsc.com	Florence	SC	29501	843-662-6301	664-8384	41
Barth Electric Company Inc 1934 N Illinois St *TF:* 800-666-6226 ■ *Web:* www.barthelectric.com	Indianapolis	IN	46202	317-924-6226	923-6938	189-4
Barth Industries Company LP 12650 Brookpark Rd *Web:* barthindustries.com	Cleveland	OH	44130	216-267-1950	267-1966	454
Bartha Visual 600 N Cassady Ave *TF:* 800-513-1209 ■ *Web:* bartha.com	Columbus	OH	43219	800-363-2698		23
Bartholomew County Public Library 536 Fifth St *TF:* 800-685-0524 ■ *Web:* www.mybcpl.org	Columbus	IN	47201	812-379-1255		434-3
Bartholomew County REMC 1697 W Deaver Rd *Web:* www.bcremc.com	Columbus	IN	47201	812-379-1670		338

Name / Address	City	State	Zip	Phone	Fax	Class
Bartizan Corp 217 Riverdale Ave *TF:* 800-899-2278 ■ *Web:* bartizan.com	Yonkers	NY	10705	914-965-7977	965-7746	534
Bartko, Zankel, Bunzel & Miller (BZBM) 1 Embarcadero Ctr Ste 800 *Web:* www.bzbm.com	San Francisco	CA	94111	415-956-1900	956-1152	445
Bartle & Gibson Company Ltd 13475 Ft Rd NW *TF:* 800-661-5615 ■ *Web:* www.bartlegibson.com	Edmonton	AB	T5A1C6	780-472-2850		612
Bartleby Press PO Box 858 *TF:* 800-953-9929 ■ *Web:* www.bartlebythepublisher.com	Savage	MD	20763	301-589-5831	725-0333	637-2
Bartlesville Area Chamber of Commerce 201 S Keeler Ave *Web:* www.bartlesville.com	Bartlesville	OK	74003	918-336-8708	337-0216	139
Bartlesville Public Library 600 S Johnstone *Web:* www.bartlesville.lib.ok.us	Bartlesville	OK	74003	918-338-4161		434-3
Bartlett & Co 600 Vine St Ste 2100 *TF:* 800-800-4612 ■ *Web:* bartlett1898.com	Cincinnati	OH	45202	513-621-4612	621-6462	401
Bartlett & West Engineers Inc 1200 SW Executive Dr *TF:* 888-200-6464 ■ *Web:* www.bartlettwest.com	Topeka	KS	66615	785-272-2252		261
Bartlett and Co 4900 Main St Ste 12 *TF:* 800-888-6300 ■ *Web:* www.bartlettandco.com	Kansas City	MO	64112	816-753-6300		296-23
Bartlett Arboretum & Gardens 151 Brookdale Rd *Web:* www.bartlettarboretum.org	Stamford	CT	06903	203-322-6971	595-9168	97
Bartlett Area Chamber of Commerce 335 S Main St *Web:* www.bartlettareachamber.com	Bartlett	IL	60103	630-830-0324	830-9724	139
Bartlett Area Chamber of Commerce 2969 Elmore Park Rd *Web:* www.bartlettchamber.org	Bartlett	TN	38134	901-372-9457	372-9488	139
Bartlett Dairy Inc 105-03 150th St *Web:* www.bartlettny.com	Jamaica	NY	11435	718-658-2299	725-2527	296-27
Bartlett Electric Co-opeartive Inc 27492 Texas 95 *TF:* 888-469-8482 ■ *Web:* bartlettec.coop	Bartlett	TX	76511	254-527-3551	527-3221	245
Bartlett High School 701 W Schick Rd *Web:* www.u-46.org	Bartlett	IL	60103	630-372-4700		685
Bartlett Instrument Company Inc 1032 Ave H *Web:* bartinst.com	Fort Madison	IA	52627	319-372-8366	372-5560	248
Bartling Insurance Group Inc 1176 Main St Ste A1 *Web:* biginsure.com	Irvine	CA	92614	714-979-6299		390
Bartolotta Ristorante diMare 3131 Las Vegas Blvd S *Web:* www.wynnlasvegas.com	Las Vegas	NV	89109	702-770-9966		671
Barton & Loguidice DPC 443 Electronics Pkwy *TF:* 800-724-1070 ■ *Web:* www.bartonandloguidice.com	Liverpool	NY	13088	315-457-5200	451-0052	261
Barton Air Fabrications Inc 394 Sherman Ave N *Web:* www.bartonairfab.com	Hamilton	ON	L8L6N7	905-524-2234	526-6580	454
Barton Brescome Inc 69 Defco Park Rd *TF:* 800-922-4840 ■ *Web:* www.brescomebarton.com	North Haven	CT	06473	203-239-4901		80-3
Barton Brimm Law Firm PA 1500 Hwy 17 Business N The Courtyard Ste 214 *Web:* bartonbrimm.com	Surfside Beach	SC	29576	803-256-6582		41
Barton College PO Box 5000 *TF:* 800-345-4973 ■ *Web:* www.barton.edu	Wilson	NC	27893	252-399-6300	399-6572	166
Barton Cotton Inc 3030 Waterview Ave **Fax Area Code: 410* ■ *TF:* 800-638-4652 ■ *Web:* www.bartoncotton.com	Baltimore	MD	21230	800-348-1102	536-0491*	317
Barton County 1400 Main St Rm 107 *Web:* www.bartoncounty.org	Great Bend	KS	67530	620-793-1800	793-1990	338
Barton County 1004 Gulf St *Web:* www.bartoncounty.com	Lamar	MO	64759	417-682-3529	682-4100	338
Barton County Community College 245 NE 30 Rd *TF:* 800-722-6842 ■ *Web:* bartonccc.edu	Great Bend	KS	67530	620-792-2701	786-1160	162
Barton County Electric Co-op 91 US-160 *TF:* 800-286-5636 ■ *Web:* www.bartonelectric.com	Lamar	MO	64759	417-682-5636		245
Barton County Feeders Inc 1164 SE 40th Rd *Web:* www.ilsbeef.com	Ellinwood	KS	67526	620-564-2200		10-1
Barton Heights Veterinary Hospital 117 Terrace Dr *Web:* www.bartonheights.com	Stroudsburg	PA	18360	570-424-6773		794
Barton Malow 26500 American Dr *Web:* www.bartonmalow.com	Southfield	MI	48034	248-436-5000	436-5001	186
Barton Solvents Inc 1920 NE Broadway Ave *TF:* 800-728-6488 ■ *Web:* www.barsol.com	Des Moines	IA	50313	515-265-7998	265-0259	146
Barton Staffing Solutions Inc 723 Aurora Ave *Web:* www.bartonstaffing.com	Aurora	IL	60505	630-897-3591	897-3935	260
Barton Supply Inc 1260 Marlkress Rd PO Box 2240 *Web:* www.bartonsupply.com	Cherry Hill	NJ	08034	856-429-6500		612
Barton W. Stone Christian Home 873 Grove St *TF:* 800-397-1313 ■ *Web:* www.heritageofcare.com	Jacksonville	IL	62650	217-479-3400	243-8553	450
Barton Warnock Visitor Ctr PO Box 375 HC 70 *Web:* tpwd.texas.gov	Terlingua	TX	79852	432-424-3327		565
Barton, Klugman & Oetting LLP 350 S Grand Ave Ste 2200 *Web:* www.bkolaw.com	Los Angeles	CA	90071	213-621-4000	625-1832	428
Bartons Club 93 1002 US Hwy 93 *Web:* www.bartonsclub93.com	Jackpot	NV	89825	775-755-2341		452
Bartow County 135 W Cherokee Ave *TF:* 800-715-4225 ■ *Web:* www.bartowga.org	Cartersville	GA	30120	770-387-5030	387-5023	338
Bartow County Public Library 429 W Main St *Web:* bartowlibrary.org	Cartersville	GA	30120	770-382-4203		434-3
Bartow Ford Co 2800 US Hwy 98 N *TF:* 800-303-4016 ■ *Web:* www.bartowford.com	Bartow	FL	33830	800-533-0425		57
Bartow-Pell Mansion Museum Pelham Bay Pk 895 Shore Rd *Web:* www.bartowpellmansionmuseum.org	Bronx	NY	10464	718-885-1461		520
Bartram's Garden 54th St & Lindbergh Blvd *Web:* www.bartramsgarden.org	Philadelphia	PA	19143	215-729-5281	729-1047	97
Barts Water Sports 7581 E 800 N *TF:* 800-348-5016 ■ *Web:* www.bartswatersports.com	North Webster	IN	46555	574-834-7666		711
Bartush-Schnitzius Foods Co 1137 N Kealy St *Web:* www.bartushfoods.com	Lewisville	TX	75057	972-219-1270		297-8
Baruch College 55 Lexington Ave at 24th St *Web:* www.baruch.cuny.edu	New York	NY	10010	646-312-3870	312-1362	166
Barudan America Inc 30901 Carter St Ste A *Web:* barudanamerica.com	Solon	OH	44139	440-248-8770		744
Bas Relief Publishing Group PO Box 645 *Web:* www.basrelief.org	Lewisburg	PA	17837	304-832-6647		637-2
Basalite Concrete Products LLC 605 Industrial Way *TF:* 800-776-6690 ■ *Web:* www.basalite.com	Dixon	CA	95620	707-678-1901	678-6268	183
Basalt Regional Library 14 Midland Ave *Web:* www.basaltlibrary.org	Basalt	CO	81621	970-927-4311		434-3
Basch Subscriptions Inc 10 Ferry St Ste 429 *Web:* www.basch.com	Concord	NH	03301	603-229-0662		366
Basco Shower Enclosures 7201 Snider Rd *TF:* 800-543-1938 ■ *Web:* bascoshowerdoor.com	Mason	OH	45040	513-573-1900		329
Bascom Maple Farms Inc 56 Sugar House Rd *Web:* www.bascommaple.com	Alstead	NH	03602	603-835-6361	835-2455	297-2
Bascom Mutual Telephone Co 5990 W Tiffin St *TF:* 800-743-5707 ■ *Web:* www.bascomtelephone.com	Bascom	OH	44809	419-937-2202	937-2299	224
Bascom Palmer Eye Institute 900 NW 17th St *TF:* 800-329-7000 ■ *Web:* umiamihealth.org	Miami	FL	33136	305-326-6000		374-7
Bascom-Turner Instrument 111 Downey St *TF:* 800-225-3298 ■ *Web:* www.bascomturner.com	Norwood	MA	02062	781-769-9660		612
BASD (Boyertown Area School District) 911 Montgomery Ave *Web:* www.boyertownasd.org	Boyertown	PA	19512	610-367-6031	369-7620	186
Base Camp Franchising 39 E Eagle Ridge Dr Ste 100 *TF:* 855-637-3211 ■ *Web:* uptowncheapskatefranchise.com	North Salt Lake	UT	84054	855-637-3211		157-1
Base Construction Inc 6980 Knott Ave Ste J *Web:* www.baseconstructionca.com	Buena Park	CA	90621	949-387-3471		194
Base One International Corp 44 E 12th St Ste 3B *Web:* www.boic.com	New York	NY	10003	212-673-2511		809
Base One Technologies Inc 30 Church St Ste 28 *Web:* www.base-one.com	New Rochelle	NY	10801	914-633-0200		180
Baseball America Magazine 4319 S Alston Ave Ste 103 *TF:* 800-845-2726 ■ *Web:* www.baseballamerica.com	Durham	NC	27713	800-845-2726		457-20
Baseball Express Inc 5750 NW Pkwy Ste 100 *TF:* 800-937-4824 ■ *Web:* www.baseballexpress.com	San Antonio	TX	78249	210-348-7000	525-9339	711
Baseball Reliquary, The PO Box 1850 *Web:* www.baseballreliquary.org	Monrovia	CA	91017	626-791-7647		522
Basecamp LLC 400 N May St Ste 301 *Web:* basecamp.com	Chicago	IL	60607	312-281-5333		177
Baseline Data Systems Inc 3655 Torrance Blvd Ste 255 *TF:* 800-429-5325 ■ *Web:* www.oa1mm.com	Torrance	CA	90503	310-214-8528		177
Baseline Engineering Corp 1950 Ford St *Web:* baselinecorp.com	Golden	CO	80401	303-940-9966		261
Baseline Tool Company Inc 8458 N Baseline Rd *Web:* baselinetool.com	Wawaka	IN	46794	260-761-4932	761-2104	567
BASF Corp 100 Campus Dr *TF:* 800-526-1072 ■ *Web:* www.basf.com	Florham Park	NJ	07932	973-245-6000		143
BASF Corporation Construction Systems 889 Valley Pk Dr *TF:* 800-433-9517 ■ *Web:* www.master-builders-solutions.com	Shakopee	MN	55379	952-496-6000		3
Bash Contracting Inc 189 Ufs Rd *Web:* bashcontracting.com	Clearfield	PA	16830	814-765-1531		752
Bash, The 50 Washington St *TF:* 866-342-9794 ■ *Web:* www.thebash.com	Norwalk	CT	06854	866-342-9794		387
Bashas Inc 22402 S Bashas Rd *TF:* 800-755-7292 ■ *Web:* www.bashas.com	Chandler	AZ	85248	480-895-9350		345
Bashlin Industries Inc PO Box 867 *Web:* www.bashlin.com	Grove City	PA	16127	724-458-8340	458-8342	351
Basi Italia 811 Highland St *Web:* www.basi-italia.com	Columbus	OH	43215	614-294-7383		671
Basic Adhesives Inc 60 Webro Rd *Web:* www.basicadhesives.com	Clifton	NJ	07012	973-614-9000		3
Basic Aluminum Castings Co 1325 E 168th St *Web:* basicaluminum.com	Cleveland	OH	44110	216-481-5606	481-7031	308
Basic Carbide Corp 900 Main St *TF:* 800-426-4291 ■ *Web:* www.basiccarbide.com	Lowber	PA	15660	724-446-1630	446-1656	1
Basic Commerce & Industries Inc 303 Harper Dr *Web:* www.bcisse.com	Moorestown	NJ	08057	856-778-1660		261
Basic Components Inc 1201 S Second Ave *TF:* 800-452-1780 ■ *Web:* www.basiccomp.com	Mansfield	TX	76063	817-473-7224	473-3388	191-2
Basic Concepts Inc 1310 Harris Bridge Rd *TF:* 800-285-4203 ■ *Web:* www.basicconcepts.com	Anderson	SC	29621	800-285-4203		287

				Phone	Fax	Class
Basic Food Flavors Inc 3950 E Craig Rd *Web:* www.basicfoodflavors.com	North Las Vegas	NV	89030	702-643-0043		275
Basic Home Infusion 1401 Valley Rd *TF:* 888-822-7428 ■ *Web:* www.basichomeinfusion.com	Wayne	NJ	07470	201-475-0500	475-9630	363
Basic ISP PO Box 511 *TF:* 800-456-3118 ■ *Web:* www.basicisp.net	Mount Vernon	OH	43050	800-456-3118		681
Basic Metals Inc W180 Nn11819 River Ln *TF:* 800-989-1996 ■ *Web:* basicmetals.com	Germantown	WI	53022	262-255-9034		492
Basic Pay LLC 231 W 29th St Ste 503 *Web:* www.basicpayllc.com	New York	NY	10001	212-684-8827	684-6036	570
Basic Plumbing Inc 1409 Mechanical Blvd *Web:* www.basicplumbinginc.com	Garner	NC	27529	919-662-1082		610
Basic Resources Inc 928 12th St Ste 700 PO Box 3191	Modesto	CA	95354	209-521-9771		188-4
Basic Rubber & Plastics Co 8700 Boulder Ct *Web:* www.basicrubber.com	Walled Lake	MI	48390	248-360-7400	360-7101	326
Basic Software Systems 905 N Kings Hwy *TF:* 800-252-4476 ■ *Web:* www.basic-software.com	Texarkana	TX	75501	903-792-4421		179
Basic Systems Inc 9255 Cadiz Rd *Web:* www.basic-systems.com	Cambridge	OH	43725	740-432-3001		192
Basil *Basil Thai Restaurant* 460 King St *Web:* www.eatatbasil.com	Charleston	SC	29403	843-724-3490		671
Basil's Restaurant & Tapas Bar 2985 Grandview Ave NE *Web:* www.basils.net	Atlanta	GA	30305	404-233-9755		671
Basilica of Saint Mary of the Immaculate Conception, The 232 Chapel St *Web:* www.basilicaofsaintmary.org	Norfolk	VA	23504	757-622-4487	625-7969	50-1
Basilica of the Assumption 409 Cathedral St *Web:* americasfirstcathedral.org	Baltimore	MD	21201	410-727-3565		50-1
Basilius Inc 1707 Cherry St *Web:* www.basilius.com	Toledo	OH	43615	419-536-5810		604
Basin Coordinated Health Care Inc 210 N Orchard Ave *TF:* 800-461-1218 ■ *Web:* www.basincoordinated.com	Farmington	NM	87401	505-324-8269	324-8387	363
Basin Disposal Inc 2021 N Commercial Ave *TF:* 888-880-0086 ■ *Web:* basindisposal.com	Pasco	WA	99301	509-547-2476		804
Basin Electric Power Co-op 1717 E Interstate Ave *Web:* www.basinelectric.com	Bismarck	ND	58503	701-223-0441	557-5110	245
Basin Harbor Club 4800 Basin Harbor Rd *TF:* 800-622-4000 ■ *Web:* www.basinharbor.com	Vergennes	VT	05491	802-475-2311	475-6545	669
Basin Holdings US LLC 200 Pk Ave Ste 5800 *Web:* basinholdings.com	New York	NY	10166	212-695-7376		256
Basin Pipe & Metal 6960 Us Hwy 70 N *Web:* www.basinpipeandmetal.com	Alamogordo	NM	88310	575-437-6272		492
Basin Printing 1437 E 2nd Ave *Web:* basinprinting.com	Durango	CO	81301	970-247-5212		627
Basin Radio Network 2810 S Dr *Web:* www.basinsradio.com	Gillette	WY	82718	307-686-2242	686-7736	645-141
Basin Tire & Auto Inc 2700 E Main St **Fax Area Code:* 970 ■ *TF:* 800-832-9832 ■ *Web:* directoryplus.com	Farmington	NM	87402	505-326-2231	385-2460*	62-5
Basis International Ltd 5901 Jefferson St NE *TF:* 800-423-1394 ■ *Web:* www.basis.com	Albuquerque	NM	87109	505-345-5232	345-5082	178-12
Basis Technology Corp 1 Alewife Ctr *TF:* 800-697-2062 ■ *Web:* www.basistech.com	Cambridge	MA	02140	617-386-2000		177
Baskerville-Donovan Inc 449 W Main St *Web:* www.baskervilledonovan.com	Pensacola	FL	32502	850-438-9661		261
Baskin Auto Truck & Tractor Inc 1844 Hwy 51 S *TF:* 877-476-2626 ■ *Web:* www.baskintrandtr.com	Covington	TN	38019	901-476-2626	476-2658	57
Baskow & Assoc 2948 E Russell Rd *Web:* www.baskow.com	Las Vegas	NV	89120	702-733-7818	733-2052	772
Basler Electric Co 12570 Rt 143 *Web:* www.basler.com	Highland	IL	62249	618-654-2341	654-2351	203
Basler Flight Service Wittman Regional Airport PO Box 2464 *TF:* 800-564-6322 ■ *Web:* baslerflightservice.com	Oshkosh	WI	54903	920-236-7827	236-7833	63
Basler Inc 855 Springdale Dr Ste 203 *Web:* www.baslerweb.com	Exton	PA	19341	610-280-0171	280-7608	392
Basler Turbo Conversions LLC 255 W 35th St *Web:* www.baslerturbo.com	Oshkosh	WI	54902	920-236-7820	235-0381	24
Basmat Inc 1531 240th St *Web:* www.mcstarlite.com	Harbor City	CA	90710	310-325-2063	325-9682	697
Basque Museum & Cultural Ctr 611 W Grove St *Web:* basquemuseum.eus	Boise	ID	83702	208-343-2671		520
Bass & Abrams Pc 109 Grand St *Web:* bassabramslaw.com	Croton-on-Hudson	NY	10520	914-271-9529		41
Bass & Associates PC 3936 E Ft Lowell Rd Ste 200 *TF:* 855-533-1107 ■ *Web:* www.bass-associates.com	Tucson	AZ	85712	520-577-1544	784-5958	41
Bass Computers Inc (BCI) 10558 Bissonnet St *TF:* 800-789-3012 ■ *Web:* www.basscomputers.com	Houston	TX	77099	281-776-6700	776-6733	174
Bass Doherty & Finks PC 40 Soldiers Field Pl *Web:* www.bassdoherty.com	Boston	MA	02135	617-787-5551		41
Bass Karen (Rep D - CA) 2059 Rayburn House Office Bldg *Web:* bass.house.gov	Washington	DC	20515	202-225-7084	225-2422	342-2
Bass Performance Hall 330 East 4th St *TF:* 877-212-4280 ■ *Web:* www.basshall.com	Fort Worth	TX	76102	817-212-4300	810-9294	572
Bass Pro Shops Outdoor World 1935 S Campbell Ave *Web:* www.basspro.com	Springfield	MO	65807	417-887-7334	885-0072	711
Bass River State Forest 762 Stage Rd *Web:* www.njparksandforests.org	Tuckerton	NJ	08087	609-296-1114		565
Bass, Nixon & Kennedy Inc 6310 Chapel Hill Rd 250 *Web:* www.bnkinc.com	Raleigh	NC	27607	919-851-4422		261
Bassett Furniture Industries Inc 3525 Fairystone Pk Hwy PO Box 626 *NASDAQ: BSET* ■ *TF:* 877-525-7070 ■ *Web:* www.bassettfurniture.com	Bassett	VA	24055	276-629-6000		319-2
Bassett Mechanical 1215 Hyland Ave *TF:* 800-236-2500 ■ *Web:* www.bassettmechanical.com	Kaukauna	WI	54130	920-759-2500	759-2525	189-10
Bassett Mirror Company Inc PO Box 627 *Web:* www.bassettmirror.com	Bassett	VA	24055	276-629-3341		332
Bassett, Discoe, Mcmains & Kargozar 1551 N Tustin Ave Ste 900 *Web:* wdbmlaw.com	Santa Ana	CA	92705	714-542-5400		41
Bassham Foods Inc 5409 Hemphill St *Web:* www.basshamfoods.com	Fort Worth	TX	76115	817-429-6910		297-8
Bassler Energy Services Inc 8050 Hwy 21 W *Web:* basslerenergyservices.com	Caldwell	TX	77836	979-535-4593		311
Bassmaster 3500 Blue Lake Dr Ste 330 *TF:* 877-227-7872 ■ *Web:* www.bassmaster.com	Birmingham	AL	35243	877-227-7872		457-20
Bass-Mollett Publishers Inc 507 Monroe St *TF:* 800-851-4046 ■ *Web:* www.bass-mollett.com	Greenville	IL	62246	800-851-4046		637-10
Basta 2195 Broad St *Web:* www.bastaonbroad.com	Cranston	RI	02905	401-461-2300		671
Bastian Co 15 Eagle St *Web:* www.bastiancompany.com	Phelps	NY	14532	315-548-2300		229
Bastian Solutions 10585 N Meridian St 3rd Fl *TF:* 800-772-0464 ■ *Web:* www.bastiansolutions.com	Indianapolis	IN	46290	317-575-9992	575-8596	55
Bastian Trucking Inc 440 S Main *TF:* 800-452-5126 ■ *Web:* www.bastiantrucking.com	Aurora	UT	84620	435-529-7453		780
Bastion Infrastructure Group 801 - 1 Richmond St W *Web:* www.bastionfunds.com	Toronto	ON	M5H3W4	416-583-2600		528
Bastion Technologies Inc 17625 El Camino Real Ste 330 *Web:* www.bastiontechnologies.com	Houston	TX	77058	281-283-9330	283-9333	256
Bastrop Chamber of Commerce 927 Main St *Web:* www.bastropchamber.com	Bastrop	TX	78602	512-303-0558		139
Bastrop County 804 Pecan St *Web:* www.co.bastrop.tx.us	Bastrop	TX	78602	512-581-4000		338
Bastrop Isd 906 Farm St *Web:* www.bisdtx.org	Bastrop	TX	78602	512-772-7100		685
Bastrop State Park 3005 Hwy 21 E *Web:* tpwd.texas.gov	Bastrop	TX	78602	512-321-2101		565
Bastrop-Morehouse Parish Chamber of Commerce 110 N Franklin St *Web:* bastroplacoc.org	Bastrop	LA	71220	318-281-3794		139
Bastyr University 14500 Juanita Dr NE *Web:* www.bastyr.edu	Kenmore	WA	98028	425-602-3000	823-6222	786
BasWare 60 Long Ridge Rd *Web:* www.basware.com	Stamford	CT	06902	203-487-7900		177
BAT Associates Inc 5151 Brook Hollow Pkwy Ste 250 *Web:* www.batassociates.com	Norcross	GA	30071	770-242-3908		256
BAT Conservation Intl (BCI) 500 N Capital of Texas Hwy *TF:* 800-538-2287 ■ *Web:* www.batcon.org	Austin	TX	78746	512-327-9721	327-9724	48-3
Batavia Container Inc 1400 Paramount Pkwy *Web:* www.bataviacontainer.com	Batavia	IL	60510	630-879-2100		100
Batavia Public Library Foundation 10 S Batavia Ave *Web:* www.batavia.lib.il.us	Batavia	IL	60510	630-879-1393	879-9118	434-3
Batavia VA Medical Ctr 222 Richmond Ave *Web:* www.buffalo.va.gov	Batavia	NY	14020	585-297-1000		374-8
Batching Systems Inc 50 Jibsail Dr *Web:* www.batchingsystems.com	Prince Frederick	MD	20678	410-414-8111	414-8121	547
BatchMaster Software 9861 Irvine Center Dr *Web:* www.batchmaster.com	Irvine	CA	92618	949-583-1646		178-10
Bateman Gordon & Sands Inc 3050 N Federal Hwy *TF:* 800-683-1964 ■ *Web:* www.bgsagency.com	Lighthouse Point	FL	33064	954-941-0900	941-2006	390
Bates & Bates Law LLC 1890 Marietta Blvd NW *Web:* bates-bates.com	Atlanta	GA	30318	404-228-7439		41
Bates Amusement Inc 1292 Bantam Ridge Rd *Web:* www.batesamusement.com	Steubenville	OH	43953	740-266-3120	266-3124	239
Bates College 2 Andrews Rd *TF:* 888-522-8371 ■ *Web:* www.bates.edu	Lewiston	ME	04240	207-786-6255	786-6025	166
Bates Communications Inc 40 Grove St Ste 310 *TF:* 800-908-8239 ■ *Web:* www.bates-communications.com	Wellesley	MA	02482	800-908-8239		195
Bates Coughtry Reiss LLP 2601 Saturn St Ste 210 *Web:* bcrcpas.com	Brea	CA	92821	714-871-2422	871-2676	2
Bates County 1 N Delaware St *Web:* www.batescounty.net	Butler	MO	64730	660-679-3371	679-9922	338
Bates Creative Group LLC 8505 Fenton St Ste 212 *Web:* batescreative.com	Silver Spring	MD	20910	301-495-8844		463
Bates Ford 1673 W Main St *TF:* 888-834-4671 ■ *Web:* www.tonybatesfordsales.com	Lebanon	TN	37087	888-834-4671		57

Name	Address	City	State	ZIP	Phone	Fax	Class	Notes
Bates Metal Products Inc	403 E Main St	Port Washington	OH	43837	740-498-8371	498-6315*	549	*Fax Area Code: 614 ■ Web: batesmetal.com
Bates Technical College	1101 S Yakima Ave	Tacoma	WA	98405	253-680-7000		162	Web: www.batestech.edu
Bates Technologies LLC	14560 Bergen Blvd Ste 800	Noblesville	IN	46060	317-841-2400	841-1200	246	Web: www.batestech.com
Bates Troy Health Care Linen Supply	151 Laurel Ave	Binghamton	NY	13905	607-723-5333		442	Web: batestroy.com
Bates White LLC	1300 Eye St N W Ste 600	Washington	DC	20005	202-408-6110		463	Web: www.bateswhite.com
Batesburg Insurance Agency Inc	657 W Columbia Ave	Batesburg	SC	29006	803-532-3864	532-2103	390	Web: batesburginsuranceagency.com
Batesville Memorial Public Library (BMPL)	131 N Walnut St	Batesville	IN	47006	812-934-4706	934-6288	434-3	Web: www.ebatesville.com
Batesville Tool & Die Inc	177 Six Pine Ranch Rd	Batesville	IN	47006	812-934-5616		483	Web: btdinc.com
Bath & Body Works	7 Limited Pkwy E	Reynoldsburg	OH	43068	877-832-9272		214	TF: 800-395-1001 ■ Web: customercare.bathandbodyworks.com
Bath + Beyond, The	77 Connecticut St	San Francisco	CA	94107	415-689-6338		362	TF: 800-696-6662 ■ Web: bathandbeyond.com
Bath County	PO Box 39	Owingsville	KY	40360	606-674-2613	674-9526	338	Web: www.bathcounty.ky.gov
Bath County	PO Box 309	Warm Springs	VA	24484	540-839-7221	839-7222	338	TF: 888-823-1710 ■ Web: www.bathcountyva.org
Bath Fitter Franchising Inc	102 Evergreen Dr	Springfield	TN	37172	800-892-2847		364	TF: 800-892-2847 ■ Web: www.bathfitter.com
Bath Iron Works Corp	700 Washington St	Bath	ME	04530	207-443-3311		698	Web: www.gdbiw.com
Bath National Cemetery	VA Medical Ctr	Bath	NY	14810	607-664-4853	664-4761	136	Web: www.cem.va.gov
Bath Regional Career & Technical Ctr	800 High St	Bath	ME	04530	207-443-8257		436	Web: www.brctc.rsu1.org
Bath Veterans Affairs Medical Ctr	76 Veterans Ave	Bath	NY	14810	607-664-4000		374-8	TF: 877-845-3247 ■ Web: www.bath.va.gov
Bathcrest Inc	3791 S 300 W	Salt Lake City	UT	84115	855-662-7220		189-11	TF: 855-662-7220 ■ Web: bathcrest.com
Bathtub Billy's	630 Ridge Rd W	Rochester	NY	14615	585-865-6510		671	Web: bathtubbillys.com
Batley Powers	316 Osuna Rd NE Ste 301	Albuquerque	NM	87107	505-246-0500		41	Web: batleypowers.com
Baton Rouge Ballet Theatre	10745 Linkwood Ct	Baton Rouge	LA	70810	225-766-8379	766-8230	573-1	Web: batonrougeballet.org
Baton Rouge Business Report	9029 Jefferson Hwy	Baton Rouge	LA	70809	225-928-1700	926-1329	457-5	Web: www.businessreport.com
Baton Rouge City Hall	222 St Louis St Ste 301	Baton Rouge	LA	70802	225-389-3100	389-5203	337	Web: www.brla.gov
Baton Rouge Community College (BRCC)	201 Community College Dr	Baton Rouge	LA	70806	225-216-8000	216-8010	162	TF: 866-217-9823 ■ Web: www.mybrcc.edu
Baton Rouge General Medical Ctr (BRGMC)	3600 Florida Blvd	Baton Rouge	LA	70806	225-387-7000		374-3	Web: www.brgeneral.org
Baton Rouge Little Theater	7155 Florida Blvd	Baton Rouge	LA	70806	225-926-3968		573-4	Web: theatrebr.org
Baton Rouge Machine Works	12612 Ronaldson Rd	Baton Rouge	LA	70807	225-775-2542	774-5928	567	TF: 844-857-2592 ■ Web: www.brmachineworks.com
Baton Rouge Metropolitan Airport	9430 Jackie Cochran Dr Ste 300	Baton Rouge	LA	70807	225-355-0333	355-2334	27	Web: www.flybtr.com
Baton Rouge Printing Inc	1130 Commercial Dr	Port Allen	LA	70767	225-343-3423	383-9937	627	Web: www.brprint.com
Baton Rouge Regional Eye Bank	7777 Hennessy Blvd Ste 1005	Baton Rouge	LA	70808	225-766-8996	765-4366	269	Web: www.eyebankbr.org
Baton Rouge Rehab Hospital	8595 United Plaza Blvd	Baton Rouge	LA	70809	225-927-0567		374-6	Web: www.brrehab.com
Batson Acctg & Tax PA	20 Washington Pk	Greenville	SC	29601	864-235-6824		2	Web: www.batsontax.net
Batson Inc	1300 Batson Dr	Little Rock	AR	72202	501-664-3311		261	Web: batson.com
Batson Printing Inc	195 Michigan St	Benton Harbor	MI	49022	269-926-6011	926-6238	627	Web: www.specialtyprintcomm.com
Batson, Himes, Norvell & Poe Partnership	4334 Papermill Dr	Knoxville	TN	37909	865-588-6472		261	Web: norvellpoe.com
Batson-Cook Co	817 Fourth Ave PO Box 151	West Point	GA	31833	706-643-2500	643-2199	186	Web: www.batson-cook.com
Batson-Cook Development Co	400 Galleria Pky Ste 1900	Atlanta	GA	30339	770-953-9600		652	Web: www.batsoncookdev.com
Batsto Historic Village	31 Batsto Rd	Hammonton	NJ	08037	609-561-0024	567-8116	50-3	Web: www.batstovillage.org
Batta Environmental Associates Inc	Delaware Industrial Pk 6 Garfield Way	Newark	DE	19713	302-737-3376	737-5764	261	Web: www.battaenv.com
Battaglia Group	221 S Knowles Ave	Winter Park	FL	32789	407-622-1700	622-1717	463	Web: www.battagliagroup.com
Battalia Winston Intl	555 Madison Ave	New York	NY	10022	212-308-8080	308-1309	266	TF: 800-570-3118 ■ Web: www.battaliawinston.com
Battambang Restaurant	850 Broadway	Oakland	CA	94607	510-839-8815		671	Web: themenupage.com
Battelle Memorial Institute Inc	505 King Ave	Columbus	OH	43201	614-424-5000		668	TF: 800-201-2011 ■ Web: www.battelle.org
Battenfeld Grease & Oil Corporation of New York	1174 Erie Ave PO Box 728	North Tonawanda	NY	14120	716-695-2100	695-0367	541	Web: www.battenfeld-grease.com
Battenkill Veterinary PC	516 SR-29	Greenwich	NY	12834	518-692-2227		794	Web: battenkillveterinary.com
Battered Women's Justice Project	1801 Nicollet Ave S Ste 102	Minneapolis	MN	55403	612-824-8768	824-8965	49-10	TF: 800-903-0111 ■ Web: www.bwjp.org
Battery Handling Systems Inc	PO Box 28990	Saint Louis	MO	63132	314-890-0953	423-5948	74	Web: www.bhs1.com
Battery Press Inc	PO Box 198885	Nashville	TN	37219	615-298-1401		637-2	Web: www.batterypress.com
Battery Specialties	3530 Cadillac Ave	Costa Mesa	CA	92626	714-755-0888	755-0889	54	TF: 800-854-5759 ■ Web: www.batteryspecialties.com
Battery Systems Inc	3051 E La Palma Ave	Anaheim	CA	92806	714-257-1705		61	Web: www.batterysystems.net
Battery Ventures	1 Marina Pk Dr Ste 1100	Boston	MA	02210	617-948-3600	948-3601	792	TF: 800-449-0645 ■ Web: battery.com
Battery Wharf Hotel, Boston Waterfront	3 Battery Wharf	Boston	MA	02109	866-898-3560	994-9092*	707	*Fax Area Code: 617 ■ TF: 866-898-3560 ■ Web: www.batterywharfhotelboston.com
BatteryMart.com	1 Battery Dr	Winchester	VA	22601	540-665-0065	665-9623	61	Web: www.batterymart.com
Battle Creek Area Chamber of Commerce	1 Riverwalk Ctr 34 W Jackson St Ste 3A	Battle Creek	MI	49017	269-962-4076	962-6309	139	Web: www.battlecreek.org
Battle Creek Enquirer	40600 Ann Arbor Rd Ste 201	Plymouth	MI	48170	269-964-7161		532-2	TF: 800-333-4139 ■ Web: static.battlecreekenquirer.com
Battle Creek/Calhoun County Convention & Visitors Bureau	1 Riverwalk Ctr 34 W Jackson St	Battle Creek	MI	49017	800-397-2240		206	TF: 800-397-2240 ■ Web: www.battlecreekvisitors.org
Battle Ground Lake State Park	18002 NE 249th St	Battle Ground	WA	98604	360-687-4621		565	Web: parks.state.wa.us
Battle Island State Park	2150 SR-48	Fulton	NY	13069	315-593-3408		565	Web: parks.ny.gov
Battle Lumber Company Inc	11261 Hwy 1 S	Wadley	GA	30477	478-252-5210	252-1364	683	Web: battlelumberco.com
Battle Medialab Inc	117 E Boca Raton Rd	Boca Raton	FL	33432	561-395-1555		180	Web: www.battlemedialab.com
Battle of Lexington State Historic Site	1101 Delaware	Lexington	MO	64067	660-259-4654		565	Web: mostateparks.com
Battle River Regional Div	5402 48A Ave	Camrose	AB	T4V0L3	780-672-6131		685	TF: 800-262-4869 ■ Web: www.brsd.ab.ca
Battle Road Research Ltd	114 Waltham St Ste 12	Lexington	MA	02421	781-863-2300		401	Web: www.battleroad.com
Battlefield Farms Inc	23190 Clarks Mtn Rd	Rapidan	VA	22733	800-722-0744	854-6486*	369	*Fax Area Code: 540 ■ TF: 800-722-0744 ■ Web: www.battlefieldfarms.com
Battlefords Chamber of Commerce	Jcts of Hws 16 & 40 E PO Box 1000	North Battleford	SK	S9A3E6	306-445-6226	445-6633	137	Web: www.battlefordschamber.com
Battlefords Union Hospital	1092 107th St	North Battleford	SK	S9A1Z1	306-446-6600		374-2	Web: buhfoundation.com
Battle-Friedman House & Gardens	1010 Greensboro Ave	Tuscaloosa	AL	35401	205-758-6138		50-3	Web: www.historictuscaloosa.org
Battleground Hospital For Animals	225 S Royal Oaks Blvd	Franklin	TN	37064	615-261-7500		794	Web: battlegroundhospital.com
Battleground National Cemetery	6625 Georgia Ave NW	Washington	DC	20012	202-829-4650		136	Web: www.nps.gov
Battleground Restaurant Group Inc	1337 Winstead Pl	Greensboro	NC	27408	336-272-9355	272-5568	670	Web: www.brginc.com
Battleship Texas SHS	3523 Independence Pkwy S	La Porte	TX	77571	281-479-2431	479-5618	520	Web: tpwd.texas.gov
Baudville Inc	5380 52nd St SE	Grand Rapids	MI	49512	616-698-0889	698-0554	178-1	TF: 800-728-0888 ■ Web: www.baudville.com
Baue Funeral Homes	620 Jefferson St	Saint Charles	MO	63301	636-940-1000		510	TF: 888-724-0073 ■ Web: www.baue.com
Bauer & Associates Attorneys	223 S Woodland Blvd	Deland	FL	32720	386-734-3313		41	Web: delandattorneys.com
Bauer & Hunter PLLC	25240 Lahser Rd Ste 2	Southfield	MI	48033	248-742-9111		41	Web: bauerhunter.com
Bauer Built Inc	PO Box 248	Durand	WI	54736	715-672-4295		755	Web: www.bauerbuilt.com
Bauer Compressors Inc	1328 Azalea Garden Rd	Norfolk	VA	23502	757-855-6006	855-6224	172	Web: www.bauercomp.com

	Phone	Fax	Class
Bauer Financial Inc 2655 LeJeune Rd ... Coral Gables FL 33134 *TF:* 800-388-6686 ■ *Web:* www.bauerfinancial.com	800-388-6686	230-9569	194
Bauer Hockey LLC 100 Domain Dr ... Exeter NH 03833 *Web:* www.bauer.com	603-430-3010		710
Bauer Howden Inc 175 Century Dr ... Bristol CT 06010 *Web:* www.bauerct.com	860-583-9100		22
Bauer Pitman Snyder Huff Lifetime Legal PLLC 1235 4th Ave E Ste 200 ... Olympia WA 98506 *Web:* www.lifetime.legal	360-754-1976	943-4427	41
Bauer Precision Inc 174 D Kinderkamack Rd ... Park Ridge NJ 07656 *Web:* www.bauerprecision.com	201-307-0369	307-1284	454
Bauer Premium Fly Reels 585 Clover Ln Ste 1 ... Ashland OR 97520 *TF:* 888-484-4165 ■ *Web:* www.bauerflyreel.com	541-488-8246	488-8244	710
Bauer Publishing 270 Sylvan Ave ... Englewood Cliffs NJ 07632 *Web:* www.bauerpublishing.com	212-764-3344	764-7255	637-9
Bauer Sheet Metal & Fabricating Inc 1550 Evanston ... Muskegon MI 49442 *Web:* bauersheetmetal.com	231-773-3244		697
Bauerle and Company PC 7887 E Belleview Ave Ste 700 ... Englewood CO 80111 *Web:* www.bauerlesolutions.com	303-759-0089		2
Bauerschmidt & Sons Inc 11920 Merrick Blvd ... Jamaica NY 11434 *Web:* www.bauerschmidtandsons.com	718-528-3500		499
Bauerware LLC 3886 17th St ... San Francisco CA 94114 *TF:* 877-864-5662 ■ *Web:* www.bauerwaresf.com	415-864-3886		362
Baugo Community School Indiana 29125 County Rd 22 W ... Elkhart IN 46517 *Web:* www.baugo.org	574-293-8583	294-2171	685
Baum Control Systems Inc 15 Thornwood Dr ... Ithaca NY 14850 *Web:* compcenter.com	607-257-3524		180
Baum Machine Inc N253 Stoney Brook Rd ... Appleton WI 54915 *Web:* baummachine.com	920-738-6613	738-0571	757
Baum Ruffolo & Marzal Ltd 33 N Lasalle St Ste 1710 ... Chicago IL 60602 *Web:* brmlaw.org	312-726-1995		41
Baum Textile Mills Inc 812 Jersey Ave ... Jersey City NJ 07310 *TF:* 866-842-7631 ■ *Web:* www.baumtextile.com	201-659-0444	659-9719	594
Bauman Associates Ltd PO Box 1225 ... Eau Claire WI 54702 *TF:* 888-952-2866 ■ *Web:* baumancpa.com	715-834-2001		2
Bauman College 10151 Main St Ste 128 PO Box 940 ... Penngrove CA 94951 *TF:* 800-987-7530 ■ *Web:* www.baumancollege.org	707-795-1284		167-3
Bauman Loewe Witt & Maxwell PLLC 8765 E Bell Rd Ste 210 ... Scottsdale AZ 85260 *Web:* blwmlawfirm.com	480-502-4664		41
Bauman Rare Books 535 Madison Ave Frnt 1 ... New York NY 10022 *Web:* www.baumanrarebooks.com	212-751-0011		95
Baumann & Baumann CPA'S 40 Walnut St Ste 301 ... Wellesley MA 02481 *Web:* www.baumanncpas.net	781-239-0190		2
Baumann & De Groot Inc 116 E Lakewood Blvd ... Holland MI 49424 *Web:* baumannanddegroot.com	616-355-6550		189-10
Baumfolder Corp 1660 Campbell Rd ... Sidney OH 45365 *TF:* 800-543-6107 ■ *Web:* www.baumfolder.com	937-492-1281	492-7280	556
Baumgarten's 144 Ottley Dr ... Atlanta GA 30324 *TF:* 800-247-5547 ■ *Web:* b3.net	404-874-7675		534
Baumhower's of Tuscaloosa 500 Harper Lee Dr ... Tuscaloosa AL 35404 *Web:* www.baumhowers.com	205-556-5658	556-5639	671
Bausch & Lomb Inc 1400 N Goodman St ... Rochester NY 14609 **Fax Area Code: 585* ■ *TF:* 800-553-5340 ■ *Web:* www.bausch.com	800-553-5340	338-6896*	542
Bau-Xi Gallery 3045 Granville St ... Vancouver BC V6H3J9 *Web:* bau-xi.com	604-733-7011		42
Bavaria Sausage Kitchen Inc 6317 Nesbitt Rd ... Madison WI 53719 *TF:* 800-733-6695 ■ *Web:* www.bavariasausage.com	608-271-1295	845-6693	296-26
Bavarian Grill 221 W Parker Rd ... Plano TX 75023 *Web:* www.bavariangrill.com	972-881-0705		671
Bavarian Inn 713 S Main St ... Frankenmuth MI 48734 *TF:* 800-228-2742 ■ *Web:* bavarianinn.com	989-652-9941		671
Bavarian Inn 855 N Fifth St ... Custer SD 57730 *Web:* www.bavarianinnsd.com	605-673-2802		379
Bavarian World 595 Valley Rd ... Reno NV 89512 *Web:* bavarianworldreno.com	775-323-7646		671
Bawa Muhaiyaddeen Fellowship (BMF) 5820 Overbrook Ave ... Philadelphia PA 19131 *TF:* 888-786-1786 ■ *Web:* www.bmf.org	215-879-6300		637-10
Bawmann Group Inc, The 2137 S Birch St ... Denver CO 80222 *Web:* goteamtbg.com	303-320-7790	320-7661	636
Bax Engineering Co 221 Point West Blvd ... Saint Charles MO 63301 *Web:* www.baxengineering.com	636-928-5552	928-1718	261
Baxter & Woodman Inc 8678 Ridgefield Rd ... Crystal Lake IL 60012 *Web:* www.baxterwoodman.com	815-459-1260	455-0450	261
Baxter Chrysler Jeep Inc 17950 Burt St ... Omaha NE 68118 *Web:* www.baxterchryslerjeepdodge.net	402-493-7800		57
Baxter Corp 7125 Mississauga Rd ... Mississauga ON L5N0C2 *TF:* 866-234-2345 ■ *Web:* www.baxter.ca	905-369-6000		231
Baxter County 1 E Seventh St Baxter County Courthouse First Fl ... Mountain Home AR 72653 *Web:* www.baxtercounty.org	870-425-3475		338
Baxter Enterprises 466 Baxter Ln ... Winchester TN 37398 *Web:* www.baxterent.com	931-962-8687		596
Baxter Healthcare Corp 1 Baxter Pkwy ... Deerfield IL 60015 *Web:* www.baxter.com	847-948-3859		476
Baxter Planning Systems Inc 7801 N Capital of Texas Hwy Ste 250 ... Austin TX 78731 *Web:* baxterplanning.com	512-323-5959		178-10
Baxter Regional Medical Ctr 624 Hospital Dr ... Mountain Home AR 72653 *Web:* www.baxterregional.org	870-508-1000		374-3
Baxter State Park 64 Balsam Dr ... Millinocket ME 04462 *Web:* baxterstatepark.org	207-723-5140		565
Baxter, Baker, Sidle, Conn & Jones PA 120 E Baltimore St Ste 2100 ... Baltimore MD 21202 *Web:* www.bbsclaw.com	410-230-3800		428
BaxterBoo 148 Cypress Ridge Crt ... Ridgeland SC 29936 *TF:* 888-887-0063 ■ *Web:* www.baxterboo.com	888-887-0063		690
Bay Agency Insurance Group Inc 93 E River Rd PO Box 543 ... Rumson NJ 07760 *Web:* bayagency.net	732-741-4637		390
Bay Alphi Manufacturing Inc 576 Beck St ... Jonesville MI 49250 *Web:* www.bayalphimfg.com	517-849-9945	849-2556	295
Bay Area Business Services Inc 610 W Main St Ste 101 ... League City TX 77573 *Web:* babs-inc.com	281-316-9246		570
Bay Area Chamber of Commerce 901 Saginaw St ... Bay City MI 48708 *Web:* www.baycityarea.com	989-893-4567	895-5594	139
Bay Area Chamber of Commerce 145 Central Ave ... Coos Bay OR 97420 *TF:* 800-944-9603 ■ *Web:* coosbaynorthbendcharlestonchamber.com	541-266-0868	267-6704	139
Bay Area Circuits Inc 44358 Old Warm Sprng Blvd ... Fremont CA 94538 *TF:* 855-811-1975 ■ *Web:* bayareacircuits.com	510-933-9000		625
Bay Area Credit Union Inc 4202 Navarre Ave ... Oregon OH 43616 *Web:* bayareacu.com	419-698-2962		219
Bay Area Discovery Museum 557 McReynolds Rd ... Sausalito CA 94965 *Web:* bayareadiscoverymuseum.org	415-339-3900		521
Bay Area Economics (BAE) 2600 Tenth St Ste 300 ... Berkeley CA 94710 *Web:* www.bae1.com	510-547-9380		194
Bay Area Health Insurance Marketing Inc 2882 Sand Hill Rd Ste 119 ... Menlo Park CA 94025 *TF:* 800-564-4476 ■ *Web:* bayareahealth.net	800-564-4476		390
Bay Area Hospital 1775 Thompson Rd ... Coos Bay OR 97420 *TF:* 800-798-0799 ■ *Web:* www.bayareahospital.org	541-269-8111		374-3
Bay Area Industrial Filtration Inc 6355 Coliseum Way ... Oakland CA 94621 *Web:* www.bayareafiltration.com	510-562-6373	562-2649	386
Bay Area Legal Aid 1735 Telegraph Ave ... Oakland CA 94612 *TF:* 800-551-5554 ■ *Web:* baylegal.org	510-663-4755	663-4740	428
Bay Area Rapid Transit District 300 Lakeside Dr ... Oakland CA 94612 *Web:* www.bart.gov	510-464-6000		468
Bay Area Renaissance Festival at Mosi 11315 N 46th St ... Tampa FL 33617 *Web:* www.bayarearenfest.com	813-983-0111		720
Bay Area Reporter 395 Ninth St ... San Francisco CA 94103 *TF:* 800-838-3006 ■ *Web:* www.ebar.com	415-861-5019		532-3
Bay Associates Group Inc 1432 Front Ave ... Lutherville Timonium MD 21093 *Web:* www.bayassociates.com	410-825-6616	825-6618	612
Bay Atlantic Federal Credit Union 101 W Elmer Rd ... Vineland NJ 08360 *Web:* bayatlanticfcu.org	856-696-2525		41
Bay Breeze Patio LLC 32 Forest Shore Dr ... Miramar FL 32550 *Web:* baybreezepatio.com	850-269-4666		321
Bay Business Credit 1407 Oakland Blvd Ste 102 ... Walnut Creek CA 94596 *TF:* 800-549-9003 ■ *Web:* www.baybizcr.com	800-549-9003		70
Bay Cast Inc 2611 Center Ave ... Bay City MI 48708 *Web:* www.baycast.com	989-892-0511		307
Bay City Flower Company Inc 2265 Cabrillo Hwy S ... Half Moon Bay CA 94019 *TF:* 800-399-5858 ■ *Web:* www.baycityflower.com	650-726-5535		369
Bay City Public Schools 910 N Walnut St ... Bay City MI 48706 *Web:* www.bcschools.net	989-686-9700	266-8202	685
Bay City Recreation Area 3582 State Pk Dr ... Bay City MI 48706 *Web:* www.michigan.org	989-684-3020		565
Bay City Tribune 2901 16th St ... Bay City TX 77414 *Web:* baycitytribune.com	979-245-5555		532-2
Bay Club at Waikoloa Beach Resort, The 69-450 Waikoloa Beach Dr ... Waikoloa HI 96738 *Web:* www.hiltongrandvacations.com	808-886-7979	886-4538	378
Bay Club Co, The 150 Greenwich St ... San Francisco CA 94111 *Web:* www.bayclubs.com	415-433-2200		354
Bay Club Hotel & Marina 2131 Shelter Island Dr ... San Diego CA 92106 *TF:* 800-672-0800 ■ *Web:* www.bayclubhotel.com	619-224-8888	225-1604	379
Bay Companies Inc, The 8500 Bell Creek Rd ... Mechanicsville VA 23116 *Web:* thebaycompanies.com	804-569-7060	569-7061	261
Bay Computer Associates Inc 136 Frances Ave ... Cranston RI 02910 *Web:* baycomp.com	401-461-1484		177
Bay Correctional Facility 5400 Bayline Dr ... Panama City FL 32404 *Web:* dc.state.fl.us	850-769-1455	769-1942	213
Bay Corrugated Container Inc 1655 W Seventh St ... Monroe MI 48161 *Web:* www.baycorr.com	734-243-5400		100
Bay County 515 Center Ave ... Bay City MI 48708 *TF:* 877-229-9960 ■ *Web:* www.baycounty-mi.gov	989-895-4280	895-4284	338
Bay County 840 W 11th St ... Panama City FL 32401 *Web:* www.baycountyfl.gov	850-248-8140	248-8343	338

Name / Address	City	State	Zip	Phone	Fax	Class
Bay County Chamber of Commerce 235 W Fifth St — *Web:* panamacity.org	Panama City	FL	32401	850-785-5206	763-6229	139
Bay County Library System 500 Center Ave — *Web:* www.baycountylibrary.org	Bay City	MI	48708	989-894-2837	894-2021	434-3
Bay County Medical Care Facility 564 W Hampton Rd — *Web:* www.baycountymcf.com	Essexville	MI	48732	989-892-3591	892-6991	450
Bay County Public Library 898 W 11th St — *Web:* www.nwrls.lib.fl.us	Panama City	FL	32401	850-522-2100	522-2138	434-3
Bay Craft Inc 1785 Langley Ave — *Web:* www.baycraftboats.com	DeLand	FL	32724	386-943-8877	943-8617	90
Bay de Noc Community College 2001 N Lincoln Rd — *TF:* 800-221-2001 ■ *Web:* www.mybay.baycollege.edu	Escanaba	MI	49829	906-786-5802		162
Bay Diesel Corp 3736 Cook Blvd — *TF:* 800-215-4005 ■ *Web:* baydiesel.com	Chesapeake	VA	23323	757-485-0075	485-0232	698
Bay Electric Company Inc 627 36th St — *Web:* www.bayelectricco.com	Newport News	VA	23607	757-595-2300	595-6112	186
Bay Electronics Inc 20805 Kraft Blvd — *Web:* www.bayelectronics.net	Roseville	MI	48066	586-296-0900	296-2141	203
Bay Glen Animal Hospital P C 1616 Clear Lake City Blvd — *Web:* www.bayglenvet.com	Houston	TX	77062	281-410-2611		794
Bay Hill Golf Club & Lodge 9000 Bay Hill Blvd — *TF:* 888-422-9445 ■ *Web:* www.bayhill.com	Orlando	FL	32819	407-876-2429	876-1035	669
Bay Houston Towing Co 2243 Milford St — *TF:* 800-324-3755 ■ *Web:* www.bayhouston.com	Houston	TX	77253	713-529-3755	529-2591	465
Bay Industries Inc 2929 Walker Dr — *Web:* www.baycompanies.com	Green Bay	WI	54311	920-406-4000		499
Bay Island Sportswear Inc 1415 Emerald Rd — *Web:* www.bayislandsportswear.com	Greenwood	SC	29646	864-229-1298	223-6685	594
Bay Landing Hotel 1550 Bayshore Hwy — *TF:* 866-783-9612 ■ *Web:* www.baylandinghotel.com	Burlingame	CA	94010	650-259-9000	259-9099	378
Bay Leaf 935 W Hamilton St — *Web:* www.allentownbayleaf.com	Allentown	PA	18101	610-433-4211		671
Bay Logistics Inc 1202 Pontaluna Rd — *Web:* www.baylogistics.com	Spring Lake	MI	49456	231-799-1015		803-1
Bay MarketForce LLC 215 N Main St Ste 140 — *Web:* baymarketforce.com	West Bend	WI	53095	262-335-1718		195
Bay Meadows 380 E 28th Ave — *Web:* baymeadows.com	San Mateo	CA	94403	650-627-0000		642
Bay Mechanical Inc 2696 Reliance Dr Ste 200 — *Web:* baymechanical.com	Virginia Beach	VA	23452	757-468-6700	468-0377	189-10
Bay Mills Community College 12214 W Lakeshore Dr — *TF:* 800-844-2622 ■ *Web:* www.bmcc.edu	Brimley	MI	49715	906-248-3354	248-3351	165
Bay Mills Resort & Casinos 11386 W Lakeshore Dr — *TF:* 888-422-9645 ■ *Web:* www.baymillscasinos.com	Brimley	MI	49715	888-422-9645		452
Bay Minette Public Library 205 W Second St — *Web:* cityofbayminette.org	Bay Minette	AL	36507	251-580-1648	937-0339	434-3
Bay News 1624 N Meadowcrest Blvd — *Web:* www.baynews9.com	Crystal River	FL	34429	352-563-2052		530
Bay Oil Co 2201 Fm 517 E — *Web:* www.bayoilfuel.com	Dickinson	TX	77539	281-337-4673	614-5949	324
Bay Paper Company Inc 1 Bay Paper Dr — *TF:* 800-476-9791 ■ *Web:* www.baypaper.com	Mobile	AL	36607	251-476-9791	476-9898	559
Bay Partners 10600 N De Anza Blvd Ste 100 — *Web:* www.baypartners.com	Cupertino	CA	95014	408-725-2444	446-4502	792
Bay Path College 588 Longmeadow St — *TF:* 800-782-7284 ■ *Web:* www.baypath.edu	Longmeadow	MA	01106	800-782-7284		166
Bay Pines National Cemetery 10000 Bay Pines Blvd — *Web:* www.cem.va.gov	Saint Petersburg	FL	33708	727-319-6479		136
Bay Pointe Nursing Pavilion 4201 31st St S — *Web:* baypointenursingpavilion.com	Saint Petersburg	FL	33712	727-867-1104	867-9837	450
Bay Pointe Technology 2662 Brecksville Rd — *TF:* 800-746-1420 ■ *Web:* baypointetechnology.com	Richfield	OH	44286	800-746-1420		525
Bay Polymer Corp 44530 S Grimmer Blvd — *Web:* www.baypolymer.com	Fremont	CA	94538	510-490-1791	490-5914	608
Bay Porte Animal Hospital LLC 10105 Fairmont Pkwy — *Web:* bay-porte.com	La Porte	TX	77571	281-471-6834		794
Bay Ship & Yacht Co 2900 Main St Ste 2100 — *Web:* www.bay-ship.com	Alameda	CA	94501	510-337-9122	337-0154	698
Bay Shore Chamber of Commerce 77 E Main St PO Box 5110 — *Web:* bayshorecommerce.com	Bay Shore	NY	11706	631-665-7003		139
Bay Shore Systems Inc 14206 N Ohio St — *Web:* www.eventbrite.com	Rathdrum	ID	83858	208-687-3311		190
Bay Standard Manufacturing Inc 24485 Marsh Creek Rd — *Web:* www.baystandard.com	Brentwood	CA	94513	925-634-1181		350
Bay State College 122 Commonwealth Ave — *TF:* 800-815-3276 ■ *Web:* www.baystate.edu	Boston	MA	02116	617-217-9000	249-0400	800
Bay State Computers Inc 16901 Melford Blvd Ste 329 — *Web:* www.bayst.com	Bowie	MD	20716	301-352-7878	352-6925	180
Bay State Envelope Inc 440 Chauncy St — *Web:* bseprint.com	Mansfield	MA	02048	508-337-8900		627
Bay State Integrated Technology Inc 43 E Grove St Ste 2 — *Web:* www.jitsolutionsit.com	Middleboro	MA	02346	508-947-1478		180
Bay State Milling Co 100 Congress St — *TF:* 800-553-5687 ■ *Web:* www.baystatemilling.com	Quincy	MA	02169	800-553-5687		296-23
Bay Technical Associates Inc 5239 Ave A — *TF:* 800-523-2702 ■ *Web:* www.baytech.net	Long Beach	MS	39560	228-563-7334		174
Bay Tek Entertainment Inc 1077 E Glenbrook Dr — *Web:* www.baytekent.com	Pulaski	WI	54162	920-822-3951		31
Bay To Bay Lending LLC 1001 W Cleveland St Ste B — *Web:* baytobaylending.com	Tampa	FL	33606	813-251-2700		652
Bay Tree Publishing 225 E Richmond Ave — **Fax Area Code:* 866 ■ *Web:* www.baytreepublish.com	Point Richmond	CA	94801	510-619-6338	552-7329*	637-2
Bay Valley Hotel & Resort 2470 Old Bridge Rd — *TF:* 888-241-4653 ■ *Web:* www.bayvalley.com	Bay City	MI	48706	989-686-3500		669
Bay View Food Products Inc 2606 N Huron Rd — *Web:* www.bayviewfoods.com	Pinconning	MI	48650	989-879-3555		296-19
Bay View State Park 10901 Bay View-Edison Rd — *Web:* parks.state.wa.us	Mount Vernon	WA	98273	360-757-0227		565
Bay Village 8400 Vamo Rd — *Web:* bayvillage.org	Sarasota	FL	34231	941-966-5611		672
Bay Watch Resort & Conference Ctr 2701 S Ocean Blvd — *Web:* www.oceanaresorts.com	North Myrtle Beach	SC	29582	843-272-4600		669
BAYADA Home Health Care 1 W Main St — *TF:* 877-591-1527 ■ *Web:* www.bayada.com	Moorestown	NJ	08057	856-231-1000	231-1955	363
Bayard Firm, The 600 N King St Ste 400 — *Web:* www.bayardlaw.com	Wilmington	DE	19801	302-655-5000	658-6395	428
Bayaud Enterprises 333 W Bayaud Ave — *Web:* www.bayaudenterprises.org	Denver	CO	80223	303-830-6885		317
Baybank Corp 104 S Tenth St — *Web:* baybank.us	Gladstone	MI	49837	906-428-4040		70
BayCare Health System 2985 Drew St — *Web:* baycare.org	Clearwater	FL	33759	727-820-8200		374-3
Bayco Products Inc 640 Sanden Blvd — *TF:* 800-233-2155 ■ *Web:* www.baycoproducts.com	Wylie	TX	75098	469-326-9400		437
Baycrest Centre For Geriatric Care 3560 Bathurst St — *Web:* www.baycrest.org	Toronto	ON	M6A2E1	416-785-2500		371
Bayer Built Woodworks Inc 24614 Hwy 71 — *Web:* www.bayerbuilt.com	Belgrade	MN	56312	320-254-3651	254-3601	191-3
Bayer Corp 100 Bayer Blvd — *Web:* www.bayer.us	Whippany	NJ	07981	862-404-3000		582
Bayer CropScience 2 TW Alexander Dr — *TF:* 800-331-2867 ■ *Web:* www.cropscience.bayer.us	Research Triangle Park	NC	27709	919-549-2000		85
Bayer Inc 77 Belfield Rd — *TF:* 800-622-2937 ■ *Web:* www.bayer.ca	Toronto	ON	M9W1G6	416-248-0771		582
Bayerkohler & Graff Ltd 11132 Zealand Ave N — *TF:* 866-315-2771 ■ *Web:* www.bayergraff.com	Champlin	MN	55316	763-427-2542		734
Bayer-Risse Engineering Inc 78 Rt 173 W — *Web:* bayer-risse.com	Hampton	NJ	08827	908-735-2255		261
Bayfield County PO Box 878 — *TF:* 800-447-4094 ■ *Web:* www.bayfieldcounty.org	Washburn	WI	54891	715-373-6100	373-6153	338
Bayfield Electric Co-opeartive Inc 68460 District St — *TF:* 800-278-0166 ■ *Web:* www.bayfieldelectric.com	Iron River	WI	54847	715-372-4287	372-4318	245
BAY-FM 94.5 (AC) 5225 Hellyer Ave Ste 245 — *TF:* 800-948-5229 ■ *Web:* www.945bayfm.com	San Jose	CA	95113	408-287-5775		645-143
Bayforce 5100 W Kennedy Blvd Ste 425 — *TF:* 877-642-4727 ■ *Web:* www.bayforce.com	Tampa	FL	33609	877-642-4727		195
Bayfront Inn 138 Avenida Menendez — *Web:* www.bayfrontinn.com	Saint Augustine	FL	32084	904-824-1681		379
Bayhead Products Corp 173 Crosby Rd — *TF:* 800-229-4323 ■ *Web:* bayheadproducts.com	Dover	NH	03820	603-742-3000	743-4701	470
Bayhealth 640 S State St — *Web:* www.bayhealth.org	Dover	DE	19901	302-674-4700		48-17
Bayjet Inc 720 W Organ — *Web:* www.bayjetinc.net	Las Cruces	NM	88005	575-526-3353	526-6003	770
Baylake Landscape Inc 1591 Orchard View Ln — *Web:* baylakelandscape.com	Brussels	WI	54204	920-825-7601		422
Bayland Buildings Inc PO Box 13571 — *Web:* www.baylandbuildings.com	Green Bay	WI	54307	920-498-9300		186
Bayless Manufacturing Inc 26100 Ave Hall — *Web:* baylessmfg.com	Valencia	CA	91355	661-257-3373	257-3522	454
Bayley Construction Co 8005 SE 28th St — *Web:* www.bayley.net	Mercer Island	WA	98040	206-621-8884	343-7728	186
Baylis & Company PA 53 Lake Morton Dr — *Web:* bayliscpas.com	Lakeland	FL	33801	863-688-8841		2
Baylis Medical Company Inc 5959 Trans-Canada Hwy — *TF:* 800-850-9801 ■ *Web:* www.baylismedical.com	Montreal	QC	H4T1A1	514-488-9801		477
Bayliss Machine & Welding Co 2901 Rev Abraham Woods Jr Blvd — *Web:* www.baylissmachine.com	Birmingham	AL	35203	205-323-6121		454
Bayloff Stamped Products 5910 Belleville Rd — *Web:* www.bayloff.com	Belleville	MI	48111	734-397-9116		489
Baylor College of Medicine 1 Baylor Plz — *TF:* 800-229-5671 ■ *Web:* www.bcm.edu	Houston	TX	77030	713-798-4951		167-2

Phone | Fax | Class

Baylor County 301 N Washington . . . Seymour TX 76380 940-889-3148 889-8882 338
TF: 800-633-0852 ■ *Web:* cityofseymour.org

Baylor Institute for Rehabilitation
909 N Washington Ave . . . Dallas TX 75246 214-820-9300 263-4599* 374-6
*Fax Area Code: 512 ■ *TF:* 888-722-9567 ■ *Web:* www.bswrehab.com

Baylor Scott & White Health
2300 Marie Curie Blvd . . . Garland TX 75042 972-487-5000 374-3
Web: www.bswhealth.com

Baylor Trucking Inc 9269 E State Rd 48 . . . Milan IN 47031 800-322-9567 780
TF: 800-322-9567 ■ *Web:* www.baylortrucking.com

Baylor University
1301 S University Parks Dr . . . Waco TX 76798 800-229-5678 710-1066* 166
*Fax Area Code: 254 ■ *TF:* 800-229-5678 ■ *Web:* www.baylor.edu

Baylor University Press (BUP)
1 Bear Pl Ste 97363 . . . Waco TX 76798 254-710-3164 710-3440 637-2
Web: www.baylorpress.com

Baylor Women's Correctional Institution
660 Baylor Blvd . . . New Castle DE 19720 302-577-3004 213
Web: www.doc.delaware.gov

Bayne Machine Works Inc
910 Fork Shoals Rd . . . Greenville SC 29605 864-288-3877 454
Web: www.baynethinline.com

Baynet World Inc
20111 Stevens Creek Blvd Ste 280 . . . Cupertino CA 95014 408-253-8090 253-8098 178-1
Web: www.baynet.com

Bayona 430 Rue Dauphine . . . New Orleans LA 70112 504-525-4455 522-0589 671
Web: www.bayona.com

Bayonne Chamber of Commerce 621 Ave C . . . Bayonne NJ 07002 201-436-4333 139
Web: www.bayonnenj.org

Bayonne Medical Ctr 29th St & Ave E . . . Bayonne NJ 07002 201-858-5000 374-3
Web: www.carepointhealth.org

Bayou Bay Seafood House
7117 Chapman Hwy . . . Knoxville TN 37920 865-573-7936 671
Web: www.bayoubayseafoodhouseknoxville.com

Bayou Bend Collection & Gardens
6003 Memorial Dr . . . Houston TX 77007 713-639-7750 520
Web: www.mfah.org

Bayou City Exploration Inc
923 College St . . . Bowling Green KY 42101 270-282-8544 282-8545 540
Web: bycex.net

Bayou Companies LLC, The
5200 Curtis Ln . . . New Iberia LA 70560 337-369-3761 539
Web: www.bayoucompanies.com

Bayou Internet Inc 1109 Hudson Ln . . . Monroe LA 71201 318-323-0011 224
TF: 888-302-2968 ■ *Web:* www.bayou.com

Bayou Manor 4141 S Braeswood Blvd . . . Houston TX 77025 713-666-2651 672
Web: houstonretirement.org

Bayou Perma-Pipe Canada Ltd
5233 39th St . . . Camrose AB T4V4R5 780-672-2345 481
Web: www.permapipe.com

Bayou Publishing 2524 Nottingham St . . . Houston TX 77005 713-526-4558 526-4342 637-10
TF: 800-340-2034 ■ *Web:* www.bayoupublishing.com

Bayou Segnette State Park
7777 Westbank Expy . . . Westwego LA 70094 504-736-7140 565
TF: 888-677-2296 ■ *Web:* crt.state.la.us

Bayou State Oil Corp 1115 Hawn Ave . . . Shreveport LA 71107 318-222-0737 536
Web: www.bayoustateoil.com

BayPort Credit Union Inc
3711 Huntington Ave . . . Newport News VA 23607 757-928-8850 219
TF: 800-928-8801 ■ *Web:* www.bayportcu.org

Bays Corp PO Box 1455 . . . Chicago IL 60690 312-346-5757 296-1
TF: 800-367-2297 ■ *Web:* bays.com

Bays Mountain Planetarium & Observatory
853 Bays Mtn Park Rd . . . Kingsport TN 37660 423-229-9447 224-2589 598
Web: www.baysmountain.com

Bayshore Concrete Products Corp
1134 Bayshore Rd . . . Cape Charles VA 23310 757-331-2300 183
Web: www.usa.skanska.com

Bayshore Recycling
75 Crows Mill Rd PO Box 290 . . . Keasbey NJ 08832 732-738-6000 738-9150 660
Web: www.bayshorerecycling.com

Bayshore Town Ctr
5800 N Bayshore Dr Ste A256 . . . Glendale WI 53217 414-963-8780 460
Web: thebayshorelife.com

Bayside Engineering Inc
600 Unicorn Park Dr . . . Woburn MA 01801 781-932-3201 261
Web: baysideengineering.com

Bayside Fuel Oil Depot Corp
1776 Shore Pkwy . . . Brooklyn NY 11214 718-372-9800 266-3744 581
Web: www.baysidedepot.com

Bayside Interiors Inc
3220 Darby Common . . . Fremont CA 94539 510-438-9171 438-9375 189-9
Web: baysideinteriors.com

Bayside Marketplace 401 Biscayne Blvd . . . Miami FL 33132 305-577-3344 50-6
Web: www.baysidemarketplace.com

Bayside Printing Inc 160 Lockhaven Dr . . . Houston TX 77073 281-209-9500 209-9569 627
Web: www.baysideprinting.com

Bayside Resort Hotel
225 Massachusetts 28 . . . West Yarmouth MA 02673 508-775-5669 775-8862 669
TF: 800-243-1114 ■ *Web:* www.baysideresort.com

Bayside Solutions Inc
3000 Executive Pkwy Ste 510 . . . San Ramon CA 94583 800-220-0074 460-8278* 260
*Fax Area Code: 925 ■ *TF:* 800-220-0074 ■ *Web:* www.baysidesolutions.com

Bayside State Prison 4293 Rt 47 . . . Leesburg NJ 08327 856-785-0040 785-2559 213
Web: state.nj.us

Bayside Surety Brokerage Inc
1621 S University Blvd Ste A4 . . . Mobile AL 36609 251-661-0745 661-0790 690
TF: 866-785-8664 ■ *Web:* baysidesurety.com

BaySpec Inc 1101 McKay Dr . . . San Jose CA 95131 408-512-5928 512-5929 246
Web: www.bayspec.com

Baystar Hotel Group
4600 W Cypress St Ste 525 . . . Tampa FL 33607 813-849-0001 286-2314 132
Web: www.baystarhotels.com

Baystate Medical Ctr
759 Chestnut St . . . Springfield MA 01199 413-794-0000 374-3
Web: www.baystatehealth.org

Baystate Wealth Management LLC
200 Clarendon St 19th Fl . . . Boston MA 02116 617-982-5200 390
Web: baystatewealth.com

Phone | Fax | Class

Bayswater Point State Park
1479 Point Breeze Pl . . . Far Rockaway NY 11691 718-471-2212 565
Web: parks.ny.gov

Baytec Service LLC 4761 Hwy 146 200 . . . Bacliff TX 77518 800-560-2334 316
TF: 800-560-2334 ■ *Web:* www.bayteccontainers.com

Baytex Energy Corp
2800 520 - Third Ave SW . . . Calgary AB T2P0R3 587-952-3000 536
TF: 800-524-5521 ■ *Web:* www.baytexenergy.com

Baytown Chamber of Commerce
1300 Rolling Brook Ste 400 . . . Baytown TX 77521 281-422-8359 428-1758 139
Web: www.baytownchamber.com

Bayview 11 W Aloha St . . . Seattle WA 98119 206-284-7330 672
Web: www.bayviewseattle.org

Bayview Capital Group LLC
214 Minnetonka Ave S . . . Wayzata MN 55391 952-345-2000 690
Web: bayviewcap.com

Bayview Custom Communications
511 Canal St . . . New York NY 10013 631-232-2520 232-2510 681
Web: www.bayviewcustom.com

Bayview Environmental Services Inc
6925 San Leandro St . . . Oakland CA 94621 510-562-6181 63
Web: www.bayviewservices.com

Bayview Furniture 2181 E Pass Rd . . . Gulfport MS 39507 228-896-4400 321
TF: 800-748-9852 ■ *Web:* www.bayviewfurniture.com

Bayview Glen Public School
42 Limcombe Dr . . . Thornhill ON L3T2V5 905-889-2448 889-2578 685
Web: www.yrdsb.ca

Bayview Limousine Service
15701 Nelson Pl S . . . Seattle WA 98188 206-223-6200 277-5895* 441
*Fax Area Code: 425 ■ *TF:* 800-606-7880 ■ *Web:* www.bayviewlimo.com

Bayview Opera House
4705 Third St . . . San Francisco CA 94124 415-824-0386 572
Web: bvoh.org

Bayview Press PO Box 153 . . . Thomaston ME 04861 207-354-9919 130
TF: 800-903-2346 ■ *Web:* www.bayviewpress.com

Bayway Lincoln 12333 Gulf Fwy . . . Houston TX 77034 866-956-0972 57
TF: 888-356-1895 ■ *Web:* www.baywaylincoln.com

Bayway Lumber & Home Center (inc)
400 Ashton Ave . . . Linden NJ 07036 908-486-4480 683
Web: www.baywaylumber.com

Bazaar del Mundo 4133 Taylor St . . . San Diego CA 92110 619-296-3161 50-6
Web: www.bazaardelmundo.com

Bazelon Less & Feldman PC
1 S Broad St Ste 1500 . . . Philadelphia PA 19107 215-568-1155 568-9319 428
Web: bazless.com

Bazon Cox & Associates Inc
1244 Executive Blvd . . . Chesapeake VA 23320 757-410-2128 180
TF: 800-769-1763 ■ *Web:* bazoncox.com

Bazooka-Farmstar Inc 800 E 7th St . . . Washington IA 52353 319-653-5080 653-5806 273
Web: www.bazookafarmstar.com

Bazz Houston Co
12700 Western Ave . . . Garden Grove CA 92841 800-385-9608 898-1389* 488
*Fax Area Code: 714 ■ *TF:* 800-385-9608 ■ *Web:* www.bazz-houston.com

Bazzirk Inc 216 Bonnieview St . . . Austin TX 78704 512-418-8500 7

BB (Big Business Inc)
420 NE Alaskan Way . . . Chehalis WA 98532 925-274-9568 984-9890* 178-1
*Fax Area Code: 206 ■ *TF:* 877-970-0022 ■ *Web:* www.bigbusiness.com

BB & T Corp
200 W 2nd St PO Box 1250 . . . Winston-Salem NC 27102 800-226-5228 360-2
NYSE: BBT ■ *TF:* 800-226-5228 ■ *Web:* www.bbt.com

BB and G Electric 3635 W Twain Ave . . . Las Vegas NV 89103 702-871-7500 189-4
Web: www.bbgelectric.com

BB King's Blues Club 143 Beale St . . . Memphis TN 38103 901-524-5464 524-5454 671
Web: www.bbkings.com

BB Riverboats Inc 101 Riverboat Row . . . Newport KY 41071 859-261-8500 749
TF: 800-261-8586 ■ *Web:* bbriverboats.com

BB's Restaurant & Bar
1019 Hendricks Ave . . . Jacksonville FL 32207 904-306-0100 671
Web: bbsrestaurant.com

BBC (Balfour Beatty Construction)
3100 McKinnon St . . . Dallas TX 75201 214-451-1177 186
Web: balfourbeattyus.com

BBC America
1120 Avenue of the Americas . . . New York NY 10036 212-705-9300 888-0576 740
Web: www.bbcamerica.com

BBCC (Brantford Brant Chamber of Commerce)
77 Charlotte St . . . Brantford ON N3T2W8 519-753-2617 753-0921 137
Web: www.brantfordbrantchamber.com

Bbdo Atlanta 3500 Lenox Rd NE Ste 1900 . . . Atlanta GA 30326 404-231-1700 4
Web: bbdoatl.com

BBDO Worldwide Inc
1285 Avenue of the Americas . . . New York NY 10019 212-459-5000 4
Web: www.bbdo.com

BBE 100 McMillan St . . . Yellowknife NT X1A3T2 867-766-8666 766-8667 314
TF: 866-746-4223 ■ *Web:* www.bbex.com

BBF (Brother's Brother Foundation)
1200 Galveston Ave . . . Pittsburgh PA 15233 412-321-3160 321-3325 48-5
Web: www.brothersbrother.org

BBFI (Baptist Bible Fellowship Intl)
720 E Kearney St . . . Springfield MO 65803 417-862-5001 865-0794 48-20
Web: www.bbfi.org

BBGM Architects & Interiors Inc
1825 K St NW Ste 300 . . . Washington DC 20006 202-452-1644 452-1647 261
Web: www.bbgm.com

BBGN Inc 283 Corporate Way . . . Upland CA 91786 909-946-5959 982-4840 22
TF: 877-877-7721 ■ *Web:* www.ja-vindustries.com

BBH (Baltimore Behavioral Health)
1101 W Pratt St . . . Baltimore MD 21223 410-962-7180 962-7194 726
TF: 800-789-2647 ■ *Web:* baltimorecity.md.networkofcare.org

BBH Consulting Inc 80 E Antelope Dr . . . Layton UT 84041 801-779-4405 317
Web: www.bbhconsulting.com

BBH Solutions Inc 121 E 24th St . . . New York NY 10010 212-475-7100 180
TF: 844-224-4968 ■ *Web:* www.bbhsolutions.com

BBIF (Black Business Investment Fund)
301 E Pine St Ste 175 . . . Orlando FL 32801 407-649-4780 649-8688 194
Web: www.bbifflorida.com

BBL (Boca Biolistics)
5001 NW 13th Ave Bay H . . . Pompano Beach FL 33064 954-449-6126 429-2998 743
Web: www.bocabio.com

	Phone	Fax	Class
BBL (BBL Construction Services Inc) 302 Washington Ave Ext........................Albany NY 12203 *Web:* www.bblinc.com	518-452-8200		186
BBL Construction Services Inc (BBL) 302 Washington Ave Ext........................Albany NY 12203 *Web:* www.bblinc.com	518-452-8200		186
BBPL (Bogue Banks Public Library) 320 Salter Path Rd Ste W .... Pine Knoll Shores NC 28512 *Web:* carteret.cpclib.org	252-247-4660	247-2802	434-3
BBR Benefits Solutions LLC 8150 Perry Hwy Ste 100.................... Pittsburgh PA 15237 *Web:* bbrbenefits.com	412-847-3100	847-3105	390
BBR Creative Inc 300 Rue Beauregard .... LaFayette LA 70508 *Web:* bbrcreative.com	337-233-1515		344
BBS Automation Chicago Inc 1580 Hecht Ct. ....Bartlett IL 60103 *Web:* www.bbsautomation.com	630-351-3000	671-2600	454
BBS Securities Inc 4100 Yonge St Ste 415......................... Toronto ON M2P2B5 *Web:* www.bbssecurities.com	416-235-0200	235-1227	690
BBTI (Broadband Technologies Inc) 255 SW 14th Pl .... Boca Raton FL 33432 *Web:* www.broadbandweb.net	561-400-3867		392
BBU (Beefmaster Breeders United) 6800 Pk Ten Blvd Ste 290-W ....San Antonio TX 78213 *Web:* www.beefmasters.org	210-732-3132	732-7711	48-2
BBVA USA Bancshares Inc 15 S 20th St ....Birmingham AL 35233 *TF:* 800-266-7277 ■ *Web:* www.bbvausa.com	205-297-1986	297-7836	360-2
BBVA Wealth Solutions Inc 2200 Post Oak Blvd ....Houston TX 77056 *TF:* 800-538-8152 ■ *Web:* www.bbvawealthsolutions.com	713-552-9277	552-0906	217
BC Clark Northpark 12042 N May Ave......................Oklahoma City OK 73120 *Web:* bcclark.com	405-755-4040		410
BC Government & Service Employees' Union 4911 Canada Way............................Burnaby BC V5G3W3 *TF:* 800-663-1674 ■ *Web:* www.bcgeu.ca	604-291-9611		414
BC Investment Management Corp (BCI) 750 Pandora Ave............................. Victoria BC V8W0E4 *Web:* www.bci.ca	778-410-7100		528
BC Lions 10605 135th St .... Surrey BC V3T4C8 *Web:* www.bclions.com	604-930-5466	583-7882	715-2
BC Maritime Employers Assn 349 Railway St ....Vancouver BC V6A1A4 *Web:* www.bcmea.com	604-688-1155		138
BC One Call Ltd 9768 3rd St..................... Sidney BC V8L3A4 *TF:* 800-474-6886 ■ *Web:* www.bc1c.ca	604-257-1900		194
BC Plumbing Co 1215 S Seventh St ....Louisville KY 40203 *Web:* www.bcplumbing.net	502-634-9725		189-10
BC Public School Employers' Assn 400-1333 W Broadway.....................Vancouver BC V6H4C1 *Web:* www.bcpsea.bc.ca	604-730-4507	730-0787	624
BC Systems Inc 200 Belle Mead Rd ....Setauket NY 11733 *Web:* bcpowersys.com	631-751-9370		668
BC Transit 520 Gorge Rd E...................... Victoria BC V8W2P3 *Web:* www.bctransit.com	250-385-2551	995-5639	468
BC Wire Rope & Rigging 2720 E Regal Park Dr .... Anaheim CA 92806 *TF:* 800-669-5919 ■ *Web:* www.bcwirerope.com	800-669-5919		492
BCA (Buddhist Churches of America) 1710 Octavia St ....San Francisco CA 94109 *Web:* www.buddhistchurchesofamerica.org	415-776-5600	771-6293	48-20
BCA (Brent Coon & Assoc) 215 Orleans St..... Beaumont TX 77701 *TF:* 866-335-2666 ■ *Web:* www.bcoonlaw.com	409-835-2666	833-4483	428
BCAA (British Columbia Automobile Assn) 4567 Canada Way.........................Burnaby BC V6C1T1 *Web:* www.bcaa.com	604 200-5000		53
BCB Bancorp Inc 595 Avenue C ....Bayonne NJ 07002 *NASDAQ: BCBP* ■ *Web:* www.bcb.bank	201-823-0700	339-0403	360-2
BCBG Max Azria 2761 Fruitland Ave..............Vernon CA 90058 *Web:* www.bcbg.com	323-589-2224		277
BCC (Benning Construction Company Inc) 4695 S Atlanta Rd............................Atlanta GA 30339 *Web:* www.benningnet.com	404-792-1911		186
BCC Engineering Inc 6401 SW 87th Ave Ste 200..................... Miami FL 33173 *Web:* bcceng.com	305-670-2350		261
BCC Software Inc 75 Josons Dr...............Rochester NY 14623 *TF:* 800-453-3130 ■ *Web:* www.bccsoftware.com	800-453-3130		225
BCCLS 21-00 Rt 208 S..............................Fair Lawn NJ 07410 *Web:* my.bccls.org	201-498-7300	489-4215	434-3
BCCR (Brown College of Court Reporting & Medical Transcription) 1900 Emery St NW Ste 200 ....Atlanta GA 30318 *TF:* 800-849-0703 ■ *Web:* www.bccr.edu	404-876-1227	876-4415	800
BCCVB (Bucks County Conference & Visitors Bureau) 3207 St Rd...............................Bensalem PA 19020 *Web:* www.visitbuckscounty.com	215-639-0300	642-3277	206
BCD (Business Cluster Development) 3186 Bryant St .... Palo Alto CA 94306 *Web:* clusterdevelopment.com	650-387-3159		393
BCD Travel USA LLC 6 Concourse Pkwy........... Atlanta GA 30328 *Web:* www.bcdtravel.com	678-441-5200		772
BCE Inc 1 Carrefour Alexander-Graham-Bell Bldg A Fourth Fl.............................Verdun QC H3E3B3 *TF:* 888-932-6666 ■ *Web:* www.bce.ca	888-932-6666		787
BCER Engineering Inc 5420 Ward Rd Ste 200........................Arvada CO 80002 *Web:* bcer.com	303-422-7400		256
BCF (Biblical Counseling Foundation) 42550 Aegean St .... Indio CA 92203 *TF:* 877-933-9333 ■ *Web:* www.bcfministries.org	760-347-4608	775-5751	48-20
BCF LLP 25th Fl 1100 Rene-Levesque Blvd W .... Montreal QC H3B5C9 *TF:* 866-511-8501 ■ *Web:* www.bcf.ca	514-397-8500		428
BCF Solutions Inc 2300 Ninth St S Ste 200.....................Arlington VA 22204 *Web:* www.bcfsolutions.com	703-717-9912		317
BCG (Buildings Consulting Group Inc) 2855 Anthony Ln S Ste 200 ....Minneapolis MN 55418 *Web:* www.bcgminnesota.com	612-789-6696	789-6397	261
BCG (Benefit Consultants Group Inc) 51 Haddonfield Rd Ste 200..................Cherry Hill NJ 08002 *TF:* 800-524-4015 ■ *Web:* www.bcgbenefits.com	856-368-2000	824-1890	390
BCG Attorney Search 175 S Lake Ave Unit 200 ....Pasadena CA 91101 *TF:* 800-298-6440 ■ *Web:* www.bcgsearch.com	800-298-6440		260
BCG Connect 755 Middlesex Tpke...............Billerica MA 01821 *TF:* 800-767-0067 ■ *Web:* www.bcgconnect.com	800-767-0067		195
BCG Engineering & Consulting Inc 3012 26th St...............................Metairie LA 70002 *Web:* ardurra.com	504-454-3866		261
BCGS (Blair County Genealogical Society) 431 Scotch Valley Rd .... Hollidaysburg PA 16648 *Web:* www.bcgslibrary.org	814-696-3492		49-19
BCGS (Bucks County Genealogical Society) PO Box 826 .... Washington Crossing PA 18977 *Web:* www.bucksgen.org	215-345-0210		49-19
BCH (Boulder Community Hospital) 1100 Balsam Ave .... Boulder CO 80301 *Web:* www.bch.org	303-440-2273		374-3
BCH Fulfillment and Distribution 33 Oakland Ave.............................Harrison NY 10528 *TF:* 800-431-1579 ■ *Web:* www.bookch.com	914-835-0015	835-0398	96
BCH Mechanical Inc 6354 118th Ave N............Largo FL 33773 *Web:* www.bchmechanical.com	727-546-3561	545-1801	189-10
BCHA (Back Country Horsemen of America) 59 Rainbow Rd.......................... East Granby CT 06026 *TF:* 888-893-5161 ■ *Web:* www.bcha.org	860-586-7540	653-1702	48-23
BCI (Benefit Communications Inc) 2977 Sidco Dr ....Nashville TN 37204 **Fax Area Code:* 615 ■ *TF:* 800-489-3786 ■ *Web:* benefitcommunications.com	800-489-3786	383-7917*	390
BCI (Bulk Chemicals Inc) 1074 Stinson Dr....... Reading PA 19605 *TF:* 800-338-2855 ■ *Web:* www.bulkchemicals.us	610-926-4128	926-6125	146
BCI (BC Investment Management Corp) 750 Pandora Ave........................... Victoria BC V8W0E4 *Web:* www.bci.ca	778-410-7100		528
BCI (BAT Conservation Intl) 500 N Capital of Texas Hwy .... Austin TX 78746 *TF:* 800-538-2287 ■ *Web:* www.batcon.org	512-327-9721	327-9724	48-3
BCI (Bass Computers Inc) 10558 Bissonnet St ....Houston TX 77099 *TF:* 800-789-3012 ■ *Web:* www.basscomputers.com	281-776-6700	776-6733	174
BCI Burke Company Inc 660 Van Dyne Rd ....Fond du Lac WI 54937 *TF:* 800-356-2070 ■ *Web:* www.bciburke.com	920-921-9220		346
BCI Inc 848 Marshall Phelps Rd.................Windsor CT 06095 *Web:* www.thebutlerco.com	860-688-8024		776
BCI Solutions Inc 500 N Baltimore St............ Bremen IN 46506 *TF:* 800-837-2411 ■ *Web:* www.bcisolutions.com	800-837-2411		307
BCInteriors 3550 Frontier Ave Ste C2 .... Boulder CO 80301 *Web:* bcinteriors.com	303-443-3666		320
BCIU (Business Council for International Understanding) 1212 Avenue of the Americas 10th Fl...........New York NY 10036 *Web:* www.bciu.org	212-490-0460	697-8526	49-12
BCJ Trucking Inc 1764 Redbrush Rd ....Mount Airy NC 27030 **Fax Area Code:* 366 ■ *TF:* 800-237-4634 ■ *Web:* www.bcjtrucking.com	800-237-4634	320-2319*	780
BCL (Bruccoli Clark Layman Inc) 2006 Sumter St.............................Columbia SC 29201 *Web:* lppub.com	803-771-4642	799-6953	637-2
BCLC (British Columbia Lottery Corp) 74 W Seymour St .... Kamloops BC V2C1E2 *TF:* 866-815-0222 ■ *Web:* www.bclc.com	250-828-5500	828-5631	452
BCM Resources Corp 1040 W Georgia St.........................Vancouver BC V6E4H1 *TF:* 888-646-0144 ■ *Web:* www.bcmresources.com	604-646-0144		502
BCM Technologies I LP 2 Greenway Plz Ste 910 ....Houston TX 77046 *Web:* www.bcmtechnologies.com	713-795-0105	795-4602	792
BCN (Bliss Clearing Niagara) 1004 E State St.......................... Hastings MI 49058 *TF:* 800-642-5477 ■ *Web:* www.bcntechserv.com	269-948-3300	948-3313	456
BCN Services Inc 3650 W Liberty Rd .... Ann Arbor MI 48103 *TF:* 800-891-9911 ■ *Web:* www.bcnservices.com	734-994-4100	994-1227	463
BCNS Technologies 116 Highwood Ave........Henderson NV 89002 *Web:* computernetworking-repair.com	702-566-5321		177
BCO Inc 799 Middlesex Tpke ....Billerica MA 01821 *Web:* www.bco-inc.com	978-663-2525		631
BCP Veterinary Pharmacy 1614 Webster St............................Houston TX 77003 *Web:* bcpvetpharm.com	713-771-1144		237
BCPL (Broome County Historical Society) 185 Court St.............................Binghamton NY 13901 *Web:* www.bclibrary.info	607-778-3572		49-19
BCRS Associates LLC 77 Water St 9th Fl.........................New York NY 10005	212-440-0800		734
BCS (Experience Bryan College Station) 715 University Dr E.................... College Station TX 77840 *TF:* 800-777-8292 ■ *Web:* www.experiencebcs.com	979-260-9898	260-9800	206
BCS (Billings Construction Supply) 5514 King Ave E............................ Billings MT 59108 *Web:* www.billingsconstructionsupply.com	406-248-8355	248-6470	523
BCS (Bulk Carrier Services Inc) 3451 Losee Rd Ste B .... North Las Vegas NV 89030 *TF:* 800-414-8785 ■ *Web:* www.bulkcarrierservices.com	702-648-9055		311
BCS Community Credit Union 4203 Wadsworth Blvd.................... Wheat Ridge CO 80033 *Web:* bcscu.com	303-425-6627		219
BCS Engineering 25 Grosvenor St............... Athens OH 45701 *Web:* www.bcsengineering.com	740-331-4481		177
BCS LLC 8920 Stephens Rd Ste 200 .... Laurel MD 20723 *Web:* www.bcs-hq.com	410-997-7778		194
BCS Prosoft Inc 2700 Lockhill Selma......................San Antonio TX 78230 *TF:* 800-882-6705 ■ *Web:* www.bcsprosoft.com	210-308-5505		179

Name / Address	City	State	ZIP	Phone	Fax	Class
BCSD (Binghamton City School District) 164 Hawley St. *Web:* binghamtonschools.org	Binghamton	NY	13901	607-762-8100		685
BCSIA (Belfer Center for Science & International Affairs) Harvard Univ John F Kennedy School of Government 79 JFK St *Web:* www.belfercenter.org	Cambridge	MA	02138	617-495-1400	495-8963	634
BCT Partners LLC 105 Lock St *Web:* www.bctpartners.com	Newark	NJ	07103	973-622-0900		463
BCVB (Bloomington Convention & Visitors Bureau) 7900 International Dr Ste 990 *TF:* 800-346-4289 ■ *Web:* www.bloomingtonmn.org	Bloomington	MN	55425	952-858-8500	858-8854	206
BCW 200 5th Ave *Web:* bcw-global.com	New York	NY	10010	212-798-9700	329-9900	636
BCW Diversified 514 E 31st St *TF:* 800-433-4229 ■ *Web:* www.bcwsupplies.com	Anderson	IN	46016	765-644-2033		627
BCWSA (Bucks County Water & Sewer Authority) 1275 Almshouse Rd **Fax Area Code:* 267 ■ *TF:* 800-222-2068 ■ *Web:* www.bcwsa.net	Warrington	PA	18976	215-343-2538	200-0339*	806
BD Biosciences 2350 Qume Dr **Fax Area Code:* 408 ■ *TF:* 800-223-8226 ■ *Web:* www.bdbiosciences.com	San Jose	CA	95131	877-232-8995	954-2347*	419
BD Diagnostics 7 Loveton Cir **Fax Area Code:* 410 ■ *TF:* 800-638-8663 ■ *Web:* www.bd.com	Sparks	MD	21152	800-638-8663	316-4066*	231
BD Energy Systems LLC 1001 S Dairy Ashford Rd Ste 410 *Web:* bdenergysystems.com	Houston	TX	77077	281-407-9812		261
BDA Sports Management 700 Ygnacio Valley Rd Ste 330 *Web:* bdasports.com	Walnut Creek	CA	94596	925-279-1040	279-1060	393
BDE Computer Services LLC 399 Lakeview Ave *TF:* 877-233-4877 ■ *Web:* www.bdecomputer.com	Clifton	NJ	07011	973-772-8507		175
BDEC (Burke-Divide Electric Co-opeartive Inc) 9549 Hwy 5 W *TF:* 800-472-2983 ■ *Web:* www.bdec.coop	Columbus	ND	58727	701-939-6671		245
BDI 5398 Manhattan Cir *Web:* bditest.com	Boulder	CO	80303	303-494-3230		261
BDL Supply 15 Sprague Rd *TF:* 888-728-9810 ■ *Web:* www.bdlsupply.com	South Charleston	OH	45368	888-728-9810		200
BDO Capital Advisors LLC 515 South Flower St 47th Fl *Web:* www.bdocap.com	Los Angeles	CA	90071	310-557-0300	557-8253	70
BDO Las Vegas 6100 Elton Ave Ste 1000 *TF:* 877-980-1120 ■ *Web:* www.bdo.com	Las Vegas	NV	89107	702-384-1120	870-2474	2
BDP Intl 510 Walnut St *Web:* www.bdpinternational.com	Philadelphia	PA	19106	215-629-8900	629-8940	449
B-D-R Transport Inc 7994 US Rt 5 *TF:* 800-421-0126 ■ *Web:* www.bdrtransport.com	Westminster	VT	05158	802-463-0606		780
BDS Engineering Inc 5575 Lake Park Way Ste 114 *Web:* www.bdsengineering.com	La Mesa	CA	91942	619-582-4992	582-7428	256
BDS Marketing LLC 10 Holland *TF:* 800-234-4237 ■ *Web:* www.bdsmktg.com	Irvine	CA	92618	800-234-4237		195
BDSI (BioDelivery Sciences International Inc) 4131 Parklake Ave Ste 225 *NASDAQ: BDSI* ■ *TF:* 877-579-4578 ■ *Web:* bdsi.com	Raleigh	NC	27612	919-582-9050	582-9051	85
BDTI (Berkeley Design Technology Inc) 1646 N California Blvd Ste 220 *Web:* bdti.com	Walnut Creek	CA	94596	925-954-1411	954-1423	196
BE & K Building Group 1031 S Caldwell St Ste 100 *Web:* www.bekbg.com	Charlotte	NC	28203	704-412-9300	659-4161	186
Be Media 655 Hawaii St *Web:* www.bemedia.com	El Segundo	CA	90245	310-725-8500		317
Be Original 1520 Lake Louella Rd *Web:* beoriginal.com	Suwanee	GA	30024	770-813-9933		344
BEA (Bureau of Economic Analysis) 4600 Silver Hill Rd *Web:* www.bea.gov	Washington	DC	20233	301-278-9004		340-2
BEA (Broadcast Education Assn) 1771 N St NW *Web:* www.beaweb.org	Washington	DC	20036	202-429-5355	609-9940	49-5
Beach & Oneill Insurance Associates Inc 7520 Greenback Ln *TF:* 800-640-0123 ■ *Web:* beachandoneill.com	Citrus Heights	CA	95610	916-676-0844		390
Beach Camera 203 Rt 22 E *TF:* 800-572-3224 ■ *Web:* www.beachcamera.com	Green Brook	NJ	08812	732-968-6400	968-7709	119
Beach Colony Resort 5308 N Ocean Blvd *TF:* 877-543-4232 ■ *Web:* www.beachcolony.com	Myrtle Beach	SC	29577	843-449-4010	449-2810	669
Beach Ford Inc 2717 Virginia Beach Blvd *TF:* 888-349-2191 ■ *Web:* www.beachford.com	Virginia Beach	VA	23452	888-349-2191		57
Beach Haven Hotel 4740 Mission Blvd *Web:* www.beachhavenpacificbeach.com	San Diego	CA	92109	858-272-3812	272-3532	379
Beach Lloyd Publishers LLC 40 Cabot Dr *Web:* www.beachlloyd.com	Wayne	PA	19087	775-254-0633		637-10
Beach Mold & Tool Inc 999 Progress Blvd *Web:* www.beachmold.com	New Albany	IN	47150	812-945-2688	944-3705	596
Beach Oil Co 631 US Hwy 76 *Web:* www.beachoil.com	Clarksville	TN	37041	931-358-9303	358-9331	579
Beach Photo & Video 604 Main St *Web:* www.beachphoto.com	Daytona Beach	FL	32118	386-252-0577		628
Beach Properties of Hilton Head 64 Arrow Rd *TF:* 800-671-5155 ■ *Web:* www.beach-property.com	Hilton Head Island	SC	29928	843-671-5155		656
Beach Realty & Construction 4826 N Croatan Hwy *TF:* 800-635-1559 ■ *Web:* www.beachrealtync.com	Kitty Hawk	NC	27949	252-261-3815		652
Beach Terrace Motor Inn 3400 Atlantic Ave *TF:* 800-841-8416 ■ *Web:* beachterrace.com	Wildwood	NJ	08260	609-522-8100		378
Beachbody LLC 3301 Exposition Blvd *Web:* www.beachbody.com	Santa Monica	CA	90404	310-883-9000		6

Name / Address	City	State	ZIP	Phone	Fax	Class
Beachcomber Resort Hotel & Villas 1200 S Ocean Blvd *TF:* 800-231-2423 ■ *Web:* www.beachcomberresort.com	Pompano Beach	FL	33062	800-231-2423		669
Beachcomber Restaurant 2 A St *Web:* www.beachcomberstaugustine.com	Saint Augustine	FL	32080	904-471-3744		671
Beacher's Lodge 6970 A1A S *TF:* 800-527-8849 ■ *Web:* www.beacherslodge.com	Saint Augustine	FL	32080	904-471-8849	471-3002	379
Beacher, The 911 Franklin St *Web:* www.thebeacher.com	Michigan City	IN	46360	219-879-0088	879-8070	532-2
Beaches Restaurant & Bar 1919 SE Columbia River Dr *Web:* beachesrestaurantandbar.com	Vancouver	WA	98661	360-699-1592		671
Beachhead Solutions 1150 S Bascom Ave Ste 7 *Web:* beachheadsolutions.com	San Jose	CA	95128	408-496-6936		180
Beachwood Systems Consulting Inc 13315 Broadway Ave *Web:* www.beachsys.com	Cleveland	OH	44125	216-823-1800	823-1806	194
Beacon Acctg Group 10 Pidgeon Hill Dr Ste 110 *Web:* beaconaccountinggroup.com	Sterling	VA	20165	703-430-7666	430-7665	2
Beacon Advanced Eye Care Ctr 1320 Shelfer St *Web:* www.beaconadvancedeyecare.com	Leesburg	FL	34748	352-728-8318		543
Beacon Application Services Corp 959 Concord St Ste 250 *Web:* www.beaconservices.com	Framingham	MA	01701	508-663-4433		41
Beacon Associates Inc 900-A S Main St Ste 102 *Web:* www.beaconassociates.net	Bel Air	MD	21014	410-638-7279	638-7662	194
Beacon Communications Inc 1944 Warwick Ave *Web:* www.warwickonline.com	Warwick	RI	02889	401-732-3100	732-3110	532-2
Beacon Container Corp 700 W First St *TF:* 800-422-8383 ■ *Web:* www.beaconcontainer.com	Birdsboro	PA	19508	610-582-2222	582-3992	100
Beacon Credit Union PO Box 627 *TF:* 800-762-3136 ■ *Web:* www.beaconcu.org	Wabash	IN	46992	260-563-7443		219
Beacon Energy Services Inc 2685 Temple Ave *Web:* www.beaconenergyservices.com	Signal Hill	CA	90755	562-997-3087		261
Beacon Fasteners & Components 198 W Carpenter Ave *TF:* 800-669-2658 ■ *Web:* www.beaconfasteners.com	Wheeling	IL	60090	847-353-2000	541-1789	350
Beacon Financial Partners 25800 Science Park Dr Ste 100 *TF:* 866-568-3951 ■ *Web:* www.beaconplanners.com	Beachwood	OH	44122	216-910-1850		194
Beacon Group Inc 6001 Broken Sound Pkwy NW Ste 500 *TF:* 800-545-9007 ■ *Web:* beacongroupinc.com	Boca Raton	FL	33487	561-994-9994		390
Beacon Health System 615 N Michigan St *TF:* 800-850-7913 ■ *Web:* www.beaconhealthsystem.org	South Bend	IN	46601	574-647-1000	647-3670	374-3
Beacon Healthcare Services Inc 710 Denbigh Blvd Ste 6C *Web:* www.beaconhealthcare.com	Newport News	VA	23608	757-833-0430		363
Beacon Hill Associates Inc 408 Park St **Fax Area Code:* 434 ■ *TF:* 855-596-2157 ■ *Web:* b-h-a.com	Charlottesville	VA	22902	855-596-2157	979-8964*	390
Beacon Hill Financial Corp 120 Water St *Web:* www.beaconhillfinancial.com	Boston	MA	02109	617-973-6900		401
Beacon Hill Staffing Group LLC 152 Bowdoin St *Web:* www.beaconhillstaffing.com	Boston	MA	02108	617-326-4000	227-1220	631
Beacon Hotel 720 Ocean Dr *TF:* 877-674-8200 ■ *Web:* www.beaconsouthbeach.com	Miami Beach	FL	33139	305-674-8200		379
Beacon Hotel & Corporate Quarters 1615 Rhode Island Ave NW *Web:* www.beaconhotelwdc.com	Washington	DC	20036	202-296-2100		379
Beacon House 19 Myrtle St *Web:* www.rogerson.org	Boston	MA	02114	617-523-8295		372
Beacon House 1301 N Third St *TF:* 800-562-9753 ■ *Web:* www.upbeaconhouse.org	Marquette	MI	49855	906-225-7100	225-4903	372
Beacon Industries Inc 12300 Old Tesson Rd *TF:* 800-454-7159 ■ *Web:* www.beacontechnology.com	Saint Louis	MO	63128	314-487-7600	487-0100	21
Beacon Learning Ctr 1311 Balboa Ave **Fax Area Code:* 850 ■ *TF:* 800-311-6437 ■ *Web:* www.beaconlearningcenter.com	Panama City	FL	32401	800-311-6437	873-7126*	167-3
Beacon Medaes 1059 Paragon Way *TF:* 888-463-3427 ■ *Web:* www.beaconmedaes.com	Rock Hill	SC	29730	803-817-5600	817-5750	250
Beacon Occupational Health & Safety Services Inc 800 Cordova St *Web:* www.beaconohss.com	Anchorage	AK	99501	907-222-7612		194
Beacon Pointe Advisors 24 Corporate Plz Dr Ste 150 *Web:* beaconpointe.com	Newport Beach	CA	92660	949-718-1600	718-0601	401
Beacon Power Corp 65 Middlesex Rd *Web:* www.beaconpower.com	Tyngsboro	MA	01879	978-661-2000		253
Beacon Press Inc 24 Farnsworth St *TF:* 800-253-9646 ■ *Web:* www.beacon.org	Boston	MA	02210	617-742-2110	723-3097	637-2
Beacon Retiree Benefits Group LLC Clock Tower Sq 710 Main St Ste 10 *TF:* 888-484-0414 ■ *Web:* beaconmedicare.aleragroup.com	Plantsville	CT	06479	860-621-5071	621-5074	390
Beacon Rock State Park 34841 State Rd 14 *Web:* www.parks.state.wa.us	Skamania	WA	98648	509-427-8265		565
Beacon Roofing Supply Inc 505 Huntmar Park Dr Ste 300 *NASDAQ: BECN* ■ *TF:* 877-645-7663 ■ *Web:* www.becn.com	Herndon	VA	20170	978-535-7668		191-4
Beacon Sporting Goods Inc 1240 Furnace Brook Pky *Web:* www.beaconsportinggoods.co	Quincy	MA	02169	617-479-8537		710
Beacon Supply Company Inc 1125 Broad Ave *Web:* www.beaconsupplyinc.com	Belle Vernon	PA	15012	724-929-6600	929-7601	191-2

				Phone	Fax	Class
Beacon Technologies Inc 1441 Donelson Pk *Web:* beacontech.net	Nashville	TN	37217	615-301-5020		179
Beacon Technologies Inc 164 Thatcher Rd *TF:* 855-877-7353 ■ *Web:* www.beacontechnologies.com	Greensboro	NC	27409	336-232-5699		261
Beacon Trust Co 163 Madison Ave Ste 600 *TF:* 866-377-8090 ■ *Web:* www.beacontrust.com	Morristown	NJ	07960	973-377-8090		401
Beacon Wealthcare Inc 1633 Glenwood Ave *Web:* beaconwc.com	Raleigh	NC	27608	919-821-5225		390
Beacon Wireless 815 Middlefield Rd Unit 1 *TF:* 866-867-7770 ■ *Web:* www.beaconinnovationsgroup.com	Toronto	ON	M1V2P9	416-696-7555		647
Beacon, The 205 SE Catawba Rd Ste G *Web:* thebeacon.net	Port Clinton	OH	43452	419-732-2154	734-5382	532-4
Bead Bazaar USA Inc 687 Lofstrand Ln	Rockville	MD	20850	301-610-6022		411
Bead Industries Inc 11 Cascade Blvd *TF:* 800-297-4851 ■ *Web:* beadindustries.com	Milford	CT	06460	203-301-0270	301-0280	487
Beaden Screen Inc 305 Melvin St *Web:* www.beadenscreen.com	Croswell	MI	48422	810-679-3119	679-4620	73
Beadle County Auditor 450 3rd St SW *Web:* beadle.sdcounties.org	Huron	SD	57350	605-353-8405		338
Beadle Smith PLC 445 S Livernois Rd Ste 305 *Web:* bbssplc.com	Rochester Hills	MI	48307	248-650-6094		41
Beaird Group 236 S Washington St *Web:* www.beairdgroup.com	Naperville	IL	60540	630-637-0430		463
Beal Bank SSB 6000 Legacy Dr *Web:* www.bealbank.com	Plano	TX	75024	469-467-5000		70
Beal College 99 Farm Rd *TF:* 800-660-7351 ■ *Web:* www.bealcollege.edu	Bangor	ME	04401	207-947-4591	947-0208	800
Beale Memorial Library 701 Truxtun Ave *Web:* www.kerncountylibrary.org	Bakersfield	CA	93301	661-868-0701	868-0799	434-3
Beale Street Historic District 203 Beale St Ste 300 *Web:* www.bealestreet.com	Memphis	TN	38103	901-526-0115		50-6
Beall Corp 9200 N Ramsey Blvd *Fax Area Code: 503 ■ *TF:* 855-219-5686 ■ *Web:* www.wabashnational.com	Portland	OR	97203	855-219-5686	289-3528*	779
Beall Woods State Park 9285 Beall Woods Ave *Web:* www2.illinois.gov	Mount Carmel	IL	62863	618-298-2442		565
Beall's Inc 1806 38th Ave E *Web:* www.beallsinc.com	Bradenton	FL	34208	941-747-2355		229
Beals Martin 2596 Bay Rd *TF:* 800-879-7730 ■ *Web:* www.bealsmartin.com	Redwood City	CA	94063	650-364-8141	367-7645	187
Beam Construction Co 601 E Main St *Web:* beamconstruction.com	Cherryville	NC	28021	704-435-3206	435-8412	685
Beam Dental 226 N 5th St 4th Fl *TF:* 800-648-1179 ■ *Web:* beam.dental	Columbus	OH	43215	800-648-1179		462
Beam Dynamics Inc 13749 Shelter Cove Dr *Web:* www.beamdynamicsinc.com	Jacksonville	FL	32225	904-221-5832	221-5896	420
Beam Engineering For Advanced 809 S Orlando Ave *Web:* www.beamco.com	Winter Park	FL	32789	407-629-1282		261
Beam Inc 510 Lake Cook Rd *Web:* www.jimbeam.com	Deerfield	IL	60015	847-948-8888		80-1
Beam Interactive 24 School St *Web:* www.beamland.com	Boston	MA	02108	617-523-0500		194
Beam Mack Sales & Service Inc 2674 W Henrietta Rd *TF:* 877-650-8789 ■ *Web:* www.beammack.com	Rochester	NY	14623	585-424-4860		780
Beam, Longest & Neff LLC 8320 Craig St *TF:* 800-382-5206 ■ *Web:* www.b-l-n.com	Indianapolis	IN	46250	800-382-5206		261
Beamalloy Technologies LLC 8270 Estates Pky *Web:* www.beamalloy.net	Plain City	OH	43064	614-873-4529	873-0167	481
Beamco Inc 20487 470th Ave Nw *Web:* www.beamco.biz	Oslo	MN	56744	218-965-4660		472
Beamers Hells Canyon Tours 1451 Bridge St *TF:* 800-522-6966 ■ *Web:* www.hellscanyontours.com	Clarkston	WA	99403	509-758-4800	758-3643	760
Beamie's At The River 865 Reynolds St *Web:* www.beamiesattheriver.com	Augusta	GA	30901	706-724-6593		671
Beamin' Lasers Inc 1741 W Rose Garden Ln Ste 4 *Web:* www.beaminlasers.com	Phoenix	AZ	85027	623-780-4668		425
BeamPines Inc 270 Madison Ave 9th Fl *Web:* beampines.com	New York	NY	10010	212-476-4100		194
Beamz Interactive Inc 15354 N 83rd Way Ste 101 *TF:* 888-724-7380 ■ *Web:* thebeamz.com	Scottsdale	AZ	85260	480-424-2053		527
Bean Creative Inc 2213 Mt Vernon Ave *Web:* www.beancreative.com	Alexandria	VA	22301	703-684-5945		177
Bean, Gentry, Wheeler & Peternell PLLC 910 Lakeridge Way SW *Web:* bgwp.net	Olympia	WA	98502	360-357-2852		41
Bean, Kinney & Korman A Professional Corp 2311 Wilson Blvd Ste 500 *Web:* www.beankinney.com	Arlington	VA	22201	703-525-4000		428
Beans & Barley 1901 E N Ave *Web:* www.beansandbarley.com	Milwaukee	WI	53202	414-278-7878		671
Beantree Learning 43629 Greenway Corporate Dr *Web:* www.beantreelearning.com	Ashburn	VA	20147	571-223-3110		685
Bear Branch Elementary School 8909 Fm 1488 Rd *Web:* www.magnoliaisd.org	Magnolia	TX	77354	281-356-4771		685
Bear Brook State Park 157 Deerfield Rd *Web:* www.nhstateparks.org	Allenstown	NH	03275	603-485-9869	271-3553	565
Bear Butte State Park 20250 Hwy 79 PO Box 688 *Web:* gfp.sd.gov	Sturgis	SD	57785	605-347-5240		565
Bear Cartage & Intermodal Inc 8600 Joliet Rd *Web:* www.bearcartage.com	Mccook	IL	60525	708-924-9093		314
Bear Cat Manufacturing Inc 3650 Sabin Brown Rd *Web:* bearcatmfg.com	Wickenburg	AZ	85390	928-684-7851	684-3241	190
Bear Creek Lake State Park 22 Bear Creek Lake Rd *Web:* www.dcr.virginia.gov	Cumberland	VA	23040	804-492-4410		565
Bear Creek Mountain Resort 101 Doe Mtn Ln *TF:* 866-754-2822 ■ *Web:* www.bcmountainresort.com	Macungie	PA	18062	610-641-7101		378
Bear Creek Nature Ctr 245 Bear Creek Rd *Web:* admin.elpasoco.com	Colorado Springs	CO	80906	719-520-6387	636-8968	50-5
Bear Forest Products Inc 4685 Brookhollow Cir *Web:* www.bearforestproducts.com	Riverside	CA	92509	951-727-1767		468
Bear Graphics Inc 2021 Floyd Blvd *TF:* 800-325-8094 ■ *Web:* www.beargraphics.com	Sioux City	IA	51104	712-252-0169	252-3042	535
Bear Head Lake State Park 9301 Bear Head State Park Rd *Web:* www.dnr.state.mn.us	Ely	MN	55731	218-235-2520		565
Bear Island Paper Company LLC 10026 Old Ridge Rd *Web:* www.paperage.com	Ashland	VA	23005	804-227-3394		557
Bear Lake County 7 E Center St PO Box 190 *Web:* www.bearlakecounty.info	Paris	ID	83261	208-945-2212		338
Bear Lake State Park 1030 N Bear Lake Blvd *Web:* stateparks.utah.gov	Garden City	UT	84028	435-946-3343		565
Bear Mountain Golf Course 43101 Gold Mine Dr PO Box 77 *TF:* 844-462-2327 ■ *Web:* www.bigbearmountainresort.com	Big Bear Lake	CA	92315	844-462-2327		669
Bear Mountain State Park Palisades Pkwy Rt 9W N *Web:* parks.ny.gov	Bear Mountain	NY	10911	845-786-2701		565
Bear Pond Books 77 Main St *Web:* www.bearpondbooks.com	Montpelier	VT	05602	802-229-0774		95
Bear River State Park 601 Bear River Dr *Web:* wyoparks.wyo.gov	Evanston	WY	82930	307-789-6547		565
Bear Staffing Services Inc 47 S Broad St *Fax Area Code: 856 ■ *TF:* 866-580-2327 ■ *Web:* www.bearstaff.com	Woodbury	NJ	08096	866-580-2327	848-0092*	260
Bear Valley Bible Institute of Denver 2707 S Lamar St *TF:* 800-766-4641 ■ *Web:* www.wetrainpreachers.com	Denver	CO	80227	303-986-5800	986-8003	167-3
Bear, The 91 Radio Park Dr *TF:* 877-232-7121 ■ *Web:* 1013thebear.com	Mount Clare	WV	26408	304-623-6546		645
BearCom Building Services 450 N University Ave Ste 201 *Web:* www.bearcomservices.com	Provo	UT	84601	801-618-0518	569-8400	152
Bearcom Inc 4009 Distribution Dr Ste 200 *TF:* 800-527-1670 ■ *Web:* bearcom.com	Garland	TX	75041	800-527-1670		246
Beard Books Inc PO Box 4250 *Fax Area Code: 301 ■ *TF:* 888-563-4573 ■ *Web:* www.beardbooks.com	Frederick	MD	21705	240-629-3300	631-0108*	637-2
Beard Implement Co 216 Frederick St *Web:* www.beardimplement.com	Arenzville	IL	62611	217-997-5514		274
Beard St Clair Gaffney PA 2105 Coronado St *Web:* www.beardstclair.com	Idaho Falls	ID	83404	208-523-5171		445
Bearden Tractor and Equipment 1680 Bankhead Hwy *Web:* www.beardentractorco.com	Carrollton	GA	30116	770-834-5656	834-8866	276
Beardsley Architects + Engineers 64 South St *Web:* www.beardsley.com	Auburn	NY	13021	315-253-7301		256
Beardsley Zoo 1875 Noble Ave *Web:* www.beardsleyzoo.org	Bridgeport	CT	06610	203-394-6565		823
Bearing Belt & Chain Inc 729 E Buckeye *Web:* www.bbcarizona.com	Phoenix	AZ	85034	602-252-6541	254-8151	770
Bearing Distributors Inc 8000 Hub Pkwy *TF:* 888-423-4872 ■ *Web:* new.bdiexpress.com	Cleveland	OH	44125	216-642-9100	642-9573	385
Bearing Engineering Company Inc 667 McCormick St *Web:* www.bearingengineering.com	San Leandro	CA	94577	510-596-4150	357-9246	385
Bearing Headquarters Co 2550 S 25th Ave *Web:* www.bearingheadquarters.com	Broadview	IL	60155	708-681-4400	681-4462	385
Bearing Inspection Inc 4500 Mt Pleasant NW *TF:* 800-416-8881 ■ *Web:* www.timken.com	North Canton	OH	44720	234-262-3000		75
Bearing Service & Supply Inc 1327 N Market *Web:* www.bearserco.com	Shreveport	LA	71107	318-424-1447		791
Bearing Service Company of Pennsylvania 630 Alpha Dr RIDC Pk *TF:* 800-783-2327 ■ *Web:* www.bearing-service.com	Pittsburgh	PA	15238	412-963-7710	963-8005	75
Bearing Technologies Ltd 1141 Jaycox Rd *TF:* 800-597-3486 ■ *Web:* www.brgtec.com	Avon	OH	44011	800-597-3486		247
Bearings & Drives Inc 607 Lower Poplar St *Web:* www.bdindustrial.com	Macon	GA	31208	478-746-7623		385
Bearings Ltd 2100 Pacific St *Web:* www.bearingslimited.com	Hauppauge	NY	11788	631-273-8200		385
Bearse Manufacturing Co 3815 W Cortland St *Web:* bearseusa.com	Chicago	IL	60647	773-235-8710	235-8716	67
Bearskin Airlines 1475 W Walsh St *TF:* 800-465-2327 ■ *Web:* www.bearskinairlines.com	Thunder Bay	ON	P7E4X6	807-577-1141		25

	Phone	Fax	Class
Beartooth Electric Co-opeartive Inc 1306 N Broadway St PO Box 1110 Red Lodge MT 59068 *TF:* 800-472-9821 ■ *Web:* beartoothec.coopwebbuilder2.com	406-446-2310	446-3934	245
Beartown State Forest 69 Blue Hill Rd Monterey MA 01245 *Web:* www.mass.gov	413-528-0904		565
Beary Landscaping Inc 15001 W 159th St Lockport IL 60491 *Web:* bearylandscaping.com	815-838-4100	838-3200	192
Beasley Allen Crow Methvin 218 Commerce St Montgomery AL 36104 *TF:* 800-898-2034 ■ *Web:* www.beasleyallen.com	334-269-2343		428
Beasley Broadcast Group Inc 3033 Riviera Dr Ste 200 Naples FL 34103 *NASDAQ: BBGI* ■ *Web:* bbgi.com	239-263-5000		643
Beasley Direct Marketing Inc 15227 Perry Ln Morgan Hill CA 95037 *Web:* beasleydirect.com	408-782-0046		225
Beasley Forest Products Inc 712 Uvalda Hwy Hazlehurst GA 31539 *Web:* www.beasleyforestproducts.com	912-375-5174	375-9541	683
Beasley Media Group Inc 55 Morrissey Blvd Boston MA 02125 *Web:* www.rock929rocks.com	617-931-1111		645-22
Beasley Mitchell Co 509 S Main St Ste A Las Cruces NM 88004 *Web:* www.bmc-cpa.com	575-528-6700		2
Beatin Path Publications LLC 302 E College St Bridgewater VA 22812 *Web:* www.beatinpathpublications.com	540-478-4833		637-2
Beatitudes Campus of Care 1610 W Glendale Ave Phoenix AZ 85021 *Web:* beatitudescampus.org	602-995-2611		672
Beatport LLC 3461 Ringsby Ct Ste 150 Denver CO 80216 *Web:* www.beatport.com	720-974-9500		526
Beatrice Concrete Company Inc 400 Scott St Beatrice NE 68310 *Web:* www.beatriceconcretecompany.com	402-223-4289		182
Beatrice Daily Sun 200 N 7th St Beatrice NE 68310 *Web:* beatricedailysun.com	402-228-3571		532-2
Beatty Group 9800 Beaverton Hillsdale Ste 105 Beaverton OR 97005 *Web:* beattygroup.com	503-644-3340		384
Beatty Joyce (Rep D - OH) 2303 Rayburn House Office Bldg Washington DC 20515 *Web:* www.beatty.house.gov	202-225-4324	225-1984	342-2
Beatty Machine & Manufacturing Company Inc 940 150th St Hammond IN 46327 *Web:* www.beattymachine.com	219-931-3000	937-1662	456
Beatty Management Company Inc 6824 Elm St Ste 200 McLean VA 22101 *Web:* www.beattycos.com	703-821-0500		652
Beau Monde College of Hair Design 1221 SW 12th Ave Portland OR 97205 *Web:* www.beaumondecollege.com	503-226-1427	241-2823	167-3
Beau Rivage Resort & Casino 875 Beach Blvd Biloxi MS 39530 *TF:* 888-750-7111 ■ *Web:* beaurivage.mgmresorts.com	228-386-7111	386-7414	669
Beauchamp Construction Co 2100 Ponce De Leon Blvd Ste 825 Coral Gables FL 33134 *Web:* www.beauchampco.com	305-445-0819	447-0941	186
Beauchamp Distributing Co 1911 S Santa Fe Ave Compton CA 90221 *Web:* www.beauchampdist.com	310-639-5320		81-1
Beaufort County Board of Education 321 Smaw Rd Washington NC 27889 *Web:* www.beaufort.k12.nc.us	252-946-6593		685
Beaufort County Clerk of Court 102 Ribaut Rd Ste 208 Beaufort SC 29902 *Web:* beaufortcountysc.gov	843-255-5050	255-9412	338
Beaufort County Community College 5337 Hwy 264 E Washington NC 27889 *Web:* beaufortccc.edu	252-946-6194	940-6393	162
Beaufort County North Carolina 121 W Third St Washington NC 27889 *Web:* co.beaufort.nc.us	252-946-0079	946-7722	338
Beaufort Memorial Hospital 955 Ribaut Rd Beaufort SC 29902 *TF:* 877-532-6472 ■ *Web:* www.bmhsc.org	843-522-5200		374-3
Beaufort National Cemetery 1601 Boundary St Beaufort SC 29902 *Web:* www.cem.va.gov	843-524-3925	524-8538	136
Beaufort-Jasper Water & Sewer Authority 6 Snake Rd Okatie SC 29909 *TF:* 888-826-7658 ■ *Web:* www.bjwsa.org	843-987-9200		806
Beaufurn LLC 5269 US Hwy 158 Advance NC 27006 *TF:* 888-766-7706 ■ *Web:* www.beaufurn.com	336-941-3446		321
Beaujolais Bistro 753 Riverside Dr Reno NV 89503 *Web:* beaujolaisbistro.com	775-323-2227		671
Beaulieu Vineyard 1960 St Helena Hwy Rutherford CA 94573 *TF:* 800-373-5896 ■ *Web:* www.bvwines.com	707-257-5749		80-3
Beaumont at Bryn Mawr 601 N Ithan Ave Bryn Mawr PA 19010 *Web:* www.beaumontretirement.com	610-526-7000	525-0293	672
Beaumont Chamber of Commerce 1110 Park St Beaumont TX 77701 *Web:* www.bmtcoc.org	409-838-6581	833-6718	139
Beaumont Chamber of Commerce 306 E Sixth St Beaumont CA 92223 *Web:* www.beaumontcachamber.com	951-845-9541	769-9080	139
Beaumont Civic Center Complex 701 Main St Beaumont TX 77701 *TF:* 800-782-3081 ■ *Web:* discoverbeaumont.com	409-838-3435		205
Beaumont Convention & Visitors Bureau 505 Willow St Beaumont TX 77701 *TF:* 800-392-4401 ■ *Web:* www.beaumontcvb.com	409-880-3749		206
Beaumont Enterprise 300 Main St Beaumont TX 77701 *Web:* www.beaumontenterprise.com	409-838-2888		532-2
Beaumont Hospital 3601 W 13-Mile Rd Royal Oak MI 48073 *Web:* www.beaumont.org	248-898-5000		353
Beaumont Library District 125 E Eigth St Beaumont CA 92223 *Web:* bld.lib.ca.us	951-845-1357		434-3
Beaumont Public Library System 801 Pearl St Beaumont TX 77701 *Web:* beaumonttexas.gov	409-838-6606	838-3838	434-3
Beaumont Rice Mills Inc 1800 Pecos St Beaumont TX 77701 *Web:* www.bmtricemills.com	409-832-2521	832-6927	296-23
Beaumont School 3301 N Park Blvd Cleveland Heights OH 44118 *Web:* www.beaumontschool.org	216-321-2954		685
Beauregard Electric Co-opeartive Inc 1010 E First St DeRidder LA 70634 *TF:* 800-367-0275 ■ *Web:* www.beci.org	337-463-6221	463-2809	245
Beauregard Parish PO Box 100 DeRidder LA 70634 *Web:* beauregardclerk.org	337-463-8595	462-3916	338
Beauregard Parish Library 205 S Washington Ave Deridder LA 70634 *TF:* 800-524-6239 ■ *Web:* www.library.beau.org	337-463-6217	462-5434	434-3
Beauregard-Keyes House 1113 Chartres St New Orleans LA 70116 *Web:* www.bkhouse.org	504-523-7257		50-3
Beautiful Restaurant, The 2260 Cascade Rd SW Atlanta GA 30311 *Web:* www.beautifulrestaurant-atlanta.com	404-752-5931	758-4767	671
Beautiful Rooms Furniture 42 Myron St West Springfield MA 01089 *TF:* 800-281-9071 ■ *Web:* www.beautifulrooms.net	413-737-4012	737-3714	320
Beauti-Vue Products Corp 8555 194th Ave Bristol WI 53104 **Fax Area Code:* 800 ■ *Web:* www.beautivue.com	262-857-2306	329-9431*	87
Beauty Bar LLC 2919 W Central Ave Toledo OH 43606 *Web:* www.beauty-bar.com	419-537-5400		77
Beauty Brands Inc 4600 Madison St Ste 400 Kansas City MO 64112 *TF:* 877-640-2248 ■ *Web:* www.beautybrands.com	816-531-2266		77
Beauty Collection 15044 Keswick St Van Nuys CA 91405 *TF:* 866-881-8393 ■ *Web:* www.beautycollection.com	866-881-8393		77
Beauty Craft Supply & Equipment Co 11110 Bren Rd W Minnetonka MN 55343 *TF:* 800-328-5010 ■ *Web:* www.beautycraft.com	952-935-4420		77
Beauty Enterprises Inc 150 Meadow St Hartford CT 06114 *Web:* www.beautyenterprises.net	860-760-1265	296-0421	238
Beauty Management Inc 270 Beavercreek Rd Oregon City OR 97045 *Web:* www.perfectlooksalons.com	503-723-3200		77
Beauty School of Middletown 225 Dolson Ave Middletown NY 10940 *TF:* 888-317-8966 ■ *Web:* www.thebeautyschoolofmiddletown.com	845-343-2171	343-0119	685
Beauty Schools of America 1176 SW 67 Ave Miami FL 33144 *Web:* www.bsa.edu	305-267-6604	267-5105	77
Beauty West Inc 13891 Nautilus Dr Garden Grove CA 92843 *TF:* 800-344-9806 ■ *Web:* beautywests.com	714-265-6100		77
Beauvais Manor On The Park 3625 Magnolia Ave Saint Louis MO 63110 *Web:* beauvaismanor.com	314-771-2990		672
Beaver Aerospace & Defense Inc 11850 Mayfield St Livonia MI 48150 *Web:* www.beaver-online.com	734-853-5003	853-5043	223
Beaver Aviation Service Inc 605 Danley Dr Fort Myers FL 33907 *Web:* www.beaveraviation.com	239-939-6010	939-6011	167-3
Beaver County PO Box 338 Beaver OK 73932 *Web:* okcounties.org	580-625-3151		338
Beaver County Courthouse 810 3rd St Beaver PA 15009 *Web:* www.beavercountypa.gov	724-728-5700	728-8853	338
Beaver County Chamber of Commerce 798 Turnpike St Beaver PA 15009 *Web:* beavercountychamber.com	724-775-3944	728-9737	139
Beaver County Times 400 Fair Ave Beaver PA 15009 *Web:* www.timesonline.com	724-775-3200	775-4180	532-2
Beaver Creek Cooperative Telephone Co 15223 Henrici Rd Oregon City OR 97045 *Web:* www.bctelco.com	503-632-3113		387
Beaver Creek Nature Area 48351 264th St Valley Springs SD 57068 *TF:* 800-710-2267 ■ *Web:* gfp.sd.gov	605-594-3824	773-6245	565
Beaver Creek State Park Winter Hike 12021 Echo Dell Rd East Liverpool OH 43920 *Web:* trails.ohiodnr.gov	330-385-3091		565
Beaver Creek Valley State Park 15954 County 1 Caledonia MN 55921 *Web:* www.dnr.state.mn.us	507-724-2107		565
Beaver Dam Community Hospital 707 S University Ave Beaver Dam WI 53916 *Web:* bdch.com	920-887-7181		374-3
Beaver Dam State Park 14548 Beaver Dam Ln Plainview IL 62685 *Web:* www2.illinois.gov	217-854-8020		565
Beaver Dunes State Park Hwy 270 N Beaver OK 73932 *TF:* 800-654-8240 ■ *Web:* www.travelok.com	580-625-3373		565
Beaver Express 4310 Oklahoma Ave Woodward OK 73802 *TF:* 800-593-2328 ■ *Web:* www.beaverexpress.net	580-256-6460	256-6239	30
Beaver Falls Beauty Academy 720 13th St Beaver Falls PA 15010 *TF:* 800-841-4247 ■ *Web:* www.bfbeauty.com	724-843-7700		167-3
Beaver Island State Park 2136 W Oakfield Rd Grand Island NY 14072 *Web:* parks.ny.gov	716-773-3271		565
Beaver Lake Nature Ctr 8477 E Mud Lake Rd Baldwinsville NY 13027 *Web:* www.onondagacountyparks.com	315-638-2519	638-7488	50-5
Beaver Lake State Park 3850 70th St SE Wishek ND 58495 *Web:* www.parkrec.nd.gov	701-452-2752		565

Company / Address	City	State	ZIP	Phone	Fax	Class
Beaver Manufacturing Company Inc 12 Ed Needham Dr *Web:* beaverloc.com	Mansfield	GA	30055	770-786-1622		548
Beaver Oil Company Inc 6037 Lenzi Ave *Web:* www.beaveroil.com	Hodgkins	IL	60525	708-354-4040	354-5627	539
Beaver Run Resort & Conference Ctr 620 Village Rd *TF:* 800-525-2253 ■ *Web:* www.beaverrun.com	Breckenridge	CO	80424	970-453-6000		669
Beaver Steel Services Inc 1200 Arch St *Web:* www.beaversteel.com	Carnegie	PA	15106	412-429-8860		492
Beaver Street Brewery 11 S Beaver St *Web:* www.beaverstreetbrewery.com	Flagstaff	AZ	86001	928-779-0079		671
Beaver Street Fisheries Inc 1741 W Beaver St *TF:* 800-874-6426 ■ *Web:* beaverstreetfisheries.com	Jacksonville	FL	32209	904-354-8533		296-13
Beavercreek Chamber of Commerce 3210 Beaver-Vu Dr *Web:* www.beavercreekchamber.org	Beavercreek	OH	45431	937-426-2202	426-2204	139
Beavercreek Florist 2173 N Fairfield Rd *TF:* 888-216-4253 ■ *Web:* www.beavercreekflorist.com	Beavercreek	OH	45431	937-426-4253		292
Beaverhead County 2400 Airport Rd *Web:* beaverheadcounty.org	Dillon	MT	59725	406-683-3725	683-3728	338
Beavers Bend Resort Park PO Box 10 *TF:* 800-435-5514 ■ *Web:* www.beaversbend.com	Broken Bow	OK	74728	580-494-6300		565
Beaverton Area Chamber of Commerce 12600 SW Crescent St Ste 160 *TF:* 888-567-8688 ■ *Web:* beaverton.org	Beaverton	OR	97005	503-644-0123	526-0349	139
Beaverton City Library 12375 SW Fifth St *Web:* www.beavertonlibrary.org	Beaverton	OR	97005	503-526-2222		434-3
Beaverton Florists Inc 4705 SW Watson Ave *Web:* beavertonflorists.com	Beaverton	OR	97005	503-644-0129		293
Beaverton Foods Inc 7100 NW Century Blvd *TF:* 800-223-8076 ■ *Web:* beavertonfoods.com	Hillsboro	OR	97124	503-646-8138		296-19
Beavertooth Oak Inc 401 S Fir St *Web:* www.beavertooth.net	Medford	OR	97501	541-779-1942		191-3
Beavertown Block Company Inc 3612 Paxtonville Rd *Web:* www.beavertownblock.com	Middleburg	PA	17842	570-837-1744	837-1591	183
Beazer Homes USA Inc 1000 Abernathy Rd Ste 1200 *NYSE:* BZH ■ *Web:* www.beazer.com	Atlanta	GA	30328	770-829-3700		653
Beazley 30 Batterson Park Rd *Web:* www.beazley.com	Farmington	CT	06032	860-677-3700		390
Beber Silverstein Group 89 NE 27th St Unit 119 *Web:* www.thinkbsg.com	Miami	FL	33137	305-856-9800		7
BEC (Broadcast Equipment Corp) 1035 44th Dr *Web:* becny.com	Long Island City	NY	11101	718-784-5540		116
BEC Consulting LLC 3660 Hartsfield Rd *Web:* www.becconsult.com	Tallahassee	FL	32303	850-558-3100	575-8454	261
BEC Legal Systems 175 Tri County Pkwy Ste 120 *TF:* 800-948-4810 ■ *Web:* www.beclegal.com	Cincinnati	OH	45246	513-948-1500		180
Bechanan & Company LLC 22226 Creekview Dr *Web:* bechanan.com	Gaithersburg	MD	20882	301-869-3747	948-4688	2
Becharas Brothers Coffee Company Inc 14501 Hamilton Ave *TF:* 800-944-9675 ■ *Web:* www.becharas.com	Highland Park	MI	48203	313-869-4700	869-7940	297-2
Bechdon Company Inc, The 300 Commerce Dr *Web:* www.bechdon.com	Upper Marlboro	MD	20774	301-249-0900		454
Becherer Kannett & Schweitzer The Water Tower 1255 Powell St *Web:* bkscal.com	Emeryville	CA	94608	510-658-3600		428
Becher-Hoppe Associates Inc 330 Fourth St *Web:* www.becherhoppe.com	Wausau	WI	54403	715-845-8000		261
Bechik Products Inc 860 Blue Gentian Rd Ste 140 **Fax Area Code:* 651 ■ *TF:* 800-328-6569 ■ *Web:* bechik.com	Eagan	MN	55121	800-328-6569	698-1009*	471
Becht Engineering Company Inc 22 Church St PO Box 300 *Web:* becht.com	Liberty Corner	NJ	07938	908-580-1119		256
Bechtel Corp 50 Beale St *Web:* www.bechtel.com	San Francisco	CA	94105	415-768-1234	768-9038	261
Bechtels Pharmacy Inc 302 Main St *Web:* bechtelspharmacyinc.com	Slatington	PA	18080	610-767-4121		237
Beck & Hofer Construction Inc 618 E Maple St *Web:* beckandhofer.com	Sioux Falls	SD	57104	605-336-0118		186
Beck Aluminum Corp 6150 Parkland Blvd Ste 260 *Web:* www.beckaluminum.com	Mayfield Heights	OH	44124	440-684-4848	684-4860	492
Beck Cultural Exchange Center Inc 1927 Dandridge Ave *Web:* www.beckcenter.net	Knoxville	TN	37915	865-524-8461	524-8462	50-2
Beck Group, The 1807 Ross Ave Ste 500 *Web:* www.beckgroup.com	Dallas	TX	75201	214-303-6200	303-6300	186
Beck Mack & Oliver LLC 565 5th Ave 19th Fl *Web:* www.beckmack.com	New York	NY	10017	212-661-2640	953-2511	401
Beck Manufacturing 330 E 9th St PO Box 510 *TF:* 800-301-2701 ■ *Web:* www.anvilintl.com	Waynesboro	PA	17268	717-762-9141	762-9153	595
Beck Oil Co 3345 Main St *Web:* gotobecks.com	Keokuk	IA	52632	319-524-9237		324
Beck Suppliers Inc 1000 N Frnt St *Web:* becksuppliers.com	Fremont	OH	43420	419-332-5527		581

Company / Address	City	State	ZIP	Phone	Fax	Class
Beck, Gogolski, Poska & Company Inc 914 Church St *Web:* bgpcpas.com	Honesdale	PA	18431	570-253-4612		2
Beck/Arnley 2375 Midway Ln *TF:* 888-464-2325 ■ *Web:* www.beckarnley.com	Smyrna	TN	37167	615-220-3200		54
Beckart Environmental Inc 6900 46th St *Web:* www.beckart.com	Kenosha	WI	53144	262-656-7680		804
Becker & Mayer 11120 NE 33rd Pl Ste 101 *Web:* beckermayer.com	Bellevue	WA	98004	425-827-7120	828-9659	626
Becker Arena Products Inc 6611 W Hwy 13 *TF:* 800-234-5522 ■ *Web:* beckerarena.com	Savage	MN	55378	952-890-2690		186
Becker Avionics Inc 10376 Usa Today Way *Web:* www.becker-avionics.com	Miramar	FL	33025	954-450-3137		22
Becker Capital Management Inc 1211 S W Fifth Ave Ste 2185 *Web:* www.beckercap.com	Portland	OR	97204	503-223-1720		401
Becker College 61 Sever St *TF:* 877-523-2537 ■ *Web:* www.becker.edu	Worcester	MA	01609	508-791-9241	890-1500	166
Becker Communications 119 Merchant St Ste 300 *Web:* www.beckercommunications.com	Honolulu	HI	96813	808-533-4165		637-9
Becker Cos 401 Main St Ste 110 *Web:* beckerbros.sitemanager.rentmanager.com	Peoria	IL	61602	309-676-1870	674-5454	186
Becker County 913 Lake Ave *Web:* www.co.becker.mn.us	Detroit Lakes	MN	56501	218-846-7305		338
Becker Media 144 Linden St *Web:* www.beckermedia.net	Oakland	CA	94607	510-465-6200		195
Becker Transportation Inc 1501 S Bulington Ave	Hastings	NE	68901	402-461-4454		314
Becker Trucking Inc 6350 S 143rd St *Web:* beckertruckinginc.com	Seattle	WA	98168	206-246-9500		311
Becker's ASC Review 35 E Wacker Dr Ste 1782 *TF:* 800-417-2035 ■ *Web:* www.beckersasc.com	Chicago	IL	60601	800-417-2035		194
Becker, Glynn, Muffly, Chassin & Hosins Llp Profit Sharing 299 Park Ave *Web:* beckerglynn.com	New York	NY	10171	212-888-3033		41
Beckerman & Beckerman 76 S Orange Ave Ste 205 *Web:* beckermanlawyers.com	South Orange	NJ	07079	973-762-7600		41
Beckerman & Co 430 Lake Ave *Web:* www.beckermanco.com	Colonia	NJ	07067	732-499-9200	499-9050	390
Becket & Lee LLP 16 General Warren Blvd *Web:* www.becket-lee.com	Malvern	PA	19355	610-644-7800		428
Becket Fund for Religious Liberty 1200 New Hampshire Ave NW Ste 700 *Web:* www.becketlaw.org	Washington	DC	20036	202-955-0095	955-0090	48-8
Beckett Air Inc 37850 Beckett Pkwy *TF:* 800-831-7839 ■ *Web:* beckettair.com	North Ridgeville	OH	44039	440-327-9999	327-3569	18
Beckett Fine Art Ltd 196 Locke St S *Web:* www.beckettfineart.com	Hamilton	ON	L8P4B4	416-922-5582		42
Beckett Football Card Monthly 4635 McEwen Rd *Web:* www.beckett.com	Dallas	TX	75244	972-991-6657		457-20
Beckfield College 16 Spiral Dr *Web:* www.beckfield.edu	Florence	KY	41042	859-371-9393		167-3
Beckham County PO Box 67 *Web:* beckham.okcounties.org	Sayre	OK	73662	580-928-2457	928-2467	338
Beckham Publications Group Inc 13019 Cedar Creek Ln **Fax Area Code:* 866 ■ *Web:* www.beckhamhouse.com	Silver Spring	MD	20904	301-384-7995	659-3306*	637-2
Beck-Lee Inc PO Box 528 *TF:* 800-235-2852 ■ *Web:* www.becklee.com	Stratford	CT	06615	800-235-2852		475
Beckley-Raleigh County Chamber of Commerce 245 N Kanawha St *Web:* www.brccc.com	Beckley	WV	25801	304-252-7328		139
Beckman & Gast Company Inc 282 W Kremer-Hoying Rd PO Box 307 *Web:* beckmangast.com	Saint Henry	OH	45883	419-678-4195	678-3005	296-20
Beckman Network Engineering 5385 Hollister Ave **Fax Area Code:* 213 ■ *TF:* 888-771-6053 ■ *Web:* www.becknet.com	Santa Barbara	CA	93111	888-771-6053	330-0210*	261
Beckman Schmalzle Plc 102 N King St *Web:* bsgrlaw.com	Leesburg	VA	20176	703-722-0717		41
Beckmann Converting Inc 14 Pk Dr PO Box 390 *Web:* www.beckmannconverting.com	Amsterdam	NY	12010	518-842-0073	842-0282	745-2
Beckmann Distribution Service 10414 Bartelso Rd *TF:* 800-527-9486 ■ *Web:* beckmanndistribution.com	Carlyle	IL	62231	618-227-8785	227-8316	780
Beckmann's Old World Bakery Ltd 104 Bronson St Ste 6 *Web:* www.beckmannsbakery.com	Santa Cruz	CA	95062	831-423-9242		345
Beckmanxmo 376 Morrison Rd *TF:* 800-864-2232 ■ *Web:* beckmanxmo.com	Columbus	OH	43213	614-864-2232	864-3305	627
Beckmill Research LLC 108 Deer Dr *Web:* www.beckmill.com	Lexington	VA	24450	540-463-6200		196
Becknell Wholesale Co 504 E 44th St *Web:* www.becknell.com	Lubbock	TX	79404	806-747-3201		350
Becks Furniture Inc 11840 Folsom Blvd *Web:* www.becksfurniture.com	Rancho Cordova	CA	95742	916-353-5000		321
Beckta Dining & Wine 150 Elgin St *Web:* www.beckta.com	Ottawa	ON	K2P1L4	613-238-7063		671
Beco Equipment Co 5555 Dahlia St *Web:* www.becoequipment.com	Commerce City	CO	80022	303-288-2613	288-5776	264-3
Beco Management Inc 5410 Edson Ln Ste 200 *TF:* 800-967-2326 ■ *Web:* www.beconet.com	Rockville	MD	20852	301-816-1500	816-1501	652
Be-Cool Inc 903 Woodside Ave *TF:* 800-691-2667 ■ *Web:* becool.com	Essexville	MI	48732	989-895-9699	892-9213	612

Company / Address	Phone	Fax	Class
BECS Technology Inc 10818 Midwest Industrial Blvd .... Saint Louis MO 63132 *Web:* www.becs.com	314-567-0088		201
Becterm Inc 4780 Boul Henri-Bourassa .... Quebec City QC G1H3A7 *Web:* becterm.com	418-622-6777		196
Becton Healthcare Resources Inc 5674 Stoneridge Dr Ste 116 .... Pleasanton CA 94588 *Web:* www.bhrcorp.org	925-520-0005		194
Bed & Breakfast Association of Downtown Toronto PO Box 190 Stn B .... Toronto ON M5T2W1 *Web:* www.bnbinfo.com	416-410-3938	483-8822	376
Bed & Breakfast Atlanta 790 N Ave .... Atlanta GA 30324 *TF:* 800-123-4567 ■ *Web:* bed-and-breakfasts.find-near-me.info	404-875-0525		376
Bed Bath & Beyond Inc 650 Liberty Ave .... Union NJ 07083 *NASDAQ:* BBBY ■ *TF:* 800-462-3966 ■ *Web:* www.bedbathandbeyond.com	908-688-0888		362
BedandBreakfast.com 700 Brazos St Ste B-700 .... Austin TX 78701 *TF:* 800-462-2632 ■ *Web:* www.bedandbreakfast.com	512-322-2700	320-0883	773
Bedco Inc 4600 Bree Rd .... East China MI 48054 *Web:* www.bedcoinc.com	810-329-2292	329-4017	456
Bedell Frazier Investment Counselling LLC 2 Walnut Creek Ctr 200 Pringle Ave Ste 555 .... Walnut Creek CA 94596 *TF:* 800-783-0344 ■ *Web:* bedellfrazier.com	925-932-0344	932-8216	401
Beden-Baugh Products Inc 105 Lisbon Rd .... Laurens SC 29360 *TF:* 866-598-5794 ■ *Web:* www.naclsolutions.com	864-682-3136		199
Bedford Area Chamber of Commerce 305 E Main St .... Bedford VA 24523 *Web:* www.bedfordareachamber.com	540-586-9401		139
Bedford Consulting Group Inc 145 Adelaide St W Ste 400 .... Toronto ON M5H4E5 *Web:* bedfordgroup.com	416-963-9000		193
Bedford County 200 S Juliana St .... Bedford PA 15522 *Web:* bedfordcountypa.org	814-623-4807	623-4831	338
Bedford County Chamber of Commerce 203 S Juliana St .... Bedford PA 15522 *Web:* www.bedfordcountychamber.com	814-623-2233	623-6089	139
Bedford County Visitors Bureau 131 S Juliana St .... Bedford PA 15522 *TF:* 800-765-3331 ■ *Web:* www.visitbedfordcounty.com	814-623-1771	623-1671	206
Bedford Farm Bureau Coop 102 Industrial Ave .... Bedford PA 15522 *TF:* 800-240-6194 ■ *Web:* www.bfbcoop.com	814-623-6194	623-1488	276
Bedford Federal Savings Bank 1030 15th St .... Bedford IN 47421 *Web:* bedfed.com	812-275-5907		70
Bedford Gazette 424 W Penn St .... Bedford PA 15522 *TF:* 800-242-4250 ■ *Web:* www.bedfordgazette.com	814-623-1151		532-3
Bedford Hills Correctional Facility 247 Harris Rd .... Bedford Hills NY 10507 *Web:* www.doccs.ny.gov	914-241-3100		213
Bedford (Independent City) 215 E Main St .... Bedford VA 24523 *Web:* www.bedfordva.gov	540-587-6001		338
Bedford Industries Inc 1659 Rowe Ave .... Worthington MN 56187 *TF:* 877-233-3673 ■ *Web:* bedford.com	507-376-4136		548
Bedford Machine & Tool Inc 2103 John Williams Blvd .... Bedford IN 47421 *Web:* www.bedfordmachine.com	812-275-1948		491
Bedford Management Co 196 Bedford Ave .... Brooklyn NY 11249 *Web:* bedfordmanagement.com	718-388-0025		463
Bedford Materials Company Inc 7676 Allegheny Rd .... Manns Choice PA 15550 *TF:* 800-773-4276 ■ *Web:* www.bedfordmaterials.com	814-623-9014	623-9199	816
Bedford Paper Inc 1891 Commerce Dr .... De Pere WI 54115 *Web:* www.bedfordpaper.com	888-336-1412		558
Bedford Public Library 1323 K St .... Bedford IN 47421 *Web:* www.bedlib.org	812-275-4471		434-3
Bedford Public Schools 1623 W Sterns Rd .... Temperance MI 48182 *Web:* www.bedford.k12.mi.us	734-850-6000	850-6099	685
Bedford Recycling Cener 904 Summit Ln .... Bedford IN 47421 *Web:* www.bedfordrecycling.com	812-275-6883		492
Bedford Reinforced Plastics Inc 264 Reynoldsdale Rd .... Bedford PA 15522 *Web:* bedfordreinforced.com	814-623-8125		596
Bedford Road Pharmacy Inc 11306 Bedford Rd NE .... Cumberland MD 21502 *TF:* 800-788-6693 ■ *Web:* www.pharmacareofcumberland.com	301-777-1771	777-0119	238
Bedford Rural Electric Co-opeartive Inc 8846 Lincoln Hwy .... Bedford PA 15522 *TF:* 800-808-2732 ■ *Web:* www.bedfordrec.com	814-623-5101	623-7983	245
Bedford Technology LLC 2424 Armour Rd PO Box 609 .... Worthington MN 56187 *TF:* 800-721-9037 ■ *Web:* plasticboards.com	507-372-5558	372-5726	661
Bedford Underwriters Ltd 315 E Mill St .... Plymouth WI 53073 *Web:* bedfordunderwriters.com	920-892-8795		390
Bedford Village Inn 2 Olde Bedford Way .... Bedford NH 03110 *TF:* 800-852-1166 ■ *Web:* www.bedfordvillageinn.com	603-472-2001		671
Bedford-Stuyvesant Community Legal Services Corp 1368 Fulton St .... Brooklyn NY 11216 *Web:* restorationplaza.org	718-636-6900		41
Bedoukian Research Inc 21 Finance Dr .... Danbury CT 06810 *Web:* www.bedoukian.com	203-830-4000	830-4010	145
Bedroc Inc 3351 Aspen Grove Dr Ste 350 .... Franklin TN 37067 *Web:* bedroc.com	615-815-1785		631
Bedrock Prime 1309 N Wilson Rd Ste A .... Radcliff KY 40160 *TF:* 866-334-5914 ■ *Web:* bedrockprime.com	270-351-8043		177
Bedroom Store Inc 2440 Adie Rd .... Maryland Heights MO 63043 *Web:* thebedroomstore.com	314-822-2617		321
BeDynamic Inc 1725 Westlake Ave N Ste 150 .... Seattle WA 98109 *Web:* bedynamic.com	206-458-6950		132
Bee County Chamber of Commerce 1705 N St Mary .... Beeville TX 78102 *Web:* members.experiencebeecounty.org	361-358-3267		139
Bee Steel Inc 2090 Celebration Dr Ste 209 .... Grand Rapids MI 49525 *Web:* www.beesteelinc.com	616-363-6694		492
Bee Trailers Inc 524 Harrell Rd .... Climax GA 39834 *TF:* 800-266-2052 ■ *Web:* www.beetrailers.com	800-266-2052		273
Bee Trucking Inc 9540 Ball St .... San Antonio TX 78217 *Web:* www.alisamtransportationsolutions.com	210-646-7211	646-6218	780
Bee Window Inc 1002 E 52nd St .... Indianapolis IN 46205 *TF:* 855-677-5530 ■ *Web:* www.beewindow.com	855-677-5530		604
Bee-alive Inc 151 North Rt 9W .... Congers NY 10920 *TF:* 800-543-2337 ■ *Web:* www.beealive.com	800-543-2337		231
Beebe Medical Ctr 424 Savannah Rd .... Lewes DE 19958 *Web:* www.beebehealthcare.org	302-645-3300		374-3
Beech Fork State Park 5601 Long Branch Rd .... Barboursville WV 25504 *Web:* wvstateparks.com	304-528-5794		565
Beech Mountain Vacation Rentals Inc 301 Pinnacle Inn Rd .... Beech Mountain NC 28604 *TF:* 800-405-7888 ■ *Web:* www.beechmountainvacationrentals.com	828-387-2231		669
Beecher Hill LLC 9991 Beecher Hill Rd .... Peshastin WA 98847 *Web:* beecherhill.com	509-548-0559		379
Beecher Investors Inc 1266 E Main St Ste 700R .... Stamford CT 06902 **Fax Area Code:* 888 ■ *Web:* beecherinvestors.com	212-779-2200	760-4093*	401
Beechmont Pet Hospital 6400 Salem Rd .... Cincinnati OH 45230 *Web:* beechmontpethospital.com	513-232-4550		794
Beech-Nut Nutrition Corp 1 Nutritious Pl .... Amsterdam NY 12010 *TF:* 800-233-2468 ■ *Web:* www.beechnut.com	800-233-2468		296-36
Beechwood Hotel 363 Plantation St .... Worcester MA 01605 *TF:* 800-344-2589 ■ *Web:* www.beechwoodhotel.com	508-754-5789		379
Beecken Petty O'Keefe & Co 131 S Dearborn St Ste 2800 .... Chicago IL 60603 *Web:* bpoc.com	312-435-0300	435-0371	792
Beed's Lake State Park 1422 165th St Pk .... Hampton IA 50441 *Web:* www.iowadnr.gov	641-456-2047		565
Beef Magazine 7900 International Dr Ste 300 .... Minneapolis MN 55425 *TF:* 800-722-5334 ■ *Web:* www.beefmagazine.com	952-851-9329	851-4601	457-1
Beef Northwest Feeders Inc 3455 Victorio Rd .... Nyssa OR 97913 *Web:* www.beefnw.com	541-898-2288		10-1
Beef O'Bradys Inc 5660 W Cypress St Ste A .... Tampa FL 33607 *TF:* 800-728-8878 ■ *Web:* www.beefobradys.com	813-226-2333		670
Beefeaters Inc 1110 Brickell Ave Ste 302 .... Miami FL 33131 *Web:* beefeaters.com	305-967-8826		366
Beefmaster Breeders United (BBU) 6800 Pk Ten Blvd Ste 290-W .... San Antonio TX 78213 *Web:* www.beefmasters.org	210-732-3132	732-7711	48-2
Beehive Botanicals Inc 16297 W Nursery Rd .... Hayward WI 54843 *TF:* 800-233-4483 ■ *Web:* www.beehivebotanicals.com	715-634-4274		799
Beehive Specialty Co 8701 Wall St Ste 900 .... Austin TX 78754 *Web:* beehivespecialty.com	512-912-7940		4
Beekley Corp 1 Prestige Ln .... Bristol CT 06010 *TF:* 800-233-5539 ■ *Web:* www.beekley.com	860-583-4700		476
Beekman Arms-delamater Inn Inc 6387 Mill St .... Rhinebeck NY 12572 *Web:* www.beekmandelamaterinn.com	845-876-7077		707
Beeler Tractor Co 887 E Onstott Rd .... Yuba City CA 95991 *Web:* www.beelertractor.com	530-673-3555		274
Beelman Truck Co 1 Racehorse Dr .... East Saint Louis IL 62205 *TF:* 800-541-5918 ■ *Web:* www.beelman.com	618-646-5300		780
Beemac Trucking 2747 Legionville Rd .... Ambridge PA 15003 *TF:* 800-282-8781 ■ *Web:* beemactrucking.com	724-266-8781		685
Beemer Precision Inc 230 New York Dr PO Box 3080 .... Fort Washington PA 19034 *TF:* 800-836-2340 ■ *Web:* oilite.com	215-646-8440	283-3397	620
Beemsterboer Slag Corp 3411 Sheffield Ave .... Hammond IN 46327 *Web:* www.beemcompanies.com	219-931-7462		779
Beena Vision Systems Inc 600 Pinnacle Ct .... Norcross GA 30071 *Web:* www.beenavision.com	678-597-3156	597-0156	544
BeenVerified Inc (BV) 48 W 38th St 8th Fl .... New York NY 10018 **Fax Area Code:* 212 ■ *TF:* 888-579-5910 ■ *Web:* www.beenverified.com	888-579-5910	813-3276*	317
Beer and Slabaugh Inc 23965 Us Hwy 6 .... Nappanee IN 46550 *Web:* www.beerandslabaugh.com	574-773-3413		189-5
Beer Industry League of Louisiana 575 N Eighth St .... Baton Rouge LA 70802 *Web:* beerleague.com	225-343-3436		414
Beer Institute 440 First St NW Ste 350 .... Washington DC 20001 *TF:* 800-379-2739 ■ *Web:* www.beerinstitute.org	202-737-2337	737-7004	49-6
Beer Marketer's Insights Inc (BMI) 49 E Maple Ave .... Suffern NY 10901 *Web:* www.beerinsights.com	845-507-0040	507-0041	637-9
Beer Nuts Inc 103 N Robinson St .... Bloomington IL 61701 *Web:* beernuts.com	309-585-6159		296-28
Beere & Purves Inc 1350 Treat Blvd Ste 470 .... Walnut Creek CA 94597 *TF:* 888-722-3373 ■ *Web:* ga.beerepurves.com	888-722-3373		390
Beere Precision Products Inc 4915 21st St .... Racine WI 53406 *TF:* 800-348-0101 ■ *Web:* www.bccrc.com	262-632-0472	632-8142	791

	Phone	Fax	Class
Beer-wells Real Estate Services-East Texas Inc 430 N Center St .... Longview TX 75601 *Web:* beerwellseasttexas.com	903-753-2191		652
Beeryard, The 218 E Lancaster Ave........ Wayne PA 19087 *Web:* www.beeryard.com	610-688-3431		81-1
Beeson & Associates Inc 7711 Cambridge Ct .... Crestwood KY 40014 *Web:* www.beesoninc.com	502-241-8460		194
Beet Sugar Development Foundation 800 Grant St Ste 300 .... Denver CO 80203 *Web:* www.bsdf-assbt.org	303-832-4460	832-4468	48-2
Beeville Independent School District 201 N St Marys St .... Beeville TX 78102 *Web:* www.beevilleisd.net	361-358-7111	358-7837	780
Beeville Publishing Company Inc 111 N Washington .... Beeville TX 78102 *Web:* mysoutex.com	361-358-2550		532-3
Beezley Management LLC 23632 Calabasas Rd Ste 105 .... Calabasas CA 91302 *Web:* www.beezleymanagement.com	818-591-8555		195
Begam Marks & Traulsen PA 11201 N Tatum Blvd Ste 110 .... Phoenix AZ 85028 *Web:* bmt-law.com	602-254-6071		41
Beggar's Banquet 218 Abbott Rd .... East Lansing MI 48823 *Web:* beggarsbanquet.com	517-351-4540		671
Beggs & Lane RLLP 501 Commendencia St .... Pensacola FL 32502 *Web:* www.beggslane.com	850-432-2451		445
Beggs Insurance Agency 323 N Main St Ste 4 .... Crookston MN 56716 *Web:* beggsagency.com	218-281-3078		390
Beghou Consulting 1880 Oak Ave .... Evanston IL 60201 *Web:* www.beghouconsulting.com	847-864-5480		463
Beginnings For Parents 156 Wind Chime Ct Ste A .... Raleigh NC 27615 *TF:* 800-541-4327 ■ *Web:* ncbegin.org	919-715-4092	715-4093	48-17
Beginnings Salon & Day Spa Inc 1120 W Maple St .... Hartville OH 44632 *Web:* beginningssalonandspa.com	330-877-2473		77
Begley, Carlin & Mandio LLP 680 Middletown Blvd .... Langhorne PA 19047 *Web:* www.begleycarlin.com	215-750-0110	750-0954	428
Begneaud Manufacturing Inc 306 E Amedee Dr .... Scott LA 70583 *TF:* 800-358-8970 ■ *Web:* www.begno.com	337-237-5069		295
Behan Communications Inc 86 Glen St .... Glens Falls NY 12801 *TF:* 877-792-3856 ■ *Web:* www.behancommunications.com	877-792-3856		636
Behavioral Health Care Consultants Inc (BHC) 12 Windham Ln .... Beverly MA 01915 *Web:* www.bhcconsult.com	978-921-5968	921-9085	196
Behavioral Health Systems Inc (BHS) PO Box 830724 .... Birmingham AL 35209 *TF:* 800-245-1150 ■ *Web:* www.behavioralhealthsystems.com	205-879-1150	879-1178	374-5
Behavioral Healthcare Inc 1290 Chambers Rd .... Aurora CO 80011 *TF:* 844-528-0372 ■ *Web:* www.bhicares.org	303-361-8100	364-2240	374-5
Behavioral Measurement Database Services (BMDS) PO Box 110287 .... Pittsburgh PA 15232 *Web:* www.bmdshapi.com	412-687-6850	687-5213	387
Behlen Building Systems 4025 E 23rd St .... Columbus NE 68601 *TF:* 800-228-0340 ■ *Web:* behlenbuildingsystems.com	800-228-0340		186
Behlen Manufacturing Co 4025 E 23rd St .... Columbus NE 68601 *Web:* www.behlenmfg.com	402-564-3111	563-7405	105
Behler-Young Co 4900 Clyde Pk SW .... Grand Rapids MI 49509 *Web:* www.behler-young.com	616-531-3400	531-1453	612
Behnke Center for Contemporary Performance 100 W Roy St PO Box 19515 .... Seattle WA 98119 *Web:* www.ontheboards.org	206-217-9886	217-9887	572
Behnke Inc 600 Helmer Rd N .... Battle Creek MI 49037 *TF:* 800-234-6531 ■ *Web:* www.behnkeinc.com	269-962-4231	966-5709	780
Behnke Lubricants Inc W134N5373 Campbell Dr .... Menomonee Falls WI 53051 *Web:* www.jax.com	262-781-8850		579
Behnke Nurseries Co 11300 Baltimore Ave .... Beltsville MD 20705 *Web:* www.behnkes.com	301-937-1100	937-8034	323
Behr Process Corp 3400 W Segerstrom Ave .... Santa Ana CA 92704 *TF:* 800-854-0133 ■ *Web:* www.behr.com	714-545-7101	241-1002	550
Behrens Manufacturing Co 1250 E Sanborn St .... Winona MN 55987 *TF:* 800-657-4939 ■ *Web:* www.behrensmfg.com	507-454-4664	452-2106	488
Behringer Corp 17 Ridge Rd .... Branchville NJ 07826 *Web:* www.behringersystems.com	973-948-0226		492
Behringer Saws Inc 721 Hemlock Rd .... Morgantown PA 19543 *Web:* www.behringersaws.com	610-286-9777	286-9699	351
Behrman House Inc 11 Edison Pl .... Springfield NJ 07081 *Web:* store.behrmanhouse.com	973-379-7200		637-2
BEI Engineering Group Inc 10511 Six Mile Cypress Pkwy .... Fort Myers FL 33966 *Web:* www.banksengfla.com	239-939-5490		261
BEI Precision Systems & Space Company Inc 1100 Murphy Dr .... Maumelle AR 72113 *Web:* www.beiprecision.com	501-851-4000	851-5452	248
BEI Technologies Inc *Industrial Encoder Div* 7230 Hollister Ave .... Goleta CA 93117 *TF:* 800-350-2727 ■ *Web:* www.beiied.com	805-968-0782	968-3154	253
Beier Radio Inc 1150 N Causeway Blvd .... Mandeville LA 70471 *Web:* www.beieris.com	504-341-0123		770
Beijing 92 Rue de la Gauchetiere O .... Montreal QC H2Z1C1 *Web:* www.restaurantbeijing.net	514-861-2003		671
Beirne & Wirthlin Company LPA 1745 Madison Rd .... Cincinnati OH 45206 *Web:* beirneandwirthlin.com	513-221-1745		41
Beirut 4082 Monroe St .... Toledo OH 43606 *Web:* www.beirutrestaurant.com	419-473-0885		671
Beirut Restaurant 1385 Robert St S .... Saint Paul MN 55118 *Web:* www.beirutrestaurantanddeli.com	651-457-4886		671
Beisel & Dunlevy PA 730 Second Ave S Ste 282 .... Minneapolis MN 55402 *Web:* bdmnlaw.com	612-436-4343		41
Beisser's Inc 3705 SE Beisser Dr .... Grimes IA 50111 *Web:* www.beisserlumber.com	515-986-4422		364
Beistle Co 1 Beistle Plz .... Shippensburg PA 17257 *TF:* 800-445-2131 ■ *Web:* www.beistle.com	717-532-2131	532-7789	566
Beiswenger Hoch & Associates Inc c/o AZTEC Engineering Group Inc 4561 E McDowell Rd .... Phoenix AZ 85008	954-334-9000		186
Beiter's Inc 560 Montgomery Pk .... South Williamsport PA 17702 *Web:* www.beiters.com	800-326-9738		321
Beitler-Mckee Optical Co 160 S 22nd St .... Pittsburgh PA 15203 *TF:* 800-989-4700 ■ *Web:* www.beitlermckee.com	412-481-4700		542
Beitzel Corp 12072 Bittinger Rd .... Grantsville MD 21536 *Web:* beitzelcorp.com	301-245-4107		186
Bekaert Corp 3200 W Market St Ste 303 .... Akron OH 44333 *TF:* 800-555-1775 ■ *Web:* www.bekaert.com	330-867-3325	873-3424	813
Bekins Van Lines LLC 8010 Castleton Rd .... Indianapolis IN 46250 *TF:* 800-456-8092 ■ *Web:* www.bekins.com	800-456-8092		519
Bekker Compliance Consulting Partners LLC 19360 Rinaldi St Ste 453 .... Porter Ranch CA 91326 *Web:* www.bccp-llc.com	818-836-1291		194
Bekum America Corp 1140 W Grand River Ave PO Box 567 .... Williamston MI 48895 *Web:* www.bekumamerica.com	517-655-4331		604
Bel Air Finishing Supply Corp 101 Circuit Dr .... North Kingstown RI 02852 *Web:* www.belairfinishing.com	401-667-7902		481
Bel Air Investment Advisors 1999 Avenue of the Stars Ste 3200 .... Los Angeles CA 90067 *Web:* www.belair-llc.com	310-229-1500		401
Bel Brands USA Inc 30 S Wacker Dr Ste 3000 .... Chicago IL 60606 *TF:* 800-831-3724 ■ *Web:* www.belbrandsusa.com	920-788-3524		296-5
Bel Fuse Inc 206 Van Vorst St .... Jersey City NJ 07302 *NASDAQ: BELFA* ■ *TF:* 800-235-3873 ■ *Web:* belfuse.com	201-432-0463	432-9542	729
Bel Mar Wire Products Inc 2343 N Damen Ave .... Chicago IL 60647 *Web:* www.belmarwire.com	773-342-3800	342-0038	73
Belair Produce Inc 7226 Pkwy Dr .... Hanover MD 21076 *Web:* www.belairproduce.us	410-782-8000		297-7
Bel-Aire Mechanical Inc 4201 N 47th Ave .... Phoenix AZ 85031 *Web:* belairemechanical.com	623-846-8600		610
Belaire Products Inc 763 S Broadway St .... Akron OH 44311	330-253-3116		9
Belamar Hotel, The 3501 Sepulveda Blvd .... Manhattan Beach CA 90266 *Web:* www.thebelamar.com	310-750-0300		707
Belar Electronics Laboratory Inc 1140 Mcdermott Dr Ste 105 .... West Chester PA 19380 *Web:* www.belar.com	610-687-5550	687-2686	647
Bel-Art Products Inc 661 Rte 23 S .... Wayne NJ 07470 *TF:* 800-423-5278 ■ *Web:* www.belart.com	973-694-0500	694-7199	420
Belarus Tractor International Inc 7842 N Faulkner Rd .... Milwaukee WI 53224 *TF:* 800-356-2336 ■ *Web:* www.belarus.com	800-356-2336		274
Belcam Inc *Delagar Div* 27 Montgomery St .... Rouses Point NY 12979 *TF:* 800-328-3006 ■ *Web:* www.belcamshop.com	518-297-3366		214
Belcan Consulting Service LLC 9000 Keystone Xing Ste 1000 .... Indianapolis IN 46240 *TF:* 866-841-3671 ■ *Web:* allegiantworks.com	866-841-3671		260
Belcan Corp 10200 Anderson Way .... Cincinnati OH 45242 *TF:* 800-423-5226 ■ *Web:* belcan.com	513-891-0972		261
Belcaro Animal Hospital Pc 5023 Leetsdale Dr .... Denver CO 80246 *Web:* belcarovets.com	303-333-8800		794
BELCO (Belco Athletic Laundry Equipment Company Inc) PO Box 473430 .... Charlotte NC 28247 *Web:* www.belcoathleticlaundry.com	704-543-6061	543-6062	76
Belco Athletic Laundry Equipment Company Inc (BELCO) PO Box 473430 .... Charlotte NC 28247 *Web:* www.belcoathleticlaundry.com	704-543-6061	543-6062	76
Belco Industries Inc 9138 W Belding Rd .... Belding MI 48809 *Web:* www.belcoind.com	616-794-0410		318
Belco Manufacturing Company Inc 2303 Taylors Valley Rd .... Belton TX 76513 *TF:* 800-251-8265 ■ *Web:* www.belco-mfg.com	254-933-9000	939-2644	199
Belco Packaging Systems Inc 910 S Mountain Ave .... Monrovia CA 91016 *TF:* 800-833-1833 ■ *Web:* www.belcopackaging.com	626-357-9566	359-3440	547
Belden Brick & Supply Company Inc 620 Leonard St NW .... Grand Rapids MI 49504 *Web:* www.beldenbrickandsupply.com	616-459-8367		362
Belden Brick Company Inc PO Box 20910 .... Canton OH 44701 *Web:* www.beldenbrick.com	330-456-0031		150
Belden Inc 2200 US Hwy 27 S .... Richmond IN 47374 *TF:* 800-235-3362 ■ *Web:* www.belden.com	765-983-5200	983-5294	814
Belden Plastics Inc 2582 Long Lake Rd .... Saint Paul MN 55113 *TF:* 888-423-5336 ■ *Web:* www.beldenplastics.com	651-389-3600		105
Belden, Hiramoto, Liu & Company LLP 3158 Red Hill Ave Ste 110 .... Costa Mesa CA 92626 *Web:* bhlcpas.com	714-556-8140	556-8144	2
Belding Tank Technologies Inc 200 N Gooding St PO Box 160 .... Belding MI 48809 *TF:* 800-253-4252 ■ *Web:* www.beldingtank.com	616-794-1130	794-3666	610
Beldon 100 S Canyonwood Dr .... Dripping Springs TX 78620 **Fax Area Code: 210* ■ *TF:* 855-971-6936 ■ *Web:* www.beldon.com	512-337-1820	341-2959*	189-12

Name / Address	City	State	ZIP	Phone	Fax	Class
Bel-Fab Co 2737 Hwy 66 S	Rogersville	TN	37857	423-235-4163		207
Web: www.bel-fab.com						
Belfair State Park 3151 NE SR 300	Belfair	WA	98528	360-275-0668		565
Web: parks.state.wa.us						
Belfast Area Chamber of Commerce						
14 Main St	Belfast	ME	04915	207-338-5900		139
TF: 877-338-9015 ■ *Web:* www.belfastmaine.org						
Belfast Free Library 106 High St	Belfast	ME	04915	207-338-3884	338-3895	434-3
Web: www.belfast.lib.me.us						
Belfer Center for Science & International Affairs (BCSIA)						
Harvard Univ John F Kennedy School of Government						
79 JFK St	Cambridge	MA	02138	617-495-1400	495-8963	634
Web: www.belfercenter.org						
Belfint Lyons & Shuman PA						
1011 Centre Rd Ste 310	Wilmington	DE	19805	302-225-0600	225-0625	2
Web: www.belfint.com						
BelFlex Staffing Network						
11591 Goldcoast Dr	Cincinnati	OH	45249	513-241-8367		260
Web: belflex.com						
Belfonte Ice Cream Co						
1625 Cleveland Ave	Kansas City	MO	64127	816-231-2000	483-1442	296-25
Web: www.belfontedairy.com						
BELFOR (Canada) Inc						
3300 Bridgeway St	Vancouver	BC	V5K1H9	604-432-1123		667
TF: 888-432-1123 ■ *Web:* www.belfor.com						
Belford's Savannah						
315 W St Julian St	Savannah	GA	31401	912-233-2626		671
Web: www.belfordssavannah.com						
Belfort Furniture Inc						
22250 & 22267 Shaw Rd	Dulles	VA	20166	703-406-7600		321
Web: www.belfortfurniture.com						
Belfort Instrument Co						
727 S Wolfe St	Baltimore	MD	21231	410-342-2626		639
Web: belfortinstrument.com						
Belgian Draft Horse Corporation of America						
125 Southwood Dr	Wabash	IN	46992	260-563-3205		48-3
Web: www.belgiancorp.com						
Belgian-American Chamber of Commerce in the US (BACC)						
1177 Avenue of the Americas 7th Fl	New York	NY	10036	212-541-0771		138
Web: www.belcham.org						
Belgium						
Consulate General						
230 Peachtree St NW Ste 2710	Atlanta	GA	30303	404-659-2150		257
Web: www.diplomatie.belgium.be						
Consulate General						
6100 Wilshire Blvd Ste 1200	Los Angeles	CA	90048	323-857-0842	936-0786	257
Web: unitedstates.diplomatie.belgium.be						
Belham Management Inc						
9307 Monroe Rd	Charlotte	NC	28270	704-815-4246	849-6913	463
Web: www.bmienergy.com						
Belhaven College						
1500 Peachtree St PO Box 153	Jackson	MS	39202	601-968-5940	968-8946	166
TF: 800-960-5940 ■ *Web:* www.belhaven.edu						
Beliefnet 999 Waterside Dr Ste 1900	Norfolk	VA	23510	800-311-2458		171
TF: 800-311-2458 ■ *Web:* www.beliefnet.com						
Believe Books 2405 49th St NW	Washington	DC	20007	202-787-1532		637-2
Web: www.believebooks.com						
Believe In Tomorrow National Children's Foundation						
6601 Frederick Rd	Baltimore	MD	21228	410-744-1032	744-1984	48-6
Web: believeintomorrow.org						
Believe Wireless LLC						
9722 Groffs Mill Dr Ste 112	Owings Mills	MD	21117	410-902-0070		225
Web: www.believebroadband.com						
Believers Bookshelf PO Box 261	Sunbury	PA	17801	570-672-2134	672-7220	637-2
Web: www.bbusa.org						
BelieversPress						
4356 Montebello Dr Ste 26287	Colorado Springs	CO	80936	719-641-7862		637-2
Web: believersbookservices.com						
Belina Interiors Inc 4540 S Adams St	Tacoma	WA	98409	253-474-0276		362
Web: www.belinainteriors.com						
Belisle Machine & Tool Inc						
3430 Hwy 70 W	Camden	TN	38320	731-584-8468	584-5564	757
Web: www.belisletool.com						
Belitec Inc						
3320 Boul Gene-H-Kruger	Trois-Rivieres	QC	G9A4M3	819-373-3880	373-8744	535
Web: belitec.ca						
Beliveau, Fradette, Doyle & Gallant PA						
91 Bay St	Manchester	NH	03104	603-623-1234		428
Web: www.beliveau-fradette.com						
Belize Embassy						
2535 Massachusetts Ave NW	Washington	DC	20008	202-332-9636	332-6888	257
Web: www.embassyofbelize.gov.bz						
Belk Farms 57800 Desert Cactus Dr	Thermal	CA	92274	760-399-5951		10-4
Belk Inc 2801 W Tyvola Rd	Charlotte	NC	28217	704-357-1000		229
OTC: BLKIB ■ *Web:* www.belk.com						
Belknap County 34 County Dr	Laconia	NH	03246	603-527-5400	527-5409	338
Web: www.belknapcounty.org						
Belknap White Group, The						
111 Plymouth St	Mansfield	MA	02048	800-283-7500	337-2727*	364
**Fax Area Code:* 508 ■ *TF:* 866-298-0708 ■ *Web:* www.belknapwhite.com						
Bell & Associates Construction LP						
1000 Health Park Dr Ste 150 PO Box 363	Brentwood	TN	37027	615-373-4343	373-9224	188-4
Web: balp.com						
Bell & Evans						
154 W Main St PO Box 39	Fredericksburg	PA	17026	717-865-6626		619
Web: www.bellandevans.com						
Bell & Hudson Insurance Agency Inc						
19 N Main St PO Box 669	Belchertown	MA	01007	413-323-9611		390
Web: bellandhudson.com						
Bell + Howell 3791 S Alston Ave	Durham	NC	27713	919-767-6400	340-8852*	173-7
**Fax Area Code:* 585 ■ *TF:* 800-961-7282 ■ *Web:* bellhowell.net						
Bell Aerospace Services Inc						
1305 Airport Fwy Ste 123	Bedford	TX	76021	817-278-0750		529
Bell Container Corp 615 Ferry St	Newark	NJ	07105	973-344-4400	344-0817	100
TF: 877-995-2355 ■ *Web:* www.bellcontainer.com						
Bell County						
101 E Central Ave PO Box 768	Belton	TX	76513	254 939 3521	933-5179	338
TF: 800-460-2355 ■ *Web:* www.bellcountytx.com						
Bell County PO Box 157	Pineville	KY	40977	606-337-6143	337-5415	338
Web: www.bellcountyclerk.ky.gov						
Bell County Chamber of Commerce						
PO Box 788	Middlesboro	KY	40965	606-248-1075	248-8851	139
Web: www.bellcountychamber.net						
Bell County Expo Ctr 301 W Loop 121	Belton	TX	76513	254-933-5353		205
Web: www.bellcountyexpo.com						
Bell Curves LLC 25 W 36th St 8th Fl	New York	NY	10018	646-414-1586		196
TF: 877-223-3828 ■ *Web:* www.bellcurves.com						
Bell Electrical Contractors						
128 Millwell Dr	Maryland Heights	MO	63043	314-739-7744		189-4
TF: 800-717-2355 ■ *Web:* www.bellelectrical.com						
Bell Equipment Inc 311 Oak St	Nezperce	ID	83543	208-937-2402	937-2118	274
Web: www.belleq.com						
Bell Firm PA, The 810 Lisbon St	Lewiston	ME	04241	207-376-3330		41
Web: bellfirmmaine.com						
Bell Ford Inc 2401 W Bell Rd	Phoenix	AZ	85023	602-560-4165		57
TF: 800-688-1776 ■ *Web:* www.bellford.com						
Bell Fork Lift Inc						
34660 Centaur Dr	Clinton Township	MI	48035	586-415-5200	415-5201	770
TF: 888-404-2575 ■ *Web:* www.bellforklift.com						
Bell Foundry Co 5310 Southern Ave	South Gate	CA	90280	323-564-5701		492
Web: www.bfco.com						
Bell Gas Inc 1811 SE Main St	Roswell	NM	88203	575-622-4800		579
Bell Geospace Inc						
400 N Sam Houston Pkwy E Ste 325	Houston	TX	77060	281-591-6900	591-1985	539
Web: bellgeo.com						
Bell Harbor International Conference Ctr						
2211 Alaskan Way Pier 66	Seattle	WA	98121	206-441-6666	441-6665	205
TF: 888-772-4422 ■ *Web:* www.bellharbor.com						
Bell Investment Advisors						
1111 Broadway Ste 1630	Oakland	CA	94607	510-433-1066		401
TF: 800-700-0089 ■ *Web:* www.bellinvest.com						
Bell Litho Inc						
370 Crossen Ave	Elk Grove Village	IL	60007	847-952-3300		781
TF: 800-952-3306 ■ *Web:* www.bell-litho.com						
Bell Lumber & Pole Co						
778 1st St NW PO Box 120786	New Brighton	MN	55112	651-633-4334	633-8852	818
TF: 877-633-4334 ■ *Web:* www.blpole.com						
Bell Machine Company Inc						
910 Grimmett Dr	Shreveport	LA	71107	318-227-2515	226-0019	454
Web: bellmachine.com						
Bell Media Inc 299 Queen St W	Toronto	ON	M5V2Z5	416-924-6664		740
Web: www.bellmedia.ca						
Bell MTS 333 Main St	Winnipeg	MB	R3C3V6	204-225-5687		224
Web: www.bellmts.ca						
Bell Museum of Natural History						
10 Church St SE	Minneapolis	MN	55455	612-626-9660		520
Web: www.bellmuseum.umn.edu						
Bell Nursery 7111 Troy Hill Dr	Elkridge	MD	21075	410-782-4500		369
Web: www.bellnursery.com						
Bell Photographers						
341 Garfield St	Idaho Falls	ID	83401	208-524-4601		590
Web: www.bellphoto.com						
Bell Processing Inc						
1326 Burkburnett Rd	Wichita Falls	TX	76306	940-322-8621		492
Web: www.bellprocessing.com						
Bell Products Inc 722 Soscol Ave	Napa	CA	94559	707-255-1811		610
Web: www.bellproducts.com						
Bell Shoals Baptist Church of Brandon Inc						
2102 Bell Shoals Rd	Brandon	FL	33511	813-689-4229		48-20
Web: bellshoals.com						
Bell Steel Co 530 S C St	Pensacola	FL	32502	850-432-1545	434-1431	480
TF: 800-272-1545 ■ *Web:* bellsteel.com						
Bell Supply Inc						
7221 Rt 130	Pennsauken Township	NJ	08110	856-663-3900	665-2196	189-13
Web: www.bellsupplyinc.com						
Bell Techlogix 4400 W 96th St	Indianapolis	IN	46268	317-333-7777	890-9494*	180
**Fax Area Code:* 888 ■ *TF:* 866-782-2355 ■ *Web:* belltechlogix.com						
Bell Tower Hotel 300 S Thayer St	Ann Arbor	MI	48104	734-769-3010	769-4339	379
Web: www.belltowerhotel.com						
Bell Training Academy PO Box 482	Fort Worth	TX	76101	817-280-2011	280-2321	167-3
Web: www.bellflight.com						
Bell Trans 1900 Industrial Rd	Las Vegas	NV	89102	702-739-7990		184
TF: 800-274-7433 ■ *Web:* www.airportshuttlelasvegas.com						
Bell, Hess & Van Zant PLLC						
2819 Ring Rd	Elizabethtown	KY	42701	270-765-4196		41
Web: bhvzlaw.com						
Bell, Nunnally & Martin						
3232 McKinney Ave Ste 1400	Dallas	TX	75204	214-740-1400	740-1499	428
Web: www.bellnunnally.com						
Bella Cosa Inc 7163 S Kingery Hwy	Willowbrook	IL	60527	630-455-1234		410
Web: bellacosajewelers.com						
Bella Distribution Services						
PO Box 10543	Tallahassee	FL	32302	800-533-1973	576-3498*	95
**Fax Area Code:* 850 ■ *TF:* 800-533-1973 ■ *Web:* www.belladistribution.com						
Bella Fresca Restaurant						
6307 Line Ave	Shreveport	LA	71106	318-865-6307		671
Web: bellafresca.com						
Bella Ink Designs						
846 W Buckingham Pl Ste 4	Chicago	IL	60657	630-576-2008		130
Web: www.bellaink.com						
Bella Italia 6407 Iron Bridge Rd	Richmond	VA	23234	804-743-1116		671
Web: visitbellaitalia.com						
Bella Monica						
3121 EdWards Mill Rd Ste 103	Raleigh	NC	27612	919-881-9778		671
Web: www.bellamonica.com						
Bella Via 47-46 Vernon Blvd	Long Island City	NY	11101	718-361-7510		671
Web: www.bellavialic.com						
Bella Vista Mexican Restaurant						
127 E 20th Ave	Denver	CO	80205	303-297-9020		671
Bella Vista Restaurant & Lounge						
53 Maryland St	Winnipeg	MB	R3G1K6	204-775-4485	651-1274*	671
**Fax Area Code:* 323						
Bella Web Design Inc						
3605 Sandy Plains Rd Ste 240-121	Marietta	GA	30066	770-509-8797		180
Web: bellawebdesign.com						

Name / Address	City	State	ZIP	Phone	Fax	Class
Bellabay Realty LLC 1685 68th St SE *Web:* bellabayrealty.com	Caledonia	MI	49316	616-871-9200		652
Bellagio - Las Vegas 3600 Las Vegas Blvd S *TF:* 866-259-7111 ■ *Web:* bellagio.mgmresorts.com	Las Vegas	NV	89109	702-693-7111		671
Bellaire Home Health Care LLC 10786-D Bellaire Blvd *Web:* www.bellairehomehealthcare.com	Houston	TX	77072	281-564-9959	564-9989	363
Bellamy Automotive Group Inc 145 Industrial Blvd *Web:* www.bellamystrickland.com	Mcdonough	GA	30253	770-954-3000		57
Bellamy Management Services LLC 901 D St SW Ste 1009 *Web:* www.bms-llc.com	Washington	DC	20024	202-863-2270		463
Bellarmine University 2001 Newburg Rd *TF:* 800-274-4723 ■ *Web:* www.bellarmine.edu	Louisville	KY	40205	502-272-8000		166
Bellasera Hotel 221 Ninth St S *TF:* 844-898-4184 ■ *Web:* www.bellaseranaples.com	Naples	FL	34102	239-649-7333		379
Bellatrix Exploration Ltd 1920 800 5th Ave SW *Web:* www.bxe.com	Calgary	AB	T2P3T6	403-266-8670		539
Bellbrook 873 W Avon Rd *Web:* www.trinityhealthseniorcommunities.org	Rochester Hills	MI	48307	248-656-6300		450
Bellco First Federal Credit Union 7600 E Orchard Rd Ste 400N *TF:* 800-235-5261 ■ *Web:* www.bellco.org	Greenwood Village	CO	80111	303-689-7800		219
Bellco Glass Inc 340 Edrudo Rd *TF:* 800-257-7043 ■ *Web:* www.bellcoglass.com	Vineland	NJ	08360	856-691-1075	691-3247	333
Belle Chasse Academy Inc 100 Fifth St *Web:* www.bellechasseacademy.com	Belle Chasse	LA	70037	504-433-5850		685
Belle Fourche Area Community Ctr 1111 National St *Web:* www.bellefourche.org	Belle Fourche	SD	57717	605-892-6345		354
Belle Fourche Pipeline PO Box 2360 *Web:* www.bridgerpipeline.com	Casper	WY	82602	307-237-9301		597
Belle Grove Historic District 623 Garrison Ave Rm 331 *TF:* 866-795-5942 ■ *Web:* www.fortsmithar.gov	Fort Smith	AR	72902	479-784-2266	784-2462	50-3
Belle Haven Country Club Inc 6023 Ft Hunt Rd *Web:* www.bellehavencc.com	Alexandria	VA	22307	703-329-1448		31
Belle Haven Investments, Lp 800 Westchester Ave Ste N607 *Web:* bellehaven.com	Rye Brook	NY	10573	914-816-4633		690
Belle Isle State Park 1632 Belle Isle Rd *Web:* www.dcr.virginia.gov	Lancaster	VA	22503	804-462-5030		565
Belle Meade Plantation 5025 Harding Pk *TF:* 800-270-3991 ■ *Web:* bellemeadeplantation.com	Nashville	TN	37205	615-356-0501		520
Belle of Baton Rouge Casino & Hotel 102 France St *TF:* 800-676-4847 ■ *Web:* belleofbatonrouge.com	Baton Rouge	LA	70802	800-676-4847		133
Belle Plaine Coop 820 E Main St *Web:* www.belleplainemn.com	Belle Plaine	MN	56011	952-873-3244	873-5509	276
Belle Tire Inc 1000 Enterprise Dr *TF:* 888-462-3553 ■ *Web:* www.belletire.com	Allen Park	MI	48101	888-462-3553		62-5
Belleclaire Hotel Corp 250 W 77th St *Web:* www.hotelbelleclaire.com	New York	NY	10024	212-362-7700		378
Bellefonte Area School District 318 N Allegheny St *Web:* www.basd.net	Bellefonte	PA	16823	814-355-4814		685
Bellefonte Intervalley Chamber of Commerce 320 W High St *Web:* www.bellefonte.com	Bellefonte	PA	16823	814-355-2917		139
Bellekeep Books 29 5th Ave Ste 7A *Web:* www.bellekeepbooks.com	New York	NY	10003	917-231-2929		637-2
Belle-Pak Packaging Inc 7465 Birchmount Rd *TF:* 800-565-2137 ■ *Web:* www.belle-pak.com	Markham	ON	L3R5X9	905-475-5151	475-9295	601
Belleplain State Forest County Rt 550 PO Box 450 *Web:* www.njparksandforests.org	Woodbine	NJ	08270	609-861-2404		565
Bellerud Transport Inc 4520 19th Ave SW *TF:* 800-737-3347 ■ *Web:* www.bellerudtransport.com	Fargo	ND	58104	701-277-8321	277-0674	780
Belletech Corp 700 W Lake Ave *Web:* www.belletechcorp.com	Bellefontaine	OH	43311	937-599-3774	599-5478	695
Belleview-South Marion Chamber of Commerce 5331 SE Abshier Blvd *Web:* belleviewsouthmarionchamber.org	Belleview	FL	34420	352 245-2178		139
Belleville Area Chamber of Commerce 248 Main St *Web:* www.bellevilleareachamber.org	Belleville	MI	48111	734-697-7151	697-1415	139
Belleville Barber College 329 N Illinois St *Web:* www.bellevillebarbercollege.net	Belleville	IL	62220	618-234-4424		167-3
Belleville Chamber of Commerce 5 Moira St E *TF:* 888-852-9992 ■ *Web:* www.bellevillechamber.ca	Belleville	ON	K8P2S3	613-962-4597	962-3911	137
Belleville General Hospital 265 Dundas St E *TF:* 800-483-2811 ■ *Web:* www.qhc.on.ca	Belleville	ON	K8N5A9	613-969-7400	968-8234	374-2
Belleville News-Democrat 120 S Illinois St *TF:* 800-642-3878 ■ *Web:* www.bnd.com	Belleville	IL	62220	618-234-1000	236-9773	532-2
Belleville Public Library & Information Ctr 221 Washington Ave *Web:* www.bellepl.org	Belleville	NJ	07109	973-450-3434		434-3
Belleville Shoe Manufacturing Co 100 Premier Dr *TF:* 800-376-6978 ■ *Web:* www.bellevilleboot.com	Belleville	IL	62220	618-233-5600	257-1112	301
Belleville Wire Cloth Inc 18 Rutgers Ave *TF:* 800-631-0490 ■ *Web:* www.bwire.com	Cedar Grove	NJ	07009	973-239-0074	239-3985	688
Bellevue Arts Museum 510 Bellevue Way NE *TF:* 800-367-2648 ■ *Web:* www.bellevuearts.org	Bellevue	WA	98004	425-519-0770	637-1799	520
Bellevue Botanical Garden 12001 Main St *Web:* www.bellevuebotanical.org	Bellevue	WA	98005	425-452-2750		97
Bellevue Chamber of Commerce 1036 Bruin Blvd Ste 119 *Web:* www.bellevuenebraska.com	Bellevue	NE	68005	402-898-3000	291-8729	139
Bellevue Chamber of Commerce 330 112th Ave NE Ste 100 *Web:* www.bellevuechamber.org	Bellevue	WA	98004	425-454-2464	462-4660	139
Bellevue Club Hotel 11200 SE Sixth St **Fax Area Code:* 425 ■ *TF:* 800-579-1110 ■ *Web:* www.bellevueclub.com	Bellevue	WA	98004	800-579-1110	688-3101*	379
Bellevue Community College 3000 Landerholm Cir SE *Web:* www.bellevuecollege.edu	Bellevue	WA	98007	425-564-1000	564-4065	162
Bellevue Drug Co 254 Bellevue Ave *Web:* bellevuedrug.com	Hammonton	NJ	08037	609-561-0825		237
Bellevue Healthcare 2112 116th Ave NE *Web:* www.bellevuehealthcare.com	Bellevue	WA	98004	425-451-2842	467-6661	475
Bellevue House National Historic Site 35 Centre St *Web:* www.pc.gc.ca	Kingston	ON	K7L4E5	613-545-8666	545-8721	563
Bellevue Leader 604 Fort Crook Rd N *Web:* www.omaha.com	Bellevue	NE	68005	402-733-7500	733-9116	532-4
Bellevue Public Library 1003 Lincoln Rd *Web:* www.bellevuelibrary.org	Bellevue	NE	68005	402-293-3157	293-3163	434-3
Bellevue State Park 800 Carr Rd *Web:* www.destateparks.com	Wilmington	DE	19809	302-761-6963	761-6951	565
Bellevue University 1000 Galvin Rd S *TF:* 800-756-7920 ■ *Web:* www.bellevue.edu	Bellevue	NE	68005	402-557-7313	557-5438	166
Bellflower Chamber of Commerce 16730 Bellflower Blvd *Web:* www.bellflowerchamber.com	Bellflower	CA	90706	562-867-1744	866-7545	139
Bellflower Health Ctr 10005 E Flower St **Fax Area Code:* 630 ■ *Web:* dhs.lacounty.gov	Bellflower	CA	90706	562-520-3000	241-0142*	374-3
Bellia Office Furniture Inc 1047 N Broad St *Web:* www.bellia.net	Woodbury	NJ	08096	856-845-2234		320
Bellin College of Nursing 3201 Eaton Rd *TF:* 800-236-8707 ■ *Web:* www.bellincollege.edu	Green Bay	WI	54311	920-433-6699	433-1922	166
Bellin Hospital 744 S Webster Ave *Web:* www.bellin.org	Green Bay	WI	54301	920-433-3500		374-3
Bellingham Herald 1155 N State St *Web:* www.bellinghamherald.com	Bellingham	WA	98225	360-650-7545		532-2
Bellingham Marine Industries Inc 1001 C St *TF:* 800-733-5679 ■ *Web:* www.bellingham-marine.com	Bellingham	WA	98225	360-676-2800	734-2417	188-5
Bellingham Public Library 100 Blackstone St *Web:* www.bellinghamlibrary.org	Bellingham	MA	02019	508-966-1660	966-3189	434-3
Bellingham Public Library 210 Central Ave *Web:* www.bellinghampubliclibrary.org	Bellingham	WA	98225	360-778 7323		434-3
Bellingham Review MS-9053 W Washington University *Web:* bhreview.org	Bellingham	WA	98225	360-650-4863		637-2
Bellingham Technical College 3028 Lindbergh Ave *Web:* www.btc.edu	Bellingham	WA	98225	360-752-7000		167-3
Bellingham/Whatcom Chamber of Commerce & Industry 119 N Commercial St Ste 110 *Web:* bellingham.com	Bellingham	WA	98225	360-734-1330	734-1332	139
Bellingrath Gardens & Home 12401 Bellingrath Garden Rd *TF:* 800-247-8420 ■ *Web:* bellingrath.org	Theodore	AL	36582	251-973-2217	973-0540	97
Bellino Fine Linens 471 S Dean St *Web:* www.bellinofinelinens.com	Englewood	NJ	07631	201-568-5255		361
Bellisio Foods Inc 1201 Harman Pl Ste 302 *Web:* www.bellisiofoods.com	Minneapolis	MN	55403	612-371-8222		296-36
Bell-Mark Corp 331 Changebridge Rd PO Box 2007 *Web:* www.bell-mark.com	Pine Brook	NJ	07058	973-882-0202	808-4616	547
Bellmont Cabinet Co 13610 52nd St E Ste 300 *Web:* bellmontcabinets.com	Sumner	WA	98390	253-321-3011		653
Bellmoor, The 6 Christian St *Web:* www.thebellmoor.com	Rehoboth Beach	DE	19971	302-227-5800		379
Bello Vita 2927 N Roan St *Web:* www.bellavitajc.com	Johnson City	TN	37601	423-282-8600		671
Bellomy Research Inc 175 Sunnynoll Ct *TF:* 800-443-7344 ■ *Web:* www.bellomy.com	Winston-Salem	NC	27106	800-443-7344		195
BellPoll Software Technologies LLC 16192 Coastal Hwy *TF:* 888-712-7872 ■ *Web:* bellpoll.com	Lewes	DE	19958	888-712-7872		180
Bellus Academy 13266 Poway Rd *TF:* 888-990-7094 ■ *Web:* www.bellusacademy.edu	Poway	CA	92064	858-748-1490		77
Bellus Health Inc 275 Armand Frappier Blvd *TSX:* BLU ■ *Web:* www.bellushealth.com	Laval	QC	H7V4A7	450-680-4500	680-4501	85
Bellwyck Packaging Inc 21 Finchdene Sq *Web:* www.bellwyck.com	Toronto	ON	M1X1A7	416-752-1210		393
Belmar 464 S Teller St *Web:* www.belmarcolorado.com	Lakewood	CO	80226	303-742-1520	987-7693	50-6
Belmark Inc 600 Heritage Rd PO Box 5310 *Web:* www.belmark.com	De Pere	WI	54115	920-336-2848	336-4577	113
Belmeade Signs 46 Simsbury Rd *TF:* 866-738-1757 ■ *Web:* www.belmeadesigns.com	West Granby	CT	06090	860-413-3569		9
Belmont Abbey College 100 Belmont-Mt Holly Rd *TF:* 888-222-0110 ■ *Web:* belmontabbeycollege.edu	Belmont	NC	28012	704-461-6700	461-6220	166

	Phone	Fax	Class
Belmont Abbey Monastery 100 Belmont Mount Holly Rd . . . Belmont NC 28012 *Web:* www.belmontabbey.org	704-461-5086		48-20
Belmont Brewing Co 25 39th Pl . . . Long Beach CA 90803 *Web:* www.belmontbrewing.com	562-433-3891	434-0604	671
Belmont Center for Comprehensive Treatment 4200 Monument Rd . . . Philadelphia PA 19131 *TF:* 800-220-4357 ■ *Web:* www.belmontbehavioral.com	800-220-4357		374-5
Belmont Chamber of Commerce 1059 Alameda De Las Pulgas . . . Belmont CA 94002 *Web:* www.belmontchamber.org	650-595-8696	204-6232	139
Belmont College 68094 Hammond Rd . . . Saint Clairsville OH 43950 *TF:* 800-423-1188 ■ *Web:* www.belmontcollege.edu	740-695-8516		167-3
Belmont County 101 W Main St . . . Saint Clairsville OH 43950 *Web:* www.belmontcountyohio.org	740-695-2121		338
Belmont Courthouse State Historic Park 16799 Lahontan Dam . . . Fallon NV 89406 *Web:* parks.nv.gov	775-867-3001		565
Belmont Hall & Restaurant 718 Grove St . . . Manchester NH 03103 *Web:* www.belmontrestaurant.com	603-625-8540		671
Belmont Icehouse LLC 3116 Commerce St Ste D . . . Dallas TX 75226 *Web:* belmonticehouse.com	972-755-3200		7
Belmont Lake State Park PO Box 247 . . . Babylon NY 11702 *Web:* parks.ny.gov	631-667-5055		565
Belmont Mansion 1900 Belmont Blvd . . . Nashville TN 37212 *Web:* www.belmontmansion.com	615-460-5459		50-3
Belmont Metals Inc 330 Belmont Ave . . . Brooklyn NY 11207 *Web:* www.belmontmetals.com	718-342-4900		492
Belmont Park 2150 Hempstead Tpke . . . Elmont NY 11003 *Web:* www.nyra.com	516-488-6000		642
Belmont Shore Land Co 201 Covina Ave Ste 7 . . . Long Beach CA 90803 *Web:* belmontshoreland.com	562-434-3066		460
Belmont Shore Veterinary Hospital 6222 E Pacific Coast Hwy . . . Long Beach CA 90803 *Web:* belmontshorevet.com	562-961-0028		794
Belmont Station 4500 SE Stark St . . . Portland OR 97215 *Web:* www.belmont-station.com	503-232-8538		297-2
Belmont Telephone Co 121 N Washington St . . . Cuba City WI 53807 *Web:* www.belmontwi.com	608-762-5800		224
Belmont Trading Company Inc 900 Corporate Grove Dr . . . Buffalo Grove IL 60089 *Web:* www.belmont-trading.com	847-412-9690	412-9692	246
Belmont University 1900 Belmont Blvd . . . Nashville TN 37212 *TF:* 800-563-6765 ■ *Web:* www.belmont.edu	615-460-6000	460-5434	166
Belmont Village LP 8554 Katy Fwy Ste 200 . . . Houston TX 77024 *Web:* www.belmontvillage.com	713-463-1700		345
Belnick Inc 4350 Ball Ground Hwy . . . Canton GA 30114 **Fax Area Code:* 770 ■ *TF:* 800-924-2472 ■ *Web:* www.bizchair.com	800-924-2472	721-8381*	320
Beloit College 700 College St . . . Beloit WI 53511 *TF:* 800-331-4943 ■ *Web:* www.beloit.edu	608-363-2500	363-2075	166
Beloit Convention & Visitors Bureau 500 Public Ave . . . Beloit WI 53511 *Web:* visitbeloit.com	608-365-4838		206
Beloit Daily News 149 State St . . . Beloit WI 53511 *Web:* www.beloitdailynews.com	608-365-8811	365-1420	532-2
Beloit Health System 1969 W Hart Rd . . . Beloit WI 53511 *TF:* 800-637-2641 ■ *Web:* beloithealthsystem.org	608-363-5724	363-5702	374-3
Beloit Pattern Works 819 Ingersoll Pl . . . South Beloit IL 61080 *Web:* beloitpatternworks.com	815-389-2578	389-4757	567
Beloit Regional Hospice 655 Third St Ste 200 . . . Beloit WI 53511 *TF:* 877-363-7421 ■ *Web:* www.beloitregionalhospice.com	608-363-7421	363-7426	371
Belpointe Capital 125 Greenwich Ave . . . Greenwich CT 06830 *Web:* belpointe.com	203-629-3300		77
Bel-Ray Company LLC PO Box 526 . . . Farmingdale NJ 07727 *Web:* www.belray.com	732-938-2421	938-4232	541
Bel-Rea Institute of Animal Technology 1681 S Dayton St . . . Denver CO 80247 *TF:* 800-950-8001 ■ *Web:* belrea.edu	303-751-8700	751-9969	800
Belshaw Adamatic Bakery 814 44th St NW Ste 103 . . . Auburn WA 98001 *TF:* 800-578-2547 ■ *Web:* www.belshaw-adamatic.com	206-322-5474		298
Belshire Environmental Services Inc 25971 Towne Centre Dr . . . Foothill Ranch CA 92610 *TF:* 800-995-8220 ■ *Web:* www.belshire.com	949-460-5200		63
Belson Outdoors Inc 111 N River Rd . . . North Aurora IL 60542 **Fax Area Code:* 630 ■ *TF:* 800-323-5664 ■ *Web:* www.belson.com	800-323-5664	897-0573*	319-4
Belstar Inc 8408 Arlington Blvd Ste 200 . . . Fairfax VA 22031 *TF:* 800-548-5921 ■ *Web:* belstar.com	703-645-0280	645-0286	261
Belstra Milling Company Inc 424 15th St . . . Demotte IN 46310 **Fax Area Code:* 219 ■ *TF:* 800-276-2789 ■ *Web:* www.belstramilling.com	800-276-2789	987-5227*	447
Belt Collins 2153 N King St Ste 200 . . . Honolulu HI 96819 *Web:* www.beltcollins.com	808-521-5361	538-7819	261
Belt Railway Company of Chicago, The 6900 S Central Ave . . . Bedford Park IL 60638 *TF:* 877-772-5772 ■ *Web:* www2.beltrailway.com	708-496-4000		651
Belt Tech Industrial Inc 1996 S 300 W . . . Washington IN 47501 *Web:* belttech1.com	812-644-7623		358
Belt Technologies Inc 11 Bowles Rd . . . Agawam MA 01001 *Web:* www.belttechnologies.com	413-786-9922	789-2786	620
Belterra Casino Resort 777 Belterra Dr . . . Florence IN 47020 *TF:* 888-235-8377 ■ *Web:* www.belterracasino.com	812-427-7777		669
Belterra Corp 1638 Fosters Way . . . Delta BC V3M6S6 *Web:* www.belterra.ca	604-540-1950		370
Belting Industries Group 1090 Lousons Rd . . . Union NJ 07083 *TF:* 800-843-2358 ■ *Web:* beltingindustries.com	908-272-8591	272-3825	370
Beltline Bar 16 28th St SE . . . Grand Rapids MI 49548 *Web:* beltlinebar.com	616-245-0494		671
Belton Foods 2701 Thunderhawk Ct . . . Dayton OH 45414 *TF:* 800-443-2266 ■ *Web:* www.beltonfoods.com	937-890-7768	890-7780	296-15
Belton Industries Inc 1205 Hanby Rd PO Box 127 . . . Belton SC 29627 *TF:* 800-845-8753 ■ *Web:* beltonindustries.com	864-338-5711	338-5594	745-3
Belton Journal 210 N Penelope St . . . Belton TX 76513 *Web:* www.beltonjournal.com	254-939-5754		96
Belton Metal Company Inc 375 Sherard Rd . . . Belton SC 29627 *Web:* www.beltonmetal.com	864-338-7426	338-7447	686
Belton School District #124 110 W Walnut St . . . Belton MO 64012 *Web:* www.beltonschools.org	816-489-7000		685
Belton Veterinary Center Dog & Cat Hospital 1001 E North Ave . . . Belton MO 64012 *Web:* beltonvetcenter.com	816-331-0061	331-0443	794
Beltone Electronics Corp 2601 Patriot Blvd . . . Glenview IL 60026 *TF:* 800-235-8663 ■ *Web:* www.beltone.com	847-832-3300		477
Beltrame Environmental Consultants Inc 14623 32nd St S . . . Afton MN 55001 *TF:* 888-476-1400 ■ *Web:* www.beltrame.com	651-222-4100	436-2496	192
Beltrami County *Department of Corrections-Probation - District Office* 619 Beltrami Ave NW Historic Courthouse Ste 200 . . . Bemidji MN 56601 *Web:* www.co.beltrami.mn.us	218-333-4169	333-8139	338
Beltrami Electric Co-opeartive Inc 4111 Technology Dr NW . . . Bemidji MN 56601 *TF:* 800-955-6083 ■ *Web:* www.beltramielectric.com	218-444-2540	444-3676	245
Beltronics Inc 124 Crescent Rd . . . Needham MA 02494 *Web:* www.beltronicsinc.com	617-244-8696		250
Beltservice Corp 4143 Rider Trl N . . . Earth City MO 63045 *TF:* 800-727-2358 ■ *Web:* www.beltservice.com	314-344-8555	344-8511	207
Beltsville Human Nutrition Research Ctr 10300 Baltimore Ave BARC-E Bldg 307-C Rm 117 . . . Beltsville MD 20705 *Web:* www.ars.usda.gov	301-504-8157		668
Beltz & West PC 405 S Cascade Ave Ste 302 . . . Colorado Springs CO 80903 *Web:* beltzandwest.com	719-694-1398		41
Beltzville State Park 2950 Pohopoco Dr . . . Lehighton PA 18235 *Web:* www.dcnr.pa.gov	610-377-0045		565
Beluga Composites Corp 6830 Av du Parc Ste 572 . . . Montreal QC H3N1W7 *Web:* www.belugacorporation.com	514-278-7856	278-8414	582
Belvac Production Machinery Inc 237 Graves Mill Rd . . . Lynchburg VA 24502 *TF:* 800-423-5822 ■ *Web:* www.belvac.com	800-423-5822		494
Belvedere Hotel 319 W 48th St . . . New York NY 10036 *Web:* www.newyorkhotel.com	212-245-7000		379
Belvedere Terminals Inc 111 NE Second Ave NE St . . . Saint Petersburg FL 33701 *TF:* 800-716-8515 ■ *Web:* belvedereterminals.com	800-716-8515		538
Belvedere USA Corp 1 Belvedere Blvd . . . Belvidere IL 61008 *TF:* 800-435-5491 ■ *Web:* www.belvedere.com	800-435-5491	626-9750	76
Belvedere-Tiburon Landmarks Society 1550 Tiburon Blvd Ste M . . . Tiburon CA 94920 *Web:* landmarkssociety.com	415-435-1853		49-19
Belvedere-Tiburon Public Library 1501 Tiburon Blvd . . . Tiburon CA 94920 *Web:* www.beltiblibrary.org	415-789-2665	789-2650	434-3
Belvest USA Inc 5 E 57th St . . . New York NY 10022 *Web:* www.belvest.com	212-317-0460		157-2
Belvidere Area Chamber of Commerce 130 S State St Ste 300 . . . Belvidere IL 61008 *Web:* www.belviderechamber.com	815-544-4357	547-7654	139
Belwave Communications PO Box 121729 Ste 115 . . . Fort Worth TX 76121	817-737-3124		225
Belwith International Ltd 3100 Broadway Ave SW . . . Grandville MI 49418 *TF:* 800-235-9484 ■ *Web:* belwith-keeler.com	800-235-9484		350
Belz Enterprises 100 Peabody Pl Ste 1400 . . . Memphis TN 38103 *Web:* www.belz.com	901-260-7348	260-7378	653
Bema Inc 744 N Oaklawn Ave . . . Elmhurst IL 60126 *Web:* bemaprint.com	630-279-7800	279-0284	66
Bemco Inc 2255 Union Pl . . . Simi Valley CA 93065 *Web:* www.bemcoinc.com	805-583-4970	583-5033	703
Beme International LLC 7333 Ronson Rd . . . San Diego CA 92111 *TF:* 877-695-8268 ■ *Web:* www.beme.net	877-695-8268		361
Bement & Company PC 39 E Eagle Ridge Dr Ste 200 . . . North Salt Lake UT 84054 *Web:* www.bementcompany.com	801-936-1900		2
Bement School 94 Main St PO Box 8 . . . Deerfield MA 01342 *TF:* 877-405-3949 ■ *Web:* www.bement.org	413-774-7061	774-7863	622
Bemidji Area Chamber of Commerce 300 Bemidji Ave . . . Bemidji MN 56601 *TF:* 800-458-2223 ■ *Web:* www.bemidji.org	218-444-3541	444-4276	139
Bemidji Ind School District 31 502 Minnesota Ave NW . . . Bemidji MN 56601 *Web:* www.bemidji.k12.mn.us	218-333-3100	333-3129	685
Bemidji State University 1500 Birchmont Dr NE . . . Bemidji MN 56601 *TF:* 800-475-2001 ■ *Web:* www.bemidjistate.edu	218-755-2001	755-4048	166
Bemidji Veterinary Hospital Inc 3610 Comfort Dr NW . . . Bemidji MN 56601 *Web:* bemidjivethospital.com	218-751-2753		794
Bemis Associates Inc 1 Bemis Way . . . Shirley MA 01464 *TF:* 800-543-1324 ■ *Web:* www.bemisworldwide.com	978-425-6761		3

Name / Address	City	State	ZIP	Phone	Fax	Class
Bemis Center for Contemporary Arts 724 S 12th St *Web:* www.bemiscenter.org	Omaha	NE	68102	402-341-7130	341-9791	50-2
Bemis Company Inc 2301 Industrial Dr *NYSE:* BMS ■ *TF:* 800-544-4672 ■ *Web:* www.bemis.com	Neenah	WI	54956	920-527-5000		548
Bemis Manufacturing Co 300 Mill St *TF:* 800-558-7651 ■ *Web:* www.bemismfg.com	Sheboygan Falls	WI	53085	920-467-4621	467-8573	319-4
Bemis Public Library 6014 S Datura St *TF:* 800-895-1999 ■ *Web:* www.littletongov.org	Littleton	CO	80120	303-795-3961	795-3996	434-3
BEMSCO Inc 1193 South 400 West *Web:* www.bemsco.com	Salt Lake City	UT	84101	801-487-7455		487
Ben & Jerry's Homemade Inc 30 Community Dr *Web:* www.benjerry.com	South Burlington	VT	05403	802-846-1500		296-25
Ben Amun Company Inc 246 W 38th St 12th A *Web:* www.ben-amun.com	New York	NY	10018	212-944-6480	944-9625	410
Ben Bridge Jeweler Inc PO Box 1908 *TF:* 888-917-9171 ■ *Web:* www.benbridge.com	Seattle	WA	98111	888-448-1912		410
Ben Davis Chevrolet 931 W 7th St *Web:* www.bendavischevrolet.com	Auburn	IN	46706	260-570-4327		57
Ben Dyer Associates Inc 11721 Woodmore Rd Ste 200 *Web:* bendyer.com	Mitchellville	MD	20721	301-430-2000		261
Ben Franklin Career Ctr 500 28th St *Web:* www.benfranklinctc.weebly.com	Dunbar	WV	25064	304-766-0369	766-0371	167-3
Ben Garelick Inc 5001 Transit Rd *Web:* bengarelick.com	Williamsville	NY	14221	716-631-1584		410
Ben Hill County 402A E Pine St *Web:* www.benhillcounty.com	Fitzgerald	GA	31750	229-426-5100	426-5630	338
Ben Hur Construction Co 3783 Rider Trail S *Web:* www.benhurconstruction.com	Earth City	MO	63045	314-298-8007		189-14
Ben J. Raia & Associates PLLC 1877 Pampas Trail Dr *Web:* raialawfirm.com	Friendswood	TX	77546	281-947-8196	333-8586	41
Ben Lippen School 7401 Monticello Rd *Web:* www.benlippen.com	Columbia	SC	29203	803-807-4000	744-1387	622
Ben Lomand Rural Telephone Cooperative Inc 311 N Chancery St *TF:* 800-974-7779 ■ *Web:* www.benlomandconnect.com	McMinnville	TN	37110	800-974-7779		224
Ben Lomond Historic Suites Hotel 2510 Washington Blvd *Web:* www.benlomondsuites.com	Ogden	UT	84401	801-627-1900		379
Ben M. Muller Realty Company Inc 1971 E Beltline Ave NE Ste 240 *Web:* mullerrealty.com	Grand Rapids	MI	49525	616-456-7114		652
Ben O'neal Company Inc 3003 Tenth Ave *Web:* www.benonealcompany.com	Chattanooga	TN	37407	423 624-3359		295
Ben Spurgin Insurance Agency 2521 Cedar Springs *TF:* 800-242-2475 ■ *Web:* spurgin.com	Dallas	TX	75201	214-871-3322	871-7351	390
Ben Taub General Hospital 1504 Taub Loop *Web:* www.harrishealth.org	Houston	TX	77030	713-873-2000		374-3
Ben Tire Distributors 207 E Madison St PO Box 158 *Fax Area Code: 217 ■ *TF:* 800-252-8961 ■ *Web:* www.bentire.com	Toledo	IL	62468	800-252-8961	849-3019*	755
Ben Yehuda Press 430 Kensington Rd *Web:* www.benyehudapress.com	Teaneck	NJ	07666	201-833-5145	917 1278	637-2
Benaka Inc 7 Lawrence St *Web:* www.benakainc.com	New Brunswick	NJ	08901	732-246-7060		186
Ben-Ari Jewelers of Exton Inc 299 Main St *TF:* 866-363-0808 ■ *Web:* benarijewelers.com	Exton	PA	19341	610-363-8450		410
Benaroya Research Institute 1201 Ninth Ave *Web:* www.benaroyaresearch.org	Seattle	WA	98101	206-342-6500	342-6580	743
Benartex LLC 132 W 36th St 4th Fl *Web:* www.benartex.com	New York	NY	10018	212-840-3250	921-8204	594
BENB (Better Endings New Beginnings) 6289 Brunswick Ave N *Web:* www.betterendings.org	Brooklyn Park	MN	55429	763-531-9548	533-3223	637-2
Benbow Lake State Recreation Area 1600 Hwy 101 *Web:* www.parks.ca.gov	Garberville	CA	95542	707-923-3238		565
Benchemark Printing Inc 1890 Maxon Rd Ext *Web:* www.benchemark.net	Schenectady	NY	12308	518-393-1361	372-1336	627
Benchling 555 Montgomery St Ste 1700 *Web:* benchling.com	San Francisco	CA	94111	415-590-2798		178-1
Benchmarc360 Inc 6340 Sugarloaf Pkwy Ste 200 *Web:* www.benchmarc360.com	Duluth	GA	30097	678-291-0011		232
Benchmark Automation LLC 1965 Statham Dr *Web:* www.benchmarkautomation.net	Statham	GA	30666	706-208-0814	208-0815	358
Benchmark Bankshares Inc 100 S Broad St *Web:* www.bcbonline.com	Kenbridge	VA	23944	434-676-8444	676-1875	360-2
Benchmark Brands Inc 1375 Peachtree St NE 6th Fl	Atlanta	GA	30309	770-242-1254		301
Benchmark Construction Company Inc 4121 Oregon Pk PO Box 806 *Web:* www.benchmarkgc.com	Brownstown	PA	17508	717-626-9559		186
Benchmark Electronics Inc 4141 N Scottsdale Rd *NYSE:* BHE ■ *TF:* 800-322-2885 ■ *Web:* www.bench.com	Scottsdale	AZ	85251	623-300-7000		625
Benchmark Group 4053 Maple Rd *TF:* 800-876-0160 ■ *Web:* www.benchmarkgrp.com	Amherst	NY	14226	716-833-4986	833-2954	654
Benchmark Hospitality Intl 1780 Hughes Landing Blvd Ste 400 *TF:* 844-258-7210 ■ *Web:* www.benchmarkresortsandhotels.com	The Woodlands	TX	77380	281-367-5757		379
Benchmark Ins 1515 Mockingbird Ln Ste 820 *Web:* benchmarkigroup.com	Charlotte	NC	28209	704-527-1211		390
Benchmark Intl 2710 W 5th Ave *Web:* www.benchmark-intl.com	Eugene	OR	97402	541-484-9212	344-2735	743
Benchmark Network Solutions Inc 1931 Evans Rd *Web:* benchmarkns.com	Cary	NC	27513	919-678-8595		180
Benchmark Plus Management LLC 820 A St Ste 700 *Web:* www.bpfunds.com	Tacoma	WA	98402	253-573-0657		401
Benchmark Products Inc 1605 Waukegan Rd *Web:* benchmarkproducts.com	Waukegan	IL	60085	847-689-9600		145
Benchmark Technologies 7 Kimball Ln Bldg E *Web:* www.benchmarktech.com	Lynnfield	MA	01940	781-246-3303	246-0308	179
Benchmark Technologies International Inc (BTI) 411 Hackensack Ave *TF:* 800-265-8254 ■ *Web:* btiworld.com	Hackensack	NJ	07601	201-996-0077		194
Benchmark Title Agency LLC 222 Bloomingdale Rd Ste 102 *Web:* benchmarkta.com	White Plains	NY	10605	914-250-2400		390
Benchworks Inc 860 High St *Web:* www.benchworks.com	Chestertown	MD	21620	410-810-8862		7
Benco Dental Co 295 CenterPoint Blvd *TF:* 800-462-3626 ■ *Web:* www.benco.com	Pittston	PA	18640	800-462-3626		475
Benco Electric Co-op 20946 549 Ave PO Box 8 *TF:* 888-792-3626 ■ *Web:* www.benco.org	Mankato	MN	56002	507-387-7963		245
Benco Steel Inc 2710 Hwy 70 S E *Web:* www.bencosteel.com	Hickory	NC	28602	828-328-1714	327-6094	492
Bend Chamber of Commerce 777 NW Wall St Ste 200 *Web:* bendchamber.org	Bend	OR	97701	541-382-3221	385-9929	139
Bend Garbage & Recycling Inc 20835 NE Montana St PO Box 504 *Web:* bendgarbage.com	Bend	OR	97709	541-382-2203	383-3640	804
Bend Honda 345 NE 3rd St *Web:* www.bendchevrolet.com	Bend	OR	97701	541-205-0717		57
Bend Metro Parks & Recreation District 18920 NW Shevlin Park Rd *Web:* www.bendparksandrec.org	Bend	OR	97701	541-389-7275		31
Bend Research Inc 64550 Research Rd *Web:* www.capsugel.com	Bend	OR	97701	541-382-4100	382-2713	668
Benda, Grace, Stulz & Company PC 38800 Van Dyke Ave *Web:* www.bgscpas.com	Sterling Heights	MI	48312	586-883-6240		2
Bendco Inc 801 Houston Ave *Web:* www.bendco.com	Pasadena	TX	77502	713-473-1557	473-1882	595
Bendel Executive Suites 213 Bendel Rd *Web:* www.bendelexec.com	Lafayette	LA	70503	337-261-0604	233-4296	379
Bender Consulting Services Inc 3 Penn Ctr W Ste 223 *TF:* 800-654-5988 ■ *Web:* www.benderconsult.com	Pittsburgh	PA	15276	412-787-8567	787-2962	180
Bender Engineering & Construction Inc 10037 E River St *Web:* benderengineering.com	Truckee	CA	96161	530-582-5578		41
Bender Group 345 Parr Cir *Fax Area Code: 775 ■ *TF:* 800-621-9402 ■ *Web:* bendergroup.com	Reno	NV	89512	800-621-9402	788-8811*	449
Bender Lumber Company Inc 6002 W State Rd 46 *Web:* www.benderlumber.com	Bloomington	IN	47404	812-339-9737		191-3
Bender Plumbing Supplies Inc 580 Grand Ave *TF:* 800-573-4288 ■ *Web:* benderplumbing.com	New Haven	CT	06511	203-787-4288	789-1699	612
Bender Rbt Inc 17 Cardinale Ln *Web:* www.benderrbt.com	Queensbury	NY	12804	518-743-8755		177
Bender/Helper Impact (BHI) 11500 W Olympic Blvd Ste 399 *Web:* www.bhimpact.com	Los Angeles	CA	90064	310-473-4147		636
Bendick Precision Inc 56 La Porte St *Web:* www.bendick.com	Arcadia	CA	91006	626-445-0217	445-0322	454
Bendigo State Park 533 State Park Rd *Web:* www.dcnr.pa.gov	Johnsonburg	PA	15845	814-778-5467		565
Bendix Commercial Vehicle Systems LLC 901 Cleveland St *TF:* 800-247-2725 ■ *Web:* www.bendix.com	Elyria	OH	44035	440-329-9000	329-9557	61
Bendon Gear & Machine Inc 100 Weymouth St Unit A *Web:* www.bendongear.com	Rockland	MA	02370	781-878-8100	878-2610	454
Bendpak Inc 1645 Lemonwood Dr *TF:* 800-253-2363 ■ *Web:* www.bendpak.com	Santa Paula	CA	93060	805-933-9970	933-9160	256
Bendsen Signs & Graphics Inc 1506 E McBride Ave *TF:* 866-275-6407 ■ *Web:* www.bsg1946.com	Decatur	IL	62526	217-877-2345	877-2347	344
BendTec Inc 366 Garfield Ave *TF:* 800-236-3832 ■ *Web:* bendtec.com	Duluth	MN	55802	218-722-0205		595
Bene's Career Academy 7027 US Highway 19 *Web:* www.benes.edu	New Port Richey	FL	34652	727-475-7690		167-3
Benecaid Health Benefit Solutions Inc 185 The W Mall Ste 800 *TF:* 877-797-7448 ■ *Web:* www.benecaid.com	Toronto	ON	M9C5L5	877-797-7448		391-3
BeneCard Services Inc 3131 Princeton Pike Bldg 2B Ste 103 *Web:* www.benecard.com	Lawrenceville	NJ	08648	609-219-0400		390
Benecon Group Inc 147 W Airport Rd *TF:* 800-400-4647 ■ *Web:* www.benecon.com	Lititz	PA	17543	717-723-4600	735-9619	390
Benedetto Guitars Inc 10 Mall Terr Ste A *Web:* benedettoguitars.com	Savannah	GA	31406	912-692-1400		194
Benedict College 1600 Harden St *TF:* 800-868-6598 ■ *Web:* www.benedict.edu	Columbia	SC	29204	803-253-5000		166
Benedict Group Inc 900 Small Dr *Web:* benedictgroup.com	Elizabeth City	NC	27909	303-747-6690		177

Phone | Fax | Class

Benedict Inn Retreat & Conference Ctr
1402 Southern Ave Beech Grove IN 46107 317-787-3287 673
Web: www.benedictine.com

Benedictine College 1020 N 2nd St Atchison KS 66002 913-367-5340 367-5462 166
TF: 800-467-5340 ■ *Web:* www.benedictine.edu

Benedictine Health System
503 E Third St Ste 400 Duluth MN 55805 218-786-2370 786-2373 353
TF: 800-833-7208 ■ *Web:* www.bhshealth.org

Benedictine University 5700 College Rd Lisle IL 60532 630-829-6300 829-6301 166
TF: 888-829-6363 ■ *Web:* www.ben.edu

Benefact Consulting Group
6285 Northam Dr Ste 200 Mississauga ON L4V1X5 855-829-2225 463
TF: 855-829-2225 ■ *Web:* www.benefact.ca

Beneficial Financial Group
55 N 300 W Salt Lake City UT 84101 801-933-1100 531-3317 391-2
TF: 800-233-7979 ■ *Web:* www.beneficialfinancialgroup.com

Benefis HealthSystems
1101 26th St S Great Falls MT 59405 406-455-5000 374-3
Web: www.benefis.org

Benefit & Risk Management Services Inc (BRMS)
80 Iron Point Cir Ste 200 PO Box 2140 Folsom CA 95763 888-326-2555 467-1401* 390
*Fax Area Code: 916 ■ *TF:* 888-326-2555 ■ *Web:* www.brmsonline.com

Benefit Administrative Services International Corp
9246 Portage Industrial Dr Portage MI 49024 269-327-1922 734
TF: 800-444-1922 ■ *Web:* www.basiconline.com

Benefit Advantage Inc
3431 Commodity Ln Green Bay WI 54304 920-339-0351 463
TF: 800-686-6829 ■ *Web:* www.benefitadvantage.com

Benefit Communications Inc (BCI)
2977 Sidco Dr Nashville TN 37204 800-489-3786 383-7917* 390
*Fax Area Code: 615 ■ *TF:* 800-489-3786 ■ *Web:* benefitcommunications.com

Benefit Concepts Inc
1173 Brittmoore Rd Houston TX 77043 713-728-7200 728-7201 390
Web: mybciteam.com

Benefit Consultants Group Inc (BCG)
51 Haddonfield Rd Ste 200 Cherry Hill NJ 08002 856-368-2000 824-1890 390
TF: 800-524-4015 ■ *Web:* www.bcgbenefits.com

Benefit Coordinators Co
2 Robinson Plz Ste 200 Pittsburgh PA 15205 412-276-1111 251
Web: www.bccbenefitsolutions.com

Benefit Express Services LLC
1700 E Golf Rd Ste 1000 Schaumburg IL 60173 877-369-2153 177
TF: 877-369-2153 ■ *Web:* www.benefitexpress.info

Benefit Plan Administrators of Eau Claire
402 Graham Ave Eau Claire WI 54702 715-832-5535 838-8507 390
TF: 800-236-7789 ■ *Web:* bpaco.com

Benefit Recovery Group
6745 Lenox Center Ct Ste 100 Memphis TN 38115 866-384-4051 445
TF: 866-384-4051 ■ *Web:* brgsubro.com

Benefit Services Group Inc, The
N25 W23050 Paul Rd Pewaukee WI 53072 262-521-5700 521-5710 401
Web: bsg.com

Benefit Watch Inc 164 S Main St Yardley PA 19067 215-321-9880 390
Web: benefitwatch.net

BenefitHelp Solutions Inc
10505 SE 17th Ave Milwaukie OR 97222 503-219-3679 535
TF: 888-398-8057 ■ *Web:* www.benefithelpsolutions.com

BenefitMall Inc 4851 LBJ Fwy Ste 1100 Dallas TX 75244 469-791-3300 791-3313 178-10
TF: 888-338-6293 ■ *Web:* www.benefitmall.com

Benefits Broker Inc
20 Club Manor Dr Unit A Pueblo CO 81008 719-545-4840 390
Web: benefitsbroker.com

Benefits Data Trust
1500 Market St Ste 2800 Philadelphia PA 19102 215-207-9100 207-9111 403
Web: bdtrust.org

Benefits Group of Haudenschield, Harrison & Blachek LLC, The
27 Johnson Rd Clarks Summit PA 18411 570-586-1859 390
Web: benegroup.net

Benefits Plus Consulting Group Inc
1807 Pine St Philadelphia PA 19103 215-564-0288 564-0286 401
Web: www.benefitsplusconsulting.com

Benefits Resource Group LLC
2530 Scottsville Rd Ste 109 Bowling Green KY 42104 270-842-8110 390
TF: 800-730-5070 ■ *Web:* brgky.com

Benefitvision Inc 4522 RFD Long Grove IL 60047 877-737-5526 196
TF: 800-810-2200 ■ *Web:* www.benefitvision.com

Beneflex Insurance Services LLC
101 W Anapamu St 3rd Fl Santa Barbara CA 93101 805-684-5100 390
Web: beneflexsb.com

Benelogic LLC 9475 Deereco Rd Ste 310 Timonium MD 21093 877-716-6615 177
TF: 877-716-6615 ■ *Web:* www.benelogic.co

Benemax Inc 7 W Mill St Medfield MA 02052 800-528-1530 194
TF: 800-528-1530 ■ *Web:* www.benemax.com

Benenati Law Firm PC 2816 Bedford Rd Bedford TX 76021 817-267-4529 684-9000 41
Web: benenatilaw.com

Benenson Strategy Group LLC
777 3rd Ave 33rd Fl New York NY 10017 212-702-8777 615
Web: www.bsgco.com

Benesch 35 W Wacker Dr Ste 3300 Chicago IL 60601 312-565-0450 261
Web: web.benesch.com

Benesyst Inc
800 Washington Ave N 8th Fl Minneapolis MN 55401 800-422-4661 256
TF: 800-422-4661 ■ *Web:* www.benesyst.net

Beneteau America Inc
24 N Market St Ste 201 Charleston SC 29401 843-805-5000 90
Web: www.beneteau.com

Benetech Inc 2245 Sequoia Dr Aurora IL 60506 630-844-1300 360-3
TF: 800-843-2625 ■ *Web:* www.benetechglobal.com

Benetrends Inc 1180 Welsh Rd North Wales PA 19454 267-498-0059 463
TF: 866-423-6387 ■ *Web:* www.benetrends.com

Benevity Social Ventures Inc
611 Meredith Rd Ste 700 Calgary AB T2E2W5 403-237-7875 195
Web: www.benevity.com

Benevolent Life Insurance Company Inc
1624 Milam St Shreveport LA 71103 318-425-1522 391-2

Benewah County 701 College Ave Saint Maries ID 83861 208-245-3212 245-9152 338
TF: 800-983-0937 ■ *Web:* www.idaho.gov

Phone | Fax | Class

Benfield Electric Supply Company Inc
25 Lafayette Ave North White Plains NY 10603 914-948-6660 993-0558 246
Web: www.benfieldelectric.com

Bengal Energy Ltd
715 Fifth Ave SW Ste 2000 Calgary AB T2P2X6 403-205-2526 263-3168 540
Web: bengalenergy.ca

Benham & Green Capital Management LLC
1299 Prospect St Ste 301 La Jolla CA 92037 858-551-3130 401

Benhart Landscaping Inc
7450 E Pinnacle Peak Rd Ste 150 Scottsdale AZ 85255 480-585-1664 422
Web: benhartlandscaping.com

Benicia Capitol State Historic Park
115 W G St Benicia CA 94510 707-745-3385 565
Web: www.parks.ca.gov

Benicia Chamber of Commerce
601 First St Ste 100 Benicia CA 94510 707-745-2628 745-2275 139
Web: www.beniciachamber.com

Benicia Fabrication & Machine Inc
101 E Channel Rd Benicia CA 94510 707-745-8111 745-8102 91
Web: www.beniciafab.com

Benicia Public Library 150 E 'L' St Benicia CA 94510 707-746-4343 747-8122 434-3
Web: www.ci.benicia.ca.us

Benicia State Recreation Area
1 State Park Rd Benicia CA 94510 707-648-1911 565
Web: www.parks.ca.gov

Benihana Inc 1100 W Eighth Ave Anchorage AK 99501 907-222-5212 671
Web: www.benihana.com

Benin Embassy 2124 Kalorama Rd NW Washington DC 20008 202-232-6656 265-1996 257
Web: beninembassy.us

Benise-Dowling & Associates Inc
5068 Snapfinger Woods Dr Decatur GA 30035 770-981-4237 593-0342 189-8
Web: www.benise-dowling.com

Benjamin Development Company Inc
377 Oak St Ste 110 Garden City NY 11530 516-745-0150 186
Web: www.benjamindevco.com

Benjamin Franklin Institute of Technology
41 Berkeley St Boston MA 02116 617-423-4630 482-3706 800
TF: 877-400-2348 ■ *Web:* www.bfit.edu

Benjamin Franklin Plumbing
12 Greenway Plz Ste 250 Houston TX 77046 713-877-3500 310
TF: 800-471-0809 ■ *Web:* www.benjaminfranklinplumbing.com

Benjamin H. Moore & Company Inc
720 N Maitland Ave Ste 105 Maitland FL 32751 407-644-3119 2
Web: www.bhmcpapa.com

Benjamin Harrison Presidential Site
1230 N Delaware St Indianapolis IN 46202 317-631-1888 632-5488 520
Web: www.presidentbenjaminharrison.org

Benjamin Manufacturing
3215 S Sweetwater Rd Lithia Springs GA 30122 770-941-1433 610
TF: 800-343-1756 ■ *Web:* www.benjaminmfg.com

Benjamin Moore & Co 101 Paragon Dr Montvale NJ 07645 855-724-6802 573-9046* 550
*Fax Area Code: 201 ■ *TF:* 800-344-0400 ■ *Web:* www.benjaminmoore.com

Benjamin N. Cardozo School of Law Yeshiva University
55 Fifth Ave 12 St New York NY 10003 212-790-0200 790-0256 167-1
Web: cardozo.yu.edu

Benjamin News Group PO Box 16147 Missoula MT 59808 800-823-6397 96
TF: 800-823-6397 ■ *Web:* bngmsla.com

Benjamin Office Supply & Services Inc
758 E Gude Dr Rockville MD 20850 301-340-1384 340-1543 535
TF: 877-439-2677 ■ *Web:* www.benjaminofficesupply.com

Benjamin Plumbing Inc
2870 Commerce Park Dr Madison WI 53719 608-271-7071 189-10
Web: benjaminplumbing.com

Benjamin Rush State Park
15001 Roosevelt Blvd Philadelphia PA 19154 215-639-4538 565
Web: www.dcnr.pa.gov

Benjamin Schlesinger & Associates LLC
3 Bethesda Metro Ctr Ste 700 Bethesda MD 20814 301-951-7266 194
Web: www.bsaenergy.com

Benjamin West 428 CTC Blvd Louisville CO 80027 303-530-3885 320
Web: www.benjaminwest.com

Benjamin, The 125 E 50th St New York NY 10022 212-715-2500 379
TF: 866-222-2365 ■ *Web:* www.thebenjamin.com

Benji's French-Basque Restaurant
4001 Rosedale Hwy Bakersfield CA 93308 661-328-0400 671
Web: www.benjisbasque.com

Benjy's 2424 Dunstan Rd Houston TX 77005 713-522-7602 522-7655 671
Web: www.benjys.com

Benko Products Inc
5350 Evergreen Pky Sheffield Village OH 44054 440-934-2180 934-4052 256
Web: www.benkoproducts.com

Benlee Dunright 30383 Ecorse Rd Romulus MI 48174 734-722-8100 120
Web: www.benlee.com

Benner Metals Corp
1220 S State College Blvd Fullerton CA 92831 714-879-6477 492
Web: bennermetals.com

Benner-Nawman Inc
3450 Sabin Brown Rd Wickenburg AZ 85390 928-684-2813 684-7041 286
TF: 800-992-3833 ■ *Web:* www.bnproducts.com

Bennet Michael F (Sen D - CO)
261 Russell Senate Office Bldg Washington DC 20510 202-224-5852 228-5097 342-2
Web: www.bennet.senate.gov

Bennett 220 NW Space Center Cir Lee's Summit MO 64064 816-379-5001 100
Web: bennettkc.com

Bennett & Assoc 100 Huronview Blvd Ann Arbor MI 48103 734-622-7000 2
Web: jimbennettcpa.com

Bennett & Hastings Publishing
2400 NW 80th St Ste 254 Seattle WA 98117 206-905-9673 789-5093 637-2
Web: www.bennetthastings.com

Bennett & Middendorf Ltd 901 York Quincy IL 62301 217-222-1142 222-2261 2
Web: www.bennettandmiddendorf.com

Bennett & Pless
47 Perimeter Ctr E Ste 500 Atlanta GA 30346 678-990-8700 990-8701 261
Web: www.bennett-pless.com

Bennett College
900 E Washington St Greensboro NC 27401 336-370-8624 517-2166 166
TF: 800-413-5323 ■ *Web:* www.bennett.edu

Bennett County 201 State St Martin SD 57551 605-685-6516 685-2255 338
Web: www.bennettcosheriff.org

Name / Address	City	State	Zip	Phone	Fax	Class
Bennett Engineering Services Inc 1082 Sunrise Ave Ste 100 *Web:* ben-en.com	Roseville	CA	95661	916-783-4100		261
Bennett Enterprises Inc PO Box 670 *Web:* www.bennett-enterprises.com	Perrysburg	OH	43552	419-874-1933		379
Bennett Hardwoods Inc 725 S 84th Ave *Web:* www.bennetthardwoods.com	Wausau	WI	54401	715-845-9663	842-1252	191-3
Bennett Jones LLP 855 Second St S W 4500 Bankers Hall E *TF:* 800-222-6479 ■ *Web:* www.bennettjones.com	Calgary	AB	T2P4K7	403-298-3100		428
Bennett Lumber Products Inc PO Box 130 *Web:* blpi.com	Princeton	ID	83857	208-875-1121	875-0191	683
Bennett Manufacturing Company Inc 13315 Railroad St *Web:* www.bennettmfg.com	Alden	NY	14004	716-937-9161	937-3137	286
Bennett Metal Products Inc 700 Rackaway St PO Box 34 *Web:* bennettmetal.com	Mount Vernon	IL	62864	618-244-1911	244-1995	481
Bennett Mineral Co PO Box 28 *Web:* bennettmineral.com	Walkerton	VA	23177	804-769-0546		761
Bennett Office Technologies 312 24th Ave SW *Web:* www.bennettoffice.com	Willmar	MN	56201	320-235-6425	231-1888	174
Bennett Oil Co 810 E Sheldon St *Web:* www.bennettoil.com	Prescott	AZ	86301	928-445-1181		581
Bennett Pointe Grill & Bar 4625 Hillsborough Rd *Web:* www.bpgrill.com	Durham	NC	27705	919-382-9431		671
Bennett Pump Co 1218 Pontaluna Rd *TF:* 800-235-7618 ■ *Web:* bennettpump.com	Spring Lake	MI	49456	231-798-1310	799-6202	639
Bennett Sharpe Delarosa Bennett & Licalsi Inc 2444 Main St Ste 150 *Web:* bennettsharpe.com	Fresno	CA	93721	559-485-0120		41
Bennett Spring State Park 26250 Hwy 64A *Web:* mostateparks.com	Lebanon	MO	65536	417-532-4338		565
Bennett Tool & Die 1550 Airport Rd *Web:* bennetttool.com	Gallatin	TN	37066	615-227-5291		697
Bennett's Bar-B-Que Inc 3538 Peoria St Ste 508 *Web:* www.bennettsbbq.com	Aurora	CO	80010	303-792-3088		670
Bennett, Boehning & Clary LLP 415 Columbia St Ste 1000 *Web:* hereforlife.com	LaFayette	IN	47901	765-742-9066		41
Bennett-Bowen & Lighthouse Inc 9844 Alburtis Ave *TF:* 800-341-5152 ■ *Web:* www.bblsafety.com	Santa Fe Springs	CA	90670	562-942-0070	942-8441	459
Bennet-Tec Information Systems Inc 50 Jericho Tpke *Web:* www.bennet-tec.com	Jericho	NY	11753	516-997-5596		177
Bennett-Thrasher PC 3300 Riverwood Pkwy Ste 700 *Web:* www.btcpa.net	Atlanta	GA	30339	770-396-2200		2
Bennigan's 5151 Beltline Rd Ste 300 *Web:* bennigans.com	Dallas	TX	75254	469-248-4419		670
Benning Construction Company Inc (BCC) 4695 S Atlanta Rd *Web:* www.benningnet.com	Atlanta	GA	30339	404-792-1911		186
Bennington Area Chamber of Commerce 100 Veterans Memorial Dr *Web:* www.bennington.com	Bennington	VT	05201	802-447-3311	447-1163	139
Bennington College 1 College Dr *TF:* 800-833-6845 ■ *Web:* www.bennington.edu	Bennington	VT	05201	802-440-4325	447-4269	166
Bennington Free Library 101 Silver St *Web:* benningtonfreelibrary.org	Bennington	VT	05201	802-442-9051		434-3
Bennon & Thorpe LLC 2100 Dudley Ave *TF:* 800-846-1805 ■ *Web:* bennonthorpe.com	Parkersburg	WV	26101	304-485-1260	422-6918	690
Benny Hinn Ministries PO Box 162000 *TF:* 888-377-7783 ■ *Web:* www.bennyhinn.org	Irving	TX	75016	888-377-7783		48-20
Benny Machine Company Inc 441 Dual Blvd *TF:* 888-400-5508 ■ *Web:* www.bennymachine.com	Isanti	MN	55040	763-444-5508	444-6481	454
Benny Whitehead Inc 3576 S Eufaula Ave *TF:* 800-633-7617 ■ *Web:* www.bwitruck.com	Eufaula	AL	36027	334-687-8055	687-1345	360-2
Benold's Jewelers 2900 W Anderson Ln *TF:* 800-460-6491 ■ *Web:* www.benolds.com	Austin	TX	78757	512-452-6491		411
BenQ America Corp 15375 Barranca Ste A205 *TF:* 866-600-2367 ■ *Web:* www.benq.com	Irvine	CA	92618	949-255-9500	255-9600	173-7
BENS (Business Executives for National Security) 1030 15th St NW Ste 200 *Web:* www.bens.org	Washington	DC	20005	202-296-2125	296-2490	49-12
Bensenville Community Public Library 200 S Church Rd *Web:* benlib.org	Bensenville	IL	60106	630-766-4642	766-0788	434-3
Bensimon Byrne Inc 225 Wellington St W *Web:* www.bensimonbyrne.com	Toronto	ON	M5V3G7	416-922-2211		7
Bensinger Consulting 625 W Deer Valley Rd Ste 103-185 *Web:* www.bensingerconsulting.com	Phoenix	AZ	85027	602-237-8500	237-8600	196
Benson & Sesser LLC 36 S Paint St *Web:* benson-law.com	Chillicothe	OH	45601	740-773-3600		41
Benson County PO Box 213 *TF:* 888-525-2104 ■ *Web:* www.bensoncountynd.com	Minnewaukan	ND	58351	701-473-5345	473-5571	338
Benson Industries LLC 1650 NW Naito Pkwy Ste 250 *Web:* www.bensonglobal.com	Portland	OR	97209	503-226-7611		189-6
Benson Marketing Group 2700 Napa Vly Corporate Dr Ste H *Web:* bensonmarketing.com	Napa	CA	94558	707-254-9292		194
Benson Steel Ltd 72 Commercial Rd *Web:* www.bensonsteel.com	Bolton	ON	L7E1K4	905-857-0684		480
Benson Stone Co 1100 Eleventh St *Web:* www.bensonstone.com	Rockford	IL	61104	815-227-2000	227-2001	724
Benson's Bakery Inc 134 Elder St *Web:* www.bensonsbakery.com	Bogart	GA	30622	770-725-5711		68
Benson's Gourmet Seasonings PO Box 638 *TF:* 800-325-5619 ■ *Web:* www.bensonsgourmetseasonings.com	Azusa	CA	91702	626-969-4443	969-2912	296-37
Benson, Piombo & Co 300 Tamal Plz Ste 180 *Web:* www.bensonpiombo.com	Corte Madera	CA	94925	415-924-2292	924-8202	2
Benson, The 309 SW Broadway *TF:* 800-663-1144 ■ *Web:* coasthotels.com	Portland	OR	97205	503-228-2000	471-3920	379
Benson, Young & Downs Insurance Agency Inc 56 Howland St *Web:* byandd.com	Provincetown	MA	02657	508-487-0500		390
Bent County 725 Bent Ave PO Box 350 *Web:* www.bentcounty.net	Las Animas	CO	81054	719-456-1600	456-0375	338
Bent Gate Mountaineering 1313 Washington Ave *TF:* 877-236-8428 ■ *Web:* www.bentgate.com	Golden	CO	80401	303-271-9382		155-2
Bent Image Lab LLC 2729 SE Division St *Web:* bentimagelab.com	Portland	OR	97202	503-228-6206		514
Bent River Machine Inc 951 Rio Torcido *Web:* www.bent-river.com	Clarkdale	AZ	86324	928-634-7568		757
Bent's Old Fort National Historic Site 35110 Hwy 194 E *Web:* www.nps.gov	La Junta	CO	81050	719-383-5010		564
Bentley College 175 Forest St *Web:* www.bentley.edu	Waltham	MA	02452	781-891-2244	891-3414	166
Bentley Historical Library 1150 Beal Ave *TF:* 866-233-6661 ■ *Web:* www.bentley.umich.edu	Ann Arbor	MI	48109	734-764-3482	936-1333	434-4
Bentley Hotel New York 500 E 62nd St *Web:* www.hotelbentleynewyork.com	New York	NY	10065	212-644-6000		379
Bentley Laboratories LLC 111 Fieldcrest Ave *Web:* www.bentleylabs.com	Edison	NJ	08837	732-512-0200	512-0208	214
Bentley Motors 12989 Research Blvd *TF:* 800-777-6923 ■ *Web:* www.bentleymotors.com	Austin	TX	78750	512-236-8539		59
Bentley Prince Street 14641 E Don Julian Rd **Fax Area Code:* 626 ■ *TF:* 800-423-4709 ■ *Web:* www.bentleymills.com	City of Industry	CA	91746	800-423-4709	956-0937*	131
Bentley Publishers 1734 Massachusetts Ave *TF:* 800-423-4595 ■ *Web:* www.bentleypublishers.com	Cambridge	MA	02138	617-547-4170	876-9235	95
Bentley Systems Inc 685 Stockton Dr *TF:* 800-236-8539 ■ *Web:* www.bentley.com	Exton	PA	19341	610-458-5000	458-1060	178-5
Bentley World Packaging Ltd 4080 N Port Washington Rd *Web:* www.bentleywp.com	Milwaukee	WI	53212	414-967-8000	967-8001	549
Bently Nevada LLC 1631 Bently Pkwy S	Minden	NV	89423	775-782-3611		536
Bento Box 584 Broadway *Web:* getbento.com	New York	NY	10038	212-748-9156		809
Benton & Associates Inc 1970 W Lafayette Ave *Web:* www.bentonassociates.com	Jacksonville	IL	62650	217-245-4146		256
Benton Air Ctr 2600 Gold St *Web:* flyhillside.com	Redding	CA	96001	530-241-4204	241-7125	167-3
Benton Convention Ctr 425 N Cherry St *Web:* twincityquarter.com	Winston-Salem	NC	27101	336-727-2976		205
Benton County 215 E Central St Rm 217 *Web:* bentoncountyar.gov	Bentonville	AR	72712	479-271-1013	271-1019	338
Benton County 205 NW Fifth St PO Box 3020 *Web:* www.co.benton.or.us	Corvallis	OR	97330	541-766-6800	766-6893	338
Benton County 615 Hwy 23 PO Box 189 *Web:* www.co.benton.mn.us	Foley	MN	56329	320-968-5205	968-5353	338
Benton County 7122 W Okanogan Pl Bldg A *Web:* www.co.benton.wa.us	Kennewick	WA	99336	509-735-3591	736-3066	338
Benton County 1231 Hirsch Pkwy PO Box 852 *Web:* www.bentoncomo.com	Warsaw	MO	65355	660-438-8412	438-8413	338
Benton County Courthouse 111 E 4th St Clerk of Court 2nd Fl *Web:* www.bentoncountyia.gov	Vinton	IA	52349	319-472-2439	472-2913	338
Benton County Schools Credit Union 2101 NW Professional Dr *TF:* 800-807-7893 ■ *Web:* bcscu.org	Corvallis	OR	97330	541-754-7765		219
Benton County State Bank 212 Locust St NE *Web:* bentoncountystatebank.com	Blairstown	IA	52209	319-454-6230		70
Benton Foundation 1625 K St NW 11th Fl *Web:* www.benton.org	Washington	DC	20006	202-638-5770		305
Benton Foundry Inc 5297 SR 487 *Web:* www.bentonfoundry.com	Benton	PA	17814	570-925-6711	925-6929	307
Benton REA 402 7th St PO Box 1150 *TF:* 800-221-6987 ■ *Web:* bentonrea.org	Prosser	WA	99350	509-786-2913	786-0291	245
Benton, Safranski & Company LLP 116 W 3rd St *Web:* bsccpas.net	Thief River Falls	MN	56701	218-681-4287		2
Bentonville Plastics Inc 607 SW A St *TF:* 800-821-2799 ■ *Web:* www.bentonvilleplastics.com	Bentonville	AR	72712	800-821-2799		608
Bentsen-Rio Grande Valley State Park 2800 S Bensen Palm Dr *Web:* www.theworldbirdingcenter.com	Mission	TX	78572	956-585-1107	584-9126	565
Bentz Whaley Flessner 7251 Ohms Ln *TF:* 800-921-0111 ■ *Web:* www.bwf.com	Minneapolis	MN	55439	952-921-0111	921-0109	317
Benucci's 3349 Monroe Ave *Web:* www.benuccis.com	Rochester	NY	14618	585-264-1300		671
Benz Oil Inc 2724 W Hampton Ave *Web:* www.benz.com	Milwaukee	WI	53209	414-442-2900		541
Benz Research & Development Corp 6447 Parkland Dr *Web:* benzrd.com	Sarasota	FL	34243	941-758-8256		544

Phone | Fax | Class

Benzel's Pretzel Bakery Inc
5200 Sixth Ave ..... Altoona PA 16602 814-942-5062 942-4133 296-9
TF: 800-344-4438 ■ *Web:* www.benzels.com

Benzie County 448 Ct Pl ..... Beulah MI 49617 231-882-9671 882-5941 338
TF: 800-315-3593 ■ *Web:* www.benzieco.net

Bep Inc 1006 W Lake St ..... Chicago IL 60607 312-850-3140 850-0740 196
Web: bepinc.com

Bepex International LLC
333 Taft St NE ..... Minneapolis MN 55413 612-331-4370 298
Web: www.bepex.com

Beppe & Gianni's Tratoria
1646 E 19th Ave ..... Eugene OR 97403 541-683-6661 671
Web: beppeandgiannis.net

BeQuick Software Inc
601 Heritage Dr Ste 442 ..... Jupiter FL 33458 561-721-9600 177
TF: 866-267-5105 ■ *Web:* bequick.com

Bera Ami (Rep D - CA)
1727 Longworth House Office Bldg ..... Washington DC 20515 202-225-5716 226-1298 342-2
Web: bera.house.gov

Beranek Inc 2340 205th St ..... Torrance CA 90501 310-328-9094 328-2764 22
Web: www.beranekinc.com

Berard & Associates CPA's PC
44 Park Ave. ..... Suffern NY 10901 845-357-5668 357-5637 2
Web: www.berardcpas.com

Berber Food Mfg
Mi Rancho Tortilla Factory
425 Hester St ..... San Leandro CA 94577 510-553-0444 123
Web: www.miranchoretail.com

Bercek & Smith Engineering Inc
358 Main St Ste 1 ..... Royersford PA 19468 610-948-8947 948-3261 261
Web: bercekandsmith.com

Berchtold Equipment Company Inc
330 E 19th St ..... Bakersfield CA 93305 661-323-7817 274
TF: 800-691-7817 ■ *Web:* www.berchtold.com

Berco Inc 111 Winnebago ..... Saint Louis MO 63118 314-772-4700 772-2744 320
TF: 888-772-4788 ■ *Web:* bercodesigns.com

Berco of America Inc
W229 N1420 Westwood Dr. ..... Waukesha WI 53186 262-524-2222 358
Web: www.thyssenkrupp-berco.com

Berding & Weil LLP
2175 N California Blvd Ste 500 ..... Walnut Creek CA 94596 925-838-2090 820-5592 428
TF: 800-838-2090 ■ *Web:* www.berding-weil.com

Berdon LLP 360 Madison Ave 8th Fl ..... New York NY 10017 212-832-0400 371-1159 2
Web: www.berdonllp.com

Berea City School District 390 Fair St ..... Berea OH 44017 216-898-8300 898-8551 685
Web: www.berea.k12.oh.us

Berea College 101 Chestnut St ..... Berea KY 40403 859-985-3500 985-3512 166
TF: 800-326-5948 ■ *Web:* www.berea.edu

Berean Baptist Church
517 Glensford Dr ..... Fayetteville NC 28314 910-868-5156 48-20
Web: www.bbcfnc.org

Bereaved Parents of the USA
PO Box 95 ..... Park Forest IL 60466 708-748-7866 48-21
Web: www.bereavedparentsusa.org

Beredco LLC 2020 N Bramblewood ..... Wichita KS 67206 316-265-2856 681-4732 536
Web: www.beredco.com

Berenbaum Weinshienk Pc
370 17th St Ste 4800 ..... Denver CO 80202 303-839-3800 41
Web: spencerfane.com

Berendsen Fluid Power
401 S Boston Ave Ste 1200 ..... Tulsa OK 74103 918-592-3781 581-5080 385
TF: 800-360-2327 ■ *Web:* www.bfpna.com

Berenergy Corp 1888 Sherman St Ste 600 ..... Denver CO 80203 303-295-2323 540

Berenson & Associates PC
415 Sixth St NW ..... Albuquerque NM 87102 505-243-4400 41
Web: nmjusticelaw.com

Berenson Corp 2495 Main St ..... Buffalo NY 14214 716-833-3100 833-2402 350
TF: 800-333-0578 ■ *Web:* www.berensonhardware.com

Beretta USA Corp 17601 Beretta Dr ..... Accokeek MD 20607 301-283-2191 283-0189 284
TF: 800-237-3882 ■ *Web:* www.berettausa.com

Berg & Associates Inc
302 W Fifth St Ste 210 ..... San Pedro CA 90731 310-548-9292 548-9195 261
Web: bergcm.com

Berg Bag Company LLC
8700 109th Ave N Ste 300 ..... Champlin MN 55316 612-332-8845 332-8847 559
TF: 800-658-7201 ■ *Web:* bergbag.com

BERG Chilling Systems Inc
51 Nantucket Blvd. ..... Toronto ON M1P2N5 416-755-2221 610
TF: 833-399-2221 ■ *Web:* berg-group.com

Berg Co 2160 Industrial Dr ..... Monona WI 53713 608-221-4281 221-1416 664
Web: www.bergliquorcontrols.com

Berg Equipment Co
2700 W Veterans Pkwy ..... Marshfield WI 54449 715-384-2151 387-6777 273
TF: 800-494-1738 ■ *Web:* www.bergequipment.com

Berg Furniture 120 E Gloucester Pk ..... Barrington NJ 08007 856-310-0511 319-2
Web: www.bergfurniture.com

Berg Hill Greenleaf & Ruscitti LLP
1712 Pearl St ..... Boulder CO 80302 303-402-1600 428
Web: www.bhgrlaw.com

Berg Lacquer Inc 3150 E Pico Blvd ..... Los Angeles CA 90023 323-261-8114 780-9940 550
TF: 800-672-4900 ■ *Web:* www.ellispaint.com

Berg Steel Pipe Corp
5315 W 19th St. ..... Panama City FL 32401 850-769-2273 763-9683 490
Web: www.bergpipe.com

Berg's Ski & Snowboard Shop
367 W 13th Ave ..... Eugene OR 97401 541-683-1300 711
TF: 800-800-1953 ■ *Web:* www.bergsskishop.com

Bergad Inc 747 Eljer Way ..... Ford City PA 16226 724-763-2883 471
TF: 888-476-8664 ■ *Web:* www.bergad.com

Bergaila & Associates Inc
1155 Dairy Ashford Rd Ste 600 ..... Houston TX 77079 281-496-0803 496-4705 721
Web: www.bergaila.com

Bergamot Inc 820 E Wisconsin St ..... Delavan WI 53115 262-728-5572 728-3750 9
TF: 800-922-6733 ■ *Web:* www.bergamot.net

Bergdorf Goodman Inc 754 Fifth Ave. ..... New York NY 10019 212-753-7300 157-4
TF: 888-774-2424 ■ *Web:* www.bergdorfgoodman.com

Bergelectric Corp
5650 W Centinela Ave. ..... Los Angeles CA 90045 310-337-1377 189-4
Web: www.bergelectric.com

Bergen Briller Group LLC, The
1787 Wrightstown Rd ..... Newtown PA 18940 215-369-4190 260
Web: www.bbgsearch.com

Bergen Community College
400 Paramus Rd ..... Paramus NJ 07652 201-447-7200 670-7973 162
TF: 877-612-5381 ■ *Web:* bergen.edu

Bergen County 1 Bergen County Plz ..... Hackensack NJ 07601 201-336-6000 338
Web: www.co.bergen.nj.us

Bergen County Zoological Park
540 Farview Ave ..... Paramus NJ 07652 201-336-7257 336-7247 823
Web: co.bergen.nj.us

Bergendal Collection of Mediaeval Manuscripts
15 Duncan St ..... Toronto ON M5H3P9 416-925-8044 925-3631 434-3
Web: www.sympatico.ca

Bergenfield Public School District
225 W Clinton Ave ..... Bergenfield NJ 07621 201-385-8801 186
Web: www.bergenfield.org

Berger & Company PA
95 Thames Blvd ..... Bergenfield NJ 07621 201-384-6667 2

Berger & Montague PC
1622 Locust St ..... Philadelphia PA 19103 215-875-3000 428
TF: 800-424-6690 ■ *Web:* bergermontague.com

Berger Associates PC 1700 Bedford St ..... Stamford CT 06905 203-325-9727 327-9035 2
Web: bergerassociatespc.com

Berger Building Products Inc
805 Pennsylvania Blvd ..... Feasterville-Trevose PA 19053 215-355-1200 355-7738 697
TF: 800-523-8852 ■ *Web:* www.bergerbp.com

Berger Engineering Co 10900 Shady Trl ..... Dallas TX 75220 214-358-4451 351-2954 189-4
Web: www.berger-engr.com

Berger Singerman
350 E Las Olas Blvd Ste 1000 ..... Fort Lauderdale FL 33301 954-525-9900 523-2872 445
Web: www.bergersingerman.com

Berger Transfer & Storage Inc
2950 Long Lake Rd ..... Saint Paul MN 55113 877-268-2101 639-2277* 519
**Fax Area Code:* 651 ■ *TF:* 877-268-2101 ■ *Web:* www.bergerallied.com

Berger, Katz, Weishaus, & Lenza PC
275 Turnpike St. ..... Canton MA 02021 781-821-6400 821-6444 2
Web: bkwpc.com

Berger, Toombs, Elam & Frank
600 Citrus Ave Ste 200 ..... Fort Pierce FL 34950 772-461-6120 2
Web: btegf.com

Bergeron Agency, The 361 Main St. ..... Nashua NH 03060 603-881-7708 390
Web: bergeronagency.com

Bergeson LLP 111 N Market St Ste 600 ..... San Jose CA 95113 408-291-6200 297-6000 445
Web: www.be-law.com

Bergey & Co 8938 Worcester Hwy ..... Berlin MD 21811 410-641-1101 641-2012 2
Web: www.bergeycpa.com

Bergey Windpower Co
2200 Industrial Blvd ..... Norman OK 73069 405-364-4212 567
Web: bergey.com

Bergey's Auto Dealerships
462 Harleysville Pk ..... Souderton PA 18964 215-723-6071 723-4963 62-5
TF: 800-237-4397 ■ *Web:* bergeys.com

Berggruen Holdings Inc
304 S Broadway Ste 550 ..... Los Angeles CA 90013 212-380-2230 360-3
Web: www.berggruenholdings.com

Berghammer Construction Corp
4750 N 132nd St ..... Butler WI 53007 262-790-4750 186
Web: berghammer.com

Berghoff Design Group Inc
7000 E Mcdowell Rd Ste 100 ..... Scottsdale AZ 85257 480-481-3433 481-3533 422
Web: berghoffdesign.com

Bergin Fruit & Nut Company Inc
2000 Energy Park Dr ..... Saint Paul MN 55108 651-642-1234 558-9702 10-11
TF: 800-486-6808 ■ *Web:* berginfruit.com

Bergin Glass Impressions Inc
451 Technology Way ..... Napa CA 94558 707-224-0111 362
Web: www.berginglass.com

Bergkamp Inc 3040 Emulsion Dr. ..... Salina KS 67401 785-825-1375 825-4269 492
TF: 800-283-7226 ■ *Web:* www.bergkampinc.com

Berglund Construction
8410 S Chicago Ave ..... Chicago IL 60617 773-374-1000 189-3
TF: 888-689-5763 ■ *Web:* www.berglundco.com

Bergman Jack (Rep R - MI)
414 Cannon House Office Bldg. ..... Washington DC 20515 202-225-4735 342-2
Web: bergman.house.gov

Bergman Luggage Co
401 NE Northgate Way Ste 914 ..... Seattle WA 98125 206-365-5775 453
TF: 800-237-4626 ■ *Web:* www.bergmanluggage.com

Bergman Real Estate Group
555 US Hwy 1 S ..... Iselin NJ 08830 732-855-8600 652
Web: www.bergmanrealty.com

Bergmann Associates Inc
280 E Broad St Ste 200 ..... Rochester NY 14614 800-724-1168 261
TF: 800-724-1168 ■ *Web:* www.bergmannpc.com

Berg-Oliver Associates Inc
14701 St Mary's Ln Ste 400 ..... Houston TX 77079 281-589-0898 261
Web: bergoliver.com

Bergquist Co, The 18930 W 78th St. ..... Chanhassen MN 55317 952-835-2322 835-4156 253
TF: 800-347-4572 ■ *Web:* www.henkel-adhesives.com

Bergseth Bros Co 1211 47th St N ..... Fargo ND 58102 701-232-8818 81-1
Web: bergsethbeer.com

Bergstresser & Pollock LLC
52 Temple Pl Ste 4 ..... Boston MA 02111 617-682-9211 41
Web: bergstresser.com

Bergstrom Automotive 1 Neenah Ctr. ..... Neenah WI 54956 920-725-4444 57
TF: 800-630-1214 ■ *Web:* www.bergstromauto.com

Bergstrom Manufacturing Co
2390 Blackhawk Rd ..... Rockford IL 61125 815-874-7821 874-2144 15
Web: www.bergstrominc.com

Bergstrom of Kaukauna 2929 Lawe St ..... Kaukauna WI 54130 866-939-0130 57
TF: 866-939-0130 ■ *Web:* www.bergstromchryslerjeep.com

Bergwall Productions Inc
PO Box 1481 ..... Chadds Ford PA 19317 800-934-8696 514
TF: 800-934-8696 ■ *Web:* www.bergwall.com

Berico Fuels Inc
2200 E Bessemer Ave ..... Greensboro NC 27405 336-273-8663 316
Web: www.berico.com

Name / Address	City	State	ZIP	Phone	Fax	Class
Bering Air 1470 Sepalla Dr PO Box 1650 *TF:* 800-478-5422 ■ *Web:* www.beringair.com	Nome	AK	99762	907-443-5464	443-5919	25
Bering Straits Information Technology LLC 4600 Debarr Rd *Web:* beringstraits.com	Anchorage	AK	99508	907-563-3788		177
Beringea LLC 32330 W 12 Mile Rd *Web:* www.beringea.com	Farmington Hills	MI	48334	248-489-9000		792
Berje Inc 700 Blair Rd *Web:* www.berjeinc.com	Carteret	NJ	07008	973-748-8980	680-9618	145
Berk Trade & Business School 33-09 Queens Blvd 2nd Fl *Web:* electricalandplumbingschool.com	Long Island City	NY	11101	718-729-0909	729-0606	685
Berkadia Commercial Mortgage LLC 323 Norristown Rd Ste 300 *Web:* www.berkadia.com	Ambler	PA	19002	215-328-3200		225
Berkebile Oil Company Inc, The 1216 Red Brant Rd *Web:* www.berkebileoil.com	Somerset	PA	15501	814-443-1656	443-2873	541
Berkel & Company Contractors Inc PO Box 335 *Web:* berkelandcompany.com	Bonner Springs	KS	66012	913-422-5125	441-0402	188-2
Berkeley Advanced Biomaterials Inc 901 Grayson St Ste 101 *Web:* www.hydroxyapatite.com	Berkeley	CA	94710	510-883-0500	883-0511	476
Berkeley Art Museum & Pacific Film Archive 2120 Oxford St Ste 2250 *Web:* bampfa.org	Berkeley	CA	94720	510-642-0808	642-4889	520
Berkeley Chamber of Commerce 1834 University Ave *TF:* 800-847-4823 ■ *Web:* www.berkeleychamber.com	Berkeley	CA	94703	510-549-7000	549-1789	139
Berkeley City College 2050 Center St *Web:* www.berkeleycitycollege.edu	Berkeley	CA	94704	510-981-2800	841-7333	162
Berkeley College 3 E 43rd St *TF:* 800-446-5400 ■ *Web:* www.berkeleycollege.edu	New York	NY	10017	212-986-4343	818-1079	800
Berkeley Communications Corp 1321 67th St *TF:* 877-237-5268 ■ *Web:* berkcom.com	Emeryville	CA	94608	510-644-1599		194
Berkeley County 1003 Hwy 52 *Web:* www.berkeleycountysc.gov	Moncks Corner	SC	29461	843-719-4234		338
Berkeley County Chamber of Commerce PO Box 968 *TF:* 800-882-0337 ■ *Web:* berkeleysc.org	Moncks Corner	SC	29461	843-761-8238	899-6491	139
Berkeley County Council 400 W Stephen St Ste 201 *Web:* www.berkeleywv.org	Martinsburg	WV	25401	304-264-1923	267-5049	338
Berkeley Design Technology Inc (BDTI) 1646 N California Blvd Ste 220 *Web:* bdti.com	Walnut Creek	CA	94596	925-954-1411	954-1423	196
Berkeley Electric Co-opeartive Inc 551 Rembert C Dennis Blvd *TF:* 888-253-4232 ■ *Web:* www.berkeleyelectric.coop	Moncks Corner	SC	29461	843-761-8200		245
Berkeley Farms Inc 25500 Clawiter Rd *Web:* www.berkeleyfarms.com	Hayward	CA	94545	510-265-8600		296-27
Berkeley Forge & Tool Inc 1331 E Shore Hwy *Web:* www.berkforge.com	Berkeley	CA	94710	510-526-5034	525-9014	483
Berkeley Hills Real Estate Inc 1714 Solano Ave *Web:* berkhills.com	Berkeley	CA	94707	510-524-9888		652
Berkeley Hotel, The 1200 E Cary St *TF:* 888-780-4422 ■ *Web:* www.berkeleyhotel.com	Richmond	VA	23219	804-780-1300		379
Berkeley International Capital Corp PO Box 591748 *Web:* www.berkeleyvc.com	San Francisco	CA	94159	415-249-0450		792
Berkeley Medevices 1330 S 51st St *TF:* 800-227-2388 ■ *Web:* www.berkeleymedevices.com	Richmond	CA	94804	510-231-2474	231-9880	475
Berkeley Public Library 2090 Kittredge St *TF:* 800-870-3663 ■ *Web:* www.berkeleypubliclibrary.org	Berkeley	CA	94704	510-981-6100	981-6111	434-3
Berkeley Pumps 293 Wright St **Fax Area Code:* 800 ■ *TF:* 888-782-7483 ■ *Web:* www.pentair.com	Delavan	WI	53115	262-728-5551	426-9446*	641
Berkeley Repertory Theatre 2025 Addison St *Web:* www.berkeleyrep.org	Berkeley	CA	94704	510-647-2949	647-2975	749
Berkeley Review PO Box 40140 *Web:* www.berkeley-review.com	Berkeley	CA	94704	510-843-8378		637-2
Berkeley Sensor & Actuator Ctr *University of California* 403 Cory Hall Ste 1764 **Fax Area Code:* 775 ■ *Web:* vcresearch.berkeley.edu	Berkeley	CA	94720	510-643-6690	833-1890*	668
Berkeley Symphony Orchestra 1942 University Ave Ste 207 *Web:* www.berkeleysymphony.org	Berkeley	CA	94704	510-841-2800	841-5422	573-3
Berkeley Varitronics Systems Inc 255 Liberty St Liberty Corporate Pk *TF:* 888-737-4287 ■ *Web:* www.bvsystems.com	Metuchen	NJ	08840	732-548-3737		177
Berkeleys Northside Travel Inc 1824 Euclid Ave *TF:* 800-575-3411 ■ *Web:* www.berkeley4travel.com	Berkeley	CA	94709	510-843-1000		772
Berkhemer Clayton Inc 241 S Figueroa St Ste 300 *Web:* www.berkhemerclayton.com	Los Angeles	CA	90012	213-621-2300	621-2309	193
Berklee College of Music 1140 Boylston St *TF:* 800-421-0084 ■ *Web:* www.berklee.edu	Boston	MA	02215	617-747-2221	747-2047	166
Berkley Medical Resources Inc 700 Mountain View Dr *Web:* www.business.com	Smithfield	PA	15478	724-564-5002		476
Berkley Risk Administrators Company LLC 222 S Ninth St Ste 2700 *Web:* www.berkleyrisk.com	Minneapolis	MN	55402	612-766-3000	766-3099	390
Berkley Screw Machine Products Inc 2100 Royce Haley Dr *Web:* www.berkleyscrew.com	Rochester Hills	MI	48309	248-853-0044	853-1532	621
Berkot Super Foods 20005 Wolf Rd *Web:* www.berkotfoods.com	Mokena	IL	60448	708-231-1623		345
Berkowits School of Electrolysis 107-25 Metropolitan Ave *TF:* 800-526-9334 ■ *Web:* www.berkowitsschool.com	Forest Hills	NY	11375	718-544-4234	544-2589	685
Berkowitz Oliver Williams Shaw & Eisenbrandt LLP Crown Ctr 2600 Grand Blvd Ste 1200 *Web:* www.berkowitzoliver.com	Kansas City	MO	64108	816-561-7007		428
Berkowitz Pollack Brant Advisors & Accountants 200 S Biscayne Blvd 7th & Eighth Fl *Web:* www.bpbcpa.com	Miami	FL	33131	305-379-7000	379-8200	2
Berkowsky & Associates Inc 2551 US Hwy 130 *Web:* berkowsky.com	Cranbury	NJ	08512	609-655-2400	655-9790	186
Berks County Law Library *Law Library* 633 Ct St Berks County Courthouse 10th Fl *Web:* www.co.berks.pa.us	Reading	PA	19601	610-478-3370	478-6375	338
Berks Packing Company Inc 307-323 Bingaman St PO Box 5919 *TF:* 800-882-3757 ■ *Web:* www.berksfoods.com	Reading	PA	19610	800-882-3757		296-26
Berks Technical Institute 2205 Ridgewood Rd *TF:* 866-481-9301 ■ *Web:* www.berks.edu	Wyomissing	PA	19610	484-855-3140		167-3
Berks Visiting Nurse Assn 1170 Berkshire Blvd **Fax Area Code:* 610 ■ *TF:* 855-843-8627 ■ *Web:* www.seniorhousingnet.com	Wyomissing	PA	19610	855-843-8627	378-9762*	371
Berkshire & Burmeister Attorneys at Law 1301 S 75th St Ste 100 *Web:* www.berkshire-law.com	Omaha	NE	68124	402-827-7000	827-7001	445
Berkshire Advisors Inc 2240 Ridgewood Rd *TF:* 800-566-4325 ■ *Web:* berkshireadvisors.net	Wyomissing	PA	19610	610-376-6970		401
Berkshire Athenaeum 1 Wendell Ave *Web:* www.berkshire.net	Pittsfield	MA	01201	413-499-9480	499-9489	434-3
Berkshire Bancorp Inc 24 North St PO Box 1308 *TF:* 800-773-5601 ■ *Web:* www.berkshirebank.com	Pittsfield	MA	01202	800-773-5601		360-2
Berkshire Blanket Inc 44 E Main St *TF:* 800-372-2018 ■ *Web:* www.berkshireblanket.com	Ware	MA	01082	413-967-5964		442
Berkshire Botanical Garden 5 W Stockbridge Rd PO Box 826 *Web:* www.berkshirebotanical.org	Stockbridge	MA	01262	413-298-3926		97
Berkshire Chamber of Commerce 66 Allen St *Web:* 1berkshire.com	Pittsfield	MA	01201	413-499-4000		139
Berkshire Community College 1350 W St *Web:* www.berkshirecc.edu	Pittsfield	MA	01201	413-499-4660	447-7840	162
Berkshire Eagle 75 S Church St PO Box 1171 *Web:* www.berkshireeagle.com	Pittsfield	MA	01202	413-447-7311	499-3419	532-2
Berkshire Gas Company Inc 115 Cheshire Rd *Web:* www.berkshiregas.com	Pittsfield	MA	01201	800-292-5012		787
Berkshire General Store, The 25 Edison Dr *Web:* www.berkshiregeneralstore.com	Wayne	NJ	07470	973-696-6204		155-10
Berkshire Hathaway HomeServices New Jersey Properties Inc 220 Davidson Ave *TF:* 800-548-3466 ■ *Web:* www.bhhsnj.com	Somerset	NJ	08873	908-273-0400		652
Berkshire Hathaway Homestates Cos (BHHC) PO Box 2048 *TF:* 888-495-8949 ■ *Web:* www.bhhc.com	Omaha	NE	68103	888-495-8949		391-4
Berkshire Hathaway Inc 3555 Farnam St Ste 1440 *NYSE:* BRK.A ■ *TF:* 800-223-2064 ■ *Web:* www.berkshirehathaway.com	Omaha	NE	68131	402-346-1400	346-3375	185
Berkshire Health & Rehabilitation Ctr 705 Clearview Dr *TF:* 800-321-1245 ■ *Web:* www.mfa.net	Vinton	VA	24179	540-982-6691		450
Berkshire Medical Ctr 725 N St *Web:* www.berkshirehealthsystems.org	Pittsfield	MA	01201	413-447-2000		374-3
Berkshire Property Advisors LLC 1150 Sanctuary Pkwy Ste 150 *Web:* www.berkshirecommunities.com	Alpharetta	GA	30009	617-646-2300		655
Berkshire Refrigerated Warehousing 4600 S Packers Ave	Chicago	IL	60609	773-254-2424		803-2
Berkshire School 245 N Undermountain Rd *Web:* www.berkshireschool.org	Sheffield	MA	01257	413-229-8511	229-1028	622
Berkshire Theatre Festival 83 E Main St *Web:* www.berkshiretheatregroup.org	Stockbridge	MA	01262	413-298-5576		749
Berlin Metals LLC 3200 Sheffield Ave *TF:* 800-754-8867 ■ *Web:* www.berlinmetals.com	Hammond	IN	46327	219-933-0111	933-0692	492
Berlin Pacific 400 W 47th Ste 3AB *Web:* berlinpacific.dreamhosters.com	New York	NY	10036	212-247-2502		463
Berlin Steel Construction Co 76 Depot Rd PO Box 428 *Web:* berlinsteel.com	Kensington	CT	06037	860-828-3531	828-5253	480
Berline 423 N Main St Ste 300 *Web:* www.berline.com	Royal Oak	MI	48067	248-593-7402		5
Berlin-Ichthyosaur State Park PO Box 61200 *Web:* www.parks.nv.gov	Austin	NV	89310	775-964-2440		565
Berlin-Wheeler Inc 2942A SW Wanamaker Dr *Web:* www.berlinwheeler.com	Topeka	KS	66614	785-271-1000		160
Berliss Bearing Co 644 Rt 10 Po Box 45 *Web:* www.berliss.com	Livingston	NJ	07039	973-992-4242	992-6669	75
Berlitz Languages Inc 7 Roszel Rd **Fax Area Code:* 609 ■ *TF:* 866-423-7548 ■ *Web:* www.berlitz.com	Princeton	NJ	08540	866-423-7548	514-9689*	423
Berman & Larson Assoc 38 E Ridgewood Ave Ste 209 *Web:* www.jobsbl.com	Ridgewood	NJ	07450	201-909-0906		260
Berman Moving & Storage Inc 23800 Corbin Dr *Web:* www.bermanmovers.com	Cleveland	OH	44128	216-663-8816		312

Company	Address	City	State	ZIP	Phone	Fax	Class	Additional
Bermant Development Co	5383 Hollister Ave Ste 150	Santa Barbara	CA	93111	805-964-7200		653	*Web:* bdcdevelopment.com
Bermar Associates Inc	433 Minnesota Dr	Troy	MI	48083	248-589-2460	589-2461	604	*Web:* www.bermarassociates.com
Bermello Ajamil & Partners	2601 S Bayshore Dr	Miami	FL	33133	305-859-2050	859-9638	261	*Web:* www.bermelloajamil.com
Bermo Inc	4501 Ball Rd NE	Circle Pines	MN	55014	763-786-7676	785-2159	488	*Web:* www.bermo.com
Bermuda Tourism	675 3rd Ave 20th Fl	New York	NY	10017	212-818-9800	983-5289	775	*TF:* 800-223-6106 ■ *Web:* www.gotobermuda.com
Bermuda Village	142 Bermuda Village Dr	Advance	NC	27006	800-843-5433		672	*TF:* 800-843-5433 ■ *Web:* www.bermudavillage.net
Bern's Steak House	1208 S Howard Ave	Tampa	FL	33606	813-251-2421		671	*Web:* bernssteakhouse.com
Bernadettes Real Estate Plus Inc	1655 W Durham Ferry Rd	Tracy	CA	95376	209-456-5200		652	*Web:* klemmpropertymanagement.com
Bernalillo County	1 Civic Plz NW 10th Fl	Albuquerque	NM	87102	505-468-1500	468-1527	338	*Web:* www.bernco.gov
Bernard Chaus Inc	530 7th Ave 18th Fl	New York	NY	10018	646-562-4700		155-21	*Web:* www.chausny.com
Bernard Food Industries Inc	PO Box 1497	Evanston	IL	60204	800-323-3663	869-5315*	296-18	**Fax Area Code:* 847 ■ *TF:* 800-323-3663 ■ *Web:* www.bernardfoods.com
Bernard L. Madoff Investment Securities Co	45 Rockefeller Ctr 11th Fl	New York	NY	10111	212-230-2424		690	*TF:* 800-334-1343 ■ *Web:* www.madofftrustee.com
Bernard N. Ackerman CPA PA	596 Herrons Ferry Rd 5th Fl	Rock Hill	SC	29730	803-366-8371		2	*Web:* www.bnacpa.com
Bernard Pavelka Trucking Inc	1215 E J St	Hastings	NE	68901	402-462-4650	462-2711	780	*TF:* 800-274-4120 ■ *Web:* www.pavelkatrucking.com
Bernard Welding Equipment	449 W Corning Rd	Beecher	IL	60401	708-946-2281		811	*Web:* www.bernardwelds.com
Bernard Zell Anshe Emet Day School	3751 N Broadway St	Chicago	IL	60613	773-281-1858	281-4709	297-7	*Web:* www.bernardzell.org
Bernard'O Restaurant	12457 Rancho Bernardo Rd	San Diego	CA	92128	858-487-7171		671	*Web:* bernardorestaurant.wordpress.com
Bernard's Grove	187 Long Pond Rd	Rochester	NY	14612	585-227-6405		671	*Web:* bernardsgrovehouse.com
Bernardo Fashions LLC	463 Seventh Ave Ste 706	New York	NY	10018	212-594-3900	594-3999	432	*Web:* bernardofashions.com
Bernards Bros Inc	555 First St	San Fernando	CA	91340	818-898-1521		186	*Web:* www.bernards.com
Bernards Inn	27 Mine Brook Rd	Bernardsville	NJ	07924	908-766-0002	766-4604	379	*TF:* 888-766-0002 ■ *Web:* www.bernardsinn.com
Bernards Township School District	101 Peachtree Rd	Basking Ridge	NJ	07920	908-204-2600		685	*Web:* www.bernardsboe.com
Bernardus Lodge & Spa	415 Carmel Valley Rd	Carmel Valley	CA	93924	831-658-3400		379	*TF:* 800-223-2533 ■ *Web:* www.bernarduslodge.com
Bernatello's	PO Box 729	Maple Lake	MN	55358	952-831-6622	831-6606	296-21	*TF:* 800-666-9455 ■ *Web:* www.bernatellos.com
Berndt & Associates PC	30500 Van Dyke Ave Ste 702	Warren	MI	48093	586-558-9000		428	*Web:* www.berndtlegal.com
Berndt Group Ltd, The	3618 Falls Rd	Baltimore	MD	21211	410-889-5854	889-5904	177	*Web:* www.berndtgroup.net
Berne Apparel Co	2501 East 850 North PO Box 530	Ossian	IN	46777	888-772-3763	622-1515*	155-19	**Fax Area Code:* 260 ■ *TF:* 800-843-7657 ■ *Web:* www.berneapparel.com
Berne Cooperative Assn	158 W Main St	Ute	IA	51060	712-885-2211		324	
Bernell Corp	4016 N Home St	Mishawaka	IN	46545	574-259-2070	259-2102	544	*TF:* 800-348-2225 ■ *Web:* www.bernell.com
Bernell Hydraulics Inc	8810 Etiwanda Ave	Rancho Cucamonga	CA	91739	909-899-1751		640	*Web:* www.bernellhydraulics.com
Berner Foods Inc	2034 E Factory Rd	Dakota	IL	61018	800-819-8199	563-4017*	296-5	**Fax Area Code:* 815 ■ *TF:* 800-819-8199 ■ *Web:* www.bernerfoodandbeverage.com
Berner Trucking Inc	5885 Crown Rd NW	Dover	OH	44622	330-343-5812	364-2935	780	*TF:* 800-346-9634 ■ *Web:* www.bernertrucking.com
Berney-Karp Inc	3350 E 26th St	Vernon	CA	90058	323-260-7122	260-7245	334	*TF:* 800-237-6395 ■ *Web:* www.ceramic-source.com
Bernhard Brothers Mechanical Contractors LLC	13641 Airline Hwy	Baton Rouge	LA	70817	225-752-0785		189-10	*Web:* www.bernhardmechanical.com
Bernhardt Furniture Co	1839 Morganton Blvd	Lenoir	NC	28645	800-638-2772		319-1	*TF:* 800-638-2772 ■ *Web:* www.bernhardt.com
Bernheim Arboretum & Research Forest	2499 Clermont Rd PO Box 130	Clermont	KY	40110	502-955-8512		97	*Web:* bernheim.org
Bernheimer-Lincoln Insurance Group	779 Farmington Ave	West Hartford	CT	06119	860-232-3810		390	*Web:* bernheimerinsurance.com
Bernicke Wealth Management	1565 Bluestem Blvd	Altoona	WI	54720	715-832-1173	832-1933	401	*TF:* 866-832-1173 ■ *Web:* www.bernicke.com
Bernie & Phyl's Furniture	308 E Main St	Norton	MA	02766	508-286-4000		321	*Web:* www.bernieandphyls.com
Bernie's Tool & Fastener Services Inc	4211 Hwy Ave	Jacksonville	FL	32254	904-384-4999	384-0626	351	*TF:* 800-940-8005 ■ *Web:* berniestools.com
Bernies Auto and Marine	5531 US 41	Champion	MI	49814	906-339-4451		57	*Web:* www.berniesautoandmarine.com
Bernina of America Inc	3702 Prairie Lake Ct	Aurora	IL	60504	630-978-2500		37	*Web:* www.bernina.com
Berns Co	1250 W 17th St	Long Beach	CA	90813	562-437-0471	436-1074	470	*TF:* 800-421-3773 ■ *Web:* www.thebernscompany.com
Bernstein & Friedland PC	16000 Ventura Blvd Ste 1000	Encino	CA	91436	818-817-7570	530-7746	41	*Web:* laemploymentcounsel.com
Bernstein & Mello PLLC	21 Temple St	Nashua	NH	03060	603-945-5000	595-1688	41	*Web:* www.bbmlawyers.com
Bernstein Crisis Management Inc	700 S Myrtle Ave Ste 404	Monrovia	CA	91016	626-825-3838		463	*Web:* www.bernsteincrisismanagement.com
Bernstein Litowitz Berger & Grossmann LLP	1251 Avenue of the Americas 44th Fl	New York	NY	10020	212-554-1400		41	*Web:* blbglaw.com
Bernstein-Rein	4600 Madison Ave Ste 1500	Kansas City	MO	64112	816-756-0640		4	*Web:* b-r.com
Berntsen Brass & Aluminum Foundry Inc	2334 Pennsylvania Ave	Madison	WI	53704	608-249-9233		492	*Web:* berntsen-foundry.com
Bernzott Capital Advisors	888 W Ventura Blvd Ste B	Camarillo	CA	93010	805-389-9445		194	*TF:* 800-856-2646 ■ *Web:* www.bernzott.com
Beroe Inc	338 Raleigh St	Holly Springs	NC	27540	919-605-3435		466	*Web:* www.beroeinc.com
Beronio Lumber Co	2525 Marin St	San Francisco	CA	94124	415-824-4300		364	*Web:* www.beronio.com
Beroth Oil Co	20 W 32nd St	Winston-Salem	NC	27105	336-757-7600	757-7612	580	*Web:* www.fourbrothersstores.com
Berren Law Firm LLC, The	197 Taunton Ave Ste 202	East Providence	RI	02914	401-437-4450		41	*Web:* berrenlaw.com
Berridge Manufacturing Co	6515 Fratt Rd	San Antonio	TX	78218	210-650-3050	650-0379	697	*TF:* 800-669-0009 ■ *Web:* www.berridge.com
Berriehill Research Corp	7735 Paragon	Dayton	OH	45459	937-435-1016	435-1018	261	*Web:* berriehill.com
Berrien County	201 N Davis St Ste 105	Nashville	GA	31639	229-686-7461	686-7819	338	*Web:* www.berriencountygeorgia.com
Berrien County	701 Main St	Saint Joseph	MI	49085	269-983-7111	982-8642	338	*Web:* www.berriencounty.org
Berrien Resa	711 St Joseph Ave PO Box 364	Berrien Springs	MI	49103	269-471-7725	471-2941	685	*Web:* www.berrienresa.org
Berry Aviation Inc	1807 Airport Dr	San Marcos	TX	78666	800-229-2379	353-2593*	13	**Fax Area Code:* 512 ■ *TF:* 800-229-2379 ■ *Web:* www.berryaviation.com
Berry Bros General Contractors Inc	1414 River Rd PO Box 253	Berwick	LA	70342	985-384-8770	384-8778	10-3	*TF:* 800-747-8771 ■ *Web:* www.bbgci.com
Berry Coffee Co	14825 Martin Dr	Eden Prairie	MN	55344	952-937-8697	937-1425	297-8	*Web:* berrycoffee.com
Berry College	2277 Martha Berry Hwy NW	Mount Berry	GA	30149	706-232-5374		166	*TF:* 800-237-7942 ■ *Web:* www.berry.edu
Berry Dunn Mcneil & Parker	100 Middle St 4th Fl	Portland	ME	04101	207-775-2387	774-2375	2	*Web:* www.berrydunn.com
Berry Global Inc	101 Oakley St	Evansville	IN	47710	413-529-2183		604	*TF:* 877-662-3779 ■ *Web:* www.berryglobal.com
Berry Mansion	700 Louisville Rd	Frankfort	KY	40601	502-564-3000		50-3	*Web:* historicproperties.ky.gov
Berry Metal Co	2408 Evans City Rd	Harmony	PA	16037	724-452-8040	452-4115	492	*Web:* www.berrymetal.com
Berry Oil	3193 Leigh Ave	Tetonia	ID	83452	208-456-2271		579	*Web:* www.berryoil.net
Berry Tractor and Equipment Co	930 SW St	Wichita	KS	67213	316-943-4246		358	*Web:* www.berrytractor.com
Berry, Verduin & Koch LLC	190 Franklin Ave	Ridgewood	NJ	07450	201-444-8800		2	*Web:* bvkcpas.com
Berry-Hill Galleries Inc	11 E 70th St	New York	NY	10021	212-744-2300	744-2838	42	*Web:* www.berry-hill.com
Berryman Products Inc	3800 E Randol Mill Rd	Arlington	TX	76011	817-640-2376	640-4850	146	*TF:* 800-433-1704 ■ *Web:* www.berrymanproducts.com
Berryville Graphics	25 Jack Enders Blvd	Berryville	VA	22611	540-955-2750	955-2633	626	*Web:* www.bpg-usa.com
Berson-Sokol Agency Inc	23500 Mercantile Rd Ste C	Cleveland	OH	44122	216-464-1542	464-6522	390	*TF:* 800-543-6000 ■ *Web:* berson-sokol.com
Bert and Ernies Dining Saloon & Grill	361 N Last Chance Gulch	Helena	MT	59601	406-443-5680		671	*Web:* www.bertanderniesofhelena.com
Bert R. Huncilman & Son	115 Security Pkwy	New Albany	IN	47150	812-945-3544		697	*Web:* huncilman.com
Bert R. Hybels Inc	3322 Grand Prairie Rd	Kalamazoo	MI	49006	800-449-2357		292	*TF:* 800-449-2357 ■ *Web:* hybels.com
Berta's	3928 Twiggs St	San Diego	CA	92110	619-295-2343		671	*Web:* www.bertasinoldtown.com
Bertch Cabinet Manufacturing Inc	4747 Crestwood Dr	Waterloo	IA	50702	319-296-2987	296-2315	115	*Web:* www.bertch.com
Bertech-Kelex	640 Maple Ave	Torrance	CA	90503	310-787-0337		246	*Web:* bertech.com
Bertelkamp Automation Inc	4716 Middle Creek Ln	Knoxville	TN	37921	865-588-7691		358	*TF:* 800-251-9134 ■ *Web:* www.bertelkamp.com
Bertelsmann SE & Co	1745 Broadway	New York	NY	10019	212-782-1000		637-9	*Web:* www.bertelsmann.com
Berthel Fisher Cos	4201 42nd St NE Ste 100	Cedar Rapids	IA	52402	319-447-5700	447-4250	690	*TF:* 800-356-5234 ■ *Web:* www.berthel.com
Bertie County	106 Dundee St PO Box 530	Windsor	NC	27983	252-794-5300	794-5327	338	*Web:* www.co.bertie.nc.us

Company / Address	City	State	ZIP	Phone	Fax	Class
Bertling Logistics Inc 19054 Kenswick Dr. *Web:* www.bertling.com	Humble	TX	77338	281-774-2300		194
Bertolinos Pharmacy 1500 S 12th St *Web:* bertolinospharmacy.net	Philadelphia	PA	19147	215-389-5917	389-8685	237
Bertone Piccini LLP 777 Terrace Ave Ste 201 *Web:* bertonepiccini.com	Hasbrouck Heights	NJ	07604	201-483-9333		41
Bertrand Products Inc 2323 Foundation Dr *Web:* www.bertrandproducts.com	South Bend	IN	46628	574-234-4181	234-9890	22
Berts Bikes & Sports 050 Southwestern Blvd *Web:* bertsbikes.com	Orchard Park	NY	14127	716-646-0028		711
Bertsche Engineering Corp 711 Dartmouth Ln *Web:* www.bertsche.com	Buffalo Grove	IL	60089	847-537-8757		261
Bertucci's Restaurant Corp 155 Otis St *Web:* www.bertuccis.com	Northborough	MA	01532	508-351-2500		670
Bertuccio Farms 2410 Airline Hwy *Web:* www.thefarmbertuccios.com	Hollister	CA	95023	831-636-0821		315-3
Berwick Electric Co 3450 N Nevada Ave Ste 100 *Web:* www.berwickelectric.com	Colorado Springs	CO	80907	719-632-7683	471-9660	189-4
Berwick Hospital Ctr, The 701 E 16th St *Web:* www.commonwealthhealth.net	Berwick	PA	18603	570-759-5000	759-3473	374-3
Berwind Group 1500 Market St 3000 Ctr Sq W *Web:* www.berwind.com	Philadelphia	PA	19102	215-563-2800	575-2314	185
Berwind Natural Resources Corp 509 15th St *Web:* www.bnrpa.com	Windber	PA	15963	814-467-4519	467-4559	501
Berwyn Development Corp 3322 S Oak Park Ave 2nd Fl *Web:* www.berwyn.net	Berwyn	IL	60402	708-788-8100	788-0966	139
Berwyn Public Library (BPL) 2701 S Harlem Ave *Web:* www.berwynlibrary.org	Berwyn	IL	60402	708-795-8000	795-8101	434-3
Bescast Inc 4600 E 355th St *Web:* www.bescast.com	Willoughby	OH	44094	440-946-5300		306
Besco Electric Supply Co 711 S 14th St *Web:* www.bescolights.com	Leesburg	FL	34748	352-787-4542	365-0554	362
Beshenich Muir & Associates LLC 121A Cherokee St *Web:* bma-1.com	Leavenworth	KS	66048	913-904-1880		463
BESI (Brantley Electronic Supply Inc) 935 Bragg Blvd *TF:* 800-682-2560 ■ *Web:* www.brantleyelectronic.com	Fayetteville	NC	28301	910-485-2100		35
Besicorp Ltd 1151 Flatbush Rd *Web:* www.besicorp.com	Kingston	NY	12401	845-336-7700		357
Besl Transfer Co 5700 Este Ave *TF:* 800-456-2375 ■ *Web:* www.besl.com	Cincinnati	OH	45232	513-242-3456	242-4013	780
Besly Cutting Tools Inc 520 Blackhawk Blvd Ste 135 *TF:* 800-435-2965 ■ *Web:* www.besly.com	South Beloit	IL	61080	815-389-2231	389-1339	493
Besnovo Inc 695 Westney Road S *Web:* www.besnovo.com	Ajax	ON	L1S6M9	905-239-9888	436-0270	256
Bess Press Inc 3565 Harding Ave *Web:* www.besspress.com	Honolulu	HI	96816	808-732-3627		637-2
Besse Forest Products Group Inc PO Box 352 *Web:* www.bessegroup.com	Gladstone	MI	49837	906-428-3113		448
Bessemer Area Chamber of Commerce 321 N 18th St *TF:* 888-423-7736 ■ *Web:* www.bessemerchamber.com	Bessemer	AL	35020	205-425-3253	425-4979	139
Bessemer Hall of History 1905 Alabama Ave *Web:* www.bhamrails.info	Bessemer	AL	35020	205-426-1633		520
Bessemer Public Library 400 19th St *Web:* www.bessemerlibrary.com	Bessemer	AL	35020	205-428-7882		434-3
Bessemer Trust Co 630 Fifth Ave *TF:* 866-271-7403 ■ *Web:* www.bessemertrust.com	New York	NY	10111	212-708-9100	265-5826	401
Bessemer Venture Partners (BVP) 1865 Palmer Ave Ste 104 *Web:* www.bvp.com	Larchmont	NY	10538	914-833-5300	833-5499	792
Besser Co 801 Johnson St **Fax Area Code:* 989 ■ *TF:* 800-530-9980 ■ *Web:* besser.com	Alpena	MI	49707	800-968-0444	354-3120*	386
Bessie Smith Cultural Ctr 200 E Martin Luther King Blvd *Web:* www.bessiesmithcc.org	Chattanooga	TN	37403	423-266-8658	267-1076	520
Bessire & Associates Inc 7621 Little Ave Ste 106 *TF:* 800-797-7355 ■ *Web:* www.bessire.com	Charlotte	NC	28226	704-341-1423		193
Bessire & Company LLC 2412 Old North Rd Bldg 101 *Web:* bessireco.com	Denton	TX	76209	940-320-6838		734
Best & Flanagan LLP 60 S 6th St Ste 2700 *Web:* www.bestlaw.com	Minneapolis	MN	55402	612-339-7121	339-5897	428
Best & Flatt PA 3016 Millwood Ave *Web:* bestandflatt.com	Columbia	SC	29205	803-252-1800		41
Best Access Systems 6161 E 75th St *TF:* 855-365-2407 ■ *Web:* www.bestaccess.com	Indianapolis	IN	46250	317-849-2250		350
Best Aire LLC 3648 Rockland Cir *TF:* 800-968-4422 ■ *Web:* www.best-aire.com	Millbury	OH	43447	419-726-0055		316
Best Bath Systems 723 Garber St *TF:* 866-333-8657 ■ *Web:* bestbath.com	Caldwell	ID	83605	208-342-6823	333-8657	375
Best Beers Inc 1100 S Strong Dr *Web:* best-beers-inc.business.site	Bloomington	IN	47403	812-332-1234		81-1
Best Best & Krieger LLP 3390 University Ave 5th Fl *Web:* www.bbklaw.com	Riverside	CA	92501	951-686-1450	686-3083	41
Best Broadcasting Inc 107 S Main *Web:* www.bestbroadcastgroup.com	Brookfield	MO	64628	660-258-3383	258-7307	645-141
Best Buy Company Inc 7601 Penn Ave S *NYSE:* BBY ■ *TF:* 888-237-8289 ■ *Web:* www.bestbuy.com	Richfield	MN	55423	612-291-1000	292-2323	35
Best Buys Direct Inc 1044 SR-23 *Web:* www.bestbuysdirect.com	Wayne	NJ	07470	973-628-8100	628-1199	514
Best Chevrolet Inc 128 Derby St *Web:* www.thebestchevy.com	Hingham	MA	02043	781-749-1950		57
Best Choice Software LLC 1404 Hatcher Dr Cir *Web:* www.bestchoicesoftware.com	Brandon	FL	33511	941-281-5943		179
Best Cleaners Inc 469 Albany Shaker Rd *Web:* www.bestcleanersny.com	Albany	NY	12211	518-459-7440		426
Best Cleaners Inc 522 S Main St *Web:* bestcleaners.com	Middletown	CT	06457	860-346-1718		426
Best Cutting Die Co 8080 McCormick Blvd *Web:* bestcuttingdie.com	Skokie	IL	60076	847-675-5522		697
Best Data Products Inc 20740 Plummer St *Web:* www.diamondmm.com	Chatsworth	CA	91311	818-773-9600	773-9619	173-3
BEST Flow Line Equipment 1329 Markum Gate Way *Web:* www.bestflowline.com	Fort Worth	TX	76126	817-850-7833		358
Best Friends Animal Care Inc 4915 Pine Ridge Dr *Web:* vetstreet.com	Columbus	IN	47201	812-342-1233		794
Best Friends Animal Hospital P 5110 Clark Rd *Web:* mybestfriendsanimalhospital.com	Sarasota	FL	34233	941-927-4567		794
Best Friends Pet Care Inc 520 Main Ave *Web:* www.bestfriendspetcare.com	Norwalk	CT	06851	203-849-1010		794
Best Friends Veterinary Ctr 2082 Cheyenne Ct *Web:* www.bestfriendsvet.com	Grafton	WI	53024	262-375-0130		794
Best Healthcare Services Inc 459 Broadway Ste 306 *Web:* besthealthservices.org	Everett	MA	02149	617-381-0050		363
Best Impressions Catalog Co 345 N Lewis Ave *TF:* 800-635-2378 ■ *Web:* www.bestimpressions.com	Oglesby	IL	61348	815-883-3532		791
Best Label Co 30803 San Clemente St *Web:* www.resourcelabel.com	Hayward	CA	94544	510-489-5400	489-2914	413
Best Lawns Inc 1435 Yorkshire Dr *Web:* bestlawns.com	Streamwood	IL	60107	630-213-7900		422
Best Life & Health Insurance Co 2505 McCabe Way *TF:* 800-433-0088 ■ *Web:* www.bestlife.com	Irvine	CA	92614	949-253-4080		391-2
Best Line Oil Company Inc 219 N 20th St *TF:* 800-382-1811 ■ *Web:* bestlineoil.com	Tampa	FL	33605	813-248-1044		579
Best Maid Products Inc 1401 S Riverside Dr *TF:* 800-447-3581 ■ *Web:* bestmaidpickles.com	Fort Worth	TX	76104	817-335-5494		296-19
Best Maids 842 Lemay Ferry Rd **Fax Area Code:* 202	Saint Louis	MO	63125	314-544-6180	338-4960*	256
Best Metal Products Co 3570 Raleigh Dr SE *Web:* www.bestmetalproducts.com	Grand Rapids	MI	49512	616-942-7141		223
Best Plumbing Specialties 3039 Ventrie Ct *TF:* 800-448-6710 ■ *Web:* www.bestplumbingspecialties.com	Myersville	MD	21773	301-695-4488		612
Best Plumbing Tile & Stone 49 Rt 138 *Web:* www.bestplg.com	Somers	NY	10589	914-232-2020	232-2345	610
Best Press Inc 4201 Airborn Dr *Web:* www.bestpress.com	Addison	TX	75001	972-930-1000	930-1030	627
Best Priced Products Inc PO Box 1174 *TF:* 800-824-2939 ■ *Web:* www.bpp2.com	White Plains	NY	10602	914-345-3800	345-0300	407
Best Provision Company Inc 144 Avon Ave *TF:* 800-631-4466 ■ *Web:* www.bestprovision.com	Newark	NJ	07108	800-631-4466		296-26
Best Registration Services Inc 1418 S Third St *TF:* 800-977-3475 ■ *Web:* www.bestregistrar.com	Louisville	KY	40208	502-637-4528		396
Best Reports Inc PO Box 546 *Web:* www.bestreports.net	Richmond	IL	60071	815-678-2703	839-7440	635
Best Telecom Inc 278 E End Ave *TF:* 888-365-2273 ■ *Web:* www.besttelecom.com	Beaver	PA	15009	888-365-2273		387
Best Theratronics Ltd 413 March Rd *TF:* 866-792-8598 ■ *Web:* www.theratronics.ca	Ottawa	ON	K2K0E4	613-591-2100		476
Best Tile 1112 Jefferson Blvd *Web:* www.besttile.com	Warwick	RI	02886	401-738-2450	738-7603	364
Best Travel Inc 6251 N Maplewood Ave	Chicago	IL	60659	773-628-6535		771
Best Vascular 4350 International Blvd Ste A *TF:* 800-668-6783 ■ *Web:* www.bestvascular.com	Norcross	GA	30093	770-717-0904	717-1283	476
Best Way Disposal 2577 Kentucky Ave *Web:* www.bestway-disposal.com	Indianapolis	IN	46221	317-390-5840		660
Best Way Transportation Inc 1195 N I-45 *Web:* www.bestwayltd.com	Palmer	TX	75152	972-845-3222	449-2052	780
Best Western Grandma's Feather Bed 9300 Glacier Hwy *TF:* 888-781-5005 ■ *Web:* www.grandmasfeatherbed.com	Juneau	AK	99801	907-789-5005		671
Best Western Heritage Inn 151 E McLeod Rd *Web:* www.bestwesternheritageinn.com	Bellingham	WA	98226	360-647-1912		378
Best Western InnTowner, The 2424 University Ave *TF:* 800-258-8321 ■ *Web:* inntowner.com	Madison	WI	53726	608-233-8778		378
Best Western International Inc 6201 N 24th Pkwy *TF:* 800-528-1234 ■ *Web:* www.bestwestern.com	Phoenix	AZ	85016	602-957-4200		379
Best Western Plus Hood River Inn 1108 E Marina Way *TF:* 800-828-7873 ■ *Web:* www.hoodriverinn.com	Hood River	OR	97031	541-386-2200		707

Name / Address	City	State	Zip	Phone	Fax	Class
Best Western Victorian Inn 487 Foam St TF: 800-232-4141 ■ Web: www.victorianinn.com	Monterey	CA	93940	831-373-8000	655-8174	379
Best Yet Market Inc 1 Lexington Ave. Web: bestmarket.com	Bethpage	NY	11714	516-570-5300		345
Best, Heyns & Schroeder PC 410 S Jackson St Web: bestlawpractice.com	Jackson	MI	49201	517-787-2620	787-1811	41
Best, Vanderlaan & Harrington 25 E Washington St Ste 800 TF: 800-351-4316 ■ Web: www.bestfirm.com	Chicago	IL	60602	312-819-1100		428
Bestar Inc 4220 Villeneuve St TF: 888-823-7827 ■ Web: www.bestar.ca	Lac-Megantic	QC	G6B2C3	819-583-1017		319-1
BestCo Inc 288 Mazeppa Rd TF: 888-211-5530 ■ Web: www.bestco.com	Mooresville	NC	28115	704-664-4300		296-8
Bestech 1040 Lorne St Unit 3 TF: 877-675-7720 ■ Web: www.bestech.com	Sudbury	ON	P3C4R9	705-675-7720	675-5507	261
Bestforms Inc 1135 Avenida Acaso TF: 800-350-0618 ■ Web: bestforms.com	Camarillo	CA	93012	805-383-6993	987-5280	110
BestIT 5716 Corsa Ave Web: www.bestit.com	Westlake Village	CA	91362	818-699-1668		196
Bestmark Inc 5500 Feltl Rd Ste 200 Web: www.bestmark.com	Minnetonka	MN	55343	952-922-3890		196
Bestolife Corp 2777 Stemmons Fwy Ste 1800 TF: 855-243-9164 ■ Web: www.bestolife.com	Dallas	TX	75207	214-583-0271	631-3047	3
Best-One Tire & Service LLC 101 N Polk St Web: www.bestonetire.com	Monroe	IN	46772	260-692-6171		755
Bestow 750 N Saint Paul St Ste 1900 TF: 833-300-0603 ■ Web: bestow.com	Dallas	TX	75201	833-300-0603		391-1
BestPass Inc 500 New Karner Rd Ste 5 TF: 888-410-9696 ■ Web: www.bestpass.com	Albany	NY	12203	518-458-1579		393
BestTel 360 E First St Ste 904 Web: www.besttel.net	Tustin	CA	92780	714-612-7333		387
BestTransportcom Inc 400 W Wilson Bridge Rd Ste 100 Web: www.besttransport.com	Columbus	OH	43085	614-888-2378		224
Best-Wade Petroleum Inc 201 Dodge Dr TF: 888-888-6457 ■ Web: www.bestwade.com	Ripley	TN	38063	731-635-9661		581
Bestway Enterprises Inc 3877 Luker Rd Web: www.bestwaylumber.com	Cortland	NY	13045	607-753-8261	753-9948	780
Bestway Inc 1201 Concord St S TF: 800-316-4567 ■ Web: www.bestwayinc.com	Saint Paul	MN	55075	214-630-6655		264-2
Bestway Systems Inc c/o Highland Park Service Corp, 28601 Chagrin Blvd Ste 600 Web: www.bestwaysystems.com	Cleveland	OH	44122	216-398-6090		449
Bestway Tours & Safaris 8678 Greenall Ave. TF: 800-663-0844 ■ Web: bestway.com	Burnaby	BC	V5J3M6	604-264-7378	264-7774	760
Bestweld Inc 40 Robinson St Web: www.bestweld.com	Pottstown	PA	19464	610-718-9700	718-9800	454
Bestwill Corp 439 Wald Web: www.bestwill.com	Irvine	CA	92618	949-502-5700		612
Beta Alpha Psi 220 Leigh Farm Rd TF: 800-362-5066 ■ Web: www.bap.org	Durham	NC	27707	919-402-4044	402-4040	48-16
Beta Analytic Inc 4985 SW 74 Ct. Web: www.betalabservices.com	Miami	FL	33155	305-667-5167	663-0964	743
Beta Beta Beta National Biological Honor Society Univ of N Alabama PO Box 5079 Web: www.tribeta.org	Florence	AL	35632	256-765-6220		167-2
Beta Cae Systems Usa Inc 29800 Middlebelt Rd Ste 100 Web: ansa-usa.com	Farmington Hills	MI	48334	248-737-9760	737-9726	177
Beta Control Systems Inc 6950 SW 111th Ave Web: www.betacontrol.com	Beaverton	OR	97008	503-646-3399		201
Beta Fluid Systems Inc 1209 Freeway Dr. Web: www.betafueling.com	Reidsville	NC	27320	336-342-0306		22
Beta Gamma Sigma Inc (BGS) 125 Weldon Pkwy TF: 800-337-4677 ■ Web: www.betagammasigma.org	Maryland Heights	MO	63043	314-432-5650	432-7083	48-16
Beta LaserMike Inc 8001 Technology Blvd TF: 800-886-9935 ■ Web: www.betalasermike.com	Dayton	OH	45424	937-233-9935	233-7284	472
Beta Phi Mu PO Box 42139 Web: www.betaphimu.org	Philadelphia	PA	19101	267-361-5018		423
Beta Research Corp 6400 Jericho Tpke Web: www.betaresearch.com	Syosset	NY	11791	516-935-3800		668
Beta Screen Corp 707 Commercial Ave TF: 800-272-7336 ■ Web: www.betascreen.com	Carlstadt	NJ	07072	201-939-2400	939-7656	591
Beta Shim Co 11 Progress Dr Web: www.betashim.com	Shelton	CT	06484	203-926-1150	929-5509	488
Beta Systems Software of North America Inc 8300 Greensboro Dr Ste L1-633 Web: www.betasystems.com	McLean	VA	22102	703-889-1240	889-1241	178-12
Beta Theta Pi 5134 Bonham Rd PO Box 6277 *Fax Area Code: 513 ■ TF: 800-800-2382 ■ Web: www.beta.org	Oxford	OH	45056	800-800-2382	523-2381*	48-16
Betach Solutions Inc 809 Manning Rd NE Ste 201 Web: www.betach.com	Calgary	AB	T2E7M9	403-984-2473		196
Betacom 9331 E Fowler Ave. Web: www.betacom.com	Thonotosassa	FL	33592	813-986-4922	982-0882	194
Betar Inc 100 Randolph Rd Web: www.betar.net	Somerset	NJ	08873	908-359-4200	359-1010	621
Beta-tech Consulting Inc 1553 Markham Way Web: www.beta-techconsulting.com	Sacramento	CA	95818	916-443-0300		194
Bete Fog Nozzle Inc 50 Greenfield St TF: 800-235-0049 ■ Web: www.bete.com	Greenfield	MA	01301	413-772-0846	772-6729	350
Betenbender Manufacturing Inc 5806 Quality Ridge Rd Web: www.betenbender.com	Coggon	IA	52218	319-435-2378	435-2262	456
Beth & Rudnicki Insurance Agency Inc 5411 E State St Ste 204 Web: brinsurance.net	Rockford	IL	61108	815-399-6690		390
Beth Ahabah Museum & Archives 1109 W Franklin St Web: www.bethahabah.org	Richmond	VA	23220	804-353-2668		520
Beth I. Silverman & Associates LLC 30 Garfield Pl Ste 750 Web: bethsilverman.com	Cincinnati	OH	45202	513-241-9844		41
Beth Israel Deaconess Hospital-Milton 199 Reedsdale Rd TF: 800-462-5540 ■ Web: www.bidmilton.org	Milton	MA	02186	617-696-4600	696-7380	374-3
Beth Israel Deaconess Medical Ctr (BIDMC) 330 Brookline Ave. TF: 800-667-5356 ■ Web: www.bidmc.org	Boston	MA	02215	617-667-7000		374-3
Beth Medrash Govoha 617 6th St Web: www.bmg.edu	Lakewood	NJ	08701	732-364-4212		48-20
Beth Ramacher Development Ctr *Ramacher School* 710 N Hughes Ave Web: fcoe.org	Fresno	CA	93728	559-497-3955		685
Bethany Bible College 26 Western St TF: 888-432-4444 ■ Web: www.kingswood.edu	Sussex	NB	E4E1E6	506-432-4400	432-4425	785
Bethany College 31 E Campus Dr. TF: 800-922-7611 ■ Web: www.bethanywv.edu	Bethany	WV	26032	304-829-7000	829-7142	166
Bethany College 335 E Swensson St TF: 800-826-2281 ■ Web: www.bethanylb.edu	Lindsborg	KS	67456	785-227-3380	227-8993	166
Bethany Lutheran College 700 Luther Dr TF: 800-944-3066 ■ Web: www.blc.edu	Mankato	MN	56001	507-344-7000	344-7376	166
Bethany Republican-Clipper 202 N 16 St Web: www.bethanyclipper.com	Bethany	MO	64424	660-425-6325	425-3441	532-4
Bethany Theological Seminary 615 National Rd W TF: 800-287-8822 ■ Web: bethanyseminary.edu	Richmond	IN	47374	765-983-1800	983-1840	167-3
Bethany Village 325 Wesley Dr Web: www.asbury.org	Mechanicsburg	PA	17055	717-213-8266		672
Bethea Baptist Retirement Community 157 Home Ave TF: 877-393-2867 ■ Web: www.bethearetirement.com	Darlington	SC	29532	843-393-2867	393-2458	672
Bethel Baptist Church 1196 N Academy St Web: www.mybethel.com	Galesburg	IL	61401	309-342-3166		48-20
Bethel College 300 E 27th St TF: 800-522-1887 ■ Web: www.bethelks.edu	North Newton	KS	67117	316-283-2500	284-5286	166
Bethel Inn & Country Club PO Box 49 Broad St *Fax Area Code: 207 ■ TF: 800-654-0125 ■ Web: www.bethelinn.com	Bethel	ME	04217	800-654-0125	824-2233*	669
Bethel Machine & Manufacturing Inc 3050 Industrial Blvd Web: www.bethelmachine.net	Bethel Park	PA	15102	412-833-5522	833-8171	454
Bethel Plastics Inc 1900 Raymer Ave Web: www.bethelplastics.com	Fullerton	CA	92833	714-533-8500		192
Bethel University 325 Cherry Ave. Web: www.bethelu.edu	McKenzie	TN	38201	731-352-4000	352-4241	166
Bethel University 3900 Bethel Dr. TF: 800-255-8706 ■ Web: www.bethel.edu	Saint Paul	MN	55112	651-638-6400	635-1490	166
Bethel University Board of Trustees 1001 Bethel Cir. TF: 800-422-4101 ■ Web: www.betheluniversity.edu	Mishawaka	IN	46545	574-807-7000		166
Bethel World Outreach Church 16227 Batchellors Forest Rd. Web: www.bethelcityofhope.com	Olney	MD	20832	301-588-8099		48-20
Bethesda Butler Hospital Sleep Ctr 3055 Hamilton Mason Rd. Web: www.cgha.com	Hamilton	OH	45011	513-454-3050		374-3
Bethesda Christian University 730 N Euclid Web: buc.edu	Anaheim	CA	92801	714-517-1945		161
Bethesda Home 408 E Main St Web: bethesdahome.org	Goessel	KS	67053	620-367-2291		371
Bethesda Hospital 2951 Maple Ave TF: 800-322-4762 ■ Web: www.genesishcs.org	Zanesville	OH	43701	740-454-4000		374-3
Bethesda Ministries Inc 2200 Peacock Rd *Fax Area Code: 978	Richmond	IN	47374	765-939-2975	369-9179*	48-20
Bethesda North Hospital 10500 Montgomery Rd. Web: www.trihealth.com	Cincinnati	OH	45242	513-865-1164		374-3
Bethesda Softworks LLC 1370 Piccard Dr Ste 120 Web: bethesda.net	Rockville	MD	20850	301-926-8300	926-8010	178-6
Bethlehem Apparatus Company Inc 890 Front St Web: www.bethlehemapparatus.com	Hellertown	PA	18055	610-838-7034	838-6333	143
Bethlehem Area Public Library 11 W Church St Web: www.bapl.org	Bethlehem	PA	18018	610-867-3761		434-3
Bethlehem Books 10194 Garfield St S Web: www.bethlehembooks.com	Bathgate	ND	58216	701-265-3725		637-2
Bethlehem Chamber of Commerce 318 Delaware Ave Ste 11 Web: www.bethlehemchamber.com	Delmar	NY	12054	518-439-0512	475-0910	139
Bethlehem Construction Inc 5505 Tichenal Rd Web: www.bethlehemconstruction.com	Cashmere	WA	98815	509-782-1001		186
Bethpage Federal Credit Union 899 S Oyster Bay Rd. *Fax Area Code: 516 ■ TF: 800-628-7070 ■ Web: www.bethpagefcu.com	Bethpage	NY	11714	800-628-7070	349-6828*	219
Bethpage State Park Bethpage Pkwy. TF: 800-456-2267 ■ Web: parks.ny.gov	Farmingdale	NY	11735	516-249-0701		565
Bethune Memorial House National Historic Site 235 John St N. Web: www.pc.gc.ca	Gravenhurst	ON	P1P1G4	705-687-4261	687-4935	563
Bethune-Cookman University 640 Dr Mary Mcleod Bethune Blvd. TF: 800-448-0228 ■ Web: www.cookman.edu	Daytona Beach	FL	32114	386-481-2900	481-2601	166
Betis Group Inc 1420 Beverly Rd Ste 330 Web: www.betis.com	McLean	VA	22101	703-532-2008		177

Name / Address	City	State	ZIP	Phone	Fax	Class
Beton Consulting Engineers 2535 Pilot Knob Rd Ste 108 *Web:* betonconsultingeng.com	Mendota Heights	MN	55120	651-330-1207		261
Beton Stahl 2003 O'Neil Rd *Web:* beton-stahl.com	Hudson	WI	54016	715-808-0213		261
Betras, Kopp & Harshman LLC 6630 Seville Dr *TF:* 800-457-2889 ■ *Web:* bhlaws.com	Canfield	OH	44406	330-746-8484		41
Betsco 233 E FM 2821 **Fax Area Code:* 936 ■ *TF:* 888-895-8189 ■ *Web:* betsco.com	Huntsville	TX	77320	888-895-8189	291-8191*	201
Betson Enterprises Inc 303 Patterson Plank Rd *TF:* 800-524-2343 ■ *Web:* www.betson.com	Carlstadt	NJ	07072	201-438-1300	438-4837	55
Betsy Hotel 1440 Ocean Dr *TF:* 866-792-3879 ■ *Web:* www.thebetsyhotel.com	Miami Beach	FL	33139	305-531-6100		379
Betsy Johnson Regional Hospital 803 Tilghman Dr *Web:* myharnetthealth.org	Dunn	NC	28334	910-892-7161		374-3
Betsy Ross House 239 Arch St *Web:* historicphiladelphia.org	Philadelphia	PA	19106	215-629-4026		50-3
Bettcher Industries Inc PO Box 336 *TF:* 800-321-8763 ■ *Web:* www.bettcher.com	Vermilion	OH	44089	440-965-4422		298
Bette & Cring LLC 22 Century Hill Dr Ste 201 *Web:* www.bettecring.com	Latham	NY	12110	518-213-1010		186
Bettendorf Community School District 3311 18th St *Web:* bettendorf.k12.ia.us	Bettendorf	IA	52722	563-359-3681	359-3685	685
Bettendorf Office Products Inc 3280 Middle Rd *Web:* www.bettoffice.com	Bettendorf	IA	52722	563-359-3487	359-8901	45
Bettendorf Public Library 2950 Learning Campus Dr *Web:* www.bettendorflibrary.com	Bettendorf	IA	52722	563-344-4175	344-4185	434-3
Bettendorf-Stanford 1370 W Main St *TF:* 800-548-2253 ■ *Web:* www.bettendorfstanford.com	Salem	IL	62881	618-548-3555		361
Better Baked Foods LLC 56 Smedley St *Web:* www.betterbaked.com	North East	PA	16428	814-725-8778		296-1
Better Banks 10225 N Knoxville Ave *Web:* www.betterbanks.com	Peoria	IL	61615	309-685-9595		70
Better Business Bureau of Quebec 1565 Boul de l'Avenir Ste 206 **Fax Area Code:* 450 ■ *Web:* www.occq-qcco.com	Laval	QC	H7S2N5	514-905-3893	663-6316*	78
Better Endings New Beginnings (BENB) 6289 Brunswick Ave N *Web:* www.betterendings.org	Brooklyn Park	MN	55429	763-531-9548	533-3223	637-2
Better Hearing Institute (BHI) 1444 I St NW Ste 700 *TF:* 800-639-3884 ■ *Web:* www.betterhearing.org	Washington	DC	20005	202-449-1100		48-17
Better Home Care LLC 1046 Bustleton Pk *Web:* www.betterhomecare.org	Feasterville	PA	19053	267-988-8978	988-8979	363
Better Home Products Ltd 534 Eccles Ave *Web:* www.betterhomeproducts.com	South San Francisco	CA	94080	650-827-9270		351
Better Homes & Gardens Real Estate Kansas City Homes 8300 College Blvd Ste 130 *Web:* kansascityhomes.com	Overland Park	KS	66210	913-981-6050		652
Better Homes & Gardens Wood Magazine 1716 Locust St *TF:* 800-374-9663 ■ *Web:* www.woodmagazine.com	Des Moines	IA	50309	800-374-9663		457-14
Better Investing PO Box 220 *TF:* 877-275-6242 ■ *Web:* www.betterinvesting.org	Royal Oak	MI	48068	248-583-6242	583-4880	49-2
Better Label & Products Inc 3333 Empire Blvd SW *TF:* 800-448-1813 ■ *Web:* betterlabel.com	Atlanta	GA	30354	404-763-8440		627
Better Living Now Inc 185 Oser Ave *Web:* www.betterlivingnow.com	Hauppauge	NY	11788	631-348-7704		352
Better Made Snack Foods Inc 10148 Gratiot Ave *TF:* 800-332-2394 ■ *Web:* bettermade.com	Detroit	MI	48213	313-925-4774	925-6028	296-35
Better Packages Inc 4 Hershey Dr *TF:* 800-237-9151 ■ *Web:* www.betterpackages.com	Ansonia	CT	06484	203-926-3700	926-3706	111
Better World Books Inc 55740 Currant Rd *Web:* www.betterworldbooks.com	Mishawaka	IN	46545	574-968-9701		95
Betteridge Jewelers Inc 117 Greenwich Ave *TF:* 888-556-2127 ■ *Web:* www.betteridge.com	Greenwich	CT	06830	203-869-0124		410
Bettinger Company Inc, The 1515 Market St Ste 935 *Web:* www.bettingerco.com	Philadelphia	PA	19102	215-564-0700		631
Bettinger Farms Inc 11602 Frankfort Rd **Fax Area Code:* 567 ■ *Web:* bettingersgreenhouse.com	Swanton	OH	43558	419-829-2771	202-2125*	369
Betts Industries Inc 1800 Pennsylvania Ave W *TF:* 800-482-2678 ■ *Web:* www.bettsind.com	Warren	PA	16365	814-723-1250	723-7030	595
Betts Patterson & Mines PS 1 Convention Pl 701 Park St Ste 1400 *Web:* www.bpmlaw.com	Seattle	WA	98101	206-292-9988	343-7053	445
Betts Tackle Ltd 1701 W Academy St *Web:* www.bettstackle.net	Fuquay-Varina	NC	27526	919-552-2226	552-3423	711
Betty Brinn Children's Museum 929 E Wisconsin Ave *Web:* www.bbcmkids.org	Milwaukee	WI	53202	414-390-5437	291-0906	521
Betty Dain Creations Inc 9701 NW 112 Ave Ste 10 *TF:* 800-327-5256 ■ *Web:* www.bettydain.com	Miami	FL	33178	305-769-3451		76
Betty Ford Alpine Gardens 183 Gore Creek Dr *Web:* bettyfordalpinegardens.org	Vail	CO	81657	970-476-0103		97
Betty Machine Company Inc 324 Freehill Rd *Web:* www.bettymachine.com	Hendersonville	TN	37075	615-826-6004	826-6262	621

Name / Address	City	State	ZIP	Phone	Fax	Class
Betz Industries Inc 2121 Bristol Ave NW *Web:* www.betzindustries.com	Grand Rapids	MI	49504	616-453-4429		492
Betz Transformers Inc 320 Industrial Ave *Web:* www.betzpower.com	Olathe	CO	81425	970-323-5177	323-5179	767
Beulah Heights University 892 Berne St SE *TF:* 888-777-2422 ■ *Web:* www.beulah.edu	Atlanta	GA	30316	404-627-2681	564-5290	161
Beusa Energy LLC 1780 Hughes Landing Blvd Ste 100 *Web:* www.beusaenergy.com	The Woodlands	TX	77380	281-296-1500		536
Beutler Air Conditioning & Plumbing 855 National Dr Ste 109 *Web:* www.ars.com	Sacramento	CA	95834	916-696-8721		189-10
Bevan & Associates, Lpa Inc 6555 Dean Memorial Pkwy *TF:* 877-873-2879 ■ *Web:* bevanlaw.com	Hudson	OH	44236	877-873-2879		41
Bevco Precision Manufacturing Co 21320 Doral Rd *TF:* 800-864-2991 ■ *Web:* www.bevco.com	Waukesha	WI	53186	262-798-9200		319-1
Bevco Sales International Inc 9354 194 St *TF:* 800-663-0090 ■ *Web:* bevco.net	Surrey	BC	V4N4E9	604-888-1455		358
Bevcomm W8108 165th Ave *Web:* www.bevcomm.net	Hager City	WI	54014	715-792-2103		224
Bevel Design Company Inc 7250 Meadow Ln *Web:* beveldesign.com	Baltimore	MD	21286	443-279-9900		358
Beverage Distributors Co 14200 E Moncrieff Pl **Fax Area Code:* 334 ■ *TF:* 888-262-9787 ■ *Web:* www.breakthrubev.com	Aurora	CO	80011	303-371-3421	270-5983*	81-3
Beverage Marketing Corp 850 Third Ave Ste 13C *TF:* 800-275-4630 ■ *Web:* www.beveragemarketing.com	New York	NY	10022	212-688-7640	826-1255	195
Beverage Works New York Inc, The 1800 Rt 34 N Ste 203 *Web:* thebeverageworks.com	Wall	NJ	07719	732-930-7000		102
Beverage World Package Store 6731 Peachtree Ind Blvd *Web:* www.bevworld.com	Doraville	GA	30360	770-441-0001		81-1
Beverage-Air Corp 3779 Champion Blvd *TF:* 800-845-9800 ■ *Web:* beverage-air.com	Winston-Salem	NC	27105	336-245-6400	245-6453	664
Beveridge & Diamond PC 1350 I St NW Ste 700 *Web:* www.bdlaw.com	Washington	DC	20005	202-789-6000		428
Beveridge Seay Inc 2000 P St NW Ste 700 *Web:* bevseay.com	Washington	DC	20036	202-822-3800		393
Beverly Animal Hospital Inc 303 Cabot St *Web:* beverlyanimalhospital.com	Beverly	MA	01915	978-927-5453		794
Beverly Beach State Park 198 NE 123rd St *Web:* oregonstateparks.reserveamerica.com	Newport	OR	97365	541-265-9278		565
Beverly Hills Cafe 7321 Miami Lakes Dr *Web:* www.thebeverlyhillscafe.com	Miami Lakes	FL	33014	305-558-8201		671
Beverly Hills Chamber of Commerce Santa Monica Blvd 2nd Fl *Web:* www.beverlyhillschamber.com	Beverly Hills	CA	90210	310-248-1000	248-1020	139
Beverly Hills Courier 9100 Wilshire Blvd Ste 360e *Web:* bhcourier.com	Beverly Hills	CA	90211	310-278-1322	271-5118	532-4
Beverly Hills Film Festival 9663 Santa Monica Blvd Ste 777 *Web:* beverlyhillsfilmfestival.com	Beverly Hills	CA	90210	310-779-1206		282
Beverly Hills Hotel 9641 Sunset Blvd *TF:* 800-650-1842 ■ *Web:* www.dorchestercollection.com	Beverly Hills	CA	90210	310-276-2251	887-2887	379
Beverly Hills Plaza Hotel 10300 Wilshire Blvd *TF:* 800-800-1234 ■ *Web:* www.beverlyhillsplazahotel.com	Los Angeles	CA	90024	310-275-5575		378
Beverly Hills Public Library 444 N Rexford Dr *TF:* 800-238-0172 ■ *Web:* www.beverlyhills.org	Beverly Hills	CA	90210	310-288-2220	278-3387	434-3
Beverly Hills Transfer & Storage Co 15500 S Main St *TF:* 800-999-7114 ■ *Web:* www.beverlyhillstransfer.com	Gardena	CA	90248	310-532-1121		519
Beverly Hills Unified School District 255 S Lasky Dr *Web:* www.bhusd.org	Beverly Hills	CA	90212	310-551-5100	277-6137	685
Beverly Hilton 9876 Wilshire Blvd *TF:* 800-605-8896 ■ *Web:* www.beverlyhilton.com	Beverly Hills	CA	90210	310-274-7777	285-1313	379
Beverly Hospital 309 W Beverly Blvd *TF:* 800-618-6664 ■ *Web:* www.beverly.org	Montebello	CA	90640	323-726-1222	725-4338	374-3
Beverly Hospital 85 Herrick St *Web:* www.beverlyhospital.org	Beverly	MA	01915	978-922-3000		374-3
Beverly Loan Co 9440 Santa Monica Blvd Ste 301 *TF:* 888-201-3303 ■ *Web:* beverlyloan.com	Beverly Hills	CA	90210	310-275-2555		217
Beverly National Cemetery 916 Bridgeboro Rd **Fax Area Code:* 609 ■ *Web:* www.cem.va.gov	Beverly	NJ	08010	215-504-5610	871-4691*	136
Beverly Pacific Company Inc 1266 SE Lake Rd *Web:* www.beverlypacific.com	Redmond	OR	97756	541-548-0810	548-0816	18
Beverly-Grant Inc 80 Peachtree Rd Ste 201 *Web:* www.beverly-grant.com	Asheville	NC	28803	828-274-7084		186
Bevilacqua Research Corp 4901 Corporate Dr NW *TF:* 877-404-9449 ■ *Web:* www.brc2.com	Huntsville	AL	35805	256-882-6229	882-6239	809
Bevill State Community College 2631 Temple Ave N *TF:* 800-648-3271 ■ *Web:* www.bscc.edu	Fayette	AL	35555	205-932-3221	932-3294	162

Name / Address	City	State	Zip	Phone	Fax	Class
Bevin Bros 10 Bevin Rd *Web:* bevinbells.com	East Hampton	CT	06424	860-267-4431		527
Bevmax Wines & Liquors 835 E Main St *Web:* www.bevmax.com	Stamford	CT	06902	203-357-9151		443
BevMo! 1401 Willow Pass Rd Ste 900 *TF:* 800-352-5267 ■ *Web:* www.bevmo.com	Concord	CA	94520	925-609-6000		443
Bewabic State Park 720 Idlewild Rd *Web:* www.michigan.org	Crystal Falls	MI	49920	906-875-3324		565
Bewley's Furniture Company Inc 900 W 70th St *Web:* bewleysfurniture.com	Shreveport	LA	71106	318-865-7151		321
Bexar Appraisal District 411 N Frio St PO Box 830248 *Web:* www.bcad.org	San Antonio	TX	78207	210-224-2432	242-2454	41
Bexar County 100 Dolorosa St *Web:* www.bexar.org	San Antonio	TX	78205	210-335-2011	335-2252	338
Bexel Corp 2701 N Ontario St *Web:* bexel.com	Burbank	CA	91504	818-565-4399		525
Bexil Corp 11 Hanover Sq *OTC:* BXLC ■ *Web:* www.bexil.com	New York	NY	10005	212-785-0900	363-1101	360-4
Bexion Pharmaceuticals LLC 632 Russell St *Web:* www.bexionpharma.com	Covington	KY	41011	859-446-7386		231
Bexley City School District 348 S Cassingham Rd *Web:* www.bexleyschools.org	Columbus	OH	43209	614-231-7611	231-8448	685
Bexley Hall Seminary 1407 E 60th St *TF:* 800-275-8235 ■ *Web:* www.bexleyseabury.edu	Chicago	IL	60637	773-380-6780	380-6788	167-3
Bexley Public Library 2411 E Main St *Web:* www.bexleylibrary.org	Bexley	OH	43209	614-231-9709		434-3
Bext Inc 1045 10th Ave *TF:* 888-239-8462 ■ *Web:* www.bext.com	San Diego	CA	92101	619-239-8462	239-8474	647
Beyer Barber Co 1136 Hamilton St Ste 103 *Web:* www.beyerbarber.com	Allentown	PA	18101	610-435-9577		77
Beyer Blinder Belle 120 Broadway 20th Fl *TF:* 800-777-7892 ■ *Web:* www.beyerblinderbelle.com	New York	NY	10271	212-777-7800	475-7424	261
Beyer Construction Ltd 3080 S Calhoun Rd *Web:* www.beyer.com	New Berlin	WI	53151	262-789-6040		186
Beyer Don (Rep D - VA) 1119 Longworth House Office Bldg *Web:* beyer.house.gov	Washington	DC	20515	202-225-4376	225-0017	342-2
Beyer Graphics Inc 30 Austin Blvd *Web:* www.beyergraphics.com	Commack	NY	11725	631-543-3900	543-3916	627
Beyers Costin Simon PC 200 Fourth St Ste 400 *Web:* beyerscostin.com	Santa Rosa	CA	95401	707-547-2000	526-2746	41
Beyond by Aerus 300 E Valley Dr *TF:* 800-243-9078 ■ *Web:* www.beyondbyaerus.com	Bristol	VA	24201	800-243-9078		37
Beyond Components 5 Carl Thompson Rd *TF:* 800-971-4242 ■ *Web:* www.beyondcomponents.com	Westford	MA	01886	800-971-4242	929-2302	246
Beyond Digital Imaging 36 Apple Creek Blvd *TF:* 888-689-1888 ■ *Web:* www.bdimaging.com	Markham	ON	L3R4Y4	905-415-1888	415-1583	701
Beyond Marketing 2001 Main St Ste 301 *Web:* www.beyondmk.com	Wheeling	WV	26003	304-232-4544		636
Beyond Pesticides 701 E St SE Ste 200 *TF:* 866-260-6653 ■ *Web:* beyondpesticides.org	Washington	DC	20003	202-543-5450	543-4791	48-13
Beyond Pix Studios 950 Battery St *Web:* beyondpix.com	San Francisco	CA	94111	415-434-1027	434-1032	512
Beyond Roi Inc 512 Brookfield Rd *Web:* www.getbeyondroi.com	Raleigh	NC	27615	919-615-4200		196
Beyond Spots & Dots 1034 Fifth Ave *Web:* www.beyondspotsanddots.com	Pittsburgh	PA	15219	412-281-6215		4
Beyond the Arc Inc 2600 Tenth St Ste 616 *TF:* 877-676-3743 ■ *Web:* beyondthearc.com	Berkeley	CA	94710	877-676-3743		463
Beyondcom Inc 1060 First Ave Ste 100 *Web:* www.beyond.com	King of Prussia	PA	19406	610-878-2800		260
Beyondroi LLC 4755 Technology Way *TF:* 800-498-4764 ■ *Web:* www.beyondroi.com	Boca Raton	FL	33431	800-498-4764		194
Bezark Lerner & De Virgilis PC 1600 Market St Ste 1600 *Web:* bldvlaw.com	Philadelphia	PA	19103	215-735-5599		41
BF Datacom Inc 391 Crest Ave *Web:* www.bfdatacom.com	Alamo	CA	94507	310-822-2439		189-4
BF Nashville 1101 Kermit Dr Ste 310 *Web:* web.nashvillechamber.com	Nashville	TN	37217	615-399-3200		194
BFA Systems Inc 3325 Triana Blvd PO Box 1527 *Web:* www.bfasystems.com	Huntsville	AL	35805	256-922-8791	922-8799	261
BFC 1051 N Kirk Rd *TF:* 800-774-6840 ■ *Web:* www.bfcprint.com	Batavia	IL	60510	630-879-9240		627
BFG 6 Anolyn Ct *Web:* bfgcom.com	Bluffton	SC	29910	843-837-9115		7
BFG Supply Company LLC 14500 Kinsman Rd PO Box 479 *TF:* 800-883-0234 ■ *Web:* www.bfgsupply.com	Burton	OH	44021	440-834-1883		276
BFGoodrich Tires Inc PO Box 19001 *TF:* 877-788-8899 ■ *Web:* www.bfgoodrichtires.com	Greenville	SC	29602	877-788-8899		755
BFI (Business Furniture Inc) 10 Lanidex Ctr W *Web:* www.bfionline.com	Parsippany	NJ	07054	973-503-0730	503-1565	320
BFMA (Business Forms Management Assn) 3800 Old Cheney Rd Ste 101-285 **Fax Area Code:* 877 ■ *TF:* 888-367-3078 ■ *Web:* www.bfma.org	Lincoln	NE	68516	888-367-3078	204-5979*	49-12
BFS (Bruceton Farm Service Inc) 116 Shannon Dr *Web:* www.bfscompanies.com	Morgantown	WV	26508	304-291-6980	291-6984	297-8
BFS Business Printing Inc 76 South St *Web:* www.bfsprinters.com	Boston	MA	02111	617-482-7770	423-2071	627
BFS Industries LLC 200 Industrial Dr *Web:* www.bfs-ind.com	Butner	NC	27509	919-575-6711	575-4275	357
BFS Publications PO Box 84231 *Web:* www.bfspublications.com	Los Angeles	CA	90073	310-820-5074		637-2
BG Financial Services Group 160 Main St *Web:* bankgloucester.com	Gloucester	MA	01930	978-675-9941		401
B-G Mechanical Service Inc 12 2nd Ave *TF:* 800-992-7386 ■ *Web:* www.engiemep.com	Chicopee	MA	01020	413-888-1500	594-2983	189-10
BG National Plumbing & Heating 200 Montrose Rd *Web:* www.bgnational.com	Westbury	NY	11590	516-334-8282		610
BG Products Inc 740 S Wichita St *TF:* 800-961-6228 ■ *Web:* www.bgprod.com	Wichita	KS	67213	800-961-6228		541
BGBC Partners LLP 300 N Meridian St Ste 1100 *Web:* www.bgbc.com	Indianapolis	IN	46204	317-633-4700	860-1065	734
BGC 199 Water St One Seaport Plz *Web:* www.bgcpartners.com	New York	NY	10038	212-829-4840		251
BGCC (Bowling Green Chamber of Commerce) 130 S Main St PO Box 31 *Web:* www.bgchamber.net	Bowling Green	OH	43402	419-353-7945	353-3693	139
BGCS (Bowling Green City Schools) 137 Clough St *Web:* www.bgcs.k12.oh.us	Bowling Green	OH	43402	419-352-3576	352-1701	685
BGD Companies Inc 5323 Lakeland Ave N *TF:* 800-699-3537 ■ *Web:* bgdcompanies.com	Minneapolis	MN	55429	612-338-6804	338-4942	319-1
BGE 10777 Westheimer Rd Ste 400 *Web:* www.bgeinc.com	Houston	TX	77042	281-558-8700	558-9701	261
BGF Industries Inc 3802 Robert Porcher Way *TF:* 800-476-4845 ■ *Web:* www.bgf.com	Greensboro	NC	27410	336-545-0011	545-0233	745-3
BGH (Buchanan General Hospital) 1535 Slate Creek Rd *Web:* www.bgh.org	Grundy	VA	24614	276-935-1000	935-1354	374-3
BGHN Associates PC 1845 51st St NE *Web:* www.bghnassociates.com	Cedar Rapids	IA	52402	319-366-8400	366-8399	2
BGIS North America 7400 Birchmount Rd *Web:* www.bgis.com	Markham	ON	L3R4E6	905-943-4100		271
BGK Finishing Systems 4131 Pheasant Ridge Dr NE *Web:* www.carlisleft.com	Minneapolis	MN	55449	763-784-0466	784-1362	470
BGL 1001 17th St Ste 1210 *Web:* bglfc.com	Denver	CO	80202	303-860-0990		271
BGL Asset Services LLC 2193 Northway Dr *Web:* www.bglas.com	Mount Pleasant	MI	48858	989-772-8888	772-7778	261
BGM Engineering Inc 14100 Simone Dr *Web:* bgmeng.com	Shelby Township	MI	48315	586-532-8670	532-8671	256
BGR Group 601 Thirteenth St NW *Web:* bgrdc.com	Washington	DC	20005	202-333-4936	833-9392	194
BGS (Beta Gamma Sigma Inc) 125 Weldon Pkwy *TF:* 800-337-4677 ■ *Web:* www.betagammasigma.org	Maryland Heights	MO	63043	314-432-5650	432-7083	48-16
BGV (Breckenridge Grand Vacations) 1627 Ski Hill Rd *TF:* 888-783-8883 ■ *Web:* www.breckenridgegrandvacations.com	Breckenridge	CO	80424	970-547-8788		378
BH (Bristol Hospital) 41 Brewster Rd *Web:* www.bristolhealth.org	Bristol	CT	06010	860-585-3000	585-3853	374-3
BH Aircraft Company Inc 2230 Smithtown Ave *Web:* www.bhaircraft.com	Ronkonkoma	NY	11779	631-981-4200	981-0221	21
BH Electronics Inc 12219 Wood Lake Dr *Web:* www.bhelectronics.com	Burnsville	MN	55337	952-894-9590	894-9380	253
BH Solutions Group Inc (BHSG) 1000 S Cleveland Massillon Rd Ste 2 *Web:* www.bhsolutionsgroup.com	Akron	OH	44333	330-666-6970	666-7380	260
B-H Transfer Co 750 Sparta Rd PO Box 151 *TF:* 800-342-6462 ■ *Web:* www.b-htransfer.com	Sandersville	GA	31082	478-552-5119		449
Bhaktivedanta Institute (BI) PO Box 3206 *Web:* www.bvinst.edu	Berkeley	CA	94703	510-841-7618		166
Bhan Thai 1324 Peabody Ave *Web:* www.bhanthairestaurant.com	Memphis	TN	38104	901-272-1538		671
Bhargava Wealth Management 609 White Pine Rd *Web:* bhargavacapital.com	Franklin Lakes	NJ	07417	201-897-0085		226
Bhb Advisors LLC 2283 Waters Dr *Web:* bhbadvisors.com	Mendota Heights	MN	55120	651-332-5101	332-5104	2
BHC (Behavioral Health Care Consultants Inc) 12 Windham Ln *Web:* www.bhcconsult.com	Beverly	MA	01915	978-921-5968	921-9085	196
BHE Consulting 276 Libbey Industrial Pkwy *Web:* www.bheconsulting.com	Weymouth	MA	02189	781-340-5871		194
BHE Environmental Inc 11733 Chesterdale Rd *Web:* www.powereng.com	Cincinnati	OH	45246	513-326-1500	326-1550	256
BHHC (Berkshire Hathaway Homestates Cos) PO Box 2048 *TF:* 888-495-8949 ■ *Web:* www.bhhc.com	Omaha	NE	68103	888-495-8949		391-4
BHI (Bender/Helper Impact) 11500 W Olympic Blvd Ste 399 *Web:* www.bhimpact.com	Los Angeles	CA	90064	310-473-4147		636
BHI (Better Hearing Institute) 1444 I St NW Ste 700 *TF:* 800-639-3884 ■ *Web:* www.betterhearing.org	Washington	DC	20005	202-449-1100		48-17
BHISD (Barbers Hill ISD) 9600 Eagle Dr PO Box 1108 *Web:* www.bhisd.net	Mont Belvieu	TX	77580	281-576-2221		685

	Phone	Fax	Class
BHK Securities LLC 2200 Lakeshore Dr Ste 250 Birmingham AL 35209 *TF:* 888-529-2610 ■ *Web:* www.bhkllc.com	205-322-2025		690
BHM (Buffalo History Museum) 1 Museum Ct. Buffalo NY 14216 *Web:* www.buffalohistory.org	716-873-9644		637-2
BHN (BioHumaNetics Inc) 1331 W Houston Ave Gilbert AZ 85233 **Fax Area Code:* 480 ■ *TF:* 800-961-1220 ■ *Web:* bhn.us	800-961-1220	961-1220*	85
BHN Corp 435 Madison Ave Memphis TN 38103 *Web:* www.bhncorp.com	901-521-9500	521-9507	189-9
BHP (Bright Hill Press) 94 Church St. Treadwell NY 13846 *Web:* www.brighthillpress.org	607-829-5055		637-2
BHP Billiton Petroleum (Americas) Inc 1500 Post Oak Blvd Houston TX 77056 *TF:* 800-359-1692 ■ *Web:* www.bhp.com	713-961-8500	961-8400	536
BHPS (Bristol Historical & Preservation Society) 48 Court St. Bristol RI 02809 *Web:* www.bhpsri.org	401-253-7223		49-19
BHPS (Bluffton Historical Preservation Society) 70 Boundary St. Bluffton SC 29910 *Web:* heywardhouse.org	843-757-6293		49-19
BHS (Behavioral Health Systems Inc) PO Box 830724 Birmingham AL 35209 *TF:* 800-245-1150 ■ *Web:* www.behavioralhealthsystems.com	205-879-1150	879-1178	374-5
BHS (Brunswick Historical Society) PO Box 1776 Cropseyville NY 12052 *Web:* www.bhs-ny.org	518-279-4024		48-6
BHS (Birmingham Historical Society) 1 Sloss Quarters Birmingham AL 35222 *Web:* www.bhistorical.org	205-251-1880	251-3260	48-13
BHSG (BH Solutions Group Inc) 1000 S Cleveland Massillon Rd Ste 2. Akron OH 44333 *Web:* www.bhsolutionsgroup.com	330-666-6970	666-7380	260
BHTC (Bloomingdale Home Telephone Co) 38 S Main St. Bloomingdale IN 47832 *Web:* bdalehtc.wixsite.com	765-498-2000	498-8000	224
BHW Sheet Metal Co 113 Johnson St PO Box 995 Jonesboro GA 30236 *Web:* bhwsheetmetal.com	770-471-9303		697
BI (Bhaktivedanta Institute) PO Box 3206 Berkeley CA 94703 *Web:* www.bvinst.edu	510-841-7618		166
BI Inc 6400 Lookout Rd. Boulder CO 80301 *TF:* 800-241-2911 ■ *Web:* bi.com	303-218-1000	218-1250	692
BI Nutraceuticals 2384 E Pacifica Pl. Rancho Dominguez CA 90220 *Web:* www.botanicals.com	310-669-2100	637-3644	479
BI Rosenhaus & Sons Inc 568 Columbus Ave Between 87 & 88 St New York NY 10023 *Web:* www.birosenhaus.com	212-873-1421		290
BIA (Bureau of Indian Affairs) 1849 C St NW MS 4004 MIB Washington DC 20240 *Web:* www.bia.gov	202-208-7163	208-5320	340-13
BIA (Brick Industry Assn) 12007 Sunrise Valley Dr Ste 430 Reston VA 20191 *TF:* 866-644-1293 ■ *Web:* www.gobrick.com	703-620-0010	620-3928	49-18
BIA (Bureau of Indian Affairs Regional Offices) *Alaska Region* 3601 C St Ste 1100 Anchorage AK 99503 *Web:* www.bia.gov	907-271-4085	271-1349	340-13
Bia Digital Partners Lp 15120 Enterprise Ct Chantilly VA 20151 *Web:* www.biadigitalpartners.com	703-227-9600		690
Biaggi's Ristorante Italiano 1705 Clearwater Ave. Bloomington IL 61704 *Web:* www.biaggis.com	309-664-2148	664-2149	670
Biagio 155 King St E. Toronto ON M5C1G9 *Web:* www.biagioristorante.com	416-366-4040		671
Bialik Hebrew Day School 2760 Bathurst St. Toronto ON M6B3A1 *Web:* bialik.ca	416-783-3346		685
Biamp Systems Inc 9300 SW Gemini Dr Beaverton OR 97008 **Fax Area Code:* 503 ■ *TF:* 800-826-1457 ■ *Web:* biamp.com	800-826-1457	626-0281*	52
Bianchi Honda 8430 Peach St. Erie PA 16509 *TF:* 866-979-8132 ■ *Web:* www.bianchihonda.com	814-864-5809	866-2921	516
Bianchi Kasavan & Pope LLP 243 Sixth St Ste 220. Hollister CA 95023 *Web:* www.bkpcpa.com	831-638-2111		2
Bianchi PR Inc 888 W Big Beaver Rd Ste 777. Troy MI 48084 *Web:* www.bianchipr.com	248-269-1122		636
Biar Inc 2506 S Philippe Ave Gonzales LA 70737 *Web:* www.biar.us	225-647-4300		358
BI-AX International Inc 596 Cedar Ave. Wingham ON N0G2W0 *Web:* www.biaxinc.com	519-357-1818		600
Biax-Fiberfilm Corp N1001 Tower View Dr. Greenville WI 54942 *Web:* www.biax-fiberfilm.com	920-757-9000		454
Biazzo Dairy Products Inc 1145 Edgewater Ave Ridgefield NJ 07657 *Web:* www.biazzo.com	201-941-6800		296-5
Biba Restauran 2801 Capitol Ave Sacramento CA 95816 *Web:* www.biba-restaurant.com	916-455-2422	455-0542	671
Bibb County 835 Walnut St Centreville AL 35042 *Web:* www.bibbal.com	205-926-3114		338
Bibb County Correctional Facility 565 Bibb Ln Brent AL 35034 *Web:* doc.alabama.gov	205-926-5252		213
Bibbero Systems Inc 1300 N McDowell Blvd. Petaluma CA 94954 **Fax Area Code:* 707 ■ *TF:* 800-242-2376 ■ *Web:* www.bibbero.com	800-242-2376	778-0824*	627
Bible Broadcasting Network Inc 11530 Carmel Commons Blvd PO Box 7300 Charlotte NC 28226 *TF:* 800-888-7077 ■ *Web:* www.bbnradio.org	704-523-5555		643
Bible League 3801 Eagle Nest Dr Crete IL 60417 *TF:* 866-825-4636 ■ *Web:* www.bibleleague.org	866-825-4636		48-20
Bible Truth Publishers 59 Industrial Rd Addison IL 60101 *Web:* bibletruthpublishers.com	630-543-1441	543-1476	637-2

	Phone	Fax	Class
Bible Way Fellowship Baptist Church 10120 Hartsook St Houston TX 77034 *Web:* bibleway1.org	713-943-2215		48-20
BibleWorks LLC 3800 Colley Ave Ste 6158 Norfolk VA 23508 *TF:* 888-747-8200 ■ *Web:* www.bibleworks.com	757-627-7100	337-2986	178-1
Bibli O'Phile Publishing Co 25199 Carlsbad Ave Davis CA 95616 *TF:* 800-255-1660 ■ *Web:* www.ggweb.com	800-255-1660		637-2
Biblical Archaeology Review 4710 41st St NW Washington DC 20016 *TF:* 800-221-4644 ■ *Web:* www.biblicalarchaeology.org	202-364-3300	364-2636	457-18
Biblical Counseling Foundation (BCF) 42550 Aegean St Indio CA 92203 *TF:* 877-933-9333 ■ *Web:* www.bcfministries.org	760-347-4608	775-5751	48-20
Biblical Research Institute (BRI) 12501 Old Columbia Pke Silver Spring MD 20904 *Web:* www.adventistbiblicalresearch.org	301-680-6790	680-6788	637-2
Bibliotheque de l'Institut Nazareth et Louis-Braille 1111 Saint Charles Ouest Longueuil QC J4K5G4 *TF:* 800-361-7063 ■ *Web:* www.inlb.qc.ca	450-463-1710	463-0243	434-3
Bibliotheques Publiques de L'Estrie Inc 4155 Rue Brodeur. Sherbrooke QC J1L1K4 *Web:* www.reseaubiblioduquebec.qc.ca	819-565-9744	565-9157	436
Biblos Foundation 196 Spring Oaks Dr Ballwin MO 63011 *TF:* 888-524-2567 ■ *Web:* www.biblosfoundation.org	636-220-4380		637-2
Biby Publishing LLC 18331 Turnberry Dr Round Hill VA 20141 *Web:* aglmediagroup.com	540-338-4363		637-9
BIC Corp 1 BIC Way Ste 1. Shelton CT 06484 *Web:* www.bicworld.com	203-783-2000		571
Bical Chevrolet of Valley Stream 709 W Merrick Rd. Valley Stream NY 11580 *TF:* 866-468-1413 ■ *Web:* www.bicalchevy.com	516-204-4119		57
Bice Ristorante 5601 Universal Blvd Orlando FL 32819 *Web:* www.bice-orlando.com	407-503-1415		670
Bicentennial Capitol Mall State Park 600 James Robertson Pkwy Nashville TN 37243 *Web:* www.state.tn.us	615-741-5280		565
Bicentennial Publishing Corp 333 W 38th St. New York NY 10018 *Web:* www.dziennik.com	212-594-2266		532-2
Bichler Oliver Longo & Fox Pll 541 S Orlando Ave Ste 310. Maitland FL 32751 *Web:* bichlerlaw.com	407-599-3777		41
Bicitis Group Inc 426 Herrick Dr. Dover NJ 07801 *Web:* www.bicitisgroup.com	631-751-3300		180
Bick Intl PO Box 854 Van Nuys CA 91408 *TF:* 866-226-0507 ■ *Web:* bickinternational.com	818-997-6496	988-4337	393
Bickel's Snack Foods PO Box 2427 York PA 17405 *TF:* 800-233-1933 ■ *Web:* www.bickelssnacks.com	800-233-1933		296-35
Bickford's Grille 37 Oak St Ext. Brockton MA 02301 **Fax Area Code:* 508 ■ *TF:* 800-969-5653 ■ *Web:* www.bickfords.com	800-969-5653	583-2120*	670
BICO Drilling Tools Inc 1604 Greens Rd Houston TX 77032 *Web:* www.bicodrillingtools.com	281-590-6966		540
Bicoastal Media Licenses IV L L C 1 Blackfield Dr Ste 333 Tiburon CA 94920 *Web:* www.bicoastalmedia.com	415-789-5035	789-5036	644
BiCoastal Media LLC 140 N Main St Lakeport CA 95453 **Fax Area Code:* 830 ■ *Web:* bicoastalmedia.com	707-263-6113	769-2721*	643
Bicon LLC 501 Arborway Boston MA 02130 *TF:* 800-882-4266 ■ *Web:* www.bicon.com	617-524-4443		228
Bi-Con Services Inc 10901 Clay Pike Rd Derwent OH 43733 *Web:* www.bi-conservices.com	740-685-2542		189-3
Bi-County Scale & Equipment Co 75 Kean St West Babylon NY 11704 *Web:* www.bicountyscale.com	631-643-2300		296-26
Bicycle Garage of Indy Inc 4340 E 82nd St. Indianapolis IN 46250 *TF:* 800-238-7389 ■ *Web:* bgifitness.com	317-842-4140		711
Bicycle Warehouse 4670 Santa Fe St San Diego CA 92109 *Web:* bicyclewarehouse.com	858-273-7300		711
Bicycling Magazine 400 S Tenth St. Emmaus PA 18098 *TF:* 800-666-2806 ■ *Web:* www.bicycling.com	800-666-2806		457-14
BID Designs 1525 Perimeter Pkwy NW Ste 125 Huntsville AL 35806 *Web:* bid-designs.com	256-489-2815		196
Bid4Assets Inc 8757 Georgia Ave Ste 520 Silver Spring MD 20910 *Web:* bid4assets.com	301-650-9193		180
Bidadoo Inc 1001 Third Ave S Kent WA 98032 *Web:* bidadoo.com	206-442-9000		366
Biddeford Blankets 300 Terr Dr Mundelein IL 60060 *TF:* 800-789-6441 ■ *Web:* biddefordblankets.com	847-566-7442	566-6431	746
Biddeford-Saco Chamber of Commerce & Industry 28 Water St Ste 101 Biddeford ME 04005 *Web:* biddefordsacochamber.org	207-282-1567		139
Biddeford-Saco-OOB Courier 295 Gannett Dr. South Portland ME 04106 *Web:* www.pressherald.com	207-282-4337		532-4
Biddison Hier Ltd 1515 15th St NW Ste 613. Washington DC 20005 *Web:* www.biddhier.com	202-882-8700	726-2251	194
Biddle & Company Inc 3650 Winding Way Ste 200 Newtown Square PA 19073 **Fax Area Code:* 484 ■ *Web:* biddleco.com	610-707-4000	427-8923*	390
Biddle Street Inn 58 W Biddle St Baltimore MD 21201 *Web:* biddlestreetinn.com	410-244-8413		671
Bidlake Agency Inc 2905 Millennium Ste 3. Billings MT 59102 *Web:* billingsinsurance.com	406-245-6224		390
BIDMC (Beth Israel Deaconess Medical Ctr) 330 Brookline Ave. Boston MA 02215 *TF:* 800-667-5356 ■ *Web:* www.bidmc.org	617-667-7000		374-3
BidMed LLC 321 N Clark St Ste 2550. Chicago IL 60654 *TF:* 866-811-1441 ■ *Web:* www.bidmed.com	773-840-8140		475

Phone | Fax | Class

Bidwell Industrial Group Inc
2055 S Main St. Middletown CT 06457 860-346-9283 347-8775 111
Web: www.bidwellinc.com

Bidwell Training Ctr
1815 Metropolitan St Pittsburgh PA 15233 412-402-9761 167-3
TF: 800-516-1800 ■ *Web:* bidwelltraining.edu

Bidwell-Sacramento River State Park
12105 River Rd. Chico CA 95973 530-342-5185 565
Web: www.parks.ca.gov

Bielecky Bros Inc 979 Third Ave New York NY 10022 212-753-2355 751-9369 319-2
Web: www.bieleckybrothers.com

Biennix Corp
2490 Black Rock Tpke Ste 354 Fairfield CT 06825 203-254-1727 254-8195 637-2
TF: 888-243-6649 ■ *Web:* www.legalcareer.com

Bienville House Hotel
320 Decatur St New Orleans LA 70130 504-529-2345 525-6079 379
TF: 800-535-7836 ■ *Web:* bienvillehouse.com

Bienville Parish 100 Courthouse Dr Arcadia LA 71001 318-263-2123 263-7426 338
Web: www.bienvilleparish.org

Bierlein Companies Inc
2000 Bay City Rd Midland MI 48642 989-496-0066 496-0144 189-16
TF: 800-336-6626 ■ *Web:* www.bierlein.com

Biernacki & Biernacki PA
2667 Enterprise Rd Orange City FL 32763 386-775-1970 41
Web: biernackilaw.com

Bierschbach Equipment & Supply Co
PO Box 1444 Sioux Falls SD 57101 605-332-4466 191-1
TF: 800-843-3707 ■ *Web:* www.bierschbach.com

Biery Cheese Co 6544 Paris Ave. Louisville OH 44641 330-875-3381 296-5
Web: bierycheese.com

Biesanz Stone Company Inc
4600 Goodview Rd Winona MN 55987 507-454-4336 454-8140 724
Web: www.biesanzstone.com

Biewer Lumber LLC 812 S Riverside Saint Clair MI 48079 800-482-5717 818
TF: 800-482-5717 ■ *Web:* www.biewerlumber.com

BIF New York Inc 465 Barell Ave. Carlstadt NJ 07072 201-933-7777 933-6261 320
Web: www.bifnewyork.com

Biff Duncan Assoc
3301 NJ-66 Ste 101 Neptune City NJ 07753 732-922-2227 876-0263 261
Web: www.biffduncan.com

Bifferato Gentilotti LLC
4250 Lancaster Pk Ste 130 Wilmington DE 19805 302-429-1900 41
Web: bglawde.com

Biflex Intimates Group LLC
180 Madison Ave 6th Fl New York NY 10016 212-532-8340 696-3485 155-18

BIFMA (Business & Institutional Furniture Manufacturers Assn)
678 Front Ave NW Ste 150 Grand Rapids MI 49504 616-285-3963 49-13
Web: www.bifma.org

BIG (Business Impact Group LLC)
2411 Galpin Ct Ste 120 Chanhassen MN 55317 952-278-7800 549
Web: impactgroup.us

Big 10 Tire Pros & Accessories
712 S State St. Jackson MS 39201 601-353-5461 948-6806 755
Web: big10tiresms.com

BIG 100 1801 Rockville Pk Rockville MD 20852 240-747-2700 645
TF: 800-493-1003 ■ *Web:* wbig.iheart.com

Big 3 Packaging LLC
4201 Torresdale Ave Philadelphia PA 19124 215-743-4201 601
TF: 866-697-2548 ■ *Web:* big3packaging.com

Big 3 Precision Products Inc
2923 S Wabash Ave Centralia IL 62801 618-533-3251 533-0167 567
Web: www.big3precision.com

Big 5 Sporting Goods Corp
2525 E El Segundo Blvd El Segundo CA 90245 310-536-0611 711
NASDAQ: BGFV ■ *TF:* 800-898-2994 ■ *Web:* www.big5sportinggoods.com

Big 6 Drilling Co 7500 San Felipe St. Houston TX 77063 713-783-2300 540
Web: www.big6drilling.com

Big 98.5 119 W Naylor Mill Rd. Salisbury MD 21801 410-202-8102 645
Web: bigclassicrock.com

Big Apple Car Inc 169 Bay 17th St Brooklyn NY 11214 718-331-9500 314
TF: 800-251-5001 ■ *Web:* www.bigapplecar.com

Big Apple Circus (BAC)
321 W 44th St Ste 400 New York NY 10036 212-257-2330 149
TF: 888-541-3750 ■ *Web:* bigapplecircus.com

Big Arm State Park
28031 Big Arm State Park Rd Big Arm MT 59910 406-849-5256 565
Web: stateparks.mt.gov

Big B Lumberteria
6600 Brentwood Blvd Brentwood CA 94513 925-634-2442 634-9839 364
Web: www.bigblumber.com

Big Bang ERP Inc
105 rue de Louvain W. Montreal QC H2N1A3 514-360-4408 196
TF: 844-361-4408 ■ *Web:* www.bigbangerp.com

Big Basin Redwoods State Park
21600 Big Basin Way Boulder Creek CA 95006 831-338-8860 565
Web: www.parks.ca.gov

Big Beam Emergency Systems Inc
290 E Prairie St. Crystal Lake IL 60014 815-459-6100 459-6126 439
Web: www.bigbeam.com

Big Bear Visitors Bureau
630 Bartlett Rd Big Bear Lake CA 92315 909-866-7000 866-8034 393
TF: 800-424-4232 ■ *Web:* www.bigbear.com

Big Ben British Pub & Restaurant
2000 S Blvd Charlotte NC 28203 704-817-9697 671
Web: www.bigbenpub.com

Big Bend Community College
7662 Chanute St. Moses Lake WA 98837 509-793-2222 762-6243 162
TF: 877-745-1212 ■ *Web:* www.bigbend.edu

Big Bend Electric Co-op
1373 N Hwy 261 Ritzville WA 99169 509-659-1700 659-1404 245
TF: 866-844-2363 ■ *Web:* www.bbec.org

Big Bend National Park
PO Box 129 Big Bend National Park TX 79834 432-477-2251 564
Web: www.nps.gov

Big Bend of the Colorado State Recreation Area
4220 S Needles Hwy Ste 3 Laughlin NV 89029 702-298-1859 565
Web: parks.nv.gov

Big Bend Ranch State Park
PO Box 2319 Presidio TX 79845 432-229-3416 565
Web: tpwd.texas.gov

Big Bend State Fish & Wildlife Area
300 E. Riverside Dr. Prophetstown IL 61277 217-782-5695 785-8565 565
Web: www2.illinois.gov

Big Bend Telephone Co 808 N 5th St Alpine TX 79830 844-592-4781 116
TF: 800-520-0092 ■ *Web:* www.bigbend.net

Big Bone Lick State Park 3380 Beaver Rd Union KY 41091 859-384-3522 565
Web: parks.ky.gov

Big Boy Restaurants International LLC
4199 Marcy St Warren MI 48091 586-759-6000 670
Web: www.bigboy.com

Big Boys Toys Automotive Specialty
1477 N Bennington Rd North Bennington VT 05257 802-447-1721 61
Web: www.bbtoys.com

Big Brand Tire & Service
805 Via Alondra Camarillo CA 93012 866-779-8473 755
TF: 866-779-8473 ■ *Web:* www.bigbrandtire.com

Big Brothers Big Sisters in San Juan County
308 N Locke Ave. Farmington NM 87401 505-326-1508 263-0939* 79
**Fax Area Code:* 707 ■ *Web:* www.bbbs-cnm.org

Big Buck Brewery & Steakhouse Inc
550 S Wisconsin Ave Gaylord MI 49735 989-732-5781 670
Web: www.bigbuckbrewery.com

Big Burrito Restaurant Group
5740 Baum Blvd Ste 2 Pittsburgh PA 15202 412-361-3272 361-4318 671
Web: www.bigburrito.com

Big Business Inc (BB)
420 NE Alaskan Way. Chehalis WA 98532 925-274-9568 984-9890* 178-1
**Fax Area Code:* 206 ■ *TF:* 877-970-0022 ■ *Web:* www.bigbusiness.com

Big C Lumber Inc
50860 Princess Way PO Box 176. Granger IN 46530 574-277-4550 191-3
TF: 888-297-0010 ■ *Web:* bigclumber.com

Big Cedar Lodge
190 Top of the Rock Rd. Ridgedale MO 65739 800-225-6343 379
TF: 800-225-6343 ■ *Web:* www.bigcedar.com

Big Ceramic Store LLC 543 Vista Blvd. Sparks NV 89434 888-513-5303 403-2241* 194
**Fax Area Code:* 775 ■ *TF:* 888-513-5303 ■ *Web:* bigceramicstore.com

Big Country Electric Co-op
1010 W S First St PO Box 518 Roby TX 79543 325-776-2244 245
TF: 888-662-2232 ■ *Web:* bigcountry.net

Big Creek Lumber Co 3564 Hwy 1 Davenport CA 95017 831-457-5015 423-2800 191-3
Web: bigcreeklumber.com

Big Creek Software LLC PO Box 50. Polk City IA 50226 515-779-0399 177
Web: www.bigcreek.com

Big Creek State Park
8794 NW 125th Ave Polk City IA 50226 515-984-6473 984-9320 565
Web: www.iowadnr.gov

Big Cypress National Preserve
33100 Tamiami Trl E. Ochopee FL 34141 239-695-2000 695-3901 564
Web: www.nps.gov

Big Cypress Tree State Park
295 Big Cypress Rd Greenfield TN 38230 731-235-2700 565
Web: www.state.tn.us

Big D Floor Covering Supplies
7261 Lampson Ave. Garden Grove CA 92841 714-894-2443 934-6078 290
Web: bigdsupply.com

Big D Ranch 7590 S 10 Mile Rd. Meridian ID 83642 208-888-1710 10-3
Web: www.bigdranch.com

Big Deahl Productions Inc
1450 N Dayton St Chicago IL 60642 424-330-1740 514
Web: www.bigdeahl.com

Big Dipper Ice Cream
631 S Higgins Rd Missoula MT 59801 406-543-5722 297-6
Web: www.bigdippericecream.com

Big Dog Logistics LLP
5177 Richmond Ave Ste 505 Houston TX 77056 713-996-8171 314

Big Dogs 519 Lincoln County Pkwy Lincolnton NC 28092 828-695-2800 155-3
TF: 800-244-3647 ■ *Web:* www.bigdogs.com

Big Dutchman Inc
3900 John F Donnelly Dr Holland MI 49424 616-392-5981 273
Web: www.bigdutchmanusa.com

Big E Drilling
4710 Bellaire Blvd Ste 350 Bellaire TX 77401 713-661-6890 540
Web: bigedrilling.com

Big Film Design 594 Broadway Ste 1001 New York NY 10012 212-627-3430 344
Web: www.bigfilmdesign.com

Big Fish Grill
20298 Coastal Hwy. Rehoboth Beach DE 19971 302-227-3474 671
Web: bigfishgrill.com

Big Five Tours & Expeditions
1551 SE Palm Ct Stuart FL 34994 800-244-3483 287-5990* 760
**Fax Area Code:* 772 ■ *TF:* 800-244-3483 ■ *Web:* www.bigfive.com

Big Flat Electric Co-opeartive Inc
333 S Seventh St Malta MT 59538 406-654-2040 245
TF: 800-242-2040 ■ *Web:* www.bigflatelectric.com

Big Foot Beach State Park
1452 Wells St Lake Geneva WI 53147 262-248-2528 565
Web: dnr.wi.gov

Big Foot Productions Inc
3709 36th Ave. Long Island City NY 11101 718-729-1900 514
Web: www.bigfootnyc.com

Big Freight Systems Inc
360 Hwy 12 N. Steinbach MB R5G1A6 204-326-3434 311
Web: www.bigfreight.com

Big Fresno Fair, The 1121 S Chance Ave. Fresno CA 93702 559-650-3247 650-3226 642
Web: www.fresnofair.com

Big Frey Promotional Products
420 Lake Cook Rd Ste 117 Deerfield IL 60015 800-888-1636 7
TF: 800-888-1636 ■ *Web:* www.bigfrey.com

Big Fun Development Corp
620 Lakeshore Dr Berkeley Lake GA 30096 770-300-0308 637-10
Web: gamesthatwork.com

Big G Express Inc 190 Hawkins Dr Shelbyville TN 37160 800-684-9140 780
TF: 800-955-9140 ■ *Web:* www.biggexpress.com

Big Girls Bras Etcetera Inc
PO Box 590250 Fort Lauderdale FL 33359 866-352-4494 157-6
TF: 866-352-4494 ■ *Web:* www.biggerbras.com

Name & Address	Phone	Fax	Class
Big Hill Pond State Park 1435 John Howell Rd .... Pocahontas TN 38061 *Web:* www.state.tn.us	731-645-7967		565
Big Hole National Battlefield 16425 Hwy 43 W .... Wisdom MT 59761 *Web:* www.nps.gov	406-689-3155	689-3151	564
Big Horn County 420 W C St.................... Basin WY 82410 *TF:* 800-500-2324 ■ *Web:* www.bighorncountywy.gov	307-568-2357	568-9375	338
Big Horn County 121 W Third St................ Hardin MT 59034 *TF:* 800-666-6899 ■ *Web:* www.bighorncountymt.gov	406-665-9830	665-9764	338
Big Horn Rural Electric Co-op 208 S Fifth St PO Box 270 .... Basin WY 82410 *TF:* 800-564-2419 ■ *Web:* www.bighornrea.com	307-568-2419		245
Big Island Publishing 11935 27th Ave N.......................... Plymouth MN 55441 *Web:* bigipub.com	612-850-4300		178-1
Big John's Moving Inc 1602 1st Ave .... New York NY 10028 *Web:* www.bigjohnsmoving.com	212-734-3300		519
Big Kaiser Precision Tooling Inc 641 Fargo Ave....................... Elk Grove Village IL 60007 *TF:* 888-866-5776 ■ *Web:* www.bigkaiser.com	847-228-7660	228-0881	493
Big L Corp 620 S Main St PO Box 134........... Sheridan MI 48884 *Web:* big-l-lumber.com	989-291-3232	291-3421	364
Big Lagoon State Park 12301 Gulf Beach Hwy..................... Pensacola FL 32507 *Web:* www.floridastateparks.org	850-492-1595		565
Big Lake Public Library 3140 S Big Lake Rd PO Box 520829 .... Big Lake AK 99652 **Fax Area Code:* 323 ■ *Web:* www.matsugov.us	907-861-7635	934-9076*	434-3
Big Lake State Park 204 Lake Shore Dr............ Craig MO 64437 *Web:* mostateparks.com	660-442-3770		565
Big League Dreams USA LLC 16333 Fairfield Ranch Rd.................. Chino Hills CA 91709 *Web:* www.bigleaguedreams.com	909-287-6900	287-6969	717
Big Lots Inc (BLI) 300 Phillipi Rd .... Columbus OH 43228 *NYSE: BIG* ■ *TF:* 877-998-1697 ■ *Web:* www.biglots.com	614-278-6800	278-8322	791
Big M Supermarkets 7252 State Fair Blvd........................ Syracuse NY 13209 *Web:* www.bigmsupermarkets.com	315-638-0291		345
Big Meadows 1000 Longmoor Ave .... Savanna IL 61074 *Web:* www.bigmeadows.biz	815-273-2238	273-7294	371
Big Moe Spring & Alignment 7190 Delta Cir .... Austell GA 30168 *Web:* www.bigmoega.com	770-948-7443	944-7046	62-7
Big Mountain Imaging 4725 Copper Sage St .... Las Vegas NV 89115 *TF:* 877-229-4030 ■ *Web:* www.bigmountain.com	877-229-4030		317
Big Muddy River Correctional Ctr 251 N Hwy 37.................................. Ina IL 62846 *Web:* www2.illinois.gov	618-437-5300	437-5627	213
Big Night Entertainment Group 186 Tremont St 2nd Fl .... Boston MA 02116 **Fax Area Code:* 857 ■ *Web:* bneg.com	617-338-4343	753-4709*	720
Big O Tires LLC 4280 Professional Center Dr Ste 400......................... Palm Beach Gardens FL 33410 *TF:* 866-834-2652 ■ *Web:* www.bigotires.com	866-834-2652		755
Big Oak Tree State Park 13640 S Hwy 102........................ East Prairie MO 63845 *Web:* mostateparks.com	573-649-3149		565
Big Pocono State Park c/o Tobyhanna State Pk Complex .... Tobyhanna PA 18466 *Web:* www.dcnr.pa.gov	570-894-8336		565
Big R 200 N Ernest Grove Pky .... Watseka IL 60970 *TF:* 844-270-2447 ■ *Web:* www.bigr.com	815-432-3440		45
Big Rapids Products 1313 Maple St .... Big Rapids MI 49307 *Web:* www.brproducts.com	231-796-3593	796-9066	247
Big Red Dog Inc 2021 E Fifth St Ste 200.......... Austin TX 78702 *Web:* bigreddog.com	512-669-5560		261
Big Red F Restaurant Group 5440 Conestoga Ct.......................... Boulder CO 80301 *Web:* www.bigredf.com	303-448-9182		670
Big Red Liquors Inc 1110 N College Ave .... Bloomington IN 47404 *Web:* bigredliquors.com	812-332-0653		443
Big Ridge State Park 1015 Big Ridge Rd...................... Maynardville TN 37807 *TF:* 800-471-5305 ■ *Web:* tnstateparks.com	865-992-5523		565
Big River Oil Company Inc 1920 Orchard Ave.......................... Hannibal MO 63401 *TF:* 800-533-0226 ■ *Web:* www.bigriveroil.com	573-221-0226		579
Big River Resources West Burlington LLC 15210 103rd St...................... West Burlington IA 52655 *Web:* www.bigriverresources.com	319-753-1100	753-1103	10-5
Big River Telephone Company LLC 24 S Minnesota St .... Cape Girardeau MO 63702 *TF:* 855-244-7483 ■ *Web:* bigrivercom.com	573-651-3373		224
Big Rock Sports LLC 173 Hankison Dr........... Newport NC 28570 *TF:* 800-334-2661 ■ *Web:* www.bigrocksports.com	252-808-3500	726-8352	710
Big Run State Park 10368 Savage River Rd...................... Swanton MD 21561 *Web:* dnr.maryland.gov	301-895-5453		565
Big Sandy Community & Technical College 1 Bert T Combs Dr .... Prestonsburg KY 41653 *TF:* 888-641-4132 ■ *Web:* bigsandy.kctcs.edu	606-886-3863		162
Big Sandy Rural Electric Cooperative Corp 504 11th St............................. Paintsville KY 41240 *TF:* 888-789-7322 ■ *Web:* www.bigsandyrecc.com	606-789-4095	789-5454	245
Big Saver Foods Inc 4260 Charter St............. Vernon CA 90058 *Web:* www.bigsaverfoods.com	323-582-7222		345
Big Shoals State Park 11330 SE County Rd 135 .... White Springs FL 32096 *TF:* 877-635-3655 ■ *Web:* www.floridastateparks.org	386-397-2733		565
Big Sioux Recreation Area 410 Park Ave.............................. Brandon SD 57005 *Web:* gfp.sd.gov	605-582-7243		565
Big Sky Construction Company Inc 507 Exposition Ave........................... Dallas TX 75226 *Web:* www.bigskyconstruction.com	972-226-4704		187

Name & Address	Phone	Fax	Class
Big Sky Engineering Inc 429 Venture Ct.......... Verona WI 53593 *Web:* www.bigskyeng.com	608-848-9898	848-9899	256
Big Sky Insulations Inc 15 Arden Dr........... Belgrade MT 59714 *TF:* 800-766-3626 ■ *Web:* www.bigskyrcontrol.com	406-388-4146	388-7223	601
Big Sky Managed Care LLC 915 First Ave S Ste 110 .... Great Falls MT 59401 *Web:* bigskymanagedcare.com	406-315-1989		237
Big Sky Publishing LLC 2820 W College St .... Bozeman MT 59718 *Web:* www.bozemandailychronicle.com	406-587-4491	587-7995	637-2
Big Sky Resort 50 Big Sky Resort Rd .... Big Sky MT 59716 *TF:* 800-548-4486 ■ *Web:* bigskyresort.com	406-995-5000	995-5001	669
Big Sky Travel Source Inc 2601 NW Expy Ste 105W .... Oklahoma City OK 73112 *TF:* 800-840-8220 ■ *Web:* www.bigskytours.com	405-840-8220	840-8233	771
Big South Fork National River & Recreation Area 4564 Leatherwood Rd......................... Oneida TN 37841 *Web:* www.nps.gov	423-569-9778	569-5505	564
Big Spring 215 W Third St PO Box 3359 .... Big Spring TX 79720 *TF:* 866-222-7100 ■ *Web:* bigspringtx.com	432-264-6032	264-6047	206
Big Spring Cafe 3507 Governors Dr .... Huntsville AL 35806 *Web:* www.bigspringcafe.com	256-539-9994		671
Big Spring Independent School District 708 E 11th Pl .... Big Spring TX 79720 *Web:* www.bsisd.esc18.net	432-264-3600	264-3646	685
Big Spring School District 45 Mount Rock Rd .... Newville PA 17241 *Web:* www.bigspringsd.org	717-776-2000	776-4428	360-2
Big Spring State Hospital 1901 N Hwy 87............................ Big Spring TX 79720 *Web:* www.dshs.texas.gov	432-267-8216	268-7263	374-5
Big Spring State Park RR 1 PO Box 486 .... Blain PA 17006 *Web:* m.dcnr.state.pa.us	717-536-3191		565
Big Spring State Park 1 Scenic Dr............ Big Spring TX 79720 *Web:* tpwd.texas.gov	432-263-4931		565
Big Stone County Courthouse 20 2nd St SE............................. Ortonville MN 56278 *Web:* www.bigstonecounty.org	320-487-1200		338
Big Stone Lake State Park 35889 Meadowbrook State Park Rd .... Ortonville MN 56278 *TF:* 888-646-6367 ■ *Web:* www.dnr.state.mn.us	320-839-3663	839-3676	565
Big Ten Conference 5440 Park Pl .... Rosemont IL 60018 *Web:* www.bigten.org	847-696-1010		206
Big Texan Steak Ranch 7701 I-40 E .... Amarillo TX 79118 *Web:* www.bigtexan.com	806-372-6000		671
Big Thicket National Preserve 6044 FM 420 .... Kountze TX 77625 *Web:* www.nps.gov	409-951-6700	951-6714	564
Big Timberworks Inc 1 Rabel Ln .... Gallatin Gateway MT 59730 *TF:* 800-763-4639 ■ *Web:* www.bigtimberworks.com	406-763-4639		286
Big Tool Store LLC 4640 E 63rd St S .... Derby KS 67037 *Web:* bigtoolstore.com	316-788-6500		351
Big W Industries Inc 200 S 5th St .... Kansas City KS 66101 *Web:* www.big-w.com	913-321-2112	321-2113	493
Big W Sales 1040 W Charter Way .... Stockton CA 95206 *Web:* www.bigwsales.com	209-464-9493		274
Big West Oil LLC 333 W Center St .... North Salt Lake UT 84054 *Web:* www.bigwestoil.com	801-296-7700		580
Big Y Foods Inc 2145 Roosevelt Ave .... Springfield MA 01102 *TF:* 800-828-2688 ■ *Web:* www.bigy.com	413-784-0600		345
Biga on the Banks 203 S St Mary's St .... San Antonio TX 78205 *Web:* biga.com	210-225-0722		671
Bigbee Steel Buildings Inc 2705 Avalon Ave....................... Muscle Shoals AL 35661 *Web:* www.bigbee.com	256-383-7322		105
Bigbend Hospice 1723 Mahan Center Blvd .... Tallahassee FL 32308 *TF:* 800-772-5862 ■ *Web:* www.bigbendhospice.org	850-878-5310		371
BigBiz Internet Services 2464 El Camino Real PMB 536 .... Santa Clara CA 95051 **Fax Area Code:* 408 ■ *TF:* 888-244-2498 ■ *Web:* www.bigbiz.com	888-244-2498	241-4615*	225
BigByte Corp 47400 Seabridge Dr.............. Fremont CA 94538 *TF:* 800-536-6425 ■ *Web:* www.bigbytecorp.com	510-249-1100		175
BigCountry 107.3 3811 Rogers Ave Ste D...................... Fort Smith AR 72903 *Web:* www.bigcountry1073.com	479-452-0681	452-0873	645-59
Big-D Construction Corp 404 West 400 South .... Salt Lake City UT 84101 *Web:* www.big-d.com	801-415-6000	415-6900	188-7
Bigelow & Co 500 N Commercial St Ste 403 .... Manchester NH 03101 *Web:* bigelowcpa.com	603-627-7659		2
Bigelow Hollow State Park & Nipmuck State Forest c/o Shenipsit State Forest 166 Chestnut Hill Rd .... Stafford Springs CT 06076 *Web:* portal.ct.gov	860-684-3430		565
Bigelow Management Inc 4640 S Eastern Ave......................... Las Vegas NV 89123 *Web:* budgetsuites.com	702-837-2000		379
Bigelow Tea 201 Black Rock Tpke .... Fairfield CT 06825 *TF:* 888-244-3569 ■ *Web:* www.bigelowtea.com	888-244-3569		296-40
Bigeye Direct Inc 13860 Redskin Dr .... Herndon VA 20171 *TF:* 866-654-2797 ■ *Web:* www.bigeyedirect.com	703-955-3017		195
BigFly Aviation Technology LLC 13940 Cedar Rd Ste 227.................... Cleveland OH 44118 *Web:* www.bigflyaviation.com	323-875-2273		21
Bigge Crane & Rigging Co 10700 Bigge Ave......................... San Leandro CA 94577 *TF:* 888-337-2444 ■ *Web:* www.bigge.com	510-277-4747	639-4053	189-1
Biggers Chevrolet 1385 E Chicago St .... Elgin IL 60120 *TF:* 866-431-1555 ■ *Web:* www.biggerschevy.com	847-742-9000	742-0061	57
Biggins Lacy Shapiro & Company LLC 47 Hulfish St Ste 400 .... Princeton NJ 08542 *TF:* 888-825-0892 ■ *Web:* www.blsstrategies.com	609-924-9775		194

Name / Address	City	State	ZIP	Phone	Fax	Class
Biggs Andy (Rep R - AZ) 1318 Longworth House Office Bldg *Web:* www.biggs.house.gov	Washington	DC	20515	202-225-2635		342-2
Biggs Cardosa Associates Inc 865 The Alameda *Web:* www.biggscardosa.com	San Jose	CA	95126	408-296-5515		261
Biggs Plumbing Co 1615 Dungan Ln *Web:* biggsplumbing.com	Austin	TX	78754	512-837-5955		189-10
Biggs, Hausserman, Thompson Dickinson Pc 356 E Main St *Web:* bhtdcpa.com	Saranac	MI	48881	616-642-9467		2
BiggsKofford & Co 630 Southpointe Ct Ste 200 *Web:* www.biggskofford.com	Colorado Springs	CO	80906	719-579-9090		2
Bigham Brothers Inc 705 E Slaton Rd *Web:* bighamag.com	Lubbock	TX	79452	806-745-0384		273
Bighorn Airways Inc 912 W Brundage Ln *Web:* www.bighornairways.com	Sheridan	WY	82801	307-672-3421		13
Bighorn Canyon National Recreation Area 5 Ave B PO Box 7458 *Web:* www.nps.gov	Fort Smith	MT	59035	406-666-2412	666-2415	564
Bighorn Resort 1801 Majestic Ln *TF:* 877-995-8999 ■ *Web:* thebighornresort.com	Billings	MT	59102	406-839-9300	839-9301	378
Biglari Holdings Inc 175 E Houston St Ste 1300 *NYSE: BH* ■ *Web:* www.biglariholdings.com	San Antonio	TX	78205	210-344-3400		360-3
BigLever Software Inc 10500 Laurel Hill Cove *Web:* www.biglever.com	Austin	TX	78730	512-426-2227		177
BIGMPG Design/Marketing 811 E Vienna Ave *TF:* 866-332-3919 ■ *Web:* www.bigmpg.com	Milwaukee	WI	53212	866-332-3919		5
Bigrentz Inc 1063 Mcgaw Ave Ste 200 *TF:* 855-999-5438 ■ *Web:* www.bigrentz.com	Irvine	CA	92614	888-325-5172		23
Bihler of America Inc 85 Industrial Rd *Web:* www.bihler.com	Phillipsburg	NJ	08865	908-213-9001		190
Bihrle Applied Research Inc 81 Research Dr *Web:* www.bihrle.com	Hampton	VA	23666	757-766-2416	766-9227	256
Bijan Boutique 420 N Rodeo Dr *Web:* www.bijan.com	Beverly Hills	CA	90210	310-273-6544	273-6535	574
Bijou Grille, The 643 Main St *Web:* www.bijougrille.com	Buffalo	NY	14203	716-847-1512	852-3041	671
Bike Friday Travel Systems 3364 W 11th Ave *TF:* 800-777-0258 ■ *Web:* www.bikefriday.com	Eugene	OR	97402	541-687-0487		775
Bike Gallery Portland Inc 5329 NE Sandy Blvd *Web:* www.bikegallery.com	Portland	OR	97213	503-281-9800		711
Bike USA Inc 2811 Brodhead Rd *TF:* 800-225-2453 ■ *Web:* www.bikeusainc.com	Bethlehem	PA	18020	800-225-2453		711
Bilbrey Insurance Services Inc 5701 Greendale Rd *TF:* 800-383-0116 ■ *Web:* www.icapiowa.com	Johnston	IA	50131	800-383-0116		390
Bilco Tool Corp 30076 Dequindre Rd *Web:* www.bilcotool.com	Warren	MI	48092	586-574-9300	574-9340	757
Bilco Tools Inc 107 Clendenning Road Houma Air Base *TF:* 800-222-1873 ■ *Web:* www.bilcotools.com	Houma	LA	70363	985-851-2240	580-0277	537
Bild Industries Inc 800 S Clearwater Loop *Web:* www.bildindustries.com	Post Falls	ID	83854	208-773-0630	773-0902	351
Bildner Center for Western Hemisphere Studies The Graduate Ctr CUNY 365 5th Ave Ste 5209 *Web:* www.gc.cuny.edu	New York	NY	10016	212-817-2096		637-2
Bilenky Cycle Works 5319 N 2nd St *Web:* www.bilenky.com	Philadelphia	PA	19120	215-329-4744		711
Bilicki Law Firm Pc, The 1285 N Main St *Web:* www.bilickilaw.com	Jamestown	NY	14701	716-664-5600		428
Bilingual Books Inc 1719 W Nickerson St *TF:* 800-488-5068 ■ *Web:* www.bbks.com	Seattle	WA	98119	206-284-4211		637-2
Bilingual Education Institute 6060 Richmond Ave Ste 180 *Web:* www.bei.edu	Houston	TX	77057	713-789-4555		764
Bilirakis Gus M (Rep R - FL) 2227 Rayburn House Office Bldg *Web:* bilirakis.house.gov	Washington	DC	20515	202-225-5755	225-4085	342-2
Bil-Jax Inc 125 Taylor Pkwy *TF:* 800-537-0540 ■ *Web:* www.biljax.com	Archbold	OH	43502	419-445-8915	445-0367	491
Bilkays Express Co 2400 Bedle Pl	Linden	NJ	07036	908-289-2400	289-6364	780
Bill & Hillary Clinton National Airport 1 Airport Dr *Web:* www.clintonairport.com	Little Rock	AR	72202	501-375-1509		27
Bill & Melinda Gates Foundation PO Box 23350 *TF:* 800-728-3843 ■ *Web:* www.gatesfoundation.org	Seattle	WA	98102	206-709-3100	709-3180	305
Bill & Ralphs Inc 118 B & R Dr *TF:* 800-406-3045 ■ *Web:* www.billandralphs.com	Sarepta	LA	71071	800-406-3045	604-0010	297-8
Bill Abbott Inc 500 W Ctr *Web:* billabbottinc.com	Monticello	IL	61856	217-762-2109		57
Bill Allen's Pocono Institute of Taxidermy 1100 Foster Ave *TF:* 888-442-4551 ■ *Web:* www.poconoinstitute.com	White Haven	PA	18661	570-443-9166		167-3
Bill Baggs Cape Florida State Park 1200 S Crandon Blvd *Web:* www.floridastateparks.org	Key Biscayne	FL	33149	305-361-5811		565
Bill Black Chevrolet Cadillac Inc 601 E Bessemer Ave *TF:* 877-352-6596 ■ *Web:* www.billblackauto.com	Greensboro	NC	27405	336-944-6555		57
Bill Collins 4220 Bardstown Rd *Web:* www.billcollinsford.net	Louisville	KY	40218	502-459-9550		57
Bill Currie Ford Inc 5815 N Dale Mabry Hwy *Web:* www.billcurrieford.com	Tampa	FL	33614	813-872-5555		57
Bill Dudley & Associates Real Estate Inc 102 E Page St *TF:* 800-848-7355 ■ *Web:* billdudleyandassociates.com	Luray	VA	22835	540-743-4663	743-1220	652
Bill Dunbar & Associates LLC 2601 Fortune Cir E Ste 301A *Web:* billdunbar.com	Indianapolis	IN	46241	317-247-8014		463
Bill Edwards Publishing 17329 Emerald Chase Dr *Web:* www.billedwards.com	Tampa	FL	33647	813-985-2689		637-10
Bill Gigler Insurance Agency Inc 526 N Washington St *Web:* billgigler.com	Naperville	IL	60563	630-355-4250		390
Bill Good Marketing Inc 6891 S 700 W Ste 100 *TF:* 800-678-1480 ■ *Web:* www.billgoodmarketing.com	Midvale	UT	84047	801-572-1480		195
Bill Graham Civic Auditorium 99 Grove St *Web:* www.sanfranciscoauditorium.com	San Francisco	CA	94102	415-624-8900		572
Bill Hwang Chinese Restaurant 879 Canton Rd *Web:* billhwangs.wixsite.com	Akron	OH	44312	330-784-7167		671
Bill Lee's Bamboo Chopsticks 1203 18th St *Web:* www.billlees.com	Bakersfield	CA	93301	661-324-9441	324-7811	671
Bill Marder 7106 SW 115 Loop *Web:* www.billmarder.com	Ocala	FL	34476	352-237-9650		637-2
Bill Miller 430 S Santa Rosa Ave *Web:* www.billmillerbbq.com	San Antonio	TX	78207	210-225-4461	302-1533	670
Bill Penney Toyota 4808 University Dr NW *Web:* www.billpenneytoyota.com	Huntsville	AL	35816	256-837-1111		57
Bill Pollard Jr CPA 79 E Eleventh St *Web:* www.billpollardcpa.com	Tracy	CA	95376	209-832-5110		2
Bill Ray Nissan 2724 N US Hwy 17-92 **Fax Area Code: 407* ■ *TF:* 866-200-5086 ■ *Web:* www.billraynissan.com	Longwood	FL	32750	866-200-5086	834-3177*	57
Bill Smith Auto Parts 400 Ash St Ste 100 *TF:* 800-252-3005 ■ *Web:* www.billsmithauto.com	Danville	IL	61832	800-252-3005		54
Bill Spoon's Barbecue 5524 S Blvd *Web:* www.spoonsbarbecue.com	Charlotte	NC	28217	704-525-8865		671
Bill Stasek Chevrolet Inc 700 W Dundee Rd *Web:* www.stasekchevrolet.com	Wheeling	IL	60090	847-537-7000		57
Bill T. Jones/Arnie Zane Dance Co 219 W 19th St *Web:* newyorklivearts.org	New York	NY	10011	212-691-6500	633-1974	573-1
Bill's Battery Co 5221 Crookshank Rd *Web:* www.billsbattery.com	Cincinnati	OH	45238	513-922-0100		74
Bill's Distributing Ltd 5900 Packer Dr NE *Web:* www.billsdist.com	Menomonie	WI	54751	715-235-5820	235-4150	297-8
Billco Manufacturing Inc 100 Halstead Blvd *Web:* www.billco-mfg.com	Zelienople	PA	16063	724-452-7390	452-0217	386
Billcom Inc 1810 Embarcadero Rd *TF:* 877-345-2455 ■ *Web:* www.bill.com	Palo Alto	CA	94303	650-621-7700		177
Billerica Public Library 15 Concord Rd *Web:* billericalibrary.org	Billerica	MA	01821	978-671-0948		434-3
BillGO 3003 E Harmony Rd 5th Fl *Web:* www.billgo.com	Fort Collins	CO	80528	970-829-0809		39
Billiard Congress of America 12303 Airport Way Ste 140 *Web:* www.bca-pool.com	Broomfield	CO	80021	303-243-5070		48-22
BILLIARD FACTORY Inc 8440 N Sam Houston Pky W *TF:* 800-641-9367 ■ *Web:* www.billiardfactory.com	Houston	TX	77064	281-943-2300		362
Billings Area Chamber of Commerce 815 S 27th St *TF:* 855-328-9116 ■ *Web:* www.billingschamber.com	Billings	MT	59101	406-245-4111	245-7333	139
Billings C'mon Inn Hotel 2020 Overland Ave *TF:* 800-655-1170 ■ *Web:* www.cmoninn.com	Billings	MT	59102	406-655-1100		379
Billings City Hall 210 N 27th St *Web:* www.ci.billings.mt.us	Billings	MT	59101	406-657-8210	657-8390	337
Billings Clinic 2800 Tenth Ave N *TF:* 800-332-7156 ■ *Web:* www.billingsclinic.com	Billings	MT	59101	406-238-2501		374-3
Billings Construction Supply (BCS) 5514 King Ave E *Web:* www.billingsconstructionsupply.com	Billings	MT	59108	406-248-8355	248-6470	523
Billings County 495 Fourth St PO Box 168 *Web:* www.billingscountynd.gov	Medora	ND	58645	701-623-4377	623-4761	338
Billings Gazette 401 N 28th St *TF:* 800-543-2505 ■ *Web:* www.billingsgazette.com	Billings	MT	59101	406-657-1580	657-1208	532-2
Billings Livestock Commission Co 2443 N Frontage Rd *Web:* www.billingslivestock.com	Billings	MT	59101	406-245-4151		446
Billings Morgan Boatwright LLC 280 W Canton Ave Ste 210 *Web:* billingslawfirm.com	Winter Park	FL	32789	407-679-9900		41
Billings Nissan 2100 King Ave W *TF:* 855-227-7058 ■ *Web:* www.billingsnissan.com	Billings	MT	59102	406-655-1111		57
Billings Studio Theatre (BST) 1500 Rimrock Rd *Web:* www.billingsstudiotheatre.com	Billings	MT	59102	406-248-1141		572
Billings Symphony 2721 Second Ave N *Web:* billingssymphony.org	Billings	MT	59101	406-252-3610		573-3
Billings Times 2919 Montana Ave *Web:* billingstimes.net	Billings	MT	59101	406-245-4994	245-5115	532-4
Billingsley House Museum 6900 Green Landing Rd *Web:* www.pgparks.com	Upper Marlboro	MD	20772	301-627-0730	627-7085	522
Billows Electric Supply 8716-A Frankford Ave *TF:* 866-398-1162 ■ *Web:* billows.com	Philadelphia	PA	19136	215-332-9700	338-8320	246

Name / Address	City	State	ZIP	Phone	Fax	Class
Billpro Management Systems Inc						
30575 Euclid Ave	Wickliffe	OH	44092	440-516-3776		177
TF: 800-736-0587 ■ *Web:* billpro.net						
Bills Engineering Inc						
1124 Ft St Mall Ste 200	Honolulu	HI	96813	808-792-2022	792-2033	261
Web: billsengineering.com						
Billups						
340 Oswego Pointe Dr Ste 101	Lake Oswego	OR	97034	503-454-0714	454-0716	6
Web: billups.com						
Billy Beson Co						
275 Market St Ste 530	Minneapolis	MN	55405	612-338-8187		393
TF: 866-999-9696 ■ *Web:* billybesonco.com						
Billy Bob's Texas 2520 Rodeo Plz	Fort Worth	TX	76164	817-624-7117		720
Web: billybobstexas.com						
Billy Graham Evangelistic Assn						
1 Billy Graham Pkwy	Charlotte	NC	28201	704-401-3200		48-20
TF: 877-247-2426 ■ *Web:* billygraham.org						
Billy Heroman's Flowerland						
10812 N Harrell 's Ferry Rd	Baton Rouge	LA	70816	225-272-7673		292
Web: www.billyheromans.com						
Billy's 1301 H St	Lincoln	NE	68508	402-474-0084		671
Web: www.billysrestaurant.com						
Bilotta Home Center Inc						
564 Mamaroneck Ave	Mamaroneck	NY	10543	914-381-7734		362
Web: bilotta.com						
Biloxi City Hall PO Box 429	Biloxi	MS	39533	228-435-6254	435-6129	337
Web: www.biloxi.ms.us						
Biloxi Little Theatre 220 Lee St	Biloxi	MS	39530	228-432-8543	392-7639	573-4
Web: www.4blt.org						
Biloxi National Cemetery						
400 Veterans Ave	Biloxi	MS	39531	228-388-6668	523-5784	136
Web: www.cem.va.gov						
Biltmore Construction Company Inc						
1055 Ponce De Leon Blvd	Belleair	FL	33756	727-585-2084	585-2088	685
Web: biltmoreconstruction.com						
Biltmore Greensboro Hotel						
111 W Washington St	Greensboro	NC	27401	336-272-3474		379
TF: 800-332-0303 ■ *Web:* thebiltmoregreensboro.com						
Biltmore Hotel & Conference Center of the Americas						
1200 Anastasia Ave	Coral Gables	FL	33134	855-311-6903		669
TF: 800-727-1926 ■ *Web:* www.biltmorehotel.com						
Biltmore Hotel & Suites						
2151 Laurelwood Rd	Santa Clara	CA	95054	408-988-8411		379
Web: www.hotelbiltmore.com						
Biltmore Hotel Oklahoma						
401 S Meridian Ave	Oklahoma City	OK	73108	405-947-7681		379
Web: www.biltmoreokc.com						
Bilt-Rite Furniture Inc						
5430 W Layton Ave	Greenfield	WI	53220	414-238-2020		321
Web: biltritefurniture.com						
Bimac 3034 Dryden Rd	Dayton	OH	45439	937-299-7333	299-7367	306
Web: bimac.com						
Bi-Mart Corp 220 S Seneca Rd	Eugene	OR	97402	541-344-0681		237
Web: www.bimart.com						
Bimbo Bakeries USA PO Box 976	Horsham	PA	19044	800-984-0989	320-9286*	296-1
**Fax Area Code:* 610 ■ *TF:* 800-984-0989 ■ *Web:* www.bimbobakeriesusa.com						
Bimeda-MTC Animal Health Inc						
420 Beaverdale Rd	Cambridge	ON	N3C2W4	519-654-8000	654-8001	584
TF: 888-524-6332 ■ *Web:* www.bimedamtc.com						
Bimini Twist						
8480 Okeechobee Blvd	West Palm Beach	FL	33411	561-784-2660		671
Web: www.mybiminitwist.com						
Bin 26 Enoteca 26 Charles St	Boston	MA	02114	617-723-5939		671
Web: bin26.com						
Binary Group Inc						
4250 N Fairfax Dr Ste 600	Arlington	VA	22203	571-480-4444	400-4445	387
TF: 855-424-0279 ■ *Web:* www.binarygroup.com						
Binary Pulse Inc 2040 Main St Ste 100	Irvine	CA	92614	949-336-7400		4
Web: www.binarypulse.com						
Bindagraphics Inc 2701 Wilmarco Ave	Baltimore	MD	21223	410-362-7200	362-7233	92
TF: 800-326-0300 ■ *Web:* www.bindagraphics.com						
Binder Metal Products Inc						
14909 S Broadway	Gardena	CA	90248	800-233-0896		295
TF: 800-233-0896 ■ *Web:* www.bindermetal.com						
Binder Park Zoo 7400 Div Dr	Battle Creek	MI	49014	269-979-1351	979-8834	823
Web: binderparkzoo.org						
Binders 284 S Sharon Amity Rd	Charlotte	NC	28211	704-442-2608		543
TF: 888-472-6866 ■ *Web:* bindersart.com						
Bindery Associates LLC						
2025 Horseshoe Rd	Lancaster	PA	17602	717-295-7443	291-1341	626
Web: www.binderyassociates.com						
Bind-Rite Services Inc						
16 Horizon Blvd	South Hackensack	NJ	07606	201-440-5585	440-7973	92
Web: www.bindrite.net						
Bindtech Inc 1232 Antioch Pk	Nashville	TN	37211	615-834-0404		92
Web: www.bindtechinc.com						
Binetti & Feerick CPAs PA						
381 Broadway Ste 45	Westwood	NJ	07675	201-664-9151		2
Bing Design						
126 E Ctr College St	Yellow Springs	OH	45387	937-767-2521		225
Web: bingdesign.com						
Bing's 1952 Kensington Ave	Buffalo	NY	14215	716-839-5788		671
Web: www.bingsrestaurant.net						
Bingham County 501 N Maple St	Blackfoot	ID	83221	208-782-3013		338
Web: www.co.bingham.id.us						
Bingham McHale LLP						
2700 Market Tower 10 W Market St	Indianapolis	IN	46204	317-635-8900	236-9907	41
Web: www.bgdlegal.com						
Bingham Osborn & Scarborough LLC						
345 California St Ste 1100	San Francisco	CA	94104	415-781-8535	291-9575	194
Web: www.bosinvest.com						
Binghamton City School District (BCSD)						
164 Hawley St	Binghamton	NY	13901	607-762-8100		685
Web: binghamtonschools.org						
Binghamton Knitting Company Inc						
11 Alice St	Binghamton	NY	13904	877-746-3368	722-4621*	155-16
**Fax Area Code:* 607 ■ *TF:* 877-746-3368 ■ *Web:* www.binghamtonknitting.com						
Binghamton University						
4400 Vestal Pkwy E	Binghamton	NY	13902	607-777-2000	777-4445	166
TF: 800-782-0289 ■ *Web:* www.binghamton.edu						
Bingolewis Inc						
5828 N Lombard St Ste A	Portland	OR	97203	503-223-2224		512
Web: www.bingolewis.com						
Binh-Le 5903 E 31st St	Tulsa	OK	74135	918-835-7722		671
Binion's Gambling Hall & Hotel						
128 E Fremont St	Las Vegas	NV	89101	702-382-1600		133
TF: 800-937-6537 ■ *Web:* www.binions.com						
Binkley & Barfield Inc						
1710 Seamist Dr	Houston	TX	77008	713-869-3433		256
Web: www.binkleybarfield.com						
Binovia Corp 3021 N 204th St	Elkhorn	NE	68022	402-331-0202	339-9010	180
TF: 877-331-0282 ■ *Web:* www.binovia.com						
Binsons Hospital Supplies Inc						
26834 Lawrence	Center Line	MI	48015	586-755-2300		475
Web: www.binsons.com						
Binstock, Rubin, Sbar, Garcia & Ellzey PA						
9100 S Dadeland Blvd Ste 1701	Miami	FL	33156	305-670-1984	670-2001	2
Web: binstockcpas.com						
Binswanger Glass						
965 Ridge Lake Blvd Ste 305	Memphis	TN	38120	800-365-9922		329
TF: 800-365-9922 ■ *Web:* www.binswangerglass.com						
Bio Agri Mix LP 11 Ellens St	Mitchell	ON	N0K1N0	519-348-9865		794
Web: www.bioagrimix.com						
Bio Compression Systems Inc						
120 W Commercial Ave	Moonachie	NJ	07074	201-939-0716		476
TF: 800-888-0908 ■ *Web:* www.biocompression.com						
Bio Dynamic Technologies						
1 Madison St Bldg A	East Rutherford	NJ	07073	800-879-2276		475
TF: 800-879-2276 ■ *Web:* www.biodynamictech.com						
Bio Home Health Services Inc						
11104 W Airport Blvd Ste 225	Stafford	TX	77477	281-980-2262		363
Web: biohhs.com						
Bio Medic Data Systems Inc 1 Silas Rd	Seaford	DE	19973	800-526-2637	628-4110*	84
**Fax Area Code:* 302 ■ *TF:* 800-526-2637 ■ *Web:* bmds.com						
Bio Medware						
3526 W Liberty Rd Ste 100	Ann Arbor	MI	48103	734-913-1098		196
Web: www.biomedware.com						
Bio/Data Corp PO Box 347	Horsham	PA	19044	215-441-4000	443-8820	419
TF: 800-257-3282 ■ *Web:* www.biodatacorp.com						
BioAdvance						
170 N Radnor Chester Rd Ste 350	Radnor	PA	19104	610-230-0544		792
Web: bioadvance.com						
Bioanalytical Systems Inc						
2701 Kent Ave	West Lafayette	IN	47906	765-463-4527	497-1102	419
NASDAQ: BASI ■ *TF:* 800-845-4246 ■ *Web:* www.basinc.com						
Bio-Botanica Inc 75 Commerce Dr	Hauppauge	NY	11788	631-231-5522	231-7332	479
TF: 800-645-5720 ■ *Web:* www.bio-botanica.com						
Biobridges LLC						
167 Worcester St Ste 211	Wellesley	MA	02481	781-416-0909		225
Web: biobridges.com						
BioCardia Inc 125 Shoreway Rd Ste B	San Carlos	CA	94070	650-226-0120		476
TF: 800-624-1179 ■ *Web:* www.biocardia.com						
Biocare Inc 122 Claire Dr	Piedmont	SC	29673	864-295-9000		83
Biocare Medical LLC 60 Berry Dr	Pacheco	CA	94553	925-603-8000	603-8080	582
TF: 800-799-9499 ■ *Web:* biocare.net						
Biocell Laboratories Inc						
2001 University Dr	Rancho Dominguez	CA	90220	310-537-3300	637-3927	231
TF: 800-222-8382 ■ *Web:* www.biocell.com						
BioCell Technology LLC						
20 Truman St Ste 105	Irvine	CA	92620	714-632-1231		345
Web: www.biocelltechnology.com						
Biocentric Inc 700 Collings Ave	Collingswood	NJ	08107	856-854-3600		403
Web: www.biocentricinc.com						
Biocept Inc						
5810 Nancy Ridge Dr Ste 150	San Diego	CA	92121	858-320-8200	320-8225	583
TF: 888-332-7729 ■ *Web:* biocept.com						
Bio-Chem Fluidics Inc 85 Fulton St	Boonton	NJ	07005	973-263-3001		201
TF: 800-541-8421 ■ *Web:* biochemfluidics.com						
Bioclimatic Inc 600 Delran Pky Ste D	Delran	NJ	08075	856-764-4300	764-4301	18
TF: 800-394-3458 ■ *Web:* www.bioclimatic.com						
Biocoat Inc 211 Witmer Rd	Horsham	PA	19044	215-734-0888		476
Web: biocoat.com						
Bio-Communications Press						
3100 N Hillside Ave	Wichita	KS	67219	316-682-3100		637-2
TF: 800-447-7276 ■ *Web:* www.riordanclinic.org						
Bio-Concepts Inc 2424 E University Dr	Phoenix	AZ	85034	602-267-7854	273-6931	477
Web: www.bio-con.com						
Biocontrol Systems Inc						
12822 SE 32nd St	Bellevue	WA	98005	425-603-1123	603-0070	668
Web: www.biocontrolsys.com						
BioCryst Pharmaceuticals Inc						
2190 Pkwy Lake Dr	Birmingham	AL	35244	205-444-4600	444-4640	85
NASDAQ: BCRX ■ *TF:* 800-361-0912 ■ *Web:* www.biocryst.com						
BioCure Inc 2975 Gateway Dr Ste 100	Norcross	GA	30071	678-966-3400	416-4331*	476
**Fax Area Code:* 770 ■ *Web:* www.biocure.com						
BioDelivery Sciences International Inc (BDSI)						
4131 Parklake Ave Ste 225	Raleigh	NC	27612	919-582-9050	582-9051	85
NASDAQ: BDSI ■ *TF:* 877-579-4578 ■ *Web:* bdsi.com						
Bio-Detek Inc						
525 Narragansett Park Dr	Pawtucket	RI	02861	401-729-1400		250
Web: www.zoll.com						
Biodex Medical Systems Inc						
20 Ramsay Rd	Shirley	NY	11967	631-924-9000	924-8355	476
TF: 800-224-6339 ■ *Web:* www.biodex.com						
Biodiversity Research Institute						
276 Canco Rd	Portland	ME	04103	207-839-7600		196
Web: www.briloon.org						
Biofeedback Press						
2166 Hayes St Ste 203	San Francisco	CA	94117	415-921-6500		637-2
Web: www.biofeedbacksf.com						
Biofilm Inc 3225 Executive Rdg	Vista	CA	92081	760-727-9030		231
Web: www.astroglide.com						
Biofit Engineered Products						
15500 Biofit Way	Bowling Green	OH	43402	419-823-1089	823-1342	319-1
TF: 800-597-0246 ■ *Web:* www.biofit.com						

	City	State	ZIP	Phone	Fax	Class
BioFlex Laser Therapy 411 Horner Ave *TF:* 888-557-4004 ■ *Web:* www.bioflexlaser.com	Etobicoke	ON	M8W4W3	416-251-1055		476
BioFlorida 6742 Forest Hill Blvd Ste 256 *Web:* www.bioflorida.com	West Palm Beach	FL	33413	561-653-3839		743
BioForce Nanosciences 1615 Golden Aspen Dr Ste 101 *Web:* bioforcenano.com	Ames	IA	50010	515-233-8333		250
Bioforest Technologies Inc 59 Industrial Park Crescent Unit 1 *TF:* 888-236-7378 ■ *Web:* www.bioforest.ca	Sault Sainte Marie	ON	P6B5P3	705-942-5824	942-8829	302
Biogen Inc 225 Binney St *NASDAQ: BIIB* ■ *Web:* www.biogen.com	Cambridge	MA	02142	781-464-2000		85
BioGenex 48810 Kato Rd Ste 200E *TF:* 800-421-4149 ■ *Web:* www.biogenex.com	San Ramon	CA	94538	510-824-1400		231
Biographical Publishing Co (BPC) 95 Sycamore Dr **Fax Area Code:* 253 ■ *Web:* biopub.us	Prospect	CT	06712	203-758-3661	793-2618*	637-2
BIOgroupUSA Inc 1059 Broadwy Ste F *Web:* biobagusa.com	Dunedin	FL	34698	727-789-1646		610
BioHorizons Inc 2300 Riverchase Ctr *TF:* 888-246-8338 ■ *Web:* www.biohorizons.com	Birmingham	AL	35244	205-967-7880	870-0304	477
BioHumaNetics Inc (BHN) 1331 W Houston Ave **Fax Area Code:* 480 ■ *TF:* 800-961-1220 ■ *Web:* bhn.us	Gilbert	AZ	85233	800-961-1220	961-1220*	85
BioIonix Inc 4603 Triangle St *Web:* www.bioionix.com	McFarland	WI	53558	608-838-0300		612
BIO-Key International Inc 3349 Hwy 138 Bldg A *Web:* www.bio-key.com	Wall	NJ	07719	732-359-1100		84
Biokinetics & Associates Ltd 2470 Don Reid Dr *Web:* www.biokinetics.com	Ottawa	ON	K1H1E1	613-736-0384		256
Biokyowa Inc 5469 Nash Rd *Web:* www.biokyowa.com	Cape Girardeau	MO	63702	573-335-4849		447
Biola University 13800 Biola Ave *TF:* 800-652-4652 ■ *Web:* www.biola.edu	La Mirada	CA	90639	562-903-6000	903-4709	166
Bio-Lab Inc 1725 N Brown Rd PO Box 30000 *Web:* www.biolabinc.com	Lawrenceville	GA	30043	678-502-4000		143
BioLase Inc 4 Cromwell *TF:* 888-424-6527 ■ *Web:* www.biolase.com	Irvine	CA	92618	888-424-6527		424
BioLegend Inc 11080 Roselle St *TF:* 877-246-5343 ■ *Web:* www.biolegend.com	San Diego	CA	92121	858-455-9588		668
BioLife Solutions Inc 3303 Monte Villa Pkwy Ste 310 *TF:* 866-424-6543 ■ *Web:* www.biolifesolutions.com	Bothell	WA	98021	425-402-1400	402-1433	85
Bioline USA Inc 305 Constitution Dr *Web:* www.bioline.com	Taunton	MA	02780	508-880-8990		194
Biolytic Lab Performance Inc 5680 Stewart Ave *Web:* biolytic.com	Fremont	CA	94538	510-795-1142		261
Biolytical Laboratories Inc 1108 - 13351 Commerce Pkwy *TF:* 866-674-6784 ■ *Web:* biolytical.com	Richmond	BC	V6V2X7	604-204-6784		668
BioMarin Pharmaceutical Inc 105 Digital Dr *NASDAQ: BMRN* ■ *Web:* www.biomarin.com	Novato	CA	94949	415-506-6700	382-7889	85
Biomarine Inc 456 Creamery Way *Web:* www.neutronicsinc.com	Exton	PA	19341	610-524-8800	524-8807	576
BioMarker Pharmaceuticals Inc 5941 Optical Ct *Web:* www.biomarkerinc.com	San Jose	CA	95138	408-257-2000	356-6661	668
BioMarker Strategies 15601 Crabbs Branch Wy *Web:* www.biomarkerstrategies.com	Rockville	MD	20855	410-522-1008	522-1009	418
BioMedical Life Systems Inc PO Box 1360 *TF:* 800-726-8367 ■ *Web:* www.bmls.com	Vista	CA	92085	760-727-5600	727-4220	475
Biomedical Publications (BP) PO Box 2876 *Web:* www.biomedicalpublications.com	Seal Beach	CA	90740	419-281-1802	281-6883	637-2
Biomere 57 Union St *Web:* biomere.com	Worcester	MA	01608	508-459-7544		10-3
Biomerica Inc 17571 Von Karman Ave *OTC: BMRA* ■ *TF:* 800-854-3002 ■ *Web:* biomerica.com	Irvine	CA	92614	949-645-2111		231
BioMerieux Inc 595 Anglum Rd *TF:* 800-634-7656 ■ *Web:* www.biomerieux.com	Hazelwood	MO	63042	314-731-8500		476
Biomerix Corp 22A Worlds Fair Dr **Fax Area Code:* 510 ■ *Web:* www.biomerix.com	Somerset	NJ	08873	732-356-5886	933-3451*	668
Biometrix Inc 2419 Ocean Ave *Web:* biometrixinc.com	San Francisco	CA	94127	415-333-0522	333-0532	418
Bio-Microbics Inc 8450 Cole Pkwy *Web:* www.biomicrobics.com	Shawnee	KS	66227	913-422-0707		427
Biomod Concepts Inc 1821B Lavoisier **Fax Area Code:* 450 ■ *Web:* biomod.com	Sainte-Julie	QC	J3E1Y6	514-905-5848	641-5491*	466
BioMotiv 20600 Chagrin Blvd Ste 210 *Web:* www.biomotiv.com	Cleveland	OH	44122	216-455-3200		238
Biomune Co 8906 Rosehill Rd *TF:* 800-999-0297 ■ *Web:* www.ceva.us	Lenexa	KS	66215	913-894-0230	894-0236	584
Biondo Investment Advisors LLC 540 Rts 6 & 209 *Web:* thebiondogroup.com	Milford	PA	18337	570-296-5525		194
Bionetics Corp, The 101 Production Dr Ste 100 *TF:* 800-868-0330 ■ *Web:* www.bionetics.com	Yorktown	VA	23693	757-873-0900		261
BioNJ 1255 Whitehorse-Mercerville Rd Bldg B-Ste 514 *Web:* bionj.org	Trenton	NJ	08619	609-890-3185	581-8244	463
Bionomic Industries Inc 777 Corporate Dr *TF:* 800-311-6767 ■ *Web:* www.bionomicind.com	Mahwah	NJ	07430	201-529-1094	529-0252	261
Bionostics Inc 7 Jackson Rd *TF:* 800-776-3856 ■ *Web:* www.bionostics.com	Devens	MA	01434	978-772-7070	772-7072	231
BioNumerik Pharmaceuticals Inc 8023 Vantage Dr Ste Lobby 1 *Web:* www.bionumerik.com	San Antonio	TX	78230	210-614-1701		85
Bioo Scientific Corp 3913 Todd Ln Ste 312 *Web:* www.biooscientific.com	Austin	TX	78744	512-707-8993		85
BIOPAC Systems Inc 42 Aero Camino *TF:* 877-524-6722 ■ *Web:* www.biopac.com	Goleta	CA	93117	805-685-0066		743
Biopass Medical Systems Inc 7401 Wiles Rd Ste 222 *Web:* www.biopass.com	Coral Springs	FL	33067	954-575-1588		476
Bio-Pharm Inc 187 S Tilley Rd *TF:* 800-443-8465 ■ *Web:* www.bphchem.com	Hatfield	AR	71945	870-389-6114	389-6604	145
Biophysical Society (BPS) 5515 Security Ln Ste 1110 **Fax Area Code:* 301 ■ *Web:* www.biophysics.org	Rockville	MD	20852	240-290-5600	634-7133*	49-19
BioPro Inc 2929 Lapeer Rd *TF:* 800-252-7707 ■ *Web:* bioproimplants.com	Port Huron	MI	48060	810-982-7777		477
BioProcess Algae LLC 1811 Aksarben Dr *Web:* www.bioprocessalgae.com	Omaha	NE	68106	402-916-9559	884-8776	580
BiOptix Diagnostics Inc 1775 38th St **Fax Area Code:* 913	Boulder	CO	80301	303-545-5550	491-7407*	419
Bioqual Corp 4 Research Ct *TF:* 800-208-3149 ■ *Web:* www.bioqual.com	Rockville	MD	20850	240-404-7654	404-7664	85
Bioquant Image Analysis Corp 5611 Ohio Ave *TF:* 800-221-0549 ■ *Web:* bioquant.com	Nashville	TN	37209	615-350-7866		514
BIOQUELL Inc 702 Electronic Dr Ste 200 *Web:* www.bioquell.com	Horsham	PA	19044	215-682-0225		743
Bio-Rad Laboratories 1000 Alfred Nobel Dr *NYSE: BIO* ■ *TF:* 800-424-6723 ■ *Web:* www.bio-rad.com	Hercules	CA	94547	510-724-7000	741-5824	231
Bio-Recovery Corp 1863 Pond Rd Ste 4 *TF:* 800-556-0621 ■ *Web:* biorecovery.com	Ronkonkoma	NY	11779	888-609-5735		83
Bio-Reference Laboratories Inc 481 Edward H Ross Dr **Fax Area Code:* 201 ■ *TF:* 800-229-5227 ■ *Web:* www.bioreference.com	Elmwood Park	NJ	07407	800-229-5227	791-1941*	416
BioReliance Corp 14920 Broschart Rd *TF:* 800-553-5372 ■ *Web:* www.bioreliance.com	Rockville	MD	20850	301-738-1000	610-2590	85
BioResource International Inc 4222 Emperor Blvd Ste 460 *Web:* briworldwide.com	Durham	NC	27703	919-993-3389		668
Bios Corp 309 E Dewey Ave *TF:* 888-920-3600 ■ *Web:* bioscorp.com	Sapulpa	OK	74066	888-920-3600		363
Biosafe Engineering 5750 W 80th St *TF:* 888-858-8099 ■ *Web:* biosafeeng.com	Indianapolis	IN	46278	317-858-8099	858-8202	111
Biosan Laboratories Inc 1950 Tobsal Ct *TF:* 800-253-6800 ■ *Web:* www.biosan.com	Warren	MI	48091	586-755-8970		743
BioSante Pharmaceuticals Inc 111 Barclay Blvd *NASDAQ: ANIP* ■ *Web:* www.biospace.com	Lincolnshire	IL	60069	847-478-0500		582
Bio-Scene Recovery 13191 Meadow St NE *TF:* 877-380-5500 ■ *Web:* bioscene.com	Alliance	OH	44601	330-823-5500		83
Bioscience Laboratories Inc 1765 S 19th Ave *Web:* www.biosciencelabs.com	Bozeman	MT	59718	406-587-5735	586-7930	743
Bioscreen Testing Services Inc 3904 Del Amo Blvd Ste 801 *Web:* bioscreen.com	Torrance	CA	90503	310-214-0043	370-3642	333
BioScrip 1600 Broadway Ste 700 *NASDAQ: BIOS* ■ *TF:* 877-409-2301 ■ *Web:* www.bioscrip.com	Denver	CO	80202	720-697-5200		586
Bioseal 167 W Orangethorpe Ave *TF:* 800-441-7325 ■ *Web:* www.biosealnet.com	Placentia	CA	92870	714-528-4695		476
Biosense Webster Inc 3333 S Diamond Canyon Rd *TF:* 800-729-9010 ■ *Web:* www.biosensewebster.com	Diamond Bar	CA	91765	909-839-8500	468-2905	476
Bio-Serv 3 Foster Ln Ste 201 *TF:* 800-996-9908 ■ *Web:* www.bio-serv.com	Flemington	NJ	08822	908-284-2155	284-4753	584
Biosonics Inc 4027 Leary Way NW *Web:* www.biosonicsinc.com	Seattle	WA	98107	206-782-2211		201
BiosPacific Inc 5980 Horton St Ste 225 *Web:* www.biospacific.com	Emeryville	CA	94608	510-652-6155	652-4531	231
Biospec Products Inc 280 N Virginia Ave *Web:* www.biospec.com	Bartlesville	OK	74003	918-336-3363		420
Biostat International Inc (BSI) 13014 N Dale Mabry Hwy Ste 745 *Web:* biostatinternational.com	Tampa	FL	33613	813-979-1619	979-1519	194
Biosynergy Inc 1940 E Devon Ave *TF:* 800-255-5274 ■ *Web:* www.biosynergyinc.com	Elk Grove Village	IL	60007	847-956-0471	956-6050	201
Biosynexus Inc 9610 Medical Center Dr Ste 100	Rockville	MD	20850	301-330-5800		231
Biotab Nutraceuticals Inc 301 N Lake Ave Ste 600	Pasadena	CA	91101	626-775-6334		345
Biotech Clinical Laboratories Inc 25775 Meadowbrook **Fax Area Code:* 517 ■ *TF:* 800-827-3797 ■ *Web:* biotechclinical.com	Novi	MI	48375	248-912-1700	913-3994*	743
BioTechLogic Inc 717 Indian Rd *Web:* www.biotechlogic.com	Glenview	IL	60025	847-730-3475		85
Biotechnology Industry Organization 1201 Maryland Ave SW Ste 900 *TF:* 866-356-5155 ■ *Web:* www.bio.org	Washington	DC	20024	202-962-9200	488-6301	49-19
BioTek Instruments Inc 100 Tigan St PO Box 998 *TF:* 888-451-5171 ■ *Web:* www.biotek.com	Winooski	VT	05404	802-655-4040	655-7941	419
BioTeknica Inc 2100 Ponce De Leon Blvd Ste 1070 *Web:* www.bioteknica.com	Coral Gables	FL	33134	305-445-2080	445-2515	466
Biothera Pharmaceuticals 3388 Mike Collins Dr Ste A *TF:* 877-699-5100 ■ *Web:* www.biothera.com	Eagan	MN	55121	651-675-0300		743
Biotheranostics Inc 9640 Towne Centre Dr Ste 200 *TF:* 877-886-6739 ■ *Web:* www.biotheranostics.com	San Diego	CA	92121	877-886-6739		743

Name	Address	City	State	ZIP	Phone	Fax	Class	Other
Bio-Tissue	7000 SW 97th Ave Ste 211	Miami	FL	33173	888-296-8858	412-4429*	545	*Fax Area Code: 305 ■ TF: 888-296-8858 ■ Web: www.biotissue.com
Biotools Inc	17546 Bee Line Hwy	Jupiter	FL	33458	561-625-0133	625-0717	583	Web: www.biotools.us
Bioturf Inc	4515 Daly Dr Ste N	Chantilly	VA	20151	703-961-9701		422	Web: bioturf-va.com
BioUrja Trading LLC	1080 Eldridge Pkwy Ste 1175	Houston	TX	77077	832-775-9000		580	Web: www.biourja.com
BioVascular Inc	12230 El Camino Real Ste 100	San Diego	CA	92130	858-455-5000		668	Web: www.biovascularinc.com
Bioventures Investors	70 Walnut St Ste 302	Wellesley	MA	02481	617-252-3443	621-7993	792	Web: www.bioventuresinvestors.com
Bioventus LLC	4721 Emperor Blvd Ste 100	Durham	NC	27703	919-474-6700		477	TF: 800-847-2381 ■ Web: www.bioventusglobal.com
Biovet Inc	4375 Ave Beaudry	Saint-Hyacinthe	QC	J2S8W2	450-771-7291	771-4158	584	TF: 888-824-6838 ■ Web: www.biovet-inc.com
BioVid Corp	10 Canal St Ste 136	Bristol	PA	19007	609-750-1400		195	Web: biovid.com
Biovision Technologies	64 E Uwchlan Ave Ste 273	Exton	PA	19341	610-524-9740		419	Web: www.biovis.com
BioWa Inc	212 Carnegie Ctr Ste 400	Princeton	NJ	08540	609-580-7340	228-5247	743	Web: www.kyowakirin.com
Bio-west Inc	1063 W 1400 N	Logan	UT	84321	435-752-4202		196	Web: www.bio-west.com
BioXcel	780 E Main St	Branford	CT	06405	203-433-4086		194	Web: bioxcel.com
BioZone Laboratories Inc	580 Garcia Ave	Pittsburg	CA	94565	925-473-1000	473-1001	418	Web: biozonelabs.com
BioZyme Inc	6010 Stockyards Expy	Saint Joseph	MO	64504	816-238-3326		447	TF: 800-821-3070 ■ Web: www.biozymeinc.com
BIPAC (Business-Industry Political Action Committee)	1707 L St NW Ste 350	Washington	DC	20036	202-833-1880	833-2338	615	Web: www.bipac.org
Bi-Petro Inc	3150 Executive Park Dr	Springfield	IL	62794	217-535-0181		581	Web: www.bipetro.com
Bi-Phase Technologies LLC	201 Mittel St	Wood Dale	IL	60191	630-350-9400	350-9900	247	Web: www.bi-phase.com
Birach Broadcasting Corp	21700 Northwestern Hwy Tower 14 Ste 1190	Southfield	MI	48075	248-557-3500	557-2950	647	Web: www.birach.com
Birbrower & Beldock PC	151 N Main St Ste 300	New City	NY	10956	845-267-4878		41	Web: bandbnylaw.com
Birch Aquarium at Scripps	2300 Expedition Way	La Jolla	CA	92037	858-534-3474	534-7114	40	Web: aquarium.ucsd.edu
Birch Bay State Park	5105 Helweg Rd	Blaine	WA	98230	360-371-2800		565	Web: parks.state.wa.us
Birch Brothers Southern Inc	9510 New Town Rd	Waxhaw	NC	28173	704-843-2111	843-3936	744	Web: www.birchbrothers.com
Birch Communications	2300 Main St Ste 340	Kansas City	MO	64108	816-300-1677	300-3350	736	TF: 866-424-5100 ■ Web: birch.com
Birch Hill Investment Advisors LLC	24 Federal St 10th Fl	Boston	MA	02110	617-502-8300		401	TF: 800-441-3453 ■ Web: www.bhboston.com
Birch Tree Promotions	5 Tyng St	Newburyport	MA	01950	978-270-3852		636	Web: www.birchtreepromotions.com
Birchard Public Library of Sandusky County	423 Croghan St	Fremont	OH	43420	419-334-7101	334-4788	434-3	Web: www.birchard.lib.oh.us
Birchbark Books	2115 W 21st St	Minneapolis	MN	55405	612-374-4023		637-2	Web: birchbarkbooks.com
Birchwood automative group	35D-3965 Portage Ave	Winnipeg	MB	R3K2H7	204-831-4214	831-4222	57	TF: 866-990-6237 ■ Web: www.birchwood.ca
Birchwood Foods	6009 Goshen Springs Rd	Norcross	GA	30071	770-448-9101		473	Web: www.bwfoods.com
Birchwood Laboratories Inc	7887 Fuller Rd Ste 100	Eden Prairie	MN	55344	952-937-7900	937-7979	145	TF: 800-328-6156 ■ Web: www.birchwoodcasey.com
Birchwood Manor	111 N Jefferson Rd	Whippany	NJ	07981	973-887-1414		671	Web: birchwoodmanor.com
Birchwood Plaza	1426 W Birchwood	Chicago	IL	60626	773-274-4405		672	
Bird Marella Boxer Wolpert Nessim Drooks & Lincenberg PC	1875 Century Pk E 23rd Fl	Los Angeles	CA	90067	310-201-2100		41	Web: www.birdmarella.com
Bird Precision	1 Spruce St PO Box 540569	Waltham	MA	02454	800-454-7369	894-6308*	620	*Fax Area Code: 781 ■ TF: 800-454-7369 ■ Web: birdprecision.com
Bird Studies Canada	115 Front St PO Box 160	Port Rowan	ON	N0E1M0	519-586-3531	586-3532	48-3	Web: www.bsc-eoc.org
Birdair Inc	65 Lawrence Bell Dr Ste 100	Amherst	NY	14221	716-633-9500	633-9850	189-12	TF: 800-622-2246 ■ Web: www.birdair.com
Birdcage Press LLC	2320 Bowdoin St	Palo Alto	CA	94306	650-462-6300	462-6305	637-9	Web: www.birdcagepress.com
Birdie Golf Balls Golf Equipment	208 Margate Ct	Margate	FL	33063	954-973-2741		711	TF: 800-333-7271 ■ Web: www.birdiegolfballstore.com
Birds & Blooms	5400 S 60th St	Greendale	WI	53129	414-423-0100		457-14	TF: 888-860-8040 ■ Web: www.birdsandblooms.com
Birdsall Tool & Gage Co	24735 Crestview Ct	Farmington Hills	MI	48335	248-474-5150		757	Web: www.birdsalltool.com
Birdsong Gregory LLC	715 N Church St Ste 101	Charlotte	NC	28202	704-332-2299		4	Web: www.birdsonggregory.com
Birdsong Peanuts	612 Madison Ave	Suffolk	VA	23434	757-539-3456		275	Web: www.birdsongpeanuts.com
BirdWatching Magazine	25 Braintree Hill Office Pk Ste 404	Braintree	MA	02184	877-252-8141		457-14	TF: 877-252-8141 ■ Web: birdwatchingdaily.com
Birk Manufacturing	14 Capitol Dr Colton Rd Industrial Park Exit 71 off I-95	East Lyme	CT	06333	860-739-4170		14	Web: www.birkmfg.com
Birken Manufacturing Co	3 Old Windsor Rd	Bloomfield	CT	06002	860-242-2211	242-2749	621	Web: www.birken.net
Birket Engineering Inc	162 W Plant St	Winter Garden	FL	34787	407-290-2000		261	Web: www.birketspecialtylighting.com
Birko Corp	9152 Yosemite St	Henderson	CO	80640	800-525-0476		146	TF: 800-525-0476 ■ Web: www.birkocorp.com
Birks	1240 du Sq-Phillips St	Montreal	QC	H3B3H4	800-758-2511		410	TF: 800-758-2511 ■ Web: www.maisonbirks.com
Birmingham Bible Institute	280 E Lincoln St	Birmingham	MI	48009	248-646-2000		167-3	Web: www.birminghambibleinstitute.org
Birmingham Board of Education	2015 Park Pl N	Birmingham	AL	35203	205-231-4600		685	TF: 800-628-6673 ■ Web: www.bhamcityschools.org
Birmingham Botanical Gardens	2612 Ln Park Rd	Birmingham	AL	35223	205-414-3900		97	Web: bbgardens.org
Birmingham Business Alliance	505 N 20th St Ste 200	Birmingham	AL	35203	205-324-2100	324-2560	139	Web: www.birminghambusinessalliance.com
Birmingham City Hall	710 N 20th St	Birmingham	AL	35203	205-254-2000	254-2926	337	Web: www.birminghamal.gov
Birmingham Civil Rights Institute	1720 University Blvd	Birmingham	AL	35203	205-328-9696	323-5219	520	TF: 866-328-9696 ■ Web: www.bcri.org
Birmingham Festival Theater	1901 1/2 11th Ave S	Birmingham	AL	35205	205-933-2383		573-4	Web: www.bftonline.org
Birmingham Historical Society (BHS)	1 Sloss Quarters	Birmingham	AL	35222	205-251-1880	251-3260	48-13	Web: www.bhistorical.org
Birmingham International Airport	5900 Messer Airport Hwy	Birmingham	AL	35212	205-595-0533	599-0538	27	Web: www.flybirmingham.com
Birmingham International Forest Products LLC	300 Riverhills Business Pk	Birmingham	AL	35242	205-972-1500	972-1461	191-3	TF: 800-767-2437 ■ Web: www.bifp.com
Birmingham Museum of Art	2000 Rev Abraham Woods Jr Blvd	Birmingham	AL	35203	205-254-2565	254-2714	520	Web: www.artsbma.org
Birmingham Public Library	2100 Pk Pl	Birmingham	AL	35203	205-226-3600		434-3	Web: www.bham.lib.al.us
Birmingham Race Course	1000 John Rogers Dr	Birmingham	AL	35210	205-838-7500	838-7407	133	TF: 800-998-8238 ■ Web: www.birminghamracecourse.com
Birmingham Rail & Locomotive Company Inc	PO Box 530157	Birmingham	AL	35253	205-424-7245	424-7436	770	TF: 800-241-2260 ■ Web: bhamrail.com
Birmingham Times	115 Third Ave W	Birmingham	AL	35204	205-251-5158	323-2294	532-4	Web: www.birminghamtimes.com
Birmingham VA Medical Ctr	700 S 19th St	Birmingham	AL	35233	205-933-8101		374-8	Web: www.birmingham.va.gov
Birmingham Vending Co	540 Second Ave N	Birmingham	AL	35204	205-324-7526	322-6639	55	TF: 800-288-7635 ■ Web: www.bhmvending.com
Birmingham Wholesale Furniture	2200 2nd Ave S	Birmingham	AL	35233	205-588-1362		321	Web: www.birminghamwholesale.com
Birmingham Zoo	2630 Cahaba Rd	Birmingham	AL	35223	205-879-0409	879-9426	823	Web: www.birminghamzoo.com
Birmingham-Bloomfield Chamber of Commerce	725 S Adams Rd Ste 130	Birmingham	MI	48009	248-644-1700	644-0286	139	Web: www.bbcc.com
Birmingham-Jefferson Convention Complex	2100 Richard Arrington Blvd N	Birmingham	AL	35203	205-458-8400		205	Web: www.bjcc.org
Birmingham-Southern College	900 Arkadelphia Rd	Birmingham	AL	35254	205-226-4600	226-3074	166	TF: 800-523-5793 ■ Web: www.bsc.edu
Birnbach Communications Inc	20 Devereux St Ste 3A	Marblehead	MA	01945	781-639-6701	639-6702	636	Web: www.birnbachcom.com
Birnbaum Interpreting Services	8730 Georgia Ave Ste 210	Silver Spring	MD	20910	301-587-8885		768	TF: 800-471-6441 ■ Web: bisworld.com
Birnie Bus Service Inc	248 Otis St	Rome	NY	13441	315-336-3950		109	TF: 800-734-3950 ■ Web: birniebus.com
BIRO Manufacturing Co	1114 W Main St	Marblehead	OH	43440	419-798-4451	798-9106	298	Web: www.birosaw.com
Biron Groupe Sante	4105-F Blvd Matte	Brossard	QC	J4Y2P4	514-866-6146		418	TF: 833-590-2715 ■ Web: www.biron.com
Birst Inc	45 Fremont St	San Francisco	CA	94105	415-766-4800	762-4115	178-1	TF: 866-940-1496 ■ Web: www.birst.com
Birtcher Anderson Realty Management	31910 Del Obispo St Ste 260	San Juan Capistrano	CA	92675	949-545-0500		652	Web: birtcheranderson.com
Birthday Direct	120 Commerce St	Muscle Shoals	AL	35661	256-381-0310		292	TF: 888-491-9185 ■ Web: www.birthdaydirect.com
Birthwise Midwifery School	24 S High St	Bridgton	ME	04009	207-647-5968	647-5919	685	Web: www.birthwisemidwifery.edu
BIS Computer Solutions Inc	2428 Foothill Blvd	La Crescenta	CA	91214	818-248-5023		177	Web: www.biscomputer.com

Name / Address	City	State	ZIP	Phone	Fax	Class
Biscayne National Park 9700 SW 328th St *Web:* www.nps.gov	Homestead	FL	33033	305-230-1144		564
Biscayne Nature Ctr 6767 Crandon Blvd *Web:* www.biscaynenaturecenter.org	Key Biscayne	FL	33149	305-361-6767	365-8434	50-5
Biscayne Rod Manufacturing Inc 425 E Ninth St *TF:* 866-969-0808 ■ *Web:* www.biscaynerod.com	Hialeah	FL	33010	305-884-0808		710
Bischoff Insurance Agency Inc 1300 Oakridge Dr Ste 100 *TF:* 888-229-5558 ■ *Web:* bradbischoff.com	Fort Collins	CO	80525	970-223-9400		390
Bisco Dental Products (Canada) Inc 2571 Smith St *TF:* 800-667-8811 ■ *Web:* www.biscocanada.com	Richmond	BC	V6X2J1	604-276-8662		475
Bisco Industries Inc 1500 N Lakeview Ave *TF:* 800-323-1232 ■ *Web:* www.biscoind.com	Anaheim	CA	92807	800-323-1232		246
Biscom Inc 321 Billerica Rd *TF:* 800-477-2472 ■ *Web:* www.biscom.com	Chelmsford	MA	01824	978-250-1800	250-4449	173-3
Biscotti's Restaurant 3556 St Johns Ave *Web:* www.biscottis.net	Jacksonville	FL	32205	904-387-2060	387-0051	671
Biscuitville Inc 1414 Yanceyville St *Web:* www.biscuitville.com	Greensboro	NC	27405	336-553-3700		670
Bisexual Resource Ctr (BRC) 29 Stanhope St *Web:* www.biresource.net	Boston	MA	02117	617-424-9595		637-10
BISG (Book Industry Study Group Inc) 232 Madison Ave Ste 1400 *Web:* bisg.org	New York	NY	10016	646-336-7141		49-16
Bishop & Associates Inc 1209 Fox Glen Dr *Web:* bishopinc.com	Saint Charles	IL	60174	630-443-2702		466
Bishop Distributing Co 5200 36th St SE *TF:* 800-748-0363 ■ *Web:* www.bishopdistributing.com	Grand Rapids	MI	49512	800-748-0363		361
Bishop Hearth & Home Inc 1948 Vanderhorn Dr *Web:* www.bishophome.com	Memphis	TN	38134	901-384-0070		362
Bishop International Airport G-3425 W Bristol Rd *Web:* www.bishopairport.org	Flint	MI	48507	810-235-6560	233-3065	27
Bishop Jr Sanford D (Rep D - GA) 2407 Rayburn House Office Bldg *Web:* bishop.house.gov	Washington	DC	20515	202-225-3631	225-2203	342-2
Bishop Kelly Foundation Inc 7009 W Franklin Rd *Web:* www.bk.org	Boise	ID	83709	208-375-6010		685
Bishop Loughlin Memorial High School 357 Clermont Ave *Web:* www.loughlin.org	Brooklyn	NY	11238	718-857-2700		685
Bishop Machine Works Inc 1780 Iris Dr SW *Web:* bishopmachineworks.com	Conyers	GA	30094	770-483-7673		697
Bishop Miege High School 5041 Reinhardt Dr *Web:* www.bishopmiege.com	Roeland Park	KS	66205	913-262-2700		685
Bishop Museum 1525 Bernice St *Web:* www.bishopmuseum.org	Honolulu	HI	96817	808-847-3511		520
Bishop O'Dowd High School 9500 Stearns Ave *Web:* www.bishopodowd.org	Oakland	CA	94605	510-577-9100	638-3259	685
Bishop Paiute Gaming Corp 2742 N Sierra Hwy *Web:* www.bishoppaiutetribe.com	Bishop	CA	93514	760-872-6005		452
Bishop Partners Ltd 28 W 44th St Ste 1120 *Web:* www.bishoppartners.com	New York	NY	10036	212-986-3419	575-1050	266
Bishop Rob (Rep R - UT) 123 Cannon House Office Bldg *Web:* robbishop.house.gov	Washington	DC	20515	202-225-0453	225-5857	342-2
Bishop Spencer Place Redevelopment Corp 4301 Madison Ave *Web:* bishopspencerplace.org	Kansas City	MO	64111	816-931-4277		672
Bishop State Community College 351 N Broad St *TF:* 800-523-7000 ■ *Web:* bishop.edu	Mobile	AL	36603	251-405-7000		162
Bishop Strachan School 298 Lonsdale Rd *Web:* www.bss.on.ca	Toronto	ON	M4V1X2	416-483-4325	481-5632	622
Bishop's 2183 W Fourth Ave *Web:* bishopsonline.com	Vancouver	BC	V6K1N7	604-738-2025		671
Bishop's College School 80 Chemin Moulton Hill *TF:* 877-570-7542 ■ *Web:* www.bishopscollegeschool.com	Sherbrooke	QC	J1M1Z8	819-566-0227		622
Bishop's Lodge 1297 Bishop *Web:* www.bishopslodge.com	Santa Fe	NM	87506	505-983-6377		707
Bishop's Ranch 5297 Westside Rd *Web:* www.bishopsranch.org	Healdsburg	CA	95448	707-433-2440	433-3431	673
Bishop's University 2600 College St *TF:* 800-567-2792 ■ *Web:* www.ubishops.ca	Sherbrooke	QC	J1M1Z7	819-822-9600	822-9661	785
Bishop-Wisecarver Corp 2104 Martin Way *TF:* 888-580-8272 ■ *Web:* www.bwc.com	Pittsburg	CA	94565	925-439-8272	439-5931	620
Bismarck Civic Ctr 315 S 5th St *Web:* www.bismarckeventcenter.com	Bismarck	ND	58504	701-355-1370		205
Bismarck Expressway Suites 180 E Bismarck Expy *TF:* 888-774-5566 ■ *Web:* www.expresswaysuites.com	Bismarck	ND	58504	701-222-3311		379
Bismarck Mandan Chamber of Commerce 1640 Burnt Boat Dr *Web:* www.bismarckmandan.com	Bismarck	ND	58502	701-223-5660	255-6125	139
Bismarck Municipal Airport 2301 University Dr Bldg 17 PO Box 991 *Web:* www.bismarckairport.com	Bismarck	ND	58502	701-355-1800		27
Bismarck State College 1500 Edwards Ave *TF:* 800-445-5073 ■ *Web:* bismarckstate.edu	Bismarck	ND	58501	701-224-5400	224-5643	162
Bismarck Tribune 707 E Front Ave *TF:* 866-476-5348 ■ *Web:* bismarcktribune.com	Bismarck	ND	58504	701-223-2500		532-2
Bismarck Veterans Memorial Public Library 515 N Fifth St *Web:* www.bismarcklibrary.org	Bismarck	ND	58501	701-355-1480		434-3
Bismarck-Burleigh Public Health 500 E Front St *Web:* www.bismarcknd.gov	Bismarck	ND	58504	701-355-1540	221-6883	337
Bismarck-Mandan Convention & Visitors Bureau 1600 Burnt Boat Dr *TF:* 800-767-3555 ■ *Web:* noboundariesnd.com	Bismarck	ND	58503	701-222-4308	222-0647	206
Bismarck-Mandan Symphony Orchestra 215 N Sixth St *Web:* www.bismarckmandansymphony.org	Bismarck	ND	58501	701-258-8345		573-3
Bison Bookbinding & Letterpress 112 Grand Ave *Web:* bisonbookbinding.com	Bellingham	WA	98225	360-734-0481		92
Bison Capital Asset Management LLC 233 Wilshire Blvd Ste 425 *Web:* www.bisoncapital.com	Santa Monica	CA	90401	310-260-6573		401
Bison Gear & Engineering Corp 3850 Ohio Ave *TF:* 800-282-4766 ■ *Web:* www.bisongear.com	Saint Charles	IL	60174	630-377-4327	377-6777	709
Bison Inc 603 L St **Fax Area Code:* 800 ■ *TF:* 800-247-7668 ■ *Web:* www.bisoninc.com	Lincoln	NE	68508	402-474-3353	638-0698*	710
Bison Pipeline LLC 717 Texas St *TF:* 800-447-8066 ■ *Web:* www.bisonpipelinellc.com	Houston	TX	77002	800-447-8066		325
Bison Turf, The 1211 N University Dr *Web:* www.thebisonturf.com	Fargo	ND	58102	701-235-9118		671
Bisque Imports 1 Belmont Ave *TF:* 888-568-5991 ■ *Web:* www.bisqueimports.com	Belmont	NC	28012	704-829-9290		361
Bissell Inc 2345 Walker NW *TF:* 800-237-7691 ■ *Web:* www.bissell.com	Grand Rapids	MI	49544	616-453-4451	791-0662	788
Bissell Professional Group Inc 3512 N Croatan Hwy *Web:* www.bissellprofessionalgroup.com	Kitty Hawk	NC	27949	252-261-3266		261
Bisso Marine 11311 Neeshaw Dr *Web:* www.bissomarine.com	Houston	TX	77065	281-897-1500		313
Bisso Towboat Company Inc 13969 River Rd	Luling	LA	70070	504-861-1411		465
Bi-State Development Agency 707 N First St *Web:* www.metrostlouis.org	Saint Louis	MO	63102	314-982-1400		468
Bistro 5 5 Playstead Rd *Web:* www.bistro5.com	West Medford	MA	02155	781-395-7464		671
Bistro 821 821 Fifth Ave S *Web:* www.bistro821.com	Naples	FL	34102	239-261-5821	261-1972	671
Bistro Aix 1440 San Marco Blvd *Web:* 3.84.76.128	Jacksonville	FL	32207	904-398-1949		671
Bistro An American Cafe 1103 E Front Ave *Web:* www.bistro1100.com	Bismarck	ND	58504	701-224-8800	224-0398	671
Bistro Bella Vita 44 Grandville Ave SW *Web:* www.bistrobellavita.com	Grand Rapids	MI	49503	616-222-4600	222-4601	671
Bistro Bis 15 East St NW *Web:* bistrobis.com	Washington	DC	20001	202-661-2700		671
Bistro by the Tracks 215 Brookview Centre Way Ste 109 *Web:* www.bistrobythetracks.com	Knoxville	TN	37919	865-558-9500		671
Bistro Enzo 1502 Rehberg Ln *Web:* bistroenzobillings.com	Billings	MT	59102	406-651-0999	651-8035	671
Bistro Jeanty 6510 Washington St *Web:* www.bistrojeanty.com	Yountville	CA	94599	707-944-0103	944-0370	671
Bistro Mezzaluna 1821 SE Tenth Ave *Web:* www.bistromezzaluna.com	Fort Lauderdale	FL	33316	954-522-9191		671
Bistro Romano 120 Lombard St *Web:* www.bistroromano.com	Philadelphia	PA	19147	215-925-8880		671
Bistro Vendome 1420 Larimer St *Web:* www.bistrovendome.com	Denver	CO	80202	303-825-3232	825-3240	671
Bit by Bit Computing 5233 Mccandlish Rd *Web:* bitbybitcomputing.com	Grand Blanc	MI	48439	810-694-7477	694-7488	177
Bit of Britain Inc 141 Union School Rd *Web:* www.bitofbritain.com	Oxford	PA	19363	610-998-0400		711
Bit Shop Inc, The 1646 Watson Ct *Web:* www.bsi-nc.com	Milpitas	CA	95035	408-262-0713	945-0852	454
BITCO Insurance Cos 3700 Market Square Cir **Fax Area Code:* 309 ■ *TF:* 800-475-4477 ■ *Web:* www.bitco.com	Davenport	IA	52807	800-475-4477	786-3847*	391-4
Bitdefender Inc 6301 NW Fifth Way Ste 4300 *Web:* bitdefender.com	Fort Lauderdale	FL	33309	954-776-6262		177
Bitflow Inc 400 W Cummings Pk Ste 5050 *Web:* www.bitflow.com	Woburn	MA	01801	781-932-2900	933-9965	178-1
bitHeads 1309 Carling Ave *TF:* 855-622-3232 ■ *Web:* www.bitheads.com	Ottawa	ON	K1Z7L3	613-722-3232		180
Bithgroup Technologies Inc 113 W Monument St *Web:* www.bithgroup.com	Baltimore	MD	21201	410-962-1188	962-6535	463
Bitlab LLC 1144 Parkwood Ave *Web:* bitlab.com	Park Ridge	IL	60068	847-823-5070		179
BitNami 900 Kearny St 5th Fl *Web:* bitnami.com	San Francisco	CA	94105	415-528-2805		387
Bitneys Furniture & Mattress Co 740 E Idaho St *Web:* bitneysfurniture.com	Kalispell	MT	59901	406-755-6033		321
Bits & Bytes Computer Services 1987 B Hendersonville Rd *Web:* bitsbyte.com	Asheville	NC	28803	828-684-8953		175
Bits N Bytes Computer Systems 3201 Double C Dr *Web:* www.bnbtech.com	Norman	OK	73069	405-292-5408		180

Name / Address	City	State	Zip	Phone	Fax	Class
Bittenbender Consruction Lp						
5 N Columbus Blvd Pier 5	Philadelphia	PA	19106	215-925-8900		186
Web: bittenbenderconstruction.com						
Bitter Creek Ale House 246 N Eigth St	Boise	ID	83702	208-429-6340		671
Web: www.bcrfl.com						
Bitterman Scales LLC						
2445-C Old Philadelphia Pke	Lancaster	PA	17602	717-464-3009		362
TF: 877-464-3009 ■ *Web:* www.bittermanscales.com						
Bitterroot Valley Chamber of Commerce						
105 E Main St	Hamilton	MT	59840	406-363-2400	363-2402	139
Web: bitterrootchamber.com						
Bittersweet Ski Resort Snowline						
600 River Rd	Otsego	MI	49078	269-694-2032		707
Web: www.skibittersweet.com						
BitWise Inc						
1515 Woodfield Rd Ste 740	Schaumburg	IL	60173	847-969-1500		177
Web: www.bitwiseglobal.com						
Bitwise Solutions Inc						
569 Aviator Dr	Fort Worth	TX	76179	817-439-1010		809
Web: www.bitwise.com						
Bitworks LLC 126 Tower Rd	Waterbury	CT	06710	203-756-9513		180
Web: www.bitworksusa.net						
Bitz-Ee Mama's 7023 N 58th Ave	Glendale	AZ	85301	623-931-0562		671
Web: www.bitz-eemamas.com						
Bix Beiderbecke Memorial Society						
PO Box 3688	Davenport	IA	52808	563-324-7170	326-1732	48-4
TF: 888-249-5487 ■ *Web:* www.bixsociety.org						
Bix Pix Entertainment Inc						
11630 Tuxford St	Sun Valley	CA	91352	818-252-7474	252-7410	33
Web: www.bixpix.com						
Bix Produce Co 1415 L'Orient St	Saint Paul	MN	55117	651-487-8000		297-7
TF: 800-642-9514 ■ *Web:* www.bixproduce.com						
Bix Restaurant 56 Gold St	San Francisco	CA	94133	415-433-6300	433-4574	671
Web: www.bixrestaurant.com						
Bixal Solutions Inc						
3050 Chain Bridge Rd Ste 420	Fairfax	VA	22030	703-634-5701		177
Web: bixal.com						
Bixby International Corp						
1 Preble Rd	Newburyport	MA	01950	978-462-4100		600
Web: www.bixbyintl.com						
Bixby Knolls Towers						
3737 Atlantic Ave	Long Beach	CA	90807	562-426-6123	426-2571	672
TF: 800-545-1833 ■ *Web:* www.bixbyknollstowers.org						
Bixel & Co						
8721 Sunset Blvd Ste 101	Los Angeles	CA	90069	310-854-3828		184
TF: 855-854-9830 ■ *Web:* bixelco.com						
Bizal Manufacturing Inc						
7880 Ranchers Rd NE	Fridley	MN	55432	763-571-4030	571-1467	454
Web: www.bizalmfg.com						
BizBen 7172 Regional St No 364	Dublin	CA	94568	866-270-6278		393
TF: 866-270-6278 ■ *Web:* www.bizben.com						
Bizco Technologies Inc 7950 "O" St	Lincoln	NE	68510	800-424-9677		179
TF: 800-424-9677 ■ *Web:* www.bizco.com						
Bizerba 1804 Fashion Ct	Piscataway	NJ	08854	732-565-6000		407
Web: www.bizerba.com						
Bizjet International Sales and Support Inc						
3515 N Sheridan Rd	Tulsa	OK	74115	918-832-7733	832-8627	62-5
Web: www.bizjet.com						
BizLand Inc 70 Blanchard Rd	Burlington	MA	01803	800-249-5263		39
TF: 800-249-5263 ■ *Web:* www.bizland.com						
Bizlink Technology Inc						
3400 Gateway Blvd	Fremont	CA	94538	510-252-0786	252-1178	815
TF: 800-326-4193 ■ *Web:* www.bizlinktech.com						
Bizmarts 222 White Eagle Dr	Waleska	GA	30183	770-345-4663		174
Web: www.bizmarts.com						
BizNet Technology Inc						
13995 SW 144th Ave Ste 208	Miami	FL	33186	305-250-2024	387-7486	180
Web: www.biznettechnology.com						
Biznetix Inc PO Box 24528	Rochester	NY	14624	585-426-6519		177
Web: www.biznetix.net						
Bizphyx Inc 1910 Poplar Dr	Wylie	TX	75098	972-429-5560		194
Web: www.bizphyx.com						
Bizport Ltd 9 N Third St	Richmond	VA	23219	804-648-7874		463
Web: www.bizportdoes.com						
BizQuest						
101 California St 43rd Fl	San Francisco	CA	94111	888-280-3815	764-1622*	393
**Fax Area Code:* 415 ■ *TF:* 844-495-3091 ■ *Web:* bizquest.com						
BizSpeed Inc						
3050 Royal Blvd S Ste 130	Alpharetta	GA	30022	678-287-3310		180
TF: 866-270-0541 ■ *Web:* www.bizspeed.com						
Bizstream Inc 11480 53rd Ave	Allendale	MI	49401	877-692-4978		180
TF: 877-692-4978 ■ *Web:* bizstream.com						
BizWest 3004 Arapahoe Ave	Boulder	CO	80301	303-440-4950	440-8954	457-5
Web: www.bizwest.com						
BizXchange Inc						
3600 136th Pl SE Ste 270	Bellevue	WA	98006	425-998-5055		691
Web: www.bizx.com						
Bizzabo 31 W 27th St fl0	New York	NY	10001	800-604-2499		178-8
TF: 800-604-2499 ■ *Web:* www.bizzabo.com						
Bizzuka Inc 105 Chapel Dr	LaFayette	LA	70506	337-216-4423		177
Web: www.bizzuka.com						
BJ Transport Inc 12720 S Hudson Rd	Afton	MN	55001	651-436-4300	436-4336	780
TF: 800-328-8163 ■ *Web:* www.bjtransport.com						
BJ's On the Water 115 75th St	Ocean City	MD	21842	410-524-7575	524-7624	671
Web: bjsonthewater.com						
BJ's Restaurants Inc						
7755 Center Ave Ste 300	Huntington Beach	CA	92647	714-500-2400	848-8287	670
Web: www.bjsrestaurants.com						
BJCC Inspections 1000 Banks Draw	Rexford	MT	59930	406-882-4825		727
TF: 877-248-6006 ■ *Web:* www.bjccinspections.com						
Bjoin Limestone Inc						
7308 W State Rd 11	Janesville	WI	53548	608-876-6959	876-6538	503-6
Web: www.bjoinlimestone.com						
Bjork Construction Company Inc						
4420 Enterprise Pl	Fremont	CA	94538	510-656-4688		378
Web: www.bjorkconstruction.com						
BJU Press 1430 Wade Hampton Blvd	Greenville	SC	29609	864-770-1317	271-8151	637-2
TF: 800-845-5731 ■ *Web:* www.bjupress.com						
BJW Berghorst & Sons 11430 James St	Holland	MI	49424	616-772-2114		612
Web: www.bjwberghorst.com						
Bkc Industries Inc						
2117 Will Suitt Rd	Creedmoor	NC	27522	919-575-6699		779
Web: www.westernsalesinc.com						
BKF Engineers						
255 Shoreline Dr Ste 200	Redwood City	CA	94065	650-482-6300	482-6399	261
Web: www.bkf.com						
Bkhm PA 1560 Orange Ave Ste 600	Winter Park	FL	32789	407-998-9000		2
Web: bkhmcpa.com						
BKI (Burk-Kleinpeter Inc)						
4176 Canal St	New Orleans	LA	70119	504-486-5901		261
Web: www.bkiusa.com						
bkm Officeworks						
9201 Spectrum Center Blvd Ste 100	San Diego	CA	92123	858-569-4700		321
Web: www.bkmofficeworks.com						
BKR Intl 19 Fulton St Ste 401	New York	NY	10038	212-964-2115	964-2133	49-1
Web: bkr.com						
BKR Studio Inc 110 E Madison St	South Bend	IN	46601	574-245-9576	245-9577	344
TF: 800-801-9576 ■ *Web:* www.bkrstudio.com						
BL Co 355 Research Pkwy	Meriden	CT	06450	203-630-1406	630-2615	261
TF: 800-301-3077 ■ *Web:* www.blcompanies.com						
BL Downey Company LLC						
2125 Gardner Rd	Broadview	IL	60155	708-345-8000		481
Web: www.bldowney.com						
BL Harbert International LLC						
820 Shades Creek Pkwy Ste 3000	Birmingham	AL	35209	205-802-2800	802-2801	256
Web: www.blharbert.com						
BLA Inc 333 Pierce Rd Ste 200	Itasca	IL	60143	630-438-6400		261
Web: www.bla-inc.com						
Blac Inc 195 Spangler Ave	Elmhurst	IL	60126	630-279-6400	279-1005	223
Web: blacinc.com						
Blach Construction Co						
469 El Cmino Real Ste 100	Santa Clara	CA	95050	408-244-7100	244-2220	186
Web: www.blach.com						
Blach Distributing Co 131 W Main St	Elko	NV	89801	775-738-7111		81-1
TF: 800-310-5099						
Blachford Corp 401 Center Rd	Frankfort	IL	60423	815-464-2100	464-2112	145
Web: blachford.com						
Blachly-Lane Inc PO Box 70	Junction City	OR	97448	541-688-8711		245
TF: 800-446-8418 ■ *Web:* www.blachlylane.coop						
Black & Soli PC CPA						
81 W Esperanza Blvd Ste E	Green Valley	AZ	85614	520-625-5988	625-5992	2
Web: www.blackandsoli.com						
Black & Veatch 11401 Lamar Ave	Overland Park	KS	66211	913-458-2000		188-7
TF: 866-496-9149 ■ *Web:* www.bv.com						
Black Angus						
10907 N Rodney Parham Rd	Little Rock	AR	72212	501-228-7800		671
Web: www.blackanguscafe.com						
Black Bart Big Game Fishing						
155 E Blue Heron Blvd	Riviera Beach	FL	33404	561-842-4550	842-4549	711
TF: 866-289-7050 ■ *Web:* www.blackbartlures.com						
Black Barts Steakhouse Saloon						
2760 E Butler Ave	Flagstaff	AZ	86004	928-779-3142		671
Web: www.blackbartssteakhouse.com						
Black Bashor & Porsch LLP						
270 E Connelly Blvd	Sharon	PA	16146	724-981-7510	342-1345	2
Web: www.bbpcpa.com						
Black Bear Casino Resort						
1785 Hwy 210 PO Box 777	Carlton	MN	55718	218-878-2418	878-2414	133
TF: 888-771-0777 ■ *Web:* www.blackbearcasinohotel.com						
Black Bear Diner 1880 Shasta St	Redding	CA	96001	602-843-1921		671
Web: blackbeardiner.com						
Black Box Distribution LLC						
2777 Loker Ave W Ste A	Carlsbad	CA	92010	760-804-3300		711
Black Business Investment Fund (BBIF)						
301 E Pine St Ste 175	Orlando	FL	32801	407-649-4780	649-8688	194
Web: www.bbifflorida.com						
Black Butte Ranch						
12930 Hawks Beard Rd PO Box 8000	Black Butte Ranch	OR	97759	541-595-1252	595-2077	669
TF: 866-901-2961 ■ *Web:* www.blackbutteranch.com						
Black Canyon Capital LLC						
2000 Avenue of the Stars 11th Fl	Los Angeles	CA	90067	310-272-1800		690
Web: www.blackcanyoncapital.com						
Black Classic Press PO Box 13414	Baltimore	MD	21203	410-242-6954	242-6959	637-2
Web: www.blackclassicbooks.com						
Black Clawson Converting Machinery Inc						
46 N First St	Fulton	NY	13069	315-598-7121	593-0396	556
Web: www.davis-standard.com						
Black Cultural Centre for Nova Scotia						
10 Cherry Brook Rd	Cherry Brook	NS	B2Z1A8	902-434-6223	434-2306	520
TF: 800-465-0767 ■ *Web:* www.bccnsweb.com						
Black Diamond Paving Inc						
41550 Boscell Rd	Fremont	CA	94538	510-770-1150		183
Web: www.blackdiamondpaving.com						
Black Enterprise Magazine						
130 Fifth Ave	New York	NY	10011	212-242-8000	886-9610	457-5
TF: 800-727-7777 ■ *Web:* www.blackenterprise.com						
Black Equipment Company Inc						
1187 Burch Dr	Evansville	IN	47725	812-477-6481	474-4346	112
TF: 866-414-7062 ■ *Web:* blackequipment.com						
Black Forest Decor LLC PO Box 297	Jenks	OK	74037	800-605-0915		791
TF: 800-605-0915 ■ *Web:* www.blackforestdecor.com						
Black Forest Inn 1 E 26th St	Minneapolis	MN	55404	612-872-0812	872-0423	671
Web: www.blackforestinnmpls.com						
Black Gold 4320 18th Ave S	Grand Forks	ND	58201	701-792-3414	772-0749	10-11
Web: blackgoldfarms.com						
Black Hat 1932 First Ave Ste 204	Seattle	WA	98101	206-443-5489	219-4143	692
TF: 866-203-8081 ■ *Web:* www.blackhat.com						
Black Hawk College 1501 State Hwy 78	Kewanee	IL	61443	309-852-5671	856-6005	162
TF: 800-233-5671 ■ *Web:* www.bhc.edu						
Black Hawk County 316 E Fifth St	Waterloo	IA	50703	319-833-3000		338
Web: www.co.black-hawk.ia.us						
Black Hawk State Park 228 S Blossom	Lake View	IA	51450	712-657-8712	657-2289	565
Web: www.iowadnr.gov						
Black Hills Bentonite PO Box 9	Mills	WY	82644	307-265-3740	235-8511	503-2
TF: 800-700-8666 ■ *Web:* www.bhbentonite.com						

Name / Address	City	State	Zip	Phone	Fax	Class
Black Hills Caverns 2600 Cavern Rd *TF:* 800-837-9358 ■ *Web:* www.blackhillscaverns.com	Rapid City	SD	57702	605-343-0542		50-5
Black Hills Corp 625 Ninth St *NYSE: BKH* ■ *TF:* 866-264-8003 ■ *Web:* www.blackhillscorp.com	Rapid City	SD	57701	605-721-1700		360-5
Black Hills Electric Co-op 25191 Co-Op Way PO Box 792 *TF:* 800-742-0085 ■ *Web:* bhec.coop	Custer	SD	57730	605-673-4461	673-3147	245
Black Hills Energy PO Box 4660 *TF:* 888-890-5554 ■ *Web:* www.blackhillsenergy.com	Carol Stream	IL	60197	888-890-5554		245
Black Hills Health & Education Ctr 13815 Battle Creek Rd PO Box 19 *TF:* 866-757-0160 ■ *Web:* bhhec.org	Hermosa	SD	57744	605-255-4101	255-4687	706
Black Hills National Cemetery 20901 Pleasant Vly Dr *Web:* www.cem.va.gov	Sturgis	SD	57785	605-347-3830	720-7298	136
Black Hills Pioneer 315 Seaton Cir *Web:* www.bhpioneer.com	Spearfish	SD	57783	605-642-2761		532-2
Black Hills Shooters Supply Inc 2875 Creek Dr *TF:* 800-289-2506 ■ *Web:* www.bhshooters.com	Rapid City	SD	57703	800-289-2506		711
Black Hills State University 1200 University St Unit 9502 *TF:* 800-255-2478 ■ *Web:* www.bhsu.edu	Spearfish	SD	57799	605-642-6343	642-6254	166
Black History Museum & Cultural Center of Virginia 122 W Leigh St *Web:* blackhistorymuseum.org	Richmond	VA	23220	804-780-9093		520
Black Horse Pike Regional School District 580 Erial Rd *Web:* www.bhprsd.org	Blackwood	NJ	08012	856-227-4105	227-6835	685
Black Light Fellowship PO Box 5369 *Web:* www.blacklightfellowship.com	Chicago	IL	60612	773-826-7790	826-7792	637-2
Black Madonna Shrine 100 St Joseph Hill Rd PO Box 181 *Web:* www.franciscancaring.org	Pacific	MO	63069	636-938-5361		50-1
Black Mann & Graham LLP 2905 Corporate Cir **Fax Area Code:* 212 ■ *Web:* www.bmandg.com	Flower Mound	TX	75028	972-353-4174	725-5061*	428
Black McCuskey Souers & Arbaugh 220 Market Ave S Ste 1000 *Web:* bmsa.com	Canton	OH	44702	330-456-8341		445
Black Mesa Casino 25 Hagon Rd *TF:* 877-529-2946 ■ *Web:* blackmesacasino.com	Algodones	NM	87001	505-867-6700		452
Black Mesa State Park & Nature Preserve County Rd 325 *Web:* www.travelok.com	Kenton	OK	73946	580-426-2222	426-2405	565
Black Millwork Company Inc 220 W Crescent Ave *Web:* www.blackmillwork.com	Allendale	NJ	07401	201-934-0100		499
Black Moshannon State Park 4216 Beaver Rd *Web:* www.dcnr.pa.gov	Philipsburg	PA	16866	814-342-5960		565
Black Mountain Ranch 4000 Conger Mesa Rd *TF:* 800-967-2401 ■ *Web:* blackmtnranch.com	McCoy	CO	80463	970-653-4226		239
Black Mountain-Swannanoa Chamber of Commerce 201 E State St *TF:* 800-669-2301 ■ *Web:* www.exploreblackmountain.com	Black Mountain	NC	28711	828-669-2300	669-1407	139
Black Olive 803 S Caroline St *Web:* theblackolive.com	Baltimore	MD	21231	410-276-7141		671
Black Pearl, The Bannister's Wharf *Web:* www.blackpearlnewport.com	Newport	RI	02840	401-846-5264		671
Black Pest Prevention Inc 605 Springbrook Rd *Web:* www.blackpest.com	Charlotte	NC	28217	704-522-9222		577
Black Point Inn Resort 510 Black Pt Rd *Web:* www.blackpointinn.com	Scarborough	ME	04074	207-883-2500	883-9976	669
Black Radio Network 375 Fifth Ave *TF:* 866-342-6892 ■ *Web:* blackradionetwork.com	New York	NY	10016	212-686-6850	686-7308	644
Black Realty Inc 107 S Howard Ste 500 *Web:* naiblack.com	Spokane	WA	99201	509-622-3524		652
Black Ridge Oil & Gas 110 N Fifth St Ste 410 *Web:* www.blackridgeoil.com	Minneapolis	MN	55401	952-426-1241		536
Black River Electric Co-op 2600 Hwy 67 PO Box 31 *TF:* 800-392-4711 ■ *Web:* www.brec.coop	Fredericktown	MO	63645	573-783-3381		245
Black River Electric Cooperative Inc 1121 N Pike Rd W *TF:* 866-731-2732 ■ *Web:* blackriver.coop	Sumter	SC	29153	803-469-8060	469-8320	245
Black River Group, The 140 Park Ave E *Web:* www.blackriverconnect.com	Mansfield	OH	44902	419-524-4312		682
Black River Manufacturing Inc (BRM) 2625 20th St *Web:* www.blackrivermfg.biz	Port Huron	MI	48060	810-982-9812	982-2074	60
Black River Technical College 1410 Hwy 304 E *TF:* 866-890-6933 ■ *Web:* www.blackrivertech.org	Pocahontas	AR	72455	870-248-4000	248-4100	162
Black Rock Mountain State Park 3085 Black Rock Mtn Pkwy *Web:* gastateparks.org	Mountain City	GA	30562	706-746-2141		565
Black Rock State Park c/o Topsmead State Forest PO Box 1081 *Web:* portal.ct.gov	Litchfield	CT	06759	860-283-8088		565
Black Srebnick Kornspan & Stumpf PA 201 S Biscayne Blvd Ste 1300 *Web:* www.royblack.com	Miami	FL	33131	305-371-6421	358-2006	428
Black Swan Energy Ltd 2700 Bow Valley Sqr Tower IV 250-6th Ave SW *TF:* 877-576-6733 ■ *Web:* www.blackswanenergy.com	Calgary	AB	T2P3H7	403-930-4400		536
Black Swan Inn 746 E Center St *Web:* www.blackswaninn.com	Pocatello	ID	83201	208-233-3051		379
Black Wing Shooting Center LLC 3722 Marysville Rd *Web:* blackwingsc.com	Delaware	OH	43015	740-363-7555		711
Black's Tire & Auto Service 610 Wicker St *Web:* www.blackstire.com	Sanford	NC	27330	919-775-7225		62-5
Black's Tire Service Inc 30 Bitmore Rd *Web:* blackstire.com	Whiteville	NC	28472	910-642-4123		54
BlackBag Technologies Inc 300 Piercy Rd *TF:* 855-844-8890 ■ *Web:* www.blackbagtech.com	San Jose	CA	95138	408-844-8890	844-8891	180
Blackbaud Inc 2000 Daniel Island Dr *NASDAQ: BLKB* ■ *TF:* 800-468-8996 ■ *Web:* www.blackbaud.com	Charleston	SC	29492	843-216-6200	216-6100	178-1
BlackBerry Ltd 2200 University Ave E *NYSE: BB* ■ *Web:* www.blackberry.com	Waterloo	ON	N2K0A7	519-888-7465	888-6906	173-2
Blackbird 619 W Randolph St *Web:* www.blackbirdrestaurant.com	Chicago	IL	60661	312-715-0708		671
Blackbird Ventures 2223 Avenida de la Playa Ste 206 *Web:* blackbirdv.com	La Jolla	CA	92037	858-754-3201		792
Blackboard Inc 1111 19th St NW Fl 9 5th Fl *TF:* 800-424-9299 ■ *Web:* www.blackboard.com	Washington	DC	20036	202-463-4860	463-4863	178-3
BlackBook 32 Union Sq E 4th Fl *Web:* bbook.com	New York	NY	10003	212-334-1800		532-3
Blackbourn Solutions 200 4th Ave N **Fax Area Code:* 507 ■ *TF:* 800-842-7550 ■ *Web:* blackbournsolutions.com	Edgerton	MN	56128	800-842-7550	442-4313*	86
Blackbridge Partners LLC 800 W Cummings Pk Ste 2000 *Web:* www.blackbridgepartners.com	Woburn	MA	01801	617-273-2404		70
BlackBrush Oil & Gas LP 18615 Tuscany Stone Ste 300 *Web:* blackbrushenergy.com	San Antonio	TX	78258	210-495-5577		536
Blackburn College 700 College Ave **Fax Area Code:* 217 ■ *TF:* 800-233-3550 ■ *Web:* blackburn.edu	Carlinville	IL	62626	800-233-3550	854-3713*	166
Blackburn Correctional Complex 3111 Spurr Rd *TF:* 800-808-1213 ■ *Web:* www.corrections.ky.gov	Lexington	KY	40511	859-246-2366	246-2376	213
Blackburn Elementary School 2285 N Anderson Ave **Fax Area Code:* 828 ■ *Web:* www.catawbaschools.net	Newton	NC	28658	704-462-1344	464-0925*	685
Blackburn Marsha (Sen R - TN) 357 Dirksen Senate Office Bldg *Web:* www.blackburn.senate.gov	Washington	DC	20510	202-224-3344		342-2
Blackburn Radio Inc 700 Richmond St Ste 102 *Web:* blackburnradio.com	London	ON	N6A5C7	519-679-8680	679-5321	360-2
Blackburn's Fabrication Inc 2467 Jackson Pk *Web:* www.blackburnsfab.com	Columbus	OH	43223	614-875-0784		492
Blackburn's Physicians Pharmacy Inc 301 Corbet St *TF:* 800-472-2440 ■ *Web:* www.blackburnsmed.com	Tarentum	PA	15084	724-224-9100	224-9124	476
Blackcomb Helicopters 9960 Heliport Rd *TF:* 800-330-4354 ■ *Web:* blackcombhelicopters.com	Whistler	BC	V0N1B0	604-938-1700		21
Blackduck Community Library 72 1st St SE *Web:* www.krls.org	Blackduck	MN	56630	218-835-6600		434-3
Blackfeet Community College 504 SE Boundary St PO Box 819 *Web:* www.bfcc.edu	Browning	MT	59417	406-338-5441	338-3272	162
Blackfoot Inn 5940 Blackfoot Trl SE *TF:* 800-661-1151 ■ *Web:* www.hotelblackfoot.com	Calgary	AB	T2H2B5	403-252-2253	252-3574	379
Blackfoot Livestock Auction 93 Rich Ln *Web:* www.blackfootlivestockauction.com	Blackfoot	ID	83221	208-785-0500		446
Blackfoot School District 55 270 E Bridge St *Web:* www.d55.k12.id.us	Blackfoot	ID	83221	208-785-8800	785-8809	685
Blackfoot Telecommunications Group 1221 N Russell St *TF:* 866-541-5000 ■ *Web:* www.blackfoot.com	Missoula	MT	59808	406-541-5000	541-5333	224
Blackford County 110 W Washington St *Web:* www.blackfordcounty.com	Hartford City	IN	47348	765-348-1620	348-7222	338
Blackhawk Bank 400 Broad St PO Box 719 *TF:* 888-769-2600 ■ *Web:* www.blackhawkbank.com	Beloit	WI	53511	608-364-8911		69
Blackhawk Equipment Co 5295 Vivian St *TF:* 888-421-3001 ■ *Web:* www.blackhawkequipment.com	Arvada	CO	80002	303-421-3000	421-0672	172
Blackhawk Machine Products Inc 6 Industrial Dr *Web:* www.blackhawk-machine.com	Smithfield	RI	02917	401-232-7563	232-0770	621
Blackhawk Management Corp 1322 Space Pk Dr *Web:* www.blackhawkmgmt.com	Houston	TX	77058	281-286-5751		463
Blackhawk Technical College 6004 S County Rd G *TF:* 800-498-1282 ■ *Web:* blackhawk.edu	Janesville	WI	53546	608-758-6900	743-4407	800
Blackhawk Veterinary Services Ltd 5548 Rt 72 E *Web:* blackhawk-vet.com	Byron	IL	61010	815-234-5424		794
BlackInk IT 1101 E 16th St Ste 300 *Web:* blackinkit.com	Indianapolis	IN	46202	317-472-8000	472-8010	225
Blackledge Furniture 233 SW Second St *TF:* 800-782-4851 ■ *Web:* www.blackledgefurniture.com	Corvallis	OR	97333	541-753-4851		321
Blacklion 10635 Park Rd *TF:* 866-466-5466 ■ *Web:* www.blacklion.com	Charlotte	NC	28210	704-541-1148		321
Blackmagic Design Inc 2875 Bayview Dr *Web:* www.blackmagic-design.com	Fremont	CA	94538	408-954-0500	954-0508	392
Blackman and Holberton Move Planning Services 201 Wilshire Blvd Ste A6 *Web:* www.blackman-holberton.com	Santa Monica	CA	90401	310-458-8898	458-8081	393
Blackman Plumbing Supply Company Inc 3480 Sunrise Hwy **Fax Area Code:* 631 ■ *Web:* www.blackman.com	Wantagh	NY	11793	516-785-6000	823-4302*	612
Blackmer 1809 Century Ave *TF:* 888-363-7886 ■ *Web:* www.psgdover.com	Grand Rapids	MI	49503	616-241-1611	241-3752	641
Blackmore Company Inc 10800 Blackmore Ave *TF:* 800-874-8660 ■ *Web:* www.blackmoreco.com	Belleville	MI	48111	734-483-8661		608

				Phone	Fax	Class
BlackPoint IT Services 20435 72nd Ave S Ste 200 *Web:* www.blackpoint-it.com	Kent	WA	98032	206-575-9511		180
BlackRock Inc 40 E 52nd St *NYSE: BLK* ■ *Web:* www.blackrock.com	New York	NY	10022	212-810-5300		401
Blacksands Petroleum Inc 800 Bering Dr Ste 250	Houston	TX	77057	713-554-4491		536
Blacksburg High School 3401 Bruin Ln *Web:* bhs.mcps.org	Blacksburg	VA	24060	540-951-5706	951-5714	685
Blackstone Advanced Technologies LLC 100 Blackstone Ave *Web:* www.blackadvtech.com	Jamestown	NY	14701	716-665-5410	665-5152	697
Blackstone Career Institute 1011 Brookside Rd Ste 300 PO Box 3717 *TF:* 800-826-9228 ■ *Web:* www.blackstone.edu	Allentown	PA	18106	610-871-0031	871-0034	167-3
Blackstone Group 345 Park Ave *TF:* 888-756-8443 ■ *Web:* www.blackstone.com	New York	NY	10154	212-583-5000	583-5749	690
Blackstone Inc 2051 Bennett Creek Rd *Web:* www.blackstoneinc.net	Cottage Grove	OR	97424	541-942-3870		194
Blackstone Industries Inc 16 Stoney Hill Rd *TF:* 800-272-2885 ■ *Web:* www.blackstoneind.com	Bethel	CT	06801	203-792-8622	796-7861	759
Blackstone River & Canal Heritage State Park 287 Oak St *Web:* www.mass.gov	Uxbridge	MA	01569	508-278-7604		565
Blackstone Valley Chamber of Commerce 110 Church St *TF:* 800-841-0919 ■ *Web:* www.blackstonevalley.org	Whitinsville	MA	01588	508-234-9090	234-5152	139
Blacktail Mountain Ski Area LLC 13990 Blacktail Rd *Web:* www.blacktailmountain.com	Lakeside	MT	59922	406-844-0999		379
Blackthorn Restaurant & Pub 2134 Seneca St *Web:* www.blackthornrestaurant.com	Buffalo	NY	14210	716-825-9327		671
Blackton Inc 1714 Alden Rd *Web:* www.blacktoninc.com	Orlando	FL	32803	407-898-2661		131
Blackwater Falls State Park PO Box 490 *Web:* wvstateparks.com	Davis	WV	26260	304-259-5216		565
Blackwater River State Park 7720 Deaton Bridge Rd *Web:* www.floridastateparks.org	Holt	FL	32564	850-983-5363		565
Blackwell & Spadaccini LLC 158 E Center St *Web:* eastcenterlaw.com	Manchester	CT	06040	860-432-0676	432-2926	41
Blackwell Burke PA 431 S Seventh St 2500 *Web:* www.blackwellburke.com	Minneapolis	MN	55415	612-343-3200		428
Blackwell Engineering 566 E Market St *Web:* www.blackwellengineering.com	Harrisonburg	VA	22801	540-432-9555		261
Blackwell Plastics Inc 5606 Cavanaugh *Web:* www.blackwellplastics.com	Houston	TX	77021	713-643-6577		596
Blackwell, The 2110 Tuttle Pk Pl *TF:* 866-247-4003 ■ *Web:* www.theblackwell.com	Columbus	OH	43210	614-247-4000	247-4040	379
Blade 541 N Superior St *TF:* 800-245-3317 ■ *Web:* www.toledoblade.com	Toledo	OH	43660	419-724-6000	724-6439	532-2
Blade Creative Branding Inc 15 Gervais Dr Ste 103 *TF:* 800-392-5233 ■ *Web:* www.bladecreativebranding.com	Toronto	ON	M3C1Y8	416-467-4770		7
Blade Energy Partners Ltd 2600 Network Blvd Ste 550 *TF:* 800-849-1545 ■ *Web:* www.blade-energy.com	Frisco	TX	75034	972-712-8407	712-8408	192
Blade HQ 400 S 1000 E Ste E *TF:* 888-252-3347 ■ *Web:* www.bladehq.com	Lehi	UT	84043	801-768-0232		362
Blade Technologies Inc 10820 Sunset Office Dr Ste 101 *Web:* www.bladetechinc.com	Saint Louis	MO	63127	314-752-7999		225
Bladen Community College 7418 NC Hwy 41W PO Box 266 *Web:* www.bladencc.edu	Dublin	NC	28332	910-879-5556	879-5513	162
Bladen County 166 E Broad St Rm 109 *Web:* bladennc.govoffice3.com	Elizabethtown	NC	28337	910-862-6700	862-6767	338
Bladensburg Barber School 4810 Annapolis Rd *Web:* www.bladensburgbarberschool.org	Bladensburg	MD	20710	301-277-8913	277-7981	685
Blades School of Hair Design 22576 MacArthur Blvd PO Box 226 *Web:* www.bladesschoolofhairdesign.com	California	MD	20619	301-862-9797		685
Blade-Tech Industries Inc 5530 184th St E *TF:* 877-331-5793 ■ *Web:* blade-tech.com	Puyallup	WA	98375	253-655-8059		711
Bladon Springs State Park 3921 Bladon Rd *Web:* www.alapark.com	Bladon Springs	AL	36919	251-754-9207		565
BlahUSA 134 W 26th St Ste 720 *Web:* www.blahusa.com	New York	NY	10001	212-627-8700		512
Blain Supply Inc 3507 E Racine St *TF:* 800-210-2370 ■ *Web:* www.farmandfleet.com	Janesville	WI	53547	608-754-2821		274
Blaine Construction Corp 6510 Deane Hill Dr *Web:* www.blaineconstruction.com	Knoxville	TN	37919	865-693-8900	691-7606	186
Blaine County 145 Lincoln Ave *TF:* 800-657-2113 ■ *Web:* www.blainecounty.ne.gov	Brewster	NE	68821	308-547-2222	547-2228	338
Blaine County 420 Ohio St *TF:* 800-666-6124 ■ *Web:* blainecounty-mt.gov	Chinook	MT	59523	406-442-9830	357-2199	338
Blaine County 206 First Ave S Blaine County Courthouse *Web:* www.co.blaine.id.us	Hailey	ID	83333	208-788-5505	788-5501	338
Blaine County 212 N Weigle *TF:* 800-513-2577 ■ *Web:* www.watonga.com	Watonga	OK	73772	580-623-5890	623-4549	338
Blaine Tech Services Inc 1680 Rogers Ave *TF:* 800-545-7558 ■ *Web:* www.blainetech.com	San Jose	CA	95112	408-573-0555		194
Blaine Warren Advertising LLC 7120 Smoke Ranch Rd *Web:* www.blainewarren.com	Las Vegas	NV	89128	702-435-6947		7
Blaine Window Hardware Inc 17319 Blaine Dr **Fax Area Code:* 888 ■ *TF:* 800-678-1919 ■ *Web:* blainewindow.com	Hagerstown	MD	21740	301-797-6500	250-3960*	351
Blaine's Art Supply 1025 Photo Ave *TF:* 866-561-4278 ■ *Web:* www.blainesart.com	Anchorage	AK	99503	907-561-5344	562-5988	45
Blair Academy 2 Park St PO Box 600 *Web:* www.blair.edu	Blairstown	NJ	07825	908-362-6121		622
Blair Agency Inc, The 1401 S Brentwood Blvd Ste 500 *TF:* 800-562-7260 ■ *Web:* capitasfinancial.com	Saint Louis	MO	63144	314-961-0013		390
Blair Candy Company Inc 3421 Beale Ave *TF:* 800-698-3536 ■ *Web:* www.blaircandy.com	Altoona	PA	16601	814-944-3581	944-8470	123
Blair Cedar & Novelty Works Inc 680 W US Hwy 54 *TF:* 800-325-3943 ■ *Web:* www.blaircedar.com	Camdenton	MO	65020	573-346-2235	346-5534	328
Blair Concrete Services 1410-B Diggs Dr *Web:* www.donleyinc.com	Raleigh	NC	27603	919-833-9088		189-3
Blair County Courthouse 423 Allegheny St Ste 011 *Web:* www.blairco.org	Hollidaysburg	PA	16648	814-693-3000		338
Blair County Genealogical Society (BCGS) 431 Scotch Valley Rd *Web:* www.bcgslibrary.org	Hollidaysburg	PA	16648	814-696-3492		49-19
Blair Dubilier & Associates Inc 4853 Cordell Ave Ste 1605 *Web:* blairdubilier.com	Bethesda	MD	20814	301-951-9131		177
Blair Museum of Lithopanes 5403 Elmer Dr *Web:* www.lithophanemuseum.org	Toledo	OH	43615	419-245-1356		520
Blair Rubber Co 5020 Panther Pkwy *TF:* 800-321-5583 ■ *Web:* blairrubber.com	Seville	OH	44273	800-321-5583		131
Blair, Church & Flynn Consulting Engineers 451 Clovis Ave Ste 200 *Web:* bcf-engr.com	Clovis	CA	93612	559-326-1400		261
Blairsville Dispatch, The 51 E Market St	Blairsville	PA	15717	724-459-6100		532-2
Blais, Halpert & Lieberman LLC 1 Financial Ctr 15th Fl *Web:* blaistaxlaw.com	Boston	MA	02111	617-918-7080		41
Blaise Alexander Chevrolet Inc 933 Broad St *Web:* www.blaisealexander.com	Montoursville	PA	17754	570-368-8677		57
Blake & Associates Law Firm 45 School St *Web:* blakelaw.com	Boston	MA	02108	617-723-3224		41
Blake Brothers International Inc 7 N Blvd *Web:* www.blakebros.com	Amherst	NH	03031	603-886-3700	882-3949	411
Blake International USA Rigs LLC 410 S Van Ave *Web:* www.blakeinternationalrigs.com	Houma	LA	70363	985-274-2200		539
Blake Law Firm PC 5225 N Central Ave Ste 101 *Web:* accidentlawyersarizona.com	Phoenix	AZ	85012	602-274-7000		41
Blake Medical Ctr 2020 59th St W *TF:* 800-523-5827 ■ *Web:* blakemedicalcenter.com	Bradenton	FL	34209	941-792-6611		374-3
Blake Real Estate Co 1150 Connecticut Ave NW *Web:* www.blakereal.com	Washington	DC	20036	202-778-0400	223-9636	186
Blake School 110 Blake Rd S *Web:* www.blakeschool.org	Hopkins	MN	55343	952-988-3405	988-3455	623
Blakely Construction Company Inc 2830 W I-20 *TF:* 800-604-9339 ■ *Web:* www.blakelycc.com	Odessa	TX	79763	432-381-3540		539
Blakely New York 136 W 55th St *TF:* 800-735-0710 ■ *Web:* www.blakelynewyork.com	New York	NY	10019	212-245-1800	582-8332	379
Blakemore & Associates 1 Greenway Plz Ste 225 *Web:* www.gophq.com	Houston	TX	77046	713-526-3399	965-9076	194
Blakeney Communications Inc 4580 Hwy 15 N PO Box 6408 *Web:* www.b95country.com	Laurel	MS	39441	601-649-0095		647
Blakeslee Advertising 916 N Charles St *Web:* www.blakesleeadv.com	Baltimore	MD	21201	410-727-8800		809
Blakeslee Arpaia Chapman Inc 200 N Branford Rd *Web:* www.bac-inc.com	Branford	CT	06405	203-488-2500	488-4538	183
Blakeslee Prestress Inc Rt 139 McDermott Rd *Web:* www.blakesleeprestress.com	Branford	CT	06405	203-481-5306	481-3562	183
Blakey, Yost, Bupp & Rausch 17 E Market St *Web:* blakeyyost.com	York	PA	17401	717-845-3674		41
Blakinger Thomas PC 28 Penn Sq *Web:* www.blakingerthomas.com	Lancaster	PA	17603	717-299-1100		428
Blalock Walters PA 802 11th St W *Web:* blalockwalters.com	Bradenton	FL	34205	941-748-0100	745-2093	428
Blanca Commercial Real Estate Inc 1450 Brickell Ave Ste 2060 *Web:* blancacre.com	Miami	FL	33131	305-577-8850		652
Blanchard Compact Equipment 1410 Ashville Hwy *TF:* 888-799-3606 ■ *Web:* www.blanchardmachinery.com	Spartanburg	SC	29303	864-582-1245		274
Blanchard Valley Hospital 1900 S Main St *Web:* www.bvhealthsystem.org	Findlay	OH	45840	419-423-4500		374-3
Blanco America Inc 110 Mt Holly By-Pass *TF:* 800-451-5782 ■ *Web:* www.blanco.com	Lumberton	NJ	08048	800-451-5782		362
Blanco County 101 E Pecan *Web:* www.co.blanco.tx.us	Johnson City	TX	78636	830-868-0973	868-2084	338
Blanco State Park PO Box 493 *Web:* tpwd.texas.gov	Blanco	TX	78606	830-833-4333		565
Bland Correctional Ctr 256 Bland Farm Rd *Web:* vadoc.virginia.gov	Bland	VA	24315	276-688-3341		213

Name / Address	City	State	ZIP	Phone	Fax	Class
Bland County 612 Main St Ste 104 TF: 800-519-3468 ■ Web: www.blandcountyva.gov	Bland	VA	24315	276-688-4622	688-9758	338
Bland Farms Inc 1126 Raymond Bland Rd TF: 800-440-9543 ■ Web: blandfarms.com	Glennville	GA	30427	800-440-9543		297-7
Blandford Nature Ctr 1715 Hillburn Ave NW Web: blandfordnaturecenter.org	Grand Rapids	MI	49504	616-735-6240		50-5
Blane Canada Ltd PO Box 4408 Web: blanecanada.com	Wheaton	IL	60189	630-462-9222		195
Blaney McMurtry LLP 2 Queen St E Ste 1500 Web: www.blaney.com	Toronto	ON	M5C3G5	416-593-1221	593-5437	428
Blank Park Zoo 7401 SW Ninth St Web: www.blankparkzoo.com	Des Moines	IA	50315	515-285-4722		823
Blank Quilting Corp 49 W 37th St 14th Fl *Fax Area Code: 212 ■ TF: 800-294-9495 ■ Web: blankquilting.net	New York	NY	10018	800-294-9495	679-4578*	594
Blank Rome LLP 1 Logan Sq 130 N 18th St Web: www.blankrome.com	Philadelphia	PA	19103	215-569-5500	569-5555	428
Blank Wesselink Cook & Associates Inc 2623 E Pershing Rd PO Box 2910 Web: www.bwcinc.com	Decatur	IL	62526	217-428-0973	428-8934	261
Blanke Industries Inc 1099 Brown St Ste 103 Web: blankeindustries.com	Wauconda	IL	60084	847-487-2780	487-2799	419
Blanks Printing & Imaging Inc 2343 N Beckley Web: www.blanks.com	Dallas	TX	75208	214-741-3905	741-6105	781
Blanks/USA Inc 7700 68th Ave N Ste 7 TF: 800-328-7311 ■ Web: blanksusa.com	Minneapolis	MN	55428	800-328-7311		560
BLANKSPACES Mid Wilshire 5405 Wilshire Blvd Web: www.blankspaces.com	Los Angeles	CA	90036	323-330-9505		23
Blanton & Associates Inc 5 Lakeway Centre Ct Ste 200 Web: www.blantonassociates.com	Austin	TX	78734	512-264-1095		194
Blanton Museum of Art University of Texas at Austin 200 E Martin Luther King Jr Blvd Web: blantonmuseum.org	Austin	TX	78701	512-471-7324	471-7023	520
Blantyre 16 Blantyre Rd PO Box 995 TF: 844-881-0104 ■ Web: blantyre.com	Lenox	MA	01240	413-637-3556		379
Blarney Castle Oil Co 12218 W St PO Box 246 Web: blarneycastleoil.com	Bear Lake	MI	49614	231-864-3111		539
Blaser Die Casting Co 5700 Third Ave S Web: www.blasercasting.com	Seattle	WA	98108	206-767-7800		308
Blaser Swisslube Inc 31 Hatfield Ln Web: www.blaser.com	Goshen	NY	10924	845-294-3200		536
Blasingame, Burch, Garrard & Ashley PC 440 College Ave Ste 320 TF: 866-354-3544 ■ Web: www.bbga.com	Athens	GA	30601	706-584-2794		428
Blast Analytics and Marketing Inc 6020 W Oaks Blvd Ste 260 TF: 888-252-7866 ■ Web: www.blastanalytics.com	Rocklin	CA	95765	916-724-6701		180
Blast Communications Inc 1444 N Farnsworth Ave Ste 304 Web: www.blastcomm.com	Aurora	IL	60505	630-375-9600		224
Blast Intermediate Unit 17 2400 Reach Rd Web: www.iu17.org	Williamsport	PA	17701	570-323-8561		685
Blast Radius 509 Richards St TF: 866-473-6800 ■ Web: www.blastradius.com	Vancouver	BC	V6B2Z6	416-214-4220		7
Blatt Billiard Corp 330 W 38th St TF: 800-252-8855 ■ Web: blattbilliards.com	New York	NY	10018	212-674-8855		761
Blattel Communications 250 Montgomery St Ste 1200 Web: blattel.com	San Francisco	CA	94104	415-397-4811	956-5125	636
Blattner Steel Company Inc 2100 Rust Ave Web: www.blattnersteel.com	Cape Girardeau	MO	63703	573-339-1129		492
Blatts Pattern Shop 760 Meckville Rd Web: blattspatternshop.com	Fredericksburg	PA	17026	717-933-5633	933-5021	567
Blau Law Firm PLLC 101 Park Ave Ste 600 Web: blaulawfirm.com	Oklahoma City	OK	73102	405-232-2528	232-2532	41
Blauch Bros Inc 911 Chicago Ave Web: blauchbrothers.com	Harrisonburg	VA	22802	540-434-2589		610
Blauer Manufacturing Company Inc 20 Aberdeen St TF: 800-225-6715 ■ Web: www.blauer.com	Boston	MA	02215	617-536-6606	536-6948	155-19
Blauvelt State Park Rte 303 North to East Greenbush Rd Web: parks.ny.gov	Blauvelt	NY	10913	845-359-0544		565
Blax Inc 9861 Colbert TF: 888-523-2529 ■ Web: blax.ca	Montreal	QC	H1J1Z9	514-523-4600		180
Blaze Fireplaces of Northern California Inc 101 Cargo Way Web: www.blazefireplaces.com	San Francisco	CA	94124	415-495-2002		361
Blaze Marketing Solutions Ltd 1000 Windmill Rd Ste 32 Web: blazemarketing.com	Dartmouth	NS	B3B1L7	902-468-0537		195
Blaze Technical Services Inc 1445 Commerce Dr *Fax Area Code: 800 ■ TF: 800-791-9874 ■ Web: www.blazeprobes.com	Stow	OH	44224	330-923-0409	218-8345*	472
Blazer Industries Inc PO Box 489 TF: 877-211-3437 ■ Web: www.blazerind.com	Aumsville	OR	97325	503-749-1900	749-3969	106
BlazeTech Corp 29B Montvale Ave TF: 888-933-5783 ■ Web: www.blazetech.com	Woburn	MA	01801	781-759-0700	759-0703	192
Blazing Editions 42 Ladd St Web: www.blazing.com	East Greenwich	RI	02818	401-885-4329		522
Blazing Technologies Inc 4631A Morgantown Rd Web: www.blazingtech.net	Mohnton	PA	19540	484-722-4800		697

Name / Address	City	State	ZIP	Phone	Fax	Class
Bleakley Platt & Schmidt 1 N Lexington Ave Web: bpslaw.com	White Plains	NY	10601	914-949-2700		41
Blecher & Collins 515 S Figueroa St Ste 1750 Web: www.blechercollins.com	Los Angeles	CA	90071	213-622-4222	622-1656	428
Bleckley County 112 N Second St Web: www.bleckley.org	Cochran	GA	31014	478-934-3200		338
Bledsoe Cattle Company LLLP 41726 US 385 PO Box 406 *Fax Area Code: 215	Wray	CO	80758	970-332-4955	324-0417*	10-1
Bledsoe County PO Box 205 Web: www.pikeville-bledsoe.com	Pikeville	TN	37367	423-447-2791		338
Bledsoe Creek State Park 400 Zieglers Ft Rd Web: www.state.tn.us	Gallatin	TN	37066	615-452-3706		565
Bledsoe Telephone Co-opeartive Corp (BTC) 338 Cumberland Ave PO Box 609 Web: bledsoe.net	Pikeville	TN	37367	423-447-2121	447-2498	736
Blencowe IT 1601 Shop Rd Ste C Web: blencowe.com	Columbia	SC	29201	803-779-5866	256-4127	35
Blendex Company Inc 11208 Electron Dr Web: www.blendex.com	Louisville	KY	40299	502-267-1003	267-1024	296-23
Blendtec Inc 1206 S 1680 W Web: www.blendtec.com	Orem	UT	84058	801-222-0888		37
Blenko Glass Co PO Box 67 TF: 877-425-3656 ■ Web: blenko.com	Milton	WV	25541	304-743-9081		334
Blennerhassett Island Historical State Park 137 Juliana St Web: wvstateparks.com	Parkersburg	WV	26101	304-420-4800		565
Blentech Corp 2899 Dowd Dr Web: blentech.com	Santa Rosa	CA	95407	707-523-5949		298
Bler Travel Inc 45 Bartlett Crescent Rd TF: 800-399-8467 ■ Web: www.bler.com	Brookline	MA	02446	617-738-0500		771
Bless Your Heart Restaurants LLC 3701 19th St PO Box 54232	Lubbock	TX	79410	806-791-2211		671
Blessey Marine Services Inc 1515 River Oaks Rd E Web: www.blessey.com	Harahan	LA	70123	504-734-1156		763
Blessing Health System Broadway at 11th St TF: 866-460-3933 ■ Web: www.blessinghealth.org	Quincy	IL	62301	217-223-8400	223-6891	374-3
Blessing Hospital School of Radiologic Technology 11th & 14th St PO Box 7005 Web: www.blessinghealth.org	Quincy	IL	62305	217-223-1200		685
Blessing White Inc 200 Clocktower Dr TF: 800-222-1349 ■ Web: blessingwhite.com	Hamilton Township	NJ	08690	609-528-3535		463
Blessingway Authors' Services 134 E Lupita Rd Web: www.blessingway.com	Santa Fe	NM	87505	505-983-2649	983-2005	637-2
BLET (Brotherhood of Locomotive Engineers & Trainmen) 7061 E Pleasant Valley Rd Web: www.ble-t.org	Independence	OH	44131	216-241-2630	241-6516	414
Bleublancrouge 780 Brewster Ave 4th Fl Web: www.bleublancrouge.ca	Montreal	QC	H4C2K1	514-875-7007		636
Bleyer Insurance Agency Inc 802 N Court St Web: bleyerinsurance.com	Marion	IL	62959	618-997-6347		390
Bleyhl Farm Service Inc 940 E Wine Country Rd TF: 800-862-6806 ■ Web: www.bleyhl.com	Grandview	WA	98930	509-882-2248	882-4208	276
Bleyl Engineering 1715 S Capital of Texas Hwy Ste 109 Web: bleylengineering.com	Austin	TX	78746	512-328-7878	328-7884	256
BLI (Bulk Lift International Inc) 1013 Tamarac Dr TF: 800-879-2247 ■ Web: www.bulklift.com	Carpentersville	IL	60110	847-428-6059	428-7180	67
BLI (Big Lots Inc) 300 Phillipi Rd NYSE: BIG ■ TF: 877-998-1697 ■ Web: www.biglots.com	Columbus	OH	43228	614-278-6800	278-8322	791
Blichmann Engineering LLC 1600 Canal Rd Ste A Web: blichmannengineering.com	LaFayette	IN	47904	765-421-2018		261
Blickman Inc 500 US Hwy 46 E Web: www.blickman.com	Clifton	NJ	07011	973-330-0557		475
Bliley Technologies Inc 2545 W Grandview Blvd Web: www.bliley.com	Erie	PA	16506	814-838-3571	833-2712	253
Blind Ctr, The 1001 N Bruce St Web: blindcenter.org	Las Vegas	NV	89101	702-642-6000		34
Blind Tiger Brewery & Restaurant 417 SW 37th St Web: www.blindtiger.com	Topeka	KS	66611	785-267-7527		671
Blink Health 1407 Broadway Ste 2100 TF: 844-265-6444 ■ Web: www.blinkhealth.com	New York	NY	10018	844-265-6444		354
Blink Press 83 Taylor St Ste 2 Web: www.blinkpress.com	Waltham	MA	02453	781-608-3210		637-10
Blinn College 902 College Ave Web: www.blinn.edu	Brenham	TX	77833	979-830-4000	830-4110	162
Blinn, Farrell & Co 60 Bailey Blvd Ste 3 Web: www.blinnfarrell.com	Haverhill	MA	01830	978-372-8518	372-6462	2
Blish-Mize Co 223 S Fifth St TF: 800-995-0525 ■ Web: www.blishmize.com	Atchison	KS	66002	913-367-1250	367-0667	351
Bliss & Nyitray Inc 5835 Blue Lagoon Dr Ste 400 Web: www.bnienginee rs.com	Miami	FL	33126	305-442-7086		261
Bliss Clearing Niagara (BCN) 1004 E State St TF: 800-642-5477 ■ Web: www.bcntechserv.com	Hastings	MI	49058	269-948-3300	948-3313	456
Bliss Communications Inc PO Box 5001 Web: www.blissnet.net	Janesville	WI	53547	608-754-3311		643
Bliss Direct Media 641 15th Ave NE TF: 800-578-7947 ■ Web: www.blissdirect.com	Saint Joseph	MN	56374	320-271-1600		387

	Phone	Fax	Class
Bliss Mcknight Inc 2801 E Empire .... Bloomington IL 61704 *Web:* blissmcknight.com	309-663-1393		390
Blistex Inc 1800 Swift Dr .... Oak Brook IL 60523 *TF:* 800-837-1800 ■ *Web:* www.blistex.com	630-571-2870		582
Blithewold Mansion Gardens & Arboretum 101 Ferry Rd Rt 114 .... Bristol RI 02809 *Web:* www.blithewold.org	401-253-2707	253-0412	97
Blitman & King LLP 16 W Main St Powers Bldg Ste 500 .... Rochester NY 14614 *Web:* bklawyers.com	585-232-5600	232-7738	445
Blitt & Gaines Pc 661 Glenn Ave .... Wheeling IL 60090 *TF:* 888-920-0620 ■ *Web:* blittandgaines.com	847-403-4900		428
Blizzard Internet Marketing Inc 1001 Grand Ave Ste 005 .... Glenwood Springs CO 81601 *TF:* 888-840-5893 ■ *Web:* www.blizzardinternet.com	970-928-7875	928-7874	225
BLJ Group LLC 5555 Glenridge Connector Ste 200 .... Atlanta GA 30342 *Web:* bljgroup.com	404-281-9056		194
BLM (Bureau of Land Management) 1849 C St NW Rm 5665 .... Washington DC 20240 *Web:* www.blm.gov	202-208-3801	208-5242	340-13
Bloated Toe Enterprises PO Box 324 .... Peru NY 12972 *TF:* 866-455-1071 ■ *Web:* www.bloatedtoe.com	518-563-9469		637-2
Block & Co 1111 S Wheeling Rd .... Wheeling IL 60090 *TF:* 800-323-7556 ■ *Web:* www.blockandcompany.com	800-323-7556	435-5707	567
Block Communications Inc 405 Madison Ave Ste 2100 .... Toledo OH 43604 *Web:* www.blockcommunications.com	419-724-6212		360-3
Block Engineering Inc 377 Simarano Dr .... Marlborough MA 01752 *Web:* www.blockeng.com	508-251-3100		419
Block Hawley Commercial Real Estate Services LLC 16253 Swingley Ridge Rd Ste 150 .... Chesterfield MO 63017 *Web:* www.blockllc.com	636-534-2900		652
Block Insurance Agency Inc 2333 Highland St .... Allentown PA 18104 *Web:* blockins.com	610-433-4131	433-1531	390
Block Insurance Agency Inc 315 E Wapakoneta St .... Waynesfield OH 45896 *TF:* 800-653-5620 ■ *Web:* blockagency.com	419-568-4801		390
Block Iron & Supply Co PO Box 557 .... Oshkosh WI 54903 *TF:* 800-236-7771 ■ *Web:* blockiron.com	920-231-8645		351
Block Law Firm, Aplc 422 E First St .... Thibodaux LA 70301 *Web:* blocklawfirm.com	985-446-0418		41
Block Scientific Inc 22 Sawgrass Dr .... Bellport NY 11713 *TF:* 866-203-5777 ■ *Web:* www.blockscientific.com	631-589-1118	589-4088	475
Block Steel Corp 6101 Oakton St .... Skokie IL 60077 *Web:* blocksteel.com	847-966-3000	966-5906	723
Blocker & Wallace Service LLC 1472 Rogers Ave .... Memphis TN 38114 *TF:* 800-843-0551 ■ *Web:* www.blockerandwallace.com	901-274-0708		791
Blodgett Supply Company Inc 100 Ave D PO Box 759 .... Williston VT 05495 *Web:* www.blodgettsupply.com	802-864-9831	229-5105	38
Bloedel Reserve, The 7571 NE Dolphin Dr .... Bainbridge Island WA 98110 *Web:* bloedelreserve.org	206-842-7631		97
Bloedorn Lumber 2120 Main St PO Box 1077 .... Torrington WY 82240 *Web:* www.bloedornlumber.com	307-532-2151	532-3760	364
Blohm Creative Partners 1331 E Grand River Ave Ste 210 .... East Lansing MI 48823 *Web:* blohmcreative.com	517-333-4900	336-9404	7
Blommer Chocolate Co 600 W Kinzie St .... Chicago IL 60610 *TF:* 800-621-1606 ■ *Web:* www.blommer.com	312-226-7700		296-8
Blomquist, Collins & Beever PC 12016 Jones Maltsberger Ste 400 .... San Antonio TX 78247 *Web:* bcb-ogmlaw.com	210-497-2600		41
Blonder Tongue Laboratories Inc 1 Jake Brown Rd .... Old Bridge NJ 08857 *NYSE:* BDR ■ *TF:* 877-407-8033 ■ *Web:* www.blondertongue.com	732-679-4000	679-4353	647
Blood & Marrow Transplant Group of Georgia (BMTGA) 5670 Peachtree Dunwoody Rd Ste 1000 .... Atlanta GA 30342 *Web:* www.bmtga.com	404-255-1930	255-1939	769
Blood Assurance Inc 705 E Fourth St .... Chattanooga TN 37403 *TF:* 800-962-0628 ■ *Web:* www.bloodassurance.org	423-756-0966		89
Blood Bank Computer Systems Inc 1002 15th St SW Ste 120 .... Auburn WA 98001 *TF:* 888-738-2227 ■ *Web:* www.bbcsinc.com	253-333-0046	217-4730	476
Blood Bank of Alaska 4000 Laurel St .... Anchorage AK 99508 *Web:* www.bloodbankofalaska.org	907-222-5600	563-1371	89
Blood Bank of Delmarva 100 Hygeia Dr .... Newark DE 19713 *TF:* 800-548-4009 ■ *Web:* www.delmarvablood.org	302-737-8405	737-8233	89
Blood Bank of Hawaii 2043 Dillingham Blvd .... Honolulu HI 96819 *TF:* 800-372-9966 ■ *Web:* www.bbh.org	808-845-9966		89
Blood Center of Northcentral Wisconsin 211 Forest St .... Wausau WI 54403 *Web:* bcnwi.org	715-842-0761		89
Blood Centers of the Pacific 250 Bush St Ste 136 .... San Francisco CA 94104 *TF:* 888-393-4483 ■ *Web:* www.bloodcenters.org	415-567-6400		89
Blood Ctr, The 2609 Canal St .... New Orleans LA 70119 *TF:* 800-862-5663 ■ *Web:* www.thebloodcenter.org	504-524-1322	592-1580	89
BloodCenter of Wisconsin 638 N 18th St .... Milwaukee WI 53233 *Web:* www.versiti.org	414-933-5000		89
Blood-Horse Magazine PO Box 911088 .... Lexington KY 40591 *TF:* 800-866-2361 ■ *Web:* www.bloodhorse.com	859-276-6743	276-4450	457-14
Bloodroot 85 Ferris St .... Bridgeport CT 06605 *Web:* www.bloodroot.com	203-576-9168		671
Bloodstock Research Information Services Inc PO Box 4097 .... Lexington KY 40544 *TF:* 800-354-9206 ■ *Web:* www.brisnet.com	859-223-4444	223-7024	387
Bloodworks Northwest 921 Terry Ave .... Seattle WA 98104 *TF:* 800-366-2831 ■ *Web:* www.bloodworksnw.org	206-292-6500		89
Bloom Engineering Company Inc 5460 Horning Rd .... Pittsburgh PA 15236 *Web:* www.bloomeng.com	412-653-3500	653-2253	318
Bloomberg LP 731 Lexington Ave .... New York NY 10022 *Web:* www.bloomberg.com	212-318-2000	893-5000	530
Bloomerang 5724 Birtz Rd .... Indianapolis IN 46216 *Web:* www.bloomerang.co	317-296-8100		180
Bloomfield Bicycle & Repair Shop Inc 38 Tunxis Ave .... Bloomfield CT 06002 *Web:* bloomfieldbike.com	860-242-9884		711
Bloomfield College 467 Franklin St .... Bloomfield NJ 07003 *TF:* 800-848-4555 ■ *Web:* www.bloomfield.edu	973-748-9000	748-0916	166
Bloomfield Public Library 90 Broad St .... Bloomfield NJ 07003 *Web:* www.bplnj.org	973-566-6200		434-3
Bloomfield Township Public Library 1099 Lone Pine Rd .... Bloomfield Hills MI 48302 *Web:* btpl.org	248-642-5800		434-3
Blooming Color Inc 230 Eisenhower Ln N .... Lombard IL 60148 *Web:* www.bloomingcolor.com	630-705-9200	705-1212	92
Blooming Rose Press PO Box 1211 .... Mount Shasta CA 96067 *Web:* www.bloomingrosepress.com	530-926-2833		637-2
Bloomingdale Florist 827 E Bloomingdale Ave .... Brandon FL 33511 *TF:* 800-940-7304 ■ *Web:* www.bloomingdaleflowers.com	813-654-7304		293
Bloomingdale Home Telephone Co (BHTC) 38 S Main St .... Bloomingdale IN 47832 *Web:* bdalehtc.wixsite.com	765-498-2000	498-8000	224
Bloomingdale's 1000 3rd Ave .... New York NY 10022 *Web:* locations.bloomingdales.com	212-705-2000		229
Bloomington Chateau Hotel & Conference Ctr 1621 Jumer Dr .... Bloomington IL 61704 *Web:* www.bloomingtonchateau.com	309-662-2020		379
Bloomington City Hall 401 N Morton St .... Bloomington IN 47404 *Web:* bloomington.in.gov	812-339-2261	349-3570	337
Bloomington Convention & Visitors Bureau (BCVB) 7900 International Dr Ste 990 .... Bloomington MN 55425 *TF:* 800-346-4289 ■ *Web:* www.bloomingtonmn.org	952-858-8500	858-8854	206
Bloomington Cooking School 115 N College Ave Ste 14 .... Bloomington IN 47404 *Web:* www.bloomingtoncookingschool.com	812-333-7100		685
Bloomington Monroe County Convention Ctr 302 S College Ave .... Bloomington IN 47403 *Web:* www.bloomingtonconvention.com	812-336-3681	349-2981	205
Bloomington Public Library 205 E Olive St .... Bloomington IL 61701 *Web:* www.bloomingtonlibrary.org	309-828-6091		434-3
Bloomington Speedway 5185 S Fairfax Rd .... Bloomington IN 47401 *Web:* www.bloomingtonspeedway.com	812-824-7400		515
Bloomington/Monroe County Convention & Visitors Bureau 2855 N Walnut St .... Bloomington IN 47404 *TF:* 800-800-0037 ■ *Web:* www.visitbloomington.com	812-334-8900	334-2344	206
Bloomington-Normal Area Convention & Visitors Bureau 3201 Cira Dr Ste 201 .... Bloomington IL 61704 *TF:* 800-433-8226 ■ *Web:* www.visitbn.org	309-665-0033	661-0743	206
BloomNation LLC 8889 W Olympic Blvd .... Beverly Hills CA 90211 *TF:* 877-702-5666 ■ *Web:* www.bloomnation.com	210-405-5050		292
BloomNet 1 Old Country Rd Ste 500 .... Carle Place NY 11514 *TF:* 866-256-6663 ■ *Web:* www.bloomnet.net	866-256-6663		387
Blooms by the Box 775 Mountain Blvd Ste 104 .... Watchung NJ 07069 *TF:* 855-289-2566 ■ *Web:* www.bloomsbythebox.com	908-791-0487		293
Bloomsburg Area Chamber of Commerce 238 Market St .... Bloomsburg PA 17815 *Web:* www.bloomsburg.org	570-784-2522	784-2661	139
Bloomsburg Carpet Industries Inc 4999 Columbia Blvd .... Bloomsburg PA 17815 *TF:* 800-233-8773 ■ *Web:* www.bloomsburgcarpet.com	570-784-9188		131
Bloomsburg University 400 E Second St .... Bloomsburg PA 17815 *TF:* 888-651-6117 ■ *Web:* www.bloomu.edu	570-389-3900	389-4795	166
Bloomsbury Bistro 509 W Whitaker Mill Rd Ste 101 .... Raleigh NC 27608 *Web:* www.bloomsburybistro.com	919-834-9011		671
Blossman Gas Inc 4601 Hanshaw Rd .... Ocean Springs MS 39564 *TF:* 800-256-7762 ■ *Web:* blossmangas.com	228-872-8747		316
Blossman Oil Company Inc 703 N Polk St .... Covington LA 70433 *Web:* www.blossmanoil.com	985-892-2401		324
Blossom Chevrolet Inc 1850 N Shadeland Ave .... Indianapolis IN 46219 *Web:* www.blossomchevrolet.com	317-357-1121		57
Blossom Restaurant 171 E Bay St .... Charleston SC 29401 *Web:* www.blossomcharleston.com	843-722-9200		671
Blossom Telephone Co (BTC) 145 Center St .... Blossom TX 75416 *Web:* www.blossomtel.net	903-982-6211		224
Blossoms Inc 33866 Woodward Ave .... Birmingham MI 48009 *Web:* www.blossomsbirmingham.com	248-644-4411		292
Blough Tech Inc 119 S Broad St .... Cairo GA 39828 *TF:* 800-957-0554 ■ *Web:* www.bloughtech.com	229-377-8825		180
Blount County 201 S Washington St .... Maryville TN 37804 *Web:* www.blounttn.org	865-273-5700	273-5705	338
Blount County Chamber of Commerce 201 S Washington St .... Maryville TN 37804 *Web:* www.blountchamber.com	865-983-2241	984-1386	139
Blount County Public Library 508 N Cusick St .... Maryville TN 37804 *Web:* www.blounttn.org	865-982-0981		434-3
Blount County Schools 204 Second Ave E .... Oneonta AL 35121 *Web:* www.blountboe.net	205-625-4102		685
Blount Fine Foods Corp 630 Currant Rd .... Fall River MA 02720 *TF:* 800-274-2526 ■ *Web:* www.blountfinefoods.com	774-888-1300	888-1399	296-14

Name / Address	City	State	Zip	Phone	Fax	Class
Blount Hospitality House 610 Madison St *Web:* www.blounthospitalityhouse.org	Huntsville	AL	35801	256-534-7014		372
Blount Mansion 200 W Hill Ave *Web:* www.blountmansion.org	Knoxville	TN	37901	865-525-2375	546-5315	50-3
Blount Memorial Hospital 907 E Lamar Alexander Pkwy *TF:* 800-448-0219 ■ *Web:* blountmemorial.org	Maryville	TN	37804	865-983-7211		374-3
Blount Outdoor Products Group 4909 SE International Way *Web:* blount.com	Portland	OR	97222	503-653-8881		429
Blount Small Ship Adventures 461 Water St *TF:* 800-556-7450 ■ *Web:* www.blountsmallshipadventures.com	Warren	RI	02885	401-247-0955		220
Blount-Oneonta Chamber of Commerce 201 1st Ave E *Web:* blountoneontachamber.org	Oneonta	AL	35121	205-274-2153	274-2099	139
Blow Fly Inn 1201 Washington Ave *Web:* www.blowflygulfport.com	Gulfport	MS	39507	228-265-8225		671
Blow Molded Products Inc 4720 Felspar St *Web:* blowmoldedproducts.com	Riverside	CA	92509	951-360-6055		608
Blow Molded Specialties Inc 222 Bronder Dr *Web:* www.blowmolded.com	Foley	MN	56329	320-968-7251		596
Blower Application Company Inc N 114 W 19125 Clinton Dr *TF:* 800-959-0880 ■ *Web:* www.bloapco.com	Germantown	WI	53022	262-255-5580	255-3446	386
Blowfish Direct LLC 6160 Bristol Pkwy Ste 100 *TF:* 877-725-6934 ■ *Web:* blowfishshoes.com	Culver City	CA	90230	310-566-5700		690
Blowfish Sushi 2170 Bryant St *Web:* www.blowfishsushi.com	San Francisco	CA	94110	415-285-3848		671
Blowing Rock Chamber of Commerce (BRCC) 132 Park Ave *TF:* 800-295-7851 ■ *Web:* www.blowingrockncchamber.com	Blowing Rock	NC	28605	828-295-7851	295-7651	139
BLR (Business & Legal Reports Inc) 141 Mill Rock Rd E *TF:* 800-727-5257 ■ *Web:* www.blr.com	Old Saybrook	CT	06475	860-510-0100	510-7225	637-9
BLT Enterprises 1714 16th St *Web:* blt-enterprises.com	Santa Monica	CA	90404	310-314-0800		358
BLT Prime 2012 Central Ave *Web:* bltrestaurants.com	New York	NY	10010	212-995-8500		671
BLU Restaurant 4 Avery St 4th Fl *Web:* www.blurestaurant.com	Boston	MA	02111	617-375-8550		671
Bluberi Gaming & Technologies inc 2120 Rue Letendre *Web:* www.bluberi.com	Drummondville	QC	J2C7E9	819-475-5155		133
Blue & Company LLC 12800 N Meridian St Ste 400 *Web:* www.blueandco.com	Carmel	IN	46032	317-848-8920	573-2458	2
Blue & Gold Sausage Inc 10101 N Hiwassee Rd *Web:* www.blueandgoldsausage.com	Jones	OK	73049	405-399-2954	399-2918	296-26
Blue & Gray Bar & Grill 2 Baltimore St *Web:* www.bluegraybargrill.com	Gettysburg	PA	17325	717-334-1999		671
Blue 9 Capital 145 Hudson St Ste 401 *Web:* www.blue9capital.com	New York	NY	10013	212-798-0400	798-0401	690
Blue Adobe Grille 10885 N Frank Lloyd Wright Blvd *Web:* www.blueadobegrille.com	Scottsdale	AZ	85259	480-314-0550		671
Blue Banner Company Inc 2601 Third St *Web:* www.pe.com	Riverside	CA	92507	951-686-2422		315-2
Blue Barn Theatre 1106 S Tenth St *Web:* bluebarn.org	Omaha	NE	68108	402-345-1576		572
Blue Beacon International Inc PO Box 856 *Web:* www.bluebeacon.com	Salina	KS	67401	785-825-2221	825-0801	62-1
Blue Bell Creameries Inc PO Box 1807 *Web:* www.bluebell.com	Brenham	TX	77834	979-836-7977		296-25
Blue Beyond Consulting 20211 Patio Dr Ste235 *Web:* www.bluebeyondconsulting.com	Castro Valley	CA	94546	510-733-5417		194
Blue Bird Bistro 1700 Summit St *Web:* bluebirdbistro.com	Kansas City	MO	64108	816-221-7559		671
Blue Bird Corp 402 Blue Bird Blvd *Web:* www.blue-bird.com	Fort Valley	GA	31030	478-825-2021		516
Blue Bird Inc 10135 Mill Rd PO Box 378 *TF:* 800-828-4106 ■ *Web:* www.bluebirdpears.com	Peshastin	WA	98847	509-548-1700	548-0288	315-3
Blue Book Services Inc 845 E Geneva Rd *Web:* bluebookservices.com	Carol Stream	IL	60188	630-668-3500		5
Blue C Advertising 3183-C Airway Ave *Web:* bluecusa.com	Costa Mesa	CA	92626	714-540-5700		7
Blue Cactus Bar & Grill 2 ByWard Market *Web:* www.bluecactusbarandgrill.com	Ottawa	ON	K1N7A1	613-241-7061		671
Blue Canoe 1198 S Van Ness Ave *Web:* www.bluecanoe.com	San Francisco	CA	94124	415-648-5000	648-5009	157-2
Blue Canoe Properties LLC 1601 21st St S **Fax Area Code:* 623	Birmingham	AL	35205	205-918-0921	386-7332*	652
Blue Care Network of Michigan PO Box 284 **Fax Area Code:* 248 ■ *TF:* 800-662-6667 ■ *Web:* www.bcbsm.com	Southfield	MI	48076	800-662-6667	799-6969*	391-3
Blue Cat Design Mastwoods Rd *Web:* www.bluecatdesign.com	Port Hope	ON	L1A3V5	905-753-1017	753-2777	7
Blue Chip Casino Inc 777 Blue Chip Dr *TF:* 888-879-7711 ■ *Web:* www.bluechipcasino.com	Michigan City	IN	46360	219-879-7711		133
Blue Chip Computer Systems 2554 Lincoln Blvd Ste 232 *TF:* 800-325-9868 ■ *Web:* www.bccs.com	Venice	CA	90291	310-410-0126		177
Blue Chip Group Inc 1911 S 3850 W *TF:* 800-878-0099 ■ *Web:* www.augasonfarms.com	Salt Lake City	UT	84104	801-269-1067		66
Blue Chip Venture Co 1308 Race St Ste 200 *Web:* bcvc.com	Cincinnati	OH	45202	513-723-2300		792
Blue Cliff Career College 2970 Cottage Hill Rd Ste 175 *Web:* www.blue.edu	Mobile	AL	36606	251-473-2220		167-3
Blue Compass Interactive 1601 48th St Ste 200 *Web:* bluecompass.com	West Des Moines	IA	50266	515-868-0010		180
Blue Corn Cafe 716 Ninth St *Web:* bluecorncafedurham.com	Durham	NC	27705	919-286-9600		671
Blue Cow Software Inc 50 Salem St **Fax Area Code:* 781 ■ *TF:* 888-499-2583 ■ *Web:* bluecowsoftware.com	Lynnfield	MA	01940	888-499-2583	623-0087*	180
Blue Cross & Blue Shield Assn 225 N Michigan Ave *TF:* 888-630-2583 ■ *Web:* www.bcbs.com	Chicago	IL	60601	312-297-6000		49-9
Blue Cross & Blue Shield of Kansas City 2301 Main St *TF:* 800-892-6048 ■ *Web:* www.bluekc.com	Kansas City	MO	64108	816-395-2222	395-2726	391-3
Blue Cross & Blue Shield of Mississippi PO Box 1043 *TF:* 800-222-8046 ■ *Web:* www.bcbsms.com	Jackson	MS	39215	601-932-3704	932-4843	391-3
Blue Cross & Blue Shield of Montana 560 N Park Ave PO Box 4309 *TF:* 800-447-7828 ■ *Web:* www.bcbsmt.com	Helena	MT	59604	406-437-5000		391-3
Blue Cross & Blue Shield of Nebraska 1919 Aksarben Dr PO Box 3248 *TF:* 800-422-2763 ■ *Web:* www.nebraskablue.com	Omaha	NE	68180	402-982-7000		391-3
Blue Cross & Blue Shield of New Mexico PO Box 27630 *TF:* 800-835-8699 ■ *Web:* www.bcbsnm.com	Albuquerque	NM	87125	505-291-3500		391-3
Blue Cross & Blue Shield of North Carolina 4615 University Dr PO Box 2291 *TF:* 800-446-8053 ■ *Web:* www.bluecrossnc.com	Durham	NC	27707	919-489-7431		391-3
Blue Cross & Blue Shield of Oklahoma 1215 S Boulder Ave *TF:* 800-942-5837 ■ *Web:* www.bcbsok.com	Tulsa	OK	74119	918-560-3500		391-3
Blue Cross & Blue Shield of Rhode Island 500 Exchange St *TF:* 800-637-3718 ■ *Web:* www.bcbsri.com	Providence	RI	02903	401-459-1000		391-3
Blue Cross & Blue Shield of Texas Inc 1001 E Lookout Dr *TF:* 800-521-2227 ■ *Web:* www.bcbstx.com	Richardson	TX	75082	972-766-6900		391-3
Blue Cross & Blue Shield of Vermont 445 Industrial Ln *TF:* 800-247-2583 ■ *Web:* www.bcbsvt.com	Montpelier	VT	05602	802-223-6131		391-3
Blue Cross and Blue Shield of Alabama 450 Riverchase Pkwy E *TF:* 800-292-8868 ■ *Web:* www.bcbsal.org	Birmingham	AL	35244	205-988-2200		391-3
Blue Cross and Blue Shield of Minnesota PO Box 64560 *TF:* 800-382-2000 ■ *Web:* www.bluecrossmn.com	Saint Paul	MN	55164	651-662-8000	662-1967	391-3
Blue Cross Blue Shield of Arizona 2444 W Las Palmaritas Dr *TF:* 800-232-2345 ■ *Web:* www.azblue.com	Phoenix	AZ	85021	602-864-4400	864-4041	391-3
Blue Cross Blue Shield of Delaware PO Box 1991 *TF:* 800-572-4400 ■ *Web:* www.highmarkbcbsde.com	Wilmington	DE	19899	800-876-7639		391-3
Blue Cross Blue Shield of Illinois 300 E Randolph St *TF:* 800-972-8382 ■ *Web:* www.bcbsil.com	Chicago	IL	60601	312-653-4019		391-3
Blue Cross Blue Shield of Kansas 1133 SW Topeka Blvd *TF:* 800-432-0216 ■ *Web:* www.bcbsks.com	Topeka	KS	66629	785-291-7000	290-0711	391-3
Blue Cross Blue Shield of Louisiana 5525 Reitz Ave **Fax Area Code:* 225 ■ *TF:* 800-599-2583 ■ *Web:* www.bcbsla.com	Baton Rouge	LA	70898	800-376-7734	295-2054*	391-3
Blue Cross Blue Shield of Massachusetts 101 Huntington Ave Ste 1300 **Fax Area Code:* 800 ■ *TF:* 800-262-2583 ■ *Web:* www.bluecrossma.com	Boston	MA	02215	617-246-5000	636-9494*	391-3
Blue Cross Blue Shield of North Dakota 4510 13th Ave S *TF:* 800-342-4718 ■ *Web:* www.bcbsnd.com	Fargo	ND	58121	701-282-1864		391-3
Blue Cross of Idaho 3000 E Pine Ave *TF:* 800-274-4018 ■ *Web:* www.bcidaho.com	Meridian	ID	83642	208-345-4550	331-7311	391-3
Blue Danube Restaurant Elm & Adeline Sts *Web:* www.bluedanuberestaurant.net	Trenton	NJ	08611	609-393-6133	393-1596	671
Blue Diamond Growers 1802 C St *TF:* 800-987-2329 ■ *Web:* www.bluediamond.com	Sacramento	CA	95811	916-442-0771		10-10
Blue Dog LLC 11939 Manchester Rd Ste 153 *Web:* www.bluedogllc.com	Des Peres	MO	63131	314-610-4262		652
Blue Dog Printing & Design 1039 Andrew Dr *Web:* www.getbluedog.com	West Chester	PA	19380	610-430-7992		627
Blue Dolphin Energy Co 801 Travis St Ste 2100 *OTC:* BDCO ■ *Web:* www.blue-dolphin-energy.com	Houston	TX	77002	713-568-4725	227-7626	536
Blue Door Consulting 50 W Sixth Ave *Web:* www.bluedoorconsulting.com	Oshkosh	WI	54902	920-230-2583		194
Blue Earth County 204 S 5th St *Web:* www.blueearthcountymn.gov	Mankato	MN	56001	507-304-4000	304-4344	338
Blue Earth Pictures Inc 5532 Code Ave *Web:* www.blueearthpictures.com	Minneapolis	MN	55436	612-619-5909		514
Blue Fin 1567 Broadway *Web:* www.bluefinnyc.com	New York	NY	10036	212-918-1400		671
Blue Foundry Bank 25 Orient Way *TF:* 888-388-7459 ■ *Web:* bluefoundrybank.com	Rutherford	NJ	07070	201-939-5000	939-3957	70
Blue Fountain Media Inc 102 Madison Ave 2nd Fl *TF:* 800-278-0816 ■ *Web:* www.bluefountainmedia.com	New York	NY	10016	212-260-1978		225
Blue Garnet Associates LLC 8055 W Manchester Ave Ste 430 *Web:* www.bluegarnet.net	Playa Del Rey	CA	90293	310-439-1930		194

	Phone	Fax	Class
Blue Generation Div of M Rubin & Sons Inc 34-01 38th Ave. . . . . Long Island City NY 11101 *Fax Area Code: 718 ■ TF: 888-336-4687 ■ Web: www.bluegeneration.com	888-336-4687	361-2680*	155-19
Blue Giant Equipment Corp 85 Heart Lake Rd S. . . . . Brampton ON L6W3K2 TF: 800-668-7078 ■ Web: www.bluegiant.com	905-457-3900		358
Blue Goose Cantina 4757 W Pk Blvd. . . . . Plano TX 75093 Web: www.bluegoosecantina.com	972-596-8882		671
Blue Granite Inc 2750 Old Centre Rd Ste 150. . . . . Portage MI 49024 TF: 877-817-0736 ■ Web: www.blue-granite.com	877-817-0736		180
Blue Grass Airport 4000 Terminal Dr. . . . . Lexington KY 40510 TF: 800-800-4000 ■ Web: bluegrassairport.com	859-425-3100	233-1822	27
Blue Grass Chemical Specialties LP 895 Industrial Blvd. . . . . New Albany IN 47150 Web: www.bluegrasschemical.com	812-948-1115	948-1561	145
Blue Grass Energy Co-opeartive Corp 1201 Lexington Rd. . . . . Nicholasville KY 40356 TF: 888-546-4243 ■ Web: www.bgenergy.com	859-885-4191	885-2854	245
Blue Grass Quality Meats 2648 Crescent Springs Pk. . . . . Covington KY 41017 Web: www.bluegrassqualitymeats.com	859-905-3431	331-7100	296-26
Blue Grass Regional Library 104 E Sixth St. . . . . Columbia TN 38401 *Fax Area Code: 865 ■ TF: 888-345-5575 ■ Web: www.tn.gov	931-388-9282	981-4587*	434-3
Blue Grass Regional Mental Health-Mental Retardation Board Inc 1351 Newtown Pk Bldg 1. . . . . Lexington KY 40511 TF: 800-928-8000 ■ Web: newvista.org	859-272-7483	233-0144	48-6
Blue Grass Stockyard 1274 Hwy 90 W PO Box 980. . . . . Albany KY 42602 *Fax Area Code: 859 ■ TF: 800-621-3972 ■ Web: www.bgstockyards.com	606-387-4681	255-5495*	446
Blue Grass Tours Inc 817 Enterprise Dr. . . . . Lexington KY 40510 Web: www.bluegrasstours.com	859-252-5744		760
Blue Grotto Technologies Inc 1000 Germantown Pk Ste C-1. . . . . Plymouth Meeting PA 19462 Web: bluegrotto.com	610-292-8088		177
Blue Harbor Resort & Conference Ctr 725 Blue Harbor Dr. . . . . Sheboygan WI 53081 Web: blueharborresort.com	920-452-2900		378
Blue Haven Resort 220 Branson Hills Pkwy. . . . . Branson MO 65616 Web: www.branson.com	417-334-3917		707
Blue Heaven 729 Thomas St. . . . . Key West FL 33040 Web: www.blueheavenkw.com	305-296-8666		671
Blue Hill 75 Washington Pl. . . . . New York NY 10011 Web: www.bluehillfarm.com	212-539-1776		671
Blue Hills Hospital 500 Vine St. . . . . Hartford CT 06112 Web: portal.ct.gov	860-293-6400		726
Blue Hills Reservation 695 Hillside St. . . . . Milton MA 02186 Web: www.mass.gov	617-698-1802		565
Blue Hills Technology Corp 33 Allerton Rd. . . . . Milton MA 02186 Web: bhtech.com	617-696-2422		177
Blue Hive Inc 7 Coppage Dr. . . . . Worcester MA 01603 Web: www.blue-hive.com	508-581-9560		8
Blue Horizon Hotel 1225 Robson St. . . . . Vancouver BC V6E1C3 TF: 800-663-1333 ■ Web: bluehorizonhotel.com	604-688-1411	688-4461	379
Blue Iceberg LLC 146 W 29th St Studio 11W. . . . . New York NY 10001 *Fax Area Code: 646 ■ Web: www.blue-iceberg.com	212-337-9920	619-4479*	7
Blue Iguana 165 SW Temple. . . . . Salt Lake City UT 84101 Web: blueiguanarestaurant.net	801-533-8900		671
Blue Interactive Agency 608 SW Fourth Ave. . . . . Fort Lauderdale FL 33315 Web: www.blueinteractiveagency.com	954-779-2801		5
Blue Ion 301B King St. . . . . Charleston SC 29401 Web: www.blueion.com	843-727-0310		180
Blue Island Newspaper Printing Inc 262 W 147th St. . . . . Harvey IL 60426 Web: www.binp.biz	708-333-1006	333-6902	627
Blue Jeans Network Inc 516 Clyde Ave. . . . . Mountain View CA 94043 TF: 800-403-9256 ■ Web: www.bluejeans.com	408-550-2828	550-2829	387
Blue Knob State Park 124 Park Rd. . . . . Imler PA 16655 Web: www.dcnr.pa.gov	814-276-3576		565
Blue Lakes Charters & Tours 12154 N Saginaw Rd. . . . . Clio MI 48420 TF: 800-282-4287 ■ Web: www.bluelakes.com	810-686-4287	686-9772	107
Blue Lan Group Inc 79 Sandwich Rd. . . . . Plymouth MA 02360 Web: www.bluelangroup.com	508-747-0433		317
Blue Lance Inc 410 Pierce St. . . . . Houston TX 77002 TF: 800-856-2583 ■ Web: bluelance.com	713-255-4800		178-12
Blue Licks Battlefield State Resort Park 10299 Maysville Rd. . . . . Carlisle KY 40311 TF: 800-443-7008 ■ Web: parks.ky.gov	859-289-5507		565
Blue Line Engineering Co 525 E Colorado Ave. . . . . Colorado Springs CO 80903 Web: www.bluelineengineering.com	719-447-1373		256
Blue Lion Restaurant 160 N Millward St. . . . . Jackson WY 83001 Web: bluelionrestaurant.com	307-733-3912		671
Blue Lotus Creative 7971 Columbia St. . . . . Vancouver BC V5Z2X5 Web: www.bluelotuscreative.com	604-306-8701		195
Blue Lotus SIDC 509 Village Rd W. . . . . Princeton Junction NJ 08550 Web: web.bluelotussidc.com	609-716-4615		180
Blue Marlin 1200 Lincoln St. . . . . Columbia SC 29201 Web: www.bluemarlincolumbia.com	803-799-3838		671
Blue Marlin Publications Ltd 823 Aberdeen Rd. . . . . West Bay Shore NY 11706 Web: www.bluemarlinpubs.com	631-666-0353		637-2
Blue Medora Inc 3225 N Evergreen Dr NE Ste 103. . . . . Grand Rapids MI 49525 Web: bluemedora.com	616-719-4550		177
Blue Mermaid Cafe & Seafood 119 Billy Mitchell Blvd. . . . . Brownsville TX 78521	956-544-2157		671
Blue Mesa Southwest Grill 612 Carroll St. . . . . Fort Worth TX 76107 Web: bluemesagrill.com	817-332-6372		671
Blue Moon Bar & Grill 2535 University Ave. . . . . Madison WI 53705 Web: www.bluemoonbar.com	608-233-0441		671
Blue Moon Fish Co 4405 W Tradewinds Ave. . . . . Lauderdale-by-the-Sea FL 33308 Web: www.bluemoonfishco.com	954-267-9888		671
Blue Moon Hotel 944 Collins Ave. . . . . Miami Beach FL 33139 TF: 800-553-7739 ■ Web: www.bluemoonhotel.com	305-673-2262	534-1546	379
Blue Moon Restaurant 35 Baltimore Ave. . . . . Rehoboth Beach DE 19971 Web: bluemoonrehoboth.com	302-227-6515		671
Blue Mound State Park 4350 Mounds Park Rd. . . . . Blue Mounds WI 53517 Web: dnr.wi.gov	608-437-5711		565
Blue Mounds State Park 1410 161st St. . . . . Luverne MN 56156 Web: www.dnr.state.mn.us	507-283-6050		565
Blue Mountain Air Inc 707 Aldridge Rd. . . . . Vacaville CA 95688 TF: 800-889-2085 ■ Web: www.bluemountainair.net	800-889-2085		610
Blue Mountain Arts Inc PO Box 4549. . . . . Boulder CO 80306 TF: 800-545-8573 ■ Web: www.sps.com	303-449-0536		130
Blue Mountain College PO Box 160. . . . . Blue Mountain MS 38610 TF: 800-235-0136 ■ Web: www.bmc.edu	662-685-4771	685-4776	166
Blue Mountain Community College 2411 NW Carden Ave PO Box 100. . . . . Pendleton OR 97801 TF: 888-441-7232 ■ Web: www.bluecc.edu	541-276-1260	278-5871	162
Blue Mountain Credit Union 520 S College Ave. . . . . College Place WA 99324 Web: bmcu.net	509-526-4562		70
Blue Mountain Quality Resources Inc 475 Rolling Ridge Dr Ste 200. . . . . State College PA 16801 TF: 800-982-2388 ■ Web: www.coolblue.com	814-234-2417	234-7077	177
Blue Mountain School District Inc PO Box 188. . . . . Orwigsburg PA 17961 Web: www.bmsd.org	570-366-0515	366-0838	685
Blue Nile 545 W Nine-Mile Rd. . . . . Ferndale MI 48220 Web: www.bluenilemi.com	248-547-6699		671
Blue Nile Inc 705 5th Ave S Ste 900. . . . . Seattle WA 98104 NASDAQ: NILE ■ TF: 800-242-2728 ■ Web: www.bluenile.com	206-336-6700		410
Blue North Fisheries Inc 2930 Westlake Ave N. . . . . Seattle WA 98109 Web: bluenorth.com	206-352-9252		285
Blue Ocean Press Inc 6299 NW 27th Way. . . . . Fort Lauderdale FL 33309 Web: www.blueoceanpress.com	954-973-1819		627
Blue Owl Restaurant & Bakery, The 6116 Second St. . . . . Kimmswick MO 63053 TF: 844-448-4340 ■ Web: www.theblueowl.com	636-464-3128		671
Blue Parrott Bar & Grille 1934 W 6th St. . . . . Wilmington DE 19805	302-655-8990	655-9488	671
Blue Pillar Inc 9025 N River Rd Ste 150. . . . . Indianapolis IN 46240 TF: 888-234-3212 ■ Web: www.bluepillar.com	888-234-3212		192
Blue Plate Communications Inc PO Box 4214. . . . . Dedham MA 02027 Web: www.blueplate.com	781-258-1710		636
Blue Plate, The 3218 Mission St. . . . . San Francisco CA 94110 Web: blueplatesf.com	415-282-6777		671
Blue Point Capital Partners 127 Public Sq Ste 5100. . . . . Cleveland OH 44114 Web: www.bluepointcapital.com	216-535-4700		401
Blue Point Coastal Cuisine 565 Fifth Ave. . . . . San Diego CA 92101 Web: www.cohnrestaurants.com	619-233-6623		671
Blue Point Grill 258 Nassau St. . . . . Princeton NJ 08542 Web: www.bluepointgrill.com	609-921-1211		671
Blue Point Grille 700 W St Clair Ave. . . . . Cleveland OH 44113 Web: hrcleveland.com	216-875-7827		671
Blue Print Automation Inc 16037 Innovation Dr. . . . . South Chesterfield VA 23834 Web: www.blueprintautomation.com	804-520-5400		547
Blue Print LLC 2707 Fairmount. . . . . Dallas TX 75201 Web: blueprintstore.com	214-954-9511		362
Blue Quill Angler Inc 1532 Bergen Pkwy. . . . . Evergreen CO 80439 TF: 800-435-5353 ■ Web: bluequillangler.com	303-674-4700		711
Blue Racer Midstream LLC 5949 Sherry Ln Ste 1300. . . . . Dallas TX 75225 Web: www.blueracermidstream.com	214-580-3700		188-10
Blue Rhino Studio Inc 3277 Sun Dr. . . . . Eagan MN 55121 Web: www.rhinocentral.com	651-287-0900		393
Blue Ribbon 97 Sullivan St. . . . . New York NY 10012 Web: www.blueribbonrestaurants.com	212-274-0404		671
Blue Ribbon Consulting 273 Poor Farm Rd. . . . . New Ipswich NH 03071 Web: www.blueribbonconsulting.com	603-878-1694		196
Blue Ribbon Home Warranty Inc 95 S Wadsworth Blvd. . . . . Lakewood CO 80226 TF: 800-571-0475 ■ Web: blueribbonhomewarranty.com	303-986-3900	986-3152	367
Blue Ribbon Meat and Butcher Shop 1436 Prater Way. . . . . Sparks NV 89431 Web: blueribbonbutchershop.com	775-358-8116		297-9
Blue Ribbon Meats Inc 3316 W 67th Pl. . . . . Cleveland OH 44102 Web: blueribbonmeats.com	216-631-8850		296-26
Blue Ribbon Tag & Label Corp 4035 N 29th Ave. . . . . Hollywood FL 33020 TF: 800-433-4974 ■ Web: blueribbonlabel.com	954-922-9292	922-9977	413
Blue Ribbon Travel-american 3601 W 76th St Ste 190. . . . . Minneapolis MN 55435 TF: 800-626-5309 ■ Web: www.blueribbontravel.com	952-835-2724		775
Blue Ridge Bank 100 E Main St. . . . . Walhalla SC 29691 Web: blueridge.bank	864-638-5444		70

Name	Address	City	State	ZIP	Phone	Fax	Class	Additional
Blue Ridge Bank & Trust Co	4240 Blue Ridge Blvd Ste 100	Kansas City	MO	64133	816-358-5000		70	*Web:* www.blueridgebank.com
Blue Ridge Beverage Company Inc	44-46 Barley Dr	Salem	VA	24153	540-380-2000		81-1	*Web:* www.blueridgebeverage.com
Blue Ridge Brewing Co	308 Trade St	Greer	SC	29651	864-232-4677		671	*Web:* www.blueridgebrewing.com
Blue Ridge Community College	180 W Campus Dr	Flat Rock	NC	28731	828-694-1700		162	*Web:* www.blueridge.edu
Blue Ridge Electric Membership Corp	1216 Blowing Rock Blvd NE	Lenoir	NC	28645	828-758-2383	758-2699	245	*TF:* 800-451-5474 ■ *Web:* www.blueridgeenergy.com
Blue Ridge Grain & Marketing Inc	4147 Cleveland Hwy Ste 400	Gainesville	GA	30506	770-535-2864		194	
Blue Ridge Grill	1261 W Paces Ferry Rd	Atlanta	GA	30327	404-233-5030		671	*Web:* www.blueridgegrill.com
Blue Ridge Industries Inc	266 Arbor Ct	Winchester	VA	22602	540-662-3900	662-3010	604	*Web:* www.blueridgeind.com
Blue Ridge Insurance Services Inc	116 Reservoir St	Harrisonburg	VA	22801	540-437-9030		390	*Web:* brisinc.com
Blue Ridge Landscape & Design Inc	172-12 Imboden Dr	Winchester	VA	22603	540-869-0000		776	*Web:* blueridgelandscape.com
Blue Ridge Mountain Cabinets	1101 Franklin St	Rocky Mount	VA	24151	540-489-1000		115	*Web:* www.blueridgemountaincabinets.com
Blue Ridge Optics LLC	1617 Longwood Ave	Bedford	VA	24523	540-586-8526		529	*Web:* www.blueridgeoptics.com
Blue Ridge Partners Management Consulting LLC	1350 Beverly Rd Ste 115	McLean	VA	22101	703-448-1881		194	*Web:* www.blueridgepartners.com
Blue Ridge Public Television	1215 McNeil Dr	Roanoke	VA	24015	540-344-0991	344-2148	632	*TF:* 888-332-7788 ■ *Web:* www.blueridgepbs.org
Blue Ridge Real Estate Co	5 Blue Ridge Ct PO Box 707	Blakeslee	PA	18610	570-443-8433	443-8412	655	*Web:* www.brreco.com
Blue Ridge Research & Consulting	29 N Market St Ste 700	Asheville	NC	28801	828-252-2209		261	*Web:* blueridgeresearch.com
Blue Ridge School	273 Mayo Dr	Saint George	VA	22935	434-985-2811	985-7215	622	*Web:* www.blueridgeschool.com
Blue Ridge Tool & Machine Company Inc	115 Hollow Oaks Ln	Easley	SC	29642	864-859-4758		454	*Web:* www.blueridgetool.com
Blue Ridge X-Ray Company Inc	120 Vista Blvd	Arden	NC	28704	800-727-7290	681-8384*	475	**Fax Area Code:* 828 ■ *TF:* 800-727-7290 ■ *Web:* www.blueridgexray.net
Blue River Technology Inc	575 N Pastoria Ave	Sunnyvale	CA	94085	408-733-2583	618-9105*	273	**Fax Area Code:* 888 ■ *Web:* www.bluerivertechnology.com
Blue Rock Advisors Inc	445 E Lake St Ste 120	Wayzata	MN	55391	952-229-8700		401	*Web:* www.blue-rock.com
Blue Rock Industries	737 Spring St	Westbrook	ME	04092	207-772-6770		189-7	*TF:* 877-772-6770 ■ *Web:* www.bluerockmaine.com
Blue Rock State Park	7924 Cutler Lake Rd	Blue Rock	OH	43720	740-674-4794		565	
Blue Rock Technologies	800 Kirts Blvd	Troy	MI	48084	248-786-6100		225	*TF:* 866-390-8200 ■ *Web:* www.bluerocktech.com
Blue Sea Capital	222 Lakeview Ave Ste 1700	West Palm Beach	FL	33401	561-655-8400		360-3	*Web:* blueseacapital.com
Blue Seal Feeds Inc	2905 US Hwy 61 N	Muscatine	IA	52761	866-647-1212		447	*TF:* 866-647-1212 ■ *Web:* blueseal.com
Blue Shield of California	50 Beale St	San Francisco	CA	94105	415-229-5000	229-6230	391-3	*TF:* 800-221-2367 ■ *Web:* www.blueshieldca.com
Blue Skies Consulting LLC	100 Blue Skies Dr	Belen	NM	87002	505-864-3700		196	
Blue Sky Agency	950 Joseph E Lowery Blvd Ste 30	Atlanta	GA	30318	404-876-0202		4	*Web:* blueskyagency.com
Blue Sky Cleaners	1111 Elliott Ave W	Seattle	WA	98119	206-838-8433		426	*Web:* www.blueskycleaners.com
Blue Sky Cycling Inc	2530 Randolph St	Huntington Park	CA	90255	323-585-3934		711	*TF:* 800-585-4137 ■ *Web:* blueskycycling.com
Blue Sky Energy Inc	2598 Fortune Way Ste K	Vista	CA	92081	760-597-1642		610	*TF:* 800-493-7877 ■ *Web:* sunforgellc.com
Blue Sky Industries Inc	595 Monterey Pass Rd	Monterey Park	CA	91754	213-620-9950	620-9953	360-3	*Web:* blueskyindustries.com
Blue Sky Pest Control	3050 S Country Club Dr Ste 7	Mesa	AZ	85210	480-635-8492	635-8489	577	*Web:* blueskypest.com
Blue Sky Productions	24021 Research Dr	Farmington Hills	MI	48335	734-542-7000	542-7014	514	*Web:* www.blueskyproductions.tv
Blue Sky Sports Center of Euless LLC	7801 Main St	The Colony	TX	75056	469-384-3400		711	*Web:* www.blueskysportscenter.com
Blue Sky Studios Inc	1 American Ln	Greenwich	CT	06831	203-992-6000		33	*Web:* blueskystudios.com
Blue Sky Swimwear	729 E International Speedway Blvd	Daytona Beach	FL	32118	386-255-2590	253-5938	155-17	*TF:* 800-799-6445 ■ *Web:* www.blueskyswimwear.com
Blue Spoon	89 Congress St	Portland	ME	04101	207-773-1116		671	*Web:* www.thebluespoon.com
Blue Spring State Park	2100 W French Ave	Orange City	FL	32763	386-775-3663		565	*Web:* www.floridastateparks.org
Blue Springs Chamber of Commerce	1000 W Main St	Blue Springs	MO	64015	816-229-8558	229-1244	139	*Web:* www.bluespringschamber.com
Blue Springs State Park	2595 Alabama 10	Clio	AL	36017	800-252-7275	397-4875*	565	**Fax Area Code:* 334 ■ *TF:* 800-252-7275 ■ *Web:* www.alapark.com
Blue Star Contemporary	116 Blue Star Rd	San Antonio	TX	78204	210-227-6960		50-2	*Web:* bluestarcontemporary.org
Blue Star Growers Inc	200 Blue Star Rd Ste I	Cashmere	WA	98815	509-782-2922		315-3	*Web:* bluestargrowers.com
Blue Star Jets Inc	880 3rd Ave 10th Fl	New York	NY	10022	212-446-9037		393	*TF:* 866-538-8463 ■ *Web:* www.bluestarjets.com
Blue Star Plastics Inc	801 Nandino Blvd	Lexington	KY	40511	859-255-0714		608	*Web:* www.bluestarplastics.com
Blue State Digital LLC	406 7th St NW 3rd Fl	Washington	DC	20004	202-449-5600		7	*Web:* www.bluestate.co
Blue Stone Strategy Group LLC	2214 N Central Ave Ste 250	Phoenix	AZ	85004	949-476-8828	861-7419	463	*Web:* bluestonestrategy.com
Blue Streak Partners Inc	825 3rd Ave 2nd Fl	New York	NY	10022	212-380-1633	937-3377	631	*Web:* www.bluestreakpartners.com
Blue Stream Fiber L.L.C	10486 SW Village Center Dr	Port Saint Lucie	FL	34987	772-345-6000		116	*Web:* www.htcplus.net
Blue Talon Bistro	420 Prince George St	Williamsburg	VA	23185	757-476-2583		671	*Web:* www.bluetalonbistro.com
Blue Tangerine Solutions LLC	2020 W Eau Gallie Blvd Ste 105	Melbourne	FL	32935	321-309-6900		180	*TF:* 800-870-4293 ■ *Web:* www.bluetangerine.com
Blue Tape Inc	16101 College Oak	San Antonio	TX	78249	210-222-0580		627	*Web:* www.blue-tape.com
Blue Technologies	5885 Grant Ave	Cleveland	OH	44105	216-271-4800		112	*Web:* www.btohio.com
Blue Telescope	236 W 30 St 7th Fl	New York	NY	10001	212-675-7702		195	*Web:* blue-telescope.com
Blue Tent	218 E Valley Rd	Carbondale	CO	81623	970-704-3240		194	*TF:* 877-716-9648 ■ *Web:* bluetent.com
Blue Tree Publishing Inc	8927 192nd St SW	Edmonds	WA	98026	425-210-4743	697-7155	637-2	*Web:* www.bluetreepublishing.com
Blue Triangle Hardwoods LLC	156 Industrial Blvd	Everett	PA	15537	814-652-9111	652-5863	191-3	*Web:* www.ahwood.com
Blue Tusk	165 Walton St	Syracuse	NY	13202	315-472-1934		671	*Web:* www.bluetusk.com
Blue Valley Machine and Manufacturing Co	6834 Truman Rd	Kansas City	MO	64126	816-231-1480	483-0059	455	*Web:* bluevalley.com
Blue Valley Public Safety Inc	509 James Rollo Dr	Grain Valley	MO	64029	816-847-7502		237	*Web:* www.bluevalleypublicsafety.com
Blue Valley Tele-Communications Inc	1559 Pony Express Hwy	Home	KS	66438	785-799-3311		737	*Web:* bluevalley.net
Blue Water Area Chamber of Commerce	512 McMorran Blvd	Port Huron	MI	48060	810-985-7101	985-7311	139	*TF:* 800-361-0526 ■ *Web:* www.bluewaterchamber.com
Blue Water Cafe	1095 Hamilton St	Vancouver	BC	V6B5T4	604-688-8078		671	*Web:* www.bluewatercafe.net
Blue Water Resort	291 S Shore Dr	South Yarmouth	MA	02664	800-367-9393		669	*TF:* 800-367-9393 ■ *Web:* redjacketresorts.com
Blue Water Sailing Magazine	747 Aquidneck Ave Ste 201	Middletown	RI	02842	401-847-7612	845-8580	457-4	*TF:* 888-800-7245 ■ *Web:* www.bwsailing.com
Blue Wave Marketing & Promotion	107 South St Ste 2F	Boston	MA	02111	617-576-3100		195	*Web:* bluewavemarketing.com
Blue Wave Solar	111 Huntington Ave Ste 650	Boston	MA	02199	844-786-4100		767	*TF:* 844-786-4100 ■ *Web:* bluewavesolar.com
Blue Williams LLP	3421 N Causeway Blvd Ste 900	Metairie	LA	70002	504-831-4091		428	*TF:* 800-326-4991 ■ *Web:* bluewilliams.com
Blue Zebra Appointment Setting	31 Corchaug Ave Ste A	Port Washington	NY	11050	800-755-0094	345-0298*	7	**Fax Area Code:* 516 ■ *TF:* 800-755-0094 ■ *Web:* www.bluezebraappointmentsetting.com
BlueAlly	8609 Westwood Center Dr Ste 100	Vienna	VA	22182	888-768-2060		260	*TF:* 888-768-2060 ■ *Web:* blueally.com
BluebellWholesale.com	163 E Union Ave	East Rutherford	NJ	07073	201-804-0111	804-7830	411	*Web:* www.bluebellwholesale.com
Bluebonnet Trail Elementary	11316 Farmhaven Rd	Austin	TX	78754	512-278-4125	278-4140	305	*Web:* www.manorisd.net
Bluechip Athletic Solutions LLC	5885 Glenridge Dr Ste 115	Atlanta	GA	30328	404-941-2510		225	*Web:* www.bluechipone.com
Bluecore	116 Nassau St Ste 7	New York	NY	10038	646-690-0490		178-1	*Web:* www.bluecore.com
BlueCross BlueShield of Tennessee Inc	1 Cameron Hill Cir	Chattanooga	TN	37402	800-565-9140		219	*TF:* 800-565-9140 ■ *Web:* www.bcbst.com
BlueCross BlueShield of Western New York	257 W Genesee St	Buffalo	NY	14202	716-887-6900		391-3	*TF:* 800-888-0757 ■ *Web:* www.bcbswny.com
Bluedial Watches	6170 W Lake Mead Blvd Ste 101	Las Vegas	NV	89108	702-645-5260		410	*Web:* www.bluedial.com

Company / Address	City	State	ZIP	Phone	Fax	Class
Bluedog Design LLC 403 N Carpenter St *Web:* www.bluedogdesign.com	Chicago	IL	60642	312-243-1101		195
Bluefield College 3000 College Ave *TF:* 800-872-0175 ■ *Web:* www.bluefield.edu	Bluefield	VA	24605	276-326-3682	326-4395	166
Bluefield Regional Medical Ctr (BRMC) 500 Cherry St *Web:* bluefieldregional.com	Bluefield	WV	24701	304-327-1100		374-3
Bluefield State College 219 Rock St *TF:* 800-654-7798 ■ *Web:* bluefieldstate.edu	Bluefield	WV	24701	304-327-4000	325-7747	166
BlueFire Capital LLC 311 S Wacker Dr Ste 2000 *Web:* www.bluefirecapital.com	Chicago	IL	60606	312-242-0500		690
BlueGenesisCom Corp 5915 Airport Rd Ste 1100 *Web:* www.bluegenesis.com	Mississauga	ON	L4V1T1	905-673-3232		387
Blue-Grace Logistics LLC 2846 S Falkenburg Rd *TF:* 800-697-4477 ■ *Web:* mybluegrace.com	Riverview	FL	33578	800-697-4477		311
Bluegrass Care Navigators 2312 Alexandria Dr *TF:* 855-492-0812 ■ *Web:* www.bgcarenav.org	Lexington	KY	40504	855-492-0812		371
Bluegrass Cellular Inc 2902 Ring Rd *TF:* 800-928-2355 ■ *Web:* bluegrasscellular.com	Elizabethtown	KY	42701	270-769-0339		736
Bluegrass Community & Technical College *Cooper Campus* 470 Cooper Dr *TF:* 866-774-4872 ■ *Web:* bluegrass.kctcs.edu	Lexington	KY	40506	859-246-6200	246-4666	162
Bluegrass Oxygen 1032 Majaun Rd *TF:* 800-404-8838 ■ *Web:* www.bluegrassoxygen.com	Lexington	KY	40511	859-277-2583		264-4
Bluegrass Scenic Railroad & Museum 175 Beasley Rd PO Box 27 *Web:* www.bgrm.org	Versailles	KY	40383	859-873-2476	873-0408	520
Bluegrassnet Development Corp 321 E Breckinridge St *Web:* www.bluegrass.net	Louisville	KY	40203	502-589-4638		225
Bluegreen Corp 4960 Conference Way N Ste 100 *NYSE: BXG* ■ *TF:* 800-456-2582 ■ *Web:* www.bluegreenvacations.com	Boca Raton	FL	33431	561-912-8000	912-8100	753
Blueharbor Bank 106 Corporate Park Dr *Web:* www.blueharborbank.com	Mooresville	NC	28117	704-662-7700		70
Bluehour 250 NW 13th Ave *Web:* www.bluehouronline.com	Portland	OR	97209	503-226-3394		671
Blueleaf Inc 57 Dresser Hill Rd *Web:* blueleafwater.com	Charlton	MA	01507	508-248-7094		261
BlueLight Analytics Inc 24-2625 Joseph Howe Dr *Web:* www.bluelightanalytics.com	Halifax	NS	B3L4G4	902-407-4242		228
BlueLine Services LLC 448 East 6400 South Ste 425 *Web:* blueline-services.com	Salt Lake City	UT	84107	801-575-8378		415
Blueline Simulations LLC 218 E Bearss Ave *Web:* www.bluelinesims.com	Tampa	FL	33613	813-269-7467		463
Bluelinx Holdings Inc 4300 Wildwood Pkwy *Web:* bluelinxco.com	Atlanta	GA	30339	770-953-7000		105
Bluenose Inn & Suites 636 Bedford Hwy *TF:* 800-553-5339 ■ *Web:* www.thebluenoseinn.com	Halifax	NS	B3M2L8	800-565-2301		379
Blueox Energy Products & Services 38 N Canal St *TF:* 877-233-8176 ■ *Web:* www.blueoxenergy.com	Oxford	NY	13830	877-233-8176		579
BluePearl Veterinary Partners LLC 3000 Busch Lake Blvd *Web:* bluepearlvet.com	Tampa	FL	33614	813-933-8944		794
Bluepoint Leadership Development Ltd 25 Whitney Dr *TF:* 888-221-8685 ■ *Web:* www.bluepointleadership.com	Milford	OH	45150	513-683-4702		194
BluePoint Venture Marketing 17 Draper Rd	Wayland	MA	01778	978-509-8444		636
BluePointe Capital Management LLC 999 Baker Way Ste 150 *Web:* www.bluepointecapital.com	San Mateo	CA	94404	650-293-4545	293-4541	690
Blueport Commerce 500 Harrison Ave Ste 3R *TF:* 855-277-0614 ■ *Web:* www.blueport.com	Boston	MA	02118	855-277-0614		459
BlueRange Technology Inc 9241 Globe Center Dr Ste 100 *TF:* 877-928-4800 ■ *Web:* www.bluerangetech.com	Morrisville	NC	27560	877-928-4800		631
BlueRun Ventures 545 Middlefield Rd Ste 250 *Web:* www.brv.com	Menlo Park	CA	94025	650-462-7250		792
BlueRush Media Group Corp 75 Sherbourne St *Web:* www.bluerush.com	Toronto	ON	M5A2P9	416-203-0618		195
Blues Audience, The 62 Cricket Hill Rd *Web:* thebluesaudience.com	Harrisville	NH	03450	603-827-3952		637-10
BlueScope Construction Inc 1540 Genessee St *Web:* www.bluescopeconstruction.com	Kansas City	MO	64102	816-245-6000	245-6099	186
Bluescope Steel Americas LLC 200 Pine Ave Ste 550	Long Beach	CA	90802	562-491-1441		492
BlueScope Steel Ltd PO Box 419917 *Web:* www.bluescopebuildings.com	Kansas	MO	64141	816-968-3000		261
BlueScreen LLC 137 N Larchmont Blvd *Web:* www.bluescreen.com	Los Angeles	CA	90004	323-467-7572		722
BlueSnap Inc 800 S St Ste 640 *Web:* home.bluesnap.com	Waltham	MA	02453	781-790-5013		178-1
Bluespec Inc 3 Speen St Ste 100 *Web:* www.bluespec.com	Framingham	MA	01701	781-250-2200	684-1119	177
BlueSpire Strategic Marketing 7650 Edinborough Way Ste 500 *TF:* 800-727-6397 ■ *Web:* www.bluespiremarketing.com	Minneapolis	MN	55435	800-727-6397		5
Bluestar Resort & Golf 8777 N Gainey Center Dr Ste 135 *Web:* www.bluestargolf.com	Scottsdale	AZ	85258	480-348-6519		707
Bluestein Nichols Thompson Delgado LLC 1614 Taylor St *Web:* bluesteinattorneys.com	Columbia	SC	29201	803-779-7599	771-8097	41
Bluestem 900 Westport Rd *Web:* www.bluestemkc.com	Kansas City	MO	64111	816-561-1101		671
Bluestem Brands Inc 7075 Flying Cloud Dr *Web:* www.bluestem.com	Eden Prairie	MN	55344	952-656-3700		737
Bluestem Electric Co-opeartive Inc 614 E Hwy 24 PO Box 5 *TF:* 800-558-1580 ■ *Web:* www.bluestemelectric.com	Wamego	KS	66547	785-456-2212		245
Bluestone & Hockley Real Estate Services 9320 SW Barbur Blvd Ste 300 *Web:* www.bluestonehockley.com	Portland	OR	97219	503-222-3800		652
Bluestone Engineering Inc 1990 N California Blvd 8th Fl *Web:* www.bluestoneeng.com	Walnut Creek	CA	94596	925-932-7053		256
Bluestone National Scenic River PO Box 246 *Web:* www.nps.gov	Glen Jean	WV	25846	304-465-0508		564
BlueStone Natural Resources 2 W Second St Ste 1700 *Web:* bluestone-nr.com	Tulsa	OK	74103	918-392-9200	392-9201	539
Bluestone State Park PO Box 3 *Web:* wvstateparks.com	Hinton	WV	25951	304-466-2805		565
Bluestorm Technologies Inc 455 Court St *Web:* www.bluestormtech.com	Binghamton	NY	13904	607-762-5401		180
BlueTie Inc 2480 Browncroft Blvd Ste 2b *TF:* 800-258-3843 ■ *Web:* www.bluetie.com	Rochester	NY	14625	585-586-2000	586-2268	225
Bluewater 4064 Peavey Rd *Web:* www.tractel.com	Chaska	MN	55318	952-448-2935		172
Bluewater Adventures 252 E 1st St Ste 3 *TF:* 888-877-1770 ■ *Web:* bluewateradventures.ca	North Vancouver	BC	V7L1B3	604-980-3800	980-1800	220
Bluewater Bay Resort 2000 Bluewater Blvd *Web:* www.bwbresort.com	Niceville	FL	32578	850-897-3241		669
Bluewater Broadcasting Company LLC 4101 Wall St *Web:* www.bluewaterbroadcasting.com	Montgomery	AL	36106	334-244-0961		632
Bluewater Energy Inc 3459 Acworth Due W Rd Ste 206 *Web:* bluewaterenergyinc.com	Acworth	GA	30101	678-594-2058		463
BlueWater Funding LLC 350 Fortune Ter 2nd Fl **Fax Area Code:* 240 ■ *Web:* bluewaterfunding.com	Rockville	MD	20854	301-656-6566	206-3228*	217
Bluewater Industries Inc 3303 FM 1960 Rd W Ste 100	Houston	TX	77068	713-802-2060		41
BlueWater Partners LLC 146 Monroe Center St NW Ste 701 *Web:* www.bluewaterpartners.com	Grand Rapids	MI	49503	616-988-9444		251
Bluewater Resort 2001 S Ocean Blvd *Web:* www.bluewaterresort.com	Myrtle Beach	SC	29577	843-626-8345		669
Bluewater Resort & Casino 11300 Resort Dr *Web:* www.bluewaterfun.com	Parker	AZ	85344	928-669-7000		378
Bluewater Ropes Inc 209 Lovvorn Rd *Web:* www.bluewaterropes.com	Carrollton	GA	30117	770-834-7515	836-1530	208
Bluewater Thermal Solutions 126 Millport Cir Ste 201 *TF:* 877-990-0050 ■ *Web:* bluewaterthermal.com	Greenville	SC	29607	864-990-0050	990-0056	484
Blue-White Industries Ltd 5300 Business Dr *Web:* www.blue-white.com	Huntington Beach	CA	92649	714-893-8529	894-9492	201
BlueWillow Biologics 2311 Green Rd *Web:* www.bluewillow.com	Ann Arbor	MI	48105	734-302-4000	302-9150	668
Bluezoo 1500 Epcot Resorts Blvd PO Box 22653 *TF:* 888-828-8850 ■ *Web:* www.swandolphin.com	Lake Buena Vista	FL	32830	407-934-1111		671
Bluff View Bank 16893 So Main St *TF:* 866-768-5844 ■ *Web:* www.bluffviewbank.com	Galesville	WI	54630	608-582-2233		70
Bluffton & Oyster Co 27 Dr Mellichamp Dr *Web:* blufftonoyster.com	Bluffton	SC	29910	843-757-4010		393
Bluffton Flying Service 1080 Navajo Dr *Web:* www.blufftonflyingservice.com	Bluffton	OH	45817	419-358-7045		13
Bluffton Historical Preservation Society (BHPS) 70 Boundary St *Web:* heywardhouse.org	Bluffton	SC	29910	843-757-6293		49-19
Bluffton Motor Works LLC 410 E Spring St *TF:* 800-579-8527 ■ *Web:* weg-cm.com	Bluffton	IN	46714	260-827-2200		518
Bluffton Today 6 Promenade St *Web:* www.blufftontoday.com	Bluffton	SC	29910	843-815-0800	815-0898	532-4
Bluffton University 1 University Dr *TF:* 800-488-3257 ■ *Web:* www.bluffton.edu	Bluffton	OH	45817	419-358-3000	358-3081	166
Blum Inc 7733 Old Plank Rd *TF:* 800-438-6788 ■ *Web:* www.blum.com	Stanley	NC	28164	704-827-1345		350
Blum Shapiro 29 S Main St PO Box 272000 *Web:* www.blumshapiro.com	West Hartford	CT	06107	860-561-4000	521-9241	2
Blumberg & Assoc 8560 Jefferson Hwy *TF:* 800-349-1442 ■ *Web:* blumbergassoc.com	Baton Rouge	LA	70809	225-767-1442	767-0806	390
Blumberg Capital 501 Folsom St Ste 400 *Web:* www.blumbergcapital.com	San Francisco	CA	94105	415-905-5000		194
BlumbergExcelsior Inc 16 Court St 14th Fl *TF:* 800-529-6278 ■ *Web:* www.blumberg.com	Brooklyn	NY	11241	212-431-5000		194
Blume Mechanical LLC 11300 43rd St N *Web:* www.blumemechanical.com	Clearwater	FL	33762	727-544-5993	330-9111	35

Name / Address	City	State	ZIP	Phone	Fax	Class
Blumen Gardens Inc 403 Edward St *Web:* blumengardens.com	Sycamore	IL	60178	815-895-3737		293
Blumenauer Earl (Rep D - OR) 1111 Longworth House Office Bldg *Web:* blumenauer.house.gov	Washington	DC	20515	202-225-4811	225-8941	342-2
Blumenthal Qualitative Research 8828 Oakham St *Web:* www.BQResearch.com	Huntersville	NC	28078	704-947-5490		194
Blumenthal Richard (Sen D - CT) 706 Hart Senate Office Bldg *Web:* www.blumenthal.senate.gov	Washington	DC	20510	202-224-2823	224-9673	342-2
Blumer USA Inc 800 Prospect Hill Rd *Web:* www.blumerusa.com	Windsor	CT	06095	860-688-1589		385
Blunt Rochester Lisa (Rep D - DE) 1519 Longworth House Office Bldg *Web:* bluntrochester.house.gov	Washington	DC	20515	202-225-4165		342-2
Blunt Roy (Sen R - MO) 260 Russell Senate Office Bldg *Web:* www.blunt.senate.gov	Washington	DC	20510	202-224-5721		342-2
Blur Studio 3960 Ince Blvd *Web:* www.blur.com	Culver City	CA	90232	424-298-4800	298-4801	33
Blutek Power Inc 300-1 SR- 17 S Ste B2 *Web:* www.blutekpower.com	Lodi	NJ	07644	973-594-1800		518
Bluware Inc 9801 Westheimer Rd Ste 950 *Web:* bluware.com	Houston	TX	77084	713-335-1500		177
BluWater Bistro 102 Lakeside Ave *Web:* www.bluwaterbistro.com	Seattle	WA	98122	206-328-2233		671
Blyth Academy 300 John St Ste 276 *Web:* blytheducation.com	Thornhill	ON	L3T5W4	905-889-8081		623
Blythe Area Chamber of Commerce 400 W Hobsonway *Web:* www.blythechamberofcommerce.com	Blythe	CA	92225	760-922-3181		139
Blythe Construction Inc 2911 N Graham St *Web:* blytheconstruction.com	Charlotte	NC	28206	704-375-8474	375-7814	188-4
Blythe Park Elementary School 735 Leesley Rd *Web:* www.district96.org	Riverside	IL	60546	708-447-2168	447-1703	685
Blytheco LLC 23161 Mill Creek Dr *TF:* 800-425-9843 ■ *Web:* www.blytheco.com	Laguna Hills	CA	92653	949-583-9500	583-0649	180
BMA (Baptist Missionary Association of America) 611 Locust Ave PO Box 878 *TF:* 800-333-1442 ■ *Web:* bmamissions.org	Conway	AR	72034	501-455-4977		48-20
BMA Communications LLC 15184 Hawk St *TF:* 800-850-4262 ■ *Web:* bmacommunications.com	Fontana	CA	92336	800-850-4262		195
BMA Software Solutions Inc 1057 E Imperial Hwy Ste 477 *Web:* www.bmasoftwaresolutions.com	Placentia	CA	92870	714-455-2717	989-8012	178-1
BMC (Business Management Consultants) 1502 Augusta Dr Ste 315 *Web:* bmc-global.com	Houston	TX	77057	713-780-2939	780-2932	194
BMC (Bryn Mawr Commentaries Inc) 101 N Merion Ave *Web:* bmcr.brynmawr.edu	Bryn Mawr	PA	19010	610-526-7475		166
BMC Software Inc 2101 City W Blvd *TF:* 800-841-2031 ■ *Web:* www.bmc.com	Houston	TX	77042	713-918-8800	918-8000	178-1
BMD (Boksa Marine Design Inc) 16627 Fishhawk Blvd Ste 101 *Web:* www.bmdinc.com	Lithia	FL	33547	813-654-9800		261
BMDA (Building Material Dealers Assn) 1006 SE Grand Ave Ste 301 *TF:* 888-960-6329 ■ *Web:* www.bmda.com	Portland	OR	97214	503-208-3763		49-3
BMDS (Behavioral Measurement Database Services) PO Box 110287 *Web:* www.bmdshapi.com	Pittsburgh	PA	15232	412-687-6850	687-5213	387
Bme Assocs 10 Liftbridge Ln E *Web:* bmepc.com	Fairport	NY	14450	585-377-7360		261
BMF (Buchanan Metal Forming Inc) 103 W Smith St *Web:* www.bmfcorp.com	Buchanan	MI	49107	269-695-3836	695-3830	483
BMF (Bawa Muhaiyaddeen Fellowship) 5820 Overbrook Ave *TF:* 888-786-1786 ■ *Web:* www.bmf.org	Philadelphia	PA	19131	215-879-6300		637-10
BMG (Buford Media Group LLC) 6125 Paluxy Dr *Web:* www.mycpa.cpa.state.tx.us	Tyler	TX	75703	903-561-4411		116
BMG Aviation Inc 984 S Kirby Rd *TF:* 888-457-3787 ■ *Web:* www.bmgaviation.com	Bloomington	IN	47403	812-825-7979	825-7978	63
BMG Communications 7810 Ballantyne Commons Pky Ste 300 *TF:* 877-264-2638 ■ *Web:* www.bmgc.net	Charlotte	NC	28277	877-264-2638		224
BMG Metals Inc 950 Masonic Ln *TF:* 800-552-1510 ■ *Web:* www.bmgmetals.com	Richmond	VA	23231	804-226-1024	222-3693	492
BMG of Kansas Inc 606 Commerce Dr *Web:* www.bmgks.com	Hesston	KS	67062	620-327-4038		697
BMH Books 1104 Kings Hwy PO Box 544 *TF:* 800-348-2756 ■ *Web:* bmhbooks.com	Winona Lake	IN	46590	800-348-2756		637-8
BMI (Book Manufacturers Institute) PO Box 731388 *Web:* www.bmibook.com	Ormond Beach	FL	32173	386-986-4552	986-4553	49-16
BMI (Broadcast Music Inc) 250 Greenwich St 7 World Trade Ctr *Web:* www.bmi.com	New York	NY	10007	212-220-3000		48-4
BMI (Brotherhood Mutual Insurance Co) 6400 Brotherhood Way *TF:* 800-333-3735 ■ *Web:* www.brotherhoodmutual.com	Fort Wayne	IN	46825	800-333-3735		391-4
BMI (Beer Marketer's Insights Inc) 49 E Maple Ave *Web:* www.beerinsights.com	Suffern	NY	10901	845-507-0040	507-0041	637-9
BMI Educational Services 4702 Benson Ave *Fax Area Code: 800 ■ *TF:* 800-222-8100 ■ *Web:* company.akjeducation.com	Halethorpe	MD	21227	732-329-6991	986-9393*	96
Bmi Gaming Inc 1350 E Newport Center Dr Ste 210 *Web:* www.bmigaming.com	Boca Raton	FL	33431	561-391-7200	892-2268	322
BMI Imaging Systems 1115 E Arques Ave *TF:* 800-359-3456 ■ *Web:* bmiimaging.com	Sunnyvale	CA	94085	408-736-7444	736-4397	496

Name / Address	City	State	ZIP	Phone	Fax	Class
BMM Testlabs 815 Pilot Rd Ste G *TF:* 800-791-6536 ■ *Web:* www.bmm.com	Las Vegas	NV	89119	702-407-2420	407-2421	463
BMO (Bank of Montreal) 100 King St W 1 First Canadian Pl 21st Fl *NYSE: BMO* ■ *TF:* 800-340-5021 ■ *Web:* www.bmo.com	Toronto	ON	M5X1A1	416-867-6785	867-6793	70
BMO Bankcorp Inc 120 S La Salle St *TF:* 888-340-2265 ■ *Web:* www.bmoharris.com	Chicago	IL	60603	888-340-2265		360-2
BMO Harris Bradley Ctr 1001 N Fourth St *Web:* www.bmoharrisbradleycenter.com	Milwaukee	WI	53203	414-227-0400		720
BMP America Inc 11625 Maple Ridge Rd *Web:* www.bmpworldwide.com	Medina	NY	14103	585-798-0950	798-4272	629
BMPL (Batesville Memorial Public Library) 131 N Walnut St *Web:* www.ebatesville.com	Batesville	IN	47006	812-934-4706	934-6288	434-3
BMS (Broadcast Microwave Services Inc) 12305 Crosthwaite Cir *TF:* 800-669-9667 ■ *Web:* www.bms-inc.com	Poway	CA	92064	858-391-3050	391-3049	224
BMS Consulting Inc 209 Starling Ave *Web:* www.bmsbenefits.com	Martinsville	VA	24112	276-666-9425		463
BMT Aerospace USA Inc 18559 Malyn Blvd *Web:* www.bmtaerospace.com	Fraser	MI	48026	586-285-7700		709
BMTGA (Blood & Marrow Transplant Group of Georgia) 5670 Peachtree Dunwoody Rd Ste 1000 *Web:* www.bmtga.com	Atlanta	GA	30342	404-255-1930	255-1939	769
BMW (Book Marketing Works LLC) 50 Lovely St Rte 177 *TF:* 800-562-4357 ■ *Web:* www.bookmarketingworks.com	Avon	CT	06001	860-675-1344		637-2
BMW Manufacturing Co 1400 Hwy 101 S *Web:* www.bmwgroup-werke.com	Greer	SC	29651	864-802-6000		59
BMW Motorcycle Owners of America PO Box 3982 *Web:* www.bmwmoa.org	Ballwin	MO	63022	636-394-7277	391-1811	48-18
BMW of Darien 140 Ledge Rd *TF:* 855-349-6240 ■ *Web:* www.bmwdarien.com	Darien	CT	06820	203-656-1804		57
BMW of Manhattan Inc 555 W 57th St *TF:* 877-855-4607 ■ *Web:* www.bmwnyc.com	New York	NY	10019	212-586-2269		54
BMW of North America LLC 300 Chestnut Ridge Rd *TF:* 800-831-1117 ■ *Web:* www.bmwusa.com	Woodcliff Lake	NJ	07677	201-307-4000	307-4095	59
Bmw Precision Machining Inc 2379 Industry St *Web:* www.bmwprecision.com	Oceanside	CA	92054	760-439-6813	439-5940	454
BMW Toronto 11 Sunlight Park Rd *TF:* 888-875-8541 ■ *Web:* www.bmwtoronto.ca	Toronto	ON	M4M1B5	416-623-4269		57
BMWC Constructors 1740 W Michigan St *Web:* www.bmwc.com	Indianapolis	IN	46222	317-267-0400		189-10
BMWED (Brotherhood of Maintenance of Way Employees) 41475 Gardenbrook Rd *Web:* bmwe.org	Novi	MI	48375	248-662-2660	662-2659	414
BNA Bank 133 E Bankhead *Web:* www.bnabank.com	New Albany	MS	38652	662-534-8171		70
BNA Consulting Inc 635 S State St *Web:* www.bnaconsulting.com	Salt Lake City	UT	84111	801-532-2196		261
BNBS Inc 11600 Otter Creek S Rd *Fax Area Code: 870 ■ *TF:* 888-842-2064 ■ *Web:* bnbsolutionsinc.com	Mabelvale	AR	72103	501-224-1992	862-8485*	535
BNBuilders Inc 2601 Fourth Ave Ste 350 *Web:* www.bnbuilders.com	Seattle	WA	98121	206-382-3443		186
BNC National Bank 322 E Main Ave *TF:* 800-262-2265 ■ *Web:* www.bncbank.com	Bismarck	ND	58501	701-250-3000	250-3028	70
BNCCORP Inc 322 E Main Ave PO Box 4050 *OTC: BNCC* ■ *Web:* www.bncbank.com	Bismarck	ND	58502	701-250-3040	222-3653	360-2
BNEINC (Boddie-Noell Enterprises Inc) 1021 Noell Ln PO Box 1908 *Web:* bneinc.com	Rocky Mount	NC	27804	252-937-2000		670
BNI Coal Ltd 1637 Burnt Boat Dr PO Box 897 *Web:* www.bnicoal.com	Bismarck	ND	58503	701-222-8828	222-1547	501
BNL (Brookhaven National Laboratory) PO Box 5000 *Web:* www.bnl.gov	Upton	NY	11973	631-344-8000	344-5832	668
BNL Industries Inc 30 Industrial Park Rd *Web:* www.bnl.com	Vernon	CT	06066	860-870-6222		789
BNL Technical Services LLC 3250 Port of Benton Blvd Ste D *Web:* bnltech.com	Richland	WA	99354	509-371-2570		261
BNN (Business News Network) 299 Queen St W *TF:* 855-326-6266 ■ *Web:* www.bnnbloomberg.ca	Toronto	ON	M5V2Z5	416-384-6600		740
BNP Paribas 787 Seventh Ave *Web:* group.bnpparibas	New York	NY	10019	212-841-3000		690
BNR (Brave New Restaurant) 2300 Cottondale Ln Ste 105 *Web:* www.bravenewrestaurant.com	Little Rock	AR	72202	501-663-2677		671
BNSF (Burlington Northern & Santa Fe Railway) 2650 Lou Menk Dr *TF:* 800-795-2673 ■ *Web:* www.bnsf.com	Fort Worth	TX	76131	800-795-2673		648
BNSF Logistics LLC 4700 S Thompson Ste A202 *TF:* 888-285-4514 ■ *Web:* www.bnsflogistics.com	Springdale	AR	72764	888-285-4514		225
BNX Shipping Inc 910 E 236th St *Web:* www.bnxinc.com	Carson	CA	90745	310-764-0999		311
BNY MELLON 225 Liberty St *NYSE: BK* ■ *Web:* www.bnymellon.com	New York	NY	10286	212-495-1784		360-2
BNZ Materials Inc 6901 S Pierce St Ste 260 *TF:* 800-999-0890 ■ *Web:* www.bnzmaterials.com	Littleton	CO	80128	303-978-1199	978-0308	662
Bo Ling's 4701 Jefferson St *Web:* bolings.com	Kansas City	MO	64112	816-753-1718		671
Bo Loong Restaurant 3922 St Clair Ave *Web:* boloongtogo.com	Cleveland	OH	44114	216-391-3113		671
BO's Fish Wagon 801 Caroline St *Web:* bosfishwagon.com	Key West	FL	33040	305-294-9272		671

Name / Address	City	State	ZIP	Phone	Fax	Class
BOA Editions Ltd 250 N Goodman St Ste 306 *Web:* www.boaeditions.org	Rochester	NY	14607	585-546-3410	546-3913	637-2
Boa Technology Inc 1760 Platte St *TF:* 844-203-1297 ■ *Web:* www.boafit.com	Denver	CO	80202	303-455-5126		194
Boa-Franc 1255-98th St *TF:* 800-463-1303 ■ *Web:* www.boa-franc.com	Saint-Georges	QC	G5Y8J5	418-227-1181	227-1188	290
Boar's Head Inn 200 Ednam Dr *TF:* 800-476-1988 ■ *Web:* www.boarsheadresort.com	Charlottesville	VA	22903	434-296-2181	972-6024	669
Boar's Head Provisions Company Inc 1819 Main St Ste 800 *Web:* boarshead.com	Sarasota	FL	34236	941-955-0994		296-26
Board of Overseers of The Bar 97 Winthrop St *Web:* mebaroverseers.org	Augusta	ME	04330	207-623-1121	623-4175	445
Board of Regents of the University of Wisconsin System 1000 Bascom Mall L107 Education Bldg (lower level) *Web:* careercenter.education.wisc.edu	Madison	WI	53706	608-262-1755	262-9074	260
Board of Supervisors 201 State St *Web:* www.boonecounty.iowa.gov	Boone	IA	50036	515-433-0500		338
BoardBookit Inc 1 Altoona Pl *Web:* boardbookit.com	Pittsburgh	PA	15228	412-436-5180		387
Boarder to Boarder Trucking Inc PO Box 328 *TF:* 800-678-8789 ■ *Web:* www.btbtrucking.com	Edinburg	TX	78541	956-316-4444		685
Boardman Inc 1135 S McKinley Ave *Web:* www.boardmaninc.com	Oklahoma City	OK	73108	405-634-5434		492
Boardman Park 375 Boardman-Poland Rd *Web:* www.cogran.io	Boardman	OH	44512	330-726-8107	726-4562	50-1
Boardman Town Crier 240 Franklin St SE *Web:* www.towncrieronline.com	Warren	OH	44483	330-629-6200	629-6210	532-4
Boardroom Communications Inc Bank of America Plz 1776 N Pine Island Rd Ste 320 *TF:* 877-773-4767 ■ *Web:* boardroompr.com	Fort Lauderdale	FL	33322	954-370-8999		636
Boardroom Insiders 1090 Assembly Dr Ste 220 *Web:* info.boardroominsiders.com	Fort Mill	SC	29708	803-560-3058		466
Boardwalk Pipeline Partners LP 3800 Frederica St *NYSE:* BWP ■ *TF:* 866-913-2122 ■ *Web:* www.bwpmlp.com	Owensboro	KY	42301	270-686-3620		325
Boardwalk Plaza Hotel 2 Olive Ave *TF:* 800-332-3224 ■ *Web:* boardwalkplaza.com	Rehoboth Beach	DE	19971	302-227-7169	227-0561	379
Boart Longyear Co 2640 W 1700 S *TF:* 800-453-8740 ■ *Web:* www.boartlongyear.com	Salt Lake City	UT	84104	801-972 6430	977-3374	190
Boat Owners Association of the US 880 S Pickett St *TF:* 800-395-2628 ■ *Web:* www.boatus.com	Alexandria	VA	22304	703-823-9550		48-22
Boathouse Group Inc 260 Charles St *Web:* www.boathouseinc.com	Waltham	MA	02453	781-663-6600		7
Boathouse, The 101 Palm Blvd *Web:* www.boathouserestaurants.com	Isle of Palms	SC	29451	843-886-8000		671
BOB 94.9 WRBT 600 Corporate Cir *Web:* bob949.iheart.com	Harrisburg	PA	17110	717-540-8800		645-68
Bob Allen Ford 9239 Metcalf Ave *TF:* 855-437-7998 ■ *Web:* www.boballenford.com	Overland Park	KS	66212	913-381-3000		57
Bob and Judy Hale Heart Ctr 830 Boylston St Ste 205 *Web:* www.lowngroup.org	Chestnut Hill	MA	02467	617-732-1318	734-5763	305
Bob Barker Company Inc PO Box 429 *TF:* 800-334-9880 ■ *Web:* www.bobbarker.com	Fuquay-Varina	NC	27526	800-334-9880		594
Bob Brown Chevrolet Inc 3600 111th St *Web:* www.bobbrownchevy.com	Urbandale	IA	50322	515-344-3786		57
Bob Bullock Texas State History Museum 1800 N Congress Ave *Web:* www.thestoryoftexas.com	Austin	TX	78701	512-936-4631		520
Bob Davidson Ford Lincoln 1845 E Joppa Rd *TF:* 877-885-7890 ■ *Web:* www.bobdavidsonford.com	Baltimore	MD	21234	410-661-6400	668-4306	57
Bob Dean Supply Inc 2624 Hanson St *Web:* bobdeansupply.com	Fort Myers	FL	33901	239-332-1131		351
Bob Feller Museum 310 Mill St PO Box 160 *Web:* bobfellermuseum.org	Van Meter	IA	50261	515-996-2644		522
Bob Fisher Chevrolet Inc 4111 Pottsville Pk *Web:* www.bobfisherchev.com	Reading	PA	19605	484-525-0904		57
Bob Gabriel Company Insurance 2325 Wilshire Blvd *Web:* bobgabrielinsurance.titaniumhosting.com	Santa Monica	CA	90403	310-829-0305	453-0302	390
Bob Hart Consulting LLC 5126 W Evans Creek Rd *Web:* bobhartconsultingllc.com	Rogue River	OR	97537	541-582-8890		194
Bob Howard Chevrolet 13130 Broadway Ext *Web:* www.bobhowardchevrolet.com	Oklahoma City	OK	73114	405-463-2524		57
Bob Hubbard Horse Transportation Inc 3730 S Riverside Ave *TF:* 800-472-7786 ■ *Web:* www.bobhubbardhorsetrans.com	Colton	CA	92324	951-369-3770	369-3205	780
Bob Johnson & Assoc 16420 W Hardy Rd Ste 100 *Web:* www.bjja.com	Houston	TX	77060	281-873-5555	873-5544	612
Bob Jones University 1700 Wade Hampton Blvd **Fax Area Code:* 800 ■ *TF:* 800-252-6363 ■ *Web:* www.bju.edu	Greenville	SC	29614	864-242-5100	232-9258*	166
Bob Jones University Museum & Gallery Bob Jones University 1700 Wade Hampton Blvd *Web:* www.bjumg.org	Greenville	SC	29614	864-770-1331		520
Bob King Insurance Agency Inc 105 SW Higgins Ave *Web:* bobkinginsuranceagency.biz	Missoula	MT	59803	406-549-2222		390
Bob Mills Furniture Company LLC 3600 W Reno Ave *Web:* www.bobmillsfurniture.com	Oklahoma City	OK	73107	405-947-6500		321
Bob Moore Cadillac Inc 13020 N Broadway Ext *Web:* www.bobmoorecadillacokc.com	Oklahoma City	OK	73114	405-749-9000		57
Bob Reeves Brass Mouthpieces 25574 Rye Canyon Rd Ste D *TF:* 800-837-0980 ■ *Web:* www.bobreeves.com	Valencia	CA	91355	661-775-8820		52
Bob Ross auto group 85 Loop Rd *TF:* 833-866-1584 ■ *Web:* www.bobrossauto.com	Centerville	OH	45459	937-433-0990		516
Bob Schmitt Homes Inc 9095 Gatestone Rd *Web:* bobschmitthomes.com	North Ridgeville	OH	44039	440-327-9495		187
Bob Sight Ford Inc 610 NW Blue Pkwy *Web:* www.bobsightford.com	Lee's Summit	MO	64063	816-524-6550		57
Bob Stall Chevrolet 7601 Alvarado Rd *TF:* 800-295-2695 ■ *Web:* www.bobstall.com	La Mesa	CA	91942	800-295-3051		57
Bob Straub State Park US Hwy 101 *Web:* stateparks.oregon.gov	Pacific City	OR	97135	503-842-3182		565
Bob Strilich Insurance Agency Inc 6751 Academy Rd NE Ste A *Web:* bobstrilich.com	Albuquerque	NM	87109	505-823-9333		390
Bob Sumerel Tire Company Inc 1257 Cox Ave *Web:* www.bobsumereltire.com	Erlanger	KY	41018	859-283-2700		755
BOB the (Big Old Bldg) 20 Monroe Ave NW *Web:* www.thebob.com	Grand Rapids	MI	49503	616-356-2000	493-2011	50-6
Bob Wagners Mill Carpet Inc 4531 W Lincoln Hwy *Web:* bobwagnerflooringdowningtown.com	Downingtown	PA	19335	610-269-7808		290
Bob Ward & Sons Inc 3015 Paxson St *TF:* 800-800-5083 ■ *Web:* www.bobwards.com	Missoula	MT	59801	406-728-3220		711
Bob Wolfe Partners Tpg 13900 Marquesas Way Ste 3115 *Web:* www.bwp-tpg.com	Marina	CA	90292	310-260-1340		7
Bob's Barricades Inc 921 Shotgun Rd *TF:* 800-432-5031 ■ *Web:* www.bobsbarricades.com	Sunrise	FL	33326	954-423-2627		295
Bob's Construction Inc 589A Lake Shady Ave N *TF:* 800-851-2627 ■ *Web:* www.bobs-construction.com	Oronoco	MN	55960	507-288-8379	282-2115	189-12
Bob's Discount Furniture Inc 428 Tolland Tpke *TF:* 800-569-1284 ■ *Web:* www.mybobs.com	Manchester	CT	06042	860-645-3208		321
Bob's Red Mill Natural Foods Inc 13521 SE Pheasant Ct *TF:* 800-553-2258 ■ *Web:* www.bobsredmill.com	Milwaukie	OR	97222	503-654-3215	653-1339	296-4
Bob's Sporting Goods 1111 Hudson St *Web:* www.bobsmerch.com	Longview	WA	98632	360-425-3870		229
Bob's Steak & Chop House 4300 Lemmon Ave *Web:* bobs-steakandchop.com	Dallas	TX	75219	214-528-9446		671
Bob's Stores Inc 160 Corporate Ct *TF:* 866-333-2627 ■ *Web:* www.bobstores.com	Meriden	CT	06450	203-379-2260		157-2
Bob's Transport & Storage Company Inc 7980 Tar Bay Dr *Web:* bobs-transport.com	Jessup	MD	20794	410-799-0832	799-0951	780
Boba House 332 S Tate St *Web:* bobahouse.com	Greensboro	NC	27403	336-379-7444		671
Bobak Sausage 4551 W Adams St *Web:* www.bobak.com	Chicago	IL	60624	773-735-5334		296-26
Bobby Brown Park 2509 Bobby Brown State Park Rd *Web:* www.bobbybrownpark.com	Elberton	GA	30635	706-283-5500		565
Bobby Jones 2625 N Berkeley Lake Rd NW Ste 100 *TF:* 888-776-0076 ■ *Web:* bobbyjones.c3style.com	Duluth	GA	30096	888-776-0076		155-3
Bobby Rahal Automotive Group 15035 Perry Hwy *TF:* 888-428-4402 ■ *Web:* www.bobbyrahal.com	Wexford	PA	15090	888-428-4402		483
Bobby Riggs Tennis Museum 875 Santa Fe Dr *Web:* www.bobbyriggs.net	Encinitas	CA	92024	760-473-2672		522
Bobby Rubino's Place for Ribs 2501 N Federal Hwy *Web:* www.bobbyrubinos.com	Pompano Beach	FL	33064	954-781-7550		670
BobCAD-CAM Inc 28200 US Hwy 19 N Ste E *TF:* 888-582-6925 ■ *Web:* bobcad.com	Clearwater	FL	33761	727-442-3554	442-9264	177
Bobcat Central Inc 3516 Newton Rd *Web:* bobcatcentral.com	Stockton	CA	95205	209-466-9631		45
Bobcat Co 250 E Beaton Dr *Web:* www.bobcat.com	West Fargo	ND	58078	701-241-8700		516
Bobcat of Atlanta 6972 Best Friend Rd *Web:* www.bobcatofatlanta.com	Atlanta	GA	30340	770-242-6500		791
Bobcat of Boston Inc 20 Concord St *Web:* bobcatboston.com	North Reading	MA	01864	978-664-3727		791
Bobcat of Springfield 4475 Camp Butler Rd *TF:* 888-464-5102 ■ *Web:* www.bobcatofspringfield.com	Springfield	IL	62707	217-525-0349	525-0375	300
Bobcat of St Louis 401 W Outer Rd *Web:* www.bobcatofstl.com	Valley Park	MO	63088	636-225-2900		470
Bobco Industries Inc 5067 David Strickland Rd Unit 104 **Fax Area Code:* 817 ■ *TF:* 866-409-3276 ■ *Web:* www.bobcoindustriesinc.com	Fort Worth	TX	76119	866-409-3276	483-8849*	625
Bobco Metals LLC 2000 S Alameda St **Fax Area Code:* 888 ■ *TF:* 800-262-2605 ■ *Web:* www.bobcometal.com	Los Angeles	CA	90058	800-262-2605	572-6226*	492
Bobeck Real Estate Company Inc 3333 W Hamilton Rd	Fort Wayne	IN	46814	260-432-1000		652
Bobit Business Media 3520 Challenger St *Web:* www.bobitbusinessmedia.com	Torrance	CA	90503	310-533-2400		637-9
Bobo Construction Inc 9728 Kent St *Web:* www.boboconstructioninc.com	Elk Grove	CA	95624	916-685-2285		187

Name / Address	City	State	Zip	Phone	Fax	Class
Bobrick Washroom Equipment Inc 11611 Hart St *Web:* www.bobrick.com	North Hollywood	CA	91605	818-764-1000	765-2700	487
BOC International Inc 21 Drydock Ave Ste 510E *Web:* www.bocintl.com	Boston	MA	02210	617-345-0050		449
BOC Partners Inc 1030 South Ave W Ste 1 *TF:* 877-310-8445 ■ *Web:* bocpartners.com	Westfield	NJ	07090	877-310-8445		7
Boc Water Hydraulics Inc 12024 Salem-Warren Rd *Web:* www.bocwaterhydraulics.com	Salem	OH	44460	330-332-4444		790
Boca Beauty Academy Inc 7820 Glades Rd *Web:* www.bocabeautyacademy.edu	Boca Raton	FL	33434	561-487-1191		167-3
Boca Biolistics (BBL) 5001 NW 13th Ave Bay H *Web:* www.bocabio.com	Pompano Beach	FL	33064	954-449-6126	429-2998	743
Boca Communications LLC 240 Stockton St F5 *Web:* bocacommunications.com	San Francisco	CA	94108	415-738-7718		636
Boca Del Lupo 1422 William St *Web:* bocadellupo.com	Vancouver	BC	V5L2P7	604-684-2622		747
Boca Raton Historical Society & Museum 71 N Federal Hwy *Web:* www.bocahistory.org	Boca Raton	FL	33432	561-395-6766		522
Boca Raton Museum of Art 501 Plaza Real Mizner Pk *TF:* 866-481-1689 ■ *Web:* www.bocamuseum.org	Boca Raton	FL	33432	561-392-2500	391-6410	520
Boca Raton Public Library 400 NW Second Ave *Web:* www.myboca.us	Boca Raton	FL	33432	561-393-7852		434-3
Boca Raton Regional Hospital 800 Meadows Rd *Web:* www.brrh.com	Boca Raton	FL	33486	561-955-7100		374-3
Boca Raton Rehabilitation Ctr 755 Meadows Rd *Web:* bocaratonhealthandrehab.com	Boca Raton	FL	33486	561-391-5200	391-0685	450
Boca Raton Resort & Club 501 E Camino Real *TF:* 888-543-1224 ■ *Web:* www.bocaresort.com	Boca Raton	FL	33432	561-447-3000	447-5073	669
Boca Systems Inc 1065 S Rogers Cir *Web:* www.bocasystems.com	Boca Raton	FL	33487	561-998-9600	998-9609	173-1
Bocada LLC 5555 Lakeview Dr Ste 201 *TF:* 866-262-2321 ■ *Web:* www.bocada.com	Kirkland	WA	98033	425-898-2400	898-2402	387
Bocarsly Emden Cowan Esmail & Arndt LLP 633 W Fifth St 64th Fl *Web:* www.bocarsly.com	Los Angeles	CA	90071	213-239-8000	239-0410	445
Boccardo Jewelers Inc 201 Jefferson Ave *Web:* boccardojewelers.com	Scranton	PA	18503	570-344-9021		410
Boccardo Law Firm Inc, The 111 W St John St Ste 400 *TF:* 800-662-9807 ■ *Web:* www.boccardo.com	San Jose	CA	95113	800-662-9807		445
Boces Lower Hudson Regional Information Ctr 44 Executive *Web:* www.lhric.org	Elmsford	NY	10523	914-592-4203		685
Boch Toyota Inc 277 Providence Hwy *TF:* 888-324-7531 ■ *Web:* www.bochtoyota.com	Norwood	MA	02062	888-324-7531		57
Bochetto & Lentz PC 1524 Locust St *Web:* bochettoandlentz.com	Philadelphia	PA	19102	215-735-3900		41
Bock & Clark Corp 3550 W Market St Ste 200 *TF:* 800-787-8397 ■ *Web:* www.bockandclark.com	Akron	OH	44333	330-665-4821		727
Bock Water Heaters Inc 110 S Dickinson St *TF:* 800-794-2491 ■ *Web:* www.bockwaterheaters.com	Madison	WI	53703	608-257-2225		36
Bockorny Group Inc 1350 I St NW Ste 800 *Web:* www.bockornygroup.com	Washington	DC	20005	202-659-9111	659-6387	194
Bockstael Construction 200-100 Paquin Rd *Web:* www.bockstael.com	Winnipeg	MB	R2J3V4	204-233-7135		186
Bocook Engineering Inc 312 10th St	Paintsville	KY	41240	606-789-5961		256
Bocotek Inc 3008 Altez NE	Albuquerque	NM	87111	505-237-0528		175
Boda Plumbing Inc 1909 Tower Industrial Dr *Web:* bodaplumbing.com	Monroe	NC	28110	704-291-9097		610
Boddie-Noell Enterprises Inc (BNEINC) 1021 Noell Ln PO Box 1908 *Web:* bneinc.com	Rocky Mount	NC	27804	252-937-2000		670
Bode Concrete 450 Amador St *Web:* centralconcrete.com	San Francisco	CA	94124	415-920-6740	920-6746	182
Bode North America Inc 660 John Dodd Rd *Web:* www.bodenorthamerica.com	Spartanburg	SC	29303	864-578-9683		60
Bodean Seafood Restaurant 3376 E 51st St *Web:* www.bodean.net	Tulsa	OK	74135	918-749-1407		671
Bodega Bay Lodge 103 Coast Hwy 1 *TF:* 888-875-2250 ■ *Web:* bodegabaylodge.com	Bodega Bay	CA	94923	707-875-3525		379
Bodega Latina Corp 14601B Lakewood Blvd *Web:* elsupermarkets.com	Paramount	CA	90723	562-616-8800		345
Bodega Restaurant 30 Baldwin St *Web:* www.bodegarestaurant.com	Toronto	ON	M5T1L3	416-977-1287	408-1941	671
Bodemuller the Printer Inc 123 S Main St *Web:* www.bodemullertheprinter.com	Opelousas	LA	70570	337-234-5002	942-6332	535
Bodhtree Bldg 3-326 7901 Cameron Rd **Fax Area Code:* 877 ■ *Web:* www.bodhtree.com	Austin	TX	78754	408-409-2568	410-0710*	177
Bodie State Historic Park PO Box 515 *Web:* www.parks.ca.gov	Bridgeport	CA	93517	760-647-6445		565
Bodine Electric Co 201 Northfield Rd *TF:* 800-726-3463 ■ *Web:* www.bodine-electric.com	Northfield	IL	60093	773-478-3515	478-3232	518
Bodine Perry LLC 3711 Starrs Centre Dr Ste 2 *Web:* bodineperry.com	Canfield	OH	44406	330-702-8100		2
Bodines Casino 5650 S Carson St *Web:* bodinescarson.com	Carson City	NV	89701	775-885-7777		452
Bodman PLC 1901 St Antoine St 6th Fl at Ford Field *Web:* www.bodmanlaw.com	Detroit	MI	48226	313-259-7777		428
Bodow Recycling Inc 1925 Park St Ste 2 *Web:* www.bodowrecycling.com	Syracuse	NY	13208	315-422-2552		686
Bodwell High School 955 Harbourside Dr *Web:* bodwell.edu	North Vancouver	BC	V7P3S4	604-924-5056		685
Body Bar Inc 1942 Broadway Ste 314 *TF:* 800-500-2030 ■ *Web:* bodybar.com	Boulder	CO	80302	800-500-2030		711
Body Shop, The 5036 One World Way *Web:* www.thebodyshop.com	Wake Forest	NC	27587	800-387-4592		214
Body Tech Total Fitness 19815 S La Grange Rd *Web:* www.bodytechtotalfitness.com	Mokena	IL	60448	708-478-5054	478-5056	354
Body Therapy Institute 300 Southwind Rd *Web:* www.bti.edu	Siler City	NC	27344	919-663-3111	663-0369	167-3
Body Wisdom Massage Therapy School 8401 Douglas Ave Ste 2 *TF:* 800-457-7339 ■ *Web:* www.bodywisdomschool.com	Urbandale	IA	50322	515-727-5100	727-5888	685
Body, The 250 W 57th St *Web:* www.thebody.com	New York	NY	10107	212-541-8500	541-4911	356
Body/Mind Restoration Retreats 56 Lieb Rd *Web:* www.bodymindretreats.com	Spencer	NY	14883	607-277-7779		706
Body-Borneman Insurance PO Box 584 *Web:* body-borneman.com	Boyertown	PA	19512	610-367-1100	367-1140	390
Bodyfelt Mount LLP 319 SW Washington St Ste 1200 *Web:* bodyfeltmount.com	Portland	OR	97204	503-243-1022		41
BODYlogic Fitness 2102 E Main Ave Ste 110 *Web:* bodylogicfit.com	Puyallup	WA	98372	253-224-7001		354
Bodymechanics School of Myotherapy & Massage 2330 Mottman Rd Ste 106 *Web:* www.bodymechanics-school.com	Tumwater	WA	98512	360-350-0015		685
Body-Solid Inc 1900 Des Plaines Ave **Fax Area Code:* 708 ■ *TF:* 800-833-1227 ■ *Web:* www.bodysolid.com	Forest Park	IL	60130	800-833-1227	427-3556*	267
Boeck & Associates Inc 930 Town Centre Dr *Web:* boeckinsurance.com	Medford	OR	97504	541-770-9400		390
BoeFly LLC 50 W 72nd St Ste C4 *TF:* 800-277-3158 ■ *Web:* boefly.com	New York	NY	10023	800-277-3158		387
Boehl Stopher & Graves LLP 400 W Market St Ste 2300 *Web:* bsg-law.com	Louisville	KY	40202	502-589-5980		428
Boehm Pressed Steel Co 5440 Wegman Dr *TF:* 800-936-3227 ■ *Web:* www.boehmstampings.com	Valley City	OH	44280	800-936-3227		488
Boehringer Ingelheim (Canada) Ltd 5180 S Service Rd *TF:* 800-263-5103 ■ *Web:* www.boehringer-ingelheim.ca	Burlington	ON	L7L5H4	905-639-0333		582
Boehringer Ingelheim Pharmaceuticals Inc 900 Ridgebury Rd *TF:* 800-243-0127 ■ *Web:* www.boehringer-ingelheim.us	Ridgefield	CT	06877	203-798-9988	791-6234	582
Boehringer Ingelheim Vetmedica Inc 2621 N Belt Hwy *TF:* 800-821-7467 ■ *Web:* www.bi-vetmedica.com	Saint Joseph	MO	64506	816-233-2571		584
Boehringer Laboratories Inc 300 Thoms Dr *TF:* 800-642-4945 ■ *Web:* boehringerlabs.com	Phoenixville	PA	19460	610-278-0900	278-0907	476
Boeing MC 11-503 7755 E Marginal Way S *Web:* www.boeing.com	Seattle	WA	98108	972-586-1985	586-1361	770
Boeing Future of Flight 8415 Paine Field Blvd *TF:* 888-467-4777 ■ *Web:* www.boeingfutureofflight.com	Mukilteo	WA	98275	425-438-8100		129
Boeing Vancouver 200-13575 Commerce Pkwy *Web:* www.boeing.ca	Richmond	BC	V6V2L1	604-232-4200	232-4201	809
Boekel Scientific 855 Pennsylvania Blvd *TF:* 800-336-6929 ■ *Web:* www.boekelsci.com	Feasterville-Trevose	PA	19053	215-396-8200	396-8264	420
Boelte-Hall Litho Inc 4710 Roe Pkwy *Web:* boelte.com	Roeland Park	KS	66205	913-766-7700		627
Boelter Companies Inc N22W23685 Ridgeview Pkwy W *TF:* 800-263-5837 ■ *Web:* www.boelter.com	Waukesha	WI	53188	262-523-6200	523-6003	300
Boelter Industries Inc 202 Galewski Dr *TF:* 877-977-5177 ■ *Web:* www.wspackaging.com	Winona	MN	55987	507-452-2315		101
Boenning & Scattergood Inc 200 Barr Harbor Dr Four Tower Bridge Ste 300 *TF:* 800-883-1212 ■ *Web:* www.boenninginc.com	West Conshohocken	PA	19428	610-832-1212		401
Boerner Botanical Gardens 9400 Boerner Dr *Web:* www.boernerbotanicalgardens.org	Hales Corners	WI	53130	414-525-5653		97
Boesen the Florist 3422 Beaver Ave *Web:* www.boesen.com	Des Moines	IA	50310	515-274-4761		292
Boething Treeland Farms Inc 23475 Long Valley Rd *Web:* www.boethingtreeland.com	Woodland Hills	CA	91367	818-316-2024	712-6979	752
Bogachiel State Park 185983 Hwy 101 *Web:* parks.state.wa.us	Forks	WA	98331	360-374-6356		565
Bogard Press 4605 N State Ln *TF:* 800-264-2482 ■ *Web:* bogardpress.org	Texarkana	TX	75503	903-792-2783	792-8128	637-2

				Phone	Fax	Class
Bogart & Brownell of MD Inc 7648 Standish Pl *Web:* www.bogartandbrownell.com	Rockville	MD	20855	301-444-4500	444-4510	390
Bogen Communications International Inc 50 Spring St *OTC:* BOGN ■ *TF:* 800-999-2809 ■ *Web:* www.bogen.com	Ramsey	NJ	07446	201-934-8500	934-6532	52
Boggs Inc 4426 Hunt Ave *Fax Area Code:* 314 ■ *TF:* 800-444-2644 ■ *Web:* www.boggsinc.com	Saint Louis	MO	63110	800-444-2644	531-1006*	815
Boggs Law Firm LLC 102 W Stone Ave *Web:* boggslawfirm.com	Greenville	SC	29609	864-233-8066	233-5067	41
Boggus Ford 1400 E Hwy 83 *TF:* 888-306-0194 ■ *Web:* www.boggusfordonline.com	McAllen	TX	78501	956-306-0194		57
Boggy Depot State Park 475 S Pk Ln *Web:* www.travelok.com	Atoka	OK	74525	580-889-5625	889-7868	565
Bogle Vineyards & Winery 37783 County Rd 144 *Web:* www.boglewinery.com	Clarksburg	CA	95612	916-744-1139	744-1187	50-7
Bogle, Deascentis & Coughlin PC 57 N Main St *Web:* b-dlaw.com	Fall River	MA	02722	508-677-2800		41
Bogner Entertainment Inc 269 S Beverly Dr Ste 8 *Web:* www.bognerentertainment.com	Beverly Hills	CA	90212	310-765-4300		572
Bognet Construction 8224 Old Courthouse Rd Ste 200 *Web:* www.bognet.com	Tysons	VA	22182	703-807-0007	807-0008	186
Bogota School District 1 Henry C Luthin Pl *Web:* www.bogotaboe.com	Bogota	NJ	07603	201-441-4800	489-5759	685
Bogue Banks Public Library (BBPL) 320 Salter Path Rd Ste W *Web:* carteret.cpclib.org	Pine Knoll Shores	NC	28512	252-247-4660	247-2802	434-3
Boh Bros Construction Company LLC 730 S Tonti St *TF:* 800-284-3377 ■ *Web:* www.bohbros.com	New Orleans	LA	70119	504-821-2400	821-0714	188-4
Bohanan's Prime Steaks & Seafood 219 E Houston St 2nd Fl *Web:* www.bohanans.com	San Antonio	TX	78205	210-472-2600	472-2276	671
Bohannan Huston Inc 7500 Jefferson St NE *TF:* 800-877-5332 ■ *Web:* www.bhinc.com	Albuquerque	NM	87109	505-823-1000	798-7988	178-5
Bohemian Cafe 1406 S 13th St *Web:* www.bohemiancafe.net	Omaha	NE	68108	402-342-9838		671
Bohler-Uddeholm North America 2505 Millenium Dr *TF:* 800-638-2520 ■ *Web:* www.voestalpine.com	Elgin	IL	60124	630-883-3000	883-3101	492
Bohn and Dawson Inc 3500 Tree Ct Industrial Blvd *Web:* www.bdiweldedtubing.com	Saint Louis	MO	63122	636-225-5011	825-6111	480
Bohnert Equipment Company Inc 1010 S Ninth St *Web:* www.bohnert.com	Louisville	KY	40203	502-584-3391		57
Bohrens Moving & Storage Inc 3 Applegate Dr *TF:* 800-326-4736 ■ *Web:* www.bohrensmoving.com	Robbinsville	NJ	08691	609-208-1470	208-1471	519
BOI (Buffalo Office Interiors Inc) 1418 Niagra St *Web:* www.boisite.com	Buffalo	NY	14213	716-883-8222	881-3359	112
Boies Schiller & Flexner LLP 1401 New York Ave NW *Web:* www.bsfllp.com	Washington	DC	20005	202-237-2727	237-6131	428
Boiling Springs State Park 207745 Boiling Springs Rd *Web:* www.travelok.com	Woodward	OK	73801	580-256-7664	256-4338	565
Boingo Graphics Inc 656 Michael Wylie Dr *Web:* www.boingographics.com	Charlotte	NC	28217	704-529-5044		627
Boingo Wireless Inc 10960 Wilshire Blvd Ste 800 *TF:* 800-880-4117 ■ *Web:* www.boingo.com	Los Angeles	CA	90024	310-586-5180		177
Boiron 6 Campus Blvd *TF:* 800-264-7661 ■ *Web:* www.boironusa.com	Newtown Square	PA	19073	610-325-7464		231
Bois Blanc Island Lighthouse National Historic Site Bois Blanc Island	Amherstburg	ON	N9V2Z2	888-773-8888		563
Bois BSL Inc 1081 Rue Industrielle CP4 *Web:* boisbsl.com	Mont-Joli	QC	G5H3T9	418-775-5360		290
Boisaco Inc 648 Chemin du Moulin *Web:* www.boisaco.com	Sacre-Coeur	QC	G0T1Y0	418-236-4633	236-4488	683
Boise Airport 3201 Airport Way *Web:* cityofboise.org	Boise	ID	83705	208-383-3110		27
Boise Art Museum 670 Julia Davis Dr *Web:* www.boiseartmuseum.org	Boise	ID	83702	208-345-8330	345-2247	520
Boise Bible College 8695 W Marigold St *TF:* 800-893-7755 ■ *Web:* www.boisebible.edu	Boise	ID	83714	208-376-7731	376-7743	161
Boise Cascade LLC 1111 W Jefferson St Ste 300 *Web:* bc.com	Boise	ID	83702	208-384-6161		557
Boise Centre on the Grove 850 W Front St *Web:* boisecentre.com	Boise	ID	83702	208-336-8900		205
Boise City Independent School District 8169 W Victory Rd *Web:* www.boiseschools.org	Boise	ID	83709	208-854-4000	854-4003	685
Boise Convention & Visitors Bureau 250 S Fifth St Ste 300 *TF:* 800-635-5240 ■ *Web:* www.boise.org	Boise	ID	83702	208-344-7777		206
Boise County 420 Main St PO Box 1300 *Web:* www.boisecounty.us	Idaho City	ID	83631	208-392-4431	392-4473	338
Boise Metro Chamber of Commerce 1101 W Front St Ste 100 *Web:* www.boisechamber.org	Boise	ID	83701	208-472-5205	472-5201	139
Boise Philharmonic Association Inc 516 S Ninth St *Web:* boisephil.org	Boise	ID	83702	208-344-7849	336-9078	573-3
Boise Public Library 715 S Capitol Blvd *TF:* 800-377-3529 ■ *Web:* www.boisepubliclibrary.org	Boise	ID	83702	208-972-8200	384-4025	434-3
Boise Refrigeration Service Co 202 W 39th St *Web:* www.brsc1.com	Garden City	ID	83714	208-344-0709		189-10
Boise State University 1910 University Dr *Web:* my.boisestate.edu	Boise	ID	83725	208-426-1011		166
Boise VA Medical Ctr 500 W Fort St *TF:* 866-437-5093 ■ *Web:* www.boise.va.gov	Boise	ID	83702	208-422-1000		374-8
Boise Weekly 523 Broad St *Web:* www.idahopress.com	Boise	ID	83702	208-344-2055	342-4733	532-5
Boiseries Raymond Inc 11880 56e Ave *TF:* 800-361-6577 ■ *Web:* www.boiseriesraymond.com	Montreal	QC	H1E2L6	514-494-1141	494-9666	499
Boise-Winnemucca Stages Inc 1230 W Bannock St *TF:* 800-448-5692 ■ *Web:* www.boise-winnemuccastages.com	Boise	ID	83702	208-336-3300	336-3303	107
Boite A. Fleur De Laval Incorporated LA 3266 Boul Sainte-Rose *TF:* 800-784-3495 ■ *Web:* alaboiteafleurs.com	Laval	QC	H7P4K8	450-622-0341		292
Boja's Foods Inc 13120 N Wintzell Ave *Web:* www.bojasfoods.com	Bayou La Batre	AL	36509	251-824-4186		296-14
Bojangles' Restaurants Inc 9432 Southern Pine Blvd *TF:* 800-366-9921 ■ *Web:* www.bojangles.com	Charlotte	NC	28273	704-335-1804		670
Bojo Tools 2283 Ringwood Ave Ste E-2 *Web:* www.bojoinc.com	San Jose	CA	95131	408-844-8211	844-8218	261
Bojorquez Law Firm PC 12325 Hymeadow Dr Ste 2-100 *Web:* texasmunicipallawyers.com	Austin	TX	78750	512-250-0411		41
BOK Financial 1044 Main St *Web:* www.bokfinancial.com	Kansas City	MO	64105	816-881-8200		70
Bokam Engineering Inc 2720 S Shannon St *Web:* www.bokam.com	Santa Ana	CA	92704	714-513-2200		261
Boker's Inc 3104 Snelling Ave *TF:* 800-927-4377 ■ *Web:* www.bokers.com	Minneapolis	MN	55406	612-729-9365		621
Boksa Marine Design Inc (BMD) 16627 Fishhawk Blvd Ste 101 *Web:* www.bmdinc.com	Lithia	FL	33547	813-654-9800		261
Boland 30 W Watkins Mill Rd *TF:* 800-552-6526 ■ *Web:* www.boland.com	Gaithersburg	MD	20878	240-306-3000		610
Boland Balloon Post Mills Airport PO Box 51 *Web:* www.myairship.com	Post Mills	VT	05058	802-333-9254		28
Boland Marine & Manufacturing Company Inc 1000 Tchoupitoulas St *Web:* www.bolandmarine.com	New Orleans	LA	70130	504-581-5800	581-5814	698
Boland Recreation Inc 2347 Oak Park Rd *TF:* 800-798-7589 ■ *Web:* www.bolandrecreation.com	Marshalltown	IA	50158	800-798-7589		711
Bolanos & Company Inc 8708 Killam Indus Blvd *Web:* www.bolanos.com	Laredo	TX	78045	956-722-0976		311
Bolay Enterprises 1880 Okeechobee Blvd Ste A *Web:* www.bolay.com	West Palm Beach	FL	33409	561-815-5185		670
Bolchazy-Carducci Publishers Inc 1570 Baskin Rd *TF:* 800-392-6453 ■ *Web:* www.bolchazy.com	Mundelein	IL	60060	847-526-4344	526-2867	637-2
Bold Beauty Academy 928 Broadwater Ste C *Web:* boldbeautyacademy.com	Billings	MT	59101	406-252-3232		166
Bold Planning Inc 4515 Harding Pk *Web:* www.boldplanning.com	Nashville	TN	37205	615-469-5558		809
Bold Spring Nursery 1366 Columbus Hwy *Web:* boldspring.com	Hawkinsville	GA	31036	478-783-4975		293
Bolden Lipkin PC 3993 Huntingdon Pk *TF:* 888-947-3750 ■ *Web:* www.blicpa.com	Huntingdon Valley	PA	19006	215-947-3750		2
Boldfocus Inc 1900 S Norfolk St Ste 350 *Web:* www.boldfocus.com	San Mateo	CA	94403	650-212-2653		180
Boldt Carlisle & Smith LLC 1255 Lee St SE Ste 210 *Web:* www.bcsllc.com	Salem	OR	97302	503-585-7751	370-3781	2
Bolduc Leroux Inc 3365 des Entreprises Blvd *Web:* www.bolducleroux.ca	Terrebonne	QC	J6X4J9	450-477-3413		492
Bolen, Robinson & Ellis LLP 202 S Franklin St 2nd Fl *Web:* brelaw.com	Decatur	IL	62523	217-429-4296		41
Boler Equipment Service Inc 4611 Sinclair Ave *Web:* www.boler.net	Midland	TX	79707	432-694-0660	694-2120	579
Bolero Associates LLC 2500 E Imperial Hwy Ste 149A 373 *Fax Area Code:* 800 ■ *Web:* www.boleroassociates.com	Brea	CA	92868	714-634-4441	634-4189*	463
Boley Tool & Machine Works Inc 1044 Spring Bay Rd *Web:* boleytool.com	East Peoria	IL	61611	309-694-2722		493
Bolger 3301 Como Ave SE *TF:* 866-264-3287 ■ *Web:* www.bolgerinc.com	Minneapolis	MN	55414	651-645-6311		627
Bolin Marketing Inc 2523 S Wayzata Blvd Ste 300 *TF:* 800-876-6264 ■ *Web:* www.bolinagency.com	Minneapolis	MN	55405	612-374-1200		7
Bolingbrook Area Chamber of Commerce & Industry 201 Canterbury Ln Unit B *Web:* www.bolingbrookchamber.org	Bolingbrook	IL	60440	630-226-8420	226-8426	139
Bolivar County 200 S Ct St *Web:* www.co.bolivar.ms.us	Cleveland	MS	38732	662-846-5877	846-5880	338
Bolivar County Library 104 S Leflore Ave *Web:* bolivar.lib.ms.us	Cleveland	MS	38732	662-843-2774	843-4701	434-3
Bolivar Medical Ctr 901 Hwy 8 E *Web:* www.bolivarmedical.com	Cleveland	MS	38732	662-846-0061	846-2380	374-3

Name / Address	City	State	Zip	Phone	Fax	Class
Bolivarian Republic of Venezuela *Consulate General* 545 Boylston St 3rd Fl *Web:* www.embavenez-us.org	Boston	MA	02116	617-266-9368		257
Bolivia *Consulate General* 800 Second Ave Ste 430 *Web:* boliviany.org	New York	NY	10017	212-687-0530		257
Bollard Group LLC, The 1 Joy St *Web:* www.bollard.com	Boston	MA	02108	617-720-5800	720-3490	194
Boller Construction Company Inc 3045 Washington St *Web:* www.bollerconstruction.com	Waukegan	IL	60085	847-662-5566		187
Bolles School 7400 San Jose Blvd *Web:* www.bolles.org	Jacksonville	FL	32217	904-733-9292	739-9929	622
Bollinger Algiers Inc 434 Powder St *Web:* www.bollingershipyards.com	New Orleans	LA	70114	504-362-7960	361-1679	698
Bollinger County 209 Mayfield Dr *Web:* bcmnh.org	Marble Hill	MO	63764	573-238-1174		338
Bollinger Insurance 101 JFK Pkwy *Web:* www.bollingerinsurance.com	Short Hills	NJ	07078	973-467-0444		390
Bollinger Mill State Historic Site 113 Bollinger Mill Rd *Web:* mostateparks.com	Burfordville	MO	63739	573-243-4591		565
Bollman Hat Co 110 E Main St *Web:* www.bollmanhats.com	Adamstown	PA	19501	717-484-4361		155-9
Bollus Lynch LLP 89 Shrewsbury St *Web:* www.bolluslynch.com	Worcester	MA	01604	508-755-7107		2
Bolon, Hart, Shives & Crisp Inc 140 E Town St Ste 1040 *Web:* www.bhsccpa.com	Columbus	OH	43215	614-228-2691		2
Bolsa Chica Ecological Reserve 3842 Warner Ave *Web:* www.bolsachica.org	Huntington Beach	CA	92649	714-846-1114	846-4065	823
Bolsan Company Inc 163 Linnwood Rd *Web:* bolsan.com	Eighty Four	PA	15330	724-225-0446		567
Bolt Enterprises 17875 Von Karman Ave Ste 150 *Web:* boltpr.com	Irvine	CA	92614	949-218-5454		636
Bolt Products Inc 16725 E Johnson Dr *TF:* 800-423-6503 ■ *Web:* www.boltproducts.com	City of Industry	CA	91745	626-961-4401	333-1908	351
Bolt Solutions Inc 100 Park Ave 16th Fl *Web:* www.boltinc.com	New York	NY	10016	212-608-4646		626
Bolt Staffing Service Inc 3427 Broadway St Ste F2 *Web:* www.boltstaffing.com	American Canyon	CA	94503	707-552-7800	552-6364	260
Boltaron Performance Products LLC 1 General St *TF:* 800-342-7444 ■ *Web:* www.boltaron.com	Newcomerstown	OH	43832	740-498-5900		601
Bolthouse Farms 7200 E Brundage Ln *TF:* 800-467-4683 ■ *Web:* www.bolthouse.com	Bakersfield	CA	93307	661-366-7201	366-2834	10-11
Bolton & Co 3475 E Foothill Blvd Ste 100 *TF:* 800-439-9337 ■ *Web:* boltonco.com	Pasadena	CA	91107	626-799-7000		390
Bolton & Hay Inc 2701 Delaware Ave *TF:* 800-362-1861 ■ *Web:* www.boltonhay.com	Des Moines	IA	50317	515-265-2554		300
Bolton & Menk Inc 1960 Premier Dr *Web:* www.bolton-menk.com	Mankato	MN	56001	507-625-4171	625-4177	261
Bolton Construction & Service of WNC Inc 169 Elk Mtn Rd *Web:* boltonservicewnc.com	Asheville	NC	28804	828-253-3621		186
Bolton Metal Products Co 2042 Axemann Rd *Web:* www.boltonmetalproducts.com	Bellefonte	PA	16823	814-355-6217	355-6219	485
Bolton Oil Company Ltd 1316 54th St *Web:* www.boltonoil.com	Lubbock	TX	79412	806-747-1629		541
Bolton, Sullivan, Taylor & Weber LLP 1023 N Mallard *Web:* bstwcpa.com	Palestine	TX	75801	903-729-2229	729-3123	2
Bolttech Mannings 501 Mosside Blvd **Fax Area Code: 412* ■ *TF:* 888-846-8827 ■ *Web:* www.bolttechmannings.com	North Versailles	PA	15137	724-872-4873	829-1834*	385
Bolzoni Auramo Inc 17635 Hoffman Way *TF:* 800-358-5438 ■ *Web:* www.bolzoni-auramo.com	Homewood	IL	60430	708-957-8809	957-8832	295
BOMA (Building Owners & Managers Association Intl) 1101 15th St NW Ste 800 *TF:* 800-426-6292 ■ *Web:* www.boma.org	Washington	DC	20005	202-408-2662	326-6377	49-17
Bo-Mac Contractors Ltd 1020 Lindbergh Dr *TF:* 800-526-6221 ■ *Web:* www.bomaccontractors.com	Beaumont	TX	77707	409-842-2125		188
Bomag Americas Inc 125 Blue Granite Pkwy *Web:* www.bomag.com	Ridgeway	SC	29130	803-337-0700	337-0800	190
Boman Kemp Basement Window Systems 2393 S 1900 W *Web:* www.boman-kemp.com	Ogden	UT	84401	801-731-0615		480
Bomanite 7862 Winding Way Ste 2649 *Web:* www.bomanite.com	Fair Oaks	CA	95628	303-369-1115		183
Bomar Inc c/o Pompanette LLC PO Box 1200 *Web:* pompanettellc.com	Charlestown	NH	03603	603-826-5791		350
Bomarko Inc 1955 N Oak Rd *Web:* www.bomarko.com	Plymouth	IN	46563	574-936-9901		548
Bomb Magazine 80 Hanson Pl Ste 703 *Web:* bombmagazine.org	Brooklyn	NY	11217	718-636-9100	636-9200	457-2
Bombard Electric LLC 4380 W Post Rd *Web:* www.bombardelectric.com	Las Vegas	NV	89118	702-263-3570		261
Bombardier Inc 800 RenT-LTvesque Blvd W *TSE: BBD.B* ■ *Web:* www.bombardier.com	Montreal	QC	H3B1Y8	514-861-9481	861-7769	20
Bombardier Recreational Products (BRP) 565 de la Montagne *Web:* www.brp.com	Valcourt	QC	J0E2L0	450-532-2211		710
Bombay Club 815 Connecticut Ave NW *Web:* bombayclubdc.com	Washington	DC	20006	202-659-3727		671
Bombay Cuisine 1420 Lake Dr *Web:* www.eatatbombay.com	Grand Rapids	MI	49506	616-456-7055		671
Bombay Curry Co 2607 Mt Vernon Ave *Web:* www.bombaycurrycompany.com	Alexandria	VA	22301	703-836-6363		671
Bombay Deluxe 555 W Northern Lights Blvd *Web:* www.bombaydeluxe.com	Anchorage	AK	99503	907-277-1200		671
Bombay House 2731 Parleys Way *Web:* bombayhouse.com	Salt Lake City	UT	84109	801-581-0222		671
Bombay Mahal 1001 Rue Jean-Talon Ouest *Web:* www.restaurantbombaymahal.ca	Montreal	QC	H3N1T2	514-273-3331		671
Bombet Cashio & Assoc 11220 N Harrells Ferry Rd *TF:* 800-256-5333 ■ *Web:* bombet.com	Baton Rouge	LA	70816	225-275-0796	272-3631	400
Bomco Inc 125 Gloucester Ave *Web:* www.bomco.com	Gloucester	MA	01930	978-283-9000	283-2882	483
Bomel Construction Company Inc 8195 E Kaiser Blvd *Web:* www.bomelconstruction.com	Anaheim Hills	CA	92808	714-921-1660	921-1943	189-3
Bomgaars 1805 Zenith *Web:* www.bomgaars.com	Sioux City	IA	51103	712-226-5000	277-1247	791
Bommarito Automotive Group 15736 Manchester Rd *TF:* 800-367-2289 ■ *Web:* www.bommarito.com	Ellisville	MO	63011	636-391-7200	394-3241	57
Bommer Industries Inc PO Box 187 *TF:* 800-334-1654 ■ *Web:* www.bommer.com	Landrum	SC	29356	864-457-3301	457-2487	350
Bomoseen State Park 22 Cedar Mtn Rd *Web:* www.vtstateparks.com	Fair Haven	VT	05743	802-265-4242		565
Bon Air Juvenile Correctional Ctr 1900 Chatsworth Ave *Web:* www.djj.virginia.gov	Bon Air	VA	23235	804-323-2550	323-2440	412
Bon Appetit Management Co 100 Hamilton Ave Ste 400 *TF:* 800-765-9419 ■ *Web:* www.bamco.com	Palo Alto	CA	94301	650-798-8000	798-8090	299
Bon Chef Inc 205 SR- 94 *TF:* 800-331-0177 ■ *Web:* www.bonchef.com	LaFayette	NJ	07848	800-331-0177		481
Bon Homme County 300 W 18th Ave PO Box 6 *Web:* www.bonhommecounty.org	Tyndall	SD	57066	605-589-4215	589-4245	338
Bon Homme Yankton Electric Association Inc 134 S Lidice St PO Box 158 *TF:* 800-925-2929 ■ *Web:* byelectric.coop	Tabor	SD	57063	605-463-2507	463-2419	245
Bon Motif Co 4045 Horton St *Web:* www.bonmotif.com	Emeryville	CA	94608	510-655-2000	655-1600	131
Bon Secour Fisheries Inc 17449 County Rd 49 S *Web:* www.bonsecourfisheries.com	Bon Secour	AL	36511	251-949-7411	949-6478	297-5
Bon Secours - Virginia Healthsource Inc 5801 Bremo Rd	Richmond	VA	23226	804-673-2727		194
Bon Secours Community Hospital 160 E Main St PO Box 1014 *Web:* www.bonsecourscommunityhosp.org	Port Jervis	NY	12771	845-858-7000		374-3
Bon Secours Health System Inc 1505 Marriottsville Rd *Web:* bonsecours.com	Marriottsville	MD	21104	410-442-5511	442-1082	353
Bon Secours Saint Francis Hospital 2095 Henry Tecklenburg Dr *TF:* 800-863-2273 ■ *Web:* www.rsfh.com	Charleston	SC	29414	843-402-1000		374-3
Bon Secours Wellness Arena 650 N Academy St *Web:* www.bonsecoursarena.com	Greenville	SC	29601	864-241-3800		720
Bon Ton Cafe 401 Magazine St *Web:* www.thebontoncafe.com	New Orleans	LA	70130	504-524-3386		671
Bon Tool Co 4430 Gibsonia Rd *TF:* 800-444-7060 ■ *Web:* www.bontool.com	Gibsonia	PA	15044	724-443-7080	443-7090	758
Bon Venture Services Inc 34 Ironia Rd *TF:* 800-883-4343 ■ *Web:* www.bonventure.net	Flanders	NJ	07836	800-883-4343		95
Bon Voyage Travel 1640 E River Rd Ste 115 *TF:* 800-439-7963 ■ *Web:* bvtravel.com	Tucson	AZ	85718	520-797-1110		771
Bonadio Group, The 171 Sully's Trl Ste 201 *TF:* 877-917-3077 ■ *Web:* www.bonadio.com	Pittsford	NY	14534	585-381-1000	381-3131	2
Bonafide Security Solutions 3605 N 126th St *Web:* www.bonafidesafe.com	Brookfield	WI	53005	262-790-9400		693
Bonair Daydreams PO Box 1522 *TF:* 888-226-6247 ■ *Web:* www.bonairdaydreams.com	Wrightsville Beach	NC	28480	910-617-3887	509-4108	130
Bonaire Government Tourist Office 80 Broad St Ste 3202 32nd Fl *Web:* www.infobonaire.com	New York	NY	10004	212-956-5912	956-5913	775
Bonal Technologies Inc 1300 N Campbell Rd *Web:* www.bonal.com	Royal Oak	MI	48067	248-582-0900		811
Bonamici Suzanne (Rep D - OR) 2231 Rayburn House Office Bldg *Web:* bonamici.house.gov	Washington	DC	20515	202-225-0855	225-9497	342-2
Bonanno, Savino & Davies PC 105 Chestnut St Ste 32 *Web:* www.bsdcpa.com	Needham	MA	02492	781-449-3919	449-7290	2
Bonanza Beverage Co 6333 Ensworth St *Web:* www.bonanzabev.com	Las Vegas	NV	89119	702-361-4166		81-1
Bonanza Creek Country Guest Ranch 523 Bonanza Creek Rd *TF:* 800-476-6045 ■ *Web:* bonanzacreekcountry.com	Martinsdale	MT	59053	406-572-3366		239
Bonanza Inc 3131 Western Ave Ste 428 *Web:* www.bonanza.com	Seattle	WA	98122	425-654-1521		393
Bonanza Press Inc 19860 141st Pl NE *TF:* 800-233-0008 ■ *Web:* www.bonanzapress.com	Woodinville	WA	98072	425-486-3399		627
Bonanza Publishing PO Box 204 **Fax Area Code: 541* ■ *TF:* 800-399-3115 ■ *Web:* www.bonanzapublishing.com	Prineville	OR	97754	800-399-3115	416-0822*	637-2

Name / Address	City	State	Zip	Phone	Fax	Class
Bonanza Trade & Supply 6853 Lankershim Blvd *TF:* 888-965-6577 ■ *Web:* www.stonetooling.com	North Hollywood	CA	91605	818-765-0686		194
Bonanzaville USA 1351 Main Ave W. *Web:* www.bonanzaville.org	West Fargo	ND	58078	701-282-2822	282-7606	520
Bonari & Company CPAS 3724 Lakeside Dr Ste 201 *Web:* bonaricpas.com	Reno	NV	89509	775-322-5850	828-6464	2
Bonaventure Tours 8 Boudreau Ln *TF:* 800-561-1213 ■ *Web:* bonaventuretours.com	Haute-Aboujagane	NB	E4P5N1	506-532-3674	532-6487	760
Bonchonsky & Zaino LLP 226 Seventh St Ste 200 *Web:* bzlawny.com	Garden City	NY	11530	516-747-1400		41
Bond & Botes of Mississippi Pc 5760 I 55 N Ste 100 *Web:* bondnbotes.com	Jackson	MS	39211	601-353-5000		41
Bond Bros Inc 10 Cabot Rd Ste 300 **Fax Area Code:* 781 ■ *Web:* www.bondbrothers.com	Medford	MA	02155	617-387-3400	874-0852*	186
Bond Consulting Services 3450 Spring St Ste 108 *Web:* bondconsultingservices.com	Long Beach	CA	90806	562-988-3451		177
Bond County 200 W College Ave *Web:* www.bondcountyil.com	Greenville	IL	62246	618-664-3208	664-2257	338
Bond Digital 2419 N Ashland Ave *Web:* bonddigital.com	Chicago	IL	60614	773-549-2710		7
Bond Optics LLC 76 Etna Rd *Web:* bondoptics.com	Lebanon	NH	03766	603-448-2300	448-5489	544
Bond Place Hotel 65 Dundas St E *TF:* 800-268-9390 ■ *Web:* www.bondplace.ca	Toronto	ON	M5B2G8	416-362-6061		379
Bond Printing Company Inc 104 Plain St *Web:* www.bondprinting.com	Hanover	MA	02339	781-871-3990		627
Bond Pro LLC 302 Knights Run Ave Ste 1160 *TF:* 888-789-4985 ■ *Web:* www.bond-pro.com	Tampa	FL	33602	813-413-7576		391-5
Bond Tool & Engineering 6190 N Riverview Dr *Web:* bondtool.com	Kalamazoo	MI	49004	269-344-5164	344-0360	256
Bondcliff Books 4 Eames Way *Web:* www.bondcliffbooks.com	Littleton	NH	03561	603-444-4880		637-2
Bondcote Corp PO Box 729 *TF:* 800-368-2160 ■ *Web:* bondcote.com	Pulaski	VA	24301	540-980-2640	980-5636	745-2
Bonded Concrete Inc PO Box 189 *TF:* 800-252-8589 ■ *Web:* www.bondedconcrete.com	Watervliet	NY	12189	518-273-5800		182
Bondfield Construction Company Ltd 407 Basaltic Rd *Web:* www.bondfield.com	Concord	ON	L4K4W8	416-667-8422		186
Bondhus Corp 1400 E Broadway St PO Box 660 *TF:* 800-328-8310 ■ *Web:* www.bondhus.com	Monticello	MN	55362	763-295-2162	295-4440	758
Bondioli & Pavesi Inc 10252 Sycamore Dr *Web:* www.bondioli-pavesi.com	Ashland	VA	23005	804-550-2224		429
Bone Bank Allografts 4808 Research Dr *TF:* 800-397-0088 ■ *Web:* bonebank.com	San Antonio	TX	78240	210-696-7616	696-7609	545
Bone McAllester Norton PLLC 511 Union St Nashville City Ctr Ste 1600 *Web:* www.bonelaw.com	Nashville	TN	37219	615-238-6300		428
Bonefish Capital LLC 13755 Hutton Dr Ste 300 *Web:* www.bonefishcapital.com	Farmers Branch	TX	75234	214-692-2900		463
Bonefish Grill 2100 Koury Blvd *Web:* www.bonefishgrill.com	Greensboro	NC	27407	336-851-8900		671
Bonell Manufacturing Co 13521 S Halsted St *Web:* www.bonellmfg.com	Riverdale	IL	60827	708-849-1770	849-3131	674
Bones Restaurant 3130 Piedmont Rd NE *Web:* www.bonesrestaurant.com	Atlanta	GA	30305	404-237-2663		671
Bonfiglioli USA 3541 Hargrave Dr *Web:* www.bonfiglioliusa.com	Hebron	KY	41048	859-334-3333		709
Bonfire, The 7009 Coastal Hwy *Web:* www.thebonfirerestaurant.com	Ocean City	MD	21842	410-524-7171		671
Bonfit America Inc 5741 Buckingham Pkwy Unit A *TF:* 800-526-6348 ■ *Web:* www.bonfit.com	Culver City	CA	90230	310-204-7880		568
Bongards' Creameries 13200 County Rd 51 *Web:* www.bongards.com	Norwood	MN	55368	952-466-3557		296-5
Bongo Room 1470 N Milwaukee Ave *Web:* thebongoroom.com	Chicago	IL	60622	773-489-0690		671
Bonham Area Chamber of Commerce 327 N Main *Web:* www.fannincountytexas.com	Bonham	TX	75418	903-583-4811	583-7972	139
Bonham State Park 1363 State Pk 24 *Web:* tpwd.texas.gov	Bonham	TX	75418	903-583-5022		565
Bonhams & Butterfields 220 San Bruno Ave *TF:* 800-223-2854 ■ *Web:* www.bonhams.com	San Francisco	CA	94103	415-861-7500	861-8951	51
Boniface Tool & Die Inc 181 Southbridge Rd *Web:* bonifacetool.com	Dudley	MA	01571	508-764-3248	764-8322	22
Bonipak 1850 W Stowell Rd **Fax Area Code:* 805 ■ *TF:* 800-328-8816 ■ *Web:* www.bonipak.com	Santa Maria	CA	93458	800-328-8816	922-7982*	10-11
Bonita Springs Area Chamber of Commerce 25071 Chamber of Commerce Dr *TF:* 800-226-2943 ■ *Web:* www.bonitaspringschamber.com	Bonita Springs	FL	34135	239-992-2943	992-5011	139
Bonitron Inc 521 Fairground Ct *Web:* www.bonitron.com	Nashville	TN	37211	615-244-2825	244-2833	425
Bonitz Contracting Company Inc 645 Rosewood Dr *Web:* www.bonitz.us	Columbia	SC	29201	803-799-0181	748-9223	189-2
Bonland Industries Inc 50 Newark-Pompton Tpke *TF:* 800-232-6600 ■ *Web:* www.bonlandhvac.com	Wayne	NJ	07470	973-694-3211	628-1120	189-12
Bonnell Aluminum 25 Bonnell St PO Box 428 *TF:* 800-846-8885 ■ *Web:* www.bonnellaluminum.com	Newnan	GA	30263	770-253-2020		485
Bonnell's 4259 Bryant Irvin Rd *Web:* bonnellstexas.com	Fort Worth	TX	76109	817-738-5489		671
Bonner Chevrolet Company Inc 694 Wyoming Ave *Web:* www.bonnerchevrolet.com	Kingston	PA	18704	570-763-4799		57
Bonner County 1500 Hwy 2 Ste 2 *Web:* www.bonnercountyid.gov	Sandpoint	ID	83864	208-255-3630	263-9084	338
Bonnet House Museum & Garden 900 N Birch Rd *Web:* www.bonnethouse.org	Fort Lauderdale	FL	33304	954-563-5393	561-4174	520
Bonnett Wholesale Florists 119 Eigth St E *Web:* www.bonnettwholesale.com	Milan	IL	61264	309-787-4401		292
Bonnette Page & Stone Corp 91 Bisson Ave *Web:* bpsnh.com	Laconia	NH	03246	603-524-3411	524-4641	186
Bonneville Collections 6026 S Fashion Point Dr *TF:* 800-660-6138 ■ *Web:* www.bonncoll.com	Ogden	UT	84403	801-621-7880		160
Bonneville County 605 N Capital Ave *Web:* www.co.bonneville.id.us	Idaho Falls	ID	83402	208-529-1350		338
Bonneville International Corp 55 N 300 W *Web:* www.bonneville.com	Salt Lake City	UT	84101	801-575-7500		643
Bonneville Transloaders Inc (BTI) 642 S Federal Blvd *Web:* www.bonntran.com	Riverton	WY	82501	307-856-7480	856-4623	648
Bonnie Castle Resort 31 Holland St PO Box 127 *TF:* 800-955-4511 ■ *Web:* www.bonniecastle.com	Alexandria Bay	NY	13607	315-482-4511		669
Bonnie Heneson Communications Inc 9891 Broken Land Pkwy Ste 304 *Web:* www.bonnieheneson.com	Columbia	MD	21046	410-740-5657		4
Bono's Pit Bar-B-Q 10645 Phillips Hwy Ste 200 *Web:* www.bonosbarbq.com	Jacksonville	FL	32256	904-886-2801	880-8373	670
Bonocore Technology Partners LLC 29 Meadow Ridge Dr *Web:* www.bonocore.com	Corte Madera	CA	94925	415-924-9991		463
Bonsai Artransport Inc 509 Mccormick Dr Ste O *Web:* www.bonsai-finearts.com	Glen Burnie	MD	21061	410-768-2787	768-5370	200
Bonsai Japanese Steak House 1925 Lakeland Dr *Web:* www.bonsaijxn.com	Jackson	MS	39216	601-981-0606		671
Bonset America Corp 6107 Corporate Pk Dr *Web:* www.bonset.com	Brown Summit	NC	27214	336-375-0234	375-6129	600
Bonstone Materials Corp 707 Swan Dr *TF:* 800-425-2214 ■ *Web:* www.bonstone.com	Mukwonago	WI	53149	262-363-9877		3
Bonten Media Group Inc Empire State Bldg 350 Fifth Ave Ste 5340 *Web:* www.bontenmedia.com	New York	NY	10118	212-710-7771	949-0909	647
Bonterra Dining & Wine Room 1829 Cleveland Ave *Web:* www.bonterradining.com	Charlotte	NC	28203	704-333-9463		671
Bonterra Energy Corp 1015 - Fourth St SW Ste 901 *Web:* www.bonterraenergy.com	Calgary	AB	T2R1J4	403-262-5307		536
Bonterra Trattoria 1016 Eigth St SW *Web:* bonterra.ca	Calgary	AB	T2R1K2	403-262-8480		671
Bon-Ton Stores Inc, The 2801 E Market St *NASDAQ:* BONTQ ■ *TF:* 800-945-4438 ■ *Web:* www.bonton.com	York	PA	17402	717-757-7660		229
Booher Carpet Sales Inc 4406 Linden Ave *Web:* boohercarpet.com	Dayton	OH	45432	937-254-1010		290
Book Country Clearing House LLC 3200 Walnut St *Web:* bookcountryclearinghouse.com	Mckeesport	PA	15132	412-678-2400		95
Book Depot 67 Front St N *TF:* 800-801-7193 ■ *Web:* www.bookdepot.com	Thorold	ON	L2V1X3	905-680-7230		96
Book Exchange Inc 152 Willey St *Web:* www.bookexchangewv.com	Morgantown	WV	26505	304-292-7354		95
Book Industry Study Group Inc (BISG) 232 Madison Ave Ste 1400 *Web:* bisg.org	New York	NY	10016	646-336-7141		49-16
Book Loft 631 S Third St *Web:* www.bookloft.com	Columbus	OH	43206	614-464-1774		95
Book Manufacturers Institute (BMI) PO Box 731388 *Web:* www.bmibook.com	Ormond Beach	FL	32173	386-986-4552	986-4553	49-16
Book Marketing Bestsellers PO Box 2887 *Web:* bookmarketingbestsellers.com	Taos	NM	87571	575-751-3398		531-10
Book Marketing Works LLC (BMW) 50 Lovely St Rte 177 *TF:* 800-562-4357 ■ *Web:* www.bookmarketingworks.com	Avon	CT	06001	860-675-1344		637-2
Book Passage 51 Tamal Vista Blvd *TF:* 800-999-7909 ■ *Web:* www.bookpassage.com	Corte Madera	CA	94925	415-927-0960		95
Book Peddlers (BP) 18925 Lake Ave *Web:* www.bookpeddlers.com	Deephaven	MN	55391	952-544-1154		637-2
Book Publishing Report 60 Long Ridge Rd Ste 300 *Web:* www.bookpublishingreport.com	Stamford	CT	06902	203-325-8193	325-8915	531-11
Book Revue 313 New York Ave *Web:* bookrevue.com	Huntington	NY	11743	631-271-1442	271-5890	95
Book Soup 8818 Sunset Blvd *Web:* www.booksoup.com	West Hollywood	CA	90069	310-659-3110	659-3410	95
Book Systems Inc 4901 University Sq Ste 3 *TF:* 800-219-6571 ■ *Web:* www.booksys.com	Huntsville	AL	35816	256-533-9746		180
Book Tree, The 3316 Adams Ave Ste A *TF:* 800-700-8733 ■ *Web:* www.thebooktree.com	San Diego	CA	92116	619-280-1263		637-2
Bookazine Company Inc 75 Hook Rd *TF:* 800-221-8112 ■ *Web:* www.bookazine.com	Bayonne	NJ	07002	201-339-7777	339-7778	96
BookBub 1 Broadway *Web:* www.bookbub.com	Cambridge	MA	02142	617-475-0782		637-2
BookBuyers 317 Castro St *Web:* www.bookbuyers.com	Mountain View	CA	94041	650-968-7323		95

	Phone	Fax	Class
Booker Cory A (Sen D - NJ) 717 Hart Senate Office Bldg .... Washington DC 20510 *Web:* www.booker.senate.gov	202-224-3224	224-8378	342-2
Booker T. Washington Insurance Co 1728 Third Ave N .... Birmingham AL 35203 *Web:* www.nolhga.com	205-328-5454		391-2
Booker T. Washington National Monument 12130 Booker T Washington Hwy .... Hardy VA 24101 *Web:* www.nps.gov	540-721-2094	721-8311	564
Bookkeeping Express Enterprises LLC 671 N Glebe Rd Ste 1610 .... Arlington VA 22203 *TF:* 844-629-8797 ■ *Web:* www.bookkeepingexpress.com	844-629-8797		2
BookLender.com Inc 44225 Mercure Cir Ste P .... Sterling VA 20166 *Web:* www.booklender.com	703-748-2390		93
BookLogix 1264 Old Alpharetta Rd .... Alpharetta GA 30005 **Fax Area Code:* 888 ■ *Web:* www.booklogix.com	470-239-8547	564-7890*	637-2
Booklyn Artists Alliance 37 Greenpoint Ave 4th Fl .... Brooklyn NY 11222 *Web:* www.booklyn.org	718-383-9621		637-2
Bookman Road Elementary School 1245 Bookman Rd .... Elgin SC 29045 *Web:* www.richland2.org	803-699-1724		685
Bookmans Entertainment Exchange 8034 N 19th Ave .... Phoenix AZ 85021 *Web:* bookmans.com	602-433-0255		95
BookPage 2143 Belcourt Ave .... Nashville TN 37212 *Web:* www.bookpage.com	615-292-8926	292-8249	637-9
BookPal LLC 18101 Von Karman Ave Ste 120 .... Irvine CA 92612 *TF:* 866-522-6657 ■ *Web:* book-pal.com	866-522-6657	522-1957	95
BookPeople 603 N Lamar .... Austin TX 78703 *TF:* 800-853-9757 ■ *Web:* www.bookpeople.com	512-472-5050	482-8495	95
Bookpress Ltd 1304 Jamestown Rd .... Williamsburg VA 23185 *Web:* www.bookpress.com	757-229-1260	229-0498	95
Books & Books 265 Aragon Ave .... Coral Gables FL 33134 *Web:* booksandbooks.com	305-442-4408		95
Books Inc 2251 Chestnut St .... San Francisco CA 94123 *Web:* www.booksinc.net	415-643-3400		95
Books of Discovery 2539 Spruce St .... Boulder CO 80302 *TF:* 800-775-9227 ■ *Web:* booksofdiscovery.com	800-775-9227		95
Books on the Square 471 Angell St .... Providence RI 02906 *TF:* 888-669-9660 ■ *Web:* www.booksq.com	401-331-9097		95
Books-A-Million Inc 402 Industrial Ln .... Birmingham AL 35211 *NASDAQ: BAMM* ■ *TF:* 800-201-3550 ■ *Web:* www.booksamillion.com	205-942-3737		95
Booksource Inc 1230 Macklind Ave .... Saint Louis MO 63110 **Fax Area Code:* 800 ■ *TF:* 800-444-0435 ■ *Web:* booksource.com	314-647-0600	647-1923*	96
Booksy Inc 148 Townsend St Ste 214 .... San Francisco CA 94107 *Web:* booksy.com	502-777-4078		178-1
Booman Floral 2302 Bautista Ave .... Vista CA 92084	760-630-4170		292
Boomer Consulting 610 Humboldt St .... Manhattan KS 66502 *Web:* www.boomer.com	785-537-2358		194
Boomerang Grille 817 SE 4th St .... Moore OK 73160 *Web:* www.boomeranggrille.com	405-676-8242		670
Boomtown Casino Biloxi 676 Bayview Ave .... Biloxi MS 39530 *TF:* 800-627-0777 ■ *Web:* www.boomtownbiloxi.com	228-435-7000		133
Boomtown Casino New Orleans 4132 Peters Rd .... Harvey LA 70058 *Web:* www.boomtownneworleans.com	504-366-7711		133
Boomtown Hotel Casino 300 Riverside Dr .... Bossier City LA 71111 *Web:* www.boomtownbossier.com	318-746-0711		133
Boomtown Inc 2100 Garson Rd .... Verdi NV 89439 *TF:* 800-648-3790 ■ *Web:* www.boomtownreno.com	775-345-6000		132
Boomtown Internet Group Inc 111 Rosemary Ln .... Glenmoore PA 19343 *TF:* 888-454-3330 ■ *Web:* www.boomtownig.com	888-454-3330		194
Boon Edam Inc 402 McKinney Pkwy .... Lillington NC 27546 *Web:* www.boonedam.us	910-814-3800		407
Boondocks Restaurant 3948 S Peninsula Dr .... Wilbur by the Sea FL 32127 *Web:* boondocks-restaurant.com	386-760-9001		671
Boone County 222 S 4th St .... Albion NE 68620 *TF:* 800-330-0755 ■ *Web:* www.co.boone.ne.us	402-395-2055	395-8531	338
Boone County 601 N Main St .... Belvidere IL 61008 *Web:* www.boonecountyil.org	815-544-0371	547-3579	338
Boone County 5958 Garrard St .... Burlington KY 41005 *Web:* www.boonecountyky.org	859-334-2117	334-3648	338
Boone County 1313 Hwy 62 65 N Ste F .... Harrison AR 72601 *Web:* www.boonecountyar.com	870-741-8428	741-9724	338
Boone County 116 W Washington St .... Lebanon IN 46052 *Web:* boonecounty.in.gov	765-483-4458	483-5243	338
Boone County 1 Avenue C Ste 101 .... Madison WV 25130 *Web:* www.boonecountywv.org	304-369-9127	369-9130	338
Boone County Chamber of Commerce 221 N Lebanon St .... Lebanon IN 46052 *Web:* www.boonechamber.org	765-482-1320	482-3114	139
Boone County Convention & Visitors Bureau PO Box 644 .... Lebanon IN 46052 *Web:* boonecvb.com	765-484-8572		206
Boone County Government Ctr 801 E Walnut St Rm 333 .... Columbia MO 65201 *TF:* 800-552-7583 ■ *Web:* www.showmeboone.com	573-886-4270	886-4254	338
Boone County Historical Society Museum 3801 Ponderosa St .... Columbia MO 65201 *Web:* boonehistory.org	573-443-8936		520
Boone County Hospital 1015 Union St .... Boone IA 50036 *Web:* www.boonehospital.com	515-432-3140	433-8926	374-3
Boone County Rural Electric Membership Corp 1207 Indianapolis Ave .... Lebanon IN 46052 *TF:* 800-897-7362 ■ *Web:* www.bremc.com	765-482-2390	482-7869	245
Boone Electric Co-op 1413 Rangeline St .... Columbia MO 65201 *TF:* 800-225-8143 ■ *Web:* www.booneelectric.coop	573-449-4181		245
Boone Graphics 70 S Kellogg .... Goleta CA 93117 *Web:* www.boonegraphics.net	805-683-2349	683-2468	627
Boone Hall Plantation & Gardens 1235 Long Pt Rd .... Mount Pleasant SC 29464 *Web:* www.boonehallplantation.com	843-884-4371	884-0475	50-3
Boone Hospital Ctr 1600 E Broadway .... Columbia MO 65201 *Web:* www.boone.org	573-815-8000	815-3763	374-3
Boone Karlberg Employee P/S Plan 201 W Main Ste 300 .... Missoula MT 59802 *Web:* boonekarlberg.com	406-543-6646		41
Boone Newspapers Inc 1060 Fairfax Pk Ste B .... Tuscaloosa AL 35406 *Web:* www.boonenewspapers.com	205-330-4100		637-8
Boone Oakley LLC 1445 S Mint St .... Charlotte NC 28203 *Web:* booneoakley.com	704-333-9797		7
Boone Publishing Inc 2136 E Mamie Eisenhower .... Boone IA 50036 *TF:* 888-270-0090 ■ *Web:* www.amestrib.com	515-432-6694	432-7811	532-2
Boone Tavern Hotel of Berea College 100 S Main St .... Berea KY 40404 *TF:* 800-366-9358 ■ *Web:* www.boonetavernhotel.com	859-985-3700		379
Boone, Rocheleau & Rodriguez PLLC 10101 Reunion Pl Ste 600 .... San Antonio TX 78216 *Web:* boonerocheleau.com	210-477-7438		41
Boonshoft Museum of Discovery 2600 DeWeese Pkwy .... Dayton OH 45414 *Web:* www.boonshoftmuseum.org	937-275-7431	275-5811	520
Boonslick Technical Education Ctr 1694 W Ashley Rd .... Boonville MO 65233	660-882-5306	882-3269	167-3
Boonville Correctional Ctr 1216 E Morgan St .... Boonville MO 65233 *Web:* doc.mo.gov	660-882-6521	882-7825	213
Boord-Henne Insurance Agency Inc 915 S Main St .... Englewood OH 45322 *Web:* boordhenne.com	937-832-4001		390
Boos Dental Laboratory 1000 Boone Ave N Ste 660 .... Golden Valley MN 55427 *TF:* 800-333-2667 ■ *Web:* www.dentalservices.net	763-544-1446	546-1392	415
Boos Products Inc 20416 Kaiser Rd .... Gregory MI 48137 *Web:* www.michigangear.com	734-498-2207	498-3523	454
Boost Engagement 811 E 4th St Ste B .... Dayton OH 45402 *TF:* 800-324-9756 ■ *Web:* engageboost.com	800-324-9756		195
Boost Motor Group Inc 3080 Yonge St .... Toronto ON M4N3N1 *Web:* www.boostmotorgroup.com	416-487-7000		177
Boost Promotional Branding 3900 Gaskins Rd .... Richmond VA 23233 *TF:* 800-582-9850 ■ *Web:* www.boostbranding.com	804-560-7000		5
Boostability Inc 2600 Ashton Blvd Ste 300 .... Lehi UT 84043 **Fax Area Code:* 801 ■ *TF:* 800-261-1537 ■ *Web:* www.boostability.com	800-261-1537	228-2546*	5
Boot Hill Casino & Resort 4000 W Comanche St .... Dodge City KS 67801 *TF:* 877-906-0777 ■ *Web:* www.boothillcasino.com	620-682-7777		452
Boot Hill Museum 500 W Wyatt Earp Blvd .... Dodge City KS 67801 *Web:* www.boothill.org	620-227-8188		520
BootBarn Inc 620 Pan American Dr .... Livingston TX 77351 *TF:* 888-440-2668 ■ *Web:* www.bootbarn.com	888-440-2668		229
Booth 4900 Nautilus Ct N Ste 220 .... Boulder CO 80301 *TF:* 800-332-6684 ■ *Web:* www.truscore.com	303-581-1408		194
Booth Bay Group 1220 Valley Forge Rd .... Valley Forge PA 19482 *Web:* www.boothbay.com	610-933-5112		195
Booth Creek Resorts 950 Red Sand Stone Rd Ste 43 .... Vail CO 81657 *Web:* www.boothcreek.com	970-476-4030		787
Booth Manufacturing Co 3101 Industrial Ave 2 .... Fort Pierce FL 34946 *TF:* 800-634-5376 ■ *Web:* www.autolabe.com	772-465-4441	465-5177	547
Booth Production Services Inc 5768 Remington Dr .... Winston-Salem NC 27104 **Fax Area Code:* 330	336-766-1961	376-7790*	514
Booth Udall Fuller PLC 1255 W Rio Salado Ste 215 .... Tempe AZ 85281 *Web:* boothudall.com	480-830-2700		41
Bootheel Area Independent Living Services Inc 719 Teaco Rd PO Box 326 .... Kennett MO 63857 *Web:* bails.org	573-888-0002		363
Bootheel Petroleum Company Inc 623 N SR-25 PO Box 187 .... Dexter MO 63841 *Web:* www.bootheelpetroleum.com	573-624-4160		580
Bootz Industries PO Box 18010 .... Evansville IN 47719 *Web:* www.bootz.com	812-423-5401	429-2254	609
Booz Allen Hamilton Inc 8283 Greensboro Dr .... McLean VA 22102 *TF:* 866-390-3908 ■ *Web:* www.boozallen.com	703-902-5000		194
Boozman John (Sen R - AR) 141 Hart Senate Office Bldg .... Washington DC 20510 *Web:* www.boozman.senate.gov	202-224-4843		342-2
Bo-Peep Productions PO Box 982 .... Eureka MT 59917 *TF:* 800-532-0420 ■ *Web:* www.bopeepproductions.com	800-532-0420		797
BOPI 1705 S Veterans Pkwy .... Bloomington IL 61701 *TF:* 800-298-2674 ■ *Web:* www.bopi.com	309-662-3395	663-0581	627
Bopp-Busch Manufacturing Co 545 E Huron Rd .... Au Gres MI 48703 *Web:* www.boppbusch.com	989-876-7121	876-6555	488
Bopti Federal Credit Union 1451 S Seaside Ave .... San Pedro CA 90731 *Web:* boptifcu.com	310-832-0227		219
Borak Inc 601 S Water St .... Northfield MN 55057	507-663-0344		237
Boral Industries Inc 200 Mansell Ct E Ste 310 .... Roswell GA 30076 *TF:* 800-255-1727 ■ *Web:* www.boral.com	800-255-1727		360-3
Borbet Alabama Inc 2 N Jackson St Ste 605 .... Montgomery AL 36104	334-502-9400		247
Borbi, Clancy & Patrizi Law LLC 999 Rt 73 N Ste 103 .... Marlton NJ 08053 *Web:* bpbclaw.com	856-424-5400		41
Borbon Inc 7312 Walnut Ave .... Buena Park CA 90620 *Web:* www.borbon.net	714-994-0170	994-0641	189-8
Borden Company Inc PO Box 1422 .... Sapulpa OK 74067 *Web:* www.bordencompanyinc.com	918-227-2600		322

Name / Address	City	State	ZIP	Phone	Fax	Class
Borden Dairy Co						
8750 N Central Expy Ste 400	Dallas	TX	75231	855-311-1583		296-25
TF: 855-311-1583 ■ *Web:* www.bordendairy.com						
Borden Ladner Gervais LLP						
40 King St W	Toronto	ON	M5H3Y4	416-367-6000		41
Web: www.blg.com						
Borden Office Equipment Co						
141 N Fifth St	Steubenville	OH	43952	740-283-3321	283-2970	320
TF: 866-283-3321 ■ *Web:* bordenofficeequipment.com						
Borden Perlman McRail						
231 Broad St	New Bethlehem	PA	16242	814-275-4999	275-1948	390
TF: 800-486-6984 ■ *Web:* mcrail.bordenperlman.com						
Border Field State Park						
1500 Monument Rd	San Diego	CA	92154	619-575-3613		565
Web: www.parks.ca.gov						
Border Gold Corp 15234 N Bluff Rd	White Rock	BC	V4B3E6	888-312-2288		691
TF: 888-312-2288 ■ *Web:* www.bordergold.com						
Border Grill Las Vegas						
Mandalay Bay Resort & Casino 3950 Las Vegas Blvd S						
	Las Vegas	NV	89119	702-632-7403	632-6945	671
Web: www.bordergrill.com						
Border States Electric Supply						
105 25th St N	Fargo	ND	58102	701-293-5834		246
TF: 800-800-0199 ■ *Web:* www.borderstates.com						
Border States Paving Inc 4101 N 32nd St	Fargo	ND	58102	701-237-4860	237-0233	188-4
Web: borderstatespaving.com						
Border Valley Trading Ltd						
604 E Mead Rd	Brawley	CA	92227	760-344-6700	344-4305	10
Web: www.bordervalley.com						
Bordercomm Partners LP						
500 W Overland Ave Ste 310	El Paso	TX	79915	915-779-3000		194
Web: bordercomm.com						
Borderland Construction Company Inc						
400 E 38 St	Tucson	AZ	85713	520-623-0900	623-0232	188-4
Web: borderland-inc.com						
Borderland State Park						
Massapoag Ave	North Easton	MA	02356	508-238-6566		565
Web: www.mass.gov						
Borderland Tours 2875 W Hilltop Rd	Portal	AZ	85632	520-558-2351		760
Web: www.borderland-tours.com						
Bordonas 102 W F St	Oakdale	CA	95361	209-719-2892		321
Web: bordonas.com						
Boreal Genomics Inc						
5150 El Camino Real	Los Altos	CA	94022	604-822-8268		231
Web: www.borealgenomics.com						
Borealis Compounds LLC						
176 Thomas Rd	Port Murray	NJ	07865	908-850-6200		77
Web: www.borealisgroup.com						
Borealis Ventures 10 Allen St	Hanover	NH	03755	603-643-1500		792
Web: www.borealis.vc						
Bored Feet Press PO Box 1832	Mendocino	CA	95460	707-964-6629	964-5953	637-2
TF: 888-336-6199 ■ *Web:* www.boredfeet.com						
Borek Construction Ltd						
9690 Rd 223 PO Box 870	Dawson Creek	BC	V1G4H8	250-782-5561		188
Web: www.borekltd.com						
Boren, Oliver & Coffey LLP						
59 N Jefferson St	Martinsville	IN	46151	765-342-0147		428
TF: 800-403-9971 ■ *Web:* boclawyers.com						
Borenson & Assoc 330 Schantz Rd	Allentown	PA	18104	610-398-6908		196
Web: borenson.com						
Borer Financial Communication Inc						
615 Fifth St Ste 210	Carlstadt	NJ	07072	201-939-9297		225
Web: www.borerfinancial.com						
Borg Compressed Steel Corp						
G & Lexington St	Tulsa	OK	74110	918-587-2511		686
Web: vaffeco.net						
Borg Indak Inc 701 Enterprise Dr	Delavan	WI	53115	262-728-5531		153
Web: www.borgindak.com						
Borgata Hotel Casino & Spa						
1 Borgata Way	Atlantic City	NJ	08401	609-317-1000		379
Web: www.theborgata.com						
Borger Independent School District						
200 E Ninth	Borger	TX	79007	806-273-6481	273-1066	685
Web: www.borgerisd.net						
Borger Matez PA						
1415 Marlton Pike E Ste 305	Cherry Hill	NJ	08034	856-424-3444		41
Web: njfamilylaw.net						
Borgeson Universal Company Inc						
91 Technology Park Dr	Torrington	CT	06790	860-482-8283	496-9320	723
Web: borgeson.com						
Borghese 3 E 54th St	New York	NY	10022	212-659-5300		214
Web: www.borghese.com						
Borghesi Building & Engineering Company Inc						
2155 E Main St	Torrington	CT	06790	860-482-7613		256
Web: www.borghesibuilding.com						
BorgWarner Inc 3850 Hamlin Rd	Auburn Hills	MI	48326	248-754-9200		60
NYSE: BWA ■ *Web:* www.borgwarner.com						
Borgwarner Turbo Systems						
1849 Brevard Rd	Arden	NC	28704	828-684-4000		247
Web: www.turbos.bwauto.com						
Boricua College 3755 Broadway	New York	NY	10032	212-694-1000	694-1015	166
Web: www.boricuacollege.edu						
Borin Manufacturing Inc						
5741 Buckingham Pkwy Unit B	Culver City	CA	90230	310-822-1000		111
Web: borin.com						
Bork Transportation of Illinois (BTI)						
7735 W 59th St	Summit	IL	60501	708-594-5551		780
TF: 800-397-2675 ■ *Web:* www.borktransport.com						
Borke Mold Specialist Inc						
9541 Glades Dr	West Chester	OH	45011	513-870-8000	870-8008	757
Web: borkemold.com						
Borkholder Buildings and Supply LLC						
786 USA 6 W	Nappanee	IN	46550	574-773-3144	773-2897	191-3
TF: 800-552-2772 ■ *Web:* borkholderbuildings.com						
Borla Performance Industries Inc						
500 Borla Dr	Johnson City	TN	37604	423-979-4000	979-4099	60
TF: 877-462-6752 ■ *Web:* www.borla.com						
Bormioli Luigi Corp						
41 Madison Ave 16 th fl	New York	NY	10010	212-719-0606		361
Web: www.bormioliluigi.com						
Boro Construction						
400 Feheley Dr	King of Prussia	PA	19406	610-272-7400		186
Web: www.boroconstruction.com						
Borrie's 1800 Smelter Ave	Black Eagle	MT	59414	406-761-0300		671
Web: www.borriesrestaurant.com						
Borro 767 3rd Ave	New York	NY	10017	888-778-7034		217
TF: 888-778-7034 ■ *Web:* www.borro.com						
Borroughs Corp 3002 N Burdick St	Kalamazoo	MI	49004	269-342-0161	342-4161	286
TF: 800-748-0227 ■ *Web:* www.borroughs.com						
Borsheim's Inc 120 Regency Pkwy	Omaha	NE	68114	402-391-0400	391-6694	410
TF: 800-642-4438 ■ *Web:* www.borsheims.com						
Bortek Industries Inc						
4713 Gettysburg Rd	Mechanicsburg	PA	17055	717-737-7162	737-7591	76
TF: 800-626-7835 ■ *Web:* www.sweeperland.com						
Borton & Sons Inc 2550 Borton Rd	Yakima	WA	98903	509-966-3905		315-3
Web: www.bortonfruit.com						
Borton LC 21 Des Moines	South Hutchinson	KS	67505	620-669-8211		685
Web: www.borton.net						
Bortstein Legal LLC						
1500 Broadway Ste 2003	New York	NY	10036	646-240-4871		41
TF: 866-955-9402 ■ *Web:* blegalgroup.com						
Bortz Media & Sports Group Inc						
5105 DTC Pkwy Ste 200	Greenwood Village	CO	80111	303-893-9902	893-9913	194
Web: www.bortz.com						
Borzynski Farms Inc						
11402 Kraut Rd PO Box 133	Franksville	WI	53126	262-886-1623	886-2111	10-11
Web: www.borzynskifarm.com						
BOS Solutions Ltd						
635-8th Ave SW Ste 1200	Calgary	AB	T2P3M3	403-234-8103		261
TF: 877-267-3434 ■ *Web:* www.bos-solutions.com						
Bosch Rexroth 14001 S Lakes Dr	Charlotte	NC	28273	330-263-3300	263-3333	790
TF: 800-739-7684 ■ *Web:* www.boschrexroth.com						
Bosch Security Systems						
130 Perinton Pkwy	Fairport	NY	14450	585-223-4060	223-9180	692
TF: 800-289-0096 ■ *Web:* www.boschsecurity.com						
Bosch Thermotechnology						
340 Mad River Pk	Waitsfield	VT	05673	800-283-3787		357
TF: 800-283-3787 ■ *Web:* www.bosch-climate.us						
Boscobel Marketing Communications Inc						
8606 Second Ave	Silver Spring	MD	20910	301-588-2900		7
Web: www.boscobel.com						
Boscogen Inc 11 Morgan	Irvine	CA	92618	949-380-4317	583-2016	791
Web: boscogen.com						
Boscos Squared 827 S Main	Memphis	TN	38106	901-278-0087		671
Web: www.boscosbeer.com						
Boscov's Department Stores						
4500 Perkiomen Ave	Reading	PA	19606	610-779-2000		229
Web: www.boscovs.com						
Bose Corp The Mountain	Framingham	MA	01701	508-766-1099	820-3465	52
TF: 800-379-2073 ■ *Web:* global.bose.com						
Bose McKinney & Evans LLP						
111 Monument Cir Ste 2700	Indianapolis	IN	46204	317-684-5000		428
Web: www.boselaw.com						
Boshco Inc 6K Dunham Rd	Billerica	MA	01821	978-667-1911	671-0011	385
Web: www.boshco.com						
Boskovich Farms Inc						
711 Diaz Ave PO Box 1352	Oxnard	CA	93030	805-487-2299	487-5189	10-11
Web: www.boskovichfarms.com						
Boslers Furniture Inc						
3820 E Morgan Ave	Evansville	IN	47715	812-476-8787		321
Web: deanboslers.com						
Bosley & Bratch Inc						
1401 Court St Ste 200	Clearwater	FL	33756	800-953-6224		41
TF: 800-953-6224 ■ *Web:* lawyers4veterans.com						
Bosley Inc						
9100 Wilshire Blvd East Twr Penthouse	Beverly Hills	CA	90212	310-288-9999		810
TF: 800-985-6405 ■ *Web:* www.bosley.com						
Bosmere Inc 323 Corban Ave SW	Concord	NC	28025	704-784-1608	784-1611	429
Web: www.bosmereusa.com						
Bosnia & Herzegovina						
Embassy 2109 E St NW	Washington	DC	20037	202-337-1500	337-1502	257
Web: www.bhembassy.org						
Bosque County 110 South St PO Box 647	Meridian	TX	76665	254-435-2382		338
Web: www.bosquecounty.us						
Boss Chair Inc 5353 Jillson St	Commerce	CA	90040	323-262-1919		321
TF: 800-593-1888 ■ *Web:* boss-chair.com						
Boss Industries Inc 1761 Genesis Dr	La Porte	IN	46350	219-324-7776		172
TF: 800-635-6587 ■ *Web:* www.bossair.com						
Boss Law Firm APLC, The						
409 Camino del Rio S Ste 201	San Diego	CA	92108	619-234-1776	444-3817*	428
**Fax Area Code:* 858 ■ *Web:* bosslawfirm.com						
Bossard Memorial Library						
7 Spruce St	Gallipolis	OH	45631	740-446-7323	446-1701	434-3
Web: www.bossardlibrary.org						
Bosse Mattingly Constructors Inc						
2116 Plantside Dr	Louisville	KY	40299	502-671-0995		186
Web: bosseconstruction.com						
Bosse Sports 141 Boston Post Rd	Sudbury	MA	01776	978-443-4613		354
Web: bossesports.com						
Bosselman Enterprises						
PO Box 4905	Grand Island	NE	68802	308-381-2800		345
Web: www.bosselman.com						
Bosshardt Realty Services LLC						
5542 NW 43rd St	Gainesville	FL	32653	352-371-6100		652
TF: 800-284-6110 ■ *Web:* www.bosshardtrealty.com						
Bossier Chamber of Commerce						
710 Benton Rd	Bossier City	LA	71111	318-746-0252	746-0357	139
Web: www.bossierchamber.com						
Bossier Civic Ctr 620 Benton Rd	Bossier City	LA	71111	318-741-8900	741-8910	205
Web: www.bossiercity.org						
Bossier Parish Community College						
6220 E Texas St	Bossier City	LA	71111	318-678-6000	678-6390	162
Web: www.bpcc.edu						
Bossier Parish Library (BPL)						
2206 Beckett St	Bossier City	LA	71111	318-746-1693	746-7768	434-3
Web: www.bossierlibrary.org						

Name	Address	City	State	ZIP	Phone	Fax	Class	Other
Bossier Press Tribune	4250 Viking Dr	Bossier City	LA	71111	318-747-7900	747-5298	532-4	*Web:* bossierpress.com
Bossong Hosiery Mills Inc	840 W Salisbury St	Asheboro	NC	27203	336-625-2175		155-10	*Web:* bossong1927.com
Bossong's Commercial Delivery	6713 Pickard Dr E	Syracuse	NY	13211	315-455-7431	455-1108	780	*TF:* 800-845-8505 ■ *Web:* www.bossongs.com
Bost Mike (Rep R - IL)	1440 Longworth House Office Bldg	Washington	DC	20515	202-225-5661	225-0285	342-2	*Web:* bost.house.gov
Boston Advisors Inc	1 Liberty Sq 10th Fl	Boston	MA	02109	617-348-3100	348-0082	401	*TF:* 800-523-5903 ■ *Web:* www.bostonadvisors.com
Boston African-American National Historic Site	14 Beacon St Ste 401	Boston	MA	02108	617-742-5415	720-0848	564	*Web:* www.nps.gov
Boston Architectural College	320 Newbury St	Boston	MA	02115	617-585-0100		800	*TF:* 877-585-0100 ■ *Web:* the-bac.edu
Boston Athenaeum	10 1/2 Beacon St	Boston	MA	02108	617-227-0270		434-4	*Web:* www.bostonathenaeum.org
Boston Ballet	19 Clarendon St	Boston	MA	02116	617-695-6950	695-6995	573-1	*Web:* www.bostonballet.org
Boston Baptist College	950 Metropolitan Ave	Boston	MA	02136	617-364-3510		166	*Web:* www.boston.edu
Boston Beanery Restaurants Inc	383 Patteson Dr	Morgantown	WV	26505	304-599-1870		670	*Web:* www.bostonbeanery.com
Boston Bed Co	1113 Commonwealth Ave	Boston	MA	02215	617-782-3830		321	*Web:* www.bostonbed.com
Boston Beer Co	1 Design Center Pl Ste 850	Boston	MA	02210	617-368-5000	368-5500	102	*NYSE: SAM* ■ *TF:* 888-661-2337 ■ *Web:* www.bostonbeer.com
Boston Benefit Partners LLC	177 Milk St 3rd Fl	Boston	MA	02109	617-570-9100		463	*Web:* www.bosben.com
Boston Bever Forrest Cross & Sickmann	27 N 8th St	Richmond	IN	47374	765-962-7527	966-4597	41	*Web:* www.bbfcslaw.com
Boston Biochem Inc	840 Memorial Dr	Cambridge	MA	02139	617-576-2210	492-3565	668	*Web:* www.bostonbiochem.com
Boston Book Company & Book Annex Inc	705 Centre St	Boston	MA	02114	617-522-2100		95	*Web:* rarebook.com
Boston Capital Ventures	84 State St Ste 320	Boston	MA	02109	617-227-6550		792	*Web:* www.bcv.com
Boston Center for the Arts	539 Tremont St	Boston	MA	02116	617-426-5000	426-5336	572	*Web:* bostonarts.org
Boston Centerless Inc	11 Presidential Way	Woburn	MA	01801	781-994-5000		454	*TF:* 800-343-4111 ■ *Web:* www.bostoncenterless.com
Boston Children's Hospital	300 Longwood Ave	Boston	MA	02115	617-355-6000		374-1	*Web:* www.childrenshospital.org
Boston Children's Museum	308 Congress St	Boston	MA	02210	617-426-6500	426-1944	521	*Web:* www.bostonchildrensmuseum.org
Boston City Hall	1 City Hall Plz	Boston	MA	02201	617-635-4601	248-1937	337	*Web:* www.boston.gov
Boston College	140 Commonwealth Ave	Chestnut Hill	MA	02467	617-552-3100	552-0798	166	*TF:* 800-360-2522 ■ *Web:* www.bc.edu
Boston Conservatory at Berklee	8 Fenway	Boston	MA	02215	617-536-6340	247-3159	166	*Web:* bostonconservatory.berklee.edu
Boston Consulting Group, The	Exchange Pl 31st Fl	Boston	MA	02109	617-973-1200		194	*Web:* www.bcg.com
Boston Convention & Exhibition Ctr	415 Summer St	Boston	MA	02210	617-954-2000	954-2299	205	*Web:* www.massconvention.com
Boston Duck Tours Ltd	4 Copley Pl Ste 4155	Boston	MA	02116	617-267-3825	450-0065	760	*TF:* 800-226-7442 ■ *Web:* www.bostonducktours.com
Boston Electronics Corp	91 Boylston St	Brookline	MA	02445	617-566-3821		179	*Web:* www.boselec.com
Boston Endoscopy Center LLC	175 Worcester St (Rte 9)	Wellesley	MA	02481	617-936-7693	754-0820	415	*Web:* www.bostonendoscopycenter.com
Boston Engineering Corp	300 Bear Hill Rd	Waltham	MA	02451	781-466-8010		261	*Web:* www.boston-engineering.com
Boston Event Guidecom	475 Hillside Ave	Needham	MA	02494	781-444-7771		194	*Web:* www.bostoneventguide.com
Boston Family Office LLC, The	88 Broad St 2nd Fl	Boston	MA	02110	617-624-0800		401	*TF:* 800-900-4401 ■ *Web:* www.bosfam.com
Boston Film Festival	126 S St	Rockport	MA	01966	617-523-8388		282	*Web:* www.bostonfilmfestival.org
Boston Foundation	75 Arlington St 10th Fl	Boston	MA	02116	617-338-1700	338-1604	303	*Web:* www.tbf.org
Boston Globe	135 Morrissey Blvd	Boston	MA	02125	617-929-7900	929-7975	532-2	*Web:* www.bostonglobe.com
Boston Group	400 Riverside Ave	Medford	MA	02155	800-225-1633		286	*TF:* 800-225-1633 ■ *Web:* www.bostonretail.com
Boston Harbor Assn, The	374 Congress St Ste 307	Boston	MA	02210	617-482-1722		804	*Web:* www.tbha.org
Boston Harbor Hotel	70 Rowes Wharf	Boston	MA	02110	617-439-7000	330-9450	379	*TF:* 800-752-7077 ■ *Web:* www.bhh.com
Boston Harbor Islands National Recreation Area	408 Atlantic Ave Ste 228	Boston	MA	02110	617-223-8666		564	*TF:* 877-874-2478 ■ *Web:* www.nps.gov
Boston House, The	229 Kent St	Brookline	MA	02446	617-734-3333	734-5239	373	*Web:* www.thebostonhouse.org
Boston Inc	2917 Business Park Dr	Stevens Point	WI	54482	715-342-2895		321	*Web:* www.furnitureappliancemart.com
Boston Industrial Consulting	89 Newbury St	Danvers	MA	01923	978-739-0399		261	*Web:* bicinc.com
Boston Jetsearch Inc	200 Hanscom Dr	Bedford	MA	01730	781-274-0074		261	*Web:* www.bostonjetsearch.com
Boston Language Institute Inc	648 Beacon St	Boston	MA	02215	617-262-3500	262-3595	768	*TF:* 877-998-3500 ■ *Web:* www.bostonlanguage.com
Boston Logic Technology Partners Inc	268 Summer St 2nd Fl	Boston	MA	02118	617-266-9166		177	*Web:* www.bostonlogic.com
Boston Market Corp	14103 Denver W Pkwy	Golden	CO	80401	303-278-9500		670	*TF:* 866-977-9090 ■ *Web:* www.bostonmarket.com
Boston Market Strategies Inc	500 Cummings Ctr Ste 3150	Beverly	MA	01915	781-245-7773	245-7774	194	*Web:* www.bmsi3.com
Boston Medical Ctr	1 Boston Medical Center Pl	Boston	MA	02118	617-638-8000		374-3	*TF:* 800-249-2007 ■ *Web:* www.bmc.org
Boston Millennia Partners	30 Rowes Wharf Ste 400	Boston	MA	02110	617-428-5150	428-5160	792	*Web:* www.bostonmillenniapartners.com
Boston Modern Orchestra Project	376 Washington St	Malden	MA	02148	781-324-0397		573-3	*Web:* www.bmop.org
Boston National Historical Park	Charlestown Navy Yard	Boston	MA	02129	617-242-5601		564	*Web:* www.nps.gov
Boston Organics	50 Terminal St Blgd 2 Ste 105	Charlestown	MA	02129	617-242-1700		297-8	*Web:* bostonorganics.grubmarket.com
Boston Park Plaza Hotel & Towers	50 Park Plz	Boston	MA	02116	617-426-2000		379	*TF:* 800-225-2008 ■ *Web:* www.bostonparkplaza.com
Boston Partners	909 Third Ave 32nd Fl	New York	NY	10022	212-908-9500		690	*Web:* www.boston-partners.com
Boston Partners Financial Group LLC	138 River Rd Ste 310	Andover	MA	01810	978-689-9303		390	*Web:* www.bostonpartnersfinancialgroup.com
Boston Philharmonic Orchestra	236 Huntington Ave Ste 209	Boston	MA	02115	617-236-0999	236-8613	573-3	*Web:* www.bostonphil.org
Boston Pizza Restaurants LP	14850 Quorum Dr Ste 201	Dallas	TX	75234	972-484-9022	484-7630	670	*TF:* 866-277-8721 ■ *Web:* www.bostons.com
Boston Pops	301 Massachusetts Ave Symphony Hall	Boston	MA	02115	617-266-1492		573-3	*TF:* 888-266-1200 ■ *Web:* www.bso.org
Boston Portfolio Advisors Inc	600 Corporate Dr Ste 502	Fort Lauderdale	FL	33334	954-938-3000		401	*Web:* www.bostonportfolio.com
Boston Private Bank & Trust Co	10 Post Office Sq	Boston	MA	02109	617-912-1900		70	*Web:* www.bostonprivate.com
Boston Properties Inc	800 Boylston St	Boston	MA	02199	617-236-3300		655	*NYSE: BXP* ■ *Web:* www.bostonproperties.com
Boston Public Library	700 Boylston St Copley Sq	Boston	MA	02116	617-536-5400		434-3	*Web:* www.bpl.org
Boston Retail Solutions	1151 19th St	Vero Beach	FL	32960	772-569-7202		295	*TF:* 866-866-0925 ■ *Web:* www.bostonbarricade.com
Boston Sand & Gravel Company Inc	100 N Washington St	Boston	MA	02114	617-227-9000		182	*OTC: BSND* ■ *TF:* 800-624-2724 ■ *Web:* www.bostonsand.com
Boston Scientific Corp	300 Boston Scientific Way	Marlborough	MA	01752	508-683-4000		476	*NYSE: BSX* ■ *TF:* 800-876-9960 ■ *Web:* www.bostonscientific.com
Boston Ship Repair Inc	32A Drydock Ave	Boston	MA	02210	617-330-5045		698	*Web:* www.northeastship.com
Boston Strategies International Inc	445 Washington St	Wellesley	MA	02482	781-250-8150		463	*Web:* www.bostonstrategies.com
Boston Systems & Solutions LLC	89 N Main St	Andover	MA	01810	978-469-0002		180	*Web:* www.bsscorp.com
Boston University	One Silber Way	Boston	MA	02215	617-353-2000		167-3	*Web:* www.bu.edu
Boston University School of Medicine	715 Albany St	Boston	MA	02118	617-638-4899	638-5258	167-2	*Web:* www.bumc.bu.edu
Boston Warehouse Trading Corp	59 Davis Ave	Norwood	MA	02062	781-769-8550	769-9468	361	*Web:* www.bwtc.com
Boston Whaler Inc	100 Whaler Way	Edgewater	FL	32141	877-294-5645		90	*TF:* 877-294-5645 ■ *Web:* www.bostonwhaler.com
Boston's Best Chimney Sweep	76 Bacon St	Waltham	MA	02451	781-893-6611		152	*TF:* 800-660-6708 ■ *Web:* www.bestchimney.com
Bostons Weekly Dig	242 E Berkeley St 5th Fl	Boston	MA	02118	617-426-8942		532-5	*Web:* digboston.com
Bostwick Laboratories	3495 Hacks Cross Rd	Memphis	TN	38125	877-545-1678	288-6568*	418	**Fax Area Code:* 804 ■ *TF:* 877-865-3262 ■ *Web:* uropathdiagnostics.com
Bostwick-Braun Co, The	7349 Crossleigh Ct	Toledo	OH	43617	800-777-9640	259-3622*	351	**Fax Area Code:* 419 ■ *TF:* 800-777-9640 ■ *Web:* www.bostwick-braun.com
Boswell Bay State Marine Park	PO Box 1247	Soldotna	AK	99669	907-262-5581		565	*Web:* dnr.alaska.gov

Name / Address	City	State	ZIP	Phone	Fax	Class
Boswell Engineering 330 Phillips Ave PO Box 3152 *Web:* boswellengineering.com	South Hackensack	NJ	07606	201-641-0770	641-1831	261
Boswell Insurance Agency 26461 Crown Valley Pkwy Ste 200 *TF:* 888-333-0147 ■ *Web:* boswellinsurance.com	Mission Viejo	CA	92691	949-855-0430	582-2983	390
Boswell's Party Supplies 1901 Cam Ramon *Web:* www.boswells-party.com	Danville	CA	94526	925-866-1644		226
Bosworth & Associates Inc 1818 Wsw Loop 323 *Web:* bosworth-associates.com	Tyler	TX	75701	903-266-1699		390
Bosworth Steel Erectors Inc 4001 Jaffee St *Web:* bosworthsteel.com	Dallas	TX	75216	214-371-3700	371-1020	189-14
Bot Home Automation Inc 1523 26th St *Web:* shop.ring.com	Santa Monica	CA	90404	310-929-7085		693
BOTA (Builders of the Adytum Ltd) 5101 N Figueroa St *Web:* www.bota.org	Los Angeles	CA	90042	323-255-7141	255-4166	48-20
Botanas 816 S Fifth St *Web:* www.botanasrestaurant.com	Milwaukee	WI	53204	414-672-3755		671
Botanic garden at Georgia Southern University 1505 Bland Ave PO Box 8039 *Web:* academics.georgiasouthern.edu	Statesboro	GA	30460	912-871-1149	871-1777	97
Botanica the Wichita Gardens 701 N Amidon Ave *Web:* botanica.org	Wichita	KS	67203	316-264-0448		97
Botanical Garden of the Ozarks 4703 N Crossover Rd PO Box 10407 *Web:* www.bgozarks.org	Fayetteville	AR	72764	479-750-2620		97
Botanical Gardens at Asheville 151 WT Weaver Blvd *Web:* www.ashevillebotanicalgardens.org	Asheville	NC	28804	828-252-5190		97
Botanical Laboratories Inc 1441 W Smith Rd PO Box 1596 *TF:* 800-232-4005 ■ *Web:* asmbs.org	Ferndale	WA	98248	360-384-5656		582
Botanical Research Institute of Texas 1700 University Dr *Web:* brit.org	Fort Worth	TX	76107	817-332-4441	332-4112	97
Botetourt County 1 W Main St *Web:* www.co.botetourt.va.us	Fincastle	VA	24090	540-473-8220		338
Botetourt County Chamber of Commerce 13 W Main St *Web:* botetourtchamber.com	Fincastle	VA	24090	540-473-8280	473-8365	139
Bothe Associates Inc 6901 46th St **Fax Area Code:* 414 ■ *Web:* www.bothe.com	Kenosha	WI	53144	262-656-1860	656-1858*	454
Bothell-Kenmore Reporter 11630 Slater Ave NE Ste 8-9 *Web:* www.bothell-reporter.com	Kirkland	WA	98034	425-483-3732		532-4
Bothe-Napa Valley State Park 3801 St Helena Hwy *Web:* www.parks.ca.gov	Calistoga	CA	94515	707-942-4575		565
Bothwell Lodge State Historic Site 19349 Bothwell State Park Rd *Web:* mostateparks.com	Sedalia	MO	65301	660-827-0510		565
Bothwell Regional Health Ctr 601 E 14th St *TF:* 800-635-9194 ■ *Web:* www.brhc.org	Sedalia	MO	65301	660-826-8833		374-3
Botkeeper 179 S St 2nd Fl *TF:* 800-388-3323 ■ *Web:* www.botkeeper.com	Boston	MA	02111	800-388-3323		39
Botnay Bay Technology Inc 390 Portsmouth Ave *Web:* www.botnaybay.com	Greenland	NH	03840	603-436-6035		196
Botswana Embassy 1531 New Hampshire Ave NW *Web:* www.botswanaembassy.org	Washington	DC	20036	202-244-4990	244-4164	257
Bott Radio Network 10550 Barkley St Ste 100 *TF:* 800-875-1903 ■ *Web:* www.bottradionetwork.com	Overland Park	KS	66212	913-642-7770	642-1319	643
Bottega 2240 Highland Ave S *Web:* bottegarestaurant.com	Birmingham	AL	35205	205-939-1000		671
Bottega Veneta Inc 699 Fifth Ave *TF:* 800-845-6790 ■ *Web:* www.bottegaveneta.com	New York	NY	10022	212-371-5511		430
Botti Marinaccio Ltd 2015 Spring Rd Ste 370 *Web:* bmltdlaw.com	Oak Brook	IL	60523	630-575-8585		41
Botticelli Italian Restaurant 523 Main St *Web:* botticelliristorante.net	Rapid City	SD	57701	605-348-0089		671
Bottineau County *Social Services Board* 314 W Fifth St Ste 1 *Web:* www.nd.gov	Bottineau	ND	58318	701-228-3613	228-3600	338
Bottini Fuel Oil Co 2785 W Main St *Web:* www.bottinifuel.com	Wappingers Falls	NY	12590	845-297-5580	297-5465	316
Bottlemate Inc 2095 Leo Ave *Web:* www.bottlemate.com	Commerce	CA	90040	323-887-9009		333
Bottom Line Inc 3 Landmark Sq Ste 201 *TF:* 800-274-5611 ■ *Web:* bottomlineinc.com	Stamford	CT	06901	203-973-5900		637-9
Bottomline Technologies 325 Corporate Dr *NASDAQ: EPAY* ■ *TF:* 800-243-2528 ■ *Web:* www.bottomline.com	Portsmouth	NH	03801	603-436-0700	436-0300	178-1
Botz Deal & Company PC 2 Wbury Dr *Web:* www.botzdeal.com	Saint Charles	MO	63301	636-946-2800		2
Bouchaine Vineyards Inc 1075 Buchli Station Rd *TF:* 800-654-9463 ■ *Web:* www.bouchaine.com	Napa	CA	94559	707-252-9065		443
Bouchard Transportation Company Inc 58 S Service Rd Ste 150 *Web:* www.bouchardtransport.com	Melville	NY	11747	631-390-4900	390-4905	314
Boucher & James Inc 1456 Ferry Rd Bldg 500 Fountainville Professional Bldg *Web:* bjengineers.com	Doylestown	PA	18901	215-345-9400	345-9401	261
Boucher Brothers Management Inc 1451 Ocean Dr Ste 205 *Web:* www.boucherbrothers.com	Miami Beach	FL	33139	305-535-8177		23
Boucher Group Inc 4141 S 108th St *Web:* www.boucher.com	Greenfield	WI	53228	414-427-4000		57
Bouchette Electronics Inc N11325 County Rd Y *TF:* 888-823-7770 ■ *Web:* www.bouchette.com	Clintonville	WI	54929	715-823-7770		203
Bouchey & Clarke Benefits Inc 1819 Fifth Ave *Web:* boucheyclarke.com	Troy	NY	12180	518-720-8888		390
Bouchey Financial Group Ltd 1819 Fifth Ave *Web:* www.boucheyfinancial.com	Troy	NY	12180	518-720-3333		401
Boudin Bakery 160 Jefferson St Lower Level *Web:* boudinbakery.com	San Francisco	CA	94133	415-882-1849		68
Boudreaux & Hebert CPAS LLC 1101 Hugh Wallis Rd S Ste 205 *Web:* boudreauxandhebertcpas.com	LaFayette	LA	70508	337-236-9992	236-9950	2
Boudro's On the Riverwalk 421 E Commerce St *Web:* www.boudros.com	San Antonio	TX	78205	210-224-8484	225-2839	671
Boulanger, Roland & Cie Ltd 235 Rue St-Louis *Web:* www.boulanger.qc.ca	Warwick	QC	J0A1M0	819-358-4100		279
Boulder Adventure Lodge (A-Lodge) 91 Four Mile Canyon Rd *Web:* a-lodge.com	Boulder	CO	80302	303-444-0882		379
Boulder Arts & Crafts 1421 Pearl St Mall *TF:* 866-656-2667 ■ *Web:* boulderartsandcrafts.com	Boulder	CO	80302	303-443-3683		460
Boulder Ballet 2590 Walnut St Ste 10 *Web:* www.boulderballet.org	Boulder	CO	80302	303-443-0028		573-1
Boulder Beach State Park 44 Stillwater Rd *Web:* www.vtstateparks.com	Groton	VT	05046	802-584-3823		565
Boulder Beer Co 2880 Wilderness Pl *Web:* boulderbeer.com	Boulder	CO	80301	303-444-8448		102
Boulder Blimp Company Inc 1208 Commerce Ct Ste 1 *Web:* boulderblimp.com	Lafayette	CO	80026	303-664-1122	664-1133	676
Boulder Book Store 1107 Pearl St *TF:* 800-244-4651 ■ *Web:* www.boulderbookstore.com	Boulder	CO	80302	303-447-2074	447-3946	95
Boulder Chamber of Commerce 2440 Pearl St *Web:* boulderchamber.com	Boulder	CO	80302	303-442-1044	938-8837	139
Boulder City/Hoover Dam Museum 1305 Arizona St *Web:* www.bchdmuseum.org	Boulder City	NV	89005	702-294-1988		520
Boulder Community Hospital (BCH) 1100 Balsam Ave *Web:* www.bch.org	Boulder	CO	80301	303-440-2273		374-3
Boulder Convention & Visitors Bureau 2440 Pearl St *TF:* 800-444-0447 ■ *Web:* www.bouldercoloradousa.com	Boulder	CO	80302	303-442-2911	938-2098	206
Boulder Cork 3295 30th St *Web:* bouldercork.com	Boulder	CO	80301	303-443-9505	443-0193	671
Boulder Country Day School 4820 Nautilus Ct N *Web:* www.bouldercountryday.org	Boulder	CO	80301	303-527-4931		685
Boulder County 1901 63rd St *Web:* www.bouldercounty.org	Boulder	CO	80301	303-413-7770	413-7775	338
Boulder Daily Camera 1048 Pearl St *Web:* www.dailycamera.com	Boulder	CO	80302	303-442-1202	449-9358	532-2
Boulder Innovation Group Inc 4824 Sterling Dr *Web:* www.boulderinnovators.com	Boulder	CO	80301	303-447-0248	447-3905	407
Boulder Museum of Contemporary Art 1750 13th St *Web:* bmoca.org	Boulder	CO	80302	303-443-2122		520
Boulder Philharmonic Orchestra 2590 Walnut St *Web:* www.boulderphil.org	Boulder	CO	80302	303-449-1343	443-9203	573-3
Boulder Public Library 1001 Arapahoe Ave *Web:* boulderlibrary.org	Boulder	CO	80302	303-441-3100		434-3
Boulder Reservoir 5565 N 51st St *Web:* bouldercolorado.gov	Boulder	CO	80301	303-441-3461	441-1807	50-5
Boulder Station Hotel & Casino 4111 Boulder Hwy *TF:* 800-683-7777 ■ *Web:* www.boulderstation.com	Las Vegas	NV	89121	702-432-7777		133
Boulder Ventures Ltd 5425 Wisconsin Ave Ste 704 *Web:* www.boulderventures.com	Chevy Chase	MD	20815	301-913-0213		792
Boulder Weekly 690 S Lashley Ln *Web:* www.boulderweekly.com	Boulder	CO	80305	303-494-5511	494-2585	532-5
Boulders Resort & Golden Door Spa 34631 N Tom Darlington Dr *TF:* 888-579-2631 ■ *Web:* www.theboulders.com	Scottsdale	AZ	85262	480-488-9009		669
Boulevard 1 Mission St *Web:* www.boulevardrestaurant.com	San Francisco	CA	94105	415-543-6084	495-2936	671
Boulevard Brewing Co 2501 SW Blvd *Web:* www.boulevard.com	Kansas City	MO	64108	816-474-7095		102
Boulevard Club, The 1491 Lake Shore Blvd W *Web:* www.boulevardclub.com	Toronto	ON	M6K3C2	416-532-3341		354
Boulevard Machine & Gear Inc 785 Page Blvd *Web:* www.boulevardmachine.com	Springfield	MA	01104	413-788-6466	734-6814	454
Boulevard Mall 3528 S Maryland Pkwy *Web:* www.boulevardmall.com	Las Vegas	NV	89169	702-735-7430		460
Boulevard Mall 730 Alberta Dr *Web:* www.boulevard-mall.com	Amherst	NY	14226	716-834-8600		460
Boulevard Vacuum Cleaner Company Inc 5086 W Pico Blvd *Web:* blvdvac.com	Los Angeles	CA	90019	323-938-2661		35
Bouley 163 Duane St *Web:* www.davidbouley.com	New York	NY	10013	212-333-1220		671

Name / Address	City	State	ZIP	Phone	Fax	Class
Bou-Matic PO Box 8050 *Web:* boumatic.com	Madison	WI	53708	608-222-3484		273
Bounce Logistics LLC 5838 Brick Rd Ste 102 *TF:* 877-677-5623 ■ *Web:* www.bouncelogistics.com	South Bend	IN	46628	574-243-1550	243-1584	311
BounceU 1166 S Gilbert Rd *Web:* www.bounceu.com	Gilbert	AZ	85296	480-632-9663		31
Bound to Stay Bound Books Inc (BTSB) 1880 W Morton Ave **Fax Area Code:* 800 ■ *TF:* 800-637-6586 ■ *Web:* www.btsb.com	Jacksonville	IL	62650	217-245-5191	747-2872*	92
Bound'ry 911 20th Ave S *Web:* boundryevents.com	Nashville	TN	37212	615-321-3043		671
Boundary County PO Box 419 *Web:* www.boundarycountyid.org	Bonners Ferry	ID	83805	208-267-5504	267-7814	338
Boundary County School District 6577 Main St Ste 101 *Web:* www.bcsd101.com	Bonners Ferry	ID	83805	208-267-3146		302
Boundless Network Inc 200 E Sixth St Ste 300 *Web:* www.boundlessnetwork.com	Austin	TX	78701	512-472-9200	472-9204	194
Bounteous 600 N King St Ste 200 *Web:* www.archer-group.com	Wilmington	DE	19801	302-429-9120		7
Bounty Print Ltd 6359 Bayne St *Web:* www.bountyprint.com	Halifax	NS	B3K2V6	902-453-0300		627
Bountyland Petroleum Inc 1510 Blue Ridge Blvd Ste 202 *Web:* mybountyland.com	Seneca	SC	29672	864-882-6876		581
Bourbon & Boots Inc 314 Main St 2th Fl *TF:* 877-435-8977 ■ *Web:* www.bourbonandboots.com	North Little Rock	AR	72114	877-435-8977		690
Bourbon County 210 S National Ave *Web:* bourboncountyks.org	Fort Scott	KS	66701	620-223-3800	223-5832	338
Bourbon House Seafood & Oyster Bar 144 Bourbon St *Web:* www.bourbonhouse.com	New Orleans	LA	70130	504-522-0111		671
Bourbon Orleans - A Wyndham Historic Hotel 717 Orleans St *TF:* 866-513-9744 ■ *Web:* www.bourbonorleans.com	New Orleans	LA	70116	504-523-2222	571-4666	379
Bourdon Forge Company Inc 99 Tuttle Rd *Web:* www.bourdonforge.com	Middletown	CT	06457	860-632-2740	632-7247	350
Bourg Insurance Agency Inc 504 Iberville St *Web:* bourginsurance.com	Donaldsonville	LA	70346	225-490-5658		390
Bourgault Industries Ltd 1 mile NE Side Hwy 368 *Web:* www.bourgault.com	Saint Brieux	SK	S0K3V0	306-275-2300		273
Bourget & Associates Inc 365 Elm St *Web:* www.bourgetgroup.com	Woonsocket	RI	02895	401-769-6762	769-2598	194
Bourn & Koch Inc 2500 Kishwaukee St *Web:* www.bourn-koch.com	Rockford	IL	61104	815-965-4013	965-0019	455
Bourne Brothers Printing Company Inc 5276 Hwy 42 *Web:* www.bournebrothers.com	Hattiesburg	MS	39401	601-582-1808		627
Bourne Industries Inc 491 S Comstock St *Web:* www.bourneindustries.com	Corunna	MI	48817	989-743-3461		599
Bourns Inc 1200 Columbia Ave *TF:* 877-426-8767 ■ *Web:* www.bourns.com	Riverside	CA	92507	951-781-5690	781-5006	625
Bouten Construction Co 627 N Napa St *Web:* boutenconstruction.com	Spokane	WA	99202	509-535-3531	535-6047	297-7
Bouthillette Parizeau 9825 Verville St *Web:* bpa.ca	Montreal	QC	H3L3E1	514-383-3747		256
Boutwell Owens & Company Inc 251 Authority Dr *Web:* www.boutwellowens.com	Fitchburg	MA	01420	978-343-3067		101
Bouvier Kelly Inc 212 S Elm St Ste 200 *Web:* www.bouvierkelly.com	Greensboro	NC	27401	336-275-7000		636
Bovie Medical Corp 5115 Ulmerton Rd *NYSE: BVX* ■ *TF:* 800-537-2790 ■ *Web:* www.boviemedical.com	Clearwater	FL	33760	800-537-2790		250
Bovine's 3979 Hwy 17 Business *Web:* www.bovinesrestaurant.com	Murrells Inlet	SC	29576	843-651-2888		671
Bow Engineering & Development Inc 1953 S Beretania St Ph A *Web:* bowengineering.com	Honolulu	HI	96826	808-941-8853	945-9299	261
Bow Plastics Ltd 5700 Cote de Liesse *TF:* 800-852-8527 ■ *Web:* www.bow-group.com	Montreal	QC	H4T1B1	514-735-5671		607
Bow Street Market Inc 79 Bow St *Web:* bowstreetmarket.com	Freeport	ME	04032	207-865-6631		345
Bowden Manufacturing Corp 4590 Beidler Rd *TF:* 800-876-8970 ■ *Web:* www.bowdenmfg.com	Willoughby	OH	44094	800-876-8970		757
Bowden Oil Company Inc PO Box 145 *TF:* 800-280-0393 ■ *Web:* www.bowdenoil.com	Sylacauga	AL	35150	256-245-5611	249-2975	316
Bowditch Ford Inc 11291 Jefferson Ave *TF:* 866-399-2616 ■ *Web:* www.bowditchford.net	Newport News	VA	23601	757-595-2211		54
Bowdoin College 5000 College Sta *Web:* www.bowdoin.edu	Brunswick	ME	04011	207-725-3100	725-3101	166
Bowdoin Group Inc, The 40 William St *Web:* www.bowdoingroup.com	Wellesley	MA	02481	781-239-9933		721
Bowe Machine Co 2527 State St *Web:* www.bowemachine.com	Bettendorf	IA	52722	563-355-4907		454
Bowen & Bowen 907 Main St *Web:* bowenandbowen.com	Hackensack	NJ	07601	201-487-3937	487-0562	2
Bowen & Bowen Certified Public Accountants 445 S Frontage Rd *Web:* bowencpa.com	Burr Ridge	IL	60527	630-325-9800	325-6621	2
Bowen & Watson Inc PO Box 877 *Web:* bowen-watson.com	Toccoa	GA	30577	706-886-3197	886-3010	186
Bowen Advisors Inc 745 Atlantic Ave 8th Fl *Web:* bowenadvisors.com	Boston	MA	02111	617-245-1666		70
Bowen Engineering Corp 8802 N Meridian St *Web:* www.bowenengineering.com	Indianapolis	IN	46260	317-842-2616	841-4257	188-7
Bowen Group 10 Center St Ste 103 *Web:* www.thebowengroup.com	Stafford	VA	22556	540-658-0490		463
Bowen Hall 5595 Kietzke Ln *Web:* bowenhall.com	Reno	NV	89511	775-323-8678		41
Bowen Machine Company Inc 3421 Fairview Dr *Web:* bowenmachine.com	Gastonia	NC	28052	704-629-9111	629-9101	454
Bowen Workforce Solutions Inc 602 12 Ave SW Ste 700 *Web:* bowenworks.ca	Calgary	AB	T2R1J3	403-262-1156		260
Bowen, Hanes & Company Inc The Forum 3290 Northside Pkwy Ste 880 *Web:* www.bowenhanes.com	Atlanta	GA	30327	404-995-0507		528
Bowers & Burrows Oil Co 213 Young St *Web:* bbfuels.net	Henderson	NC	27536	252-492-0181		316
Bowers Museum 2002 N Main St *Web:* www.bowers.org	Santa Ana	CA	92706	714-567-3600		520
Bowerston Shale Co 515 Main St PO Box 199 *Web:* www.bowerstonshale.com	Bowerston	OH	44695	740-269-2921		150
Bowhead 4900 Seminary Rd Ste 1200 *Web:* www.bowheadsupport.com	Alexandria	VA	22311	703-931-2451		22
Bowie Bolt & Supply Inc 617 Market St Ste 3 *TF:* 800-337-9650 ■ *Web:* www.bowiebolt.com	Bridgeville	DE	19933	800-337-9650	597-3911	351
Bowie County 710 James Bowie Dr *Web:* www.co.bowie.tx.us	New Boston	TX	75570	903-628-6700	628-6729	338
Bowie Industries Inc 1004 E Wise St *TF:* 800-433-0934 ■ *Web:* www.bowieindustries.com	Bowie	TX	76230	940-872-1106	872-4792	273
Bowie State University 14000 Jericho Park Rd *TF:* 877-772-6943 ■ *Web:* www.bowiestate.edu	Bowie	MD	20715	301-860-4000	860-3518	166
Bowie-Cass Electric Co-opeartive Inc 117 N St *TF:* 800-794-2919 ■ *Web:* www.bcec.com	Douglassville	TX	75560	903-846-2311		245
Bowl America Inc 6446 Edsall Rd PO Box 1288 *NYSE: BWL.A* ■ *Web:* www.bowl-america.com	Alexandria	VA	22312	703-941-6300		99
Bowl-A-Roll Lanes 1560 Jefferson Rd *Web:* www.bowl-a-roll.com	Rochester	NY	14623	585-427-7250		99
Bowler Dixon & Twitchell LLP 3137 E Warm Springs Rd Ste 100 *Web:* nevadalegalcounsel.com	Las Vegas	NV	89120	702-703-6998		41
Bowles & Associates LLC 911 W Eighth Ave Ste 202 *Web:* bowlescpa.com	Anchorage	AK	99501	907-274-9720		2
Bowles Mattress Company Inc 1220 Watt St *TF:* 800-223-7509 ■ *Web:* www.bowlesmattress.com	Jeffersonville	IN	47130	812-288-8614		471
Bowles Rice LLP 600 Quarrier St *Web:* www.bowlesrice.com	Charleston	WV	25301	304-347-1100	343-2867	41
Bowlin Travel Centers Inc 150 Louisiana Blvd NE *OTC: BWTL* ■ *TF:* 800-716-8413 ■ *Web:* www.bowlintc.com	Albuquerque	NM	87108	800-716-8413		579
Bowling Green Area Chamber of Commerce 710 College St *TF:* 866-330-2422 ■ *Web:* www.bgchamber.com	Bowling Green	KY	42101	270-781-3200	843-0458	139
Bowling Green Chamber of Commerce (BGCC) 130 S Main St PO Box 31 *Web:* www.bgchamber.net	Bowling Green	OH	43402	419-353-7945	353-3693	139
Bowling Green City Schools (BGCS) 137 Clough St *Web:* www.bgcs.k12.oh.us	Bowling Green	OH	43402	419-352-3576	352-1701	685
Bowling Green Independent School District 1211 Center St *Web:* www.b-g.k12.ky.us	Bowling Green	KY	42101	270-746-2200		685
Bowling Green Public Library 201 W Locust St *Web:* www.bowlinggreen-mo.gov	Bowling Green	MO	63334	573-324-5030	324-6367	434-3
Bowling Green State University 1001 E Wooster St *TF:* 866-246-6732 ■ *Web:* www.bgsu.edu	Bowling Green	OH	43403	419-372-2531	372-6955	166
Bowling Green State University Firelands 1 University Dr *Web:* www.firelands.bgsu.edu	Huron	OH	44839	419-433-5560	433-9696	162
Bowling Portfolio Management LLC 4030 Smith Rd Ste 140 *Web:* www.bowlingpm.com	Cincinnati	OH	45209	513-871-7776	871-7791	401
Bowling Proprietors' Association of America (BPAA) 621 Six Flags Dr PO Box 5802 **Fax Area Code:* 817 ■ *TF:* 800-343-1329 ■ *Web:* www.bpaa.com	Arlington	TX	76011	800-343-1329	633-2940*	48-23
Bowlmor 222 W 44th St *Web:* www.bowlmor.com	New York	NY	10036	212-777-2214		31
Bowls USA Inc 1050 Burning Tree Rd *Web:* www.bowlsusa.us	Pinehurst	NC	28374	910-295-2831		48-6
Bowman & Associates Insurance 16042 N 32nd St Bldg A **Fax Area Code:* 480 ■ *TF:* 800-456-0241 ■ *Web:* bowmaninsurance.com	Phoenix	AZ	85032	602-482-3300	838-4445*	390
Bowman & Company LLP 601 White Horse Rd *Web:* www.bowmanllp.com	Voorhees	NJ	08043	856-435-6200		2
Bowman and Brooke LLP 970 W 190th St Ste 700 *Web:* www.bowmanandbrooke.com	Torrance	CA	90502	310-768-3068	719-1019	41
Bowman Animal Hospital Cat Clinic Inc 8308 Creedmoor Rd *Web:* bowmananimalhospital.com	Raleigh	NC	27613	919-847-6216		794
Bowman Barrett & Associates Inc 130 E Randolph St Ste 2650	Chicago	IL	60601	312-228-0100	228-0706	261
Bowman Books c/o Joseph Bruchac PO Box 308 *Web:* www.josephbruchac.com	Greenfield Center	NY	12833	518-584-1728	583-9741	637-2
Bowman Consulting Group 13461 Sunrise Valley Dr Ste 500 *Web:* www.bowmanconsulting.com	Herndon	VA	20171	703-464-1000		727

Name / Address	City	State	Zip	Phone	Fax	Class
Bowman County 104 First St NW Ste 3 *TF:* 866-752-2691 ■ *Web:* www.bowmannd.com	Bowman	ND	58623	701-523-3450	523-5443	338
Bowman Foster & Associates Inc 6353 Center Dr Ste 101 *Web:* www.bfa-eng.com	Norfolk	VA	23502	757-466-7400	466-7887	261
Bowman Hollis Manufacturing Inc 2925 Old Steele Creek Rd *TF:* 888-269-2358 ■ *Web:* www.bowmanhollis.com	Charlotte	NC	28208	704-374-1500	333-5520	744
Bowman Lake State Park 745 Bliven Sherman Rd *Web:* parks.ny.gov	Oxford	NY	13830	607-334-2718		565
Bowman Manufacturing Company Inc 17301 51st Ave NE *TF:* 800-962-4660 ■ *Web:* www.bowmandispensers.com	Arlington	WA	98223	360-435-5005		608
Bowman Plating Company Inc 2631 126th St *Web:* www.bowmanplating.com	Compton	CA	90222	310-639-4343	639-3577	481
Bowman's Agency, The PO Box 4071 *Web:* www.thebowmanagency.com	Lancaster	PA	17604	717-898-7716	898-6084	167-3
Bowman's Hill Wildflower Preserve 1635 River Rd PO Box 685 *Web:* bhwp.org	New Hope	PA	18938	215-862-2924	862-1846	97
Bowne House Historical Society, The 3701 Bowne St *Web:* www.bownehouse.org	Flushing	NY	11354	718-359-0528		637-2
Bowperson Publishing PO Box 564 *Web:* www.bowperson.com	Glenbrook	NV	89413	775-749-5247	749-1891	637-10
Bowring Ranch State Historical Park Highway 61 *Web:* outdoornebraska.gov	Merriman	NE	69218	308-684-3428		565
Bowser Manufacturing 1302 Jordan Ave *TF:* 800-327-5126 ■ *Web:* www.bowser-trains.com	Montoursville	PA	17754	570-368-2379	368-5046	44
Bowser Morner Inc 1419 Miami St *Web:* www.bowser-morner.com	Toledo	OH	43605	419-691-4800		261
Bowser's Lucky Dog Casino 3140 Dredge Dr	Helena	MT	59602	406-442-1555		443
Box Butto County 7006 Otoe Rd PO Box 802 *Web:* boxbuttecounty.us	Alliance	NE	69301	308-762-4607	762-2867	338
Box Elder County 1 S Main St *TF:* 877-390-2326 ■ *Web:* www.boxeldercounty.org	Brigham City	UT	84302	435-734-3300	723-7562	338
Box Turtle Press 184 Franklin St Ground Fl *Web:* www.mudfish.org	New York	NY	10013	212-219-9278		637-2
Boxer Blake & Moore PLLC PO Box 948 *Web:* boxerblake.com	Springfield	VT	05156	802-885-2141		41
Boxer Hotel, The 107 Merrimac St *Web:* www.theboxerboston.com	Boston	MA	02114	617-624-0202	624-0211	707
Boxer Software PO Box 14545 *TF:* 800-982-6937 ■ *Web:* www.boxersoftware.com	Scottsdale	AZ	85267	602-485-1635		178-1
Boxerwood Nature Center & Woodland Garden 963 Ross Rd *Web:* boxerwood.org	Lexington	VA	24450	540-463-2697		97
Boxes Inc 1833 Knox Ave *Web:* www.boxesinc.com	Saint Louis	MO	63139	314-781-2600		100
Boxwood Hall State Historic Site 1073 E Jersey St *Web:* www.state.nj.us	Elizabeth	NJ	07201	908-282-7617		565
Boxworks Technologies Inc 2065 Pkwy Blve *TF:* 877-495-2250 ■ *Web:* www.boxworks.com	Salt Lake City	UT	84119	801-214-6100		180
BOXX Modular Inc 555 Jubilee Ln Bldg A *Web:* www.blackdiamondgroup.com	Lewisville	TX	75056	972-492-4040		106
Boy Scouts of America (BSA) 1325 W Walnut Hill Ln PO Box 152079 *TF:* 800-323-0732 ■ *Web:* www.scouting.org	Irving	TX	75015	972-580-2000		48-15
Boyajian Inc 144 Will Dr *TF:* 800-965-0665 ■ *Web:* www.boyajianinc.com	Canton	MA	02021	781-828-9966		296-41
Boyar's Research 32 W 39th St 9th Fl *Web:* boyarresearch.com	New York	NY	10016	212-995-8300	995-5636	401
Boyarski Fritz LLP 1330 Avenue of the Americas Ste 1800 *TF:* 877-606-7211 ■ *Web:* boyarskifritz.com	New York	NY	10019	212-920-4925		41
Boyarsky, Silbert, Silverman, Vas & Pasternak, CPA's, PA 6151 Executive Blvd	Rockville	MD	20852	301-231-0535		2
Boyce & Bynum Pathology Laboratories 200 Portland St *TF:* 800-392-2748 ■ *Web:* www.bbpllab.com	Columbia	MO	65201	573-886-4600	886-4695	415
Boyce Thompson Arboretum 37615 US Hwy 60 *TF:* 877-763-5315 ■ *Web:* cals.arizona.edu	Superior	AZ	85273	520-689-2723	689-5858	97
Boyce Thompson Institute for Plant Research Inc 533 Tower Rd *Web:* btiscience.org	Ithaca	NY	14853	607-254-1234	254-1242	668
Boyd & Associates Inc 6319 Colfax Ave *Web:* www.boydsecurity.com	North Hollywood	CA	91606	818-752-1888		693
Boyd & Boyd PC 101 W Main St Ste 4900 *Web:* boydlaw.org	Norfolk	VA	23510	757-622-3611		41
Boyd and Sons Inc 1312 E 200 N *TF:* 800-648-9915 ■ *Web:* www.boydandsons.com	Washington	IN	47501	812-254-6858	254-2035	780
Boyd Bros Transportation Inc 3275 Alabama 30 *TF:* 800-700-2693 ■ *Web:* www.boydbros.com	Clayton	AL	36016	334-775-1400		780
Boyd Coffee Co 19730 NE Sandy Blvd *TF:* 800-545-4077 ■ *Web:* www.boydscoffeestore.com	Portland	OR	97230	503-666-4545		296-7
Boyd County PO Box 26 *Web:* boydcounty.ne.gov	Butte	NE	68722	402-775-2391	775-2146	338
Boyd County Public Library 1740 Central Ave *Web:* thebookplace.org	Ashland	KY	41101	606-329-0518	329-0578	434-3
Boyd F. Buckingham Inc PS 321 Burnett Ave S Ste 200 *Web:* boydbuckingham.com	Renton	WA	98057	425-228-6662		41
Boyd Gaming Corp 3883 Howard Hughes Pkwy 9th Fl *NYSE: BYD* ■ *Web:* www.boydgaming.com	Las Vegas	NV	89169	702-792-7200		132
Boyd Grain Inc 1957 E 200 N *Web:* www.boydgrain.com	Washington	IN	47501	812-254-5599	254-6706	780
Boyd Group Inc, The 3570 Portage Ave *TF:* 800-385-5451 ■ *Web:* www.boydgroup.com	Winnipeg	MB	R3K0Z8	204-895-1244		62
Boyd Jones Construction 950 S Tenth St Ste 100 *Web:* www.boydjones.biz	Omaha	NE	68108	402-553-1804	561-7705	186
Boyd Lake State Park 3720 N County Rd 11-C *Web:* cpw.state.co.us	Loveland	CO	80538	970-669-1739	669-0071	565
Boyd Lighting Co 944 Folsom St *TF:* 800-224-2693 ■ *Web:* www.boydlighting.com	San Francisco	CA	94107	415-778-4300	778-4319	439
Boyd Special Commodities Inc 2000 Paulson Rd *Web:* safer.fmcsa.dot.gov	Turlock	CA	95380	209-632-0221		311
Boydell Development Co 1600 Clay St **Fax Area Code: 440*	Detroit	MI	48211	313-964-0333	232-6264*	652
Boyden & Youngblutt Adv & Marketing Inc 120 W Superior St *Web:* b-y.net	Fort Wayne	IN	46802	260-422-4499		4
Boyden World Corp 50 Broadway *Web:* www.boyden.com	Hawthorne	NY	10532	914-747-0093	747-0108	266
Boyds Philadelphia 1818 Chestnut St *Web:* www.boydsphila.com	Philadelphia	PA	19103	215-564-9000		157-3
Boyer Candy Inc 821 17th St *Web:* www.boyercandies.com	Altoona	PA	16602	814-944-9401		296-8
Boyer Steel Inc 26532 Groesbeck *TF:* 800-280-8167 ■ *Web:* www.boyersteel.com	Warren	MI	48089	586-541-8355	541-8363	492
Boyer's Food Markets Inc 301 S Warren St *Web:* www.boyersfood.com	Orwigsburg	PA	17961	570-366-1477		345
Boyertown Area Historical Society Library 43 S Chestnut St *Web:* www.boyertownhistory.org	Boyertown	PA	19512	610-367-5255		434-3
Boyertown Area School District (BASD) 911 Montgomery Ave *Web:* www.boyertownasd.org	Boyertown	PA	19512	610-367-6031	369-7620	186
Boyertown Furnace Co 156 Holly Rd *Web:* www.boyertownfurnace.com	Boyertown	PA	19512	610-369-1450	367-6800	318
Boyett Petroleum 601 McHenry Ave *TF:* 800-545-9212 ■ *Web:* boyett.net	Modesto	CA	95350	209-577-6000	577-6040	579
Boyhood Home of President Woodrow Wilson 419 Seventh St *Web:* www.wilsonboyhoodhome.org	Augusta	GA	30901	706-722-9828		50-3
Boykin Contracting Inc 167 Lott Ct	West Columbia	SC	29172	803-926-4930		610
Boykin Management Co 8015 W Kenton Cir Ste 220 *Web:* www.boykin.com	Huntersville	NC	28078	704-896-2880		194
Boylan Indoor Tennis 4000 St Francis Dr *Web:* www.boylan.org	Rockford	IL	61103	815-877-4273		354
Boyle & Anderson PC 110 Genesee St *Web:* boylefirm.com	Auburn	NY	13021	315-253-0326	253-4968	41
Boyle & Stoll CPAs PC 3755 Brickway Blvd *Web:* www.boyle-stoll.com	Santa Rosa	CA	95403	707-571-1951	571-1817	2
Boyle Brendan (Rep D - PA) 1133 Longworth House Office Bldg *Web:* boyle.house.gov	Washington	DC	20515	202-225-6111	226-0611	342-2
Boyle County 321 W Main St Rm 111 *Web:* boyleky.com	Danville	KY	40422	859-238-1110	238-1108	338
Boyle County Public Library 307 W Broadway *Web:* boylepublib.org	Danville	KY	40422	859-238-7323	236-7692	434-3
Boyle Energy Services & Technology Inc 28 Locke Rd *Web:* boyleenergy.com	Concord	NH	03301	603-227-5200		256
Boyle Fredrickson SC 840 N Plankinton Ave *Web:* www.boylefred.com	Milwaukee	WI	53203	414-225-9755		428
Boyle Investment Co 5900 Poplar Ave *Web:* www.boyle.com	Memphis	TN	38119	901-767-0100	766-4299	655
Boyle Ogata Bregman 17461 Derian Ave Ste 202 *Web:* www.bobsearch.com	Irvine	CA	92614	949-471-6200		260
Boyle Software Inc 42 W 24th St *Web:* www.boylesoftware.com	New York	NY	10010	212-691-0776		180
Boyne Country Sports 1200 Bay View Rd *TF:* 800-462-6963 ■ *Web:* boynecountrysports.com	Petoskey	MI	49770	231-439-4906		711
Boyne Highlands Resort 600 Highlands Dr **Fax Area Code: 231* ■ *TF:* 855-688-7022 ■ *Web:* www.boyne.com	Harbor Springs	MI	49740	855-688-7022	526-3100*	669
Boyne Mountain Resort 3951 Charlevoix Ave *Web:* www.boyneresorts.com	Petoskey	MI	49770	231-439-4750	439-4786	669
Boynton Beach City Library 208 S Seacrest Blvd *Web:* www.boynton-beach.org	Boynton Beach	FL	33435	561-742-6390		434-3
Boynton Restaurant & Spirits 117 Highland St *Web:* www.boyntonrestaurant.com	Worcester	MA	01609	508-756-5432		671
Boys & Girls Club of Boone County 1575 Mulberry St *Web:* www.bgcboone.org	Zionsville	IN	46077	317-873-6670		652
Boys & Girls Clubs of America 1275 Peachtree St NE *Web:* www.bgca.org	Atlanta	GA	30309	404-487-5700		48-15
Boys Arnold Wealth Management 1272 Hendersonville Rd *Web:* www.boysarnold.com	Asheville	NC	28803	828-274-1542		401
Boys Town 14100 Crawford St *TF:* 800-217-3700 ■ *Web:* www.boystown.org	Boys Town	NE	68010	402-498-1300		48-6

Name / Address	City	State	ZIP	Phone	Fax	Class
Boys Town Press 13603 Flanagan Blvd *TF:* 800-282-6657 ■ *Web:* www.boystownpress.org	Boys Town	NE	68010	800-282-6657		637-2
Bozard Ford Co 540 Outlet Mall Blvd *TF:* 866-488-9252 ■ *Web:* bozardford.com	Saint Augustine	FL	32084	904-824-1641		57
Bozeman Area Chamber of Commerce 2000 Commerce Way *Web:* www.bozemanchamber.com	Bozeman	MT	59715	406-586-5421	586-8286	139
Bozeman Deaconess Hospital 915 Highland Blvd *Web:* www.bozemanhealth.org	Bozeman	MT	59715	406-414-5000		374-3
Bozeman Public Library 626 E Main St *Web:* www.bozemanlibrary.org	Bozeman	MT	59715	406-582-2400	582-2424	434-3
Bozeman School District 7 PO Box 520 *Web:* www.bsd7.org	Bozeman	MT	59771	406-522-6000		685
Bozzuto Group 7850 Walker Dr Ste 400 *Web:* www.bozzuto.com	Greenbelt	MD	20770	301-220-0100		187
Bozzuto's Inc 275 School House Rd *OTC:* BOZZ ■ *TF:* 800-458-5114 ■ *Web:* www.bozzutos.com	Cheshire	CT	06410	203-272-3511	250-2880	297-8
BP (Backcountry Publishing) 3303 Dick George Rd *TF:* 888-443-3826 ■ *Web:* www.braintan.com	Cave Junction	OR	97523	541-592-3778		637-2
BP (Biomedical Publications) PO Box 2876 *Web:* www.biomedicalpublications.com	Seal Beach	CA	90740	419-281-1802	281-6883	637-2
BP (Book Peddlers) 18925 Lake Ave *Web:* www.bookpeddlers.com	Deephaven	MN	55391	952-544-1154		637-2
BP Environmental Inc 8615 Commerce Dr Unit 1 *Web:* bpenvironmental.net	Easton	MD	21601	410-819-0919		192
BP Logix Inc 410 S Melrose Dr Ste 100 *TF:* 800-431-1450 ■ *Web:* www.bplogix.com	Vista	CA	92081	760-643-4121	643-4122	225
BP MotorClub PO Box 4441 *TF:* 800-334-3300 ■ *Web:* www.bpmotorclub.com	Carol Stream	IL	60197	800-334-3300		53
BP PLC 501 Westlake Park Blvd *Web:* www.bp.com	Houston	TX	77079	281-366-2000		316
BP Solutions Group Inc 24 Wilmington St *TF:* 888-252-4476 ■ *Web:* bpsg.us	Asheville	NC	28806	828-252-4476	252-3038	627
BP Studios 2100 Gateway Centre Blvd Ste 105 *Web:* www.bpstudios.com	Morrisville	NC	27560	919-484-9522		177
BPA *Bonneville Power Administration* 905 NE 11th Ave *TF:* 800-282-3713 ■ *Web:* www.bpa.gov	Portland	OR	97232	503-230-3000		340-9
BPA Worldwide 100 Beard Sawmill Rd 6th Fl *Web:* www.bpaww.com	Shelton	CT	06484	203-447-2800	447-2900	49-18
BPAA (Bowling Proprietors' Association of America) 621 Six Flags Dr PO Box 5802 **Fax Area Code:* 817 ■ *TF:* 800-343-1329 ■ *Web:* www.bpaa.com	Arlington	TX	76011	800-343-1329	633-2940*	48-23
BPC (Biographical Publishing Co) 95 Sycamore Dr **Fax Area Code:* 253 ■ *Web:* biopub.us	Prospect	CT	06712	203-758-3661	793-2618*	637-2
BPG Wealth Management LLC 12901 SE 97th Ave Ste 240 *Web:* bpgnetwork.com	Clackamas	OR	97015	503-654-7676		390
BPI (Broadband Products Inc) 1951 Old Cuthbert Rd Ste 301 *TF:* 800-956-8898 ■ *Web:* www.broadbandproducts.com	Cherry Hill	NJ	08034	800-956-8898		681
BPI Communications LLC 13700 Oakland Ave *Web:* www.bpicommunications.com	Highland Park	MI	48203	313-957-5155		5
BPI Inc 612 S Trenton Ave *Web:* www.bpiminerals.com	Pittsburgh	PA	15221	412-371-8554	371-9984	192
BPI Information Systems 6055 W Snowville Rd *Web:* www.bpiohio.com	Brecksville	OH	44141	440-717-4112		138
BPI Media Group Inc 340 Denson Ave *Web:* www.bpimediagroup.com	Boaz	AL	35957	256-593-2048		92
BPL (Brentwood Public Library) 34 Second Ave *Web:* brentwoodnylibrary.org	Brentwood	NY	11717	631-273-7883		434-3
BPL (Brooklyn Public Library) 496 Franklin Ave *Web:* www.bklynlibrary.org	Brooklyn	NY	11238	718-623-2134		434-3
BPL (Berwyn Public Library) 2701 S Harlem Ave *Web:* www.berwynlibrary.org	Berwyn	IL	60402	708-795-8000	795-8101	434-3
BPL (Bossier Parish Library) 2206 Beckett St *Web:* www.bossierlibrary.org	Bossier City	LA	71111	318-746-1693	746-7768	434-3
BPM (Burr Pilger & Mayer) 600 California St Ste 600 *Web:* www.bpmcpa.com	San Francisco	CA	94108	415-421-5757	288-6288	2
BPM Inc 200 W Front St *TF:* 800-826-0494 ■ *Web:* www.bpmpaper.com	Peshtigo	WI	54157	715-582-4551	582-4853	557
BPPI (Broadway Play Publishing Inc) 224 E 62nd St *Web:* www.broadwayplaypub.com	New York	NY	10065	212-772-8334		637-2
BPR Inc 4655 Wilfrid-Hamel Blvd	Quebec City	QC	G1P2J7	418-871-8151		668
BPS (Biophysical Society) 5515 Security Ln Ste 1110 **Fax Area Code:* 301 ■ *Web:* www.biophysics.org	Rockville	MD	20852	240-290-5600	634-7133*	49-19
BR (Business Roundtable) 300 New Jersey Ave NW Ste 800 *Web:* www.businessroundtable.org	Washington	DC	20001	202-872-1260	466-3509	49-12
BR Anchor Publishing LLC 4596 Capital Dome Dr *Web:* www.branchor.com	Jacksonville	FL	32246	904-642-1667		637-2
BR Fries & Associates Inc 34 W 32nd St *Web:* brfries.com	New York	NY	10001	212-563-3300	629-6029	261
BR Funsten & Co 5200 Watt Ct Ste B *TF:* 888-261-2871 ■ *Web:* www.brfunsten.com	Fairfield	CA	94534	209-825-5375	825-4916	361
BR Kreider & Son Inc 63 Kreider Ln *Web:* www.brkreider.com	Manheim	PA	17545	717-898-7651		189-5
BR Printers Inc 10154 Toebben Dr *Web:* www.brprinters.com	Independence	KY	41051	859-292-1700		627
BR Williams Trucking Inc 2339 Hwy 21 S *TF:* 800-523-7963 ■ *Web:* www.brwilliams.com	Oxford	AL	36203	256-831-5580	831-8059	780
Brabazon Pumps & Compressor 2484 Century Rd *TF:* 800-825-3222 ■ *Web:* www.brabazon.com	Green Bay	WI	54303	920-498-6020		172
BrabenderCox Inc 108 S St *Web:* www.brabendercox.com	Leesburg	VA	20175	703-896-5300		194
Brabham Oil Company Inc 525 Midway St **Fax Area Code:* 514	Bamberg	SC	29003	803-245-2471	932-9701*	581
Brabo & Carlsen LLP 1111 E Tahquitz Canyon Way *Web:* www.brabo-carlsen.com	Palm Springs	CA	92262	760-320-0848	322-4626	2
Bracalente Manufacturing Group 20 W Creamery Rd *Web:* www.bracalente.com	Trumbauersville	PA	18970	215-536-3077	536-4844	621
Bracco Diagnostics Inc 259 Prospect Plains Rd Bldg H *TF:* 800-631-5245 ■ *Web:* imaging.bracco.com	Monroe Township	NJ	08831	609-514-2200		582
Brace Management Group Inc 9500 Arena Dr Ste 270 *Web:* www.bracemgmt.com	Largo	MD	20774	301-772-7600		193
Bracewell & Giuliani LLP 711 Louisiana St Ste 2300 *TF:* 800-404-3970 ■ *Web:* bracewell.com	Houston	TX	77002	713-223-2300		428
Bracewell Engineering Inc 155 Mast St Ste 114 *Web:* bracewellengineering.com	Morgan Hill	CA	95037	669-258-5820		261
Brach Eichler LLC 101 Eisenhower Pkwy *Web:* bracheichler.com	Roseland	NJ	07068	973-228-5700		41
Bracing Systems Inc 4N350 Old Gary Ave *Web:* www.bracingsystems.com	Hanover Park	IL	60133	630-665-2732		480
Brack Capital Real Estate 853 Broadway 2nd Fl *Web:* www.brack-capital.com	New York	NY	10003	212-308-7200	308-1231	652
Bracken County 116 W Miami St PO Box 264 *Web:* www.brackencounty.ky.gov	Brooksville	KY	41004	606-735-2300	735-2615	338
Brackett Builders Inc 185 Marybill Dr S *Web:* www.brackettbuilders.com	Troy	OH	45373	937-339-7505		186
Brackett Inc 7115 SE Forbes Ave Bldg 451 J St *TF:* 800-255-3506 ■ *Web:* brackett-inc.com	Topeka	KS	66619	785-862-2205	862-1127	629
Brackmann Tax & Accounting Service PC 727 N Cross Pointe Blvd Ste B *Web:* brackmanncpa.net	Evansville	IN	47715	812-476-9801		2
Braco Window Cleaning Service Inc 1 Braco International Blvd *TF:* 800-969-4300 ■ *Web:* www.bracowindowcleaning.com	Wilder	KY	41076	859-442-6000	442-6001	152
Brad Montgomery Productions Inc 6574 S Zeno Ct *Web:* bradmontgomery.com	Aurora	CO	80016	303-691-0726		196
Brad Young & Associates Inc 345 Pollasky Ave *Web:* byaengineering.com	Clovis	CA	93612	559-323-9600		261
Brada Manufacturing Inc 46 Warwick Industrial Dr *Web:* www.bradamfg.com	Warwick	RI	02886	401-739-3774	738-4634	621
Bradbury & Stamm Construction Company Inc 7110 Second St NW *Web:* www.bradburystamm.com	Albuquerque	NM	87107	505-765-1200	842-5419	186
Bradbury Company Inc 1200 E Cole *TF:* 800-397-6394 ■ *Web:* bradburygroup.com	Moundridge	KS	67107	620-345-6394		456
Bradbury Mountain State Park 528 Hallowell Rd *Web:* www.maine.gov	Pownal	ME	04069	207-528-2215		565
Bradbury Science Museum 1350 Central PO Box 1663 *Web:* www.lanl.gov	Los Alamos	NM	87545	505-667-4444		520
Braddock Hospital 12500 Willowbrook Rd *TF:* 888-369-1122 ■ *Web:* www.wmhs.com	Cumberland	MD	21502	240-964-7000		374-3
Braden Farms Inc 6940 Hughson Ave PO Box 1022	Hughson	CA	95326	209-883-4061		10-10
Braden Insurance Agency Inc 3069 Breckenridge Ln *Web:* bradeninsurance.com	Louisville	KY	40220	502-454-9191	454-2766	390
Braden Manufacturing LLC 5199 N Mingo Rd **Fax Area Code:* 918 ■ *TF:* 800-272-3360 ■ *Web:* www.braden.com	Tulsa	OK	74117	800-272-3360	272-7414*	480
Braden's Furniture 11105 Turkey Dr *Web:* www.bradens.com	Knoxville	TN	37934	865-777-4059		321
BradenCarco Gearmatic Paccar Winch Div 800 E Dallas St *Web:* www.paccarwinch.com	Broken Arrow	OK	74012	918-251-8511	259-1575	190
Bradenton Area Convention Ctr 1 Haben Blvd *Web:* www.bradentongulfislands.com	Palmetto	FL	34221	941-722-3244		205
Bradenton Insurance LLC 1400 Ballard Park Dr *Web:* bradentoninsurance.com	Bradenton	FL	34205	941-748-0511		390
Bradford & Barthel LLP 2518 River Plaza Dr *Web:* bradfordbarthel.com	Sacramento	CA	95833	916-569-0790		428
Bradford & Bigelow Inc 3 Perkins Way *Web:* www.bradford-bigelow.com	Newburyport	MA	01950	978-904-3100		626
Bradford & Galt Inc 11457 Olde Cabin Rd Ste 200 *TF:* 800-997-4644 ■ *Web:* bradfordandgalt.com	Saint Louis	MO	63141	314-997-4644		196
Bradford Allen 200 S Michigan Ave 18th Fl *Web:* www.bradfordallen.com	Chicago	IL	60604	312-994-5700		652
Bradford Area School District Inc 150 Lorana Ave *Web:* www.bradfordareaschools.org	Bradford	PA	16701	814-362-3841		685

Name / Address	City	State	ZIP	Phone	Fax	Class
Bradford Cos 3100 McKinnon St Ste 400	Dallas	TX	75231	972-776-7000	776-7083	655
TF: 866-261-9713 ■ *Web:* www.bradford.com						
Bradford County						
Courthouse 301 Main St	Towanda	PA	18848	570-265-1727	265-1729	338
Web: www.bradfordcountypa.org						
Bradford County Florida						
945 N Temple Ave PO Box B	Starke	FL	32091	904-966-6220	964-4454	338
Web: www.bradfordcountyfl.gov						
Bradford Era, The 43 Main St	Bradford	PA	16701	814-368-3173		532-2
Web: www.bradfordera.com						
Bradford Health Services						
2101 Magnolia Ave S Ste 518	Birmingham	AL	35205	205-251-7753		726
TF: 800-217-2849 ■ *Web:* bradfordhealth.com						
Bradford Labs LLC 216 River St	Haverhill	MA	01832	978-372-9091		261
Web: bradfordlabsllc.com						
Bradford Licensing Assoc						
7 Oak Pl Ste 1	Montclair	NJ	07042	973-509-0200		618
Web: www.bradfordlicensing.com						
Bradford Regional Medical Ctr						
116 Interstate Pk	Bradford	PA	16701	814-368-4143		374-3
Web: www.brmc.com						
Bradford School 2469 Stelzer Rd	Columbus	OH	43219	614-416-6200		800
TF: 800-678-7981 ■ *Web:* www.bradfordschoolcolumbus.edu						
Bradford Scott Data Corp						
1001 Chestnut Hills Pkwy Ste 1	Fort Wayne	IN	46814	260-625-5107		396
TF: 800-430-5120 ■ *Web:* www.bradfordscott.com						
Bradford Soap Works Inc						
200 Providence St	West Warwick	RI	02893	401-821-2141		214
Web: www.bradfordsoap.com						
Bradford Supply Co 801 E Main St	Robinson	IL	62454	618-544-3171	544-3729	385
TF: 800-851-6817 ■ *Web:* www.bradfordsupplycompany.com						
Bradford Technologies Inc						
302 Piercy Rd	San Jose	CA	95138	408-360-8520		177
TF: 866-445-8367 ■ *Web:* www.bradfordsoftware.com						
Bradford White Corp 725 Talamore Dr	Ambler	PA	19002	215-641-9400	641-1612	36
TF: 800-523-2931 ■ *Web:* www.bradfordwhite.com						
Bradford-O'Keefe Funeral Homes Inc						
075 E Howard Ave	Biloxi	MS	39530	228-374-5650		510
Web: www.bradfordokeefe.com						
Bradham Bros Inc						
6128 Rozzelles Ferry Rd	Charlotte	NC	28214	704-323-8038		189-10
Web: www.bradhambrothers.com						
Bradhart Products Inc						
7747 Lochlin Dr	Brighton	MI	48116	248-437-8700		454
Web: www.bradhart.com						
Bradington-Young 1340 14th Ave Ct SW	Hickory	NC	28602	704-435-5881	435-4276	319-2
Web: www.bradington-young.com						
Bradley & Riley PC PO Box 2804	Cedar Rapids	IA	52406	319-363-0101		428
Web: bradleyriley.com						
Bradley Arant Boult Cummings LLP						
1819 Fifth Ave N	Birmingham	AL	35203	205-521-8000		428
Web: www.bradley.com						
Bradley Associates PC						
201 S Capitol Ave Ste 700	Indianapolis	IN	46225	317-237-5500	237-5503	734
Web: www.bradleycpa.com						
Bradley Boulder Inn 2040 16th St	Boulder	CO	80302	303-545-5200		379
Web: www.thebradleyboulder.com						
Bradley Caldwell Inc						
200 Kiwanis Blvd	Hazleton	PA	18202	570-455-7511	455-0385	276
TF: 800-257-9100 ■ *Web:* www.bradleycaldwell.com						
Bradley Corp						
W 142 N 9101 Fountain Blvd	Menomonee Falls	WI	53051	262-251-6000	251-5817	609
TF: 800-272-3539 ■ *Web:* www.bradleycorp.com						
Bradley County 155 N Ocoee St	Cleveland	TN	37311	423-728-7226		338
Web: clevelandtn.gov						
Bradley County 104 N Myrtle PO Box 352	Warren	AR	71671	870-226-6743		338
TF: 870-226-8301 ■ *Web:* bradleycountyarkansas.com						
Bradley Graphic Solutions Inc						
941 Mill Rd	Bensalem	PA	19020	215-638-8771		627
TF: 800-638-8223 ■ *Web:* www.bradleygraphics.net						
Bradley Hospital						
1011 Veterans Memorial Pkwy	Riverside	RI	02915	401-432-1000		374-1
Web: www.bradleyhospital.org						
Bradley House 11321 Old Seward Hwy	Anchorage	AK	99515	907-336-7177	336-7178	671
Web: alaskabradleyhouse.com						
Bradley Inn 3063 Bristol Rd	New Harbor	ME	04554	207-677-2105		379
Web: www.bradleyinn.com						
Bradley Law Firm 13 E Henderson	Cleburne	TX	76031	817-645-3993	517-2522	41
Web: bradleylawyers.com						
Bradley Lifting Corp 1030 Elm St	York	PA	17403	717-848-3121	843-7102	190
Web: www.bradleylifting.com						
Bradley Mj & Associates Inc						
47 Jct Sq Dr	Concord	MA	01742	978-369-5533		196
Web: www.mjbradley.com						
Bradley Petroleum Inc						
7268 S Tucson Way	Centennial	CO	80112	303-733-4627		580
Web: www.bradleygas.com						
Bradley Plumbing & Heating						
431 Hackel Dr	Montgomery	AL	36117	334-271-0700	542-3965*	189-10
**Fax Area Code:* 602 ■ *Web:* www.bradleyph.com						
Bradley Pulverizer Company Inc						
123 S Third St	Allentown	PA	18105	610-434-5191		491
Web: www.bradleypulverizer.com						
Bradley University 1501 W Bradley Ave	Peoria	IL	61625	309-676-7611	677-2797	166
TF: 800-447-6460 ■ *Web:* www.bradley.edu						
Bradley Welborn 800 W Church St	Livingston	TX	77351	936-327-2541		390
Web: bradleywelborn.com						
Bradley-Sciocchetti Inc						
4420 N Crescent Blvd	Pennsauken Township	NJ	08109	856-663-3022	663-5579	196
Web: www.bsihvac.com						
Bradmark Technologies Inc						
4265 San Felipe St Ste 700	Houston	TX	77027	713-621-2808	621-1639	178-1
TF: 800-621-2808 ■ *Web:* www.bradmark.com						
Brad-Pak Enterprises Inc 124 S Ave	Garwood	NJ	07027	908-233-1234		76
Web: brad-pak.com						
Bradshaw Advertising 811 NW 19th Ave	Portland	OR	97209	503-221-5000		7
Web: bradshawads.com						

Name / Address	City	State	ZIP	Phone	Fax	Class
Bradshaw Consulting Services Inc						
2170 Woodside Exec Ct	Aiken	SC	29803	803-641-0960		180
Web: www.bcs-gis.com						
Bradshaw Home						
9409 Buffalo Ave	Rancho Cucamonga	CA	91730	909-476-3884	476-3616	730
Web: bradshawhome.com						
Bradshaw Smith & Company Entertainment Management LLC						
5851 W Charleston	Las Vegas	NV	89146	702-878-9788		2
Brady & Kosofsky PA 3065 B Senna Dr	Matthews	NC	28105	704-849-8008		41
Web: bandklaw.com						
Brady Campaign to Prevent Gun Violence						
840 1st St NE Ste 400	Washington	DC	20002	202-370-8100	371-9615	48-7
Web: www.bradyunited.org						
Brady Chapman Holland & Associates Inc						
10055 W Gulf Bank	Houston	TX	77040	713-688-1500	688-7967	390
Web: bch-insurance.com						
Brady Connolly & Masuda Pc						
211 Landmark Dr Ste C2	Normal	IL	61761	309-862-4914		428
Web: www.bcm-law.com						
Brady Corp 6555 W Good Hope Rd	Milwaukee	WI	53223	888-250-3082	292-2289*	413
NYSE: BRC ■ **Fax Area Code:* 800 ■ *TF:* 800-541-1686 ■ *Web:* www.bradyid.com						
Brady Enterprises Inc						
167 Moore Rd	East Weymouth	MA	02189	781-337-5000		296-15
Web: www.bradyenterprises.com						
Brady Fischel & Daily LLC						
721 Melvin Ave	Annapolis	MD	21401	410-216-9054	216-9034	41
Web: bfdlegal.com						
Brady Industries Inc						
7055 Lindell Rd	Las Vegas	NV	89118	702-876-3990	876-1580	406
TF: 800-293-4698 ■ *Web:* www.bradyindustries.com						
Brady Kevin (Rep R - TX)						
1011 Longworth House Office Bldg	Washington	DC	20515	202-225-4901	225-5524	342-2
Web: kevinbrady.house.gov						
Brady Martz & Associates PC						
401 Demers Ave Ste 300	Grand Forks	ND	58201	701-775-4685	795-7498	2
Web: www.bradymartz.com						
Brady Oilfield Services LP						
23 Marion Ave PO Box 83	Oxbow	SK	S0C2B0	306-458-2344		539
Web: www.brady.sk.ca						
Brady Risk Management Inc						
24 W Carver St 2nd Fl	Huntington	NY	11743	631-549-8561		390
Web: bradyrisk.com						
Brady Sullivan Properties LLC						
670 N Commercial St	Manchester	NH	03101	603-622-6223	622-7342	652
Web: bradysullivan.com						
Brady, Connolly & Masuda PC						
10 S Lasalle St Ste 900	Chicago	IL	60603	312-425-3131		41
Web: bcm-law.com						
Brady, Klein, Weissman LLP						
501 Fifth Ave Ste 1900	New York	NY	10017	212-949-5800		41
Web: bkwlegal.com						
Brady, Radcliff & Brown LLP						
1201 Riverview Plaza Office Bldg						
63 S Royal St	Mobile	AL	36602	251-405-0077		41
Web: brblawyers.com						
Braen Stone Co						
400 Central Ave PO Box 8310	Haledon	NJ	07508	973-720-7090	595-7087	503-5
Web: www.braenstone.com						
Braff Group, The						
1665 Washington Rd Ste 3	Pittsburgh	PA	15228	412-833-5733		476
TF: 888-922-5169 ■ *Web:* thebraffgroup.com						
Braff Harris & Sukoneck						
305 Broadway 7th Fl	New York	NY	10007	212-599-2085		445
Web: bhsm-law.com						
Bragar Eagel & Squire PC						
885 Third Ave Ste 3040	New York	NY	10022	212-308-5858	486-0462	41
Web: bespc.com						
Bragg Financial Advisors Inc						
1031 S Caldwell St Ste 200	Charlotte	NC	28203	704-377-0261		401
Web: www.braggfinancial.com						
Bragg Live Food Products Inc						
PO Box 7	Santa Barbara	CA	93102	800-446-1990	968-1001*	297-8
**Fax Area Code:* 805 ■ *TF:* 800-446-1990 ■ *Web:* bragg.com						
Bragg-Mitchell Mansion						
1906 Springhill Ave	Mobile	AL	36607	251-471-6364		520
Web: braggmitchellmansion.com						
Braille Battery Inc 6935 15th St E	Sarasota	FL	34243	941-312-5047		74
Web: braillebattery.com						
Braille Institute of America Inc						
741 N Vermont Ave	Los Angeles	CA	90029	323-663-1111	663-0867	48-11
TF: 800-272-4553 ■ *Web:* www.brailleinstitute.org						
Brain Injury Association of America						
1608 Spring Hill Rd Ste 110	Vienna	VA	22182	703-761-0750	761-0755	48-17
TF: 800-444-6443 ■ *Web:* www.biausa.org						
Brain Power Inc 4470 SW 74th Ave	Miami	FL	33155	305-264-4465	264-1467	476
TF: 800-225-5274 ■ *Web:* www.callbpi.com						
Brain Research Institute						
695 Charles Young Dr S	Los Angeles	CA	90095	310-825-5061	206-5855	668
Web: www.bri.ucla.edu						
Brain Sync PO Box 3120	Ashland	OR	97520	541-488-8078	488-7870	514
TF: 800-444-7962 ■ *Web:* www.brainsync.com						
Brain Technologies Corp (BTC)						
PO Box 358655	Gainesville	FL	32635	352-792-1036	639-2814*	637-2
**Fax Area Code:* 888 ■ *Web:* www.braintechnologies.com						
Brainerd Baptist Church						
300 Brookfield Ave	Chattanooga	TN	37411	423-624-2606		48-20
Web: www.brainerdbaptist.org						
Brainerd Compressor 3034 Sandbrook St	Memphis	TN	38116	800-228-4138		14
TF: 800-228-4138 ■ *Web:* bcr.us.com						
Brainerd Industries Inc						
680 Precision Ct	Miamisburg	OH	45342	937-228-0488	449-8057	483
Web: www.brainerdindustries.com						
Brainerd International Raceway						
5523 Birchdale Rd	Brainerd	MN	56401	218-824-7223	824-7240	515
TF: 866-444-4455 ■ *Web:* www.brainerdraceway.com						
Brainerd Lakes Area Chamber of Commerce						
7393 State Hwy 371 PO Box 356	Brainerd	MN	56401	218-829-2838	829-8199	139
TF: 800-450-2838 ■ *Web:* www.explorebrainerdlakes.com						

Phone | Fax | Class

Brainin 48 Frank Mossberg Dr . . . Attleboro MA 02703 508-226-1200 226-8703 815
Web: brainin.wpengine.com
BrainLAB Inc
5 Westbrook Corporate Ctr . . . Westchester IL 60154 708-409-1343 409-1619 382
TF: 800-784-7700 ■ *Web:* www.brainlab.com
Brains II 165 Konrad Crescent . . . Markham ON L3R9T9 888-272-4672 946-1949* 175
**Fax Area Code:* 905 ■ *TF:* 888-272-4672 ■ *Web:* brainsiisolutions.com
Brains On Fire 1263 Pendleton St . . . Greenville SC 29611 864-676-9663 195
Web: brainsonfire.com
Brainshark Inc
130 Turner St Bldg 1 Ste 100 . . . Waltham MA 02453 781-370-8000 177
TF: 866-276-7427 ■ *Web:* www.brainshark.com
Brainsport 616 10th St E . . . Saskatoon SK S7N1B5 306-244-0955 711
Web: brainsport.ca
Brainstorm Internet Inc
640 Main Ave Ste 201 . . . Durango CO 81301 970-247-1442 225
Web: www.gobrainstorm.net
Braintree Laboratories Inc
60 Columbian St W . . . Braintree MA 02185 781-843-2202 843-7932 476
TF: 800-874-6756 ■ *Web:* www.braintreelabs.com
Brainworks Software Inc
100 S Main St . . . Sayville NY 11782 631-563-5000 178-1
TF: 800-755-1111 ■ *Web:* www.brainworks.com
BrainX Inc 45 Rincon Dr . . . Camarillo CA 93012 844-927-2469 177
TF: 844-927-2469 ■ *Web:* www.brainx.com
Brake and Clutch Inc 63 Bridge St . . . Salem MA 01970 978-745-2500 745-4484 61
TF: 800-322-1111 ■ *Web:* www.brakeandclutch.com
Brake Masters 6179 E Broadway . . . Tucson AZ 85711 520-512-0000 512-1000 62-5
TF: 800-888-5545 ■ *Web:* www.brakemasters.com
Brake Roller Company Inc
730 E Michigan Ave . . . Battle Creek MI 49016 269-965-2371 965-2389 456
TF: 800-537-9940 ■ *Web:* brakeroller.com
Brake Supply Company Inc
5501 Foundation Blvd . . . Evansville IN 47725 812-467-1000 385
TF: 800-457-5788 ■ *Web:* www.brake.com
Brake Systems Inc 2221 NE Hoyt St . . . Portland OR 97232 503-236-2116 239-5005 454
Web: www.brakesystemsinc.com
Brakebush Bros Inc N4993 Sixth Dr . . . Westfield WI 53964 608-296-2121 296-3192 619
TF: 800-933-2121 ■ *Web:* www.brakebush.com
Brakeley Briscoe Inc
322 W Bellevue Ave . . . San Mateo CA 94402 650-344-8883 317
TF: 800-416-3086 ■ *Web:* www.brakeleybriscoe.com
Brakewell Steel Fabricator Inc
55 Leone Ln . . . Chester NY 10918 845-469-9131 469-7618 482
TF: 888-914-9131 ■ *Web:* brakewell.com
Brakke Consulting Inc
12005 Ford Rd Ste 530 . . . Dallas TX 75234 972-243-4033 194
Web: www.brakkeconsulting.com
Brakur Custom Cabinetry 18656 Rt 59 . . . Shorewood IL 60404 815-436-4970 115
Web: brakur.com
Bramble Books
3002 NE 5th Ter Ste 212B . . . Wilton Manors FL 33334 954-533-3325 637-2
Web: www.bramblebooks.com
Bramble Park Zoo
800 Tenth St NW PO Box 910 . . . Watertown SD 57201 605-882-6269 882-5232 823
Web: www.brambleparkzoo.com
Bramco Inc 1801 Watterson Trl . . . Louisville KY 40299 502-493-4380 219
Web: www.bramco.com
Brame Specialty Company Inc PO Box 271 . . . Durham NC 27702 919-598-1500 598-5623 559
TF: 800-672-0011 ■ *Web:* www.bramespecialty.com
Brammer Engineering Inc
401 Edwards St Ste 1510 . . . Shreveport LA 71101 318-429-2345 429-2340 539
Web: brammer.com
Brampton Board of Trade
36 Queen St E Ste 101 . . . Brampton ON L6V1A2 905-451-1122 450-0295 137
Web: www.bramptonbot.com
Brampton Brick Ltd 225 Wanless Dr . . . Brampton ON L7A1E9 905-840-1011 840-1535 150
TSX: BBL.A ■ *TF:* 800-709-6257 ■ *Web:* bramptonbrick.com
Brampton (City of) 2 Wellington St W . . . Brampton ON L6Y4R2 905-874-2000 707
Web: www.brampton.ca
Branagh Inc 750 Kevin Ct . . . Oakland CA 94621 510-638-6455 562-8371 186
Web: www.branaghinc.com
Branbury State Park
3570 Lake Dunmore Rd Rt 53 . . . Brandon VT 05733 802-247-5925 565
Web: www.vtstateparks.com
Branch County 31 Div St . . . Coldwater MI 49036 517-279-4301 278-4130 338
Web: www.countyofbranch.com
Branch Group Inc
442 Rutherford Ave NE . . . Roanoke VA 24016 540-982-1678 982-4217 186
Web: www.branchgroup.com
Branch Manufacturing Co
6420 Pine St . . . North Branch MN 55056 651-674-4441 674-4442 697
Web: www.branchmfg.com
Branch Metrics
1400 Seaport Blvd Bldg B 2nd Fl . . . Redwood City CA 94063 650-209-6461 178-8
Web: branch.io
Branched Oak State Recreation Area
12000 W Branched Oak Rd . . . Raymond NE 68428 402-783-3400 565
Web: outdoornebraska.gov
BranchPattern 2820 N 48th St . . . Lincoln NE 68504 402-464-3833 187
Web: branchpattern.com
Brand Advisor 512 Union St . . . San Francisco CA 94133 415-393-0800 194
Web: www.brandadvisors.com
Brand Electric Inc 6274 E 375 S . . . LaFayette IN 47905 765-296-3437 194
Web: brandelectric.com
Brand Energy & Infrastructure Services Inc
1325 Cobb International Dr Ste A-1 . . . Kennesaw GA 30152 678-285-1400 514-0285* 491
**Fax Area Code:* 770 ■ *TF:* 855-746-4477 ■ *Web:* www.beis-deutschland.de
Brand Hydraulics Co
2332 S 25th St PO Box 6069 . . . Omaha NE 68105 402-344-4434 341-5419 790
Web: www.brand-hyd.com
Brand Innovation Group
8902 Airport Dr Ste A . . . Fort Wayne IN 46809 260-469-4060 7
Web: gotobig.com
Brand Institute Inc
200 SE First St 12th Fl . . . Miami FL 33131 305-374-2500 466
Web: www.brandinst.com
Brand Iron 931 Santa Fe Dr Ste 200 . . . Denver CO 80204 303-534-1901 195
TF: 800-343-6405 ■ *Web:* brandiron.net

Phone | Fax | Class

Brand Launcher Inc 4703 Falls Rd . . . Baltimore MD 21209 410-235-7070 7
Web: www.brandlauncher.com
Brand Library & Art Ctr
1601 W Mountain St . . . Glendale CA 91201 818-548-2051 520
Web: www.glendaleca.gov
Brand Protection Agency LLC
8750 N Central Expwy Ste 720 . . . Dallas TX 75231 866-339-5657 534-1756* 195
**Fax Area Code:* 972 ■ *TF:* 866-339-5657 ■ *Web:* brandprotectionagency.com
Brand Sense Partners LLC
3250 Ocean Park Blvd Ste 160 . . . Santa Monica CA 90405 310-867-7222 195
Web: bspbackup.wpengine.com
Brand Thunder LLC 6588 Dalmore Ln . . . Dublin OH 43016 614-408-8202 387
Web: brandthunder.com
Brand X Internet PO Box 7248 . . . Santa Monica CA 90406 310-395-5500 225
Web: www.brandx.net
Brandamplitude LLC
3467 Notre Dame Path . . . Stevensville MI 49127 269-429-6526 195
Web: brandamplitude.com
Branded Emblem Company Inc
7920 Foster St . . . Overland Park KS 66204 913-648-0573 258
Web: www.campdavid.com
Brandeis University 415 S St . . . Waltham MA 02454 781-736-3500 736-3536 166
TF: 800-622-0622 ■ *Web:* www.brandeis.edu
BrandEquity Intl 7 Great Meadow Rd . . . Newton MA 02462 800-969-3150 344
TF: 800-969-3150 ■ *Web:* www.brandequity.com
Brander Engineering Inc
975 Hansen Rd . . . Green Bay WI 54304 920-499-0260 261
Web: www.brandercti.com
Brandermill Woods
14311 Brandermill Woods Trl . . . Midlothian VA 23112 804-744-1173 744-4894 672
Web: www.brandermillwoods.com
Brandes Investment Partners LP
11988 El Camino Real Ste 600 . . . San Diego CA 92191 858-755-0239 755-0916 401
TF: 800-237-7119 ■ *Web:* www.brandes.com
Branding Brand 2313 E Carson St . . . Pittsburgh PA 15203 888-979-5018 387
TF: 888-979-5018 ■ *Web:* www.brandingbrand.com
Branding Farm, The (TBF) 1378 Main St . . . Venice CA 90291 310-396-4025 5
Web: branding.farm
BrandingBusiness 1 Wrigley . . . Irvine CA 92618 949-438-5174 7
Web: www.brandingbusiness.com
BrandJuice Consulting Inc
1700 E 17th Ave Ste 200 . . . Denver CO 80218 303-629-0560 466
Web: www.brandjuice.com
Brandman University 325 Mall Dr . . . Hanford CA 93230 559-587-1454 587-1604 786
TF: 800-746-0082 ■ *Web:* www.brandman.edu
Brandmovers Inc 590 Means St Ste 250 . . . Atlanta GA 30318 678-718-1850 718-1851 631
TF: 888-463-4933 ■ *Web:* brandmovers.com
Brand-Nu Laboratories Inc
377 Research Pky Ste 2 . . . Meriden CT 06450 203-235-7989 235-7163 145
Web: www.brandnu.com
Brandon Advertising
3023 Church St . . . Myrtle Beach SC 29577 843-916-2000 7
Web: www.thebrandonagency.com
Brandon Business Machines Inc
505 W Robertson St . . . Brandon FL 33511 813-689-1950 684-8051 175
Web: bbmusa.com
Brandon Chamber of Commerce
1043 Rosser Ave . . . Brandon MB R7A0L5 204-571-5340 571-5347 137
Web: brandonchamber.ca
Brandon Financial Planning
5101 Wheelis Rd Ste 112 . . . Memphis TN 38117 901-324-6600 324-5743 401
Web: brandonplanning.com
Brandon Hall School
1701 Brandon Hall Dr . . . Atlanta GA 30350 770-394-8177 622
Web: brandonhall.org
Brandon Meats & Sausage Inc
117 S Commercial St . . . Brandon WI 53919 920-346-2227 346-2532 345
Web: www.brandonmeats.com
Brandon Regional Health Ctr
150 McTavish Ave E . . . Brandon MB R7A2B3 204-578-4000 374-2
Web: www.prairiemountainhealth.ca
Brandon Regional Hospital
119 Oakfield Dr . . . Brandon FL 33511 813-681-5551 374-3
TF: 800-733-0429 ■ *Web:* brandonhospital.com
Brandon School Division 1031 Sixth St . . . Brandon MB R7A4K5 204-729-3100 727-2217 685
Web: www.bsd.ca
Brandon Systems
c/o A Brandon Associates Co 26 Sarah Dr . . . Farmingdale NY 11735 631-293-1414 256
Web: brandonsystems.com
Brandon University 270 18th St . . . Brandon MB R7A6A9 204-728-9520 728-7346 785
Web: www.brandonu.ca
Brandpoint 850 Fifth St S . . . Hopkins MN 55343 877-374-5270 5
TF: 877-374-5270 ■ *Web:* www.brandpoint.com
Brandstand Group Inc
686 Yorktown Rd . . . Lewisberry PA 17339 717-932-4178 671
Brandstream 8353 160th Ave NE . . . Redmond WA 98052 425-497-1404 497-1804 463
Web: www.brandstream.com
Brandt Box & Paper Company Inc
6 W Crisman Rd . . . Columbia NJ 07832 908-496-4500 100
Web: www.brandtboxnj.com
Brandt Consolidated Inc
211 IL-125 . . . Pleasant Plains IL 62677 217-476-3438 280
Web: brandt.co
Brandt Holdings Co 4650 26th Ave S Ste E . . . Fargo ND 58104 701-237-6000 360-3
Web: www.brandtholdings.com
Brandt Information Services Inc
501 N Duval St . . . Tallahassee FL 32301 850-577-4900 177
Web: www.brandtinfo.com
Brandt Precision Machining Inc
11116 N Lamar Blvd . . . Austin TX 78753 512-339-7251 339-0225 488
Web: www.brandtprecision.com
Brandt Ronat & Co 60 McLeod St . . . Merritt Island FL 32953 321-453-3101 7
Web: www.brc60.com
Brandt Technologies Inc
231 W Grand Ave . . . Bensenville IL 60106 630-787-1800 146
Web: www.brandttech.com
Brandt Tractor Ltd Hwy 1 E PO Box 3856 . . . Regina SK S4P3R8 306-791-7777 111
TF: 888-227-2638 ■ *Web:* www.brandt.ca

Name / Address	City	State	Zip	Phone	Fax	Class
Brandtailers						
1501 Quail St Ste 210	Newport Beach	CA	92660	949-442-0500		7
Web: brandtailers.com						
Brandtjen & Kluge Inc						
539 Blanding Woods Rd	Saint Croix Falls	WI	54024	715-483-3265	483-1640	629
TF: 800-826-7320 ■ *Web:* kluge.biz						
Brandy's 1500 E Cedar Ave Ste 40	Flagstaff	AZ	86004	928-779-2187		671
Web: www.brandysrestaurant.com						
Brandylane Publishers Inc 5 S 1st St	Richmond	VA	23219	804-644-3090	644-3092	637-2
Web: brandylanepublishers.com						
Brandywine Capital Associates Inc						
100 S Church St	West Chester	PA	19382	610-344-2910	344-0955	401
TF: 888-344-2920 ■ *Web:* www.brandywinecap.com						
Brandywine Conservancy & Museum of Arts						
1 Hoffman's Mill Rd PO Box 141	Chadds Ford	PA	19317	610-388-2700		520
Web: www.brandywine.org						
Brandywine Creek State Park						
PO Box 3782	Greenville	DE	19807	302-577-3534		565
Web: www.destateparks.com						
Brandywine Financial Services Corp						
2 Ponds Edge Dr PO Box 500	Chadds Ford	PA	19317	610-388-9600		653
Web: brandywine-financial.com						
Brandywine Global Investment Management LLC						
1735 Market St Ste 1800	Philadelphia	PA	19103	215-609-3500	609-3501	401
TF: 800-348-2499 ■ *Web:* brandywineglobal.com						
Brandywine Hospital						
201 Reeceville Rd	Coatesville	PA	19320	610-383-8000		374-3
TF: 800-430-3762 ■ *Web:* brandywine.towerhealth.org						
Brandywine Machine Company Inc						
300 Creek Rd	Downingtown	PA	19335	800-523-7128		454
TF: 800-523-7128 ■ *Web:* www.bramcostainless.com						
Brandywine Nursing & Rehabilitation Center Inc						
505 Greenbank Rd	Wilmington	DE	19808	302-998-0101		363
Web: www.brandywinenursing.org						
Brandywine Realty Trust						
555 E Lancaster Ave Ste 100	Radnor	PA	19087	610-325-5600	325-5622	655
NYSE: BDN ■ *TF:* 866-426-5400 ■ *Web:* www.brandywinerealty.com						
Brandywine Valley Baptist Church						
7 Mt Lebanon Rd	Wilmington	DE	19803	302-478-4255		48-20
Web: brandywineonline.org						
Brandywine Valley Fabricators Inc						
Brandywine Vly Fab	Coatesville	PA	19320	610-384-7440	384-7042	480
Web: www.brandywinevalleyfab.com						
Brandywine Zoo 1001 N Pk Dr	Wilmington	DE	19802	302-571-7747	571-7787	823
Web: brandywinezoo.org						
Branford Academy of Hair & Cosmetology						
251 W Main	Branford	CT	06405	203-315-2985		214
Web: www.branfordacademy.com						
Branford Hall Career Institute						
1 Summit Pl	Branford	CT	06405	203-488-2525	488-2920	167-3
TF: 800-959-7599 ■ *Web:* www.branfordhall.edu						
Branford Hills Health Care Ctr						
189 Alps Rd	Branford	CT	06405	203-481-6221	483-1893	450
Web: www.bhhcc.com						
Branham Corp 207 Eiler Ave	Louisville	KY	40214	502-366-0326	366-3234	207
TF: 800-331-6643 ■ *Web:* www.branhamcorp.com						
Branksome Hall 10 Elm Ave	Toronto	ON	M4W1N4	416-920-9741	920-5390	622
Web: www.branksome.on.ca						
Brann & Isaacson 184 Main St	Lewiston	ME	04243	207-786-3566		428
TF: 800-225-6964 ■ *Web:* www.brannlaw.com						
Brann's Steakhouse & Grille						
401 Leonard St NW	Grand Rapids	MI	49504	616-454-9368		671
Web: www.branns.com						
Brannan Island State Recreation Area						
17645 State Hwy 160	Rio Vista	CA	94571	916-777-6671		565
Web: www.parks.ca.gov						
Brannan Paving Company Ltd						
111 Elk Dr PO Box 3403	Victoria	TX	77903	361-573-3130	573-6211	186
TF: 800-626-7064 ■ *Web:* www.brannanpaving.com						
Brannan Sand & Gravel Co						
2500 Brannan Way	Denver	CO	80229	303-534-1231	534-1236	46
Web: www.brannan1.com						
Brannan Veterinary Clinic						
120 E Dudley St	Maumee	OH	43537	419-893-0552		794
Web: brannanvet.com						
Brannen Banks of Florida Inc						
PO Box 1929	Inverness	FL	34451	352-726-1221	726-1156	360-2
Web: www.brannenbanks.com						
Brannen Brothers-flutemakers Inc						
58 Dragon Ct	Woburn	MA	01801	781-935-9522		527
Web: www.brannenflutes.com						
Brannons Rentals & Sales						
2052 Lincoln Ave	San Jose	CA	95125	408-448-3000	448-2076	363
Web: brannonsmedical.com						
Branom Instrument Co						
5500 Fourth Ave So	Seattle	WA	98108	206-762-6050		358
TF: 800-767-6051 ■ *Web:* www.branom.com						
Branson Cafe 120 W Main St	Branson	MO	65616	417-334-3021		671
Web: www.downtownbransoncafe.com						
Branson City Hall 110 W Maddux St	Branson	MO	65616	417-334-3345	335-4354	337
Web: www.cityofbranson.org						
Branson Daily News						
200 Industrial Pk Dr	Hollister	MO	65672	417-334-3161		532-2
Web: bransontrilakesnews.com						
Branson Fowlkes & Company Inc						
19 Briar Hollow Ln Ste 130	Houston	TX	77027	713-780-0606		401
Web: www.bransonfowlkes.com						
Branson's Best Reservations						
3431 W 76 Country Blvd	Branson	MO	65616	417-335-2555		376
TF: 800-800-2019 ■ *Web:* branson-missouri.com						
Branson/Lakes Area Lodging Assn						
PO Box 430	Branson	MO	65615	417-559-3869		376
Web: www.bransonarealodging.com						
Brant Securities Ltd						
220 Bay St Ste 300	Toronto	ON	M5J2W4	416-596-4545	596-4546	690
TF: 888-544-9318 ■ *Web:* brantsec.com						
Branter Thibodeau & Associate						
674 Mt Hope Ave Ste 1	Bangor	ME	04401	207-947-3325	945-3400	2
Web: btacpa.com						
Brantford Brant Chamber of Commerce (BBCC)						
77 Charlotte St	Brantford	ON	N3T2W8	519-753-2617	753-0921	137
Web: www.brantfordbrantchamber.com						
Brantley Electronic Supply Inc (BESI)						
935 Bragg Blvd	Fayetteville	NC	28301	910-485-2100		35
TF: 800-682-2560 ■ *Web:* www.brantleyelectronic.com						
Brantley Janson Yost & Ellison CPA						
1617 S 325th St	Federal Way	WA	98003	253-838-3484	874-6831	2
Web: www.brantleyjanson.com						
Brantley-Jordan Animal Hospital PC						
5698 Thomaston Rd	Macon	GA	31220	478-757-1600		794
Web: bjahpc.net						
Brasfield & Gorrie LLC						
3021 Seventh Ave S	Birmingham	AL	35233	205-328-4000	251-1304	186
TF: 800-239-8017 ■ *Web:* www.brasfieldgorrie.com						
Brasher Motor Company of Weimar Inc						
1700 I- 10	Weimar	TX	78962	800-375-2438	725-8118*	57
**Fax Area Code:* 979 ■ *TF:* 800-783-1746						
Brasitas 954 E Main St	Stamford	CT	06902	203-323-3176		671
Web: brasitas.com						
Braskem 1735 Market St 28th Fl	Philadelphia	PA	19103	215-841-3100		144
Web: www.braskem.com.br						
Brass Reminders Company Inc PO Box 160	Keene	KY	40339	859-881-0556	887-5394	322
TF: 888-272-7773 ■ *Web:* www.brassreminders.com						
Brass Ring Capital Inc						
301 Carlson Pkwy Ste 265	Minnetonka	MN	55305	952-473-2710		401
Web: www.brassringcapital.com						
Brass-Craft Manufacturing Co						
39600 Orchard Hill Pl	Novi	MI	48375	248-305-6000	305-6011	609
TF: 877-272-7755 ■ *Web:* www.brasscraft.com						
Brasseler USA 1 Brasseler Blvd	Savannah	GA	31419	800-841-4522		228
TF: 800-841-4522 ■ *Web:* brasselerusa.com						
Brasserie Margaux 401 Lenora St	Seattle	WA	98121	206-219-2224		671
Web: www.margauxseattle.com						
Brasstech Inc 2001 Carnegie Ave	Santa Ana	CA	92705	949-417-5207		609
Web: www.brasstech.com						
Brasstown Valley Resort						
6321 Hwy 76	Young Harris	GA	30582	800-201-3205	379-9999*	669
**Fax Area Code:* 706 ■ *TF:* 800-201-3205 ■ *Web:* www.brasstownvalley.com						
Braswell Food Co						
226 N Zetterower Ave	Statesboro	GA	30458	912-764-6191		296-20
TF: 800-673-9388 ■ *Web:* braswells.com						
Bratcher Heating & Air Conditioning						
1210 Ft Jesse Rd	Normal	IL	61761	309-807-4733		189-10
Web: bratchercomfort.com						
Bratslavsky Consulting Engineers Inc						
500 W 27th Ave Ste A	Anchorage	AK	99503	877-844-5264	272-5214*	261
**Fax Area Code:* 907 ■ *TF:* 877-844-5264 ■ *Web:* bce-ak.com						
Bratt Decor Inc 5 N Haven St	Baltimore	MD	21224	703-448-6833		321
Web: www.brattdecor.com						
Brattle Book Shop Inc 9 West St	Boston	MA	02111	617-542-0210		95
Web: brattlebookshop.com						
Brattle Group Inc, The						
44 Brattle St	Cambridge	MA	02138	617-864-7900		194
Web: www.brattle.com						
Brattleboro Area Chamber of Commerce						
180 Main St	Brattleboro	VT	05301	802-254-4565	254-5675	139
TF: 877-254-4565 ■ *Web:* www.brattleborochamber.org						
Brattleboro Memorial Hospital Inc						
17 Belmont Ave	Brattleboro	VT	05301	802-257-0341		374-3
TF: 866-972-5266 ■ *Web:* www.bmhvt.org						
Bratton Corp 2801 E 85th St	Kansas City	MO	64132	816-363-1014		189-14
Web: www.brattonsteel.com						
Bratton, Mcmorrow & Associates LLP						
1841 Knoll Dr	Ventura	CA	93003	805-654-1040	654-1445	2
Web: bmk-cpa.com						
Brauer Material Handling Systems Inc						
226 Molly Walton Dr	Hendersonville	TN	37075	800-645-6083	859-2937*	385
**Fax Area Code:* 615 ■ *TF:* 800-645-6083 ■ *Web:* www.braueronline.com						
Braun Industries Inc						
1170 Production Dr	Van Wert	OH	45891	877-344-9990		59
TF: 877-344-9990 ■ *Web:* www.braunambulances.com						
Braun Intertec Corp						
11001 Hampshire Ave S	Minneapolis	MN	55438	952-995-2000	995-2020	261
TF: 800-279-6100 ■ *Web:* braunintertec.com						
Braun Mike (Sen R - IN)						
374 Russell Senate Office Bldg	Washington	DC	20510	202-224-4814		342-2
Web: www.braun.senate.gov						
Braun's Express Inc 10 Tandem Way	Hopedale	MA	01747	508-473-8405	473-8284	780
TF: 800-654-0055 ■ *Web:* www.braunsexpress.com						
Brause Realty Inc 52 Vanderbilt Ave	New York	NY	10017	212-697-5454		652
Web: www.brauserealty.com						
Bravado International Group Merchandising Services Inc						
1755 Broadway 2nd Fl	New York	NY	10019	212-445-3400		7
Web: www.bravadousa.com						
Brave 512 Second St 2nd Fl	San Francisco	CA	94107	650-200-3351		788
Web: brave.com						
Brave New Restaurant (BNR)						
2300 Cottondale Ln Ste 105	Little Rock	AR	72202	501-663-2677		671
Web: www.bravenewrestaurant.com						
Brave River Solutions Inc						
875 Centerville Rd Bldg 3	Warwick	RI	02886	401-828-6611	828-4834	180
TF: 888-828-8911 ■ *Web:* www.braveriver.com						
Braverman & Co 110 E 42nd St 17th Fl	New York	NY	10017	212-682-2900	682-7718	41
Web: www.braverlaw.net						
Braverman Financial Assoc						
2173 Embassy Dr	Lancaster	PA	17603	717-399-4030		194
Web: www.bravermanfinancial.com						
Bravo						
4500 I-55 Frontage Rd Highland Vlg Ste 244	Jackson	MS	39211	601-982-8111		671
Web: bravobuzz.com						
Bravo 98-115 Kaonohi St	Aiea	HI	96701	808-487-5544		671
Web: www.bravorestaurant.com						
Bravo Brio Restaurant Group Inc						
777 Goodale Blvd Ste 100	Columbus	OH	43212	614-326-7944	326-7943	670
Bravo Sports Corp						
12801 Carmenita Rd	Santa Fe Springs	CA	90670	562-484-5100		710
TF: 800-234-9737 ■ *Web:* www.bravosportscorp.com						

Name / Address	City	State	Zip	Phone	Fax	Class
Bravo Wellness LLC						
20445 Emerald Pkwy Dr SW Ste 400	Cleveland	OH	44135	877-662-7286		363
TF: 877-662-7286 ■ *Web:* www.bravowell.com						
Brawner Paper Company Inc						
5702 Armour Dr	Houston	TX	77020	713-675-6584		553
TF: 800-962-9384 ■ *Web:* www.brawnerpaper.com						
Braxton Automotive Group Inc						
1604 Howell Mill Rd	Atlanta	GA	30318	404-367-4767		57
Web: www.braxtonautogroup.com						
Braxton County 300 Main St PO Box 486	Sutton	WV	26601	304-765-2833	765-2947	338
Web: www.braxtoncounty.wv.gov						
Braxton Design Group						
PO Box 5524	Charlottesville	VA	22905	434-977-7999		187
Web: braxtondesigngroup.com						
Braxton Manufacturing Company Inc						
858 Echo Lake Rd	Watertown	CT	06795	860-274-6781	274-9195	483
Web: www.braxtonmfg.com						
Braxton Technologies LLC						
559 E Pikes Peak Ave Ste 300	Colorado Springs	CO	80903	719-380-8488		196
Web: www.braxtontech.com						
Bray and Scarff Inc 3801 Evergreen Pky	Bowie	MD	20716	301-464-0085		361
Web: www.brayandscarff.com						
Bray International Inc						
13333 Westland E Blvd	Houston	TX	77041	281-894-5454	894-9499	789
TF: 800-800-2729 ■ *Web:* www.bray.com						
Bray Real Estate 637 N Ave	Grand Junction	CO	81501	970-242-8450		652
TF: 888-760-4251 ■ *Web:* www.brayandco.com						
Braymar Precision Inc 641 Lunar Ave	Brea	CA	92821	714-674-0846	674-1965	386
Web: www.braymar.com						
Brayton Energy LLC 75 Lafayette Rd	Hampton	NH	03842	603-601-0450		261
Web: www.braytonenergy.net						
BraytonHughes Design Studios						
465 California St Ste 350	San Francisco	CA	94104	415-291-8100		393
Web: www.bhdstudios.com						
Braze 330 W 34th St 18th Fl	New York	NY	10001	504-327-7269		178-8
Web: www.braze.com						
Brazi's Italian Restaurant						
201 Food Terminal Plz	New Haven	CT	06511	203-498-2488		671
Web: brazis.com						
Brazil						
Consulate General						
1233 W Loop S Ste 1150	Houston	TX	77027	713-961-3063		257
Web: houston.itamaraty.gov.br						
Consulate General						
300 Montgomery St Ste 300	San Francisco	CA	94104	415-981-8170		257
Web: saofrancisco.itamaraty.gov.br						
Consulate General						
8484 Wilshire Blvd Ste 300	Beverly Hills	CA	90211	323-651-2664		257
Web: losangeles.itamaraty.gov.br						
Brazilian Court, The						
301 Australian Ave	Palm Beach Gardens	FL	33480	561-655-7740	655-0801	379
TF: 800-552-0335 ■ *Web:* www.thebraziliancourt.com						
Brazilian Grill 680 Main St	Hyannis	MA	02601	508-771-0109		671
Web: braziliangrillrestaurants.com						
Brazilian Travel Service (BTS)						
16 W 46th St 2nd Fl	New York	NY	10036	212-764-6161	719-4142	16
TF: 800-342-5746 ■ *Web:* www.btstravel.com						
Brazilian-American Chamber of Commerce Inc						
485 Madison Ave 52nd St Ste 401	New York	NY	10022	212-751-4691	751-7692	138
Web: www.brazilcham.com						
Brazilian-American Chamber of Commerce of Florida						
PO Box 310038	Miami	FL	33231	305-579-9030	579-9756	138
Web: www.brazilchamber.org						
Brazoria County 111 E Locust St	Angleton	TX	77515	979-849-5711		338
Web: brazoriacountytx.gov						
Brazoria County Library System						
451 N Velasco Ste 250	Angleton	TX	77515	979-864-1505		434-3
Web: bcls.lib.tx.us						
Brazoria Telephone Co 314 W Texas St	Brazoria	TX	77422	979-798-2121		736
TF: 844-849-1514 ■ *Web:* www.btel.com						
Brazos Bend State Park 21901 FM 762	Needville	TX	77461	409-553-5101		565
Web: tpwd.texas.gov						
Brazos Bookstore 2421 Bissonnet	Houston	TX	77005	713-523-0701		95
Web: www.brazosbookstore.com						
Brazos County 300 E 26th St Ste 120	Bryan	TX	77803	979-361-4224		338
Web: www.brazoscountytx.gov						
Brazos Telecommunications Inc						
109 N Ave D	Olney	TX	76374	940-564-5659		196
TF: 800-687-3222 ■ *Web:* www.brazosnet.com						
Brazos Urethane Inc						
1031 Sixth St N	Texas City	TX	77590	866-527-2967	948-1511*	189-12
**Fax Area Code:* 409 ■ *TF:* 866-527-2967 ■ *Web:* www.brazosurethane.com						
Brazos Valley Radio						
1240 E Villa Maria Rd	Bryan	TX	77802	979-776-1240		643
Web: www.brazosradio.com						
Brazosport Area Chamber of Commerce						
300 Abner Jackson Pkwy	Lake Jackson	TX	77566	979-285-2501	285-2505	139
Web: www.brazosport.org						
Brazosport College						
500 College Dr	Lake Jackson	TX	77566	979-230-3000	230-3443	162
TF: 877-717-7873 ■ *Web:* www.brazosport.edu						
Brazosport Facts 720 S Main St	Clute	TX	77531	979-265-7411	265-9052	532-2
TF: 800-864-8340 ■ *Web:* www.thefacts.com						
BRB Contractors Inc 3805 NW 25th St	Topeka	KS	66618	785-232-1245	235-8045	188-10
Web: www.brbcontractors.com						
BRB Publications Inc PO Box 27869	Tempe	AZ	85285	480-829-7475		637-2
TF: 800-929-3811 ■ *Web:* www.brbpub.com						
BRC (Bisexual Resource Ctr)						
29 Stanhope St	Boston	MA	02117	617-424-9595		637-10
Web: www.biresource.net						
Brc Advisors Inc						
700 S Flower St Ste 2650	Los Angeles	CA	90017	213-226-8700	226-8767	652
Web: www.brcadvisors.com						
BRC Imagination Arts 2711 Winona Ave	Burbank	CA	91504	818-841-8084		514
Web: www.brcweb.com						
BRC Rubber Group Inc PO Box 227	Churubusco	IN	46723	260-693-2171	693-6511	677
Web: www.brcrp.com						
BRCC (Baton Rouge Community College)						
201 Community College Dr	Baton Rouge	LA	70806	225-216-8000	216-8010	162
TF: 866-217-9823 ■ *Web:* www.mybrcc.edu						
BRCC (Blowing Rock Chamber of Commerce)						
132 Park Ave	Blowing Rock	NC	28605	828-295-7851	295-7651	139
TF: 800-295-7851 ■ *Web:* www.blowingrockncchamber.com						
BRD Solutions 101 Trenton Cir	Canonsburg	PA	15601	724-941-6375		195
Brea Chamber of Commerce						
1 Civic Center Cir	Brea	CA	92821	714-529-3660		139
Web: www.breachamber.com						
Bread for the World						
425 Third St SW Ste 1200	Washington	DC	20024	202-639-9400	639-9401	48-5
TF: 800-822-7323 ■ *Web:* www.bread.org						
Bread Loaf Corp 1293 Rt 7 S	Middlebury	VT	05753	802-388-9871	388-3815	194
Web: breadloaf.com						
Breadsmith						
420 E Silver Spring Dr	Whitefish Bay	WI	53217	414-962-6203		68
Web: www.breadsmith.com						
Breakaway Books PO Box 24	Halcottsville	NY	12438	800-548-4348		637-2
TF: 800-548-4348 ■ *Web:* www.breakawaybooks.com						
Breakaway Press Inc						
9620 Topanga Canyon Pl	Chatsworth	CA	91311	818-727-7388	727-7432	627
Web: www.breakawaypress.com						
Breakaway Tours 337 Queen St W	Toronto	ON	M5V2A4	800-465-4257		760
TF: 800-465-4257 ■ *Web:* www.breakawaytours.com						
Breakers at Waikiki, The						
250 Beach Walk	Honolulu	HI	96815	808-923-3181	923-7174	379
TF: 800-426-0494 ■ *Web:* www.breakers-hawaii.com						
Breakers Hotel & Restaurant						
1507 Ocean Ave	Spring Lake	NJ	07762	732-449-7700		378
Web: breakershotel.com						
Breakers Hotel & Suites						
105 Second St	Rehoboth Beach	DE	19971	302-227-6688	227-2013	379
TF: 800-441-8009 ■ *Web:* www.thebreakershotel.com						
Breakers Palm Beach, The						
1 S County Rd	Palm Beach Gardens	FL	33480	561-655-6611		707
TF: 888-273-2537 ■ *Web:* www.thebreakers.com						
Breakers Resort						
3002 N Ocean Blvd	Myrtle Beach	SC	29577	843-448-8082	626-5001	669
TF: 800-952-4507 ■ *Web:* www.breakers.com						
Breakers Resort Inn						
16th & Oceanfront	Virginia Beach	VA	23451	757-428-1821	422-9602	669
TF: 800-237-7532 ■ *Web:* www.breakersresort.com						
Breakeven Inc						
355 Apple Creek Blvd Ste 200	Markham	ON	L3R9X7	905-752-1500		305
TF: 877-752-1590 ■ *Web:* www.causeview.com						
Breaks Interstate Park						
627 Commission Cir	Breaks	VA	24607	276-865-4413		565
Web: www.breakspark.com						
Breakthrough Collaborative						
PO Box 71420 Ste 700	Oakland	CA	94612	415-442-0600	935-2357	48-11
Web: www.breakthroughcollaborative.org						
Breakthrough Technologies LLC						
1880 Oak Ave Ste 300	Evanston	IL	60201	847-864-0033		177
Web: breaktech.com						
Breakthrough Urban Ministries						
3330 W Carroll Ave	Chicago	IL	60624	773-722-1144		48-20
Web: www.breakthrough.org						
Breakthrough Version Publishing						
1725 Faulders Ln	Wichita	KS	67218	929-273-2568		637-2
Web: www.breakthroughversion.com						
Breakthru Beverage South Carolina						
101 Beverage Blvd	Ridgeway	SC	29130	803-337-3500		81-3
Web: www.breakthrubev.com						
Breakwater Inn 1711 Glacier Ave	Juneau	AK	99801	907-586-6303	541-7746*	379
**Fax Area Code:* 212 ■ *Web:* www.breakwaterinn.com						
Brearley School 610 E 83rd St	New York	NY	10028	212-744-8582		623
Web: www.brearley.org						
Breathe Technologies Inc						
175 Technology Dr Ste 100	Irvine	CA	92618	949-988-7700		475
Web: www.breathetechnologies.com						
Breathing Color Inc						
18552 MacArthur Blvd	Irvine	CA	92612	866-722-6567		552-1
TF: 866-722-6567 ■ *Web:* www.breathingcolor.com						
Breathitt County PO Box 227	Jackson	KY	41339	606-666-5060	666-7018	338
Web: www.breathittcounty.com						
Breault Industrial Group Inc						
5400 SW Meadows Rd Ste 350	Lake Oswego	OR	97035	503-924-4801	924-4803	448
TF: 800-460-7816 ■ *Web:* breaultindustrial.com						
Breault Research Organization Inc						
6400 E Grant Rd Ste 350	Tucson	AZ	85715	520-721-0500		261
Web: www.breault.com						
Breaux Machine Works LP						
13842 Hirschfield Rd	Tomball	TX	77377	281-351-4042	351-2640	454
Web: www.breauxmachine.com						
BREC (Butler Rural Electric Co-opeartive Inc)						
3888 Still-Beckett Rd	Oxford	OH	45056	513-867-4400		245
TF: 800-255-2732 ■ *Web:* www.butlerrural.coop						
BREC'S Baton Rouge Zoo						
3601 Thomas Rd	Baton Rouge	LA	70807	225-775-3877	775-3931	823
Web: www.brzoo.org						
Brechan Construction LLC						
2705 Mill Bay Rd	Kodiak	AK	99615	907-486-3215	486-4889	188-4
Web: www.brechan.com						
Brecher and Choate Business Advisors LLC						
4529 Quail Lakes Dr Ste C	Stockton	CA	95207	209-235-1040	235-1044	2
Web: www.bcbatax.com						
Breck's PO Box 65	Guilford	IN	47022	513-354-1511	354-1505	323
TF: 800-644-5505 ■ *Web:* www.brecks.com						
Breckenridge Grand Vacations (BGV)						
1627 Ski Hill Rd	Breckenridge	CO	80424	970-547-8788		378
TF: 888-783-8883 ■ *Web:* www.breckenridgegrandvacations.com						
Breckenridge Village						
36851 Ridge Rd	Willoughby	OH	44094	440-942-4342		672
Web: www.ohioliving.org						
Breckinridge Capital Advisors Inc						
125 High St Oliver St Tower 4th Fl	Boston	MA	02110	617-443-0779		401
Web: www.breckinridge.com						

				Phone	Fax	Class
Breckinridge County School District						
86 Airport Rd	Hardinsburg	KY	40143	270-756-3000		685
Web: www.breck.kyschools.us						
Breckinridge Inn						
2800 Breckinridge Ln	Louisville	KY	40220	502-456-5050	451-1577	379
Web: www.breckinridgeinn.com						
Brecksville Broadview Hts Csd						
6638 Mill Rd.	Brecksville	OH	44141	440-740-4000		685
Web: www.bbhcsd.org						
Bredet Services Inc						
1660 N Service Rd E Ste 105	Oakville	ON	L6H7G3	905-337-7233		180
Web: www.bredetservices.com						
Bredy Consulting Services 50 Union St.	Andover	MA	01810	978-482-2020	932-8997*	179
**Fax Area Code:* 781 ■ *Web:* www.bnmc.net						
Breeden & Associates Ltd						
4924 N Renwood	Peoria	IL	61614	309-691-3654	691-6315	2
Web: breedencpa.com						
Breeden Homes Inc 366 E 40th Ave	Eugene	OR	97405	541-686-9431	686-0918	187
Web: breedenhomes.com						
Breeden Insurance Services Inc						
312 W Center St	Lexington	NC	27292	336-249-8616		390
Web: breedeninsurance.com						
B-Reel 77 Sands St 12th Fl	Brooklyn	NY	11201	212-966-6186		514
Web: www.b-reel.com						
Breen Energy Solutions LLC						
104 Broadway St.	Carnegie	PA	15106	412-431-4499		250
Web: breenes.com						
Breen Engineering Inc						
1983 W 190th St.	Torrance	CA	90504	310-464-8404		261
Web: www.breeneng.com						
Breese Publishing Co						
8060 Old US Hwy 50	Breese	IL	62230	618-526-7211	526-2590	637-8
Web: breesepub.com						
Breeze Newspaper						
2510 Del Prado Blvd.	Cape Coral	FL	33904	239-574-1110		637-8
Web: www.breezenewspapers.com						
Breeze Publications Inc						
6 Blackstone Valley Pl Ste 204	Lincoln	RI	02865	401-334-9555		532-3
Web: valleybreeze.com						
Breeze-Eastern Corp 35 Melanie Ln	Whippany	NJ	07981	973-602-1001		470
TF: 800-929-1919 ■ *Web:* www.breeze-eastern.com						
BreezeGo Inc						
6622 Southside Blvd Ste 180	Jacksonville	FL	32216	904-374-3760		174
Breezy Hill Nursery Inc 7530 288th Ave	Salem	WI	53168	262-537-2111	537-3434	776
Web: www.breezyhillnursery.com						
Breezy Point Resort						
9252 Breezy Pt Dr.	Breezy Point	MN	56472	800-432-3777	562-4510*	669
**Fax Area Code:* 218 ■ *TF:* 800-432-3777 ■ *Web:* breezypointresort.com						
Breg Inc 2885 Loker Ave E	Carlsbad	CA	92010	800-897-2734	329-2734	48-2
TF: 800-897-2734 ■ *Web:* www.breg.com						
Brehm Communications Inc						
16644 W Bernardo Dr Ste 300	San Diego	CA	92127	858-451-6200	451-3814	637-8
Web: www.brehmcommunications.com						
Brehm Inc 1030 High St.	Auburn	CA	95604	530-885-2471	885-4902	532-2
Web: www.goldcountrymedia.com						
Brehm Preparatory School						
950 S Brehm Ln	Carbondale	IL	62901	618-457-0371	529-1248	622
Web: www.brehm.org						
Breiholz Construction Co						
1527 Maine St	Des Moines	IA	50314	515-280-9920	288-6335	186
Web: www.breiholz.com						
Breitburn Operating LP						
707 Wilshire Blvd 46th Fl.	Los Angeles	CA	90017	213-225-5900		538
NASDAQ: BBEP ■ *Web:* www.mavresources.com						
Brek Manufacturing Co 1513 W 132nd St	Gardena	CA	90249	310-329-7638	329-5601	529
Web: www.brek.aero						
Bremer County 415 E Bremer Ave	Waverly	IA	50677	319-352-0130		338
Web: www.co.bremer.ia.us						
Bremer Financial Corp						
380 Saint Peter St Ste 500	Saint Paul	MN	55102	651-288-3751		69
TF: 800-908-2265 ■ *Web:* www.bremer.com						
Bremer Whyte Brown & O'Meara LLP						
20320 SW Birch St 2nd Fl	Newport Beach	CA	92660	949-221-1000	221-1001	428
Web: bremerwhyte.com						
Bremerton Area Chamber of Commerce						
286 Fourth St	Bremerton	WA	98337	360-479-3579	479-1033	139
Web: www.bremertonchamber.org						
Bremerton Washington						
345 6th St Ste 100	Bremerton	WA	98337	360-473-5290		706
Web: www.bremertonwa.gov						
Bremner Biscuit Co 4600 Joliet St.	Denver	CO	80239	855-972-0535		296-9
TF: 800-668-3273 ■ *Web:* www.bremnerbiscuitco.com						
Bren Events Ctr 100 Bren Events Ctr.	Irvine	CA	92697	949-824-5050		572
Web: www.ucirvinesports.com						
Brenau University						
500 Washington St	Gainesville	GA	30501	770-534-6299	538-4701	166
TF: 800-252-5119 ■ *Web:* www.brenau.edu						
Brendan T. Byrne State Forest						
PO Box 215	New Lisbon	NJ	08064	609-726-1191		565
Web: www.njparksandforests.org						
Brendan Vacations 801 E Katella Ave	Anaheim	CA	92805	800-687-1002	973-8994*	760
**Fax Area Code:* 866 ■ *TF:* 800-687-1002 ■ *Web:* www.brendanvacations.com						
Brenden Theatres 531 Davis St	Vacaville	CA	95688	866-857-5191		748
TF: 866-857-5191 ■ *Web:* www.brendentheatres.com						
Brendle Sprinkler Company Inc						
3635 Montgomery St	Montgomery	AL	36109	334-270-8571	277-7967	189-13
Web: www.brendlesprinkler.com						
Breneman & Company PC						
14382 Woodlake Dr	Chesterfield	MO	63017	314-469-7007		2
Web: brenemancpa.com						
Brenham Wholesale Grocery Co						
602 W First St.	Brenham	TX	77833	979-836-7925		297-8
TF: 800-392-4869 ■ *Web:* www.brenhamwholesale.com						
Brenham/Washington County Convention & Visitor Bureau						
314 S Austin St.	Brenham	TX	77833	979-836-8927	836-2540	206
Web: www.brenhamtexas.com						
Brennan & Clark LLC						
721 E Madison Ste 200	Villa Park	IL	60181	630-279-7600		160
TF: 800-858-7600 ■ *Web:* www.brennanclark.com						
Brennan Manna & Diamond LLC						
75 E Market St	Akron	OH	44308	330-253-5060		428
Web: www.bmdllc.com						
Brennan's of Houston 3300 Smith St.	Houston	TX	77006	713-522-9711		671
Web: www.brennanshouston.com						
Brenneman Printing Inc						
1909 Olde Homestead Ln	Lancaster	PA	17601	717-299-2847		627
TF: 800-222-2423 ■ *Web:* www.brennemaninc.com						
Brenner by Wabash National Corp						
450 Arlington Ave	Fond du Lac	WI	54935	800-558-9750		779
TF: 800-558-9750 ■ *Web:* www.wabashnational.com						
Brenner Group Inc, The						
2735 Sand Hill Rd Ste 205	Menlo Park	CA	94025	408-873-3400		401
Web: www.thebrennergroup.com						
Brenner Oil Co 12948 Quincy St	Holland	MI	49424	616-399-9742		538
TF: 800-642-3029 ■ *Web:* www.brenneroil.com						
Brenner Printing Inc						
1234 Triplett St	San Antonio	TX	78216	210-349-4024		627
TF: 877-349-4024 ■ *Web:* www.brennerprinting.com						
Brenner's Steakhouse 10911 Katy Fwy	Houston	TX	77079	713-465-2901		671
Web: www.brennerssteakhouse.com						
Brenner-Fiedler & Associates Inc						
4059 Flat Rock Dr	Riverside	CA	92505	800-843-5558		358
TF: 800-843-5558 ■ *Web:* www.brenner-fiedler.com						
Brenntag North America Inc						
5083 Pottsville Pk	Reading	PA	19605	610-926-6100	916-3782	146
TF: 877-363-5843 ■ *Web:* www.brenntag.com						
Brent Adams & Assoc 119 Lucknow Sq.	Dunn	NC	28334	910-892-8177		445
Web: www.brentadams.com						
Brent Coon & Assoc (BCA) 215 Orleans St	Beaumont	TX	77701	409-835-2666	833-4483	428
TF: 866-335-2666 ■ *Web:* www.bcoonlaw.com						
Brent House Hotel						
1512 Jefferson Hwy	New Orleans	LA	70121	504-842-4140	842-4160	379
TF: 800-535-3986 ■ *Web:* www.brenthouse.com						
Brent Meyer, CPA & Assoc						
16133 Ventura Blvd Ste 625	Encino	CA	91436	818-501-8427		2
Web: brentmeyercpa.com						
Brent's Place 11980 E 16th Ave	Aurora	CO	80010	720-343-2800	831-4567*	372
**Fax Area Code:* 303 ■ *Web:* www.brentsplace.org						
Brentech Inc						
9340 Carmel Mtn Rd Ste C	San Diego	CA	92129	858-484-7314		175
TF: 800-709-0440 ■ *Web:* www.brentech-inc.com						
Brenton Arboretum						
25141 260th St	Dallas Center	IA	50063	515-992-4211	992-3303	97
Web: www.thebrentonarboretum.org						
Brenton LLC 4750 County Rd 13 NE	Alexandria	MN	56308	320-852-7705	852-7621	547
TF: 800-535-2730 ■ *Web:* www.brentonengineering.com						
Brenton Productions Inc						
179 Gasoline Alley Ste 102A	Mooresville	NC	28117	800-572-7798		60
TF: 800-572-7798 ■ *Web:* brentontv.com						
Bren-Tronics Inc 10 Brayton Ct.	Commack	NY	11725	631-499-5155	499-5504	74
Web: www.bren-tronics.com						
Brentwood Assoc						
11150 Santa Monica Blvd Ste 1200	Los Angeles	CA	90025	310-477-6611	477-1011	403
Web: www.brentwood.com						
Brentwood Capital Advisors LLC						
5000 Meridian Blvd Ste 350	Franklin	TN	37067	615-224-3830	224-3831	401
Web: www.brentwoodcap.com						
Brentwood Christian School						
11908 N Lamar Blvd	Austin	TX	78753	512-835-2184		685
Web: www.brentwoodchristian.org						
Brentwood College School						
2735 Mt Baker Rd	Mill Bay	BC	V0R2P1	250-743-5521	743-2911	622
Web: www.brentwood.bc.ca						
Brentwood Corp						
453 Industrial Way PO Box 265	Molalla	OR	97038	503-829-7366	829-7367	115
TF: 800-331-6013 ■ *Web:* www.brentwoodcorp.com						
Brentwood Development (California) Inc						
5800 Stanford Ranch Rd Ste 210	Rocklin	CA	95765	916-435-4180		653
Web: brentwooddev.com						
Brentwood Group Ltd, The						
1980 Willamette Falls Dr Ste 260	West Linn	OR	97068	503-697-8136	697-8161	721
Web: www.brentwoodgroup.com						
Brentwood High School Pto						
5304 Murray Ln	Brentwood	TN	37027	615-472-4220		685
Web: brentwoodpto.membershiptoolkit.com						
Brentwood Hospital						
1006 Highland Ave	Shreveport	LA	71101	318-678-7500	558-8022*	374-5
**Fax Area Code:* 800 ■ *TF:* 877-678-7500 ■ *Web:* brentwoodbehavioral.com						
Brentwood Industries Inc						
Polychem Systems Div						
500 Spring Ridge Dr	Reading	PA	19610	610-374-5109		806
Web: www.brentwoodindustries.com						
Brentwood Originals Inc						
20639 S Fordyce Ave	Carson	CA	90810	310-637-6804	639-9710	746
Web: www.brentwoodoriginals.com						
Brentwood Plastics Inc						
8734 Suburban Tracks	Saint Louis	MO	63144	314-968-1135	968-4276	596
Web: www.brentwoodplastics.com						
Brentwood Public Library (BPL)						
34 Second Ave	Brentwood	NY	11717	631-273-7883		434-3
Web: brentwoodnylibrary.org						
Brentwood School						
100 S Barrington Pl	Los Angeles	CA	90049	310-476-9633		685
Web: www.bwscampus.com						
Brentwood Veterinary Group Inc						
4519 O'Hara Ave	Brentwood	CA	94513	925-634-1177		794
Web: brentwoodvet.net						
Brescia University 717 Frederica St.	Owensboro	KY	42301	270-685-3131	686-4314	166
TF: 877-273-7242 ■ *Web:* www.brescia.edu						
Brescia University College						
1285 Western Rd	London	ON	N6G1H2	519-432-8353	858-5137	785
Web: www.brescia.uwo.ca						
Breslov Research Institute (BRI)						
44 St Nicholas Ave	Lakewood	NJ	08701	732-534-7263	608-8461	637-2
TF: 800-332-7375 ■ *Web:* www.breslov.org						
Bresser's Cross Index Directory Co						
684 W Baltimore St	Detroit	MI	48202	313-874-0570	874-3510	637-6
TF: 800-995-0570 ■ *Web:* www.bressers.com						

Phone | Fax | Class

Bresslergroup 1216 Arch St 7th Fl ... Philadelphia PA 19107 215-561-5100 261
Web: www.bresslergroup.com

Bresson Flying Service Incorporated Rochelle
2760 US Hwy 30 ... Compton IL 61318 815-628-7431 167-3
Web: www.bressonflying.com

Bretford Manufacturing Inc
11000 Seymour Ave ... Franklin Park IL 60131 847-678-2545 343-1779* 319-3
**Fax Area Code:* 800 ■ *TF:* 800-521-9614 ■ *Web:* www.bretford.com

Brethren Press 1451 Dundee Ave ... Elgin IL 60120 800-441-3712 667-8188 637-3
TF: 800-441-3712 ■ *Web:* www.brethrenpress.com

Breton Industries Inc
1 Sam Stratton Rd ... Amsterdam NY 12010 518-842-3030 842-1031 733
Web: bretonindustries.com

Bretthauer Oil Co 453 SW Washington ... Hillsboro OR 97123 503-648-2531 579
TF: 800-359-3113 ■ *Web:* www.bretthauer.com

Brevard College 1 Brevard College Dr ... Brevard NC 28712 828-883-8292 884-3790 166
TF: 800-527-9090 ■ *Web:* brevard.edu

Brevard Correctional Institution
855 Camp Rd ... Cocoa FL 32927 321-634-6000 213
Web: dc.state.fl.us

Brevard County
2725 Judge Fran Jamieson Way ... Viera FL 32940 321-633-2016 338
Web: www.brevardfl.gov

Brevard Eye Center Inc
665 Apollo Blvd ... Melbourne FL 32901 321-984-3200 984-0032 237
Web: www.brevardeye.com

Brevard Zoo 8225 N Wickham Rd ... Melbourne FL 32940 321-254-9453 259-5966 823
Web: brevardzoo.org

Brevard-Transylvania Chamber of Commerce
175 E Main St ... Brevard NC 28712 828-883-3700 139
Web: www.brevardncchamber.org

Brevium Inc 947 S 500 E Ste 250 ... American Fork UT 84003 801-854-5400 854-5404 261
Web: www.brevium.com

Brew Media Relations
603 Greenwich St ... New York NY 10014 212-677-4835 636
Web: www.brewpr.com

Brewco Inc 607 Front St ... Central City KY 42330 270-754-5847 754-9249 821
TF: 800-237-6880 ■ *Web:* www.brewcoinc.com

Brewer Co 25 Whitney Dr Ste 104 ... Milford OH 45150 513-576-6300 46
TF: 800-394-0017 ■ *Web:* www.thebrewerco.com

Brewer Lang Veach PC
920 S Main St Ste 100 ... Grapevine TX 76051 972-870-9898 41
Web: blvlawfirm.com

Brewer Machine & Manufacturing Inc
1501 Miller Ave ... Shelbyville IN 46176 317-398-3505 454
Web: www.brewermachine.com

Brewer Oil Co 2701 Candelaria NE ... Albuquerque NM 87107 505-884-2040 884-1987 579
Web: www.breweroil.com

Brewer Science Inc 2401 Brewer Dr ... Rolla MO 65401 573-364-0300 368-3318 550
Web: www.brewerscience.com

Brewer, Krause, Brooks & Chastain PLLC
545 Mainstream Dr Ste 101 ... Nashville TN 37228 615-256-8787 256-8985 41
Web: bkblaw.com

Brewer, Pritchard & Buckley PC
770 S Post Oak Ln Ste 620A ... Houston TX 77056 713-209-2950 428
Web: www.bplaw.com

Brewer-Cantelmo Company Inc
109 W 27th St ... New York NY 10001 212-244-4600 453
Web: www.brewer-cantelmo.com

Brewer-Garrett Company (Inc)
6800 Eastland Rd ... Cleveland OH 44130 440-243-3535 243-9993 189-10
Web: www.brewer-garrett.com

Brewer-Hendley Oil Co
207 N Forest Hills School Rd ... Marshville NC 28103 704-233-2600 579
Web: www.brewerhendley.com

Brewers Art 1106 N Charles St ... Baltimore MD 21201 410-547-6925 671
Web: www.thebrewersart.com

Brewers Publications 1327 Spruce St ... Boulder CO 80302 303-447-0816 338-4550* 637-2
**Fax Area Code:* 800 ■ *TF:* 888-822-6273 ■ *Web:* www.brewerspublications.com

Brewery Arts Ctr 449 W King St ... Carson City NV 89703 775-883-1976 572
Web: www.breweryarts.org

Brewery Products Co 1017 N Sherman St ... York PA 17402 717-757-3515 81-1
Web: www.breweryproducts.com

Brewhouse Brew Pub & Grill
939 Getchell St ... Helena MT 59601 406-457-9390 457-9296 671
Web: www.atthebrewhouse.com

Brewpub Design Services Inc
1130 Dublin Rd ... Columbus OH 43215 614-485-0227 485-0166 671
Web: www.smokehousebrewing.com

Brewster Academy 80 Academy Dr ... Wolfeboro NH 03894 603-569-7200 569-7272 622
TF: 800-842-9961 ■ *Web:* www.brewsteracademy.org

Brewster Adventures PO Box 370 ... Banff AB T1L1A5 403-762-5454 673-2100 760
TF: 800-691-5085 ■ *Web:* www.brewsteradventures.com

Brewster County 201 W Ave E ... Alpine TX 79830 432-837-6200 837-6217 338
Web: www.brewstercountytx.com

Brewster Place 1205 SW 29th St ... Topeka KS 66611 785-274-3350 672
Web: brewsterliving.org

Brewster Technical College
2222 N Tampa St ... Tampa FL 33602 813-276-5464 276-5769 167-3
Web: www.brewstertech.org

Brewster Technology
16 Mt Ebo Rd S Ste 18 ... Brewster NY 10509 845-279-9400 225
Web: www.brewstertech.com

Brewster Village 3300 W Brewster St ... Appleton WI 54914 920-832-5400 832-4922 450
Web: www.outagamie.org

Brewster WaLLPaper Corp
67 Pacella Park Dr ... Randolph MA 02368 781-963-4800 986-0650 550
Web: www.brewsterwallcovering.com

Brewton Iron Works Inc 132 Mildred St ... Brewton AL 36426 251-867-3603 867-9524 454
Web: www.biwinc.net

Brewton-Parker College
201 David-Eliza Fountain Cir Hwy 280
PO Box 197 ... Mount Vernon GA 30445 912-583-2241 583-3598 166
TF: 800-342-1087 ■ *Web:* www.bpc.edu

Brex 405 Howard St Ste 200 ... San Francisco CA 94105 844-725-9569 178-1
TF: 844-725-9569 ■ *Web:* brex.com

BRG (Business Resource Group)
10440 N Central Expy Ste 1150 ... Dallas TX 75231 214-777-5100 194
TF: 888-391-9166 ■ *Web:* www.brg.com

BRGMC (Baton Rouge General Medical Ctr)
3600 Florida Blvd ... Baton Rouge LA 70806 225-387-7000 374-3
Web: www.brgeneral.org

BRHS (CHI St Luke's Health - Brazosport Hospital)
100 Medical Dr ... Lake Jackson TX 77566 979-297-4411 374-3
Web: www.stlukeshealth.org

BRI (Biblical Research Institute)
12501 Old Columbia Pke ... Silver Spring MD 20904 301-680-6790 680-6788 637-2
Web: www.adventistbiblicalresearch.org

BRI (Breslov Research Institute)
44 St Nicholas Ave ... Lakewood NJ 08701 732-534-7263 608-8461 637-2
TF: 800-332-7375 ■ *Web:* www.breslov.org

BRI Works 300 E Main St ... Charlottesville VA 22902 434-817-0707 387
Web: bri.works

Briad Group, The 78 Okner Pkwy ... Livingston NJ 07039 973-597-6433 597-6422 670
Web: www.briad.com

Brian A. Sutton PC
53 Old Kings Hwy N Ste 203 ... Darien CT 06820 203-655-3990 2
Web: suttoncpa.com

Brian Berg Insurance Services
23101 Lake Center Dr Ste 335 ... Lake Forest CA 92630 888-791-7069 243-0891* 390
**Fax Area Code:* 949 ■ *TF:* 888-791-7069 ■ *Web:* bbisinc.com

Brian Frederick Funk PA
24 Polly Drummond Hill Rd ... Newark DE 19711 302-368-6233 41
Web: funkattorneys.com

Brian Gavin Diamonds
7322 SW Frwy Ste 1810 - Arena One ... Houston TX 77074 866-611-4465 410
TF: 866-611-4465 ■ *Web:* www.briangavindiamonds.com

Brian Lee Law Firm PLLC
18 Division St Ste 102 ... Saratoga Springs NY 12866 518-587-1380 41
Web: brianleelaw.com

Brian Patrick Conry PC
534 SW Third Ave Ste 711 ... Portland OR 97204 503-274-4430 428
Web: www.brianpatrickconry.com

Brian Taylor International LLC (BTI)
100 Cheshire Dr ... Griffin GA 30223 770-294-4653 506-9835* 393
**Fax Area Code:* 404 ■ *Web:* www.btillc.com

Brian's Toys W730 State Rd 35 ... Fountain City WI 54629 608-687-7572 687-7573 292
Web: www.brianstoys.com

Briar Cliff University
3303 Rebecca St ... Sioux City IA 51104 712-279-5321 279-1632 166
TF: 800-662-3303 ■ *Web:* www.briarcliff.edu

Briar Hill Stone Co, The
12470 SR-520 PO Box 457 ... Glenmont OH 44628 330-377-5100 377-5110 724
Web: www.briarhillstone.com

Briar Ridge Country Club
123 Country Club Dr ... Schererville IN 46375 219-322-3660 706
Web: www.briarridgecc.com

Briarcliffe College 1055 Stewart Ave ... Bethpage NY 11714 516-918-3600 165
Web: www.briarcliffe.edu

Briarhurst Manor
404 Manitou Ave ... Manitou Springs CO 80829 719-685-1864 685-9638 671
TF: 877-685-1448 ■ *Web:* www.briarhurst.com

Briarlane Rental Property Management Inc
85 Spy Ct Ste 100 ... Markham ON L3R4Z4 905-944-9406 944-9083 652
Web: www.briarlane.ca

BriarTek Inc 3129 Mt Vernon Ave ... Alexandria VA 22305 703-548-7892 180
Web: www.briartek.com

Briarwood College
2279 Mt Vernon Rd ... Southington CT 06489 860-628-4751 628-6444 166
TF: 800-952-2444 ■ *Web:* www.lincolncollegene.edu

Briarwood Veterinary Hospital PC
8213 S Saginaw St ... Grand Blanc MI 48439 810-695-6055 794
Web: briarwoodveterinaryhosp.com

Bricco 241 Hanover St ... Boston MA 02113 617-248-6800 671
Web: bricco.com

Bricco 1 W Exchange St ... Akron OH 44308 330-475-1600 671
Web: www.briccoakron.com

Brick Alley Pub & Restaurant
140 Thames St ... Newport RI 02840 401-849-6334 848-5640 671
Web: www.brickalley.com

Brick Bodies Fitness Services Inc
212 W Padonia Rd ... Timonium MD 21093 410-252-8058 560-3299 354
TF: 866-952-7425 ■ *Web:* www.brickbodies.com

Brick Gentry Law Firm
6701 Westown Pkwy Ste 100 ... West Des Moines IA 50266 515-274-1450 428
Web: www.brickgentrylaw.com

Brick Industry Assn (BIA)
12007 Sunrise Valley Dr Ste 430 ... Reston VA 20191 703-620-0010 620-3928 49-18
TF: 866-644-1293 ■ *Web:* www.gobrick.com

Brick Oven 111 East 800 North ... Provo UT 84606 801-374-8800 671
Web: www.brickovenrestaurants.com

Brick Store Museum 117 Main St ... Kennebunkport ME 04043 207-985-4802 520
Web: www.brickstoremuseum.org

Brick Township Chamber of Commerce
270 Chambers Bridge Rd ... Brick NJ 08723 732-477-4949 477-5788 139
Web: brickchamber.com

Brickell Financial Services Motor Club Inc
7300 Corporate Center Dr ... Miami FL 33126 305-392-4300 392-4301 53
TF: 800-262-7262 ■ *Web:* www.road-america.com

Bricker & Eckler LLP 100 S Third St ... Columbus OH 43215 614-227-2300 428
Web: www.bricker.com

Brickforce Staffing Inc
2 Ethel Rd Ste 204-B ... Edison NJ 08817 732-819-7770 650-0714 260
Web: brickforce.com

BrickKicker, The
849 N Ellsworth St ... Naperville IL 60563 800-821-1820 420-2270* 365
**Fax Area Code:* 630 ■ *TF:* 800-821-1820 ■ *Web:* www.brickkicker.com

Brickner Motors Inc
16450 County Rd A ... Marathon WI 54448 715-842-5611 57
Web: www.bricknermotors.net

Bricks 1695 S Virginia St ... Reno NV 89502 775-786-2277 671
Web: bricksrestaurant.com

Bricktown 2 S Mickey Mantle Dr ... Oklahoma City OK 73104 405-236-8666 50-6
Web: welcometobricktown.com

Bricktown Brewery
1 N Oklahoma Ave ... Oklahoma City OK 73104 405-232-2739 671
Web: bricktownbrewery.com

Name / Address	City	State	ZIP	Phone	Fax	Class
Brickyard Crossing Golf Resort & Inn 4400 W 16th St *Web:* www.brickyardcrossing.com	Indianapolis	IN	46222	317-492-6417		669
Brickyard VFX 2054 Broadway *Web:* www.brickyardvfx.com	Santa Monica	CA	90404	310-453-5722		530
Bridal Guide Magazine 228 E 45th St 11th Fl *TF:* 800-472-7744 ■ *Web:* www.bridalguide.com	New York	NY	10017	212-838-7733	308-7165	457-11
Bridal Veil Falls State Scenic Viewpoint I-84 *Web:* stateparks.oregon.gov	Bridal Veil	OR	97010	503-695-2261		565
Brides n Blooms 15708 Pinto Pl *TF:* 800-963-5977 ■ *Web:* www.bridesnblooms.com	Tampa	FL	33602	813-852-2052		293
Bridgcom 11388 W Olympic Blvd *TF:* 855-455-5522 ■ *Web:* bridg.com	Los Angeles	CA	90064	323-510-3860		5
Bridge Bank 55 Almaden Blvd Ste 200 *NASDAQ: BDGE* ■ *TF:* 866-273-4265 ■ *Web:* www.westernalliancebancorporation.com	San Jose	CA	95113	408-423-8500	423-8520	360-2
Bridge Capital LLC Micro Beach Rd *Web:* www.bccnmi.com	Saipan	MP	96950	670-322-2222		186
Bridge Community Bank 200 S Cherry *Web:* www.bridge.bank	Mechanicsville	IA	52306	563-432-7291	432-7294	360-2
Bridge Kitchenware Inc B 198 Mt Pleasant Ave *Web:* www.bridgekitchenware.com	East Hanover	NJ	07936	973-884-9000		362
Bridge Law Group Ltd 2900 Washington Ave N **Fax Area Code:* 612 ■ *Web:* bridgeattorneys.com	Minneapolis	MN	55411	763-201-1200	345-4220*	41
Bridge Personnel Services 2800 W Higgins Rd Ste 680 *Web:* bridgepersonnel.com	Hoffman Estates	IL	60195	847-885-9696		260
Bridge Restaurant 31 Locust St *Web:* www.bridgerest.com	Dubuque	IA	52001	563-557-7280		671
Bridge world Language Center Inc, The 110 2nd St S Ste 213 *TF:* 800-835-6870 ■ *Web:* www.bridgelanguage.com	Waite Park	MN	56387	320-259-9239	654-1698	768
Bridgeborn 448 Viking Dr Ste 390 *Web:* www.bridgeborn.com	Virginia Beach	VA	23452	757-437-5000		434-3
Bridgecom Solutions LLC 22895 Eastpark Dr *TF:* 888-685-7100 ■ *Web:* www.bridgecomsolutions.com	Yorba Linda	CA	92887	909-361-7100		627
Bridgeforce Inc 101 Ponds Edge Dr Ste 300 *Web:* www.bridgeforce.com	Chadds Ford	PA	19317	610-616-3106		196
Bridgehead IT 2810 N Flores St *Web:* www.bridgeheadit.com	San Antonio	TX	78212	210-477-7900		225
BridgeHead Software Ltd 400 W Cummings Pk Ste 6050 *Web:* www.bridgeheadsoftware.com	Woburn	MA	01801	781-939-0780	939-5607	178-1
Bridgeline Digital 80 Blanchard Rd *TF:* 800-603-9936 ■ *Web:* www.bridgeline.com	Burlington	MA	01803	781-376-5555	376-5033	180
Bridgeman Art Library Intl 274 Madison Ave Ste 1604 *Web:* www.bridgemanimages.com	New York	NY	10016	212-828-1238		393
Bridgepoint Investment Banking 816 P St Ste 200 *Web:* www.bridgepointib.com	Lincoln	NE	68508	402-817-7900		690
Bridgeport City Hall 999 Broad St *TF:* 800-978-2828 ■ *Web:* bridgeportct.gov	Bridgeport	CT	06604	203-576-7201	576-3913	337
Bridgeport Fittings Inc 705 Lordship Blvd *Web:* www.bptfittings.com	Stratford	CT	06615	203-377-5944	381-3488	816
Bridgeport Hospital 267 Grant St *TF:* 800-688-4954 ■ *Web:* www.bridgeporthospital.org	Bridgeport	CT	06610	203-384-3000	384-3046	374-3
Bridgeport National Bindery Inc 662 Silver St *Web:* www.bnbindery.com	Agawam	MA	01001	413-789-1981		92
Bridgeport News 3506 S Halsted St *Web:* www.bridgeportnews.net	Chicago	IL	60609	773-927-0025		532-4
Bridgeport News 1000 Bridgeport Ave *TF:* 855-247-8573 ■ *Web:* www.thebridgeportnews.com	Shelton	CT	06484	860-491-9988		532-4
Bridgeport Public Library 925 Broad St *Web:* www.bportlibrary.org	Bridgeport	CT	06604	203-576-7403	576-8255	434-3
Bridgeport Regional Business Council 10 Middle St 14th Fl *Web:* www.brbc.org	Bridgeport	CT	06604	203-335-3800		139
Bridger Scientific Inc 114 State Rd Bldg B7 *Web:* www.bridgersci.com	Sagamore Beach	MA	02562	508-888-6699	888-5919	201
Bridger Steel Inc 1558 Amsterdam Rd *Web:* www.bridgersteel.com	Belgrade	MT	59714	406-388-9555		697
Bridger Valley Extreme Access 40014 Business Loop 1-80 PO Box 399 *TF:* 800-276-3481 ■ *Web:* bvea.coop	Mountain View	WY	82939	307-786-2800	786-4362	245
Bridgerland Technical College 1301 N 600 W *TF:* 800-346-4128 ■ *Web:* btech.edu	Logan	UT	84321	435-753-6780	752-2016	167-3
Bridgers & Paxton Consulting Engineers Inc 4600-C Montgomery Blvd NE *Web:* www.bpce.com	Albuquerque	NM	87109	505-883-4111		256
Bridges 209 Pine Creek Rd *Web:* www.bridgespbt.com	Wexford	PA	15090	412-837-1381	837-1385	186
Bridges Consulting Inc 7880 Milestone Pkwy *Web:* www.bridges-inc.com	Hanover	MD	21076	301-974-6200		463
Bridges Investment Counsel Inc 256 Durham Plz 8401 W Dodge Rd Ste 256 *TF:* 866-934-4700 ■ *Web:* www.bridgesfund.com	Omaha	NE	68114	866-934-4700		528
Bridges Public Charter School 100 Gallatin St NE *Web:* bridgespcs.org	Washington	DC	20011	202-545-0515		685
Bridges Restaurant 1696 Duranleau St *Web:* www.bridgesrestaurant.com	Vancouver	BC	V6H3S4	604-687-4400		671
Bridges USA Inc 477 N Fifth St *Web:* bridgesusa.org	Memphis	TN	38105	901-452-5600		260

Name / Address	City	State	ZIP	Phone	Fax	Class
Bridgestone Aircraft Tire USA Inc 802 S Ayersville Rd *Web:* www.bridgestone.com	Mayodan	NC	27027	336-548-8100	548-7441	24
Bridgestone Americas Holding Inc 535 Marriott Dr *TF:* 877-201-2373 ■ *Web:* www.bridgestoneamericas.com	Nashville	TN	37214	615-937-1000	937-3621	754
Bridgestone Arena 501 Broadway *TF:* 800-356-4840 ■ *Web:* www.bridgestonearena.com	Nashville	TN	37203	615-770-2000		720
Bridgestone Canada Inc 5770 Hurontario St Ste 400 *Web:* www.bridgestoneamericas.com	Mississauga	ON	L5R3G5	905-890-1990		755
Bridgestone Golf Inc 15320 Industrial Pk Blvd NE *TF:* 800-358-6319 ■ *Web:* www.bridgestonegolf.com	Covington	GA	30014	770-787-7400		710
Bridgestone Multimedia Group Inc 300 N McKemy Ave *TF:* 866-774-3774 ■ *Web:* www.gobmg.com	Chandler	AZ	85226	866-774-3774		511
BridgeSTOR LLC 18060 Old Coach Dr *TF:* 800-280-8204 ■ *Web:* bridgestor.com	Poway	CA	92064	858-375-7076	613-9141	173-8
Bridgeton Area Chamber of Commerce 76 Magnolia Ave *Web:* www.cumberlandgrows.com	Bridgeton	NJ	08302	856-455-1312	453-9795	139
Bridgetown Printing Co 5300 N Channel Ave *Web:* www.bridgetown.com	Portland	OR	97217	503-863-5300		627
Bridgevine Inc 2770 Indian River Blvd Ste 400 *Web:* www.bridgevine.com	Vero Beach	FL	32960	470-719-4535		393
Bridgewater & Area Chamber of Commerce 373 King St *Web:* www.bridgewaterchamber.com	Bridgewater	NS	B4V1B1	902-543-4263	543-1156	137
Bridgewater Associates Inc 1 Glendinning Pl *Web:* www.bridgewater.com	Westport	CT	06880	203-226-3030		401
Bridgewater College 402 E College St *TF:* 800-759-8328 ■ *Web:* www.bridgewater.edu	Bridgewater	VA	22812	540-828-5375		166
Bridgewater Foods LLC 519 N Main St *Web:* bridgewaterfoods.com	Bridgewater	VA	22812	540-828-3010		345
Bridgewater Interiors LLC 4617 W Fort St *Web:* bridgewater-interiors.com	Detroit	MI	48209	313-842-3300		689
Bridgewater State College 131 Summer St *Web:* www.bridgew.edu	Bridgewater	MA	02325	508-531-2922	531-1746	166
Bridgewater State College Maxwell Library 10 Shaw Rd *Web:* www.library.bridgew.edu	Bridgewater	MA	02325	508-531-1392		434-6
Bridgewater State Hospital 20 Admin Rd *Web:* www.mass.gov	Bridgewater	MA	02324	508-279-4500		374-5
BridgeWave Communications Inc 3350 Thomas Rd *Web:* bridgewave.com	Santa Clara	CA	95054	408-567-6908		647
Bridgford Foods Corp 1308 N Patt St *NASDAQ: BRID* ■ *TF:* 800-854-3255 ■ *Web:* www.bridgford.com	Anaheim	CA	92801	714-526-5533	526-4360	296-26
Bridgton Academy PO Box 292 *Web:* bridgtonacademy.org	North Bridgton	ME	04057	207-647-3322		622
Bridgton News Corp PO Box 244 *Web:* www.bridgton.com	Bridgton	ME	04009	207-647-2851	647-5001	532-2
Bridon USA LLC PO Box 841 *TF:* 800-533-6002 ■ *Web:* www.bridon-usa.com	Dubuque	IA	52004	507-377-1601		208
Briefingcom Inc 401 N Michigan Ste 2910 *TF:* 800-752-3013 ■ *Web:* www.briefing.com	Chicago	IL	60611	312-670-4463		404
Briercrest College & Seminary 510 College Dr *Web:* www.briercrest.ca	Caronport	SK	S0H0S0	306-756-3200	756-5500	167-3
Brierley & Partners 5465 Legacy Dr Ste 300 *TF:* 800-899-8700 ■ *Web:* www.brierley.com	Plano	TX	75024	214-760-8700	743-5511	5
Brierley Associates LLC 990 S Broadway Ste 222 *Web:* www.brierleyassociates.com	Denver	CO	80209	303-703-1405		261
Briess Malting Co 625 S Irish Rd *TF:* 800-657-0806 ■ *Web:* www.briess.com	Chilton	WI	53014	920-849-7711	849-4277	461
Brigade LLC 195 Russell St Ste A1 *Web:* brigadebranding.com	Hadley	MA	01035	413-387-0307		180
Brigantine Media 211 N Ave *Web:* brigantinemedia.com	Saint Johnsbury	VT	05819	802-751-8802	751-8804	637-2
Brigantine Restaurants Inc 7889 Ostrow St *Web:* www.brigantine.com	San Diego	CA	92111	858-268-5727		670
Briggs & Stratton Corp 12301 W Wirth St *NYSE: BGG* ■ *TF:* 800-444-7774 ■ *Web:* www.briggsandstratton.com	Milwaukee	WI	53222	414-259-5333		262
Briggs & Veselka Co 9 Greenway Plz Ste 1700 *Web:* bvccpa.com	Houston	TX	77046	713-667-9147		2
Briggs Auto Group Inc 2312 Stagg Hill Rd *TF:* 800-257-4004 ■ *Web:* www.briggsauto.com	Manhattan	KS	66502	785-537-8330		54
Briggs Boat Works Inc 370 Harbor Rd *Web:* www.briggsboatworks.com	Wanchese	NC	27981	252-473-2393	473-2392	90
Briggs Capital LLC 858 Washington St Ste 303 *Web:* www.briggscapital.com	Dedham	MA	02026	781-493-6581		401
Briggs Equipment 10540 N Stemmons Fwy *TF:* 800-606-1833 ■ *Web:* www.briggsequipment.us	Dallas	TX	75220	214-630-0808	631-3560	385
Briggs Equipment 10550 N Stemmons Fwy *TF:* 800-516-9206 ■ *Web:* briggsindustrial.com	Dallas	TX	75220	214-351-4511		385
Briggs Lawrence County Public Library 321 S 4th St *Web:* www.briggslibrary.com	Ironton	OH	45638	740-532-1124		434-3
Briggs Plumbing 597 Old Mt Holly Rd *TF:* 800-888-4458 ■ *Web:* www.briggsplumbing.com	Goose Creek	SC	29445	800-888-4458	627-4449	611

	Phone	Fax	Class
Brigham & Women's Hospital 75 Francis St .... Boston MA 02115 *TF:* 800-294-9999 ■ *Web:* www.brighamandwomens.org	617-732-5500		374-7
Brigham Property Rights Law Firm PLLC 2963 Dupont Ave Ste 3 .... Jacksonville FL 32217 *Web:* propertyrights.com	904-730-9001		41
Brigham Young University			
Lee Library Wilkinson Student Center (WSC) Brigham Young University .... Provo UT 84602 *Web:* lib.byu.edu	801-422-2905	422-0466	434-6
Office of the General Counsel A-357 ASB PO Box 1333 .... Provo UT 84604 *Web:* ogc.byu.edu	801-422-3089	422-0265	166
Brigham Young University Hawaii 55-220 Kulanui St .... Laie HI 96762 *Web:* www.byuh.edu	808-675-3211	293-3741	166
Brigham Young University Idaho 525 S Ctr .... Rexburg ID 83460 **Fax Area Code:* 208 ■ *TF:* 866-672-2984 ■ *Web:* www.byui.edu	866-672-2984	496-1220*	166
Bright Chair Co 51 Railroad Ave .... Middletown NY 10940 *TF:* 888-524-5997 ■ *Web:* www.brightchair.com	845-343-2196		319-1
Bright Communications Inc 11120 N Stemmons Fwy .... Dallas TX 75229 *Web:* www.brightcommunications.com	972-406-0303	406-0345	681
Bright Community Trust Inc 2605 Enterprise Rd E Ste 230 .... Clearwater FL 33759 *Web:* thebrightway.org	727-475-1366		653
Bright Co-opeartive Inc 803 W Seale St .... Nacogdoches TX 75964 *TF:* 800-562-0730 ■ *Web:* www.brightcoop.com	936-564-8378	564-3281	763
Bright Hill Press (BHP) 94 Church St .... Treadwell NY 13846 *Web:* www.brighthillpress.org	607-829-5055		637-2
Bright Horizon Resources LLC 6120 S Yale Ave Ste 900 .... Tulsa OK 74136 *Web:* www.bhrep.com	918-879-3200	879-3232	536
Bright Horizons Family Solutions LLC 200 Talcott Ave S .... Watertown MA 02472 *TF:* 800-324-4386 ■ *Web:* www.brighthorizons.com	617-673-8000	673-8001	148
Bright Ideas in Broad Ripple Inc 7425 Westfield Blvd .... Indianapolis IN 46240 *Web:* www.bright-ideas.org	317-257-4111		328
Bright Image Corp 2830 S18th Ave .... Broadview IL 60155 **Fax Area Code:* 708 ■ *TF:* 888-449-5656 ■ *Web:* www.touchandglow.com	888-449-5656	449-1155*	203
Bright of America Inc 300 Greenbrier Rd .... Summersville WV 26651	304-872-3000		558
Bright Pest Control Co 4340 Sanita Ct .... Louisville KY 40213 *Web:* brightpest.com	502-452-9600		577
Bright Ring Publishing Inc PO Box 31338 .... Bellingham WA 98228 *TF:* 800-480-4278 ■ *Web:* www.brightring.com	800-480-4278		637-2
Bright Sky Press (BSP) 2365 Rice Blvd Ste 202 .... Houston TX 77005 *TF:* 866-933-6133 ■ *Web:* www.brightskypress.com	713-533-9300	528-2432	637-2
Bright Trading LLC 4850 Harrison Dr .... Las Vegas NV 89121 *Web:* www.stocktrading.com	702-739-1393	739-1398	113
Bright View Technologies Corp 4022 Stirrup Creek Dr Ste 301 .... Durham NC 27703 *Web:* www.brightviewtechnologies.com	919-228-4370	228-4371	253
Bright Wood Corp 335 NW Hess St .... Madras OR 97741 *Web:* www.brightwood.com	541-475-2234	475-7086	499
Brightergy LLC 1627 Main St Ste 201 .... Kansas City MO 64108 *Web:* brightergy.com	816-866-0555		192
BrightHouse LLC 675 Ponce de Leon Ave Ste 9700 .... Atlanta GA 30308 *Web:* thinkbrighthouse.com	404-240-2500		195
Brightleaf Square 905 W Main St Ste 24 .... Durham NC 27701 *Web:* historicbrightleaf.com	919-682-9229	688-1953	50-6
Brightlight Pictures Inc 2400 Boundary Rd The Bridge Studios .... Burnaby BC V5M3Z3 *Web:* www.brightlightpictures.com	604-628-3000		514
BrightMove Inc 320 High Tide Dr Ste 201 .... Saint Augustine FL 32080 *TF:* 877-482-8840 ■ *Web:* www.brightmove.com	877-482-8840		196
Brighton Animal Hospital 723 Linden Ave .... Rochester NY 14625 *Web:* brightonanimalhospital.com	585-586-1462		794
Brighton Bank 7101 S Highland Dr .... Salt Lake City UT 84121 *TF:* 877-763-5678 ■ *Web:* www.brightonbank.com	801-943-6500	943-4406	70
Brighton Chrysler Plymouth Dodge Inc 9827 E Grand River .... Brighton MI 48116 *Web:* www.brightonchrysler.com	810-229-4100		57
Brighton College 8777 E Via de Ventura .... Scottsdale AZ 85258 *TF:* 800-354-1254 ■ *Web:* www.brightoncollege.edu	602-212-0501	212-0502	167-3
Brighton Cromwell LLC 111 Canfield Ave Bldg C 1-10 .... Randolph NJ 07869 *Web:* brightoncromwell.com	973-252-4100		314
Brighton Ford Inc 8240 W Grand River .... Brighton MI 48114 *TF:* 888-644-9991 ■ *Web:* www.brightonford.com	810-227-1171		57
Brighton Institute of Cosmetology 10543 Citation Dr .... Brighton MI 48116 *Web:* www.brightoninstitute.net	810-229-5066		167-3
Brighton Jones LLC 2030 1st Ave 3rd Fl .... Seattle WA 98121 *Web:* www.brightonjones.com	206-258-5000		401
Brighton Memorial Library 2300 Elmwood Ave .... Rochester NY 14618 *Web:* www.brightonlibrary.org	585-784-5300	784-5333	434-3
Brighton Recreation Area 6360 Chilson Rd .... Howell MI 48843 *Web:* www.michigan.org	810-229-6566		565
Brighton Securities Corp 1703 Monroe Ave .... Rochester NY 14610 *TF:* 800-388-1703 ■ *Web:* www.brightonsecurities.com	585-473-3590		690
Brighton State Park 102 State Park Rd .... Island Pond VT 05846 *Web:* www.vtstateparks.com	802-723-4360		565
Brighton-Pittsford Agency Inc 30 Grove St .... Pittsford NY 14534 *Web:* brightonpittsfordagency.com	585-381-1463		390
Brightside for Families and Children - Holyoke 1233 Main St .... Holyoke MA 01040 *Web:* www.trinityhealthofne.org	413-536-5111		726
BrightSign LLC 983-A University Ave .... Los Gatos CA 95032 *Web:* www.brightsign.biz	408-852-9263		407
Brightsource Energy Inc 1999 Harrison St Ste 2150 .... Oakland CA 94612 *Web:* www.brightsourceenergy.com	510-550-8161	550-8165	245
Brightstar Care of Austin 7703 N Lamar Blvd Ste 418 .... Austin TX 78752 *Web:* brightstarcare.com	512-452-9800		363
Brightstar Corp 9725 NW 117th Ave Ste 300 .... Miami FL 33178 *TF:* 866-277-6325 ■ *Web:* www.brightstar.com	305-421-6000		246
Brightwell Payments Inc 6860 N Frontage Rd Ste 100 .... Burr Ridge IL 60527 *TF:* 855-858-1983 ■ *Web:* www.brightwellpayments.com	855-858-1983		225
Brightwood College 8205 Spain Rd NE .... Albuquerque NM 87109 *TF:* 888-450-4690 ■ *Web:* www.kapre.com	888-450-4690		653
Brigtsen's 723 Dante St .... New Orleans LA 70118 *Web:* www.brigtsens.com	504-861-7610		671
Brilex Industries Inc PO Box 749 .... Youngstown OH 44501 *Web:* www.brilex.com	330-744-1114	744-1125	480
Briljent LLC 7615 W Jefferson Blvd .... Fort Wayne IN 46804 *TF:* 877-434-0990 ■ *Web:* briljent.com	260-434-0990	434-0991	765
Brill Hygienic Products Inc 601 N Congress Ave Bldg 306 .... Delray Beach FL 33445 *TF:* 800-330-6696 ■ *Web:* www.brillseat.com	561-278-5600	272-3542	610
Brill Securities Inc 152 W 57th St 16th Fl .... New York NY 10019 *TF:* 800-933-0800 ■ *Web:* www.brillsec.com	212-957-5700		690
Brillacademic Publishers Inc 2 Liberty Sq 11th Fl .... Boston MA 02109 *TF:* 800-337-9255 ■ *Web:* brill.com	617-263-2323	263-2324	637-2
Brilliance Audio 1704 Eaton Dr Door No 4 .... Grand Haven MI 49417 *TF:* 800-648-2312 ■ *Web:* www.brillianceaudio.com	616-846-5256		658
Brilliance Web Design Inc 229 E Wisconsin Ave Ste 300 .... Milwaukee WI 53202 *Web:* brillianceweb.com	414-247-3101		177
Brilliant Digital Entertainment Inc 14011 Ventura Blvd Ste 501 .... Sherman Oaks CA 91423 *Web:* www.globalfileregistry.com	818-386-2179		178-8
Brillio 5201 Great America Pkwy Ste 100 .... Santa Clara CA 95054 *TF:* 800-317-0575 ■ *Web:* www.brillio.com	800-317-0575		463
Brim's Snack Foods 3045 Bartlett Corporate Dr Ste 101 .... Bartlett TN 38133 *Web:* brimsnacks.com	901-377-9016		297-8
Brimar Industries Inc 64 Outwater Ln .... Garfield NJ 07026 *TF:* 800-274-6271 ■ *Web:* www.brimar.com	800-274-6271		627
Bri-Mar Manufacturing LLC 1002 Wayne Ave .... Chambersburg PA 17201 *Web:* www.bri-mar.com	717-261-0922		779
Brimberry, Kaplan & Brimberry PC 408 N Jackson St .... Albany GA 31701 *TF:* 877-757-7730 ■ *Web:* bkblawyers.com	229-436-0537		41
Brimfield State Forest 86 Dearth Hill Rd .... Brimfield MA 01010 *Web:* www.mass.gov	413-267-9687		565
Brimley State Park 9200 W 6-Mile Rd .... Brimley MI 49715 *Web:* www.michigan.org	906-248-3422		565
Brimmer Burek & Keelan LLP 5601 Mariner St Ste 200 .... Tampa FL 33609 *Web:* www.bbkm.com	813-282-3400		2
Brindisi Anthony (Rep D - NY) 329 Cannon House Office Bldg .... Washington DC 20515 *Web:* www.brindisi.house.gov	202-225-3665		342-2
Brine Group Staffing Solutions Inc 800 District Ave Ste 120 .... Burlington MA 01803 *Web:* brinegroup.com	781-272-3400		260
Briney Foret Corry LLP 413 Travis St Ste 200 .... LaFayette LA 70503 *Web:* brineyforet.com	337-237-4070		41
Brinjac Engineering Inc 114 N Second St .... Harrisburg PA 17101 *TF:* 877-274-6526 ■ *Web:* www.brinjac.com	717-233-4502	233-0833	261
Brink Constructors Inc 2950 N Plaza Dr .... Rapid City SD 57702 *Web:* www.brinkred.com	605-342-6966	342-5905	189-4
Brink's Inc 1801 Bayberry Ct PO Box 18100 .... Richmond VA 23226 *NYSE:* BCO ■ *TF:* 877-527-4657 ■ *Web:* us.brinks.com	804-289-9600		185
Brink, Key & Chludzinski PC 1300 W Centre Ave Ste 200 .... Portage MI 49024 *Web:* bkccpa.com	269-321-9200		2
Brinker International Inc 6820 LBJ Fwy .... Dallas TX 75240 *NYSE:* EAT ■ *TF:* 800-983-4637 ■ *Web:* www.brinker.com	972-980-9917	770-9593	670
Brinkman International Group Inc 167 Ames St .... Rochester NY 14611 *Web:* brinkmanig.com	585-235-4545	235-6568	295
Brinkman Tool & Die Inc 325 Kiser St .... Dayton OH 45404 *Web:* www.brinkmantool.com	937-222-1161	222-2079	757
Brinkmann Instruments Inc 1819 Underwood Blvd .... Delran NJ 08075 *Web:* www.lauda-brinkmann.com	856-764-7300		419
Brinks Hofer Gilson & Lione Library 455 N Cityfront Plaza Dr NBC Twr Ste 3600 .... Chicago IL 60611 *Web:* www.brinksgilson.com	312-321-4200	321-4299	434-3
Brinly-Hardy Co 3230 Industrial Pkwy .... Jeffersonville IN 47130 *TF:* 877-728-8224 ■ *Web:* www.brinly.com	812-218-7200	218-6085	429

	Phone	Fax	Class
Brin-Northwestern Glass Co 2300 N 2nd St .... Minneapolis MN 55411 *Web:* www.bringlass.com	612-529-9671		191-2
Brinton's Paint Co 200 Park St .... Jacksonville FL 32204 *Web:* www.brintonspaint.com	904-354-7707	358-6934	802
Brintons USA 1000 Cobb Pl Blvd Bldg 200 Ste 200 .... Kennesaw GA 30144 *Web:* www.brintons.net	678-594-9300		131
Brio Tuscan Grille 3993 Easton Stn St .... Columbus OH 43219 *Web:* www.brioitalian.com	614-416-4745		671
Briohn Building Corp 3885 N Brookfield Rd Ste 200 .... Brookfield WI 53045 *Web:* www.briohn.com	262-790-0500		186
Briones Consulting & Engineering Ltd 8118 Broadway .... San Antonio TX 78209 *Web:* brionesengineering.com	210-828-1431	828-1432	261
Brioni Roman Style USA Corp 595 Madison Ave 6th Fl .... New York NY 10022 *Web:* www.brioni.com	212-332-6900	332-6902	157-6
Brisar Industries Inc 150 E 7th St .... Paterson NJ 07524 *Web:* www.brisar.com	973-278-2500		88
Brisbee & Stockton LLC 139 NE Lincoln St .... Hillsboro OR 97123 *Web:* brisbeeandstockton.com	503-648-6677	648-1091	41
Briscoe Burke & Grigsby LLP 4120 E 51st St Ste 100 .... Tulsa OK 74135 *Web:* bbgcpa.com	918-749-8337	748-8585	2
Briscoe County PO Box 555 .... Silverton TX 79257 *Web:* www.co.briscoe.tx.us	806-823-2134	823-2359	338
BriskHeat Corp 1055 Gibbard Ave .... Columbus OH 43201 *TF:* 800-848-7673 ■ *Web:* www.briskheat.com	614-294-3376	294-3807	318
Brismet 390 Bristol Metals Rd .... Bristol TN 37620 *Web:* brismet.com	423-989-4700		490
Bristol Aluminum 5514 Bristol Emilie Rd .... Levittown PA 19057 *TF:* 800-338-5532 ■ *Web:* bristolaluminum.com	215-946-3160		362
Bristol Bar & Grille Inc 1321 Bardstown Rd .... Louisville KY 40204 *Web:* www.bristolbarandgrille.com	502-456-1702		670
Bristol Bay Borough PO Box 189 .... Naknek AK 99633 *Web:* www.bristolbayboroughak.us	907-246-4224	246-6633	338
Bristol Bay Native Corp 111 W 16th Ave Ste 400 .... Anchorage AK 99501 *Fax Area Code: 907 ■ *TF:* 800-426-3602 ■ *Web:* www.bbnc.net	800-426-3602	276-3924*	360-3
Bristol Broadcasting Company Inc 901 E Valley Dr .... Bristol VA 24201 *Web:* www.bristolbroadcasting.com	276-669-8112	669-0541	643
Bristol Chamber of Commerce 20 Volunteer Pkwy .... Bristol TN 37620 *Web:* www.bristolchamber.com	423-989-4850	989-4867	139
Bristol Community College 11 Field St .... Attleboro MA 02703 *Web:* www.bristolcc.edu	508-226-2484		162
Bristol Construction Services LLC 111 W 16th Ave 3rd Fl .... Anchorage AK 99501 *Web:* www.bristol-companies.com	907-743-9310		186
Bristol County 9 Court St .... Taunton MA 02780 *Web:* countyofbristol.net	508-824-9681	821-3101	338
Bristol County 10 Ct St .... Bristol RI 02809 *Web:* www.bristolri.us	401-253-7000	253-3080	338
Bristol County Veterinary Hospital 288 Fall River Ave .... Seekonk MA 02771 *Web:* bristolcountyvet.com	508-336-3381	336-4528	794
Bristol Environmental Inc 1123 Beaver St .... Bristol PA 19007 *Web:* www.beigroup.com	215-788-6040		667
Bristol Farms 915 E 230th St .... Carson CA 90745 *Web:* www.bristolfarms.com	310-233-4700		345
Bristol Financial Services PC 36 Main St PO Box 387 .... Bristol VT 05443 *Web:* bristolfinancial.com	802-453-2378		690
Bristol Harbor Group Inc 99 Poppasquash Rd Unit H .... Bristol RI 02809 *Web:* bristolharborgroup.com	401-253-4318		261
Bristol Herald-Courier 320 Bob Morrison Blvd .... Bristol VA 24201 *TF:* 888-228-2098 ■ *Web:* www.heraldcourier.com	276-669-2181	669-3696	532-2
Bristol Historical & Preservation Society (BHPS) 48 Court St .... Bristol RI 02809 *Web:* www.bhpsri.org	401-253-7223		49-19
Bristol Hospice - California LLC 374 E Yosemite Ave Ste 200 .... Merced CA 95340 *Web:* www.bristolhospice.com	209-384-1415	384-1449	363
Bristol Hospital (BH) 41 Brewster Rd .... Bristol CT 06010 *Web:* www.bristolhealth.org	860-585-3000	585-3853	374-3
Bristol Hotel 1055 First Ave .... San Diego CA 92101 *TF:* 800-662-4477 ■ *Web:* www.thebristolsandiego.com	619-232-6141	232-0118	379
Bristol (Independent City) 497 Cumberland St Rm 210 .... Bristol VA 24201 *Web:* www.bristolva.org	276-645-7321	821-6097	338
Bristol Industries 630 E Lambert Rd .... Brea CA 92821 *Web:* www.camaerospace.com	714-990-4121	529-6726	278
Bristol Instruments Inc 770 Canning Pkwy .... Victor NY 14564 *Web:* www.bristol-inst.com	585-924-2620		544
Bristol Memorial Works 797 King St .... Bristol CT 06010 *Web:* www.bristolmemorialworks.com	860-583-1654		724
Bristol Motor Speedway 151 Speedway Blvd .... Bristol TN 37620 *TF:* 866-415-4158 ■ *Web:* www.bristolmotorspeedway.com	423-989-6933	764-1646	515
Bristol Public Library 701 Goode St .... Bristol VA 24201 *Web:* bristol-library.org	276-645-8780	669-5593	434-3
Bristol Public Library 5 High St .... Bristol CT 06010 *TF:* 877-603-7323 ■ *Web:* www.bristollib.com	860-584-7787	584-7696	434-3
Bristol Technical Education Ctr 431 Minor St .... Bristol CT 06010 *Web:* bristol.cttech.org	860-584-8433	584-0795	167-3
Bristol West Insurance Group 900 S Pine Island Rd Ste 600 .... Plantation FL 33324 *TF:* 888-888-0080 ■ *Web:* www.bristolwest.com	888-888-0080	888-0070	391-2
Bristol-Donald Company Inc 50 Roanoke Ave .... Newark NJ 07105 *Web:* www.bristoldonald.com	973-589-2640	589-2610	516
Bristol-Myers Squibb Co 345 Park Ave .... New York NY 10154 *NYSE:* BMY ■ *TF:* 800-332-2056 ■ *Web:* www.bms.com	212-546-4000		582
Bristol-Plymouth Regional Technical School 207 Hart St .... Taunton MA 02780 *Web:* bptech.org	508-823-5151	822-2687	685
Bristol-Warren Regional School District 151 State St .... Bristol RI 02809 *Web:* www.bwrsd.org	401-253-4000		685
Briston Construction LLC 309 E 10th Dr .... Mesa AZ 85210 *Web:* www.bristonconstruction.com	480-776-5810	776-5813	186
Bristow Alaska Inc 1915 Donald Ave .... Fairbanks AK 99701 *Web:* app01.bristowgroup.com	907-452-1197	452-4539	13
BRIT Systems Inc 1909 Hi Line Dr .... Dallas TX 75207 *Web:* www.brit.com	214-630-0636		475
Brit's Pub & Eating Establishment 1110 Nicollet Mall .... Minneapolis MN 55403 *Web:* britspub.com	612-332-3908	332-8032	671
Brita Products Co 1221 Broadway .... Oakland CA 94612 *TF:* 800-242-7482 ■ *Web:* www.brita.com	510-271-7000	832-1463	806
Britax Child Safety Inc 4140 Pleasant Rd .... Fort Mill SC 29708 *TF:* 888-427-4829 ■ *Web:* us.britax.com	704-409-1700		64
Brite Pharmacy Inc 83-19 37th Ave .... Jackson Heights NY 11372 *Web:* npino.com	718-424-1101	424-1299	237
Briteline Extrusions Inc 575 Beech Hill Rd .... Summerville SC 29485 *Web:* www.briteline.net	843-873-4410	873-8129	492
Brite-Line LLC 10660 E 51st Ave .... Denver CO 80239 *TF:* 888-201-6448 ■ *Web:* brite-line.com	888-201-6448	208-0758	732
Brito O Matic Manufacturing Inc 527 W Algonquin Rd .... Arlington Heights IL 60005 *TF:* 800-323-0577 ■ *Web:* briteomatic.com	847-956-1100	956-1225	806
Britestar Business 1305-B Governor Ct .... Abingdon MD 21009 *TF:* 888-409-6227 ■ *Web:* britestarbusiness.com	410-679-0441	679-1275	317
BriteVision Media LLC 350 Frank H Ogawa Plz Ste 310 .... Oakland CA 94612 *Fax Area Code: 888 ■ *TF:* 877-479-7777 ■ *Web:* britevision.com	877-479-7777	755-5282*	8
Britex Fabrics LLC 117 Post St .... San Francisco CA 94108 *Web:* www.britexfabrics.com	415-392-2910	392-3906	270
British Airways Executive Club PO Box 300743 .... Jamaica NY 11430 *Fax Area Code: 212 ■ *TF:* 800-452-1201 ■ *Web:* www.britishairways.com	800-452-1201	251-6767*	26
British Columbia Automobile Assn (BCAA) 4567 Canada Way .... Burnaby BC V5G4T1 *Web:* www.bcaa.com	604-268-5000		53
British Columbia Chamber of Commerce 750 W Pender St .... Vancouver BC V6C1G8 *Web:* www.bcchamber.org	604-683-0700	683-0416	137
British Columbia Lottery Corp (BCLC) 74 W Seymour St .... Kamloops BC V2C1E2 *TF:* 866-815-0222 ■ *Web:* www.bclc.com	250-828-5500	828-5631	452
British Columbia Place Stadium 777 Pacific Blvd .... Vancouver BC V6B4Y8 *Web:* www.bcplace.com	604-669-2300		720
British Columbia Wildlife Park 9077 Dallas Dr .... Kamloops BC V2C6V1 *Web:* www.bcwildlife.org	250-573-3242	573-2406	823
British Columbia's Women's Hospital & Health Ctr 4500 Oak St .... Vancouver BC V6H3N1 *TF:* 888-300-3088 ■ *Web:* www.bcwomens.ca	604-875-2424		374-2
British Precision Inc 20 Sequin Dr .... Glastonbury CT 06033 *TF:* 800-364-8787 ■ *Web:* www.britishprecision.com	860-785-4908	633-9395	493
British Standards Institution, The 12110 Sunset Hills Rd Ste 200 .... Reston VA 20190 *TF:* 800-862-4977 ■ *Web:* www.bsigroup.com	345-086-9001		457-5
British-American Business Council (BABC) 52 Vanderbilt Ave 20th Fl .... New York NY 10017 *Web:* www.babc.org	212-661-4060	661-4074	138
British-American Business Council of Los Angeles 15303 Ventura Blvd Ste 1040 .... Sherman Oaks CA 91403 *Fax Area Code: 818 ■ *Web:* www.babcla.org	310-312-1962	995-4124*	138
British-American Chamber of Commerce Great Lakes Region (BACC) PO Box 360707 .... Strongsville OH 44136 *Web:* www.baccohio.org	216-621-0222		138
Britt Carter & Company Inc 1350 S Skokie Hwy .... Lake Forest IL 60045 *Web:* brittcarter.net	847-735-1180		321
Britt Trucking & Construction Co 1900 Seminole Rd .... Lamesa TX 79331	806-872-3353		780
Brittain & Crawford 3908 South Fwy .... Fort Worth TX 76110 *Web:* brittain-crawford.com	817-926-0211		261
Brittain Engineering 56 Third St NW PO Box 939 .... Hickory NC 28601 *Web:* brittainengineering.com	828-328-1813	328-1814	256
Brittain Resorts & Hotels 407 30th Ave N .... Myrtle Beach SC 29577 *Web:* www.brittainresorts.com	843-282-7300		379
Brittany Beauty Academy Ltd 210 E 188th St 2nd Fl .... Bronx NY 10458 *Web:* brittanyacademy.edu	718-220-0040		685
Britten Woodworks 1954 N Betsie River Rd .... Interlochen MI 49643 *Web:* www.brittenwoodworks.com	231-275-5457		115
Britto Agency, The 277 Broadway Ste 110 .... New York NY 10007 *Web:* thebrittoagency.com	212-977-6772	977-4350	195
Britto Central Inc 1102 Lincoln Rd .... Miami Beach FL 33139 *Web:* www.britto.com	305-531-8821	531-8831	522

	Phone	Fax	Class
Britton Building Maintenance Inc 6404 International Pkwy Ste 1350 . . . . . Plano TX 75093 *Web:* britton-bmi.com	214-888-2155		104
Britton Lumber Company Inc 7 Ely Rd PO Box 389 . . . . . Fairlee VT 05045 *Web:* www.brittonlumber.com	802-333-4388	333-4295	191-3
Brivo Systems LLC 7700 Old Georgetown Rd Ste 300. . . . . Bethesda MD 20814 *TF:* 866-692-7486 ■ *Web:* www.brivo.com	301-664-5242		692
Brixmor Property Group 450 Lexington Ave 13th Fl . . . . . New York NY 10017 *TF:* 800-468-7526 ■ *Web:* www.brixmor.com	212-869-3000		655
BRM (Black River Manufacturing Inc) 2625 20th St. . . . . . Port Huron MI 48060 *Web:* www.blackrivermfg.biz	810-982-9812	982-2074	60
BRMC (Bluefield Regional Medical Ctr) 500 Cherry St . . . . . Bluefield WV 24701 *Web:* bluefieldregional.com	304-327-1100		374-3
BRMS (Benefit & Risk Management Services Inc) 80 Iron Point Cir Ste 200 PO Box 2140 . . . . . Folsom CA 95763 **Fax Area Code:* 916 ■ *TF:* 888-326-2555 ■ *Web:* www.brmsonline.com	888-326-2555	467-1401*	390
Broaching Industries Inc 25755 Dhondt Ct . . . . . Chesterfield MI 48051 *Web:* www.broachingindustries.com	586-949-3775		454
Broad Oak Energy II LLC 1707 Market Pl Ste 320 . . . . . Irving TX 75063	972-444-8808		192
Broad River Correctional Institution 4460 Broad River Rd. . . . . . Columbia SC 29210 *Web:* www.doc.sc.gov	803-896-2234		213
Broad River Electric Co-opeartive Inc 811 Hamrick St. . . . . . Gaffney SC 29342 *TF:* 866-687-2667 ■ *Web:* www.broadriverelectric.com	864-489-5737	487-7808	245
Broad River Review Gardner-Webb University PO Box 7224 . . . . Boiling Springs NC 28017 *Web:* broadriverreview.org	704-406-3224		637-9
Broad Street Grille at the Chattanoogan 1201 Broad St. . . . . . Chattanooga TN 37402 *Web:* www.chattanooganhotel.com	423-424-3700		671
BroadBand Communications Inc 207 N County Rd 3 Ft. . . . . . Fort Collins CO 80524 *Web:* www.broadbandcomm.net	970-484-6713		224
Broadband Dynamics LLC 8757 E Via De Commercio . . . . . Scottsdale AZ 85258 *TF:* 888-801-1034 ■ *Web:* www.broadbanddynamics.com	888-801-1034	801-1038	387
Broadband Express LLC 374 Westdale Ave . . . . . Westerville OH 43082 *Web:* www.broadbandexpress.com	614-823-6464		260
Broadband Forum 5177 Brandin Ct . . . . . Fremont CA 94538 *Web:* www.broadband-forum.org	510-492-4020		48-9
Broadband Products Inc (BPI) 1951 Old Cuthbert Rd Ste 301 . . . . . Cherry Hill NJ 08034 *TF:* 800-956-8898 ■ *Web:* www.broadbandproducts.com	800-956-8898		681
Broadband Solutions Inc 1886 Commerce Dr . . . . . De Pere WI 54115 *Web:* broadband-solutions.com	920-339-8056		116
Broadband Technologies Inc (BBTI) 255 SW 14th Pl . . . . . Boca Raton FL 33432 *Web:* www.broadbandweb.net	561-400-3867		392
Broadbeach Records 3465 Encinal Canyon Rd . . . . . Malibu CA 90265 *Web:* www.nauert.com	310-457-4405		657
Broadcast Communications Media Inc 3101 Ocean Park Blvd Ste 309 . . . . . Santa Monica CA 90405 *Web:* www.bcmedia.tv	310-452-6585	452-6766	393
Broadcast Ctr 2360 Hampton Ave. . . . . . Saint Louis MO 63139 *TF:* 877-334-8429 ■ *Web:* www.broadcastcenterinfo.com	314-647-8181	647-1575	167-3
Broadcast Education Assn (BEA) 1771 N St NW. . . . . . Washington DC 20036 *Web:* www.beaweb.org	202-429-5355	609-9940	49-5
Broadcast Electronics Inc 4100 N 24th St. . . . . . Quincy IL 62305 *Web:* www.bdcast.com	217-224-9600	224-9607	647
Broadcast Equipment Corp (BEC) 1035 44th Dr . . . . . Long Island City NY 11101 *Web:* becny.com	718-784-5540		116
Broadcast International Group 10458 NW 31st Terr . . . . . Doral FL 33172 *Web:* www.bigmiami.com	305-599-2112		647
Broadcast Microwave Services Inc (BMS) 12305 Crosthwaite Cir . . . . . Poway CA 92064 *TF:* 800-669-9667 ■ *Web:* www.bms-inc.com	858-391-3050	391-3049	224
Broadcast Music Inc (BMI) 250 Greenwich St 7 World Trade Ctr. . . . . . New York NY 10007 *Web:* www.bmi.com	212-220-3000		48-4
Broadcast South LLC 509 B S Columbia Ave . . . . . Douglas GA 31533 *Web:* www.broadcastsouth.com	912-389-0995	383-8552	645-141
Broadcast Sports International LLC 7455 Race Rd . . . . . Hanover MD 21076 *Web:* broadcastsportsinc.com	410-564-2600		514
Broadcast Technical Services Inc 7219 Gessner Dr. . . . . . Houston TX 77040 *Web:* www.btshouston.com	832-467-0002		224
Broadcaster Press Inc, The 201 W Cherry St. . . . . . Vermillion SD 57069 *Web:* www.broadcasteronline.com	605-624-4429		532-3
Broadcasters Letter 1400 Independence Ave SW. . . . . . Washington DC 20228 *Web:* www.usda.gov	202-720-4623		531-11
Broadcasting Board of Governors *International Broadcasting Bureau* 330 Independence Ave SW . . . . . Washington DC 20237 *Web:* www.bbg.gov	202-203-4000		340-20
Voice of America 330 Independence Ave SW . . . . . Washington DC 20237 *Web:* www.voanews.com	202-203-4545		340-20
Broadcom Corp 1320 Ridder Park Dr . . . . . San Jose CA 95131 *NASDAQ: AVGO* ■ **Fax Area Code:* 949 ■ *Web:* www.broadcom.com	408-433-8000	926-5203*	696
Broaddus & Assoc 1301 S Capital of Texas Hwy Ste A 302 . . . . . Austin TX 78746 *Web:* broaddusassociates.com	512-329-8822	329-8242	261
Broadfield Distributing Inc 67A Glen Cove Ave. . . . . . Glen Cove NY 11542 *TF:* 800-634-5178 ■ *Web:* www.broadfield.com	516-676-2378	671-3092	246
Broadgate Consultants LLC 48 Wall St . . . . . New York NY 10005 *Web:* www.broadgate.com	212-232-2222	232-3232	196
Broadgate Inc 830 Kirts Blvd Ste 400. . . . . . Troy MI 48084 *Web:* www.broadgateinc.com	248-918-0110		463
Broadhurst Theatre 235 W 44th St . . . . . New York NY 10036 *Web:* www.shubert.nyc	212-944-3700		747
Broadjam Inc 6401 Odana Rd . . . . . Madison WI 53719 *Web:* www.broadjam.com	608-271-3633		225
Broadlawns Medical Ctr 1801 Hickman Rd. . . . . . Des Moines IA 50314 *Web:* www.broadlawns.org	515-282-2200	282-3589	374-3
Broadleaf Services Inc 6 Fortune Dr. . . . . . Billerica MA 01821 *TF:* 866-337-7733 ■ *Web:* www.broadleafservices.com	866-337-7733		180
Broadley-James Corp 19 Thomas . . . . . Irvine CA 92618 *Web:* www.broadleyjames.com	949-829-5555		475
Broadman & Holman Publishers One LifeWay Plaza . . . . . Nashville TN 37234 **Fax Area Code:* 615 ■ *TF:* 800-448-8032 ■ *Web:* www.bhpublishinggroup.com	800-448-8032	251-3914*	637-3
Broadmead 13801 York Rd . . . . . Cockeysville MD 21030 *Web:* www.broadmead.org	410-527-1900		672
Broadmoor LLC 2740 N Arnoult Rd . . . . . Metairie LA 70002 *Web:* www.broadmoorllc.com	504-885-5400		187
Broadmoor, The 1 Lake Ave . . . . . Colorado Springs CO 80906 *TF:* 866-837-9520 ■ *Web:* www.broadmoor.com	719-577-5775	577-5738	669
Broadnet Teleservices LLC 1805 Shea Center Dr Ste 160 . . . . . Highlands Ranch CO 80129 *TF:* 877-579-4929 ■ *Web:* www.broadnet.com	877-579-4929		116
BroadSpan Capital 1450 Brickell Ave Ste 1550. . . . . . Miami FL 33131 *Web:* www.brocap.com	305-424-3400		70
Broadstone Real Estate LLC 530 Clinton Sq . . . . . Rochester NY 14604 *Web:* www.broadstone.com	585-287-6500	625-3680	655
Broadstreet Inc 242 W 30 St Fl 2. . . . . . New York NY 10001 *Web:* www.broadstreet.com	212-780-5700		7
Broadus Oil Corporation of Illinois 201 Dannys Dr Ste 5. . . . . . Streator IL 61364 *Web:* www.broadusoil.com	815-673-5515		579
Broadview Networks Holdings Inc 800 Westchester Ave Ste N-501 . . . . . Rye Brook NY 10573 *TF:* 800-260-8766 ■ *Web:* www.broadviewnet.com	914-922-7000		736
Broadview University - West Jordan Campus 1902 W 7800 S. . . . . . West Jordan UT 84088 *TF:* 866-304-4224 ■ *Web:* www.broadviewuniversity.edu	801-542-7600	542-7601	786
BroadVision Inc 1700 Seaport Blvd Ste 210. . . . . . Redwood City CA 94063 *NASDAQ: BVSN* ■ *Web:* www.broadvision.com	650-295-0716		39
BroadVoice Inc 9221 Corbin Ave Ste 155 . . . . . Northridge CA 91324 *TF:* 866-247-3194 ■ *Web:* www.broadvoice.com	888-325-5875		387
Broadwater Hot Springs & Fitness 4920 W US Hwy 12 . . . . . Helena MT 59601 *Web:* broadwatermt.com	406-443-5777		354
Broadway at the Beach 1325 Celebrity Cir . . . . . Myrtle Beach SC 29577 *TF:* 800-386-4662 ■ *Web:* www.broadwayatthebeach.com	843-444-3200		50-6
Broadway Bank PO Box 17001. . . . . . San Antonio TX 78217 **Fax Area Code:* 888 ■ *TF:* 800-531-7650 ■ *Web:* broadway.bank	210-283-6505	242-3344*	70
Broadway Electric Service Company Inc 1800 N Central St. . . . . . Knoxville TN 37917 *Web:* besco.com	865-524-1851		189-4
Broadway Financial Corp 5055 Wilshire Blvd Ste 100 . . . . . Los Angeles CA 90036 *NASDAQ: BYFC* ■ *TF:* 888-988-2265 ■ *Web:* www.broadwayfederalbank.com	888-988-2265		360-2
Broadway Ford Truck Sales Inc 1506 S 7th St . . . . . Saint Louis MO 63104 *Web:* www.broadwaytruck.net	314-241-9140		57
Broadway In Chicago 24 W Randolph St. . . . . . Chicago IL 60601 *TF:* 800-359-2525 ■ *Web:* www.broadwayinchicago.com	312-977-1700	977-0519	572
Broadway League, The 729 Seventh Ave 5th Fl. . . . . . New York NY 10019 *TF:* 866-442-9878 ■ *Web:* www.broadwayleague.com	212-764-1122	944-2136	48-4
Broadway Marketing Ltd 80 Fuller Rd . . . . . Albany NY 12205 *TF:* 866-757-5050 ■ *Web:* www.broadwaymarketing.com	518-489-3226		195
Broadway Mechanical 873 81st Ave. . . . . . Oakland CA 94621 *Web:* www.broadwaymechanical.com	510-746-4000		610
Broadway Oyster Bar 736 S Broadway . . . . . Saint Louis MO 63102 *Web:* www.broadwayoysterbar.com	314-621-8811	621-1995	671
Broadway Play Publishing Inc (BPPI) 224 E 62nd St. . . . . . New York NY 10065 *Web:* www.broadwayplaypub.com	212-772-8334		637-2
Broadway Plaza Hotel 1155 Broadway . . . . . New York NY 10001 *TF:* 800-249-7135 ■ *Web:* www.broadwayplazahotel.com	212-679-7665		378
Broadway School of Real Estate 339 Springwood Rd . . . . . Hot Springs AR 71913 *TF:* 877-332-2630 ■ *Web:* www.keahey.com	501-623-3029	623-8632	685
Broadway Services Inc 3709 E Monument St . . . . . Baltimore MD 21205 *Web:* www.broadwayservices.com	410-563-6900	563-6960	104
Broadway Video Inc 1619 Broadway . . . . . New York NY 10019 *Web:* www.broadwayvideo.com	212-265-7600		512
Broadway.com 729 Seventh Ave 6th Fl. . . . . . New York NY 10019 *TF:* 800-276-2392 ■ *Web:* www.broadway.com	212-541-8457	541-4892	750
Broan-NuTone LLC 926 W State St . . . . . Hartford WI 53027 *TF:* 800-558-1711 ■ *Web:* www.broan-nutone.com	262-673-4340	673-8709	37
Broaster Company LLC, The 2855 Cranston Rd. . . . . . Beloit WI 53511 *Web:* broaster.com	608-365-0193		296
Brochsteins Inc 11530 Main St . . . . . Houston TX 77025 *Web:* brochsteins.com	713-666-2881		499

	Phone	Fax	Class
Brock & Company Inc 257 Great Vly Pkwy.......... Malvern PA 19355 *TF:* 866-468-2783 ■ *Web:* www.brockco.com	610-647-5656	647-0867	670
Brock & Scott PLLC 4550 Country Club Rd.......... Winston-Salem NC 27104 *TF:* 844-856-6646 ■ *Web:* www.brockandscott.com	336-354-1797	354-1588	428
Brock Cabinets Inc 2218 Wingate Rd.......... Fayetteville NC 28304 *Web:* www.brockcabinets.com	910-424-1776		115
Brock Capital Group LLC 505 Park Ave 16th Fl.......... New York NY 10022 *Web:* brockcapital.com	212-209-3000		41
Brock Grain Systems 611 N Higbee St PO Box 2000.......... Milford IN 46542 *Web:* www.brockgrain.com	574-658-4191	658-4133	273
Brock Grain Systems 1750 W State Rd 28.......... Frankfort IN 46041 *TF:* 800-541-7900 ■ *Web:* www.graindryers.com	765-654-8517	654-8510	273
Brock Group 10343 Sam Houston Park Dr Ste 200.......... Houston TX 77064 *TF:* 800-600-9675 ■ *Web:* www.brockgroup.com	281-807-8200	807-8201	189-8
Brock Solutions Inc 86 Ardelt Ave.......... Kitchener ON N2C2C9 *TF:* 877-702-7625 ■ *Web:* www.brocksolutions.com	519-571-1522		261
Brock University 1812 Sir Isaac Brock Way.......... Saint Catharines ON L2S3A1 *Web:* brocku.ca	905-688-5550	988-5488	785
Brocker Law Firm, The 5540 Centerview Dr Ste 200.......... Raleigh NC 27606 *Web:* brockerlawfirm.com	919-854-2461		41
Brock-McVey Co 1100 Brock-McVey Dr.......... Lexington KY 40509 *Web:* www.ferguson.com	859-255-1412	233-7592	612
Brockport Animal Hospital 6352 Brockport - Spencerport Rd.......... Brockport NY 14420 *Web:* brockportanhosp.com	585-637-6190	637-5581	794
Brockton Area Workforce Investment Board Inc 34 School St 2nd Fl.......... Brockton MA 02301	508-584-3234	584-3235	260
Brockton Hospital 680 Centre St.......... Brockton MA 02302 *Web:* www.signature-healthcare.org	508-941-7000		374-3
Brockton Public Library 304 Main St.......... Brockton MA 02301 *Web:* www.brocktonpubliclibrary.org	508-580-7890	580-7898	434-3
Brockton Symphony Orchestra PO Box 1407.......... Brockton MA 02303 *Web:* www.brocktonsymphony.org	508-588-3841		573-3
Brockville General Hospital 75 Charles St.......... Brockville ON K6V1S8 *TF:* 800-567-7415 ■ *Web:* www.brockvillegeneralhospital.ca	613-345-5649		374-2
Brockway-Smith Co 146 Dascomb Rd.......... Andover MA 01810 **Fax Area Code:* 732 ■ *Web:* www.brosco.com	978-475-7100	826-0606*	499
Broco Inc 10868 Bell Ct.......... Rancho Cucamonga CA 91730 *TF:* 800-845-7259 ■ *Web:* www.broco-rankin.com	909-483-3222	483-3233	485
Broco Products Inc 18624 Syracuse Ave.......... Cleveland OH 44110 *TF:* 800-321-0837 ■ *Web:* brocoproducts.com	216-531-0880		411
Broda Construction Ltd 4271 - Fifth Ave E.......... Prince Albert SK S6V7V6 *Web:* www.brodagroup.com	306-764-5337		188
Brodart Co 500 Arch St.......... Williamsport PA 17701 *Web:* www.brodart.com	570-326-2461		178-10
Broders' Cucina 2308 W 50th St.......... Minneapolis MN 55410 *Web:* www.broders.com	612-925-3113		671
Brodeur Partners 535 Boylston St.......... Boston MA 02116 *Web:* www.brodeur.com	617-587-2800		317
Brodock Press Inc 502 Court St.......... Utica NY 13502 *TF:* 800-765-3536 ■ *Web:* www.brodock.com	315-735-9577		627
Brodsky School of Real Estate 720 S Craycroft Rd.......... Tucson AZ 85711 *Web:* www.brodskyschool.com	520-747-1485		685
Brody & Associates LLC 120 Post Rd W Ste 101.......... Westport CT 06880 *Web:* brodyandassociates.com	203-454-0560		41
Brody Transportation Company Inc 621 S Bentalou St.......... Baltimore MD 21223 *Web:* www.brodytransportation.com	410-947-7000		778
Broedell Plumbing Supply Inc 1601 Commerce Ln.......... Jupiter FL 33458 *TF:* 800-683-6363 ■ *Web:* www.broedell.com	561-743-6663	743-4644	612
Broetje Orchards 1111 Fishhook Park Rd.......... Prescott WA 99348 *Web:* firstfruits.com	509-749-2217		315-3
Brogan & Partners Advertising Consultancy Inc 800 N Old Woodward Ave Ste 100.......... Birmingham MI 48009 *Web:* brogan.com	248-341-8200		195
Brogan Cadillac Co 112 Rt 46 E.......... Totowa NJ 07512 *Web:* www.brogancadillac.com	973-200-6342		57
Brogan Tennyson Group Inc 2245 US Hwy 130 Ste 102.......... Dayton NJ 08810 *Web:* www.brogantennyson.com	732-355-0700		7
Brogdon Machine Inc 304 NW 12th St.......... Blue Springs MO 64015 *Web:* www.brogdonmachine.com	816-229-1171	229-6991	757
Brogli, Lane, Weaver & Brogli Animal Hospital PC 1807 NW Broad St.......... Murfreesboro TN 37129 *Web:* broglilaneweaver.com	615-893-1728		794
Broich Enterprises Inc 6440 City W Pkwy.......... Eden Prairie MN 55344 *TF:* 800-853-3508 ■ *Web:* www.arcticairco.com	952-941-2270	941-3066	665
Brokaw Credit Union 2006 Schofield Ave PO Box 199.......... Weston WI 54476 *Web:* brokawcu.com	715-359-7012		219
Broken Arrow Chamber of Commerce 210 N Main Ste C.......... Broken Arrow OK 74012 *Web:* www.brokenarrow.org	918-893-2100	251-1777	139
Broken Arrow Communications Inc 8316 Corona Loop NE.......... Albuquerque NM 87113 *Web:* www.bacom-inc.com	505-877-2100	877-2101	681
Broken Arrow Electric Supply Inc 2350 W Vancouver.......... Broken Arrow OK 74012 *Web:* www.baes.com	918-258-3581	251-3799	246

	Phone	Fax	Class
Broker One Realty Inc 3400 N High St Ste 200.......... Columbus OH 43202 *Web:* brokerone.us	614-246-7153		652
Brokerage Professionals Inc 7910 E Thompson Peak Pkwy.......... Scottsdale AZ 85255 *TF:* 800-733-7729 ■ *Web:* brokeragepros.com	480-505-2500	505-2501	390
Brokers Group LLC, The 50 Millstone Rd Bldg 200 Ste 180.......... East Windsor NJ 08520 *Web:* www.talonpro.com	609-924-8900	924-8929	260
Brokers International Financial Services LLC 4135 NW Urbandale Dr.......... Urbandale IA 50322 **Fax Area Code:* 800 ■ *TF:* 877-886-1939 ■ *Web:* brokersifs.com	877-886-1939	541-7986*	693
Brokers Logistics Ltd 1000 Hawkins Blvd.......... El Paso TX 79915 *Web:* brokerslogistics.com	915-778-7751		194
Brokers Real Estate Group Inc 8600 Commodity Cir 105.......... Orlando FL 32819 *Web:* bregroups.com	407-770-1464		652
Brokers Worldwide 701C Ashland Ave.......... Folcroft PA 19032 *TF:* 800-624-5287 ■ *Web:* www.asendiausa.com	610-461-3661		459
Brolite Products Inc 1900 S Park Ave.......... Streamwood IL 60107 *TF:* 888-276-5483 ■ *Web:* www.bakewithbrolite.com	630-830-0340		296-42
Bromelkamp Company LLC 106 E 24th St.......... Minneapolis MN 55404 *TF:* 877-767-6703 ■ *Web:* akoyago.com	612-767-6701		180
Bromley Group LLC, The 15 W 26th St 3rd Fl.......... New York NY 10010 *Web:* www.the-bromley-group.com	212-696-1100		195
Bromley Mountain Ski Resort 3984 Vt Rt 11.......... Peru VT 05152 *Web:* www.bromley.com	802-824-5522		378
Bromma Inc 4400 Ben Franklin Blvd Ste 200.......... Durham NC 27704 *Web:* www.bromma.com	919-471-4000		295
Bronco Billy's Casino 233 E Bennett Ave.......... Cripple Creek CO 80813 *TF:* 877-989-2142 ■ *Web:* broncobillyscasino.com	719-689-2142		133
Bronco Manufacturing LLC 4953 S 48th W Ave.......... Tulsa OK 74107 *Web:* www.broncomfg.com	918-446-7196		539
Bronco Oilfield Services Inc 88 E Buffalo Church Rd.......... Washington PA 15301 *Web:* www.broncoservices.com	724-222-1219	222-4915	539
Bronco Wine Co 6342 Bystrum Rd.......... Ceres CA 95307 *TF:* 855-874-2394 ■ *Web:* broncowine.com	209-538-3131	538-2178	80-3
Brondell Inc 1159 Howard St.......... San Francisco CA 94103 *TF:* 888-542-3355 ■ *Web:* www.brondell.com	888-542-3355		320
Broniec Assoc 4855 Peachtree Industrial Blvd Ste 215.......... Berkeley Lake GA 30092 *Web:* www.broniec.com	770-729-9664	729-9764	2
Bronner Bros Inc 2141 Powers Ferry Rd.......... Marietta GA 30067 *TF:* 800-241-6151 ■ *Web:* bronnerbros.com	770-988-0015	953-0848	214
Bronson & Kahn LLC 150 N Wacker Dr Ste 1400.......... Chicago IL 60606 *Web:* bronson-kahn.com	312-553-1700		41
Bronson Healthcare 601 John St.......... Kalamazoo MI 49007 *Web:* www.bronsonhealth.com	269-341-7654		374-3
Bronx Chamber of Commerce 1200 Waters Pl.......... Bronx NY 10461 *Web:* www.bronxmall.com	718-828-3900		139
Bronx Charter School for Excellence 1960 Benedict Ave.......... Bronx NY 10462 *Web:* www.excellencecommunityschools.org	718-828-7301		685
Bronx Community College 2155 University Ave.......... Bronx NY 10453 *TF:* 866-888-8777 ■ *Web:* www.bcc.cuny.edu	718-289-5100	289-6003	162
Bronx Council on the Arts 1738 Hone Ave.......... Bronx NY 10461 *TF:* 866-564-5226 ■ *Web:* bronxarts.org	718-931-9500	409-6445	460
Bronx County 851 Grand Concourse 3rd Fl.......... Bronx NY 10451 *Web:* bronxboropres.nyc.gov	718-590-3500		338
Bronx County Historical Society 3309 Bainbridge Ave.......... Bronx NY 10467 *Web:* www.bronxhistoricalsociety.org	718-881-8900	881-4827	520
Bronx Defenders, The 860 Courtlandt Ave.......... Bronx NY 10451 *Web:* www.bronxdefenders.org	718-838-7878	665-0100	708
Bronx Library Ctr 310 E Kings Bridge Rd.......... Bronx NY 10458 **Fax Area Code:* 212 ■ *TF:* 800-342-3688 ■ *Web:* www.nypl.org	718-579-4244	930-0983*	434-3
Bronx Museum of the Arts 1040 Grand Concourse.......... Bronx NY 10456 *Web:* www.bronxmuseum.org	718-681-6000	681-6181	520
Bronx Psychiatric Ctr 1500 Waters Pl.......... Bronx NY 10461 *Web:* omh.ny.gov	718-931-0600	862-4858	374-5
BronxCare Family Wellness Ctr 1276 Fulton Ave.......... Bronx NY 10456 *TF:* 877-451-9361 ■ *Web:* www.bronxcare.org	718-590-1800		374-3
Bronze Craft Corp 37 Will St.......... Nashua NH 03060 **Fax Area Code:* 603 ■ *TF:* 800-488-7747 ■ *Web:* www.bronzecraft.com	800-488-7747	883-0222*	350
Brook Consulting Services Inc 203 Main St Ste 393.......... Flemington NJ 08822 *Web:* brookconsultingservice.com	908-391-5778		196
Brook Farm Veterinary Ctr 2371 Rt 22.......... Patterson NY 12563 *Web:* brookfarmveterinarycenter.com	845-878-4833		794
Brook Forest Voices 32440 Aspen Meadow Dr.......... Evergreen CO 80439 *Web:* www.brookforestvoices.com	303-670-4145		637-10
Brook Furniture Rental Inc 100 N Field Dr Ste 220.......... Lake Forest IL 60045 *TF:* 877-285-7368 ■ *Web:* bfr.com	877-285-7368		264-2
Brook Ledge Inc 12 Gotwals Ln.......... Oley PA 19547 *TF:* 800-523-8143 ■ *Web:* www.brookledge.com	610-987-6284		780
Brook Mays Music Co 8605 John Carpenter Fwy.......... Dallas TX 75247 *TF:* 800-637-8966 ■ *Web:* www.brookmays.com	214-631-0928	905-4964	526
Brook Warehousing Systems 18 Van Veghten Dr.......... Bridgewater NJ 08807 *Web:* www.brookwarehouse.com	908-725-4343		581

				Phone	Fax	Class
Brookdale Animal Hospital PA 13521 Plaza Road Ext *Web:* brookdaleanimalhospital.com	Charlotte	NC	28215	704-598-1095	598-3595	794
Brookdale Community College 765 Newman Springs Rd *TF:* 866-767-9512 ■ *Web:* www.brookdalecc.edu	Lincroft	NJ	07738	732-224-2345	224-2271	162
Brookdale Group, The 3455 Peachtree Rd NE Ste 700 *Web:* www.brookdalegroup.com	Atlanta	GA	30326	404-364-8080		528
Brookdale Senior Living Inc 111 Westwood Pl Ste 400 **Fax Area Code:* 615 ■ *TF:* 888-221-7317 ■ *Web:* www.brookdale.com	Brentwood	TN	37027	888-221-7317	221-2289*	303
Brookdale University Hospital & Medical Ctr 1 Brookdale Plz *Web:* www.brookdalehospital.org	Brooklyn	NY	11212	718-240-5000		374-3
Brooke Alexander Editions 59 Wooster St *Web:* www.baeditions.com	New York	NY	10012	212-925-4338	941-9565	42
Brooke Army Medical Ctr (BAMC) 3551 Roger Brooke Dr *TF:* 800-443-2262 ■ *Web:* www.bamc.health.mil	Fort Sam Houston	TX	78234	210-916-9900		374-4
Brooke Chase Associates Inc 1543 Second St *TF:* 877-374-0039 ■ *Web:* www.brookechase.com	Sarasota	FL	34236	877-374-0039		721
Brooke County 632 Main St *Web:* www.brookewv.org	Wellsburg	WV	26070	304-737-3661		338
Brooke County Schools 1201 Pleasant Ave *TF:* 866-632-9992 ■ *Web:* www.brooke.k12.wv.us	Wellsburg	WV	26070	304-737-3481	737-3480	780
Brooke Private Equity Assoc 20 Custom House St Ste 610 *Web:* www.bpea-pe.com	Boston	MA	02110	617-227-3160	227-4128	401
Brooker Insurance Agency Inc 10749 Pearl Rd *Web:* brooker-ins.com	Strongsville	OH	44136	440-238-5454		390
Brookfield Engineering Lab Inc 11 Commerce Blvd *TF:* 800-628-8139 ■ *Web:* www.brookfieldengineering.com	Middleboro	MA	02346	508-946-6200	946-6262	201
Brookfield Fabricating Corp 111 Stanbury Industrial Dr *Web:* www.brookfieldfabricating.com	Brookfield	MO	64628	660-258-2214		480
Brookfield Properties Corp 181 Bay St Ste 330 *NYSE: BPO* ■ *Web:* www.brookfieldproperties.com	Toronto	ON	M5J2T3	416-369-2300	369-2301	655
Brookfield Public Library 1900 N Calhoun Rd *Web:* www.ci.brookfield.wi.us	Brookfield	WI	53005	262-782-4140	796-6670	434-3
Brookfield Sand & Gravel Inc 8587 N 850 W *Web:* brookfieldsandandgravel.com	Fairland	IN	46126	317-835-2235	862-3773	503-4
Brookfield Square 95 N Moorland Rd *Web:* www.shopbrookfieldsquaremall.com	Brookfield	WI	53005	262-797-7245		655
Brookfield Zoo 3300 Golf Rd *Web:* www.czs.org	Brookfield	IL	60513	708-688-8000		823
Brookgreen Gardens 1931 Brookgreen Dr *TF:* 800-849-1931 ■ *Web:* www.brookgreen.org	Murrells Inlet	SC	29576	843-235-6000	235-6039	97
Brookhaven at Lexington 1010 Waltham St *Web:* brookhavenatlexington.org	Lexington	MA	02421	781-863-9660		672
Brookhaven National Laboratory (BNL) PO Box 5000 *Web:* www.bnl.gov	Upton	NY	11973	631-344-8000	344-5832	668
Brookhaven School District 326 E Ct St *Web:* www.brookhavenschools.org	Brookhaven	MS	39601	601-833-6661	833-4154	685
Brookhaven-Lincoln County Chamber of Commerce 230 S Whitworth Ave *TF:* 800-613-4667 ■ *Web:* brookhavenchamber.org	Brookhaven	MS	39601	601-833-1411	833-1412	139
Brookhurst Mill 3315 Van Buren Blvd *Web:* www.brookhurstmill.com	Riverside	CA	92503	951-688-3511		447
Brookings County 314 Sixth Ave *Web:* www.brookingscountysd.gov	Brookings	SD	57006	605-696-8205		338
Brookings Institution 1775 Massachusetts Ave NW *Web:* www.brookings.edu	Washington	DC	20036	202-797-6236	797-6004	634
Brookings Public Library 515 Third St *Web:* www.brookingslibrary.org	Brookings	SD	57006	605-692-9407		434-3
Brookings Register, The 312 Fifth St *Web:* www.brookingsregister.com	Brookings	SD	57006	605-692-6271	692-2979	532-2
Brookland Federal Credit Union 1058 Sunset Blvd *Web:* brooklandfcu.org	West Columbia	SC	29169	803-794-9201		219
Brookline Bank 131 Clarendon St PO Box 470469 *TF:* 877-668-2265 ■ *Web:* www.brooklinebank.com	Boston	MA	02116	617-425-4600		360-2
Brookline Booksmith 279 Harvard St *Web:* www.brooklinebooksmith.com	Brookline	MA	02446	617-566-6660	734-9125	95
Brookline Chamber of Commerce 251 Harvard St Ste 1 *Web:* www.brooklinechamber.com	Brookline	MA	02446	617-739-1330	739-1200	139
Brookline College 2445 W Dunlap Ave Ste 100 *TF:* 800-793-2428 ■ *Web:* brooklinecollege.edu	Phoenix	AZ	85021	602-242-6265		685
Brookline Public Library 361 Washington St *TF:* 800-447-8844 ■ *Web:* www.brooklinelibrary.org	Brookline	MA	02445	617-730-2370		434-3
Brooklyn Academy of Music (BAM) 30 Lafayette Ave *Web:* www.bam.org	Brooklyn	NY	11217	718-636-4100		572
Brooklyn Ascend Charter School 205 Rockaway Pkwy *Web:* www.ascendlearning.org	Brooklyn	NY	11212	347-464-7600		685
Brooklyn Botanic Garden 1000 Washington Ave *Web:* www.bbg.org	Brooklyn	NY	11225	718-623-7200		97
Brooklyn Bottling Co 643 S Rd	Milton	NY	12547	845-795-2171		296-20
Brooklyn Brewery, The 79 N 11th St *Web:* www.brooklynbrewery.com	Brooklyn	NY	11211	718-486-7422	486-7440	102
Brooklyn Chamber of Commerce 335 Adams St Ste 2700 *Web:* www.brooklynchamber.com	Brooklyn	NY	11201	718-875-1000	237-4274	139
Brooklyn College 2900 Bedford Ave *Web:* www.brooklyn.cuny.edu	Brooklyn	NY	11210	718-951-5000	951-4506	166
Brooklyn Correctional Institution 59 Hartford Rd *Web:* portal.ct.gov	Brooklyn	CT	06234	860-779-2600		213
Brooklyn Cyclones 1904 Surf Ave MCU Pk *Web:* www.brooklyncyclones.com	Brooklyn	NY	11224	718-449-8497		717
Brooklyn Fashion + Design Accelerator 630 Flushing Ave Ste 704 *Web:* bkaccelerator.com	Brooklyn	NY	11206	718-687-5700		393
Brooklyn Gallery of Coins & Stamps Inc 8725 Fourth Ave *Web:* brooklyngallery.com	Brooklyn	NY	11209	718-745-5701	745-2775	160
Brooklyn Historical Society 128 Pierrepont St *Web:* www.brooklynhistory.org	Brooklyn	NY	11201	718-222-4111		520
Brooklyn Hospital Ctr 121 DeKalb Ave *TF:* 833-824-2669 ■ *Web:* www.tbh.org	Brooklyn	NY	11201	718-250-8000		374-3
Brooklyn International Film Festival 180 S Fourth St Ste 2S *Web:* www.brooklynfilmfestival.org	Brooklyn	NY	11211	718-486-8181		282
Brooklyn Law School 250 Joralemon St *Web:* www.brooklaw.edu	Brooklyn	NY	11201	718-780-7906	780-0395	167-1
Brooklyn Legal Services Corp 105 Court St 3rd Fl *Web:* www.legalservicesnyc.org	Brooklyn	NY	11201	718-237-5500		428
Brooklyn Legal Services Corp 260 Broadway 2nd Fl *Web:* bka.org	Brooklyn	NY	11211	718-487-2305		41
Brooklyn Museum of Art 200 Eastern Pkwy *Web:* www.brooklynmuseum.org	Brooklyn	NY	11238	718-638-5000	501-6136	520
Brooklyn Mutual Telecommunications Coop 129 Jackson St *TF:* 877-610-0330 ■ *Web:* www.brooklyntelco.com	Brooklyn	IA	52211	641-522-9211	522-5001	681
Brooklyn Navy Yard Development Corp 63 Flushing Ave Bldg 292 Unit 300 *Web:* brooklynnavyyard.org	Brooklyn	NY	11205	718-907-5900	643-9296	655
Brooklyn Products Inc 171 Wamplers Lake Rd *Web:* www.brooklynproducts.com	Brooklyn	MI	49230	517-592-2185		247
Brooklyn Public Library (BPL) 496 Franklin Ave *Web:* www.bklynlibrary.org	Brooklyn	NY	11238	718-623-2134		434-3
Brooklyn Seafood Steak & Oyster House 1212 Second Ave *Web:* www.thebrooklyn.com	Seattle	WA	98101	206-224-7000		671
Brooklyn Tabernacle 17 Smith St *Web:* www.brooklyntabernacle.org	Brooklyn	NY	11201	718-290-2000		48-20
Brooklyn-Irish Hills Chamber of Commerce 131 N Main St PO Box 805 *Web:* irishhills.com	Brooklyn	MI	49230	517-592-8907		139
Brookman LLC 61 Rhode Island Ave NW *Web:* www.brookman.com	Washington	DC	20001	301-515-0450		196
Brookmont Capital Management LLC 2000 McKinney Ave Ste 1230 *Web:* www.brookmont.com	Dallas	TX	75201	214-953-0190		401
Brooks & Brooks CPAS 110 Pleasant Hill Rd *Web:* brookscpamaine.com	Scarborough	ME	04074	207-883-8810		2
Brooks & District Chamber of Commerce 403-2 Ave W Ste 4 *Web:* www.brookschamber.ab.ca	Brooks	AB	T1R1B4	403-362-7641	362-6893	137
Brooks & Freund LLC 5661 Independence Cir Ste 1 *Web:* brooksandfreund.com	Fort Myers	FL	33912	239-939-5251	939-5117	187
Brooks & Sparks Inc 21020 Park Row Dr *Web:* www.brooksandsparks.com	Katy	TX	77449	281-578-9595		261
Brooks Automation Inc 15 Elizabeth Dr *NASDAQ: BRKS* ■ *TF:* 800-698-6149 ■ *Web:* www.brooks.com	Chelmsford	MA	01824	978-262-2400	262-2500	695
Brooks Borg Skiles Architecture Engineering 317 Sixth Ave Ste 400 *Web:* www.bbsae.com	Des Moines	IA	50309	515-244-7167		256
Brooks Construction Company Inc 6525 Ardmore Ave *Web:* www.brooks1st.com	Fort Wayne	IN	46809	260-478-1990		191-2
Brooks County 100 E Miller St *Web:* co.brooks.tx.us	Falfurrias	TX	78355	361-325-5604		338
Brooks Elementary School 2700 Stonebridge Blvd *Web:* brooks.ipsd.org	Aurora	IL	60502	630-375-3200		685
Brooks Equipment Company Inc 10926 David Taylor Dr Ste 300 PO Box 481888 *TF:* 800-826-3473 ■ *Web:* brooksequipment.com	Charlotte	NC	28262	800-826-3473	433-9265	679
Brooks Group, The 10 W 37th St 5th Fl *Web:* brookspr.com	New York	NY	10018	212-768-0860		195
Brooks Instrument LLC 407 W Vine St *TF:* 888-554-3569 ■ *Web:* www.brooksinstrument.com	Hatfield	PA	19440	888-554-3569		407
Brooks Intl 3531 S Logan St Ste D 127 *Web:* www.brooksinternational.com	Englewood	CO	80113	303-825-8700		708
Brooks Jeffrey Computer Services 971 Coley Dr *Web:* www.brooksjeffreycomputerstore.com	Mountain Home	AR	72653	870-425-8064		175
Brooks Lake Lodge & Guest Ranch 458 Brooks Lake Rd *TF:* 866-213-4022 ■ *Web:* www.brookslake.com	Dubois	WY	82513	866-213-4022		239
Brooks Law Firm PC 3725 Blackhawk Rd Ste 200 *Web:* brookslawfirmpc.com	Rock Island	IL	61201	309-786-4900	786-4940	41

Name	Address	City	State	ZIP	Phone	Fax	Class
Brooks Law Group PA, The	123 First St N *Web:* brookslawgroup.com	Winter Haven	FL	33881	863-299-1962		41
Brooks Manufacturing Co	2120 Pacific St *Web:* www.brooksmfg.com	Bellingham	WA	98229	360-733-1700	734-6668	818
Brooks Memorial Hospital	529 Central Ave *Web:* www.brookshospital.org	Dunkirk	NY	14048	716-366-1111		374-3
Brooks Memorial State Park	2465 Hwy 97 *Web:* parks.state.wa.us	Goldendale	WA	98620	509-773-4611		565
Brooks Mo (Rep R - AL)	2246 Rayburn House Office Bldg *Web:* brooks.house.gov	Washington	DC	20515	202-225-4801		342-2
Brooks Rand Labs LLC	18804 N Crk Pkwy Ste 100 *Web:* brooksapplied.com	Bothell	WA	98011	206-632-6206		743
Brooks Resources Corp	409 NW Franklin Ave *Web:* brooksresources.com	Bend	OR	97701	541-382-1662	385-3285	653
Brooks School	1160 Great Pond Rd *Web:* www.brooksschool.org	North Andover	MA	01845	978-725-6300		622
Brooks Sports Inc	19910 N Creek Pkwy Ste 200 *TF:* 800-227-6657 ■ *Web:* www.brooksrunning.com	Bothell	WA	98011	800-227-6657		301
Brooks Susan W (Rep R - IN)	2211 Rayburn House Office Bldg *Web:* susanwbrooks.house.gov	Washington	DC	20515	202-225-2276	225-0016	342-2
Brooks Tactical Systems	865 9th Ave *Web:* www.brookstactical.com	Fox Island	WA	98333	253-549-2703		155-8
Brooks Tropicals Inc	18400 SW 256th St *TF:* 800-327-4833 ■ *Web:* www.brookstropicals.com	Homestead	FL	33090	305-247-3544	246-5827	315-4
Brooks Utility Products Group	23847 Industrial Park Dr *TF:* 888-687-3008 ■ *Web:* www.brooksutility.com	Farmington Hills	MI	48335	248-477-0250		639
Brooks, McGinnis & Company LLC	2 Premier Plz 5607 Glenridge Dr Ste 650 *Web:* www.brooksmcginnis.com	Atlanta	GA	30342	404-531-4940		2
Brooks, Pierce, McLendon, Humphrey & Leonard LLP	230 N Elm St 2000 Renaissance Plz PO Box 26000 *Web:* www.brookspierce.com	Greensboro	NC	27401	336-373-8850	378-1001	428
Brookshire Bros Inc	1201 Ellen Trout Dr *Web:* www.brookshirebrothers.com	Lufkin	TX	75904	936-634-8155		345
Brookshire Grocery Co	1600 W SW Loop 323 *Web:* www.brookshires.com	Tyler	TX	75701	903-534-3000		345
Brookshire Suites	120 E Lombard St *TF:* 855-345-5033 ■ *Web:* www.brookshiresuites.com	Baltimore	MD	21202	410-625-1300		379
Brookside by Day	3313 S Peoria Ave *Web:* brooksidebyday.com	Tulsa	OK	74105	918-745-9989		671
Brookside Equipment sales inc	3715 S Sam Houston Pkwy E **Fax Area Code:* 281 ■ *Web:* www.brooksideusa.com	Houston	TX	77047	713-943-7100	501-3994*	755
Brookside Gardens	1800 Glenallan Ave *Web:* www.montgomeryparks.org	Wheaton	MD	20902	301-962-1400		97
Brookside Group, The	1 Stamford Forum 201 Tresser Blvd Ste 320 *Web:* www.brooksideequity.com	Stamford	CT	06901	203-595-4520		604
Brookside Inn	1297 S Perry St *Web:* bsisnf.com	Castle Rock	CO	80104	303-688-2500		379
Brookside Lumber & Supply Co	500 Logan Rd PO Box 327 *Web:* www.brooksidelumber.com	Bethel Park	PA	15102	412-835-7610	835-8672	191-3
Brookside Resort	463 E Pkwy *TF:* 800-251-9597 ■ *Web:* www.brooksideresort.com	Gatlinburg	TN	37738	865-436-5611		669
Brooks-Ransom Assn	7415 N Palm Ave Ste 100 *Web:* www.brooksransom.com	Fresno	CA	93711	559-449-8444		256
Brookstone Capital Management	1745 S Naperville Rd Ste 200 *TF:* 866-425-3003 ■ *Web:* www.brookstonecm.com	Wheaton	IL	60189	630-653-1400		194
Brookstone Inc	1 Innovation Way *TF:* 800-846-3000 ■ *Web:* www.brookstone.com	Merrimack	NH	03054	800-846-3000		327
Brookstown Inn	200 Brookstown Ave *TF:* 800-845-4262 ■ *Web:* www.brookstowninn.com	Winston-Salem	NC	27101	336-725-1120	773-0147	379
Brooksville Regional Hospital	17240 Cortez Blvd *Web:* www.bayfrontbrooksville.com	Brooksville	FL	34601	352-796-5111		374-3
Brookville Building & Savings Assn	510 Arlington Rd *Web:* brookvillesavings.com	Brookville	OH	45309	937-833-2176		70
Brookville Lake	PO Box 100 *Web:* www.in.gov	Brookville	IN	47012	765-647-2657		565
Brookwood Companies Inc	485 Madison Ave Ste 500 **Fax Area Code:* 646 ■ *TF:* 800-247-6658 ■ *Web:* www.brookwoodcos.net	New York	NY	10022	212-551-0100	472-0294*	594
Brookwood Laminating	275 Putnam Rd *Web:* www.brookwoodcos.com	Wauregan	CT	06387	860-774-5001	774-5002	745-2
Brookwood Middle School	1020 Hunters Ridge Dr *Web:* www.genoacityschools.org	Genoa City	WI	53128	262-279-1053		685
Brookwood Program Management LLC	100 Hartsfield Centre Pkwy Ste 500 *Web:* www.brookwoodgroup.com	Atlanta	GA	30354	404-350-9988	605-8906	463
Brookwoods Group Inc	1225 N Loop W Ste 1111 *TF:* 800-426-3900 ■ *Web:* www.brookwoods.com	Houston	TX	77008	713-934-0532	934-0589	260
Broom Street Theatre	1119 Williamson St *Web:* www.bstonline.org	Madison	WI	53703	608-244-8338		572
Broome Community College	901 Front St *TF:* 800-836-0689 ■ *Web:* www.sunybroome.edu	Binghamton	NY	13905	607-778-5000	778-5442	162
Broome County	44 Hawley St *Web:* www.gobroomecounty.com	Binghamton	NY	13902	607-778-2114	778-2243	338
Broome County Historical Society (BCPL)	185 Court St *Web:* www.bclibrary.info	Binghamton	NY	13901	607-778-3572		49-19
Broome County Veterans Memorial Arena	1 Stuart St *Web:* broomearenaforum.com	Binghamton	NY	13901	607-778-1528		720
Broome-Tioga Workforce New York	171 Front St *Web:* www.broometiogaworks.com	Binghamton	NY	13901	607-778-2136		260
Broomfield Chamber of Commerce	105 Edgeview Dr Ste 410 *Web:* www.broomfieldchamber.com	Broomfield	CO	80021	303-466-1775	466-4481	139
Broomfield Colorado	1 DesCombes Dr *Web:* www.broomfield.org	Broomfield	CO	80020	303-469-3301	438-6296	338
Broomfield Laboratories Inc	164 Still River Rd *Web:* www.broomfieldusa.com	Bolton	MA	01740	978-779-6600	779-2954	494
Brophy, Dailey & Incardona LLP	140 Allens Creek Rd *Web:* brophydailey.com	Rochester	NY	14618	585-256-1550	256-3295	2
Brose North America Inc	3933 Automation Ave *Web:* www.brose.com	Auburn Hills	MI	48326	248-339-4000	339-4099	360-3
Brosius, Johnson & Griggs LLC	1600 Dublin Rd Ste 100 *Web:* bjglaw.net	Columbus	OH	43215	614-464-3563	224-6221	41
Bross & Frankel PA	102 Browning Ln Bldg C-1 *Web:* brossfrankel.com	Cherry Hill	NJ	08003	856-795-8880		41
Bro-Tex Inc	800 Hampden Ave *TF:* 800-328-2282 ■ *Web:* www.brotex.com	Saint Paul	MN	55114	651-645-5721	646-1876	508
Brother International Corp	100 Somerset Corporate Blvd *TF:* 877-552-6255 ■ *Web:* www.brother-usa.com	Bridgewater	NJ	08807	908-704-1700	704-8235	111
Brother Sebastian's Steak House	1350 S 119th St *Web:* brothersebastians.com	Omaha	NE	68144	402-330-0300	330-4814	671
Brother's Brother Foundation (BBF)	1200 Galveston Ave *Web:* www.brothersbrother.org	Pittsburgh	PA	15233	412-321-3160	321-3325	48-5
Brotherhood Bank & Trust	756 Minnesota Ave *TF:* 855-522-6722 ■ *Web:* www.bankoflabor.com	Kansas City	KS	66101	913 321-4242		70
Brotherhood Credit Union	75 Market St *Web:* brotherhoodcu.org	Lynn	MA	01901	781-598-5555		219
Brotherhood Mutual Insurance Co (BMI)	6400 Brotherhood Way *TF:* 800-333-3735 ■ *Web:* www.brotherhoodmutual.com	Fort Wayne	IN	46825	800-333-3735		391-4
Brotherhood of Locomotive Engineers & Trainmen (BLET)	7061 E Pleasant Valley Rd *Web:* www.ble-t.org	Independence	OH	44131	216-241-2630	241-6516	414
Brotherhood of Maintenance of Way Employees (BMWED)	41475 Gardenbrook Rd *Web:* bmwe.org	Novi	MI	48375	248-662-2660	662-2659	414
Brotherhood of Railroad Signalmen	917 Shenandoah Shores Rd *Web:* www.brs.org	Front Royal	VA	22630	540-622-6522	622-6532	49-21
Brotherhood Winery	100 Brotherhood Plaza Dr PO Box 190 *TF:* 800-724-3960 ■ *Web:* www.brotherhood-winery.com	Washingtonville	NY	10992	845-496-3661		80-3
Brothers & Co	4860 S Lewis Ave *Web:* www.broco.com	Tulsa	OK	74105	918-743-8822		4
Brothers Assoc. Landscaping Garden Center LLC	2281 Albany Ave *Web:* brothersassociates.net	West Hartford	CT	06117	860-232-9794		422
Brothers Inc	1000 Sussex Blvd *Web:* brotherselectric.com	Broomall	PA	19008	610-328-0670	328-6218	189-4
Brothers Produce Inc	3173 Produce Row *Web:* www.brothersproduce.com	Houston	TX	77023	713-924-4196	921-3060	297-7
Brotherston Homecare Inc	1412 Wells Dr *Web:* brotherstonhomecare.com	Bensalem	PA	19020	215-633-7300		363
Brotherton Ford Berry & Weaver PLLC	5509A W Friendly Ave Ste 204 *Web:* brothertonford.com	Greensboro	NC	27410	336-346-1116		41
Brotherton Seed Company Inc	451 S Milwaukee Ave *Web:* www.brothertonseed.com	Moses Lake	WA	98837	509-765-1816	765-1817	276
Brotman Financial Group Inc	16 Greenmeadow Dr Ste 201 *Web:* bfgfa.com	Timonium	MD	21093	410-252-4555		528
Broudy Precision Equipment Co	9 Union Hill Rd *Web:* www.broudyprecision.com	West Conshohocken	PA	19428	610-825-7200		111
Brough, Chadrow & Levine PA	2149 N Commerce Pkwy *Web:* www.bclattorneys.com	Weston	FL	33326	954-384-0732	384-0846	41
Broughal & Devito LLP	38 W Market St *Web:* broughal-devito.com	Bethlehem	PA	18018	610-865-3664		41
Broughton Foods LLC	1701 Green St *TF:* 800-303-3400 ■ *Web:* www.broughtonfoods.com	Marietta	OH	45750	740-373-4121		296-27
Broughton Hospital	1000 S Sterling St *Web:* www.ncdhhs.gov	Morganton	NC	28655	828-433-2111		374-5
Broussard Brothers Inc	501A South Main St *Web:* www.broussardbrothers.com	Abbeville	LA	70510	337-893-5303	893-7148	264-3
Broussard's Restaurant	819 Rue Conti *Web:* broussards.com	New Orleans	LA	70112	504-581-3866	581-3873	671
Brouwer and Janachowski	100 Shoreline Hwy Ste B-101 *Web:* www.bandjadvisors.com	Mill Valley	CA	94941	415-435-8330	289-0192	401

Name	Address	City	State	ZIP	Phone	Fax	Class	Other
Broward County	115 S Andrews Ave Annex B	Fort Lauderdale	FL	33301	954-357-7000		338	*Web:* www.broward.org
Broward County Chamber of Commerce	2000 W Commercial Blvd Ste 229	Fort Lauderdale	FL	33309	954-565-5750	334-9617	139	*Web:* www.browardbiz.com
Broward County Public Schools	600 SE Third Ave	Fort Lauderdale	FL	33301	754-321-0000	321-2701	685	*Web:* www.browardschools.com
Broward Fire Equipment & Service Inc	101 SW Sixth St	Fort Lauderdale	FL	33301	954-467-6625	467-6640	679	*TF:* 800-866-3473 ■ *Web:* www.browardfire.com
Broward Health Imperial Point	6401 N Federal Hwy	Fort Lauderdale	FL	33308	954-776-8500		48-17	*Web:* www.browardhealth.org
Brower Mechanical Inc	4060 Alvis Ct	Rocklin	CA	95677	916-624-0808		610	*TF:* 877-816-6649 ■ *Web:* www.browermechanical.com
Brower Timing Systems	12660 S Fort St Ste 102	Draper	UT	84020	801-572-5540		203	*Web:* www.browertiming.com
Brown & Bigelow Inc	345 Plato Blvd E	Saint Paul	MN	55107	651-293-7000		9	*TF:* 800-628-1755 ■ *Web:* www.brownandbigelow.com
Brown & Brown Agency of Insurance Professionals Inc	208 N Mill	Pryor	OK	74361	918-825-3295		390	*Web:* www.bbinsurance.com
Brown & Brown Insurance	2106 Pacific Ave Ste 501	Tacoma	WA	98402	253-396-5500	396-4500	391-4	*Web:* www.bbtacoma.com
Brown & Brown of Indiana LLC	11555 N Meridian St Ste 200	Carmel	IN	46032	317-574-5000	470-1968*	260	**Fax Area Code:* 877 ■ *Web:* www.brownandbrownindiana.com
Brown & Bunch PLLC	101 N Columbia St	Chapel Hill	NC	27514	919-968-1111	968-1444	41	*Web:* brownandbunch.com
Brown & Caldwell	201 N Civic Dr Ste 300	Walnut Creek	CA	94596	925-937-9010	937-9026	261	*Web:* brownandcaldwell.com
Brown & Charbonneau LLP	420 Exchange Ste 270	Irvine	CA	92602	714-505-3000		428	*Web:* www.bc-llp.com
Brown & Company Inc	1700 Broadway Ste 500	Denver	CO	80290	303-863-7112		401	*Web:* brownandco.com
Brown & Connery LLP	360 Haddon Ave	Westmont	NJ	08108	856-854-8900		428	*Web:* brownconnery.com
Brown & Crona LLC	7900 E Union Ave Ste 1012	Denver	CO	80237	303-339-3750		41	*Web:* brownandcrona.com
Brown & Haley	PO Box 1596	Tacoma	WA	98401	800-426-8400		296-8	*TF:* 800-426-8400 ■ *Web:* www.brown-haley.com
Brown & Michaels PC	118 N Tioga St 400 M T Bank Bldg	Ithaca	NY	14850	607-256-2000	256-3628	428	*Web:* www.bpmlegal.com
Brown & Miller Racing Solutions LLC	4005 Dearborn Pl NW	Concord	NC	28027	704-793-4319		609	*Web:* www.bmrs.net
Brown & Streza LLP	40 Pacifica 15th Fl	Irvine	CA	92618	949-453-2900		41	*Web:* www.brownandstreza.com
Brown and James PC	800 Market St Ste 1100	Saint Louis	MO	63101	314-421-3400	421-3128	41	*Web:* www.brownjames.com
Brown Anthony (Rep D - MD)	1323 Longworth House Office Bldg	Washington	DC	20515	202-225-8699		342-2	*Web:* anthonybrown.house.gov
Brown Armstrong Accountancy Corp	4200 Truxtun Ave Ste 300	Bakersfield	CA	93309	661-324-4971		2	*Web:* bacpas.com
Brown Automotive Group LP	4300 S Georgia	Amarillo	TX	79110	806-353-7211		57	*TF:* 888-388-6728 ■ *Web:* www.smallerprofit.com
Brown Aveda Institute	8816 Mentor Ave	Mentor	OH	44060	440-255-9494		214	*Web:* www.brownaveda.com
Brown Bros Harriman & Co	140 Broadway	New York	NY	10005	212-483-1818		70	*Web:* www.bbh.com
Brown Brown & Associates PA	551 Ave K SE	Winter Haven	FL	33880	312-967-6100		2	*Web:* brownbrowncpas.com
Brown Bus Co	2111 E Sherman Ave	Nampa	ID	83686	208-466-4181	466-2861	109	*TF:* 800-574-1580 ■ *Web:* www.brownbuscompany.com
Brown Coach Inc	50 Venner Rd	Amsterdam	NY	12010	518-843-4700	843-3600	107	*TF:* 800-424-4700 ■ *Web:* www.browntours.com
Brown College of Court Reporting & Medical Transcription (BCCR)	1900 Emery St NW Ste 200	Atlanta	GA	30318	404-876-1227	876-4415	800	*TF:* 800-849-0703 ■ *Web:* www.bccr.edu
Brown County	25 Market St Ste 1	Aberdeen	SD	57401	605-626-7105	626-4010	338	*Web:* www.brown.sd.us
Brown County	800 Mt Orab Pk Ste 101	Georgetown	OH	45121	937-378-3956	378-6324	338	*Web:* www.browncountyohio.gov
Brown County	305 E Walnut Rm 620	Green Bay	WI	54301	920-448-4016	448-4498	338	*TF:* 800-362-9082 ■ *Web:* www.browncountywi.gov
Brown County	601 Oregon St	Hiawatha	KS	66434	785-742-2581	742-7705	338	*Web:* www.browncountywi.gov
Brown County	200 Ct St Rm 5	Mount Sterling	IL	62353	217-773-2713	773-3648	338	*Web:* www.bccircuitclerk.com
Brown County	PO Box 164	Nashville	IN	47448	812-988-0234		338	*Web:* thebrowncountychamber.org
Brown County	14 S State St PO Box 248	New Ulm	MN	56073	507-233-6600	359-1430	338	*Web:* www.co.brown.mn.us
Brown County Chamber of Commerce	9301 Hamer Rd	Georgetown	OH	45121	937-378-4784	378-1634	139	*Web:* browncountyohiochamber.com
Brown County Convention & Visitors Bureau	PO Box 840	Nashville	IN	47448	812-988-7303		206	*TF:* 800-753-3255 ■ *Web:* www.browncounty.com
Brown County Court	148 W Fourth St	Ainsworth	NE	69210	402-387-2864	382-3374	338	*Web:* supremecourt.nebraska.gov
Brown County Inn	51 State Rd 46	Nashville	IN	47448	812-988-2291		379	*TF:* 800-772-5249 ■ *Web:* www.browncountyinn.com
Brown County Library	515 Pine St	Green Bay	WI	54301	920-448-4400		434-3	*Web:* www.browncountylibrary.org
Brown County Rural Electric Assn	24386 State Hwy 4 PO Box 529	Sleepy Eye	MN	56085	507-794-3331	794-4282	245	*TF:* 800-658-2368 ■ *Web:* www.browncountyrea.coop
Brown County State Park	1405 State Rd 46 W PO Box 608	Nashville	IN	47448	812-988-6406		565	*Web:* www.in.gov
Brown Dairy Equipment	6500 W Gerwoude Dr	McBain	MI	49657	231-825-4144		429	*Web:* www.browndairyequip.com
Brown Distributing Co	1300 Allendale Rd	West Palm Beach	FL	33405	561-655-3791	655-3099	81-1	*Web:* www.brown.com
Brown Dog Cafe, The	1000 Summit Pl Ste A	Cincinnati	OH	45242	513-794-1610		671	*Web:* www.browndogcafe.com
Brown Engineering Co	5525 Meredith Dr Ste D	Des Moines	IA	50310	515-331-1325		261	*Web:* brownengineeringcompany.com
Brown Family Law Group PLC	9201 N 25th Ave Ste 250	Phoenix	AZ	85021	602-589-5110		41	*Web:* brucedbrownlaw.com
Brown Financial Services Group	1930 Del Paso Rd Ste 122	Sacramento	CA	95834	916-928-2207		690	*Web:* brownfsg.com
Brown Flying School Inc	6898 N Clinton St	Terre Haute	IN	47805	812-466-2229	466-7428	685	*Web:* www.brownflyingschool.com
Brown Foundation, The	2217 Welch St	Houston	TX	77019	713-523-6867	523-2917	305	*Web:* www.brownfoundation.org
Brown Fox Books	1090 Eugenia Pl Ste 102	Carpinteria	CA	93013	805-684-5951	684-1628	637-2	*Web:* www.brownfoxbooks.com
Brown Gibbons Lang & Company LLC	1375 E Ninth St Ste 2500	Cleveland	OH	44114	216-241-2800		403	*Web:* www.bglco.com
Brown Graham & Company PC	7431 Continental Pkwy	Amarillo	TX	79114	806-355-8241	355-6415	2	*Web:* www.bgc-cpa.com
Brown Greer PLC	250 Rocketts Way	Richmond	VA	23231	804-521-7200	521-7299	445	*Web:* browngreer.com
Brown Hay & Stephens LLP	205 S Fifth St Ste 700	Springfield	IL	62701	888-666-8491	544-9609*	445	**Fax Area Code:* 217 ■ *TF:* 888-666-8491 ■ *Web:* www.bhslaw.com
Brown Hotel, The	335 W Broadway St	Louisville	KY	40202	502-209-7346		379	*Web:* www.brownhotel.com
Brown Industrial Inc	311 W S St	Botkins	OH	45306	937-693-3838	693-4121	516	*Web:* brownindustrial.com
Brown Industries Inc	205 W Industrial Blvd	Dalton	GA	30720	706-277-1977		627	*Web:* www.brownind.com
Brown International Corporation LLC	333 Ave M NW	Winter Haven	FL	33881	863-299-2111	299-2688	296	*Web:* www.brown-intl.com
Brown Investment Advisory & Trust Co	901 S Bond St Ste 400	Baltimore	MD	21231	410-537-5400		401	*TF:* 800-645-3923 ■ *Web:* www.brownadvisory.com
Brown Jordan Co	9860 Gidley St	El Monte	CA	91731	626-279-5537		319-4	*TF:* 800-743-4252 ■ *Web:* www.brownjordan.com
Brown Jug	4140 Old Seward Hwy	Anchorage	AK	99503	907-563-3008		81-1	*Web:* www.brownjugalaska.net
Brown Law Firm PC	315 N 24th St	Billings	MT	59101	406-248-2611		41	*Web:* brownfirm.com
Brown Law PLLC	109 N Henry St Ste 203	Alexandria	VA	22314	703-778-6531		41	*Web:* brownlawpllc.com
Brown Machine LLC	330 N Ross St	Beaverton	MI	48612	989-435-7741		146	*TF:* 877-702-4142 ■ *Web:* brownmachinegroup.com
Brown Machine Works Inc	8459 Wards Rd	Rustburg	VA	24588	434-821-5008	821-4805	454	*Web:* www.brownmachine.com
Brown Mackie College	3454 Douglas Rd	South Bend	IN	46635	574-237-0774	237-3585	800	*TF:* 800-743-2447 ■ *Web:* www.brownmackie.edu
Brown Manufacturing Corp	6001 E Hwy 27	Ozark	AL	36360	800-633-8909	795-3029*	273	**Fax Area Code:* 334 ■ *TF:* 800-633-8909 ■ *Web:* www.brownmfgcorp.com
Brown Metals Co	8635 White Oak Ave	Rancho Cucamonga	CA	91730	909-484-3124		492	*Web:* www.brownmetals.com
Brown Packing Company Inc	116 Willis St	Gaffney	SC	29341	864-489-5723		296-26	*Web:* www.brownpacking.com
Brown Palace Hotel	321 17th St	Denver	CO	80202	303-297-3111		379	*TF:* 800-321-2599 ■ *Web:* www.brownpalace.com
Brown Parker & Demarinis Adv	1825 NW Corporate Blvd Ste 250	Boca Raton	FL	33431	276-770-1206		4	*Web:* bpdadvertising.com
Brown Precision Inc	90 Shields Rd	Huntsville	AL	35811	256-746-0533	746-0511	21	*Web:* www.brownprecisioninc.com
Brown Produce Co	IL Hwy 37	Farina	IL	62838	618-245-3301		619	*Web:* www.illinois.food-us.org
Brown Room at Congress Hall	25 Jackson St	Cape May	NJ	08204	609-884-8421		377	*Web:* www.caperesorts.com
Brown Schultz Sheridan & Fritz	210 Grandview Ave	Camp Hill	PA	17011	717-761-7171	737-6655	2	*Web:* www.bssf.com
Brown Sherrod (Sen D - OH)	503 Hart Senate Office Bldg	Washington	DC	20510	202-224-2315	228-6321	342-2	*Web:* www.brown.senate.gov
Brown Smith Wallace LLC	6 Cityplace Dr Ste 900	Saint Louis	MO	63141	314-983-1200		390	*Web:* www.bswllc.com
Brown Sprinkler Corp	4705 Pinewood Rd	Louisville	KY	40218	502-968-6274		189-10	*Web:* www.brownsprinkler.com

Phone | Fax | Class

Brown Stove Works Inc
1422 Carolina Ave PO Box 2490 Cleveland TN 37320 423-476-6544 476-6599 36
TF: 800-251-7485 ■ *Web:* www.brownstoveworksinc.com
Brown Strauss Inc 2495 Uravan St Aurora CO 80011 303-371-2200 492
TF: 800-677-2778 ■ *Web:* brownstrauss.com
Brown Sugar Cafe 1033 Commonwealth Ave Boston MA 02215 617-787-4242 671
Web: www.brownsugarcafe.com
Brown Swiss Cattle Breeders Association of the USA
800 Pleasant St Beloit WI 53511 608-365-4474 365-5577 48-2
Web: www.brownswissusa.com
Brown University 45 Prospect St Providence RI 02912 401-863-2378 863-9300 166
Web: www.brown.edu
Brown Vs Board of Education National Historic Site
1515 SE Monroe St Topeka KS 66612 785-354-4273 354-7213 564
Web: www.nps.gov
Brown Wood Preserving Company Inc
6201 Camp Ground Rd Louisville KY 40216 502-448-2337 448-9944 818
TF: 800-537-1765 ■ *Web:* www.bwpole.com
Brown Wood Products Co
7040 N Lawndale Ave Lincolnwood IL 60712 800-328-5858 884-0423 820
TF: 800-328-5858 ■ *Web:* www.brownwoodinc.com
Brown's Cleaners
1223 Montana Ave Santa Monica CA 90403 310-451-8531 426
Web: www.brownscleaners.net
Brown's Wharf Inn
121 Atlantic Ave Boothbay Harbor ME 04538 207-633-5440 379
TF: 800-334-8110 ■ *Web:* www.brownswharfinn.com
Brown, Lisle/Cummings Inc
1 Turks Head Pl Ste 800 Providence RI 02903 401-421-8900 690
Web: brownlc.com
Brown-Atchison Electric Cooperative Association Inc
1712 Central Ave PO Box 230 Horton KS 66439 785-486-2117 245
Web: www.baelectric.com
Brown-Campbell Co
11800 Investment Dr Shelby Township MI 48315 800-472-8464 884-2181* 492
**Fax Area Code:* 586 ■ *TF:* 800-472-8464 ■ *Web:* www.brown-campbell.com
Browne & Co
505 Apple Creek Blvd Unit 2 Markham ON L3R5B1 905-475-6104 849-4719* 300
**Fax Area Code:* 866 ■ *TF:* 866-300-3072 ■ *Web:* www.browneco.com
Browne & Miller Literary Associates LLC
52 Village Pl Hinsdale IL 60521 312-922-3063 444
Web: www.browneandmiller.com
Browne Academy 5917 Telegraph Rd Alexandria VA 22310 703-960-3000 685
Web: www.browneacademy.org
Browne Foodservice
1122 US Rt 22 Ste 203 Mountainside NJ 07092 973-232-1065 232-1066 300
TF: 888-289-1005 ■ *Web:* brownefoodservice.com
Brown-Eagle Group Inc
5330 Dijon Dr Baton Rouge LA 70808 225-769-1111 769-1175 260
Web: www.browneagle.com
Brownell World Travel
216 Summit Blvd Ste 220 Birmingham AL 35243 205-802-6222 771
TF: 800-999-3960 ■ *Web:* www.brownelltravel.com
Brownfield Ag News
505 Hobbs Rd Jefferson City MO 65109 573-893-5700 893-8094 647
Web: www.brownfieldagnews.com
Brown-Forman 850 Dixie Hwy Louisville KY 40210 502-585-1100 774-7188 185
NYSE: BFA ■ *TF:* 800-831-9146 ■ *Web:* www.brown-forman.com
Brown-Heatly Library 4900 N Lamar Blvd Austin TX 78751 512-424-4240 434-3
Web: www.main.org
Brownie Baker, The
4870 W Jacquelyn Ave Fresno CA 93722 559-277-7070 297-8
Web: www.browniebaker.com
Browning Arms Co 1 Browning Pl Morgan UT 84050 801-876-2711 229
TF: 800-333-3288 ■ *Web:* www.browning.com
Browning Equipment Inc
800 E Main St Purcellville VA 20132 540-338-7123 338-5035 274
Web: www.browningequipment.com
Browning Kaleczyc Berry & Hoven P C
800 N Last Chance Gulch Ste 101 Helena MT 59601 406-443-6820 453-1634 445
Web: www.bkbh.com
Browning School Inc 52 E 62nd St New York NY 10065 212-838-6280 355-5602 685
Web: www.browning.edu
Brownlee Distributing Company Inc
34401 Groesbeck Hwy Clinton Township MI 48035 586-792-9100 54
Brownlee Fryett 396 11th Ave SW 7th Fl Calgary AB T2R0C5 403-232-8408 428
TF: 800-661-9069 ■ *Web:* brownleelaw.com
Brownlee Lighting Inc
4600 Dardanelle Dr Orlando FL 32808 407-297-3677 297-3705 439
TF: 800-318-6768 ■ *Web:* www.brownlee.com
Brownley Julia (Rep D - CA)
2262 Rayburn House Office Bldg Washington DC 20515 202-225-5811 225-1100 342-2
Web: juliabrownley.house.gov
Brownlie & Braden LLC
2820 Ross Tower 500 N Akard Dallas TX 75201 214-219-4650 194
TF: 888-339-4650 ■ *Web:* www.brownliebraden.com
Brownlow gifts 6309 Airport Fwy Fort Worth TX 76117 817-831-3831 831-7025 637-2
TF: 800-433-7610 ■ *Web:* www.brownlowgift.com
Browns Corner Short Stop
5550 Auburn Way S Auburn WA 98092 253-833-7185 297-8
Browns Medical Imaging 9880 Pflumm Rd Lenexa KS 66215 800-701-9729 475
TF: 800-701-9729 ■ *Web:* www.brownsmedicalimaging.com
Brownson Technical School
1110 Technology Cir Ste D Anaheim CA 92805 800-799-9891 685
TF: 800-799-9891 ■ *Web:* www.brownson.edu
Brownstein Group Inc
215 S Broad St Philadelphia PA 19107 215-735-3470 7
Web: m.brownsteingroup.com
Brownstone Agency Inc
32 Old Slip 8th Fl New York NY 10005 212-962-5620 742-7934 390
Web: brownstoneagency.com
Brownstone Furniture
3435 Regatta Blvd Richmond CA 94804 510-236-0703 236-0772 321
Web: www.brownstonefurniture.com
Brownstone House 351 W Broadway Paterson NJ 07522 973-595-8582 671
Web: thebrownstone.com
Brownstone Real Estate Co
1840 Fishburn Rd Hershey PA 17033 717-533-6222 652
TF: 877-533-6222 ■ *Web:* www.brwnstone.com

Brownstown Electric Supply Company Inc
690 E State Rd 250 Brownstown IN 47220 800-742-8492 787
TF: 800-742-8492 ■ *Web:* www.brownstown.com
Brownstown Sports Ctr
21902 Telegraph Rd Brownstown Charter Township MI 48183 734-676-5500 711
Web: www.brownstownsportscenter.com
Brownsville Area School Dist
5 Falcon Dr Brownsville PA 15417 724-785-2021 785-4333 685
Web: www.basd.org
Brownsville Chamber of Commerce
1600 University Blvd Brownsville TX 78520 956-542-4341 504-3348 139
Web: brownsvillechamber.com
Brownsville City Hall
1001 E Elizabeth St Brownsville TX 78520 956-548-6000 546-4021 337
Web: www.cob.us
Brownsville Convention & Visitors Bureau
650 Ruben M Torres Sr Blvd Brownsville TX 78521 956-546-3721 206
TF: 800-626-2639 ■ *Web:* brownsville.org
Brownsville Herald, The
1135 E Van Buren St Brownsville TX 78520 956-542-4301 542-0840 532-2
TF: 800-488-4301 ■ *Web:* www.brownsvilleherald.com
Brownsville Independent School District
1900 Price Rd Brownsville TX 78521 956-548-8000 574-6497 685
Web: www.bisd.us
Browntown-Cadiz Springs State Recreation Area
PO Box 36 Browntown WI 53522 608-966-3777 565
Web: www.cadizsprings.com
Browntrout Publishers Inc
201 Continental Blvd El Segundo CA 90245 310-607-9010 607-9011 637-2
TF: 800-777-7812 ■ *Web:* www.browntrout.com
Brown-Wilbert Inc
2280 Hamline Ave N Saint Paul MN 55113 800-672-0709 134
TF: 800-672-0709 ■ *Web:* www.brownwilbert.com
Brownwinick Law Firm
666 Grand Ave Ruan Ctr Des Moines IA 50309 515-242-2400 41
TF: 888-282-3515 ■ *Web:* brownwinick.com
Brownwood Area Chamber of Commerce
600 E Depot St Brownwood TX 76801 325-646-9535 643-6686 139
Web: www.brownwoodchamber.org
Brownwood Public Library
600 Carnegie Blvd Brownwood TX 76801 325-646-0155 646-6503 434-3
Web: www.brownwoodpubliclibrary.com
Brownwood Regional Medical Ctr
1501 Burnet Dr Brownwood TX 76801 325-646-8541 374-3
Web: www.brmc-cares.com
Brox Industries Inc 1471 Methuen St Dracut MA 01826 978-454-9105 805-9720 188-4
Web: www.broxindustries.com
Broydrick and Associates
1150 Connecticut Ave NW Ste 615 Washington DC 20036 202-637-0637 888-7458 317
Web: www.broydrick.com
Broyhill Asset Management LLC
800 Hickory Blvd SW Lenoir NC 28645 828-610-5360 401
Web: www.broyhillasset.com
Broyhill Co
1 N Market Sq PO Box 475 Dakota City NE 68731 402-987-3412 987-3601 273
TF: 800-228-1003 ■ *Web:* www.broyhill.com
Broyhill Furniture Industries Inc
3483 Hickory Blvd Hudson NC 28638 800-225-0265 319-2
TF: 800-225-0265 ■ *Web:* www.broyhillfurniture.com
Broyles Kight & Ricafort PC
8250 Haverstick Rd Ste 100 Indianapolis IN 46240 317-571-3600 428
TF: 888-834-2692 ■ *Web:* www.bkrlaw.com
BRP (Bombardier Recreational Products)
565 de la Montagne Valcourt QC J0E2L0 450-532-2211 710
Web: www.brp.com
BRP Manufacturing Co 637 N Jackson St Lima OH 45801 419-228-4441 222-5010 676
TF: 800-858-0482 ■ *Web:* brpmfg.com
BRProud 10000 Perkins Rd Baton Rouge LA 70810 225-766-3233 768-9293 741-13
Web: www.brproud.com
BRS Produce 6700 Essington Ave Philadelphia PA 19153 215-336-5454 297-7
Web: brs-produce-company.business.site
BRT Apartments Corp
60 Cutter Mill Rd Ste 303 Great Neck NY 11021 516-466-3100 509
NYSE: BRT ■ *TF:* 800-450-5816 ■ *Web:* brtapartments.com
BRT Extrusions Inc 1818 N Main St Niles OH 44446 330-544-0244 544-0377 492
Web: www.brtextrusions.com
Brubacher Excavating Inc
825 Reading Rd Bowmansville PA 17507 717-445-4571 445-7789 189-5
Web: www.brubacher.net
Brubaker & Associates Inc
7626 Hammerly Blvd Houston TX 77055 713-464-4666 464-4669 196
Web: www.brubakerandassociates.com
Brubaker-Mann Inc 36011 Soap Mine Rd Barstow CA 92311 760-256-2520 256-0127 500
Web: www.brubakermann.com
Bruccoli Clark Layman Inc (BCL)
2006 Sumter St Columbia SC 29201 803-771-4642 799-6953 637-2
Web: lpppub.com
Bruce & Merrilees Electric Co
930 Cass St New Castle PA 16101 724-652-5566 652-8290 189-4
TF: 800-652-5560 ■ *Web:* www.bruceandmerrilees.com
Bruce Aerospace 101 Evans Ave Dayton NV 89403 775-246-0101 438
Web: www.bruce.aero
Bruce Clay Inc
2245 First St Ste 101 Simi Valley CA 93065 805-517-1900 517-1919 225
TF: 866-517-1900 ■ *Web:* bruceclay.com
Bruce E. Brooks & Associates Inc
2209 Chestnut St Philadelphia PA 19103 215-569-0400 261
Web: www.brucebrooks.com
Bruce Foods Corp
221 Southpark Plz PO Box 1030 LaFayette LA 70508 337-365-8101 369-9026 296-20
TF: 800-299-9082 ■ *Web:* brucefoods.com
Bruce Fox Inc 1909 McDonald Ln New Albany IN 47150 812-945-3511 777
Web: brucefox.com
Bruce Hersh CPA Accountancy Corp
17547 Ventura Blvd Encino CA 91316 818-905-0533 2
Web: www.brucehershcpa.com
Bruce Junior High 111 Bruce St Gilmer TX 75645 903-841-7600 685
Web: www.gilmerisd.org

	Phone	Fax	Class
Bruce Mau Design Inc 340 King St E Ste 500 . . . Toronto ON M5A1K8 *Web:* www.brucemaudesign.com	416-306-6401		344
Bruce Mckittrick Rare Books Inc 43 Sabine Ave . . . Narberth PA 19072 *Web:* mckittrickrarebooks.com	610-660-0132		95
Bruce Michael Redlin CPA LLC 2323 S 109th St Ste 135 . . . West Allis WI 53227 *Web:* www.accountingmilwaukee.com	414-543-1550		194
Bruce Museum of Arts & Science 1 Museum Dr . . . Greenwich CT 06830 *Web:* brucemuseum.org	203-869-0376	869-0963	520
Bruce Nilson Associates Inc 3511 N Front St Ste 201 . . . Harrisburg PA 17110 *Web:* www.futuredirection.com	717-232-1515		194
Bruce Squire Law LLC 1212 E Baseline Rd Ste 105 . . . Tempe AZ 85283 *TF:* 888-412-6896 ■ *Web:* brucesquirelaw.com	480-247-3890		41
Bruce Supply Corp 8805 18th Ave . . . Brooklyn NY 11214 *Web:* www.brucesupplyplumbing.com	718-259-4900	256-5082	612
Bruce Telecom 3145 Hwy 21 PO Box 80 . . . Tiverton ON N0G2T0 *TF:* 866-517-2000 ■ *Web:* www.brucetelecom.com	519-368-2000		736
Brucemore 2160 Linden Dr SE . . . Cedar Rapids IA 52403 *Web:* www.brucemore.org	319-362-7375		50-3
Bruceton Farm Service Inc (BFS) 116 Shannon Dr . . . Morgantown WV 26508 *Web:* www.bfscompanies.com	304-291-6980	291-6984	297-8
Bruckmann Rosser Sherrill & Company LLC 126 E 56th St 29th Fl . . . New York NY 10022 *Web:* www.brs.com	212-521-3700	521-3799	360-3
Bruderer Machinery Inc 1200 Hendricks Cswy . . . Ridgefield NJ 07657 *Web:* www.brudereramericas.com	201-941-2121	886-2010	456
Bruegger's Enterprises 8008 Herb Kelleher Way Love Field Terminal Bldg . . . Dallas TX 75235 *Web:* www.brueggers.com	972-629-9255		68
Bruel & Kjaer 3079 Premiere Pkwy Ste 120 . . . Duluth GA 30097 *Web:* www.bksv.com	770-209-6907	448-3246	248
Brueton Industries Inc 146 Hanse Ave . . . Freeport NY 11520 *TF:* 800-221-6783 ■ *Web:* www.brueton.com	516-379-3400	543-4520	319-2
Bruin Plastics Company Inc 61 Joslin Rd . . . Glendale RI 02826 *TF:* 800-556-7764 ■ *Web:* www.bruinplastics.com	401-568-3081	568-0019	600
Bruker Daltonics Inc 40 Manning Rd . . . Billerica MA 01821 *TF:* 800-672-7676 ■ *Web:* www.bruker.com	978-663-3660	667-5993	419
Brule County 300 S Courtland St Ste 111 . . . Chamberlain SD 57325 *TF:* 866-592-0846 ■ *Web:* brulecounty.org	605-734-4580		338
Brule River State Forest 6250 S Ranger Rd . . . Brule WI 54820 *Web:* dnr.wi.gov	715-372-5678		565
Brulin Holding Co 2920 Dr AJ Brown Ave . . . Indianapolis IN 46205 *TF:* 800-776-7149 ■ *Web:* bhcinc.com	317-923-3211	925-4596	145
Brumback Library 215 W Main St . . . Van Wert OH 45891 *Web:* www.brumbacklib.com	419-238-2168	238-3180	434-3
Bruml Capital Corp 1801 E Ninth St Ste 1620 . . . Cleveland OH 44114	216-771-6660	771-6673	690
Brumlow Mills Inc 734 S River St PO Box 1779 . . . Calhoun GA 30701 *TF:* 855-427-8656 ■ *Web:* www.brumlowcarpet.com	855-427-8656		131
Brumm & Associates Inc 257 S Fair Oaks Ave Ste 204 . . . Pasadena CA 91105 *Web:* brummassociates.com	626-219-7002		2
Brundage Jewelers Inc 141 Chenoweth Ln . . . Louisville KY 40207 *Web:* brundagejewelers.com	502-895-7717		410
Brundage Management Company Inc 254 Spencer Ln . . . San Antonio TX 78201 *Web:* www.brundagemgt.com	210-735-9393		803-1
Bruneau Dunes State Park 27608 Sand Dunes Rd . . . Mountain Home ID 83647 *Web:* parksandrecreation.idaho.gov	208-366-7919		565
Brunei Darussalam *Embassy* 3520 International Ct NW . . . Washington DC 20008 *Web:* www.bruneiembassy.org	202-237-1838	885-0560	257
Bruner Corp 3637 Lacon Rd . . . Hilliard OH 43026 *Web:* www.brunercorp.com	614-334-9000	334-9001	14
Brunet Island State Park 23125 255th St . . . Cornell WI 54732 *Web:* dnr.wi.gov	715-239-6888		565
Brunet-Garcia Advertising Inc 1510 Hendricks Ave . . . Jacksonville FL 32207 *TF:* 866-346-1977 ■ *Web:* www.brunetgarcia.com	904-346-1977		7
Bruning & Federle Manufacturing Co 2503 Northside Dr . . . Statesville NC 28625 *Web:* www.bruning-federle.com	704-873-7237		18
Bruning Law Firm, The 555 Washington Ave Ste 600A . . . Saint Louis MO 63101 *Web:* bruninglegal.com	314-735-8100		41
Brunini 190 E Capitol St The Pinnacle Bldg Ste 100 . . . Jackson MS 39201 *Web:* www.brunini.com	601-948-3101		445
Brunk House 5705 Salem-Dallas Hwy NW . . . Salem OR 97304 *Web:* www.polkcountyhistoricalsociety.org	503-371-8586		50-3
Brunk Industries Inc 1225 Sage St PO Box 310 . . . Lake Geneva WI 53147 *Web:* www.brunk.com	262-248-8873		483
Brunkenhoefer, PC Injury Attorneys 500 N Shoreline Blvd Ste 1100 . . . Corpus Christi TX 78401 *Web:* www.brunklaw.com	361-254-8021		41
Brunner Inc 11 Stanwix St 5th Fl . . . Pittsburgh PA 15222 *Web:* www.brunnerworks.com	412-995-9500		7
Brunner International Inc 3959 Bates Rd . . . Medina NY 14103 *Web:* www.brunnerinc.com	585-798-6000		516
Bruno Skorheim 9665 Chesapeake Dr Ste 470 . . . San Diego CA 92123 *Web:* www.brunoskorheim.com	858-300-3141	300-3142	2
Bruno's 9462 N MacArthur Blvd . . . Irving TX 75063 *Web:* www.brunosristorante.com	972-556-2465		671
Bruns Gutzwiller Construction Co 305 John St . . . Batesville IN 47006 *Web:* www.bruns-gutzwiller.com	812-934-2105	934-2107	189-7
Brunsell Bros Ltd 4611 W Beltline Hwy . . . Madison WI 53711 *Web:* brunsell.com	608-275-7171		364
Brunson Instrument Co 8000 E 23rd St . . . Kansas City MO 64129 *TF:* 877-632-7873 ■ *Web:* www.brunson.us	816-483-3187	241-1945	544
BRUNS-PAK Corp 999 New Durham Rd . . . Edison NJ 08817 *TF:* 888-704-1400 ■ *Web:* bruns-pak.com	732-248-4455	248-3644	261
Brunswick & The Golden Isles of Georgia Visitors Bureau 529 Beachview Dr . . . Saint Simons Island GA 31522 *TF:* 800-933-2627 ■ *Web:* www.goldenisles.com	912-638-9014		206
Brunswick Area Chamber of Commerce PO Box 192 . . . Brunswick MD 21716 *Web:* gbacc.net	240-415-8790		139
Brunswick Bank & trust 439 Livingston Ave . . . New Brunswick NJ 08901 *Web:* www.brunswickbank.com	732-247-5800		360-2
Brunswick Boat Group 1st Tennessee Plz Bldg 800 S Gay St Ste 1200 . . . Knoxville TN 37929 *Web:* brunswick.com	865-582-2200	582-2301	90
Brunswick City School District 3643 Center Rd . . . Brunswick OH 44212 *Web:* www.bcsoh.org	330-225-7731	273-0507	685
Brunswick Community College 50 College Rd . . . Bolivia NC 28422 *TF:* 800-754-1050 ■ *Web:* www.brunswickcc.edu	910-755-7300		162
Brunswick Corp *Mercury Marine Div* W 6250 Pioneer Rd . . . Fond du Lac WI 54935 *TF:* 866-408-6372 ■ *Web:* www.mercurymarine.com	920-929-5040		262
Brunswick Corporation Sea Ray Group 26125 N Riverwoods Blvd Ste 500 . . . Mettawa IL 60045 *Web:* www.brunswick.com	847-735-4700	735-4765	90
Brunswick County 30 Government Center Dr NE . . . Bolivia NC 28422 *TF:* 800-442-7033 ■ *Web:* www.brunswickcountync.gov	910-253-2657	253-2022	338
Brunswick County 228 N Main St . . . Lawrenceville VA 23868 *Web:* www.brunswickco.com	434-848-3107	848-4307	338
Brunswick County Board of Education 35 Referendum Dr . . . Bolivia NC 28422 *TF:* 800-662-7030 ■ *Web:* www.bcswan.net	910-253-2900		685
Brunswick County Chamber of Commerce 114 Wall St . . . Shallotte NC 28459 *TF:* 800-426-6644 ■ *Web:* brunswickcountychamber.org	910-754-6644		139
Brunswick County Library 109 W Moore St . . . Southport NC 28461 *Web:* www.brunswickcountync.gov	910-457-6237	371-1856	434-3
Brunswick Cove Inc 1478 River Rd SE . . . Winnabow NC 28479 *Web:* www.brunswickcove.com	910-371-9894		186
Brunswick Electric Membership Corp 795 Ocean Hwy PO Box 826 . . . Shallotte NC 28459 *TF:* 800-842-5871 ■ *Web:* www.bemc.org	910-754-4391	755-4299	245
Brunswick Floors 3550 Darien Hwy . . . Brunswick GA 31525 *Web:* brunswickfloors.com	912-265-0222		191-4
Brunswick Historical Society (BHS) PO Box 1776 . . . Cropseyville NY 12052 *Web:* www.bhs-ny.org	518-279-4024		48-6
Brunswick Instrument LLC 21535 County Hwy X . . . Kiel WI 53042 *Web:* www.brunswickinstrument.com	920-894-1176		493
Brunswick Laboratories LLC 200 Turnpike Rd . . . Southborough MA 01772 *Web:* brunswicklabs.com	508-281-6660		743
Brunswick News PO Box 1557 . . . Brunswick GA 31521 *Web:* thebrunswicknews.com	912-265-8320	280-0926	532-2
Brunswick School Inc 100 Maher Ave . . . Greenwich CT 06830 *TF:* 800-546-9425 ■ *Web:* brunswickschool.org	203-625-5800		41
Brunswick-Glynn County Library 208 Gloucester St . . . Brunswick GA 31520 *Web:* www.moglibraries.org	912-279-3740	261-3849	434-3
Brunswick-Golden Isles Chamber of Commerce 1505 Richmond St 2nd Fl . . . Brunswick GA 31520 *Web:* www.brunswickgoldenisleschamber.com	912-265-0620	265-0629	139
Brunton Enterprises Inc 8815 S Sorensen Ave . . . Santa Fe Springs CA 90670 *Web:* www.plas-tal.com	562-945-0013	696-7620	189-14
Brush Art Corp 343 W US Hwy 24 . . . Downs KS 67437 *Web:* www.brushart.com	785-454-3383		7
Brush Creek Ranch 66 Brush Creek Ranch Rd . . . Saratoga WY 82331 *Web:* www.brushcreekranch.com	307-327-5284		239
Brush Research Manufacturing Company Inc 4642 Floral Dr . . . Los Angeles CA 90022 *TF:* 800-572-6501 ■ *Web:* brushresearch.com	323-261-2193	268-6587	103
Brushes Corp 5400 Smith Rd . . . Cleveland OH 44142 *Web:* www.malinco.com	216-267-8084	267-9077	103
Brushfire Inc 2 Wing Dr . . . Cedar Knolls NJ 07927 *Web:* www.brushfireinc.com	973-871-1700		4
Brushfoil LLC 1 Shoreline Dr Unit 6 . . . Guilford CT 06437 *TF:* 800-493-2321 ■ *Web:* www.brushfoil.com	203-453-7403		601
Brushtech Inc 4 Matt Ave . . . Plattsburgh NY 12901 *Web:* brushtechbrushes.com	518-563-8420	563-0581	103
Brushy Creek State Recreation Area 2820 Brushy Creek Rd . . . Lehigh IA 50557 *Web:* www.iowadnr.gov	515-543-8298	843-8395	565
Bruss North American Inc 600 Progress Dr . . . Russell Springs KY 42642 *Web:* www.bruss.de	270-858-2600		247
Brutger Equities Inc 100 4th Ave S PO Box 399 . . . Saint Cloud MN 56302 *Web:* brutgerequities.com	320-252-6262		377

Company / Address	City	State	ZIP	Phone	Fax	Class
Bruton & Berube PLLC 601 Central Ave *Web:* brutonlaw.com	Dover	NH	03820	603-749-4529	343-2986	41
Brutzkus Gubner 21650 Oxnard St Ste 500 *Web:* www.bg.law	Woodland Hills	CA	91367	818-827-9000	827-9099	41
Bry-Air Inc 10793 SR 37 W *TF:* 877-427-9247 ■ *Web:* www.bry-air.com	Sunbury	OH	43074	740-965-2974	965-5470	14
Bryan Broadcasting Inc 2700 Rudder Fwy Ste 5000 *Web:* www.bryanbroadcasting.com	College Station	TX	77845	979-695-9595	695-1933	647
Bryan City School District 1350 Fountain Grove Dr *Web:* www.bryan.k12.oh.us	Bryan	OH	43506	419-636-6973	633-6280	48-11
Bryan College 140 Landes Way *TF:* 800-277-9522 ■ *Web:* www.bryan.edu	Dayton	TN	37321	423-775-2041	775-7199	166
Bryan Company Inc PO Box 379 *Web:* thebryancompany.com	Jackson	NH	03846	603-383-8200		757
Bryan Construction Co 1007 N Earl Rudder Fwy *Web:* www.bryan-construction-co.com	Bryan	TX	77802	979-776-6000	776-6008	186
Bryan County 402 W Evergreen St *Web:* ltap.okstate.edu	Durant	OK	74701	580-924-2202	924-3094	338
Bryan County 51 N Courthouse St *Web:* www.bryancountyga.org	Pembroke	GA	31321	912-653-5252	653-4691	338
Bryan Health 1600 S 48th St *TF:* 800-742-7844 ■ *Web:* www.bryanhealth.com	Lincoln	NE	68506	402-481-7333		374-3
Bryan Hospital 433 W High St *Web:* www.chwchospital.org	Bryan	OH	43506	419-636-1131	630-2155	374-3
Bryan Michaels State Farm Insurance 219 E Broadway *Web:* bryanmichaels.net	Bel Air	MD	21014	410-638-0101		390
Bryan Steam LLC 783 Chili Ave *Web:* bryanboilers.com	Peru	IN	46970	765-473-6651	473-3074	91
Bryan Systems 14020 US 20A Hwy *TF:* 800-745-2796 ■ *Web:* www.bryansystems.com	Montpelier	OH	43543	800-745-2796		780
Bryan University 4255 S Nature Center Way *TF:* 855-500-0850 ■ *Web:* www.bryanu.edu	Springfield	MO	65804	417-862-5700		700
Bryan W. Whitfield Memorial Hospital 105 Hwy 80 E PO Box 890 *TF:* 800-453-2395 ■ *Web:* www.bwwmh.com	Demopolis	AL	36732	334-289-4000		374-3
Bryan World Productions PO Box 74033 *Web:* www.graffitiverite.com	Los Angeles	CA	90004	323-856-9256		514
Bryan+College Station Public Library System 201 E 26th St *Web:* www.bcslibrary.org	Bryan	TX	77803	979-209-5600		434-3
Bryan-College Station Chamber of Commerce 4001 E 29th St Ste 175 *Web:* www.bcschamber.org	Bryan	TX	77802	979-260-5200		139
Bryan-College Station Eagle 1729 Briarcrest Dr *TF:* 800-299-7355 ■ *Web:* www.theeagle.com	Bryan	TX	77802	979-776-4444		532-2
Bryant Asset Protection Inc 1280 New Scotland Rd *TF:* 800-439-6051 ■ *Web:* bryantasset.com	Slingerlands	NY	12159	518-439-1141	475-0030	390
Bryant Bureau 18600 Florence St Ste C-1 *Web:* bryantbureau.net	Roseville	MI	48066	586-772-6452	772-6788	260
Bryant Chastain Insurance Agency Inc 720 W Broadway *Web:* bryantchastain.com	Bolivar	MO	65613	417-326-5825		390
Bryant Christie Inc 1418 Third Ave Ste 300 *Web:* www.bryantchristie.com	Seattle	WA	98101	206-292-6340	292-6341	196
Bryant Grinder 65 Pearl St	Springfield	VT	05156	802-885-5161	885-9444	455
Bryant Katt & Associates PC 6211 O St *Web:* www.bka-cpa.com	Lincoln	NE	68510	402-486-1040	489-8150	2
Bryant Label Company Inc 2240 Hwy 75 *Web:* www.bryantlabel.com	Blountville	TN	37617	423-323-5440	323-6671	554
Bryant Park Hotel 40 W 40th St *TF:* 877-640-9300 ■ *Web:* www.bryantparkhotel.com	New York	NY	10018	212-869-0100	869-4446	379
Bryant Rubber Corp 1112 Lomita Blvd *Web:* www.bryantrubber.com	Harbor City	CA	90710	310-530-2530	530-9143	605-3
Bryant Staffing 377 Hoes Ln *Web:* www.bryantstaffing.com	Piscataway	NJ	08854	732-981-0440	981-0248	260
Bryant University 1150 Douglas Pk *TF:* 800-622-7001 ■ *Web:* www.bryant.edu	Smithfield	RI	02917	401-232-6000	232-6741	166
Bryce Canyon National Park PO Box 640201 *Web:* www.nps.gov	Bryce Canyon	UT	84764	435-834-5322	834-4102	564
Bryce Corp 4505 Old Lamar Ave *TF:* 800-238-7277 ■ *Web:* www.brycecorp.com	Memphis	TN	38118	901-369-4400		548
BryCoat Inc 207 Vollmer Ave *TF:* 800-989-8788 ■ *Web:* www.brycoat.com	Oldsmar	FL	34677	727-490-1000		550
Brycon Corp 134 Rio Rancho Blvd NE *Web:* www.brycon.com	Rio Rancho	NM	87124	505-892-6163		186
Brydan Solutions Inc 8550 W Desert Inn Rd Ste 102-176 *Web:* www.brydansolutions.com	Las Vegas	NV	89117	702-966-2774	966-2758	175
Bryley Systems Inc 12 Main St *Web:* www.bryley.com	Hudson	MA	01749	978-562-6077		175
BryLin Hospitals 1263 Delaware Ave *TF:* 800-727-9546 ■ *Web:* www.brylin.com	Buffalo	NY	14209	716-886-8200		374-5
Bryn Mawr Bank Corp 801 Lancaster Ave *NASDAQ: BMTC* ■ *Web:* www.bmt.com	Bryn Mawr	PA	19010	610-525-1700	520-7278	360-2
Bryn Mawr Capital Management Inc 1 Town Pl Ste 200 *Web:* www.brynmawrcap.com	Bryn Mawr	PA	19010	484-380-8100	380-8150	194
Bryn Mawr College 101 N Merion Ave *Web:* www.brynmawr.edu	Bryn Mawr	PA	19010	610-526-5000	526-7471	166
Bryn Mawr Commentaries Inc (BMC) 101 N Merion Ave *Web:* bmcr.brynmawr.edu	Bryn Mawr	PA	19010	610-526-7475		166
Bryn Mawr Jewelry Company Inc 1125 W Bryn Mawr Ave *Web:* brynmawrjewelry.com	Chicago	IL	60660	773-271-6263		410
Brynwood Partners 8 Sound Shore Dr Ste 265 *Web:* www.brynwoodpartners.com	Greenwich	CT	06830	203-622-1790	622-0559	402
Brytex Building Systems Inc 5610 97 St *Web:* brytex.com	Edmonton	AB	T6E3J1	780-437-7970		186
BS & B Safety Systems LLC 7455 E 46th St *Web:* www.bsbsystems.com	Tulsa	OK	74145	918-622-5950	665-3904	789
BS Xpress Inc 4703 S 169 Hwy **Fax Area Code:* 816 ■ *TF:* 800-821-9016 ■ *Web:* www.dbrant.com	Saint Joseph	MO	64507	800-821-9016	364-5482*	780
BSA (Boy Scouts of America) 1325 W Walnut Hill Ln PO Box 152079 *TF:* 800-323-0732 ■ *Web:* www.scouting.org	Irving	TX	75015	972-580-2000		48-15
BSA Life Structures 9365 Counselors Row *Web:* www.bsalifestructures.com	Indianapolis	IN	46240	317-819-7878		261
BSC (Business Systems Consulting) 15 Lincoln St *Web:* www.bizsysconsulting.com	Wakefield	MA	01880	781-683-4040		196
BSC America Inc 803 Bel Air Rd *TF:* 800-764-7400 ■ *Web:* www.bscamerica.com	Bel Air	MD	21014	800-764-7400		463
BSCAI (Building Service Contractors Association Intl) 330 N Wabash Ave Ste 2000 **Fax Area Code:* 312 ■ *TF:* 800-368-3414 ■ *Web:* www.bscai.org	Chicago	IL	60611	800-368-3414	673-6735*	49-13
BSG Team Ventures Inc 224 Clarendon St Ste 41 *Web:* www.bostonsearchgroup.com	Boston	MA	02116	617-266-4333		260
BSI (Badger State Industries) 3099 E Washington Ave PO Box 8990 *TF:* 800-862-1086 ■ *Web:* buybsi.com	Madison	WI	53708	608-240-5200	240-3320	630
BSI (Building Service Inc) W222 N630 Cheaney Rd *Web:* buildingservice.com	Waukesha	WI	53186	262-955-6400		393
BSI (Biostat International Inc) 13014 N Dale Mabry Hwy Ste 745 *Web:* biostatinternational.com	Tampa	FL	33613	813-979-1619	979-1519	194
BSI (Business Software Inc) 155 Technology Pky Ste 100 Peachtree *TF:* 888-293-3413 ■ *Web:* www.bsi.com	Norcross	GA	30092	770-449-3200		178-1
BSI Constructors Inc 6767 SW Ave *Web:* www.bsistl.com	Saint Louis	MO	63143	314-781-7820	781-1354	186
BSK & Assoc 550 W Locust Ave *TF:* 800-669-3201 ■ *Web:* www.bskassociates.com	Fresno	CA	93650	559-497-2880	497-2864	261
BSM A Geotab Co 75 International Blvd Ste 100 *TF:* 866-768-4771 ■ *Web:* www.bsmtechnologies.com	Toronto	ON	M9W6L9	866-768-4771		178-11
Bsm Engineering 865 NE Tomahawk Island Dr Ste 101 *Web:* bsmengineering.com	Portland	OR	97217	503-325-8065		261
BSM Media Inc 1002 NE First St *Web:* www.bsmmedia.com	Pompano Beach	FL	33060	954-261-2145		195
BSN Medical Inc 5825 Carnegie Blvd *TF:* 800-552-1157 ■ *Web:* www.bsnmedical.com	Charlotte	NC	28209	704-554-9933		477
BSP (Bright Sky Press) 2365 Rice Blvd Ste 202 *TF:* 866-933-6133 ■ *Web:* www.brightskypress.com	Houston	TX	77005	713-533-9300	528-2432	637-2
BSQUARE Corp 110 110th Ave NE Ste 300 *NASDAQ: BSQR* ■ *TF:* 888-820-4500 ■ *Web:* www.bsquare.com	Bellevue	WA	98004	425-519-5900		178-2
BST (Billings Studio Theatre) 1500 Rimrock Rd *Web:* www.billingsstudiotheatre.com	Billings	MT	59102	406-248-1141		572
BT Bones 193 Honeybee Dr Ste 300	Branson	MO	65616	417-335-2002		671
BT Conferencing Inc 30 Braintree Hill Office Pk Ste 301 *TF:* 866-766-8777 ■ *Web:* www.btconferencing.com	Braintree	MA	02184	617-801-6700		360-3
BT Mancini Company Inc *Brookman Div* 876 S Milpitas Blvd *Web:* www.btmancini.com	Milpitas	CA	95036	408-942-7900		186
BTA (Business Technology Assn) 12411 Wornall Rd Ste 200 *TF:* 800-325-7219 ■ *Web:* www.bta.org	Kansas City	MO	64145	816-941-3100		49-18
BTA Oil Producers LLC 104 S Pecos *Web:* www.btaoil.com	Midland	TX	79701	432-682-3753		536
BTAS 4391 Dayton-Xenia Rd Ste 210 *Web:* btas.com	Beavercreek	OH	45432	937-431-9431	431-9413	194
BTC 1450 N Jim Wright Fwy Ft Worth *Web:* btcbuilds.com	White Settlement	TX	76108	817-467-4981	467-5619	186
BTC (Bledsoe Telephone Co-opeartive Corp) 338 Cumberland Ave PO Box 609 *Web:* bledsoe.net	Pikeville	TN	37367	423-447-2121	447-2498	736
BTC (Blossom Telephone Co) 145 Center St *Web:* www.blossomtel.net	Blossom	TX	75416	903-982-6211		224
BTC (Brain Technologies Corp) PO Box 358655 **Fax Area Code:* 888 ■ *Web:* www.braintechnologies.com	Gainesville	FL	32635	352-792-1036	639-2814*	637-2
BTD Manufacturing 1111 13th Ave SE *TF:* 866-562-3986 ■ *Web:* www.btdmfg.com	Detroit Lakes	MN	56501	866-562-3986		488
BTE Technologies Inc 7455-L New Ridge Rd *TF:* 800-331-8845 ■ *Web:* www.btetech.com	Hanover	MD	21076	410-850-0333		250
B-tec Solutions Inc 913 Cedar Ave *Web:* www.btecsolutions.com	Croydon	PA	19021	215-785-2400		454
BTECH Inc 10 Astro Pl *Web:* www.btechinc.com	Rockaway	NJ	07866	973-983-1120		74
BTF Enterprises Inc 3121 Park Ave Ste C *Web:* www.btfenterprises.com	Soquel	CA	95073	831-464-4880	464-4881	47
BTI (Bonneville Transloaders Inc) 642 S Federal Blvd *Web:* www.bonntran.com	Riverton	WY	82501	307-856-7480	856-4623	648
BTI (Benchmark Technologies International Inc) 411 Hackensack Ave *TF:* 800-265-8254 ■ *Web:* btiworld.com	Hackensack	NJ	07601	201-996-0077		194

Name / Address	City	State	ZIP	Phone	Fax	Class
BTI (Brian Taylor International LLC) 100 Cheshire Dr *Fax Area Code: 404 ■ Web: www.btillc.com	Griffin	GA	30223	770-294-4653	506-9835*	393
BTI (Bork Transportation of Illinois) 7735 W 59th St TF: 800-397-2675 ■ Web: www.borktransport.com	Summit	IL	60501	708-594-5551		780
BTIG LLC 600 Montgomery St 6th Fl Web: www.btig.com	San Francisco	CA	94111	415-248-2200		690
BTL Machine 1168 Sherborn St	Corona	CA	92879	951-808-9929		454
BTM Global Consulting 330 S Second Ave Ste 450 Web: www.btmglobal.com	Minneapolis	MN	55401	612-238-8800		225
BTM Solutions Inc 572 Yorkville Rd E TF: 800-909-9381 ■ Web: www.btmsolutions.com	Columbus	MS	39702	662-328-2400		177
BTR Capital Management Inc 550 Kearny St Ste 510 Web: www.btrcap.com	San Francisco	CA	94108	415-989-0100		528
BTS (Brazilian Travel Service) 16 W 46th St 2nd Fl TF: 800-342-5746 ■ Web: www.btstravel.com	New York	NY	10036	212-764-6161	719-4142	16
BTS Asset Management Inc 420 Bedford St Ste 340 TF: 800-343-3040 ■ Web: www.btsmanagement.com	Lexington	MA	02420	800-343-3040		401
BTS Consulting Group Ltd 355 Glen Arms Dr Web: btsconsultinggroup.com	Danville	CA	94526	925-837-1730		196
BTS USA Inc 222 Kearny St Ste 1000 TF: 800-445-7089 ■ Web: www.bts.com	San Francisco	CA	94108	415-362-4200	449-6119	194
BTSB (Bound to Stay Bound Books Inc) 1880 W Morton Ave *Fax Area Code: 800 ■ TF: 800-637-6586 ■ Web: www.btsb.com	Jacksonville	IL	62650	217-245-5191	747-2872*	92
BTU International Inc 23 Esquire Rd NASDAQ: BTUI ■ TF: 800-998-0666 ■ Web: www.btu.com	North Billerica	MA	01862	978-667-4111	667-9068	695
BTU Management Inc 534 La Crosse St Web: btumanagement.com	Mauston	WI	53948	608-847-4600		189-10
Bubba Gump Shrimp Co 401 Biscayne Blvd Web: www.bubbagump.com	Miami	FL	33132	305-379-8866		671
Bubba's 100 Flat Creek Dr Web: bubbasjh.com	Jackson	WY	83001	307-733-2288		671
Bubble Technology Industries Inc 31278 Hwy 17 Web: bubbletech.ca	Chalk River	ON	K0J1J0	613-589-2456		639
BubbleLife Media LLC 7850 Collin McKinney Pkwy Ste 300 Web: www.bubblelife.com	McKinney	TX	75070	214-233-0740		5
Buca Inc 1204 Harmon Pl Web: bucadibeppo.com	Minneapolis	MN	55403	612-288-0138	341-0496	670
Buca's Tuscan Roadhouse 4 Depot Rd Web: www.bucastuscanroadhouse.com	Harwich	MA	02645	508-432-6900		671
Buccaneer State Park 1150 S Beach Blvd Web: www.mdwfp.com	Waveland	MS	39576	228-467-3822		565
Buchalter Nemer Pc 1000 Wilshire Blvd Web: www.buchalter.com	Los Angeles	CA	90017	213-891-0700	896-0400	428
Buchanan Automotive Group 707 S Washington Blvd TF: 888-349-4989 ■ Web: buchananautogroup.com	Sarasota	FL	34236	888-349-4989		57
Buchanan County 1012 Walnut St Ste 104 Web: www.buchanancountyonline.com	Grundy	VA	24614	276-935-6550	935-1802	338
Buchanan County 210 Fifth Ave NE Web: www.buchanancountyiowa.org	Independence	IA	50644	319-334-5989		338
Buchanan County 411 Jules St Web: www.co.buchanan.mo.us	Saint Joseph	MO	64501	816-271-1437	271-1535	338
Buchanan County Public Library 1185 Poe Town St Web: bcplnet.org	Grundy	VA	24614	276-935-5721	935-6292	434-3
Buchanan General Hospital (BGH) 1535 Slate Creek Rd Web: www.bgh.org	Grundy	VA	24614	276-935-1000	935-1354	374-3
Buchanan Hardwoods Inc 600 Baptist Line Rd Web: www.buchananhardwoods.com	Aliceville	AL	35442	205-373-8710	373-6982	291
Buchanan Hauling & Rigging 4625 Industrial Rd TF: 888-544-4285 ■ Web: www.buchananhauling.com	Fort Wayne	IN	46825	260-471-1877		780
Buchanan Ingersoll & Rooney PC 301 Grant St 1 Oxford Ctr 20th Fl Web: www.bipc.com	Pittsburgh	PA	15219	412-562-8800	562-1041	428
Buchanan Metal Forming Inc (BMF) 103 W Smith St Web: www.bmfcorp.com	Buchanan	MI	49107	269-695-3836	695-3830	483
Buchanan Technologies Inc 1026 Texan Trl TF: 888-730-2774 ■ Web: www.buchanan.com	Grapevine	TX	76051	972-869-3966	869-3975	180
Buchanan Vern (Rep R - FL) 2427 Rayburn House Office Bldg Web: buchanan.house.gov	Washington	DC	20515	202-225-5015	226-0828	342-2
Buchberger & Gloudeman CPA LLC 3415 Commerce Ct Web: bgh-cpa.com	Appleton	WI	54911	920-731-6028		2
Buchbinder Tunick & Company LLP One Penn Plaza Ste 5335 Web: www.buchbinder.com	New York	NY	10119	212-695-5003	695-4638	711
Bucher & Christian Consulting Inc 9777 N College TF: 866-363-1132 ■ Web: www.bcforward.com	Indianapolis	IN	46280	866-363-1132		194
Buchheit Inc 1011 S Perryville Blvd Web: www.buchheitonline.com	Perryville	MO	63775	573-547-1010		191-2
Buck & Knobby Equipment Co 6220 Sterns Rd TF: 855-213-2825 ■ Web: www.buckandknobby.com	Ottawa Lake	MI	49267	734-856-2811	856-2709	264-3
Buck Company Inc 897 Lancaster Pk Web: www.buckcompany.com	Quarryville	PA	17566	717-284-4114	284-3737	307
Buck Distributing Company Inc 15827 Commerce Ct TF: 800-750-2825 ■ Web: www.buckdistributing.com	Upper Marlboro	MD	20774	301-952-0400		81-1
Buck Ken (Rep R - CO) 2455 Rayburn House Office Bldg Web: buck.house.gov	Washington	DC	20515	202-225-4676	225-5870	342-2
Buck Knives Inc 660 S Lochsa St TF: 800-326-2825 ■ Web: www.buckknives.com	Post Falls	ID	83854	208-262-0500		222
Buck Owens' Crystal Palace Steakhouse 2800 Buck Owens Blvd Web: www.buckowens.com	Bakersfield	CA	93308	661-328-7560		671
Buck's Pizza Franchising Corporation Inc PO Box 405 TF: 800-310-8848 ■ Web: buckspizza.com	DuBois	PA	15801	800-310-8848		670
Buck's Pocket State Park 393 County Rd 174 Web: www.alapark.com	Grove Oak	AL	35975	256-659-2000		565
Buck's Restaurant 425 W Ormsby Ave Web: www.buckslou.com	Louisville	KY	40203	502-637-5284	637-7883	671
Buckert Patent & Trademark Law Firm PC 2731 S Adams Rd Ste 109 Web: buckertlawfirm.com	Rochester Hills	MI	48309	248-853-1422	606-4298	41
Buckeye Book Fair 205 W Liberty St Web: www.buckeyebookfair.com	Wooster	OH	44691	330-262-3244		281
Buckeye Boxes Inc 601 N Hague Ave Web: www.buckeyeboxes.com	Columbus	OH	43204	614-274-8484	274-7381	66
Buckeye Broadband 5566 Southwick Blvd Web: www.buckeyebroadband.com	Toledo	OH	43614	419-724-9802	724-7074	116
Buckeye Business Products Inc 3830 Kelley Ave *Fax Area Code: 216 ■ TF: 800-837-4323 ■ Web: www.buckeyebusiness.com	Cleveland	OH	44114	800-837-4323	881-6105*	628
Buckeye Career Ctr 545 University Dr NE TF: 800-227-1665 ■ Web: www.buckeyecareercenter.org	New Philadelphia	OH	44663	330-339-2288		162
Buckeye Community Federal Credit Union 1825 S Jefferson St Web: bcfcu.coop	Perry	FL	32348	850-223-7100		219
Buckeye Corrugated Inc 822 Kumho Dr Ste 400 Web: www.bcipkg.com	Fairlawn	OH	44333	330-576-0590	576-0600	100
Buckeye Fabric Finishing Co 1260 E Main St Web: be-fabric.com	Coshocton	OH	43812	740-622-3251	622-9317	745-7
Buckeye Fire Equipment Co 110 Kings Rd Web: www.buckeyefire.com	Kings Mountain	NC	28086	704-739-7415	739-7418	482
Buckeye Hills Career Center Practical Nursing Program 351 Buckeye Hills Rd Web: www.buckeyehills.net	Rio Grande	OH	45674	740-245-5334	245-9465	167-3
Buckeye Home Health Care 7700 Paragon Rd TF: 877-291-3780 ■ Web: buckeyehomehealthcare.com	Dayton	OH	45459	937-291-3780	291-3789	363
Buckeye International Inc 2700 Wagner Pl TF: 800-321-2583 ■ Web: www.buckeyeinternational.com	Maryland Heights	MO	63043	314-291-1900	298-2850	151
Buckeye Lake State Park 2905 Liebs Island Rd Web: ohiodnr.gov	Millersport	OH	43046	740-467-2690		565
Buckeye Machine Fabricators Inc 610 E Lima St Web: www.buckeyemachine.com	Forest	OH	45843	419-273-2521		757
Buckeye Nissan Inc 3820 Pkwy Ln TF: 800-686-4391 ■ Web: www.buckeyenissan.com	Hilliard	OH	43026	614-771-2345		57
Buckeye Nutrition 330 E Schultz Ave TF: 800-417-6460 ■ Web: www.buckeyenutrition.com	Dalton	OH	44618	800-417-6460		447
Buckeye Pacific LLC 4386 SW Macadam Ave Ste 200 TF: 800-767-9191 ■ Web: www.buckeyepacific.com	Portland	OR	97207	503-274-2284		191-3
Buckeye Partners LP 1 Greenway Plz Ste 600 TF: 877-774-9673 ■ Web: www.buckeye.com	Houston	TX	77046	832-615-8600		597
Buckeye Payroll Services 5749 Park Center Ct Web: buckeyepayroll.com	Toledo	OH	43615	419-472-7377		2
Buckeye Power Sales Company Inc 6850 Commerce Ct Dr TF: 800-523-3587 ■ Web: buckeyepowersales.com	Blacklick	OH	43004	614-861-6000		620
Buckeye Pumps Inc 1311 Freese Works Pl TF: 866-900-7867 ■ Web: www.buckeyepumps.com	Galion	OH	44833	866-900-7867		358
Buckeye Rural Electric Co-op 4848 SR-325 PO Box 200 TF: 800-231-2732 ■ Web: www.buckeyerec.coop	Patriot	OH	45658	740-379-2025		245
Buckeye ShapeForm 555 Marion Rd TF: 800-728-0776 ■ Web: www.buckeyeshapeform.com	Columbus	OH	43207	614-445-8433	445-8224	254
Buckeye Tools & Supply Company Inc 400 Gargrave Rd Web: www.buckeyetools.com	Dayton	OH	45449	937-847-8888		351
Buckfire & Buckfire PC 29000 Inkster Rd Ste 150 TF: 800-606-1717 ■ Web: buckfirelaw.com	Southfield	MI	48034	248-569-4646		41
Buckham Memorial Library 11 Div St E TF: 800-658-2354 ■ Web: www.ci.faribault.mn.us	Faribault	MN	55021	507-334-2089		434-3
Buckhannon-Upshur Chamber of Commerce 14 E Main St Web: www.buchamber.com	Buckhannon	WV	26201	304-472-1722		139
Buckhead Capital Management LLC 3100 Cumberland Blvd Ste 1450 Web: buckheadcapital.com	Atlanta	GA	30339	404-720-8800	720-8802	401
Buckhead Life Restaurant Group 265 Pharr Rd NE Web: www.buckheadrestaurants.com	Atlanta	GA	30305	404-237-2060		670
Buckhorn Inc 55 W Techne Center Dr TF: 800-543-4454 ■ Web: www.buckhorninc.com	Milford	OH	45150	513-831-4402	831-5474	199
Buckhorn Lake State Resort Park 4441 Ky Hwy 1833 TF: 800-325-0058 ■ Web: parks.ky.gov	Buckhorn	KY	41721	606-398-7510		565

Name / Address	City	State	ZIP	Phone	Fax	Class
Buckhorn Saloon & Museum 318 E Houston St *Web:* www.buckhornmuseum.com	San Antonio	TX	78205	210-247-4000	247-4020	520
Buckhorn State Park W8450 Buckhorn Park Ave *Web:* dnr.wi.gov	Necedah	WI	54646	608-565-2789		565
Buckingham & Company Inc 6856 Loop Rd *Web:* buckinghamfinancial.com	Dayton	OH	45459	937-435-2742		690
Buckingham Branch Railroad Co PO Box 336 *Web:* buckinghambranch.com	Dillwyn	VA	23936	434-983-3300		649
Buckingham Browne & Nichols School 46 Belmont St *Web:* www.bbns.org	Watertown	MA	02472	617-547-6100		685
Buckingham Correctional Ctr 1349 Correctional Center Rd *Web:* vadoc.virginia.gov	Dillwyn	VA	23936	434-983-4400		213
Buckingham County 13360 W James Anderson Hwy *TF:* 800-440-6116 ■ *Web:* buckinghamcountyva.org	Buckingham	VA	23921	434-969-4242	969-1638	338
Buckingham Hotel 101 W 57th St *Web:* www.tripadvisor.com.au	New York	NY	10019	212-246-1500		379
Buckingham's BBQ 2002 S Campbell Ave *Web:* buckinghambbq.com	Springfield	MO	65807	417-886-9979		671
Buckingham's Restaurant & Oasis 2820 W Hwy 76 *TF:* 800-725-2236 ■ *Web:* clarionhotelbranson.com	Branson	MO	65616	417-337-7777		671
Buckland Telephone Co 105 S Main St *Web:* www.btccom.net	Buckland	OH	45819	419-657-2222		224
Buckle Inc 2407 W 24th St *NYSE:* BKE ■ *TF:* 800-626-1255 ■ *Web:* www.buckle.com	Kearney	NE	68845	308-236-8491	236-4493	157-4
Buckles-Smith 540 Martin Ave *TF:* 800-833-7362 ■ *Web:* www.buckles-smith.com	Santa Clara	CA	95050	408-280-7777		246
Buckley Associates Inc 385 King St *Web:* www.buckleyonline.com	Hanover	MA	02339	781-878-5000	871-9435	14
Buckley Energy Group Ltd 154 Admiral St *TF:* 800-937-2682 ■ *Web:* www.santaenergy.com	Bridgeport	CT	06605	800-937-2682		310
Buckley Gent Macdonald & Cary PC 100 Great Oaks Blvd Ste 121 *Web:* bgmccpa.com	Albany	NY	12203	518-437-0430	437-1157	2
Buckley Graphics Inc 4980 Monroe St *TF:* 800-525-1075 ■ *Web:* www.buckleygraphics.com	Denver	CO	80216	303-321-6833	388-7585	393
Buckley Industries Inc 1850 E 53rd St N *TF:* 800-835-2779 ■ *Web:* www.buckleyind.com	Wichita	KS	67219	316-744-7587	744-8463	603
Buckley Oil Company Inc 1809 Rock Island St *TF:* 800-721-4147 ■ *Web:* www.buckleyoil.com	Dallas	TX	75207	214-421-4147		581
Buckley Powder Co 42 Inverness Dr E *TF:* 800-333-2266 ■ *Web:* www.buckleypowder.com	Englewood	CO	80112	303-790-7007		268
Buckley School, The 3900 Stansbury Ave *TF:* 800-655-1610 ■ *Web:* www.buckley.org	Sherman Oaks	CA	91423	818-783-1610		685
Buckley's 5355 Poplar Ave *Web:* www.buckleysgrill.com	Memphis	TN	38119	901-683-4538		671
Buckley, Mendleson & Criscione PC 29 Wards Ln *Web:* bmcqlaw.com	Albany	NY	12204	518-449-3107		41
Buckley, Miller, Wright & Raizk 145 N South St *Web:* bmwlaw.net	Wilmington	OH	45177	937-382-0946		41
Bucklin Tractor & Implement Co 115 W Railroad PO Box 127 *TF:* 800-334-4823 ■ *Web:* www.btiequip.com	Bucklin	KS	67834	620-826-3271	826-3760	273
Buckman Enochs Coss & Assoc 590 Enterprise Dr *Web:* becsearch.com	Lewis Center	OH	43035	614-825-6215		260
Buckman Laboratories Inc 1256 N McLean Blvd *Web:* www.buckman.com	Memphis	TN	38108	901-278-0330	276-5343	145
Buckman, Buckman & Reid Inc 44 Church St *Web:* buckmanbuckman.com	Little Silver	NJ	07739	732-530-0303		690
Bucknell University 701 Moore Ave *Web:* www.bucknell.edu	Lewisburg	PA	17837	570-577-2000		166
Buckner Intl 700 N Pearl St Ste 1200 *TF:* 800-442-4800 ■ *Web:* www.buckner.org	Dallas	TX	75201	214-758-8000		48-6
Bucks County 55 E Ct St *TF:* 888-942-8257 ■ *Web:* www.buckscounty.org	Doylestown	PA	18901	215-348-6000		338
Bucks County Community College 275 Swamp Rd *Web:* www.bucks.edu	Newtown	PA	18940	215-968-8000	968-8110	162
Bucks County Conference & Visitors Bureau (BCCVB) 3207 St Rd *Web:* www.visitbuckscounty.com	Bensalem	PA	19020	215-639-0300	642-3277	206
Bucks County Free Library 150 S Pine St *Web:* www.buckslib.org	Doylestown	PA	18901	215-348-9081	348-4760	434-3
Bucks County Genealogical Society (BCGS) PO Box 826 *Web:* www.bucksgen.org	Washington Crossing	PA	18977	215-345-0210		49-19
Bucks County Water & Sewer Authority (BCWSA) 1275 Almshouse Rd **Fax Area Code:* 267 ■ *TF:* 800-222-2068 ■ *Web:* www.bcwsa.net	Warrington	PA	18976	215-343-2538	200-0339*	806
Buckskin Mountain State Park 5476 N US Hwy 95 *Web:* azstateparks.com	Parker	AZ	85344	928-667-3231		565
Bucktail State Park c/o Region 1 Ofc 260 Sizerville Rd *Web:* www.dcnr.pa.gov	Emporium	PA	15834	814-486-3365		565
Bucshon Larry (Rep R - IN) 2313 Rayburn House Office Bldg *Web:* bucshon.house.gov	Washington	DC	20515	202-225-4636	225-3284	342-2
Bucyrus Precision Tech Inc 200 Crossroads Blvd *Web:* www.bucyrusprecisiontech.com	Bucyrus	OH	44820	419-563-9950	563-9949	60
Bud Industries Inc 4605 E 355th St *Web:* www.budind.com	Willoughby	OH	44094	440-946-3200	951-4015	254
Bud K. Worldwide 475 US Hwy 319 S *Web:* www.budk.com	Moultrie	GA	31768	229-985-1667		350
Bud Weiser Motors Inc 2676 Milwaukee Rd *Web:* www.budweisermotors.com	Beloit	WI	53511	608-466-4172		57
Bud Werner Memorial Library 1289 Lincoln Ave *Web:* www.steamboatlibrary.org	Steamboat Springs	CO	80487	970-879-0240		434-3
Bud's Best Cookies Inc 2070 Pkwy Office Cir *Web:* www.budsbestcookies.com	Hoover	AL	35244	205-987-4840		297-8
Bud's Seafood Grill 314 Lincoln Ctr *Web:* www.budsseafood.com	Stockton	CA	95207	209-956-0270		671
Budco 2004 N Yellowood Ave **Fax Area Code:* 888 ■ *Web:* www.budcocable.com	Broken Arrow	OK	74012	918-252-3420	827-5625*	73
Budco Inc PO Box 3065 *TF:* 800-747-7307 ■ *Web:* budcobank.com	Tulsa	OK	74101	800-747-7307		459
Budd Bay Cafe 525 Columbia St NW *Web:* www.buddbaycafe.com	Olympia	WA	98501	360-357-6963		671
Budd Larner PC 150 John F Kennedy Pkwy CN	Short Hills	NJ	07078	973-379-4800	379-7734	428
Budd Ted (Rep R - NC) 118 Cannon House Office Bldg *Web:* www.budd.house.gov	Washington	DC	20515	202-225-4531		342-2
Budd Van Lines 24 Schoolhouse Rd *TF:* 800-833-2833 ■ *Web:* www.buddvanlines.com	Somerset	NJ	08873	800-833-2833		519
Buddakan 325 Chestnut St *Web:* buddakan.com	Philadelphia	PA	19106	215-574-9440	574-8994	671
Buddhist Churches of America (BCA) 1710 Octavia St *Web:* www.buddhistchurchesofamerica.org	San Francisco	CA	94109	415-776-5600	771-6293	48-20
Buddy Davis Yachts 801 Philadelphia Ave PO Box 702 *Web:* www.eggharboryachts.us	Egg Harbor City	NJ	08215	609-965-2300	965-3517	90
Buddy Group Inc, The 7 Studebaker *Web:* www.thebuddygroup.com	Irvine	CA	92618	949-468-0042		5
Buddy H. Coffey CPA PC PO Box 1029	Dalton	GA	30720	706-226-7924		2
Buddy Moore Trucking Inc 925 34th St N **Fax Area Code:* 205 ■ *TF:* 877-366-6566 ■ *Web:* www.buddymooretrucking.com	Birmingham	AL	35222	877-366-6566	327-5178*	780
Buddy Rogers Music Inc 6891 Simpson Ave *TF:* 800-536-2263 ■ *Web:* www.buddyrogers.com	Cincinnati	OH	45239	513-729-1950	728-6010	526
Buddy's Bar-B-Q 5806 Kingston Pk *Web:* buddysbarbq.com	Knoxville	TN	37919	865-584-1924	588-7211	670
Buddy's Home Furnishings 4705 S Apopka Vineland Rd *TF:* 855-298-9325 ■ *Web:* www.buddyrents.com	Orlando	FL	32819	866-779-5058		264-2
Buddy's Italian Restaurant 626 E Lewis St *Web:* www.buddysitalian.com	Pocatello	ID	83201	208-233-1172		671
Buddy's Kitchen Inc 12105 Nicollet Ave *Web:* buddyskitchen.com	Burnsville	MN	55337	952-894-2540		296-36
Budget *House Budget Committee* 207 Cannon House Office Bldg *Web:* www.budget.house.gov	Washington	DC	20515	202-226-7270		342-1
Budget 1 Hour Signs Inc 2535 E Indian School Rd *Web:* budgetsignsaz.com	Phoenix	AZ	85016	602-955-4686	957-3032	701
Budget Blinds Inc 1927 N Glassell St *TF:* 800-800-9250 ■ *Web:* www.budgetblinds.com	Orange	CA	92865	714-637-2100		87
Budget Finance Co 1849 Sawtelle Blvd *TF:* 800-225-6267 ■ *Web:* www.bfcloans.com	Los Angeles	CA	90025	310-696-4050		217
Budget Host Inn 116 Kenyon Rd W *Web:* budgethost.com	Fort Dodge	IA	50501	515-955-8501		379
Budget Host Intl 2307 Roosevelt Dr *TF:* 800-283-4678 ■ *Web:* www.budgethost.com	Arlington	TX	76016	817-861-6088	861-6089	379
Budget Rent A Car System Inc 6 Sylvan Way *TF:* 800-283-4382 ■ *Web:* www.budget.com	Parsippany	NJ	07054	800-283-4382		126
Budget Suites of America 3500 NE Loop 820 *Web:* www.budgetsuites.com	Grand Prairie	TX	75050	972-647-2500		379
BudgetSurf PO Box 22310 *TF:* 866-440-0419 ■ *Web:* www.budgetsurf.com	Salt Lake City	UT	84122	866-440-0419		681
Budney Industries Inc PO Box 8316 *Web:* www.budney.com	Berlin	CT	06037	860-828-1950	828-7528	21
Budreck Truck Lines Inc 2642 Joseph Ct *TF:* 800-621-0013 ■ *Web:* www.budreck.com	University Park	IL	60484	708-496-0522	496-0568	186
Buds Salads 2428 Harrison Ave *Web:* budssalads.com	Dallas	TX	75215	214-428-1200		345
Budzar Industries Inc 38241 Willoughby Pkwy *Web:* www.budzar.com	Willoughby	OH	44094	440-918-0505		201
BUECI (Barrow Utilities & Electric Co-opeartive Inc) 1295 Agvik St PO Box 449 *Web:* www.bueci.org	Barrow	AK	99723	907-852-6166		245
Buecomp Inc 7016 S State Rte 19 *Web:* buecomp.com	Bloomville	OH	44818	419-284-3840	284-3881	604
Buehler Cos 16456 E Airport Cir Ste 100 *TF:* 800-234-6683 ■ *Web:* www.buehlercompanies.com	Aurora	CO	80011	303-388-4000	388-0296	519
Buehler Engineering Inc 600 Q St Ste 200 *Web:* buehlerengineering.com	Sacramento	CA	95811	916-443-0303		261
Buehler Food Markets Inc 1401 Old Mansfield Rd *TF:* 800-998-4438 ■ *Web:* www.buehlers.com	Wooster	OH	44691	330-264-4355		345
Buehler Ltd 41 Waukegan Rd *TF:* 800-283-4537 ■ *Web:* www.buehler.com	Lake Bluff	IL	60044	847-295-6500	295-7979	419
Buehler Motor Inc 860 Aviation Pkwy Ste 300 *Web:* www.buehlermotor.com	Morrisville	NC	27560	919-380-3333	380-3256	518

Name / Address	Phone	Fax	Class
Buehler Planetarium & Observatory 3501 SW Davie Rd .... Davie FL 33314 *Web:* www.broward.edu	954-201-6681		598
Buell Consulting Inc 1360 Energy Park Dr Ste 210 .... Saint Paul MN 55108 *Web:* www.buellconsulting.com	651-361-8110		180
Buena Park Convention & Visitors Office 6601 Beach Blvd......................... Buena Park CA 90621 *TF:* 800-541-3953 ■ *Web:* www.visitbuenapark.com	800-541-3953		206
Buena Park Downtown 8308 On The Mall......................... Buena Park CA 90620 *Web:* www.buenaparkdowntown.com	714-503-5000	761-0748	460
Buena Vista Hospitality Group Inc 6750 Forum Dr Ste 316 .... Orlando FL 32821 *Web:* www.bvhg.com	407-352-7161	352-2413	669
Buena Vista Inn 1599 Lombard St .... San Francisco CA 94123 *TF:* 800-835-4980 ■ *Web:* www.buenavistainnsf.com	415-923-9600		378
Buena Vista Museum of Natural History and Science 2018 Chester Ave..........................Bakersfield CA 93301 *Web:* www.buenavistamuseum.org	661-324-6350	324-7522	520
Buena Vista Regional Medical Ctr PO Box 309 .... Storm Lake IA 50588 *TF:* 877-401-8030 ■ *Web:* www.bvrmc.org	712-732-4030		374-3
Buena Vista University 610 W Fourth St......................... Storm Lake IA 50588 *TF:* 800-383-9600 ■ *Web:* www.bvu.edu	712-749-2253	749-2035	166
Buescher State Park PO Box 75 .... Smithville TX 78957 *Web:* tpwd.texas.gov	512-237-2241		565
Buettner Bros Lumber Co 700 Seventh Ave SW.........................Cullman AL 35055 *Web:* www.bblumber.net	256-734-4221		817
Buff & Shine Manufacturing 2139 E Del Amo Blvd .... Rancho Dominguez CA 90220 *TF:* 800-659-2833 ■ *Web:* www.buffandshine.com	310-886-5111	886-5099	295
Buff Restaurant 2600 Canyon Blvd .... Boulder CO 80302 *Web:* www.buffrestaurant.com	303-442-9150		671
Buffa Louie's 114 S Indiana Ave .... Bloomington IN 47408 *Web:* buffalouies.com	812-333-3030	334-3945	671
Buffalo & Erie County Botanical Gardens 2655 S Park Ave.............................Buffalo NY 14218 *Web:* buffalogardens.com	716-827-1584		97
Buffalo & Erie County Naval & Military Park 1 Naval Park Cove ....Buffalo NY 14202 *Web:* buffalonavalpark.org	716-847-1773		50-4
Buffalo & Erie County Public Library 1 Lafayette Sq...............................Buffalo NY 14203 *Web:* www.buffalolib.org	716-858-8900	858-6211	434-3
Buffalo Abrasives Inc 960 Erie Ave........................North Tonawanda NY 14120 *TF:* 888-311-3856 ■ *Web:* www.buffaloabrasives.com	716-693-3856	693-4092	295
Buffalo Air Handling Co 467 Zane Snead Dr..........................Amherst VA 24521 *Web:* www.buffaloair.com	434-946-7455	946-0226	18
Buffalo Bill Center of the West 720 Sheridan Ave .... Cody WY 82414 *Web:* centerofthewest.org	307-587-4771		520
Buffalo Bill Memorial Museum 987 1/2 Lookout Mtn Rd.......................Golden CO 80401 *Web:* www.buffalobill.org	303-526-0744	526-0197	520
Buffalo Bill Ranch State Historical Park 2921 Scouts Rest Ranch Rd ....North Platte NE 69147 *Web:* outdoornebraska.gov	308-535-8035		565
Buffalo Bill's Resort & Casino 31900 Las Vegas Blvd S....................... Primm NV 89019 *TF:* 888-774-6668 ■ *Web:* www.primmvalleyresorts.com	702-386-7867		133
Buffalo Bills 1 Bills Dr.................... Orchard Park NY 14127 *TF:* 877-228-4257 ■ *Web:* www.buffalobills.com	716-648-1800		715-3
Buffalo City Hall 65 Niagara Sq ....Buffalo NY 14202 *TF:* 800-541-2437 ■ *Web:* www.buffalony.gov	716-851-4200	851-4360	337
Buffalo Computer Graphics Inc 4185 Bayview Rd .... Blasdell NY 14219 *Web:* www.buffalocomputergraphics.com	716-822-8668		180
Buffalo Conrail Federal Credit Union 1481 Harlem Rd ....Cheektowaga NY 14206 *Web:* www.bufconfcu.com	716-897-2383		219
Buffalo Corp 950 Hoff Rd................... Saint Louis MO 63132 *Web:* www.buffalotools.com	636-532-9888	537-1055	361
Buffalo County 407 S Second St.................. Alma WI 54610 *Web:* www.buffalocounty.com	608-685-6209	685-6213	338
Buffalo County Nebraska 1512 Central Ave PO Box 1270 .... Kearney NE 68848 *Web:* buffalocounty.ne.gov	308-236-1224	233-3649	338
Buffalo Dental Manufacturing Company Inc 159 Lafayette Dr .... Syosset NY 11791 *TF:* 800-828-0203 ■ *Web:* www.buffalodental.com	516-496-7200		228
Buffalo Design & Printing 2620 Elmwood Ave.......................... Kenmore NY 14217 *Web:* buffalodesignandprinting.com	716-877-9444		627
Buffalo Design Collaborative Group, The 443 Delaware Ave............................Buffalo NY 14202 *Web:* www.schneiderdesign.com	716-923-7000		226
Buffalo Engineering PC 4245 Union Rd ....Cheektowaga NY 14225 *Web:* buffaloengineering.com	716-633-5300	633-5598	261
Buffalo Feeders LLC US Hwy 64 PO Box 409 ....Buffalo OK 73834 *Web:* www.buffalofeeders.com	580-735-2511		10-1
Buffalo Filter LLC 5900 Genesee St ....Lancaster NY 14086 *TF:* 800-343-2324 ■ *Web:* www.buffalofilter.com	716-835-7000	835-3414	476
Buffalo Fire Historical Museum 1850 William St ....Buffalo NY 14206 *Web:* www.bfhsmuseum.com	716-892-8400		520
Buffalo Games Inc 220 James E Casey Dr.........................Buffalo NY 14206 *TF:* 855-895-4290 ■ *Web:* buffalogames.com	855-895-4290		762
Buffalo Grand Hotel & Event Ctr 120 Church St ....Buffalo NY 14202 *Web:* www.thebuffalogrand.com	716-845-5100		379
Buffalo Grill 1611 Rebsamen Park Rd.................... Little Rock AR 72202 *Web:* buffalogrilllr.net	501-296-9535		671
Buffalo Grove Park District 530 Bernard Dr.........................Buffalo Grove IL 60089 *Web:* bgparks.org	847-850-2100	459-5741	31
Buffalo History Museum (BHM) 1 Museum Ct..... Buffalo NY 14216 *Web:* www.buffalohistory.org	716-873-9644		637-2
Buffalo Hospital Supply Company Inc 4039 Genesee St.............................Buffalo NY 14225 *Web:* www.buffalohospital.com	716-626-9400	626-4307	475
Buffalo Industries Inc 99 S Spokane St.............................. Seattle WA 98134 *TF:* 800-683-0052 ■ *Web:* www.buffaloindustries.com	206-682-9900	682-9907	745-8
Buffalo Lodging Associates LLC 570 Delaware Ave............................Buffalo NY 14202 *Web:* www.buffalolodging.com	781-344-4435		378
Buffalo Museum of Science 1020 Humboldt Pkwy..........................Buffalo NY 14211 *TF:* 866-291-6660 ■ *Web:* www.sciencebuff.org	716-896-5200	897-6723	520
Buffalo National River 402 N Walnut St Ste 136 ....Harrison AR 72601 *TF:* 800-447-7538 ■ *Web:* www.nps.gov	870-439-2502		564
Buffalo News 200 Broadway PO Box 100 ....Buffalo NY 14240 *TF:* 800-777-8640 ■ *Web:* buffalonews.com	716-849-4444	856-5150	532-2
Buffalo Niagara Convention & Visitors Bureau 403 Main St Ste 630..........................Buffalo NY 14203 *TF:* 800-283-3256 ■ *Web:* www.visitbuffaloniagara.com	716-852-2356	852-0131	206
Buffalo Niagara Convention Ctr 153 Franklin St..............................Buffalo NY 14202 *TF:* 800-995-7570 ■ *Web:* www.buffaloconvention.com	716-855-5555	855-3158	205
Buffalo Niagara International Airport 4200 Genesee St........................Cheektowaga NY 14225 *TF:* 877-359-2642 ■ *Web:* www.buffaloairport.com	716-630-6000	630-6070	27
Buffalo Niagara Partnership 665 Main St ....Buffalo NY 14203 *TF:* 844-308-9165 ■ *Web:* www.thepartnership.org	716-566-5400	852-2761	139
Buffalo Office Interiors Inc (BOI) 1418 Niagra St ....Buffalo NY 14213 *Web:* www.boisite.com	716-883-8222	881-3359	112
Buffalo Pharmacies Inc 1479 Kensington Ave ....Buffalo NY 14215 *Web:* buffalopharmacies.com	716-832-0599	332-9310	237
Buffalo Phil's 1149 University Blvd ....Tuscaloosa AL 35401 *Web:* www.buffalophils.com	205-758-3318	758-3310	671
Buffalo Philharmonic Orchestra 499 Franklin St..............................Buffalo NY 14202 *Web:* bpo.org	716-885-0331		573-3
Buffalo Psychiatric Ctr 400 Forest Ave ....Buffalo NY 14213 *Web:* omh.ny.gov	716-885-2261	885-4852	374-5
Buffalo Public Schools 712 City Hall ....Buffalo NY 14202 *Web:* www.buffaloschools.org	716-816-3500		685
Buffalo Pumps 874 Oliver St...........North Tonawanda NY 14120 *Web:* www.buffalopumps.com	716-693-1850	693-6303	641
Buffalo Raceway 5600 McKinley Pkwy .... Hamburg NY 14075 *Web:* www.buffaloraceway.com	716-649-1280	649-0033	642
Buffalo River Services Inc 410 Old Hog Creek Rd ....Waynesboro TN 38485 *Web:* www.brstn.org	931-722-5401		393
Buffalo River State Park 565 155th St S ....Glyndon MN 56547 *Web:* www.dnr.state.mn.us	218-498-2124	498-2583	565
Buffalo Rock Co 111 Oxmoor Rd ....Birmingham AL 35209 *Web:* www.buffalorock.com	205-942-3435		81-2
Buffalo Rock State Park 1300 N 27th Rd PO Box 2034................... Ottawa IL 61350 *Web:* www2.illinois.gov	815-433-2224		565
Buffalo Run Casino 1000 Buffalo Run Blvd .... Miami OK 74354 *Web:* buffalorun.com	918-542-7140	542-7160	132
Buffalo Seminary 205 Bidwell Pkwy.............Buffalo NY 14222 *Web:* www.buffaloseminary.org	716-885-6780		165
Buffalo Services Inc 747 S Broadway St........ Mccomb MS 39648 *Web:* buffaloservices.com	601-249-3013		345
Buffalo Specialties Inc 10706 Craighead Dr ....Houston TX 77025 *TF:* 800-256-0838 ■ *Web:* buffspec.com	713-271-6107		687
Buffalo Spree Magazine 100 Corporate Pkwy Ste 220 ....Buffalo NY 14226 *TF:* 855-697-7733 ■ *Web:* www.buffalospree.com	716-783-9119	783-9983	457-22
Buffalo State College EH Butler Library 1300 Elmwood Ave............................Buffalo NY 14222 *Web:* suny.buffalostate.edu	716-878-6314	878-3134	434-6
Buffalo Supply Inc 1650A Coal Creek Dr ....LaFayette CO 80026 *TF:* 800-366-1812 ■ *Web:* buffalosupply.com	303-666-6333		238
Buffalo Veneer & Plywood 501 Sixth Ave NE ....Buffalo MN 55313 *Web:* buffaloveneerandplywood.com	763-682-1822	682-9769	613
Buffalo Wild Wings Inc 5500 Wayzata Blvd Ste 1600 ....Minneapolis MN 55416 *NASDAQ: BWLD* ■ *Web:* www.buffalowildwings.com	952-593-9943	593-9787	670
Buffalo Wire Works Co 1165 Clinton St ....Buffalo NY 14206 *TF:* 800-828-7028 ■ *Web:* www.buffalowire.com	716-826-4666	826-8271	688
Buffalo Zoological Gardens 300 Parkside Ave ....Buffalo NY 14214 *Web:* buffalozoo.org	716-837-3900		823
Buffamante Whipple Buttafaro PC 130 S Union St Ste 200 ....Olean NY 14760 *TF:* 800-233-7585 ■ *Web:* bwbcpa.com	716-372-1620	372-2316	2
Buffelen Woodworking Co 1901 Taylor Way............................ Tacoma WA 98421 *TF:* 800-423-8810 ■ *Web:* www.buffelendoor.com	253-627-1191		499
Buffington Capital Holdings LLC 8601 Ranch Rd 2222 Bldg I Ste 150............. Austin TX 78730 *Web:* mybuffington.com	512-579-4800		653

Company / Address	City	State	ZIP	Phone	Fax	Class
Buford Goff & Associates Inc 1331 Elmwood Ave; *Web:* bgainc.com	Columbia	SC	29201	803-254-6302		261
Buford Media Group LLC (BMG) 6125 Paluxy Dr; *Web:* www.mycpa.cpa.state.tx.us	Tyler	TX	75703	903-561-4411		116
Bug Off Exterminators Inc 1064 NW 54th St; *Web:* bugoffexterminatorsflorida.com	Fort Lauderdale	FL	33309	954-772-8338		577
Bugcrowd 921 Front St 1st Fl; *TF:* 888-361-9734 ■ *Web:* www.bugcrowd.com	San Francisco	CA	94111	888-361-9734		196
Buglisi Dance Theatre 229 W 42nd St Ste 502; *TF:* 800-754-0797 ■ *Web:* www.buglisi-foreman.org	New York	NY	10036	212-719-3301	719-3302	573-1
BUG-O Systems Inc 161 Hillpointe Dr; *TF:* 800-245-3186 ■ *Web:* www.bugo.com	Canonsburg	PA	15317	412-331-1776	331-0383	811
Bug-Out Service Inc 5951 Arlington Expwy; *Web:* bugoutservice.com	Jacksonville	FL	32211	904-743-8272		577
Buhl, Little, Lynwood & Harris PLC 271 Woodland Pass Ste 115; *Web:* bllhlaw.com	East Lansing	MI	48823	517-853-6900		41
Buhler Inc 13105 12th Ave N; *TF:* 800-722-7483 ■ *Web:* www.buhlergroup.com	Plymouth	MN	55441	763-847-9900	847-9911	201
Buhler Versatile Inc 1260 Clarence Ave; *Web:* www.buhlerindustries.com	Winnipeg	MB	R3T1T2	204-661-8711	654-2503	273
Build-A-Bear Workshop Inc 1954 Innerbelt Business Center Dr; *NYSE:* BBW ■ *TF:* 877-789-2327 ■ *Web:* www.buildabear.com	Saint Louis	MO	63114	877-789-2327		761
BuildASign.com 11525B Stonehollow Dr Ste 100; *Fax Area Code: 866 ■ *TF:* 800-330-9622 ■ *Web:* www.buildasign.com	Austin	TX	78758	512-374-9850	807-5867*	177
BuildBlock Building Systems LLC 9701 N Broadway Ext; *Web:* buildblock.com	Oklahoma City	OK	73114	405-840-3386		183
BuildCentral Inc 200 W Madison St Ste 1110; *Web:* www.buildcentral.com	Chicago	IL	60606	312-223-1600		5
Builder Homesite Inc 11900 Ranch Rd 620 N; *Web:* www.builderhomesite.com	Austin	TX	78750	512-371-3800		195
Builder Magazine 1 Thomas Cir NW Ste 600; *TF:* 800-325-6180 ■ *Web:* www.builderonline.com	Washington	DC	20005	202-452-0800	785-1974	457-21
BuilderGuru Contracting Inc 2124 Priest Bridge Dr Ste 14; *Web:* www.builderguru.com	Crofton	MD	21114	410-923-1379		186
Builders Design & Leasing Inc 7601 Lindbergh Dr; *Web:* www.buildersdesign.com	Gaithersburg	MD	20879	301-590-1100		393
Builders Exchange Inc, The 9555 Rockside Rd Ste 300; *TF:* 866-907-6304 ■ *Web:* www.bxohio.com	Valley View	OH	44125	216-393-6300	393-6304	463
Builders FirstSource Inc 2001 Bryan St Ste 1600; *NASDAQ:* BLDR ■ *Web:* bldr.com	Dallas	TX	75201	214-880-3500	880-3599	191-3
Builders General Supply Co 15 Sycamore Ave; *TF:* 800-570-7227 ■ *Web:* buildersgeneral.com	Little Silver	NJ	07739	800-570-7227		191-3
Builders Hardware & Specialty Company Inc 2002 W 16th St; *Web:* www.builders-hardware.net	Erie	PA	16505	814-455-4799	454-0275	191-2
Builders Hardware & Supply Company Inc 1516 15th Ave W; *TF:* 800-828-1437 ■ *Web:* www.builders-hardware.com	Seattle	WA	98119	206-281-3700		351
Builders of the Adytum Ltd (BOTA) 5101 N Figueroa St; *Web:* www.bota.org	Los Angeles	CA	90042	323-255-7141	255-4166	48-20
Builders Redi-Mix Inc 30701 W 10 Mile Rd Ste 500; PO Box 2900; *TF:* 888-988-4400 ■ *Web:* www.superiormaterialsllc.com	Farmington Hills	MI	48333	888-988-4400		182
Buildex Electronics Inc 1734 Elmhurst Rd; *Web:* www.buildexelectronics.com	Elk Grove Village	IL	60007	847-437-2299	437-0885	625
Building & Earth Sciences Inc 5545 Derby Dr; *Fax Area Code: 205 ■ *TF:* 800-775-2468 ■ *Web:* www.buildingandearth.com	Birmingham	AL	35210	800-775-2468	836-9007*	256
Building & Fire Code Academy 2420 Vantage Dr; *Fax Area Code: 847 ■ *TF:* 800-488-7057 ■ *Web:* www.bfcacademy.com	Elgin	IL	60124	800-488-7057	428-2911*	166
Building Block Computer 3209 Terminal Dr Ste 100; *TF:* 800-272-2650 ■ *Web:* www.bbcusa.com	Eagan	MN	55121	651-687-9435	687-9448	734
Building Design & Construction Magazine 3030 W Salt Creek Ln Ste 201; *Web:* www.bdcnetwork.com	Arlington Heights	IL	60005	847-954-7929	390-0408	457-21
Building Industry Credit Assn 10601 Civic Center Dr; *Fax Area Code: 213 ■ *TF:* 800-722-2422 ■ *Web:* www.bicanet.com	Rancho Cucamonga	CA	91730	909-303-2300	986-3903*	218
Building Inspector's Career Institute c/o David Goldstein 1200 Rte 130; *Web:* inspectoreducation.com	Robbinsville	NJ	08691	609-490-0022	426-1230	167-3
Building Leaders Inc PO Box 408263; *Web:* buildingleaders.com	Chicago	IL	60640	773-769-4409		261
Building Maintenance Services LLC 1542 Young St Ste 206; *Web:* bmsnationwide.com	Honolulu	HI	96826	808-983-1250	983-1245	104
Building Material Dealers Assn (BMDA) 1006 SE Grand Ave Ste 301; *TF:* 888-960-6329 ■ *Web:* www.bmda.com	Portland	OR	97214	503-208-3763		49-3
Building Owners & Managers Association Intl (BOMA) 1101 15th St NW Ste 800; *TF:* 800-426-6292 ■ *Web:* www.boma.org	Washington	DC	20005	202-408-2662	326-6377	49-17
Building Performance Institute Inc 107 Hermes Rd Ste 210; *TF:* 877-274-1274 ■ *Web:* www.bpihomeowner.org	Malta	NY	12020	518-899-2727		194
Building Products Corp 950 Freeburg Ave; *TF:* 800-233-1996 ■ *Web:* www.buildingproductscorp.com	Belleville	IL	62220	618-233-4427	233-2031	182
Building Products Plus 12317 Almeda Rd; *TF:* 800-460-8627 ■ *Web:* www.buildingproductsplus.com	Houston	TX	77045	713-434-8008	433-7068	818
Building Restoration Inc 2423 Ravine Rd; *Web:* www.gobri.com	Kalamazoo	MI	49004	269-345-0567		104
Building Service Contractors Association Intl (BSCAI) 330 N Wabash Ave Ste 2000; *Fax Area Code: 312 ■ *TF:* 800-368-3414 ■ *Web:* www.bscai.org	Chicago	IL	60611	800-368-3414	673-6735*	49-13
Building Service Inc (BSI) W222 N630 Cheaney Rd; *Web:* buildingservice.com	Waukesha	WI	53186	262-955-6400		393
Building Technology Consultants Inc 1845 E Rand Rd Ste L-100; *Web:* btc.expert	Arlington Heights	IL	60004	847-454-8800	454-8801	261
Building Trades Federal Credit Union 12080 73rd Ave N; *TF:* 800-496-2460 ■ *Web:* buildingtradescu.com	Maple Grove	MN	55369	763-315-3888		219
Buildings Consulting Group Inc (BCG) 2855 Anthony Ln S Ste 200; *Web:* www.bcgminnesota.com	Minneapolis	MN	55418	612-789-6696	789-6397	261
BuildingSearchcom Inc 90 Railway Ave; *Web:* www.buildingsearch.com	Campbell	CA	95008	408-426-8424		387
BuildingStars Inc 33 Worthington Access Dr; *TF:* 866-991-3356 ■ *Web:* www.buildingstars.com	Maryland Heights	MO	63043	314-991-3356		310
Builtrite Handlers & Attachments 530 Recycle Center Dr; *Web:* builtrite.com	Two Harbors	MN	55616	218-834-5555		295
Buker Inc 800 Main St; *Fax Area Code: 630 ■ *Web:* www.buker.com	Antioch	IL	60002	847-395-3050	868-2969*	194
Bukit Energy Inc 1436 202 - 6th Ave SW Ste 1436; *Web:* www.bukitenergy.com	Calgary	AB	T2P2R9	403-930-2250	930-2251	536
Bula Forge & Machine Inc 3001 W 121st St; *Web:* www.bulaforge.com	Cleveland	OH	44111	216-252-7600		483
Bulbman 3101 Orange Grove Ave; *TF:* 800-648-1163 ■ *Web:* bulbman.com	North Highlands	CA	95660	916-920-3234		752
Bulfinch Companies Inc 250 First Ave Ste 200; *Web:* www.bulfinch.com	Needham	MA	02494	781-707-4000	707-4001	652
Bulgaria 767 3rd Ave	New York	NY	10028	212-737-4790		784
Consulate General 121 E 62nd St; *Web:* www.bulgaria-embassy.org	New York	NY	10065	212-935-4646	319-5955	257
Bul-Go-Gi House 8813 92 St NW; *Web:* edmontonkoreanfood.com	Edmonton	AB	T6C3P9	780-466-2330		671
Bulk Carrier Services Inc (BCS) 3451 Losee Rd Ste B; *TF:* 800-414-8785 ■ *Web:* www.bulkcarrierservices.com	North Las Vegas	NV	89030	702-648-9055		311
Bulk Chemicals Inc (BCI) 1074 Stinson Dr; *TF:* 800-338-2855 ■ *Web:* www.bulkchemicals.us	Reading	PA	19605	610-926-4128	926-6125	146
Bulk Connection Inc 15 Allen St; *TF:* 800-543-2855 ■ *Web:* www.bulkconnection.com	Mystic	CT	06355	860-572-9111		311
Bulk Foodscom 3040 Hill Ave; *Web:* www.bulkfoods.com	Toledo	OH	43607	419-537-1713		345
Bulk Lift International Inc (BLI) 1013 Tamarac Dr; *TF:* 800-879-2247 ■ *Web:* www.bulklift.com	Carpentersville	IL	60110	847-428-6059	428-7180	67
Bulk Solutions Inc 4040 Waring Rd; *Web:* bulksol.com	Lakeland	FL	33811	863-248-1136		463
Bulk Transit Corp 7177 Industrial Pkwy; *TF:* 800-345-2855 ■ *Web:* www.bulktransit.com	Plain City	OH	43064	614-873-4632	873-3393	780
Bulkmatic Transport Co 2001 N Cline Ave; *Fax Area Code: 219 ■ *TF:* 800-535-8505 ■ *Web:* www.bulkmatic.com	Griffith	IN	46319	800-535-8505	972-7655*	780
Bulkmatic Transport Co 205 Butler Cir SW	Vernon	AL	35592	205-695-7132		780
BulkOfficeSupply.com 1614 Hereford Rd; *Fax Area Code: 516 ■ *TF:* 800-658-1488 ■ *Web:* www.bulkofficesupply.com	Hewlett	NY	11557	800-658-1488	252-1527*	459
Bulk-Pack Inc 1025 N Ninth St; *Web:* www.bulk-pack.com	Monroe	LA	71201	318-387-3260		100
Bull & Bear Capital Advisors LLC 6817 Southpoint Pkwy Ste 1003; *Web:* www.bullbearcapital.com	Jacksonville	FL	32216	904-363-3600	224-0441	194
Bull Auto Parts 2715 W Warren Ave; *Web:* www.bullsautoparts.com	Detroit	MI	48208	313-894-4488	894-1537	61
Bull HN Information Systems Inc 285 Billerica Rd; *Web:* www.atos.net	Chelmsford	MA	01824	978-294-6000	244-0085	180
Bull Island Realty Inc 44 Holloway Rd; *Web:* bullislandrealty.com	Poquoson	VA	24342	757-868-4663		652
Bull Marketing Group LLC 79 S Milwaukee Ave	Wheeling	IL	60090	847-520-1182		194
Bull Metal Products Inc 191 Saybrook Rd; *Web:* www.bullmetal.com	Middletown	CT	06457	860-346-9691	346-2722	286
Bull Moose Tube Co 1819 Clarkson Rd Ste 100; *TF:* 800-325-4467 ■ *Web:* www.bullmoosetube.com	Chesterfield	MO	63017	636-537-2600		490
Bull Publishing Co PO Box 1377; *TF:* 800-676-2855 ■ *Web:* www.bullpub.com	Boulder	CO	80306	303-545-6350	545-6354	637-2
Bull Ring of Santa Fe, The 150 Washington Ave; *Web:* santafebullring.com	Santa Fe	NM	87501	505-983-3328		671
Bull Shoals-White River State Park 153 Dam Overlook Ln; *TF:* 877-879-2741 ■ *Web:* www.arkansasstateparks.com	Bull Shoals	AR	72619	877-879-2741		565
Bull Wealth Management Group Inc 4100 Yonge St Ste 612; *TF:* 866-623-2053 ■ *Web:* bullwealth.com	Toronto	ON	M2P2B5	416-223-2053		690
Bull's Eye Saloon & Restaurant 3734 Kirkwood Hwy; *Web:* bullseyesaloon.com	Wilmington	DE	19808	302-633-6557		671

Name / Address	City	State	Zip	Phone	Fax	Class
Bull's Island Recreation Area 2185 Daniel Bray Hwy — Web: www.njparksandforests.org	Stockton	NJ	08559	609-397-2949		565
Bullard Abrasives Inc 6 Carol Dr. — TF: 800-227-4469 ■ Web: www.bullardabrasives.com	Lincoln	RI	02865	401-333-3000		1
Bullard Construction Inc 4371 Lindbergh — Web: www.bullardconstruction.com	Addison	TX	75001	972-661-8474	661-8985	186
Bullard Law 200 SW Market St Ste 1900 — Web: bullardlaw.com	Portland	OR	97201	503-248-1134		41
Bullard-Havens Technical High School 500 Palisade Ave — Web: bullard-havens.cttech.org	Bridgeport	CT	06610	203-579-6333	579-6904	685
Bullards Beach State Park PO Box 569 — Web: oregonstateparks.org	Bandon	OR	97411	541-347-2209		565
Bullaro & Carton PC 200 N Lasalle St Ste 2420 — Web: bullarocarton.com	Chicago	IL	60601	312-831-1000		41
Bulldog Automation 653 Riverside St — Web: bulldogautomation.com	Portland	ME	04103	207-772-9561	772-9563	261
Bulldog Bag Ltd 13631 Vulcan Way — TF: 800-665-1944 ■ Web: www.bulldogbag.com	Richmond	BC	V6V1K4	604-273-8021		601
Bulldog Federal Credit Union 580 Northern Ave — Web: bdfcu.com	Hagerstown	MD	21742	301-797-6318		219
Bulldog Hiway Express 3390 Buffalo Ave. — TF: 800-331-9515 ■ Web: www.bulldoghiway.com	Charleston	SC	29418	843-744-1651	529-3345	449
Bulldog Marine 1133 Lake Oconee Pkwy — Web: www.bulldog-marine.biz	Eatonton	GA	31024	706-923-0404		261
Bullen Cos 1640 Delmar Dr PO Box 37 — TF: 800-444-8900 ■ Web: www.bullenonline.com	Folcroft	PA	19032	610-534-8900	534-8912	151
Bullet Guard Corp 3963 Commerce Dr — TF: 800-233-5632 ■ Web: www.bulletguard.com	West Sacramento	CA	95691	916-373-0402	373-0208	320
Bullet Weights Inc 182 S Apollo Dr — TF: 800-872-0131 ■ Web: www.bulletweights.com	Alda	NE	68810	308-382-7436	382-2906	710
Bulletin Daily 211 N Main St. — Web: www.colfax.com	Colfax	WA	99111	509-397-3332		532-3
Bulletin, The 1777 Chandler Ave. — TF: 800-503-3933 ■ Web: www.bendbulletin.com	Bend	OR	97702	541-382-1811	385-5804	532-2
BulletinHealthcare 11190 Sunrise Valley Dr Ste 20 — Web: www.bulletinhealthcare.com	Reston	VA	20191	703-483-6100		225
Bulley & Andrews LLC 1755 W Armitage Ave — Web: www.bulley.com	Chicago	IL	60622	773-235-2433	235-2471	186
Bullfrog Films Inc 372 Dautrich Rd — TF: 800-543-3764 ■ Web: www.bullfrogfilms.com	Reading	PA	19606	610-779-8226		514
Bullhead Area Chamber of Commerce 1251 Hwy 95 — Web: bullheadareachamber.com	Bullhead City	AZ	86429	928-754-4121	754-5514	139
Bullhorn Inc 33-41 Farnsworth St 5th Fl — TF: 800-206-7934 ■ Web: www.bullhorn.com	Boston	MA	02210	617-478-9100		177
Bullis Charter School 102 W Portola Ave — Web: bullischarterschool.com	Los Altos	CA	94022	650-947-4939		685
Bullitt County 300 S Buckman St — Web: bullitt.kysheriff.org	Shepherdsville	KY	40165	502-543-2514	543-2710	338
Bullitt County Chamber of Commerce 162 S Buckman St PO Box 1656 — Web: www.bullittchamber.org	Shepherdsville	KY	40165	502-543-6727	543-1765	139
Bullivant Houser Bailey PC 888 SW Fifth Ave Ste 300 — TF: 800-654-8972 ■ Web: www.bullivant.com	Portland	OR	97204	503-228-6351	295-0915	428
Bulloch & Bulloch Inc 309 Cash Memorial Blvd — TF: 800-339-8177 ■ Web: www.jphallexpress.com	Forest Park	GA	30297	404-762-5063		25
Bulloch County 20 Siebald St — Web: www.bullochcounty.net	Statesboro	GA	30458	912-764-6245	764-8634	338
Bulloch County Schools 150 Williams Rd Ste A — Web: bcss-ga.schoolloop.com	Statesboro	GA	30458	912-212-8500	764-8436	685
Bulloch Fertilizer Company Inc 205 W Main St — Web: bullochfertilizer.com	Statesboro	GA	30458	912-764-9084	489-2783	276
Bullock County Correctional Facility 104 Bullock Dr PO Box 5107 — Web: www.alabama.gov	Union Springs	AL	36089	334-738-5625		213
Bullock County Development Authority, The 106 Conecuh Ave E. — Web: www.unionspringsalabama.com	Union Springs	AL	36089	334-738-5411	738-5310	338
Bullock Creek Public Schools 1420 S Badour — Web: www.bcreek.k12.mi.us	Midland	MI	48640	989-631-9022	631-2882	685
Bullock's Bar-B-Que 3330 Quebec Dr — Web: www.bullocks-bbq.com	Durham	NC	27705	919-383-3211		671
Bullseye Analytics Group LLC PO Box 565 — Web: www.bullseyegroup.biz	Croton Falls	NY	10519	914-242-8288		195
Bullseye Database Marketing LLC 5546 S 104th E Ave — Web: www.bullseyedm.com	Tulsa	OK	74146	918-587-1731	587-0450	194
Bullseye Glass Co 3722 SE 21st Ave — TF: 888-220-3002 ■ Web: www.bullseyeglass.com	Portland	OR	97202	503-232-8887		329
Bullseye Strategy 110 E Broward Blvd Ste 1550 — Web: bullseyestrategy.com	Fort Lauderdale	FL	33301	954-591-8999		194
Bullseye Wholesale 1854 S MacDonald Dr — Web: www.bullseyewholesale.com	Mesa	AZ	85210	480-306-6135		44
BullseyeDisc 5247 SE 79th Ste B — TF: 800-652-7194 ■ Web: www.bullseyedisc.com	Portland	OR	97206	503-233-2313		658
Bulltick Capital Markets 701 Brickell Ave Ste 2550 — Web: bulltick.com	Miami	FL	33131	305-533-1541	533-1008	691
Bully Hill Vineyards 8043 Greyton H Taylor Memorial Dr — Web: www.bullyhillvineyards.com	Hammondsport	NY	14840	607-868-3610	868-3205	80-3
Bulova Corp Empire State Bldg 350 5th Ave — *Fax Area Code: 718 ■ TF: 800-228-5682 ■ Web: www.bulova.com	New York	NY	10118	212-497-1875	204-3546*	153
Bulow Plantation Ruins Historic State Park 3501 Old Kings Rd — Web: www.floridastateparks.org	Flagler Beach	FL	32136	386-517-2084		565
Bumble Bee Seafoods Inc PO Box 85362 — TF: 800-800-8572 ■ Web: www.bumblebee.com	San Diego	CA	92186	858-715-4000		296-13
Bumpers & Co 1104 Philadelphia Pk. — Web: bumpersco.com	Wilmington	DE	19809	302-798-3300		2
Bunbury & Associates Inc 2970 Chapel Valley Rd Ste 104 — TF: 877-233-7356 ■ Web: bunburyrealtors.com	Madison	WI	53711	608-441-7777		570
Bunches 14 1/2 N Santa Cruz Ave — Web: www.buncheslosgatos.com	Los Gatos	CA	95030	408-395-5451		292
Bunduki Publishing 39384 WCR 19. — Web: www.bundukipublishing.com	Fort Collins	CO	80524	970-686-5220		637-2
Bundy Group 24 Walnut Ave. — Web: bundygroup.com	Roanoke	VA	24016	540-342-2151		194
Bungalow 1 Letterman Dr. — Web: bungalow.com	San Francisco	CA	94129	415-501-0981		49-17
Bunge Ltd 50 Main St. — NYSE: BG ■ Web: www.bunge.com	White Plains	NY	10606	914-684-2800		296-29
Bunim/Murray Productions 6007 Sepulveda Blvd — Web: www.bunim-murray.com	Van Nuys	CA	91411	818-756-5100		514
Bunker Engineering & Construct 120 N Federal Hwy Ste 305 — Web: bunkerengineering.com	Lake Worth	FL	33460	561-585-5696		261
Bunker Hill Community College 250 New Rutherford Ave — TF: 877-218-8829 ■ Web: www.bhcc.edu	Boston	MA	02129	617-228-2000	228-2082	162
Bunker Hill Monument Charlestown Navy Yard — Web: www.nps.gov	Boston	MA	02129	617-242-5642		50-4
Bunkers International Corp 4300 W Lake Mary Blvd Ste 1010	Lake Mary	FL	32746	407-328-7757		579
Bunkie Trinite Trophies Inc 12 E Grace St — TF: 800-698-4077 ■ Web: bunkietrinitetrophies.com	Richmond	VA	23219	804-648-2416	788-4814	45
Bunnell Inc 436 Lawndale Dr — TF: 800-800-4358 ■ Web: www.bunl.com	Salt Lake City	UT	84115	801-467-0800		476
Bunnery Bakery & Restaurant, The 130 N Cache Dr — Web: www.bunnery.com	Jackson	WY	83001	307-733-5474		671
Bunn-O-Matic Corp 1400 Stevenson Dr — TF: 800-637-8606 ■ Web: www.bunn.com	Springfield	IL	62703	217-529-6601		37
Buns Over Texas 6045 SW 34th — Web: bunsovertexas.com	Amarillo	TX	79109	806-358-6808		671
Buntin Group, The 716 Division St. — Web: www.buntingroup.com	Nashville	TN	37203	615-244-5720	244-6511	4
Bunting Bearings Corp 1001 Holland Pk Blvd — TF: 888-286-8464 ■ Web: www.buntingbearings.com	Holland	OH	43528	419-866-7000	866-0653	308
Bunting Door & Hardware Company Inc 6650 Business Pkwy Ste C — Web: www.buntingdoor.com	Elkridge	MD	21075	410-574-8123	574-8171	351
Bunting Magnetics Co 500 S Spencer Ave — TF: 800-835-2526 ■ Web: buntingmagnetics.com	Newton	KS	67114	316-284-2020	283-4975	485
Bunzl Distribution 4501 W Vly Hwy E — Web: www.bunzldistribution.com	Sumner	WA	98390	253-321-3300	321-3302	96
Buon Appetito 1609 India St — Web: www.sandiegouniontribune.com	San Diego	CA	92101	619-238-9880		671
Buona Terra 2535 N California Ave — Web: www.buona-terra.com	Chicago	IL	60647	773-289-3800		671
Buona Vita Inc 1 S Industrial Blvd — Web: www.buonavitainc.com	Bridgeton	NJ	08302	856-453-7972	453-7978	297-8
BUP (Baylor University Press) 1 Bear Pl Ste 97363 — Web: www.baylorpress.com	Waco	TX	76798	254-710-3164	710-3440	637-2
Burbank Central Library 110 N Glenoaks Blvd — Web: www.burbank.lib.ca.us	Burbank	CA	91502	818-238-5600		434-3
Burbank Chamber of Commerce 200 W Magnolia Blvd — TF: 800-495-5005 ■ Web: burbankchamber.org	Burbank	CA	91502	818-846-3111	846-0109	139
Burbank Shipping Ctr 1812 W Burbank Blvd — Web: burbank-shipping-center.business.site	Burbank	CA	91506	818-846-1400		264-2
Burbank Town Ctr 201 E Magnolia Blvd — Web: www.burbanktowncenter.com	Burbank	CA	91502	818-566-8556	566-7936	460
Burbank Veterinary Center Apc 2118 W Burbank Blvd — Web: burbankvetcenter.com	Burbank	CA	91506	818-736-5334	736-5338	794
Burbank Water & Power 164 W Magnolia Blvd — Web: www.burbankwaterandpower.com	Burbank	CA	91502	818-238-3700		539
Burberry Ltd (New York) 444 Madison Ave — TF: 877-217-4085 ■ Web: us.burberry.com	New York	NY	10022	212-407-7100		157-4
Burch & Company Inc 4151 N Mulberry Dr Ste 235 — Web: www.burchco.com	Kansas City	MO	64116	816-842-4660		690
Burch & Cracchiolo PA 702 E Osborn Rd Ste 200 — Web: www.bcattorneys.com	Phoenix	AZ	85014	602-274-7611	234-0341	428
Burch Fabrics Group 4200 Brockton Dr SE — TF: 800-841-8111 ■ Web: burchfabrics.com	Grand Rapids	MI	49512	616-698-2800		594
Burch Industries Inc 21381 Charles Craft Ln PO Box 1049 — Web: www.burchindustries.com	Laurinburg	NC	28352	910-844-3688	844-3689	664
Burch Porter & Johnson PLLC 130 N Court Ave — Web: www.bpjlaw.com	Memphis	TN	38103	901-524-5000	524-5024	428

Name / Address	City	State	Zip	Phone	Fax	Class
Burchell Nursery Inc, The						
12000 Hwy 120	Oakdale	CA	95361	209-845-8733	847-0284	292
TF: 800-828-8733 ■ *Web:* www.burchellnursery.com						
Burchett Tim (Rep R - TN)						
1122 Longworth House Office Bldg	Washington	DC	20515	202-225-5435		342-2
Web: www.burchett.house.gov						
Burchfield Group Inc, The						
1295 Northland Dr Ste 350	Saint Paul	MN	55120	651-389-5640		194
TF: 800-778-1359 ■ *Web:* www.burchfieldgroup.com						
Burchfield-Penney Art Ctr						
Buffalo State College						
1300 Elmwood Ave	Buffalo	NY	14222	716-878-6011	878-6003	50-2
Web: www.burchfieldpenney.org						
Burckhardt Compression (US) Inc						
19750 FM 362 Rd	Waller	TX	77484	281-582-1050	582-1060	358
Web: www.burckhardtcompression.com						
Burco Molding Inc						
15015 Herriman Blvd	Noblesville	IN	46060	317-773-5699		608
TF: 888-883-6656 ■ *Web:* www.burco-molding.com						
Burd & Fletcher						
5151 E Geospace Dr	Independence	MO	64056	800-821-2776		101
TF: 800-821-2776 ■ *Web:* burdfletcher.com						
Burd Street Press 73 W Burd St	Shippensburg	PA	17257	717-532-2237	532-6110	637-2
TF: 888-948-6263 ■ *Web:* www.whitemane.com						
Burdeshaw Associates LLC						
11230 Waples Mill Rd Ste 105	Fairfax	VA	22030	703-567-7346		194
Web: www.burdeshaw.com						
Burdette Beckmann Inc						
5851 Johnson St	Hollywood	FL	33021	954-983-4360		123
TF: 888-575-7413 ■ *Web:* www.bbiteam.com						
Burdette Ketchum 1023 Kings Ave	Jacksonville	FL	32207	904-645-6200		7
Web: burdetteketchum.com						
Burdine-Anderson Corp						
1528 Resource Dr	Burlington	KY	41005	859-371-4985		454
Web: www.burdine-andersoninc.com						
Burdiss Lettershop Services Co						
9765 Widmer Rd	Lenexa	KS	66215	913-492-0545		5
Web: burdiss.com						
Burdman Law Group LLP						
6370 Lusk Blvd Ste F203	San Diego	CA	92121	888-350-9080		41
Web: burdmanlaw.com						
Bureau County 205 S Fifth St	Princeton	IL	61356	815-866-3606		338
Web: www.bureaucounty-il.com						
Bureau of Alcohol Tobacco Firearms & Explosives (ATF)						
650 Massachusetts Ave NW	Washington	DC	20226	202-927-8210		340-14
Web: www.atf.gov						
Boston Field Div 10 Causeway St Ste 791	Boston	MA	02222	617-557-1200	557-1201	340-14
Web: www.atf.gov						
Denver Field Div						
99 New York Ave NE	Washington	DC	20226	202-648-7080		340-14
Web: www.atf.gov						
New Orleans Field Div						
1 Galleria Blvd Ste 1700	Metairie	LA	70001	504-841-7000	841-7039	340-14
Web: www.atf.gov						
Bureau of Alcohol Tobacco Firearms & Explosives Regional Offices						
Atlanta Field Div						
2600 Century Pkwy NE	Atlanta	GA	30345	404-417-2600	417-2601	340-14
Web: www.atf.gov						
Baltimore Field Div						
31 Hopkins Plz 5th Fl	Baltimore	MD	21201	443-965-2000	965-2001	340-14
Web: www.atf.gov						
Charlotte Field Div						
6701 Carmel Rd Ste 200	Charlotte	NC	28226	704-716-1800	716-1801	340-14
Web: www.atf.gov						
Chicago Field Div						
525 W Van Buren St Ste 600	Chicago	IL	60607	312-846-7200	846-7201	340-14
Web: www.atf.gov						
Columbus Field Div						
230 West St Ste 400	Columbus	OH	43215	614-827-8400	827-8401	340-14
Web: www.atf.gov						
Dallas Field Div						
1114 Commerce St Rm 303	Dallas	TX	75242	469-227-4300	227-4330	340-14
Web: www.atf.gov						
Detroit Field Div						
1155 Brewery Pk Blvd Ste 300	Detroit	MI	48207	313-202-3400	202-3445	340-14
Web: www.atf.gov						
Houston Field Div						
5825 N Sam Houston Pkwy W	Houston	TX	77086	281-716-8200	716-8219	340-14
Web: www.atf.gov						
Kansas City Group V						
2600 Grand Ave Ste 280	Kansas City	MO	64108	816-559-0850	559-0831	340-14
Web: www.atf.gov						
Louisville Field Div						
600 Martin Luther King Pl Ste 322	Louisville	KY	40202	502-753-3400	753-3401	340-14
Web: www.atf.gov						
Miami Field Div 11410 NW 20 St Ste 201	Miami	FL	33172	305-597-4800	597-4801	340-14
Web: www.atf.gov						
Nashville Field Div						
5300 Maryland Way Ste 200	Brentwood	TN	37027	615-565-1400	565-1401	340-14
Web: www.atf.gov						
Philadelphia Field Div						
601 Walnut St	Philadelphia	PA	19106	215-446-7800	446-7811	340-14
Web: www.atf.gov						
Phoenix Field Div						
201 E Washington St Ste 940	Phoenix	AZ	85004	602-776-5400	776-5429	340-14
Web: www.atf.gov						
Saint Paul Field Div						
30 E Seventh St Ste 1900	Saint Paul	MN	55101	651-726-0200	726-0201	340-14
Web: www.atf.gov						
Tampa Field Div 400 N Tampa St Ste 2100	Tampa	FL	33602	813-202-7300	202-7301	340-14
Web: www.atf.gov						
Bureau of Child Support Enforcement						
PO Box 8018	Harrisburg	PA	17105	717-787-9706		339-39
Web: www.childsupportoffice.net						
Bureau of Consular Affairs						
2201 C St NW SA 17 Ninth Fl	Washington	DC	20522	202-501-4444		340-16
TF: 888-407-4747 ■ *Web:* www.travel.state.gov						
Bureau of Diplomatic Security						
DS Public Affairs	Washington	DC	20522	571-345-3146		340-16
TF: 866-217-2089 ■ *Web:* www.state.gov						
Bureau of Economic Analysis (BEA)						
4600 Silver Hill Rd	Washington	DC	20233	301-278-9004		340-2
Web: www.bea.gov						
Bureau of Engraving & Printing						
14th & C Sts SW	Washington	DC	20228	877-874-4114	874-3177*	340-18
**Fax Area Code:* 202 ■ *TF:* 877-874-4114 ■ *Web:* moneyfactory.gov						
Bureau of Indian Affairs (BIA)						
1849 C St NW MS 4004 MIB	Washington	DC	20240	202-208-7163	208-5320	340-13
Web: www.bia.gov						
Bureau of Indian Affairs Regional Offices (BIA)						
Alaska Region 3601 C St Ste 1100	Anchorage	AK	99503	907-271-4085	271-1349	340-13
Web: www.bia.gov						
Eastern Oklahoma Region						
3100 W Peak Blvd PO Box 8002	Muskogee	OK	74402	918-781-4600	781-4604	340-13
Web: www.bia.gov						
Eastern Region						
545 Marriott Dr Ste 700	Nashville	TN	37214	202-513-7641	564-6701*	340-13
**Fax Area Code:* 615 ■ *Web:* www.bia.gov						
Great Plains Region						
115 Fourth Ave SE	Aberdeen	SD	57401	605-226-7343	226-7446	340-13
Web: www.bia.gov						
Midwest Region						
5600 American Blvd W Ste 500	Minneapolis	MN	55437	612-713-4400	713-4401	340-13
Web: www.bia.gov						
Navajo Region 301 W Hill St	Gallup	NM	87301	505-863-8314	863-8324	340-13
Web: www.bia.gov						
Northwest Region 911 NE 11th Ave	Portland	OR	97232	503-231-6702	231-2201	340-13
Web: www.bia.gov						
Pacific Region 2800 Cottage Way	Sacramento	CA	95825	916-978-6000	978-6099	340-13
TF: 800-645-8397 ■ *Web:* www.bia.gov						
Rocky Mountain Region 316 N 26th St	Billings	MT	59101	406-247-7943	247-7976	340-13
Web: www.bia.gov						
Southern Plains Region PO Box 368	Anadarko	OK	73005	405-247-6673	247-5611	340-13
TF: 800-645-0405 ■ *Web:* www.indianaffairs.gov						
Southwest Region						
1001 Indian School Rd NW	Albuquerque	NM	87104	505-563-3103	563-3101	340-13
Web: www.bia.gov						
Western Region						
2600 N Central Ave Ste 310 Eighth Fl	Phoenix	AZ	85008	602-379-6958	379-6462	340-13
Web: www.bia.gov						
Bureau of International Labor Affairs						
200 Constitution Ave NW	Washington	DC	20210	202-693-4770	693-4780	340-15
Web: www.dol.gov						
Bureau of Labor Statistics						
Consumer Price Index						
2 Massachusetts Ave NE	Washington	DC	20002	202-691-5200		340-15
Web: www.bls.gov						
Mountain-Plains Information Office						
2 Pershing Sq Bldg 2300 Main St Ste 1190	Kansas City	MO	64108	816-285-7000	285-7009	340-15
Web: www.bls.gov						
Southeast Information Office						
61 Forsyth St SW Rm 7T25	Atlanta	GA	30303	404-893-4222	893-4221	340-15
TF: 800-347-3764 ■ *Web:* www.bls.gov						
Bureau of Labor Statistics Regional Offices						
Mid-Atlantic Information Office						
170 S Independence Mall W Ste 610 E	Philadelphia	PA	19106	215-597-3282	861-5720	340-15
Web: www.bls.gov						
Midwest Information Office						
230 S Dearborn St Ste 960	Chicago	IL	60604	312-353-1880	353-1886	340-15
Web: www.bls.gov						
New England Information Office						
JFK Federal Bldg Ste E-310	Boston	MA	02203	617-565-2327	565-4182	340-15
Web: www.bls.gov						
New York-New Jersey Information Office						
201 Varick St Rm 808	New York	NY	10014	646-264-3600	337-2532*	340-15
**Fax Area Code:* 212 ■ *Web:* www.bls.gov						
Southwest Information Office						
525 Griffin St Rm 221 Federal Bldg	Dallas	TX	75202	972-850-4800		340-15
Web: www.bls.gov						
Western Information Office						
PO Box 193766	San Francisco	CA	94119	415-625-2270	625-2351	340-15
Web: www.bls.gov						
Bureau of Land Management (BLM)						
1849 C St NW Rm 5665	Washington	DC	20240	202-208-3801	208-5242	340-13
Web: www.blm.gov						
Bureau of Land Management Regional Offices						
Alaska State Office						
222 W Seventh Ave Ste 13	Anchorage	AK	99513	907-271-5960	271-3684	340-13
Web: www.blm.gov						
Arizona State Office						
1 N Central Ave Ste 800	Phoenix	AZ	85004	602-417-9200	417-9556	340-13
Web: www.blm.gov						
California State Office						
2800 Cottage Way Ste W-1623	Sacramento	CA	95825	916-978-4400	978-4416	340-13
Web: www.blm.gov						
Colorado State Office						
2850 Youngfield St	Lakewood	CO	80215	303-239-3600	239-3933	340-13
Web: www.blm.gov						
Eastern States Office						
7450 Boston Blvd	Springfield	VA	22153	703-440-1600		340-13
TF: 800-370-3936 ■ *Web:* www.blm.gov						
Idaho State Office 1387 S Vinnell Way	Boise	ID	83709	208-373-4000	373-3899	340-13
Web: www.blm.gov						
Montana State Office						
5001 Southgate Dr	Billings	MT	59101	406-896-5000		340-13
Web: www.blm.gov						
Nevada State Office 1340 Financial Blvd	Reno	NV	89502	775-861-6400	861-6606	340-13
Web: www.blm.gov						
Oregon/Washington State Office						
333 SW First Ave	Portland	OR	97204	503-808-6001	808-6422	340-13
Web: www.blm.gov						
Wyoming State Office						
5353 Yellowstone Rd PO Box 1828	Cheyenne	WY	82003	307-775-6256	775-6129	340-13
Web: www.blm.gov						

Name	Address	City	State	ZIP	Phone	Fax	Class	Other
Bureau of National Affairs Inc, The	1801 S Bell St	Arlington	VA	22202	703-341-5777		531-7	TF: 800-960-1220 ■ Web: www.bna.com
Bureau of Reclamation Regional Offices *Great Plains Region*	2021 Fourth Ave	Billings	MT	59107	406-247-7600	247-7793	340-13	Web: www.usbr.gov
Lower Colorado Region	PO Box 61470	Boulder City	NV	89006	702-293-8411	293-8333	340-13	Web: www.usbr.gov
Mid-Pacific Region	2800 Cottage Way Federal Bldg	Sacramento	CA	95825	916-978-5001	978-5005	340-13	Web: www.usbr.gov
Pacific Northwest Region	1150 N Curtis Rd Ste 100	Boise	ID	83706	208-378-5012	378-5019	340-13	Web: www.usbr.gov
Upper Colorado Region	125 S State St Rm 8100	Salt Lake City	UT	84138	801-524-3600	524-5499	340-13	Web: www.usbr.gov
Bureau of the Fiscal Service	401 14th St SW	Washington	DC	20227	202-874-6950		340-18	Web: www.fiscal.treasury.gov
Bureau of the Public Debt	PO Box 7015	Parkersburg	WV	26106	800-722-2678		340-18	TF: 800-722-2678 ■ Web: thepeoplegov.org
Bureau of the Public Debt *TreasuryDirect*	PO Box 7015	Parkersburg	WV	26106	844-284-2676		340-18	TF: 844-284-2676 ■ Web: www.savingsbonds.gov
Bureau of Vital Records & Health Statistics	PO Box 83720	Boise	ID	83720	208-334-5980		339-13	Web: healthandwelfare.idaho.gov
Bureau Veritas Primary Integration	8180 Greensboro Dr Ste 700	McLean	VA	22102	703-356-2200	356-2206	186	Web: www.bvpi.com
Burg Simpson Eldredge Hersh Jardine PC	40 Inverness Dr E	Englewood	CO	80112	303-792-5595	708-0527	428	TF: 888-895-2080 ■ Web: www.burgsimpson.com
Burge & Burge PC	2001 Park Pl Ste 850	Birmingham	AL	35203	205-251-9000	323-0512	41	TF: 800-633-3733 ■ Web: burge-law.com
Burger & Brown Engineering Inc	4500 E 142nd St	Grandview	MO	64030	816-878-6675		454	TF: 800-764-3518 ■ Web: www.smartflow-usa.com
Burger King Corp	5505 Blue Lagoon Dr	Miami	FL	33126	305-378-3000		670	TF: 866-394-2493 ■ Web: www.bk.com
Burger's Ozark Country Cured Hams Inc	32819 Hwy 87	California	MO	65018	573-796-3134	796-3137	296-26	TF: 800-203-4424 ■ Web: www.smokehouse.com
Burgerville USA	109 W 17th St	Vancouver	WA	98660	888-827-8369		670	TF: 888-827-8369 ■ Web: www.burgerville.com
Burgess & Niple Inc	5085 Reed Rd	Columbus	OH	43220	614-459-2050		261	TF: 800-282-1761 ■ Web: www.burgessniple.com
Burgess Advertising & Marketing	6 Fundy Rd Ste 300	Portland	ME	04105	207-775-5227	835-0339	4	Web: www.burgessadv.com
Burgess Aviation Consultants	12533 Avondale Ridge Dr	Fort Worth	TX	76179	817-236-3144	236-3563	194	TF: 888-905-4040 ■ Web: www.jurispro.com
Burgess Falls State Natural Area	4000 Burgess Falls Dr	Sparta	TN	38583	931-432-5312		565	Web: www.state.tn.us
Burgess Group LLC, The	1701 Duke St Ste 300	Alexandria	VA	22314	703-894-1800		809	TF: 800-637-2004 ■ Web: www.burgessgroup.com
Burgess Law Firm PC	4310 Madison Ave Ste 100	Kansas City	MO	64111	816-471-1700		41	Web: burgesslawkc.com
Burgess Michael (Rep R - TX)	2161 Rayburn House Office Bldg	Washington	DC	20515	202-225-7772	225-2919	342-2	Web: burgess.house.gov
Burgess Pigment Company Inc	525 Beck Blvd PO Box 349	Sandersville	GA	31082	478-552-2544	552-4274	500	TF: 800-841-8999 ■ Web: www.burgesspigment.com
Burgess Sales & Supply Inc	2121 W Morehead St	Charlotte	NC	28208	704-333-8933		351	Web: www.burgesssales.com
Burgess Speciality Fabrication Inc	8222 Fawndale Ln	Houston	TX	77040	713-462-0293		697	Web: www.burgessfab.com
Burgess Steel LLC	200 W Forest Ave	Englewood	NJ	07631	201-871-3500	871-8750	690	TF: 800-871-3501 ■ Web: burgesssteel.com
Burgess-Norton Manufacturing Co	737 Peyton St	Geneva	IL	60134	630-232-4100	232-3734	621	Web: www.burgessnorton.com
Burghardt Sporting Goods	14660 W Capitol Dr	Brookfield	WI	53005	262-790-1170		711	TF: 866-790-6606 ■ Web: www.burghardtsportinggoods.com
Burgiss Group LLC, The	111 River St 10th Fl	Hoboken	NJ	07030	201-427-9600		180	Web: www.burgiss.com
Burgoyne and Burgoyne Publishers	PO Box 17095	Salt Lake City	UT	84117	801-277-8977	277-7789*	637-2	*Fax Area Code: 877 ■ TF: 877-278-8977 ■ Web: www.burgoyneandburgoynepublishers.com
Burgundy Asset Management Ltd	Bay Wellington Tower Brookfield Pl 181 Bay St Ste 4510	Toronto	ON	M5J2T3	416-869-3222		690	TF: 888-480-1790 ■ Web: www.burgundyasset.com
Burgundy Group Inc, The	2420 S Power Rd Ste 103	Mesa	AZ	85209	480-444-7744		180	Web: www.tbginc.com
Burien Toyota Collision Ctr	15025 First Ave S	Burien	WA	98148	206-243-0700		54	Web: www.burientoyota.com
Burkart-Phelan Inc	2 Shaker Rd	Shirley	MA	01464	978-425-4500	425-9800	527	Web: www.burkart.com
Burke & Herbert Bank & Trust Co	100 S Fairfax St	Alexandria	VA	22314	703-684-1655		70	TF: 877-440-0800 ■ Web: www.burkeandherbertbank.com
Burke & Lamb Pc	300 Union St	New Bedford	MA	02740	508-984-4800		2	Web: burkelambcpa.com
Burke & Schindler PLL	901 Adams Crossing	Cincinnati	OH	45202	513-455-8200		2	Web: burkecpa.com
Burke Beverages Inc	4900 S Vernon Ave	McCook	IL	60525	708-688-2000		81-1	Web: www.burkebev.com
Burke County	PO Box 310	Bowbells	ND	58721	701-377-2718		338	Web: burkecountynd.com
Burke County	602 Liberty St	Waynesboro	GA	30830	706-554-2324	554-0350	338	Web: www.burkecounty-ga.gov
Burke County Chamber of Commerce	110 E Meeting St	Morganton	NC	28655	828-437-3021	437-1613	139	Web: burkecountychamber.org
Burke County Public Library	204 S King St	Morganton	NC	28655	828-437-5638	433-1914	434-3	Web: www.bcpls.org
Burke County Public Schools	789 Burke Veterans Pkwy	Waynesboro	GA	30830	706-554-5101	554-8051	685	Web: www.burke.k12.ga.us
Burke E. Porter Machinery Co	730 Plymouth Ave NE	Grand Rapids	MI	49505	616-234-1200	459-1032	386	TF: 800-562-9133 ■ Web: bepco.com
Burke Handling Systems	431 Hwy 49 S	Jackson	MS	39218	601-939-6600		770	TF: 800-222-5400 ■ Web: burkehandling.com
Burke Inc	500 W Seventh St	Cincinnati	OH	45203	513-241-5663	684-7500	466	TF: 800-688-2674 ■ Web: burke.com
Burke Inc	1800 Merriam Ln	Kansas City	KS	66106	800-255-4147		477	TF: 800-255-4147 ■ Web: burkebariatric.com
Burke International Tours Inc	PO Box 890	Newton	NC	28658	828-465-3900		760	TF: 800-476-3900 ■ Web: www.burkechristiantours.com
Burke Lake Recreation Area	29145 Burke Lake Rd	Burke	SD	57523	605-337-2587		565	Web: gfp.sd.gov
Burke Mountain Operating Co	223 Sherburne Lodge Rd	East Burke	VT	05832	802-626-7300		378	Web: skiburke.com
Burke Museum of Natural History & Culture	17th Ave NE & NE 45th St	Seattle	WA	98195	206-543-5590	685-3039	520	TF: 800-411-9671 ■ Web: www.burkemuseum.org
Burke Rehabilitation Hospital	785 Mamaroneck Ave	White Plains	NY	10605	914-597-2500		374-6	TF: 888-992-8753 ■ Web: www.burke.org
Burke-Divide Electric Co-opeartive Inc (BDEC)	9549 Hwy 5 W	Columbus	ND	58727	701-939-6671		245	TF: 800-472-2983 ■ Web: www.bdec.coop
Burkett & Wong Engineers	9449 Balboa Ave Ste 270	San Diego	CA	92123	619-299-5550		261	Web: bwesd.com
Burkett Engineering Inc	105 E Robinson St Ste 501	Orlando	FL	32801	407-246-1260		261	Web: burkettengineering.com
Burkett Oil Company Inc	6788 Best Friend Rd	Norcross	GA	30071	770-447-8030		579	TF: 800-228-1786 ■ Web: www.burkettoil.com
Burkett's Office Supplies Inc	8520 Younger Creek Dr	Sacramento	CA	95828	916-387-8900		535	Web: burkettsoffice.com
Burkhalter Travel Agency	6501 Mineral Pt Rd	Madison	WI	53705	608-833-5200		771	TF: 800-556-9286 ■ Web: www.burkhaltertravel.com
Burkhart Advertising Inc	1335 Mishawaka Ave	South Bend	IN	46615	574-233-2101		7	TF: 800-777-8122 ■ Web: www.burkhartadv.com
Burkhart Dental Supply Co	2502 S 78th St	Tacoma	WA	98409	253-474-7761	472-4773	475	TF: 800-562-8176 ■ Web: www.burkhartdental.com
Burkhart Group Ltd, The	412 S Broadleigh Rd	Columbus	OH	43209	614-397-8788		180	Web: burkhartgrp.com
Burkina Faso	866 UN Plz 1st Ave Ste 326	New York	NY	10017	212-308-4720	308-4690	784	Web: burkina-usa.org
Burkina Faso Embassy	2340 Massachusetts Ave NW	Washington	DC	20008	202-332-5577	667-1882	257	Web: burkina-usa.org
Burk-Kleinpeter Inc (BKI)	4176 Canal St	New Orleans	LA	70119	504-486-5901		261	Web: www.bkiusa.com
Burkland Inc	6520 S State Rd	Goodrich	MI	48438	810-636-2233		489	Web: burklandinc.com
Burkle North America Inc	11105 Knott Ave	Cypress	CA	90630	714-379-5090		770	Web: burkleamerica.com
Burklund Distributors Inc	2500 N Main St Ste 3	East Peoria	IL	61611	309-694-1900	694-6788	297-3	TF: 800-322-2876 ■ Web: www.burklund.com
Burks Tractor Company Inc	3140 Kimberly Rd	Twin Falls	ID	83301	208-733-5543	734-9852	274	TF: 800-247-7419 ■ Web: www.burkstractor.com
Burleigh County	514 E Thayer Ave PO Box 1055	Bismarck	ND	58502	701-222-6690	222-6758	338	TF: 877-222-6682 ■ Web: www.ndcourts.gov
Burleson Area Chamber of Commerce	1044 SW Wilshire Blvd	Burleson	TX	76028	817-295-6121	295-6192	139	Web: burlesonchamber.com
Burleson County	100 W Buck	Caldwell	TX	77836	979-567-0000	567-2376	338	Web: co.burleson.tx.us
Burley Tobacco Growers Cooperative Assn	620 S Broadway	Lexington	KY	40508	859-252-3561		48-2	Web: www.burleytobacco.com
Burlingame Chamber of Commerce	417 California Dr	Burlingame	CA	94010	650-344-1735	344-1763	139	Web: burlingamechamber.org
Burlington & Rockenbach PA	444 W Railroad Ave Courthouse Commons Ste 350	West Palm Beach	FL	33401	561-721-0400		41	Web: flappellatelaw.com

Name / Address	City	State	Zip	Phone	Fax	Class
Burlington Chamber of Commerce 414 Locust St Ste 201 *Web:* burlingtonchamber.com	Burlington	ON	L7S1T7	905-639-0174	333-3956	137
Burlington City Hall 149 Church St *Web:* www.burlingtonvt.gov	Burlington	VT	05401	802-865-7000	865-7014	337
Burlington Coat Factory 1830 Rt 130 N *TF:* 855-355-2875 ■ *Web:* www.burlington.com	Burlington	NJ	08016	609-387-7800		362
Burlington County 49 Rancocas Rd *Web:* www.co.burlington.nj.us	Mount Holly	NJ	08060	609-265-5122	265-0696	338
Burlington County Library 5 Pioneer Blvd *Web:* www.bcls.lib.nj.us	Mount Holly	NJ	08060	609-267-9660	267-4091	434-3
Burlington County Times 4284 US-130 *Web:* www.phillyburbs.com	Willingboro	NJ	08046	609-871-8000		532-2
Burlington Engineering Inc 220 W Grove Ave *Web:* www.burlingtoneng.com	Orange	CA	92865	714-921-4045	921-4029	256
Burlington Free Press 100 Bank St *TF:* 800-427-3124 ■ *Web:* www.burlingtonfreepress.com	Burlington	VT	05401	802-660-1819	660-1802	532-2
Burlington Furniture Co 747 Pine St *Web:* burlingtonfurniture.us	Burlington	VT	05401	802-862-5056		321
Burlington International Airport 1200 Airport Dr *Web:* www.btv.aero	South Burlington	VT	05403	802-863-2874	863-7947	27
Burlington Medical Supplies Inc 3 Elmhurst St *TF:* 800-221-3466 ■ *Web:* burmed.com	Newport News	VA	23603	800-221-3466		475
Burlington Northern & Santa Fe Railway (BNSF) 2650 Lou Menk Dr *TF:* 800-795-2673 ■ *Web:* www.bnsf.com	Fort Worth	TX	76131	800-795-2673		648
Burlington Public Library 22 Sears St *TF:* 800-422-2462 ■ *Web:* www.burlington.org	Burlington	MA	01803	781-270-1690	229-0406	434-3
Burlington Public Library 210 Ct St *Web:* www.burlington.lib.ia.us	Burlington	IA	52601	319-753-1647		434-3
Burlington Record 202 S 14th St *Web:* www.burlington-record.com	Burlington	CO	80807	719-346-5381	346-5514	532-2
Burlington Technical Ctr 52 Institute Rd *Web:* btc.bsdvt.org	Burlington	VT	05408	802-864-8426		167-3
Burlington/Alamance County Convention & Visitors Bureau 200 S Main St PO Box 519 *TF:* 800-637-3804 ■ *Web:* www.visitalamance.com	Burlington	NC	27216	336-570-1444	228-1330	206
Burlington/West Burlington Area Chamber of Commerce 610 N Fourth St Ste 200 *Web:* www.greaterburlington.com	Burlington	IA	52601	319-752-6365	752-6454	139
Burma Bibas Inc 597 Fifth Ave 10th Fl *Web:* burmabibas.com	New York	NY	10017	212-750-2500		155-13
Burmax Co 28 Barretts Ave *Fax Area Code: 631 ■ *TF:* 800-645-5118 ■ *Web:* www.burmax.com	Holtsville	NY	11742	800-645-5118	289-7590*	76
Burnaby Board of Trade 4555 Kings Way Ste 201 *Web:* www.bbot.ca	Burnaby	BC	V5H4T8	604-412-0100	412-0102	137
Burnaby Lake Greenhouses Ltd 17250 80 Ave *TF:* 800-663-0149 ■ *Web:* burlake.com	Surrey	BC	V4N6J6	604-576-2088	576-2475	192
Burnac Corp 44 St Clair Ave W *Web:* www.burnac.com	Toronto	ON	M4V3C9	416-964-3600		652
Burner Law Group PC 12 Research Way *Web:* burnerlaw.com	East Setauket	NY	11733	631-941-3434		41
Burness Communications Inc 7910 Woodmont Ave Ste 700 *Web:* www.burness.com	Bethesda	MD	20814	301-652-1558		317
Burnet Consolidated Independent School District 208 E Brier *Web:* www.burnetcisd.net	Burnet	TX	78611	512-756-2124	756-7498	800
Burnet County 220 S Pierce St *Web:* www.burnetcountytexas.org	Burnet	TX	78611	512-756-5406	756-5410	338
Burnet Middle School 8401 Hathaway Dr *Web:* www.austinisd.org	Austin	TX	78757	512-414-3225		685
Burnett & Kastran PC 313 Hubbard St *TF:* 866-361-2537 ■ *Web:* law-bk.com	Allegan	MI	49010	269-673-8407	673-2764	41
Burnett & Son Meat Company Inc 1420 S Myrtle Ave *Web:* www.burnettandson.com	Monrovia	CA	91016	626-357-2165		473
Burnett County 7410 County Rd K *TF:* 800-788-3164 ■ *Web:* www.burnettcounty.com	Siren	WI	54872	715-349-2181	349-2830	338
Burnett Dairy Co-op 11681 State Rd 70 *TF:* 800-854-2716 ■ *Web:* www.burnettdairy.com	Grantsburg	WI	54840	715-689-2468	689-2135	296-5
Burnett Specialists 9800 Richmond Ave Ste 800 *Web:* www.burnettspecialists.com	Houston	TX	77042	713-977-4777	977-7533	631
Burnette Foods Inc 701 US-31 S PO Box 128 *Web:* www.burnettefoods.com	Elk Rapids	MI	49629	231-264-8116		296-20
Burnette Insurance Agency Inc 3447 Lawrenceville Suwanee Rd *Web:* burnetteinsurance.com	Suwanee	GA	30024	770-339-8888		390
Burnetti PA 211 S Florida Ave *TF:* 888-287-6388 ■ *Web:* burnetti.com	Lakeland	FL	33801	863-688-8288		41
Burnetts Staffing Inc 2710 Ave E E *Web:* www.burnetts.com	Arlington	TX	76011	817-640-5255		260
Burney Co 1800 Alexander Bell Dr Ste 510 *TF:* 866-928-7639 ■ *Web:* www.burney.com	Reston	VA	20191	866-928-7639		403
Burnham & Flower Group Inc 315 S Kalamazoo Mall *TF:* 888-748-7966 ■ *Web:* bfgroup.com	Kalamazoo	MI	49007	269-381-1173		390
Burnham Composite Structures Inc 6262 W 34th St S *Web:* www.burnhamcs.com	Wichita	KS	67215	316-946-5900	219-6893	22
Burnham Financial Services LLC 2038 Saranac Ave *Web:* www.burnhambenefitadvisors.com	Lake Placid	NY	12946	518-523-8100		390
Burnham Holdings Inc 1241 Harrisburg Ave PO Box 3245 *Web:* www.burnhamholdings.com	Lancaster	PA	17604	717-390-7800		357
Burnham Industrial Contractors Inc 3229 Babcock Blvd *Web:* www.burnhamindustrial.net	Pittsburgh	PA	15237	412-366-6622		189-9
Burnham Nationwide Inc The Burnham Ctr 111 W Washington St Ste 450 *TF:* 800-407-7990 ■ *Web:* www.burnhamnationwide.com	Chicago	IL	60602	312-407-7990		194
Burnham Park Animal Hospital 1025 S State St *Web:* www.burnhamparkvet.com	Chicago	IL	60605	312-663-9200	971-1001	794
Burnham Point State Park 340765 NYS Rt 12E *Web:* parks.ny.gov	Cape Vincent	NY	13618	315-654-2522		565
Burnham Polymeric Inc 1408 Rte 9 *TF:* 800-833-8783 ■ *Web:* www.burnhams.com	Fort Edward	NY	12828	518-792-3040	792-4680	604
Burning Glass International Inc 1 Lewis Wharf *Web:* www.burning-glass.com	Boston	MA	02110	617-227-4800		260
Burning Man 1900 Third St *Web:* burningman.org	San Francisco	CA	94158	415-865-3800		520
Burns & McBride Inc 18 Boulden Cir Ste 30 *TF:* 800-756-5110 ■ *Web:* www.burnsandmcbride.com	New Castle	DE	19720	302-656-5110	656-7560	316
Burns & McDonnell 9400 Ward Pkwy *Web:* www.burnsmcd.com	Kansas City	MO	64114	816-333-9400		261
Burns Bog Conservation Society 7953 120 St *TF:* 888-850-6264 ■ *Web:* www.burnsbog.org	Delta	BC	V4C6P6	604-572-0373		138
Burns Burns Walsh & Walsh PA 704 Topeka Ave *TF:* 888-528-3186 ■ *Web:* www.bbwwlaw.com	Lyndon	KS	66451	785-828-4418		428
Burns Controls Co 13735 Beta Rd *TF:* 800-442-2010 ■ *Web:* www.burnscontrols.com	Dallas	TX	75244	972-233-6712		358
Burns Cooley Dennis Inc 551 Sunnybrook Rd *Web:* bcdgeo.com	Ridgeland	MS	39157	601-856-9911		256
Burns Engineering Inc 10201 Bren Rd E *TF:* 800-328-3871 ■ *Web:* www.burnsengineering.com	Minnetonka	MN	55343	952-935-4400		256
Burns Mailing & Printing Inc 6131 Industrial Heights Dr PO Box 52730 *TF:* 866-288-5618 ■ *Web:* burnsmp.com	Knoxville	TN	37909	865-584-2265	584-4871	627
Burns Motor Freight Inc 18750 Seneca Trl N *TF:* 800-598-5674 ■ *Web:* www.burnsmotorfreight.com	Marlinton	WV	24954	304-799-6106	799-4257	780
Burns Pest Elimination Inc 2620 Grovers Ave *TF:* 877-971-4782 ■ *Web:* burnspestelimination.com	Phoenix	AZ	85053	602-971-4782		577
Burns Power Tools 350 Mariano S Bishop Blvd *Web:* www.burnstools.com	Fall River	MA	02721	508-675-0381		190
Burns Times-Herald 355 N Broadway Ave *Web:* btimesherald.com	Burns	OR	97720	541-573-2022		532-2
Burns, Delatte & Mccoy Inc 320 Westcott St Ste 100 *Web:* www.bdmi-ce.com	Houston	TX	77007	713-861-3016		261
Burnsteads, The 11980 NE 24th St Ste 200 *Web:* www.burnstead.com	Bellevue	WA	98005	425-454-1900		187
Burnsville Chamber of Commerce 350 W Burnsville Pkwy Ste 425 *TF:* 800-521-6055 ■ *Web:* burnsvillechamber.com	Burnsville	MN	55337	952-435-6000	435-6972	139
Burnsville Ctr 1178 Burnsville Ctr *Web:* www.burnsvillecenter.com	Burnsville	MN	55306	952-435-8182		460
Burpee Museum of Natural History 737 N Main St *Web:* www.burpee.org	Rockford	IL	61103	815-965-3433		520
Burr & Brown 101 S Salina St 7th Fl *Web:* burrandbrown.com	Syracuse	NY	13202	315-233-8300		41
Burr & Co 3351 Claystone St SE *Web:* burrcompany.com	Grand Rapids	MI	49546	616-977-7750		390
Burr & Cole Consulting Engineers Inc 3485 Poplar Ave Ste 200 *Web:* burrcole.com	Memphis	TN	38111	901-452-9676		261
Burr & Forman LLP 420 N 20th St Ste 3400 *Web:* www.burr.com	Birmingham	AL	35203	205-251-3000		41
Burr & Smith LLP 9800 4th St N Ste 1100 *Web:* burrandsmithlaw.com	Saint Petersburg	FL	33701	813-253-2010		41
Burr Oak Tool Inc 405 W S St *TF:* 800-861-8864 ■ *Web:* burroak.com	Sturgis	MI	49091	269-651-9393		455
Burr Pilger & Mayer (BPM) 600 California St Ste 600 *Web:* www.bpmcpa.com	San Francisco	CA	94108	415-421-5757	288-6288	2
Burr Pond State Park 384 Burr Mountain Rd *Web:* portal.ct.gov	Torrington	CT	06790	860-482-1817		565
Burr Richard (Sen R - NC) 217 Russell Senate Office Bldg *TF:* 888-848-1833 ■ *Web:* www.burr.senate.gov	Washington	DC	20510	202-224-3154		342-2
Burr Truck & Trailer Sales Inc 2901 Vestal Rd *Web:* www.burrtruck.com	Vestal	NY	13850	607-729-2211		57
Burrell 233 N Michigan Ave Ste 2900 *Web:* www.burrell.com	Chicago	IL	60601	312-297-9600		4
Burrell Consultng Group Inc 1001 Enterprise Way Ste 100 *Web:* burrellcg.com	Roseville	CA	95678	916-783-8898		256
Burrell Imaging 1311 Merrillville Rd *TF:* 800-348-8732 ■ *Web:* www.burrellprolabs.com	Crown Point	IN	46307	219-663-3210	662-0915	588

Phone Fax Class

Burrelles
30 B Vreeland Rd PO Box 674 .... Florham Park NJ 07932 973-992-6600 992-7675 387
TF: 800-631-1160 ■ *Web:* burrelles.com
Burris Company Inc 331 E Eighth St .... Greeley CO 80631 970-356-1670 356-8702 544
TF: 888-228-7747 ■ *Web:* www.burrisoptics.com
Burris Law PLLC
300 River Place Dr Ste 1775 .... Detroit MI 48207 313-393-5400 41
Web: burrisiplaw.com
Burris Logistics 501 SE Fifth St .... Milford DE 19963 302-839-5157 839-5175 803-2
TF: 800-805-8135 ■ *Web:* www.burrislogistics.com
Burris Machine Company Inc
1631 Main Ave Dr NW .... Hickory NC 28601 828-322-6914 324-2793 493
Web: burrismachineco.com
Burritt on the Mountain
3101 Burritt Dr .... Huntsville AL 35801 256-536-2882 532-1784 520
Web: www.burrittonthemountain.com
Burroughs Diesel Inc
3626 Industrial Blvd .... Laurel MS 39440 601-399-4515 57
TF: 877-628-2668 ■ *Web:* www.burroughscompanies.com
Burroughs Wellcome Fund
21 TW Alexander Dr
PO Box 13901 .... Research Triangle Park NC 27709 919-991-5100 991-5160 304
Web: www.bwfund.org
Burrow Global LLC
6200 Savoy Dr Ste 800 .... Houston TX 77036 713-963-0930 186
Web: www.burrowglobal.com
Burrow Lee PLLC
611 Commerce St Ste 2603 .... Nashville TN 37203 615-540-1004 866-6927 41
Web: burrowlee.com
Burrows Aviation
W3244 County Rd O .... Sheboygan Falls WI 53085 920-467-6151 467-1337 167-3
Web: www.burrowsaviation.com
Burrtec Waste Industries Inc
9890 Cherry Ave .... Fontana CA 92335 909-429-4200 429-4291 804
TF: 888-287-7832 ■ *Web:* www.burrtec.com
Burruezo & Burruezo PLLC
941 Lake Baldwin Ln Ste 102 .... Orlando FL 32814 407-754-2904 754-2905 41
Web: burruezolaw.com
Burrus Research Associates Inc
557 Cottonwood Ave .... Hartland WI 53029 262-367-0949 367-7163 463
Web: www.burrus.com
Bursich Associates Inc
2129 E High St .... Pottstown PA 19464 610-323-4040 323-8240 261
Web: www.bursich.com
Bursma Electronic Distributing Inc
4727 Clyde Park Ave SW Ste 1 .... Wyoming MI 49509 616-831-0080 38
TF: 800-777-2604 ■ *Web:* www.bursma.com
Burson Center, The
500 Old Bremen Rd .... Carrollton GA 30117 678-890-2333 393
Web: bursoncenter.com
Burst Marketing LLC 297 River St .... Troy NY 12180 518-279-7945 5
Web: www.burstmarketing.net
Burstek 9240 Bonita Beach Rd .... Bonita Springs FL 34135 239-495-5900 174
TF: 800-709-2551 ■ *Web:* www.burstek.com
Burt and Associates
Dallas Ft Worth Metropolitan Area .... Carrollton TX 75007 877-740-7839 401
TF: 877-740-7839 ■ *Web:* www.burtcollect.com
Burt County Economic Development Corp
111 N 13th St Ste 12 .... Tekamah NE 68061 402-374-2955 374-2956 338
Web: www.burtcounty.ne.gov
Burt County Public Power District
613 N 13th St .... Tekamah NE 68061 402-374-2631 245
TF: 888-835-1620 ■ *Web:* www.burtcoppd.com
Burt Lake State Park
6635 State Pk Dr .... Indian River MI 49749 231-238-9392 565
Web: www.michigan.org
Burt Lumber Co
911 Greensboro Rd PO Box 220 .... Washington GA 30673 706-678-1531 678-4040 683
Web: www.burtlumbercompany.com
Burt Martin Arnold Securities Inc
2321 Rosecrans Ave Ste 3285 .... El Segundo CA 90245 310-544-3545 544-6626 690
Web: www.bmasecurities.com
Burtco Inc PO Box 40 .... Westminster VT 05159 802-722-3358 183
TF: 800-451-4401 ■ *Web:* burtcoselfstorage.com
Burtech Plumbing 102 Second St .... Encinitas CA 92024 760-634-5134 634-5154 261
Web: burtechplumbing.com
Burton & Mayer Inc
W140 N9000 Lilly Rd .... Menomonee Falls WI 53051 262-781-0770 627
TF: 800-236-1770 ■ *Web:* www.burtonmayer.com
Burton Computer Resources Inc
400 N 16th Ave .... Laurel MS 39440 601-428-0205 180
Web: www.burtoncomputer.com
Burton Cummings Theatre 364 Smith St .... Winnipeg MB R3B2H2 204-987-7825 572
TF: 855-985-5000 ■ *Web:* burtoncummingstheatre.ca
Burton Industries Inc
9821 Cedar Falls Rd .... Hazelhurst WI 54531 715-356-5767 729
Web: www.burtonindustries.com
Burton Industries Inc
243 Wyandanch Ave .... West Babylon NY 11704 631-643-6660 643-6665 695
Web: www.heatreat.com
Burton J. Haynes PC
9273 Old Keene Mill Rd .... Burke VA 22015 703-913-7500 866-2427 41
Web: haynestaxlaw.com
Burton Lumber Corp 835 Wilson Rd .... Chesapeake VA 23324 757-545-4613 545-8852 236
Web: www.burton-lumber.com
Burton Neil & Associates PC
1060 Andrew Dr Ste 170 .... West Chester PA 19380 610-696-2120 696-4111 445
TF: 866-696-2120 ■ *Web:* www.burt-law.com
Burton-Taylor International Consulting LLC
1319 Thornapple Dr Mezzanine Level .... Osprey FL 34229 646-201-4152 194
Web: burton-taylor.com
Burundi Embassy
2233 Wisconsin Ave NW Ste 408 .... Washington DC 20007 202-342-2574 342-2578 257
Web: www.burundiembassy-usa.org
Bus Andrews Truck Equipment Inc
2828 E Kearney St .... Springfield MO 65803 417-869-1541 869-1656 57
TF: 800-273-0733 ■ *Web:* busandrews.com
Busald, Funk, Zevely Psc 226 Main St .... Florence KY 41042 859-371-3600 525-1040 41
Web: bfzlaw.com

Buscemi Co, International LLC
PO Box 88065 .... Los Angeles CA 90009 310-568-1011 311
Web: buscemico.com
Buscemi Hallett LLP
555 W Beech St Ste 450 .... San Diego CA 92101 619-821-9163 41
Web: buhalaw.com
Busch Distributors Inc 7603 SR-270 .... Pullman WA 99163 509-339-6600 339-6616 581
TF: 800-752-2295 ■ *Web:* www.buschdist.com
Busch Electronics
739 Kasota Ave SE .... Minneapolis MN 55414 651-288-2580 791
Web: www.buschelectronics.com
Busch Gardens Williamsburg
1 Busch Gardens Blvd .... Williamsburg VA 23185 757-229-4386 32
Web: buschgardens.com
Busch Industries Inc
900 E Paris Ave SE .... Grand Rapids MI 49546 616-957-3737 480
Busch Jewelry Company Inc
1960 Pawlisch Dr .... Rockford IL 61112 815-332-2222 410
Web: buschjewelry.com
Busch LLC 516 Viking Dr .... Virginia Beach VA 23452 757-463-7800 358
Web: www.buschvacuum.com
Busch Precision Inc
8200 N Faulkner Rd .... Milwaukee WI 53224 414-362-7300 757
Web: www.buschprecision.com
Busch Vacuum Technics Inc
1740 Lionel Bertrand .... Boisbriand QC J7H1N7 450-435-6899 641
TF: 800-363-6360 ■ *Web:* www.buschvacuum.com
Busch's Inc 2240 S Main St .... Ann Arbor MI 48103 734-214-8088 345
Web: www.buschs.com
Buschbach Insurance Agency Inc
5615 W 95th St .... Oak Lawn IL 60453 708-423-2350 390
Web: buschbach.com
Busche Performance Group
1563 E State Rd 8 .... Albion IN 46701 260-636-7030 295
Web: www.buschegroup.com
Buschman 4100 Payne Ave .... Cleveland OH 44103 216-431-6633 431-5037 557
Web: buschman.com
Buscomm Inc 11696 Lilburn Park Rd .... Saint Louis MO 63146 314-567-7755 177
TF: 800-283-7755 ■ *Web:* buscomminc.com
BUSE Industries Inc
177 NW Industrial Ct .... Bridgeton MO 63044 314-344-1166 344-1131 246
TF: 800-999-2873 ■ *Web:* www.buseinc.com
Buse Timber & Sales Inc
3812 28th Pl NE .... Everett WA 98201 425-258-2577 683
TF: 800-305-2577 ■ *Web:* www.busetimber.com
Busek Company Inc 11 Tech Cir .... Natick MA 01760 508-655-5565 194
Web: www.busek.com
Bush & Ramirez LLC
5615 Kirby Dr Ste 900 .... Houston TX 77005 713-626-1555 622-8077 41
Web: bushramirez.com
Bush Barn Art Ctr 600 Mission St SE .... Salem OR 97302 503-581-2228 371-3342 50-2
Web: salemart.org
Bush Bros & Co 1016 E Weisgarber Rd .... Knoxville TN 37909 865-509-3077 296-20
Web: www.bushbeans.com
Bush Construction Corp
4029 Ironbound Rd Ste 100 .... Williamsburg VA 23188 757-220-2874 187
Bush Consulting Group 34 S Main St .... Cleveland OH 44022 330-337-6104 194
Web: bushconsultinggroup.com
Bush House Museum 600 Mission St SE .... Salem OR 97302 503-363-4714 520
Web: www.oregonlink.com
Bush Inc 2581 Hickory Blvd SE .... Lenoir NC 28645 828-728-4224 57
Web: www.roosterbush.com
Bush Industries Inc 1 Mason Dr .... Jamestown NY 14701 716-665-2000 319-2
TF: 800-950-4782 ■ *Web:* www.bushfurniture.com
Bush Intercontinental Airport
2800 N Terminal Rd .... Houston TX 77032 281-233-3000 27
Web: www.fly2houston.com
Bush Ross PA 1801 N Highland Ave .... Tampa FL 33602 813-224-9255 428
Web: www.bushross.com
Bush Rudnicki Shelton PC
200 N Mesquite St Ste 200 .... Arlington TX 76011 817-274-5992 41
Web: brstexas.com
Bush School, The 3400 E Harrison St .... Seattle WA 98112 206-322-7978 685
Web: www.bush.edu
Bushline Inc
707 Industrial Park Rd .... New Tazewell TN 37825 423-626-5246 319-2
Web: bushline.com
Bushnell Center for the Performing Arts
166 Capitol Ave .... Hartford CT 06106 860-987-6000 987-6070 572
TF: 888-824-2874 ■ *Web:* www.bushnell.org
Bushnell Corp 9200 Cody St .... Overland Park KS 66214 913-752-3400 752-3550 544
TF: 800-423-3537 ■ *Web:* www.bushnell.com
Bushnell Illinois Tank Co
380 E Main St .... Bushnell IL 61422 309-772-3106 772-2045 273
Web: schuldbushnell.com
Bushnell University 828 E 11th Ave .... Eugene OR 97401 541-684-7201 684-7317 166
TF: 877-463-6622 ■ *Web:* www.bushnell.edu
Bushnells Basin Veterinary Clinic Pc
1311 Marsh Rd .... Pittsford NY 14534 585-248-9590 794
Web: catsexclusively.com
Bushwacker Inc 6710 N Catlin Ave .... Portland OR 97203 503-283-4335 283-3007 60
TF: 800-234-8920 ■ *Web:* www.bushwacker.com
Bushwick Metals LLC
560 N Washington Ave .... Bridgeport CT 06604 888-399-4070 723
TF: 888-399-4070 ■ *Web:* www.bushwickmetals.com
Business & Escrow Service Center Inc
3031 Tisch Way .... San Jose CA 95128 408-296-7373 653
Web: business-escrow.net
Business & Government Continuity Services Inc
13404 Princeton Ln .... Edmond OK 73013 405-286-1649 194
Web: businesscontinuity.info
Business & Institutional Furniture Manufacturers Assn (BIFMA)
678 Front Ave NW Ste 150 .... Grand Rapids MI 49504 616-285-3963 49-13
Web: www.bifma.org
Business & Legal Reports Inc (BLR)
141 Mill Rock Rd E .... Old Saybrook CT 06475 860-510-0100 510-7225 637-9
TF: 800-727-5257 ■ *Web:* www.blr.com

Name / Address	City	State	Zip	Phone	Fax	Class
Business Advancement Inc 178 Sycamore Terr *Web:* businessadvance.com	Glen Rock	NJ	07452	201-612-1228	251-8265	194
Business Benefits Group Inc, The 4069 Chain Bridge Rd Top Fl **Fax Area Code:* 703 ■ *TF:* 844-201-3612 ■ *Web:* bbgbroker.com	Fairfax	VA	22030	844-201-3612	385-3444*	390
Business Card Service Inc 3200 143rd Cir *Web:* www.bcsinet.com	Burnsville	MN	55306	952-895-6750		627
Business Cluster Development (BCD) 3186 Bryant St *Web:* clusterdevelopment.com	Palo Alto	CA	94306	650-387-3159		393
Business Communication 2379 NE Loop 410 Ste 1b *Web:* bcs-ip.com	San Antonio	TX	78217	210-485-1915		681
Business Computer Design International Inc 20 Fall Pippin Ln Ste 202 *Web:* www.bcdsoftware.com	Asheville	NC	28803	630-986-0800	986-0926	178-1
Business Consumer Alliance 315 N La Cadena Dr **Fax Area Code:* 562 ■ *Web:* www.checkbca.org	Colton	CA	92324	909-825-7280	216-9241*	79
Business Council for International Understanding (BCIU) 1212 Avenue of the Americas 10th Fl *Web:* www.bciu.org	New York	NY	10036	212-490-0460	697-8526	49-12
Business Council of Alabama 2 N Jackson St PO Box 76 *TF:* 800-665-9647 ■ *Web:* www.bcatoday.org	Montgomery	AL	36101	334-834-6000		140
Business Council of Fairfield County (SACIA) 888 Washington Blvd *Web:* www.businessfairfield.com	Stamford	CT	06901	203-359-3220	967-8294	139
Business Council of New York State Inc 152 Washington Ave *TF:* 800-358-1202 ■ *Web:* www.bcnys.org	Albany	NY	12210	518-465-7511	465-4389	140
Business Council of Westchester 800 Westchester Ave Ste S-310 *Web:* thebcw.org	Rye Brook	NY	10573	914-948-2110	948-0122	139
Business Efficacy 6130 Blue Cir Dr Ste 100A *Web:* www.businessefficacy.com	Hopkins	MN	55343	952-217-0425		195
Business Equipment Unlimited 275 Read St *TF:* 800-452-4657 ■ *Web:* www.beu.net	Portland	ME	04103	207-878-8500		112
Business Executives for National Security (BENS) 1030 15th St NW Ste 200 *Web:* www.bens.org	Washington	DC	20005	202-296-2125	296-2490	49-12
Business Facilities Magazine 44 Apple St Ste 3 *TF:* 800-524-0337 ■ *Web:* businessfacilities.com	Tinton Falls	NJ	07724	732-842-7433	758-6634	457-5
Business Forms Management Assn (BFMA) 3800 Old Cheney Rd Ste 101-285 **Fax Area Code:* 877 ■ *TF:* 888-367-3078 ■ *Web:* www.bfma.org	Lincoln	NE	68516	888-367-3078	204-5979*	49-12
Business Furniture Corp 8421 Bearing Dr Ste 200 *TF:* 800-774-5544 ■ *Web:* businessfurniture.net	Indianapolis	IN	46278	317-216-1600	216-1602	320
Business Furniture Inc (BFI) 10 Lanidex Ctr W *Web:* www.bfionline.com	Parsippany	NJ	07054	973-503-0730	503-1565	320
Business High Point - Chamber of Commerce 1634 N Main St *Web:* www.bhpchamber.org	High Point	NC	27262	336-882-5000	889-9499	139
Business Impact Group LLC (BIG) 2411 Galpin Ct Ste 120 *Web:* impactgroup.us	Chanhassen	MN	55317	952-278-7800		549
Business Inn 180 MacLaren St *TF:* 800-363-1777 ■ *Web:* thebusinessinn.com	Ottawa	ON	K2P0L3	613-232-1121	232-8143	379
Business Innovation Ctr 5230 W US Hwy 98 *Web:* www.bicpc.com	Panama City	FL	32401	850-913-2904		393
Business Insurers of The Carolinas Inc 800 Eastowne Dr Ste 208 *TF:* 877-834-4467 ■ *Web:* business-insurers.com	Chapel Hill	NC	27514	919-968-4611	537-0750	390
Business Interiors Inc 146 Market Ridge Dr *TF:* 800-568-9281 ■ *Web:* bijackson.com	Ridgeland	MS	39157	601-969-1000		321
Business Interiors Northwest Inc 10848 E Marginal Way S *Web:* catalystactivation.com	Seattle	WA	98168	206-762-8818	763-4078	320
Business Journal, The 25 E Boardman St *TF:* 800-837-6397 ■ *Web:* businessjournaldaily.com	Youngstown	OH	44501	330-744-5023	744-5838	457-5
Business Leaders for Michigan 600 Renaissance Ctr Ste 1760 *Web:* businessleadersformichigan.com	Detroit	MI	48243	313-259-5400		194
Business Lenders LLC 225 Asylum St Goodwin Sq 16th Fl *Web:* www.businesslenders.com	Hartford	CT	06103	860-244-9202		217
Business Management Consultants (BMC) 1502 Augusta Dr Ste 315 *Web:* bmc-global.com	Houston	TX	77057	713-780-2939	780-2932	194
Business News Network (BNN) 299 Queen St W *TF:* 855-326-6266 ■ *Web:* www.bnnbloomberg.ca	Toronto	ON	M5V2Z5	416-384-6600		740
Business News Publishing Co 2401 W Big Beaver Rd Ste 700 *TF:* 800-837-7370 ■ *Web:* www.bnpmedia.com	Troy	MI	48084	248-362-3700	362-0317	637-9
Business Performance Systems LLC 7808 Trevino Ln *Web:* bpsconsulting.com	Falls Church	VA	22043	703-286-2813	940-8310	180
Business Professionals of America 5454 Cleveland Ave *TF:* 800-334-2007 ■ *Web:* www.bpa.org	Columbus	OH	43231	614-895-7277	895-1165	49-5
Business Protection Specialists Inc 1296 E Victor Rd *TF:* 800-560-2199 ■ *Web:* www.securingpeople.com	Victor	NY	14564	800-560-2199		693
Business Resource Group (BRG) 10440 N Central Expy Ste 1150 *TF:* 888-391-9166 ■ *Web:* www.brg.com	Dallas	TX	75231	214-777-5100		194
Business Roundtable (BR) 300 New Jersey Ave NW Ste 800 *Web:* www.businessroundtable.org	Washington	DC	20001	202-872-1260	466-3509	49-12
Business Software Inc (BSI) 155 Technology Pky Ste 100 Peachtree *TF:* 888-293-3413 ■ *Web:* www.bsi.com	Norcross	GA	30092	770-449-3200		178-1
Business Software Solutions 334 N Marshall Way Ste H *Web:* www.businessoftware.com	Layton	UT	84041	801-336-3303	336-3313	178-1
Business Stationery LLC 4944 Commerce Pkwy *Web:* www.identitygroup.com	Cleveland	OH	44128	216-514-1277		534
Business Systems & Consultants Inc 113 Little Vly Ct *Web:* www.bscsolutions.com	Birmingham	AL	35244	205-988-3300	208-0459	45
Business Systems Consulting (BSC) 15 Lincoln St *Web:* www.bizsysconsulting.com	Wakefield	MA	01880	781-683-4040		196
Business Talent Group LLC 260 W 39th St 4th Fl *Web:* www.businesstalentgroup.com	New York	NY	10018	646-530-8404		260
Business Technology Assn (BTA) 12411 Wornall Rd Ste 200 *TF:* 800-325-7219 ■ *Web:* www.bta.org	Kansas City	MO	64145	816-941-3100		49-18
Business Training Library Inc 14500 S Outer Forty Ste 500 *TF:* 888-432-3077 ■ *Web:* www.bizlibrary.com	Town and Country	MO	63017	888-432-3077		194
Business Valuation Center LLC 1717 Pennsylvania Ave NW Ste 1025 *TF:* 800-856-6780 ■ *Web:* businessvaluationcenter.com	Washington	DC	20006	703-787-0012		463
Business Wire 101 California St 20th Fl *TF:* 800-227-0845 ■ *Web:* www.businesswire.com	San Francisco	CA	94111	415-986-4422		530
Business Wise Inc 6190 Powers Ferry Rd Ste 190 *TF:* 888-414-8651 ■ *Web:* www.businesswise.com	Atlanta	GA	30339	770-956-1955		627
BusinessBroker Network LLC 375 Northridge Rd Ste 475 *TF:* 877-342-9786 ■ *Web:* www.businessbroker.net	Atlanta	GA	30350	877-342-9786		194
BusinessGenetics Inc 8494 W Fork Rd *Web:* www.businessgenetics.com	Boulder	CO	80302	720-213-4500		196
Business-Higher Education Forum 2025 M St NW Ste 800 *Web:* www.bhef.com	Washington	DC	20036	202-367-1189		49-5
Business-Industry Political Action Committee (BIPAC) 1707 L St NW Ste 350 *Web:* www.bipac.org	Washington	DC	20036	202-833-1880	833-2338	615
Businesspersons Between Jobs Inc 601 Claymont Dr *Web:* bbj.org	Ballwin	MO	63011	636-394-1440		194
BusinessPlans Inc 432 E Pearl St *TF:* 800-865-4485 ■ *Web:* www.businessplansinc.com	Miamisburg	OH	45342	800-865-4485		463
Business-to-Business Marketing Communications Inc 900 Ridgefield Dr Ste 135 *Web:* www.btbmarketing.com	Raleigh	NC	27609	919-872-8172		195
Buske Logistics 7 Gateway Commerce Ctr W *TF:* 800-879-2258 ■ *Web:* www.buske.com	Edwardsville	IL	62025	618-931-6091	931-6387	311
Busken Bakery Inc 2675 Madison Rd *Web:* www.busken.com	Cincinnati	OH	45208	513-871-2114		68
Buskirk Lumber Co 319 Oak St **Fax Area Code:* 616 ■ *TF:* 800-860-9663 ■ *Web:* www.buskirklumber.com	Freeport	MI	49325	800-860-9663	765-3380*	683
Busler Enterprises Inc 2601 N St Joseph Ave *Web:* buslerlubricants.com	Evansville	IN	47720	812-424-7511		324
BUSlink Media 440 Cloverleaf Dr *Web:* buslink.com	Baldwin Park	CA	91706	626-336-1888		104
Buss Mechanical Services Inc PO Box 190476 *Web:* www.bussmechanical.com	Boise	ID	83709	208-562-0600		612
Busse Design USA Inc 5857 Chabot Ct *Web:* www.bussedesign.com	Oakland	CA	94618	415-689-8090		344
Bustos Cheri (Rep D - IL) 1233 Longworth House Office Bldg *Web:* bustos.house.gov	Washington	DC	20515	202-225-5905		342-2
Busy Beaver 3130 William Pitt Way *Web:* www.busybeaver.com	Pittsburgh	PA	15238	412-828-2323		364
Busy Bee Cleaning Company Inc 18 Wilson Ave *Web:* www.busybeecleaningcompany.com	West Chester	PA	19382	610-430-6888		104
Busy Bee Group PO Box 327 *Web:* www.busybeegroup.com	Lawrence	NY	11559	815-366-8138		637-2
Buta Ramen 5190 Morris St *Web:* www.hamachirestaurants.com	Halifax	NS	B3J1B3	902-422-0245		671
Butano State Park 1500 Cloverdale Rd *Web:* www.parks.ca.gov	Pescadero	CA	94060	650-879-2040		565
Butch Quinn Rosemurgy Jardis Burkhart Lewandowski & Miller Pc 816 Ludington St *Web:* www.bqrlaw.com	Escanaba	MI	49829	906-786-4422		428
Butchart Gardens, The 800 Benvenuto Ave *TF:* 866-652-4422 ■ *Web:* www.butchartgardens.com	Brentwood Bay	BC	V8M1J8	250-652-4422	652-7751	97
Butcher Air Conditioning Company Inc 101 Boyce St *Web:* www.butcherac.com	Broussard	LA	70518	337-837-2000		189-10
Butcher Block 15 Booth Dr *Web:* butcherblockrestaurant.com	Plattsburgh	NY	12901	518-563-0920		671
Butcher Block Inc, The 35 Food Mart Rd *Web:* www.butcherblocksauces.com	Boston	MA	02118	617-269-1105		619
Butcher Box 20 Guest St Ste 300 *TF:* 855-981-8568 ■ *Web:* www.butcherbox.com	Boston	MA	02135	855-981-8568		546
Butcher Distributors Inc 101 Boyce Rd *TF:* 800-960-0008 ■ *Web:* www.butcherdistributors.com	Broussard	LA	70518	337-837-2088	837-2069	612
Butcher Shop, The 552 Tremont St *Web:* www.thebutchershopboston.com	Boston	MA	02118	617-423-4800		671
Butech Bliss Inc 550 S Ellsworth Ave *TF:* 888-285-6433 ■ *Web:* www.butechbliss.com	Salem	OH	44460	888-285-6433		485

Name / Address	City	State	ZIP	Phone	Fax	Class
Butera & Jones LLP 130 W Lancaster Ave *Web:* buterajoneslaw.com	Wayne	PA	19087	610-964-9770		41
Butier Engineering Inc 17822 E 17th St Ste 404 *Web:* butier.com	Tustin	CA	92780	714-832-7222		256
Butler Associates Financial Planners Inc 10733 Sunset Office Dr Ste 259A *TF:* 800-547-2382 ■ *Web:* b-a-f-p.com	Saint Louis	MO	63127	314-842-6555	287-6049	690
Butler Automatic Inc 41 Leona Dr *Web:* www.butlerautomatic.com	Middleboro	MA	02346	508-923-0544		547
Butler Avionics Inc 280 Gardner Dr Ste 3 *Web:* www.butleravionics.com	New Century	KS	66031	913-829-4606	829-4326	22
Butler Brothers Supply Division Inc 2001 Lisbon St *TF:* 888-784-6875 ■ *Web:* www.butlerbros.com	Lewiston	ME	04240	207-784-6875		186
Butler Capital Investments LLC 151 Post Rd *Fax Area Code: 434 ■ *Web:* www.butlercap.com	Old Westbury	NY	11568	516-333-2100	293-7057*	690
Butler Color Press Inc 116 W Diamond St Box 271 *Web:* www.butlercp.com	Butler	PA	16001	724-283-9132		627
Butler Community College 901 S Haverhill Rd *Web:* www.butlercc.edu	El Dorado	KS	67042	316-321-2222	322-3316	162
Butler County 428 Sixth St *Web:* www.butlercoiowa.org	Allison	IA	50602	319-267-2487	267-2488	338
Butler County 124 W Diamond St PO Box 1208 *Web:* www.butlercountypa.gov	Butler	PA	16003	724-284-5233	284-5244	338
Butler County 205 W Central Ave *TF:* 800-822-6104 ■ *Web:* www.bucoks.com	El Dorado	KS	67042	316-322-4300	322-4387	338
Butler County 104 S Tyler St Ste B *Web:* www.revenue.ky.gov	Morgantown	KY	42261	270-526-5676		338
Butler County 100 N Main St Rm 202 *Web:* butler.countyportal.net	Poplar Bluff	MO	63901	573-686-8050	686-8066	338
Butler County Board of Education 211 School Highlands Rd *Web:* www.butlerco.k12.al.us	Greenville	AL	36037	334-382-2665	382-1845	685
Butler County Chamber of Commerce 101 E Diamond St Ste 116 *Web:* www.butlercountychamber.com	Butler	PA	16001	724-283-2222	283-0224	139
Butler County Community College 107 College Dr *TF:* 888-826-2829 ■ *Web:* bc3.edu	Butler	PA	16002	724-287-8711	285-6047	162
Butler County Ford 400 S Main St *Web:* www.butlercountyford.net	Butler	PA	16001	724-287-2766		57
Butler County Radio Network Inc 252 Pillow St *Web:* wisr680.com	Butler	PA	16001	724-283-1500	282-9188	645-141
Butler County REC 521 N Main PO Box 98 *TF:* 888-267-2726 ■ *Web:* www.butlerrec.coop	Allison	IA	50602	319-267-2726	267-2566	245
Butler County Revenue Commission 700 Ct Sq *Web:* revenue.alabama.gov	Greenville	AL	36037	334-382-3221	382-0385	338
Butler Eagle 114 W Diamond St *TF:* 800-842-8098 ■ *Web:* www.butlereagle.com	Butler	PA	16001	724-282-8000	282-4180	532-2
Butler Fairman & Seufert Inc 8450 Wfield Blvd Ste 300 *TF:* 800-553-0863 ■ *Web:* bfsengr.com	Indianapolis	IN	46240	317-713-4615		261
Butler Health System 1 Hospital Way *Web:* www.butlerhealthsystem.org	Butler	PA	16001	724-283-6666		374-3
Butler Home Products LLC 237 Cedar Hill St *Web:* www.cleanerhomeliving.com	Marlborough	MA	01752	508-597-8000	597-8010	508
Butler Hospital 345 Blackstone Blvd *TF:* 844-401-0111 ■ *Web:* www.butler.org	Providence	RI	02906	401-455-6200		374-5
Butler Institute of American Art 524 Wick Ave *Web:* butlerart.com	Youngstown	OH	44502	330-743-1107	743-9567	520
Butler Library 535 W 114th St *Web:* library.columbia.edu	New York	NY	10027	212-854-7309	854-9099	434-6
Butler National Corp 19920 W 161st St *OTC: BUKS* ■ *Web:* www.butlernational.com	Olathe	KS	66062	913-780-9595	780-5088	529
Butler Paper Recycling Inc 324 Newport St *Web:* www.butlerpaper.com	Suffolk	VA	23434	757-539-2351	925-0874	686
Butler Pappas Weihmuller Katz Craig LLP 80 SW Eighth St Ste 3300 *Web:* www.butler.legal	Miami	FL	33130	305-416-9998		466
Butler Public Power District 1331 N Fourth St *TF:* 800-230-0569 ■ *Web:* butlerppd.com	David City	NE	68632	402-367-3081		245
Butler Rural Electric Co-opeartive Inc (BREC) 3888 Still-Beckett Rd *TF:* 800-255-2732 ■ *Web:* www.butlerrural.coop	Oxford	OH	45056	513-867-4400		245
Butler Rural Electric Cooperative Association Inc 216 S Vine St PO Box 1242 *TF:* 800-464-0060 ■ *Web:* www.butler.coop	El Dorado	KS	67042	316-321-9600	321-9980	245
Butler Shine Stern & Partners 20 Liberty Ship Way *Web:* bssp.com	Sausalito	CA	94965	415-331-6049		7
Butler Supply Inc 965 Horan Dr *TF:* 800-850-9949 ■ *Web:* www.butlersupply.com	Fenton	MO	63026	636-349-9000	349-7877	246
Butler Technologies Inc 231 W Wayne St *TF:* 800-494-6656 ■ *Web:* butlertechnologies.com	Butler	PA	16001	724-283-6656		174
Butler Technology & Career Development Schools 3603 Hamilton-Middletown Rd *Web:* www.butlertech.org	Hamilton	OH	45011	513-645-8200	844-8916	685
Butler Transport Inc 347 N James St *TF:* 800-345-8158 ■ *Web:* www.butlertransport.com	Kansas City	KS	66118	800-345-8158		780
Butler University 4600 Sunset Ave *TF:* 800-368-6852 ■ *Web:* www.butler.edu	Indianapolis	IN	46208	317-940-8100	940-8150	166
Butler Winery 1022 N College Ave *Web:* www.butlerwinery.com	Bloomington	IN	47404	812-339-7233		50-7
Butler, Lavanceau & Sober LLC 10450 Shaker Dr Ste 112 *Web:* blscpafirm.com	Columbia	MD	21046	410-997-9299	992-7929	2
Butler/Newco Printing & Laminating Inc 250 Hamburg Tpke *Web:* www.butlerprinting.com	Butler	NJ	07405	973-838-8550		802
Butler-Dearden Paper Service Inc PO Box 1069 *TF:* 800-634-7070 ■ *Web:* www.butlerdearden.com	Boylston	MA	01505	508-869-9000	869-0211	559
Butt, Thornton & Baehr PC 4101 Indian School NE Ste 300-S *TF:* 800-322-6883 ■ *Web:* btblaw.com	Albuquerque	NM	87110	505-884-0777	889-8870	41
Butte College 3536 Butte Campus Dr *TF:* 800-933-8322 ■ *Web:* www.butte.edu	Oroville	CA	95965	530-895-2511	879-4313	162
Butte County County Courthouse *Web:* www.idaho.gov	Arco	ID	83213	208-587-2130	527-3295	338
Butte County 25 County Center Dr *Web:* www.buttecounty.net	Oroville	CA	95965	530-538-7691	538-7975	338
Butte County Extension Office 117 Fifth Ave *Web:* www.buttesd.org	Belle Fourche	SD	57717	605-892-4456	892-9064	338
Butte County Public Law Library 1675 Montgomery St *Web:* www.buttecountylawlibrary.org	Oroville	CA	95965	530-538-7122	534-1499	434-3
Butte Electric Co-op 109 Dartmouth Ave *TF:* 800-928-8839 ■ *Web:* www.butteelectric.com	Newell	SD	57760	605-456-2494		245
Butte Home Health and Hospice 10 Constitution Dr *TF:* 800-655-0462 ■ *Web:* www.buttehomehealth.com	Chico	CA	95973	530-895-0462		363
Butterball Farms Inc 1435 Buchanan Ave SW *TF:* 888-828-8837 ■ *Web:* butterballfarms.com	Grand Rapids	MI	49507	616-243-0105		296-25
Butterfield Foods Co 225 Hubbard Ave *Web:* www.butterfieldfoods.com	Butterfield	MN	56120	507-956-5103	956-5751	619
Butterfield G. K. (Rep D - NC) 2080 Rayburn House Office Bldg *Web:* www.butterfield.house.gov	Washington	DC	20515	202-225-3101		342-2
Butterfield Trail Village 1923 E Joyce Blvd *Web:* butterfieldtrailvillage.org	Fayetteville	AR	72703	479-442-7220		672
Butterfly House 11455 Obee Rd *Web:* www.wheelerfarms.com	Whitehouse	OH	43571	419-877-2733		50-5
Butterfly House - Faust Park, The 15193 Olive Blvd *TF:* 800-642-8842 ■ *Web:* www.missouribotanicalgarden.org	Chesterfield	MO	63017	636-530-0076		50-5
Butterfly Pavilion & Insect Ctr 6252 W 104th Ave *Web:* www.butterflies.org	Westminster	CO	80020	303-469-5441	657-5944	823
Butterfly World 3600 W Sample Rd *Web:* www.butterflyworld.com	Coconut Creek	FL	33073	954-977-4400	977-4501	50-5
ButterflyMX 127 W 26th St 6th Fl *Web:* www.butterflymx.com	New York	NY	10001	571-480-6579		178-1
Buttermilk Falls State Park 112 E Buttermilk Falls Rd 105 Enfield Falls Rd *Web:* parks.ny.gov	Ithaca	NY	14850	607-273-5761		565
Butters Construction & Development Inc 6820 Lyons Technology Cir Ste 100 *Web:* butters.com	Coconut Creek	FL	33073	954-312-2400	570-8844	186
Butters-Fetting Company Inc 1669 S First St *TF:* 800-361-6154 ■ *Web:* www.buttersfetting.com	Milwaukee	WI	53204	414-645-1535	645-7622	189-10
Butte-Silver Bow Chamber of Commerce 1000 George St *TF:* 800-735-6814 ■ *Web:* www.buttechambersite.org	Butte	MT	59701	406-723-3177		139
Butte-Silver Bow Public Library 226 West Broadway *Web:* buttepubliclibrary.info	Butte	MT	59701	406-723-3361		434-3
Butt-Holdsworth Memorial Library 505 Water St *Web:* www.kerrvilletx.gov	Kerrville	TX	78028	830-257-8422		434-3
Button Bay State Park 5 Button Bay State Park Rd *Web:* www.vtstateparks.com	Vergennes	VT	05491	802-475-2377		565
Buttonwood Park Zoo 425 Hawthorn St *Web:* www.bpzoo.org	New Bedford	MA	02740	508-991-6178		823
Butts County 625 W Third St Ste 4 *Web:* buttscountyga.com	Jackson	GA	30233	770-775-8200	775-8211	338
Butts County Board of Education 181 N Mulberry St *Web:* www.butts.k12.ga.us	Jackson	GA	30233	770-504-2300	504-2305	685
Butts Foods Inc 2596 Bransford Ave *TF:* 800-962-8570 ■ *Web:* www.buttsfoods.com	Nashville	TN	37204	615-292-5562		297-10
Butts Ticket Company Inc 151 Hood Rd *TF:* 800-642-7051 ■ *Web:* www.buttsticket.com	Cochranville	PA	19330	610-869-7450	869-7454	627
Butzel Long PC 150 W Jefferson Ste 100 *Web:* www.butzel.com	Detroit	MI	48226	313-225-7000	225-7080	41
Buurma Farms Inc 3909 Kok Rd *TF:* 888-428-8762 ■ *Web:* www.buurmafarms.com	Willard	OH	44890	419-935-6411	935-1918	10-11
Buursma Agency 238 Hoover Blvd Ste 10 *Web:* www.buursmaagency.com	Holland	MI	49423	616-392-2105	392-1619	390
Buxton Co 245 Cadwell Dr *TF:* 800-426-3638 ■ *Web:* buxton.co	Springfield	MA	01104	413-734-5900	785-1367	430
Buxton Co 2651 S Polaris Dr *TF:* 888-228-9866 ■ *Web:* www.buxtonco.com	Fort Worth	TX	76137	888-228-9866		656
Buxy's Salty Dog 2707 Philadelphia Ave *Web:* buxys.com	Ocean City	MD	21842	410-289-0973	289-0038	671
Buy Gitomer 310 Arlington Ave *Web:* www.gitomer.com	Charlotte	NC	28203	704-333-1112		463
Buy Me Beauty 4221 NE 12th Terr *Web:* www.buymebeauty.com	Oakland Park	FL	33334	954-568-7150	568-7177	77
Buy Owner Inc 1192 E Newport Center Dr Ste 200 *Web:* www.buyowner.com	Deerfield Beach	FL	33442	954-202-7777		5

	Phone	Fax	Class
Buy Rite Liquidators 1076 Park Rd . . . . Blandon PA 19510 *Web:* buyriteliquidators.com	610-926-4444	921-0268	41
Buyatab Online Inc B1 - 788 Beatty St. . . . . Vancouver BC V6B2M1 *TF:* 888-267-0447 ■ *Web:* web.buyatab.com	888-267-0447		224
Buyer Advertising Inc 189 Wells Ave. . . . . Newton MA 02459 *Web:* www.buyerads.com	617-969-4646		193
Buyer Group, The 950 Celebration Blvd Ste F . . . . Celebration FL 34747 *Web:* www.thebuyergroup.com	407-964-1383		5
Buzas Greenhouses 3927 Newburg Rd. . . . . Easton PA 18045 *Web:* www.buzasgreenhouses.com	610-252-5289		192
Buzgon Davis Law Offices 525 S Eighth St. . . . . Lebanon PA 17042 *Web:* buzgondavis.com	717-274-1421	274-1752	41
Buzz Company Inc, The 220 N Green St . . . . Chicago IL 60607 *Web:* www.buzzco.com	312-255-0808		260
Buzz Marketing Group 132 Kings Hwy E Ste 202 . . . . Haddonfield NJ 08033 *Web:* buzzmg.com	856-433-8579		195
Buzz Oates Construction LP 8615 Elder Creek Rd. . . . . Sacramento CA 95828 *Web:* www.buzzoates.com	916-379-3800		653
Buzz Products Inc 4818 Kanawha Blvd E. . . . . Charleston WV 25306 *Web:* buzzfoodsvc.com	304-925-4781	925-1502	297-6
BV (BeenVerified Inc) 48 W 38th St 8th Fl. . . . . New York NY 10018 **Fax Area Code:* 212 ■ *TF:* 888-579-5910 ■ *Web:* www.beenverified.com	888-579-5910	813-3276*	317
BV Unitron Manufacturing Inc 707 Robins St Ste 115 . . . . Conway AR 72034 *Web:* www.unitron.com	501-231-4034		729
BVK Inc 250 W Coventry Ct Ste 300. . . . . Milwaukee WI 53217 *Web:* www.bvk.com	414-228-1990		7
BVM Corp 430 S Navajo St. . . . . Denver CO 80223 *Web:* www.bvmcorp.com	303-975-0981		537
BVP (Bessemer Venture Partners) 1865 Palmer Ave Ste 104 . . . . Larchmont NY 10538 *Web:* www.bvp.com	914-833-5300	833-5499	792
BVS Inc 949 Poplar Rd . . . . Honey Brook PA 19344 *TF:* 877-877-4821 ■ *Web:* www.bvssamplers.com	610-273-2841	273-2843	454
BVS Performance Systems Inc 4060 Glass Rd NE. . . . . Cedar Rapids IA 52402 *Web:* www.bvs.com	319-378-1807		463
BVT Equity Holdings Inc 400 Interstate North Pkwy Ste 700 . . . . Atlanta GA 30339 *Web:* www.bvt.com	770-618-3500	618-3578	655
BW (Baker - Wotring LLP) 700 JPMorgan Chase Tower 600 Travis St . . . . Houston TX 77002 *Web:* www.bakerwotring.com	713-980-1700	980-1701	428
B-W Graphics Inc 101 Westview St. . . . . Versailles MO 65084 *Web:* www.bwgraphics.com	573-378-6363	378-5337	627
BW Offshore Management USA Inc 2925 Briar Pk Ste 1295. . . . . Houston TX 77042 *Web:* www.bwoffshore.com	713-781-0670	781-1216	194
BW Papersystems 3333 Crocker Ave . . . . Sheboygan WI 53082 *TF:* 888 310-1898 ■ *Web:* www.bwpapersystems.com	920-458-2500	458-1265	556
BW Rogers Co 195 S Main St Ste 400. . . . . Akron OH 44308 *Web:* www.kamanfluidpower.com	330-315-3100		295
BWAY Corp 375 Northridge Rd Ste 600 . . . . Atlanta GA 30350 *TF:* 800-527-2267 ■ *Web:* www.mauserpackaging.com	770-645-4800	645-4810	124
Bwbacon Group 621 Kalamath St . . . . Denver CO 80204 *Web:* www.bwbacon.com	303-800-8897		260
BWD Group LLC 45 Executive Dr . . . . Plainview NY 11803 *Web:* www.bwd.us	516-327-2700	327-2800	390
BWI (Baltimore/Washington International Thurgood Marshall Airport) PO Box 8766 . . . . Baltimore MD 21240 *TF:* 800-435-9294 ■ *Web:* www.bwiairport.com	410-859-7111		27
Byard F. Brogan Inc PO Box 0369 . . . . Glenside PA 19038 *TF:* 800-232-7642 ■ *Web:* www.bfbrogan.com	215-885-3550	885-1366	409
Byars Machine Company Inc 167 Byars Rd . . . . Laurens SC 29360 *Web:* byarsmachine.com	864-682-3146	682-3147	385
Bybee Stone Company Inc 6293 N Matthews Dr. . . . . Ellettsville IN 47429 *TF:* 800-457-4530 ■ *Web:* www.bybeestone.com	812-876-2215		724
Bybel Rutledge LLP 1017 Mumma Rd . . . . Lemoyne PA 17043 *Web:* www.bybelrutledge.com	717-731-1700		428
Byblos 3218 Magazine St . . . . New Orleans LA 70115 *Web:* www.byblosrestaurants.com	504-894-1233	894-1239	671
Byblos Byblos Lebanese Restaurant 1406 N Main St . . . . Fort Worth TX 76106 *Web:* www.byblostx.com	817-625-9667		671
Byblos Cafe 2832 S MacDill Ave. . . . . Tampa FL 33629 *Web:* www.byblostampa.com	813-805-7977		671
Byblos Restaurant 3332 S Mill Ave . . . . Tempe AZ 85282 *Web:* www.byblostempe.com	480-894-1945		671
Byce & Associates Inc 487 Portage St . . . . Kalamazoo MI 49007 *Web:* byce.com	269-381-6170	381-6176	261
Bycor General Contractors Inc 6490 Marindustry Pl. . . . . San Diego CA 92121 *Web:* www.bycor.com	858-587-1901		186
By-Crete 517 King St . . . . Lebanon PA 17042 *Web:* www.bycrete.com	717-866-7690		183
Bye Aerospace Inc 7395 S Peoria St Ste 206 PO Box C3 . . . . Englewood CO 80112 *Web:* byeaerospace.com	303-459-2862		261
Byer California 66 Potrero Ave . . . . San Francisco CA 94103 *Web:* byerca.com	415-626-7844		155-4
Byerly Aviation 6100 EM Dirkson Pkwy . . . . Peoria IL 61607 *Web:* www.byerlyaviation.com	309-697-6300		24
Byerly Ford 4041 Dixie Hwy. . . . . Louisville KY 40216 *TF:* 888-436-0819 ■ *Web:* www.byerlyford.com	502-448-1661		57
Byers Choice Ltd 4355 County Line Rd . . . . Chalfont PA 18914 *Web:* www.byerschoice.com	215-822-6700		362
Byers Engineering Co 6285 Barfield Rd. . . . . Atlanta GA 30328 *Web:* www.byers.com	404-843-1000	843-2000	261

	Phone	Fax	Class
Byers-Evans House Museum 1310 Bannock St . . . . Denver CO 80204 *TF:* 800-824-0150 ■ *Web:* www.historycolorado.org	303-620-4933		520
Byford Machine-Tool Inc 2038 State Hwy 6 N . . . . Valley Mills TX 76689 *Web:* www.byfordmachine.com	254-932-6111	932-6577	454
Bygone Designs PO Box 229. . . . . Newport MN 55055 *Web:* www.bygones.com	651-451-6737		593
BYK USA Inc 4285 Rider Trl N Ste 200 . . . . Earth City MO 63045 *Web:* www.byk.com	314-506-3135	506-3200	596
Byler, Wolf, Lutsch & Kampfer CPAS Inc 360 E State St. . . . . Salem OH 44460 *Web:* bwlkcpa.com	330-332-4646		2
Byline Bank 180 N LaSalle St . . . . Chicago IL 60601 *TF:* 800-236-2442 ■ *Web:* www.bylinebank.com	773-244-7000		70
Bypass Pharmacy Inc 104 S Eisenhower Dr . . . . Beckley WV 25801 *Web:* bypassrx.com	304-256-2006		237
Byram Laboratories Inc 1 Columbia Rd . . . . Branchburg NJ 08876 *TF:* 800-766-1212 ■ *Web:* byramlabs.com	908-252-0852		246
Byrd Cookie Company Inc 6700 Waters Ave. . . . . Savannah GA 31406 *TF:* 800-291-2973 ■ *Web:* www.byrdcookiecompany.com	912-355-1716		345
Byrd Instruments Inc 3611 Hwy 90 . . . . Westlake LA 70669 *Web:* byrdinst.com	337-882-0704	882-0706	189-4
Byrd Maintenance Services Inc 3172 Hwy 20 W . . . . Decatur AL 35601 *Web:* bmsi1.com	256-355-1627	355-0170	393
Byrne Bradley (Rep R - AL) 119 Cannon House Office Bldg. . . . . Washington DC 20515 *Web:* byrne.house.gov	202-225-4931	225-0562	342-2
Byrne Insurance Agency Inc 98 Homochitto St . . . . Natchez MS 39120 *Web:* www.byrneagency.com	601-442-2511	445-5375	390
Byrne Software Technologies Inc 16091 Swingley Ridge Rd Ste 200 . . . . Chesterfield MO 63017 *Web:* www.byrnesoftware.com	636-537-2505		177
Byrne, Byrne & Co 120 S Lasalle St Ste 1710. Chicago IL 60603 *Web:* byrnebyrne.com	312-346-2150		390
Byrnes & Kiefer Co 131 Kline Ave . . . . Callery PA 16024 *Web:* www.bkcompany.com	724-538-5200		296-1
Byrnes Agency Inc 394 Lake Rd. . . . . Dayville CT 06241 *Web:* www.byrnesagency.com	860-774-8549	779-3799	390
Byron & Edwards, Apc 530 B St Ste 610. . . . . San Diego CA 92101 *Web:* bemapc.com	619-400-5880		41
Byron Originals Fuel Sales 119 E State Hwy 175 PO Box 279. . . . . Ida Grove IA 51445 *TF:* 800-594-9421 ■ *Web:* byronfuels.com	800-594-9421		579
Byron Products Inc 3781 Port Union Rd . . . . Fairfield OH 45014 *Web:* byronproducts.com	513-870-9111		484
Bystronic Inc 200 Airport Rd. . . . . Elgin IL 60123 *Web:* www.bystronic.com	847-214-0300		454
Byte Right Support Inc 335 N Charles St . . . . Baltimore MD 21201 *TF:* 855-736-4437 ■ *Web:* www.byterightsupport.com	410-347-2983		175
Byte Systems LLC 2201 Cooperative Way Ste 600. . . . . Herndon VA 20171 *Web:* bytesys.net	703-436-8616		180
Bytemobile Inc 4988 Great America Pkwy. . . . . Santa Clara CA 95054 *TF:* 800-424-8749 ■ *Web:* www.citrix.com	408-790-8000		681
Bytespeed LLC 3131 24th Ave S . . . . Moorhead MN 56560 *TF:* 877-553-0777 ■ *Web:* www.bytespeed.com	218-227-0445		173-2
Bytewyze 120 Iowa LN Ste 101 . . . . Cary NC 27511 *Web:* www.bytewyze.com	919-465-1916		177
Bytown Museum 1 Canal Ln PO Box 423 Sta B. . . . . Ottawa ON K1P5P6 *Web:* www.bytownmuseum.com	613-234-4570	234-4846	520
BYU Museum of Peoples & Cultures 2201 N Canyon Rd . . . . Provo UT 84602 *Web:* mpc.byu.edu	801-422-0020	422-0026	520
Byzantine Catholic Seminary of SS Cyril & Methodius 3605 Perrysville Ave. . . . . Pittsburgh PA 15214 *Web:* www.bcs.edu	412-321-8383		167-3
BZ Media LLC 1 Shore Ave Unit 218 Ste 211 E . . . . Melville NY 11747 *Web:* www.bzmedia.com	631-421-4158		532-3
BZBM (Bartko, Zankel, Bunzel & Miller) 1 Embarcadero Ctr Ste 800. . . . . San Francisco CA 94111 *Web:* www.bzbm.com	415-956-1900	956-1152	445

C

	Phone	Fax	Class
C & A Financial Group 2111 Rt 34 S . . . . Wall NJ 07719 *Web:* www.ca-strategy.com	732-528-4800		390
C & A Industries Inc 13609 California St. . . . . Omaha NE 68154 *TF:* 800-574-9829 ■ *Web:* www.ca-industries.com	402-891-0009	891-9461	721
C & A Tool Engineering Inc 4100 North US 33 PO Box 94. . . . . Churubusco IN 46723 *Web:* www.catool.com	260-693-2167	693-3633	757
C & B Books Distribution 65-77 160th St No 3A. . . . . Flushing NY 11365 *Web:* www.cbbooksdistribution.com	718-591-4525		96
C & B Piping Inc 8804 Pkwy Dr . . . . Leeds AL 35094 *Web:* cbpiping.com	205-699-0455		480

Company	City	State	ZIP	Phone	Fax	Class
C & C Boiler Sales & Service Inc 3401 Rotary Dr *TF:* 800-333-1631 ■ *Web:* www.ccboiler.com	Charlotte	NC	28269	704-597-0003	598-2242	610
C & C Fabrication Company Inc 30 Fabrication Dr *TF:* 888-485-5130 ■ *Web:* www.ccfab.com	Laceys Spring	AL	35754	256-881-7300		198
C & C Machine Inc 159 Buchner Pl *Web:* www.ccmachineinc.com	La Crosse	WI	54603	608-784-4427		454
C & C Market Research Inc 1115 S Waldron Rd Ste 207 *Web:* www.ccmarketresearch.com	Fort Smith	AR	72903	479-785-5637		668
C & C Metal Products Corp 456 Nordhoff Pl *Web:* www.ccmetal.com	Englewood	NJ	07631	201-569-7300		295
C & C Reservoirs Inc 13831 NW Fwy Ste 450 *Web:* www.ccreservoirs.com	Houston	TX	77040	713-776-3872		194
C & D Insurance Service Inc 53 S Broad St E *Web:* canddinsurance.com	Angier	NC	27501	919-639-2990		390
C & D Technologies Inc 1400 Union Meeting Rd PO Box 3053 *TF:* 800-543-8630 ■ *Web:* www.cdtechno.com	Blue Bell	PA	19422	215-619-2700	619-7899	74
C & D Valve LLC 201 NW 67th St *TF:* 800-654-9233 ■ *Web:* www.cdvalve.com	Oklahoma City	OK	73116	800-654-9233	840-0443	789
C & D Zodiac Inc 5701 Bolsa Ave *Web:* www.safran-cabin.com	Huntington Beach	CA	92647	714-934-0000	934-0088	529
C & E Computers 165 Ramona Ave *Web:* cdgrp.com	South San Francisco	CA	94080	650-222-3857		175
C & E Plastics Inc 2500 State Rte 168 *TF:* 877-742-5531 ■ *Web:* ceplastics.com	Georgetown	PA	15043	724-947-4949	947-5150	604
C & E Specialities 2530 Laude Dr *Web:* www.cespecialties.com	Rockford	IL	61109	815-229-9230		627
C & E Tooling Inc 2560 W Brooks Ave *Web:* www.cetooling.com	North Las Vegas	NV	89032	702-736-2958	736-3038	757
C & F Enterprises Inc 819 Bluecrab Rd *TF:* 888-889-9868 ■ *Web:* www.cnfei.com	Newport News	VA	23606	757-873-5688		361
C & F Financial Co 1313 E Main St Ste 400 *NASDAQ: CFFI* ■ *TF:* 855-602-2001 ■ *Web:* www.cffc.com	Richmond	VA	23219	855-602-2001		360-2
C & F Packing Company Inc 515 Park Ave *Web:* www.cfpacking.com	Lake Villa	IL	60046	847-245-2000	245-2100	473
C & F Tool & Die Co 7206 Eckhert Rd *Web:* c-ftool.com	San Antonio	TX	78238	210-522-9310		454
C & G Plastics 12729 Foothill Blvd *Web:* www.cgplastics.net	Sylmar	CA	91342	818-837-3773	837-3770	604
C & G Systems Corp 320 E Main St *Web:* www.cgsystems.com	Lake Zurich	IL	60047	847-816-9700	816-9777	480
C & H Bus Lines Inc 448 Pine St candhbuslines.com	Macon	GA	31201	478-746-6441		107
C & H Hardware Inc 1403 Fruitvale Blvd *Web:* chhardwareyakima.com	Yakima	WA	98902	509-453-1912		351
C & H Intl 4751 Wilshire Blvd Ste 201 *TF:* 800-833-8888 ■ *Web:* www.cnhintl.com	Los Angeles	CA	90010	323-933-2288	939-2286	16
C & H Machine Inc 943 S Andreasen Dr *Web:* www.c-hmachine.com	Escondido	CA	92029	760-746-6459		757
C & H Stone Company Inc PO Box 147 *Web:* www.chstoneinc.com	Clear Creek	IN	47426	812-336-2560	331-7292	724
C & H Testing Service LLC 6224 Price Way *Web:* www.candhtesting.com	Bakersfield	CA	93308	661-589-4030	589-5390	539
C & I Engineering 1930 Bishop Ln Ste 800 *Web:* www.cieng.com	Louisville	KY	40218	502-451-4977	451-9574	261
C & J Clark America Inc 60 Tower Rd *TF:* 800-211-5461 ■ *Web:* www.clarksusa.com	Waltham	MA	02451	800-211-5461		301
C & J Forms & Label Inc 5115 Wheeler Ave *Web:* www.cjforms.com	Fort Smith	AR	72901	479-646-8716	646-8809	627
C & J Industries Inc 760 Water St *Web:* www.cjindustries.com	Meadville	PA	16335	814-724-4950	724-4959	604
C & J Jewelry Co 100 Dupont Dr *Web:* www.candjjewelry.com	Providence	RI	02907	401-944-2200		408
C & K Components Inc 15 Riverdale Ave *Web:* www.ckswitches.com	Newton	MA	02458	617-969-3700		729
C & K Industrial Services Inc 5617 Schaaf Rd *Web:* www.ckindustrial.com	Independence	OH	44131	216-642-0055		553
C & K Johnson Industries Inc 1061 Samoa Blvd *Web:* www.ckjohnsonind.com	Arcata	CA	95521	707-822-7688		492
C & K Markets Inc 615 5th St *Web:* www.ckmarket.com	Brookings	OR	97415	541-412-3550	469-6717	345
C & K Plastics Inc 159 Liberty St *Web:* www.candkplastics.com	Metuchen	NJ	08840	732-549-0011	549-1889	604
C & L Bus Company Inc 12200 W Broward Blvd	Plantation	FL	33325	954-472-7800		108
C & L Electric Co-opeartive Corp 900 Church St PO Box 9 *Web:* www.clelectric.com	Star City	AR	71667	870-628-4221	628-4676	245
C & L Supply Co PO Box 578 *TF:* 800-256-6411 ■ *Web:* clsupplyinc.com	Vinita	OK	74301	800-256-6411		38
C & l Value Advisors LLC 4805 W Laurel St Ste 100 *TF:* 888-876-4939 ■ *Web:* clvalue.com	Tampa	FL	33607	813-286-7373		2
C & M Conveyor 4598 State Rd 37 *TF:* 800-551-3195 ■ *Web:* cmconveyor.com	Mitchell	IN	47446	812-849-5647	849-5015	207
C & M Corp 349 Lake Rd *Web:* www.winconn.com	Dayville	CT	06241	860-774-4812		814
C & N Tractors 496 Salinas Rd *TF:* 800-499-0833 ■ *Web:* candntractors.com	Watsonville	CA	95076	831-722-2733		274
C & O United Credit Union Inc 3029 Dixie Hwy *Web:* co-united.org	Edgewood	KY	41017	859-331-3447		219
C & R Distributing Inc 8528 Alameda Ave *Web:* candrdistributing.com	El Paso	TX	79907	915-860-4205		579
C & R Mechanical 12825 Pennridge Dr *TF:* 800-524-3828 ■ *Web:* www.crmechanical.com	Bridgeton	MO	63044	314-739-1800	739-1721	189-10
C & R Racing Inc 6950 Guion Rd *Web:* www.crracing.com	Indianapolis	IN	46268	317-293-4100		54
C & R Research Services Inc 500 N Michigan Ave Ste 1100 *Web:* www.crresearch.com	Chicago	IL	60611	312-828-9200	527-3113	466
C & S Antennas Inc 1123 Industrial Dr SW *Web:* www.csantennas.com	Conover	NC	28613	828-324-2454		647
C & S Cos (CSCOS) 499 Col Eileen Collins Blvd *Web:* www.cscos.com	Syracuse	NY	13212	315-455-2000	455-9667	261
C & S Engineering Inc 956 Old Colony Rd *Web:* www.c-sengineering.com	Meriden	CT	06451	203-235-5727		75
C & S Sales Inc 12947 Chadron Ave *Web:* www.cssales.com	Hawthorne	CA	90250	310-538-1219	538-2814	534
C & S Wholesale Grocers Inc 47 Old Ferry Rd PO Box 821 *Web:* www.cswg.com	Brattleboro	VT	05301	802-464-6333		297-8
C & T Design & Equipment Company Inc 2750 Tobey Dr *TF:* 800-966-3374 ■ *Web:* www.c-tdesign.com	Indianapolis	IN	46219	800-966-3374		406
C & W Technologies 2522 SE Federal Hwy *TF:* 844-241-6442 ■ *Web:* cwnow.com	Stuart	FL	34994	772-287-5215		175
C A I Insurance Agency Inc 2035 Reading Rd *Web:* cai-insurance.com	Cincinnati	OH	45202	513-221-1140		390
C and S Specialty Inc 1181 Old Smithfield Rd *TF:* 800-321-0325 ■ *Web:* www.csspecialty.com	North Smithfield	RI	02896	401-769-2260	769-2270	76
C Bennett Building Supply Inc 1700 W Terra Ln *Web:* www.cbennett.net	O'Fallon	MO	63366	636-379-9886		361
C C M H Federal Credit Union 801 Ann St *Web:* ccmhfcu.org	Parkersburg	WV	26101	304-424-2255		219
C Cowles & Company Inc 83 Water St *Web:* www.ccowles.com	New Haven	CT	06511	203-865-3117		489
C Cretors & Co 176 Mittel Dr *TF:* 800-228-1885 ■ *Web:* www.cretors.com	Wood Dale	IL	60191	847-616-6900	616-6970	298
C D Barnes Associates Inc 3437 E Ave SE *Web:* www.cdbarnes.com	Grand Rapids	MI	49508	616-241-4491		463
C Dental X Ray 1050 Northgate Dr Ste 110 *Web:* www.cdental.com	San Rafael	CA	94903	415-472-1323		415
C Enterprises LP 2445 Cades Way *TF:* 800-334-3815 ■ *Web:* www.centerprises.com	Vista	CA	92081	760-599-5111	599-5120	174
C Erickson & Sons Inc 2200 Arch St Ste 200 *Web:* www.cerickson.com	Philadelphia	PA	19103	215-568-3120	496-9460	186
C H Garmong & Son Inc 3050 Poplar St **Fax Area Code:* 317 ■ *Web:* www.garmong.net	Terre Haute	IN	47803	812-234-3714	821-0266*	610
C I Thornburg Company Inc, The 4034 Altizer Ave *Web:* cithornburg.com	Huntington	WV	25705	304-523-3484	523-0510	595
C J Horner Company Inc 105 W Grand Ave *TF:* 800-426-4261 ■ *Web:* www.cjhornerinc.com	Hot Springs	AR	71901	501-321-9600	321-9623	182
C J Nolte Co, The 49 Village Ct *Web:* cjnolte.com	Hazlet	NJ	07730	732-739-1800	739-1814	112
C J Schlosser & Company LLC 233 E Center Dr PO Box 416 *Web:* cjsco.com	Alton	IL	62002	618-465-7717	465-7710	2
C L Smith 1311 S 39th St *TF:* 855-551-2625 ■ *Web:* www.clsmith.com	Saint Louis	MO	63110	855-551-2625		608
C Lazy U Ranch 3640 Colorado Hwy 125 PO Box 379 *Web:* www.clazyu.com	Granby	CO	80446	970-887-3344	887-3917	239
C M Buck & Associates Inc 6850 Guion Rd *TF:* 800-382-3961 ■ *Web:* cmbuck.com	Indianapolis	IN	46268	317-293-5704		393
C M School Supply Inc 940 N Central Ave *TF:* 800-464-6681 ■ *Web:* cmschoolsupply.com	Upland	CA	91786	909-982-9695		535
C Martin Company Inc 3395 W Cheyenne Ave *Web:* www.cmartin.com	North Las Vegas	NV	89032	702-656-8080		186
C Myers Corp 8222 S 48th St Ste 275 *TF:* 800-238-7475 ■ *Web:* www.cmyers.com	Phoenix	AZ	85044	800-238-7475		194
C Overaa & Company Inc 200 Parr Blvd *Web:* www.overaa.com	Richmond	CA	94801	510-234-0926	237-2435	186
C P H & Assoc 711 S Dearborn St Unit 205 *TF:* 800-875-1911 ■ *Web:* www.cphins.com	Chicago	IL	60605	312-987-9823	987-0902	390
C R & A Custom Inc 312 W Pico Blvd *Web:* www.cracustom.com	Los Angeles	CA	90015	213-749-4440		627
C R Hipp Construction Inc 4981 Dorchester Rd *Web:* www.crhippconstruction.com	North Charleston	SC	29418	843-744-4477	747-3399	261
C R International Inc 9105 Whiskey Bottom Rd *Web:* cri-inc.net	Laurel	MD	20723	301-210-1540		246
C R Laurence Company Inc 2503 E Vernon Ave *TF:* 800-421-6144 ■ *Web:* www.crlaurence.com	Los Angeles	CA	90058	800-421-6144		351

Company / Address	City	State	ZIP	Phone	Fax	Class
C R T & Associates Inc						
806 Hastings St Ste 8	Traverse City	MI	49686	231-946-1680		387
Web: www.crt-a.com						
C S Davidson Inc 38 N Duke St	York	PA	17401	717-846-4805		261
Web: www.csdavidson.com						
C S Precision Manufacturing Inc						
140028 Lockwood Rd	Gering	NE	69341	308-436-2099		358
Web: csprecisionmfg.com						
C Spire						
1018 Highland Colony Pkwy Ste 300	Ridgeland	MS	39157	855-277-4735		387
TF: 855-277-4735 ■ *Web:* www.cspire.com						
C Steinweg Inc 1201 Wallace St	Baltimore	MD	21230	410-752-8254		581
Web: www.steinweg.com						
C T S Services Inc 260 Maple St	Bellingham	MA	02019	508-528-7720	966-9734	175
Web: www.ctsservices.com						
C Thorrez Industries Inc						
4909 W Michigan Ave	Jackson	MI	49201	517-750-3160	750-1792	621
Web: www.thorrez.com						
C W I Inc						
650 Three Springs Raod	Bowling Green	KY	42104	888-626-7576		711
TF: 888-626-7576 ■ *Web:* www.campingworld.com						
C W Thomas Inc 8000 State Rd	Philadelphia	PA	19136	215-335-0200	335-4310	596
TF: 800-523-0856 ■ *Web:* www.cwthomas.com						
C Walters Intercoastal Corporation Inc						
20081 Ellipse	Foothill Ranch	CA	92610	949-448-9940	448-7008	711
TF: 800-500-8292 ■ *Web:* www.destinationwater.com						
C. Basil Grossnickle Inc						
415 Main St	Myersville	MD	21773	301-293-1755		390
Web: cbgrossnickle.com						
C. D. Denison Orthopaedic Appliance Corp						
32 W Rd Ste 120	Towson	MD	21204	410-235-9645	243-7413	477
Web: www.cddenison.com						
C. E. Bradley Laboratories Inc						
56 Bennett Dr	Brattleboro	VT	05304	802-257-7971	257-7070	550
Web: www.cebradley.com						
C. E. Conover & Company Inc						
4100 Blanche Rd	Bensalem	PA	19020	215-639-8888	639-1799	326
Web: conoverseals.com						
C. F. Bean LLC 619 Engineers Rd	Belle Chasse	LA	70037	504-587-8700		192
Web: www.cfbean.com						
C. H. Briggs Co PO Box 15188	Reading	PA	19612	610-929-6969	355-3131*	350
**Fax Area Code:* 800 ■ *Web:* www.chbriggs.com						
C. H. Guernsey & Co						
5555 N Grand Blvd	Oklahoma City	OK	73112	405-416-8100	416-8111	261
Web: guernsey.us						
C. H. Martin Co 329 Marietta St NW	Atlanta	GA	30313	404-525-1533	525-9819	477
Web: www.chmartinco.com						
C. J. Driscoll & Assoc						
2636 Via Carrillo	Palos Verdes Estates	CA	90274	310-544-5046		195
Web: www.cjdriscoll.com						
C. K. Smith & Company Inc						
99 Crescent St	Worcester	MA	01605	508-753-1475		581
Web: www.cksmithsuperior.com						
C. M. Cleaning Company Inc						
1024 Turnpike St	Canton	MA	02021	781-828-2014		104
Web: cmcleaning.com						
C. Martinez Insurance Agency Inc						
878 S Dixie Hwy Ste 100	Coral Gables	FL	33146	305-663-4921		390
Web: carmartinez.com						
C. S. McKee LP						
420 Ft Duquesne Blvd 8th Fl	Pittsburgh	PA	15222	412-566-1234	566-1557	528
Web: www.csmckee.com						
C. W. Brown Inc 1 Labriola Ct	Armonk	NY	10504	914-741-1212		186
C. W. Howard Insurance Agency Inc						
405 W Jefferson St	Butler	PA	16001	724-283-8181	431-2835	390
TF: 800-533-5151 ■ *Web:* howardinsurance.com						
C.A. Murren & Sons Company Inc						
2275 Loganville Hwy	Grayson	GA	30017	770-682-2940		186
TF: 866-912-8906 ■ *Web:* camurren.com						
C.A. Precision Inc						
1004 NW 51st Pl	Fort Lauderdale	FL	33309	954-491-4356	491-4369	454
Web: www.caprecision.com						
C.A.P.S. Inc 13080 Hollenberg Dr	Bridgeton	MO	63044	314-739-2002	739-7889	604
TF: 800-216-2993 ■ *Web:* www.capsincorporated.com						
C.B. Development Services Inc						
1617 Jfk Blvd Ste 1090	Philadelphia	PA	19103	215-569-0156		653
Web: cbdsi.com						
C.B.S. Boring & Machine Company Inc						
33750 Riviera Dr	Fraser	MI	48026	586-294-7540		757
Web: www.cbsboring.com						
C.C. Clark Inc						
300 Oakland-Flatrock Rd	Oakland	KY	42159	270-563-4735	563-4529	360-3
Web: www.ccclark.com						
C.D. Haugen Inc 5049 Scribner Rd NW	Bemidji	MN	56601	218-751-2738	751-0426	780
Web: www.cdhaugen.com						
C.D. Plus Inc 8400 N Magnolia Ave Ste K	Santee	CA	92071	619-405-3938	486-2591*	411
**Fax Area Code:* 866 ■ *Web:* www.orientalpearls.net						
C.E. Beckman Co						
11-35 Commercial St	New Bedford	MA	02741	508-994-9674	990-2785	61
Web: www.cebeckman.com						
C.F. Maier Composites Inc						
16351 Table Mountain Pky	Golden	CO	80403	800-962-6079	278-0940*	125
**Fax Area Code:* 303 ■ *TF:* 800-962-6079 ■ *Web:* www.cfmaier.com						
C.J. Hughes Construction Co						
75 W 3rd Ave	Huntington	WV	25701	304-522-3868	522-2729	188-10
Web: www.cjhughes.com						
C.J. Link Lumber Co 11711 E 8 Mile Rd	Warren	MI	48089	586-773-1200	773-9611	191-3
TF: 800-462-9716 ■ *Web:* www.cjlinklumber.com						
C.L. Pugh & Associates Inc (CLP)						
1157 Pearl Rd	Brunswick	OH	44212	330-220-4404	220-4434	246
Web: www.pugh.com						
C.O.W. Industries Inc						
1875 Progress Ave	Columbus	OH	43207	614-443-6537	443-9600	482
Web: www.cowind.com						
C.R. Newton Company Ltd						
1575 S Beretania St	Honolulu	HI	96826	808-949-8389	955-4721	475
TF: 800-545-2078 ■ *Web:* www.crnewton.com						
C.S. Bancshares Inc						
600 Washington St	Chillicothe	MO	64601	660-646-5120	646-6903	360-2
Web: www.gostatebank.com						
C.S. Garber & Sons Inc						
7928 Boyertown Pke	Boyertown	PA	19512	610-367-2861	367-5560	189-15
Web: csgarber.com						
C.S.S. Publishing Co 5450 N Dixie Hwy	Lima	OH	45802	419-227-1818		637-2
TF: 800-537-1030 ■ *Web:* www.csspub.com						
C.V. Starr and Co 399 Park Ave 8th Fl	New York	NY	10022	646-227-6300		391-4
Web: www.starrcompanies.com						
C.W. O'Conner & Associates Inc						
655 Engineering Dr Ste 110	Peachtree Corners	GA	30092	770-368-9919		690
Web: cwoconner.com						
C12 Group LLC, The						
4101 Piedmont Pkwy	Greensboro	NC	27410	336-841-7100		317
Web: www.c12group.com						
C14 Consulting Group LLC						
1307 Summerhill Dr	Malvern	PA	19355	610-644-2243		261
Web: c14consultinggroup.com						
C1S Group Inc 4231 Sigma Rd Ste 110	Dallas	TX	75244	972-386-7005		186
Web: c1sinc.com						
C2 Group LLC						
325 7th St NW Liberty Pl Ste 400	Washington	DC	20004	202-567-2900	393-7887	463
Web: www.thec2group.com						
C21 Investments Inc						
595 Howe St Ste 303	Vancouver	BC	V6C2T5	604-336-8613		536
Web: www.curlew-lake.com						
C2AE 106 W Allegan St Ste 500	Lansing	MI	48933	866-454-3923		261
TF: 866-454-3923 ■ *Web:* www.c2ae.com						
C2C Outdoor						
32 Avenue of the Americas 25th Fl	New York	NY	10013	917-677-3032		8
Web: www.c2c-outdoor.com						
C2ER (Council for Community & Economic Research)						
1700 N Moore St Ste 2225	Arlington	VA	22209	703-522-4980	393-5098*	49-12
**Fax Area Code:* 480 ■ *Web:* www.c2er.org						
C2F Inc 6600 SW 111th Ave	Beaverton	OR	97008	503-643-9050		96
TF: 800-544-8825 ■ *Web:* www.c2f.com						
C2it Consulting Inc						
9107 State Rd 142	Martinsville	IN	46151	317-721-2248		463
TF: 866-217-7478 ■ *Web:* c2itconsulting.net						
C3 Corp 3300 E Venture Dr	Appleton	WI	54911	920-749-9944		261
TF: 888-835-9653 ■ *Web:* c3ingenuity.com						
C3 Tech Services 1536 E Warner Ave	Santa Ana	CA	92705	714-689-1700		366
Web: c3technology.services						
C3LS 941 Clint Moore Rd	Boca Raton	FL	33487	561-995-9004		177
Web: www.c3ls.com						
C-4 Analytics LLC 999 Broadway Ste 500	Saugus	MA	01906	617-250-8888		195
Web: c-4analytics.com						
C4 Planning Solutions LLC						
4914 Deans Bridge Rd	Blythe	GA	30805	706-592-1520		194
TF: 800-715-5436 ■ *Web:* www.c4plans.com						
C5 Group Inc 1329 Bay St 3 Fl	Toronto	ON	M5R2C4	416-927-0718		224
Web: c5groupinc.com						
C5 Insight Inc						
9319 Robert D Snyder Rd Ste 348	Charlotte	NC	28223	704-895-2500		463
Web: www.c5insight.com						
CA (Cocaine Anonymous World Services Inc)						
PO Box 492000	Los Angeles	CA	90049	310-559-5833	559-2554	48-21
TF: 800-347-8998 ■ *Web:* ca.org						
CA Child Support Services						
PO Box 419064	Rancho Cordova	CA	95741	916-464-5000		339-5
TF: 866-901-3212 ■ *Web:* childsupport.ca.gov						
CA Lawton Company Inc						
1950 Enterprise Way	De Pere	WI	54115	920-337-2470		456
Web: www.calawton.com						
Ca Lindman Inc 10401 Guilford Rd	Jessup	MD	20794	301-470-4700	470-4708	186
TF: 877-737-8675 ■ *Web:* www.calindman.com						
CA Rasmussen Inc						
28548 Livingston Ave	Valencia	CA	91355	661-367-9040	367-9099	188-4
Web: www.carasmussen.com						
CA Spalding Co 1011 Cedar Ave	Croydon	PA	19021	267-550-9000		757
Web: www.caspalding.com						
CA Walker Research Solutions Inc						
100 W Broadway Ste 1170	Glendale	CA	91210	626-584-8180	584-8199	466
Web: www.cawalker.com						
Ca'del Sole 4100 Cahuenga Blvd	Toluca Lake	CA	91602	818-985-4669		671
Web: www.cadelsole.com						
CAA (Creative Artists Agency Inc)						
2000 Avenue of the Stars	Los Angeles	CA	90067	424-288-2000	288-2900	731
Web: www.caa.com						
CAA (Council on Aviation Accreditation)						
Aviation Accreditation Board International						
3410 Skyway Dr	Auburn	AL	36830	334-844-2431	844-2432	48-1
Web: www.aabi.aero						
CAA Club Group						
60 Commerce Valley Dr E	Thornhill	ON	L3T7P9	905-771-3000	771-3101	53
TF: 866-988-8878 ■ *Web:* www.caasco.com						
CAA Manitoba 870 Empress St	Winnipeg	MB	R3C2Z3	204-262-6166		53
TF: 800-222-4357 ■ *Web:* www.caamanitoba.com						
CAA Maritimes Ltd						
378 Westmorland Rd	Saint John	NB	E2J2G4	506-634-1400	653-9500	53
TF: 800-471-1611 ■ *Web:* www.atlantic.caa.ca						
CAA North & East Ontario PO Box 8350	Ottawa	ON	K1G3T2	613-820-1890	820-4646	53
TF: 800-267-8713 ■ *Web:* caaneo.ca						
CAA Quebec 444 Bouvier St	Quebec City	QC	G2J1E3	418-624-8222		53
TF: 800-686-9243 ■ *Web:* www.caaquebec.com						
CAA Saskatchewan 200 N Albert St	Regina	SK	S4R5E2	306-791-4314		390
TF: 800-564-6222 ■ *Web:* caask.ca						
CAAHEP (Commission on Accreditation of Allied Health Education Programs)						
1361 Park St	Clearwater	FL	33756	727-210-2350	210-2354	48-1
Web: caahep.org						
CAAS (Connecticut Academy of Arts & Sciences, The)						
310 Prospect St	New Haven	CT	06511	203-432-3113	432-5712	637-2
Web: caas.yale.edu						
CAAS (Classical Association of the Atlantic States)						
Valley Forge Military Academy & College						
1001 Eagle Rd	Wayne	PA	19087	610-896-8903		49-19
Web: caas-cw.org						

Name / Address	City	State	Zip	Phone	Fax	Class
Caasco Signs 2719 Texas Ave *Web:* creativesigntc.com	Texas City	TX	77590	409-945-4929		701
CAB (Video Advertising Bureau) 830 Third Ave 2nd Fl *Web:* www.thevab.com	New York	NY	10022	212-508-1200	832-3268	49-18
Cab Signs 38 Livonia Ave *TF:* 800-394-1690 ■ *Web:* cabsignsinc.com	Brooklyn	NY	11212	800-394-1690		627
Caballo Blanco Restaurante Inc 5604 Franklin Blvd	Sacramento	CA	95824	916-428-6706		671
Caballo Energy LLC 2007 E 15th St	Tulsa	OK	74104	918-794-8800		580
Caban Resources LLC 130 Arena St *TF:* 877-880-1600 ■ *Web:* www.cabanresources.com	El Segundo	CA	90245	877-880-1600		463
Cabana 533 Clematis St *Web:* www.cabanarestaurant.com	West Palm Beach	FL	33401	561-833-4773		671
Cabaniss, Johnston, Gardner, Dumas & O'Neal LLP 2001 Park Pl N Ste 700 *Web:* www.cabaniss.com	Birmingham	AL	35203	205-716-5200		428
Cabaret Systems Inc 6923 Shannon Willow Rd *Web:* www.cabaretsystems.com	Charlotte	NC	28226	704-333-1100		174
Cabarrus County 65 Church St S PO Box 707 *Web:* www.cabarruscounty.us	Concord	NC	28025	704-920-2100	920-2820	338
Cabarrus County Convention & Visitors Bureau 10099 Weddington Road Ext Ste 102 *TF:* 800-848-3740 ■ *Web:* www.visitcabarrus.com	Concord	NC	28027	704-782-4340	782-4333	206
Cabarrus County School District 4401 Old Airport Rd *Web:* www.cabarrus.k12.nc.us	Concord	NC	28025	704-786-6191	786-6141	685
Cabarrus Regional Chamber of Commerce 3003 Dale Earnhardt Blvd *Web:* www.cabarrus.biz	Kannapolis	NC	28083	704-782-4000	782-4050	139
Cabedge 1310 Clinton St Ste 200 *Web:* www.cabedge.com	Nashville	TN	37203	615-942-9937	942-9976	631
Cabela's Inc 1 Cabela Dr *NYSE: CAB* ■ *TF:* 800-237-8888 ■ *Web:* www.cabelas.com	Sidney	NE	69160	800-850-8402		711
Cabell County 750 Fifth Ave Ste 300 *Web:* www.cabellcounty.org	Huntington	WV	25701	304-526-8634	526-8648	338
Cabell County Public Library 455 9th St *Web:* www.cabell.lib.wv.us	Huntington	WV	25701	304-528-5700		434-3
Cabell Huntington Hospital (CHH) 1340 Hal Greer Blvd *Web:* www.cabellhuntington.org	Huntington	WV	25701	304-526-2000		374-3
Cabell-Huntington Convention & Visitors Bureau PO Box 347 *TF:* 800-635-6329 ■ *Web:* www.visithuntingtonwv.org	Huntington	WV	25708	304-525-7333	525-7345	206
Cabello Assoc 8340 Little Eagle Ct Ste 2 *Web:* www.cabelloassociates.com	Indianapolis	IN	46234	317-209-9991		7
CabelTel International Corp 1603 Lyndon B Johnson Fwy **Fax Area Code:* 469 ■ *Web:* www.newconceptenergy.com	Dallas	TX	75234	972-407-8400	522-4240*	451
Cabem Technologies LLC 2000 Commonwealth Ave Ste 410 *Web:* www.cabem.com	Auburndale	MA	02466	617-244-6609		261
Caber Sure Fit Inc 25A E Pearce St Unit 2 *Web:* www.cabersurefit.com	Richmond Hill	ON	L4B2M9	905-886-5849		361
Cabin Crafters 1225 W First St *TF:* 800-699-3920 ■ *Web:* www.cabincrafters.com	Nevada	IA	50201	515-382-5406	382-3106	523
Cabinet Components & Distribution Inc 760 Beltline Rd	Sauk Centre	MN	56378	320-352-5404		115
Cabinet Discounters Inc 9500 Berger Rd *TF:* 800-843-3732 ■ *Web:* www.cabinetdiscounters.com	Columbia	MD	21046	410-793-1265	266-9287	321
Cabinet Press, The 167 Elm St *Web:* www.cabinet.com	Milford	NH	03055	603-673-3100		532-3
Cabinet Tronix 280 Trousdale Dr Ste A *TF:* 866-876-6199 ■ *Web:* www.cabinet-tronix.com	Chula Vista	CA	91910	866-876-6199		819
Cabinetry By Karman 6000 S Stratler St *TF:* 800-255-3581 ■ *Web:* cabinetrybykarman.com	Salt Lake City	UT	84107	801-268-3581		115
Cabinetry Concepts Inc 14410 Azurite St NW *Web:* cabinetryconcepts.com	Anoka	MN	55303	763-427-4600		115
Cabinetry Ideas Inc 6113 Allisonville Rd *Web:* cabinetryideas.com	Indianapolis	IN	46220	317-722-1300		362
Cabinets 2000 Inc 11100 Firestone Blvd *Web:* www.cabinets2000.com	Norwalk	CA	90650	562-868-0909		115
Cabinets By Michael 4301 Murray Ave *Web:* cabinetsbymichael.com	Fort Worth	TX	76117	817-485-1962	485-9034	115
Cabinets To Go LLC 6901 Crestwood Blvd *Web:* cabinetstogo.com	Birmingham	AL	35210	205-623-2209		393
Cabins Usa Gatlinburg LLC 849 Glades Rd Unit 1A1 *TF:* 800-584-9872 ■ *Web:* www.cabinsusagatlinburg.com	Gatlinburg	TN	37738	865-436-5031		377
Cable Aml Inc 2271 W 205th St Ste 101 *Web:* cableaml.com	Torrance	CA	90501	310-222-5599	222-5593	261
Cable Com Inc 12115 Roxie Dr *Web:* www.cablecominc.com	Austin	TX	78729	512-250-5901		116
Cable Connection, The 52 Heppner Dr *TF:* 800-851-2961 ■ *Web:* www.thecableconnection.com	Carson City	NV	89706	775-885-1443	885-2734	116
Cable Coop 27 E College St *Web:* www.oberlin.net	Oberlin	OH	44074	440-775-4001		116
Cable Ctr, The 2000 Buchtel Blvd *Web:* www.cablecenter.org	Denver	CO	80210	720-502-7500		116
Cable Huston Benedic 1001 SW Fifth Ave Ste 2000 *Web:* www.cablehuston.com	Portland	OR	97204	503-224-3092		428
Cable Line Inc 460 Ax Handle Rd *Web:* www.cable-line.com	Quakertown	PA	18951	267-772-1779		116
Cable Manufacturing & Assembly Co 10896 Industrial Pkwy NW *Web:* www.cmacable.com	Bolivar	OH	44612	330-874-2900		203
Cable Markers Company Inc 13805-C Alton Pkwy **Fax Area Code:* 949 ■ *TF:* 800-746-7655 ■ *Web:* www.cablemarkers.com	Irvine	CA	92618	800-746-7655	699-1642*	467
Cable One Inc 210 E Earll Dr *TF:* 877-692-2253 ■ *Web:* www.cableone.net	Phoenix	AZ	85012	602-364-6000	364-6010	116
Cable Public Affairs Channel (CPAC) PO Box 81099 **Fax Area Code:* 613 ■ *TF:* 877-287-2722 ■ *Web:* www.cpac.ca	Ottawa	ON	K1P1B1	877-287-2722	567-2749*	740
Cable Satellite Public Affairs Network (C-SPAN) 400 N Capitol St NW Ste 650 *Web:* www.c-span.org	Washington	DC	20001	202-737-3220		740
Cable Technologies Inc 3209 Ave E East *Web:* www.cabletechnologiesinc.com	Arlington	TX	76011	817-633-9181	633-2472	815
Cable Technology Laboratories Inc (CTL) 625 Jersey Ave Unit 14 *Web:* www.cabtl.com	New Brunswick	NJ	08901	732-846-3133	846-5531	194
Cable Television Laboratories Inc 858 Coal Creek Cir *Web:* www.cablelabs.com	Louisville	CO	80027	303-661-9100	661-9199	49-14
Cable USA LLC 2584 S Horseshoe Dr *Web:* cableusallc.com	Naples	FL	34104	239-643-6400	643-4230	814
Cableair Inc 1749 W 13th St *Web:* cableairport.com	Upland	CA	91786	909-982-6021	920-0705	167-3
CableAmerica Corp 7822 E Gray Rd *TF:* 866-871-4492 ■ *Web:* www.cableamerica.com	Scottsdale	AZ	85260	480-315-1820		116
CableCom LLC 6070 N Flint Rd *Web:* www.cablecomllc.com	Glendale	WI	53209	414-226-2205		116
Cable-Comm Technologies Inc 800 Enterprise Ct *TF:* 800-544-1330 ■ *Web:* www.cable-comm.com	Naperville	IL	60563	630-717-7179	717-5758	116
Cablecraft Motion Controls LLC 2110 Summit St *Web:* www.cablecraft.com	New Haven	IN	46774	260-749-5105	493-2387	620
Cable-Dahmer Chevrolet Inc 1834 S Noland Rd *TF:* 866-650-1809 ■ *Web:* www.cabledahmer.com	Independence	MO	64055	866-918-1427		57
Cables and Chips Inc 121 Fulton St *Web:* www.cablesandchipsinc.com	New York	NY	10038	212-619-3132	619-3982	174
Cables to Go Inc 3599 Dayton Pk Dr *TF:* 800-826-7904 ■ *Web:* www.cablestogo.com	Dayton	OH	45414	937-224-8646		814
Cableworks Communications 3112 Main St Unit 3 *Web:* cableworks.co	Salisbury	NB	E4J2L6	506-372-9542		681
Cabo Drilling (Ontario) Corp 20 Sixth St *Web:* www.cabo.ca	New Westminster	BC	V3L2Y8	604-527-4201		540
Cabo Seafood Grill & Cantina 1041 S Oxnard Blvd *Web:* www.caboox.com	Oxnard	CA	93030	805-487-6933		671
Cabo's Island Grill & Bar 1221 Apalachee Pkwy *Web:* www.cabosgrill.com	Tallahassee	FL	32301	850-878-7707		671
Cabot Coach Builders Inc 99 Newark St *TF:* 800-544-5587 ■ *Web:* www.royalelimo.com	Haverhill	MA	01832	978-374-4530		647
Cabot Corp 2 Seaport Ln Ste 1300 *NYSE: CBT* ■ *TF:* 800-322-1236 ■ *Web:* www.cabotcorp.com	Boston	MA	02210	617-345-0100	342-6103	145
Cabot Creamery 193 Home Farm Way *TF:* 888-792-2268 ■ *Web:* www.cabotcheese.coop	Waitsfield	VT	05673	888-792-2268		296-5
Cabot House Furniture 10 Industrial Way *Web:* cabothousefurniture.com	Amesbury	MA	01913	207-761-1999		321
Cabot Microelectronics Corp 870 N Commons Dr *NASDAQ: CCMP* ■ *TF:* 800-811-2756 ■ *Web:* www.cabotcmp.com	Aurora	IL	60504	630-375-6631	375-5539	145
Cabot Oil & Gas Corp 840 Gessner Rd Ste 1400 *NYSE: COG* ■ *TF:* 800-434-3985 ■ *Web:* www.cabotog.com	Houston	TX	77024	281-848-2799		787
Cabot Wealth Management Inc 216 Essex St *TF:* 800-888-6468 ■ *Web:* ecabot.com	Salem	MA	01970	978-745-9233		528
Cabot Wealth Network 176 N St PO Box 2049 **Fax Area Code:* 978 ■ *TF:* 800-326-8826 ■ *Web:* cabotwealth.com	Salem	MA	01970	800-326-8826	745-1283*	531-9
Cabot's Pueblo Museum 67616 E Desert View Ave *Web:* www.cabotsmuseum.org	Desert Hot Springs	CA	92240	760-329-7610		520
CabotWrenn 405 Rink Dam Rd PO Box 1767 *Web:* www.cabotwrenn.com	Hickory	NC	28603	828-495-4607	495-1294	319-1
Cabrera Capital Markets LLC 10 S La Salle St Ste 1050 *Web:* www.cabreracapital.com	Chicago	IL	60603	312-236-8888	236-8936	690
Cabrillo Advisors LLC 1200 Prospect St Ste 550 *Web:* www.cabrilloadvisors.com	La Jolla	CA	92037	858-452-9500		70
Cabrillo College 6500 Soquel Dr *Web:* www.cabrillo.edu	Aptos	CA	95003	831-479-6100	479-5782	162
Cabrillo Marine Aquarium 3720 Stephen M White Dr *Web:* www.cabrillomarineaquarium.org	San Pedro	CA	90731	310-548-7562	548-2649	40
Cabrillo National Monument 1800 Cabrillo Memorial Dr *Web:* www.nps.gov	San Diego	CA	92106	619-557-5450	226-6311	564
Cabrillo Unified School District 498 Kelly Ave *Web:* www.cabrillo.k12.ca.us	Half Moon Bay	CA	94019	650-712-7100	726-0279	685
Cabrini College 610 King of Prussia Rd *TF:* 800-848-1003 ■ *Web:* www.cabrini.edu	Radnor	PA	19087	610-902-8552	902-8508	166
CABT (Coalition Against Bigger Trucks) 109 N Fairfax St 2nd Fl *TF:* 888-222-8123 ■ *Web:* cabt.org	Alexandria	VA	22314	703-535-3131		49-21
Cabwaylingo State Forest 4279 Cabwaylingo Park Rd *Web:* wvstateparks.com	Dunlow	WV	25511	304-385-4255		565

Phone | Fax | Class

CAC (Cement Association of Canada)
1105-350 Sparks St . . . Ottawa ON K1R7S8 613-236-9471 49-3
Web: www.cement.ca

CAC (Coating & Adhesive Corp)
1901 Popular St PO Box 1080 . . . Leland NC 28451 910-371-3184 371-5580 550
TF: 800-410-2999 ■ *Web:* www.cacoatings.com

CAC China 30 Camptown Rd . . . Maplewood NJ 07040 973-371-4300 371-4611 361
Web: www.cacchinausa.com

Cacapon Resort State Park
818 Cacapon Lodge Dr . . . Berkeley Springs WV 25411 304-258-1022 565
Web: wvstateparks.com

CACC (Charleston Area Convention Center Complex)
5000 Coliseum Dr . . . North Charleston SC 29418 843-529-5050 205
Web: www.charlestonconventioncenter.com

Cache Cache Bistro 205 S Mill St . . . Aspen CO 81611 970-925-3835 671
Web: cachecache.com

Cache Chamber of Commerce 160 N Main St . . . Logan UT 84321 435-752-2161 753-5825 139
Web: www.cachechamber.com

Cache County School District
2063 N 1200 E . . . North Logan UT 84341 435-752-3925 753-2168 685
Web: www.ccsdut.org

Cache Creek Casino Resort 14455 Hwy 16 . . . Brooks CA 95606 530-796-3118 133
TF: 800-992-8686 ■ *Web:* www.cachecreek.com

Cache Creek Foods LLC
411 Pioneer Ave . . . Woodland CA 95776 530-662-1764 345
Web: www.cachecreekfoods.com

Cache River State Natural Area
930 Sunflower Ln . . . Belknap IL 62908 618-657-2064 565
Web: www2.illinois.gov

Cache Valley Electric Inc 875 N 1000 W . . . Logan UT 84321 435-752-6405 752-9111 189-4
TF: 888-558-0600 ■ *Web:* www.cve.com

Cachet Financial Services
175 S Lake Ave Ste 200 . . . Pasadena CA 91101 855-591-9865 2
TF: 855-591-9865 ■ *Web:* www.cachetservices.com

Cachuma Press PO Box 560 . . . Los Olivos CA 93441 805-688-0413 637-2
Web: cachumapress.com

CACI Inc 12855 Tesson Ferry Rd . . . Saint Louis MO 63128 800-777-7971 160
TF: 800-777-7971 ■ *Web:* cacionline.net

CACI International Inc
1100 N Glebe Rd . . . Arlington VA 22201 703-841-7800 841-7882 180
NYSE: CACI ■ *TF:* 866-606-3471 ■ *Web:* www.caci.com

Cacique Inc 14923 Procter Ave . . . La Puente CA 91746 626-961-3399 369-8083 296-5
TF: 800-521-6987 ■ *Web:* www.caciqueinc.com

Cacl Federal Credit Union
1800 W Market St . . . Pottsville PA 17901 570-628-2400 628-0488 219
Web: caclfcu.org

Caco-Pacific Corp 813 N Cummings Rd . . . Covina CA 91724 626-331-3361 966-4219 757
Web: www.cacopacific.com

Cactus 4220 E Madison . . . Seattle WA 98112 206-324-4140 671
Web: www.cactusrestaurants.com

Cactus Cantina
3300 Wisconsin Ave NW . . . Washington DC 20016 202-686-7222 671
Web: www.cactuscantina.com

Cactus Car Wash
2777 Chapel Hill Rd . . . Douglasville GA 30135 770-726-7716 62-1
Web: www.cactuscarwash.com

Cactus Computer Inc
1120 Metrocrest Dr Ste 222 . . . Carrollton TX 75006 972-416-0525 447-9511* 180
**Fax Area Code:* 214 ■ *Web:* www.cactuscomputerinc.com

Cactus Feeders Inc
2209 W Seventh Ave . . . Amarillo TX 79106 806-373-2333 10-1
Web: www.cactusfeeders.com

Cactus Flower Florists
10822 N Scottsdale Rd . . . Scottsdale AZ 85254 480-483-9200 292
TF: 800-922-2887 ■ *Web:* www.cactusflower.com

Cactus International Inc 211 S Main St . . . Moscow ID 83843 208-883-5500 224
TF: 800-310-5554 ■ *Web:* www.cactuscomputer.com

Cactus Jack Marketing
420 N Carson St . . . Carson City NV 89701 775-882-8770 133
Web: cactusjackmarketing.com

Cactus Jacks Southwest Grill
782 S Willow St . . . Manchester NH 03103 603-627-8600 434-3200 671
Web: www.cactusjacksnh.com

Cactus Mailing Co 16020 N 77th St . . . Scottsdale AZ 85260 866-443-1442 5
TF: 888-633-7939 ■ *Web:* www.cactusmailing.com

Cactus Punch Inc
1224 Heil Quaker Blvd . . . La Vergne TN 37086 800-446-2333 344
TF: 800-446-2333 ■ *Web:* www.myembroideries.com

Cactus Ya Ya
15704 SE Mill Plain Blvd . . . Vancouver WA 98684 360-944-9292 671
Web: www.cactusyayarestaurant.com

CACU (Community America Credit Union)
9777 Ridge Dr . . . Lenexa KS 66219 913-905-7000 905-7111 219
TF: 800-892-7957 ■ *Web:* www.communityamerica.com

CAD (Cartridge Actuated Devices Inc)
51 Dwight Pl . . . Fairfield NJ 07004 973-575-1312 268
Web: cartactdev.com

CAD & Graphic Supply Inc
2410 Luna Rd Ste 114 . . . Carrollton TX 75006 972-409-7333 175

CAD Control Systems
1017 Frenchman Dr . . . Broussard LA 70518 337-369-3737 538
TF: 800-543-1968 ■ *Web:* www.cadoil.com

CAD Enterprises Inc 302 N 52nd Ave . . . Phoenix AZ 85043 602-278-4407 278-7262 454
Web: www.cadmachining.com

CAD Railway Industries Ltd
155 Boul Montreal-Toronto (Hwy 2-20) . . . Lachine QC H8S1B4 514-634-3131 650
Web: www.cadrail.ca

CAD/CAM Consulting Services Inc (CCCS)
1525 Rancho Conejo Blvd Ste 103 . . . Newbury Park CA 91320 805-375-7676 375-7678 174
TF: 888-375-7676 ■ *Web:* www.cad-cam.com

Cadalog Inc 1448 King St . . . Bellingham WA 98229 360-647-2426 647-2890 178-5
Web: www.cadalog-inc.com

Cadbury at Home 2317 Church Rd . . . Cherry Hill NJ 08002 800-422-3287 672
TF: 800-422-3287 ■ *Web:* cadbury.org

Cadco Ltd 145 Colebrook River Rd . . . Winsted CT 06098 860-738-2500 362
Web: cadco-ltd.com

Caddell Construction Company Inc
2700 Lagoon Pk Dr . . . Montgomery AL 36109 334-272-7723 272-8844 186
Web: www.caddell.com

Phone | Fax | Class

Cadden & Fuller LLP
114 Pacifica Ste 450 . . . Irvine CA 92618 949-416-0245 445
Web: www.caddenfuller.com

Caddo County PO Box 68 . . . Anadarko OK 73005 405-247-6609 338
Web: ok.gov

Caddo Kiowa Technology Ctr
1415 N 7th St PO Box 190 . . . Fort Cobb OK 73038 405-643-5511 643-3014 167-3
Web: mycktc.com

Caddo Lake State Park 245 Park Rd 2 . . . Karnack TX 75661 903-679-3351 565
Web: tpwd.texas.gov

Caddo Mills ISD 100 Fox Ln . . . Caddo Mills TX 75135 903-527-6056 685
Web: www.caddomillsisd.org

Caddo Parish School Board
1961 Midway Ave PO Box 32000 . . . Shreveport LA 71130 318-603-6300 603-6559 685
Web: www.caddoschools.org

Caddoan Mounds State Historic Site
1649 Texas 21 . . . Alto TX 75925 936-858-3218 565
Web: www.thc.texas.gov

Caddy Corporation of America
509 Sharptown Rd . . . Bridgeport NJ 08014 856-467-4222 467-5511 207
Web: www.caddycorp.com

Caddy Printing & Graphics Inc
13701 Neutron Rd . . . Dallas TX 75244 972-991-1770 627
Web: www.caddyprinting.com

CADE (Commission on Accreditation for Dietetics Education)
120 S Riverside Plz Ste 2000 . . . Chicago IL 60606 312-899-0040 48-1
TF: 800-877-1600 ■ *Web:* www.eatright.org

Cade & Associates Adv Inc
1645 Metropolitan Blvd . . . Tallahassee FL 32308 850-385-0300 4
Web: cade1.com

Cadeau Express Inc 3494 E Sunset Rd . . . Las Vegas NV 89120 702-433-1333 238

Cadence Capital Management
265 Franklin St 4th Fl . . . Boston MA 02110 617-624-3500 624-3591 401
Web: cadencecapital.com

Cadence Design Systems Inc
2655 Seely Ave . . . San Jose CA 95134 408-943-1234 428-5001 178-5
NASDAQ: CDNS ■ *TF:* 800-746-6223 ■ *Web:* www.cadence.com

Cadence Environmental Energy Inc
One Cadence Park Plz . . . Michigan City IN 46360 219-879-0371 196
Web: cadenceenvironmental.com

Cadence Group Inc
1095 Zonolite Rd Ste 105 . . . Atlanta GA 30306 888-346-8125 225
TF: 888-346-8125 ■ *Web:* www.cadence-group.com

Cadence Marketing LLC 509 Lake Ct . . . Basalt CO 81621 970-618-1789 195
Web: www.cadencemarketing.net

Cadence Mcshane Corp
5057 Keller Springs Rd Ste 500 . . . Addison TX 75001 972-239-2336 186
Web: cadencemcshane.com

Cadence Research & Consulting
360 Via Las Brisas Ste 210 . . . Thousand Oaks CA 91320 805-499-8603 466
Web: testcadres.com

Cadence Technologies Inc
1075 Windward Ridge Pkwy Ste 100 . . . Alpharetta GA 30005 678-894-1136 180
Web: www.cadencetechnologies.com

Cadet Manufacturing Company Inc
2500 W Fourth Plain Blvd . . . Vancouver WA 98660 360-693-2505 37
TF: 800-442-2338 ■ *Web:* cadetheat.com

Cadex Electronics Inc
22000 Fraserwood Way . . . Richmond BC V6W1J6 604-231-7777 231-7755 246
TF: 800-565-5228 ■ *Web:* www.cadex.com

Cadie Products Corp 151 E 11th St . . . Paterson NJ 07524 973-278-8300 278-0303 508
Web: www.cadie.com

Cadillac Area Chamber of Commerce
222 N Lake St . . . Cadillac MI 49601 231-775-9776 775-1440 139
Web: www.cadillac.org

Cadillac Area Public Schools
421 S Mitchell St . . . Cadillac MI 49601 231-876-5000 876-5021 685
Web: www.cadillacschools.org

Cadillac Area Visitors Bureau
201 N Mitchell St . . . Cadillac MI 49601 231-775-0657 779-5933 206
TF: 800-325-2525 ■ *Web:* www.cadillacmichigan.com

Cadillac Casting Inc 1500 Fourth Ave . . . Cadillac MI 49601 231-779-9600 779-9640 723
Web: cadillaccasting.com

Cadillac Coffee Co 194 E Maple Rd . . . Troy MI 48083 248-545-2266 296-7
TF: 800-438-6900 ■ *Web:* www.cadillaccoffee.com

Cadillac Fairview Ltd
20 Queen St W 5th Fl . . . Toronto ON M5H3R4 416-598-8200 655
Web: www.cadillacfairview.com

Cadillac Oil Co 13650 Helen St . . . Detroit MI 48212 313-365-6200 365-4420 541
Web: www.cadillacoil.com

Cadillac Printing Co
214 S Mitchell St . . . Cadillac MI 49601 231-775-2488 627
Web: www.cadillacprintingco.com

Cadillac Products Inc
5800 Crooks Rd Ste 100 . . . Troy MI 48098 248-813-8200 813-8282 60
Web: www.cadprodauto.com

Cadillac Products Packaging Co
5800 Crooks Rd . . . Troy MI 48098 248-879-5000 247
Web: www.cadprod.com

Cadillac-Wexford County Public Library
411 S Lake St . . . Cadillac MI 49601 231-775-6541 434-3
Web: www.cadillaclibrary.org

Cadiz Inc 550 S Hope St Ste 2850 . . . Los Angeles CA 90071 213-271-1600 271-1614 787
NASDAQ: CDZI ■ *Web:* www.cadizinc.com

Cadman Inc 7554 185th Ave NE . . . Redmond WA 98052 425-961-7100 861-9282 182
TF: 888-322-6847 ■ *Web:* www.cadman.com

Cadmium Cd LLC
19 Newport Dr Ste 101 . . . Forest Hill MD 21050 410-638-9239 195
TF: 877-426-6323 ■ *Web:* www.cadmiumcd.com

Cadmus Group Inc 100 Fifth Ave Ste 100 . . . Waltham MA 02451 617-673-7000 673-7001 193
Web: cadmusgroup.com

Cadnet Services 100 Carl Dr Ste 12 . . . Manchester NH 03103 866-522-3638 296-2370* 180
**Fax Area Code:* 603 ■ *TF:* 866-522-3638 ■ *Web:* www.cadnetservices.com

Cadnetics 400 Holiday Dri Ste 102 . . . Pittsburgh PA 15220 412-642-2701 180
TF: 855-494-0043 ■ *Web:* www.cadnetics.com

Cadore-Miller Printing Inc
9901 S 78th Ave . . . Hickory Hills IL 60457 708-430-7091 430-5989 627
TF: 800-382-2963 ■ *Web:* cadoremiller.com

Phone | Fax | Class

Cadre Computer Resources Co
201 E Fifth St Ste 1800 ..... Cincinnati OH 45202 513-762-7350 762-6502 180
TF: 866-762-6700 ■ *Web:* www.cadre.net

Cadwell Laboratories Inc
909 N Kellogg St ..... Kennewick WA 99336 509-735-6481 783-6503 476
TF: 800-245-3001 ■ *Web:* www.cadwell.com

CAE (Center of the American Experiment)
8441 Wayzata Blvd Ste 350 ..... Golden Valley MN 55426 612-338-3605 634
Web: www.americanexperiment.org

CAE Inc 8585 Cote de Liesse ..... Saint-Laurent QC H4T1G6 514-341-6780 341-7699 703
NYSE: CAE ■ *TF:* 866-999-6223 ■ *Web:* www.cae.com

Caelum Research Corp
30 W Gude Dr Ste 200 ..... Rockville MD 20850 301-424-8205 424-8183 668
Web: www.caelum.com

Caen Engineering Inc 337 Hwy 7 N ..... Oxford MS 38655 714-456-0800 256
Web: caeneng.com

CAEP (Canadian Association of Emergency Physicians)
1785 Alta Vista Dr Ste 104 ..... Ottawa ON K1G3Y6 613-523-3343 523-0190 49-8
TF: 800-463-1158 ■ *Web:* caep.ca

CAEP (Council for the Accreditation of Educator Preparation)
1140 19th St NW Ste 400 ..... Washington DC 20036 202-223-0077 48-1
Web: caepnet.org

Caesar Creek State Park
8570 E SR-73 ..... Waynesville OH 45068 513-897-1092 565
Web: www.caesarcreekstatepark.com

Caesar's Steak House
512 Fourth Ave SW ..... Calgary AB T2P0J6 403-264-1222 671
Web: www.caesarssteakhouse.com

Caesar, Rivise, Bernstein, Cohen & Pokotilow Ltd
1635 Market St 12th Fl ..... Philadelphia PA 19103 215-567-2010 428
Web: www.caesar.law

Caesars Head State Park
8155 Geer Hwy ..... Cleveland SC 29635 864-836-6115 565
Web: southcarolinaparks.com

Caesars License Company LLC
3655 Las Vegas Blvd S ..... Las Vegas NV 89109 702-946-7000 379
TF: 877-796-2096 ■ *Web:* www.caesars.com

Cafa Corporate Finance
4269 Sainte-Catherine W Office 200 ..... Westmount QC H3Z1P7 514-989-5508 401
Web: cafafinance.com

Cafardi Ferguson Wyrick Weis + Gabriel LLC
2605 Nicholson Rd Ste 2101 Bldg 11 ..... Sewickley PA 15143 412-515-8900 41
Web: cfwwg.com

Cafaro Corporate 2445 Belmont Ave ..... Youngstown OH 44504 330-747-2661 743-2902 653
Web: www.cafarocompany.com

Cafe 1217 1217 Malvern Ave ..... Hot Springs AR 71901 501-318-1094 671
Web: cafe1217.net

Cafe 1912 243 S Cooper at Peabody ..... Memphis TN 38104 901-722-2700 671
Web: www.cafe1912.com

Cafe 302 2700 Winchester Rd NE ..... Huntsville AL 35811 256-852-3442 671

Cafe 615 615 Dauphin St ..... Mobile AL 36602 251-432-8434 671
Web: cafe615mobile.com

Cafe 668 885 Dundas St W ..... Toronto ON M6J1V9 416-703-0668 671
Web: www.cafe668.com

Cafe Aladdin 1609 32nd Ave S ..... Fargo ND 58103 701-232-4200 671
Web: cafealaddinfargomoorhead.com

Cafe Amici 2301 Airport Thwy E2 ..... Columbus GA 31904 706-653-6361 671
Web: www.amicicolumbus.com

Cafe Amici 1371 Main St ..... Sarasota FL 34236 941-951-6896 671
Web: cafeamicisrq.com

Cafe at Adele's 1112 N Carson St ..... Carson City NV 89701 775-882-3353 671
Web: www.adelesrestaurantandlounge.com

Cafe Bacchus 76 High St ..... Morgantown WV 26505 304-296-9234 671
Web: cafebacchus.net

Cafe Baci 4001 S Tamiami Trl ..... Sarasota FL 34231 941-921-4848 923-8643 671
Web: www.cafebacisarasota.com

Cafe Bel Ami 229 E William St Ste 101 ..... Wichita KS 67202 316-267-3433 671
Web: www.cafebelami.biz

Cafe Boulud 20 E 76th St ..... New York NY 10021 212-772-2600 671
Web: www.cafeboulud.com

Cafe Boulud
301 Australian Ave ..... Palm Beach Gardens FL 33480 561-655-6060 671
Web: www.cafeboulud.com

Cafe Brazil 4408 Lowell Blvd ..... Denver CO 80211 303-480-1877 671
Web: www.cafebrazildenver.com

Cafe Capriccio 49 Grand St ..... Albany NY 12207 518-465-0439 671
Web: www.cafecapriccio.com

Cafe Carlo 243 Lilac St ..... Winnipeg MB R3M2S2 204-477-5544 477-1652 671
Web: cafecarlo.com

Cafe Central 109 N Oregon St ..... El Paso TX 79901 915-545-2233 671
Web: www.cafecentral.com

Cafe Chardonnay
4533 PGA Blvd ..... Palm Beach Gardens FL 33418 561-627-2662 671
Web: www.cafechardonnay.com

Cafe de Thai 7499 Longly Ln ..... Reno NV 89511 775-829-8424 671
Web: cafedethaireno.net

Cafe Degas 3127 Esplanade Ave ..... New Orleans LA 70119 504-945-5635 943-5255 671
Web: www.cafedegas.com

Cafe du Berry 6439 SW MacAdam Ave ..... Portland OR 97239 503-244-5551 671
Web: cafe-du-berry.business.site

Cafe du Jour 1107 E Carson St ..... Pittsburgh PA 15203 412-488-9695 671
Web: www.cafedujourpgh.com

Cafe Express LLC 19443 Gulf Fwy ..... Webster TX 77598 281-554-6999 670
Web: www.cafe-express.com

Cafe Fina 47 Fisherman's Wharf Ste 1 ..... Monterey CA 93940 831-372-5200 372-5209 671
TF: 800-843-3462 ■ *Web:* www.cafefina.com

Cafe Flora 2901 E Madison St ..... Seattle WA 98112 206-325-9100 671
Web: cafeflora.com

Cafe Istanbul 3983 Worth Ave ..... Columbus OH 43219 614-473-9144 671
Web: www.cafeistanbul.com

Cafe Istanbul 5450 W Lovers Ln ..... Dallas TX 75209 214-902-0919 671
Web: www.cafe-istanbul.net

Cafe Izmir 211 N Ervay St ..... Dallas TX 75201 469-998-0123 671
Web: cafeizmir.com

Cafe L'Europe
331 S County Rd ..... Palm Beach Gardens FL 33480 561-655-4020 671
Web: www.cafeleurope.com

Cafe Lago 2305 24th Ave E ..... Seattle WA 98122 206-329-8005 671
Web: www.cafelago.com

Cafe Lurcat 1624 Harmon Pl ..... Minneapolis MN 55403 612-486-5500 671
Web: lurcatminneapolis.com

Cafe Madrid 5244 S Highland Dr ..... Salt Lake City UT 84117 801-273-0837 671
Web: www.cafemadrid.net

Cafe Madrid 4501 Travis St ..... Dallas TX 75205 214-528-1731 671
Web: cafemadrid-dallas.com

Cafe Marquesa 600 Fleming St ..... Key West FL 33040 305-292-1244 671
TF: 800-869-4631 ■ *Web:* www.marquesa.com

Cafe Martorano
3343 E Oakland Pk Blvd ..... Fort Lauderdale FL 33308 954-561-2554 671
Web: www.cafemartorano.com

Cafe Maxx 2601 E Atlantic Blvd ..... Pompano Beach FL 33062 954-782-0606 782-0648 671
Web: www.cafemaxx.com

Cafe Mosaics 10844 82nd Ave ..... Edmonton AB T6E2B3 780-433-9702 671
Web: mosaicsandmotharchive.com

Cafe Normandie 185 Main St ..... Annapolis MD 21401 410-263-3382 671
Web: www.cafenormandie.com

Cafe on Park 3831 Pk Blvd ..... San Diego CA 92103 619-293-7275 671
Web: cafeonpark.com

Cafe One 11 111 Broyles St Ste 1 ..... Johnson City TN 37601 423-283-4633 671
Web: www.cafeone11jc.com

Cafe Pacific 24 Highland Pk Vlg ..... Dallas TX 75205 214-526-1170 671
Web: cafepacificdallas.com

Cafe Pasta 305 State St ..... Greensboro NC 27408 336-272-1308 671
Web: www.cafepasta.com

Cafe Piccolo 3222 E Broadway ..... Long Beach CA 90803 562-438-1316 671
Web: cafepiccolo.com

Cafe Poca Cosa 110 E Pennington St ..... Tucson AZ 85701 520-622-6400 671
Web: cafepocacosatucson.com

Cafe Prima Pasta 414 71st St ..... Miami Beach FL 33141 305-867-0106 671
Web: cafeprimapasta.com

Cafe Rabelais 2442 Times Blvd ..... Houston TX 77005 713-520-8841 524-0071 671
Web: www.caferabelais.com

Cafe Rio
215 N Admiral Byrd Rd Ste 100 ..... Salt Lake City UT 84116 801-441-5000 671
TF: 800-223-3746 ■ *Web:* www.caferio.com

Cafe Seville
2768 E Oakland Pk Blvd ..... Fort Lauderdale FL 33306 954-565-1148 671
Web: www.cafeseville.com

Cafe Society 212 N Evergreen St ..... Memphis TN 38112 901-722-2177 671
Web: www.cafesocietymemphis.com

Cafe Sole 1029 Southard St ..... Key West FL 33040 305-294-0230 671
Web: www.cafesole.com

Cafe Soriah 384 W 13th Ave ..... Eugene OR 97401 541-342-4410 671
Web: soriah.com

Cafe Stella 3932 W Sunset Blvd ..... Los Angeles CA 90029 323-666-0265 666-0258 671
Web: cafestella.com

Cafe Sunflower 2140 Peachtree Rd ..... Atlanta GA 30309 404-352-8859 671
Web: www.cafesunflower.com

Cafe Tandoor
2096 S Taylor Rd ..... Cleveland Heights OH 44118 216-371-8500 371-8560 671
Web: www.cafetandoorcleveland.com

Cafe Tu Tu Tango
8625 International Dr ..... Orlando FL 32819 407-248-2222 352-3696 671
Web: www.cafetututango.com

Cafe Vermilionville
1304 W Pinhook Rd ..... LaFayette LA 70503 337-237-0100 671
Web: www.cafev.com

Cafe Vico 1125 N Federal Hwy ..... Fort Lauderdale FL 33304 954-565-9681 671
Web: www.cafevicorestaurant.com

Cafe Zucchero 1731 India St ..... San Diego CA 92101 619-531-1731 671
Web: www.nonnasd.com

Cafepresscom Inc
1850 Gateway Dr Ste 300 ..... Foster City CA 94404 502-822-7501 240-0260* 204
**Fax Area Code:* 650 ■ *TF:* 877-809-1659 ■ *Web:* www.cafepress.com

CAFF (Community Alliance with Family Farmers)
TS Glide Ranch 36355 Russell Blvd ..... Davis CA 95616 530-756-8518 48-13
Web: www.caff.org

Caffe Boa 398 S Mill Ave ..... Tempe AZ 85281 480-968-9112 671
Web: www.cafeboa.com

Caffe Italia Ristorante
662 Central Ave ..... Albany NY 12206 518-459-8029 671
Web: www.caffeitaliaalbany.com

Caffe La Strada 4716 E Second St ..... Long Beach CA 90803 562-433-8100 671
Web: www.lastradalongbeach.com

Caffe Luna 136 E Hargett St ..... Raleigh NC 27601 919-832-6090 671
Web: www.cafeluna.com

Caffe Mingo 807 NW 21st Ave ..... Portland OR 97209 503-226-4646 671
Web: caffemingonw.com

Caffe Molise 55 West 100 South ..... Salt Lake City UT 84101 801-364-8833 671
Web: www.caffemolise.com

Caffe Paridiso 4205 S MacDill Ave ..... Tampa FL 33611 813-835-6622 671
Web: www.paradisotampa.com

Caffe Vialetto 4019 Le Jeune Rd ..... Coral Gables FL 33134 305-446-5659 671
Web: www.caffevialetto.com

Cafritz Interests
1660 L St NW Ste 600 ..... Washington DC 20036 202-331-3800 785-3205 653
Web: www.cafritzinterests.com

Cagan Management Group Inc
16554 Cagan Crossings Blvd Ste 4 ..... Clermont FL 34714 352-242-2444 652
Web: www.cagan.com

Cage Inc 6440 N Beltline Rd Ste 125 ..... Irving TX 75063 972-550-1001 196
Web: www.cage-inc.com

Cagle Steaks & BBQ 8732 Fourth St ..... Lubbock TX 79416 806-795-3879 671
Web: www.caglesteaks.com

Cagles Appliance Ctr 114 S Campus Ave ..... Ontario CA 91761 909-986-9789 362
Web: cagles.com

Cagles Mill Lake
1317 W Lieber Rd Ste 1 ..... Cloverdale IN 46120 765-795-4576 565
Web: www.in.gov

CAGW (Citizens Against Government Waste)
1301 Pennsylvania Ave NW Ste 1075 ..... Washington DC 20004 202-467-5300 467-4253 48-7
Web: www.cagw.org

Cagwin & Dorward Inc
1565 S Novato Blvd Ste B ..... Novato CA 94947 415-892-7710 897-7864 422
TF: 800-891-7710 ■ *Web:* www.cagwin.com

Name / Address	City	State	ZIP	Phone	Fax	Class
Cahaba Pressure Treated Forest Products Inc PO Box 160 *Web:* www.cahabapressure.com	Brierfield	AL	35035	205-926-9888	926-7625	683
CAHI (Council for Affordable Health Coverage) 127 S Peyton St Ste 210 *Web:* www.cahi.org	Alexandria	VA	22314	703-836-6200	836-6550	49-9
Cahill & Cahill P C 142 Joralemon St Ste 9 B *Web:* cahillcahill.com	Brooklyn	NY	11201	718-855-4076		41
Cahill Contractors Inc 425 California St Ste 2200 *Web:* www.cahill-sf.com	San Francisco	CA	94104	415-986-0600	986-4406	186
CAHME (Commission on Accreditation of Healthcare Management Education) 6110 Executive Blvd Ste 614 *Web:* www.cahme.org	Rockville	MD	20852	301-298-1820		48-1
Cahokia Mounds State Historic Site 30 Ramey St *Web:* cahokiamounds.org	Collinsville	IL	62234	618-346-5160		565
CAI (Community Associations Institute) 6402 Arlington Blvd Ste 500 *TF:* 888-224-4321 ■ *Web:* www.caionline.org	Falls Church	VA	22042	703-970-9220	970-9558	48-7
CAI (Chrysler Aviation Inc) 7120 Hayvenhurst Ave Ste 309 *TF:* 800-995-0825 ■ *Web:* www.chrysleraviation.com	Van Nuys	CA	91406	818-989-7900		13
CAI (Computer Aid Inc) 1390 Ridgeview Dr *Web:* www.cai.io	Allentown	PA	18104	610-530-5000		177
CAI-CLAC 1809 S St Ste 101-245 *TF:* 888-909-7403 ■ *Web:* caiclac.com	Sacramento	CA	95811	916-791-4750		533
CAIG Laboratories Inc 12200 Thatcher Ct *TF:* 800-224-4123 ■ *Web:* www.caig.com	Poway	CA	92064	858-486-8388	486-8398	145
Cailor Fleming & Associates Inc 4610 Market St *TF:* 800-796-8495 ■ *Web:* www.cailorfleming.com	Youngstown	OH	44512	330-782-8068		390
Caiman Consulting 15127 NE 24th St Ste 547 *Web:* www.caimanconsulting.com	Redmond	WA	98052	425-296-9254		196
Cain & Bultman Inc 2145 Dennis St *TF:* 800-356-2687 ■ *Web:* www.cainbultman.com	Jacksonville	FL	32204	904-356-4812		361
Cain Food Industries Inc 8401 Sovereign Row *Web:* www.cainfood.com	Dallas	TX	75247	214-630-4511		123
Cain Lamarre Sengrl 630 Boul Rene-Levesque Ouest Ste 2780 *Web:* www.cainlamarre.ca	Montreal	QC	H3B1S6	514-393-4580	393-9590	428
Cain Millwork Inc 1 Cain Pkwy *Web:* cainmillwork.com	Rochelle	IL	61068	815-561-9700		499
Cain Park Theatre 40 Severance Cir *Web:* cainpark.com	Cleveland Heights	OH	44118	216-371-3000	371-6995	572
Cain Steel and Supply Inc 2650 20th St *Web:* www.cainsteel.com	Tuscaloosa	AL	35401	205-349-2751	759-5515	492
Cain, Ackerman & Mccormick PC 2 Chatham Ctr Ste 1410 *Web:* cainackermanmccormickpc.com	Pittsburgh	PA	15219	412-281-8541	281-9850	41
Cair National 453 New Jersey Ave SE *TF:* 800-728-1266 ■ *Web:* www.cair.com	Washington	DC	20003	202-488-8787	488-0833	48-7
Cairncross & Hempelmann PS 524 Second Ave Ste 500 *Web:* www.cairncross.com	Seattle	WA	98104	206-587-0700	587-2308	428
Caithness Energy LLC 565 5th Ave 29th Fl *Web:* www.caithnessenergy.com	New York	NY	10017	212-921-9099	921-9239	245
Cajun Boilers 2000 Albert Pike Rd *Web:* cajunboilers.com	Hot Springs	AR	71913	501-767-5695		671
Cajun Chef Products Inc 519 Joseph Rd *Web:* www.cajunchefshop.com	Saint Martinville	LA	70582	337-394-7112		296-19
Cajun Computers 107 6th St (corner of 6th & Front *Web:* www.cajuncomputers.com	Evanston	WY	82930	307-789-8145		179
Cajun Constructors Inc 15635 Airline Hwy *TF:* 800-944-5857 ■ *Web:* www.cajunusa.com	Baton Rouge	LA	70817	225-753-5857	751-9777	188-7
Cajun Cutters Inc 205 Cajun Rd *Web:* www.cajuncutters.com	Houma	LA	70363	985-868-2112	876-6032	455
Cajun Queen 1800 E 7th St *Web:* www.cajunqueen.com	Charlotte	NC	28204	704-377-9017		671
Cajun's Wharf 2400 Cantrell Rd *Web:* www.cajunswharf.com	Little Rock	AR	72202	501-375-5351		671
Cajundome & Convention Ctr 444 Cajundome Blvd *Web:* www.cajundome.com	LaFayette	LA	70506	337-265-2100	265-2311	205
Cake Development Corp 1785 E Sahara Ave Ste 490-423 *Web:* www.cakedc.com	Las Vegas	NV	89104	702-425-5085		177
Cakewalk Inc 268 Summer St 8th Fl *Web:* www.cakewalk.com	Boston	MA	02210	617-423-9004		174
Cal Check LLC 11600 Black Horse Run *Web:* www.calcheck.com	Raleigh	NC	27613	919-847-1898	847-8005	668
Cal Coast Telecom 886 Faulstich Ct *Web:* cctcom.net	San Jose	CA	95112	408-275-8888		525
Cal Dive International Inc 400 N Sam Houston Pkwy E Ste 400	Houston	TX	77042	713-361-2600		539
Cal Farley's PO Box 1890 *TF:* 800-687-3722 ■ *Web:* www.calfarley.org	Amarillo	TX	79174	800-687-3722		48-6
Cal Fasteners Inc 4300 E Miraloma Ave *Web:* www.cfi1.com	Anaheim	CA	92807	714-854-1715	854-1716	350
Cal Herbold Nursery 9403 E Ave *Web:* www.affordabledecorativerock.com	Hesperia	CA	92345	760-244-6125		323
Cal Info 316 W Second St Ste 1102 *Web:* www.calinfo.net	Los Angeles	CA	90012	213-687-8710	687-8778	387
Cal Insurance & Associates Inc 2311 Taraval St *Web:* mycalteam.com	San Francisco	CA	94116	415-661-6500		390
Cal Poly Pomona Foundation Inc 3801 W Temple Ave Bldg 55 *Web:* foundation.cpp.edu	Pomona	CA	91768	909-869-2950	869-3716	49-11
Cal Quality Electronics 2700 S Fairview St *Web:* www.calquality.com	Santa Ana	CA	92704	714-545-8886	545-4975	625
Cal Spas Inc 1462 E Ninth St *TF:* 800-225-7727 ■ *Web:* www.calspas.com	Pomona	CA	91766	909-629-3890	629-0751	375
Cal State La Federal Credit Unio 2445 Mariondale Ave *Web:* calstatela-fcu.org	Los Angeles	CA	90032	323-505-2600		219
Cal Tech Precision Inc 1830 N Lemon St *Web:* www.caltechprecision.com	Anaheim	CA	92801	714-992-4130		21
Calabash Animation Inc 4809 N Ravenswood Ave Ste 217 **Fax Area Code:* 872 ■ *Web:* www.calabashanimation.com	Chicago	IL	60640	312-243-3433	208-7849*	514
Calabrese Management 2207 Forest Hills Dr *Web:* www.calabresemgt.com	Harrisburg	PA	17112	717-238-9989	238-9985	47
Calabro Cheese Corp 580 Coe Ave *Web:* www.calabrocheese.com	East Haven	CT	06512	203-469-1311	469-6929	296-5
Caladesi Island State Park 1 Cswy Blvd *Web:* www.floridastateparks.org	Dunedin	FL	34698	727-469-5918		565
Calamari's Squid Row 1317 State St *Web:* www.calamaris-squidrow.com	Erie	PA	16501	814-459-4276		671
CALAMCO (California Ammonia Co) 1776 W March Ln Ste 420 *TF:* 800-624-4200 ■ *Web:* www.calamco.com	Stockton	CA	95207	209-982-1000	983-0822	280
Calamos Asset Management Inc 2020 Calamos Ct *NASDAQ: CLMS* ■ *TF:* 800-582-6959 ■ *Web:* www.calamos.com	Naperville	IL	60563	630-245-7200		401
CalAmp Corp 1401 N Rice Ave *NASDAQ: CAMP* ■ *Web:* www.calamp.com	Oxnard	CA	93030	805-987-9000		647
Cal-ark Inc PO Box 990 *TF:* 888-200-0303 ■ *Web:* www.calark.com	Mabelvale	AR	72103	501-455-3399		780
CALARVC (California Association of RV Parks and Campgrounds) 319 Nevada St *Web:* www.calarvc.com	Auburn	CA	95603	530-885-1624	823-6331	48-13
Calaveras Big Trees State Park 1170 State Hwy 4 *Web:* www.parks.ca.gov	Arnold	CA	95223	209-795-2334		565
Calaveras County 891 Mountain Ranch Rd *Web:* calaverasgov.us	San Andreas	CA	95249	209-754-6370	754-6733	338
Cal-a-Vie Spa 29402 Spa Havens Way *TF:* 866-772-4283 ■ *Web:* www.cal-a-vie.com	Vista	CA	92084	760-945-2055	630-0074	706
Calavista Systems Inc 3700 N Capial of Texas Ste 450 *Web:* calavista.com	Austin	TX	78746	512-231-0500		177
Calavo Growers Inc 1141-A Cummings Rd *NASDAQ: CVGW* ■ *TF:* 800-654-8758 ■ *Web:* www.calavo.com	Santa Paula	CA	93060	805-525-1245	921-3287	315-4
Calaway Systems Inc 32 Lindburgh St *Web:* www.calawaysystems.com	Courtland	AL	35618	256-637-2736		687
Calbag Metals Co 2495 NW Nicolai St *TF:* 800-398-3441 ■ *Web:* www.calbag.com	Portland	OR	97210	503-226-3441		686
CALC Institute of Technology 141 Market Pl Dr Ste 180 *Web:* www.calc.edu	Fairview Heights	IL	62208	618-398-2252		167-3
Calcasieu Parish Police Jury 1015 Pithon St 2nd Fl PO Box 1583 *Web:* www.calcasieuparish.gov	Lake Charles	LA	70601	337-721-3500	437-3399	338
Calcasieu Parish Public Library System 301 W Claude St *Web:* www.calcasieulibrary.org	Lake Charles	LA	70605	337-721-7116		434-3
Calcasieu Refining Co 4359 W Tank Farm Rd *Web:* www.calcasieurefining.com	Lake Charles	LA	70605	337-478-2130	474-2505	580
Cal-Chip Electronics Inc 59 Steam Whistle Dr *Web:* www.calchipelectronics.com	Ivyland	PA	18974	215-942-8900	942-6400	246
Cal-Chlor Corp 627 Jefferson St *Web:* www.cal-chlor.com	LaFayette	LA	70501	337-264-1449	264-9359	146
Calco Applications Inc 2820 N Roxboro Rd *Web:* www.calcoapps.com	Durham	NC	27704	919-220-2558	220-2531	261
Calco Sprouts Inc 2751 Minnehaha Ave *Web:* www.calcosprouts.com	Minneapolis	MN	55406	612-724-0276		297-7
Cal-Coast Dairy Systems Inc 424 S Tegner Rd *TF:* 800-732-6826 ■ *Web:* www.calcoastinc.com	Turlock	CA	95380	209-634-9026	634-3458	273
Calcon Constructors Inc 2270 W Bates Ave *Web:* www.calconci.com	Englewood	CO	80110	303-762-1554		187
Calcot Ltd 1900 E Brundage Ln *Web:* www.calcot.net	Bakersfield	CA	93307	661-327-5961		275
Calculated Industries Inc 4840 Hytech Dr *TF:* 800-854-8075 ■ *Web:* www.calculated.com	Carson City	NV	89706	775-885-4900	885-4949	118
Calder Casino & Race Course 21001 NW 27th Ave *Web:* www.caldercasino.com	Miami Gardens	FL	33056	305-625-1311		642
Calder Richards Consulting Engineers 634 South 400 West Ste 100 *Web:* crceng.com	Salt Lake City	UT	84101	801-466-1699		261
Caldera Engineering 695 S 320 W *Web:* www.calderaengineering.com	Provo	UT	84601	801-356-2862	356-2892	256
Cal-Disc Grinding Company Inc 1741 Potrero Ave *Web:* caldisc.com	South El Monte	CA	91733	626-444-9576	444-9683	393
Caldwell & Dean LLP 4268 Cahaba Heights Ct Ste 118 *Web:* caldwelldean.com	Birmingham	AL	35243	205-969-8550	409-7798	41
Caldwell Associates Architects Inc 116 N Tarragona St *Web:* www.caldwell-assoc.com	Pensacola	FL	32502	850-432-9500		261

Name / Address	City	State	Zip	Phone	Fax	Class
Caldwell Chamber of Commerce 704 Blaine St *TF:* 866-206-6944 ■ *Web:* www.cityofcaldwell.org	Caldwell	ID	83605	208-459-7493	454-1284	139
Caldwell Community College & Technical Institute 2855 Hickory Blvd *Web:* www.cccti.edu	Hudson	NC	28638	828-726-2200	726-2216	162
Caldwell Consumer Health LLC 8 Elmer St *TF:* 888-317-4402 ■ *Web:* www.bleedinggums.com	Madison	NJ	07940	973-360-1090	360-1091	231
Caldwell County 49 E Main St PO Box 67 *Web:* www.caldwellcountymissouri.com	Kingston	MO	64650	816-586-2571	586-3001	338
Caldwell County 905 W Ave NW *Web:* www.caldwellcountync.org	Lenoir	NC	28645	828-757-1300	757-1295	338
Caldwell County 110 S Main St *Web:* www.co.caldwell.tx.us	Lockhart	TX	78644	512-398-1824		338
Caldwell County Chamber of Commerce 1909 Hickory Blvd SE *Web:* caldwellchambernc.com	Lenoir	NC	28645	828-726-0616	726-0385	139
Caldwell Hospice & Palliative Care 902 Kirkwood St NW *Web:* www.caldwellhospice.org	Lenoir	NC	28645	828-754-0101	757-0402	371
Caldwell Manufacturing Inc 2605 Manitou Rd *Web:* www.caldwellmfgco.com	Rochester	NY	14624	585-352-3790		743
Caldwell Memorial Hospital 321 Mulberry St SW *Web:* www.caldwellmemorial.org	Lenoir	NC	28645	828-757-5100	757-5247	374-3
Caldwell Partners International Inc, The 165 Ave Rd *Web:* www.caldwellpartners.com	Toronto	ON	M5R3S4	416-920-7702		193
Caldwell Public Library 1010 Dearborn St *Web:* www.caldwellpubliclibrary.org	Caldwell	ID	83605	208-459-3242		434-3
Caldwell Securities Ltd 150 King St W Ste 1710 *TF:* 800-387-0859 ■ *Web:* www.caldwellsecurities.com	Toronto	ON	M5H1J9	416-862-7755		690
Caldwell Tanks Inc 4000 Tower Rd *Web:* caldwellwatertanks.com	Louisville	KY	40219	502-964-3361	966-8732	91
Caldwell Trust Co 1400 Center Rd *TF:* 800-338-9476 ■ *Web:* www.ctrust.com	Venice	FL	34292	941-493-3600	496-4660	401
Caldwell University 120 Bloomfield Ave *TF:* 888-864-9516 ■ *Web:* www.caldwell.edu	Caldwell	NJ	07006	973-618-3500	618-3600	166
Caldwell Wholesale Company Inc 9630 St Vincent Ave	Shreveport	LA	71106	318-869-3101		756
Caldwell Zoo 2203 ML King Blvd *Web:* www.caldwellzoo.org	Tyler	TX	75702	903-593-0121		823
Caldwell, Wenzel, & Asthana PC 218 N Alston St *TF:* 855-390-5566 ■ *Web:* cwalawfirm.com	Foley	AL	36535	251-948-2168		41
CALEA (Commission on Accreditation for Law Enforcement Agencies) 13575 Heathcote Blvd Ste 320 *TF:* 877-789-6904 ■ *Web:* www.calea.org	Gainesville	VA	20155	703-352-4225	890-3126	49-7
Calea Ltd 2785 Skymark Ave Unit 2 *TF:* 888-909-3299 ■ *Web:* www.calea.ca	Mississauga	ON	L4W4Y3	905-238-1234		363
Caleb Smith State Park Preserve 581 W Jericho Tpke PO Box 963 *Web:* parks.ny.gov	Smithtown	NY	11787	631-265-1054		565
Caled 550 Bercut Dr Ste G *Web:* caled.org	Sacramento	CA	95811	916-448-8252		463
Caledon Chamber of Commerce 23 Mill St *Web:* www.caledonchamber.com	Bolton	ON	L7E1C1	905-857-7393	857-7405	137
Caledon Laboratories Ltd 40 Armstrong Ave *TF:* 877-225-3366 ■ *Web:* www.caledonlabs.com	Georgetown	ON	L7G4R9	905-877-0101		226
Caledon State Park 11617 Caledon Rd *Web:* www.dcr.virginia.gov	King George	VA	22485	540-663-3861		565
Caledonia County 1153 Main St Ste 4 *Web:* prosecutors.vermont.gov	Saint Johnsbury	VT	05819	802-748-6657	748-6659	338
Caledonia Haulers LLC 420 W Lincoln St PO Box 31 *TF:* 800-325-4728 ■ *Web:* www.caledoniahaulers.com	Caledonia	MN	55921	507-725-9000	725-9015	468
Caledonia State Park 101 Pine Grove Rd *Web:* www.dcnr.pa.gov	Fayetteville	PA	17222	717-352-2161		565
Calegari & Morris 650 California St 3rd Fl *Web:* calegariandmorris.com	San Francisco	CA	94105	415-981-8766		2
Calendar Press Inc 28 Winter St *Web:* www.calendarpressinc.com	Peabody	MA	01960	978-531-1860	531-3715	627
Calendarscom LLC 6411 Burleson Rd *TF:* 800-366-3645 ■ *Web:* www.calendars.com	Austin	TX	78744	800-366-3645		292
Calendly 271 17th St NW *TF:* 800-979-9850 ■ *Web:* calendly.com	Atlanta	GA	30363	800-979-9850		39
Caler Group, The 23337 Lago Mar Cir *Web:* www.calergroup.com	Boca Raton	FL	33433	561-394-8045	394-4645	260
Calera Capital 580 California St Ste 2200 *Web:* www.caleracapital.com	San Francisco	CA	94104	415-632-5200		401
Calero Software LLC Northridge Ctr II 375 Northridge Rd Ste 450 *TF:* 866-769-5992 ■ *Web:* www.calero.com	Sandy Springs	GA	30350	866-769-5992		463
Calev Systems 5575 NW 36th St *Web:* calevsystems.com	Miami Springs	FL	33166	305-672-2900	672-4044	627
Calex ISCS 58 Pittston Ave *TF:* 800-292-2539 ■ *Web:* www.calexiscs.com	Pittston	PA	18640	570-603-0180	603-0940	780
CALEX Manufacturing Co 2401 Stanwell Dr *TF:* 800-542-3355 ■ *Web:* www.calex.com	Concord	CA	94520	925-687-4411	687-3333	518
Calfrac Well Services Ltd 411 8 Ave SW *TF:* 866-770-3722 ■ *Web:* www.calfrac.com	Calgary	AB	T2P1E3	403-266-6000		539
Calgary Chamber of Commerce 600 237 8 Ave SE *Web:* www.calgarychamber.com	Calgary	AB	T2G5C3	403-750-0400	266-3413	137
Calgary City Hall 800 Macleod Trail SE PO Box 2100 *Web:* www.calgary.ca	Calgary	AB	T2P2M5	403-268-2489	538-6111	337
Calgary College of Holistic Health & Clinics Inc 412 Silver Valley Rd NW *Web:* www.calgarycollegeofholistic.com	Calgary	AB	T3B4B9	403-288-4511		167-2
Calgary Co-Operative Association Ltd 151-86th Ave SE Ste 110 *Web:* www.calgarycoop.com	Calgary	AB	T2H3A5	403-219-6025		237
Calgary Economic Development 731 First St SE *TF:* 888-222-5855 ■ *Web:* www.calgaryeconomicdevelopment.com	Calgary	AB	T2G2G9	403-221-7831		342
Calgary Exhibition & Stampede Ltd 1410 Olympic Way S E *Web:* www.calgarystampede.com	Calgary	AB	T2G2W1	403-261-0101		642
Calgary Herald 215-16th St SE *TF:* 800-372-9219 ■ *Web:* calgaryherald.com	Calgary	AB	T2E7P5	403-235-7100	235-7379	532-1
Calgary International Airport 2000 Airport Rd NE *TF:* 877-254-7427 ■ *Web:* www.yyc.com	Calgary	AB	T2E6W5	403-735-1200	735-1281	27
Calgary Laboratory Services 3535 Research Rd NW *TF:* 800-661-3450 ■ *Web:* www.calgarylabservices.com	Calgary	AB	T2L2K8	403-770-3500		415
Calgary Philharmonic Orchestra 205 Eigth Ave SE *Web:* calgaryphil.com	Calgary	AB	T2G0K9	403-571-0270	294-7424	573-3
Calgary Stampeders McMahon Stadium 1817 Crowchild Trail NW *Web:* www.stampeders.com	Calgary	AB	T2M4R6	403-289-0205		715-2
Calgary Sun 2615 12th St NE *Web:* www.calgarysun.com	Calgary	AB	T2E7W9	403-410-1010		532-1
Calgary Winter Club 4611 14 St NW *Web:* www.calgarywinterclub.com	Calgary	AB	T2K1J7	403-289-5511		354
Calgary Zoo Botanical Garden & Prehistoric Park 1300 Zoo Rd NE *TF:* 800-588-9993 ■ *Web:* www.calgaryzoo.com	Calgary	AB	T2E7V6	403-232-9300	237-7582	823
Calhoun & Company Communications LLC 3275 Sacramento St *Web:* www.calhounwine.com	San Francisco	CA	94115	415-346-2929		636
Calhoun City of Schools Superintendents Office 380 Barrett Rd *Web:* www.calhounschools.org	Calhoun	GA	30701	706-629-2900		685
Calhoun Community College PO Box 2216 *TF:* 800-626-3628 ■ *Web:* www.calhoun.edu	Decatur	AL	35609	256-306-2500	306-2941	162
Calhoun Correctional Institution 19562 SE Institutional Dr Unit 1 *Web:* dc.state.fl.us	Blountstown	FL	32424	850-237-6500	237-6508	213
Calhoun County 1702 Noble St Ste 103 *Web:* www.calhounchamber.com	Anniston	AL	36201	256-241-2800	231-1744	338
Calhoun County 20859 Central Ave E 1st Fl *Web:* calhounco.org	Blountstown	FL	32424	850-674-4545	674-5553	338
Calhoun County PO Box 230 *Web:* www.calhouncounty.wv.gov	Grantsville	WV	26147	304-354-6725		338
Calhoun County 309 W Main St *Web:* calhouncounty.arkansas.gov	Hampton	AR	71744	870-798-4818		338
Calhoun County 315 W Green St *Web:* www.calhouncountymi.gov	Marshall	MI	49068	269-781-0700		338
Calhoun County PO Box 226 *Web:* calhouncountyga.com	Morgan	GA	39866	229-849-4835	849-2100	338
Calhoun County 416 Fourth St Ste 5 *Web:* www.calhouncountyiowa.com	Rockwell City	IA	50579	712-297-8122	297-5082	338
Calhoun County 102 Courthouse Dr *Web:* www.calhouncounty.sc.gov	Saint Matthews	SC	29135	803-874-2435	874-1034	338
Calhoun County *Sheriff's Office* 178 S Murphree St *Web:* www.calhounso.org	Pittsboro	MS	38951	662-412-3149	412-3199	338
Calhoun County Electric Cooperative Assn 1015 Tonawanda St PO Box 312 *TF:* 800-821-4879 ■ *Web:* www.calhounrec.coop	Rockwell City	IA	50579	712-297-7112		245
Calhoun County Journal PO Box 278 *Web:* www.calhouncountyjournal.com	Bruce	MS	38915	662-983-2570	983-7667	532-2
Calhoun County School District 4400 McClellan Blvd PO Box 2084 *Web:* al01901382.schoolwires.net	Anniston	AL	36202	256-741-7400	237-5332	685
Calhoun Falls State Recreation Area 46 Maintenance Shop Rd *Web:* southcarolinaparks.com	Calhoun Falls	SC	29628	864-447-8267		565
Calhoun Plastics and Chemicals Inc 1139 Newtown Loop NE *Web:* www.calhounplastics.com	Calhoun	GA	30701	706-629-9077		144
Calhoun Satellite Communications 1914 Tigertail Blvd *Web:* www.calhounsat.com	Dania Beach	FL	33004	305-655-2629	655-3023	681
Calhoun School Inc, The 160 W 74th St *Web:* www.calhoun.org	New York	NY	10023	212-497-6500		685
Calhoun State Prison 27823 Main St *Web:* www.dcor.state.ga.us	Morgan	GA	39866	229-849-5000	849-5017	213
Calhoun's 10020 Kingston Pk *Web:* calhouns.com	Knoxville	TN	37922	865-673-3444		671
Calian Technology Ltd 340 Legget Dr Ste 101 *TSX:* CGY ■ *TF:* 877-225-4264 ■ *Web:* www.calian.com	Ottawa	ON	K2K1Y6	613-599-8600	599-8650	721
Caliber Advisors Inc 514 Via De La Valle Ste 210 *Web:* caliberadvisors.com	Solana Beach	CA	92075	858-792-8990		401
Caliber Construction Inc 240 N Orange Ave *Web:* caliberconstructioninc.com	Brea	CA	92821	714-255-2700	255-2730	186
Calibre Computer Solutions LLC 405 W State St *Web:* www.calibreforhome.com	Princeton	IN	47670	812-386-8919		196

Name / Address	City	State	Zip	Phone	Fax	Class
Calibre CPA Group						
7501 Wisconsin Ave Ste 1200 W	Bethesda	MD	20814	202-331-9880	331-9890	2
TF: 866-464-2839 ■ *Web:* www.calibrecpa.com						
Calibre Door Closers Inc						
1481 N Main St	Orange	CA	92867	714-633-5100	633-5102	351
TF: 800-560-0012 ■ *Web:* www.calibredoorclosers.com						
Calibre Engineering Inc						
9090 S Ridgeline Blvd Ste 105	Highlands Ranch	CO	80129	303-730-0434		261
Web: calibre-engineering.com						
Calibre International Co						
6250 N Irwindale Ave	Irwindale	CA	91702	626-969-4660		636
Web: highcaliberline.com						
Calibre Systems Inc						
6354 Walker Ln Ste 300	Alexandria	VA	22310	703-797-8500	797-8501	180
TF: 888-225-4273 ■ *Web:* www.calibresys.com						
Caliche Jr Sr High School						
301 Hagen St	Sterling	CO	80751	970-522-8200		685
Web: www.re1valleyschools.org						
CALICO (Computer Assisted Language Instruction Consortium)						
214 Centennial Hall	San Marcos	TX	78666	512-245-1417		48-9
Web: calico.org						
Calico Building Services Inc						
15550-C Rockfield Blvd	Irvine	CA	92618	800-576-7313		104
TF: 800-576-7313 ■ *Web:* www.calicoweb.com						
Calico Restaurant & Bar						
2650 Moose Wilson Rd	Wilson	WY	83014	307-733-2460		671
Web: www.calicorestaurant.com						
Calient Technologies 25 Castilian Dr	Goleta	CA	93117	805-562-5500		387
Web: www.calient.net						
Caliente Resorts LLC						
21240 Gran Via Blvd	Land O' Lakes	FL	34637	813-996-3700		239
TF: 833-879-7399 ■ *Web:* calienteresorts.com						
Califone International Inc						
9135 Alabama Ave Ste B	Chatsworth	CA	91311	818-407-2400	407-2405	253
TF: 800-722-0500 ■ *Web:* www.califone.com						
California						
Aging Dept 1300 National Dr Ste 200	Sacramento	CA	95834	916-419-7500	928-2267	339-5
TF: 800-510-2020 ■ *Web:* www.aging.ca.gov						
Arts Council 1300 'I' St Ste 930	Sacramento	CA	95814	916-322-6555	322-6575	339-5
TF: 800-201-6201 ■ *Web:* www.cac.ca.gov						
Athletic Commission						
2005 Evergreen St Ste 2010	Sacramento	CA	95815	916-263-2195	263-2197	712
TF: 800-326-2297 ■ *Web:* www.dca.ca.gov						
Attorney General 1300 I St	Sacramento	CA	95814	916-445-9555		339-5
Web: oag.ca.gov						
Bureau of Real Estate						
1651 Exposition Blvd	Sacramento	CA	95815	877-373-4542	263-8943*	339-5
**Fax Area Code:* 916 ■ *TF:* 877-373-4542 ■ *Web:* www.dre.ca.gov						
Consumer Affairs Dept						
1625 N Market Blvd Ste N 112	Sacramento	CA	95834	916-445-1254		339-5
TF: 800-952-5210 ■ *Web:* www.dca.ca.gov						
Corrections Dept PO Box 942883	Sacramento	CA	94283	916-324-7308		339-5
TF: 877-256-6877 ■ *Web:* cdcr.ca.gov						
Cuyamaca Rancho State Park						
13652 Hwy 79	Julian	CA	92036	760-765-0755		565
Web: www.parks.ca.gov						
Department of Conservation						
801 K St MS 24-01	Sacramento	CA	95814	916-322-1080	445-0732	339-5
Web: www.conservation.ca.gov						
Economic Development Dept						
915 I St 3rd Fl	Sacramento	CA	95814	916-808-7223		339-5
Web: www.cityofsacramento.org						
Education Dept 1430 N St	Sacramento	CA	95814	916-319-0800		339-5
Web: www.cde.ca.gov						
Emergency Services Office						
3650 Schriever Ave	Mather	CA	95655	916-845-8510		339-5
Web: www.caloes.ca.gov						
Employment Development Dept						
PO Box 826880 MIC 83	Sacramento	CA	94280	916-654-8210		259
Web: www.edd.ca.gov						
Energy Commission 1516 9th St	Sacramento	CA	95814	916-654-4287		339-5
Web: www.energy.ca.gov						
Environmental Protection Agency						
1001 I St	Sacramento	CA	95814	916-323-2514		339-5
Web: calepa.ca.gov						
Fair Political Practices Commission						
428 J St Ste 620	Sacramento	CA	95814	916-322-5660	322-0886	265
TF: 866-275-3772 ■ *Web:* www.fppc.ca.gov						
Finance Dept State Capitol Rm 1145	Sacramento	CA	95814	916-445-3878		339-5
Web: www.dof.ca.gov						
Fish & Game Commission						
1416 Ninth St Ste 1320	Sacramento	CA	95814	916-653-4899		339-5
Web: www.fgc.ca.gov						
Food & Agriculture Dept 1220 N St	Sacramento	CA	95814	916-654-0466	657-4240	339-5
Web: www.cdfa.ca.gov						
Health Care Services Dept						
PO Box 997413 MS 8502	Sacramento	CA	95899	800-735-2929		339-5
TF: 800-735-2929 ■ *Web:* www.dhcs.ca.gov						
Historic Preservation Office						
PO Box 942896	Sacramento	CA	94296	916-445-7000		339-5
Web: www.ohp.parks.ca.gov						
Horse Racing Board						
1010 Hurley Way Ste 300	Sacramento	CA	95825	916-263-6000	263-6042	339-5
Web: www.chrb.ca.gov						
Housing Finance Agency						
500 Capitol Mall Ste 1400	Sacramento	CA	95814	877-922-5432		339-5
TF: 877-922-5432 ■ *Web:* www.calhfa.ca.gov						
Industrial Relations Dept						
455 Golden Gate Ave 2nd Fl	San Francisco	CA	94102	415-557-0100	703-5058	339-5
Web: www.dir.ca.gov						
Insurance Dept						
300 Capitol Mall Ste 1700	Sacramento	CA	95814	916-492-3500		339-5
Web: www.insurance.ca.gov						
Judicial Council of California						
455 Golden Gate Ave	San Francisco	CA	94102	415-865-4200	865-4205	339-5
TF: 800-900-5980 ■ *Web:* www.courts.ca.gov						
Lieutenant Governor						
State Capitol Ste 1114	Sacramento	CA	95814	916-445-8994		339-5
Web: www.ltg.ca.gov						
Medical Board						
2005 Evergreen St Ste 1200	Sacramento	CA	95815	916-263-2382	263-2944	339-5
TF: 800-633-2322 ■ *Web:* www.mbc.ca.gov						
Military Dept 9800 Goethe Rd	Sacramento	CA	95827	916-854-3000		339-5
Web: calguard.ca.gov						
Morro Bay State Park						
Morro Bay State Park Rd	Morro Bay	CA	93442	805-772-2560		565
TF: 800-777-0369 ■ *Web:* www.parks.ca.gov						
Office of the Governor						
Governor Gavin Newsom 1303 10th St Ste 1173	Sacramento	CA	95814	916-445-2841	558-3160	339-5
Web: www.gov.ca.gov						
Office of Vital Records						
PO Box 997410	Sacramento	CA	95899	916-445-2684		339-5
Web: www.cdph.ca.gov						
Parks & Recreation Dept						
PO Box 942896	Sacramento	CA	94296	916-653-6995	657-3903	339-5
Web: www.parks.ca.gov						
Point Sur State Historic Park						
Big Sur Sta Ste 1	Big Sur	CA	93920	831-625-4419		565
Web: www.parks.ca.gov						
Public Utilities Commission						
505 Van Ness Ave	San Francisco	CA	94102	415-703-2782	703-1758	339-5
TF: 800-848-5580 ■ *Web:* www.cpuc.ca.gov						
Secretary of State 1500 11th St	Sacramento	CA	95814	916-653-6814	653-4620	339-5
TF: 800-833-8683 ■ *Web:* www.sos.ca.gov						
Supreme Court						
333 W Santa Clara St Ste 1060	San Jose	CA	95113	408-277-1004		339-5
TF: 800-660-8144 ■ *Web:* www.courts.ca.gov						
Teacher Credentialing Commission						
1900 Capitol Ave	Sacramento	CA	95811	916-322-4974		339-5
Web: www.ctc.ca.gov						
Transportation Dept 1120 N St	Sacramento	CA	95814	916-654-4245		339-5
Web: www.dot.ca.gov						
Treasurer 915 Capitol Mall Rm 110	Sacramento	CA	95814	916-653-2995	653-3125	339-5
Web: www.treasurer.ca.gov						
Veterans Affairs Dept 1227 'O' St	Sacramento	CA	95814	916-653-1402		339-5
Web: www.calvet.ca.gov						
Workers' Compensation Div						
PO Box 420603	San Francisco	CA	94142	415-703-4600		339-5
Web: www.dir.ca.gov						
California African American Museum						
Exposition Pk 600 State Dr	Los Angeles	CA	90037	213-744-7432		520
Web: caamuseum.org						
California Amforge Corp						
750 N Vernon Ave	Azusa	CA	91702	626-334-4931		21
Web: www.cal-amforge.com						
California Ammonia Co (CALAMCO)						
1776 W March Ln Ste 420	Stockton	CA	95207	209-982-1000	983-0822	280
TF: 800-624-4200 ■ *Web:* www.calamco.com						
California Analytical Instruments Inc						
1312 W Grove Ave	Orange	CA	92865	714-974-5560		419
TF: 800-959-0949 ■ *Web:* www.gasanalyzers.com						
California Association of Realtors						
525 S Virgil Ave	Los Angeles	CA	90020	213-739-8200	480-7724	656
Web: car.org						
California Association of RV Parks and Campgrounds (CALARVC)						
319 Nevada St	Auburn	CA	95603	530-885-1624	823-6331	48-13
Web: www.calarvc.com						
California Ballet Co (CBC)						
4819 Ronson Ct	San Diego	CA	92111	858-560-5676	560-0072	573-1
Web: www.californiaballet.org						
California Bank & Trust						
11622 El Camino Real Ste 200	San Diego	CA	92130	858-793-7400	793-7438	70
TF: 800-400-6080 ■ *Web:* www.calbanktrust.com						
California Baptist University						
8432 Magnolia Ave	Riverside	CA	92504	951-689-5771	343-4525	166
TF: 877-228-8866 ■ *Web:* calbaptist.edu						
California Beauty College						
1115 15th St	Modesto	CA	95354	209-524-5184		167-3
Web: www.calbeautycollege.edu						
California Butcher Supply Inc						
841 Yosemite Way	Milpitas	CA	95035	408-946-2820	946-3247	300
Web: www.cbsfoodequipment.com						
California Capital Insurance Co						
2300 Garden Rd	Monterey	CA	93940	831-233-5500	233-5883	391-4
TF: 800-682-9255 ■ *Web:* www.ciginsurance.com						
California Cascade Industries						
7512 14th Ave	Sacramento	CA	95820	916-736-3353		683
Web: www.californiacascade.com						
California Casualty Insurance Group						
1900 Alameda De Las Pulgas	San Mateo	CA	94403	650-574-4000		391-4
Web: www.calcas.com						
California Cedar Products Co						
2385 Arch Airport Rd Ste 500	Stockton	CA	95206	209-932-5001		571
Web: www.calcedar.com						
California Center for the Arts						
340 N Escondido Blvd	Escondido	CA	92025	760-839-4138		572
TF: 800-988-4253 ■ *Web:* www.artcenter.org						
California Chamber of Commerce						
1215 K St Ste 1400 PO Box 1736	Sacramento	CA	95812	916-444-6670	325-1272	140
TF: 800-649-4921 ■ *Web:* www.calchamber.com						
California Christian College						
5364 E Belmont Ave	Fresno	CA	93727	559-251-4215		166
Web: www.calchristiancollege.edu						
California Closet Co 1716 Fourth St	Berkeley	CA	94710	510-763-2033	256-8501*	189-11
**Fax Area Code:* 415 ■ *TF:* 888-336-9707 ■ *Web:* www.californiaclosets.com						
California Coast Limousine						
PO Box 1501	Anaheim	CA	92815	714-524-6500		468
Web: www.calcoastlimo.com						
California College of the Arts						
San Francisco 1111 Eigth St	San Francisco	CA	94107	415-703-9500		164
Web: www.cca.edu						
California Combining Corp						
5607 S Santa Fe Ave	Los Angeles	CA	90058	323-589-5727	585-8078	599
Web: www.californiacombining.com						
California Community Foundation						
445 S Figueroa St Ste 3400	Los Angeles	CA	90071	213-413-4130	383-2046	303
Web: www.calfund.org						

Name	Address	City	State	ZIP	Phone	Fax	Class	Toll-Free / Web
California Controlled Atmosphere	39138 Rd 56	Dinuba	CA	93618	559-591-8874	591-8896	14	*TF:* 888-591-8874 ■ *Web:* www.calca.com
California Correctional Institution	24900 Hwy 202 PO Box 1031	Tehachapi	CA	93581	661-822-4402		213	*Web:* cdcr.ca.gov
California Cryobank Inc	11915 La Grange Ave	Los Angeles	CA	90025	310-443-5244	826-1605	545	*TF:* 866-927-9622 ■ *Web:* cryobank.com
California Culinary Academy - Le Cordon Bleu	350 Rhode Island St	San Francisco	CA	94103	415-771-3500		167-3	*TF:* 888-897-3222 ■ *Web:* www.chefs.edu
California Custom Carpets Inc	6815 Dublin Blvd	Dublin	CA	94568	925-828-7810		290	*Web:* cacustomcarpets.com
California Custom Fruits & Flavors Inc	15800 Tapia St	Irwindale	CA	91706	626-736-4130		123	*Web:* www.ccff.com
California Dairies Inc	2000 N Plaza Dr	Visalia	CA	93291	559-625-2200	625-5433	296-27	*Web:* www.californiadairies.com
California Democratic Party	1401 21st St Ste 200	Sacramento	CA	95811	916-442-5707		616-1	*Web:* cadem.org
California Dental Assn	1201 K St 14th Fl	Sacramento	CA	95814	916-443-0505	443-2943	227	*TF:* 800-736-7071 ■ *Web:* www.cda.org
California Department of Motor Vehicles	4700 Broadway	Sacramento	CA	95820	916-657-6437		339-5	*Web:* www.dmv.ca.gov
San Clemente State Beach	225 W Califia Ave	San Clemente	CA	92672	949-492-3156		565	*Web:* www.parks.ca.gov
California Department of Rehabilitation	721 Capitol Mall	Sacramento	CA	95814	916-324-1313		339-5	*TF:* 800-952-5544 ■ *Web:* www.dor.ca.gov
California Department of State Hospitals	1600 9th St Rm 151	Sacramento	CA	95814	916-573-2059		374-3	*Web:* www.dsh.ca.gov
California Department of Veterans Affairs	1227 O St	Sacramento	CA	95814	800-952-5626		793	*TF:* 800-952-5626 ■ *Web:* www.calvet.ca.gov
California District Attorneys Assn	921 11th St Ste 300	Sacramento	CA	95814	916-443-2017	443-0540	41	*Web:* www.cdaa.org
California Dreaming	1 Ashley Pointe Dr	Charleston	SC	29407	843-766-1644		671	*Web:* centraarchy.com
California Eastern Laboratories Inc (CEL)	4590 Patrick Henry Dr	Santa Clara	CA	95054	408-919-2500	988-0279	246	*TF:* 800-390-3232 ■ *Web:* www.cel.com
California Educator Magazine	1705 Murchison Dr	Burlingame	CA	94010	650-697-1400	552-5002	457-8	*Web:* www.cta.org
California Exposition & State Fair	1600 Exposition Blvd	Sacramento	CA	95815	916-263-3000		31	*Web:* calexpostatefair.com
California Flexrake Corp	9620 Gidley St	Temple City	CA	91780	626-443-4026	443-6887	429	*TF:* 800-266-4200 ■ *Web:* flexrake.com
California Flower Art Academy	7280 Blue Hill Dr ste 7	San Jose	CA	95129	408-859-7812		167-3	*Web:* www.california-academy.com
California Flower Market Inc	640 Brannan St	San Francisco	CA	94107	415-392-1298		293	*Web:* sanfranciscoflowermart.com
California Foundation for Agriculture in the Classroom (CFAITC)	2300 River Plaza Dr	Sacramento	CA	95833	916-561-5625	561-5697	423	*TF:* 800-700-2482 ■ *Web:* learnaboutag.org
California Gasket & Rubber Corp	533 W Collins Ave	Orange	CA	92867	714-202-8500	912-1241	326	*TF:* 800-635-7084 ■ *Web:* www.calgasket.com
California Giant Inc	75 Sakata Ln	Watsonville	CA	95076	831-728-1773	728-0613	315-1	*Web:* www.calgiant.com
California Historical Society (CHS)	678 Mission St	San Francisco	CA	94105	415-357-1848	357-1850	48-13	*Web:* www.californiahistoricalsociety.org
California Hobby Distributors	415 S Palm Ave	Alhambra	CA	91803	626-289-8857		44	*TF:* 800-242-4440 ■ *Web:* www.calhobbydist.com
California Hospital Assn (CHA)	1215 K St Ste 800	Sacramento	CA	95814	916-443-7401	552-7596	48-13	*Web:* www.calhospital.org
California Hot Water Supply Inc	15705 Condon Ave Ste D-2	Lawndale	CA	90260	310-725-5144	643-8499	612	*TF:* 888-249-7244 ■ *Web:* www.calhot.com
California Hotel & Casino	12 E Ogden Ave	Las Vegas	NV	89101	702-385-1222		133	*TF:* 800-634-6505 ■ *Web:* www.thecal.com
California Human Development Corp — *Anthony Soto Employment Training Ctr*	1015 Center Dr Ste B	Santa Rosa	CA	95403	707-523-1155		193	*Web:* www.californiahumandevelopment.org
California Hydroforming Company Inc	850 S Lawson St	City of Industry	CA	91748	626-912-0036	965-5944	697	*Web:* californiahydroforming.com
California Institute of Technology	1200 E California Blvd	Pasadena	CA	91125	626-395-6811		166	*Web:* www.caltech.edu
California Institute of the Arts	24700 McBean Pkwy	Valencia	CA	91355	661-255-1050	253-7710	164	*TF:* 800-545-2787 ■ *Web:* calarts.edu
California International Bank NA	15606 Brookhurst St Ste C-D	Westminster	CA	92683	714-338-8700		70	*Web:* calibankna.com
California International University	3130 Wilshire Blvd	Los Angeles	CA	90010	213-381-3710	381-6990	166	*Web:* www.ciula.edu
California ISO	151 Blue Ravine Rd PO Box 639014	Folsom	CA	95630	916-351-4400	608-7222	787	*TF:* 800-220-4907 ■ *Web:* www.caiso.com
California Kitchen Cabinet Door Corp	400 Cochrane Cir	Morgan Hill	CA	95037	408-782-5700	782-9000	115	*Web:* www.caldoor.com
California Lawyer Magazine	44 Montgomery St Ste 250	San Francisco	CA	94104	415-296-2400		457-15	*Web:* www.dailyjournal.com
California Lighting Sales Inc (CLS)	4900 Rivergrade Rd Ste D110	Irwindale	CA	91706	626-775-6000	775-6001	439	*TF:* 800-853-5094 ■ *Web:* www.californialightingsales.com
California Living Museum (CALM)	10500 Alfred Harrell Hwy	Bakersfield	CA	93306	661-872-2256	872-2205	520	*Web:* www.calmzoo.org
California Lutheran University	60 W Olsen Rd	Thousand Oaks	CA	91360	805-493-3135	493-3114	166	*TF:* 877-258-3678 ■ *Web:* www.callutheran.edu
California Magnetics	7898 Ostrow St Ste H	San Diego	CA	92111	858-576-0291		657	*Web:* www.californiamagnetics.com
California Manufacturing Co	2302 Weldon Pkwy	Saint Louis	MO	63146	314-567-4404	567-5062	155-3	*Web:* www.cmcbrands.com
California Maritime Academy	200 Maritime Academy Dr	Vallejo	CA	94590	707-654-1330	654-1336	166	*TF:* 800-561-1945 ■ *Web:* www.csum.edu
California Market Ctr	110 E Ninth St	Los Angeles	CA	90079	213-630-3600	630-3708	205	*Web:* www.californiamarketcenter.com
California Medical Assn	1201 K St Ste 800	Sacramento	CA	95814	916-444-5532		474	*TF:* 800-300-1506 ■ *Web:* www.cmadocs.org
California Men's Colony (CMC)	Colony Dr PO Box 8101	San Luis Obispo	CA	93409	805-547-7900		213	*Web:* www.cdcr.ca.gov
California Military Museum	1119 Second St	Sacramento	CA	95814	916-854-1900		520	*Web:* www.militarymuseum.org
California Mortgage Advisors Inc	4304 Redwood Hwy Ste 100	San Rafael	CA	94903	415-451-4888		653	*TF:* 800-927-6560 ■ *Web:* calmtg.com
California Museum for History Women & the Arts	1020 'O' St	Sacramento	CA	95814	916-653-7524	653-0314	520	*Web:* www.californiamuseum.org
California Museum of Photography	3824 Main St	Riverside	CA	92501	951-827-4787		520	*Web:* artsblock.ucr.edu
California Newspaper Service Bureau	915 E First St	Los Angeles	CA	90012	213-229-5500	229-5481	530	*TF:* 800-788-7840 ■ *Web:* dailyjournal.com
California Nurses Assn (CNA)	2000 Franklin St	Oakland	CA	94612	510-273-2200	663-1625	533	*Web:* www.nationalnursesunited.org
California Office Furniture	3480 Industrial Blvd Ste 100	West Sacramento	CA	95691	916-442-6959	442-3480	320	*TF:* 877-442-6959 ■ *Web:* caloffice.com
California Oregon Broadcasting Inc	125 S Fir St	Medford	OR	97501	541-779-5555	779-5564	738	*Web:* kobi5.com
California Pacific Homes	38 Executive Pk Ste 200	Irvine	CA	92614	949-833-6000	833-6133	653	*Web:* www.calpacifichomes.com
California Pacific International LLC	1801 Murchison Dr Ste 310	Burlingame	CA	94010	650-692-6200		345	*Web:* calpacsf.com
California Pajarosa	133 Hughes Rd PO Box 684	Watsonville	CA	95077	831-722-6374	722-1316	369	*Web:* www.pajarosa.com
California Panel & Veneer Co	14055 Artesia Blvd	Cerritos	CA	90703	562-926-5834	926-3139	613	*TF:* 800-451-1745 ■ *Web:* www.calpanel.com
California Parlor Car Tours	500 Sutter St Ste 401	San Francisco	CA	94102	415-474-7500	673-1539	760	*TF:* 800-227-4250 ■ *Web:* www.calpartours.com
California Pet Pharmacy	3157 Corporate Pl	Hayward	CA	94545	877-554-4797		637-2	*TF:* 800-624-1765 ■ *Web:* www.californiapetpharmacy.com
California Pharmacists Assn (CPHA)	4030 Lennane Dr	Sacramento	CA	95834	916-779-1400	779-1401	585	*TF:* 866-365-7472 ■ *Web:* cpha.com
California Philharmonic Orchestra	600 Playhouse Alley	Pasadena	CA	91101	626-304-0333		573-3	*Web:* www.calphil.com
California Pizza Kitchen Inc	18601 Airport Way	Santa Ana	CA	92707	949-252-6125		670	*NASDAQ: CPKI* ■ *TF:* 800-919-3227 ■ *Web:* www.cpk.com
California Polytechnic State University	1 Grand Ave	San Luis Obispo	CA	93407	805-756-1111	756-5400	166	*Web:* www.calpoly.edu
California Portland Cement Co	2025 E Financial Way	Glendora	CA	91741	626-852-6200		135	*TF:* 800-272-1891 ■ *Web:* www.calportland.com
California Precision Products Inc	6790 Flanders Dr	San Diego	CA	92121	858-638-7300	638-7600	697	*Web:* www.cal-precision.com
California Primary Care Assn	1231 I St Ste 400	Sacramento	CA	95814	916-440-8170		194	*Web:* www.cpca.org
California Prison Industry Authority (CALPIA)	560 E Natoma St	Folsom	CA	95630	916-358-2733	358-2660	630	*TF:* 877-276-7290 ■ *Web:* www.calpia.ca.gov
California Public Interest Research Group (CAPIRG)	1111 H St Ste 207	Sacramento	CA	95814	916-448-4516		633	*Web:* calpirg.org
California Public Radio	4100 Vachell Ln	San Luis Obispo	CA	93401	805-549-8855		632	*TF:* 800-549-8055 ■ *Web:* www.kcbx.org

	City	State	Zip	Phone	Fax	Class
California Quality Plastics Inc 2226 Castle Harbor Pl S *Web:* www.calplastics.com	Ontario	CA	91761	909-930-5535	930-5540	604
California Regional Multiple Listing Service Inc 180 Via Verde Ste 200 *Web:* go.crmls.org	San Dimas	CA	91773	909-859-2040		387
California Republican Party 1903 W Magnolia Blvd *Web:* www.cagop.org	Burbank	CA	91506	818-841-5210		616-2
California Rollin II 100 N River St *Web:* www.californiarollin.com	Rochester	NY	14612	585-271-8920		671
California Saw & Knife Works 721 Brannan St *TF:* 888-729-6533 ■ *Web:* www.calsaw.com	San Francisco	CA	94103	415-861-0644	861-0406	682
California Science Ctr 700 Exposition Park Dr *Web:* californiasciencecenter.org	Los Angeles	CA	90037	213-744-7400		520
California Sidecar Inc 100 Motorcycle Run *TF:* 800-824-1523 ■ *Web:* www.californiasidecar.com	Arrington	VA	22922	434-263-6500	263-8421	82
California Society of Association Executives (CALSAE) 775 Sunrise Ave Ste 270 *Web:* www.calsae.org	Roseville	CA	95661	916-443-8980	749-3369	260
California Solar Energy Industries Assn (CALSEIA) 1107 9th St Ste 820 *Web:* www.calseia.org	Sacramento	CA	95814	916-228-4567		139
California Southern Baptist Convention 678 E Shaw Ave *Web:* www.csbc.com	Fresno	CA	93710	559-229-9533	229-2824	48-20
California Stamp Co 3341 Hancock St *TF:* 800-373-5614 ■ *Web:* www.olstamp.com	San Diego	CA	92110	800-373-5614		467
California State Archives 1020 'O' St *TF:* 800-633-5155 ■ *Web:* www.sos.ca.gov	Sacramento	CA	95814	916-653-7715	653-7134	520
California State Library 900 N St *TF:* 800-952-5666 ■ *Web:* www.library.ca.gov	Sacramento	CA	95814	916-654-0261		434-5
California State Mining & Mineral Museum 5005 Fairgrounds Rd *Web:* www.parks.ca.gov	Mariposa	CA	95338	209-742-7625	966-3597	505
California State Polytechnic University Pomona 3801 W Temple Ave *Web:* www.cpp.edu	Pomona	CA	91768	909-869-7659	869-4555	166
California State Prison Corcoran 4001 King Ave PO Box 8800 *Web:* cdcr.ca.gov	Corcoran	CA	93212	559-992-8800	386-7461	213
California State Prison Los Angeles County 44750 60th St W *Web:* cdcr.ca.gov	Lancaster	CA	93536	661-729-2000		213
California State Prison Solano 2100 Peabody Rd PO Box 4000 *Web:* cdcr.ca.gov	Vacaville	CA	95696	707-451-0182		213
California State Railroad Museum 125 "I" St *TF:* 800-825-5464 ■ *Web:* www.californiarailroad.museum	Sacramento	CA	95814	916-323-9280	327-5655	565
California State University 401 Golden Shore *TF:* 800-325-4000 ■ *Web:* www2.calstate.edu	Long Beach	CA	90802	562-951-4000		786
California State University 6000 J St *TF:* 800-667-7531 ■ *Web:* www.csus.edu	Sacramento	CA	95819	916-278-6011	278-7473	166
California State University						
Channel Islands 1 University Dr *Web:* www.csuci.edu	Camarillo	CA	93012	805-437-8400		166
Chico 400 W 1st St *TF:* 800-542-4426 ■ *Web:* www.csuchico.edu	Chico	CA	95929	530-898-6321	898-6456	166
Dominguez Hills 1000 E Victoria St *TF:* 888-545-6512 ■ *Web:* www.csudh.edu	Carson	CA	90747	310-243-3696		166
East Bay 25800 Carlos Bee Blvd *TF:* 800-884-1684 ■ *Web:* www.csueastbay.edu	Hayward	CA	94542	510-885-3000	885-4059	166
Fullerton 800 N State College Blvd *TF:* 888-433-9406 ■ *Web:* www.fullerton.edu	Fullerton	CA	92834	657-278-7859		166
Los Angeles 5151 State University Dr *Web:* www.calstatela.edu	Los Angeles	CA	90032	323-343-3000	343-6306	166
Monterey Bay 100 Campus Ctr *Web:* csumb.edu	Seaside	CA	93955	831-582-3000	582-3738	166
Northridge 18111 Nordhoff St *TF:* 800-399-4529 ■ *Web:* www.csun.edu	Northridge	CA	91330	818-677-1200	677-3766	166
San Bernardino 5500 University Pkwy *Web:* www.csusb.edu	San Bernardino	CA	92407	909-537-5188	537-7034	166
San Marcos 333 S Twin Oaks Valley Rd *Web:* www.csusm.edu	San Marcos	CA	92096	760-750-4000	750-3248	166
Stanislaus 1 University Cir *TF:* 800-235-9292 ■ *Web:* www.csustan.edu	Turlock	CA	95382	209-667-3152	667-3788	166
California Steel & Tube 16049 Stephens St *TF:* 800-338-8823 ■ *Web:* www.californiasteelandtube.com	City of Industry	CA	91745	626-968-5511		490
California Steel Industries Inc 14000 San Bernardino Ave *Web:* www.californiasteel.com	Fontana	CA	92335	909-350-6300	350-6398	480
California Steel Services Inc 1212 S Mtn View Ave *TF:* 800-323-7227 ■ *Web:* calsteel.com	San Bernardino	CA	92408	909-796-2222		492
California Supermarket 127 E Second St *Web:* superbikeschool.com	Calexico	CA	92231	760-357-4061		345
California Sushi Academy 11310 Nebraska Ave Ste 1 *Web:* www.sushi-academy.com	Los Angeles	CA	90025	310-231-4499	478-8613	167-3
California Technology Ventures LLC 670 N Rosemead Blvd Ste 201 *Web:* ctventures.com	Pasadena	CA	91107	626-351-3700		401
California Theatre of Performing Arts 562 W Fourth St *Web:* www.californiatheatre.net	San Bernardino	CA	92401	909-885-5152	885-8948	572
California TrusFrame 23665 Cajalco Rd *Web:* caltrusframe.com	Perris	CA	92570	951-657-7491		817
California University of Pennsylvania 250 University Ave *TF:* 888-412-0479 ■ *Web:* www.calu.edu	California	PA	15419	724-938-4000	938-4564	166
California Veterinary Supply 891 W Indole St **Fax Area Code:* 775 ■ *TF:* 800-366-3047 ■ *Web:* www.calvetsupply.com	Pahrump	NV	89048	800-366-3047	727-4498*	76
California Victim Compensation Board PO Box 3036 **Fax Area Code:* 866 ■ *TF:* 800-777-9229 ■ *Web:* victims.ca.gov	Sacramento	CA	95812	800-777-9229	902-8669*	339-5
California Water Service Group 1720 N First St *NYSE:* CWT ■ *TF:* 866-734-0743 ■ *Web:* www.calwater.com	San Jose	CA	95112	408-367-8200		787
California Wellness Foundation (CWF) 6320 Canoga Ave Ste 1700 *Web:* www.calwellness.org	Woodland Hills	CA	91367	818-702-1900	702-1999	303
California Western School of Law 225 Cedar St *TF:* 800-255-4252 ■ *Web:* www.cwsl.edu	San Diego	CA	92101	619-239-0391		167-1
California's Great America 4701 Great America Pkwy *TF:* 800-660-4287 ■ *Web:* www.cagreatamerica.com	Santa Clara	CA	95054	408-988-1776		32
Californian, The 123 W Alisal St *Web:* www.thecalifornian.com	Salinas	CA	93901	831-754-4133		532-2
Calipatria State Prison 7018 Blair Rd *Web:* cdcr.ca.gov	Calipatria	CA	92233	760-348-7000		213
Caliper Corporation Inc 506 Carnegie Ctr Ste 300 *Web:* www.calipercorp.com	Princeton	NJ	08543	609-524-1200		193
Caliper Life Sciences Inc 68 Elm St **Fax Area Code:* 508 ■ *TF:* 800-762-4000 ■ *Web:* www.perkinelmer.com	Hopkinton	MA	01748	877-522-2447	435-3439*	419
Calise & Sons Bakery Inc 2 Quality Dr *TF:* 800-225-4737 ■ *Web:* www.calisebakery.com	Lincoln	RI	02865	401-334-3444	334-0938	296-1
Calista Corp 301 Calista Ct Ste A *TF:* 800-277-5516 ■ *Web:* www.calistacorp.com	Anchorage	AK	99518	907-279-5516	272-5060	655
Calistoga Massage Therapy of Santa Rosa 2801 Yulupa Ave Unit B *Web:* www.calistogamassagetherapy.com	Santa Rosa	CA	95405	707-542-4577		685
Calistoga Spa Hot Springs 1006 Washington St *TF:* 866-822-5772 ■ *Web:* www.calistogaspa.com	Calistoga	CA	94515	707-942-6269	942-4214	706
Caliva 1695 S 7th St *TF:* 888-688-0303 ■ *Web:* caliva.com	San Jose	CA	95112	888-688-0303		582
Calix Society, The 239 Selby Ave *Web:* www.calixsociety.org	Saint Paul	MN	55102	651-773-3117		48-21
Calkins Creek 815 Church St *TF:* 800-490-5111 ■ *Web:* www.boydsmillspress.com	Honesdale	PA	18431	570-253-1164	253-0179	637-2
Call for Action 11820 Parklawn Dr Ste 340 *Web:* www.callforaction.org	Rockville	MD	20852	240-747-0225		48-10
Callaghan Tire 1511 38th Ave E *Web:* www.callaghantire.com	Bradenton	FL	34208	941-746-6188		754
Callahan Chemical Co Broad St & Filmore Ave *TF:* 800-257-7967 ■ *Web:* www.calchem.com	Palmyra	NJ	08065	800-257-7967		146
Callahan Consulting Group (CCG) 3557 Maryhill Ln NW *Web:* www.callahanconsultinggroup.com	Kennesaw	GA	30152	770-715-5036		196
Callahan County Courthouse 100 W 4th St *Web:* www.callahancounty.org	Baird	TX	79504	325-854-5873		338
Callahan Eye Foundation Hospital PO Box 55309 *Web:* uabmedicine.org	Birmingham	AL	35233	205-325-8100		374-7
Callahan Financial Planning Co 3157 Farnam St Ste 7111 *TF:* 800-991-5195 ■ *Web:* callahanplanning.com	Omaha	NE	68131	402-341-2000		194
Callahan Inc 80 First St *Web:* callahan-inc.com	Bridgewater	MA	02324	508-279-0012		186
Callahan Thompson Sherman & Caudill 2601 Main St Ste 800 *Web:* ctsclaw.com	Irvine	CA	92614	949-261-2872		41
Callahan, Barraco & Inman PC 1700 W Park Dr Ste 160 *Web:* callahanbarraco.com	Westborough	MA	01581	508-372-1200		41
Call-A-Head Corp 304 Cross Bay Blvd *TF:* 800-634-2085 ■ *Web:* www.callahead.com	Broad Channel	NY	11693	800-634-2085		610
Callan & Woodworth Moving & Storage 900 Hwy 212 *TF:* 800-584-0551 ■ *Web:* www.callanmoving.com	Michigan City	IN	46360	219-874-3274		519
Callan Associates Inc 600 Montgomery St Ste 800 *TF:* 800-227-3288 ■ *Web:* www.callan.com	San Francisco	CA	94111	516-150-2772		401
Callanwolde Fine Arts Ctr 980 Briarcliff Rd NE *Web:* www.callanwolde.org	Atlanta	GA	30306	404-872-5338	872-5175	50-2
Callas Contractors Inc 10549 Downsville Pk *Web:* www.callascontractors.com	Hagerstown	MD	21740	301-739-8400		188-10
Callaway Cars Inc 3 High St *TF:* 866-927-9400 ■ *Web:* www.callawaycars.com	Old Lyme	CT	06371	860-434-9002		57
Callaway County Clerk 10 E Fifth St *Web:* callawaycountyclerk.com	Fulton	MO	65251	573-642-0730	642-7181	338
Callaway Electric Co-op 1313 Co-op Dr PO Box 250 *TF:* 888-642-4840 ■ *Web:* www.callawayelectric.com	Fulton	MO	65251	573-642-3326		245
Callaway Gardens 17800 Hwy 27 *TF:* 800-225-5292 ■ *Web:* www.callawaygardens.com	Pine Mountain	GA	31822	706-663-2281	663-5122	669
Callaway Golf Co 2180 Rutherford Rd *NYSE:* ELY ■ *TF:* 800-588-9836 ■ *Web:* www.callawaygolf.com	Carlsbad	CA	92008	760-931-1771	931-8013	710
Callaway Partners LLC 600 Galleria Pkwy SE Ste 1400 *Web:* www.warbirdconsulting.com	Atlanta	GA	30339	404-496-5230	252-9078	292
Callbright Corp 6700 Hollister *TF:* 877-462-2552 ■ *Web:* www.callbright.com	Houston	TX	77040	855-225-5274		390
CallDirek 4770 Biscayne Blvd Ste 1480	Miami	FL	33137	305-434-7072		387
Callenor Company Inc N 60 W 15725 Kohler Ln *Web:* www.callenor.com	Menomonee Falls	WI	53051	262-252-3343		125

Name / Address	City	State	ZIP	Phone	Fax	Class
Callero & Callero LLP 7800 N Milwaukee Ave *Web:* www.callero.com	Niles	IL	60714	847-966-2040	966-2179	2
Caller-Times 820 N Lower Broadway *TF:* 800-827-2011 ■ *Web:* www.caller.com	Corpus Christi	TX	78401	361-884-2011		532-2
Calling Solutions By Phone Power Inc 2200 McCullough Ave *TF:* 800-683-5500 ■ *Web:* www.callingsolutions.org	San Antonio	TX	78212	210-801-9630		737
Calliope Learning 1581H Hillside Ave PO Box 151 *Web:* www.calliopelearning.com	Victoria	BC	V8T2C1	250-213-6239	370-0436	194
Callisto Integration 635 Fourth Line Ste 16 *TF:* 800-387-0467 ■ *Web:* www.callistointegration.com	Oakville	ON	L6L5B3	905-339-0059		194
Callisto Media 6005 Shellmound St Ste 175 *Web:* www.callistomedia.com	Emeryville	CA	94608	717-896-6437		514
Callocchia Law Firm PLLC 56 Bidwell Pkwy *Web:* callocchialaw.com	Buffalo	NY	14222	716-883-3953		41
Callon Petroleum Co 200 N Canal St *NYSE: CPE* ■ *TF:* 800-451-1294 ■ *Web:* www.callon.com	Natchez	MS	39120	601-442-1601	446-1410	540
Callos 1375 S Main St Ste 101 *TF:* 877-240-0529 ■ *Web:* www.callos.com	North Canton	OH	44720	330-499-1299	499-1315	260
Calloway County 101 S Fifth St Ste 5 *Web:* calloway.clerkinfo.net	Murray	KY	42071	270-753-3923	759-9611	338
Calloway's Nursery Inc 4200 Airport Fwy Ste 200 *OTC: CLWY* ■ *Web:* www.calloways.com	Fort Worth	TX	76117	817-222-1122		323
CallRail Inc 100 Peachtree St NW Ste 2700 *TF:* 888-663-0997 ■ *Web:* www.callrail.com	Atlanta	GA	30303	888-663-0997		788
Callware Technologies Inc 8871 S Sandy Pkwy Ste 200 *TF:* 800-888-4226 ■ *Web:* www.callware.com	Sandy	UT	84070	801-988-6800		178-7
CALM (California Living Museum) 10500 Alfred Harrell Hwy *Web:* www.calmzoo.org	Bakersfield	CA	93306	661-872-2256	872-2205	520
Calm 77 Geary St 3rd Fl *Web:* www.calm.com	San Francisco	CA	94108	650-988-8500		42
CALMAC Manufacturing Corp 3-00 Banta Pl *Web:* www.calmac.com	Fair Lawn	NJ	07410	201-797-1511		194
Calmare Therapeutics Inc 1375 Kings Hwy *Web:* calmaretherapeutics.com	Fairfield	CT	06824	203-368-6044	368-5399	195
Calmark Inc 1400 W 44th St *Web:* calmarkgroup.com	Chicago	IL	60609	773-247-7200		5
Calmax Technology Inc 526 Laurelwood Rd *Web:* www.calmaxtechnology.com	Santa Clara	CA	95054	408-748-8660		757
CalMet Services Inc 7202 Petterson Ln *Web:* calmetservices.com	Paramount	CA	90723	562-259-1239	529-7958	804
Calmetto Management Group Inc 883 NE Main St 2nd Fl PO Box 1237 *Web:* www.calmetto.com	Simpsonville	SC	29681	864-962-2201	962-2483	195
Calmont Beverage Inc 308 Industrial Ln *TF:* 800-649-3143 ■ *Web:* www.calmontbeverage.com	Berlin	VT	05641	802-223-3281	223-5615	81-1
Calmont Leasing Ltd 14610 Yellowhead Trail NW *TF:* 855-474-2568 ■ *Web:* www.calmont.ca	Edmonton	AB	T5L3C5	855-474-2568		778
Calmoseptine Inc 16602 Burke Ln *TF:* 800-800-3405 ■ *Web:* www.calmoseptine.com	Huntington Beach	CA	92647	714-840-3405		231
Calnet Inc 12359 Sunrise Vly Dr Ste 270 *TF:* 877-322-5638 ■ *Web:* www.calnet.com	Reston	VA	20191	703-547-6800	547-6806	194
Calnetix Technologies LLC 16323 Shoemaker Ave *Web:* www.calnetix.com	Cerritos	CA	90703	562-293-1660	293-1689	518
Calolympic Glove & Safety Company Inc 1720 Delilah St *TF:* 800-421-6630 ■ *Web:* www.caloly-safety.com	Corona	CA	92879	951-340-2229	340-3337	679
Caloris Engineering LLC 8649 Commerce Dr *Web:* caloris.com	Easton	MD	21601	410-822-6900		261
Calox Inc 3034 Fierro St *Web:* www.caloxinc.com	Los Angeles	CA	90065	323-255-5175	872-5135	264-4
Cal-Pac Chemical Company Inc 6231 Maywood Ave *Web:* www.calpacchem.com	Huntington Park	CA	90255	323-585-2178	585-3087	145
Calphalon Corp PO Box 583 **Fax Area Code:* 419 ■ *TF:* 800-809-7267 ■ *Web:* www.calphalon.com	Toledo	OH	43697	800-809-7267	666-2859*	486
CALPIA (California Prison Industry Authority) 560 E Natoma St *TF:* 877-276-7290 ■ *Web:* www.calpia.ca.gov	Folsom	CA	95630	916-358-2733	358-2660	630
Calpico Inc 1387 San Mateo Ave *TF:* 800-998-9115 ■ *Web:* www.calpicoinc.com	South San Francisco	CA	94080	650-588-2241		326
Calpine Containers Inc 380 W Spruce Ave *Web:* calpinecontainers.com	Clovis	CA	93611	559-519-7199	421-9198	101
Calrad Electronics Inc 819 N Highland Ave *Web:* www.calrad.com	Los Angeles	CA	90038	323-465-2131		246
Cal-Royal Products Inc 6605 Flotilla St *TF:* 800-876-9258 ■ *Web:* www.cal-royal.com	Commerce	CA	90040	323-888-6601	888-6699	350
CALSAE (California Society of Association Executives) 775 Sunrise Ave Ste 270 *Web:* www.calsae.org	Roseville	CA	95661	916-443-8980	749-3369	260
Calsak Corp 1411 W 190th St Ste 400 *Web:* www.calsak.com	Gardena	CA	90248	310-719-9500	719-1300	603
CALSEIA (California Solar Energy Industries Assn) 1107 9th St Ste 820 *Web:* www.calseia.org	Sacramento	CA	95814	916-228-4567		139
Cal-Sierra Pipe LLC 3033 S 99 Hwy W Frontage Rd *TF:* 800-366-0988 ■ *Web:* calsierrapipe.com	Stockton	CA	95215	209-466-0988		690
CalsonicKansei North America Inc 1 Calsonic Way *Web:* www.calsonic.com	Shelbyville	TN	37160	931-684-4490	684-2724	15
Calstrip Steel Corp 3030 Dulles Dr *Web:* calstripsteel.com	Mira Loma	CA	91752	323-726-1345	722-8269	723
CalSurance 681 S Parker St Ste 300 *TF:* 800-762-7800 ■ *Web:* www.calsurance.com	Orange	CA	92868	714-939-0800	939-1641	390
CalTel (CT) 665 Main St *Web:* www.caltel.com	Copperopolis	CA	95228	209-785-2211		224
Calton & Associates Inc 2701 N Rocky Point Dr Ste 1000 *TF:* 800-942-0262 ■ *Web:* www.calton.com	Tampa	FL	33607	813-264-0440		690
Cal-Trade Welding School of Modesto 424 Kansas Ave *Web:* www.caltradeweldingschool.com	Modesto	CA	95351	209-523-0753	523-8826	685
Calumet Armature & Electric Company Inc 1050 W 134th St *Web:* www.calumetarmature.com	Riverdale	IL	60827	708-841-6880		518
Calumet Breweries Inc 6535 Osborn Ave *Web:* www.calbrew.com	Hammond	IN	46320	219-845-2338		81-1
Calumet City Chamber of Commerce 80 River Oaks Ctr PO Box 2406 *Web:* www.calumetcitychamber.com	Calumet City	IL	60409	708-891-5888		139
Calumet City Public Library 660 Manistee Ave *Web:* calumetcitypl.org	Calumet City	IL	60409	708-862-6220	862-0872	434-3
Calumet College of Saint Joseph 2400 New York Ave *TF:* 877-700-9100 ■ *Web:* ccsj.edu	Whiting	IN	46394	219-473-4215	473-4336	166
Calumet County 206 Ct St *TF:* 833-620-2730 ■ *Web:* www.co.calumet.wi.us	Chilton	WI	53014	920-849-1442	849-1469	338
Calumet Diversified Meats Inc 10000 80th Ave *TF:* 800-752-7427 ■ *Web:* www.porkchops.com	Pleasant Prairie	WI	53158	262-947-7200	947-7209	297-9
Calumet Specialty Products Partners LP 2780 Waterfront Pkwy E Dr Ste 200 *NASDAQ: CLMT* ■ *TF:* 800-437-3188 ■ *Web:* www.calumetspecialty.com	Indianapolis	IN	46214	317-328-5660	328-5668	580
Cal-Van Tools 7918 Industrial Village Rd *TF:* 800-537-1077 ■ *Web:* cal-vantools.com	Greensboro	NC	27409	800-537-1077	537-1717	758
Calvary Baptist Christian Academy 543 Randolph St *Web:* calvarymeadville.com	Meadville	PA	16335	814-724-8099		48-20
Calvary Bible College & Theological Seminary 15800 Calvary Rd *TF:* 800-326-3960 ■ *Web:* www.calvary.edu	Kansas City	MO	64147	816-322-3960	331-4474	161
Calvary Chapel 13500 Philmont Ave *Web:* www.ccphilly.org	Philadelphia	PA	19116	215-969-1520		48-20
Calvary Chapel of Costa Mesa Inc 3800 S Fairview St *Web:* www.calvarychapelcostamesa.com	Santa Ana	CA	92704	714-979-4422		48-20
Calvary Church of Pacific 701 Palisades Dr *Web:* calvarypalisades.org	Pacific Palisades	CA	90272	310-454-6537		685
Calvert Cliffs State Park 10540 H G Trueman Rd *Web:* www.dnr.maryland.gov	Lusby	MD	20657	443-975-4360		565
Calvert Company Inc 3559 Truman St *Web:* calvertglulam.com	Washougal	WA	98671	360-693-0971	693-3389	817
Calvert County 175 Main St *TF:* 800-492-7122 ■ *Web:* www.calvertcountymd.gov	Prince Frederick	MD	20678	410-535-1600		338
Calvert County Chamber of Commerce PO Box 9 **Fax Area Code:* 443 ■ *TF:* 800-972-4389 ■ *Web:* www.calvertchamber.org	Prince Frederick	MD	20678	410-535-2577	295-7213*	139
Calvert County Nursing Center Inc 85 Hospital Rd *Web:* www.calvertcountynursingcenter.org	Prince Frederick	MD	20678	410-535-2300		371
Calvert County Public Library 850 Costley Way *Web:* calvertlibrary.info	Prince Frederick	MD	20678	410-535-0291		434-3
Calvert Eaves Clarke & Stelly LLP 2615 Calder Ste 1070 *Web:* calvert-eaves.com	Beaumont	TX	77702	409-832-8885		41
Calvert Investment Counsel LLC 4 N Park Dr Ste 201 *Web:* www.calvertinvestmentcounsel.com	Hunt Valley	MD	21030	410-435-3270		401
Calvert Ken (Rep R - CA) 2205 Rayburn House Office Bldg *Web:* calvert.house.gov	Washington	DC	20515	202-225-1986	225-2004	342-2
Calvert Labs 1225 Crescent Green Ste 460 *TF:* 800-300-8114 ■ *Web:* calvertlabs.com	Cary	NC	27518	919-854-4453		418
Calvert Marine Museum 14200 Solomons Island Rd PO Box 97 *Web:* www.calvertmarinemuseum.com	Solomons	MD	20688	410-326-2042	326-6691	520
Calvert Plumbing & Heating Company Inc 8801 Mylander Ln *Web:* www.calvertinc.com	Towson	MD	21286	410-323-5400		189-10
Calvert Systems Engineering Inc 85 Sherry Ln Ste 3A *Web:* calvertsystemsengineering.com	Prince Frederick	MD	20678	443-968-2471		177
Calvert Wealth Management Inc 3175 W Ward Rd Ste 120 *TF:* 800-637-3211 ■ *Web:* www.calvertwealth.com	Dunkirk	MD	20754	301-812-1550		690
Calvert's Restaurant 475 Highland Ave *Web:* www.calvertsrestaurant.net	Augusta	GA	30909	706-738-4514		671
Calverton National Cemetery 210 Princeton Blvd *Web:* www.cem.va.gov	Calverton	NY	11933	631-727-5410	369-4397	136
Calvin B. Taylor House Museum 208 N Main St *Web:* taylorhousemuseum.org	Berlin	MD	21811	410-641-1019		520
Calvin College 3201 Burton St SE *TF:* 800-688-0122 ■ *Web:* calvin.edu	Grand Rapids	MI	49546	616-526-6000	526-6777	166

				Phone	Fax	Class
Calvin Dean Homolka Ii 200 E First St N Ste 542 *Web:* homolkalaw.com	Wichita	KS	67202	316-263-6950		41
Calvin Giordano & Associates Inc 1800 Eller Dr Ste 600 *Web:* www.cgasolutions.com	Fort Lauderdale	FL	33316	954-921-7781		261
Calvin Theological Seminary 3233 Burton St SE *TF:* 800-388-6034 ■ *Web:* www.calvinseminary.edu	Grand Rapids	MI	49546	616-957-6036	957-8621	167-3
Calypso 595 Market St Ste 1800 *Web:* www.calypso.com	San Francisco	CA	94105	415-817-2400	284-1222	178
Calypte Biomedical Corp 15875 SW 72nd Ave *OTC:* CBMC ■ *Web:* www.calypte.com	Portland	OR	97224	503-726-2227	601-6299	231
Calyx Transportation Group Inc *National Fast Freight* 107 Alfred Kuehne Blvd *TF:* 800-563-2223 ■ *Web:* www.nationalfastfreight.com	Brampton	ON	L6T4K3	905-494-4808	494-4809	314
Calzone Case Co 225 Black Rock Ave **Fax Area Code:* 203 ■ *TF:* 800-243-5152 ■ *Web:* www.calzoneandanvil.com	Bridgeport	CT	06605	800-243-5182	336-4406*	453
CAM (CAM Raleigh) 409 W Martin St *Web:* camraleigh.org	Raleigh	NC	27603	919-261-5920		520
CAM (Cincinnati Asset Management Inc) 8845 Governor's Hill Dr *Web:* www.cambonds.com	Cincinnati	OH	45249	513-554-8500		401
CAM Administrative Services Inc 25800 Northwestern Hwy Ste 700 *TF:* 800-732-8906 ■ *Web:* www.camads.com	Southfield	MI	48075	248-827-1050	827-2112	390
CAM Audio Inc 2210 Executive Dr *TF:* 800-527-3458 ■ *Web:* www.camaudio.com	Garland	TX	75041	972-271-2800		35
CAM Commerce Solutions Inc 17075 Newhope St Ste A *Web:* www.camcommerce.com	Fountain Valley	CA	92708	714-338-0200	241-9893	178-10
CAM Consulting Group LLC 10 Tudor Ct *Web:* cam4consulting.com	Chesterfield	NJ	08515	609-291-1937		196
CAM Innovation Inc 215 Philadelphia St *Web:* www.caminnovation.com	Hanover	PA	17331	717-637-5988	637-9329	295
CAM International LLC 503 Space Pk S *TF:* 800-251-8544 ■ *Web:* caminternational.com	Nashville	TN	37211	800-251-8544		61
CAM Raleigh (CAM) 409 W Martin St *Web:* camraleigh.org	Raleigh	NC	27603	919-261-5920		520
CAM Services Inc 5664 Selmaraine Dr *TF:* 800-576-3050 ■ *Web:* www.camservices.com	Culver City	CA	90230	310-390-3552		256
CAM Superline Inc 4763 Zane A Miller Dr *TF:* 800-378-7623 ■ *Web:* www.camsuperline.com	Waynesboro	PA	17268	717-749-3369		120
CAM Tran Company Ltd 203 Purdy Rd *TF:* 844-379-3224 ■ *Web:* www.camtran.com	Colborne	ON	K0K1S0	905-355-3224		767
Cama Inc 31 Audubon St *Web:* www.camainc.com	New Haven	CT	06511	203-777-9921		393
CAMAC Inc 1330 Post Oak Blvd Ste 2200 *Web:* www.camac.com	Houston	TX	77056	713-965-5100	965-5128	538
CAMACOL (Latin Chamber of Commerce of the US) 1401 W Flagler St *Web:* www.camacol.org	Miami	FL	33135	305-642-3870	642-3961	138
Camadro Inc 508 Mohawk St Ste A *Web:* freearcade.com	Tecumseh	MI	49286	517-423-0523		180
Camag Scientific Inc 515 Cornelius Harnett Dr *Web:* www.camag.com	Wilmington	NC	28401	910-343-1830		250
Camalloy Inc 1960 N Main St *Web:* camalloy.com	Washington	PA	15301	724-222-2022	222-0336	492
Camano Island State Park 2269 S Lowell Pt Rd *Web:* www.parks.state.wa.us	Camano Island	WA	98282	360-387-3031		565
Camar Aircraft Parts Co 1987 Via Montecito *Web:* www.camarac.com	Camarillo	CA	93012	805-389-8944	389-0416	24
Camarillo Chamber of Commerce 2400 Ventura Blvd *Web:* www.camarillochamber.org	Camarillo	CA	93010	805-484-4383	484-1395	139
Camas County 501 Soldier Rd *Web:* camascounty.id.gov	Fairfield	ID	83327	208-764-2242	764-2349	338
Camas-Washougal Chamber of Commerce 422 NE Fourth Ave *TF:* 844-262-1100 ■ *Web:* www.cwchamber.com	Camas	WA	98607	360-834-2472	834-9171	139
Cambay Group Inc, The 1676 N California Blvd Ste 420 *Web:* www.cambaygroup.com	Walnut Creek	CA	94596	925-933-1405	933-1404	194
Cambelt International Corp 2820 West 1100 South *TF:* 855-226-2358 ■ *Web:* www.cambelt.com	Salt Lake City	UT	84104	801-972-5511	972-5522	207
Cambex Corp 337 Tpke Rd *OTC:* CBEX ■ *TF:* 800-325-5565 ■ *Web:* www.cambex.com	Southborough	MA	01772	508-281-0209	281-0214	176
Cambey & West Inc 120 N Rt 9W *Web:* home.cambeywest.com	Congers	NY	10920	845-267-3490		225
Cambiar Investors Inc 2401 E Second Ave Ste 500 *TF:* 888-673-9950 ■ *Web:* www.cambiar.com	Denver	CO	80206	888-673-9950		401
Cambium Learning Group Inc 17855 Dallas Pkwy Ste 400 *Web:* www.cambiumlearning.com	Dallas	TX	75287	214-932-9500		242
Cambodia Embassy 4530 16th St NW *Web:* www.embassyofcambodiadc.org	Washington	DC	20011	202-726-7742	726-8381	257
Cambrex Charles City Inc 1205 11th St *Web:* www.cambrex.com	Charles City	IA	50616	641-257-1000		479
Cambria 31496 Cambria Ave Ste 220 *Web:* www.cambriausa.com	Le Sueur	MN	56058	507-665-5003		115
Cambria Bicycle Outfitter 1645 Commerce Way *TF:* 888-937-4331 ■ *Web:* www.cambriabike.com	Paso Robles	CA	93446	805-221-2602		711
Cambria Capital LLC 488 E Winchester St Ste 200 *TF:* 877-226-0477 ■ *Web:* www.cambriacapital.com	Salt Lake City	UT	84107	801-320-9606		401
Cambria Consulting Inc 50 Milk St *Web:* www.cambriaconsulting.com	Boston	MA	02114	617-523-7500		194
Cambria Corp 3723 Haven Ave Ste 130 *Web:* www.cambria.com	Menlo Park	CA	94025	650-549-8911		809
Cambria County 216 Plank Rd *Web:* www.cambriacountypa.gov	Ebensburg	PA	15931	814-472-1540	472-0761	338
Cambria County Library System 248 Main St *Web:* www.cclsys.org	Johnstown	PA	15901	814-536-5131	536-6905	434-3
Cambria Group, The 300 Crescent Ct Ste 1175 *Web:* www.cambriagroup.com	Dallas	TX	75201	469-513-2200	513-2201	792
Cambria Music PO Box 374 *Web:* www.cambriamus.com	Lomita	CA	90717	310-831-1322	833-7442	657
Cambria Pines Realty Inc 746-A Main St *TF:* 800-676-8616 ■ *Web:* cambriapinesrealty.com	Cambria	CA	93428	805-927-8616		652
Cambria Solutions Inc 1050 20th St Ste 275 *Web:* www.cambriasolutions.com	Sacramento	CA	95811	916-326-4446		194
Cambria Truck Ctr 116 Talmadge Rd **Fax Area Code:* 732 ■ *TF:* 800-680-6225 ■ *Web:* www.cambrias.com	Edison	NJ	08817	800-680-6225	491-2152*	57
Cambrian Management 415 W Wall St Ste 900 *Web:* cambrianmgmt.com	Midland	TX	79701	432-620-9181		540
Cambridge Advisors Inc 17330 Wright St Ste 205 *Web:* cambridgeadvisors.net	Omaha	NE	68130	402-697-1166	697-9271	690
Cambridge Area Chamber of Commerce 607 Wheeling Ave *Web:* cambridgeohiochamber.com	Cambridge	OH	43725	740-439-6688	439-6689	139
Cambridge Associates LLC 125 High St *Web:* www.cambridgeassociates.com	Boston	MA	02110	617-457-7500		401
Cambridge BioMarketing Group LLC 245 First St *Web:* cambridgebmg.com	Cambridge	MA	02142	617-225-0001		4
Cambridge Chamber of Commerce 1 Kendall Sq *Web:* www.cambridgechamber.org	Cambridge	MA	02139	617-876-4100		139
Cambridge Chamber of Commerce 750 Hespeler Rd *TF:* 800-749-7560 ■ *Web:* www.cambridgechamber.com	Cambridge	ON	N3H5L8	519-622-2221	622-0177	137
Cambridge Chemical Technologies Inc 625 Mt Auburn St *Web:* cambchemtech.com	Cambridge	MA	02138	617-868-0670		261
Cambridge College Inc 360 Merrimack St 4th Fl *TF:* 800-829-4723 ■ *Web:* www.cambridgecollege.edu	Lawrence	MA	01843	617-868-1000		800
Cambridge Construction Management Inc 97 Grayrock Rd *Web:* cambridgecm.com	Clinton	NJ	08809	908-638-9700		653
Cambridge Financial Group Inc 4100 Horizons Dr Ste 200 *Web:* www.cfginc.net	Columbus	OH	43220	614-457-1530		401
Cambridge Historical Society (CHS) Hooper-Lee-Nichols House 159 Brattle St *Web:* www.cambridgehistory.org	Cambridge	MA	02138	617-547-4252		49-19
Cambridge Hospital 1493 Cambridge St *Web:* www.challiance.org	Cambridge	MA	02139	617-665-1000		374-3
Cambridge Innovation Institute 250 First Ave Ste 300 *TF:* 888-999-6288 ■ *Web:* www.cambridgeinnovationinstitute.com	Needham	MA	02494	781-972-5400		668
Cambridge Innovations Inc (CIC) *Cambridge Innovation Ctr* 1 Broadway Kendall Sq 14th Fl *Web:* cic.com	Cambridge	MA	02142	617-758-4100		792
Cambridge Intl 105 Goodwill Rd *TF:* 800-638-9560 ■ *Web:* www.cambridge-intl.com	Cambridge	MD	21613	410-901-4979		207
Cambridge Isotope Laboratories Inc 3 Highwood Dr **Fax Area Code:* 978 ■ *TF:* 800-322-1174 ■ *Web:* www.isotope.com	Tewksbury	MA	01876	800-322-1174	749-2768*	145
Cambridge Lasers Laboratories Inc 853 Brown Rd *Web:* www.lexellaser.com	Fremont	CA	94539	510-651-0110		535
Cambridge Memorial Hospital 700 Coronation Blvd *Web:* www.cmh.org	Cambridge	ON	N1R3G2	519-621-2330	740-4938	374-2
Cambridge Meridian Group Inc (CMG) 2 Hancock Pk *Web:* cambridge-meridian.com	Cambridge	MA	02139	617-876-7400	497-2501	194
Cambridge Office for Tourism Inc 4 Brattle St Ste 208 *Web:* www.cambridgeusa.org	Cambridge	MA	02138	617-441-2884		206
Cambridge Pro Fab Inc 470 Franklin Blvd *Web:* www.cambridgeprofab.com	Cambridge	ON	N1R8G6	519-740-6033		518
Cambridge Public Library 449 Broadway *TF:* 800-327-5050 ■ *Web:* www.cambridgema.gov	Cambridge	MA	02138	617-349-4040		434-3
Cambridge Realty Capital LLC 1 N LaSalle St 37th Fl *Web:* www.cambridgecap.com	Chicago	IL	60602	312-357-1601	357-1611	652
Cambridge Resources Corp 960 Alabama Ave *Web:* www.cambridgeresources.com	Brooklyn	NY	11207	718-927-0009		605-2
Cambridge Savings Bank 1374 Massachusetts Ave *TF:* 888-418-5626 ■ *Web:* cambridgesavings.com	Cambridge	MA	02138	617-441-4155	520-5306	70
Cambridge School of Culinary Arts 2020 Massachusetts Ave *Web:* cambridgeculinary.com	Cambridge	MA	02140	617-354-2020	576-1963	163
Cambridge School of Weston 45 Georgian Rd *Web:* www.csw.org	Weston	MA	02493	781-642-8650		622
Cambridge Silversmith Ltd 116 Lehigh Dr *TF:* 800-890-3366 ■ *Web:* www.cambridgesilversmiths.com	Fairfield	NJ	07004	973-227-4400	227-5600	361

Name / Address	City	State	Zip	Phone	Fax	Class
Cambridge Street Metal Corp (CSM) 82 Stevens St — TF: 800-254-7580 ■ Web: www.csmetal.net	East Taunton	MA	02718	508-822-2278	822-4667	492
Cambridge Suites Hotel Halifax 1583 Brunswick St — TF: 800-565-1263 ■ Web: www.cambridgesuiteshalifax.com	Halifax	NS	B3J3P5	902-420-0555	420-9379	379
Cambridge Suites Hotel Toronto 15 Richmond St E — TF: 800-463-1990 ■ Web: www.cambridgesuitestoronto.com	Toronto	ON	M5C1N2	416-368-1990	601-3751	379
Cambridge Technology 125 Middlesex Tpke — Web: www.cambridgetechnology.com	Bedford	MA	01730	781-266-5800	266-5123	472
Cambridge Technology Consulting Group Inc (CTCG) 201 Wilshire Blvd Ste 41 — Web: www.ctcg.com	Santa Monica	CA	90401	310-229-8947		180
Cambridge Telephone Co (CTC) 611 Patterson St — TF: 800-793-2788 ■ Web: www.pnpt.com	Cambridge	NE	69022	800-793-2788		224
Cambridge Telephone Company Inc (CTC) 130 N Superior — Web: www.ctcweb.net	Cambridge	ID	83610	208-257-3314	257-3310	224
Cambridge Trust Co 1336 Massachusetts Ave — TF: 800-876-6406 ■ Web: www.cambridgetrust.com	Cambridge	MA	02138	617-876-5500	812-2403	70
Cambridge Valley Machining Inc 28 Perry Ln — Web: www.cvmusa.com	Cambridge	NY	12816	518-677-5617	677-5974	454
Cambridge Viscosity Inc 101 Stn Landing — Web: www.cambridgeviscosity.com	Medford	MA	02155	781-393-6500		203
Cambridge Whos Who Publishing Inc 498 RXR Plz — TF: 866-933-1555 ■ Web: cambridgewhoswho.com	Uniondale	NY	11556	516-535-1515	535-1514	637-9
Cambridge World 34 Franklin Ave — TF: 800-221-2253 ■ Web: www.cambridgeworld.com	Brooklyn	NY	11205	718-858-5002	858-5437	119
Cambridgeport Air Systems 8 Fanaras Dr — TF: 877-648-2872 ■ Web: www.cambridgeport.net	Salisbury	MA	01952	978-465-8481		610
CambridgeSoft Corp 100 CambridgePark Dr — TF: 800-315-7300 ■ Web: www.cambridgesoft.com	Cambridge	MA	02140	617-588-9100	588-9190	178-5
Cambro Manufacturing Co 5801 Skylab Rd — TF: 800-833-3003 ■ Web: www.cambro.com	Huntington Beach	CA	92647	714-848-1555	842-3430	300
Camcad Technologies Inc 5840 Red Bug Lake Rd Ste 175 — Web: camcadtech.com	Winter Springs	FL	32708	407-327-4975	650-2874	177
Camco Chemical Co 8145 Holton Dr — TF: 800-354-1001 ■ Web: www.camco-chem.com	Florence	KY	41042	859-727-3200	727-1508	151
Camco Manufacturing Inc 121 Landmark Dr — TF: 800-334-2004 ■ Web: www.camco.net	Greensboro	NC	27409	336-668-7661		247
Camco Pacific Construction Company Inc 19712 MacArthur Blvd Ste 200	Irvine	CA	92612	949-251-1300	251-1333	186
Camcor Partners Inc 734-7th Ave SW Ste 1310 — Web: www.camcorpartners.com	Calgary	AB	T2P3P8	403-508-2950		401
Camcraft Inc 1080 Muirfield Dr — Web: www.camcraft.com	Hanover Park	IL	60133	630-582-6000	582-6019	621
Camden Children's Garden 3 Riverside Dr — Web: www.camdenchildrensgarden.org	Camden	NJ	08103	856-365-8733		97
Camden County 117 N NC 343 PO Box 190 — TF: 877-885-7968 ■ Web: camdencountync.gov	Camden	NC	27921	252-338-1919	333-1603	338
Camden County 520 Market St Ste 306 — TF: 866-226-3362 ■ Web: www.camdencounty.com	Camden	NJ	08102	856-225-5300		338
Camden County 1 Court Cir Ste 8 — Web: www.camdenmo.org	Camdenton	MO	65020	573-346-4440		338
Camden County 200 E 4th St PO Box 99 — Web: www.camdencountyga.gov	Woodbine	GA	31569	912-576-5601	576-5647	338
Camden County Chamber of Commerce 2603 Osborne Rd Unit CC — Web: www.camdenchamber.com	Saint Marys	GA	31558	912-673-3101	673-3109	139
Camden County College 200 College Dr — Web: camdencc.edu	Blackwood	NJ	08012	856-227-7200	374-4917	162
Camden County Library 203 Laurel Rd — TF: 877-222-3737 ■ Web: www.camdencountylibrary.org	Voorhees	NJ	08043	856-772-1636	772-6105	434-3
Camden County Library District 89 Rodeo Rd PO Box 1320 — Web: www.ccld.us	Camdenton	MO	65020	573-346-5954	346-1263	434-3
Camden Fairview School District 625 Clifton St — Web: cfsd.k12.ar.us	Camden	AR	71701	870-836-4193		685
Camden Hills State Park 280 Belfast Rd — Web: www.maine.gov	Camden	ME	04843	207-236-3109		565
Camden House 668 Mount Hope Ave	Rochester	NY	14620	585-275-0419	271-8778	637-2
Camden Law LLP 20 Mechanic St — Web: camdenlaw.com	Camden	ME	04843	207-236-8836		41
Camden National Corp 2 Elm St — NASDAQ: CAC ■ TF: 800-860-8821 ■ Web: www.camdennational.com	Camden	ME	04843	207-236-8821		360-2
Camden Property Trust 11 Greenway Plz Ste 2400 — NYSE: CPT ■ TF: 800-922-6336 ■ Web: www.camdenliving.com	Houston	TX	77046	713-354-2500	354-2700	655
Camden Public Library (CPL) 55 Main St — Web: www.librarycamden.org	Camden	ME	04843	207-236-3440	236-6673	434-3
Camden State Park 1897 County Rd — Web: www.dnr.state.mn.us	Lynd	MN	56157	507-865-4530	865-4608	565
Came Americas Automation LLC 11345 NW 122nd St — Web: www.came.com	Medley	FL	33178	305-433-3307		358
Cameco Corp 2121 11th St W — NYSE: CCO ■ Web: www.cameco.com	Saskatoon	SK	S7M1J3	306-956-6200		502
Camel Grinding Wheels 7525 N Oak Park Ave — TF: 800-447-3731 ■ Web: www.cgwheels.com	Niles	IL	60714	800-447-3731		1
Camelback Mountain 301 Resort Dr — Web: www.skicamelback.com	Tannersville	PA	18372	570-629-1661		31
Camelbeach Mountain Waterpark 309 Resort Dr — Web: www.camelbeach.com	Tannersville	PA	18372	570-629-1662		32
Cameli & Hoag PC 105 W Adams Ste 1430 — Web: camelihoaglaw.com	Chicago	IL	60603	312-726-7300	726-7302	41
Camellia Symphony Orchestra 1731 Howe Ave Ste 499 — Web: www.camelliasymphony.org	Sacramento	CA	95825	916-929-6655		573-3
Camelot 3PI Software 10020 Park Cedar Dr — Web: www.3plsoftware.com	Charlotte	NC	28210	704-554-1670		178-1
Camelot Cleaners Co 8590 Frederick St — Web: camelotcleanersomaha.com	Omaha	NE	68124	402-393-5257		426
Camelot Community Care Inc 4910 D Creekside Dr — Web: www.camelotcommunitycare.org	Clearwater	FL	33760	727-593-0003	595-0735	48-6
Camelot Entertainment Group 300 Spectrum Center Dr Ste 400 — Web: www.camelotfilms.com	Irvine	CA	92618	949-754-3030		514
Camelot Homes 6607 N Scottsdale Rd Ste H100 — Web: www.camelothomes.com	Scottsdale	AZ	85250	480-367-4300	367-4350	652
Camelot Technology 30 Snowflake Rd — Web: www.camelottechnology.com	Huntingdon Valley	PA	19006	215-357-3416	469-5200	52
Cameo 400 N Aberdeen St — Web: cameo.com	Chicago	IL	60642	847-529-5202		6
Cameo Beauty Academy 9714 S Cicero Ave — Web: www.cameobeautyacademy.com	Oak Lawn	IL	60453	708-636-4660		167-3
Cameo College of Essential Beauty 124 East 5770 South — TF: 888-334-1897 ■ Web: www.cameocollege.com	Murray	UT	84107	801-747-5700	747-5701	167-3
Camera Corner Inc PO Box 1899 — TF: 800-868-2462 ■ Web: www.camcor.com	Burlington	NC	27216	336-228-0251	222-8011	119
Camerican International Inc 45 Eisenhower Dr — Web: camerican.com	Paramus	NJ	07652	201-587-0101		297-11
Cameron & Marroney PLLC 901 N Olive Ave — Web: attorneysofwestpalmbeach.com	West Palm Beach	FL	33401	561-659-5522		41
Cameron & Mittleman LLP 301 Promenade St — Web: www.cm-law.com	Providence	RI	02908	401-331-5700	331-5787	445
Cameron & Moresco CPA LLP 865 Aerovista Pl Ste 220 — Web: cameronmorescocpas.com	San Luis Obispo	CA	93401	805-592-2860		2
Cameron + Co 149 Kentucky St Ste 7 — *Fax Area Code: 415 ■ Web: www.cameronbooks.com	Petaluma	CA	94952	707-769-1617	223-8520*	637-2
Cameron Ashley Building Products 979 Batesville Rd Ste A — TF: 800-569-4262 ■ Web: www.guardianbp.com	Greer	SC	29651	864-297-6101	281-3558	191-3
Cameron Balloons US PO Box 3672 — TF: 866-423-6178 ■ Web: www.cameronballoons.com	Ann Arbor	MI	48106	734-426-5525	426-5026	28
Cameron Broadcasting Inc 2350 Miracle Mile Rd Ste 300 — Web: www.cameronbroadcasting.com	Bullhead City	AZ	86442	928-763-5586		645-141
Cameron Construction 573 W 3560 S Ste 1 — Web: www.cameronconstruction.com	Salt Lake City	UT	84115	801-268-3584		261
Cameron County 20 E Fifth St — Web: www.pacourts.us	Emporium	PA	15834	814-486-2315		338
Cameron Engineering & Associates LLP 177 Crossways Park Dr — Web: www.cameronengineering.com	Woodbury	NY	11797	516-827-4900	827-4920	256
Cameron Glass Inc 3550 W Tacoma St — Web: www.camglass.com	Broken Arrow	OK	74012	918-254-6000	252-4665	329
Cameron Holdings Corp 1200 Prospect St — Web: www.cameron-holdings.com	La Jolla	CA	92037	858-551-1335	551-1343	360-3
Cameron Instruments Inc 173 Woolwich St — TF: 888-863-8010 ■ Web: cameroninstruments.com	Guelph	ON	N1H3V4	519-824-7111		358
Cameron Missouri 205 N Main St — Web: www.cameron-mo.com	Cameron	MO	64429	816-632-2177	632-1067	251
Cameron Mitchell Restaurants 390 W Nationwide Blvd — Web: www.cameronmitchell.com	Columbus	OH	43215	614-621-3663		671
Cameron Parish Police Jury 148 Smith Cir PO Box 1280 — TF: 844-503-7283 ■ Web: parishofcameron.net	Cameron	LA	70631	337-775-5718	775-5567	338
Cameron Park Zoo 1701 N Fourth St — Web: www.cameronparkzoo.com	Waco	TX	76707	254-750-8400	750-8430	823
Cameron Smith & Associates Inc 3350 Pinnacle Hills Pkwy Ste 101 — Web: www.csarecruiters.com	Rogers	AR	72758	479-271-6042		260
Cameron Thomson Group Ltd 390 Bay St Ste 1706 — Web: www.cameronthomson.com	Toronto	ON	M5H2Y2	416-350-5009		401
Cameron University 2800 W Gore Blvd — TF: 888-454-7600 ■ Web: www.cameron.edu	Lawton	OK	73505	580-581-2289	581-5514	166
Cameron, Hodges, Coleman, LaPointe & Wright PA 111 N Magnolia Ave Ste 1350 — TF: 888-841-5030 ■ Web: www.cameronhodges.com	Orlando	FL	32801	407-841-5030		428
Cameron-cole LLC 200 E Government St Ste 100 — Web: www.cameron-cole.com	Pensacola	FL	32502	850-434-1011	434-2168	196
Cameroon Embassy 3400 International Dr NW — Web: www.cameroonembassyusa.org	Washington	DC	20008	202-265-8790	387-3826	257
Cameroon Mission TO-UN 22 E 73rd St — Web: www.delecam.us	New York	NY	10021	646-850-1826	850-1820	784
Camesa Inc 1131 Blume Rd — TF: 800-866-0001 ■ Web: www.camesaemc.com	Rosenberg	TX	77471	281-342-4492		253
Camex Equipment Sales & Rental Inc 1806 Second St — TF: 877-955-2770 ■ Web: www.camex.com	Nisku	AB	T9E0W8	780-955-2770		539

Name / Address	City	State	ZIP	Phone	Fax	Class
Camfour Inc 65 Westfield Industrial Park Rd *Web:* www.camfour.com	Westfield	MA	01085	413-564-2300	568-9663	690
CAM-I (Consortium for Advanced Manufacturing Intl) 6836 Bee Cave Ste 256 *Web:* www.cam-i.org	Austin	TX	78746	512-296-6872		49-13
Camie Campbell Inc 2651 Warrenville Rd *Web:* www.camie.com	Downers Grove	IL	60515	800-325-9572		3
Camille Players Inc 1 Dean Porter Pk *Web:* www.camilleplayhouse.net	Brownsville	TX	78520	956-542-8900		572
Camille's Sidewalk Cafe 9637 S Riverside *Web:* www.camillescafe.com	Tulsa	OK	74137	918-299-5997		670
Camilles Restaurant 71 Bradford St *Web:* www.camillesonthehill.com	Providence	RI	02903	401-751-4812		671
Camillus Octagon House 5420 W Genesee St *Web:* octagonhouseofcamillus.org	Camillus	NY	13031	315-488-7800		50-3
Camin Cargo Control Inc 230 Marion Ave *Web:* www.camincargo.com	Linden	NJ	07036	908-862-1899	523-0616	743
Camino Agave Inc 314 US Hwy 181 N PO Box 129 *Web:* www.caminoagave.com	Floresville	TX	78114	830-393-1051	393-1052	539
Camino Books Inc PO Box 59026 *Web:* www.caminobooks.com	Philadelphia	PA	19102	215-413-1917	413-3255	637-2
Camino Modular Systems - Global IFS Co 3175 Airway Dr *Web:* www.globalifs.com	Mississauga	ON	L4V1C2	416-936-5900	675-2424	360-3
Camino Real Foods Inc 2638 E Vernon Ave *Web:* www.caminorealkitchens.com	Vernon	CA	90058	323-585-6599		296-36
Camino Real Hotel LLC 2856 E Main St *Web:* www.caminorealhoteleaglepass.business.site	Eagle Pass	TX	78852	830-757-8111		379
Cammenga Company LLC 2011 Bailey St *Web:* cammenga.com	Dearborn	MI	48124	313-914-7160	914-7153	807
Camnet Inc 3201 Fourth St NW *Web:* camnet.us	Albuquerque	NM	87107	505-761-4500		175
Camosun College 3100 Foul Bay Rd *Web:* camosun.ca	Victoria	BC	V8P5J2	250-370-3018		162
Camosy Construction Inc 43451 N US Hwy 41 *Web:* www.camosy.com	Zion	IL	60099	847-395-6800	395-6891	186
Camp Arrowhead 20 Arrowhead Rd *Web:* rochesterymca.org	Pittsford	NY	14534	585-383-4590		239
Camp Butler National Cemetery 5063 Camp Butler Rd *TF:* 877-907-8585 ■ *Web:* www.cem.va.gov	Springfield	IL	62707	217-492-4070	492-4072	136
Camp Chase gazette PO Box 625 *Fax Area Code: 423 ■ *TF:* 800-624-0281 ■ *Web:* www.campchase.com	Morristown	TN	37814	800-624-0281	581-3061*	637-9
Camp Chevrolet 101 E Montgomery *TF:* 866-373-7644 ■ *Web:* www.campchevrolet.com	Spokane	WA	99207	509-590-1342		57
Camp Conferences Inc 4905 Old Orchard Rd Ste 509 *Fax Area Code: 847 ■ *Web:* www.campconferences.com	Skokie	IL	60077	224-251-8889	881-0747*	239
Camp County 126 Church St *Web:* www.co.camp.tx.us	Pittsburg	TX	75686	903-856-2731	856-2309	338
Camp Creek State Park & Forest 2390 Camp Creek Rd *Web:* wvstateparks.com	Camp Creek	WV	25820	304-425-9481		565
Camp Florence 4859 S Jetty Rd *TF:* 800-588-9003 ■ *Web:* www.oregon.gov	Florence	OR	97439	541-997-2076		412
Camp Floyd/Stagecoach Inn State Park & Museum 18035 W 1540 N *Web:* stateparks.utah.gov	Fairfield	UT	84013	801-768-8932		565
Camp Helen State Park 23937 Panama City Beach Pkwy *Web:* www.floridastateparks.org	Panama City Beach	FL	32413	850-233-5059	236-3204	565
Camp Hilbert 5403 Monument Ave *Web:* weinsteinjcc.org	Richmond	VA	23226	804-285-6500		239
Camp Hill Presbyterian Church 101 N 23rd St *Web:* www.thechpc.org	Camp Hill	PA	17011	717-737-0488		48-20
Camp Lebanon 1205 Acorn Rd *TF:* 800-816-1502 ■ *Web:* camplebanon.org	Burtrum	MN	56318	320-573-2125		239
Camp Moring & Brendle LLC 1418 Laurel St	Columbia	SC	29201	803-252-9375		2
Camp Nelson National Cemetery 6980 Danville Rd *Web:* www.cem.va.gov	Nicholasville	KY	40356	859-885-5727	887-4860	136
Camp Ocean Pines Inc 1473 Randall Dr *Web:* campoceanpines.org	Cambria	CA	93428	805-927-0254		239
Camp Olympia 723 Olympia Dr *TF:* 800-735-6190 ■ *Web:* www.campolympia.com	Trinity	TX	75862	936-594-2541	594-8143	297-8
Camp Oty'okwa 24799 Purcell Rd *Web:* campotyokwa.org	South Bloomingville	OH	43152	740-385-5279		239
Camp Ozark 155 Camp Ozark Dr *Web:* campozark.com	Mount Ida	AR	71957	870-867-4131	867-4344	239
Camp Plymouth State Park 2008 Scout Camp Rd *Web:* www.vtstateparks.com	Ludlow	VT	05149	802-228-2025		565
Camp Randall Stadium 1440 Monroe St *Web:* uwbadgers.com	Madison	WI	53711	608-262-1866		720
Camp Rocky Point 1586 Hanna Dr *Web:* www.gsnetx.org	Denison	TX	75020	903-465-5270		239
Camp Simcha 430 White Rd *TF:* 888-756-1432 ■ *Web:* www.campsimcha.org	Glen Spey	NY	12737	845-856-1432		239
Camp Summit Boot Camp 2407 N 500 W *Web:* www.in.gov	La Porte	IN	46350	219-326-1188	326-9218	412
Camp Sunshine 35 Acadia Rd *Web:* www.campsunshine.org	Casco	ME	04015	207-655-3800		239
Camp Tawonga 131 Steuart St Ste 460 *Web:* tawonga.org	San Francisco	CA	94105	415-543-2267	543-5417	239
Camp Tillamook 6820 Barracks Cir *Web:* www.oregon.gov	Tillamook	OR	97141	503-842-4243	842-1476	412
Camp Ventures Inc 280 2nd St Ste 280 *Web:* www.campventures.com	Los Altos	CA	94022	650-949-0804	618-1719	792
Campagne 1600 Post Alley *Web:* cafecampagne.com	Seattle	WA	98101	206-728-2233		671
Campagnia 1185 E Champlain Dr *Web:* campagnia.net	Fresno	CA	93720	559-285-6900	433-3066	671
Campaign Consultation Inc 1817 N St Paul St *Web:* campaignconsultation.com	Baltimore	MD	21202	410-243-7979		194
Campaign for Tobacco-Free Kids 1400 'I' St NW Ste 1200 *Web:* www.tobaccofreekids.org	Washington	DC	20005	202-296-5469	296-5427	48-17
Campaign for Working Families (CWF) PO Box 1222 *Web:* www.cwfpac.com	Merrifield	VA	22116	703-671-8800		615
Campaign Legal Ctr 1101 14th St NW Ste 400 *Web:* campaignlegal.org	Washington	DC	20005	202-736-2200	736-2222	48-7
Campaign Marketing Strategies Inc (CMS) 3240 Wilson Blvd Ste 202 *TF:* 877-267-0030 ■ *Web:* www.cmsconnects.com	Arlington	VA	22201	877-267-0030		194
Campaign Services 117 N St Asaph St *Web:* www.campaignsolutions.com	Alexandria	VA	22314	703-684-1072		196
Campania Intl 2452 Quakertown Rd *Web:* www.campaniainternational.com	Pennsburg	PA	18073	215-541-4627	541-4628	183
Campbell & Associates Inc 3485 Fortuna Dr Ste 100 *TF:* 800-233-4117 ■ *Web:* www.campbellsurvey.com	Akron	OH	44312	330-945-4117		727
Campbell & George Co 1100 Industrial Rd Ste 12 *TF:* 800-682-4224 ■ *Web:* www.cgco.com	San Carlos	CA	94070	650-654-5000		253
Campbell & Grooms PLLC 8500 W Markham Ste 105 *Web:* campbellgrooms.com	Little Rock	AR	72205	501-313-4967		41
Campbell Blueprint & Supply Company Inc 3124 Broad Ave *Web:* www.memphisreprographics.com	Memphis	TN	38112	901-327-7385		240
Campbell Chamber of Commerce 267 E Campbell Ave Ste C *Web:* campbellchamber.net	Campbell	CA	95008	408-378-6252	378-0192	139
Campbell Christian Schools 1075 W Campbell Ave *TF:* 800-264-7955 ■ *Web:* www.campbellchristian.org	Campbell	CA	95008	408-370-4900		685
Campbell County 1635 Reata Dr *TF:* 800-457-9312 ■ *Web:* www.ccgov.net	Gillette	WY	82718	307-682-0552	682-8418	338
Campbell County PO Box 305 *Web:* campbellcountytn.gov	Jacksboro	TN	37757	423-562-4985	566-3852	338
Campbell County 1098 Monmouth St PO Box 72340 *Web:* www.campbellcountyky.org	Newport	KY	41071	859-292-3838		338
Campbell County 87 Courthouse Ln PO Box 280 *Web:* www.co.campbell.va.us	Rustburg	VA	24588	434-332-9517	332-9518	338
Campbell County Board of Education 2500 Grandview Rd *Web:* www.campbell.k12.ky.us	Alexandria	KY	41001	859-635-2173	448-2428	685
Campbell County Chamber of Commerce 314 S Gillette Ave *Web:* www.gillettechamber.com	Gillette	WY	82716	307-682-3673	682-0538	139
Campbell County Department of Education 172 Valley St *Web:* www.campbell.k12.tn.us	Jacksboro	TN	37757	423-562-8377	566-7562	685
Campbell County Memorial Hospital 501 S Burma PO Box 3011 *TF:* 800-247-5381 ■ *Web:* www.cchwyo.org	Gillette	WY	82717	307-688-1000	688-1516	374-3
Campbell County Public Library 684 Village Hwy PO Box 310 *Web:* campbellcountylibraries.org	Rustburg	VA	24588	434-332-9560		434-3
Campbell Farms 15111 Hwy 17 *TF:* 800-222-7783 ■ *Web:* www.tricampbellfarms.com	Grafton	ND	58237	701-352-3116	352-2008	10-11
Campbell Foundry Co 800 Bergen St *Web:* www.campbellfoundry.com	Harrison	NJ	07029	973-483-5480	483-1843	307
Campbell Grinder Co 1226 Pontaluna Rd *Web:* www.campbellgrinder.com	Spring Lake	MI	49456	231-798-6464	798-6466	261
Campbell Grinding & Machine Inc 582 Benjamins Way *Web:* www.campbellgrinding.com	Lewisville	TX	75057	972-221-2211	221-5432	454
Campbell Hausfeld 100 Production Dr *Web:* campbellhausfeld.com	Harrison	OH	45030	513-367-4811		172
Campbell Historical Museum 51 N Central Ave *Web:* www.ci.campbell.ca.us	Campbell	CA	95008	408-866-2757		520
Campbell Historical Museum & Ainsley House 51 N Central Ave *Web:* www.campbellmuseums.com	Campbell	CA	95008	408-866-2119		520
Campbell Manufacturing Inc 127 E Spring St *TF:* 800-523-0224 ■ *Web:* www.bakerwatersystems.com	Bechtelsville	PA	19505	610-367-2107	369-3580	595
Campbell Marketing & Communications 3200 Greenfield St Ste 280 *Web:* www.campbellmarketing.com	Dearborn	MI	48120	313-336-9000		636
Campbell Pet Co 9606 NE 126th Ave *TF:* 800-228-6364 ■ *Web:* www.campbellpet.com	Vancouver	WA	98682	360-892-9786	944-9999	431
Campbell Printing Co 2017 Cleveland Hwy *Web:* campbellprintingco.com	Dalton	GA	30721	706-259-3344		627
Campbell Rappold & Yurasits LLP 1033 S Cedar Crest Blvd *Web:* www.crycpas.com	Allentown	PA	18103	610-435-7489		2
Campbell River & District Chamber of Commerce Enterprise Ctr 900 Alder St *Web:* www.campbellriverchamber.ca	Campbell River	BC	V9W2P6	250-287-4636	286-6490	137
Campbell Scientific Inc 815 W 1800 N *Fax Area Code: 435 ■ *TF:* 844-454-2505 ■ *Web:* www.campbellsci.com	Logan	UT	84321	844-454-2505	750-9540*	201

Phone | Fax | Class

Campbell Sevey Inc
15350 Minnetonka Blvd ... Minnetonka MN 55345 952-935-2345 789
Web: www.campbell-sevey.com

Campbell Solberg Associates Inc
129 W 27th St 6th Fl ... New York NY 10001 800-874-6172 693-2064* 390
**Fax Area Code:* 212 ■ *TF:* 800-874-6172 ■ *Web:* campbellsolberg.com

Campbell Soup Co 1 Campbell Pl ... Camden NJ 08103 856-342-4800 342-3878 296-36
NYSE: CPB ■ *TF:* 800-257-8443 ■ *Web:* www.campbellsoupcompany.com

Campbell Union High School District
3235 Union Ave ... San Jose CA 95124 408-371-0960 685
Web: www.cuhsd.org

Campbell Union School District
155 N Third St ... Campbell CA 95008 408-364-4200 685
Web: www.campbellusd.org

Campbell University
450 Leslie Campbell Ave PO Box 546 ... Buies Creek NC 27506 910-893-1290 893-1288 166
TF: 800-334-4111 ■ *Web:* www.campbell.edu

Campbell University Norman Adrian Wiggins School of Law
225 Hillsborough St ... Raleigh NC 27603 919-865-4650 167-1
Web: law.campbell.edu

Campbell Wrapper Corp
1415 Fortune Ave ... De Pere WI 54115 920-983-7100 547
TF: 800-727-4210 ■ *Web:* www.campbellwrapper.com

Campbell's Resort
104 W Woodin Ave PO Box 278 ... Chelan WA 98816 509-682-2561 682-2177 669
TF: 800-553-8225 ■ *Web:* campbellsresort.com

Campbell-Ewald 2000 Brush St Ste 601 ... Detroit MI 48226 586-574-3400 4
Web: www.c-e.com

Campbellsville University
1 University Dr ... Campbellsville KY 42718 270-789-5000 789-5071 166
TF: 800-264-6014 ■ *Web:* www.campbellsville.edu

Camperos Grill & Bar
2500 N Expy 77 ... Brownsville TX 78521 956-546-8172 671
Web: camperosgrillandbar.com

Campers Inn Inc
35 Robert Milligan Pkwy ... Merrimack NH 03054 603-883-1082 262-2077 360-3
Web: www.campersinn.com

Campfire Grill 3003 Walden Ave ... Depew NY 14043 716-725-9969 121
Web: www.campfiregrilldepewny.com

Camphill School, The
1784 Fairview Rd ... Glenmoore PA 19343 610-469-9236 685
Web: camphillschool.org

Camphor Technologies Inc
1584 Independence Blvd ... Sarasota FL 34234 941-360-0025 360-0035 238
Web: camphortech.com

Campiello 1177 Third St S ... Naples FL 34102 239-435-1166 671
Web: www.campiello.damico.com

Camping Investigations
4427 N 27th Ave ... Phoenix AZ 85017 602-864-7860 400
TF: 800-862-8458 ■ *Web:* www.campingcompanies.com

Camping World RV Sales
8155 Rivers Ave ... Charleston SC 29406 888-471-3171 791
TF: 888-586-5446 ■ *Web:* rv.campingworld.com

Campino Restaurant 70 Jabez St ... Newark NJ 07105 973-589-4004 671
Web: www.campinorestaurant.com

Campion College at the University of Regina
3737 Wascana Pkwy ... Regina SK S4S0A2 306-586-4242 359-1200 785
TF: 800-667-7282 ■ *Web:* www.campioncollege.sk.ca

Campion Renewal Ctr 319 Concord Rd ... Weston MA 02493 781-419-1337 894-5864 673
Web: www.campioncenter.org

Campisano Insurance Agency
839 Kearny Ave ... Kearny NJ 07032 201-997-0060 390
Web: campisanoinsurance.com

Campito Plumbing & Heating Inc
3 Hemlock St ... Latham NY 12110 518-785-0994 785-0769 189-10
Web: www.web.ecainc.org

Campmor Inc 400 Corporate Dr PO Box 680 ... Mahwah NJ 07430 800-226-7667 711
TF: 800-226-7667 ■ *Web:* www.campmor.com

Campo de Fiori 205 S Mill St ... Aspen CO 81611 970-920-7717 671
Web: campodefiori.net

Campofresco Corp PO Box 755 ... Santa Isabel PR 00757 787-845-4747 845-3490 80-2
Web: campofresco.com

Campora Inc
2525 E Mariposa Rd PO Box 31625 ... Stockton CA 95205 209-941-2994 466-7421 316
Web: www.campora.com

Campos Creative Works
1715 14th St ... Santa Monica CA 90404 310-453-1511 514
Web: www.ccwla.com

Campos Engineering Inc
1331 River Bend Dr ... Dallas TX 75231 214-696-6291 256
Web: www.camposengineering.com

Campos Market Research
216 Blvd of the Allies ... Pittsburgh PA 15222 412-471-8484 196
Web: campos.com

Campton Place Restaurant
340 Stockton St ... San Francisco CA 94108 415-955-5555 671
Web: www.tajcamptonplace.com

Campus Circle Inc
5042 Willshire Blvd ... Los Angeles CA 90036 323-823-8548 532-2
Web: www.campuscircle.com

Campus Crusade for Christ Intl
100 Lake Hart Dr ... Orlando FL 32832 407-826-2500 48-20
Web: www.cru.org

Campus Federal Credit Union
PO Box 98036 ... Baton Rouge LA 70898 225-769-8841 219
TF: 888-769-8841 ■ *Web:* www.campusfederal.org

Campus Inn & Suites Eugene Downtown
390 E Broadway ... Eugene OR 97401 541-636-9376 485-9392 379
Web: www.campus-inn.com

Campus Outreach PO Box 43737 ... Birmingham AL 35243 205-776-5500 48-20
Web: cobirmingham.org

Campus Televideo Inc
100 First Stamford Pl ... Stamford CT 06902 203-983-5400 116
Web: campustelevideo.com

Campus Text Inc 814 Montgomery Ave ... Narberth PA 19072 888-606-8398 664-6976* 96
**Fax Area Code:* 610 ■ *TF:* 888-606-8398 ■ *Web:* www.campustext.com

Campus USA Credit Union
PO Box 147029 ... Gainesville FL 32614 352-335-9090 219
TF: 800-367-6440 ■ *Web:* www.campuscu.com

Campus2careers Inc 4700 Guadalupe St ... Austin TX 78751 512-354-7690 260
Web: www.campus2careers.com

CampusCareerCenter Inc
110 Rockview St Ste 1 ... Boston MA 02130 617-661-2613 812-8585 260
Web: www.campuscareercenter.com

Campustours Inc 110 Jacques Rd ... Auburn ME 04210 207-753-0136 180
Web: campustours.com

Camron-Stanford House
1418 Lakeside Dr ... Oakland CA 94612 510-874-7802 874-7803 50-3
Web: cshouse.org

Camshaft Machine Co 717 Woodworth Rd ... Jackson MI 49202 517-787-2040 247
Web: camshaftmachine.com

Cam-Wal Electric Co-opeartive Inc
PO Box 135 ... Selby SD 57472 605-649-7676 245
TF: 800-269-7676 ■ *Web:* www.cam-walnet.com

Can Corporation of America Inc
326 June Ave ... Blandon PA 19510 610-926-3044 926-5041 124
Web: cancorpam.com

Can Lines Engineering
9839 Downey Norwalk Rd PO Box 7039 ... Downey CA 90241 562-861-2996 869-5293 207
Web: www.canlines.com

Can Manufacturers Institute (CMI)
1730 Rhode Island Ave NW Ste 1000 ... Washington DC 20036 202-232-4677 232-5756 49-13
Web: www.cancentral.com

CANA (Cremation Association of North America)
499 Northgate Pkwy ... Wheeling IL 60090 312-245-1077 321-4098 49-4
Web: www.cremationassociation.org

Canaan Printing
4820 Jefferson Davis Hwy ... North Chesterfield VA 23234 804-271-4820 627
TF: 800-332-3580 ■ *Web:* canaanprinting.net

Canaan Valley Resort & Conference Ctr
230 Main Lodge Rd ... Davis WV 26260 304-866-4121 669
TF: 800-622-4121 ■ *Web:* www.canaanresort.com

CANAC Inc
6505 Trans-Canada Hwy Ste 405 ... Saint-Laurent QC H4T1S3 514-734-4700 734-4850 650
TF: 800-588-4387 ■ *Web:* www.canac.com

Canaccord Genuity, Research Division
Pacific Centre 609 Granville St Ste 2200
PO Box 10337 ... Vancouver BC V7Y1H2 604-643-7300 401
Web: www.canaccordgenuity.com

Canad Inns 930 Jefferson Ave 3rd Fl ... Winnipeg MB R2P1W1 204-697-1495 694-9427 379
Web: www.canadinns.com

Canada 885 Second Ave 14th Fl ... New York NY 10017 212-848-1100 848-1195 784
Web: www.international.gc.ca

Canada
Consulate General
1175 Peachtree St NE Ste 1700 ... Atlanta GA 30361 404-532-2000 532-2050 257
Web: www.international.gc.ca
Consulate General 5505 Blue Lagoon Dr ... Miami FL 33131 305-579-1600 257
Web: canadainternational.gc.ca
Consulate General
500 N Akard St Ste 2900 ... Dallas TX 75201 214-922-9806 257
Web: international.gc.ca
Consulate General
1251 Avenue of the Americas Concourse Level New York NY 10020 212-596-1628 596-1790 257
TF: 800-267-8376 ■ *Web:* international.gc.ca
Consulate General
2 Prudential Plz 180 N Stetson Ave Ste 2400 ... Chicago IL 60601 312-616-1860 616-1877 257
Web: international.gc.ca
Consulate General
701 Fourth Ave S Ste 900 ... Minneapolis MN 55415 612-333-4641 332-4061 257
Web: international.gc.ca
Embassy 501 Pennsylvania Ave NW ... Washington DC 20001 844-880-6519 682-7726* 257
**Fax Area Code:* 202 ■ *TF:* 800-647-5463 ■ *Web:* www.international.gc.ca

Canada Agriculture & Food Museum
901 Prince of Wales Dr ... Ottawa ON K2C3K1 613-991-3044 993-7923 520
Web: ingeniumcanada.org

Canada Alloy Casting Co
529 Manitou Dr ... Kitchener ON N2C1S2 519-895-1161 895-1169 307
Web: www.cac.ca

Canada Aviation Museum & Space Museum
11 Aviation Pkwy ... Ottawa ON K1K2X5 613-993-2010 990-3655 520
Web: ingeniumcanada.org

Canada College
4200 Farm Hill Blvd ... Redwood City CA 94061 650-306-3100 306-3113 162
Web: canadacollege.edu

Canada Colors & Chemicals Ltd
175 Bloor St E Ste 1300 N Twr ... Toronto ON M4W3R8 416-443-5500 449-9039 146
TF: 800-461-1638 ■ *Web:* www.ccc-group.com

Canada Deposit Insurance Corp
50 O'Connor St 17th Fl ... Ottawa ON K1P6L2 613-996-2081 509
TF: 800-461-2342 ■ *Web:* www.cdic.ca

Canada Energy Partners Inc
669 Howe St Ste 650 ... Vancouver BC V6C0B4 778-725-1489 428-1124* 539
**Fax Area Code:* 604 ■ *Web:* www.canadaenergypartners.com

Canada Flowers
4073 Longhurst Ave ... Niagara Falls ON L2E6G5 905-354-2713 374-8708 292
TF: 888-705-9999 ■ *Web:* www.canadaflowers.ca

Canada Forgings Inc 130 Hagar St ... Welland ON L3B5P8 905-735-1220 541
TF: 800-263-0440 ■ *Web:* www.canforge.com

Canada Labour Congress
2841 Riverside Dr ... Ottawa ON K1V8X7 613-521-3400 521-4655 414
Web: canadianlabour.ca

Canada Life Assurance Co, The
330 University Ave ... Toronto ON M5G1R8 416-597-1456 391-4
TF: 888-252-1847 ■ *Web:* www.canadalife.com

Canada Media Fund
50 Wellington St E Ste 202 ... Toronto ON M5E1C8 416-214-4400 393
TF: 877-975-0766 ■ *Web:* www.cmf-fmc.ca

Canada Mortgage & Housing Corp
700 Montreal Rd ... Ottawa ON K1A0P7 613-748-2000 509
Web: www.cmhc-schl.gc.ca

Canada Olympic Hall of Fame
88 Canada Olympic Rd SW ... Calgary AB T3B5R5 403-247-5607 286-7213 522
Web: www.winsport.ca

Canada Pipe Co 1757 Burlington St E ... Hamilton ON L8H3L5 905-547-3251 547-7369 492
Web: www.canadapipe.com

Company	Address	City	State	ZIP	Phone	Fax	Class	Notes
Canada School of Public Service	373 Sussex Dr	Ottawa	ON	K1N6Z2	819-953-5400		623	*TF:* 866-703-9598 ■ *Web:* www.csps-efpc.gc.ca
Canada Science & Technology Museum	2421 Lancaster Rd	Ottawa	ON	K1G5A3	613-327-4611	990-3654	520	*Web:* ingeniumcanada.org
Canada Sportswear Corp	230 Barmac Dr	North York	ON	M9L2Z3	416-740-8020		157-6	*Web:* www.canadasportswear.com
Canada's Children's Hospital Foundations	8001 Weston Rd Ste 200	Vaughan	ON	L4L9C8	905-265-9750		48-5	*Web:* childrensmiraclenetwork.ca
Canada's Sports Hall of Fame	169 Canada Olympic Rd SW	Calgary	AB	T3B6B7	403-776-1040		522	*Web:* www.sportshall.ca
Canada's Wonderland	9580 Jane St	Vaughan	ON	L6A1S6	905-832-8131		32	*Web:* www.canadaswonderland.com
Canada-Israel Industrial Research & Development Foundation	371A Richmond Rd Ste 3	Ottawa	ON	K2A0E7	613-724-1284		305	*Web:* www.ciirdf.ca
Canadel Furniture Inc	700 Canadel Ave	Louiseville	QC	J5V2L6	819-228-8471	228-8389	319-2	*Web:* canadel.com
Canadian Academy of Sport Medicine (CASM)	55 Metcalfe St Ste 300	Ottawa	ON	K1P6L5	613-748-5851	912-0128	49-8	*TF:* 877-585-2394 ■ *Web:* casem-acmse.org
Canadian American Restoration Supplies Inc	2600 Bond St	Rochester Hills	MI	48309	248-227-7462		54	*Web:* www.carsinc.com
Canadian Architectural Certification Board	1 Nicholas St Ste 710	Ottawa	ON	K1N7B7	613-241-8399	241-7991	48-1	*Web:* www.cacb.ca
Canadian Association of Emergency Physicians (CAEP)	1785 Alta Vista Dr Ste 104	Ottawa	ON	K1G3Y6	613-523-3343	523-0190	49-8	*TF:* 800-463-1158 ■ *Web:* caep.ca
Canadian Association of Occupational Therapists (CAOT)	1125 Colonel By Dr	Ottawa	ON	K1S5R1	613-523-2268		48-1	*TF:* 800-434-2268 ■ *Web:* www.caot.ca
Canadian Association of Petroleum Producers	350 - Seventh Ave S W Ste 2100	Calgary	AB	T2P3N9	403-267-1100		78	*Web:* www.capp.ca
Canadian Bank Note Company Ltd (CBNC)	145 Richmond Rd	Ottawa	ON	K1Z1A1	613-722-3421		627	*Web:* www.cbnco.com
Canadian Bar Assn	500-865 Carling Ave	Ottawa	ON	K1S5S8	613-237-2925	237-0185	138	*TF:* 800-267-8860 ■ *Web:* www.cba.org
Canadian Bearings Ltd	1600 Drew Rd	Mississauga	ON	L5S1S5	905-670-6700	670-0459	385	*TF:* 800-229-2327 ■ *Web:* www.canadianbearings.com
Canadian Broadcasting Corp (CBC)	PO Box 3220	Ottawa	ON	K1Y1E4	613-724-1200		643	*Web:* www.cbc.radio-canada.ca
Canadian Business for Social Responsibility	215 Spadina Ave Ste 300	Toronto	ON	M5T2C7	416-703-7435		78	*Web:* www.cbsr.ca
Canadian Cancer Society	55 St Clair Ave W Ste 300	Toronto	ON	M4V2Y7	416-961-7223		138	*Web:* www.cancer.ca
Canadian Centre for Architecture	1920 Baile St	Montreal	QC	H3H2S6	514-939-7000	939-7020	520	*Web:* www.cca.qc.ca
Canadian Chamber of Commerce	360 Albert St Ste 420	Ottawa	ON	K1R7X7	613-238-4000	238-7643	137	*Web:* www.chamber.ca
Canadian College of Naturopathic Medicine	1255 Sheppard Ave E	Toronto	ON	M2K1E2	416-498-1255		785	*TF:* 866-241-2266 ■ *Web:* www.ccnm.edu
Canadian Council for International Co-op (CCIC)	39 McArthur Ave	Ottawa	ON	K1L8L7	613-241-7007	241-5302	48-5	*Web:* ccic.ca
Canadian County	1800 S Shepard Ave	El Reno	OK	73036	405-262-1070	422-2411	338	*Web:* www.canadiancounty.org
Canadian Dental Assn	1815 Alta Vista Dr	Ottawa	ON	K1G3Y6	613-523-7114	523-7736	48-1	*TF:* 866-521-2322 ■ *Web:* www.cda-adc.ca
Canadian Electricity Assn	275 Slater St Ste 1500	Ottawa	ON	K1P5H9	613-230-9263	230-9326	138	*Web:* electricity.ca
Canadian Enerdata Ltd	86 Ringwood Dr Ste 201	Stouffville	ON	L4A1C3	905-642-8167		194	*Web:* www.enerdata.com
Canadian Federation of Humane Societies (CFHS)	30 Concourse Gate Ste 102	Ottawa	ON	K2E7V7	613-224-8072		48-3	*TF:* 888-678-2347 ■ *Web:* www.humanecanada.ca
Canadian Finance & Leasing Assn	15 Toronto St	Toronto	ON	M5C2E3	416-860-1133		138	*TF:* 877-213-7373 ■ *Web:* www.cfla-acfl.ca
Canadian Fishing Co	301 E Waterfront Rd E	Vancouver	BC	V6A2Y7	604-681-0211	681-3277	285	*Web:* www.canfisco.com
Canadian Football Hall of Fame & Museum	58 Jackson St W	Hamilton	ON	L8P1H4	905-528-7566	528-9781	522	*Web:* www.cfhof.ca
Canadian Football League	50 Wellington St E 3rd Fl	Toronto	ON	M5E1C8	416-322-9650	322-9651	715-2	*TF:* 855-264-4242 ■ *Web:* www.cfl.ca
Canadian Forest Products Ltd	5162 Northwood Pulp Mill Rd PO Box 9000	Prince George	BC	V2L4W2	250-962-3414	962-3473	638	*Web:* www.canfor.com
Canadian Forestry Accreditation Board	18 Pommel Cres	Kanata	ON	K2M1A2	613-599-7259	599-8107	48-1	*Web:* www.cfa-international.org
Canadian Golf Hall of Fame & Museum	1333 Dorval Dr Ste 1	Oakville	ON	L6M4X7	905-849-9700	845-7040	522	*TF:* 800-263-0009 ■ *Web:* golfcanada.ca
Canadian Health Libraries Assn (CHLA)	39 River St	Toronto	ON	M5A3P1	416-646-1600	646-9460	49-11	*Web:* www.chla-absc.ca
Canadian Honker Restaurant	1203 2nd St SW	Rochester	MN	55902	507-282-6572		671	*Web:* canadianhonker.com
Canadian Hospital Specialties ULC	2810 Coventry Rd	Oakville	ON	L6H6R1	905-825-9300		475	*TF:* 800-461-1423 ■ *Web:* www.chsltd.com
Canadian Imperial Bank of Commerce (CIBC)	199 Bay St Commerce Ct W	Toronto	ON	M5L1A2	800-465-2422		70	*NYSE:* CM ■ *TF:* 800-465-2422 ■ *Web:* www.cibc.com
Canadian Information Processing Society (CIPS)	5090 Explorer Dr Ste 801	Mississauga	ON	L4W4T9	905-602-1370	602-7884	48-1	*TF:* 877-275-2477 ■ *Web:* www.cips.ca
Canadian Institute, The	1329 Bay St	Toronto	ON	M5R2C4	416-927-7936		387	*Web:* www.canadianinstitute.com
Canadian Kennel Club (CKC)	200 Ronson Dr Ste 400	Etobicoke	ON	M9W5Z9	416-675-5511	675-6506	48-3	*TF:* 800-250-8040 ■ *Web:* www.ckc.ca
Canadian Library Assn (CLA)	1150 Morrison Dr Ste 400	Ottawa	ON	K2H8S9	613-232-9625	563-9895	49-11	*Web:* cla.ca
Canadian Manufacturers & Exporters	1 Nicholas St Ste 1500	Ottawa	ON	K1N7B7	647-556-5818		138	*Web:* cme-mec.ca
Canadian Medical Assn (CMA)	1867 Alta Vista Dr	Ottawa	ON	K1G5W8	613-731-9331		49-8	*TF:* 800-663-7336 ■ *Web:* www.cma.ca
Canadian Memorial Chiropractic College	6100 Leslie St	Toronto	ON	M2H3J1	416-482-2340		785	*TF:* 800-463-2923 ■ *Web:* www.cmcc.ca
Canadian Mental Health Assn	250 Dundas St W Ste 500	Toronto	ON	M5T2Z5	416-646-5557		138	*TF:* 800-616-8816 ■ *Web:* cmha.ca
Canadian Museum of Civilization	100 Laurier St	Gatineau	QC	K1A0M8	819-776-7000	776-8300	520	*TF:* 800-555-5621 ■ *Web:* www.historymuseum.ca
Canadian Museum of Flight	5333 216th St Hanger No 3	Langley	BC	V2Y2N3	604-532-0035	532-0056	520	*Web:* www.canadianflight.org
Canadian Museum of Nature	240 McLeod St	Ottawa	ON	K2P2R1	613-566-4700	364-4021	520	*TF:* 800-263-4433 ■ *Web:* nature.ca
Canadian Musical Reproduction Rights Agency Ltd, The	56 Wellesley St W Ste 320	Toronto	ON	M5S2S3	416-926-1966		138	*Web:* www.cmrra.ca
Canadian Musician (CM)	4056 Dorchester Rd Ste 202	Niagara Falls	ON	L2E6M9	905-374-8878	665-1307*	457-9	**Fax Area Code:* 888 ■ *Web:* www.canadianmusician.com
Canadian National Railway Co	935 Rue de la Gauchetiere O	Montreal	QC	H3B2M9	888-888-5909		648	*NYSE:* CNI ■ *TF:* 888-668-4626 ■ *Web:* www.cn.ca
Canadian Natural Resources Ltd (CNRL)	855 Second St SW Ste 2100	Calgary	AB	T2P4J8	403-517-6700	517-7350	536	*NYSE:* CNQ ■ *TF:* 888-878-3700 ■ *Web:* www.cnrl.com
Canadian Pacific	7550 Ogden Dale Rd SE	Calgary	AB	T2C4X9	888-333-6370	704-3000*	648	**Fax Area Code:* 800 ■ *TF:* 888-333-6370 ■ *Web:* www.cpr.ca
Canadian Parks & Recreation Assn (CPRA)	1180 Walkley Rd PO Box 83069	Ottawa	ON	K1V2M5	613-523-5315		48-23	*Web:* www.cpra.ca
Canadian Parks & Wilderness Society (CPAWS)	250 City Center Ave Ste 506	Ottawa	ON	K1R6K7	613-569-7226	569-7098	48-13	*TF:* 800-333-9453 ■ *Web:* www.cpaws.org
Canadian Payroll Assn	250 Bloor St E	Toronto	ON	M4W1E6	416-487-3380		138	*TF:* 800-387-4693 ■ *Web:* www.payroll.ca
Canadian Peregrine Foundation	25 Crouse Rd Unit 20	Toronto	ON	M1R5P8	416-481-1233	481-7158	48-3	*TF:* 888-709-3944 ■ *Web:* www.peregrine-foundation.ca
Canadian Press Ltd, The	36 King St E	Toronto	ON	M5C2L9	416-364-0321		532-3	*Web:* www.thecanadianpress.com
Canadian Professional Sales Assn	310 Front St W Ste 800	Toronto	ON	M5V3B5	416-408-2685		196	*TF:* 888-267-2772 ■ *Web:* www.cpsa.com
Canadian School of Natural Nutrition	11685 Yonge St Unit B108	Richmond Hill	ON	L4E0K7	905-737-0284	737-1994	685	*Web:* www.csnn.ca
Canadian Seed Growers' Assn	240 Catherine St	Ottawa	ON	K2P2G8	613-236-0497		138	*Web:* seedgrowers.ca
Canadian Society of Customs Brokers	55 Murray St Ste 320	Ottawa	ON	K1N5M3	613-562-3543		138	*TF:* 800-668-6870 ■ *Web:* cscb.ca
Canadian Solar Solutions Inc	545 Speedvale Ave W	Guelph	ON	N1K1E6	519-837-1881		253	*Web:* www.canadiansolar.com
Canadian Southern Baptist Seminary	200 Seminary View	Cochrane	AB	T4C2G1	403-932-6622	932-7049	167-3	*TF:* 877-922-2727 ■ *Web:* csbs.ca
Canadian Sport Centre Atlantic	26 Thomas Raddall Dr	Halifax	NS	B3S0E2	902-425-0942		78	*Web:* cscatlantic.ca
Canadian Tire Corporation Ltd	2180 Yonge St PO Box 770 Stn K	Toronto	ON	M4P2V8	416-480-3000		185	*TSX:* CTC.A ■ *TF:* 800-387-8803 ■ *Web:* corp.canadiantire.ca
Canadian Tool & Die Ltd	1331 Chevrier Blvd	Winnipeg	MB	R3T1Y4	204-453-6833		757	*TF:* 800-204-4150 ■ *Web:* www.canadiantool.com
Canadian Transportation Research Forum	PO Box 23033	Woodstock	ON	N4T1R9	519-421-9701	421-9319	167-3	*Web:* www.ctrf.ca
Canadian Urban Institute	30 St Patrick St Ste 500	Toronto	ON	M5T3A3	416-365-0816	365-0650	194	*TF:* 888-845-0516 ■ *Web:* www.canurb.org
Canadian Valley Electric Cooperative	11277 Hwy 99 N PO Box 751	Seminole	OK	74868	405-382-3680		245	*TF:* 877-382-3680 ■ *Web:* www.mycvec.coop
Canadian Valley Technology Ctr	6505 E US Hwy 66	El Reno	OK	73036	405-262-2629		507	*Web:* cvtech.edu

	Phone	Fax	Class
Canadian Valley Telephone Co 194 Telephone Rd. Crowder OK 74430 *TF:* 888-527-3096 ■ *Web:* www.cvok.net	918-334-3700	334-3202	224
Canadian Veterinary Medical Assn (CVMA) 339 Booth St. Ottawa ON K1R7K1 *TF:* 800-567-2862 ■ *Web:* www.canadianveterinarians.net	613-236-1162	236-9681	49-8
Canadian Warplane Heritage Museum 9280 Airport Rd Mount Hope ON L0R1W0 *Web:* www.warplane.com	905-679-4183		522
Canadian Water Resources Assn (CWRA) 176 Gloucester St Ste 320 Ottawa ON K2P0A6 *Web:* www.cwra.org	613-237-9363	594-5190	48-13
Canadian Western Bank 10303 Jasper Ave Ste 3000 Edmonton AB T5J3X6 *TSE: CWB* ■ *Web:* www.cwbank.com	780-423-8888		70
Canadian Wildlife Federation (CWF) 350 Michael Cowpland Dr Kanata ON K2M2W1 *TF:* 800-563-9453 ■ *Web:* www.cwf-fcf.org	613-599-9594	599-4428	48-13
Canadian Wood Council 99 Bank St Ste 400 Ottawa ON K1P6B9 *Web:* cwc.ca	613-747-5544		78
CanaDream Corp Rocky View County 292154 Crosspointe Dr Calgary AB T4A0V2 *TF:* 800-461-7368 ■ *Web:* www.canadream.com	403-291-1000	291-5509	121
Canal Barge Company Inc 835 Union St New Orleans LA 70112 *Web:* www.canalbarge.com	504-581-2424	584-1505	314
Canal Insurance Co 400 E Stone Ave PO Box 7 Greenville SC 29601 *TF:* 800-452-6911 ■ *Web:* canalinsurance.com	800-452-6911		391-4
Canal Park Lodge 250 Canal Pk Dr Duluth MN 55802 *TF:* 800-777-8560 ■ *Web:* www.canalparklodge.com	218-279-6000		379
Canal Wood LLC 2430 Main St Conway SC 29526 *TF:* 866-587-1460 ■ *Web:* www.canalwood.com	843-488-9663		448
Canales & Simonson PC 2601 Morgan Ave PO Box 5624 Corpus Christi TX 78405 *Web:* canalessimonson.com	361-883-0601	884-7023	41
Canals & Trails Credit Union 838 State St Lockport IL 60441 *Web:* canals-trailscu.org	815-838-7159		219
Canam Group Inc 11535 First Ave Bureau 500 Saint-Georges QC G5Y7H5 *TSX: CAM* ■ *TF:* 877-499-6049 ■ *Web:* www.groupecanam.com	418-228-8031		723
Can-am Plumbing Inc 151 Wyoming St. Pleasanton CA 94566 *TF:* 800-786-9797 ■ *Web:* www.canamplumbing.com	925-846-1833		610
Canamax Energy Ltd 7th Ave SW Ste 2500 Calgary AB T2P2Z1 *TF:* 866-716-8557 ■ *Web:* canamaxenergy.ca	587-349-5186		536
Canamer International Inc 5701 Industrial Park Rd Winona MN 55987 *TF:* 800-533-8020 ■ *Web:* www.canamer.com	507-452-1700		733
Canamould Extrusions Inc 101a Roytec Rd. Woodbridge ON L4L8A9 *TF:* 866-874-6762 ■ *Web:* canamould.com	905-264-4436		499
Canandaigua City School District 143 N Pearl St Canandaigua NY 14424 *Web:* www.canandaiguaschools.org	585-396-3700		685
Canandaigua Federal Credit Union 3210 Eastern Blvd. Canandaigua NY 14424 *Web:* canandaiguafcu.com	585-394-2436	394-2837	219
Canandaigua Insurance Agency LLC 470 S Pearl St. Canandaigua NY 14424 *Web:* canandaiguainsurance.com	585-394-5544		390
Canandaigua Lake State Marine Park 620 S Main St. Canandaigua NY 14424 *Web:* parks.ny.gov	585-394-9420		565
Canandaigua National Corp 72 S Main St. Canandaigua NY 14424 *OTC: CNND* ■ *Web:* www.cnbank.com	585-394-4260		70
Canard Aerospace Corp 1157 Valley Park Dr Ste 115 Shakopee MN 55379 *Web:* www.canardaero.com	952-944-7990	944-9149	256
Canarie 45 O'Connor St Ste 500 Ottawa ON K1P1A4 *TF:* 800-959-5525 ■ *Web:* www.canarie.ca	613-943-5454	943-5443	48-9
Canary Connect Publications 605 Holiday Rd. Coralville IA 52241 **Fax Area Code: 612* ■ *Web:* www.canaryconnect.com	319-338-3827	435-3340*	637-2
Canary Hotel 31 W Carrillo Santa Barbara CA 93101 *TF:* 866-999-5401 ■ *Web:* www.canarysantabarbara.com	805-884-0300	884-8153	379
Canary Marketing Inc 2700 Camino Ramon Ste 110 San Ramon CA 94583 *Web:* www.canarymarketing.com	925-314-1888	314-9184	195
Canatal Industries Inc 2885 Boul Frontenac E Thetford Mines QC G6G6P6 *Web:* www.canatal.net	418-338-6044		105
Canaudit Inc 100 N First St Ste 201 Burbank CA 91502 *TF:* 800-774-1717 ■ *Web:* www.canaudit.com	805-583-3723		194
Canaveral National Seashore 212 S Washington Ave Titusville FL 32796 *Web:* www.nps.gov	321-267-1110	264-2906	564
Canberra Corp 3610 Holland Sylvania Rd Toledo OH 43615 *TF:* 800-832-8992 ■ *Web:* www.canberracorp.com	419-841-6616	841-7597	151
Can-Blast Inc 755 Wallace Rd Unit 3 North Bay ON P1B8K4 *Web:* www.can-blast.com	705-474-3431	476-7643	268
Canby School District 1130 S Ivy Canby OR 97013 *Web:* www.canby.k12.or.us	503-266-7861	266-0022	685
Cancap Pharmaceutical Ltd 13111 Vanier Pl Unit 180 Richmond BC V6V2J1 *TF:* 877-998-2378 ■ *Web:* www.cancappharma.com	604-278-2188	278-2210	231
Cancer Care Inc 275 Seventh Ave 22nd Fl New York NY 10001 *TF:* 800-813-4673 ■ *Web:* www.cancercare.org	212-712-8400	712-8495	48-17
Cancer Genetics Inc Meadows Office Complex 201 Rt 17 N 2nd Fl Rutherford NJ 07070 *TF:* 888-334-4988 ■ *Web:* www.cancergenetics.com	201-528-9200		231
Cancer Letter PO Box 9905 Washington DC 20016 *Web:* cancerletter.com	202-362-1809	379-1787	531-8
Cancun Grill 15406 NW 77th Ct. Miami FL 33016 *Web:* cancungrillmiamilakes.com	305-826 8571		671
Candela Controls Inc 751 Business Park Blvd Ste 101 Winter Garden FL 34787 *Web:* www.candelacontrols.com	407-654-2420		362
Candela Corp 530 Boston Post Rd. Wayland MA 01778 *TF:* 800-733-8550 ■ *Web:* shop.candelamedical.com	508-358-7400	358-5602	424
Candelis Inc 18821 Bardeen Ave Irvine CA 92612 *Web:* www.candelis.com	949-852-1000		415
Candid 32 Old Slip 24th Fl New York NY 10005 *TF:* 800-424-9836 ■ *Web:* candid.org	212-620-4230	807-3691	48-11
Candid Color Systems Inc 1300 Metropolitan Ave Oklahoma City OK 73108 *TF:* 800-336-4550 ■ *Web:* www.candid.com	405-947-8747	951-7353	588
Candid Worldwide 210 Rte 109 Long Island City NY 11735 *Web:* www.candidww.com	212-431-3800		344
Candlelight Cabinetry Inc 24 Michigan St. Lockport NY 14094 *Web:* www.candlelightcab.com	716-434-6543	434-6748	115
Candlelight Inn 2200 First Ave Rock Falls IL 61071 *Web:* candlelightinnrestaurant.com	815-626-1897		378
Candlelighters Childhood Cancer Foundation 10920 Connecticut Ave Suuite A PO Box 498 Kensington MD 20895 *TF:* 800-366-2223 ■ *Web:* www.acco.org	301-962-3520	962-3521	48-17
Candler County 705 N Lewis St. Metter GA 30439 *Web:* georgia.gov	912-685-2835	685-4823	338
Candler Hospital 5353 Reynolds St Savannah GA 31405 *TF:* 800-622-6877 ■ *Web:* www.sjchs.org	912-819-6000		374-3
Candlewick Press Inc 99 Dover St Somerville MA 02144 *Web:* www.candlewick.com	617-661-3330	661-0565	637-2
Can-do Promotions Inc 6517 Wise Ave NW North Canton OH 44720 *TF:* 800-325-7981 ■ *Web:* www.candopromo.com	800-325-7981		184
Cando Railway Services Ltd Unit 400 - 740 Rosser Ave Brandon MB R7A0K9 *TF:* 866-989-5310 ■ *Web:* www.candorail.com	204-725-2627	725-4100	650
Candoris Technologies LLC 475 N Weaber St. Annville PA 17003 *Web:* candoris.com	717-228-1600		196
Candy & Schonwald PLLC 3116 Live Oak St Dallas TX 75204 *Web:* cscpa.com	214-826-6660	826-6925	2
Candy Basket Inc, The 1924 Ne 181st Ave Portland OR 97230 *Web:* www.candybasketinc.com	503-666-2000		296-8
Candy Bouquet International Inc 510 Mclean St Little Rock AR 72202 *TF:* 877-226-3901 ■ *Web:* www.candybouquet.com	501-375-9990	375-9998	123
Candy Express 3320 Greencastle Rd. Burtonsville MD 20866 *Web:* candyexpress.com	301-384-5889		123
Candy Manufacturing Company Inc 5633 W Howard St Niles IL 60714 *TF:* 800-927-6776 ■ *Web:* www.candycontrols.com	847-588-2639	588-0055	202
Cane Creek Cycling Components 355 Cane Creek Rd. Fletcher NC 28732 *TF:* 800-234-2725 ■ *Web:* www.canecreek.com	828-684-3551	684-1057	82
Cane Creek State Park 50 State Park Rd Star City AR 71667 *Web:* www.arkansasstateparks.com	870-628-4714		565
Cane River Creole National Historical Park 400 Rapides Dr. Natchitoches LA 71457 *Web:* www.nps.gov	318-356-8441		564
Cane River Pecan Co 1415 Easy St New Iberia LA 70560 *TF:* 800-293-8710 ■ *Web:* www.caneriverpecan.com	337-365-4136	365-4137	328
Caneel Bay Resort PO Box 720 Saint John VI 00831 **Fax Area Code: 340* ■ *TF:* 855-226-3358 ■ *Web:* www.caneelbay.com	212-845-0581	693-8280*	378
Caneel Group LLC 59 N Lakeview Dr. Gibbsboro NJ 08026 *TF:* 800-632-6977 ■ *Web:* caneelgroup.com	800-632-6977		653
Can-Eng Furnaces International Ltd 6800 Montrose Rd PO Box 628 Niagara Falls ON L2E6V5 *Web:* www.can-eng.com	905-356-1327		610
Canepa & Vidal PA 200 W Devargas St Ste 7 Santa Fe NM 87501 *Web:* canepavidal.com	505-982-9229		41
Canerector Inc 1 Sparks Ave. North York ON M2H2W1 *Web:* www.canerector.com	416-225-6240		490
Caney Fork Electric Co-opeartive Inc 920 Smithville Hwy PO Box 272 McMinnville TN 37110 *TF:* 888-505-3030 ■ *Web:* www.caneyforkec.com	931-473-3116	473-4939	245
Caney Valley Electric Cooperative Association Inc, The 401 Lawrence St PO Box 308 Cedar Vale KS 67024 *TF:* 800-310-8911 ■ *Web:* www.caneyvalley.com	620-758-2262	758-2926	245
Canfield & Tack Inc 925 Exchange St Rochester NY 14608 *TF:* 800-246-0158 ■ *Web:* www.canfieldtack.com	585-235-7710		627
Canfield Connector Div 8510 Foxwood Ct Youngstown OH 44514 *TF:* 800-554-5071 ■ *Web:* www.canfieldconnector.com	800-554-5071		201
Canfield Equipment Service 21533 Mound Rd Warren MI 48091 *TF:* 800-637-3956 ■ *Web:* www.canfieldequipment.com	800-637-3956		59
Canfield Machine & Tool LLC 121 Howard Rd. Fulton NY 13069 *Web:* www.canfieldmachine.com	315-593-8062		454
Canfield Scientific Inc 253 Passaic Ave Fairfield NJ 07004 *Web:* www.canfieldsci.com	973-276-0336		179
Cangro Industries Long Island Transmission Co 495 Smith St. Farmingdale NY 11735 *TF:* 800-422-9210 ■ *Web:* www.cangroindustries.com	631-454-9000	454-9155	620
Canidium LLC 3801 Kirby Dr S456 Houston TX 77024 *TF:* 877-651-1837 ■ *Web:* canidium.com	877-651-1837		196
Canine Companions for Independence Inc (CCI) 2965 Dutton Ave PO Box 446 Santa Rosa CA 95402 *TF:* 800-572-2275 ■ *Web:* www.cci.org	707-577-1700		48-17
Canine Country Club Kennel & Pet Resort, The 33306 Tract 43 Rd. Los Fresnos TX 78566 *Web:* www.caninecountryclub.com	956-233-1746		794
Canisius College 2001 Main St Buffalo NY 14208 *TF:* 800-843-1517 ■ *Web:* www.canisius.edu	716-888-2200	888-3230	166

Name / Address	City	State	ZIP	Phone	Fax	Class
Cankdeska Cikana Community College PO Box 269 TF: 888-783-1463 ■ Web: www.littlehoop.edu	Fort Totten	ND	58335	701-766-4415	766-4077	165
Canlan Ice Sports Corp 6501 Sprott St Web: www.icesports.com	Burnaby	BC	V5B3B8	604-736-9152		354
Canlis Restaurant 2576 Aurora Ave N Web: canlis.com	Seattle	WA	98109	206-283-3313		671
CAN-med Healthcare 99 Susie Lake Crescent TF: 800-565-7553 ■ Web: www.canmedhealthcare.com	Halifax	NS	B3S1C3	902-455-4649	455-1028	475
Cannagrow Holdings Inc 8101 E Prentice Ave Ste 500 Web: www.cannagrowholdings.com	Greenwood Village	CO	80111	720-486-5309		45
Canndescent 128 W Canon Perdido St Web: www.canndescent.com	Santa Barbara	CA	93101	760-205-2087		293
Cannella Response Television LLC 848 Liberty Dr Web: drtv.com	Burlington	WI	53105	262-763-4810	763-2875	195
Cannella School of Hair Design 117 W Chicago Web: www.cannellabeautyschools.com	Elgin	IL	60120	847-742-6611		685
Cannery Casino & Hotel, The *Cannery Casino Resorts LLC* 2121 E Craig Rd TF: 866-999-4899 ■ Web: www.cannerycasino.com	North Las Vegas	NV	89030	702-507-5700		379
CanNet Internet Services Inc PO Box 36696 Web: www.cannet.com	Canton	OH	44735	330-484-2260	493-9771	224
Cannon & Dunphy Sc 595 N Barker Rd TF: 855-570-2676 ■ Web: www.cannon-dunphy.com	Brookfield	WI	53045	855-570-2676		428
Cannon & Wendt Electric Co 4020 N 16th St Web: www.cannon-wendt.com	Phoenix	AZ	85016	602-279-1681	230-8464	189-4
Cannon Air Force Base 110 Alison Ave Ste 1150 Web: www.cannon.af.mil	Cannon AFB	NM	88103	575-784-4131	784-8101	497-1
Cannon Building Svc Inc 1640 Sierra Madre Cir Web: www.cannonbuilding.com	Placentia	CA	92870	714-630-9570		256
Cannon Cochran Management Services Inc 2 E Main St Towne Centre Bldg Ste 208 TF: 800-252-5059 ■ Web: www.ccmsi.com	Danville	IL	61832	217-446-1089		463
Cannon Constructors Inc 17000 Ventura Blvd Ste 301 Web: www.cannongroup.com	Encino	CA	91316	818-906-6200	906-6220	189-9
Cannon County 1424 John Bragg Hwy Web: www.cannontn.com	Woodbury	TN	37190	615-563-2222		338
Cannon Design 2170 Whitehaven Rd Web: www.cannondesign.com	Grand Island	NY	14072	716-773-6800	773-5909	261
Cannon Equipment 324 Washington St W TF: 800-825-8501 ■ Web: www.cannonequipment.com	Cannon Falls	MN	55009	507-263-6400		233
Cannon Instrument Co 2139 High Tech Rd TF: 800-676-6232 ■ Web: www.cannoninstrument.com	State College	PA	16803	814-353-8000		653
Cannon IV Inc 950 Dorman St TF: 800-825-7779 ■ Web: www.cannon4.com	Indianapolis	IN	46202	317-951-0500		179
Cannon Marketing Inc 4684 US Hwy 70 W Web: www.1cmi.com	Kinston	NC	28504	252-527-3361		665
Cannon Muskegon Corp 2875 Lincoln St TF: 800-253-0371 ■ Web: cannonmuskegon.com	Muskegon	MI	49441	231-755-1681	755-4975	485
Cannon Sports Inc 12701 Van Nuys Blvd Ste P TF: 800-223-0064 ■ Web: www.cannonsports.com	Pacoima	CA	91331	800-223-0064	388-1993	711
Cannon USA Inc 1235 Freedom Rd Web: cannonusa.com	Cranberry Township	PA	16066	724-772-5600	776-1070	695
Cannon Wright Blount (CWB) 756 Ridge Lake Blvd TF: 888-681-9392 ■ Web: www.cannonwrightblount.com	Memphis	TN	38120	901-685-7500	685-7569	2
Cannon, Aveni & Malchesky Company LPA 41 E Erie St Web: csalawgroup.com	Painesville	OH	44077	440-357-5537		41
Cannonball Advertising & Promotion 8251 Maryland Ave Ste 200 Web: www.cannonballagency.com	Saint Louis	MO	63105	314-445-6400		7
Cannonball Express Transportation LLC 10064 S 134th St Web: www.cannonball-express.com	Omaha	NE	68138	402-894-4882		780
Cannonball Trucking Inc 6815 Lindbergh St Web: cannonballtrucking.com	Houston	TX	77087	713-644-7300		311
Cano Container Corp 3920 Enterprise Ct Web: www.canocontainer.com	Aurora	IL	60504	630-585-7500	585-7501	100
Canoe 4199 Paces Ferry Rd NW Web: www.canoeatl.com	Atlanta	GA	30339	770-432-2663		671
Canoe Bay PO Box 28 Web: www.canoebay.com	Chetek	WI	54728	715-924-4594		379
Canoe Creek State Park 205 Canoe Creek Rd Web: www.dcnr.pa.gov	Hollidaysburg	PA	16648	814-695-6807		565
Canoe Island Lodge 3820 Lakeshore Dr Web: www.canoeislandlodge.com	Diamond Point	NY	12824	518-668-5592	668-2012	669
Canoga Park/West Hills Chamber of Commerce 7248 Owensmouth Ave Web: www.cpwhchamber.org	Canoga Park	CA	91303	818-884-4222		139
Canoga Perkins Corp 20600 Prairie St TF: 800-360-6642 ■ Web: www.canoga.com	Chatsworth	CA	91311	818-718-6300	718-6312	173-3
Canon Business Solutions-Central 425 N Martingale Rd Ste 100 Web: csa.canon.com	Schaumburg	IL	60173	847-706-3400		112
Canon Capital Management Group LLC 357 N Main St PO Box 64160 Web: canoncapital.com	Souderton	PA	18964	215-723-4881		2
Canon City Chamber of Commerce 403 Royal Gorge Blvd TF: 800-876-7922 ■ Web: www.canoncity.com	Canon City	CO	81212	719-275-2331		139
Canon Information Technology Services Inc 850 Greenbrier Cir Web: www.cits.canon.com	Chesapeake	VA	23320	757-579-7100		196
Canon Law Society of America (CLSA) 415 Michigan Ave Ste 101 Web: canonlawsocietyofamerica.org	Washington	DC	20017	202-832-2350		48-20
Canon Press 207 N Main St TF: 800-488-2034 ■ Web: canonpress.com	Moscow	ID	83843	800-488-2034		637-2
Canon Recruiting Group LLC 26531 Summit Cir Web: www.canonrecruiting.com	Santa Clarita	CA	91350	661-252-7400		260
Canon Solutions America Inc One Canon Pk TF: 844-443-4636 ■ Web: www.csa.canon.com	Melville	NY	11747	844-443-4636		804
Canoochee Electric Membership Corp 342 E Brazell St TF: 800-342-0134 ■ Web: www.canoocheeemc.com	Reidsville	GA	30453	912-557-4391		245
Canopach Inc 48 Wall St 11th Fl Web: canopach.com	New York	NY	10005	347-694-7809		463
Canopies Party Rental 7234 N 60th St Web: canopiesevents.com	Milwaukee	WI	53223	414-760-0770		62
Canopy 333 S 520 W Web: canopyproperties.info	Lindon	UT	84042	801-932-6120	229-2458	655
Canplas Industries Ltd 500 Veterans Dr TF: 800-461-1771 ■ Web: www.canplas.com	Barrie	ON	L4M4V3	705-726-3361		605-2
Canpotex Ltd 111 2nd Ave S Ste 400 PO Box 1600 Web: www.canpotex.com	Saskatoon	SK	S7K1K6	306-931-2200	653-5505	146
Cansec Systems Ltd 3105 Unity Dr Unit 9 TF: 877-545-7755 ■ Web: www.cansec.com	Mississauga	ON	L5L4L2	905-820-2404		693
Canso Islands National Historic Site 1465 Union St Web: www.pc.gc.ca	Canso	NS	B0E1B0	902-366-3136	295-3496	563
Canson Inc 21 Industrial Dr Web: www.cansonstudio.com	South Hadley	MA	01075	413-538-9250		43
CanTalk (Canada) Inc 250-70 Arthur St TF: 800-480-9686 ■ Web: cantalk.com	Winnipeg	MB	R3B1G7	800-480-9686		768
Canteen Service Co 712 Industrial Dr TF: 800-467-2471 ■ Web: www.canteenatyourservice.com	Owensboro	KY	42301	270-683-2471		299
Cantel Medical Corp 150 Clove Rd 9th Fl NYSE: CMN ■ TF: 800-714-4152 ■ Web: www.cantelmedical.com	Little Falls	NJ	07424	973-890-7220	890-7270	476
Cantella & Company Inc 28 State St 40th Fl TF: 800-333-3502 ■ Web: www.cantella.com	Boston	MA	02109	617-521-8630		390
Canter & Associates LLC 12975 Coral Tree Pl TF: 800-669-9011 ■ Web: www.canter.net	Los Angeles	CA	90066	310-578-4700		766
Canterbury & Parkside PO Box 130823 Web: www.louderthanthunder.com	Ann Arbor	MI	48113	734-237-6614		637-2
Canterbury Designs 6195 Maywood Ave TF: 800-935-7111 ■ Web: canterbury-designs.com	Huntington Park	CA	90255	323-936-7111	936-7115	153
Canterbury Park Holding Corp 1100 Canterbury Rd NASDAQ: CPHC ■ TF: 800-340-6361 ■ Web: www.canterburypark.com	Shakopee	MN	55379	952-445-7223		642
Canterbury School 101 Aspetuck Ave Web: www.cbury.org	New Milford	CT	06776	860-210-3800		622
Canterbury Shaker Village 288 Shaker Rd Web: www.shakers.org	Canterbury	NH	03224	603-783-9511		520
CANTEX Inc 301 Commerce St Ste 2700 Web: www.cantexinc.com	Fort Worth	TX	76102	817-215-7000	215-7001	596
Cantey Hanger LLP 600 W Sixth St Ste 300 Web: canteyhanger.com	Fort Worth	TX	76102	817-877-2863	877-2807	226
Cantina Italiana 346 Hanover St Web: cantinaitaliana.com	Boston	MA	02113	617-723-4577	723-6357	671
Cantler's Riverside Inn 458 Forest Beach Rd Web: www.cantlers.com	Annapolis	MD	21409	410-757-1311	757-6784	671
Canton Chamber of Commerce 45525 Hanford Rd Web: www.cantonchamber.com	Canton	MI	48187	734-453-4040	453-4503	139
Canton Drop Forge Inc 4575 Southway St SW Web: cantondropforge.com	Canton	OH	44706	330-477-4511	477-2046	483
Canton Food Co 750 S Alameda St Web: cantonfoodco.com	Los Angeles	CA	90021	213-688-7707	688-1121	297-8
Canton Free Library (CFL) 8 Park St Web: www.cantonfreelibrary.org	Canton	NY	13617	315-386-3712	386-4131	434-3
Canton Grill 2610 SE 82nd Ave Web: canton-grill.com	Portland	OR	97266	503-774-1135		671
Canton Group LLC, The 2400 Boston St Web: cantongroup.com	Baltimore	MD	21224	410-675-5708	675-5111	177
Canton Historical Society, The 1022 N Canton Center Rd Web: www.cantonhistoricalsociety.org	Canton	MI	48188	734-397-0088		522
Canton Inn Restaurant 947 N Pk Dr Web: cantoninnevansville.com	Evansville	IN	47710	812-428-6611		671
Canton Palace Theatre 605 Market Ave N Web: www.cantonpalacetheatre.org	Canton	OH	44702	330-454-8172	454-8171	572
Canton Public Library 1200 S Canton Center Rd TF: 888-988-6300 ■ Web: www.cantonpl.org	Canton	MI	48188	734-397-0999	397-1130	434-3
Canton Public School District 403 Lincoln St Web: www.cantonschools.net	Canton	MS	39046	601-859-4110		685

Name / Address	City	State	ZIP	Phone	Fax	Class
Canton Regional Chamber of Commerce 222 Market Ave N *TF:* 800-533-4302 ■ *Web:* www.cantonchamber.org	Canton	OH	44702	330-456-7253	452-7786	139
Canton Symphony Orchestra 1001 Market Ave N *Web:* www.cantonsymphony.org	Canton	OH	44702	330-452-3434	452-4429	573-3
Canton Veterinary Clinic Inc 1010 W Dallas St *Web:* cantontxvet.com	Canton	TX	75103	903-567-6581		794
Canton/Stark County Convention & Visitors Bureau 227 Second St NW *TF:* 800-552-6051 ■ *Web:* www.visitcanton.com	Canton	OH	44702	330-454-1439		206
Cantor Colburn LLP 20 Church St 22nd Fl *Web:* www.cantorcolburn.com	Hartford	CT	06103	860-286-2929		428
Cantor Fitzgerald 110 East 59th St *Web:* www.cantor.com	New York	NY	10022	212-938-5000		69
Cantos Para Todos 2250 N Rock Rd Ste 118-127 *Web:* www.cantos.org	Wichita	KS	67226	316-689-0495		637-2
Cantrell Gainco Group 1635 Oakbrook Dr *TF:* 800-922-1232 ■ *Web:* cantrellgainco.com	Gainesville	GA	30501	770-534-0703	531-0832	296
Cantu Pest Control 4950 Keller Springs Rd Ste 340 *Web:* cantupestcontrol.com	Addison	TX	75001	972-885-3618		192
Cantwell Maria (Sen D - WA) 511 Hart Senate Office Bldg *Web:* www.cantwell.senate.gov	Washington	DC	20510	202-224-3441	228-0514	342-2
Canusa Hershman Recycling Co 45 NE Industrial Rd *Web:* www.chrecycling.com	Branford	CT	06405	203-488-0887		660
Canvs 85 Broad St 27th Fl *Web:* canvs.tv	New York	NY	10004	646-201-9124		466
Canvys 40 W 267 Keslinger Rd *TF:* 800-291-1344 ■ *Web:* www.canvys.com	Lafox	IL	60147	508-460-5400	460-5470	201
Canweb Internet Services 1086 Modeland Rd *TF:* 877-422-6932 ■ *Web:* www.canweb.ca	Sarnia	ON	N7S6L2	519-332-6900		180
CanWel Building Materials Group Ltd West Georgia St Ste 1100 - 1055 *TF:* 877-656-6166 ■ *Web:* www.canwel.com	Vancouver	BC	V6E3P3	604-432-1400	436-6670	364
CanWest DHI 660 Speedvale Ave W *TF:* 800-549-4373 ■ *Web:* www.canwestdhi.com	Guelph	ON	N1K1E5	519-824-2320		743
Canyon Air Service Inc 416 S Vermont Ave *Web:* www.canyonair.com	Glendora	CA	91741	626-335-1116	914-1088	610
Canyon Chamber of Commerce 1518 Fifth Ave *TF:* 800-999-9481 ■ *Web:* www.canyonchamber.org	Canyon	TX	79015	806-655-7815		139
Canyon Concert Ballet 1031 Conifer St *Web:* ccballet.org	Fort Collins	CO	80524	970-472-4156		573-1
Canyon County 1115 Albany St *Web:* www.canyonco.org	Caldwell	ID	83605	208-454-7300	454-7525	338
Canyon Creek Cabinet Co 16726 Tye St SE *TF:* 800-228-1830 ■ *Web:* www.canyoncreek.com	Monroe	WA	98272	360-348-4600		115
Canyon Creek Travel Inc 333 W Campbell Rd Ste 440 *TF:* 800-952-1998 ■ *Web:* www.canyoncreektravel.com	Richardson	TX	75080	972-238-1998		775
Canyon de Chelly National Monument PO Box 588 *Web:* www.nps.gov	Chinle	AZ	86503	928-674-5500		564
Canyon Explorations Inc 675 W Clay Ave *TF:* 800-654-0723 ■ *Web:* www.canyonexplorations.com	Flagstaff	AZ	86001	928-774-4559	774-4655	536
Canyon Graphics Inc 6680 Cobra Way *Web:* www.canyongraphics.com	San Diego	CA	92121	858-646-0444	646-0440	344
Canyon Marketing & Media PO Box 2223 *Web:* canyoninternational.com	Folsom	CA	95763	916-933-3026		5
Canyon Media Broadcasting 619 S Bluff St Tower 1 Tower 1 Ste 300 *Web:* www.canyonmedia.net	Saint George	UT	84770	435-628-3643	673-1210	645-141
Canyon Ranch 165 Kemble St *TF:* 800-742-9000 ■ *Web:* www.canyonranch.com	Lenox	MA	01240	413-637-4100	637-0057	669
Canyon Ridge Christian Church 6200 W Lone Mtn Rd *Web:* www.canyonridge.org	Las Vegas	NV	89130	702-658-2722		48-20
Canyon Specialty Foods Inc 3251 Tom Braniff	Dallas	TX	75238	214-352-1771		297-8
Canyon State Wireless 8 Corral Rd	Sierra Vista	AZ	85635	520-458-4772		647
Canyon Tax & Bookkeeping Service Inc PO Box 80429 *Web:* www.canyontax.com	Rancho Santa Margarita	CA	92688	949-888-2829	888-2831	734
Canyonlands National Park 2282 SW Resource Blvd *TF:* 800-394-9978 ■ *Web:* www.nps.gov	Moab	UT	84532	435-719-2313		564
Canyonville Christian Academy 250 E First St *Web:* www.canyonville.net	Canyonville	OR	97417	541-839-4401	839-6228	622
CAO Group Inc 4628 Skyhawk Dr *TF:* 877-877-9778 ■ *Web:* www.caogroup.com	West Jordan	UT	84084	801-256-9282	256-9287	419
CAOT (Canadian Association of Occupational Therapists) 1125 Colonel By Dr *TF:* 800-434-2268 ■ *Web:* www.caot.ca	Ottawa	ON	K1S5R1	613-523-2268		48-1
CAP (College of American Pathologists) 325 Waukegan Rd *TF:* 800-323-4040 ■ *Web:* www.cap.org	Northfield	IL	60093	847-832-7000	832-8168	49-8
CAP (Children Awaiting Parents) 274 N Goodman St *TF:* 888-835-8802 ■ *Web:* www.childrenawaitingparents.org	Rochester	NY	14610	585-232-5110	232-2634	48-6
CAP (Carolina Academic Press) 700 Kent St *Web:* www.cap-press.com	Durham	NC	27701	919-489-7486	493-5668	637-2
CAP Barbell Inc 10820 Westpark *Web:* capbarbell.com	Houston	TX	77042	713-977-3090		711
Cap Collet & Tool Company Inc 4082 6th St *Web:* capcollet.com	Wyandotte	MI	48192	734-283-4040	283-0084	493
CAP Index Inc 150 John Robert Thomas Dr The Commons at Lincoln C *TF:* 800-227-7475 ■ *Web:* capindex.com	Exton	PA	19341	610-903-3000		196
Cap N. Cork 1031 Broadway *Web:* www.capncork.com	Fort Wayne	IN	46802	260-423-1496		443
CAP Rock Telephone Co-opeartive Inc 121 E Third St PO Box 300 *Web:* www.caprock-spur.com	Spur	TX	79370	806-271-3336		736
CAP Systems Inc 16 Market St Ste 204 *Web:* www.capsystems.com	Ipswich	MA	01938	781-341-5440	341-5441	178-1
Cap's 4325 Myrtle St *Web:* www.capsonthewater.com	Saint Augustine	FL	32084	904-824-8794		671
Cap's Place Island Restaurant 2765 NE 28th Ct *Web:* www.capsplace.com	Lighthouse Point	FL	33064	954-941-0418		671
Capability Co 8300 Clark Branch Dr *Web:* www.capabilitycompany.com	Raleigh	NC	27613	919-410-6263		631
Capacity 6665 Delmar Blvd Ste 300 *Web:* capacity.com	University City	MO	63130	314-502-9412		178-1
Capasso & Associates LLC 215 State St *Web:* vcapassolaw.com	Schenectady	NY	12305	518-374-1800		41
Capax Global LLC 410 N Michigan Ave *TF:* 866-780-0385 ■ *Web:* www.capaxglobal.com	Chicago	IL	60611	866-780-0385		225
Capco Inc 1328 Winters Ave *Web:* capcoinc.com	Grand Junction	CO	81501	970-243-8750		268
Capco LLC 1349 Arcadia Dr *Web:* capco-llc.com	Columbus	IN	47201	812-375-1700	375-1800	488
Capcom USA Inc 185 Berry St Ste 1200 *Web:* www.capcom.com	San Mateo	CA	94402	650-350-6500		178-6
Capdevila at Lateresita 3248 W Columbus Dr *Web:* www.lateresitarestaurant.com	Tampa	FL	33607	813-879-9704		671
Cape & Island Kitchens 99 State Rd Rte 3A *Web:* www.capekitchens.com	Sagamore Beach	MA	02562	508-888-4762	833-1442	362
Cape Air 660 Barnstable Rd *TF:* 800-227-3247 ■ *Web:* www.capeair.com	Hyannis	MA	02601	508-771-6944		25
Cape Ann Chamber of Commerce 33 Commercial St *Web:* capeannchamber.com	Gloucester	MA	01930	978-283-1601	283-4740	139
Cape Arago State Park Cape Arago Hwy *Web:* stateparks.oregon.gov	Coos Bay	OR	97420	541-888-3778		565
Cape Breton Post 255 George St PO Box 1500 *Web:* www.capebretonpost.com	Sydney	NS	B1P6K6	902-562-7077	564-6280	532-1
Cape Breton Regional Library 50 Falmouth St *Web:* cbrl.ca	Sydney	NS	B1P6X9	902-562-3279	564-0765	436
Cape Breton University (CBU) 1250 Grand Lake Rd PO Box 5300 *TF:* 888-959-9995 ■ *Web:* www.cbu.ca	Sydney	NS	B1P6L2	902-539-5300	562-0119	785
Cape Christian Academy 10 Oyster Rd *Web:* capechristianacademy.com	Cape May	NJ	08210	609-465-4132	465-0170	148
Cape Cod Canal Regional Chamber of Commerce 70 Main St *TF:* 888-332-2732 ■ *Web:* www.capecodcanalchamber.org	Buzzards Bay	MA	02532	508-759-6000	759-6965	139
Cape Cod Chamber of Commerce 5 Shoot Flying Hill Rd *Web:* www.capecodchamber.org	Centerville	MA	02632	508-362-3225	362-3698	139
Cape Cod Children's Museum 577 Great Neck Rd S *Web:* www.capecodchildrensmuseum.org	Mashpee	MA	02649	508-539-8788		521
Cape Cod Community College 2240 Iyanough Rd *TF:* 877-846-3672 ■ *Web:* www.capecod.edu	West Barnstable	MA	02668	508-362-2131	375-4089	162
Cape Cod Five Cents Savings Bank 532 Rte 28 PO Box 20 *TF:* 800-678-1855 ■ *Web:* www.capecodfive.com	Harwich	MA	02646	508-430-0400	430-0403	70
Cape Cod Healthcare Inc 25 Communication Way *TF:* 844-275-2242 ■ *Web:* www.capecodhealth.org	Hyannis	MA	02601	844-275-2242		374-3
Cape Cod Irish Village 822 Rt 28 *Web:* www.capecod-irishvillage.com	South Yarmouth	MA	02664	508-771-0100		379
Cape Cod Life Magazine 13 Steeple St Ste 204 PO Box 1439 *TF:* 800-698-1717 ■ *Web:* capecodlife.com	Mashpee	MA	02649	508-419-7381	477-1225	457-22
Cape Cod Lumber Company Inc 225 Groveland St *Web:* capecodlumber.com	Abington	MA	02351	781-878-0715	871-6726	364
Cape Cod Maritime Museum 135 S St PO Box 443 *Web:* www.capecodmaritimemuseum.org	Hyannis	MA	02601	508-775-1723	775-1706	520
Cape Cod Museum of Natural History 869 Main St *Web:* www.ccmnh.org	Brewster	MA	02631	508-896-3867	896-8844	520
Cape Cod Potato Chip Co 100 Breed's Hill Rd *TF:* 888-881-2447 ■ *Web:* www.capecodchips.com	Hyannis	MA	02601	888-881-2447		296-35
Cape Cod Regional Transit Authority (CCRTA) 215 Iyannough Rd PO Box 1988 *TF:* 800-352-7155 ■ *Web:* www.capecodtransit.org	Hyannis	MA	02601	508-775-8504	775-8513	468
Cape Cod Shipbuilding Co 7 Narrows Rd PO Box 152 *Web:* www.capecodshipbuilding.com	Wareham	MA	02571	508-295-3550	295-3551	90
Cape Cod Times 319 Main St *TF:* 800-451-7887 ■ *Web:* www.capecodonline.com	Hyannis	MA	02601	508-775-1200	771-3292	532-2
Cape Codder Resort & Spa 1225 Iyanough Rd Rt 132 Bearse's Way *TF:* 888-297-2200 ■ *Web:* www.capecodderresort.com	Hyannis	MA	02601	508-771-3000		669
Cape Coral Plumbing Inc 5812 Enterprise Pkwy *Web:* capecoralplumbing.com	Fort Myers	FL	33905	239-693-4714		189-10

Name / Address	City	State	ZIP	Phone	Fax	Class
Cape Dairy LLC 44 Bodick Rd *Web:* capedairy.com	Hyannis	MA	02601	508-771-4700		297-4
Cape Design Engineering Co 775 E Merritt Island Cswy Ste 230 *Web:* www.cdeco.com	Merritt Island	FL	32952	321-799-2970	799-0375	256
Cape Disappointment State Park PO Box 488 *Web:* capedisappointment.org	Ilwaco	WA	98624	360-642-3078	642-4216	565
Cape Electronics 19 Dupont Ave *Web:* capeelectronics.com	South Yarmouth	MA	02664	508-394-2405		54
Cape Fear Botanical Garden 536 N Eastern Blvd PO Box 53485 *Web:* www.capefearbg.org	Fayetteville	NC	28301	910-486-0221	486-4209	97
Cape Fear Community College 411 N Front St *TF:* 877-799-2322 ■ *Web:* www.cfcc.edu	Wilmington	NC	28401	910-362-7000	362-7080	162
Cape Fear Hospital 5301 Wrightsville Ave *Web:* www.nhrmc.org	Wilmington	NC	28403	910-452-8100		374-3
Cape Fear Valley Medical Ctr (CFVMC) 1638 Owen Dr PO Box 2000 *Web:* www.capefearvalley.com	Fayetteville	NC	28304	910-615-4000		374-3
Cape Fox Corp PO Box 8558 *Web:* www.capefoxcorp.com	Ketchikan	AK	99901	907-225-5163		194
Cape Gazette 17585 Nassau Commons Blvd PO Box 213 *Web:* www.capegazette.com	Lewes	DE	19958	302-645-7700	645-1664	532-4
Cape Girardeau Area Chamber of Commerce 220 N Fountain *Web:* www.capechamber.com	Cape Girardeau	MO	63701	573-335-3312	335-4686	139
Cape Girardeau County 1 Barton Sq Ste 301 *Web:* www.capecounty.us	Jackson	MO	63755	573-243-3547	204-2418	338
Cape Girardeau Public Library 711 N Clark St *Web:* www.capelibrary.org	Cape Girardeau	MO	63701	573-334-5279		434-3
Cape Hatteras Electric Co-op 47109 Light Plant Rd PO Box 9 *TF:* 800-454-5616 ■ *Web:* www.chec.coop	Buxton	NC	27920	252-995-5616	995-4088	245
Cape Hatteras National Seashore 1401 National Pk Dr *Web:* www.nps.gov	Manteo	NC	27954	252-473-2111	473-2595	564
Cape Henlopen State Park 42 Cape Henlopen Dr *Web:* www.destateparks.com	Lewes	DE	19958	302-645-8983		565
Cape Henry Associates Inc 2877 Guardian Ln Ste 300 *Web:* cape-henry.com	Virginia Beach	VA	23452	757-502-7424	961-0944	463
Cape Henry Lighthouse 583 Atlantic Ave *Web:* www.preservationvirginia.org	Fort Story	VA	23459	757-422-9421		50-3
Cape Jourimain Nature Centre Inc 5039 Rt 16 *Web:* www.capejourimain.ca	Bayfield	NB	E4M3Z8	506-538-2220		138
Cape Krusenstern National Monument PO Box 1029 *Web:* www.nps.gov	Kotzebue	AK	99752	907-442-3890	442-8316	564
Cape Lookout National Seashore 131 Charles St *Web:* www.nps.gov	Harkers Island	NC	28531	252-728-2250	728-2160	564
Cape May County 7 N Main St PO Box 5000 *TF:* 800-621-5388 ■ *Web:* capemaycountynj.gov	Cape May	NJ	08210	609-465-1010	465-8625	338
Cape May County Chamber of Commerce 13 Crest Haven Rd PO Box 74 *Web:* www.capemaycountychamber.com	Cape May	NJ	08210	609-465-7181	465-5017	139
Cape May Point State Park PO Box 107 *Web:* www.njparksandforests.org	Cape May Point	NJ	08212	609-884-2159		565
Cape Medical Supply Inc 28 Jan Sebastian Dr *TF:* 800-339-3322 ■ *Web:* www.capemedical.com	Sandwich	MA	02563	800-339-3322		363
Cape Project Management Inc 14 Bay View Ave *Web:* www.capeprojectmanagement.com	Plymouth	MA	02360	508-728-3614		463
Cape Regional Medical Center Inc (CRMC) 2 Stone Harbor Blvd *Web:* www.caperegional.com	Cape May	NJ	08210	609-463-2000		374-3
Cape Rod Regional Technical High School 351 Pleasant Lake Ave *Web:* www.capetech.us	Harwich	MA	02645	508-432-4500		685
Cape Securities Inc 2005 Pennsylvania Ave *Web:* www.capesecurities.com	Mcdonough	GA	30253	678-583-1120		691
Cape Verde *Embassy* 3415 Massachusetts Ave NW *Web:* www.embcv-usa.gov.cv	Washington	DC	20007	202-965-6820		257
Cape Vincent Correctional Facility 36560 New York 12E *Web:* www.doccs.ny.gov	Cape Vincent	NY	13618	315-654-4100		213
Capel Inc 8000 Winchester Dr **Fax Area Code:* 910 ■ *TF:* 800-334-3711 ■ *Web:* www.capelrugs.com	Troy	NC	27371	800-334-3711	572-7040*	131
Capell & Howard PC 150 S Perry St *Web:* capellhoward.com	Montgomery	AL	36104	334-241-8000		428
Capella Education Co 225 S Sixth St 9th Fl *NASDAQ: CPLA* ■ *TF:* 888-227-3552 ■ *Web:* www.capella.edu	Minneapolis	MN	55402	612-339-8650		242
Capella Group Inc 4929 W Royal Ln Ste 200 **Fax Area Code:* 888 ■ *TF:* 888-411-3888 ■ *Web:* www.careentree.com	Irving	TX	75063	214-259-0445	626-0833*	393
Capella Hotel Group 3384 Peachtree Rd Ste 375 *Web:* www.capellahotels.com	Atlanta	GA	30326	404-842-7280		379
Capellon Pharmaceuticals Ltd 7509 Flagstone St *Web:* www.capellon.com	Fort Worth	TX	76118	817-595-5820		238
Capen Hill Nature Sanctuary 56 Capen Rd PO Box 218 *Web:* capenhill.org	Charlton	MA	01507	508-248-5516		50-5

Name / Address	City	State	ZIP	Phone	Fax	Class
Capers 14502 Cantrell Rd *Web:* www.capersrestaurant.com	Little Rock	AR	72223	501-868-7600		671
Capezio 1 Campus Rd *TF:* 888-227-3946 ■ *Web:* www.capezio.com	Totowa	NJ	07512	973-595-9000	595-9120	301
Capgemini US LLC 623 Fifth Ave Ste 33 *Web:* www.capgemini.com	New York	NY	10022	212-314-8000		180
CapGen Financial Group 120 W 45th St Ste 1010 *Web:* www.capgen.com	New York	NY	10036	212-542-6868		194
Capilano University 2055 Purcell Way *Web:* www.capilanou.ca	North Vancouver	BC	V7J3H5	604-986-1911		162
Capilo Institute 43 Bridge St *Web:* www.capilo.com	Augusta	ME	04330	207-621-9941		167-3
Capintec Inc 7 Vreeland Rd *TF:* 800-631-3826 ■ *Web:* capintec.com	Florham Park	NJ	07932	201-825-9500	825-1336	153
CAPIRG (California Public Interest Research Group) 1111 H St Ste 207 *Web:* calpirg.org	Sacramento	CA	95814	916-448-4516		633
Capital Access Group 150 California St Ste 250 *Web:* capitalaccess.com	San Francisco	CA	94111	415-217-7600		217
Capital Advantage Inc 3708 Mount Diablo Blvd Ste 200 *Web:* www.capitaladvantage.com	Lafayette	CA	94549	925-299-1500		401
Capital Advisors Group Inc Chatham Ctr 29 Crafts St Ste 270 *Web:* www.capitaladvisors.com	Newton	MA	02458	617-630-8100		401
Capital Advisors Inc 2200 S Utica Pl Ste 150 *TF:* 866-230-5879 ■ *Web:* www.capitaladv.com	Tulsa	OK	74114	918-599-0045	584-8866	401
Capital Advisors Limited LLC 20600 Chagrin Blvd *TF:* 888-295-7908 ■ *Web:* www.capitaladvisorsltd.com	Shaker Heights	OH	44122	216-295-7900		194
Capital Agricultural Property Services Inc 801 Warrenville Rd Ste 150 *TF:* 800-243-2060 ■ *Web:* www.capitalag.com	Lisle	IL	60532	630-434-9150	434-9343	315-3
Capital Alliance Corp 2777 N Stemmons Fwy Ste 1220 *Web:* www.cadallas.com	Dallas	TX	75207	214-638-8280	638-8009	70
Capital Alpha Partners LLC 600 Pennsylvania Ave SE Ste 220 *Web:* www.capalphadc.com	Washington	DC	20003	202-548-0111		401
Capital Analysts Inc 218 Glenside Ave *TF:* 800-242-1421 ■ *Web:* www.capitalanalysts.com	Wyncote	PA	19095	800-242-1421		390
Capital Area District Libraries 401 S Capitol Ave *TF:* 866-561-2500 ■ *Web:* www.cadl.org	Lansing	MI	48933	517-367-6300	374-1068	434-3
Capital Assets Inc 8002 S 101st E Ave *Web:* www.capitalassetsok.com	Tulsa	OK	74133	918-481-1700	481-5363	652
Capital Automobile Co 2210 Cobb Pkwy SE *Web:* www.capitalcadillac.com	Smyrna	GA	30080	770-952-2277	989-8439	57
Capital Automotive Real Estate Services Inc 8484 Westpark Dr Ste 200 *Web:* www.capitalautomotive.com	McLean	VA	22102	703-288-3075		654
Capital Brewery 7734 Terr Ave *TF:* 800-598-6352 ■ *Web:* capitalbrewery.com	Middleton	WI	53562	608-836-7100		102
Capital Candy Company Inc 32 Burnham St **Fax Area Code:* 802 ■ *TF:* 800-639-2224 ■ *Web:* www.capitalcandy.com	Barre	VT	05641	800-639-2224	476-6929*	297-3
Capital Christian Ctr 9470 Micron Ave *Web:* www.capitalonline.cc	Sacramento	CA	95827	916-856-5683		48-20
Capital City Bank 217 N Monroe St *TF:* 888-671-0400 ■ *Web:* www.ccbg.com	Tallahassee	FL	32301	850-402-7700		70
Capital City Club Inc 7 John Portman Blvd *Web:* www.capitalcityclub.org	Atlanta	GA	30303	404-523-8221		354
Capital City Press Inc PO Box 588 *TF:* 800-960-6397 ■ *Web:* www.theadvocate.com	Baton Rouge	LA	70821	225-388-0297		637-8
Capital City Restaurant Supply Inc 1414 Interstate Loop *TF:* 800-279-4576 ■ *Web:* www.capitalcityrestaurantsupply.com	Bismarck	ND	58503	800-279-4576		300
Capital City Trust Co 304 E Tennessee St *TF:* 866-820-9671 ■ *Web:* www.capitalcitytrust.com	Tallahassee	FL	32301	866-820-9671		401
Capital Commercial Flooring Inc 3709 Bradview Dr *Web:* ccfinc.net	Sacramento	CA	95827	916-569-1960	569-1970	290
Capital Community College 950 Main St *TF:* 800-894-6126 ■ *Web:* www.capitalcc.edu	Hartford	CT	06103	860-906-5000	906-5129	162
Capital Concepts Group Inc 1030-4720 Kingsway *Web:* www.capitalconceptsgroup.ca	Burnaby	BC	V5H4N2	604-432-7743		401
Capital Consulting Corp 11821 Parklawn Dr Ste 100 **Fax Area Code:* 703 ■ *Web:* www.capconcorp.com	Rockville	MD	20852	301-468-6001	876-0496*	194
Capital Corrugated Inc 8333 24th Ave *TF:* 800-916-3010 ■ *Web:* capitalcorrugated.com	Sacramento	CA	95826	916-388-7848		100
Capital Crime Press PO Box 272904 *Web:* www.capitalcrimepress.com	Fort Collins	CO	80527	970-481-4894		637-2
Capital Datacorp 3600 Madison Ave Ste 65 *Web:* www.capdata.com	North Highlands	CA	95660	916-529-4063		180
Capital Design Inc 1 Richmond Sq Ste 210E *Web:* www.freemiums.com	Providence	RI	02906	401-270-6777		5
Capital District Physicians' Health Plan 500 Patroon Creek Blvd *TF:* 888-258-0477 ■ *Web:* www.cdphp.com	Albany	NY	12206	518-641-3000	641-3507	391-3
Capital District Psychiatric Ctr 75 New Scotland Ave *Web:* omh.ny.gov	Albany	NY	12208	518-549-6000	434-0041	374-5
Capital District Transportation Authority (CDTA) 110 Watervliet Ave *Web:* www.cdta.org	Albany	NY	12206	518-482-8822	437-8318	468

	Phone	Fax	Class
Capital Electric Construction Company Inc			
600 Broadway Ste 600 ... Kansas City MO 64105	816-472-9500	421-4244	189-4
Web: www.capitalelectric.com			
Capital Electric Co-opeartive Inc			
4111 State St ... Bismarck ND 58503	701-223-1513	223-1557	245
TF: 888-223-1513 ■ *Web:* www.capitalelec.com			
Capital Equipment & Handling Inc			
1100 Cottonwood Ave ... Hartland WI 53029	262-369-5500		358
Web: cehwi.com			
Capital Estate Advisors Inc			
116 Central Pk S Ste 6 ... New York NY 10019	212-489-8443		390
Web: paulreback.com			
Capital Excavation Co			
2967 Business Park Dr ... Buda TX 78610	512-440-1717		261
Web: www.capitalexcavation.com			
Capital Farm Credit Aca 7000 Woodway Dr ... Waco TX 76712	866-845-3977	776-8112*	69
**Fax Area Code:* 254 ■ *TF:* 877-944-5500 ■ *Web:* www.capitalfarmcredit.com			
Capital Financial & Insurance			
1500 Townside Dr 2nd Fl ... Apex NC 27502	919-657-4201		390
Web: capitalfinancialusa.com			
Capital Ford Inc 4900 Capital Blvd ... Raleigh NC 27616	919-790-4600		57
TF: 877-659-2496 ■ *Web:* www.capitalford.com			
Capital Ford of Charlotte			
5411 N Tryon St ... Charlotte NC 28213	844-242-1515		57
TF: 844-242-1515 ■ *Web:* capitalfordcharlotte.com			
Capital Forensics Inc (CFI)			
1530 E Dundee Rd Ste 333 ... Palatine IL 60074	847-392-0900	392-2990	194
TF: 888-970-1700 ■ *Web:* www.capitalforensics.com			
Capital Gallery of Contemporary Art			
314 Lewis St ... Frankfort KY 40601	502-223-2649		50-2
Web: ellenglasgow.com			
Capital Grille, The			
1000 Darden Center Dr ... Orlando FL 32837	202-737-6200		671
Web: www.thecapitalgrille.com			
Capital Group Companies Inc			
333 S Hope St ... Los Angeles CA 90071	213-615-0514		401
Web: www.capitalgroup.com			
Capital Growth Management LP			
1 International Pl ... Boston MA 02110	617-737-3225		401
TF: 800-345-4048 ■ *Web:* www.cgmfunds.com			
Capital Growth Planning Inc			
405 E Lexington Ave Ste 201 ... El Cajon CA 92020	619-440-7023		691
Web: www.capplan.com			
Capital Health One Capital Way ... Pennington NJ 08534	800-637-2374		374-3
TF: 800-637-2374 ■ *Web:* www.capitalhealth.org			
Capital Health Plan PO Box 15349 ... Tallahassee FL 32317	850-383-3333	383-3339	391-3
TF: 800-390-1434 ■ *Web:* capitalhealth.com			
Capital High School			
1500 Greenbrier St ... Charleston WV 25311	304-348-6500		685
Web: chs.kana.k12.wv.us			
Capital Hill Group			
45 O'Connor St Ste 1540 ... Ottawa ON K1P1A4	613-235-0221		196
Web: capitalhillgroup.ca			
Capital Hill Hotel & Suites			
88 Albert St ... Ottawa ON K1P5E9	613-235-1413	235-6047	379
TF: 800-463-7705 ■ *Web:* www.capitalhill.com			
Capital Home Healthcare Inc			
211 Gibson St NW Ste 207 ... Leesburg VA 20176	703-737-6310		363
Web: capitalhomehealth.com			
Capital Hospice Inc			
2900 Telestar Ct ... Falls Church VA 22042	703-538-2065		371
TF: 855-571-5700 ■ *Web:* www.capitalcaring.org			
Capital Hotel 111 W Markham St ... Little Rock AR 72201	501-374-7474	370-7091	379
TF: 877-637-0037 ■ *Web:* www.capitalhotel.com			
Capital Imaging Inc			
2521 E Michigan Ave ... Lansing MI 48912	517-482-2292		627
Web: capital-imaging.com			
Capital Innovations LLC			
325 Forest Grove Dr Ste 100 ... Pewaukee WI 53072	262-746-3100		401
Web: www.capinnovations.com			
Capital Institutional Services Inc			
1700 Pacific Ave Ste 1100 ... Dallas TX 75201	214-720-0055	922-3220	401
TF: 800-247-6729 ■ *Web:* www.capis.com			
Capital Investment Advisors Inc			
200 Sandy Springs Pl NE Ste 300 ... Atlanta GA 30328	404-531-0018		194
TF: 888-531-0018 ■ *Web:* www.yourwealth.com			
Capital Journal 333 W Dakota Ave ... Pierre SD 57501	605-224-7301	224-9210	532-2
TF: 800-537-0025 ■ *Web:* www.capjournal.com			
Capital Link Inc			
230 Park Ave Ste 1536 ... New York NY 10169	212-661-7566		401
Web: www.capitallink.com			
Capital Lumber Company Inc			
5110 N 40th St Ste 242 ... Phoenix AZ 85018	602-381-0709	824-5675	690
TF: 877-479-5077 ■ *Web:* www.capital-lumber.com			
Capital Machine Company Inc			
2801 Roosevelt Ave ... Indianapolis IN 46218	317-638-6661	636-5122	821
Web: www.capitalmachineco.com			
Capital Management Corp, The			
4101 Cox Rd Ste 110 ... Glen Allen VA 23060	804-270-4000		401
Web: www.cmcva.com			
Capital Management Enterprises Inc			
1111 W Dekalb Pk ... Wayne PA 19087	610-265-9600		391-3
Web: www.cms-advisors.com			
Capital Management Group			
934 S Flintridge Way ... Anaheim CA 92808	714-439-9600		401
Web: cm-group.com			
Capital Manor 1955 Dallas Hwy NW ... Salem OR 97304	503-967-3086		672
Web: www.capitalmanor.com			
Capital Markets Advisors LLC (CMA)			
11 Grace Ave Ste 308 ... Great Neck NY 11021	516-487-9815	487-2575	345
Web: www.capmark.org			
Capital Markets Cooperative LLC			
814 A1A N Ste 303 ... Ponte Vedra Beach FL 32082	904-543-0052		345
Web: www.capmkts.org			
Capital Medical Ctr			
3900 Capital Mall Dr SW ... Olympia WA 98502	360-754-5858	956-2574	374-3
TF: 888-677-9757 ■ *Web:* www.capitalmedical.com			
Capital Merchant Solutions Inc			
3005 Gill St ... Bloomington IL 61704	309-452-5990	313-0716*	251
**Fax Area Code:* 866 ■ *TF:* 877-495-2419 ■ *Web:* holyprocessing.com			
Capital Mercury Apparel			
105 Mulberry Ave ... New York NY 11530	212-704-4800		155-12
Capital Mortgages Inc			
260 Hearst Way Ste 200 ... Kanata ON K2L3H1	613-228-3888		509
Web: capitalmortgages.com			
Capital Network Inc, The			
281 Summer St 2nd Fl ... Boston MA 02210	781-591-0291		792
Web: www.thecapitalnetwork.org			
Capital Newspapers Inc			
1901 Fish Hatchery Rd ... Madison WI 53713	608-252-6400		532-2
TF: 800-362-8333 ■ *Web:* madison.com			
Capital Office Systems			
3201 Industrial Ave ... Fairbanks AK 99701	907-777-1500		321
Web: www.capital-office.com			
Capital One Arena 601 F St NW ... Washington DC 20004	202-628-3200		720
Web: www.capitalonearena.com			
Capital One Auto Finance Inc			
PO Box 60511 ... City of Industry CA 91716	800-946-0332		70
TF: 800-946-0332 ■ *Web:* www.capitalone.com			
Capital Pacific Partners			
180 Montgomery St Ste 1250 ... San Francisco CA 94104	415-274-2709		652
Web: capitalpacific.com			
Capital Premium Financing Inc			
12235 South 800 East ... Draper UT 84020	800-767-0705	470-2628*	401
**Fax Area Code:* 855 ■ *TF:* 877-730-1906 ■ *Web:* www.capitalpremium.net			
Capital Printing Corp 420 South Ave ... Middlesex NJ 08846	732-560-1515		627
Web: www.capitalprintingcorp.com			
Capital Properties Management LTD			
12929 Shaker Blvd ... Cleveland OH 44120	216-991-3057		260
Web: cpm-ltd.com			
Capital Public Radio Inc			
7055 Folsom Blvd ... Sacramento CA 95826	916-278-8900	278-8989	645-137
TF: 877-480-5900 ■ *Web:* www.capradio.org			
Capital Realty Advisors Inc			
600 Sandtree Dr Ste 109 ... Palm Beach Gardens FL 33403	561-624-5888		463
TF: 800-940-1088 ■ *Web:* capitalrealtyadvisors.nabrnetwork.com			
Capital Region International Airport			
4100 Capital City Blvd ... Lansing MI 48906	517-321-6121	321-6197	27
Web: www.flylansing.com			
Capital Region Medical Ctr			
1125 Madison St ... Jefferson City MO 65101	573-632-5000	632-5880	374-3
Web: www.crmc.org			
Capital Regional Medical Ctr (CRMC)			
2626 Capital Medical Blvd ... Tallahassee FL 32308	850-325-5000		374-3
Web: capitalregionalmedicalcenter.com			
Capital Repertory Theatre			
432 State St ... Schenectady NY 12305	518-462-4531		749
Web: www.capitalrep.org			
Capital Research Ctr			
1513 16th St NW ... Washington DC 20036	202-483-6900		634
Web: capitalresearch.org			
Capital Resin Corp 324 Dering Ave ... Columbus OH 43207	614-445-7177	445-7290	605-2
Web: capitalresin.com			
Capital Resource Partners			
31 State St 6th Fl ... Boston MA 02109	617-478-9600	478-9605	792
Web: crp.com			
Capital Restaurant Concepts Ltd (CRC)			
1305 Wisconsin Ave NW ... Washington DC 20007	202-339-6800	339-6801	670
Web: www.capitalrestaurants.com			
Capital Review Group (CRG)			
214 E Roosevelt St ... Phoenix AZ 85004	877-666-5539		463
TF: 877-666-5539 ■ *Web:* capitalreviewgroup.com			
Capital Senior Living Corp			
14160 Dallas Pkwy Ste 300 ... Dallas TX 75254	972-770-5600	770-5666	672
NYSE: CSU ■ *TF:* 800-635-1232 ■ *Web:* www.capitalsenior.com			
Capital Southwest Corp			
5400 Lyndon B Johnson Fwy Ste 1300 ... Dallas TX 75240	214-238-5700	238-5701	792
NASDAQ: CSWC ■ *Web:* www.capitalsouthwest.com			
Capital Spectrum Inc 502 S Loop 4 ... Buda TX 78610	512-478-3448	443-2196	92
Web: www.csiprinting.com			
Capital Springs 3101 Lake Farm Rd ... Madison WI 53711	608-224-3606		565
Web: www.friendsofcapitalsprings.org			
Capital Strategies Group Inc			
850 Shades Creek Pkwy Ste 300 ... Birmingham AL 35209	205-263-2400	263-2300	390
Web: capitalstrategies.net			
Capital Tower & Communications Inc			
13330 Amberly Rd ... Waverly NE 68462	402-786-3334		480
Web: capitaltower.com			
Capital Transportation Solutions LLC			
1915 Vaughn Rd ... Kennesaw GA 30144	770-690-8684		311
Web: www.odysseylogistics.com			
Capital University College & Main St ... Columbus OH 43209	614-236-6101	236-6926	166
TF: 866-544-6175 ■ *Web:* www.capital.edu			
Capital University Law School			
303 E Broad St ... Columbus OH 43215	614-236-6500	236-6972	167-1
Web: law.capital.edu			
Capital Valuation Group Inc			
1 N Pinckney St Ste 200 ... Madison WI 53703	608-257-2757	257-7741	41
Web: www.capvalgroup.com			
Capital Veneer Works Inc			
2550 Jackson Ferry Rd ... Montgomery AL 36104	334-264-1401	264-6923	613
Web: capitalmat.com			
Capital Workforce Partners			
1 Union Pl ... Hartford CT 06103	860-522-1111	722-2486	260
Web: capitalworkforce.org			
Capital X-Ray Inc 2189 Notasulga Rd ... Tallassee AL 36078	334-283-8410		475
Web: www.capitalxray.com			
Capital Z Partners (CZIP)			
142 W 57th St 3rd Fl ... New York NY 10019	212-965-2400	965-2301	792
Web: www.capitalz.com			
Capital-Plus Inc (CPI)			
3250 W Henderson Rd Ste 201 ... Columbus OH 43220	614-848-7620		272
Web: www.capplus.com			
Capitalsoft Inc			
1702 N Collins Blvd Ste 532 ... Richardson TX 75080	972-220-1560		180
Web: www.capitalsoft.com			

Name	Address	City	State	ZIP	Phone	Fax	Class
CapitalSouth Partners SBIC F-III LLC	4201 Congress St Ste 360 *Web:* www.capitalagroup.com	Charlotte	NC	28209	704-376-5502	376-5877	401
Capito Shelley Moore (Sen R - WV)	172 Russell Senate Office Bldg *Web:* www.capito.senate.gov	Washington	DC	20510	202-224-6472		342-2
Capitol Aggregates Ltd	2330 N Loop 1604 W *TF:* 855-422-7244 ■ *Web:* www.capitolaggregates.com	San Antonio	TX	78248	210-871-6100		46
Capitol Aluminum & Glass Corp	1276 W Main St *TF:* 800-331-8268 ■ *Web:* www.capitol-windows.com	Bellevue	OH	44811	800-331-8268		330
Capitol Archives & Record Storage Inc	133 Laurel St *TF:* 800-381-2277 ■ *Web:* www.capitolarchives.com	Hartford	CT	06106	860-951-8981		194
Capitol Auto Group	783 Auto Group Ave *TF:* 800-888-1391 ■ *Web:* www.capitolauto.com	Salem	OR	97301	503-585-4141		57
Capitol Baptist Church	401 Kesselring Ave *Web:* www.cbcofdover.com	Dover	DE	19904	302-734-2410		48-20
Capitol Benefits LLC	364 Main St 2nd Fl *Web:* www.capitolbenefits.com	Gaithersburg	MD	20878	301-431-0000		193
Capitol Beverage Sales	6982 Hwy 65 NE *Web:* capitolbeverage.com	Fridley	MN	55432	763-571-4115	571-9785	81-1
Capitol Broadcasting Company Inc	2619 Western Blvd *TF:* 800-234-4857 ■ *Web:* www.capitolbroadcasting.com	Raleigh	NC	27606	919-890-6000	890-6095	738
Capitol Business Interiors	711 Indiana Ave *Web:* cbiwv.com	Charleston	WV	25302	304-343-7551		320
Capitol Center for the Arts	44 S Main St *Web:* ccanh.com	Concord	NH	03301	603-225-1111	224-3408	572
Capitol Chevrolet Montgomery	711 Eastern Blvd *TF:* 800-410-1137 ■ *Web:* www.capitolchevrolet.com	Montgomery	AL	36117	888-311-4644		57
Capitol City Bolt & Screw Company Inc	1003 Third Ave S *Web:* ccbstn.com	Nashville	TN	37210	615-254-8707		350
Capitol City Container Corp	8240 Zionsville Rd *TF:* 800-233-5145 ■ *Web:* www.capcitycont.com	Indianapolis	IN	46268	317-875-0290		100
Capitol City Produce	16550 Commercial Ave *TF:* 800-349-1583 ■ *Web:* www.capitolcityproduce.com	Baton Rouge	LA	70816	225-272-8153	272-8152	296-21
Capitol City Speakers Bureau	1620 S Fifth St *TF:* 800-397-3183 ■ *Web:* www.capcityspeakers.com	Springfield	IL	62703	217-544-8552	544-1496	708
Capitol Computers Inc	151 Water St *Web:* capcomp.com	Augusta	ME	04330	207-623-2700		180
Capitol Connection	4400 University Dr MSN 1D2 *TF:* 844-504-7161 ■ *Web:* www.capitolconnection.org	Fairfax	VA	22030	703-993-3100		116
Capitol Construction Services Inc	11051 Village Square Ln *Web:* www.capitolconstruct.com	Fishers	IN	46038	317-574-5488	574-5482	186
Capitol Copy Service	116 W State St *Web:* capitol-copy.com	Trenton	NJ	08608	609-989-8776		113
Capitol Core Group Inc	600 Congress Ave 3rd Fl *Web:* www.capitolcore.com	Austin	TX	78701	512-568-3084		194
Capitol Creag LLC	1300 Penn Ave NW	Washington	DC	20004	202-355-1028		463
Capitol Detective Agency	2922 N 18th Pl	Phoenix	AZ	85016	602-264-9771		400
Capitol Distributing Inc	3500 E Commercial Ct *Web:* www.capitoldist.com	Meridian	ID	83642	208-888-5112	888-5989	345
Capitol Federal Financial	700 Kansas Ave *NASDAQ:* CFFN ■ *TF:* 888-822-7333 ■ *Web:* capfed.com	Topeka	KS	66603	785-235-1341		360-2
Capitol Fishing Tackle	132 W 36th St Broadway & 7th Ave *TF:* 800-528-0853 ■ *Web:* www.capitolfishing.com	New York	NY	10018	800-528-0853		711
Capitol Foam Products Inc	75 E Union Ave *Web:* www.capitolfoamproducts.com	East Rutherford	NJ	07073	201-933-5277	933-7684	45
Capitol Granite & Marble	1700 Oak Lake Blvd *Web:* www.capitolgranite.net	Midlothian	VA	23112	804-265-4751		115
Capitol Hill Hotel	200 C St SE *TF:* 800-491-2525 ■ *Web:* capitolhillhotel-dc.com	Washington	DC	20003	202-543-6000	547-2608	379
Capitol Hill Publishing Corp	1625 K St NW Ste 900 *Web:* thehill.com	Washington	DC	20006	202-628-8500		532-3
Capitol Lien Records & Research Inc	1010 N Dale St *TF:* 800-845-4077 ■ *Web:* www.capitollien.com	Saint Paul	MN	55117	651-488-0100	488-0200	635
Capitol Petroleum Equipment Inc	11319 Old Baltimore Pk *Web:* www.cpe123.com	Beltsville	MD	20705	301-931-9090		539
Capitol Pharmacy Inc	2923 W Capitol Ave *Web:* cpi-rx.com	West Sacramento	CA	95691	916-617-4321		237
Capitol Plaza Hotel	415 W McCarty St *TF:* 800-338-8088 ■ *Web:* www.capitolplazajeffersoncity.com	Jefferson City	MO	65101	573-635-1234	635-4565	671
Capitol Plaza Hotel & Conference Ctr	100 State St *TF:* 800-274-5252 ■ *Web:* www.capitolplaza.com	Montpelier	VT	05602	802-223-5252		379
Capitol Reef National Park	PO Box 15 *Web:* www.nps.gov	Torrey	UT	84775	435-425-3791	425-3026	564
Capitol Resources LLC	200 N Congress St Ste 500 *Web:* capitolresourcesllc.com	Jackson	MS	39201	601-948-6020		41
Capitol Risk Management	55 Old Turnpike Rd Ste 110 *Web:* capitolrisk.com	Nanuet	NY	10954	845-627-7111		390
Capitol Sales Company Inc	1245 Trapp Rd Ste 130 *TF:* 800-467-8255 ■ *Web:* www.capitolsales.com	Eagan	MN	55121	800-467-8255	440-4077	38
Capitol School of Hairstyling	10803 John Galt Blvd *TF:* 800-352-1331 ■ *Web:* www.capitollook.com	Omaha	NE	68137	402-333-3329		685
Capitol Securities Management Inc	100 Concourse Blvd *Web:* www.capitolsecurities.com	Glen Allen	VA	23059	804-612-9700		690
Capitol Security Police Inc	703 Calle Victor Lopez *Web:* capitol-security-police-inc.negocio.site	San Juan	PR	00909	787-727-1700		393
Capitol Services Inc	206 E Ninth St Ste 1300 *TF:* 800-345-4647 ■ *Web:* www.capitolservices.com	Austin	TX	78701	800-345-4647	432-3622	635
Capitol Stampings Corp	2700 W N Ave *Web:* capitolstampings.com	Milwaukee	WI	53208	414-372-3500	372-3535	488
Capitol Steps Productions Inc	210 N Washington St *TF:* 800-733-7837 ■ *Web:* www.capsteps.com	Alexandria	VA	22314	703-683-8330		632
Capitol Technology University	11301 Springfield Rd *TF:* 800-950-1992 ■ *Web:* www.captechu.edu	Laurel	MD	20708	301-369-2800	953-1442	166
Capitol Theatre, The	149 Westchester Ave *TF:* 877-987-6487 ■ *Web:* www.thecapitoltheatre.com	Port Chester	NY	10573	914-937-4126		572
Capitol Tunneling Inc	2216 Refugee Rd *Web:* capitoltunneling.com	Columbus	OH	43207	614-444-0255		188
Capitol Uniform & Linen Service	195 Commerce Way *TF:* 800-822-7352 ■ *Web:* www.capitollinen.com	Dover	DE	19904	302-674-1511		442
Capitol-Husting Company Inc	12001 W Carmen Ave *Web:* www.capitol-husting.com	Milwaukee	WI	53225	414-353-1000	353-0768	81-3
CapitolWorks Inc	2000 P St NW *Web:* capitolworks.com	Washington	DC	20036	202-785-2020		260
Caplan & Earnest LLC	1800 Broadway Ste 200 *Web:* www.celaw.com	Boulder	CO	80302	303-443-8010		445
Caplan's Inc	916 Third St *Web:* www.shopcaplans.com	Alexandria	LA	71301	318-427-7700		157-3
Caplugs LLC	2150 Elmwood Ave *TF:* 888-227-5847 ■ *Web:* www.caplugs.com	Buffalo	NY	14207	716-876-9855	874-1680	154
Capone's	PO Box 914 *Web:* www.capones.com	Richmond	ON	K2G1W2	613-226-6947		671
Capone's Cucina	19688 Beach Blvd Ste 10 *Web:* www.caponescucina.com	Huntington Beach	CA	92646	714-593-2888		671
CAPP/USA Inc	201 Marple Ave *TF:* 800-356-8000 ■ *Web:* www.cappusa.com	Clifton Heights	PA	19018	800-356-8000		202
Cappa & Graham Inc	401 Terry A Francois Blvd Ste 128 *Web:* www.cappa-graham.com	San Francisco	CA	94158	415-512-6967		184
Cappaert Manufactured Housing Inc	6200 Hwy 61 S *Web:* cappaert.biz	Vicksburg	MS	39180	601-636-5401		505
Cappelli Organization	7 Renaissance Sq 4th Fl *Web:* www.cappelli-inc.com	White Plains	NY	10601	914-769-6500		653
Cappellino Cadillac	4130 Sheridan Dr *Web:* www.cappellinocadillac.com	Williamsville	NY	14221	716-568-7045		57
Cappello & Noel LLP	831 State St *Web:* cappellonoel.com	Santa Barbara	CA	93101	805-564-2444		41
Cappello Capital Corp	100 Wilshire Blvd Ste 1200 *Web:* www.cappellocorp.com	Santa Monica	CA	90401	310-393-6632		401
Capps Manufacturing Inc	2121 S Edwards *Web:* www.cappsmfg.com	Wichita	KS	67213	316-942-9351	942-6771	22
Cappy's	5011 Broadway St *Web:* www.cappysrestaurant.com	San Antonio	TX	78209	210-828-9669		671
CAPREIT	11200 Rockville Pk Ste 100 *Web:* www.capreit.com	Rockville	MD	20852	301-231-8700		655
Capri	313 E State St *Web:* caprirockford.com	Rockford	IL	61104	815-965-6341		671
Capri Beauty College	1938 E Lincoln Hwy *Web:* www.capri.edu	New Lenox	IL	60451	815-485-3020		167-3
Capri College	2945 Williams Pkwy SW *Web:* capricollege.edu	Cedar Rapids	IA	52404	319-364-1541		167-3
Capri Cosmetology Learning Ctr	251 W Rt 59 *Web:* www.caprinow.edu	Nanuet	NY	10954	845-623-6339		766
Capri IGA	224 E Harris St *Web:* capriiga.com	Greenville	IL	62246	618-664-0022		345
Capri Institute Cosmetology Training Ctr	1595 Main Ave *Web:* www.capriinstitute.com	Clifton	NJ	07011	973-772-4610	772-8732	765
Capri Investment Group	875 N Michigan Ave Ste 3430 *Web:* www.capricap.com	Chicago	IL	60611	312-573-5300	475-2457	194
Capriccio	2 Pine St *Web:* www.capriccios.com	Providence	RI	02903	401-421-1320	331-8732	671
Capriccio	2424 N University Dr *Web:* capriccios.net	Pembroke Pines	FL	33024	954-432-7001		671
Capricorn Coffees Inc	353 10th St *TF:* 800-541-0758 ■ *Web:* www.capricorncoffees.com	San Francisco	CA	94103	415-621-8500	621-9875	297-2
Capricorn Products LLC	12 Rice St *Web:* www.capricornproducts.com	Portland	ME	04103	207-321-0014	321-0015	231
Capricorn Systems Inc	3569 Habersham At N *Web:* www.capricornsys.com	Tucker	GA	30084	678-514-1080	514-1081	225

Company / Address	Phone	Fax	Class
Capris Furniture Industries Inc 1401 NW 27th Ave, Ocala FL 34475 *Web:* www.caprisfurniture.com	352-629-8889		319-2
Caprock Canyons State Park & Trailway 850 Caprock Canyon Park Rd, Quitaque TX 79255 *Web:* tpwd.texas.gov	806-455-1492		565
Caprock Mfg 2303 120th St, Lubbock TX 79423 *Web:* www.caprock-mfg.com	806-745-6454		596
Capron & Avgerinos PC 55 W Monroe Ste 900, Chicago IL 60603 *Web:* capronlaw.com	312-346-6444		41
Capron Company Inc 411 N Stonestreet Ave, Rockville MD 20850 *Web:* capron.com	301-424-9500		189-10
Capron Park Zoo 201 County St, Attleboro MA 02703 **Fax Area Code:* 508 ■ *Web:* www.capronparkzoo.com	774-203-1840	223-2208*	823
Capsilon Corp 1 Sansome St Ste 1800, San Francisco CA 94104 *TF:* 877-362-8356 ■ *Web:* www.capsilon.com	877-362-8356		2
Capsmith Inc 2240 Old Lake Mary Rd, Sanford FL 32771 *TF:* 800-228-3889 ■ *Web:* capsmith.com	407-328-7660		157-6
Capsonic Group 460 Second St, Elgin IL 60123 *Web:* www.capsonic.com	847-888-7300		604
CapSouth Partners Inc 2216 W Main St, Dothan AL 36301 *TF:* 800-929-1001 ■ *Web:* capsouthwm.com	334-673-8600		463
Capstead Mortgage Corp 8401 N Central Expy Ste 800, Dallas TX 75225 *NYSE: CMO* ■ *TF:* 800-358-2323 ■ *Web:* www.capstead.com	214-874-2323	874-2398	654
Capstone College 1200 N Fair Oaks Ave No 32, Pasadena CA 91103 **Fax Area Code:* 626 ■ *TF:* 888-991-1580 ■ *Web:* www.capstonecollege.edu	888-991-1580	486-1001*	167-3
Capstone Development LLC 4445 Willard Ave Ste 600, Chevy Chase MD 20815 *Web:* www.capstonedevco.com	202-470-3122		377
Capstone Hotel Ltd 320 Paul W Bryant Dr, Tuscaloosa AL 35401 *Web:* www.hotelcapstone.com	205-752-3200		378
Capstone Metering LLC 1600 Capital Ave Ste 200, Plano TX 75074 *Web:* capstonemetering.com	214-469-1065	469-2504	407
Capstone Press Inc 1710 Roe Crest Dr, Mankato MN 56003 **Fax Area Code:* 888 ■ *TF:* 800-747-4992 ■ *Web:* www.capstonepub.com	800-747-4992	262-0705*	637-2
Capstone Production Group 1030 Nowell Rd, Raleigh NC 27603 *TF:* 800-951-4005 ■ *Web:* www.capstoneproductiongroup.com	919-838-8030		344
Capstone Real Estate Investments LLC 402 Office Park Dr Ste 150, Birmingham AL 35223 *Web:* capstonerealestateinvestments.com	205-949-2060		655
Capstone Technology Corp 14300 SE 1st St Ste 200, Vancouver WA 98684 *Web:* www.capstonetechnology.com	360-619-5010		177
Capstone Therapeutics Corp 1275 W Washington St Ste 101, Tempe AZ 85281 *OTC: CAPS* ■ *TF:* 800-937-5520 ■ *Web:* capstonethx.com	602-286-5520		477
Capstone Turbine Corp 21211 Nordhoff St, Chatsworth CA 91311 *NASDAQ: CPST* ■ *TF:* 866-422-7786 ■ *Web:* www.capstoneturbine.com	818-734-5300	734-5320	262
Capstone Underwriters LLC 4144 N Central Expy Ste 920, Dallas TX 75204 *Web:* capstoneunderwriters.com	214-520-1388		390
CAPT (Celina Aluminum Precision Technology Inc) 7059 Staeger Rd, Celina OH 45822 *Web:* www.capt-celina.com	419-586-2278	586-6474	621
Capt Harrys Fishing Supply Company Inc 8501 NW Seventh Ave, Miami FL 33150 *TF:* 800-327-4088 ■ *Web:* www.captharry.com	305-374-4661		711
Capt Hirams Resort 1580 US Hwy 1, Sebastian FL 32958 *Web:* www.hirams.com	772-589-4345	589-4346	379
Captain Bangs Hallett House 11 Strawberry Ln PO Box 11, Yarmouth Port MA 02675 *Web:* www.hsoy.org	508-362-3021		50-3
Captain Bijou PO Box 7307, Houston TX 77248 *Web:* www.captainbijou.com	713-864-8101		525
Captain Bill's Seafood Co 2701 Century Harbor Rd, Middleton WI 53562 *Web:* capbills.com	608-831-7327		671
Captain Brian's Seafood Market & Restaurant 8421 N Tamiami Trl, Sarasota FL 34243 *Web:* www.captainbriansseafood.com	941-351-4492		671
Captain D's LLC 624 Grassmere Park Dr Ste 30, Nashville TN 37211 *TF:* 800-314-4819 ■ *Web:* www.captainds.com	615-391-5461	231-2309	670
Captain Daniel Stone Inn 10 Water St, Brunswick ME 04011 *Web:* www.thedanielhotel.com	207-373-1824		379
Captain Fiddle Publications 94 Wiswall Rd, Lee NH 03861 *Web:* www.captainfiddle.com	603-659-2658		637-2
Captain George's 1401 29th Ave, Myrtle Beach SC 29577 *Web:* www.captaingeorges.com	843-916-2278		671
Captain Gosnold Village 230 Gosnold St, Hyannis MA 02601 *Web:* www.captaingosnold.com	508-775-9111		669
Captain Kens Foods Inc 344 Robert St S, Saint Paul MN 55107 *Web:* captainkens.com	651-298-0071		297-8
Captain Linnell House 137 Skaket Beach Rd, Orleans MA 02653 *Web:* www.linnell.com	508-255-3400		671
Captain Slates Atlantis Dive Ctr 90791 Overseas Hwy Ste 1, Tavernier FL 33070 *TF:* 800-331-3483 ■ *Web:* www.captainslate.com	305-451-3020		167-3
Captain's Cove Seaport 1 Bostwick Ave, Bridgeport CT 06605 *Web:* www.captainscoveseaport.com	203-335-1433		671
Captain's Tavern Restaurant Inc 9625 S Dixie Hwy, Miami FL 33156 *Web:* www.captainstavernmiami.com	305-666-5979		671
CaptainU LLC PO Box 40002, Denver CO 80204 *Web:* www.captainu.com	773-800-0476		387
CAPTE (Commission on Accreditation in Physical Therapy Education) 1111 N Fairfax St, Alexandria VA 22314 *Web:* www.capteonline.org	703-706-3245	838-8910	48-1
Captec Engineering Inc 301 NW Flagler Ave, Stuart FL 34994 *Web:* gocaptec.com	772-692-4344	692-4341	261
Captek Softgel Int'l Inc 16218 Arthur St, Cerritos CA 90703 *Web:* capteksoftgel.com	562-921-9511		583
CaptionMax Inc 2438 27th Ave S, Minneapolis MN 55406 *Web:* www.captionmax.com	612-341-3566		116
Captiv 8 102 W 38th St 5th Fl, New York NY 10018 *Web:* captiv8promos.com	212-473-2440	473-2739	129
Captive Fastener Corp 19 Thornton Rd, Oakland NJ 07436 *TF:* 800-526-4430 ■ *Web:* www.captive-fastener.com	201-337-6800	337-1012	278
Captive-aire Systems Inc 4641 Paragon Park Rd, Raleigh NC 27616 *TF:* 800-334-9256 ■ *Web:* www.captiveaire.com	919-882-2410	882-5204	697
Captools Co Tiger Mtn Prof Bldg 14401 Issaquah-Hobart Rd Ste 203, Issaquah WA 98027 *TF:* 800-826-8082 ■ *Web:* www.captools.com	425-391-4250	313-5647	177
Captree State Park PO Box 247, Babylon NY 11702 *Web:* parks.ny.gov	631-669-0449		565
Captrust 4208 Six Forks Rd Ste 1700, Raleigh NC 27609 *TF:* 800-216-0645 ■ *Web:* www.captrust.com	800-216-0645		401
Capulin Volcano National Monument 46 Volcano Rd, Capulin NM 88414 *Web:* www.nps.gov	505-278-2201		564
Caputo & Associates Inc 5580 Monroe St Ste 102, Sylvania OH 43560 *Web:* caputoagency.com	419-537-5588	537-1630	390
CapWealth Advisors LLC 3000 Meridian Blvd Ste 250, Franklin TN 37067 *Web:* capwealthgroup.com	615-778-0740		463
Car Care Council 7101 Wisconsin Ave, Bethesda MD 20814 *Web:* www.carcare.org	240-333-1088		49-21
Car City Motor Company Inc 3100 S US Hwy 169, Saint Joseph MO 64503 *TF:* 800-525-7008 ■ *Web:* carcitymotors.com	816-233-9149		57
Car Clinic Productions 5675 N Davis Hwy, Pensacola FL 32503 *TF:* 888-227-2546 ■ *Web:* www.carclinicnetwork.com	850-478-3139	477-0862	646
Car Parts Warehouse Inc 5200 W 130th St, Brook Park OH 44142 *Web:* carpartswarehouse.net	216-676-5100	676-5516	60
Car People Marketing Inc 3818 S Nova Rd Ste C, Port Orange FL 32127 *TF:* 866-227-7337 ■ *Web:* carpeoplemarketing.com	866-227-7337		195
Car Rental Reservation System 29 - 50778 Ledgestone Pl, Chilliwack BC V2P0E7 *TF:* 888-557-8188 ■ *Web:* www.agencies.carrentalexpress.com	604-714-5911		126
Car Rentals Inc 1570 S Washington Ave, Piscataway NJ 08854 *TF:* 888-230-9387 ■ *Web:* www.avisnj.com	732-752-6800		126
Car Toys Inc 400 Fairview Ave N Ste 900, Seattle WA 98109 *TF:* 888-227-8697 ■ *Web:* www.cartoys.com	888-227-8697		52
CARA Group 2215 York Rd Ste 300, Oak Brook IL 60523 *TF:* 866-401-2272 ■ *Web:* www.thecaragroup.com	866-401-2272		180
Carabin & Shaw Pc 630 Broadway, San Antonio TX 78215 *TF:* 800-862-1260 ■ *Web:* carabinshaw.com	210-222-2288	222-1480	41
Carahsoft Technology Corp 11493 Sunset Hills Rd Ste 100, Reston VA 20190 *TF:* 888-662-2724 ■ *Web:* www.carahsoft.com	703-871-8500	871-8505	225
Caramagno Foods Co 14255 Dequindre St, Detroit MI 48212 *Web:* www.caramagnofoods.com	313-869-8200		345
Caramba 5421 W Glendale Ave, Glendale AZ 85301 *Web:* carambamex.com	623-934-8888		671
Caramel Cookie Waffles 1707 17th St W, Billings MT 59102 *Web:* www.caramelcookiewaffles.com	406-252-1960		68
Caramoor Center for Music & The Arts Inc 149 Girdle Ridge Rd, Katonah NY 10536 *Web:* www.caramoor.org	914-232-5035		522
Carana Corp 4350 Fairfax Dr Ste 900, Arlington VA 22203 *Web:* www.carana.com	703-243-1700	243-0471	194
Caravan Facilities Management LLC 1400 Weiss St, Saginaw MI 48602 *TF:* 855-211-7450 ■ *Web:* www.caravanfm.com	855-211-7450		192
Caravelle Resort Hotel & Villas 6900 N Ocean Blvd, Myrtle Beach SC 29572 *TF:* 800-297-3413 ■ *Web:* www.thecaravelle.com	843-310-3420		669
Carbajal Law Firm PC, The 1180 Avenue of the Americas St, New York NY 10036 *Web:* globalbusinessattorney.com	212-382-4652		41
Carbajal Salud (Rep D - CA) 1431 Longworth House Office Bldg, Washington DC 20515 *Web:* carbajal.house.gov	202-225-3601		342-2
Carbide Grinding Inc 9317 Gamebird Ln, Houston TX 77034 *TF:* 844-325-2791 ■ *Web:* www.carbidegrinding.com	844-325-2791		143
Carbide Industries LLC 4400 Bells Ln, Louisville KY 40211 *TF:* 800-626-2578 ■ *Web:* www.carbidellc.com	502-775-4100	775-4107	440
Carbide Metals Inc 176 Cherry St, Blairsville PA 15717 *Web:* www.psicmi.com	724-459-6355		1
Carbide Probes Inc 1328 Research Park Dr, Dayton OH 45432 *Web:* www.carbideprobes.com	937-429-1235	429-2103	815
Carbide Products Inc 800 Clayton Ave, Georgetown KY 40324 *TF:* 877-863-2340 ■ *Web:* www.carbidepros.com	877-863-2340		493
Carbo Ceramics Inc 575 N Dairy Ashford Rd Ste 300, Houston TX 77079 *NYSE: CRR* ■ *TF:* 800-551-3247 ■ *Web:* www.carboceramics.com	281-921-6400		537
Carboline Co 350 Hanley Industrial Ct, Saint Louis MO 63144 *TF:* 800-848-4645 ■ *Web:* www.carboline.com	314-644-1000	644-4617	550

Phone Fax Class

Carbon County
2 Hazard Sq PO Box 129 .... Jim Thorpe PA 18229 570-325-3611 325-3622 338
TF: 800-441-1315 ■ *Web:* www.carboncounty.com

Carbon County PO Box 1017 .... Rawlins WY 82301 800-228-3547 338
TF: 800-228-3547 ■ *Web:* www.wyomingcarboncounty.com

Carbon Credit Capital LLC
561 Broadway Ste 6A .... New York NY 10012 212-925-5697 251
Web: www.carboncreditcapital.com

Carbon Medical Technologies Inc
1290 Hammond Rd .... Saint Paul MN 55110 651-653-8512 476
TF: 877-227-1788 ■ *Web:* www.carbonmed.com

Carbon Power & Light Inc
100 E Willow Ave PO Box 579 .... Saratoga WY 82331 307-326-5206 245
TF: 800-359-0249 ■ *Web:* www.carbonpower.com

Carbon Resources of Florida Inc
5206 Paylor Ln .... Sarasota FL 34240 941-747-2630 311
Web: www.carbonresourcesofflorida.com

Carbondale Chamber of Commerce
131 S Illinois Ave .... Carbondale IL 62901 618-549-2146 529-5063 139
Web: www.carbondalechamber.com

Carbondale Elementary School District 95
925 S Giant City Rd .... Carbondale IL 62902 618-457-3591 186
Web: www.ces95.org

Carbondale Public Library
405 W Main St .... Carbondale IL 62901 618-457-0354 457-0353 434-3
Web: carbondalepubliclibrary.org

Carbone Metal Fabricator Inc
240 Marginal St .... Chelsea MA 02150 617-884-0237 697
Web: www.cmfi.com

Carbone's Ristorante
588 Franklin Ave .... Hartford CT 06114 860-296-9646 671
Web: www.carbonesct.com

Carbonyx Inc 645 S Custer Rd Ste 300 .... Allen TX 75013 972-943-3355 127
Web: www.carbonyx.com

Carbro Corp
15724 Condon Ave PO Box 278 .... Lawndale CA 90260 310-643-8400 643-9703 493
TF: 888-738-4400 ■ *Web:* www.carbrousa.com

Carcinoid Cancer Foundation Inc
333 Mamaroneck Ave Ste 492 .... White Plains NY 10605 888-722-3132 683-1083* 48-17
**Fax Area Code:* 914 ■ *TF:* 888-722-3132 ■ *Web:* www.carcinoid.org

Carco Inc 10333 Shoemaker PO Box 13859 .... Detroit MI 48213 313-925-9000 925-9602 467
Web: www.carcousa.com

Carco International Inc
2721 Midland Blvd .... Fort Smith AR 72904 479-441-3270 274
TF: 800-824-3215 ■ *Web:* www.carcoint.com

Carco National Lease Inc
2905 N 32nd St .... Fort Smith AR 72904 479-441-3200 778
TF: 800-643-2596 ■ *Web:* carcotrans.com

Carcoustics USA Inc 1400 Durant Dr .... Howell MI 48843 517-548-6700 52
Web: www.carcoustics.com

Card Player Media LLC
6940 O'Bannon Dr Ste 8 .... Las Vegas NV 89117 702-871-1720 637-9
Web: www.cardplayer.com

Card USA Inc 201 N Ocean Dr 2nd Fl .... Hollywood FL 33019 954-862-1300 344
Web: www.cardusa.com

Cardaro & Peek LLC
201 N Charles St Ste 2100 .... Baltimore MD 21201 410-752-6166 752-6013 41
TF: 800-810-6780 ■ *Web:* cardarolaw.com

Cardenas Marketing Network Inc
1459 W Hubbard St .... Chicago IL 60642 312-492-6424 5
Web: cmnevents.com

Cardenas Markets Inc 2501 E Guasti Rd .... Ontario CA 91761 909-923-7426 345
Web: cardenasmarkets.com

Cardenas Tony (Rep D - CA)
2438 Rayburn House Office Bldg .... Washington DC 20515 202-225-6131 342-2
Web: www.cardenas.house.gov

Cardero's 1583 Coal Harbour Quay .... Vancouver BC V6G3E7 604-669-7666 671
Web: www.vancouverdine.com

Carderock Capital Management Inc
2 Wisconsin Cir Ste 600 .... Chevy Chase MD 20815 301-951-5288 401
Web: www.carderockcapital.com

Cardi Corp 400 Lincoln Ave .... Warwick RI 02888 401-739-8300 736-2977 188-4
Web: cardi.com

Cardi's Furniture 1 Furniture Way .... Swansea MA 02777 508-379-7510 321
Web: www.cardis.com

Cardiac Dimensions Inc
5540 Lake Washington Blvd NE .... Kirkland WA 98033 425-605-5900 475
Web: www.cardiacdimensions.com

Cardiac Science Corp
3303 Monte Villa Pkwy .... Bothell WA 98021 800-426-0337 402-2001* 250
**Fax Area Code:* 425 ■ *TF:* 800-426-0337 ■ *Web:* www.cardiacscience.com

CardiacAssist Inc 240 Alpha Dr .... Pittsburgh PA 15238 412-963-7770 476
TF: 800-373-1607 ■ *Web:* www.tandemlife.com

Cardiff Park Advisors
2257 Vista La Nisa .... Carlsbad CA 92009 760-635-7526 196
TF: 888-332-2238 ■ *Web:* www.cardiffpark.com

Cardigan Mountain School 62 Alumni Dr .... Canaan NH 03741 603-523-4321 622
Web: www.cardigan.org

Cardigan State Park
658 Cardigan Mtn Rd .... Orange NH 03741 603-227-8745 565
Web: www.nhstateparks.org

Cardillo Law Firm
2707 W Azeele St Ste 100 .... Tampa FL 33609 813-801-9050 41
Web: cardillolaw.com

Cardin Benjamin L (Sen D - MD)
509 Hart Senate Office Bldg .... Washington DC 20510 202-224-4524 342-2
Web: www.cardin.senate.gov

Cardinal / Detecto Scale
102 East Daugherty St .... Webb City MO 64870 417-673-4631 350
Web: www.cardinalscale.com

Cardinal Aluminum Co
6910 Preston Hwy .... Louisville KY 40219 502-969-9302 485
TF: 800-398-7833 ■ *Web:* cardinalaluminum.com

Cardinal Capital Management LLC
4 Greenwich Office Pk .... Greenwich CT 06831 203-863-8990 861-4112 401
Web: www.cardcap.com

Cardinal Carryor Inc 1055 Grade Ln .... Louisville KY 40213 502-363-6641 770
TF: 800-666-5600 ■ *Web:* www.cardinalcarryor.com

Cardinal Color Inc 50-56 First Ave .... Paterson NJ 07524 973-684-1919 684-0865 146
Web: www.cardinalcolor.com

Cardinal Construction Inc
1246 Martin Rd .... Waterloo IA 50701 319-232-5400 186
Web: cardinalconst.com

Cardinal Distributing Company LLC
269 Jackrabbit Ln .... Bozeman MT 59718 406-586-0241 587-1156 81-3
Web: www.cardinaldistributing.com

Cardinal Escrow
6615 E Pacific Coast Hwy Ste 240 .... Long Beach CA 90803 562-493-9393 652
Web: www.cardinalescrow.com

Cardinal Gates 79 Amlajack Way .... Newnan GA 30265 770-252-4200 64
TF: 800-318-3380 ■ *Web:* cardinalgates.com

Cardinal Glass Industries
775 Prairie Center Dr .... Eden Prairie MN 55344 952-229-2600 935-5538 329
Web: www.cardinalcorp.com

Cardinal Group Inc, The 406 King St E .... Toronto ON M5A1L4 416-971-4494 192
Web: cardinalgroup.ca

Cardinal Hayes High School
650 Grand Concourse .... Bronx NY 10451 718-292-6100 685
Web: www.cardinalhayes.org

Cardinal Health Inc 7000 Cardinal Pl .... Dublin OH 43017 614-757-5000 757-6000 360-3
NYSE: CAH ■ *TF:* 800-926-0834 ■ *Web:* www.cardinalhealth.com

Cardinal Hill Healthcare System
2050 Versailles Rd .... Lexington KY 40504 859-254-5701 374-6
Web: cardinalhill.org

Cardinal Homes Inc
525 Barnesville Hwy .... Wylliesburg VA 23976 434-735-8111 735-8824 106
Web: www.cardinalhomes.com

Cardinal Honda 531 Rt 12 .... Groton CT 06340 860-449-0411 57
Web: www.cardinalhonda.com

Cardinal Ice Equipment Inc
3311 Gilmore Industrial B .... Louisville KY 40213 502-966-4579 665
TF: 800-467-0448 ■ *Web:* iceguys.com

Cardinal Industries Inc
21-01 51st Ave .... Long Island City NY 11101 718-784-3000 482-7877 762
Web: www.cardinalgames.com

Cardinal Intl 43 RT 46 E Ste 70 .... Pine Brook NJ 07058 973-628-0900 633-5555 361
Web: www.cardinalfoodservice.com

Cardinal Logistics Management Corp
5333 Davidson Hwy .... Concord NC 28027 704-786-6125 788-6618 449
Web: www.cardlog.com

Cardinal Machine Co 860 Tacoma Ct .... Clio MI 48420 810-686-1190 494
Web: www.cardinalmachine.biz

Cardinal Machinery Inc
7535 Appling Center Dr .... Memphis TN 38133 901-377-3107 358
Web: www.cardinalmachinery.com

Cardinal Management Group
3704 Golf Trl Ln .... Fairfax VA 22033 703-591-1818 866-3156 652
TF: 800-356-3294 ■ *Web:* www.cardinalmanagementgroup.com

Cardinal Manufacturing Company Inc
225 Eiler Ave PO Box 14127 .... Louisville KY 40214 502-363-2661 363-5905 490
Web: www.cardinalmfg.com

Cardinal Meat Specialists Ltd
155 Hedgedale Rd .... Brampton ON L6T5P3 905-459-4436 297-9
TF: 800-363-1439 ■ *Web:* www.cardinalmeats.com

Cardinal O'hara High School
39 Ohara Rd .... Tonawanda NY 14150 716-695-2600 685
Web: www.cardinalohara.com

Cardinal Office Products Inc
576 E Main St .... Frankfort KY 40601 502-875-3300 539-4325* 534
**Fax Area Code:* 800 ■ *TF:* 800-589-5886 ■ *Web:* www.cardinaloffice.com

Cardinal Partners 230 Nassau St .... Princeton NJ 08542 609-924-6452 683-0174 792
Web: www.cardinalpartners.com

Cardinal Path LLC
301 W Warner Rd Ste 136 .... Tempe AZ 85284 480-285-1622 631
Web: www.cardinalpath.com

Cardinal Publishers Group (CPG)
2402 Shadeland Ave Ste A .... Indianapolis IN 46219 800-296-0481 96
TF: 800-296-0481 ■ *Web:* www.cardinalpub.com

Cardinal Ritter Senior Services
7601 Watson Rd .... Saint Louis MO 63119 314-961-8000 451
Web: www.ccstl.org

Cardinal Rubber Company Inc
939 Wooster Rd N .... Barberton OH 44203 330-745-2191 676
Web: www.cardinalrubbercompany.com

Cardinal Services Inc
1721 Indian Wood Cir A .... Maumee OH 43537 419-893-5400 893-8596 260
Web: www.cardinalstaffing.com

Cardinal Shoe Corp 468 Canal St .... Lawrence MA 01840 603-401-7557 301
Web: cardinalshoe.com

Cardinal Steel Supply Inc
6335 Mckissock Ave .... Saint Louis MO 63147 314-382-6500 382-4035 492
TF: 800-328-5150 ■ *Web:* cardinalsteel.com

Cardinal Stritch University
6801 N Yates Rd .... Milwaukee WI 53217 414-410-4000 166
TF: 800-347-8822 ■ *Web:* www.stritch.edu

Cardinal Transport Inc
7180 E Reed Rd .... Coal City IL 60416 815-634-4443 634-8267 780
TF: 800-435-9302 ■ *Web:* www.cardinaltransport.com

Cardinal Wealth Services Inc
8270 Greensboro Dr Ste 500 .... McLean VA 22102 703-584-3470 584-3471 401
Web: www.cardinalbank.com

CardioCommand Inc
4920 W Cypress St Ste 110 .... Tampa FL 33607 813-289-5555 289-5454 475
TF: 800-231-6370 ■ *Web:* www.cardiocommand.com

CardioFocus Inc
500 Nickerson Rd Ste 500-200 .... Marlborough MA 01752 508-658-7200 480-0600 476
Web: www.cardiofocus.com

Cardiogenesis Corp 11 Musick .... Irvine CA 92618 949-420-1800 250
Web: www.cryolife.com

CardioGenics Holdings Inc
6295 Northam Dr Unit 8 .... Mississauga ON L4V1W8 905-673-8501 419
Web: www.cardiogenics.com

CardioKinetix Inc 925 Hamilton Ave .... Menlo Park CA 94025 650-364-7016 364-7038 668
Web: www.cardiokinetix.com

CardioMed Supplies Inc
199 St David St .... Lindsay ON K9V5K7 705-328-2518 328-9747 475
TF: 800-387-9757 ■ *Web:* cardiomed.com

Company	Phone	Fax	Class
Cardiosolutions Inc 375 W St West Bridgewater MA 02379 *Web:* www.cardiosolutionsinc.com	781-344-0801		194
Cardiovascular Research Foundation 111 E 59th St New York NY 10022 *Web:* www.crf.org	646-434-4500		743
Cardiovascular Systems Inc 1225 Old H 8 NW Saint Paul MN 55112 *TF:* 877-274-0360 ■ *Web:* csi360.com	651-259-1600		476
CardLogix 16 Hughes Ste 100 Irvine CA 92618 *TF:* 866-392-8326 ■ *Web:* www.cardlogix.com	949-380-1312	380-1428	704
Cardlytics Inc 675 Ponce de Leon Ave NE Ste 6000 Atlanta GA 30308 *TF:* 888-798-5802 ■ *Web:* www.cardlytics.com	866-269-1020		5
Cardno ChemRisk 235 Pine St 23rd Fl San Francisco CA 94104 *Web:* www.cardnochemrisk.com	415-896-2400		463
Cardolite Corp 11 Deer Park Dr Ste 124 Monmouth Junction NJ 08852 **Fax Area Code:* 732 ■ *Web:* www.cardolite.com	609-436-0902	823-1063*	144
Cardon & Associates Inc 2749 E Covenanter Dr Bloomington IN 47401 *Web:* cardon.us	812-332-2265		463
Cardone Industries Inc 5501 Whitaker Ave Philadelphia PA 19124 **Fax Area Code:* 215 ■ *TF:* 800-777-4780 ■ *Web:* www.cardone.com	800-777-4304	912-3700*	60
CardScan Inc 25 1st St Ste 107 Cambridge MA 02141 *TF:* 800-942-6739 ■ *Web:* www.cardscan.com	617-492-4200		173-7
CardSmart Retail Corp 11 Executive Ave Edison NJ 08817 *TF:* 888-782-7050 ■ *Web:* www.cardsmart.com	800-654-6960		310
Cardtronics GP Inc 3110 Hayes Rd Ste 300 Houston TX 77082 *Web:* www.cardtronics.com	281-596-9988		225
Cardwell Group 24481 Detroit Rd Ste 300 Cleveland OH 44145 *Web:* www.connectionsonline.net	440-892-1410		196
Cardwell Printing & Advertising 15470 Warwick Blvd Newport News VA 23608 *Web:* cardwellprinting.com	757-888-0674		627
CARE (Coalition for Auto Repair Equality) 105 Oronoco St Ste 115 Alexandria VA 22314 *TF:* 800-229-5380 ■ *Web:* www.careauto.org	703-519-7555	519-7747	49-21
Care 1st Health Plan Inc 601 Potrero Grande Dr 2nd Fl Monterey Park CA 91755 *Web:* www.care1st.com	323-889-6638	889-6255	391-3
Care Center of Honolulu, The 1900 Bachelot St Honolulu HI 96817 *TF:* 844-421-7023 ■ *Web:* www.ccoh.us	844-421-7023		371
Care Choice Home Health 7840 Lincoln Ave Ste 103 Skokie IL 60077 *Web:* carechoicehomehealth.com	847-329-0648	329-0360	363
Care Edge, The 5151 Bonney Rd Virginia Beach VA 23462 *Web:* www.the-care-edge.net	757-769-7136		393
Care Finders Inc 754 Rte 18 N Ste 203 East Brunswick NJ 08816 *Web:* carefinders.org	732-390-1630	390-1639	260
Care Force 5801 NW 151 St Ste 304 Miami Lakes FL 33014 *Web:* careforceinc.net	305-362-4980	362-4981	363
Care Hope College 901 N Congress Ave Ste C-201 Boynton Beach FL 33426 *Web:* www.chcollege.org	561-966-0551	965-7948	167-3
Care Industries Inc 27312-68 Twp Rd 394 Blackfalds AB T0M0J0 *Web:* www.careindustries.ca	403-885-5442		538
Care One Home Health Services 2660 44th St SW Ste 500 Wyoming MI 49519 *Web:* www.careonehhs.com	616-719-4440	719-4406	363
Care Partners 68 Sweeten Creek Rd Asheville NC 28803 *TF:* 800-627-1533 ■ *Web:* missionhealth.org	828-274-6151		363
Care Pet Inc 785 E Main St Columbus OH 43205 *Web:* carepetclinic.com	614-252-4353		794
Care Resources Inc 1026 Cromwell Bridge Rd Towson MD 21286	410-583-1515		260
Care Solutions Inc 176 E Main St Ste 1 Westborough MA 01581 *Web:* homecaresolutionsma.com	508-366-1766		363
Care Systems Inc 1 Research Crt Ste 120 Rockville MD 20850 **Fax Area Code:* 301 ■ *Web:* www.caresystemsinc.com	240-404-0355	987-7423*	194
Care Training Ctr 142 Temple St Ste 303 New Haven CT 06510 *TF:* 877-227-3524 ■ *Web:* www.care-ct.com	203-782-0055	782-0059	167-3
CARE USA 151 Ellis St NE Atlanta GA 30303 *TF:* 800-521-2273 ■ *Web:* www.care.org	404-681-2552	577-5977	48-5
Care Wise LabLogic Systems Inc 1911 N US Hwy 301 Ste 140 Tampa FL 33619 *Web:* carewise.com	813-626-6848		45
Care Zone Inc 1463 E Republican St Ste 198 Seattle WA 98112 *TF:* 888-407-7785 ■ *Web:* www.carezone.com	888-407-7785		387
Care/of 75 Varick St 9th Fl New York NY 10013 *TF:* 877-227-3631 ■ *Web:* takecareof.com	877-227-3631		459
Careage Inc 4411 Point Fosdick Dr NW Gig Harbor WA 98335 *Web:* www.careage.com	253-853-4457	853-5280	186
Care-A-Lot Pet Supply 1617 Diamond Springs Rd Virginia Beach VA 23455 **Fax Area Code:* 866 ■ *TF:* 800-343-7680 ■ *Web:* www.carealotpets.com	757-460-9771	379-3604*	45
CareCentric Inc 20 Church St 12th Fl Hartford CT 06103 *TF:* 800-808-1902 ■ *Web:* www.carecentrix.com	800-808-1902		178-10
Carecycle Solutions LLC 17480 Dallas Pkwy Dallas TX 75287 *TF:* 866-345-4343	214-698-0600		363
Career Academy Inc 160 Gould St Ste 208 Needham MA 02494 *TF:* 800-538-9193 ■ *Web:* www.careeracademy.com	781-453-3900		167-3
Career Academy of Beauty 12471 Valley View St Garden Grove CA 92845 *Web:* www.caofb.com	714-897-3010		167-3
Career Academy of Hair Design 346 E Robinson Ave Springdale AR 72764 *TF:* 866-845-1618 ■ *Web:* www.beautynwa.com	479-756-6060		167-3
Career Care Institute 2151 Alessandro Dr Ste 150 Ventura CA 93001 *Web:* www.ccicolleges.edu	805-477-0660		166
Career Choices 59 South 100 East Saint George UT 84770 **Fax Area Code:* 800 ■ *TF:* 800-967-8016 ■ *Web:* www.careerchoices.com	435-673-0843	967-4027*	167-3
Career College Assn (CCA) 1101 Connecticut Ave NW Ste 900 Washington DC 20036 *Web:* www.career.org	202-336-6700		49-5
Career College of Northern Nevada 1421 Pullman Dr Sparks NV 89434 *Web:* www.ccnn.edu	775-856-2266		166
Career Exposure Inc 805 SW Broadway Portland OR 97205 *Web:* www.careerexposure.com	503-221-7779		260
Career Foundations Inc 4011 Westchase Blvd Ste 200 Raleigh NC 27607 *Web:* careerfoundations.com	919-828-1000		260
Career Networks Institute 702 W Town and Country Rd Orange CA 92868 **Fax Area Code:* 714 ■ *TF:* 888-976-5120 ■ *Web:* www.cnicollege.edu	888-976-5120	437-9356*	167-3
Career Solutions International Inc 400 Lexington Green Ln Sanford FL 32771 *TF:* 866-484-4752 ■ *Web:* csigroup.net	407-688-6727		260
Career Step LLC 4692 N 300 W Ste 150 Provo UT 84604 *TF:* 800-246-7837 ■ *Web:* www.careerstep.com	801-489-9393		764
Career Team LLC 3580 Main St Hartford CT 06120 *Web:* careerteam.com	203-407-8800	407-8801	41
Career Training Academy 4314 Old William Penn Hwy Ste 103 Monroeville PA 15146 *TF:* 866-673-7773 ■ *Web:* www.careerta.edu	412-206-5514		167-3
CareerBoard LLC 23245 Mercantile Rd Beachwood OH 44122 *Web:* www.careerboard.com	216-781-5311	595-3688	260
CareerBuilder Employment Screening LLC Atrium Corporate Ctr 3800 Golf Rd Ste 120 Rolling Meadows IL 60008 *TF:* 866-255-1852 ■ *Web:* screen.careerbuilder.com	866-255-1852		400
CareerBuilder Inc 200 N LaSalle St Ste 1100 Chicago IL 60601 *Web:* www.careerbuilder.com	773-527-3600		395
CareerCurve LLC 5005 Rockside Rd Ste 600-076 Cleveland OH 44131 **Fax Area Code:* 440 ■ *TF:* 800-314-8230 ■ *Web:* www.careercurve.com	800-314-8230	423-0997*	41
Careerpros LLC 2065 Holliday Dr Dubuque IA 52002 *Web:* careerpros.com	563-556-3040	556-3041	41
Careers Express Inc 234 Mall Blvd Ste 120 King of Prussia PA 19406 *Web:* careersexpress.com	610-768-1788	768-1789	631
Careers Inc 208 Ave Ponce De Leon Ste 1100 San Juan PR 00918 *Web:* careersincpr.com	787-764-2298		463
Careers The Next Generation Foundation 18256-102 Ave NW Edmonton AB T5S1S7 *TF:* 888-757-7172 ■ *Web:* www.careersnextgen.ca	780-426-3414		305
careerSMITH Inc 537 Newport Center Dr Ste 364 Newport Beach CA 92660 *Web:* www.careersmith.com	949-760-8666		260
CareerSource Flagler Volusia 359 Bill France Blvd Daytona Beach FL 32114 *TF:* 800-476-7574 ■ *Web:* www.careersourcefv.com	386-323-7001		260
CareerSource Polk 500 E Lake Howard Dr Winter Haven FL 33881 *Web:* www.careersourcepolk.com	863-508-1100		260
CareerStaff Unlimited Inc 6363 N State Hwy 161 Ste 100 Irving TX 75038 *TF:* 888-993-4599 ■ *Web:* www.careerstaff.com	972-812-3200		721
CareEvolution Inc 320 Miller Ave Ste 195 Ann Arbor MI 48104 *Web:* www.careevolution.com	734-678-4788		177
CareFirst Inc 10455 Mill Run Cir Owings Mills MD 21117 *Web:* www.carefirst.com	410-581-3000		390
Carefirst Seniors & Community Services Assn 3601 Victoria Park Ave Scarborough ON M1W3Y3 *TF:* 800-268-7708 ■ *Web:* carefirstontario.ca	416-502-2323		138
CareFlite 3110 S Great SW Pkwy Grand Prairie TX 75052 *Web:* www.careflite.org	972-339-4200		30
Careforde Inc 233 S Wacker Dr Ste 8400 Chicago IL 60606 *TF:* 800-830-4050 ■ *Web:* www.careforde.com	800-830-4050		475
Carefree of Colorado 2145 W 6th Ave Broomfield CO 80020 *Web:* www.carefreeofcolorado.com	303-469-3324		733
Carefree Resort & Conference Ctr 37220 Mule Train Rd Carefree AZ 85377 *TF:* 888-692-4343 ■ *Web:* www.civanacarefree.com	888-692-4343		707
Carefree Vacations Inc 11885 Carmel Mountain Rd Ste 906 San Diego CA 92128 *TF:* 800-266-3476 ■ *Web:* www.carefreevacations.com	800-795-0720		771
Careful Courier Service Inc PO Box 51118 Palo Alto CA 94306 **Fax Area Code:* 628 ■ *Web:* carefulcourier.com	650-903-9393	239-0194*	546
Caregivers Home Health Service 431 Park Ave Falls Church VA 22046 *Web:* www.caregivershhs.com	703-532-6210	532-6718	363
CareGo Holdings Inc 3600 Dundas St Ste 300 Burlington ON L7M4B8 *Web:* carego.com	905-592-4900	336-9429	314
CareGroup Inc 109 Brookline Ave Ste 300 Boston MA 02215 *Web:* www.caregroup.org	617-667-1715		353
CAREington Intl 7400 Gaylord Pky Frisco TX 75034 **Fax Area Code:* 800 ■ *TF:* 800-441-0380 ■ *Web:* www.careington.com	972-335-6970	247-4450*	352
Carelinc Medical Equipment & Supply Company LLC 89 - 54th St SW Grand Rapids MI 49548 *Web:* www.carelincmed.com	616-249-2273		363
Carelink Inc 25 S Tyson Ave Floral Park NY 11001 *TF:* 888-665-1526 ■ *Web:* carelinkhomecareny.com	888-665-1526		363
Carelli's of Boulder 645 30th St Boulder CO 80303 *Web:* carellis.com	303-938-9300		671

Name / Address	City	State	Zip	Phone	Fax	Class
Caremark Rx Inc PO Box 832407 *TF:* 877-460-7766 ■ *Web:* www.caremark.com	Richardson	TX	75083	877-460-7766		586
Carenbauer Distributing Corp 1900 Jacob St	Wheeling	WV	26003	304-232-3000		81-1
Carenet Healthcare Services 11845 I-10 W Ste 400 *TF:* 800-809-7000 ■ *Web:* carenethealthcare.com	San Antonio	TX	78230	800-809-7000		393
CareOne at Concord 57 Old Rd to Nine Acre Cor *TF:* 855-277-8550 ■ *Web:* ma.care-one.com	Concord	MA	01742	855-277-8550		450
CareOne at Newton 2101 Washington St *TF:* 877-992-2731 ■ *Web:* ma.care-one.com	Newton	MA	02462	617-969-4660	928-0737	450
CareOne At Valley 300 Old Hook Rd *Web:* www.care-one.com	Westwood	NJ	07675	201-664-8888		450
CarePartners Home Care & Hospice and Solace Ctr 68 Sweeten Creek Rd *Web:* missionhealth.org	Asheville	NC	28813	828-255-0231	255-2944	371
CarePlus Health Plans Inc 11430 NW 20th St Ste 300 *TF:* 855-605-6171 ■ *Web:* www.care-plus-health-plans.com	Doral	FL	33172	855-605-6171		391-3
CarePoint Health 10 Exchange Pl 15th Fl *Web:* www.carepointhealth.org	Jersey City	NJ	07302	201-884-5329		374-3
Carepoint Health Inc 7324 SW Fwy **Fax Area Code:* 832 ■ *TF:* 888-436-5261 ■ *Web:* www.carepointus.com	Houston	TX	77074	713-771-7990	218-0050*	352
Carepoint Inc 215 E Bay St Ste 304 *TF:* 800-296-1825 ■ *Web:* www.carepoint.com	Charleston	SC	29401	843-853-6999		237
Carepro Health Services 1014 5th Ave SE *TF:* 800-575-8810 ■ *Web:* careprohs.com	Cedar Rapids	IA	52403	800-575-8810		194
Caresoft Inc 220 Lincoln Blvd Ste 300 *Web:* caresoftinc.com	Middlesex	NJ	08846	732-248-7825		177
CareSource 230 N Main St *TF:* 800-488-0134 ■ *Web:* www.caresource.com	Dayton	OH	45402	937-224-3300		352
CareStack 2954 Mallory Cir Ste 209 *Web:* www.carestack.com	Kissimmee	FL	34747	407-833-6123		178-8
Carestar Inc 5566 Cheviot Rd *Web:* carestar.com	Cincinnati	OH	45247	513-618-8300		363
Carestream Health 150 Verona St *TF:* 888-777-2072 ■ *Web:* www.carestream.com	Rochester	NY	14608	585-627-1800		476
CAREstream Medical Ltd 20133 102 Ave Units 1 *TF:* 888-310-2186 ■ *Web:* carestreammedical.com	Langley	BC	V1M4B4	888-310-2186	310-2187	475
Care-Tech Laboratories Inc 3224 S Kingshighway Blvd *TF:* 800-325-9681 ■ *Web:* www.caretechlabs.com	Saint Louis	MO	63139	314-772-4610	772-4613	582
CareTrust Publications LLC PO Box 10283 **Fax Area Code:* 415 ■ *TF:* 800-565-1533 ■ *Web:* www.comfortofhome.com	Portland	OR	97296	800-565-1533	673-2205*	637-2
Caretti Inc 4590 Industrial Park Rd PO Box 331 *Web:* www.carettimasonry.com	Camp Hill	PA	17001	717-737-6759	737-6880	189-7
CareWatch Inc 3483 Satellite Blvd Ste 211 S *TF:* 800-901-2454 ■ *Web:* www.carewatch.com	Duluth	GA	30096	770-409-0244		177
CareWorks Technologies Ltd 5555 Glendon Ct *TF:* 800-669-9623 ■ *Web:* www.careworkstech.com	Dublin	OH	43016	800-669-9623		196
Carey & Hanna CPAS 1000 Town Center Dr Ste 200 *Web:* taxwealthplan.com	Oxnard	CA	93036	805-644-0697	981-0698	2
Carey Color Inc 6835 Ridge Rd *TF:* 800-555-3142 ■ *Web:* careyweb.com	Wadsworth	OH	44281	330-239-1835		195
Carey Digital 1718 Central Pkwy *TF:* 800-707-8071 ■ *Web:* www.careydigital.com	Cincinnati	OH	45214	513-241-5210	241-2205	781
Carey Executive Limousine 245 University Ave *TF:* 800-241-3943 ■ *Web:* www.careyatlanta.com	Atlanta	GA	30315	404-223-2000		441
Carey Hilliard's Restaurants 11111 Abercom St *Web:* careyhilliards.com	Savannah	GA	31419	912-925-3225		670
Carey International Inc 4530 Wisconsin Ave NW *TF:* 800-336-4646 ■ *Web:* www.carey.com	Washington	DC	20016	301-698-3900		441
Carey Poverello Federal Credit Union 201 N Vance St *Web:* careycu.com	Carey	OH	43316	419-396-6071		219
Carey Sales & Services Inc 3141-47 Frederick Ave *TF:* 800-848-7748 ■ *Web:* www.careysales.com	Baltimore	MD	21229	410-945-7878		35
Carey Theological College 5920 Iona Dr *TF:* 844-862-2739 ■ *Web:* carey-edu.ca	Vancouver	BC	V6T1J6	604-224-4308	224-5014	167-3
CARF (Commission on Accreditation of Rehabilitation Facilities Intl) 6951 E Southpoint Rd *TF:* 888-281-6531 ■ *Web:* www.carf.org	Tucson	AZ	85756	520-325-1044	318-1129	48-1
Carfair Composites 837 Cedar St *Web:* carfaircomposites.com	Wausaukee	WI	54177	715-856-6321	856-5567	608
Cargill Associates Inc 4701 Altamesa Blvd *Web:* www.cargillassociates.com	Fort Worth	TX	76133	817-292-9374		317
Cargill Energy PO Box 9300 *TF:* 800-227-4455 ■ *Web:* www.cargill.com	Minneapolis	MN	55440	800-227-4455		579
Cargill Ltd 300-240 Graham Ave PO Box 5900 *Web:* www.cargillag.ca	Winnipeg	MB	R3C4C5	204-947-0141	947-6444	275
Cargille-Sacher Laboratories Inc 55 Commerce Rd *Web:* www.cargille.com	Cedar Grove	NJ	07009	973-239-6633	239-6096	419
Cargo Airline Assn 1620 L St NW Ste 610 *Web:* www.cargoair.org	Washington	DC	20036	202-293-1030		49-21
Cargo Carriers PO Box 5608 *Web:* www.ccibarge.com	Minneapolis	MN	55440	952-742-6763	742-1021	637-10
Cargo Control USA Inc PO Box 2806 *TF:* 888-775-5059 ■ *Web:* www.cargocontrolusa.com	Sanford	NC	27331	919-775-5059	718-1599	366
Cargo Equipment Corp 13700 George Bush Ct *Web:* www.cargoequipmentcorp.com	Huntley	IL	60142	847-741-7272		770
Cargo Management Systems LLC 827 E Main St *TF:* 855-484-9235 ■ *Web:* www.cmscargo.com	Richmond	KY	40475	855-484-9235		195
Cargo Network Services Corp 703 Waterford Way Ste 680 *Web:* www.cnsc.net	Miami	FL	33126	786-413-1000	413-1005	393
Cargo Pacific Logistics 800 Mark St *Web:* www.cargopacificlogistics.com	Elk Grove Village	IL	60007	847-750-1230		314
Cargo Solution Express Inc 14589 Valley Blvd *TF:* 800-582-5014 ■ *Web:* www.cargosolutionexpress.com	Fontana	CA	92335	909-350-1644		449
Cargo Transport Logistics Inc 6055 E Washington Blvd Ste 110 *Web:* safer.fmcsa.dot.gov	Commerce	CA	90040	323-887-8603	722-4254	311
Cargo Transporters Inc 3390 N Oxford St PO Box 850 *Web:* www.cargotransporters.com	Claremont	NC	28610	828-459-3282		780
Carhartt Inc 5750 Mercury Dr *TF:* 800-833-3118 ■ *Web:* www.carhartt.com	Dearborn	MI	48126	313-271-8460		155-19
Caribbean Gardens 1590 Goodlette-Frank Rd *Web:* napleszoo.org	Naples	FL	34102	239-262-5409	262-6866	823
Caribbean Jack's 721 Ballough Rd *Web:* www.caribbeanjacks.com	Daytona Beach	FL	32114	386-523-3000	252-7362	671
Caribbean Products Ltd 3624 Falls Rd *TF:* 888-689-5068 ■ *Web:* caribbeanproductsltd.com	Baltimore	MD	21211	888-689-5068		296-26
Caribbean Resort & Villas 3000 N Ocean Blvd *TF:* 800-552-8509 ■ *Web:* www.caribbeanresort.com	Myrtle Beach	SC	29577	800-552-8509		669
Caribbean Tourism Organization 80 Broad St 32nd Fl *Web:* www.onecaribbean.org	New York	NY	10004	212-635-9530	635-9511	775
Caribbean Travel & Life Magazine 460 N Orlando Ave Ste 200 *Web:* www.bonniercorp.com	Winter Park	FL	32789	407-628-4802	628-7061	457-22
Caribe Federal Credit Union 195 Oneil St *Web:* www.caribefederal.com	San Juan	PR	00918	787-474-5151		219
Caribe Hilton 1 San Geronimo St *Web:* www.caribehilton.com	San Juan	PR	00901	787-721-0303	725-8849	669
Cariboo Regional District 180 N Third Ave Ste D *TF:* 800-665-1636 ■ *Web:* cariboord.bc.ca	Williams Lake	BC	V2G2A4	250-392-3351		435
Caribou Coffee Company Inc 3900 Lakebreeze Ave N *NASDAQ: CBOU* ■ *TF:* 888-227-4268 ■ *Web:* www.cariboucoffee.com	Minneapolis	MN	55429	763-592-2200	592-2300	159
Caribou County 159 S Main *Web:* www.cariboucounty.us	Soda Springs	ID	83276	208-547-4324	547-4759	338
Caribou Highlands Lodge 371 Ski Hill Rd *TF:* 800-642-6036 ■ *Web:* odysseyresorts.com	Lutsen	MN	55612	218-663-7241		669
Caribou Road Services Ltd 5110 52nd Ave *TF:* 800-667-2322 ■ *Web:* www.caribouroads.com	Pouce Coupe	BC	V0C2C0	250-786-5440		261
Caridad & Louie's Restaurant 187 S Broadway *Web:* www.caridadlouiesyonkers.com	Yonkers	NY	10701	914-375-9777		671
Carilion Clinic 102 Highland Ave SE *Web:* www.carilionclinic.org	Roanoke	VA	24013	540-985-8032		353
Carillon ERP 13601 Preston Rd Ste E300 *Web:* carillonerp.com	Dallas	TX	75240	972-437-2230		177
Carillon Group Inc 641 Cepi Dr *Web:* carillongroup.com	Chesterfield	MO	63005	636-777-7001		390
Carillon Historical Park 1000 Carillon Blvd *Web:* www.daytonhistory.org	Dayton	OH	45409	937-293-2841		520
Carillon Properties 4100 Carillon Point *Web:* www.carillon-point.com	Kirkland	WA	98033	425-822-1700	828-3094	655
Carina Lounge 410 NW 21st Ave *Web:* www.carinalounge.com	Portland	OR	97209	503-274-1572		671
Carina Technology Inc 2366 Whitesburg Dr *TF:* 866-915-5464 ■ *Web:* www.carinatek.com	Huntsville	AL	35801	256-704-0422		177
Carinet 8929 Complex Dr *TF:* 888-221-5902 ■ *Web:* www.cari.net	San Diego	CA	92123	858-974-5080		396
Caring Choice Network Inc 23800 W Ten Mile Rd Ste 155 *Web:* www.caringchoicenetwork.com	Southfield	MI	48033	248-356-7525	356-7522	363
Caring Hands Animal Hospital of Arlington LLC 5659 Stone Rd *Web:* caringhandsvet.com	Centreville	VA	20120	703-830-5700		794
Caring Hands Veterinary Hospital 1020 E Avenida De Los Arboles *Web:* caringhandsvethosp.com	Thousand Oaks	CA	91360	805-492-4951		794
Caring Home Health 2515 N Belt Line Rd *Web:* www.caringhomehealth.net	Sunnyvale	TX	75182	972-226-2929	226-1141	363
Caring House Inc 2625 Pickett Rd *Web:* www.caringhouse.com	Durham	NC	27705	919-490-5449		372
Caring Nature LLC 237 E Aurora St *Web:* caringnaturedispensary.com	Waterbury	CT	06708	203-437-8477	437-8621	237
Caring Professionals Home Care Inc 3456 W Peterson Ave *Web:* cphcinc.com	Chicago	IL	60659	773-588-5700		363
Caringo Inc 6801 N Capital of Texas Hwy Bldg 2 Ste 200 *Web:* www.caringo.com	Austin	TX	78731	512-782-4490		177
Carino's Italian 150 Cascade Mall Dr *Web:* www.carinos.com	Burlington	WA	98233	360-757-4535		670

Name / Address	City	State	ZIP	Phone	Fax	Class
Carithers Wallace Courtenay Co 4343 NE Expy *TF:* 800-292-8220 ■ *Web:* www.c-w-c.com	Atlanta	GA	30340	770-493-8200	491-6374	320
Carl Albert State College 1507 S McKenna *Web:* www.carlalbert.edu	Poteau	OK	74953	918-647-1300		162
Carl Belt Inc 11521 Milnor Ave PO Box 1210 *TF:* 888-729-1616 ■ *Web:* www.thebeltgroup.com	Cumberland	MD	21502	301-729-8900		186
Carl Bloom Associates Inc 81 Main St Ste 126 *Web:* carlbloom.com	White Plains	NY	10601	914-761-2800	761-2744	5
Carl Bolander & Sons Company Inc 251 Starkey St *Web:* bolander.com	Saint Paul	MN	55107	651-224-6299		189-5
Carl Buddig & Co 950 175th St *TF:* 888-633-5684 ■ *Web:* www.buddig.com	Homewood	IL	60430	708-798-0900	798-1284	296-26
Carl Diebold Lumber Co 725 NW Dunbar Ave *Web:* dieboldlumber.com	Troutdale	OR	97060	503-669-8226		683
Carl E. Mellen & Co 601 W Greenwood Ave *Web:* www.carlmellen.com	Waukegan	IL	60087	847-244-3500		390
Carl Elliott Regional Library 98 E 18th St *Web:* www.youseemore.com	Jasper	AL	35501	205-221-2568		434-3
Carl Fischer 48 Wall St 28th Fl *Web:* www.carlfischer.com	New York	NY	10005	212-777-0900	477-6996	637-7
Carl Group Inc 282 Dry Creek Rd *Web:* www.thecarlgroup.com	Aptos	CA	95003	831-708-2610		177
Carl Marks Advisory Group LLC 900 3rd Ave 33rd Fl *Web:* www.carlmarks.com	New York	NY	10022	212-909-8400		690
Carl Nelson Insurance Agency I 1519 N 11th Ave *TF:* 800-582-4264 ■ *Web:* carlnelsonins.com	Hanford	CA	93230	559-584-4495		390
Carl Rittberger Sr Inc 1900 Lutz Ln *Web:* www.rittbergers.com	Zanesville	OH	43701	740-452-2767		473
Carl Rosenberry & Sons Lumber Inc 7446 Path Valley Rd *Web:* rosenberrylumber.com	Fort Loudon	PA	17224	717-349-2289		448
Carl Sandburg College 2400 Tom L Wilson Blvd *TF:* 877-236-1862 ■ *Web:* www.sandburg.edu	Galesburg	IL	61401	309-344-2518	344-3291	162
Carl Sandburg Home National Historic Site 81 Carl Sadburg Ln *Web:* www.nps.gov	Flat Rock	NC	28731	828-693-4178	693-4179	564
Carl Sandburg Jr High School 2600 Martin Ln *Web:* www.ccsd15.net	Rolling Meadows	IL	60008	847-963-7800		685
Carl Vinson Veterans Affairs Medical Ctr 1826 Veterans Blvd *TF:* 800-595-5229 ■ *Web:* va.gov	Dublin	GA	31021	478-272-1210		374-8
Carl Warren & Co 17862 E 17th St Ste 111 **Fax Area Code:* 866 ■ *Web:* www.carlwarren.com	Tustin	CA	92780	657-622-4200	254-4423*	390
Carl Zeiss Canada Ltd 45 Valleybrook D *Web:* www.zeiss.ca	Toronto	ON	M3B2S6	416-449-4660	449-0641	475
Carl Zeiss Inc 1 Zeiss Dr *TF:* 800-233-2343 ■ *Web:* www.zeiss.com	Thornwood	NY	10594	914-747-1800	681-7446	544
Carl's Golfland Inc 1976 S Telegraph Rd *TF:* 877-412-2757 ■ *Web:* www.carlsgolfland.com	Bloomfield Hills	MI	48302	248-335-8095		711
Carla's Pasta Inc 50 Talbot Ln *Web:* www.carlaspasta.com	South Windsor	CT	06074	860-436-4042		296-31
Carle Foundation Hospital 611 W Park St *Web:* carle.org	Urbana	IL	61801	217-383-3311	383-3137	374-3
Carle, Mackie, Power & Ross LLP 100 B St Ste 400 *Web:* cmprlaw.com	Santa Rosa	CA	95401	707-526-4200		41
Carleen Bright Arboretum 9001 Bosque Blvd *Web:* www.woodway-texas.com	Woodway	TX	76712	254-399-9204	772-6092	97
Carlen Controls Inc 6560 Commonwealth Dr *Web:* carlencontrols.com	Roanoke	VA	24018	540-772-1736	772-1737	472
Carleton College 100 S College St *TF:* 800-995-2275 ■ *Web:* www.carleton.edu	Northfield	MN	55057	507-222-4000		166
Carleton Insurance Agency 383 Kings Hwy N *Web:* www.carletoninsurance.com	Cherry Hill	NJ	08034	856-482-6200		390
Carleton Life Support Systems Inc 2734 Hickory Grove Rd *Web:* www.cobham.com	Davenport	IA	52804	563-383-6000	383-6430	22
Carleton University 1125 Colonel By Dr *TF:* 888-354-4414 ■ *Web:* carleton.ca	Ottawa	ON	K1S5B6	613-520-7400	520-3847	785
Norman Paterson School of International Affairs 5306 River Bldg 1125 Colonel By Dr *Web:* www.carleton.ca	Ottawa	ON	K1S5B6	613-520-6655	520-2889	167-3
Carleton-Willard Village (CWV) 100 Old Billerica Rd *Web:* www.cwvillage.org	Bedford	MA	01730	781-275-8700	275-5787	672
Carlex Glass Co 77 Excellence Way *Web:* carlex.com	Vonore	TN	37885	423-884-1105		330
Carley Foundry Inc 8301 Coral Sea St NE *Web:* www.carleyfoundry.com	Blaine	MN	55449	763-780-5123		492
Carley Lamps Inc 1502 W 228th St *Web:* carleylamps.com	Torrance	CA	90501	310-325-8474	534-2912	437
Carlie C's IGA Inc 10 Carlie C'S Dr *Web:* carliecs.com	Dunn	NC	28334	910-892-4124		297-8
Carlile Macy 15 3rd St *Web:* www.carlilemacy.com	Santa Rosa	CA	95403	707-542-6451		256
Carlile Patchen & Murphy LLP 366 E Broad St *Web:* www.cpmlaw.com	Columbus	OH	43215	614-228-6135	221-0216	428
Carlile Transportation Systems 1800 E 1st Ave *TF:* 800-478-1853 ■ *Web:* www.carlile.biz	Anchorage	AK	99501	907-276-7797	278-7301	780
Carlin & Buchsbaum LLP 555 E Ocean Blvd Ste 818 *TF:* 866-915-3589 ■ *Web:* workdiscriminationlawyer.com	Long Beach	CA	90802	562-432-8933	435-1656	41
Carlin Manufacturing Inc 466 W Fallbrook Ave Ste 106 *Web:* www.carlinmfg.com	Fresno	CA	93711	559-276-0123	222-1538	488
Carlin Systems Inc 31 Floyds Run *TF:* 800-222-2717 ■ *Web:* www.carlinsystems.com	Bohemia	NY	11716	631-471-2000	471-2109	246
Carling Technologies Inc 60 Johnson Ave *Web:* www.carlingtech.com	Plainville	CT	06062	860-793-9281	793-9231	815
Carlinville Primary School 18456 Shipman Rd *Web:* www.cusd1.com	Carlinville	IL	62626	217-854-9823		685
Carlisle & Company Inc 30 Monument Sq Ste 225 *Web:* www.carlisle-co.com	Concord	MA	01742	978-318-0500		194
Carlisle & Finch Co, The 4562 W Mitchell Ave *TF:* 800-828-3186 ■ *Web:* carlislefinch.com	Cincinnati	OH	45232	513-681-6080	681-6226	439
Carlisle Brake & Friction 6180 Cochran Rd *TF:* 800-873-6361 ■ *Web:* www.carlislecbf.com	Solon	OH	44139	440-528-4000	528-4099	60
Carlisle Companies Inc 16430 N Scottsdale Rd Ste 400 *NYSE: CSL* ■ **Fax Area Code:* 602 ■ *Web:* www.carlisle.com	Scottsdale	AZ	85254	480-781-5000	313-4300*	60
Carlisle Corp 263 Wagner Pl *Web:* www.carlislecorp.com	Memphis	TN	38103	901-526-5000		653
Carlisle County PO Box 279 *Web:* www.carlislecountyclerk.com	Bardwell	KY	42023	270-628-5451	628-0191	338
Carlisle Energy Group 104 Ridona St *Web:* www.ceg-usa.com	LaFayette	LA	70508	337-237-4941		539
Carlisle FoodService Products Inc 4711 E Hefner Rd *TF:* 800-654-8210 ■ *Web:* www.carlislefsp.com	Oklahoma City	OK	73131	405-475-5600	475-5607	300
Carlisle Interconnect Technologies 7911 S 188th St Ste 100 *TF:* 800-458-9960 ■ *Web:* www.carlisleit.com	Kent	WA	98032	425-251-0700	251-8826	815
Carlisle Medical Inc 501 Boulevard Pk E **Fax Area Code:* 800 ■ *TF:* 800-553-1783 ■ *Web:* www.carlislemedical.com	Mobile	AL	36609	251-344-7988	488-8543*	475
Carlisle Plastics Co 320 S Ohio Ave *Web:* www.carlisleplastics.com	New Carlisle	OH	45344	937-845-9411		596
Carlisle Productions Inc 1000 Bryn Mawr Rd *Web:* www.carlisleevents.com	Carlisle	PA	17013	717-243-7855		184
Carlisle SynTec 1285 Ritner Hwy PO Box 7000 **Fax Area Code:* 717 ■ *TF:* 800-479-6832 ■ *Web:* www.carlislesyntec.com	Carlisle	PA	17013	800-479-6832	245-7053*	191-4
Carlisle Tax Credit Advisors 263 Summer St 6th Fl *Web:* www.carlisletaxcredits.com	Boston	MA	02210	617-500-8620	500-9920	734
Carlisle Wide Plank Floors Inc 1676 Rt 9 *TF:* 800-595-9663 ■ *Web:* www.wideplankflooring.com	Stoddard	NH	03464	603-446-3937		364
Carlitos Gardel 7963 Melrose Ave *Web:* www.carlitosgardel.com	Los Angeles	CA	90046	323-655-0891		671
Carlo Gavazzi Inc 750 Hastings Ln *TF:* 800-222-2659 ■ *Web:* www.gavazzionline.com	Buffalo Grove	IL	60089	847-465-6100		729
Carlos & Pepe's 1420 Peel St *Web:* www.carlospepes.com	Montreal	QC	H3A1S8	514-288-3090		671
Carlos Brazilian International Cuisine 4167 Electric Rd SW *Web:* carlosbrazilian.com	Roanoke	VA	24018	540-776-1117		671
Carlow University 3333 5th Ave *TF:* 800-333-2275 ■ *Web:* www.carlow.edu	Pittsburgh	PA	15213	412-578-6000	578-6689	166
Carlsbad Chamber of Commerce 5934 Priestly Dr *Web:* www.carlsbad.org	Carlsbad	CA	92008	760-931-8400	931-9153	139
Carlsbad Chamber of Commerce 302 S Canal St *Web:* www.carlsbadchamber.com	Carlsbad	NM	88220	575-887-6516	885-1455	139
Carlsbad Current Argus 620 S Main St *Web:* static.currentargus.com	Carlsbad	NM	88220	575-887-5501		532-2
Carlsbad Medical Ctr 2430 W Pierce St *Web:* www.carlsbadmedicalcenter.com	Carlsbad	NM	88220	575-887-4100		374-3
Carlsbad State Beach c/o San Diego Coast District Ofc 4477 Pacific Hwy *Web:* www.parks.ca.gov	San Diego	CA	92110	760-438-3143		565
Carlsbad Strawberry Co 1205 Aviara Pky *Web:* www.carlsbadstrawberrycompany.com	Carlsbad	CA	92011	760-603-9608		297-7
Carlsbad Technology Inc 5922 Farnsworth Ct *Web:* carlsbadtech.com	Carlsbad	CA	92008	760-431-8284	448-4459	231
Carlsen & Assoc 1439 Grove St *Web:* carlsenassociates.com	Healdsburg	CA	95448	707-431-2000		297
Carlsen Resources 312 W Riverwoods Dr *Web:* www.carlsenresources.com	New Hope	PA	18938	970-242-9462		193
Carlsmith Ball LLP 1001 Bishop St Ste 2100 *Web:* www.carlsmith.com	Honolulu	HI	96813	808-523-2500	523-0842	428
Carlson						
Radisson Blu Hotels & Resorts 701 Carlson Pkwy *Web:* www.carlson.com	Minnetonka	MN	55305	763-762-2222		379
Carlson & Messer LLP 5901 W Century Blvd Ste 1200 *Web:* www.cmtlaw.com	Los Angeles	CA	90045	310-242-2200		41

	Phone	Fax	Class
Carlson and Beauloye 2141 Newton Ave San Diego CA 92113 *TF:* 866-926-1350 ■ *Web:* www.cbmachineandair.com	619-234-2256	234-2095	385
Carlson Capital Management LLC 11 Bridge Sq. Northfield MN 55057 *Web:* carlsoncap.com	507-645-8887		194
Carlson Craft Inc 1750 Tower Blvd North Mankato MN 56003 *TF:* 800-774-6848 ■ *Web:* www.carlsoncraft.com	800-774-6848		627
Carlson Ctr 2010 Second Ave Fairbanks AK 99701 *Web:* www.carlson-center.com	907-451-7800	451-1195	205
Carlson Manufacturing Inc 1495 90th St SE Kerkhoven MN 56252 *Web:* www.carlsonmfg.com	320-264-8101	264-8122	454
Carlson Mccain Inc 3890 Pheasant Ridge Dr Ste 100 Blaine MN 55449 *Web:* carlsonmccain.com	763-489-7900		261
Carlson Paving Products Inc 18425 50th Ave E Tacoma WA 98446 *Web:* www.carlsonpavingproducts.com	253-875-8000		190
Carlson Real Estate Co 301 Carlson Pky Ste 100 Hopkins MN 55305 *Web:* www.carlsonrealestate.org	952-404-5000		652
Carlson Software Inc 33 E Second St Maysville KY 41056 *TF:* 800-942-2540 ■ *Web:* www.carlsonsw.com	606-564-5028		177
Carlson Testing Inc 8430 SW Hunziker Tigard OR 97223 *Web:* www.carlsontesting.com	503-684-3460	684-0954	743
Carlson Tool & Machine Co 2300 Gary Ln Geneva IL 60134 *Web:* www.carlson-tool.com	630-232-2460	232-2016	455
Carlson Tool & Manufacturing Corp W57 N14386 Doerr Way Cedarburg WI 53012 *TF:* 800-532-2252 ■ *Web:* www.carlsontool.com	262-377-2020		757
Carlson Wagonlit Travel Inc 701 Carlson Pkwy Minnetonka MN 55305 **Fax Area Code:* 763 ■ *TF:* 800-213-7295 ■ *Web:* www.mycwt.com	800-213-7295	212-2409*	772
Carlson, Brigance & Doering Inc 5501 W William Cannon Dr Austin TX 78749 *Web:* cbdeng.com	512-280-5160		261
Carlson, Caspers, Vandenburgh & Lindquist 225 S Sixth St Ste 4200 Minneapolis MN 55402 *Web:* www.carlsoncaspers.com	612-436-9600		428
Carlson, Gaskey & Olds A Professional Corp 400 W Maple Rd Ste 350 Birmingham MI 48009 *Web:* www.cgolaw.com	248-988-8360		428
Carlstar Group LLC, The 725 Cool Springs Blvd Ste 500 Franklin TN 37067 *TF:* 800-889-7367 ■ *Web:* www.carlstargroup.com	615-503-0220	503-0228	370
Carlthorp School 438 San Vicente Blvd Santa Monica CA 90402 *Web:* www.carlthorp.org	310-451-1332	451-8559	685
Carlton Arms 160 E 25th St New York NY 10010 *Web:* www.carltonarms.com	212-679-0680		379
Carlton Bates Co 3600 W 69th St Little Rock AR 72209 *TF:* 866-600-6040 ■ *Web:* www.carltonbates.com	501-562-9100		246
Carlton Co 3901 SE Naef Rd Milwaukie OR 97267 *Web:* carltonproducts.com	503-659-8911		682
Carlton County PO Box 130 Carlton MN 55718 *Web:* www.co.carlton.mn.us	218-384-9166		338
Carlton Farms Inc 10600 NW Westside Rd Carlton OR 97111 *TF:* 800-932-0946 ■ *Web:* www.carltonfarms.com	503-852-7166	852-6263	473
Carlton Fields PA 4221 W Boy Scout Blvd Corporate Ctr Three Ste 1000 Tampa FL 33607 *TF:* 888-223-9191 ■ *Web:* www.carltonfields.com	813-223-7000	229-4133	428
Carlton Forge Works Inc 7743 E Adams St Paramount CA 90723 *Web:* www.carltonforgeworks.com	562-633-1131		483
Carlton Group Inc 120 Landmark Dr Greensboro NC 27409 *TF:* 800-722-7824 ■ *Web:* www.carltonscale.com	336-668-7677		361
Carlton Restaurant, The BNY Mellon Ctr 500 Grant St Pittsburgh PA 15219 *Web:* www.thecarltonrestaurant.com	412-391-4099	281-1704	671
Carlton Staffing 24 E Greenway Plz Ste 1207 Houston TX 77046 *Web:* www.carltonstaffing.com	713-629-0116		631
Carluccio, Leone, Dimon, Doyle & Sacks LLC 9 Robbins St Toms River NJ 08753 *Web:* www.cldds.com	732-797-1600		428
Carlyle 4000 Campbell Ave Arlington VA 22206 *Web:* www.greatamericanrestaurants.com	703-931-0777	931-9420	671
Carlyle Capital Markets Inc 14755 Preston Rd Ste 510 Dallas TX 75254 *Web:* www.ccmi-dallas.com	972-404-8686		690
Carlyle House Historic Park 121 N Fairfax St Alexandria VA 22314 *TF:* 800-877-0954 ■ *Web:* www.novaparks.com	703-549-2997		520
Carlyle Johnson Machine Co (CJM) 291 Boston Tpke Bolton CT 06043 *TF:* 888-629-4867 ■ *Web:* www.cjmco.com	860-643-1531	646-2645	620
Carlyle Lake State Fish & Wildlife Area RR 2 Vandalia IL 62471 *Web:* www.stateparks.com	618-425-3533		565
Carlyle Van Lines Inc 801 W Young Ave Warrensburg MO 64093 *TF:* 888-749-0010 ■ *Web:* www.carlylevanlines.com	660-747-8128	747-9327	519
Carlynton School District 435 Kings Hwy Carnegie PA 15106 *Web:* www.carlynton.k12.pa.us	412-429-8400		685
Carma Laboratories Inc 5801 W Airways Ave Franklin WI 53132 *Web:* www.mycarmex.com	414-421-7707		231
Carman Callahan & Ingham LLP 266 Main St Farmingdale NY 11735 *Web:* www.carmancallahan.com	516-249-3450		428
Carman Industries Inc 1005 W Riverside Dr Jeffersonville IN 47130 *Web:* www.carmanindustries.com	812-288-4710	288-4707	207
Carman-Dunne PC 2 Lakeview Ave Lynbrook NY 11563 *Web:* www.carman-dunne.com	516-599-5563	593-4873	261
CarMax Inc 12800 Tuckahoe Creek Pkwy Richmond VA 23238 *NYSE: KMX* ■ *TF:* 800-519-1511 ■ *Web:* www.carmax.com	800-519-1511		57
Carmel Clay Public Library 55 4th Ave SE Carmel IN 46032 *TF:* 800-908-4490 ■ *Web:* carmelclaylibrary.org	317-844-3361		434-3
Carmel Contractors 8030 England St Charlotte NC 28273 *Web:* carmelcontractors.com	704-552-2338		186
Carmel Engineering Inc 413 E Madison St Kirklin IN 46050 *TF:* 888-472-0497 ■ *Web:* carmeleng.com	765-279-8955	279-8966	189-11
Carmel Mission 3080 Rio Rd Carmel By The Sea CA 93923 *Web:* carmelmission.org	831-624-1271		50-1
Carmel Mission Inn 3665 Rio Rd Carmel By The Sea CA 93923 *TF:* 800-348-9090 ■ *Web:* www.carmelmissioninn.com	831-624-1841		378
Carmel River Inn 26600 Oliver Rd Carmel By The Sea CA 93923 *TF:* 800-882-8142 ■ *Web:* carmelriverinn.com	831-624-1575		379
Carmel Valley Manor 8545 Carmel Valley Rd Carmel By The Sea CA 93923 *TF:* 800-544-5546 ■ *Web:* www.cvmanor.com	831-624-1281	622-4543	672
Carmel Valley Ranch Resort 1 Old Ranch Rd Carmel By The Sea CA 93923 *TF:* 866-405-5037 ■ *Web:* www.carmelvalleyranch.com	855-687-7262		669
Carmelite Monastery Library & Archives 1318 Dulaney Valley Rd Baltimore MD 21286 *Web:* www.baltimorecarmel.org	410-823-7415	823-7418	434-3
Carmell Therapeutics Corp 2403 Sidney St Ste 300 Pittsburgh PA 15203 *Web:* www.carmellrx.com	412-894-8248		668
Carmen & Family Bar-B-Q 41986 Fremont Blvd Fremont CA 94538 *Web:* carmenandfamilybbq.com	510-657-5464		671
Carmeuse North America 11 Stanwix St Pittsburgh PA 15222 *TF:* 866-780-0974 ■ *Web:* www.carmeuse.com	412-995-5500	995-5570	440
Carmichael Brasher Tuvell & Co 1647 Mt Vernon Rd Atlanta GA 30338 *Web:* www.cbtcpa.com	678-443-9200	443-9700	2
Carmichael Chamber of Commerce 6825 Fair Oaks Blvd Ste 100 Carmichael CA 95608 *TF:* 800-991-6147 ■ *Web:* www.carmichaelchamber.com	916-481-1002	481-1003	139
Carmichael Lynch Relate 110 N 5th St Minneapolis MN 55403 *Web:* spongpr.com	612-334-6000	334-6090	636
Carmine Vella & Company Inc 25 Leroy Pl Ste 411 New Rochelle NY 10805 *Web:* vellacpa.com	914-632-1695		2
Carmine's on Penn 92 S Pennsylvania Denver CO 80209 *Web:* www.carminescolorado.com	303-777-6443	777-4129	671
Carmine's Steak House 20 S Fourth St Saint Louis MO 63102 *Web:* lombardosrestaurants.com	314-241-1631		671
Carmines Gourmet Market 2401 Pga Blvd Palm Beach Gardens FL 33410 *Web:* www.carmines.com	561-775-0105	775-9233	345
Carmody Torrance Sandak & Hennessey LLP 50 Leavenworth St Waterbury CT 06721 *Web:* www.carmodylaw.com	203-573-1200		428
CarnaBio USA Inc 209 W Central St Ste 307 Natick MA 01760 *TF:* 888-645-1233 ■ *Web:* www.carnabio.com	508-650-1244	650-1722	238
Carnahan Group Inc 5005 W Laurel St Ste 204 Tampa FL 33607 *Web:* carnahangroup.com	813-289-2588		463
Carnahan Proctor & Cross Inc 604 Courtland St Ste 101 Orlando FL 32804 *Web:* carnahan-proctor.com	954-972-3959		256
Carnation Software Inc PO Box 318 Driftwood TX 78619 *Web:* www.carnationsoftware.com	512-858-9234		178-1
Carnations Home Fashions Inc 53 Jeanne Dr Newburgh NY 12550 *TF:* 800-866-8949 ■ *Web:* www.carnationhomefashions.com	212-679-6017		361
Carneghi-Nakasako & Assn 1602 The Alameda Ste 103 San Jose CA 95126 *Web:* cbpappraisal.com	408-535-0900		655
Carnegie Art Museum Cornerstones 424 S 'C' St Oxnard CA 93030 *Web:* www.carnegieartcornerstones.com	805-385-8158	483-3654	520
Carnegie Corporation of New York 437 Madison Ave New York NY 10022 *Web:* www.carnegie.org	212-371-3200	754-4073	305
Carnegie Council for Ethics in International Affairs (CCEIA) Merrill House 170 E 64th St New York NY 10065 *Web:* www.carnegiecouncil.org	212-838-4120	752-2432	634
Carnegie East House For Seniors 1844 Second Ave New York NY 10128 *TF:* 888-410-0033 ■ *Web:* www.carnegieeast.org	212-410-0033		196
Carnegie Endowment for International Peace 1779 Massachusetts Ave NW Washington DC 20036 *TF:* 877-866-3070 ■ *Web:* www.carnegieendowment.org	202-483-7600	483-1840	634
Carnegie Fabrics LLC 110 N Centre Ave Rockville Centre NY 11570 *TF:* 800-727-6770 ■ *Web:* www.carnegiefabrics.com	516-678-6770	678-6848	87
Carnegie Hall Corp, The 881 Seventh Ave New York NY 10019 *Web:* www.carnegiehall.org	212-247-7800	581-6539	572
Carnegie Hotel 1216 W State of Franklin Rd Johnson City TN 37604 *TF:* 866-757-8277 ■ *Web:* www.carnegiehotel.com	423-979-6400	979-6424	379
Carnegie Institution of Washington 1530 P St NW Washington DC 20005 *Web:* carnegiescience.edu	202-387-6400	387-8092	668
Carnegie Learning Inc 501 Grant St Ste 1075 Pittsburgh PA 15219 **Fax Area Code:* 412 ■ *TF:* 888-851-7094 ■ *Web:* www.carnegielearning.com	888-851-7094	690-2444*	177

Entry	City	State	ZIP	Phone	Fax	Class
Carnegie Library of Pittsburgh 4400 Forbes Ave *Web:* www.carnegielibrary.org	Pittsburgh	PA	15213	412-622-3114		434-3
Carnegie Mellon University 5000 Forbes Ave *TF:* 844-625-4600 ■ *Web:* www.cmu.edu	Pittsburgh	PA	15213	412-268-2000	268-7838	166
Carnegie Museum of Art 4400 Forbes Ave *Web:* cmoa.org	Pittsburgh	PA	15213	412-622-3131	622-3112	520
Carnegie Observatories 813 Santa Barbara St *Web:* obs.carnegiescience.edu	Pasadena	CA	91101	626-577-1122	795-8136	466
Carnegie Public Library 127 S N St *Web:* www.cplwcho.org	Washington Court House	OH	43160	740-335-2540	335-2928	434-3
Carnegie Public Library of Clarksdale and Coahoma County 114 Delta Ave *Web:* www.cplclarksdale.lib.ms.us	Clarksdale	MS	38614	662-624-4461	627-4344	434-3
Carnegie Regional Library 630 Griggs Ave *Web:* graftonndlibrary.com	Grafton	ND	58237	701-352-2754	352-2757	434-3
Carnegie Science Ctr 1 Allegheny Ave *Web:* www.carnegiesciencecenter.org	Pittsburgh	PA	15212	412-237-3400	237-3375	520
Carnegie-Stout Public Library 360 W 11th St *Web:* www.dubuque.lib.ia.us	Dubuque	IA	52001	563-589-4225	589-4217	434-3
Carneros Resort & Spa 4048 Sonoma Hwy *TF:* 888-400-9000 ■ *Web:* www.carnerosresort.com	Napa	CA	94559	707-299-4900	299-4950	707
Carnes Co 448 S Main St *Web:* www.carnes.com	Verona	WI	53593	608-845-6411	845-6470	14
Carney Group, The 925 Harvest Dr Ste 240 *Web:* www.carneyjobs.com	Blue Bell	PA	19422	215-646-6200		260
Carney, Sandoe & Associates, Limited Partnersh 44 Bromfield St *TF:* 800-225-7986 ■ *Web:* www.carneysandoe.com	Boston	MA	02108	617-542-0260		242
Carnicerias Jimenez 4204 W N Ave *Web:* www.carniceriasjimenez.com	Chicago	IL	60639	773-486-5805		297-8
Carnifex Ferry Battlefield State Park 1194 Carnifex Ferry Rd *Web:* wvstateparks.com	Summersville	WV	26651	304-872-0825		565
Carnival Cruise Lines 3655 NW 87th Ave *TF:* 800-764-7419 ■ *Web:* www.carnival.com	Miami	FL	33178	305-599-2600		220
Carnow Conibear & Associates Ltd 600 W Van Buren Ste 500 *Web:* www.ccaltd.com	Chicago	IL	60607	312-782-4486		193
Caro Ctr 2000 Chambers Rd *Web:* www.michigan.gov	Caro	MI	48723	989-673-3191	673-6749	374-5
Caro Foods Inc 2324 Bayou Blue Rd *TF:* 800-395-2276 ■ *Web:* www.performancefoodservice.com	Houma	LA	70364	985-872-1483	876-0825	297-7
Carol Ann Wilson LLC 906 Cranberry Ct **Fax Area Code:* 720 ■ *TF:* 888-332-3342 ■ *Web:* www.carolannwilson.com	Longmont	CO	80503	303-774-1225	600-5134*	41
Carol Drake 1913 N Green Vly Pkwy *Web:* caroldrake.com	Henderson	NV	89074	702-361-0300	361-4387	390
Carol Fox & Assoc 1412 W Belmont Ave *Web:* www.carolfoxassociates.com	Chicago	IL	60657	773-327-3830		636
Carol H. Williams Advertising 1625 Clay St Ste 800 *Web:* www.carolhwilliams.com	Oakland	CA	94612	510-763-5200	763-9266	4
Carol House Furniture 38 Marshall Rd *Web:* www.carolhouse.com	Valley Park	MO	63088	314-427-4200		321
Carol Mendel PO Box 6022 *Web:* www.carolmendelmaps.com	San Diego	CA	92166	619-226-1406		637-2
Carol Stream Public Library 616 Hiawatha Dr *Web:* www.cslibrary.org	Carol Stream	IL	60188	630-653-0755	653-6809	434-3
Carol Woods Retirement Community 750 Weaver Dairy Rd *TF:* 800-518-9333 ■ *Web:* www.carolwoods.org	Chapel Hill	NC	27514	919-968-4511		672
Carol's Carpet Inc 1640 NE Blvd *Web:* www.carolscarpetmontgomery.com	Montgomery	AL	36117	334-603-8713		290
Carol's Corner Cafe 7800 NE St Johns Blvd *Web:* www.carolscornercafe.com	Vancouver	WA	98665	360-573-6357		671
Carolace Embroidery Company Inc 325 Sylvan Ave *Web:* trimplace.com	Englewood Cliffs	NJ	07632	608-709-8746		258
Carolando Press Inc (CP) 6545 W N Ave *TF:* 866-366-2668 ■ *Web:* www.carolando.com	Oak Park	IL	60302	866-366-2668		637-2
Carole Fabrics Inc 633 NW Frontage Rd *TF:* 800-241-0920 ■ *Web:* www.carolefabrics.com	Augusta	GA	30903	706-863-4742		746
Carole Maggio Facercise Inc 1713 S Catalina Ave *TF:* 800-597-3555 ■ *Web:* www.facercise.com	Redondo Beach	CA	90277	310-316-1818		214
Carole Wren Inc 30-30 47th Ave *Web:* www.carolewren.com	Long Island City	NY	11101	718-552-3800		155-21
Carolina PO Box 4398 **Fax Area Code:* 336 ■ *TF:* 800-763-0212 ■ *Web:* carolina.ofs.com	Archdale	NC	27263	800-763-0212	431-9511*	319-1
Carolina Academic Press (CAP) 700 Kent St *Web:* www.cap-press.com	Durham	NC	27701	919-489-7486	493-5668	637-2
Carolina Advanced Digital Inc 133 Triangle Trade Dr *TF:* 800-435-2212 ■ *Web:* cadinc.com	Cary	NC	27513	919-460-1313		463
Carolina Aeronautical Testing & Certification Ctr 202 N Maple St Ste 111 *TF:* 888-878-4443 ■ *Web:* www.carolina-aero.com	Simpsonville	SC	29681	864-228-9588	228-9838	764
Carolina Apothecary Inc 726 S Scales St *TF:* 800-633-1447 ■ *Web:* www.carolinaapothecary.com	Reidsville	NC	27320	336-342-0071		475
Carolina Ballet Inc 3401-131 Atlantic Ave *Web:* carolinaballet.com	Raleigh	NC	27604	919-719-0800	719-0910	573-1
Carolina Beach State Park 1010 State Park Rd PO Box 475 *Web:* www.ncparks.gov	Carolina Beach	NC	28428	910-458-0206		565
Carolina Biological Supply Co 2700 York Rd *TF:* 800-334-5551 ■ *Web:* www.carolina.com	Burlington	NC	27215	336-584-0381	584-7686	243
Carolina Brush Manufacturing Company Inc 3093 Northwest Blvd PO Box 2469 *Web:* www.carolinabrush.com	Gastonia	NC	28052	704-867-0286		362
Carolina Cabinet Co 3363 Hwy 301 N *Web:* www.3c-inc.net	Wilson	NC	27893	252-291-5181	291-8039	286
Carolina Canners Inc PO Box 1628 *Web:* www.carolinacanners.com	Cheraw	SC	29520	843-537-5281	537-6743	81-2
Carolina Carports Inc 187 Cardinal Ridge Trl *TF:* 800-670-4262 ■ *Web:* carolinacarportsinc.com	Dobson	NC	27017	800-670-4262		487
Carolina Casualty Insurance Co 5011 Gate Pkwy Ste 200 *TF:* 800-874-8053 ■ *Web:* www.carolinacas.com	Jacksonville	FL	32256	904-363-0900	363-8098	391-4
Carolina College of Hair Design 3420 Clemson Blvd *Web:* carolinacollege.com	Anderson	SC	29621	864-332-0031		167-3
Carolina Color Corp 100 E 17th St *TF:* 800-437-7012 ■ *Web:* www.carocolor.com	Salisbury	NC	28144	704-637-7000		596
Carolina Container Co 909 Prospect St *TF:* 800-627-0825 ■ *Web:* www.carolinacontainer.com	High Point	NC	27260	336-883-7146	883-7576	100
Carolina Crown Inc 227 A Main St *Web:* carolinacrown.org	Fort Mill	SC	29715	803-547-2270		526
Carolina Designs Realty Inc 1197 Duck Rd *TF:* 800-368-3825 ■ *Web:* www.carolinadesigns.com	Duck	NC	27949	252-261-3934		656
Carolina Dragway 302 Dragstrip Rd *TF:* 877-471-7223 ■ *Web:* www.carolinadragway.com	Aiken	SC	29803	803-471-2285		515
Carolina Espinoza Insurance & Financial Services Inc 343 Scott Ct *Web:* carolinaespinoza.com	Iowa City	IA	52245	319-337-7000		390
Carolina Eye Associates PA 2170 Midland Rd *TF:* 800-733-5357 ■ *Web:* www.carolinaeye.com	Southern Pines	NC	28387	910-295-2100	295-5339	798
Carolina Eyecare Physicians 2060 Charlie Hall Blvd Ste 201 *Web:* www.carolinaeyecare.com	Charleston	SC	29414	843-722-2010		543
Carolina Fabricators Inc 3831 Hwy 321 *Web:* carolinafab.com	West Columbia	SC	29172	803-794-4906		124
Carolina Farms Real Estate 547 S Main St *Web:* carolinafarms.com	King	NC	27021	336-983-5263		652
Carolina Federal Credit Union 1200 E Church St *Web:* carolinafcu.org	Cherryville	NC	28021	704-435-0186		219
Carolina Filters Inc 109 E Newberry Ave *TF:* 800-849-5646 ■ *Web:* carolinafilters.com	Sumter	SC	29150	800-849-5646		806
Carolina Foods Inc 1807 S Tryon St *TF:* 800-234-0441 ■ *Web:* carolinafoodsinc.com	Charlotte	NC	28203	704-333-9812		296-1
Carolina Foothills Chamber of Commerce 2753 Lynn Rd Ste A *TF:* 888-296-0711 ■ *Web:* carolinafoothillschamber.com	Tryon	NC	28782	828-859-6236		139
Carolina Forest Veterinary Hospital 209 Ronnie Ct *Web:* carolinaforestveterinary.com	Myrtle Beach	SC	29579	843-236-7383		794
Carolina Forge Company LLC 2401 Stantonsburg Rd *Web:* www.meadforge.com	Wilson	NC	27893	252-237-8181		75
Carolina Glove Co 116 Mclin Creek Rd PO Box 999 *TF:* 800-335-1918 ■ *Web:* www.carolinaglove.com	Conover	NC	28613	828-464-1132	485-2416	155-8
Carolina Herrera 501 Seventh Ave 17th Fl *TF:* 866-254-7660 ■ *Web:* www.carolinaherrera.com	New York	NY	10018	866-254-7660		277
Carolina Holdings Inc 40 W Broad St Ste 410 *Web:* www.choldings.com	Greenville	SC	29601	864-272-0088	272-0078	654
Carolina Hosiery Mills Inc 710 Plantation Dr *Web:* carolinahosiery.com	Burlington	NC	27215	336-226-5581		155-10
Carolina International Trucks Inc 1619 Bluff Rd *TF:* 800-868-4923 ■ *Web:* www.carolinainternational.com	Columbia	SC	29201	800-868-4923		57
Carolina Loom Reed Company Inc 3503 Holts Chapel Rd **Fax Area Code:* 336 ■ *TF:* 888-257-3337 ■ *Web:* www.loomreeds.com	Greensboro	NC	27401	888-257-3337	275-1407*	744
Carolina Meadows 100 Carolina Meadows *TF:* 800-458-6756 ■ *Web:* carolinameadows.org	Chapel Hill	NC	27517	919-942-4014		672
Carolina Medical Lab 1815 Back Creek Dr *Web:* www.cmedlab.com	Charlotte	NC	28213	704-598-8818	598-7477	415
Carolina Mfg 7025 Augusta Rd **Fax Area Code:* 864 ■ *TF:* 800-845-2744 ■ *Web:* thebandannacompany.com	Greenville	SC	29605	800-845-2744	299-0603*	155-13
Carolina Mills Inc 618 N Carolina Ave *Web:* www.carolinamills.com	Maiden	NC	28650	828-428-9911		745-9
Carolina Narrow Fabric Co 1100 N Patterson Ave *TF:* 877-631-3077 ■ *Web:* www.carolinanarrowfabric.com	Winston-Salem	NC	27101	336-631-3000	631-3060	745-5
Carolina Office Systems Inc 13245 Reese Blvd W Ste 130 *Web:* carolinaosonline.com	Huntersville	NC	28078	704-337-8900	337-8901	112
Carolina Opry 8901 Hwy 17 N *TF:* 800-843-6779 ■ *Web:* www.thecarolinaopry.com	Myrtle Beach	SC	29572	800-843-6779		572
Carolina Packers Inc 2999 S Bright Leaf Blvd *TF:* 800-682-7675 ■ *Web:* www.carolinapackers.com	Smithfield	NC	27577	800-682-7675		473
Carolina Peacemaker 807 Summit Ave *Web:* peacemakeronline.com	Greensboro	NC	27405	336-274-6210		532-2
Carolina Pines Regional Medical Ctr 1304 W Bobo Newsome Hwy *Web:* www.cprmc.com	Hartsville	SC	29550	843-339-2100		374-3
Carolina Place Mall 11025 Carolina Pl Pkwy *Web:* www.carolinaplace.com	Pineville	NC	28134	704-543-9300		460

Phone | Fax | Class

Carolina Pride Foods Inc
1 Packer Ave ... Greenwood SC 29646 864-229-5611 296-26
Web: carolinapride.com

Carolina Raptor Ctr
6000 Sample Rd ... Huntersville NC 28078 704-875-6521 522
Web: carolinaraptorcenter.org

Carolina Rim & Wheel Co
1308 Upper Asbury Ave ... Charlotte NC 28206 704-334-7276 61
TF: 800-247-4337 ■ *Web:* truckpro.com

Carolina Scales Inc
929 N Lucas St ... West Columbia SC 29169 803-739-4360 739-4365 361
TF: 800-277-2439 ■ *Web:* www.carolinascales.com

Carolina Skiff Inc 3231 Fulford Rd ... Waycross GA 31503 912-287-0547 90
TF: 800-422-7282 ■ *Web:* www.carolinaskiff.com

Carolina Stair Supply Inc
316 Herrick St ... Uhrichsville OH 44683 740-922-3333 499
Web: www.carolinastair.com

Carolina Supplyhouse Inc
218 Second Loop Rd ... Florence SC 29504 843-662-0702 362
Web: www.thesupplyhouse.com

Carolina Swatching Inc
725 14th St Dr Sw ... Hickory NC 28603 828-327-9499 92
Web: www.carolinaswatching.com

Carolina Theatre 310 S Greene St ... Greensboro NC 27401 336-333-2600 572
Web: carolinatheatre.com

Carolina Theatre of Durham, The
309 W Morgan St ... Durham NC 27701 919-560-3040 560-3065 572
Web: www.carolinatheatre.org

Carolina Training Associates (CTA)
3623 Latrobe Ste 120 ... Charlotte NC 28211 704-366-6309 423
TF: 800-962-8815 ■ *Web:* www.carolinatraining.com

Carolina Veterinary Specialists
2225 Township Rd ... Charlotte NC 28273 704-504-9608 794
Web: www.carolinavet.com

Carolina Village
600 Carolina Village Rd ... Hendersonville NC 28792 828-692-6275 233-6273 672
Web: www.carolinavillage.com

Carolina Woman Inc PO Box 3520 ... Cary NC 27519 919-852-5900 852-5910 637-9
Web: www.carolinawoman.com

Carolina's 12045 Chapman Ave ... Garden Grove CA 92840 714-971-5551 671
Web: www.carolinasitalianrestaurant.com

Carolina's 10 Exchange St ... Charleston SC 29401 843-724-3800 722-9493 671
Web: www.carolinasrestaurant.com

CarolinaEast Health System
2000 Neuse Blvd ... New Bern NC 28561 252-633-8111 374-3
Web: www.carolinaeasthealth.com

Carolinas Auto Supply House Inc
2135 Tipton Dr ... Charlotte NC 28206 704-334-4646 377-7016* 61
**Fax Area Code:* 800 ■ *TF:* 800-438-4070 ■ *Web:* www.autosupplyhouse.com

Carolinas HealthCare System Blue Ridge
2201 S Sterling St ... Morganton NC 28655 828-580-5000 374-3
TF: 800-624-3004 ■ *Web:* www.carolinashealthcareblueridge.org

Carolinas Hospital System
805 Pamplico Hwy ... Florence SC 29505 843-674-5000 374-3
Web: www.carolinashospital.com

Carolinas Investment Consulting LLC
5605 Carnegie Blvd Ste 400 ... Charlotte NC 28209 704-643-2455 401
TF: 800-255-2904 ■ *Web:* www.carolinasinvest.com

Caroline County
212 N Main St PO Box 447 ... Bowling Green VA 22427 804-633-5380 633-4970 338
Web: co.caroline.va.us

Caroline County 109 Market St ... Denton MD 21629 410-479-0660 479-4060 338
Web: www.carolinemd.org

Caroline County Chamber of Commerce
9194 Legion Rd Ste 1 ... Denton MD 21629 410-479-4638 479-4862 139
Web: www.carolinechamber.org

Caroline County Public Library
100 Market St ... Denton MD 21629 410-479-1343 479-1443 434-3
Web: www.carolib.org

Caroline Distribution 150 5th Ave ... New York NY 10011 212-886-7500 523
Web: www.caroline.com

Carollo Engineers
2700 Ygnacio Valley Rd Ste 300 ... Walnut Creek CA 94598 925-932-1710 930-0208 261
TF: 800-523-5826 ■ *Web:* www.carollo.com

Carolyn Dorfman Dance Co (CDDC)
2780 Morris Ave Ste 1-A ... Union NJ 07083 908-687-8855 686-5245 573-1
Web: carolyndorfman.dance

Carolyn Fabrics Inc (CF)
1948 W Green Dr ... High Point NC 27261 800-333-8400 887-2895* 594
**Fax Area Code:* 336 ■ *TF:* 800-333-8400 ■ *Web:* www.carolynfabrics.com

Caron Compactor Co 1204 Ullrey Ave ... Escalon CA 95320 209-838-2062 190
TF: 800-542-2766 ■ *Web:* www.caroncompactor.com

Caron Engineering Inc
116 Willie Hill Rd ... Wells ME 04090 207-646-6071 180
Web: www.caroneng.com

Carondelet Saint Joseph's Hospital
350 N Wilmot Rd ... Tucson AZ 85711 520-873-3000 374-3
Web: www.carondelet.org

Caroplast Inc PO Box 668405 ... Charlotte NC 28266 704-394-4191 612
TF: 800-327-5797 ■ *Web:* www.caroplast.com

Carotek Inc
700 Sam Newell Rd PO Box 1395 ... Matthews NC 28106 704-844-1100 844-8432 358
Web: www.carotek.com

Carousel Beachfront Hotel & Suites
11700 Coastal Hwy ... Ocean City MD 21842 410-524-1000 524-7766 379
Web: carouselhotel.com

Carousel Industries of North America Inc
659 S County Trl ... Exeter RI 02822 800-401-0760 224
TF: 800-401-0760 ■ *Web:* www.carouselindustries.com

Carousel Restaurant 304 N Brand Blvd ... Glendale CA 91203 818-246-7775 246-6627 671
Web: www.carouselrestaurant.com

Carousel Signs & Designs Inc
2312 Commerce Center Dr Ste B ... Rockville VA 23146 804-620-3200 620-3211 701
Web: carouselsigns.com

Carparts.com 761 Progress Pkwy ... LaSalle IL 61301 866-529-0412 431-6095* 459
**Fax Area Code:* 312 ■ *TF:* 866-529-5530 ■ *Web:* www.carparts.com

Carpe Diem 1535 Elizabeth Ave ... Charlotte NC 28204 704-377-7976 671
Web: www.carpediemrestaurant.com

Phone | Fax | Class

Carpedia International Ltd
75 Navy St ... Oakville ON L6J2Z1 877-445-8288 463
TF: 877-445-8288 ■ *Web:* carpedia.com

Carpenter & Schumacher PC
2701 N Dallas Pkwy Parkway Ctr IV ... Plano TX 75093 972-403-1133 403-0311 41
TF: 844-370-1133 ■ *Web:* www.cstriallaw.com

Carpenter Co 5016 Monument Ave ... Richmond VA 23230 804-359-0800 353-0694 601
TF: 800-288-3830 ■ *Web:* www.carpenter.com

Carpenter Contractors of America Inc
3900 Ave D NW ... Winter Haven FL 33880 863-294-6449 299-9940 189-2
TF: 800-959-8806 ■ *Web:* www.carpentercontractors.com

Carpenter Law Offices
2039 N Kavaney Dr ... Bismarck ND 58501 701-223-3080 41
Web: ndcourts.gov

Carpenter Lipps & Leland LLP
280 N High St Ste 1300 ... Columbus OH 43215 614-365-4100 428
Web: carpenterlipps.com

Carpenter Powder Products
682 Mayer St ... Bridgeville PA 15017 833-584-1052 257-5058* 595
**Fax Area Code:* 412 ■ *TF:* 866-790-9092 ■ *Web:* www.carpentertechnology.com

Carpenter Technology Corp
1735 Market St 15th Fl ... Philadelphia PA 19103 610-208-2000 208-3716 449
Web: www.carpentertechnology.com

Carpenter Technology Corporation - Latrobe Operations (PA)
2626 Ligonier St ... Latrobe PA 15650 724-537-7711 492
TF: 800-241-8527 ■ *Web:* www.carpentertechnology.com

Carpenter's Motor Transport Inc
413 Commerce St ... Williston VT 05495 802-862-9669 862-5802 780
Web: www.carpentersmotor.com

Carpenters Apprentice School of Philadelphia & Vicinity
10401 Decatur Rd ... Philadelphia PA 19154 215-824-2300 824-2313 685
Web: www.carpentersofphila.com

Carpenters' Hall 320 Chestnut St ... Philadelphia PA 19106 215-925-0167 50-3
Web: www.ushistory.org

Carper Thomas R (Sen D - DE)
513 Hart Senate Office Bldg ... Washington DC 20510 202-224-2441 228-2190 342-2
Web: www.carper.senate.gov

Carpet & Rug Institute (CRI)
100 S Hamilton St PO Box 2048 ... Dalton GA 30720 706-278-3176 278-8835 49-4
Web: web.carpet-rug.org

Carpet Cushions & Supplies
855 N Wood Dale Rd Unit A ... Wood Dale IL 60191 847-364-6760 364-6785 131
Web: www.carpetcushions.com

Carpet Exchange 1133 S Platte River Dr ... Denver CO 80223 303-744-3300 744-3324 131
Web: carpetexchange.com

Carpet House 1320 Woodlawn ... Lincoln IL 62656 217-735-2531 290
Web: thecarpethouselincolnil.com

Carpet King Inc 1815 W River Rd N ... Minneapolis MN 55411 612-588-7600 290
TF: 800-375-3608 ■ *Web:* www.carpetking.com

Carpet Maintenance Solutions
1116 Paloma Ave ... Burlingame CA 94010 650-861-2050 931-4736 104
Web: cmscleaners.com

Carpet Specialists Inc
2101 Stanley Gault Pky ... Louisville KY 40223 502-245-0221 290
Web: carpetspecialistsonline.com

Carpet Studio Inc 2865 Jolly Rd ... Okemos MI 48864 517-325-5799 290
Web: flooringamericalansing.com

Carpet Tech 6613 19th St ... Lubbock TX 79407 806-795-5142 290
Web: callcarpettech.com

Carpetland Usa 7851 Plantation Rd ... Roanoke VA 24019 540-265-1919 290
Web: carpetlandusava.com

Carpets Plus by Design 330 Lockwood ... Woodville WI 54028 715-698-2200 131
Web: carpetsplusbydesign.com

Carpin Manufacturing Inc
411 Austin Rd ... Waterbury CT 06705 203-574-2556 753-8771 154
Web: www.carpin.com

Carr & Assoc 5251 W 116th Pl Ste 200 ... Leawood KS 66211 913-451-9220 451-9228 393
Web: carrassessments.com

Carr & Duff Inc
2100 Byberry Rd ... Huntingdon Valley PA 19006 215-672-4200 261
Web: carrduff.com

Carr & Ferrell LLP
120 Constitution Dr ... Menlo Park CA 94025 650-812-3400 812-3444 428
Web: www.carrferrell.com

Carr Auto Group 11635 SW Canyon Rd ... Beaverton OR 97006 503-644-2161 57
TF: 888-679-3827 ■ *Web:* www.carrauto.com

Carr Business Systems
130 Spagnoli Rd ... Melville NY 11747 631-249-9880 112
TF: 800-720-2277 ■ *Web:* www.carrxerox.com

Carr Co 6000 Park of Commerce Blvd ... Boca Raton FL 33487 800-578-2277 612
TF: 800-578-2277 ■ *Web:* www.carrcompany.com

Carr Communications 4325 S Masten Rd ... Branch MI 49402 231-898-2244 898-3900 224
TF: 800-431-1213 ■ *Web:* site.carrinter.net

Carr Concrete Corp
362 Waverly Rd ... Williamstown WV 26187 304-464-4441 464-4013 183
TF: 800-837-8918 ■ *Web:* www.carrconcrete.com

Carr Corp 1547 11th St ... Santa Monica CA 90401 310-587-1113 395-9751 591
TF: 800-952-2398 ■ *Web:* www.carrcorporation.com

Carr Creek State Park
2086 Smithboro Rd, Highway 15 ... Sassafras KY 41759 606-642-4050 565
Web: parks.ky.gov

Carr Engineering Inc
12500 Castlebridge Dr ... Houston TX 77065 281-894-8955 894-5455 256
Web: www.carrengineeringinc.com

Carr Lane Mfg 4200 Carr Ln Ct ... Saint Louis MO 63119 314-647-6200 647-5736 757
Web: www.carrlane.com

Carr Machine & Tool Inc
1301 Jarvis Ave ... Elk Grove Village IL 60007 847-593-8003 454
Web: www.carrmachine.com

Carr McClellan Ingersall Thompson
216 Park Rd ... Burlingame CA 94010 650-342-9600 428
Web: www.carr-mcclellan.com

Carr Riggs & Ingram LLC
1117 Boll Weevil Cir ... Enterprise AL 36330 334-347-0088 2
Web: www.cricpa.com

Carr's Restaurant 50 W Grant St ... Lancaster PA 17603 717-299-7090 671
Web: carrsrestaurant.com

Name / Address	Phone	Fax	Class
Carr, Riggs & Ingram LLC 1601 Second Ave E .... Oneonta AL 35121 *Web:* cpasmc.com	205-625-3472	274-0182	2
Carrasquillo Associates, Lp 5113 Southwest Pkwy Ste 250 .... Austin TX 78735 *Web:* carrasquilloassociates.com	512-358-7020		261
Carrell Blanton Ferris & Associates PLC 7275 Glen Forest Dr Ste 310 .... Richmond VA 23226 *TF:* 866-479-2900 ■ *Web:* carrellblanton.com	804-285-7900	285-8925	41
Carrera & Partners Inc 600 Fairway Dr Ste 208 .... Deerfield Beach FL 33441 *Web:* www.carreraadvertising.com	954-360-9111		7
Carreta's Grill 2320 Veterans Memorial Blvd. .... Metairie LA 70002 *Web:* www.carretasgrillrestaurant.com	504-837-6696		671
Carriage House 24460 Adams Rd .... South Bend IN 46628 *Web:* www.carriagehousediningroomandgardens.com	574-272-9220		671
Carriage House Timeshare Association Inc 105 E Harmon Ave .... Las Vegas NV 89109 *Web:* carriagehouselasvegas.com	702-798-1020		378
Carriage Services Inc 3040 Post Oak Blvd Ste 300 .... Houston TX 77056 *NYSE:* CSV ■ *TF:* 866-332-8400 ■ *Web:* www.carriageservices.com	713-332-8400		510
Carriage Works Inc 6600 Arnold Ave .... Klamath Falls OR 97603 *Web:* carriageworks.com	541-882-0700	882-9661	820
Carrico Implement Company Inc 3160 US 24 Hwy .... Beloit KS 67420 *TF:* 877-542-4099 ■ *Web:* www.carricoimplement.com	785-738-5744	738-2648	274
Carrico Maldegen LLC 41000 W Seven Mile Rd Ste 140 .... Northville MI 48167 *Web:* carricomaldegen.com	248-773-7930		390
Carrier Clinic 252 County Rd 601 .... Belle Mead NJ 08502 *TF:* 800-933-3579 ■ *Web:* carrierclinic.org	800-933-3579		374-5
Carrier Interamerica 10801 NW 103rd St Ste 1 .... Miami FL 33178 *Web:* www.carriercca.com	305-880-5450		610
Carrier Logistics Inc 220 White Plains Rd Ste 6 .... Tarrytown NY 10591 *Web:* carrierlogistics.com	914-332-0300		180
Carrier Lumber Ltd 4722 Continental Way .... Prince George BC V2N5S5 *Web:* www.carrierlumber.bc.ca	250-563-9271		683
Carrier Vibrating Equipment Inc 3400 Fern Valley Rd .... Louisville KY 40213 *TF:* 800-547-7278 ■ *Web:* www.carriervibrating.com	502-969-3171	969-3172	207
Carriercom Lp 200 S 10th St Ste 708 .... McAllen TX 78501 *Web:* www.carriercom.net	956-682-3656		387
Carriere Bernier Ltee 25 Petit Bernier CP 548 .... Saint-Jean-sur-Richelieu QC J3B6Z8 *Web:* www.carrierebernier.com	450-545-2000		135
Carrillo Business Technologies Inc 770 The City Dr S Ste 5300 .... Orange CA 92868 *TF:* 888-241-7585 ■ *Web:* www.cbtechinc.com	888-241-7585		387
Carrington College 5883 Rue Ferrari Ste 125 .... San Jose CA 95138 *Web:* www.carrington.edu	408-337-3829		167-2
Carrington Convention & Visitors Bureau 871 Main St .... Carrington ND 58421 *TF:* 800-641-9668 ■ *Web:* www.cgtn-nd.com	701-652-2524	652-2391	206
Carrington Foods Company Inc 200 Jacintoport Blvd. .... Saraland AL 36571 *Web:* www.carringtonfoods.com	251-675-9700	679-8721	297-8
Carris Reels Inc 46 Ripley Rd .... Rutland VT 05701 *Web:* www.carris.com	802-773-9111	770-3551	279
Carroll & Co 425 N Canon Dr Ste 108 .... Beverly Hills CA 90210 *TF:* 800-238-9400 ■ *Web:* carrollcustom.com	310-273-9060	273-7974	157-3
Carroll Air Systems Inc 3711 W Walnut St .... Tampa FL 33607 *Web:* www.carrollair.com	813-879-5790	874-9553	14
Carroll Apothecary Inc 425 Hwy 30 W Ste 140 .... Carroll IA 51401 *TF:* 800-736-8248 ■ *Web:* carrollapothecary.com	712-792-2671	792-0894	237
Carroll Clean 2900 W Kingsley Rd .... Garland TX 75041 **Fax Area Code:* 972 ■ *TF:* 800-527-5722 ■ *Web:* carrollclean.com	800-527-5722	840-0678*	151
Carroll College 1601 N Benton Ave .... Helena MT 59625 *TF:* 800-992-3648 ■ *Web:* www.carroll.edu	406-447-4300	447-4533	166
Carroll Communications Inc PO Box 186 .... Spring Lake NJ 07762 *Web:* www.carrollcommunications.com	732-280-3200		681
Carroll Community College 1601 Washington Rd .... Westminster MD 21157 *TF:* 888-221-9748 ■ *Web:* www.carrollcc.edu	410-386-8000		162
Carroll Companies Inc 1640 Old Hwy 421 S .... Boone NC 28607 *TF:* 800-884-2521 ■ *Web:* www.clgco.com	828-264-2521	264-2633	431
Carroll Concrete Co 8 Reeds Mill Rd .... Newport NH 03773 *TF:* 800-622-4100 ■ *Web:* www.carrollconcrete.com	603-863-1000	863-3660	182
Carroll County 114 E 6th St .... Carroll IA 51401 *Web:* www.co.carroll.ia.us	712-792-4923		338
Carroll County 423 College St Rm 408 PO Box 338 .... Carrollton GA 30112 *Web:* www.carrollcountyga.com	770-830-5800	830-5992	338
Carroll County 105 B E Washington St PO Box 59 .... Carrollton MS 38917 *Web:* carrollcountyms.org	662-237-4413		338
Carroll County 119 S Lisbon St Ste 201 .... Carrollton OH 44615 *Web:* carrollcountyohio.us	330-627-4869	627-6656	338
Carroll County PO Box 195 .... Delphi IN 46923 *TF:* 866-374-6813 ■ *Web:* www.carrollcountyindiana.com	765-564-6757	564-2207	338
Carroll County 605-1 Pine St .... Hillsville VA 24343 *Web:* carrollcountyva.gov	276-730-3070	730-3071	338
Carroll County 8215 Black Oak Rd .... Mount Carroll IL 61053 *TF:* 800-485-0145 ■ *Web:* www.gocarrollcounty.com	815-244-2035		338
Carroll County 225 N Center St .... Westminster MD 21157 *TF:* 800-735-2258 ■ *Web:* www.carrollcountymd.gov	410-386-2011	840-8932	338
Carroll County Chamber of Commerce 700 Corporate Center Ct Ste L .... Westminster MD 21157 *Web:* carrollcountychamber.org	410-848-9050	876-1023	139
Carroll County Chamber of Commerce 200 Northside Dr .... Carrollton GA 30117 *Web:* www.carroll-ga.org	770-832-2446	832-1300	139
Carroll County Chamber of Commerce 20740 Main St E .... Huntingdon TN 38344 *Web:* www.carrollcounty-tn-chamber.com	731-986-4664	986-2029	139
Carroll County Chamber of Commerce & Economic Development 30 S Lisbon St 30 Public Sq. .... Carrollton OH 44615 *TF:* 877-727-0103 ■ *Web:* www.carrollohchamber.com	330-627-4811	627-3674	139
Carroll County Clerk 8 S Main .... Carrollton MO 64633 *Web:* www.carrollcomo.org	660-542-0615		338
Carroll County District Library 70 Second St NE .... Carrollton OH 44615 *Web:* carrolllibrary.org	330-627-2613	627-2523	434-3
Carroll County Economic Development 101 Eastridge Dr Ste A .... Carrollton MO 64633	660-542-0922		194
Carroll County public schools 125 N Court St Ste 101 .... Westminster MD 21157 *Web:* www.carrollk12.org	410-751-3000	751-3677	685
Carroll County School District 605-9 Pine St .... Hillsville VA 24343 *Web:* www.ccpsd.k12.va.us	276-730-3200	728-3195	186
Carroll County Sheriff's Office 95 Water Village Rd PO Box 190 .... Ossipee NH 03864 *TF:* 800-552-8960 ■ *Web:* www.carrollcountynh.net	603-539-2284		338
Carroll County Times, The PO Box 169 .... Westminster MD 21158 *Web:* www.baltimoresun.com	410-848-4400		532-2
Carroll CountyClerk 210 W Church St .... Berryville AR 72616 *Web:* co.carroll.ar.us	870-423-2022		338
Carroll Electric Co-opeartive Corp 920 Hwy 62 Spur .... Berryville AR 72616 *TF:* 800-432-9720 ■ *Web:* www.carrollecc.com	870-423-2161	423-4815	245
Carroll Electric Co-opeartive Inc 350 Canton Rd NW .... Carrollton OH 44615 *TF:* 800-232-7697 ■ *Web:* cecpower.coop	330-627-2116		245
Carroll Electric Membership Corp (EMC) 155 N Hwy 113 .... Carrollton GA 30117 *Web:* www.cemc.com	770-832-3552		245
Carroll Engineering Corp 949 Easton Rd .... Warrington PA 18976 *Web:* carrollengineering.com	215-343-5700	343-0875	261
Carroll Engineering Inc 1101 S Winchester Blvd Ste H-184 .... San Jose CA 95128 *Web:* carroll-engineering.com	408-261-9800		261
Carroll Fulmer Logistics Corp 8340 American Way .... Groveland FL 34736 *Web:* www.cfulmer.com	352-429-5000	429-1010	780
Carroll Independent Fuel Co 2700 Loch Raven Rd. .... Baltimore MD 21218 *Web:* www.carrollhomeservices.com	410-246-6988		316
Carroll Industrial Molds Inc 202 N Washington St .... Milledgeville IL 61051 *Web:* carrollmolds.com	815-225-7250	225-7260	757
Carroll Insurance Agency Ltd 14906 Fm 529 .... Houston TX 77095 *Web:* carrollins.com	281-656-3000		390
Carroll Lutheran Village 200 St Luke Cir. .... Westminster MD 21157 *TF:* 877-848-0095 ■ *Web:* www.carrolllutheranvillage.org	410-848-0090		672
Carroll Papers Inc PO Box 26 .... Flora IN 46929 *Web:* www.carrollcountycomet.com	574-967-4135	967-3384	532-2
Carroll Properties Partnership 12734 Kenwood Ln Ste 35 .... Fort Myers FL 33907 *Web:* www.carroll-properties.com	239-278-5900		379
Carroll Publishing 4701 Sangamore Rd Ste S-155 .... Bethesda MD 20816 *Web:* www.carrollpublishing.com	301-263-9800	263-9801	637-2
Carroll Seating Company Inc 10 Lincoln St .... Kansas City KS 66103 *TF:* 800-972-3779 ■ *Web:* www.carrollseating.com	816-471-2929	471-3001	320
Carroll Service Co 505 W Illinois Rt 64 .... Lanark IL 61046 *Web:* carrollsvc.com	815-493-2181	493-6173	276
Carroll Tool and Die Co 46650 Erb Dr .... Macomb MI 48042 *Web:* www.carrolltool.com	586-949-7670	949-3150	757
Carroll University 100 NE Ave .... Waukesha WI 53186 *TF:* 800-227-7655 ■ *Web:* www.carrollu.edu	262-547-1211	951-3037	166
Carrollton Public Library 4220 N Josey Ln. .... Carrollton TX 75010 *TF:* 888-727-2978 ■ *Web:* www.cityofcarrollton.com	972-466-4800	466-4722	434-3
Carrols Restaurant Group Inc 968 James St .... Syracuse NY 13203 *NASDAQ:* TAST ■ *TF:* 800-348-1074 ■ *Web:* www.carrols.com	315-424-0513		670
Carrom 218 E Dowland St .... Ludington MI 49431 *TF:* 800-223-6047 ■ *Web:* carrom.com	231-845-1263		319-2
Carron Net Company Inc 1623 17th St PO Box 177 .... Two Rivers WI 54241 *TF:* 800-558-7768 ■ *Web:* www.carronnet.com	920-793-2217	793-2122	208
Carrot & Stick Inc 115 New St Ste A .... Decatur GA 30030 *Web:* www.carrotandstick.com	404-371-1891		636
Carrot Medical LLC 22122 20th Ave SE Ste H-166 .... Bothell WA 98021 *TF:* 866-492-3533 ■ *Web:* carrotmedical.com	425-318-8089		743
Cars & Trucks r Us 7676 Happy Valley Rd. .... Cave City KY 42127 *Web:* www.ucarsandtrucks.com	270-773-2886		57
Carscom 175 W Jackson Blvd Ste 800 .... Chicago IL 60604 *TF:* 888-246-6298 ■ *Web:* www.cars.com	312-601-5000	601-5755	58
CarsDirectcom Inc 909 N Sepulveda Blvd 11th Fl .... El Segundo CA 90245 *TF:* 888-227-7347 ■ *Web:* www.carsdirect.com	888-227-7347		58
Carsey-Werner LLC 16027 Ventura Blvd Ste 600 .... Encino CA 91436 *Web:* www.carseywerner.com	818-464-9600	464-9650	511

Name / Address	City	State	ZIP	Phone	Fax	Class
Carson 3125 NW 35th Ave *TF:* 800-998-7767 ■ *Web:* carsonteam.com	Portland	OR	97210	503-224-8500		579
Carson & Coil PC 515 E High St *TF:* 877-442-3049 ■ *Web:* carsoncoil.com	Jefferson City	MO	65101	573-636-2177	636-7119	41
Carson Andre (Rep D - IN) 2135 Rayburn House Office Bldg *Web:* www.carson.house.gov	Washington	DC	20515	202-225-4011		342-2
Carson Bank 122 W Main St *Web:* carsonbank.com	Mulvane	KS	67110	316-777-1171		70
Carson Boxberger LLP 301 W Jefferson Blvd Ste 200 *TF:* 800-900-4250 ■ *Web:* www.carsonllp.com	Fort Wayne	IN	46802	260-423-9411		445
Carson Chamber of Commerce 530 E Del Amo Blvd *Web:* www.carsonchamber.com	Carson	CA	90746	310-217-4590	217-4591	139
Carson City - City Hall 201 N Carson St *Web:* carson.org	Carson City	NV	89701	775-887-2100	887-2139	337
Carson City Area Chamber of Commerce 1900 S Carson St Ste 200 *Web:* www.carsoncitychamber.com	Carson City	NV	89701	775-882-1565	882-4179	139
Carson City Correctional Facility 10274 Boyer Rd *Web:* www.michigan.gov	Carson City	MI	48811	989-584-3941		213
Carson City Library 900 N Roop St *Web:* www.carsoncitylibrary.org	Carson City	NV	89701	775-887-2244		434-3
Carson City Nugget 507 N Carson St *TF:* 800-426-5239 ■ *Web:* ccnugget.com	Carson City	NV	89701	775-882-1626		133
Carson City Symphony PO Box 2001 *Web:* www.ccsymphony.com	Carson City	NV	89702	775-883-4154	883-4371	573-3
Carson County 501 Main St PO Box 487 *Web:* www.co.carson.tx.us	Panhandle	TX	79068	806-537-3873	537-3623	338
Carson Ctr 801 E Carson St *Web:* www.carsoncenter.com	Carson	CA	90745	310-835-0212	835-0160	205
Carson Dunlop Home Inspection 120 Carlton St Ste 407 *TF:* 800-268-7070 ■ *Web:* carsondunlop.com	Toronto	ON	M5A4K2	416-964-9415	964-0683	652
Carson Group Advertising, The 1708 Hwy 6 S *Web:* www.carsongroupadvertising.com	Houston	TX	77077	281-496-2600		7
Carson Helicopters 952 Blooming Glen Rd *Web:* www.carsonhelicopters.com	Perkasie	PA	18944	215-249-3535		359
Carson Hot Springs 1500 Hot Springs Rd *TF:* 888-917-3711 ■ *Web:* carsonhotsprings.com	Carson City	NV	89706	775-885-8844		50-5
Carson Long Military Institute 200 N Carlisle St *Web:* www.carsonlong.org	New Bloomfield	PA	17068	717-582-2121		622
Carson Masonry and Steel Supply (CMS) 4783 Hwy 50 E *Web:* www.carsonmasonry.com	Carson City	NV	89701	775-882-3832	882-1654	191-1
Carson Tahoe Hospital 1600 Medical Pkwy *Web:* www.carsontahoe.com	Carson City	NV	89703	775-445-8000		374-3
Carson Valley Chamber of Commerce 1477 Hwy 395 N Ste A *TF:* 800-727-7677 ■ *Web:* www.carsonvalleynv.org	Gardnerville	NV	89410	775-782-8144	782-1025	139
Carson Valley Museum & Cultural Ctr 1477 Old US Hwy 395 S Ste B *Web:* www.historicnv.org	Gardnerville	NV	89410	775-782-2555		520
Carson's Inc PO Box 14186 *Web:* www.carsonshospitality.com	Archdale	NC	27263	336-397-4339		319-2
Carson's Nut-Bolt & Tool Co 301 Hammett St Ext *Web:* www.carsons-nbt.com	Greenville	SC	29609	864-242-4720	242-6821	351
Carson-Dellosa Publishing Company Inc 7027 Albert Pick Rd *TF:* 800-321-0943 ■ *Web:* www.carsondellosa.com	Greensboro	NC	27409	336-632-0084		243
Carsonite Composites LLC 19845 US Hwy 76 *TF:* 800-648-7916 ■ *Web:* www.carsonite.com	Newberry	SC	29108	803-321-1185	276-8940	678
Carson-Newman College 1646 Russell Ave *TF:* 800-678-9061 ■ *Web:* www.cn.edu	Jefferson City	TN	37760	865-471-2000	471-3502	166
CARSTAR Quality Collision Service 13750 W 108th St *TF:* 800-227-7827 ■ *Web:* www.carstar.com	Lenexa	KS	66215	913-696-0003		62-4
Carsten Institute of Cosmetology 3345 S Rural Rd *Web:* www.carsteninstitute.com	Tempe	AZ	85282	480-491-0449		167-3
Carstens Industries Inc 733 W Main St *Web:* www.carstensindustries.com	Melrose	MN	56352	320-256-3919	256-4052	710
Carswell Distributing Co 3750 N Liberty St *TF:* 800-929-1948 ■ *Web:* carswelldist.com	Winston-Salem	NC	27105	800-929-1948		429
CARTA (Charleston Area Regional Transportation Authority) 1362 McMillan Ave Ste 100 *Web:* www.ridecarta.com	North Charleston	SC	29405	843-724-7420		468
Carta 333 Bush St *Web:* carta.com	San Francisco	CA	94105	650-669-8381		113
Cartec International Inc 106 Powder Mill Rd *TF:* 800-821-4434 ■ *Web:* www.cartec.com	Canton	CT	06019	860-693-9395		605-2
Carten Controls 604 W Johnson Ave *Web:* www.cartenus.com	Cheshire	CT	06410	203-699-2100		790
Carter & Sloope Inc 6310 Peake Rd *Web:* cartersloope.com	Macon	GA	31210	478-477-3923		261
Carter Agri-System (AGCO) 45 W 1st N *Web:* www.carterag.com	Lund	NV	89317	775-238-5295	238-5410	274
Carter Bank & Trust 1300 Kings Mountain Rd *Web:* www.cbtcares.com	Martinsville	VA	24112	276-656-1776		70
Carter BloodCare 2205 Hwy 121 *Web:* www.carterbloodcare.org	Bedford	TX	76021	817-412-5385		89
Carter Broadcast Group Inc 11131 Colorado Ave *Web:* www.kprs.com	KANSAS CITY	MO	64137	816-763-2040	966-1055	645-80
Carter Bros LLC 3015 RN Martin St *TF:* 888-818-0152 ■ *Web:* www.carterbrothers.com	East Point	GA	30344	888-818-0152		692
Carter Buddy (Rep R - GA) 2432 Rayburn House Office Bldg *Web:* buddycarter.house.gov	Washington	DC	20515	202-225-5831	226-2269	342-2
Carter Business Service Inc 150A Andover St *Web:* www.carterbusiness.com	Danvers	MA	01923	781-246-4300		160
Carter Composition Corp 2007 N Hamilton St *TF:* 800-344-9206 ■ *Web:* carterprinting.com	Richmond	VA	23230	804-359-9206		627
Carter County 3600 W Broadway *TF:* 800-231-8668 ■ *Web:* cartercountyok.us	Ardmore	OK	73401	580-223-8162		338
Carter County 214 Park St *Web:* www.cartercountymt.info	Ekalaka	MT	59324	406-775-8749	775-8750	338
Carter County 300 W Main St Rm 227 *Web:* www.cartercounty.ky.gov	Grayson	KY	41143	606-474-5366	474-6991	338
Carter Ctr 1 Copenhill Ave 453 Freedom Pkwy *TF:* 800-550-3560 ■ *Web:* www.cartercenter.org	Atlanta	GA	30307	404-420-5100	331-0283	634
Carter Day International Inc 500 73rd Ave NE *Web:* www.carterday.com	Minneapolis	MN	55432	763-571-1000	571-3012	273
Carter Express Inc 4020 W 73rd St *TF:* 800-738-7705 ■ *Web:* carter-express.com	Anderson	IN	46011	800-738-7705		194
Carter Group LLC, The 1621 University Blvd S Ste B2 *Web:* www.thecartergroup.com	Mobile	AL	36609	251-342-0999		260
Carter Healthcare 3105 S Meridian Ave *TF:* 888-951-1112 ■ *Web:* www.carterhealthcare.com	Oklahoma City	OK	73119	405-947-7700	947-7300	363
Carter John (Rep R - TX) 2110 Rayburn House Office Bldg *Web:* carter.house.gov	Washington	DC	20515	202-225-3864		342-2
Carter Ledyard & Milburn LLP 2 Wall St *Web:* www.clm.com	New York	NY	10005	212-732-3200	732-3232	428
Carter Lumber Company Inc 601 Tallmadge Rd *Web:* www.carterlumber.com	Kent	OH	44240	330-673-6100		364
Carter Machinery Company Inc 1330 Lynchburg Tpk *TF:* 800-768-4200 ■ *Web:* cartermachinery.com	Salem	VA	24153	540-387-1111	375-9390	190
Carter Mario Injury Lawyers 176 Wethersfield Ave *TF:* 844-634-5656 ■ *Web:* www.cartermario.com	Hartford	CT	06114	844-634-5656		428
Carter Motor Co 400 S Railroad St *TF:* 866-745-2100 ■ *Web:* www.cartermotor.com	Warren	IL	61087	815-745-2100	745-2135	57
Carter Oil Company Inc 2201 E Huntington Dr *TF:* 800-430-5419 ■ *Web:* www.carteroil.com	Flagstaff	AZ	86004	928-774-7600	774-0763	579
Carter Printing Company Inc 1739 E Grand Ave *Web:* carterprinting.net	Des Moines	IA	50316	515-265-6139		627
Carter Schwartze CPAS PLLC 16300 Mill Creek Blvd *Web:* millcreekcpa.com	Mill Creek	WA	98012	425-481-1040		2
Carter, Conboy, Case, Blackmore, Maloney & Laird PC 20 Corporate Woods Blvd Ste 23 *Web:* carterconboy.com	Albany	NY	12211	518-465-3484		41
CarterBaldwin Inc 200 Mansell Ct E Ste 450 *Web:* carterbaldwin.com	Roswell	GA	30076	678-448-0000		193
Carteret Community College 3505 Arendell St *Web:* www.carteret.edu	Morehead City	NC	28557	252-222-6000	222-6265	162
Carteret County Courthouse Sq *Web:* carteretcountync.gov	Beaufort	NC	28516	252-728-8485	728-2092	338
Carteret County Chamber of Commerce 801 Arendell St Ste 1 *TF:* 800-622-6278 ■ *Web:* nccoastchamber.com	Morehead City	NC	28557	252-726-6350	726-3505	139
Carteret Health Care 3500 Arendell St *Web:* www.carterethealth.org	Morehead City	NC	28557	252-247-2013		374-3
Carteret-Craven Electric Co-op (CCEC) 1300 Hwy 24 W PO Box 1490 *TF:* 800-682-2217 ■ *Web:* www.ccemc.com	Newport	NC	28570	252-247-3107		245
Carter-Hoffmann Corp 1551 Mccormick Ave *TF:* 800-323-9793 ■ *Web:* www.carter-hoffmann.com	Mundelein	IL	60060	847-362-5500	367-8981	427
Carter-Lee ProBuild 1717 W Washington St *TF:* 800-344-9242 ■ *Web:* probuildindy.com	Indianapolis	IN	46222	317-639-5431	639-6982	499
Cartersville City Schools 15 Nelson St PO Box 3310 *Web:* www.cartersvilleschools.org	Cartersville	GA	30120	770-382-5880	387-7476	685
Cartersville-Bartow County Chamber of Commerce 122 W Main St PO Box 307 *TF:* 800-527-9395 ■ *Web:* www.cartersvillechamber.com	Cartersville	GA	30120	770-382-1466	382-2704	139
Carthage College 2001 Alford Pk Dr *TF:* 800-351-4058 ■ *Web:* www.carthage.edu	Kenosha	WI	53140	262-551-8500	551-5762	166
Carthage Mills 4243 Hunt Rd **Fax Area Code:* 513 ■ *TF:* 800-543-4430 ■ *Web:* carthagemills.com	Cincinnati	OH	45242	800-543-4430	794-3434*	745-3
Carthage Technical Ctr 609 S River St *Web:* www.ctc-carthage-mo.schoolloop.com	Carthage	MO	64836	417-359-7095	359-7419	167-3
Carthage Veterinary Service Ltd 34 W Main St *Web:* www.hogvet.com	Carthage	IL	62321	217-357-2811	357-6665	794
Carthage Water & Electric Plant 627 W Centennial Ave PO Box 611 *Web:* cwep.com	Carthage	MO	64836	417-237-7300		787
Cartier Place Suite Hotel 180 Cooper St *TF:* 800-236-8399 ■ *Web:* www.suitedreams.com	Ottawa	ON	K2P2L5	613-236-5000	238-3842	379
CarTika Medical Inc 6550 Wedgwood Rd N Ste 300 *Web:* www.cartikamedical.com	Maple Grove	MN	55311	763-545-5188		477

Name / Address	Phone	Fax	Class
Cartmell Communities 2212 W Reagan St . . . . Palestine TX 75801 *Web:* www.cartmellcommunities.org	903-727-8500		371
Cartner Glass Systems Inc 2508 Westinghouse Blvd . . . . Charlotte NC 28273	704-588-1976		189-6
Carton Service Inc First Quality Dr PO Box 702 . . . . Shelby OH 44875 *TF:* 800-533-7744 ■ *Web:* www.cartonservice.com	419-342-5010	342-4804	101
Cartoon Art Museum 655 Mission St . . . . San Francisco CA 94105 *Web:* www.cartoonart.org	415-227-8666	243-8666	520
Cartoon Cuts LP 927 N University Dr . . . . Coral Springs FL 33071 *Web:* www.cartooncuts.com	954-341-4221		77
Cartridge Actuated Devices Inc (CAD) 51 Dwight Pl . . . . Fairfield NJ 07004 *Web:* cartactdev.com	973-575-1312		268
Cartus Corp 40 Apple Ridge Rd . . . . Danbury CT 06810 *TF:* 888-767-9357 ■ *Web:* www.cartus.com	203-205-3400	205-6575	666
Cartwright Cos, The 11901 Cartwright Ave . . . . Grandview MO 64030 **Fax Area Code:* 816 ■ *TF:* 800-821-2334 ■ *Web:* cartwrightcompanies.com	800-821-2334	442-6360*	519
Cartwright Matt (Rep D - PA) 1034 Longworth House Office Bldg . . . . Washington DC 20515 *Web:* www.cartwright.house.gov	202-225-5546		342-2
Carty & Company Inc 6263 Poplar Ave Ste 800 . . . . Memphis TN 38119 *TF:* 800-767-8940 ■ *Web:* cartyco.com	901-767-8940		401
Carus Corp 315 5th St . . . . Peru IL 61354 *TF:* 800-435-6856 ■ *Web:* www.carusllc.com	815-223-1500	224-6697	143
Caruso Affiliated Holdings LLC 101 The Grove Dr . . . . Los Angeles CA 90036 *Web:* caruso.com	323-900-8100		360-2
Caruso Inc 3465 Hauck Rd . . . . Cincinnati OH 45241 *TF:* 800-759-7659 ■ *Web:* www.carusologistics.com	513-860-9200		10-11
Caruso Turley Scott Inc 1215 W Rio Salado Pkwy Ste 200 . . . . Tempe AZ 85281 *Web:* www.ctsaz.com	480-774-1700		256
Caruthers Raisin Packing Company Inc 12797 S Elm Ave . . . . Caruthers CA 93609 *Web:* caruthersraisinpacking.com	559-864-9448	864-3849	297-8
CarVal Investors LLC 9320 Excelsior Blvd 7th Fl . . . . Hopkins MN 55343 *Web:* carvalinvestors.com	952-444-4780		401
Carvel Express 200 Glenridge Point Pkwy Ste 200 . . . . Atlanta GA 30342 *TF:* 800-322-4848 ■ *Web:* www.carvel.com	800-322-4848		381
Carver & Associates Inc 4177 Northeast Expy . . . . Atlanta GA 30340 *Web:* www.carverassoc.com	770-446-2677		317
Carver Aero Inc Davenport Municipal Airport 9230 Harrison St . . . . Davenport IA 52806 *Web:* www.carveraero.com	563-391-5650		167-3
Carver Bancorp Inc 75 W 125th St . . . . New York NY 10027 *NASDAQ: CARV* ■ *Web:* www.carverbank.com	718-230-2900		360-2
Carver Bible College 3870 Cascade Rd . . . . Atlanta GA 30331 *Web:* www.carver.edu	404-527-4520	527-4524	166
Carver Boat Corporation LLC 790 Markham Dr . . . . Pulaski WI 54162 *Web:* www.carveryachts.com	920-822-1600	822-8820	90
Carver Brewing Co 1022 Main Ave . . . . Durango CO 81301 *Web:* carverbrewing.com	970-259-2545		671
Carver Career & Technical Ctr 4799 Midland Dr . . . . Charleston WV 25306 *Web:* ccc.kana.k12.wv.us	304-348-1965		167-3
Carver Community Cultural Ctr 226 N Hackberry St . . . . San Antonio TX 78202 *Web:* www.thecarver.org	210-207-7211		50-2
Carver County 606 E Fourth St . . . . Chaska MN 55318 *Web:* www.co.carver.mn.us	952-361-1105		338
Carver County Historical Society (CCHS) 555 W 1st St . . . . Waconia MN 55387 *Web:* www.carvercountyhistoricalsociety.org	952-442-4234		49-19
Carver County Library 4 City Hall Plz . . . . Chaska MN 55318 *Web:* www.carverlib.org	952-448-9395	448-9392	434-3
Carver Financial Services Inc 7473 Center St . . . . Mentor OH 44060 *TF:* 800-627-7279 ■ *Web:* carverfinancialservices.com	440-974-0808	974-3371	401
Carver Florek & James LLC 2246 University Park Blvd . . . . Layton UT 84041 *Web:* cfjcpa.com	801-926-1177	926-1178	2
Carver Inc 1569 Morris St . . . . Wabash IN 46992 *Web:* www.carverpress.com	260-563-7577	563-7625	420
Carver Law LLC 600 17th St Ste 2800 S . . . . Denver CO 80202 *Web:* johndcarver.com	720-932-8510		41
Carver Law Office PLLC 2800 NW 36th St Ste 225 . . . . Oklahoma City OK 73112 *Web:* oklataxrelief.com	405-256-2619		41
Carver Machine Works 129 Christian Service Camp Rd . . . . Washington NC 27889 *Web:* cmwglobal.com	252-975-3101		454
Carver Pump Co 2415 Park Ave . . . . Muscatine IA 52761 *Web:* www.carverpump.com	563-263-3410		641
Carvers Steak & Chops 11940 Bernardo Plaza Dr . . . . San Diego CA 92128 *Web:* www.carverssteak.com	858-485-1262		670
Carvin Corp 12340 World Trade Dr . . . . San Diego CA 92128 **Fax Area Code:* 760 ■ *TF:* 800-854-2235 ■ *Web:* carvinaudio.com	858-487-8700	487-7620*	527
Carvin French Jewelers Inc 515 Madison Ave Ste 1605 . . . . New York NY 10022 *Web:* www.carvinfrench.com	212-755-6474		409
Car-X Associates Corp 1375 E Woodfield Rd Ste 500 . . . . Schaumburg IL 60173 *Web:* www.carx.com	847-273-8920		310
Cary Academy 1500 N Harrison Ave . . . . Cary NC 27513 *TF:* 800-948-2557 ■ *Web:* www.caryacademy.org	919-677-3873		685
Cary Chamber of Commerce 307 N Academy St . . . . Cary NC 27513 *Web:* www.carychamber.com	919-467-1016	469-2375	139
Cary Concrete Products Inc 370 Lincoln Ave . . . . Woodstock IL 60098 *Web:* www.caryconcrete.com	815-338-2301	337-5801	183
Cary Kopczynski & Company Incorporated PS Bellevue Pl 10500 Eighth St Ste 800 . . . . Bellevue WA 98004 *Web:* www.ckcps.com	425-455-2144		256
Cary Memorial Library 1874 Massachusetts Ave . . . . Lexington MA 02420 *Web:* www.carylibrary.org	781-862-6288	862-7355	434-3
Cary Oil Company Inc 110 Mackenan Dr . . . . Cary NC 27511 *TF:* 800-227-9645 ■ *Web:* www.caryoil.com	919-462-1100	481-6862	581
Cary Pharmaceuticals Inc 9903 Windy Hollow Rd . . . . Great Falls VA 22066 *Web:* www.carypharma.com	703-759-7460		582
Cary Towne Ctr 1105 Walnut St . . . . Cary NC 27511 *Web:* www.shopcarytownecentermall.com	919-467-0145		460
Cary, Trlica & Wood Pc 11612 Fm2244 . . . . Austin TX 78738 *Web:* ctwpc.com	512-373-8239		2
CAS (Center for Auto Safety) 1825 Connecticut Ave NW Ste 330 . . . . Washington DC 20009 *Web:* www.autosafety.org	202-328-7700		49-21
CAS (Chemical Abstracts Service) 2540 Olentangy River Rd . . . . Columbus OH 43202 *TF:* 800-848-6538 ■ *Web:* www.cas.org	614-447-3600	447-3713	387
CAS (Coastal Administrative Services) PO Box 3070 . . . . Bellingham WA 98227 **Fax Area Code:* 360 ■ *TF:* 800-870-1831 ■ *Web:* www.casbenefits.com	800-870-1831	746-8386*	260
CAS (Casualty Actuarial Society) 4350 Fairfax Dr Ste 250 . . . . Arlington VA 22203 *TF:* 800-766-0070 ■ *Web:* www.casact.org	703-276-3100	276-3108	49-9
CAS Constructors LLC 3500 SW Fairlawn Dr Ste 200 . . . . Topeka KS 66614 *Web:* casconstructors.com	785-354-9953		187
CAS Severn Inc 6201 Chevy Chase Dr . . . . Laurel MD 20707 *TF:* 800-252-4715 ■ *Web:* www.cassevern.com	301-776-3400	776-3444	178-1
CASA (National CASA Assn) 100 W Harrison St N Tower Ste 500 . . . . Seattle WA 98119 *TF:* 800-628-3233 ■ *Web:* www.casaforchildren.org	206-270-0072	270-0078	48-6
Casa Alvarez 106 Dawson Pl . . . . Longmont CO 80504 *Web:* casaalvarezfoods.com	720-491-1985		671
Casa Baez 1292 Lancaster Dr NE . . . . Salem OR 97301 *Web:* www.casabaez.com	503-371-3867		671
Casa Bonita 6715 W Colfax Ave . . . . Lakewood CO 80214 *Web:* www.casabonitadenver.com	303-232-5115		671
Casa Colina Hospital & Centers for Healthcare 255 E Bonita Ave . . . . Pomona CA 91767 *TF:* 866-724-4127 ■ *Web:* www.casacolina.org	866-724-4127		450
Casa D'Amici 485 High St . . . . Morgantown WV 26505 *Web:* www.casadamiciwv.com	304-292-4400		671
Casa D'Angelo 1201 N Federal Hwy . . . . Fort Lauderdale FL 33304 *Web:* casa-d-angelo.com	954-564-1234		671
Casa Dante 737 Newark Ave . . . . Jersey City NJ 07306 *Web:* www.casadante.com	201-795-2750	795-1225	671
Casa De La Luz Hospice 7740 N Oracle Rd . . . . Tucson AZ 85704 *Web:* www.casahospice.com	520-544-9890	544-9894	450
Casa de Luz 1701 Toomey Rd . . . . Austin TX 78704 *Web:* www.casadeluz.org	512-476-2535		671
Casa De Soto 8562 Garden Grove Blvd . . . . Garden Grove CA 92844 *Web:* www.casadesoto.com	714-530-4200		671
Casa del Herrero 1387 E Valley Rd . . . . Montecito CA 93108 *Web:* www.casadelherrero.com	805-565-5653	969-2371	97
Casa Di Mir Montessori School 90 E Latimer Ave . . . . Campbell CA 95008 *Web:* www.casadimir.org	408-370-3073	370-3153	685
Casa Dorinda 300 Hot Springs Rd . . . . Santa Barbara CA 93108 *Web:* www.casadorinda.org	805-969-8011	969-8686	672
Casa Esperanza 1005 Yale NE . . . . Albuquerque NM 87106 *TF:* 866-654-1338 ■ *Web:* casanm.org	505-246-2700	277-9876	372
Casa Fiesta 801 Louisville Rd . . . . Frankfort KY 40601 *Web:* www.links2thebluegrass.com	502-226-5010		671
Casa Fuentes 1107 W Hwy 76 . . . . Branson MO 65616 *Web:* www.casafuentes.com	417-339-3888		671
Casa Garcia 8814 Veterans Memorial Blvd . . . . Metairie LA 70003 *Web:* casagarcianola.com	504-464-0354		671
Casa Grande Beach House, The 834 Ocean Dr . . . . Miami Beach FL 33139 *Web:* www.thecasagrandebeachhouse.com	305-423-0608		379
Casa Grande Ruins National Monument 1100 W Ruins Dr . . . . Coolidge AZ 85128 *TF:* 877-642-4743 ■ *Web:* www.nps.gov	520-723-3172		564
Casa Grande Valley Newspaper Inc 200 W Second St . . . . Casa Grande AZ 85122 *Web:* www.pinalcentral.com	520-836-7461	836-0343	637-8
Casa Herrerra Inc 2655 N Pine St . . . . Pomona CA 91767 *TF:* 800-624-3916 ■ *Web:* www.casaherrera.com	909-392-3930	392-0231	298
Casa Juancho 2436 SW Eigth St . . . . Miami FL 33135 *Web:* www.opentable.com	305-642-2452	642-2524	671
Casa Linda Furniture Inc 4815 Whittier Blvd . . . . Los Angeles CA 90022 *TF:* 888-783-0631 ■ *Web:* www.furniturecasalinda.com	323-263-3851	263-1292	321
Casa Loma College 6725 Kester Ave . . . . Van Nuys CA 91405 *TF:* 800-270-5052 ■ *Web:* www.casalomacollege.com	818-785-2726		167-3
Casa Madrona Hotel 801 Bridgeway . . . . Sausalito CA 94965 *TF:* 800-288-0502 ■ *Web:* www.casamadrona.com	415-332-0502	331-3125	379
Casa Manana Theatre 3101 W Lancaster Ave . . . . Fort Worth TX 76107 *Web:* www.casamanana.org	817-332-2272		572
Casa Marina Hotel & Restaurant 691 First St N . . . . Jacksonville Beach FL 32250 *Web:* casamarinahotel.com	904-270-0025		707

Name / Address	City	State	ZIP	Phone	Fax	Class
Casa Marina Resort & Beach Club 1500 Reynolds St — *TF:* 888-303-5719 ■ *Web:* www.casamarinaresort.com	Key West	FL	33040	305-296-3535	296-4633	669
Casa Mexicana Tile Distributors 5603 S Main St — *Web:* www.casamexicana.com	Mesilla Park	NM	88047	575-523-2777		290
Casa Mia 716 Plum St — *Web:* www.casamiarestaurants.com	Olympia	WA	98501	360-352-0440		671
Casa Molina 3001 N Campbell Ave	Tucson	AZ	85712	520-886-5468		671
Casa Mono 52 Irving Pl — *Web:* casamononyc.com	New York	NY	10003	212-253-2773		671
Casa Munras Hotel 700 Munras Ave — *TF:* 800-222-2446 ■ *Web:* www.hotelcasamunras.com	Monterey	CA	93940	831-375-2411	375-1365	379
Casa Navarro State Historic Site 228 S Laredo St — *Web:* www.thc.texas.gov	San Antonio	TX	78207	210-226-4801		565
Casa Palmera 14750 El Camino Real — *Web:* Www.casapalmera.com	Del Mar	CA	92014	858-481-4411		450
Casa Payroll Service LLC 3120 Fire Rd — *Web:* www.casapayroll.com	Egg Harbor Township	NJ	08234	609-383-0677	383-0907	734
Casa Ristoranti Italiano 7539 W Jefferson Blvd — *Web:* www.casarestaurants.com	Fort Wayne	IN	46804	260-399-2455		671
Casa Romero 30 Gloucester St — *Web:* www.casaromero.com	Boston	MA	02115	617-536-4341		671
Casa Rondena Winery 733 Chavez Rd NW — *Web:* www.casarondena.com	Albuquerque	NM	87107	505-344-5911	343-1823	50-7
Casa Via Mar Inn & Tennis Club 377 W Ch Islands Blvd — *Web:* www.casaviamar.com	Port Hueneme	CA	93041	805-984-6222		379
Casa Ybel Resort 2255 W Gulf Dr — *TF:* 800-276-4753 ■ *Web:* www.casaybelresort.com	Sanibel	FL	33957	239-472-3145		669
Casablanca Cafe 3049 Alhambra St — *Web:* www.casablancacafeonline.com	Fort Lauderdale	FL	33304	954-764-3500		671
Casablanca Hotel 147 W 43rd St — *Web:* casablancahotel.com	New York	NY	10036	212-869-1212	391-7585	379
Casablanca Resort 950 W Mesquite Blvd — *TF:* 800-459-7529 ■ *Web:* casablancaresort.com	Mesquite	NV	89027	702-346-7529		669
Casahl Technology Inc 2400 Camino Ramon Bldg K Ste 355 — *TF:* 800-324-4284 ■ *Web:* www.casahl.com	San Ramon	CA	94583	925-328-2828	328-1188	177
Casal Aveda Institute 6000 Mahoning Ave — *Web:* www.casalaveda.com	Austintown	OH	44515	330-792-6504	792-6509	167-3
Casale Engineering 13030 E Telegraph Rd — *Web:* www.casalev-drive.com	Santa Fe Springs	CA	90670	562-906-4825	906-4827	709
Casani Candy Co 7905 Browning Rd Ste 208 — *Web:* www.casanicandyco.com	Pennsauken	NJ	08109	856-488-0045		123
Casanova 5th between Mission & San Carlos — *Web:* www.casanovacarmel.com	Carmel By The Sea	CA	93921	831-625-0501		671
Casavant Freres Inc 900 Girouard Est — *Web:* www.casavant.ca	Saint-Hyacinthe	QC	J2S2Y2	450-773-5001		526
Casbah 229 S Highland Ave — *Web:* casbah.kitchen	Pittsburgh	PA	15206	412-661-5656		671
Cascade Analytic LLC 1705 Gill Rd — *Fax Area Code: 832 ■ *Web:* cascademvs.com	Dickinson	TX	77539	281-482-2727	201-0346*	261
Cascade Autocenter 148 Easy St — *Web:* www.cascadeautocenter.com	Wenatchee	WA	98801	509-639-7993		57
Cascade Bicycle Club 7400 Sand Point Way NE Ste 101s — *Web:* www.cascade.org	Seattle	WA	98115	206-522-3222		326
Cascade Brewing Company LLC 7424 SW Beaverton Hillsdale Hwy — *Web:* lodgeatcascade.com	Portland	OR	97225	503-296-0110		102
Cascade Caverns 226 Cascade Caverns Rd — *Web:* www.cascadecaverns.com	Boerne	TX	78015	830-755-8080		50-5
Cascade Central Credit Union 1206 12th St — *Web:* cascadecentral.com	Hood River	OR	97031	541-387-9297		219
Cascade Computer Maintenance Inc 750 Front St NE — *TF:* 800-421-7934 ■ *Web:* www.ccmaint.com	Salem	OR	97302	503-581-0081	585-0991	175
Cascade Controls 19785 NE San Raffael St — *Web:* cascadecontrolsinc.com	Portland	OR	97230	503-252-3116		358
Cascade Corp 2201 NE 201st Ave — *NYSE: CASC* ■ *TF:* 800-227-2233 ■ *Web:* www.cascorp.com	Fairview	OR	97024	503-669-6300		470
Cascade County 325 Second Ave N — *Web:* www.cascadecountymt.gov	Great Falls	MT	59401	406-454-6795	454-6797	338
Cascade Credit Services Inc 1635 SE Malden St Ste D — *Fax Area Code: 971 ■ *Web:* www.cascadecredit.com	Portland	OR	97202	503-722-2009	230-0090*	70
Cascade Dafo Inc 1360 Sunset Ave — *Web:* cascadedafo.com	Ferndale	WA	98248	360-543-9306		475
Cascade Data Solutions PO Box 2677 — *TF:* 800-280-2090 ■ *Web:* www.cascadeds.com	Albany	OR	97321	541-924-5714	924-1870	178-1
Cascade Designs Inc 4000 First Ave S — *TF:* 800-531-9531 ■ *Web:* www.cascadedesigns.com	Seattle	WA	98134	206-505-9500	505-9525	710
Cascade Earth Sciences (CES) 2902 W Main St — *Web:* www.cascade-earth.com	Visalia	CA	93291	559-732-3665	732-3720	538
Cascade Federal Credit Union 18020 80th Ave S — *TF:* 800-562-2853 ■ *Web:* www.cascadefcu.org	Kent	WA	98032	425-251-8888	251-0299	216
Cascade Financial Management Inc 950 17th St Ste 950 — *TF:* 800-353-0008 ■ *Web:* cascade-inc.com	Denver	CO	80202	800-353-0008		194
Cascade Hardwoods Inc 158 Ribelin Rd — *Web:* www.cascadehardwood.com	Chehalis	WA	98532	360-748-3317		683
Cascade Lodge 3719 W Hwy 61 — *TF:* 800-322-9543 ■ *Web:* cascadelodgemn.com	Lutsen	MN	55612	218-387-1112		669
Cascade Lumber Co 1000 First Ave E — *Web:* www.caslbr.com	Cascade	IA	52033	563-852-3232		817
Cascade Lumber Co 109 Madison St SE — *Web:* www.cascade-mfg-co.com	Cascade	IA	52033	563-852-3231	852-7391	191-3
Cascade Machinery & Electric Inc 4600 E Marginal Way S — *TF:* 800-289-0500 ■ *Web:* www.cascade-machinery.com	Seattle	WA	98134	206-762-0500	767-5122	385
Cascade Microtech Inc 2430 NW 206th Ave — *NASDAQ: CSCD* ■ *Web:* www.cascademicrotech.com	Beaverton	OR	97006	503-601-1000		248
Cascade Natural Gas Corp (CNGC) 8113 W Grandridge Blvd — *Fax Area Code: 206 ■ *TF:* 888-522-1130 ■ *Web:* www.cngc.com	Kennewick	WA	99336	888-522-1130	624-7215*	787
Cascade Networks Inc 1111-11th Ave PO Box 887 — *Web:* cni.net	Longview	WA	98632	360-414-5990		180
Cascade Orthopedic Supply Inc 2638 Aztec Dr — *TF:* 800-888-0865 ■ *Web:* www.cascade-usa.com	Chico	CA	95928	800-888-0865		475
Cascade Pacific Pulp LLC 30480 American Dr — *Web:* www.cascadepulp.com	Halsey	OR	97348	541-369-2841		638
Cascade Pioneer PO Box 901 — *Web:* www.cascadechamber.org	Cascade	IA	52033	563-690-8611		532-2
Cascade Plastics Company Inc 7009 45th St Ct E — *Web:* www.cfmconsolidated.com	Fife	WA	98424	253-922-3460		499
Cascade Policy Institute 4850 SW Scholls Ferry Rd Ste 103 — *Web:* www.cascadepolicy.org	Portland	OR	97225	503-242-0900	242-3822	634
Cascade Precision Inc 35700 SE Bluff Rd — *Web:* www.cascadeprecision.com	Boring	OR	97009	503-663-9506		454
Cascade Pump Co 10107 Norwalk Blvd — *Web:* www.cascadepump.com	Santa Fe Springs	CA	90670	562-946-1414		641
Cascade Regional Blood Services 220 S 'I' St — *Web:* www.crbs.net	Tacoma	WA	98405	253-383-2553		89
Cascade River State Park 3481 W Hwy 61 — *Web:* www.dnr.state.mn.us	Lutsen	MN	55612	218-387-6000		565
Cascade Rubber Products Inc 1828 NW Quimby St — *Web:* www.cascaderubber.com	Portland	OR	97209	503-248-1992		326
Cascade Steel Rolling Mills Inc (CSRM) 3200 N Hwy 99 W PO Box 687 — *TF:* 800-283-2776 ■ *Web:* www.cascadesteel.com	McMinnville	OR	97128	503-472-4181	434-5739	723
Cascade Timber Consulting Inc 3210 Hwy 20 — *Web:* cascadetimber.com	Sweet Home	OR	97386	541-367-2111	367-2117	302
Cascade Title Co 811 Willamette St — *Web:* cascadetitle.com	Eugene	OR	97401	541-687-2233	485-0307	653
Cascade Waterworks Manufacturing 1213 Badger St — *TF:* 800-426-4301 ■ *Web:* www.cascademfg.com	Yorkville	IL	60560	630-553-0840	553-0181	595
Cascade Wholesale Hardware Inc 5650 NW Wagon Way — *TF:* 800-877-9987 ■ *Web:* www.cascade.com	Hillsboro	OR	97124	503-614-2600	629-5793	351
Cascade Wood Products Inc PO Box 2429 — *TF:* 800-423-3311 ■ *Web:* www.cascadewood.com	White City	OR	97503	541-826-2911		499
Cascade Yacht Works LLC 485 SE 5th St — *Web:* cascadeyachtworks.com	Warrenton	OR	97146	503-440-0233		393
Cascade365 1070 Corporate Cir Ste 202 — *TF:* 888-417-1531 ■ *Web:* www.cascade365.com	Petaluma	CA	94954	707-981-4002		393
Cascades Inc 404 Marie-Victorin Blvd — *TSX: CAS* ■ *TF:* 800-361-4070 ■ *Web:* www.cascades.com	Kingsey Falls	QC	J0A1B0	819-363-5100	363-5155	561
Cascadia College 18345 Campus Way NE — *Web:* www.cascadia.edu	Bothell	WA	98011	425-352-8000		167-3
Cascadia Managing Brands 1109 First Ave Ste 400 — *Web:* www.cascadiaconsulting.com	Seattle	WA	98101	206-343-9759		463
Cascadia Motivation 4646 Riverside Dr Ste 14 — *TF:* 800-661-8360 ■ *Web:* www.cascadiamotivation.com	Red Deer	AB	T4N6Y5	403-340-8687	346-6220	772
Cascadia State Park PO Box 549 — *Web:* stateparks.oregon.gov	Detroit	OR	97342	541-367-6021		565
Cascadian Building Maintenance Ltd 1331 118th Ave SE Ste 100 — *Web:* www.cascadian.org	Bellevue	WA	98005	425-455-8404	454-7978	256
Cascio Interstate Music 13819 W National Ave — *TF:* 800-462-2263 ■ *Web:* www.interstatemusic.com	New Berlin	WI	53151	262-789-7600		526
Cascio's Steak House 1620 S Tenth St — *Web:* www.casciossteakhouse.com	Omaha	NE	68108	402-345-8313		671
Casco Bay Engineering Inc 424 Fore St — *Web:* cascobayengineering.com	Portland	ME	04101	207-842-2800		261
Casco Circuits Inc 10039 Canoga Ave Unit D — *Web:* www.cascocircuits.com	Chatsworth	CA	91311	818-882-0972	882-3728	625
Casco Equipment Corp 4141 Flat Rock Dr — *Web:* cascoequip.com	Riverside	CA	92505	951-324-8500		358
Casco Federal Credit Union 375 Main St PO Box 87 — *TF:* 888-395-5588 ■ *Web:* cascofcu.com	Gorham	ME	04038	207-839-5588	839-3971	219
Casco International Inc 4205 E Dixon Blvd — *TF:* 800-535-5690 ■ *Web:* www.cashort.com	Shelby	NC	28152	800-535-5690		260
Cascone & Kluepfel LLP 1399 Franklin Ave Ste 302 — *Web:* cklaw.com	Garden City	NY	11530	516-747-1990		41
Cascone's 8131 N OAK — *Web:* www.cascones.com	Kansas City	MO	64116	816-454-7977		671

Name / Address	Phone	Fax	Class
CASE (Council of Administrators of Special Education) Osigian Office Centre 101 Katelyn Cir Ste E ... Warner Robins GA 31088 *TF:* 800-585-1753 ■ *Web:* www.casecec.org	478-333-6892	333-2453	49-5
CASE (Council for Advancement & Support of Education) 1307 New York Ave NW Ste 1000 ... Washington DC 20005 *TF:* 800-554-8536 ■ *Web:* www.case.org	202-328-5900	387-4973	49-5
Case Construction LLC 56 Midtown Park W ... Mobile AL 36606	251-338-2400		186
Case Consulting Inc 18425 Rustling Woods Ct ... Leesburg VA 20175 *Web:* consultwithcase.com	703-728-0294		177
Case Contracting Co 2311 Turkey Creek Rd ... Plant City FL 33566 *Web:* www.casecontracting.com	813-754-3477	752-6732	186
Case Design Corp 333 School Ln ... Telford PA 18969 *TF:* 800-847-4176 ■ *Web:* www.casedesigncorp.com	215-703-0130	703-0139	199
Case Ed (Rep D - HI) 2443 Rayburn House Office Bldg ... Washington DC 20515 *Web:* www.case.house.gov	202-225-2726		342-2
Case Farms Inc 121 Rand St ... Morganton NC 28655 *Web:* www.casefarms.com	828-438-6900		619
Case Foundation Co 1350 W Lake St ... Roselle IL 60172 *TF:* 800-999-4087 ■ *Web:* www.keller.com	630-529-2911	529-4802	188-2
Case Logic Inc 6303 Dry Creek Pkwy ... Longmont CO 80503 *TF:* 800-925-8111 ■ *Web:* www.caselogic.com	303-652-1000		534
Case Management Society of America (CMSA) 6301 Ranch Dr ... Little Rock AR 72223 *TF:* 800-216-2672 ■ *Web:* www.cmsa.org	501-225-2229	221-9068	49-8
Case Medical Inc 65 Railroad Ave ... Ridgefield NJ 07657 *Web:* www.casemed.com	201-313-1999		488
Case Paper Company Inc 500 Mamaroneck Ave ... Harrison NY 10528 **Fax Area Code:* 914 ■ *TF:* 800-222-2922 ■ *Web:* www.casepaper.com	888-227-3178	777-1028*	554
Case Sabatini 470 Sts Run Rd ... Pittsburgh PA 15236 *Web:* www.casesabatini.com	412-881-4411	881-4421	2
Case Systems Inc 2700 James Savage Rd ... Midland MI 48642 *Web:* www.casesystems.com	989-496-9510		803-1
Case Western Reserve University 10900 Euclid Ave ... Cleveland OH 44106 *TF:* 800-967-8898 ■ *Web:* www.case.edu	216-368-2000	368-5111	166
Casella Waste Systems Inc 25 Greens Hill Ln ... Rutland VT 05701 *NASDAQ: CWST* ■ *TF:* 800-227-3552 ■ *Web:* www.casella.com	802-775-0325		804
Caselle Inc 1656 S East Bay Blvd Ste 100 ... Provo UT 84606 *TF:* 800-228-9851 ■ *Web:* www.caselle.com	801-850-5000		179
Casemate Academic 1950 Lawrence Rd ... Havertown PA 19083 *Web:* www.oxbowbooks.com	610-853-9131		637-2
Casepro Inc 19122 Autumn Garden Ste 1005 ... San Antonio TX 78258	210-496-8050		363
Caserta 501 5th Ave 11th Fl ... New York NY 10017 *TF:* 855-755-2246 ■ *Web:* caserta.com	855-755-2246		180
Cases By Source Inc 215 Island Rd ... Mahwah NJ 07430 *TF:* 888-515-5255 ■ *Web:* www.casesbysource.com	888-515-5255		557
Casey & Son Horseshoeing School 14013 E Hwy 136 ... La Fayette GA 30728 *Web:* www.caseyhorseshoeingschool.com	706-397-8909	397-8047	685
Casey Communications Inc 8301 Maryland Ave Ste 350 ... Saint Louis MO 63105 *Web:* www.caseycomm.com	314-721-2828		636
Casey Gerry Schenk Francavilla Blatt & Penfield LLP 110 Laurel St ... San Diego CA 92101 *TF:* 800-292-5865 ■ *Web:* caseygerry.com	619-238-1811	544-9232	428
Casey Moores Oyster House 850 S Ash Ave ... Tempe AZ 85281 *Web:* www.caseymooresoysterhouse.godaddysites.com	480-968-9935		671
Casey Mutual Telephone Co 108 E Logan St ... Casey IA 50048 *Web:* www.caseytelco.com	641-746-2222	746-2221	224
Casey Neilon & Associates LLC 503 N Division St ... Carson City NV 89703 *Web:* caseyneilon.com	775-283-5555		2
Casey Printing Inc 398 E San Antonio Dr ... King City CA 93930 *Web:* www.caseyprinting.com	831-385-3222		627
Casey Products 11230 Katherine Crossing ... Woodridge IL 60517 *Web:* www.caseyproducts.com	630-960-3360		351
Casey Quirk 17 Old King's Hwy S Ste 200 ... Darien CT 06820 *Web:* www2.deloitte.com	203-899-3000		196
Casey R. Stevens Pc 4311 Ridgewood Center Dr ... Woodbridge VA 22192 *Web:* stevenscarusolaw.com	703-897-1777	897-0077	41
Casey Research LLC 55 NE 5th Ave ... Delray Beach FL 33483 *TF:* 888-512-2739 ■ *Web:* www.caseyresearch.com	602-445-2736		401
Casey Robert P Jr (Sen D - PA) 393 Russell Senate Office Bldg ... Washington DC 20510 *Web:* www.casey.senate.gov	202-224-6324		342-2
Casey State Bank 305-307 N Central Ave ... Casey IL 62420 *TF:* 866-666-2754 ■ *Web:* www.caseystatebank.com	217-932-2136	932-4370	70
Casey's Foods 124 W Gartner Rd ... Naperville IL 60540 *Web:* caseysfoods.com	630-369-1686		345
Casey's General Stores 1 SE Convenience Blvd ... Ankeny IA 50021 *NASDAQ: CASY* ■ *Web:* www.caseys.com	515-965-6100		204
Casgrain & Company Ltd 1200 Mcgill College 21st Fl ... Montreal QC H3B4G7 *Web:* www.casgrain.ca	514-871-8080		401
Cash Acme Inc 2727 Paces Ferry Rd SE Ste 1800 ... Atlanta GA 30339 *TF:* 877-700-4242 ■ *Web:* www.cashacme.com	877-700-4242		789
Cash Control Business Systems 9101 Lackland Rd ... Overland MO 63114 *Web:* www.cashcontrolbiz.com	314-427-6143		535
Cash Flow Solutions Inc 5166 College Corner Pk ... Oxford OH 45056 *TF:* 800-736-5123 ■ *Web:* www.followthefrog.com	800-736-5123		196
Cash Management Solutions Inc 14450 46th St N Ste 112 ... Clearwater FL 33762 *Web:* www.lockboxpayments.com	727-524-1103		174
Cash Plus Inc PO Box 2185 ... Anaheim CA 92814 *TF:* 877-227-4758 ■ *Web:* cashplusinc.com	714-731-2274	731-2099	141
Cashco Inc 607 W 15th St PO Box 6 ... Ellsworth KS 67439 *Web:* www.cashco.com	785-472-4461	472-3539	790
Cashdollar & Associates LLC 115 Erie St ... Grove City PA 16127 *Web:* cashdollarandassociates.com	724-458-5233	458-4870	690
Cashiers Historical Society 1940 Hwy 107 S ... Cashiers NC 28717 *Web:* www.cashiershistoricalsociety.org	828-743-7710		50-3
Cashin Associates PC 1200 Veterans Memorial Hwy Ste 200 ... Hauppauge NY 11788 *Web:* www.cashinassociates.com	631-348-7600	348-7601	261
Cashion Co, The 321 Scott St ... Little Rock AR 72201 *Web:* cashionco.com	501-376-0716		390
Cashion's Eat Place 1819 Columbia Rd NW ... Washington DC 20009 *Web:* www.cashionseatplace.com	202-797-1819		671
Cashland Holdings LLC 10417 N May Ave ... Oklahoma City OK 73120 *Web:* cashlandok.com	405-748-5510		217
Cashman Equipment Co 3300 St Rose Pkwy ... Henderson NV 89052 *TF:* 800-937-2326 ■ *Web:* www.cashmanequipment.com	702-649-8777		45
CashmanKatz 76 E Blvd ... Glastonbury CT 06033 *Web:* cashmankatz.com	860-652-0300		344
Cashtown Inn Restaurant 1325 Old Rt 30 PO Box 103 ... Cashtown PA 17310 *TF:* 800-367-1797 ■ *Web:* cashtowninn.com	717-334-9722	334-4679	671
Cash-Wa Distributing Co 401 W Fourth St ... Kearney NE 68845 *TF:* 800-652-0010 ■ *Web:* web.cashwa.com	308-237-3151	234-6018	297-8
Cashwell Appliance Parts Inc 3485 Clinton Rd ... Fayetteville NC 28312 **Fax Area Code:* 800 ■ *TF:* 800-277-1220 ■ *Web:* www.cashwells.com	910-323-1111	277-2811*	38
Casino Arizona at Salt River 524 N 92nd St ... Scottsdale AZ 85256 *TF:* 866-877-9897 ■ *Web:* www.casinoarizona.com	480-850-7777		133
Casino City Network 95 Wells Ave ... Newton Center MA 02459 *TF:* 800-490-1715 ■ *Web:* www.casinocitypress.com	617-332-2850		637-10
Casino Fandango 3800 S Carson St ... Carson City NV 89701 *Web:* www.casinofandango.com	775-885-7000		133
Casino KC 1800 E Front St ... Kansas City MO 64120 *Web:* www.isleofcaprikansascity.com	816-855-7777		133
Casino NB 21 Casino Dr ... Moncton NB E1G0R7 **Fax Area Code:* 506 ■ *TF:* 877-859-7775 ■ *Web:* www.casinonb.ca	877-859-7775	859-7771*	133
Casino Nova Scotia 1983 Upper Water St ... Halifax NS B3J3Y5 *Web:* casinonovascotia.com	902-425-7777		133
Casino Pauma 777 Pauma Reservation Rd PO Box 1067 ... Pauma Valley CA 92061 *TF:* 877-687-2862 ■ *Web:* www.casinopauma.com	760-742-2177		31
Casino Pier & Water Works 800 Ocean Terr ... Seaside Heights NJ 08751 *Web:* casinopiernj.com	732-793-6488		32
Casino Queen 200 S Front St ... East Saint Louis IL 62201 *TF:* 800-777-0777 ■ *Web:* www.casinoqueen.com	618-874-5000		133
Casino Royale Hotel 3411 Las Vegas Blvd S ... Las Vegas NV 89109 *TF:* 800-854-7666 ■ *Web:* www.casinoroyalehotel.com	702-737-3500		379
Casio Cumputer Company Ltd 570 Mt Pleasant Ave ... Dover NJ 07801 *Web:* www.casio.com	973-361-5400		591
Cask 'n' Cleaver 8689 Ninth St ... Rancho Cucamonga CA 91730 *TF:* 800-995-4452 ■ *Web:* www.caskncleaver.com	909-982-7108	981-9734	670
Cask LLC PO Box 927170 ... San Diego CA 92192 *TF:* 866-535-8915 ■ *Web:* casknx.com	866-535-8915		196
Casket Shells Inc 432 1st St PO Box 172 ... Eynon PA 18403 *Web:* www.casketshellsinc.com	570-876-2642	876-5613	134
Caskey Printing Inc 850 Vogelsong Rd ... York PA 17404 *TF:* 800-864-2040 ■ *Web:* www.caskeygroup.com	717-764-4500		627
Casle Corp, The 200 Fisher Dr ... Avon CT 06001 *Web:* casle.com	860-674-9000		653
CASM (Canadian Academy of Sport Medicine) 55 Metcalfe St Ste 300 ... Ottawa ON K1P6L5 *TF:* 877-585-2394 ■ *Web:* casem-acmse.org	613-748-5851	912-0128	49-8
Casne Engineering Inc 3545 Factoria Blvd SE Ste 200 ... Kirkland WA 98033 *Web:* casne.com	425-522-1000		256
Casner & Edwards LLP 303 Congress St ... Boston MA 02210 *Web:* www.casneredwards.com	617-426-5900	426-8810	428
Casnet 45 Goodyear Blvd ... Akron OH 44314 *Web:* www.casnet.com	330-848-8800		317
Caspari Inc 100 W Main St ... Charlottesville VA 22902 *TF:* 800-227-7274 ■ *Web:* www.casparionline.com	434-817-7880		637-10
Casper Area Chamber of Commerce 500 N Center St ... Casper WY 82601 *Web:* casperwyoming.org	307-234-5311	265-2643	139
Casper Area Convention & Visitors Bureau 139 W Second St Ste 1B ... Casper WY 82601 *TF:* 800-852-1882 ■ *Web:* visitcasper.com	307-234-5362		206
Casper City Hall 200 N David St ... Casper WY 82601 *Web:* www.casperwy.gov	307-235-8264	235-7575	337
Casper College 125 College Dr ... Casper WY 82601 *TF:* 800-442-2963 ■ *Web:* www.caspercollege.edu	307-268-2100	268-2611	162
Casper Events Ctr 1 Events Dr ... Casper WY 82601 *TF:* 800-442-2256 ■ *Web:* www.casperwy.gov	307-235-8441		205
Casper Planetarium 904 N Poplar St ... Casper WY 82601 *Web:* www.casperplanetarium.com	307-577-0310		598
Caspian Energy Inc 649 Varsity Estates Crescent NW ... Calgary AB T3B3C5 **Fax Area Code:* 727 ■ *Web:* www.caspianenergyinc.com	701-537-1306	244-2819*	536
CASS (CASS Tech) 37000 Grand River Ave Ste 130 ... Farmington Hills MI 48335 *Web:* www.cass-tech.com	248-538-7374		177
Cass Arrieta PO Box 309 ... El Cajon CA 92022 *Web:* cassarrieta.com	619-590-0929		261

Name / Address	City	State	Zip	Phone	Fax	Class
Cass Career Ctr 1600 E Elm St Web: www.harrisonvilleschools.org	Harrisonville	MO	64701	816-380-3253	884-3179	167-3
Cass Communications Management Inc 100 Redbud Rd TF: 800-252-1799 ■ Web: www.home.casscomm.com	Virginia	IL	62691	217-452-7725		224
Cass County 5 W Seventh St Web: www.atlanticiowa.com	Atlantic	IA	50022	712-243-5503		338
Cass County 120 N Broadway Web: casscountymi.org	Cassopolis	MI	49031	269-445-4420		338
Cass County 211 Ninth St S Web: www.casscountynd.gov	Fargo	ND	58103	701-241-5600	241-5728	338
Cass County PO Box 449 Web: www.co.cass.tx.us	Linden	TX	75563	903-756-5071	756-8057	338
Cass County 200 Court Pk Web: co.cass.in.us	Logansport	IN	46947	574-753-7740	722-1556	338
Cass County 346 Main St TF: 855-658-5736 ■ Web: www.cassne.org	Plattsmouth	NE	68048	402-296-1028		338
Cass County 100 E Springfield St Web: www.illinoiscourts.gov	Virginia	IL	62691	217-452-7225		338
Cass County Electric Cooperartive 4100 32nd Ave SW TF: 800-248-3292 ■ Web: casscountyelectric.com	Fargo	ND	58104	701-356-4400		245
Cass County Public Library 400 E Mechanic St Web: www.casscolibrary.org	Harrisonville	MO	64701	816-380-4600	884-2301	434-3
Cass County Publishing Company Inc 301 S Lexington Web: www.kansascity.com	Harrisonville	MO	64701	816-380-3228		532-3
Cass County-Sun 122 W Houston St Web: www.casscountynow.com	Linden	TX	75563	903-756-7396		532-2
Cass Information Systems Inc 13001 Hollenberg Dr NASDAQ: CASS ■ TF: 888-569-4707 ■ Web: www.cassinfo.com	Bridgeton	MO	63044	314-506-5500	506-5560	225
Cass Precision Machining 4800 N Lilac Dr Web: cassprecisionmachining.com	Brooklyn Center	MN	55429	763-535-0501	535-9238	621
Cass Scenic Railroad State Park 242 Main St Web: wvstateparks.com	Cass	WV	24927	304-456-4300		565
Cass School of Floral Design 531 Mt Auburn St TF: 800-920-1222 ■ Web: www.cassflowers.com	Watertown	MA	02472	617-920-1222		685
CASS Tech (CASS) 37000 Grand River Ave Ste 130 Web: www.cass-tech.com	Farmington Hills	MI	48335	248-538-7374		177
Cassandra Ballet of Toledo 3157 Sylvania Ave Web: cassandraballet.com	Toledo	OH	43613	419-475-0458		573-1
Cassarino's Restaurant 177 Atwells Ave Web: www.cassarinosri.com	Providence	RI	02903	401-751-3333		671
Casscom Media 6000 Industrial Dr Web: www.casscommedia.com	Greenville	TX	75402	903-455-2555	455-4448	657
Casselman River Bridge State Park 580 Taylor Ave TF: 877-620-8367 ■ Web: dnr.maryland.gov	Annapolis	MD	21401	877-620-8367		565
Cassels Brock & Blackwell LLP Scotia Plz 40 King St W Ste 2100 Web: cassels.com	Toronto	ON	M5H3C2	416-869-5300		428
Cassemco Inc 1595 Lemon Farris Rd TF: 800-844-3626 ■ Web: www.cassemco.com	Cookeville	TN	38506	931-528-6588	528-2290	601
Cassens Transport Co 145 N Kansas St Web: www.cassens.com	Edwardsville	IL	62025	618-656-3006	692-7316	780
Cassia County Fairgrounds 1101 Elba Ave Web: cassiacountyfair.com	Burley	ID	83318	208-678-9150		642
Cassia County, Idaho 1459 Overland Ave Web: www.cassiacounty.org	Burley	ID	83318	208-878-7302		338
Cassidy & Assoc 733 Tenth St NW Ste 400 Web: cassidy.com	Washington	DC	20001	202-347-0773	347-0785	636
Cassidy Associates Insurance 234 Humphrey St Web: cassidyins.com	Swampscott	MA	01907	781-598-4300	599-1530	390
Cassidy Bill (Sen R - LA) 520 Hart Senate Office Bldg Web: www.cassidy.senate.gov	Washington	DC	20510	202-224-5824		342-2
Cassidy Cataloguing Services Inc 248 W Main St Web: www.cassidycataloguing.com	Rockaway	NJ	07866	973-586-3200	586-3201	393
Cassidy Connor & Pitchford L 295 E Swedesford Rd *Fax Area Code: 484 ■ Web: ccplegal.com	Wayne	PA	19087	610-783-3515	390-5848*	41
Cassidy-Tricker Industrial Sales 1608 Hwy 13 W Web: cassidytricker.com	Burnsville	MN	55337	952-882-6338		350
Cassin & Cassin LLP 711 Third Ave 20th Fl Web: www.cassinllp.com	New York	NY	10017	212-972-6161		428
Cassina Group LLC, The 309 Coleman Blvd Web: thecassinagroup.com	Mount Pleasant	SC	29464	843-628-0008		652
Cassling Diagnostic Imaging Inc 13808 F St Web: www.cassling.com	Omaha	NE	68137	402-334-5000		475
Casson-Mark Corp 10515 Markison Rd Web: cmarkcorp.com	Dallas	TX	75238	214-340-0880		196
Cassville Area Chamber of Commerce 504 Main St Web: www.cassville.com	Cassville	MO	65625	417-847-2814		139
Casswood Insurance Agency Ltd 5 Executive Pk Dr TF: 800-972-2242 ■ Web: casswood.com	Clifton Park	NY	12065	518-373-8700	373-8799	390
Cast & Crew Entertainment Services LLC 2300 Empire Ave Web: www.castandcrew.com	Burbank	CA	91504	818-848-6022		2
Cast Products Inc 4200 N Nordica Web: www.castproducts.com	Norridge	IL	60706	708-457-1500		358
Cast Software Inc 321 W 44th St Ste 501 TF: 877-852-2278 ■ Web: www.castsoftware.com	New York	NY	10036	212-871-8330	759-3845	178-1
Cast Specialties Inc 26711 Miles Ave Web: castspecialties.com	Warrensville Heights	OH	44128	216-292-7393		308
Cast Systems LLC 19400 Peachland Blvd Web: www.castsystemsllc.com	Port Charlotte	FL	33948	941-625-3474		183
Cast Technologies Inc 1100 SW Washington St Web: casttechnologies.net	Peoria	IL	61602	309-676-2157	676-2167	308
Cast Transportation 9850 Havana St TF: 800-369-6374 ■ Web: www.casttrans.com	Henderson	CO	80640	303-534-6376	853-3377	780
Castagna 1752 SE Hawthorne Blvd Web: www.castagnarestaurant.com	Portland	OR	97214	503-231-7373		671
Castalloy Inc 1701 Industrial Ln PO Box 827 TF: 800-211-0900 ■ Web: www.castalloygroup.com	Waukesha	WI	53189	262-547-0070	547-2215	307
Castan & Lecca PC 51 Lenox Pointe NE Web: caslec-law.com	Atlanta	GA	30324	404-998-4285		41
Cast-Crete USA Inc 6324 County Rd 579 TF: 800-999-4641 ■ Web: www.castcrete.com	Seffner	FL	33584	813-621-4641		183
Castellan Inc 16255 Ventura Blvd Ste 930 Web: www.castellan.net	Encino	CA	91436	818-789-0088	789 2674	177
Castellano, Korenberg & Company CPA PC 313 W Old Country Rd Web: castellanokorenberg.com	Hicksville	NY	11801	516-937-9500		2
Castelli Marble Inc 3958 Superior Ave E Web: castellimarbleinc.com	Cleveland	OH	44114	216-361-1222	361-1797	191-1
Casten Sean (Rep D - IL) 429 Cannon House Office Bldg Web: www.casten.house.gov	Washington	DC	20515	202-225-4561		342-2
Caster Concepts Inc 10000 E Michigan Ave TF: 800-800-0036 ■ Web: www.casterconcepts.com	Albion	MI	49224	517-629-8838		358
Caster Technology Corp 11552 Markon Dr TF: 866-547-8090 ■ Web: www.castertech.com	Garden Grove	CA	92841	714-893-6886		351
CastiaRx 2275 Half Day Rd Ste 210 Web: www.castiarx.com	Bannockburn	IL	60015	314-652-2121	652-2126	231
Castile Ventures 65 William St Ste 205 Web: www.castileventures.com	Wellesley	MA	02481	781 890-0060		792
Castilleja School Foundation 1310 Bryant St Web: www.castilleja.org	Palo Alto	CA	94301	650-328-3160		685
Castillo de San Marcos National Monument 1 S Castillo Dr Web: www.nps.gov	Saint Augustine	FL	32084	904-829-6506		564
Castine Moving & Storage 1235 Chestnut St TF: 800-225-8068 ■ Web: www.castinemovers.com	Athol	MA	01331	978-249-9105	249-5337	519
Casting Solutions LLC 2345 Licking Rd Web: www.burnhamfoundry.com	Zanesville	OH	43701	740-452-9371		307
Castle & Cooke Inc One Dole Dr Web: www.castlecooke.com	Westlake Village	CA	91362	310-209-3550		653
Castle Bank NA 121 W Lincoln Hwy TF: 800-990-5713 ■ Web: www.castlebank.com	DeKalb	IL	60115	800-990-5713		70
Castle Branch Inc 1844 Sir Tyler Dr Web: www.castlebranch.com	Wilmington	NC	28405	888-723-4263		435
Castle Brands Inc 122 E 42nd St Ste 4700 NYSE: ROX ■ TF: 800-882-8140 ■ Web: castlebrandsinc.com	New York	NY	10168	646-356-0200	356-0222	81-3
Castle Breckenridge Management 5185 Comanche Dr Ste D Web: www.cbmgmt.com	La Mesa	CA	91942	619-697-3191	697-3164	256
Castle Contracting LLC 345 Marshall Ave Ste 302 Web: www.digcastle.com	Webster Groves	MO	63119	314-421-0042	231-9157	188
Castle Creek Capital LLC 6051 El Tordo Web: castlecreek.com	Rancho Santa Fe	CA	92067	858-756-8300		401
Castle Harlan Inc 150 E 58th St Web: www.castleharlan.com	New York	NY	10155	212-644-8600	207-8042	403
Castle High School 3344 SR-261 Web: www.warrick.k12.in.us	Newburgh	IN	47630	812-853-3331		685
Castle Hill Inn & Resort 590 Ocean Dr TF: 888-466-1355 ■ Web: www.castlehillinn.com	Newport	RI	02840	401-849-3800		669
Castle Impact Windows 7089 Hemstreet Pl TF: 800-643-6371 ■ Web: www.castleimpactwindows.com	West Palm Beach	FL	33413	561-683-4811	640-8204	234
Castle In The Clouds 455 Old Mountain Rd Web: www.castleintheclouds.org	Moultonborough	NH	03254	603-476-5900		671
Castle in the Sand Hotel 3701 Atlantic Ave TF: 800-552-7263 ■ Web: castleinthesand.com	Ocean City	MD	21842	410-289-6846		379
Castle Inn & Suites 1734 S Harbor Blvd Web: www.castleinn.com	Anaheim	CA	92802	714-774-8111	956-4736	379
Castle Keepers of Charleston Inc 2030 Harley St Web: castle-keepers.com	North Charleston	SC	29406	843-569-4400		104
Castle Kitchens 137 Pleasant Hill Rd Web: www.castlekitchens.com	Scarborough	ME	04074	207-883-8901		191-3
Castle McCulloch 3925 Kivett Dr Web: www.castlemcculloch.com	Jamestown	NC	27282	336-887-5413		50-3
Castle Park 3500 Polk St Web: www.castlepark.com	Riverside	CA	92505	951-785-3000		32
Castle Pierce 2247 Ryf Rd *Fax Area Code: 920 ■ TF: 800-227-8537 ■ Web: www.castlepierce.com	Oshkosh	WI	54904	800-227-8537	235-4763*	627

				Phone	Fax	Class
Castle Rock Computing Inc 12930 Saratoga Ave *Web:* www.castlerock.com	Saratoga	CA	95070	408-366-6540		178-1
Castle Rock State Park 1365 W Castle Rd *Web:* www2.illinois.gov	Oregon	IL	61061	815-732-7329		565
Castle Sprinkler & Alalarm 5114 College Ave *Web:* www.csafire.com	College Park	MD	20740	301-927-7300		406
Castle Valley Consultants Inc 10 Beulah Rd *Web:* casval.com	New Britain	PA	18901	215-348-8257		261
Castle Wholesalers Inc 3450 Bladensburg Rd *Web:* www.castlewholesalers.com	Brentwood	MD	20722	301-699-2206	699-2137	351
Castlebay Irish Pub 193-A Main St *Web:* www.castlebayirishpub.com	Annapolis	MD	21401	410-626-0165		671
Castlegarde Inc 4911 S W Shore Blvd *TF:* 866-751-3203 ■ *Web:* www.castlegarde.com	Tampa	FL	33611	813-872-4844		693
Castlemoyle Books The Hotel Revere Bldg 7th Main St *TF:* 888-773-5586 ■ *Web:* www.castlemoyle.com	Pomeroy	WA	99347	509-843-5009	843-3183	95
Castles Information Network 301 Alamo Dr *Web:* www.castles.com	Vacaville	CA	95688	707-455-3401		225
Castles N. Coasters 9445 N Metro Pkwy E *Web:* www.castlesncoasters.com	Phoenix	AZ	85051	602-997-7575		31
Castleton State College 86 Seminary St *TF:* 800-639-8521 ■ *Web:* www.csc.vsc.edu	Castleton	VT	05735	802-468-5611	468-1476	166
Castletop Capital 3600 N Capital of Texas Hwy Bldg Ste B320 *Web:* www.castletopcapital.com	Austin	TX	78746	512-329-6600		528
Castlewood State Park 1401 Kiefer Creek Rd *Web:* mostateparks.com	Ballwin	MO	63021	636-227-4433		565
Casto 250 Civic Center Dr Ste 500 *Web:* www.castoinfo.com	Columbus	OH	43215	614-228-5331	469-8376	655
Casto & Harris Inc 109 Market St *TF:* 800-678-8683 ■ *Web:* casto-harris.com	Spencer	WV	25276	304-927-2222	927-2236	626
Casto Technical Services Inc 540 Leon Sullivan Way *TF:* 800-232-2221 ■ *Web:* www.castotech.com	Charleston	WV	25301	304-346-0549		610
Casto Travel Inc 2560 N First St Ste 150 **Fax Area Code:* 408 ■ *TF:* 800-832-3445 ■ *Web:* www.casto.com	San Jose	CA	95131	800-832-3445	984-7007*	771
Castor Kathy (Rep D - FL) 2052 Rayburn House Office Bldg *Web:* castor.house.gov	Washington	DC	20515	202-225-3376	225-5652	342-2
Castparts Employees Federal Credit Union 8120 SE Luther Rd *TF:* 800-973-3328 ■ *Web:* castpartsfcu.org	Portland	OR	97206	503-771-2464	536-6516	219
Cast-Rite Corp 515 E Airline Way *Web:* www.cast-rite.com	Gardena	CA	90248	310-532-2080	532-0605	308
Castro County Texas Castro County Courthouse 100 E Bedford St *Web:* www.co.castro.tx.us	Dimmitt	TX	79027	806-647-3338	647-5438	338
Castro Joaquin (Rep D - TX) 2241 Rayburn House Office Bldg *Web:* castro.house.gov	Washington	DC	20515	202-225-3236	225-1915	342-2
Castro Valley Chamber of Commerce 3160 Castro Vly Blvd *Web:* www.edenareachamber.com	Castro Valley	CA	94546	510-537-5300	537-5335	139
Castrol Industrial North America Inc 150 W Warrenville Rd *TF:* 877-641-1600 ■ *Web:* www.castrol.com	Naperville	IL	60563	877-641-1600	648-9801	541
Casual Cushion Corp 1686 Overview Dr *Web:* www.casualcushion.com	Rock Hill	SC	29730	803-329-2932	329-3041	361
Casual Designs Furniture Inc 36523 Lighthouse Rd *TF:* 888-629-1717 ■ *Web:* www.casualdesignsfurniture.com	Selbyville	DE	19975	302-436-8224		321
Casualty Actuarial Society (CAS) 4350 Fairfax Dr Ste 250 *TF:* 800-766-0070 ■ *Web:* www.casact.org	Arlington	VA	22203	703-276-3100	276-3108	49-9
Caswell Developmental Ctr 2415 W Vernon Ave *Web:* www.ncdhhs.gov	Kinston	NC	28504	252-208-4000		230
Caswood Group Inc, The 811 Ayrault Rd Ste 2 *Web:* www.caswood.com	Fairport	NY	14450	585-425-0332	223-2601	463
Cat Clinic of Seattle PS 3842 Stone Way N *Web:* catclinicofseattle.com	Seattle	WA	98103	206-633-1133		794
Cat Doctor, The 535 N 22nd St *Web:* www.thecatdr.com	Philadelphia	PA	19130	215-561-7668		794
Cat Practice Inc, The 1809 Magazine St *Web:* catpractice.com	New Orleans	LA	70130	504-525-6369		794
CAT Publishing Inc 10793 Northgate Dr **Fax Area Code:* 530 ■ *TF:* 800-767-0511 ■ *Web:* www.catpublishing.com	Palo Cedro	CA	96073	800-767-0511	549-5167*	637-2
Cat Pumps 1681 94th Ln NE *Web:* www.catpumps.com	Minneapolis	MN	55449	763-780-5440	780-2958	641
Cat Rental Store, The 9520 - 51 Ave *TF:* 866-285-5550 ■ *Web:* www.finning.com	Edmonton	AB	T6E5A6	780-989-1301		23
Cat Tales Zoological Park 17020 Newport Hwy *Web:* www.cattales.org	Mead	WA	99021	509-238-4126		823
CAT Technology Inc 411 Hackensack Ave 7th Fl *Web:* www.catamerica.com	Hackensack	NJ	07601	201-727-9299		463
CATAAlliance 207 Bank St Ste 416 *Web:* cata.ca	Ottawa	ON	K2P2N2	613-236-6550		138
Catahoula Correctional Ctr 499 Columbia Rd *Web:* www.lasallecorrections.com	Harrisonburg	LA	71340	318-744-2121	744-2126	213
Catalano Gallardo & Petropoulos LLP 100 Jericho Quadrangle Ste 326 *Web:* cgpllp.com	Jericho	NY	11753	516-931-1800		41
Catalant Technologies 25 Thomson Pl *Web:* gocatalant.com	Boston	MA	02210	617-446-3734		178-1
Cataldi Public Relations Inc 143 W 29th St Ste 904 *Web:* www.cataldipr.com	New York	NY	10001	212-244-9797		317
Cataldo Ambulance Service Inc 137 Washington St *Web:* cataldoambulance.com	Somerville	MA	02143	617-625-0126		30
Catalent Pharma Solutions Inc 14 Schoolhouse Rd *Web:* www.catalent.com	Somerset	NJ	08873	732-537-6200	537-6480	231
Catalina Express Berth 95 *TF:* 800-481-3470 ■ *Web:* www.catalinaexpress.com	San Pedro	CA	90731	310-519-1212		468
Catalina Graphic Films Inc 27001 Agoura Rd Ste 100 *TF:* 800-333-3136 ■ *Web:* www.catalinagraphicfilms.com	Calabasas	CA	91301	818-880-8060	880-1144	600
Catalina High School 3645 E Pima St *Web:* www.catalina.tusd1.schooldesk.net	Tucson	AZ	85716	520-232-8400		685
Catalina Island Visitor Ctr 1 Green Pier PO Box 217 *Web:* www.lovecatalina.com	Avalon	CA	90704	310-510-1520	510-7607	206
Catalina Marketing Corp 200 Carillon Pkwy *TF:* 877-210-1917 ■ *Web:* www.catalina.com	Saint Petersburg	FL	33716	727-579-5000	556-2700	5
Catalina Mechanical Contracting Inc 2702 S Alvernon Way *Web:* www.btucson.com	Tucson	AZ	85713	520-745-3000		610
Catalina Post Acute Care & Rehabiliation 2611 N Warren Ave *Web:* catalinacare.com	Tucson	AZ	85719	520-795-9574		450
Catalina State Park 11570 N Oracle Rd *Web:* www.azstateparks.com	Tucson	AZ	85737	520-628-5798		565
Catalina Yachts Inc 21200 Victory Blvd *Web:* www.catalinayachts.com	Woodland Hills	CA	91367	818-884-7700		90
Catalogcom Inc 14000 Quail Springs Pkwy Ste 3600 *TF:* 888-932-4376 ■ *Web:* www.webhero.com	Oklahoma City	OK	73134	405-753-9300	753-9353	808
Catalpa Systems Inc 53 W Jackson Blvd Ste 552 *Web:* www.catalpa-systems.com	Chicago	IL	60604	312-663-3658		177
Catalpha Advertising & Design Inc 6801 Loch Raven Blvd *TF:* 888-337-0066 ■ *Web:* www.catalpha.com	Towson	MD	21286	410-337-0066		7
Catalyst Biosciences Inc 260 Littlefield Ave *Web:* www.catalystbiosciences.com	South San Francisco	CA	94080	650-871-0761		743
Catalyst Communications Technologies Inc 2107 Graves Mill Rd MS D *Web:* www.catcomtec.com	Forest	VA	24551	434-582-6146		224
Catalyst Energy Inc 424 S 27th St Ste 304 *Web:* www.catalystenergyinc.com	Pittsburgh	PA	15203	412-325-4350	325-4356	536
Catalyst Marketing Design Inc 624 W Wayne St *Web:* catalystgetsit.com	Fort Wayne	IN	46802	260-422-4888		194
Catalyst Paper Corp 3600 Lysander Ln 2nd Fl *TSX:* CYT ■ *Web:* www.catalystpaper.com	Richmond	BC	V7B1C3	604-247-4400	247-0512	557
Catalyte 502 S Sharp St *Web:* www.catalyte.io	Baltimore	MD	21201	410-385-2500		196
Catalytic Combustion Corp 709 21st Ave *TF:* 888-285-5940 ■ *Web:* www.catalyticcombustion.com	Bloomer	WI	54724	715-568-2882		194
Catalytic Products International Inc 980 Ensell Rd *Web:* www.cpilink.com	Lake Zurich	IL	60047	847-438-0334		804
Catamount Constructors Inc 1527 Cole Blvd *Web:* www.catamountinc.com	Lakewood	CO	80401	303-679-0087		186
Catamount Energy Corp 71 Allen St Ste 101	Rutland	VT	05701	802-773-6684		196
Catamount Ventures 400 Pacific Ave 3rd Fl *Web:* www.catamountventures.com	San Francisco	CA	94133	415-277-0300	277-0301	792
Catanese Group PC 307 State St *Web:* catanesegroup.com	Johnstown	PA	15905	814-255-8400		2
Catania-Spagna Corp 3 Nemco Way *Web:* cataniaoils.com	Ayer	MA	01432	978-772-7900	722-7970	297-8
Catapult Me Inc 2229 Edgewood Ave S *TF:* 877-453-9117 ■ *Web:* www.catapult-me.com	Minneapolis	MN	55426	612-359-5600		627
Catapult Systems Inc 1221 S MoPac Expwy Ste 350 *TF:* 800-528-6248 ■ *Web:* www.catapultsystems.com	Austin	TX	78746	512-328-8181		180
Cataract Elementary School 6070 WI-27 *Web:* www.spartan.org	Sparta	WI	54656	608-366-3453	366-3455	685
Catastrophe Risk Exchange Inc 902 Carnegie Ctr Ste340 *Web:* www.catex.com	Princeton	NJ	08540	609-683-0888	683-0808	391-4
Catawba College 2300 W Innes St *TF:* 800-228-2922 ■ *Web:* www.catawba.edu	Salisbury	NC	28144	704-637-4772	637-4222	166
Catawba Correctional Ctr 1347 Prison Camp Rd *Web:* www.ncdps.gov	Newton	NC	28658	828-466-5521		213
Catawba County PO Box 389 *Web:* www.catawbacountync.gov	Newton	NC	28658	828-465-8201	465-8392	338
Catawba County Chamber of Commerce 1055 Southgate Corporate Pk SW *Web:* www.catawbachamber.org	Hickory	NC	28602	828-328-6111	328-1175	139
Catawba County Library 115 W C St *Web:* www.catawbacountync.gov	Newton	NC	28658	828-465-8664		434-3
Catawba Hospital 5525 Catawba Hospital Dr *TF:* 800-451-5544 ■ *Web:* www.catawba.dbhds.virginia.gov	Catawba	VA	24070	540-375-4200		374-5

Phone Fax Class

Catawba Valley Community College
2550 US Hwy 70 SE Hickory NC 28602 828-327-7000 327-7276 162
Web: www.cvcc.edu

Catawba Valley Hospice House
3975 Robinson Rd Newton NC 28658 828-466-0466 466-8862 371
Web: www.carolinacaring.org

Catawba Valley Medical Ctr
810 Fairgrove Church Rd SE Hickory NC 28602 828-326-3000 374-3
Web: www.catawbavalleyhealth.org

Catawissa Wood & Components Inc
1015 W Valley Ave Elysburg PA 17824 570-644-1928 486-2800 683
Web: www.catlmbr.com

Catbird Press 16 Windsor Rd North Haven CT 06473 203-230-2548 637-2
Web: catbirdpress.com

CATC (Central Arkansas Telephone Cooperative Inc)
4036 Hwy 7 Bismarck AR 71929 501-865-2282 224
Web: www.catc.net

Catch, The 2100 E Katella Ave Anaheim CA 92806 714-935-0101 671
Web: www.catchanaheim.com

Cate School 1960 Cate Mesa Rd Carpinteria CA 93013 805-684-4127 622
Web: www.cate.org

CaTECH Systems Ltd
201 Whitehall Dr Unit 4 Markham ON L3R9Y3 905-944-0000 224
TF: 800-267-1919 ■ *Web:* catech-systems.com

Caterina's Ristorante
9104 W Oklahoma Ave Milwaukee WI 53227 414-541-4200 671
Web: www.caterinasristorante.com

Caterpillar 501 S W Jefferson Ave Peoria IL 61630 309-675-2337 449
TF: 888-614-4328 ■ *Web:* www.caterpillar.com

Caterpillar Financial Services Corp
2120 W End Ave Nashville TN 37203 615-341-1000 390
Web: www.catfinancial.com

Caterpillar Incorporated Employees PAC
100 NE Adams St Peoria IL 61629 309-675-4549 615
Web: caterpillar.com

Caterpillar Paving Products Inc
9401 85th Ave N Brooklyn Park MN 55445 763-425-4100 190
Web: www.cat.com

Cate-Russell Insurance Inc
415 High St Maryville TN 37804 865-982-4111 390
Web: caterussell.com

Cates Engineering Ltd
13575 Heathcote Blvd Ste 170 Gainesville VA 20155 571-261-9280 261-9286 261
Web: www.cateseng.com

Catfish Bend Casinos II LLC
3001 Winegard Dr Burlington IA 52601 866-792-9948 452
TF: 866-792-9948 ■ *Web:* www.thepzazz.com

Catfish Corner 780 S Treadaway Blvd Abilene TX 79602 325-672-3620 671
Web: catfish-corner.business.site

Cathay General Bancorp Inc
777 N Broadway Los Angeles CA 90012 213-625-4700 625-1368 360-2
NASDAQ: CATY ■ *TF:* 800-922-8429 ■ *Web:* www.cathaybank.com

Cathay Inn 3714 N Division St Spokane WA 99207 509-326-2226 671
Web: www.cathayinn.com

Cathay Pacific Cargo
6040 Avion Dr Ste 338 Los Angeles CA 90045 310-417-0052 348-9789 12
TF: 800-628-6960 ■ *Web:* www.cathaypacificcargo.com

Cathedral Basilica of Saint Joseph
80 S Market St San Jose CA 95113 408-283-8100 50-1
Web: www.stjosephcathedral.org

Cathedral Basilica of Saint Louis (New Cathedral)
4431 Lindell Blvd Saint Louis MO 63108 314-373-8200 373-8290 50-1
Web: www.cathedralstl.org

Cathedral Basilica of the Sacred Heart
89 Ridge St Newark NJ 07104 973-484-4600 483-8253 50-1
Web: www.cathedralbasilica.org

Cathedral Caverns State Park
637 Cave Rd Woodville AL 35776 256-728-8193 565
Web: www.alapark.com

Cathedral Church of All Saints
1330 Cathedral Ln Halifax NS B3H2Z1 902-423-6002 423-1437 50-1
Web: www.cathedralchurchofallsaints.com

Cathedral Church of Saint John the Divine
1047 Amsterdam Ave New York NY 10025 212-316-7490 932-7347 50-1
Web: www.stjohndivine.org

Cathedral Church of Saint Mark
231 E 100 S Salt Lake City UT 84111 801-322-3400 50-1
Web: www.stmarksutah.org

Cathedral Corp
632 Ellsworth Rd Griffis Technology Pk Rome NY 13441 315-338-0021 627
TF: 800-698-0299 ■ *Web:* www.cathedralcorporation.com

Cathedral Energy Services
6030 Third St SE Calgary AB T2H1K2 403-265-2560 540
TF: 866-276-8201 ■ *Web:* www.cathedralenergyservices.com

Cathedral Gorge State Park PO Box 176 Panaca NV 89042 775-728-8101 565
Web: www.parks.nv.gov

Cathedral High School
1253 Bishops Rd Los Angeles CA 90012 323-225-2438 222-7223 685
Web: www.cathedralhighschool.org

Cathedral of Christ the King
299 Colony Blvd Lexington KY 40502 859-268-2861 268-8061 50-1
Web: cathedralctk.org

Cathedral of Our Lady of the Angels
555 W Temple St Los Angeles CA 90012 213-680-5200 620-1982 50-1
Web: www.olacathedral.org

Cathedral of Saint John the Evangelist Museum
515 Cathedral St LaFayette LA 70501 337-232-1322 232-1379 520
Web: saintjohncathedral.org

Cathedral of Saint Paul
239 Selby Ave Saint Paul MN 55102 651-228-1766 50-1
Web: www.cathedralsaintpaul.org

Cathedral of Saints Peter & Paul
30 Fenner St Providence RI 02903 401-331-2434 50-1
Web: www.providencecathedral.org

Cathedral of the Blessed Sacrament
1019 11th St Sacramento CA 95814 916-444-3071 443-2749 50-1
Web: www.cathedralsacramento.org

Cathedral of the Immaculate Conception
2 S Claiborne St Mobile AL 36602 251-434-1565 434-1588 50-1
Web: www.mobilecathedral.org

Cathedral of the Immaculate Conception
125 Eagle St Albany NY 12202 518-463-4447 436-5177 50-1
Web: cathedralic.com

Cathedral of the Madeleine
331 E S Temple St Salt Lake City UT 84111 801-328-8941 50-1
Web: www.utcotm.org

Cathedral Press Inc
600 NE Sixth St Long Prairie MN 56347 320-732-6143 732-3457 637-10
TF: 800-874-8332 ■ *Web:* www.cathedralpress.com

Cathedral School for Boys
1275 Sacramento St San Francisco CA 94108 415-771-6600 771-2547 48-20
Web: www.cathedralschool.net

Cathedral State Park
Rt 1 12 Cathedral Way Aurora WV 26705 304-735-3771 565
Web: wvstateparks.com

Cathedral Village
600 E Cathedral Rd Philadelphia PA 19128 215-487-1300 393
TF: 800-382-1385 ■ *Web:* www.presbyterianseniorliving.org

Catherine H. Voit, Esquire
1221 W Chester Pk West Chester PA 19382 610-692-9768 41
Web: voitfamilylaw.com

Catherine Hinds Institute of Esthetics
300 Wildwood Ave Woburn MA 01801 781-935-3344 167-3
Web: www.catherinehinds.edu

Catholic Biblical Association of America
433 Caldwell Hall Washington DC 20064 202-319-5519 319-4799 48-20
Web: catholicbiblical.org

Catholic Book Publishing Corp
77 W End Rd Totowa NJ 07512 877-228-2665 890-2410* 637-2
**Fax Area Code:* 973 ■ *Web:* www.catholicbookpublishing.com

Catholic Charities of Buffalo New York Inc
741 Delaware Ave Buffalo NY 14209 716-218-1400 49-15
Web: www.ccwny.org

Catholic Charities USA
2050 Ballenger Ave Ste 400 Alexandria VA 22314 703-549-1390 549-1656 48-5
TF: 800-919-9338 ■ *Web:* www.catholiccharitiesusa.org

Catholic Courses
c/o Saint Benedict Press LLC PO Box 410487 Charlotte NC 28241 704-731-0651 226-7770* 637-10
**Fax Area Code:* 815 ■ *TF:* 800-437-5876 ■ *Web:* www.tanbooks.com

Catholic Digest
1 Montauk Ave No 200 New London CT 06320 800-678-2836 457-18
TF: 800-678-2836 ■ *Web:* www.catholicdigest.com

Catholic Diocese of Buffalo
795 Main St Buffalo NY 14203 716-847-8700 847-8797 673
Web: www.buffalodiocese.org

Catholic Diocese of Evansville
4200 N Kentucky Ave Evansville IN 47711 812-424-5536 48-20
TF: 800-637-1731 ■ *Web:* www.evdio.org

Catholic Diocese of Peoria, The
607 NE Madison Ave Peoria IL 61603 309-682-5823 671-1579 50-1
Web: cdop.org

Catholic Extension
150 S Wacker Dr Ste 2000 Chicago IL 60606 800-842-7804 236 5276* 48-20
**Fax Area Code:* 312 ■ *TF:* 800-842-7804 ■ *Web:* www.catholicextension.org

Catholic Family Credit Union
9237 Ward Pkwy Ste 114 Kansas City MO 64114 816-444-7440 444-6360 219
Web: catholicfamilycu.com

Catholic Family Federal Credit Union
717 N Socora St Wichita KS 67212 316-264-9163 219
Web: cffcu.com

Catholic Health Association of the US (CHA)
4455 Woodson Rd Saint Louis MO 63134 314-427-2500 427-0029 49-8
TF: 800-230-7823 ■ *Web:* www.chausa.org

Catholic Health Home Care
144 Genesee St Fl 2 Buffalo NY 14203 716-685-4870 374-3
Web: www.chsbuffalo.org

Catholic Health Initiatives
11045 East Lansing Cir Englewood CO 80112 720-875-7100 875-7102 374-3
Web: www.catholichealthinitiatives.org

Catholic Health Services
4790 N State Rd 7 Lauderdale Lakes FL 33319 877-247-4632 353
TF: 877-247-4632 ■ *Web:* www.catholichealthservices.org

Catholic High School
855 Hearthstone Dr Baton Rouge LA 70806 225-383-0397 685
Web: catholichigh.org

Catholic Medical Ctr (CMC)
100 McGregor St Manchester NH 03102 603-668-3545 374-3
TF: 800-437-9666 ■ *Web:* www.catholicmedicalcenter.org

Catholic Medical Mission Board (CMMB)
100 Wall St 9th Fl New York NY 10005 212-242-7757 48-5
TF: 800-678-5659 ■ *Web:* www.cmmb.org

Catholic Memorial High School
235 Baker St West Roxbury MA 02132 617-469-8000 713
Web: www.catholicmemorial.org

Catholic Mutual Group 10843 Old Mill Rd Omaha NE 68154 402-551-8765 551-2943 391-5
TF: 800-228-6108 ■ *Web:* www.catholicmutual.org

Catholic News Publishing Co
420 Railroad Way Mamaroneck NY 10543 800-433-7771 632-3412* 637-2
**Fax Area Code:* 914 ■ *TF:* 800-433-7771 ■ *Web:* catholicguides.com

Catholic Order of Foresters
355 Shuman Blvd PO Box 3012 Naperville IL 60566 630-983-4900 391-2
TF: 800-552-0145 ■ *Web:* www.catholicforester.org

Catholic Press Assn (CPA)
205 W Monroe St Ste 470 Chicago IL 60606 312-380-6789 361-0256 49-14
Web: www.catholicpress.org

Catholic Relief Services (CRS)
228 W Lexington St Baltimore MD 21201 410-625-2220 685-1635 48-5
TF: 800-235-2772 ■ *Web:* www.crs.org

Catholic Social Services
12431 Stony Plain Rd Edmonton AB T5N3N3 780-432-1137 439-3154 48-20
TF: 877-994-4673 ■ *Web:* www.cssalberta.ca

Catholic Spirit, The PO Box 230 Wheeling WV 26003 304-233-0880 637-9
Web: thecatholicspiritwv.org

Catholic Supply of st Louis Inc
6759 Chippewa St Saint Louis MO 63109 314-644-0643 48-20
TF: 800-325-9026 ■ *Web:* shop.catholicsupply.com

Listing	Phone	Fax	Class
Catholic Theological Union 5416 S Cornell Ave. . . . . Chicago IL 60615 *Web:* ctu.edu	773-324-8000		167-3
Catholic United Financial 3499 Lexington Ave N. . . . . Saint Paul MN 55126 *TF:* 800-568-6670 ■ *Web:* www.catholicunitedfinancial.org	651-490-0170		390
Catholic University of America 620 Michigan Ave NE. . . . . Washington DC 20064 *TF:* 800-673-2772 ■ *Web:* www.catholic.edu	202-319-5000	319-6533	166
Catholic University of America Columbus School of Law 3600 John McCormack Rd NE . . . . . Washington DC 20064 *Web:* www.law.edu	202-319-5140	319-4459	167-1
CatholicMatch.com PO Box 154. . . . . Zelienople PA 16063 *TF:* 888-605-3977 ■ *Web:* www.catholicmatch.com	888-605-3977		387
Cathy's Concepts Inc 6900 E 30th St . . . . . Indianapolis IN 46219 *Web:* www.cathysconcepts.com	317-860-1700		292
Catlow Inc 2750 US Rt 40 . . . . . Tipp City OH 45371 *TF:* 855-324-3998 ■ *Web:* www.catlow.com	855-324-3998		295
Cato Corp, The 8100 Denmark Rd. . . . . Charlotte NC 28273 *TF:* 800-758-2286 ■ *Web:* info.catofashions.com	704-554-8510		157-6
Cato Institute 1000 Massachusetts Ave NW . . . . . Washington DC 20001 *Web:* www.cato.org	202-842-0200	842-3490	634
Cato Research Ltd 4364 S Alston Ave . . . . . Durham NC 27713 *Web:* www.cato.com	919-361-2286	361-2290	194
Catoctin Mountain Park 6602 Foxville Rd. . . . . Thurmont MD 21788 *Web:* www.nps.gov	301-663-9330		564
Caton Connector Corp 26 Wapping Rd . . . . . Kingston MA 02364 *Web:* caton.com	781-585-4315		815
Catonsville Builders Inc 11175 Stratfield Ct . . . . . Marriottsville MD 21104 *Web:* catonsvillehomes.com	410-442-2211		653
Catoosa County 800 Lafayette St. . . . . Ringgold GA 30736 *Web:* www.catoosa.com	706-965-2500	935-3112	338
Catoosa County Area Chamber of Commerce 264 Catoosa Cir . . . . . Ringgold GA 30736 *Web:* catoosachamberofcommerce.com	706-965-5201	965-8224	139
Cator Ruma & Associates Co 896 Tabor St. . . . . Lakewood CO 80401 *Web:* catorruma.com	303-232-6200		256
Catral Doyle Creative Co 231 E Buffalo St Ste 301. . . . . Milwaukee WI 53202 *Web:* www.catraldoylecreative.com	414-276-3075		7
Catriona Jeffries Gallery 274 E First Ave . . . . . Vancouver BC V5T1A6 *Web:* www.catrionajeffries.com	604-736-1554		42
Cats Co 1607 E Big Beaver Rd Ste 110. . . . . Troy MI 48083 *Web:* www.catscompany.com	248-816-2287	528-0757	177
Cats Preferred Veterinary Hospital 16795 County Rd 24 Ste 4 . . . . . Plymouth MN 55447 *Web:* catspreferred.com	763-383-8865		794
Catskill Regional Medical Ctr 68 Harris-Bushville Rd PO Box 800 . . . . . Harris NY 12742 *Web:* www.crmcny.org	845-794-3300	794-3240	374-3
Cattaneo Bros Inc 769 Caudill St. . . . . San Luis Obispo CA 93401 **Fax Area Code:* 805 ■ *TF:* 800-243-8537 ■ *Web:* www.cattaneobros.com	800-243-8537	543-4698*	296-26
Cattaraugus Allegany-Erie-Wyoming Board of Cooperative Educational Services 1825 Windfall Rd . . . . . Olean NY 14760 *Web:* www.caboces.org	716-376-8200	376-8450	167-3
Cattaraugus County 303 Court St . . . . . Little Valley NY 14755 *Web:* www.cattco.org	716-938-9111		338
Cattle Baron Restaurants Inc 1113 N Main. . . . . Roswell NM 88201 *Web:* www.cattlebaron.com	575-622-2465		671
Cattle Empire LLC 1174 Empire Cir . . . . . Satanta KS 67870 *Web:* www.cattle-empire.net	620-649-2235	649-2218	446
Cattle Raisers Museum 1600 Gendy St . . . . . Fort Worth TX 76107 *Web:* www.cattleraisersmuseum.org	817-332-8551		520
CattleDog Publishing PO Box 4516. . . . . Davis CA 95617 *Web:* cattledogpublishing.com	530-757-2383		637-2
CattleLog 10305 102nd Terr. . . . . Sebastian FL 32958 *TF:* 866-239-2665 ■ *Web:* www.cattlelog.com	866-239-2665		466
Cattleman's Club Steakhouse & Lounge 29608 SD Hwy 34. . . . . Pierre SD 57501 *Web:* www.cattlemansclub.com	605-224-9774		671
Cattleman's Steakhouse 3450 S Fabens Carlsbad Rd . . . . . Fabens TX 79838 *Web:* www.cattlemanssteakhouse.com	915-544-3200		671
Cattlemen's Cut Supper Club 369 Vaughn Frontage Rd S. . . . . Great Falls MT 59404 *Web:* cattlemenscut.com	406-452-0702		671
Cattrell Companies Inc 906 Franklin St. . . . . Toronto OH 43964 *Web:* cattrell.com	740-537-2481	537-1528	189-10
Cattron Group Intl 58 W Shenango St . . . . . Sharpsville PA 16150 *Web:* www.cattron.com	724-962-3571	962-4310	647
Catty Corp 6111 White Oaks Rd. . . . . Harvard IL 60033 *Web:* www.cattycorp.com	815-943-2288	943-4473	548
CAU (Community Association Underwriters of America) 2 Caufield Pl. . . . . Newtown PA 18940 *Web:* www.cauinsure.com	267-757-7100		391-4
Caufield & Flood 407 E Congress Pkwy Ste A . . . . . Crystal Lake IL 60014 *Web:* www.cfcpas.com	847-669-5950		2
Cauldwell Wingate Company LLC 380 Lexington Ave . . . . . New York NY 10168 *Web:* www.cauldwellwingate.com	212-983-7150		41
Caumsett State Historic Park Preserve 25 Lloyd Harbor Rd . . . . . Huntington NY 11743 *Web:* parks.ny.gov	631-423-1770		565
Causeit Inc 1631 NE Broadway Ste 249. . . . . Portland OR 97232 *Web:* causeit.org	503-493-7332		466
Cautela-Solutions Ltd 8 Tiburon Ct. . . . . Austin TX 78730 *Web:* www.cautela-solutions.com	972-772-8020		196
Cauthorne Paper Co 12124 S Washington Hwy. . . . . Ashland VA 23005 *TF:* 800-552-3011 ■ *Web:* www.cauthornepaper.com	804-798-6999	798-6466	557
Cauttrell Enterprises Inc 7618 N Broadway . . . . . Saint Louis MO 63147 *Web:* www.cauttrellenterprises.com	314-385-4270		480
CAV Distributing Corp 253 Utah Ave . . . . . South San Francisco CA 94080 *Web:* www.cavd.com	650-588-2228		514
CAV Restaurant 14 Imperial Pl . . . . . Providence RI 02903 *Web:* www.cavrestaurant.com	401-751-9164	274-9107	671
Cavaform 2700 72nd St N . . . . . Saint Petersburg FL 33710 *Web:* cavaform.com	727-384-3676	384-0523	757
Cavalier County Job Development Authority 901 Third St Ste 5. . . . . Langdon ND 58249 *Web:* www.ccjda.org	701-256-3475	256-3536	338
Cavalier Energy Inc 5 Ave SW Ste 2500-255 . . . . . Calgary AB T2P3G6 *Web:* cavalierenergy.com	403-268-3940	268-3987	579
Cavalier Homes Alabama 32 Wilson Blvd 100 PO Box 300 . . . . . Addison AL 35540 *TF:* 800-465-7923 ■ *Web:* cavalieralabama.com	800-465-7923		505
Cavalier Hotel 4200 Atlantic Ave . . . . . Virginia Beach VA 23451 *Web:* www.cavalierhotel.com	757-425-8555		669
Cavalier Logistics Management Inc 45085 Old Ox Rd . . . . . Dulles VA 20166 **Fax Area Code:* 571 ■ *TF:* 800-445-1020 ■ *Web:* www.cavlog.com	703-733-4010	252-3119*	194
Cavallino LLC PO Box 1117. . . . . Tiburon CA 94920 *Web:* www.cavallinollc.com	415-890-2074	789-4479	401
Cavanagh Co 610 Putnam Pke. . . . . Greenville RI 02828 *TF:* 800-635-0568 ■ *Web:* www.cavanaghco.com	800-635-0568	949-0680	296-9
Cavanagh Law Firm, The 1850 N Central Ave. . . . . Phoenix AZ 85004 *TF:* 888-824-3476 ■ *Web:* www.cavanaghlaw.com	602-322-4000	322-4100	428
Cavanal Hill Investment Management Inc 1 Williams Ctr 15th Fl. . . . . Tulsa OK 74172 *Web:* cavanalhillfunds.com	918-588-8688		401
Cavanaugh Flight Museum, The 4572 Claire Chennault . . . . . Addison TX 75001 *Web:* www.cavflight.org	972-380-8800		520
Cavanaugh Tocci Associates Inc 327 Boston Post Rd . . . . . Sudbury MA 01776 *Web:* www.cavtocci.com	978-443-7871		463
Cavanaugh Trucking Inc 318 Everson Valley Rd . . . . . Connellsville PA 15425 *TF:* 800-541-4497 ■ *Web:* www.cavanaughtrucking.com	724-628-1018	628-3114	780
Cavco Industries Inc 1001 N Central Ave 8th Fl. . . . . Phoenix AZ 85004 *NASDAQ: CVCO* ■ *TF:* 800-790-9111 ■ *Web:* www.cavco.com	602-256-6263	256-6189	505
Cave & Mine Adventures/Sierra Nevada Recreation Corp 5350 Moaning Cave Rd . . . . . Vallecito CA 95251 *TF:* 866-762-2837 ■ *Web:* moaningcaverns.com	209-736-2708	736-0330	50-5
Cave Canem Foundation Inc 20 Jay St Ste 310-A . . . . . Brooklyn NY 11201 *Web:* cavecanempoets.org	718-858-0000	858-0002	48-13
Cave City Convention Ctr 502 Mammoth Cave St. . . . . Cave City KY 42127 *Web:* cavecity.com	270-773-3131		232
Cave Hill Cemetery & Arboretum 701 Baxter Ave . . . . . Louisville KY 40204 *Web:* www.cavehillcemetery.com	502-451-5630		97
Cave of the Mounds 2975 Cave of the Mounds Rd PO Box 148 . . . . Blue Mounds WI 53517 *Web:* www.caveofthemounds.com	608-437-3038	437-4181	50-5
Cave of the Winds 100 Cave of the Winds Rd . . . . . Manitou Springs CO 80829 *Web:* caveofthewinds.com	719-685-5444	685-1712	50-5
Cave Vin 5555 Xerxes Ave S. . . . . Minneapolis MN 55410 *Web:* cave-vin.net	612-922-0100		671
Cave-In-Rock State Park 1 New State Park Rd . . . . . Cave-In-Rock IL 62919 *Web:* www2.illinois.gov	618-289-4325		565
Cavell Mertz & Associates Inc 7724 Donegan Dr . . . . . Manassas VA 20109 *Web:* cavellmertz.com	703-392-9090		261
Cavender Cadillac 7625 N Loop 1604 E. . . . . San Antonio TX 78233 *Web:* www.cavendercadillac.com	210-807-9079		57
Cavender's 2025 SW Loop 323 . . . . . Tyler TX 75701 *TF:* 844-283-8423 ■ *Web:* www.cavenders.com	903-561-2510		157-5
Caveon LLC 6905 S 1300 E Ste 468. . . . . Midvale UT 84047 *Web:* www.caveon.com	801-208-0103		693
Cavetown Storage 22425 Old Georgetown Rd & 12121 Mapleville Rd . . . . . Smithsburg MD 21783 *Web:* cavetown.com	301-733-7940	824-2022	683
Caviar Russe 538 Madison Ave. . . . . New York NY 10022 *Web:* www.caviarrusse.com	212-980-5908		671
Caviness Beef Packers Ltd 3255 US Hwy 60. . . . . Hereford TX 79045 *Web:* cavinessbeefpackers.com	806-357-2443		473
Caviness Lambert Engineering LLC 508 E N St Ste 202 . . . . . Greenville SC 29601 *Web:* www.cl-e.com	864-242-5844		261
Cawley Gillespie and Associates Inc 306 W 7th St Ste 302 . . . . . Fort Worth TX 76102 *Web:* www.cgaus.com	817-336-2461	877-3728	261
Cawthorn, Deskevich & Gavin PC 9701 Metropolitan Ct Ste C . . . . . Richmond VA 23236 *Web:* cawthorn.net	804-320-7186	288-9015	41
C-Axis Inc 800 Tower Dr. . . . . Hamel MN 55340 *Web:* c-axis.com	763-478-8982		454
Caxton Growth Partners 5755 Granger Rd Ste 100 . . . . . Independence OH 44131	216-867-9780		194
Caxton Printers Ltd 312 Main St . . . . . Caldwell ID 83605 *TF:* 800-657-6465 ■ *Web:* www.caxtonprinters.com	208-459-7421	459-7450	559

Company	City	State	ZIP	Phone	Fax	Class
Cay Insurance Services Inc 22 Barnard St Ste 210 *Web:* cayinsurance.com	Savannah	GA	31401	912-238-0098	232-6564	390
Cayce Historical Museum 1800 12th St *Web:* www.caycesc.gov	Cayce	SC	29033	803-796-9020		520
Cayce/Reilly School of Massage 215 67th St *Web:* www.caycereilly.edu	Virginia Beach	VA	23451	757-457-7270	428-0398	685
Cayenta Canada Corp 4200 N Fraser Way Ste 201 *Web:* www.cayenta.com	Burnaby	BC	V5J5K7	604-570-4300		39
Caylor Industrial Sales Inc PO Box 4659 *Web:* www.caylorindustrial.com	Dalton	GA	30721	706-226-3198	278-4104	612
Cayman Airways Cargo Services 6103 NW 72nd Ave *TF:* 800-252-2746 ■ *Web:* www.caymanairways.com	Miami	FL	33166	305-526-3190	455-5616	12
Cayman Islands Department of Tourism 350 Fifth Ave *TF:* 800-235-5888 ■ *Web:* www.visitcaymanislands.com	New York	NY	10118	212-889-9009	889-9125	775
Cayman Islands Department of Tourism 8300 NW 53rd St Ste 103 *TF:* 800-553-4939 ■ *Web:* www.visitcaymanislands.com	Miami	FL	33166	305-599-9033	599-3766	775
Cayman Technologies Inc 12954 Stonecreek Dr Ste E *TF:* 877-370-9470 ■ *Web:* www.caymantech.com	Pickerington	OH	43147	614-759-9461		180
Cayuga Community College 197 Franklin St *TF:* 866-598-8883 ■ *Web:* www.cayuga-cc.edu	Auburn	NY	13021	315-255-1743	255-2117	162
Cayuga Correctional Facility 2202 SR-38A PO Box 1150 *Web:* www.doccs.ny.gov	Moravia	NY	13118	315-497-1110		213
Cayuga County 160 Genesee St 1st Fl *TF:* 800-771-7755 ■ *Web:* www.cayugacounty.us	Auburn	NY	13021	315-253-1271		338
Cayuga County Chamber of Commerce 2 State St *Web:* www.cayugacountychamber.com	Auburn	NY	13021	315-252-7291	255-3077	139
Cayuga Lake State Park 2678 Lower Lake Rd *Web:* parks.ny.gov	Seneca Falls	NY	13148	315-568-5163		565
Cayuga Medical Ctr 101 Dates Dr *Web:* www.cayugamed.org	Ithaca	NY	14850	607-274-4011		374-3
Cayuse Technologies LLC 72632 Coyote Rd *Web:* www.cayusetechnologies.com	Pendleton	OR	97801	541-278-8200		177
Cazarin Interactive 7064 E Fish Lake Rd *Web:* www.cazarin.com	Maple Grove	MN	55311	763-420-9992	322-9020	180
Cazenovia College 8 Sullivan St *TF:* 800-654-3210 ■ *Web:* cazenovia.edu	Cazenovia	NY	13035	315-655-7208		166
Cazenovia Equipment Company Inc 2 Remington Park Dr *Web:* www.cazenoviaequipment.com	Cazenovia	NY	13035	315-655-8620		45
CB (Cofer Brothers Inc) 2300 Main St *Web:* www.coferbros.com	Tucker	GA	30084	770-938-3200	493-3624	364
CB Bovenkamp Inc 9002 SW 152nd St *Web:* cbbovenkamp.com	Miami	FL	33157	305-233-4438	254-1098	390
CB Displays Intl 5141 S Procyon *Web:* www.cbdisplays.com	Las Vegas	NV	89118	702-739-9301		232
CB Distributing 3075 Kathryn Ave NE *TF:* 800-553-1027 ■ *Web:* www.cbdistributing.com	Albany	OR	97321	541-926-1027	926-7640	246
CB Engineering Pacific Inc 909 Seventh Ave Ste 201 *Web:* www.cb-pacific.com	Kirkland	WA	98033	425-822-1702	827-3482	256
CB Engineers 449 10th St *Web:* www.cbengineers.com	San Francisco	CA	94103	415-437-7330		256
CB Information Services Inc 498 Seventh Ave 17th Fl *Web:* www.cbinsights.com	New York	NY	10018	212-292-3148		387
CB Kaupp & Sons Inc 6-10 Newark Way *Web:* www.kaupp.com	Maplewood	NJ	07040	973-761-4000	761-0253	483
CB Ragland Co 2720 Eugenia Ave *Web:* www.cbragland.com	Nashville	TN	37211	615-254-2841		297-8
CB Ram Electronics Inc 9665 SW Allen Blvd Ste 117 *Web:* www.cbram.com	Beaverton	OR	97005	503-626-8374		625
CBA (Critical Business Analysis Inc) 133 W Second St *TF:* 800-874-8080 ■ *Web:* cbainc.com	Perrysburg	OH	43551	800-874-8080		463
Cbaia 1125 Jefferson Davis Hwy Ste 380 *Web:* cbaia.com	Fredericksburg	VA	22401	540-604-9731		475
CBB (Citizens Business Bank) 701 N Haven Ave *TF:* 888-222-5432 ■ *Web:* www.cbbank.com	Ontario	CA	91764	909-980-4030	481-2130	70
CBC (California Ballet Co) 4819 Ronson Ct *Web:* www.californiaballet.org	San Diego	CA	92111	858-560-5676	560-0072	573-1
CBC (Children's Book Council) 54 W 39th St 14th Fl *Web:* www.cbcbooks.org	New York	NY	10018	212-966-1990		49-16
CBC (Canadian Broadcasting Corp) PO Box 3220 *Web:* www.cbc.radio-canada.ca	Ottawa	ON	K1Y1E4	613-724-1200		643
CBC (Crawford Broadcasting Co) 2821 S Parker Rd Ste 1205 *Web:* crawfordmediagroup.net	Aurora	CO	80014	303-481-1800	433-1555	643
CBC (Community Blood Ctr) 4040 Main St *TF:* 888-647-4040 ■ *Web:* www.savealifenow.org	Kansas City	MO	64111	816-753-4040	968-4047	89
CBC Advertising 56 Industrial Park Rd Ste 103 *TF:* 800-222-2682 ■ *Web:* www.cbcads.com	Saco	ME	04072	207-283-9191		4
CBC Intl PO Box 30655 *TF:* 888-434-9227 ■ *Web:* www.cbcintl.com	Tucson	AZ	85751	520-298-7980		637-2
CBC Mortgage at First Federal Bank 1891 S 14th St *Web:* www.cbcnationalbankmortgage.com	Fernandina Beach	FL	32034	904-321-0400		70
CBC Radio Canada 181 Queen St PO Box 3220 *Web:* www.cbc.ca	Ottawa	ON	K1P1K9	613-288-6000		644
CBCInnovis Inc 3 Executive Park Dr *TF:* 877-284-8322 ■ *Web:* www.cbcinnovis.com	Columbus	OH	43215	877-284-8322		218
CBCL Ltd 1489 Hollis St *Web:* www.cbcl.ca	Halifax	NS	B3J2R7	902-421-7241		256
CBE (Center for Biofilm Engineering) Montana State University PO Box 173980 *Web:* www.biofilm.montana.edu	Bozeman	MT	59717	406-994-4770	994-6098	668
CBE Companies Inc 1309 Technology Pkwy *TF:* 800-925-6686 ■ *Web:* www.cbecompanies.com	Cedar Falls	IA	50613	800-925-6686		393
CBG Corp 4616 W Howard Ln Ste 900 *Web:* cbgcorp.com	Austin	TX	78728	512-491-7541	491-7561	538
C-B-Gear & Machine Inc 4232 Mooney Rd *Web:* www.cbgear.com	Houston	TX	77093	281-449-0777	590-9127	454
CBH Homes 1977 E Overland Rd *Web:* cbhhomes.com	Meridian	ID	83642	208-288-5560		655
Cbhf Engineers PLLC 2246 Yaupon Dr *Web:* cbhfengineers.com	Wilmington	NC	28401	910-791-4000	791-5266	261
CBI 70 Blanchard Rd *TF:* 800-817-8601 ■ *Web:* www.cbinet.com	Burlington	MA	01803	339-298-2100		194
CBI Group LLC Casho Mill Professional Ctr 1501 Casho Mill Rd Ste 9 *Web:* myplacers.com	Newark	DE	19711	302-266-0860		194
CBI Laboratories 4201 Diplomacy Rd **Fax Area Code:* 800 ■ *TF:* 800-822-7546 ■ *Web:* www.cbiskincare.com	Fort Worth	TX	76155	972-241-7546	352-1094*	214
CBIZ Benefits & Insurance Services of Maryland Inc 44 Baltimore St *Web:* www.cbiz.com	Cumberland	MD	21502	301-777-1500		390
CBIZ Life Insurance Solutions Inc 10616 Scripps Summit Ct Ste 210 *TF:* 800-422-7536 ■ *Web:* www.cbizlife.com	San Diego	CA	92131	858-444-3100	444-3157	796
CBK Partners 156 W 56th St 18th Fl *Web:* cbkpartners.com	New York	NY	10019	212-755-7051		200
CBLPath Inc 2100 SE 17th St *Web:* www.cblpath.com	Ocala	FL	34471	352-732-9990		415
Cbm Chartered Accountants 152 Jackson St E Ste 200 *Web:* www.cbmca.com	Hamilton	ON	L8N1L3	905-572-7220	572-7225	2
CBM Inc 2614 Hickory St *Web:* www.cbme.net	Santa Ana	CA	92707	714-424-9250		693
CBM of America Inc 1455 W Newport Center Dr *TF:* 800-881-8202 ■ *Web:* cbmusa.com	Deerfield Beach	FL	33442	954-698-9104		180
CBMC (Christian Business Men's Connection) 5746 Marlin Rd Ste 602 Osborne Ctr *TF:* 800-566-2262 ■ *Web:* www.cbmc.com	Chattanooga	TN	37411	423-698-4444	629-4434	48-20
CBMR (Crested Butte Mountain Resort) 12 Snowmass Rd PO Box 5700 **Fax Area Code:* 970 ■ *TF:* 877-547-5143 ■ *Web:* www.skicb.com	Crested Butte	CO	81225	877-547-5143	349-2250*	669
CBN Radio Christian Broadcasting Network 977 Centerville Tpke *TF:* 800-823-6053 ■ *Web:* www1.cbn.com	Virginia Beach	VA	23463	757-226-7000		647
CBNC (Canadian Bank Note Company Ltd) 145 Richmond Rd *Web:* www.cbnco.com	Ottawa	ON	K1Z1A1	613-722-3421		627
CBOE (Chicago Board Options Exchange) 400 S La Salle St *Web:* www.cboe.com	Chicago	IL	60605	312-786-5600	786-8818	691
CBOL Corp 19850 Plummer St *Web:* www.cbol.com	Chatsworth	CA	91311	818-704-8200	704-4336	21
CBORD Group Inc, The 950 Danby Rd Ste 100C *TF:* 844-462-2673 ■ *Web:* www.cbord.com	Ithaca	NY	14850	844-462-2673		180
CBOSS Inc 827 Southwestern Run *TF:* 866-726-0429 ■ *Web:* www.cboss.com	Poland	OH	44514	330-726-0429	726-0499	224
CBR International Corp 2905 Wilderness Pl Ste 202 *Web:* cbrintl.com	Boulder	CO	80301	720-746-1190	746-1192	466
CBR Laser Inc 340 Rt 116 W *Web:* www.cbrlaser.com	Plessisville	QC	G6L2Y2	819-362-9339		295
CBRE Group Inc 11150 Santa Monica Blvd Ste 1600 *NYSE:* CBRE ■ *Web:* www.cbre.us	Los Angeles	CA	90025	310-405-8900		652
CBR-Technology Corp 15581 Sunburst Ln *TF:* 800-227-0700 ■ *Web:* www.cbrtechnology.com	Huntington Beach	CA	92647	714-901-5740		463
CBS 42 News 2075 Golden Crest Dr *Web:* wiat.com	Birmingham	AL	35209	205-322-4200	320-2722	116
CBS Construction Ltd 150 MacKay Crescent *Web:* www.cbsconstruction.ca	Fort McMurray	AB	T9H4W8	780-743-1810		186
CBS Corp 51 W 52nd St *NYSE:* CBS ■ *TF:* 877-227-0787 ■ *Web:* www.cbscorporation.com	New York	NY	10019	212-975-4321		739
CBS Denver 1044 Lincoln St *Web:* denver.cbslocal.com	Denver	CO	80203	303-861-4444	830-6537	741-39
CBS Interactive Inc 235 Second St **Fax Area Code:* 949 ■ *Web:* www.cbsinteractive.com	San Francisco	CA	94105	415-344-2000	399-8740*	808
CBS Manufacturing Co, The 35 Kripes Rd *Web:* www.cbsmfg.com	East Granby	CT	06026	860-653-8100		21
CBS News 524 W 57th St *Web:* www.cbsnews.com	New York	NY	10019	212-975-5005		514
Cbs Payroll Service Inc 1950 Cordell Ct Ste 106 *Web:* cbspayrollservice.com	El Cajon	CA	92020	619-448-2800		570
CBS SPORTS 1430 AM 9245 N Meridian St Ste 300 *Web:* www.radiostationusa.fm	Indianapolis	IN	46260	317-816-4000		645-74
CBS Studio City Broadcast Ctr 4200 Radford Ave *Web:* losangeles.cbslocal.com	Studio City	CA	91604	818-655-2000		741
CBS Studio Ctr 4024 Radford Ave *Web:* www.cbssc.com	Studio City	CA	91604	818-655-5000		514

	Phone	Fax	Class
CBS Television Distribution 2450 Colorado Ave Ste 500E .... Santa Monica CA 90404 *Web:* www.cbstvd.com	310-264-3300		514
CBS4 WTTV-TV 6910 Network Pl .... Indianapolis IN 46278 *Web:* cbs4indy.com	317-687-6584		741-62
CBSL Transportation Services Inc 4750 S Merrimac Ave .... Chicago IL 60638 *Web:* www.cbsltrans.com	708-496-1100		311
CBT Bank 11 N Second St PO Box 171 .... Clearfield PA 16830 *TF:* 888-765-7551 ■ *Web:* www.cbtbank.bank	814-765-7551	765-2943	70
CBU (Cape Breton University) 1250 Grand Lake Rd PO Box 5300 .... Sydney NS B1P6L2 *TF:* 888-959-9995 ■ *Web:* www.cbu.ca	902-539-5300	562-0119	785
CBUF-FM PO Box 4600 .... Vancouver BC V6B2R5 *Web:* www.ici.radio-canada.ca	604-662-6000	662-6161	647
CBV Collection Services Ltd 1490 Denison St Ste 100 .... Markham ON L3R9T7 **Fax Area Code:* 905 ■ *TF:* 866-877-9323 ■ *Web:* www.cbvcollections.com	416-482-9323	474-0328*	160
CBY Systems Inc 33 S Duke St .... York PA 17401 *TF:* 800-717-4229 ■ *Web:* cby.com	800-717-4229		160
CC Coaching & Consulting Inc 5595 S Sycamore St .... Littleton CO 80120 *Web:* www.cccandc.com	303-984-9000	797-6310	196
CC Communications 1750 W Williams Ave .... Fallon NV 89406 *Web:* www.cccomm.net	775-423-7171		224
CC Pollen Co 3627 E Indian School Rd Ste 209 .... Phoenix AZ 85018 *TF:* 800-875-0096 ■ *Web:* www.beepollen.com	800-875-0096		799
CCA (Career College Assn) 1101 Connecticut Ave NW Ste 900 .... Washington DC 20036 *Web:* www.career.org	202-336-6700		49-5
CCA (Coastal Conservation Assn) 6919 Portwest Dr Ste 100 .... Houston TX 77024 *Web:* www.joincca.org	713-626-4234	626-5852	48-13
CCA Global Partners 4301 Earth City Expy .... Saint Louis MO 63045 **Fax Area Code:* 603 ■ *TF:* 800-466-6984 ■ *Web:* www.ccaglobalpartners.com	800-466-6984	626-3444*	361
CCA Industries Inc 193 Conshohocken State Rd .... Penn Valley PA 19072 *NYSE: CAW* ■ *TF:* 800-595-6230 ■ *Web:* ccaindustries.com	800-595-6230		214
CCA Medical Inc 6 Southridge Ct .... Greenville SC 29607 *TF:* 800-775-2556 ■ *Web:* www.ccamedical.com	864-233-2700		180
CCAII (Computer Consulting Associates International Inc) 200 Pequot Ave .... Southport CT 06890 *Web:* www.ccaii.com	203-255-8966		721
CCAR Press 355 Lexington Ave 8th Fl .... New York NY 10017 *Web:* www.ccarpress.org	212-972-3636		637-2
CCAS (Cross Country Automotive Services) 1 Cabot Rd .... Medford MA 02155 *Web:* www.agero.com	781-393-9300	395-6706	53
CCB Community Bank 225 E Three Notch St .... Andalusia AL 36420 *Web:* www.bankccb.com	334-222-2561		70
CCB Packaging Inc 1905 N Center Point Rd .... Hiawatha IA 52233 *Web:* www.ccbpackaging.com	319-378-0114		393
CCBC (Community College of Baltimore County) *Hunt Valley* 11101 McCormick Rd .... Hunt Valley MD 21031 *Web:* www.ccbcmd.edu	443-840-5830		162
CCC (Center for Community Change) 1536 U St NW .... Washington DC 20009 *Web:* communitychange.org	202-339-9300	387-4891	48-5
CCC (Copyright Clearance Center Inc) 222 Rosewood Dr .... Danvers MA 01923 *TF:* 855-239-3415 ■ *Web:* www.copyright.com	978-750-8400	646-8600	49-16
CCC (Clovis Community College) 417 Schepps Blvd .... Clovis NM 88101 *TF:* 800-769-1409 ■ *Web:* www.clovis.edu	575-769-2811	769-4190	162
CCC Group Inc 5797 Dietrich Rd .... San Antonio TX 78219 *Web:* www.cccgroupinc.com	210-661-4251	661-6060	188-7
CCC Information Services Inc 222 Merchandise Mart Plz .... Chicago IL 60654 *TF:* 800-621-8070 ■ *Web:* www.cccis.com	800-621-8070		225
CCC Investment Banking 155 Wellington St W Ste 3720 .... Toronto ON M5V3H1 *Web:* cccinvestmentbanking.com	416-599-4206		70
CCCC (Cherokee County Chamber of Commerce) 805 W US 64 Hwy .... Murphy NC 28906 *Web:* www.cherokeecountychamber.com	828-837-2242	837-6012	139
CCCS (CAD/CAM Consulting Services Inc) 1525 Rancho Conejo Blvd Ste 103 .... Newbury Park CA 91320 *TF:* 888-375-7676 ■ *Web:* www.cad-cam.com	805-375-7676	375-7678	174
CCCS (Community Counseling & Correctional Service) 471 E Mercury St .... Butte MT 59701 *Web:* www.cccscorp.com	406-782-0417		48-15
CCCU (Council for Christian Colleges & Universities) 321 Eigth St NE .... Washington DC 20002 *Web:* www.cccu.org	202-546-8713	546-8913	49-5
CCCVB (Clermont County Convention & Visitors Bureau) 410 E Main St PO Box 100 .... Batavia OH 45103 *TF:* 800-796-4282 ■ *Web:* discoverclermont.com	513-732-3600		206
CCD (Consortium for Citizens with Disabilities) 1660 L St NW Ste 701 .... Washington DC 20036 *TF:* 800-669-7079 ■ *Web:* www.c-c-d.org	202-783-2229		48-6
CCE (Cost Containment Engineering Inc) 9222 Linbrooke St .... San Antonio TX 78250 *Web:* www.costcontainmentengr.com	210-722-7278		261
CCEC (Carteret-Craven Electric Co-op) 1300 Hwy 24 W PO Box 1490 .... Newport NC 28570 *TF:* 800-682-2217 ■ *Web:* www.ccemc.com	252-247-3107		245
CCEIA (Carnegie Council for Ethics in International Affairs) Merrill House 170 E 64th St .... New York NY 10065 *Web:* www.carnegiecouncil.org	212-838-4120	752-2432	634
CCF (Clarity Coverdale Fury) 120 S Sixth St Ste 1300 .... Minneapolis MN 55402 *Web:* claritycoverdalefury.com	612-339-3902		4
CCFA (Crohn's & Colitis Foundation of America) 733 Third Ave Ste 510 .... New York NY 10017 **Fax Area Code:* 212 ■ *TF:* 800-932-2423 ■ *Web:* www.crohnscolitisfoundation.org	800-932-2423	679-3567*	48-17
CCG (Community Consulting Group) 5008 Morgan Ave S .... Minneapolis MN 55419 *Web:* www.ccgpartnership.com	612-926-0122		194
CCG (Callahan Consulting Group) 3557 Maryhill Ln NW .... Kennesaw GA 30152 *Web:* www.callahanconsultinggroup.com	770-715-5036		196
CCG Automation Inc 3868 Congress Pkwy .... Richfield OH 44286 *Web:* www.ccgautomation.com	330-659-5082		463
CCGA (Chicago Council on Global Affairs, The) 332 S Michigan Ave Ste 1100 .... Chicago IL 60604 *Web:* www.thechicagocouncil.org	312-726-3860	821-7555	634
CCGS (Clark County Genealogical Society) 717 Grand Blvd .... Vancouver WA 98661 *Web:* www.ccgs-wa.org	360-750-5688		48-13
CCH Small Firm Services 225 Chastain Meadows Ct NW Ste 200 .... Kennesaw GA 30144 *TF:* 866-345-4171 ■ *Web:* taxna.wolterskluwer.com	866-345-4171		178-10
CCHA (Clarke County Historical Assn) 32 E Main St .... Berryville VA 22611 *Web:* www.clarkehistory.org	540-955-2600		48-13
CCHC Southern Gastroenterology Assoc 3100 Wellons Blvd .... New Bern NC 28562 *Web:* www.cchchealthcare.com	252-634-9000	634-9001	543
CCHS (Clark County Historical Society) Heritage Center of Clark County 117 S Fountain Ave .... Springfield OH 45502 *Web:* heritage.center	937-324-0657	324-1992	49-19
CCHS (Carver County Historical Society) 555 W 1st St .... Waconia MN 55387 *Web:* www.carvercountyhistoricalsociety.org	952-442-4234		49-19
CCI (Canine Companions for Independence Inc) 2965 Dutton Ave PO Box 446 .... Santa Rosa CA 95402 *TF:* 800-572-2275 ■ *Web:* www.cci.org	707-577-1700		48-17
CCI (Charlestown Retirement Community) 715 Maiden Choice Ln .... Catonsville MD 21228 *TF:* 800-917-8649 ■ *Web:* www.ericksonliving.com	410-242-2880		672
CCI (Columbia Collectors Inc) 1104 Main St Ste 311 .... Vancouver WA 98660 *TF:* 800-694-7585 ■ *Web:* www.columbiacollectors.com	360-694-7585		160
CCI (Columbus Cir Investors Inc) 1 Stn Pl Metro Ctr .... Stamford CT 06902 *Web:* www.columbuscircle.com	203-353-6000		401
CCI (CCI Crane & Transport Inc) PO Box 52237 .... Idaho Falls ID 83402 *TF:* 800-388-0334 ■ *Web:* www.ccicrane.com	208-324-1128	522-7259	393
CCI (Certified Communications Inc) 5213 Coconut Creek Pky .... Margate FL 33063 *Web:* www.certifiedcommunications.com	954-974-4000	974-4701	194
CCI Crane & Transport Inc (CCI) PO Box 52237 .... Idaho Falls ID 83402 *TF:* 800-388-0334 ■ *Web:* www.ccicrane.com	208-324-1128	522-7259	393
CCI Mechanical Inc 2345 S CCI Way PO Box 25788 .... Salt Lake City UT 84119 *Web:* ccimechanical.com	801-973-9000	975-7204	189-10
CCI Network Services 155 North 400 West Ste 100 .... Salt Lake City UT 84103 *TF:* 877-592-8049 ■ *Web:* www.ccicom.com	801-994-4100	994-2960	387
CCI Thermal Technologies Inc 5918 Roper Rd .... Edmonton AB T6B3E1 *TF:* 800-661-8529 ■ *Web:* www.ccithermal.com	780-466-3178	468-5904	318
CCIA (Computer & Communications Industry Assn) 666 11th St NW .... Washington DC 20001 *Web:* www.ccianet.org	202-783-0070	783-0534	49-20
CCIC (Canadian Council for International Co-op) 39 McArthur Ave .... Ottawa ON K1L8L7 *Web:* ccic.ca	613-241-7007	241-5302	48-5
CCIM Institute 430 N Michigan Ave Ste 800 .... Chicago IL 60611 *TF:* 800-621-7027 ■ *Web:* www.ccim.com	312-321-4460	321-4530	49-17
CCL Container Corp 1 Llodio Dr .... Hermitage PA 16148 *Web:* cclcontainer.com	724-981-4420	981-7226	124
CCL Industries Corp 161 Worcester Rd Ste 603 .... Framingham MA 01701 *Web:* www.cclind.com	508-872-4511		413
CCLS (Cultural Center for Language School) 3191 Coral Way Ste 114 .... Miami FL 33145 *Web:* www.cclsmiami.edu	305-529-2257	443-8538	423
CCM (Comprehensive Care Management Corp) 1250 Waters Pl Tower 1 Ste 602 .... Bronx NY 10461 *TF:* 877-226-8500 ■ *Web:* www.centerlighthealthcare.org	877-226-8500		450
CCMC (Crozer-Chester Medical Ctr) 1 Medical Center Blvd .... Upland PA 19013 *TF:* 800-254-3258 ■ *Web:* www.crozerkeystone.org	610-447-2000		374-3
CCMG (Clark Capital Management Group Inc) 1650 Market St 1 Liberty Pl 53rd Fl .... Philadelphia PA 19103 *TF:* 800-766-2264 ■ *Web:* www.ccmg.com	215-569-2224	569-3639	401
CCOM (CCOM Group Inc) 275 Wagaraw Rd ..... Hawthorne NJ 07506 *OTC: CCOM* ■ *Web:* ccom-group.com	973-427-8224		14
CCOM Group Inc (CCOM) 275 Wagaraw Rd ..... Hawthorne NJ 07506 *OTC: CCOM* ■ *Web:* ccom-group.com	973-427-8224		14
CCP (Continental Commercial Products) 11840 Westline Industrial Dr .... Saint Louis MO 63146 *TF:* 800-325-1051 ■ *Web:* www.continentalcommercialproducts.com	800-325-1051	327-5492	508
CCP (Cypress Cove Publishing) PO Box 91195 .... Lafayette LA 70509 *TF:* 888-606-3257 ■ *Web:* cypresscovepublishing.com	888-606-3257		637-2
CCP Global Inc 4220 Shawnee Mission Pkwy Ste B350 .... Fairway KS 66205 *Web:* www.ccpglobal.com	913-948-7400		809
CCPL (Collier County Public Library) 2385 Orange Blossom Dr .... Naples FL 34109 *Web:* www.colliercountyfl.gov	239-593-0177		434-3
CCPL (Cecil County Public Library) 301 Newark Ave .... Elkton MD 21921 *Web:* www.cecil.ebranch.info	410-996-1055	996-5604	434-3
CCR (Council for Chemical Research Inc) 1550 M St NW Ste 300 .... Washington DC 20005 *Web:* ccrhq.org	202-429-3971	429-3976	49-19

Phone | Fax | Class

CCR (Communications Credit & Recovery)
20 Broad Hollow Rd Ste 1002 Melville NY 11747 631-923-2200 923-2784 160
Web: www.ccrcollect.com

CCRA Travel Commerce Network
320 Hemphill St Fort Worth TX 76104 800-771-7327 393
TF: 800-771-7327 ■ *Web:* www.ccra.com

CCRKBA (Citizens Committee for the Right to Keep & Bear Arms)
Liberty Pk 12500 NE Tenth Pl Bellevue WA 98005 425-454-4911 48-7
TF: 800-486-6963 ■ *Web:* www.ccrkba.org

CCRTA (Cape Cod Regional Transit Authority)
215 Iyannough Rd PO Box 1988 Hyannis MA 02601 508-775-8504 775-8513 468
TF: 800-352-7155 ■ *Web:* www.capecodtransit.org

CCS (Cleveland Chamber Symphony, The)
The Music School Settlement 11125 Magnolia Dr
Cleveland OH 44106 216-202-4227 573-3
Web: www.clevelandchambersymphony.org

CCS (Custom Computer Specialists Inc)
70 Suffolk Ct Hauppauge NY 11788 800-598-8989 986-5518 180
TF: 800-598-8989 ■ *Web:* www.customonline.com

CCS (Check Cashing Store)
6340 NW Fifth Way Fort Lauderdale FL 33309 800-361-1407 141
TF: 800-361-1407 ■ *Web:* www.thecheckcashingstore.com

CCS (Continental Currency Services Inc)
PO Box 10970 Santa Ana CA 92711 714-667-6699 569-0882 217
Web: www.ccurr.com

CCS (Craven County School)
3600 Trent Rd New Bern NC 28562 252-514-6300 514-6351 685
Web: www.cravenk12.org

CCS (Converged Communication Systems)
2930 Central St Evanston IL 60201 877-598-3999 180
TF: 877-598-3999 ■ *Web:* www.convergedsystems.com

CCS (Comprehensive Computer Services Inc)
169 Commack Rd Ste H-233 Commack NY 11725 631-755-2250 755-2254 180
Web: www.comprehensive.com

CCS (Cooper Consulting Service)
211 E Parkwood Ave Ste 200 Friendswood TX 77546 281-482-9786 261
Web: www.cooperconsultingservice.com

CCS Medical Inc
1505 LBJ Fwy Ste 550 Farmers Branch TX 75234 972-628-2100 475
TF: 800-726-9811 ■ *Web:* www.ccsmed.com

CCS of South Carolina Inc
2325 Prosperity Way Ste 8 Florence SC 29501 843-669-2273 104
Web: www.southcarolinabids.us

CCS Plas-Tech 180 Shepard Ave Wheeling IL 60090 847-459-8320 704
TF: 800-747-1269 ■ *Web:* www.ccsplastech.com

CCS Presentation Systems Inc
17350 N Hartford Dr Scottsdale AZ 85255 480-348-0100 196
TF: 800-742-5036 ■ *Web:* www.ccsprojects.com

CCSCE (Center for Continuing Study of the California Economy)
385 Homer Ave Palo Alto CA 94301 650-321-8550 321-5451 466
Web: www.ccsce.com

CCSD (Charleston County School District)
75 Calhoun St Charleston SC 29401 843-937-6300 937-6307 685
TF: 800-241-8898 ■ *Web:* www.ccsdschools.com

CCSD (Clark County School District)
5100 W Sahara Ave Las Vegas NV 89146 702-799-8111 799-5125 685
TF: 866-799-8997 ■ *Web:* ccsd.net

CCSE Federal Credit Union
417 Broad St Salamanca NY 14779 716-945-5340 219
Web: ccseonline.com

CCSI (Computer Consulting Services Inc)
409A Walker Rd Jackson TN 38305 731-668-0303 554-3359 180
Web: www.ccsi.me

CCSNH (Community College System of New Hampshire)
26 College Dr Concord NH 03301 603-230-3500 271-2725 162
TF: 866-945-2255 ■ *Web:* www.ccsnh.edu

CCSSO (Council of Chief State School Officers)
1 Massachusetts Ave NW Ste 700 Washington DC 20001 202-336-7000 408-8072 49-5
Web: www.ccsso.org

CCT Technologies Inc
482 W San Carlos St San Jose CA 95110 408-519-3200 174
Web: www.cland.com

CCT Telecomm 1106 E Turner Rd Lodi CA 95240 209-365-9500 387
Web: www.4cct.com

CCTC (Cochrane Cooperative Telephone Co)
103 W 5th St Cochrane WI 54622 608-248-2323 224
Web: www.cochranetel.com

CCTEC (Cuba City Telephone Exchange Co)
104 S Main St Cuba City WI 53807 608-744-2154 224
Web: www.cubacity.org

CCTF Corp 5407 - 53 Ave NW Edmonton AB T6B3G2 780-463-8700 111
TF: 800-661-3633 ■ *Web:* www.cctf.com

CCTV Agent Inc
1300 N Florida Mango Rd Ste 1 West Palm Beach FL 33409 561-249-4511 261
Web: cctvagent.com

C-Cube Consulting Inc
1238 Ridge Oak Ct San Jose CA 95120 408-268-4886 180
Web: ccubeconsulting.net

CCUSD (Culver City Unified School District)
4034 Irving Pl Culver City CA 90232 310-842-4220 842-4205 685
TF: 855-446-2673 ■ *Web:* www.ccusd.org

CCWF (Central California Women's Facility)
23370 Rd 22 PO Box 1501 Chowchilla CA 93610 559-665-5531 213
Web: www.cdcr.ca.gov

CCX Corp 1399 Horizon Ave LaFayette CO 80026 303-666-5206 111
Web: www.ccxcorp.com

CD Aero LLC
167 John Vertente Blvd New Bedford MA 02745 508-994-9661 995-3000 253
Web: www.cd-aero.com

CD Commercial Agency Inc
300 Wheeler Rd Ste 108 Hauppauge NY 11788 631-582-4400 390
Web: cdinsagency.com

CD Diagnostics Inc
650 Naamans Rd Ste 100 Claymont DE 19703 302-367-7770 743
Web: cddiagnostics.com

CD Ford & Sons Inc 16243 Ford Rd Geneseo IL 61254 309-944-4661 944-3703 369
TF: 800-383-4661 ■ *Web:* www.cdford.com

CD Hartnett Co 302 N Main St Weatherford TX 76086 817-594-3813 594-9714 297-8
Web: esite.cd-hartnett.com

CD Moody Construction Company Inc
6017 Redan Rd Lithonia GA 30058 770-482-7778 482-7727 186
Web: www.cdmoodyconstruction.com

CD Smith Construction Inc
889 E Johnson St Fond du Lac WI 54935 920-924-2900 186
Web: www.cdsmith.com

CD Solutions Inc
100 W Monument St Pleasant Hill OH 45359 937-676-2376 676-2478 179
TF: 800-860-2376 ■ *Web:* www.cds.com

CD Stampley Enterprises Inc
6100 Orr Rd Charlotte NC 28213 704-333-6631 336-6932 96
Web: www.stampley.com

CD Universe
101 N Plains Industrial Rd Wallingford CT 06492 203-294-1648 294-0391 525
TF: 800-231-7937 ■ *Web:* www.cduniverse.com

CDA (Chemically Dependent Anonymous)
PO Box 423 Severna Park MD 21146 888-232-4673 48-21
TF: 888-232-4673 ■ *Web:* cdawebsitedev.com

CDA Technical Institute
91 Trout River Dr Jacksonville FL 32208 904-766-7736 766-7764 167-3
TF: 888-974-2232 ■ *Web:* www.commercialdivingacademy.com

CDC (Cookie Dough Creations)
22 W Chicago Ave Naperville IL 60540 630-369-4833 369-2833 297-3
Web: www.cookiedoughcreations.com

CDC (ChemDesign) 2 Stanton St Marinette WI 54143 715-735-9033 735-5304 145
Web: www.chemdesigncorp.com

CDC Distributors
10511 Medallion Dr Cincinnati OH 45241 513-771-3100 771-2920 361
TF: 800-678-2321 ■ *Web:* www.cdcdist.com

CDC Small Business Finance Corp
2448 Historic Decatur Rd Ste 200 San Diego CA 92106 619-291-3594 216
TF: 800-611-5170 ■ *Web:* cdcloans.com

CDCHY (Chambre de Commerce Haute-Yamaska Region)
90 Rue Robinson S Ste 102 Granby QC J2G7L4 450-372-6100 372-3161 137
Web: cchy.ca

CDD 11603 Crosswinds Way Ste 100 San Antonio TX 78233 210-590-3033 415
Web: www.cddmedical.com

CDDC (Carolyn Dorfman Dance Co)
2780 Morris Ave Ste 1-A Union NJ 07083 908-687-8855 686-5245 573-1
Web: carolyndorfman.dance

CDE Career Institute
2942 Rte 611 Tannersville PA 18372 570-629-2690 167-3
Web: cde.edu

CDEC (Continental Divide Electric Co-opeartive Inc)
200 E High St PO Box 1087 Grants NM 87020 505-285-6656 287-2234 245
TF: 877-775-5211 ■ *Web:* www.cdec.coop

CDF (Children's Defense Fund)
25 E St NW Washington DC 20001 202-628-8787 662-3510 48-6
TF: 800-233-1200 ■ *Web:* www.childrensdefense.org

CDF Corp 77 Industrial Park Rd Plymouth MA 02360 800-443-1920 601
TF: 800-443-1920 ■ *Web:* www.cdf1.com

CDG Engineers Inc
1 Campbell Plz Ste 3A Saint Louis MO 63139 314-781-7770 781-9075 261
Web: cdgengineers.com

CDI (Consolidated Devices Inc)
19220 San Jose Ave City of Industry CA 91748 626-965-0668 810-2759 758
TF: 800-525-6319 ■ *Web:* www.cditorque.com

CDI (Charles D. Sheehy Inc)
675 Bodwell St Ext Avon MA 02322 508-583-7612 586-2312 612
Web: www.cdsi.com

CDI Contractors LLC
3000 Cantrell Rd Little Rock AR 72202 501-666-4300 666-4741 186
Web: www.cdicon.com

CDI Corp 1735 Market St Ste 200 Philadelphia PA 19103 216-202-0300 030-1233 261
TF: 866-472-2203 ■ *Web:* www.cdiengineeringsolutions.com

CDI Credit Inc
6160 Peachtree Dunwoody Rd NE Ste B-210 Atlanta GA 30328 770-350-5070 394-2197 635
TF: 800-633-3961 ■ *Web:* www.cdicredit.com

CDI Nuclear Technologies Inc
6400 Brooktree Ct Ste 320 Wexford PA 15090 724-933-5570 363
Web: cdlnuclear.com

CDIA (Consumer Data Industry Assn)
1090 Vermont Ave NW Ste 200 Washington DC 20005 202-371-0910 371-0134 49-2
Web: www.cdiaonline.org

CDLS (Cornelia de Lange Syndrome Foundation Inc)
302 W Main St Ste 100 Avon CT 06001 860-676-8166 676-8337 48-17
TF: 800-753-2357 ■ *Web:* www.cdlsusa.org

CDM (Cline Davis & Mann Inc)
220 E 42nd St 8Th Fl New York NY 10017 212-907-4300 4
Web: www.clinedavis.com

CDM Smith Inc 75 State St Ste 701 Boston MA 02109 617-452-6000 345-3901 261
TF: 800-243-2677 ■ *Web:* www.cdmsmith.com

CDMA (Chain Drug Marketing Assn)
43157 W Nine-Mile Rd PO Box 995 Novi MI 48376 248-449-9300 449-9396 49-18
TF: 800-935-2362 ■ *Web:* www.chaindrug.com

CDMS Inc
550 Sherbrooke W West Tower Ste 250 Montreal QC H3A1B9 514-286-2367 180
TF: 866-337-2367 ■ *Web:* www.cdmsfirst.com

CDNetworks Inc
1919 S Bascom Ave Ste 600 Campbell CA 95008 408-228-3700 387
TF: 877-937-4236 ■ *Web:* www.cdnetworks.com

CDO Technologies Inc
5200 Springfeld St Ste 320 Dayton OH 45431 937-258-0022 258-1614 449
TF: 866-307-6616 ■ *Web:* www.cdotech.com

C-Double Web Development
7000 College Ave Bakersfield CA 93306 661-735-7309 180
Web: c-double.com

CDR Assessment Group Inc
1644 S Denver Ave Tulsa OK 74119 918-488-0722 195
TF: 888-406-0100 ■ *Web:* www.cdrassessmentgroup.com

CDR Data 1028 N Lake Ave Ste 105 Pasadena CA 91104 626-791-9700 791-4658 116
Web: www.cdrdata.com

CDR Fundraising Group
16900 Science Dr Ste 210 Bowie MD 20715 301-858-1500 721-5795* 393
*Fax Area Code: 410 ■ *Web:* www.cdrfg.com

CDR of NC Inc 109 Waters Dr Moyock NC 27958 252-232-3932 175
Web: www.probay.com

Name / Address	City	State	ZIP	Phone	Fax	Class
CDRI (Chihuahuan Desert Research Institute) 43869 State Hwy 118 PO Box 905 *Web:* www.cdri.org	Fort Davis	TX	79734	432-364-2499		97
CDS - Networks & Services Inc 672 Stratford Blvd *Web:* www.cdsnetworks.com	Kinston	NC	28504	252-523-6664		175
CDS Analytical Inc 465 Limestone Rd *TF:* 800-541-6593 ■ *Web:* www.cdsanalytical.com	Oxford	PA	19363	610-932-3636		419
CDS Engineering Inc 4461 Peralta Blvd Ste 3 *Web:* www.cdsengineeringinc.com	Fremont	CA	94538	510-252-2100		454
CDS Logistics Management Inc 1225 Bengies Rd Ste A *TF:* 866-649-9559 ■ *Web:* www.cdslogistics.net	Baltimore	MD	21220	410-314-8000		311
CDSPI 155 Lesmill Rd *TF:* 800-561-9401 ■ *Web:* www.cdspi.com	Toronto	ON	M3B2T8	416-296-9401		391-3
CDT (Center for Democracy & Technology) 1401 K St NW Ste 200 *TF:* 800-869-4499 ■ *Web:* cdt.org	Washington	DC	20005	202-637-9800	637-0968	48-7
CDT (Community Development Trust) 1350 Broadway Ste 700 *Web:* www.cdt.biz	New York	NY	10018	212-271-5080	271-5079	655
CDT Micrographics Inc 137 Water St *Web:* cdtmicrographics.com	Exeter	NH	03833	603-778-6140		180
CDTA (Capital District Transportation Authority) 110 Watervliet Ave *Web:* www.cdta.org	Albany	NY	12206	518-482-8822	437-8318	468
CDTS (Continental Divide Trail Society) 3704 N Charles St Ste 601 *Web:* www.cdtsociety.org	Baltimore	MD	21218	410-235-9610		48-23
CDW Corp 200 N Milwaukee Ave *TF:* 800-800-4239 ■ *Web:* www.cdw.com	Vernon Hills	IL	60061	847-465-6000	465-6800	179
CE (Cordell Expeditions) 4295 Walnut Blvd *Web:* www.cordell.org	Walnut Creek	CA	94596	925-934-3735		48-6
CE Electronics Inc 2107 Industrial Dr *Web:* www.ceelectronics.com	Bryan	OH	43506	419-636-6705	636-2516	253
CE Holden Inc 938 Rt 910 *Web:* www.ceholden.com	Cheswick	PA	15024	412-767-5050	767-9922	621
CE National Inc 1003 Presidential Dr *Web:* www.cenational.org	Winona Lake	IN	46590	574-267-6622		48-20
CE Niehoff & Co 2021 Lee St *TF:* 800-643-4633 ■ *Web:* www.ceniehoff.com	Evanston	IL	60202	847-866-6030	492-1242	247
CE Print Solutions Inc 564 Dixon St *Web:* www.ceprint.com	Lexington	NC	27292	336-956-6327		627
CE Ready Mix 185 N Washington Rd *Web:* www.cticoordinators.com	Apollo	PA	15613	724-727-3331	639-3059	182
CE Resource Inc PO Box 997581 *TF:* 800-707-5644 ■ *Web:* www.paragoncet.com	Sacramento	CA	95899	800-707-5644		463
CE Thurston & Sons Inc 3550 East Virginia Beach Blvd *TF:* 800-444-7713 ■ *Web:* www.cethurston.com	Norfolk	VA	23513	757-855-7700		189-9
CE Toland & Son 5300 Industrial Way *Web:* cetoland.com	Benicia	CA	94510	707-747-1000	747-5300	189-14
CEA (CEA Study Abroad) 2999 N 44th St Ste 200 **Fax Area Code:* 480 ■ *TF:* 866-987-8906 ■ *Web:* www.ceastudyabroad.com	Phoenix	AZ	85018	800-266-4441	557-7926*	760
CEA (Commission on English Language Program Accreditation) 801 N Fairfax St Ste 402A *Web:* cea-accredit.org	Alexandria	VA	22314	703-665-3400	519-2071	48-1
CEA (Chmura Economics & Analytics) 1309 E Cary St *Web:* www.chmuraecon.com	Richmond	VA	23219	804-554-5400	644-2828	466
CEA Study Abroad (CEA) 2999 N 44th St Ste 200 **Fax Area Code:* 480 ■ *TF:* 866-987-8906 ■ *Web:* www.ceastudyabroad.com	Phoenix	AZ	85018	800-266-4441	557-7926*	760
CEA-HOW (Compulsive Eaters Anonymous - HOW) 3371 Glendale Blvd Ste 104 *Web:* www.ceahow.org	Los Angeles	CA	90039	323-660-4333	660-4334	48-21
Ceavco Audio-visual Co 6240 W 54th Ave *Web:* ceavco.com	Arvada	CO	80002	303-539-3500		38
CEBOS Ltd 5936 Ford Ct Ste 203 *Web:* www.cebos.com	Brighton	MI	48116	810-534-2222		463
CEC Controls Company Inc 14555 Barber Ave *TF:* 877-924-0303 ■ *Web:* www.ceccontrols.com	Warren	MI	48088	586-779-0222	779-0266	201
CEC Entertainment Inc 3903 W Airport Frwy *NYSE:* CEC ■ *TF:* 888-778-7193 ■ *Web:* www.chuckecheese.com	Irving	TX	75062	972-258-8507		670
CEC Industries Ltd 599 Bond St *TF:* 800-572-4168 ■ *Web:* cecindustries.com	Lincolnshire	IL	60069	847-821-1199		54
Cecchin Plumbing & Heating Inc 4N275 Cavalry Dr *Web:* cecchin-inc.com	Bloomingdale	IL	60108	630-529-4046		610
Cecconi Simone Inc 1335 Dundas St W *Web:* www.cecconisimone.com	Toronto	ON	M6J1Y3	416-588-5900		393
Cecelia Packing Corp 24780 E South Ave *Web:* ceceliapack.com	Orange Cove	CA	93646	559-626-5000		11-1
Ceci New York 255 W 36th St Ste 14B *Web:* www.cecinewyork.com	New York	NY	10018	212-989-0695		627
Cecil A. Ross Inc 5301 Knickerbocker Rd Ste 110 *Web:* cecilaross.com	San Angelo	TX	76904	325-949-3200		690
Cecil Community College 1 Seahawk Dr *TF:* 866-966-1001 ■ *Web:* www.cecil.edu	North East	MD	21901	410-287-6060	287-1001	162
Cecil County 129 E Main St Ste 300 *Web:* www.ccgov.org	Elkton	MD	21921	410-996-5375		338
Cecil County Chamber of Commerce 106 E Main St Ste 101 *Web:* www.cecilchamber.com	Elkton	MD	21921	410-392-3833		139
Cecil County Public Library (CCPL) 301 Newark Ave *Web:* www.cecil.ebranch.info	Elkton	MD	21921	410-996-1055	996-5604	434-3
Cecil M. Harden Lake 1588 S Raccoon Pkwy *Web:* www.in.gov	Rockville	IN	47872	765-344-1412		565
CECO (Compressor Engineering Corp) 5440 Alder Dr *TF:* 800-879-2326 ■ *Web:* www.tryceco.com	Houston	TX	77081	713-664-7333	664-6444	172
Ceco Building Systems 2400 Hwy 45 N *TF:* 800-474-2326 ■ *Web:* www.cecobuildings.com	Columbus	MS	39705	662-243-6400		105
Ceco Concrete Construction LLC 9135 Barton *Web:* www.cecoconcrete.com	Overland Park	KS	66214	913-362-1855		189-3
Ceco Door 9159 Telecom Dr *TF:* 888-264-7474 ■ *Web:* www.cecodoor.com	Milan	TN	38358	731-686-8345	686-4211	234
CECO Environmental 700 Emlen Way *Web:* www.cecoenviro.com	Telford	PA	18969	215-723-8155	723-2197	18
CED (Committee for Economic Development) 1530 Wilson Blvd Ste 400 *TF:* 800-676-7353 ■ *Web:* www.ced.org	Arlington	VA	22209	202-296-5860	223-0776	634
CED (CED Omaha) 2000 Judson St *Web:* www.cedlincoln.com	Lincoln	NE	68127	402-465-5151		246
CED Omaha (CED) 2000 Judson St *Web:* www.cedlincoln.com	Lincoln	NE	68127	402-465-5151		246
Cedar Bluff State Park 32001 147 Hwy *Web:* ksoutdoors.com	Ellis	KS	67637	785-726-3212		565
Cedar Breaks National Monument 2390 W Hwy 56 Ste 11 *Web:* www.nps.gov	Cedar City	UT	84720	435-586-9451	586-3813	564
Cedar Brook Financial Partners LLC 5885 Landerbrook Dr Ste 200 *TF:* 800-922-6931 ■ *Web:* cedarbrookfinancial.com	Cleveland	OH	44124	440-683-9200	683-9100	401
Cedar City-Brian Head Tourism & Convention Bureau 581 N Main St *TF:* 800-354-4849 ■ *Web:* www.visitcedarcity.com	Cedar City	UT	84721	435-586-5124		206
Cedar County 400 Cedar St *Web:* www.cedarcounty.org	Tipton	IA	52772	563-886-2101	886-3594	338
Cedar Courthouse 101 S Broadway *Web:* www.co.cedar.ne.us	Hartington	NE	68739	402-254-7411	254-7410	338
Cedar Creek & Belle Grove National Historical Park 7718 1/2 Main St *Web:* www.nps.gov	Middletown	VA	22645	540-868-9176	869-4527	564
Cedar Creek Correctional Ctr 12200 Bordeaux Rd PO Box 37 *Web:* www.doc.wa.gov	Littlerock	WA	98556	360-359-4100		213
Cedar Creek Lake Area Chamber of Commerce 604 S Third St Ste E *TF:* 800-443-0131 ■ *Web:* www.cedarcreeklakechamber.com	Mabank	TX	75147	903-887-3152	887-3695	139
Cedar Creek State Park 2947 Cedar Creek Rd *Web:* wvstateparks.com	Glenville	WV	26351	304-462-7158		565
Cedar Crest College 100 College Dr *TF:* 800-360-1222 ■ *Web:* www.cedarcrest.edu	Allentown	PA	18104	610-437-4471	606-4647	166
Cedar Crest Specialties Inc 7269 Hwy 60 PO Box 260 *TF:* 800-877-8341 ■ *Web:* www.cedarcresticecream.com	Cedarburg	WI	53012	262-377-7252	377-5554	296-25
Cedar Fair LP 1 Cedar Pt Dr *NYSE:* FUN ■ *Web:* www.cedarfair.com	Sandusky	OH	44870	419-627-2233	627-2260	31
Cedar Fair Parks 14523 Carowinds Blvd *Web:* www.carowinds.com	Charlotte	NC	28273	704-588-2600		32
Cedar Falls Public Library 524 Main St *Web:* www.cedarfallspubliclibrary.org	Cedar Falls	IA	50613	319-273-8643		434-3
Cedar Farms 2100 Hornig Rd *TF:* 800-220-2217 ■ *Web:* cedarfarms.com	Philadelphia	PA	19116	215-934-7100		297-6
Cedar Financial Advisors Inc 3853 SW Hall Blvd *Web:* www.cedaradvisors.com	Beaverton	OR	97005	503-512-5890		401
Cedar Fort Inc (CFI) 2373 W 700 S *TF:* 800-759-2665 ■ *Web:* www.cedarfort.com	Springville	UT	84663	801-489-4084	489-1097	637-2
Cedar Graphics Inc 311 Parsons Dr **Fax Area Code:* 866 ■ *TF:* 800-393-2399 ■ *Web:* www.cedargraphicsinc.com	Hiawatha	IA	52233	319-395-6900	238-0467*	393
Cedar Grove Composting Inc 7343 E Marginal Way S **Fax Area Code:* 206 ■ *TF:* 888-832-3008 ■ *Web:* cedar-grove.com	Seattle	WA	98108	877-764-5748	832-3030*	186
Cedar Hill State Park 1570 W FM 1382 *Web:* tpwd.texas.gov	Cedar Hill	TX	75104	972-291-3900		565
Cedar Key Museum State Park 12231 SW 166 Ct *Web:* www.floridastateparks.org	Cedar Key	FL	32625	352-543-5350		565
Cedar Lake Nursing Home 1611 W Royall Blvd *Web:* cedarlakenursing.com	Malakoff	TX	75148	903-489-1702		371
Cedar Management Consulting International LLC 250 Park Ave 7th Fl *Web:* www.cedar-consulting.com	New York	NY	10177	212-572-6314		194
Cedar Petrochemicals Inc 203 E 72ND St APT Ste 12E	New York	NY	10021	212-288-4320		169
Cedar Point Amusement Park 1 Cedar Point Dr *Web:* www.cedarpoint.com	Sandusky	OH	44870	419-609-5997		32
Cedar Rapids & Iowa City Railway Co 2330 12th St SW *Web:* www.aetransportation.com	Cedar Rapids	IA	52404	319-786-3698		648
Cedar Rapids Area Chamber of Commerce 424 First Ave NE *Web:* www.cedarrapids.org	Cedar Rapids	IA	52401	319-398-5317	398-5228	139
Cedar Rapids City Hall 3851 River Ridge Dr NE *Web:* www.cedar-rapids.org	Cedar Rapids	IA	52402	319-286-5670	286-5130	337
Cedar Rapids Museum of Art 410 Third Ave SE *Web:* www.crma.org	Cedar Rapids	IA	52401	319-366-7503	366-4111	520
Cedar Rapids Public Library 2600 Edgewood Rd SW Ste 330 *Web:* www.crlibrary.org	Cedar Rapids	IA	52404	319-398-5123	398-0476	434-3
Cedar Realty Trust Inc 44 S Bayles Ave *NYSE:* CDR ■ *Web:* www.cedarrealtytrust.com	Port Washington	NY	11050	516-767-6492		655

	Phone	Fax	Class
Cedar Rock 2611 Quasqueton Diagonal Blvd Buch Co Hwy W-35 Independence IA 50644 *Web:* www.iowadnr.gov	319-934-3572		565
Cedar Shake & Shingle Bureau 7101 Horne St Ste 2 Mission BC V2V7A2 *Web:* www.cedarbureau.org	604-820-7700	820-0266	49-3
Cedar Springs Hospital 2135 Southgate Rd Colorado Springs CO 80906 *TF:* 888-456-0968 ■ *Web:* www.cedarspringsbhs.com	719-633-4114	578-0857	374-5
Cedar Springs Post 36 E Maple PO Box 370 Cedar Springs MI 49319 *TF:* 888-937-4514 ■ *Web:* cedarspringspost.com	616-696-3655	696-9010	532-4
Cedar Valley Arboretum & Botanic Gardens 1927 E Orange Rd Waterloo IA 50701 *Web:* www.cedarvalleyarboretum.org	319-226-4966		97
Cedar Valley Cheese Inc W3115 Jay Rd Belgium WI 53004 *Web:* www.cedarvalleycheesestore.com	920-994-9500	994-9595	296-5
Cedar Valley College 3030 N Dallas Ave Lancaster TX 75134 *Web:* www.dcccd.edu	972-860-8201		162
Cedar Valley Hospice 2101 Kimball Ave Ste 401 Waterloo IA 50702 *TF:* 800-617-1972 ■ *Web:* www.cvhospice.org	319-272-2002	272-2071	371
Cedar Ventures LLC 2870 Peachtree Rd Ste 450 Atlanta GA 30305 *Web:* cedarventures.com	404-239-8416	239-8417	691
Cedarberg Industries Inc 1960 Seneca Rd Eagan MN 55122 *TF:* 800-328-2279 ■ *Web:* www.cedarberg.com	651-452-5012	452-5350	493
Cedarburg Cultural Ctr W62 N546 Washington Ave Cedarburg WI 53012 *Web:* cedarburgculturalcenter.org	262-375-3676		520
Cedar-Knox Public Power District 56272 W Hwy 84 PO Box 947 Hartington NE 68739 *Web:* www.cedarknoxppd.com	402-254-6291		245
Cedarlane Laboratories Inc 4410 Paletta Ct Burlington ON L7L5R2 **Fax Area Code:* 289 ■ *TF:* 800-268-5058 ■ *Web:* www.cedarlanelabs.com	905-878-8891	288-0020*	231
Cedarome Canada Inc 21 Rue Paul-Gauguin Candiac QC J5R3X8 *Web:* cedarome.com	450-659-8000	659-8010	296-37
Cedaron Medical Inc 1644 Da Vinci Ct Davis CA 95618 *Web:* www.cedaron.com	530-758-7007	759-1699	668
Cedarpoint Trucking Inc 1272 N Yellowstone Hwy Rexburg ID 83440 *TF:* 800-543-4042 ■ *Web:* www.cedarpointtrucking.com	208-356-8095	356-9785	780
Cedars Business Services LLC 5230 Las Virgenes Ste 210 Calabasas CA 91302 *TF:* 800-804-3353 ■ *Web:* cedarfinancial.com	818-224-3800		160
Cedars Mediterranean Foods Inc 50 Foundation Ave Ward Hill MA 01835 *Web:* www.cedarsfoods.com	978-372-8010		805
Cedars of Lebanon State Park 328 Cedar Forest Rd Lebanon TN 37090 *Web:* www.state.tn.us	615-443-2769		565
Cedars Wholesale Floral Imports 6151 B St Anchorage AK 99518 *Web:* www.cedarsfloralwholesale.com	907-563-5566	561-5566	293
Cedars-Sinai Medical Ctr (CSMC) 8700 Beverly Blvd Los Angeles CA 90048 *TF:* 800-233-2771 ■ *Web:* www.cedars-sinai.org	310-423-3277		374-3
Cedarstone 209 E Liberty Dr Wheaton IL 60187 *Web:* cedarstone.us	630-580-5750	580-5757	193
CedarStone Bank 900 W Main St Lebanon TN 37087 *Web:* www.cedarstonebank.com	615-443-1411		70
CedarStore.com 5410 Rt 8 Gibsonia PA 15044 *TF:* 888 293-2339 ■ *Web:* www.cedarstore.com	724 444-5300	444-5301	106
Cedarville State Forest 10201 Bee Oak Rd Brandywine MD 20613 *Web:* www.dnr.maryland.gov	301-888-1410		565
Cedarville University 251 N Main St Cedarville OH 45314 *TF:* 800-233-2784 ■ *Web:* www.cedarville.edu	937-766-7700	766-7575	166
Cedarwood Plaza 12504 Cedar Rd Cleveland Heights OH 44106 *Web:* www.lhshealth.com	216-371-3600	371-4661	450
Cedarwood Veterinary Hospital PC 1111 E Hwy 25/70 Newport TN 37821 *Web:* cedarwoodvet.com	423-623-4362		794
CEDC (Central European Distribution Corp) 3000 Atrium Way Ste 265 Mount Laurel NJ 08054 *NASDAQ: CEDC* ■ *Web:* www.cedc.com	856-273-6980		81-1
Ceder's Restaurant 7732 W Sand Lake Rd Orlando FL 32819 *Web:* www.orlandocedars.com	407-351-6000		671
Cederdahl Consulting and Coaching 4109 Nabal Dr La Mesa CA 91941 *Web:* www.cederdahl.com	619-670-1122	670-9363	194
Cederstrom Inc 7663 79th St S Cottage Grove MN 55016 *Web:* parkgrovepethospital.com	651-459-9663		794
CEDIA (Custom Electronic Design & Installation Assn) 7150 Winton Dr Ste 300 Indianapolis IN 46268 *TF:* 800-669-5329 ■ *Web:* cedia.net	317-328-4336	735-4012	49-19
Cedrus Digital 530 5th Ave 9th Fl New York NY 10036 *Web:* cedrus.digital	929-224-3860		178-1
Cee Kay Supply Co 5835 Manchester Ave Saint Louis MO 63110 *Web:* ceekay.com	314-644-3500		385
CEEMCO 3330 E Kemper Rd Cincinnati OH 45241 *Web:* www.ceemco.com	513-563-8822	563-8830	697
Ceeva Inc 643 First Ave Ste 300 Pittsburgh PA 15219 *Web:* www.ceeva.com	412-690-2300		194
CEF (Committee for Education Funding) 1800 M St NW Ste 500 Washington DC 20036 *Web:* cef.org	202-383-0083		48-11
CEF Industries Inc 320 S Church St Addison IL 60101 *TF:* 800-888-6419 ■ *Web:* www.cefindustries.com	630-628-2299	628-1386	22
Cefco Convenience Stores 6261 Central Pointe Pkwy Temple TX 76504 *Web:* cefcostores.com	254-791-0009	791-0018	345
CeFO Inc 88 Inverness Cir E Ste L107 Englewood CO 80112 *Web:* www.cefo.net	720-506-4105	506-4106	734
CEG Technologies 5 Reeve Rd Rockville Center NY 11570 *Web:* www.cegtech.com	516-678-0275	594-0049	178-1
Cegep Andre Laurendeau 1111 Rue Lapierre LaSalle QC H8N2J4 *Web:* www.claurendeau.qc.ca	514-364-3320		165
Cegep De L'outaouais 333 boul de la Cite-des-Jeunes Gatineau QC J8Y6M4 *TF:* 866-770-4012 ■ *Web:* www.cegepoutaouais.qc.ca	819-770-4012		165
Cegep De Matane 616 Ave Saint-Redempteur Matane QC G4W1L1 *TF:* 800-463-4299 ■ *Web:* www.cegep-matane.qc.ca	418-562-1240	566-2115	167
Cegep De Sainte-Foy 2410 Sainte-Foy Rd Quebec City QC G1V1T3 *Web:* www.cegep-ste-foy.qc.ca	418-659-6600	659-4563	162
Cegep De Thetford 671 Boul Frontenac O Thetford Mines QC G6G1N1 *TF:* 855-338-8591 ■ *Web:* www.cegepthetford.ca	418-338-8591		162
Cegep Marie-Victorin 7000 Rue Marie-Victorin Montreal QC H1G2J6 *Web:* www.collegemv.qc.ca	514-325-0150		165
CEI (Computer Enterprises Inc) 1000 Omega Dr Ste 1150 Pittsburgh PA 15205 *Web:* www.ceiamerica.com	215-621-6814		721
CEI (Construction Enterprises Inc) 2179 Edward Curd Ln Ste 100 Franklin TN 37067 *Web:* constructionenterprises.com	615-332-8880	771-0818	187
CEI 801 NW St Mary Dr Ste 205 Blue Springs MO 64014 *TF:* 800-473-1976 ■ *Web:* www.thinkcei.com	816-228-2976		225
CEI (Communications Engineering LLC) PO Box 108 Cresskill NJ 07626 *Web:* www.ce-inc.com	917-282-1814		194
CEI Enterprises Inc 245 Woodward Rd SE Albuquerque NM 87102 **Fax Area Code:* 505 ■ *TF:* 800-545-4034 ■ *Web:* www.ceienterprises.com	800-545-4034	243-1422*	14
CEI Equipment Company Inc 5555 16th Ave SW Cedar Rapids IA 52404 *Web:* www.ceipacer.com	319-396-7336	396-2462	650
Ceia USA Ltd 9155 Dutton Dr Twinsburg OH 44087 *Web:* www.ceia-usa.com	330-405-3190	405-3196	691
Ceilings & Interior Systems Construction Assn (CISCA) 1010 Jorie Blvd Ste 30 Oak Brook IL 60523 **Fax Area Code:* 866 ■ *Web:* www.cisca.org	630-584-1919	560-8537*	49-3
CEIPAL Corp 687 Lee Rd Ste 208a Rochester NY 14606 *Web:* ceipal.com	585-326-1312		657
CEIR (Center for Exhibition Industry Research) 12700 Park Central Dr Ste 308 Dallas TX 75251 *Web:* www.ceir.org	972-687-9242	692-6020	49-18
Ceis Review Inc 8 Tannery Ln Camden ME 04843 *Web:* www.ceisreview.com	207-230-2515		652
Ceiva Logic Inc 214 E Magnolia Blvd Burbank CA 91502 *TF:* 877-693-7263 ■ *Web:* www.ceiva.com	818-562-1495	562-1491	591
Cejka Search Inc 4 Cityplace Dr Ste 300 Saint Louis MO 63141 **Fax Area Code:* 314 ■ *TF:* 800-678-7858 ■ *Web:* www.cejkasearch.com	800-678-7858	726-0026*	721
CEL (California Eastern Laboratories Inc) 4590 Patrick Henry Dr Santa Clara CA 95054 *TF:* 800-390-3232 ■ *Web:* www.cel.com	408-919-2500	988-0279	246
Cel Oil Products Corp 5402 Dutton Ave Charleston SC 29406 *Web:* www.celoil.com	843-744-2525	554-1412	539
CelAccess Systems Inc 13619 Inwood Rd Ste 360 Dallas TX 75244 *Web:* cell-gate.com	972-231-1999		693
Celadon Spa 1180 F St NW Frnt 1 Washington DC 20004 *Web:* www.celadonspa.com	202-347-3333		77
Celanese Corp 1601 W LBJ Fwy Dallas TX 75234 *NYSE: CE* ■ *TF:* 800-627-9581 ■ *Web:* celanese.com	972-443-4000		144
Celdara Medical LLC 16 Cavendish Ct Lebanon NH 03766 *Web:* www.celdaramedical.com	617-320-8521		415
Celebration Publications 115 E Armour Blvd Kansas City MO 64111 **Fax Area Code:* 816 ■ *TF:* 800-333-7373 ■ *Web:* celebrationpublications.org	800-333-7373	968-2293*	637-9
Celebration Restaurant 4503 W Lovers Ln Dallas TX 75209 *Web:* celebrationrestaurant.com	214-351-5681	904-1716	671
Celebration Town Hall 851 Celebration Ave Celebration FL 34747 *Web:* www.celebration.fl.us	407-566-1200		50-6
Celebration! Cinema 2121 Celebration Ave Grand Rapids MI 49525 *Web:* celebrationcinema.com	616-530-7469		748
Celebritees Inc 1014 Atlantic Ave Savannah GA 31401 *Web:* www.celebritees.net	912-233-9941		184
Celebrity Health Services Inc 16600 Sherman Way Ste 200 Van Nuys CA 91406 *Web:* celebrityhomehealth.com	818-343-4001		363
Celebrity Helicopters 961 W Alondra Blvd Compton CA 90220 *TF:* 877-999-2099 ■ *Web:* www.celebheli.com	877-999-2099		167-3
Celebrity Hotel Inc 629 Main St Deadwood SD 57732 *TF:* 888-399-1885 ■ *Web:* www.celebrityhotel.com	605-578-1909		378
Celebrity Theatre 440 N 32nd St Phoenix AZ 85008 *Web:* www.celebritytheatre.com	602-267-1600		572
Celenia 7887 E Belleview Ave Englewood CO 80111 *Web:* www.celenia.com	303-469-2346		463
Celentano, Stadtmauer & Walentowicz 1035 Rt 46 E Clifton NJ 07015 *Web:* csandw-llp.com	973-778-1771		41
Celergo LLC 750 Estate Dr Ste 110 Deerfield IL 60015 *Web:* www.adp.com	847-512-2600	512-2650	570
Celerity Consulting Group Inc 2 Gough St Ste 300 San Francisco CA 94103 *TF:* 866-224-4333 ■ *Web:* www.consultcelerity.com	415-986-8850		196

Company / Address	City	State	ZIP	Phone	Fax	Class
Celerity Staffing Solutions 6255 University Ave *Web:* www.celeritystaffing.com	Middleton	WI	53562	608-238-3410		260
Celerity Systems Inc 8401 Greensboro Dr 5th Fl *Web:* www.celerity.com	McLean	VA	22102	703-848-1900	848-2139	647
Celery LLC 501 Bloomfield Ave *TF:* 866-692-3537 ■ *Web:* www.mycelery.com	Montclair	NJ	07042	518-833-6807		681
Celestial Seasonings Inc 4600 Sleepytime Dr *TF:* 800-351-8175 ■ *Web:* www.celestialseasonings.com	Boulder	CO	80301	800-351-8175		296-40
Celestial Software LLC 6641 E Mercer Way *Web:* www.celestial.com	Mercer Island	WA	98040	206-236-1676	232-9186	180
Celestica Inc 844 Don Mills Rd *NYSE:* CLS ■ *TF:* 888-899-9998 ■ *Web:* www.celestica.com	Toronto	ON	M3C1V7	416-448-5800	448-4810	253
Celestron LLC 2835 Columbia St *Web:* www.celestron.com	Torrance	CA	90503	310-328-9560	212-5835	419
Celex Laboratories Inc 21600 Westminster Hwy Ste 115 *Web:* celexlaboratories.com	Richmond	BC	V6V0A2	604-231-6077	231-6078	799
Celgard LLC 13800 S Lakes Dr *TF:* 800-235-4273 ■ *Web:* www.celgard.com	Charlotte	NC	28273	704-588-5310	587-8585	600
Celgene Corp 86 Morris Ave *NASDAQ:* CELG ■ *TF:* 888-771-0141 ■ *Web:* www.celgene.com	Summit	NJ	07901	908-673-9000	673-9001	85
Celigo LLC 230 Twin Dolphin Dr Ste A *Web:* www.celigo.com	Redwood City	CA	94065	650-579-0210		196
Celina Aluminum Precision Technology Inc (CAPT) 7059 Staeger Rd *Web:* www.capt-celina.com	Celina	OH	45822	419-586-2278	586-6474	621
Celina-Mercer County *Chamber of Commerce* 121 E Logan St *Web:* www.celinamercer.com	Celina	OH	45822	419-586-2219	586-8645	139
Celino South Beach 640 Ocean Dr *Web:* www.thecelinohotel.com	Miami Beach	FL	33139	786-574-4090		379
Cell Marque Corp 6600 Sierra College Blvd *TF:* 800-665-7284 ■ *Web:* www.cellmarque.com	Rocklin	CA	95677	916-746-8900	746-8989	479
Cell Point Systems Inc 44931 Industrial Dr *Web:* www.cellpointsystems.com	Fremont	CA	94538	510-270-2280		261
Cell Signaling Technology Inc 3 Trask Ln *TF:* 877-678-8324 ■ *Web:* www.cellsignal.com	Danvers	MA	01923	978-867-2300	867-2400	418
Cella Consulting LLC 4350 E W Hwy Ste 307 *Web:* www.cellainc.com	Bethesda	MD	20814	301-280-0313		196
CellAegis Devices Inc 6711 Mississauga Rd Ste 109 *Web:* cellaegis.com	Toronto	ON	L5N2W3	647-722-9601	722-9553	475
Cellar Restaurant, The 220 Magnolia Ave *Web:* thecellarrestaurant.com	Daytona Beach	FL	32114	386-258-0011		671
Cell-con Inc 305 Commerce Dr Ste 300 *TF:* 800-771-7139 ■ *Web:* cell-con.com	Exton	PA	19341	800-771-7139		74
Cellectar Biosciences Inc 3301 Agriculture Dr *Web:* www.cellectar.com	Madison	WI	53716	608-441-8120		231
Cellhire USA LLC 3520 W Miller Rd Ste 100 *TF:* 877-244-7242 ■ *Web:* www.cellhire.com	Garland	TX	75041	877-244-7242		736
Cellino & Barnes PC 2500 Main Place Twr *TF:* 800-888-8888 ■ *Web:* www.cellinoandbarnes.com	Buffalo	NY	14202	800-888-8888		428
Cello & Maudru Construction Company Inc 2505 Oak St *Web:* cello-maudru.com	Napa	CA	94559	707-257-0454		186
Cellofoam North America Inc 1917 Rockdale Industrial Blvd *TF:* 800-241-3634 ■ *Web:* www.cellofoam.com	Conyers	GA	30012	770-929-3688	929-3608	601
Cellotape Inc 47623 Fremont Blvd *TF:* 800-231-0608 ■ *Web:* www.cellotape.com	Fremont	CA	94538	510-651-5551	651-8091	413
Cellox Inc 1200 Industrial St *Web:* www.cellox.com	Reedsburg	WI	53959	608-524-2316	524-2362	601
Celltron Inc 1110 W 7th St *Web:* www.celltron.com	Galena	KS	66739	620-783-1333		61
CellTrust Corp 14822 N 73rd St Bldg B Ste 113 *Web:* www.celltrust.com	Scottsdale	AZ	85260	480-515-5200		195
Cellular Dynamics International Inc 525 Science Dr *TF:* 877-310-6688 ■ *Web:* www.cellulardynamics.com	Madison	WI	53711	608-310-5100		668
CellularOne 1500 S White Mtn Rd Ste 3 *Web:* www.cellularoneonline.com	Show Low	AZ	85901	928-537-0690		387
Celluphone Inc 6119 E Washington Blvd **Fax Area Code:* 323 ■ *TF:* 800-367-8822 ■ *Web:* www.secure.celluphone.com	Commerce	CA	90040	800-367-8822	727-7004*	224
Cellusuede Products Inc 500 N Madison St *Web:* www.cellusuede.com	Rockford	IL	61107	815-964-8619	964-7949	745-2
Cels Enterprises Inc 3485 S La Cienega Blvd *Web:* www.chineselaundry.com	Los Angeles	CA	90016	310-945-3299		301
CEL-SCI Corp 8229 Boone Blvd Ste 802 *NYSE:* CVM ■ *Web:* www.cel-sci.com	Vienna	VA	22182	703-506-9460	506-9471	85
Celsion Corp 10220-L Old Columbia Rd *NASDAQ:* CLSN ■ *Web:* celsion.com	Columbia	MD	21046	410-290-5390	290-5394	476
Celtech Corp 1300 Terminal Dr *TF:* 877-514-2218 ■ *Web:* celtech.com	Carlsbad	NM	88220	575-887-2044	885-6976	201
Celtic Cat Publishing 5111 Green Valley Dr *Web:* www.celticcatpublishing.com	Knoxville	TN	37914	865-248-3133		637-2
Celtic Commercial Finance 4 Park Plz Ste 300 **Fax Area Code:* 949 ■ *TF:* 866-323-5842 ■ *Web:* www.53.com	Irvine	CA	92614	866-323-5842	263-1331*	264-2
Celtic Crossing Irish Pub & Restaurant 903 S Cooper St *Web:* www.celticcrossingmemphis.com	Memphis	TN	38104	901-274-5151		671
Celtic Financial Group LLC 60 Cutter Mill Rd Ste 600	Great Neck	NY	11021	516-466-0550		215
Celtic House Venture Partners Inc 239 Argyle Ave Ste 100 *Web:* www.celtic.vc	Ottawa	ON	K2P1B8	613-569-7200		528
Celtic Inc 316 N Milwaukee St Ste 350 *Web:* www.celticinc.com	Milwaukee	WI	53202	414-316-2100		4
Celtic Marine Corp 3888 S Sherwood Forest Blvd Celtic Ctr Bldg 1 *TF:* 877-752-2359 ■ *Web:* celticmarine.com	Baton Rouge	LA	70816	225-752-2490	752-2582	314
Celtic Tavern, The 1801 Blake St *Web:* www.thecelticttavern.com	Denver	CO	80202	303-308-1795	308-1576	671
Celtrade Canada Inc 7566 Bath Rd *Web:* celtrade.ca	Mississauga	ON	L4T1L2	905-678-1322		296-37
CEM (Conference Event Management) 1045 76th St Ste 3025 *Web:* www.myCEM.com	West Des Moines	IA	50266	515-254-0289		393
CEM Corp 3100 Smith Farm Rd *TF:* 800-726-3331 ■ *Web:* www.cem.com	Matthews	NC	28104	704-821-7015	821-7894	419
Cem Insurance Co 21805 Field Pkwy Ste 320 *Web:* cemic.com	Deer Park	IL	60010	847-307-6300		390
Cembell Industries Inc 740 CCC Rd (Hwy 628) *Web:* www.cembell.com	Montz	LA	70068	985-652-1188		14
CEMCO 263 N Covina Ln **Fax Area Code:* 626 ■ *TF:* 800-775-2362 ■ *Web:* www.cemcosteel.com	City of Industry	CA	91744	800-775-2362	330-7598*	105
Cemco Partitions Inc 5340 US Hwy 220 N *TF:* 800-643-4052 ■ *Web:* www.cemcopartitions.com	Summerfield	NC	27358	800-643-4052		321
Cemcon Ltd 2280 White Oak Cir Ste 100 *Web:* www.cemcon.com	Aurora	IL	60502	630-862-2100	862-2199	256
Cemen Tech Inc 1700 N 14th St *TF:* 800-247-2464 ■ *Web:* cementech.com	Indianola	IA	50125	515-961-7407		190
Cement Association of Canada (CAC) 1105-350 Sparks St *Web:* www.cement.ca	Ottawa	ON	K1R7S8	613-236-9471		49-3
Cement Industries Inc 2925 Hanson St PO Box 823 *TF:* 800-332-1440 ■ *Web:* www.cementindustries.com	Fort Myers	FL	33902	239-332-1440	332-0370	183
Cement Products & Supply Company Inc PO Box 12 *Web:* cementproductsusa.com	Lakeland	FL	33815	863-686-5141		183
Cement Test Equipment Inc 4001 W Edison St *Web:* www.ctetulsa.com	Tulsa	OK	74127	918-835-4454	835-4475	472
Cemex USA 929 Gessner Rd Ste 1900 *NYSE:* CX ■ *TF:* 800-999-8529 ■ *Web:* www.cemex.com	Houston	TX	77024	713-650-6200		135
Cemline Corp 808 Freeport Rd *Web:* www.cemline.com	Cheswick	PA	15024	724-275-1168		427
Cemo Commercial Inc 950 Glenn Dr Ste 130 *Web:* quirozcre.com	Folsom	CA	95630	916-933-2300		652
Cems Engineering Inc 108 Bentons Lodge Rd Ste B *Web:* www.cems-ae.com	Summerville	SC	29485	843-875-3637		261
Cemstone 2025 Centre Pt Blvd Ste 300 *TF:* 800-642-3887 ■ *Web:* cemstone.com	Mendota Heights	MN	55120	651-688-9292	688-0124	182
Cemtrol Inc 3035 E La Jolla St *Web:* cemtrol.com	Anaheim	CA	92806	714-666-6606	666-6616	173-2
Cen-Cal Fire Systems Inc PO Box 1284 *TF:* 800-655-9136 ■ *Web:* cen-calfire.com	Lodi	CA	95240	209-334-9119	334-2923	45
Cencir Inc 24124 Lakeside Trl *Web:* www.cencir.com	Crete	IL	60417	708-672-3957	672-4473	194
Cendec Systems Inc 1615 Tenth Ave SW Ste 315 *Web:* cendec.com	Calgary	AB	T3C0J7	403-215-9936		179
Cendrex 11303 26th Ave *TF:* 800-479-1489 ■ *Web:* www.cendrex.com	Montreal	QC	H1E6N6	514-493-1489		198
Cendyn 4550 N Point Pkwy Ste 400 *Web:* www.cendyn.com	Alpharetta	GA	30022	678-578-5700		403
Cenergistic Inc 5950 Sherry Ln *TF:* 855-798-7779 ■ *Web:* cenergistic.com	Dallas	TX	75225	855-798-7779		194
Cengage Learning PTR 10650 Toebben Dr *TF:* 800-354-9706 ■ *Web:* www.cengageptr.com	Independence	KY	41051	800-354-9706	487-8488	637-2
Cenla Broadcasting 1115 Texas Ave *Web:* cenlabroadcasting.com	Alexandria	LA	71301	318-445-1234	445-7231	645-141
Cenovus Energy Inc 500 Centre St SE PO Box 766 *Web:* www.cenovus.com	Calgary	AB	T2P0M5	403-766-2000		536
Cenpatico 12515-8 Research Blvd Ste 400 *TF:* 877-264-6550 ■ *Web:* www.cenpatico.com	Austin	TX	78759	512-406-7200		374-5
Centaur Products Inc 3145 Thunderbird Crescent *Web:* www.centaurproducts.com	Burnaby	BC	V5A3G1	604-430-3088	430-1393	711
Centaur Tool & Die Inc 2019 Wood Bridge Blvd *Web:* www.centaurtool.com	Bowling Green	OH	43402	419-352-7704		757
Centaurus Financial 2300 E Katella Ave Ste 200 *TF:* 800-880-4234 ■ *Web:* www.centaurusfinancial.com	Anaheim	CA	92806	800-880-4234		690
Centenary College 400 Jefferson St *TF:* 800-236-8679 ■ *Web:* www.centenaryuniversity.edu	Hackettstown	NJ	07840	908-852-1400		166
Centenary College of Louisiana 2911 Centenary Blvd *TF:* 800-234-4448 ■ *Web:* www.centenary.edu	Shreveport	LA	71104	318-869-5131	869-5005	166
Centenary State Historic Site 3522 College St *TF:* 888-677-2364 ■ *Web:* crt.state.la.us	Jackson	LA	70748	225-634-7925		565
Centene Corp 7700 Forsyth Blvd *NYSE:* CNC ■ *TF:* 800-293-0056 ■ *Web:* www.centene.com	Saint Louis	MO	63105	314-725-4477		391-3
Centennial Conferences 908 Main St Ste 350 *Web:* www.centennialconferences.com	Louisville	CO	80027	303-499-2299	499-2599	184

Phone | Fax | Class

Centennial Hall Convention Ctr
101 Egan Dr . . . . . Juneau AK 99801 907-586-5283 586-1135 205
TF: 800-478-4176 ■ *Web:* www.juneau.org

Centennial Hotel 96 Pleasant St . . . . . Concord NH 03301 603-227-9000 225-5031 379
Web: www.thecentennialhotel.com

Centennial Olympic Park
265 Park Ave W NW . . . . . Atlanta GA 30313 404-223-4412 223-4499 50-5
Web: www.gwcca.org

Centennial Optical Ltd
158 Norfinch Dr . . . . . Toronto ON M3N1X6 416-739-8539 475
Web: centennialoptical.com

Centennial School District
18135 SE Brooklyn . . . . . Portland OR 97236 503-760-7990 762-3689 685
Web: csd28j.org

Centennial School District
48 Swan Way . . . . . Warminster PA 18974 215-441-6000 441-6101 685
Web: www.centennialsd.org

Centennial School ISD 12
4707 North Rd . . . . . Circle Pines MN 55014 763-792-6000 392-6943 685
Web: www.isd12.org

Centennial Travelers
7697 S Roslyn Ct . . . . . Centennial CO 80112 303-741-6685 760
TF: 800-223-0675 ■ *Web:* www.centennialtravel.com

Centennial Windows Ltd
687 Sovereign Rd . . . . . London ON N5V4K8 519-451-0508 499
TF: 800-265-1995 ■ *Web:* centennialwindows.com

Center BMW 5201 Van Nuys Blvd . . . . . Sherman Oaks CA 91401 818-907-9995 364
Web: www.centerbmw.com

Center Church 60 Gold St . . . . . Hartford CT 06103 860-249-5631 246-3915 50-1
Web: www.centerchurchhartford.org

Center City Film & Video
1635 Market St 19th Fl . . . . . Philadelphia PA 19103 267-597-3500 514
Web: www.ccfv.com

Center City Pretzel Co
816 Washington Ave . . . . . Philadelphia PA 19147 215-463-5664 297-3
Web: www.centercitypretzel.com

Center Court Key West 916 Center St . . . . . Key West FL 33040 305-295-7313 379
Web: www.centercourtkeywest.com

Center Enterprises Inc
30 Shield St . . . . . West Hartford CT 06110 860-953-4423 953-2948 243
TF: 800-542-2214 ■ *Web:* www.centerenterprises.com

Center Financial Corp
651 Pennsylvania Ave SE . . . . . Washington DC 20003 202-546-8500 360-2
Web: www.taxpayer.net

Center for Action & Contempla
1823 Five Points Rd SW . . . . . Albuquerque NM 87105 505-242-9588 48-20
Web: cac.org

Center for Advanced Biotechnology & Medicine
Rutgers The State University of New Jersey
679 Hoes Ln . . . . . Piscataway NJ 08854 848-445-9898 235-5318* 668
**Fax Area Code:* 732 ■ *Web:* www.cabm.rutgers.edu

Center for American Progress
1333 H St NW 10th Fl . . . . . Washington DC 20005 202-682-1611 682-1867 634
Web: www.americanprogress.org

Center for Animals & Public Policy
Cummings School of Veterinary Medicine at Tufts University 200 Westboro Rd
. . . . . North Grafton MA 01536 508-839-7991 839-3337 634
Web: vet.tufts.edu

Center for Art & Education
104 N 13th St . . . . . Van Buren AR 72956 479-474-7767 50-2
Web: www.art-ed.org

Center for Association Growth, The (TCAG)
1926 Waukegan Rd Ste 300 . . . . . Glenview IL 60025 847-657-6700 657-6819 47
TF: 800-492-6462 ■ *Web:* www.tcag.us

Center for Association Resources Inc
1901 N Roselle Rd Ste 920 . . . . . Schaumburg IL 60195 888-705-1434 885-8393* 47
**Fax Area Code:* 847 ■ *TF:* 888-705-1434 ■ *Web:* www.association-resources.com

Center for Auto Safety (CAS)
1825 Connecticut Ave NW Ste 330 . . . . . Washington DC 20009 202-328-7700 49-21
Web: www.autosafety.org

Center for Automation Research
University of Maryland
Av Williams Bldg 115 Rm 4413 . . . . . College Park MD 20742 301-405-4526 314-9115 668
Web: www.cfar.umd.edu

Center for Behavioral Health Inc, The
175 Cedar Ln Ste A . . . . . Teaneck NJ 07666 201-692-9500 543
Web: www.njpsychologist.com

Center for Biofilm Engineering (CBE)
Montana State University PO Box 173980 . . . . . Bozeman MT 59717 406-994-4770 994-6098 668
Web: www.biofilm.montana.edu

Center for Career Development
199 Chambers St S-342 . . . . . New York NY 10007 212-220-8170 166
Web: www.bmcc.cuny.edu

Center for Civic Education
5145 Douglas Fir Rd . . . . . Calabasas CA 91302 818-591-9321 194
TF: 800-350-4223 ■ *Web:* www.civiced.org

Center for Cognitive Liberty & Ethics
PO Box 73481 . . . . . Davis CA 95617 530-750-7912 839-6835* 634
**Fax Area Code:* 213 ■ *Web:* www.cognitiveliberty.org

Center for Collaborative
33 Harrison Ave Ste 6 . . . . . Boston MA 02111 617-421-0134 421-9016 194
Web: cce.org

Center for Community Change (CCC)
1536 U St NW . . . . . Washington DC 20009 202-339-9300 387-4891 48-5
Web: communitychange.org

Center For Comprehensive Care and Diagnosis of Inherited Blood Di, The
2670 N Main St Ste 150 . . . . . Santa Ana CA 92705 949-748-7521 237
Web: cibd-ca.org

Center for Contemporary Arts, The
220 Cypress St . . . . . Abilene TX 79601 325-677-8389 677-1171 50-2
Web: www.center-arts.com

Center for Continuing Study of the California Economy (CCSCE)
385 Homer Ave . . . . . Palo Alto CA 94301 650-321-8550 321-5451 466
Web: www.ccsce.com

Center for Creative Leadership
1 Leadership Pl . . . . . Greensboro NC 27410 336-545-2810 282-3284 765
Web: www.ccl.org

Center for Creative Photography
1030 N Olive Rd . . . . . Tucson AZ 85721 520-621-7968 621-9444 520
TF: 888-472-4732 ■ *Web:* kennerly.ccp.arizona.edu

Center for Crops Utilization Research
Iowa State University 536 Farm House Ln
1041 Food Sciences Bldg . . . . . Ames IA 50011 515-294-0160 294-6261 668
Web: www.ccur.iastate.edu

Center for Cuban Studies
231 W 29th St Ste 401 . . . . . New York NY 10001 212-242-0559 48-14
Web: centerforcubanstudies.org

Center for Democracy & Technology (CDT)
1401 K St NW Ste 200 . . . . . Washington DC 20005 202-637-9800 637-0968 48-7
TF: 800-869-4499 ■ *Web:* cdt.org

Center for Diagnostic Imaging
5775 Wayzata Blvd Ste 190 . . . . . Saint Louis Park MN 55416 952-541-1840 847-1152 383
TF: 800-537-0005 ■ *Web:* www.mycdi.com

Center for Education
Rice University 320 IBC Bldg PO Box 1892 . . . . . Houston TX 77251 713-348-4827 668
Web: www.centerforeducation.rice.edu

Center for Electromechanics
University of Texas at Austin
10100 Burnet Rd Bldg 133 . . . . . Austin TX 78758 512-471-4496 471-0781 668
Web: www.cem.utexas.edu

Center for Engineering Logistics & Distribution
University of Arkansas Dept of Industrial Engineer 4207 Bell Engineering Ctr
. . . . . Fayetteville AR 72701 479-575-2124 668
Web: celdi.org

Center for Equal Opportunity (CEO)
14 Pidgeon Hill Dr Ste 500 . . . . . Sterling VA 20165 703-421-5443 421-6401 634
Web: www.ceousa.org

Center for Exhibition Industry Research (CEIR)
12700 Park Central Dr Ste 308 . . . . . Dallas TX 75251 972-687-9242 692-6020 49-18
Web: www.ceir.org

Center for Genetic Testing at Saint Francis
6465 S Yale Ave . . . . . Tulsa OK 74136 918-502-1720 417
TF: 877-789-6001 ■ *Web:* www.saintfrancis.com

Center for Global Change Science
77 Massachusetts Ave 54-1312 . . . . . Cambridge MA 02139 617-253-4902 253-0354 668
Web: cgcs.mit.edu

Center for Grain & Animal Health Research
1515 College Ave . . . . . Manhattan KS 66502 800-627-0388 776-2789* 668
**Fax Area Code:* 785 ■ *TF:* 800-627-0388 ■ *Web:* www.ars.usda.gov

Center For Health Equity Inc
231 E Jefferson St . . . . . Quincy FL 32351 850-875-4959 363
Web: centerforhealthequity.com

Center for High Performance Software Research
HiPerSoft 6100 Main St MS-41 . . . . . Houston TX 77005 713-348-5186 348-3111 668
Web: www.hipersoft.rice.edu

Center for Hope 1900 Raritan Rd . . . . . Scotch Plains NJ 07076 908-889-7780 889-5172 371
Web: www.cfhh.org

Center for Hospice Care Inc
111 Sunnybrook Ct . . . . . South Bend IN 46637 574-243-3100 243-3134 371
TF: 800-413-9083 ■ *Web:* www.cfhcare.org

Center for Immigration Studies
1522 K St NW Ste 820 . . . . . Washington DC 20005 202-466-8185 466-8076 634
Web: cis.org

Center for Indigenous Knowledge for Agriculture and Rural Development (CIKARD)
Iowa State University 318 Curtiss Hall . . . . . Ames IA 50011 515-294-0938 294-6058 423
Web: www.ciesin.org

Center for Individual Rights (CIR)
1100 Connecticut Ave NW Ste 625 . . . . . Washington DC 20036 202-833-8400 833-8410 48-8
TF: 877-426-2665 ■ *Web:* www.cir-usa.org

Center for Information Systems Research (CISR)
Massachusetts Institute of Technology 245 First St
E94-15th Fl . . . . . Cambridge MA 02142 617-253-2348 253-4424 668
Web: cisr.mit.edu

Center for Innovation
4200 James Ray Dr . . . . . Grand Forks ND 58202 701-777-3132 777-2339 402
Web: www.innovators.net

Center for Integrative Toxicology
1129 Farm Ln Rm 165 . . . . . East Lansing MI 48824 517-353-6469 355-4603 668
Web: iit.msu.edu

Center for International Private Enterprise
1155 15th St NW Ste 700 . . . . . Washington DC 20005 202-721-9200 721-9250 634
Web: www.cipe.org

Center for International Trade in Forest Products (CINTRAFOR)
University of Washington 126 Anderson Hall
PO Box 352100 . . . . . Seattle WA 98195 206-543-1918 685-0790 668
Web: www.cintrafor.org

Center for Lasik Ophthalmology Consultants, The
5800 Colonial Dr Ste 103 . . . . . Margate FL 33063 954-969-0090 798
Web: www.bestvision.com

Center for Law & Social Policy (CLASP)
1015 15th St NW Ste 400 . . . . . Washington DC 20005 202-906-8000 842-2885 634
TF: 800-821-4367 ■ *Web:* www.clasp.org

Center for Literacy (CFL)
399 Market St Ste 201 . . . . . Philadelphia PA 19106 215-474-1235 48-6
Web: www.centerforliteracy.org

Center for Media Literacy
23852 Pacific Coast Hwy Ste 472 . . . . . Malibu CA 90265 310-456-1225 49-14
Web: www.medialit.org

Center for Medical Agricultural & Veterinary Entomology (CMAVE)
1700 SW 23rd Dr . . . . . Gainesville FL 32608 352-374-5901 374-5852 668
Web: www.ars.usda.gov

Center for Migration Studies (CMS)
Archives Intern 307 E 60th St 4th Fl . . . . . New York NY 10022 212-337-3080 434-4
Web: www.cmsny.org

Center for Nanophysics & Advanced Materials
University of Maryland . . . . . College Park MD 20742 301-405-8285 405-3779 668
Web: cnam.umd.edu

Center for Neighborhood Technology
2125 W N Ave . . . . . Chicago IL 60647 773-278-4800 278-3840 634
Web: www.cnt.org

Center for Organ Recovery & Education (CORE)
204 Sigma Dr RIDC Pk . . . . . Pittsburgh PA 15238 412-963-3550 269
TF: 800-366-6777 ■ *Web:* www.core.org

Center for Policy Research
Syracuse University 426 Eggers Hall . . . . . Syracuse NY 13244 315-443-3114 443-1081 634
Web: www.maxwell.syr.edu

	Phone	Fax	Class
Center for Practical Bioethics 1111 Main St Ste 500 Kansas City MO 64105 *Web:* www.practicalbioethics.org	816-221-1100	221-2002	48-17
Center for Professional 1 Liberty Blvd Malvern PA 19355 *TF:* 800-575-1776 ■ *Web:* www.cfpie.com	610-648-7550	889-9869	194
Center for Public Integrity 910 17th St NW 7th Fl Washington DC 20006 *Web:* www.publicintegrity.org	202-466-1300	466-1101	634
Center for Puppetry Arts 1404 Spring St NW Atlanta GA 30309 *Web:* www.puppet.org	404-873-3089	873-9907	50-2
Center for Radiophysics & Space Research Cornell University 616A Space Science Bldg Ithaca NY 14853 *Web:* www.astro.cornell.edu	607-255-6789	255-3433	668
Center for Reproductive Rights 199 Water St 14th Fl New York NY 10038 *Web:* beta.reproductiverights.org	917-637-3600	637-3666	48-8
Center for Research in Mathematics & Science Education (CRMSE) San Diego State University 6505 Alvarado Rd Ste 201 San Diego CA 92120 *Web:* www.sci.sdsu.edu	619-594-3977		668
Center for Responsive Politics, The 1300 L St NW Ste 200 Washington DC 20005 *Web:* www.opensecrets.org	202-857-0044	857-7809	634
Center for Science in the Public Interest 1220 L St N W Ste 300 Washington DC 20005 *TF:* 866-293-2774 ■ *Web:* www.cspinet.org	202-332-9110	265-4954	634
Center for Security Policy 1920 L St NW Washington DC 20036 *Web:* www.centerforsecuritypolicy.org	202-835-9077		634
Center for Southern Folklore 119 S Main St Memphis TN 38103 *Web:* www.southernfolklore.com	901-525-3655		520
Center for Space Research *University of Texas at Austin* 3925 W Braker Ln Ste 200 Austin TX 78759 *Web:* www.csr.utexas.edu	512-471-5573	471-3570	668
Center for Strategic & International Studies 1616 Rhode Island Ave NW Washington DC 20036 *Web:* www.csis.org	202-887-0200	775-3199	634
Center for the Arts 103 Center for the Arts Buffalo NY 14260 *Web:* www.ubcfa.org	716-645-2787	645-6973	572
Center for the Collaborative Classroom 1001 Marina Village Pky Ste 110 Alameda CA 94501 *TF:* 800-666-7270 ■ *Web:* www.collaborativeclassroom.org	510-533-0213	464-3670	423
Center for the Study of Language & Information Stanford University Cordura Hall 210 Panama St Stanford CA 94305 *Web:* www-csli.stanford.edu	650-725-3286		668
Center for Touch Drawing PO Box 1089 Langley WA 98260 *TF:* 800-989-6334 ■ *Web:* www.touchdrawing.com	360-221-5745	221-5931	637-2
Center for Visual Arts - Greensboro 200 N Davie St PO Box 13 Greensboro NC 27401 *Web:* www.greensboroart.org	336-333-7475	333-7477	50-2
Center for Women Policy Studies 1776 Masachusetts Ave NW Ste 450 Washington DC 20036 *Web:* centerwomenpolicy.org	202-872-1770	296-8962	48-24
Center for Wooden Boats 1010 Valley St Seattle WA 98109 *Web:* www.cwb.org	206-382-2628	382-2699	520
Center for Workforce Research and Information *Labor Dept* 54 State House Sta Augusta ME 04333 *TF:* 800-593-7660 ■ *Web:* www.maine.gov	207-623-7900		339-20
Center in the Square 1 Market Sq SE Roanoke VA 24011 *Web:* www.centerinthesquare.org	540-342-5700		50-6
Center Independent School Dist 404 Mosby St Center TX 75935 *Web:* www.centerisd.org	936-598-5642		685
Center Industries Corp 2505 S Custer Wichita KS 67217 *Web:* www.centerindustries.com	316-942-8255		697
Center Line Electric Inc 26554 Lawrence Center Line MI 48015 *Web:* centerline-elec.com	586-757-5505	759-2453	189-4
Center Municipal Revenue Collection PO Box 195387 San Juan PR 00919 *Web:* www.crimpr.net	787-625-2746	289-7660	535
Center of Contemporary Arts 524 Trinity Ave Saint Louis MO 63130 *Web:* www.cocastl.org	314-725-6555	725-6222	50-2
Center of Southwest Studies 1000 Rim Dr Durango CO 81301 *Web:* swcenter.fortlewis.edu	970-247-7456	247-7422	520
Center of the American Experiment (CAE) 8441 Wayzata Blvd Ste 350 Golden Valley MN 55426 *Web:* www.americanexperiment.org	612-338-3605		634
Center of Vocational Alternative For Men 3770 N High St Columbus OH 43214 *TF:* 877-521-2682 ■ *Web:* www.cova.org	614-294-7117		242
Center of Workforce Innovations Inc 2804 Boilermaker Ct Ste E Valparaiso IN 46383 *TF:* 877-607-0680 ■ *Web:* www.cwicorp.com	219-462-2940		463
Center Oil Co 600 Mason Ridge Center Dr Fl 2 Saint Louis MO 63141 *Web:* www.centeroil.com	314-682-3500		579
Center on Budget & Policy Priorities 820 First St NE Ste 510 Washington DC 20002 *Web:* www.cbpp.org	202-408-1080	408-1056	634
Center on Education & Training for Employment Ohio State University 1900 Kenny Rd Columbus OH 43210 *Web:* cete.osu.edu	614-292-6869	292-3742	668
Center on Human Policy 805 S Crouse Ave Syracuse NY 13244 *Web:* thechp.syr.edu	315-443-3851		48-17
Center Partners Inc 4401 Innovation Dr Fort Collins CO 80525 *Web:* www.qualfon.com	970-206-9000		317

	Phone	Fax	Class
Center Press 2045 Francisco St Berkeley CA 94709 *Web:* www.centerpress.com	510-845-8373	841-3884	637-2
Center Rock Inc 118 Schrock Dr Berlin PA 15530 *TF:* 888-267-9004 ■ *Web:* centerrock.com	814-267-7100		480
Center Stage 700 N Calvert St Baltimore MD 21202 *Web:* www.centerstage.org	410-986-4000		749
Center Stage Productions Inc 20-10 Maple Ave Fair Lawn NJ 07410 *TF:* 800-955-1663 ■ *Web:* cspdisplay.com	973-423-5000		393
Center Theatre Group 601 W Temple St Los Angeles CA 90012 *Web:* www.centertheatregroup.org	213-628-2772	972-3107	573-4
Center to Support Excellence in Teaching 520 Galvez Mall 5th Fl Ste 531 Stanford CA 94305 *Web:* cset.stanford.edu	650-721-1660	723-3654	668
Center Township Trustee 863 Massachusetts Ave Indianapolis IN 46204 *Web:* www.centergov.org	317-633-3610		48
CenterCal Properties LLC 7455 SW Bridgeport Rd Tigard OR 97224 *Web:* www.centercal.com	503-968-8940		653
Centerchem Inc 20 Glover Ave Merritt On The River Norwalk CT 06850 *Web:* www.centerchem.com	203-822-9800		146
Centered Networks Inc 1527 Stockton St 2nd Fl San Francisco CA 94133 *Web:* www.centerednetworks.com	415-294-7776		174
CenterGate Research Group LLC 420 S Smith Rd Tempe AZ 85281 *Web:* www.centergate.com	480-804-8100	804-8235	179
Centerless Rebuilders Inc 57877 Main St New Haven MI 48048 *Web:* centerlessrebuildersinc.com	586-749-6529		454
Centerline Machine Inc 777 S Industrial Dr Waupaca WI 54981 **Fax Area Code:* 715 ■ *TF:* 800-367-9122 ■ *Web:* centerlinemachine.com	800-367-9122	258-8220*	482
Centerplate 2187 Atlantic St Stamford CT 06902 *TF:* 800-698-6992 ■ *Web:* www.centerplate.com	203-975-5900		299
CenterPoint Energy Inc 1111 Louisiana St Houston TX 77002 *NYSE:* CNP ■ *TF:* 800-495-9880 ■ *Web:* www.centerpointenergy.com	713-207-1111		360-5
Centerpoint Insurance Group 3900 E Mexico Ave Ste 850 Denver CO 80210 *Web:* centerpointins.com	303-333-0375		390
CenterPoint Properties Trust 1808 Swift Dr Oak Brook IL 60523 *Web:* centerpoint.com	630-586-8000	586-8010	655
CenterPoint Ventures 6300 Bridge Pt Pkwy Bldg 1 Ste 500 Austin TX 78730 *Web:* www.cpventures.com	512-795-5800	795-5849	792
CenterPointe Inc 2633 P St Lincoln NE 68503 *Web:* www.centerpointe.org	402-475-8717		726
Centers for Disease Control & Prevention			
National Center for Health Statistics 6525 Belcrest Rd Hyattsville MD 20782 *Web:* www.cdc.gov	301-436-8500		340-10
National Center for Injury Prevention & Control (NCIPC) 4770 Buford Hwy NE Atlanta GA 30341 *TF:* 800-232-4636 ■ *Web:* www.cdc.gov	800-232-4636		340-10
National Institute for Occupational Safety & Health 200 Independence Ave SW Washington DC 20201 *TF:* 800-356-4674 ■ *Web:* www.cdc.gov	404-639-3286		340-10
Centers for Medicare & Medicaid Services Regional Offices			
New York Regional Office 26 Federal Plz Rm 3812 New York NY 10278 **Fax Area Code:* 443 ■ *Web:* www.cms.gov	212-616-2439	380-8855*	340-10
Region I JFK Federal Bldg Rm 2325 Boston MA 02203 *Web:* www.cms.gov	617-565-1188	565-1339	340-10
Region III 150 S Independence Mall W Ste 216 Philadelphia PA 19106 *Web:* www.cms.gov	215-861-4140		340-10
Region IV 61 Forsyth St SW Ste 4T20 Atlanta GA 30303 **Fax Area Code:* 443 ■ *Web:* www.cms.gov	404-562-1738	380-8945*	340-10
Region IX 90 Seventh St Ste 5-300 San Francisco CA 94103 **Fax Area Code:* 443 ■ *Web:* www.cms.gov	415-744-3502	380-8863*	340-10
Region V 233 N Michigan Ave Ste 600 Chicago IL 60601 *Web:* www.cms.gov	312-886-5344	353-0252	340-10
Region VI 1301 Young St Ste 714 Dallas TX 75202 *Web:* www.cms.gov	214-767-6427		340-10
Region VII 601 E 12th St Rm 227 Richard Bolling Federal Bldg Kansas City MO 64106 *Web:* www.cms.gov	303-844-7481		340-10
Region VIII 1600 Broadway Ste 700 Denver CO 80202 *Web:* www.cms.gov	303-844-7035	844-3753	340-10
Region X 2201 Sixth Ave Ste 801 Seattle WA 98121 *Web:* www.cms.gov	206-615-2306		340-10
CenterSite LLC (CS) PO Box 20709 Columbus OH 43220 *Web:* www.centersite.net	614-448-4055		637-10
CenterSource Systems LLC 60 Commerce Ln Ste D Cloverdale CA 95425 *TF:* 800-810-1701 ■ *Web:* www.tribes.com	707-838-1061	894-2355	637-2
CenterSquare Investment Management 630 W Germantown Pk Ste 300 Plymouth Meeting PA 19462 *Web:* www.centersquare.com	610-834-9500		652
CenterStaging Corp 3407 Winona Ave Burbank CA 91504 *Web:* www.centerstaging.com	818-559-4333		514
Centerstate Banks Inc 42725 US Hwy 27 Davenport FL 33837 *TF:* 855-863-2265 ■ *Web:* www.centerstatebank.com	855-863-2265		70
Centerville Public Library 585 Main St Centerville MA 02632 *Web:* www.centervillelibrary.org	508-790-6220	790-6218	434-3
CenTex Foundation Repair Austin 1120 E 52nd St Austin TX 78723 *TF:* 888-425-5438 ■ *Web:* www.centexhouseleveling.com	512-444-5438		186

Company / Address	City	State	ZIP	Phone	Fax	Class
Centex Materials Inc 3019 Alvin Devane Blvd Ste 100 *Web:* www.eaglematerials.com	Austin	TX	78741	512-460-3003		182
Centimark Corp 12 Grandview Cir. *TF:* 800-558-4100 ■ *Web:* www.centimark.com	Canonsburg	PA	15317	724-743-7777		189-12
Centinela Elementary School 1123 Marlborough Ave *TF:* 800-942-2761 ■ *Web:* centinela.inglewoodusd.com	Inglewood	CA	90302	310-680-5440		685
Centinela Hospital Medical Ctr 555 E Hardy St *Web:* www.centinelamed.com	Inglewood	CA	90301	310-673-4660		374-3
Centinela State Prison 2302 Brown Rd PO Box 731 *Web:* www.cdcr.ca.gov	Imperial	CA	92251	760-337-7900	337-7665	213
Centipede Press 2565 Teller Ct *Web:* www.centipedepress.com	Lakewood	CO	80214	303-231-9720		637-10
Cento Fine Foods Inc 100 Cento Blvd *Web:* www.cento.com	West Deptford	NJ	08086	856-853-7800		296-25
Centon Electronics Inc 27412 Aliso Viejo Pkwy *Web:* www.centon.com	Aliso Viejo	CA	92656	949-855-9111		625
Centra Financial Holdings Inc 990 Elmer Prince Dr *Web:* www.bankwithunited.com	Morgantown	WV	26505	304-598-2000		780
Centra Health Inc 1920 Atherholt Rd *TF:* 800-947-5442 ■ *Web:* www.centrahealth.com	Lynchburg	VA	24501	434-200-3000		353
Centra Southside Community Hospital (CSCH) 800 Oak St *TF:* 800-400-7247 ■ *Web:* www.centrahealth.com	Farmville	VA	23901	434-392-8811	200-2994	374-3
Centra Technology Inc 25 Burlington Mall Rd *Web:* www.centratechnology.com	Burlington	MA	01803	781-272-7887	272-7836	261
CentraArchy Restaurants 236 Albemarle Rd *Web:* www.centraarchy.com	Charleston	SC	29407	843-571-0096		670
CenTrak 125 Pheasant Run *Web:* www.centrak.com	Newtown	PA	18940	215-860-2928		475
Central Address Systems Inc 10303 Crown Point Ave *TF:* 800-482-7705 ■ *Web:* www.cas-online.com	Omaha	NE	68134	402-964-9998		7
Central Alabama Community College 1675 Cherokee Rd *Web:* www.cacc.edu	Alexander City	AL	35010	256-234-6346		162
Central Alabama Electric Co-op 1802 Hwy 31 N *TF:* 800-545-5735 ■ *Web:* cacc.coop	Prattville	AL	36067	334-365-6762		245
Central Allied Enterprises Inc 1243 Raff Rd SW PO Box 80449 *Web:* www.central-allied.com	Canton	OH	44710	330-477-6751	477-1660	188-4
Central Aluminum Co 2045 Broehm Rd *TF:* 800-542-2105 ■ *Web:* www.centralaluminum.com	Columbus	OH	43207	614-491-5700	491-8478	480
Central Animal Hospital 317 Ardsley Rd *Web:* bestvets.net	Scarsdale	NY	10583	914-723-1250		794
Central Arizona College 8470 N Overfield Rd *TF:* 800-237-9814 ■ *Web:* centralaz.edu	Coolidge	AZ	85228	520-494-5444	494-5083	162
Central Arizona Fire & Medical Authority 8603 E Eastridge Dr *Web:* www.centralyavapaifire.org	Prescott Valley	AZ	86314	928-772-7711		302
Central Arizona Supply 208 S Country Club Dr *Web:* centralazsupply.com	Mesa	AZ	85210	480-834-5817		612
Central Arkansas Telephone Cooperative Inc (CATC) 4036 Hwy 7 *Web:* www.catc.net	Bismarck	AR	71929	501-865-2282		224
Central Audio Visual Equipment Inc 375 Roma Jean Pky *TF:* 800-636-2284 ■ *Web:* www.cavinc.com	Streamwood	IL	60107	630-372-8100		246
Central Bag Co 4901 S 4th St *Web:* centralbagcompany.com	Leavenworth	KS	66048	913-250-0325	727-1760	559
Central Bancshares Inc 300 W Vine St *TF:* 800-637-6884 ■ *Web:* www.centralbank.com	Lexington	KY	40507	859-253-6222	253-6003	360-2
Central Bank 238 Madison St *Web:* www.centralbank.net	Jefferson City	MO	65101	573-634-1234		70
Central Bank 2400 Prairie View Rd PO Box 1250 *Web:* www.centralbank.net	Platte City	MO	64079	816-858-5400		70
Central Bank of Kansas City 2301 Independence Ave *Web:* www.centralbankkc.com	Kansas City	MO	64124	816-483-1210	483-2586	70
Central Baptist College 1501 College Ave *TF:* 800-205-6872 ■ *Web:* www.cbc.edu	Conway	AR	72034	501-329-6872		166
Central Baptist Theological Seminary 6601 Monticello Rd **Fax Area Code:* 412 ■ *Web:* www.cbts.edu	Shawnee	KS	66226	913-667-5700	788-6510*	167-3
Central Baptist Village 4747 N Canfield Ave *TF:* 855-264-9355 ■ *Web:* cbvillage.org	Norridge	IL	60706	708-583-8500		48-20
Central BBQ 2249 Central Ave *Web:* eatcbq.com	Memphis	TN	38104	901-272-9377		671
Central Boiler Inc 20502 160th St *TF:* 800-248-4681 ■ *Web:* centralboiler.com	Greenbush	MN	56726	218-782-2575	782-2580	362
Central Boston Elder Services Inc 2315 Washington St *TF:* 800-922-2275 ■ *Web:* www.centralboston.org	Boston	MA	02119	617-277-7416	277-2005	450
Central Brevard Library 308 Forest Ave *Web:* www.brevardfl.gov	Cocoa	FL	32922	321-633-1792		434-3
Central Bucks Chamber of Commerce 252 W Swamp Rd Ste 23 *Web:* www.centralbuckschamber.com	Doylestown	PA	18901	215-348-3913	348-7154	139
Central Builders Supply Company Inc 125 Bridge Ave PO Box 152 *TF:* 800-326-9361 ■ *Web:* centralbuilderssupply.com	Sunbury	PA	17801	570-286-6461	286-5108	182
Central California Blood Ctr 4343 W Herndon Ave *TF:* 800-649-5399 ■ *Web:* donateblood.org	Fresno	CA	93722	559-389-5433	225-1602	89
Central California Parent 7638 N Ingram Ste 101 *Web:* ccparent.com	Fresno	CA	93711	559-435-1409		5
Central California Traction Co 2201 W Washington St Ste 12 *Web:* www.cctrailroad.com	Stockton	CA	95203	209-466-6927		651
Central California Women's Facility (CCWF) 23370 Rd 22 PO Box 1501 *Web:* www.cdcr.ca.gov	Chowchilla	CA	93610	559-665-5531		213
Central Career School 126 Corporate Blvd *Web:* www.centralcareer.edu	South Plainfield	NJ	07080	908-412-8600	462-3801	685
Central Carolina Community College 1105 Kelly Dr *TF:* 800-682-8353 ■ *Web:* www.cccc.edu	Sanford	NC	27330	919-775-5401	718-7380	162
Central Carolina Hospital 1135 Carthage St *TF:* 800-292-2262 ■ *Web:* www.centralcarolinahosp.com	Sanford	NC	27330	919-774-2100	774-2295	374-3
Central Carolina Products Inc 250 W Old Glencoe Rd *Web:* www.ccair.com	Burlington	NC	27217	336-226-0005		596
Central Carolina Technical College 506 N Guignard Dr *TF:* 800-221-8711 ■ *Web:* www.cctech.edu	Sumter	SC	29150	803-778-1961	778-6696	800
Central Ceilings Inc 36 Norfolk Ave *Web:* www.centralceilings.com	South Easton	MA	02375	508-238-6985	238-2191	189-9
Central Christian College PO Box 1403 *TF:* 800-835-0078 ■ *Web:* www.centralchristian.edu	McPherson	KS	67460	620-241-0723	241-6032	166
Central Christian College of the Bible 911 E Urbandale Dr *TF:* 888-263-3900 ■ *Web:* cccb.edu	Moberly	MO	65270	660-263-3900	263-3936	161
Central City Integrated Health 10 Peterboro St *Web:* www.centralcityhealth.com	Detroit	MI	48201	313-831-3160		726
Central City Opera 400 S Colorado Blvd Ste 530 *Web:* centralcityopera.org	Denver	CO	80246	303-292-6500	292-4958	573-2
Central Coast Federal Credit Union 4242 Gigling Rd *TF:* 800-558-3424 ■ *Web:* centcoastfcu.com	Seaside	CA	93955	831-393-3480	899-2572	219
Central Coast Home Health Inc 253 Granada Ste D *Web:* www.mycchh.com	San Luis Obispo	CA	93401	805-543-2244	543-2224	363
Central Coast Pharmacy Specialists 590A So Main St *Web:* www.ccpsrx.com	Templeton	CA	93465	805-434-5999	434-5968	584
Central College 812 University St *TF:* 877-462-3687 ■ *Web:* www.central.edu	Pella	IA	50219	641-628-5285	628-5983	166
Central Community College 4500 63rd St PO Box 1027 *Web:* www.cccneb.edu	Columbus	NE	68602	402-564-7132	562-1201	162
Central Computer Systems Inc 3777 Stevens Creek Blvd *Web:* www.centralcomputer.com	Santa Clara	CA	95051	650-345-5888		180
Central Concrete Supermix Inc 4300 SW 74th Ave *Web:* www.supermix.com	Miami	FL	33155	305-262-3250	267-0698	182
Central Connecticut State University 1615 Stanley St Davidson Hall Rm 115 *Web:* www.ccsu.edu	New Britain	CT	06050	860-832-3200	832-2295	166
Central Consolidated Inc 3435 W Harry St *Web:* www.centralconsolidated.net	Wichita	KS	67213	316-945-0797		189-10
Central Container Corp 3901 85th Ave N *TF:* 800-523-2697 ■ *Web:* www.centralpackage.com	Minneapolis	MN	55443	763-425-7444	425-7917	100
Central Crude Inc 4187 Hwy 3059 PO Box 1863 *TF:* 800-245-8408 ■ *Web:* www.centralcrude.com	Lake Charles	LA	70602	337-436-1000	436-9602	581
Central Defense Security 50 Vantage Way Ste 251 *Web:* www.centdef.com	Nashville	TN	37228	615-256-0300		693
Central Dispatch Inc 1800 4th St *Web:* www.centraldispatchinc.net	Harvey	LA	70058	504-362-3282	362-4029	311
Central Distributing Co 609 N 108th Cir *TF:* 800-253-8212 ■ *Web:* gamesales.com	Omaha	NE	68154	402-493-5600	493-8510	328
Central Distributors Inc 15 Foss Rd *TF:* 800-427-5757 ■ *Web:* www.centraldistributors.com	Lewiston	ME	04240	207-784-4026		81-1
Central Electric Cooperative 3305 S Boomer Rd PO Box 1809 *TF:* 800-375-2884 ■ *Web:* www.mycentral.coop	Stillwater	OK	74076	405-372-2884	372-8559	245
Central Electric Cooperative Inc 2098 N Hwy 97 *TF:* 866-459-8651 ■ *Web:* www.cec.coop	Redmond	OR	97756	541-548-2144	548-0366	245
Central Electric Cooperative Inc 716 Rte 368 *TF:* 800-521-0570 ■ *Web:* www.central.coop	Parker	PA	16049	724-399-2931	399-2300	245
Central Electric Membership Corp 128 Wilson Rd *TF:* 800-446-7752 ■ *Web:* cemcpower.com	Sanford	NC	27331	919-774-4900		245
Central Electric Power Assn 107 E Main St *Web:* www.centralepa.com	Carthage	MS	39051	601-267-5671		245
Central European Distribution Corp (CEDC) 3000 Atrium Way Ste 265 *NASDAQ: CEDC* ■ *Web:* www.cedc.com	Mount Laurel	NJ	08054	856-273-6980		81-1
Central Extrusion Die Company Inc PO Box 3209	Muscle Shoals	AL	35662	256-381-3620		757
Central Fairfax Chamber of Commerce 4031 University Dr Ste 100 *Web:* www.cfcc.org	Fairfax	VA	22030	703-591-2450	591-2820	139
Central Florida Community College 114 Rodgers Blvd *Web:* www.cf.edu	Chiefland	FL	32626	352-493-9533	493-9994	162

Name / Address	Phone	Fax	Class
Central Florida Electric Cooperative Inc 11491 NW 50th Ave........................Chiefland FL 32626 *TF:* 800-227-1302 ■ *Web:* www.cfec.com	352-493-2511		245
Central Florida Investments Inc 5601 Windhover Dr ....Orlando FL 32819 *TF:* 888-852-2959 ■ *Web:* www.westgateresorts.com	407-351-3351		753
Central Florida Publishing Inc 700 W Fulton St ....Sanford FL 32771 *Web:* www.centralfloridapublishing.com	407-365-6604	366-0729	532-2
Central Florida Regional Hospital 1401 W Seminole Blvd.......................Sanford FL 32771 *Web:* centralfloridaregional.com	407-321-4500		374-3
Central Florida Regional Transportation Authority (Inc) 455 N Garland Ave ....Orlando FL 32801 *Web:* www.golynx.com	407-841-2279		468
Central Florida Visitors & Convention Bureau 101 Adventure Ct ....Davenport FL 33837 *TF:* 800-828-7655 ■ *Web:* visitcentralflorida.org	863-420-2586	420-2593	206
Central Florida Zoological Park 3755 NW Hwy 17-92 & I-4 PO Box 470309...Lake Monroe FL 32747 *Web:* www.centralfloridazoo.org	407-323-4450	321-0900	823
Central Flying Service Inc 1501 Bond Ave...........................Little Rock AR 72202 *TF:* 800-888-5387 ■ *Web:* www.central.aero.com	501-375-3245		63
Central Freight Lines Inc PO Box 2638 ....Waco TX 76702 **Fax Area Code:* 254 ■ *TF:* 800-782-5036 ■ *Web:* www.centralfreight.com	800-782-5036	741-5370*	780
Central Garden & Pet Co 1340 Treat Blvd Ste 600..................Walnut Creek CA 94597 *NASDAQ: CENT* ■ *TF:* 800-356-2017 ■ *Web:* www.central.com	925-948-4000		293
Central Georgia Electric Membership Corp 923 S Mulberry St ....Jackson GA 30233 *TF:* 800-222-4877 ■ *Web:* www.cgemc.com	770-775-7857	504-7877	245
Central Georgia Technical College 3300 Macon Tech Dr.........................Macon GA 31206 *TF:* 866-430-0135 ■ *Web:* www.centralgatech.edu	478-757-3400	757-3454	800
Central Group, The 5526 Timberlea Blvd.....................Mississauga ON L4W2T7 *Web:* centralgrp.com	905-238-8400	238-8127	100
Central Heating & Air Conditioning 2317 Nc Hwy 11 N ....Kinston NC 28501 *Web:* centralheataircondiitioning.com	252-527-6676		189-10
Central Holidays 250 Moonachie Rd ....Moonachie NJ 07074 **Fax Area Code:* 800 ■ *TF:* 800-935-5000 ■ *Web:* www.centralholidays.com	201-228-5200	329-4248*	771
Central Home Health Care Inc 20245 W 12 Mile Rd Ste 100 ....Southfield MI 48076 *TF:* 800-698-5410 ■ *Web:* www.centralhomecare.com	248-569-5410	569-5412	363
Central Hudson Enterprises Corp 284 S Ave............................Poughkeepsie NY 12601 *TF:* 800-527-2714 ■ *Web:* www.chenergygroup.com	845-452-2000		316
Central Hudson Gas & Electric Corp 284 S Ave............................Poughkeepsie NY 12601 *Web:* www.cenhud.com	845-452-2700		787
Central Illinois Community Blood Ctr 1999 Wabash Ave.........................Springfield IL 62703 *TF:* 866-448-3253 ■ *Web:* www.bloodcenter.org	217-753-1530		89
Central Illinois Credit Union 2106 W John St ....Champaign IL 61821 *TF:* 866-374-6975 ■ *Web:* cicu.com	217-356-9721	356-0044	219
Central Illinois Loan 435 S Fifth Ave.............Canton IL 61520 *Web:* centralillinoisloans.com	309-647-6663		217
Central Illinois Tourism Development Office 700 E Adams St ....Springfield IL 62701 *Web:* www.visitcentralillinois.com	217-525-7980		206
Central Indiana Hardware Company Inc 9190 Corporation Dr.....................Indianapolis IN 46256 *Web:* www.cih-inc.com	317-558-5700		350
Central Industries Inc 11438 Cronridge Dr Ste W................Owings Mills MD 21117 *TF:* 800-304-8484 ■ *Web:* www.centralindustriesusa.com	800-304-8484	932-1222	539
Central Ink Corp 1100 Harvester Rd ....West Chicago IL 60185 *TF:* 800-345-2541 ■ *Web:* www.cicink.com	630-231-6500	231-6554	388
Central Institute for the Deaf (CID) 825 S Taylor Ave.........................Saint Louis MO 63110 *TF:* 877-444-4574 ■ *Web:* www.cid.edu	314-977-0132	977-0023	49-19
Central Insulation Systems Inc 300 Murray Rd ....Cincinnati OH 45217 *TF:* 800-544-7502 ■ *Web:* www.centralinsulation.com	513-242-0600		667
Central Insurance Companies, The 800 S Washington St ....Van Wert OH 45891 *TF:* 800-736-7000 ■ *Web:* www.central-insurance.com	419-238-1010	238-7626	391-4
Central Intelligence Agency (CIA) Office of Public Affairs ....Washington DC 20505 *Web:* www.cia.gov	703-482-0623		340-20
Central Iowa Power Coop 1400 Hwy 13 SE.......................Cedar Rapids IA 52403 *TF:* 800-373-8011 ■ *Web:* www.cipco.net	319-366-8011	366-8626	787
Central IQ Inc 14527 Cotswolds Dr...............Tampa FL 33626 *Web:* www.centraliq.com	813-920-4001		463
Central Jersey Blood Ctr 494 Sycamore Ave ....Shrewsbury NJ 07702 *Web:* www.cjbcblood.org	732-842-5750		89
Central Jersey Pro Medical Corp 1970 Swarthmore Ave Ste 2 ....Lakewood NJ 08701 *Web:* homeinstead.com	732-901-5500		363
Central Jersey Supply Company Inc 201 Second St PO Box 549 ....Perth Amboy NJ 08862 *Web:* www.centraljerseysupply.com	732-826-7400		612
Central Lakes College 501 W College Dr..........................Brainerd MN 56401 *TF:* 800-933-0346 ■ *Web:* www.clcmn.edu	218-855-8199	855-8057	162
Central Library of Rochester & Monroe County 115 S Ave................................Rochester NY 14604 *Web:* www.libraryweb.org	585-428-7300	428-8353	434-3
Central Louisiana Chamber of Commerce 1118 Third St PO Box 992 ....Alexandria LA 71300 *Web:* www.cenlachamber.org	318-442-6671	442-6734	139
Central Louisiana State Hospital 242 W Shamrock St ....Pineville LA 71360 *TF:* 888-342-6207 ■ *Web:* ldh.la.gov	318-484-6200	484-6501	374-5
Central Lumber Sales Inc (CLS) 439 A St ....Lincoln NE 68542 *Web:* www.centrallumber.com	402-474-4441	474-0595	364
Central Maine Community College 1250 Turner St ....Auburn ME 04210 *TF:* 800-891-2002 ■ *Web:* www.cmcc.edu	207-755-5100	755-5493	800
Central Maine Medical Ctr 300 Main St ....Lewiston ME 04240 *Web:* www.cmhc.org	207-795-0111		374-3
Central Maine Power Co 83 Edison Dr..........Augusta ME 04336 **Fax Area Code:* 207 ■ *TF:* 800-565-0121 ■ *Web:* www.cmpco.com	800-696-1000	621-4778*	787
Central Maine Title Company Inc 78 Winthrop St.............................Augusta ME 04330 *Web:* cmetitle.com	207-622-7505	622-7507	41
Central Maintenance & Welding Inc (CMW) 2620 E Keysville Rd ....Lithia FL 33547 *TF:* 877-704-7411 ■ *Web:* www.cmw.cc	813-737-1402	737-1820	189-14
Central Management Inc (CMI) 820 Gessner Rd Ste 1525....................Houston TX 77024 *Web:* www.cmirealestate.com	713-961-9777		652
Central Mass Oil Company Inc 451 Main St PO Box 276 ....Rutland MA 01543 *Web:* centralmassoilinc.com	508-886-6823		316
Central Mass Web Design Inc 70 Snake Pond Rd ....Gardner MA 01440 *Web:* www.centralmasswebdesign.com	978-632-5300		179
Central Mechanical Construction Company Inc 631 Pecan Cir...........................Manhattan KS 66502 *TF:* 800-631-6999 ■ *Web:* centralmechanical.com	785-537-2437	537-2491	189-10
Central Mechanical Systems Inc 3218 S Cherry Ave ....Marshfield WI 54449 *Web:* www.cmsmfld.com	715-387-4568		189-10
Central Metal Fabricators Inc 900 SW 70th Ave ....Miami FL 33144 *Web:* www.centralmetalfab.com	305-261-6262		492
Central Metal Finishing Inc 80 Flagship Dr ....North Andover MA 01845 *Web:* www.cenmet.com	978-291-0500		481
Central Metals Inc 1054 S Second St ....Camden NJ 08103 *Web:* www.centralmetals.com	856-963-5844	963-1789	492
Central Methodist University 411 Central Methodist Sq......................Fayette MO 65248 *TF:* 877-268-1854 ■ *Web:* www.centralmethodist.edu	660-248-3391	248-1872	166
Central Michigan Correctional Facility 320 N Hubbard..........................Saint Louis MI 48880 *Web:* www.michigan.gov	989-681-6668		213
Central Michigan University 102 Warriner Hall ....Mount Pleasant MI 48859 *TF:* 888-292-5366 ■ *Web:* www.cmich.edu	989-774-4000	774-7267	166
Central Mine Equipment Company Inc 4215 Rider Trl N...........................Earth City MO 63045 *TF:* 800-325-8827 ■ *Web:* www.cmeco.com	314-291-7700	291-4880	190
Central Minnesota Fabricating Inc 2725 W Gorton Ave..........................Willmar MN 56201 *TF:* 800-839-8857 ■ *Web:* www.cmf-inc.com	320-235-4181		480
Central Mississippi Correctional Facility 3794 Hwy 468 ....Pearl MS 39208 *Web:* www.mdoc.ms.gov	601-932-2880	932-6202	213
Central Missouri Electric Co-opeartive Inc 22702 Hwy 65 PO Box 939....................Sedalia MO 65302 *TF:* 855-875-7165 ■ *Web:* www.cmecinc.com	660-826-2900		245
Central Moloney Inc 2400 W Sixth Ave ....Pine Bluff AR 71601 *Web:* www.centralmoloneyinc.com	870-534-5332	536-4002	767
Central Montcalm Public School 1480 S Sheridan Rd PO Box 9 ....Stanton MI 48888 *Web:* central-montcalm.org	989-831-2000		685
Central Motive Power Inc (CMP) 6301 N Broadway ....Denver CO 80216 *TF:* 800-822-4332 ■ *Web:* centralmotivepower.com	303-428-3611	428-6785	262
Central National Bank 800 SE Quincy St ....Topeka KS 66612 *Web:* centralnational.com	785-234-2265	234-9660	70
Central National Bank, Waco, Texas 8320 W Hwy 84 ....Waco TX 76712 *Web:* cnbwaco.com	254-776-3800		70
Central Nebraska Home Care 221 W 44th St.............................Kearney NE 68845 *Web:* www.cnhconline.com	308-865-2936		363
Central Nebraska Packing Inc 2800 E Eigth St PO Box 550...............North Platte NE 69103 *TF:* 800-445-2881 ■ *Web:* www.nebraskabrand.com	308-532-1250	532-2744	473
Central New Mexico Community College 10549 Universe Blvd NW ....Albuquerque NM 87114 *TF:* 888-453-1304 ■ *Web:* www.cnm.edu	505-224-3000	224-3237	800
Central New Mexico Correctional Facility 1525 Morris Rd ....Los Lunas NM 87031 *Web:* cd.nm.gov	505-865-1622		213
Central New York Business Journal, The 269 W Jefferson St.........................Syracuse NY 13202 *TF:* 800-836-3539 ■ *Web:* www.cnybj.com	315-579-3919		457-5
Central New York Regional Transportation Authority (Centro) 200 Cortland Ave PO Box 820 ....Syracuse NY 13205 *Web:* www.centro.org	315-442-3400		468
Central Office 1275 4th St..................Santa Rosa CA 95404 *Web:* thecentraloffice.net	707-576-1155	576-7041	549
Central Ohio Lions Eye Bank 262 Neil Ave Ste 140 ....Columbus OH 43215 *Web:* www.coleb.org	614-545-2057		269
Central Ohio Technical College 1179 University Dr...........................Newark OH 43055 *Web:* www.cotc.edu	740-366-9494		800
Central Ohio Transit Authority (COTA) 33 N High St............................Columbus OH 43215 *Web:* www.cota.com	614-228-1776		468
Central Oil & Supply Corp 2300 Booth St..............................Monroe LA 71201 *TF:* 800-883-8081 ■ *Web:* www.central-oil.com	318-388-2602		581

Name / Address	City	State	ZIP	Phone	Fax	Class
Central Oklahoma Detention Juvenile Ctr 700 S 9th St *Web:* oja.ok.gov	Tecumseh	OK	74873	405-598-2135	598-8713	412
Central Oklahoma Telephone Co (COTC) 223 Broadway *TF:* 800-252-8854 ■ *Web:* www.cotc.net	Davenport	OK	74026	918-377-2241	377-2506	224
Central One Federal Credit Union 714 Main St *TF:* 800-527-1017 ■ *Web:* centralfcu.com	Shrewsbury	MA	01545	800-527-1017		219
Central Oregon Association of Realtors 2112 NE Fourth St *Web:* coar.com	Bend	OR	97701	541-382-6027		653
Central Oregon Community College 2600 NW College Way *Web:* www.cocc.edu	Bend	OR	97701	541-383-7700	383-7506	162
Central Oregon Mall on The Internet, The 25 NW Minnesota Ave Ste 8 *Web:* www.coinet.com	Bend	OR	97701	541-389-1303		396
Central Oregon Visitors Assn 57100 Beaver Dr Bldg 6 Ste 130 *TF:* 800-800-8334 ■ *Web:* visitcentraloregon.com	Sunriver	OR	97707	800-800-8334		206
Central Pacific Financial Corp PO Box 3590 *NYSE: CPF* ■ *TF:* 800-342-8422 ■ *Web:* www.cpb.bank	Honolulu	HI	96811	808-544-0500		360-2
Central Palm Beach County Chamber of Commerce 12794 W Forest Hill Blvd Ste 19 *Web:* www.cpbchamber.com	Wellington	FL	33414	561-790-6200		139
Central Paper Company Inc 1201 Newell Pky *TF:* 800-854-0619 ■ *Web:* www.centralpaper-al.com	Montgomery	AL	36110	334-244-0555	244-1198	559
Central Paper Products Company Inc John C Mongan Industrial Pk 350 Gay St *TF:* 800-339-4065 ■ *Web:* www.centralpaper.com	Manchester	NH	03103	603-624-4065	624-8795	559
Central Park Group LLC 805 Third Ave *Web:* centralparkgroup.com	New York	NY	10022	212-317-9200	813-1543	401
Central Park Zoo 64th St & Fifth Ave *Web:* centralparkzoo.com	New York	NY	10021	212-439-6500		823
Central Pennsylvania Blood Bank 8167 Adams Dr *TF:* 800-771-0059 ■ *Web:* www.cpbb.org	Hummelstown	PA	17036	717-566-6161		89
Central Pennsylvania College 600 Valley Rd PO Box 309 *TF:* 800-759-2727 ■ *Web:* www.centralpenn.edu	Summerdale	PA	17093	717-732-0702	732-5254	800
Central Petroleum Transport Inc (CPT) 6115 Mitchell St *TF:* 800-798-6357 ■ *Web:* www.cptrans.com	Sioux City	IA	51111	712-258-6357	258-8592	780
Central Piedmont Community College 1201 Elizabeth Ave *TF:* 877-530-8815 ■ *Web:* www.cpcc.edu	Charlotte	NC	28204	704-330-2722	330-6136	162
Central Pinellas Chamber of Commerce 801 W Bay Ctr Ste 602 *Web:* www.centralchamber.biz	Largo	FL	33770	727-584-2321	586-3112	139
Central Pipe Supply Inc 101 Ware Rd PO Box 5470 *TF:* 800-844-7700 ■ *Web:* centralpipe.com	Pearl	MS	39288	601-939-3322	932-8944	595
Central Power Electric Co-op 525 20th Ave SW *TF:* 866-852-4407 ■ *Web:* www.centralpwr.com	Minot	ND	58701	701-852-4407	852-4401	245
Central Power Systems & Services 9200 W Liberty Dr *TF:* 800-444-0442 ■ *Web:* www.cpower.com	Liberty	MO	64068	816-781-8070	781-2207	385
Central Prairie Co-op 225 S Broadway *TF:* 800-861-3207 ■ *Web:* www.cpcoop.us	Sterling	KS	67579	620-278-2141		11-1
Central Pre-Mix Concrete Co 5111 E Broadway *Web:* cpminland.com	Spokane	WA	99212	509-534-6221		183
Central Prison 1300 Western Blvd *Web:* www.ncdps.gov	Raleigh	NC	27606	919-733-0800	716-2045	213
Central Products LLC 7750 Georgetown Rd *TF:* 800-215-9293 ■ *Web:* www.centralrestaurant.com	Indianapolis	IN	46268	800-215-9293		14
Central Puget Sound Regional Transit Authority 401 S Jackson St *TF:* 800-201-4900 ■ *Web:* www.soundtransit.org	Seattle	WA	98104	206-398-5000		468
Central Reach 371 S Federal Hwy *TF:* 800-939-5414 ■ *Web:* www.centralreach.com	Pompano Beach	FL	33062	800-939-5414		39
Central Record PO Box 1027 *TF:* 800-825-7653 ■ *Web:* www.southjerseylocalnews.com	Medford	NJ	08055	609-654-5000		532-4
Central Recovery Press (CRP) 3321 N Buffalo Dr Ste 275 *TF:* 888-855-7199 ■ *Web:* www.centralrecoverypress.com	Las Vegas	NV	89129	702-868-5830		637-2
Central Resources Inc 1775 Sherman St Ste 2600 *Web:* centralresources.com	Denver	CO	80203	303-830-0100	830-9297	538
Central Rhode Island Chamber of Commerce 3288 Post Rd *Web:* www.centralrichamber.com	Warwick	RI	02886	401-732-1100	732-1107	139
Central Rubber & Plastics 17416 County Rd 34 *Web:* www.centralrubbercompany.com	Goshen	IN	46528	574-534-6411		677
Central Sales & Service Inc 110 Industrial Ct *TF:* 800-467-0568 ■ *Web:* www.centralsales-service.com	Waverly	TN	37185	931-296-1940	296-1944	650
Central School of Practical Nursing 4700 Rockside Rd Summit 1 Ste 250 *Web:* www.cspnohio.edu	Independence	OH	44131	216-901-4400	901-2040	685
Central Scott Telephone Co 125 N 2nd St *TF:* 800-292-8989 ■ *Web:* www.centralscott.com	Eldridge	IA	52748	563-285-9611	285-9648	224
Central Security Life Insurance Co PO Box 833879 *Web:* www.cslic.com	Richardson	TX	75083	972-699-2770	699-2788	391-2
Central Service Assn 93 S Coley Rd *TF:* 877-842-5962 ■ *Web:* www.csa1.com	Tupelo	MS	38801	662-842-5962	840-1329	225
Central Signaling 2033 Hamilton Rd *TF:* 800-554-1101 ■ *Web:* www.censignal.com	Columbus	GA	31904	800-554-1101		692
Central Specialties Ltd 220 Exchange Dr *TF:* 800-873-4370 ■ *Web:* www.csltd.com	Crystal Lake	IL	60014	815-459-6000	459-6562	64
Central State Enterprises Inc 1331 Freese Works Pl *Web:* www.centralstateent.net	Galion	OH	44833	419-468-8191		454
Central State Hospital 26317 W Washington St *Web:* www.csh.dbhds.virginia.gov	Petersburg	VA	23803	804-524-7000		374-5
Central State Hospital 10510 LaGrange Rd *Web:* dbhdid.ky.gov	Louisville	KY	40223	502-253-7060	253-7049	374-5
Central State Prison 4600 Fulton Mill Rd *Web:* www.dcor.state.ga.us	Macon	GA	31208	478-471-2906	471-2068	213
Central State University 1400 Brush Row Rd PO Box 1004 *TF:* 800-388-2781 ■ *Web:* www.centralstate.edu	Wilberforce	OH	45384	937-376-6011	376-6648	166
Central States Bus Sales Inc 2450 Cassens Dr *Web:* www.centralstatesbus.com	Fenton	MO	63026	636-343-6050		59
Central States Health & Life Company of Omaha 1212 N 96th St *TF:* 800-826-6587 ■ *Web:* www.cso.com	Omaha	NE	68114	800-826-6587		391-2
Central States Indemnity Company of Omaha (CSI) 1212 N 96th St *Web:* www.csi-omaha.com	Omaha	NE	68114	402-997-8000		391-5
Central States Industrial Supply Inc 8720 S 137th Cir *Web:* www.centralstatesgroup.com	Omaha	NE	68138	763-531-2222		492
Central Steel Fabricators Inc 1843 S 54th Ave *TF:* 855-652-7010 ■ *Web:* www.centralsteelfab.com	Cicero	IL	60804	708-652-2037		480
Central Susquehanna LPN Career Ctr 1339 St Mary St *Web:* www.csiu.org	Lewisburg	PA	17837	570-768-4960	768-4961	167-3
Central Tech 1720 S Main St *Web:* www.centraltech.edu	Sapulpa	OK	74066	918-224-9300		167-3
Central Texas College PO Box 1800 *TF:* 800-792-3348 ■ *Web:* www.online.ctcd.edu	Killeen	TX	76540	254-526-1296		162
Central Texas Communications Inc (CTC) 1012 Reilly St *TF:* 877-212-2598 ■ *Web:* www.centex.net	Goldthwaite	TX	76844	325-648-2237		224
Central Texas Corrugated LP 7200 Mars Dr	Waco	TX	76712	254-776-6902		548
Central Texas Electric Co-opeartive Inc (CTEC) 386 Friendship Ln PO Box 553 *TF:* 800-900-2832 ■ *Web:* www.ctec.coop	Fredericksburg	TX	78624	830-997-2126		245
Central Texas Iron Works 1100 Winchell Dr *Web:* www.ctiw.com	Waco	TX	76712	254-776-8000	772-5811	480
Central Texas Veterans Health Care System 1901 Veterans Memorial Dr *TF:* 800-423-2111 ■ *Web:* www.centraltexas.va.gov	Temple	TX	76504	254-778-4811		374-8
Central Textiles Inc 237 Mill Ave *Web:* ctextiles.com	Central	SC	29630	864-639-2491	639-4513	745-1
Central Transportation Systems 4105 Rio Bravo Ste 100 *TF:* 855-636-9780 ■ *Web:* www.centralsystems.com	El Paso	TX	79902	855-636-9780		449
Central Union High School District 351 W Ross Ave *Web:* www.cuhsd.net	El Centro	CA	92243	760-336-4500	353-3606	685
Central Utah Correctional Facility 255 E 300 N *Web:* corrections.utah.gov	Gunnison	UT	84634	435-528-6000		213
Central Valley Builders Supply 7030 Canby Blvd *Web:* www.cvbs.com	Reseda	CA	91335	818-343-4614	343-2904	191-1
Central Valley Community Bancorp 7100 N Financial Dr Ste 101 *NASDAQ: CVCY* ■ *TF:* 866-294-9588 ■ *Web:* www.cvcb.com	Fresno	CA	93720	559-298-1775		360-2
Central Valley Electric Co-opeartive Inc 1403 N 13th St PO Box 230 *Web:* www.cvecoop.org	Artesia	NM	88210	575-746-3571		245
Central Valley Financial Services 1822 W Kettleman Ln Ste 2A *Web:* www.centralvalleyfinancialservices.com	Lodi	CA	95242	209-992-4279	370-8152	393
Central Valley Machine Inc 1886 N 100 E *Web:* www.cvm-inc.com	North Logan	UT	84341	435-752-0934	752-0935	454
Central Van and Storage Inc 301 Jacobson Dr *TF:* 800-753-1898 ■ *Web:* www.centralvan.com	Poca	WV	25159	304-755-1904	755-1910	519
Central Vermont Chamber of Commerce 33 Stewart Rd *TF:* 877-887-3678 ■ *Web:* www.centralvt.com	Berlin	VT	05641	802-229-5711	229-5713	139
Central Vermont Home Health & Hospice 600 Granger Rd *TF:* 800-286-1219 ■ *Web:* www.cvhhh.org	Barre	VT	05641	802-223-1878		363
Central Vermont Medical Ctr (CVMC) 130 Fisher Rd *Web:* www.cvmc.org	Berlin	VT	05602	802-371-4100		374-3
Central Virginia Community College 3506 Wards Rd *Web:* centralvirginia.edu	Lynchburg	VA	24502	434-832-7600	832-7793	162
Central Virginia Electric Co-op 800 Co-op Way PO Box 247 *TF:* 800-367-2832 ■ *Web:* www.mycvec.com	Lovingston	VA	22949	434-263-8336	263-8339	245
Central Virginia Training Ctr 521 Colony Rd *TF:* 866-897-6095 ■ *Web:* www.cvtc.dbhds.virginia.gov	Madison Heights	VA	24572	434-947-6000		230
Central Washington Comprehensive Mental Health PO Box 959 *Web:* www.comphc.org	Yakima	WA	98907	509-575-4084		352
Central Washington Hospital 1201 S Miller St *TF:* 800-365-6428 ■ *Web:* www.confluencehealth.org	Wenatchee	WA	98801	509-662-1511		374-5
Central Washington University 400 E University Way *TF:* 866-298-4968 ■ *Web:* www.cwu.edu	Ellensburg	WA	98926	509-963-1111	963-3022	166
Central West Ballet Co (CWB) 5039 Pentecost Dr Ste B2 *Web:* cwballet.org	Modesto	CA	95356	209-576-8957	576-1308	573-1

Company / Address	Phone	Fax	Class
Central Woodwork Inc 870 Keough Rd Collierville TN 38017 *TF:* 800-788-3775 ■ *Web:* www.centralwoodwork.com	901-363-4141		499
Central Wyoming College 2660 Peck Ave Riverton WY 82501 *TF:* 800-735-8418 ■ *Web:* www.cwc.edu	307-855-2000	855-2092	162
Central Wyoming Fairgrounds 1700 Fairgrounds Rd Casper WY 82604 *Web:* www.centralwyomingfair.com	307-235-5775	266-4224	642
Central Wyoming Hospice & Transitions 319 S Wilson St Casper WY 82601 *Web:* cwhp.org	307-577-4832	577-4841	371
Centralia College 600 Centralia College Blvd Centralia WA 98531 *Web:* www.centralia.edu	360-736-9391	330-7503	162
Centralia Correctional Ctr 9330 Shattuc Rd PO Box 1266 Centralia IL 62801 *TF:* 844-258-9071 ■ *Web:* www2.illinois.gov	618-533-4111	533-4112	213
Centralia Square 201 S Pearl Centralia WA 98531 *Web:* www.myantiquemall.com	360-736-6406		460
Centralia-Chehalis Chamber of Commerce 500 NW Chamber of Commerce Way Chehalis WA 98532 *TF:* 800-525-3323 ■ *Web:* chamberway.com	360-748-8885	748-8763	139
Centralized Supply Chain Services LLC 8140 Ward Pkwy Kansas City MO 64114 *Web:* cscscoop.com	913-438-5552		466
CentralVac Intl 23455 Hellman Ave PO Box 259 Dollar Bay MI 49922 *TF:* 800-666-3133 ■ *Web:* www.centralvac.com	800-666-3133		788
CentraState Medical Ctr 901 W Main St Freehold NJ 07728 *Web:* www.centrastate.com	732-431-2000		374-3
Centratel 141 NW Greenwood Ave Ste 200 Bend OR 97701 *TF:* 800-664-7159 ■ *Web:* www.centratel.com	541-385-2616	388-2351	736
Centrav Inc 511 E Travelers Trl Burnsville MN 55337 *TF:* 800-874-2033 ■ *Web:* www.centrav.com	952-886-7650	886-7640	16
Centre at Salisbury 2300 N Salisbury Blvd Salisbury MD 21801 *Web:* www.centreatsalisbury.com	410-548-1600		460
Centre College 600 W Walnut St Danville KY 40422 *TF:* 800-423-6236 ■ *Web:* www.centre.edu	859-238-5350	238-5373	166
Centre County 420 Holmes St Ste 334 Bellefonte PA 16823 *Web:* centrecountypa.gov	814-355-6748	355-8742	338
Centre County Convention & Visitors Bureau 800 E Park Ave State College PA 16803 *TF:* 800-358-5466 ■ *Web:* happyvalley.com	814-231-1400	231-8123	206
Centre Daily Times 3400 E College Ave State College PA 16801 *TF:* 800-327-5500 ■ *Web:* www.centredaily.com	814-238-5000		532-2
Centre de sant et de services sociaux d'Argenteuil 145 Boul Providence Lachute QC J8H4C7 *Web:* www.santelaurentides.gouv.qc.ca	450-566-8558		374-2
Centre for Skills Development & Training, The 3350 S Service Rd Burlington ON L7N3M6 *TF:* 888-315-5521 ■ *Web:* www.centreforskills.ca	905-333-3499	634-2775	148
Centre for Well-Being at the Phoenician 6000 E Camelback Rd Scottsdale AZ 85251 *TF:* 800-843-2392 ■ *Web:* www.thephoenician.com	800-843-2392		707
Centre Hospitalier Hotel-Dieu d'Amos 622 4e Rue Ouest Amos QC J9T2S2 *Web:* csssea.ca	819-732-3341		374-2
Centre Hospitalier Mount Sinai 5690 Cavendish Blvd Montreal QC H4W1S7 *Web:* sinaimontreal.ca	514-369-2222	369-2225	374-2
Centre in the Square 101 Queen St N Kitchener ON N2H6P7 *TF:* 800-265-8977 ■ *Web:* centreinthesquare.com	519-578-1570		572
Centre Lane Partners LLC 1 Grand Central Pl 60 E 42nd St Ste 1250 New York NY 10165 *Web:* centrelanepartners.com	646-843-0710		528
Centre Street United Methodist Church 217 N Centre St Cumberland MD 21502 *Web:* centrestreetumc.com	301-722-5370		48-20
Centreville Savings Bank 1218 Main St West Warwick RI 02893 *Web:* www.centrevillebank.com	401-821-9100		70
CENTRIA 1005 Beaver Grade Rd Moon Township PA 15108 *TF:* 800-759-7474 ■ *Web:* www.centria.com	412-299-8000		480
Centric Business Systems Inc 10702 Red Run Blvd Owings Mills MD 21117 *TF:* 877-902-3301 ■ *Web:* centricbiz.com	410-902-3300		179
Centric Health Resources Inc 17877 Chesterfield Airport Rd Chesterfield MO 63005 *Web:* www.centrichealthresources.com	636-519-2400		237
Centric Parts Inc 14528 Bonelli St City of Industry CA 91746 *Web:* www.apcautotech.com	626-961-5775		60
Centric Software Inc 655 Campbell Technology Pkwy Ste 200 Campbell CA 95008 *Web:* www.centricsoftware.com	408-574-7802	866-5869	39
Centriq University 8700 State Line Rd Ste 200 Leawood KS 66206 *Web:* www.centriq.com	913-322-7000		631
Centris Consulting Inc 800 James Ave Scranton PA 18510 *Web:* centrisconsulting.com	570-963-1136		194
Centrix Builders Inc 160 S Linden Ave Ste 100 S San Francisco South San Francisco CA 94080 *Web:* www.centrixbuilders.com	650-876-9400	876-9404	186
Centrix Inc 770 River Rd Shelton CT 06484 *Web:* www.centrixdental.com	203-929-5582		228
Centrix Pharmaceutical Inc 951 Clint Moore Rd Ste A Boca Raton FL 33487 *TF:* 866-991-9870 ■ *Web:* www.cenrx.com	205-991-9870	991-9420	231
Centro De Servicios 525 "H" St Union City CA 94587 *Web:* www.centrodeservicios.org	510-489-4100		48-6
Centro Inc 950 N Bend Dr North Liberty IA 52317 *Web:* www.centroinc.com	319-626-3200	626-3203	604
Centro Ybor 1600 E Eigth Ave Tampa FL 33605 *Web:* centroybor.com	813-242-4660		50-6

Company / Address	Phone	Fax	Class
Centron Data Services Inc 1175 Devin Dr Norton Shores MI 49441 **Fax Area Code:* 231 ■ *TF:* 800-732-8787 ■ *Web:* www.centrondata.com	800-732-8787	799-0092*	5
Centron Industries Inc 441 W Victoria St Gardena CA 90248 *Web:* www.centronind.com	310-324-6443	324-7708	246
Centronia 1420 Columbia Rd NW Washington DC 20009 *Web:* centronia.org	202-332-4200	745-2562	685
Centrose LLC 918 Deming Way Madison WI 53717 *Web:* www.centrosepharma.com	608-836-0207		668
CENTROSOLAR America Inc 14350 N 87th St Ste 105 Scottsdale AZ 85260 **Fax Area Code:* 480 ■ *TF:* 877-348-2555 ■ *Web:* centrosolaramerica.com	877-348-2555	348-2556*	253
Centrus Energy Corp 6903 Rockledge Dr Bethesda MD 20817 *NYSE: LEU* ■ *TF:* 800-273-7754 ■ *Web:* www.centrusenergy.com	301-564-3200	564-3201	143
Centrus Group Inc 1653 Merriman Rd Ste 211 Akron OH 44313 *Web:* www.centrusllc.com	330-864-5800	865-9222	195
Centura College 8084 Rivers Ave North Charleston SC 29406 *TF:* 877-604-2121 ■ *Web:* www.centuracollege.edu	843-569-0889		167-3
Centura Health 9100 E Mineral Cir Centennial CO 80112 *Web:* www.centura.org	303-561-5000		371
Centuria Corp 1851 Alexander Bell Dr Ste 440 Reston VA 20191 *Web:* centuria.com	703-435-4600	435-9974	463
Centurion Counsel Inc 1282 Pacific Oaks Pl Escondido CA 92029 *Web:* centurioncounsel.com	760-471-8536		690
Centurion Data Systems N27w23957 Paul Rd Ste 100 Pewaukee WI 53072 *Web:* www.cendatsys.com	262-524-9290	524-1555	180
Centurion Industries Inc 1107 N Taylor Rd Garrett IN 46738 *TF:* 888-832-4466 ■ *Web:* www.centurionind.com	260-357-6665	357-6761	190
Centurion Investments Inc 18377 Edison Ave Chesterfield MO 63005 *Web:* www.avmats.com	636-532-2674		770
Centurion Products Inc 50 Van Buren St Nashville TN 37208 *Web:* www.centurionstone.com	615-256-6694		183
Centurion Service Group LLC 3325 Mt Prospect Rd Franklin Park IL 60131 *Web:* www.centurionservice.com	708-761-6655		475
Century 21 A Property Shoppe 2033 N Main St Salinas CA 93906 *Web:* apropertyshoppe.c21.com	831-443-2121	443-9436	652
CENTURY 21 Bolte Real Estate 124 E 2nd St Port Clinton OH 43452 *Web:* c21bolterealestate.com	419-732-3111		390
Century 21 Consolidated 2820 Flamingo Rd Las Vegas NV 89121 *Web:* homesforsale.century21.com	702-732-7282		652
Century 21 Department Stores 22 Cortlandt St New York NY 10007 *Web:* www.c21stores.com	212-227-9092		229
Century 21 Percy Fulton Ltd 2911 Kennedy Rd Toronto ON M1V1S8 *Web:* www.century21toronto.com	416-298-8200	298-6602	652
CENTURY 21 Sweyer & Assoc 1612 Military Cutoff Rd Ste 200 Wilmington NC 28403 *Web:* www.century21sweyer.com	910-256-0021	256-0000	652
Century 3-Plus LLC 2410 W Aero Park Ct Traverse City MI 49686 *Web:* www.centinc.com	231-946-7500		295
Century Aluminum 1 S Wacker Dr Ste 1000 Chicago IL 60606 *Web:* centuryaluminum.com	312-696-3101	696-3102	485
Century Bancorp Inc 400 Mystic Ave Medford MA 02155 *NASDAQ: CNBKA* ■ *TF:* 866-823-6887 ■ *Web:* www.centurybank.com	781-393-4160		360-2
Century Casinos Inc 2860 S Cir Dr Ste 350 Colorado Springs CO 80906 *NASDAQ: CNTY* ■ *TF:* 888-966-2257 ■ *Web:* www.cnty.com	719-527-8300		132
Century City Chamber of Commerce 2029 Century Pk E Los Angeles CA 90067 *Web:* centurycitycc.com	310-553-2222	553-4623	139
Century City Fitness Club & Spa 10250 Santa Monica Century City CA 90067 *Web:* www.equinox.com	310-552-0420		707
Century City Flower Mart 9551 W Pico Blvd Los Angeles CA 90035 *Web:* centurycityflowermarket.com	310-277-6737		292
Century College 3300 Century Ave N White Bear Lake MN 55110 *TF:* 800-228-1978 ■ *Web:* www.century.edu	651-779-3300	773-1796	162
Century Companies Inc 510 1st Ave N Lewistown MT 59457 *Web:* www.centuryci.com	406-535-1200	535-1205	188-4
Century Concrete Inc 1364 Air Rail Ave Virginia Beach VA 23455 *Web:* www.centuryconcreteinc.com	757-460-5366	460-3296	186
Century Ctr Martin Luther King Jr Blvd 120 South Dr South Bend IN 46601 *Web:* www.centurycenter.org	574-235-9711	235-9185	205
Century Direct LLC 15 Enter Ln Islandia NY 11749 **Fax Area Code:* 718 ■ *Web:* www.centurydirect.net	212-763-0600	349-9528*	5
Century Distributors Inc 15710 Crabbs Branch Way Rockville MD 20855 *Web:* centurydist.com	301-212-9100	212-9681	335
Century Engineering Inc 10710 Gilroy Rd Hunt Valley MD 21031 *TF:* 800-318-6867 ■ *Web:* www.centuryeng.com	443-589-2400		261
Century Equipment Inc 5959 Angola Rd PO Box 352889 Toledo OH 43615 *TF:* 800-346-0066 ■ *Web:* www.centuryequip.com	419-865-7400	865-8215	472
Century Fasteners Corp 50-20 Ireland St Elmhurst NY 11373 *TF:* 800-221-0769 ■ *Web:* www.centuryfasteners.com	718-446-5000	426-8119	246

Phone | Fax | Class

Century Foods Intl 400 Century Ct. Sparta WI 54656 608-269-1900 296-27
Web: www.centuryfoods.com

Century Foundation, The
1 Whitehall St 15th Fl. New York NY 10004 212-535-4441 535-7534 634
Web: tcf.org

Century Foundry Inc 339 W Hovey Ave. Muskegon MI 49444 231-733-1572 739-5572 492
Web: centuryfoundry.com

Century Furniture LLC 401 11th St NW. Hickory NC 28601 828-328-1851 328-2176 319-2
TF: 800-852-5552 ■ *Web:* www.centuryfurniture.com

Century Graphics & Metals Inc
550 S N Lake Blvd Ste 1000. Altamonte Springs FL 32701 800-373-5330 701
TF: 800-373-5330 ■ *Web:* www.centurygraphics.com

Century Group Inc, The
1106 W Napoleon St PO Box 228. Sulphur LA 70664 337-527-5266 527-8028 183
TF: 800-527-5232 ■ *Web:* www.centurygrp.com

Century Home Healthcare
1601 Rainbow Dr. Richardson TX 75081 972-235-6700 699-7598 363
Web: centuryhomehealth.com

Century Hotel South Beach
140 Ocean Dr. Miami Beach FL 33139 305-674-8855 379
Web: www.centurymiamibeach.com

Century II Performing Arts & Convention Ctr
225 W Douglas Ave. Wichita KS 67202 316-303-8000 205
Web: www.century2.org

Century Industries Inc
1130 W Grove Ave. Orange CA 92865 714-637-3691 637-9542 454
Web: centuryindustriesinc.com

Century Industries Inc PO Box C. Sellersburg IN 47172 812-246-3371 246-5446 499
Web: www.centuryindustries.com

Century Insurance Group Inc
550 Polaris Pkwy Ste 300. Westerville OH 43082 614-895-2000 832-8793* 391-5
*Fax Area Code: 800 ■ *TF:* 800-878-7389 ■ *Web:* www.home.centurysurety.com

Century Junior High School
10801 W 159th St. Orland Park IL 60467 708-364-3500 685
Web: www.orland135.org

Century Kitchen Inc 106 Bethlehem Pk. Colmar PA 18915 215-822-1300 286
Web: www.centurykitchens.com

Century Maintenance & Supply Corp
4309 Broadway 184th St. New York NY 10033 212-927-9000 351
Web: centuryhardware.com

Century Manufacturing Inc
9750 E 50th St N. Wichita KS 67226 316-636-5423 608
Web: centurymfg.com

Century Marketing Solutions LLC
100 Centurylink Dr. Monroe LA 71203 800-256-6000 627
TF: 800-256-6000 ■ *Web:* www.centurymarketingsolutions.com

Century Martial Art Supply Inc
1000 Century Blvd. Oklahoma City OK 73110 405-732-2226 711
TF: 800-626-2787 ■ *Web:* www.centurymartialarts.com

Century Mechanical Contractors Inc
3008 Wichita Ct. Fort Worth TX 76140 817-293-3803 610
Web: centurymech.com

Century Media
2323 W El Segundo Blvd. Hawthorne CA 90250 323-418-1400 657
Web: www.centurymedia.com

Century Metal Spinning Company Inc
430 Meyer Rd. Bensenville IL 60106 630-595-3900 595-3933 483
Web: www.centurymetalspinning.com

Century Mold Company Inc
25 Vantage Point Dr. Rochester NY 14624 585-352-8600 596
Web: www.centurymold.com

Century Mortgage
14 Corporate Plz Ste 120. Newport Beach CA 92660 949-759-3610 759-3543 509
Web: www.fixyourmortgage.com

Century National Bank 14 S 5th St. Zanesville OH 43701 740-454-2521 70
TF: 800-548-3557 ■ *Web:* parknationalbank.com

Century Packaging Inc
42 Edgeboro Rd. East Brunswick NJ 08816 732-249-6600 561
Web: www.centurypackaginginc.com

Century Plaza Hotel & Spa
1015 Burrard St. Vancouver BC V6Z1Y5 604-687-0575 379
TF: 800-663-1818 ■ *Web:* www.century-plaza.com

Century Plumbing Inc 901 SW 69th Ave. Miami FL 33144 305-261-4731 612
Web: www.centurywholesale.us

Century Ready-Mix Corp
3250 Armand St PO Box 4420. Monroe LA 71211 318-322-4444 322-7299 182
TF: 800-732-3969 ■ *Web:* centuryreadymix.com

Century Roof Tile 23135 Saklan Rd. Hayward CA 94545 510-780-9489 191-1
TF: 888-233-7548 ■ *Web:* www.centuryrooftile.com

Century Snacks 5560 E Slauson Ave. Commerce CA 90040 323-278-9578 297-8
Web: www.newcenturysnacks.com

Century Spring Corp 222 E 16th St. Los Angeles CA 90015 213-749-1466 749-3802 719
TF: 800-237-5225 ■ *Web:* www.centuryspring.com

Century Steel Erectors Co
210 Washington Ave. Dravosburg PA 15034 412-469-8800 469-0813 189-14
TF: 888-601-8801 ■ *Web:* www.centurysteel.com

Century Suites Hotel 300 SR-446. Bloomington IN 47401 812-336-7777 379
TF: 800-766-5446 ■ *Web:* www.centurysuites.com

Century Tile Supply Co
747 E Roosevelt Rd. Lombard IL 60148 630-495-2300 237-8257* 290
*Fax Area Code: 773 ■ *TF:* 888-845-3968 ■ *Web:* www.century-tile.com

Century Tire Inc 5355 E 39th Ave. Denver CO 80207 303-455-3302 455-2037 755
TF: 800-634-8473 ■ *Web:* www.centurytireinc.com

Century Tool & Gage Co 200 S Alloy Dr. Fenton MI 48430 810-629-0784 629-9284 60
Web: www.toolingtechgroup.com

Century Tool Inc 21495 147th Ave N. Rogers MN 55374 763-428-2168 454
Web: www.century-tool.com

Century Village
14653 E Park St PO Box 153. Burton OH 44021 440-834-1492 520
Web: www.centuryvillagemuseum.org

Century Wealth Management LLC
1770 Kirby Pkwy Ste 117. Memphis TN 38138 901-850-5532 401
TF: 855-850-5532 ■ *Web:* www.centurywealth.com

Century Wireline Services
1223 S 71st E Ave. Tulsa OK 74112 918-838-9811 838-1532 536
Web: www.centurywirelineservices.com

CenturyTel Inc 100 Centurylink Dr. Monroe LA 71203 318-388-9000 176
NYSE: CTL ■ *Web:* www.centurylink.com

Cenveo Inc
200 First Stamford Pl 2nd Fl. Stamford CT 06902 203-595-3000 263
OTC: CVOVQ ■ *Web:* www.cenveo.com

Cenvill Recreation Inc
1601 Forum Pl Ste 500. West Palm Beach FL 33401 561-640-3114 463
Web: www.cenrec.com

CEO (Center for Equal Opportunity)
14 Pidgeon Hill Dr Ste 500. Sterling VA 20165 703-421-5443 421-6401 634
Web: www.ceousa.org

CEO Inc 412 Louise Ave. Charlotte NC 28204 704-372-4701 193
TF: 888-242-1755 ■ *Web:* ceoinc.com

CEOExpress Company LLC
1 Boston Pl Ste 2600. Boston MA 02108 617-482-1200 299-8649 397
Web: www.ceoexpress.com

CEP Forensic Inc
1345 Boul Louis-xiv Blvd. Quebec City QC G2L1M4 418-622-4480 622-6002 261
TF: 855-622-4480 ■ *Web:* cep-experts.ca

CEPA Gallery 617 Main St. Buffalo NY 14203 716-856-2717 270-0184 520
Web: www.cepagallery.org

Cepeda Systems & Software Analysis Inc
2225 Drake Ave SW Ste 8. Huntsville AL 35805 256-428-8186 179
Web: www.cepedasystems.com

Cephasonics Inc
160 Saratoga Ave Ste 180. Santa Clara CA 95051 408-249-4629 201
Web: www.cephasonics.com

Cepheid 904 E Caribbean Dr. Sunnyvale CA 94089 408-541-4191 541-4192 419
TF: 888-838-3222 ■ *Web:* www.cepheid.com

Cepstral LLC
1801 E Carson St 2nd Fl. Pittsburgh PA 15203 412-432-0400 177
Web: www.cepstral.com

Ceptaris Therapeutics Inc
101 Lindenwood Dr Ste 400. Malvern PA 19355 610-975-9290 231

Cequence Energy Ltd
215 Ninth Ave SW Ste 1400. Calgary AB T2P1K3 403-229-3050 536
TF: 866-764-4569 ■ *Web:* www.cequence-energy.com

Cequent Towing Products
47774 Anchor Ct W. Plymouth MI 48170 800-521-0510 763
TF: 800-521-0510 ■ *Web:* www.draw-tite.com

Cequint Inc 1011 W Ave Ste 800. Seattle WA 98104 206-264-1909 177
Web: www.cequint.com

CERAGEM Company Inc
3699 Wilshire Blvd Ste 930. Los Angeles CA 90010 213-480-7070 480-7071 475
TF: 800-903-9333 ■ *Web:* www.ceragem.com

Ceragon Networks Ltd
851 International Pkwy Ste 130. Richardson TX 75081 201-845-6955 494-6080* 735
NASDAQ: CRNT ■ *Fax Area Code: 214 ■ *Web:* www.ceragon.com

Ceraml & Associates Inc
404 Fifth Ave. New York NY 10018 212-370-1776 370-1736 261
Web: www.ceramiassociates.com

Ceramic Industry Inc (CI) 6075-B Glick Rd. Powell OH 43065 847-763-9538 637-9
Web: www.ceramicindustry.com

Ceramic Tech Inc 46211 Research Ave. Fremont CA 94539 510-252-8500 252-8700 454
Web: www.ceramictechinc.com

Ceramic Technology Inc
606 Wardell Industrial Pk. Cedar Bluff VA 24609 800-437-1142 567
TF: 800-437-1142 ■ *Web:* ceramictech.com

Ceramo Company Inc 681 Kasten Dr. Jackson MO 63755 573-243-3138 243-3130 334
TF: 800-325-8303 ■ *Web:* www.ceramousa.com

CeramTec North America Corp
Technology Pl. Laurens SC 29360 864-682-3215 682-1140 249
TF: 800-752-7325 ■ *Web:* www.ceramtec.com

Cerberus Capital Management LP
875 3rd Ave. New York NY 10022 212-891-2100 405
Web: www.cerberus.com

CERC (Columbia Environmental Research Ctr)
4200 New Haven Rd. Columbia MO 65201 573-875-5399 876-1896 668
TF: 888-283-7626 ■ *Web:* www.usgs.gov

Cereal Byproducts Co
14500 S Outer Forty Rd Ste 502. Town and Country MO 63017 314-781-9600 781-9601 276
TF: 800-237-3258 ■ *Web:* www.cerealbyproducts.com

Ceredo-Kenova Public Library
1200 Oak St. Kenova WV 25530 304-453-2462 434-3
Web: www.wcpl.lib.wv.us

Ceres Chamber of Commerce
2491 Lawrence St. Ceres CA 95307 209-537-2601 139
Web: www.cereschamber.com

Ceres Consulting LLC
3808 Cookson Rd. East Saint Louis IL 62201 618-271-7903 313
Web: www.ceresbarge.com

Ceres Courier 138 S Center St. Turlock CA 95380 209-537-5032 532-4
Web: www.cerescourier.com

Ceres Environmental Services Inc
3825 85th Ave N. Minneapolis MN 55443 800-218-4424 228-5636* 683
*Fax Area Code: 866 ■ *TF:* 800-218-4424 ■ *Web:* www.ceresenvironmental.com

Ceres Terminals Inc
2 Tower Center Blvd. East Brunswick NJ 08816 201-974-3800 974-3850 465
Web: www.ceresglobal.com

Cereus Graphics Printing Co
2950-2 E Bldg Broadway Rd. Phoenix AZ 85040 602-445-0680 627
Web: www.cereusgraphics.com

Cerex Advanced Fabrics Inc
610 Chemstrand Rd. Cantonment FL 32533 850-937-3365 937-3328 745-6
TF: 800-572-3739 ■ *Web:* www.cerex.com

Ceri Boutique 103 Union St. Newton Center MA 02459 617-527-6710 157-6
Web: www.ceriboutique.com

Ceridian Benefits Services Inc
3201 34th St S. Saint Petersburg FL 33711 800-729-7655 865-3648* 195
*Fax Area Code: 727 ■ *TF:* 800-689-7893 ■ *Web:* www.ceridian.com

Cerini & Assoc
3340 Veterans Memorial Hwy. Bohemia NY 11716 631-582-1600 582-1714 2
Web: ceriniandassociates.com

Cerium Networks Inc 1636 W 1st. Spokane WA 99201 877-423-7486 35
TF: 877-423-7486 ■ *Web:* www.ceriumnetworks.com

Cermak Nakajima LLP
127 S Peyton St Ste 200. Alexandria VA 22314 703-717-9350 717-9392 41
Web: cnmiplaw.com

Cermetek Microelectronics Inc
374 Turquoise St. Milpitas CA 95035 408-752-5000 942-1346 173-3
TF: 800-882-6271 ■ *Web:* www.cermetek.com

	City	State	ZIP	Phone	Fax	Class
Cerner Corp 2800 Rockcreek Pkwy *NASDAQ:* CERN ■ *Web:* www.cerner.com	Kansas City	MO	64117	816-221-1024	579-0550	178-11
Ceros Financial Services Inc 1445 Research Blvd Ste 530 *TF:* 866-842-3356 ■ *Web:* www.cerosfs.com	Rockville	MD	20850	866-842-3356		690
Cerow & Company CPAS PA 422 Miami Ave Ste 3	Indialantic	FL	32903	321-242-2511		2
Cerrell Associates Inc 320 N Larchmont Blvd *Web:* www.cerrell.com	Los Angeles	CA	90004	323-466-3445		636
Cerritos Center for the Performing Arts 18000 Park Plaza Dr *Web:* www.cerritoscenter.com	Cerritos	CA	90703	562-916-8501	916-8514	572
Cerritos Chamber of Commerce 13259 South St *Web:* www.cerritos.org	Cerritos	CA	90703	562-467-0800	467-0840	139
Cerritos College 11110 Alondra Blvd *Web:* www.cerritos.edu	Norwalk	CA	90650	562-860-2451	467-5068	162
Cerro Coso Community College 101 College Pkwy *TF:* 888-537-6932 ■ *Web:* www.cerrocoso.edu	Mammoth Lakes	CA	93546	760-934-2875	924-1613	162
Cerro Fabricated Products Inc 300 Triangle Dr *Web:* www.cerrofabricated.com	Weyers Cave	VA	24486	540-234-9252	234-8416	482
Cerro Flow Products Inc PO Box 66800 *TF:* 888-237-7611 ■ *Web:* www.cerroflow.com	Saint Louis	MO	63166	618-337-6000	337-6958	490
Cerro Gordo County 220 N Washington Ave *Web:* www.cgcounty.org	Mason City	IA	50401	641-421-3065	421-3139	338
Cerro Wire & Cable Company Inc 1099 Thompson Rd SE *TF:* 800-523-3869 ■ *Web:* www.cerrowire.com	Hartselle	AL	35640	256-773-2522		813
Cerrone, Graham & Shepherd PC 446 Main St 10th Fl *Web:* cgscpas.com	Worcester	MA	01608	508-754-8512		2
Cersosimo Lumber Company Inc 1103 Vernon St *Web:* www.cersosimolumber.com	Brattleboro	VT	05301	802-254-4508	254-5691	683
Certa Law Group Incorporated PS 320 Dayton St Ste 108 *Web:* certalaw.com	Edmonds	WA	98020	206-838-2500		41
Certain Affinity Inc 7620 Guadalupe St *Web:* www.certainaffinity.com	Austin	TX	78752	512-524-8510		322
CertainTeed Corp 750 E Swedesford Rd *TF:* 800-782-8777 ■ *Web:* www.certainteed.com	Valley Forge	PA	19482	610-341-7000		389
CertaPro Painters Ltd 150 Green Tree Rd Ste 1003 *TF:* 800-689-7271 ■ *Web:* certapro.com	Oaks	PA	19456	800-689-7271		189-8
Certec Consulting Inc 4037 N Harvard Ave *Web:* www.certecinc.com	Arlington Heights	IL	60004	847-253-8968		180
Certex USA Inc 1721 W Culver St *TF:* 800-225-2103 ■ *Web:* www.certex.com	Phoenix	AZ	85007	602-271-9048		492
Certicom Corp 4701 Tahoe Blvd Bldg A *TF:* 800-561-6100 ■ *Web:* blackberry.certicom.com	Mississauga	ON	L4W0B5	905-507-4220	507-4230	178-12
Certif-a-gift Co, The 1625 E Algonquin Rd *TF:* 800-545-5156 ■ *Web:* certif-a-gift.com	Arlington Heights	IL	60005	800-545-5156		459
Certified Alloy Products Inc 3245 Cherry Ave PO Box 90 *Web:* doncasters.com	Long Beach	CA	90801	562-595-6621		485
Certified Business Brokers Ltd 12141 Wickchester Ln Ste 200 *Web:* certifiedbb.com	Houston	TX	77092	713-680-1200		41
Certified Communications Inc (CCI) 5213 Coconut Creek Pky *Web:* www.certifiedcommunications.com	Margate	FL	33063	954-974-4000	974-4701	194
Certified Enameling Inc 3342 Emery St *Web:* www.certifiedenameling.com	Los Angeles	CA	90023	323-264-4403		481
Certified Financial Planner Board of Standards Inc 1425 K St NW Ste 500 *TF:* 800-487-1497 ■ *Web:* www.cfp.net	Washington	DC	20005	202-379-2200	379-2299	49-2
Certified Freight Logistics Inc 1344 White Ct *TF:* 800-592-5906 ■ *Web:* driveforcfl.com	Santa Maria	CA	93458	805-925-9900	346-7803	311
Certified Grinding and Machine Inc 47 Scrantom St *Web:* www.certifiedgrinding.com	Rochester	NY	14605	585-423-0990	423-0728	393
Certified Horsemanship Assn (CHA) 1795 Alysheba Way Ste 7102 *TF:* 800-399-0138 ■ *Web:* cha.horse	Lexington	KY	40509	859-259-3399	255-0726	48-3
Certified Languages International LLC 4800 SW Macadam Ave Ste 400 *TF:* 800-362-3241 ■ *Web:* www.certifiedlanguages.com	Portland	OR	97239	800-362-3241		768
Certified Metal Finishing Inc 1420 SW 28th Ave *Web:* www.certifiedmetalfinishing.com	Pompano Beach	FL	33069	954-979-0707	979-4158	481
Certified Mint Inc 3800 N Central Ave 11th Fl *TF:* 800-528-1380 ■ *Web:* www.certifiedmint.com	Phoenix	AZ	85012	602-234-2300		792
Certified Oil Corp 949 King Ave *Web:* www.certifiedoil.com	Columbus	OH	43212	614-421-7500		68
Certified Plumbing of Brevard 1434 Norman St NE Ste 101	Palm Bay	FL	32907	321-676-0812		610
Certified Power Inc 970 Campus Dr *TF:* 888-905-7411 ■ *Web:* www.certifiedpower.com	Mundelein	IL	60060	847-573-3800	573-3832	620
Certified Restoration DryCleaning Network LLC 2060 Coolidge Hwy *TF:* 800-963-2736 ■ *Web:* www.crdn.com	Berkley	MI	48072	800-963-2736		310
Certified Safety Manufacturing Inc 1400 Chestnut Ave *TF:* 800-854-7474 ■ *Web:* certifiedsafetymfg.com	Kansas City	MO	64127	800-854-7474		476
Certified Slings & Supply Inc PO Box 180127 *TF:* 800-486-5542 ■ *Web:* www.certifiedslings.com	Casselberry	FL	32718	407-331-6677	260-9196	385
Certified Stainless Service Inc 2704 Railroad Ave *Web:* www.west-mark.com	Ceres	CA	95307	209-537-4747		480
Certified Transmission 1801 S 54th St *Web:* certifiedtransmission.com	Omaha	NE	68106	402-558-2117		62-6
Certified Transportation Services Inc 1038 N Custer St *Web:* ctsbus.com	Santa Ana	CA	92701	714-835-8676		107
Certipay 199 Ave B NW Ste 270 *TF:* 800-422-3782 ■ *Web:* www.certipay.com	Winter Haven	FL	33881	863-299-2400	299-2131	2
Certis USA LLC 9145 Guilford Rd Ste 175 **Fax Area Code:* 301 ■ *TF:* 800-250-5024 ■ *Web:* www.certisusa.com	Columbia	MD	21046	800-250-5024	604-7015*	280
Certus Financial Services 7650 SW Beveland Ste 110 *Web:* certusfs.com	Tigard	OR	97223	503-906-5220		390
Certus Intl 9 Cedarwood Dr Ste 8 *TF:* 800-969-3218 ■ *Web:* certusintl.com	Bedford	NH	03110	603-627-1212	627-8484	194
Cerus Corp 2550 Stanwell Dr *NASDAQ:* CERS ■ *Web:* www.cerus.com	Concord	CA	94520	925-288-6000	288-6001	85
Cerwin-Vega Inc 3000 SW 42nd St *Web:* www.cerwinvega.com	Hollywood	FL	33312	954-316-1501	316-1590	52
CES (Community Eldercare Services LLC) PO Box 3667 *TF:* 877-461-1062 ■ *Web:* www.cesltc.com	Tupelo	MS	38803	877-461-1062		463
CES (Cascade Earth Sciences) 2902 W Main St *Web:* www.cascade-earth.com	Visalia	CA	93291	559-732-3665	732-3720	538
CES (Computer Enhancement Systems Inc) 8038-D Liberty Rd *Web:* www.cesitservice.com	Frederick	MD	21701	301-620-1580	620-1586	174
CES Machine Products Inc 8880 Double Diamond Pkwy *Web:* www.cesmachine.com	Reno	NV	89521	775-852-0900		454
CES Mail Communications Inc 2319 Atlantic Ave *Web:* www.cesmail.com	Raleigh	NC	27604	919-833-5785	833-4649	5
CES USA Inc 235 Remington Blvd Ste H *Web:* www.cesltd.com	Bolingbrook	IL	60440	630-296-8939	296-8940	463
Cesar Chavez Foundation, The 4300 Stine Rd Ste 209 *Web:* www.campesina.net	Bakersfield	CA	93313	661-837-0745		645-14
Cesare Inc 7108 S Alton Way Bldg B *Web:* cesareinc.com	Centennial	CO	80112	303-220-0300		261
Cesco Inc 7251 Cross County Rd *Web:* www.blastandpaint.com	North Charleston	SC	29418	843-760-3000	760-3500	385
CESD Talent Agency Inc 10635 Santa Monica Blvd Ste 130 *Web:* www.cesdtalent.com	Los Angeles	CA	90025	310-475-2111		731
CESI Civil-Geotechnical-Surveying 45 Spring St *Web:* www.cesicgs.com	Concord	NC	28025	704-786-5404		727
Cesium Telecom Inc 5798 Ferrier *TF:* 877-798-8686 ■ *Web:* shop.cesiumonline.com	Montreal	QC	H4P1M7	514-798-8686		736
Ceso Inc 3601 Rigby Rd Ste 300 *Web:* www.cesoinc.com	Miamisburg	OH	45342	937-435-8584		261
Cessco Fabrication & Engineering Ltd 7310-99 St *TF:* 800-272-9698 ■ *Web:* cessco.ca	Edmonton	AB	T6E3R8	780-433-9531	432-7899	480
Cessford Construction Co 3808 Old Hwy 61 *Web:* www.omgmidwest.com	Burlington	IA	52601	319-753-2297	753-0926	503-5
Cessna Aircraft Co 1 Cessna Blvd *Web:* cessna.txtav.com	Wichita	KS	67215	316-517-6000		20
CET 1223 Central Pkwy *TF:* 800-808-0445 ■ *Web:* www.cetconnect.org	Cincinnati	OH	45214	513-381-4033	381-7520	741-30
Cetac Technologies Inc 14306 Industrial Rd *TF:* 800-369-2822 ■ *Web:* www.teledynecetac.com	Omaha	NE	68144	402-733-2829	733-5292	419
CETCO Energy Services 1001 Ochsner Blvd Ste 425 *TF:* 800-527-9948 ■ *Web:* www.mineralstech.com	Covington	LA	70433	985-871-4700		538
CETECH-Triumph 11325 Random Hills Rd Ste 340 **Fax Area Code:* 571 ■ *Web:* www.cetech-triumph.com	Fairfax	VA	22030	703-563-4400	432-0559*	177
Cetek Inc 2235 W 76th St *Web:* cetekinc.com	Davenport	IA	52806	563-386-4800		261
Cetera Financial Group Inc 200 N Sepulveda Blvd Ste 1200 *TF:* 866-489-3100 ■ *Web:* www.cetera.com	El Segundo	CA	90245	866-489-3100		690
Ceto and Associates 3325 Paddocks Pky Ste 400 *TF:* 866-227-1361 ■ *Web:* www.ceto.com	Suwanee	GA	30024	678-297-1151	297-1127	194
Cetylite Industries 9051 River Rd *TF:* 800-257-7740 ■ *Web:* www.cetylite.com	Pennsauken Township	NJ	08110	856-665-6111		231
Cev Multimedia Ltd 1020 SE Loop 289 *TF:* 877-610-5017 ■ *Web:* www.icevonline.com	Lubbock	TX	79404	877-610-5017		514
CEVA Ground US LP 15390 Vickery Dr **Fax Area Code:* 866	Houston	TX	77032	281-227-5000	766-0165*	311
CEVA Inc 1174 Castro St Ste 210 *Web:* www.ceva-dsp.com	Mountain View	CA	94040	650-417-7900	417-7995	696
Ceva Logistics US Holdings Inc 10751 Deerwood Park Blvd 201 *Web:* www.cevalogistics.com	Jacksonville	FL	32256	904-928-1400		311
CF (Carolyn Fabrics Inc) 1948 W Green Dr **Fax Area Code:* 336 ■ *TF:* 800-333-8400 ■ *Web:* www.carolynfabrics.com	High Point	NC	27261	800-333-8400	887-2895*	594
CF Bank 7000 N High St *Web:* cfbankonline.com	Worthington	OH	43085	330-532-5070		70
CF Energy Inc 32 S Unionville Ave Unit 2036-2038 *Web:* www.cfenergy.com	Markham	ON	L3R9S6	647-313-0066	313-0088	536
CF Evans Construction 125 Regional Pkwy Ste 200 *Web:* cfevans.com	Orangeburg	SC	29118	803-536-6443		186

Phone | Fax | Class

CF Industries Inc 4 Pkwy N Ste 400 .... Deerfield IL 60015 847-405-2400 405-2711 280
TF: 800-462-8565 ■ *Web:* www.cfindustries.com

CF Jordan Construction LLC
221 N Kansas St Ste 1300 .... El Paso TX 79901 915-877-3333 877-3999 186
Web: www.jordanfosterconstruction.com

CF Martin & Company Inc
510 Sycamore St PO Box 329.................Nazareth PA 18064 610-759-2837 759-5757 527
TF: 888-433-9177 ■ *Web:* www.martinguitar.com

CF Napa 2787 Napa Valley Coporate Dr .... Napa CA 94558 707-265-1891 265-1899 393
Web: cfnapa.com

CF Roark Welding & Engineering Company Inc
136 N Green St ....Brownsburg IN 46112 317-852-3163 256
Web: www.roarkfab.com

CFA (Consumer Federation of America)
1620 I St NW Ste 200.....................Washington DC 20006 202-387-6121 265-7989 48-10
Web: consumerfed.org

CFA Institute 915 E High St.............. Charlottesville VA 22902 434-951-5499 951-5262 49-2
TF: 800-247-8132 ■ *Web:* www.cfainstitute.org

CFAI-FM 17 rue Costigan .... Edmundston NB E3V1W7 506-737-5060 737-5084 647
Web: www.cfai.fm

CFAITC (California Foundation for Agriculture in the Classroom)
2300 River Plaza Dr .... Sacramento CA 95833 916-561-5625 561-5697 423
TF: 800-700-2482 ■ *Web:* learnaboutag.org

CFAN Co 1000 Technology Way .... San Marcos TX 78666 512-353-2832 22
Web: c-fan.com

CFAR-AM 316 Green St....................... Flin Flon MB R8A0H2 204-687-3469 647
Web: www.flinflononline.com

CFBank 7000 N High St ....Worthington OH 43085 614-334-7979 666-7959* 360-2
NASDAQ: CFBK ■ **Fax Area Code:* 330 ■ *TF:* 866-668-4606 ■ *Web:* www.cfbankonline.com

CFBC-AM 226 Union St .... Saint John NB E2L1B1 506-658-5100 647
Web: www.cfbcradio.com

CFBV-AM 1139 Queen St .... Smithers BC V0J2N0 250-847-2521 647
Web: www.mybulkleylakesnow.com

CFC Canadoil Inc
8000 Market St Ste 100 ....Houston TX 77029 713-676-0077 492
Web: www.cfcfittings.com

CFC Inc 320 W Eigth St Ste 200 .... Bloomington IN 47402 812-332-0053 333-4680 653
Web: www.cfcproperties.com

CFC International Inc
500 State St .... Chicago Heights IL 60411 708-891-3456 758-5989 3
TF: 800-393-4505 ■ *Web:* www.cfcintl.com

CFCA (Christian Foundation for Children & Aging)
1 Elmwood Ave..........................Kansas City KS 66103 913-384-6500 384-2211 48-6
TF: 800-875-6564 ■ *Web:* www.unbound.org

CFCC (Cuyahoga Falls Chamber of Commerce)
151 Portage Trl Ste 1 .... Cuyahoga Falls OH 44221 330-929-6756 929-4278 139
TF: 800-248-4040 ■ *Web:* www.cfchamber.com

CFCO-AM 117 Keil Dr S .... Chatham-Kent ON N7M3H3 519-354-2200 354-2880 647
Web: www.country929.com

CFCP-FM 202-910 Fitzgerald Ave.............. Courtenay BC V9N2R5 250-334-2421 334-1977 647
Web: www.mycomoxvalleynow.com

CFCU Community Credit Union
1030 Craft Rd................................Ithaca NY 14850 607-257-8500 219
TF: 800-428-8340 ■ *Web:* mycfcu.com

CFDA Fashion Incubator
65 Bleecker St 11th Fl.......................New York NY 10012 212-302-1821 393
Web: cfda.com

CFDV-FM 2840 Bremmer Ave.................. Red Deer AB T4R1M9 403-343-7105 343-2573 647
Web: www.1067thedrive.fm

CFE Equipment Corp 818 Widgeon Rd............Norfolk VA 23513 757-858-2660 853-4280 358
Web: www.cfeequipment.com

CFFR-AM 535 7th Ave SW .... Calgary AB T2P0Y4 403-291-0000 647
Web: www.660citynews.com

CFG (Creative Financial Group)
16 Campus Blvd..................... Newtown Square PA 19073 610-325-6100 325-6240 401
TF: 800-893-4824 ■ *Web:* www.1creative.com

CFG Community Bank
1422 Clarkview Rd ....Baltimore MD 21209 410-823-0500 70
Web: www.thecfgbank.com

CFG Investments Inc
17220 Newhope St 224 .... Fountain Valley CA 92708 714-299-4096 652
Web: cfginvestments.com

CFGQ-FM 200 3320 17th Ave SW................ Calgary AB T3E0B4 403-444-4319 647
Web: www.q107fm.ca

CFHS (Canadian Federation of Humane Societies)
30 Concourse Gate Ste 102 .... Ottawa ON K2E7V7 613-224-8072 48-3
TF: 888-678-2347 ■ *Web:* www.humanecanada.ca

CFI (Coatings For Industry Inc)
319 Township Line Rd .... Souderton PA 18964 215-723-0919 723-0911 481
TF: 877-723-0919 ■ *Web:* www.coating4ind.com

CFI (Capital Forensics Inc)
1530 E Dundee Rd Ste 333..................... Palatine IL 60074 847-392-0900 392-2990 194
TF: 888-970-1700 ■ *Web:* www.capitalforensics.com

CFI (Cedar Fort Inc) 2373 W 700 S ....Springville UT 84663 801-489-4084 489-1097 637-2
TF: 800-759-2665 ■ *Web:* www.cedarfort.com

CFI Group 625 Avis Dr .... Ann Arbor MI 48108 734-930-9090 194
Web: cfigroup.com

CFI Mechanical Inc 6109 Brittmoore Rd ....Houston TX 77041 832-467-8200 467-8203 610
Web: cfimechanical.com

CFI Tire Service
1520 E S Omaha Bridge Rd .... Council Bluffs IA 51503 712-388-9744 751
Web: cfitirecb.com

CFJ Manufacturing
701 820 Blvd Ste 145.......................Fort Worth TX 76106 800-964-6308 226
TF: 800-964-6308 ■ *Web:* www.cfjmanufacturinglp.com

CFJC Today 460 Pemberton Ter .... Kamloops BC V2C1T5 250-372-3322 647
Web: www.cfjctoday.com

CFL (Canton Free Library) 8 Park St.............Canton NY 13617 315-386-3712 386-4131 434-3
Web: www.cantonfreelibrary.org

CFL (Center for Literacy)
399 Market St Ste 201 ....Philadelphia PA 19106 215-474-1235 48-6
Web: www.centerforliteracy.org

CFL Inc PO Box 358 ....Pebble Beach CA 93953 831-622-0946 45
Web: www.fragrancewholesale.com

CFM Partners Inc
1701 Rhode Island Ave NW ....Washington DC 20036 202-364-2380 194
Web: www.cfmpartners.com

CFMA (Construction Financial Management Assn)
100 Village Blvd Ste 200 ....Princeton NJ 08540 609-452-8000 452-0474 49-1
TF: 888-421-9996 ■ *Web:* www.cfma.org

CFMH-FM
100 Tucker Park Rd TJ Condon Student Ctr Rm 235
....Saint John NB E2L4L5 506-648-5667 647
Web: www.localfm.ca

CFMI-FM 700 W Georgia St Ste 2000........... Vancouver BC V7Y1K9 604-331-2808 331-2722 647
TF: 877-762-5101 ■ *Web:* www.rock101.com

CFML-FM 3700 Willingdon Ave ....Burnaby BC V5G3H2 604-953-3333 647
Web: www.commons.bcit.ca

CFMY-FM Media Ctr 10 Boundary Rd............. Redcliff AB T0J2P0 403-548-8282 548-8270 647
Web: www.my96fm.com

CFNA-FM 102-5316 54 Ave .... Bonnyville AB T9N2C9 780-812-3997 573-1746 647
Web: www.mylakelandnow.com

CFNI-AM 7035 A Market St................... Port Hardy BC V0N2P0 250-949-6500 949-6580 647
Web: www.mytriportnow.com

CFNY-FM 102.1 (Alt) 25 Dock Side Dr .... Toronto ON M5A0B5 416-870-3343 645-163
Web: edge.ca

CFO Connection LLC, The
15 Oakland St.......................... Newburyport MA 01950 978-255-1236 41
Web: thecfoconnection.com

CFO Selections LLC
310 120th Ave NE Ste 101 ....Bellevue WA 98005 206-686-4480 260
TF: 800-931-6557 ■ *Web:* www.cfoselections.com

CFOB-FM 210 Scott St ....Fort Frances ON P9A1G7 807-274-5341 647
Web: www.931theborder.ca

Cfocus Software Inc 10536 Joyceton Dr...........Largo MD 20774 301-499-2650 499-2651 396
Web: cfocussoftware.com

CFOs 2Go Inc
500 Ygnacio Valley Rd Ste 410.............Walnut Creek CA 94596 925-299-4450 463
Web: www.2gocompanies.com

CFOU-FM 3351 Blvd Des Forges.............Trois-Rivieres QC G9A5H7 819-376-5184 376-5239 647
Web: www.cfou.ca

CFP (Christian Fellowship Publishers Inc)
11515 Allecingie Pky .... Richmond VA 23235 804-794-5333 637-2
Web: www.c-f-p.com

CFP (Crystal Fountain Publications)
PO Box 4434 .... Diamond Bar CA 91765 909-396-1201 860-7803 637-10
Web: www.crystalfountain.org

CFPL-TV One Communications Rd .... London ON N6J4Z1 519-686-8810 668-3288 647
TF: 800-668-7754 ■ *Web:* www.london.ctvnews.ca

CFQC-TV 216 1st Ave N .... Saskatoon SK S7K3W3 306-665-8600 665-0450 647
Web: www.saskatoon.ctvnews.ca

CFRC-FM
Queen's University Lower Carruthers Hall........ Kingston ON K7L3N6 613-533-2121 647
Web: www.cfrc.ca

CFRK-FM 495-A Prospect St................. Fredericton NB E3B9M4 506-455-0923 455-3602 647
Web: www.newcountry923.com

CFRN-AM 18520 Stony Plain Rd Ste 100 .... Edmonton AB T5S2E2 780-486-2800 647
TF: 800-243-1945 ■ *Web:* www.tsn.ca

CFS II Inc PO Box 690417 .... Tulsa OK 74169 888-394-3951 393
TF: 888-394-3951 ■ *Web:* www.cfstwo.com

CFS Investment Advisory Services LLC
97 Lackawanna Ave Ste 101 ....Totowa NJ 07512 973-826-8800 256-8688 401
Web: www.cfsias.com

CFTK-TV 4625 Lazelle Ave ....Terrace BC V8G1S4 250-635-6316 638-6320 647
Web: www.cftktv.com

CFTV-TV 3165 S Talbot Rd ....Cottam ON N0R1B0 519-839-3400 647
Web: www.cftvdt.net

CFU (Croatian Fraternal Union of America)
100 Delaney Dr........................... Pittsburgh PA 15235 412-843-0380 823-1594 48-14
Web: cfu.org

CFUR-FM 3333 University Way............. Prince George BC V2N4Z9 250-960-7664 960-5006 647
Web: www.cfur.ca

CFUV-FM
University of Victoria PO Box 3035.............. Victoria BC V8W3P3 250-721-8704 647
Web: www.cfuv.uvic.ca

CFVMC (Cape Fear Valley Medical Ctr)
1638 Owen Dr PO Box 2000.................Fayetteville NC 28304 910-615-4000 374-3
Web: www.capefearvalley.com

CFVR-FM 9904 Franklin Ave...............Fort McMurray AB T9H2K5 780-791-0103 791-1448 647
Web: www.broadcasting-history.ca

CFW Associated Engineers Inc
9200 Leesgate Rd Ste 200 ....Louisville KY 40222 502-423-0805 423-0806 256
Web: www.cfwengineers.com

CFWD-FM 105 21st St E Ste 200 .... Saskatoon SK S7K0B3 306-938-0963 653-2634 647
Web: www.cruzfm.com

CFX Inc 55 Broadway Ste 2608.................New York NY 10006 212-431-5800 431-6520 463
Web: www.cfx.com

CFZM-AM 70 Jefferson Ave..................... Toronto ON M6K1Y4 416-544-0740 647
TF: 866-740-4740 ■ *Web:* www.zoomerradio.ca

CG Automation 60 Fadem Rd ....Springfield NJ 07081 973-379-7400 379-2138 173-2
Web: www.qeiinc.com

CG Design Concepts
1150 N Highland Ave .... Fullerton CA 92835 714-871-7342 344
Web: cgdesignconcepts.com

CG Life 657 W Lake St.........................Chicago IL 60661 312-997-2436 7
Web: cglife.com

CG Power Systems USA Inc
1 Pauwels Dr ....Washington MO 63090 636-239-9300 239-9398 767
Web: www.cgglobal.com

CG Schmidt 11777 W Lake Pk Dr............. Milwaukee WI 53224 414-577-1177 577-1155 186
Web: www.cgschmidt.com

CGA (Compressed Gas Association CGA)
14501 George Carter Way Ste 103 .... Chantilly VA 20151 703-788-2700 961-1831 49-13
Web: www.cganet.com

CGA Engineers Inc 8179 E 41st St .... Tulsa OK 74145 918-749-5800 256
Web: www.cgaengineers.com

CGA Law Firm 106 Harrisburg St.............. East Berlin PA 17316 717-848-4900 843-9039 428
Web: www.cgalaw.com

CGCC (Columbia-Greene Community College)
4400 Rt 23 .... Hudson NY 12534 518-828-4181 822-2015 162
Web: www.sunycgcc.edu

CGF Industries Inc
2420 N Woodlawn Bldg 100 Ste A.............. Wichita KS 67220 316-691-4500 691-4545 360-3
Web: www.cgcpi.com

Name / Address	City	State	Zip	Phone	Fax	Class
CGH (Coral Gables Hospital Inc) 3100 Douglas Rd *TF:* 866-728-3677 ■ *Web:* www.coralgableshospital.com	Coral Gables	FL	33134	305-445-8461	441-6879	374-3
CGH Medical Ctr (CGHMC) 100 E LeFevre Rd *TF:* 800-625-4790 ■ *Web:* www.cghmc.com	Sterling	IL	61081	815-625-0400		374-3
CGHMC (CGH Medical Ctr) 100 E LeFevre Rd *TF:* 800-625-4790 ■ *Web:* www.cghmc.com	Sterling	IL	61081	815-625-0400		374-3
CGHS (Coastal Georgia Historical Society) A.W. Jones Heritage Ctr 601 Beachview Dr *Web:* www.saintsimonslighthouse.org	Saint Simons Island	GA	31522	912-638-4666	638-6609	637-2
CGI Communications Inc 130 E Main St The Granite Blvd *Web:* www.cgicommunications.com	Rochester	NY	14604	585-427-0020		514
CGI Federal Inc 12601 Fair Lks Cir *Web:* www.cgi.com	Fairfax	VA	22033	703-227-6000		196
CGI Interactive Communications 76 Otis St *Web:* cgiinteractive.com	Westborough	MA	01581	508-898-2500		809
CGLA Infrastructure Inc 1827 Jefferson Pl NW *Web:* www.cg-la.com	Washington	DC	20036	202-776-0990		194
CGM Inc 1445 Ford Rd *Web:* www.cgmbuildingproducts.com	Bensalem	PA	19020	215-638-4400	638-7949	135
CGN & Associates Inc 415 SW Washington St *Web:* www.cgnglobal.com	Peoria	IL	61602	309-672-6400	213-2126	194
CGO (Concordia Gospel Outreach) 3558 S Jefferson Ave *TF:* 800-325-3040 ■ *Web:* www.concordiagospeloutreach.org	Saint Louis	MO	63118	314-268-1076		48-20
CGR Products Inc 4655 US Hwy 29 N *TF:* 877-313-6785 ■ *Web:* www.cgrproducts.com	Greensboro	NC	27405	336-621-4568	375-5324	326
CGS (Council of Graduate Schools) 1 Dupont Cir NW Ste 230 *Web:* cgsnet.org	Washington	DC	20036	202-223-3791	331-7157	49-5
CGS Motorsports 3227 Producer Way Ste 134 *Web:* www.cgsmotorsports.com	Pomona	CA	91768	909-444-5536		393
CGS Technology Associates Inc 1001 Durham Ave Ste 300 *Web:* www.cgsonline.com	South Plainfield	NJ	07080	732-750-4141		180
CGX Energy Inc 333 Bay St Ste 1100 *Web:* www.cgxenergy.com	Toronto	ON	M5H2R2	416-364-5569		536
CH (Clarion Hospital) 1 Hospital Dr *TF:* 800-522-0505 ■ *Web:* www.clarionhospital.org	Clarion	PA	16214	814-226-9500	226-1224	374-3
CH (Cold Headers Inc) 5514 N Elston Ave *Web:* www.coldheaders.com	Chicago	IL	60630	773-775-7900	775-0779	278
CH Ellis Company Inc 2432 SE Ave *TF:* 800-466-3351 ■ *Web:* chellis.com	Indianapolis	IN	46201	317-636-3351	635-5140	453
CH Evans Brewing Company at the Albany Pump Station 19 Quackenbush Sq *Web:* www.evansale.com	Albany	NY	12207	518-447-9000		671
CH Fenstermaker & Associates LLC 135 Regency Sq *Web:* www.fenstermaker.com	LaFayette	LA	70508	337-237-2200	232-3299	302
CH Hanson Co 2000 N Aurora Rd *TF:* 800-827-3398 ■ *Web:* www.chhanson.com	Naperville	IL	60563	800-827-3398		467
CH Perez & Associates Consulting Engineers in 9594 NW 41st St Ste 201 *Web:* p-a.cc	Doral	FL	33178	305-592-1070		256
CH Powell Co 75 Shawmut Rd *Web:* chpowell.com	Canton	MA	02021	781-302-7300		311
CH Products 970 Park Center Dr *Web:* www.chproducts.com	Vista	CA	92081	760-598-2518	598-2524	173-1
CH Robinson Worldwide Inc 14701 Charlson Rd *NASDAQ:* CHRW ■ *TF:* 855-229-6128 ■ *Web:* www.chrobinson.com	Eden Prairie	MN	55347	952-683-3950		449
CH Technologies (USA) Inc 263 Center Ave Ste 1 *Web:* chtechusa.com	Westwood	NJ	07675	201-666-2335		419
CHA (Certified Horsemanship Assn) 1795 Alysheba Way Ste 7102 *TF:* 800-399-0138 ■ *Web:* cha.horse	Lexington	KY	40509	859-259-3399	255-0726	48-3
CHA (Catholic Health Association of the US) 4455 Woodson Rd *TF:* 800-230-7823 ■ *Web:* www.chausa.org	Saint Louis	MO	63134	314-427-2500	427-0029	49-8
CHA (Craft & Hobby Assn) 319 E 54th St *TF:* 800-822-0494 ■ *Web:* craftandhobby.org	Elmwood Park	NJ	07407	201-835-1200	797-0657	48-18
CHA 33 Wilbur Cross Way Ste 105 *Web:* www.chacompanies.com	Mansfield	CT	06268	860-885-1055		256
CHA (Community Hospital Anderson) 1515 N Madison Ave *TF:* 800-777-7775 ■ *Web:* www.ecommunity.com	Anderson	IN	46011	765-298-4242		374-3
CHA (California Hospital Assn) 1215 K St Ste 800 *Web:* www.calhospital.org	Sacramento	CA	95814	916-443-7401	552-7596	48-13
CHA Canada 80 King St Ste 404 *TF:* 800-268-9242 ■ *Web:* www.chacanada.com	Saint Catharines	ON	L2R7G1	905-984-8383		256
Cha Cha Cha 656 N Virgil Ave *Web:* www.theoriginalchachacha.com	Los Angeles	CA	90004	323-664-7723	664-7769	671
CHA Hollywood Presbyterian Medical Ctr 1300 N Vermont Ave *TF:* 800-465-3203 ■ *Web:* www.hollywoodpresbyterian.com	Los Angeles	CA	90027	213-413-3000		374-3
CHA Industries 4201 Business Center Dr *Web:* www.chaindustries.com	Fremont	CA	94538	510-683-8554	683-3848	386
Chaat Cafe 1902 University Ave *Web:* www.chaatcafes.com	Berkeley	CA	94704	510-845-1431		671
Chabot College 25555 Hesperian Blvd *Web:* www.chabotcollege.edu	Hayward	CA	94545	925-485-5215		162
Chabot Space & Science Ctr 10000 Skyline Blvd *Web:* www.chabotspace.org	Oakland	CA	94619	510-336-7300	336-7491	520
Chabot Steve (Rep R - OH) 2408 Rayburn House Office Bldg *Web:* www.chabot.house.gov	Washington	DC	20515	202-225-2216	225-3012	342-2
Chace Ruttenberg & Freedman LLP Wayland Bldg 1 Park Row Ste 300 *Web:* www.crfllp.com	Providence	RI	02903	401-453-6400	453-6411	445
Chaco Culture National Historical Park PO Box 220 *Web:* www.nps.gov	Nageezi	NM	87037	505-786-7014	786-7061	564
CHADD (Children & Adults with Attention-Deficit/Hyperactivity Disorder) 4601 Presidents Dr Ste 300 **Fax Area Code:* 301 ■ *TF:* 800-233-4050 ■ *Web:* www.chadd.org	Lanham	MD	20706	800-233-4050	306-7090*	48-17
Chadderton Trucking Inc 40 Stewart Way PO Box 687 *TF:* 800-327-6868 ■ *Web:* chaddertontrucking.com	Sharon	PA	16146	724-981-5050	981-1615	780
Chaddsford Winery 632 Baltimore Pk *Web:* www.chaddsford.com	Chadds Ford	PA	19317	610-388-6221		50-7
Chadick Ellig Inc 300 Park Ave *Web:* www.chadickellig.com	New York	NY	10022	212-688-8671		266
Chadron State College 1000 Main St *Web:* www.csc.edu	Chadron	NE	69337	308-432-6000	432-6229	166
Chadron State Park 15951 Hwy 385 *Web:* outdoornebraska.gov	Chadron	NE	69337	308-432-6167		565
Chadwick Martin Bailey Inc 179 South St *Web:* www.cmbinfo.com	Boston	MA	02111	617-350-8922		466
Chadwick Optical Inc 117 Allen Town Rd **Fax Area Code:* 800 ■ *TF:* 800-410-1618 ■ *Web:* www.chadwickoptical.com	Souderton	PA	18964	267-203-8665	468-9301*	542
Chadwick's of Boston 75 Aircraft Rd *TF:* 877-330-3393 ■ *Web:* www.chadwicks.com	Southington	CT	06489	877-330-3393		459
Chaffe McCall LLP 2300 Energy Ctr 1100 Poydras St *Web:* www.chaffe.com	New Orleans	LA	70163	504-585-7000	585-7075	41
Chaffee and Partners 310 Maple St Ste L02 *Web:* www.chaffeecommunications.com	Barrington	RI	02806	401-247-2300	247-2002	4
Chaffee County 104 Crestone Ave PO Box 249 *Web:* www.chaffeecounty.org	Salida	CO	81201	719-539-4004	539-8588	338
Chaffetz Lindsey LLP 1700 Broadway 33rd Fl *Web:* www.chaffetzlindsey.com	New York	NY	10019	212-257-6960	257-6950	428
Chaffey College 5885 Haven Ave *TF:* 800-535-2421 ■ *Web:* www.chaffey.edu	Rancho Cucamonga	CA	91737	909-652-6000		162
Chafin Law Firm PC 44 E Main St PO Box 1210 *Web:* www.chafinlaw.net	Lebanon	VA	24266	276-889-0143		41
Chagrin Consulting Services 24800 Chagrin Blvd Ste 207	Beachwood	OH	44122	216-514-3301		463
Chagrin Valley Chamber of Commerce 83 N Main St *Web:* www.cvcc.org	Chagrin Falls	OH	44022	440-247-6607		139
Chahinkapa Zoo Park & Carousel 1004 RJ Hughes Dr PO Box 1325 *TF:* 800-342-4671 ■ *Web:* www.chahinkapazoo.org	Wahpeton	ND	58075	701-642-8709	642-9285	823
Chaikin Sherman Cammarata Siegel Pc 1232 17th St NW *Web:* chaikinandsherman.com	Washington	DC	20036	202-659-8600		41
Chain Drug Marketing Assn (CDMA) 43157 W Nine-Mile Rd PO Box 995 *TF:* 800-935-2362 ■ *Web:* www.chaindrug.com	Novi	MI	48376	248-449-9300	449-9396	49-18
Chain O'Lakes State Park 8916 Wilmot Rd *Web:* www.dnr.illinois.gov	Spring Grove	IL	60081	847-587-5512		565
Chain O'Lakes State Park 2355 E 75 S *Web:* www.in.gov	Albion	IN	46701	260-636-2654		565
Chain Store Guide 10117 Princess Palm Ave Ste 375 **Fax Area Code:* 813 ■ *TF:* 800-927-9292 ■ *Web:* www.chainstoreguide.com	Tampa	FL	33610	800-927-9292	627-6888*	637-6
Chair King Inc, The 5405 W Sam Houston Pkwy N *Web:* www.chairking.com	Houston	TX	77041	713-690-1919		321
Chair-man Mills Inc 501 Consumers Rd *Web:* www.chairmanmills.com	Toronto	ON	M2J5E2	416-391-0400		205
Chairside Dental Academy 2830 E Brown Rd Ste 9 *Web:* www.chairside.com	Mesa	AZ	85213	480-830-3546	830-9584	167-3
Chaitman LLP 465 Park Ave *TF:* 888-759-1114 ■ *Web:* chaitmanllp.com	New York	NY	10022	908-303-4568		41
Chakeres Theatres Inc 200 N Murray St	Springfield	OH	45503	937-324-0002		748
Chakra Communications Inc 80 W Drullard Ave *Web:* chakracentral.com	Lancaster	NY	14086	716-505-7300		627
Chaleff Rehwald Peterson 5855 Topanga Canyon Blvd Ste 400 *Web:* www.caregiverovertime.com	Woodland Hills	CA	91367	818-703-7500	703-7498	41
Chalet Basque Restaurant 200 Oak St *Web:* www.basquerestaurantbakersfield.com	Bakersfield	CA	93304	661-327-2915		671
Chalfant Manufacturing Co 50 Pearl Rd Ste 212 *Web:* www.chalfant-obo.com	Brunswick	OH	44212	330-273-3510	273-8149	816
Chalfin Group Inc 45 Bridge St *TF:* 800-321-1099 ■ *Web:* www.chalfin.com	Metuchen	NJ	08840	732-321-1099	321-1066	393
Chalice Press 3280 Summit Ridge Pky *TF:* 800-366-3383 ■ *Web:* www.chalicepress.com	Duluth	GA	30096	770-280-4026		96
Chalk & Vermilion LLC 55 Old Post Rd Ste 2 *TF:* 800-877-2250 ■ *Web:* www.chalk-vermilion.com	Greenwich	CT	06830	203-869-9500		637-10
Chalkboard, The 1324 S Main St *Web:* chalkboardtulsa.com	Tulsa	OK	74119	918-582-1964		671
Chalker Flores LLP 14951 N Dallas Pkwy Ste 400 *Web:* www.chalkerflores.com	Dallas	TX	75254	214-866-0001	866-0010	428
Challenge Dairy Products Inc PO Box 2369 **Fax Area Code:* 925 ■ *TF:* 800-733-2479 ■ *Web:* challengedairy.com	Dublin	CA	94568	800-733-2479	551-7591*	296-3

Phone | Fax | Class

Challenge Engineering & Testing Inc
4234 Halls Mill Rd ... Mobile AL 36693 251-666-1435 261
Web: challengetesting.com

Challenge Enterprises of North Florida Inc
3530 Enterprise Way ... Green Cove Springs FL 32043 904-284-9859 631
Web: www.challengeenterprises.org

Challenge Graphics Corp
16611 Roscoe Pl ... North Hills CA 91343 818-892-0123 892-0331 532-3
Web: www.challenge-graphics.com

Challenge Management Company Inc (CMI)
4000 1st National Bank Bldg ... Dallas TX 75202 972-755-2560 47
Web: www.challenge-management.com

Challenge Plastic Products Inc
110 W Industrial Dr ... Edinburgh IN 46124 812-526-0582 526-0590 604
Web: challengeplastics.com

Challenge Printing Co, The
2 Bridewell Pl ... Clifton NJ 07014 973-471-4700 627
TF: 800-654-1234 ■ *Web:* www.challengeprintingco.com

Challenge Publications Inc
21835 Nordhoff St ... Chatsworth CA 91311 818-700-6868 700-6282 637-9
TF: 800-562-9182 ■ *Web:* www.challengeweb.com

Challenged Athletes Foundation
9591 Waples St ... San Diego CA 92121 858-866-0959 866-0958 305
Web: www.challengedathletes.org

Challenger Center for Space Science Education
422 First St SE 3rd Fl ... Washington DC 20003 202-827-1580 48-11
TF: 800-969-5747 ■ *Web:* www.challenger.org

Challenger Gray & Christmas Inc
150 S Wacker Dr Ste 2800 ... Chicago IL 60606 312-332-5790 193
TF: 855-242-3424 ■ *Web:* www.challengergray.com

Challenger Industries Inc 743 Hill Rd ... Dalton GA 30721 706-278-7707 278-3432 131
TF: 800-334-8873 ■ *Web:* www.challengerturf.com

Challenger Learning Ctr
2600-A Barhamville Rd ... Columbia SC 29204 803-929-3951 520
Web: www.richlandone.org

Challenger Lighting Company Inc
1400 Kingsland Dr ... Batavia IL 60510 847-717-4700 482-9591* 362
**Fax Area Code: 630* ■ *Web:* www.challengerlighting.com

Challenger Water International Inc
41588 Eastman Dr ... Murrieta CA 92562 951-600-3880 806
Web: www.challengerwater.com

Chally Group Worldwide Inc
3123 Research Blvd ... Dayton OH 45420 800-254-5995 463
TF: 800-254-5995 ■ *Web:* growthplay.com

Chalmers & Kubeck Inc 150 Commerce Dr ... Aston PA 19014 610-494-4300 485-1484 454
TF: 800-242-5637 ■ *Web:* www.candk.com

Chalmers Group 6400 Northam Dr ... Mississauga ON L4V1J1 905-362-6400 61
Web: www.chalmersgroup.com

Chalmette Refining LLC
500 W St Bernard Hwy ... Chalmette LA 70043 504-281-1212 580
Web: www.chalmetterefining.com

Chambar Restaurant 568 Beatty St ... Vancouver BC V6B2L3 604-879-7119 671
Web: www.chambar.com

Chamber Collaborative of Greater Portsmouth, The
PO Box 239 ... Portsmouth NH 03802 603-610-5510 436-5118 139
Web: portsmouthchamber.org

Chamber Discoveries Inc
1300 E Shaw Ave Ste 127 ... Fresno CA 93710 559-244-6600 772
TF: 800-339-7781 ■ *Web:* www.chamberdiscoveries.com

Chamber Music America (CMA)
305 Seventh Ave 5th Fl ... New York NY 10001 212-242-2022 242-7955 48-4
TF: 888-221-9836 ■ *Web:* www.chamber-music.org

Chamber Music Society of Lincoln Ctr
70 Lincoln Center Plz ... New York NY 10023 212-875-5788 42
Web: www.chambermusicsociety.org

Chamber of Business & Industry of Centre County
200 Innovation Blvd Ste 150 ... State College PA 16803 814-234-1829 234-5869 139
TF: 877-234-5050 ■ *Web:* www.cbicc.org

Chamber of Commerce
101 Bill Smith Blvd ... King of Prussia PA 19406 610-265-1776 265-0473 139
Web: montgomerycountychamber.org

Chamber of Commerce 195 Water St ... Naugatuck CT 06770 203-729-4511 729-4512 139
Web: www.waterburychamber.com

Chamber of Commerce - Grand Haven-Spring Lake-Ferrysburg
1 S Harbor Dr ... Grand Haven MI 49417 616-842-4910 842-0379 139
TF: 800-277-6774 ■ *Web:* grandhavenchamber.org

Chamber of Commerce - Murray-Calloway County, The
805 N 12th St ... Murray KY 42071 270-753-5171 139
Web: www.mymurray.com

Chamber of Commerce Hawaii (COCHI)
1132 Bishop St Ste 2105 ... Honolulu HI 96813 808-545-4300 545-4369 139
Web: www.cochawaii.org

Chamber of Commerce Mountain View
580 Castro St ... Mountain View CA 94041 650-968-8378 968-5668 139
TF: 800-576-3279 ■ *Web:* www.chambermv.org

Chamber of Commerce of Eastern Connecticut Inc
914 Hartford Tpke ... Waterford CT 06385 860-701-9113 139
Web: www.chamberect.com

Chamber of Commerce of Fargo Moorhead
202 First Ave N ... Moorhead MN 56560 218-233-1100 233-1200 139
Web: fmwfchamber.com

Chamber of Commerce of Greater Cape May
PO Box 556 ... Cape May NJ 08204 609-884-5508 884-2054 139
Web: www.capemaychamber.com

Chamber of Commerce of Harrison County
111 W Walnut St ... Corydon IN 47112 812-738-0120 738-0500 139
Web: www.harrisonchamber.org

Chamber of Commerce of Huntsville/Madison County
225 Church St ... Huntsville AL 35801 256-535-2000 535-2015 139
Web: hsvchamber.org

Chamber of Commerce of Kitchener & Waterloo
80 Queen St N PO Box 2367 ... Kitchener ON N2H6L4 519-576-5000 742-4760 137
Web: greaterkwchamber.com

Chamber of Commerce of New Rochelle
417 N Ave PO Box 140 ... New Rochelle NY 10801 914-632-5700 632-0708 139
Web: newrochellechamber.org

Chamber of Commerce of Northwest Connecticut
333 Kennedy Dr Ste R101 PO Box 59 ... Torrington CT 06790 860-482-6586 489-8851 139
Web: nwctchamberofcommerce.org

Chamber of Commerce of Sandusky County
215 Croghan St ... Fremont OH 43420 419-332-1591 332-8666 139
Web: www.scchamber.org

Chamber of Commerce of Smyth County
214 W Main St Po Box 924 ... Marion VA 24354 276-783-3298 139

Chamber of Commerce of Southern New Jersey
4015 Main St ... Voorhees NJ 08043 856-424-7776 424-8180 139
Web: www.chambersnj.com

Chamber of Commerce of Southwest Indiana
318 Main St Ste 401 ... Evansville IN 47708 812-425-8147 421-5883 139
Web: swinchamber.com

Chamber of Commerce of Southwestern Madison County
3600 Nameoki Rd Ste 202 ... Granite City IL 62040 618-876-6400 876-6448 139
Web: chamberswmc.org

Chamber of Commerce of the Massapequas Inc
674 Broadway ... Massapequa NY 11758 516-541-1443 541-8625 139
Web: massapequachamber.org

Chamber of Commerce of the Palm Beaches
401 N Flagler Dr ... West Palm Beach FL 33401 561-833-3711 833-5582 139
Web: www.palmbeaches.org

Chamber of Commerce of the Tonawandas
254 Sweeney St ... North Tonawanda NY 14120 716-692-5120 692-1867 139
Web: www.the-tonawandas.com

Chamber of Commerce of Ulster County
55 Albany Ave ... Kingston NY 12401 845-338-5100 338-0968 139
Web: www.ulsterchamber.org

Chamber of Commerce of West Alabama
2201 Jack Warner Blvd Bldg C ... Tuscaloosa AL 35401 205-758-7588 391-0565 139
Web: www.tuscaloosachamber.com

Chamber of Commerce Serving Lexington, Buena Vista & Rockbridge County
18 E Nelson St Ste 101 ... Lexington VA 24450 540-463-5375 139
Web: www.lexrockchamber.com

Chamber of Commerce serving Middletown Monroe & Trenton
1500 Central Ave ... Middletown OH 45044 513-422-4551 422-6831 139
Web: www.thechamberofcommerce.org

Chamber of Medford/Jackson County
101 E Eigth St ... Medford OR 97501 541-779-4847 776-4808 139
Web: www.medfordchamber.com

Chamber of Southwest Florida
5621 Banner Dr ... Fort Myers FL 33912 239-433-4111 139
Web: chamberswfl.com

Chamber Orchestra of Philadelphia
1520 Locust St Ste 500 ... Philadelphia PA 19102 215-545-5451 545-3868 573-3
Web: chamberorchestra.org

Chamber South 6410 SW 80th St ... South Miami FL 33143 305-661-1621 666-0508 139
Web: www.chambersouth.com

Chamber, The (SWLA)
Southwest Louisiana 4310 Ryan St ... Lake Charles LA 70605 337-433-3632 139
Web: allianceswla.org

Chamber630 5 Plaza Dr Ste 212 ... Woodridge IL 60517 630-960-7080 719-0021 139
Web: www.chamber630.com

Chamberlain College of Nursing
11830 Westline Industrial Ste 106 ... Saint Louis MO 63146 314-991-6200 166
TF: 888-556-8226 ■ *Web:* www.chamberlain.edu

Chamberlain Group 845 Larch Ave ... Elmhurst IL 60126 630-279-3600 350
Web: www.chamberlaingroup.com

Chamberlain Machine LLC
17 Huntington Ln ... Walpole NH 03608 603-756-2560 60
Web: www.chamberlainmachine.com

Chamberlain West Hollywood
1000 Westmount Dr ... West Hollywood CA 90069 310-657-7400 379
TF: 877-686-2082 ■ *Web:* www.chamberlainwesthollywood.com

Chamberlin & Keaster LLP
16000 Ventura Blvd Ste 700 ... Encino CA 91436 818-385-1434 41
Web: ckbllp.com

Chamberlin Rubber Co
3333 Brighton-Henrietta Townline Rd ... Rochester NY 14623 585-427-7780 370
Web: www.chamberlinrubber.com

Chamberlin Tax Advisory Group Inc
12444 Powerscourt Dr Ste 200 ... Saint Louis MO 63131 314-909-1100 390
Web: chamberlin-group.com

ChamberRVA
SunTrust Bldg 919 E Main St Ste 1700 ... Richmond VA 23219 804-648-1234 139
TF: 888-207-3027 ■ *Web:* www.chamberrva.com

Chambers & Aholt LLC
150 E Ponce De Leon Ave Ste 260 ... Decatur GA 30030 404-253-7860 41
Web: carllp.com

Chambers County 404 Washington Ave ... Anahuac TX 77514 409-267-8309 267-8315 338
Web: www.co.chambers.tx.us

Chambers County Library
H. Grady Bradshaw Library
3419 20th Ave ... Valley AL 36854 334-768-2161 434-3
Web: www.chamberscountylibrary.org

Chambers Gasket & Manufacturing Co
4701 W Rice St ... Chicago IL 60651 773-626-8800 626-1430 326
Web: www.chambersgasket.com

Chambers Group Inc
5 Hutton Centre Dr Ste 750 ... Santa Ana CA 92707 949-261-5414 194
TF: 866-261-3100 ■ *Web:* chambersgroupinc.com

Chambers Hotel 15 W 56th St ... New York NY 10019 212-974-5656 974-5657 379
Web: www.chambershotel.com

Chambers Lopez LLC PO Box 5539 ... Arlington VA 22205 304-876-2706 194
Web: chamberslopez.com

Chambers of Commerce / Tourism
106 E Jefferson St ... Tallahassee FL 32301 850-606-2305 606-2301 206
TF: 800-628-2866 ■ *Web:* www.visittallahassee.com

Chambers Prairie Veterinary Service
3100 Yelm Hwy SE ... Olympia WA 98501 360-491-3800 794
Web: chambersprairie.com

ChamberWest
3540 S 4000 W Ste 240 ... West Valley City UT 84120 801-977-8755 977-8329 139
Web: chamberwest.com

Chambre de commerce de Sherbrooke
9 Rue Wellington S ... Sherbrooke QC J1H5C8 819-822-6151 822-6156 137
Web: ccisherbrooke.com

Chambre de Commerce et d'Industrie du Quebec Metropolitain
17 Rue Saint-Louis ... Quebec City QC G1R3Y8 418-692-3853 694-2286 137
Web: www.cciquebec.ca

Name / Address	City	State	ZIP	Phone	Fax	Class
Chambre de Commerce Haute-Yamaska Region (CDCHY) 90 Rue Robinson S Ste 102 *Web:* cchy.ca	Granby	QC	J2G7L4	450-372-6100	372-3161	137
Chameleon Group LLC 951 Islington St *TF:* 800-773-9182 ■ *Web:* www.chameleonsales.com	Portsmouth	NH	03801	603-570-4305		196
Chameleon Like Inc 345 Kishimura Dr *Web:* www.chameleonlike.com	Gilroy	CA	95020	408-847-3661		627
Chameleon Technologies Inc 520 Kirkland Way Ste 101 *Web:* chameleontechnologiesinc.com	Kirkland	WA	98033	425-827-1173		260
Chaminade College Preparatory School 425 S Lindbergh Blvd *TF:* 877-378-6847 ■ *Web:* www.chaminade-stl.org	Saint Louis	MO	63131	314-993-4400		622
Chaminade Resort & Spa 1 Chaminade Ln *TF:* 800-283-6569 ■ *Web:* www.chaminade.com	Santa Cruz	CA	95065	831-475-5600	476-4798	377
Chaminade University 3140 Waialae Ave *TF:* 800-735-3733 ■ *Web:* chaminade.edu	Honolulu	HI	96816	808-735-4711		166
Chamizal National Memorial 800 S San Marcial St *Web:* www.nps.gov	El Paso	TX	79905	915-532-7273	532-7240	564
Chamlin & Associates Inc 3017 Fifth St *Web:* chamlin.com	Peru	IL	61354	815-223-3344		261
Chamness Technology Inc 2255 Little Wall Lake Rd *Web:* www.chamnesstechnology.com	Blairsburg	IA	50034	515-325-6133		196
Champ's Barber School 54 and 56 W King St *Web:* www.champsbarberschool.com	Lancaster	PA	17603	717-394-0422		685
Champagne Metals LLC 429 W 158th St S *Web:* www.champagnemetals.com	Glenpool	OK	74033	918-322-1131	322-2121	492
Champaign County 303 W Kirby Ave *Web:* www.co.champaign.il.us	Urbana	IL	61802	217-384-3776	384-3896	338
Champaign County 1512 S US Hwy 68 Ste A100 *Web:* www.co.champaign.oh.us	Urbana	OH	43078	937-484-1611	484-1609	338
Champaign County Chamber of Commerce 1817 S Neil St Ste 201 *Web:* champaigncounty.org	Champaign	IL	61820	217-359-1791	359-1809	139
Champaign County Chamber of Commerce 107 N Main St *TF:* 877-873-5764 ■ *Web:* champaignohio.com	Urbana	OH	43078	937-653-5764	652-1599	139
Champaign County Convention & Visitors Bureau 108 S Neil St *Web:* www.visitchampaigncounty.org	Champaign	IL	61820	217-351-4133		206
Champaign County School Employees Credit Union 1203 S Mattis Ave *TF:* 800-322-8472 ■ *Web:* ccsecu.org	Champaign	IL	61821	217-351-3100	351-7360	219
Champaign-Urbana Mass Transit District 1101 E University Ave *Web:* mtd.org	Urbana	IL	61802	217-384-8188	384-8215	468
Champaign-Urbana Symphony Orchestra (CUSO) 701 Devonshire Dr Ste C-24 *Web:* cusymphony.org	Champaign	IL	61820	217-351-9139		573-3
Champion Aerospace LLC 1230 Old Norris Rd *Web:* www.championaerospace.com	Liberty	SC	29657	864-843-1162		22
Champion Aluminum Corp 140 Eileen Way *Web:* www.championwindows.com	Syosset	NY	11791	516-921-6200		234
Champion America Inc PO Box 3092 *TF:* 877-242-6709 ■ *Web:* www.champion-america.com	Branford	CT	06405	877-242-6709		392
Champion Awards & Apparel Inc 3649 Winplace Rd *Web:* www.tshirtchampions.com	Memphis	TN	38118	901-365-4830		344
Champion Beauty College 3920 FM 1960 Rd W Ste 210 *TF:* 800-784-9117 ■ *Web:* www.championbeautycollege.com	Houston	TX	77068	281-583-9117	583-7275	167-3
Champion Bus Inc 331 Graham Rd *TF:* 800-776-4943 ■ *Web:* www.championbus.com	Imlay City	MI	48444	810-724-6474		516
Champion Chevrolet Cadillac of Johnson City LLC 3606 Bristol Hwy *Web:* www.championjc.com	Johnson City	TN	37601	423-218-0317		57
Champion Cleaners 2548 Rocky Ridge Rd *Web:* championcleaners.com	Vestavia Hills	AL	35243	205-824-7737		426
Champion Co 400 Harrison St *TF:* 800-328-0115 ■ *Web:* www.thechampioncompany.com	Springfield	OH	45505	937-324-5681	324-2397	198
Champion College Services Inc 7776 S Pointe Pkwy W Ste 250 **Fax Area Code:* 800 ■ *TF:* 800-761-7376 ■ *Web:* championcollegeservices.com	Phoenix	AZ	85044	480-947-7375	761-7854*	194
Champion Container Corp 180 Essex Ave E *TF:* 877-574-6522 ■ *Web:* www.championcontainer.com	Avenel	NJ	07001	732-636-6700	855-8663	199
Champion Electric Inc 3950 Garner Rd *Web:* www.championelec.com	Riverside	CA	92501	951-276-9619		121
Champion Energy Corp 175 Sunnyside Blvd *Web:* www.championenergy.com	Plainview	NY	11803	914-576-6190		14
Champion Enterprises Management Co 755 W Big Beaver Rd Ste 1000 *Web:* www.championhomes.com	Troy	MI	48084	910-814-4256		505
Champion Fasteners Inc 707 Smithville Rd **Fax Area Code:* 609 ■ *TF:* 800-755-2693 ■ *Web:* www.champfast.com	Lumberton	NJ	08048	800-755-2693	267-2745*	621
Champion Ford Lincoln Inc 140 Southtown Blvd *Web:* www.championowensboro.com	Owensboro	KY	42303	270-684-1441		57
Champion Gasket & Rubber Inc 3225 Haggerty Rd *Web:* championgasket.com	Walled Lake	MI	48390	248-624-6140	624-3069	326
Champion Graphics Corp 3100 Service Corp 600 Vine St Ste 2700 *Web:* champion-graphics.com	Cincinnati	OH	45202	513-271-3800	271-5963	627
Champion Hi-Tech Manufacturing Inc 5565 Maudlin St *Web:* www.chmpgrp.com	Houston	TX	77087	713-644-2181	644-1257	326
Champion Hotels & Development 3048 N Grand Blvd *Web:* championhotels.com	Oklahoma City	OK	73107	405-606-7400		378
Champion Industrial Contractors Inc 1420 Coldwell Ave PO Box 4399 *Web:* championindustrial.com	Modesto	CA	95350	209-524-6601	524-6931	189-10
Champion Industries Inc PO Box 2968 *OTC: CHMP* ■ *TF:* 800-624-3431 ■ *Web:* chapmanprinting.com	Huntington	WV	25728	304-528-2791	528-2746	627
Champion Laboratories Inc 200 S Fourth St *Web:* www.champlabs.com	Albion	IL	62806	618-445-6011		60
Champion Lumber Co 1313 Chicago Ave Ste 100 *Web:* www.championlumber.net	Riverside	CA	92507	951-684-5670		191-3
Champion Packaging & Distribution Inc 1840 Internationale Pky *Web:* www.champakinc.com	Woodridge	IL	60517	630-972-0100	972-1020	151
Champion Photochemistry 7895 Tranmere Dr *TF:* 800-387-3430 ■ *Web:* www.championphotochemistry.com	Mississauga	ON	L5S1V9	905-670-7900	670-2581	591
Champion Power Equipment 12039 Smith Ave *TF:* 877-338-0999 ■ *Web:* www.championpowerequipment.com	Santa Fe Springs	CA	90670	877-338-0999		61
Champion Precast Inc 2441 N Hwy 61 *Web:* championprecast.com	Troy	MO	63379	573-384-5855		183
Champion Preferred Automotive 2020 Lexington Rd *TF:* 800-990-8497 ■ *Web:* www.championautos.com	Nicholasville	KY	40356	859-269-4141		57
Champion Safe Company Inc 2055 S Larsen Pkwy *Web:* championsafe.com	Provo	UT	84606	801-377-7199	377-7195	361
Champion Sales & Manufacturing Inc 32510 Decker Prairie Rd *Web:* www.championgaskets.com	Magnolia	TX	77355	281-356-6162	259-8104	326
Champion Site Prep LP 455-A Hwy 195 *Web:* idigdirt.com	Georgetown	TX	78633	512-863-3453	863-3463	186
Champion Solutions Group 791 Pk of Commerce Blvd Ste 200 *Web:* www.championsg.com	Boca Raton	FL	33487	561-997-2900	997-4043	174
Champion Technologies Inc 845 Mckinley St *TF:* 800-547-6180 ■ *Web:* www.stillchampion.com	Eugene	OR	97402	800-547-6180		247
Champion Window Manufacturing Inc 12121 Champion Way *TF:* 877-424-2674 ■ *Web:* www.championwindow.com	Cincinnati	OH	45241	513-346-4600	346-4614	235
Champion-Arrowhead LLC 5147 Alhambra Ave *TF:* 800-332-4267 ■ *Web:* champion-arrowhead.com	Los Angeles	CA	90032	323-221-9137	221-2579	609
Champions for Life Sports Ctr 453 Grant Ave Rd *Web:* www.championsforlife.org	Auburn	NY	13021	315-252-9305		711
Champions Printing & Publishing Inc 6608 Fm 1960 Rd W Ste G *Web:* www.championsprinting.com	Houston	TX	77069	281-583-7661	583-2669	637-10
Champions Real Estate Group LLC 6117 Richmond Ave Ste 120 *Web:* www.creg1.com	Houston	TX	77057	713-785-6666		652
Champlain Cable Corp 175 Hercules Dr *TF:* 800-451-5162 ■ *Web:* www.champcable.com	Colchester	VT	05446	800-451-5162		814
Champlain College 163 S Willard St *TF:* 800-570-5858 ■ *Web:* www.champlain.edu	Burlington	VT	05401	802-860-2700	860-2767	166
Champlain National Bank 3900 NY Rt 22 *Web:* champlainbank.com	Willsboro	NY	12996	518-963-4201		70
Champlain Oil Company Inc 45 San Remo Dr *TF:* 800-649-3229 ■ *Web:* www.champlainoil.com	South Burlington	VT	05403	802-222-9294	864-0535	579
Champlain Radio Group 336 Water Tower Cir Ste 900 *Web:* www.champlainradio.com	Colchester	VT	05446	802-863-1010		645-141
Champlain Valley Educational Services PO Box 455 *Web:* www.cves.org	Plattsburgh	NY	12901	518-561-0100		800
Champlain Valley Equipment Inc 453 Exchange St *Web:* www.champlainvalleyequipment.com	Middlebury	VT	05753	802-388-4967	388-9656	323
Champlain Valley Exposition 105 Pearl St *Web:* www.cvph.org	Essex Junction	VT	05452	802-878-5545		32
Champlin Foundations, The 2000 Chapel View Blvd *Web:* champlinfoundation.org	Cranston	RI	02920	401-944-9200		305
Champps Entertainment Inc 650 Hwy 287 N Ste 180 **Fax Area Code:* 708 ■ *Web:* champps.com	Dallas	TX	75287	972-581-1171	564-2282*	670
Chan & Company Inc 5701 W Slauson Ave Ste 108 *Web:* chancocpa.com	Culver City	CA	90230	310-216-0066		2
Chance Rides Manufacturing Inc 4219 Irving *Web:* www.chancerides.com	Wichita	KS	67209	316-945-6555		454
Chancellor Hotel on Union Square 433 Powell St *TF:* 800-428-4748 ■ *Web:* www.chancellorhotel.com	San Francisco	CA	94102	415-362-2004	362-1403	379
Chancellor Publications 249 W 34th St Ste 605 *Web:* www.chancellorpublications.com.php	New York	NY	10001	212-214-0825		637-10
Chand 157 Hwy 654 *Web:* www.chand.com	Mathews	LA	70375	985-532-2512	532-3262	770
Chander Software Solutions Inc 1622 Saint Regis Dr *TF:* 800-714-4882 ■ *Web:* www.chandersoft.com	San Jose	CA	95124	408-406-5624		178-1

Name / Address	City	State	ZIP	Phone	Fax	Class
Chandler Asset Management Inc 6225 Lusk Blvd. *TF:* 800-317-4747 ■ *Web:* chandlerasset.com	San Diego	CA	92121	800-317-4747		528
Chandler Center for the Arts 250 N Arizona Ave *Web:* chandlercenter.org	Chandler	AZ	85225	480-782-2680	782-2684	572
Chandler Chamber of Commerce 25 S Arizona Pl Ste 201 *TF:* 800-963-4571 ■ *Web:* www.chandlerchamber.com	Chandler	AZ	85225	480-963-4571	963-0188	139
Chandler Chicco Agency 200 Vesey St. *Web:* www.ccapr.com	New York	NY	10281	212-229-8400		636
Chandler Concrete Company Inc 1006 S Church St PO Box 131 *Web:* www.chandlerconcrete.com	Burlington	NC	27216	336-226-1181	226-2969	182
Chandler Equipment Co 1111 E Ridge Rd. *Web:* www.chandlerequipment.net	Gainesville	GA	30501	770-536-8891	535-1265	516
Chandler Group Executive Search 4165 Shoreline Dr Ste 220 *Web:* www.chandgroup.com	Spring Park	MN	55384	952-471-3000		260
Chandler Hall Hospice 99 Barclay St. *TF:* 888-603-1973 ■ *Web:* ch.kendal.org	Newtown	PA	18940	215-860-4000		371
Chandler Industries Inc 1654 N Ninth St *Web:* www.chandlerindustries.com	Montevideo	MN	56265	320-269-8893	269-5827	482
Chandler Innovations 249 E Chicago St *Web:* innovationsincubator.com	Chandler	AZ	85225	480-884-0336		393
Chandler Instruments Company LLC 2001 N Indianwood Ave *Web:* www.chandlereng.com	Broken Arrow	OK	74012	918-250-7200	459-0165	358
Chandler Medical Center Library 500 S Limestone St *Web:* libraries.uky.edu	Lexington	KY	40506	859-323-5300	323-1040	434-1
Chandler Properties 2799 California St. *Web:* chandlerproperties.com	San Francisco	CA	94115	415-921-5733		652
Chandler Public Library 176 E Arizona Ave. *Web:* www.chandlerlibrary.org	Chandler	AZ	85225	480-782-2000	782-2823	434-3
Chandler's Crabhouse 901 Fairview Ave N. *Web:* www.schwartzbros.com	Seattle	WA	98109	206-223-2722		671
Chandler-Gilbert Community College 7360 E Tahoe Ave *Web:* www.cgc.edu	Mesa	AZ	85212	480-988-8000	988-8993	162
Chandlers Plywood Products Inc 3716 Waverly Rd. *Web:* www.chandlerkitchens.com	Huntington	WV	25704	304-429-1311		115
Chanel Inc 15 E 57th St *TF:* 800-550-0005 ■ *Web:* www.chanel.com	New York	NY	10022	212-355-5050		574
Chanen Construction Company Inc 3300 N Third Ave *Web:* www.srchanen.com	Phoenix	AZ	85013	602-266-3600	285-9268	186
Chaney & Assn 230 Highview Ave. *Web:* www.chaneyassoc.com	Pittsburgh	PA	15238	412-767-0307		196
Chaney Enterprises 2410 Evergreen Rd Ste 201 *TF:* 888-244-0411 ■ *Web:* www.chaneyenterprises.com	Gambrills	MD	21054	301-932-5000		183
Chaney Instrument Co 965 Wells St *TF:* 877-221-1252 ■ *Web:* www.acurite.com	Lake Geneva	WI	53147	262-729-4852		201
Chaney Systems Inc 5100 S Calhoun Rd *Web:* www.chaney.net	New Berlin	WI	53151	262-679-6000	679-3715	180
Chang & Boos 1305 11th St Ste 301 *Web:* www.americanlaw.com	Bellingham	WA	98225	360-671-5945		428
Change Companies, The 5221 Sigstrom Dr. *Web:* www.changecompanies.net	Carson City	NV	89706	775-885-2610		196
Changed Healthcare 3055 Lebanon Pk *TF:* 800-735-8254 ■ *Web:* www.changehealthcare.com	Nashville	TN	37214	615-932-3000		39
Changes Salon & Day Spa Inc 1475 N Broadway *Web:* changessalon.com	Walnut Creek	CA	94596	925-947-1814		77
ChangeScape Inc 220 N Glengarry *Web:* www.changescapeinc.com	Bloomfield Hills	MI	48301	248-561-5063		194
Changing Church Forum Inc 13901 Fairview Dr *Web:* popmn.org	Burnsville	MN	55337	952-898-9317		637-2
Changing Hands Bookstore 6428 S McClintock Dr *Web:* www.changinghands.com	Tempe	AZ	85283	480-730-0205	730-1196	95
Changing Lives Press PO Box 140189 *Web:* www.changinglivespress.org	Howard Beach	NY	11414	718-835-8546		637-2
Changing Our World Inc 220 E 42nd St 5th Fl. *Web:* www.changingourworld.com	New York	NY	10017	212-499-0866		317
Channahon State Park PO Box 54. *Web:* www.dnr.illinois.gov	Channahon	IL	60410	815-467-4271		565
Channel 96.1 801 Wood Ridge Center Dr. *Web:* 1029thelake.iheart.com	Charlotte	NC	28217	704-714-9444		645-32
Channel Building Company Inc 355 Middlesex Ave *Web:* www.channelbuilding.com	Wilmington	MA	01887	978-657-7300	657-7788	186
Channel Islands Aviation 305 Durley Ave *Web:* flycia.com	Camarillo	CA	93010	805-987-1301	987-8301	63
Channel Islands National Park 1901 Spinnaker Dr *Web:* www.nps.gov	Ventura	CA	93001	805-658-5730	658-5799	564
Channel Islands Surfboards Inc 36 Anacapa St. *TF:* 866-642-7843 ■ *Web:* www.cisurfboards.com	Santa Barbara	CA	93101	805-966-7213	564-1143	711
Channel Methods Partners LLC 1913 Atlantic Ave Ste 5. **Fax Area Code: 732 ■ TF: 877-739-1152 ■ Web:* www.channelmethods.com	Manasquan	NJ	08736	877-739-1152	223-2081*	393
Channel Photographics 980 Lincoln Ave Ste 200 B *Web:* www.channelphotographics.com	San Rafael	CA	94901	415-456-2934	456-4124	590
Channel Products Inc 7100 Wilson Mills Rd. *Web:* www.channelproducts.com	Chesterland	OH	44026	440-423-0113	423-1502	202
Channel Solutions LLC 3145 E Chandler Blvd Ste 110 *TF:* 866-501-9690 ■ *Web:* www.channelsolutionsgroup.com	Phoenix	AZ	85048	866-501-9690		196
Channel Systems Inc 74 98th Ave *Web:* www.channelsystems.com	Oakland	CA	94603	510-568-7170	568-4619	186
Channel Zero Inc PO Box 6143 Sta A *Web:* www.chz.com	Toronto	ON	M5W1P6	416-492-1595	492-9539	647
Channell 26040 Ynez Rd *OTC: CHNL ■ TF:* 800-423-1863 ■ *Web:* www.channell.com	Temecula	CA	92591	951-719-2600	296-2322	647
Channellock Inc 1306 S Main St *TF:* 800-724-3018 ■ *Web:* www.channellock.com	Meadville	PA	16335	800-724-3018	962-2583	758
ChannelMeter Inc 1061 Market St Ste 508 *Web:* channelmeter.com	San Francisco	CA	94103	415-578-0714		387
Channelnet 1 Harbor Dr Ste 106 *Web:* www.channelnet.com	Sausalito	CA	94965	415-332-4704		177
Channing House 850 Webster St. *Web:* channinghouse.org	Palo Alto	CA	94301	650-327-0950		672
Chant Engineering 59 Industrial Dr. *Web:* chantengineering.com	New Britain	PA	18901	215-230-4260		454
Chanticleer Garden 786 Church Rd. *Web:* www.chanticleergarden.org	Wayne	PA	19087	610-687-4163	293-0149	97
Chanticleer Inn 1458 E Dollar Lake Rd *TF:* 800-752-9193 ■ *Web:* www.chanticleerinn.com	Eagle River	WI	54521	715-479-4486	479-0004	669
Chantiers Chibougamau Ltd 521 Chemin Merrill PO Box 216. *Web:* www.chibou.com	Chibougamau	QC	G8P2K7	418-748-6481	748-2469	817
Chantland-MHS 502 Seventh St N. *Web:* www.chantland.com	Dakota City	IA	50529	515-332-4045		697
Chao & Associates Inc 7 Clusters Ct *Web:* chaoinc.com	Columbia	SC	29210	803-772-8420		261
Chao Pra Ya Thai Cuisine 580 Adams St *Web:* www.cpythai.com	Eugene	OR	97402	541-344-1706		671
Chaosity LLC 1918 Stone Ridge Way *Web:* chaosity.com	Boise	ID	83712	602-315-7623		196
CHAP (Community Health Accreditation Program Inc) 1275 K St NW Ste 800 *TF:* 800-656-9656 ■ *Web:* www.chapinc.org	Washington	DC	20005	202-862-3413	862-3419	48-1
Chapa Elementary School 5670 N Doffing Rd *Web:* www.lajoyaisd.com	Mission	TX	78574	956-580-6150		685
Chapala 136 Oakway Ctr. *Web:* chapalamex.com	Eugene	OR	97401	541-434-6113		671
Chaparral Boats Inc 300 Industrial Park Blvd *Web:* www.chaparralboats.com	Nashville	GA	31639	229-686-7481	686-3660	90
Chaparral Elementary School 451 Chaparral Dr *Web:* www.ces-claremont-ca.schoolloop.com	Claremont	CA	91711	909-398-0305	398-0306	685
Chaparral Energy Inc 701 Cedar Lake Blvd. *TF:* 888-830-4659 ■ *Web:* www.chaparralenergy.com	Oklahoma City	OK	73114	405-478-8770		538
Chaparral High School 1600 N Cuyamaca St *Web:* chaparral.guhsd.net	El Cajon	CA	92020	619-956-4600		685
Chaparral Technologies Inc 2600 Gravel Dr Bldg 7 *Web:* www.chaparraltech.net	Fort Worth	TX	76118	972-988-0067	660-1790	523
Chapco Inc 10 Denlar Dr *Web:* www.chapcoinc.com	Chester	CT	06412	860-526-9535		697
Chapel Hill Historical Society (CHHS) 100 Library Dr *Web:* www.chapelhillhistoricalsociety.org	Chapel Hill	NC	27514	919-929-1793		637-2
Chapel Hill Public Library 100 Library Dr *Web:* chapelhillpubliclibrary.org	Chapel Hill	NC	27514	919-968-2777		434-3
Chapel Hill/Orange County Visitors Bureau 501 W Franklin St. **Fax Area Code: 919 ■ TF:* 888-968-2060 ■ *Web:* www.visitchapelhill.org	Chapel Hill	NC	27516	888-968-2060	968-2062*	206
Chapel Hill-Carrboro Chamber of Commerce 104 S Estes Dr *TF:* 800-694-9784 ■ *Web:* www.carolinachamber.org	Chapel Hill	NC	27515	919-967-7075	968-6874	139
Chapel Hills Mall 1710 Briargate Blvd *Web:* www.chapelhillsmall.com	Colorado Springs	CO	80920	719-594-0111		460
Chapel Steel Co 590 N Bethlehem Pk. *TF:* 800-570-7674 ■ *Web:* www.chapelsteel.com	Lower Gwynedd	PA	19002	215-793-0899	793-0919	454
Chapel Valley Landscape Co 3275 Jennings Chapel Rd. *TF:* 888-285-5355 ■ *Web:* www.chapelvalley.com	Woodbine	MD	21797	301-924-5400		422
Chapelwood United Methodist Church 11140 Greenbay St *Web:* www.chapelwood.org	Houston	TX	77024	713-465-3467		366
Chapin & Bangs Co, The 165 River St *TF:* 800-972-9615 ■ *Web:* www.cbsteel.com	Bridgeport	CT	06604	800-972-9615		492
Chapin Davis Investments 1411 Clarkview Rd *TF:* 800-222-3246 ■ *Web:* chapindavis.com	Baltimore	MD	21209	410-435-3200		691
Chapin Hall Center For Children 1313 E 60th St *Web:* www.chapinhall.org	Chicago	IL	60637	773-256-5100		652
Chapin International Inc 700 Ellicott St. *TF:* 888-209-1193 ■ *Web:* www.chapinmfg.com	Batavia	NY	14021	888-209-1193		172
Chapin Memorial Library 400 14th Ave N. *Web:* www.cityofmyrtlebeach.com	Myrtle Beach	SC	29577	843-918-1275		434-3
Chapin School 100 E End Ave *Web:* www.chapin.edu	New York	NY	10028	212-744-2335		623

Phone | Fax | Class

Chaplaincy Health Care
2108 W Entiat Ave. . . . . Kennewick WA 99336 509-783-7417 735-7850 371
Web: chaplaincyhealthcare.org

Chapman & Intrieri LLP
2236 Mariner Sq Dr Ste 300. . . . . Alameda CA 94501 510-864-3600 428
Web: www.cnilawfirm.com

Chapman Assoc
16 E Schaumburg Rd Ste 3. . . . . Schaumburg IL 60194 847-884-0010 41
Web: chapman-usa.com

Chapman Consulting Inc
338 Thoroughbred Dr. . . . . LaFayette LA 70507 337-896-1721 261
Web: chapmanconsulting.net

Chapman Corp 331 S Main St. . . . . Washington PA 15301 724-228-1900 189-10
Web: www.chapmancorporation.com

Chapman Cubine Adams + Hussey
2000 15th St N Ste 550 . . . . . Arlington VA 22201 703-248-0025 248-0029 317
Web: www.ccah.com

Chapman Engineering Corp
2321 Cape Cod Way. . . . . Santa Ana CA 92703 714-542-1942 697
Web: www.chapmanengineering.com

Chapman Ford Lancaster
5201 Main St . . . . . East Petersburg PA 17520 855-457-8267 57
TF: 855-457-8267 ■ *Web:* www.chapmanfordlancaster.net

Chapman Global Medical Ctr
2601 E Chapman Ave. . . . . Orange CA 92869 714-633-0011 374-3
Web: chapmanglobalmedicalcenter.com

Chapman Homes Inc
43600 Rodeo Ln Ste B . . . . . Santa Fe NM 87507 505-983-8100 983-9660 187
Web: www.chapmanhomes.com

Chapman Manufacturing Company Inc
PO Box 359 . . . . . Avon MA 02322 508-588-3200 587-7592 439
Web: www.chapmanco.com

Chapman School of Seamanship
4343 SE St Lucie Blvd . . . . . Stuart FL 34997 772-283-8130 283-2019 685
TF: 800-225-2841 ■ *Web:* www.chapman.org

Chapman State Park
4790 Chapman Dam Rd . . . . . Clarendon PA 16313 814-723-0250 565
Web: www.dcnr.pa.gov

Chapman Technical Group
200 6th Ave. . . . . Saint Albans WV 25177 304-727-5501 727-5580 261
Web: chaptech.com

Chapman University 1 University Dr . . . . . Orange CA 92866 714-997-6815 997-6713 166
TF: 888-282-7759 ■ *Web:* chapman.edu

Chapman/Leonard Studio Equipment Inc
12950 Raymer St . . . . . North Hollywood CA 91605 818-764-6726 764-6730 722
TF: 888-883-6559 ■ *Web:* www.chapman-leonard.com

Chappaqua Public Library
195 S Greeley Ave. . . . . Chappaqua NY 10514 914-238-4779 238-3597 434-3
Web: www.chappaqualibrary.org

Chappell Farms Inc
166 Boiling Springs Rd . . . . . Barnwell SC 29812 803-584-2565 584-3676 315-3
Web: www.chappellfarms.com

Chappell's Restaurant & Sports Museum
323 Armour Rd. . . . . North Kansas City MO 64116 816-421-0002 671
Web: www.chappellsrestaurant.com

Chapter & Verse 111 N Post St Ste 400 . . . . . Spokane WA 99201 509-688-2200 688-2299 7
Web: www.chapterandver.se

Chapter 2 Inc 305 S CP Ave . . . . . Lake Mills WI 53551 920-648-8125 648-8298 454
Web: www.chap2.com

Chapters Health System
12470 Telecom Dr W Ste 300. . . . . Temple Terrace FL 33637 813-871-8111 371
Web: chaptershealth.org

Char Glo School of Beauty
1418 S Pioneer Way. . . . . Moses Lake WA 98837 509-765-5309 685
Web: www.char-gloschoolofbeauty.com

Char Thai 5039 Fifth St. . . . . Tucson AZ 85711 520-795-1715 671
Web: www.charsthaitucson.com

CharacTell Inc 34 Wessex Rd . . . . . Newton MA 02459 617-965-0010 387
Web: www.charactell.com

Charbon Steakhouse
450 Gare du Palais (Old Port). . . . . Quebec City QC G1K3X2 418-522-0133 671
Web: charbonsteakhouse.com

Char-Broil 1442 Belfast Ave . . . . . Columbus GA 31902 800-241-7548 36
TF: 800-241-7548 ■ *Web:* www.charbroil.com

Chardon Laboratories Inc
7300 Tussing Rd. . . . . Reynoldsburg OH 43068 888-660-1724 743
TF: 888-660-1724 ■ *Web:* www.chardonlabs.com

Chardon Oil Company Inc 420 Water St . . . . . Chardon OH 44024 440-285-7711 316
TF: 800-686-6451 ■ *Web:* chardonoil.com

CHARGED.fm 10 Jay St . . . . . Brooklyn NY 11201 646-490-2700 224
Web: www.charged.fm

Chargeurs Wool USA 178 Wool Rd. . . . . Jamestown SC 29453 843-257-2212 745-9
Web: www.chargeurswoolusa.com

Chariho Regional School District
455 Switch Rd . . . . . Wood River Junction RI 02894 401-364-7575 415-6076 685
Web: www.chariho.k12.ri.us

Chariot Eagle Inc 931 NW 37th Ave . . . . . Ocala FL 34475 352-629-7007 629-6920 505
Web: www.charioteagle.com

Charisma Magazine 600 Rinehart Rd. . . . . Lake Mary FL 32746 407-333-0600 333-7100 457-18
TF: 800-749-6500 ■ *Web:* www.charismamag.com

Chariton County 306 S Cherry St . . . . . Keytesville MO 65261 660-288-3200 288-3403 338
Web: www.marcelinemo.us

Chariton Review
Truman State University Press
100 E Normal Ave. . . . . Kirksville MO 63501 660-785-7336 785-4480 637-2
TF: 800-916-6802 ■ *Web:* www.tsup.truman.edu

Chariton Valley Electric Co-op
2090 Hwy 5 PO Box 486. . . . . Albia IA 52531 641-932-7126 245
TF: 800-475-1702 ■ *Web:* www.cvrec.com

Charity Cultural Services Ctr
747 Commercial St. . . . . San Francisco CA 94108 415-989-8224 391-0525 167-3
Web: www.sfccsc.org

Charity Home Health Services Inc
500 Carson Plz Ste 228 . . . . . Carson CA 90746 310-527-4339 363
Web: charityhhs.com

CharityUSAcom LLC
600 University St Ste 1000 One Union Sq . . . . . Seattle WA 98101 206-268-5454 264-8448 387
TF: 888-811-5271 ■ *Web:* greatergood.com

Charkit Chemical Corp
32 Haviland St Unit 1 . . . . . Norwalk CT 06854 203-299-3220 299-1355 146
Web: www.charkit.com

Charles & Colvard Ltd
170 Southport Dr . . . . . Morrisville NC 27560 919-468-0399 411
NASDAQ: CTHR ■ *TF:* 800-210-4367 ■ *Web:* www.charlesandcolvard.com

Charles & Emma Frye Free Public Art Museum
704 Terry Ave . . . . . Seattle WA 98104 206-622-9250 223-1701 520
Web: www.fryemuseum.org

Charles & Helen Schwab Foundation
201 Mission St Ste 1950 . . . . . San Francisco CA 94105 415-795-4920 795-4921 305
Web: www.schwabfoundation.org

Charles & Sue's School of Hair Design
1711 Briarcrest Dr . . . . . Bryan TX 77802 979-776-4375 685
Web: www.charlesandsues.com

Charles A. Hones Inc
355 Rte 49 PO Box 405 . . . . . Cleveland NY 13042 631-842-8886 842-9300 357
Web: charlesahones.com

Charles A. Lindbergh State Park
1615 Lindbergh Dr S . . . . . Little Falls MN 56345 320-616-2525 616-2526 565
Web: www.dnr.state.mn.us

Charles A. Rogers Enterprises Inc
51 Victor Heights Pky. . . . . Victor NY 14564 585-924-6400 924-6408 488
Web: www.car-eng.com

Charles Agapiou Ltd
9017 Santa Monica Blvd. . . . . West Hollywood CA 90069 310-274-6201 62
Web: www.rollsandbentley.com

Charles Allis Art Museum
1801 N Prospect Ave . . . . . Milwaukee WI 53202 414-278-8295 520
Web: www.cavtmuseums.org

Charles Bailey Trucking Inc
7052 Roberts Matthews Hwy . . . . . Cookeville TN 38506 931-738-5065 780
TF: 800-467-5065 ■ *Web:* www.cb-trucking.com

Charles Bond Co
11 Green St PO Box 105. . . . . Christiana PA 17509 610-596-5171 922-0125* 709
**Fax Area Code:* 888 ■ *TF:* 800-922-0125 ■ *Web:* www.bondmachine.com

Charles Bowman & Company Inc
3328 John F Donnelly Dr . . . . . Holland MI 49424 616-786-4000 786-2864 238
Web: www.charlesbowman.com

Charles C. Brandt Construction Co
1505 N Sherman Dr . . . . . Indianapolis IN 46201 317-375-1111 375-4321 186
Web: www.ccbrandt.com

Charles C. Parks Co
388 N Belvedere Dr. . . . . Gallatin TN 37066 615-452-2406 451-4212 297-11
TF: 800-873-2406 ■ *Web:* www.charlescparks.com

Charles C. Thomas Publisher
2600 S First St . . . . . Springfield IL 62704 217-789-8980 789-9130 637-2
TF: 800-258-8980 ■ *Web:* www.ccthomas.com

Charles City Forest Products
2200 Barnetts Rd . . . . . Providence Forge VA 23140 804-966-2336 683

Charles Cole Memorial Hospital
1001 E Second St. . . . . Coudersport PA 16915 814-274-9300 374-3
Web: www.colememorial.org

Charles County 200 Baltimore St . . . . . La Plata MD 20646 301-645-0600 645-0560 338
Web: www.charlescountymd.gov

Charles County Chamber of Commerce
101 Centennial St Ste A . . . . . La Plata MD 20646 301-932-6500 932-3945 139
TF: 800-992-3194 ■ *Web:* www.charlescountychamber.org

Charles Craft Inc
21381 Charles Craft Ln. . . . . Laurinburg NC 28352 910-844-3521 844-9333 745-9
Web: www.charlescraftinc.com

Charles D. Hankey Law Office PC
434 E New York St . . . . . Indianapolis IN 46202 317-634-8565 428
Web: www.hankeylawoffice.com

Charles D. Sheehy Inc (CDI)
675 Bodwell St Ext . . . . . Avon MA 02322 508-583-7612 586-2312 612
Web: www.cdsi.com

Charles DeWeese Construction Inc
765 Industrial By Pass PO Box 504 . . . . . Franklin KY 42135 270-586-9122 186
Web: www.charlesdeweeseconstruction.com

Charles Dolce Inc 4714 Canal St . . . . . New Orleans LA 70119 504-486-2772 4
Web: www.dolceadvertising.com

Charles Dunn Company Inc
800 W Sixth St 6th Fl . . . . . Los Angeles CA 90017 213-683-0500 652
Web: charlesdunn.com

Charles E. Egeler Correctional Facility
3855 Cooper St . . . . . Jackson MI 49201 517-780-5600 780-5814 213
Web: www.michigan.gov

Charles E. Gillman Co
907 E Frontage Rd . . . . . Rio Rico AZ 85648 520-281-1141 281-1372 815
TF: 800-783-2589 ■ *Web:* www.gillman.com

Charles E. Jarrell Contracting
4208 Rider Trail N. . . . . Earth City MO 63045 314-291-0100 291-2803 697
TF: 800-729-4822 ■ *Web:* jarrellcontracting.com

Charles E. Larson and Sons Inc
2645-65 N Keeler Ave. . . . . Chicago IL 60639 773-772-9700 772-9785 483
Web: www.larsonforgings.com

Charles E. Reed & Associates PC
3636 Professional Dr . . . . . Port Arthur TX 77642 409-983-3277 2

Charles Eisen & Assoc
595 S Broadway 103-W . . . . . Denver CO 80209 303-744-3200 744-3203 321
Web: www.eisenassociates.com

Charles F. Evans Company Inc
800 Canal St. . . . . Elmira NY 14901 607-734-8151 733-5422 189-12
Web: evansroofingcompany.com

Charles F. Foster PC 1445 Main St . . . . . Tewksbury MA 01876 978-851-8300 41
Web: attyfoster.com

Charles G. Lawson Trucking
4366 Mt Pleasant St NW. . . . . North Canton OH 44720 334-284-3220 780

Charles G.G. Schmidt & Comapany Inc
301 W Grand Ave . . . . . Montvale NJ 07645 800-724-6438 391-3565* 758
**Fax Area Code:* 201 ■ *TF:* 800-724-6438 ■ *Web:* www.cggschmidt.net

Charles Gabus Ford Inc
4545 Merle Hay Rd. . . . . Des Moines IA 50310 515-270-0707 57
TF: 800-934-2287 ■ *Web:* www.charlesgabusford.com

Charles Gojer & Associates Inc
11615 Forest Central Dr Ste 303 . . . . . Dallas TX 75243 214-340-1199 348-8053 261
Web: www.cgojer.com

	Phone	Fax	Class
Charles H. West Farms Inc 2953 Tub Mill Pond Rd. Milford DE 19963	302-335-3936		10-11
Charles H. Wright Museum of African American History 315 E Warren Ave Detroit MI 48201 *Web:* thewright.org	313-494-5800	494-5855	520
Charles Hayden Foundation 140 Broadway New York NY 10005 *Web:* charleshaydenfoundation.org	212-785-3677		305
Charles Hayden Planetarium 1 Science Pk Boston MA 02114 *Web:* www.mos.org	617-723-2500	589-0362	598
Charles Hosmer Morse Museum of American Art 445 N Park Ave Winter Park FL 32789 *Web:* www.morsemuseum.org	407-645-5311		520
Charles Hotel Harvard Square 1 Bennett St Cambridge MA 02138 *TF:* 800-882-1818 ■ *Web:* www.charleshotel.com	617-864-1200	864-5715	379
Charles Ifergan Coiffures Ltd 106 E Oak St Chicago IL 60611 *Web:* charlesifergan.com	312-642-4484		77
Charles Industries Ltd 5600 Apollo Dr Rolling Meadows IL 60008 *TF:* 800-458-4747 ■ *Web:* www.charlesindustries.com	847-806-6300	806-6231	735
Charles Inn, The 20 Broad St Bangor ME 04401 *Web:* thecharlesinn.com	207-992-2820		379
Charles J. Arena 583 Skippack Pk Ste 100 Blue Bell PA 19422 *Web:* charlesarena.com	215-540-0300		41
Charles J. Becker & Bro. Inc 1500 Melrose Hwy Pennsauken Township NJ 08110 *TF:* 800-523-1490 ■ *Web:* shopbecker.com	800-523-1490		535
Charles Jacquinet Cie Inc 2633 Trenton Ave Philadelphia PA 19125	215-425-9300		80-1
Charles Jones LLC PO Box 8488 Trenton NJ 08650 *TF:* 800-792-8888 ■ *Web:* www.charlesjones.com	800-792-8888		635
Charles L. Crane Agency Co 100 N Broadway Ste 900 Saint Louis MO 63102 *TF:* 800-264-8722 ■ *Web:* www.craneagency.com	314-241-8700	444-1970	300
Charles Leonard Inc 145 Kennedy Dr Hauppauge NY 11788 *TF:* 800-999-7202 ■ *Web:* www.charlesleonard.com	631-273-6700	273-6777	350
Charles Loomis Inc 11828 NE 112th St Kirkland WA 98033 *TF:* 800-755-0471 ■ *Web:* www.charlesloomis.com	425-823-4560	823-8654	439
Charles Mcmurray Co 2520 N Argyle Ave Fresno CA 93727 *Web:* www.charlesmcmurray.com	559-292-5751		350
Charles Mix Electric Association Inc 440 Lake St Lake Andes SD 57356 *TF:* 800-208-8587 ■ *Web:* www.cme.coop	605-487-7321		245
Charles N. White Construction Company Inc 613 Crescent Cir Ste 100 Ridgeland MS 39157 *Web:* www.whiteconst.com	601-898-5180		186
Charles O. Morgan Jr PA 2121 Ponce De Leon Blvd Ste 900 Coral Gables FL 33134 *Web:* morganhortonlaw.com	305-624-0011		41
Charles of Italy Beauty College & Massage Therapy School 1987 McCulloch Blvd Lake Havasu City AZ 86403 *Web:* www.charlesofitaly.edu	928-453-6666		685
Charles P. Blouin Inc 203 New Zealand Rd Seabrook NH 03874 *Web:* cpblouin.com	603-474-3400	474-7118	189-10
Charles P. Romaker PC 211 W Wacker Dr Ste 1450 Chicago IL 60606 *Web:* romakerlaw.com	312-377-7000		41
Charles Paddock Zoo 9305 Pismo Ave Atascadero CA 93422 *Web:* charlespaddockzoo.org	805-461-5080		823
Charles Pankow Builders Ltd 199 S Los Robles Ave Ste 300 Pasadena CA 91101 *TF:* 888-815-8518 ■ *Web:* www.pankow.com	626-304-1190	696-1782	186
Charles Pinckney National Historic Site 1214 Middle St Sullivans Island SC 29482 *Web:* www.nps.gov	843-881-5516	881-7070	564
Charles Playhouse 74 Warrenton St Boston MA 02116 *Web:* blueman.com	617-426-6912		572
Charles R. Drew University of Medicine & Science 1731 E 120th St Los Angeles CA 90059 *Web:* www.cdrewu.edu	323-563-4800	563-4957	166
Charles Ritter Inc 3333 S 3rd St Philadelphia PA 19148 *Web:* www.charlesritterinc.com	215-320-5000	320-5057	297-10
Charles River Analytics Inc 625 Mt Auburn St Cambridge MA 02138 *Web:* www.cra.com	617-491-3474	868-0780	177
Charles River CFO Inc Two Newton Executive Park Newton MA 02462 *Web:* crcfo.com	781-431-0420		2
Charles River Development Inc 700 District Ave Burlington MA 01803 *Web:* www.crd.com	781-238-0099	238-0088	178-10
Charles River Insurance Brokerage Inc 5 Whittier St 4th Fl Framingham MA 01701 *Web:* charlesriverinsurance.com	508-656-1400		390
Charles River Laboratories Inc 251 Ballardvale St Wilmington MA 01887 *NYSE:* CRL ■ **Fax Area Code:* 978 ■ *TF:* 800-772-3271 ■ *Web:* www.criver.com	781-222-6000	658-7132*	668
Charles Ross & Son Co 710 Old Willets Path Hauppauge NY 11788 *TF:* 800-243-7677 ■ *Web:* www.mixers.com	631-234-0500	234-0691	386
Charles Ryan Associates Inc 601 Morris St Ste 301 Charleston WV 25301 *TF:* 877-342-0161 ■ *Web:* www.charlesryan.com	877-342-0161		636
Charles S. Nacol Jewelry Co 4320 Dowlen Rd Beaumont TX 77706 *Web:* chasnacol.com	409-866-3847		411
Charles Schwab & Company Inc 211 Main St San Francisco CA 94105 *TF:* 800-648-5300 ■ *Web:* www.schwab.com	415-667-1009		690
Charles Stark Draper Laboratory Inc 555 Technology Sq Cambridge MA 02139 *Web:* www.draper.com	617-258-1000		668

	Phone	Fax	Class
Charles Stewart Mott Community College 1401 E Ct St Flint MI 48503 *Web:* www.mcc.edu	810-762-0200	762-5611	162
Charles Stewart Mott Foundation 503 S Saginaw St Ste 1200 Flint MI 48502 *Web:* www.mott.org	810-238-5651	766-1753	305
Charles Tombras Advertising Inc 620 S Gay St Knoxville TN 37902 *Web:* tombras.com	865-524-5376		4
Charles Towne Landing State Historic Site 1500 Old Towne Rd Charleston SC 29407 *Web:* southcarolinaparks.com	843-852-4200		565
Charlesmead Pharmacy Inc 6242 Bellona Ave Baltimore MD 21212 *Web:* stores.healthmart.com	410-435-0210		237
Charleston 1000 Lancaster St Baltimore MD 21202 *Web:* www.charlestonrestaurant.com	410-332-7373		671
Charleston Area Chamber of Commerce 501 Jackson Ave Charleston IL 61920 *Web:* www.charlestonchamber.com	217-345-7041	345-7042	139
Charleston Area Convention & Visitors Bureau 423 King St Charleston SC 29403 **Fax Area Code:* 843 ■ *TF:* 800-868-8118 ■ *Web:* www.charlestoncvb.com	800-774-4444	853-0444*	206
Charleston Area Convention Center Complex (CACC) 5000 Coliseum Dr North Charleston SC 29418 *Web:* www.charlestonconventioncenter.com	843-529-5050		205
Charleston Area Regional Transportation Authority (CARTA) 1362 McMillan Ave Ste 100 North Charleston SC 29405 *Web:* www.ridecarta.com	843-724-7420		468
Charleston Ballet 100 Capitol St Ste 302 Charleston WV 25301 *Web:* www.thecharlestonballet.com	304-342-6541		573-1
Charleston City Paper 1049 Morrison Dr Ste B Charleston SC 29403 *Web:* www.charlestoncitypaper.com	843-577-5304		532-5
Charleston Civic Center & Coliseum 200 Civic Center Dr Charleston WV 25301 *Web:* www.chaswvccc.com	304-345-1500	345-3492	205
Charleston Coast Guard Base 196 Tradd St Charleston SC 29401 *Web:* www.uscg.mil	843-724-7600		158
Charleston Convention & Visitors Bureau 601 Morris St Ste 204 Charleston WV 25301 *Web:* www.charlestonwv.com	304-344-5075		206
Charleston Cosmetology Institute 8484 Dorchester Rd Charleston SC 29420 *Web:* www.charlestoncosmetology.com	843-552-3670	760-0976	167-3
Charleston County 4045 Bridge View Dr North Charleston SC 29405 *TF:* 800-735-2905 ■ *Web:* charlestoncounty.org	843-958-4030	958-4035	338
Charleston County Public Library 68 Calhoun St Charleston SC 29401 *TF:* 800-768-3676 ■ *Web:* ccpl.org	843-805-6930	727-3741	434-3
Charleston County School District (CCSD) 75 Calhoun St Charleston SC 29401 *TF:* 800-241-8898 ■ *Web:* www.ccsdschools.com	843-937-6300	937-6307	685
Charleston Crab House 145 Wappoo Creek Dr Charleston SC 29412 *Web:* charlestoncrabhouse.com	843-795-1963		671
Charleston Express PO Box 39 Charleston AR 72933 *Web:* www.charlestonexpress.com	479-252-6351	996-4494	532-2
Charleston Gazette 1001 Virginia St E Charleston WV 25301 *Web:* www.wvgazettemail.com	304-348-5140	348-1233	532-2
Charleston Grill 224 King St Charleston SC 29401 *Web:* www.charlestongrill.com	843-577-4522		671
Charleston Harbor Resort & Marina 20 Patriots Pt Rd Mount Pleasant SC 29464 *TF:* 888-856-0028 ■ *Web:* charlestonharborresort.com	843-856-0028	856-8333	669
Charleston International Airport 5500 International Blvd Ste 101 Charleston SC 29418 *Web:* www.iflychs.com	843-767-7000	760-3020	27
Charleston Marine Containers Inc 2301 Noisette Blvd North Charleston SC 29405 **Fax Area Code:* 843 ■ *TF:* 877-775-3795 ■ *Web:* www.cmci.com	877-775-3795	745-0302*	482
Charleston Metal Products Inc 350 Grant St Waterloo IN 46793 *Web:* www.charlestonmetal.com	260-837-8211	837-8101	621
Charleston Metro Chamber of Commerce 4500 Leeds Ave Ste 100 North Charleston SC 29405 *Web:* www.charlestonchamber.org	843-577-2510	723-4853	139
Charleston Museum 360 Meeting St Charleston SC 29403 *Web:* www.charlestonmuseum.org	843-722-2996	722-1784	520
Charleston Newspapers Ltd 1001 Virginia St E Charleston WV 25301 *TF:* 800-982-6397 ■ *Web:* www.cnpapers.com	304-348-4848		532-3
Charleston Place 205 Meeting St Charleston SC 29401 *TF:* 888-635-2350 ■ *Web:* www.belmond.com	843-722-4900		379
Charleston Regional Chamber of Commerce 1116 Smith St Charleston WV 25301 *TF:* 800-792-4326 ■ *Web:* www.charlestonareaalliance.org	304-340-4253	340-4275	139
Charleston (SC) City Hall 50 Broad St Charleston SC 29401 *Web:* www.charleston-sc.gov	843-577-6970	720-3959	337
Charleston School of Law LLC, The 81 Mary St Charleston SC 29403 *Web:* charlestonlaw.edu	843-329-1000		685
Charleston Southern University 9200 University Blvd Charleston SC 29423 *TF:* 800-947-7474 ■ *Web:* www.charlestonsouthern.edu	843-863-7050	863-7070	166
Charleston Steel & Metal Co 2700 Spruill Ave Charleston SC 29405 *Web:* www.charlestonsteelandmetal.com	843-722-7278		723
Charleston Symphony Orchestra 756 St Andrews Blvd Charleston SC 29407 *Web:* charlestonsymphony.org	843-723-7528		573-3
Charleston (WV) City Hall 200 Civic Center Dr Charleston WV 25301 *Web:* www.charlestonwv.gov	304-348-8000	348-8157	337

	Phone	Fax	Class
Charleston's 5907 NW Expy St . . . . Oklahoma City OK 73132 *Fax Area Code: 918 ■ Web: charlestons.com	405-721-0060	355-9181*	671
Charlestown Clark County Public Library 51 Clark Rd. . . . . Charlestown IN 47111 Web: clarkco.lib.in.us	812-256-3337		434-3
Charlestown Retirement Community (CCI) 715 Maiden Choice Ln . . . . Catonsville MD 21228 TF: 800-917-8649 ■ Web: www.ericksonliving.com	410-242-2880		672
Charlestown State Park 12500 Indiana 62 . . . . Charlestown IN 47111 Web: www.in.gov	812-256-5600		565
Charlevoix County 203 Antrim St. . . . . Charlevoix MI 49720 TF: 800-548-9157 ■ Web: www.charlevoixcounty.org	231-547-7200	547-7217	338
Charlevoix Public Schools 104 E St Marys Dr . . . . Charlevoix MI 49720 Web: www.rayder.net	231-547-3200	547-0556	685
Charley G's Seafood Grill 3809 Ambassador Caffery Pkwy . . . . LaFayette LA 70503 Web: www.charleygs.com	337-981-0108		671
Charley's Concrete 700 Katy Rd. . . . . Keller TX 76244 Web: www.charleysconcrete.com	817-431-2016	431-5337	182
Charley's Crab Restaurant 63 Market St SW. . . . . Grand Rapids MI 49503 Web: www.muer.com	616-459-2500	459-8142	671
Charley's Steak House 1260 Central Florida Pkwy . . . . Orlando FL 32837 Web: www.talkofthetownrestaurants.com	407-363-0228		671
Charleys Philly Steaks 2500 Farmers Dr Ste 140 . . . . Columbus OH 43235 TF: 800-437-8325 ■ Web: www.charleys.com	614-923-4700		670
Charlie Bravo Aviation LLC 160 Terminal Rd . . . . Georgetown TX 78628 Web: www.wepushtin.com	512-868-9000		261
Charlie Palmer Steak D.C. LLC 1090 Vermont Ave NW . . . . Washington DC 20005	202-547-8100		671
Charlie's Charts PO Box 352 . . . . Seal Beach CA 90740 Web: www.charliescharts.com	562-787-5653	430-6969	637-2
Charlie's L'Etoile Verte 8 New Orleans Rd. . . . . Hilton Head Island SC 29928 Web: www.charliesgreenstar.com	843-785-9277		671
Charlie's on the Lake 4150 S 144th St . . . . Omaha NE 68137 Web: www.charliesonthelake.net	402-894-9411		671
Charlie's Steak-Ribs-Ale 3009 W State Hwy 76 . . . . Branson MO 65616 Web: charliesbranson.com	417-334-6090		671
Charloma Inc 727 N Liberty St. . . . . Cherryvale KS 67335 Web: www.charloma.com	620-336-2124	336-2127	604
Charlotte Ann Albertson's Cooking School PO Box 27 . . . . Wynnewood PA 19096 Web: www.albertsoncookingschool.com	610-649-9290	649-2939	685
Charlotte Anodizing Products Inc 591 E Packard Hwy. . . . . Charlotte MI 48813 TF: 800-818-6945 ■ Web: www.charlotte-anodizing.com	517-543-1911		481
Charlotte Appliances Inc 3200 Lake Ave . . . . Rochester NY 14612 TF: 800-244-0405 ■ Web: www.charlotteappliance.com	585-663-5050		321
Charlotte Chamber of Commerce 330 S Tryon St PO Box 32785 . . . . Charlotte NC 28202 Web: charlotteregion.com	704-378-1300	374-1903	139
Charlotte Convention & Visitors Bureau 500 S College St. . . . . Charlotte NC 28202 TF: 800-722-1994 ■ Web: www.charlottesgotalot.com	704-334-2282	342-3972	206
Charlotte Convention Ctr 501 S College St. . . . . Charlotte NC 28202 Web: www.charlottemeetings.com	704-339-6000		205
Charlotte Correctional Institution 33123 Oil Well Rd. . . . . Punta Gorda FL 33955 Web: dc.state.fl.us	941-833-8100		213
Charlotte County 250 LeGrande Ave Ste A PO Box 608 . . . . Charlotte Court House VA 23923 Web: www.charlotteva.com	434-542-5117	542-5248	338
Charlotte County 18500 Murdoch Cir . . . . Port Charlotte FL 33948 Web: www.charlottecountyfl.gov	941-743-1300		338
Charlotte County Chamber of Commerce 311 W Retta Esplanade. Punta Gorda FL 33950 Web: www.charlottecountychamber.org	941-639-6330		139
Charlotte Hall Veterans Home 29449 Charlotte Hall Rd . . . . Charlotte Hall MD 20622 Web: charhall.org	301-884-8171		793
Charlotte Hawkins Brown Museum 6136 Burlington Rd . . . . Gibsonville NC 27249 TF: 800-767-1560 ■ Web: historicsites.nc.gov	336-449-4846	449-0176	520
Charlotte Hungerford Hospital (CHH) 540 Litchfield St . . . . Torrington CT 06790 Web: www.charlottehungerford.org	860-496-6666		374-3
Charlotte Latin Schools Inc 9502 Providence Rd . . . . Charlotte NC 28277 Web: www.charlottelatin.org	704-846-1100		685
Charlotte Mecklenburg Library 310 N Tryon St . . . . Charlotte NC 28202 Web: cmlibrary.org	704-416-0100		434-3
Charlotte Motor Speedway 5555 Concord Pkwy S . . . . Concord NC 28027 TF: 800-455-3267 ■ Web: www.charlottemotorspeedway.com	704-455-3200	455-2547	642
Charlotte Museum of History & Hezekiah Alexander Homesite 3500 Shamrock Dr . . . . Charlotte NC 28215 Web: www.charlottemuseum.org	704-568-1774		520
Charlotte Observer 550 S Caldwell St. . . . . Charlotte NC 28202 TF: 800-532-5350 ■ Web: www.charlotteobserver.com	704-358-5000		532-2
Charlotte Pipe & Foundry Co 2109 Randolph Rd . . . . Charlotte NC 28207 TF: 800-438-6091 ■ Web: www.charlottepipe.com	704-372-5030	348-6450	490
Charlotte Radiological PA 1701 E Blvd . . . . Charlotte NC 28203 Web: www.charlotteradiology.com	704-334-7800		418

	Phone	Fax	Class
Charlotte Russe Inc 5910 Pacific Center Blvd . . . . San Diego CA 92121 TF: 888-211-7271 ■ Web: www.charlotterusse.com	888-211-7271		157-6
Charlotte Street Grill & Pub 157 Charlotte St . . . . Asheville NC 28801 Web: charlottestreetpub.com	828-252-2948		671
Charlotte Technical College 18150 Murdock Cir . . . . Port Charlotte FL 33948 Web: www.yourcharlotteschools.net	941-255-7500	255-7509	167-3
Charlotte-Mecklenburg Schools 701 E ML King Jr Blvd . . . . Charlotte NC 28202 Web: www.cms.k12.nc.us	980-343-5139	343-5661	685
Charlottesville (Independent City) 605 E Main St. . . . . Charlottesville VA 22902 Web: www.charlottesville.gov	434-970-3101	970-3890	338
Charlottesville Regional Chamber of Commerce 209 Fifth St NE . . . . Charlottesville VA 22902 Web: cvillechamber.com	434-295-3141	295-3144	139
Charlson & Wilson Bonded Abstracters Inc 111 N Fourth St . . . . Manhattan KS 66502 Web: charlsonandwilson.com	785-565-4800		653
Charlton Memorial Hospital 363 Highland Ave . . . . Fall River MA 02720 TF: 800-276-0103 ■ Web: www.southcoast.org	508-679-3131		374-3
Charlton Weeks LLP 1031 West Ave M 14 Ste A . . . . Palmdale CA 93551 Web: charltonweeks.com	661-265-0969		41
Charm Jewelry Ltd 140 Portland St . . . . Dartmouth NS B2Y1J1 Web: charmdiamondcentres.com	902-463-7177		410
Charm Sciences Inc 659 Andover St . . . . Lawrence MA 01843 TF: 800-343-2170 ■ Web: www.charm.com	978-687-9200	687-9216	479
Charmac Inc 452 S Park Ave W . . . . Twin Falls ID 83301 Web: www.charmactrailers.com	208-733-5241	733-5557	763
Charmaine School & Model Agency 3538 Stellhorn Rd. . . . . Fort Wayne IN 46815 Web: www.charmainemodels.com	260-485-8421	485-1873	685
Charming Shoppes Inc 933 MacArthur Blvd . . . . Mahwah NJ 07430 NASDAQ: ASNA ■ Web: www.ascenaretail.com	551-777-6700		157-6
Charnstrom 5391 12th Ave E . . . . Shakopee MN 55379 TF: 800-328-2962 ■ Web: www.charnstrom.com	800-328-2962	916-3215	470
Chart House Restaurant 1 Cameron St . . . . Alexandria VA 22314 Web: www.chart-house.com	703-684-5080		671
Chart Industries Air-X-Changers/Hammco 5616 S 129th E Ave . . . . Tulsa OK 74134 TF: 800-404-3904 ■ Web: www.airx.com	918-619-8000	384-5000	91
Chart Industries Inc 1 Infinity Corporate Centre Dr Ste 300 . . . . Garfield Heights OH 44125 Web: www.chartindustries.com	440-753-1490	753-1491	91
Chart Tech Tool Inc 4060 Lisa Dr. . . . . Tipp City OH 45371 Web: ctti-inc.com	937-667-3543	667-3613	455
Chartbeat Inc 826 Broadway 12th St 6th Fl. . . . . New York NY 10003 Web: chartbeat.com	646-786-8472		387
Charter at Beaver Creek 120 Offerson Rd . . . . Beaver Creek CO 81620 Web: www.wyndhamvacationrentals.com	970-949-6660		379
Charter Brokerage 383 Main Ave Ste 400 . . . . Norwalk CT 06851 Web: www.charterbrokerage.net	203-840-7500	840-7525	690
Charter College 2221 E Northern Lights Blvd Ste 120 . . . . Anchorage AK 99508 TF: 888-200-9942 ■ Web: www.chartercollege.edu	907-277-1000		166
Charter Communications Inc 12405 Powerscourt Dr . . . . Saint Louis MO 63131 NASDAQ: CHTR ■ TF: 888-438-2427 ■ Web: www.spectrum.com	314-965-0555	965-9745	116
Charter Dura-Bar 2100 W Lake Shore Dr . . . . Woodstock IL 60098 Web: www.charterdura-bar.com	815-338-3900	338-3950	307
Charter Enterprises LLC 1255 Corporate Center Dr Ste PH402. . . . . . . Monterey Park CA 91754 Web: www.charterbbq.com	323-269-6868		360-2
Charter Films Inc 1901 Winter St PO Box 277 . . . . Superior WI 54880 TF: 877-411-3456 ■ Web: charternex.com	715-395-8258		548
Charter Industries LLC 3900 S Greenbrooke Dr SE. . . . . Kentwood MI 49512 TF: 800-538-9088 ■ Web: charterindustries.com	800-538-9088		351
Charter Manufacturing Company Inc 1212 W Glen Oaks Ln. . . . . Mequon WI 53092 TF: 800-437-8789 ■ Web: www.chartermfg.com	262-243-4700		723
Charter Medical Ltd 3948-A Westpoint Blvd. . . . . Winston-Salem NC 27103 *Fax Area Code: 336 ■ TF: 866-458-3116 ■ Web: chartermedical.com	866-458-3116	714-4241*	475
Charter Oak Cultural Ctr 21 Charter Oak Ave. . . . . Hartford CT 06106 Web: www.charteroakcenter.org	860-524-8014		50-2
Charter Oak State College 55 Paul J Manafort Dr. . . . . New Britain CT 06053 TF: 800-235-6559 ■ Web: charteroak.edu	860-515-3800		166
Charter of Lynchburg Inc 139 Winebarger Cir . . . . Lynchburg VA 24501 Web: www.charterinc.com	434-239-9000		319-4
Charter One Hotels & Resorts Inc 5464 Lena Rd . . . . Bradenton FL 34211 Web: charteronehotels.com	941-907-9017		379
Charter Plastics 221 S Perry St . . . . Titusville PA 16354 Web: www.charterplastics.com	814-827-9665		608
Charter School Business Management (CSBM) 237 W 35th St Ste 301 . . . . New York NY 10001 TF: 888-710-2726 ■ Web: www.csbm.com	888-710-2726		393
Charter Schools USA 6245 N Federal Hwy Ste 500 . . . . Fort Lauderdale FL 33308 Web: charterschoolsusa.com	954-202-3500	202-3512	242
Charter Steel Trading Company Inc 4401 W Roosevelt Rd . . . . Chicago IL 60624 Web: www.chartersteeltrading.com	773-522-3100		492

Name / Address	City	State	Zip	Phone	Fax	Class
Charter Trust Co 90 N Main St *Web:* www.chartertrust.com	Concord	NH	03301	603-224-1350		194
Charter UP 3340 Peachtree Rd NE Ste 100 *TF:* 855-920-2287 ■ *Web:* www.charterup.com	Atlanta	GA	30326	855-920-2287		788
Charter Wire 3700 W Milwaukee Rd *TF:* 800-436-9074 ■ *Web:* www.charterwire.com	Milwaukee	WI	53208	414-390-3000	390-3031	813
Chartered Business Valuators 277 Wellington St W Ste 808 *TF:* 866-770-7315 ■ *Web:* cbvinstitute.com	Toronto	ON	M5V3E4	416-977-1117	977-7066	772
Chartis Group LLC 220 W Kinzie St 3rd Fl *TF:* 877-667-4700 ■ *Web:* www.chartis.com	Chicago	IL	60654	877-667-4700		463
Chartist Newsletter PO Box 758 *TF:* 800-942-4278 ■ *Web:* www.thechartist.com	Seal Beach	CA	90740	562-596-2385		531-9
Charton Management Inc 373 Timberline Pkwy *Web:* charton.biz	Vienna	WV	26105	304-865-2222	865-2231	463
Chartpak Inc 1 River Rd *TF:* 800-628-1910 ■ *Web:* www.chartpak.net	Leeds	MA	01053	413-584-5446	584-6781	43
Chartrand Imports PO Box 1319 *TF:* 800-473-7307 ■ *Web:* www.chartrandimports.com	Rockland	ME	04841	207-594-7300		81-3
Chartway Federal Credit Union 5700 Cleveland St *TF:* 800-678-8765 ■ *Web:* www.chartway.com	Virginia Beach	VA	23462	757-552-1000	671-7691	219
Chartwell Hospitality 5000 Meridian Blvd Ste 750 *Web:* www.chartwellhospitality.com	Franklin	TN	37067	615-550-1270	550-1271	379
Chartwell Master Care LP 100 Milverton Dr Ste 700 *TF:* 855-461-0685 ■ *Web:* chartwell.com	Mississauga	ON	L5R4H1	905-501-9219		371
Chas G. Allen Inc 25 Williamsville Rd *Web:* www.chasgallen.com	Barre	MA	01005	978-355-2911	355-2917	455
Chas Roberts Air Conditioning Inc 9828 N 19th Ave *Web:* www.chasroberts.com	Phoenix	AZ	85021	602-943-3426		189-10
Chasan Leyner & Lamparello A Professional Corp 300 Harmon Meadow Blvd *Web:* www.chasanlaw.com	Secaucus	NJ	07094	201-348-6000		428
Chasan LLC 15185 Industrial Park Rd *TF:* 855-601-0894 ■ *Web:* www.chasantn.com	Bristol	VA	24202	276-466-4121		14
Chasco Constructors Limited LLP 2801 E Old Settlers Blvd *Web:* www.chasco.com	Round Rock	TX	78665	512-244-0600		186
Chase & Sons Inc 295 University Ave *TF:* 800-323-4182 ■ *Web:* www.chasecorp.com	Westwood	MA	02090	781-332-0700		816
Chase Bank 28 Liberty St *TF:* 800-935-9935 ■ *Web:* www.chase.com	New York	NY	10005	800-935-9935		70
Chase Brexton Health Services Inc 1111 N Charles St *TF:* 866-392-4483 ■ *Web:* www.chasebrexton.org	Baltimore	MD	21201	410-837-2050	234-8177	353
Chase Collegiate School 565 Chase Pkwy *Web:* www.chasecollegiate.org	Waterbury	CT	06708	203-236-9500		148
Chase County 318 Broadway St *Web:* www.chasecountychamber.org	Cottonwood Falls	KS	66845	620-273-8469		338
Chase County 341 W 3 St PO Box 1299 *Web:* www.co.chase.ne.us	Imperial	NE	69033	308-882-7500	882-7552	338
Chase Design Group 99 Pasadena Ave Ste 9 *Web:* www.chasedesigngroup.com	South Pasadena	CA	91030	323-668-1055		344
Chase Enterprises Inc 6509 W Reno Ave *TF:* 800-525-4970 ■ *Web:* www.chappellsupply.com	Oklahoma City	OK	73127	405-495-1722		196
Chase Home Museum of Utah Folk Art 617 E S Temple *Web:* heritage.utah.gov	Salt Lake City	UT	84102	801-533-5760	533-4202	520
Chase Industries Inc 10021 Commerce Park Dr *TF:* 800-543-4455 ■ *Web:* www.chasedoors.com	Cincinnati	OH	45246	513-860-5565		480
Chase Law Group LLC, The 1447 York Rd Ste 505 *Web:* chaserelaw.com	Lutherville Timonium	MD	21093	410-928-7991		41
Chase Paymentech Solutions LLC 14221 Dallas Pkwy *TF:* 800-708-3740 ■ *Web:* merchantservices.chase.com	Dallas	TX	75254	800-708-3740		255
Chase Plastic Services Inc 6467 Waldon Center Dr *TF:* 800-232-4273 ■ *Web:* chaseplastics.com	Clarkston	MI	48346	248-620-2120		599
Chase Publishing PO Box 1200 *Web:* www.chasepublishing.com	Glen	NH	03838	603-383-4166	383-8162	637-2
Chase, Alex & Charles Emporium Inc 202 McGrath	Battle Creek	MI	49014	269-963-4131		567
Chase-Lloyd House 22 Maryland Ave *Web:* www.chaselloydhouse.org	Annapolis	MD	21401	410-263-2723		50-3
Chase-Logeman Corp 303 Friendship Dr *Web:* chaselogeman.com	Greensboro	NC	27409	336-665-0754		358
ChaseSource LP 3311 W Alabama *Web:* www.chasesource.com	Houston	TX	77098	713-874-5800		260
Chastain Homer L & Associates LLP 5 N Country Club Rd *Web:* www.chastainengineers.com	Decatur	IL	62521	217-422-8544		727
Chastain, The 4320 Powers Ferry Rd *Web:* www.horseradishgrill.com	Atlanta	GA	30342	404-255-7277		671
Chastain-Skillman Inc 4705 Old Rd 37 *Web:* www.chastainskillman.com	Lakeland	FL	33813	863-646-1402	647-3806	261
Chateau at Brooklyn Rehabilitation & Nursing Ctr, The 3457 Nostrand Ave *Web:* thechateaurehab.com	Brooklyn	NY	11229	718-535-5100		371
Chateau De Mores State Historic Site 3426 Chateau Rd *Web:* history.nd.gov	Medora	ND	58645	701-623-4355	623-4921	565
Chateau du Sureau 48688 Victoria Ln *Web:* www.chateausureau.com	Oakhurst	CA	93644	559-683-6860		379
Chateau Elan Resort & Conference Ctr 100 Rue Charlemagne *Web:* www.chateauelan.com	Braselton	GA	30517	678-425-0900		377
Chateau La Jolla Inn 233 Prospect St *Web:* chateaulajollainn.com	La Jolla	CA	92037	858-459-4451		378
Chateau Lacombe Hotel 10111 Bellamy Hill *TF:* 800-661-8801 ■ *Web:* www.chateaulacombe.com	Edmonton	AB	T5J1N7	780-428-6611	425-6564	379
Chateau Louis Hotel & Conference Ctr 11727 Kingsway *TF:* 800-661-9843 ■ *Web:* www.chateaulouis.com	Edmonton	AB	T5G3A1	780-452-7770	454-3436	379
Chateau Marmont Hotel 8221 Sunset Blvd *Web:* www.chateaumarmont.com	Los Angeles	CA	90046	323-656-1010	655-5311	379
Chateau Montelena Winery 1429 Tubbs Ln *Web:* montelena.com	Calistoga	CA	94515	707-942-5105	942-4221	80-3
Chateau Morrisette Winery 287 Winery Rd SW *TF:* 866-695-2001 ■ *Web:* www.thedogs.com	Floyd	VA	24091	540-593-2865	593-2868	50-7
Chateau on the Lake 415 N State Hwy 265 *TF:* 888-333-5253 ■ *Web:* www.chateauonthelake.com	Branson	MO	65616	417-334-1161	339-5566	379
Chateau Resort & Conference Ctr, The 475 Camelback Rd *TF:* 800-245-5900 ■ *Web:* chateauresort.com	Tannersville	PA	18372	570-629-5900		707
Chateau Rouge 1505 S Broadway Ave *TF:* 800-926-1601 ■ *Web:* chateaurouge.com	Red Lodge	MT	59068	406-446-1601		707
Chateau Saint Jean 8555 Sonoma Hwy *Web:* www.chateaustjean.com	Kenwood	CA	95452	707-257-5784		50-7
Chateau Ste Michelle Winery 14111 NE 145th St *TF:* 800-267-6793 ■ *Web:* www.ste-michelle.com	Woodinville	WA	98072	425-488-1133		50-7
Chateau Vaudreuil Hotel & Suites 21700 Rt Transcanada Hwy *TF:* 800-363-7896 ■ *Web:* www.chateau-vaudreuil.com	Vaudreuil-Dorion	QC	J7V8P3	450-455-0955	455-6617	379
Chateau Versailles 1659 Sherbrooke St W *TF:* 888-933-8111 ■ *Web:* www.chateauversaillesmontreal.com	Montreal	QC	H3H1E3	514-933-3611		379
Chateau-Sur-Mer 474 Bellevue Ave *TF:* 800-326-6030 ■ *Web:* www.newportmansions.org	Newport	RI	02840	401-847-1000	847-1361	50-3
Chatfield Hollow State Park 381 Rt 80 *Web:* portal.ct.gov	Killingworth	CT	06419	860-663-2030		565
Chatfield Lumber Company Inc 4707 County Rd 7 SE *TF:* 877-669-9120 ■ *Web:* www.chatfieldlumber.com	Eyota	MN	55934	507-545-3900	545-3901	364
Chatham Bars Inn 297 Shore Rd *TF:* 800-527-4884 ■ *Web:* www.chathambarsinn.com	Chatham	MA	02633	800-527-4884		669
Chatham Central School District 50 Woodbridge Ave *Web:* www.chathamcentralschools.com	Chatham	NY	12037	518-392-2400		685
Chatham Chamber of Commerce 531 E Third St *TF:* 800-329-7466 ■ *Web:* www.ccucc.net	Siler City	NC	27344	919-742-3333	742-1333	139
Chatham County 124 Bull St *Web:* www.chathamcountyga.gov	Savannah	GA	31401	912-652-7869	652-7874	338
Chatham Daily News 138 King St W *Web:* www.chathamdailynews.ca	Chatham-Kent	ON	N7M1E3	519-354-2000		532-1
Chatham Financial Corp 235 Whitehorse Ln *Web:* www.chathamfinancial.com	Kennett Square	PA	19348	610-925-3120		403
Chatham Hall 800 Chatham Hall Cir *TF:* 877-644-2941 ■ *Web:* www.chathamhall.org	Chatham	VA	24531	434-432-2941	432-2405	622
Chatham Imports Inc 245 5th Ave Ste 1402 *Web:* www.chathamimports.com	New York	NY	10016	212-473-1100		80-3
Chatham Lodging Trust 222 Lakeview Ave Ste 200 *Web:* chathamlodgingtrust.com	West Palm Beach	FL	33401	561-802-4477		403
Chatham Search International Inc 3 Lion Gardiner *Web:* www.chathamct.com	Cromwell	CT	06416	860-635-5538		260
Chatham Steel Corp 501 W Boundary St *TF:* 800-800-1337 ■ *Web:* www.chathamsteel.com	Savannah	GA	31401	912-233-5751	944-0236	492
Chatham University 1 Woodland Rd *TF:* 800-837-1290 ■ *Web:* www.chatham.edu	Pittsburgh	PA	15232	412-365-1100	365-1609	166
Chatham's Place Restaurant 7575 Doctor Philips Blvd *Web:* chathamsplace.com	Orlando	FL	32819	407-345-2992		671
Chatham-Kent Chamber of Commerce 54 Fourth St *Web:* www.chatham-kentchamber.ca	Chatham-Kent	ON	N7M2G2	519-352-7540	352-8741	137
Chatham-Kent Health Alliance 80 Grand Ave W PO Box 2030 *Web:* www.ckha.on.ca	Chatham-Kent	ON	N7M5L9	519-352-6400	436-2522	374-2
Chatillon-DeMenil Mansion & Museum 3352 DeMenil Pl *Web:* www.demenil.org	Saint Louis	MO	63118	314-771-5828		520
Chatlos Foundation PO Box 915048 *Web:* www.chatlos.org	Longwood	FL	32791	407-862-5077		305
Chatr Mobile 333 Bloor St E 8th Fl *TF:* 800-485-9745 ■ *Web:* www.chatrwireless.com	Toronto	ON	M4W1G9	800-485-9745		224
Chatsworth Chamber of Commerce 10038 Old Depot Plaza Rd *TF:* 800-613-5903 ■ *Web:* www.chatsworthchamber.com	Chatsworth	CA	91311	818-341-2428	341-4930	139
Chatsworth Data Corp 9735 Lurline Ave *Web:* www.chatsworthdata.com	Chatsworth	CA	91311	818-350-5072	350-5090	248
Chatsworth Products Inc 31425 Agoura Rd *TF:* 800-834-4969 ■ *Web:* www.chatsworth.com	Westlake Village	CA	91361	818-735-6100	735-6199	176
Chatsworth Securities LLC 95 E Putnam Ave *Web:* chatsworthgroup.com	Greenwich	CT	06830	203-629-2612	629-2375	690
Chatsworth-Murray County Chamber of Commerce 1001 Green Rd *TF:* 800-969-9490 ■ *Web:* www.murraycountychamber.org	Chatsworth	GA	30705	706-695-6060	517-0198	139
Chattahoochee Hospice 6 Medical Park N *TF:* 800-770-8043 ■ *Web:* www.chattahoocheehospice.com	Valley	AL	36854	334-756-8043	756-8059	363

Name / Address	City	State	Zip	Phone	Fax	Class
Chattahoochee Nature Ctr 9135 Willeo Rd *Web:* www.chattnaturecenter.org	Roswell	GA	30075	770-992-2055	552-0926	50-5
Chattahoochee River National Recreation Area 1978 Island Ford Pkwy **Fax Area Code: 770 ■ Web:* www.nps.gov	Atlanta	GA	30350	678-538-1200	399-8087*	564
Chattahoochee Technical College - Appalachian Campus 100 Campus Dr *Web:* www.chattahoocheetech.edu	Jasper	GA	30143	706-253-4500		167-3
Chattahoochee Valley Community College 2602 College Dr *Web:* www.cv.edu	Phenix City	AL	36869	334-291-4900	291-4994	162
Chattanooga Area Chamber of Commerce 811 Broad St *TF:* 877-756-1684 ■ *Web:* www.chattanoogachamber.com	Chattanooga	TN	37402	423-756-2121		139
Chattanooga Area Convention & Visitors Bureau 215 Broad St *TF:* 800-322-3344 ■ *Web:* www.visitchattanooga.com	Chattanooga	TN	37402	423-756-8687	265-1630	206
Chattanooga City Hall 101 E 11th St Rm 100 *TF:* 866-894-5026 ■ *Web:* www.chattanooga.gov	Chattanooga	TN	37402	423-643-6311	643-7278	337
Chattanooga Convention Ctr One Carter Plz *TF:* 800-962-5213 ■ *Web:* www.chattanoogaconventioncenter.org	Chattanooga	TN	37402	423-756-0001		205
Chattanooga Group 4717 Adams Rd *TF:* 800-592-7329 ■ *Web:* www.djoglobal.com	Hixson	TN	37343	423-870-2281	875-5497	477
Chattanooga Labeling Systems Inc 120 Parmenas Ln *Web:* www.clsdeco.com	Chattanooga	TN	37405	423-825-2125		331
Chattanooga Metropolitan Airport 1001 Airport Rd Ste 14 *Web:* www.chattairport.com	Chattanooga	TN	37421	423-855-2202	855-2212	27
Chattanooga National Cemetery 1200 Bailey Ave *Web:* www.cem.va.gov	Chattanooga	TN	37404	423-855-6590	855-6597	136
Chattanooga public Library 1001 Broad St *Web:* www.lib.chattanooga.gov	Chattanooga	TN	37402	423-757-5310		434-3
Chattanooga State Technical Community College 4501 Amnicola Hwy *TF:* 866-547-3733 ■ *Web:* www.chattanoogastate.edu	Chattanooga	TN	37406	423-697-4400	697-4709	162
Chattanooga Symphony & Opera (CSO) 701 Broad St *Web:* chattanoogasymphony.org	Chattanooga	TN	37402	423-267-8583	265-6520	573-3
Chattanooga Theatre Ctr 400 River St *Web:* www.theatrecentre.com	Chattanooga	TN	37405	423-267-8534		572
Chattanooga Times Free Press 400 E 11th St *Web:* www.timesfreepress.com	Chattanooga	TN	37403	423-756-6900	757-6383	532-2
Chattanooga Zoo 301 N Holtzclaw Ave *Web:* www.chattzoo.org	Chattanooga	TN	37404	423-697-1322	697-1329	823
Chattaway 358 22nd Ave S *Web:* www.thechattaway.com	Saint Petersburg	FL	33705	727-823-1594		671
Chattem Inc 1715 W 38th St PO Box 2219 *Web:* www.chattem.com	Chattanooga	TN	37409	423-821-2037	821-0395	214
Chatten-Brown & Carstens LLP 2200 Pacific Coast Hwy Ste 318 *Web:* cbcearthlaw.com	Hermosa Beach	CA	90254	310-798-2400	798-2402	41
Chatterton & Associates The Wealth Management Team Inc 3061 E La Palma Ave *TF:* 800-490-4988 ■ *Web:* chattertoninc.com	Anaheim	CA	92806	714-572-2050	572-2056	690
Chaucer's Books 3321 State St *Web:* www.chaucersbooks.com	Santa Barbara	CA	93105	805-682-6787		95
Chaudhary & Associates Inc 211 Gateway Rd W Ste 204 *Web:* chaudhary.com	Napa	CA	94558	707-255-2729		261
Chauncey Conference Ctr 1 Chauncey Rd *Web:* www.acc-chaunceyconferencecenter.com	Princeton	NJ	08541	609-921-3600	683-4958	377
Chautauqua County 3 N Erie St *TF:* 800-252-8748 ■ *Web:* chqgov.com	Mayville	NY	14757	716-753-4000	753-4756	338
Chautauqua County 215 N Chautauqua St *Web:* chautauquacountyks.com	Sedan	KS	67361	620-725-5800	725-5801	338
Chautauqua County Chamber of Commerce 10785 Bennett Rd *Web:* www.chautauquachamber.org	Dunkirk	NY	14048	716-366-6200	366-4276	139
Chautauqua County Visitors Bureau Chautauqua Main Gate Rt 394 PO Box 1441 *TF:* 800-242-4569 ■ *Web:* www.tourchautauqua.com	Chautauqua	NY	14722	716-357-4569	357-2284	206
Chautauqua Dining Hall 900 Baseline Rd *Web:* www.chautauqua.com	Boulder	CO	80302	303-440-3776	449-0790	671
Chautauqua Region Community Foundation Inc 418 Spring St *Web:* crcfonline.org	Jamestown	NY	14701	716-661-3390	488-0387	305
Chautauqua-Cattaraugus Library System 106 W 5th St *Web:* www.cclsny.org	Jamestown	NY	14701	716-664-6675		434-3
Chauvin Arnoux Inc 15 Faraday Dr *Web:* www.aemc.com	Dover	NH	03820	603-749-6434		407
Chauvin Arnoux Inc 200 Foxborough Blvd *TF:* 800-343-1391 ■ *Web:* www.chauvin-arnoux.us	Foxborough	MA	02035	508-698-2115	698-2118	201
Chavez Grieves Consulting Engrs Inc 4700 Lincoln Rd NE *Web:* cg-engrs.com	Albuquerque	NM	87109	505-344-4080		261
Chavigny 365 Rue Chavigny St *Web:* www.chavigny.qc.ca	Trois-Rivieres	QC	G9B1A7	819-840-0400	377-1119	623
Chax Press 1517 N Wilmot Rd *Web:* www.chax.org	Tucson	AZ	85712	520-275-4330		637-2
Chaya Brasserie 110 Navy St *Web:* www.thechaya.com	Venice	CA	90291	310-396-1179		671
Chayet & Danzo LLC 650 S Cherry St Ste 710 *Web:* coloradoelderlaw.com	Denver	CO	80246	303-872-5980		41
Chaz Consulting PO Box 1853 *Web:* www.chazconsulting.com	Boulder	CO	80306	303-859-0934		196
Chazen Museum of Art University of Wisconsin 800 University Ave *Web:* www.chazen.wisc.edu	Madison	WI	53706	608-263-2246	263-8188	520
CHBN-FM 5915 Gateway Blvd *Web:* www.kiss917.com	Edmonton	AB	T5J5A3	780-423-2005	437-5129	647
CHC Consulting 1845 W Orangewood Ave Ste 300 *Web:* chcconsulting.com	Orange	CA	92868	949-250-0004		194
CHC Health 5550 Wild Rose Ln Ste 400 *TF:* 800-705-2930 ■ *Web:* chchealth.com	West Des Moines	IA	50266	800-705-2930		89
CHC Helicopter Corp 4740 Agar Dr *Web:* www.chcheli.com	Richmond	BC	V7B1A3	604-276-7500		359
CHCH-TV 163 Jackson St W PO Box 2230 *Web:* www.chch.com	Hamilton	ON	L8N3A6	905-522-1101	523-8011	647
CHCP 2656 S Loop W Ste 380 *TF:* 800-850-0255 ■ *Web:* www.chcp.edu	Houston	TX	77054	713-664-5300	664-7951	167-3
CHEA (Council for Higher Education Accreditation) 1 Dupont Cir NW Ste 510 *Web:* www.chea.org	Washington	DC	20036	202-955-6126	955-6129	48-1
Cheaha Regional Library 935 Coleman St *Web:* www.cheaharegionallibrary.org	Heflin	AL	36264	256-463-7125		434-3
Cheaha Resort State Park 19644 Hwy 281 *TF:* 800-610-5801 ■ *Web:* www.alapark.com	Delta	AL	36258	256-488-5111	488-5885	565
Cheap Joe's Art Stuff Inc 374 Industrial Park Dr *TF:* 800-227-2788 ■ *Web:* www.cheapjoes.com	Boone	NC	28607	828-262-5459		522
Cheatham County 100 Public Sq *Web:* cheathamcountytn.gov	Ashland City	TN	37015	615-792-4316		338
Cheatham County Chamber of Commerce 108 N Main St PO Box 354 *Web:* www.cheathamchamber.org	Ashland City	TN	37015	615-792-6722	792-5001	139
Cheatham County Public Library 188 County Services Dr Ste 200 *Web:* www.cheathamcountytn.gov	Ashland City	TN	37015	615-792-4828		434-3
Cheboygan County 870 S Main St *Web:* www.cheboygancounty.net	Cheboygan	MI	49721	231-627-8855		338
Cheboygan State Park 4490 Beach Rd *Web:* www.michigan.org	Cheboygan	MI	49721	231-627-2811		565
Checchi & Company Consulting Inc 1899 L St NW Ste 800 *Web:* www.checchiconsulting.com	Washington	DC	20036	202-452-9700	466-9070	194
Checchi Capital Advisors LLC 190 N Canon Dr Ste 402 *Web:* www.checchicapital.com	Beverly Hills	CA	90210	310-432-0010		514
Check Cashing Place Inc, The 945 Fifth Ave *TF:* 800-479-6677 ■ *Web:* thecheckcashingplaceinc.com	San Diego	CA	92101	619-239-6151		251
Check Cashing Store (CCS) 6340 NW Fifth Way *TF:* 800-361-1407 ■ *Web:* www.thecheckcashingstore.com	Fort Lauderdale	FL	33309	800-361-1407		141
Check Cashing USA Inc 899 NW 37th Ave *TF:* 833-352-2274 ■ *Web:* www.checkcashingusa.com	Miami	FL	33125	305-644-1840		141
Check Gallery PO Box 40006 *TF:* 800-995-9925 ■ *Web:* www.checkgallery.com	Colorado Springs	CO	80935	800-995-9925		142
Check Point Software Technologies Ltd 800 Bridge Pkwy *NASDAQ: CHKP ■ TF:* 800-429-4391 ■ *Web:* www.checkpoint.com	Redwood City	CA	94065	650-628-2000	654-4233	178-12
Checkbox Survey Inc 44 Pleasant St *TF:* 866-430-8274 ■ *Web:* www.checkbox.com	Watertown	MA	02472	617-231-8890	231-8815	396
Checker Distributors 400 W Dussel Dr Ste B *Web:* www.checkerdist.com	Maumee	OH	43537	419-893-2422		594
Checker Industrial Ltd 3345 Wyandotte St *Web:* www.checkerindustrial.com	East Windsor	ON	N8Y4S2	519-258-2022		111
Checkerboard Ltd 216 W Boylston St *TF:* 800-735-2475 ■ *Web:* checkerboardltd.com	West Boylston	MA	01583	800-735-2475		130
Checkered Flag Motor Car Corp 5225 Virginia Beach Blvd *TF:* 866-414-7820 ■ *Web:* www.checkeredflag.com	Virginia Beach	VA	23462	757-687-3486		57
Checkers Drive-In Restaurants Inc 4300 W Cypress St Ste 600 *TF:* 800-800-8072 ■ *Web:* checkers.com	Tampa	FL	33607	813-283-7000		670
Checkpoint Systems Inc 101 Wolf Dr *NYSE: CKP ■ TF:* 800-257-5540 ■ *Web:* www.checkpointsystems.com	Thorofare	NJ	08086	856-848-1800	848-0937	692
Checkr Inc 1 Montgomery St *TF:* 844-824-3257 ■ *Web:* www.checkr.com	San Francisco	CA	94108	844-824-3257		180
Checks In The Mail Inc 2435 Goodwin Ln *TF:* 800-733-4443 ■ *Web:* www.secure.checksinthemail.com	New Braunfels	TX	78135	800-733-4443		142
Checks Unlimited PO Box 19000 *TF:* 800-210-0468 ■ *Web:* www.checksunlimited.com	Colorado Springs	CO	80935	800-210-0468		142
ChecksByDeluxe.com LLC 3680 Victoria St N *TF:* 866-653-9471 ■ *Web:* www.checksbydeluxe.com	Shoreview	MN	55126	866-653-9471		86
Checon Corp 30 Larsen Way *Web:* www.checon.com	North Attleboro	MA	02763	508-809-5112	809-5163	815
Cheddar's Scratch Kitchen 700 I- 635 *Web:* cheddars.com	Irving	TX	75063	972-409-0300		670
Cheeca Lodge & Spa 81801 Overseas Hwy Mile Marker 82 *TF:* 800-327-2888 ■ *Web:* www.cheeca.com	Islamorada	FL	33036	305-664-4651		707
Cheek & Scott Drugs Inc 1520 Ohio Ave S *Web:* cheekandscott.com	Live Oak	FL	32064	386-362-2591		237
Cheeks International Academy 207 W 18th St *Web:* www.cheeksbeautyacademy.com	Cheyenne	WY	82001	307-637-8700	634-4944	167-3
Cheektowaga Chamber of Commerce 2875 Union Rd Ste 50 *Web:* www.cheektowaga.org	Cheektowaga	NY	14227	716-684-5838	684-5571	139
Cheekwood estate & gardens 1200 Forrest Pk Dr *Web:* cheekwood.org	Nashville	TN	37205	615-356-8000		97

Name / Address	City	State	Zip	Phone	Fax	Class
Cheer Inc 546 S Bedford St *Web:* www.cheerde.com	Georgetown	DE	19947	302-856-5187		363
Cheers 17 Depot St *Web:* www.cheersnh.com	Concord	NH	03301	603-228-0180	226-3459	671
Cheers Liquor Mart 1105 N Circle Dr *Web:* www.cheersliquormart.com	Colorado Springs	CO	80909	719-574-2244		443
Cheese Importers Warehouse 103 Main St *Web:* www.cheeseimporters.com	Longmont	CO	80501	303-772-9599		296-5
Cheeseburger in Paradise 10562 US Hwy 98W *Web:* www.cheeseburgerinparadise.com	Miramar	FL	32550	850-837-0197	837-0866	671
Cheesecake Factory Inc 26901 Malibu Hills Rd *NASDAQ:* CAKE ■ *Web:* www.thecheesecakefactory.com	Calabasas	CA	91301	818-871-3000		670
Cheesecake Factory, The 789 W Harbor Dr	San Diego	CA	92101	619-231-0036		296-5
Cheesequake State Park 300 Gordon Rd *Web:* www.njparksandforests.org	Matawan	NJ	07747	732-566-2161		565
Chef Allen's 19088 NE 29th Ave *Web:* www.chefallens.com	Aventura	FL	33180	305-935-2900		671
Chef Jean-Pierre Cooking School 1436 N Federal Hwy *Web:* www.chefjeanpierre.com	Fort Lauderdale	FL	33304	954-563-2700		685
Chef Joe Randall's Cooking School 5409 Waters Ave *Web:* www.chefjoerandall.com	Savannah	GA	31404	912-303-0409	303-0947	685
Chef John Folse & Company Inc 2517 S Philippe Ave *Web:* www.jfolse.com	Gonzales	LA	70737	225-644-6000		296-14
Chef Mavro 1969 S King St *Web:* mbychefmavrorestaurant.com	Honolulu	HI	96826	808-944-4714		671
Chef Wayne's Big Mamou 63 Liberty St *Web:* chefwaynes-bigmamou.com	Springfield	MA	01103	413-732-1011		671
Chef's Workshop 3439 Lorna Ln *Web:* chefsworkshop.com	Birmingham	AL	35216	205-637-1055		196
Chefs International Inc 62 Broadway *Web:* www.chefsinternationalnj.com	Point Pleasant Beach	NJ	08742	732-295-0350		670
Chefs' Warehouse Inc, The 100 East Ridge Rd *Web:* www.chefswarehouse.com	Ridgefield	CT	06877	203-894-1345		803-1
Chehayeb & Associates Inc 3702 W Azeele St *Web:* chehayeb.com	Tampa	FL	33609	813-876-1415	876-0913	261
Cheim & Read 547 W 25th St *Web:* www.cheimread.com	New York	NY	10001	212-242-7727	242-7737	42
CHEK-TV 780 King's Rd *TF:* 866-639-7241 ■ *Web:* www.cheknews.ca	Victoria	BC	V8T5A2	250-383-2435	384-7766	647
Chelan County Deputy Sheriff's Assn 401 Washington Ste 1 *Web:* www.co.chelan.wa.us	Wenatchee	WA	98801	509-667-6380	667-6611	338
Chelan Fruit Marketing 8 Howser Rd PO Box 669 *Web:* www.chelanfruit.com	Chelan	WA	98816	509-682-2591	682-4620	315-3
Cheley Colorado Camps Inc 601 Steele St *TF:* 800-359-7200 ■ *Web:* www.cheley.com	Denver	CO	80206	303-377-3616		239
Chella Professional Skin Care 507 Calle San Pablo *TF:* 877-424-3552 ■ *Web:* www.chella.com	Camarillo	CA	93012	805-383-7711		77
Chelmsford Public Library 25 Boston Rd *Web:* www.chelmsfordlibrary.org	Chelmsford	MA	01824	978-256-5521	256-8511	434-3
Chelo's Inc 1725 Mendon Rd Ste 200 *Web:* www.chelos.com	Cumberland	RI	02864	401-312-6500	312-6501	670
Chelsea Building Products 565 Cedar Way *TF:* 800-424-3573 ■ *Web:* www.chelseabuildingproducts.com	Oakmont	PA	15139	800-424-3573		235
Chelsea District Library 221 S Main St *Web:* chelseadistrictlibrary.org	Chelsea	MI	48118	734-475-8732	475-6190	434-3
Chelsea Green Publishing Co 85 N Main St *TF:* 800-639-4099 ■ *Web:* www.chelseagreen.com	White River Junction	VT	05001	802-295-6300	295-6444	637-2
Chelsea Investment Corp 6339 Paseo Del Lago *Web:* www.chelseainvestco.com	Carlsbad	CA	92011	760-456-6000	456-6001	653
Chelsea Lumber Co 1 Old Barn Cir *TF:* 800-875-9126 ■ *Web:* www.chelsealumber.com	Chelsea	MI	48118	734-475-9126		191-3
Chelsea Milling Co 201 W N St PO Box 460 *TF:* 800-727-2460 ■ *Web:* site.jiffymix.com	Chelsea	MI	48118	734-475-1361	475-4630	296-23
Chelsea Pictures Inc 343 E 18th St 3rd Fl *Web:* www.chelsea.com	New York	NY	10003	212-431-3434		514
Chelsea Piers Sports & Entertainment Complex 23rd St & Hudson River *Web:* www.chelseapiers.com	New York	NY	10011	212-336-6400	336-6130	354
Chelsea Savoy Hotel 204 W 23rd St *TF:* 866-929-9353 ■ *Web:* www.chelseasavoynyc.com	New York	NY	10011	212-929-9353	741-6309	379
Chelsea Soldiers Home 91 Crest Ave *Web:* www.mass.gov	Chelsea	MA	02150	617-884-5660	884-1162	793
Chelsio Communications Inc 209 N Fair Oaks Ave *Web:* www.chelsio.com	Sunnyvale	CA	94085	408-962-3600		225
Chelten House Products Inc 607 Heron Dr *Web:* www.cheltenhouse.com	Swedesboro	NJ	08085	856-467-1600		296-33
Chem Processing Inc 3910 Linden Oaks Dr *TF:* 800-262-2119 ■ *Web:* www.chemprocessing.com	Rockford	IL	61109	800-262-2119		481
Chem Quip Inc 2551 Land Ave *TF:* 800-821-1678 ■ *Web:* www.chemquip.com	Sacramento	CA	95815	916-923-5091	920-4611	146
CHEM Rx 750 Park Pl *Web:* www.chemrx.net	Long Beach	NY	11561	516-889-8770		237
Chem Space Associates Inc 655 William Pitt Way *Web:* www.lcms.com	Pittsburgh	PA	15238	412-828-3191	828-3192	194
Chem USA Corp 38507 Cherry St *TF:* 800-866-2436 ■ *Web:* www.chemusa.com	Newark	CA	94560	510-608-8818	608-8828	173-2
Chem/Serv Inc 715 SE 8th St *Web:* www.chemserv.com	Minneapolis	MN	55414	612-379-4411	379-8244	146
ChemADVISOR Inc 811 Camp Horne Rd Ste 220	Pittsburgh	PA	15237	412-847-2000	847-2010	194
Chemart Co 15 New England Way *Web:* chemart.com	Lincoln	RI	02865	401-333-9200		481
Chematics Inc PO Box 293 *TF:* 800-348-5174 ■ *Web:* chematics.com	North Webster	IN	46555	574-834-2406	834-7427	231
Chembio Diagnostics Inc 3661 Horseblock Rd *NASDAQ:* CEMI ■ *TF:* 844-243-6246 ■ *Web:* chembio.com	Medford	NY	11763	631-924-1135		582
Chemco Federal Credit Union 4200 Bells Ln *TF:* 888-785-1890 ■ *Web:* chemcofcu.com	Louisville	KY	40211	502-772-5780		219
Chemcoat Inc 2790 Canfields Ln *Web:* www.chemcoat.com	Montoursville	PA	17754	570-368-8631	368-8635	550
ChemDesign (CDC) 2 Stanton St *Web:* www.chemdesigncorp.com	Marinette	WI	54143	715-735-9033	735-5304	145
Chemed Corp 255 E Fifth St Ste 2600 *NYSE:* CHE ■ *TF:* 800-224-3633 ■ *Web:* www.chemed.com	Cincinnati	OH	45202	513-762-6900		185
Chemeketa Community College 4000 Lancaster Dr NE PO Box 14007 *Web:* www.chemeketa.edu	Salem	OR	97305	503-399-5006	399-3918	162
Chemetal 39 O'Neil St **Fax Area Code:* 413 ■ *TF:* 800-807-7341 ■ *Web:* www.chemetal.com	Easthampton	MA	01027	800-807-7341	529-9898*	295
CHEMetrics Inc 4295 Catlett Rd **Fax Area Code:* 540 ■ *TF:* 800-356-3072 ■ *Web:* www.chemetrics.com	Midland	VA	22728	800-356-3072	788-4856*	419
ChemGenes Corp 33 Industrial Way *Web:* www.chemgenes.com	Wilmington	MA	01887	978-694-4500		231
Chemgro Fertilizer Company Inc 1550 State St *TF:* 800-346-4769 ■ *Web:* chemgro.com	East Petersburg	PA	17520	717-560-1174	560-0117	276
Chemgrout Inc 805 E 31st St *Web:* www.chemgrout.com	LaGrange	IL	60526	708-354-7112	354-3881	190
Chemic Engineers & Constructors Inc 4820 FM 2004 *Web:* www.chemic.com	Hitchcock	TX	77563	409-986-6504		261
Chemical Abstracts Service (CAS) 2540 Olentangy River Rd *TF:* 800-848-6538 ■ *Web:* www.cas.org	Columbus	OH	43202	614-447-3600	447-3713	387
Chemical Bank 333 E Main St *NASDAQ:* CHFC ■ *TF:* 800-867-9757 ■ *Web:* www.chemicalbank.com	Midland	MI	48640	989-488-9219		360-2
Chemical Processing Magazine 1501 E Woodfield Rd Ste 400N *TF:* 800-343-4048 ■ *Web:* www.chemicalprocessing.com	Schaumburg	IL	60173	630-467-1300		457-21
Chemical Products Corp 102 Old Mill Rd *TF:* 877-210-9814 ■ *Web:* www.chemicalproductscorp.com	Cartersville	GA	30120	770-382-2144		143
Chemical Safety Corp 5901 Christie Ave *TF:* 888-594-1100 ■ *Web:* chemicalsafety.com	Emeryville	CA	94608	510-594-1000	594-1100	39
Chemical Safety Technology Inc 2461 Autumnvale Dr *Web:* www.kemsafe.com	San Jose	CA	95131	408-263-0984	263-2640	695
Chemical Solvents Inc 3751 Jennings Rd *Web:* chemicalsolvents.com	Cleveland	OH	44109	216-741-9310		541
Chemical Week 450 W 33rd St 5th Fl *TF:* 866-501-7540 ■ *Web:* chemweek.com	New York	NY	10001	212-884-9528	884-9514	457-21
Chemically Dependent Anonymous (CDA) PO Box 423 *TF:* 888-232-4673 ■ *Web:* cdawebsitedev.com	Severna Park	MD	21146	888-232-4673		48-21
Chemico Systems Inc 25200 Telegraph Rd *Web:* www.chemicosystems.com	Southfield	MI	48034	248-723-3263		144
Chemin-A-Haut State Park 14656 State Park Rd *TF:* 888-677-2436 ■ *Web:* crt.state.la.us	Bastrop	LA	71220	318-283-0812		565
ChemIndustry.com Inc 730 E Cypress Ave *Web:* www.chemweb.com	Monrovia	CA	91016	626-930-0808		681
Chemineer Inc 5870 Poe Ave *TF:* 800-643-0641 ■ *Web:* chemineer.com	Dayton	OH	45414	937-454-3200	454-3379	386
Chemistry Store, The 1133 Walter Price St *TF:* 800-224-1430 ■ *Web:* www.chemistrystore.com	Cayce	SC	29033	803-926-5385	926-5389	238
Chemithon Corp 5430 W Marginal Way SW *Web:* www.chemithon.com	Seattle	WA	98106	206-937-9954	932-3786	386
Chemline Inc 5151 Natural Bridge Rd *Web:* www.chemline.net	Saint Louis	MO	63115	314-664-2230		481
Chemlink Laboratories Inc 3960 Royal Dr *Web:* chemlinklabs.com	Kennesaw	GA	30144	770-499-8008		476
Chemmasters Inc 300 Edwards St *Web:* www.chemmasters.net	Madison	OH	44057	440-428-2105		145
Chem-Met Co, The 6419 Yochelson Pl *Web:* www.chem-metco.com	Clinton	MD	20735	301-868-3355	868-8946	143
Chemonics International Inc 1717 H St NW *TF:* 888-955-6881 ■ *Web:* www.chemonics.com	Washington	DC	20006	202-955-3300	955-3400	194
Chempacific Corp 6200 Freeport Ctr *Web:* www.chempacific.com	Baltimore	MD	21224	410-633-5771		146
Chem-pak Inc 242 Corning Way *TF:* 800-336-9828 ■ *Web:* chem-pak.com	Martinsburg	WV	25405	800-336-9828		295
Chem-plate Industries Inc 1800 Touhy Ave *Web:* www.chemplateindustries.com	Elk Grove Village	IL	60007	847-640-1600	640-1699	484
Chemprene Inc 483 Fishkill Ave *TF:* 800-431-9981 ■ *Web:* www.chemprene.com	Beacon	NY	12508	845-831-2800	831-4639	370
ChemQuest Group Inc, The 8150 Corporate Dr Ste 250 *Web:* chemquest.com	Cincinnati	OH	45242	513-469-7555		463

Name / Address	City	State	ZIP	Phone	Fax	Class
Chemresearch Company Inc 1101 W Hilton Ave *TF:* 877-457-5283 ■ *Web:* chemresearchco.com	Phoenix	AZ	85007	602-253-4175	254-0428	481
ChemRite CoPac 19725 W Edgewood Dr Bldg A101 *Web:* www.chemritecopac.com	Lannon	WI	53046	262-255-3880		393
Chemroy Canada Inc 106 Summerlea Rd *Web:* azeliscanada.com	Brampton	ON	L6T4X3	905-789-0701	789-7170	146
Chemsolv Inc 1140 Industry Ave SE *Web:* www.chemsolv.com	Roanoke	VA	24013	540-427-4000	427-3207	146
Chemstar Products Co 3915 Hiawatha Ave *TF:* 800-328-5037 ■ *Web:* www.chemstar.com	Minneapolis	MN	55406	612-722-0079	722-2473	144
Chemstress Consultant Co 39 S Main St *Web:* www.chemstress.com	Akron	OH	44308	330-434-3400	535-1431	261
Chem-Tainer Industries Inc 361 Neptune Ave *TF:* 800-275-2436 ■ *Web:* www.chemtainer.com	West Babylon	NY	11704	631-661-8300	661-8209	199
ChemTech Consultants Inc 1370 Washington Pk	Bridgeville	PA	15017	412-221-1360		261
Chemtech Plastics Inc 765 Church Rd *Web:* www.chemtechplastics.com	Elgin	IL	60123	847-742-6800	742-6884	604
Chemtex Print Usa Inc 3061 E Maria St *Web:* chemtexprint.com	Compton	CA	90221	310-900-1818		258
Chemtool Inc 801 W Rockton Rd *Web:* chemtool.com	Rockton	IL	61072	815-957-4140	624-0381	145
Chemtrans 14700 S Avalon Blvd *Web:* www.chemtrans.com	Gardena	CA	90248	310-523-2555	523-2552	780
Chem-Trend LP 1445 McPherson Pk Dr *TF:* 800-727-7730 ■ *Web:* www.chemtrend.com	Howell	MI	48843	517-546-4520		541
Chemtron Corp 35850 Schneider Ct *TF:* 800-676-5091 ■ *Web:* www.chemtron-corp.com	Avon	OH	44011	440-937-6348		660
Chemtron Inc 7350 C Lockport Pl *TF:* 800-536-7773 ■ *Web:* chemtroninc.com	Lorton	VA	22079	703-550-7772	339-7512	151
Chemtronics Inc 8125 Cobb Centre Dr *TF:* 800-645-5244 ■ *Web:* www.chemtronics.com	Kennesaw	GA	30152	770-424-4888		145
Chemtrusion Inc 7115 Clinton Dr *Web:* www.chemtrusion.com	Houston	TX	77020	713-675-1616	675-3944	604
Chemung County 210 Lake St PO Box 588 *Web:* www.chemungcountyny.gov	Elmira	NY	14902	607-737-2920		338
Chemung County Chamber of Commerce 400 E Church St *Web:* www.chemungchamber.org	Elmira	NY	14901	607-734-5137		139
Chemung Supply Corp PO Box 527 *TF:* 800-733-5508 ■ *Web:* www.chemungsupply.com	Elmira	NY	14903	607-733-5506	732-5379	191-2
ChemWerth Inc 1764 Litchfield Tpke *Web:* www.chemwerth.com	Woodbridge	CT	06525	203-387-7794	397-8132	479
Chen Dance Ctr 70 Mulberry St 2nd Fl *Web:* www.chendancecenter.org	New York	NY	10013	212-349-0126	349-0494	573-1
Chen Ling Palace 9856 Magnolia Ave *Web:* chenlingpalace.com	Riverside	CA	92503	951-351-8511		671
Chen PR Inc 71 Summer St *Web:* www.chenpr.com	Boston	MA	02110	781-466-8282	466-8989	636
Chena Hot Springs Resort 2040 Richardson Hwy *Web:* chenahotsprings.com	North Pole	AK	99705	907-488-1505	488-4058	378
Chena River State Recreation Area 3700 Airport Way *Web:* www.dnr.alaska.gov	Fairbanks	AK	99709	907-451-2705	451-2706	565
Chenango County 26 Conkey Ave Ste 125 *Web:* www.co.chenango.ny.us	Norwich	NY	13815	607-337-1450	337-1455	338
Chenango Valley State Park 153 State Park Rd *Web:* parks.ny.gov	Chenango Forks	NY	13746	607-648-5251		565
Chenango Valley Technologies Inc 328 Rte 12b *Web:* www.chenangovalleytech.com	Sherburne	NY	13460	607-674-4115		757
Cheney Liz (Rep R - WY) 416 Cannon House Office Bldg *Web:* cheney.house.gov	Washington	DC	20515	202-225-2311	225-3057	342-2
Cheney Pulp & Paper Co 1000 Anderson St *Web:* www.cheneypulp.com	Franklin	OH	45005	937-746-9991	746-3884	638
Cheney State Park 16000 NE 50th St *Web:* ksoutdoors.com	Cheney	KS	67025	316-542-3664		565
Cheng Cohen LLC 311 N Aberdeen Ste 400 *Web:* www.chengcohen.com	Chicago	IL	60607	312-243-1701		428
Cheniere Energy Inc 700 Milam St Ste 800 *NYSE: LNG* ■ *Web:* www.cheniere.com	Houston	TX	77002	713-375-5000	375-6000	325
Chenomx Inc 10230 Jasper Ave Ste 4350 *Web:* www.chenomx.com	Edmonton	AB	T5J4P6	780-432-0033		179
Chenoweth Ford Inc 1564 E Pike St *TF:* 877-289-8348 ■ *Web:* www.chenford.com	Clarksburg	WV	26301	877-289-8348		57
CHEP USA 8517 S Pk Cir *TF:* 866-855-2437 ■ *Web:* www.chep.com	Orlando	FL	32819	407-370-2437		648
Chepenik Financial Services 1010 Orange Ave *Web:* www.chepenikfinancial.com	Winter Park	FL	32789	407-660-1010		251
CHEQ-FM 373 Rte Cameron *Web:* www.pagesjaunes.ca	Sainte-Marie	QC	G6E3E2	418-387-1013		647
Cheraw State Park 100 State Park Rd *Web:* southcarolinaparks.com	Cheraw	SC	29520	843-537-9656		565
Cherette Group LLC 333 Washington Ave Ste 200 *Web:* cherettegroup.com	Grand Haven	MI	49417	616-842-6300		652
Cher-Make Sausage Co 2915 Calumet Ave **Fax Area Code:* 920 ■ *TF:* 800-242-7679 ■ *Web:* www.cher-make.com	Manitowoc	WI	54220	800-242-7679	683-5990*	296-26
Chernay Printing Inc 7483 S Main St *Web:* www.chernay.com	Coopersburg	PA	18036	610-282-3774	282-2982	627
Cherney Microbiological Services Ltd 1110 S Huron Rd *Web:* www.cherneymicro.com	Green Bay	WI	54311	920-406-8300		743
Chernoff Diamond & Company LLC 725 RXR Plz East Tower *Web:* www.chernoffdiamond.com	Uniondale	NY	11556	516-683-6100		193
Cherokee Brick & Tile Company Inc 3250 Waterville Rd *TF:* 800-277-2745 ■ *Web:* www.cherokeebrick.com	Macon	GA	31206	478-781-6800		150
Cherokee Consulting LLC 5057 Bear Mtn Dr *Web:* www.cherokeeconsultingllc.com	Evergreen	CO	80439	303-674-4857		180
Cherokee County 90 North St *Web:* www.cherokeega.com	Canton	GA	30114	678-493-6511		338
Cherokee County 260 Cedar Bluff Rd Ste 103 *Web:* www.cherokee-chamber.org	Centre	AL	35960	256-927-3668		338
Cherokee County 520 W Main St *Web:* www.cherokeecountyiowa.com	Cherokee	IA	51012	712-225-6744		338
Cherokee County 110 W Maple PO Box 14 *Web:* cherokeecountyks.gov	Columbus	KS	66725	620-429-2042		338
Cherokee County 110 Railroad Ave *Web:* cherokeecountysc.gov	Gaffney	SC	29340	864-487-2560	487-2594	338
Cherokee County 75 Peachtree St *Web:* cherokeecounty-nc.gov	Murphy	NC	28906	828-837-5527	837-9684	338
Cherokee County 213 W Delaware St *Web:* www.oklahomacounty.org	Tahlequah	OK	74464	918-456-0691		338
Cherokee County Chamber of Commerce 3605 Marietta Hwy *Web:* cherokeechamber.com	Canton	GA	30114	770-345-0400		139
Cherokee County Chamber of Commerce (CCCC) 805 W US 64 Hwy *Web:* www.cherokeecountychamber.com	Murphy	NC	28906	828-837-2242	837-6012	139
Cherokee County Chamber of Commerce 225 S Limestone St *Web:* www.cherokeechamber.org	Gaffney	SC	29340	864-489-5721		139
Cherokee County Public Library 300 E Rutledge Ave *Web:* cherokeecountylibrary.org	Gaffney	SC	29340	864-487-2711		434-3
Cherokee County School District 1205 Bluffs Pkwy *Web:* cherokeek12.net	Canton	GA	30114	770-479-1871		685
Cherokee County School District One 141 Twin Lake Rd PO Box 460 *Web:* www.cherokee1.org	Gaffney	SC	29342	864-206-2201		685
Cherokee Distributing Company Inc 200 Miller Main Cir *Web:* www.cherokeedistributing.com	Knoxville	TN	37919	865-588-7641	558-8941	81-1
Cherokee Electric Cooperative 1550 Clarence Chestnut Bypass PO Box O *TF:* 800-952-2667 ■ *Web:* www.cherokee.coop	Centre	AL	35960	256-927-5524	927-2278	245
Cherokee Enterprises Inc 14474 Commerce Way *Web:* www.cherokeecorp.com	Miami Lakes	FL	33016	305-828-3353		463
Cherokee Heritage Center & National Museum 21192 S Keeler Dr *TF:* 888-999-6007 ■ *Web:* www.cherokeeheritage.org	Park Hill	OK	74451	918-456-6007		520
Cherokee Inc 5990 Sepulveda Blvd Ste 600 *NASDAQ: CHKE* ■ *Web:* www.apexglobalbrands.com	Sherman Oaks	CA	91411	818-908-9868		301
Cherokee Investment Partners LLC 111 E Hargett St Ste 300 *Web:* cherokeefund.com	Raleigh	NC	27601	919-743-2500		401
Cherokee Landing State Park 28610 Pk 20 *Web:* www.travelok.com	Park Hill	OK	74451	918-457-5716	457-4871	565
Cherokee Ledger News, The 521 E Main St *Web:* www.ledgernews.com	Canton	GA	30114	770-479-1441		532-3
Cherokee Nation Businesses 10838 E Marshall St Ste 220 *Web:* cherokee-federal.com	Tulsa	OK	74116	918-582-9110		196
Cherokee Nation Entertainment LLC 3307 Seven Clans Ave *Web:* www.cherokeecasino.com	Tahlequah	OK	74464	918-207-3600		132
Cherokee Park Ranch 436 Cherokee Hills Dr *Web:* www.cherokeeparkranch.com	Livermore	CO	80536	970-493-6522	493-5802	239
Cherokee State Park N 4475 Rd *TF:* 866-602-4653 ■ *Web:* www.travelok.com	Langley	OK	74350	918-435-8727		565
Cherokee Steel Supply 196 Leroy Anderson Dr *TF:* 800-729-0334 ■ *Web:* cherokeesteel.com	Monroe	GA	30655	770-207-4621		492
Cherokee Telephone Co 403 N Service Rd *TF:* 844-424-3765 ■ *Web:* www.cherokeecomm.com	Calera	OK	74730	580-434-5375		224
Cherokee Welcome Ctr 498 Tsali Blvd *Web:* www.visitcherokeenc.com	Cherokee	NC	28719	828-359-6490		206
Cherry Aerospace LLC 1224 E Warner Ave *Web:* www.cherryaerospace.com	Santa Ana	CA	92705	714-545-5511	850-6095	621
Cherry Bekaert & Holland LLP 200 S Tenth St Ste 900 *Web:* www.cbh.com	Richmond	VA	23219	804-673-5700	673-4290	2
Cherry Carpet Inc 2915 London Blvd *Web:* cherrycarpet.com	Portsmouth	VA	23707	757-397-5811		290
Cherry Central Cooperative Inc 1771 N US 31 S *Web:* www.cherrycentral.com	Traverse City	MI	49684	231-946-1860	941-4167	296-20
Cherry City Electric 1596 22nd St SE *TF:* 800-755-7609 ■ *Web:* www.cherrycityelectric.com	Salem	OR	97302	503-566-5600	362-2468	41
Cherry Corp 11200 88th Ave *TF:* 800-510-1689 ■ *Web:* cherryamericas.com	Pleasant Prairie	WI	53158	262-942-6500		815
Cherry County Fairgrounds, The 120 S Green St *Web:* www.cherrycofairgrounds.com	Valentine	NE	69201	402-376-2771	376-3095	338
Cherry Creek Grill 3104 E 26th St *Web:* www.cherrycreek-grill.com	Sioux Falls	SD	57103	605-336-2333		671
Cherry Creek Media 501 S Cherry St Ste 480 *Web:* www.cherrycreekmedia.com	Denver	CO	80246	303-468-6500	468-6555	643
Cherry Creek Mortgage Company Inc 7600 E Orchard Rd Ste 250N *TF:* 888-303-2262 ■ *Web:* www.cherrycreekmortgage.com	Greenwood Village	CO	80111	888-303-2262		509

	Phone	Fax	Class
Cherry Creek Shopping Ctr 3000 E First Ave . . . . Denver CO 80206 *Web:* www.shopcherrycreek.com	303-388-3900		460
Cherry Demolition 6131 Selinsky Rd . . . . Houston TX 77048 *TF:* 800-444-1123 ■ *Web:* www.cherrycompanies.com	713-987-0000	987-0629	189-16
Cherry Grove Animal Hospital 8407 Beechmont Ave . . . . Cincinnati OH 45255 *Web:* www.cherrygroveanimalhospital.vet	513-474-4111		794
Cherry Hill Construction Inc 8211 Washington Blvd . . . . Jessup MD 20794 *Web:* www.cherryhillconstruction.com	410-799-3577	799-5483	188-4
Cherry Hill Photo Enterprises Inc 4 E Stow Rd . . . . Marlton NJ 08053 *TF:* 800-969-2440 ■ *Web:* www.cherryhillphoto.com	856-663-1616		590
Cherry Hill Winery 7867 Crowley Rd PO Box 66 . . . . Rickreall OR 97371 *Web:* www.cherryhillwinery.com	503-623-7867	623-7878	50-7
Cherry Hospital 1401 W Ash St . . . . Goldsboro NC 27530 *Web:* www.ncdhhs.gov	919-947-7000		374-5
Cherry House Inc 2419 S Hwy 53 . . . . LaGrange KY 40031 *Web:* cherryhouse.com	502-222-0343		321
Cherry Lake Publishing 1750 Northway Dr Ste 101 . . . . North Mankato MN 56003 *TF:* 866-918-3956 ■ *Web:* cherrylakepublishing.com	866-918-3956	489-6490	637-10
Cherry Lake Tree Farm 7836 Cherry Lake Rd . . . . Groveland FL 34736 *Web:* cherrylake.com	352-429-2171		752
Cherry Meat Packers Inc 4750 S California Ave . . . . Chicago IL 60632	773-927-1200		473
Cherry Plain State Park 10 State Park Rd . . . . Petersburg NY 12138 *Web:* www.parks.ny.gov	518-733-5400		565
Cherry Springs State Park c/o Lyman Run State Pk 4639 Cherry Springs Rd . . . . Coudersport PA 16915 *Web:* www.dcnr.pa.gov	814-435-1037		565
Cherry Systems Inc 2270 Northwest Pkwy Ste 125 . . . . Marietta GA 30067 *TF:* 800-500-2040 ■ *Web:* cherrysystems.com	770-955-2395		624
Cherry Tree Investment Co 301 Carlson Pkwy Ste 103 . . . . Minnetonka MN 55305 *Web:* www.cherrytree.com	952-893-9012	893-9036	792
Cherry's Industrial Equipment 600 Morse Ave . . . . Elk Grove Village IL 60007 *TF:* 800-350-0011 ■ *Web:* cherrysind.com	847-364-0200		358
Cherrydale Farms Fundraising 707 N Vly Forge Rd . . . . Lansdale PA 19446 *TF:* 877-619-4822 ■ *Web:* www.cherrydale.com	877-619-4822		296-8
Cherryfield Foods Inc 320 Ridge Rd . . . . Cherryfield ME 04622 *Web:* oxfordfrozenfoods.com	207-546-7573	546-2713	315-1
Cherryland Electric Co-op 5930 US 31 S PO Box 298 . . . . Grawn MI 49637 *TF:* 800-442-8616 ■ *Web:* www.cherrylandelectric.coop	231-486-9200		245
Cherryman Industries 5690 Lindbergh Ln . . . . Bell CA 90201 *Web:* www.cherrymanindustries.com	323-780-0859		321
Cherryroad Technologies Inc 301 Gibraltar Dr Ste 2C . . . . Morris Plains NJ 07950 *TF:* 877-402-7804 ■ *Web:* www.cherryroad.com	973-402-7802		177
Cherrystoneit Inc 7632 Woodwind Dr Ste 101 . . . . Huntington Beach CA 92647 *Web:* cherrystoneit.com	714-596-0505		366
Cherry-Todd Electric Co-opeartive Inc 625 W 2nd St . . . . Mission SD 57555 *TF:* 800-856-4417 ■ *Web:* cherry-todd.com	605-856-4416		245
Cherryville Animal Hospital PA 1412 Shelby Hwy . . . . Cherryville NC 28021 *Web:* cherryvilleanimalhospital.net	704-435-5475		794
Cherubini Metal Works Ltd 570 Wilkinson Ave . . . . Dartmouth NS B3B0J4 *Web:* www.cherubinigroup.com	902-468-5630	468-5742	480
Cheryl & Co 646 McCorkle Blvd . . . . Westerville OH 43082 **Fax Area Code:* 614 ■ *TF:* 800-443-8124 ■ *Web:* www.cheryls.com	800-443-8124	891-8699*	68
Chesapeake & Ohio Canal National Historical Park 1850 Dual Hwy Ste 100 . . . . Hagerstown MD 21740 *Web:* www.nps.gov	301-739-4200		564
Chesapeake Arts Ctr 194 Hammonds Ln . . . . Brooklyn Park MD 21225 *Web:* www.chesapeakearts.org	410-636-6597		572
Chesapeake Bank of Maryland 2001 E Joppa Rd . . . . Baltimore MD 21234 *TF:* 800-746-2375 ■ *Web:* www.chesapeakebank.com	410-661-1141	665-8604	70
Chesapeake Bay Magazine 601 6th St Ste 180 . . . . Annapolis MD 21403 *TF:* 877-804-8624 ■ *Web:* www.chesapeakebaymagazine.com	410-263-2662	267-6924	457-22
Chesapeake Bay Maritime Museum 213 N Talbot St . . . . Saint Michaels MD 21663 *Web:* www.cbmm.org	410-745-2916	745-6088	520
Chesapeake Bay Packing LLC 800 Terminal Ave . . . . Newport News VA 23607 *Web:* www.chesapeakebaypacking.com	757-244-8400	244-8500	296-14
Chesapeake Bay Seafood House Associates LLC 1960 Gallows Rd Ste 200 . . . . Vienna VA 22182 *Web:* www.chesapeakerestaurants.com	703-827-0320	893-1536	670
Chesapeake Children's Museum 25 Silopanna Rd . . . . Annapolis MD 21403 *Web:* www.theccm.org	410-990-1993		521
Chesapeake College PO Box 8 . . . . Wye Mills MD 21679 *Web:* www.chesapeake.edu	410-758-1537	827-5878	162
Chesapeake Convention & Visitors Bureau 1224 Progressive Dr . . . . Chesapeake VA 23320 *TF:* 888-889-5551 ■ *Web:* www.visitchesapeake.com	757-382-6411	502-8016	206
Chesapeake Energy Corp 6100 N Western Ave . . . . Oklahoma City OK 73118 *NYSE:* CHK ■ *TF:* 877-245-1427 ■ *Web:* www.chk.com	405-848-3000		536
Chesapeake Gateway *Chamber of Commerce* 405 Williams Ct Ste 108 . . . . Baltimore MD 21220 *Web:* www.chesapeakechamber.org	443-317-8763	317-8772	139
Chesapeake Lodging Trust (CLT) 1997 Annapolis Exchange Pkwy Ste 410 . . . . . . Annapolis MD 21401 *NYSE:* CHSP ■ *TF:* 800-698-2820 ■ *Web:* www.chesapeakelodgingtrust.com	571-349-9450		654
Chesapeake Medical Systems Inc 118 Cedar St . . . . Cambridge MD 21613 **Fax Area Code:* 410 ■ *TF:* 800-333-5643 ■ *Web:* chesapeakemedicalsystems.com	800-333-5643	228-4561*	353
Chesapeake Planetarium 312 Cedar Rd . . . . Chesapeake VA 23322 *Web:* www.virginia.org	757-547-0153		598
Chesapeake Public Library 298 Cedar Rd . . . . Chesapeake VA 23322 *Web:* chesapeakelibrary.org	757-410-7100		434-3
Chesapeake Regional Medical Ctr 736 Battlefield Blvd N . . . . Chesapeake VA 23320 *TF:* 800-456-8121 ■ *Web:* chesapeakeregional.com	757-312-8121		374-3
Chesapeake Seafood House 3045 Clear Lake Ave . . . . Springfield IL 62702 *Web:* www.chesapeakeseafoodhouse.com	217-522-5220		671
Chesapeake Spice Company LLC 4613 Mercedes Dr . . . . Belcamp MD 21017 *Web:* chesapeakespice.com	410-272-6100		123
Chesapeake Utilities Corp 909 Silver Lake Blvd . . . . Dover DE 19904 *NYSE:* CPK ■ *TF:* 888-742-5275 ■ *Web:* www.chpk.com	302-734-6799	734-6750	787
Chesapeake Woodworking Inc 125 N Kresson St . . . . Baltimore MD 21224 *Web:* www.chesapeakewoodworking.net	410-276-1060		200
Chesapeake's 600 Union Ave . . . . Knoxville TN 37902 *Web:* www.chesapeakes.com	865-673-3433		671
Chesbro Music Co 327 Broadway St . . . . Idaho Falls ID 83402 *Web:* chesbroretail.com	208-522-8691		527
Cheshire Academy 10 Main St . . . . Cheshire CT 06410 *Web:* www.cheshireacademy.org	203-272-5396	250-7209	622
Cheshire Center Pediatric Comm 2500 N Church St . . . . Greensboro NC 27405 *TF:* 800-360-1099 ■ *Web:* www.cheshirecenter.net	336-375-2240		356
Cheshire Chamber of Commerce 195 S Main St . . . . Cheshire CT 06410 *Web:* www.cheshirechamber.org	203-272-2345	271-3044	139
Cheshire Medical Ctr 590 Ct St . . . . Keene NH 03431 *Web:* www.cheshire-med.com	603-354-5400		374-3
Cheshire Public Library 104 Main St . . . . Cheshire CT 06410 *TF:* 800-275-2273 ■ *Web:* www.cheshirelibrary.org	203-272-2245	272-7714	434-3
Cheshire, The 6300 Clayton Rd . . . . Saint Louis MO 63117 *Web:* www.cheshirestl.com	314-647-7300	647-0442	379
Chesnee Communications PO Box 430 . . . . Chesnee SC 29323 *Web:* www.chesnet.net	864-461-2211		225
Chester Bross Construction Co 6739 CR 423 . . . . Palmyra MO 63461 *Web:* www.cbrossgroup.com	573-221-5958	221-1892	780
Chester Career College 751 W Hundred Rd . . . . Chester VA 23836 *Web:* www.chestercareercollege.edu	804-751-9191	751-2599	167-3
Chester Charter Inc 61 Winthrop Rd . . . . Chester CT 06412 *TF:* 800-752-6371 ■ *Web:* www.chester-charter.com	860-526-4321	526-4322	167-3
Chester County 140 Main St PO Box 580 . . . . Chester SC 29706 *TF:* 855-935-3708 ■ *Web:* www.chestercounty.org	803-385-2605		338
Chester County 313 W Market St Ste 6202 PO Box 2748 . . . . . West Chester PA 19380 *TF:* 800-692-1100 ■ *Web:* www.chesco.org	610-344-6100	344-5995	338
Chester County Bar Assn, The 15 W Gay St 2nd Fl . . . . West Chester PA 19380 *TF:* 800-701-5161 ■ *Web:* www.chescobar.org	610-692-1889		533
Chester County Chamber of Commerce 109 Gadsden St . . . . Chester SC 29706 *Web:* www.chesterchamber.com	803-581-4142	581-2431	139
Chester County Historical Society 225 N High St . . . . West Chester PA 19380 *Web:* www.chestercohistorical.org	610-692-4800		520
Chester County Hospital 701 E Marshall St . . . . West Chester PA 19380 *Web:* www.chestercountyhospital.org	610-431-5000	430-2958	374-3
Chester County Independent Inc 218 S Church Ave . . . . Henderson TN 38340 *Web:* www.chestercountyindependent.com	731-989-4624	989-5008	532-2
Chester County Library 450 Exton Sq Pkwy . . . . Exton PA 19341 *Web:* www.ccls.org	610-280-2600		434-3
Chester County Library 100 Center St . . . . Chester SC 29706 *Web:* www.chesterlibsc.org	803-377-8145	377-8146	434-3
Chester County School District 509 District Office Dr . . . . Chester SC 29706 *Web:* www.chester.k12.sc.us	803-385-6122		685
Chester County Tourist Bureau 300 Greenwood Rd . . . . Kennett Square PA 19348 *Web:* www.brandywinevalley.com	484-770-8550	770-8557	206
Chester Engineers Inc 1555 Coraopolis Heights Rd . . . . Moon Township PA 15108 *Web:* www.hatch.com	412-809-6600	809-6611	256
Chester Inc 555 Eastport Center Dr . . . . Valparaiso IN 46383 *Web:* chesterinc.com	219-465-7555		296-35
Chester River Press 117 N Water St . . . . Chestertown MD 21620 *Web:* www.chesterriverpress.com	443-480-5830		637-2
Chester State Park 759 State Pk Dr . . . . Chester SC 29706 *Web:* southcarolinaparks.com	803-385-2680		565
Chester Technical Services Inc 10 White Wood Ln . . . . North Branford CT 06471 *TF:* 800-342-5285 ■ *Web:* www.ctslabs.com	203-315-1496		174
Chester Valley Engineers Inc 83 Chestnut Rd . . . . Paoli PA 19301 *Web:* chesterv.com	610-644-4623		261
Chester Water Authority PO Box 467 . . . . Chester PA 19016 *TF:* 800-793-2323 ■ *Web:* www.chesterwater.com	610-876-8185		805
Chester's International LLC 2020 Cahaba Rd . . . . Birmingham AL 35223 *Web:* www.chestersinternational.com	205-949-4690	298-0332	310

	City	State	Zip	Phone	Fax	Class
Chesterfield Chamber of Commerce 101 Chesterfield Business Pkwy *Web:* www.chesterfieldmochamber.com	Chesterfield	MO	63005	636-532-3399	532-7446	139
Chesterfield County Library 119 Main St *Web:* chesterfield.lib.sc.us	Chesterfield	SC	29709	843-623-7489	623-3295	434-3
Chesterfield Gorge Natural Area 1823 Rt 9 *Web:* www.nhstateparks.org	Chesterfield	NH	03443	603-363-8373		565
Chesterfield Hotel 363 Cocoanut Row *Web:* www.chesterfieldpb.com	Palm Beach Gardens	FL	33480	561-659-5800		379
Chesterfield Yarn Mills Inc 201 N Maple St *Web:* www.chesterfieldwraps.com	Pageland	SC	29728	843-672-7211	672-7210	745-9
Chester-Jensen Company Inc PO Box 908 *TF:* 800-685-3750 ■ *Web:* www.chester-jensen.com	Chester	PA	19016	610-876-6276	876-0485	298
Chesterman Co 4700 S Lewis Blvd *TF:* 800-831-2653 ■ *Web:* www.chesterman.com	Sioux City	IA	51106	800-831-2653		805
Chesterton Tribune 193 S Calumet Rd *Web:* www.chestertontribune.com	Chesterton	IN	46304	219-926-1131		532-3
Chestnut Hill College 9601 Germantown Ave *TF:* 800-248-0052 ■ *Web:* www.chc.edu	Philadelphia	PA	19118	215-248-7001	248-7082	166
Chestnut Hill Hospital 8835 Germantown Ave *Web:* www.chestnuthill.towerhealth.org	Philadelphia	PA	19118	215-248-8200		374-3
Chestnut Hill Hotel 8229 Germantown Ave *TF:* 800-628-9744 ■ *Web:* www.chestnuthillhotel.com	Philadelphia	PA	19118	215-242-5905	242-8778	379
Chestnut Investment Advisory 402 Bethlehem Pk *Web:* www.regardingyourmoney.com	Erdenheim	PA	19038	215-836-4880		796
Chestnut Mountain Resort 8700 W Chestnut Mountain Rd *TF:* 800-397-1320 ■ *Web:* www.chestnutmtn.com	Galena	IL	61036	800-397-1320		378
Chestnut Ridge Foam Inc PO Box 781 *TF:* 800-234-2734 ■ *Web:* www.chestnutridgefoam.com	Latrobe	PA	15650	724-537-9000		601
Chet Johnson Drug Inc 204 Keller Ave N *Web:* chetjohnsondrug.com	Amery	WI	54001	715-268-8121		237
Chet Morrison Contractors LLC 9 Bayou Dularge Rd *Web:* chetmorrison.com	Houma	LA	70363	985-868-1950		188
Chetan Sharma Consulting LLC 1778 12th Ave NE **Fax Area Code:* 703 ■ *Web:* www.chetansharma.com	Issaquah	WA	98029	425-657-0555	848-2981*	196
Cheval Publishing Inc 1049 Swarthmore Ave *TF:* 877-243-8251 ■ *Web:* www.chevalpublishing.com	Pacific Palisades	CA	90272	877-243-8251		637-2
Cheverus High School 267 Ocean Ave *Web:* www.cheverus.org	Portland	ME	04103	207-774-6238		685
Chevo Consulting LLC 2275 Research Blvd Ste 100 *Web:* www.chevoconsulting.com	Rockville	MD	20850	301-309-0040		196
Chevrolet of Naperville 1515 W Ogden Ave *Web:* www.chevroletofnaperville.com	Naperville	IL	60540	630-246-4639		57
Chevron Canada Ltd 1500 1050 W Pender St *TF:* 800-663-1650 ■ *Web:* canada.chevron.com	Vancouver	BC	V6E3T4	604-668-5300		580
Chevron Corp 6001 Bollinger Canyon Rd *NYSE:* CVX ■ *TF:* 800-368-8357 ■ *Web:* www.chevron.com	San Ramon	CA	94583	925-842-1000		536
Chevron Global Marine Products LLC 9401 Williamsburg Plz Ste 201 *TF:* 800-283-9582 ■ *Web:* www.chevronmarineproducts.com	Louisville	KY	40222	914-285-7390		580
Chevron Phillips Chemical Co *Performance Pipe Div* 5085 W Pk Blvd Ste 500 *TF:* 800-527-0662 ■ *Web:* www.cpchem.com	Plano	TX	75093	972-599-6600		596
Chevron Phillips Chemical Company LP 10001 Six Pines Dr *TF:* 800-231-1212 ■ *Web:* www.cpchem.com	The Woodlands	TX	77380	832-813-4100		144
Chevron Texaco Credit Card Ctr PO Box P **Fax Area Code:* 925 ■ *TF:* 800-243-8766 ■ *Web:* www.chevrontexacocards.com	Concord	CA	94524	800-243-8766	827-6367*	215
Chevy Chase Presbyterian Church Library 1 Chevy Chase Cir NW *Web:* www.chevychasepc.org	Washington	DC	20015	202-363-2202		434-3
Chevy Chase Trust Co 7501 Wisconsin Ave Ste 1500W *Web:* www.chevychasetrust.com	Bethesda	MD	20814	240-497-5000		401
Chevys Inc 31100 Courthouse Dr *Web:* locations.chevys.com	Union City	CA	94587	510-675-9620		670
Chewacla State Park 124 Shell Toomer Pkwy *Web:* www.alapark.com	Auburn	AL	36830	334-887-5621	821-2439	565
Chewonki Foundation 485 Chewonki Neck Rd *Web:* chewonki.org	Wiscasset	ME	04578	207-882-7323	882-4074	239
Cheyenne Area Convention & Visitors Bureau 121 W 15th St Ste 202 *TF:* 800-426-5009 ■ *Web:* www.cheyenne.org	Cheyenne	WY	82001	307-778-3133	778-3190	206
Cheyenne Botanic Gardens 710 S Lions Pk Dr *Web:* www.botanic.org	Cheyenne	WY	82001	307-637-6458		97
Cheyenne City Hall 2101 O'Neil Ave *TF:* 855-491-1859 ■ *Web:* www.cheyennecity.org	Cheyenne	WY	82001	307-637-6200	637-6454	337
Cheyenne County PO Box 567 *Web:* www.co.cheyenne.co.us	Cheyenne Wells	CO	80810	719-767-5685	767-8730	338
Cheyenne County 212 E Washington *Web:* www.cheyennecounty.org	Saint Francis	KS	67756	785-332-8850		338
Cheyenne Depot Museum 121 W 15th St Ste 300 *Web:* www.cheyennedepotmuseum.org	Cheyenne	WY	82001	307-632-3905	632-0614	520
Cheyenne Frontier Days Old West Museum 4610 Carey Ave *TF:* 800-227-6336 ■ *Web:* www.cfdrodeo.com	Cheyenne	WY	82001	307-778-7290		520
Cheyenne Little Theatre Players PO Box 20087 *Web:* www.cheyennelittletheatre.org	Cheyenne	WY	82003	307-638-6543		572
Cheyenne Mountain Conference Resort 3225 Broadmoor Valley Rd *TF:* 800-428-8886 ■ *Web:* www.cheyennemountain.com	Colorado Springs	CO	80906	719-538-4000		377
Cheyenne Mountain Zoological Park 4250 Cheyenne Mtn Zoo Rd *Web:* www.cmzoo.org	Colorado Springs	CO	80906	719-633-9925	633-2254	823
Cheyenne Regional Airport 4000 Airport Pkwy PO Box 2210 *Web:* www.cheyenneairport.com	Cheyenne	WY	82001	307-634-7071	632-1206	27
Cheyenne Regional Medical Ctr (CRMC) 214 E 23rd St *Web:* www.cheyenneregional.org	Cheyenne	WY	82001	307-634-2273		374-3
Cheyenne State Recreation Area Cheyenne SRA I-80 Exit 300 *Web:* outdoornebraska.gov	Wood River	NE	68883	308-385-6211		565
Cheyenne Symphony Orchestra (CSO) 1904 Thomes Ave *Web:* www.cheyennesymphony.org	Cheyenne	WY	82001	307-778-8561	634-7512	573-3
Cheyenne-Laramie County Efcu 4523 Driftwood Dr *Web:* clcefcu.org	Cheyenne	WY	82009	307-638-6476		219
Cheyney University of Pennsylvania 1837 University Cir PO Box 200 *TF:* 800-243-9639 ■ *Web:* www.cheyney.edu	Cheyney	PA	19319	610-399-2275	399-2099	166
Chez Boucher Cooking School 32 Depot Sq *Web:* www.chezboucher.com	Hampton	NH	03842	603-926-2202		685
Chez Jean-Pierre Bistro 132 N County Rd *Web:* www.chezjean-pierre.com	Palm Beach Gardens	FL	33480	561-833-1171		671
Chez Leveque 1030 Laurier Ave W *Web:* www.chezleveque.ca	Outremont	QC	H2V2K8	514-279-7355		671
Chez Nous 510 Neches St *Web:* cheznousaustin.com	Austin	TX	78701	512-473-2413		671
Chez Pascal 960 Hope St *Web:* chez-pascal.com	Providence	RI	02906	401-421-4422		671
Chez Spencer 82 14th St *Web:* chezspencer.net	San Francisco	CA	94103	415-864-2191		671
Chez Thuy Restaurant 2655 28th St *Web:* www.chezthuy.com	Boulder	CO	80301	303-442-1700		671
Chez Zee American Bistro 5406 Balcones Dr *Web:* www.chez-zee.com	Austin	TX	78731	512-454-2666		671
Chezgal Merchandising Creations PO Box 5274 *Web:* www.cmc-promotional-merchandising.com	Culver City	CA	90231	310-841-5874	841-5893	241
CHF Home Furnishings 104 S Orchard St *Web:* www.shopchf.com	Boise	ID	83705	208-343-7769		362
CHF Industries Inc 1 Park Ave 9th Fl *TF:* 800-243-7090 ■ *Web:* www.chfindustries.com	New York	NY	10016	212-951-7800		746
CHFD-TV 87 Hill St N *Web:* www.dougallmedia.com	Thunder Bay	ON	P7A5V6	807-346-2600	345-9923	647
CHFM-FM 95.9 535 Seventh Ave SW *Web:* www.959chfm.com	San Francisco	AB	T2P0Y4	403-246-9696		645-26
CHH (Cabell Huntington Hospital) 1340 Hal Greer Blvd *Web:* www.cabellhuntington.org	Huntington	WV	25701	304-526-2000		374-3
CHH (Charlotte Hungerford Hospital) 540 Litchfield St *Web:* www.charlottehungerford.org	Torrington	CT	06790	860-496-6666		374-3
Chhandam School of Kathak 2325 3rd St Ste 320 *Web:* www.kathak.org	San Francisco	CA	94107	415-333-9000		573-1
Chhe Federal Credit Union 1204 Hal Greer Blvd *Web:* chhe.org	Huntington	WV	25701	304-525-4145		219
CHHS (Chapel Hill Historical Society) 100 Library Dr *Web:* www.chapelhillhistoricalsociety.org	Chapel Hill	NC	27514	919-929-1793		637-2
CHI (Children's Hospice Intl) 500 Montgomery St Ste 400 *Web:* www.chionline.org	Alexandria	VA	22314	703-684-0330		49-8
CHI Corp 5265 Naiman Pkwy *TF:* 800-828-0599 ■ *Web:* chicorporation.com	Cleveland	OH	44139	440-498-2300		180
CHI Dynasty 1813 Hillhurst Ave *Web:* chidynasty.com	Los Angeles	CA	90027	323-667-3388		671
CHI Health 12809 W Dodge Rd *TF:* 855-515-9372 ■ *Web:* www.chihealth.com	Omaha	NE	68154	402-343-4411	717-7960	352
CHI Omega Fraternity 3395 Players Club Pkwy *Web:* chiomega.com	Memphis	TN	38125	901-748-8600	748-8686	48-16
CHI Overhead Doors Inc 1485 Sunrise Dr *Web:* www.chiohd.com	Arthur	IL	61911	860-628-2042		480
CHI Phi Fraternity 1160 Satellite Blvd *Web:* chiphi.org	Suwanee	GA	30024	404-231-1824		48-16
CHI Psi Fraternity 45 Rutledge St *Web:* www.chipsi.org	Nashville	TN	37210	615-736-2520	736-2366	48-16
CHI Solutions Inc 5414 Oberlin Dr Ste 202 **Fax Area Code:* 734 ■ *TF:* 800-860-5454 ■ *Web:* www.chisolutionsinc.com	San Diego	CA	92121	800-860-5454	662-7118*	668
CHI St Alexius Health Bismarck 900 E Broadway Ave *TF:* 877-530-5550 ■ *Web:* www.chistalexiushealth.org	Bismarck	ND	58501	701-530-7000	530-8984	374-3
CHI St Joseph Health Regional Hospital - Bryan, TX 2801 Franciscan Dr *Web:* www.stjoseph.stlukeshealth.org	Bryan	TX	77802	979-776-3777		374-3
CHI St Luke's Health - Brazosport Hospital (BRHS) 100 Medical Dr *Web:* www.stlukeshealth.org	Lake Jackson	TX	77566	979-297-4411		374-3
CHI St Vincent No 2 St Vincent Cir *Web:* www.chistvincent.com	Little Rock	AR	72205	501-552-3000		374-3

Name / Address	City	State	ZIP	Phone	Fax	Class
Chia Shiang 2016 Packard Rd *Web:* chiashiangannarbor.com	Ann Arbor	MI	48104	734-741-0778		671
Chiado 864 College St *Web:* www.chiadorestaurant.com	Toronto	ON	M6H1A3	416-538-1910	588-8383	671
Chiampou Travis Besaw & Kershner LLP 45 Bryant Woods N. *Web:* ctbk.com	Amherst	NY	14228	716-630-2400		2
Chiante Cafe & Restaurant 2805 - 32 Ave NE *Web:* www.chianticafe.ca	Calgary	AB	T1Y6J1	403-291-2707	291-1615	671
Chianti Restaurant 6535 Line Ave *Web:* www.chiantirestaurant.net	Shreveport	LA	71106	318-868-8866		671
Chiba Bank Ltd, The 1133 Avenue of the Americas 15th Fl *Web:* www.chibabank.co.jp	New York	NY	10036	212-354-7777	354-8575	70
Chicago Architecture Foundation 224 S Michigan Ave *Web:* www.architecture.org	Chicago	IL	60604	312-922-3432		95
Chicago Area Express 5504 W 47th St. *TF:* 800-621-8538 ■ *Web:* chicagosuburban.com	Forest View	IL	60638	708-496-3300	496-1811	311
Chicago Association of Realtors 430 N Michigan Ave Ste 800 *Web:* chicagorealtor.com	Chicago	IL	60611	312-803-4900	803-4905	653
Chicago Automobile Trade Assn 18 W 200 Butterfield Rd *Web:* www.cata.info	Oakbrook Terrace	IL	60181	630-495-2282		138
Chicago Bears 1920 Football Dr *Web:* www.chicagobears.com	Lake Forest	IL	60045	847-295-6600		715-3
Chicago Board of Education 125 S Clark St *Web:* www.cps.edu	Chicago	IL	60603	773-553-1600	553-3543	685
Chicago Board Options Exchange (CBOE) 400 S La Salle St *Web:* www.cboe.com	Chicago	IL	60605	312-786-5600	786-8818	691
Chicago Boiler Co 1300 Northwestern Ave. *TF:* 800-522-7343 ■ *Web:* cbmills.com	Gurnee	IL	60031	847-662-4000	662-4003	91
Chicago Botanic Garden 1000 Lake Cook Rd *Web:* www.chicagobotanic.org	Glencoe	IL	60022	847-835-5440	835-4484	97
Chicago Children's Museum 700 E Grand Ave. *Web:* www.chicagochildrensmuseum.org	Chicago	IL	60611	312-527-1000	527-9082	521
Chicago Chop House 60 W Ontario St *Web:* chicagochophouse.com	Chicago	IL	60654	312-787-7100		671
Chicago Citizen Newspaper Group 8741 S Greenwood Ave Ste 107 *Web:* thechicagocitizen.com	Chicago	IL	60619	773-783-1251	783-1301	532-2
Chicago City Limits 46 W 96Th Street Studio 4W *Web:* www.chicagocitylimits.com	New York	NY	10025	212-888-5233		572
Chicago Community Trust & Affiliates 111 E Wacker Dr Ste 1400 *Web:* cct.org	Chicago	IL	60601	312-616-8000		303
Chicago Cornea Consultants Ltd 806 S Central Ave Ste 300 *Web:* www.chicagocornea.com	Highland Park	IL	60035	847-882-5900	882-6028	798
Chicago Council on Global Affairs, The (CCGA) 332 S Michigan Ave Ste 1100 *Web:* www.thechicagocouncil.org	Chicago	IL	60604	312-726-3860	821-7555	634
Chicago Cutting Die Co 3555 Woodhead Dr. *TF:* 800-747-3437 ■ *Web:* www.chicagocuttingdie.com	Northbrook	IL	60062	847-509-5800	509-0355	757
Chicago Defender 4445 S King Dr *Web:* chicagodefender.com	Chicago	IL	60653	312-225-2400	225-9231	532-2
Chicago Department of Aviation 10510 W Zemk 2nd Fl *Web:* www.flychicago.com	Chicago	IL	60666	773-686-3522		340-4
Chicago Display Marketing Corp 2021 W St. **Fax Area Code:* 800 ■ *TF:* 800-681-4340 ■ *Web:* www.chicagodisplay.com	River Grove	IL	60171	708-842-0001	681-0010*	233
Chicago Dowel Company Inc 4700 W Grand Ave *Web:* www.chicagodowel.com	Chicago	IL	60639	773-622-2000	622-2047	820
Chicago Dryer Co 2200 N Pulaski Rd *Web:* www.chidry.com	Chicago	IL	60639	773-235-4430	235-4439	427
Chicago Equity Partners LLC 180 N LaSalle St Ste 3800 *Web:* www.chicagoequity.com	Chicago	IL	60601	312-629-8200	629-2701	528
Chicago Executive Airport 1020 Plant Rd *Web:* www.chiexec.com	Wheeling	IL	60090	847-537-2580		63
Chicago Extruded Metals Co (CXM) 1601 S 54th Ave **Fax Area Code:* 708 ■ *TF:* 800-323-8102 ■ *Web:* www.cxm.com	Cicero	IL	60804	800-323-8102	780-3479*	485
Chicago Faucets A Geberit Co 2100 S Clearwater Dr *TF:* 800-323-5060 ■ *Web:* www.chicagofaucets.com	Des Plaines	IL	60018	847-803-5000	298-3101	609
Chicago Firefighters Credit Union 6230 S Central Ave *TF:* 866-604-0381 ■ *Web:* chicagofirefighterscu.com	Chicago	IL	60638	773-581-5253	581-5712	219
Chicago Flame Hardening Company Inc 5200 Railroad Ave. *Web:* www.cflame.com	East Chicago	IN	46312	219-397-6475	397-4029	484
Chicago Gasket Co 1285 W N Ave *TF:* 800-833-5666 ■ *Web:* www.chicagogasket.com	Chicago	IL	60642	773-486-3060	486-3784	326
Chicago Gear-DO James Corp 2823 W Fulton St *Web:* www.oc-gear.com	Chicago	IL	60612	773-638-0508	638-7161	709
Chicago Hardware & Fixture Co 9100 Parklane Ave *Web:* www.chicagohardware.com	Franklin Park	Il	60131	847-455-6609	455-0012	350
Chicago Heights Steel 211 E Main St. *TF:* 800-424-4487 ■ *Web:* www.chs.com	Chicago Heights	IL	60411	708-756-5648		723
Chicago History Museum 1601 N Clark St *Web:* www.chicagohistory.org	Chicago	IL	60614	312-642-4600		520
Chicago Import Inc 3811 W Lawrence Ave. *TF:* 800-854-0881 ■ *Web:* www.chicagoimportinc.net	Chicago	IL	60625	773-482-3200	478-4974	328
Chicago Institute for Psychoanalysis 122 S Michigan Ave Ste 1300 *Web:* www.chicagoanalysis.org	Chicago	IL	60603	312-922-7474	922-5656	637-2
Chicago International Film Festival Cinema Chicago 212 W Van Buren St Ste 400 *Web:* www.chicagofilmfestival.com	Chicago	IL	60607	312-683-0121	683-0122	282
Chicago Joe's 820 S Fourth St *Web:* www.chicagojoesrestaurant.com	Las Vegas	NV	89101	702-382-5637		671
Chicago Lakeshore Hospital 4840 N Marine Dr *TF:* 800-888-0560 ■ *Web:* www.chicagolakeshorehospital.com	Chicago	IL	60640	773-878-9700		374-5
Chicago Laminating Inc 125 Weiler Rd *Web:* chicagolam.com	Arlington Heights	IL	60005	847-437-6850	437-9809	344
Chicago Legal Search Ltd 180 N LaSalle St *Web:* chicagolegalsearch.com	Chicago	IL	60601	312-251-2580	251-0223	266
Chicago Life Magazine PO Box 11311 *Web:* www.chicagolife.net	Chicago	IL	60611	773-549-1523		457-22
Chicago Lighthouse, The 1850 W Roosevelt Rd *Web:* www.chicagolighthouse.org	Chicago	IL	60608	312-997-3686		242
Chicago Magazine 435 N Michigan Ave Ste 1100 *TF:* 800-999-0879 ■ *Web:* www.chicagomag.com	Chicago	IL	60611	312-222-8999		457-22
Chicago Mailing Tube Co 400 N Leavitt St *Web:* www.mailing-tube.com	Chicago	IL	60612	312-243-6050	243-6545	125
Chicago Meat Authority Inc (CMA) 1120 W 47th Pl. *TF:* 800-383-3811 ■ *Web:* www.chicagomeat.com	Chicago	IL	60609	773-254-3811	254-5851	296-26
Chicago Metal Fabricators Inc 3724 S Rockwell St. *TF:* 877-400-5995 ■ *Web:* www.chicagometal.com	Chicago	IL	60632	773-523-5755	523-8680	482
Chicago Midway Airport 6500 S Cicero Ave *Web:* www.flychicago.com	Chicago	IL	60638	773-838-0600		27
Chicago Mold Engineering Co 615 Stetson Ave *Web:* www.chicagomold.com	Saint Charles	IL	60174	630-584-1311	584-8695	757
Chicago Nannies Inc 101 N Marion St Ste 300 *TF:* 866-900-9605 ■ *Web:* www.chicagonanniesinc.com	Oak Park	IL	60301	708-524-2101		260
Chicago Nut & Bolt Inc 150 Covington Dr *TF:* 888-529-8600 ■ *Web:* www.cnb-inc.com	Bloomingdale	IL	60108	630-529-8600		350
Chicago Oakbrook Financial Group 903 Commerce Dr Ste 300 *Web:* www.cofgroup.com	Oak Brook	IL	60523	630-954-5572		403
Chicago Office of Tourism & Culture 78 E Washington St 4th Fl *TF:* 888-871-5311 ■ *Web:* www.choosechicago.com	Chicago	IL	60602	312-744-2400		206
Chicago Office Technology Group 3 Territorial Ct. *Web:* www.cotg.com	Bolingbrook	IL	60440	630-771-2600	771-2601	112
Chicago Opera Theater 70 E Lake St Ste 415 *Web:* www.chicagooperatheater.org	Chicago	IL	60601	312-704-8414		573-2
Chicago Parking Meters LLC 205 N Michigan Ave Ste 1910 *TF:* 877-242-7901 ■ *Web:* parkchicago.com	Chicago	IL	60601	877-242-7901		192
Chicago Patrolmen's Federal Credit Union 1407 W Washington Blvd *Web:* www.cpdfcu.com	Chicago	IL	60607	312-726-8814		219
Chicago Pneumatic Tool Co 1800 Overview Dr **Fax Area Code:* 800 ■ *TF:* 800-624-4735 ■ *Web:* www.cp.com	Rock Hill	SC	29730	877-861-2722	228-9096*	759
Chicago Public Library 400 S State St *Web:* www.chipublib.org	Chicago	IL	60605	312-747-4300		434-3
Chicago Reader 11 E Illinois St *Web:* www.chicagoreader.com	Chicago	IL	60611	312-828-0350	828-9926	532-5
Chicago Records Management Inc 3815 Carnation St. *Web:* chicagorecords.com	Franklin Park	IL	60131	847-678-0002	678-0065	186
Chicago Rivet & Machine Co 901 Frontenac Rd *AMEX:* CVR ■ *Web:* www.chicagorivet.com	Naperville	IL	60563	630-357-8500	983-9314	278
Chicago Scenic Studios Inc 1315 N Branch St *Web:* www.chicagoscenic.com	Chicago	IL	60642	312-274-9900		8
Chicago School of Flower Design 452 N Ashland *TF:* 877-322-5666 ■ *Web:* www.chicagoflowerdesign.com	Chicago	IL	60622	877-322-5666		685
Chicago Shakespeare Theater 800 E Grand Ave Navy Pier *Web:* www.chicagoshakes.com	Chicago	IL	60611	312-595-5600	595-5644	572
Chicago Shimpo 2045 S Arlington Heights Rd Ste 108C *Web:* Chicagoshimpo.Com	Arlington Heights	IL	60005	847-437-7700		532-2
Chicago Sinfonietta 70 E Lake St Ste 1430 *Web:* www.chicagosinfonietta.org	Chicago	IL	60601	312-236-3681	236-5429	573-3
Chicago Slitter Company Inc, The 1025 W Thorndale Ave *Web:* www.therdigroup.com	Itasca	IL	60143	630-875-9800	773-3414	190
Chicago South Loop Hotel 11 W 26th St. *Web:* www.chicagosouthloophotel.com	Chicago	IL	60616	312-225-7000	225-2396	378
Chicago South Shore & South Bend Railroad 505 N Carroll Ave *TF:* 800-356-2079 ■ *Web:* www.anacostia.com	Michigan City	IN	46360	219-874-9000	879-3754	648
Chicago Southland Chamber of Commerce 920 W 175th St. *Web:* www.chicagosouthlandchamber.com	Homewood	IL	60430	708-957-6950	957-6968	139
Chicago Southland CVB 2304 173rd St. *TF:* 888-895-8233 ■ *Web:* www.visitchicagosouthland.com	Lansing	IL	60438	708-895-8200	895-8288	206

Name / Address	City	State	Zip	Phone	Fax	Class
Chicago State University 9501 S King Dr *TF:* 800-937-3898 ■ *Web:* www.csu.edu	Chicago	IL	60628	773-995-2513	995-3820	166
Chicago Steel Container Corp 1846 S Kilbourn Ave **Fax Area Code:* 773 ■ *TF:* 800-633-4933 ■ *Web:* chicagosteelcontainer.com	Chicago	IL	60623	800-633-4933	277-1585*	198
Chicago Stock Exchange 440 S LaSalle St *Web:* www.nyse.com	Chicago	IL	60605	312-663-2222		691
Chicago Sun-Times 350 N Orleans St *Web:* chicago.suntimes.com	Chicago	IL	60654	312-321-3000		532-2
Chicago Symphony Orchestra Assn 220 S Michigan Ave *Web:* www.cso.org	Chicago	IL	60604	312-294-3000		48-5
Chicago Teachers Union 1901 W Carroll Ave Ste 400 *Web:* www.ctulocal1.org	Chicago	IL	60654	312-329-9100	329-6200	414
Chicago Tire 16001 S Van Drunen Rd *Web:* www.chicagotire.com	South Holland	IL	60473	708-514-3974	331-9059	755
Chicago Title & Trust Co 171 N Clark St *TF:* 800-621-1919 ■ *Web:* www.ctic.com	Chicago	IL	60601	312-223-2000		391-6
Chicago Title Company of Oregon 10135 SE Sunnyside Rd Ste 300 *Web:* www.chicagotitleoregon.com	Clackamas	OR	97015	503-794-5860		391-6
Chicago Transit Authority (CTA) 567 W Lake St *TF:* 888-578-7275 ■ *Web:* www.transitchicago.com	Chicago	IL	60661	312-664-7200	681-5035	468
Chicago Tribune 160 N Stetson Ave *TF:* 800-874-2863 ■ *Web:* www.chicagotribune.com	Chicago	IL	60601	312-222-3232		532-4
Chicago Tube & Iron Co 1 Chicago Tube Dr *TF:* 800-972-0217 ■ *Web:* www.chicagotube.com	Romeoville	IL	60446	815-834-2500	588-3958	492
Chicago Vocational Career Academy 2100 E 87th St *Web:* www.cvcacademy.org	Chicago	IL	60617	773-535-6100	535-6633	800
Chicago White Metal Casting Inc 649 IL Rt 83 *Web:* www.cwmdiecast.com	Bensenville	IL	60106	630-595-4424	595-4474	308
Chicago Wilcox Manufacturing Company Inc 16928 State St *TF:* 800-323-5282 ■ *Web:* www.chicagowilcox.com	South Holland	IL	60473	708-339-5000	339-9876	326
Chicago Wine Co 835 N Central Ave *Web:* www.tcwc.com	Wood Dale	IL	60191	630-594-2972		443
Chicago's Pizza 1031 N State St *Web:* www.chicagospizza.com	Greenfield	IN	46140	317-462-3131		670
Chicago's WSHE 100.3 130 E Randolph St No 2700 Ste 2780 *Web:* wshechicago.com	Chicago	IL	60601	312-297-5100	297-5155	645-34
Chicago-Kent College of Law Illinois Institute of Technology 565 W Adams St *Web:* www.kentlaw.iit.edu	Chicago	IL	60661	312-906-5000	906-5280	167-1
Chicagoland Chamber of Commerce 410 N Michigan Ave Ste 900 *Web:* chicagolandchamber.org	Chicago	IL	60611	312-494-6700	861-0660	139
Chicagoland Speedway 500 Speedway Blvd *TF:* 888-629-7223 ■ *Web:* www.chicagolandspeedway.com	Joliet	IL	60433	815-722-5500	727-7895	515
Chicanos Por La Causa Inc 1112 E Buckeye Rd *Web:* www.cplc.org	Phoenix	AZ	85034	602-257-0700		192
Chick & Nello's Homestead Inn 800 Kuser Rd *Web:* www.homestead1939.com	Trenton	NJ	08619	609-890-9851		671
Chick Master Incubator Co 945 Lafayette Rd *TF:* 800-727-8726 ■ *Web:* www.chickmaster.com	Medina	OH	44256	330-722-5591	723-0233	273
Chick Publications Inc 8780 Archibald Ave *Web:* www.chick.com	Rancho Cucamonga	CA	91730	909-987-0771	941-8128	637-2
Chick Workholding Solutions Inc 500 Keystone Dr *Web:* chickworkholding.com	Warrendale	PA	15086	724-772-1644	772-1633	493
Chick's 18011 S Dupont Hwy *Web:* www.chicksaddlery.com	Harrington	DE	19952	302-398-4630		711
Chickamauga & Chattanooga National Military Park 3370 Lafayette Rd **Fax Area Code:* 423 ■ *Web:* www.nps.gov	Fort Oglethorpe	GA	30742	706-866-9241	752-5215*	564
Chickasaw Community Bank 909 S Meridian *Web:* ccb.bank	Oklahoma City	OK	73108	405-946-2265		70
Chickasaw Container Co 219 S Carter St *Web:* www.chickasawboxes.com	Okolona	MS	38860	662-447-3339		100
Chickasaw County 1 Pinson Sq *Web:* chickasaw.msghn.org	Houston	MS	38851	662-456-2513		338
Chickasaw Distributors Inc 800 Bering Dr Ste 330 *Web:* www.chickasawdistributors.com	Houston	TX	77057	713-974-2905		492
Chickasaw Electric Co-op 17970 US Hwy 64 E PO Box 459 *Web:* billing.cecpowerup.com	Somerville	TN	38068	901-465-3591		245
Chickasaw Holding Co 124 W Vinita *Web:* www.chickasawholding.com	Sulphur	OK	73086	580-622-2111		787
Chickasaw Nation, The 520 Arlington St PO Box 1548 *Web:* www.chickasaw.net	Ada	OK	74820	580-436-2603		48-11
Chickasaw National Recreation Area 1008 W Second St *Web:* www.nps.gov	Sulphur	OK	73086	580-622-7234		564
Chickasaw Personal Communications Inc 717 S Dewey Ave *TF:* 800-259-2929 ■ *Web:* www.chickasawpersonal.com	Oklahoma City	OK	73116	405-677-5382		246
Chickasaw State Park 26955 US Hwy 43 *Web:* www.alapark.com	Gallion	AL	36742	334-295-8230		565
Chickasaw State Park 20 Cabin Ln *Web:* www.state.tn.us	Henderson	TN	38340	731-989-5141		565
Chickasaw Telecom Inc 5 N McCormick *Web:* www.chickasawtel.com	Oklahoma City	OK	73127	405-946-1200		393
Chickasaw Voting Information 8 E Prospect St *Web:* www.chickasawcoia.org	New Hampton	IA	50659	641-394-2100	394-5541	338
Chickasha Manufacturing Company Inc 5501 Hwy 81 S *Web:* www.chickashamfg.com	Chickasha	OK	73018	405-224-5200	224-4464	482
Chicken Soup Press Inc (CSP) PO Box 164 *Web:* www.chickensouppress.com	Circleville	NY	10919	845-692-6320	692-7574	637-2
Chick-fil-A 5200 Buffington Rd *Web:* www.chick-fil-a.com	Atlanta	GA	30349	404-765-8000		670
Chico Chamber of Commerce 441 Main St *Web:* www.chicochamber.com	Chico	CA	95928	530-891-5556	891-3613	139
Chico Enterprise Record 400 E Park Ave PO Box 9 *Web:* www.chicoer.com	Chico	CA	95927	530-891-1234	891-9204	532-2
Chico Homes Real Estate Sales Inc 2571 California Park Dr Ste 200 *Web:* chicohomesearch.net	Chico	CA	95928	530-864-5407		652
Chico News & Review 353 E Second St *TF:* 866-703-3873 ■ *Web:* www.newsreview.com	Chico	CA	95928	530-894-2300		532-5
Chico Unified School District 1163 E Seventh St *Web:* www.bcoe.org	Chico	CA	95928	530-891-3000		685
Chico's FAS Inc 11215 Metro Pkwy *NYSE: CHS* ■ *TF:* 888-855-4986 ■ *Web:* www.chicosfas.com	Fort Myers	FL	33966	888-855-4986		157-6
Chicoine Law Group PLLC 66 S Hanford St Ste 300 *Web:* www.robertchicoinelaw.com	Seattle	WA	98134	206-467-9000		41
Chicony America Inc 53 Parker *Web:* www.chicony.com.tw	Irvine	CA	92618	949-380-0928		173-1
Chicopee Chamber of Commerce 264 Exchange St *Web:* www.chicopeechamber.org	Chicopee	MA	01013	413-594-2101	594-2103	139
Chicopee Memorial State Park 570 Burnett Rd *Web:* www.mass.gov	Chicopee	MA	01020	413-594-9416		565
Chicopee Provision Company Inc 19 Sitarz St *TF:* 800-924-6328 ■ *Web:* bluesealkielbasa.com	Chicopee	MA	01013	413-594-4765		296-26
Chicopee Public Library 449 Front St *Web:* www.chicopeepubliclibrary.org	Chicopee	MA	01013	413-594-1800	594-1819	434-3
Chicora Alley 608B S Main St *Web:* chicoraalley.com	Greenville	SC	29601	864-232-4100		671
Chicora Foundation Inc 861 Arbutus Dr *Web:* www.chicora.org	Columbia	SC	29205	803-787-6910		668
Chicory Blue Press Inc 795 E St N *Web:* www.chicorybluepress.com	Goshen	CT	06756	860-491-2271	491-8619	637-2
Chicot County 417 Main St *Web:* chicotcounty.arkansas.gov	Lake Village	AR	71663	870-265-8040	265-8018	338
Chicot State Park 3469 Chicot Park Rd *Web:* crt.state.la.us	Ville Platte	LA	70586	337-363-2403		565
Chief Architect Inc 6500 N Mineral Dr *Web:* www.chiefarchitect.com	Coeur d'Alene	ID	83815	208-292-3400		174
Chief Automotive Systems Inc 1924 E 4th St *TF:* 800-445-9262 ■ *Web:* chieftechnology.com	Grand Island	NE	68802	308-384-9747	384-8966	386
Chief Custom Homes 111 Grant St PO Box 127 *Web:* www.bonnavilla.com	Aurora	NE	68818	402-694-5250	694-5873	505
Chief Dull Knife College PO Box 98 *Web:* www.cdkc.edu	Lame Deer	MT	59043	406-477-6215	477-6219	165
Chief Executive Magazine 9 W Broad St Ste 430 *Web:* www.chiefexecutive.net	Greenwich	CT	06830	203-930-2700	930-2701	457-5
Chief Logan State Park 376 Little Buffalo Creek Rd *Web:* wvstateparks.com	Logan	WV	25601	304-792-7125		565
Chief Manufacturing 301 Mcintosh Pkwy **Fax Area Code:* 706 ■ *TF:* 800-722-2061 ■ *Web:* www.chiefmanufacturing.net	Thomaston	GA	30286	800-722-2061	647-2790*	350
Chief Manufacturing Inc 6436 City W Pkwy Ste 700 *Web:* www.legrandav.com	Eden Prairie	MN	55344	952-894-6280		194
Chief Super Market Inc 1340 W High St Ste E *Web:* www.chiefmarkets.com	Defiance	OH	43512	419-782-0950		345
Chief Vann House State Historic Site 82 Georgia 225 *Web:* gastateparks.org	Chatsworth	GA	30705	706-695-2598		565
Chief White Crane Recreation Area 31323 Toe Rd *Web:* gfp.sd.gov	Yankton	SD	57078	605-668-2985		565
Chiefland Citizen 624 W Park Ave *Web:* www.chieflandcitizen.com	Chiefland	FL	32626	352-493-4796		532-2
Chieftain Wild Rice Co 1210 Basswood Ave *TF:* 800-262-6368 ■ *Web:* www.chieftainwildrice.com	Spooner	WI	54801	715-635-6401		123
Chignecto-central Regional 60 Lorne St *TF:* 800-770-0008 ■ *Web:* www.ccrce.ca	Truro	NS	B2N3K3	800-770-0008		685
Chihuahuan Desert Research Institute (CDRI) 43869 State Hwy 118 PO Box 905 *Web:* www.cdri.org	Fort Davis	TX	79734	432-364-2499		97
Chilangos 447 Manton Ave	Providence	RI	02909	401-383-4877		671
Child & Jackson - A Professional Law Corp 101 Parkshore Dr Ste 205 *Web:* childjackson.com	Folsom	CA	95630	916-932-2170	932-2171	41
Child Development Associates Inc 180 Otay Lakes Rd Ste 310 *TF:* 888-755-2445 ■ *Web:* cdasd.org	Bonita	CA	91902	619-427-4411	434-5323	148
Child Evangelism Fellowship Inc 17482 Hwy M *TF:* 800-748-7710 ■ *Web:* www.cefonline.com	Warrenton	MO	63383	636-456-4321		48-20

Name / Address	City	State	ZIP	Phone	Fax	Class
Child Guidance Resource Centers 2000 Old W Chester Pk *Web:* cgrc.org	Havertown	PA	19083	484-454-8700		726
Child Health Foundation 110 E Ridgely Rd *Web:* www.childhealthfoundation.org	Timonium	MD	21093	410-992-5512	992-5641	48-5
Child Lures Prevention 5166 Shelburne Rd *TF:* 800-552-2197 ■ *Web:* childluresprevention.com	Shelburne	VT	05482	802-985-8458	985-8418	48-6
Child Welfare Information Gateway Children's Bureau/ACYF 330 C St SW *TF:* 800-394-3366 ■ *Web:* www.childwelfare.gov	Washington	DC	20201	703-385-7565	385-3206	340-10
Child Welfare League of America (CWLA) 727 15th St NW 12th Fl *Web:* www.cwla.org	Washington	DC	20005	202-688-4200	833-1689	48-6
Child's Gift of Lullabyes PO Box 120278 *TF:* 800-965-2229 ■ *Web:* www.lullabyes.com	Nashville	TN	37212	615-385-0022	386-9988	657
Child's Play 250 Minot Ave *Fax Area Code: 800 ■ *TF:* 800-639-6404 ■ *Web:* www.childs-play.com	Auburn	ME	04210	207-784-7252	854-6989*	637-2
Child's World Inc 1980 Lookout Dr *TF:* 800-599-7323 ■ *Web:* www.childsworld.com	North Mankato	MN	56003	800-599-7323		637-2
Child1st Publications LLC PO Box 150226 *Fax Area Code: 888 ■ *TF:* 800-881-0912 ■ *Web:* www.child1st.com	Grand Rapids	MI	49515	800-881-0912	886-1636*	637-10
Childcare Network 3009 University Ave *TF:* 866-521-5437 ■ *Web:* www.childcarenetwork.com	Columbus	GA	31909	706-819-6297		148
Childers Hanlon & Hudson PLC 722 E Osborn Ste 100 *Web:* chhazlaw.com	Phoenix	AZ	85014	602-254-1444		41
Childers Oil Co 51 Hwy 2034 *Web:* www.doublekwik.com	Whitesburg	KY	41858	606-633-2525		581
Childhaven 316 Broadway *Web:* childhaven.org	Seattle	WA	98122	206-624-6477	621-8374	353
Childhelp USA 4350 E Camelback Rd Bldg F250 *TF:* 800-422-4453 ■ *Web:* www.childhelp.org	Phoenix	AZ	85018	480-922-8212	922-7061	48-6
Children & Adults with Attention-Deficit/Hyperactivity Disorder (CHADD) 4601 Presidents Dr Ste 300 *Fax Area Code: 301 ■ *TF:* 800-233-4050 ■ *Web:* www.chadd.org	Lanham	MD	20706	800-233-4050	306-7090*	48-17
Children Awaiting Parents (CAP) 274 N Goodman St *TF:* 888-835-8802 ■ *Web:* www.childrenawaitingparents.org	Rochester	NY	14610	585-232-5110	232-2634	48-6
Children Inc 4205 Dover Rd *TF:* 800-538-5381 ■ *Web:* childrenincorporated.org	Richmond	VA	23221	804-359-4562		48-6
Children Intl 2000 E Red Bridge Rd *TF:* 800-888-3089 ■ *Web:* www.children.org	Kansas City	MO	64131	816-942-2000	942-3714	48-5
Children of Lesbians & Gays Everywhere (COLAGE) 3815 S Othello St Ste 100 *Web:* www.colage.org	Seattle	WA	98118	828-782-1938		48-21
Children of Mary PO Box 350333 *Web:* www.catholicbook.com	Fort Lauderdale	FL	33335	954-583-5108		637-2
Children of the Night 14530 Sylvan St *TF:* 800-551-1300 ■ *Web:* www.childrenofthenight.org	Van Nuys	CA	91411	818-908-4474	908-1468	48-6
Children's Book Council (CBC) 54 W 39th St 14th Fl *Web:* www.cbcbooks.org	New York	NY	10018	212-966-1990		49-16
Children's Book Insider 901 Columbia Rd *Web:* www.cbiclubhouse.com	Fort Collins	CO	80525	970-495-0056		531-11
Children's Bureau of Southern California 1910 Magnolia Ave *TF:* 800-730-3933 ■ *Web:* www.all4kids.org	Los Angeles	CA	90004	213-342-0100		352
Children's Defense Fund (CDF) 25 E St NW *TF:* 800-233-1200 ■ *Web:* www.childrensdefense.org	Washington	DC	20001	202-628-8787	662-3510	48-6
Children's Discovery Museum of San Jose 180 Woz Way *Web:* www.cdm.org	San Jose	CA	95110	408-298-5437	298-6826	521
Children's Discovery Museum of the Desert 71701 Gerald Ford Dr *Web:* www.cdmod.org	Rancho Mirage	CA	92270	760-321-0602	321-1605	521
Children's Eye Care 11800 NE 128th Ste 430 *Web:* www.childrenseyefoundation.org	Kirkland	WA	98034	425-823-3937	823-7479	48-17
Children's Fairyland Theme Park 699 Bellevue Ave *Web:* www.fairyland.org	Oakland	CA	94610	510-452-2259	452-2261	32
Children's Hands-On Museum 2213 University Blvd *Web:* www.chomonline.org	Tuscaloosa	AL	35401	205-349-4235	349-4276	521
Children's Healthcare of Atlanta at Egleston 1405 Clifton Rd NE *TF:* 888-785-7778 ■ *Web:* www.choa.org	Atlanta	GA	30322	404-785-6000		374-1
Children's Historical Publishing (CHPS) 1616 Turnberry Village Dr *Web:* www.childrenshistoricalpublishing.org	Dayton	OH	45458	937-643-0502		637-2
Children's Home + Aid 125 S Wacker Dr 14th Fl *Web:* www.childrenshomeandaid.org	Chicago	IL	60606	312-424-0200		148
Children's Hope House 7922 W Jefferson Blvd *Web:* childrenshopefw.org	Fort Wayne	IN	46804	260-459-8550		372
Children's Hospice Intl (CHI) 500 Montgomery St Ste 400 *Web:* www.chionline.org	Alexandria	VA	22314	703-684-0330		49-8
Children's Hospital 200 Henry Clay Ave *TF:* 800-299-9511 ■ *Web:* www.chnola.org	New Orleans	LA	70118	504-899-9511		374-1
Children's Hospital & Medical Ctr 8200 Dodge St *Web:* www.childrensomaha.org	Omaha	NE	68114	402-955-5400	955-4046	374-1
Children's Hospital & Research Center at Oakland 747 52nd St *Web:* www.childrenshospitaloakland.org	Oakland	CA	94609	510-428-3000	658-1923	374-1
Children's Hospital Association of Texas 823 Congress Ave Ste 1500 *Web:* www.chatexas.com	Austin	TX	78701	512-320-0910		414
Children's Hospital at OU Medical Ctr, The 1200 N Everett Dr *Web:* www.oumedicine.com	Oklahoma City	OK	73104	405-271-4700		374-3
Children's Hospital Medical Center of Akron 1 Perkins Sq *TF:* 800-262-0333 ■ *Web:* www.akronchildrens.org	Akron	OH	44308	330-543-1000	543-3146	374-1
Children's Hospital of Alabama 1600 Seventh Ave S *TF:* 800-504-9768 ■ *Web:* www.childrensal.org	Birmingham	AL	35233	205-638-9100		374-1
Children's Hospital of Eastern Ontario 401 Smyth Rd *TF:* 866-797-0007 ■ *Web:* www.cheo.on.ca	Ottawa	ON	K1H8L1	613-737-7600	738-4866	374-2
Children's Hospital of Pittsburgh 4401 Penn Ave *Web:* www.chp.edu	Pittsburgh	PA	15224	412-692-5325		374-1
Children's Hospital of the King's Daughters 601 Children's Ln *TF:* 800-395-2453 ■ *Web:* www.chkd.org	Norfolk	VA	23507	757-668-7000		374-1
Children's Hospital of Wisconsin 9000 W Wisconsin Ave *TF:* 800-266-0366 ■ *Web:* childrenswi.org	Milwaukee	WI	53226	414-266-2000	266-2547	374-1
Children's Hospitals & Clinics Minneapolis 2525 Chicago Ave *TF:* 866-225-3251 ■ *Web:* www.childrensmn.org	Minneapolis	MN	55404	612-813-6000		374-1
Children's Institute of Pittsburgh 1405 Shady Ave *TF:* 877-433-1109 ■ *Web:* www.amazingkids.org	Pittsburgh	PA	15217	412-420-2400	420-2200	374-1
Children's Leukemia Research Assn 585 Stewart Ave Ste 18 *Web:* www.childrensleukemia.org	Garden City	NY	11530	516-222-1944	222-0457	48-17
Children's Medical Center of Dallas 1935 Medical District Dr *Web:* www.childrens.com	Dallas	TX	75235	214-456-7000		374-1
Children's Medical Ctr 1 Children's Plz *TF:* 800-228-4055 ■ *Web:* www.childrensdayton.org	Dayton	OH	45404	937-641-3000	641-3326	374-1
Children's Memorial Hospital 2300 Children's Plz *Web:* www.luriechildrens.org	Chicago	IL	60614	312-227-4000		374-1
Children's Mercy Hospital & Clinics 2401 Gillham Rd *TF:* 866-512-2168 ■ *Web:* www.childrensmercy.org	Kansas City	MO	64108	816-234-3000		374-1
Children's Museum 498 Crawford Blvd *Web:* www.cmboca.org	Boca Raton	FL	33432	561-368-6875		521
Children's Museum of Acadiana 201 E Congress St *Web:* www.childrensmuseumofacadiana.com	LaFayette	LA	70501	337-232-8500	232-8167	521
Children's Museum of Atlanta, The 275 Centennial Olympic Pk Dr NW *Web:* childrensmuseumatlanta.org	Atlanta	GA	30313	404-659-5437	223-3675	521
Children's Museum of Cleveland 3813 Euclid Ave *Web:* cmcleveland.org	Cleveland	OH	44115	216-791-7114	791-8838	521
Children's Museum of Denver 2121 Children's Museum Dr *Web:* www.mychildsmuseum.org	Denver	CO	80211	303-433-7444	433-9520	521
Children's Museum of History Natural History Science & Technology Pkwy District Holland Ave *Web:* www.uticacm.org	Utica	NY	13501	315-731-2627	724-6120	521
Children's Museum of Houston 1500 Binz St *Web:* www.cmhouston.org	Houston	TX	77004	713-522-1138	522-5747	521
Children's Museum of Indianapolis 3000 N Meridian St *TF:* 800-820-6214 ■ *Web:* www.childrensmuseum.org	Indianapolis	IN	46208	317-334-4000	920-2001	520
Children's Museum of Lake Charles 327 Broad St *Web:* www.swlakids.org	Lake Charles	LA	70601	337-433-9420		521
Children's Museum of Maine 142 Free St PO Box 4041 *Web:* www.kitetails.org	Portland	ME	04101	207-828-1234	828-5726	521
Children's Museum of Manhattan 212 W 83rd St *Web:* www.cmom.org	New York	NY	10024	212-721-1223	721-1127	521
Children's Museum of Memphis 2525 Central Ave *Web:* www.cmom.com	Memphis	TN	38104	901-458-2678	458-4033	521
Children's Museum of Montana 22 Railroad Sq *Web:* www.childrensmuseumofmontana.org	Great Falls	MT	59401	406-452-6661		520
Children's Museum of New Hampshire 6 Washington St *Web:* www.childrens-museum.org	Dover	NH	03820	603-742-2002		521
Children's Museum of Northern Nevada 813 N Carson St *Web:* www.cmnn.org	Carson City	NV	89701	775-884-2226	884-2179	521
Children's Museum of Oak Ridge 461 W Outer Dr *TF:* 877-524-1223 ■ *Web:* www.childrensmuseumofoakridge.org	Oak Ridge	TN	37830	865-482-1074	481-4889	521
Children's Museum of Pittsburgh 10 Children's Way *Web:* pittsburghkids.org	Pittsburgh	PA	15212	412-322-5058		521
Children's Museum of Science & Technology 250 Jordan Rd *Web:* www.cmost.org	Troy	NY	12180	518-235-2120	235-6836	520
Children's Museum of South Carolina 2204 N Oak St *Web:* www.cmsckids.org	Myrtle Beach	SC	29577	843-946-9469	946-7011	521
Children's Museum of Stockton 402 W Weber Ave *Web:* www.stocktongov.com	Stockton	CA	95202	209-465-4386		521

				Phone	Fax	Class
Children's Museum of Tacoma 1501 Pacific Ave *Web:* www.playtacoma.org	Tacoma	WA	98402	253-627-6031	627-2436	521
Children's Museum of the Arts 103 Charlton St *Web:* cmany.org	New York	NY	10014	212-274-0986	274-1776	521
Children's Museum of the Lowcountry 25 Ann St *Web:* explorecml.org	Charleston	SC	29403	843-853-8962		521
Children's Museum of Virginia 221 High St *Web:* childrensmuseumvirginia.com	Portsmouth	VA	23704	757-393-5258		521
Children's Museum Seattle 305 Harrison St *Web:* www.thechildrensmuseum.org	Seattle	WA	98109	206-441-1768	448-0910	521
Children's Music Network, The (CMN) 10 Court St *Web:* www.cmnonline.org	Arlington	MA	02476	339-707-0277		423
Children's Musical Theater San Jose (CMTS) 1401 Parkmoor Ave Ste 100 *Web:* www.cmtsj.org	San Jose	CA	95126	408-288-5437		573-4
Children's National Health System 111 Michigan Ave NW *Web:* www.childrensnational.org	Washington	DC	20010	202-476-5000		353
Children's Organ Transplant Assn (COTA) 2501 W Cota Dr *TF:* 800-366-2682 ■ *Web:* cota.org	Bloomington	IN	47403	812-336-8872		48-17
Children's Place Retail Stores Inc 500 Plaza Dr *NASDAQ: PLCE* ■ *TF:* 877-752-2387 ■ *Web:* www.childrensplace.com	Secaucus	NJ	07094	201-558-2400		157-1
Children's Science Explorium 300 S Military Trl *Web:* sugarsandpark.org	Boca Raton	FL	33486	561-347-3912	347-3910	521
Children's Specialized Hospital 150 New Providence Rd **Fax Area Code:* 908 ■ *TF:* 888-244-5373 ■ *Web:* www.childrens-specialized.org	Mountainside	NJ	07092	888-244-5373	233-4967*	374-1
Children's Tumor Foundation 120 Wall St 16th Fl *TF:* 800-323-7938 ■ *Web:* www.ctf.org	New York	NY	10005	212-344-6633	747-0004	48-17
Children's Wish Foundation Intl 8615 Roswell Rd *TF:* 800-323-9474 ■ *Web:* www.childrenswish.org	Atlanta	GA	30350	770-393-9474	393-0683	48-17
ChildrenFirst Health Care System 4448 Edgewater Dr *TF:* 800-207-0802 ■ *Web:* childrenfirst.com	Orlando	FL	32804	407-513-3000		260
Children's Discovery Museum, The 177 Main St *TF:* 800-544-6666 ■ *Web:* www.discoveryacton.org	Acton	MA	01720	978-264-4200		520
Children's Hopechest PO Box 63842 *Web:* www.hopechest.org	Colorado Springs	CO	80962	719-487-7800		48-20
Children's Plus Inc 1387 Dutch American Way *TF:* 800-230-1279 ■ *Web:* hellocpi.com	Beecher	IL	60401	800-230-1279		95
Childress Ahlheim Cary LLC 1010 Market St Ste 500 *Web:* jchildresslaw.com	Saint Louis	MO	63101	314-621-9800		41
Childress County 1710 Ave F NW *Web:* www.childresscad.org	Childress	TX	79201	940-937-6062	937-3386	338
Childs & Company Inc 2311 N Larkin Ave *Web:* childshdw.com	Fresno	CA	93727	559-485-0520	485-6965	351
Childs Company LLC Three Alliance Ctr 3550 Lenox Rd Ste 1200-B *Web:* www.childscompany.com	Atlanta	GA	30326	404-461-4649		401
Childs/Dreyfus Group 70 W Hubbard St Ste 300 *Web:* www.childsdreyfus.com	Chicago	IL	60654	312-222-0098		393
Childventures Early Learning Academy Inc Burlington Campus 2180 Itabashi Way *TF:* 877-797-9534 ■ *Web:* childventures.ca	Burlington	ON	L7M5A5	905-637-8481		685
Chile						
Consulate General 866 UN Plz Ste 603 *Web:* www.chile.gob.cl	New York	NY	10017	212-980-3366	888-5288	257
Consulate General 870 Market St Ste 1058 *Web:* chile.gob.cl	San Francisco	CA	94102	415-982-7662		257
Chile-US Chamber of Commerce 8333 NW 53rd St Ste 450 *Web:* www.chileus.org	Doral	FL	33166	786-762-4155		138
Chili Public Library 3333 Chili Ave *Web:* www.libraryweb.org	Rochester	NY	14624	585-889-2200		434-3
Chilito's 2405 S Valley Dr *Web:* chilitos.net	Las Cruces	NM	88005	575-526-4184		671
Chilivis Cochran Larkins & Bever LLP 3127 Maple Dr NE *Web:* cglawfirm.com	Atlanta	GA	30305	404-233-4171		428
Chiller Solutions LLC 101 Alexander Ave *Web:* www.edwards-eng.com	Pompton Plains	NJ	07444	973-835-2800		14
Chillicothe & Ross County Public Library 140 S Paint St *Web:* www.crcpl.org	Chillicothe	OH	45601	740-702-4145		434-3
Chillicothe Beauty Academy 505 Elm St *Web:* www.chillicothebeautyacademy.com	Chillicothe	MO	64601	660-646-4198	646-9983	167-3
Chillicothe Correctional Ctr 3151 Litton Rd *Web:* doc.mo.gov	Chillicothe	MO	64601	660-646-4032	646-1217	213
Chillicothe Gazette 50 W Main St *TF:* 877-424-0215 ■ *Web:* www.chillicothegazette.com	Chillicothe	OH	45601	740-773-2111		532-2
Chillicothe-Ross Chamber of Commerce 45 E Main St *Web:* chillicotheohio.com	Chillicothe	OH	45601	740-702-2722	702-2727	139
Chillingsworth Restaurant 2449 Main St *Web:* www.chillingsworth.com	Brewster	MA	02631	508-896-3640		671
Chilliwack Chamber of Commerce 46093 Yale Rd Ste 201 *Web:* www.chilliwackchamber.com	Chilliwack	BC	V2P2L8	604-793-4323	793-4303	137
Chillybears 6 Brook Rd *Web:* chillybears.com	Needham	MA	02494	781-455-6321		5
Chiltern Inn 11 Cromwell Harbor Rd *TF:* 800-709-0114 ■ *Web:* chilterninnbarharbor.com	Bar Harbor	ME	04609	207-288-3371		379
Chilton County Commission 500 Second Ave N *Web:* www.chiltoncounty.org	Clanton	AL	35045	205-755-1551	280-7204	338
Chimacum Valley Veterinary Hos 820 Chimacum Rd *Web:* chimacumvet.com	Port Hadlock	WA	98339	360-385-4488		794
Chime PO Box 417 *TF:* 844-244-6363 ■ *Web:* chime.com	San Francisco	CA	94108	844-244-6363		69
Chime Education Foundation 710 Avis Dr Ste 200 *Web:* chimecentral.org	Ann Arbor	MI	48108	734-665-0000	665-4922	166
Chime Master Systems PO Box 936 *TF:* 800-344-7464 ■ *Web:* www.chimemaster.com	Lancaster	OH	43130	740-746-9181	746-9566	527
Chimes Inc, The 4815 Seton Dr *Web:* chimes.org	Baltimore	MD	21215	410-358-6400	358-1747	687
Chimes Restaurant & Tap Room 3357 Highland Rd *Web:* www.thechimes.com	Baton Rouge	LA	70802	225-383-1754		671
Chimi's 1304 E 15th St *Web:* chimismexican.com	Tulsa	OK	74120	918-587-4411		671
Chimney Rock Inn 800 Thompson Ave *Web:* www.chimneyrockinn.com	Bound Brook	NJ	08805	732-469-4600		378
Chimney Rock Park 431 Main St **Fax Area Code:* 828 ■ *TF:* 800-277-9611 ■ *Web:* www.chimneyrockpark.com	Chimney Rock	NC	28720	800-277-9611	625-9610*	97
Chimney Rock Public Power District 128 Eighth St PO Box 608 *TF:* 877-773-6300 ■ *Web:* www.crppd.com	Bayard	NE	69334	308-586-1824		245
Chin Music Press 1501 Pike Pl Ste 329 *Web:* www.chinmusicpress.com	Seattle	WA	98101	206-380-1947		637-10
CHIN Radio 622 College St 4th Fl *Web:* www.chinradio.com	Toronto	ON	M6G1B6	416-531-9991	531-5274	645-163
China						
Consulate General 1450 Laguna St *Web:* www.chinaconsulatesf.org	San Francisco	CA	94115	415-872-9091	852-5940	257
Consulate General 55 W Monroe St Ste 630 *Web:* www.chinaconsulatechicago.org	Chicago	IL	60654	312-803-0095	803-0110	257
Consulate General 3417 Montrose Blvd *Web:* houston.china-consulate.org	Houston	TX	77006	713-520-1462		257
Consulate General 443 Shatto Pl *Web:* losangeles.china-consulate.org	Los Angeles	CA	90020	213-807-8088	807-8091	257
Embassy 2201 Wisconsin Ave NW Ste 110 *Web:* www.china-embassy.org	Washington	DC	20007	202-337-1956	588-9760	257
China Airlines Cargo Sales & Service 11201 Aviation Blvd **Fax Area Code:* 907 ■ *Web:* www.china-airlines.com	Los Angeles	CA	90045	310-646-4293	248-4176*	12
China Buffet 1300 US Hwy 127 S *Web:* www.eatchinabuffet.com	Frankfort	KY	40601	502-226-3400		671
China Camp State Park 101 Peacock Gap Trl *Web:* www.parks.ca.gov	San Rafael	CA	94901	415-456-0766		565
China Capital 530 N Gloster St *Web:* www.chinacapitaltupelo.com	Tupelo	MS	38804	662-841-0484		671
China Chef 4335 Lake Michigan Dr NW *Web:* www.chinachef49534.com	Grand Rapids	MI	49534	616-791-4488		671
China Daily Press 2121 W Mission Rd *Web:* www.uschinapress.com	Alhambra	CA	91803	626-281-8500		532-2
China Dragon 27 E Queen Ave *Web:* chinadragonspokane.com	Spokane	WA	99207	509-483-5209		671
China East 1810 E William St	Carson City	NV	89701	775-885-6996		671
China East Restaurant 1086 S Virginia St *Web:* www.chinaeastreno.com	Reno	NV	89502	775-348-7020		671
China Garden 1929 N Washington St *Web:* www.chinagardenbis.com	Bismarck	ND	58501	701-224-0698		671
China Gourmet 3340 Erie Ave *Web:* thechinagourmet.com	Cincinnati	OH	45208	513-871-6612		671
China Institute in America 100 Washington St *Web:* www.chinainstitute.org	New York	NY	10006	212-744-8181	628-4159	48-14
China Jade 2190 Brookpark Rd *Web:* www.chinajadecleveland.com	Cleveland	OH	44134	216-749-4720		671
China Light 571 Broadway *Web:* www.chinalightbangor.com	Bangor	ME	04401	207-947-6750		671
China National Tourist Office 370 Lexington Ave Ste 912 *Web:* www.cnto.org	New York	NY	10017	212-760-8218	760-8809	775
China Ocean Shipping Company Americas Inc (COSCO) 100 Lighting Way *TF:* 800-242-7354 ■ *Web:* www.na.coscoshipping.com	Secaucus	NJ	07094	201-422-0500	422-8956	220
China Palace 213 N Washington St *Web:* chinapalacegreenbay.com	Green Bay	WI	54301	920-433-0688		671
China Rose Restaurant 228 28th St SE *Web:* www.chinarose.ca	Calgary	AB	T2A6J9	403-248-2711	248-6810	671
China Star 2425 W Walnut St *Web:* www.garlandchinastar.com	Garland	TX	75042	972-487-8311		671
China Star Chinese Restaurant 11-15 Main St *Web:* www.chinastarvt.com	Montpelier	VT	05602	802-223-0808		671
China Town 326 S Nevada Ave *Web:* chinatown-restaurant.com	Colorado Springs	CO	80903	719-632-5151		671
China Travel Service Chicago Inc 2145b S China Pl *TF:* 800-793-8856 ■ *Web:* www.nexusholidays.com	Chicago	IL	60616	312-328-0688		775
Chinati Foundation PO Box 1135 *Web:* chinati.org	Marfa	TX	79843	432-729-4362	729-4597	95
Chinatown 3900 Hillsboro Pk *Web:* www.nashvillechinatown.com	Nashville	TN	37215	615-269-3275		671
Chinatrust Bank USA 801 S Figueroa St Ste 2300 *TF:* 888-308-0986 ■ *Web:* www.chinatrustusa.com	Los Angeles	CA	90017	310-791-2828		70

Name / Address	City	State	ZIP	Phone	Fax	Class
Chincoteague Seafood Company Inc 7056 Forest Grove Rd PO Box 88 *Fax Area Code: 443 ■ Web: chincoteagueseafood.com	Parsonsburg	MD	21849	410-260-4800	260-4900*	805
Chinese Chamber of Commerce of Hawaii 8 S King St Ste 201 TF: 877-533-2444 ■ Web: www.chinesechamber.com	Honolulu	HI	96813	808-533-3181		138
Chinese Chamber of Commerce of Los Angeles 977 N Broadway Ground Fl Ste E Web: www.lachinesechamber.org	Los Angeles	CA	90012	213-617-0396	617-2128	138
Chinese Chamber of Commerce of San Francisco 730 Sacramento St Web: www.chineseparade.com	San Francisco	CA	94108	415-982-3000		138
Chinese Community Health Plan 445 Grant Ave Ste 700 Web: www.cchphmo.com	San Francisco	CA	94108	415-955-8800		391-3
Chino Champion PO Box 607 Web: www.championnewspapers.com	Chino	CA	91708	909-628-5501	590-1217	532-4
Chino Hills Ford 4480 Chino Hills Pkwy TF: 866-261-0153 ■ Web: www.chinohillsford.com	Chino	CA	91710	866-261-0153		57
Chino Hills High School 16150 Pomona Rincon Rd Web: www.chino.k12.ca.us	Chino Hills	CA	91709	909-606-7540		685
Chino Valley Chamber of Commerce 13150 Seventh St Web: chinovalleychamberofcommerce.com	Chino	CA	91710	909-627-6177	627-4180	139
Chino Valley Ranchers 331 W Citrus St TF: 800-354-4503 ■ Web: www.chinovalleyranchers.com	Colton	CA	92324	800-354-4503		297-10
Chino Works America Inc 22301 S Wstn Ave Ste 105 TF: 888-321-9118 ■ Web: www.chinoamerica.com	Torrance	CA	90501	310-787-8899	787-8898	201
Chinois on Main 2709 Main St TF: 888-646-3387 ■ Web: www.wolfgangpuck.com	Santa Monica	CA	90405	310-392-9025	396-5102	671
Chinook Lumber Inc 17606 SR- 9 SE Web: www.chinooklumber.com	Snohomish	WA	98296	360-668-8800	668-2633	364
Chinook Winds Casino Resort 1777 NW 44th St TF: 888-244-6665 ■ Web: www.chinookwindscasino.com	Lincoln City	OR	97367	888-244-6665		452
Chintz & Co 1720 Store St Web: chintz.com	Victoria	BC	V8W1V5	250-381-2404		362
Chip Systems Intl 10953 Norscott St TF: 888-672-4477 ■ Web: www.chipsystemsintl.com	Scotts	MI	49088	269-626-8000	626-8080	207
ChipChat Technology Group 24224 Michigan Ave Web: www.chipchat.com	Dearborn	MI	48124	313-565-4000	565-4001	178-1
Chipola College 3094 Indian Cir Web: www.chipola.edu	Marianna	FL	32446	850-526-2761	718-2287	166
Chipotle Mexican Grill Inc 1401 Wynkoop St NYSE: CMG ■ Web: www.chipotle.com	Denver	CO	80202	303-595-4000		670
Chippendales USA LLC 4 Expressway Plz Ste 218 Web: www.chippendales.com	Roslyn Heights	NY	11577	516-454-0981		149
Chippewa Correctional Facility 4269 W M-80 Web: www.michigan.gov	Kincheloe	MI	49784	906-495-2275		213
Chippewa County 711 N Bridge St Web: www.co.chippewa.wi.us	Chippewa Falls	WI	54729	715-726-7980	726-7987	338
Chippewa County 629 N 11th St Web: www.co.chippewa.mn.us	Montevideo	MN	56265	320-269-7447	269-7412	338
Chippewa Falls Area Chamber of Commerce 10 S Bridge St TF: 888-723-0024 ■ Web: www.chippewachamber.org	Chippewa Falls	WI	54729	715-723-0331	723-0332	139
Chippewa Falls Public Library 105 W Central St Web: www.chippewafallslibrary.org	Chippewa Falls	WI	54729	715-723-1146		434-3
Chippewa Moraine Ice Age State Recreation Area 13394 County Hwy M Web: dnr.wi.gov	New Auburn	WI	54757	715-967-2800		565
Chippewa Trucking 510 E S Ave Web: www.chippewatrails.com	Chippewa Falls	WI	54729	715-726-2457	726-2455	107
Chippewa Valley Electric Co-op 317 S Eigth St TF: 800-300-6800 ■ Web: www.cvecoop.com	Cornell	WI	54732	715-239-6800		245
Chippewa Valley Ethanol Company LLC 270 20th St NW Web: cvec.com	Benson	MN	56215	320-843-4813	843-4800	145
Chippewa Valley Technical College 620 W Clairemont Ave TF: 800-547-2882 ■ Web: www.cvtc.edu	Eau Claire	WI	54701	715-833-6200	833-6470	800
Chippewa Veterinary Clinic SC 14961 81st Ave Web: chippewavet.com	Chippewa Falls	WI	54729	715-723-3655	723-5245	794
Chippokes Plantation State Park 695 Chippokes Park Rd Web: www.dcr.virginia.gov	Surry	VA	23883	757-294-3728		565
CHIPS Computer Services 4600 Churchill St Web: www.chipscs.com	Shoreview	MN	55126	651-407-8555		175
CHIPS Technology Group LLC 5 Aerial Way Ste 400 Web: www.chipstechnologygroup.com	Syosset	NY	11791	516-377-6585	470-9214	174
Chipton-Ross Inc 343 Main St TF: 800-927-9318 ■ Web: www.chiptonross.com	El Segundo	CA	90245	310-414-7800		631
Chiral Quest Inc 7 Deer Park Dr Ste C1 Web: www.chiralquest.com	Monmouth Junction	NJ	08852	732-274-0399		231
Chiral Technologies Inc 800 N Five Points Rd TF: 800-624-4725 ■ Web: www.chiraltech.com	West Chester	PA	19380	610-594-2286	594-2325	476
Chirch Global Manufacturing LLC 1150 Ridgeview Dr	Mchenry	IL	60050	815-385-5600		697
ChiRhoClin Inc 4000 Blackburn Ln Ste 270 Web: www.chirhoclin.com	Burtonsville	MD	20866	301-476-8388		231
Chiricahua National Monument 12856 E Rhyolite Creek Rd TF: 877-444-6777 ■ Web: www.nps.gov	Willcox	AZ	85643	520-824-3560		564
Chiro Inc 2260 S Vista Ave TF: 800-237-2778 ■ Web: mrcleansystems.com	Bloomington	CA	92316	909-879-1160	879-1155	291
Chiron Data Systems Inc 1802 Regent Ct Web: www.chirondata.com	Corinth	TX	76210	866-855-9330		396
Chiropractic Health Plan of California PO Box 190 *Fax Area Code: 925 ■ TF: 800-995-2442 ■ Web: www.chpc.com	Clayton	CA	94517	800-995-2442	844-3124*	391-3
Chirpify 317 SW Alder St Ste 1100 Web: www.chirpify.com	Portland	OR	97204	503-208-3068		387
Chisago County 313 N Main St TF: 888-234-1246 ■ Web: www.chisagocounty.us	Center City	MN	55012	651-257-1300	213-8876	338
Chisesi Bros Meat Packing Co 5221 Jefferson Hwy TF: 800-966-3550 ■ Web: www.chisesibros.com	New Orleans	LA	70123	504-822-3550		473
Chisholm Fleming & Assoc 317 Renfrew Dr Ste 301 TF: 888-241-4149 ■ Web: chisholmfleming.com	Markham	ON	L3R9S8	905-474-1458		256
Chistell Publishing 3300 Neshaminy Blvd Ste 589 Web: www.chistell.com	Bensalem	PA	19020	215-869-3469		637-2
Chisum High School 3250 Church St Web: www.chisumisd.org	Paris	TX	75462	903-737-2800	737-2831	685
Chitiva's Salsa & Sports Bar & Grille 445 W Weber Ave Ste 122 Web: www.chitiva.net	Stockton	CA	95203	209-941-8605		671
Chittenango Falls State Park 2300 Rathbun Rd Web: parks.ny.gov	Cazenovia	NY	13035	315-492-1756		565
Chittenden County 110 W Canal St Ste 202 Web: www.ccrpcvt.org	Winooski	VT	05404	802-846-4490		338
Chittenden Regional Correctional Facility 7 Farrell St Web: www.doc.state.vt.us	South Burlington	VT	05403	802-863-7356	863-7473	213
Chives Canadian Bistro 1537 Barrington St Web: www.chives.ca	Halifax	NS	B3J1Z4	902-420-9626		671
Chiyoda International Corp 2050 W Sam Houston Pky S Ste 850 Web: www.chiyoda-us.com	Houston	TX	77042	713-965-9005		261
CHKF 94.7 FM No 109 2723 37-Ave NE Web: www.fm947.com	Calgary	AB	T1Y5R8	403-717-1940	717-1945	643
CHL Medical Partners 2507 Post Rd Web: www.chlmedical.com	Southport	CT	06890	203-324-7700	324-3636	792
CHL Systems 476 Meetinghouse Rd Web: chlsystems.com	Souderton	PA	18964	215-723-7284	723-9115	261
CHLA (Canadian Health Libraries Assn) 39 River St Web: www.chla-absc.ca	Toronto	ON	M5A3P1	416-646-1600	646-9460	49-11
CHLC-FM 907 Rue de Puyjalon Web: www.chlc.com	Baie Comeau	QC	G5C1N3	418-589-3771	589-9086	647
Chloe 232 Arch St Web: www.chloebyob.com	Philadelphia	PA	19106	215-629-2337		671
Chlorine Institute Inc 1300 Wilson Blvd Ste 525 Web: www.chlorineinstitute.org	Arlington	VA	22209	703-894-4140	894-4130	49-13
CHM (Clearwater Historical Museum) 315 College Ave Web: www.clearwatermuseum.org	Orofino	ID	83544	208-476-5033		520
CHME Inc 289 Foster City Blvd Ste A Web: www.chme.org	Foster City	CA	94404	650-357-8550		475
Chmura Economics & Analytics (CEA) 1309 E Cary St Web: www.chmuraecon.com	Richmond	VA	23219	804-554-5400	644-2828	466
Chmura's Bakery Inc 12 Pulaski St Web: www.chmurasbakery.com	Indian Orchard	MA	01151	413-543-2521		68
CHMWarnick 548 Cabot St Web: chmwarnick.com	Beverly	MA	01915	978-522-7000		379
CHMY-FM 321-B Raglan St S TF: 855-946-6936 ■ Web: www.renfrewtoday.ca	Renfrew	ON	K7V4H4	613-432-6936	432-1086	647
CHN (Coalition on Human Needs) 1120 Connecticut Ave NW TF: 888-668-8919 ■ Web: www.chn.org	Washington	DC	20036	202-223-2532	223-2538	48-5
Choate Construction Co 8200 Roberts Dr Ste 600 Web: www.choateco.com	Atlanta	GA	30350	678-892-1200	892-1202	186
Choate Rosemary Hall 333 Christian St Web: www.choate.edu	Wallingford	CT	06492	203-697-2239	697-2629	622
Chocklett Press Inc 2922 Nicholas Ave TF: 800-533-4146 ■ Web: chocklettpress.com	Roanoke	VA	24012	540-345-1820	342-6526	627
Chocolate Factory Theater 549 49th Ave Web: chocolatefactorytheater.org	Long Island City	NY	11101	718-482-7069		297
Chocolate Shoppe Ice Cream 2221 Daniels St TF: 800-466-8043 ■ Web: www.chocolateshoppeicecream.com	Madison	WI	53718	608-221-8640	221-8650	296-25
Chocolates A la Carte 24836 Ave Rockefeller *Fax Area Code: 661 ■ TF: 800-818-2462 ■ Web: www.candymaker.com	Valencia	CA	91355	800-818-2462	257-4999*	296-8
Chocolates by Leopold 170 Church St Web: www.chocolatesbyleopold.com	Montrose	PA	18801	570-278-1230		297-3
Choctaw Casino Resorts 3735 Choctaw Rd TF: 888-652-4628 ■ Web: www.choctawcasinos.com	Durant	OK	74701	580-920-0160		452
Choctaw County 55 E Quinn St Web: choctawcountyms.com	Ackerman	MS	39735	662-285-3778		338
Choctaw County Choctaw County Courthouse 117 S Mulberry St Ste 8 Web: paroles.alabama.gov	Butler	AL	36904	205-459-2684	459-8554	338
Choctaw County Public Library 124 N Academy Ave	Butler	AL	36904	205-459-2542		434-3
Choctaw Electric Co-opeartive Inc Hwy 93 N PO Box 758 TF: 800-780-6486 ■ Web: choctawelectric.net	Hugo	OK	74743	580-326-6486	326-2492	245

Phone | Fax | Class

Choctaw Management Services Enterprise
2101 W Arkansas St . . . . Durant OK 74701 866-326-1000 260
TF: 866-326-1000

Choctaw Transportation Company Inc
1311 E Ct PO Box 527 . . . . Dyersburg TN 38025 731-286-0012 286-1528 188-5
Web: choctawtrans.com

Choctawhatchee Electric Co-opeartive Inc
1350 W Baldwin Ave. . . . . DeFuniak Springs FL 32435 850-892-2111 892-9243 245
TF: 800-342-0990 ■ Web: www.chelco.com

Choctaw-Kaul Distribution Co
3540 Vinewood Ave . . . . Detroit MI 48208 313-894-9494 894-7977 576
Web: www.choctawkaul.com

Choffin Career & Technical Ctr
200 E Wood St . . . . Youngstown OH 44503 330-744-8700 744-8705 250
Web: www.choffincareer.com

Choi Bros Inc 3401 W Div St. . . . . Chicago IL 60651 773-489-2800 489-3030 155-1
TF: 800-524-2464 ■ Web: www.choibrothers.com

Choice Books LLC
2387 Grace Chapel Rd . . . . Harrisonburg VA 22801 540-434-1827 434-9894 96
TF: 800-827-1894 ■ Web: www.choicebooks.org

Choice Brands Inc 310 Powell Ave. . . . . Monroe LA 71201 318-387-0432 81-1
Web: www.choice-brands.net

Choice Financial Group 645 Hill Ave . . . . Grafton ND 58237 701-352-0242 70
Web: bankwithchoice.com

Choice Genetics
1415 28th St Ste 400 . . . . West Des Moines IA 50266 515-225-9420 11-2
Web: www.choice-genetics.com

Choice Granite & Marble
803 Geyer Rd . . . . Pittsburgh PA 15212 412-821-3900 362
Web: choicegraniteandmarble.com

Choice Group 2265 Livernois Rd Ste 500 . . . . Troy MI 48084 248-362-4150 362-4154 654
Web: www.choiceproperties.com

Choice Hotels International Inc
1 Choice Hotels Cir Ste 400 . . . . Rockville MD 20850 301-592-5000 379
NYSE: CHH ■ TF: 800-424-6423 ■ Web: www.choicehotels.com

Choice Medical Inc 400 Erin Dr. . . . . Knoxville TN 37919 877-588-1643 588-4355* 475
*Fax Area Code: 865 ■ TF: 877-588-1643 ■ Web: choicemedinc.com

Choice Metals Inc 36 Cote Ave . . . . Goffstown NH 03045 603-626-5500 626-5502 492
TF: 800-621-6267 ■ Web: choicemet.com

Choice One Engineering Corp
440 E Hoewisher Rd . . . . Sidney OH 45365 937-497-0200 256
Web: choiceoneengineering.com

Choice Precision Machine Inc
4380 Commerce Dr . . . . Whitehall PA 18052 610-502-1111 502-1109 454
Web: www.choiceprecision.com

Choice Respiratory Care Inc
657 Morganza Rd . . . . Canonsburg PA 15317 724-745-9401 704-9066* 352
*Fax Area Code: 866 ■ TF: 866-404-7377 ■ Web: www.choicerespiratorycare.com

Choice Telecommunications Inc
7640 Dixie Hwy Ste 150 . . . . Clarkston MI 48346 248-922-1150 196
TF: 800-815-3320 ■ Web: choicetel.com

Choice Translating Inc
112 S Tryon St Ste 1500. . . . . Charlotte NC 28284 704-717-0043 393
Web: www.choicetranslating.com

Choices Software Inc
200 Broadway Ste 203 . . . . Lynnfield MA 01940 800-873-4757 180
TF: 800-873-4757 ■ Web: acords.com

Choke Canyon State Park PO Box 2. . . . . Calliham TX 78007 361-786-3868 565
Web: tpwd.texas.gov

CHOMP (Community Hospital of the Monterey Peninsula)
23625 Holman Hwy . . . . Monterey CA 93940 831-624-5311 625-4948 374-3
TF: 888-452-4667 ■ Web: www.chomp.org

Choochai Thai Restaurant 2330 19th St . . . . Lubbock TX 79401 806-747-1767 671
Web: choochai.com

Chooljian Brothers Packing Company Inc
3192 S Indianola Ave PO Box 395 . . . . Sanger CA 93657 559-875-5501 875-1582 11-1
Web: www.chooljianbrothers.com

Chooseco LLC PO Box 46 . . . . Waitsfield VT 05673 802-496-2595 637-2
TF: 800-564-3468 ■ Web: www.cyoa.com

Chop House 9700 Kingston Pk. . . . . Knoxville TN 37922 865-531-2467 693-4814 671
Web: thechophouse.com

Chop House Ann Arbor, The
322 S Main St. . . . . Ann Arbor MI 48104 734-669-9977 671
Web: thechophouseannarbor.com

Chop House, The 2011 Gunbarrel Rd . . . . Chattanooga TN 37421 423-892-1222 671
Web: www.thechophouse.com

Chop's City Grill 837 Fifth Ave S. . . . . Naples FL 34102 239-262-4677 671
Web: www.chopscitygrill.com

Chophouse '47 36 Beacon Dr . . . . Greenville SC 29615 864-286-8700 671
Web: chophouse47.com

Chopra Center at La Costa Resort & Spa
2013 Costa del Mar Rd. . . . . Carlsbad CA 92009 760-494-1600 494-1608 673
TF: 888-424-6772 ■ Web: chopra.com

Chopstick House 5412 E Indiana St . . . . Evansville IN 47715 812-473-5551 671
Web: www.chopstickhouserestaurant.net

Choptank Electric Co-opeartive Inc
24820 Meeting House Rd PO Box 430 . . . . Denton MD 21629 877-892-0001 479-3516* 245
*Fax Area Code: 410 ■ TF: 877-892-0001 ■ Web: www.choptankelectric.com

Choristers Guild 2834 W Kingsley Rd. . . . . Garland TX 75041 469-398-3606 48-4
TF: 800-246-7478 ■ Web: www.choristersguild.org

Chortek LLP
N16W23217 Stone Ridge Dr Ste 350 . . . . Waukesha WI 53188 262-522-8227 2
Web: chortek.com

Chorus America
1156 15th St NW Ste 310. . . . . Washington DC 20005 202-331-7577 331-7599 48-4
Web: www.chorusamerica.org

Chorus Aviation Inc
3 Spectacle Lake Dr . . . . Dartmouth NS B3B1W8 902-873-5000 787
Web: www.flyjazz.ca

Chouteau County Courthouse
1308 Franklin St. . . . . Fort Benton MT 59442 406-622-5151 622-3012 338
Web: www.co.chouteau.mt.us

Chow's Contemporary Chinese Food
720 St Michaels Dr. . . . . Santa Fe NM 87505 505-471-7120 671
Web: mychows.com

Chowan County PO Box 1030. . . . . Edenton NC 27932 252-482-8431 482-4925 338
Web: www.chowancounty-nc.gov

Chowan University
1 University Pl . . . . Murfreesboro NC 27855 252-398-6535 166
TF: 888-424-6926 ■ Web: chowan.edu

Chowly Inc 225 W Wacker Dr Ste 550 . . . . Chicago IL 60606 888-628-0823 178-1
TF: 888-628-0823 ■ Web: www.chowly.com

CHOX-FM 601 1ere rue Bureau 50 . . . . La Pocatiere QC G0R1Z0 418-856-1310 856-3747 647
Web: www.chox97.com

Choyce Peterson Inc 383 Main Ave. . . . . Norwalk CT 06851 203-356-9600 652
Web: choycepeterson.com

CHP Group, The
6600 SW 105th Ave Ste 115. . . . . Beaverton OR 97008 503-203-8333 644-0442 352
TF: 800-449-9479 ■ Web: www.chpgroup.com

CHP International Inc
1040 N Blvd Ste 220. . . . . Oak Park IL 60301 708-848-9650 196
TF: 800-449-2614 ■ Web: www.chpinternational.com

CHPA (Consumer Healthcare Products Assn)
1625 Eye St NW Ste 600. . . . . Washington DC 20036 202-429-9260 223-6835 49-4
Web: www.chpa.org

CHPS (Children's Historical Publishing)
1616 Turnberry Village Dr. . . . . Dayton OH 45458 937-643-0502 637-2
Web: www.childrenshistoricalpublishing.org

CHR Solutions Inc
9700 Bissonnet Ste 2800 . . . . Houston TX 77036 713-351-5111 196
Web: www.chrsolutions.com

CHRIE (International Council on Hotel Restaurant & Institutional Education)
2810 N Parham Rd Ste 230 . . . . Richmond VA 23294 804-346-4800 346-5009 49-5
Web: www.chrie.org

Chris A. Owens Attorney at Law
22 W Pennsylvania Ave Ste 606 . . . . Towson MD 21204 410-339-7313 41
Web: hfflegal.com

Chris Alston Chassisworks Inc
8661 Younger Creek Dr . . . . Sacramento CA 95828 916-388-0288 54
TF: 800-722-2269 ■ Web: www.cachassisworks.com

Chris Hart & Partners Inc
115 N Market St . . . . Wailuku HI 96793 808-242-1955 422
Web: chpmaui.com

Chris Madrid's 830 W Hollywood . . . . San Antonio TX 78212 210-735-3552 671
Web: chrismadrids.com

Chris Palmer Agency Inc
3215 E Main St. . . . . Endwell NY 13760 607-484-8400 390
Web: chrispalmeragency.com

Chris Smith Realty 1204 Third Ave . . . . Spring Lake NJ 07762 732-449-3777 449-7790 652
Web: www.chrissmithrealty.com

Chris Woods Construction Company Inc
8068 US Hwy 70. . . . . Memphis TN 38133 901-386-3182 382-0454 186
Web: www.chriswoodsconstruction.com

Chris Young Consulting Co
83 N 64th St. . . . . Harrisburg PA 17111 717-561-9742 180

Chrisad Inc
11 Professional Center Pkwy . . . . San Rafael CA 94903 415-924-8575 7
TF: 800-505-4150 ■ Web: chrisad.com

Chrisanntha Construction Corp
4661 Dewey Ave PO Box 165. . . . . Gorham NY 14461 585-526-6376 187
Web: www.chrisanntha.com

Chris-Craft Boats 8161 15th St E. . . . . Sarasota FL 34243 941-351-4900 90
Web: www.chriscraft.com

Chrisian Inc 17561 Hillside Ave. . . . . Jamaica NY 11432 718-465-9151 225
Web: www.chrisian.com

Chrisken Property Management LLC
345 N Canal St Ste 201 . . . . Chicago IL 60606 312-454-1626 454-1627 655
Web: www.chrisken.com

Chrisman Manufacturing Inc
7399 Beatline Rd . . . . Long Beach MS 39560 228-864-6293 864-1381 470
Web: www.navigatorforklift.com

ChrisNik Inc
7461-A Cincinnati Brookville Rd . . . . Okeana OH 45053 513-738-2920 738-5817 187
TF: 800-262-4992 ■ Web: www.chrisnik.com

Christ & Grace Episcopal Church
1545 S Sycamore St. . . . . Petersburg VA 23805 804-733-7202 48-20
Web: christandgrace.org

Christ Church Cathedral
125 Monument Cir . . . . Indianapolis IN 46204 317-636-4577 50-1
Web: www.cccindy.org

Christ Church Cathedral 45 Church St. . . . . Hartford CT 06103 860-527-7231 50-1
Web: www.cccathedral.org

Christ Church Cathedral
1210 Locust St. . . . . Saint Louis MO 63103 314-231-3454 231-3142 50-1
Web: www.christchurchcathedral.us

Christ Church Cathedral
690 Burrard St . . . . Vancouver BC V6C2L1 604-682-3848 50-1
Web: thecathedral.ca

Christ Church Episcopal
10 N Church St. . . . . Greenville SC 29601 864-271-8773 242-0879 50-1
Web: www.ccgsc.org

Christ Church in Philadelphia
20 N American St . . . . Philadelphia PA 19106 215-922-1695 922-3578 50-1
Web: www.christchurchphila.org

Christ Church of Universal Love, The
11699 130th Ave. . . . . Largo FL 33778 727-585-5088 48-20

Christ Church Xp 8800 Vaughn Rd. . . . . Montgomery AL 36117 334-387-0566 48-20
Web: www.christchurchmgm.net

Christ Episcopal Church
501 S State St PO Box 1374. . . . . Dover DE 19903 302-734-5731 50-1
Web: www.christchurchdover.org

Christ For The Nations Institute
3404 Conway St . . . . Dallas TX 75224 214-302-6420 302-6529 167-3
TF: 800-477-2364 ■ Web: www.cfni.org

Christ Hospital 176 Palisade Ave . . . . Jersey City NJ 07306 201-795-8200 374-3
Web: carepointhealth.org

Christ Hospital Health Network, The
2139 Auburn Ave . . . . Cincinnati OH 45219 513-585-2000 374-3
Web: www.thechristhospital.com

Christ in Youth PO Box B . . . . Joplin MO 64802 417-781-2273 781-5958 48-20
Web: new.ciy.com

Christ School 500 Christ School Rd . . . . Arden NC 28704 828-684-6232 684-4869 622
TF: 800-422-3212 ■ Web: www.christschool.org

Christ the King Retreat Ctr
621 First Ave S. . . . . Buffalo MN 55313 763-682-1394 682-3453 673
Web: kingshouse.com

Name / Address	City	State	ZIP	Phone	Fax	Class
Christ the King School 1920 Barberry Dr *Web:* www.ctkcougars.com	Springfield	IL	62704	217-546-2159		685
Christ The King Seminary 711 Knox Rd *Web:* www.cks.edu	East Aurora	NY	14052	716-652-8900	652-8903	167-3
Christ Universal Temple 11901 S Ashland Ave Apt S *Web:* cutemple.org	Chicago	IL	60643	773-568-2282		48-20
Christa Construction LLC 600 E Ave Ste 201 *Web:* www.christa.com	Rochester	NY	14607	585-924-3050		186
Christa McAuliffe Planetarium 2 Institute Dr *Web:* www.starhop.com	Concord	NH	03301	603-271-7827	271-7832	598
Christchurch School 49 Seahorse Ln *Web:* www.christchurchschool.org	Christchurch	VA	23031	804-758-2306	758-0721	622
Christendom College 134 Christendom Dr *TF:* 800-877-5456 ■ *Web:* www.christendom.edu	Front Royal	VA	22630	540-636-2900	636-1655	166
Christensen Computer Company Inc 12005 N Panorama Dr *TF:* 800-222-6102 ■ *Web:* www.cccsoft.com	Fountain Hills	AZ	85268	800-222-6102		177
Christensen Farms 23971 County Rd 10 *Web:* www.christensenfarms.com	Sleepy Eye	MN	56085	507-794-5310		10-6
Christensen Industries 2990 S Main St *Web:* www.christensenindustries.com	Salt Lake City	UT	84115	801-466-3334	466-1441	697
Christensen O'Connor Johnson & Kindness PLLC 1201 Third Ave Ste 3600 *Web:* www.cojk.com	Seattle	WA	98101	206-682-8100		428
Christensen Roberts Solutions 60 Pond St *Web:* www.crsol.com	Milford	CT	06460	203-389-4440	389-4480	194
Christensen Shipyards LLC 4400 SE Columbia Way *Web:* www.christensenyachts.com	Vancouver	WA	98661	360-831-9800		770
Christenson Communication PO Box 61627 *Web:* www.chriscom.net	Sunnyvale	CA	94088	408-744-9400	744-9410	224
Christenson Transportation Inc 2301 W Old Rt 66 *Web:* www.christensontrans.com	Strafford	MO	65757	417-866-5993	447-0864	780
Christian & Associates LLC 1006 Poyntz Ave *Web:* movemanhattan.com	Manhattan	KS	66502	785-587-5222		652
Christian & Missionary Alliance 8595 Explorer Dr *TF:* 800-700-2651 ■ *Web:* www.cmalliance.org	Colorado Springs	CO	80920	719-599-5999		48-20
Christian & Smith 2302 Fannin Ste 500 *Web:* csj-law.com	Houston	TX	77002	713-659-7617		41
Christian Aid Ministries PO Box 360 *Web:* christianaidministries.org	Berlin	OH	44610	330-893-2428	893-2305	48-20
Christian Alliance for Humanitarian Aid Inc 1525 Main St L-3 *Web:* christian-alliance.org	Pearland	TX	77581	281-412-2285		743
Christian Appalachian Project 485 Ponderosa Dr PO Box 1768 *TF:* 800-755-5322 ■ *Web:* www.christianapp.org	Paintsville	KY	41240	800-755-5322		48-5
Christian Blue Pages 521 Byers Rd Ste 102 *TF:* 800-860-2583 ■ *Web:* www.trustbluereview.com	Miamisburg	OH	45342	800-860-2583		637-2
Christian Brothers University 650 E Pkwy S *TF:* 800-288-7576 ■ *Web:* www.cbu.edu	Memphis	TN	38104	901-321-3000	321-3494	166
Christian Brothers Retreat 4401 Redwood Rd *Web:* www.christianbrosretreat.com	Napa	CA	94558	707-252-3810		378
Christian Business Men's Connection (CBMC) 5746 Marlin Rd Ste 602 Osborne Ctr *TF:* 800-566-2262 ■ *Web:* www.cbmc.com	Chattanooga	TN	37411	423-698-4444	629-4434	48-20
Christian Church (Disciples of Christ) 130 E Washington St *TF:* 800-668-8016 ■ *Web:* www.disciples.org	Indianapolis	IN	46204	317-635-3100	635-3700	48-20
Christian Coalition of America PO Box 37030 *Fax Area Code: 808 ■ *Web:* www.cc.org	Washington	DC	20013	202-479-6900	586-0006*	48-7
Christian County 511 S Main St *Web:* www.christiancountyky.gov	Hopkinsville	KY	42240	270-887-4100	885-7501	338
Christian County 100 W Church St Rm 206 *Web:* www.christiancountymo.gov	Ozark	MO	65721	417-582-4300	581-8331	338
Christian County 101 S Main St PO Box 647 *Web:* christiancountyil.com	Taylorville	IL	62568	217-824-4969	824-5105	338
Christian County Library 1005 N Fourth Ave *Web:* christiancountylibrary.org	Ozark	MO	65721	417-581-2432	581-8855	434-3
Christian County Public Schools 200 Glass Ave *Web:* www.christian.kyschools.us	Hopkinsville	KY	42240	270-887-7000	887-1316	685
Christian Dior Inc 19 East 57th St 37th Fl *Web:* dior.com	New York	NY	10019	212-582-0500		277
Christian Disaster Response Intl PO Box 3339 *Web:* cdresponse.org	Winter Haven	FL	33885	863-967-4357		48-5
Christian Fellowship Church Foundation 21673 Beaumeade Cir *Web:* www.cfellowshipc.org	Ashburn	VA	20147	703-729-3900		48-20
Christian Fellowship Publishers Inc (CFP) 11515 Allecingie Pky *Web:* www.c-f-p.com	Richmond	VA	23235	804-794-5333		637-2
Christian Foundation for Children & Aging (CFCA) 1 Elmwood Ave *TF:* 800-875-6564 ■ *Web:* www.unbound.org	Kansas City	KS	66103	913-384-6500	384-2211	48-6
Christian Growth Publishers Inc PO Box 999 *Web:* www.christiangrowth.com	Atascadero	CA	93423	805-466-5555		637-2
Christian Horizons 200 N Postville Dr *TF:* 800-535-8717 ■ *Web:* christianhorizonsliving.org	Lincoln	IL	62656	217-732-9651	732-8686	363
Christian Leadership Alliance (CLA) 635 Camino De Los Mares Ste 216 *Web:* www.christianleadershipalliance.org	San Clemente	CA	92673	949-487-0900	487-0927	49-12
Christian Legal Society (CLS) 8001 Braddock Rd Ste 300 *TF:* 800-225-4008 ■ *Web:* www.christianlegalsociety.org	Springfield	VA	22151	703-642-1070	642-1075	49-10
Christian Media Inc 209 E 15th St *Web:* kcmifm.org	Scottsbluff	NE	69361	308-632-5264		645-141
Christian Medical & Dental Assn (CMDA) 2604 Hwy 421 PO Box 7500 *TF:* 888-231-2637 ■ *Web:* www.cmda.org	Bristol	TN	37620	423-844-1000	844-1005	49-8
Christian Publishers PO Box 248 *TF:* 844-841-6387 ■ *Web:* www.christianpub.com	Cedar Rapids	IA	52406	319-368-8009	368-8011	637-10
Christian Reformed Church in North America (CRC) 2850 Kalamazoo Ave SE *TF:* 800-272-5125 ■ *Web:* www.crcna.org	Grand Rapids	MI	49560	616-241-1691	224-0834	48-20
Christian Schools Intl (CSI) 3350 E Paris Ave SE *TF:* 800-635-8288 ■ *Web:* www.csionline.org	Grand Rapids	MI	49512	616-957-1070	957-5022	49-5
Christian Science Monitor 210 Massachusetts Ave *Web:* www.csmonitor.com	Boston	MA	02115	617-450-2356		532-3
Christian Television Network Inc (CTN) 6922 142nd Ave N *TF:* 800-716-7729 ■ *Web:* www.ctnonline.com	Largo	FL	33771	727-535-5622	531-2497	738
Christian Theological Seminary 1000 W 42nd St *Web:* www.cts.edu	Indianapolis	IN	46208	317-924-1331		167-3
Christian Witness Theological Seminary 1975 Concourse Dr *Web:* www.cwts.edu	San Jose	CA	95131	408-433-2280	433-9855	167-3
Christiana Care Health System 501 W 14th St *TF:* 855-250-9594 ■ *Web:* christianacare.org	Wilmington	DE	19801	302-366-1929		353
Christiana Mall 132 Christiana Mal *Web:* www.christianamall.com	Newark	DE	19702	302-731-9815		460
Christianity Today 465 Gundersen Dr *TF:* 800-222-1840 ■ *Web:* www.christianitytoday.com	Carol Stream	IL	60188	630-260-6200	260-0114	457-11
Christiansen Aviation Inc 200 Lear Jet Ln *Web:* www.christiansenaviation.com	Tulsa	OK	74132	918-298-6650	298-6656	24
Christianson Air Conditioning & Plumbing 1950 Louis Henna Blvd *Web:* www.christiansonco.com	Round Rock	TX	78664	512-246-5200	246-5201	189-10
Christianson Systems Inc 20421 15th St SE PO Box 138 *TF:* 800-328-8896 ■ *Web:* www.christianson.com	Blomkest	MN	56216	320-995-6141	995-6145	207
Christie Cookie Co 1205 Third Ave N *TF:* 800-458-2447 ■ *Web:* www.christiecookies.com	Nashville	TN	37208	615-242-3817	242-5572	296-9
Christie L. Fraser A Law Corp 50 Osgood Pl Ste 110 *Web:* cfraserlawcorp.com	San Francisco	CA	94133	415-394-8880		41
Christie Law Group PLLC 2100 Westlake Ave N Ste 206 *Web:* christielawgroup.com	Seattle	WA	98109	206-957-9669		41
Christie Lodge PO Box 1196 *TF:* 888-325-6343 ■ *Web:* www.christielodge.com	Avon	CO	81620	970-845-4504		378
Christie Medical Holdings Inc 1256 Union Ave 3rd Fl *TF:* 877-733-8346 ■ *Web:* www.christiedigital.com	Memphis	TN	38104	901-721-0330	721-0350	476
Christina & Company Inc 2901 Northwestern Ave *Web:* christinaspa.com	West Lafayette	IN	47906	765-449-4448		77
Christina Cultural Arts Ctr 705 N Market St *Web:* ccacde.org	Wilmington	DE	19801	302-652-0101	652-7480	572
Christina I. Collins 1 N Wacker Ste 4600 *Web:* christina-collins.com	Chicago	IL	60606	312-641-8950		390
Christine Valmy International School of Esthetics & Cosmetology 285 Changebridge Rd *TF:* 800-526-5057 ■ *Web:* www.christinevalmy.com	Pine Brook	NJ	07058	973-575-1050	575-1355	685
Christini's 7600 Doctor Phillips Blvd *Web:* www.christinis.com	Orlando	FL	32819	407-545-6867	345-8700	671
Christman Co 208 N Capitol Ave The Christman Bldg *Web:* www.christmanco.com	Lansing	MI	48933	517-482-1488	482-3520	186
Christmas Classics Ltd PO Box 1184 *TF:* 866-552-7742 ■ *Web:* www.christmasclassics.com	North Cape May	NJ	08204	609-886-6540	886-8004	637-10
Christmas Decor Inc 2301 Crown Crt *Web:* www.christmasdecor.net	Irving	TX	75038	806-722-1225		310
Christmas Lumber Company Inc 101 Roane St *Web:* www.christmaslumber.com	Harriman	TN	37748	865-882-2362	882-1973	191-3
Christo's 2632 Nicollet Ave *Web:* www.christos.com	Minneapolis	MN	55408	612-871-2111	871-8129	671
Christopher & Banks Corp 2400 Xenium Ln N *NYSE: CBK* ■ *TF:* 800-890-9601 ■ *Web:* www.christopherandbanks.com	Plymouth	MN	55441	763-551-5000	551-5198	157-6
Christopher & Weisberg PA 1232 N University Dr *TF:* 800-978-2947 ■ *Web:* cwiplaw.com	Plantation	FL	33322	954-828-1488		41
Christopher Cutts Gallery 21 Morrow Ave *Web:* www.cuttsgallery.com	Toronto	ON	M6R2H9	416-532-5566		42
Christopher D. Smith PA 5391 Lakewood Ranch Blvd N Ste 203 *TF:* 855-746-3900 ■ *Web:* chrissmith.com	Sarasota	FL	34240	941-202-2222	907-3040	41
Christopher D. Soto PLC 4500 S Lakeshore Dr Ste 5 *Web:* sotolawfirm.com	Tempe	AZ	85282	480-456-6267		41

Name / Address	Phone	Fax	Class
Christopher Enterprises 155 W 2050 N .... Spanish Fork UT 84660 *Fax Area Code: 801 ■ TF: 800-453-1406 ■ Web: www.drchristopher.com	800-453-1406	794-6801*	355
Christopher Guy 8900 Beverly Blvd. .... West Hollywood CA 90048 TF: 800-476-9505 ■ Web: www.christopherguy.com	323-509-4034	628-6929	361
Christopher L. Giddings PC 1880 Jfk Blvd Ste 1710 .... Philadelphia PA 19103 Web: chrisgiddingslaw.com	215-243-3450		41
Christopher Martin's 860 State St .... New Haven CT 06511 Web: www.christophermartins.com	203-776-8835		671
Christopher Newport University 1 University Pl .... Newport News VA 23606 TF: 800-333-4268 ■ Web: www.cnu.edu	757-594-7015	594-7333	166
Christopher R. Stein Comprehensive Wealth Management Inc 4711 Golf Rd Ste 705 .... Skokie IL 60076 Web: crscompwealth.com	847-677-3108	789-9400	690
Christopher Ranch 305 Bloomfield Ave .... Gilroy CA 95020 TF: 800-779-1156 ■ Web: primuslabs.com	408-847-1100		10-11
Christopher Reeve Foundation 636 Morris Tpke Ste 3A .... Short Hills NJ 07078 TF: 800-225-0292 ■ Web: www.christopherreeve.org	973-379-2690		48-17
Christopher Smith Leonard Bristow Stanell & Wells PA Suntrust Bank Bldg 1001 Third Ave W Ste 700 .... Bradenton FL 34205 Web: www.cslcpa.com	941-748-1040		734
Christopher's Crush 2502 E Camelback Rd .... Phoenix AZ 85016 Web: www.wrigleymansion.com	602-522-2344		671
Christopher's Seafood & Steak House 134 W Pierpont Ave .... Salt Lake City UT 84101	801-519-8515		671
Christophers, The 5 Hanover Sq .... New York NY 10004 TF: 888-298-4050 ■ Web: www.christophers.org	212-759-4050	838-5073	48-20
Christos Mediterranean Grille 130 6th St .... Pittsburgh PA 15222 Web: christospitt.com	412-261-6442		671
Christown Spectrum Mall 7511 E McDonald Dr .... Phoenix AZ 85015 Web: www.christownspectrum.com	602-249-0670		460
CHRISTUS Health 919 Hidden Rdg Ste 450 .... Irving TX 75038 Web: christushealth.org	469-282-2000		353
Christus Victor Lutheran Church Incorporated of Knox County Tennessee 4110 Central Ave Pk .... Knoxville TN 37912 Web: christusvictorknoxville.org	865-687-6622		48-20
Christy Capital Management Inc 2939 Mcmanus Rd .... Macon GA 31220 Web: www.christycapital.com	478-314-2160		765
Christy Lane Enterprises PO Box 4040 .... Palm Springs CA 92263 TF: 800-555-0206 ■ Web: www.christylane.com	800-555-0206		810
Christy Refractories Co 4641 McRee Ave .... Saint Louis MO 63110 Web: www.christyco.com	314-773-7500	773-8371	500
Christy Sports LLC 875 Parfet St .... Lakewood CO 80215 TF: 888-413-6966 ■ Web: christysports.com	303-237-6321		711
Christy's 3101 Ponce de Leon Blvd .... Coral Gables FL 33134 Web: christysrestaurant.com	305-446-1400	446-3257	671
CHRK-FM 500 Kings Rd Ste 300 .... Sydney NS B1L1BB Web: www.giant1019.com	902-270-1019	270-3566	647
Chrom Tech Inc PO Box 240248 .... Apple Valley MN 55124 TF: 800-822-5242 ■ Web: www.chromtech.com	952-431-6000	431-6345	419
Chroma Technology Corp 10 Imtec Ln .... Bellows Falls VT 05101 TF: 800-824-7662 ■ Web: www.chroma.com	802-428-2500	428-2525	544
ChromaGen Vision LLC 657 Swedesford Rd .... Malvern PA 19335 TF: 855-473-2323 ■ Web: www.ireadbetternow.com	855-473-2323		544
Chromaline Corp 4832 Grand Ave .... Duluth MN 55807 TF: 800-328-4261 ■ Web: www.chromaline.com	218-628-2217	628-3245	628
Chromalloy Gas Turbine LLC 3999 RCA Blvd .... Palm Beach Gardens FL 33410 Web: www.chromalloy.com	561-935-3571		21
Chromalox Inc 103 Gamma Dr Ext .... Pittsburgh PA 15238 Web: www.chromalox.com	412-967-3800		14
Chromaprobe Inc 10 Kimler Dr .... Maryland Heights MO 63043 Web: www.chromaprobe.com	314-738-0001		231
Chromatech Printing Inc 16 Mary St .... Des Plaines IL 60016 Web: www.chromatech.com	847-699-0333		627
Chromcraft Revington Inc 1330 Win Hentschel Blvd .... West Lafayette IN 47906 OTC: CRCV ■ Web: www.chromcraft-revington.com	765-807-2640		319-2
Chronicle Books 680 Second St .... San Francisco CA 94107 TF: 800-722-6657 ■ Web: www.chroniclebooks.com	415-537-4200	537-4460	637-2
Chronicle Herald, The PO Box 610 .... Halifax NS B3J2T2 TF: 800-563-1187 ■ Web: thechronicleherald.ca	902-426-2811	426-1158	532-1
Chronicle Independent 909 W Dekalb St .... Camden SC 29020 Web: www.chronicle-independent.com	803-432-6157	432-7609	532-4
Chronicle of Higher Education, The 1255 23rd St NW Ste 700 .... Washington DC 20037 TF: 800-728-2803 ■ Web: www.chronicle.com	202-466-1000	452-1033	457-8
Chronicle, The 225 E Ave .... Elyria OH 44035 Web: www.chroniclet.com	440-329-7000	329-7282	532-2
Chronicle, The 15 Ridge St .... Glens Falls NY 12801 Web: www.glensfallschronicle.com	518-792-1126	793-1587	532-4
Chronicle-Journal, The 75 S Cumberland St .... Thunder Bay ON P7B1A3 TF: 800-465-3914 ■ Web: www.chroniclejournal.com	807-343-6200		532-1
Chronicle-Tribune 610 S Adams St .... Marion IN 46953 Web: www.chronicle-tribune.com	765-664-5111	668-4256	532-2
Chrysalis Consulting LLC 11711 N Pennsylvania St .... Carmel IN 46032 Web: www.chrysalisglobal.com	317-844-1400		194
Chrysalis Inn & Spa 804 10th St .... Bellingham WA 98225 TF: 888-808-0005 ■ Web: curiocollection3.hilton.com	360-756-1005		379
Chrysalis Packaging & Assembly Corp 130 W Edgerton Ave Ste 130 .... Milwaukee WI 53207 Web: www.chryspac.com	414-744-8550		88
Chrysalis Ventures 101 S Fifth St Ste 1650 .... Louisville KY 40202 Web: chrysalisventures.com	502-583-7644		792
Chrysler Aviation Inc (CAI) 7120 Hayvenhurst Ave Ste 309 .... Van Nuys CA 91406 TF: 800-995-0825 ■ Web: www.chrysleraviation.com	818-989-7900		13
Chrysler Group LLC 1000 Chrysler Dr .... Auburn Hills MI 48326 TF: 800-423-6343 ■ Web: www.dodge.com	800-423-6343		59
Chrysler Museum of Art One Memorial Pl .... Norfolk VA 23510 Web: www.chrysler.org	757-664-6200		520
Chrysostom Press PO Box 752 .... Manchester MO 63011 TF: 877-377-4333 ■ Web: chrysostompress.org	877-377-4333		637-2
CHS (Cambridge Historical Society) Hooper-Lee-Nichols House 159 Brattle St .... Cambridge MA 02138 Web: www.cambridgehistory.org	617-547-4252		49-19
CHS (California Historical Society) 678 Mission St .... San Francisco CA 94105 Web: www.californiahistoricalsociety.org	415-357-1848	357-1850	48-13
CHS Inc 5500 Cenex Dr .... Inver Grove Heights MN 55077 NASDAQ: CHSCP ■ TF: 800-232-3639 ■ Web: www.chsinc.com	651-355-6000		276
CHSLD Papineau Hospital 198 Presland Rd .... Gatineau QC J9L0C2 Web: cisss-outaouais.gouv.qc.ca	819-986-3341		374-2
CHST-FM 1 Communictions Rd .... London ON N6J4Z1 Web: www.jack1023.com	519-690-0102		647
CHT Global Corp 2107 N First St Ste 580 .... San Jose CA 95131 Web: www.chtglobal.com	408-988-1898		387
CHTN-FM 176 Great George St .... Charlottetown PE C1A4K9 Web: www.ocean100.com	902-569-1003	569-8693	647
CHU de Quebec 1050 Ch Sainte-Foy .... Quebec City QC G1S4L8 Web: www.chudequebec.ca	418-682-7511	682-7877	374-2
Chu Judy (Rep D - CA) 2423 Rayburn House Office Bldg .... Washington DC 20515 Web: chu.house.gov	202-225-5464	225-5467	342-2
CHU Sainte-Justine 3175 Ch de la Cote-Sainte-Catherine .... Montreal QC H3T1C5 TF: 888-235-3667 ■ Web: www.chusj.org	514-345-4931	345-4760	374-2
Chubb 202 Halls Mill Rd .... Whitehouse Station NJ 08889 Web: www.chubb.com	908-572-2000		391-2
Chubb Group of Insurance Cos 15 Mtn View Rd .... Warren NJ 07059 Web: www.chubb.com	908-903-2000		391-4
Chubu Electric Power Company Inc 900 17th St NW Ste 1220 .... Washington DC 20006 Web: www.chuden.co.jp	202-775-1960	331-9256	787
Chuck Patterson Inc 200 E Ave .... Chico CA 95926 TF: 866-417-8520 ■ Web: www.chuckpattersontoyota.net	530-895-1771		57
Chuck Schubert & Assoc 17197 N Laurel Park Dr Ste 145 .... Livonia MI 48152 Web: csasoftware.com	734-953-5600	953-5604	311
Chuck's Cellar 150 Kaiulani Ave .... Honolulu HI 96815 Web: www.chuckshawaii.com	808-923-4488		671
Chuck's Restaurant 3610 Sixth Ave .... Des Moines IA 50313 Web: www.chucksdsm.com	515-244-4104		671
Chuck's Steak House Inc 20 Segar St .... Danbury CT 06810 Web: www.chuckssteakhouse.com	203-792-5555		670
Chuckawalla Valley State Prison (CVSP) 19025 Wiley's Well Rd PO Box 2289 .... Blythe CA 92226 Web: cdcr.ca.gov	760-922-5300	922-6855	213
Chugach Electric Association Inc 5601 Electron Dr .... Anchorage AK 99518 TF: 800-478-7494 ■ Web: www.chugachelectric.com	907-563-7494	562-0027	245
Chugach Management Services Inc 3800 Centerpoint Dr Ste 601 .... Anchorage AK 99503 Web: www.chugach.com	907-563-8866		463
Chugach State Park 18620 Seward Hwy .... Anchorage AK 99516 TF: 800-478-6196 ■ Web: www.dnr.alaska.gov	907-345-5014	345-6982	565
Chukchansi Gold Resort & Casino 711 Lucky Ln .... Coarsegold CA 93614 TF: 866-794-6946 ■ Web: chukchansigold.com	866-794-6946		378
Chula Vista Convention & Visitors Bureau 233 Fourth Ave .... Chula Vista CA 91910 Web: www.chulavistaconvis.com	619-426-2882	420-1269	206
Chula Vista Public Library 365 F St .... Chula Vista CA 91910 Web: www.chulavistaca.gov	619-691-5069	427-4246	434-3
Chula Vista Resort 2501 River Rd .... Wisconsin Dells WI 53965 TF: 800-388-4782 ■ Web: www.chulavistaresort.com	608-254-8366	254-7653	669
Chumash Casino Resort 3400 E Hwy 246 .... Santa Ynez CA 93460 TF: 800-248-6274 ■ Web: www.chumashcasino.com	805-686-0855		452
Chumney & Assoc 660 US-1 2nd Fl .... North Palm Beach FL 33408 TF: 877-816-7347 ■ Web: www.chumneyads.com	561-768-5818	249-7243	7
Chung Oak Korean Restaurant 15320 A & B Warwick Blvd .... Newport News VA 23608 Web: chung-oak-korean-restaurant.business.site	757-874-3505		671
Chungs Gourmet Foods 3907 Dennis St .... Houston TX 77004 Web: www.chungsfoods.com	713-741-2118		296-36
Church & Chapel Metal Arts Inc 2616 W Grand Ave .... Chicago IL 60612 TF: 800-992-1234 ■ Web: www.church-chapel.com	800-992-1234	626-3299	510
Church & Dwight Canada Corp 635 Secretariat Ct .... Mississauga ON L5S0A5 Web: www.churchdwight.ca	905-696-6570		583
Church & Dwight Company Inc 469 N Harrison St .... Princeton NJ 08543 NYSE: CHD ■ TF: 800-617-4220 ■ Web: churchdwight.com	800-617-4220		214
Church & Murdock Electric Inc 5709 Wattsburg Rd .... Erie PA 16509 Web: www.churchandmurdock.com	814-825-3456	825-4043	189-4
Church Brew Works 3525 Liberty Ave .... Pittsburgh PA 15201 Web: churchbrew.com	412-688-8200		671

Name / Address	City	State	ZIP	Phone	Fax	Class
Church Divinity School of the Pacific 2451 Ridge Rd *Web:* cdsp.edu	Berkeley	CA	94709	510-204-0700	644-0712	167-3
Church Metal Spinning Co 5050 N 124th St *Web:* www.churchmetal.com	Milwaukee	WI	53225	414-461-6460		757
Church Mutual Insurance Co 3000 Schuster Ln *TF:* 800-554-2642 ■ *Web:* www.churchmutual.com	Merrill	WI	54452	715-536-5577	539-4650	391-4
Church of God in Christ Inc 930 Mason St *TF:* 877-746-8578 ■ *Web:* www.cogic.org	Memphis	TN	38126	901-947-9300		48-20
Church of God in Christ Publishing House 2500 Lamar Ave *Web:* www.cogicpublishinghouse.net	Memphis	TN	38114	901-744-0477	743-1555	637-2
Church of God Ministries 1201 E Fifth St *TF:* 800-848-2464 ■ *Web:* www.jesusisthesubject.org	Anderson	IN	46012	765-642-0256	642-5652	48-20
Church of God World Missions (COGWM) 2490 Keith St *TF:* 800-345-7492 ■ *Web:* cogwm.org	Cleveland	TN	37311	800-345-7492		48-20
Church of Jesus Christ of Latter-Day Saints 50 E N Temple St *TF:* 800-453-3860 ■ *Web:* www.churchofjesuschrist.org	Salt Lake City	UT	84150	801-240-1000		48-20
Church of Light 2119 Gold Ave SE *TF:* 800-500-0453 ■ *Web:* www.light.org	Albuquerque	NM	87106	505-247-1338	814-7318	48-20
Church of Our Lady of Lourdes 901 Atwells Ave *Web:* www.parishesonline.com	Providence	RI	02909	401-272-8127		48-20
Church of Scientology Flag Service Organization 500 Cleveland St *Web:* www.scientology-fso.org	Clearwater	FL	33755	727-467-5000		48-20
Church of the Brethren 1451 Dundee Ave *TF:* 800-323-8039 ■ *Web:* www.brethren.org	Elgin	IL	60120	847-742-5100	742-1407	48-20
Church of The Holy Communion 218 Ashley Ave *Web:* www.holycomm.org	Charleston	SC	29403	843-722-2024		48-20
Church of the Nazarene 17001 Prairie Star Pkwy *Web:* www.nazarene.org	Lenexa	KS	66220	913-577-0500		48-20
Church of the Transfiguration 1 E 29th St *Web:* www.littlechurch.org	New York	NY	10016	212-684-6770		50-1
Church Offset Printing Inc 1731 Margaretha Ave *Web:* www.churchoffsetprinting.com	Albert Lea	MN	56007	507-373-6485	373-2716	92
Church Women United (CWU) 475 Riverside Dr Ste 243 *TF:* 800-298-5551 ■ *Web:* www.churchwomenunited.net	New York	NY	10115	212-870-2347	870-2338	48-20
Church World Service 28606 Phillips St PO Box 968 *TF:* 800-297-1516 ■ *Web:* cwsglobal.org	Elkhart	IN	46515	574-264-3102	262-0966	48-5
Church, Harris, Johnson, Williams PC 114 Third St S *Web:* chjw.com	Great Falls	MT	59401	406-761-3000	453-2313	41
Churchill & Harriman LLC 239 Wall St *Web:* chus.com	Princeton	NJ	08540	609-921-3551		225
Churchill Cabinet Co 4616 W 19th St *TF:* 800-379-9776 ■ *Web:* www.chicago-gaming.com	Cicero	IL	60804	708-780-0070	780-9762	286
Churchill Corporate Services 56 Utter Ave *TF:* 800-941-7458 ■ *Web:* www.furnishedhousing.com	Hawthorne	NJ	07506	973-636-9400	636-0179	210
Churchill County 155 N Taylor St *Web:* nv-churchillcounty.civicplus.com	Fallon	NV	89406	775-423-6584		338
Churchill County Museum & Archives 1050 S Maine St *Web:* www.ccmuseum.org	Fallon	NV	89406	775-423-3677	423-3662	520
Churchill County School District 690 S Maine St *Web:* churchill.k12.nv.us	Fallon	NV	89406	775-423-0462	423-9581	685
Churchill Development Corp 1395 Piccard Dr Ste 170 *Web:* www.churchillbuilders.com	Rockville	MD	20850	240-243-1000	243-0715	187
Churchill Downs Inc 600 N Hurstbourne Pkwy Ste 400 *NASDAQ: CHDN* ■ *TF:* 800-283-3729 ■ *Web:* www.churchilldownsincorporated.com	Louisville	KY	40222	502-636-4400		642
Churchill Hotel 1914 Connecticut Ave NW *TF:* 800-424-2464 ■ *Web:* www.thechurchillhotel.com	Washington	DC	20009	202-797-2000	462-0944	379
Churchill Nature Tours PO Box 429 *TF:* 877-636-2968 ■ *Web:* www.churchillnaturetours.com	Erickson	MB	R0J0P0	204-636-2968	636-2557	760
Churchill School & Ctr, The 301 E 29th St *Web:* www.churchillschoolnyc.org	New York	NY	10016	212-722-0610		148
Churchill's Food & Spirits 340 S Saginaw St *Web:* churchillsflint.com	Flint	MI	48502	810-238-3800		671
Churchville Fire Equipment Corp 340 Sanford Rd S *TF:* 800-462-6143 ■ *Web:* www.churchvillefire.com	Churchville	NY	14428	585-293-1688		791
Churchwell Co 814 S Edgewood Ave *TF:* 877-537-6166 ■ *Web:* www.churchwellcompany.com	Jacksonville	FL	32205	904-356-5721		9
Churrascaria Plataforma 316 W 49th St *Web:* plataformaonline.com	New York	NY	10019	212-245-0505	974-8250	671
Churrasco's 2055 Westheimer *Web:* www.cordua.com	Houston	TX	77098	713-527-8300	527-0847	671
Chuy's Mesquite Broiler 2500 New Stine Rd *Web:* bajachuys.com	Bakersfield	CA	93309	661-833-3469		671
CHVC-TV 99 Gorse St *Web:* www.vctv.ca	Valemount	BC	V0E2Z0	250-566-8288		647
CHYM-FM 305 King St W *Web:* www.chymfm.com	Kitchener	ON	N2G4E4	519-743-2611		647
Chyron Corp 5 Hub Dr *NASDAQ: CHYR* ■ *Web:* chyronhego.com	Melville	NY	11747	631-845-2000		178-8
CHYZ-FM 2305 Rue de l'universite Local 0236 *Web:* www.chyz.ca	Pavillon Maurice-Pollack	QC	G1V0A6	418-656-2215		647
CI (Conservation Intl) 2011 Crystal Dr Ste 500 *TF:* 800-406-2306 ■ *Web:* www.conservation.org	Arlington	VA	22202	703-341-2400	553-0654	48-13
CI (Commercial Interior Decor Inc) 3617 W Teem Dr *Web:* cidinc.net	Sioux Falls	SD	57107	605-334-9288	334-2706	393
CI (Ceramic Industry Inc) 6075-B Glick Rd *Web:* www.ceramicindustry.com	Powell	OH	43065	847-763-9538		637-9
CI Financial Corp 20 Second Queen St E *TF:* 800-268-9374 ■ *Web:* www.theglobeandmail.com	Toronto	ON	M5C3G5	416-862-2222		787
CI Metal Fabrication 6205 St Louis St *Web:* cimetalfab.com	Meridian	MS	39307	601-483-6281	693-6529	697
CI Radar LLC 40 Technology Pkwy S Ste 150 *TF:* 888-421-0617 ■ *Web:* www.ciradar.com	Peachtree Corners	GA	30092	678-680-2103		393
CIA (Central Intelligence Agency) Office of Public Affairs *Web:* www.cia.gov	Washington	DC	20505	703-482-0623		340-20
CIA (Constitution Island Assn) PO Box 126 *Web:* www.constitutionisland.org	Cold Spring	NY	10516	845-265-2501		49-19
Cianbro Corp 101 Cianbro Sq *TF:* 866-242-6276 ■ *Web:* www.cianbro.com	Pittsfield	ME	04967	207-487-3311		188-4
Cianci Engineering LLC 53 Hurlbut St *Web:* cianciengineering.com	West Hartford	CT	06110	860-527-6415		261
CIANJ (Commerce & Industry Association of New Jersey) 61 S Paramus Rd *Web:* www.cianj.org	Paramus	NJ	07652	201-368-2100	368-3438	139
Ciao Italia 6149 Westwood Blvd *Web:* www.ciaoitaliaonline.com	Orlando	FL	32821	407-354-0770		671
Ciao Systems Inc 4326 Lorcom Ln *Web:* www.ciaosoftware.com	Arlington	VA	22207	703-524-9356		225
Cibar Inc 4575 Hilton Pky Ste 201 *Web:* www.cibar.com	Colorado Springs	CO	80907	719-260-6700		177
CIBC (Canadian Imperial Bank of Commerce) 199 Bay St Commerce Ct W *NYSE: CM* ■ *TF:* 800-465-2422 ■ *Web:* www.cibc.com	Toronto	ON	M5L1A2	800-465-2422		70
CIBC Mellon Global Securities Services Co 320 Bay St PO Box 1 *Web:* www.cibcmellon.com	Toronto	ON	M5H4A6	416-643-5000		528
CIBER Inc 5990 Greenwood Plaza Blvd Ste 255 *NYSE: CBR* ■ *TF:* 800-242-3799 ■ *Web:* www.ciber.com	Greenwood Village	CO	80111	303-220-0100	220-7100	180
CIBM-FM 64 Hotel de Ville *Web:* www.cibm107.com	Riviere-du-Loup	QC	G5R1L5	418-867-1071		647
CIBO (Council of Industrial Boiler Owners) 6801 Kennedy Rd Ste 102 *Web:* www.cibo.org	Warrenton	VA	20187	540-349-9043	349-9850	49-13
Cibo Global LLC 1000 Sansome St Ste 200 *Web:* ciboglobal.com	San Francisco	CA	94111	415-233-8357		195
Cibola County 700 E Roosevelt Ste 50 *Web:* www.cibolacountynm.com	Grants	NM	87020	505-287-9431		338
Cibola Systems Corp 180 S Cypress St *Web:* cibolasystems.com	Orange	CA	92866	714-480-0272		196
Cibus 6455 Nancy Ridge Dr *Web:* www.cibus.com	San Diego	CA	92121	858-450-0008		668
CIBW-FM 5164 52 Ave *TF:* 888-884-2448 ■ *Web:* www.bigwestcountry.ca	Drayton Valley	AB	T7A1V3	780-542-9290		647
CIC (Cambridge Innovations Inc) *Cambridge Innovation Ctr* 1 Broadway Kendall Sq 14th Fl *Web:* cic.com	Cambridge	MA	02142	617-758-4100		792
CIC Group Inc 530 Maryville Centre Dr Ste 100 *Web:* www.cicgroup.com	Saint Louis	MO	63141	314-682-2900		360-3
CIC Photonics Inc 6310 Edith Blvd NE Ste A *Web:* cicp.com	Albuquerque	NM	87107	505-343-9500		711
Cic Plus Inc 7321 Ridgeway Ave *Web:* www.cicplus.com	Skokie	IL	60076	847-677-9800		138
CICA Life Insurance Company of America PO Box 149151 *Web:* www.cicalife.com	Austin	TX	78714	512-837-7100	836-9785	796
Cicada Club 617 S Olive St *Web:* www.cicadaclub.com	Los Angeles	CA	90014	213-488-9488	488-9546	671
Cicatelli Associates Inc-ccd 505 Eighth Ave Ste 1900 *Web:* www.caiglobal.org	New York	NY	10018	212-594-7741	629-3321	305
Cicchetti, Tansley & Mcgrath LLP 500 Chase Pkwy *Web:* ctm-law.com	Waterbury	CT	06708	203-574-4700		41
Ciccio Cafe 875 Claire-Fontaine *Web:* www.cicciocafe.com	Quebec City	QC	G1R3A8	418-525-6161		671
Ciccolini & Associates Company LPA 2715 Manchester Rd *Web:* ciccolinilawfirm.com	Akron	OH	44319	330-753-1051		41
Cicero Group 35 N Rio Grande St *Web:* www.cicerogroup.com	Salt Lake City	UT	84101	801-456-6700		463
Cicero Inc 8000 Regency Pkwy Ste 542 *TF:* 866-538-3588 ■ *Web:* www.ciceroinc.com	Cary	NC	27518	919-380-5000		178-1
Cicero Plastic Products Inc 121 Anton Dr *Web:* www.ciceroplastics.com	Romeoville	IL	60446	815-886-9522	886-9277	488
Cicero Public Library 5225 W Cermak Rd *Web:* cicerolibrary.org	Cicero	IL	60804	708-652-8084	652-8095	434-3
Ciceron Inc 126 N Third St Ste 200 *Web:* www.ciceron.com	Minneapolis	MN	55401	612-204-1919		4
CiCi Enterprises LP 1080 W Bethel Rd *Web:* www.cicis.com	Coppell	TX	75019	972-745-4200		670

				Phone	Fax	Class
Cicilline David (Rep D - RI) 2233 Rayburn House Office Bldg *Web:* cicilline.house.gov	Washington	DC	20515	202-225-4911	225-3290	342-2
Cicinelli & Dippolito CPAs PC 1858 Commerce St *Web:* cdcpas.com	Yorktown Heights	NY	10598	914-302-2290	302-2292	2
Cicogna Electric and Sign Co 4330 N Bend Rd *TF:* 800-242-6462 ■ *Web:* cicognasign.com	Ashtabula	OH	44004	440-998-2637	992-8021	9
Cicoil Corp 24960 Ave Tibbitts *Web:* www.cicoil.com	Valencia	CA	91355	661-295-1295	295-0813	814
Cicon Engineering 6633 Odessa Ave *Web:* cicon.com	Van Nuys	CA	91406	818-909-6060		529
CID (Central Institute for the Deaf) 825 S Taylor Ave *TF:* 877-444-4574 ■ *Web:* www.cid.edu	Saint Louis	MO	63110	314-977-0132	977-0023	49-19
CID Bio-Science Inc 4845 NW Camas Meadows Dr *TF:* 800-767-0119 ■ *Web:* www.cid-inc.com	Camas	WA	98607	360-833-8835		639
CID Capital Inc 10201 N Illinois St Ste 200 *Web:* www.cidcap.com	Indianapolis	IN	46290	317-818-5030	644-2914	792
CID Performance Tooling Inc 6 Willey Rd *TF:* 800-964-2331 ■ *Web:* www.cidtools.com	Saco	ME	04072	800-964-2331		697
CIDA (Council for Interior Design Accreditation) 206 Grandville Ave Ste 350 *Web:* accredit-id.org	Grand Rapids	MI	49503	616-458-0400	458-0460	48-1
Cideon America Inc 92 W Lancaster Ave Ste 120 *Web:* cideon.com	Devon	PA	19333	484-532-7800		261
Cidesign 20 Odyssey *TF:* 800-576-5487 ■ *Web:* www.cidesign.com	Irvine	CA	92618	949-872-2555	679-1572	173-1
CiDRA Corp 50 Barnes Pk N *TF:* 877-243-7277 ■ *Web:* www.cidra.com	Wallingford	CT	06492	203-265-0035	294-4211	735
CIEE (Council on International Educational Exchange) 300 Fore St *TF:* 888-268-6245 ■ *Web:* www.ciee.org	Portland	ME	04101	207-553-4000	553-5272	49-5
CIENA Corp 7035 Ridge Rd *TF:* 800-207-3714 ■ *Web:* www.ciena.com	Hanover	MD	21076	410-694-5700	694-5750	176
CIES (Council for International Exchange of Scholars) 1400 K St NW Ste 700 *Web:* www.cies.org	Washington	DC	20005	202-686-4000		49-5
CIG 888 Seventh Ave 17th Fl *Web:* www.cig.com	New York	NY	10019	212-897-6635	897-6640	637-11
Cigarcom Inc 1911 Spillman Dr Ste 26 **Fax Area Code: 877* ■ *TF:* 800-357-9800 ■ *Web:* www.cigar.com	Bethlehem	PA	18015	800-357-9800	464-2872*	756
Cigarette Racing Team LLC 4355 NW 128th St *Web:* www.cigaretteracing.com	Opa Locka	FL	33054	305-931-4564	769-4355	90
Cigas Machine Shop Inc 1245 Manor Rd *Web:* www.cigasmachine.com	Coatesville	PA	19320	610-384-5239	384-7362	454
CIGNA 900 Cottage Grove Rd **Fax Area Code: 800* ■ *TF:* 800-244-6224 ■ *Web:* www.cigna.com	Bloomfield	CT	06002	860-226-3535	351-3616*	391-2
CIGNA Behavioral Health Inc 11095 Viking Dr Ste 350 *TF:* 800-753-0540 ■ *Web:* apps.cignabehavioral.com	Eden Prairie	MN	55344	800-433-5768		462
Cigniti Inc 433 E Las Colinas Blvd Ste 1300 *Web:* www.cigniti.com	Irving	TX	75039	972-756-0622	756-0644	180
CIGNYS 68 Williamson St *Web:* www.cignys.com	Saginaw	MI	48601	989-753-1411	753-4386	207
CIKARD (Center for Indigenous Knowledge for Agriculture and Rural Development) Iowa State University 318 Curtiss Hall *Web:* www.ciesin.org	Ames	IA	50011	515-294-0938	294-6058	423
CILB-FM 10107-102 Ave Ste 201 PO Box 86 *Web:* www.boom1035.com	Lac La Biche	AB	T0A2C0	780-623-3701	623-3740	647
CILV-FM Six Antares Dr Phase 1 Unit 100 *Web:* www.live885.com	Ottawa	ON	K2E8A9	613-727-8850		647
CIM (Inter-American Commission of Women) 1889 F St NW *Web:* www.oas.org	Washington	DC	20006	202-458-6084	458-6094	48-24
CIM Concepts Inc 100 W Commons Blvd Ste 101 *Web:* cimconcepts.com	New Castle	DE	19720	302-613-5400	613-5411	180
CIMA Technologies 1035 Eastside Rd *Web:* cima-technologies.com	El Paso	TX	79915	915-775-1919		261
Cimarron Correctional Facility 3200 S Kings Hwy *Web:* www.corecivic.com	Cushing	OK	74023	918-225-3336	225-3363	213
Cimarron County County Courthouse PO Box 145 *Web:* ltap.okstate.edu	Boise City	OK	73933	580-544-2251	544-3420	338
Cimarron Electric Co-op PO Box 299 *TF:* 800-375-4121 ■ *Web:* www.cimarronelectric.com	Kingfisher	OK	73750	405-375-4121	375-4209	245
Cimarron Energy Inc 1012 24th Ave NW Ste 100 PO Box 722110 *TF:* 844-746-1676 ■ *Web:* www.cimarron.com	Norman	OK	73070	405-928-7373		539
Cimarron Software Services Inc 18050 Saturn Ln Ste 280 *Web:* www.cimarroninc.com	Houston	TX	77058	281-226-5100		177
Cimbrian 114 E Chestnut St Ste 200 *Web:* www.cimbrian.com	Lancaster	PA	17602	717-368-2563		4
CIMCO Refrigeration 65 Villiers St *TF:* 800-267-1418 ■ *Web:* www.cimcorefrigeration.com	Toronto	ON	M5A3S1	416-465-7581		664
CIMdata Inc 3909 Research Park Dr *Web:* www.cimdata.com	Ann Arbor	MI	48108	734-668-9922		194
Ciment Quebec Inc 145 Du Centenaire Blvd Rr 1 *Web:* bcr.cc	Saint Basile	QC	G0A3G0	418-329-2100		183
Cimetrics Inc 141 Tremont St 1st Fl *Web:* www.cimetrics.com	Boston	MA	02111	617-350-7550		177
CIMplify 720 Cool Springs Blvd Ste 500 *TF:* 888-232-7026 ■ *Web:* www.cimplify.net	Franklin	TN	37067	615-261-6700	261-6050	194
Cimro of Nebraska 1200 Libra Dr Ste 102	Lincoln	NE	68512	402-476-1399		463
CIMT-TV 15 Rue De La Chute *Web:* www.cimt.teleinterrives.com	Riviere-du-Loup	QC	G5R5B7	418-867-1341	867-4710	647
Cinc Systems LLC 3055 Breckinridge Blvd Ste 310 *Web:* cincsystems.com	Duluth	GA	30096	678-205-1465		180
Cinch Home Services Inc 1625 NW 136th Ave Ste 200 *TF:* 800-778-8000 ■ *Web:* www.cinchhomeservices.com	Sunrise	FL	33323	800-475-9679		367
Cinchseal Associates Inc 23b Roland Ave *Web:* www.cinchseal.com	Mount Laurel	NJ	08054	856-662-5162		326
Cincilingua International Language Ctr 322 E 4th St *Web:* www.cincilingua.com	Cincinnati	OH	45202	513-721-8782	721-8819	167-3
CinCin Ristorante 1154 Robson St *Web:* cincin.net	Vancouver	BC	V6E1B2	604-688-7338	688-7339	671
Cincinnati Art Museum 953 Eden Pk Dr *TF:* 877-472-4226 ■ *Web:* www.cincinnatiartmuseum.org	Cincinnati	OH	45202	513-721-2787		520
Cincinnati Asset Management Inc (CAM) 8845 Governor's Hill Dr *Web:* www.cambonds.com	Cincinnati	OH	45249	513-554-8500		401
Cincinnati Ballet 1555 Central Pkwy *Web:* www.cballet.org	Cincinnati	OH	45214	513-621-5219	621-4844	573-1
Cincinnati Bell Inc 221 E Fourth St *NYSE: CBB* ■ *TF:* 866-565-2210 ■ *Web:* www.cincinnatibell.com	Cincinnati	OH	45202	513-565-2210		736
Cincinnati Bengals 1 Paul Brown Stadium *TF:* 866-621-8383 ■ *Web:* www.bengals.com	Cincinnati	OH	45202	513-621-3550	621-3570	715-3
Cincinnati Casualty Co 6200 S Gilmore Rd *Web:* www.cinfin.com	Fairfield	OH	45014	513-870-2000		391-5
Cincinnati Children's Hospital Medical Ctr 3333 Burnet Ave *TF:* 800-344-2462 ■ *Web:* www.cincinnatichildrens.org	Cincinnati	OH	45229	513-636-4200		374-1
Cincinnati Christian University 2700 Glenway Ave *TF:* 800-949-4228 ■ *Web:* www.ccuniversity.edu	Cincinnati	OH	45204	513-244-8100		161
Cincinnati City Hall 801 Plum St *Web:* www.cincinnati-oh.gov	Cincinnati	OH	45202	513-352-3334		337
Cincinnati CityBeat 811 Race St *Web:* www.citybeat.com	Cincinnati	OH	45202	513-665-4700		532-5
Cincinnati College of Mortuary Science 645 W N Bend Rd *TF:* 888-377-8433 ■ *Web:* www.ccms.edu	Cincinnati	OH	45224	513-761-2020	761-3333	800
Cincinnati Enquirer 312 Elm St *TF:* 800-876-4500 ■ *Web:* www.cincinnati.com	Cincinnati	OH	45202	513-721-2700	768-8340	532-2
Cincinnati Equitable Life Insurance Co PO Box 3428 *Web:* www.cineqlife.com	Cincinnati	OH	45202	513-621-1826		796
Cincinnati Eye Bank 4015 Executive Pk Dr Ste 330 *Web:* www.cintieb.org	Cincinnati	OH	45241	513-861-3716	483-3984	269
Cincinnati Fan & Ventilator 7697 Snider Rd *Web:* www.cincinnatifan.com	Mason	OH	45040	513-573-1000	573-0640	18
Cincinnati Fire Museum 315 W Court St Ste 1 *Web:* www.cincyfiremuseum.com	Cincinnati	OH	45202	513-621-5553		521
Cincinnati Floor Company Inc 5162 Broerman Ave *TF:* 800-886-4501 ■ *Web:* cincinnatifloor.com	Cincinnati	OH	45217	513-641-4500	482-4204	189-2
Cincinnati Gardens 2250 Seymour Ave *Web:* www.cincygardens.com	Cincinnati	OH	45212	513-631-7793	351-5898	720
Cincinnati Gasket Packing & Manufacturing Inc 40 Illinois Ave *Web:* www.cgindustrialglass.com	Cincinnati	OH	45215	513-761-3458	761-2994	326
Cincinnati Gilbert Machine Tool Company LLC 3366 Beekman St *Web:* www.cincinnatigilbert.com	Cincinnati	OH	45223	513-541-4815	541-4885	493
Cincinnati History Museum 1301 Western Ave Cincinnati Museum Ctr *TF:* 800-733-2077 ■ *Web:* www.cincymuseum.org	Cincinnati	OH	45203	513-287-7000		520
Cincinnati Inc 7420 Kilby Rd *Web:* www.e-ci.com	Harrison	OH	45030	513-367-7100	367-7552	456
Cincinnati Magazine 441 Vine St Ste 200 *TF:* 866-660-6247 ■ *Web:* www.cincinnatimagazine.com	Cincinnati	OH	45202	513-421-4300		457-22
Cincinnati Metropolitan Housing Authority 1627 Western Ave *TF:* 800-750-0750 ■ *Web:* cintimha.com	Cincinnati	OH	45214	513-721-4580	977-5606	210
Cincinnati Opera 1243 Elm St *Web:* www.cincinnatiopera.org	Cincinnati	OH	45202	513-768-5500		573-2
Cincinnati Playhouse in the Park 962 Mt Adams Cir *TF:* 800-582-3208 ■ *Web:* www.cincyplay.com	Cincinnati	OH	45202	513-345-2242	345-2250	572
Cincinnati Psychoanalytic Institute (CPI) 3001 Highland Ave *Web:* www.cps-i.org	Cincinnati	OH	45219	513-961-8886		48-6
Cincinnati Public Radio Inc 1223 Central Pky *Web:* www.cinradio.org	Cincinnati	OH	45214	513-352-9185	419-7145	645-141
Cincinnati School of Barbering & Hair Design Inc 6500 Colerain Ave *Web:* www.cincinnatischoolofbarbering.com	Cincinnati	OH	45239	513-923-3385	923-3595	685
Cincinnati State Technical & Community College 3520 Central Pkwy *TF:* 877-569-0115 ■ *Web:* www.cincinnatistate.edu	Cincinnati	OH	45223	513-569-1500	569-1562	162
Cincinnati Symphony Orchestra 1241 Elm St *Web:* www.cincinnatisymphony.org	Cincinnati	OH	45202	513-621-1919	744-3535	573-3
Cincinnati Tool Steel Co 5190 28th Ave *Web:* www.cintool.com	Rockford	IL	61109	815-226-8800	226-4388	492

Company	Phone	Fax	Class
Cincinnati United Contractors Inc 7143 E Kemper Rd . . . Cincinnati OH 45249 *Web:* www.cintiunited.com	513-677-0060	677-1121	189-11
Cincinnati USA Regional Chamber 3 E Fourth St. . . . Cincinnati OH 45202 *Web:* www.cincinnatichamber.com	513-579-3100	579-3101	139
Cincinnati VA Medical Ctr 3200 Vine St. . . . Cincinnati OH 45220 *Web:* www.cincinnati.va.gov	513-861-3100	487-6661	374-8
Cincinnati Ventilating Company Inc 7410 Industrial Rd . . . Florence KY 41042 *Web:* cvc-fab.com	859-371-1320		697
Cincinnati Zoo & Botanical Garden 3400 Vine St. . . . Cincinnati OH 45220 *TF:* 800-944-4776 ■ *Web:* www.cincinnatizoo.org	513-281-4700	559-7790	823
Cincinnatian Hotel 601 Vine St . . . Cincinnati OH 45202 *TF:* 800-942-9000 ■ *Web:* www.cincinnatianhotel.com	513-381-3000	651-0256	379
Cincinnati-Northern Kentucky International Airport PO Box 752000 . . . Cincinnati OH 45275 *TF:* 800-990-8841 ■ *Web:* www.cvgairport.com	859-767-3151		27
Cincinnatus Consulting LLC 1721 Spruce St. . . . Philadelphia PA 19103 *Web:* www.cincinnatus-consulting.com	267-872-0313		693
Cinco Energy Management Group 1616 S Voss Rd Ste 100. . . . Houston TX 77057 **Fax Area Code:* 877 ■ *Web:* cincoland.com	713-463-6009	888-1686*	690
Cincom Systems Inc 55 Merchant St. . . . Cincinnati OH 45246 *TF:* 800-224-6266 ■ *Web:* www.cincom.com	513-612-2300	612-2000	178-1
Cindrich & Co 1368 Marsh St . . . San Luis Obispo CA 93401 *Web:* cindrichcocpa.com	805-543-5800		2
Cind-R-Lite Block Co 4745 Mitchell St. . . . North Las Vegas NV 89081 *Web:* cind-r-lite.com	702-651-1550		183
Cindus Corp 515 Stn Ave. . . . Cincinnati OH 45215 **Fax Area Code:* 513 ■ *TF:* 800-543-4691 ■ *Web:* www.cindus.com	800-543-4691	948-8805*	554
Cindy's Canine Companions Salon & Services 12 Chestnut St PO Box 75 . . . Rehrersburg PA 19550 *Web:* www.cindyscaninecompanions.com	717-933-1333		570
Cine Magnetics Inc (CMI) 9 W Broad St. . . . Stamford CT 06902 *TF:* 800-431-1102 ■ *Web:* www.cminyla.com	203-989-9955	316-8353	658
Cinecraft Productions Inc 2515 Franklin Blvd . . . Cleveland OH 44113 *Web:* cinecraft.com	216-781-2300		514
Cineflix Media Inc 3510 St Laurent Blvd Ste 202. . . . Montreal QC H2X2V2 *Web:* www.cineflix.com	514-278-3140		514
Cinema Epoch 2600 W Olive Ave 5th Fl . . . Burbank CA 91505 *Web:* www.cinemaepoch.com	818-753-2345		748
Cinema Libre Studio 120 S Victory Blvd . . . Burbank CA 91502 *Web:* www.cinemalibrestudio.com	818-588-3033	349-9922	512
Cinema Makeup School 3780 Wilshire Blvd Ste 202 . . . Los Angeles CA 90010 *Web:* www.cinemamakeup.com	213-368-1234	739-0819	685
Cinemark USA Inc 3900 Dallas Pkwy Ste 500 . . . Plano TX 75093 *TF:* 800-246-3627 ■ *Web:* www.cinemark.com	972-665-1000	665-1004	748
Cinemax 1100 Avenue of the Americas. . . . New York NY 10036 *Web:* www.cinemax.com	212-512-1002		740
Cineplex Entertainment LP 1303 Yonge St . . . Toronto ON M4T2Y9 *TF:* 800-333-0061 ■ *Web:* www.cineplex.com	416-323-6600		748
Cinespace Film Studios 2621 W 15th Pl. . . . Chicago IL 60608 *Web:* cinespace.com	773-521-8000		514
Cine-tal Systems Inc PO Box 6086 . . . Fishers IN 46038	317-576-0091		33
Cinetel Films 8484 Wilshire Blvd Ste 850C . . . Beverly Hills CA 90210 *Web:* www.cinetelfilms.com	323-654-4000	650-6400	514
Cinetic Media Inc 555 W 25th St 4th Fl. . . . New York NY 10001 *Web:* www.cineticmedia.com	212-204-7979		194
Cinfab Mechanical Inc 5240 Lester Rd . . . Cincinnati OH 45213 *Web:* www.cinfab.com	513-396-6100	396-7574	189-10
Cingo 106 Roosevelt St PO Box 891 . . . Dublin GA 31021 *TF:* 855-919-9090 ■ *Web:* www.cingopest.com	478-272-6271		577
Cinmar LLC 5566 W Chester Rd. . . . West Chester OH 45069 **Fax Area Code:* 513 ■ *TF:* 888-263-9850 ■ *Web:* www.frontgate.com	888-263-9850	603-1492*	459
Cinnabar California Inc 4571 Electronics Pl. . . . Los Angeles CA 90039 *Web:* cinnabar.com	818-842-8190	842-0563	181
Cinnaire Corp 1118 S Washington . . . Lansing MI 48910 *Web:* cinnaire.com	517-482-8555		653
Cinquini & Passarino Inc 1360 N Dutton Ave Ste 150 . . . Santa Rosa CA 95401 **Fax Area Code:* 510 ■ *Web:* cinquinipassarino.com	707-542-6268	645-1561*	727
Cinta Aveda Institute 305 Kearny St. . . . San Francisco CA 94108 *Web:* www.cintaaveda.edu	415-989-4400		167-3
Cinta Salon 23 Grant Ave. . . . San Francisco CA 94108 *Web:* cinta.com	415-989-1000		77
Cintar Inc 1667 E Sutter Rd PO Box 478. . . . Glenshaw PA 15116 *Web:* cintar.com	412-753-1018		261
Cintas Canada Ltd 6300 Kennedy Rd. . . . Mississauga ON L5T2X5 *Web:* www.cintas.ca	513-573-4155		393
Cintas Corp PO Box 625737 . . . Cincinnati OH 45262 *NASDAQ:* CTAS ■ *TF:* 800-786-4367 ■ *Web:* www.cintas.com	513-459-1200		442
CINTRAFOR (Center for International Trade in Forest Products) University of Washington 126 Anderson Hall PO Box 352100 . . . Seattle WA 98195 *Web:* www.cintrafor.org	206-543-1918	685-0790	668
Cintrex Audio Visual 656 Axminister Dr . . . Fenton MO 63026 *TF:* 800-325-9541 ■ *Web:* www.cintrexav.com	636-343-0178		514
CIO Association of Canada 7270 Woodbine Ave Ste 204. . . . Markham ON L3R4B9 *Web:* www.ciocan.ca	905-752-1899		138

Company	Phone	Fax	Class
CIO Magazine 492 Old Connecticut Path PO Box 9208. . . . Framingham MA 01701 *Web:* www.cio.com	508-872-0080		457-5
CIO Solutions 5425 Hollister Ave Ste 150. . . . Santa Barbara CA 93111 *Web:* www.ciosolutions.com	805-692-6709		180
CIOG-FM 645 Pinewood Rd Unit 4 . . . Riverview NB E1B5R6 *TF:* 855-330-0335 ■ *Web:* www.harvestersfm.com	506-872-2901		647
Cioppino's Mediterranean Grill & Enoteca 1133 Hamilton St . . . Vancouver BC V6B5P6 *Web:* www.cioppinosyaletown.com	604-688-7466		671
Ciorba Group Inc 5507 N Cumberland Ave. . . . Chicago IL 60656 *Web:* www.ciorba.com	773-775-4009		261
CIP Group, The 799 Cambridge St . . . Cambridge MA 02141 *Web:* www.askcip.com	617-354-0866	354-1137	463
Cip Real Estate Property Services Inc 19762 Macarthur Blvd Ste 300. . . . Irvine CA 92612 *Web:* ciprealestate.com	949-474-7030		652
Cipher Systems LLC 185 Admiral Cochrane Dr Ste 210 . . . Annapolis MD 21401 *TF:* 888-899-1523 ■ *Web:* www.cipher-sys.com	410-412-3326		194
Cipherspace LLC 376 Main St Ste 100. . . . Bedminster NJ 07921 *Web:* www.cipherspace.com	973-630-1050		177
Cipriani Corp 30271 Tomas St . . . Rancho Santa Margarita CA 92688 *Web:* www.ciprianiharrisonvalves.com	949-589-3978	589-3979	789
Ciproms Inc 3600 Woodview Trce . . . Indianapolis IN 46268 *Web:* www.ciproms.com	317-870-0480	870-0499	463
CIPS (Canadian Information Processing Society) 5090 Explorer Dr Ste 801 . . . Mississauga ON L4W4T9 *TF:* 877-275-2477 ■ *Web:* www.cips.ca	905-602-1370	602-7884	48-1
CIR (Center for Individual Rights) 1100 Connecticut Ave NW Ste 625. . . . Washington DC 20036 *TF:* 877-426-2665 ■ *Web:* www.cir-usa.org	202-833-8400	833-8410	48-8
CIR (Commercial Interior Resources Inc) 1781 Reynolds Ave. . . . Irvine CA 92614 *Web:* cir-resource.com	949-752-1470	752-6103	290
CIR Law Offices International LLP 2650 Camino Del Rio N Ste 308. . . . San Diego CA 92108 *TF:* 800-496-8909 ■ *Web:* www.cirlaw.com	858-496-8909	496-5977	41
Ciranda Inc 221 Vine St. . . . Hudson WI 54016 *Web:* www.ciranda.com	715-386-1737		297-8
Circa 1801 1 Jacquard Dr. . . . Connelly Springs NC 28612	828-397-7003		745-1
Circa 1886 149 Wentworth St. . . . Charleston SC 29401 *Web:* www.circa1886.com	843-853-7828		671
Circa Corp 1330 Fitzgerald Ave . . . San Francisco CA 94124	415-822-1600		155-2
Circa Enterprises Inc 535-10333 Southport Rd SW. . . . Calgary AB T2W3X6 *TF:* 877-257-4588 ■ *Web:* www.circaent.com	403-258-2011	255-2595	736
Circa Inc 415 Madison Ave 19th Fl . . . New York NY 10017 *TF:* 877-876-5493 ■ *Web:* www.circajewels.com	212-486-6013	688-0605	411
Circa Information Technology 12001 Woodruff Ave Ste H . . . Downey CA 90241 *Web:* www.circausa.com	562-803-1594		178-10
Circa39 Hotel 3900 Collins Ave . . . Miami Beach FL 33140 *TF:* 877-824-7223 ■ *Web:* www.circa39.com	305-538-4900	538-4998	379
Circadian Technologies Inc 2 Main St Ste 310. . . . Stoneham MA 02180 *TF:* 800-284-5001 ■ *Web:* www.circadian.com	781-439-6300	439-6399	194
Circle "S" Ranch Inc 1604 Cir S Ranch Rd . . . Monroe NC 28112	704-764-7414		447
Circle 1 Network Inc 131 W Seeboth St. . . . Milwaukee WI 53204 *Web:* www.circle1network.com	414-271-5437		387
Circle B Company Inc 5636 S Meridian St. . . . Indianapolis IN 46217 *Web:* circlebco.com	317-787-5746	780-2654	189-9
Circle Bolt & Nut Company Inc 158 Pringle St. . . . Kingston PA 18704 *TF:* 800-548-2658 ■ *Web:* circlebolt.com	570-718-6001		350
Circle Buick Gmc Inc 2440 45th St. . . . Highland IN 46322 *Web:* www.circleautomotive.com	219-227-4410		57
Circle Business Equipment 7340 E Washington St . . . Indianapolis IN 46219 *Web:* www.circlebusinessequipment.com	317-293-9916		300
Circle City Software Solutions LLC 5868 E 71st St Ste E330. . . . Indianapolis IN 46220 *Web:* ccssindy.com	317-523-8229		177
Circle Commerce Inc 50 Avon Meadow Ln . . . Avon CT 06001 **Fax Area Code:* 860 ■ *TF:* 800-554-2472 ■ *Web:* www.circlecommerce.com	800-554-2472	255-7490*	177
Circle Federal Credit Union 507 E Main St. . . . Niles MI 49120 *Web:* www.circlefcu.org	269-684-6005		219
Circle Floors Inc 1911 Revere Beach Pkwy . . . Everett MA 02149 *Web:* www.circlefloors.com	617-381-6600		290
Circle Furniture Inc 19 Craig Rd . . . Acton MA 01720 *Web:* www.circlefurniture.com	978-263-4509		321
Circle Gear & Machine Company Inc 1501 S 55th Ct . . . Cicero IL 60804 *TF:* 800-637-9335 ■ *Web:* circlegear.com	708-652-1000	652-1100	709
Circle Graphics LLC 120 Ninth Ave . . . Longmont CO 80501 *TF:* 800-367-2472 ■ *Web:* www.circlegraphicsonline.com	303-532-2370		627
Circle Group, The 1275 Alderman Dr. . . . Alpharetta GA 30005 *Web:* www.thecirclegroup.com	678-356-1000		189-9
Circle Media Inc 5817 Old Leeds Rd . . . Irondale AL 35210 *TF:* 800-356-9916 ■ *Web:* www.ncregister.com	800-356-9916		532-3
Circle Mold Inc 85 S Thomas Rd . . . Tallmadge OH 44278 *Web:* circlemold.com	330-633-7017	633-7025	757
Circle Plumbing & Heating 2317 Raspberry Rd. . . . Anchorage AK 99502 *Web:* www.circleplumbingandheating.com	907-243-2171		612
Circle Publishing PO Box 4238 . . . Sedona AZ 86340 *Web:* www.circleofa.org	928-282-0790		637-2
Circle S Studio LLC 201 W Seventh St. . . . Richmond VA 23224 *Web:* www.circlesstudio.com	804-232-2908		7

Name / Address	City	State	ZIP	Phone	Fax	Class
Circle Theatre 230 W Fourth St *Web:* www.circletheatre.com	Fort Worth	TX	76102	817-877-3040	877-3536	572
Circle Theatre 1703 Robinson Rd SE *Web:* circletheatre.org	Grand Rapids	MI	49506	616-456-6656	456-8540	573-4
Circle V Specialized Inc 11301 W 57th Pl S *TF:* 800-654-1464 ■ *Web:* www.rasmussengroup.com	Sand Springs	OK	74063	918-245-2400	245-4798	780
Circle X Land & Cattle Company Ltd Hwy 6 & OSR PO Box 4747 *Web:* www.circlexcountrystore.com	Bryan	TX	77805	979-776-5760	776-4818	446
Circle Z Ranch PO Box 194 *TF:* 888-854-2525 ■ *Web:* circlez.com	Patagonia	AZ	85624	520-394-2525		239
Circle-Prosco Inc 401 N Gates Dr *Web:* www.circleprosco.com	Bloomington	IN	47404	812-339-3653		143
Circleville City School District 388 Clark Dr *TF:* 800-418-6423 ■ *Web:* www.circlevillecityschools.org	Circleville	OH	43113	740-474-4340	474-6600	685
Circor Aerospace Inc 2301 Wardlow Cir *TF:* 800-344-8724 ■ *Web:* www.circoraerospace.com	Corona	CA	92880	951-270-6200		350
CIRCOR International Inc 30 Corporate Dr Ste 200 *NYSE: CIR* ■ *Web:* www.circor.com	Burlington	MA	01803	781-270-1200	270-1299	641
Circuit Assembly Corp 18 Thomas St *Web:* www.circuitassembly.com	Irvine	CA	92618	949-855-7887	855-4298	253
Circuit Automation Inc 5292 System Dr *Web:* s585017606.onlinehome.us	Huntington Beach	CA	92647	714-763-4180		253
Circuit Breaker Sales Company Inc 1315 Columbine Dr *TF:* 800-232-5809 ■ *Web:* www.circuitbreaker.com	Gainesville	TX	76241	940-665-4444		729
Circuit Graphics Inc 1120 S Swaner Rd *Web:* circuitboard.com	Salt Lake City	UT	84104	801-974-5164		625
Circuit Shop Inc, The 8512 San Joaquin Ave SE *Web:* www.cktshop.com	Albuquerque	NM	87108	505-266-3970	266-3932	625
Circuit World Inc 751 Hilltop Dr *Web:* www.circuitw.com	Itasca	IL	60143	630-250-1100	250-4159	625
Circuitronics LLC 223 Hickman Dr *Web:* www.circuitronics.org	Sanford	FL	32771	407-322-8300		625
Circuits West Inc 410 S Sunset St Ste D *TF:* 877-650-5321 ■ *Web:* www.circuitswest.com	Longmont	CO	80501	303-772-9261	772-0490	625
Circular Congregational Church 150 Meeting St *Web:* www.circularchurch.org	Charleston	SC	29401	843-577-6400		50-1
Circular Technologies 3275 Prairie Ave *TF:* 800-215-1831 ■ *Web:* www.circulartech.com	Boulder	CO	80301	303-443-8512	443-0232	820
Circus Circus Hotel & Casino Reno 500 N Sierra St *TF:* 800-648-5010 ■ *Web:* www.circusreno.com	Reno	NV	89503	775-329-0711	328-9652	133
Circus Circus Hotel Casino & Theme Park Las Vegas 2880 Las Vegas Blvd S *Web:* www.circuscircus.com	Las Vegas	NV	89109	702-734-0410		133
Circus World Museum 550 Water St *TF:* 866-693-1500 ■ *Web:* www.circusworldbaraboo.org	Baraboo	WI	53913	608-356-8341	356-1800	520
Cirilli Law Offices SC 116 E Davenport St *TF:* 888-844-3443 ■ *Web:* cirillilaw.com	Rhinelander	WI	54501	715-369-3443		41
Ciro's Cote Sud 7918 Maple St *Web:* www.cotesudrestaurant.com	New Orleans	LA	70118	504-866-9551		671
Cirque Corp 2463 South 3850 West *TF:* 800-454-3375 ■ *Web:* www.cirque.com	Salt Lake City	UT	84120	801-467-1100	467-0208	173-1
Cirque du Soleil Inc 8400 Second Ave *Web:* www.cirquedusoleil.com	Montreal	QC	H1Z4M6	514-722-2324	722-3692	149
Cirrascale Corp 12140 Community Rd *TF:* 888-942-3800 ■ *Web:* www.cirrascale.com	Poway	CA	92064	858-874-3800		173-8
Cirro Energy 2745 Dallas Pkwy Ste 200 *TF:* 800-692-4776 ■ *Web:* www.cirroenergy.com	Plano	TX	75093	800-692-4776		463
Cirro Inc 31920 Del Obispo Ste 100 *Web:* www.cirro.com	San Juan Capistrano	CA	92675	949-373-9600		196
Cirrus Associates LLC 600 S Sherman St Ste 102 *Web:* www.cirrusassociates.com	Richardson	TX	75081	972-680-8555		194
Cirrus Design Corp 4515 Taylor Cir *TF:* 800-279-4322 ■ *Web:* www.cirrusaircraft.com	Duluth	MN	55811	218-727-2737		20
Cirrus Healthcare Products LLC 60 Main St PO Box 220 *Web:* cirrushealthcare.com	Cold Spring	NY	11724	631-692-7600		582
Cirrus Logic Inc 2901 Via Fortuna *NASDAQ: CRUS* ■ *TF:* 800-888-5016 ■ *Web:* www.cirrus.com	Austin	TX	78746	512-851-4000	851-4977	696
Cirrus Research LLC 303 S Broadway Ste 212 *Web:* www.cirrus-res.com	Tarrytown	NY	10591	914-289-1400		401
Cirtec Medical Systems LLC 9200 Xylon Ave N *Web:* cirtecmed.com	Brooklyn Park	MN	55445	763-493-8556		476
CIS (Clinical Immunology Society) 555 E Wells St Ste 1100 *Web:* www.clinimmsoc.org	Milwaukee	WI	53202	414-224-8095	272-6070	49-8
CIS (Citadel Information Services Inc) 33 Wood Ave S Ste 720 *TF:* 888-862-4823 ■ *Web:* www.citadelinc.com	Iselin	NJ	08830	732-238-0072	967-1891	180
CIS Biotech Inc 2701 N Decatur Rd *Web:* www.cisbiotech.com	Decatur	GA	30033	404-576-8856		418
CIS Group 55 Castonguay St Ste 301 *TF:* 888-432-1550 ■ *Web:* www.cis-group.com	Saint-Jerome	QC	J7Y2H9	450-432-1550	436-8801	2
CISCA (Ceilings & Interior Systems Construction Assn) 1010 Jorie Blvd Ste 30 **Fax Area Code: 866* ■ *Web:* www.cisca.org	Oak Brook	IL	60523	630-584-1919	560-8537*	49-3
Cisco Air Systems Inc 214 27th St *TF:* 800-813-6763 ■ *Web:* www.ciscoair.com	Sacramento	CA	95816	916-444-2525		358
Cisco Brewers Inc 5 Barrett Farm Rd *Web:* ciscobrewers.com	Nantucket	MA	02554	508-325-5929		102
CISCO Inc 1702 Townhurst *TF:* 800-231-3686 ■ *Web:* www.ciscocollect.com	Houston	TX	77043	713-461-9407	461-2432	393
Cisco Junior College 101 College Hts *Web:* www.cisco.edu	Cisco	TX	76437	254-442-5000		162
Cisco Systems Inc 170 W Tasman Dr *NASDAQ: CSCO* ■ *TF:* 800-553-6387 ■ *Web:* www.cisco.com	San Jose	CA	95134	408-526-4000	526-4100	176
Cisco-Eagle 2120 Valley View Ln *TF:* 888-877-3861 ■ *Web:* www.cisco-eagle.com	Dallas	TX	75234	972-406-9330	406-9577	385
Cision US Inc 130 E Randolph St 7th Fl *TF:* 800-588-3827 ■ *Web:* www.cision.com	Chicago	IL	60601	866-639-5087		637-6
CISM-FM 2332 Edouard-Montpetit bureau C-1509 PO Box 6128 Stn Downtown *Web:* cism893.ca	Montreal	QC	H3C3J7	514-343-7511		647
Cisneros Gilbert Ray Jr (Rep D - CA) 431 Cannon House Office Bldg *Web:* www.cisneros.house.gov	Washington	DC	20515	202-225-4111		342-2
CISP (Community ISP Inc) 3035 Moffat Rd *Web:* www.cisp.com	Toledo	OH	43615	419-724-5300		225
CISR (Center for Information Systems Research) Massachusetts Institute of Technology 245 First St E94-15th Fl *Web:* cisr.mit.edu	Cambridge	MA	02142	617-253-2348	253-4424	668
Cistera Networks Inc 5045 Lorimar Dr Ste 180 *TF:* 866-965-8646 ■ *Web:* www.cisteralmr.com	Plano	TX	75024	972-381-4699	381-4635	177
Cisys LifeSciences 8386 Six Forks Rd *TF:* 888-476-3133 ■ *Web:* www.cisys.com	Raleigh	NC	27615	888-476-3133		177
CIT Group Inc 505 Fifth Ave *NYSE: CIT* ■ *Web:* www.cit.com	New York	NY	10017	212-771-0505		216
Citadel Federal Credit Union 520 Eagleview Blvd **Fax Area Code: 610* ■ *Web:* www.citadelbanking.com	Exton	PA	19341	800-666-0191	380-6070*	219
Citadel Information Services Inc (CIS) 33 Wood Ave S Ste 720 *TF:* 888-862-4823 ■ *Web:* www.citadelinc.com	Iselin	NJ	08830	732-238-0072	967-1891	180
Citadel Insurance Services, Lc 826 E State Rd Ste 100 *TF:* 877-247-4468 ■ *Web:* citadelus.com	American Fork	UT	84003	801-610-2700		390
Citadel Mall 2070 Sam Rittenberg Blvd *Web:* www.citadelmall.net	Charleston	SC	29407	843-766-8321		460
Citadel Mall, The 750 Citadel Dr E *Web:* www.shopthecitadel.com	Colorado Springs	CO	80909	719-591-2900		460
Citadel, The 171 Moultrie St *TF:* 800-868-1842 ■ *Web:* go.citadel.edu	Charleston	SC	29409	843-953-5230	953-7036	166
Citagenix Inc 1111 Autoroute Chomedy *Web:* www.citagenix.com	Laval	QC	H7W5J8	450-688-8699		475
Citarella 2135 Broadway *Web:* www.citarella.com	New York	NY	10023	212-874-0383		297-8
Citation Communications Inc 1855 Indian Rd Ste 207 *TF:* 800-286-5109 ■ *Web:* citation2way.com	West Palm Beach	FL	33409	561-688-0330		387
Citation Oil & Gas Corp 14077 Cutten Rd *Web:* www.cogc.com	Houston	TX	77069	281-891-1000		536
Citation Solutions Inc 5535 Memorial Dr Ste F802 *Web:* www.citationsolutions.com	Houston	TX	77092	713-895-8261		396
Citco Fund Services San Francisco Inc 560 Mission St Ste 2950 *Web:* www.citco.com	San Francisco	CA	94105	415-228-0390	228-0335	401
Citent Inc 3420 Bristol St 6th Fl *Web:* www.citent.com	Costa Mesa	CA	92626	714-436-6100		463
CITGO Petroleum Corp 1293 Eldridge Pkwy *TF:* 866-926-5615 ■ *Web:* www.citgo.com	Houston	TX	77077	832-486-4700		580
CITI (Columbia Institute for Tele-Information) 3022 Broadway Uris Hall *Web:* www8.gsb.columbia.edu	New York	NY	10027	212-854-4222	854-1471	668
Citi Trends Inc 104 Coleman Blvd *NASDAQ: CTRN* ■ *Web:* www.cititrends.com	Savannah	GA	31408	912-236-1561		157-2
Citibank NA 399 Park Ave *TF:* 800-627-3999 ■ *Web:* www.citigroup.com	New York	NY	10022	800-627-3999		70
Citibank (South Dakota) NA 701 E 60th St N *Web:* www.online.citi.com	Sioux Falls	SD	57104	605-331-2626		70
Cities of Gold Casino 10-A Cities of Gold Rd *TF:* 800-455-3313 ■ *Web:* www.citiesofgold.com	Santa Fe	NM	87506	505-455-4232		133
CITI-FM 92.1 4-166 Osborne St *Web:* www.921citi.ca	Winnipeg	MB	R3L1Y8	204-788-3400		645-175
CitiMortgage Inc 1000 Technology Dr *TF:* 800-283-7918 ■ *Web:* www.citimortgage.com	O'Fallon	MO	63368	800-283-7918		509
CitiusTech Inc 2 Research Way *TF:* 877-248-4871 ■ *Web:* www.citiustech.com	Princeton	NJ	08540	877-248-4871		225
Citivest Inc 4340 Von Karman Ave Ste 110 *Web:* citivestgroup.com	Newport Beach	CA	92660	714-788-9644		653
Citizant Inc 15000 Conference Center Dr Ste 500 *TF:* 877-248-4926 ■ *Web:* citizant.com	Chantilly	VA	20151	703-667-9420		177
Citizen Auto Stage Co 3594 E Lincoln St *TF:* 800-276-1528 ■ *Web:* graylinearizona.com	Tucson	AZ	85714	520-622-8811		107
Citizen National Bank of Bluffton, The 102 S Main St PO Box 88 *TF:* 800-262-4663 ■ *Web:* www.cnbohio.com	Bluffton	OH	45817	419-358-8040		70
Citizen Publishing Company Inc 260 Tenth St *Web:* www.windomnews.com	Windom	MN	56101	507-831-3455	831-3740	637-8
Citizen Systems America Corp 363 Van Ness Way Ste 404 *TF:* 800-421-6516 ■ *Web:* www.citizen-systems.com	Torrance	CA	90501	310-781-1460	781-9152	173-6

Name / Address	City	State	Zip	Phone	Fax	Class
Citizen Tribune 1609 W First N St PO Box 625 *Web:* www.citizentribune.com	Morristown	TN	37815	423-581-5630	581-8863	532-2
Citizen Watch Company of America Inc 1000 W 190th St *TF:* 800-321-1023 ■ *Web:* us.citizenwatch.com	Torrance	CA	90502	310-532-8463		153
Citizens & Northern Corp 90-92 Main St *NASDAQ: CZNC* ■ *TF:* 877-838-2517 ■ *Web:* www.cnbankpa.com	Wellsboro	PA	16901	570-724-3411	724-6395	360-2
Citizens Against Government Waste (CAGW) 1301 Pennsylvania Ave NW Ste 1075 *Web:* www.cagw.org	Washington	DC	20004	202-467-5300	467-4253	48-7
Citizens Bank 275 SW 3rd St *TF:* 800-577-1778 ■ *Web:* www.citizensebank.com	Corvallis	OR	97339	541-752-5161		70
Citizens Bank 114 W Main St *TF:* 800-780-4808 ■ *Web:* www.tcbanytime.com	Morehead	KY	40351	606-780-0000	784-4616	70
Citizens Bank & Trust 711 Gunter Ave *Web:* citizensbanktrust.com	Guntersville	AL	35976	256-505-4600		70
Citizens Bank of Ada 123 W 12th St *Web:* citizensada.bank	Ada	OK	74820	580-332-6100		70
Citizens Bank of Clovis 420 Wheeler *TF:* 844-657-3553 ■ *Web:* www.citizensbankofclovis.com	Texico	NM	88135	575-482-3381	482-3208	70
Citizens Bank of Greensboro, The 1300 State St *Web:* greensborocitizensbank.com	Greensboro	AL	36744	334-624-8888		70
Citizens Bank of Las Cruces 505 S Main St *Web:* www.citizenslc.com	Las Cruces	NM	88004	575-647-4100		70
Citizens Bank of Massachusetts 28 State St *TF:* 800-610-7300 ■ *Web:* www.citizensbank.com	Boston	MA	02109	800-610-7300		70
Citizens Bank of Mukwonago 301 N Rochester St PO Box 223 *TF:* 877-546-5868 ■ *Web:* www.citizenbank.bank	Mukwonago	WI	53149	262-363-6500	363-6515	70
Citizens Bank, The 301 S Edwards St *Web:* tcbenterprise.com	Enterprise	AL	36330	334-347-3411		70
Citizens Business Bank (CBB) 701 N Haven Ave *TF:* 888-222-5432 ■ *Web:* www.cbbank.com	Ontario	CA	91764	909-980-4030	481-2130	70
Citizens Committee for New York City 77 Water St Ste 202 *Web:* www.citizensnyc.org	New York	NY	10005	212-989-0909	989-0983	48-13
Citizens Committee for the Right to Keep & Bear Arms (CCRKBA) Liberty Pk 12500 NE Tenth Pl *TF:* 800-486-6963 ■ *Web:* www.ccrkba.org	Bellevue	WA	98005	425-454-4911		48-7
Citizens Equity First Credit Union 5401 W Dirksen Pkwy *TF:* 800-633-7077 ■ *Web:* www.cefcu.com	Peoria	IL	61607	309-633-7000		219
Citizens Federal Savings & Loan Assn 110 N Main St PO Box 9 *Web:* www.citizensfederalsl.com	Bellefontaine	OH	43311	937-593-0015	593-6577	69
Citizens Federal Savings & Loan Association of Covington 433 Madison Ave *Web:* citizens-federal.com	Covington	KY	41012	859-431-0087		70
Citizens Fidelity Insurance Co PO Box 25440 *Web:* www.citizensfidelityinsurance.com	Little Rock	AR	72221	501-228-5134	223-0181	796
Citizens Financial Services 707 Ridge Rd *TF:* 800-205-3464 ■ *Web:* www.firstmerchants.com	Munster	IN	46321	219-836-5500		70
Citizens For Citizens Inc 264 Griffin St *Web:* cfcinc.org	Fall River	MA	02724	508-679-0041	324-7503	48-15
Citizens for Tax Justice (CTJ) 1616 P St NW Ste 200 *Web:* www.ctj.org	Washington	DC	20036	202-299-1066	299-1065	48-7
Citizens Gas & Coke Utility 2020 N Meridian St *TF:* 800-427-4217 ■ *Web:* www.citizensenergygroup.com	Indianapolis	IN	46202	317-924-3311	927-4395	787
Citizens Gas Fuel Co 127 N Main St *TF:* 800-482-7171 ■ *Web:* www.citizensgasfuel.com	Adrian	MI	49221	517-265-2144		536
Citizens Guaranty Bank 25 River Dr *Web:* mycgb.com	Irvine	KY	40336	606-723-2139	723-2142	70
Citizens Holding Co 521 Main St PO Box 209 *NASDAQ: CIZN* ■ *Web:* www.thecitizensbankphila.com	Philadelphia	MS	39350	601-656-4692		360-2
Citizens Medical Ctr 2701 Hospital Dr *Web:* citizensmedicalcenter.org	Victoria	TX	77901	361-573-9181		374-3
Citizens Mutual Telephone (CMTEL) 114 W Jefferson St *TF:* 800-746-4268 ■ *Web:* www.cmtel.com	Bloomfield	IA	52537	641-664-2074	664-9780	224
Citizens Network for Foreign Affairs (CNFA) 1828 L St NW Ste 710 *Web:* www.cnfa.org	Washington	DC	20036	202-296-3920	296-3948	48-5
Citizens News 389 Meadow St *Web:* www.mycitizensnews.net	Waterbury	CT	06722	203-729-2228	729-9099	532-2
Citizens of Humanity Inc 5715 Bickett St *Web:* www.citizensofhumanity.com	Huntington Park	CA	90255	323-923-1240		157-6
Citizens Property Insurance Corp 6676 Corporate Center Pkwy *Web:* www.citizensfla.com	Jacksonville	FL	32216	904-296-6105		390
Citizens Security Life Insurance Co 12910 Shelbyville Rd Ste 300 *TF:* 800-843-7752 ■ *Web:* www.citizenssecuritylife.com	Louisville	KY	40243	502-244-2420	254-4059	391-2
Citizens State Bank 1300 W Hildebrand Ave PO Box 5970 *Web:* www.csbsa.com	San Antonio	TX	78201	210-785-2300	785-2301	70
Citizens State Bank 329 W Harris Ave *Web:* citizensstatebk.com	San Angelo	TX	76903	325-657-0099		70
Citizens State Bank & Trust Co 203 N Douglas PO Box 518 *TF:* 800-472-3145 ■ *Web:* secure.csbanc.com	Ellsworth	KS	67439	785-472-3141		70
Citizens State Bank of Roseau 118 Main Ave S *Web:* citizensros.com	Roseau	MN	56751	218-463-2135		70
Citizens Telephone Co 26 S Main St *Web:* www.cit-tele.com	Hammond	NY	13646	315-324-5911	324-5917	116
Citizens Telephone Co-op PO Box 137 *TF:* 800-941-0426 ■ *Web:* citizens.coop	Floyd	VA	24091	540-745-2111	745-3791	736
Citizens Trust Bank 1700 3rd Ave N *TF:* 888-214-3099 ■ *Web:* ctbconnect.com	Birmingham	AL	35203	205-328-2041		70
Citizens' Electric Co 1775 Industrial Blvd PO Box 551 *TF:* 877-487-9384 ■ *Web:* www.citizenselectric.com	Lewisburg	PA	17837	570-524-2231	524-5887	245
Citizens' Voice, The 75 N Washington St *Web:* www.citizensvoice.com	Wilkes-Barre	PA	18701	570-821-2000	821-2247	532-2
Citizens-Direct 18431 Yorba Linda Blvd **Fax Area Code:* 714 ■ *TF:* 888-572-3002 ■ *Web:* citizens-direct.com	Yorba Linda	CA	92886	888-572-3002	572-2700*	652
Citizen-Times, The PO Box 310 *Web:* www.thecitizen-times.com	Scottsville	KY	42164	270-237-3441	237-4943	775
CITO-TV 681 Pine St N *Web:* www.ctvnews.ca	Timmins	ON	P4N7G3	705-264-4211		647
Citrin Cooperman & Company LLP 529 Fifth Ave *Web:* www.citrincooperman.com	New York	NY	10017	212-697-1000	697-1004	2
Citris Grill 3977 S Wasatch Blvd *Web:* citrisgrill.com	Salt Lake City	UT	84124	801-277-6113		671
Citrus & Allied Essences Ltd 65 S Tyson Ave *Web:* www.citrusandallied.com	Floral Park	NY	11001	516-354-1200	354-1262	145
Citrus College 1000 W Foothill Blvd *Web:* www.citruscollege.edu	Glendora	CA	91741	626-963-0323	914-8613	162
Citrus County 110 N Apopka Ave *TF:* 800-955-8771 ■ *Web:* www.citrusclerk.org	Inverness	FL	34450	352-341-6400	341-6491	338
Citrus County Chamber of Commerce 106 W Main St *Web:* www.citruscountychamber.com	Inverness	FL	34450	352-726-2801		139
Citrus County Chronicle 1624 N Meadowcrest Blvd *Web:* www.chronicleonline.com	Crystal River	FL	34429	352-563-6363	563-5665	532-2
Citrus County Library System 425 W Roosevelt Blvd *Web:* www.citruslibraries.org	Beverly Hills	FL	34465	352-746-9077	746-9493	434-3
Citrus County School District 1007 W Main St *Web:* www.citrusschools.org	Inverness	FL	34450	352-726-1931		685
Citrus Heights Chamber 7920 Alta Sunrise Dr Ste 100 *Web:* www.chchamber.com	Citrus Heights	CA	95610	916-722-4545	722-4543	139
Citrus Salon & Day Spa Inc 1201 Dekalb Pk *Web:* citrussalonspa.com	Blue Bell	PA	19422	610-277-4247		77
Citrus Systems Inc 415 11th Ave S *Web:* www.citrussystems.com	Hopkins	MN	55343	952-935-0410		296-20
CITS-TV 1295 N Service Rd *Web:* www.yestv.com	Burlington	ON	L7R4X5	905-331-7333		647
Citterio USA Corp 2008 SR- 940 *TF:* 800-435-8888 ■ *Web:* www.usa.citterio.com	Freeland	PA	18224	570-636-3171	636-5340	296-26
City & Borough of Sitka 100 Lincoln St *Web:* www.cityofsitka.com	Sitka	AK	99835	907-747-3294	747-4779	338
City & County of Butte-Silver Bow 155 W Granite St *Web:* www.co.silverbow.mt.us	Butte	MT	59701	406-497-6200	497-6328	338
City Auto Glass Inc 116 S Concord Exchange *TF:* 888-552-4272 ■ *Web:* www.cityautoglass.com	South Saint Paul	MN	55075	651-552-1000		62-2
City Auto Sales 4932 Elmore Rd *Web:* www.cityauto.com	Memphis	TN	38128	901-377-9502		57
City Barbeque Inc 6175 Emerald Pkwy *Web:* www.citybbq.com	Dublin	OH	43016	614-583-0999	583-0998	670
City Beverage 8283 State Rte 66 N *TF:* 888-283-2739 ■ *Web:* beercocitybev.com	Defiance	OH	43512	419-782-7065	782-9426	81-1
City Beverage 915 Burke St *Web:* www.citybeverage.com	Winston-Salem	NC	27101	336-722-2774	725-1481	81-1
City Beverages of Orlando 10928 Florida Crown Dr *Web:* citybeverages.wpengine.com	Orlando	FL	32824	407-851-7100		81-1
City Bikes 2501 Champlain St NW *Web:* citybikes.com	Washington	DC	20009	202-265-1564		711
City Brewery-Latrobe 100 33rd St *Web:* www.citybrewery.com	Latrobe	PA	15650	724-537-5545	537-4035	102
City Cafe 5757 W Lovers Ln *Web:* www.thecitycafedallas.com	Dallas	TX	75209	214-351-2233		671
City Cellar Wine Bar & Grill 400 Clematis St Ste 205 *Web:* www.bigtimerestaurants.com	West Palm Beach	FL	33401	561-659-1940		671
City Center Parking 514 SW Sixth Ave *Web:* www.citycenterparking.com	Portland	OR	97204	503-221-1666	517-0915	562
City College of New York 160 Convent Ave *Web:* www.ccny.cuny.edu	New York	NY	10031	212-650-7000		166
City College of San Francisco 50 Phelan Ave *Web:* www.ccsf.edu	San Francisco	CA	94112	415-239-3000	239-3936	162
City Colleges of Chicago 180 N Wabash *Web:* www.ccc.edu	Chicago	IL	60601	773-265-5343		166
City Dash 949 Laidlaw Ave *Web:* www.citydash.com	Cincinnati	OH	45237	513-562-2000		187
City Directory Inc 524 River Ave N *TF:* 800-374-4691 ■ *Web:* www.citydirectoryinc.com	Belmond	IA	50421	641-444-4468	444-5150	637-10
City Escape Holidays 13470 Washington Blvd Ste 101 **Fax Area Code:* 310 ■ *TF:* 800-222-0022 ■ *Web:* www.cityescapeholidays.com	Marina	CA	90292	800-222-0022	827-5575*	771
City Flowers Inc 10500 NE Eighth St Ste 950 *TF:* 888-513-3043 ■ *Web:* cityflowers.com	Bellevue	WA	98004	425-454-0882		292

	Phone	Fax	Class
City Foods Inc 4230 S Racine Ave. . . . . Chicago IL 60609 *Web:* www.beasbest.com	773-523-1566		473
City Furniture Inc 6701 N Hiatus Rd . . . . Tamarac FL 33321 *TF:* 866-930-4233 ■ *Web:* www.cityfurniture.com	954-597-2200		321
City Glass Co 8037 H St . . . . Omaha NE 68127 *Web:* www.cityglasscompany.com	402-593-1242		329
City Glass Company of Colorado Springs 414 W Colorado Ave. . . . . Colorado Springs CO 80905 *Web:* www.cityglasscompany.net	719-634-2891		330
City Holding Co 25 Gatewater Rd. . . . . Charleston WV 25313 *NASDAQ: CHCO* ■ *Web:* www.bankatcity.com	304-769-1100		360-2
City Lights Booksellers 261 Columbus Ave . . . . San Francisco CA 94133 *Web:* www.citylights.com	415-362-8193	362-4921	95
City Lights of China 1731 Connecticut Ave NW . . . . Washington DC 20009 *Web:* www.citylightsofchina.com	202-265-6688	265-1369	671
City Lights Theatre 529 S Second St. . . . . San Jose CA 95112 *Web:* cltc.org	408-295-4200	295-8318	573-4
City Line Distributers 20 Industry Dr. . . . . West Haven CT 06516 *Web:* www.citylinefoods.com	203-931-3707		186
City Machine Technologies Inc 773 W Rayen Ave . . . . Youngstown OH 44502 *Web:* www.cmtcompanies.com	330-747-2639	747-3205	454
City Market 219 W Bryan St . . . . Savannah GA 31401 *Web:* www.savannahcitymarket.com	912-232-4903		50-6
City Market 555 Sandhill Ln . . . . Grand Junction CO 81505 *Web:* www.citymarket.com	970-241-0750		345
City Mattress Inc 12660 Bonita Beach Rd . . . . Bonita Springs FL 34135 *Web:* www.citymattress.com	239-908-2700		321
City Mill Company Ltd 660 N Nimitz Hwy. . . . . Honolulu HI 96817 *Web:* www.citymill.com	808-533-3811	529-5871	364
City National Bank 400 N Roxbury Dr. . . . . Beverly Hills CA 90210 *TF:* 800-773-7100 ■ *Web:* www.cnb.com	310-888-6000		70
City National Bank of Florida 450 E Las Olas Blvd . . . . Fort Lauderdale FL 33301 *TF:* 800-762-2489 ■ *Web:* www.citynationalcm.com	954-467-6667		70
City National Bank of New Jersey (CNB) 900 Broad St. . . . . Newark NJ 07102 *TF:* 877-350-3524 ■ *Web:* www.citynatbank.com	973-624-0865		70
City National Bank of Sulphur Springs, The 201 Connally . . . . Sulphur Springs TX 75482 *Web:* www.bankatcnb.bank	903-885-7523		70
City Newspaper 250 N Goodman St Ste 1 . . . . Rochester NY 14607 *Web:* www.rochestercitynewspaper.com	585-244-3329		532-5
City of Alameda 2263 Santa Clara Ave . . . . Alameda CA 94501 *Web:* www.alamedaca.gov	510-747-7400		337
City of Albany GA *Dougherty County* 222 Pine Ave Ste 560. . . . . Albany GA 31701 *Web:* www.albanyga.gov	229-431-2161		338
City of Albuquerque, The 1 Civic Plz NW . . . . Albuquerque NM 87102 *Web:* www.cabq.gov	505-242-2677		337
City of Asheville, The 70 Court Plaza PO Box 7148 . . . . Asheville NC 28802 *Web:* www.ashevillenc.gov	828-259-5690		337
City of Austin Employees' Retirement System 418 E Highland Mall Blvd. . . . . Austin TX 78752 *Web:* www.coaers.org	512-458-2551		528
City of Baton Rouge Parish of East Baton Rouge PO Box 1471 . . . . Baton Rouge LA 70821 *Web:* www.brla.gov	225-389-3000		337
City of Bay Village Ohio 350 Dover Center Rd . . . . Bay Village OH 44140 *Web:* www.cityofbayvillage.com	440-899-3412		734
City of Birmingham, Alabama 331 Cotton Ave SW. . . . . Birmingham AL 35211 *Web:* www.birminghamal.gov	205-780-5656		520
City of Boulder 1777 Broadway PO Box 791. . . . . Boulder CO 80302 *Web:* bouldercolorado.gov	303-441-3388	441-4478	337
City of Buena Vista 2039 Sycamore Ave . . . . Buena Vista VA 24416 *Web:* www.buenavistava.org	540-261-6121		338
City of Carlsbad Library 1250 Carlsbad Village Dr . . . . Carlsbad CA 92008 *Web:* carlsbadca.gov	760-434-2870	929-0256	434-3
City of Cerritos 18125 Bloomfield Ave PO Box 3130. . . . . Cerritos CA 90703 *Web:* www.cerritos.us	562-860-0311	916-1375	434-3
City of Champaign 102 N Neil St . . . . Champaign IL 61820 *Web:* www.ci.champaign.il.us	217-403-8700		337
City of Charlotte *Mecklenburg County* Charlotte-Mecklenburg Government Ctr 600 E 4th St . . . . Charlotte NC 28202 *Web:* www.charmeck.org	704-336-7600		338
City of Chicago 121 N LaSalle St . . . . Chicago IL 60602 *Web:* www.chicago.gov	312-744-5000		50-2
City of Chula Vista 276 4th Ave. . . . . Chula Vista CA 91910 *TF:* 877-478-5478 ■ *Web:* www.chulavistaca.gov	619-691-5044		52
City of Clarksville 199 Tenth St . . . . Clarksville TN 37040 *TF:* 800-342-1003 ■ *Web:* www.cityofclarksville.com	931-645-7464		256
City of Clinton Sheriff Dept 184 Detention Dr PO Box 451. Clinton AR 72031 *Web:* www.vbcso.com	501-745-2112		338
City of Coleraine 302 Roosevelt Ave . . . . Coleraine MN 55722 *Web:* cityofcoleraine.com	218-245-2112	245-2123	433
City of Com, The 1559 S Brownlee Blvd . . . . Corpus Christi TX 78404 *TF:* 888-785-0500 ■ *Web:* www.cityof.com	888-785-0500		7
City of Dayton Ohio, The 101 W 3rd St. . . . . Dayton OH 45402 *Web:* www.daytonohio.gov	937-333-3600		337

	Phone	Fax	Class
City of Deadwood Archives 108 Sherman St . . . . Deadwood SD 57732 *Web:* www.cityofdeadwood.com	605-578-2082		434-3
City of Dearborn 16099 Michigan Ave . . . . Dearborn MI 48126 *Web:* cityofdearborn.org	313-563-4653		31
City of Emporia, Virginia, The 201 S Main St. . . . . Emporia VA 23847 *Web:* www.ci.emporia.va.us	434-634-3332	634-0003	338
City of Eugene 125 East 8th Ave 2nd Fl . . . . Eugene OR 97401 *Web:* www.eugene-or.gov	541-682-5010		337
City of Falls Church 400 N Washington St Ste 300-05. . . . . Falls Church VA 22046 *Web:* www.fallschurchva.gov	703-248-5001	248-5146	338
City of Fargo 225 4th St N. . . . . Fargo ND 58102 *Web:* www.fargond.gov	701-241-1474		337
City of Farmers Branch 13000 William Dodson Pkwy . . . . Farmers Branch TX 75234 *Web:* www.farmersbranchtx.gov	972-247-3131		434-3
City of Flandreau, South Dakota, The 1005 W Elm Ave. . . . . Flandreau SD 57028 *Web:* www.cityofflandreau.com	605-997-2492		338
City of Fort Lauderdale 100 N Andrews Ave 5th Fl . . . . Fort Lauderdale FL 33301 *Web:* www.fortlauderdale.gov	954-828-8658		337
City of Galax 111 E Grayson St . . . . Galax VA 24333 *Web:* www.galaxva.com	276-236-5773	236-2889	338
City of Glendale City Hall 5850 West Glendale Ave. . . . . Glendale AZ 85301 *Web:* www.glendaleaz.com	623-930-2000		337
City of Glendora 140 S Glendora Ave . . . . Glendora CA 91741 *Web:* www.cityofglendora.org	626-852-4891	852-4899	434-3
City of Great Falls PO Box 5021 . . . . Great Falls MT 59403 *Web:* greatfallsmt.net	406-771-0885		205
City of Helena 316 N Park Ave . . . . Helena MT 59623 *Web:* www.helenamt.gov	406-447-8000		337
City of Henderson *Henderson Convention Ctr* 200 S Water St. . . . . Henderson NV 89015 *TF:* 877-775-5252 ■ *Web:* www.cityofhenderson.com	702-267-2171		205
City of High Point Public Library (HPPL) 901 N Main St . . . . High Point NC 27262 *Web:* www.highpointnc.gov	336-883-3660	883-3636	434-3
City of Homer 491 E Pioneer Ave. . . . . Homer AK 99603 *Web:* www.cityofhomer-ak.gov	907-235-8121		337
City of Hope National Medical Center Hematology & Hematopoietic Cell Transplantation Div 1500 E Duarte Rd . . . . Duarte CA 91010 *TF:* 800-826-4673 ■ *Web:* www.cityofhope.org	626-256-4673		769
City of Hopewell 300 N Main St . . . . Hopewell VA 23860 *TF:* 800-552-7096 ■ *Web:* hopewellva.gov	804-541-2243	541-2248	338
City of Jackson, The 219 S President St . . . . Jackson MS 39201 *Web:* www.jacksonms.gov	601-960-1084	960-2193	337
City of Johnson City 601 E Main St. . . . . Johnson City TN 37601 *Web:* www.johnsoncitytn.org	423-434-6000	434-6295	337
City of Kamloops 105 Seymour St . . . . Kamloops BC V2C2C6 *Web:* www.kamloops.ca	250-828-3439		354
City of Kodiak Alaska City of Kodiak 710 Mill Bay Rd. . . . . Kodiak AK 99615 *Web:* www.city.kodiak.ak.us	907-486-8640	486-8014	618
City of Leawood, Kansas 4800 Town Center Dr . . . . Leawood KS 66211 *Web:* www.leawood.org	913-339-6700		393
City of Lewiston City Hall 1134 F St. . . . . Lewiston ID 83501 *Web:* www.cityoflewiston.org	208-746-3671		434-3
City of Little Rock 500 W Markham St. . . . . Little Rock AR 72201 *Web:* www.littlerock.gov	501-371-4770	371-4498	337
City of Logan Recreation Ctr 195 S 100 W. . . . . Logan UT 84321 *Web:* loganutah.org	435-716-9250		564
City of Lompoc 100 Civic Center Plz. . . . . Lompoc CA 93436 *Web:* www.cityoflompoc.com	805-736-1261		434-3
City of Longview 300 W Cotton St PO Box 1952 . . . . Longview TX 75606 *Web:* www.longviewtexas.gov	903-237-1000		337
City of Louisville Kentucky 527 W Jefferson St. . . . . Louisville KY 40202 *Web:* www.louisvilleky.gov	502-574-5000		337
City of Manchester One City Hall Plaza. . . . . Manchester NH 03101 *Web:* www.manchesternh.gov	603-624-6500	624-6576	337
City of Monroe, Louisiana 400 Lea Joyner Expy. . . . . Monroe LA 71201 *Web:* monroela.us	318-329-2585	329-2548	205
City of Naples 735 Eigth St S . . . . Naples FL 34102 *Web:* www.naplesgov.com	239-213-1015	213-1025	337
City of New Westminster 511 Royal Ave. . . . . New Westminster BC V3L1H9 *Web:* www.newwestcity.ca	604-527-4605		194
City of Newark 920 Broad St. . . . . Newark NJ 07102 *Web:* www.ci.newark.nj.us	973-733-8004	733-5352	337
City of Norfolk, The 810 Union St . . . . Norfolk VA 23510 *Web:* www.norfolk.gov	757-664-6510		337
City of Orlando 400 S Orange Ave. . . . . Orlando FL 32801 *Web:* www.orlando.gov	407-246-2121		337
City of Palm Springs 300 S Sunrise Way. . . . . Palm Springs CA 92262 *TF:* 800-611-1911 ■ *Web:* www.palmspringsca.gov	760-322-7323		434-3
City of Palm Springs 3200 E Tahquitz Canyon Way . . . . Palm Springs CA 92262 *Web:* www.palmspringsca.gov	760-323-8299		337
City of Pendleton 500 SW Dorion Ave . . . . Pendleton OR 97801 *TF:* 800-238-5355 ■ *Web:* www.pendleton.or.us	541-966-0201	966-0251	205
City of Phoenix 200 W Washington St . . . . Phoenix AZ 85003 *Web:* www.phoenix.gov	602-262-6011		337
City of Pierre 2301 Patron Pkwy . . . . Pierre SD 57501 *Web:* ci.pierre.sd.us	605-773-7407	773-7406	337

Name / Address	City	State	ZIP	Phone	Fax	Class
City of Portland, Oregon 1221 SW 4th Ave Rm 110	Portland	OR	97204	503-823-4000	823-3588	337
TF: 800-729-8807 ■ *Web:* www.portland.gov						
City of Quebec 2 Rue des Jardins	Quebec City	QC	G1R4S9	418-641-6651		337
Web: www.ville.quebec.qc.ca						
City of Rahway, The 1 City Hall Plz	Rahway	NJ	07065	732-827-2000		562
Web: www.cityofrahway.com						
City of Rancho Cucamonga califonia 7368 Archibald Ave	Rancho Cucamonga	CA	91730	909-477-2720		434-3
Web: www.cityofrc.us						
City of Rapid City 300 6th St	Rapid City	SD	57701	605-394-9300		337
Web: www.rcgov.org						
City of Riverside 3900 Main St	Riverside	CA	92501	951-826-5311		337
Web: www.riversideca.gov						
City of Rochester Parks & Recreation 201 4th St SE Rm 150	Rochester	MN	55904	507-328-2525	328-2535	565
Web: www.rochestermn.gov						
City of Rocks National Reserve PO Box 169	Almo	ID	83312	208-824-5901		564
Web: www.nps.gov						
City of Salem 101 S Broadway	Salem	IL	62881	618-548-2222	548-5330	206
TF: 800-755-5000 ■ *Web:* www.salemil.us						
City of Salem 114 N Broad St PO Box 869	Salem	VA	24153	540-375-3000	375-3003	338
Web: salemva.gov						
City of San Antonio 315 S Santa Rosa Ave	San Antonio	TX	78207	210-735-2989		337
Web: www.sanantonio.gov						
City of San Diego 202 C St	San Diego	CA	92101	619-236-5555		337
Web: www.sandiego.gov						
City of San Leandro Public Library, The 835 E 14th St	San Leandro	CA	94577	510-577-3351	278-3095	434-3
Web: www.sanleandro.org						
City of Saskatoon 222 3rd Ave N	Saskatoon	SK	S7K0J5	306-975-2476		564
Web: www.saskatoon.ca						
City of Seward, AK 410 Adams St City Hall Bldg PO Box 167	Seward	AK	99664	907-224-3331	224-7187	618
Web: www.cityofseward.us						
City of Shreveport 505 Travis St	Shreveport	LA	71101	318-673-5010		337
Web: www.shreveportla.gov						
City of Spokane 808 W Spokane Falls Blvd	Spokane	WA	99201	509-625-6677		50-2
Web: my.spokanecity.org						
City of St Petersburg PO Box 2842	Saint Petersburg	FL	33731	727-893-7111	892-5102	337
Web: www.stpete.org						
City of Sterling Heights Library 40255 Dodge Park Rd	Sterling Heights	MI	48313	586-446-2665		434-3
Web: www.sterling-heights.net						
City of Thomasville Tourism Authority 144 E Jackson St	Thomasville	GA	31792	229-226-3424	228-4188	206
Web: thomasvillega.com						
City of Toronto 100 Queen St W	Toronto	ON	M5H2N2	416-338-0889		337
Web: www.toronto.ca						
City of Torrance City Hall 3301 Torrance Blvd	Torrance	CA	90503	310-328-5310		337
Web: www.torranceca.gov						
City of Truth or Consequences 505 Sims	Truth Or Consequences	NM	87901	575-894-6673	894-7767	48
Web: www.torcnm.org						
City of Vacaville Inc, The 650 Merchant St	Vacaville	CA	95688	707-449-5100		256
TF: 800-759-7159 ■ *Web:* www.ci.vacaville.ca.us						
City of Valdez, The 212 Chenega Ave PO Box 307	Valdez	AK	99686	907-835-4313	835-4479	618
Web: www.valdezak.gov						
City of West Palm Beach 401 Clematis St	West Palm Beach	FL	33401	561-822-2222		337
Web: www.wpb.org						
City of Wetaskiwin Recreation 4705-50 Ave	Wetaskiwin	AB	T9A2E9	780-361-4446		706
TF: 800-419-2913 ■ *Web:* www.wetaskiwin.ca						
City Pages 300 Third St PO Box 942	Wausau	WI	54402	715-845-5171	848-5887	532-5
Web: www.thecitypages.com						
City Plumbing & Electric Supply Co 730 EE Butler Pkwy	Gainesville	GA	30501	770-532-4123		612
TF: 800-260-2024 ■ *Web:* www.cpesupply.com						
City Point National Cemetery 10th Ave & Davis St	Hopewell	VA	23860	804-795-2031	795-1064	136
Web: www.cem.va.gov						
City Press Inc W238 N1650 Rockwood Dr	Waukesha	WI	53188	262-523-3000		174
Web: www.citypressinc.com						
City Printing Company Inc 122 Oakhill Ave	Youngstown	OH	44502	330-747-5691		627
Web: cityprinting.com						
City Property Management Co 4645 E Cotton Gin Loop	Phoenix	AZ	85040	602-437-4777		652
Web: cityproperty.com						
City Psych Wellness Inc 333 Lee Burbank Hwy Ste 2	Revere	MA	02151	617-242-1000		363
Web: citypsych.net						
City Public Service Board PO Box 1771	San Antonio	TX	78296	210-353-2222		787
TF: 800-870-1006 ■ *Web:* www.cpsenergy.com						
City Public Service IBEW Federal Credit Union 1002 Camden St	San Antonio	TX	78215	210-353-2376		219
Web: cpsibewfcu.org						
City State Bank 1012 Hwy 69	Fort Scott	KS	66701	620-223-1600		70
Web: citysb.com						
City Steam Brewery Cafe 942 Main St	Hartford	CT	06103	860-548-1589		671
Web: www.citysteambrewerycafe.com						
City Suites Hotel 933 W Belmont Ave	Chicago	IL	60657	773-404-3400		379
Web: chicagocitysuites.com						
City Supply Corp 2326 Bell Ave	Des Moines	IA	50321	515-288-3211		612
TF: 800-400-2377 ■ *Web:* www.citysupplycorp.com						
City Theatre Co 1300 Bingham St	Pittsburgh	PA	15203	412-431-4400	431-5535	749
Web: www.citytheatrecompany.org						
City Union Mission Inc 1100 E 11th St	Kansas City	MO	64106	816-474-9380		48-20
Web: cityunionmission.org						
City University 521 Wall St Ste100	Seattle	WA	98121	888-422-4898		166
TF: 800-426-5596 ■ *Web:* www.cityu.edu						
City University of New York (CUNY) 205 East 42nd St	New York	NY	10017	212-997-2869	794-5397	786
TF: 800-286-9937 ■ *Web:* www.cuny.edu						
City University of New York School of Law 65-21 Main St	Flushing	NY	11367	718-340-4200	340-4435	167-1
Web: www.law.cuny.edu						
City Utilities of Springfield (CU) 301 E Central St	Springfield	MO	65801	417-831-8400		245
TF: 888-863-9001 ■ *Web:* www.cityutilities.net						
City Water, Light & Power 800 E Monroe St 4th Fl Municipal Ctr E	Springfield	IL	62701	217-789-2116	789-2136	539
Web: www.cwlp.com						
CityDesk 350 S Miami Ave	Miami	FL	33130	786-623-3882		393
Web: citydeskmiami.com						
Cityfeetcom Inc 101 California St 43rd Fl	San Francisco	CA	94111	212-924-6450	764-1622*	652
**Fax Area Code:* 415 ■ *TF:* 866-527-0540 ■ *Web:* www.cityfeet.com						
CityFiles Press 2618 W Farwell	Chicago	IL	60645	847-722-9244		637-2
Web: www.cityfilespress.com						
Cityfone PO Box 19372	Burnaby	BC	V5H4J8	888-499-7566		387
TF: 888-499-7566 ■ *Web:* www.cityfone.net						
Citygate Associates LLC 600 Coolidge Dr Ste 150	Folsom	CA	95630	916-318-3684		194
Web: www.citygateassociates.com						
Citygate GIS LLC 125 Cathedral St	Annapolis	MD	21401	410-295-3333		261
Web: www.citygategis.com						
CityKids Foundation 601 W 26th St Ste 325	New York	NY	10001	212-925-3320		48-6
Web: www.citykids.com						
Cityline Partners LLC 1651 Old Meadow Rd Ste 650	Tysons	VA	22102	703-556-3777		653
Web: citylinepartners.com						
City-Pro Group Inc 2625 E 14th St	Brooklyn	NY	11235	718-769-2698		148
Web: cityprogroup.com						
Cityrealty.Com LLC 275 Seventh Ave 20th Fl Ste 2001	New York	NY	10001	212-755-5544		653
Web: cityrealty.com						
Cityside Subaru 790 Pleasant St	Belmont	MA	02478	617-826-5000		57
Web: www.citysidesubaru.com						
Cityspan Technologies Inc 2054 University Ave 5th Fl	Berkeley	CA	94704	510-665-1700		809
Web: www.cityspan.com						
Citystaff Inc 1701 K St NW Ste 500	Washington	DC	20006	202-861-4200	861-4209	193
Web: www.citystaffdc.com						
Cityview 414 61st St	Des Moines	IA	50312	515-953-4822	953-1394	532-5
Web: www.dmcityview.com						
Ciulla Group LLC, The 6364 Pearl Rd	Cleveland	OH	44130	440-884-2036		2
Web: theciullagroup.com						
CIVC Partners 191 N Wacker Dr Ste 1100	Chicago	IL	60606	312-873-7300	873-7301	792
Web: www.civc.com						
CIVCO Medical Solutions 102 First St	Kalona	IA	52247	319-248-6757	248-6660	382
TF: 877-329-2482 ■ *Web:* www.civco.com						
Cives Corp 3700 Mansell Rd Ste 500	Alpharetta	GA	30022	770-993-4424	998-2361	188-10
Web: www.cives.com						
Civic Center Music Hall 201 N Walker St	Oklahoma City	OK	73102	405-297-2584		572
Web: okcciviccenter.com						
Civic Center of Greater Des Moines 221 Walnut St	Des Moines	IA	50309	515-246-2300	246-2305	572
Web: desmoinesperformingarts.org						
Civic Opera House 20 N Wacker Dr	Chicago	IL	60606	312-332-2244	332-8120	572
Web: www.lyricopera.org						
Civic Orchestra of Tucson (COT) PO Box 42764	Tucson	AZ	85733	520-730-3371		573-3
Web: www.cotmusic.org						
Civic Plaza Hotel 505 Pine St	Abilene	TX	79601	325-676-0222		379
Web: civicplazahotel.net						
Civic Theatre of Allentown 527 N 19th St	Allentown	PA	18104	610-432-8943		572
Web: www.civictheatre.com						
CivicConnect 915 Wilshire Blvd Ste 2175	Los Angeles	CA	90017	213-225-1170		196
Web: civicconnect.com						
Civil & Environmental Consultants Inc 333 Baldwin Rd	Pittsburgh	PA	15205	412-429-2324	429-2114	261
TF: 800-365-2324 ■ *Web:* www.cecinc.com						
Civil Constructors Inc 2283 US-20 BUS	Freeport	IL	61032	815-235-2200		188-4
Web: www.helmgroup.com						
Civil Consulting Group PLLC 1575 Heritage Dr Ste 308	Mckinney	TX	75069	972-569-9193		261
Web: civilgroup.net						
Civil Design Solutions LLC 371 Main St	Warrenton	GA	30828	706-465-0900		261
Web: civildesignsolutions.com						
Civil Dynamics Inc 109a Rt 515	Stockholm	NJ	07460	973-697-3496		261
Web: civildynamics.com						
Civil Engineering Consultants Inc 2400 - 86th St Ste 12	Des Moines	IA	50322	515-276-4884		261
Web: civilengineeringconsultantsinc.com						
Civil Works Engineers Inc 3151 Airway Ave	Costa Mesa	CA	92626	714-966-9060	966-9085	261
Web: civilworksengineers.com						
Civilcorp LLC 4611 E Airline Rd Ste 300	Victoria	TX	77904	361-570-7500		261
Web: civilcorp.us						
Civil-Surv Land Surveying LC 10590 Westoffice Dr Ste 100	Houston	TX	77042	713-839-9181		261
Web: civil-surv.com						
Civiltec Engineering Inc 118 W Lime Ave	Monrovia	CA	91016	626-357-0588		261
Web: www.civiltec.com						

				Phone	Fax	Class
Civiltech Engineering Inc 450 E Devon Ave Ste 300 *Web:* www.civiltechinc.com	Itasca	IL	60143	630-773-3900	773-3975	261
Civiltech Engineering Inc 11821 Telge Rd. *Web:* civiltecheng.com	Cypress	TX	77429	281-304-0200		261
Civista Bank 100 E Water St *TF:* 888-645-4121 ■ *Web:* www.civista.bank	Sandusky	OH	44870	419-625-4121		69
Civitan Intl PO Box 130744 *TF:* 800-248-4826 ■ *Web:* www.civitan.org	Birmingham	AL	35213	205-591-8910		48-15
Civtech Designs Inc 11012 Rhodenda Pl **Fax Area Code:* 240 ■ *Web:* www.civtechdesigns.com	Upper Marlboro	MD	20772	301-440-1747	244-5517*	261
CIXK-FM 270 Nineth St E PO Box 280 *TF:* 800-265-3742 ■ *Web:* www.mix106.ca	Owen Sound	ON	N4K5P5	519-376-2030	371-4242	647
CIXN-FM 1010 Hanwell Rd Ste 10.	Fredericton	NB	E3B6A4	506-443-0991		647
CIYM-FM PO Box 1522. *Web:* www.brightontoday.ca	Brighton	ON	K0K1H0	613-475-6936	475-9026	647
CJ & Associates Inc 16915 W Victor Rd *Web:* cjassociatesinc.com	New Berlin	WI	53151	262-786-1772		321
CJ Brown Energy PC 4245 Union Rd Ste 204 *Web:* cjbrownenergy.com	Buffalo	NY	14225	716-565-9190	633-5598	196
CJ Erickson Plumbing Co 4141 W 124th Pl *Web:* www.cjerickson.com	Alsip	IL	60803	708-371-4900	371-3885	610
CJ Mahan Construction Co 250 N Hartford Ave *Web:* cjmahan.com	Columbus	OH	43222	614-875-8200	875-1175	188-4
CJ's in Tiger Country 704 E Broadway *Web:* www.cjshotwings.com	Columbia	MO	65201	573-442-7777		671
CJA & Associates Inc 791 Tenth St S Ste 202 *Web:* cjamarketing.com	Naples	FL	34102	239-298-8210		390
CJAV-FM 3296 3rd Ave *Web:* www.933thepeak.com	Port Alberni	BC	V9Y4E1	250-723-2455	723-0797	647
CJBQ-AM 10 S Front St PO Box 488 *Web:* www.mix97.com	Belleville	ON	K8N5B2	613-969-5555	969-8122	647
CJBS LLC 2100 Sanders Rd Ste 200 *Web:* www.cjbs.com	Northbrook	IL	60062	847-945-2888		2
CJCB-TV 1283 George St *Web:* www.atlantic.ctvnews.ca	Sydney	NS	B1P1N7	902-562-5511		647
CJCI-FM 1940 3rd Ave *Web:* www.myprincegeorgenow.com	Prince George	BC	V2M1G7	250-564-2524	562-6611	647
CJCL-AM One Ted Rogers Way *TF:* 888-666-0590 ■ *Web:* www.sportsnet.ca	Toronto	ON	M4Y3B7	416-870-0590		647
CJDV-FM 50 Sportsworld Crossing Rd Ste 210 *Web:* www.davefm.com	Kitchener	ON	N2P0A4	519-772-1212	772-1213	647
CJE SeniorLife 3003 W Touhy Ave *Web:* www.cje.net	Chicago	IL	60645	773-508-1000	508-1028	48-17
CJEC-FM 815 Boulevard Lebourgneuf Ste 505 *Web:* www.wknd.fm	Quebec City	QC	G2J0C1	418-688-0919		647
CJEM-FM 64 Rue Rice *Web:* frontiere.fm	Edmundston	NB	E3V1T2	506-735-3351	739-5803	647
CJFO-FM 245 Av McArthur *Web:* www.uniquefm.ca	Ottawa	ON	K1L6P3	613-745-5529		647
CJIL-TV 450-31 St N *TF:* 800-414-2545 ■ *Web:* www.miraclechannel.ca	Lethbridge	AB	T1H3Z3	800-414-2545		647
CJK 3962 Virginia Ave *TF:* 800-598-7808 ■ *Web:* www.cjkusa.com	Cincinnati	OH	45227	513-271-6035	271-6082	626
CJKX-FM 1200 Airport Blvd Ste 207 *TF:* 877-302-9696 ■ *Web:* www.kx96.fm	Oshawa	ON	L1J8P5	905-428-9600	571-1150	647
CJL Engineering 1550 Coraopolis Heights Rd Ste 4200 *Web:* www.cjlengineering.com	Moon Township	PA	15108	412-262-1220	262-2972	261
CJLO-AM 7141 Sherbrooke St Ouest Ste CC-430 *Web:* www.cjlo.com	Montreal	QC	H4B1R6	514-848-8663		647
CJM (Carlyle Johnson Machine Co) 291 Boston Tpke *TF:* 888-629-4867 ■ *Web:* www.cjmco.com	Bolton	CT	06043	860-643-1531	646-2645	620
CJMO-FM Moncton Industrial Pk 27 Arsenault Ct *Web:* www.c103.com	Moncton	NB	E1E4J8	506-858-5525		647
CJMP-FM 4476C Marine Ave *Web:* www.cjmp.ca	Powell River	BC	V8A2K2	604-485-0088		647
CJMQ-FM 184 Queen St *Web:* www.cjmq.fm	Sherbrooke	QC	J1M1J9	819-822-1838		647
CJRT-FM 4 Pardee Ave Ste 100 *TF:* 888-595-0404 ■ *Web:* www.jazz.fm	Toronto	ON	M6K3H5	416-595-0404	575-9413	647
CJRW 300 Main St *Web:* www.cjrw.com	Little Rock	AR	72201	501-975-6251		4
CJS Securities Inc 50 Main St *Web:* www.cjssecurities.com	White Plains	NY	10606	914-287-7600		690
CJSE-FM 51 chemin Cornwall *Web:* www.cjse.ca	Shediac	NB	E4P8T8	506-532-0120		647
CJSF-FM TC 216 Simon Fraser University *Web:* www.cjsf.ca	Burnaby	BC	V5A1S6	778-782-3727	782-3695	647
CJSI-FM 4510 MacLeod Trl S *Web:* www.cjsi.ca	Calgary	AB	T2G0A4	403-276-1111	276-1114	647
CJSW-FM University of Calgary MacEwan Hall Rm 312 *Web:* www.cjsw.com	Calgary	AB	T2N1N4	403-220-3902	289-8212	647
CJT Koolcarb Inc 494 Mission St *TF:* 800-323-2299 ■ *Web:* www.cjtkoolcarb.com	Carol Stream	IL	60188	630-690-5933	690-6355	493
CJVA-AM 270 Avenue Douglas Ste 301 *Web:* www.ckle.fm	Bathurst	NB	E2A1M9	506-727-4605	546-6611	647
CJWF-FM 2090 Wyandotte St E *TF:* 877-488-2593 ■ *Web:* www.country959.com	Windsor	ON	N8Y5B2	519-944-4400	944-3747	647
CJYM 1330-AM 208 Hwy Ste 4 PO Box 490 *TF:* 800-882-4545 ■ *Web:* www.westcentralonline.com	Rosetown	SK	S0L2V0	306-882-2686		647
CK Associates 33 Hammond Ste 204 *Web:* www.ckassoc.com	Irvine	CA	92618	949-457-7800	457-7801	194
C-K Composites Company LLC 361 Bridgeport St *Web:* www.ckcomposites.com	Mount Pleasant	PA	15666	724-547-4581	547-2890	599
CK Technologies Inc 3629 Vista Mercado *Web:* ckt.com	Camarillo	CA	93012	805-987-4801		246
CK Technologies LLC 1701 Magda Dr *Web:* www.cktech.biz	Montpelier	OH	43543	419-485-1110		62-4
CK Worldwide Inc 3501 C St NE *TF:* 800-426-0877 ■ *Web:* www.ckworldwide.com	Auburn	WA	98002	253-854-5820	939-1746	811
CKAP-FM 22 Queen St Ste 2A *Web:* www.ckap.moosefm.com	Kapuskasing	ON	P5N1G8	705-335-2379	337-6391	647
CKB (CKB Products Wholesale) 8900 Directors Row **Fax Area Code:* 817 ■ *Web:* www.ckbproducts.com	Dallas	TX	75247	214-951-0488	887-1921*	328
CKB Products Wholesale (CKB) 8900 Directors Row **Fax Area Code:* 817 ■ *Web:* www.ckbproducts.com	Dallas	TX	75247	214-951-0488	887-1921*	328
CKBK-FM 14760 School House Line RR No 3 *TF:* 877-294-4435 ■ *Web:* www.delawarenation.on.ca	Thamesville	ON	N0P2K0	519-692-3936	692-5522	647
CKBW-FM 135 N St Ste 200 *Web:* www.ckbw.ca	Bridgewater	NS	B4V2V7	902-543-2401		647
CKC (Canadian Kennel Club) 200 Ronson Dr Ste 400 *TF:* 800-250-8040 ■ *Web:* www.ckc.ca	Etobicoke	ON	M9W5Z9	416-675-5511	675-6506	48-3
Ckc Laboratories Inc 5046 Sierra Pines Dr *TF:* 800-500-4362 ■ *Web:* www.ckc.com	Mariposa	CA	95338	209-966-5240		180
CKCG Health Care Services 5995 Oakbrook Pky *Web:* www.ckcghealth.com	Norcross	GA	30093	770-209-9998	674-5290	363
CKCO-TV 864 King St W PO Box 91026 *Web:* www.kitchener.ctvnews.ca	Kitchener	ON	N2G4E9	519-578-1314		647
CKCU-FM Rm 517 University Ctr 1125 Colonel By Dr *Web:* www.ckcufm.com	Ottawa	ON	K1S5B6	613-520-2898	520-4060	647
CKCW-FM 1000 St George Blvd Ste 102 *Web:* www.k945.ca	Moncton	NB	E1E4M7	506-858-1220	858-1209	647
CKDK-FM 290 Dundas St *TF:* 877-643-1039 ■ *Web:* www.country104.com	Woodstock	ON	N4S1B2	519-931-6000		647
CKDM-AM 1735 Main St S *Web:* www.730ckdm.com	Dauphin	MB	R7N2V4	204-638-3230	638-8891	647
CKGE-FM 1200 Airport Blvd Ste 207 *TF:* 855-432-7625 ■ *Web:* www.therock.fm	Oshawa	ON	L1J8P5	905-571-0949	571-1150	647
CKGP PW & Associates Inc 989 Chicago Rd *Web:* www.ckgppw.com	Troy	MI	48083	248-577-0400	589-8379	261
CKM Staffing 500 Giuseppe Ct Ste 1 *Web:* www.ckmstaffing.com	Roseville	CA	95678	916-297-6815		41
CKMB-FM 431 Huronia Rd Ste 10 *Web:* www.1075koolfm.com	Barrie	ON	L4N9B3	705-725-7304	792-7858	647
CKMN-FM 323 Montee Industrielle et Commerciale *Web:* www.ckmn.fm	Rimouski	QC	G5M1A7	418-722-2566	724-7815	647
CKMP-FM 1110 Centre St NE Ste 100 *Web:* www.ampcalgary.com	Calgary	AB	T2E2R2	403-271-6366		647
CKNX-TV 215 Carling Ter PO Box 300 *TF:* 800-265-3030 ■ *Web:* www.cknx.ca	Wingham	ON	N0G2W0	519-357-1310	357-1897	647
CKNY-TV 245 Oak St E *Web:* www.ctv.ca	North Bay	ON	P1B8P8	705-476-3111	495-4474	647
CKPG-TV 1810 3rd Ave 2nd Fl *Web:* www.ckpg.com	Prince George	BC	V2M1G4	250-564-8861	562-8768	647
CKPK-FM No 300-1401 W 8th Ave *Web:* www.thepeak.fm	Vancouver	BC	V6H1C9	604-731-7772		647
CKS Packaging Inc 445 Great SW Pkwy *Web:* www.ckspackaging.com	Atlanta	GA	30336	404-691-8900		601
CKSA-AM 5026 50th St *TF:* 800-565-2572 ■ *Web:* www.realcountrylloydminster.ca	Lloydminster	AB	T9V1P3	780-875-3321	875-4704	647
CKTP-FM 401 Bishop Dr Ste 101B *Web:* www.957thewolf.ca	Fredericton	NB	E3C2M6	506-474-2795	206-3301	647
CKUW-FM University of Winnipeg 515 Portage Ave *Web:* www.ckuw.ca	Winnipeg	MB	R3B2E9	204-786-9782	783-7080	647
CKVR-TV 33 Beacon Rd *TF:* 800-461-5820 ■ *Web:* www.barrie.ctvnews.ca	Barrie	ON	L4N9J9	705-734-3300	733-0302	647
CKXC-FM 863 Princess St Ste 301 *Web:* www.country935.ca	Kingston	ON	K7L5N4	613-549-1057	549-5302	647
CKXM-FM 145 Thames Rd W Ste 6 *Web:* www.exetertoday.ca	Exeter	ON	N0M1S3	519-235-3000	235-6262	647
CKXS-FM 520 James St *Web:* www.ckxsfm.com	Wallaceburg	ON	N8A2N9	519-627-0007		647
CKXU-FM SU 164 4401 University Dr W *Web:* www.ckxu.com	Lethbridge	AB	T1K3M4	403-329-2180		647
CKYE-FM 201 8383A 128th St *Web:* www.vancouver.redfm.ca	Surrey	BC	V3W4G1	604-591-9311	599-6063	647
CKYM-FM 11 Market Sq *Web:* www.napaneetoday.ca	Napanee	ON	K7R1J4	613-354-4554		647
CKZM-FM 2-300 Talbot St *Web:* www.stthomastoday.ca	Saint Thomas	ON	N5P4E2	519-633-6936	637-8410	647
CL (Contract Lumber Inc) 1590 W Northfield Dr *Web:* www.contractlumber.com	Brownsburg	IN	46112	317-852-8996	852-8999	191-3
CL Hauthaway & Sons Corp 638 Summer St *Web:* www.hauthaway.com	Lynn	MA	01905	781-592-6444	599-9565	605-2
CL King & Associates Inc 9 Elk St *Web:* www.clking.com	Albany	NY	12207	518-431-3555		690
CL Services Inc 4245 International Pkwy Ste 125 *TF:* 800-533-3922 ■ *Web:* www.clservicesinc.com	Atlanta	GA	30354	678-686-0933	686-0935	194
CLA (Christian Leadership Alliance) 635 Camino De Los Mares Ste 216 *Web:* www.christianleadershipalliance.org	San Clemente	CA	92673	949-487-0900	487-0927	49-12
CLA (Canadian Library Assn) 1150 Morrison Dr Ste 400 *Web:* cla.ca	Ottawa	ON	K2H8S9	613-232-9625	563-9895	49-11

Name / Address	City	State	Zip	Phone	Fax	Class
CLA (Coin Laundry Assn) 1s660 Midwest Rd Ste 205 *TF:* 800-570-5629 ■ *Web:* www.coinlaundry.org	Oakbrook Terrace	IL	60181	630-953-7920		49-4
CLA Engineers Inc 317 Main St *Web:* claengineers.com	Norwich	CT	06360	860-886-1966		261
CLAAS of America Inc 8401 S 132nd St *Web:* www.claasofamerica.com	Omaha	NE	68138	402-861-1000	861-1003	273
Clack Corp 4462 Duraform Ln *Web:* www.clackcorp.com	Windsor	WI	53598	608-846-3010	846-2586	806
Clackamas Community College 19600 Molalla Ave *Web:* www.clackamas.edu	Oregon City	OR	97045	503-594-6000		162
Clackamas County 2051 Kaen Rd *Web:* www.clackamas.us	Oregon City	OR	97045	503-655-8459	742-5468	338
Clackamas Town Ctr 12000 SE 82nd Ave *Web:* www.clackamastowncenter.com	Happy Valley	OR	97086	503-653-6913		460
Clacton Press 122 Berkley Dr *Web:* www.clactonpress.com	Palestine	TX	75801	903-729-1606		637-2
Clad Metal Specialities Inc 1516 Fifth Industrial Ct *Web:* cladmetal.com	Bay Shore	NY	11706	631-666-7750		488
Cladach Publishing PO Box 336144 *Web:* www.cladach.com	Greeley	CO	80633	970-371-9530		637-2
CLAdirect Inc 8600 NW 17th St Ste 140 *Web:* www.cladirect.com	Miami	FL	33126	305-418-4253		180
Claffey Printing Co 748 Greene St *Web:* claffeyprinting.com	Augusta	GA	30901	706-724-3040	722-2447	627
Claflin University 400 Magnolia St *TF:* 800-922-1276 ■ *Web:* www.claflin.edu	Orangeburg	SC	29115	803-535-5000	535-5385	166
CLAGS (CTR for LGBTQ Studies) CUNY Graduate Ctr 365 Fifth Ave Rm 7115 *Web:* www.clags.org	New York	NY	10016	212-817-1955	817-1567	668
Claiborne County 404 Market St *Web:* www.claiborne.k12.ms.us	Port Gibson	MS	39150	601-437-4232		338
Claiborne County Chamber of Commerce 1732 Main St Ste 1	Tazewell	TN	37879	423-626-4149		139
Claiborne County Public Library 1304 Old Knoxville Rd PO Box 139 *Web:* clabornelibrary.org	Tazewell	TN	37879	423-626-5414		434-3
Claiborne Electric Co-opeartive Inc 12525 Hwy 9 PO Box 719 *TF:* 800-900-9406 ■ *Web:* www.our.coop	Homer	LA	71040	318-927-3504		245
Claiborne Farm 703 Winchester Rd *Web:* clabornefarm.com	Paris	KY	40361	859-233-4252	987-0008	368
Claiborne Medical Ctr 1850 Old Knoxville Rd *Web:* www.clabornemedicalcenter.com	Tazewell	TN	37879	423-626-4211		374-3
Claiborne Parish Clerk of Court 512 E Main St PO Box 330 *Web:* clairborneclerkorg.ipage.com	Homer	LA	71040	318-927-9601	927-2345	338
Claim Technologies Inc 100 Court Ave Ste 306 *Web:* www.claimtechnologies.com	Des Moines	IA	50309	515-244-7322		390
Claims Providers of America PO Box 270529 *TF:* 800-735-6660 ■ *Web:* www.national-experts.com	San Diego	CA	92198	800-735-6660		390
Claims Verification Inc 6700 N Andrews Ave Ste 200 *TF:* 888-284-2000 ■ *Web:* www.cvi.com	Fort Lauderdale	FL	33309	888-284-2000		400
Claimsnetcom Inc 14860 Montfort Dr Ste 250 *TF:* 800-356-1511 ■ *Web:* www.claimsnet.com	Dallas	TX	75254	972-458-1701	458-1737	225
Claire Manufacturing Co 1005 S Westgate Ave *TF:* 800-252-4731 ■ *Web:* www.clairemfg.com	Addison	IL	60101	630-543-7600	543-4310	145
Claire's Accessories 3 SW 129th Ave *TF:* 800-252-4737 ■ *Web:* www.claires.com	Pembroke Pines	FL	33027	954-433-3000	433-3999	157-6
Claire's Corner Copia 1000 Chapel St *Web:* www.clairescornercopia.com	New Haven	CT	06510	203-562-3888		671
Clairmont Place 2100 Clairmont Lk *Web:* clairmontplace.org	Decatur	GA	30033	404-633-8875	633-9417	672
Clairmount Group Plc, The 28 W Adams *Web:* clairmount.com	Detroit	MI	48226	313-642-1102	456-9400	734
Clairon Metals Corp 11194 Alcovy Rd *Web:* www.claironmetals.com	Covington	GA	30014	770-786-9681	786-4183	488
Claitor's Law Books & Publishing Division PO Box 261333 *TF:* 800-274-1403 ■ *Web:* www.claitors.com	Baton Rouge	LA	70826	225-344-0476	344-0480	626
Clallam Bay Corrections Ctr 1830 Eagle Crest Way *Web:* doc.wa.gov	Clallam Bay	WA	98326	360-963-2000		213
Clallam County 223 E Fourth St *TF:* 800-424-5555 ■ *Web:* www.clallam.net	Port Angeles	WA	98362	360-417-2318	417-2493	338
Clamp Swing Pricing Company Inc 8386 Capwell Dr *TF:* 800-227-7615 ■ *Web:* www.clampswing.com	Oakland	CA	94621	510-567-1600		413
Clampco Products Inc 1743 Wall Rd *Web:* clampco.com	Wadsworth	OH	44281	330-336-8857		350
Clampitt Paper Company of Dallas 9207 Ambassador Row *Web:* www.clampitt.com	Dallas	TX	75247	214-638-3300		553
Clamshell Structures Inc 1101 Maulhardt Ave *TF:* 800-360-8853 ■ *Web:* www.clamshell.com	Oxnard	CA	93030	805-988-1340	988-2266	733
Clancy & Theys Construction Co 516 W Cabarrus St *Web:* www.clancytheys.com	Raleigh	NC	27603	919-834-3601	834-2439	186
Clancy's 6100 Annunciation St *Web:* www.clancysneworleans.com	New Orleans	LA	70118	504-895-1111		671
Clara Barton National Historic Site 5801 Oxford Rd *Web:* www.nps.gov	Glen Echo	MD	20812	301-320-1410		564
Clara City Farmers Elevator 110 SW 1st Ave *Web:* www.prccoop.com	Clara City	MN	56222	320-367-2300		275
Clara's 637 E Michigan Ave *Web:* www.claras.com	Lansing	MI	48912	517-372-7120		671
Clare Computer Solutions Inc 2400 Camino Ramon Ste 195 *TF:* 800-339-0690 ■ *Web:* www.clarecomputer.com	San Ramon	CA	94583	925-277-0690	277-0694	180
Clare County 225 W Main St PO Box 438 *Web:* www.clareco.net	Harrison	MI	48625	989-539-2510	539-6616	338
Clare Inc 78 Cherry Hill Dr *TF:* 800-272-5273 ■ *Web:* www.ixysic.com	Beverly	MA	01915	978-524-6700	524-4700	696
Clare Oaks 825 Carillon Dr *Web:* www.clareoaks.com	Bartlett	IL	60103	630-372-1983		371
Clare Rose Inc 100 Rose Executive Blvd *Web:* www.clarerose.com	East Yaphank	NY	11967	631-475-1840		81-1
Claremont Animal Hospital Inc 446 Charlestown Rd *Web:* www.claremontanimalhospital.com	Claremont	NH	03743	603-543-0117		794
Claremont Chamber of Commerce 205 Yale Ave *Web:* www.claremontchamber.org	Claremont	CA	91711	909-624-1681	624-6629	139
Claremont Companies Inc 1 Lakeshore Ctr *TF:* 800-848-9077 ■ *Web:* www.claremontcorp.com	Bridgewater	MA	02324	508-279-4300		528
Claremont Flock 107 Scott Dr *Web:* www.claremontflock.com	Leominster	MA	01453	978-534-6191	534-7352	745-8
Claremont Institute 937 W Foothill Blvd Ste E *Web:* www.claremont.org	Claremont	CA	91711	909-621-6825		634
Claremont McKenna College 500 E Ninth St *Web:* www.cmc.edu	Claremont	CA	91711	909-621-8088	621-8516	166
Claremont Sales Corp 35 Winsome Dr PO Box 430 *TF:* 800-222-4448 ■ *Web:* www.claremontcorporation.com	Durham	CT	06422	860-349-4499	349-7977	389
Claremont School of Theology 1325 N College Ave *Web:* cst.edu	Claremont	CA	91711	909-447-2500	447-6380	167-3
Claremore Progress PO Box 248 *Web:* www.claremoreprogress.com	Claremore	OK	74018	918-341-1131		532-2
Claremore Regional Hospital LLC 1202 N Muskogee Pl *Web:* hillcrestclaremore.com	Claremore	OK	74017	918-341-2556		374-3
Clarence Brown Theatre *University of Tennessee* 206 McClung Tower *Web:* clarencebrowntheatre.com	Knoxville	TN	37996	865-974-5161	974-4867	572
Clarence Fahnestock State Park 1498 Rt 301 *Web:* parks.ny.gov	Carmel	NY	10512	845-225-7207		565
Clarendon College 1122 College Dr PO Box 968 *TF:* 800-687-9737 ■ *Web:* www.clarendoncollege.edu	Clarendon	TX	79226	806-874-3571	874-5080	162
Clarendon County Chamber of Commerce 19 N Brooks St *Web:* www.clarendoncounty.com	Manning	SC	29102	803-435-4405		338
Clarendon Hall School 1140 S Dukes St PO Box 609 *Web:* www.clarendonhall.org	Summerton	SC	29148	803-485-3550	485-3205	685
Clarendon Hotel & Suites 401 W Clarendon Ave *Web:* goclarendon.com	Phoenix	AZ	85013	602-252-7363		379
Claret Canada Inc 1400 Rue Joliot-Curie *TF:* 800-567-7442 ■ *Web:* groupeclaret.com	Boucherville	QC	J4B7L9	450-449-5774		757
Claridge Products & Equipment Inc 601 Hwy 62 65 PO Box 910 *TF:* 800-434-4610 ■ *Web:* claridgeproducts.com	Harrison	AR	72602	870-743-2200	743-1908	243
Clarinda Correctional Facility 2000 N 16th St Ste 1 *Web:* doc.iowa.gov	Clarinda	IA	51632	712-542-5634		213
Clarion Area Chamber of Business & Industry 650 Main St *Web:* www.clarionpa.com	Clarion	PA	16214	814-226-9161	226-4903	139
Clarion Associates Inc 30W Monore St Ste 810 *Web:* www.clarionassociates.com	Chicago	IL	60603	312-630-9400		449
Clarion Bathware Inc 44 Amsler Ave *Web:* www.clarionbathware.com	Shippenville	PA	16254	814-226-5374		362
Clarion Capital Partners LLC 527 Madison Ave 10th Fl *Web:* www.clarion-capital.com	New York	NY	10022	212-821-0111	371-7597	690
Clarion Construction Inc 21067 Commerce Pointe Dr *Web:* www.clarionconst.com	Walnut	CA	91789	909-598-4060		186
Clarion Corporation of America 6200 Gateway Dr *TF:* 800-347-8667 ■ *Web:* www.clarion.com	Cypress	CA	90630	310-327-9100	327-1999	52
Clarion County Courthouse 421 Main St *Web:* www.co.clarion.pa.us	Clarion	PA	16214	814-226-4000	226-9824	338
Clarion Federal Credit Union 144 Holiday Inn Rd *Web:* clarionfcu.org	Clarion	PA	16214	814-226-5032		219
Clarion Forest Vna Inc 271 Perkins Rd *Web:* cfvna.org	Clarion	PA	16214	814-297-8400		363
Clarion Hospital (CH) 1 Hospital Dr *TF:* 800-522-0505 ■ *Web:* www.clarionhospital.org	Clarion	PA	16214	814-226-9500	226-1224	374-3
Clarion Medical Technologies Inc 125 Fleming Dr *Web:* www.clarionmedical.com	Cambridge	ON	N1T2B8	519-620-3900		475
Clarion Sintered Metals Inc 3472 Montmorenci Rd *Web:* www.clarionsintered.com	Ridgway	PA	15853	814-773-3124		485
Clarion Technologies Inc 170 College Ave Ste 300 *Web:* www.clariontechnologies.com	Holland	MI	49423	616-698-7277		256
Clarion-Ledger, The 201 S Congress St *TF:* 877-850-5343 ■ *Web:* www.clarionledger.com	Jackson	MS	39201	601-961-7000		532-2

Name / Address	City	State	Zip	Phone	Fax	Class
Claris Construction Inc 53 Church Hill Rd *Web:* www.clarisconstruction.com	Newtown	CT	06470	203-364-9460		186
Claris Health 11500 W Olympic Blvd Ste 570 *Web:* www.clarishealth.org	Los Angeles	CA	90064	310-268-8400		354
Claris International Inc 5201 Patrick Henry Dr *Web:* www.claris.com	Santa Clara	CA	95054	408-987-7000		178-1
Claritee Group 1259 PA-113 *Web:* clariteegroup.com	Perkasie	PA	18944	267-338-3300		194
Clarity Coverdale Fury (CCF) 120 S Sixth St Ste 1300 *Web:* claritycoverdalefury.com	Minneapolis	MN	55402	612-339-3902		4
Clarity Innovations Inc 1001 SE Water Ave Ste 400 *TF:* 877-683-3187 ■ *Web:* www.clarity-innovations.com	Portland	OR	97214	503-248-4300		256
Clarity Partners LLC 20 N Clark St Ste 3600 *Web:* www.claritypartners.com	Chicago	IL	60602	312-920-0550	920-0554	463
Clarity Press Inc 2625 Piedmont Rd NE Ste 56 *TF:* 877-613-1495 ■ *Web:* www.claritypress.com	Atlanta	GA	30324	404-647-6501		637-2
Clarity Software Solutions Inc 92 Wall St Ste 1 *Web:* www.clarityssi.com	Madison	CT	06443	203-453-3999		177
Clark & Morrison Insurance Agency Inc 84 Broadway *Web:* clarkmorrison.com	Denville	NJ	07834	973-627-3600		390
Clark & Smith Law Firm LLC 150 College St *Web:* www.clarksmithsizemore.com	Macon	GA	31201	478-254-5040	254-5041	41
Clark Appler & Optical 7301 York Rd *Web:* clarkappleroptical.com	Towson	MD	21204	410-825-4454	825-4456	543
Clark Atlanta University 223 James P Brawley Dr SW *TF:* 800-688-3228 ■ *Web:* www.cau.edu	Atlanta	GA	30314	404-880-8000	880-6174	166
Clark Brothers Instrument Company Inc 56680 Mound Rd *Web:* www.clarkbrothers.net	Shelby Township	MI	48316	586-781-7000		54
Clark Builders Ltd 4703 - 52 Ave *TF:* 844-301-4340 ■ *Web:* www.clarkbuilders.com	Edmonton	AB	T6B3R6	780-395-3300		261
Clark Capital Management Group Inc (CCMG) 1650 Market St 1 Liberty Pl 53rd Fl *TF:* 800-766-2264 ■ *Web:* www.ccmg.com	Philadelphia	PA	19103	215-569-2224	569-3639	401
Clark College 1933 Fort Vancouver Way *Web:* www.clark.edu	Vancouver	WA	98663	360-699-6398		162
Clark Construction Co 3535 Moores River Dr *Web:* www.clarkcc.com	Lansing	MI	48911	517-372-0940	372-0668	188-7
Clark Construction Group LLC 7500 Old Georgetown Rd *TF:* 800-655-1330 ■ *Web:* www.clarkconstruction.com	Bethesda	MD	20814	301-272-8100		186
Clark Container Inc 6895 Industrial Rd *Web:* www.clarkcontainer.com	Lyles	TN	37098	931-670-4400	670-3041	66
Clark County Courthouse Sq 401 Clay St *Web:* www.clarkcountyarkansas.com	Arkadelphia	AR	71923	870-246-4491	246-6505	338
Clark County 913 Highland St PO Box 222 *Web:* clarkcountyks.publicaccessnow.com	Ashland	KS	67831	620-635-2813	635-2051	338
Clark County 501 E Ct Ave *Web:* www.co.clark.in.us	Jeffersonville	IN	47130	812-285-6275	285-6366	338
Clark County 111 E Court St *Web:* clarkcountymo.org	Kahoka	MO	63445	660-727-8240	727-2617	338
Clark County 500 S Grand Central Pkwy *Web:* www.clarkcountynv.gov	Las Vegas	NV	89155	702-455-0000		338
Clark County 501 Archer Ave County Courthouse *Web:* www.clarkcountyil.org	Marshall	IL	62441	217-826-8311		338
Clark County 517 Court St Rm 301 *Web:* www.co.clark.wi.us	Neillsville	WI	54456	715-743-5148	743-5154	338
Clark County 101 N Limestone St *Web:* www.clarkcountyohio.gov	Springfield	OH	45501	937-521-1680	328-2436	338
Clark County 1300 Franklin St-5th Fl PO Box 5000 **Fax Area Code:* 360 ■ *Web:* www.clark.wa.gov	Vancouver	WA	98666	564-397-2456	397-6099*	338
Clark County 34 S Main St *Web:* www.clarkcoky.com	Winchester	KY	40391	859-745-0200	737-5678	338
Clark County Event Center at The Fairgrounds 17402 NE Delfel Rd *Web:* www.clarkcofair.com	Ridgefield	WA	98642	360-397-6180		720
Clark County Genealogical Society (CCGS) 717 Grand Blvd *Web:* www.ccgs-wa.org	Vancouver	WA	98661	360-750-5688		48-13
Clark County Historical Museum 1511 Main St *Web:* www.cchmuseum.org	Vancouver	WA	98660	360-993-5679	993-5683	520
Clark County Historical Society (CCHS) Heritage Center of Clark County 117 S Fountain Ave *Web:* heritage.center	Springfield	OH	45502	937-324-0657	324-1992	49-19
Clark County Museum 1830 S Boulder Hwy *Web:* www.clarkcountynv.gov	Henderson	NV	89002	702-455-7955	455-7948	520
Clark County Public Library 201 S Fountain Ave *Web:* ccplohio.org	Springfield	OH	45501	937-328-6903	328-6908	434-3
Clark County REMC 7810 State Rd 60 PO Box 411 *TF:* 800-462-6988 ■ *Web:* www.theremc.com	Sellersburg	IN	47172	812-246-3316		245
Clark County School District (CCSD) 5100 W Sahara Ave *TF:* 866-799-8997 ■ *Web:* ccsd.net	Las Vegas	NV	89146	702-799-8111	799-5125	685
Clark Dietz Inc 125 W Church St *Web:* www.clarkdietz.com	Champaign	IL	61820	217-373-8900		256
Clark Distributing Company Inc 1300 Hwy 51 S *Web:* www.clarkdistributingco.com	Dyersburg	TN	38024	731-285-1500		443
Clark Dodge Asset Management 2 Westchester Park Dr Ste 107 *Web:* www.clarkdodgewealth.com	White Plains	NY	10604	914-641-4900		528
Clark Electric Co-op 124 N Main St PO Box 190 *TF:* 800-272-6188 ■ *Web:* www.cecoop.com	Greenwood	WI	54437	800-927-5707		245
Clark Energy Co-opeartive Inc 2640 Ironworks Rd *Web:* www.clarkenergy.com	Winchester	KY	40391	859-744-4251		245
Clark Engineering Corp 12755 Hwy 55 Ste 100 *Web:* clark-eng.com	Minneapolis	MN	55441	763-545-9196	541-0056	261
Clark Foam Products Corp 655 Remington Blvd *TF:* 888-284-2290 ■ *Web:* clarkfoam.net	Bolingbrook	IL	60440	630-226-5900	226-5959	601
Clark Food Service Equipment 2209 Old Philadelphia Pk *Web:* www.clarkfoodserviceequipment.biz	Lancaster	PA	17602	717-392-7363		300
Clark Freight Lines Inc 5129 Pine Ave *Web:* www.clarkfreight.com	Pasadena	TX	77503	281-487-3160		314
Clark Frost Williams Zucchi Pc 7320 N Alpine Rd *Web:* clarkfrost.com	Loves Park	IL	61111	815-315-9357	962-6153	41
Clark Grave Vault Co, The 375 E Fifth Ave *TF:* 800-848-3570 ■ *Web:* www.clarkvault.com	Columbus	OH	43201	800-848-3570		134
Clark Industries Inc 816 E Callan St *TF:* 800-743-9727 ■ *Web:* clark-ind.com	Monett	MO	65708	417-235-7182	235-8262	454
Clark Insurance 1945 Congress St Bldg A *Web:* www.clarkinsurance.com	Portland	ME	04104	207-774-6257	774-2994	390
Clark Katherine (Rep D - MA) 2448 Rayburn House Office Bldg *Web:* katherineclark.house.gov	Washington	DC	20515	202-225-2836		342-2
Clark Lami Hembree Inc 14288 Manchester Rd *Web:* clhins.com	Manchester	MO	63011	636-391-0700		390
Clark Martire & Bartolomeo 3 Winthrop Pl *Web:* www.cmbinc.com	Leonia	NJ	07605	201-568-0011		668
Clark Material Handling Co 700 Enterprise Dr *TF:* 866-252-5275 ■ *Web:* clarkmhc.com	Lexington	KY	40510	859-422-6400		470
Clark Mc Dowall 404 E 11th St *Web:* clarkmcdowall.com	New York	NY	10009	212-473-3737		463
Clark Mechanical Services Inc 2445A Old Philadelphia Pke *Web:* clarkmechanicalinc.com	Lancaster	PA	17602	717-396-0545	396-0549	189-4
Clark Memorial Hospital (CMH) 1220 Missouri Ave *Web:* www.clarkmemorial.org	Jeffersonville	IN	47130	812-282-6631	283-6330	374-3
Clark Metal Products Co 100 Serrell Dr *Web:* www.clark-metal.com	Blairsville	PA	15717	724-459-7550	459-0207	489
Clark Nuber PS 10900 NE Fourth St Ste 1400 *TF:* 800-504-8747 ■ *Web:* clarknuber.com	Bellevue	WA	98004	425-454-4919	454-4620	2
Clark Patterson Lee 205 St Paul St Ste 500 *Web:* cplteam.com	Rochester	NY	14604	919-833-6064		256
Clark Personnel Service 1180 Montlimar Dr *Web:* www.clarkpersonnel.com	Mobile	AL	36609	251-471-6777	471-4123	260
Clark Planetarium 110 S 400 W *TF:* 800-501-2885 ■ *Web:* slco.org	Salt Lake City	UT	84101	385-468-7827		598
Clark Precision Machined Components LLC 320 Fourth St *Web:* www.clarkprecision.com	Blawnox	PA	15238	412-828-1210		490
Clark Public Library 303 Westfield Ave *Web:* clarklibrary.org	Clark	NJ	07066	732-388-5999		434-3
Clark Regional Medical Center Inc 175 Hospital Dr *Web:* www.clarkregional.org	Winchester	KY	40391	859-745-3500		374-3
Clark Reservation State Park 6105 E Seneca Tpke *Web:* parks.ny.gov	Jamesville	NY	13078	315-492-1590		565
Clark Schaefer Hackett & Co 1 E Fourth St Ste 1200 *TF:* 800-772-8144 ■ *Web:* cshco.com	Cincinnati	OH	45202	513-241-3111		2
Clark Specialty Company Inc 6824 Industrial Park Rd *Web:* www.clarkspecialty.com	Bath	NY	14810	607-776-3193	776-3190	697
Clark State Community College 570 E Leffel Ln *Web:* www.clarkstate.edu	Springfield	OH	45505	937-325-0691	328-6097	162
Clark Steel Fabricators Inc 12610 Vigilante Rd *Web:* www.clarksteelfab.com	Lakeside	CA	92040	619-390-1502		480
Clark Street Grill 811 Spruce St *Web:* www.clarkstreetgrill.com	Saint Louis	MO	63102	314-552-5850		671
Clark Technology Systems Inc 159 Harveys Ln *Web:* www.clarkts.com	Milton	PA	17847	570-742-1819		295
Clark Transfer Inc 800A Paxton St *TF:* 800-488-7585 ■ *Web:* clarktransfer.com	Harrisburg	PA	17104	800-488-7585		186
Clark University 950 Main St *TF:* 800-462-5275 ■ *Web:* www.clarku.edu	Worcester	MA	01610	508-793-7711	793-8821	166
Clark Wilson LLP 900 885 W Georgia St *Web:* www.cwilson.com	Vancouver	BC	V6C3H1	604-687-5700	687-6314	41
Clark, Fountain, La Vista, Prather, Keen & Littky-Rubin LLP 1919 N Flagler Dr *Web:* clarkfountain.com	West Palm Beach	FL	33407	561-922-0258		41

Phone | Fax | Class

Clark, Gagliardi & Miller PC
99 Court St ... White Plains NY 10601 800-734-5694 428
TF: 800-734-5694 ■ *Web:* www.cgmlaw.com

Clark/Sullivan Construction
905 Industrial Way Ste 26 ... Sparks NV 89431 775-355-8500 186
Web: clarksullivan.com

Clarkco State Park 386 Clarkco Rd ... Quitman MS 39355 601-776-6651 565
Web: www.mdwfp.com

Clark-Dunbar Flooring Superstore
3232 Empire Dr ... Alexandria LA 71301 318-445-0262 290
TF: 800-256-1467 ■ *Web:* www.clarkdunbarsuperstore.com

Clarke & Rush 4411 Auburn Blvd ... Sacramento CA 95841 916-609-2667 610
Web: www.clarke-rush.com

Clarke College 1550 Clarke Dr ... Dubuque IA 52001 563-588-6300 588-6789 166
TF: 888-825-2753 ■ *Web:* www.clarke.edu

Clarke County 101 N Church Ct Ste B ... Berryville VA 22611 540-955-5100 338
Web: www.clarkecounty.gov

Clarke County PO Box 548 ... Grove Hill AL 36451 251-275-3507 275-8517 338
Web: clarkecountyal.com

Clarke County 100 S Main ... Osceola IA 50213 641-342-3315 338
Web: www.clarkecountyiowa.org

Clarke County Historical Assn (CCHA)
32 E Main St ... Berryville VA 22611 540-955-2600 48-13
Web: www.clarkehistory.org

Clarke Historical Museum 240 E St ... Eureka CA 95501 707-443-1947 520
Web: www.clarkemuseum.org

Clarke Inc PO Box 10936 ... Lynchburg VA 24506 434-847-5561 627
Web: bebetterdomore.com

Clarke Leiper PLLC
6265 Franconia Rd ... Alexandria VA 22310 703-922-7622 2
Web: clarkeleiper.com

Clarke Power Services Inc
3133 E Kemper Rd ... Cincinnati OH 45241 513-771-2200 358
TF: 800-513-9591 ■ *Web:* www.clarkepowerservices.com

Clarke Silverglate PA
799 Brickell Plz Ste 900 ... Miami FL 33131 305-377-0700 428
Web: www.cspalaw.com

Clarke Yvette D (Rep D - NY)
2058 Rayburn House Office Bldg ... Washington DC 20515 202-225-6231 226-0112 342-2
Web: www.clarke.house.gov

Clarke-Hess Communications Research Corp
3243 Rte 112 ... Medford NY 11763 631-698-3350 698-3356 248
Web: clarke-hess.com

Clark-Floyd Counties Convention & Tourism Bureau
315 Southern Indiana Ave ... Jeffersonville IN 47130 812-282-6654 282-1904 206
TF: 800-552-3842 ■ *Web:* www.gosoin.com

Clark-Lindsey Village 101 W Windsor Rd ... Urbana IL 61802 217-344-2144 672
TF: 800-998-2581 ■ *Web:* www.clark-lindsey.com

Clark-Pacific Corp
1980 S River Rd ... West Sacramento CA 95691 916-371-0305 372-0323 187
Web: www.clarkpacific.com

Clark-Reliance Corp
16633 Foltz Pkwy ... Strongsville OH 44149 440-572-1500 495
TF: 800-238-4027 ■ *Web:* clarkreliance.com

Clarksburg Exponent Telegram
324 Hewes Ave ... Clarksburg WV 26301 304-626-1400 624-4188 532-2
TF: 800-982-6034 ■ *Web:* www.wvnews.com

Clarksburg State Park
1199 Middle Rd ... Clarksburg MA 01247 413-664-8345 565
Web: www.mass.gov

Clarksdale Municipal School District
135 Washington Ave PO Box 1088 ... Clarksdale MS 38614 662-627-8500 624-9405 186
Web: www.cmsdschools.org

Clarksdale-Coahoma County Chamber of Commerce & Industrial Foundation
1540 DeSoto Ave PO Box 160 ... Clarksdale MS 38614 662-627-7337 627-1313 139
TF: 800-626-3764 ■ *Web:* www.clarksdale-ms.com

Clarkson College 101 S 42nd St ... Omaha NE 68131 402-552-3100 552-6057 166
TF: 800-647-5500 ■ *Web:* www.clarksoncollege.edu

Clarkson Construction Co
4133 Gardner Ave ... Kansas City MO 64120 816-483-8800 188-4
Web: clarksonconstruction.com

Clarkson University 10 Clarkson Ave ... Potsdam NY 13699 315-268-6480 268-7647 166
TF: 800-527-6577 ■ *Web:* www.clarkson.edu

Clarkston Area Chamber of Commerce
5856 S Main St ... Clarkston MI 48346 248-625-8055 625-8041 139
Web: clarkston.org

Clarkston Consulting
Research Triangle Pk 2655 Meridian Pkwy ... Durham NC 27713 919-484-4400 484-4450 180
TF: 800-652-4274 ■ *Web:* www.clarkstonconsulting.com

Clarkston Specialty Healthcare Ctr
4800 Clintonville Rd ... Clarkston MI 48346 248-674-0903 450
Web: www.savaseniorcare.com

Clarksville Area Chamber of Commerce
25 Jefferson St Ste 300 ... Clarksville TN 37040 931-647-2331 645-1574 139
TF: 800-530-2487 ■ *Web:* www.clarksvillechamber.com

Clarksville Foundry Inc
1140 Red River St ... Clarksville TN 37040 931-647-1538 645-7207 480
Web: clarksvillefoundry.com

Clarksville Montgomery County Public Library
350 Pageant Ln ... Clarksville TN 37040 931-648-8826 648-8831 434-3
TF: 877-239-6635 ■ *Web:* www.mcgtn.org

ClarkWestern Dietrich Building Systems LLC
9100 Centre Pointe Dr Ste 210 ... West Chester OH 45069 513-870-1100 191-1
Web: www.clarkdietrich.com

Claro Group LLC, The
321 N Clark St Ste 1200 ... Chicago IL 60654 312-546-3400 554-8085 194
Web: www.theclarogroup.com

Clarus Marketing Group LLC
500 Enterprise Dr 2nd Fl ... Rocky Hill CT 06067 860-358-9198 194
TF: 855-226-7047 ■ *Web:* www.claruscommerce.com

Clarus Technologies LLC
3145 Mercer Ave Unit 104 ... Bellingham WA 98225 360-715-1356 647-3882 386
Web: www.clarustechnologies.com

Clarus Therapeutics Inc
555 Skokie Blvd Ste 340 ... Northbrook IL 60062 847-562-4300 231
Web: www.clarustherapeutics.com

Clary Corp 150 E Huntington Dr ... Monrovia CA 91016 626-359-4486 305-0254 253
TF: 800-551-6111 ■ *Web:* www.clary.com

CLASP (Center for Law & Social Policy)
1015 15th St NW Ste 400 ... Washington DC 20005 202-906-8000 842-2885 634
TF: 800-821-4367 ■ *Web:* www.clasp.org

Class 1 Controls Inc 1720 Elmview Dr ... Houston TX 77080 713-467-8397 467-8398 261
Web: www.class1controls.com

Class Act Federal Credit Union
3620 Fern Valley Rd ... Louisville KY 40219 502-964-7575 966-2061 219
TF: 800-292-2960 ■ *Web:* www.classact.org

Class Action Litigation Report
1801 S Bell St ... Arlington VA 22202 800-372-1033 531-7
TF: 800-372-1033 ■ *Web:* pro.bloomberglaw.com

Classic Arts Showcase PO Box 828 ... Burbank CA 91503 323-878-0283 878-0329 740
Web: www.classicartsshowcase.org

Classic Blind Ltd
2801 Brasher Ln Ste 100 ... Bedford TX 76021 817-540-9300 540-1304 361
TF: 800-961-9867 ■ *Web:* www.classicsameday.com

Classic Brands LLC 8214 Wellmoor Ct ... Jessup MD 20794 877-707-7533 471
TF: 877-707-7533 ■ *Web:* www.classicbrands.com

Classic Brass Inc 2051 Stoneman Cir ... Lakewood NY 14750 716-763-1400 350
TF: 800-869-3173 ■ *Web:* www.classic-brass.com

Classic Cafe 865 Westminster St ... Providence RI 02903 401-273-0707 671
Web: classiccaferi.com

Classic Care Pharmacy Corp
1320 Heine Ct ... Burlington ON L7L6L9 905-631-9027 237
TF: 866-773-1354 ■ *Web:* www.classiccare.ca

Classic Carriers Inc
151 Industrial Pky ... Versailles OH 45380 937-526-5100 780
TF: 800-348-6244 ■ *Web:* www.classiccarriers.com

Classic Cinemas 603 Rogers St ... Downers Grove IL 60515 630-968-1600 968-1626 748
Web: www.classiccinemas.com

Classic City Beverages LLC
530 Calhoun Dr ... Athens GA 30601 706-353-1650 353-1655 81-1
Web: bevsouth.com

Classic Components Corp
23605 Telo Ave ... Torrance CA 90505 310-539-5500 246
Web: www.class-ic.com

Classic Containers Inc
1700 S Hellman Ave ... Ontario CA 91761 909-930-3610 930-3640 362
Web: classiccontainers.com

Classic Custom Vacations
5893 Rue Ferrari ... San Jose CA 95138 800-635-1333 771
TF: 800-635-1333 ■ *Web:* www.classicvacations.com

Classic Die Inc
610 Plymouth Ave Ne ... Grand Rapids MI 49505 616-454-3760 604
Web: www.classicdie.com

Classic Die Services Inc PO Box 106 ... New Haven IN 46774 260-748-6907 41
Web: www.classicdieservices.com

Classic Distributing & Beverage Group Inc
120 N Puente Ave ... City of Industry CA 91746 626-934-3700 80-2
Web: classicdist.com

Classic Floors Inc 13725 S Mur Len Rd ... Olathe KS 66062 913-780-2171 780-0117 291
Web: www.classicfloors.com

Classic Golf Management Inc
2295 Towne Lake Pkwy Ste 116 ... Woodstock GA 30189 770-928-1600 706
Web: www.cgmgolf.com

Classic Hits 93.1 WNOX
1533 Amherst Rd ... Knoxville TN 37909 865-824-1021 645-82
Web: www.931wnox.com

Classic Industrial Services Inc
456 Highlandia Dr ... Baton Rouge LA 70809 225-756-4450 261
Web: www.classicindustrial.com

Classic Leather Inc PO Box 2404 ... Hickory NC 28603 828-328-2046 324-6212 319-2
Web: www.classic-leather.com

Classic Medallics Inc
520 S Fulton Ave ... Mount Vernon NY 10550 914-530-6250 530-0250 777
TF: 800-221-1040 ■ *Web:* classic-medallics.com

Classic Optical Laboratories Inc
3710 Belmont Ave ... Youngstown OH 44505 330-759-8245 759-8300 237
TF: 888-522-2020 ■ *Web:* www.classicoptical.com

Classic Packaging Co
5570 Bethania Rd ... Pfafftown NC 27040 336-922-4224 601
Web: www.classicpackaging.com

Classic Parking Inc 3208 Royal St ... Los Angeles CA 90007 213-742-1238 295-9745* 562
**Fax Area Code:* 408 ■ *Web:* classicparking.com

Classic Residence Management LP
71 S Wacker Dr ... Chicago IL 60606 312-803-8800 672
TF: 800-421-1442 ■ *Web:* www.viliving.com

Classic Rock 100.3 the FOX
660 Flormann St Ste 100 ... Rapid City SD 57701 605-394-4487 343-9012 645-129
Web: www.foxradio.com

Classic Sheet Metal Inc
1065 Sesame St ... Franklin Park IL 60131 866-918-0995 492
TF: 866-918-0995 ■ *Web:* www.classic-sheet-metal.com

Classic Solutions
22365 El Toro Rd Ste 420 ... Lake Forest CA 92630 877-870-6961 597-1994* 178-1
**Fax Area Code:* 949 ■ *TF:* 877-870-6961 ■ *Web:* www.classicsolutions.com

Classic Student Tours
75 Rhoads Center Dr ... Dayton OH 45458 937-439-0032 439-0041 760
TF: 800-860-0246 ■ *Web:* classicstudenttours.com

Classic Touch Limousine Inc
908 N Walnut St ... Bloomington IN 47404 812-339-7269 441
TF: 800-319-0082 ■ *Web:* www.classictouchlimo.com

Classic Travel Inc 4767 Okemos Rd ... Okemos MI 48864 517-349-6200 772
TF: 800-643-3449 ■ *Web:* classictravelusa.com

Classic Tube 80 Rotech Dr ... Lancaster NY 14086 716-759-1800 595
TF: 800-882-3711 ■ *Web:* www.classictube.com

Classic Turning Inc 3000 E S St ... Jackson MI 49201 517-764-1335 764-6161 757
Web: classicturning.com

Classic Warships Publishing
PO Box 57591 ... Tucson AZ 85732 520-748-2992 637-2
Web: www.classicwarships.com

Classic Wines LLC 6489 E 39th Ave ... Denver CO 80207 303-825-1360 80-3
Web: www.classicwines.net

Classical 91.5 280 State St ... Rochester NY 14614 585-325-7500 645-135
Web: www.classical915.org

Classical 95.5 KHFM
4125 Carlisle Blvd NE ... Albuquerque NM 87107 505-878-0980 878-0098 645-4
Web: www.khfm.org

Name / Address	City	State	Zip	Phone	Fax	Class
Classical Academy 975 Stout Rd. *Web:* www.tcatitans.org	Colorado Springs	CO	80921	719-484-0091		449
Classical Association of the Atlantic States (CAAS) Valley Forge Military Academy & College 1001 Eagle Rd *Web:* caas-cw.org	Wayne	PA	19087	610-896-8903		49-19
Classical Marketing LLC 2300 Cabot Dr Ste 390 *TF:* 800-613-3489 ■ *Web:* www.classicalmarketing.com	Lisle	IL	60532	847-969-1696		195
Classroom Inc 245 Fifth Ave 20th Fl *Web:* www.classroominc.org	New York	NY	10016	212-545-8400		194
Classy 100 417 Robison Rd *Web:* www.classy100.com	Erie	PA	16509	814-868-9100	868-1876	645-53
Classy Llama Studios LLC 4064 S Lone Pine *Web:* www.classyllama.com	Springfield	MO	65804	417-866-8887		180
Clatsop Community College 1653 Jerome Ave *TF:* 855-252-8767 ■ *Web:* www.clatsopcc.edu	Astoria	OR	97103	503-325-0910	325-5738	162
Clatsop County 820 Exchange St Ste 100 *Web:* www.co.clatsop.or.us	Astoria	OR	97103	503-325-8511	325-9307	338
Claude Howard Lumber Company Inc 600 Park Ave. *Web:* www.sbcontract.com	Statesboro	GA	30458	912-764-5407	764-6279	683
Clausing Industrial Inc 3963 Emerald Dr. **Fax Area Code:* 269 ■ *TF:* 800-323-0972 ■ *Web:* www.clausing-industrial.com	Kalamazoo	MI	49001	800-323-0972	345-5945*	358
Clausman & Associates PC 1980 E 116th St	Carmel	IN	46032	317-844-3110		2
Claverack Rural Electric Co-opeartive Inc 32750 W US 6 *TF:* 800-326-9799 ■ *Web:* www.claverack.com	Wysox	PA	18854	570-265-2167	265-6019	245
Claws 'n' Paws Wild Animal Park 1475 Ledgedale Rd. *Web:* www.clawsnpaws.com	Lake Ariel	PA	18436	570-698-6154		823
Claxton Poultry Farms 8816 Hwy 301 N *TF:* 888-739-3181 ■ *Web:* www.claxtonpoultry.com	Claxton	GA	30417	912-739-3181		619
Claxton Printing Company Inc 1118 Culpepper Dr *Web:* www.claxtonprinting.com	Conyers	GA	30094	404-521-0933		627
Claxton-Hepburn Medical Ctr 214 King St. *Web:* www.claxtonhepburn.org	Ogdensburg	NY	13669	315-393-3600		374-3
Clay & Land Insurance Inc 866 Ridgeway Loop Rd Ste 200 *Web:* clayandland.com	Memphis	TN	38120	901-767-3600		390
Clay Center for the Arts & Sciences 1 Clay Sq *Web:* www.theclaycenter.org	Charleston	WV	25301	304-561-3570		572
Clay County 25 Court Sq PO Box 1120 *Web:* claycountyprobate.com	Ashland	AL	36251	256-354-2198	354-4778	338
Clay County 609 E National Ave Rm 211 *Web:* www.claycountyin.gov	Brazil	IN	47834	812-448-9023	446-9602	338
Clay County 424 Brown St *Web:* www.dalehollowlake.org	Celina	TN	38551	931-243-3338	243-6809	338
Clay County 712 Fifth St *Web:* claycountykansas.org	Clay Center	KS	67432	785-632-2552	632-5856	338
Clay County PO Box 519 **Fax Area Code:* 229 ■ *TF:* 800-436-7442 ■ *Web:* georgia.gov	Fort Gaines	GA	39851	478-934-3303	768-3672*	338
Clay County 477 Houston St *Web:* www.claycountygov.com	Green Cove Springs	FL	32043	904-278-4708	284-9780	338
Clay County 100 N Bridge St *Web:* www.co.clay.tx.us	Henrietta	TX	76365	940-538-4631		338
Clay County 1 Courthouse Sq *Web:* claycountymo.gov	Liberty	MO	64068	816-407-3600		338
Clay County PO Box 160 *Web:* www.claycountyillinois.org	Louisville	IL	62858	618-665-3626	665-3607	338
Clay County 807 11th St N. *Web:* claycountymn.gov	Moorhead	MN	56560	218-299-5012	299-5195	338
Clay County 215 W Fourth St. *Web:* www.co.clay.ia.us	Spencer	IA	51301	712-262-9438		338
Clay County 211 W Main St Ste 200 *Web:* www.claycountysd.org	Vermillion	SD	57069	605-677-7120	677-7104	338
Clay County PO Box 815 *Web:* www.claycountyms.com	West Point	MS	39773	662-494-3124	492-4059	338
Clay County Chamber of Commerce 1734 Kingsley Ave *Web:* www.claychamber.com	Orange Park	FL	32073	904-264-2651	264-0070	139
Clay County Electric Co-opeartive Corp 3111 US-67 *TF:* 800-521-2450 ■ *Web:* www.claycountyelectric.com	Corning	AR	72422	870-857-3521	857-3523	245
Clay County Savings Bank 1178 W Kansas St PO Box 277. *Web:* www.claycountysavings.com	Liberty	MO	64069	816-781-4500	781-1668	70
Clay Dunn Enterprises Inc 1606 E Carson St *Web:* www.airtecperforms.com	Carson	CA	90745	310-549-1698		35
Clay Electric Co-operative Inc 10 Citrus Dr PO Box 308 *TF:* 800-224-4917 ■ *Web:* www.clayelectric.com	Keystone Heights	FL	32656	352-473-4917	473-1403	245
Clay Hill Lodge PO Box 544 *Web:* www.clayhilllodge.com	Lyons	OR	97358	503-859-3772		379
Clay Ingels Company LLC 914 Delaware Ave *Web:* www.clayingels.com	Lexington	KY	40505	859-252-0836		191-1
Clay Lacy Aviation 7435 Valjean Ave *TF:* 800-423-2904 ■ *Web:* www.claylacy.com	Van Nuys	CA	91406	818-989-2900	904-3450	13
Clay Pit 1601 Guadalupe St *Web:* www.claypit.com	Austin	TX	78701	512-322-5131		671
Clay Pit Ponds State Park Preserve 83 Nielsen Ave *Web:* parks.ny.gov	Staten Island	NY	10309	718-967-1976		565
Clay Today 3513 US Hwy 17 *TF:* 888-434-9844 ■ *Web:* www.claytodayonline.com	Fleming Island	FL	32003	904-264-3200		532-4
Clay William Jr (Rep D - MO) 2428 Rayburn House Office Bldg *Web:* www.lacyclay.house.gov	Washington	DC	20515	202-225-2406	226-3717	342-2
Claybar Constracting Inc 424 MacNab St *TF:* 866-801-9305 ■ *Web:* claybar.ca	Dundas	ON	L9H2L3	905-627-8000		610
Clayton & Mckervey PC 2000 Town Ctr Ste 1800 *Web:* claytonmckervey.com	Southfield	MI	48075	248-208-8860		2
Clayton Aquariums Inc 12031 Northup Way Ste 106 *Web:* www.claytonaquariums.com	Bellevue	WA	98005	425-644-7222	644-7219	189-6
Clayton Block Co PO Box 3015 *TF:* 800-662-3044 ■ *Web:* www.claytonco.com	Lakewood	NJ	08701	800-662-3044		183
Clayton Capital Partners 8112 Maryland Ave Ste 250 *Web:* www.claytoncapitalpartners.com	Saint Louis	MO	63105	314-725-9939		317
Clayton Corp 866 Horan Dr *TF:* 800-729-8220 ■ *Web:* www.claytoncorp.com	Fenton	MO	63026	636-349-5333	349-5335	601
Clayton County 111 High St NE PO Box 418 *Web:* www.claytoncountyia.gov	Elkader	IA	52043	563-245-2204	245-1175	338
Clayton County 112 Smith St *Web:* www.claytoncountyga.gov	Jonesboro	GA	30236	770-477-3569	477-3217	338
Clayton County Chamber of Commerce 2270 Mt Zion Rd. *Web:* www.claytonchamber.org	Jonesboro	GA	30236	678-610-4021	610-4025	139
Clayton County Library System 865 Battle Creek Rd *Web:* claytonpl.org	Jonesboro	GA	30236	770-473-3850		434-3
Clayton Dubilier & Rice Inc 375 Park Ave 18th Fl *Web:* www.cdr-inc.com	New York	NY	10152	212-407-5200	407-5252	403
Clayton Industries 17477 Hurley St *TF:* 800-423-4585 ■ *Web:* www.claytonindustries.com	City of Industry	CA	91744	626-435-1200	435-0180	472
Clayton Lake State Park 170591 US Hwy 271 *Web:* www.travelok.com	Clayton	OK	74536	918-569-7981		565
Clayton Metals Inc 546 Clayton Ct **Fax Area Code:* 630 ■ *TF:* 800-323-7628 ■ *Web:* www.claytonmetals.com	Wood Dale	IL	60191	800-323-7628	860-1053*	492
Clayton Neighbor 5442 Frontage Rd Ste 130 *Web:* www.mdjonline.com	Forest Park	GA	30297	404-363-8484		532-4
Clayton on the Park 7343 Scottsdale Mall *Web:* www.theclaytonvenues.com	Scottsdale	AZ	85251	480-990-7300		379
Clayton State University (CSU) 2000 Clayton State Blvd *Web:* www.clayton.edu	Morrow	GA	30260	678-466-4000	466-4149	166
Clayton Tile 535 Woodruff Rd *Web:* claytontile.com	Greenville	SC	29607	864-288-6290		290
Clayton's Crab Company Inc 5775 S US Hwy 1 *Web:* claytonscrabcompany.com	Rockledge	FL	32955	321-639-0161	636-4631	297-5
Claytor Lake State Park 6620 Ben H Boden Dr *Web:* www.dcr.virginia.gov	Dublin	VA	24084	540-643-2500		565
Clay-Union Electric Corp 1410 E Cherry St PO Box 317 *TF:* 800-696-2832 ■ *Web:* www.clayunionelectric.coop	Vermillion	SD	57069	605-624-2673		245
Clayworks Ltd 629 Bedford Hwy *Web:* clayworks.ca	Halifax	NS	B3M2L6	902-445-4453		361
CLC Inc 3001 Lava Ridge Ct *Web:* www.clcincorporated.com	Roseville	CA	95661	916-789-7600		2
CLC Lubricants Co 0N902 Old Kirk Rd *TF:* 800-543-0505 ■ *Web:* clclubricants.com	Geneva	IL	60134	630-232-7900	232-7915	541
Clean Air Engineering Inc 500 W Wood St. *TF:* 800-553-5511 ■ *Web:* www.cleanair.com	Palatine	IL	60067	847-991-3300		41
Clean Air Report 1919 S Eads St Ste 201 *TF:* 800-424-9068 ■ *Web:* insideepa.com	Arlington	VA	22202	703-416-8505	416-8543	531-5
Clean Air Solutions Inc 826 Bayridge Pl *Web:* www.cleanroomspecialists.com	Fairfield	CA	94534	707-864-9499		246
Clean Air Technology Inc 41105 Capital Dr **Fax Area Code:* 734 ■ *TF:* 800-459-6320 ■ *Web:* www.cleanairtechnology.com	Canton	MI	48187	800-459-6320	459-9437*	449
Clean and Happy Windows 10019 Des Moines Memorial Dr. *TF:* 866-762-7617 ■ *Web:* www.cleanhappy.com	Seattle	WA	98168	206-762-7617	762-7637	152
Clean Coal Technologies Inc 295 Madison Ave *Web:* www.cleancoaltechnologiesinc.com	Manhattan	NY	10017	646-710-3549		202
Clean Cuts Inc 2901 Chestnut Ave *Web:* cleancuts.cccl.tv	Baltimore	MD	21211	410-467-4231	467-4642	657
Clean Design Inc 6601 Six Forks Rd Ste 400 *Web:* cleaninc.com	Raleigh	NC	27615	919-544-2193		4
Clean Diesel Technologies Inc 4567 Telephone Rd Ste 206 *NASDAQ: CDTI* ■ *TF:* 800-661-9963 ■ *Web:* www.cdti.com	Ventura	CA	93003	805-639-9458		386
Clean Earth of North Jersey Inc 115 Jacobus Ave. *TF:* 877-445-3478 ■ *Web:* cleanearthinc.com	South Kearny	NJ	07032	973-344-4004	344-8652	660
Clean Foods Inc 4561 Market St Ste B **Fax Area Code:* 805 ■ *TF:* 800-526-8328 ■ *Web:* cafealtura.com	Ventura	CA	93003	800-526-8328	933-9367*	297-8
Clean Fuels Ohio 530 W Spring St Ste 250 *Web:* www.cleanfuelsohio.org	Columbus	OH	43215	614-884-7336		580
Clean Harbors Inc 42 Longwater Dr PO Box 9149 *NYSE: CLH* ■ *TF:* 800-282-0058 ■ *Web:* www.cleanharbors.com	Norwell	MA	02061	781-792-5000		667
Clean Master 1572 Nord Ave *Web:* www.cleanmasterservices.com	Chico	CA	95926	530-343-0123	343-0101	577
Clean Ones Corp 317 SW Alder St Ste 350 *TF:* 800-367-4587 ■ *Web:* www.cleanones.com	Portland	OR	97204	800-367-4587		151
Clean Power LLC 124 N 121st St *TF:* 800-588-1000 ■ *Web:* www.cleanpower1.com	Milwaukee	WI	53226	414-302-3000		152

	Phone	Fax	Class
Clean Rooms West Inc 1392 Industrial Dr. Tustin CA 92780 *TF:* 800-772-6634 ■ *Web:* www.cleanroomswest.com	714-258-7700		385
Clean Seal Inc (CS) 20900 W Ireland Rd South Bend IN 46614 *TF:* 800-366-3682 ■ *Web:* www.cleanseal.com	574-299-1888	299-8044	676
Clean Street Inc 1937 W 169th St Gardena CA 90247 **Fax Area Code:* 310 ■ *TF:* 800-225-7316 ■ *Web:* cleanstreet.com	800-225-7316	538-8015*	667
Clean Tech Inc 500 Dunham St. Dundee MI 48131 *Web:* www.cleantechrecycling.com	734-529-2475		596
Clean Uniform Co 1316 S Seventh St Saint Louis MO 63104 *Web:* www.cleanuniform.com	314-421-1220		393
Clean Water Action 4455 Connecticut Ave NW Washington DC 20008 *Web:* www.cleanwateraction.org	202-895-0420	895-0438	48-13
Clean Water Systems Intl (CWS) 2322 Marina Dr Klamath Falls OR 97601 *Web:* www.cleanwatersysintl.com	541-882-9993	882-9994	806
Clean Yield Asset Management Inc 16 Beaver Meadow Rd Norwich VT 05055 *TF:* 800-809-6439 ■ *Web:* www.cleanyield.com	802-526-2525	526-2528	401
Cleaning Authority 7230 Lee DeForest Dr Columbia MD 21046 *TF:* 888-658-0659 ■ *Web:* www.thecleaningauthority.com	443-602-9154		310
Cleanmark Labels *LGI* 6700 SW Bradbury Ct Portland OR 97224 *TF:* 800-345-0534 ■ *Web:* cleanmarklabels.com	503-968-8303	620-3290	413
CleanNet USA 9861 Broken Land Pkwy Ste 208 Columbia MD 21046 *TF:* 800-735-8838 ■ *Web:* www.cleannetusa.com	410-720-6444	720-5307	152
Cleanroom Systems 7000 Performance Dr North Syracuse NY 13212 *TF:* 800-825-3268 ■ *Web:* airinnovations.com	315-452-7400	452-7420	18
Cleantec Enterprises Inc 1232 Tulip St Liverpool NY 13088 *Web:* cleantec.us	315-463-5353		104
Clean-Tech Co 211 S Jefferson Ave. Saint Louis MO 63103 *Web:* www.cleantechcompany.com	314-652-2388		152
Cleanwise LLC 1100 E Woodfield Rd Ste 200 Schaumburg IL 60173 *TF:* 877-255-5230	877-255-5230		393
CLEAR (Council on Licensure Enforcement & Regulation) 403 Marquis Ave. Lexington KY 40502 *Web:* www.clearhq.org	859-269-1289		49-7
Clear Align LLC 2550 Blvd of the Generals Ste 280 Eagleville PA 19403 *Web:* www.clearalign.com	484-956-0510		256
Clear Brook Manor 1100 E Northampton St Laurel Run PA 18706 *TF:* 800-582-6241 ■ *Web:* www.clearbrookinc.com	800-582-6241		726
Clear Capital 10266 Truckee Airport Rd Truckee CA 96161 *Web:* www.clearcapital.com	530-550-2500		652
Clear Ch Outdoor Inc 2325 E Camelback Rd Ste 400 Phoenix AZ 85016 *Web:* clearchanneloutdoor.com	602-381-5700		8
Clear Comfort Water 3063 Sterling Cir Unit 8 Boulder CO 80301 *Web:* clearcomfort.com	303-872-4477		192
Clear Creek Baptist Bible College 300 Clear Creek Rd. Pineville KY 40977 *TF:* 866-340-3196 ■ *Web:* www.ccbbc.edu	606-337-3196	337-2372	161
Clear Creek Communications 18238 S Fischers Mill Rd Oregon City OR 97045 *Web:* www.ccmtc.com	503-631-2101	631-2098	681
Clear Creek County 405 Argentine St Georgetown CO 80444 *Web:* www.clearcreekcounty.us	303-679-2312	679-2440	338
Clear Creek State Park 38 Clear Creek State Park Rd Sigel PA 15860 *Web:* www.dcnr.pa.gov	814-752-2368		565
Clear Cut Plastics Inc 507 N 36th St. Seattle WA 98103 *Web:* www.clearcutplastics.com	206-545-9131	545-7316	604
Clear Edge Technical Fabrics 7160 Northland Cir N Minneapolis MN 55428 *TF:* 800-328-3036 ■ *Web:* www.clear-edge.com	763-535-3220	535-6040	745-3
Clear Harbor LLC 3030 Royal Blvd S Ste 150 Alpharetta GA 30022 *Web:* www.clearharbor.biz	678-566-3212	566-3120	393
Clear Image Printing Inc 12744 San Fernando Rd Bldg 2 Sylmar CA 91342 *Web:* clearimageprinting.com	818-547-4684		627
Clear Labs 2529 Central Ave Saint Petersburg FL 33713 *Web:* clearlabs.org	727-289-7204		7
Clear Labs 3565 Haven Ave Ste 2 Menlo Park CA 94025 *Web:* www.clearlabs.com	650-257-3304		178-8
Clear Lake Area Chamber of Commerce 1201 NASA Pkwy Houston TX 77058 *Web:* www.clearlakearea.com	281-488-7676	488-8981	139
Clear Lake Convention & Visitors Bureau 205 Main Ave PO Box 188 Clear Lake IA 50428 *TF:* 800-285-5338 ■ *Web:* www.clearlakeiowa.com	641-357-2159	357-8141	206
Clear Lake State Park 2730 S Lakeview Dr Clear Lake IA 50428 *Web:* www.iowadnr.gov	641-357-4212		565
Clear Lake State Park 20500 M-33 N Atlanta MI 49709 *Web:* www.michigan.org	989-785-4388		565
Clear Link Technologies LLC 5202 W Douglas Corrigan Way Ste 300 Salt Lake City UT 84116 *Web:* www.clearlink.com	801-424-0018		195
Clear Path For Veterans Inc 1223 Salt Springs Rd Chittenango NY 13037 *Web:* clearpath4vets.com	315-687-3300		363
Clear Perspectives Inc 431 Ohio Pke Ste 212 Cincinnati OH 45255 *Web:* www.clearperspectivesinc.com	513-489-4040	489-4115	196
Clear Resolution Consulting LLC 5523 Research Park Dr Ste 240 Baltimore MD 21228 *Web:* www.crctoday.com	443-543-5260		196
Clear Seas Research 2401 W Big Beaver Rd Troy MI 48084 *TF:* 800-811-6640 ■ *Web:* clearseasresearch.com	248-786-1683		466
Clear Spring Publishing PO Box 91 Greene NY 13778 *Web:* www.clearspringpublishing.com	607-656-5848		637-2
Clear Technologies Inc Addison Tower 16415 Addison Rd Ste 300 Addison TX 75001 *Web:* www.cleartechnologies.net	972-906-7543		525
Clear View Bag Co 5 Burdick Dr. Albany NY 12205 *TF:* 800-458-7153 ■ *Web:* www.clearviewbag.com	518-458-7153	458-1401	66
Clear View Sanitarium & Convalescent Ctr 15823 S Western Ave Gardena CA 90247 *Web:* www.clearviewcare.com	310-538-2323	538-3509	450
Clear Water Outdoor LLC 744 W Main St Lake Geneva WI 53147 *Web:* www.clearwateroutdoor.com	262-348-2422		711
Clear Water Press (CWP) PO Box 62 Olathe KS 66051 **Fax Area Code:* 970 ■ *TF:* 888-481-4550 ■ *Web:* www.clearwaterpress.com	888-481-4550	692-2241*	637-2
Clearbit 90 Sheridan San Francisco CA 94103 *Web:* clearbit.com	415-555-1212		39
ClearBridge Compensation Group LLC 515 Madison Ave 32nd Fl. New York NY 10022 *Web:* www.clearbridgecomp.com	212-886-1022		194
Clearbridge Technology Group 6 Fortune Dr Billerica MA 01821 *TF:* 877-808-2284 ■ *Web:* clearbridgetech.com	781-916-2284		260
Clearcadence LLC 3030 N Rocky Point Dr Ste 150 Tampa FL 33607 *Web:* clearcadence.com	813-659-5405		180
Clear-Com USA 850 Marina Village Pkwy Alameda CA 94501 *TF:* 800-462-4357 ■ *Web:* www.clearcom.com	510-337-6600		392
ClearCreek Partners 1165 Delaware St Ste 130 Denver CO 80204 *Web:* clearcreekpartners.com	303-383-1100		194
Cleardata Networks Inc 101 W Sixth St Ste 310 Austin TX 78701 *TF:* 800-804-6052 ■ *Web:* cleardata.com	800-804-6052		225
ClearEdge IT Solutions LLC 10620 Guilford Rd Ste 200 Jessup MD 20794 *Web:* www.clearedgeit.com	443-212-4700		196
Clearedge Marketing LLC 415 N Lasalle St Ste 202 Chicago IL 60654 *Web:* www.clearedgemarketing.com	312-731-3149		194
ClearEdge Partners Inc 254 2nd Ave Ste 140 Needham MA 02494 *Web:* www.clearedgepartners.com	617-527-2022	527-8022	631
CLEAResult 4301 Westbank Dr Ste 300 Austin TX 78746 *TF:* 888-812-6146 ■ *Web:* www.clearesult.com	512-327-9200		194
Clearfield County 230 E Market St Clearfield PA 16830 *Web:* www.clearfieldco.org	814-765-2641	765-2640	338
Clearfield Hospital 809 Tpke Ave PO Box 992 Clearfield PA 16830 *TF:* 800-281-8000 ■ *Web:* www.phhealthcare.org	814-765-5341		374-3
ClearFreight Inc 880 Apollo St Ste 101 El Segundo CA 90245 *Web:* www.clearfreight.com	310-726-0400		345
Clearinghouse Community Development Financial Institution 23861 El Toro Rd Ste 401 Lake Forest CA 92630 *TF:* 800-445-2142 ■ *Web:* www.clearinghousecdfi.com	949-859-3600	859-8534	41
Clearlake Veterinary Corp 3424 Emerson St Clearlake CA 95422 *Web:* clearlakevetclinic.com	707-994-9100		794
Clearlight Glass & Mirror Inc 1310 Shields Rd Kernersville NC 27284 *Web:* www.clearlightglass.com	336-993-7300		362
ClearOne Communications Inc 5225 Wiley Post Way Salt Lake City UT 84116 *TF:* 800-945-7730 ■ *Web:* www.clearone.com	801-975-7200	977-0087	735
Clearpath Capital Partners 222 Front St 3rd Fl San Francisco CA 94111 *Web:* www.clearpathcapital.com	415-682-6900		627
ClearPoint Inc 19 W College Ave Ste 350 Yardley PA 19067 *Web:* www.clearpointlearning.com	201-683-9944		177
ClearSail Communications LLC 3950 Braxton Houston TX 77063 *TF:* 888-905-0888 ■ *Web:* www.clearsail.net	713-230-2800		398
Clearsign Combustion Corp 12870 Interurban Ave S Seattle WA 98168 *Web:* www.clearsign.com	206-673-4848		201
Clearspan Components Inc PO Box 4195 Meridian MS 39304 *Web:* 173.10.197.225	601-483-3941	693-7493	105
Clearspring Capital Group 11000 Richmond Ste 550 Houston TX 77042 *Web:* www.clearspringcapitalgroup.com	713-339-1903	339-1931	401
ClearStaff Inc 251 N Bolingbrook Dr. Bolingbrook IL 60440 *Web:* www.clearstaff.net	630-759-2900	759-2919	260
Clearstone Venture Partners 725 Arizona Ave Ste 304 Santa Monica CA 90401 *Web:* www.clearstone.com	310-460-7900		792
ClearStream Energy Services 311 - 6 Ave SW Ste 415 Calgary AB T2P3H2 *TF:* 855-410-9835 ■ *Web:* clearstreamenergy.ca	587-318-0997		536
ClearTech Industries Inc 2302 Hanselman Ave Saskatoon SK S7L5Z3 *Web:* www.cleartech.ca	306-664-2522		146
Cleartrack Information Network Inc 5301 Virginia Way Ste 110 Brentwood TN 37027 *TF:* 877-377-4400 ■ *Web:* www2.cleartrack.com	615-377-4400		177
ClearTrade Inc 5415 N Sheridan Rd Ste 5512 Chicago IL 60640 *Web:* www.cleartrade.com	773-561-9777		169
Clear-Vu Products Inc 29 New York Ave. Westbury NY 11590 *Web:* www.clear-vu.com	516-333-8880		601

Name / Address	City	State	Zip	Phone	Fax	Class
Clearwater County 213 Main Ave N *Web:* www.co.clearwater.mn.us	Bagley	MN	56621	218-694-6520	694-6244	338
Clearwater County 150 Michigan Ave *Web:* www.clearwatercounty.org	Orofino	ID	83544	208-476-3615	476-8902	338
Clearwater Credit Union 320 15th St *Web:* lewisclarkcu.org	Lewiston	ID	83501	208-746-9836		219
Clearwater Federal Credit Union 3600 Brooks St *Web:* missoulafcu.org	Missoula	MT	59801	406-523-3300		219
Clearwater Historical Museum (CHM) 315 College Ave *Web:* www.clearwatermuseum.org	Orofino	ID	83544	208-476-5033		520
Clearwater Marine Aquarium 249 Windward Passage *Web:* www.cmaquarium.org	Clearwater	FL	33767	727-441-1790		40
Clearwater Packaging Inc 615 Grand Central St B *TF:* 800-299-2596 ■ *Web:* www.clearwaterpackaging.com	Clearwater	FL	33756	727-442-2596	447-3587	548
Clearwater Power Co 4230 Hatwai Rd PO Box 997 *TF:* 888-743-1501 ■ *Web:* www.clearwaterpower.com	Lewiston	ID	83501	208-743-1501	746-3902	245
Clearwater Progress Inc, The PO Box 428 *Web:* www.clearwaterprogress.com	Kamiah	ID	83536	208-935-0838	935-0973	532-2
Clearwater Public Library 100 N Osceola Ave *Web:* www.myclearwater.com	Clearwater	FL	33755	727-562-4970	562-4977	434-3
Clearwater Spas 18800 Woodinville Snohomish Rd *Web:* www.clearwaterspas.com	Woodinville	WA	98072	425-481-1918		610
Clearwater-Polk Electric Co-op 315 Main Ave N *TF:* 877-881-7673 ■ *Web:* www.clearwater-polk.com	Bagley	MN	56621	218-694-6241		245
Cleary Building Corp 190 Paoli St *TF:* 800-373-5550 ■ *Web:* clearybuilding.com	Verona	WI	53593	608-845-9700		186
Cleary Gottlieb Steen & Hamilton 1 Liberty Plz *Web:* www.clearygottlieb.com	New York	NY	10006	212-225-2000		41
Cleary Millwork Company Inc 1255B Grand Army Hwy *TF:* 800-486-7600 ■ *Web:* www.clearymillwork.com	Somerset	MA	02726	800-899-4533		191-3
Cleary University 3750 Cleary Dr **Fax Area Code:* 734 ■ *TF:* 800-686-1883 ■ *Web:* www.cleary.edu	Howell	MI	48843	800-686-1883	332-4646*	800
Cleary Zimmermann Engineers Inc 1344 S Flores St *Web:* clearyzimmermann.com	San Antonio	TX	78204	210-447-6100		261
Cleasby Manufacturing Inc 1414 Bancroft Ave *TF:* 800-253-2729 ■ *Web:* www.cleasby.com	San Francisco	CA	94124	415-822-6565	822-1843	191-4
Cleaveland Price Inc 14000 Rt 993 *Web:* www.cleavelandprice.com	Trafford	PA	15085	724-864-4177	864-9040	729
Cleaver Brooks 11950 W Lake Pk Dr *Web:* www.cleaverbrooks.com	Milwaukee	WI	53224	414-359-0600		91
Cleaver Emanuel (Rep D - MO) 2335 Rayburn House Office Bldg *Web:* www.cleaver.house.gov	Washington	DC	20515	202-225-4535	225-4403	342-2
CleaverBrooks Inc 221 Law St *TF:* 800-250-5883 ■ *Web:* www.cleaver-brooks.com	Thomasville	GA	31792	229-226-3024		91
Cleburne Chamber of Commerce 1511 W Henderson St *TF:* 800-621-8566 ■ *Web:* www.cleburnechamber.com	Cleburne	TX	76033	817-645-2455	641-3069	139
Cleburne County 300 W Main St *Web:* www.cleburnecountyar.com	Heber Springs	AR	72543	501-362-8141	362-4605	338
Cleburne County 120 Vickery St *Web:* cleburnecounty.us	Heflin	AL	36264	256-463-2651		338
Cleburne State Park 5800 Park Rd 21 *Web:* tpwd.texas.gov	Cleburne	TX	76033	817-645-4215		565
Cleco Corp 2030 Donahue Ferry Rd PO Box 5000 *TF:* 800-622-6537 ■ *Web:* www.cleco.com	Pineville	LA	71361	800-622-6537		787
Cleft Palate Foundation (CPF) 1504 E Franklin St Ste 102 *TF:* 800-242-5338 ■ *Web:* www.cleftline.org	Chapel Hill	NC	27514	919-933-9044	933-9604	48-17
Cleftstone Manor 92 Eden St *Web:* www.cleftstone.com	Bar Harbor	ME	04609	207-288-8086		379
Clegg's Termite & Pest Control LLC 2401 Reichard St *Web:* www.cleggs.com	Durham	NC	27705	919-477-2134		577
Cleland Site Prep Inc PO Box 3822 *Web:* www.clelandsiteprep.com	Bluffton	SC	29910	843-987-0500	987-0600	261
Clell Wade Coaches Directory Inc 701 Main St **Fax Area Code:* 417 ■ *TF:* 877-386-4840 ■ *Web:* www.coachesdirectory.com	Cassville	MO	65625	877-386-4840	847-5920*	637-9
Clem J. Butsch General Insurance Inc 195 N Main *Web:* butschinsurance.com	Mount Angel	OR	97362	503-845-6811		390
Clemco Industries Corp I Cable Car Dr **Fax Area Code:* 800 ■ *Web:* www.clemcoindustries.com	Washington	MO	63090	636-239-4300	726-7559*	386
Clemens Construction Company Inc 1435 Walnut St 2nd Fl Drexel Bldg *Web:* www.clemensconstruction.com	Philadelphia	PA	19102	215-567-5757		186
Clement Communications Inc 3 Creek Pkwy *TF:* 800-253-6368 ■ *Web:* www.clement.com	Upper Chichester	PA	19061	610-459-4200	459-5092	637-10
Clement Industries Inc PO Box 914 *TF:* 800-562-5948 ■ *Web:* www.clementind.com	Minden	LA	71058	318-377-2776		779
Clement Manor 3939 S 92nd St *Web:* www.clementmanor.com	Greenfield	WI	53228	414-321-1800		450
Clementon Park & Splash World PO Box 125 *Web:* www.clementonpark.com	Clementon	NJ	08021	856-783-0263	783-5387	31
Clements Environmental Corp 15230 Burbank Blvd Ste 103 *Web:* clementsenvironmental.com	Sherman Oaks	CA	91411	818-267-5100		261
Clements Foods Co 6601 N Harvey Pl *Web:* www.clementsfoods.com	Oklahoma City	OK	73116	405-842-3308	843-6894	296-19
Clements Intl 1301 K St NW Ste 1200 W *TF:* 800-872-0067 ■ *Web:* www.clements.com	Washington	DC	20005	202-872-0060		390
Clements Marketplace Inc 2575 E Main Rd *Web:* www.clementsmarket.com	Portsmouth	RI	02871	401-683-0180		345
Clements, Taylor, Butkovich & Cohen Lpa Co 125 E Court St Ste 800 *Web:* ctbclawyers.com	Cincinnati	OH	45202	513-721-6500	763-6415	41
Clemm & Associates LLC 488 Norristown Rd Ste 140 *Web:* clemmlaw.com	Blue Bell	PA	19422	484-539-1300		41
Clemson University 201 Sikes Hall *Web:* www.clemson.edu	Clemson	SC	29634	864-656-3311		434-6
Cleo Parker Robinson Dance 119 Park Ave W *Web:* cleoparkerdance.org	Denver	CO	80205	303-295-1759		573-1
Clerkin, Sinclair & Mahfouz LLP 530 B St 8th Fl *Web:* clerkinlaw.com	San Diego	CA	92101	619-308-6550		41
Clermont Chamber of Commerce 4355 Ferguson Dr Ste 150 *Web:* clermontchamber.com	Cincinnati	OH	45245	513-576-5000	576-5001	139
Clermont County 101 E Main St *Web:* www.clermontcountyohio.gov	Batavia	OH	45103	513-732-7300	732-7921	338
Clermont County Convention & Visitors Bureau (CCCVB) 410 E Main St PO Box 100 *TF:* 800-796-4282 ■ *Web:* discoverclermont.com	Batavia	OH	45103	513-732-3600		206
Clermont County Public Library System 326 Broadway St *Web:* www.clermontlibrary.org	Batavia	OH	45103	513-732-2736	732-3177	434-3
Clermont State Historic Site 1 Clermont Ave *Web:* parks.ny.gov	Germantown	NY	12526	518-537-4240	537-6240	565
Clermont Steel Fabricators LLC 2565 Old SR 32 *Web:* www.clermontsteel.com	Batavia	OH	45103	513-732-6033	732-5344	480
Clermont Sun, The 465 E Main St *Web:* www.clermontsun.com	Batavia	OH	45103	513-732-2511	732-6344	532-2
Clerysys Inc 10 S Riverside Plz Ste 875 *Web:* www.clerysys.com	Chicago	IL	60606	312-474-6034		809
Cleveland Biolabs Inc 73 High St *NASDAQ: CBLI* ■ *Web:* www.cbiolabs.com	Buffalo	NY	14203	716-849-6810	849-6820	668
Cleveland Botanical Garden 11030 E Blvd *Web:* www.cbgarden.org	Cleveland	OH	44106	216-721-1600	721-2056	97
Cleveland Bradley County Public Library 795 N Church St NE *Web:* www.clevelandlibrary.org	Cleveland	TN	37311	423-472-2163		434-3
Cleveland Bros Equipment Company Inc 5300 Paxton St *TF:* 866-551-4602 ■ *Web:* www.clevelandbrothers.com	Harrisburg	PA	17111	717-564-2121		358
Cleveland Browns 76 Lou Groza Blvd *Web:* www.clevelandbrowns.com	Berea	OH	44017	440-824-3434		715-3
Cleveland Cement Contractors Inc 4823 Van Epps Rd *Web:* www.clevelandcement.com	Cleveland	OH	44131	216-741-3954	741-9278	189-3
Cleveland Chamber Symphony, The (CCS) The Music School Settlement 11125 Magnolia Dr *Web:* www.clevelandchambersymphony.org	Cleveland	OH	44106	216-202-4227		573-3
Cleveland City Hall 601 Lakeside Ave *TF:* 800-589-3101 ■ *Web:* www.cleveland-oh.gov	Cleveland	OH	44114	216-664-2000		337
Cleveland Clinic Hospital 2950 Cleveland Clinic Blvd *Web:* my.clevelandclinic.org	Weston	FL	33331	954-689-5000		374-3
Cleveland Community College 137 S Post Rd *Web:* clevelandcc.edu	Shelby	NC	28152	704-484-4000		162
Cleveland Construction Inc 8620 Tyler Blvd *Web:* www.clevelandconstruction.com	Mentor	OH	44060	440-255-8000	205-1138	189-9
Cleveland Corp 42810 N Green Bay Rd *TF:* 800-281-3464 ■ *Web:* www.clevelandcorp.com	Zion	IL	60099	847-872-7200		686
Cleveland County 2550 W Franklin Rd *Web:* clevelandcountyok.com	Norman	OK	73069	405-701-8888		338
Cleveland County PO Box 368 *Web:* www.argenweb.net	Rison	AR	71665	870-325-6214		338
Cleveland County 311 E Marion St *Web:* www.clevelandcounty.com	Shelby	NC	28150	704-484-4800	484-4930	338
Cleveland County Chamber of Commerce 200 S Lafayette St *Web:* clevelandchamber.org	Shelby	NC	28150	704-487-8521	487-7458	139
Cleveland Die & Manufacturing Co 20303 First Ave *Web:* www.clevelanddie.com	Middleburg Heights	OH	44130	440-243-3404		483
Cleveland Electric Labortories 1776 Enterprise Pkwy *Web:* www.clevelandelectriclabs.com	Twinsburg	OH	44087	330-425-4747		201
Cleveland Foundation 1422 Euclid Ave Ste 1300 *TF:* 877-554-5054 ■ *Web:* www.clevelandfoundation.org	Cleveland	OH	44115	216-861-3810		303
Cleveland Gear Co 3249 E 80th St *TF:* 800-423-3169 ■ *Web:* www.clevelandgear.com	Cleveland	OH	44104	216-641-9000	641-2731	709
Cleveland Golf Co 5601 Skylab Rd *TF:* 800-999-6263 ■ *Web:* www.clevelandgolf.com	Huntington Beach	CA	92647	800-999-6263		710
Cleveland Group CPAS & Business Advisors LLC, The 3740 Executive Center Dr *Web:* clevelandgroup.net	Augusta	GA	30907	706-288-2800		2
Cleveland Group Inc 1281 Fulton Industrial Blvd *Web:* www.clevelandelectric.com	Atlanta	GA	30336	404-696-4550		189-4
Cleveland Health Network 6000 W Creek Rd Ste 20 *Web:* www.chnetwork.com	Independence	OH	44131	216-986-1100		352

Name / Address	City	State	ZIP	Phone	Fax	Class
Cleveland HeartLab Inc 6701 Carnegie Ave Ste 500 *TF:* 866-358-9828 ■ *Web:* www.clevelandheartlab.com	Cleveland	OH	44103	866-358-9828		415
Cleveland Heights-University Heights Public Library 2345 Lee Rd *Web:* heightslibrary.org	Cleveland Heights	OH	44118	216-932-3600	932-0932	434-3
Cleveland Hopkins International Airport 5300 Riverside Dr *Web:* www.clevelandairport.com	Cleveland	OH	44135	216-265-6000	265-6021	27
Cleveland Industrial Training Ctr 1311 Brookpark Rd *Web:* www.clevelandindustrialtraining.com	Cleveland	OH	44109	216-459-9292		167-3
Cleveland Institute of Art 11141 E Blvd **Fax Area Code: 216* ■ *TF:* 800-223-4700 ■ *Web:* www.cia.edu	Cleveland	OH	44106	800-223-4700	754-3634*	164
Cleveland Institute of Electronics 1776 E 17th St *TF:* 800-243-6446 ■ *Web:* cie-wc.edu	Cleveland	OH	44114	216-781-9400	781-0331	800
Cleveland Institute of Music 11021 E Blvd *Web:* www.cim.edu	Cleveland	OH	44106	216-791-5000	791-3063	166
Cleveland International Film Festival 2510 Market Ave *Web:* www.clevelandfilm.org	Cleveland	OH	44113	216-623-3456	623-0103	282
Cleveland Metroparks Zoo 3900 Wildlife Way *Web:* www.clevelandmetroparks.com	Cleveland	OH	44109	216-661-6500		823
Cleveland Motion Controls Inc 7550 Hub Pkwy *TF:* 800-321-8072 ■ *Web:* www.cmccontrols.com	Cleveland	OH	44125	216-524-8800	642-2199	203
Cleveland Municipal School District (CMSD) 1380 E Sixth St *Web:* www.clevelandmetroschools.org	Cleveland	OH	44114	216-838-0000		685
Cleveland Museum of Art, The 11150 E Blvd *TF:* 877-262-4748 ■ *Web:* www.clevelandart.org	Cleveland	OH	44106	216-421-7350	707-6679	520
Cleveland Museum of Natural History 1 Wade Oval Dr *TF:* 800-317-9155 ■ *Web:* www.cmnh.org	Cleveland	OH	44106	216-231-4600	231-5010	520
Cleveland Orchestra, The 11001 Euclid Ave Severance Hall *TF:* 800-686-1141 ■ *Web:* www.clevelandorchestra.com	Cleveland	OH	44106	216-231-1111	231-4029	573-3
Cleveland Plant & Flower Co 12920 Corporate Dr *TF:* 888-231-7569 ■ *Web:* www.cpfco.com	Cleveland	OH	44130	216-898-3500		293
Cleveland Plumbing Supply Company Inc 143 E Washington St *TF:* 800-331-1078 ■ *Web:* www.clevelandplumbing.com	Chagrin Falls	OH	44022	440-247-2555	247-2116	612
Cleveland Pops Orchestra 24000 Mercantile Rd Unit 8 *Web:* www.clevelandpops.com	Cleveland	OH	44122	216-765-7677	765-1931	573-3
Cleveland Public Library 325 Superior Ave *TF:* 800-362-1262 ■ *Web:* cpl.org	Cleveland	OH	44114	216-623-2800	623-7015	434-3
Cleveland Public Theatre 6415 Detroit Ave *Web:* www.cptonline.org	Cleveland	OH	44102	216-631-2727	631-2575	573-4
Cleveland Punch & Die Co 666 Pratt St PO Box 769 *TF:* 888-451-4342 ■ *Web:* clevelandpunch.com	Ravenna	OH	44266	888-451-4342	451-6877	757
Cleveland Range Co 1333 E 179th St *TF:* 800-338-2204 ■ *Web:* www.clevelandrange.com	Cleveland	OH	44110	216-481-4900	481-3782	298
Cleveland Research Co 1375 E Ninth St Ste 2700 *Web:* www.clevelandresearch.com	Cleveland	OH	44114	216-649-7250		401
Cleveland Scene 737 Bolivar Rd Ste 4100 *Web:* www.clevescene.com	Cleveland	OH	44113	216-241-7550	802-7212	532-5
Cleveland Selfreliance Federal Credit Union 6108 State Rd *Web:* clevelandselfreliance.com	Parma	OH	44134	440-884-9111	884-1719	219
Cleveland State Community College 3535 Adkisson Dr *TF:* 800-604-2722 ■ *Web:* clevelandstatecc.edu	Cleveland	TN	37312	423-472-7141	478-6255	162
Cleveland State University 2121 Euclid Ave *TF:* 888-278-6446 ■ *Web:* www.csuohio.edu	Cleveland	OH	44115	216-687-2000	687-9210	166
Cleveland State University Cleveland-Marshall College of Law 1801 Euclid Ave LB 138 *TF:* 866-687-2304 ■ *Web:* www.law.csuohio.edu	Cleveland	OH	44115	216-687-2344	687-6881	167-1
Cleveland Steel Container Corp 30310 Emerald Valley Pkwy Ste 400 *Web:* www.cscpails.com	Glenwillow	OH	44139	440-349-8000	349-8101	492
Cleveland Tool & Machine 5240 Smith Rd *TF:* 800-253-4502 ■ *Web:* www.clevtool.com	Brook Park	OH	44142	216-267-6010		454
Cleveland Track Material Inc 6917 Bessemer Ave *Web:* www.clevelandtrack.com	Cleveland	OH	44127	216-641-4000	641-0882	480
Cleveland Wire Cloth & Manufacturing Co 3573 E 78th St *TF:* 800-321-3234 ■ *Web:* www.wirecloth.com	Cleveland	OH	44105	216-341-1832	341-1876	688
Cleveland/Bradley Chamber of Commerce 225 Keith St *TF:* 800-533-9930 ■ *Web:* clevelandchamber.com	Cleveland	TN	37311	423-472-6587	472-2019	139
Cleveland-Bolivar County Chamber of Commerce 101 S Bayou Ave PO Box 490 *Web:* www.clevelandmschamber.com	Cleveland	MS	38732	662-843-2712	843-2718	139
Cleveland-Cliffs Inc 200 Public Sq Ste 3300 *Web:* www.clevelandcliffs.com	Cleveland	OH	44114	216-694-5700		502
Cleveland-Cuyahoga County Port Authority 1375 E Ninth St Ste 2300 *Web:* www.portofcleveland.com	Cleveland	OH	44114	216-241-8004		618
Clever Devices Ltd 300 Crossways Pk Dr *TF:* 800-872-6129 ■ *Web:* www.cleverdevices.com	Woodbury	NY	11797	516-433-6100		180
Clever Inc 1263 Mission St *Web:* clever.com	San Francisco	CA	94103	415-701-0405		788
CleverTap 607 W Dana St *Web:* clevertap.com	Mountain View	CA	94041	415-513-5756		39
Clevest Solutions Inc 13911 Wireless Way Ste 100 *TF:* 866-915-0088 ■ *Web:* www.clevest.com	Richmond	BC	V6V3B9	604-214-9700		224
ClevrU Corp 1-564 Weber St N *Web:* www.clevru.com	Waterloo	ON	N2L5C6	519-746-1898		242
Clewiston Public Library System 120 W Osceola Ave *Web:* www.hendrylibraries.org	Clewiston	FL	33440	863-983-1493	983-9194	434-3
CLIA (Cruise Lines International Assn) 1201 F St NW Ste 250 *TF:* 855-444-2542 ■ *Web:* cruising.org	Washington	DC	20004	202-759-9370		48-23
Click Funnels 3443 W Bavaria St *Web:* www.clickfunnels.com	Eagle	ID	83616	208-323-9451		178-1
Click Model Management 129 W 27th St PH *Web:* www.clickmodelnyc.com	New York	NY	10001	212-206-1414	206-6228	506
Click2mail 3103 Tenth St N Ste 201 *TF:* 866-665-2787 ■ *Web:* click2mail.com	Arlington	VA	22201	703-521-9029		627
ClickAway Corp 457 E McGlincy Ln Ste 1 *TF:* 800-960-9030 ■ *Web:* www.clickaway.com	Campbell	CA	95008	408-626-9400		175
ClickCulture Inc 9121 Anson Way Ste 200 *Web:* www.clickculture.com	Raleigh	NC	27615	919-987-1055		7
CLICK-into Inc 8300 Woodbine Ave Ste 301 *Web:* www.click-into.com	Markham	ON	L3R9Y7	905-477-8853		180
Clicks Billiards 3100 Monticello Ave Ste 350 *Web:* clicks.com	Dallas	TX	75205	214-521-7001		659
ClickSafetycom Inc 2185 N California Blvd Ste 425 *TF:* 800-971-1080 ■ *Web:* www.clicksafety.com	Walnut Creek	CA	94596	800-971-1080		765
Clickworkercom Inc PO Box 601 *Web:* www.clickworker.com	Penfield	NY	14526	585-210-3912		307
Client Focused Media Inc 1611 San Marco Blvd *Web:* cfmedia.net	Jacksonville	FL	32207	904-232-3001		195
Client Marketing Systems Inc 880 Price St	Pismo Beach	CA	93449	805-773-7981		194
Client Services Inc 3451 Harry S Truman Blvd *Web:* www.clientservices.com	Saint Charles	MO	63301	636-947-2321		160
Client Solution Architects 52 Gettysburg Pk *Web:* csaassociates.com	Mechanicsburg	PA	17055	717-795-9104		113
Client Success Group Inc 5166 Sunny Creek Dr *Web:* www.clientsuccessgroup.com	San Jose	CA	95135	408-531-1907		194
Clientize com Inc 160 W Camino Real Ste 250 *Web:* www.clientize.com	Boca Raton	FL	33432	561-417-5533		195
Clients First Business Solutions LLC 670 N Beers St Bldg 4 *TF:* 866-677-6290 ■ *Web:* www.clientsfirst-us.com	Holmdel	NJ	07733	866-677-6290		177
Cliff Castle Casino 555 W Middle Verde Rd *TF:* 800-381-7568 ■ *Web:* www.cliffcastlecasinohotel.com	Camp Verde	AZ	86322	928-567-7999		452
Cliff House at Pikes Peak 306 Canyon Ave *TF:* 888-212-7000 ■ *Web:* www.thecliffhouse.com	Manitou Springs	CO	80829	719-785-1000		379
Cliff House Maine 591 Shore Rd *Web:* www.cliffhousemaine.com	Cape Neddick	ME	03902	207-361-1000		660
Cliff Spa at Snowbird PO Box 929000 *TF:* 800-453-3000 ■ *Web:* www.snowbird.com	Snowbird	UT	84092	801-933-2225		707
Cliff Viessman Inc 215 First Ave PO Box 175 *TF:* 800-328-2408 ■ *Web:* viessmantrucking.com	Gary	SD	57237	605-272-5241		468
Cliff Weil Inc 8043 Industrial Park Rd *TF:* 800-446-9345 ■ *Web:* www.cliffweil.com	Mechanicsville	VA	23116	804-746-1321	746-2595	543
Cliff's Amusement Park Inc 4800 Osuna Rd NE *Web:* www.cliffsamusementpark.com	Albuquerque	NM	87109	505-881-9373	881-7807	31
Cliffbreakers River Restaurant 700 W Riverside Blvd *Web:* www.cliffbreakers.com	Rockford	IL	61103	815-282-3033		671
Clifford & Rano Associates Inc 57 Cedar St *TF:* 800-660-8284 ■ *Web:* www.cliffordrano.com	Worcester	MA	01609	508-752-8284		390
Clifford Chance LLP 31 W 52nd St *Web:* www.cliffordchance.com	New York	NY	10019	212-878-8000	878-8375	428
Clifford Insurance Center Inc 9790 SE 160th Ln *Web:* cliffordinsurance.net	Summerfield	FL	34491	352-245-5455	245-9866	390
Clifford Paper Inc 600 E Crescent Ave *Web:* www.cliffordpaper.com	Upper Saddle River	NJ	07458	201-934-5115	934-5188	553
Clifford-Jacobs Forging Co 2410 N Fifth St PO Box 830 *Web:* clifford-jacobs.com	Champaign	IL	61822	217-352-5172	352-4629	483
Cliffs Club Interval Owners Assn 3811 Edward Rd *TF:* 800-367-8024 ■ *Web:* cliffsatprinceville.com	Princeville	HI	96722	808-826-6219	826-2140	653
Cliffs of the Neuse State Park 240 Park Entrance Rd *Web:* www.ncparks.gov	Seven Springs	NC	28578	919-778-6234		565
Cliffwater LLC 4640 Admiralty Way 11th Fl *Web:* www.cliffwater.com	Marina	CA	90292	310-448-5000		194
Clifton Associates Ltd 340 Maxwell Cres *Web:* www.clifton.ca	Regina	SK	S4N5Y5	306-721-7611		256
Clifton Public Library 292 Piaget Ave *Web:* www.cliftonpl.org	Clifton	NJ	07011	973-772-5500		434-3

Name / Address	Phone	Fax	Class
Clifton Savings Bancorp Inc 1433 Van Houten Ave, Clifton NJ 07013 *NASDAQ: CSBK* ■ *TF:* 888-562-6727 ■ *Web:* www.csbk.bank	973-473-2200		360-2
Clifton T. Perkins Hospital Ctr (CTPHC) 1 Renaissance Blvd, Oakbrook Terrace IL 60181 **Fax Area Code:* 630 ■ *TF:* 800-994-6610 ■ *Web:* health.maryland.gov	800-994-6610	792-5636*	374-5
CliftonLarsonAllen - CLA 301 SW Adams St Ste 1000, Peoria IL 61602 *TF:* 888-529-2648 ■ *Web:* www.claconnect.com	309-671-4500	671-4508	2
Clifty Engineering & Tool Company Inc 2949 Clifty Dr, Madison IN 47250 *Web:* www.cliftyengineering.com	812-273-3272		757
Clifty Falls State Park 1501 Green Rd, Madison IN 47250 *Web:* www.in.gov	812-273-8885		565
ClimaCool Corp 15 S Virginia, Oklahoma City OK 73106 *Web:* www.climacoolcorp.com	405-815-3000		14
Climate Design Air Conditioningln 12530 47th Way N, Clearwater FL 33762 *TF:* 888-572-7245 ■ *Web:* www.climatedesign.com	888-572-7245		189-10
Climate Engineers Inc 3005 Robins Rd, Hiawatha IA 52233 *Web:* www.climate-engr.com	319-364-1569		189-10
Climate Registry, The PO Box 811488, Los Angeles CA 90081 *TF:* 866-523-0764 ■ *Web:* www.theclimateregistry.org	866-523-0764		192
Climatec Inc 2851 W Kathleen Rd, Phoenix AZ 85053 *Web:* www.climatec.com	602-944-3330	674-1279	186
Clima-Tech 504 N Phillippi St, Boise ID 83706 *Web:* www.clima-tech.com	208-377-9755	378-8075	189-10
ClimateCraft Inc 518 N Indiana Ave, Oklahoma City OK 73106 *Web:* www.climatecraft.com	405-415-9230		610
ClimateMaster Inc 7300 SW 44th St, Oklahoma City OK 73179 *TF:* 800-299-9747 ■ *Web:* www.climatemaster.com	405-745-6000	745-2006	14
Climatemp Service Group LLC 2315 Gardner Rd, Broadview IL 60155 **Fax Area Code:* 312 ■ *Web:* climatempservice.com	708-449-8888	829-7510*	189-10
Climatronics Corp 140 Wilbur Pl, Bohemia NY 11716 *Web:* www.climatronics.com	631-567-7300		668
Climax Molybdenum Co PO Box 220, Fort Madison IA 52627 *Web:* www.climaxmolybdenum.com	602-366-8100	366-7318	502
Climbing Magazine 5720 Flatiron Pkwy, Boulder CO 80301 *TF:* 800-829-5895 ■ *Web:* www.climbing.com	303-253-6412		457-20
Clinch County 46 S College St, Homerville GA 31634 *Web:* www.clinchcounty.com	912-487-5321	487-5068	338
Cline Ben (Rep R - VA) 1009 Longworth House Office Bldg, Washington DC 20515 *Web:* www.cline.house.gov	202-225-5431		342-2
Cline Davis & Mann Inc (CDM) 220 E 42nd St 8Th Fl, New York NY 10017 *Web:* www.clinedavis.com	212-907-4300		4
Cline Design Associates of Wilmington PLLC 125 N Harrington St, Raleigh NC 27603 *Web:* www.clinedesignassoc.com	919-833-6413		314
Cline Mining Corp Heritage Bldg 181 Bay St Brookfield Pl 3rd Fl, Toronto ON M5J2T3 *Web:* www.clinemining.com	416-504-7600		501
C-Line Products Inc 1100 E Business Center Dr, Mount Prospect IL 60056 *TF:* 800-323-6084 ■ *Web:* www.c-lineproducts.com	847-827-6661	827-3329	534
Cline Resource & Development Co 430 Harper Park Dr, Beckley WV 25801	304-255-7458		194
Cline Tool & Service Co PO Box 866, Newton IA 50208 **Fax Area Code:* 641 ■ *TF:* 866-561-3022 ■ *Web:* www.clinetool.com	866-561-3022	792-0309*	493
Cline Williams Wright Johnson & Oldfather L L P 1900 USBank Bldg 233 S 13th St, Lincoln NE 68508 *Web:* www.clinewilliams.com	402-474-6900		445
Cline-Sigmon Publishers PO Box 367, Hickory NC 28603 *Web:* www.clinesigmonpublishers.com	704-528-6964	528-9563	637-2
Cling's Aerospace LLC 700 W 22nd St, Tempe AZ 85282 *Web:* clingsaz.com	480-968-1778	968-0576	454
Clingen Callow & Mclean LLC 2300 Cabot Dr Ste 500, Lisle IL 60532 *Web:* ccmlawyer.com	630-871-2600		41
Clinic Drug Store 1001 E Forsyth St, Americus GA 31709 *Web:* clinicdrugstore.net	229-924-2783		237
Clinic Service Corp 3464 S Willow St, Denver CO 80231 *TF:* 800-929-5395 ■ *Web:* clinicservice.com	303-755-2900		2
Clinical & Laboratory Standards Institute (CLSI) 950 W Valley Rd Ste 2500, Wayne PA 19087 *TF:* 877-447-1888 ■ *Web:* clsi.org	610-688-0100	688-0700	49-8
Clinical 1 Home Medical 65 Mathewson Dr Ste E, East Weymouth MA 02189 *TF:* 800-261-5737 ■ *Web:* www.clinical1.com	781-331-6856	331-4783	264-4
Clinical Immunology Society (CIS) 555 E Wells St Ste 1100, Milwaukee WI 53202 *Web:* www.clinimmsoc.org	414-224-8095	272-6070	49-8
Clinical Laboratories of Hawaii LLP 91-2135 Ft Weaver Rd Ste 195, Ewa Beach HI 96706 *Web:* www.clinicallabs.com	808-671-6191	677-2484	415
Clinical Laboratory Management Assn (CLMA) 330 N Wabash Ave Ste 2000, Chicago IL 60611 *Web:* www.clma.org	312-321-5111	673-6927	49-19
Clinical Meeting Management Inc 313 Cedar St, Bastrop TX 78602 *Web:* www.cmmglobal.com	512-303-6610		196
Clinical Pathology Laboratories Inc 9200 Wall St, Austin TX 78754 *TF:* 800-595-1275 ■ *Web:* www.cpllabs.com	512-339-1275		415
Clinical Reference Laboratory Inc 8433 Quivira Rd, Lenexa KS 66215 *Web:* www.crlcorp.com	913-492-3652	492-4308	415
Clinical Science Laboratory Inc 51 Francis Ave, Mansfield MA 02048 *TF:* 800-255-6106 ■ *Web:* clinicalsciencelab.com	508-339-6106		415
Clinicient Inc 708 SW Third Ave Ste 400, Portland OR 97204 *TF:* 855-900-9227 ■ *Web:* www.clinicient.com	503-525-0275		177
CliniComp Intl 9655 Towne Center Dr, San Diego CA 92121 *TF:* 800-350-8202 ■ *Web:* www.clinicomp.com	858-546-8202	546-1801	178-10
Clinilabs Inc 423 W 55th St, New York NY 10019 *Web:* clinilabs.com	646-215-6400	215-6401	231
CLINIQA Corp 288 Distribution St, San Marcos CA 92078 *Web:* www.cliniqa.com	760-744-1900		231
Clinique Laboratories Inc 767 Fifth Ave, New York NY 10153 *TF:* 800-419-4041 ■ *Web:* www.clinique.com	212-572-3983		214
Clinkerdagger 621 W Mallon Ave, Spokane WA 99201 *Web:* clinkerdagger.com	509-328-5965		671
Clinton Area Chamber of Commerce 721 S Second St, Clinton IA 52732 *Web:* www.clintonia.com	563-242-5702	242-5803	139
Clinton Community College 136 Clinton Pt Dr, Plattsburgh NY 12901 *TF:* 800-552-1160 ■ *Web:* www.clinton.edu	518-562-4200	562-4158	162
Clinton Correctional Facility 1156 Cook St, Dannemora NY 12929 *Web:* www.doccs.ny.gov	518-492-2511		213
Clinton County 810 Franklin St, Carlyle IL 62231 *Web:* www.clintonco.illinois.gov	618-594-2464	594-5574	338
Clinton County 1900 N Third St PO Box 2957, Clinton IA 52733 *TF:* 866-227-9040 ■ *Web:* www.clintoncounty-ia.gov	563-243-6210	242-3154	338
Clinton County 265 Courthouse Sq, Frankfort IN 46041 *Web:* www.clintonco.com	765-659-6335	659-6347	338
Clinton County 232 E Main St 3rd Fl, Lock Haven PA 17745 *Web:* www.clintoncountypa.com	570-893-4000	893-4041	338
Clinton County 207 N Main St Ste 6, Plattsburg MO 64477 *Web:* sheriff.clintoncomo.org	816-539-2156	539-2346	338
Clinton County 137 Margaret St Ste 208, Plattsburgh NY 12901 *TF:* 877-873-7283 ■ *Web:* clintoncountygov.com	518-565-4600	565-4616	338
Clinton County 100 E State St, Saint John MI 48879 *TF:* 877-543-2660 ■ *Web:* www.clinton-county.org	989-224-5140	224-5102	338
Clinton County 46 S S St, Wilmington OH 45177 *Web:* co.clinton.oh.us	937-382-2316	383-3455	338
Clinton County *Fiscal Court* 100 S Cross St, Albany KY 42602 *Web:* www.clintoncounty.ky.gov	606-387-5234	387-7651	338
Clinton County Economic Partnership 212 N Jay St, Lock Haven PA 17745 *TF:* 888-388-6991 ■ *Web:* www.clintoncountyinfo.com	570-748-5782	893-0433	139
Clinton County Electric Co-opeartive Inc 475 N Main St PO Box 40, Breese IL 62230 *TF:* 800-526-7282 ■ *Web:* www.cceci.com	618-526-7282	526-4561	245
Clinton County Historical Society Archives PO Box 174, Saint John MI 48879 *Web:* dewittlibrary.org	517-482-5117		434-3
Clinton County Regional Educatonal Service Agency Resa 1013 S US Hwy 27, Saint John MI 48879 *Web:* www.ccresa.org	989-224-6831		244
Clinton Electronics Corp 6701 Clinton Rd, Loves Park IL 61111 *TF:* 800-549-6393 ■ *Web:* clintonelectronics.com	815-633-1444		253
Clinton Family Ford Lincoln Mercury of Rock Hill Inc 1884 Canterbury Glen Ln, Rock Hill SC 29730 *Web:* www.clintonfamilyford.com	803-366-3181		57
Clinton Fences Company Inc 2630 Old Washington Rd, Waldorf MD 20601 *TF:* 800-323-6869 ■ *Web:* fencesouthernmd.com	301-645-8808		186
Clinton House State Historic Site 549 Main St PO Box 88, Poughkeepsie NY 12602 *Web:* parks.ny.gov	845-471-1630		565
Clinton Industries Inc 525 E Market St Office Bldg 1, York PA 17403 *TF:* 800-441-9131 ■ *Web:* clinton-ind.com	717-848-2391	843-5871	476
Clinton Inn Hotel 145 Dean Dr, Tenafly NJ 07670 *TF:* 800-275-4411 ■ *Web:* www.clinton-inn.com	201-871-3200	871-3435	379
Clinton Junior College 1029 Crawford Rd, Rock Hill SC 29730 *Web:* www.clintoncollege.edu	803-327-7402	327-3261	162
Clinton Lake State Recreation Area 7251 Ranger Rd, De Witt IL 61735 *Web:* www2.illinois.gov	217-935-8722		565
Clinton Local, The 108 Tecumseh St, Clinton MI 49236 *Web:* www.villageofclinton.org	517-456-4100		532-2
Clinton Memorial Hospital (CMH) 610 W Main St, Wilmington OH 45177 *TF:* 800-803-9648 ■ *Web:* www.cmhregional.com	937-382-6611		374-3
Clinton National Bank PO Box 1510, Clinton IA 52732 *Web:* clintonnational.com	563-243-1243		70
Clinton Public Library 118 S Hicks St, Clinton TN 37716 *Web:* clintonpubliclibrary.org	865-457-0519		434-3
Clinton Public Library 306 Eigth Ave S, Clinton IA 52732 *Web:* www.clintonpubliclibrary.us	563-242-8441		434-3
Clinton Public School District 201 Easthaven Dr, Clinton MS 39060 *Web:* www.clintonpublicschools.com	601-924-7533		685
Clinton Rubin LLC 5 Neshaminy Interplex Ste 205, Trevose PA 19053 *Web:* www.clintonrubin.com	215-245-2212	245-4705	180
Clinton State Park 798 N 1415 Rd, Lawrence KS 66049 *Web:* ksoutdoors.com	785-842-8562		565
Clintondale Aviation Inc 652 Rt 299 Ste 201, Highland Falls NY 12528	845-883-9657	883-5277	13
Clinton-Essex-Franklin Library System 33 Oak St, Plattsburgh NY 12901 *Web:* cefls.org	518-563-5190	563-0421	434-3
Clintonville Veterinary Hospital 300 S Main St, Clintonville WI 54929 *Web:* clintonvillevethospital.com	715-823-4747	823-1431	794
Clintrak Clinical Labeling Services LLC 2800 Veterans Hwy, Bohemia NY 11716 *Web:* www.fisherclinicalservices.com	631-467-3900		627
Clio Area School District 430 N Mill St, Clio MI 48420 *Web:* www.clioschools.org	810-591-0500		685

Name / Address	City	State	Zip	Phone	Fax	Class
Clio Awards Inc 104 W 27th St 10th Fl *Web:* clios.com	New York	NY	10001	212-683-4300		49-18
ClioSoft Inc 39500 Stevenson Pl Ste 110 *Web:* www.cliosoft.com	Fremont	CA	94539	510-790-4732	790-4740	177
Clip Shop, The 42 Spring St PO Box 697 *Web:* theclipshop.com	Williamstown	MA	01267	413-458-2411		77
Clippard Instrument Lab 7390 Colerain Ave *TF:* 877-245-6247 ■ *Web:* www.clippard.com	Cincinnati	OH	45239	513-521-4261	521-4464	223
Clipper Americas Inc 750 Town & Country Blvd Ste 550 *Web:* www.clipper-group.com	Houston	TX	77024	713-953-2200	953-2201	780
Clipper Fund 2949 E Elvira Rd Ste 101 *TF:* 800-432-2504 ■ *Web:* www.clipperfund.com	Tucson	AZ	85756	800-432-2504		528
Clipper Magazine LLC 3708 Hempland Rd *TF:* 888-569-5100 ■ *Web:* www.clippermagazine.com	Mountville	PA	17554	717-569-5100	569-5101	532-3
Clipper Navigation Inc 2701 Alaskan Way Pier 69 *TF:* 800-888-2535 ■ *Web:* www.clippervacations.com	Seattle	WA	98121	206-443-2560		771
Clipper Oil Co 2040 Harbor Island Dr Ste 203 *Web:* www.clipperoil.com	San Diego	CA	92101	619-692-9701	398-0810	580
Clips & Clamps Industries 15050 Keel St *Web:* www.clipsclamps.com	Plymouth	MI	48170	734-455-0880		488
Clixo LLC 222 Milwaukee St Ste 307 *Web:* www.clixosearch.com	Denver	CO	80206	303-632-8722		5
CLLA (Commercial Law League of America) 3005 Tollview Dr **Fax Area Code:* 847 ■ *TF:* 800-978-2552 ■ *Web:* www.clla.org	Rolling Meadows	IL	60008	312-240-1400	584-3939*	49-10
Clm Equipment Company Inc 3135 Hwy 90 E *TF:* 800-256-0490 ■ *Web:* www.clmequipment.com	Broussard	LA	70518	337-837-6693		190
CLMA (Clinical Laboratory Management Assn) 330 N Wabash Ave Ste 2000 *Web:* www.clma.org	Chicago	IL	60611	312-321-5111	673-6927	49-19
CLMI Safety Training 15800 32nd Ave N Ste 106 *Web:* www.clmi-training.com	Minneapolis	MN	55447	763-551-1022		194
Clock Family Restaurant 2010 N Main St *Web:* www.clockrestaurantfl.com	Gainesville	FL	32609	352-375-1411		671
Clock Mobility 6700 Clay Ave *TF:* 800-732-5625 ■ *Web:* www.clockmobility.com	Grand Rapids	MI	49548	616-698-9400	698-9495	62-7
Clocktower Inn Hotel 181 E Santa Clara St *Web:* www.clocktowerinn.com	Ventura	CA	93001	805-652-0141	643-1432	379
Clocktower Technology Services Inc 308 W Central St PO Box 664 *Web:* clocktowertech.com	Franklin	MA	02038	508-541-6143		525
Clockwork 4120 Yonge St *Web:* www.clockwork.ca	North York	ON	M2P2B8	416-222-8990		180
Clockwork Active Media Systems LLC 1501 E Hennepin Ave *Web:* clockwork.com	Minneapolis	MN	55414	612-746-1850		177
Clockwork Marketing Services Inc 4337 Pablo Oaks Ct Ste 103 *Web:* www.clockworkmarketing.com	Jacksonville	FL	32224	904-280-7960		636
Cloeren Inc 401 16th St *Web:* www.cloeren.com	Orange	TX	77630	409-886-5820		454
Clofine Dairy Products Inc 1407 New Rd *TF:* 800-441-1001 ■ *Web:* www.clofinedairy.com	Linwood	NJ	08221	609-653-1000	653-0127	297-4
Cloisters Museum Fort Tryon Pk *TF:* 800-662-3397 ■ *Web:* www.metmuseum.org	New York	NY	10040	212-923-3700	795-3640	520
Cloneys Pharmacy Inc 525 Fifth St *Web:* www.cloneys.com	Eureka	CA	95501	707-443-1614		237
Cloninger, Barbour, Searson, Jones, & Cash PLLC 21 Battery Park Ave Ste 201 *Web:* lawyersasheville.com	Asheville	NC	28801	828-252-5555		41
Clopay Building Products Inc 8585 Duke Blvd *TF:* 800-225-6729 ■ *Web:* www.clopaydoor.com	Mason	OH	45040	800-225-6729		234
Cloppert, Latanick, Sauter & Washburn 225 E Broad St 4th Fl *Web:* www.cloppertlaw.com	Columbus	OH	43215	614-461-4455		428
Cloquet Area Chamber of Commerce 225 Sunnyside Dr *TF:* 800-554-4350 ■ *Web:* www.cloquet.com	Cloquet	MN	55720	218-879-1551	878-0223	139
Clore Automotive 8600 NE Underground Dr Pillar 248 *Web:* www.cloreautomotive.com	Kansas City	MO	64161	816-459-2200		811
Clos du Bois 19410 Geyserville Ave *TF:* 800-222-3189 ■ *Web:* www.closdubois.com	Geyserville	CA	95441	800-222-3189		80-3
Close Family Law 727 W Hargett St Ste 205 *Web:* closefamilylaw.com	Raleigh	NC	27603	919-834-8484		41
Close Jensen & Miller PC 1137 Silas Deane Hwy *Web:* www.ctengineers.org	Wethersfield	CT	06109	860-563-9375		261
Close To My Heart 1199 W 700 S *TF:* 888-655-6552 ■ *Web:* www.closetomyheart.com	Pleasant Grove	UT	84062	888-655-6552		157-6
Close Up Foundation 1330 Braddock Pl Ste 400 *TF:* 800-256-7387 ■ *Web:* www.closeup.org	Alexandria	VA	22314	703-706-3300		48-7
Closerlook Inc 212 W Superior St Ste 300 *Web:* www.closerlook.com	Chicago	IL	60654	312-640-3700		463
Closet Factory 12800 S Broadway *TF:* 800-838-7995 ■ *Web:* www.closetfactory.com	Los Angeles	CA	90061	310-516-7000		189-11
Closets by Design Franchising 3850 Capitol Ave *TF:* 800-500-9210 ■ *Web:* www.closetsbydesign.com	Whittier	CA	90601	800-500-9210		320
Closing USA LLC 7665 Omnitech Pl *Web:* www.closingusa.com	Victor	NY	14564	585-454-1730		652
ClosingCorp Inc 6165 Greenwich Dr Ste 300 *Web:* www.closing.com	San Diego	CA	92122	858-551-1500		772
Closson Press 257 Delilah St *Web:* www.clossonpress.com	Apollo	PA	15613	724-337-4482		637-2
Clothes Out Factory Inc 34 Grazza Blvd *TF:* 877-443-7377 ■ *Web:* www.clozeout.com	Farmingdale	NY	11735	631-777-7330	777-7322	157-6
Clothing Cove, The 414 N Main St *Web:* www.theclothingcove.com	Milford	MI	48381	248-685-2500		157-6
Clothworks 6301 W Marginal Way SW *TF:* 800-874-0541 ■ *Web:* www.clothworks.com	Seattle	WA	98106	206-762-7886		258
Cloud 9 Living 11101 W 120th Ave Ste 150 *TF:* 866-525-6839 ■ *Web:* www.cloud9living.com	Broomfield	CO	80021	866-525-6839		196
Cloud 9 Wine Bar 25 E 10th St *Web:* www.cloud9erie.com	Erie	PA	16501	814-870-9007		671
Cloud Cap Technology Inc 205 N Wasco Loop Ste 103 *Web:* www.cloudcaptech.com	Hood River	OR	97031	541-387-2120	387-2030	529
Cloud County Community College 2221 Campus Dr *TF:* 800-729-5101 ■ *Web:* www.cloud.edu	Concordia	KS	66901	785-243-1435		162
Cloud Creek Systems Inc 2955 E Hillcrest Dr Ste 101 *TF:* 800-977-4130 ■ *Web:* cloudcreek.com	Westlake Village	CA	91362	818-865-2800	865-8793	180
Cloud Michael (Rep R - TX) 1314 Longworth House Office Bldg *Web:* www.cloud.house.gov	Washington	DC	20515	202-225-7742		342-2
Cloud Packaging Solutions LLC 424 Howard Ave *TF:* 888-221-0700 ■ *Web:* www.cloudeg.com	Des Plaines	IL	60018	847-390-9410	390-6170	123
Cloud Peak Energy Inc 505 S Gillette Ave PO Box 3009 **Fax Area Code:* 303 ■ *TF:* 866-470-4300 ■ *Web:* www.cloudpeakenergy.com	Gillette	WY	82717	307-687-6000	262-0604*	501
Cloudbank Books PO Box 610 *TF:* 877-782-6762 ■ *Web:* www.cloudbankbooks.com	Corvallis	OR	97339	877-782-6762		637-2
Cloudbeds 3033 Fifth Ave Ste 100 *Web:* www.cloudbeds.com	San Diego	CA	92103	858-345-5316		178-1
CloudBolt Software 6130 Executive Blvd Ste 310 *Web:* www.cloudbolt.io	Rockville	MD	20852	703-665-1060		657
CloudCheckr Inc 342 N Goodman St *TF:* 833-253-2425 ■ *Web:* cloudcheckr.com	Rochester	NY	14607	833-253-2425		387
Cloudland Canyon State Park 122 Cloudland Canyon Pk *Web:* gastateparks.org	Rising Fawn	GA	30738	706-657-4050		565
Cloud-rider Designs Ltd 1260 Eighth Ave *TF:* 800-632-1255 ■ *Web:* www.cloud-rider.com	Regina	SK	S4R1C9	306-761-2119		350
CloudVisit Telemedicine 3182 Rte 9 Ste 107A *TF:* 888-503-3009 ■ *Web:* www.cloudvisittm.com	Cold Spring	NY	10516	888-503-3009		178-1
Cloudwerx Data Solutions Inc 1440 28th St NE Ste 2 *Web:* www.cloudwerx.com	Calgary	AB	T2A7W6	403-538-6659		396
Clough State Park 455 Clough Park Rd *Web:* www.nhstateparks.org	Weare	NH	03281	603-529-7112		565
Clouse Engineering Inc 5010 E Shea Blvd *Web:* clouseaz.com	Phoenix	AZ	85028	602-395-9300		256
Cloutier Supply Co 10 Deerfield Rd *Web:* www.cloutiersupply.com	Harwich	MA	02645	508-398-2136		290
Clove Lakes Health Care & Rehabilitation Ctr 25 Fanning St *Web:* www.clovelakes.com	Staten Island	NY	10314	718-289-7900		450
Clover Farms Dairy PO Box 14627 *TF:* 800-323-0123 ■ *Web:* www.cloverfarms.com	Reading	PA	19612	610-921-9111		296-27
Clover Knits Inc 1075 Jackson Hts *Web:* www.cloverknits.com	Clover	SC	29710	803-222-3021		745-4
Clover Park Technical College 4500 Steilacoom Blvd SW *Web:* www.cptc.edu	Lakewood	WA	98499	253-589-5800		162
Clover Wireless 2700 W Higgins Rd Ste 100 *TF:* 866-734-6548 ■ *Web:* www.cloverwireless.com	Hoffman Estates	IL	60169	800-863-8023		393
Cloverdale Equipment Co 13133 Cloverdale St *TF:* 888-415-8502 ■ *Web:* www.cloverdaleequipment.com	Oak Park	MI	48237	248-399-6600	399-7730	264-3
Cloverdale Foods Co 3015 34th St NW **Fax Area Code:* 701 ■ *TF:* 800-669-9511 ■ *Web:* www.cloverdalefoods.com	Mandan	ND	58554	800-669-9511	663-0690*	296-26
Cloverhill Bakery Inc 2035 N Narragansett Ave *Web:* www.cloverhill.com	Chicago	IL	60639	773-745-9800	745-1647	296-1
Cloverland Green Spring Dairy Inc 2701 Loch Raven Rd *TF:* 800-492-0094 ■ *Web:* www.cloverlanddairy.com	Baltimore	MD	21218	410-235-4477		296-27
Clover-Stornetta Farms Inc PO Box 750369 *TF:* 800-237-3315 ■ *Web:* cloversonoma.com	Petaluma	CA	94975	800-237-3315		297-4
Clovis Adult Education 1452 David E Cook Way *Web:* clovisadult.cusd.com	Clovis	CA	93611	559-327-2800		685
Clovis Botanical Garden 945 N Clovis Ave *Web:* clovisbotanicalgarden.org	Clovis	CA	93611	559-298-3091		97
Clovis Chamber of Commerce 325 Pollasky Ave *Web:* clovischamber.com	Clovis	CA	93612	559-299-7363	299-2969	139
Clovis Community College (CCC) 417 Schepps Blvd *TF:* 800-769-1409 ■ *Web:* www.clovis.edu	Clovis	NM	88101	575-769-2811	769-4190	162
Clovis Insurance Agency Inc 2147 Herndon Ave Ste 101 *Web:* clovisinsuranceagency.com	Clovis	CA	93611	559-203-7345		390
Clovis Livestock Auction 504 S Hull St *Web:* clovislivestock.auction	Clovis	NM	88101	575-762-4422	762-4421	446

Name	Address	City	State	Zip	Phone	Fax	Class
Clovis Unified School District	1450 Herndon Ave *TF:* 877-544-6664 ■ *Web:* www.cusd.com	Clovis	CA	93611	559-327-9300	327-9339	685
Clovis/Curry County Chamber of Commerce	105 E Third St *TF:* 800-261-7656 ■ *Web:* www.clovisnm.org	Clovis	NM	88101	575-763-3435	763-7266	139
Clow Stamping Co	23103 County Rd 3 *Web:* clowstamping.com	Merrifield	MN	56465	218-765-3111		488
Clow Valve Co	902 S 2nd St **Fax Area Code:* 641 ■ *TF:* 800-829-2569 ■ *Web:* www.clowvalve.com	Oskaloosa	IA	52577	800-829-2569	673-8269*	789
Cloward H2o	2696 N University Ave *Web:* clowardh2o.com	Provo	UT	84604	801-375-1223		261
Cloyd's Beauty School	603 Natchitoches St *Web:* www.cloydsbeautyschool.com	West Monroe	LA	71291	318-322-5465		685
CLP (C.L. Pugh & Associates Inc)	1157 Pearl Rd *Web:* www.pugh.com	Brunswick	OH	44212	330-220-4404	220-4434	246
CLS (Christian Legal Society)	8001 Braddock Rd Ste 300 *TF:* 800-225-4008 ■ *Web:* www.christianlegalsociety.org	Springfield	VA	22151	703-642-1070	642-1075	49-10
CLS (California Lighting Sales Inc)	4900 Rivergrade Rd Ste D110 *TF:* 800-853-5094 ■ *Web:* www.californialightingsales.com	Irwindale	CA	91706	626-775-6000	775-6001	439
CLS (Central Lumber Sales Inc)	439 A St *Web:* www.centrallumber.com	Lincoln	NE	68542	402-474-4441	474-0595	364
CLS Group	609 S Kelly Ave Ste D *Web:* www.clsgroup.com	Edmond	OK	73003	405-348-5460		188-1
CLS Investments LLC	17605 Wright St *TF:* 888-455-4244 ■ *Web:* www.clsinvest.com	Omaha	NE	68130	402-493-3313		690
CLS Strategies	1615 L St NW 10th Fl *Web:* www.clsstrategies.com	Washington	DC	20036	202-289-5900		196
CLSA (Canon Law Society of America)	415 Michigan Ave Ste 101 *Web:* canonlawsocietyofamerica.org	Washington	DC	20017	202-832-2350		48-20
CLSI (Clinical & Laboratory Standards Institute)	950 W Valley Rd Ste 2500 *TF:* 877-447-1888 ■ *Web:* clsi.org	Wayne	PA	19087	610-688-0100	688-0700	49-8
CLT (Chesapeake Lodging Trust)	1997 Annapolis Exchange Pkwy Ste 410 *NYSE:* CHSP ■ *TF:* 800-698-2820 ■ *Web:* www.chesapeakelodgingtrust.com	Annapolis	MD	21401	571-349-9450		654
Club Cal Neva Hotel Casino, The	38 E Second St PO Box 2071 *TF:* 877-777-7303 ■ *Web:* www.clubcalneva.com	Reno	NV	89501	775-323-1046		669
Club Colors Inc	420 E State Pkwy *Web:* www.clubcolors.com	Schaumburg	IL	60173	847-490-3636		701
Club Cruise	851 Sterling Pkwy *Web:* clubcruise.com	Auburn	CA	95603	530-889-2582		772
Club Donatello Owners Assoc	501 Post St *Web:* clubdonatello.org	San Francisco	CA	94102	415-885-8847		378
Club Ed Surf School and Camps	2350 Paul Minnie Ave *Web:* www.club-ed.com	Santa Cruz	CA	95062	831-464-0177		800
Club Europa	802 W Oregon St *TF:* 800-331-1882 ■ *Web:* www.clubeuropatravel.com	Urbana	IL	61801	217-344-5863	344-4072	760
Club Furniture	11535 Carmel Commons Blvd Ste 202 *TF:* 888-378-8383 ■ *Web:* www.clubfurniture.com	Charlotte	NC	28226	888-378-8383		791
Club Greenwood	5801 S Quebec St *Web:* clubgreenwood.com	Greenwood Village	CO	80111	303-770-2582	850-9219	354
Club Managers Association of America (CMAA)	CMAA - 1733 King St *TF:* 800-409-7755 ■ *Web:* www.cmaa.org	Alexandria	VA	22314	703-739-9500	739-0124	49-12
Club Marketing Services Inc	101 W Central *Web:* www.clubmarketing.com	Bentonville	AR	72712	479-696-3100		5
Club Med Sandpiper	4500 SE Pine Valley St *Web:* www.clubmed.asia	Port Saint Lucie	FL	34952	772-398-5100		669
Club One Casino	1033 Van Ness Ave *Web:* clubonecasino.com	Fresno	CA	93721	559-497-3000		133
Club Paris	417 W 5th Ave *Web:* www.clubparisrestaurant.com	Anchorage	AK	99501	907-277-6332		671
Club Quarters Hotels	40 W 45th St *Web:* clubquartershotels.com	New York	NY	10036	212-354-6400		377
Club Soda	235 E Superior St *Web:* clubsodafortwayne.com	Fort Wayne	IN	46802	260-426-3442	426-4214	671
ClubCorp Inc	3030 Lyndon B Johnson Fwy Ste 600 *TF:* 800-433-5079 ■ *Web:* www.clubcorp.com	Dallas	TX	75234	972-243-6191		655
ClubHouse Hotel & Suites Sioux Falls	2320 S Louise Ave *Web:* siouxfalls.clubhouseinn.com	Sioux Falls	SD	57106	605-361-8700		379
ClubLink Corp	15675 Dufferin St **Fax Area Code:* 905 ■ *TF:* 800-661-1818 ■ *Web:* clublink.ca	King City	ON	L7B1K5	800-661-1818	841-1134*	655
Clubsport of San Ramon	350 Bollinger Canyon Ln *Web:* www.clubsportsr.com	San Ramon	CA	94582	925-735-8500	735-7916	354
Clusters & Hops	707 N Monroe St *Web:* www.winencheese.com	Tallahassee	FL	32303	850-222-2669	222-0469	671
Clutter Cutters LLC	9208 E State Rd 46 *TF:* 877-823-4455 ■ *Web:* www.clutter-cutters.com	Sunman	IN	47041	812-623-4455		519
Clutter Inc	3526 Hayden Ave *Web:* www.clutter.com	Culver City	CA	90232	424-343-1088		449
CLUW (Coalition of Labor Union Women)	815 16th St NW 2nd Fl *Web:* www.cluw.org	Washington	DC	20006	202-508-6969	508-6968	48-24
CLV Group Inc	485 Bank St Ste 200 *Web:* www.clvgroup.com	Ottawa	ON	K2P1Z2	613-728-2000		390
CLX Engineering	645 Hickman Cir *Web:* clxengineering.com	Sanford	FL	32771	407-878-2774		180
CLX Logistics LLC	1777 Sentry Pkwy W Abington Hall Ste 300 *TF:* 800-288-4851 ■ *Web:* www.clxlogistics.com	Blue Bell	PA	19422	215-461-3805		194
Clyburn James E (Rep D - SC)	200 Cannon House Office Bldg *Web:* clyburn.house.gov	Washington	DC	20515	202-225-3315	225-2313	342-2
Clyde Bergemann Bachmann Inc	416 Lewiston Junction Rd *Web:* www.bachmannusa.com	Auburn	ME	04210	207-784-1903	784-1904	261
Clyde Companies Inc	730 N 1500 W *Web:* www.clydeinc.com	Orem	UT	84057	801-802-6900		191-2
Clyde Cooper's BBQ	327 S Wilmington St *Web:* www.clydecoopersbbq.com	Raleigh	NC	27601	919-832-7614		671
Clyde Duneier Inc	415 Madison Ave *Web:* www.clydeduneier.com	New York	NY	10017	212-398-1122		411
Clyde Industrial LLC	36445 S Reserve Cir *Web:* www.clydeindustrial.com	Avon	OH	44011	440-653-1062		463
Clyde Machines Inc	1150 State Hwy 55 N PO Box 194 *Web:* www.clydemachines.com	Glenwood	MN	56334	320-634-4503	634-4506	470
Clyde Otis Music Group Inc	PO Box 325 *Web:* www.tcomg.com	Englewood	NJ	07631	845-425-8198		393
Clyde Peeling's Reptiland	18628 US Rt 15 *TF:* 800-737-8452 ■ *Web:* www.reptiland.com	Allenwood	PA	17810	570-538-1869		823
Clyde's Restaurant Group	3236 M St NW *Web:* www.clydes.com	Washington	DC	20007	202-333-9180	625-7429	670
Clyde's Transfer Inc	8015 Industrial Park Rd *TF:* 800-342-8758 ■ *Web:* clydestransfer.com	Mechanicsville	VA	23116	804-746-1135	746-8898	685
Clyfford Still Museum	1250 Bannock St *Web:* clyffordstillmuseum.org	Denver	CO	80204	720-354-4880		522
CM (Canadian Musician)	4056 Dorchester Rd Ste 202 **Fax Area Code:* 888 ■ *Web:* www.canadianmusician.com	Niagara Falls	ON	L2E6M9	905-374-8878	665-1307*	457-9
CM ALMY	28 Kaysal Ct **Fax Area Code:* 800 ■ *TF:* 800-225-2569 ■ *Web:* www.almy.com	Armonk	NY	10504	207-487-3232	426-2569*	155-14
CM Artists New York	127 W 96th St Ste 13 B *Web:* www.cmartists.com	New York	NY	10025	212-864-1005	864-1066	731
CM Automotive Systems Inc	120 Commerce Way *Web:* www.cmautomotive.com	Walnut	CA	91789	909-869-7912	444-1155	60
CM Bidwell & Associates Ltd	20 Old Pali Pl *Web:* www.cmbidwellandassociates.com	Honolulu	HI	96817	808-595-1099		401
CM Company Inc	431 W McGregor Ct *Web:* www.cmcompany.com	Boise	ID	83705	208-384-0800		186
CM Construction Company Inc	12215 Nicollet Ave *Web:* www.cmconstructionco.com	Burnsville	MN	55337	952-895-8223		186
CM Paula Co	6049 Hi-Tek Ct *TF:* 800-543-4464 ■ *Web:* www.cmpaula.com	Mason	OH	45040	800-543-4464		327
CM Ranch	167 Fish Hatchery Rd PO Box 217 *TF:* 800-455-0721 ■ *Web:* cmranch.com	Dubois	WY	82513	307-455-2331		239
CM Russell Museum	400 13th St N *Web:* cmrussell.org	Great Falls	MT	59401	406-727-8787	727-2402	520
CM Services Inc	800 Roosevelt Rd Bldg C Ste 312 **Fax Area Code:* 630 ■ *TF:* 800-613-6672 ■ *Web:* www.cmservices.com	Glen Ellyn	IL	60137	800-613-6672	790-3095*	47
CM Solutions Inc	2674 S Harper Rd PO Box 670 *Web:* www.cm-solutions.biz	Corinth	MS	38835	662-287-8810	287-9434	625
CM Trailers Inc	200 County Rd *TF:* 888-268-7577 ■ *Web:* www.cmtrailers.com	Madill	OK	73446	888-268-7577		779
CMA (Chicago Meat Authority Inc)	1120 W 47th Pl *TF:* 800-383-3811 ■ *Web:* www.chicagomeat.com	Chicago	IL	60609	773-254-3811	254-5851	296-26
CMA (Chamber Music America)	305 Seventh Ave 5th Fl *TF:* 888-221-9836 ■ *Web:* www.chamber-music.org	New York	NY	10001	212-242-2022	242-7955	48-4
CMA (Canadian Medical Assn)	1867 Alta Vista Dr *TF:* 800-663-7336 ■ *Web:* www.cma.ca	Ottawa	ON	K1G5W8	613-731-9331		49-8
CMA (Country Music Association Inc)	35 Music Sq E Ste 201 *Web:* www.cmaworld.com	Nashville	TN	37203	615-244-2840	726-0314	48-4
CMA (Crystal Meth Anonymous)	4470 W Sunset Blvd Ste 107 PO Box 555 *TF:* 877-262-6691 ■ *Web:* crystalmeth.org	Los Angeles	CA	90027	855-638-4373		48-21
CMA (Capital Markets Advisors LLC)	11 Grace Ave Ste 308 *Web:* www.capmark.org	Great Neck	NY	11021	516-487-9815	487-2575	345
CMA Consulting Services Inc	700 Troy Schenectady Rd *TF:* 800-276-6101 ■ *Web:* cma.com	Latham	NY	12110	518-783-9003	783-5093	177
CMA Dishmachines	12700 Knott St *TF:* 800-854-6417 ■ *Web:* www.cmadishmachines.com	Garden Grove	CA	92841	714-898-8781		386
CMA Electric LLC	Monmouth County *Web:* www.cmaelectricllc.com	Middletown	NJ	07748	732-758-8300	758-8301	189-4
Cma Engineers	35 Bow St *Web:* cmaengineers.com	Portsmouth	NH	03801	603-431-6196		261
CMAA (Club Managers Association of America)	CMAA - 1733 King St *TF:* 800-409-7755 ■ *Web:* www.cmaa.org	Alexandria	VA	22314	703-739-9500	739-0124	49-12
CMAVE (Center for Medical Agricultural & Veterinary Entomology)	1700 SW 23rd Dr *Web:* www.ars.usda.gov	Gainesville	FL	32608	352-374-5901	374-5852	668
Cmbs Medical Business Services	223 N First Ave Ste 201 *Web:* cmbsllc.net	Arcadia	CA	91006	626-821-1411		113
CMC (Catholic Medical Ctr)	100 McGregor St *TF:* 800-437-9666 ■ *Web:* www.catholicmedicalcenter.org	Manchester	NH	03102	603-668-3545		374-3
CMC (Commercial Metals Co)	6565 N MacArthur Blvd Ste 800 *NYSE:* CMC ■ *Web:* www.cmc.com	Irving	TX	75039	214-689-4300		723
CMC (Communications Manufacturing Co)	2239 Colby Ave *TF:* 800-462-5532 ■ *Web:* www.gotocmc.com	Los Angeles	CA	90064	310-828-3200		248

Company / Address	City	State	ZIP	Phone	Fax	Class
CMC (Concrete Materials Corp) 106 Industry Rd *Web:* www.concretematerialscompany.net	Richmond	KY	40475	859-623-4238	623-4255	182
CMC (California Men's Colony) Colony Dr PO Box 8101 *Web:* www.cdcr.ca.gov	San Luis Obispo	CA	93409	805-547-7900		213
CMC (Colleton Medical Ctr) 501 Robertson Blvd *TF:* 866-492-9083 ■ *Web:* colletonmedical.com	Walterboro	SC	29488	843-782-2000		374-3
CMC (Cumberland Medical Ctr) 421 S Main St *Web:* www.cmchealthcare.org	Crossville	TN	38555	931-484-9511		374-3
CMC America Corp 210 S Center St *Web:* cmc-america.com	Joliet	IL	60436	815-726-4337		362
CMC Construction Services 9103 E Almeda Rd *TF:* 877-297-9111 ■ *Web:* www.cmcconstructionservices.com	Houston	TX	77054	713-799-1150	799-8431	385
CMC Energy Services 1301 Virginia Dr Ste 250 *TF:* 800-540-5800 ■ *Web:* www.cmcenergy.com	Fort Washington	PA	19034	215-611-4856		194
CMC Howell Metal 574 New Market Depot Rd *TF:* 800-247-2048 ■ *Web:* www.howellmetal.com	New Market	VA	22844	540-740-4700	740-4778	723
CMC-KUHNKE 90 State St Ste 601 *Web:* www.cmc-kuhnke.com	Albany	NY	12207	518-694-3310		41
CMD 1631 NW Thurman St *Web:* www.cmdagency.com	Portland	OR	97209	503-223-6794	223-2430	4
CMD Corp 2901-3005 E Pershing St PO Box 1279 *TF:* 800-438-7912 ■ *Web:* www.cmd-corp.com	Appleton	WI	54912	920-730-6888		111
CMD Outsourcing Solutions Inc 729 E Pratt St Ste 700 *TF:* 888-817-7575 ■ *Web:* www.cmdosi.com	Baltimore	MD	21202	410-347-5544	347-3132	393
CMD Products 1410 Flightline Dr Ste D *TF:* 800-210-9949 ■ *Web:* www.cmdproducts.com	Lincoln	CA	95648	916-434-0228	434-0214	429
CMDA (Christian Medical & Dental Assn) 2604 Hwy 421 PO Box 7500 *TF:* 888-231-2637 ■ *Web:* www.cmda.org	Bristol	TN	37620	423-844-1000	844-1005	49-8
CME Associates Inc PO Box 5490 *Web:* www.cmeassociates.com	Syracuse	NY	13220	315-437-0050	437-0023	743
CME Group Inc 20 S Wacker Dr *NASDAQ: CME* ■ *TF:* 866-716-7274 ■ *Web:* www.cmegroup.com	Chicago	IL	60606	312-930-1000	466-4410	691
Cme Printing Inc 8181 Commerce Park Dr *Web:* cmeprinting.com	Houston	TX	77036	713-271-7700		627
CMG (Cambridge Meridian Group Inc) 2 Hancock Pk *Web:* cambridge-meridian.com	Cambridge	MA	02139	617-876-7400	497-2501	194
CMG (Color Marketing Group) 1908 Mt Vernon Ave *Web:* colormarketing.org	Alexandria	VA	22301	703-329-8500		49-18
CMG (Computer Measurement Group Inc) 3501 Rt 42 Ste 130 & 121 *Web:* www.cmg.org	Turnersville	NJ	08012	856-401-1700		48-9
CMG Environmental Inc 67 Hall Rd *TF:* 866-304-7625 ■ *Web:* www.cmgenv.com	Sturbridge	MA	01566	774-241-0901		261
CMG Worldwide Inc 10500 Crosspoint Blvd *Web:* www.cmgworldwide.com	Indianapolis	IN	46256	317-570-5000		7
CMH (Clark Memorial Hospital) 1220 Missouri Ave *Web:* www.clarkmemorial.org	Jeffersonville	IN	47130	812-282-6631	283-6330	374-3
CMH (Clinton Memorial Hospital) 610 W Main St *TF:* 800-803-9648 ■ *Web:* www.cmhregional.com	Wilmington	OH	45177	937-382-6611		374-3
CMH (Community Memorial Hospital) W 180 N 8085 Town Hall Rd *Web:* www.froedtert.com	Menomonee Falls	WI	53051	262-251-1000		374-3
CMHIFL (Colorado Mental Health Institute at Fort Logan) 3520 W Oxford Ave *Web:* www.colorado.gov	Denver	CO	80236	303-866-7066		374-5
CMHIP (Colorado Mental Health Institute at Pueblo) 1600 W 24th St *Web:* www.colorado.gov	Pueblo	CO	81003	719-546-4000		374-5
CMI (Can Manufacturers Institute) 1730 Rhode Island Ave NW Ste 1000 *Web:* www.cancentral.com	Washington	DC	20036	202-232-4677	232-5756	49-13
CMI (Cine Magnetics Inc) 9 W Broad St *TF:* 800-431-1102 ■ *Web:* www.cminyla.com	Stamford	CT	06902	203-989-9955	316-8353	658
CMI (Challenge Management Company Inc) 4000 1st National Bank Bldg *Web:* www.challenge-management.com	Dallas	TX	75202	972-755-2560		47
CMI (Central Management Inc) 820 Gessner Rd Ste 1525 *Web:* www.cmirealestate.com	Houston	TX	77024	713-961-9777		652
CMI Credit Mediators Inc 414 Sansom St *TF:* 800-456-3328 ■ *Web:* www.cmiweb.com	Upper Darby	PA	19082	610-352-5151		160
CMI Inc 316 E Ninth St **Fax Area Code: 270* ■ *TF:* 866-835-0690 ■ *Web:* www.alcoholtest.com	Owensboro	KY	42303	866-835-0690	685-6678*	529
CMI Industry Americas Inc 435 W Wilson St *TF:* 877-225-2674 ■ *Web:* johncockerill.com	Salem	OH	44460	330-332-4661		318
CMI Plastics Inc 222 Pepsi Way *TF:* 877-395-1920 ■ *Web:* www.cmiplastics.com	Ayden	NC	28513	252-746-2171		608
CMI Promex Inc 7 Benjamin Green Rd *TF:* 800-381-5808 ■ *Web:* cmi-promex.com	Pedricktown	NJ	08067	856-351-1000	351-1659	723
CMIC (Connecticut Medical Insurance Co) 80 Glastonbury Blvd 3rd Fl *TF:* 800-228-0287 ■ *Web:* www.cmic.biz	Glastonbury	CT	06033	860-633-7788	633-8237	391-5
CMJ Engineering Inc 7636 Pebble Dr *Web:* cmjengineering.com	Fort Worth	TX	76118	817-284-9400		261
CMJ LLP 276 Dix Ave PO Box 4680 *Web:* cmjllp.com	Queensbury	NY	12804	518-798-3330	798-0163	2
CMJ Marian Publishers and Distributors 10745 S Kolmar Ave *TF:* 888-636-6799 ■ *Web:* www.cmjbooks.com	Oak Lawn	IL	60453	708-636-2995	636-2855	637-2
CML (Colorado Municipal League) 1144 Sherman St *Web:* www.cml.org	Denver	CO	80203	303-831-6411	860-8175	48-6
CMLS Financial Ltd 2110 - 1066 W Hastings St Oceanic Plaza Bldg *TF:* 888-995-2657 ■ *Web:* www.cmls.ca	Vancouver	BC	V6E3X2	604-687-2118		509
CMMB (Catholic Medical Mission Board) 100 Wall St 9th Fl *TF:* 800-678-5659 ■ *Web:* www.cmmb.org	New York	NY	10005	212-242-7757		48-5
CMMG Inc 620 County Rd 118 *Web:* www.cmmginc.com	Fayette	MO	65248	660-248-2293		711
CMN (Children's Music Network, The) 10 Court St *Web:* www.cmnonline.org	Arlington	MA	02476	339-707-0277		423
CMOE Press 9146 S 700 E *TF:* 888-262-2499 ■ *Web:* www.cmoe.com	Sandy	UT	84070	801-569-3444	569-3449	637-2
C-MOR LLC 2626 W Broad St *Web:* www.childrensmuseumofrichmond.org	Richmond	VA	23220	804-474-7000	474-7099	521
CMP (Central Motive Power Inc) 6301 N Broadway *TF:* 800-822-4332 ■ *Web:* centralmotivepower.com	Denver	CO	80216	303-428-3611	428-6785	262
CMP Pharma Inc 8026 Hwy 264 Alternate *TF:* 800-227-6637 ■ *Web:* cmppharma.com	Farmville	NC	27828	252-753-7111	753-3882	582
CMPPG (Country Messenger Press Publishing Group LLC) 27657 US Hwy 97 *Web:* www.cmppg.com	Okanogan	WA	98840	253-216-6364		637-2
CMS (College Music Society) 312 E Pine St *TF:* 800-729-0235 ■ *Web:* www.music.org	Missoula	MT	59802	406-721-9616	721-9419	49-5
CMS (Carson Masonry and Steel Supply) 4783 Hwy 50 E *Web:* www.carsonmasonry.com	Carson City	NV	89701	775-882-3832	882-1654	191-1
CMS (Campaign Marketing Strategies Inc) 3240 Wilson Blvd Ste 202 *TF:* 877-267-0030 ■ *Web:* www.cmsconnects.com	Arlington	VA	22201	877-267-0030		194
CMS (Cost Management Services Inc) 2737 78th Ave SE Ste 203 *Web:* www.cmsnaturalgas.com	Mercer Island	WA	98040	206-236-8808	237-8807	196
CMS (Center for Migration Studies) *Archives Intern* 307 E 60th St 4th Fl *Web:* www.cmsny.org	New York	NY	10022	212-337-3080		434-4
Cms Communications Inc 722 Goddard Ave *TF:* 800-755-9169 ■ *Web:* www.cmsc.com	Chesterfield	MO	63005	800-755-9169		246
CMS Electric Co-opeartive Inc 509 E Carthage St *TF:* 800-794-2353 ■ *Web:* www.cmselectric.com	Meade	KS	67864	620-873-2184		245
CMS Innovative Consultants 8 Fletcher Pl *Web:* www.cmsav.com	Melville	NY	11747	631-425-3000		194
CMS Mechanical Services Inc 609 Technology Cir Ste A *Web:* www.mechanicalservicesco.com	Windsor	CO	80550	970-686-6800		610
CMS Mid-Atlantic Inc 295 Totowa Rd *TF:* 800-267-1981 ■ *Web:* www.cmsmidatlantic.com	Totowa	NJ	07512	800-267-1981		393
CMS North America 4095 Korona Ct *TF:* 800-931-6083 ■ *Web:* www.scmgroup.com	Caledonia	MI	49316	616-698-9970		358
CMS Peripherals Inc 12 Mauchly Unit E *TF:* 800-327-5773 ■ *Web:* cmsproducts.com	Irvine	CA	92618	714-424-5520		173-8
CMSA (Case Management Society of America) 6301 Ranch Dr *TF:* 800-216-2672 ■ *Web:* www.cmsa.org	Little Rock	AR	72223	501-225-2229	221-9068	49-8
CMSA Inc 2142 Palm Harbor Blvd Ste A *Web:* cmsa.com	Palm Harbor	FL	34683	727-447-3396		7
CMSD (Cleveland Municipal School District) 1380 E Sixth St *Web:* www.clevelandmetroschools.org	Cleveland	OH	44114	216-838-0000		685
CMSE (Communications Marketing Southeast Inc) 442 Cadillac Pky *Web:* cmse1.com	Dallas	GA	30157	770-443-9514	443-9513	523
CMT (Country Music Television) 330 Commerce St *Web:* www.cmt.com	Nashville	TN	37201	615-335-8400		740
CMT (Core Molding Technologies Inc) 800 Manor Pk Dr *NYSE: CMT* ■ *Web:* www.coremt.com	Columbus	OH	43228	614-870-5000	870-4029	604
CMTEL (Citizens Mutual Telephone) 114 W Jefferson St *TF:* 800-746-4268 ■ *Web:* www.cmtel.com	Bloomfield	IA	52537	641-664-2074	664-9780	224
CMTS (Children's Musical Theater San Jose) 1401 Parkmoor Ave Ste 100 *Web:* www.cmtsj.org	San Jose	CA	95126	408-288-5437		573-4
CMW (Central Maintenance & Welding Inc) 2620 E Keysville Rd *TF:* 877-704-7411 ■ *Web:* www.cmw.cc	Lithia	FL	33547	813-737-1402	737-1820	189-14
CMX Systems Inc 11161 E State Rd 70 Ste 110-127 *Web:* www.cmx.com	Lakewood Ranch	FL	34202	941-799-5640	799-5641	174
CN Staffing Inc 1201 Richardson Dr Ste 150 *Web:* www.cnstaffing.com	Richardson	TX	75080	972-484-3922		260
CNA (California Nurses Assn) 2000 Franklin St *Web:* www.nationalnursesunited.org	Oakland	CA	94612	510-273-2200	663-1625	533
CNA (Colorado Nurses Assn) 2851 S Parker Rd Ste 1210 *Web:* www.coloradonurses.org	Aurora	CO	80014	720-457-1194		533
CNA (Connecticut Nurses Assn) 377 Research Pkwy Ste 2D *Web:* www.ctnurses.org	Meriden	CT	06450	203-238-1207	238-3437	533
CNA Corp 4825 Mark Center Dr *Web:* www.cna.org	Alexandria	VA	22311	703-824-2000		668
CNA Financial Corp 333 S Wabash Ave *NYSE: CNA* ■ *TF:* 800-262-4357 ■ *Web:* www.cna.com	Chicago	IL	60604	312-822-1926		360-4

	Phone	Fax	Class
CNA National Warranty Corp 4150 N Drinkwater Blvd Ste 400 . . . . . Scottsdale AZ 85251 *TF:* 800-345-0191 ■ *Web:* www.cnanational.com	800-345-0191		390
CNB (City National Bank of New Jersey) 900 Broad St. . . . . . Newark NJ 07102 *TF:* 877-350-3524 ■ *Web:* www.citynatbank.com	973-624-0865		70
CNB Financial Corp 1 S Second St PO Box 42. . . . . . Clearfield PA 16830 *NASDAQ: CCNE* ■ *TF:* 800-492-3221 ■ *Web:* www.cnbbank.bank	814-765-9621	765-8294	360-2
CNB Technology USA Inc 2310 E Artesia Blvd . . . . . . Long Beach CA 90805 *Web:* www.cnbusa.com	562-728-8500	728-8600	693
CNBC Inc 900 Sylvan Ave. . . . . . Englewood Cliffs NJ 07632 *Web:* www.cnbc.com	201-735-2622		740
CNC Associates NY Inc 101 Kentile Rd . . . . . . South Plainfield NJ 07080 *Web:* www.cncassociates.com	718-416-3853		191-3
CNC Engineering Inc 19 Bacon Rd. . . . . . Enfield CT 06082 *Web:* www.cnc1.com	860-749-1780		256
CNC Engineering Inc 255 N Hacienda Blvd Ste 222. . . . . . City of Industry CA 91744 *Web:* cnc-eng.com	626-333-0336	369-4306	261
CNC Industries Inc 3810 Fourier Dr. . . . . . Fort Wayne IN 46818 *Web:* cncind.com	260-490-5700		111
CNC Industries Ltd 9331 39 Ave. . . . . . Edmonton AB T6E5T3 *TF:* 877-262-2343 ■ *Web:* www.cncindustries.com	780-469-2346		454
CNC Machine Products Inc 1709 W 20th St. . . . . . Joplin MO 64804 *Web:* www.cncmp.com	417-782-2627	782-3793	757
CNC Software Inc 671 Old Post Rd. . . . . . Tolland CT 06084 *TF:* 800-228-2877 ■ *Web:* www.mastercam.com	860-875-5006		225
CNE (Communication Network Engineering) 210 27th St N . . . . . . Fargo ND 58102 *Web:* cnefargo.com	701-237-3433		194
CNF (Cornell NanoScale Science & Technology Facility) Cornell University 250 Duffield Hall . . . . . . Ithaca NY 14853 *Web:* www.cnf.cornell.edu	607-255-2329	255-8601	668
CNFA (Citizens Network for Foreign Affairs) 1828 L St NW Ste 710 . . . . . . Washington DC 20036 *Web:* www.cnfa.org	202-296-3920	296-3948	48-5
CNG (Connecticut Natural Gas Corp) 76 Meadow St. . . . . . East Hartford CT 06108 *Web:* www.cngcorp.com	860-727-3000		787
CNG Engineering PLLC 1917 N New Braunfels Ave Ste 201 . . . . . . San Antonio TX 78208 *Web:* cngengineering.com	210-224-8841		261
CNGC (Cascade Natural Gas Corp) 8113 W Grandridge Blvd . . . . . . Kennewick WA 99336 **Fax Area Code: 206* ■ *TF:* 888-522-1130 ■ *Web:* www.cngc.com	888-522-1130	624-7215*	787
CNI Ag 800 Business Pk Dr Hwy 82 W . . . . . . Leesburg GA 31763 *Web:* www.cniag.com	229-883-7050	439-0842	276
CNI Distribution 5584 Mt View Rd . . . . . . Antioch TN 37013 *Web:* www.cnidist.com	615-641-5550	641-5566	523
Cnic Inc 4418 Monroe Rd E . . . . . . Charlotte NC 28205 *Web:* www.cnic-inc.com	704-344-0090		175
CNL Financial Group Inc 450 S Orange Ave. . . . . . Orlando FL 32801 **Fax Area Code: 800* ■ *Web:* www.cnl.com	407-650-1000	522-3863*	360-2
CNME (Council on Naturopathic Medical Education) PO Box 178 . . . . . . Great Barrington MA 01230 *Web:* cnme.org	413-528-8877		48-1
CNP Signs & Graphics 4530 Mission Gorge Pl. . . . . . San Diego CA 92120 *Web:* www.cnpsigns.com	619-283-2191		701
CNP Technologies LLC 806 Tyvola Rd Ste 102 . . . . . . Charlotte NC 28217 *TF:* 888-973-3737 ■ *Web:* www.cnp.net	704-927-6600		180
CNRL (Canadian Natural Resources Ltd) 855 Second St SW Ste 2100. . . . . . Calgary AB T2P4J8 *NYSE: CNQ* ■ *TF:* 888-878-3700 ■ *Web:* www.cnrl.com	403-517-6700	517-7350	536
CNS Response Inc 85 Enterprise Ste 410. . . . . . Aliso Viejo CA 92656 *Web:* www.cnsresponse.com	949-420-4400		250
CNS Therapeutics Inc 332 Minnesota St W1750. . . . . . Saint Paul MN 55101 *Web:* www.gablofen.com	651-207-6959		231
CNY Biotech Accelerator 841 E Fayette St . . . . . . Syracuse NY 13210 *Web:* cnybac.com	315-464-9288		196
Co Do Vietnamese 1411 17th Ave SW . . . . . . Calgary AB T2T0C6 *Web:* www.codovietnamese.com	403-228-7798		671
COA (Council on Accreditation) 45 Broadway 29th Fl. . . . . . New York NY 10006 *TF:* 866-262-8088 ■ *Web:* www.coanet.org	212-797-3000	797-1428	48-1
Coach & Equipment Manufacturing Corp 130 Horizon Pk Dr PO Box 36 . . . . . . Penn Yan NY 14527 *TF:* 800-724-8464 ■ *Web:* www.coachandequipment.com	315-536-2321		516
Coach & Four Restaurant 5206 Williamson Rd. . . . . . Roanoke VA 24012 *Web:* www.coachandfour.com	540-362-4220		671
Coach House Inc 3480 Technology Dr . . . . . . Nokomis FL 34275 *TF:* 800-235-0984 ■ *Web:* www.coachhouserv.com	941-485-0984		120
Coach House Theatre 732 W Exchange St. . . . . . Akron OH 44302 *Web:* www.akronwomanscityclub.org	330-434-7741		572
Coach Inc 342 Madison Ave. . . . . . New York NY 10173 *NYSE: COH* ■ *TF:* 800-444-3611 ■ *Web:* world.coach.com	212-599-4777	594-1682	430
Coach Stop Inn 715 State Hwy 3. . . . . . Bar Harbor ME 04609 *Web:* coachstopinn.com	207-288-9886		378
Coach Tours Ltd 475 Federal Rd. . . . . . Brookfield CT 06804 *TF:* 800-822-6224 ■ *Web:* www.coachtour.com	203-740-1118		760
Coach USA 160 S Rt 17 N. . . . . . Paramus NJ 07652 *TF:* 800-877-1888 ■ *Web:* www.coachusa.com	201-225-7500		468
Coachella Valley History Museum 82616 Miles Ave. . . . . . Indio CA 92201 *Web:* www.cvhm.org	760-342-6651	863-5232	520
Coachella Valley Unified School District 87-225 Church St. . . . . . Thermal CA 92274 *Web:* www.cvusd.us	760-399-5137	399-1052	685
Coachman Inn 32959 SR-Hwy 20 . . . . . . Oak Harbor WA 98277 *Web:* www.thecoachmaninn.com	360-675-0727		379
CoachNow 80 E Rio Salado Pkwy. . . . . . Tempe AZ 85281 *TF:* 888-414-7276 ■ *Web:* coachnow.io	888-414-7276		387
Coact Associates Ltd 2748 Centennial Rd . . . . . . Toledo OH 43617 *TF:* 866-646-4400 ■ *Web:* teamcoact.com	866-646-4400		196
COACT Inc 9140 Guilford Rd Ste N. . . . . . Columbia MD 21046 *Web:* coact.com	301-498-0150		743
Co-Advantage Resources 3350 Buschwood Park Dr Ste 200 . . . . . . Tampa FL 33618 *TF:* 800-868-1016 ■ *Web:* www.coadvantage.com	855-351-4731		631
CoAEMSP 8301 Lakeview Pkwy Ste 111-312 . . . . . . Rowlett TX 75088 **Fax Area Code: 214* ■ *Web:* www.coaemsp.org	817-330-0080	703-8992*	48-1
Coahoma Community College 3240 Friars Point Rd. . . . . . Clarksdale MS 38614 *Web:* www.coahomacc.edu	662-627-2571		162
Coahoma County 115 First St PO Box 98. . . . . . Clarksdale MS 38614 *Web:* www.coahomacounty.net	662-624-3000	624-3040	338
Coahoma Electric Power Assn 340 Hopson St . . . . . . Lyon MS 38645 *Web:* www.coahomaepa.com	662-624-8321		245
Coair Industrial Air Compressor & Sandblasting 5405 Sarosto St . . . . . . Levis QC G6V5B6 *TF:* 888-835-0141 ■ *Web:* www.coair.qc.ca	418-835-0141	835-0297	358
Coakley & Williams Construction Inc 7475 Wisconsin Ave Ste 900 . . . . . . Bethesda MD 20814 *Web:* coakleywilliams.com	301-963-5000		187
Coakley & Williams Hotel Management 6404 Ivy Ln Ste 720 . . . . . . Greenbelt MD 20770 *Web:* cwhotels.com	301-474-6200	614-8836	378
Coal Leader Inc 222 Sunny Hills Dr. . . . . . Cedar Bluff VA 24609 *Web:* www.coalleader.com	276-964-6363	964-6342	532-2
Coal Valley News 350 Main St. . . . . . Madison WV 25130 *Web:* www.loganbanner.com	304-369-1165	369-1166	532-4
Coalesce Corp 447 Miller Ave Ste E . . . . . . Mill Valley CA 94941 *Web:* www.coalesce.com	415-384-3040		195
Coalesce Marketing & Design Inc 4321 W College Ave Ste 250 . . . . . . Appleton WI 54914 *Web:* coalescemarketing.com	920-380-4444		194
Coalfire Systems Inc 361 Centennial Pkwy Ste 150. . . . . . Louisville CO 80027 *Web:* www.coalfire.com	303-554-6333		180
Coalition Against Bigger Trucks (CABT) 109 N Fairfax St 2nd Fl. . . . . . Alexandria VA 22314 *TF:* 888-222-8123 ■ *Web:* cabt.org	703-535-3131		49-21
Coalition Against Insurance Fraud 1012 14th St NW Ste 200. . . . . . Washington DC 20005 *TF:* 800-835-6422 ■ *Web:* www.insurancefraud.org	202-393-7330	318-9189	49-9
Coalition for Auto Repair Equality (CARE) 105 Oronoco St Ste 115 . . . . . . Alexandria VA 22314 *TF:* 800-229-5380 ■ *Web:* www.careauto.org	703-519-7555	519-7747	49-21
Coalition for Buzzards Bay Inc, The 114 Front St . . . . . . New Bedford MA 02740 *Web:* www.savebuzzardsbay.org	508-999-6363		804
Coalition for Government Procurement 1990 M St NW Ste 450. . . . . . Washington DC 20036 *Web:* thecgp.org	202-331-0975	822-9788	49-18
Coalition for Networked Information 21 Dupont Cir. . . . . . Washington DC 20036 *Web:* www.cni.org	202-296-5098	872-0884	48-9
Coalition for Responsible Waste Incineration (CRWI) 1615 L St NW Ste 1350 . . . . . . Washington DC 20036 *Web:* www.crwi.org	202-452-1241		48-13
Coalition of Health Services Inc 301 S Polk St Ste 740. . . . . . Amarillo TX 79101 *TF:* 800-442-7893 ■ *Web:* www.cohs.net	806-337-1700		463
Coalition of Labor Union Women (CLUW) 815 16th St NW 2nd Fl. . . . . . Washington DC 20006 *Web:* www.cluw.org	202-508-6969	508-6968	48-24
Coalition on Human Needs (CHN) 1120 Connecticut Ave NW . . . . . . Washington DC 20036 *TF:* 888-668-8919 ■ *Web:* www.chn.org	202-223-2532	223-2538	48-5
Coalition to Stop Gun Violence 805 15th St NW . . . . . . Washington DC 20005 *Web:* www.csgv.org	202-408-0061		48-7
Co-Alliance LLP 5250 E US Hwy 36 Bldg 1000 . . . . . . Avon IN 46123 *TF:* 800-525-0272 ■ *Web:* www.co-alliance.com	317-745-4491	718-1850	275
Coan Construction Company Inc 1481 E Grand Ave. . . . . . Pomona CA 91766 *Web:* www.coanconstruction.com	909-868-6812		121
Coan Engineering LLC 2277 E North St. . . . . . Kokomo IN 46901 *Web:* www.coanracing.com	765-456-3957		54
Co-Anon Family Groups PO Box 3664. . . . . . Gilbert AZ 85299 *Web:* www.co-anon.org	480-442-3869		48-21
Coast 1054 Alberni St. . . . . . Vancouver BC V6E1A3 *Web:* www.glowbalgroup.com	604-685-5010		671
Coast 102 10250 Lorraine Rd. . . . . . Gulfport MS 39503 *TF:* 800-813-6884 ■ *Web:* coast102.com	228-896-5500		645-66
Coast 2 Coast 7704 Basswood Dr. . . . . . Chattanooga TN 37416 *Web:* www.coast2coast.net	423-296-9000		701
Coast Aluminum & Architectural Inc 30551 Huntwood Ave . . . . . . Hayward CA 94544 *Web:* coastaluminum.com	510-441-6600		492
Coast Appliance Parts Co 2606 Lee Ave . . . . . . South El Monte CA 91733 *TF:* 800-821-0244 ■ *Web:* www.coastparts.com	626-579-1500		246
Coast Capital Savings 800-9900 King George Blvd. . . . . . Surrey BC V3T0K7 *TF:* 888-517-7000 ■ *Web:* www.coastcapitalsavings.com	250-483-7000		70
Coast Central Credit Union Inc 2650 Harrison Ave . . . . . . Eureka CA 95501 *TF:* 800-974-9727 ■ *Web:* www.coastccu.org	707-445-8801		219
Coast Communications Company Inc 349 Damon Rd . . . . . . Ocean Shores WA 98569 *Web:* www.coastaccess.com	360-289-2252		116

Name / Address	City	State	Zip	Phone	Fax	Class
Coast Dental Services Inc 4010 W Boy Scout Blvd Ste 1100 *Web:* www.coastdental.com	Tampa	FL	33607	813-288-1999	289-4500	463
Coast Electric Power Assn 18020 Hwy Ste 603 *TF:* 877-769-2372 ■ *Web:* coastepa.com	Kiln	MS	39556	228-363-7000		245
Coast Guard Exchange System 510 Independence Pkwy Ste 500 *TF:* 800-572-0230 ■ *Web:* shopcgx.com	Chesapeake	VA	23320	800-572-0230		791
Coast Guard Sector Detroit 110 Mt Elliott Ave *Web:* www.uscg.mil	Detroit	MI	48207	313-568-9525		158
Coast Hotels 600 Stewart St Ste 1920 *Web:* www.coasthotels.com	Seattle	WA	98101	206-826-2700	826-2701	379
Coast Industrial Sales Inc 1630 S Sunkist St Unit T *Web:* coastindustrialsales.com	Anaheim	CA	92806	714-282-6711		366
Coast Packing Co 3275 E Vernon Ave *Web:* coastpacking.com	Vernon	CA	90058	323-277-7700		296-12
Coast Personnel 2295 De La Cruz Blvd *Web:* www.coastjobs.com	Santa Clara	CA	95050	408-653-2100		260
Coast Plaza Doctors Hospital Inc 13100 Studebaker Rd *Web:* avantihospitals.com	Norwalk	CA	90650	562-868-3751		374-3
Coast Plaza Hotel 1316 33 St NE *Web:* www.calgaryplaza.com	Calgary	AB	T2A6B6	403-248-8888		379
Coast Pneumatics 8055 E Crystal Dr *TF:* 888-918-8432 ■ *Web:* www.coastpneumatics.com	Anaheim	CA	92807	714-921-2255		358
Coast Powder Coating 227 Calle Pintoresco *Web:* www.coastpowdercoating.com	San Clemente	CA	92672	949-492-9037	492-9038	481
Coast Produce Co 1791 Bay St *Web:* coastproduce.com	Los Angeles	CA	90021	213-955-4900		10-11
COAST Products Inc 8033 NE Holman St *TF:* 800-426-5858 ■ *Web:* coastportland.com	Portland	OR	97218	800-426-5858		362
Coast Professional Inc 214 Expo Cir Ste 7 *TF:* 800-231-0225 ■ *Web:* www.coastprofessional.net	West Monroe	LA	71202	318-807-4500	807-6398	160
Coast Property Management 2829 Rucker Ave *TF:* 800-339-3634 ■ *Web:* www.coastmgt.com	Everett	WA	98201	800-339-3634		652
Coast Pump Water Technologies Inc 210 Center Ct *Web:* www.coastpumpwatertechnology.com	Venice	FL	34285	941-484-3738		429
Coast Sign Inc 1500 W Embassy St *Web:* www.coastsign.com	Anaheim	CA	92802	714-520-9144	520-5847	9
Coast Surveying Inc 15031 Pkwy Loop Ste B *Web:* coastsurvey.com	Tustin	CA	92780	714-918-6266		727
Coast to Coast Business Equipment Inc 8 Vanderbilt *Web:* www.ctcbe.com	Irvine	CA	92619	949-457-7300		589
Coast to Coast Corporate Housing 10773 Los Alamitos Blvd **Fax Area Code:* 562 ■ *TF:* 800-451-9466 ■ *Web:* www.ctchousing.com	Los Alamitos	CA	90720	800-451-9466	795-0251*	210
Coast to Coast Moving & Storage Co 136 41st St *TF:* 800-872-6683 ■ *Web:* www.ctcvanlines.com	Brooklyn	NY	11232	718-443-5800		519
Coast2Coast Diagnostics Inc 600 N Tustin Ave Ste 110 *TF:* 800-730-9263 ■ *Web:* www.c2cdiagnostics.net	Santa Ana	CA	92705	800-730-9263		415
Coastal Administrative Services (CAS) PO Box 3070 **Fax Area Code:* 360 ■ *TF:* 800-870-1831 ■ *Web:* www.casbenefits.com	Bellingham	WA	98227	800-870-1831	746-8386*	260
Coastal Agrobusiness Inc 112 Staton Rd *TF:* 800-758-1828 ■ *Web:* www.coastalagro.com	Greenville	NC	27834	252-756-1126	756-3282	280
Coastal Alabama Community College 1900 Hwy 31 S *TF:* 800-381-3722 ■ *Web:* www.coastalalabama.edu	Bay Minette	AL	36507	800-381-3722		162
Coastal Bend Blood Ctr 209 N Padre Island Dr *TF:* 800-299-4943 ■ *Web:* www.coastalbendbloodcenter.org	Corpus Christi	TX	78406	361-855-4943		89
Coastal Bend College *Beeville* 3800 Charco Rd *TF:* 866-722-2838 ■ *Web:* coastalbend.edu	Beeville	TX	78102	361-358-2838	354-2254	162
Coastal Bend Tooling & Automation 510 S Staples St *Web:* www.coastalbendtooling.com	Corpus Christi	TX	78401	361-883-0376	883-2346	494
Coastal Beverage Company Inc 461 N Corporate Dr *Web:* www.coastalbev.com	Wilmington	NC	28405	910-799-3011	392-3674	81-1
Coastal Bridge Company LLC 4825 Jamestown Ave PO Box 14715 *Web:* www.coastalbridge.com	Baton Rouge	LA	70808	225-766-0244	766-0423	46
Coastal Building Maintenance 8651 NW 70th St *TF:* 800-357-7790 ■ *Web:* www.cbmflorida.com	Miami	FL	33166	305-681-6100	681-3584	104
Coastal Carolina Community College 444 Western Blvd *Web:* www.coastalcarolina.edu	Jacksonville	NC	28546	910-455-1221	455-7027	162
Coastal Carolina University PO Box 261954 *TF:* 800-277-7000 ■ *Web:* www.coastal.edu	Conway	SC	29528	843-349-2170	349-2127	166
Coastal Carriers Inc 120 Hammer Ln **Fax Area Code:* 636 ■ *TF:* 877-848-8726 ■ *Web:* www.coastalcarriers.com	Troy	MO	63379	877-848-8726	528-5879*	780
Coastal Casting Service Inc 2903 Gano St *TF:* 800-433-6223 ■ *Web:* coastalcasting.com	Houston	TX	77009	713-223-4439		757
Coastal Cement Corp 36 Drydock Ave *Web:* www.dragonproducts.com	Boston	MA	02210	617-350-0183		135
Coastal Community & Teachers Credit Union 6810 Saratoga Blvd *Web:* myccatcu.com	Corpus Christi	TX	78414	361-985-6810		219
Coastal Conservation Assn (CCA) 6919 Portwest Dr Ste 100 *Web:* www.joincca.org	Houston	TX	77024	713-626-4234	626-5852	48-13
Coastal Corrosion Control Surveys LLC 10172 Mammoth Ave *TF:* 800-894-2120 ■ *Web:* coastalcorrosion.com	Baton Rouge	LA	70814	225-275-6131		492
Coastal Electric Co-op 1265 S Coastal Hwy *TF:* 800-421-2343 ■ *Web:* coastalelectriccooperative.com	Midway	GA	31320	912-884-3311		245
Coastal Electric Co-opeartive Inc 2269 Jefferies Hwy *Web:* www.coastal.coop	Walterboro	SC	29488	843-538-5700		245
Coastal Elite Veterinary Services 3701 Rte 9 *Web:* www.coastalelitevet.com	Howell Township	NJ	07731	732-780-7563	780-5265	794
Coastal Engineering Consultants Inc 3106 S Horseshoe Dr *Web:* coastalengineering.com	Naples	FL	34104	239-643-2324	643-1143	196
Coastal Environmental Systems Inc 820 First Ave S *TF:* 800-488-8291 ■ *Web:* www.coastalenvironmental.com	Seattle	WA	98134	206-682-6048	682-5658	407
Coastal Federal Credit Union 1000 St Albans Dr *TF:* 800-868-4262 ■ *Web:* www.coastal24.com	Raleigh	NC	27609	919-420-8000		219
Coastal Flow Measurement Inc 2222 Bay Area Blvd Ste 200 *TF:* 800-231-9741 ■ *Web:* www.coastalflow.com	Houston	TX	77058	281-282-0622	282-0792	201
Coastal Georgia Historical Society (CGHS) A.W. Jones Heritage Ctr 601 Beachview Dr *Web:* www.saintsimonslighthouse.org	Saint Simons Island	GA	31522	912-638-4666	638-6609	637-2
Coastal Harbor Treatment Ctr 1150 Cornell St *TF:* 844-657-2638 ■ *Web:* coastalharbor.com	Savannah	GA	31406	912-354-3911		374-5
Coastal Healthcare Consulting Inc 6808 220th St SW Ste 204 *Web:* www.coastalhealthcare.com	Mountlake Terrace	WA	98043	206-324-6540		196
Coastal Helicopters Inc 8995 Yandukin Dr *TF:* 800-789-5610 ■ *Web:* www.coastalhelicopters.com	Juneau	AK	99801	907-789-5600		359
Coastal Hospice & Palliative Care 2604 Old Ocean City Rd PO Box 1733 *TF:* 800-780-7886 ■ *Web:* coastalhospice.org	Salisbury	MD	21804	410-742-8732		371
Coastal Inn Concorde 379 Windmill Rd *TF:* 800-565-1565 ■ *Web:* coastalinns.com	Dartmouth	NS	B3A1J6	800-565-1565		379
Coastal Logistics Group Inc 5715 Distribution Dr *Web:* www.clg-sav.com	Garden City	GA	31408	912-964-0707		194
Coastal Maine Botanical Gardens PO Box 234 *Web:* www.mainegardens.org	Boothbay	ME	04537	207-633-4333	633-2366	97
Coastal Manufacturing Inc 6700 Hardeson Rd Ste 103 *Web:* www.coastal-mfg.com	Everett	WA	98203	425-407-0624		105
Coastal Mechanical Services LLC 394 E Dr *TF:* 866-584-9528 ■ *Web:* www.coastalmechanical.com	Melbourne	FL	32904	321-725-3061	984-0718	189-10
Coastal Mountain Fuels 501 Industrial Park Pl *TF:* 800-798-3835 ■ *Web:* www.cmfuels.ca	Gold River	BC	V0P2G0	800-798-3835		536
Coastal Outdoor Advertising 2024 Corporate Centre Dr Ste 206 *Web:* youroutdoorvoice.com	Myrtle Beach	SC	29577	843-692-2334		8
Coastal Pacific Food Distributors Inc (CPFD) 1015 Performance Dr *TF:* 800-500-2611 ■ *Web:* www.cpfd.com	Stockton	CA	95206	209-983-2454		297-8
Coastal Palms Hotel 120th St Coastal Hwy *TF:* 800-641-0011 ■ *Web:* coastalpalmshotel.com	Ocean City	MD	21842	800-641-0011		379
Coastal Plain Ventures LLC 211 Broad Hollow Rd *Web:* www.amsteelpro.com	Swainsboro	GA	30401	706-413-3806		234
Coastal Plastics Inc 35 Mechanic St *Web:* www.coastalplasticsinc.com	Hope Valley	RI	02832	401-539-2446	539-0055	605-2
Coastal Printing 1730 Independence Blvd *Web:* coastalprint.com	Sarasota	FL	34234	941-351-1515		627
Coastal Reprographics Services 880 Via Esteban Ste B *Web:* gocrs.com	San Luis Obispo	CA	93401	805-543-5247		113
Coastal Software & Consulting Inc PO Box 872106 *Web:* www.coastalsoftware.com	Vancouver	WA	98687	360-891-6174		177
Coastal Steel Inc 870 Cidco Rd *Web:* www.coastalsteel.com	Cocoa	FL	32923	407-827-4309		480
Coastal Supply Group 480 Bay St *Web:* www.coastalsupplygroup.com	Staten Island	NY	10304	718-447-2692		612
Coastal Tag & Label Inc 13233 Barton Cir *Web:* www.coastaltag.com	Santa Fe Springs	CA	90670	562-946-4318		627
Coastal Technologies 615 Valley Rd *Web:* www.coastaltech.com	Montclair	NJ	07043	973-744-2900		177
Coastal Television Broadcasting Co 2700 East Tudor Rd *Web:* www.youralaskalink.com	Anchorage	AK	99507	907-561-1313		739
Coastal Timbers Inc 1310 Jane St *Web:* www.coastaltimbers.com	New Iberia	LA	70563	337-369-3017	365-0003	683
Coastal Tractor Inc 10 Harris Pl *Web:* www.coastaltractor.com	Salinas	CA	93901	831-757-4101		57
Coastal Training Technologies Corp 500 Studio Dr *TF:* 866-333-6888 ■ *Web:* www.coastal.com	Virginia Beach	VA	23452	757-498-9014		513
Coastal Transport Company Inc 1603 Ackerman Rd *TF:* 800-523-8612 ■ *Web:* coastaltransport.com	San Antonio	TX	78219	210-661-4287		780
Coastal Transportation Inc 4025 13th Ave W *TF:* 800-544-2580 ■ *Web:* www.coastaltransportation.com	Seattle	WA	98119	206-282-9979	283-9121	312

Name / Address	Phone	Fax	Class
Coastal Truck Driving School 4016 Canal St New Orleans LA 70119 TF: 800-486-3639 ■ Web: www.coastaltruckdriving.net	504-486-3639	486-3562	685
Coastal View 4856 Carpinteria Ave Carpinteria CA 93013 Web: www.coastalview.com	805-684-4428		532-2
Coastline Community College 11460 Warner Ave Fountain Valley CA 92708 TF: 866-422-2645 ■ Web: www.coastline.edu	714-546-7600	241-6288	162
Coastline Equipment 1930 Lockwood St Oxnard CA 93036 Web: www.coastlineequipment.com	805-485-2106		57
Coastline Law Group PLLC 4015 Ruston Way Ste 200 Tacoma WA 98402 Web: coastlinelaw.com	253-203-6226	276-2642	41
Coates & Davenport PC 5206 Markel Rd Richmond VA 23230 Web: coateslaw.com	804-285-7000	285-2849	41
Coates Field Service Inc 4800 N Santa Fe Oklahoma City OK 73118 Web: www.coatesfs.com	405-528-5676		194
Coates Kokes 421 SW 6th Ave Ste 1300 Portland OR 97204 Web: www.coateskokes.com	503-241-1124	241-1326	4
Coating & Adhesive Corp (CAC) 1901 Popular St PO Box 1080 Leland NC 28451 TF: 800-410-2999 ■ Web: www.cacoatings.com	910-371-3184	371-5580	550
Coating Place Inc 200 Paoli St Verona WI 53593 Web: www.coatingplace.com	608-845-9521	845-9526	582
Coating Systems Laboratories Inc 211 E Chilton Dr Chandler AZ 85225 TF: 888-777-0898 ■ Web: www.coatingsystemslaboratories.com	480-503-0267	503-4628	536
Coating Technology Inc 800 Saint Paul St Rochester NY 14605 Web: www.ctiroc.com	585-546-7170	546-7202	481
Coatings For Industry Inc (CFI) 319 Township Line Rd Souderton PA 18964 TF: 877-723-0919 ■ Web: www.coating4ind.com	215-723-0919	723-0911	481
Coatings Resource Corp 15541 Commerce Ln Huntington Beach CA 92649 Web: www.coatingsresource.com	714-894-5252	893-2322	550
Coats North America 14120 Ballantyne Corporate Pl Ste 300 Charlotte NC 28277 TF: 800-631-0965 ■ Web: www.coats.com	704-329-5800		745-9
Coaxial Dynamics 6800 Lake Abrams Dr Middleburg Heights OH 44130 TF: 800-262-9425 ■ Web: www.coaxial.com	440-243-1100	243-1101	647
Coaxis Inc 1515 SE Water Ave Ste 300 Portland OR 97214 TF: 800-333-3197 ■ Web: viewpoint.com	800-333-3197		177
Coaxis Intl 1816 Old St Augustine Rd Tallahassee FL 32301 Web: www.coaxiscloud.com	850-391-1022	391-1023	180
Coba Cosmetology Academy 102 N Glassell St Orange CA 92866 Web: www.coba.edu	714-633-5950	633-4139	167-3
COBA/Select Sires Inc 1224 Alton Darby Creek Rd Columbus OH 43228 TF: 800-837-2621 ■ Web: www.cobaselect.com	614-878-5333	870-2622	11-2
Cobalt Boats LLC 1715 N Eigth St Neodesha KS 66757 TF: 800-468-5764 ■ Web: cobaltboats.com	620-325-2653	325-2361	90
Cobalt Digital Inc 2506 Galen Dr Champaign IL 61821 TF: 800-669-1691 ■ Web: www.cobaltdigital.com	217-344-1243	344-1245	647
Cobalt Software Inc 2 Financial Ctr 60 S St Ste 820 Boston MA 02111 Web: www.cobalt.pe	617-752-1921		387
Cobalt Truck Equipment 4620 E Trent Ave Spokane WA 99212 TF: 800-733-0342 ■ Web: www.critzer.com	800-733-0342		57
Cobb & Cole 149 S Ridgewood Ave Ste 700 Daytona Beach FL 32114 Web: www.cobbcole.com	386-255-8171		428
Cobb Architects LLC 67 Washington St Charleston SC 29403 Web: www.cobbarchitecture.com	843-856-7333		256
Cobb Chamber of Commerce 1100 Cr 75 Pkwy Ste 1000 Atlanta GA 30339 Web: www.cobbchamber.org	770-980-2000	980-9510	139
Cobb County 100 Cherokee St Marietta GA 30090 Web: cobbcounty.org	770-528-1000	528-2606	338
Cobb County Public Library System 266 Roswell St Marietta GA 30060 Web: www.cobbcat.org	770-528-2320		434-3
Cobb EMC 1000 EMC Pkwy PO Box 369 Marietta GA 30061 *Fax Area Code: 678 ■ Web: www.cobbemc.com	770-429-2100	355-3363*	245
Cobb Fendley & Associates Inc 13430 Northwest Fwy Ste 1100 Houston TX 77040 Web: www.cobbfendley.com	713-462-3242	462-3262	256
Cobb Galleria Ctr 2 Galleria Pkwy Atlanta GA 30339 Web: cobbgalleria.com	770-955-8000		205
Cobb Mechanical Contractors 2906 W Morrison Colorado Springs CO 80904 Web: www.cobbmechanical.com	719-471-8958	389-0127	189-10
Cobb Planning Group 1206 N Broadway Santa Ana CA 92701 Web: cobbplanninggroup.com	714-550-7242		528
Cobb Strecker Dunphy & Zimmermann 225 S 6th St Ste 1900 Minneapolis MN 55402 Web: www.csdz.com	612-349-2400		390
Cobb Travel & Tourism 1 Galleria Pkwy Atlanta GA 30339 TF: 800-451-3480 ■ Web: travelcobb.org	678-303-2622		206
Cobbleheads Bar & Grill 3154 Central Blvd Brownsville TX 78520 Web: www.cobbleheads.com	956-546-6224		671
Cobblestone Capital Advisors LLC 140 Allens Creek Rd Rochester NY 14618 TF: 800-264-2769 ■ Web: www.cobblestonecap.com	585-473-3333		690
Cobblestone Hotels LLC 980 American Dr Neenah WI 54956 Web: whgco.com	920-237-0233		378
Cobbs Allen & Hall of Louisiana Inc 2250 Hospital Dr Ste 120 Bossier City LA 71111 Web: cahinsla.com	318-524-3501		390
Cobb-Vantress Inc PO Box 1030 Siloam Springs AR 72761 TF: 800-748-9719 ■ Web: www.cobb-vantress.com	479-524-3166	524-3043	11-2

Name / Address	Phone	Fax	Class
Cober Evolving Solutions 1351 Strasburg Rd Kitchener ON N2R1H2 TF: 800-263-7136 ■ Web: cobersolutions.com	519-745-7136		627
Cobham Mission Systems Orchard Park Inc 10 Cobham Dr Orchard Park NY 14127 Web: resources.carltech.com	716-662-0006	662-0747	576
Coble Intl 1420 Steeple Chase Dover PA 17315 Web: www.importexporthelp.com	717-467-1835		196
Coble-Cravens Financial Services 504 W Main St Arlington TX 76010 TF: 800-709-4279 ■ Web: coblecravens.com	817-462-4200	462-4250	390
Coblentz Patch Duffy & Bass LLP 1 Montgomery St Ste 3000 San Francisco CA 94104 Web: www.coblentzlaw.com	415-391-4800	989-1663	41
Cobleskill-Richmondville Central School District 155 Washington Ave Cobleskill NY 12043 Web: www.crcs.k12.ny.us	518-234-4032		685
Cobon Plastics Corp 90 South St Newark NJ 07114 TF: 800-360-1324 ■ Web: www.cobonplastics.com	973-344-6330		370
Coborn's Inc 1921 Coborn Blvd Saint Cloud MN 56301 Web: www.cobornsinc.com	763-971-4900		345
Cobra Anchors Corp 504 Mount-Laurel Ave Temple PA 19560 Web: www.cobraanchors.com	610-929-5764		350
Cobra Electronics 6500 W Cortland St Chicago IL 60707 Web: www.cobra.com	773-889-8870		647
Cobra Engineering Inc 23801 La Palma Ave Yorba Linda CA 92887 Web: cobrausa.com	714-692-8180	692-5019	256
Cobra Manufacturing Company Inc 7909 E 148th St S Bixby OK 74008 TF: 800-352-6272 ■ Web: www.cobraarchery.com	800-352-6272		710
Cobra Oil & Gas Corp 2201 Kell Blvd PO Box 8206 Wichita Falls TX 76308 Web: www.cobraogc.com	940-716-5100	716-5190	536
Cobra Plastics Inc 1244 Highland Rd E Macedonia OH 44056 Web: www.cobraplastics.com	330-425-3669	425-7338	604
Cobra Solutions Inc 4500 S Lakeshore Dr Tempe AZ 85282 TF: 800-325-1957 ■ Web: www.cobra-solutions.com	480-831-6078		734
Cobra Wire & Cable Inc 2930 Turnpike Dr Hatboro PA 19040 Web: www.cobrawire.com	215-674-8773	674-9530	253
Coburn Co, The PO Box 147 Whitewater WI 53190 TF: 800-776-7042 ■ Web: www.coburn.com	262-473-2822	473-3522	600
Coburn Supply Company Inc 390 Park St Ste 100 Beaumont TX 77701 TF: 800-832-8492 ■ Web: www.coburns.com	409-838-6363	838-1920	612
Coburn Technologies Inc 55 Gerber Rd E South Windsor CT 06074 TF: 800-843-1479 ■ Web: www.coburntechnologies.com	800-843-1479	648-6601	542
CocaCola 121 Baker St NW Atlanta GA 30313 TF: 800-676-2653 ■ Web: www.worldofcoca-cola.com	404-676-5151		80-2
Coca-Cola Consolidated 4100 Coca-Cola Plz PO Box 31487 Charlotte NC 28211 NASDAQ: COKE ■ TF: 800-866-2653 ■ Web: www.cokeconsolidated.com	704-557-4000		81-2
Coca-Cola Export Corp, The 1 Coca Cola Plz NW Atlanta GA 30313 Web: www.coca-colacompany.com	404-676-2121		805
Cocaine Anonymous World Services Inc (CA) PO Box 492000 Los Angeles CA 90049 TF: 800-347-8998 ■ Web: ca.org	310-559-5833	559-2554	48-21
CoCal Landscape Services Inc 12570 E 39th Ave Denver CO 80229 Web: www.cocal.com	303-578-4788		776
Cocalico Biologicals Inc 449 Stevens Rd Reamstown PA 17567 TF: 877-357-7217 ■ Web: www.cocalicobiologicals.com	717-336-1990	336-1993	85
Cocca's Inn & Suites 42 Wolf Rd Albany NY 12205 TF: 888-426-2227 ■ Web: coccahotels.com	518-459-5670		379
Cocciardi & Associates Inc 4 Kacey Ct Mechanicsburg PA 17055 TF: 800-377-3024 ■ Web: www.cocciardi.com	717-766-4500		194
COCHI (Chamber of Commerce Hawaii) 1132 Bishop St Ste 2105 Honolulu HI 96813 Web: www.cochawaii.org	808-545-4300	545-4369	139
Cochise College 4190 W Hwy 80 Douglas AZ 85607 TF: 800-966-7943 ■ Web: www.cochise.edu	520-364-7943		162
Cochise County 100 Quality Hill Rd PO Box CK Bisbee AZ 85603 Web: www.cochise.az.gov	520-432-9200	432-5016	338
Cochlear Americas 13059 E Peakview Ave Centennial CO 80111 TF: 800-523-5798 ■ Web: www.cochlear.com	303-790-9010	792-9025	475
Cochon Dingue Le 46 Champlain Blvd Quebec City QC G1K4H7 Web: www.cochondingue.com	418-692-2013		671
Cochran Abstract Co 314 W Choctaw Chickasha OK 73018 Web: cochranabstract.com	405-224-6360		653
Cochran County 100 N Main St Morton TX 79346 Web: www.co.cochran.tx.us	806-266-5508	266-9027	338
Cochran Davis & Associates P C 36 Malaga Cove Plz Ste 206 Palos Verdes Estates CA 90274 Web: cochranlaw1.com	310-373-0900	373-0244	445
Cochran Firm LLC 111 E Main St Dothan AL 36301 TF: 800-843-3476 ■ Web: www.cochranfirm.com	334-673-1555		428
Cochran Inc 12500 Aurora Ave N Seattle WA 98133 Web: www.cochraninc.com	206-367-1900		189-4
Cochran School of Nursing 967 N Broadway Yonkers NY 10701 Web: www.riversidehealth.org	914-964-4444		800
Cochran, Cochran & Yale LLC 955 E Henrietta Rd Rochester NY 14623 Web: www.ccy.com	585-424-6060		463
Cochran, Kroll & Associates PC 15510 Farmington Rd Livonia MI 48154 TF: 800-322-5543 ■ Web: www.cochranlaw.com	800-322-5543		445

Name / Address	City	State	Zip	Phone	Fax	Class
Cochrane Cooperative Telephone Co (CCTC) 103 W 5th St *Web:* www.cochranetel.com	Cochrane	WI	54622	608-248-2323		224
Cochrane Technologies Inc 317 Thibodeaux Dr *TF:* 800-346-3745 ■ *Web:* www.cochranetech.com	Lafayette	LA	70598	337-837-3334	837-7134	727
Cocina Superior 587 Brookwood Vlg *Web:* www.thecocinasuperior.com	Birmingham	AL	35209	205-259-1980		671
Cock of the Walk 2624 Music Vly Dr *Web:* www.cockofthewalkrestaurant.com	Nashville	TN	37214	601-856-5500		671
Cocke County Tourism 433 B Prospect Ave *Web:* www.cockecounty.com	Newport	TN	37821	423-625-9675		338
Coco Creative Wellness LLC 4021 Eastern Ave Stev7 *Web:* cococreativewellness.com	Cincinnati	OH	45226	513-713-1448		77
Coco Pazzo 300 W Hubbard St *Web:* www.cocopazzochicago.com	Chicago	IL	60654	312-836-0900		671
Cocoa Beach Area Chamber of Commerce 400 Fortenberry Rd *TF:* 800-248-5955 ■ *Web:* cocoabeachchamber.com	Merritt Island	FL	32952	321-459-2200	459-2232	139
Cocola Broadcasting Companies LLC 706 W Herndon Ave *Web:* www.cocolatv.com	Fresno	CA	93650	559-435-7000	435-3201	647
Coconino County 219 E Cherry Ave *TF:* 800-559-9289 ■ *Web:* www.coconino.az.gov	Flagstaff	AZ	86001	928-679-7120		338
Coconino Federal Credit Union 2800 S Woodlands Village Blvd *Web:* coconinofcu.org	Flagstaff	AZ	86001	928-913-8100		219
Coconis Furniture Inc 4 S Maysville Ave *TF:* 800-479-6139 ■ *Web:* coconisfurniture.com	South Zanesville	OH	43701	740-452-1231		321
Coconut Grove Gallery Inc 2884 Bird Ave *Web:* grovegalleryinteriors.com	Miami	FL	33133	305-445-7401		42
Coconut Mallory Resort & Marina 1445 S Roosevelt Blvd *TF:* 866-316-1843 ■ *Web:* mallorykeywest.com	Key West	FL	33040	800-958-2628		377
Coconut Malorie Resort 200 59th St *TF:* 855-826-6361 ■ *Web:* www.vacationcondos.com	Ocean City	MD	21842	855-826-6361		669
Cocoro Bistro & Sushi Bar 2105 Pacific Ave	Stockton	CA	95204	209-941-6053		671
CocoWalk 3015 Grand Ave *Web:* www.cocowalk.net	Coconut Grove	FL	33133	305-444-0777	441-8936	50-6
CODA (Co-Dependents Anonymous Inc) PO Box 33577 *TF:* 888-444-2359 ■ *Web:* www.codependents.org	Phoenix	AZ	85067	602-277-7991		48-21
CODA Enterprises 465 Van Duzer St *Web:* www.nearbycafe.com	Staten Island	NY	10304	718-447-3280		637-2
CODA Inc 30 Industrial Ave *Web:* www.codamount.com	Mahwah	NJ	07430	201-825-7400	825-8133	629
Coda Signature 1580 Lincoln St *Web:* codasignature.com	Denver	CO	80203	617-818-2480		486
Codale Electric Supply Inc 5225 West 2400 South PO Box 702070 *TF:* 800-300-6634 ■ *Web:* www.codale.com	Salt Lake City	UT	84120	801-975-7300	977-8833	246
CODAN US Corp 3511 W Sunflower Ave *TF:* 800-332-6326 ■ *Web:* www.codanusa.com	Santa Ana	CA	92704	714-545-2111	545-9111	166
Codding Enterprises 1400 Valley House Dr Ste 100 PO Box 3550 *Web:* www.codding.com	Rohnert Park	CA	94928	707-795-3550	665-2882	655
Coddington Group LLC, The 115 W St Ste 300 *Web:* www.coddingtongroup.com	Annapolis	MD	21401	410-263-6200		260
Code & Theory Inc 1 World Trade Ctr 62nd Fl *Web:* www.codeandtheory.com	New York	NY	10007	212-358-0717		5
Code Blue Corp 259 Hedcor St *TF:* 800-205-7186 ■ *Web:* codeblue.com	Holland	MI	49423	616-392-8296		693
Code Consultants Inc 2043 Woodland Pky Ste 300 *Web:* www.codeconsultants.com	Saint Louis	MO	63146	314-991-2633	991-4614	261
Code Credit Union 355 W Monument Ave *Web:* codecu.org	Dayton	OH	45402	937-222-8971		219
Code Environmental Services Inc 400 Middlesex Ave *Web:* www.codeenvironmental.com	Carteret	NJ	07008	732-969-2700	969-2701	261
Code Green Networks Inc 385 Moffett Park Dr Ste 105 *Web:* codegreennetworks.com	Sunnyvale	CA	94089	408-716-4200		177
Code Ninjas 11200 W Broadway St Ste 2731 *TF:* 855-446-4652 ■ *Web:* www.codeninjas.com	Pearland	TX	77584	855-446-4652		113
Codemettle LLC 6 Concourse Pkwy Ste 1050 *Web:* codemettle.com	Atlanta	GA	30328	678-336-8590		177
Co-Dependents Anonymous Inc (CODA) PO Box 33577 *TF:* 888-444-2359 ■ *Web:* www.codependents.org	Phoenix	AZ	85067	602-277-7991		48-21
Codilis & Associates PC 15W030 N Frontage Rd *Web:* www.codilis.com	Burr Ridge	IL	60527	630-794-5300		428
Codington County 14 First Ave SE Rm 110 *Web:* www.codington.org	Watertown	SD	57201	605-882-6300		338
Codington-Clark Electric Co-op 3520 Ninth Ave SW PO Box 880 *TF:* 800-463-8938 ■ *Web:* www.codingtonclarkelectric.coop	Watertown	SD	57201	605-886-5848		245
Codino's Foods Inc 704 Corporations Pk *Web:* www.codinos.com	Scotia	NY	12302	518-372-3308	372-2787	68
Cody & Pfursich 53 N Duke St Ste 420 *Web:* codylegal.com	Lancaster	PA	17602	717-299-7374	291-0998	41
Cody Company Inc 4200 N I-45 *Web:* www.codycompany.com	Ennis	TX	75119	972-875-5884	875-0308	697
Cody Laboratories Inc 601 Yellowstone Ave *Web:* codylabs.com	Cody	WY	82414	307-587-7099		231
Cody Pools Inc 2300 W Parmer Ln *Web:* codypools.com	Austin	TX	78727	512-835-4966		45
COE & Van Loo Consultants Inc 4550 N 12th St *Web:* cvlci.com	Phoenix	AZ	85014	602-264-6831	264-0928	261
COE College 1220 First Ave NE *TF:* 877-225-5263 ■ *Web:* www.coe.edu	Cedar Rapids	IA	52402	319-399-8500	399-8816	166
COE Review Press (CRP) 1220 1st Ave NE *Web:* www.public.coe.edu	Cedar Rapids	IA	52402	319-399-8557		637-2
COECO Office Systems Co 2521 N Church St *TF:* 800-682-6844 ■ *Web:* www.coeco.com	Rocky Mount	NC	27804	252-977-1121		320
Coeur Business Group Inc 18 Hawk Ridge Blvd Ste 150 *TF:* 800-335-9029 ■ *Web:* www.coeurgroup.com	Lake Saint Louis	MO	63367	800-335-9029		196
Coeur d'Alene Area Chamber of Commerce 105 N First St Ste 100 *Web:* www.cdachamber.com	Coeur d'Alene	ID	83814	208-664-3194	667-9338	139
Coeur d'Alene Convention & Visitor Bureau Inc 105 N 1st Ste 100 *TF:* 877-782-9232 ■ *Web:* www.coeurdalene.org	Coeur d'Alene	ID	83814	877-782-9232		623
Coeur d'Alene Press 201 N Second St *Web:* www.cdapress.com	Coeur d'Alene	ID	83814	208-664-8176		532-2
Coeur d'Alene Public Library 702 East Frnt *Web:* www.cdalibrary.org	Coeur d'Alene	ID	83814	208-769-2315	769-2381	434-3
Coeur d'Alene Resort Spa, The 115 S Second St *TF:* 855-703-4648 ■ *Web:* www.cdaresort.com	Coeur d'Alene	ID	83814	855-703-4648		706
Coeur Inc 209 Creekside Dr *Web:* coeurinc.com	Washington	NC	27889	252-946-1963		608
Cofa Media Inc 2251 Las Palmas Dr Ste 201 *TF:* 877-293-2007 ■ *Web:* cofamedia.com	Carlsbad	CA	92011	877-293-2007		463
Coface Services North America Inc 50 Millstone Rd *TF:* 877-626-3223 ■ *Web:* www.coface-usa.com	East Windsor	NJ	08520	609-469-0400	490-1582	218
Cofer Brothers Inc (CB) 2300 Main St *Web:* www.coferbros.com	Tucker	GA	30084	770-938-3200	493-3624	364
Coffee Beanery Ltd, The 3429 Pierson Pl *TF:* 800-441-2255 ■ *Web:* www.coffeebeanery.com	Flushing	MI	48433	810-733-1020	733-1536	159
Coffee City USA 13195 Hwy 155 S *TF:* 888-583-9526 ■ *Web:* www.coffeecityusa.com	Tyler	TX	75703	888-583-9526		297-2
Coffee County 101 S Peterson Ave Ste A-15 *Web:* coffeecountygov.com	Douglas	GA	31533	912-384-4895	389-1375	338
Coffee County 2 County Complex *Web:* www.coffeecounty.us	New Brockton	AL	36351	334-894-5556		338
Coffee County 1329 McArthur Dr *Web:* www.coffeecountytn.gov	Manchester	TN	37355	931-723-5106	723-8248	338
Coffee Creek Correctional Facility 24499 SW Grahams Ferry Rd *Web:* www.oregon.gov	Wilsonville	OR	97070	503-570-6400	570-6417	213
Coffee Exchange 207 Wickenden St *Web:* thecoffeeexchange.com	Providence	RI	02903	401-273-1198		379
Coffee Holding Company Inc 3475 Victory Blvd *NASDAQ: JVA* ■ *TF:* 800-458-2233 ■ *Web:* coffeeholding.com	Staten Island	NY	10314	718-832-0800	832-0892	296-7
Coffee Masters Inc 7606 Industrial Ct *TF:* 800-334-6485 ■ *Web:* www.coffeemasters.com	Spring Grove	IL	60081	815-675-0088	675-3166	297-2
Coffee Memorial Blood Ctr 7500 Wallace Dr *Web:* www.thegiftoflife.org	Amarillo	TX	79124	806-358-4563		89
Coffee Regional Medical Ctr (CRMC) 1101 Ocilla Rd *TF:* 800-555-4444 ■ *Web:* www.coffeeregional.org	Douglas	GA	31533	912-384-1900		374-3
Coffee Solutions Inc 14 Fanaras Dr *Web:* www.coffeesolutions.net	Hopedale	MA	01747	508-422-9233		463
CoffeeAM 12230 Cumming Hwy *TF:* 800-803-7774 ■ *Web:* www.coffeeam.com	Canton	GA	30115	678-494-1915		159
Coffeen Lake State Fish & Wildlife Area 15084 N 4th Ave *Web:* www2.illinois.gov	Coffeen	IL	62017	217-537-3351		565
Coffey Communications Inc 1505 Business One Cir *TF:* 888-805-9101 ■ *Web:* www.coffeycomm.com	Walla Walla	WA	99362	509-525-0101		637-9
Coffey County 520 Cross St *Web:* www.coffeycountyks.org	Burlington	KS	66839	620-364-2191	364-8975	338
Coffey Law PLLC 152 E Kinderton Way Ste 100 *Web:* coffeylawpllc.com	Bermuda Run	NC	27006	336-940-3009		41
Coffeyville Community College 400 W 11th St *Web:* www.coffeyville.edu	Coffeyville	KS	67337	620-251-7700		162
Coffeyville Regional Medical Ctr 1400 W Fourth St *TF:* 800-540-2762 ■ *Web:* crmcinc.org	Coffeyville	KS	67337	620-251-1200		374-3
Coffeyville Sektam Inc 509 N Cline Rd *Web:* www.coffeyvillesektam.com	Coffeyville	KS	67337	620-251-3880	251-0404	454
Coffin Turbo Pump Inc 326 S Dean St *TF:* 800-568-9798 ■ *Web:* www.coffinturbopump.com	Englewood	NJ	07631	201-568-4700	568-4716	641
Coffman Engineers Inc 1455 Frazee Rd Ste 600 *Web:* www.coffman.com	San Diego	CA	92108	619-232-4673		256
Coffman Truck Sales 1149 W Lake St *TF:* 800-255-7641 ■ *Web:* www.coffmantrucks.com	Aurora	IL	60507	630-892-7093	892-1080	57
Cofinity 28588 NW Hwy *TF:* 800-831-1166 ■ *Web:* www.cofinity.net	Southfield	MI	48034	800-831-1166		391-3
COG 1731 Technology Dr Ste 100 *Web:* www.cog.com	San Jose	CA	95110	408-213-1790		393
Cogar Manufacturing Inc 951 Lester Hwy *Web:* www.cogarmanufacturing.com	Glen White	WV	25849	304-252-4435		358

Company / Address	City	State	ZIP	Phone	Fax	Class
Cogeco Connexion 5 Pl Ville-Marie Office 1700 *Web:* corpo.cogeco.com	Montreal	QC	H3B0B3	514-764-4700		116
Cogeco Peer 1 413 Horner Ave *TF:* 877-720-2228 ■ *Web:* aptum.com	Etobicoke	ON	M8W4W3	877-504-0091		225
Cogenix Consulting Ltd 50 Burnhamthorpe Rd W Ste 401 **Fax Area Code:* 905 ■ *Web:* www.cogenix-bpm.com	Mississauga	ON	L5B3C2	416-807-9042	896-9380*	194
Cogent Communications Group Inc 1015 31st St NW *NASDAQ: CCOI* ■ *TF:* 877-875-4432 ■ *Web:* www.cogentco.com	Washington	DC	20007	202-295-4200	338-8798	394
Cogent Industrial Technologies Ltd 13775 Commerce Pkwy Ste 300 *Web:* www.cogentind.com	Richmond	BC	V6V2V4	604-207-8880		261
Cogentic LLC 1834 Collins St Ste E *Web:* www.cogentic.com	Tarzana	CA	91356	818-578-6930		463
Cogentrix Energy Inc 9405 Arrowpoint Blvd *Web:* www.cogentrix.com	Charlotte	NC	28273	704-525-3800		245
Coghill Composition Company Inc 7640 Whitepine Rd *Web:* coghillcomposition.com	North Chesterfield	VA	23237	804-714-1100	714-1103	781
Coghlan's Ltd 121 Irene St *TF:* 877-264-4526 ■ *Web:* www.coghlans.com	Winnipeg	MB	R3T4C7	204-284-9550		711
Cogistics Inc 2485 Drane Field Rd *Web:* www.cogistics.com	Lakeland	FL	33811	863-647-9389		194
Cognify PO Box 69337 *TF:* 888-264-6439 ■ *Web:* www.cognify.com	Oro Valley	AZ	85737	888-264-6439		224
CogniTech Corp 1060 E 100 S Ste 306 *Web:* www.cognitech-ut.com	Salt Lake City	UT	84102	801-322-0101		177
Cognitim Codeworks Inc 2860 Zanker Rd Ste 100 *Web:* www.cognitim.com	San Jose	CA	95134	408-434-6400		177
Cognitive Medical Systems Inc 9444 Waples St Ste 300 *Web:* cognitivemedicalsystems.com	San Diego	CA	92121	858-509-4949		177
Cognitive Technologies Inc 16333 S Great Oaks Dr Ste 201 *Web:* www.cog-ps.com	Round Rock	TX	78681	703-562-0600		180
Cognizant Technology Solutions Corp 500 Frank W Burr Blvd *NASDAQ: CTSH* ■ *TF:* 888-937-3277 ■ *Web:* www.cognizant.com	Teaneck	NJ	07666	201-801-0233	801-0243	180
Cogo's *Property Div* 2589 Boyce Plaza Rd *Web:* cogos.com	Pittsburgh	PA	15241	412-257-1550		345
Cogswell Polytechnical College 1175 Bordeaux Dr *Web:* cogswell.edu	Sunnyvale	CA	94089	408-541-0100	747-0764	166
COGWM (Church of God World Missions) 2490 Keith St *TF:* 800-345-7492 ■ *Web:* cogwm.org	Cleveland	TN	37311	800-345-7492		48-20
Cohasset Associates Inc 505 N Lake Shore Dr Apt 3806 *Web:* www.cohasset.com	Chicago	IL	60611	312-527-1550		194
Cohasset Harbor Inn 124 Elm St *Web:* cohassetharborresort.com	Cohasset	MA	02025	781-383-6650		379
Cohber Press PO Box 93100 *TF:* 800-724-3032 ■ *Web:* www.cohber.com	Rochester	NY	14692	585-475-9100	475-9406	781
Cohelan, Khoury & Singer, A Partnership of Pcs 605 C St Ste 200 *TF:* 888-808-8358 ■ *Web:* ckslaw.com	San Diego	CA	92101	888-808-8358		41
Cohen & Associates LLC 49 Richmondville Ave Ste 105 *Web:* cohenandassociates.com	Westport	CT	06880	203-454-2210	454-9632	2
Cohen & Co 1350 Euclid Ave Ste 800 *Web:* www.cohencpa.com	Cleveland	OH	44115	216-579-1040		734
Cohen & Cohen LLP 16130 Ventura Blvd Ste 140 *Web:* cohenlaw.net	Encino	CA	91436	818-981-2300		41
Cohen & Gresser LLP 800 Third Ave *Web:* www.cohengresser.com	New York	NY	10022	212-957-7600		428
Cohen & Sinowski Pc 30 Trammell St SW *Web:* cohensinowski.com	Marietta	GA	30064	404-351-8888		41
Cohen & Steers Inc 280 Park Ave 10th Fl *NYSE: CNS* ■ *TF:* 800-330-7348 ■ *Web:* www.cohenandsteers.com	New York	NY	10017	800-330-7348		401
Cohen and Lombardo PC 343 Elmwood Ave *Web:* www.cn-lo.com	Buffalo	NY	14213	716-262-8428	881-2755	41
Cohen Asset Management Inc 1900 Avenue of the Stars 3rd Fl *Web:* www.cohenasset.com	Los Angeles	CA	90067	310-860-0598		194
Cohen Brown Management Group 11835 Olympic Blvd Ste 920 *TF:* 888-288-5955 ■ *Web:* cohenbrown.com	Los Angeles	CA	90064	310-966-1001	966-4700	631
Cohen Financial A Division of SunTrust Bank 227 W Monroe St Ste 1000 *TF:* 866-315-6212 ■ *Web:* www.cohenfinancial.com	Chicago	IL	60606	312-346-5680	346-6669	652
Cohen Group, The 500 Eighth St NW Ste 200 *Web:* www.cohengroup.net	Washington	DC	20004	202-863-7200		317
Cohen Highley LLP 255 Queens Ave *TF:* 800-563-1020 ■ *Web:* cohenhighley.com	London	ON	N6A5R8	519-672-9330		428
Cohen Lexington 1520 14th Ave *Web:* www.cohenusa.com	Middletown	OH	45044	859-255-5676	252-3590	686
Cohen Placitella & Roth P C 2001 Market St Ste 2900 *Web:* cprlaw.com	Philadelphia	PA	19103	215-567-3500		445
Cohen Seglias Pallas Greenhall & Furman PC 30 S 17th St 19th Fl United Plz *Web:* cohenseglias.com	Philadelphia	PA	19103	215-564-1700		428
Cohen Steve (Rep D - TN) 2104 Rayburn House Office Bldg *Web:* cohen.house.gov	Washington	DC	20515	202-225-3265	225-5663	342-2
Cohen, Hurkin, Ehrenfeld, Pomerantz & Tenenbaum 25 Chapel St Ste 705 *Web:* www.cohenhurkin.com	Brooklyn	NY	11201	718-596-9000		428
Coherent Inc 5100 Patrick Henry Dr *NASDAQ: COHR* ■ *TF:* 800-527-3786 ■ *Web:* www.coherent.com	Santa Clara	CA	95054	408-764-4000		425
Coherent Solutions Inc 1600 Utica Ave S Ste 120 *TF:* 877-502-5619 ■ *Web:* www.coherentsolutions.com	Minneapolis	MN	55416	612-279-6262		177
Coherex Medical Inc 3598 W 1820 S	Salt Lake City	UT	84104	801-433-9900		743
Cohesion Corp 5151 Pfeiffer Rd Ste 105 *Web:* cohesion.com	Cincinnati	OH	45242	513-587-7700		196
Cohesionforce Inc 360C Quality Cir *Web:* cohesionforce.com	Huntsville	AL	35806	256-562-0600		261
Cohn & Gregory Inc 5450 Midway Rd *Web:* www.cgsupply.com	Fort Worth	TX	76117	817-831-9998		385
COHN Marketing Group 2434 W Caithness Pl *Web:* cohnmarketing.com	Denver	CO	80211	303-839-1415		195
Coho Partners Ltd 801 Cassatt Rd Ste 100 *Web:* www.cohopartners.com	Berwyn	PA	19312	484-318-7575		401
Cohoes Fashions Inc 1830 Rte 130 N *Web:* www.cohoesfashions.com	Burlington	NJ	08016	401-946-7740		157-4
Cohu Inc 12367 Crosthwaite Cir *NASDAQ: COHU* ■ *Web:* www.cohu.com	Poway	CA	92064	858-848-8000		248
Coil Construction Inc 209 E Broadway *Web:* www.coilconstruction.com	Columbia	MO	65203	573-874-1444	443-3039	685
Coil Tec of Arizona Inc 17617 N 25th Ave *TF:* 888-264-5746 ■ *Web:* www.coiltec.net	Phoenix	AZ	85023	602-547-0016	547-8726	767
Coil Tubing Technology Holding Inc (CTT) 3002 Farrell Rd *Web:* www.coiltubingtechnology.com	Houston	TX	77073	281-651-0200		539
Coilcraft Inc 1102 Silver Lake Rd *TF:* 800-322-2645 ■ *Web:* www.coilcraft.com	Cary	IL	60013	847-639-2361	639-1469	253
Coilhose Pneumatics Inc 19 Kimberly Rd *TF:* 800-526-2100 ■ *Web:* www.coilhose.com	East Brunswick	NJ	08816	732-390-8480	390-9693	370
Coiling Technologies Inc 7777 Wright Rd *TF:* 800-969-2645 ■ *Web:* www.coilingtech.com	Houston	TX	77041	713-849-4000		718
Coilmaster Corp 440 Industrial Dr *TF:* 888-302-6049 ■ *Web:* coilmastercorp.com	Moscow	TN	38057	901-877-3333		35
Coilplus Inc 6250 N River Rd Ste 6050 *Web:* www.coilplus.com	Rosemont	IL	60018	847-384-3000		487
Coin Acceptors Inc 300 Hunter Ave *TF:* 800-325-2646 ■ *Web:* www.coinco.com	Saint Louis	MO	63124	314-725-0100		55
Coin Laundry Assn (CLA) 1s660 Midwest Rd Ste 205 *TF:* 800-570-5629 ■ *Web:* www.coinlaundry.org	Oakbrook Terrace	IL	60181	630-953-7920		49-4
COINage Magazine 3585 Maple St Ste 232 *TF:* 800-764-6278 ■ *Web:* coinagemag.com	Ventura	CA	93003	800-764-6278		457-14
Coinco Inc 23727 US Hwy 322 *Web:* www.coinco.org	Cochranton	PA	16314	814-425-7407	425-7489	488
Coining Technologies Inc 400 Kuller Rd *Web:* www.coining.com	Clifton	NJ	07011	973-253-0500		483
Coinstar Inc 1800 114th Ave SE *TF:* 800-928-2274 ■ *Web:* www.coinstar.com	Bellevue	WA	98004	425-943-8000		55
Coit Services of Ohio Inc 23580 Miles Rd *Web:* coit.com	Bedford Heights	OH	44128	216-626-0040		426
Cok Kinzler Pllp 35 N Bozeman Ave *TF:* 800-677-6263 ■ *Web:* cokkinzlerlaw.com	Bozeman	MT	59771	800-677-6263		41
Coke County 13 E Seventh St *Web:* www.co.coke.tx.us	Robert Lee	TX	76945	325-453-2631	453-2650	338
COKeM International Inc 3880 4th Ave E **Fax Area Code:* 763 ■ *TF:* 866-816-7085 ■ *Web:* www.cokem.com	Shakopee	MN	55379	952-358-6000	544-4100*	246
Coker & Palmer Inc 1667 Lelia Dr *Web:* www.cokerpalmer.com	Jackson	MS	39216	601-354-0860		691
Coker College 300 E College Ave *TF:* 800-950-1908 ■ *Web:* www.coker.edu	Hartsville	SC	29550	843-383-8000	383-8056	166
Coker Consulting 2400 Lakeview Pkwy Ste 400 *TF:* 800-345-5829 ■ *Web:* cokergroup.com	Alpharetta	GA	30009	800-345-5829		463
Coker Tire Co 1317 Chestnut St *TF:* 866-516-3215 ■ *Web:* www.cokertire.com	Chattanooga	TN	37402	866-516-3215		754
Cokeva Inc 9000 Foothills Blvd *Web:* www.cokeva.com	Roseville	CA	95747	916-462-6000		196
Cokinos | Young 1221 Lamar 16th Fl *Web:* cokinoslaw.com	Houston	TX	77010	713-535-5500		428
Col Pump Company Inc 131 E Railroad St *Web:* www.col-pump.net	Columbiana	OH	44408	330-482-1029		492
COLA 9881 Broken Land Pkwy Ste 200 *TF:* 800-981-9883 ■ *Web:* www.cola.org	Columbia	MD	21046	410-381-6581	381-8611	49-8
COLA (ABA Commission on Law & Aging) 1050 Connecticut Ave NW Ste 400 *Web:* www.americanbar.org	Washington	DC	20036	202-662-1000	662-8698	49-10
COLAB (Company Lab, The) 1100 Market St Ste 100 *Web:* colab.co	Chattanooga	TN	37402	423-648-2195		393
Colad Group 801 Exchange St *TF:* 800-950-1755 ■ *Web:* www.colad.com	Buffalo	NY	14210	716-961-1776	961-1753	555
COLAGE (Children of Lesbians & Gays Everywhere) 3815 S Othello St Ste 100 *Web:* www.colage.org	Seattle	WA	98118	828-782-1938		48-21
Colaianni Construction Inc 2141 SR-150 *Web:* www.colaianniconst.com	Dillonvale	OH	43917	740-769-2362	769-2069	186
Colao's Ristorante 2826 Plum St *Web:* www.colaos.com	Erie	PA	16508	814-866-9621		671
Colarelli Construction Inc 111 S Tejon St Ste 112 *Web:* www.colarelliconstruction.com	Colorado Springs	CO	80903	719-475-7997	475-7994	186
Colautti Construction Ltd 2575 Sheffield Rd	Ottawa	ON	K1B3V6	613-822-1440		463

				Phone	Fax	Class
ColbaNet 6465 TransCanada Hwy *Web:* colba.net	Montreal	QC	H4T1S3	514-856-3500		224
Colbert County 201 N Main St *Web:* www.colbertcounty.org	Tuscumbia	AL	35674	256-386-8500	386-8510	338
Colbert Packaging Corp 28355 N Bradley Rd *Web:* www.colbertpkg.com	Lake Forest	IL	60045	847-367-5990	367-4403	101
Colbert, Matz, Rosenfelt Inc 2835 Smith Ave Ste G *Web:* cmrengineers.com	Baltimore	MD	21209	410-653-3838	653-7953	261
Colborne Foodbotics LLC 28495 N Ballard Dr *TF:* 800-626-9501 ■ *Web:* colbornefoodbotics.com	Lake Forest	IL	60045	847-371-0101	371-0199	298
Colby & Thornes PLLC 4800 N Scottsdale Rd Ste 1900 *Web:* colbythornes.com	Scottsdale	AZ	85251	480-443-1990		41
Colby Attorneys Service Company Inc 111 Washington Ave Ste 703 *TF:* 800-832-1220 ■ *Web:* www.colbyservice.com	Albany	NY	12210	800-832-1220		635
Colby Community College 1255 S Range *TF:* 888-634-9350 ■ *Web:* www.colbycc.edu	Colby	KS	67701	785-462-3984	460-4691	162
Colby Convention & Visitors Bureau 350 S Range Ave *TF:* 800-499-7928 ■ *Web:* www.oasisontheplains.com	Colby	KS	67701	785-460-7643	460-4509	206
Colby Equipment Company Inc 3048 Ridgeview Dr *TF:* 800-443-2981 ■ *Web:* colbyequipment.com	Indianapolis	IN	46226	317-545-4221		358
Colby Hill Inn 33 The Oaks PO Box 779 *TF:* 800-531-0330 ■ *Web:* www.colbyhillinn.com	Henniker	NH	03242	603-428-3281	428-9218	379
Colby Instruments Inc 15375 SE 30th Pl Ste 320 *Web:* www.colbyinstruments.com	Bellevue	WA	98007	425-452-8889	452-8802	472
Colby Metal Inc 701 Industrial Dr *Web:* www.colbymetal.com	Colby	WI	54421	715-223-2334		492
Colby-Sawyer College 541 Main St *TF:* 800-272-1015 ■ *Web:* www.colby-sawyer.edu	New London	NH	03257	603-526-3700	526-3452	166
Colchester Christian Academy 15 Elm St *Web:* colchesterchristianacademy.ca	Truro	NS	B2N3H5	902-895-6520		623
Colchester Veterinary Hospital LLC 364 Old Hartford Rd *Web:* colchestervet.net	Colchester	CT	06415	860-537-3435		794
Colcord Hotel 15 N Robinson Ave *Web:* colcordhotel.com	Oklahoma City	OK	73102	405-601-4300		379
Cold Air Distributors Warehouse of Florida Inc 3053 Industrial 31st St *Web:* www.coldairdistributors.com	Fort Pierce	FL	34946	772-466-3036		61
Cold Bore Technology Inc 5970 Centre St SE Ste 200 *Web:* coldboretechnology.com	Calgary	AB	T2H0C1	403-991-7295		538
Cold Headers Inc (CH) 5514 N Elston Ave *Web:* www.coldheaders.com	Chicago	IL	60630	773-775-7900	775-0779	278
Cold Heading Co 21777 Hoover Rd *Web:* www.coldheading.com	Warren	MI	48089	586-497-7000		278
Cold Open Inc 1313 Innes Pl *Web:* www.coldopen.com	Venice	CA	90291	310-399-3307		7
Cold Shot Chillers 2730 Maximilian St *TF:* 800-473-9178 ■ *Web:* www.waterchillers.com	Houston	TX	77032	281-227-8400		14
Cold Spring Brewing Co 219 Red River Ave N *Web:* www.coldspringbrewery.com	Cold Spring	MN	56320	320-685-8686		102
Cold Spring Harbor Laboratory (CSHL) 1 Bungtown Rd *Web:* www.cshl.edu	Cold Spring	NY	11724	516-367-8800	367-8455	668
Cold Water Area Chamber of Commerce 20 Div St *Web:* www.coldwaterchamber.com	Coldwater	MI	49036	517-278-5985		139
Colder Products Co 1001 Westgate Dr *Web:* www.cpcworldwide.com	Saint Paul	MN	55114	651-645-0091		596
Colder's Inc 333 S 108th St *Web:* www.colders.com	West Allis	WI	53214	414-476-1574		321
Coldiron Companies Inc 200 N Sooner Rd *TF:* 800-293-4369 ■ *Web:* coldironcompanies.com	Edmond	OK	73034	405-562-2910		311
Coldmatic 61 Baywood Rd *Web:* www.coldmatic.com	Etobicoke	ON	M9V3Y8	416-744-7600	744-7601	664
ColDoc Publishing PO Box 50682 *Web:* www.coldoc.com	Sparks	NV	89435	775-424-6333		637-2
Coldspring 17482 Granite W Rd *TF:* 800-328-5040 ■ *Web:* www.coldspringusa.com	Cold Spring	MN	56320	800-328-5040	473-4881	724
ColdStar Solutions Inc 101-937 Dunford Ave *TF:* 800-201-1277 ■ *Web:* www.coldstarsolutions.com	Victoria	BC	V9B6B2	250-381-3399		311
Coldwater Community Schools 401 Sauk River Dr *Web:* www.coldwaterschools.org	Coldwater	MI	49036	517-279-5910	279-7651	685
Coldwater Lake State Park Copeland Rd *Web:* www.michigan.org	Coldwater	MI	49036	517-780-7866		565
Coldwell Banker 320 Water Stone Way *Web:* www.coldwellhomes.com	Joliet	IL	60435	815-744-1000		652
Coldwell Banker 1217 Fayette St *Web:* www.coldwellbankerhomes.com	Conshohocken	PA	19428	610-828-9558		652
Coldwell Banker Howard Perry & Walston 1001 Wade Ave *Web:* www.hpw.com	Raleigh	NC	27605	919-781-4663		652
Coldwell Banker Mountain West 235 Union St NE *Web:* coldwellbankermountainwest.com	Salem	OR	97301	503-364-9596		652
Coldwell Banker Platinum Partners 6349 Abercorn St *Web:* www.mycbhomes.com	Savannah	GA	31405	912-352-1222		652
Coldwell Banker Prime Properties Inc 621 Columbia St *Web:* coldwellbankerprime.com	Cohoes	NY	12047	518-456-8950		652
Coldwell Banker Rmr 790 Peachtree Ind Blvd *Web:* remaxregencyatl.com	Suwanee	GA	30024	678-318-7900		652
Coldwell Banker Schmidt Realtors 7841 Underwood Rdg *Web:* www.cbgreatlakes.com	Traverse City	MI	49686	231-922-2350		652
Coldwell Banker Select Professionals 1000 N Prince St *Web:* www.jeannewalkrealestate.com	Lancaster	PA	17603	717-735-8400		652
Coldwell, Sclafani & Company LLP 3239 N Verdugo Rd *Web:* csccpa.com	Glendale	CA	91208	818-249-2085		2
Cole & Company PC 5518 Telegraph Rd Ste 201 *Web:* cole-cpa.com	Saint Louis	MO	63129	314-892-6700	894-3614	2
Cole & Reed PC 531 Couch Dr *Web:* www.rsmus.com	Oklahoma City	OK	73102	405-239-7961		2
Cole Carbide Industries Inc 4930 S Lapeer Rd *Web:* www.colecarbide.com	Lake Orion	MI	48359	586-757-8700	757-8701	493
Cole Chemical & Distributing Inc 1500 S Dairy Ashford St Ste 450 *Web:* www.colechem.com	Houston	TX	77077	713-465-2653	461-3462	146
Cole County 301 E High St *TF:* 800-392-3738 ■ *Web:* www.colecounty.org	Jefferson City	MO	65101	573-634-9150	634-8031	338
Cole County Historical Museum 109 Madison St *Web:* www.colecohistsoc.org	Jefferson City	MO	65101	573-635-1850		520
Cole Gavlas PC 2401 W Centre Ave *Web:* colegavlas.com	Portage	MI	49024	269-329-6600		2
Cole Hardwood Inc 1611 W Market St *TF:* 800-536-3151 ■ *Web:* www.colehardwood.com	Logansport	IN	46947	800-536-3151		191-3
Cole Industrial Inc 5924 203rd St SW *TF:* 800-627-2653 ■ *Web:* coleindust.com	Lynnwood	WA	98036	425-774-6602		610
Cole Information Services 17041 Lakeside Hills Plz Ste 2 *TF:* 800-283-2855 ■ *Web:* www.coleinformation.com	Omaha	NE	68130	877-414-3332		637-6
Cole Instrument Corp 2650 S Croddy Way *Web:* www.cole-switches.com	Santa Ana	CA	92704	714-556-3100	241-9061	729
Cole International Inc 3033 - 34th Ave NE *Web:* www.coleintl.com	Calgary	AB	T1Y6X2	403-262-2771		314
Cole Kepro International LLC 4170-103 Distribution Cir *Web:* colekepro.com	North Las Vegas	NV	89030	702-633-4270		115
Cole Land Transportation Museum 405 Perry Rd *Web:* www.colemuseum.org	Bangor	ME	04401	207-990-3600	990-2653	520
Cole Martinez Curtis & Assoc 4040 Del Rey Ave Ste 7 *Web:* www.cmcadesign.com	Marina	CA	90292	310-827-7200		393
Cole Media Group 237 Park Ave *Web:* www.colemediagroup.com	Lockport	NY	14094	716-433-6592	433-6609	657
Cole Papers Inc 1300 N 38th St *TF:* 800-800-8090 ■ *Web:* www.colepapers.com	Fargo	ND	58102	701-282-5311	282-5513	553
Cole Scott & Kissane PA 617 Whitehead St *Web:* www.csklegal.com	Key West	FL	33040	305-294-4440		428
Cole Sport Inc 1615 Park Ave *TF:* 800-345-2938 ■ *Web:* www.colesport.com	Park City	UT	84060	435-649-4800		711
Cole Tom (Rep R - OK) 2207 Rayburn House Office Bldg *Web:* www.cole.house.gov	Washington	DC	20515	202-225-6165	225-3512	342-2
Cole Tool & Die Co 333 Redwood *TF:* 800-837-2653 ■ *Web:* www.coletool.com	Mansfield	OH	44905	419-522-1272	522-5506	757
Cole Veterinary Services PC 2757 Rayford Rd *Web:* colevet.com	Spring	TX	77386	281-465-0880		704
Cole, Cole, Anderson & Newman PSC 108 Knox St *Web:* coleandersonnewman.com	Barbourville	KY	40906	606-546-3116		41
Colehour & Cohen 1011 Wern Ave Ste 702 *Web:* cplusc.com	Seattle	WA	98104	206-262-0363		636
Coleman A. Young International Airport 11499 Conner *TF:* 800-874-9426 ■ *Web:* www.detroitmi.gov	Detroit	MI	48213	313-628-2146	372-2448	27
Coleman Company Inc 3600 N Hydraulic *TF:* 800-835-3278 ■ *Web:* www.coleman.com	Wichita	KS	67219	800-835-3278		710
Coleman County 100 W Live Oak *Web:* www.co.coleman.tx.us	Coleman	TX	76834	325-625-2889		338
Coleman County Electric Co-opeartive Inc 3300 N Hwy 84 PO Box 860 *TF:* 800-560-2128 ■ *Web:* www.colemanelectric.org	Coleman	TX	76834	325-625-2128	625-4600	245
Coleman Dairy Inc 6901 I-30 *TF:* 800-365-1551 ■ *Web:* www.hilanddairy.com	Little Rock	AR	72209	501-748-1700		296-27
Coleman E. Adler & Sons Inc 722 Canal St *TF:* 800-925-7912 ■ *Web:* www.adlersjewelry.com	New Orleans	LA	70130	504-523-5292	568-0610	410
Coleman Equipment Inc 24000 W 43rd St *TF:* 877-851-3647 ■ *Web:* www.colemanequip.com	Bonner Springs	KS	66012	913-422-3040	422-3044	274
Coleman Instrument Co 11575 Goldcoast Dr *TF:* 800-899-5745 ■ *Web:* www.colemaninstrument.com	Cincinnati	OH	45249	513-489-5745		358
Coleman Isd 2400 S Concho St *Web:* www.colemanisd.net	Coleman	TX	76834	325-625-4369		685
Coleman Lew Canny Bowen 375 Park Ave Ste 2607 *Web:* www.cannybowen.com	New York	NY	10152	212-949-6611		266
Coleman Lew Canny Bowen 6101 Carnegie Blvd Ste 300 *Web:* clcbsearch.com	Charlotte	NC	28209	704-377-0362		193
Coleman Oil Co 335 Mill Rd *Web:* www.colemanoil.com	Lewiston	ID	83501	208-799-2000		581
Coleman Professional Services 3920 Lovers Ln *TF:* 800-673-1347 ■ *Web:* www.colemanservices.org	Ravenna	OH	44266	330-296-3555		726
Coleman Research Inc 909 Aviation Pkwy Ste 400 *Web:* colemaninsights.com	Morrisville	NC	27560	919-571-0000		466

Phone | Fax | Class

Coleman State Park
1166 Diamond Pond Rd .... Stewartstown NH 03576 603-237-5382 565
Web: www.nhstateparks.org

Coleman University 8888 Balboa Ave .... San Diego CA 92123 858-499-0202 499-0233 166
Web: www.coleman.edu

Coleman Worldwide Moving
PO Box 960 .... Midland City AL 36350 877-693-7060 780
TF: 877-693-7060 ■ *Web:* www.colemanallied.com

Coleman's Fish Market
2226 Centre Market .... Wheeling WV 26003 304-232-8510 671

Coleman-Adams Construction Inc
1031 Performance Rd .... Forest VA 24551 434-525-4700 186
Web: www.coleman-adams.com

Cole-Parmer Instrument Co
625 E Bunker Ct .... Vernon Hills IL 60061 847-549-7600 247-2929 420
TF: 800-323-4340 ■ *Web:* www.coleparmer.com

Coles Creek State Park 13003 NY-37 .... Waddington NY 13694 315-388-5636 565
Web: parks.ny.gov

Coles Marketing Communications Inc
3950 Priority Way S Dr Ste 106 .... Indianapolis IN 46240 317-571-0051 194
Web: www.colesmarketing.com

Coles Quality Foods Inc
25 Ottawa SW 4th Fl .... Grand Rapids MI 49503 616-975-0081 68
Web: www.coles.com

Coles-Moultrie Electric Co-op
104 DeWitt Ave E PO Box 709 .... Mattoon IL 61938 217-235-0341 234-8342 245
TF: 888-661-2632 ■ *Web:* www.cmec.coop

Colette Phillips Communications Inc (CPC)
177 State St Ste 6 .... Boston MA 02109 617-357-5777 357-7114 636
Web: www.cpcglobal.com

Coley & Associates Inc
140 Heimer Rd Ste 400 .... San Antonio TX 78232 210-402-6766 402-6829 396
Web: www.coleygsa.com

Colfax Corp
8730 Stony Pt Pkwy Ste 150 .... Richmond VA 23235 804-560-4076 641
Web: www.colfaxcorp.com

Colfax County 230 N Third St PO Box 1498 .... Raton NM 87740 575-445-9661 445-2902 338
Web: www.co.colfax.nm.us

Colfax County 411 E 11th St .... Schuyler NE 68661 402-352-8504 276-0206 338
Web: www.colfaxne.com

Colfax Elementary School
24825 Ben Taylor Rd .... Colfax CA 95713 530-346-2202 685
Web: www.colfax.k12.ca.us

Colgate Inn 1 Payne St .... Hamilton NY 13346 315-824-2300 824-4500 379
Web: www.colgateinn.com

Colgate Rochester Crozer Divinity School
1100 S Goodman St .... Rochester NY 14620 585-271-1320 271-8013 167-3
TF: 888-937-3732 ■ *Web:* www.crcds.edu

Colgate University 13 Oak Dr .... Hamilton NY 13346 315-228-1000 228-7544 166
Web: www.colgate.edu

Colibri Ltd
419 E Crossville Rd Ste 102 .... Roswell GA 30075 678-352-1001 180
Web: www.colibrilimited.com

Colich & Assn 10 S 5th St Ste 420 .... Minneapolis MN 55402 612-333-7007 41
Web: colichlaw.com

Colima Inc 130 N Fairview St .... Santa Ana CA 92703 714-836-1254 671
Web: colimarestaurant.com

Coliseum Medical Ctr 350 Hospital Dr .... Macon GA 31217 478-765-7000 374-3
TF: 877-467-0481 ■ *Web:* coliseumhealthsystem.com

Colite International Ltd
5 Technology Cir .... Columbia SC 29203 803-926-7926 610
TF: 800-760-7926 ■ *Web:* colite.com

CollabNet Inc
8000 Marina Blvd Ste 600 .... Brisbane CA 94005 650-228-2500 228-2501 177
TF: 888-532-6823 ■ *Web:* www.collab.net

Collabrus Inc
111 Sutter St Ste 900 .... San Francisco CA 94104 415-288-1826 734
Web: www.collabrus.com

CollabWorks 1695 Broadway .... Redwood City CA 94063 650-368-2523 393
Web: collabworks.com

Collado Engineering PC
2 Holland Ave .... White Plains NY 10603 914-332-7658 261
Web: collado-eng.com

Collarini Corp
11111 Richmond Ave Ste 126 .... Houston TX 77082 504-887-7127 539
Web: www.collarini.com

Colle & McVoy Inc
400 First Ave N Ste 700 .... Minneapolis MN 55401 612-305-6000 4
Web: collemcvoy.com

Collectcents Inc
1450 Meyerside Dr 2nd Fl .... Mississauga ON L5T2N5 905-670-7575 160
TF: 800-256-8964 ■ *Web:* www.collectcents.com

Collective Technologies LLC
9433 Bee Caves Rd Bldg III Ste 200 .... Austin TX 78733 512-263-5500 263-0606 225
Web: www.collectivegroup.com

Collective[i] 130 Madison Ave .... New York NY 10016 888-890-0020 466
TF: 888-890-0020 ■ *Web:* www.collectivei.com

Collectiveview Inc
3333 S Bannock St Ste 425 .... Englewood CO 80110 303-268-3800 806-0924 180
Web: www.collectiveview.com

Collector Car Network Inc
1345 E Chandler Blvd Ste 101 .... Phoenix AZ 85048 480-285-1600 285-1601 387
Web: classiccars.com

Collectors Alliance Inc
1942 Swarthmore Ave .... Lakewood NJ 08701 732-730-3580 292
Web: www.collectorsalliance.com

Collectors Universe Inc
PO Box 6280 .... Newport Beach CA 92658 949-567-1234 833-7955 51
TF: 800-325-1121 ■ *Web:* www.collectors.com

College & University Professional Association for Hum Res (CUPA-HR)
1811 Commons Pt Dr .... Knoxville TN 37932 865-637-7673 637-7674 49-5
TF: 877-287-2474 ■ *Web:* www.cupahr.org

College America
399 S Malpais 2nd Fl .... Flagstaff AZ 86001 928-774-1934 167-3
TF: 800-622-2894 ■ *Web:* www.collegeamerica.edu

College Board 45 Columbus Ave .... New York NY 10023 212-713-8000 244
TF: 800-927-4302 ■ *Web:* www.collegeboard.org

College De Maisonneuve
3800 Rue Sherbrooke St E .... Montreal QC H1X2A2 514-254-7131 165
Web: www.cmaisonneuve.qc.ca

College De Rosemont 6400 16e Ave .... Montreal QC H1X2S9 514-376-1620 376-1440 162
Web: www.crosemont.qc.ca

College De Valleyfield (cegep)
169 Rue Champlain .... Salaberry-de-Valleyfield QC J6T1X6 450-373-9441 165
Web: www.colval.qc.ca

College for Appraisers
12301 Whittier Blvd .... Whittier CA 90602 714-952-2727 167-3
Web: www.cfacollege.org

College Health Services LLC
112 Turnpike Rd Ste 304 .... Westborough MA 01581 866-636-8336 177
TF: 866-636-8336 ■ *Web:* he.studenthealth101.com

College Hospital Cerritos
10802 College Pl .... Cerritos CA 90703 562-924-9581 809-0981 374-5
TF: 800-352-3301 ■ *Web:* www.chc.la

College Houses Co-ops
1906 Pearl St Ofc 101 .... Austin TX 78705 512-476-5678 379
Web: collegehouses.org

College Internship Program Inc
199 South St .... Pittsfield MA 01201 413-344-4109 238-2122* 148
**Fax Area Code:* 617 ■ *Web:* cipworldwide.org

College Jacques-prevert
12349 Rue De Serres .... Montreal QC H4J2H1 514-336-2330 336-7091 623
Web: collegejacquesprevert.ca

College Jean De Brebeuf
3200 Cote-Sainte-Catherine Rd .... Montreal QC H3T1C1 514-342-9342 685
Web: www.brebeuf.qc.ca

College Marketing Group
7760 France Ave S Ste 1050 .... Bloomington MN 55435 866-721-1357 7
Web: collegemarketinggroup.com

College Merici
755 Grande Allee Ouest .... Quebec City QC G1S1C1 418-683-1591 682-8938 162
TF: 800-208-1463 ■ *Web:* www.merici.ca

College Militaire Royal de Saint-Jean Bibliotheque
15 Jacques Cartier Nord
Lahaie Pavilion Rm 210 .... Saint-Jean-sur-Richelieu QC J3B8R8 450-358-6777 358-7580 434-3
Web: www.cmrsj-rmcsj.forces.gc.ca

College Music Society (CMS)
312 E Pine St .... Missoula MT 59802 406-721-9616 721-9419 49-5
TF: 800-729-0235 ■ *Web:* www.music.org

College Nannies & Tutors Inc
850 Mill St .... Wayzata MN 55391 952-285-7667 260
Web: www.collegenanniesandtutors.com

College Notre Dame
3791 Chemin Queen Mary .... Montreal QC H3V1A8 514-739-3371 739-4833 685
Web: collegenotredame.com

College of Alameda
555 Ralph Appezzato Meml Pkwy .... Alameda CA 94501 510-522-7221 769-6019 162
Web: www.alameda.peralta.edu

College of American Pathologists (CAP)
325 Waukegan Rd .... Northfield IL 60093 847-832-7000 832-8168 49-8
TF: 800-323-4040 ■ *Web:* www.cap.org

College of Biblical Studies-Houston
7000 Regency Sq Blvd Ste 110 .... Houston TX 77036 713-785-5995 161
TF: 844-227-9673 ■ *Web:* www.cbshouston.edu

College of Charleston 66 George St .... Charleston SC 29424 843-805-5507 953-6322 166
Web: www.cofc.edu

College of Court Reporting Inc
111 W Tenth St Ste 111 .... Hobart IN 46342 866-294-3974 942-1631* 800
**Fax Area Code:* 219 ■ *TF:* 866-294-3974 ■ *Web:* www.ccr.edu

College of DuPage 425 Fawell Blvd .... Glen Ellyn IL 60137 630-942-2380 790-2686 162
Web: www.cod.edu

College of Eastern Idaho
1600 S 25th E .... Idaho Falls ID 83404 208-524-3000 525-7026 800
TF: 800-662-0261 ■ *Web:* www.cei.edu

College of Eastern Utah
San Juan 639 W 100 S .... Blanding UT 84511 435-678-2201 678-2220 162
TF: 800-395-2969 ■ *Web:* usueastern.edu

College of Family Physicians of Canada, The
2630 Skymark Ave .... Mississauga ON L4W5A4 905-629-0900 167
Web: www.cfpc.ca

College of Idaho 2112 Cleveland Blvd .... Caldwell ID 83605 208-459-5011 459-5757 166
TF: 800-224-3246 ■ *Web:* www.collegeofidaho.edu

College of Lake County
33 N Genessee St .... Waukegan IL 60085 847-543-2191 543-2170 162
Web: www.clcillinois.edu

College of Marin 835 College Ave .... Kentfield CA 94904 415-485-9502 162
Web: www1.marin.edu

College of Menominee Nation
PO Box 1179 .... Keshena WI 54135 715-799-5600 799-4392 165
TF: 800-567-2344 ■ *Web:* www.menominee.edu

College of Mount Saint Joseph
5701 Delhi Rd .... Cincinnati OH 45233 513-244-4200 244-4601 166
TF: 800-654-9314 ■ *Web:* www.msj.edu

College of Mount Saint Vincent
6301 Riverdale Ave .... Riverdale NY 10471 718-405-3304 166
TF: 800-722-4867 ■ *Web:* mountsaintvincent.edu

College of Nurses of Ontario
101 Davenport Rd .... Toronto ON M5R3P1 416-928-0900 162
TF: 800-387-5526 ■ *Web:* www.cno.org

College of Registered Nurses of Manitoba
890 Pembina Hwy .... Winnipeg MB R3M2M8 204-774-3477 165
TF: 800-665-2027 ■ *Web:* www.crnm.mb.ca

College of Saint Catherine
2004 Randolph Ave .... Saint Paul MN 55105 651-690-6000 166
TF: 800-945-4599 ■ *Web:* www.stkate.edu

College of Saint Mary 7000 Mercy Rd .... Omaha NE 68106 402-399-2400 399-2412 166
TF: 800-926-5534 ■ *Web:* www.csm.edu

College of Saint Rose 979 Madison Ave .... Albany NY 12203 800-637-8556 166
TF: 800-637-8556 ■ *Web:* www.strose.edu

College of Saint Scholastica
1200 Kenwood Ave .... Duluth MN 55811 218-723-6046 723-5991 166
TF: 800-447-5444 ■ *Web:* www.css.edu

College of San Mateo
1700 W Hillsdale Blvd .... San Mateo CA 94402 650-574-6161 574-6506 162
Web: www.collegeofsanmateo.edu

Name / Address	City	State	ZIP	Phone	Fax	Class
College of Santa Fe 1600 St Michaels Dr	Santa Fe	NM	87505	877-732-5977		166
TF: 800-862-7759 ■ *Web:* www.mycollegeoptions.org						
College of Southern Idaho PO Box 1238	Twin Falls	ID	83303	208-733-9554	736-3014	162
TF: 800-680-0274 ■ *Web:* www.csi.edu						
College of Southern Maryland 115 J W Williams Rd	Prince Frederick	MD	20678	443-550-6000	550-6100	162
TF: 800-933-9177 ■ *Web:* www.csmd.edu						
College of Southern Nevada 3200 E Cheyenne Ave	North Las Vegas	NV	89030	702-651-4000		162
Web: www.csn.edu						
College of Staten Island 2800 Victory Blvd	Staten Island	NY	10314	718-982-2000	982-2500	166
Web: www.csi.cuny.edu						
College of the Albemarle PO Box 2327	Elizabeth City	NC	27906	252-335-0821	335-2011	162
TF: 800-335-9050 ■ *Web:* www.albemarle.edu						
College of the Atlantic 105 Eden St	Bar Harbor	ME	04609	207-288-5015	288-4126	166
TF: 800-528-0025 ■ *Web:* www.coa.edu						
College of the Canyons 26455 Rockwell Canyon Rd	Santa Clarita	CA	91355	661-259-7800	362-5566	162
TF: 800-695-4858 ■ *Web:* www.canyons.edu						
College of the Desert 43-500 Monterey Ave	Palm Desert	CA	92260	760-346-8041	862-1379	162
Web: www.collegeofthedesert.edu						
College of the Holy Cross 1 College St	Worcester	MA	01610	508-793-2407	793-3888	166
TF: 800-442-2421 ■ *Web:* www.holycross.edu						
College of the Mainland 1200 N Amburn Rd	Texas City	TX	77591	409-938-1211		162
TF: 888-258-8859 ■ *Web:* www.com.edu						
College of the Ozarks PO Box 17	Point Lookout	MO	65726	417-334-6411	335-2618	166
TF: 800-222-0525 ■ *Web:* www.cofo.edu						
College of the Redwoods 7351 Tompkins Hill Rd	Eureka	CA	95501	707-476-4100	476-4406	162
TF: 800-641-0400 ■ *Web:* www.redwoods.edu						
College of the Sequoias 915 S Mooney Blvd	Visalia	CA	93277	559-730-3700		162
Web: www.cos.edu						
College of the Siskiyous 800 College Ave	Weed	CA	96094	530-938-5237	938-5367	162
TF: 888-397-4339 ■ *Web:* www.siskiyous.edu						
College of the Southwest 6610 N Lovington Hwy	Hobbs	NM	88240	575-392-6561		166
TF: 800-530-4400 ■ *Web:* www.usw.edu						
College of Westchester (CW) 325 Central Ave	White Plains	NY	10606	800-660-7093	948-5441*	800
**Fax Area Code:* 914 ■ *TF:* 800-660-7093 ■ *Web:* www.cw.edu						
College of Wooster 1189 Beall Ave	Wooster	OH	44691	330-263-2000	263-2621	166
TF: 800-877-9905 ■ *Web:* www.wooster.edu						
College Outlook & Career Opportunities Magazine 20 E Gregory Blvd	Kansas City	MO	64114	816-361-0616		457-11
TF: 800-274-8867 ■ *Web:* www.mymajors.com						
College Parents of America (CPA) 2200 Wilson Blvd Ste 102-396	Arlington	VA	22201	888-761-6702		48-11
TF: 888-761-6702 ■ *Web:* collegeparents.org						
College Pharmacy Inc 3505 Austin Bluffs Pkwy Ste 101	Colorado Springs	CO	80918	719-262-0022		237
TF: 800-888-9358 ■ *Web:* collegepharmacy.com						
College Recruiter Inc 7201 York Ave S Ste 410	Minneapolis	MN	55435	952-848-2211		260
Web: www.collegerecruiter.com						
College Regina Assumpta 1750 Rue Sauriol E	Montreal	QC	H2C1X4	514-382-4121		685
Web: www.reginaassumpta.qc.ca						
College Savings Bank PO Box 3769	Princeton	NJ	08543	800-888-2723	907-3760*	70
**Fax Area Code:* 609 ■ *TF:* 800-888-2723 ■ *Web:* www.collegesavings.com						
College Station Ford 1351 Earl Rudder Fwy	College Station	TX	77845	979-431-3394		57
TF: 888-508-0241 ■ *Web:* www.collegestationford.com						
College Station Medical Ctr 1604 Rock Prairie Rd	College Station	TX	77845	979-764-5100	764-5261	374-3
Web: www.csmedcenter.com						
College Village Animal Clinic Inc 2036 E Northern Lights Blvd	Anchorage	AK	99508	907-274-5623		794
Web: collegevillageanimalclinic.com						
CollegeBound Network 1200 S Ave Ste 202	Staten Island	NY	10314	718-761-4800	761-3300	637-9
Web: www.collegebound.net						
CollegeDegrees.com 1001 McKinney St Ste 400	Houston	TX	77002	713-534-1948	534-1949	387
Web: www.collegedegrees.com						
CollegeNET Inc 805 SW Broadway Ste 1600	Portland	OR	97205	503-973-5200	973-5252	423
Web: corp.collegenet.com						
Colleges Ontario 20 Bay St Ste 1600	Toronto	ON	M5J2N8	647-258-7670	258-7699	242
Web: www.collegesontario.org						
Collegiate Directories Inc (NACDA) PO Box 450640	Cleveland	OH	44145	440-835-1172	835-8835	637-2
TF: 800-426-2232 ■ *Web:* www.collegiatedirectories.com						
Collegiate Funding Services LLC 10304 Spotsylvania Ave	Fredericksburg	VA	22408	540-374-1600		217
Web: htyp.org						
Collegium Pharmaceutical Inc 400 Highland Corporate Dr	Cumberland	RI	02864	401-762-2000		231
Web: collegiumpharma.com						
Collen IP Intellectual Property Law P C 80 S Highland Ave	Ossining	NY	10562	914-941-5668		445
Web: collenip.com						
Colleton County 31 Klein St Harrelson Bldg Rm 109	Walterboro	SC	29488	843-782-4282	549-7215	338
Web: www.colletoncounty.org						
Colleton County Memorial Library 600 Hampton St	Walterboro	SC	29488	843-549-5621	549-5122	434-3
Web: www.colletonlibrary.org						
Colleton Medical Ctr (CMC) 501 Robertson Blvd	Walterboro	SC	29488	843-782-2000		374-3
TF: 866-492-9083 ■ *Web:* colletonmedical.com						
Colleton State Park 147 Wayside Ln	Walterboro	SC	29488	843-538-8206		565
Web: southcarolinaparks.com						
Collett & Associates LLC 1111 Metropolitan Ave Ste 700	Charlotte	NC	28204	704-206-8300		652
Web: www.collettre.com						
Colletti-fiss LLC 8423 E Charter Oak Dr	Scottsdale	AZ	85260	480-483-1480		195
Web: collettifiss.com						
Collicutt Energy Services Ltd 8133 Edgar Industrial Close	Red Deer	AB	T4P3R4	403-309-9250		112
Web: www.collicutt.com						
Collie Drugs Inc 21728 Harper Ave	Saint Clair Shores	MI	48080	586-776-6122		237
Web: colliedrugs.com						
Collier County Museum 3331 Tamiami Trl E	Naples	FL	34112	239-252-8476		520
Web: www.colliermuseums.com						
Collier County Public Library (CCPL) 2385 Orange Blossom Dr	Naples	FL	34109	239-593-0177		434-3
Web: www.colliercountyfl.gov						
Collier County School Board 5775 Osceola Trl	Naples	FL	34109	239-377-0001	377-0336	685
Web: www.collierschools.com						
Collier Enterprises Management Inc 2550 Goodlette Rd N Ste 100	Naples	FL	34103	239-261-4455		652
Web: www.collierenterprises.com						
Collier Gobel Homann LLC 100 W Main St PO Box 838	Crawfordsville	IN	47933	765-362-1099		41
Web: cghlegal.com						
Collier Insurance 606 S Mendenhall Rd Ste 200	Memphis	TN	38117	901-529-2900	529-2916	390
TF: 866-600-2655 ■ *Web:* www.collierinsurance.com						
Collier Memorial State Park 46000 Hwy 97 N	Chiloquin	OR	97624	541-783-2471		565
Web: stateparks.oregon.gov						
Colliers Intl 6606 W Broad St Ste 400	Richmond	VA	23226	804-788-1000		652
Web: www2.colliers.com						
Colliers Intl 1 Almaden Blvd Ste 300	San Jose	CA	95113	408-282-4000	282-4001	652
Web: www.colliersparrish.com						
Collier-Seminole State Park 20200 E Tamiami Trl	Naples	FL	34114	239-394-3397	394-5113	565
Web: www.floridastateparks.org						
Collierville Chamber of Commerce 485 Halle Pk Dr	Collierville	TN	38017	901-853-1949	853-2399	139
Web: www.colliervillechamber.com						
Colliflower Inc 9320 Pulaski Hwy	Baltimore	MD	21220	410-686-1200		295
Web: www.colliflower.com						
Colligo Networks Inc 400-1152 Mainland St	Vancouver	BC	V6B4X2	604-685-7962		179
TF: 866-685-7962 ■ *Web:* www.colligo.com						
Collin County 2300 Bloomdale Rd Ste 2106	McKinney	TX	75071	972-548-4185	547-5731	338
TF: 800-974-2437 ■ *Web:* www.collincountytx.gov						
Collin County Community College 9700 Wade Blvd	Frisco	TX	75035	972-377-1582	377-1723	162
Web: www.collin.edu						
Collin Creek Mall 811 N Central Expy	Plano	TX	75075	972-422-1070		460
Web: www.collincreekmall.com						
Collin Street Bakery Inc 401 W Seventh Ave	Corsicana	TX	75110	800-267-4657	872-6879*	68
**Fax Area Code:* 903 ■ *TF:* 800-267-4657 ■ *Web:* www.collinstreet.com						
Colling, Gilbert, Wright & Carter 801 N Orange Ave Ste 830	Orlando	FL	32801	407-712-7300		41
Web: thefloridafirm.com						
Collings & Associates LLC 260 Maple Ct Ste 241	Ventura	CA	93003	805-658-0003		261
Web: collingsandassociates.com						
Collingswood Nursing Facilities Inc 299 Hurley Ave	Rockville	MD	20850	301-762-8900		371
Web: www.collingswoodnursing.com						
Collingsworth County 800 W Ave	Wellington	TX	79095	806-447-5408	447-5418	338
Web: co.collingsworth.tx.us						
Collington Episcopal Community 10450 Lottsford Rd	Mitchellville	MD	20721	888-257-9468		672
TF: 888-257-9468 ■ *Web:* collington.kendal.org						
Collins & Hermann Inc 1215 Dunn Rd	Saint Louis	MO	63138	314-869-8000		492
Web: collinsandhermann.com						
Collins & Lacy PC 1330 Lady St 6th Fl	Columbia	SC	29201	803-256-2660		428
TF: 888-648-0526 ■ *Web:* www.collinsandlacy.com						
Collins Bowling Centers Inc 205 Southland Dr	Lexington	KY	40505	859-277-5746		99
Web: www.collinsbowling.com						
Collins Bus Corp 415 W Sixth Ave	South Hutchinson	KS	67505	620-662-9000		59
Web: www.collinsbus.com						
Collins Communications Inc 1009 W Jackson St	Demopolis	AL	36732	334-289-0439		246
Web: www.westal.net						
Collins Community Credit Union 1150 42nd St NE	Cedar Rapids	IA	52402	319-393-9000		219
Web: www.collinscu.org						
Collins Computing Inc 26050 Acero St	Mission Viejo	CA	92691	949-457-0500		177
Web: www.collinscomputing.com						
Collins Consulting 630 Woofter Ave	Colby	KS	67701	785-462-8352		194
Web: www.collins.net						
Collins Correctional Facility Middle Rd PO Box 490	Collins	NY	14034	716-532-4588		213
Web: www.doccs.ny.gov						
Collins Cos 3113 S Taft Hill Rd Ste 500	Portland	OR	97201	800-329-1219	227-5349*	683
**Fax Area Code:* 503 ■ *TF:* 800-329-1219 ■ *Web:* www.collinsco.com						
Collins Crane and Rigging Service Inc 408 Spring St	East Bridgewater	MA	02333	508-378-3435	378-1526	190
Web: www.collinscrane.com						
Collins Digital Imaging 1218 B Old Chattahoochee Ave	Atlanta	GA	30318	404-525-0406		627
Web: collinsdigital.com						

Name / Address	City	State	Zip	Phone	Fax	Class
Collins Doug (Rep R - GA) 1504 Longworth House Office Bldg *Web:* dougcollins.house.gov	Washington	DC	20515	202-225-9893	226-1224	342-2
Collins Electric Company Inc 53 Second Ave *TF:* 877-553-2810 ■ *Web:* www.collinselectricco.com	Chicopee	MA	01020	413-592-9221	592-4157	189-4
Collins Hannafin PC 148 Deer Hill Ave *Web:* chgjtlaw.com	Danbury	CT	06810	203-885-1938		41
Collins Industries Ltd 3740-73 Ave *Web:* www.collins-industries-ltd.com	Edmonton	AB	T6B2Z2	780-440-1414		480
Collins Irish Pub 2 N Leroux St *Web:* collinsirishpub.com	Flagstaff	AZ	86001	928-214-7363		671
Collins Law Firm PC, The 1770 Park St Ste 200 *TF:* 866-480-8223 ■ *Web:* www.collinslaw.com	Naperville	IL	60563	630-687-9838	527-1193	445
Collins Manufacturing Co 2000 Bowser Rd *TF:* 800-292-6450 ■ *Web:* collins.co	Cookeville	TN	38506	931-528-5151	528-5472	76
Collins Plumbing Inc 8130 Commercial St *Web:* www.collinsplumbing.com	La Mesa	CA	91942	619-469-0800	469-0930	189-10
Collins Susan M (Sen R - ME) 413 Dirksen Senate Office Bldg *Web:* www.collins.senate.gov	Washington	DC	20510	202-224-2523	224-2693	342-2
Collins, Fitzpatrick & Schoene LLP 34 S Broadway Ste 407 *Web:* cfsllp-law.com	White Plains	NY	10601	914-437-8020		41
Collinsville Chamber of Commerce 221 W Main St *Web:* www.discovercollinsville.com	Collinsville	IL	62234	618-344-2884	344-7499	139
Collinsville Community 201 W Clay St *Web:* www.kahoks.org	Collinsville	IL	62234	618-343-2878		148
Collis & Griffor Pc 1851 Washtenaw Ave *Web:* collisandgriffor.com	Ypsilanti	MI	48197	734-827-1337		41
Colloidal Dynamics Pty Ltd 5150 Palm Valley Rd Ste 303 *Web:* www.colloidal-dynamics.com	Ponte Vedra Beach	FL	32082	904-686-1536		201
Collum's Lumber Products LLC 1723 Barnwell Hwy *Web:* collumlumber.com	Allendale	SC	29810	803-584-3451		683
Colmac Coil Manufacturing Inc 370 N Lincoln St PO Box 571 *TF:* 800-845-6778 ■ *Web:* www.colmaccoil.com	Colville	WA	99114	509-684-2595	684-8331	14
Colmac Industries Inc PO Box 72 *TF:* 800-926-5622 ■ *Web:* www.colmacind.com	Colville	WA	99114	509-684-4505	684-4500	427
Colman Wolf Sanitary Supply Co 15201 E 11-Mile Rd *Web:* www.theprofgroup.com	Roseville	MI	48066	586-779-5500		508
Colmery-O'Neil Veterans Affairs Medical Ctr 2200 SW Gage Blvd *TF:* 800-574-8387 ■ *Web:* www.topeka.va.gov	Topeka	KS	66622	785-350-3111		374-8
Col-Met Spray Booths Inc 1635 Innovation Dr *Web:* www.colmetsb.com	Rockwall	TX	75032	972-772-1919		111
Cologix Inc 225 E 16th Ave *TF:* 800-638-6336 ■ *Web:* www.cologix.com	Denver	CO	80202	720-230-7000		224
Colography Group Inc, The 47 Perimeter Ctr E Ste 600 *Web:* www.colography.com	Atlanta	GA	30346	678-385-2500	385-2501	466
Coloma Frozen Foods Inc 4145 Coloma Rd *TF:* 800-642-2723 ■ *Web:* www.colomafrozen.com	Coloma	MI	49038	269-849-0500	849-0886	296-21
Colombia 140 E 57th St *Web:* nuevayork-onu.mision.gov.co	New York	NY	10022	212-355-7776	371-2813	784
Colombia						
Consulate General 5851 San Felipe Ste 300 *Web:* www.colhouston.org	Houston	TX	77057	713-527-8919	529-3395	257
Embassy 1724 Massachusetts Ave NW *Web:* www.colombiaemb.org	Washington	DC	20036	202-387-8338	232-8643	257
General Consulate of Colombia in Chicago 500 N Michigan Ave Ste 1960 *TF:* 888-764-3326 ■ *Web:* chicago.consulado.gov.co	Chicago	IL	60611	312-923-1196	923-1197	257
Colombo, Kitchin, Dunn, Ball & Porter LLP 1698 E Arlington Blvd *Web:* ck-attorneys.com	Greenville	NC	27858	252-321-2020		41
Colonel Florence A Blanchfield Army Community Hospital 650 Joel Dr *Web:* www.blanchfield.amedd.army.mil	Fort Campbell	KY	42223	270-798-8400		374-4
Colonial Air 1605 Airport Rd *Web:* www.colonial-air.com	New Bedford	MA	02746	508-997-0620	990-2582	63
Colonial Bag Company Inc PO Box 929 *TF:* 800-392-4875 ■ *Web:* www.colonial-bag.com	Lake Park	GA	31636	229-559-8484	559-0085	65
Colonial Bag Corp 205 E Fullerton Ave *TF:* 800-445-7496 ■ *Web:* www.colonialbag.com	Carol Stream	IL	60188	630-690-3999	690-1571	66
Colonial Bronze Co 511 Winsted Rd **Fax Area Code:* 800 ■ *Web:* www.colonialbronze.com	Torrington	CT	06790	860-489-9233	355-7903*	350
Colonial Circuits Inc 1026 Warrenton Rd **Fax Area Code:* 540 ■ *TF:* 800-578-9602 ■ *Web:* www.colonialcircuits.com	Fredericksburg	VA	22406	800-578-9602	752-2109*	625
Colonial Dorchester State Historic Site 300 State Park Rd *Web:* southcarolinaparks.com	Summerville	SC	29485	843-873-1740		565
Colonial DPP 2055 Forrest St *TF:* 800-303-3606 ■ *Web:* www.colonialdpp.com	Dyersburg	TN	38024	731-287-3636		677
Colonial Engineering Inc 6400 Corporate Ave *TF:* 800-374-0234 ■ *Web:* colonialengineering.com	Portage	MI	49002	269-323-2495	323-0630	595
Colonial Farm Credit Aca 7104 Mechanicsville Tpke *TF:* 800-777-8908 ■ *Web:* www.colonialfarmcredit.com	Mechanicsville	VA	23111	804-746-1252		216
Colonial Ford Truck Sales Inc 1833 Commerce Rd *TF:* 800-234-8782 ■ *Web:* www.colonialtruck.net	Richmond	VA	23224	804-232-3492		780
Colonial Freight Systems Inc 10924 McBride Ln *TF:* 800-826-1402 ■ *Web:* www.cfsi.com	Knoxville	TN	37932	865-966-9711	966-3649	780
Colonial Garage & Distributors Ltd 59 Majors Path *Web:* www.colonialautoparts.ca	Saint John	NL	A1A4Z9	709-576-7278	576-3389	61
Colonial Group Inc 101 N Lathrop Ave *TF:* 800-944-3835 ■ *Web:* www.colonialgroupinc.com	Savannah	GA	31415	800-944-3835		324
Colonial Heights (Independent City) 201 James Ave PO Box 3401 *Web:* www.colonialheightsva.gov	Colonial Heights	VA	23834	804-520-9265	520-9207	338
Colonial Hills Baptist Church 8140 Union Chapel Rd *Web:* www.colonialindy.org	Indianapolis	IN	46240	317-253-5597	254-2847	48-20
Colonial House 2315 Mt Rushmore Rd *Web:* www.colonialhousernb.com	Rapid City	SD	57701	605-342-4640		671
Colonial Intermediate Unit 20 6 Danforth Rd *Web:* www.ciu20.org	Easton	PA	18045	610-252-5550	252-5740	148
Colonial Life & Accident Insurance Co 1200 Colonial Life Blvd *TF:* 800-325-4368 ■ *Web:* www.coloniallife.com	Columbia	SC	29210	800-345-4368		391-2
Colonial Lloyds PO Box 2988 *TF:* 800-937-6001 ■ *Web:* www.gocolonial.com	Fort Worth	TX	76113	817-390-2000		796
Colonial Loan Assn 2645 W Andrew Johnson Hwy Ste B *Web:* www.colonialloan.com	Morristown	TN	37814	423-586-1125		217
Colonial Machine Co 1041 Mogadore Rd *Web:* www.colonial-machine.com	Kent	OH	44240	330-673-5859		757
Colonial Materials of Fayetteville Inc 570 Belt Blvd *Web:* www.colonialmaterials.com	Fayetteville	NC	28301	910-485-5099		191-1
Colonial Medical Supplies 915 S Orange Ave *TF:* 800-747-0246 ■ *Web:* www.colonialmed.com	Orlando	FL	32806	407-849-6455	849-6458	475
Colonial Metal Products Inc 2350 Quality Ln *Web:* www.colonialmetalproducts.com	Hermitage	PA	16148	724-346-6379		492
Colonial Metals Co 217 Linden St PO Box 311 *Web:* www.colonialmetalsco.com	Columbia	PA	17512	717-684-2311	684-9555	485
Colonial Mills Inc 560 Mineral Spring Ave *Web:* www.colonialmills.com	Pawtucket	RI	02860	401-724-6279		364
Colonial Millwork Ltd PO Box 436 *TF:* 800-833-7612 ■ *Web:* colonialmillwork.com	Beverly	WV	26253	800-833-7612		499
Colonial National Historical Park PO Box 210 *TF:* 866-945-7920 ■ *Web:* www.nps.gov	Yorktown	VA	23690	757-898-3400	898-6346	564
Colonial Nursing & Rehabilitation Inc 125 Broad St *TF:* 800-245-8389 ■ *Web:* www.welchhrg.com	Weymouth	MA	02188	781-337-3121		450
Colonial Opticians 4942 St Elmo Ave *Web:* colonialopticians.com	Bethesda	MD	20814	301-657-3332		543
Colonial Parking Inc 1050 Thomas Jefferson St NW Ste 100 *Web:* www.ecolonial.com	Washington	DC	20007	202-295-8100	295-8111	562
Colonial Parking Inc 715 Orange St *TF:* 888-672-7536 ■ *Web:* www.colonialparking.com	Wilmington	DE	19801	302-651-3600		562
Colonial Patterns Inc 920 Overholt Rd *Web:* www.colonialpatt.com	Kent	OH	44240	330-673-6475	673-7577	567
Colonial Pemaquid State Historic Site PO Box 304 *Web:* www.maine.gov	New Harbor	ME	04554	207-677-2423		565
Colonial Penn Life Insurance Co 399 Market St *TF:* 800-523-9100 ■ *Web:* colonialpenn.com	Philadelphia	PA	19181	877-877-8052		391-2
Colonial Pipeline Co 1185 Sanctuary Pkwy Ste 100 *TF:* 800-275-3004 ■ *Web:* www.colpipe.com	Alpharetta	GA	30009	678-762-2200	762-2883	597
Colonial Press Inc, The 10607 Harrison St *Web:* www.thecolonialpress.net	La Vista	NE	68128	402-593-0580		627
Colonial Press International Inc 3690 NW 50th St *TF:* 800-767-1581 ■ *Web:* www.colonialpressintl.com	Miami	FL	33142	305-633-1581		627
Colonial Quarter 33 St George St *TF:* 888-991-0933 ■ *Web:* www.colonialquarter.com	Saint Augustine	FL	32084	888-991-0933		520
Colonial Saw Company Inc 122 Pembroke St *Web:* www.csaw.com	Kingston	MA	02364	781-585-4364	585-9375	358
Colonial Society of Massachusetts (CSM) 87 Mount Vernon St *Web:* www.colonialsociety.org	Boston	MA	02108	617-227-2782		48-13
Colonial Spirits of Stow 117 Great Rd *Web:* colonialstow.com	Stow	MA	01775	978-897-2303		443
Colonial Spirits, The 87 Great Rd *Web:* www.colonialspirits.com	Acton	MA	01720	978-263-7775		443
Colonial Systems Inc 326 Ballardvale St Ste 200 *Web:* colonialsystems.com	Wilmington	MA	01887	978-657-6508		179
Colonial Van and Storage Inc 6001 88th St *TF:* 888-581-6667 ■ *Web:* www.colonialvan.com	Sacramento	CA	95828	916-546-3600		519
Colonial Williamsburg Foundation PO Box 1776 *Web:* www.history.org	Williamsburg	VA	23187	757-229-1000		305
Colonial Williamsburg Foundation, The 101 Visitor Center Dr *TF:* 800-447-8679 ■ *Web:* colonialwilliamsburg.com	Williamsburg	VA	23185	888-965-7254		520
ColonialWebb Contractors Co 3719 E Virginia Beach Blvd *TF:* 877-208-3894 ■ *Web:* www.colonialwebb.com	Richmond	VA	23228	804-916-1400		189-10
Colonie Ctr 131 Colonie Ctr *Web:* shopatcoloniecenter.com	Albany	NY	12205	518-459-9020		460
Colonna Bros Inc 4102 Bergen Tpke *Web:* www.colonnabrothers.com	North Bergen	NJ	07047	201-864-1115	864-0144	296-5
Colonna's Shipyard Inc 400 E Indian River Rd *TF:* 800-265-6627 ■ *Web:* www.colonnaship.com	Norfolk	VA	23523	757-545-2414	543-2480	698

				Phone	Fax	Class
Colonnade Hotel 120 Huntington Ave *TF:* 800-962-3030 ■ *Web:* www.colonnadehotel.com	Boston	MA	02116	617-424-7000	424-1717	379
Colony Brands Inc 1112 7th Ave *Web:* www.swisscolony.com	Monroe	WI	53566	608-328-8400	328-8457	459
Colony Capital Management 3050 Peachtree Rd NW Ste 200 *Web:* www.colonycapital.com	Atlanta	GA	30305	404-365-5050	523-7877	401
Colony Group LLC, The 2 Atlantic Ave *Web:* www.thecolonygroup.com	Boston	MA	02110	617-723-8200	723-6338	194
Colony Group, The 11 S Main St Ste 501 *Web:* www.harvestcap.com	Concord	NH	03301	603-224-6994		528
Colony Hotel 140 Ocean Ave *TF:* 800-552-2363 ■ *Web:* www.thecolonyhotel.com	Kennebunkport	ME	04046	207-967-3331		669
Colony Inc 2500 Galvin Dr *TF:* 800-735-1300 ■ *Web:* www.colonydisplay.com	Elgin	IL	60123	847-426-5300		233
Colony Palms Hotel 572 N Indian Canyon Dr *TF:* 800-557-2187 ■ *Web:* www.colonypalmshotel.com	Palm Springs	CA	92262	760-969-1800		132
Colony Pub & Grille 2670 W Eigth St *Web:* www.colonypub.com	Erie	PA	16505	814-838-2162		671
Colony Public Library, The 5151 N Colony Blvd *Web:* www.thecolonytx.gov	The Colony	TX	75056	972-625-1900	624-2281	434-3
Colony South Hotel 7401 Surratts Rd *Web:* www.colonysouth.com	Clinton	MD	20735	301-856-4500		379
Color Ad Inc 18601 S Santa Fe Ave *TF:* 888-264-6991 ■ *Web:* www.gocolorad.com	Compton	CA	90221	888-264-6991		627
Color Art Integrated Interiors 1325 N Warson Rd *Web:* www.color-art.com	Saint Louis	MO	63132	314-432-3000		320
Color Communication Inc 4000 W Fillmore St **Fax Area Code:* 773 ■ *TF:* 800-458-5743 ■ *Web:* www.ccicolor.com	Chicago	IL	60624	800-458-5743	638-0887*	781
Color House Graphics Inc 3505 Eastern Ave SE *TF:* 800-454-1916 ■ *Web:* www.colorhousegraphics.com	Grand Rapids	MI	49508	616-241-1916		781
Color Imaging Inc 4350 Peachtree Industrial Blvd Ste 100 **Fax Area Code:* 000 ■ *TF:* 800-783-1090 ■ *Web:* www.colorimaging.com	Norcross	GA	30071	770-840-1090	783 0010*	620
Color Inc 1600 Flower St *Web:* www.colorincorporated.com	Glendale	CA	91201	818-240-1350		627
Color Ink Inc W250 N6681 Hwy 164 PO Box 360 *Web:* www.colorink.com	Sussex	WI	53089	262-246-5000		627
Color Kinetics Distribution Inc 1247 Norwood Ave *Web:* www.colorkinetics.com	Itasca	IL	60143	630-285-9772		253
Color Marketing Group (CMG) 1908 Mt Vernon Ave *Web:* colormarketing.org	Alexandria	VA	22301	703-329-8500		49-18
Color Me Beautiful 7000 Infantry Ridge Rd Ste 200 *TF:* 800-265-6763 ■ *Web:* www.colormebeautiful.com	Manassas	VA	20109	800-265-6763		366
Color Me Mine Enterprises Inc 3722 San Fernando Rd **Fax Area Code:* 858 ■ *Web:* www.colormemine.com	Glendale	CA	91204	818-291-5900	312-5501*	310
Color Merchants 6 E 45th St Rm 1704 *TF:* 800-356-3851 ■ *Web:* www.colormerchants.com	New York	NY	10017	212-682-4788		410
Color Optics 40 Green Pond Rd *Web:* www.coloroptics.com	Rockaway	NJ	07866	973-664-3100		92
Color Pigments Manufacturers Association Inc 1400 Crystal Dr Ste 630 **Fax Area Code:* 703 ■ *TF:* 888-233-9527 ■ *Web:* www.pigments.org	Arlington	VA	22202	571-348-5130	684-1795*	49-13
Color Putty Company Inc PO Box 738 *Web:* www.colorputty.com	Monroe	WI	53566	608-325-6033	325-6397	550
Color Reflections 10795 Rockley Rd *Web:* www.colorreflections.com	Houston	TX	77099	713-626-4045		113
Color Room 1155 Wentzville Pkwy *Web:* wentzvillecolorroom.com	Wentzville	MO	63385	636-856-1400		77
Color Spot Nurseries Inc 2575 Olive Hill Rd **Fax Area Code:* 800 ■ *TF:* 800-554-4065 ■ *Web:* www.colorspot.com	Fallbrook	CA	92028	760-695-1480	250-5135*	369
Color Voodoo Publications 3907 Maunahilu Pl Ste C *Web:* www.colorvoodoo.com	Honolulu	HI	96816	707-709-8988		637-2
Color Web Printers Inc 4700 Bowling St SW *TF:* 888-265-1511 ■ *Web:* www.colorwebprinters.com	Cedar Rapids	IA	52404	888-265-1511		627
Colorado						
Agriculture Dept 305 Interlocken Pkwy *Web:* www.colorado.gov	Broomfield	CO	80021	303-869-9000		339-6
Attorney General 1300 Broadway 10th Fl *Web:* www.coloradoattorneygeneral.gov	Denver	CO	80203	720-508-6000	508-6030	339-6
Banking Div 1560 Broadway St Ste 975 *Web:* www.colorado.gov	Denver	CO	80202	303-894-7575		339-6
Child Support Enforcement Div 1575 Sherman St 5th Fl *TF:* 800-374-6558 ■ *Web:* childsupport.state.co.us	Denver	CO	80203	303-866-4300	866-4360	339-6
Children Youth & Families Office 1575 Sherman St *Web:* www.colorado.gov	Denver	CO	80203	303-866-4119		339-6
CollegeInvest 1560 Broadway Ste 1700 *TF:* 800-448-2424 ■ *Web:* www.collegeinvest.org	Denver	CO	80202	303-376-8800	296-4811	725
Corrections Dept 2862 S Cir Dr *Web:* www.colorado.gov	Colorado Springs	CO	80906	719-579-9580		339-6
Division of Criminal Justice 700 Kipling St Ste 1000 *TF:* 888-282-1080 ■ *Web:* www.colorado.gov	Denver	CO	80215	303-239-4442	239-4491	339-6
Education Dept 201 E Colfax Ave *Web:* www.cde.state.co.us	Denver	CO	80203	303-866-6600	830-0793	339-6
Emergency Management Office 9195 E Mineral Ave *Web:* www.coemergency.com	Centennial	CO	80112	720-279-0026		339-6
General Assembly 200 E Colfax Ave *Web:* www.leg.state.co.us	Denver	CO	80203	303-866-3521		339-6
Governor 136 State Capitol Bldg *Web:* www.colorado.gov	Denver	CO	80203	303-866-2471		339-6
Higher Education Commission 1380 Lawrence St Ste 470 *Web:* www.colorado.gov	Denver	CO	80202	303-556-2448	315-2048	339-6
Housing & Finance Authority 1313 Sherman St Rm 500 *Web:* www.colorado.gov	Denver	CO	80203	303-864-7810	864-7856	339-6
Human Services Dept 1575 Sherman St *Web:* www.colorado.gov	Denver	CO	80203	303-866-5700	866-5563	339-6
Insurance Div 1560 Broadway Ste 850 *TF:* 800-930-3745 ■ *Web:* www.colorado.gov	Denver	CO	80202	303-894-7499	894-7455	339-6
Labor & Employment Dept 633 17th St Ste 201 *TF:* 800-388-5515 ■ *Web:* www.colorado.gov	Denver	CO	80202	303-318-8000		259
Lieutenant Governor 130 State Capitol Bldg *Web:* www.colorado.gov	Denver	CO	80203	303-866-2087		339-6
Lottery 225 N Main St *TF:* 800-999-2959 ■ *Web:* www.coloradolottery.com	Pueblo	CO	81003	719-546-2400	546-5208	452
Measurements Standards Section 3125 Wyandot St *Web:* www.colorado.gov	Denver	CO	80211	303-477-4220	477-4248	339-6
Medical Examiners Board 1560 Broadway Ste 1350 *Web:* www.colorado.gov	Denver	CO	80202	303-894-2121	894-7692	339-6
Motor Vehicle Div 1881 Pierce St *Web:* www.colorado.gov	Lakewood	CO	80214	303-205-5600		339-6
Natural Resources Dept 1313 Sherman St Rm 718 *TF:* 800-536-5308 ■ *Web:* www.dnr.state.co.us	Denver	CO	80203	303-866-3311		339-6
Office of Information Technology 601 E 18th Ave Ste 250 *Web:* www.colorado.gov	Denver	CO	80203	303-764-7700		339-6
Parks & Wildlife 1313 Sherman St Rm 618 *TF:* 800-678-2267 ■ *Web:* www.cpw.state.co.us	Denver	CO	80203	303-866-3437		339-6
Public Health & Environment Dept (CDPHE) 4300 Cherry Creek Dr S *Web:* www.colorado.gov	Denver	CO	80246	303-692-2000		339-6
Public Utilities Commission 1560 Broadway Ste 250 *TF:* 800-888-0170 ■ *Web:* www.colorado.gov	Denver	CO	80202	303-894-2000	894-2065	339-6
Real Estate Commission 1560 Broadway Ste 925 *Web:* www.colorado.gov	Denver	CO	80202	303-894-2166	894-2683	339-6
Regulatory Agencies Dept 1560 Broadway Ste 110 *TF:* 800-886-7675 ■ *Web:* www.colorado.gov	Denver	CO	80202	303-894-7855		339-6
Secretary of State 1700 Broadway Ste 200 *TF:* 855-428-3555 ■ *Web:* www.sos.state.co.us	Denver	CO	80290	303-894-2200	869-4867	339-6
Securities Div 1560 Broadway Ste 900 *Web:* www.colorado.gov	Denver	CO	80202	303-894-2320	861-2126	339-6
State Court Administrator 1300 Broadway Ste 210 *TF:* 800-888-0001 ■ *Web:* www.courts.state.co.us	Denver	CO	80203	720-625-5000		339-6
State Government Information 1525 Sherman St 4th Fl *Web:* www.colorado.gov	Denver	CO	80203	303-866-2000	866-5909	339-6
State Patrol 700 Kipling St *Web:* www.colorado.gov	Lakewood	CO	80215	303-239-4500		339-6
Supreme Court 1300 Broadway Ste 500 *TF:* 877-888-1370 ■ *Web:* www.coloradosupremecourt.com	Denver	CO	80203	303-457-5800		339-6
Tourism Office 1625 Broadway St Ste 2700 *Web:* www.colorado.com	Denver	CO	80202	303-892-3840	892-3848	339-6
Transportation Dept 4201 E Arkansas Ave *Web:* www.codot.gov	Denver	CO	80222	303-757-9228	757-9669	339-6
Treasurer 200 E Colfax Ave State Capitol Ste 140 *Web:* www.colorado.gov	Denver	CO	80203	303-866-2441	866-2123	339-6
Vital Records Section 4300 Cherry Creek Dr S *Web:* www.colorado.gov	Denver	CO	80246	303-692-2200		339-6
Vocational Rehabilitation Div 2211 W Evans *Web:* www.colorado.gov	Denver	CO	80223	720-595-6747		339-6
Workers Compensation Div 633 17th St Ste 400 *Web:* www.colorado.gov	Denver	CO	80202	303-318-8700		339-6
Colorado Academy 3800 S Pierce St *Web:* www.coloradoacademy.org	Denver	CO	80235	303-986-1501		685
Colorado Access 10065 E Harvard Ave Ste 600 *TF:* 877-441-6032 ■ *Web:* www.coaccess.com	Denver	CO	80231	303-751-2657	751-9048	391-3
Colorado Advanced Esthetics Inc 13111 E Briarwood Ave Ste 310 *Web:* www.coloradoesthetictraining.com	Centennial	CO	80112	303-768-8811		167-3
Colorado Asphalt Services Inc 3700 E 56th Ave *Web:* www.coloradoasphalt.com	Commerce City	CO	80022	303-292-3434	292-6267	189-3
Colorado Association of Commerce & Industry 1600 Broadway Ste 1000 *Web:* www.cochamber.com	Denver	CO	80202	303-831-7411	860-1439	140
Colorado Association of Realtors 309 Inverness Way S *TF:* 800-944-6550 ■ *Web:* www.coloradorealtors.com	Englewood	CO	80112	303-790-7099	790-7299	656
Colorado Ballet 1278 Lincoln St *Web:* www.coloradoballet.org	Denver	CO	80203	303-837-8888	861-7174	573-1
Colorado Bar Assn 1290 Broadway Ste 1700 *TF:* 800-332-6736 ■ *Web:* www.cobar.org	Denver	CO	80203	303-860-1115	894-0821	72
Colorado Belle Hotel & Casino 2100 S Casino Dr *TF:* 877-460-0777 ■ *Web:* www.coloradobelle.com	Laughlin	NV	89029	702-298-4000		133
Colorado Bend State Park PO Box 118 *Web:* tpwd.texas.gov	Bend	TX	76824	325-628-3240		565
Colorado Boxed Beef Co 302 Progress Rd *Web:* coloradoboxedbeef.com	Auburndale	FL	33823	863-967-0636		297-9

Name / Address	Phone	Fax	Class
Colorado Cattle Company & Guest Ranch 70008 County Rd 132 ..... New Raymer CO 80742 *Web:* coloradocattlecompany.com	970-437-5345		239
Colorado Christian University 8787 W Alameda Ave ..... Lakewood CO 80226 *TF:* 800-443-2484 ■ *Web:* www.ccu.edu	303-963-3000	963-3201	166
Colorado College 14 E Cache La Poudre St ..... Colorado Springs CO 80903 *TF:* 800-542-7214 ■ *Web:* coloradocollege.edu	719-389-6344	389-6816	166
Colorado Community College System 9101 E Lowry Blvd ..... Denver CO 80230 *Web:* www.cccs.edu	303-620-4000	620-4030	162
Colorado Container Corp 4221 Monaco St ..... Denver CO 80216 *Fax Area Code: 303 ■ *TF:* 800-456-4725 ■ *Web:* www.packagingcorp.com	800-456-4725	331-9455*	100
Colorado Convention Ctr 700 14th St ..... Denver CO 80202 *Web:* www.denverconvention.com	303-228-8000	228-8103	205
Colorado Correctional Industries 4999 Oakland St ..... Denver CO 80239 *TF:* 800-685-7891 ■ *Web:* www.coloradoci.com	719-226-4206	226-4220	211
Colorado County 318 Springs St Rm 103 ..... Columbus TX 78934 *Web:* www.co.colorado.tx.us	979-732-2155	732-8852	338
Colorado Credit Union 8331 Continental Divide Rd ..... Littleton CO 80127 *Web:* ccu.org	303-978-2274		219
Colorado Daily 5450 Western Ave ..... Boulder CO 80301 *Web:* www.coloradodaily.com	303-473-1111		532-2
Colorado Data Mail Inc 2525 W 4th Ave ..... Denver CO 80219 *Web:* www.coloradodatamail.com	303-629-6155	592-1554	5
Colorado Democratic Party 789 Sherman St Ste 110 ..... Denver CO 80203 *Web:* www.coloradodems.org	303-623-4762		616-1
Colorado Dental Assn 8301 E Prentice Ave Ste 400 ..... Greenwood Village CO 80111 *Web:* cdaonline.org	303-740-6900	740-7989	227
Colorado Energy Management LLC 2575 Park Ln Ste 200 ..... LaFayette CO 80026 *Web:* www.coloradoenergy.com	303-442-5112		256
Colorado Farm Bureau Mutual Insurance Co PO Box 5647 ..... Denver CO 80217 *TF:* 800-315-5998 ■ *Web:* cfbinsurance.com	303-749-7500	660-1694	391-4
Colorado Fasteners Inc 570 Turner Dr Ste C ..... Durango CO 81303 *TF:* 800-332-1514 ■ *Web:* www.coloradofasteners.com	970-749-2992		351
Colorado Governor Jared Polis 200 E Colfax Ave Rm 136 ..... Denver CO 80203 *Web:* www.colorado.gov	303-866-2885		213
Colorado Home Mortgages 621 Southpark Dr Ste 300 ..... Littleton CO 80120 *TF:* 888-344-5193 ■ *Web:* comtgs.com	303-471-4445		653
Colorado Institute of Massage Therapy 1490 W Fillmore St ..... Colorado Springs CO 80904 *Fax Area Code: 719 ■ *TF:* 888-634-7347 ■ *Web:* www.cimt.edu	888-634-7347	447-9198*	167-3
Colorado Insurance Advisors LLC 323 W Drake Rd Ste 104 ..... Fort Collins CO 80526 *Web:* coloradoinsuranceadvisors.com	970-204-0044		390
Colorado Medical Society 7351 Lowry Blvd ..... Denver CO 80230 *TF:* 800-654-5653 ■ *Web:* www.cms.org	720-859-1001	859-7509	474
Colorado Mental Health Institute at Fort Logan (CMHIFL) 3520 W Oxford Ave ..... Denver CO 80236 *Web:* www.colorado.gov	303-866-7066		374-5
Colorado Mental Health Institute at Pueblo (CMHIP) 1600 W 24th St ..... Pueblo CO 81003 *Web:* www.colorado.gov	719-546-4000		374-5
Colorado Mesa University 1100 North Ave ..... Grand Junction CO 81501 *TF:* 800-982-6372 ■ *Web:* www.coloradomesa.edu	970-248-1020		786
Colorado Municipal League (CML) 1144 Sherman St ..... Denver CO 80203 *Web:* www.cml.org	303-831-6411	860-8175	48-6
Colorado National Monument 1750 Rim Rock Dr ..... Fruita CO 81521 *Web:* www.nps.gov	970-858-3617	858-0372	564
Colorado National Speedway 4281 Speedway Blvd ..... Dacono CO 80514 *Web:* www.coloradospeedway.com	303-665-4173	828-2403	515
Colorado Network Staffing Inc 8787 Turnpike Dr ..... Westminster CO 80031 *Web:* www.conetstaff.com	303-430-1441	430-1443	396
Colorado Northwestern Community College 500 Kennedy Dr ..... Rangely CO 81648 *TF:* 800-562-1105 ■ *Web:* www.cncc.edu	970-675-3335	675-3343	162
Colorado Nurses Assn (CNA) 2851 S Parker Rd Ste 1210 ..... Aurora CO 80014 *Web:* www.coloradonurses.org	720-457-1194		533
Colorado Outdoor Adventure Guide School 50158 Eagles Way ..... Mesa CO 81643 *Web:* www.guideschool.com	790-268-5205		685
Colorado Petroleum 5590 N High St ..... Denver CO 80216 *Web:* www.colopetro.com	303-294-0302		541
Colorado Pharmacists Society 2851 S Parker Rd Ste 1210 ..... Aurora CO 80014 *Fax Area Code: 303 ■ *Web:* www.copharm.org	720-250-9585	200-7099*	585
Colorado Precast Concrete Inc 1820 14th St SE ..... Loveland CO 80537 *Web:* www.coloprecast.com	970-669-0535		183
Colorado Public Interest Research Group (COPIRG) 1543 Wazee St Ste 330 ..... Denver CO 80202 *Web:* copirg.org	303-573-7474		633
Colorado Railroad Museum 17155 W 44th Ave ..... Golden CO 80403 *TF:* 800-365-6263 ■ *Web:* coloradorailroadmuseum.org	303-279-4591	279-4229	520
Colorado Rapids 6000 Victory Way ..... Commerce City CO 80022 *TF:* 800-979-3370 ■ *Web:* www.coloradorapids.com	303-727-3500	727-3536	717
Colorado Rapids Youth Soccer Club 2619 Canton Ct Ste C ..... Fort Collins CO 80525 *Web:* rapidsyouthsoccer.org	303-399-5858		717
Colorado Republican Party 5950 S Willow Dr Ste 210 ..... Greenwood Village CO 80111 *Web:* cologop.org	303-758-3333		616-2
Colorado River Animal Medical Center Inc 2079 Hwy 95 ..... Bullhead City AZ 86442 *Web:* www.cramcvet.com	928-763-7387		794
Colorado Rocky Mountain School 1493 County Rd 106 ..... Carbondale CO 81623 *Web:* www.crms.org	970-963-2562	963-9865	622
Colorado School of English 331 14th St ..... Denver CO 80202 *TF:* 877-234-0654 ■ *Web:* www.englishamerica.com	720-932-8900	932-0315	423
Colorado School of Mines 1600 Maple St ..... Golden CO 80401 *Web:* www.mines.edu	303-273-3000	273-3509	166
Colorado School of Mines Foundation 1812 Illinois St ..... Golden CO 80401 *TF:* 800-446-9488 ■ *Web:* weare.mines.edu	303-273-3275	273-3165	305
Colorado Serum Co 4950 York St PO Box 16428 ..... Denver CO 80216 *TF:* 800-525-2065 ■ *Web:* www.thepeakofquality.com	303-295-7527	295-1923	85
Colorado Ski Country USA Inc 3773 Cherry Creek North Dr Ste 955 ..... Denver CO 80209 *Web:* www.coloradoski.com	303-837-0793		711
Colorado Sports Hall of Fame 1701 Mile High Stadium ..... Denver CO 80204 *Web:* www.coloradosports.org	720-258-3888		522
Colorado Springs 30 S Nevada Ave Ste 202 ..... Colorado Springs CO 80903 *Web:* www.coloradosprings.gov	719-385-5912	385-5200	339-6
Colorado Springs Chamber & EDC 102 S Tejon St Ste 430 ..... Colorado Springs CO 80903 *Web:* www.coloradospringsbusinessalliance.com	719-471-8183		139
Colorado Springs City Auditorium 221 E Kiowa St Ste 702 ..... Colorado Springs CO 80903 *Web:* www.springsgov.com	719-385-5969	385-6584	205
Colorado Springs City Hall 30 S Nevada Ste 203 ..... Colorado Springs CO 80903 *Web:* coloradosprings.gov	719-385-5900	385-5488	337
Colorado Springs Convention & Visitors Bureau 515 S Cascade Ave ..... Colorado Springs CO 80903 *TF:* 800-888-4748 ■ *Web:* www.visitcos.com	719-635-7506	635-4968	206
Colorado Springs Independent 235 S Nevada Ave ..... Colorado Springs CO 80903 *Web:* www.csindy.com	719-577-4545	577-4107	532-5
Colorado Springs Philharmonic 111 S Tejon St PO Box 1266 ..... Colorado Springs CO 80903 *Web:* www.csphilharmonic.org	719-575-9632		573-3
Colorado Springs School District #11 1115 N El Paso St ..... Colorado Springs CO 80903 *Web:* www.d11.org	719-520-2000		685
Colorado Springs Utilities 111 S Cascade Ave ..... Colorado Springs CO 80903 *TF:* 800-238-5434 ■ *Web:* www.csu.org	719-448-4800		787
Colorado State University 200 W Lake St ..... Fort Collins CO 80523 *TF:* 800-491-4366 ■ *Web:* www.colostate.edu	970-491-1595	491-7799	166
Colorado State University			
Morgan Library 1201 Center Avenue Mall 1019 Campus Delivery ..... Fort Collins CO 80523 *Web:* lib.colostate.edu	970-491-1841	491-1195	434-6
Pueblo 2200 Bonforte Blvd ..... Pueblo CO 81001 *Web:* www.csupueblo.edu	719-549-2100	549-2419	166
Colorado State University System 410 17th St Ste 2440 ..... Denver CO 80202 *Web:* www.csusystem.edu	303-534-6290	534-6298	786
Colorado Symphony Orchestra 1245 Champa St ..... Denver CO 80204 *TF:* 877-292-7979 ■ *Web:* coloradosymphony.org	303-292-5566	293-2649	573-3
Colorado Technical University 4435 N Chestnut St ..... Colorado Springs CO 80907 *TF:* 855-230-0555 ■ *Web:* www.coloradotech.edu	719-598-0200		166
Colorado Time Systems 1551 E 11th St ..... Loveland CO 80537 *TF:* 800-279-0111 ■ *Web:* www.coloradotime.com	970-667-1000	667-5876	701
Colorado Trails Ranch 12161 County Rd 240 ..... Durango CO 81301 *Fax Area Code: 970 ■ *TF:* 800-323-3833 ■ *Web:* coloradotrails.com	800-323-3833	385-7372*	239
Colorado Trust 1600 Sherman St ..... Denver CO 80203 *TF:* 888-847-9140 ■ *Web:* www.coloradotrust.org	303-837-1200	839-9034	303
Colorado Valley Transit Inc 108 Cardinal Ln PO Box 940 ..... Columbus TX 78934 *TF:* 800-548-1068 ■ *Web:* gotransit.org	979-732-6281	732-6283	108
Colorado Veterinary Medical Assn 191 Yuma St ..... Denver CO 80223 *Web:* www.colovma.org	303-318-0447	318-0450	795
Colorado Video Inc 3335 Airport Rd Ste E ..... Boulder CO 80301 *Fax Area Code: 303 ■ *Web:* www.colorado-video.com	720-893-0081	530-9569*	52
Colorado WaterJet Co 5186 Longs Peak Rd Ste F ..... Berthoud CO 80513 *Web:* www.coloradowaterjet.com	970-532-5404		322
Colorado West Investments Inc 1731 E Niagara Rd ..... Montrose CO 81401 *Web:* www.wealthwithapurpose.com	970-249-9882	249-0830	690
ColorCentric Corp 100 Carlson Rd ..... Rochester NY 14610 *Web:* www.colorcentriccorp.com	585-413-9200		627
Colorcon Inc 415 Moyer Blvd ..... West Point PA 19486 *Web:* www.colorcon.com	215-699-7733	661-2605	144
ColorDynamics Inc 200 E Bethany Dr ..... Allen TX 75002 *Web:* www.colordynamics.com	972-390-6500		627
Coloredge Inc 132 W 31st St ..... New York NY 10001 *TF:* 800-321-8864 ■ *Web:* www.merisel.com	212-594-4800		174
Color-Fi Inc 320 Neeley St ..... Sumter SC 29150 *Web:* www.colorfi.com	803-436-4200	436-4220	605-1
Colorfx Inc 10776 Aurora Ave ..... Des Moines IA 50322 *TF:* 800-348-9044 ■ *Web:* mittera.com	800-348-9044		174
Color-Glo Intl 7111-7115 Ohms Ln ..... Minneapolis MN 55439 *Web:* colorglo.com	952-835-1338		62-1
ColorGraphics Inc 150 N Myers St ..... Los Angeles CA 90033 *Web:* www.colorgraphics.com	323-261-7171	261-7077	627

Name	Address	City	State	Zip	Phone	Fax	Class	Notes
Colorid LLC	20480 Chartwls Center Dr	Cornelius	NC	28031	704-987-2238		358	TF: 888-682-6567 ■ Web: www.colorid.com
Colormark LC	1840 Hutton Dr Bldg 208	Carrollton	TX	75006	972-243-1919		627	Web: www.colormark-lc.com
Colors of The West LLC	201 W Rt 66	Williams	AZ	86046	928-635-9559		327	Web: www.colorsofthewestusa.com
Colors on Parade	125 Daytona St PO Box 50940	Conway	SC	29526	843-347-8818		62-4	TF: 866-756-4207 ■ Web: www.colorsonparade.com
Colortech Graphics Inc	28700 Hayes Rd	Roseville	MI	48066	586-779-7800	779-7809	627	Web: www.colortechgraphics.com
Colosseum Online Inc	800 Petrolia Rd	Toronto	ON	M3J3K4	416-739-7873		225	TF: 877-739-7873 ■ Web: www.colosseum.com
Colourbox Hairdressing	305 Cordova St W	Vancouver	BC	V6B1E5	604-669-6354		77	Web: colourboxhair.com
Colpitts World Travel	875 Providence Hwy	Dedham	MA	02026	781-326-7800	326-2921	772	Web: www.colpittswt.com
Colquitt County	PO Box 517	Moultrie	GA	31776	229-616-7056	616-7498	338	Web: www.ccboc.com
Colquitt Regional Medical Ctr (CRMC)	3131 S Main St PO Box 40	Moultrie	GA	31768	229-985-3420		374-3	TF: 888-262-2762 ■ Web: colquittregional.com
COLSA Corp	6728 Odyssey Dr	Huntsville	AL	35806	256-964-5555		180	Web: www.colsa.com
Colson & Colson Construction Co	2260 McGilchrist St SE	Salem	OR	97302	503-586-7401		187	Web: www.colson-colson.com
Colson Associates Inc	1 N Franklin St 2420	Chicago	IL	60606	630-613-2955		475	Web: colsongroup.com
Colson Caster Corp	3700 Airport Rd	Jonesboro	AR	72401	870-932-4501		596	TF: 800-643-5515 ■ Web: www.colsoncaster.com
Colt Defense LLC	547 New Park Ave	West Hartford	CT	06110	860-232-4489	244-1442	807	Web: www.colt.com
Colt Inc	1223 Delhomme Ave	Scott	LA	70583	337-235-0353		660	TF: 800-259-8311 ■ Web: www.coltscraptire.com
Colt International Inc	300 Flint Ridge Rd	Webster	TX	77598	281-280-2100		194	Web: www.coltinternational.com
Colt State Park	Route 114, Hope St	Bristol	RI	02809	401-253-7482	253-6766	565	Web: www.riparks.com
Colt Tech LLC	14830 W 117th St	Olathe	KS	66062	913-839-8198		393	Web: www.colttech.com
Colt's Plastics Co	969 N Main St	Dayville	CT	06241	860-774-2301	779-0782	98	TF: 800-222-2658 ■ Web: www.coltsplastics.com
Col-Tab Inc	1919 SE Belmont St	Portland	OR	97214	503-233-2248	230-7901	554	Web: www.coltab.com
Coltene/Whaledent Inc	235 Ascot Pkwy	Cuyahoga Falls	OH	44223	330-916-8800	916-7077	228	TF: 800-221-3046 ■ Web: ap.coltene.com
Colton Chamber of Commerce	655 N La Cadena Dr	Colton	CA	92324	909-825-2222	824-1650	139	Web: coltonchamber.org
Colton Hall Museum	Colton Hall Museum City Hall	Monterey	CA	93940	831-646-5648	646-3917	520	Web: www.monterey.org
Colton Point State Park	c/o Leonard Harrison State Pk 4797 Rt 660	Wellsboro	PA	16901	570-724-3061		565	Web: www.dcnr.pa.gov
Colton Public Library	656 N Ninth St	Colton	CA	92324	909-370-5083		434-3	Web: ci.colton.ca.us
Coltontel	20983 S Hwy 211	Colton	OR	97017	503-824-3211	824-9944	681	Web: www.colton.com
Colts Neck High School	59 Five Points Rd	Colts Neck	NJ	07722	732-761-0190	761-0193	685	Web: www.frhsd.com
Coltwell Industries Inc	55 Winans Ave	Cranford	NJ	07016	908-276-7600		697	Web: www.coltwell.com
Colucci & Umans Inc	218 E 50th St	New York	NY	10022	212-935-5700	935-5728	428	Web: www.colucci-umans.com
Columbia Air Services	175 Tower Ave Groton-New London Airport	Groton	CT	06340	860-449-1400	405-7269	63	TF: 800-787-5001 ■ Web: www.columbiaaironline.com
Columbia Analytical Services Inc	1317 S 13th Ave	Kelso	WA	98626	360-577-7222		743	Web: www.caslab.com
Columbia Area Career Ctr	4203 S Providence Rd	Columbia	MO	65203	573-214-3800	214-3801	167-3	Web: www.career-center.org
Columbia Artists Management LLC	1790 Broadway	New York	NY	10019	212-841-9500	841-9744	731	Web: www.columbia-artists.com
Columbia Bank	1301 A St Ste 800	Tacoma	WA	98402	253-305-1900		360-2	NASDAQ: COLB ■ TF: 800-305-1905 ■ Web: www.columbiabank.com
Columbia Basin College	2600 N 20th Ave	Pasco	WA	99301	509-547-0511	546-0401	162	Web: www.columbiabasin.edu
Columbia Basin Electric Co-op	171 W Linden Way	Heppner	OR	97836	541-676-9146		245	Web: cbec.cc
Columbia Bible College	2940 Clearbrook Rd	Abbotsford	BC	V2T2Z8	604-853-3358	853-3063	785	TF: 800-283-0881 ■ Web: www.columbiabc.edu
Columbia Boiler Co	390 Old Reading Pk PO Box 1070	Pottstown	PA	19464	610-323-2700	323-7292	91	Web: www.columbiaboiler.com
Columbia Capital	204 S Union St	Alexandria	VA	22314	703-519-2000	519-5870	792	Web: colcap.com
Columbia Cascade Co	1300 SW 6th Ave Ste 310	Portland	OR	97201	503-223-1157	223-4530	346	TF: 800-547-1940 ■ Web: www.columbia-cascade.com
Columbia Chamber of Commerce	300 S Providence Rd	Columbia	MO	65203	573-874-1132		139	Web: columbiamochamber.com
Columbia City Ballet	1545 Main St	Columbia	SC	29201	803-799-7605		573-1	TF: 800-899-7408 ■ Web: www.columbiacityballet.com
Columbia Collectors Inc (CCI)	1104 Main St Ste 311	Vancouver	WA	98660	360-694-7585		160	TF: 800-694-7585 ■ Web: www.columbiacollectors.com
Columbia College	1001 Rogers St	Columbia	MO	65216	573-875-8700	875-7209	166	TF: 800-231-2391 ■ Web: www.ccis.edu
Columbia College	1301 Columbia College Dr	Columbia	SC	29203	800-277-1301	786-3674*	166	*Fax Area Code: 803 ■ TF: 800-277-1301 ■ Web: www.columbiasc.edu
Columbia College	11600 Columbia College Dr	Sonora	CA	95370	209-588-5100	588-5104	162	TF: 888-722-2873 ■ Web: www.gocolumbia.edu
Columbia College Chicago	600 S Michigan Ave	Chicago	IL	60605	312-369-7507		166	TF: 866-705-0200 ■ Web: www.colum.edu
Columbia College Hollywood	18618 Oxnard St	Tarzana	CA	91356	818-345-8414	345-9053	166	TF: 800-785-0585 ■ Web: www.columbiacollege.edu
Columbia Community Mental Health	58646 McNulty Way	Saint Helens	OR	97051	503-397-5211		726	TF: 800-294-5211 ■ Web: www.ccmh1.com
Columbia Correctional Institution	2925 Columbia Dr	Portage	WI	53901	608-742-9100	742-9111	213	Web: www.doc.wi.gov
Columbia Corrugated Box Company Inc	12777 SW Tualatin Sherwood Rd	Tualatin	OR	97062	503-692-3344		100	Web: ccbox.com
Columbia County	35 W Main St	Bloomsburg	PA	17815	570-389-5600	784-0257	338	Web: www.columbiapa.org
Columbia County	341 E Main St	Dayton	WA	99328	509-382-4542	382-2490	338	Web: www.columbiaco.com
Columbia County	PO Box 498	Evans	GA	30809	706-868-3379	868-3348	338	Web: www.columbiacountyga.gov
Columbia County	560 Warren St	Hudson	NY	12534	518-828-3339		338	Web: www.columbiacountyny.com
Columbia County	112 E Edgewater St	Portage	WI	53901	608-742-9654	742-9602	338	Web: www.co.columbia.wi.us
Columbia County	230 Strand St	Saint Helens	OR	97051	503-397-3796	397-7266	338	TF: 888-397-7210 ■ Web: www.columbiacountyor.gov
Columbia County Chamber of Commerce	507 Warren St	Hudson	NY	12534	518-828-4417	822-9539	139	Web: columbiachamber-ny.com
Columbia County Public Library	308 NW Columbia Ave	Lake City	FL	32055	386-758-2101	758-2135	434-3	Web: www.columbiacountyfla.com
Columbia Crest Winery	178810 SR-221 PO Box 231	Paterson	WA	99345	509-875-4227	415-3657*	80-3	*Fax Area Code: 425 ■ TF: 888-309-9463 ■ Web: www.columbiacrest.com
Columbia Daily Tribune	101 N Fourth St	Columbia	MO	65201	573-815-1640		532-2	TF: 800-333-6799 ■ Web: www.columbiatribune.com
Columbia Data Systems Inc	2002 Oakland Pky	Columbia	TN	38401	931-381-7695	380-1212	174	Web: www.cdsmicro.com
Columbia Distributing Co	6840 N Cutter Cir	Portland	OR	97217	503-289-9600		81-1	Web: www.coldist.com
Columbia Elevator Products Company Inc	380 Horace St	Bridgeport	CT	06610	888-858-1558		189-1	TF: 888-858-1558 ■ Web: www.columbiaelevator.com
Columbia Empire Farms Inc	31461 Ne Bell Rd	Sherwood	OR	97140	503-538-2156		10-10	Web: www.columbiaempirefarms.com
Columbia Energy & Environmental Services Inc	1806 Terminal Dr	Richland	WA	99354	509-946-7111		256	Web: www.columbia-energy.com
Columbia Environmental Research Ctr (CERC)	4200 New Haven Rd	Columbia	MO	65201	573-875-5399	876-1896	668	TF: 888-283-7626 ■ Web: www.usgs.gov
Columbia Forest Products Inc	*Columbia Plywood Div* 7900 McCloud Dr Ste 200	Greensboro	NC	27409	800-637-1609		613	TF: 800-637-1609 ■ Web: www.columbiaforestproducts.com
Columbia Fruit Packers Inc	2575 Euclid Ave PO Box 920	Wenatchee	WA	98801	509-662-7153	662-0933	546	Web: www.columbiafruit.com
Columbia Gas of Ohio Inc	50 W Broad St Ste 1330	Columbus	OH	43215	800-344-4077		787	TF: 800-807-9781 ■ Web: www.columbiagasohio.com
Columbia Gas of Virginia Inc	1809 Coyote Dr	Chester	VA	23836	800-543-8911		787	TF: 800-544-5606 ■ Web: www.columbiagasva.com
Columbia Gear Corp	530 County Rd 50	Avon	MN	56310	320-356-7301	356-2131	709	TF: 800-323-9838 ■ Web: www.columbiagear.com
Columbia Gorge Hotel	4000 Westcliff Dr	Hood River	OR	97031	541-386-5566		379	Web: www.columbiagorgehotel.com
Columbia Gorge Premium Outlets	450 NW 257th Way	Troutdale	OR	97060	503-669-8060		460	Web: shopcolumbiagorgeoutlets.com
Columbia Helicopters Inc	14452 Arndt Rd NE	Aurora	OR	97002	503-678-1222	678-5841	359	Web: www.colheli.com
Columbia Hills State Park	85 Hwy 14	Dallesport	WA	98617	509-767-1159		565	Web: parks.state.wa.us
Columbia Hospitality	2223 Alaskan Way Ste 200	Seattle	WA	98121	206-239-1800	239-1801	379	Web: www.columbiahospitality.com
Columbia Impex LC	6073 NW 167th St Ste C14	Hialeah	FL	33015	305-819-7116	819-7029	328	Web: www.colimpex.com
Columbia Institute for Tele-Information (CITI)	3022 Broadway Uris Hall	New York	NY	10027	212-854-4222	854-1471	668	Web: www8.gsb.columbia.edu

Name / Address	Phone	Fax	Class
Columbia Insurance Group Inc 2102 White Gate Dr ... Columbia MO 65205 TF: 800-877-3579 ■ Web: www.colinsgrp.com	573-474-6193		390
Columbia International University 7435 Monticello Rd ... Columbia SC 29203 TF: 800-777-2227 ■ Web: www.ciu.edu	803-754-4100	786-4209	161
Columbia Legal Services 6 S Second St 600 Larson Bldg ... Yakima WA 98901 TF: 800-631-1323 ■ Web: www.columbialegal.org	509-575-5593		445
Columbia Lutheran Home 4700 Phinney Ave N ... Seattle WA 98103 Web: www.columbialutheranhome.org	206-632-7400		48-20
Columbia Machine Works 934 75th Ave ... Oakland CA 94621 Web: www.columbiamachine.net	510-568-0808	568-0810	454
Columbia Manufacturing Inc 1 Cycle St ... Westfield MA 01085 Web: www.columbiamfginc.com	413-562-3664	568-5345	319-3
Columbia Memorial Hospital 71 Prospect Ave ... Hudson NY 12534 TF: 866-539-1370 ■ Web: www.columbiamemorialhealth.org	518-828-7601	828-9980	374-3
Columbia Metal Spinning Company Inc 4351 N Normandy Ave ... Chicago IL 60634 Web: www.cmspinning.com	773-685-2800	685-4328	198
Columbia Metropolitan Airport 3250 Airport Blvd ... West Columbia SC 29170 Web: flycae.com	803-822-5000		27
Columbia Missourian 221 S Eigth St ... Columbia MO 65201 TF: 855-270-6572 ■ Web: www.columbiamissourian.com	573-882-5700		532-2
Columbia (MO) City Hall 701 E Broadway PO Box 6015 ... Columbia MO 65205 Web: www.como.gov	573-874-7111		337
Columbia Museum of Art 1515 Main St ... Columbia SC 29201 Web: www.columbiamuseum.org	803-799-2810		520
Columbia Northwest Engineering 249 N Elder St ... Moses Lake WA 98837 Web: www.cnweng.com	509-766-1226		256
Columbia Okura LLC 301 Grove St Ste A ... Vancouver WA 98661 TF: 877-204-7444 ■ Web: columbiaokura.com	877-204-7444		207
Columbia Omnicorp 14 W 33rd St ... New York NY 10001 Web: www.columbiaomni.com	212-279-6161		535
Columbia Packing Company Inc 2807 E 11th St ... Dallas TX 75203 Web: www.columbiapacking.com	214-946-8171		473
Columbia Panel Manufacturing Co 100 Giles St ... High Point NC 27263 Web: columbiapanel.com	336-861-4100		613
Columbia Pike Library 816 S Walter Reed Dr ... Arlington VA 22204 Web: library.arlingtonva.us	703-228-5710		434-3
Columbia Pipe & Supply Co 1120 W Pershing Rd ... Chicago IL 60609 TF: 888-429-4635 ■ Web: www.columbiapipe.com	773-927-6600	927-8415	492
Columbia Place 7201 Two Notch Rd ... Columbia SC 29223 Web: columbiaplacemall.com	803-788-4678	736-9168	460
Columbia Power Cooperative Assn 311 Wilson St ... Monument OR 97864	541-934-2311		245
Columbia Printing & Cleanroom Inc 835 SE Hawthorne Blvd ... Portland OR 97214 Web: www.colprinting.com	503-232-2212	232-7974	627
Columbia Regional Airport 11200 S Airport Dr ... Columbia MO 65201 Web: www.flycou.com	573-874-7508		27
Columbia Restaurant 2025 E Seventh Ave ... Tampa FL 33605 Web: www.columbiarestaurant.com	904-824-3341		671
Columbia River Carbonates 300 N Pekin Rd ... Woodland WA 98674 Web: www.carbonates.com	360-225-6505		143
Columbia River Correctional Institution 2575 Center St NE ... Salem OR 97301 Web: www.oregon.gov	503-280-6646	280-6012	213
Columbia River Inter-Tribal Fish Commission (CRITFC) 700 NE Multnomah St Ste 1200 ... Portland OR 97232 Web: www.critfc.org	503-238-0667	235-4228	48-13
Columbia River Knife & Tool Inc 18348 SW 126th Pl ... Tualatin OR 97062 TF: 800-891-3100 ■ Web: www.crkt.com	503-685-5015		350
Columbia River Log Scaling & Grading Bureau 260 Oakway Ctr ... Eugene OR 97401 Web: www.crls.com	541-342-6007		302
Columbia River Maritime Museum 1792 Marine Dr ... Astoria OR 97103 Web: www.crmm.org	503-325-2323		520
Columbia Rubber Mills Inc 14800 SE 82nd Dr ... Clackamas OR 97015 TF: 800-547-5557 ■ Web: www.columbiarubbermills.com	503-557-9919	557-9923	677
Columbia Rural Electric Association Inc 115 E Main St ... Dayton WA 99328 TF: 800-642-1231 ■ Web: www.columbiarea.com	509-382-2578		245
Columbia Savings Bank 19-01 Rt 208 ... Fair Lawn NJ 07410 TF: 800-747-4428 ■ Web: www.columbiabankonline.com	800-522-4167		70
Columbia Scholastic Press Assn (CSPA) Columbia University 90 Morningside Dr Ste B01 ... New York NY 10027 Web: cspa.columbia.edu	212-854-9400	854-9401	48-11
Columbia Specialty Company Inc 5875 Obispo Ave ... Long Beach CA 90805 Web: www.columbiaspecialty.com	562-634-6425		358
Columbia Sportswear Co 14375 NW Science Park Dr ... Portland OR 97229 NASDAQ: COLM ■ TF: 800-622-6953 ■ Web: www.columbia.com	503-985-4000	985-5800	155-1
Columbia Star PO Box 5955 ... Columbia SC 29250 Web: www.thecolumbiastar.com	803-771-0219		637-8
Columbia State Community College 1665 Hampshire Pk ... Columbia TN 38401 TF: 800-848-0298 ■ Web: www.columbiastate.edu	931-540-2722	540-2830	162
Columbia State Historic Park 11255 Jackson St ... Columbia CA 95310 Web: www.parks.ca.gov	209-588-9128		565

Name / Address	Phone	Fax	Class
Columbia Steel Casting Company Inc 10425 N Bloss Ave ... Portland OR 97203 TF: 800-547-9471 ■ Web: www.columbiasteel.com	503-286-0685	286-1743	307
Columbia Steel Inc 2175 N Linden Ave ... Rialto CA 92377 Web: www.csirialto.com	909-874-8840		492
Columbia Sussex Corp 740 Centre View Blvd ... Crestview Hills KY 41017 Web: www.columbiasussex.com	859-578-1100	578-1154	379
Columbia Telecommunications Corp 10613 Concord St ... Kensington MD 20895 Web: www.ctcnet.us	301-933-1488		261
Columbia Theological Seminary 701 S Columbia Dr ... Decatur GA 30030 TF: 888-601-8916 ■ Web: www.ctsnet.edu	404-378-8821	377-9696	167-3
Columbia Threadneedle Investments PO Box 8081 ... Boston MA 02266 TF: 800-426-3750 ■ Web: www.columbiathreadneedleus.com	800-345-6611		401
Columbia University 2960 Broadway ... New York NY 10027 Web: www.columbia.edu	212-854-4065		166
Columbia University Press 61 W 62nd St ... New York NY 10023 Web: cup.columbia.edu	212-459-0600		637-2
Columbia University School of Law 435 W 116th St ... New York NY 10027 Web: www.law.columbia.edu	212-854-2640	854-1109	167-1
Columbia Utilities Heating Corp 8751 18th Ave ... Brooklyn NY 11214 TF: 877-726-5862 ■ Web: columbiautilities.com	718-851-6655	851-2427	316
Columbia Ventures Corp (CVC) 14301 SE 1st St Ste 201 ... Vancouver WA 98684 Web: colventures.com	360-816-1840		405
Columbia West Capital LLC 14624 N Scottsdale Rd Ste 124 ... Scottsdale AZ 85254 Web: www.columbiawestcap.com	480-664-3949	664-3952	690
Columbia Winery 14030 NE 145th St ... Woodinville WA 98072 TF: 800-488-2347 ■ Web: www.columbiawinery.com	425-482-7490		50-7
Columbia Woodworking Inc 935 Brentwood Rd NE ... Washington DC 20018 Web: www.cwwcorp.com	202-526-2387	526-5163	499
Columbia-Greene Community College (CGCC) 4400 Rt 23 ... Hudson NY 12534 Web: www.sunycgcc.edu	518-828-4181	822-2015	162
Columbia-Montour Visitors Bureau 121 Papermill Rd ... Bloomsburg PA 17815 TF: 800-847-4810 ■ Web: www.itourcolumbiamontour.com	570-784-8279		206
Columbian 701 W Eigth St PO Box 180 ... Vancouver WA 98660 TF: 800-743-3391 ■ Web: www.columbian.com	360-694-3391		532-2
Columbian Chemicals Co 1800 W Oak Commons Ct ... Marietta GA 30062 TF: 800-235-4003 ■ Web: birlacarbon.com	770-792-9400		145
Columbian Mutual Life Insurance Co Vestal Pkwy E ... Binghamton NY 13902 TF: 800-423-9765 ■ Web: www.cfglife.com	607-724-2472		390
Columbian Park Zoo 1915 Scott St ... LaFayette IN 47904 Web: www.lafayette.in.gov	765-807-1540	807-1547	823
Columbiana Centre Mall 100 Columbiana Cir ... Columbia SC 29212 Web: www.columbianacentre.com	803-732-6255		460
Columbiana County 105 S Market St ... Lisbon OH 44432 Web: www.columbianacounty.org	330-424-9514		338
Columbiana Hi Tech LLC 1621 Old Greensboro Rd ... Kernersville NC 27284 Web: www.chtnuclear.com	336-497-3600		295
Columbine Plastics Corp 1815 Boxelder St ... Louisville CO 80027 Web: www.columbineplastics.com	303-442-0051	444-0316	604
Columbus Air Force Base 555 Seventh St ... Columbus AFB MS 39710 Web: www.columbus.af.mil	662-434-7068	434-7009	497-1
Columbus Area Chamber of Commerce 500 Franklin St ... Columbus IN 47201 Web: www.columbusareachamber.com	812-379-4457		139
Columbus Area Visitors Ctr 506 Fifth St ... Columbus IN 47201 TF: 800-468-6564 ■ Web: columbus.in.us	812-378-2622		206
Columbus Association for the Performing Arts 39 East State St ... Columbus OH 43215 Web: www.capa.com	614-469-0939		48-5
Columbus Bank & Trust Co 1148 Broadway ... Columbus GA 31901 TF: 800-334-9007 ■ Web: www.synovus.com	706-641-3483		70
Columbus Chamber of Commerce 150 S Front St Ste 200 ... Columbus OH 43215 Web: www.columbus.org	614-221-1321	221-1408	139
Columbus Chemical Industries Inc N4335 Temkin Rd ... Columbus WI 53925 Web: www.columbuschemical.com	920-623-2140	623-2577	146
Columbus Cir Investors Inc (CCI) 1 Stn Pl Metro Ctr ... Stamford CT 06902 Web: www.columbuscircle.com	203-353-6000		401
Columbus City Schools 270 E State St ... Columbus OH 43215 Web: www.ccsoh.us	614-365-5000	365-5652	685
Columbus Civic Ctr 400 Fourth St ... Columbus GA 31901 Web: civiccenter.columbusga.gov	706-653-4482		720
Columbus College of Art & Design 60 Cleveland Ave ... Columbus OH 43215 TF: 877-997-2223 ■ Web: www.ccad.edu	614-224-9101	222-4040	164
Columbus Consolidated Government Ctr 100 Tenth St ... Columbus GA 31901 Web: www.columbusga.gov	706-653-4000		337
Columbus Convention & Visitors Bureau 900 Front Ave ... Columbus GA 31901 TF: 800-999-1613 ■ Web: www.visitcolumbusga.com	706-322-1613	322-0701	206
Columbus County PO Box 1587 ... Whiteville NC 28472 TF: 800-553-9759 ■ Web: www.columbusco.org	910-641-3000		338
Columbus County Schools PO Box 729 ... Whiteville NC 28472 Web: www2.columbus.k12.nc.us	910-642-5168	640-1010	685
Columbus Crew SC 1 Black & Gold Blvd ... Columbus OH 43211 Web: www.thccrow.com	614-447-2739	447-4109	714-1

Name	City	State	Zip	Phone	Fax	Class
Columbus Dispatch 62 E Broad St *Web:* www.dispatch.com	Columbus	OH	43215	614-461-5000		532-2
Columbus Distributing Co, The 4949 Freeway E Dr *Web:* www.columbusdistributing.com	Columbus	OH	43229	614-846-1000		81-1
Columbus Door Company Inc 1884 Elmwood Ave *Web:* www.columbusdoor.com	Warwick	RI	02888	401-781-7792		234
Columbus Electric Co-opeartive Inc 900 N Gold St PO Box 631 *TF:* 800-950-2667 ■ *Web:* www.columbusco-op.org	Deming	NM	88031	575-546-8838		245
Columbus Foundation, The 1234 E Broad St *Web:* columbusfoundation.org	Columbus	OH	43205	614-251-4000	251-4009	303
Columbus Georgia Convention & Trade Ctr 801 Front Ave *Web:* www.columbusga.gov	Columbus	GA	31901	706-327-4522		205
Columbus Hospice 7020 Moon Rd *Web:* www.columbushospice.com	Columbus	GA	31909	706-569-7992		371
Columbus Hospital 495 N 13th St *Web:* www.columbusltach.org	Newark	NJ	07107	973-587-7777	587-7829	374-3
Columbus Humanities Arts & Technology Academy 1333 Morse Rd *Web:* columbushumanitiesata.org	Columbus	OH	43229	614-261-1200		685
Columbus Hydraulics Co PO Box 250 *Web:* www.columbushydraulics.com	Columbus	NE	68601	402-564-8544	564-0129	223
Columbus Industries Inc 2938 SR-752 PO Box 257 *Web:* www.colind.com	Ashville	OH	43103	740-983-2552	983-4622	18
Columbus Jack Corp 2222 S Third St *TF:* 800-426-6301 ■ *Web:* www.columbusjack.com	Columbus	OH	43207	614-443-7492	444-9337	454
Columbus Jewish Foundation 1175 College Ave *Web:* jewishcolumbus.org	Columbus	OH	43209	614-237-7686	237-2221	305
Columbus Ledger-Enquirer 945 Broadway Ste 102 *TF:* 800-282-7859 ■ *Web:* www.ledger-enquirer.com	Columbus	GA	31901	706-324-5526	576-6290	532-2
Columbus Marble Works Corp 2415 Hwy 45 N *TF:* 800-647-1055 ■ *Web:* www.columbusmarbleworks.net	Columbus	MS	39705	662-328-1477		724
Columbus McKinnon Corp 205 Crosspoint Pkwy *NASDAQ: CMCO* ■ *TF:* 800-888-0985 ■ *Web:* www.columbusmckinnon.com	Getzville	NY	14228	716-689-5400		470
Columbus Metropolitan Airport 3250 W Britt David Rd *Web:* www.flycolumbusga.com	Columbus	GA	31909	706-324-2449		27
Columbus Metropolitan Library 96 S Grant Ave *Web:* www.columbuslibrary.org	Columbus	OH	43215	614-645-2275		434-3
Columbus Monthly Magazine 62 E Broad St PO Box 1289 *Web:* www.columbusmonthly.com	Columbus	OH	43216	614-888-4567		457-22
Columbus Museum 1251 Wynnton Rd *Web:* www.columbusmuseum.com	Columbus	GA	31906	706-748-2562	748-2570	520
Columbus Museum of Art 480 E Broad St *Web:* www.columbusmuseum.org	Columbus	OH	43215	614-221-6801		520
Columbus Paper Company Inc 807 Joy Rd **Fax Area Code:* 706 ■ *TF:* 800-277-1361 ■ *Web:* www.copacoinc.com	Columbus	GA	31906	800-277-1361	689-1452*	553
Columbus Park Trattoria 205 Main St *Web:* www.columbusparktrattoria.com	Stamford	CT	06901	203-967-9191		671
Columbus Pipe & Equipment Co 773 E Markison Ave *Web:* www.columbuspipe.com	Columbus	OH	43207	614-444-7871		492
Columbus Productions Inc 4580 Cargo Dr *Web:* www.columbusproductionsinc.com	Columbus	GA	31907	706-644-1595		174
Columbus Public Library 3000 Macon Rd *TF:* 800-652-0782 ■ *Web:* www.cvlga.org	Columbus	GA	31906	706-243-2669		434-3
Columbus Public Library 2504 14th St *Web:* www.columbusne.us	Columbus	NE	68601	402-564-7116		434-3
Columbus Regional Healthcare System 500 Jefferson St *Web:* www.crhealthcare.org	Whiteville	NC	28472	910-642-8011	642-9305	374-3
Columbus Regional Hospital 2400 E 17th St *TF:* 800-841-4938 ■ *Web:* www.crh.org	Columbus	IN	47201	812-379-4441		374-3
Columbus Rehabilitation & Subacute Institute 44 S Souder Ave *Web:* columbusrehabskillednursing.com	Columbus	OH	43222	614-228-5900		450
Columbus Scrap Material Company Inc 973 Island Rd *Web:* www.columbusrecycling.com	Columbus	MS	39701	662-328-8176	328-1058	686
Columbus State Community College 550 E Spring St *TF:* 800-621-6407 ■ *Web:* www.cscc.edu	Columbus	OH	43215	614-287-2400	287-6019	162
Columbus State University 4225 University Ave *TF:* 866-264-2035 ■ *Web:* www.columbusstate.edu	Columbus	GA	31907	706-507-8800		166
Columbus Symphony Orchestra 935 First Ave *Web:* www.csoga.org	Columbus	GA	31901	706-323-5059	323-7051	573-3
Columbus Symphony Orchestra 55 E State St *Web:* www.columbussymphony.com	Columbus	OH	43215	614-228-9600	224-7273	573-3
Columbus Technical College 928 Manchester Expy *Web:* www.columbustech.edu	Columbus	GA	31904	706-649-1800		800
Columbus Telephone Company Inc 224 S Kansas Ave *Web:* www.columbus-telephone.com	Columbus	KS	66725	620-429-3132	429-1704	224
Columbus United Federal Credit Union 2472 39th Ave PO Box 585 *Web:* bankingwithyou.com	Columbus	NE	68602	402-563-4597		219
Columbus Zoo & Aquarium 4850 W Powell Rd *Web:* www.columbuszoo.org	Powell	OH	43065	614-645-3400	645-3465	823
Columbus-Belmont State Park 350 Park Rd *Web:* parks.ky.gov	Columbus	KY	42032	270-677-2327		565
Columbus-Lowndes Convention & Visitors Bureau 117 Third St S PO Box 789 *TF:* 800-327-2686 ■ *Web:* www.visitcolumbusms.org	Columbus	MS	39703	662-329-1191		206
Columbus-Lowndes County Library 314 N Seventh St *Web:* www.lowndes.lib.ms.us	Columbus	MS	39701	662-329-5300		434-3
Column Technologies Inc 10 E 22nd St Ste 300 *TF:* 866-265-8665 ■ *Web:* www.columnit.com	Lombard	IL	60148	630-515-6660	271-1508	174
Columns, The 3811 St Charles Ave *TF:* 800-445-9308 ■ *Web:* www.thecolumns.com	New Orleans	LA	70115	504-899-9308	899-8170	379
Colusa Casino & Bingo 3770 Hwy 45 *Web:* www.colusacasino.com	Colusa	CA	95932	530-458-8844		707
Colusa County 546 Jay St *Web:* countyofcolusa.org	Colusa	CA	95932	530-458-0500	458-0512	338
Colusa Elevator Co PO Box 354 *Web:* www.colusaelevator.com	Colusa	IL	62329	217-755-4221		10-5
Colusa Industrial Properties 50 Sunrise Blvd *Web:* cipcorp.com	Colusa	CA	95932	530-458-2118		653
Colussy Chevrolet 3073 Washington Pk *Web:* www.colussy.com	Bridgeville	PA	15017	412-564-4132		57
Colvin Engineering Associates Inc 505 E S Temple Ste 100 *Web:* www.cea-ut.com	Salt Lake City	UT	84103	801-322-2400		261
Colwell Construction Company Inc 587 Rock Rd *Web:* colwellconstruction.com	Blairsville	GA	30514	706-745-6239	745-9582	188-4
Colwell Flower Shop 2448 Brightwood Rd SE *Web:* www.colwellflowershop.com	New Philadelphia	OH	44663	330-204-1100		292
Colwell Inc 2605 Marion Dr PO Box 300 *Web:* www.colwellcolour.com	Kendallville	IN	46755	260-347-1981		627
Colwell Industries Inc 123 N Third St *Web:* www.colwellindustries.com	Minneapolis	MN	55401	612-340-0365		86
Colwill Engineering Mep & Fp 4750 E Adamo Dr *Web:* www.colwillengineering.com	Tampa	FL	33605	813-241-2525		256
Comag Marketing Group 155 Village Blvd Ste 300 *TF:* 866-790-9353 ■ *Web:* www.i-cmg.com	Princeton	NJ	08540	609-524-1800	524-1629	96
Comaintel Inc 121 Second Ave Ste 100 *Web:* www.comaintel.com	Grand-Mere	QC	G9T7G1	819-538-6583		196
Comal County 199 Main Plz *TF:* 877-724-9475 ■ *Web:* www.co.comal.tx.us	New Braunfels	TX	78130	830-221-1100	620-5506	338
Comanche Chamber of Commerce & Agriculture 304 S Austin St *Web:* comanchechamber.org	Comanche	TX	76442	325-356-3233		338
Comanche County 315 SW Fifth St Ste 304 *Web:* www.comanchecounty.us	Lawton	OK	73501	580-355-5214		338
Comanche County Memorial Hospital 3401 NW Gore Blvd *Web:* www.ccmhhealth.com	Lawton	OK	73505	580-355-8620		374-3
Comanche Electric Cooperative Assn 201 W Wrights Ave *TF:* 800-915-2533 ■ *Web:* www.ceca.coop	Comanche	TX	76442	325-356-2533		245
Comanco 4301 Sterling Commerce Dr *Web:* comanco.com	Plant City	FL	33566	813-988-8829	988-8779	186
Co-Mar Aviation 1020 Woodhurst St *Web:* www.comaraviation.com	Bowling Green	KY	42103	270-781-9797	793-0525	63
Comar Inc 1 Comar Pl *TF:* 800-962-6627 ■ *Web:* www.comar.com	Buena	NJ	08310	856-692-6100		199
Comarch Inc 9450 W Bryn Mawr Ave Ste 325 *Web:* www.comarch.com	Rosemont	IL	60018	847-260-5500	260-5501	177
Comarco Inc 28202 Cabot Rd Ste 300 *OTC: CMRO* ■ *Web:* www.comarco.com	Laguna Niguel	CA	92677	949-599-7400		735
Comarco Products 7100 PRC Way **Fax Area Code:* 856 ■ *TF:* 800-524-2128 ■ *Web:* comarco.net	Palatka	FL	32177	800-524-2128	342-8448*	123
COMARK Communications 104 Feeding Hills Rd *TF:* 800-288-8364 ■ *Web:* www.comarktv.com	Southwick	MA	01077	413-998-1100		647
Comark Corp 93 West St *TF:* 800-280-8522 ■ *Web:* comarkcorp.com	Medfield	MA	02052	508-359-8161	359-2267	173-2
Comark Direct 507 S Main St *TF:* 888-742-0405 ■ *Web:* www.comarkdirect.com	Fort Worth	TX	76104	888-742-0405		5
Comark Instruments Inc PO Box 500 *TF:* 800-555-6658 ■ *Web:* www.comarkinstruments.net	Beaverton	OR	97077	503-643-5204	627-5311	407
Comau LLC 21000 Telegraph Rd *TF:* 888-888-8998 ■ *Web:* www.comau.com	Southfield	MI	48033	248-353-8888		60
ComAv Technical Services LLC 18438 Readiness St *Web:* www.comav.com	Victorville	CA	92394	760-530-2400	246-1186	24
Combat Air Museum 7016 SE Forbes Ave Forbes Field *Web:* www.combatairmuseum.org	Topeka	KS	66619	785-862-3303	862-3304	520
Combe Inc 1101 Westchester Ave **Fax Area Code:* 914 ■ *TF:* 800-431-2610 ■ *Web:* www.combe.com	White Plains	NY	10604	800-431-2610	461-4402*	214
CombiMatrix Corp 300 Goddard Ste 100 *NASDAQ: CBMX* ■ *TF:* 800-710-0624 ■ *Web:* combimatrix.com	Irvine	CA	92618	949-753-0624	753-1504	85
Combination Door Co 1000 Morris St *Web:* www.combinationdoor.com	Fond du Lac	WI	54935	920-922-2050	922-2917	236
Combine International Inc 354 Indusco Ct *Web:* www.combine.com	Troy	MI	48083	248-809-5560		411
Combined Employees Credit Union 593 Russell Pkwy *Web:* combinedecu.com	Warner Robins	GA	31088	478-929-5700		219

Company	Address	City	State	ZIP	Phone	Fax	Class	Details
Combined Express Inc	3685 Marshall Ln	Bensalem	PA	19020	800-777-0458		311	TF: 800-777-0458 ■ Web: www.combinedexpress.com
Combined Insurance Services	1701 NE 42nd Ave Ste 200	Ocala	FL	34470	352-237-2181		390	Web: combinedinsuranceservices.com
Combined Properties Inc	300 Commercial St Ste 25	Malden	MA	02148	781-321-7800	321-5144	655	Web: www.combinedproperties.com
Combined Refrigeration Resources Inc	1036-A 1st St	Humble	TX	77338	281-540-7552		610	Web: www.combinedrefrigeration.com
Combined Rose List	PO Box 677	Mantua	OH	44255	330-296-2618		637-9	Web: www.combinedroselist.com
Combined Systems Inc	388 Kinsman Rd	Jamestown	PA	16134	724-932-2177		268	Web: www.combinedsystems.com
Combined Technologies Inc	13970 W Polo Trl Dr	Lake Forest	IL	60045	847-968-4855		561	Web: ctipack.com
Combined Transport Inc	5656 Crater Lake Ave	Central Point	OR	97502	541-734-7418	826-2001	780	TF: 800-547-2870 ■ Web: www.combinedtransport.com
Combs Insurance Agency Inc	341 S Alaska St	Palmer	AK	99645	907-745-2144		390	Web: www.combsinsurance.com
CoMc LLC	13423 F St	Omaha	NE	68137	402-505-7627		364	Web: www.snapstone.com
ComCanada Communications Inc	232-1027 Davie St	Vancouver	BC	V6E4L2	604-998-4500		224	TF: 877-697-8647 ■ Web: www.comcanada.ca
Comcar Industries Inc	502 E Bridgers Ave	Auburndale	FL	33823	800-524-1101	965-6896*	780	*Fax Area Code: 863 ■ TF: 800-524-1101 ■ Web: comcar.com
Comcast Corp	1701 JFK Blvd	Philadelphia	PA	19103	215-665-1700	981-7790	360-3	NASDAQ: CMCSA ■ TF: 800-266-2278 ■ Web: corporate.comcast.com
Comcast Technology Solutions	1899 Wynkoop St Ste 550	Denver	CO	80202	206-436-7900	257-6060	116	TF: 800-824-1776 ■ Web: www.comcasttechnologysolutions.com
Comcentric Inc	10463 Park Meadows Dr Ste 208	Lone Tree	CO	80124	303-805-4700	805-4701	193	Web: www.comcentric.com
Comco Inc	2151 N Lincoln St	Burbank	CA	91504	818-841-5500	955-8365	1	TF: 800-796-6626 ■ Web: www.comcoinc.com
Comco Plastics Inc	98-31 Jamaica Ave	Woodhaven	NY	11421	718-849-9000		602	TF: 800-221-9555 ■ Web: comcoplastics.com
Comcor Environmental Ltd	320 Pinebush Rd Ste 12	Cambridge	ON	N1T1Z6	519-621-6669		668	Web: www.comcor.com
COMCOR Event and Meeting Production Inc	1040 Bayview Drilve Ste 407	Fort Lauderdale	FL	33308	954-491-3233		184	Web: www.comcorevents.com
Comdata Corp	5301 Maryland Way	Brentwood	TN	37027	615-370-7000		69	TF: 800-266-3282 ■ Web: www.comdata.com
Come Back in	508 E Wilson St	Madison	WI	53703	608-258-8619		379	Web: comebackintavern.com
Comedical Inc	7100 Roosevelt Way NE	Seattle	WA	98115	206-524-7424		475	Web: www.comedical.com
Comedy Central	345 Hudson St	New York	NY	10014	212-767-8600		395	Web: www.cc.com
Comedy Works Inc	1226 15th St	Denver	CO	80202	720-274-6866		749	Web: www.comedyworks.com
Comer Holdings LLC	21624 Melrose Ave	Southfield	MI	48075	248-663-5700		247	Web: www.comerholdings.com
Comer Industries Inc	12730 Virkler Dr	Charlotte	NC	28273	704-588-8400		188	Web: www.comerindustries.com
Comer James (Rep R - KY)	1037 Longworth House Office Bldg	Washington	DC	20515	202-225-3115		342-2	TF: 800-328-5629 ■ Web: comer.house.gov
Comerica Bank	411 W Lafayette	Detroit	MI	48226	313-222-4000		70	TF: 800-292-1300 ■ Web: www.comerica.com
Comet Consultants Inc	150 Keating Dr	Belle Chasse	LA	70037	504-392-3196		261	Web: cometcon.com
Comet Die & Engraving Co	909 Larch Ave	Elmhurst	IL	60126	630-833-5600	833-2644	757	Web: www.cometdie.com
Comet Micro System Inc	390 Swift Ave Unit 24	South San Francisco	CA	94080	650-615-9123		180	Web: www.cometmicro.com
COMET Technologies USA Inc	3400 Gilchrist Rd	Akron	OH	44260	330-798-4800		420	Web: www.yxlon.com
Cometic Gasket Inc	8090 Auburn Rd	Painesville	OH	44077	440-354-0777		326	TF: 800-752-9850 ■ Web: www.cometic.com
Com-Fab Inc	4657 Price Hilliards Rd	Plain City	OH	43064	740-857-1107	857-1757	763	TF: 866-522-1794 ■ Web: www.comfab-inc.com
ComForCare Home Care	2520 Telegraph Rd Ste 100	Bloomfield Hills	MI	48302	248-499-5190	745-9763	310	TF: 800-886-4044 ■ Web: comforcare.com
Comfort - Air Engineering Inc	11403 Jones Maltsberger Rd	San Antonio	TX	78216	210-494-1691		256	Web: www.comfort-air.com
Comfort Care Home Health LLC	245 Cahaba Valley Pky Ste 100	Pelham	AL	35124	877-231-0321		363	TF: 877-231-0321 ■ Web: www.comfortcarehomehealth.com
Comfort Caregivers Inc	6501 E Greenway Pkwy Ste 103	Scottsdale	AZ	85254	602-482-7777		363	Web: comfortcaregivers.com
Comfort Group Inc, The	659 Thompson Ln	Nashville	TN	37204	615-263-2900		189-10	Web: www.thecomfortgroup.com
Comfort Products Distributing LLC	13202 I St	Omaha	NE	68137	402-334-7777		612	TF: 800-779-8299 ■ Web: comfortproducts.com
Comfort Research	1719 Elizabeth Ave NW	Grand Rapids	MI	49548	616-475-5000		601	Web: comfortresearch.com
Comfort Systems USA Inc	675 Bering Ste 400	Houston	TX	77057	713-830-9600	830-9696	189-10	NYSE: FIX ■ TF: 800-723-8431 ■ Web: www.comfortsystemsusa.com
Comfortex Inc	1680 Wilkie Dr	Winona	MN	55987	507-454-6579	454-6581	471	TF: 800-445-4007 ■ Web: www.comfortexinc.com
Comfortex Window Fashions Inc	21 Elm St	Maplewood	NY	12189	800-843-4151	336-4580	87	TF: 800-843-4151 ■ Web: www.comfortex.com
Comforting Hands Hospice	1366 SE Washington Blvd Ste A	Bartlesville	OK	74006	918-331-0003	331-9556	450	Web: comfortinghandshospice.com
Comgraphics Inc	329 W 18th St 10th Fl	Chicago	IL	60616	312-226-0900		496	Web: ww3.cgichicago.com
COMHAR Inc	100 W Lehigh Ave	Philadelphia	PA	19133	215-203-3000	203-3011	726	Web: www.comhar.org
Comic Strip Live	1568 2nd Ave Frnt	New York	NY	10028	212-861-9386		95	Web: www.comicstriplive.com
Coming Attractions Theatres	1644 Ashland St Unit 5	Ashland	OR	97520	541-488-4040		748	Web: www.catheatres.com
Comint Apparel Group LLC	463 7th Ave 11th Fl	New York	NY	10018	212-947-7474		96	
Comit Developers	1325 Eraste Landry Rd	LaFayette	LA	70506	337-326-5479		180	Web: www.comitdevelopers.com
Comitz Law Firm LLC	46 Public Sq Ste 101	Wilkes-Barre	PA	18701	570-829-1111		41	Web: comitzlaw.com
Comlink Network Services	4009 S Meridian St	Indianapolis	IN	46217	317-786-3496		180	Web: comlinkns.com
COMM Group Inc	2003 S Easton Rd Ste 100	Doylestown	PA	18901	215-348-8775		376	Web: www.cheapcaribbean.com
Comm Source Data	200 Waler Way Bldg 1 Unit 1	Saint Augustine	FL	32086	800-434-5750	718-4149	180	TF: 800-434-5750 ■ Web: www.comm-source-data.com
Command Alkon Inc	1800 International Pk Dr Ste 400	Birmingham	AL	35243	205-879-3282		178-10	TF: 800-624-1872 ■ Web: commandalkon.com
Command Companies	100 Castle Rd	Secaucus	NJ	07096	201-863-8100	863-5443	626	Web: www.commandweb.com
Command Consulting Group LLC	1919 M St NW Ste 200	Washington	DC	20036	202-207-2930		194	Web: www.commandcg.com
Command Financial Press Corp	345 Hudson St	New York	NY	10014	212-274-0070		626	Web: www.commandfinancial.com
Command Medical Products Inc	15 Signal Ave	Ormond Beach	FL	32174	386-672-8116	677-7781	476	Web: www.commandmedical.com
Command Nutritionals LLC	10 Washington Ave Ste 1	Fairfield	NJ	07004	973-227-8210		296-10	Web: www.commandnutritionals.com
Command Plastic Corp	124 W Ave	Tallmadge	OH	44278	330-434-3497	434-8316	548	TF: 800-321-8001 ■ Web: www.commandplastic.com
Command Post Technologies Inc	1039 Champions Way	Suffolk	VA	23435	757-394-1311		256	Web: commandposttech.com
Command Security Corp	512 Herndon Pkwy Ste A	Herndon	VA	20170	703-464-4735	543-0631	693	Web: www.commandsecurity.com
Command Spanish Inc	PO Box 1091	Petal	MS	39465	601-582-8378	582-5177	96	TF: 800-250-8637 ■ Web: www.commandspanish.com
Command Technology Inc (CTI)	404 Thames St	Groton	CT	06340	860-445-0156	446-2010	174	Web: www.commandtech.com
Command Tooling Systems LLC	13931 Sunfish Lk Blvd	Ramsey	MN	55303	800-328-2197	576-6911*	493	*Fax Area Code: 763 ■ Web: www.commandtool.com
Commander Buildings Inc	22223 Hwy 38 N	Monticello	IA	52310	319-465-5961		480	Web: www.commanderbuildings.com
Commander Electric Inc	500 Johnson Ave PO Box 526	Bohemia	NY	11716	631-563-3223	563-8322	189-4	Web: www.commanderelectric.com
Commander Hotel	1401 Atlantic Ave	Ocean City	MD	21842	888-289-6166		379	TF: 888-289-6166 ■ Web: www.commanderhotel.com
Commander Navy Installations Command (CNIC)	716 Sicard St SE Ste 1000	Washington Navy Yard	DC	20374	800-362-4704		340-6	TF: 800-362-4704 ■ Web: www.cnic.navy.mil
Commando Products Inc	420A Blue Ridge Ext	Grandview	MO	64030	816-966-8889		351	Web: www.commandoproducts.com
CommCare Corp	601 Poydras St 2755 Pan American Life Ctr	New Orleans	LA	70130	504-324-8950		371	TF: 877-792-5434 ■ Web: www.commcare.com
Commcare Pharmacy	2817 E Oakland Park Blvd Ste 100	Fort Lauderdale	FL	33306	888-203-7973		237	TF: 888-203-7973 ■ Web: www.commcarepharmacy.com
Commenco Inc	4901 Bristol Ave	Kansas City	MO	64129	816-753-2166		736	TF: 800-292-9725 ■ Web: commenco.com
Commentary Magazine	561 Seventh Ave 16th Fl	New York	NY	10018	212-891-1400		457-10	Web: www.commentarymagazine.com
Commerce & Industry Association of New Jersey (CIANJ)	61 S Paramus Rd	Paramus	NJ	07652	201-368-2100	368-3438	139	Web: www.cianj.org
Commerce Bank of Washington, The (TCBWA)	2 Union Sq 601 Union St Ste 3600	Seattle	WA	98101	206-292-3900	625-9457	70	TF: 800-877-8021 ■ Web: www.tcbwa.com
Commerce Casino	6131 Telegraph Rd	Commerce	CA	90040	323-721-2100		133	Web: www.commercecasino.com

Name / Address	Phone	Fax	Class
Commerce Printing Service 322 N 12th St ... Sacramento CA 95811 *Web:* commerceprinting.com	916-442-8100	448-2727	627
Commercewest Bank NA 2111 Business Center Dr ... Irvine CA 92612 *OTC:* CWBK ■ *Web:* www.cwbk.com	949-251-6959		70
Commercial & Architectural Products Inc PO Box 250 ... Dover OH 44622 *TF:* 800-377-1221 ■ *Web:* www.marlite.com	330-343-6621	343-7296	499
Commercial Agency Inc, The 141 Kinderkamack Rd ... Park Ridge NJ 07656 *Web:* thecommercialagency.com	201-391-1324		390
Commercial Air 601 Ransdell Rd ... Lebanon IN 46052 *Web:* www.commercialair.com	765-482-8121		186
Commercial Appeal 495 Union Ave ... Memphis TN 38103 *TF:* 800-444-6397 ■ *Web:* www.commercialappeal.com	901-529-2345		532-2
Commercial Bank 301 N State St PO Box 638 ... Alma MI 48801 *OTC:* CEFC ■ *TF:* 800-547-8531 ■ *Web:* www.commercial-bank.com	989-463-2185		70
Commercial Bank 401 S Main St PO Box 388 ... Nelson NE 68961 *Web:* gotocb.com	402-225-3381		70
Commercial Brokers Assn 12131 113th Ave NE Ste 101 ... Kirkland WA 98034 *TF:* 800-275-2522 ■ *Web:* commercialmls.com	800-275-2522		652
Commercial Contracting Corp 4260 N Atlantic Blvd ... Auburn Hills MI 48326 *Web:* www.cccnetwork.com	248-209-0500	209-0501	189-1
Commercial Contractors Inc 4920 Fairbanks St ... Anchorage AK 99503 *Web:* www.alaskacci.com	907-563-1911		290
Commercial Distributing Company Inc 46 S Broad St ... Westfield MA 01085 *Web:* www.commercialdist.com	413-562-9691	562-7302	81-1
Commercial Driver Training 600 Patton Ave ... West Babylon NY 11704 *TF:* 800-649-7447 ■ *Web:* cdtschool.com	631-249-1330		800
Commercial Enameling Co 1310 E Borchard Ave ... Santa Ana CA 92705 *Web:* www.cecosinks.com	714-058-1950	656-1969	481
Commercial Energy Specialists Inc 952 Jupiter Park Ln Ste 1 ... Jupiter FL 33458 *TF:* 800-940-1557 ■ *Web:* www.ceswaterquality.com	561-744-1557	746-5898	612
Commercial Flooring Inc 3418 E Pershing Blvd ... Cheyenne WY 82001 *Web:* carpetonecommercialflooring.com	307-222-3094		290
Commercial Furniture Interiors Inc 1154 Rt 22 W ... Mountainside NJ 07092 *Web:* cfioffice.com	908-518-1670	654-8436	393
Commercial Honing Company Inc 8608 Sultana Ave ... Fontana CA 92335 *Web:* www.commercialhoning.com	909-829-1211	829-7631	223
Commercial Honing LLC 2997 Progress St ... Dover OH 44622 **Fax Area Code:* 330 ■ *TF:* 800-346-2601 ■ *Web:* www.commercialfluidpower.com	800-346-2601	343-6391*	454
Commercial Insurance Associates Inc 250 State St Unit K-1 ... North Haven CT 06473 *Web:* ciaonline.com	203-281-5911		390
Commercial Interior Decor Inc (CI) 3617 W Teem Dr ... Sioux Falls SD 57107 *Web:* cidinc.net	605-334-9288	334-2706	393
Commercial Interior Resources Inc (CIR) 1761 Reynolds Ave ... Irvine CA 92614 *Web:* cir-resource.com	949-752-1470	752-6103	290
Commercial Jet Inc 4600 NW 36 St Miami International Airport Bldg 896 ... Miami FL 33166 *Web:* www.commercialjet.com	305-341-5150		454
Commercial Law League of America (CLLA) 3005 Tollview Dr ... Rolling Meadows IL 60008 **Fax Area Code:* 847 ■ *TF:* 800-978-2552 ■ *Web:* www.clla.org	312-240-1400	584-3939*	49-10
Commercial Lighting Industries 81161 Indio Blvd ... Indio CA 92201 *TF:* 800-755-0155 ■ *Web:* www.commercial-lighting.net	800-755-0155		439
Commercial Lumber & Pallet Co 135 Long Ln ... City of Industry CA 91746 *TF:* 800-252-4968 ■ *Web:* clcpallets.com	800-252-4968		200
Commercial Mailing Accessories Inc 28220 Playmor Beach Rd ... Rocky Mount MO 65072 *TF:* 800-325-7303 ■ *Web:* dispensamatic.com	800-325-7303		413
Commercial Manufacturing & Assembly Inc 17087 Hayes St ... Grand Haven MI 49417 *Web:* www.callcma.com	616-847-9980	847-3570	488
Commercial Metal Fabricators Company Inc 150 Commerce Park Dr ... Dayton OH 45404 *Web:* www.commercialmetalfabricators.com	937-233-4911		480
Commercial Metals Co (CMC) 6565 N MacArthur Blvd Ste 800 ... Irving TX 75039 *NYSE:* CMC ■ *Web:* www.cmc.com	214-689-4300		723
Commercial National Financial Corp 900 Ligonier St ... Latrobe PA 15650 *OTC:* CNAF ■ *TF:* 800-803-2265 ■ *Web:* www.cnbthebankonline.com	724-539-3501		360-2
Commercial Plastics Co (CPC) 800 Allanson Rd ... Mundelein IL 60060 *Web:* www.ecommercialplastics.com	847-566-1700		604
Commercial Programming Systems Inc 4400 Coldwater Canyon Ave ... Studio City CA 91604 **Fax Area Code:* 818 ■ *TF:* 888-277-4562 ■ *Web:* www.cpsinc.com	323-851-2681	301-1996*	177
Commercial Properties Realty Trust 100 North St ... Baton Rouge LA 70802 *TF:* 800-648-9064 ■ *Web:* www.cprt.com	225-924-7206	924-1235	654
Commercial Ready Mix Products Inc PO Box 189 ... Winton NC 27986 *Web:* www.crmpinc.com	252-358-5461	358-4912	191-1
Commercial Realty & Resources Corp 1415 Wyckoff Rd PO Box 1468 ... Wall NJ 07719 *Web:* njresources.com	732-938-1111		652
Commercial Refrigerator Door Company Inc 6200 Porter Rd ... Sarasota FL 34240 *TF:* 800-237-3940 ■ *Web:* www.styleline.com	941-371-8110	377-2850	234
Commercial Resins Company Inc 8100 E 96th Ave ... Henderson CO 80640 *Web:* www.commercialresins.com	303-288-3914		480
Commercial Savings Bank 627 N Adams St ... Carroll IA 51401 *TF:* 800-383-8000 ■ *Web:* csbcarroll.com	712-792-4346		70
Commercial Siding & Maintenance Co, The 8059 Crile Rd ... Painesville OH 44077 *TF:* 800-229-4276 ■ *Web:* www.commercialsiding.com	440-352-7800	352-7048	189-12
Commercial Software Inc 5214 Western Blvd ... Raleigh NC 27606 *TF:* 800-849-3838 ■ *Web:* comsoft.com	919-851-2010	851-3471	177
Commercial State Bank 519 E Broadway ... Wausa NE 68786 *Web:* wausabank.com	402-586-2266		70
Commercial Steel Treating Corp 31440 Stephenson Hwy ... Madison Heights MI 48071 *Web:* www.commercialsteel.com	248-588-3300	588-3534	484
Commercial Storage & Distribution Co 4103 Metro Dr ... Texarkana TX 75503	903-794-2202		780
Commercial Transport Inc 121 Premier Dr ... Belleville IL 62220 *TF:* 800-851-7541 ■ *Web:* cti-bulk.com	618-233-5260	233-5263	780
Commercial Utility Consultants Inc (CUC) 1556 McDaniel Dr ... West Chester PA 19380 **Fax Area Code:* 610 ■ *TF:* 800-296-2821 ■ *Web:* www.commercialutility.com	800-296-2821	431-1023*	393
Commercial Vehicle Group Inc 7800 Walton Pkwy ... New Albany OH 43054 *NASDAQ:* CVGI ■ *Web:* cvgrp.com	614-289-5360		60
Commercial Wood Products Co 10007 Yucca Rd ... Adelanto CA 92301 *Web:* cwp.cab	760-246-4530	246-8226	115
Commercial-News 17 W North ... Danville IL 61832 *TF:* 877-732-8258 ■ *Web:* www.commercial-news.com	217-446-1000	446-6648	532-2
Commerx Computer Systems Inc 2880 Argentia Rd Unit 1 ... Mississauga ON L5N7X8 *TF:* 855-907-0116 ■ *Web:* www.commerx.ca	905-542-9400		224
Commerzbank AG 2 World Financial Ctr ... New York NY 10281 *Web:* www.corporates.commerzbank.com	212-266-7200		70
Commission Junction Inc 530 E Montecito St ... Santa Barbara CA 93103 **Fax Area Code:* 805 ■ *TF:* 800-761-1072 ■ *Web:* www.cj.com	800-761-1072	730-8001*	7
Commission of Fine Arts 401 F St NW Ste 312 ... Washington DC 20001 *Web:* www.cfa.gov	202-504-2200	504-2195	340-20
Commission on Accreditation for Dietetics Education (CADE) 120 S Riverside Plz Ste 2000 ... Chicago IL 60606 *TF:* 800-877-1600 ■ *Web:* www.eatright.org	312-899-0040		48-1
Commission on Accreditation for Law Enforcement Agencies (CALEA) 13575 Heathcote Blvd Ste 320 ... Gainesville VA 20155 *TF:* 877-789-6904 ■ *Web:* www.calea.org	703-352-4225	890-3126	49-7
Commission on Accreditation in Physical Therapy Education (CAPTE) 1111 N Fairfax St ... Alexandria VA 22314 *Web:* www.capteonline.org	703-706-3245	838-8910	48-1
Commission on Accreditation of Allied Health Education Programs (CAAHEP) 1361 Park St ... Clearwater FL 33756 *Web:* caahep.org	727-210-2350	210-2354	48-1
Commission on Accreditation of Healthcare Management Education (CAHME) 6110 Executive Blvd Ste 614 ... Rockville MD 20852 *Web:* www.cahme.org	301-298-1820		48-1
Commission on Accreditation of Rehabilitation Facilities Intl (CARF) 6951 E Southpoint Rd ... Tucson AZ 85756 *TF:* 888-281-6531 ■ *Web:* www.carf.org	520-325-1044	318-1129	48-1
Commission on English Language Program Accreditation (CEA) 801 N Fairfax St Ste 402A ... Alexandria VA 22314 *Web:* cea-accredit.org	703-665-3400	519-2071	48-1
Commission on Massage Therapy Accreditation (COMTA) 2101 Wilson Blvd Ste 302 ... Arlington VA 22201 *Web:* comta.org	202-888-6790	888-6787	48-1
Commission on Presidential Scholars *U.S. Presidential Scholars Program* 400 Maryland Ave SW US Department of Education ... Washington DC 20202 *TF:* 800-872-5327 ■ *Web:* www.ed.gov	202-401-0961	260-7464	340-20
Commission on Security & Cooperation in Europe 3rd & D Sts SW 234 Ford House Office Bldg ... Washington DC 20515 *Web:* www.csce.gov	202-225-1901	226-4199	340-20
Commissioners of Public Works 121 W Ct Ave ... Greenwood SC 29646 *Web:* www.greenwoodcpw.com	864-942-8100	942-8114	787
Committed Home Healthcare 4217 Marsh Ridge Rd Ste 100 ... Carrollton TX 75010 *Web:* www.committedcare.com	972-306-5060	307-6699	363
Committee for Economic Development (CED) 1530 Wilson Blvd Ste 400 ... Arlington VA 22209 *TF:* 800-676-7353 ■ *Web:* www.ced.org	202-296-5860	223-0776	634
Committee for Education Funding (CEF) 1800 M St NW Ste 500 ... Washington DC 20036 *Web:* cef.org	202-383-0083		48-11
Committee for Purchase from People Who Are Blind or Severely Disabled 1401 S Clark St Ste 715 ... Arlington VA 22202 *Web:* www.abilityone.gov	703-603-7740	603-0655	340-20
Commnet Wireless LLC 400 Northridge Rd Ste 325 ... Atlanta GA 30350 *TF:* 877-510-4357 ■ *Web:* www.commnetwireless.com	678-338-5960	338-5961	387
Commodity Components International Inc 100 Summit St ... Peabody MA 01960 *Web:* cci-inc.com	978-538-0020	538-3633	246
Commodity Futures Trading Commission 1155 21 St NW ... Washington DC 20581 *TF:* 866-366-2382 ■ *Web:* www.cftc.gov	202-418-5000	418-5521	340-20
Commodity Futures Trading Commission Regional Offices			
Central Region 525 W Monroe St ... Chicago IL 60661 *TF:* 800-621-3570 ■ *Web:* www.cftc.gov	312-596-0700	596-0713	340-20
Eastern Region 140 Broadway 19th Fl ... New York NY 10005 *Web:* www.cftc.gov	646-746-9700	746-9938	340-20
Southwestern Region 2 Emanuel Cleaver II Blvd Ste 300 ... Kansas City MO 64112 *Web:* www.cftc.gov	816-960-7700	960-7750	340-20

	Phone	Fax	Class
Commodity Information Systems Inc 3030 NW Expy Ste 725 .... Oklahoma City OK 73112 *TF:* 800-231-0477 ■ *Web:* www.cis-okc.com	405-604-8726		637-9
Commodity Marketing Co 8480 Holcomb Bridge Rd Ste D200 .... Alpharetta GA 30022 **Fax Area Code:* 678 ■ *TF:* 877-566-9196 ■ *Web:* commoditymarketing.com	877-566-9196	566-7821*	169
Commodity Systems Inc 200 W Palmetto Park Rd Ste 200 .... Boca Raton FL 33432 *TF:* 800-274-4727 ■ *Web:* www.csidata.com	561-392-8663		224
Commodore Builders 80 Bridge St. .... Newton MA 02458 *Web:* commodorebuilders.com	617-614-3500		186
Commodore Corp 1423 Lincolnway E .... Goshen IN 46526 *Web:* www.commodorehomes.com	574-533-7100		505
Commodore Plastics LLC 26 Maple Ave .... Bloomfield NY 14469 *Web:* www.commodoresolutions.com	585-657-7777		599
Common Bond 1080 Montreal Ave. .... St. Paul MN 55116 *Web:* www.commonbond.org	651-291-1750		113
Common Cause 1133 19th St NW 9th Fl .... Washington DC 20036 *Web:* www.commoncause.org	202-833-1200	659-3716	48-7
Common Census Inc 90 Bridge St Ste 105 .... Westbrook ME 04092 *TF:* 800-552-7373 ■ *Web:* www.commoncensus.com	207-854-5454	854-3154	390
Common Ground Distributors Inc PO Box 25249 .... Asheville NC 28813 *TF:* 800-654-0626 ■ *Web:* www.comground.com	828-274-5575	274-1955	96
Common Interest Management Services Inc 315 Diablo Rd Ste 221 .... Danville CA 94526 *TF:* 866-673-5414 ■ *Web:* www.commoninterest.com	925-743-3080	743-3084	195
Common Living 335 Madison Ave Ste 6A .... New York NY 10017 *TF:* 844-612-6697 ■ *Web:* www.common.com	844-612-6697		652
Common Man, The 25 Water St .... Concord NH 03301 *Web:* www.thecman.com	603-228-3463		671
Common Sensing Inc 2216 Mosquito Creek Rd .... Clark Fork ID 83811 *Web:* www.commonsensinginc.com	208-266-1541	266-1428	201
Common Source LP, The 14500 N Fwy .... Houston TX 77090 *Web:* www.commonsource.com	281-260-9220		445
Commonfund Inc 15 Old Danbury Rd .... Wilton CT 06897 *TF:* 888-823-6246 ■ *Web:* www.commonfund.org	203-563-5000		401
CommonGrounds Workplace 6790 Embarcadero Ln Ste 100 .... Carlsbad CA 92011 *Web:* www.cgworkplace.com	760-206-7861		188-9
Commons at Orlando Lutheran Towers, The 300 E Church St .... Orlando FL 32801 *TF:* 800-859-1033 ■ *Web:* orlandoseniorhealth.org	407-422-4103		48-20
Commons Capital LP 320 Washington St 4th Fl .... Brookline MA 02445 *Web:* www.commonscapital.com	617-739-3500		792
Commons, The 1928 S Commons .... Federal Way WA 98003 *Web:* www.shopthecommonsmall.com	253-839-6150	946-1413	460
Commonweal Magazine 475 Riverside Dr Rm 405 .... New York NY 10115 *Web:* www.commonwealmagazine.org	212-662-4200		457-17
Commonwealth Annuity and Life Insurance Co 132 Turnpike Rd Ste 210 .... Southborough MA 01772 *Web:* www.commonwealthannuity.com	508-460-2400	460-2401	796
Commonwealth Associates Inc PO Box 1124 .... Jackson MI 49204 *Web:* www.cai-engr.com	517-788-3000		261
Commonwealth Bank of Australia 599 Lexington Ave Ste 1701 .... New York NY 10022 *Web:* www.commbank.com.au	212-848-9200		70
Commonwealth Biotechnologies Inc 601 Biotech Dr .... Richmond VA 23235 *TF:* 800-735-9224 ■ *Web:* cbi-biotech.com	804-648-3820	648-2641	417
Commonwealth Canvas Inc 5 Perkins Way .... Newburyport MA 01950 *TF:* 877-922-6827 ■ *Web:* www.commonwealthcanvas.com	978-499-3900	499-3933	733
Commonwealth Capital LLC 30 S Wacker Dr 22nd Fl .... Chicago IL 60606 *Web:* commonwealthcapital.co	419-724-7327		401
Commonwealth Capital Ventures 400 W Cummings Pk Ste 1725-134 .... Woburn MA 01801 *Web:* www.commonwealthvc.com	781-890-5554		792
Commonwealth Club, The 555 Post St .... San Francisco CA 94102 *TF:* 800-847-7730 ■ *Web:* www.commonwealthclub.org	415-597-6700	597-6729	632
Commonwealth Credit Union PO Box 978 .... Frankfort KY 40602 *TF:* 800-228-6420 ■ *Web:* www.ccuky.org	502-564-4775		219
Commonwealth Electric Company of Midwest 1901 Y St Ste 100 PO Box 80638 .... Lincoln NE 68501 *Web:* www.commonwealthelectric.com	402-474-1341	473-2200	189-4
Commonwealth Financial Corp 101 Federal St Ste 800 .... Boston MA 02110 *Web:* commonwealthfinancialgroup.com	617-439-4389		390
Commonwealth Financial Network 29 Sawyer Rd .... Waltham MA 02453 **Fax Area Code:* 866 ■ *TF:* 800-237-0081 ■ *Web:* www.commonwealth.com	781-736-0700	316-8357*	401
Commonwealth Fund 1 E 75th St .... New York NY 10021 *Web:* www.commonwealthfund.org	212-606-3800	606-3500	305
Commonwealth Health Corporation Inc 800 Park St .... Bowling Green KY 42101 *TF:* 800-786-1581 ■ *Web:* www.chc.net	270-745-1500		363
Commonwealth Hosiery Mills Inc 4964 Island Ford Rd .... Randleman NC 27317 *Web:* www.commonwealth-hosiery.com	336-498-2621		155-10
Commonwealth Hotels LLC 100 E Rivercenter Blvd Ste 1050 .... Covington KY 41011 *Web:* commonwealthhotels.com	859-261-5522		378
Commonwealth Institute 186 Hampshire St .... Cambridge MA 02139 *Web:* comw.org	617-547-4474	868-1267	634
Commonwealth Laminating & Coating Inc 345 Beaver Creek Dr .... Martinsville VA 24112 *TF:* 888-321-5111 ■ *Web:* www.suntekfilms.com	276-632-4991	632-0173	699
Commonwealth Land Title Insurance Co 601 Riverside Ave .... Jacksonville FL 32204 *TF:* 888-866-3684 ■ *Web:* www.cltic.com	888-866-3684		391-6
Commonwealth Mailing Systems Inc 1700 Venable St .... Richmond VA 23223 *TF:* 800-336-6245 ■ *Web:* www.cms-mpc.com	804-780-1700	782-9876	5
Commonwealth National Bank 2214 St Stephens Rd .... Mobile AL 36617 *Web:* www.ecommonwealthbank.com	251-476-5938	476-5946	70
Commonwealth of Massachusetts *Schooner Ernestina-Morrissey* New Bedford State Pier .... New Bedford MA 02740 *Web:* www.mass.gov	508-992-4900		565
Skinner State Park 10 Skinner State Park Rd .... Hadley MA 01035 *Web:* www.mass.gov	413-586-0350		565
Commonwealth of Pennsylvania 302 North Office Bldg 401 North St .... Harrisburg PA 17120 *Web:* www.dos.pa.gov	717-787-6458	787-1734	339-39
Commonwealth Park Suites Hotel 901 Bank St .... Richmond VA 23219 *TF:* 888-343-7301 ■ *Web:* www.thecommonwealthsuites.com	804-343-7300		379
Commonwealth Technology Inc 5875 Barclay Dr .... Alexandria VA 22315 *Web:* www.cti1.net	703-719-6800	719-6631	261
Commonwealth Telephone Co 1 Newbury St Ste 103 .... Peabody MA 01960 *TF:* 800-439-7170 ■ *Web:* www.commonwealthtel.com	978-536-9500		736
Commonwealth Toy & Novelty Company Inc 980 Sixth Ave 3rd Fl .... New York NY 10018 *Web:* commonwealthtoy.com	212-242-4070	645-4279	762
Comm-Pro Associates Inc 25852 McBean Pky Ste 611 .... Santa Clarita CA 91355 *Web:* www.comm-pro.com	661-284-3650		178-1
CommScope Inc 1100 Commscope Pl SE PO Box 339 .... Hickory NC 28603 *TF:* 800-982-1708 ■ *Web:* www.commscope.com	828-324-2200	328-3400	814
CommStructures Inc 101 E Roberts Rd .... Pensacola FL 32534 *Web:* www.commstructures.com	850-968-9293	968-9283	188-1
Communauto Inc 335 Rue St-Joseph Est Ste 310 .... Quebec City QC G1K3B4 *TF:* 877-496-1116 ■ *Web:* www.communauto.com	418-523-1788		126
Communi Care At Waterford 955 Garden Lake Pkwy .... Toledo OH 43614 *Web:* www.communicarehealth.com	419-382-2200		450
Communica 31 N Erie St .... Toledo OH 43604 *TF:* 800-800-7890 ■ *Web:* www.communica.world	800-800-7890		514
Communication Arts 110 Constitution Dr .... Menlo Park CA 94025 *Web:* www.commarts.com	650-326-6040	326-1648	637-9
Communication Consulting Services Inc 1605 Colburn St .... Honolulu HI 96817 *Web:* www.ccsi-solutions.net	808-842-7800		177
Communication Data Services 1901 Bell Ave .... Des Moines IA 50315 *TF:* 866-897-7987 ■ *Web:* www.cds-global.com	515-246-6837	246-6687	225
Communication Devices Inc 85 Fulton St .... Boonton NJ 07005 *Web:* www.commdevices.com	973-334-1980	334-0545	392
Communication Network Engineering (CNE) 210 27th St N .... Fargo ND 58102 *Web:* cnefargo.com	701-237-3433		194
Communication Research Consultants Inc (CRC) 1170 Rte 17M Ste 3 .... Chester NY 10918 *Web:* www.crcglobal.com	845-774-1231	774-1492	196
Communication Technologies Inc 14151 Newbrook Dr Ste 400 .... Chantilly VA 20151 *TF:* 888-266-8358 ■ *Web:* www.comtechnologies.com	703-961-9080		735
Communication Technologies Inc 18110-E Chesterfield Airport Rd .... Chesterfield MO 63005 *Web:* www.cti-stl.com	636-537-7200		224
Communication Unlimited (CU) 185 Shevelin Rd .... Novato CA 94948 *TF:* 800-563-1454 ■ *Web:* www.gordonburgett.com	415-884-2941	883-5707	637-2
Communication Wiring Specialists Inc 8909 Complex Dr Ste F .... San Diego CA 92123 *Web:* cwssandiego.com	858-278-7709		387
Communications & Power Industries Inc (CPI-BMD) *Beverly Microwave Div* 150 Sohier Rd. .... Beverly MA 01915 *Web:* www.cpii.com	978-922-6000	922-2736	647
Communications & Power Industries LLC 811 Hansen Way .... Palo Alto CA 94304 *Web:* www.cpii.com	650-846-2900	846-3276	253
Communications Concepts Inc 7481 Huntsman Blvd No 720 .... Springfield VA 22153 *Web:* www.apexawards.com	703-643-2200	643-2329	647
Communications Conveyor Company Inc 306 W Overly Dr .... Lake Dallas TX 75065 *TF:* 800-533-3794 ■ *Web:* www.comcosystems.com	940-230-2943	222-2699	207
Communications Credit & Recovery (CCR) 20 Broad Hollow Rd Ste 1002 .... Melville NY 11747 *Web:* www.ccrcollect.com	631-923-2200	923-2784	160
Communications Design Associates Inc 437 Turnpike St .... Canton MA 02021 *Web:* cdaconsultants.com	339-502-6551		261
Communications Engineering LLC (CEI) PO Box 108 .... Cresskill NJ 07626 *Web:* www.ce-inc.com	917-282-1814		194
Communications Manufacturing Co (CMC) 2239 Colby Ave .... Los Angeles CA 90064 *TF:* 800-462-5532 ■ *Web:* www.gotocmc.com	310-828-3200		248
Communications Marketing Southeast Inc (CMSE) 442 Cadillac Pky .... Dallas GA 30157 *Web:* cmse1.com	770-443-9514	443-9513	523
Communications Media Inc 2200 Renaissance Blvd Ste 160 .... King of Prussia PA 19406 *Web:* www.cmimedia.com	484-322-0880		4
Communications News PO Box 866 .... Osprey FL 34229 *TF:* 800-827-9715 ■ *Web:* www.comnews.com	941-539-7579		457-5

	Phone	Fax	Class
Communications Research Associates Inc (CRA) 8190A Beechmont Ave Ste 336 . . . Cincinnati OH 45255 *Web:* www.commres.com	513-618-5223	618-5203	393
Communications Resource Inc 8280 Greensboro Dr Ste 500 . . . McLean VA 22102 *TF:* 888-900-9757 ■ *Web:* www.cri-solutions.com	703-245-4120	356-4860	177
Communications Supply Service Association CSSA (CSSA) 5700 Murray St. . . . Little Rock AR 72209 *TF:* 800-252-2772 ■ *Web:* www.cssa.net	501-562-7666	562-7616	49-20
Communications Systems Inc (CSI) 10900 Red Cir Dr . . . Minnetonka MN 55343 *NASDAQ: JCS* ■ *Web:* www.commsystems.com	952-941-2322		735
Communications Test Design Inc 1339 Enterprise Dr . . . West Chester PA 19380 *TF:* 800-223-3910 ■ *Web:* www.ctdi.com	610-436-5203		735
Communications Unlimited 5013 W Irving Park Rd . . . Chicago IL 60641 *Web:* www.com-unlimited.com	773-282-6222	282-1198	224
Communications Workers of America (CWA) 501 Third St NW . . . Washington DC 20001 *Web:* www.cwa-union.org	202-434-1100		414
Communico Ltd 19 Ludlow Rd . . . Westport CT 06880 *Web:* www.communico.com	203-226-7117		463
Communicorp Inc 1001 Lockwood Ave. . . . Columbus GA 31999 *TF:* 800-775-7998 ■ *Web:* communicorp.com	706-324-1182		627
CommuniGate Systems Inc 388 Market St Ste 1300 . . . San Francisco CA 94111 *TF:* 800-262-4722 ■ *Web:* communigate.com	415-569-2280	383-7461	178-12
Communique Conferencing Inc 1558 Brookshire Ct Ste 100 . . . Reston VA 20190 **Fax Area Code: 703* ■ *TF:* 866-332-2255 ■ *Web:* www.communiqueconferencing.com	202-266-0058	579-6833*	393
Communispond Inc 12 Barns Ln. . . . East Hampton NY 11937 *TF:* 800-529-5925 ■ *Web:* communispond.com	631-907-8010		194
Communist Party USA 235 W 23rd St 7th Fl . . . New York NY 10011 *Web:* www.cpusa.org	212-989-4994		616
Communities Foundation of Texas Inc 5500 Caruth Haven Ln . . . Dallas TX 75225 *Web:* www.cftexas.org	214-750-4222	750-4210	303
Community Action Partnership 1140 Connecticut Ave NW Ste 1210 . . . Washington DC 20036 *Web:* www.communityactionpartnership.com	202-265-7546	265-5048	48-5
Community Alliance with Family Farmers (CAFF) TS Glide Ranch 36355 Russell Blvd . . . Davis CA 95616 *Web:* www.caff.org	530-756-8518		48-13
Community America Credit Union (CACU) 9777 Ridge Dr . . . Lenexa KS 66219 *TF:* 800-892-7957 ■ *Web:* www.communityamerica.com	913-905-7000	905-7111	219
Community Asphalt Corp 9675 NW 117 Ave Ste 108 . . . Miami FL 33178 *Web:* www.cacorp.net	305-884-9444		46
Community Association Underwriters of America (CAU) 2 Caufield Pl. . . . Newtown PA 18940 *Web:* www.cauinsure.com	267-757-7100		391-4
Community Associations Institute (CAI) 6402 Arlington Blvd Ste 500 . . . Falls Church VA 22042 *TF:* 888-224-4321 ■ *Web:* www.caionline.org	703-970-9220	970-9558	48-7
Community Banc Investments Inc 26 E Main St. . . . New Concord OH 43762 *TF:* 800-224-1013 ■ *Web:* www.cbibankstocks.com	800-224-1013		690
Community Bank 875 National Rd . . . Wheeling WV 26003 *Web:* www.communitybank.tv	304-233-0060	238-0045	70
Community Bank 118 N Main St. . . . Avon SD 57315 *Web:* communitybankavon.com	605-286-3213		70
Community Bank 101 Community Blvd . . . Longview TX 75605 *Web:* www.cbanktexas.com	903-236-4422		70
Community Bank of Midwest 2220 Broadway Ave . . . Great Bend KS 67530 *Web:* www.communitybankmidwest.com	620-792-5111		70
Community Bank of Oelwein 150 First St SE . . . Oelwein IA 50662 *Web:* bankoelwein.com	319-283-4000		70
Community Bank of Raymore PO Box 200. . . . Raymore MO 64083 *Web:* www.cbronline.net	816-322-2100	322-5915	70
Community Bank of Snyder 1715 25th St. . . . Snyder TX 79549 *Web:* cbankofsnyder.com	325-573-2681		70
Community Bank System Inc 5790 Widewaters Pkwy . . . Syracuse NY 13214 *NYSE: CBU* ■ *TF:* 866-764-8638 ■ *Web:* www.communitybankna.com	315-445-2282		360-2
Community Bank, The 507 US Hwy 380 . . . Bridgeport TX 76426 *Web:* onlinewithtcb.com	940-683-4191		70
Community Bankers Merchant Services Inc 908 S Old Missouri Rd . . . Springdale AR 72764 *Web:* www.merchantprocessing.com	479-725-1000		218
Community Bankshares Inc 4950 S Yosemite St Ste F2 . . . Greenwood Village CO 80111 *Web:* www.cobnks.com	720-529-3336		360-2
Community Blood Bank of Northwest Pennsylvania 2646 Peach St . . . Erie PA 16508 *TF:* 877-842-0631 ■ *Web:* fourhearts.org	814-456-4206		89
Community Blood Center Inc 4406 W Spencer St . . . Appleton WI 54914 *TF:* 800-280-4102 ■ *Web:* www.communityblood.org	920-738-3131		89
Community Blood Center of the Ozarks 220 W Plainview Rd . . . Springfield MO 65810 *TF:* 800-280-5337 ■ *Web:* www.cbco.org	417-227-5000		89
Community Blood Ctr 349 S Main St. . . . Dayton OH 45402 *TF:* 800-388-4483 ■ *Web:* www.cbccts.org	800-388-4483		89
Community Blood Ctr (CBC) 4040 Main St . . . Kansas City MO 64111 *TF:* 888-647-4040 ■ *Web:* www.savealifenow.org	816-753-4040	968-4047	89
Community Blood Services 102 Chestnut Ridge Rd . . . Montvale NJ 07645 *TF:* 866-228-1500 ■ *Web:* communitybloodservices.org	201-444-3900		89
Community Broadcasters LLC 199 Wealtha Ave . . . Watertown NY 13601 *Web:* www.commbroadcasters.com	315-782-1240		645-11
Community Care Center Inc 201 Fir Rd . . . Carl Junction MO 64834 *Web:* comm-care.com	417-782-5659	659-8880	391-3
Community Care Inc 1555 S Layton Blvd . . . Milwaukee WI 53215 *TF:* 866-992-6600 ■ *Web:* www.communitycareinc.org	414-385-6600		194
Community Coffee Co 3332 Partridge Ln Bldg A . . . Baton Rouge LA 70809 *TF:* 800-688-0990 ■ *Web:* www.communitycoffee.com	800-884-5282	643-8199	296-7
Community College Foundation, The 1901 Royal Oaks Dr Ste 100. . . . Sacramento CA 95815 *Web:* www.communitycollege.org	916-418-5115		305
Community College of Allegheny County 808 Ridge Ave. . . . Pittsburgh PA 15212 *Web:* ccac.edu	412-237-2525	237-4581	162
Community College of Aurora 16000 E Centretech Pkwy . . . Aurora CO 80011 *TF:* 844-493-8255 ■ *Web:* www.ccaurora.edu	303-360-4700	361-7432	162
Community College of Baltimore County (CCBC) *Hunt Valley* 11101 McCormick Rd. . . . Hunt Valley MD 21031 *Web:* www.ccbcmd.edu	443-840-5830		162
Community College of Beaver County 1 Campus Dr . . . Monaca PA 15061 *TF:* 800-335-0222 ■ *Web:* www.ccbc.edu	724-775-8561	728-7599	162
Community College of Denver 1111 E Colfax Ave. . . . Denver CO 80204 *Web:* www.ccd.edu	303-556-2600	556-2431	162
Community College of Philadelphia 1700 Spring Garden St. . . . Philadelphia PA 19130 *Web:* www.ccp.edu	215-751-8000		162
Community College of Vermont 10 Merchants Row Ste 223. . . . Middlebury VT 05753 *TF:* 800-431-0025 ■ *Web:* www.ccv.edu	802-388-3032	388-4686	162
Community College System of New Hampshire (CCSNH) 26 College Dr . . . Concord NH 03301 *TF:* 866-945-2255 ■ *Web:* www.ccsnh.edu	603-230-3500	271-2725	162
Community Consulting Group (CCG) 5008 Morgan Ave S . . . Minneapolis MN 55419 *Web:* www.ccgpartnership.com	612-926-0122		194
Community Counseling & Correctional Service (CCCS) 471 E Mercury St . . . Butte MT 59701 *Web:* www.cccscorp.com	406-782-0417		48-15
Community Culinary School of Charlotte 9315-D Monroe Rd. . . . Charlotte NC 28270 *Web:* www.communityculinary.org	704-375-4500	347-0258	685
Community Development Partnership 256 W Beacon Str. . . . Philadelphia MS 39350 *Web:* www.neshoba.org	601-656-1000	656-1066	139
Community Development Trust (CDT) 1350 Broadway Ste 700 . . . New York NY 10018 *Web:* www.cdt.biz	212-271-5080	271-5079	655
Community Educational Television 10902 S Wilcrest Dr . . . Houston TX 77099 *Web:* myedutv.org	281-561-5828		738
Community Eldercare Services LLC (CES) PO Box 3667 . . . Tupelo MS 38803 *TF:* 877-461-1062 ■ *Web:* www.cesltc.com	877-461-1062		463
Community Electric Co-op 52 W Windsor Blvd. . . . Windsor VA 23487 *TF:* 855-700-2667 ■ *Web:* www.comelec.coop	757-242-6181		245
Community Financial Services Federal Credit Union 149 St George Ave . . . Roselle NJ 07203 *Web:* cfsfcu.com	908-245-1650	245-1651	219
Community First Bank 925 Wisconsin Ave. . . . Boscobel WI 53805 *Web:* www.cfbank.com	608-375-4117	375-4119	70
Community First Bank 915 W Fort Scott St . . . Butler MO 64730 *Web:* communityfirstbank.net	660-679-3135		70
Community First Bank Na PO Box 39. . . . Forest OH 45843 *Web:* www.com1stbank.com	419-273-2595		360-2
Community First Bank of The Heartland 117 N 10th St . . . Mount Vernon IL 62864 *Web:* www.cfbh.bank	618-244-3000		70
Community First Health Plans Inc 1410 Guadalupe St Ste 222 . . . San Antonio TX 78207 *TF:* 800-434-2347 ■ *Web:* www.cfhp.com	210-227-2347		352
Community Focus Federal Credit Union 18925 Telegraph . . . Brownstown MI 48174 *Web:* communityfocusfcu.org	734-281-3900		219
Community Food Bank of New Jersey Inc 31 Evans Terminal. . . . Hillside NJ 07205 *Web:* www.cfbnj.org	908-355-3663	355-0270	48-5
Community Food Coop 908 W Main St . . . Bozeman MT 59715 *Web:* www.bozo.coop	406-587-4039		345
Community Foundation for Greater Atlanta Inc 191 Peachtree St NE Ste 1000 Tenth Fl. . . . Atlanta GA 30303 *Web:* www.cfgreateratlanta.org	404-688-5525	688-3060	303
Community Foundation for Greater New Haven 70 Audubon St . . . New Haven CT 06510 *Web:* www.cfgnh.org	203-777-2386	787-6584	303
Community Foundation of Greater Memphis 1900 Union Ave . . . Memphis TN 38104 *Web:* www.cfgm.org	901-728-4600	722-0010	303
Community Foundation Serving Richmond & Central Virginia, The 7501 Boulders View Dr Ste 110 . . . Richmond VA 23225 *Web:* www.cfrichmond.org	804-330-7400	330-5992	303
Community Foundation Silicon Valley 60 S Market St Ste 1000. . . . San Jose CA 95113 *Web:* www.siliconvalleycf.org	408-278-2200		303
Community Health Accreditation Program Inc (CHAP) 1275 K St NW Ste 800 . . . Washington DC 20005 *TF:* 800-656-9656 ■ *Web:* www.chapinc.org	202-862-3413	862-3419	48-1
Community Health Charities 1199 N Fairfax St . . . Alexandria VA 22314 *TF:* 800-654-0845 ■ *Web:* healthcharities.org	703-528-1007		48-5
Community Health Systems Inc 4000 Meridian Blvd . . . Franklin TN 37067 *NYSE: CYH* ■ *TF:* 888-373-9600 ■ *Web:* www.chs.net	615-465-7000		353

Phone | Fax | Class

Community Healthcare Credit Union Inc
48 Haynes St ... Manchester CT 06040 860-643-3420 643-3049 219
TF: 866-283-3420 ■ *Web:* chcu.org

Community Healthcare System
901 MacArthur Blvd ... Munster IN 46321 219-836-1600 353
TF: 866-836-3477 ■ *Web:* www.comhs.org

Community High School District 99
6301 Springside Ave. ... Downers Grove IL 60516 630-795-7100 795-7199 685
Web: www.csd99.org

Community Hospice 1480 Carter Ave. ... Ashland KY 41101 606-329-1890 329-0018 371
TF: 800-926-6184 ■ *Web:* www.chospice.org

Community Hospice & Palliative Care
4266 Sunbeam Rd ... Jacksonville FL 32257 904-268-5200 371
TF: 866-253-6681 ■ *Web:* www.communityhospice.com

Community Hospice Inc 4368 Spyres Way ... Modesto CA 95356 209-578-6300 371
TF: 866-645-4567 ■ *Web:* hospiceheart.org

Community Hospice of Albany
445 New Karner Rd. ... Albany NY 12205 518-724-0200 724-0299 371
Web: communityhospice.org

Community Hospice of Texas
6100 Western Pl Ste 105 ... Fort Worth TX 76107 800-226-0373 371
TF: 800-226-0373 ■ *Web:* www.chot.org

Community Hospital Anderson (CHA)
1515 N Madison Ave ... Anderson IN 46011 765-298-4242 374-3
TF: 800-777-7775 ■ *Web:* www.ecommunity.com

Community Hospital East
1500 N Ritter Ave ... Indianapolis IN 46219 317-355-1411 374-3
Web: www.ecommunity.com

Community Hospital of the Monterey Peninsula (CHOMP)
23625 Holman Hwy ... Monterey CA 93940 831-624-5311 625-4948 374-3
TF: 888-452-4667 ■ *Web:* www.chomp.org

Community Imports Inc
8340 W 159th St. ... Orland Park IL 60462 708-364-2600 755
Web: www.communityhonda.com

Community Investors Bancorp Inc
119 S Sandusky Ave. ... Bucyrus OH 44820 419-562-7055 562-5516 360-2
OTC: CIBN ■ *TF:* 800-222-4955 ■ *Web:* ffcb.com

Community ISP Inc (CISP) 3035 Moffat Rd ... Toledo OH 43615 419-724-5300 225
Web: www.cisp.com

Community Link Inc 1665 N Fourth St. ... Breese IL 62230 618-526-8800 242
Web: www.commlink.org

Community Marketing Inc
584 Castro St Ste 834. ... San Francisco CA 94114 415-437-3800 552-5104 466
Web: www.communitymarketinginc.com

Community Matters Inc PO Box 5900. ... Frisco TX 75035 800-380-2450 370-1766* 637-2
**Fax Area Code:* 972 ■ *TF:* 800-380-2450 ■ *Web:* communitymattersinc.com

Community Medical Ctr
2827 Ft Missoula Rd ... Missoula MT 59804 406-728-4100 374-3
Web: www.communitymed.org

Community Memorial Healthcenter
412 Bracey Ln. ... South Hill VA 23970 434-447-3151 374-3
Web: www.vcuhealth.org

Community Memorial Hospital
147 N Brent St ... Ventura CA 93003 805-652-5011 374-3
Web: www.cmhshealth.org

Community Memorial Hospital (CMH)
W 180 N 8085 Town Hall Rd. ... Menomonee Falls WI 53051 262-251-1000 374-3
Web: www.froedtert.com

Community Mortgage Corp
142 Timber Creek Dr. ... Cordova TN 38018 901-759-4400 759-4489 403
Web: www.communitymtg.com

Community National Bank
100 Main St Ste 110. ... Newport VT 05855 802-334-7915 70
Web: www.communitynationalbank.com

Community Newspaper Company Inc
72 Cherry Hill Dr ... Beverly MA 01915 978-739-1300 637-8
Web: www.wickedlocal.com

Community Newspapers Inc
6605 SE Lake Rd ... Portland OR 97222 503-684-0360 620-3433 637-8
Web: pamplinmedia.com

Community of Christ
1001 W Walnut St. ... Independence MO 64050 816-833-1000 521-3085 48-20
TF: 800-825-2806 ■ *Web:* www.cofchrist.org

Community One Credit Union of Ohio Inc
6583 Frank Ave NW ... North Canton OH 44720 330-305-3050 219
TF: 800-469-0497 ■ *Web:* c1cu.com

Community Options Inc 16 Farber Rd ... Princeton NJ 08540 609-951-9900 951-9112 48-6
TF: 877-875-1212 ■ *Web:* www.comop.org

Community Oriented Policing Services (COPS)
145 N St NE ... Washington DC 20530 800-421-6770 340-14
TF: 800-421-6770 ■ *Web:* cops.usdoj.gov

Community Partnership of the Ozarks
330 N Jefferson Ave Ste A ... Springfield MO 65806 417-888-2020 726
Web: www.cpozarks.org

Community Pharmacies
16 Commerce Dr Ste 1 PO Box 528 ... Augusta ME 04332 800-730-4840 622-3264* 237
**Fax Area Code:* 207 ■ *TF:* 800-730-4840 ■ *Web:* communityrx.com

Community Plus Federal Credit Union
526 E Champaign Ave. ... Rantoul IL 61866 217-893-8201 219
Web: cplusfcu.org

Community Preservation Corp, The (CPC)
28 E 28th St 9th Fl ... New York NY 10016 212-869-5300 509
Web: communityp.com

Community Professional Loudspeakers
333 E Fifth St ... Chester PA 19013 610-876-3400 874-0190 52
TF: 800-523-4934 ■ *Web:* www.communitypro.com

Community Regional Credit Union
584 Wyoming Ave. ... Kingston PA 18704 570-288-2326 288-0448 219
TF: 800-698-0101 ■ *Web:* crcu.info

Community Regional Medical Ctr
2823 Fresno St. ... Fresno CA 93721 559-459-6000 374-3
Web: www.communitymedical.org

Community Renewal Team Inc
555 Windsor St. ... Hartford CT 06120 860-560-5600 560-5722 48-5
Web: www.crtct.org

Community Resource Federal Credit Union
20 Wade Rd ... Latham NY 12110 518-783-2211 783-2266 219
TF: 888-783-2211 ■ *Web:* communityresourcefcu.com

Phone | Fax | Class

Community Services Group (CSG)
320 Highland Dr PO Box 597 ... Mountville PA 17554 717-285-7121 285-2658 353
TF: 877-907-7970 ■ *Web:* csgonline.org

Community Shores Bank Corp
1030 W Norton Ave. ... Muskegon MI 49441 231-780-1800 360-2
NASDAQ: CSHB ■ *TF:* 888-853-6633 ■ *Web:* communityshores.com

Community Star Credit Union
832 Cleveland St ... Elyria OH 44035 440-365-7342 219
Web: commstar.org

Community State Bancorp 1812 Hwy Blvd. ... Spencer IA 51301 712-262-6444 70
Web: ecommunitybank.org

Community State Bank 208 N Ctr ... Shelbina MO 63468 573-588-4101 588-4408 360-2
Web: www.commbankonline.com

Community State Bank
1414 W 11th St PO Box 219. ... Coffeyville KS 67337 620-251-1313 70
Web: www.ourlocalbank.com

Community State Bank of Missouri
117 W Church St ... Bowling Green MO 63334 573-324-2233 70
Web: c-s-b.com

Community Suffolk Inc 304 Second St ... Everett MA 02149 617-389-5200 389-6680 297-7
Web: community-suffolk.com

Community Surgical Supply Inc
1390 Rt 37 W ... Toms River NJ 08755 732-349-2990 477
TF: 800-349-2990 ■ *Web:* www.communitysurgical.com

Community Teamwork Inc
155 Merrimack St. ... Lowell MA 01852 978-459-0551 48-21
Web: www.commteam.org

Community Telephone Company Inc (CTC)
10184 S Hwy 25E. ... Windthorst TX 76389 940-423-6201 423-2111 224
TF: 800-794-6407 ■ *Web:* comcell.net

Community Television Network
516 Congress St. ... Portland ME 04101 207-775-2900 741-99
Web: www.ctn5.org

Community Theater 100 South St ... Morristown NJ 07960 973-455-1607 748
Web: www.mayoarts.org

Community Tissue Services
2900 College Dr ... Kettering OH 45420 800-684-7783 461-4237* 545
**Fax Area Code:* 937 ■ *TF:* 800-684-7783 ■ *Web:* www.communitytissue.org

Community Title & Escrow Ltd
1207 Thouvenot Ln Ste 800 ... Shiloh IL 62269 618-234-1400 234-8275 391-6
Web: communitytitle.net

Community Transportation Association of America (CTAA)
1341 G St NW 10th Fl. ... Washington DC 20005 800-891-0590 737-9197* 49-21
**Fax Area Code:* 202 ■ *TF:* 800-891-0590 ■ *Web:* www.ctaa.org

Community Trust Bank NA
346 N Mayo Trl PO Box 2947 ... Pikeville KY 41501 606-432-1414 70
TF: 800-422-1090 ■ *Web:* www.ctbi.com

Community Unit School District 200
130 W Park Ave ... Wheaton IL 60189 630-682-2000 682-2227 685
TF: 800-421-3481 ■ *Web:* www.cusd200.org

Community Unit School District 308
4175 Rt 71 ... Oswego IL 60543 630-636-3080 636-3688 685
Web: www.sd308.org

Community United Credit Union
10883 Pearl Rd Ste 203 ... Strongsville OH 44136 440-572-9950 572-9914 219
Web: cu-cu.org

Community VNA 10 Emory St ... Attleboro MA 02703 508-222-0118 226-8939 371
TF: 800-220-0110 ■ *Web:* www.communityvna.com

Community Voice PO Box 2038 ... Rohnert Park CA 94927 707-584-2222 584-2233 532-4
Web: www.thecommunityvoice.com

Community Waste Disposal Inc
2010 California Crossing ... Dallas TX 75220 972-392-9300 392-9301 804
Web: www.communitywastedisposal.com

Community West Bancshares 445 Pine Ave ... Goleta CA 93117 805-692-5821 360-2
NASDAQ: CWBC ■ *Web:* www.communitywest.com

Community WISP Inc (CWISP)
235 Bear Hill Rd Ste 102A ... Waltham MA 02451 866-863-1035 658-2087* 224
**Fax Area Code:* 781 ■ *TF:* 866-863-1035 ■ *Web:* www.communitywisp.com

Communitywide Federal Credit Union
1555 W Western Ave. ... South Bend IN 46619 574-239-2700 219
Web: comwide.com

CommutAir
24950 Country Club Blvd Ste 300 ... North Olmsted OH 44070 440-779-4588 779-4688 25
Web: www.flycommutair.com

Comm-Works Holdings LLC
1405 Xenium Ln N Ste 120. ... Minneapolis MN 55441 763-475-1300 475-6656 252
TF: 800-853-8090 ■ *Web:* www.comm-works.com

Comnexia Corp 590 W Crssvlle Rd ... Roswell GA 30075 877-600-6550 196
TF: 877-600-6550 ■ *Web:* www.comnexia.com

Co-Mo Electric Co-opeartive Inc
29868 Hwy 5 PO Box 220. ... Tipton MO 65081 660-433-5521 245
TF: 800-781-0157 ■ *Web:* www.co-mo.coop

Como Industrial Equipment Inc
130 Freedom Ln ... Janesville WI 53546 608-756-3838 756-1262 386
TF: 800-451-0028 ■ *Web:* www.comofiltration.com

Como Park Zoo & Conservatory
1225 Estabrook Dr ... Saint Paul MN 55103 651-487-8200 823
Web: www.comozooconservatory.org

Comox Air Force Museum
19 Wing Comex PO Box 1000 Stn Forces ... Lazo BC V0R2K0 250-339-8162 520
Web: comoxairforcemuseum.ca

Comox Valley Chamber of Commerce
2040 Cliffe Ave ... Courtenay BC V9N2L3 250-334-3234 334-4908 137
TF: 888-357-4471 ■ *Web:* www.comoxvalleychamber.com

Com-Pac International Inc
800 W Industrial Park Rd ... Carbondale IL 62901 800-824-0817 553
TF: 800-824-0817 ■ *Web:* com-pac.com

Compact Excavator Sales LLC
400 Production Ct ... Elizabethtown KY 42701 270-737-1447 737-1857 358
TF: 800-538-1447 ■ *Web:* www.ihicompactexcavator.com

Compact Information Systems Inc
7120 185th Ave NE Ste 150 ... Redmond WA 98052 425-869-1379 885-4617 225
Web: www.compactlists.com

Compact Membrane Systems Inc
335 Water St. ... Newport DE 19804 302-999-7996 743
Web: compactmembrane.com

Compacting Tooling Inc 403 Wide Dr. ... McKeesport PA 15135 412-751-3535 751-0510 757
Web: compactingtooling.com

Company / Address	City	State	ZIP	Phone	Fax	Class
Compaction Technologies Inc 8324 89th Ave N *TF:* 877-860-6900 ■ *Web:* www.compactiontechnologies.com	Brooklyn Park	MN	55445	877-860-6900		192
Compadre Labs 2105 Donley Dr Ste 100 *Web:* www.compadrelabs.com	Austin	TX	78758	512-337-8378		393
Compagnie Beaulieu Canada 335 Ch Roxton *Web:* www.beaulieucanada.com	Acton Vale	QC	J0H1A0	450-546-5000		131
Compak Asset Management 1801 Dove St *TF:* 800-388-9700 ■ *Web:* www.compak.com	Newport Beach	CA	92660	800-388-9700		401
Companion Animal Clinic 201 S Hill Dr *Web:* companion-vets.com	Blacksburg	VA	24060	540-552-6800	552-1974	794
Companion Animal Eye Center Ltd 4708 Olson Memorial Hwy *Web:* www.companionanimaleyecenter.com	Golden Valley	MN	55422	763-529-7591		794
COMPanion Corp 1831 Ft Union Blvd *TF:* 800-347-6439 ■ *Web:* www.companioncorp.com	Salt Lake City	UT	84121	801-943-7277		177
Companion Health Services LLC PO Box 1095 *Web:* www.companionhealth.net	Guthrie	OK	73044	405-282-6285		475
Companion Life Insurance Co 7909 Parklane Rd Ste 200 *TF:* 800-753-0404 ■ *Web:* www.companionlife.com	Columbia	SC	29223	803-735-1251	735-0736	391-2
Companion Pet Clinic of Klamath Falls Inc 2343 Gettle St *Web:* cpckfalls.com	Klamath Falls	OR	97603	541-882-7674		794
Companion Pet Clinic of Southwest Washington PS 211 NE Crestwood Ct *Web:* companionpetclinic.net	Vancouver	WA	98684	360-254-8811		794
Companion Pets Inc (CPI) 2001 N Black Canyon Hwy *TF:* 800-646-3611 ■ *Web:* www.cpipets.com	Phoenix	AZ	85009	602-255-0166	255-0841	578
Companion Professional Services LLC 1301 Gervais St Ste 1700 *Web:* www.tmfloyd.com	Columbia	SC	29201	803-765-1310	780-1170	177
Companions & Homemakers Inc 613 New Britain Ave *TF:* 800-348-4663 ■ *Web:* companionsandhomemakers.com	Farmington	CT	06032	860-677-4948		810
Company C Inc 102 Old Tpke Rd *TF:* 800-818-8288 ■ *Web:* www.companyc.com	Concord	NH	03301	603-226-4460		361
Company Car Chauffeured Transportation 7138 Envoy Ct *TF:* 888-559-0708 ■ *Web:* limodfw.com	Dallas	TX	75247	214-824-0011	827-0136	441
Company Lab, The (COLAB) 1100 Market St Ste 100 *Web:* colab.co	Chattanooga	TN	37402	423-648-2195		393
Company of the Cauldron 5 India St *Web:* www.companyofthecauldron.com	Nantucket	MA	02554	508-228-4016		671
Company Voice 930 Harvest Dr Union Meeting Corporate Ctr Ste 100 *Web:* companyvoice.com	Blue Bell	PA	19422	215-525-5016		393
Compare Foods 1457 Fairfield Ave *Web:* www.galasupermarkets.com	Bridgeport	CT	06605	203-330-1094		345
Compas Inc 3 Executive Campus Ste 430 *Web:* www.compasonline.com	Cherry Hill	NJ	08002	856-667-8577		4
Compass Books PO Box 3091 *Web:* www.spiritualsurvivalbook.com	Linden	NJ	07036	908-868-1023		637-2
Compass Capital Management Inc 400 Baker Bldg 706 Second Ave S *Web:* www.compasscap.com	Minneapolis	MN	55402	612-338-4051		528
Compass Career Management Solutions LLC 8509 Crown Crescent Ct *Web:* www.compasscareer.com	Charlotte	NC	28227	704-849-2500		194
Compass Collective 2150 Button Gwinnett Dr *Web:* www.compasscollective.com	Atlanta	GA	30340	404-875-6543		8
Compass College of Cinematic Arts 41 Sheldon Blvd SE *Web:* www.compass.edu	Grand Rapids	MI	49503	616-988-1000		167-3
Compass Computer Group Inc 9408 Ravenna Rd *Web:* www.compasscomputergroup.com	Twinsburg	OH	44087	330-963-0800		196
Compass Cove Ocean Resort 2311 S Ocean Blvd *TF:* 800-331-0934 ■ *Web:* compasscove.com	Myrtle Beach	SC	29577	843-448-8373	448-5444	669
Compass Electronics Group LLC 6201 Bury Dr *Web:* compasses.com	Eden Prairie	MN	55346	952-941-8071		393
Compass Enterprise Solutions Inc 223 E State St *Web:* www.compass-solutions.com	Geneva	IL	60134	630-208-0200		631
Compass Federal Credit Union 131 George St *Web:* compassfcu.com	Oswego	NY	13126	315-342-5300		219
Compass Health Inc 200 S 13th St Ste 208 *Web:* compass-health.com	Grover Beach	CA	93433	805-474-7010	474-7013	371
Compass Marketing Inc 222 Severn Ave *Web:* compassmarketinginc.net	Annapolis	MD	21403	410-268-0030		7
Compass Marketing Solutions LLC 808 P St Ste 300 *Web:* www.compassventures.com	Lincoln	NE	68508	402-438-3222	438-3439	194
Compass Minerals Intl 9900 W 109th St Ste 100 *NYSE:* CMP ■ *TF:* 866-755-1743 ■ *Web:* www.compassminerals.com	Overland Park	KS	66210	913-344-9200		680
Compass Office Solutions LLC 3320 Enterprise Way *Web:* www.compass-office.com	Miramar	FL	33025	954-430-4590	430-4591	321
Compass Point Research & Trading LLC 1055 Thomas Jefferson St NW Ste 303 *Web:* www.compasspointllc.com	Washington	DC	20007	202-540-7300		690
Compass Systems Inc 21471 Great Mills Rd *Web:* compass-sys-inc.com	Lexington Park	MD	20653	301-737-4640		261
Compassion & Choices PO Box 101810 *TF:* 800-247-7421 ■ *Web:* www.compassionandchoices.org	Denver	CO	80250	800-247-7421		48-17
Compassion Canada 985 Adelaide St S *TF:* 800-563-5437 ■ *Web:* www.compassion.ca	London	ON	N6E4A3	519-668-0224		48-20
Compassion Hospice Inc 3775 Milam St *Web:* compassionhospice.org	Beaumont	TX	77701	409-835-8357		363
Compassion Intl 12290 Voyager Pkwy *TF:* 800-336-7676 ■ *Web:* www.compassion.com	Colorado Springs	CO	80921	719-487-7000	481-1893	48-5
Compassionate Friends PO Box 3696 *TF:* 877-969-0010 ■ *Web:* www.compassionatefriends.org	Oak Brook	IL	60522	630-990-0010	990-0246	48-21
Compassionate Passages Inc 29869 White Hall Dr *Web:* compassionatepassages.org	Farmington Hills	MI	48331	919-969-9512		636
CompassLearning Inc 203 Colorado St *TF:* 800-232-9556 ■ *Web:* www.edgenuity.com	Austin	TX	78701	512-478-9600		178-3
Compassus 4242 Piedras Dr E Ste 200 *Web:* compassus.com	San Antonio	TX	78228	210-731-0505	731-3905	450
Compassus 8 Wyoming St Ste 102 *Web:* compassus.com	Welch	WV	24801	304-409-3055	436-2306	450
Compatible Manufacturing Inc 11600 Us Hwy 2 W *Web:* www.compatiblemanufacturing.com	Marion	MT	59925	406-858-2016		454
Compatico Inc 5005 Kraft Ave SE Ste A *TF:* 800-336-1772 ■ *Web:* www.compatico.com	Grand Rapids	MI	49512	616-940-1772		351
Compax Inc 1210 N Blue Gum St *Web:* www.compaxinc.com	Anaheim	CA	92806	714-630-3670	632-1344	482
Compciti Business Solutions Inc 261 W 35th St Ste 603 *Web:* compciti.com	New York	NY	10001	212-594-4374	594-6714	175
Compensation Resources Inc 310 Rt 17 N *TF:* 877-934-0505 ■ *Web:* www.compensationresources.com	Upper Saddle River	NJ	07458	201-934-0505	934-0737	194
Compensation Systems Inc 900 E 96th St Ste 325 *Web:* compensationsystems.com	Indianapolis	IN	46240	317-844-6466		390
Compensia Inc 1731 Technology Dr Ste 810 *Web:* compensia.com	San Jose	CA	95110	408-876-4025		194
Competency & Credentialing Institute 2170 S Parker Rd Ste 295 *TF:* 888-257-2667 ■ *Web:* www.cc-institute.org	Denver	CO	80231	888-257-2667		148
Competition Bureau Canada 50 Victoria St *TF:* 866-997-1936 ■ *Web:* www.competitionbureau.gc.ca	Gatineau	QC	K1A0C9	819-997-4282		393
Competition Cams Inc 3406 Democrat Rd *TF:* 800-999-0853 ■ *Web:* www.compcams.com	Memphis	TN	38118	901-795-2400	366-1807	60
Competitive Computing Inc 354 Mountain View Dr Ste 400 *Web:* competitive.com	Colchester	VT	05446	802-764-1700		180
Competitive Edge Consulting 3235 Lakeview Dr *Web:* www.shopsuey.biz	Allegan	MI	49010	616-218-6374		196
Competitive Engineering Inc 3371 E Hemisphere Loop *Web:* www.ceiglobal.com	Tucson	AZ	85706	520-746-0270		454
Competitive Innovations LLC 2724 Dorr Ave Ste 100G *Web:* www.cillc.com	Fairfax	VA	22031	703-698-5000		177
Compex 110 Second St **Fax Area Code:* 866 ■ *Web:* compextech.com	Silverton	OR	97381	503-873-0188	746-0634*	176
Compex Legal Services Inc 325 S Maple Ave *TF:* 800-426-6739 ■ *Web:* cpxlegal.com	Torrance	CA	90503	800-426-6739	479-3365	445
CompHealth Inc 7259 S Bingham Junction Blvd *TF:* 800-466-0637 ■ *Web:* www.chghealthcare.com	Midvale	UT	84047	800-466-0637		721
Complemar Partners 500 Lee Rd *TF:* 800-388-7254 ■ *Web:* www.complemar.com	Rochester	NY	14606	585-647-5800		555
Complete Care at Linwood 201 New Rd *Web:* www.cclinwood.com	Linwood	NJ	08221	609-927-6131	927-5899	450
Complete Data Solutions LLC 7115 Leesburg Pk Ste 317 *Web:* know-your-data.com	Falls Church	VA	22043	703-536-3282		225
Complete Dewatering Pumps & Wellpoints Inc 710 W Park Ave *TF:* 800-800-9562 ■ *Web:* cdpwinc.com	Edgewater	FL	32132	386-767-3400	426-1835	23
Complete Genomics Inc 2904 Orchard Pkwy *Web:* www.completegenomics.com	San Jose	CA	95134	650-943-2800		634
Complete Home Concepts Inc 4380 Beljoum Blvd *Web:* completehomeconcepts.com	Riverside	MO	64150	816-471-4663		183
Complete Linen Services 290 S Maple St *Web:* www.completelinen.com	South San Francisco	CA	94080	650-873-1221	873-3676	442
Complete Network Management 649 Enterprise Dr *Web:* www.completenetwork.com	Houma	LA	70360	985-580-3040		196
Complete Payroll Processing Inc 7488 SR- 39 Po Box 190 *TF:* 888-237-5800 ■ *Web:* www.completepayroll.com	Perry	NY	14530	585-237-5800		2
Complete Printer, The 1920 Jim Neu Dr *Web:* www.thecompleteprinter.com	Plymouth	IN	46563	574-936-9505	936-5028	627
Complete Property Services Inc 140 Pine Ave S *Web:* completeproperty.com	Oldsmar	FL	34677	727-793-9777		186
Complete Prototype Services Inc 44783 Morley Dr *Web:* www.completeprototype.com	Clinton Township	MI	48036	586-469-9155	469-9156	454
Complete Pump Service 461 S Irmen Dr *Web:* www.completepump.com	Addison	IL	60101	630-628-1600		641

Phone | Fax | Class

Complete Rx Ltd
3100 S Gessner Rd Ste 640 ... Houston TX 77063 713-355-1196 355-5404 237
Web: www.completerx.com

Complete Systems Support Inc
2 Rosemar Cir Ste A ... Parkersburg WV 26104 304-428-2143 428-2145 177
Web: www.cssiwv.com

Completech Inc 5502 Serenity Terr ... Pleasanton CA 94588 925-462-9600 260
Web: www.completech.com

Complex Steel & Wire Corp
36254 Annapolis St ... Wayne MI 48184 734-326-1600 326-7421 307
TF: 800-521-0666 ■ *Web:* www.complexsteel.com

Complex Technologies
726 US Rte 202 S Ste 320-175 ... Bridgewater NJ 08807 732-709-5180 180
Web: www.complextech.com

Complexe Les Ailes
705 Rue Sainte-Catherine Ouest ... Montreal QC H3B4G5 514-288-3708 460
Web: www.centreeatondemontreal.com

Compli 711 SW Alder Ste 200 ... Portland OR 97205 800-481-8309 270-2338* 177
**Fax Area Code:* 877 ■ *TF:* 877-522-4276 ■ *Web:* www.compli.com

Complia Health
1827 Walden Office Sq Ste 104 ... Schaumburg IL 60173 866-802-7704 525
TF: 866-802-7704 ■ *Web:* www.compliahealth.com

Compliance Associates LP
6704 Guada Coma Dr ... Schertz TX 78154 210-967-6169 967-9233 418
TF: 800-840-1070 ■ *Web:* www.cmi-satx.com

Compliance Corp
21617 S Essex Dr Ste 34 ... Lexington Park MD 20653 301-863-8070 194
Web: www.compliancecorporation.com

Compliance Services Group Inc
5202 County Rd 7350 Ste A ... Lubbock TX 79424 806-748-0040 748-0030 194
Web: www.csg.net

Compmanagement Inc PO Box 884 ... Dublin OH 43017 614-376-5300 766-6888 463
TF: 800-825-6755 ■ *Web:* www.compmgt.com

Component Control Inc
1731 Kettner Blvd ... San Diego CA 92101 619-696-5400 177
Web: www.componentcontrol.com

Component Design Northwest Inc
2355 NW Vaughn St ... Portland OR 97210 503-225-0900 361
TF: 800-338-5594 ■ *Web:* cdnkitchen.com

Component Engineers Inc
108 N Plains Industrial Rd ... Wallingford CT 06492 203-269-0557 269-1357 454
Web: ceiprecision.com

Component Enterprises Company Inc
235 E Penn St PO Box 189 ... Norristown PA 19401 877-232-7253 272-7040* 815
**Fax Area Code:* 610 ■ *TF:* 877-232-7253 ■ *Web:* www.componententerprises.com

Component Hardware Group Inc
1890 Swarthmore Ave ... Lakewood NJ 08701 732-363-4700 364-8110 350
TF: 800-526-3694 ■ *Web:* www.componenthardware.com

Component InterTechnologies Inc
2426 Perry Hwy ... Hadley PA 16130 724-253-3161 246
Web: www.cit-hadley.com

Component West Inc 620 Fifth Ave ... Pelham NY 10803 914-738-5400 738-5934 189-9
Web: www.componentwest.com

ComponentOne LLC
201 S Highland Ave 3rd Fl ... Pittsburgh PA 15206 412-681-4343 681-4384 178-12
TF: 800-858-2739 ■ *Web:* www.grapecity.com

Components Corporation of America
5950 Berkshire Ln Ste 1550 ... Dallas TX 75225 214-969-0166 969-5905 729
Web: www.ccoadallas.com

Components Distributors Inc
2601 Blake St Ste 200 ... Denver CO 80205 800-777-7334 246
TF: 800-777-7334 ■ *Web:* www.cdiweb.com

Comporium Communications PO Box 470 ... Rock Hill SC 29731 888-403-2667 326-5703* 736
**Fax Area Code:* 803 ■ *TF:* 888-403-2667 ■ *Web:* www.comporium.com

Comport Consulting Corp 78 Orchard St ... Ramsey NJ 07446 201-236-0505 180
TF: 888-696-0706 ■ *Web:* www.comport.com

Composidie Inc 1295 Rt 380 ... Apollo PA 15613 724-727-3466 727-3788 757
Web: www.composidie.com

Composiflex Inc 8100 Hawthorne Dr ... Erie PA 16509 814-866-8616 596
TF: 800-673-2544 ■ *Web:* www.composiflex.com

Composite Engineering Inc
277 Baker Ave ... Concord MA 01742 978-371-3132 369-3162 90
Web: www.composite-eng.com

Composite Manufacturing Inc
970 D Calle Amanecer ... San Clemente CA 92673 949-361-7580 361-7586 476
Web: www.carbonfiber.com

Composite Motors Acquisition Inc
15460 Aviation Loop Dr ... Brooksville FL 34604 352-799-2599 518
Web: compositemotors.com

Composite Panel Assn
19465 Deerfield Ave Ste 306 ... Leesburg VA 20176 703-724-1128 49-3
TF: 866-426-6767 ■ *Web:* www.compositepanel.org

Composite Resources Inc
485 Lakeshore Pkwy ... Rock Hill SC 29730 803-366-9700 20
Web: composite-resources.com

Composite Solutions Corp
14810 Puyallup St Ste 100 ... Sumner WA 98390 253-833-1878 939-4617 57
Web: www.compositesolutions.com

Composite Technology Development Inc
2600 Campus Dr Ste D ... LaFayette CO 80026 303-664-0394 664-0392 261
Web: www.ctd-materials.com

Compositech Inc 5315 Walt Pl ... Indianapolis IN 46254 317-481-1120 517
TF: 800-447-8372

Composites Horizons Inc
1471 W Industrial Park St ... Covina CA 91722 626-331-0861 113
Web: chi-covina.com

Composites Innovation Ctr
158 Commerce Dr ... Winnipeg MB R3P0Z6 204-262-3400 261
Web: www.compositesinnovation.ca

Composites Unlimited Inc
53770 Airport Rd ... Scappoose OR 97056 503-543-7031 543-7091 20
Web: www.compositesunlimited.com

Composition Materials Company Inc
249 Pepes Farm Rd ... Milford CT 06460 203-874-6500 874-6505 1
TF: 800-262-7763 ■ *Web:* compomat.com

Compounding Pharmacy of Beverly Hills, The
9629 W Olympic Blvd ... Beverly Hills CA 90212 310-284-8675 237
Web: compoundingexpert.com

Compounding Solutions LLC
258 Goddard Rd ... Lewiston ME 04240 207-777-1122 777-1566 596
Web: compoundingsolutions.net

Compqsoft Inc
505N Sam Houston Pkwy E Ste 682 ... Houston TX 77060 281-668-8461 196
Web: www.compqsoft.com

Comprehensive Care Management Corp (CCM)
1250 Waters Pl Tower 1 Ste 602 ... Bronx NY 10461 877-226-8500 450
TF: 877-226-8500 ■ *Web:* www.centerlighthealthcare.org

Comprehensive Computer Services Inc (CCS)
169 Commack Rd Ste H-233 ... Commack NY 11725 631-755-2250 755-2254 180
Web: www.comprehensive.com

Comprehensive Consulting Group
1800 Walt Whitman Rd ... Melville NY 11747 631-249-0500 694-6209 194
TF: 800-231-7269 ■ *Web:* www.ccg1800.com

Comprehensive EAP 4 Mt Royal Ave ... Marlborough MA 01752 800-344-1011 462
TF: 800-344-1011 ■ *Web:* compeap.com

Comprehensive Energy Services Inc
777 Bennett Dr ... Longwood FL 32750 407-682-1313 682-5166 610
TF: 800-393-1261 ■ *Web:* www.cesmechanical.com

Comprehensive Financial Planning Inc
900 Main Ave Ste 200 ... Durango CO 81301 970-385-5227 194
TF: 877-901-5227 ■ *Web:* www.compfinancial.com

Comprehensive Health Service
8600 Astronaut Blvd ... Cape Canaveral FL 32920 321-783-2720 363
TF: 800-638-8083 ■ *Web:* www.chsmedical.com

Comprehensive Nursing Services Inc
8817 Bel Air Rd Ste 203 ... Baltimore MD 21236 410-529-0078 529-4511 363
Web: www.compnursing.com

Comprehensive Pharmacy Services Inc (CPS)
6409 N Quail Hollow Rd ... Memphis TN 38120 901-748-0470 194
TF: 800-968-6962 ■ *Web:* www.cpspharm.com

Comprehensive Quality Care Inc
3517 S King Dr ... Chicago IL 60653 773-924-5900 924-5933 363
Web: comprehensivequalitycare.homestead.com

Comprehensive Systems Inc
1700 Clark St ... Charles City IA 50616 641-228-4842 228-4675 451
Web: comprehensivesystems.org

Comprehensive Traffic Systems Inc
4300 Harlan St ... Wheat Ridge CO 80033 888-353-9002 174
TF: 888-353-9002 ■ *Web:* cts-worldwide.net

Comprehensive Wealth Management LLC
3500 188th St SW Ste 102 ... Lynnwood WA 98037 425-778-6160 690
Web: cwmnw.com

Compressed Air Systems Inc
9303 Stannum St ... Tampa FL 33619 813-626-8177 628-0187 172
TF: 800-626-8177 ■ *Web:* www.compressedairsystems.com

Compressed Gas Association CGA (CGA)
14501 George Carter Way Ste 103 ... Chantilly VA 20151 703-788-2700 961-1831 49-13
Web: www.cganet.com

Compression Leasing Services Inc
1935 N Loop Ave ... Casper WY 82601 307-265-3242 172
TF: 855-355-3242 ■ *Web:* www.compressionleasing.com

Compressor Controls Corp
4725 121st St ... Des Moines IA 50323 515-270-0857 270-1331 201
Web: www.cccglobal.com

Compressor Engineering Corp (CECO)
5440 Alder Dr ... Houston TX 77081 713-664-7333 664-6444 172
TF: 800-879-2326 ■ *Web:* www.tryceco.com

Compressor Products Intl
4410 Greenbriar Dr ... Stafford TX 77477 281-207-4600 207-4612 128
TF: 800-675-6646 ■ *Web:* www.cpicompression.com

Compressor World LLC 32 Riverside Dr ... Pembroke MA 02359 508-230-7118 366
TF: 866-778-6572 ■ *Web:* compressorworld.com

Compressors Unlimited International LLC
2531 S Belt Line Rd ... Dallas TX 75253 972-286-2264 286-5545 385
TF: 800-789-9890 ■ *Web:* compressorsunlimited.com

Comprint Military Publications
29088 Airpark Dr ... Easton MD 21601 301-342-4163 627
Web: www.dcmilitary.com

Compro Computer Services Inc
105 E Dr ... Melbourne FL 32904 321-727-2211 727-7009 175
Web: www.compro.net

Comprobe Inc 9632 Crowley Rd ... Fort Worth TX 76134 817-293-7333 529
Web: www.comprobeinc.com

ComPsych Corp
455 N City Front Plaza Dr 13th Fl ... Chicago IL 60611 312-595-4000 462
TF: 800-851-1714 ■ *Web:* www.compsych.com

Compsys Inc 800 Wilcrest ... Houston TX 77042 713-961-3999 180
Web: www.datacorp.net

Comp-Tac Victory Gear LLC/Minotaur Gear LLC
3003 Farrell Rd ... Houston TX 77073 281-209-3040 711
Web: comp-tac.com

COMPTIA (Computing Technology Industry Assn)
3500 Lacey Rd Ste 100 ... Downers Grove IL 60515 630-678-8300 678-8384 48-9
Web: www.comptia.org

Compton Engineering 156 Nixon St ... Biloxi MS 39530 228-432-2133 432-8149 256
Web: www.comptonengineering.com

Comptroller of the Currency
250 E St SW ... Washington DC 20219 202-874-5301 874-5221 340-18
TF: 800-613-6743 ■ *Web:* occ.treas.gov

Comptron Data Inc
37450 Enterprise Crt ... Farmington Hills MI 48331 248-477-5215 477-5311 180
Web: www.comptekinc.com

Compu- Vision Consulting Inc
Brunswick Plz I 2050 Rte 27 Ste 202 ... North Brunswick NJ 08902 732-422-1500 194
Web: www.compuvis.com

Compu-Aire Inc 8167 Byron Rd ... Whittier CA 90606 562-945-8971 664
Web: www.compu-aire.com

Comp-U-Build Computers Inc
45 S Maine St ... Fallon NV 89406 775-423-8229 173-2
Web: www.cub.net

Compucolor Associates Inc
2200 Marcus Ave ... New Hyde Park NY 11042 516-358-0000 627
Web: www.compucolor.com

CompuCom Systems Inc 7171 Forest Ln ... Dallas TX 75230 972-856-3600 176
TF: 800-597-0555 ■ *Web:* www.compucom.com

Compucover Inc PO Box 972 ... Defuniak Springs FL 32435 850-892-5752 892-9259 173-1
TF: 877-743-4217 ■ *Web:* compucover.com

Name / Address	City	State	ZIP	Phone	Fax	Class
CompuCure New Orleans Inc 3528 Holiday Dr Ste B *Web:* www.compucure.com	New Orleans	LA	70114	504-486-7741		180
CompuCycle Inc 7700 Kempwood Dr *TF:* 888-314-7922 ■ *Web:* www.compucycle.com	Houston	TX	77055	713-869-6700	866-8033	175
Compu-data International LLC 431 Nursery Rd Ste A300 *Web:* www.cdlac.com	Spring	TX	77380	281-292-1333		177
Compudent Systems Inc 10345 Keele St Ste 6 *TF:* 888-470-3593 ■ *Web:* compudentinc.com	Maple	ON	L6A3Y9	905-417-9345		175
CompuDyne Corp 306 W Michigan St Ste 200 *Web:* www.compudyne.com	Duluth	MN	55802	218-729-0920		692
Compu-Gard Inc 1432 Grand Army Hwy **Fax Area Code:* 508 ■ *TF:* 800-333-6810 ■ *Web:* www.compu-gard.com	Swansea	MA	02777	800-333-6810	679-1114*	425
Compugen Inc 100 Via Renzo Dr *TF:* 800-387-5045 ■ *Web:* www.compugen.com	Richmond Hill	ON	L4S0B8	905-707-2000		395
Compulink Inc 1205 Gandy Blvd N *TF:* 800-231-6685 ■ *Web:* www.compulink.com	Saint Petersburg	FL	33702	727-579-1500	578-8420	814
Compulink Technologies Inc 260 W 39th St Ste 302 *Web:* www.compu-link.com	New York	NY	10018	212-695-5465	695-5560	177
Compulsive Eaters Anonymous - HOW (CEA-HOW) 3371 Glendale Blvd Ste 104 *Web:* www.ceahow.org	Los Angeles	CA	90039	323-660-4333	660-4334	48-21
Compu-Mail LLC 3235 Grand Island Blvd *TF:* 800-255-0670 ■ *Web:* compu-mail.com	Grand Island	NY	14072	716-775-8001	775-5681	195
Compumation Inc 205 W Grand Ave *Web:* www.compumation.com	Bensenville	IL	60106	630-860-1921		261
CompuMed Inc 5777 W Century Blvd Ste 360 *Web:* compumedinc.com	Los Angeles	CA	90045	310-258-5000		419
Compu-Med Vocational Careers 2900 W 12th Ave 3rd Fl *Web:* www.compumed.edu	Hialeah	FL	33012	305-888-9200		000
CompuNet Consulting Group Inc 6535 Shiloh Rd Ste 300 *Web:* www.ccgi.net	Alpharetta	GA	30005	678-965-6500		180
Compunetics Inc 700 Seco Rd *Web:* www.compunetics.com	Monroeville	PA	15146	412-373-8110	373-8060	625
Compunetix Inc 2420 Mosside Blvd **Fax Area Code:* 412 ■ *TF:* 800-879-4266 ■ *Web:* www.compunetix.com	Monroeville	PA	15146	800-879-4266	373-2720*	735
Compunnel Software Group Inc 103 Morgan Ln Ste 102 *TF:* 800-696-8128 ■ *Web:* www.compunnel.com	Plainsboro	NJ	08536	800-696-8128		721
CompuOne Corp 9888 Carroll Centre Rd Ste 201 *TF:* 888-226-6781 ■ *Web:* www.compuone.com	San Diego	CA	92126	858-404-7000		196
Compusearch Software Systems Inc 21251 Ridgetop Cir **Fax Area Code:* 703 ■ *TF:* 855-817-2720 ■ *Web:* www.compusearch.com	Dulles	VA	20166	571-449-4000	481-3442*	177
Compusoft Integrated Solutions Inc 31500 W 13 Mile Rd Ste 200 *Web:* www.compusoft-is.com	Farmington Hills	MI	48334	248-538-9494		196
Comp-U-Sultants Inc 131 Waterford Rd *Web:* www.comp-u-sultants.com	Island Park	NY	11558	516-897-8477		175
Computac Inc 162 N Main St *Web:* www.computac.com	West Lebanon	NH	03784	603-298-5721	298-6189	178-10
Computan 3350 Merrittville Hwy *Web:* www.computan.com	Thorold	ON	L2V4Y6	905-984-8388		180
Computech 2155 Orchard Dr Ste 201 *Web:* www.computech.biz	Bountiful	UT	84010	801-298-2155	410-1557	194
Computech Corp 100 W Kirby St Ste 101 *Web:* computechcorp.com	Detroit	MI	48202	248-594-6500	594-4855	177
Computech International Inc 525 Northern Blvd *Web:* www.cti-intl.com	Great Neck	NY	11021	516-487-0101		174
Computech Systems Inc 400 C Southlake Blvd *Web:* computechsystemsinc.com	North Chesterfield	VA	23236	804-897-7917		195
Computechnique 407 Stonebrook Dr *Web:* computechnique.com	Benton	IL	62812	618-439-4000		175
Computek 9580 Commerce Center Dr *Web:* www.computek.com	Rancho Cucamonga	CA	91730	909-987-8515		180
Computek Inc 355 Crawford St Ste 214 *Web:* www.e-computek.com	Portsmouth	VA	23704	757-399-0320		177
Computer & Communications Industry Assn (CCIA) 666 11th St NW *Web:* www.ccianet.org	Washington	DC	20001	202-783-0070	783-0534	49-20
Computer Advantage 358 Newnan Crossing Bypass *Web:* www.computeradvantage.us	Newnan	GA	30265	770-461-2147		175
Computer Age Engineering Inc 867 E 38th St *Web:* www.caeweb.com	Marion	IN	46953	765-674-8551		256
Computer Aid Inc (CAI) 1390 Ridgeview Dr *Web:* www.cai.io	Allentown	PA	18104	610-530-5000		177
Computer Aided Technology Inc 165 N Arlington Heights Rd Ste 101 *TF:* 888-308-2284 ■ *Web:* www.cati.com	Buffalo Grove	IL	60089	888-308-2284		174
Computer Arts Inc 320 SW 5th Ave *TF:* 800-365-9335 ■ *Web:* www.gocai.com	Meridian	ID	83642	208-385-9335		177
Computer Assisted Language Instruction Consortium (CALICO) 214 Centennial Hall *Web:* calico.org	San Marcos	TX	78666	512-245-1417		48-9
Computer Business Applications Inc 507 N Mulberry St *Web:* cbatech.com	Elizabethtown	KY	42701	270-737-1888		2
Computer Centerline 1500 Broad St *Web:* www.cclprotech.com	Greensburg	PA	15601	724-838-0852		175
Computer Clinic Center Inc 4427 Wisconsin Ave NW *Web:* www.cccits.com	Washington	DC	20016	202-362-9702		175
Computer Components Corp 2751 S Hampton Rd *Web:* compcomp.com	Philadelphia	PA	19154	215-676-7600	464-7876	697
Computer Composition Corp 1401 W Girard Ave *Web:* www.computercomposition.com	Madison Heights	MI	48071	248-545-4330	544-1611	781
Computer Connection of Central New York Inc 11206 Cosby Manor Rd	Utica	NY	13502	315-724-2209		174
Computer Connections Inc 1241-2 E Dixon Blvd *TF:* 844-369-3993 ■ *Web:* painlesspc.net	Shelby	NC	28152	704-482-0057		180
Computer Consulting Associates International Inc (CCAII) 200 Pequot Ave *Web:* www.ccaii.com	Southport	CT	06890	203-255-8966		721
Computer Consulting Services Inc (CCSI) 409A Walker Rd *Web:* www.ccsi.me	Jackson	TN	38305	731-668-0303	554-3359	180
Computer Crafts Inc 57 Thomas Rd *Web:* www.computer-crafts.com	Hawthorne	NJ	07506	973-423-3500		174
Computer Credit Inc 7996 N Point Blvd Ste 200	Winston-Salem	NC	27106	336-761-1524	201-0590	160
Computer Designs Inc 5235 W Coplay Rd *Web:* www.computer-designs.com	Whitehall	PA	18052	610-261-2100		535
Computer Dynamics Inc 3030 Whitehall Pk Dr **Fax Area Code:* 704 ■ *TF:* 866-599-6512 ■ *Web:* www.cdynamics.com	Charlotte	NC	28273	866-599-6512	583-9671*	174
Computer Economics Inc 2082 Business Center Dr Ste 240 *Web:* www.computereconomics.com	Irvine	CA	92612	949-831-8700	442-7688	637-9
Computer Enhancement Systems Inc (CES) 8038-D Liberty Rd *Web:* www.cesitservice.com	Frederick	MD	21701	301-620-1580	620-1586	174
Computer Enterprises Inc (CEI) 1000 Omega Dr Ste 1150 *Web:* www.ceiamerica.com	Pittsburgh	PA	15205	215-621-6814		721
Computer Equip Svces 261 W Main St *Web:* www.netces.com	Bay Shore	NY	11706	631-666-1234		175
Computer Explorers 12715 Telge Rd *TF:* 800-531-5053 ■ *Web:* computerexplorers.com	Cypress	TX	77429	800-531-5053		148
Computer Forms Inc 12111 SW Herman Rd **Fax Area Code:* 503 ■ *TF:* 800-547-8027 ■ *Web:* www.computerforms.biz	Tualatin	OR	97062	800-547-8027	620-0277*	110
Computer Frontiers Inc 5970 Frederick Crossing Ln Ste 101 *Web:* www.computerfrontiers.com	Frederick	MD	21704	301-601-0624		177
Computer Fulfillment 24 Cook St *Web:* www.computerfulfillment.com	Billerica	MA	01821	978-671-0440	671-0450	225
Computer Generated Solutions Inc 200 Vesey St Three World Financial Ctr 27th Fl *Web:* www.cgsinc.com	New York	NY	10281	212-408-3800		180
Computer Guidance Corp 15035 N 75th St *TF:* 888-361-4551 ■ *Web:* computerguidance.com	Scottsdale	AZ	85260	480-444-7000		177
Computer Guys Inc, The 851 Burlway Rd Ste 168 *Web:* www.computerguys.com	Burlingame	CA	94010	650-692-6888	692-6890	180
Computer Heaven 577 Oak Villa Blvd *Web:* www.computerheaven.com	Baton Rouge	LA	70815	225-923-0999		175
Computer Helper Publishing Inc 450 Beecher Rd *Web:* www.churchwindows.com	Columbus	OH	43230	614-939-9004		178-1
Computer History Museum, The 1401 N Shoreline Blvd *Web:* www.computerhistory.org	Mountain View	CA	94043	650-810-1010	810-1055	520
Computer Lab International Inc 735 Challenger St *Web:* www.computerlab.com	Brea	CA	92821	714-572-8000		350
Computer Logix Inc 268 Aldrich Rd *TF:* 800-220-8211 ■ *Web:* www.clogix.com	Howell Township	NJ	07731	732-919-3131		174
Computer Management Technologies Inc 731 Gratiot Ave *Web:* www.cmtonline.com	Saginaw	MI	48602	989-791-4860	791-4928	194
Computer Manager Inc 19885 7th Ave **Fax Area Code:* 360 ■ *TF:* 800-552-8397 ■ *Web:* www.debtnet5.com	Poulsbo	WA	98370	800-552-8397	697-2053*	178-1
Computer Measurement Group Inc (CMG) 3501 Rt 42 Ste 130 & 121 *Web:* www.cmg.org	Turnersville	NJ	08012	856-401-1700		48-9
Computer Modelling Group Ltd 3710 33rd St NW *Web:* www.cmgl.ca	Calgary	AB	T2L2M1	403-531-1300		539
Computer Modules Inc 11409 W Bernardo Ct *Web:* www.dveo.com	San Diego	CA	92127	858-613-1818	613-1815	625
Computer Office Solutions 7266 SW 48th St *Web:* www.snappydsl.com	Miami	FL	33155	305-663-5518		177
Computer Options Inc 1470 Maria Ln Ste 320	Walnut Creek	CA	94596	925-933-4800		180
Computer Parts Warehouse 4681 Calle Bolero *Web:* www.thecpw.com	Camarillo	CA	93012	805-987-5882		177
Computer Power Solutions Inc 4644 Katella Ave *TF:* 800-444-1938 ■ *Web:* www.computerpowersolutions.com	Los Alamitos	CA	90720	562-493-4487		180
Computer Products Inc 1221 Avenida Acaso Ste F *Web:* cpisolutions.com	Camarillo	CA	93012	805-987-2222		180
Computer Professionals for Social Responsibility (CPSR) 1370 Mission St 4th Fl **Fax Area Code:* 415 ■ *Web:* www.cpsr.org	San Francisco	CA	94103	650-989-1294	839-8617*	49-19

Company	Phone	Fax	Class
Computer Professionals Unlimited 401 E Collins Dr. Casper WY 82601 *Web:* www.cpuiit.com	307-235-6212		174
Computer Programmers Unlimited Inc 500 Valence St. New Orleans LA 70115 *Web:* www.computer-programmers.com	504-269-4492		177
Computer Programs & Systems Inc (CPSI) 6600 Wall St. Mobile AL 36695 *NASDAQ: CPSI* ■ *TF:* 877-424-1777 ■ *Web:* www.cpsi.com	251-639-8100	639-8214	39
Computer Repair & Sales 2930 W Main St. Rapid City SD 57702 *Web:* www.computerrepair.org	605-399-0278	342-6141	175
Computer Resource Solutions 1 Pierce Pl. Itasca IL 60143 *Web:* www.crscorp.com	630-467-1010		194
Computer Science & Artificial Intelligence Laboratory (CSAIL) 32 Vassar St Bldg 32. Cambridge MA 02139 *Web:* www.csail.mit.edu	617-253-5851	258-8682	668
Computer Security Products Inc 100 Factory St Ste D3. Nashua NH 03060 *Web:* www.computersecurity.com	603-889-9899	889-9822	196
Computer Services Inc 3901 Technology Dr. Paducah KY 42001 *OTC: CSVI* ■ *TF:* 800-545-4274 ■ *Web:* www.csiweb.com	270-442-7361		225
Computer Solutions 814 Arion Pkwy Ste 101. San Antonio TX 78216 *TF:* 800-326-4304 ■ *Web:* www.comsoltx.com	210-369-0300	369-0389	177
Computer Source Inc (SC) 2623 Wayne Sullivan Dr. Paducah KY 42003 *Web:* www.computer-source.com	270-442-9726	442-5058	179
Computer Spectrum Inc 200 Distillery Commons Ste 250. Louisville KY 40206 *TF:* 866-585-8844 ■ *Web:* www.computerspectrum.com	502-585-8866		180
Computer Support Services Inc 145 N 15th St. Lewisburg PA 17837 *Web:* cssi.com	570-524-4424		180
Computer Support Systems Inc (CSS) 3418 Hooper Ln. Decatur AL 35602 *TF:* 800-925-9860 ■ *Web:* www.computersupportsystems.com	256-355-5973	340-0675	180
Computer Systems Plus Inc 605 Sevier Ave. Knoxville TN 37920 *Web:* compsysplus.com	865-573-5303		180
Computer Task Group Inc (CTG) 800 Delaware Ave. Buffalo NY 14209 *OTC: CTG* ■ *TF:* 800-992-5350 ■ *Web:* www.ctg.com	716-882-8000	887-7464	180
Computer Team Inc 1049 State St. Bettendorf IA 52722 *TF:* 800-355-0450 ■ *Web:* www.computerteam.com	563-355-0426		177
Computer Technology Services Inc 200 Great Oaks Blvd Ste 211. Albany NY 12203 *Web:* www.ctsalbany.com	518-869-3591		177
Computer Training Systems 200 W Douglas Ave Ste 230. Wichita KS 67202 *Web:* www.ctsys.com	316-265-1585		194
Computer Troubleshooters USA 7100 E Pleasant Valley Rd Ste 300. Independence OH 44131 *TF:* 877-704-1702 ■ *Web:* www.technology-solved.com	216-674-0645		310
Computer Visionaries Inc 1075 Oak St. Pittston PA 18640 *Web:* www.computervisionaries.com	570-891-0220	891-0224	180
Computer Workshop Inc, The 5200 Upper Metro Pl. Dublin OH 43017 *TF:* 800-639-3535 ■ *Web:* www.tcworkshop.com	614-798-9505		764
Computer Wrangler On-site Service 4937 320th St. Stacy MN 55079 *Web:* www.computerwrangler.net	651-462-8809		809
Computerized Inventory Systems Specialists Ltd 2512 Eberhart Rd. Whitehall PA 18052 *Web:* cissltd.com	610-266-7200		177
Computerized Screening Inc 9550 Gateway Dr. Reno NV 89521 *TF:* 800-533-9230 ■ *Web:* www.computerizedscreening.com	775-359-1191	359-7879	476
Computerized Structural Design SC 8989 N Port Washington Rd. Milwaukee WI 53217 *Web:* csd-eng.com	414-351-5588		261
ComputerJobscom Inc 1995 N Pk Pl SE. Atlanta GA 30339 *TF:* 800-850-0045 ■ *Web:* www.computerjobs.com	770-850-0045		260
ComputerLogic Inc 4951 Forsyth Rd. Macon GA 31210 *TF:* 800-933-6564 ■ *Web:* www.computerlogic.com	478-474-5593		177
ComputerPlus Sales & Service Inc 5 Northway Ct. Greer SC 29651 *TF:* 800-849-4426 ■ *Web:* www.computer-plus.com	864-801-9003		175
Computers Unlimited 2407 Montana Ave. Billings MT 59101 *TF:* 800-763-0308 ■ *Web:* www.cu.net	406-255-9500	255-9595	178-10
Computerway Food Systems 2700 Westchester Dr. High Point NC 27260 *Web:* www.mycfs.com	336-841-7289		296
Computerwise Inc 302 N Winchester Ln. Olathe KS 66062 *TF:* 800-255-3739 ■ *Web:* www.computerwise.com	913-829-0600	829-0810	173-7
Computerworks of Chicago Inc 5153 N Clark St. Chicago IL 60640 *TF:* 800-977-8212 ■ *Web:* www.booklog.com	773-275-4437		177
Computerworks Technologies 711 S Victory Blvd. Burbank CA 91502 *TF:* 800-255-5045 ■ *Web:* www.computerworkstech.com	818-244-4484		610
Computing Integrity Inc 60 Belvedere Ave. Richmond CA 94801 *Web:* cintegrity.com	510-233-5400		177
Computing Research Assn 1828 L St NW. Washington DC 20036 *Web:* cra.org	202-234-2111	667-1066	48-9
Computing Technologies Inc (COTS) 6372 Mechanicsville Tpk Ste 112. Mechanicsville VA 23111 **Fax Area Code: 571* ■ *Web:* www.cots.com	703-280-8800	386-4959*	178-1
Computing Technology Industry Assn (COMPTIA) 3500 Lacey Rd Ste 100. Downers Grove IL 60515 *Web:* www.comptia.org	630-678-8300	678-8384	48-9
Computrition Inc 8521 Fallbrook Ave Ste 100. West Hills CA 91304 *TF:* 800-222-4488 ■ *Web:* www.computrition.com	800-222-4488		177
Computype Inc 2285 W County Rd C. Saint Paul MN 55113 *TF:* 800-328-0852 ■ *Web:* www.computype.com	800-328-0852		627
Compuware Corp 1 Campus Martius St. Detroit MI 48226 *NASDAQ: CPWR* ■ *TF:* 800-266-7892 ■ *Web:* www.compuware.com	313-227-7300		178-1
CompuWeather Inc 2566 Rte 52. Hopewell Junction NY 12533 **Fax Area Code: 800* ■ *TF:* 800-825-4445 ■ *Web:* www.compuweather.com	845-227-8500	825-4441*	192
Compuweigh Corp 50 Middle Quarter Rd. Woodbury CT 06798 *Web:* www.compuweigh.com	203-262-9400	262-9488	684
Compuworks Ltd 1 Fenn St. Pittsfield MA 01201 *Web:* compuworks.biz	413-499-0607		177
CompX International Inc 5430 LBJ Fwy Ste 1700. Dallas TX 75240 *NYSE: CIX* ■ *Web:* www.compx.com	972-448-1400	448-1408	350
Compx Security Products Inc 200 Old Mill Rd. Mauldin SC 29662 *Web:* www.compxnet.com	864-297-6655		295
COMRES Inc 424 SW 12th Ave. Deerfield Beach FL 33442 *TF:* 877-379-9600 ■ *Web:* comresusa.com	954-462-9600		179
ComResource Inc 1159 Dublin Rd Ste 200. Columbus OH 43215 *Web:* comresource.com	614-221-6348		180
ComSci LLC 401 Congress Ave Ste 1850. Austin TX 78701 *Web:* uplandsoftware.com	732-632-8000		196
Comscore Inc 11950 Democracy Dr Ste 600. Reston VA 20190 *TF:* 866-276-6972 ■ *Web:* www.comscore.com	703-438-2000	438-2051	466
Comsearch 19700 Janelia Farm Blvd. Ashburn VA 20147 *Web:* www.comsearch.com	703-726-5500	726-5600	261
COMSERV Inc 105 Scroggs Ct. Morganton NC 28680 *Web:* comserve.org	828-430-7194	430-7001	180
COMSO Inc 7075 Samuel Morse Dr Ste 110. Columbia MD 21046 *Web:* www.comso.com	301-345-0046		177
ComSonics Inc 1350 Port Republic Rd PO Box 1106. Harrisonburg VA 22801 *TF:* 800-336-9681 ■ *Web:* www.comsonics.com	540-434-5965	432-9794	639
Comspark International Inc 3265 W Sarazens Cir Ste 201. Memphis TN 38125 *Web:* www.comsparkint.com	901-758-0261		177
Comspec Corp 822 N Elm St. Greensboro NC 27401 *Web:* www.comspeccorp.com	336-370-1456		194
Comstar Enterprises Inc 169 Industrial Cir PO Box 6698. Springdale AR 72766 *TF:* 800-533-2343 ■ *Web:* comstar-inc.com	479-361-2111	361-1069	48-11
ComStar Networks LLC 1820 NE Jensen Beach Blvd Ste 564. Jensen Beach FL 34957 *TF:* 800-516-1595 ■ *Web:* www.newclientgenerator.com	800-516-1595		195
Comstock Holding Companies Inc 1886 Metro Center Dr 4th Fl. Reston VA 20190 *NASDAQ: CHCI* ■ *Web:* comstockhomes.com	703-883-1700	760-1520	653
Comstock Resources Inc 5300 Town & Country Blvd Ste 500. Frisco TX 75034 *NYSE: CRK* ■ *TF:* 800-929-4884 ■ *Web:* crkfrisco.com	972-668-8800	668-8812	536
Comstock Telcom 5445 Equity Ave. Reno NV 89502 *Web:* www.comstocktel.com	775-856-2227		246
Comstor Productivity Center Inc 441 W Sharp Ave. Spokane WA 99201 *TF:* 800-776-2451 ■ *Web:* www.comstorinc.com	509-534-5080	536-0281	496
COMTA (Commission on Massage Therapy Accreditation) 2101 Wilson Blvd Ste 302. Arlington VA 22201 *Web:* comta.org	202-888-6790	888-6787	48-1
Comtec Manufacturing Inc 1012 Delaum Rd. Saint Marys PA 15857 *Web:* www.comtecmfg.com	814-834-9300		295
Comtech EF Data Corp 2114 W Seventh St. Tempe AZ 85281 *Web:* www.comtechefdata.com	480-333-2200	333-2540	173-3
Comtech Inc 1001 S Reilly Rd Ste 639 Reilly Road Industrial Pk. Fayetteville NC 28314 *TF:* 800-868-5295 ■ *Web:* www.comtechfay.com	910-864-8787	864-4444	817
Comtech Network Systems Inc 1320 Lincoln Ave Ste 4. Holbrook NY 11741 *TF:* 877-267-0750 ■ *Web:* comtechnetworks.com	631-981-2694		180
Comtech PST Corp 105 Baylis Rd. Melville NY 11747 *Web:* www.comtechpst.com	631-777-8900	777-8877	647
Comtech Systems Inc 212 Outlook Point Dr Ste 100. Orlando FL 32809 *Web:* www.comtechsystems.com	407-854-1950	851-6960	647
Comtech Telecommunications Corp 68 S Service Rd Ste 230. Melville NY 11747 *NASDAQ: CMTL* ■ *Web:* www.comtechtel.com	631-962-7000		647
Comtech Xicom Technology Inc 3550 Bassett St. Santa Clara CA 95054 *Web:* xicomtech.com	408-213-3000	213-3001	647
Comtel 750 Ensminger Rd. Tonawanda NY 14150 *Web:* www.comtel.us	716-874-5500	874-6500	194
Comtel Corp 34029 Schoolcraft Rd. Livonia MI 48150 **Fax Area Code: 248* ■ *TF:* 800-335-2505 ■ *Web:* www.comtel.com	800-335-2505	888-4743*	246
Comtrac Services Inc 2250 Lithonia Industrial Blvd. Lithonia GA 30058 *Web:* comtracinc.com	770-934-9595		261
Comtrade International Inc 2 Bowers Dr. Freehold NJ 07728 *Web:* www.comtradeintl.com	201-337-0014	337-7860	328
Comtran Cable 330A Turner St. Attleboro MA 02703 *TF:* 800-842-7809 ■ *Web:* comtrancorp.com	508-399-7004		814
Comtrans 2336 E Magnolia St. Phoenix AZ 85034 *Web:* www.gocomtrans.com	602-231-0102		478
Comtrex Systems Corp 101B Foster Rd. Moorestown NJ 08057 *Web:* www.comtrex.com	770-955-1223		614
Comtrol 100 Fifth Ave NW. Maple Grove MN 55369 *TF:* 800-926-6876 ■ *Web:* comtrol.com	763-957-6000	957-6001	176
Comus International Inc 454 Allwood Rd. Clifton NJ 07012 *Web:* www.comus-intl.com	973-777-6900	777-8405	729
Comvox Systems LLC 5570-403 Florida Mining Blvd S. Jacksonville FL 32257 *Web:* www.comvox.com	904-309-6300		196

Name / Address	Phone	Fax	Class
Comware Technical Services Inc 17922 Sky Park Cir Ste E, Irvine CA 92614 — *TF:* 800-460-1970 ■ *Web:* comwaretech.com	949-851-9600		175
Comwave Networks Inc 61 Wildcat Rd, Toronto ON M3J2P5 — *TF:* 877-474-6638 ■ *Web:* www.comwave.net	416-663-9700		387
Comyns, Smith, McCleary & Deaver LLP 1777 Botelho Dr Ste 350, Walnut Creek CA 94596 — *Web:* csmllp.com	925-299-1040		2
Con Cast Pipe LP 299 Brock Rd S, Puslinch ON N0B2J0 — *TF:* 800-668-7473 ■ *Web:* www.concastpipe.com	519-763-8655	763-1956	183
Con Forms 777 Maritime Dr, Port Washington WI 53074 — *TF:* 800-223-3676 ■ *Web:* conforms.com	262-284-7800	284-7878	183
Conagra Brands Inc 1 Conagra Dr, Omaha NE 68102 — *NYSE:* CAG ■ *TF:* 877-266-2472 ■ *Web:* www.conagrabrands.com	402-240-4000	595-4707	360-3
Conair Corp 1 Cummings Point Rd, Stamford CT 06902 — *OTC:* CNGA ■ *TF:* 800-326-6247 ■ *Web:* www.conair.com	203-351-9000		37
Conair Group Inc 1510 Tower St, Abbotsford BC V2T6H5 — *Web:* conair.ca	604-855-1171		20
ConAm Management Corp 3990 Ruffin Rd Ste 100, San Diego CA 92123 — *Web:* www.conam.com	858-614-7200		652
Conan Law Offices LLC 755 N Monroe St, Media PA 19063 — *Web:* conanlawoffices.com	610-565-6688	891-1645	41
Conaway K. Michael (Rep R - TX) 2469 Rayburn House Office Bldg, Washington DC 20515 — *Web:* conaway.house.gov	202-225-3605	225-1783	342-2
Conax Buffalo Technologies LLC 2300 Walden Ave, Buffalo NY 14225 — *TF:* 800-223-2389 ■ *Web:* www.conaxtechnologies.com	716-684-4500	684-7433	201
Conbraco Industries Inc 701 Matthew-Mint Hill Rd, Matthews NC 28105 — **Fax Area Code:* 843 ■ *Web:* www.apollovalves.com	704-841-6000	672-1511*	609
Concannon & Charles 810 Asbury Ave Ste 212, Ocean City NJ 08226 — *Web:* davidconcannon.com	610-293-8084		41
Concast Inc 1010 N Star Dr, Zumbrota MN 55992 — *Web:* www.concastinc.com	507-732-4095		183
Concast Metal Products Co 131 Myoma Rd PO Box 816, Mars PA 16046 — *TF:* 800-626-7071 ■ *Web:* www.concast.com	724-538-4000	538-3956	295
Concensus Consulting LLC 51 Dutilh Rd Ste 140, Cranberry Township PA 16066 — **Fax Area Code:* 412 ■ *TF:* 888-349-1014 ■ *Web:* www.concensus.com	888-349-1014	291-2934*	194
Concentra Inc 5080 Spectrum Dr Ste 1200 W, Addison TX 75001 — *TF:* 866-944-6046 ■ *Web:* www.concentra.com	866-944-6046		463
Concentric Energy Advisors Inc 293 Boston Post Rd W Ste 500, Marlborough MA 01752 — *Web:* ceadvisors.com	508-263-6200		194
Concentrix Corp 44201 Nobel Dr, Fremont CA 94538 — *TF:* 800-747-0583 ■ *Web:* www.concentrix.com	800-747-0583		195
Concept 1604 Medina Rd Ste A, Wadsworth OH 44281 — *Web:* conceptltd.com	330-336-2571		737
Concept Art House Inc 785 Market St Ste 1100, San Francisco CA 94103 — *Web:* www.conceptarthouse.com	415-707-1500		514
Concept Boats Corp 2410 NW 147th St, Opa Locka FL 33054 — *Web:* www.conceptboats.com	305-635-8712	635-9543	90
Concept Display & Packaging Corp 20 River Terr, New York NY 10282 — *Web:* www.conceptdisplaycorp.com	212-566-2359		233
Concept Dynamics Ltd 1101 Hwy 69, New Glarus WI 53574 — *Web:* www.cdlweb.net	815-880-8630		177
Concept Electronics Inc 6243 Renoir Ave, Baton Rouge LA 70806 — *Web:* www.ceibr.com	225-927-8614		351
Concept Molds Inc 12273 N Us 131, Schoolcraft MI 49087 — *Web:* conceptmolds.com	269-679-2100	679-2157	604
Concept Studio LLC, The 165 Kings Hwy N, Westport CT 06880 — *Web:* www.tcspromo.com	203-227-7444		195
Concept Systems Inc 1957 Fescue St SE, Albany OR 97322 — *TF:* 866-791-8140 ■ *Web:* conceptsystemsinc.com	866-791-8140		261
Conception Abbey PO Box 501, Conception MO 64433 — *Web:* www.conceptionabbey.org	660-944-3100	944-2811	673
Conception To Reality Inc 6020 W 91 Ave, Westminster CO 80031 — *Web:* www.ctr-inc.com	303-225-0230	225-0231	463
Concepts and Designs Inc 2100 Park Dr, Owatonna MN 55060 — *Web:* www.cdihvac.com	507-451-2198	451-1177	14
Concepts Av Integration 4610 S 133rd St Ste 106, Omaha NE 68137 — *TF:* 877-422-3933 ■ *Web:* conceptsav.com	402-298-5011		253
Concepts NREC 217 Billings Farm Rd, White River Junction VT 05001 — *Web:* www.conceptsnrec.com	802-296-2321	296-2325	261
Concepts of Independence Inc 120 Wall St 9th Fl, New York NY 10005 — *TF:* 844-692-3727 ■ *Web:* www.coiny.org	212-293-9999		196
Concepts to Operations Inc 801 Compass Way Ste 217, Annapolis MD 21401 — *Web:* www.concepts2ops.com	301-249-2007		196
Concepts Tv Production 53 Indian Ln E, Towaco NJ 07082 — *Web:* conceptstv.com	973-331-1500	331-1550	514
Conceptual Financial Planning Inc 2561 E Calumet St, Appleton WI 54915 — *TF:* 866-809-6411 ■ *Web:* ontrackadvisor.com	920-731-9500	731-9504	690
Concern America 2015 N Broadway, Santa Ana CA 92706 — *TF:* 800-266-2376 ■ *Web:* www.concernamerica.org	714-953-8575	953-1242	48-5
Concerned United Birthparents Inc (CUB) PO Box 503475, San Diego CA 92150 — **Fax Area Code:* 858 ■ *TF:* 800-822-2777 ■ *Web:* www.cubirthparents.org	800-822-2777	712-3317*	48-21
Concerns of Police Survivors Inc (COPS) 846 Old S 5 PO Box 3199, Camdenton MO 65020 — *TF:* 800-784-2677 ■ *Web:* www.concernsofpolicesurvivors.org	573-346-4911	346-1414	48-21
ConcertAI 631 Park Ave, King of Prussia PA 19406 — *Web:* www.concertai.com	610-265-6344		463
Concerto Marketing Group Inc 250 128 W Hastings St, Vancouver BC V6B1G8 — *TF:* 877-873-2738 ■ *Web:* www.concertomarketing.com	604-642-5901		7
Conch House Heritage Inn 625 Truman Ave, Key West FL 33040 — *TF:* 800-207-5806 ■ *Web:* www.conchhouse.com	305-293-0020		379
Conch House Marina Resort 57 Comares Ave, Saint Augustine FL 32080 — *TF:* 800-940-6256 ■ *Web:* www.conch-house.com	904-829-8646	829-5414	379
Conchita Foods Inc 10051 NW 99th Ave Ste 3, Medley FL 33178 — *Web:* www.conchita-foods.com	305-888-9703	887-8817	296
Concho County PO Box 98, Paint Rock TX 76866 — *Web:* www.co.concho.tx.us	325-732-4322		338
Concho Resources Inc 600 W Illinois Ave, Midland TX 79701 — *NYSE:* CXO ■ *TF:* 877-201-5449 ■ *Web:* www.concho.com	432-683-7443	683-7441	538
Concho Valley Electric Co-opeartive Inc 2530 Pulliam St PO Box 3388, San Angelo TX 76902 — *Web:* www.cvec.coop	325-655-6957	655-6950	245
Concierge Publications 365 E Main St, Harbor Springs MI 49740 — *Web:* www.myconciergepublications.com	231-526-9422		637-9
Concinnity Services 109 Washington Ave, Hastings-on-Hudson NY 10706 — *Web:* www.concinnityservices.com	914-478-9000		194
Concklin Insurance Agency Inc 240 S Wmore Ave, Lombard IL 60148 — *Web:* concklin.com	630-268-1600		390
Conco 5141 Commercial Cir, Concord CA 94520 — *Web:* www.conconow.com	925-685-6799	685-6851	183
Conco Inc 4000 Oaklawn Dr, Louisville KY 40219 — *Web:* www.concocontainers.com	502-969-1333	962-2190	198
Conconully State Park 119 W Broadway Ave, Conconully WA 98819 — *Web:* parks.state.wa.us	509-826-7408		565
Concord Academy 166 Main St, Concord MA 01742 — *Web:* concordacademy.org	978-402-2200	402-2210	622
Concord Care and Rehabilitation Center of Toledo 3121 Glanzman Rd, Toledo OH 43614 — *Web:* www.concordcarecenters.com	419-385-7091		371
Concord City Hall 41 Green St, Concord NH 03301 — *Web:* www.concordnh.gov	603-225-8610	225-8592	337
Concord Coalition 1011 Arlington Blvd Ste 300, Arlington VA 22209 — *Web:* www.concordcoalition.org	703-894-6222	894-6231	48-7
Concord Companies Inc 4215 E McDowell Rd Ste 201, Mesa AZ 85215 — *Web:* www.concordinc.com	480-962-8080	962-0707	186
Concord Custom Cleaners PO Box 54910, Lexington KY 40555 — *Web:* www.concordcustomcleaners.com	859-422-4800	422-4801	426
Concord Direct 92 Old Tpke Rd, Concord NH 03301 — *TF:* 800-258-3662 ■ *Web:* www.concordlitho.com	603-225-3328		627
Concord Document Services Inc 1321 W 12th St, Los Angeles CA 90015 — *TF:* 800-246-7881 ■ *Web:* www.copying.la	213-745-3175		225
Concord Engineering Group 520 S Burnt Mill Rd, Voorhees NJ 08043 — *Web:* www.concord-engineering.com	856-427-0200	427-6529	256
Concord Foods Inc 10 Minuteman Way, Brockton MA 02301 — *Web:* www.concordfoods.com	508-580-1700		296-18
Concord Group Insurance Cos 4 Bouton St, Concord NH 03301 — *TF:* 800-852-3380 ■ *Web:* www.concordgroupinsurance.com	800-852-3380		391-4
Concord Grove Press 1407 Chapala St, Santa Barbara CA 93101 — *Web:* www.concordgrovepress.org	805-966-3941		637-2
Concord Home Health Care 424 N Lake Ave Ste 202, Pasadena CA 91101 — *Web:* www.concordhhc.com	626-792-0911	792-8911	363
Concord Hospital 250 Pleasant St, Concord NH 03301 — *Web:* www.concordhospital.org	603-225-2711		374-3
Concord International Investments Group LP 6 E 45th St 10th Fl, New York NY 10017 — *Web:* www.concordus.com	212-759-2375		690
Concord Iron Works Inc 1501 Loveridge Rd Ste 15, Pittsburg CA 94565 — *Web:* www.concordiron.com	925-432-0136		480
Concord Mall 4737 Concord Pk, Wilmington DE 19803 — *Web:* www.concordmall.com	302-478-9271	479-8314	460
Concord Marketing Solutions Inc 195 Exchange Blvd, Glendale Heights IL 60139 — *TF:* 800-648-8588 ■ *Web:* www.store.concordms.com	630-893-6453		463
Concord Monitor 1 Monitor Dr PO Box 1177, Concord NH 03302 — *Web:* www.concordmonitor.com	603-224-5301	224-8120	532-2
Concord Oil Company Inc 147 Lowell Rd, Concord MA 01742 — *Web:* concordoilco.com	978-369-3333		579
Concord Public Library 45 Green St, Concord NH 03301 — *Web:* www.concordnh.gov	603-225-8670		434-3
Concord Regional Visiting Nurse Associates Hospice Program 30 Pillsbury St, Concord NH 03301 — *TF:* 800-924-8620 ■ *Web:* www.crvna.org	603-224-4093	227-7525	371
Concord Road Equipment Manufacturing Inc 348 Chester St, Painesville OH 44077 — *TF:* 800-942-7623 ■ *Web:* www.concordroadequipment.com	440-357-5344		60
Concord School of Pet Grooming 9232 Kingston Pke, Knoxville TN 37922 — *Web:* www.concord-inc.com	865-769-0598	769-0579	685
Concord Servicing Corp 4150 N Drinkwater Blvd, Scottsdale AZ 85251 — *TF:* 866-493-6393 ■ *Web:* www.concordservicing.com	866-493-6393		317
Concord Speedway 7940 US Hwy 601, Concord NC 28025 — *Web:* www.concordspeedway.net	704-782-4221	782-4420	515
Concord Steel Centre Ltd 147 Ashbridge Cir, Woodbridge ON L4L3R5 — *Web:* www.concordsteel.com	905-856-1717		295

	Phone	Fax	Class
Concord Tool & Mfg 118 N Groesbeck Hwy ....Mount Clemens MI 48043 *Web:* www.concordtool.com	586-465-6537	465-7301	489
Concord University PO Box 1000................Athens WV 24712 *TF:* 800-344-6679 ■ *Web:* www.concord.edu	304-384-3115	384-3218	166
Concord Wealth Partners *Lopez Wealth Management Group LLC* 955 W Main St...........................Abingdon VA 24210 *TF:* 800-838-4370 ■ *Web:* www.concordwealthpartners.com	276-628-5910	623-1593	690
Concorde Asset Management LLC 1120 E Long Lake Rd Ste 250....................Troy MI 48085 *Web:* www.concordefinancial.com	248-740-8500		401
Concorde Battery Corp 2009 W San Bernardino Rd .... West Covina CA 91790 *Web:* www.concordebattery.com	626-813-1234	813-1235	20
Concorde Career Colleges Inc 5800 Foxridge Dr Ste 500.....................Mission KS 66202 *TF:* 800-693-7010 ■ *Web:* www.concorde.edu	913-831-9977	831-6556	800
Concorde Inc 1835 Market St Ste 1200 ....Philadelphia PA 19103 **Fax Area Code:* 215 ■ *TF:* 800-662-1676 ■ *Web:* www.concorde2000.com	800-662-1676	563-1269*	592
Concorde Management & Development Inc 1314 O St Ste 101 .... Lincoln NE 68508 *Web:* concordemgmt.com	402-476-0086		652
Concorde Management Services Inc 9 Gerhard Rd ....Plainview NY 11803 *Web:* concorde-li.com	516-433-9000		653
Concordia College 901 Eigth St S .... Moorhead MN 56562 *TF:* 800-699-9897 ■ *Web:* concordiacollege.edu	218-299-4000	299-4720	166
Concordia College New York 171 White Plains Rd....................... Bronxville NY 10708 *TF:* 800-937-2655 ■ *Web:* www.concordia-ny.edu	914-337-9300	395-4636	166
Concordia Electric Co-opeartive Inc 1865 Hwy 84 W PO Box 98 .... Jonesville LA 71343 *TF:* 800-617-6282 ■ *Web:* concordiaelectric.com	318-339-7969	339-7462	245
Concordia Gospel Outreach (CGO) 3558 S Jefferson Ave .... Saint Louis MO 63118 *TF:* 800-325-3040 ■ *Web:* www.concordiagospeloutreach.org	314-268-1076		48-20
Concordia Historical Institute 804 Seminary Pl......................... Saint Louis MO 63105 *Web:* concordiahistoricalinstitute.org	314-505-7900	505-7901	520
Concordia Hospital 1095 Concordia Ave........................Winnipeg MB R2K3S8 *TF:* 888-315-9257 ■ *Web:* www.concordiahospital.mb.ca	204-667-1560	667-1049	374-2
Concordia International Forwarding Inc 70 E Sunrise Hwy Ste 605 ....Valley Stream NY 11581 *Web:* www.concordiafreight.com	516-561-1100	561-1323	311
Concordia Language Villages 8659 Thorsonveien Rd .... Bemidji MN 56601 *TF:* 800-450-2214 ■ *Web:* www.concordialanguagevillages.org	800-222-4750		239
Concordia Lutheran Seminary 7040 Ada Blvd .... Edmonton AB T5B4E3 *Web:* www.concordiasem.ab.ca	780-474-1468	479-3067	167-3
Concordia Parish 4001 Carter St Rm 5............Vidalia LA 71373 *Web:* www.concordiaclerk.org	318-336-4204	336-8777	338
Concordia Publishing House Inc 3558 S Jefferson Ave .... Saint Louis MO 63118 *Web:* www.cph.org	314-268-1384	268-1329	637-3
Concordia Seminary 801 Seminary Pl......................... Saint Louis MO 63105 *TF:* 800-822-9545 ■ *Web:* www.csl.edu	314-505-7000		167-3
Concordia Theological Seminary 6600 N Clinton St........................ Fort Wayne IN 46825 *TF:* 800-481-2155 ■ *Web:* www.ctsfw.edu	260-452-2100		167-3
Concordia University 1455 de Maisonneuve Blvd W .... Montreal QC H3G1M8 *TF:* 866-333-2271 ■ *Web:* www.concordia.ca	514-848-2424	848-2621	785
Concordia University Ann Arbor 4090 Geddes Rd.......................... Ann Arbor MI 48105 *Web:* www.cuaa.edu	734-995-7300		166
Concordia University Chicago 7400 Augusta St.........................River Forest IL 60305 *TF:* 888-258-6773 ■ *Web:* cuchicago.edu	708-771-8300		166
Concordia University College of Alberta 7128 Ada Blvd NW........................ Edmonton AB T5B4E4 *TF:* 866-479-5200 ■ *Web:* www.concordia.ab.ca	780-479-8481	378-8460	785
Concordia University Irvine 1530 Concordia W ....Irvine CA 92612 *TF:* 800-229-1200 ■ *Web:* www.cui.edu	949-854-8002	854-6894	166
Concordia University Nebraska 800 N Columbia Ave..........................Seward NE 68434 *TF:* 800-535-5494 ■ *Web:* www.cune.edu	402-643-3651	643-4073	166
Concordia University Portland 2811 NE Holman St ....Portland OR 97211 *TF:* 800-321-9371 ■ *Web:* www.cu-portland.edu	503-288-9371	280-8531	166
Concordia University Texas 11400 Concordia University Dr .... Austin TX 78726 *TF:* 800-865-4282 ■ *Web:* www.concordia.edu	512-313-3000		166
Concordia University Wisconsin 12800 N Lake Shore Dr ....Mequon WI 53097 *TF:* 888-628-9472 ■ *Web:* www.cuw.edu	262-243-5700		166
Conco-west Inc 322 E Wetmore St PO Box 1360................Manteca CA 95337 *Web:* www.concowest.com	209-239-2110		261
Concrete Company of Springfield 431 S Jefferson Ste 250....................Springfield MO 65806 *Web:* concocompanies.com	417-831-7622	831-7236	182
Concrete Contractors Interstate 12599 Stotler Ct .... Poway CA 92064 *Web:* seicci.com	858-679-5550		377
Concrete Coring Co 4024 Jason St ....Denver CO 80211 *TF:* 800-333-8768 ■ *Web:* www.ccc-co.com	303-433-8818		189-11
Concrete Equipment Company Inc 237 N 13th St ....Blair NE 68008 *Web:* con-e-co.com	402-426-4181		183
Concrete General Inc 8000 Beechcraft Ave..................... Gaithersburg MD 20879 *Web:* www.concretegeneral.com	301-948-4450	940-0273	188 4

	Phone	Fax	Class
Concrete Materials Corp (CMC) 106 Industry Rd .... Richmond KY 40475 *Web:* www.concretematerialscompany.net	859-623-4238	623-4255	182
Concrete Materials Inc 1500 N Sweetman Pl ....Sioux Falls SD 57105 *Web:* concretematerialscompany.com	605-336-5760	334-6221	188-4
Concrete Reinforcing Steel Institute (CRSI) 933 N Plum Grove Rd.................... Schaumburg IL 60173 *Web:* www.crsi.org	847-517-1200	517-1206	49-3
Concrete Sealants Inc 9325 SR- 201 .... Tipp City OH 45371 *Web:* conseal.com	937-845-8776		3
Concrete Structures Inc 12100 NW 58 St .... Miami FL 33010 *Web:* www.concretestructures.net	305-597-9393		183
Concrete Supply Co 155 Greencastle Rd .... Tyrone GA 30290 *Web:* concretesupplyco.net	770-692-2620	692-2626	182
Concrete Supply Co 3823 Raleigh St........... Charlotte NC 28206 *Web:* www.concretesupplyco.com	704-372-2930		182
Concrete Supply of Topeka Inc 2450 Waterworks Dr..........................Topeka KS 66606 *Web:* cst-bc.com	785-235-1585	235-9071	182
Concrete Systems Inc 9 Commercial St .... Hudson NH 03051 *TF:* 800-342-3374 ■ *Web:* www.csigroup.com	603-889-4163	889-0039	183
Concrete Technology Corp 1123 Port of Tacoma Rd PO Box 2259 .... Tacoma WA 98401 *Web:* www.concretetech.com	253-383-3545		183
Concrete Tie Industries 1512 N Tamarind Ave .... Compton CA 90222 *Web:* www.concretetie.net	310-735-9970		183
Concurrent EDA LLC 5001 Baum Blvd Ste 640 .... Pittsburgh PA 15213 *Web:* www.concurrenteda.com	412-687-8800		177
Condado Vanderbilt Hotel Towers 1055 Ashford Ave.......................... San Juan PR 00907 *Web:* www.condadovanderbilt.com	787-721-5500		707
Condal Distributors 531-541 Dupont St............Bronx NY 10474	718-589-1100		297-11
Conde Group Inc 1804 Garnet Ave Ste 386 ....San Diego CA 92109 *TF:* 800-838-0819 ■ *Web:* www.condegroup.com	858-337-0187		196
Conde-Charlotte Museum House 104 Theatre St ....Mobile AL 36602 *Web:* condecharlotte.com	251-432-4722		50-3
Condenast 1166 Ave of the Americas 15th Fl..............New York NY 10036 *Web:* www.condenet.com	212-286-2860		387
Conder Flag Co 4705 Dwight Evans Rd.......... Charlotte NC 28217 *TF:* 855-344-1500 ■ *Web:* www.conderflags.com	704-529-1976		557
Condit Exhibits LLC 5151 Bannock St ....Denver CO 80216 *Web:* condit.com	303-744-7167		232
Condley & Company LLP 993 N Third St......... Abilene TX 79601 *Web:* www.condley.com	325-677-6251	677-0006	2
Condo Control Central 2 Carlton St Ste 1000....................... Toronto ON M5B1J3 **Fax Area Code:* 877 ■ *TF:* 888-762-6636 ■ *Web:* www.condocontrolcentral.com	416-961-7884	306-0138*	224
Condon & Cook LLC 745 N Dearborn St..........Chicago IL 60654 *Web:* condoncook.com	312-266-1313		41
Condon & Forsyth LLP 7 Times Sq ....New York NY 10036 *Web:* condonlaw.com	212-490-9100		445
Condon Oil Co 126 E Jackson St ....Ripon WI 54971 *TF:* 800-452-1212 ■ *Web:* www.condoncompanies.com	920-748-3186	748-3201	579
Condon-Johnson & Associates Inc 480 Roland Way Ste 200 ....Oakland CA 94621 *Web:* condon-johnson.com	510-636-2100	568-9316	186
Condor Capital Management Inc 1973 Washington Valley Rd .... Martinsville NJ 08836 *Web:* www.condorcapital.com	732-356-7323	356-5875	194
Condor Earth Technologies Inc 21663 Brian Ln.............................Sonora CA 95370 *TF:* 800-800-0490 ■ *Web:* condorearth.com	209-532-0361		194
Condor Outdoor Products 5268 Rivergrade Rd .... Irwindale CA 91706 *TF:* 800-552-2554 ■ *Web:* www.condoroutdoor.com	800-552-2554		711
Condor Reliability Services Inc 3400 De La Cruz Blvd Unit R .... Santa Clara CA 95054 *Web:* www.crsigroup.com	408-486-9600		45
Condortech Services Inc 6621-A Electronic Dr ....Springfield VA 22151 *TF:* 800-842-9171 ■ *Web:* www.condortech.com	703-916-9200		180
Condotte America Inc 10790 NW 127th St........Medley FL 33178 *Web:* www.condotteamerica.com	305-670-7585		186
Conduant Corp 1501 S Sunset St Ste D .... Longmont CO 80501 *TF:* 888-497-7327 ■ *Web:* conduant.com	303-485-2721		658
Conducive Consulting Inc 3445 Executive Center Dr Ste 216 .... Austin TX 78731 *Web:* www.conducivesi.com	512-551-0660		463
Conductive Containers Inc 4500 Quebec Ave N .... New Hope MN 55428 *Web:* www.corstat.com	763-537-2090	537-1738	548
Conductix 10102 F St..........................Omaha NE 68127 *TF:* 800-521-4888 ■ *Web:* www.conductix.us	402-339-9300	339-9627	117
Conductors Guild Inc 15 E Market St Ste 22....................... Leesburg VA 20178 *Web:* www.conductorsguild.org	202-643-4791		48-4
Conduit Corp 3212 W End Ave Ste 500.......... Nashville TN 37203	615-269-5710		180
Conduit Pipe Products Co 1501 W Main St.........................West Jefferson OH 43162 *TF:* 800-848-6125 ■ *Web:* www.conduitpipe.com	614-879-9114	879-5185	816
Condusiv Technologies Corp 611 S Fort Harrison Ave Ste 357 .... Clearwater FL 33756 *TF:* 800-829-6468 ■ *Web:* condusiv.com	818-771-1600	252-5512	178-12
Condustrial Inc 514 E North St............... Greenville SC 29601 *TF:* 888-794-7798 ■ *Web:* www.condustrial.com	864-235-3619		260
Condux Intl 145 Kingswood Rd ....Mankato MN 56001 *Web:* www.condux.com	507-387-6576		190
Cone Denim LLC 804 Green Valley Rd Ste 300 .... Greensboro NC 27408 *Web:* www.conedenim.com	336-379-2903		745-1
Cone Drive Operations Incorporated - A Textron Co 240 E 12th St .... Traverse City MI 49684 **Fax Area Code:* 888 ■ *TF:* 888-994-2663 ■ *Web:* conedrive.com	231-946-8410	907-2663*	709

Phone | Fax | Class

Cone Inc 855 Boylston St Boston MA 02116 617-227-2111 636
Web: www.conecomm.com

Cone Solvents Inc
6185 Cockrill Bend Cir Nashville TN 37209 615-350-6166 324
Web: www.conesolvents.com

Coneco Engineers & Scientists Inc
4 First St Bridgewater MA 02324 508-697-3191 261
TF: 800-548-3355 ■ *Web:* www.coneco.com

Conejo Valley Adult School
1025 Old Farm Rd Thousand Oaks CA 91360 805-497-2761 374-1167 685
Web: www.conejoadultschool.org

Conejos County 6683 County Rd 13 Conejos CO 81129 719-376-2014 338
Web: conejoscounty.org

Conenza 1411 4th Ave Ste 1000 Seattle WA 98101 206-792-4247 225
Web: www.conenza.com

Conergy Inc 2480 W 26th Ave Ste 26B Denver CO 80211 720-305-0700 787
Web: www.conergy.com

Conery Manufacturing Inc
1380 Enterprise Pky Ashland OH 44805 419-289-1444 281-0366 202
Web: conerymfg.com

ConEst Software Systems Inc
592 Harvey Rd Manchester NH 03103 603-437-9353 177
Web: www.conest.com

Conestoga Capital Advisors LLC'
CrossPoint at Valley Forge 550 E Swedesford Rd
Ste 120 Radnor PA 19087 484-654-1380 225-0533* 401
**Fax Area Code:* 610 ■ *TF:* 800-320-7790 ■ *Web:* www.conestogacapital.com

Conestoga Energy Partners LLC
1701 N Kansas Ave Ste 101 Liberal KS 67901 620-624-2901 41
Web: www.conestogaenergy.com

Conestoga Supply Corp
11011 Sheldon Rd Houston TX 77044 832-391-9431 456-7574* 492
**Fax Area Code:* 281 ■ *Web:* www.conestogasupply.com

Conestoga Tours Inc 1619 Manheim Pk Lancaster PA 17601 717-569-1111 107
TF: 800-538-2222 ■ *Web:* conestogatours.com

Conestoga Valley School District
2110 Horseshoe Rd Lancaster PA 17601 717-397-2421 397-0442 685
TF: 800-732-0025 ■ *Web:* www.conestogavalley.org

Conestoga Wood Specialties Inc
245 Reading Rd East Earl PA 17519 800-964-3667 115
TF: 800-964-3667 ■ *Web:* www.conestogawood.com

Conesys Inc 2280 208th St Torrance CA 90501 310-618-3737 618-3738 253
Web: www.conesys.com

Conetic Software Systems Inc
10860 Gulfdale St San Antonio TX 78216 210-225-5185 178-1
TF: 800-541-4580 ■ *Web:* www.conetic.com

CoNetrix LLC 5214 68th St Ste 200 Lubbock TX 79424 806-687-8600 177
TF: 800-356-6568 ■ *Web:* conetrix.com

Conewago Enterprises Inc
660 Edgegrove Rd Hanover PA 17331 717-632-7722 632-5045 261
Web: www.conewago.com

Conexess Group LLC
4336 Kenilwood Dr Nashville TN 37204 615-242-1014 260
Web: conexess.com

Conexnet Corp
477 E Butterfield Rd Ste 200 Lombard IL 60148 312-692-0898 525
Web: www.conexnet.com

Coney Island Hospital
2601 Ocean Pkwy Brooklyn NY 11235 718-616-3000 374-3
Web: www1.nyc.gov

Coney Island Park 6201 Kellogg Ave Cincinnati OH 45230 513-232-8230 231-1352 32
Web: coneyislandpark.com

Confederate Memorial Hall Museum
929 Camp St New Orleans LA 70130 504-523-4522 520
Web: confederatemuseum.com

Confederate Memorial State Historic Site
211 W First St Higginsville MO 64037 660-584-2853 565
Web: mostateparks.com

Confederate Reunion Grounds State Historic Site
1738 FM 2705 Mexia TX 76667 254-472-0959 565
Web: www.thc.texas.gov

Confer Plastics Inc (CPI)
97 Witmer Rd North Tonawanda NY 14120 716-693-2056 694-3102 604
TF: 800-635-3213 ■ *Web:* www.conferplastics.com

Conference & Logistics Consultants Inc
31 Old Solomans Island Rd Annapolis MD 21401 410-571-0590 571-0592 184
Web: www.gomeeting.com

Conference & Visitors Bureau of Montgomery County MD Inc
1801 Rockville Pk Ste 320 Rockville MD 20852 240-641-6750 641-6720 206
Web: www.visitmontgomery.com

Conference Board Inc 845 Third Ave New York NY 10022 212-759-0900 980-7014 49-12
TF: 866-711-2262 ■ *Web:* www.conference-board.org

Conference Center at NorthPointe
100 Green Meadows Dr S Lewis Center OH 43035 614-880-4300 377
TF: 844-475-5045 ■ *Web:* www.nwhotelandconferencecenter.com

Conference Event Management (CEM)
1045 76th St Ste 3025 West Des Moines IA 50266 515-254-0289 393
Web: www.myCEM.com

Conference Group, The
254 Chapman Rd Topkis Bldg Ste 200 Newark DE 19702 302-224-8255 179
TF: 877-716-8255 ■ *Web:* conferencegroup.com

Conference Hotels Unlimited
51 Harborview Rd Hull MA 02045 781-925-4000 925-2474 184
Web: www.conferencehotels.com

Conference Management Associates Inc
45 Lyme Rd Ste 304 Hanover NH 03755 603-643-2325 184

Conference Management Services
PO Box 2506 Monterey CA 93942 831-622-7772 622-0711 184
Web: www.conferencemanagement.net

Conference of Radiation Control Program Directors (CRCPD)
1030 Burlington Ln Ste 4B Frankfort KY 40601 502-227-4543 227-7862 49-7
Web: www.crcpd.org

Conference of State Bank Supervisors (CSBS)
1129 20th St NW 9th Fl Washington DC 20036 202-296-2840 296-1928 49-7
Web: www.csbs.org

Conference Plus Inc
1051 E Woodfield Rd Schaumburg IL 60173 847-619-6100 736
Web: conferenceplus.com

Conference Recording Service Inc (CRS)
2317 Carquinez Ave El Cerrito CA 94530 510-527-3600 637-10
Web: www.conferencerecording.com

Conference Solutions Inc
1033 SE Main St Ste 4 Portland OR 97214 503-244-4294 244-2401 184
Web: www.conferencesolutionsinc.com

Conference Technologies Inc
11653 Adie Rd Maryland Heights MO 63043 314-993-1400 41
TF: 800-743-6051 ■ *Web:* www.conferencetech.com

Confident Care Corp
3 University Plaza Dr Ste 340 Hackensack NJ 07601 201-498-9400 498-1556 363
Web: www.confidentcarecorp.com

Configure Inc
1800 Hamilton Ave Ste 200 San Jose CA 95123 408-269-1122 174
TF: 877-408-2636 ■ *Web:* www.configureinc.com

Configure One Inc
900 Jorie Blvd Ste 190 Oak Brook IL 60523 630-368-9950 178-5
TF: 800-798-2802 ■ *Web:* www.configureone.com

Confluence Advisors LLC
200 Wallace Rd Wexford PA 15090 724-940-1900 940-1930 70
Web: www.confluenceadvisorsllc.com

Confluence Energy LLC 1809 Hwy 9 Kremmling CO 80459 970-724-9839 724-9905 820
Web: www.confluenceenergy.com

Confluent 899 W Evelyn Ave Mountain View CA 94041 800-439-3207 788
TF: 800-439-3207 ■ *Web:* www.confluent.io

Conforma Clad Inc 501 Park E Blvd New Albany IN 47150 812-948-2118 481
TF: 888-289-4590 ■ *Web:* www.conformaclad.com

Conforma Laboratories Inc
4705 Colley Ave Norfolk VA 23508 800-426-1700 321-0201* 542
**Fax Area Code:* 757 ■ *TF:* 800-426-1700 ■ *Web:* www.conforma.com

Confrerie de la Chaine des Rotisseurs
285 Madison Ave Madison NJ 07940 973-360-9200 360-9330 49-6
Web: www.chaineus.org

Congaree National Park
100 National Park Rd Hopkins SC 29061 803-776-4396 783-4241 564
Web: www.nps.gov

Congdon's Aids To Daily Living Ltd
10550 - Mayfield Rd Edmonton AB T5P4X4 780-483-1762 489-6813 45
TF: 800-252-9368 ■ *Web:* congdons.ca

Congleton Hacker Co PO Box 22640 Lexington KY 40522 859-254-6481 186
Web: congleton-hacker.com

Conglom Inc
2600 Marie-Curie Ave Saint-Laurent QC H4S2C3 514-333-6666 601
TF: 877-333-0098 ■ *Web:* www.conglom.com

Congoleum Corp
3500 Quakerridge Rd PO Box 3127 Mercerville NJ 08619 609-584-3601 291
TF: 800-274-3266 ■ *Web:* www.congoleum.com

Congregation Beth Elohim
90 Hasell St Charleston SC 29401 843-723-1090 723-0537 50-1
Web: www.kkbe.org

Congregation Mikveh Israel
44 N Fourth St Philadelphia PA 19106 215-922-5446 922-1550 50-1
Web: www.mikvehisrael.org

Congregation Rodeph Sholom
7 W 83rd St New York NY 10024 212-362-8800 877-6526 48-20
Web: rodephsholom.org

Congregation Sha'ar Zahav (CSZ)
290 Dolores St San Francisco CA 94103 415-861-6932 48-20
Web: www.shaarzahav.org

Congress Daily
600 New Hampshire Ave The Watergate Washington DC 20037 202-266-7000 531-7
Web: www.nationaljournal.com

Congress of Racial Equality (CORE)
730 W Cheyenne Ave Ste 150 North Las Vegas NV 89030 702-637-7968 637-7953 48-8
Web: www.thecongressofracialequality.org

Congress of Russian-Americans
2460 Sutter St San Francisco CA 94115 415-928-5841 48-14
Web: www.russian-americans.org

Congress Plaza Hotel & Convention Ctr
520 S Michigan Ave Chicago IL 60605 312-427-3800 427-2919 379
Web: www.congressplazahotel.com

Congress Watch
215 Pennsylvania Ave SE Washington DC 20003 202-546-4996 547-7392 48-7
TF: 800-289-3787 ■ *Web:* www.citizen.org

Congressional Budget Office
4th Fl Second & D St SW
Ford House Office Bldg Washington DC 20515 202-226-2602 342
Web: www.cbo.gov

Congressional Quarterly House Action Reports
1625 Eye St Ste 200 Washington DC 20006 202-650-6500 531-7
Web: cqrollcall.com

Congruent Investment Partners LLC
3400 Carlisle St Ste 430 Dallas TX 75204 214-760-7411 302-5063 528
Web: www.congruentinv.com

Conifer Park 79 Glenridge Rd Schenectady NY 12302 518-399-6446 952-8228 726
TF: 800-989-6446 ■ *Web:* www.coniferpark.com

Conifex Timber Inc
980-700 W Georgia St PO Box 10070 Vancouver BC V7Y1B6 604-216-2949 279
TF: 866-301-2949 ■ *Web:* www.conifex.com

Conimar Group LLC 1724 NE 22nd Ave Ocala FL 34470 800-874-9735 596
TF: 877-395-3473 ■ *Web:* conimar.com

Conine Clubhouse
1005 Joe DiMaggio Dr Hollywood FL 33021 954-265-5324 372
TF: 866-532-4362 ■ *Web:* www.jdch.com

Conitex-Sonoco Usainc
1302 Industrial Pk Gastonia NC 28052 704-864-5406 125
Web: www.conitex.com

ConJelCo LLC 1460 Bennington Ave Pittsburgh PA 15217 412-621-6040 621-6214 637-2
TF: 800-492-9210 ■ *Web:* www.conjelco.com

Conklin & de Decker 62B Cranberry Hwy Orleans MA 02653 508-255-5975 463
Web: www.site.conklindd.com

Conklin Associates Inc
29 Church St PO Box 282 Ramsey NJ 07446 201-327-0443 261
Web: conklinassociates.net

Conklin Company Inc 551 Valley Pk Dr Shakopee MN 55379 952-445-6010 366
TF: 800-888-8838 ■ *Web:* www.conklin.com

Conklin Metal Industries
684 Antone St NW Atlanta GA 30318 404-688-4511 522-7439 697
Web: conklinmetal.com

Phone | Fax | Class

Conklin Office Furniture
56 N Canal St . . . . Holyoke MA 01040 413-315-6777 315-6454 320
TF: 800-817-1187 ■ *Web:* www.conklinoffice.com

Conklin, Woodcock & Ziegler PC
320 Gold Ave SW Ste 800 . . . . Albuquerque NM 87102 505-224-9160 224-9161 41
Web: conklinfirm.com

ConklinScott 14 10th St NE . . . . Washington DC 20002 202-744-8498 194
Web: www.conklinscott.com

Conlan Co, The 1800 Pkwy Pl Ste 1010 . . . . Marietta GA 30067 770-423-8000 423-8010 186
Web: www.conlancompany.com

Conlee College of Cosmetology
320 W Water St Ste E . . . . Kerrville TX 78028 830-896-2380 896-0470 167-3
Web: www.conleescollegeofcosmetology.com

Conley Engineering Inc
1301 S Cap of Tx Hwy Unit A 230 . . . . Austin TX 78746 512-328-3506 261
Web: conleyengineering.com

Conley Insurance Group Inc
13421 Manchester Rd Ste 204 . . . . Saint Louis MO 63131 314-909-9100 390
Web: conleyinsurance.com

Conley Publishing Group Ltd
119 Monroe St PO Box 478 . . . . Beaver Dam WI 53916 920-885-7800 887-0439 627
Web: www.gmtoday.com

Conley Transport Ii Inc
2104 Eastline Rd . . . . Searcy AR 72143 800-338-8700 449
TF: 800-338-8700 ■ *Web:* www.conleytransport.com

Conlin Travel Inc
3270 Washtenaw Ave . . . . Ann Arbor MI 48104 734-677-0900 677-0901 771
TF: 800-426-6546 ■ *Web:* www.conlintravel.com

Conlin's Furniture Inc
739 S 20th St W . . . . Billings MT 59102 406-656-4900 321
Web: www.conlins.com

Conlin's Print 52 W Lancaster Ave . . . . Malvern PA 19355 610-647-6100 113
Web: conlinsprint.com

Conlins Pharmacy Inc 30 Lawrence St . . . . Methuen MA 01844 978-552-1700 552-1785 237
Web: conlinspharmacy.com

Conlon & Company CPAS PLLC
1635 Brooks Ave W . . . . Rochester NY 14624 585-328-4990 328-1498 2
Web: conlonandcompany.com

Conlon Construction Company Inc
1100 Rockdale Rd . . . . Dubuque IA 52003 563-583-1724 588-3939 186
Web: www.conlonco.com

Conmaco/Rector LP
1602 Engineers Rd . . . . Belle Chasse LA 70037 504-394-7330 393-8715 358
Web: www.conmaco.com

Con-Mat Supply 822 N Sargent . . . . Glendive MT 59330 800-452-8449 191-4
TF: 800-452-8449 ■ *Web:* www.conmatsupply.com

Conmed Corp 525 French Rd . . . . Utica NY 13502 315-797-8375 438-3051* 476
NASDAQ: CNMD ■ **Fax Area Code:* 800 ■ *TF:* 800-448-6506 ■ *Web:* www.conmed.com

Conn's Inc 3295 College St . . . . Beaumont TX 77701 409-832-1696 35
NASDAQ: CONN ■ *TF:* 800-511-5750 ■ *Web:* www.conns.com

Connacher Oil and Gas Ltd
215 9th Ave SW Ste 500 . . . . Calgary AB T2P1K3 403-538-6201 538-6225 536
Web: www.connacheroil.com

Conneaut Lake Park
12382 Center St . . . . Conneaut Lake PA 16316 814-382-5115 32
Web: www.conneautlakepark.com

Conneaut Savings Bank
305 Main St PO Box 740 . . . . Conneaut OH 44030 440-599-8121 593-6446 70
TF: 888-453-2311 ■ *Web:* www.conneautsavings.com

Conneaut School District
219 W School Dr . . . . Linesville PA 16424 814-683-5900 685
Web: www.conneautsd.org

Connect America LLC 1 Belmont Ave . . . . Bala Cynwyd PA 19004 800-815-5809 475
TF: 800-283-2300 ■ *Web:* www.connectamerica.com

Connect Marketing Inc
One Market St 36th Fl . . . . San Francisco CA 94105 415-222-9691 195
TF: 800-455-8855 ■ *Web:* www.connectmarketing.com

Connect One Semiconductors Inc
95 S Market St 3rd Fl . . . . San Jose CA 95113 408-572-5675 572-5601 696
Web: www.connectone.com

Connect Tech Inc 42 Arrow Rd . . . . Guelph ON N1K1S6 519-836-1291 180
TF: 800-426-8979 ■ *Web:* connecttech.com

Connect802 Corp
111 Deerwood Rd Ste 200 . . . . San Ramon CA 94583 925-552-0802 116
Web: www.maui-communications.net

Connect-Air International Inc
4240 'B' St NW . . . . Auburn WA 98001 253-813-5599 492
TF: 800-247-1978 ■ *Web:* www.connect-air.com

ConnectCare 4000 Wellness Dr . . . . Midland MI 48670 989-839-1629 839-1626 363
TF: 888-646-2429 ■ *Web:* www.connectcare.com

Connectec Company Inc
1701 Reynolds Ave . . . . Irvine CA 92614 949-252-1077 252-1299 815
TF: 800-800-7000 ■ *Web:* www.connectecco.com

Connected Dots Media
155 Montgometry St No 507 . . . . San Francisco CA 94104 415-235-9360 637-2
Web: connecteddotsmedia.com

Connected Nation
191 W Professional Park Ct B . . . . Bowling Green KY 42104 270-781-4320 466
TF: 877-846-7710 ■ *Web:* connectednation.org

ConnectED: The National Center for College and Career
2150 Shattuck Ste 1200 . . . . Berkeley CA 94704 510-849-4945 305
Web: connectednational.org

Connected2Fiber 53 Sumner St . . . . Milford MA 01757 508-202-1807 39
Web: www.connected2fiber.com

ConnectiCare Inc
175 Scott Swamp Rd . . . . Farmington CT 06032 860-674-5700 674-5728 391-3
TF: 800-251-7722 ■ *Web:* www.connecticare.com

Connecticut

Aging Commission
210 Capitol Ave
State Capitol Building, Rm 011 . . . . Hartford CT 06106 860-240-5200 339-7
TF: 866-218-6631 ■ *Web:* www.cga.ct.gov

Agriculture Dept
450 Columbus Blvd Ste 701 . . . . Hartford CT 06103 860-713-2500 713-2515 339-7
Web: portal.ct.gov

Attorney General 55 Elm St . . . . Hartford CT 06106 860-808-5318 808-5387 339-7
Web: portal.ct.gov

Banking Dept 260 Constitution Plz . . . . Hartford CT 06103 860-240-8230 240-8295 339-7
TF: 800-831-7225 ■ *Web:* portal.ct.gov

Chief Medical Examiner
11 Shuttle Rd . . . . Farmington CT 06032 860-679-3980 679-1257 339-7
TF: 800-842-8820 ■ *Web:* portal.ct.gov

Child Support Assistance
55 Farmington Ave . . . . Hartford CT 06106 800-228-5437 339-7
TF: 800-228-5437 ■ *Web:* portal.ct.gov

Commission on Culture & Tourism
1 Constitution Plz . . . . Hartford CT 06103 860-256-2800 256-2811 339-7

Consumer Protection Dept
450 Columbus Blvd Ste 1404 . . . . Hartford CT 06106 860-713-5107 707-1966 339-7
TF: 800-838-6554 ■ *Web:* portal.ct.gov

Correction Dept
24 Wolcott Hill Rd . . . . Wethersfield CT 06109 860-692-7780 692-7783 339-7
Web: www.portal.ct.gov

Department of Education
PO Box 150471 . . . . Hartford CT 06115 860-713-6969 713-7017 339-7
Web: portal.ct.gov

Emergency Management & Homeland Security Div
25 Sigourney St 6th Fl . . . . Hartford CT 06106 860-256-0800 256-0815 339-7
TF: 800-397-8876 ■ *Web:* portal.ct.gov

Environmental & Energy Protection Dept
79 Elm St . . . . Hartford CT 06106 860-424-3000 339-7
Web: portal.ct.gov

Ethics Commission
18-20 Trinity St Ste 205 . . . . Hartford CT 06106 860-263-2400 263-2402 265
Web: portal.ct.gov

General Assembly 300 Capitol Ave . . . . Hartford CT 06106 860-240-0100 339-7
Web: www.cga.ct.gov

Higher Education Dept
450 Columbus Blvd Ste 510 . . . . Hartford CT 06103 860-947-1800 947-1310 339-7
Web: www.ctdhe.org

Housing Finance Authority 999 W St . . . . Rocky Hill CT 06067 860-721-9501 339-7
Web: www.chfa.org

Insurance Dept 153 Market St . . . . Hartford CT 06103 860-297-3800 566-7410 339-7
TF: 800-203-3447 ■ *Web:* portal.ct.gov

Judicial Branch 231 Capitol Ave . . . . Hartford CT 06106 860-757-2200 757-2130 339-7
Web: www.jud.ct.gov

Labor Dept 200 Folly Brook Blvd . . . . Wethersfield CT 06109 860-263-6000 259
Web: www.ctdol.state.ct.us

Motor Vehicles Dept 60 State St . . . . Wethersfield CT 06161 860-263-5700 339-7
Web: portal.ct.gov

Office of Tourism
Connecticut Office of Tourism 450 Columbus Blvd
Ste 5 . . . . Hartford CT 06103 888-288-4748 339-7
TF: 888-288-4748 ■ *Web:* www.ctvisit.com

Parole Board 55 W Main St . . . . Waterbury CT 06702 203-805-7400 805-6652 339-7
Web: portal.ct.gov

Public Health Dept 410 Capitol Ave . . . . Hartford CT 06134 860-509-8000 509-7111 339-7
Web: portal.ct.gov

Public Utility Control Dept
10 Franklin Sq . . . . New Britain CT 06051 860-685-8127 339-7
TF: 800-382-4586 ■ *Web:* portal.ct.gov

Rehabilitation Services Bureau
55 Farmington Ave 1st Fl . . . . Hartford CT 06105 860-424-4844 424-4850 339-7
TF: 800-537-2549 ■ *Web:* portal.ct.gov

Secretary of State 30 Trinity St . . . . Hartford CT 06106 860-509-6200 509-6209 339-7
Web: portal.ct.gov

State Police Div
1111 Country Club Rd . . . . Middletown CT 06457 860-685-8000 685-8354 339-7
Web: portal.ct.gov

Transportation Dept
2800 Berlin Tpke . . . . Newington CT 06111 860-594-2000 339-7
Web: portal.ct.gov

Veterans Affairs Dept 287 W St . . . . Rocky Hill CT 06067 860-616-3600 339-7
TF: 800-447-0961 ■ *Web:* portal.ct.gov

Victim Services Office
225 Spring St 4th Fl . . . . Wethersfield CT 06109 800-822-8428 339-7
TF: 800-822-8428 ■ *Web:* jud.ct.gov

Workers' Compensation Commission
21 Oak St 4th Fl . . . . Hartford CT 06106 860-493-1500 247-1361 339-7
TF: 800-223-9675 ■ *Web:* www.wcc.state.ct.us

Connecticut Academy of Arts & Sciences, The (CAAS)
310 Prospect St . . . . New Haven CT 06511 203-432-3113 432-5712 637-2
Web: caas.yale.edu

Connecticut Aero Tech School
Brainard Airport 500 Lindbergh Dr . . . . Hartford CT 06114 860-566-1234 566-1350 685
Web: ctaero.cttech.org

Connecticut Association of Realtors
111 Founders Plz Ste 1101 . . . . East Hartford CT 06108 860-290-6601 290-6615 656
TF: 800-335-4862 ■ *Web:* www.ctrealtors.com

Connecticut Audubon Society Birdcraft Museum & Sanctuary
314 Unquowa Rd . . . . Fairfield CT 06824 203-259-0416 520
Web: www.ctaudubon.org

Connecticut Ballet 20 Acosta St . . . . Stamford CT 06902 203-964-1211 573-1
Web: connecticutballet.org

Connecticut Bar Assn
30 Bank St PO Box 350 . . . . New Britain CT 06050 860-223-4400 72
Web: www.ctbar.org

Connecticut Business & Industry Assn
350 Church St . . . . Hartford CT 06103 860-244-1900 278-8562 140
Web: www.cbia.com

Connecticut Business Systems Inc
240 Pane Rd . . . . Newington CT 06111 860-667-2900 666-6866 112
TF: 800-842-0009 ■ *Web:* www.cbs-gisx.com

Connecticut Center for Massage Therapy
1154 Poquonnock Rd . . . . Groton CT 06340 860-446-2299 446-9410 706
Web: www.unigo.com

Connecticut Center for Universal Reflexology
800 Woodtick Rd . . . . Wolcott CT 06716 203-879-5551 167-3
Web: www.universalreflexology.net

Connecticut Children's Medical Ctr
282 Washington St . . . . Hartford CT 06106 860-545-9000 374-1
TF: 833-733-7669 ■ *Web:* www.connecticutchildrens.org

Connecticut Children's Museum
22 Wall St . . . . New Haven CT 06511 203-562-5437 787-9414 521
Web: www.childrensbuilding.org

Connecticut College
270 Mohegan Ave . . . . New London CT 06320 860-439-4587 439-4301 166
TF: 800-892-3363 ■ *Web:* www.conncoll.edu

Name / Address	Phone	Fax	Class
Connecticut Democratic Party 30 Arbor St Ste 103 Hartford CT 06106 *Web:* ctdems.org	860-560-1775	387-0147	616-1
Connecticut Historical Society Museum 1 Elizabeth St Hartford CT 06105 *Web:* chs.org	860-236-5621	236-2664	520
Connecticut Hospice 100 Double Beach Rd Branford CT 06405 *Web:* www.hospice.com	203-315-7500	315-7561	371
Connecticut Hypodermics Inc 519 Main St Yalesville CT 06492 *Web:* connhypo.com	203-265-4881	284-1520	477
Connecticut Industrial Gauging Inc 3460 Crystal St Gotha FL 34734 *Web:* www.xraygauge.com	401-556-9444		201
Connecticut Innovations Inc 865 Brook St 3rd Fl Rocky Hill CT 06067 *Web:* ctinnovations.com	860-563-5851	563-4877	792
Connecticut Institute for Herbal Studies 912 Corbin Ave New Britain CT 06052 *Web:* www.ctherbschool.com	860-826-2705	666-5064	167-3
Connecticut K-9 Education Ctr 239 Maple Hill Ave Newington CT 06111 *Web:* www.ctk9.com	860-666-4646	666-1566	167-3
Connecticut Laminating Company Inc 162 James St New Haven CT 06513 *TF:* 800-753-9119 ■ *Web:* www.ctlaminating.com	203-787-2184	787-4073	599
Connecticut Lighting Center Inc 160 Brainard Rd Hartford CT 06114 *Web:* ctlighting.com	860-249-7631	249-8994	362
Connecticut Magazine 100 Gando Dr New Haven CT 06513 *TF:* 877-396-8937 ■ *Web:* www.connecticutmag.com	203-789-5300	789-5255	457-22
Connecticut Medical Insurance Co (CMIC) 80 Glastonbury Blvd 3rd Fl Glastonbury CT 06033 *TF:* 800-228-0287 ■ *Web:* www.cmic.biz	860-633-7788	633-8237	391-5
Connecticut Natural Gas Corp (CNG) 76 Meadow St East Hartford CT 06108 *Web:* www.cngcorp.com	860-727-3000		787
Connecticut Nurses Assn (CNA) 377 Research Pkwy Ste 2D Meriden CT 06450 *Web:* www.ctnurses.org	203-238-1207	238-3437	533
Connecticut On-Line Computer Center Inc 100 Executive Blvd Southington CT 06489 *Web:* www.cocc.com	860-678-0444	677-1169	225
Connecticut Pharmacists Assn 35 Cold Spring Rd Ste 121 Rocky Hill CT 06067 *Web:* www.ctpharmacists.org	860-563-4619	257-8241	585
Connecticut Post 410 State St Bridgeport CT 06604 *TF:* 800-542-2517 ■ *Web:* www.ctpost.com	203-333-0161	367-8158	532-2
Connecticut Public Interest Research Group (CONNPIRG) 2074 Park St Hartford CT 06106 *Web:* connpirg.org	860-233-7554		633
Connecticut Radio Holding Inc 1208 Cromwell Ave PO Box 487 Rocky Hill CT 06067 *TF:* 800-527-8855 ■ *Web:* www.connradio.com	860-563-4867	563-1179	647
Connecticut Republican Party 31 Pratt St Hartford CT 06103 *Web:* ct.gop	860-422-8211		616-2
Connecticut River Greenway State Park 136 Damon Rd Northampton MA 01060 *Web:* www.mass.gov	413-586-8706		565
Connecticut Science Center Inc 250 Columbus Blvd Hartford CT 06103 *Web:* ctsciencecenter.org	860-520-2112		520
Connecticut Spring & Stamping Corp 48 Spring Ln Farmington CT 06032 *Web:* www.ctspring.com	860-677-1341	677-7199	719
Connecticut State Department of Correction *Manson Youth Institution* 42 Jarvis St Cheshire CT 06410 *Web:* www.portal.ct.gov	203-806-2500	699-1845	412
Connecticut State Library 231 Capitol Ave Hartford CT 06106 *TF:* 866-886-4478 ■ *Web:* ctstatelibrary.org	860-757-6510	757-6503	434-5
Connecticut State Medical Society 127 Washington Ave East Bldg 3rd Fl North Haven CT 06473 *Web:* www.csms.org	203-865-0587		474
Connecticut State Museum of Natural History UConn Unit 4023 Storrs CT 06269 *Web:* mnh.uconn.edu	860-486-4460	486-0827	520
Connecticut State University System 39 Woodland St Hartford CT 06105 *Web:* www.ct.edu	860-493-0000		786
Connecticut Transit 100 Leibert Rd Hartford CT 06141 *Web:* www.cttransit.com	860-522-8101	247-1810	468
Connecticut Valley Arms (CVA) 1270 Progress Center Ave Ste 1 Lawrenceville GA 30043 *Web:* cva.com	770-449-4687		284
Connecticut Valley Biological Supply Company Inc 82 Valley Rd Southampton MA 01073 *TF:* 800-628-7748 ■ *Web:* www.connecticutvalleybiological.com	800-628-7748	355-6813	459
Connecticut Valley Hospital 1000 Silver St Middletown CT 06457 *Web:* portal.ct.gov	860-569-2669	262-5989	374-5
Connecticut Valley Railroad State Park 1 Railroad Ave PO Box 452 Essex CT 06426 *Web:* essexsteamtrain.com	860-767-0103	767-0104	565
Connecticut Veterinary Medical Assn PO Box 107 Glastonbury CT 06033 *Web:* ctvet.org	860-635-7770		795
Connecticut Water Service Inc 93 W Main St Clinton CT 06413 *NASDAQ: CTWS* ■ **Fax Area Code: 860* ■ *TF:* 800-286-5700 ■ *Web:* www.ctwater.com	800-286-5700	664-8081*	360-5
Connecting Generations 100 W Tenth St Ste 1115 Wilmington DE 19801 *Web:* connecting-generations.org	302-656-2122	656-2123	48-6
Connecting Point Computer Centers 1251 E McAndrews Rd Ste 114 Medford OR 97504 *TF:* 888-245-9861 ■ *Web:* connectingpointonline.com	541-773-9861		174
Connection Bank 636 Ave G Fort Madison IA 52627 *Web:* myconnectionbank.com	319-372-5164		70
Connection Culture Group 104 Brookside Dr Greenwich CT 06831 *Web:* www.sia-partners.com	203-422-6511		196
Connection Pointe Christian Church of Brownsburg 1800 N Green St Brownsburg IN 46112 *Web:* www.connectionpointe.org	317-852-2221		48-20
Connection Wholesale Florist, The 2733 W 7th St Fort Worth TX 76107 *Web:* www.theflowermarketon7th.com	817-377-3660		293
Connection, The 11351 Rupp Dr Burnsville MN 55337 *TF:* 800-883-5777 ■ *Web:* www.theconnectioncc.com	952-948-5488		737
Connections USA Inc 2288 Marietta Hwy Ste 200 Canton GA 30114 *Web:* www.connections-usa.com	770-479-7508	479-7510	180
Connectit Networks Inc 4603 NE St Johns Rd Ste B Vancouver WA 98661 *Web:* www.connectitnetworks.com	360-450-0860		393
Connective Capital Management LLC 385 Homer Ave Palo Alto CA 94301 *Web:* connectcap.com	650-321-4545	618-0385	528
ConnectLife 4444 Bryant & Stratton Way Buffalo NY 14203 *TF:* 800-227-4771 ■ *Web:* www.connectlife.org	716-853-6667	853-6674	269
ConnectOne Bank 301 Sylvan Ave Englewood Cliffs NJ 07632 *NASDAQ: CNOB* ■ *TF:* 844-266-2548 ■ *Web:* connectonebank.com	844-266-2548		360-2
Connector Specialists Inc 175 James Dr E Saint Rose LA 70087 *TF:* 800-666-8620 ■ *Web:* www.connectorspecialists.com	504-469-1659	469-8545	492
Connectria Hosting 10845 Olive Blvd Ste 300 Saint Louis MO 63141 *TF:* 800-781-7820 ■ *Web:* www.connectria.com	314-587-7000	587-7090	39
connectRN Inc 203 Crescent St Ste 403 Waltham MA 02453 *Web:* www.connectrn.com	617-944-1515		178-1
Connectronics Corp 2745 Avondale Ave Toledo OH 43607 *TF:* 800-965-0020 ■ *Web:* www.connectronicscorp.com	419-537-0020	537-0007	815
ConnectU Consulting 2880 David Walker Dr Ste 123 Eustis FL 32726 **Fax Area Code: 866* ■ *Web:* connectuconsulting.wordpress.com	352-702-0354	936-1369*	177
Connecture Inc 18500 W Corporate Dr Ste 250 Brookfield WI 53045 *Web:* www.connecture.com	262-432-8282		390
ConnectWise Inc 4110 George Rd Ste 200 Tampa FL 33634 *TF:* 800-671-6898 ■ *Web:* www.connectwise.com	813-463-4700		179
Connell Chevrolet 2828 Harbor Blvd Costa Mesa CA 92626 *Web:* www.connellchevrolet.com	714-546-1200		57
Connell Finance Company Inc 300 Connell Dr Berkeley Heights NJ 07922 *Web:* www.connellfinance.com	908-673-3700	673-3800	216
Connell Foley LLP 56 Livingston Ave Roseland NJ 07068 *Web:* www.connellfoley.com	973-535-0500		428
Connell LP 1 International Pl 31st Fl Boston MA 02110 *Web:* connell-lp.com	617-737-2700	737-1617	686
Connell Oil Incorporated Co *CO-Energy* 1015 N Oregon Ave Pasco WA 99301 *TF:* 888-806-7676 ■ *Web:* www.connelloil.com	509-547-3326		581
Connell USA 345 California St 27th Fl San Francisco CA 94104 *Web:* www.connellworld.com	415-772-4000	772-4100	146
Connell's Map Lee Flowers & Gifts 3014 E Broad St Columbus OH 43209 *Web:* www.cmlflowers.com	614-237-8653		292
Connelly & Associates Inc 1513 Tilco Dr Frederick MD 21704 *Web:* connellyandassociates.com	301-696-8820	696-0327	261
Connelly & Wicker Inc 10060 Skinner Lake Dr Ste 500 Jacksonville FL 32246 *Web:* cwieng.com	904-265-3030		261
Connelly Law Offices Ltd 372 Broadway Ste A Pawtucket RI 02860 *Web:* connellylaw.com	401-724-9400		41
Connelly Law Offices PLLC 2301 N 30th St Tacoma WA 98403 *Web:* connelly-law.com	253-593-5100		41
Connelly Partners LLC 46 Waltham St 4th Fl Boston MA 02118 *Web:* www.connellypartners.com	617-521-5400		4
Connelly Skis Inc 20621 52nd Ave W Lynnwood WA 98036 *Web:* www.connellyskis.com	425-775-5416	778-9590	710
Conner & Winters 1700 One Leadership Sq 211 N Robinson Oklahoma City OK 73102 *Web:* www.cwlaw.com	405-272-5711		445
Conner Ash PC 12101 Woodcrest Exec Dr 300 Saint Louis MO 63141 *Web:* www.connerash.com	314-205-2510		2
Conner Homes Co 12600 SE 38th St Bellevue WA 98006 *Web:* www.connerhomes.com	425-455-9280		653
Conner Industries Inc 3800 Sandshell Dr Ste 235 Fort Worth TX 76137 *Web:* www.connerindustries.com	817-847-0361		683
Conner Insurance Inc 8445 Keystone Crossing Ste 200 Indianapolis IN 46240 *Web:* connerins.com	317-808-7711		390
Conner Prairie Living History Museum 11140 E 106th St Fishers IN 46038 *TF:* 800-966-1836 ■ *Web:* www.connerprairie.org	317-776-6000	776-6014	520
Conner Rosenkranz LLC 19 E 74th St New York NY 10021 *Web:* www.crsculpture.com	212-517-3710	734-7678	42
Conners Publications 503 Tahoe St Natchitoches LA 71457 *Web:* www.music-usa.org	318-357-0924		637-10
Connersville Fayette County *Chamber of Commerce* 504 Central Ave Connersville IN 47331 *Web:* www.fayettechamber.com	765-825-2561	825-4613	338

				Phone	Fax	Class
Connestee Falls Property Owners Assn 33 Connestee Trail *Web:* connesteefalls.com	Brevard	NC	28712	828-885-2001		653
Connetquot River State Park Preserve PO Box 505 *Web:* parks.ny.gov	Oakdale	NY	11769	631-581-1005		565
Connexio Media LLC 904 Fournie Ln *Web:* connexiomedia.com	Collinsville	IL	62234	618-628-8888		5
Connexity Inc 12200 W Olympic Blvd Ste 300 *Web:* connexity.com	Los Angeles	CA	90064	310-571-1235		178-1
Connexsys Engineering Inc 1320 Willow Pass Rd Ste 500 *Web:* www.connexsysinc.com	Concord	CA	94520	925-471-0700		261
Connexus Energy Co-op 14601 Ramsey Blvd *Web:* www.connexusenergy.com	Ramsey	MN	55303	763-323-2650	323-2603	245
Connexus Inc 6510 Abrams Rd Ste 350 *Web:* connexusvideo.com	Dallas	TX	75231	214-443-2600	443-2620	390
Conney Safety Products LLC 3202 Latham Dr *TF:* 800-462-1947 ■ *Web:* www.conney.com	Madison	WI	53744	800-462-1947		535
Connie Wilson Consulting Inc 2721-302 Glenwood Gardens Ln **Fax Area Code:* 866 ■ *Web:* www.lobbync.com	Raleigh	NC	27608	919-274-0557	386-3280*	317
Conning Holdings Ltd 1 Financial Plz *Web:* www.conning.com	Hartford	CT	06103	860-299-2000		401
Connoisseur Media LLC 180 Post Rd E Ste 201 *Web:* connoisseurmedia.com	Westport	CT	06880	203-227-1978	227-2373	645-141
Connolly Gerald E (Rep D - VA) 2238 Rayburn House Office Bldg *Web:* connolly.house.gov	Washington	DC	20515	202-225-1492		342-2
Connolly Krause LLC 500 W Madison St Ste 2430 *Web:* www.cktrials.com	Chicago	IL	60661	312-253-6200		41
Connor Co 2800 N E Adams *Web:* www.connorco.com	Peoria	IL	61603	309-688-1068		612
Connor Corp 10633 Coldwater Rd Ste 200 *TF:* 866-920-7115 ■ *Web:* www.connorcorp.com	Fort Wayne	IN	46845	260-424-1601		604
Connors Investor Services Inc 1210 Broadcasting Rd Ste 200 *TF:* 877-376-7418 ■ *Web:* connorsinvestor.com	Wyomissing	PA	19610	610-376-7418		401
Connors State College 700 College Rd *Web:* connorsstate.edu	Warner	OK	74469	918-463-2931	463-6324	162
Connor-Winfield Corp 2111 Comprehensive Dr *Web:* www.conwin.com	Aurora	IL	60505	630-851-4722	851-5040	203
CONNPIRG (Connecticut Public Interest Research Group) 2074 Park St *Web:* connpirg.org	Hartford	CT	06106	860-233-7554		633
Conn-Selmer Inc 600 Industrial Pkwy *TF:* 800-348-7426 ■ *Web:* www.bachbrass.com	Elkhart	IN	46516	574-522-1675		527
Conntrol International Inc 135 Park Rd *Web:* www.conntrol.com	Putnam	CT	06260	860-928-0567	963-2147	729
ConnXus Inc 5155 Financial Way *Web:* connxus.com	Mason	OH	45040	513-204-2873		387
ConocoPhillips Co PO Box 2197 *Web:* www.conocophillips.com	Houston	TX	77252	281-293-1000		538
Conolog Corp 5 Columbia Rd *NASDAQ: CNLG* ■ *TF:* 800-526-3984 ■ *Web:* iniven.com	Somerville	NJ	08876	908-722-3770		647
Conopco Project Management 5448 Prairie Stone Pkwy *Web:* www.conopco.com	Hoffman Estates	IL	60192	847-645-5000	645-5050	652
Conoptics International Sales Corp 19 Eagle Rd *TF:* 800-748-3349 ■ *Web:* www.conoptics.com	Danbury	CT	06810	203-743-3349	790-6145	544
Conproco Corp 17 Production Dr *TF:* 800-258-3500 ■ *Web:* conproco.com	Dover	NH	03820	800-258-3500		182
Conquest Technologies Inc 9250 Rumsey Rd Ste B *Web:* www.conquesttechnologies.com	Columbia	MD	21045	410-740-4448	740-1492	463
Conquip Inc 11255 Pyrites Way	Rancho Cordova	CA	95670	916-379-8200		454
Conrad & Bischoff Inc 2251 N Holmes Ave *Web:* www.conradbischoff.com	Idaho Falls	ID	83401	208-522-4217		581
Conrad & Scherer LLP 633 S Federal Hwy *Web:* www.conradscherer.com	Fort Lauderdale	FL	33301	954-462-5500	463-9244	428
Conrad Acceptance Corp 476 W Vermont Ave *TF:* 888-904-8963 ■ *Web:* www.conradco.com	Escondido	CA	92025	760-735-5000	735-5010	160
Conrad Bros Inc 800 Industrial Ave *Web:* www.conradbrothersinc.com	Chesapeake	VA	23324	757-543-3521		187
Conrad Caldwell House Museum, The 1402 St James Ct *Web:* conrad-caldwell.org	Louisville	KY	40208	502-636-5023		520
Conrad Capital Management Inc 1377 Motor Pkwy Ste 406 *Web:* www.conradcapital.com	Islandia	NY	11749	631-439-7878	439-7879	401
Conrad Co, The 1304 Farmville Rd *Web:* www.theconradcompany.com	Memphis	TN	38122	901-323-5926	323-5948	22
Conrad Forest Products 68765 Wildwood Dr **Fax Area Code:* 541 ■ *TF:* 800-356-7146 ■ *Web:* www.conradfp.com	North Bend	OR	97459	800-356-7146	756-0131*	818
Conrad Machine Inc 1627 E 27th Ter *Web:* www.conradmachineinc.com	Pittsburg	KS	66762	620-231-9458		537
Conrad N. Hilton Foundation 30440 Agoura Rd *Web:* www.hiltonfoundation.org	Agoura Hills	CA	91301	818-851-3700		305
Conrad Schmitt Studios Inc 2405 S 162nd St *TF:* 800-969-3033 ■ *Web:* www.conradschmitt.com	New Berlin	WI	53151	262-786-3030		186
Conrad Shipyards 1501 Front St *Web:* www.conradindustries.com	Morgan City	LA	70380	985-384-3060	385-4090	698

				Phone	Fax	Class
Conrad, Trosch & Kemmy PA 5821 Fairview Rd Ste 405 *Web:* www.ctklawyers.com	Charlotte	NC	28204	704-553-8221	331-0595	428
Conrad-American Inc 609 Main St *TF:* 800-553-1791 ■ *Web:* conradamerican.com	Houghton	IA	52631	319-469-4141	469-6012	273
Conrad-Jarvis Corp 217 Conant St *Web:* conrad-jarvis.com	Pawtucket	RI	02860	401-722-8700	726-8860	745-5
Con-Real Support Group LP 1900 Ballpark Way *Web:* www.con-real.com	Arlington	TX	76006	817-640-4420	640-4430	186
Conroe Business Furniture 2305 Airport Rd *Web:* www.conroebusinessfurniture.com	Conroe	TX	77303	936-441-3375	760-3376	320
Conroe/Lake Conroe Chamber of Commerce 505 W Davis *Web:* www.conroe.org	Conroe	TX	77301	936-756-6644	756-6462	139
Conroy & Knowlton Inc 320 S Montebello Blvd *Web:* www.conroyknowlton.com	Montebello	CA	90640	323-665-5288	722-4670	602
Conroy Media Ltd 6713 Kingery Hwy *Web:* conroymedialtd.squarespace.com	Willowbrook	IL	60527	630-920-7800		7
Conroy, Conroy & Durant PA 2210 Vanderbilt Beach Rd Ste 1201 *Web:* naplespropertylaw.com	Naples	FL	34109	239-649-5200	649-8140	41
Conroy, Simberg, Krevans, Abel, Lurvey, Morrow, Kraft, Klein, Goldberg PA 3440 Hollywood Blvd 2nd Fl *Web:* www.conroysimberg.com	Hollywood	FL	33021	954-961-1400		428
Consarc Corp 100 Indel Ave *Web:* www.consarc.com	Rancocas	NJ	08073	609-267-8000	267-1366	318
Conscious Teaching LLC 21 Crest Rd *TF:* 800-667-6062 ■ *Web:* www.consciousteaching.com	Fairfax	CA	94930	415-456-9190		423
Conseil Des Ecoles Publique De L'est De L'ontario 2445 St Laurent Blvd *Web:* www.cepeo.on.ca	Ottawa	ON	K1G6C3	613-742-8960		685
Consensus Advisory Services LLC 100 River Rdg Dr Ste 202 *Web:* www.consensusadvisors.com	Norwood	MA	02062	617-437-6500		41
Consensus Inc PO Box 520526 *Web:* www.consensus-inc.com	Independence	MO	64052	816-373-3700	373-3701	532-2
Consensus Intl 3905 NW 107 Ave *Web:* www.consensusintl.net	Doral	FL	33178	786-206-0034		809
Consensus Orthopedics Inc 1115 Windfield Way Ste 100 *Web:* www.consensusortho.com	El Dorado Hills	CA	95762	916-355-7100		477
Conserv FS Inc 1110 McConnell Rd *Web:* www.conservfs.com	Woodstock	IL	60098	815-334-5950		791
Conservation & Production Research Laboratory (CPRL) USDA/ARS PO Box 10 *Web:* www.ars.usda.gov	Bushland	TX	79012	806-356-5749	356-5750	668
Conservation Fund 1655 N Fort Myer Dr Ste 1300 *Web:* www.conservationfund.org	Arlington	VA	22209	703-525-6300	525-4610	48-13
Conservation Intl (CI) 2011 Crystal Dr Ste 500 *TF:* 800-406-2306 ■ *Web:* www.conservation.org	Arlington	VA	22202	703-341-2400	553-0654	48-13
Conservatory Garden Central Pk 14 E 60th St *Web:* www.centralparknyc.org	New York	NY	10022	212-310-6600		97
Conservatory of Flowers 100 John F Kennedy Dr *Web:* conservatoryofflowers.org	San Francisco	CA	94118	415-831-2090		97
Conservatory of Recording Arts & Sciences 2300 E Broadway Rd *TF:* 888-930-1991 ■ *Web:* www.audiorecordingschool.com	Tempe	AZ	85282	480-858-9400		166
Conservco Water Conservation Products LLC 550 W Plumb Ln Ste B-147 **Fax Area Code:* 860 ■ *Web:* www.conservco.us	Reno	NV	89509	775-747-3333	540-8762*	326
Considine & Considine 8989 Rio San Diego Dr Ste 250 *Web:* www.cccpa.com	San Diego	CA	92108	619-231-1977	231-8244	2
Consiglio's 165 Wooster St *Web:* www.consigliosrestaurant.com	New Haven	CT	06511	203-865-4489		671
CONSOL Energy Inc 1000 Consol Energy Dr *NYSE: CNX* ■ *TF:* 800-544-8024 ■ *Web:* www.consolenergy.com	Canonsburg	PA	15317	724-485-4000		360-3
ConSol Inc 1610 R St Ste 200 *Web:* consol.org	Sacramento	CA	95811	209-473-5000		463
Console Mattiacci Law Offices LLC 1525 Locust St *Web:* consolelaw.com	Philadelphia	PA	19102	215-545-7676		41
Consolidated Beverages Inc 12 St Mark St *Web:* www.consolidatedbeverages.weebly.com	Auburn	MA	01501	508-832-5311		81-1
Consolidated Bottle Corp 77 Union St *Web:* consolidatedbottle.com	Toronto	ON	M6N3N2	416-656-7777		454
Consolidated Brick 650 Bodwell St Ext **Fax Area Code:* 508 ■ *TF:* 800-321-0021 ■ *Web:* www.consolidatedbrick.com	Avon	MA	02322	800-321-0021	559-8910*	191-1
Consolidated Carpet Associates LLC 16 W 22nd St 12th Fl *Web:* www.consolidatedcarpet.com	New York	NY	10010	212-226-4600	675-1973	131
Consolidated Catfish Inc 299 S St PO Box 271 *TF:* 800-228-3474 ■ *Web:* deltapride.com	Isola	MS	38754	662-962-3101	962-0114	296-14
Consolidated Chassis Management LLC 500 International Dr *Web:* www.ccmpool.com	Budd Lake	NJ	07828	973-298-8900	298-8939	194
Consolidated Communications Holdings Inc 121 S 17th St *NASDAQ: CNSL* ■ *Web:* www.consolidated.com	Mattoon	IL	61938	217-235-3311		360-3
Consolidated Devices Inc (CDI) 19220 San Jose Ave *TF:* 800-525-6319 ■ *Web:* www.cditorque.com	City of Industry	CA	91748	626-965-0668	810-2759	758
Consolidated Disposal Services Inc 12949 Telegraph Rd *TF:* 800-299-4898 ■ *Web:* www.republicservices.com	Santa Fe Springs	CA	90670	800-299-4898		804
Consolidated Distribution Corp 1285 101st St *Web:* www.cdcsupply.com	Lemont	IL	60439	630-972-9800	972-9876	186

Name / Address	City	State	ZIP	Phone	Fax	Class
Consolidated Edison Inc 4 Irving Pl *NYSE:* ED ■ *TF:* 800-752-6633 ■ *Web:* www.coned.com	New York	NY	10003	212-460-4600		360-5
Consolidated Electric Co-op 3940 E Liberty St *TF:* 800-621-0091 ■ *Web:* www.consolidatedelectric.com	Mexico	MO	65265	573-581-3630	581-0990	245
Consolidated Electronic Wire & Cable Co 11044 King St *TF:* 800-621-4278 ■ *Web:* www.conwire.com	Franklin Park	IL	60131	847-455-8830	455-8837	814
Consolidated Energy Co 910 Main St **Fax Area Code:* 319 ■ *TF:* 800-338-3021 ■ *Web:* www.cecgas.com	Jesup	IA	50648	800-338-3021	827-3154*	579
Consolidated Engineering Company Inc 1971 Mccollum Pkwy NW *TF:* 800-486-6836 ■ *Web:* www.cec-intl.com	Kennesaw	GA	30144	770-422-5100		256
Consolidated Environmental Engineering LLC 2515 N Wickham Rd *Web:* ceefl.com	Melbourne	FL	32935	321-242-7100		261
Consolidated Fabricators Corp 14620 Arminta St *Web:* www.con-fab.com	Van Nuys	CA	91402	818-901-1005		124
Consolidated Facility Service Inc 1376 Chattahoochee Ave *Web:* cfsserv.com	Atlanta	GA	30318	404-355-9137	355-9139	104
Consolidated Federal Credit Union 1033 NE Sixth Ave *Web:* consolidatedccu.com	Portland	OR	97232	503-232-8070		219
Consolidated Fiberglass Products Co 3801 Standard St *Web:* www.conglas.com	Bakersfield	CA	93308	661-323-6026		46
Consolidated Fibers 8100 S Blvd *TF:* 800-243-8621 ■ *Web:* www.consolidatedfibers.com	Charlotte	NC	28273	704-554-8621		605-1
Consolidated Graphics Group Inc 1614 E 40th St *Web:* www.csinc.com	Cleveland	OH	44103	216-881-9191		627
Consolidated Hinge and Manufactured Products 1150b Dell Ave *Web:* www.champcompany.com	Campbell	CA	95008	408-379-6550	378-2570	454
Consolidated Industries Inc 677 Mixville Rd *Web:* www.forgemetal.com	Cheshire	CT	06410	203-272-5371	272-5672	483
Consolidated Metal Products Inc 1028 Depot St *Web:* www.cmpubolt.com	Cincinnati	OH	45204	513-251-2625		455
Consolidated Metco Inc 5701 SE Columbia Way *TF:* 800-547-9473 ■ *Web:* www.conmet.com	Vancouver	WA	98661	800-547-9473		60
Consolidated Pipe & Supply Inc 1205 Hilltop Pkwy *Web:* www.consolidatedpipe.com	Birmingham	AL	35204	205-323-7261	251-7838	492
Consolidated Precision Products 8333 Wilcox Ave *Web:* www.cppcorp.com	Cudahy	CA	90201	323-773-2363	562-3174	308
Consolidated Printers Inc 2630 Eigth St *Web:* www.consoprinters.com	Berkeley	CA	94710	510-843-8524	486-0580	626
Consolidated Publishing Co 4305 McClellan Blvd PO Box 189 *Web:* www.annistonstar.com	Anniston	AL	36206	256-236-1551	241-1991	637-8
Consolidated Rail Corp 1717 Arch St 13th Fl *TF:* 800-272-0911 ■ *Web:* www.conrail.com	Philadelphia	PA	19103	215-209-2000		648
Consolidated Shoe Company Inc 22290 Timberlake Rd *TF:* 800-368-7463 ■ *Web:* www.consolidatedshoe.com	Lynchburg	VA	24502	434-239-0391		301
Consolidated Steel Services Inc 632 Glendale Vly Blvd *TF:* 800-237-8783 ■ *Web:* www.csteel.com	Fallentimber	PA	16639	814-944-5890	943-8278	492
Consolidated Supply Co 7337 SW Kable Ln *TF:* 800-929-5810 ■ *Web:* www.consolidatedsupply.com	Tigard	OR	97224	503-620-7050	684-3254	612
Consolidated Utility & Equipment Service Inc (CUES) 53 Lebanon Rd N *TF:* 800-526-3916 ■ *Web:* www.cuesequip.com	Franklin	CT	06254	860-886-7081	886-6546	385
CONSOR Inc 7342 Girard Ave Ste 8 *TF:* 800-454-9091 ■ *Web:* www.consor.com	La Jolla	CA	92037	858-454-9091		463
Consortia Consulting Inc 233 S 13th St Ste 1225 *Web:* www.consortiaconsulting.com	Lincoln	NE	68508	402-441-4315		194
Consortium Book Sales & Distribution Inc The Keg House 34 Thirteenth Ave NE Ste 101 *Web:* www.cbsd.com	Minneapolis	MN	55413	612-746-2600		96
Consortium for Advanced Manufacturing Intl (CAM-I) 6836 Bee Cave Ste 256 *Web:* www.cam-i.org	Austin	TX	78746	512-296-6872		49-13
Consortium for Citizens with Disabilities (CCD) 1660 L St NW Ste 701 *TF:* 800-669-7079 ■ *Web:* www.c-c-d.org	Washington	DC	20036	202-783-2229		48-6
Consortium for Policy Research in Education (CPRE) 3440 Market St Ste 560 *Web:* www.cpre.org	Philadelphia	PA	19104	215-573-0700	573-7914	634
Consortium for School Networking (COSN) 1025 Vermont Ave NW Ste 1010 *TF:* 866-267-8747 ■ *Web:* cosn.org	Washington	DC	20005	202-861-2676	393-2011	48-9
ConSova Corp 1536 Cole Blvd Ste 350 *TF:* 866-529-9107 ■ *Web:* consova.com	Lakewood	CO	80401	866-529-9107		196
Conspectus Inc 2231 Rt 50 PO Box 248 *Web:* www.conspectusinc.com	Tuckahoe	NJ	08250	609-628-2390		193
Constangy, Brooks & Smith LLC 230 Peachtree St N W Ste 2400 *Web:* www.constangy.com	Atlanta	GA	30303	404-525-8622		428
Constantine's Wood Ctr 1040 E Oakland Pk Blvd *TF:* 800-443-9667 ■ *Web:* www.constantines.com	Fort Lauderdale	FL	33334	954-561-1716	565-8149	613
Constellation Brands Inc 207 High Pt Dr Bldg 100 *NYSE:* STZ ■ *TF:* 888-724-2169 ■ *Web:* www.cbrands.com	Victor	NY	14564	888-724-2169		81-3
Constellation Technology Corp 7887 Bryan Dairy Rd Ste 100 *TF:* 800-335-7355 ■ *Web:* www.contech.com	Largo	FL	33777	727-547-0600		218
Constellium Automotive USA LLC 46555 Magellan Dr *Web:* www.constellium.com	Novi	MI	48377	248-668-3211		492
Constitution Convention Museum State Park 200 Allen Memorial Way *Web:* www.floridastateparks.org	Port Saint Joe	FL	32456	850-229-8029		565
Constitution Island Assn (CIA) PO Box 126 *Web:* www.constitutionisland.org	Cold Spring	NY	10516	845-265-2501		49-19
Constitution Square State Historic Site 134 S Second St *Web:* www.danvillekentucky.com	Danville	KY	40422	859-236-7794		565
Constitutional Rights Foundation 601 S Kingsley Dr *TF:* 800-488-4273 ■ *Web:* www.crf-usa.org	Los Angeles	CA	90005	213-487-5590	386-0459	48-7
Construction Albert Jean Ltd 4045 Parthenais St *Web:* www.albertjean.com	Montreal	QC	H2K3T8	514-522-2121		186
Construction Book Express Inc 990 Park Center Dr Ste E *TF:* 800-253-0541 ■ *Web:* www.constructionbook.com	Vista	CA	92081	800-253-0541		690
Construction Enterprises Inc (CEI) 2179 Edward Curd Ln Ste 100 *Web:* constructionenterprises.com	Franklin	TN	37067	615-332-8880	771-0818	187
Construction Financial Management Assn (CFMA) 100 Village Blvd Ste 200 *TF:* 888-421-9996 ■ *Web:* www.cfma.org	Princeton	NJ	08540	609-452-8000	452-0474	49-1
Construction Industry Training Council of Washington 1930 116th Ave NE *TF:* 877-707-2482 ■ *Web:* citcwa.org	Bellevue	WA	98004	425-454-2482	462-7391	167-3
Construction Journal Ltd 400 SW 7th St *Web:* www.constructionjournal.com	Stuart	FL	34994	772-781-2144		637-9
Construction Outfitters International Inc 37450 I-10 W Ste 101 *Web:* coiworld.com	Boerne	TX	78006	830-816-2104	816-2464	186
Construction Products Inc 1631 Ashport Rd *TF:* 800-238-8226 ■ *Web:* www.cpi-tn.com	Jackson	TN	38305	731-668-7305	668-1361	183
Construction Specialties Inc 3 Werner Way *TF:* 800-972-7214 ■ *Web:* c-sgroup.com	Lebanon	NJ	08833	908-236-0800	236-0801	491
Construction Systems Software Inc PO Box 203184 *TF:* 800-531-1035 ■ *Web:* www.cssisw.com	Austin	TX	78720	800-531-1035		178-10
Construction Testing & Engineering Inc 1441 Montiel Rd Ste 115 *TF:* 800-576-4955 ■ *Web:* www.cte-inc.net	Escondido	CA	92026	760-746-4955	746-9806	743
Construction Trades Press LLC 2265 SE Blvd *TF:* 800-462-6487 ■ *Web:* www.pipefitter.com	Clinton	NC	28328	910-592-1310	592-9266	637-2
Construction Trailer Specialists Inc 2535 Rose Pkwy *Web:* www.constructiontrailerspecialists.com	Sikeston	MO	63801	573-481-0941		779
Constructors Association of Western Pennsylvania 800 Cranberry Woods Dr Ste 110 *TF:* 877-343-2297 ■ *Web:* www.cawp.org	Cranberry Township	PA	16066	412-343-8000		138
Constructors Inc 1815 Y St *Web:* www.constructorslincoln.com	Lincoln	NE	68508	402-434-1764		188-4
Construx Software 10900 NE 8th St Ste 1300 *TF:* 866-296-6300 ■ *Web:* www.construx.com	Bellevue	WA	98005	425-636-0100	636-0159	177
Consulado General de Mexico en Chicago 204 S Ashland Ave *Web:* consulmex.sre.gob.mx	Chicago	IL	60607	312-738-2383	491-9143	257
Consulado General del Peru en San Francisco *Consulate General* 870 Market St Ste 1075 *Web:* www.consulado.pe	San Francisco	CA	94102	415-362-5185	362-2836	257
Consulate General Of Italy 150 S Independence Mall W 1026 Public Ledger Bldg *TF:* 800-531-0840 ■ *Web:* consfiladelfia.esteri.it	Philadelphia	PA	19106	215-592-7329	592-9808	257
Consulate General of Argentina in New York 12 W 56th St *Web:* cnyor.cancilleria.gob.ar	New York	NY	10019	212-603-0400		257
Consulate General of Brazil in Miami 3150 SW 38th Ave Ste 100 *Web:* miami.itamaraty.gov.br	Miami	FL	33146	305-285-6200		257
Consulate General of El Salvador 46 Park Ave *Web:* www.consuladonuevayork.rree.gob.sv	New York	NY	10016	212-889-3608		784
Consulate General of Finland *Consulate General* 11900 W Olympic Blvd Ste 580 *Web:* finlandabroad.fi	Los Angeles	CA	90064	310-203-9903	481-8981	257
Consulate General of India 455 N Cityfront Plaza Dr Ste 850 *Web:* www.cgichicago.gov.in	Chicago	IL	60611	312-595-0405		257
Consulate General of Japan in San Francisco 275 Battery St Ste 2100 *Web:* www.sf.us.emb-japan.go.jp	San Francisco	CA	94105	415-780-6000	767-4200	257
Consulate General of Paraguay 801 Second Ave Ste 600 **Fax Area Code:* 212 ■ *Web:* www.mre.gov.py	New York	NY	10017	347-260-0013	682-9443*	257
Consulate General of Romania 11766 Wilshire Blvd Ste 560 *Web:* www.losangeles.mae.ro	Los Angeles	CA	90025	310-444-0043	445-0043	257
Consulate General of Switzerland 633 Third Ave 30th Fl *Web:* www.eda.admin.ch	New York	NY	10017	212-599-5700		257
Consulate General of the Republic of Liberia in New York, The 228 E 45th St & 2nd Ave Ste 602 *Web:* liberiaconsulate-ny.com	New York	NY	10017	212-687-1025	599-3189	257
Consulate General of the Slovak Republic in New York 801 Second Ave 12th Fl *Web:* www.mzv.sk	New York	NY	10017	212-286-8434	286-8439	784
Consulate Health Care 800 Concourse Pkwy S Ste 200 *Web:* www.consulatehealthcare.com	Maitland	FL	32751	407-571-1550	571-1599	353

Name / Address	City	State	ZIP	Phone	Fax	Class
Consulate Health Care at Lake Parker 2020 W Lake Parker Dr *Web:* www.consulatemgt.com	Lakeland	FL	33805	863-682-7580		450
Consulate of St Vincent and the Grenadines New York USA *Consulate General* 801 2nd Ave 21st Fl *Web:* www.ny.consulate.gov.vc	New York	NY	10017	212-687-4490	949-5946	257
Consulate-General of Japan 737 N Michigan Ave Ste 1100 *Web:* www.chicago.us.emb-japan.go.jp	Chicago	IL	60611	312-280-0400	280-9568	257
Consulate-General of Japan in Atlanta 3438 Peachtree Rd Phipps Tower Ste 850 *Web:* www.atlanta.us.emb-japan.go.jp	Atlanta	GA	30326	404-240-4300	240-4311	257
Consult Dynamics Inc 1016 Delaware Ave *TF:* 800-784-4788 ■ *Web:* www.dca.net	Wilmington	DE	19806	302-654-1019		180
Consult Usa Inc 634 Alpha Dr *TF:* 866-963-8621 ■ *Web:* www.consultusa.com	Pittsburgh	PA	15238	412-963-8621		177
Consultant Engineering Service Inc 1111 S Marshall St Ste 250 *Web:* www.ceseng.net	Winston-Salem	NC	27101	336-724-0139		261
Consultants & Builders Inc 3100 Medlock Bridge Rd Ste 420 *Web:* www.consultantsandbuilders.com	Norcross	GA	30071	770-729-8183	416-9619	194
Consultants in Laboratory Medicine of Greater Toledo Inc 3170 W Central Ave *Web:* www.clm-pml.com	Toledo	OH	43606	419-535-9629		415
ConsultKAP Inc 3115 Woodchuck Way SW Ste 101 *Web:* www.consultkap.com	Conyers	GA	30094	770-918-9390		317
Consultnet LLC 10813 S River Front Pkwy Ste 150 *Web:* www.consultnet.com	South Jordan	UT	84095	801-208-3700	208-3643	721
Consumer Attorneys of California 770 L St Ste 1200 *Web:* www.caoc.org	Sacramento	CA	95814	916-442-6902		428
Consumer Brands LLC 4600 Campus Dr Ste 107 *Web:* www.consumerbrands.com	Newport Beach	CA	92660	949-267-4117		366
Consumer Data Industry Assn (CDIA) 1090 Vermont Ave NW Ste 200 *Web:* www.cdiaonline.org	Washington	DC	20005	202-371-0910	371-0134	49-2
Consumer Depot LLC 3332 Powell Ave *Web:* www.consumerdepot.com	Nashville	TN	37204	615-263-0282	851-2126	174
Consumer Federation of America (CFA) 1620 I St NW Ste 200 *Web:* consumerfed.org	Washington	DC	20006	202-387-6121	265-7989	48-10
Consumer Healthcare Products Assn (CHPA) 1625 Eye St NW Ste 600 *Web:* www.chpa.org	Washington	DC	20036	202-429-9260	223-6835	49-4
Consumer Law Books Publishing House 12725 W Indian School Rd Ste E-101 *Web:* www.arizonalandlordsdeskbook.com	Avondale	AZ	85392	602-255-0101	255-0431	637-2
Consumer Marine Supply 88 Royal Dr *Web:* www.consumermarinesupply.com	Brick	NJ	08723	732-477-0119		196
Consumer News 110 Main St *Web:* www.cortlandstandard.net	Cortland	NY	13045	607-756-5665		532-2
Consumer Oil & Supply Co 100 Railroad St	Braymer	MO	64624	660-645-2215		316
Consumer Product Safety Commission (CPSC) 4340 E W Hwy Ste 502 *Web:* www.cpsc.gov	Bethesda	MD	20814	301-504-7923		340-20
Consumer Reports Inc 101 Truman Ave *TF:* 800-333-0663 ■ *Web:* www.consumerreports.org	Yonkers	NY	10703	800-333-0663		634
Consumer Reports On Health 101 Truman Ave *Web:* www.consumerreports.org	Yonkers	NY	10703	914-378-2881		531-8
Consumer Safety Technology LLC 666 Walnut St Ste 2000 *TF:* 888-283-5899 ■ *Web:* www.intoxalock.com	Des Moines	IA	50309	515-331-7643		57
Consumer Textile Corp 123 N fourth St PO Box 1597 *TF:* 800-926-5646 ■ *Web:* www.ctc-corp.net	Clinton	OK	73601	580-323-3111	323-7229	426
Consumer's Beverages Company Inc 2765 Genesee St *Web:* www.consumersbeverages.com	Buffalo	NY	14225	716-893-7040		443
ConsumerMetrics Inc 2299 Perimeter Park Dr **Fax Area Code:* 770 ■ *TF:* 888-311-0936 ■ *Web:* home.cmiresearch.com	Atlanta	GA	30341	678-805-4000	936-0714*	605-2
Consumers Energy 2074 242nd St *TF:* 800-696-6552 ■ *Web:* consumersenergy.coop	Marshalltown	IA	50158	641-752-1593	752-5738	245
Consumers Energy Co 1 Energy Plz *TF:* 800-477-5050 ■ *Web:* www.consumersenergy.com	Jackson	MI	49201	517-788-0550		787
Consumers Life Insurance Co 15885 W Sprague Rd *TF:* 866-925-2542 ■ *Web:* www.consumerslife.com	Strongsville	OH	44136	866-925-2542		796
Consumers Packing Company Inc 1301 Carson Dr *TF:* 800-356-9876 ■ *Web:* consumerspacking.com	Melrose Park	IL	60160	708-345-6780		297-9
Consumers Pipe & Supply Co 13424 Arrow Blvd *TF:* 800-338-7473 ■ *Web:* www.consumerspipe.com	Fontana	CA	92335	909-728-4828		492
Consumers Power Inc (CPI) 6990 W Hills Rd *TF:* 800-872-9036 ■ *Web:* www.cpi.coop	Philomath	OR	97370	541-929-3124	929-8673	245
Consumers Produce Co 1 21st St *Web:* www.consumersproduce.com	Pittsburgh	PA	15222	412-281-0722	281-6541	297-7
Consumers Vinegar & Spice Company Inc 4723 S Washtenaw Ave *Web:* cvsco.com	Chicago	IL	60632	773-376-4100	376-6224	296-41
Consumers' Checkbook 1625 K St NW 8th Fl *TF:* 800-213-7283 ■ *Web:* www.checkbook.org	Washington	DC	20006	800-213-7283		637-2
Consumers' Research Council of America (CRCA) 2020 Pennsylvania Ave NW Ste 300-A *TF:* 877 774-6337 ■ *Web:* www.consumersresearchcncl.org	Washington	DC	20006	202-835-9698	835-9739	48-10
Consutech Systems LLC PO Box 15119 *Web:* www.consutech.com	Richmond	VA	23227	804-746-4120	730-9056	318
Contact America Inc 2325 Maryland Rd Ste 150 *TF:* 800-887-6837 ■ *Web:* www.contact-america.com	Willow Grove	PA	19090	800-887-6837		393
Contact Castle Hotel & Spa 400 Benedict Ave *Web:* castlehotelandspa.com	Tarrytown	NY	10591	914-631-1980		379
Contact Industries Inc 9200 SE Sunnybrook Blvd Ste 200 *TF:* 800-547-1038 ■ *Web:* www.contactind.com	Clackamas	OR	97015	503-228-7361	221-1340	499
Contact Industries Inc 25 Lex-Industrial Dr *Web:* contactindustriesinc.com	Lexington	OH	44904	419-884-9788	884-9767	203
Contact Lens Manufacturers Assn PO Box 29398 *TF:* 800-344-9060 ■ *Web:* www.clma.net	Lincoln	NE	68529	402-465-4122	465-4187	49-4
Contact Solutions LLC 11950 Democracy Dr Ste 250 *TF:* 866-979-3339 ■ *Web:* www.contactsolutions.com	Reston	VA	20190	866-979-3339		393
Contactability-Com LLC 1901 Newport Blvd Ste 300B *TF:* 877-323-7750 ■ *Web:* contactability.com	Costa Mesa	CA	92627	877-323-7750		390
Contactpointe of Pittsburgh 2593 Wexford Bayne Rd Ste 200 *TF:* 877-255-4916 ■ *Web:* www.contactpointe.com	Sewickley	PA	15143	412-788-0680		379
Container Consulting Service Inc 455 Mayock Rd *Web:* www.ccs-packaging.com	Gilroy	CA	95020	408-842-1919	842-5339	194
Container Graphics Corp 114 Edinburgh S Dr Ste 104 *Web:* containergraphics.com	Cary	NC	27511	919-481-4200	469-4897	781
Container Manufacturing Inc 50 Baekeland Ave *Web:* www.containermfg.com	Middlesex	NJ	08846	732-563-0100	563-0704	333
Container Port Group Inc 1340 Depot St 2nd Fl *Web:* www.containerport.com	Cleveland	OH	44116	440-333-1330	333-1520	780
Container Products Corp 112 N College Rd *Web:* www.c-p-c.com	Wilmington	NC	28405	910-392-6100		124
Container Research Corp (CRC) 2 New Rd *TF:* 844-220-9574 ■ *Web:* www.crc-flex.com	Aston	PA	19014	844-220-9574		198
Container Store, The 500 Freeport Pkwy *TF:* 800-733-3532 ■ *Web:* www.containerstore.com	Coppell	TX	75019	972-538-6000		362
Container Supply Company Inc 12571 Western Ave *Web:* www.containersupplycompany.com	Garden Grove	CA	92841	714-892-8321	892-3824	124
ContainerWorld Forwarding Services Inc 16133 Blundell Rd *TF:* 877-838-8880 ■ *Web:* www.containerworld.com	Richmond	BC	V6W0A3	604-276-1300		311
Containment Solutions Inc 5150 Jefferson Chemical Rd *Web:* containmentsolutions.com	Conroe	TX	77301	936-756-7731		600
Contaminant Control Inc 3434 Black & Decker Rd **Fax Area Code:* 910 ■ *TF:* 888-624-6555 ■ *Web:* www.cci-env.com	Hope Mills	NC	28348	888-624-6555	484-4978*	189-16
Contango Oil & Gas Co 3700 Buffalo Speedway Ste 960 *NYSE: MCF* ■ *Web:* www.contango.com	Houston	TX	77098	713-960-1901	960-1065	536
CONTAX Inc 893 Yonge St *Web:* www.contax.com	Toronto	ON	M4W2H2	416-927-1913		193
Contec Systems Industrial Corp 1566 Medical Dr Ste 310 *Web:* contecsystems.com	Pottstown	PA	19464	610-326-3235	326-3238	180
Contech Construction Products Inc 9025 Centre Pt Dr Ste 400 **Fax Area Code:* 513 ■ *TF:* 800-338-1122 ■ *Web:* www.conteches.com	West Chester	OH	45069	919-858-7820	645-7993*	697
Con-Tech Cos 366 W Fourth St *Web:* www.contech-mo.com	Eureka	MO	63025	636-938-4748	938-9603	261
Con-Tech International Inc 1046 Annunciation St *Web:* www.con-techinternational.com	New Orleans	LA	70130	504-523-4785	522-7332	758
Con-Tech Lighting 2783 Shermer Rd *TF:* 800-728-0312 ■ *Web:* www.contechlighting.com	Northbrook	IL	60062	847-559-5500	559-5505	439
Contecture International Ltd 17252 Armstrong Ave Ste A *Web:* www.contextureintl.com	Irvine	CA	92614	949-250-0811		514
Con-tek Machine Inc 3575 Hoffman Rd E *TF:* 800-968-9801 ■ *Web:* con-tek.com	Saint Paul	MN	55110	651-779-6058	779-6571	111
Contemar Silo Systems Inc 30 Pennsylvania Ave Unit 8 *TF:* 800-567-2741 ■ *Web:* contemar.com	Concord	ON	L4K4A5	905-669-3604		296
Contempo Ceramic Tile Corp 3732 South 300 West *Web:* contempotile.com	Salt Lake City	UT	84115	801-262-1717		191-1
Contempora Fabrics Inc 351 Contempora Dr *Web:* www.contemporafabrics.com	Lumberton	NC	28358	910-738-7131	738-9575	745-4
Contemporary Art Museum Saint Louis 3750 Washington Blvd *Web:* camstl.org	Saint Louis	MO	63108	314-535-4660		520
Contemporary Arts Ctr 44 E Sixth St *Web:* www.contemporaryartscenter.org	Cincinnati	OH	45202	513-345-8400		50-2
Contemporary Arts Ctr 900 Camp St *Web:* www.cacno.org	New Orleans	LA	70130	504-528-3805	528-3828	572
Contemporary Arts Museum Houston 5216 Montrose Blvd *Web:* camh.org	Houston	TX	77006	713-284-8250	284-8275	520
Contemporary Control Systems Inc 2431 Curtiss St *Web:* www.ccontrols.com	Downers Grove	IL	60515	630-963-7070	963-0109	176
Contemporary Dance Theatre 1805 Larch Ave *Web:* www.cdt-dance.org	Cincinnati	OH	45224	513-591-1222		573-1
Contemporary Dayton, The 118 N Jefferson St *Web:* thecontemporarydayton.org	Dayton	OH	45402	937-224-3822		50-2

Phone | Fax | Class

Contemporary Electrical Services Inc
1954 Isaac Newton Sq W Reston VA 20190 703-255-9226 189-4
Web: www.cont-elec.com

Contemporary Galleries of KY Inc
220 N Hurstbourne Pky Louisville KY 40222 502-426-9273 321
Web: www.contemporarygalleries.com

Contemporary MicroSystems
5262 King St. Riverside CA 92506 626-487-7034 888-4425 174
Web: www.ipctechnology.com

Contemporary Productions LLC
190 Carondelet Plz Ste 1111 Saint Louis MO 63105 314-721-9090 181
Web: contemporaryproductions.com

Contemporary Software Concepts Inc
650 Park Ave Ste 205 Fort Washington PA 19456 610-687-6000 177
Web: www.consoftware.com

Contemporary Tours
100 Crossways Park Dr W Ste 400 Woodbury NY 11797 516-484-5032 760
TF: 800-627-8873 ■ *Web:* www.contemporarytours.com

Content Firm LLC, The
26 Academy Dr E Whippany NJ 07981 973-993-8098 195
Web: www.thecontentfirm.com

Content Is Queen Productions
6701 Old 28th St Ste Q Grand Rapids MI 49546 616-915-8444 177
Web: www.contentisqueen.com

Content Management Corp
4287 Technology Dr Fremont CA 94538 510-505-1100 627
TF: 877-495-3720 ■ *Web:* cmcondemand.com

Content Solutions 1413 E Mckinney St Denton TX 76209 940-384-9407 317
Web: www.yourcontentsolutions.com

Contenti Co, The
515 Narragansett Park Dr Pawtucket RI 02861 401-305-3000 305-3005 411
TF: 800-343-3364 ■ *Web:* contenti.com

Conterra Ultra Broadband LLC
2101 Rexford Rd Ste 200E Charlotte NC 28211 704-936-1806 652
TF: 800-634-1374 ■ *Web:* www.conterra.com

Con-Test Analytical Laboratory
39 Spruce St 2 East Longmeadow MA 01028 413-525-2332 743
Web: contestlabs.com

Contex Americas Inc
15737 Crabbs Branch Way Derwood MD 20855 240-399-5600 268-1118 196
Web: www.contex.com

Context Creative Inc
317 Adelaide St W Toronto ON M5V1P9 416-972-1439 195
Web: contextcreative.com

Context Publications
2448 Guerneville Rd Ste 800 Santa Rosa CA 95403 707-576-0100 575-6830 637-2
Web: www.contextpub.com

Contigo 2700 Production Way Ste 300 Burnaby BC V5A4X1 604-683-3106 648-9886 525
Web: www.contigo.com

Contiki Holidays 801 E Katella Ave Anaheim CA 92805 866-266-8454 760
TF: 800-944-5708 ■ *Web:* www.contiki.com

Continental Academie of Hair Design
102 Derry St Rte 102 Hudson NH 03051 603-889-1614 167-3
Web: www.continentalacademie.com

Continental Aerospace Technologies
2039 Broad St Mobile AL 36615 251-436-8292 21
TF: 800-326-0089 ■ *Web:* www.continental.aero

Continental Agency of Ct Inc
105 Sanford St Hamden CT 06518 203-281-6800 390
Web: canewengland.com

Continental Airlines Inc PO Box 4607 Houston TX 77067 713-952-1630 26
TF: 800-621-7467 ■ *Web:* www.united.com

Continental American Insurance Company Inc
PO Box 427 Columbia SC 29202 866-849-0011 390
Web: www.caicworksite.com

Continental Art Supplies
7041 Reseda Blvd Reseda CA 91335 818-345-1044 45
Web: www.continentalart.com

Continental Auctioneers School
2409 Hwy 9 Buffalo Center IA 50424 507-625-5595 625-6929 685
TF: 800-373-2255 ■ *Web:* www.auctioneerschool.com

Continental Battery Corp
4919 Woodall St Dallas TX 75247 214-631-5701 634-7846 74
TF: 800-442-0081 ■ *Web:* www.continentalbattery.com

Continental Binder & Specialty Corp
407 W Compton Blvd Gardena CA 90248 310-324-8227 715-6740 86
TF: 800-872-2897 ■ *Web:* www.continentalbinder.com

Continental Bindery Corp
1250 Pratt Blvd Elk Grove Village IL 60007 847-439-6811 439-6847 92

Continental Book Company Inc
7000 Broadway Ste 102 Denver CO 80221 303-289-1761 279-1764* 95
**Fax Area Code:* 800 ■ *TF:* 800-364-0350 ■ *Web:* www.continentalbook.com

Continental Cabinet Inc 2841 Pierce St Dallas TX 75233 214-467-4444 115

Continental Cast Stone Manufacturing Inc
22001 W 83rd St Shawnee KS 66227 800-989-7866 422-7272* 724
**Fax Area Code:* 913 ■ *TF:* 800-989-7866 ■ *Web:* www.continentalcaststone.com

Continental Cement Company LLC
16401 Swingley Ridge Rd Ste 610 Chesterfield MO 63017 636-532-7440 532-7445 135
TF: 800-625-1144 ■ *Web:* www.continentalcement.com

Continental Coatings Inc
10938 Beech Ave Fontana CA 92337 909-355-1200 355-2061 550
Web: continentalyca.com

Continental Coin & Jewlery Co
5627 Sepulveda Blvd Van Nuys CA 91411 818-781-4232 782-6779 411
TF: 800-552-6467 ■ *Web:* dmndlimited.com

Continental Colorcraft
1166 W Garvey Ave Monterey Park CA 91754 323-283-3000 283-3206 781
Web: www.continentalcolorcraft.com

Continental Commercial Products (CCP)
11840 Westline Industrial Dr Saint Louis MO 63146 800-325-1051 327-5492 508
TF: 800-325-1051 ■ *Web:* www.continentalcommercialproducts.com

Continental Cordage 75 Burton St Cazenovia NY 13035 315-655-9800 655-9686 492
Web: www.iwgcontinentalcordage.com

Continental Currency Services Inc (CCS)
PO Box 10970 Santa Ana CA 92711 714-667-6699 569-0882 217
Web: www.ccurr.com

Continental Development Corp
2041 Rosecrans Ave Ste 200 El Segundo CA 90245 310-640-1520 414-9279 685
Web: www.continentaldevelopment.com

Continental Disc Corp
3160 W Heartland Dr Liberty MO 64068 816-792-1500 792-2277 789
Web: www.contdisc.com

Continental Divide Electric Co-opeartive Inc (CDEC)
200 E High St PO Box 1087 Grants NM 87020 505-285-6656 287-2234 245
TF: 877-775-5211 ■ *Web:* www.cdec.coop

Continental Divide Trail Society (CDTS)
3704 N Charles St Ste 601 Baltimore MD 21218 410-235-9610 48-23
Web: www.cdtsociety.org

Continental Electric Company Inc
9501 E Fifth Ave PO Box 2710 Gary IN 46403 219-938-3460 938-3469 189-4
Web: www.continentalelectric.com

Continental Electric Motors Inc
23 Sebago St Clifton NJ 07013 800-335-6718 518
TF: 800-335-6718 ■ *Web:* www.cecoinc.com

Continental Electronics Corp
4212 S Buckner Blvd Dallas TX 75227 214-381-7161 381-4949 647
TF: 800-733-5011 ■ *Web:* contelec.com

Continental Fabricators Inc
5601 W Park Ave Saint Louis MO 63110 314-781-6300 781-1290 91
Web: confabinc.com

Continental Fire Sprinkler Co
4518 S 133rd St Omaha NE 68137 402-330-5170 610
TF: 800-543-5170 ■ *Web:* www.continental-fire.com

Continental Flowers Inc 8101 NW 21 St Miami FL 33122 800-327-2715 292
TF: 800-327-2715 ■ *Web:* www.continentalflowers.com

Continental Forge Company Inc
412 E El Segundo Blvd Compton CA 90222 310-603-1014 483
Web: www.cforge.com

Continental Glass Systems Inc
325 W 74th Pl Hialeah FL 33014 305-231-1101 256
Web: www.cgsfl.com

Continental Health Care Inc
205 Wild Basin Rd S Austin TX 78746 512-906-1756 906-1877 363
Web: continentalhealthcareinc.com

Continental Heritage Insurance
200 Park Ave Ste 400 Orange Village OH 44122 440-229-3420 390
Web: continentalheritage.com

Continental Inc 1524 Jackson St Anderson IN 46016 765-298-8020 302
TF: 800-875-4557 ■ *Web:* www.continentalinc.com

Continental Linen Services
4200 Manchester Rd Kalamazoo MI 49001 800-878-4357 442
TF: 800-878-4357 ■ *Web:* www.clsimage.com

Continental Machines Inc
5505 W 123rd St Savage MN 55378 888-362-5572 895-6450* 455
**Fax Area Code:* 952 ■ *TF:* 888-362-5572 ■ *Web:* www.doallsaws.com

Continental Metal Products Co
35 Olympia Ave Woburn MA 01888 781-935-4400 427
Web: continentalmetal.com

Continental Mineral Processing Corp
11817 Mosteller Rd Cincinnati OH 45241 513-771-7190 771-9153 500
Web: www.continentalmineral.com

Continental Office Furniture & Supply Corp
2601 Silver Dr Columbus OH 43211 614-262-5010 320
Web: www.continentaloffice.com

Continental Paper Grading Company Inc
1623 S Lumber St Chicago IL 60616 312-226-2010 226-2025 660
Web: www.cpgco.com

Continental Pump Co
29425 State Hwy B Warrenton MO 63383 636-456-6006 456-4337 641
Web: www.continentalultrapumps.com

Continental Resources Inc
175 Middlesex Tpke Bedford MA 01730 781-275-0850 176
TF: 800-937-4688 ■ *Web:* www.conres.com

Continental Safety Equipment
2935 Waters Rd Ste 140 Eagan MN 55121 651-454-7233 454-3217 679
TF: 800-844-7003 ■ *Web:* www.csesafety.com

Continental School of Beauty Culture
215 Main St Batavia NY 14020 585-344-0886 685
TF: 877-317-7170 ■ *Web:* continentalschoolofbeauty.edu

Continental Service Group Inc
200 Cross Keys Office Pk Fairport NY 14450 585-421-1000 160
TF: 800-724-7500 ■ *Web:* www.conserve-arm.com

Continental Shelf Associates Inc
8502 SW Kansas Ave Stuart FL 34997 772-219-3000 219-3010 194
Web: www.conshelf.com

Continental Stock Transfer & Trust Company Inc
17 Battery Pl New York NY 10004 212-509-4000 690
Web: www.continentalstock.com

Continental Studwelding Ltd
35 Devon Rd Brampton ON L6T5B6 905-792-3650 792-3711 481
TF: 800-848-9442 ■ *Web:* www.constud.ca

Continental Tire the Americas LLC
PO Box 3010 Fort Mill SC 29716 704-588-1600 754
Web: www.continentaltire.com

Continental Traffic Service Inc (CTSI)
5100 Poplar Ave 15th Fl Memphis TN 38137 901-766-1500 766-1520 311
TF: 888-836-5135 ■ *Web:* www.ctsi-global.com

Continental Van Lines Inc
4501 W Marginal Way SW Seattle WA 98106 800-426-0286 780
TF: 800-426-0286 ■ *Web:* www.continentalvan.com

Continental Web Press Inc
1430 Industrial Dr Itasca IL 60143 630-773-1903 627
Web: www.continentalweb.com

Continental Western Group
11201 Douglas Ave Urbandale IA 50322 515-473-3000 391-4
TF: 800-235-2942 ■ *Web:* www.cwgins.com

Continental, The 138 Market St Philadelphia PA 19106 215-923-6069 671
Web: continentalmartinibar.com

Continental-Capri Inc
250 Jackson St Englewood NJ 07631 201-568-7100 296-26

Contingent Workforce Solutions Inc
2430 Meadowpine Blvd Ste 101 Mississauga ON L5N6S2 866-837-8630 2
TF: 866-837-8630 ■ *Web:* www.cwsolutions.ca

Continuent Inc
535 Mission St 14th Fl San Francisco CA 94105 800-270-9035 178-1
TF: 800-270-9035 ■ *Web:* www.continuent.com

Name / Address	City	State	Zip	Phone	Fax	Class
Continuous Metal Technology Inc 439 W Main St	Ridgway	PA	15853	814-772-9274	772-4345	697
Web: www.powdered-metal.com						
Continuum 532 Gibraltar Dr	Milpitas	CA	95035	408-727-3240	727-3550	425
TF: 888-532-1064 ■ *Web:* amplitude-laser.com						
Continuum Legal 1700 Old Meadow Rd Ste 100	McLean	VA	22102	703-734-7474		721
Web: continuumlegal.com						
Contour Hardening Inc 8401 NW Blvd	Indianapolis	IN	46278	317-876-1530	879-2484	318
TF: 888-867-2184 ■ *Web:* contourhardening.com						
Contour Products Inc 1430 W Pointe Dr Ste K	Charlotte	NC	28214	704-527-6133		366
Web: contourliving.com						
Contour Saws Inc 900 Graceland Ave	Des Plaines	IL	60016	800-259-6834		682
TF: 800-259-6834 ■ *Web:* www.contoursawsinc.com						
Contour Tool Inc 38830 Taylor Pkwy	North Ridgeville	OH	44039	440-365-7333	365-7335	621
Web: www.contourprecisionmilling.com						
Contoural Inc 5150 El Camino Real Ste D-30	Los Altos	CA	94022	650-390-0800		194
Web: www.contoural.com						
Contra Costa College 2600 Mission Bell	San Pablo	CA	94806	510-235-7800	412-0769	162
Web: www.contracosta.edu						
Contra Costa County 651 Pine St 10th Fl	Martinez	CA	94553	925-335-1080	335-1098	338
Web: www.contracosta.ca.gov						
Contra Costa County Library 75 Santa Barbara Rd	Pleasant Hill	CA	94523	800-984-4636	646-6461*	434-3
**Fax Area Code:* 925 ■ *TF:* 800-984-4636 ■ *Web:* www.ccclib.org						
Contra Costa Health Services 2500 Alhambra Ave	Martinez	CA	94553	925-370-5000	370-5138	374-3
TF: 877-661-6230 ■ *Web:* cchealth.org						
Contract Converting LLC W6580 Quality Ct	Greenville	WI	54942	800-734-0990	734-0994	92
TF: 800-734-0990 ■ *Web:* www.contractconverting.com						
Contract Design Magazine 100 Broadway 14th Fl	New York	NY	10005	800-697-8859	564-9453*	457-5
**Fax Area Code:* 847 ■ *TF:* 800-697-8859 ■ *Web:* www.contractdesign.com						
Contract Environments Inc 1020 W 18th St	Wilmington	DE	19802	302-658-0668		393
Web: www.contractenvironments.us						
Contract Fabrication & Design LLC 5427 Fm 546	Princeton	TX	75407	972-736-2260		529
Web: cfdintl.com						
Contract Fabricators Inc 105 Rolfing Rd	Holly Springs	MS	38635	662-252-6330		480
Web: contractfab.com						
Contract Filling Inc 10 Cliffside Dr	Cedar Grove	NJ	07009	973-239-6608	239-6692	214
Web: www.contractfillinginc.com						
Contract Furnishers of Hawaii Inc 50 S Beretania St C-208B	Honolulu	HI	96813	808-599-2411		321
Web: op-hawaii.com						
Contract Furnishings Mart 22230 84th Ave S Ste 110	Kent	WA	98032	253-234-2040	234-2039	290
Web: www.cfmfloors.com						
Contract Land Staff LLC 2245 Texas Dr Ste 200	Sugar Land	TX	77479	281-240-3370		194
TF: 800-874-4519 ■ *Web:* www.contractlandstaff.com						
Contract Lumber Inc (CL) 1590 W Northfield Dr	Brownsburg	IN	46112	317-852-8996	852-8999	191-3
Web: www.contractlumber.com						
Contract Manufacturers Inc 729 N Fleishel Ave	Tyler	TX	75702	903-597-8297		664
Web: www.cmitx.net						
Contract Packaging Resources Inc 8009 Industrial Village Rd	Greensboro	NC	27409	336-665-1300		582
Web: www.aenova-group.com						
Contract Pharmacal Corp 135 Adams Ave	Hauppauge	NY	11788	631-231-4610		479
Web: cpc.com						
Contract Pharmacy Services Inc 125 Titus Ave	Warrington	PA	18976	267-487-9000	487-9050	238
TF: 800-555-8062 ■ *Web:* www.contractpharmacy.com						
Contractors Cargo Co 500 S Alameda St	Compton	CA	90221	310-609-1957	609-1767	358
Web: contractorscargo.com						
Contractors Material Co 10320 S Medallion Dr	Cincinnati	OH	45241	513-733-3000		480
TF: 844-323-7623 ■ *Web:* cmcmmi.com						
Contractors Register Inc 800 E Main St	Jefferson Valley	NY	10535	800-431-2584	243-0287*	637-6
**Fax Area Code:* 914 ■ *TF:* 800-431-2584 ■ *Web:* www.thebluebook.com						
Contractors Scaffold Supply Inc 229 Harbor Way	South San Francisco	CA	94080	650-871-8190	871-8193	290
Web: contractorsscaffold.com						
Contractors State License Service 6347 Mission St	Daly City	CA	94014	650-244-9377		167-3
TF: 800-409-8237 ■ *Web:* www.contractorslicensingschools.com						
Contractors Steel Co 36555 Amrhein Rd	Livonia	MI	48150	734-464-4000	452-3939	492
TF: 800-521-3946 ■ *Web:* www.contractorssteel.com						
Contractual Carriers Inc 104 Alan Dr	Newark	DE	19711	302-453-1420		780
TF: 888-594-4771 ■ *Web:* www.contractualcarriers.com						
Contrans Corp 1179 Ridgeway Rd	Woodstock	ON	N4V1E3	519-421-4600		360-2
Web: www.contrans.ca						
Contrast Creative 2598 Highstone Rd	Cary	NC	27519	919-469-9151		514
Web: www.contrastcreative.com						
Contrex Inc 8900 Zachary Ln N	Maple Grove	MN	55369	763-424-7800		203
TF: 800-342-4411 ■ *Web:* www.contrexinc.com						
Control Alt Design Ltd 1760 Britannia Dr Ste 8	Elgin	IL	60124	847-695-4050		454
Web: controlalt.com						
Control Cable Inc 7261 Ambassador Rd	Baltimore	MD	21244	800-296-4411		173-1
TF: 800-296-4411 ■ *Web:* www.controlcable.com						
Control Design Inc 211 Ridc Pk W Dr	Pittsburgh	PA	15275	412-788-2280	424-0135	729
Web: controldesigninc.com						
Control Electronics Inc 148 Brandamore Rd	Brandamore	PA	19316	610-942-3190	942-3672	472
Web: www.controlelectronics.com						
Control Engineering Magazine 2000 Clearwater Dr	Oak Brook	IL	60523	630-288-8000	288-8580	457-21
Web: www.controleng.com						
Control Flow Inc 9201 Fairbanks N Houston Rd	Houston	TX	77064	281-890-8300	890-3947	790
TF: 800-231-9922 ■ *Web:* www.controlflow.com						
Control Gaging Inc 5200 Venture Dr	Ann Arbor	MI	48108	734-668-6750		201
Web: www.controlgaging.com						
Control Industries Inc 1700 Fostoria Ave Ste 300	Findlay	OH	45840	419-800-0129	500-9015	647
Web: www.controlindustriesinc.com						
Control Line Equipment Inc 14750 Industrial Pkwy	Cleveland	OH	44135	216-433-7766		223
TF: 888-895-1440 ■ *Web:* www.control-line.com						
Control Logistics Inc 1213 Pope Ln	Lake Worth	FL	33460	561-641-2031		60
Web: www.aerowindows.com						
Control Masters Inc 5235 Katrine Ave	Downers Grove	IL	60515	630-968-2390	968-3260	203
Web: www.controlmasters.com						
Control Micro Systems Inc 4420-A Metric Dr	Winter Park	FL	32792	407-679-9716	657-6883	425
Web: cmslaser.com						
Control Module Inc 89 Phoenix Ave	Enfield	CT	06082	860-745-2433		407
TF: 800-722-6654 ■ *Web:* controlmod.com						
Control Printing Group Inc 4212 S Hocker Dr Ste 150	Independence	MO	64055	816-350-8100		627
TF: 800-333-2820 ■ *Web:* www.controlgroup.biz						
Control Resources Inc 11 Beaver Brook Rd	Littleton	MA	01460	978-486-4160		203
Web: controlresources.com						
Control Risks Group Ltd 1600 K St NW Ste 700	Washington	DC	20006	202-449-3330		194
Web: www.controlrisks.com						
Control Southern Inc 3850 Lakefield Dr	Suwanee	GA	30024	770-495-3100	623-3663	358
Web: www.controlsouthern.com						
Control Specialists Inc 2021 W Lloyd Expy	Evansville	IN	47712	812-425-9249	425-9250	385
TF: 800-765-4274 ■ *Web:* www.gocsi.biz						
Control Stuff Inc 10550 County Rd 50	Cologne	MN	55322	952-466-2175	466-2177	203
Web: www.controlstuff.com						
Control Systems International Inc 8040 Nieman Rd	Lenexa	KS	66214	913-599-5010		177
Control Techniques Americas 7078 Shady Oak Rd	Eden Prairie	MN	55344	952-995-8000		709
TF: 800-893-2321 ■ *Web:* acim.nidec.com						
Control Technology Inc 5734 Middlebrook Pk	Knoxville	TN	37921	865-584-0440	584-5720	203
TF: 800-537-8398 ■ *Web:* www.controltechnology.com						
Controlled Access Inc 1515 W 130th St	Hinckley	OH	44233	330-273-6185		639
TF: 800-942-0829 ■ *Web:* www.controlledaccess.com						
Controlled Automation Inc 15421 Stony Creek Way	Noblesville	IN	46060	317-776-1099	776-1280	729
Web: www.controlledautomationinc.com						
Controlled Contamination Services LLC 6150 Lusk Blvd Ste B205	San Diego	CA	92121	888-263-9886		256
TF: 888-979-9608 ■ *Web:* cleanroomcleaning.com						
Controlled Kinematics Inc 46740 Lakeview Blvd	Fremont	CA	94538	408-945-1616		350
Web: www.ckinematics.com						
Controlled Magnetics Inc 10766 Plz Dr	Whitmore Lake	MI	48189	734-449-7225	449-7229	767
Web: www.controlledmagnetics.com						
Controlled Power Co 1955 Stephenson Hwy	Troy	MI	48083	248-528-3700	528-0411	767
TF: 800-521-4792 ■ *Web:* www.controlledpwr.com						
Controlled Power Inc 17909 Bothell Everett Hwy Ste 102	Bothell	WA	98012	425-485-1778	485-0658	729
Web: www.controlledpowerinc.com						
Controlled Release Technologies Inc 1016 Industry Dr	Shelby	NC	28152	704-487-0878		151
TF: 800-766-9057 ■ *Web:* cleanac.com						
Controllers Group Inc 1818 The Alameda	San Jose	CA	95126	408-294-0004		260
Web: www.controllersgroup.net						
Controls Corporation of America 1501 Harpers Rd	Virginia Beach	VA	23454	757-422-8330		45
TF: 800-225-0473 ■ *Web:* www.concoa.com						
Controls Southeast Inc PO Box 7500	Charlotte	NC	28241	704-588-3030	644-5100	595
Web: www.csiheat.com						
Convaid Products LLC 2830 California St	Torrance	CA	90503	310-618-0111	618-2166	477
TF: 888-266-8243 ■ *Web:* www.convaid.com						
Conval Inc 265 Field Rd	Somers	CT	06071	860-749-0761	763-3557	789
TF: 800-839-2117 ■ *Web:* www.conval.com						
Convenient Food Mart 123 Gateway Blvd N	Elyria	OH	44035	440-322-6301		345
Web: www.myconvenient.com						
Convention & Visitors Bureau of Marion County 1000 Cole St Ste A	Fairmont	WV	26554	304-368-1123		206
Web: marioncvb.com						
Convention Consultants Historic Savannah Foundation 117 W Perry St	Savannah	GA	31401	912-234-4088		184
TF: 800-559-6627 ■ *Web:* www.conventionconsultants.net						
Conventus 516 N Ogden Ave Ste 115	Chicago	IL	60642	312-421-3270		180
Web: www.northstar.io						
Conventus Orthopaedics Inc 10200 73rd Ave N Ste 122	Maple Grove	MN	55369	763-515-5000		477
TF: 855-418-6466 ■ *Web:* www.conventusortho.com						
Converged Communication Systems (CCS) 2930 Central St	Evanston	IL	60201	877-598-3999		180
TF: 877-598-3999 ■ *Web:* www.convergedsystems.com						

	Phone	Fax	Class
Convergence LLC 6 Journey Ste 160 . . . Aliso Viejo CA 92656 *Web:* www.convergence.net	949-716-8322		225
Convergent 190 Bluegrass Valley Pkwy . . . Alpharetta GA 30005 *Web:* www.convergent.com	770-369-9000	369-9100	736
Convergent Laser Technologies 1660 S Loop Rd . . . Alameda CA 94502 *Web:* www.convergentlaser.com	510-832-2130	832-1600	424
Convergent Photonics LLC 711 E Main St . . . Chicopee MA 01020 *Web:* www.primaelectro.com	413-598-5200	598-5201	425
Convergenz LLC 8260 Greensboro Dr Ste 200 . . . McLean VA 22102 **Fax Area Code:* 800 ■ *Web:* www.conv.com	703-584-3700	965-2691*	631
ConvergeOne LLC 3344 Hwy 149 . . . Eagan MN 55121 *TF:* 888-321-6227 ■ *Web:* www.convergeone.com	888-321-6227		387
Convergint Technologies LLC 1651 Wilkening Rd . . . Schaumburg IL 60173 *Web:* www.convergint.com	847-229-0222		693
Conversant LLC 101 North Wacker 23rd Fl . . . Chicago IL 60606 *Web:* www.conversantmedia.com	312-588-3600	588-3671	466
Conversation Arts Media PO Box 715 . . . Brooklyn NY 11215 *Web:* www.dongabor.com	718-768-0824		637-10
Converse College 580 E Main St . . . Spartanburg SC 29302 *TF:* 800-766-1125 ■ *Web:* www.converse.edu	864-596-9000	596-9225	166
Converse Consultants 717 S Myrtle Ave . . . Monrovia CA 91016 *Web:* www.converseconsultants.com	626-930-1200	930-1212	261
Converse County 107 N Fifth St . . . Douglas WY 82633 **Fax Area Code:* 866 ■ *Web:* www.conversecounty.org	307-358-2244	770-3590*	338
Converse International School of Languages 636 Broadway Ste 210 . . . San Diego CA 92101 *Web:* cisl.edu	619-239-3363	239-3778	423
Conversion Components Inc 2605 Decio Dr . . . Elkhart IN 46514 *Web:* www.conversioncomponents.com	574-264-4181	264-2823	60
Conversion Devices Inc 15481 Electronic Ln . . . Huntington Beach CA 92649 *Web:* www.cdipower.com	714-898-6551	894-9248	250
Convertech Inc 353 Richard Mine Rd . . . Wharton NJ 07885 *Web:* www.convertech.com	973-328-1850		628
Convexx 6865 S Ea Ste 101 . . . Las Vegas NV 89119 *Web:* convexx.com	702-450-7662		760
Convey Health Solutions 13621 NW 12th St Ste 100 . . . Sunrise FL 33323 *Web:* www.conveyhealthsolutions.com	954-903-5000	903-5002	352
Con-Vey Keystone Inc 526 NE Chestnut PO Box 1399 . . . Roseburg OR 97470 *Web:* www.con-vey.com	541-672-5506	672-2513	207
Convey Technology Inc 2 Campbell Dr . . . Somers NY 10589 *Web:* www.conveytechnology.com	914-277-7502		180
Conveyco Technologies Inc PO Box 1000 . . . Bristol CT 06011 *TF:* 800-229-8215 ■ *Web:* www.conveyco.com	860-589-8215	583-1384	385
Conveyer & Caster Corp 3501 Detroit Ave . . . Cleveland OH 44113 *TF:* 800-777-0600 ■ *Web:* www.cc-efi.com	216-631-4448		351
Conveyor Belt Service Inc 400 S 1st Ave . . . Virginia MN 55792 *TF:* 888-821-5939 ■ *Web:* www.cbsrubber.com	218-741-5939	741-5953	207
Conveyor Components Co 130 Seltzer Rd . . . Croswell MI 48422 *TF:* 800-233-3233 ■ *Web:* www.conveyorcomponents.com	810-679-4211		207
Conveyor Dynamics Inc 1111 W Holly St Ste A . . . Bellingham WA 98225 *Web:* conveyor-dynamics.com	360-671-2200		256
Conveyor Handling Company Inc 6715 Santa Barbara Ct . . . Elkridge MD 21075 *TF:* 877-553-2296 ■ *Web:* conveyorhandling.com	877-553-2296		358
Conveyor Technologies Inc 5313 Womack Rd . . . Sanford NC 27330 *Web:* www.conveyor-technologies.com	919-776-7227	774-3097	207
Conveyors Inc 620 S Fourth Ave . . . Mansfield TX 76063 *TF:* 800-243-9327 ■ *Web:* conveyorsinc.net	817-473-4645	473-3024	207
Convince & Convert 899 S College Mall Rd Ste 376 . . . Bloomington IN 47401 *Web:* www.convinceandconvert.com	602-616-1895		393
Convio Inc 11501 Domain Dr Ste 200 . . . Austin TX 78758 *TF:* 888-528-9501 ■ *Web:* www.convio.com	512-652-2600		180
Convoy 1700 7th Ave Ste 116 . . . Seattle WA 98101 *TF:* 855-526-6869 ■ *Web:* convoy.com	855-526-6869		311
Convoy Servicing Company Inc 3323 Jane Ln . . . Dallas TX 75247 *Web:* www.convoyservicing.com	214-638-3050		610
Conway & Greenwood 766 E Whitaker Mill Rd . . . Raleigh NC 27608 *Web:* www.conwaygreenwood.com	919-833-9000		260
Conway & Owen Inc 1455 Bluegrass Lakes Pkwy . . . Alpharetta GA 30004 *Web:* www.conway-owen.com	678-350-9000	350-9010	256
Conway Area Chamber of Commerce 900 Oak St . . . Conway AR 72032 *TF:* 800-750-8155 ■ *Web:* www.conwaychamber.org	501-327-7788	327-7790	139
Conway Area Chamber of Commerce 203 Main St . . . Conway SC 29526 *Web:* conwayscchamber.com	843-248-2273	248-0003	139
Conway Cemetery State Park 1 Capitol Mall . . . Little Rock AR 72201 *TF:* 888-287-2757 ■ *Web:* www.arkansasstateparks.com	888-287-2757		565
Conway County 117 S Moose St . . . Morrilton AR 72110 *Web:* conwaycountyar.com	501-354-9640		338
Conway Daily Sun 64 Seavey St PO Box 1940 . . . North Conway NH 03860 *Web:* www.conwaydailysun.com	603-356-3456		532-3
Conway Glass Tinting Plus 701 Sixth St . . . Conway AR 72032 *Web:* conwayglasstinting.net	501-450-7587		362
Conway Homer PC 16 Shawmut St . . . Boston MA 02116 *TF:* 855-880-5324 ■ *Web:* ccandh.com	617-695-1990	695-0880	41
Conway Import Company Inc 11051 W Addison St . . . Franklin Park IL 60131 **Fax Area Code:* 800 ■ *TF:* 800-323-8801 ■ *Web:* conwaydressings.com	847-455-5600	304-4021*	296-19
Conway MacKenzie Inc 401 S Old Woodward Ave Ste 340 . . . Birmingham MI 48009 *Web:* conwaymackenzie.com	248-433-3100		194
Conway Management Co 547 Amherst St Ste 106 . . . Nashua NH 03063 *TF:* 800-359-0099 ■ *Web:* www.conwaymgmt.com	603-889-1130		463
Conway Marketing Communications 6400 Baum Dr . . . Knoxville TN 37919 *TF:* 800-882-7875 ■ *Web:* conwaymktg.com	865-588-5731		7
Conway Medical Ctr 300 Singleton Ridge Rd . . . Conway SC 29526 *Web:* www.conwaymedicalcenter.com	843-347-7111		374-3
Conway Regional Medical Ctr 2302 College Ave . . . Conway AR 72034 *Web:* www.conwayregional.org	501-329-3831		374-3
Conway Services LLC 1220 Big Orange Rd . . . Cordova TN 38018 *Web:* www.conwayservices.net	901-384-3511		610
Conway, Olejniczak & Jerry SC 231 S Adams St . . . Green Bay WI 54301 *Web:* www.lcojlaw.com	920-437-0476	437-2868	428
Conxxus LLC 330 W Ottawa . . . Paxton IL 60957 *Web:* www.conxxus.com	217-379-2026		224
Conybeare Law Office PC 519 Main St . . . Saint Joseph MI 49085 *Web:* conybearelaw.com	269-983-0561		41
Conyers-Rockdale Chamber of Commerce 1186 Scott St . . . Conyers GA 30012 *Web:* conyers-rockdale.com	770-483-7049	922-8415	139
Cooch & Taylor 1000 W St The Brandywine Bldg 10th Fl . . . Wilmington DE 19801 *Web:* www.coochtaylor.com	302-984-3800		428
Cook & Boardman Inc 9347 D Ducks Ln Ste A . . . Charlotte NC 28273 **Fax Area Code:* 336 ■ *TF:* 855-447-8600 ■ *Web:* www.cookandboardman.com	704-334-8683	837-0678*	234
Cook Aviation Inc 970 S Kirby Rd . . . Bloomington IN 47403 *TF:* 800-880-3499 ■ *Web:* www.cookaviation.com	812-825-2392	825-3701	63
Cook Biotech Inc 1425 Innovation Pl . . . West Lafayette IN 47906 *TF:* 888-299-4224 ■ *Web:* www.cookbiotech.com	765-497-3355		85
Cook Brothers Inc 1740 N Kostner Ave . . . Chicago IL 60639 *Web:* www.cookbrothers.com	773-770-1200		321
Cook Brothers Insulation Inc 1405 St Louis Ave . . . Kansas City MO 64101 *TF:* 800-624-3043 ■ *Web:* cookbro.com	816-421-6300	842-4031	601
Cook Children's Medical Ctr 801 Seventh Ave . . . Fort Worth TX 76104 *TF:* 888-852-6635 ■ *Web:* www.cookchildrens.org	682-885-4000		374-1
Cook Coggin Engineers Inc 703 Crossover Rd PO Box 1526 . . . Tupelo MS 38802 *TF:* 877-807-4667 ■ *Web:* cookcoggin.com	662-842-7381	844-4564	261
Cook Concrete Products Inc 5461 Eastside Rd . . . Redding CA 96001 *Web:* www.cookconcreteproducts.com	530-243-2562	243-6881	183
Cook County 69 W Washington Ste 500 . . . Chicago IL 60602 *Web:* www.cookcountyclerk.com	312-603-5656	603-6767	338
Cook County 411 W Second St . . . Grand Marais MN 55604 *Web:* www.co.cook.mn.us	218-387-3610		338
Cook County College Teachers' Union 1901 W Carroll Ave Ste 200 . . . Chicago IL 60612 *Web:* ccctu.org	312-755-9400	614-4381	219
Cook Flatt & Strobel Engineers 2930 SW Woodside Dr . . . Topeka KS 66614 *Web:* cfse.com	785-272-4706		261
Cook Flavoring Co 200 Sherwood Rd . . . Paso Robles CA 93446 **Fax Area Code:* 805 ■ *TF:* 800-735-0545 ■ *Web:* www.cooksvanilla.com	800-735-0545	238-0111*	296-15
Cook Forest State Park PO Box 120 . . . Cooksburg PA 16217 *Web:* www.dcnr.pa.gov	814-744-8407		565
Cook Gm Super Store 1193 W Saginaw Rd . . . Vassar MI 48768 *Web:* www.cookgm.com	989-882-4074		57
Cook Hotel & Conference Ctr 3848 W Lakeshore Dr . . . Baton Rouge LA 70808 *TF:* 866-610-2665 ■ *Web:* www.thecookhotel.com	225-383-2665		377
Cook Inc PO Box 4195 . . . Bloomington IN 47402 *TF:* 800-457-4500 ■ *Web:* www.cookmedical.com	812-339-2235		476
Cook Inlet Region Inc 725 E Fireweed Ln Ste800 PO Box 93330 . . . Anchorage AK 99503 *TF:* 800-764-2474 ■ *Web:* www.ciri.com	907-274-8638		760
Cook M & A 212 W Kinzie St Ste 600 . . . Chicago IL 60654 *Web:* www.cookma.com	312-755-5750		266
Cook Medical Travel 1025 Acuff Rd . . . Bloomington IN 47404 *TF:* 800-542-1687 ■ *Web:* www.cookmedicaltravel.com	812-336-6811		771
Cook Memorial Public Library District 413 N Milwaukee Ave . . . Libertyville IL 60048 *Web:* www.cooklib.org	847-362-2330		434-3
Cook Paul (Rep R - CA) 1027 Longworth House Office Bldg . . . Washington DC 20515 *Web:* cook.house.gov	202-225-5861		342-2
Cook Pine Capital LLC 2 Sound View Dr 2nd Fl . . . Greenwich CT 06830 *Web:* www.cookpinecapital.com	203-861-2930		401
Cook School of Real Estate 4305 Freeport Blvd . . . Sacramento CA 95822 *Web:* www.cookrealty.net	916-451-6702	451-2754	685
Cook Security Group Inc 5841 SE International Way . . . Milwaukie OR 97222 *TF:* 844-305-2665 ■ *Web:* cooksecuritygroup.com	844-305-2665		693
Cook Street School of Fine Cooking 1937 Market St . . . Denver CO 80202 *Web:* cookstreet.com	303-308-9300	308-9400	163
Cook Systems Inc 6799 Great Oaks Rd Atrium II Ste 200 . . . Memphis TN 38138 *Web:* cooksys.com	901-757-8877		180
Cook Truck Equipment & Tools 2517 Starita Rd . . . Charlotte NC 28208 *TF:* 800-241-4210 ■ *Web:* www.cooktruck.com	704-392-4138		57

				Phone	Fax	Class
Cook's Corner 19152 Santiago Canyon Rd *Web:* cookscorners.com	Trabuco Canyon	CA	92679	949-858-0266		361
Cook's Ham Inc 200 S 2nd St *TF:* 800-332-8400 ■ *Web:* www.mycooksham.com	Lincoln	NE	68508	402-475-6700	475-4772	296-26
Cook's Illustrated Magazine PO Box 470739 *TF:* 800-526-8442 ■ *Web:* www.cooksillustrated.com	Brookline	MA	02447	617-232-1000		457-11
Cook's Pest Control Inc 1624 Fourth Ave SE *TF:* 800-239-9898 ■ *Web:* www.cookspest.com	Decatur	AL	35601	256-353-6461		577
Cookbook Publishers 11633 W 83rd Ter *TF:* 800-227-7282 ■ *Web:* cookbookpublishers.com	Lenexa	KS	66214	913-492-5900	492-5947	626
Cooke & Bieler LP 1700 Market St Ste 3222 *Web:* www.cooke-bieler.com	Philadelphia	PA	19103	215-567-1101	567-1681	401
Cooke County 101S Dixon *Web:* www.co.cooke.tx.us	Gainesville	TX	76240	940-668-5500	668-5522	338
Cooke County Electric Co-op 11799 W US Hwy 82 PO Box 530 *TF:* 800-962-0296 ■ *Web:* www.cceca.com	Muenster	TX	76252	940-759-2211	759-4122	245
Cooke Stationery Co 370 State St *Web:* cookestationery.com	Salem	OR	97301	503-581-1404		535
Cooke Trucking Company Inc 1759 S Andy Griffith Pkwy *TF:* 800-888-9502 ■ *Web:* www.cooketrucking.com	Mount Airy	NC	27030	336-786-5181	789-7132	780
Cooke's Crating Inc 3124 E 11th St *Web:* www.cookescrating.com	Los Angeles	CA	90023	323-268-5101	262-2001	549
Cooke's Seafood 1120 Iyannough Rd *Web:* cookesseafood.com	Hyannis	MA	02601	508-775-0450		671
Cookeville Area-Putnam County Chamber of Commerce 1 W First St *TF:* 800-264-5541 ■ *Web:* cookevillechamber.com	Cookeville	TN	38501	931-526-2211	526-4023	139
Cookeville Newspapers Inc 1300 Neal St *Web:* www.herald-citizen.com	Cookeville	TN	38501	931-526-9715		532-3
Cookeville Regional Medical Ctr (CRMC) 1 Medical Center Blvd *TF:* 800-897-1898 ■ *Web:* www.crmchealth.org	Cookeville	TN	38501	931-528-2541		374-3
Cookie Dough Creations (CDC) 22 W Chicago Ave *Web:* www.cookiedoughcreations.com	Naperville	IL	60540	630-369-4833	369-2833	297-3
Cookie Jar 1006 Cadillac Ct *Web:* cookiejarfairbanks.com	Fairbanks	AK	99701	907-479-8319		671
Cookies By Design Inc 1865 Summit Ave Ste 605 *TF:* 800-945-2665 ■ *Web:* www.cookiesbydesign.com	Plano	TX	75074	972-398-9536	398-9542	310
Cookies The Kids Department Store 510 Fulton St *TF:* 877-942-6654 ■ *Web:* www.cookieskids.com	Brooklyn	NY	11201	718-797-3300		229
Cook-Illinois Corp 2100 Clearwater Dr *Web:* cookillinois.com	Oak Brook	IL	60523	708-560-9840		109
Cookin' Cajun co Creole Delicacies 533 St Ann St *Web:* www.cookincajun.com	New Orleans	LA	70116	504-523-6425		167-3
Cooking Fools 1916 W North Ave *Web:* www.cookingfools.net	Chicago	IL	60622	773-276-5565		167-3
Cooking Light Magazine 2100 Lakeshore Dr *TF:* 800-366-4712 ■ *Web:* www.cookinglight.com	Birmingham	AL	35209	205-445-6000	445-6600	457-13
Cooks Pharmacy of Kingston Inc 777 Wyoming Ave *Web:* cookspharmacykingston.com	Kingston	PA	18704	570-288-3633		237
Cooksey Toolen Gage Duffy & Woog 535 Anton Blvd 10 Fl *Web:* cookseylaw.com	Costa Mesa	CA	92626	714-431-1002		41
Cookshack 2304 N Ash St *TF:* 800-423-0698 ■ *Web:* www.cookshack.com	Ponca City	OK	74601	580-765-3669		361
Cookson Co 2417 S 50th Ave *TF:* 800-294-4358 ■ *Web:* www.cooksondoor.com	Phoenix	AZ	85043	602-272-4244		234
Cookson Hills Electric Cooperative Inc 1002 E Main St **Fax Area Code:* 918 ■ *TF:* 800-328-2368 ■ *Web:* www.cooksonhills.com	Stigler	OK	74462	800-328-2368	967-2610*	245
Cookson Peirce & Company Inc 555 Grant St Ste 380 *Web:* www.cooksonpeirce.com	Pittsburgh	PA	15219	412-471-5320		401
CookTek LLC 156 N Jefferson St Ste 300 *TF:* 888-266-5835 ■ *Web:* www.cooktek.com	Chicago	IL	60661	312-563-9600		36
Cool Amphibious Manufacturers International LLC 714 Okeetee Rd *Web:* www.camillc.com	Ridgeland	SC	29936	843-717-2444	717-2424	120
Cool Check 25 Coronet Rd Unit 4 *Web:* coolcheck.ca	Etobicoke	ON	M8Z2L8	416-236-1000	236-4323	610
Cool Earth Solar Inc 4659 Las Positas Rd Ste C *Web:* www.coolearthsolar.com	Livermore	CA	94551	925-454-8506		357
Cool Energy Inc 5541 Central Ave Ste 172 *Web:* coolenergy.com	Boulder	CO	80301	303-442-2121		357
Cool Gear International LLC 10 Cordage Park Cir *TF:* 855-393-2665 ■ *Web:* shop.coolgearinc.com	Plymouth	MA	02360	855-393-2665		361
Cool River Cafe 1045 Hidden Rdg *Web:* www.coolrivercafe.com	Irving	TX	75038	972-871-8881	871-8882	671
Coolant Control Inc 5353 Spring Grove Ave *TF:* 800-535-3885 ■ *Web:* coolantcontrol.com	Cincinnati	OH	45217	513-471-8770		146
Cooley Dickinson Hospital 30 Locust St *Web:* www.cooleydickinson.org	Northampton	MA	01060	413-582-2000		374-3
Cooley Gallery Inc, The 25 Lyme St *Web:* cooleygallery.com	Old Lyme	CT	06371	860-434-8807	434-7526	42
Cooley Group 50 Esten Ave *TF:* 800-992-0072 ■ *Web:* www.cooleygroup.com	Pawtucket	RI	02860	401-724-9000		745-2
Cooley LLP 3000 El Camino Real *Web:* www.cooley.com	Palo Alto	CA	94306	650-843-5000	849-7400	428
Cooley Motors Corp 401 N Greenbush Rd *Web:* www.cooleyvw.com	Rensselaer	NY	12144	518-283-2902		57
Coolidge State Park 855 Coolidge State Park Rd *Web:* www.vtstateparks.com	Plymouth	VT	05056	802-672-3612		565
Cooling Technology Inc 1800 Orr Industrial Ct *Web:* www.coolingtechnology.com	Charlotte	NC	28213	704-596-4109	597-8697	14
Cooling Technology Institute (CTI) 3845 Cypress Creek Pkwy Ste 420 *Web:* www.coolingtechnology.org	Houston	TX	77068	281-583-4087	537-1721	48-12
Cooling Tower Technologies 52410 Clark Rd *TF:* 800-882-1361 ■ *Web:* www.cttillc.com	White Castle	LA	70788	225-545-3970	545-4151	596
Coolmore America 5095 Frankfort Rd *Web:* coolmore.com	Versailles	KY	40383	859-873-7088		368
Cool-Rite Cooler Company Inc 3316 Conti St **Fax Area Code:* 866 ■ *TF:* 866-754-2738 ■ *Web:* coolrite.net	New Orleans	LA	70119	504-822-4886	402-6893*	665
CoolSprings Galleria 1800 Galleria Blvd *Web:* www.coolspringsgalleria.com	Franklin	TN	37067	615-771-2050		460
CoolTronics 220 E Madison St Ste 1220 *Web:* www.cooltronics.com	Tampa	FL	33602	813-259-4407		791
Coon Memorial Home Health 1411 Denver Ave *Web:* www.dhchd.org	Dalhart	TX	79022	806-244-8738		363
Coon Valley Telecommunications 105 Central Ave *Web:* www.coonvalleytel.com	Coon Valley	WI	54623	608-452-3101		225
Cooner Wire Co 9265 Owensmouth Ave *Web:* www.coonerwire.com	Chatsworth	CA	91311	818-882-8311	709-8281	813
Cooney State Park PO Box 254 *Web:* stateparks.mt.gov	Joliet	MT	59041	406-445-2326		565
Cooney Trybus Kwavnick Peets LLC 1600 W Commercial Blvd Ste 200 *Web:* ctkplaw.com	Fort Lauderdale	FL	33309	954-568-6669		41
Coons Christopher A (Sen D - DE) 218 Russell Senate Office Bldg *Web:* www.coons.senate.gov	Washington	DC	20510	202-224-5042		342-2
Coontail 5466 Park St *TF:* 888-874-0885 ■ *Web:* coontail.com	Boulder Junction	WI	54512	888-874-0885		711
Coop Ale Works LLC 4745 Council Heights Rd *Web:* coopaleworks.com	Oklahoma City	OK	73179	405-842-2667		102
Co-op Elevator Co 7211 E Michigan Ave *TF:* 800-968-0601 ■ *Web:* www.coopelev.com	Pigeon	MI	48755	989-453-4500	453-3942	275
Coop Purdel LA 155 Rue Saint-Jean-Baptiste *Web:* www.purdel.qc.ca	Le Bic	QC	G0L1B0	418-736-4363		111
Co-opeartive America 1612 K St NW Ste 600 *TF:* 800-584-7336 ■ *Web:* www.greenamerica.org	Washington	DC	20006	202-872-5307	331-8166	48-13
Co-opeartive Feed Dealers Inc 380 Broome Corporate Pkwy PO Box 670 *TF:* 800-333-0895 ■ *Web:* www.cfd.coop	Conklin	NY	13748	607-651-9078		276
Co-opeartive Financial Services Inc 9692 Haven Ave *TF:* 800-782-9042 ■ *Web:* www.co-opfs.org	Rancho Cucamonga	CA	91730	800-782-9042		393
Co-opeartive Gas Inc PO Box 27 *TF:* 888-578-5752 ■ *Web:* www.ballooncountry.com	Pauline	SC	29374	864-583-6546	948-0623	316
Cooper & Company Inc 10179 Commerce Park Dr *Web:* www.dakotawatchsales.com	Cincinnati	OH	45246	513-671-6067		410
Cooper Aerial Survey Co 1692 W Grant Rd *TF:* 800-229-2279 ■ *Web:* cooperaerial.com	Tucson	AZ	85745	520-884-7580		727
Cooper Aerobics 12200 Preston Rd *TF:* 866-906-2667 ■ *Web:* www.cooperaerobics.com	Dallas	TX	75230	972-560-2667		48-17
Cooper Atkins Corp 33 Reeds Gap Rd *TF:* 800-835-5011 ■ *Web:* www.cooper-atkins.com	Middlefield	CT	06455	860-349-3473	349-8994	201
Cooper Carry Inc 191 Peachtree St NE Ste 2400 *Web:* www.coopercarry.com	Atlanta	GA	30303	404-237-2000	237-0276	261
Cooper Companies Inc, The 6140 Stoneridge Mall Rd Ste 590 *Web:* www.coopercos.com	Pleasanton	CA	94588	925-460-3600		353
Cooper Consulting Service (CCS) 211 E Parkwood Ave Ste 200 *Web:* www.cooperconsultingservice.com	Friendswood	TX	77546	281-482-9786		261
Cooper County 200 Main St *Web:* www.coopercountymo.gov	Boonville	MO	65233	660-882-2114	882-5645	338
Cooper Drug Inc 509 State St *Web:* cooperdrugstore.com	Augusta	KS	67010	316-775-2289	775-2280	237
Cooper Engineering Company Inc 2600 College Dr *Web:* www.cooperengineering.net	Rice Lake	WI	54868	715-234-7008		261
Cooper Farms 22348 County Rd 140 PO Box 547 *Web:* www.cooperfarms.com	Oakwood	OH	45873	419-594-3325	594-3372	10-8
Cooper Green Hospital 1515 Sixth Ave S *Web:* www.coopergreen.org	Birmingham	AL	35233	205-930-3200		374-3
Cooper High School 3639 Sayles Blvd *Web:* www.abileneisd.org	Abilene	TX	79605	325-691-1000		685
Cooper Hosiery Mills Inc 4005 Gault Ave N *Web:* cooperhosiery.com	Fort Payne	AL	35967	256-845-1491		155-10
Cooper Hotel & Conference Ctr 12230 Preston Rd *Web:* cooperaerobics.com	Dallas	TX	75230	972-386-0306		379
Cooper Hotels 1661 Arrion Brainner Dr Ste 200 *Web:* www.cooperhotels.com	Memphis	TN	38120	901-322-1400	322-1403	379
Cooper Jim (Rep D - TN) 1536 Longworth House Office Bldg *Web:* cooper.house.gov	Washington	DC	20515	202-225-4311	226-1035	342-2

	Phone	Fax	Class
Cooper Lake State Park 1664 Farm Rd 1529 S. . . . . Cooper TX 75432 *Web:* tpwd.texas.gov	903-395-3100		565
Cooper Learning Systems PO Box 642679 . . . . . Los Angeles CA 90064 *TF:* 866-499-0900 ■ *Web:* www.englishskills.com	866-499-0900		637-2
Cooper Legal Services Dwayne E Cooper Attorney at Law 718 S Washinton St . . . . . Marion IN 46953 *TF:* 800-959-1825 ■ *Web:* cooperlegalservices.com	765-573-3133		428
Cooper Machine Company Inc 50 W Smith St . . . . . Wadley GA 30477 *Web:* www.coopermachine.com	478-252-5885	252-1866	821
Cooper Motors Lincoln 985 York St . . . . . Hanover PA 17331 *TF:* 866-414-2809 ■ *Web:* www.coopermotorslincoln.com	866-414-2809		57
Cooper Perkins Inc 10 Maguire Rd . . . . . Lexington MA 02421 *Web:* cooperperkins.com	781-538-5536		463
Cooper Pugeda Management Inc 65 Mccoppin St . . . . . San Francisco CA 94103 *Web:* www.cpmservices.com	415-543-6515		186
Cooper Smith Advertising 3500 Granite Cir. . . . . Toledo OH 43617 *TF:* 800-215-8812 ■ *Web:* cooper-smith.com	419-470-5900	470-5912	4
Cooper Split Roller Bearing Corp, The 5365 Robin Hood Rd Ste B. . . . . Norfolk VA 23513 *Web:* www.cooperbearings.com	757-460-0925		75
Cooper Standard 39550 Orchard Hill Place . . . . . Novi MI 48375 *Web:* www.cooperstandard.com	248-596-5900	596-6535	60
Cooper Steel Inc 503 N Hillcrest Dr. . . . . Shelbyville TN 37160 *Web:* www.coopersteel.com	931-684-7962		480
Cooper Street Correctional Facility 3100 Cooper St . . . . . Jackson MI 49201 *Web:* www.michigan.gov	517-780-6175		213
Cooper Thomas LLC 923 V St NW . . . . . Washington DC 20001 *Web:* cooperthomas.com	202-387-8366		195
Cooper Tire & Rubber Co 701 Lima Ave . . . . . Findlay OH 45840 *NYSE: CTB* ■ *TF:* 800-854-6288 ■ *Web:* www.coopertire.com	419-423-1321		754
Cooper Union for the Advancement of Science & Art, The 30 Cooper Sq . . . . . New York NY 10003 *Web:* www.cooper.edu	212-353-4100	353-4327	166
Cooper University Hospital 3 Cooper Plz. . . . . Camden NJ 08103 *TF:* 800-826-6737 ■ *Web:* www.cooperhealth.org	856-342-2000		374-3
Cooper Zietz Engineers Inc 620 S W 5th Ave Ste 1225 . . . . . Portland OR 97204	503-253-5429		261
Cooper's Ale House 8065 Lake City Way NE. . . . . Seattle WA 98115 *Web:* www.coopersalehouse.com	206-522-2923		671
Cooper'S Furniture House Inc 820 E Chatham St. . . . . Cary NC 27511 *Web:* coopersfurniturenc.com	919-467-2401		321
Cooper's Seafood House 701 N Washington Ave . . . . . Scranton PA 18509 *Web:* www.coopers-seafood.com	570-346-6883		671
Cooper, Adel, Vu & Associated LPA 36 W Main St . . . . . Centerburg OH 43011 *TF:* 800-798-5297 ■ *Web:* cooperandadel.com	800-798-5297		41
Cooper, Moss, Resnick, Klein & Company LLP 15165 Ventura Blvd Ste 330 . . . . . Sherman Oaks CA 91403 *Web:* cmrkcpa.com	818-728-9868	728-9822	2
Cooper, Travis & Company PLC 3008 Poston Ave. . . . . Nashville TN 37203 *Web:* www.coopertravis.com	615-329-4500		2
Cooper/T Smith Stevedoring Co 118 N Royal St . . . . . Mobile AL 36602 *TF:* 833-260-4500 ■ *Web:* www.coopertsmith.com	251-431-6100		465
Cooperative Center Federal Credit Union 2001 Ashby Ave . . . . . Berkeley CA 94703 *TF:* 877-599-9586 ■ *Web:* coopfcu.org	510-845-6428		219
Cooperative Choice Network Credit Union 3919 N University St. . . . . Peoria IL 61614 *TF:* 800-757-7432 ■ *Web:* www.ccncu.com	309-672-5230	672-1990	219
Cooperative Communciations Inc 412 Washington Ave. . . . . Belleville NJ 07109 **Fax Area Code:* 201 ■ *Web:* www.cooperativenet.com	973-969-9680	531-0150*	736
Cooperative Energy 7037 US Hwy 49 . . . . . Hattiesburg MS 39402 *Web:* cooperativeenergy.com	601-268-2083		245
Cooperative Finance Association, The 11500 N Ambassador Dr Ste 300 . . . . . Kansas City MO 64153 *TF:* 877-835-5232 ■ *Web:* www.cfafs.com	816-214-4200	214-4221	216
Cooperative Forestiere Des Hautes-Laurentides 395 Boul Des Ruisseaux. . . . . Mont-Laurier QC J9L0H6 *Web:* www.cfhl.qc.ca	819-623-4422	623-6287	302
Cooperative Telephone Exchange 425 Parker St . . . . . Stanhope IA 50246 *TF:* 800-205-1110 ■ *Web:* www.cooptelexchange.com	515-826-3206	826-3200	224
Cooper-Hewitt National Design Museum (Smithsonian Institution) 2 E 91st St . . . . . New York NY 10128 *Web:* www.cooperhewitt.org	212-849-8400		520
Cooperman Lester Miller Carus LLP 1129 Northern Blvd Ste 402 . . . . . Manhasset NY 11030 *Web:* clmclaw.com	516-365-1400	365-1404	41
Coopers Creek Chemical Corp 884 River Rd. . . . . West Conshohocken PA 19428 *Web:* www.cooperscreekchemical.com	610-828-0375	828-9720	46
Coopers Rock State Forest 61 County Line Dr . . . . . Bruceton Mills WV 26525 *Web:* wvstateparks.com	304-594-1561		565
Coopersburg Plumbing Corp 203 Charles St . . . . . Coopersburg PA 18036 *TF:* 800-718-1256 ■ *Web:* www.coopersburgconstruction.com	610-282-4717	282-2951	612
CooperSurgical Inc 95 Corporate Dr . . . . . Trumbull CT 06611 **Fax Area Code:* 800 ■ *TF:* 800-645-3760 ■ *Web:* www.coopersurgical.com	203-929-6321	262-0105*	476
Cooptel 5521 Valcourt Airport Rd. . . . . Valcourt QC J0E2L0 *TF:* 888-532-2667 ■ *Web:* www.cooptel.ca	450-532-2667		224
Coordinated Equipment Co 1707 E Anaheim St. . . . . Wilmington CA 90744 *Web:* www.coordinatedcompanies.com	310-834-8535		385
Coordinating Council on Juvenile Justice & Delinquency Prevention 810 Seventh St NW. . . . . Washington DC 20531 *Web:* juvenilecouncil.gov	202-514-0582	307-2093	340-20
Coordinating Research Council Inc (CRC) 5755 N Point Pkwy Ste 265 . . . . . Alpharetta GA 30022 *Web:* crcao.org	678-795-0506	795-0509	49-19
Coors Distributing Co 5400 N Pecos St. . . . . Denver CO 80221 *Web:* www.cdccoors.com	303-433-6541	964-5577	81-1
CoorsTek Inc 600 Ninth St. . . . . Golden CO 80401 *TF:* 800-821-6110 ■ *Web:* www.coorstek.com	303-278-4000	271-7009	249
Coos Bay Public Library 525 W Anderson Ave . . . . . Coos Bay OR 97420 *Web:* www.coosbaylibrary.org	541-269-1101		434-3
Coos Bay-North Bend Visitor & Convention Bureau 200 S Bayshore Dr . . . . . Coos Bay OR 97420 *TF:* 800-824-8486 ■ *Web:* www.oregonsadventurecoast.com	541-269-0215	269-2861	206
Coos County 250 N Baxter St. . . . . Coquille OR 97423 *TF:* 800-452-6010 ■ *Web:* www.co.coos.or.us	541-396-3121	396-4861	338
Coos County PO Box 10. . . . . West Stewartstown NH 03597 *Web:* www.cooscountynh.us	603-246-3321	246-8117	338
Coosa County 9709 US Hwy 231 PO Box 10. . . . . Rockford AL 35136 *Web:* www.coosacountyal.com	256-377-2420	377-2524	338
Coosa Pines Federal Credit Union 17591 Plant Rd. . . . . Childersburg AL 35044 *TF:* 800-237-9789 ■ *Web:* www.coosapinesfcu.org	256-378-5559	378-3881	219
Coosa Valley Electric Cooperative Inc 69220 Alabama Hwy 77 N . . . . . Talladega AL 35161 *TF:* 800-273-7210 ■ *Web:* www.billing.coosavalleyec.com	256-362-4180		245
Coosa Valley HomeCare 209 W Spring St. . . . . Sylacauga AL 35150 *Web:* lhcgroup.com	256-208-0087		374-3
Coos-Curry Electric Co-opeartive Inc 43050 Hwy 101 PO Box 1268. . . . . Port Orford OR 97465 *Web:* www.ccec.coop	541-332-3931	332-3501	245
COP Communications Inc 620 W Elk Ave . . . . . Glendale CA 91204 *Web:* www.copprints.com	818-291-1100	291-1192	627
COPE Inc 1120 G St NW Ste 550 . . . . . Washington DC 20005 *TF:* 800-247-3054 ■ *Web:* www.cope-inc.com	202-628-5100	628-5111	462
Cope Little LLC 14045 Ballantyne Corporate Pl Ste 375 . . . . . Charlotte NC 28277 *Web:* lclirm.com	980-406-5988		390
Cope Plastics Inc 4441 Industrial Dr . . . . . Alton IL 62002 *TF:* 800-851-5510 ■ *Web:* www.copeplastics.com	618-466-0221	466-7975	603
Cope's Knotty Pine Cafe 1530 Norris Rd. . . . . Bakersfield CA 93308 *Web:* copes-knotty-pine-cafe.cafe-inspector.com	661-399-0120		671
Copeland Capital Management LLC 8 Tower Bridge 161 Washington St Ste 1325. . . . . Conshohocken PA 19428 *Web:* www.copelandcapital.com	484-351-3665		401
Copeland Industries 6841 Ave U . . . . . Houston TX 77011 *Web:* www.copelandballvalves.com	713-926-7481	926-9806	454
Copeland Law Firm PC 212 Valley St NW . . . . . Abingdon VA 24210 *Web:* www.rcopelandlaw.com	276-628-9525	628-4711	445
Copeland's of New Orleans 1665 E Industrial Loop . . . . . Shreveport LA 71106 *Web:* copelandsofneworleans.com	318-797-0143		671
Copenhagen 1701 E Camelback Rd . . . . . Phoenix AZ 85016 *Web:* www.copenhagenliving.com	602-266-8060		321
Copernicus Group Independent Review Board 5000 CentreGreen Way Ste 200 . . . . . Cary NC 27513 *TF:* 888-303-2224 ■ *Web:* www.cgirb.com	919-465-4310	465-4311	743
Copesan Services Inc W175 N5711 Technology Dr. . . . . Menomonee Falls WI 53051 *TF:* 800-267-3726 ■ *Web:* www.copesan.com	800-267-3726		577
Copia International Ltd 1220 Iroquois Dr Ste 180 . . . . . Naperville IL 60563 *TF:* 800-689-8898 ■ *Web:* www.copia.com	630-778-8898	778-8848	173-3
Copiah-Lincoln Community College *Natchez* 1028 JC Redd Dr . . . . . Wesson MS 39191 *Web:* www.colin.edu	601-442-9111		162
Copic Insurance Co 7351 Lowry Blvd . . . . . Denver CO 80230 *TF:* 800-421-1834 ■ *Web:* www.callcopic.com	720-858-6000	858-6001	391-5
Copiers Northwest Inc 601 Dexter Ave N . . . . . Seattle WA 98109 *TF:* 866-692-0700 ■ *Web:* copiersnw.com	206-282-1200	282-2010	112
Copies Plus Printing Inc 717 N Main St . . . . . Springville UT 84663 *Web:* www.copiesplusprinting.com	801-489-3456		240
COPIRG (Colorado Public Interest Research Group) 1543 Wazee St Ste 330. . . . . Denver CO 80202 *Web:* copirg.org	303-573-7474		633
Coplan and Co 1107 First Ave Ste 907 . . . . . Seattle WA 98101 *Web:* www.coplan.com	206-715-2142		194
Co-Planar Inc 88 Ford Rd . . . . . Denville NJ 07834 *Web:* www.co-planar.com	973-625-3500	625-1849	488
Copley Controls Corp 20 Dan Rd. . . . . Canton MA 02021 *Web:* www.copleycontrols.com	781-828-8090	828-6547	472
Copley Hospital System 528 Washington Hwy . . . . . Morrisville VT 05661 *TF:* 800-564-1612 ■ *Web:* www.copleyvt.org	802-888-8888		374-3
Copley Square Hotel 47 Huntington Ave . . . . . Boston MA 02116 *TF:* 800-225-7062 ■ *Web:* www.copleysquarehotel.com	617-536-9000		379
Copoco Credit Union 4265 Wilder Rd . . . . . Bay City MI 48706 *Web:* copoco.org	989-684-1873		219
Coppel Corp 503 Scaroni Ave . . . . . Calexico CA 92231 *TF:* 800-220-7735 ■ *Web:* www.coppel.com	760-357-3707		96
Coppell Chamber of Commerce 509 W Bethel Rd Ste 200 . . . . . Coppell TX 75019 *Web:* coppellchamber.org	972-393-2829	393-0659	139
Copper Beech Inn, The 46 Main St. . . . . Ivoryton CT 06442 *Web:* www.copperbeechinn.com	860-767-0330		378
Copper Breaks State Park 777 Park Rd 62. . . . . Quanah TX 79252 *Web:* tpwd.texas.gov	940-839-4331		565

				Phone	Fax	Class
Copper Brite Inc 1482 E Valley Rd Ste 29 *Web:* www.copperbrite.com	Santa Barbara	CA	93108	805-565-1566		151
Copper Creek Canyon 3953 E 82nd St *Web:* www.coppercreekcanyon.com	Indianapolis	IN	46240	317-577-2990		321
Copper Development Association Inc 260 Madison Ave 16th Fl *TF:* 800-232-3282 ■ *Web:* www.copper.org	New York	NY	10016	212-251-7200	251-7234	49-13
Copper Falls State Park 36764 Copper Falls Rd *Web:* dnr.wi.gov	Mellen	WI	54546	715-274-5123		565
Copper Hills Youth Ctr 5899 Rivendell Dr **Fax Area Code:* 801 ■ *TF:* 800-776-7116 ■ *Web:* copperhillsyouthcenter.com	West Jordan	UT	84081	800-776-7116	569-2959*	374-1
Copper Mountain College 6162 Rotary Way *Web:* www.cmccd.edu	Joshua Tree	CA	92252	760-366-3791	366-5255	162
Copper Mountain Resort 209 Ten Mile Cir *TF:* 888-219-2441 ■ *Web:* www.coppercolorado.com	Frisco	CO	80443	866-841-2481		669
Copper Queen Hotel, The 11 Howell Ave *Web:* www.copperqueen.com	Bisbee	AZ	85603	520-432-2216	432-3819	379
Copper River Information Technology LLC 1577 C St Ste 201 *Web:* www.copperriverit.com	Anchorage	AK	99501	703-234-9000		631
Copper State Rubber of Arizona Inc 750 S 59th Ave *Web:* copperstaterubber.com	Phoenix	AZ	85043	713-644-1491		370
Copper Valley Electric Association Inc (CVEA) Mile 187 Glenn Hwy PO Box 45 *TF:* 866-835-2832 ■ *Web:* www.cvea.org	Glennallen	AK	99588	907-822-3211	822-5586	245
Copper Valley Telephone Cooperative Inc 329 Fairbanks Dr *Web:* www.cvinternet.net	Valdez	AK	99686	907-835-2231		224
Copper.Net Inc 895 Harcourt Rd *TF:* 888-336-3318 ■ *Web:* www.copper.net	Mount Vernon	OH	43050	888-336-3318		225
Copperas Cove Chamber of Commerce 204 E Robertson Ave *Web:* copperascove.com	Copperas Cove	TX	76522	254-547-7571	547-5015	139
Copperas Cove Independent School District 703 W Ave D *Web:* www.ccisd.com	Copperas Cove	TX	76522	254-547-1227		685
CopperGifts.com LLC 900 N 32nd St *Web:* www.coppergifts.com	Parsons	KS	67357	620-421-0654	421-0668	697
CopperLeaf Technologies Inc 2920 Virtual Wy Ste 140 *Web:* www.copperleaf.com	Vancouver	BC	V5M0C4	604-639-9700	639-9699	179
Coppersmith Consulting Inc 2121 N California Blvd Ste 290 *Web:* coppersmithconsulting.com	Walnut Creek	CA	94596	925-974-3335	932-3506	261
Copperstone Connect Inc 3308 Cindy Cres Ste 200 *Web:* www.copperstoneconnect.com	Mississauga	ON	L4Y3J6	416-849-2320	849-2316	196
CopperWynd Resort & Club 13225 N Eagle Ridge Dr *TF:* 877-707-7760 ■ *Web:* www.copperwynd.com	Scottsdale	AZ	85268	480-333-1900	333-1901	669
Coppi 3363 Yonge St *Web:* www.coppi.ca	Toronto	ON	M4N2M6	416-484-4464		671
Coppin State University 2500 W N Ave *TF:* 800-635-3674 ■ *Web:* www.coppin.edu	Baltimore	MD	21216	410-951-3600	523-7351	166
Copple Insurance Agency Inc 1640 L St *Web:* coppleinsurance.com	Lincoln	NE	68508	402-475-3213		390
Copple, Rockey, Mckeever & Schlecht PC LLO 2425 Taylor Ave *TF:* 888-860-2425 ■ *Web:* www.greatadvocates.com	Norfolk	NE	68701	402-371-4300		428
Copps Industries Inc 10600 N Industrial Dr *Web:* coppsindustries.com	Mequon	WI	53092	262-238-1700		290
COPS (Community Oriented Policing Services) 145 N St NE *TF:* 800-421-6770 ■ *Web:* cops.usdoj.gov	Washington	DC	20530	800-421-6770		340-14
COPS (Concerns of Police Survivors Inc) 846 Old S 5 PO Box 3199 *TF:* 800-784-2677 ■ *Web:* www.concernsofpolicesurvivors.org	Camdenton	MO	65020	573-346-4911	346-1414	48-21
Copy Cat Printing 365 N Broadwell Ave *TF:* 800-400-8520 ■ *Web:* www.copycatprinting.com	Grand Island	NE	68803	308-384-8520		627
Copy Products Inc 2103 W Vista *TF:* 800-337-2679 ■ *Web:* www.copyproductsinc.com	Springfield	MO	65807	417-889-5665		535
Copylite Products Corp 4491 S State Rd 7 Ste 210 *TF:* 800-989-6000 ■ *Web:* www.copylite.com	Fort Lauderdale	FL	33314	954-581-2470	581-2606	358
Copymat Digibranch 191 Battery St *Web:* www.copymat3.com	San Francisco	CA	94111	415-981-1300	981-1311	113
CopyPage Inc 11826 Stanwood Dr PO Box 64457	Los Angeles	CA	90066	310-822-1620		627
Copyright Clearance Center Inc (CCC) 222 Rosewood Dr *TF:* 855-239-3415 ■ *Web:* www.copyright.com	Danvers	MA	01923	978-750-8400	646-8600	49-16
Copyright Society of the USA 1 E 53rd St *Web:* www.csusa.org	New York	NY	10022	212-354-6401	354-2847	49-16
Copy-Rite Inc 1108 W 2nd Ave *TF:* 877-624-8503 ■ *Web:* www.copy-rite.com	Spokane	WA	99201	509-624-8503	456-0789	627
Copyworks 4837 First Ave SE Ste 103 *Web:* www.copyworks.com	Cedar Rapids	IA	52402	319-373-5335	373-5436	184
Coquitlam Public Library 1169 Pinetree Way *Web:* www.coqlibrary.ca	Coquitlam	BC	V3B0Y1	604-554-7323		434
Corad Technology Inc 3080 Olcott St Ste B202 *Web:* corad.com	Santa Clara	CA	95054	408-496-5511	496-1211	625
Coradix Technology Consulting Ltd 151 Slater St *Web:* www.coradix.com	Ottawa	ON	K1P5H3	613-234-0000	234-0988	194
Coral Beach Resort & Suites 1105 S Ocean Blvd *TF:* 800-843-2684 ■ *Web:* www.coralbeachmyrtlebeachresort.com	Myrtle Beach	SC	29577	800-314-8060		669
Coral Chemical Co 1915 Industrial Ave *TF:* 800-228-4646 ■ *Web:* www.coral.com	Zion	IL	60099	847-246-6666	246-6667	145
Coral Color Process Ltd 50 Mall Dr *TF:* 800-564-7303 ■ *Web:* www.coralcolor.com	Commack	NY	11725	631-543-5200		627
Coral Community Federal Credit Union 1930 NE 47th St Ste 120 *Web:* coralfcu.org	Fort Lauderdale	FL	33308	954-772-2330		219
Coral Gables Chamber of Commerce 224 Catalonia *Web:* coralgableschamber.org	Coral Gables	FL	33134	305-446-1657	446-9900	139
Coral Gables Hospital Inc (CGH) 3100 Douglas Rd *TF:* 866-728-3677 ■ *Web:* www.coralgableshospital.com	Coral Gables	FL	33134	305-445-8461	441-6879	374-3
Coral Hospitality LLC 9180 Galleria Ct Ste 600 *Web:* www.coralhospitality.com	Naples	FL	34109	239-449-1800		378
Coral Industries Inc 3010 Rice Mine Rd NE *Web:* coralind.com	Tuscaloosa	AL	35406	205-345-1013		610
Coral Productions Inc 100 Bickford St *Web:* www.coralproductions.com	Rochester	NY	14606	585-254-2580	458-1511	129
Coral Reef Restaurant 106 N Baltimore Ave *TF:* 866-627-8483 ■ *Web:* www.ocmdhotels.com	Ocean City	MD	21842	410-289-2612	289-3381	671
Coral Ridge Mall 1451 Coral Ridge Ave *Web:* www.coralridgemall.com	Coralville	IA	52241	319-625-5522		460
Coral Ridge Presbyterian Church Inc 5555 N Federal Hwy *Web:* www.crpc.org	Fort Lauderdale	FL	33308	954-771-8840		48-20
Coral Springs Auto Mall 9400 W Atlantic Blvd *TF:* 800-353-8660 ■ *Web:* www.coralspringsautomall.com	Coral Springs	FL	33071	954-369-1016		57
Coral Springs Center for the Arts 2855 Coral Springs Dr *Web:* www.thecentercs.com	Coral Springs	FL	33065	954-344-5990	344-5980	572
Coral Springs Coconut Creek Regional Chamber of Commerce 9500 W Sample Rd *TF:* 800-816-1256 ■ *Web:* www.csccrchamber.com	Coral Springs	FL	33065	954-752-4242		139
Coral Springs Medical Ctr 3000 Coral Hills Dr *Web:* browardhealth.org	Coral Springs	FL	33065	954-344-3000		374-3
Coram Healthcare Corp 555 17th St Ste 1500 **Fax Area Code:* 303 ■ *TF:* 800-267-2642 ■ *Web:* www.coramhc.com	Denver	CO	80202	800-267-2642	298-0043*	363
Coranet Corp 2 Washington St Ste 701 *Web:* www.coranet.com	New York	NY	10004	212-635-2770		224
Cora-Texas Manufacturing Co PO Box 280 *Web:* www.coratexas.com	White Castle	LA	70788	225-545-3679	545-8360	296-38
Corathers' Health Consulting LLC 119 Northwoods Dr *TF:* 800-952-1716 ■ *Web:* corathers.com	Morgantown	WV	26508	304-594-3574		194
Corbally, Gartland & Rappleyea LLP 35 Market St *Web:* cgrlaw.com	Poughkeepsie	NY	12601	845-240-7308	454-4857	41
Corban Onesource 235 Third St S Ste 300 *TF:* 844-267-2261 ■ *Web:* corbanone.com	Saint Petersburg	FL	33701	844-267-2261		251
Corban University 5000 Deer Pk Dr SE *Web:* www.corban.edu	Salem	OR	97317	503-581-8600		166
Corbett Duncan & Hubly PC 100 E Pierce Rd Ste 100 *Web:* cdhcpa.com	Itasca	IL	60143	630-285-0215	285-1166	2
Corbett Public Relations Inc 111 S Tyson Ave *TF:* 877-240-7821 ■ *Web:* www.corbettpr.com	Floral Park	NY	11001	516-775-0435	328-2545	317
Corbett Technology Solutions 4151 Lafeyette Center Dr Ste 700 *TF:* 888-401-0647 ■ *Web:* www.ctsi-usa.com	Chantilly	VA	20151	703-631-3377		180
Corbin 2360 Technology Pkwy **Fax Area Code:* 831 ■ *TF:* 800-538-7035 ■ *Web:* www.corbin.com	Hollister	CA	95023	800-538-7035	634-1059*	517
Corbin Area Technology Ctr 1901 Snyder St *Web:* www.corbinhigh.org	Corbin	KY	40701	606-528-3902		167-3
Corbin Manufacturing & Supply Inc 600 Industrial Cir *Web:* www.corbins.com	White City	OR	97503	541-826-8669		454
Corbin Russwin Inc 225 Episcopal Rd *TF:* 800-543-3658 ■ *Web:* www.corbinrusswin.com	Berlin	CT	06037	860-225-7411		350
Corbin Turf & Ornamental Supply 1105 Old Buncombe Rd *Web:* www.corbinturf.com	Greenville	SC	29617	864-233-2113	610-6338	366
Corbitt Manufacturing 854 NW Guerdon St *Web:* www.cypress-mulch.com	Lake City	FL	32055	386-755-2555		323
Corbo Jewelers Inc 58 Park Ave *Web:* www.corbojewelers.com	Rutherford	NJ	07070	201-438-4454	438-3108	410
Corby Industries Inc 1501 E Pennsylvania St *TF:* 800-652-6729 ■ *Web:* www.corby.com	Allentown	PA	18109	610-433-1412	435-1963	692
Corbyn Investment Management Inc 2330 W Joppa Rd Ste 108 *Web:* www.corbyn.com	Lutherville Timonium	MD	21093	410-832-5500		401
Corcept Therapeutics Inc 149 Commonwealth Dr *NASDAQ: CORT* ■ *Web:* www.corcept.com	Menlo Park	CA	94025	650-327-3270	327-3218	85
Corchran Inc 1340 State St S *Web:* www.corchran.com	Waseca	MN	56093	507-835-3910	835-1382	697
Corcoran 660 Madison Ave 12th Fl *TF:* 800-544-4055 ■ *Web:* www.corcoran.com	New York	NY	10065	212-355-3550		652
Corcoran Ender & Assoc 4010 S California Av *Web:* www.cpa-chicago.com	Chicago	IL	60632	773-247-7132		2

Name / Address	City	State	Zip	Phone	Fax	Class
Corcoran Jennison Development Co 150 Mt Vernon St Bayside Ofc Ctr Ste 500 *Web:* www.corcoranjennison.com	Boston	MA	02125	617-822-7350		653
Corcoran Journal, The 1012 Hale *Web:* www.thecorcoranjournal.net	Corcoran	CA	93212	559-992-3115	992-5543	532-2
Corcoran School of the Arts & Design 500 17th St NW *Web:* corcoran.gwu.edu	Washington	DC	20006	202-994-1700		164
Cord Moving & Storage 4101 Rider Trl N *TF:* 866-742-1558 ■ *Web:* www.cordmoving.com	Earth City	MO	63045	314-291-7440	291-6127	449
Cord Sets Inc 1015 N 5th St *TF:* 800-752-0580 ■ *Web:* www.cordsetsinc.com	Minneapolis	MN	55411	612-337-9700	337-0800	815
Cord Specialties Co 10632 Grand Ave *Web:* www.cordspecialties.com	Franklin Park	IL	60131	847-455-3503		815
Cordage Institute 994 Old Eagle School Rd Ste 1019 *Web:* www.ropecord.com	Wayne	PA	19087	610-971-4854	971-4859	49-13
Cordano Severson & Associates Ltd 2321 Plainfield Rd *Web:* www.csatax.com	Crest Hill	IL	60403	815-744-1900	744-1330	734
Cordell Expeditions (CE) 4295 Walnut Blvd *Web:* www.cordell.org	Walnut Creek	CA	94596	925-934-3735		48-6
Cordell Hull Birthplace State Park 1300 Cordell Hull Memorial Dr *Web:* www.state.tn.us	Byrdstown	TN	38549	931-864-3247		565
CordenPharma Colorado 2075 55th St *Web:* www.cordenpharma.com	Boulder	CO	80301	303-442-1926	938-6413	582
Corder Associates Inc 2602 W Baseline Rd Ste 22 *TF:* 877-303-7575 ■ *Web:* www.cordernet.com	Mesa	AZ	85202	480-752-8533	752-8534	177
Cordev Inc 146 B Hillwood Ave Ste 146 B *Web:* www.cordev.net	Falls Church	VA	22046	703-237-2802		196
Cordiant Capital Inc 1002 Sherbrooke St W Ste 2800 *Web:* cordiantcap.com	Montreal	QC	H3A3L6	514-286-1142		528
Cordis Corp 14201 NW 60th Ave *TF:* 800-327-7714 ■ *Web:* www.cordis.com	Miami Lakes	FL	33014	786-313-2000		476
Cordoba Corp 1401 N Broadway **Fax Area Code:* 415 ■ *Web:* www.cordobacorp.com	Los Angeles	CA	90012	213-895-0224	930-9986*	174
Cordova Bolt Inc 5601 Dolly Ave *Web:* www.cordovabolt.com	Buena Park	CA	90621	714-739-7500	994-2661	350
Cordova Electric Co-opeartive Inc 705 Second St PO Box 20 *Web:* www.cordovaelectric.com	Cordova	AK	99574	907-424-5555		245
Cordova High School 1800 Berryhill Rd *Web:* www.scsk12.org	Cordova	TN	38016	901-416-4540		685
Cordova Recreation & Park District 2197 Chase Dr *Web:* crpd.com	Rancho Cordova	CA	95670	916-362-1841	362-9602	31
Corduroy 1122 9th St NW *Web:* corduroydc.com	Washington	DC	20001	202-589-0699		671
Cordy Oilfield Services Inc 5366 55 St SE *Web:* www.cordy.ca	Calgary	AB	T2C3G9	403-266-2067		539
CORE (Congress of Racial Equality) 730 W Cheyenne Ave Ste 150 *Web:* www.thecongressofracialequality.org	North Las Vegas	NV	89030	702-637-7968	637-7953	48-8
CORE (Center for Organ Recovery & Education) 204 Sigma Dr RIDC Pk *TF:* 800-366-6777 ■ *Web:* www.core.org	Pittsburgh	PA	15238	412-963-3550		269
Core & Main LP PO Box 28446 *Web:* coreandmain.com	Saint Louis	MO	63146	314-432-4700		385
Core Brands LLC 1800 S McDowell Blvd 2nd Fl **Fax Area Code:* 707 ■ *TF:* 800-472-5555 ■ *Web:* www.corebrands.com	Petaluma	CA	94954	800-472-5555	283-5901*	173-1
Core Bts Inc 5875 Castle Creek Pkwy N Dr Ste 320 *TF:* 855-267-3287 ■ *Web:* www.corebts.com	Indianapolis	IN	46250	855-267-3287		113
Core Care Technologies Inc 136 Hurffville-Crosskeys Rd *Web:* www.corecarenj.com	Sewell	NJ	08080	856-629-0400	629-8441	475
Core Club, The 66 E 55th St *Web:* www.thecoreclub.com	New York	NY	10022	212-486-6600		354
Core Construction Services of Arizona Inc 3036 E Greenway Rd *Web:* www.coreconstruction.com	Phoenix	AZ	85032	602-494-0800		186
Core Design Inc 12100 NE 195th St Ste 300 *Web:* www.coredesigninc.com	Bothell	WA	98011	425-885-7877		727
Core Health & Fitness LLC 4400 NE 77th Ave Ste 300 *TF:* 888-678-2476 ■ *Web:* corehandf.com	Vancouver	WA	98662	360-326-4090		706
Core Inc 6590 W Rogers Cir *Web:* www.core-aerospace.com	Boca Raton	FL	33487	561-241-4580		770
Core Laboratories 6316 Windfern Rd *NYSE:* CLB ■ *Web:* corelab.com	Houston	TX	77040	713-328-2673	328-2150	539
Core Management Resources Group Inc 515 Mulberry St *TF:* 888-741-2673 ■ *Web:* www.corehealthbenefits.com	Macon	GA	31201	478-741-3521		196
Core Medical Imaging Inc 6161 NE 175th St Ste 201 *Web:* www.coremedicalimaging.com	Kenmore	WA	98028	425-485-4330		475
Core Molding Technologies Inc (CMT) 800 Manor Pk Dr *NYSE:* CMT ■ *Web:* www.coremt.com	Columbus	OH	43228	614-870-5000	870-4029	604
Core Office Interiors 7108 Old Katy Rd Ste 150 *Web:* www.coreoi.com	Houston	TX	77024	713-803-0100		321
Core Partners LLC 30100 Telegraph Rd Ste 366 *Web:* www.corepartners.net	Bingham Farms	MI	48025	248-399-9999		652
Core Power Services Inc 37428 Centralmont Pl *Web:* cpspower.com	Fremont	CA	94536	510-796-6682		767
Core Realty Holdings LLC 1600 Dove St Ste 450 *Web:* www.corerealtyholdings.com	Newport Beach	CA	92660	949-863-1031		403
Core Six Precision Glass 1737 Endeavor Dr *Web:* coresix.com	Williamsburg	VA	23185	757-888-1361	888-1366	329
Core Twelve Inc 600 W Van Buren Ste 1010 *Web:* www.core12.com	Chicago	IL	60607	312-274-1270		7
Core Vision IT Solutions 1266 NW Hwy *TF:* 855-788-5835 ■ *Web:* www.cvits.com	Palatine	IL	60067	855-788-5835		196
CoreCivic 5501 Virginia Way Ste 110 *Web:* www.corecivic.com	Brentwood	TN	37027	615-263-3000	263-3140	337
Coregistics 240 Northpoint Pkwy *Web:* www.coregistics.com	Acworth	GA	30102	678-453-5900		393
Corel Corp 1600 Carling Ave *TF:* 800-772-6735 ■ *Web:* www.corel.com	Ottawa	ON	K1Z8R7	613-728-8200	761-9176	178-8
Corelight Inc 22 4th St 6th Fl *Web:* www.corelight.com	San Francisco	CA	94103	510-281-0760		692
Corelis Inc Alondra Corporate Ctr 13100 Alondra Blvd *Web:* www.corelis.com	Cerritos	CA	90703	562-926-6727		201
CoreLogic 40 Pacifica Ste 900 *NYSE:* CLGX ■ *TF:* 800-426-1466 ■ *Web:* www.corelogic.com	Irvine	CA	92618	949-214-1000		69
CoreMedia Systems Inc 695 Rte 46 W Ste 403 *Web:* www.coremedia-systems.com	Fairfield	NJ	07004	973-276-0882	276-0891	177
CoreNet Global Inc 260 Peachtree St NW Ste 1500 *TF:* 800-726-8111 ■ *Web:* www.corenetglobal.org	Atlanta	GA	30303	404-589-3200	589-3201	49-17
Coresco Inc 1407 Airport Rd *Web:* www.coresco.com	Monroe	NC	28110	704-296-5600		5
Coreslab Structures 150 W Placentia Ave *Web:* www.coreslab.com	Perris	CA	92571	951-943-9119	943-7571	183
CoreSource Inc 400 Field Dr *Web:* www.coresource.com	Lake Forest	IL	60045	847-604-9200		586
Corestaff Services 1775 St James Pl *Web:* www.corestaff.com	Houston	TX	77056	713-438-1400		721
Corestar International Corp 1044 Sandy Hill Rd *Web:* www.corestar-corp.com	Irwin	PA	15642	724-744-4094		180
Corestates Inc 3039 Premiere Pkwy *Web:* core-states.com	Duluth	GA	30097	770-242-9550		261
CoreTech 660 American Ave Ste 103 *TF:* 800-220-3337 ■ *Web:* xsellresources.com	King of Prussia	PA	19406	800-220-3337		194
Coretelligent 34 SW Pk *Web:* coretelligent.com	Westwood	MA	02090	781-247-4900		180
CoreTitle 1300 NJ-73 Ste 112 *Web:* coretitle.com	Mount Laurel	NJ	08054	800-248-0341		690
Core-Vens & Company Inc 2301 N Second St *TF:* 800-796-9907 ■ *Web:* www.corevensguninsurance.com	Clinton	IA	52732	563-242-5423	242-5242	390
Corey Steel Co 2800 S 61st Ct *TF:* 800-323-2750 ■ *Web:* www.coreysteel.com	Cicero	IL	60804	708-735-8000	735-8100	723
Corgan Associates Inc 401 N Houston St *Web:* www.corgan.com	Dallas	TX	75202	214-748-2000		261
Coriander 282 Kent St *Web:* www.corianderthaiottawa.com	Ottawa	ON	K2P2A4	613-233-2828		671
Coriant 220 Mill Rd *Web:* www.coriant.com	Chelmsford	MA	01824	978-250-2900		176
Coridian Technologies Inc 1725 Lake Dr W *Web:* www.coridian.com	Chanhassen	MN	55317	952-361-9980	361-0081	174
Coriell Institute for Medical Research 403 Haddon Ave *TF:* 800-752-3805 ■ *Web:* coriell.org	Camden	NJ	08103	856-966-7377		668
Corinth Area Convention & Visitors Bureau 215 N Fillmore St *Web:* corinth.net	Corinth	MS	38834	662-287-8300	286-0102	206
Corinthian Media 500 Eigth Ave 5th Fl *Web:* www.mediabuying.com	New York	NY	10018	212-279-5700		6
Corinthian Partners LLC 850 Third Ave Ste 16C *TF:* 800-899-8950 ■ *Web:* corinthianpartners.com	New York	NY	10022	212-287-1500		690
Corium International Inc 4558 50th St SE *Web:* www.coriumintl.com	Grand Rapids	MI	49512	616-656-4563	698-5070	582
Corix Utilities (US) Inc 11020 W Plank Crt Ste 100 *TF:* 877-678-3842 ■ *Web:* www.corix.com	Milwaukee	WI	53226	414-203-8700	203-8807	393
Corizon 105 Westpark Dr Ste 200 *TF:* 800-729-0069 ■ *Web:* www.corizonhealth.com	Brentwood	TN	37027	800-729-0069		463
Cork Industries Inc 500 Kaiser Dr *TF:* 800-394-9550 ■ *Web:* www.corkind.com	Folcroft	PA	19032	800-394-9550		481
Cork Supply USA Inc 531 Stone Rd *Web:* www.corksupply.com	Benicia	CA	94510	707-746-0353	746-7471	124
Cork'N Cleaver 221 E Washington Center Rd *Web:* corkncleaveronline.com	Fort Wayne	IN	46825	260-484-7772		671
Corken Inc 3805 NW 36th St *TF:* 800-631-4929 ■ *Web:* www.corken.com	Oklahoma City	OK	73112	405-946-5576	948-6664	641
Corkhill Insurance Agency LLC 20 S Bumby Ave *Web:* corkhillinsurance.com	Orlando	FL	32803	407-898-8891		390
Corkin Gallery Distillery District 7 Tank House Ln *Web:* www.corkingallery.com	Toronto	ON	M5A3C4	416-979-1980		42
Corky's 100 Franklin Rd *TF:* 800-926-7597 ■ *Web:* www.corkysbbq.com	Brentwood	TN	37027	615-373-1020		671
Corland Co 327 S Isis Ave *Web:* www.coreland.com	Inglewood	CA	90301	310-670-3720		770
Corley Manufacturing Co PO Box 471 *Web:* www.corleymfg.com	Chattanooga	TN	37401	423-698-0284	622-3258	821
Corma Inc 10 McCleary Ct Concord *Web:* corma.com	Toronto	ON	L4K2Z3	905-669-9397		111

	Phone	Fax	Class
CORMAC Corp 5950 Symphony Woods Rd Ste 500 Columbia MD 21044 *Web:* www.cormac-corp.com	443-864-5880	319-5483	396
Corman Bag Co 32 Arlington St. Chelsea MA 02150 *Web:* www.cormanbag.com	617-884-7600	437-7917	67
Cormark Securities Inc 200 Bay St Royal Bank Plz S Tower Ste 2800 Toronto ON M5J2J2 *Web:* www.cormark.com	416-362-7485		195
Cormetech Inc 5000 International Dr Durham NC 27712 *Web:* www.cormetech.com	919-620-3000	620-3001	143
Cormier Jewelers 42 Central St Southbridge MA 01550 *Web:* cormiers.com	508-764-7415		410
Cormier Rice Milling Company Inc 501 W 3rd St De Witt AR 72042 *Web:* www.cormierrice.com	870-946-1479	946-3029	296-23
Corn Belt Energy Corp 1 Energy Way Bloomington IL 61705 *TF:* 800-879-0339 ■ *Web:* www.cornbeltenergy.com	309-662-5330	663-4516	245
Corn Belt Power Co-op 1300 13th St N PO Box 508 Humboldt IA 50548 *Web:* www.cbpower.coop	515-332-2571	332-1375	245
Corn Heritage Village 106 W Adams St Apt 1 Corn OK 73024 *Web:* cornheritage.org	580-343-2295		672
Corn Palace 604 N Main St Mitchell SD 57301 *TF:* 800-289-7469 ■ *Web:* cornpalace.com	605-995-8430		50-3
Corn Plus 711 6th Ave SE Winnebago MN 56098 *Web:* www.cornplus.com	507-893-4747		144
Corn Refiners Association Inc (CRA) 1701 Pennsylvania Ave. Washington DC 20006 *Web:* corn.org	202-331-1634	331-2054	48-2
Corn Stock Theatre 1700 Park Rd Peoria IL 61604 *Web:* www.cornstocktheatre.com	309-676-2196		573-4
Corna/Kokosing Construction Co 6235 Westerville Rd Westerville OH 43081 *Web:* www.corna.com	614-901-8844		186
Cornelia Connelly School of The Holy Child 2323 West Broadway Anaheim CA 92804 *Web:* connellyschoolanaheim.org	714-776-1717		685
Cornelia de Lange Syndrome Foundation Inc (CDLS) 302 W Main St Ste 100 Avon CT 06001 *TF:* 800-753-2357 ■ *Web:* www.cdlsusa.org	860-676-8166	676-8337	48-17
Cornelius & Associates Inc 141 Pelham Dr Ste F Columbia SC 29205 *Web:* www.corneliusassoc.com	803-779-3354	254-0183	194
Cornelius Seed Corn Co 14760 317th Ave. Bellevue IA 52031 *TF:* 800-218-1862 ■ *Web:* www.corneliusseed.com	800-218-1862		296-20
Cornelius Systems Inc (CS) 3966 Eleven Mile Rd. Berkley MI 48072 *TF:* 877-545-5558 ■ *Web:* www.mycornelius.com	877-545-5558	545-0022	535
Cornell & Associates Inc 2633 Eastlake Ave E Ste 307 Seattle WA 98102 *Web:* www.cornellandassociates.com	206-329-0085	329-4110	655
Cornell & Company Inc 224 Cornell Ln Westville NJ 08093 *Web:* www.cornellcraneandsteel.com	856-742-1900	742-8186	264-3
Cornell Botanic Gardens 1 Plantations Rd Ithaca NY 14850 *TF:* 800-269-8368 ■ *Web:* www.cornellbotanicgardens.org	607-255-2400		97
Cornell College 600 First St SW Mount Vernon IA 52314 *TF:* 800-747-1112 ■ *Web:* www.cornellcollege.edu	319-895-4215	895-4451	166
Cornell Forge Co 6666 W 66th St Chicago IL 60638 *Web:* www.cornellforge.com	708-458-1582	728-9883	483
Cornell Iron Works Inc 24 Elmwood Rd Mountain Top PA 18707 **Fax Area Code:* 570 ■ *TF:* 800-233-8366 ■ *Web:* www.cornelliron.com	800-233-8366	474-9973*	234
Cornell Law School 226 Myron Taylor Hall Ithaca NY 14853 *Web:* www.lawschool.cornell.edu	607-255-5141	255-7193	167-1
Cornell Mayo Associates Inc 600 Lanidex Plz Parsippany NJ 07054 *Web:* www.ncr.com	973-887-3069	887-0383	174
Cornell NanoScale Science & Technology Facility (CNF) Cornell University 250 Duffield Hall Ithaca NY 14853 *Web:* www.cnf.cornell.edu	607-255-2329	255-8601	668
Cornell Paper & Box Co 162 - 168 Van Dyke Brooklyn NY 11231 *Web:* cornellpaper.com	201-863-8844	863-7799	101
Cornell Pump Co 16261 SE 130th Ave Clackamas OR 97015 *Web:* www.cornellpump.com	503-653-0330	653-0338	641
Cornell Roofing & Sheet Metal Co 901 S Northern Independence MO 64053 *Web:* www.cornellroofingkansascity.com	816-252-8300		697
Cornell School of Hotel Administration Statler Hall Cornell University Ithaca NY 14853 *Web:* sha.cornell.edu	607-255-8702		434-3
Cornell Storefront Systems Inc 140 Maffet St Wilkes-Barre PA 18705 *TF:* 800-882-6772 ■ *Web:* storefronts.cornelliron.com	800-882-6773		234
Cornell Technical Services LLC 9700 Patuxent Woods Dr Ste 140 Columbia MD 21046 *Web:* www.cts-llc.com	301-560-2544		463
Cornell University 410 Thurston Ave Ithaca NY 14850 *Web:* www.cornell.edu	607-255-5241	255-0659	166
Cornell University Olin Library 2018 Cornell University Library Ithaca NY 14853 *Web:* olinuris.library.cornell.edu	607-255-4144		434-6
Cornell University Press 512 E State St Ithaca NY 14850 *TF:* 800-666-2211 ■ *Web:* www.cornellpress.cornell.edu	607-277-2338	277-6292	637-4
Corner Alliance Inc 1620 L St NW Ste 200 Washington DC 20036 *Web:* www.corneralliance.com	202-754-8120		194
Corner Bakery Cafe 5225 Beltline Rd Ste 58 Dallas TX 75254 *Web:* cornerbakerycafe.com	469-547-0019		68
Corner Bistro 3604 Silverside Rd Wilmington DE 19810 *Web:* www.mybistro.com	302-477-1778		671
Corner Music Inc 3048 Dickerson Pk Nashville TN 37207 *Web:* www.cornermusic.com	615-297-9559		526
Corner Stone Credit Union 130 Historic Town Sq Lancaster TX 75146 *TF:* 800-345-5690 ■ *Web:* cornerstonecreditunion.net	972-218-9266	218-5887	219
CornerCap Investment Counsel Inc 1355 Peachtree St NE The Peachtree Ste 1700 Atlanta GA 30309 *TF:* 800-728-0670 ■ *Web:* www.cornercap.com	404-870-0700		528
Cornerstar Inc 10145 NW Ash St Portland OR 97229 *Web:* www.cornerstar.com	503-546-0500		226
Cornerstone Advisors Asset Management Inc 74 W Broad St Ste 340 Bethlehem PA 18018 *TF:* 800-923-0900 ■ *Web:* www.cornerstone-companies.com	610-694-0900		401
Cornerstone Alliance Chamber Services 38 W Wall St. Benton Harbor MI 49022 *Web:* www.cstonealliance.org	269-925-6100	925-4471	139
Cornerstone Commissioning Inc 11 Cold Spring Dr Boxford MA 01921 *Web:* www.cornerstonecx.com	978-887-8177		256
Cornerstone Communications Inc PO Box 1244 Plainfield IL 60544 *TF:* 866-483-4094 ■ *Web:* www.cornerstonecomm.com	815-439-9108	828-0920	681
Cornerstone Community Bank 192 Hartnell Ave Redding CA 96002 *TF:* 877-529-1861 ■ *Web:* bankcornerstone.com	530-222-1460	222-4501	70
Cornerstone Composites Inc 900 E Vienna Ave Milwaukee WI 53212 *Web:* cornerstonecomposites.com	414-964-5200	964-9677	596
Cornerstone Consulting & Technology 44 Montgomery St Ste 3360 San Francisco CA 94104 *Web:* www.cornerstoneconcilium.com	415-705-7800		194
Cornerstone Escrow Inc 110 N Lincoln Ave Ste 303 Corona CA 92882 *Web:* cornerstoneescrow.com	951-734-8221		653
Cornerstone Financial Group Inc 51 Main St Succasunna NJ 07876 *Web:* cornerstonefg.com	973-584-0031		390
Cornerstone Global Commodities LLC 34 Broad St Unit 2C Red Bank NJ 07701 *Web:* cornerstoneglobalcommodities.com	212-206-6611		169
Cornerstone Home Healthcare 5 E High St Mooresville IN 46158 *Web:* www.cornerstonehhc.com	317-834-8034	584-3016	363
Cornerstone Hospice & Palliative Care 2445 Ln Park Rd Tavares FL 32778 *TF:* 866-742-6655 ■ *Web:* cornerstonehospice.org	866-742-6655	303-1184	371
Cornerstone Hospital of Austin 4207 Burnet Rd Austin TX 78756 *Web:* chghospitals.com	512-706-1900		374-7
Cornerstone Information Systems Inc 300 W 6th St Bloomington IN 47404 *Web:* www.ciswired.com	812-330-4361		178-1
Cornerstone Interlocking Inc PO Box 91299 Lakeland FL 33804 *Web:* www.cornerstoneinterlocking.com	863-816-1749	816-1742	189-2
Cornerstone Law Firm 8350 N St Clair Ave Ste 225 Kansas City MO 64151 *Web:* cornerstonefirm.com	816-581-4040		41
Cornerstone Medical Arts Center Hospital 159-05 Union Tpke Fresh Meadows NY 11366 *TF:* 800-233-9999 ■ *Web:* www.cornerstoneny.com	718-906-6700		726
Cornerstone Medical Inc 900 Ashwood Pky Ste 200 Atlanta GA 30358 *TF:* 800-741-4078 ■ *Web:* www.cornerstonemedical.net	770-399-7337		475
Cornerstone Mortgage 1494 Midvalley Dr De Pere WI 54115 *Web:* csm-wi.com	920-347-1638		217
Cornerstone National Insurance Co 3100 Falling Leaf Ct Ste 200 PO Box 6040 Columbia MO 65201 *Web:* cornerstonenational.com	573-817-2481		390
Cornerstone Research 699 Boylston St 5th Fl Boston MA 02116 *Web:* www.cornerstone.com	617-927-3000	927-3100	196
Cornerstone residential management LLC 2100 Hollywood Blvd Hollywood FL 33020 *TF:* 800-809-4099 ■ *Web:* www.theapartmentcorner.com	800-809-4099		653
Cornerstone Services Inc 777 Joyce Rd. Joliet IL 60436 *Web:* www.cornerstoneservices.org	815-741-7600		592
Cornerstone SMR Inc 1001 W Cyress Creek Rd Ste 410 Fort Lauderdale FL 33309 *Web:* www.cornerstonesmr.com	954-714-7030		387
Cornerstone Systems Inc 3250 Players Club Pkwy Memphis TN 38125 *TF:* 800-278-7677 ■ *Web:* www.cornerstone-systems.com	901-842-0660		194
Cornerstone Systems Inc 820 E Terra Cotta Ave Ste 156 Crystal Lake IL 60014 *TF:* 800-275-4274 ■ *Web:* csivisualshop.com	815-356-8110		180
Cornerstone United Methodist Church Inc 8200 Immokalee Rd Naples FL 34119 *Web:* www.cornerstonenaples.org	239-354-9160		48-20
Cornerstone University 1001 E Beltline Ave NE Grand Rapids MI 49525 *TF:* 800-787-9778 ■ *Web:* www.cornerstone.edu	616-222-1426	222-1418	166
Cornet Technology Inc 6800 Versar Ctr Ste 216 Springfield VA 22151 *Web:* cornet.com	703-658-3400	658-3440	52
Corney Transportation Inc 19214 US Hwy 301 N Saint Pauls NC 28384 *Web:* www.corneytransportation.com	910-865-4045		780
Cornhusker Bank 1101 Cornhusker Hwy Lincoln NE 68521 *TF:* 877-837-4481 ■ *Web:* www.cornhuskerbank.com	402-434-2265		70
Cornhusker Public Power District 23169 235th Ave PO Box 9 Columbus NE 68602 *TF:* 800-955-2773 ■ *Web:* cornhusker-power.com	402-564-2821	564-9907	245
Cornhusker State Industries 800 Pioneers Blvd Lincoln NE 68502 *TF:* 800-348-7537 ■ *Web:* www.nebraska.gov	402-471-4597	471-1236	630
Cornice 615 N Benson Ave Ste B Upland CA 91786 *Web:* www.cornicemac.com	909-985-8323		175

Name / Address	City	State	ZIP	Phone	Fax	Class
Corniche Furs Inc 345 Seventh Ave 20th Fl *Web:* www.nycfur.com	New York	NY	10001	212-239-8655		155-7
Corniche Group Inc, The 8721 W Sunset Blvd Ste 200 *Web:* www.corniche.com	West Hollywood	CA	90069	310-854-6000		772
Corning Area Chamber of Commerce 1 W Market St Ste 202 *TF:* 866-463-6264 ■ *Web:* www.corningny.com	Corning	NY	14830	607-936-4686	936-4685	139
Corning Community College 1 Academic Dr *Web:* www.corning-cc.edu	Corning	NY	14830	607-962-9251	962-9582	162
Corning Data Services Inc PO Box 1187 **Fax Area Code:* 607 ■ *TF:* 800-455-5996 ■ *Web:* www.corningdata.com	Corning	NY	14830	800-455-5996	936-0495*	177
Corning Ford Inc 2280 Short Dr *TF:* 888-378-5961 ■ *Web:* www.corningford.com	Corning	CA	96021	530-824-5434		57
Corning Museum of Glass 1 Museum Way *TF:* 800-732-6845 ■ *Web:* home.cmog.org	Corning	NY	14830	607-937-5371	438-5410	520
Cornish College of the Arts 1000 Lenora St *TF:* 800-726-2787 ■ *Web:* www.cornish.edu	Seattle	WA	98121	206-726-5141	720-1011	164
Cornucopia Software 1205 Brighton Ave *Web:* www.practicemagic.com	Albany	CA	94706	510-528-7000		178-1
Cornucopia Tool & Plastics Inc 448 Sherwood Rd PO Box 1915 *TF:* 800-235-4144 ■ *Web:* www.cornucopiaplastics.com	Paso Robles	CA	93447	805-369-0030	369-0033	253
Cornwall & Area Chamber of Commerce 113 Second St E *Web:* www.cornwallchamber.com	Cornwall	ON	K6H1Y5	613-933-4004	933-8466	137
Cornwall Community Hospital 840 McConnell Ave *TF:* 866-263-1560 ■ *Web:* www.cornwallhospital.ca	Cornwall	ON	K6H5S5	613-938-4240	930-4502	374-2
Cornwall Lebanon School District 105 E Evergreen Rd *Web:* www.clsd.k12.pa.us	Lebanon	PA	17042	717-272-2031		685
Cornwall Manor 1 Boyd St *TF:* 800-222-2476 ■ *Web:* cornwallmanor.org	Cornwall	PA	17016	717-273-2647		672
Cornwall Standard Freeholder, The 1150 Montreal Rd *Web:* www.standard-freeholder.com	Cornwall	ON	K6H1E2	613-933-3160		532-1
Cornwell & Sample 7045 N Fruit *Web:* cornwellsample.com	Fresno	CA	93711	559-431-3142		41
Cornwell Data Services Inc 352 Evelyn St Ste B *Web:* cornwelldirect.com	Paramus	NJ	07652	201-261-1050		225
Cornwell Quality Tools 667 Seville Rd *TF:* 800-321-8356 ■ *Web:* www.cornwelltools.com	Wadsworth	OH	44281	330-336-3506	336-3337	758
Cornyn John (Sen R - TX) 517 Hart Senate Office Bldg *Web:* www.cornyn.senate.gov	Washington	DC	20510	202-224-2934		342-2
Corona Brushes Inc 5065 Savarese Cir *TF:* 800-458-3483 ■ *Web:* www.coronabrushes.com	Tampa	FL	33634	813-885-2525	882-9810	103
Corona Chamber of Commerce 904 E Sixth St *Web:* www.mychamber.org	Corona	CA	92879	951-737-3350	737-3531	139
Corona Clipper Inc 22440 Tomasco Canyon Rd *TF:* 800-234-2547 ■ *Web:* www.coronatoolsusa.com	Corona	CA	92883	951-737-6515		429
Corona College Heights Orange & Lemon Assn 8000 Lincoln Ave *Web:* www.cchcitrus.com	Riverside	CA	92504	951-688-1811	689-5115	315-2
Corona Del Mar Animal Hospital 2948 E Coast Hwy *Web:* cdmah.com	Corona Del Mar	CA	92625	949-644-8160		794
Corona del Mar State Beach 3001 Ocean Blvd *Web:* www.parks.ca.gov	Corona Del Mar	CA	92625	949-644-3151		565
Corona Public Library 650 S Main St *Web:* www.coronaca.gov	Corona	CA	92882	951-736-2381	736-2499	434-3
Coronado Chamber of Commerce 875 Orange Ave Ste 102 *Web:* www.coronadochamber.com	Coronado	CA	92118	619-435-9260	522-6577	139
Coronado Ctr 6600 Menaul Blvd NE Ste 1 *Web:* www.coronadocenter.com	Albuquerque	NM	87110	505-881-2700		460
Coronado Healthcare Ctr 11411 N 19th Ave *Web:* coronadocare.com	Phoenix	AZ	85029	602-256-7500		450
Coronado Manufacturing Inc 8991 Glenoaks Boulvard *Web:* www.coronadomfg.com	Sun Valley	CA	91352	818-768-5010	504-9564	22
Coronado National Memorial 4101 E Montezuma Canyon Rd *Web:* www.nps.gov	Hereford	AZ	85615	520-366-5515	366-5705	564
Coronado Public Library 640 Orange Ave *Web:* www.coronado.ca.us	Coronado	CA	92118	619-522-7300	435-4205	434-3
Coronado State Monument 485 Kuaua Rd *Web:* www.nmhistoricsites.org	Bernalillo	NM	87004	505-867-5351	867-1733	50-3
Coronado Theatre 314 N Main St *Web:* www.coronadopac.org	Rockford	IL	61101	815-968-2722	968-1318	572
Coronado Unified School District 201 Sixth St *Web:* coronadousd.net	Coronado	CA	92118	619-522-8900	437-6570	808
Corona-Norco Unified School District 2820 Clark Ave *Web:* www.cnusd.k12.ca.us	Norco	CA	92860	951-736-5000		685
Coronation Sheet Metal Company Inc 2198 Stanley Terr *Web:* www.coronationsheetmetal.com	Union	NJ	07083	908-686-0930	686-1534	697
Coronet Books Inc 311 Bainbridge St *Web:* www.coronetbooks.com	Philadelphia	PA	19147	215-925-2762	925-1912	95
Coronet Lighting 16210 S Avalon Blvd *Web:* coronetlighting.com	Gardena	CA	90248	310-593-9561		439
Corotec Corp 145 Hyde Rd *TF:* 800-423-0348 ■ *Web:* www.corotec.com	Farmington	CT	06032	860-678-0038	674-5229	386
Corp for National & Community Service *Learn & Serve America* 1201 New York Ave NW *TF:* 800-833-3722 ■ *Web:* www.nationalservice.gov	Washington	DC	20525	202-606-5000		340-20
CORPAC Steel Products Corp 20803 Biscayne Blvd Ste 502 *TF:* 888-799-5869 ■ *Web:* corpacsteel.com	Miami	FL	33180	305-918-0540	931-2251	492
CorpCare Associates Inc 1050 Crown Pointe Pkwy Ste 500 *TF:* 800-728-9444 ■ *Web:* www.corpcareeap.com	Atlanta	GA	30338	770-200-8085		462
Corpfinance International Ltd 229 Niagara St *Web:* www.corpfinance.ca	Toronto	ON	M6J2L5	416-364-6191		217
Corporate Accountability Intl 10 Milk St Ste 610 *TF:* 800-688-8797 ■ *Web:* www.corporateaccountability.org	Boston	MA	02108	617-695-2525	695-2626	48-8
Corporate Air LLC 15 Allegheny County Airport *Web:* www.travelredefined.com	West Mifflin	PA	15122	412-469-6800		63
Corporate Air Technology 1250 Aviation Ave Ste 125 *Web:* corpairtech.com	San Jose	CA	95110	408-977-0990		359
Corporate Business Solutions 1523 Johnson Ferry Rd Ste 200 *TF:* 800-239-8182 ■ *Web:* www.cbshro.com	Marietta	GA	30062	404-521-6030		570
Corporate Chefs Inc 22 Parkridge Rd *Web:* www.corporatechefs.com	Haverhill	MA	01835	978-372-7400		670
Corporate Construction Ltd 8517 Excelsior Dr Ste 203 *Web:* www.corporate-construction.com	Madison	WI	53717	608-827-6001	827-6066	186
Corporate Development Associates Inc 5335 Far Hills Ave Ste 304 *Web:* www.cda-inc.net	Dayton	OH	45429	937-439-4227	439-5593	401
Corporate Disk Co 4610 Crime Pkwy *TF:* 800-634-3475 ■ *Web:* www.disk.com	McHenry	IL	60050	800-634-3475		240
Corporate Dynamics Inc 4320 Winfield Rd Ste 200 *Web:* corporatedynamicsinc.com	Warrenville	IL	60563	630-778-9991		194
Corporate Eagle Management Services Inc 6320 Highland Rd *Web:* corporateeagle.com	Waterford	MI	48327	248-461-9000		21
Corporate Environments 1636 NE Expwy *Web:* www.corporateenvironments.com	Atlanta	GA	30329	404-679-8999		320
Corporate Executive Board Co 1919 N Lynn St *TF:* 866-913-2632 ■ *Web:* www.cebglobal.com	Arlington	VA	22209	571-303-3000	303-3100	194
Corporate Facilities Inc 2129 Chestnut St *Web:* cfi-knoll.com	Philadelphia	PA	19103	215-279-9999	279-9445	321
Corporate Farmer Inc 1307 Sixth St SW Ste 1 *Web:* corporatefarmer.com	Mason City	IA	50401	641-424-4170		2
Corporate Finance Group Inc 15 Broad St 5th Fl *Web:* www.cfgi.com	Boston	MA	02109	617-531-8270		194
Corporate Fitness Works Inc 1200 16th St N *Web:* corporatefitnessworks.com	Saint Petersburg	FL	33705	301-417-9697		354
Corporate Flight Inc 6150 Highland Rd *Web:* corporateflight.com	Waterford	MI	48327	248-666-8800		13
Corporate Four Insurance 7220 Metro Blvd *Web:* www.corporatefour.com	Edina	MN	55439	952-893-9218		390
Corporate Graphics International Inc 1885 Northway Dr *Web:* www.cgintl.com	North Mankato	MN	56003	507-625-4400		627
Corporate Image Maintenance 2116 S Wright St *TF:* 866-977-9811 ■ *Web:* www.cim-janitorial.com	Santa Ana	CA	92705	714-966-5325	966-5329	256
Corporate Incentive Travel Inc 685 S Washington St *Web:* www.corporateincentivetravel.net	Alexandria	VA	22314	703-683-0123		772
Corporate Information Technologies Inc 14 Brick Walk Ln *Web:* www.corpit.com	Farmington	CT	06032	860-676-2720		174
Corporate Ink Public Relations Ltd 90 Washington St *Web:* www.corporateink.com	Newton	MA	02458	617-969-9192		194
Corporate Interior Systems 3311 E Broadway Rd *Web:* www.cisinphx.com	Phoenix	AZ	85040	602-304-0100		321
Corporate It Solutions Inc 661 Pleasant St *TF:* 888-521-2487 ■ *Web:* www.corpitsol.com	Norwood	MA	02062	888-521-2487		196
Corporate Jet Support Inc 1 Graphic Pl *TF:* 800-486-2376 ■ *Web:* www.corpjetsupport.com	Moonachie	NJ	07074	201-807-0784	807-0950	770
Corporate Living.Com Inc 8972 Darrow Rd Ste A202A *Web:* corporateliving.com	Twinsburg	OH	44087	330-405-0525		653
Corporate Mailing Services Inc 1625 Knecht Ave *Web:* whycms.com	Halethorpe	MD	21227	410-242-7356		5
Corporate Office Properties Trust 6711 Columbia Gateway Dr Ste 300 *NYSE:* OFC ■ *Web:* www.copt.com	Columbia	MD	21046	443-285-5400	285-7650	655
Corporate Payroll Services Inc 1000 Miller Ct W *Web:* www.corpay.com	Norcross	GA	30071	770-446-7289		734
Corporate Reports Inc 3610 Piedmont Rd NE Ste 200 *Web:* corporatereport.com	Atlanta	GA	30305	404-233-2230		393
Corporate Resources 704-B Plaza Blvd *TF:* 800-277-7666 ■ *Web:* www.corporateresources.net	Kinston	NC	28501	252-523-5164	523-3884	627
Corporate Strategies 21021 Ventura Blvd Ste 200 *TF:* 800-914-3564 ■ *Web:* corpstrat.com	Woodland Hills	CA	91364	818-377-7260	377-7263	390

Phone | Fax | Class

Corporate Strategy Institute Inc
9103 Lytham Ct ... Orlando FL 32819 407-342-6507 194
Web: www.corporatestrategy.com

Corporate Synergies Group LLC
5000 Dearborn Cir Ste 100 ... Mount Laurel NJ 08054 856-813-1500 390
Web: www.corpsyn.com

Corporate Systems Engineering LLC
1215 Brookville Way ... Indianapolis IN 46239 317-375-3600 375-3610 177
Web: www.corporatesystems.com

Corporate Technology Partners Inc
10281 Bentwood Ct ... Littleton CO 80126 877-287-2874 177
TF: 877-287-2874 ■ *Web:* ctpartners.com

Corporate Traffic Logistics
6500 Bowden Rd Ste 202 ... Jacksonville FL 32216 904-727-0051 727-6804 311
Web: www.corporatetraffic.com

Corporate Travel Management Group
450 E 22nd St ... Lombard IL 60148 630-691-8000 771
Web: www.corptrav.com

Corporate Travel Service
23420 Ford Rd Ste 1 ... Dearborn Heights MI 48127 313-565-8888 772
Web: www.ctscentral.net

Corporate University Xchange
4900 Ritter Rd Ste 103 ... Mechanicsburg PA 17055 717-395-9267 463
Web: www.corpu.com

Corporate Visions
1020 19th St NW Ste LL20 ... Washington DC 20036 202-833-4333 833-4332 344
Web: www.corpvisions.com

Corporate West Computer Systems
1610 Dell Ave Ste F ... Campbell CA 95008 408-374-4655 196
TF: 800-870-5454 ■ *Web:* www.corpwest.com

Corporate Writer & Editor
111 E Wacker Dr Ste 500 ... Chicago IL 60601 312-960-4140 531-2
TF: 800-878-5331 ■ *Web:* www.ragan.com

Corporation for Public Broadcasting (CPB)
401 Ninth St NW ... Washington DC 20004 202-879-9600 879-9700 305
TF: 800-272-2190 ■ *Web:* www.cpb.org

Corporation Service Co
2711 Centerville Rd Ste 400 ... Wilmington DE 19808 302-636-5400 636-5454 113
TF: 866-403-5272 ■ *Web:* www.cscglobal.com

Corps Network, The
1275 K St NW Ste 1050 ... Washington DC 20005 202-737-6272 737-6277 48-6
Web: www.corpsnetwork.org

Corps Solutions LLC
235 Garrisonville Rd Ste 202 ... Stafford VA 22554 540-300-1274 891-9570* 463
**Fax Area Code:* 703 ■ *Web:* corps-solutions.com

Corptax LLC
1751 Lake Cook Rd Ste 100 ... Deerfield IL 60015 800-966-1639 236-8011* 177
**Fax Area Code:* 847 ■ *TF:* 800-966-1639 ■ *Web:* corptax.com

Corpus Christi Ballet
1621 N Mesquite St ... Corpus Christi TX 78401 361-882-4588 881-9291 573-1
Web: www.corpuschristiballet.com

Corpus Christi City Hall
1201 Leopard St PO Box 9277 ... Corpus Christi TX 78469 361-826-2489 337
Web: www.cctexas.com

Corpus Christi Convention & Visitors Bureau
101 N Shoreline Blvd Ste 430 ... Corpus Christi TX 78401 361-881-1888 887-9023 206
TF: 800-678-6232 ■ *Web:* www.visitcorpuschristitx.org

Corpus Christi Gasket & Fastener Inc
PO Box 4074 ... Corpus Christi TX 78469 361-884-6366 884-0695 326
TF: 800-460-6366 ■ *Web:* www.ccgasket.com

Corpus Christi International Airport
1000 International Dr ... Corpus Christi TX 78406 361-289-0171 289-0251 27
Web: www.corpuschristiairport.com

Corpus Christi Museum of Science & History
1900 N Chaparral St ... Corpus Christi TX 78401 361-826-4667 520
Web: ccmuseum.com

Corpus Christi Symphony Orchestra
555 N Carancahua St Tower II Ste 410 ... Corpus Christi TX 78401 361-883-6683 573-3
Web: ccsymphony.org

Corr Tech Inc 4545 Homestead Rd ... Houston TX 77028 713-674-7887 674-0840 612
Web: www.corr-tech.com

Corra Group
13011 W Washington Blvd ... Los Angeles CA 90066 310-822-7788 774-3970 466
Web: www.corragroup.com

Corradino Group 200 S Fifth St ... Louisville KY 40202 502-587-7221 587-2636 256
TF: 800-880-8241 ■ *Web:* www.corradino.com

Correa J. Luis (Rep D - CA)
1039 Longworth House Office Bldg ... Washington DC 20515 202-225-2965 342-2
Web: correa.house.gov

Correct Craft Inc
14700 Aerospace Pkwy ... Orlando FL 32832 407-855-4141 90
TF: 800-346-2092 ■ *Web:* www.nautique.com

Correct Rx Pharmacy Services Inc
1352-C Charwood Rd ... Hanover MD 21076 800-636-0501 238
TF: 800-636-0501 ■ *Web:* correctrxpharmacy.com

Correct Temp Inc 268 Hampstead Rd ... Methuen MA 01844 978-688-8700 189-10
Web: correcttemp.com

Correctional Enterprises of Connecticut
24 Wolcott Hill Rd ... Wethersfield CT 06109 860-263-6839 263-6838 630
TF: 800-842-1146 ■ *Web:* portal.ct.gov

Correctional Institute
18601 Roxbury Rd ... Hagerstown MD 21746 240-420-1000 790-4939* 213
**Fax Area Code:* 301 ■ *Web:* msa.maryland.gov

Corrections Dept 52 Main St ... Bridgeport CT 06604 475-225-8000 225-8050 213
Web: portal.ct.gov

Corrective Eye Center
35010 Chardon Rd Bldg IV Ste 102 ... Willoughby Hills OH 44094 216-574-8900 374-3
Web: www.correctiveeye.com

Corredor, Husseini & Snedaker PA
3905 NW 107th Ave Ste 502 ... Doral FL 33178 305-670-1880 41
Web: corredorlaw.com

Correira & Correira LLP 1010 Gar Hwy ... Swansea MA 02777 508-679-5040 41
Web: correiralaw.com

Correlated Products Inc
5616 Progress Rd ... Indianapolis IN 46242 317-243-3248 244-8461 151
TF: 800-428-3266 ■ *Web:* cpiroadsolutions.com

Correll Associates PC
26026 Telegraph Rd Ste 200 ... Southfield MI 48033 248-355-5151 355-0106 2
Web: www.correllcpa.com

Correvio Pharma Corp
1441 Creekside Dr 6th Fl ... Vancouver BC V6J4S7 604-677-6905 677-6915 85
NASDAQ: CORV ■ *TF:* 800-330-9928 ■ *Web:* correvio.com

Corridor Capital LLC
12400 Wilshire Blvd Ste 645 ... Los Angeles CA 90025 310-442-7000 194
Web: www.corridorcapital.com

Corridor Group Inc, The
6405 Metcalf Ste 108 ... Overland Park KS 66202 866-263-3795 194
TF: 866-263-3795 ■ *Web:* www.corridorgroup.com

Corridor Title LLC
171 Benney Ln Ste 200 ... Dripping Springs TX 78620 512-894-0187 390
Web: corridortitleco.com

Corriente Resources Inc
5811 Cooney Rd Unit S209 ... Richmond BC V6X3M1 604-282-7212 282-7568 502
Web: www.corriente.com

Corrigan Co 3545 Gratiot St ... Saint Louis MO 63103 314-771-6200 771-8537 189-10
Web: www.corriganco.com

Corrigan Correctional Institution
986 Norwich-New London Tpke ... Uncasville CT 06382 860-848-5700 213
Web: portal.ct.gov

Corrigan Moving Systems
23923 Research Dr ... Farmington Hills MI 48335 800-267-7442 519
TF: 800-267-7442 ■ *Web:* www.corriganmoving.com

Corrigan, Krause, Harrison, Long, Harsar CPAS LLC
2055 Crocker Rd Ste 300 ... Westlake OH 44145 440-471-0800 2
Web: corrigankrause.com

Corrosion Companies Inc
3725 Grant St ... Washougal WA 98671 360-835-2171 835-2173 605-2
Web: www.ccifrp.com

Corrosion Engineering Inc PO Box 5670 ... Mesa AZ 85211 480-890-0203 890-0589 676
TF: 888-501-2047 ■ *Web:* www.corroeng.com

Corrosion Monitoring Services Inc
902 Equity Dr ... Saint Charles IL 60174 800-637-6592 481
TF: 800-637-6592 ■ *Web:* www.cmsinc.us

Corrosion Probe Inc
12 Industrial Park Rd ... Centerbrook CT 06409 860-767-4402 261
Web: www.cpiengineering.com

Corrugated Gear & Services Inc
100 Anderson Rd ... Alpharetta GA 30004 770-475-8929 442-3371 547
Web: www.corrugatedgear.com

Corrugated Replacements Inc
161 Lee Industrial Dr ... Blairsville GA 30512 706-781-6650 781-6649 556
TF: 800-969-0881 ■ *Web:* corrugatedreplacements.com

Corr-Williams Co, The
110 Airport Rd S Ste B ... Pearl MS 39208 601-420-5121 756
Web: www.corrwilliams.com

Corry Contract Inc 21 Maple Ave ... Corry PA 16407 814-665-8221 320
Web: corrycontract.com

Corry Federal Credit Union 728 Worth St ... Corry PA 16407 814-663-3263 664-2387 219
TF: 855-628-2328 ■ *Web:* corryfcu.org

Corry Redevelopment Authority
1524 Enterprise Rd ... Corry PA 16407 814-664-3884 393
Web: corryredevelopment.com

Cors & Bassett
201 E 5th St PNC Ctr Ste 900 ... Cincinnati OH 45202 513-852-8200 428
Web: www.corsbassett.com

Corsair 46221 Landing Pkwy ... Fremont CA 94538 510-657-8747 657-8748 173-5
TF: 888-222-4346 ■ *Web:* www.corsair.com

Corsaro & Associates Company LPA
28039 Clemens Rd ... Westlake OH 44145 440-871-4022 41
Web: corsarolaw.com

Corsemax 900 W Valley Rd Ste 502 ... Wayne PA 19087 610-687-9701 177
Web: corsemax.com

Corsicana & Navarro County Chamber of Commerce
120 N 12th St ... Corsicana TX 75110 469-988-0839 874-4187* 139
**Fax Area Code:* 903 ■ *Web:* www.corsicana.org

Corsicana Mattress Co PO Box 1050 ... Corsicana TX 75151 903-872-2591 471
TF: 800-323-4349 ■ *Web:* www.corsicanamattress.com

Corsicana Public Library
100 N 12th St ... Corsicana TX 75110 903-874-4731 434-3
TF: 877-648-2836 ■ *Web:* www.cityofcorsicana.com

Corson & Johnson Law Firm PC, The
940 Willamette St Ste 500 ... Eugene OR 97401 541-484-2525 484-2929 41
Web: corsonjohnsonlaw.com

Corstar Communications LLC
40 Saw Mill River Rd ... Hawthorne NY 10532 914-347-2700 347-5547 180
Web: corstar.com

Cortac Group
609 Deep Valley Dr Ste 200 ... Rolling Hills Estates CA 90274 877-216-1717 216-1911 195
TF: 877-216-1717 ■ *Web:* www.cortacgroup.com

Cortec Corp 4119 White Bear Pkwy ... Saint Paul MN 55110 651-429-1100 429-1122 145
TF: 800-426-7832 ■ *Web:* www.cortecvci.com

Cortec Group 140 E 45th St 43rd Fl ... New York NY 10017 212-370-5600 360-3
Web: www.cortecgroup.com

Cortec Precision Sheet Metal Inc
2231 Will Wool Dr ... San Jose CA 95112 408-278-8540 278-8548 697
Web: www.cortecprecision.com

Cortech Engineering Inc
22785 Savi Ranch Pkwy ... Yorba Linda CA 92887 714-779-0911 693-1715 536
TF: 866-472-3959 ■ *Web:* cortecheng.com

Cortech Solutions Inc
1409 Audubon Blvd Ste B1 ... Wilmington NC 28403 910-362-1143 378-3443 475
Web: cortechsolutions.com

Cortek Inc 12 E V Hogan Dr ... Hamlet NC 28345 910-582-0100 548
Web: www.cortek.us

Cortelco Inc 1703 Sawyer Rd ... Corinth MS 38834 662-287-5281 287-3889 246
TF: 800-288-3132 ■ *Web:* www.cortelco.com

Cortera 901 Yamato Rd Ste 210 E ... Boca Raton FL 33431 877-569-7376 178-1
TF: 877-569-7376 ■ *Web:* www.cortera.com

Cortex Consultants Inc
1027 Pandora Ave ... Victoria BC V8V3P6 250-360-1492 463
TF: 866-931-1192 ■ *Web:* www.cortex.ca

Cortez Masto Catherine (Sen D - NV)
516 Hart Senate Office Bldg ... Washington DC 20510 202-224-3542 342-2
Web: www.cortezmasto.senate.gov

Cortina Tool & Molding Co
10706 W Grand Ave ... Franklin Park IL 60131 847-455-2800 451-7247 604
TF: 800-225-5206 ■ *Web:* www.cortinaco.com

Name / Address	City	State	Zip	Phone	Fax	Class
Cortiva Institute 211 S Gulph Rd *TF:* 866-267-8482 ■ *Web:* www.cortiva.com	King of Prussia	PA	19406	484-690-1400	690-1423	352
Cortiva Institute 425 Pontius Ave N Ste 100 *Web:* www.cortiva.com	Seattle	WA	98109	206-204-3165		167-3
Florida School of Massage Therapy 2370 34th St N *Web:* www.cortiva.com	Saint Petersburg	FL	33713	727-865-4940	545-0053	166
Cortiva Institute - Scottsdale 8010 E McDowell Rd Ste 214 *Web:* www.cortiva.edu	Scottsdale	AZ	85257	480-945-9461	425-8247	352
Cortland County 46 Greenbush St Ste 101 *Web:* www.cortland-co.org	Cortland	NY	13045	607-753-5021	753-5378	338
Cortland Line Company Inc 3736 Kellogg Rd *Web:* www.cortlandline.com	Cortland	NY	13045	607-756-2851		710
Cortland Plastics International LLC 211 Main St *Web:* www.cortlandplastics.com	Cortland	NY	13045	607-662-0120	662-0139	98
Cortlandt Recreation Dept 1 Heady St *Web:* www.townofcortlandt.com	Cortlandt Manor	NY	10567	914-734-1050		564
Cortron Inc 59 Technology Dr *Web:* www.cortroninc.com	Lowell	MA	01851	978-975-5445	975-0357	173-1
Corum Group Ltd 19805 N Creek Pkwy Ste 300 *TF:* 800-228-8281 ■ *Web:* www.corumgroup.com	Bothell	WA	98011	425-455-8281		463
Corum Real Estate Group Inc 600 S Cherry St Ste 625 *Web:* www.corumrealestate.com	Glendale	CO	80246	303-796-2000	796-2065	653
Corunna Public School District 124 N Shiawassee St *Web:* www.corunna.k12.mi.us	Corunna	MI	48817	989-743-6338	743-4474	685
Corus Entertainment Inc Corus Quay 25 Dockside Dr *Web:* www.corusent.com	Toronto	ON	M5A0B5	416-479-7000	479-7006	738
Corus Group LLC 130 Technology Pkwy *Web:* corus360.com	Norcross	GA	30092	770-300-4700		180
Corus Realty Holdings Inc 6726 Curran St *TF:* 888-812-6787 ■ *Web:* www.corushome.com	McLean	VA	22101	703-827-0075	827-0074	652
Corvallis Area Chamber of Commerce 420 NW Second St *TF:* 800-562-8526 ■ *Web:* www.corvallischamber.com	Corvallis	OR	97330	541-757-1505		139
Corvallis Microtechnology Inc 413 SW Jefferson Ave *Web:* www.cmtinc.com	Corvallis	OR	97333	541-752-5456	752-4117	173-2
Corvallis Peter Productions 2200 N Interstate Ave *Web:* www.petercorvallis.com	Portland	OR	97227	503-222-1665		226
Corvallis School District 509 J 1555 SW 35th St PO Box 3509J *Web:* www.csd509j.net	Corvallis	OR	97333	541-757-5811		780
Corvallis Tourism 420 NW Second St *TF:* 800-334-8118 ■ *Web:* www.visitcorvallis.com	Corvallis	OR	97330	541-757-1544	753-2664	206
Corvallis-Benton County Library 645 NW Monroe Ave *Web:* cbcpubliclibrary.net	Corvallis	OR	97330	541-766-6793	766-6915	434-3
CorVel Corp 2010 Main St Ste 600 *NASDAQ: CRVL* ■ *TF:* 888-726-7835 ■ *Web:* www.corvel.com	Irvine	CA	92614	949-851-1473	851-1469	463
Corvirtus 4360 Montebello Dr Ste 400 *TF:* 800-322-5329 ■ *Web:* corvirtus.com	Colorado Springs	CO	80918	800-322-5329		463
Cory Watson Attorneys 2131 Magnolia Ave *TF:* 800-852-6299 ■ *Web:* www.corywatson.com	Birmingham	AL	35205	205-328-2200		428
Corybant Inc 3800 Arapahoe Ave Ste 205 *Web:* www.corybant.com	Boulder	CO	80303	303-447-1988		194
Coryell County Courthouse 620 E Main St 1st Fl PO Box 237 *Web:* coryellcounty.org	Gatesville	TX	76528	254-865-5911	865-5064	338
COSA Xentaur Corp 84G Horseblock Rd *Web:* cosaxentaur.com	Yaphank	NY	11980	631-345-3434		407
Cosabella 12186 SW 128th St *TF:* 888-836-1628 ■ *Web:* www.cosabella.com	Miami	FL	33186	888-675-0828		157-6
Co-Sales Co 3410 E University Dr Ste 100 *Web:* www.co-sales.com	Phoenix	AZ	85034	602-254-5555		194
Cosanti Originals Inc 6433 Doubletree Ranch Rd *TF:* 800-752-3187 ■ *Web:* www.cosanti.com	Paradise Valley	AZ	85253	480-948-6145	998-4312	50-3
COSCO (China Ocean Shipping Company Americas Inc) 100 Lighting Way *TF:* 800-242-7354 ■ *Web:* www.na.coscoshipping.com	Secaucus	NJ	07094	201-422-0500	422-8956	220
Cosco Fire Protection 1075 W Lambert Rd Bldg D *TF:* 800-485-3795 ■ *Web:* www.coscofire.com	Brea	CA	92821	714-989-1800	989-1801	189-13
Cosco Industries Inc 7220 W Wilson Ave *TF:* 800-296-8970 ■ *Web:* www.coscoindustries.com	Harwood Heights	IL	60706	800-296-8970		467
Cosco International Inc Cumberland Business Pk 1633 Sands Pl SE *Web:* www.coscous.com	Marietta	GA	30067	770-303-0797	303-0795	80-2
Cosentini Associates Inc 2 Pennsylvania Plz 3rd Fl *Web:* www.cosentini.com	New York	NY	10121	212-615-3600	615-3700	256
CoServ Electric 7701 S Stemmons Fwy *TF:* 800-274-4014 ■ *Web:* www.coserv.com	Corinth	TX	76210	940-321-7800	270-6640	245
Cosfibel Inc 369 Lexington Ave Ste 322-323	New York	NY	10017	212-867-4133		711
Cosgrove Aircraft Service Inc 70 Oser Ave *Web:* www.cosgroveaircraft.com	Hauppauge	NY	11788	631-231-6111		770
Cosgrove Assoc 81 Main St *Web:* www.cosgroveny.com	White Plains	NY	10601	212-888-7202	888-7201	344
Cosgrove Computer Systems 7411 Earldom Ave *Web:* cosgrovecomputer.com	Playa Del Rey	CA	90293	310-823-9448		261
Cosgrove Distributors Inc 120 S Greenwood St *Web:* www.cosgrovedistributors.com	Spring Valley	IL	61362	815-664-4121		559
Coshocton County Chamber of Commerce 401 Main St *Web:* www.coshoctoncounty.net	Coshocton	OH	43812	740-622-5411	622-9902	139
Coshocton County Medical Ctr 1460 Orange St *Web:* ccmh.com	Coshocton	OH	43812	740-622-6411		374-3
COSI Columbus 333 W Broad St *TF:* 888-819-2674 ■ *Web:* cosi.org	Columbus	OH	43215	614-228-2674		520
COSI Cucina 1975 NW 86th St *Web:* www.cosicucina.com	Clive	IA	50325	515-278-8148		671
COSI Inc 1751 Lake Cook Rd Ste 600 *NASDAQ: COSI* ■ *Web:* www.getcosi.com	Deerfield	IL	60015	847-597-8800		670
COSI Toledo 1 Discovery Way *TF:* 800-590-9755 ■ *Web:* www.imaginationstationtoledo.org	Toledo	OH	43604	419-244-2674	255-2674	520
Cosley Zoo 1356 N Gary Ave *Web:* cosleyzoo.org	Wheaton	IL	60187	630-665-5534	260-6408	823
Cosmed Group Inc 28 Narragansett Ave *Web:* www.cosmedgroup.com	Jamestown	RI	02835	908-583-5500		743
COSMED USA Inc 2211 N Elston Ave Ste 305 *Web:* www.cosmed.com	Chicago	IL	60614	773-645-8113		250
Cosmetic Specialty Labs Inc 210 SW Texas Ave *TF:* 800-364-2182 ■ *Web:* www.aloe-vera.com	Lawton	OK	73501	800-364-2182		214
Cosmetics Corner 2050 Stemmons Fwy Ste 7256 *Web:* www.cosmeticscorner.com	Dallas	TX	75207	214-434-0344	573-7655	238
Cosmetology Careers Unlimited 121 W Superior St *Web:* www.ccucollege.net	Duluth	MN	55802	218-722-7484		167-3
Cosmetology Training Ctr 5520 Johnston St Ste H2 *TF:* 877-237-6833 ■ *Web:* www.cosmetlafayettela.com	Lafayette	LA	70503	337-237-6868		167-3
Cosmic Cafe 2912 Oak Lawn *Web:* www.cosmiccafedallas.com	Dallas	TX	75219	214-521-6157	521-9195	671
Cosmic Pictures Inc 1345 Major St *Web:* cosmicpictures.com	Salt Lake City	UT	84115	801-463-3880		514
Cosmix School of Beauty Sciences 181 Cedar Hill St *TF:* 866-903-3457 ■ *Web:* www.cosmixschoolofbeautysciences.com	Marlboro	MA	01752	508-787-0099		685
Cosmix School of Makeup Artistry 3440 N Andrews Ave *Web:* www.cosmixinc.com	Fort Lauderdale	FL	33309	954-564-4181	564-0156	685
Cosmo 12 Kent Way Ste 201 PO Box 737 *Web:* cosmofabric.net	Byfield	MA	01922	978-462-7311	465-6223	745-7
Cosmo Bio USA Inc 2792 Loker Ave W Ste 101 *Web:* cosmobiousa.com	Carlsbad	CA	92010	760-431-4600	431-4604	145
Cosmo Corp 30201 Aurora Rd *Web:* www.cosmocorp.com	Cleveland	OH	44139	440-498-7500	498-7515	604
Cosmo Specialty Fibers Inc 1701 First St *Web:* www.cosmospecialtyfibers.com	Cosmopolis	WA	98537	360-500-4600		638
Cosmo's Food Products Inc 200 Callegari Dr **Fax Area Code: 203* ■ *TF:* 800-942-6766 ■ *Web:* www.cosmosfoods.com	West Haven	CT	06516	800-942-6766	937-7283*	296-19
Cosmodyne LLC 3010 Old Ranch Pky Ste 300 *Web:* www.cosmodyne.com	Seal Beach	CA	90740	562-795-5990	320-5688	695
Cosmopolitan Hotel Toronto 8 Colborne St *TF:* 800-958-3488 ■ *Web:* www.cosmotoronto.com	Toronto	ON	M5E1E1	416-350-2000	350-2460	379
Cosmopolitan Intl PO Box 7351 *TF:* 800-648-4331 ■ *Web:* www.cosmopolitan.org	Lancaster	PA	17604	717-295-7142	295-7143	48-15
Cosmos Cafe 575 Grande Allee E *Web:* lecosmos.com	Quebec City	QC	G1R2K5	418-640-0606		671
Cosmos Communications Inc 11-05 44th Dr *TF:* 800-223-5751 ■ *Web:* www.cosmoscommunications.com	Long Island City	NY	11101	718-482-1800	482-1968	627
Cosmos Consulting Group Inc 22 W Washington St Ste 1500 *Web:* cosmosconsulting.com	Chicago	IL	60602	800-439-6132		194
Cosmos Electronic Machine Corp 140 Schmitt Blvd *Web:* www.cosmos-kabar.com	Farmingdale	NY	11735	631-249-2535	694-6846	318
Cosmos Sports 1690 Bonhill Rd *Web:* www.cosmossports.com	Mississauga	ON	L5T1C8	905-564-4660	564-4881	194
Cosmotech School of Cosmetology 39 Mechanic St *Web:* www.cosmotechschool.com	Westbrook	ME	04038	207-591-4122		685
COSN (Consortium for School Networking) 1025 Vermont Ave NW Ste 1010 *TF:* 866-267-8747 ■ *Web:* cosn.org	Washington	DC	20005	202-861-2676	393-2011	48-9
Cospolich Inc 14695 US 61 *TF:* 800-423-7761 ■ *Web:* cospolich.com	Norco	LA	70079	985-725-0222	725-1564	14
Cosrich Group Inc 12243 Branford St *TF:* 800-831-7210 ■ *Web:* www.ouchiesonline.com	Sun Valley	CA	91352	818-686-2500		214
Cossatot Community College of the University of Arkansas 183 College Dr *TF:* 800-844-4471 ■ *Web:* www.cccua.edu	De Queen	AR	71832	870-584-4471		786
Cossatot River State Park-Natural Area 1980 Hwy 278 W *TF:* 877-665-6343 ■ *Web:* www.arkansasstateparks.com	Wickes	AR	71973	870-385-2201		565
COST (Council on State Taxation) 122 C St NW Ste 330 *Web:* www.cost.org	Washington	DC	20001	202-484-5222	484-5229	49-12
Cost Containment Engineering Inc (CCE) 9222 Linbrooke St *Web:* www.costcontainmentengr.com	San Antonio	TX	78250	210-722-7278		261

	Phone	Fax	Class
Cost Control Associates Inc 310 Bay Rd.......Queensbury NY 12804 *TF:* 800-836-3787 ■ *Web:* costcontrolassociates.com	518-798-4437		196
Cost Effective Computers 2955 C-Cleveland Hwy.......Dalton GA 30721 *Web:* www.quickscrip.net	706-259-6091	259-2278	175
Cost Management Services Inc (CMS) 2737 78th Ave SE Ste 203.......Mercer Island WA 98040 *Web:* www.cmsnaturalgas.com	206-236-8808	237-8807	196
Cost Plus Inc 200 Fourth St.......Oakland CA 94607 *NASDAQ: CPWM* ■ *TF:* 877-967-5362 ■ *Web:* www.worldmarket.com	510-893-7300	893-3681	362
Costa Cruise Lines Inc 880 SW 145th Ave Ste 102.......Pembroke Pines FL 33021 *TF:* 800-462-6782 ■ *Web:* www.costacruises.com	954-266-5600		220
Costa Del Mar 2361 Mason Ave Ste 100.......Daytona Beach FL 32117 *TF:* 800-447-3700 ■ *Web:* www.costadelmar.com	386-274-4000	274-4001	542
Costa Fruit & Produce 18 Bunker Hill Industrial Pk.......Boston MA 02129 *TF:* 800-322-1374 ■ *Web:* www.freshideas.com	617-241-8007		297-7
Costa Jim (Rep D - CA) 2081 Rayburn House Office Bldg.......Washington DC 20515 *Web:* costa.house.gov	202-225-3341		342-2
Costa Mesa Chamber of Commerce 1700 Adams Ave Ste 101.......Costa Mesa CA 92626 *Web:* www.costamesachamber.com	714-885-9090	885-9094	139
Costa Nursery Farms Inc 21800 SW 162nd Ave.......Miami FL 33170 *TF:* 800-327-7074 ■ *Web:* www.costafarms.com	800-327-7074		369
Costa Rica *Consulate General* 1605 W Olympic Blvd Ste 400.......Los Angeles CA 90015 *Web:* www.costarica-embassy.org	213-380-7915	380-5639	257
Costanoa Coastal Lodge & Camp 2001 Rossi Rd.......Pescadero CA 94060 *TF:* 877-262-7848 ■ *Web:* www.costanoa.com	650-879-1100	879-2275	669
Costanzo's Bakery Inc 30 Innsbruck Dr.......Buffalo NY 14227 *TF:* 844-354-7783 ■ *Web:* www.costanzosbakery.com	716-656-9093		296-1
CoStar Group Inc 1331 L St NW.......Washington DC 20005 *NASDAQ: CSGP* ■ *TF:* 888-226-7404 ■ *Web:* www.costargroup.com	800-204-5960		653
Costar Video Systems LLC 101 Wrangler Dr Ste 201.......Coppell TX 75019 *TF:* 888-694-7827 ■ *Web:* www.costarvideo.com	469-635-6800	635-6822	652
Costco Wholesale Corp 999 Lake Dr.......Issaquah WA 98027 *NASDAQ: COST* ■ *TF:* 800-774-2678 ■ *Web:* www.costco.com	425-313-8100		812
Costello Inc 2107 CityWest Blvd Third Fl.......Houston TX 77042 *Web:* www.costelloinc.com	713-783-7788		261
Costello, Porter, Hill, Heisterkamp, Bushnell & Carpenter LLP 704 St Joseph St Security Bldg.......Rapid City SD 57709 *Web:* www.costelloporter.com	605-343-2410		428
Costich Engineering & Land Surveying PC 217 Lake Ave.......Rochester NY 14608 *Web:* costich.com	585-458-3020		261
Costilla County 233 Main St Ste C PO Box 99.......San Luis CO 81152 **Fax Area Code:* 719 ■ *TF:* 866-509-9302 ■ *Web:* www.colorado.gov	866-509-9302	672-3856*	338
Costner & Greene 315 High St.......Maryville TN 37801 *Web:* costnergreene.com	865-983-7642		41
Costume Gallery 700 Creek Rd.......Delanco NJ 08075 *TF:* 800-222-8125 ■ *Web:* www.costumegallery.net	609-386-6601	386-0677	155-6
Costume Specialists Inc 211 N Fifth St.......Columbus OH 43215 *TF:* 800-596-9357 ■ *Web:* costumespecialists.com	614-464-2115	464-2114	155-6
COSUD Intellectual Property Solutions PC. 15 Chester Ave.......White Plains NY 10601 *Web:* www.patentassets.com	203-366-3560	335-6779	445
Cosumnes River College 8401 Center Pkwy.......Sacramento CA 95823 *Web:* www.crc.losrios.edu	916-691-7410	691-7467	162
COT (Civic Orchestra of Tucson) PO Box 42764.......Tucson AZ 85733 *Web:* www.cotmusic.org	520-730-3371		573-3
COTA (Children's Organ Transplant Assn) 2501 W Cota Dr.......Bloomington IN 47403 *TF:* 800-366-2682 ■ *Web:* cota.org	812-336-8872		48-17
COTA (Central Ohio Transit Authority) 33 N High St.......Columbus OH 43215 *Web:* www.cota.com	614-228-1776		468
Cota & Cota Inc 56 Bridge St.......Bellows Falls VT 05101 *TF:* 888-268-2645 ■ *Web:* www.cotaoil.com	802-463-9149		316
Cota & Cota Inc 4 Green St.......Bellows Falls VT 05101 *Web:* cotaoil.com	802-463-0000	460-3429	316
COTC (Central Oklahoma Telephone Co) 223 Broadway.......Davenport OK 74026 *TF:* 800-252-8854 ■ *Web:* www.cotc.net	918-377-2241	377-2506	224
Cotchett Pitre & McCarthy LLP San Francisco Airport Office Ctr 840 Malcolm Rd Ste 200.......Burlingame CA 94010 *Web:* www.cpmlegal.com	650-697-6000		41
Coteau Properties Co 204 County Rd 15.......Beulah ND 58523 *Web:* www.nacoal.com	701-873-2281	873-7226	501
COTEC Offshore Engineering Solutions 738 S Tx Hwy 6 Ste 901.......Houston TX 77079 *Web:* cotecinc.com	281-760-3108		261
Coterie Theatre, The 2450 Grand Blvd Ste 144.......Kansas City MO 64108 *Web:* thecoterie.org	816-474-6785	474-7112	572
Cothern Computer Systems Inc 1640 Lelia Dr Ste 200.......Jackson MS 39216 **Fax Area Code:* 601 ■ *TF:* 800-844-1155 ■ *Web:* www.ccslink.com	800-844-1155	969-1184*	178-7
Cothrun & Lucido 3401 Allen Pkwy STE 100.......Houston TX 77002 *Web:* cothrunlucido.com	713-228-2858		41
Cotiviti Corp 1 Glenlake Pkwy Ste 1400.......Atlanta GA 30328 *TF:* 800-530-1013 ■ *Web:* www.cotiviti.com	770-379-2800		734
Coto Technology USA 66 Whitecap Dr.......North Kingstown RI 02052 *Web:* cotorelay.com	401-943-2686	942-0920	203
Co-Tronics Inc 2935 W 100 N.......Peru IN 46970 *Web:* www.cotronicsinc.com	574-722-3850		604
COTS (Computing Technologies Inc) 6372 Mechanicsville Tpk Ste 112.......Mechanicsville VA 23111 **Fax Area Code:* 571 ■ *Web:* www.cots.com	703-280-8800	386-4959*	178-1
Cott Systems Inc 2800 Corporate Exchange Dr Ste 300.......Columbus OH 43231 *Web:* www.cottsystems.com	614-847-4405		225
Cotta Transmission Company LLC 1301 Prince Hall Dr.......Beloit WI 53511 *Web:* www.cotta.com	608-368-5600	368-5605	709
Cottage Grove Area Chamber of Commerce 8617 W Point Douglas Rd Ste 150.......Cottage Grove MN 55016 *Web:* www.cottagegrovechamber.org	651-458-8334	458-8383	139
Cottage Place 5181 E Hawthorne Dr.......Flagstaff AZ 86004 *Web:* www.cottageplace.com	928-774-8431		671
Cottage Press PO Box 6135.......Lincoln MA 01773 *Web:* www.thecottagepress.com	781-259-8270		637-2
Cotter High School 1115 West Broadway St.......Winona MN 55987 *Web:* www.cotterschools.org	507-453-5000		622
Cotter Machine Company Inc 7 Little Brook Rd.......West Wareham MA 02576 *Web:* www.cottermachine.com	508-291-7400	291-7401	488
Cotterman Co 130 Seltzer Rd.......Croswell MI 48422 *TF:* 800-552-3337 ■ *Web:* www.cotterman.com	810-679-4400	679-4510	421
Cottey College 1000 W Austin Blvd.......Nevada MO 64772 *TF:* 888-526-8839 ■ *Web:* www.cottey.edu	417-667-8181	667-8103	162
Cottle County PO Box 717.......Paducah TX 79248 *Web:* www.co.cottle.tx.us	806-492-3823	492-2625	338
Cottman Animal Hospital PC 1012 Cottman Ave.......Philadelphia PA 19111 *Web:* cottmanah.com	215-745-9030	745-3055	794
Cotton & Co 633 SE Fifth St.......Stuart FL 34994 *Web:* thecottonsolution.com	772-287-6612		4
Cotton Belt Inc 401 E Sater St.......Pinetops NC 27864 *TF:* 800-849-4192 ■ *Web:* www.edgecombe.com	252-827-4192	827-5683	471
Cotton Council Intl 1521 New Hampshire Ave NW.......Washington DC 20036 *Web:* www.cottonusa.org	202-745-7805	483-4040	48-2
Cotton Electric Co-opeartive Inc 226 N Broadway.......Walters OK 73572 *TF:* 855-730-8711 ■ *Web:* www.cottonelectric.com	580-875-3351		245
Cotton Exchange Tavern 201 E River St.......Savannah GA 31401 *Web:* www.exchangetavernsavannah.com	912-232-7088		671
Cotton Exchange, The 115 E 3rd St.......Wendell NC 27591 *Web:* thirdstreetscreen.com	919-365-2725		155-3
Cotton Goods Manufacturing Co 259 N California Ave.......Chicago IL 60612 *Web:* www.cottongoodsmfg.com	773-265-0088	265-0096	746
Cotton Inc 6399 Weston Pkwy.......Cary NC 27513 *TF:* 800-334-5868 ■ *Web:* www.cottoninc.com	919-678-2220	678-2230	48-2
Cotton Patch Cafe 3302 S Clack St.......Abilene TX 79606 *Web:* www.cottonpatch.com	325-691-0509		671
Cotton Tom (Sen R - AR) 326 Russell Senate Office Bldg.......Washington DC 20510 *Web:* www.cotton.senate.gov	202-224-2353		342-2
Cotton's All Lines Insurance Inc 1222 NW 16th Ave.......Gainesville FL 32601 *Web:* cottonsalllines.com	352-338-1222		390
CottonimagesCom Inc 10481 NW 28th St.......Miami FL 33172 *TF:* 888-642-7999 ■ *Web:* cottonimages.com	305-251-2560		344
Cottonwood Chamber of Commerce 1010 S Main St.......Cottonwood AZ 86326 *Web:* www.cottonwoodchamberaz.org	928-634-7593	634-7594	139
Cottonwood Chronicle 503 King St.......Cottonwood ID 83522 *Web:* www.cottonwoodchronicle.com	208-962-3851	962-7131	532-2
Cottonwood County Historical Society 812 4th Ave.......Windom MN 56101 *Web:* www.cchsmn1901.org	507-831-1134		637-2
Cottonwood Grille 913 W River St.......Boise ID 83702 *Web:* cottonwoodgrille.com	208-333-9800		671
Cottonwood Livestock Auction 2151 Hwy 95 N.......Cottonwood ID 83522 *Web:* www.cottonwoodlivestock.com	208-983-7400	962-3778	446
Cottonwood Public Library 100 S Sixth St.......Cottonwood AZ 86326 *Web:* ctwpl.info	928-634-7559	634-0253	434-3
Cottonwood Software PO Box 657.......Litchfield Park AZ 85340 *TF:* 877-414-8384 ■ *Web:* www.cottonwoodsw.com	877-414-8384		178-1
Cottonwood Technology Funds (CTF) 422 Old Santa Fe Trail.......Santa Fe NM 87505 *Web:* cottonwoodtechnologyfund.com	505-412-8537		792
Cottrell Inc 2125 Candler Rd.......Gainesville GA 30507 *TF:* 800-827-0132 ■ *Web:* www.cottrelltrailers.com	770-532-7251	535-2831	779
Cottrell Paper Company Inc 1135 Rock City Rd PO Box 35.......Rock City Falls NY 12863 *TF:* 800-948-3559 ■ *Web:* www.cottrellpaper.com	518-885-1702		816
Coty Inc 350 Fifth Ave 17th Fl.......New York NY 10118 *Web:* www.coty.com	212-389-7300		574
Couch Distributing Company Inc 104 Lee Rd.......Watsonville CA 95076 *Web:* www.couchdistributing.com	831-724-0649	724-4293	81-1
Couch White LLP 540 Broadway PO Box 22222.......Albany NY 12201 *Web:* couchwhite.com	518-426-4600		41
Cougar Drilling Solutions Inc 7319 - 17 St.......Edmonton AB T6P1P1 *TF:* 877-439-3376 ■ *Web:* www.cougards.com	877-439-3376		539
Cougar Helicopters Inc St John's International Airport 40 Craig Dobbins' Way ....Saint John NL A1A4Y3 *Web:* www.cougar.ca	709-758-4800	758-4850	359
Cougar Mountain Zoo 19525 SE 54th St.......Issaquah WA 98027 *Web:* www.cougarmountainzoo.org	425-392-6278	392-1076	823
Coughlin & CO 140 E 19th Ave Ste 700.......Denver CO 80203 *Web:* www.coughlinandcompany.com	303-863-1900	863-7100	401

Name / Address	City	State	Zip	Phone	Fax	Class
Coughlin Equipment Company Inc						
2221 E Hwy 66	El Reno	OK	73036	405-262-9101		358
Web: coughlinequipment.com						
Cougle Commission Co						
345 N Aberdeen St	Chicago	IL	60607	312-666-7861	666-6434	473
TF: 800-568-2240 ■ *Web:* www.couglefoods.com						
Cougle's Recycling Inc 1000 S 4th St	Hamburg	PA	19526	610-562-8336	562-8381	660
Web: www.couglesrecycling.com						
Coulson Group of Cos						
4890 Cherry Creek Rd	Port Alberni	BC	V9Y8E9	250-724-7600		787
TF: 800-663-3456 ■ *Web:* www.coulsongroup.com						
Coulter & Justus PC						
9717 Cogdill Rd Ste 201	Knoxville	TN	37932	865-637-4161		2
Web: cj-pc.com						
Coulter Cadillac phoenix						
1188 E Camelback Rd	Phoenix	AZ	85014	602-626-9493		57
Web: www.coultercadillacphoenix.com						
Coulter Forge Technology Inc						
1494 67th St	Emeryville	CA	94608	510-420-3500	420-3555	483
TF: 800-648-4884 ■ *Web:* www.coulter-forge.com						
Coulter Lake Guest Ranch						
80 County Rd 273	Rifle	CO	81650	970-625-1473		239
TF: 800-858-3046 ■ *Web:* www.coulterlake.com						
Coulter's Furniture 1324 Windsor Ave	Windsor	ON	N8X3L9	519-253-7422	253-3744	321
Web: www.coulters.com						
Council Bluffs Area Chamber of Commerce						
149 W Broadway	Council Bluffs	IA	51503	712-325-1000	322-5698	139
TF: 800-228-6878 ■ *Web:* www.councilbluffsiowa.com						
Council Bluffs Public Library						
400 Willow Ave	Council Bluffs	IA	51503	712-323-7553		434-3
Web: www.councilbluffslibrary.org						
Council for Advancement & Support of Education (CASE)						
1307 New York Ave NW Ste 1000	Washington	DC	20005	202-328-5900	387-4973	49-5
TF: 800-554-8536 ■ *Web:* www.case.org						
Council for Affordable Health Coverage (CAHI)						
127 S Peyton St Ste 210	Alexandria	VA	22314	703-836-6200	836-6550	49-9
Web: www.cahi.org						
Council for Chemical Research Inc (CCR)						
1550 M St NW Ste 300	Washington	DC	20005	202-429-3971	429-3976	49-19
Web: ccrhq.org						
Council for Christian Colleges & Universities (CCCU)						
321 Eigth St NE	Washington	DC	20002	202-546-8713	546-8913	49-5
Web: www.cccu.org						
Council for Community & Economic Research (C2ER)						
1700 N Moore St Ste 2225	Arlington	VA	22209	703-522-4980	393-5098*	49-12
**Fax Area Code:* 480 ■ *Web:* www.c2er.org						
Council For Economic Opportunities In Greater Cleveland						
1801 Superior Ave 4th Fl	Cleveland	OH	44114	216-696-9077	696-0770	48-11
Web: www.ceogc.org						
Council for Equal Rights in Adoption						
444 E 76th St	New York	NY	10021	212-988-0110		48-6
Web: www.adoptionhealing.com						
Council for Higher Education Accreditation (CHEA)						
1 Dupont Cir NW Ste 510	Washington	DC	20036	202-955-6126	955-6129	48-1
Web: www.chea.org						
Council for Interior Design Accreditation (CIDA)						
206 Grandville Ave Ste 350	Grand Rapids	MI	49503	616-458-0400	458-0460	48-1
Web: accredit-id.org						
Council for International Exchange of Scholars (CIES)						
1400 K St NW Ste 700	Washington	DC	20005	202-686-4000		49-5
Web: www.cies.org						
Council for Opportunity in Education						
1025 Vermont Ave NW Ste 400	Washington	DC	20005	202-347-7430	347-0786	48-11
Web: www.coenet.org						
Council for Professional Recognition						
2460 16th St NW	Washington	DC	20009	202-265-9090	265-9161	49-5
TF: 800-424-4310 ■ *Web:* www.cdacouncil.org						
Council for Responsible Genetics (CRG)						
5 Upland Rd Ste 3	Cambridge	MA	02140	617-868-0870	491-5344	49-19
Web: www.councilforresponsiblegenetics.org						
Council for Responsible Nutrition (CRN)						
1828 L St NW Ste 510	Washington	DC	20036	202-204-7700	204-7701	49-6
Web: www.crnusa.org						
Council for the Accreditation of Educator Preparation (CAEP)						
1140 19th St NW Ste 400	Washington	DC	20036	202-223-0077		48-1
Web: caepnet.org						
Council Grove State Park						
3201 Spurgin Rd	Missoula	MT	59804	406-542-5500	542-5517	565
Web: stateparks.mt.gov						
Council Grove/Morris County Chamber of Commerce & Tourism						
207 W Main St	Council Grove	KS	66846	620-767-5413		206
Web: www.councilgrove.com						
Council of Administrators of Special Education (CASE)						
Osigian Office Centre 101 Katelyn Cir						
Ste E	Warner Robins	GA	31088	478-333-6892	333-2453	49-5
TF: 800-585-1753 ■ *Web:* www.casecec.org						
Council of Better Business Bureaus						
3033 Wilson Blvd Ste 600	Arlington	VA	22201	800-621-8096		78
TF: 800-621-8096 ■ *Web:* www.bbb.org						
Council of Canadians						
170 Laurier Ave W Ste 700	Ottawa	ON	K1P5V5	613-233-2773		48-7
TF: 800-387-7177 ■ *Web:* canadians.org						
Council of Chief State School Officers (CCSSO)						
1 Massachusetts Ave NW Ste 700	Washington	DC	20001	202-336-7000	408-8072	49-5
Web: www.ccsso.org						
Council of Ethical Organizations						
1727 King St Ste 300	Alexandria	VA	22314	703-683-7916		533
Web: councilofethicalorganizations.com						
Council of Graduate Schools (CGS)						
1 Dupont Cir NW Ste 230	Washington	DC	20036	202-223-3791	331-7157	49-5
Web: cgsnet.org						
Council of Industrial Boiler Owners (CIBO)						
6801 Kennedy Rd Ste 102	Warrenton	VA	20187	540-349-9043	349-9850	49-13
Web: www.cibo.org						
Council of Institutional Investors						
1717 Pennsylvania Ave NW Ste 350	Washington	DC	20006	202-822-0800	822-0801	49-2
Web: www.cii.org						
Council of Insurance Agents & Brokers						
701 Pennsylvania Ave NW Ste 750	Washington	DC	20004	202-783-4400	783-4410	49-9
Web: www.ciab.com						
Council of Residential Specialists						
430 N Michigan Ave Ste 300	Chicago	IL	60611	312-321-4400		49-17
TF: 800-462-8841 ■ *Web:* crs.com						
Council of State & Territorial Epidemiologists (CSTE)						
2872 Woodcock Blvd Ste 303	Atlanta	GA	30341	770-458-3811	458-8516	49-7
Web: www.cste.org						
Council of Supply Chain Management Professionals						
333 E Butterfield Rd Ste 140	Lombard	IL	60148	630-574-0985	574-0989	49-18
Web: cscmp.org						
Council of the Great City Schools						
1301 Pennsylvania Ave NW Ste 702	Washington	DC	20004	202-393-2427	393-2400	49-5
Web: www.cgcs.org						
Council on Accreditation (COA)						
45 Broadway 29th Fl	New York	NY	10006	212-797-3000	797-1428	48-1
TF: 866-262-8088 ■ *Web:* www.coanet.org						
Council on Aviation Accreditation (CAA)						
Aviation Accreditation Board International						
3410 Skyway Dr	Auburn	AL	36830	334-844-2431	844-2432	48-1
Web: www.aabi.aero						
Council on Chiropractic Education Commission on Accreditation						
8049 N 85th Way	Scottsdale	AZ	85258	480-443-8877	483-7333	48-1
TF: 888-443-3506 ■ *Web:* www.cce-usa.org						
Council on Education for Public Health						
1010 Wayne Ave Ste 220	Silver Spring	MD	20910	202-789-1050	789-1895	48-1
Web: ceph.org						
Council on Environmental Quality						
730 Jackson Pl NW	Washington	DC	20503	202-395-5750	456-0753	340
Web: www.whitehouse.gov						
Council on Foundations						
2121 Crystal Dr Ste 700	Arlington	VA	22202	703-879-0600	879-0800	48-5
TF: 800-673-9036 ■ *Web:* www.cof.org						
Council on International Educational Exchange (CIEE)						
300 Fore St	Portland	ME	04101	207-553-4000	553-5272	49-5
TF: 888-268-6245 ■ *Web:* www.ciee.org						
Council on Licensure Enforcement & Regulation (CLEAR)						
403 Marquis Ave	Lexington	KY	40502	859-269-1289		49-7
Web: www.clearhq.org						
Council on Naturopathic Medical Education (CNME)						
PO Box 178	Great Barrington	MA	01230	413-528-8877		48-1
Web: cnme.org						
Council on Occupational Education						
7840 Roswell Rd Bldg 300 Ste 325	Atlanta	GA	30350	770-396-3898		48-1
Web: www.council.org						
Council on Quality & Leadership, The (CQL)						
100 W Rd Ste 300	Towson	MD	21204	410-583-0060		48-1
Web: c-q-l.org						
Council on Size & Weight Discrimination (CSWD)						
PO Box 305	Mount Marion	NY	12456	845-679-1209	679-1206	48-17
Web: cswd.org						
Council on Social Work Education (CSWE)						
1701 Duke St Ste 200	Alexandria	VA	22314	703-683-8080	683-8099	49-5
Web: cswe.org						
Council on Southeast Asia Studies						
Henry R. Luce Hall 34 Hillhouse Ave						
Ste 311	New Haven	CT	06520	203-432-3431	432-3432	393
Web: cseas.yale.edu						
Council on State Taxation (COST)						
122 C St NW Ste 330	Washington	DC	20001	202-484-5222	484-5229	49-12
Web: www.cost.org						
Council Rock School District						
30 N Chancellor St	Newtown	PA	18940	215-944-1000		685
Web: www.crsd.org						
Councilor, Buchanan and Mitchell PC						
7910 Woodmont Ave Ste 500	Bethesda	MD	20814	301-986-0600	986-0432	2
Web: www.cbmcpa.com						
Counselors of Real Estate (CRE)						
430 N Michigan Ave	Chicago	IL	60611	312-329-8427	329-8881	49-17
Web: www.cre.org						
Count Basie Center for the Arts						
99 Monmouth St	Red Bank	NJ	07701	732-842-9000		572
Web: thebasie.org						
Count Me In 5955 Edmond St	Las Vegas	NV	89118	866-514-5888	958-8779*	84
**Fax Area Code:* 800 ■ *TF:* 866-514-5888 ■ *Web:* www.countmeinllc.com						
Counter Pro Inc 210 Lincoln St	Manchester	NH	03103	603-647-2444		191-3
TF: 800-899-2444 ■ *Web:* counterproincusa.com						
Counter-Fit Inc 1 Ironside Ct	Willingboro	NJ	08046	609-871-8888	820-2779	189-7
Web: www.counterfit.biz						
Counterforce Inc						
2740 Matheson Blvd E Unit 2A	Mississauga	ON	L4W4X3	905-282-6200		693
TF: 800-591-7374 ■ *Web:* www.counterforce.com						
Counterpane Montessori Inc						
839 Hwy 314	Fayetteville	GA	30214	770-461-2304		685
Web: www.counterpane.org						
Counterparts 1400 Douglas St MS 0110	Omaha	NE	68179	402-932-2220		226
Web: www.mycounterparts.com						
Counterstrike Corp						
10535 Jordon Ave	Chatsworth	CA	91311	818-906-1596		693
Web: www.counterstrike.com						
Country 106.7 5026 Cliff Gookin Blvd	Tupelo	MS	38801	662-842-1067		645-167
Web: wizard106.iheart.com						
Country 96 KWWR 1705 E Liberty St	Mexico	MO	65265	573-581-5500		645
Country 97.1 HANK FM						
40 Monument Cir Ste 600	Indianapolis	IN	46204	317-266-9700	684-2021	645-74
Web: www.hankfm.com						
Country Aircheck						
1102 17th Ave S Ste 205	Nashville	TN	37212	615-320-1450		194
Web: countryaircheck.com						
Country Bank for Savings 75 Main St	Ware	MA	01082	413-967-6221	967-3289	70
TF: 800-322-8233 ■ *Web:* www.countrybank.com						
Country Bank Shares Inc 617 1st St	Milford	NE	68405	402-761-7600		360-2
TF: 800-695-2045 ■ *Web:* www.bankfmb.com						
Country Cablevision Inc						
9449 State Hwy 197 S	Burnsville	NC	28714	828-682-4074		116
TF: 800-722-4074 ■ *Web:* ccvn.com						

				Phone	Fax	Class
Country Caterers Inc 1775 Marion Waldo Rd *TF:* 800-743-1013 ■ *Web:* www.countrycaterers.net	Marion	OH	43302	740-595-3095		670
Country Club Bank 2310 S 4th St *Web:* www.ccbfinancial.com	Leavenworth	KS	66048	913-682-2300		360-2
Country Club Nissan 55 Oneida St *TF:* 888-685-1081 ■ *Web:* www.countryclubnissan.com	Oneonta	NY	13820	607-432-2800		57
Country Court Nursing Ctr 1076 Coshocton Ave *Web:* countrycourt.com	Mount Vernon	OH	43050	740-397-4125		371
Country Financial / Country Trust Bank 1701 N Towanda Ave *TF:* 866-268-6879 ■ *Web:* www.countryfinancial.com	Bloomington	IL	61701	866-268-6879		70
Country Floors Inc 15 E 16th St *Web:* www.countryfloors.com	New York	NY	10003	212-627-8300	242-1604	291
Country Fresh Mushroom Co 289 Chambers Rd PO Box 490 *Web:* www.countryfreshmushrooms.com	Toughkenamon	PA	19374	610-268-3043	268-0479	297-7
Country Hills Health Care Inc 1580 Broadway *Web:* www.countryhills.com	El Cajon	CA	92021	619-441-8745		371
Country Home Furniture LLC 1352 Main St *Web:* www.chfs1.com	East Earl	PA	17519	717-354-2329		321
Country Inn at the Mall 936 Stillwater Ave *TF:* 800-244-3961 ■ *Web:* www.countryinnatthemall.net	Bangor	ME	04401	207-941-0200		379
Country Inn Lake Resort 1332 Airport Rd *Web:* www.countryinnlakeresort.com	Hot Springs	AR	71913	501-767-3535		379
Country Kitchen SweetArt 4621 Speedway Dr *Web:* www.countrykitchensa.com	Fort Wayne	IN	46825	260-482-4835		167-3
Country Lane Flower Shop 729 S Michigan Ave *TF:* 800-764-7673 ■ *Web:* www.countrylaneflowers.com	Howell	MI	48843	517-546-1111		292
Country Life Farm 319 Old Joppa Rd *Web:* www.countrylifefarm.com	Bel Air	MD	21014	410-879-1952	879-6207	368
Country Living Magazine 300 W 57th St *Web:* www.countryliving.com	New York	NY	10019	212-649-3204		457-11
Country Maid Inc 1919 S Kinnickinnic Ave *Web:* www.countrymaid.com	Milwaukee	WI	53204	414-383-3970		123
Country Mark Co-op 1200 Refinery Rd **Fax Area Code: 812* ■ *TF:* 800-832-5490 ■ *Web:* www.countrymark.com	Mount Vernon	IN	47620	800-832-5490	838-8196*	597
Country Messenger Press Publishing Group LLC (CMPPG) 27657 US Hwy 97 *Web:* www.cmppg.com	Okanogan	WA	98840	253-216-6364		637-2
Country Music Association Inc (CMA) 35 Music Sq E Ste 201 *Web:* www.cmaworld.com	Nashville	TN	37203	615-244-2840	726-0314	48-4
Country Music Hall of Fame & Museum 222 Fifth Ave S *TF:* 800-852-6437 ■ *Web:* countrymusichalloffame.org	Nashville	TN	37203	615-416-2001	255-2245	520
Country Music Television (CMT) 330 Commerce St *Web:* www.cmt.com	Nashville	TN	37201	615-335-8400		740
Country Pride Services Coop 144 9th St *TF:* 800-228-1667 ■ *Web:* www.countryprideservices.com	Bingham Lake	MN	56118	507-831-2580	831-3651	276
Country Pure Foods Inc 681 W Waterloo Rd *Web:* countrypure.com	Akron	OH	44314	330-753-2293	848-4287	296-20
Country Radio Broadcasters Inc (CRB) 819 18th Ave S *Web:* www.countryradioseminar.com	Nashville	TN	37203	615-327-4487	329-4492	49-14
Country Sampler Magazine 707 Kautz Rd *Web:* www.countrysampler.com	Saint Charles	IL	60174	630-377-8000		457-14
Country Silk Inc 2147 State Rte 27 S Ste 402 *Web:* www.countrysilk.com	Edison	NJ	08817	732-752-5556	752-7550	293
Country Today 701 S Farwell St *Web:* www.leadertelegram.com	Eau Claire	WI	54701	715-833-9270		532-4
Country Treasures 216 N Bridge St *Web:* countrytreasureshallmark.com	Chippewa Falls	WI	54729	715-723-8883		327
Country Way 5325 Mowry Ave	Fremont	CA	94536	510-797-3188		671
Country's Barbecue 2016 12th Ave *TF:* 800-285-4267 ■ *Web:* www.countrysbarbecue.com	Columbus	GA	31901	706-327-7702		671
Countrycare Animal Complex Inc 4235 Elmview Rd *Web:* countrycareac.com	Green Bay	WI	54311	920-863-3220		794
CountryPlace Mortgage Ltd 15301 Spectrum Dr Ste 550 *Web:* www.countryplaceloans.com	Addison	TX	75001	800-228-1828		509
Countryside Bank 6734 Joliet Rd *Web:* www.bankcountryside.com	Countryside	IL	60525	708-485-3100	485-3106	70
Countryside Co-op 514 E Main St *TF:* 800-236-7585 ■ *Web:* www.countrysidecoop.com	Durand	WI	54736	715-672-8947	672-5131	276
Countryside Federal Credit Union 5720 Commons Park Dr *Web:* countryside.org	East Syracuse	NY	13057	315-445-2300		219
Countryside Large Animal Veterinary Services PLLC 3765 W O St *Web:* csidevet.com	Greeley	CO	80631	970-351-7045		794
Countryside Veterinary Services of The Fox Valley SC W3022 Edgewood Trail *Web:* countrysidevets.net	Appleton	WI	54913	920-968-3322		794
Countryside Vineyards and Winery 658 Henry Harr Rd *Web:* www.cvwineryandsupply.com	Blountville	TN	37617	423-323-1660		50-7
CountryTyme Inc 3451 Cincinnati-Zanesville Rd SW *TF:* 800-213-8365 ■ *Web:* www.countrytyme.com	Lancaster	OH	43130	740-475-6001		653
Countrywide Tire & Rubber Inc 17200 Medina Rd Ste 100 *Web:* www.countrywidetire.com	Plymouth	MN	55447	763-546-1636		755
County & Circuit Clerk 206 W 3rd St	Fordyce	AR	71742	870-352-2307		338
County Beverage Company Inc 1290 SE Hamblen Rd	Lee's Summit	MO	64081	816-525-4550		297-8
County Business Systems Inc 1574 Reed Rd *Web:* cbs-nj.com	Pennington	NJ	08534	609-935-0180		225
County Clare 1234 N Astor St *Web:* www.countyclare-inn.com	Milwaukee	WI	53202	414-272-5273	290-6300	671
County College of Morris 214 Ctr Grove Rd *TF:* 888-726-3260 ■ *Web:* www.ccm.edu	Randolph	NJ	07869	973-328-5000		162
County Concrete Corp 50 Railroad Ave *Web:* www.countyconcretenj.com	Kenvil	NJ	07847	973-584-7122		182
County Courthouse 255 N Forbes St *Web:* www.lakecountyca.gov	Lakeport	CA	95453	707-263-2371	263-2207	338
County Credit Union 130 S Bemiston Ave Ste 100 *TF:* 844-383-8650 ■ *Web:* countycu.org	Saint Louis	MO	63105	314-725-1113		219
County Educators Federal Credit Union 16 E Lincoln Ave *Web:* countyedfcu.org	Roselle Park	NJ	07204	908-245-0173		219
County Engineers Association of Ohio 6500 Busch Blvd Ste 100 *Web:* www.ceao.org	Columbus	OH	43229	614-221-0707		256
County Line 9600 Tramway Blvd NE *Web:* www.countyline.com	Albuquerque	NM	87122	505-856-7477		671
County of Bedford Virginia 122 E Main St Ste 202 *Web:* www.bedfordcountyva.gov	Bedford	VA	24523	540-586-7601	586-0406	338
County of Greene 93 E High St *TF:* 888-852-5399 ■ *Web:* www.co.greene.pa.us	Waynesburg	PA	15370	724-852-5399	852-5327	338
County of Kauai *Office of the County Clerk, Council Services Division* 4396 Rice St Ste 209 *Web:* www.kauai.gov	Lihue	HI	96766	808-241-4188	241-6349	338
County of San Bernardino 2024 Orange Tree Ln *Web:* www.sbcounty.gov	Redlands	CA	92374	909-307-2669	307-0539	520
County of Santa Cruz 701 Ocean St Rm 230 *Web:* www.co.santa-cruz.ca.us	Santa Cruz	CA	95060	831-454-2800	454-2660	338
County Press 1521 Imlay City Rd PO Box 220 *Web:* thecountypress.mihomepaper.com	Lapeer	MI	48446	810-664-0811		532-4
County Rescue Services 1765 Allouez Ave *Web:* www.countyrescue.com	Green Bay	WI	54311	920-469-9779		30
Coup, The 924 17th Ave SW *Web:* www.thecoup.ca	Calgary	AB	T2T0A2	403-541-1041		671
Coupland-Moran Engineers Inc 6001 Indian School Rd NE Ste 200 *Web:* www.cmenm.com	Albuquerque	NM	87110	505-884-8868		48-20
CouponMom Inc, The 3901 Roswell Rd *Web:* www.couponmom.com	Marietta	GA	30062	770-485-6569		393
Courage Kenny Cards 1750 Tower Blvd *TF:* 800-992-6872 ■ *Web:* www.couragecards.org	North Mankato	MN	56003	800-992-6872		241
Courier 117 E Oak St *Web:* www.sissetoncourier.com	Sisseton	SD	57262	605-698-7642	698-3641	532-2
Courier Cafe 111 N Race St *Web:* couriercafe.squarespace.com	Urbana	IL	61801	217-328-1811		671
Courier Capital Corp 1114 Delaware Ave *Web:* www.couriercapital.com	Buffalo	NY	14209	716-883-9595		401
Courier Graphics Corp 2621 S 37th St *TF:* 800-454-6381 ■ *Web:* couriergraphics.com	Phoenix	AZ	85034	602-437-9700		627
Courier Journal 219 W Tennessee St *Web:* www.courierjournal.net	Florence	AL	35630	256-764-4268	760-9618	532-4
Courier Life Publications 1 Metrotech Ctr Ste 1001 *Web:* www.cnglocal.com	Brooklyn	NY	11201	718-260-2500		360-3
Courier Systems Inc 180 Pulaski St *TF:* 800-252-0353 ■ *Web:* www.csweb.biz	Bayonne	NJ	07002	201-432-0550		803-1
Courier, The 701 W Sandusky St PO Box 609 *Web:* www.thecourier.com	Findlay	OH	45839	419-422-5151		532-2
Courier-Journal 525 W Broadway PO Box 740031 *TF:* 800-765-4011 ■ *Web:* www.courier-journal.com	Louisville	KY	40201	502-582-4011		532-2
Courier-Post 301 Cuthbert Blvd *TF:* 800-677-6289 ■ *Web:* www.courierpostonline.com	Cherry Hill	NJ	08002	856-663-6000		532-2
Courier-Tribune 500 Sunset Ave *TF:* 800-488-0444 ■ *Web:* www.courier-tribune.com	Asheboro	NC	27203	336-625-2101		532-2
Courion Industries 3044 Lambdin Ave *Web:* www.couriondoors.com	Saint Louis	MO	63115	314-533-5700		647
Couronne Company Inc 12617 Beltex Rd *TF:* 800-573-4367 ■ *Web:* www.couronneco.com	Manor	TX	78653	512-339-7808		361
Coursera 381 E Evelyn Ave *Web:* www.coursera.org	Mountain View	CA	94041	650-963-9884		725
Court Avenue Brewing Co 309 Ct Ave *Web:* www.courtavebrew.com	Des Moines	IA	50309	515-282-2739	282-3789	671
Court House Cafe 350 S Battlefield Blvd *Web:* gbcourthousecafe.com	Chesapeake	VA	23322	757-482-7077		671
Court Reporting Institute of Louisiana 5700 Florida Blvd *Web:* www.niche.com	Baton Rouge	LA	70806	225-292-1950	612-6949	167-3
Court Services & Offender Supervision Agency for the District of Columbia 633 Indiana Ave NW *Web:* www.csosa.gov	Washington	DC	20004	202-220-5300	220-5350	340-20
Court Square Ventures 427 Park St *Web:* courtsquareventures.com	Charlottesville	VA	22902	434-817-3300		792

Name / Address	City	State	ZIP	Phone	Fax	Class
Court Street Ford Inc 558 William Latham Dr *Web:* www.courtstreetfordbourbonnais.com	Bourbonnais	IL	60914	815-939-9600		57
Court Theatre 5535 S Ellis Ave *Web:* www.courttheatre.org	Chicago	IL	60637	773-702-7005		749
Court Thomas Wingert 11800 Monarch St PO Box 6207 *TF:* 800-359-7337 ■ *Web:* www.jlwingert.com	Garden Grove	CA	92841	714-379-5519	379-5549	806
CourtCall 6383 Arizona Cir *TF:* 888-882-6878 ■ *Web:* www.courtcall.com	Los Angeles	CA	90045	310-342-0888	743-1850	445
Courtesy Building Services Inc 2154 W Northwest Hwy Ste 214 *TF:* 800-479-3853 ■ *Web:* www.courtesybldgservices.com	Dallas	TX	75220	972-831-1444		104
Courtesy Chevrolet 1233 E Camelback Rd *TF:* 877-295-4648 ■ *Web:* www.houseofcourtesy.com	Phoenix	AZ	85014	602-235-0255		57
Courtesy Chevrolet Ctr 750 Camino Del Rio N *Web:* www.courtesysandiego.com	San Diego	CA	92108	619-297-4321		516
Courtesy Chrysler Jeep Dodge 9207 Adamo Dr E *TF:* 866-343-9730 ■ *Web:* www.courtesychryslerjeepdodge.com	Tampa	FL	33619	813-685-4511		57
Courtesy Insurance Agency 324 W Hefner Rd *Web:* ciaokc.com	Oklahoma City	OK	73114	405-755-4571		390
Courthouse Fitness 451 Division St Ste 200 *Web:* courthousefit.com	Salem	OR	97301	503-588-2582		354
Courtney Honda 767 Bridgeport Ave *Web:* www.hondaofmilford.com	Milford	CT	06460	203-877-2888		57
Courtney Joe (Rep D - CT) 2332 Rayburn House Office Bldg *Web:* courtney.house.gov	Washington	DC	20515	202-225-2076	225-4977	342-2
Courtroom Sciences Inc 4950 N O'Connor Rd *TF:* 800-514-5879 ■ *Web:* www.courtroomsciences.com	Irving	TX	75062	972-717-1773	717-3985	445
Courts Plus Fitness Ctr 3491 University Dr S *Web:* courtsplus.org	Fargo	ND	58104	701-237-4805		42
CourtSmart Digital Systems Inc 51 Middlesex St **Fax Area Code:* 978 ■ *TF:* 800-235-8690 ■ *Web:* www.courtsmart.com	North Chelmsford	MA	01863	800-235-8690	251-4488*	392
Coushatta Casino Resort 777 Coushatta Dr PO Box 1510 *TF:* 800-584-7263 ■ *Web:* www.coushattacasinoresort.com	Kinder	LA	70648	800-584-7263		133
Cousin Corporation of America 12333 Enterprise Blvd *Web:* www.cousin.com	Largo	FL	33773	727-536-3568		96
Cousin's Restaurant 3545 Robie St *Web:* www.cousinsrestaurant.webs.com	Halifax	NS	B3K4S7	902-455-8931		671
Cousineau Inc 3 Valley Rd PO Box 58 *TF:* 877-268-7463 ■ *Web:* www.cousineaus.com	North Anson	ME	04958	207-635-4445		448
Cousino's Steak House 1842 Woodville Rd *Web:* www.cousinossteakhouse.com	Oregon	OH	43616	419-693-0862		671
Cousins Properties Inc 191 Peachtree St NE Ste 500 *NYSE: CUZ* ■ *TF:* 844-862-7983 ■ *Web:* www.cousins.com	Atlanta	GA	30303	404-407-1000		655
Cousins Submarines Inc N83 W13400 Leon Rd *TF:* 800-238-9736 ■ *Web:* cousinssubs.com	Menomonee Falls	WI	53051	262-253-7700	253-7710	670
Couts Heating & Cooling Inc 1693 Rimpau Ave *Web:* www.couts.com	Corona	CA	92881	951-278-5560		610
Couturier Iron Craft Inc 5050 W River Dr NE *Web:* www.couturierironcraft.com	Comstock Park	MI	49321	616-784-6780		492
Couzens Lansky Fealk Ellis & Lazar P C 39395 Twelve Mile Rd Ste 200 *Web:* couzens.com	Farmington Hills	MI	48331	248-489-8600		445
Cova Hotel 655 Ellis St *Web:* www.covahotel.com	San Francisco	CA	94109	415-771-3000		393
Covalar Design LLC 1850 N Greenville Ave Ste 164 *Web:* covalar.com	Richardson	TX	75081	214-710-1045		261
Covalent Medical Inc 4750 S State Rd Ste 301 *Web:* www.covamed.com	Ann Arbor	MI	48108	734-604-0688		3
Covalent Partners LLC Reservoir Woods 930 Winter St Ste 2800 *Web:* www.covalentpartnersllc.com	Waltham	MA	02451	617-658-5500		528
Covalon Technologies Ltd 405 Britannia Rd E Ste 106 *TF:* 877-711-6055 ■ *Web:* www.covalon.com	Mississauga	ON	L4Z3E6	905-568-8400		582
Covance Inc 210 Carnegie Ctr *NYSE: CVD* ■ *TF:* 888-268-2623 ■ *Web:* www.covance.com	Princeton	NJ	08540	609-452-4440		85
Covanta Energy Corp 445 South St *NYSE: CVA* ■ *TF:* 800-950-8749 ■ *Web:* www.covanta.com	Morristown	NJ	07960	862-345-5000		787
Cove Haven Pocono Palace 5222 Milford Rd *TF:* 800-432-9932 ■ *Web:* www.covepoconoresorts.com	East Stroudsburg	PA	18302	800-432-9932		669
Cove Inn 900 Broad Ave S *TF:* 800-255-4365 ■ *Web:* www.coveinnnaples.com	Naples	FL	34102	239-262-7161	261-6905	379
Cove Lake State Park 110 Cove Lake Ln *TF:* 800-250-8615 ■ *Web:* tnstateparks.com	Caryville	TN	37714	423-566-9701		565
Cove Palisades State Park 7300 Jordan Rd *Web:* stateparks.oregon.gov	Culver	OR	97734	541-546-3412		565
Cove Point Holdings LLC 60 E 42nd St Ste 3210 *Web:* covepointholdings.net	New York	NY	10165	212-599-3388		360-3
Cove West 335 S Hale Ave *Web:* covewestusa.com	Fullerton	CA	92831	714-525-2930	525-2928	813
Cove, The 606 W Cypress St *Web:* thecove.us	San Antonio	TX	78212	210-227-2683		671
Covello Group Inc, The 1660 Olympic Blvd Ste 300 *Web:* covellogroup.com	Walnut Creek	CA	94596	925-933-2300		194
Covenant Aviation Security LLC 400 Quadrangle Dr Ste A *Web:* www.covenantsecurity.com	Bolingbrook	IL	60440	630-771-0800		693
Covenant Care 27071 Aliso Creek Rd Ste 100 **Fax Area Code:* 949 ■ *TF:* 800-861-0086 ■ *Web:* www.covenantcare.com	Aliso Viejo	CA	92656	800-861-0086	349-1900*	374-3
Covenant Care Home 5700 Old Orchard Rd *TF:* 877-708-7689 ■ *Web:* www.covenantcareathome.org	Skokie	IL	60077	877-708-7689		371
Covenant College 14049 Scenic Hwy *TF:* 888-451-2683 ■ *Web:* www.covenant.edu	Lookout Mountain	GA	30750	706-820-1560	820-0893	166
Covenant Health 100 Fort Sanders West Blvd *Web:* www.covenanthealth.com	Knoxville	TN	37922	865-374-1000		353
Covenant Health Systems Inc 100 Ames Pond Dr Ste 102 **Fax Area Code:* 978 ■ *Web:* www.covenanthealth.net	Tewksbury	MA	01876	781-861-3535	851-0828*	353
Covenant Hospice 5041 N 12th Ave *TF:* 800-541-3072 ■ *Web:* www.choosecovenant.org	Pensacola	FL	32504	850-433-2155		371
Covenant Insurance Group Inc 732 W Collins Dr *Web:* covenantgroupinc.com	Casper	WY	82601	307-265-0885		390
Covenant Living 700 W Fabyan Pkwy *TF:* 877-420-5046 ■ *Web:* www.covlivingholmstad.org	Batavia	IL	60510	630-879-4000		672
Covenant Living of Cromwell 52 Missionary Rd *TF:* 800-255-8989 ■ *Web:* www.covenantvillageofcromwell.org	Cromwell	CT	06416	860-635-2690	632-2407	672
Covenant Living of Florida 9215 W Broward Blvd *Web:* www.covenantflorida.org	Plantation	FL	33324	954-472-2860		672
Covenant Living of Golden Valley 5800 St Croix Ave *TF:* 877-825-9763 ■ *Web:* www.covlivinggoldenvalley.org	Minneapolis	MN	55422	763-546-6125		672
Covenant Living of Turlock 2125 N Olive Ave **Fax Area Code:* 617 ■ *TF:* 877-395-4851 ■ *Web:* www.covlivingturlock.org	Turlock	CA	95382	209-216-5610	565-3809*	672
Covenant Medical Center Cooper 700 Cooper Ave *Web:* www.covenanthealthcare.com	Saginaw	MI	48602	989-583-0000		374-3
Covenant Medical Ctr 3421 W Ninth St *Web:* www.wheatoniowa.org	Waterloo	IA	50702	319-272-8000		374-3
Covenant Retirement Communities Inc 5700 Old Orchard Rd *TF:* 888-401-6459 ■ *Web:* www.covliving.org	Skokie	IL	60077	773-878-2294		672
Covenant Technology Services 4900 Woodway Ste 520 *Web:* www.covenant.com	Houston	TX	77056	713-358-7500		175
Covenant Transport Inc 400 Birmingham Hwy *NASDAQ: CVTI* ■ *TF:* 800-334-9686 ■ *Web:* www.covenanttransport.com	Chattanooga	TN	37419	423-821-1212		780
Covenant United Methodist Church 6824 Tuckaseegee Rd *Web:* www.covenantcharlotte.com	Charlotte	NC	28214	704-392-3925		48-20
Covenant Village 1351 Robinwood Rd *Web:* www.covenantvillagenc.com	Gastonia	NC	28054	704-867-2319		672
Covenant Woods 7090 Covenant Woods Dr *Web:* covenantwoods.com	Mechanicsville	VA	23111	804-569-8000		672
Coventry First LLC 7111 Vly Green Rd **Fax Area Code:* 215 ■ *TF:* 877-836-8300 ■ *Web:* coventry.com	Fort Washington	PA	19034	877-836-8300	233-3201*	796
Coventry Health Care of Louisiana Inc 1720 S Sykes Dr *Web:* coventrycaresoh.coventryhealthcare.com	Bismarck	ND	58504	800-341-6613		391-3
Coventry Lumber Inc 2030 Nooseneck Hill Rd *TF:* 800-390-0919 ■ *Web:* www.coventrylumber.com	Coventry	RI	02816	401-821-2800		191-3
Coventry Public Library 1672 Flat River Rd *Web:* coventrylibrary.org	Coventry	RI	02816	401-822-9100	822-9133	434-3
Cover Publishing Co PO Box 1092 *TF:* 800-441-8398 ■ *Web:* www.ionadventure.com	Tampa	FL	33601	800-441-8398		637-2
Coverage Inc 14130-J Sullyfield Cir *Web:* www.coverageinc.com	Chantilly	VA	20151	703-631-8000		390
Coverall of Palm Beach 2541 Metrocentre Blvd St 1 Ste 1 *TF:* 800-537-3371 ■ *Web:* www.coverall.com	West Palm Beach	FL	33407	561-732-3100	922-2423	152
Coverbind Corp 3200 Corporate Dr *TF:* 800-366-6060 ■ *Web:* www.coverbind.com	Wilmington	NC	28405	910-799-4116	799-3935	608
Covered Wagon Tours LLC 1000 State St Rte 96 *Web:* www.coveredwagontours.net	Hornell	NY	14843	585-438-3063		107
Covert Manufacturing Inc 328 S East St *Web:* www.covertmfg.com	Galion	OH	44833	419-468-1761		454
Covestic Inc 5555 Lakeview Dr Ste 100 *Web:* www.covestic.com	Kirkland	WA	98033	425-803-9889		180
Covestro LLC 1 Covestro Cir *Web:* www.covestro.us	Pittsburgh	PA	15205	412-415-1199		605-2
Covia 2185 N California Blvd Ste 215 *Web:* www.covia.org	Walnut Creek	CA	94596	925-956-7400		50-4
Covina Chamber of Commerce 935 W Badillo St Ste 100 *Web:* covina.org	Covina	CA	91722	626-334-9695	966-9660	139
Covina Public Library 234 N Second Ave *Web:* covinaca.gov	Covina	CA	91723	626-967-4191		434-3
Covington & Burling LLP 1 City Ctr 850 Tenth St NW *Web:* www.cov.com	Washington	DC	20001	202-662-6000	662-6291	428
Covington Capital Management 601 S Figueroa St Ste 2000 *Web:* www.covingtoncapitalmanagement.com	Los Angeles	CA	90017	213-629-7500	629-2990	401
Covington County PO Box 1679 *Web:* www.msgw.org	Collins	MS	39428	601-765-4242		338

Name / Address	City	State	ZIP	Phone	Fax	Class
Covington County Commission 260 Hillcrest Dr *Web:* www.covcounty.com	Andalusia	AL	36420	334-428-2610		338
Covington County Market 301 3rd St *Web:* www.mycountymarket.com	Covington	IN	47932	765-793-2352		345
Covington Electric Co-opeartive Inc 18836 US Hwy 84 *TF:* 800-239-4121 ■ *Web:* covington.coop	Andalusia	AL	36421	334-222-4121		245
Covington Flooring Co 709 1st Ave N *Web:* www.covington.com	Birmingham	AL	35203	205-328-2330	328-2496	189-2
Covington House 4201 Main St *Web:* www.clark.wa.gov	Vancouver	WA	98663	360-397-2000		50-3
Covington (Independent City) 333 W Locust St *Web:* www.covington.va.us	Covington	VA	24426	540-965-6300	965-6303	338
Covington Industries Inc 470 Seventh Ave Ste 900 *Web:* www.covingtonfabric.com	New York	NY	10018	212-689-2200		745-1
Covington Patrick Hagins Stern & Lewis PA 211 Pettigru St *Web:* www.covpatlaw.com	Greenville	SC	29601	864-242-9000		428
Covington Planter Co 410 Hodges Ave *Web:* www.covingtonplanter.com	Albany	GA	31701	229-888-2032	888-0448	273
Covington Travel 4800 Cox Rd Ste 200 *TF:* 800-922-9218 ■ *Web:* www.covingtontravel.com	Glen Allen	VA	23060	804-747-7077	747-5170	771
Covingtonleader.com 111 S Munford St *Web:* www.covingtonleader.com	Covington	TN	38019	901-476-7116		532-3
Covington-Tipton County Chamber of Commerce PO Box 683 *Web:* www.covington-tiptoncochamber.com	Covington	TN	38019	901-476-9727	476-0056	139
Covino's 3265 Independence Pkwy *Web:* www.covinos.com	Plano	TX	75075	972-519-0345		671
Cow Palace 2600 Geneva Ave *Web:* www.cowpalace.com	Daly City	CA	94014	415-404-4100	404-4111	205
Cowan Costumes Inc 108 S Caddo St *Web:* www.cowancostumes.com	Cleburne	TX	76031	817-641-3126	641-3149	157-4
Cowan Graphics Inc 4864 - 93 Ave NW *TF:* 800-661-6996 ■ *Web:* cowan.ca	Edmonton	AB	T6B2R9	780-577-5700		627
Cowan Hardware Co 1264 Green St PO Box 1437 *Web:* cowanhardware.com	Conyers	GA	30012	770-483-8818		351
Cowan Lake State Park 1750 Osborn Rd *Web:* www.cowanlakestatepark.com	Wilmington	OH	45177	937-382-1096		565
Cowans Gap State Park 6235 Aughwick Rd *Web:* www.dcnr.pa.gov	Fort Loudon	PA	17224	717-485-3948		565
Cowboy Ciao Wine Bar & Grill 7133 E Stetson Dr *Web:* cowboyciao.com	Scottsdale	AZ	85251	480-946-3111		671
Cowboy Maloney's Electric City 1313 Harding St *Web:* www.cowboymaloneys.com	Jackson	MS	39202	601-948-5600		38
Cowelco A. California Corp 1634 W 14th St *Web:* www.cowelco.com	Long Beach	CA	90813	562-432-5766		480
Cowen Truck Line Inc 2697 SR-39 PO Box 480 *TF:* 800-537-1669 ■ *Web:* cowentruckline.com	Perrysville	OH	44864	419-938-3401	938-5491	311
Coweta County 22 E Broad St *Web:* www.coweta.ga.us	Newnan	GA	30263	770-254-2601	254-2606	338
Coweta-Fayette Electric Membership Corp 807 Collinsworth Rd *TF:* 877-746-4362 ■ *Web:* utility.org	Palmetto	GA	30268	770-502-0226	251-9788	245
Cowiche Growers Inc 251 Cowiche City Rd *Web:* cowichegrowers.com	Cowiche	WA	98923	509-678-4168		315-3
Cowin & Company Inc 301 Industrial Dr *Web:* www.cowin-co.com	Birmingham	AL	35211	205-945-1300	945-1441	194
Cowles & Thompson A Professional Corp 901 Main St Ste 3900 *Web:* www.cowlesthompson.com	Dallas	TX	75202	214-672-2000	672-2020	428
Cowles Publishing Co 999 W Riverside Ave *Web:* www.spokesman.com	Spokane	WA	99201	509-459-3815		532-3
Cowles, Murphy, Glover & Assoc 457 St Michael St *Web:* cmg-a.com	Mobile	AL	36602	251-433-1611		261
Cowley County Community College & Area Vocational-Technical School PO Box 1147 *TF:* 800-593-2222 ■ *Web:* www.cowley.edu	Arkansas City	KS	67005	620-442-0430	441-5350	162
Cowley County Courthouse 311 E 9th Ave *TF:* 800-876-3469 ■ *Web:* www.cowleycounty.org	Winfield	KS	67156	620-221-5400	221-5498	338
Cowlitz County 312 SW 1st Ave *TF:* 800-883-6388 ■ *Web:* www.co.cowlitz.wa.us	Kelso	WA	98626	360-577-3016	414-5506	338
Cowlitz County Tourism 2920 Douglas St *Web:* www.visitmtsthelens.com	Longview	WA	98632	360-577-3137		206
Cowne & Weybright Inc 10559 Crestwood Dr *Web:* cawins.com	Manassas	VA	20109	703-368-2151		390
Cowork Tampa 3104 N Armenia Ave Ste 2 *TF:* 800-531-2986 ■ *Web:* coworktampa.com	Tampa	FL	33607	800-531-2986		393
CoWorx Staffing Services LLC 1375 Plainfield Ave *TF:* 800-754-7000 ■ *Web:* www.coworxstaffing.com	Watchung	NJ	07069	908-757-5300		260
Cowpens National Battlefield 4001 Chesnee Hwy PO Box 308 *Web:* www.nps.gov	Gaffney	SC	29341	864-461-2828	461-7795	564
Cowtown Boots 11451 Gateway W (I-10) *TF:* 800-580-2698 ■ *Web:* cowtownboots.com	El Paso	TX	79936	915-593-2929	593-2249	301
Cowtown Bus Charters Inc 5504 Forest Hill Dr *Web:* www.cowtowncharters.com	Fort Worth	TX	76119	817-531-3287		107
Cowtown Coliseum 121 E Exchange Ave *Web:* stockyardsrodeo.com	Fort Worth	TX	76164	817-625-1025		720
Cox & Company Inc 1664 Old Country Rd *Web:* www.coxandco.com	Plainview	NY	11803	212-366-0200		22
Cox & Dinkins Inc 724 Beltline Blvd *Web:* www.coxanddinkins.com	Columbia	SC	29205	803-254-0518		261
Cox & Palmer LLP 1100-1959 Upper Water St Purdy's Wharf Tower I *Web:* www.coxandpalmerlaw.com	Halifax	NS	B3J3N2	902-421-6262		41
Cox Brewing Co 274 Heisey Quarry Rd *Web:* www.coxbrewingcompany.com	Elizabethtown	PA	17022	717-449-9926		647
Cox Communications Inc 1400 Lake Hearn Dr *TF:* 866-961-0027 ■ *Web:* www.cox.com	Atlanta	GA	30319	404-843-5000		116
Cox Construction Co 3170 Scott St *Web:* www.coxconstructionco.com	Vista	CA	92081	760-727-9020	727-9229	186
Cox Convention Ctr 1 Myriad Gardens *Web:* www.coxconventioncenter.com	Oklahoma City	OK	73102	405-602-8500	602-8505	205
Cox Elearning Consultants LLC 4047 1st St Ste 203 *TF:* 866-240-3540 ■ *Web:* www.coxec.com	Livermore	CA	94551	925-344-6459		721
Cox Engineering Co 21 Pacella Park Dr *TF:* 800-232-1846 ■ *Web:* coxengineering.com	Randolph	MA	02368	781-302-3300	302-3444	189-10
Cox Health Plans 3200 S National Ste B *Web:* www.coxhealthplans.com	Springfield	MO	65807	417-269-4679	269-4667	391-3
Cox Hospital North 1423 N Jefferson Ave *TF:* 800-711-9455 ■ *Web:* www.coxhealth.com	Springfield	MO	65802	417-269-3000		374-3
Cox Interior Inc 1751 Old Columbia Rd **Fax Area Code:* 270 ■ *TF:* 800-733-1751 ■ *Web:* www.coxinterior.com	Campbellsville	KY	42718	800-733-1751	465-7977*	499
Cox Manufacturing Co 5500 N Loop 1604 E *TF:* 800-900-7981 ■ *Web:* www.coxmanufacturing.com	San Antonio	TX	78247	210-657-7731	657-2345	621
Cox Matthews & Associates Inc 10520 Warwick Ave Ste B-8 *Web:* diverseeducation.com	Fairfax	VA	22030	703-385-2981		514
Cox Mclain Environmental Consulting Inc 6010 Balcones Dr Ste 210 *Web:* www.coxmclain.com	Austin	TX	78731	512-338-2223		192
Cox Media Group 6205 Peachtree Dunwoody Rd *Web:* www.coxmediagroup.com	Atlanta	GA	30328	678-645-0000	645-5002	637-8
Cox Media Group Tampa 11300 Fourth St N Ste 300 *TF:* 888-723-9388 ■ *Web:* www.wduv.com	Saint Petersburg	FL	33716	727-579-2000		645-160
Cox Schepp Construction 2410 Dunavant St *TF:* 800-954-0823 ■ *Web:* www.coxschepp.com	Charlotte	NC	28203	704-716-2100		186
Cox TJ (Rep D - CA) 1728 Longworth House Office Bldg *Web:* www.cox.house.gov	Washington	DC	20515	202-225-4695		342-2
Cox Transfer Inc 1065 W Center St *TF:* 800-728-1269 ■ *Web:* www.coxtransfer.com	Eureka	IL	61530	309-467-4614	467-4089	780
Cox Transportation Services Inc 10448 Dow Gil Rd *TF:* 800-288-8118 ■ *Web:* www.truckingforamerica.com	Ashland	VA	23005	804-798-1477	798-1299	780
Cox, Cox & Estes PLLC 3900 Front St Ste 203 PO Box 9630 *Web:* coxfirm.com	Fayetteville	AR	72703	479-251-7900		41
Coxsackie Correctional Facility 11260 Rt 9W PO Box 200 *Web:* www.doccs.ny.gov	Coxsackie	NY	12051	518-731-2781		213
Coy Industries Inc 2970 E Maria St *Web:* www.ercco.com	East Rancho Dominguez	CA	90221	310-603-2970	603-0165	697
Coyle Carpet One Inc 250 W Beltline Hwy *Web:* www.coylecarpet.com	Madison	WI	53713	608-257-0291		290
Coyle Financial Counsel LLC 2700 Patriot Dr Ste 440 *Web:* coylefinancial.com	Glenview	IL	60026	847-441-5644		690
Coyle Group of New York Inc, The 30 S Main St *Web:* thecoylegroup.com	New City	NY	10956	845-634-3606		390
Coyle Hospitality Group 244 Madison Ave Ste 369 *TF:* 800-891-9292 ■ *Web:* www.coylehospitality.com	New York	NY	10016	212-629-2083		463
Coyle Reproductions Inc 2850 Orbiter St *TF:* 866-269-5373 ■ *Web:* www.coylerepro.com	Brea	CA	92821	714-690-8200	690-8219	627
Coyne College Inc 1 N State St Ste 400 *TF:* 800-707-1922 ■ *Web:* www.coynecollege.edu	Chicago	IL	60607	773-577-8100		764
Coyne Public Relations LLC 5 Wood Hollow Rd *Web:* www.coynepr.com	Parsippany	NJ	07054	973-588-2000		636
Coyote Bluff Cafe 2417 S Grand St *Web:* coyotebluffcafe.com	Amarillo	TX	79103	806-373-4640		671
Coyote Cafe 132 W Water St *Web:* www.coyotecafe.com	Santa Fe	NM	87501	505-983-1615		671
Coyote Creek State Park Hwy 434 Mile Marker 17 *Web:* www.emnrd.state.nm.us	Guadalupita	NM	87722	575-387-2328		565
Coyote Flaco 635 New Britain Ave *Web:* www.coyoteflacoct.com	Hartford	CT	06106	860-953-1299		671
Coyote Lake Feedyard Inc 1287 FM 1731 *Web:* coyotelakefeedyard.com	Muleshoe	TX	79347	806-946-3321		10-1
Coyote Logistics LLC 2545 W Diversey Ave *TF:* 877-626-9683 ■ *Web:* www.coyote.com	Chicago	IL	60647	877-626-9683		449

Name / Address	City	State	Zip	Phone	Fax	Class
Coyote Ridge Corrections Ctr 1301 N Ephrata St. *Web:* www.doc.wa.gov	Connell	WA	99326	509-543-5800	543-5801	213
Coyote Software Corp 3425 Harvester Rd Ste 216 *Web:* coyotecorp.com	Burlington	ON	L7N3N1	905-639-8533		177
Cozad Asset Management Inc 2501 Galen Dr *TF:* 800-437-1686 ■ *Web:* www.cozadassetmgmt.com	Champaign	IL	61821	217-356-8363		528
Cozen O'Connor 1900 Market St *TF:* 800-523-2900 ■ *Web:* www.cozen.com	Philadelphia	PA	19103	215-665-2000	665-2013	428
Cozi Inc 506 Second Ave Ste 800 *Web:* www.cozi.com	Seattle	WA	98104	206-957-8447		387
Cozmo Beauty School 10347 Bonita Beach Rd Unit 103 *Web:* www.cozmo.edu	Bonita Springs	FL	34135	239-495-1810		685
Cozy Harbor Seafood Inc 35 Union Wharf *TF:* 800-225-2586 ■ *Web:* www.cozyharbor.com	Portland	ME	04112	207-879-2665		296-14
Cozymels Restaurant 2655 Grapevine Mills *Web:* www.cozymels.com	Grapevine	TX	76051	972-724-0277		670
Cozzini Inc 4300 W Bryn Mawr Ave *Web:* www.cozzini.com	Chicago	IL	60646	773-478-9700	478-8669	470
CP (Carolando Press Inc) 6545 W N Ave *TF:* 866-366-2668 ■ *Web:* www.carolando.com	Oak Park	IL	60302	866-366-2668		637-2
CP & Y 1820 Regal Row Ste 200 *Web:* www.cpyi.com	Dallas	TX	75235	214-638-0500	638-3723	261
CP Aviation 830 E Santa Maria St No 301 *Web:* www.cpaviation.com	Santa Paula	CA	93060	805-525-2138		167-3
CP Bourg Inc 50 Samuel Barnet Blvd *Web:* www.cpbourg.com	New Bedford	MA	02745	508-998-2171		111
CP Communications 2010 Crow Canyon Pl Ste 100 *TF:* 800-796-3683 ■ *Web:* www.cpcom.com	San Ramon	CA	94583	951-694-4830		177
CP Direct Inc 4600 Boston Way A *Web:* www.cpdirectinc.com	Lanham	MD	20706	301-918-4084		627
CP Engineers LLC 35 Sparta Ave. *Web:* cppsc.com	Sparta	NJ	07871	973-300-9003		261
CP Federal Credit Union 1100 Clinton Rd *TF:* 800-554-7101 ■ *Web:* www.cpfederal.com	Jackson	MI	49202	517-784-7101	784-6677	219
CP Flexible Packaging 15 Grumbacher Rd *TF:* 800-815-0667 ■ *Web:* www.cpflexpack.com	York	PA	17406	717-764-1193	764-2039	554
CP Franchising LLC 3300 University Dr *TF:* 800-683-0206 ■ *Web:* www.cruiseplanners.com	Coral Springs	FL	33065	954-344-8060		772
CP Industries Inc (CPI) 2214 Walnut St. *Web:* www.cp-industries.com	McKeesport	PA	15132	412-664-6604	664-6653	91
CP Industries Inc PO Box 690 *Web:* www.cpind.com	Granger	IN	46530	574-273-3000	273-4000	91
CP Manufacturing Inc 6795 Calle de Linea *TF:* 800-462-5311 ■ *Web:* www.cpmfg.com	San Diego	CA	92154	619-477-3175	477-2215	695
CP Medical Inc 1775 Corporate Dr Ste 150 *TF:* 800-950-2763 ■ *Web:* www.cpmedical.com	Norcross	GA	30093	678-710-2016		476
CP Software Group Inc (CPSG) 716 Figueroa St *Web:* www.cpsoftwaregroup.com	Folsom	CA	95630	916-985-4445	985-3557	178-1
CP Ward Inc PO Box 900 *Web:* www.cpward.com	Scottsville	NY	14546	585-889-8800		189-5
CPA (College Parents of America) 2200 Wilson Blvd Ste 102-396 *TF:* 888-761-6702 ■ *Web:* collegeparents.org	Arlington	VA	22201	888-761-6702		48-11
CPA (Catholic Press Assn) 205 W Monroe St Ste 470 *Web:* www.catholicpress.org	Chicago	IL	60606	312-380-6789	361-0256	49-14
CPA Associates International Inc 301 Rt 17 N *Web:* cpaai.mgiworld.com	Rutherford	NJ	07070	201-804-8686		49-1
CPA Consulting Group PLLC 109 Kenner Ave Ste 100 *Web:* cpacg.com	Nashville	TN	37205	615-322-1225		2
CPA Financial Advantage PC 798 W 28th St *Web:* cpafapc.com	Yuma	AZ	85364	928-344-3003		2
CPA Okc PLLC 780 E Britton Rd *TF:* 866-340-5652 ■ *Web:* cpaokc.net	Oklahoma City	OK	73114	405-843-1011	843-9748	2
CPA School of Washington 3819 Lee St 2nd Fl *Web:* www.cmaschool.com	Fairfax	VA	22030	703-273-5745	591-1194	685
CPAC (Cable Public Affairs Channel) PO Box 81099 *Fax Area Code: 613 ■ *TF:* 877-287-2722 ■ *Web:* www.cpac.ca	Ottawa	ON	K1P1B1	877-287-2722	567-2749*	740
CPAdirect Marketing Inc 2001 Grove St. *Web:* www.cpadirectory.com	Wantagh	NY	11793	516-409-8357	977-0643	681
CPAWS (Canadian Parks & Wilderness Society) 250 City Center Ave Ste 506 *TF:* 800-333-9453 ■ *Web:* www.cpaws.org	Ottawa	ON	K1R6K7	613-569-7226	569-7098	48-13
CPB (Corporation for Public Broadcasting) 401 Ninth St NW *TF:* 800-272-2190 ■ *Web:* www.cpb.org	Washington	DC	20004	202-879-9600	879-9700	305
CPC (Commercial Plastics Co) 800 Allanson Rd *Web:* www.ecommercialplastics.com	Mundelein	IL	60060	847-566-1700		604
CPC (Community Preservation Corp, The) 28 E 28th St 9th Fl *Web:* communityp.com	New York	NY	10016	212-869-5300		509
CPC (Colette Phillips Communications Inc) 177 State St Ste 6 *Web:* www.cpcglobal.com	Boston	MA	02109	617-357-5777	357-7114	636
CPC Aeroscience Inc 1005 S Westgate St. *TF:* 800-327-1835 ■ *Web:* www.cpcaeroscience.com	Addison	IL	60101	800-327-1835		151

Name / Address	City	State	Zip	Phone	Fax	Class
CPC Logistics Inc 14528 S Outer 40 Rd Ste 210 *TF:* 800-274-3746 ■ *Web:* callcpc.com	Chesterfield	MO	63017	314-542-2266	542-0666	721
CPCU Society 720 Providence Rd *Fax Area Code: 610 ■ *TF:* 800-932-2728 ■ *Web:* www.cpcusociety.org	Malvern	PA	19355	800-932-2728	251-2780*	49-9
CPE HR Inc 9000 Sunset Blvd Ste 900 *Web:* www.cpehr.com	West Hollywood	CA	90069	310-270-9800		193
CPF (Cleft Palate Foundation) 1504 E Franklin St Ste 102 *TF:* 800-242-5338 ■ *Web:* www.cleftline.org	Chapel Hill	NC	27514	919-933-9044	933-9604	48-17
CPFD (Coastal Pacific Food Distributors Inc) 1015 Performance Dr *TF:* 800-500-2611 ■ *Web:* www.cpfd.com	Stockton	CA	95206	209-983-2454		297-8
CPG (Cardinal Publishers Group) 2402 Shadeland Ave Ste A *TF:* 800-296-0481 ■ *Web:* www.cardinalpub.com	Indianapolis	IN	46219	800-296-0481		96
CPH Engineers 500 W Fulton St *Fax Area Code: 407 ■ *TF:* 866-609-0688 ■ *Web:* www.cphengineers.com	Sanford	FL	32771	866-609-0688	330-0639*	261
CPHA (California Pharmacists Assn) 4030 Lennane Dr *TF:* 866-365-7472 ■ *Web:* cpha.com	Sacramento	CA	95834	916-779-1400	779-1401	585
CPI (Companion Pets Inc) 2001 N Black Canyon Hwy *TF:* 800-646-3611 ■ *Web:* www.cpipets.com	Phoenix	AZ	85009	602-255-0166	255-0841	578
CPI (Capital-Plus Inc) 3250 W Henderson Rd Ste 201 *Web:* www.capplus.com	Columbus	OH	43220	614-848-7620		272
CPI (CP Industries Inc) 2214 Walnut St. *Web:* www.cp-industries.com	McKeesport	PA	15132	412-664-6604	664-6653	91
CPI (Consumers Power Inc) 6990 W Hills Rd *TF:* 800-872-9036 ■ *Web:* www.cpi.coop	Philomath	OR	97370	541-929-3124	929-8673	245
CPI (Confer Plastics Inc) 97 Witmer Rd *TF:* 800-635-3213 ■ *Web:* www.conferplastics.com	North Tonawanda	NY	14120	716-693-2056	694-3102	604
CPI (CPIcocom) 1210 Hickory Chapel Rd *Web:* www.cpico.com	High Point	NC	27261	336-889-2001	889-5752	608
CPI (Cincinnati Psychoanalytic Institute) 3001 Highland Ave *Web:* www.cps-i.org	Cincinnati	OH	45219	513-961-8886		48-6
CPI Aerostructures Inc 91 Heartland Blvd *NYSE: CVU* ■ *Web:* www.cpiaero.com	Edgewood	NY	11717	631-586-5200	586-5840	621
CPI Corp 1706 Washington Ave *OTC: CPIC* ■ *Web:* www.cpicorp.com	Saint Louis	MO	63103	314-231-1575		590
CPI Daylighting Inc 28662 N Ballard Dr *TF:* 800-759-6985 ■ *Web:* www.cpidaylighting.com	Lake Forest	IL	60045	847-816-1060	816-0425	590
CPI Group Inc, The 112 Fifth St N PO Box 828 *TF:* 888-566-8303 ■ *Web:* www.cpi-group.com	Columbus	MS	39703	662-328-1042	329-1017	260
CPI Human Resources Solutions Inc 5203 Maverick Dr	Austin	TX	78727	512-335-9347		317
CPI International Inc 5580 Skylane Blvd *TF:* 800-878-7654 ■ *Web:* www.cpiinternational.com	Santa Rosa	CA	95403	707-525-5788		419
CPI Manufacturing LLC 108 Ledyard St *Web:* www.cpimanufacturing.com	Hartford	CT	06114	860-296-7980		20
CPI Wire Cloth & Screens Inc 2425 Roy Rd *Web:* www.cpiwirecloth.com	Pearland	TX	77581	281-485-2300		360-3
CPI-BMD (Communications & Power Industries Inc) *Beverly Microwave Div* 150 Sohier Rd. *Web:* www.cpii.com	Beverly	MA	01915	978-922-6000	922-2736	647
CPIcocom (CPI) 1210 Hickory Chapel Rd *Web:* www.cpico.com	High Point	NC	27261	336-889-2001	889-5752	608
CPI-HR Inc 6830 Cochran Rd *TF:* 877-542-7833 ■ *Web:* cpihr.aleragroup.com	Solon	OH	44139	440-542-7800		390
CPL (Camden Public Library) 55 Main St. *Web:* www.librarycamden.org	Camden	ME	04843	207-236-3440	236-6673	434-3
C-Plastics Inc 12463 Cleveland St *Web:* www.cplasticsinc.com	Nunica	MI	49448	616-837-7396	837-5074	604
C-Plex Inc 520 Two Notch Rd. *Web:* www.c-plexinc.com	Lexington	SC	29073	803-951-0628		604
CPM Constructors Inc 30 Bonney St. *Web:* www.cpmconstructors.com	Freeport	ME	04032	207-865-0000		186
CPM Group 168 Seventh St Ste 310 *Web:* www.cpmgroup.com	Brooklyn	NY	11215	212-785-8320		401
CPM Wolverine Proctor LLC 251 Gibraltar Rd *TF:* 800-428-0846 ■ *Web:* www.cpm.net	Horsham	PA	19044	215-443-5200	443-5206	298
CPP Global 405 Commerce Pl *Web:* cppglobal.com	Asheboro	NC	27203	336-498-2654		596
CPP Inc 185 N Wolfe Rd *Web:* www.cpp.com	Sunnyvale	CA	94086	650-969-8901	969-8608	178-1
CPR Institute for Dispute Resolution 30 E 33rd St 6th Fl *Web:* www.cpradr.org	New York	NY	10016	212-949-6490	949-8859	41
CPR Savers & First Aid Supply 7904 E Chaparral Rd Ste A110-242 *TF:* 800-480-1277 ■ *Web:* www.cpr-savers.com	Scottsdale	AZ	85250	800-480-1277		507
CPRA (Canadian Parks & Recreation Assn) 1180 Walkley Rd PO Box 83069 *Web:* www.cpra.ca	Ottawa	ON	K1V2M5	613-523-5315		48-23
CPRE (Consortium for Policy Research in Education) 3440 Market St Ste 560 *Web:* www.cpre.org	Philadelphia	PA	19104	215-573-0700	573-7914	634
CPRL (Conservation & Production Research Laboratory) USDA/ARS PO Box 10 *Web:* www.ars.usda.gov	Bushland	TX	79012	806-356-5749	356-5750	668
CPS (Comprehensive Pharmacy Services Inc) 6409 N Quail Hollow Rd *TF:* 800-968-6962 ■ *Web:* www.cpspharm.com	Memphis	TN	38120	901-748-0470		194
CPS Cards 7520 Morris Ct *TF:* 888-817-8121 ■ *Web:* cpscards.com	Allentown	PA	18106	610-231-1860	231-1881	627

Phone | Fax | Class

CPS Investment Advisors
205 E Orange St ... Lakeland FL 33801 | 863-688-1725 | 972-5548* | 401
Fax Area Code: 888 ■ *Web:* www.cpalliance.com

CPS Polytechnic LLC 200 E Big Beaver Rd ... Troy MI 48084 | 248-844-9090 | 250-5897 | 167-3
Web: www.cpspoly.com

CPS Technologies Corp
111 S Worcester St ... Norton MA 02766 | 508-222-0614 | | 249
OTC: CPSH ■ *Web:* www.alsic.com

CPS Technology Solutions Inc
3949 County Rd 116 ... Hamel MN 55340 | 763-553-1514 | 553-9058 | 174
TF: 800-438-4202 ■ *Web:* www.cpsts.com

CPSC (Consumer Product Safety Commission)
4340 E W Hwy Ste 502 ... Bethesda MD 20814 | 301-504-7923 | | 340-20
Web: www.cpsc.gov

CPSG (CP Software Group Inc)
716 Figueroa St ... Folsom CA 95630 | 916-985-4445 | 985-3557 | 178-1
Web: www.cpsoftwaregroup.com

CPSI (Computer Programs & Systems Inc)
6600 Wall St ... Mobile AL 36695 | 251-639-8100 | 639-8214 | 39
NASDAQ: CPSI ■ *TF:* 877-424-1777 ■ *Web:* www.cpsi.com

CPSI Consulting Inc
720-A Maiden Choice Ln ... Baltimore MD 21228 | 410-455-0005 | 455-0311 | 260
Web: www.cpsiconsulting.com

CPSR (Computer Professionals for Social Responsibility)
1370 Mission St 4th Fl ... San Francisco CA 94103 | 650-989-1294 | 839-8617* | 49-19
Fax Area Code: 415 ■ *Web:* www.cpsr.org

CPT (Central Petroleum Transport Inc)
6115 Mitchell St ... Sioux City IA 51111 | 712-258-6357 | 258-8592 | 780
TF: 800-798-6357 ■ *Web:* www.cptrans.com

CPT Group Inc 50 Corporate Pk ... Irvine CA 92606 | 877-705-5021 | 419-3446* | 225
Fax Area Code: 949 ■ *TF:* 800-542-0900 ■ *Web:* www.cptgroup.com

CPT of South Florida Inc
2699 Stirling Rd Ste A 101 ... Fort Lauderdale FL 33312 | 954-963-2775 | 963-5781 | 175
Web: www.cpt-florida.com

CPTE Health Group Inc 522 Amherst St ... Nashua NH 03063 | 603-880-0448 | | 360-3
Web: cpte.net

Parks & Wildlife 1313 Sherman St Rm 618 ... Denver CO 80203 | 303-866-3437 | | 339-6
TF: 800-678-2267 ■ *Web:* www.cpw.state.co.us

CQ's Restaurant
Harbour Town 140-A Lighthouse Rd ... Hilton Head Island SC 29928 | 843-671-2779 | | 671
Web: www.cqsrestaurant.com

CQL (Council on Quality & Leadership, The)
100 W Rd Ste 300 ... Towson MD 21204 | 410-583-0060 | | 48-1
Web: c-q-l.org

CR Bard Inc
Urological Div 8195 Industrial Blvd ... Covington GA 30014 | 770-784-6100 | | 476
TF: 800-526-4455 ■ *Web:* www.crbard.com

CR Daniels Inc
3451 Ellicott Center Dr ... Ellicott City MD 21043 | 410-461-2100 | | 733
Web: www.crdaniels.com

CR England & Sons Inc
4701 W 2100 S ... Salt Lake City UT 84120 | 801-972-2712 | | 780
TF: 800-453-8826 ■ *Web:* www.crengland.com

CR Magnetics Inc
3500 Scarlet Oak Blvd ... Saint Louis MO 63122 | 636-343-8518 | | 248
Web: crmagnetics.com

CR Meyer & Sons Co 895 W 20th Ave ... Oshkosh WI 54902 | 920-235-3350 | | 186
Web: www.crmeyer.com

CRA (CRAssociates Inc)
8580 Cinderbed Rd Ste 2400 ... Newington VA 22122 | 877-272-8960 | 550-1880* | 463
Fax Area Code: 703 ■ *TF:* 877-272-8960 ■ *Web:* www.crassoc.com

CRA (Corn Refiners Association Inc)
1701 Pennsylvania Ave ... Washington DC 20006 | 202-331-1634 | 331-2054 | 48-2
Web: corn.org

CRA (Communications Research Associates Inc)
8190A Beechmont Ave Ste 336 ... Cincinnati OH 45255 | 513-618-5223 | 618-5203 | 393
Web: www.commres.com

CRA International Inc 200 Clarendon St ... Boston MA 02116 | 617-425-3000 | 425-3132 | 194
NASDAQ: CRAI ■ *Web:* www.crai.com

Crab Alley
9703 Golf Course Rd ... West Ocean City MD 21842 | 410-213-7800 | 213-1048 | 671
Web: craballeyoc.com

Crab Pot Restaurant & Bar, The
215 N Marina Dr ... Long Beach CA 90803 | 562-430-0272 | | 671
Web: www.crabpotlongbeach.com

Crab Shell 46 Southfield Ave ... Stamford CT 06902 | 203-967-7229 | 967-7233 | 671
Web: www.crabshell.com

Crab Trap, The 2 Broadway ... Somers Point NJ 08244 | 609-927-7377 | | 671
Web: www.thecrabtrap.com

Crabapple Financial Services Inc
12220 Birmingham Hwy Bldg 30 ... Milton GA 30004 | 770-667-0043 | 667-8905 | 734
Web: crabapplecpa.com

Crabby Mike's Calabash Seafood
290 Hwy 17 N ... Surfside Beach SC 29575 | 843-238-3524 | | 671
Web: www.crabbymikes.com

Crabtree & Evelyn Ltd
102 Peake Brook Rd ... Woodstock CT 06281 | 860-928-2761 | | 214
TF: 800-272-2873 ■ *Web:* www.crabtree-evelyn.com

Crabtree Financial Services LLC
1713 Fort Jesse Rd Ste F ... Normal IL 61761 | 309-454-1200 | | 690
Web: crabtreefinancial.com

Crabtree Valley Mall
4325 Glenwood Ave ... Raleigh NC 27612 | 919-787-2506 | | 460
TF: 800-762-0419 ■ *Web:* shopcrabtree.com

Cracker Barrel Old Country Store Inc
PO Box 787 ... Lebanon TN 37088 | 615-235-4054 | 444-5533 | 670
NASDAQ: CBRL ■ *TF:* 800-333-9566 ■ *Web:* www.crackerbarrel.com

Cracker Box, The 6682 Hwy 7 ... Bismarck AR 71929 | 501-865-2249 | | 297-8

Craddock Finishing Corp
1400 W Illinois St ... Evansville IN 47710 | 812-425-2691 | 429-1370 | 481
Web: www.craddockfinishing.com

Craden Peripherals Corp
7860 Airport Hwy ... Pennsauken Township NJ 08109 | 856-488-0700 | 488-0925 | 173-6
Web: www.craden.com

Cradle Solution Inc
16000 Park Ten Pl Ste 501 ... Houston TX 77084 | 713-776-8510 | | 180
Web: cradlesolution.com

Cradlerock Group LLC, The
65 High Ridge Rd ... Stamford CT 06905 | 203-324-0088 | | 194
Web: www.cradlerock.com

Crafco Inc 420 N Roosevelt Ave ... Chandler AZ 85226 | 602-276-0406 | 961-0513* | 46
Fax Area Code: 480 ■ *TF:* 800-528-8242 ■ *Web:* www.crafco.com

Craft 43 E 19th St ... New York NY 10003 | 212-780-0880 | | 671
Web: www.craftrestaurant.com

Craft & Hobby Assn (CHA)
319 E 54th St ... Elmwood Park NJ 07407 | 201-835-1200 | 797-0657 | 48-18
TF: 800-822-0494 ■ *Web:* craftandhobby.org

Craft Brew Alliance 929 N Russell St ... Portland OR 97227 | 503-331-7270 | | 102
NASDAQ: BREW ■ *Web:* craftbrew.com

Craft Emergency Relief Fund
535 Stone Cutters Way Ste 202 ... Montpelier VT 05602 | 802-229-2306 | 223-6484 | 522
Web: cerfplus.org

Craft Inc
1929 County St PO Box 3049 ... South Attleboro MA 02703 | 800-827-2388 | 399-7240* | 350
Fax Area Code: 508 ■ *TF:* 800-827-2388 ■ *Web:* craft-inc-asia.com

Craft Machine Works Inc 2102 48th St ... Hampton VA 23661 | 757-380-8615 | 380-9120 | 454
Web: www.craftmachine.com

Craft Manufacturing & Tooling Inc
7152 Central Ave ... Hot Springs AR 71913 | 501-525-0268 | 525-8642 | 22
Web: cmtair.com

Craft Memorial Library
600 Commerce St ... Bluefield WV 24701 | 304-325-3943 | 325-3702 | 434-3
Web: craftmemorial.lib.wv.us

Craft Pattern & Mold Inc 60 3rd St S ... Montrose MN 55363 | 763-675-3169 | 675-3177 | 567
Web: www.craftpattern.com

Craftcorps Inc 3401 Manor Rd ... Austin TX 78723 | 512-476-8886 | | 186
Web: www.craftcorps.com

Craftech Corp 2941 E La Jolla St ... Anaheim CA 92806 | 714-630-8117 | 630-7959 | 608
Web: craftechcorp.com

Craftech Metal Forming Inc
24100 Water St Ste B ... Perris CA 92570 | 951-940-6444 | 940-6446 | 697
Web: www.craftechmetal.com

Craft-E-Corner 5715 Green Valley Rd ... Oshkosh WI 54904 | 800-236-3877 | | 366
TF: 800-236-3877 ■ *Web:* craft-e-corner.com

Crafted Plastics Inc
1822 Martin Ave ... Sheboygan WI 53083 | 920-457-5593 | 457-6261 | 604
Web: www.craftedplastics.com

Crafter's Workshop Inc, The
116 S Central Ave ... Elmsford NY 10523 | 914-345-2838 | | 42
Web: store.thecraftersworkshop.com

Craftmade 650 S Royal Ln ... Coppell TX 75019 | 972-393-3800 | | 37
OTC: CRFT ■ *TF:* 800-486-4892 ■ *Web:* www.craftmade.com

Craftmaster Furniture Corp
221 Craftmaster Rd ... Hiddenite NC 28636 | 828-632-9786 | | 319-2
Web: www.cmfurniture.com

Crafton Hills College
11711 Sand Canyon Rd ... Yucaipa CA 92399 | 909-794-2161 | 389-9141 | 162
Web: www.craftonhills.edu

Crafts Frames & Things
108 Owen Dr ... Fayetteville NC 28304 | 910-485-4833 | | 45
Web: www.craftsframesandthings.com

Crafts Technology
91 Joey Dr ... Elk Grove Village IL 60007 | 847-758-3100 | 758-0162 | 455
TF: 800-323-6802 ■ *Web:* www.craftstech.net

Craftsman Custom Metals LLC
3838 N River Rd ... Schiller Park IL 60176 | 847-655-0040 | | 697
Web: www.ccm.com

Craftsman Inn 7300 E Genesee St ... Fayetteville NY 13066 | 315-637-8000 | | 379
Web: www.craftsmaninn.com

Craftsman Printing Inc
120 Citation Ct ... Birmingham AL 35209 | 205-942-3939 | | 627
TF: 800-543-1051 ■ *Web:* craftsmanprintinginc.com

Craftsmen Developers LLC
7524 Wb & A Rd Ste 101 ... Glen Burnie MD 21061 | 410-766-6565 | | 653
Web: craftsmendevelopers.com

Craftsmen Machinery Company Inc
1257 Worcester Rd Unit 167 ... Framingham MA 01701 | 508-376-2001 | 376-2003 | 629
Web: www.craftsmenmachinery.com

Craftsteak 3799 Las Vegas Blvd S ... Las Vegas NV 89109 | 800-929-1111 | | 671
TF: 800-929-1111 ■ *Web:* www.craftedhospitality.com

Craftstones 505 Elm St ... Ramona CA 92065 | 760-789-1620 | | 407
Web: craftstones.com

Craggy Correctional Ctr
2992 Riverside Dr ... Asheville NC 28804 | 828-645-5315 | 658-2183 | 213
Web: www.ncdps.gov

Cragun's Conference & Golf Resort
11000 Cragun's Dr ... Brainerd MN 56401 | 800-272-4867 | 829-9188* | 669
Fax Area Code: 218 ■ *TF:* 800-272-4867 ■ *Web:* www.craguns.com

CRAIC Technologies Inc
948 N Amelia Ave ... San Dimas CA 91773 | 310-573-8180 | 573-8182 | 419
TF: 877-882-7242 ■ *Web:* www.microspectra.com

Craig & Hall Insurance Agency Inc
158 E Main St PO Box 249 ... Georgetown KY 40324 | 502-863-0755 | | 390
Web: craigandhallinsurance.com

Craig A. Davis Aplc 111 Mercury St ... Lafayette LA 70503 | 337-231-5351 | 289-1219 | 41
Web: craigadavis.com

Craig Angie (Rep D - MN)
1523 Longworth House Office Bldg ... Washington DC 20515 | 202-225-2271 | | 342-2
Web: www.craig.house.gov

Craig Baker Marble Company Inc
1918 Baker Rd ... Houston TX 77094 | 281-492-2365 | 578-0940 | 724
Web: iwantgranite.com

Craig Construction Co 835 Wall St ... Florence AL 35630 | 256-766-3350 | | 186
Web: bhcraigconst.com

Craig County PO Box 308 ... New Castle VA 24127 | 540-864-5010 | 864-5590 | 338
Web: www.craigcountyva.gov

Craig D. Carter & Associates PC
772 N Santa Fe Ave ... Edmond OK 73003 | 405-340-5971 | | 2
Web: craigcarterassociates.com

Craig Donoff PA
2999 NE 191st St Ste 702 ... Aventura FL 33180 | 305-935-0496 | | 41
Web: craigdonofftrustandestates.com

Craig E. Schroeder CPA Group
4404 N Franklin Rd ... Indianapolis IN 46226 | 317-546-1167 | | 2
Web: schroedercpas.com

Name / Address	City	State	Zip	Phone	Fax	Class
Craig Envelope Corp 12-01 44th Ave *TF:* 888-272-4436 ■ *Web:* www.craigenvelope.com	Long Island City	NY	11101	888-272-4436		263
Craig Frames Inc 140 Industrial Pkwy *Web:* www.craigframes.com	Ithaca	MI	48847	989-875-8600		200
Craig Hospital 3425 S Clarkson St *TF:* 800-247-0257 ■ *Web:* craighospital.org	Englewood	CO	80113	303-789-8000	789-8219	374-6
Craig Lake State Park 851 County Rd AKE *Web:* www.michigan.org	Champion	MI	49814	906-339-4461		565
Craig Manufacturing Ltd 96 Mclean Ave *TF:* 800-565-5007 ■ *Web:* www.craigattachments.com	Hartland	NB	E7P2K5	800-565-5007		480
Craig Roberts Associates Inc 4230 Avondale Ave Ste 202 *Web:* www.craigroberts.com	Dallas	TX	75219	214-526-6470		196
Craig Technologies Inc 103 Davis Dr *Web:* www.craigtechnologies.com	Seaford	DE	19973	302-628-9900		604
Craig Test Boring Company Inc 5230 Atlantic Ave *TF:* 800-584-2277 ■ *Web:* craigtestboring.com	Mays Landing	NJ	08330	609-625-4862		261
Craig Thomas Pest Control Inc 2170 Piedmont Rd NE *Web:* callcraig.com	Hyde Park	NY	12538	800-255-6777		577
Craig Transportation Co 819 Kingsbury St *TF:* 800-521-9119 ■ *Web:* www.craigtransportation.com	Maumee	OH	43537	419-872-3333	874-9372	780
Craig W. Drummond PC 810 S Casino Center Blvd Ste 10 *Web:* drummondfirm.com	Las Vegas	NV	89101	702-366-9966	508-9440	41
Craig-Botetourt Electric Coop 26198 Craigs Creek Rd PO Box 265 *TF:* 800-760-2232 ■ *Web:* www.cbec.coop	New Castle	VA	24127	540-864-5121	864-5461	245
Craig-Hallum Capital Group LLC 222 S Ninth St Ste 350 *TF:* 800-752-1476 ■ *Web:* www.craig-hallum.com	Minneapolis	MN	55402	612-334-6300		401
Craighead County 511 S Main St Ste 202 *Web:* www.craigheadcounty.org	Jonesboro	AR	72401	870-933-4520	933-4514	338
Craighead Electric Co-opeartive Corp 4314 Stadium Blvd PO Box 7503 *TF:* 800-794-5012 ■ *Web:* www.craigheadelectric.coop	Jonesboro	AR	72403	870-932-8301	972-5674	245
Crailo State Historic Site 9 1/2 Riverside Ave *Web:* parks.ny.gov	Rensselaer	NY	12144	518-463-8738		565
Crain Bros Inc 300 Rita Dr *Web:* www.crainbrothers.com	Bell City	LA	70630	337-905-2411	905-2700	539
Crain Chemical Co 2624 Andjon Dr	Dallas	TX	75220	214-358-3301		151
Crain Communications Inc 1155 Gratiot Ave *TF:* 888-288-6954 ■ *Web:* www.crain.com	Detroit	MI	48207	313-446-6000		637-9
Crain's Chicago Business Magazine 150 N Michigan Ave 16th Fl *TF:* 877-812-1590 ■ *Web:* www.chicagobusiness.com	Chicago	IL	60601	312-649-5200	280-3150	457-5
Crain's Cleveland Business Magazine 700 W St Clair Ave Ste 310 *TF:* 888-909-9111 ■ *Web:* www.crainscleveland.com	Cleveland	OH	44113	216-522-1383	694-4264	457-5
Cramco Inc 2200 E Ann St *Web:* cramco.net	Philadelphia	PA	19134	215-427-9500	427-9528	319-2
Cramer 425 University Ave *Web:* cramer.com	Norwood	MA	02062	781-278-2300		4
Cramer & Assoc 18 S High St *Web:* www.cramerphilanthropy.com	Dublin	OH	43017	614-766-4483		317
Cramer Fish Sciences 7525 NE Ambassador Pl Ste C *TF:* 888-224-1221 ■ *Web:* www.fishsciences.net	Portland	OR	97220	503-491-9577		192
Cramer Inc 1523 Grand Blvd *TF:* 800-366-6700 ■ *Web:* www.cramerinc.com	Kansas City	MO	64108	800-366-6700	607-2821	319-1
Cramer Johnson Wiggins & Assoc 1420 Edgewater Dr Ste 200 *Web:* cjw-assoc.com	Orlando	FL	32804	407-849-0044		390
Cramer Kevin (Sen R - ND) 400 Russell Senate Office Bldg *Web:* www.cramer.senate.gov	Washington	DC	20510	202-224-2043		342-2
Cramer Products Inc 153 W Warren St *TF:* 800-345-2231 ■ *Web:* www.cramersportsmed.com	Gardner	KS	66030	913-856-7511		477
Cramer Rosenthal Mcglynn LLC 520 Madison Ave 20th Fl *Web:* www.crmllc.com	New York	NY	10022	212-838-3830		401
Cramer, Price & De Armas PA 1411 Edgewater Dr Ste 200 *Web:* cramerprice.com	Orlando	FL	32804	407-843-3300	843-6300	41
Cramer-Krasselt 246 E Chicago St *Web:* c-k.com	Milwaukee	WI	53202	414-227-3500		4
Cranberry Country Chamber of Commerce 40 N Main St *Web:* cranberrycountry.org	Middleboro	MA	02346	508-947-1499	947-1446	139
Cranbrook Art Museum 39221 Woodward Ave *Web:* cranbrookartmuseum.org	Bloomfield Hills	MI	48304	248-645-3323	645-3324	520
Cranbrook Educational Community 39221 Woodward Ave PO Box 801 *TF:* 877-462-7262 ■ *Web:* www.cranbrook.edu	Bloomfield Hills	MI	48303	877-462-7262		668
Cranbrook History Ctr 57 Van Horne St S PO Box 400 *Web:* www.cranbrookhistorycentre.com	Cranbrook	BC	V1C1Y7	250-489-3918		520
Cranbrook Institute of Science 39221 Woodward Ave PO Box 801 *Web:* science.cranbrook.edu	Bloomfield Hills	MI	48303	248-645-3000		520
Cranbrook Schools 39221 Woodward Ave *Web:* schools.cranbrook.edu	Bloomfield Hills	MI	48304	248-645-3610	645-3025	622
Crandall Associates Inc 6 Litchfield Rd Ste 316 *Web:* www.crandallassociates.com	Port Washington	NY	11050	516-767-6800		260
Crandall Engineering Ltd 1077 St George Blvd Ste 400 *TF:* 866-857-2777 ■ *Web:* crandallengineering.ca	Moncton	NB	E1E4C9	506-857-2777	857-2753	194
Crandall Historical Printing Museum 275 E Center St	Provo	UT	84606	801-377-7777		520
Crandall Public Library 251 Glen St *Web:* www.crandalllibrary.org	Glens Falls	NY	12801	518-792-6508		434-3
Crandall University 333 Gorge Rd *TF:* 888-968-6228 ■ *Web:* www.crandallu.ca	Moncton	NB	E1G3H9	506-858-8970		785
Crandall, Crandall & Baert PC 423 Williamsburg Ave *TF:* 800-361-0707 ■ *Web:* theretirementnetwork.com	Geneva	IL	60134	630-232-8995		2
Crane & Company Inc 30 South St *TF:* 800-268-2281 ■ *Web:* www.crane.com	Dalton	MA	01226	800-268-2281		552-2
Crane Aerospace & Electronics 3000 Winona Ave *Web:* www.craneae.com	Burbank	CA	91504	818-526-2600		22
Crane Cams Inc 530 Fentress Blvd *Web:* www.cranecams.com	Daytona Beach	FL	32114	386-310-4875		247
Crane Carrier (Canada) Ltd 11523 186 St *TF:* 800-263-7619 ■ *Web:* pacifictruck.com	Edmonton	AB	T5S2W6	780-443-2493		190
Crane Carrier Co 12536 E 52nd St *Web:* www.cranecarrier.com	Tulsa	OK	74146	918-286-2300	286-2944	516
Crane ChemPharma 1 Quality Way *Web:* www.cranecpe.com	Marion	NC	28752	828-724-4000	724-4783	596
Crane Co 100 First Stamford Pl *NYSE: CR* ■ *Web:* www.craneco.com	Stamford	CT	06902	203-363-7300		641
Crane Composites Inc 23525 W Eames St *TF:* 800-435-0080 ■ *Web:* www.cranecomposites.com	Channahon	IL	60410	815-467-8600	467-8666	606
Crane Consulting 11052 Picaza Pl *Web:* www.craneconsulting.com	San Diego	CA	92127	858-487-9017	592-0689	196
Crane Country Day School 1795 San Leandro Ln *Web:* www.craneschool.org	Santa Barbara	CA	93108	805-969-7732		685
Crane County Courthouse 201 W 6th St *Web:* www.co.crane.tx.us	Crane	TX	79731	432-558-1101	558-1185	338
Crane Creek State Park 2045 Morse Rd Bldg C *Web:* www.maumeebaystatepark.org	Columbus	OH	43229	614-265-6561		565
Crane Engineering Inc 707 Ford St *Web:* www.craneengineering.net	Kimberly	WI	54136	920-733-4425		385
Crane Group 330 W Spring St Ste 200 *Web:* www.cranegroup.com	Columbus	OH	43215	614-754-3000		360-3
Crane Hill Machine & Fabrication Inc 2476 E US Hwy 50 *Web:* www.cranehillmachine.com	Seymour	IN	47274	812-358-3534	358-2351	480
Crane Interiors Inc 200 Alexander Dr *Web:* www.crane-interiors.com	Woodbury	TN	37190	615-563-4800		746
Crane Merchandising Systems 3330 Crane Way PO Box 719 **Fax Area Code: 803* ■ *TF:* 800-628-8363 ■ *Web:* cranems.com	Williston	SC	29853	800-621-7278	266-5150*	111
Crane Mills Inc 22938 S Ave PO Box 318	Corning	CA	96021	530-824-5427		448
Crane Nuclear Inc 2825 Cobb International Blvd *TF:* 800-795-8013 ■ *Web:* www.cranenuclear.com	Kennesaw	GA	30152	770-424-6343	429-4750	472
Crane Pest Control Inc 2700 Geary Blvd *TF:* 800-592-7777 ■ *Web:* www.cranepestcontrol.com	San Francisco	CA	94118	415-922-1666	922-1789	577
Crane Press 3510 NE 3rd Ave Ste 172 *TF:* 800-745-6273 ■ *Web:* www.cranepress.com	Camas	WA	98607	360-210-5982	210-5983	637-2
Crane Pumps & Systems 420 Third St *Web:* www.cranepumps.com	Piqua	OH	45356	937-778-0947		641
Crane Tech Solutions LLC 2030 Ponderosa St *Web:* cranetechsolutions.com	Portsmouth	VA	23701	757-405-0311	405-0313	470
Crane Worldwide Logistics LLC 1500 Rankin Rd *TF:* 888-870-2726 ■ *Web:* www.craneww.com	Houston	TX	77073	281-443-2777		449
Crane's Tavern & Steakhouse 26 New Orleans Rd *Web:* cranestavern.com	Hilton Head Island	SC	29928	843-341-2333		671
Cranel Inc 4400 Easton Commons Way Ste 125 *Web:* www.cranel.com	Columbus	OH	43219	614-431-8000	431-8388	174
Cranes Software Inc 1133 E Maple Rd Ste 200 *Web:* www.nisasoftware.com	Troy	MI	48083	248-689-0077	689-7479	178-1
Cranesmart Systems Inc 4908 97 St NW *TF:* 888-562-3222 ■ *Web:* cranesmart.com	Edmonton	AB	T6E5S1	780-437-2986		407
Cranesville Block Company Inc 1250 Riverfront Ctr *Web:* www.cranesville.com	Amsterdam	NY	12010	518-684-6000		183
Craneveyor Corp 1524 Potrero Ave **Fax Area Code: 626* ■ *TF:* 888-501-0050 ■ *Web:* www.craneveyor.com	South El Monte	CA	91733	888-501-0050	442-7308*	470
Cranfill Sumner & Hartzog LLP 5420 Wade Park Blvd Ste 300 *Web:* www.cshlaw.com	Raleigh	NC	27607	919-828-5100		428
Crankshaft Machine Co 314 N Jackson St *Web:* www.crankshaft.net	Jackson	MI	49201	517-787-3791	787-5326	223
Cranmore Mountain Resort 239 Skimobile Rd *Web:* www.cranmore.com	North Conway	NH	03860	603-356-5543	356-8526	669
Cranston Machinery Company Inc 2251 SE Oak Grove Blvd *TF:* 800-547-1012 ■ *Web:* www.cranston-machinery.com	Oak Grove	OR	97267	503-654-7751		556
Cranston Municipal Employees Credit Union 1615 Pontiac Ave Ste 2 *TF:* 877-442-6328 ■ *Web:* cranstonmecu.org	Cranston	RI	02920	401-463-3010	463-3319	219
Cranston Print Works Co 1381 Cranston St *TF:* 800-876-2756 ■ *Web:* www.cpw.com	Cranston	RI	02920	401-943-4800		745-7
Cranston Public Library 140 Sockanosset Cross Rd *Web:* www.cranstonlibrary.org	Cranston	RI	02920	401-943-9080	946-5079	434-3
Crapo Ltd 535 N 2500 E *Web:* crapoltd.business.site	Saint Anthony	ID	83445	208-624-3293		780

Name / Address	City	State	ZIP	Phone	Fax	Class
Crapo Mike (Sen R - ID) 239 Dirksen Senate Office Bldg *Web:* www.crapo.senate.gov	Washington	DC	20510	202-224-6142	228-1375	342-2
Crary Buchanan Attorneys At Law 759 SW Federal Hwy Ste 106 *TF:* 888-899-8161 ■ *Web:* www.crarybuchanan.com	Stuart	FL	34994	772-287-2600		445
Crary Co 237 12th St NW *Web:* www.crary.com	West Fargo	ND	58078	701-282-5520		429
Crary Huff Ringgenberg Hartnett & Storm Pc 329 Pierce St Ste 200 *Web:* craryhuff.com	Sioux City	IA	51101	712-277-4561		41
Crash Hotel 10266 103 St NW *Web:* crashhotel.com	Edmonton	AB	T5J0Y8	780-719-3807		379
CRAssociates Inc (CRA) 8580 Cinderbed Rd Ste 2400 **Fax Area Code:* 703 ■ *TF:* 877-272-8960 ■ *Web:* www.crassoc.com	Newington	VA	22122	877-272-8960	550-1880*	463
Crate 1960 Greentree Rd *Web:* www.cratecook.com	Pittsburgh	PA	15220	412-341-5700		167-3
Crater Lake National Park PO Box 7 *Web:* www.nps.gov	Crater Lake	OR	97604	541-594-3000		564
Crater of Diamonds State Park 209 State Park Rd *Web:* www.arkansasstateparks.com	Murfreesboro	AR	71958	870-285-3113		565
Craters & Freighters 331 Corporate Cir Ste J *TF:* 800-736-3335 ■ *Web:* www.cratersandfreighters.com	Golden	CO	80401	303-399-8190		310
Craters of the Moon National Monument & Preserve PO Box 29 *TF:* 800-562-3408 ■ *Web:* www.nps.gov	Arco	ID	83213	208-527-1300	527-3073	564
Cravath Swaine & Moore LLP 825 Eigth Ave Worldwide Plz *Web:* www.cravath.com	New York	NY	10019	212-474-1000	474-3700	428
Craven Community College 800 College Ct *Web:* www.cravencc.edu	New Bern	NC	28562	252-638-4131	638-4649	162
Craven County 406 Craven St *TF:* 800-437-5767 ■ *Web:* www.cravencountync.gov	New Bern	NC	28560	252-636-6600	637-0526	338
Craven County Convention & Visitors Bureau 203 S Front St *Web:* www.visitnewbern.com	New Bern	NC	28560	252-637-9400		206
Craven County School (CCS) 3600 Trent Rd *Web:* www.cravenk12.org	New Bern	NC	28562	252-514-6300	514-6351	685
Craven Thompson & Associates Inc 3563 NW 53rd St *Web:* www.craventhompson.com	Fort Lauderdale	FL	33309	954-739-6400		261
Crawdaddy's 317 N Mesquite St	Corpus Christi	TX	78401	361-883-5432		671
Crawford Ausable School District 1135 N Old 27 *Web:* www.casdk12.net	Grayling	MI	49738	989-344-3500		685
Crawford Broadcasting Co (CBC) 2821 S Parker Rd Ste 1205 *Web:* crawfordmediagroup.net	Aurora	CO	80014	303-481-1800	433-1555	643
Crawford Central School District 11280 Mercer Pk *Web:* www.craw.org	Meadville	PA	16335	814-724-3960		685
Crawford Consulting Services Inc 239 Highland Ave *TF:* 800-365-9010 ■ *Web:* www.crawfordcs.com	East Pittsburgh	PA	15112	412-823-0400		261
Crawford County 112 E Mansfield St *Web:* www.crawford-co.org	Bucyrus	OH	44820	419-562-5876	562-3491	338
Crawford County 1202 Broadway Ste 5 *Web:* www.crawfordcounty.org	Denison	IA	51442	712-263-3045	263-8382	338
Crawford County 715 Judicial Plaza Dr PO Box 375 *Web:* www.in.gov	English	IN	47118	812-338-2565	338-2507	338
Crawford County 111 E Forest Ave *Web:* www.crawfordcountykansas.org	Girard	KS	66743	620-724-6115	724-6007	338
Crawford County 200 W Michigan Ave *Web:* www.crawfordco.org	Grayling	MI	49738	989-344-3206	344-3223	338
Crawford County 39 Wright Ave *Web:* www.crawfordcountyga.org	Roberta	GA	31078	478-836-3782	836-5818	338
Crawford County 225 N Beaumont Rd *TF:* 877-794-2372 ■ *Web:* www.crawfordcountywi.org	Prairie du Chien	WI	53821	608-326-0200		338
Crawford County 100 Douglas St PO Box 616 *Web:* crawfordcountyil.org	Robinson	IL	62454	618-546-1212	546-0140	338
Crawford County 302 Main St PO Box AS *TF:* 866-566-8267 ■ *Web:* crawfordcountymo.net	Steelville	MO	65565	573-775-2376	775-3066	338
Crawford County 300 Main St Rm 25 *Web:* crawford-county.org	Van Buren	AR	72956	479-474-1312	471-3236	338
Crawford County Fair 903 Diamond Sq *TF:* 800-585-3737 ■ *Web:* www.crawfordcountyfairpa.com	Meadville	PA	16335	814-333-7465	337-0457	338
Crawford County State Fish & Wildlife Area 12609 E 1700th Ave *Web:* www2.illinois.gov	Hutsonville	IL	62433	618-563-4405		565
Crawford Electric Co-opeartive Inc 10301 N Service Rd PO Box 10 *TF:* 800-677-2667 ■ *Web:* www.crawfordelec.com	Bourbon	MO	65441	573-732-4415		245
Crawford Industries 1414 Crawford Dr *TF:* 800-428-0840 ■ *Web:* crawford-industries.com	Crawfordsville	IN	47933	800-428-0840	962-3343	548
Crawford Investment Counsel Inc 600 Galleria Pkwy Ste 1650 *Web:* www.crawfordinvestment.com	Atlanta	GA	30339	770-859-0045	859-0049	401
Crawford Merz Anderson Construction Co 2316 Fourth Ave S *Web:* crawfordmerz.com	Minneapolis	MN	55404	612-874-9011		186
Crawford Murphy & Tilly Inc 2750 W Washington St *TF:* 844-426-8364 ■ *Web:* www.cmtengr.com	Springfield	IL	62702	217-787-8050		261
Crawford Nautical School 801 NW 42nd St Ste 206 *Web:* www.crawfordnautical.com	Seattle	WA	98107	206-667-9377		685
Crawford Notch State Park 1464 US Rt 302 *Web:* www.nhstateparks.org	Harts Location	NH	03812	603-374-2272		565
Crawford Rick (Rep R - AR) 2422 Rayburn House Office Bldg *Web:* crawford.house.gov	Washington	DC	20515	202-225-4076	225-5602	342-2
Crawford Sausage Company Inc 2310 S Pulaski Rd *Web:* daisybrandsausage.net	Chicago	IL	60623	773-277-3095	277-7749	296-26
Crawford Sprinkler Co 1814 US Hwy 70 SW *Web:* www.crawfordhickory.com.html	Hickory	NC	28602	828-327-4116	327-4115	386
Crawford State Park 1 Lake Rd *Web:* ksoutdoors.com	Farlington	KS	66734	620-362-3671		565
Crawford Strategy 200 E Camperdown Way *Web:* crawfordstrategy.com	Greenville	SC	29601	864-232-2302		4
Crawford Supply Co 8150 Lehigh Ave *Web:* www.crawfordsupply.com	Morton Grove	IL	60053	847-967-1414		612
Crawford Technologies Inc 60 St Clair Ave E Ste 1002 *TF:* 866-679-0864 ■ *Web:* www.crawfordtech.com	Toronto	ON	M4T1N5	416-923-0080		179
Crawfordsville Electric Light & Power 808 Lafayette Ave *Web:* www.metronetinc.com	Crawfordsville	IN	47933	765-362-1900		245
Crawfordsville-Montgomery County Chamber of Commerce 200 S Washington St Ste 304 *Web:* www.crawfordsvillechamber.com	Crawfordsville	IN	47933	765-362-6800	362-6900	139
Crawley Petroleum Corp 105 N Hudson Ste 800 *Web:* www.crawleypetroleum.com	Oklahoma City	OK	73102	405-232-9700		536
Cray Inc 901 Fifth Ave Ste 1000 *NASDAQ: CRAY* ■ *Web:* www.cray.com	Seattle	WA	98164	206-701-2000	701-2500	173-2
Crazy Crab 104 William Hilton Pkwy *Web:* www.thecrazycrab.com	Hilton Head Island	SC	29926	843-681-5021		671
Crazy Horse 214 W Kirkwood Ave *Web:* www.crazyhorseindiana.com	Bloomington	IN	47404	812-336-8877		671
Crazy Horse Memorial Avenue of the Chiefs *Web:* crazyhorsememorial.org	Crazy Horse	SD	57730	605-673-4681	673-2185	50-4
Crazy Horse SF Gentlemens Club 980 Market St *Web:* theworldfamouscrazyhorse.com	San Francisco	CA	94102	415-771-6259		149
Crazy Shirts Inc 99-969 Iwaena St *TF:* 800-771-2720 ■ *Web:* www.crazyshirts.com	Aiea	HI	96701	808-487-9919		155-3
Crazy Woman Creek Bancorp Inc PO Box 1020 *TF:* 877-684-2766 ■ *Web:* www.buffalofed.com	Buffalo	WY	82834	307-684-5591		360-2
CRB (Country Radio Broadcasters Inc) 819 18th Ave S *Web:* www.countryradioseminar.com	Nashville	TN	37203	615-327-4487	329-4492	49-14
CRC (Christian Reformed Church in North America) 2850 Kalamazoo Ave SE *TF:* 800-272-5125 ■ *Web:* www.crcna.org	Grand Rapids	MI	49560	616-241-1691	224-0834	48-20
CRC (Container Research Corp) 2 New Rd *TF:* 844-220-9574 ■ *Web:* www.crc-flex.com	Aston	PA	19014	844-220-9574		198
CRC (Coordinating Research Council Inc) 5755 N Point Pkwy Ste 265 *Web:* crcao.org	Alpharetta	GA	30022	678-795-0506	795-0509	49-19
CRC (Capital Restaurant Concepts Ltd) 1305 Wisconsin Ave NW *Web:* www.capitalrestaurants.com	Washington	DC	20007	202-339-6800	339-6801	670
CRC (Communication Research Consultants Inc) 1170 Rte 17M Ste 3 *Web:* www.crcglobal.com	Chester	NY	10918	845-774-1231	774-1492	196
CRC Evans Pipeline International Inc 10700 E Independence St *TF:* 800-664-9224 ■ *Web:* www.crc-evans.com	Tulsa	OK	74116	918-438-2100		190
CRC Industries Inc 885 Louis Dr *TF:* 800-556-5074 ■ *Web:* www.crcindustries.com	Warminster	PA	18974	215-674-4300	674-2196	541
CRC Press LLC 6000 Broken Sound Pkwy NW Ste 300 **Fax Area Code:* 800 ■ *TF:* 800-272-7737 ■ *Web:* www.routledge.com	Boca Raton	FL	33487	561-994-0555	374-3401*	637-9
CRCA (Consumers' Research Council of America) 2020 Pennsylvania Ave NW Ste 300-A *TF:* 877-774-6337 ■ *Web:* www.consumersresearchcncl.org	Washington	DC	20006	202-835-9698	835-9739	48-10
CRCPD (Conference of Radiation Control Program Directors) 1030 Burlington Ln Ste 4B *Web:* www.crcpd.org	Frankfort	KY	40601	502-227-4543	227-7862	49-7
CRE (Counselors of Real Estate) 430 N Michigan Ave *Web:* www.cre.org	Chicago	IL	60611	312-329-8427	329-8881	49-17
CreaGen Inc 299 Washington St *Web:* www.creagenbio.com	Woburn	MA	01801	781-938-1122		479
Cream City Music 12505 W Bluemound Rd *TF:* 800-800-0087 ■ *Web:* www.creamcitymusic.com	Brookfield	WI	53005	262-860-1800		526
Cream Wine Co 1035 W Lake St 3rd Fl E *Web:* www.creamwine.com	Chicago	IL	60607	312-421-1900	421-1977	81-3
Creamer Metal Products Inc 77 S Madison Rd *TF:* 800-362-1603 ■ *Web:* www.creamermetal.com	London	OH	43140	740-852-1752		295
Creamland Dairies 10 Indian School Rd NW *Web:* www.deanfoods.com	Albuquerque	NM	87102	505-247-0721		296-25
Cream-O-Land Dairy Inc 529 Cedar Ln *TF:* 800-220-6455 ■ *Web:* www.creamoland.com	Florence	NJ	08518	609-499-3601	499-3896	297-4
Creare Inc 16 Great Hollow Rd *Web:* www.creare.com	Hanover	NH	03755	603-643-3800	643-4657	668
Create A. Pack Foods Inc W1344 Industrial Dr *Web:* www.create-a-pack.com	Ixonia	WI	53036	262-567-6069		297-8
Create One for Me Inc 4416 NW 99th Ave *Web:* createoneforme.com	Sunrise	FL	33351	954-746-5199		344
Create-a-card Inc 16 Brasswood Rd *TF:* 800-753-6867 ■ *Web:* www.createacardinc.com	Saint James	NY	11780	631-584-2273	584-3214	535

Company	Address	City	State	Zip	Phone	Fax	Class	Details
Creatherm Building Products	17715 Commerce Dr Ste 100	Westfield	IN	46074	888-925-5484		189-2	*TF:* 888-925-5484 ■ *Web:* www.creatherm.com
Creating Results Inc	14000 Crown Ct Ste 211	Woodbridge	VA	22193	703-494-7888		189-9	*TF:* 888-205-8899 ■ *Web:* www.creatingresults.com
Creation Engine	425 N Whisman Rd Ste 300	Mountain View	CA	94043	650-934-0176		180	*TF:* 800-431-8713 ■ *Web:* www.creationengine.com
Creative Advantage Inc	620 Union St	Schenectady	NY	12305	518-370-0312		194	*Web:* www.thecreativeadvantage.com
Creative Age Publications Inc	7628 Densmore Ave	Van Nuys	CA	91406	818-782-7328		457-11	*Web:* www.creativeage.com
Creative Allies Inc	1730 Varsity Dr Ste 200	Raleigh	NC	27606	828-252-6300		48-4	*Web:* creativeallies.com
Creative Approaches	PO Box 91	Bloomfield	NY	14469	800-934-6299		196	*Web:* www.creativeapproachesinc.com
Creative Artists Agency Inc (CAA)	2000 Avenue of the Stars	Los Angeles	CA	90067	424-288-2000	288-2900	731	*Web:* www.caa.com
Creative Arts Theatre And School Inc	602 E S St	Arlington	TX	76010	817-861-2287	274-0793	572	*Web:* www.creativearts.org
Creative Associates International Inc	5301 Wisconsin Ave NW Ste 700	Washington	DC	20015	202-966-5804	363-4771	194	*Web:* www.creativeassociatesinternational.com
Creative Automation Inc	1175 E N Territorial Rd	Whitmore Lake	MI	48189	734-780-3175	780-3189	386	*Web:* www.cautomation.com
Creative Bath Products	250 Creative Dr	Central Islip	NY	11722	631-582-8000	582-2020	746	*Web:* www.creativebath.com
Creative Breakthroughs Inc	2075 W Big Beaver Rd Ste 700	Troy	MI	48084	248-519-4000	519-5555	225	*Web:* cbisecure.com
Creative Business	101 Tremont St Ste 300	Boston	MA	02108	617-451-0041	338-6570	637-2	*Web:* www.creativebusiness.com
Creative Business Interiors	1535 S 101st St	Milwaukee	WI	53214	414-545-8500		186	*Web:* creativebusinessinteriors.com
Creative Circus	812 Lambert Dr	Atlanta	GA	30324	404-477-6700		167-3	*TF:* 866-685-8349 ■ *Web:* www.creativecircus.edu
Creative Co, The	PO Box 227	Mankato	MN	56002	800-445-6209	388-2746*	637-2	**Fax Area Code:* 507 ■ *TF:* 800-445-6209 ■ *Web:* www.thecreativecompany.us
Creative Colors International Inc	19015 S Jodi Rd Ste E	Mokena	IL	60448	708-478-1437	478-1636	310	*TF:* 800-933-2656 ■ *Web:* www.wecanfixthat.com
Creative Communication for Kids	880 E Campbell Ave Ste 203	Campbell	CA	95008	408-371-4004	371-5024	48-6	*Web:* www.creativecommunicationforkids.com
Creative Communications For The Parish Inc	1564 Fencorp Dr	Fenton	MO	63026	636-305-9777		637-2	*TF:* 800-325-9414 ■ *Web:* www.creativecommunications.com
Creative Continuum	325 E Commonwealth Ave	Fullerton	CA	92832	714-801-9973		637-2	*Web:* www.creativecontinuum.com
Creative Contractors Inc	620 Drew St	Clearwater	FL	33755	727-461-5522	447-4808	685	*Web:* www.creativecontractors.com
Creative Ctr, The	10850 Emmet St	Omaha	NE	68164	402-898-1000		167-3	*TF:* 888-898-1789 ■ *Web:* www.thecreativecenter.com
Creative Data Services Inc	440 Quadrangle Dr Ste E	Bolingbrook	IL	60440	630-739-0900		225	*Web:* cds1976.net
Creative Design & Machining Inc	Ivy Industrial Pk 969 Griffin Pond Rd	Clarks Summit	PA	18411	570-587-3077	587-3075	454	*Web:* www.cdmi.cc
Creative Design and Machine Inc	197 Stone Castle Rd	Rock Tavern	NY	12575	845-778-9001	778-9086	806	*Web:* www.cdmlift.com
Creative Dining Services	1 Royal Pk Dr Ste 3	Zeeland	MI	49464	616-748-1700	748-1900	271	*Web:* creativedining.com
Creative Discovery Museum	321 Chestnut St	Chattanooga	TN	37402	423-756-2738	267-9344	521	*Web:* www.cdmfun.org
Creative Door Services Ltd	14904 - 135 Ave	Edmonton	AB	T5V1R9	780-483-1789		480	*Web:* www.creativedoor.com
Creative Educational Concepts Inc	501 Darby Creek Dr Unit 15	Lexington	KY	40509	859-260-1717	276-6118	194	*TF:* 866-226-9650 ■ *Web:* www.ceconcepts.com
Creative Energy Options Inc	1735 Calle Ranchero Dr	Petaluma	CA	94954	570-233-1042		194	*Web:* ceoptions.com
Creative Engineering LLC	38 Milburn St	Bronxville	NY	10708	914-771-5540		256	*Web:* www.creativeengineering.com
Creative Engineers Inc	15425 Elm Dr	New Freedom	PA	17349	443-807-1202		256	*Web:* www.creativeengineers.com
Creative Environments	8920 S Hardy Dr	Tempe	AZ	85284	480-777-9305	777-9296	422	*Web:* www.creativeenvironments.com
Creative Extrusion & Technologies Inc	230 Elliot St	Brockton	MA	02302	508-587-2290		432	*Web:* www.creativeet.com
Creative Financial Group (CFG)	16 Campus Blvd	Newtown Square	PA	19073	610-325-6100	325-6240	401	*TF:* 800-893-4824 ■ *Web:* www.1creative.com
Creative Financial Group Ltd	1000 Abernathy Rd Bldg 400 Ste 1500	Atlanta	GA	30328	770-913-9704	913-9619	401	*TF:* 800-435-8526 ■ *Web:* www.cfgltd.com
Creative Fire	313 Ontario Ave	Saskatoon	SK	S7K1S3	306-934-3337		4	*Web:* creative-fire.com
Creative Foam Corp	300 N Alloy Dr	Fenton	MI	48430	810-629-4149		601	*TF:* 800-529-4149 ■ *Web:* creativefoam.com
Creative Foods Corp	200 Garden City Plz Ste 505	Garden City	NY	11530	516-746-6800	746-3464	345	*Web:* www.bkcfcny.com
Creative Glass Center of America	1501 Glasstown Rd	Millville	NJ	08332	856-825-6800		520	*TF:* 800-998-4552 ■ *Web:* www.wheatonarts.org
Creative Global Investments LLC	*Research Div* 115 E 57th St 11th Fl	New York	NY	10022	212-939-7256		401	*Web:* cg-inv.com
Creative Group Inc	619 N Lynndale Dr	Appleton	WI	54914	920-739-8850		193	*TF:* 800-236-2800 ■ *Web:* www.creativegroupinc.com
Creative Health Capital LLC	1101 W Lake St 1st Fl	Chicago	IL	60607	312-574-3740		70	*Web:* www.chcapital.com
Creative Imaging Group	64 Mussey Rd	Scarborough	ME	04074	207-883-2999		627	*Web:* www.creative-ig.com
Creative Impact Group Inc	801 Skokie Blvd Ste 108	Northbrook	IL	60062	800-445-2171		184	*TF:* 800-445-2171 ■ *Web:* creativeimpactgroup.com
Creative Kid Stuff	3939 E 46th St	Minneapolis	MN	55406	888-811-5271		761	*TF:* 800-353-0710 ■ *Web:* store.creativekidstuff.greatergood.com
Creative Kids Magazine	PO Box 8813	Waco	TX	76714	254-756-3337		457-6	*TF:* 800-998-2208 ■ *Web:* www.prufrock.com
Creative Laboratories Inc	1325 Eagandale Ct Ste 110	Saint Paul	MN	55121	651-681-7740		214	*Web:* www.creativelabsinc.com
Creative Labs Inc	1901 McCarthy Blvd	Milpitas	CA	95035	408-428-6600		625	*Web:* us.creative.com
Creative Loafing Atlanta	115 Martin Luther King Jr Dr SW Ste 301	Atlanta	GA	30303	404-688-5623		532-5	*TF:* 888-278-9866 ■ *Web:* www.creativeloafing.com
Creative Loafing Tampa	1911 N 13th St Ste W200	Tampa	FL	33605	813-739-4856	730 4801	532-5	*Web:* www.cltampa.com
Creative Logistics Solutions Inc	980 Mercantile Dr Ste J	Hanover	MD	21076	410-793-0708		180	*Web:* www.creativelogistics.com
Creative Machining Systems Inc	124 Youngs Rd	Mercerville	NJ	08619	609-586-3932	586-5633	695	*Web:* www.creativemachining.com
Creative Marketing Alliance Inc	191 Clarksville Rd	Princeton Junction	NJ	08550	609-297-2235	799-7032	4	*Web:* cmasolutions.com
Creative Marketing International Corp	11460 Tomahawk Creek Pkwy	Leawood	KS	66211	913-814-0510		391-2	*TF:* 800-992-2642 ■ *Web:* creativeone.com
Creative Metal Products	1101 S Kilbourn Ave	Chicago	IL	60624	800-728-6386		286	*Web:* www.kaganind.com
Creative Monograms	122 N 30th St	Billings	MT	59101	406-259-9925		226	*Web:* www.creativemonograms.com
Creative Outdoor Advertising	2402 Stouffville Rd	Stouffville	ON	L4A2J4	800-661-6088	426-2237*	7	**Fax Area Code:* 866 ■ *TF:* 800-661-6088 ■ *Web:* www.creativeoutdoor.com
Creative Paradise Inc	415 Industrial Rd	Goddard	KS	67052	316-794-8621		757	*Web:* www.creativeparadiseglass.com
Creative Playthings Ltd	33 Loring Dr	Framingham	MA	01702	508-620-0900		710	*Web:* www.creativeplaythings.com
Creative Precision Inc	1801 W Parkside Ln	Phoenix	AZ	85027	623-724-1294	742-1296*	757	**Fax Area Code:* 844 ■ *TF:* 844-742-1294 ■ *Web:* cpeast.com
Creative Producers Group Inc	200 N Broadway Ste 1400	Saint Louis	MO	63102	314-313-3151	367-5510	4	*Web:* cpgagency.com
Creative Publishing Co	409 Timber St	College Station	TX	77840	979-693-0808	764-7758	637-2	*TF:* 800-245-5841 ■ *Web:* www.creativepublishing.com
Creative Pultrusions Inc	214 Industrial Ln	Alum Bank	PA	15521	814-839-4186	839-4276	191-3	*TF:* 888-274-7855 ■ *Web:* www.creativepultrusions.com
Creative Security Company Inc	150 S Autumn St	San Jose	CA	95110	408-295-2600		693	*Web:* creativesecurity.com
Creative Sign Designs	12801 Commodity Pl	Tampa	FL	33626	800-804-4809	749-2311*	317	**Fax Area Code:* 813 ■ *TF:* 800-804-4809 ■ *Web:* www.creativesigndesigns.com
Creative Stage Lighting Company Inc	149 Rt 28 N PO Box 567	North Creek	NY	12853	518-251-3302		722	*Web:* www.creativestagelighting.com
Creative Support Solutions	5508 W Hwy 290 Ste 203	Austin	TX	78735	512-330-0701	330-0801	463	*Web:* www.solutionsbycss.com
Creative Teaching Press Inc	6262 Katella Ave	Cypress	CA	90630	714-895-5047	895-6547	243	*TF:* 800-444-4287 ■ *Web:* www.creativeteaching.com
Creative Technical Services Inc	3901 GE Rd Ste 3B	Bloomington	IL	61704	309-662-4090	662-4011	192	*Web:* www.ctechservices.com
Creative Techniques Inc	200 Northpointe Dr	Orion	MI	48359	248-373-3050		596	*Web:* www.creativetechniques.com
Creative Technology of Sarasota Inc	5959 Palmer Blvd	Sarasota	FL	34232	941-371-2743	371-3343	637-2	*Web:* creative-technology.com
Creative Training Techniques International Inc	14530 Martin Dr	Eden Prairie	MN	55344	952-829-1954	829-0260	765	*TF:* 800-383-9210 ■ *Web:* www.bobpikegroup.com
Creative Trust Inc	210 Jamestown Park Dr Ste 200	Brentwood	TN	37027	615-297-5010		506	*Web:* creativetrust.com
CreativeDrive	3850 N 29th Terr Ste 107	Hollywood	FL	33020	954-322-7600		5	*Web:* www.creativedrive.com

	Phone	Fax	Class
Creativelive Inc 757 Thomas St ... Seattle WA 98109 *Web:* www.creativelive.com	206-403-1395		387
Creativity for Kids 9450 Allen Dr ... Cleveland OH 44125 *TF:* 800-311-8684 ■ *Web:* www.fabercastell.com	216-643-4660	643-4663	762
CreatorIQ 600 Corporate Pointe ... Culver City CA 90230 *TF:* 866-448-7624 ■ *Web:* creatoriq.com	866-448-7624		657
Creators Syndicate Inc 5777 W Century Blvd Ste 700 ... Los Angeles CA 90045 *Web:* www.creators.com	310-337-7003		530
Credent Technologies LLC 30 Brookfield St Ste A ... South Windsor CT 06074 *Web:* www.credenttech.com	860-436-6391	371-2779	196
Credent Wealth Management 721 W Centre Ave ... Portage MI 49024 *Web:* www.credentwealth.com	269-532-1901		690
Credere Associates LLC 776 Main St ... Westbrook ME 04092 *Web:* crederellc.com	207-828-1272		261
Credit Acceptance Corp 25505 W 12 Mile Rd ... Southfield MI 48034 *TF:* 800-634-1506 ■ *Web:* creditacceptance.com	248-353-2700		217
Credit Bureau of Connecticut Inc, The 600 Saw Mill Rd ... West Haven CT 06516 *Web:* www.avantus.com	203-931-2000		218
Credit Consulting Services Inc 201 John St Ste E ... Salinas CA 93901 *TF:* 800-679-6888 ■ *Web:* www.creditconsultingservices.com	831-424-0606		160
Credit Human Federal Credit Union PO Box 1356 ... San Antonio TX 78295 *TF:* 800-234-7228 ■ *Web:* www.credithuman.com	210-258-1234	258-1543	219
Credit Management LP 4200 International Pkwy ... Carrollton TX 75007 *TF:* 800-377-7713 ■ *Web:* www.thecmigroup.com	800-377-7713		160
Credit Plus Inc 31550 Winterplace Pkwy ... Salisbury MD 21804 *TF:* 800-258-3287 ■ *Web:* www.creditplus.com	800-258-3488		226
Credit Professionals Intl PO Box 220714 ... Saint Louis MO 63122 *Web:* www.creditprofessionals.org	314-821-9393	821-7171	49-2
Credit Repair Consultants 122 Hialeah Dr ... Hialeah FL 33010 *TF:* 877-402-7334 ■ *Web:* www.creditrepairconsultants.com	877-402-7334		810
Credit Research Foundation (CRF) 1812 Baltimore Blvd Ste H ... Westminster MD 21157 *Web:* www.crfonline.org	443-821-3000	821-3627	49-2
Credit Suisse 11 Madison Ave ... New York NY 10010 *Web:* www.credit-suisse.com	212-325-2000	325-6665	690
Credit Union Acceptance Company LLC 9601 Jones Rd Ste 108 ... Houston TX 77065 *TF:* 866-970-2822 ■ *Web:* www.cuac.com	281-970-2822		219
Credit Union Directors Newsletter 5710 Mineral Pt Rd ... Madison WI 53705 *TF:* 800-356-9655 ■ *Web:* www.cuna.org	608-231-4000		531-1
Credit Union Executives Society (CUES) 5510 Research Pk Dr ... Madison WI 53711 *TF:* 800-252-2664 ■ *Web:* www.cues.org	608-271-2664	271-2303	49-2
Credit Union of Denver 9305 W Alameda Ave ... Lakewood CO 80226 *Web:* www.cudenver.com	303-234-1700	239-1108	70
Credit Union of Dodge City 1200 W Frontview St ... Dodge City KS 67801 *TF:* 877-227-6171 ■ *Web:* cudodge.com	620-227-7181	227-7180	219
Credit Union of Richmond 1601 Ownby Ln ... Richmond VA 23220 *Web:* curich.org	804-355-9684		219
Credit Union of Southern California PO Box 200 ... Whittier CA 90608 **Fax Area Code: 714* ■ *TF:* 866-287-6225 ■ *Web:* www.cusocal.org	562-698-8326	990-5492*	219
Credit Union of Texas PO Box 517028 ... Dallas TX 75251 *TF:* 800-314-3828 ■ *Web:* www.cutx.org	972-263-9497	301-1980	219
Credit Valley Hospital 2200 Eglinton Ave W ... Mississauga ON L5M2N1 *Web:* www.cvh.on.ca	905-813-1550		374-2
Credit.net 1020 E 1st St ... Papillion NE 68046 *TF:* 800-993-5323 ■ *Web:* www.credit.net	800-993-5323		215
Creditcom Inc 160 Spear St Ste 1020 ... San Francisco CA 94105 *Web:* www.credit.com	415-901-1550		219
Creditors Adjustment Bureau 14226 Ventura Blvd ... Sherman Oaks CA 91423 *TF:* 800-800-4523 ■ *Web:* cabcollects.com	818-990-4800	780-3112	160
Creditors Bureau Assoc 112 Ward St ... Macon GA 31201 *TF:* 866-949-4213 ■ *Web:* www.cbamacon.com	478-750-1111		218
Creditors Service Bureau Inc 3410 SW Van Buren St Ste 101 ... Topeka KS 66611	785-266-4567		160
CREDO Long Distance P O Box 7015 ... San Francisco CA 94120 *TF:* 800-788-0898 ■ *Web:* www.credolongdistance.com	800-788-0898		192
Cree Inc 4600 Silicon Dr ... Durham NC 27703 *NASDAQ: CREE* ■ *TF:* 800-533-2583 ■ *Web:* www.cree.com	919-313-5300		696
Cree Nation of Eastmain 78 Nouchimi PO Box 90 ... Eastmain QC J0M1W0 *Web:* eastmain.ca	819-977-0211	977-0281	78
Creed & Creed 1805 Tower Dr ... Monroe LA 71201 *Web:* creedlaw.com	318-387-5800		41
Creed-Monarch Inc 1 Pucci Pk ... New Britain CT 06051 *Web:* www.creedmonarch.com	860-826-4000	224-8762	454
Creedmoor Psychiatric Ctr 79-25 Winchester Blvd ... Queens Village NY 11427 *Web:* omh.ny.gov	718-464-7500	264-3636	374-5
Creek County 317 E Lee St Ste 100 ... Sapulpa OK 74066 *Web:* www.creekcountyclerk.org	918-224-4084		338
Creekside Cellars 28036 Hwy 74 ... Evergreen CO 80439 *Web:* www.creeksidecellars.net	303-674-5460		443
Creekside Dinery 160 Nix Boat Yard Rd ... Saint Augustine FL 32084 *Web:* www.creeksidedinery.com	904-829-6113		671
Creekside Inn 3400 El Camino Real ... Palo Alto CA 94306 *TF:* 800-492-7335 ■ *Web:* www.greystonehotels.com	650-493-2411	493-6787	379
Creekside Insurance Advisors 167 Creekside Ln ... Winchester VA 22602 *TF:* 800-467-5425 ■ *Web:* creeksideadvisors.net	540-722-2529		390
Creekstone Farms Premium Beef LLC 604 Goff Industrial Park Rd ... Arkansas City KS 67005 *Web:* www.creekstonefarms.com	620-741-3100		473
Creel Printing LLC 6330 W Sunset Rd ... Las Vegas NV 89118 *TF:* 866-494-6155 ■ *Web:* www.creelprint.com	702-735-8161		627
Creform Corp PO Box 830 ... Greer SC 29652 *TF:* 800-839-8823 ■ *Web:* creform.com	864-989-1700	877-3863	723
Cregger Company Inc 629 12th St Extn ... West Columbia SC 29169 *Web:* www.creggercompany.com	803-791-5195	794-8375	610
Creighton Bros LLC PO Box 220 ... Atwood IN 46502 *Web:* www.creightonbrothersllc.com	574-267-3101		10-8
Creighton University 2500 California Plz ... Omaha NE 68178 *TF:* 800-282-5835 ■ *Web:* www.creighton.edu	402-280-2700	280-2685	166
Cremac LLC 78 Delevan St ... Brooklyn NY 11231 *Web:* www.cremac.com	718-222-4500		401
Cremach Tech Inc 369 Meyers Cir ... Corona CA 92879 *Web:* www.cmtus.com	951-735-3194	735-3051	454
Cremation Association of North America (CANA) 499 Northgate Pkwy ... Wheeling IL 60090 *Web:* www.cremationassociation.org	312-245-1077	321-4098	49-4
Creme Curls Bakery Inc 5292 Lawndale Ave PO Box 276 ... Hudsonville MI 49426 *TF:* 800-466-1219 ■ *Web:* www.cremecurls.com	616-669-6230	669-2469	297-8
Crenlo LLC 1600 Fourth Ave NW ... Rochester MN 55901 *Web:* www.crenlo.com	507-289-3371	287-3405	254
Crenshaw Consulting Engineers Inc 3516 Bush St Ste 200 ... Raleigh NC 27609 *Web:* www.crenshawconsulting.com	919-871-1070		261
Crenshaw County 245 Saint James Church Rd ... Luverne AL 36049 *Web:* sos.alabama.gov	334-335-6575		338
Crenshaw Dan (Rep R - TX) 413 Cannon House Office Bldg ... Washington DC 20515 *Web:* www.crenshaw.house.gov	202-225-6565		342-2
Crenshaw, Ware & Martin PLC 150 W Main St Ste 1500 ... Norfolk VA 23510 *Web:* cwm-law.com	757-623-3000		41
Creor Group 952 School St Ste 310 ... Napa CA 94559 *TF:* 877-774-4312 ■ *Web:* www.creorgroup.com	877-774-4312		195
Creperie, The 10220 103rd St NW ... Edmonton AB T5J4C9 *Web:* www.thecreperie.com	780-420-6656		671
Creps United Publications 4185 Rte 286 Hwy W ... Indiana PA 15701 *TF:* 800-752-0555 ■ *Web:* www.crepsunited.com	724-463-8522		627
Crescendo Consulting Group 48 Free St Ste 206 ... Portland ME 04101 *Web:* www.crescendocg.com	207-774-2345		194
Crescendo Designs 641 County Rd 39A ... Southampton NY 11968 *Web:* www.crescendodesigns.com	631-283-2133		52
Crescendo Systems Corp 1600 Montgolfier ... Laval QC H7T0A2 *TF:* 800-724-2930 ■ *Web:* www.crescendo.com	450-973-8029		177
Crescendo Venture Management LLP 405 El Camino Real Ste 206 ... Menlo Park CA 94025 *Web:* www.crescendoventures.com	650-470-1200		792
Crescent Bank & Trust 1100 Poydras St Ste 100 ... New Orleans LA 70163 *Web:* cbtno.com	504-556-5950		70
Crescent Cardboard Company LLC 100 W Willow Rd ... Wheeling IL 60090 *TF:* 888-293-3956 ■ *Web:* www.crescentcardboard.com	847-537-3400	537-7153	560
Crescent City Coca-Cola Bottling Co 5601 Citrus Blvd ... Harahan LA 70123 *TF:* 844-733-2653 ■ *Web:* cocacolaunited.com	504-818-7000		805
Crescent City Consultants 1010 Common St Ste 3010 ... New Orleans LA 70112 *Web:* www.ccc-nola.com	504-561-1191	568-0783	184
Crescent City-Del Norte County Chamber of Commerce 1001 Front St ... Crescent City CA 95531 *TF:* 800-343-8300 ■ *Web:* visitdelnortecounty.com	707-464-3174	464-3561	206
Crescent Communities 400 S Tryon Ste 2900 ... Charlotte NC 28202 *Web:* www.crescentcommunities.com	980-321-6000		653
Crescent Crown Distributing 5900 Almonaster Ave ... New Orleans LA 70126 *Web:* crescentcrown.com	504-240-5900		81-1
Crescent Design Inc 6370 Nancy Ridge Dr Ste 105 ... San Diego CA 92121 *Web:* crescentdesign.com	858-452-3240	452-3241	396
Crescent Directional Drilling LP 2040 Aldine Western Rd ... Houston TX 77038 *Web:* www.crescentdirectional.com	281-668-9500	668-9539	540
Crescent Electric Supply Co 7750 Dunleith Dr ... East Dubuque IL 61025 *Web:* www.cesco.com	815-747-3145	747-7720	246
Crescent Energy Services LLC 1304 Engineers Rd ... Belle Chasse LA 70037 *Web:* www.crescentes.com	504-433-4188	433-9159	540
Crescent Ford Truck Sales 6121 Jefferson Hwy ... Harahan LA 70123 *Web:* www.crescentfordtrucksharahan.com	504-818-1818		57
Crescent Hill Books 2410 Frankfort Ave ... Louisville KY 40206 *TF:* 800-401-6838 ■ *Web:* www.crescenthillbooks.com	800-401-6838		637-2
Crescent Hotel 403 N Crescent Dr ... Beverly Hills CA 90210 *Web:* crescentbh.com	310-247-0505		379
Crescent Hotels & Resorts LLC 10306 Eaton Pl Ste 430 ... Fairfax VA 22030 *Web:* www.crescenthotels.com	703-279-7820		379
Crescent Industries Inc 70 E High St ... New Freedom PA 17349 *Web:* crescentind.com	717-235-3844		596

Company / Address	City	State	ZIP	Phone	Fax	Class
Crescent Manufacturing Co 1310 Majestic Dr; TF: 800-537-1330 ■ Web: www.crescentblades.com	Fremont	OH	43420	419-332-6484	332-6564	222
Crescent Marketing Inc 10285 Eagle Dr PO Box 1500; Web: www.crescentmfg.net	North Collins	NY	14111	716-337-0145		3
Crescent Plastics Inc 955 E Diamond Ave; Web: www.crescentplastics.com	Evansville	IN	47711	812-428-9305		596
Crescent Point Energy Corp 585 Eighth Ave SW Ste 2000; Web: www.crescentpointenergy.com	Calgary	AB	T2P1G1	403-693-0020		536
Crescent Printing Company Inc 1001 Commercial Ct; TF: 800-658-9032 ■ Web: www.cpcprintpromo.com	Onalaska	WI	54650	608-781-1050	781-6158	627
Crescent Real Estate 777 Main St Ste 2260; Web: crescent.com	Fort Worth	TX	76102	817-321-1566	321-2090	655
Crescent School of Gaming & Bartending 1306 29th Ave; Web: crescent.edu	Gulfport	MS	39501	228-822-2444		685
Crescent Sock Co 527 E Willson St; Web: www.crescentsockco.com	Niota	TN	37826	423-568-2101	568-2104	155-10
Crescent Systems Inc 1801 Gateway Blvd Ste 105; Web: csitx.com	Richardson	TX	75080	972-437-0400		261
Crescent Woolen Mills Co 1016 School St; Web: crescentwoolenmills.com	Two Rivers	WI	54241	920-793-3331	793-3818	745-9
Crescenta Valley Chamber of Commerce 3131 Foothill Blvd Ste D; Web: www.crescentavalleychamber.org	La Crescenta	CA	91214	818-248-4957	248-9625	139
Crescent-News, The 624 W Second St; Web: www.crescent-news.com	Defiance	OH	43512	419-784-5441		532-2
Cresco Lines Inc 15220 S Halsted St; TF: 800-323-4476 ■ Web: www.crescolines.com	Harvey	IL	60426	708-339-1186		780
Cres-Cor 5925 Heisley Rd; TF: 877-273-7267 ■ Web: www.crescor.com	Mentor	OH	44060	440-350-1100	350-7267	286
Cresent Fine Furniture PO Box 1438; Web: www.cresent.com	Gallatin	TN	37066	615-452-1671		319-2
Cresleigh Homes Corp 433 California St Ste 700; Web: cresleigh.com	San Francisco	CA	94104	415-982-7777	982-7781	186
Cresline-West Inc 600 Crosspointe Blvd; Web: www.cresline.com	Evansville	IN	47715	812-428-9300	428-9353	596
Crespi Carmelite High School Inc 5031 Alonzo Ave; TF: 800-540-4000 ■ Web: www.crespi.org	Encino	CA	91316	818-345-1672		685
Cress Photo PO Box 4262; Web: www.flashbulbs.com	Wayne	NJ	07474	973-694-1280	694-6965	119
Cressey Development Corp 555 W Eighth Ave Ste 200; Web: cressey.com	Vancouver	BC	V5Z1C6	604-683-1256		186
Cresskill Animal Hospital 39 Spring St; Web: www.cresskillanimalhosp.com	Cresskill	NJ	07626	201-568-7700		794
Cressman Tubular Products Corp 3939 Beltline Rd Ste 460; Web: www.cressmantubular.com	Addison	TX	75001	214-352-5252		358
Cressy & Everett Inc 332 N Ironwood Dr; Web: cressyeverett.com	South Bend	IN	46615	574-532-8779		652
Crest Beverage 8870 Liquid Ct; Web: www.crestbeverage.com	San Diego	CA	92121	858-452-2300		81-1
Crest Coating Inc 1361 S Allec St; Web: www.crestcoating.com	Anaheim	CA	92805	714-635-7090	758-8752	481
Crest Craft Co 3860 Virginia Ave; TF: 800-860-1662 ■ Web: www.crestcraft.com	Cincinnati	OH	45227	513-271-4858		627
Crest Electronics Inc 3706 Alliance Dr; Web: www.crestelectronics.com	Greensboro	NC	27407	336-855-6422	855-6676	52
Crest Foam Industries Inc 100 Carol Pl; Web: www.inoacusa.com	Moonachie	NJ	07074	201-807-0809	807-1113	601
Crest Foods Company Inc 905 Main St; TF: 877-273-7893 ■ Web: crestfoods.com	Ashton	IL	61006	800-435-6972		296-17
Crest Foods Inc 101 W Renner Rd Ste 240; Web: nestlecafe.com	Richardson	TX	75082	214-495-9533		68
Crest Healthcare Supply 195 Third St; *Fax Area Code: 320 ■ TF: 800-328-8908 ■ Web: www.cresthealthcare.com	Dassel	MN	55325	800-328-8908	275-2306*	392
Crest Industries Inc 231 Larkin Williams Industrial Ct; TF: 800-733-2737 ■ Web: www.crestindustries.com	Fenton	MO	63026	636-349-4800	349-4888	690
Crest Manufacturing Co 5 Hood Dr; Web: www.crestmfg.com	Lincoln	RI	02865	401-333-1350	333-0821	488
Crest Publications PO Box 481022; Web: www.christianpublishers.net	Charlotte	NC	28269	704-277-7194	717-2928	637-2
Crest Publishers 111 Burnham St; Web: crestpublishers.com	Birmingham	AL	35242	205-527-7785		637-2
Crest Services 3015 Merle Hay Rd Ste 6; Web: crestservices.org	Des Moines	IA	50310	515-331-1200	331-1220	475
Crest Theater 1013 K St; Web: www.crestsacramento.com	Sacramento	CA	95814	916-476-3356		748
Crest Ultrasonics Corp 18 Graphics Dr; Web: www.crest-ultrasonics.com	Ewing Township	NJ	08628	609-883-4000		782
Crest Ultrasonics Corp 14000 NW 4th St; *Fax Area Code: 609 ■ TF: 800-992-7378 ■ Web: www.thecrestgroupincorporated.com	Sunrise	FL	33325	954-724-2730	883-6452*	425
Crest/Good Manufacturing Company Inc 90 Gordon Dr Ste A; TF: 800-645-1251 ■ Web: www.crestgood.com	Syosset	NY	11791	800-645-1251		612
Cresta Technology Corp 3900 Freedom Cir Ste 201; Web: www.crestatech.com	Santa Clara	CA	95054	408-486-5610	486-5615	201
Crestcom International Ltd 6900 E Belleview Ave; TF: 800-333-7680 ■ Web: crestcom.com	Greenwood Village	CO	80111	303-267-8200		765
Crestec USA Inc 2410 Mira Mar Ave; Web: www.crestecusa.com	Long Beach	CA	90815	310-327-9000	532-0361	627
Crested Butte Mountain Resort (CBMR) 12 Snowmass Rd PO Box 5700; *Fax Area Code: 970 ■ TF: 877-547-5143 ■ Web: www.skicb.com	Crested Butte	CO	81225	877-547-5143	349-2250*	669
Cresthill Suites Hotel 1415 Washington Ave; Web: cresthillsuites.com	Albany	NY	12206	518-454-0007		379
Cresting Wave 260 Harristown Rd; Web: www.crestingwave.com	Glen Rock	NJ	07452	201-444-0084		463
Crestline Hotels & Resorts 3950 University Dr Ste 301; Web: www.crestlinehotels.com	Fairfax	VA	22030	571-529-6100	529-6095	379
Crestliner Inc 9040 Quaday Ave NE; *Fax Area Code: 320 ■ TF: 866-301-8544 ■ Web: www.crestliner.com	Otsego	MN	55330	866-301-8544	256-4676*	90
Crestmark Bank 5480 Corporate Dr Ste 350; *Fax Area Code: 248 ■ TF: 888-999-8050 ■ Web: www.crestmark.com	Troy	MI	48098	888-999-8050	641-5101*	272
Crestmont Health Care Ctr 111 Trealout Dr; Web: savaseniorcare.com	Fenton	MI	48430	810-629-4105		450
Crestview Area Chamber of Commerce 1447 Commerce Dr; Web: www.crestviewchamber.com	Crestview	FL	32539	850-682-3212	682-7413	139
Crestview Baptist Church Georgetown Texas 2300 Williams Dr; Web: peoplesharingjesus.com	Georgetown	TX	78628	512-863-6576		48-20
Crestview Partners LP 667 Madison Ave 10th Fl; Web: www.crestview.com	New York	NY	10065	212-906-0700		360-3
Crestwood Advisors LLC 50 Federal St Ste 810; TF: 877-273-7896 ■ Web: www.crestwoodadvisors.com	Boston	MA	02110	617-523-8880		401
Crestwood Animal Hospital 28822 Pacific Hwy S; Web: crestwoodanhosp.com	Federal Way	WA	98003	253-839-4744	941-1650	794
Crestwood Equity Partners LP 811 Main St Ste 3400; TF: 877-446-3749 ■ Web: www.crestwoodlp.com	Houston	TX	77002	832-519-2200	519-2250	579
Crestwood Inc 601 E Water Well Rd; Web: www.crestwooddesigncenter.com	Salina	KS	67401	785-823-1532	827-0084	115
Crestwood Manor 50 Lacey Rd; TF: 877-467-1652 ■ Web: crestwoodmanoronline.org	Whiting	NJ	08759	732-849-4900		672
Crestwood Medical Ctr 1 Hospital Dr; Web: www.crestwoodmedcenter.com	Huntsville	AL	35801	256-429-4000		374-3
Crestwood Tubulars Inc PO Box 6950; *Fax Area Code: 314 ■ TF: 800-238-7473 ■ Web: www.crestwoodtubulars.com	Saint Louis	MO	63123	800-238-7473	842-9064*	492
Creswell Richardson 900 Appling St; Web: www.mycreswell.com	Chattanooga	TN	37406	423-894-4117		253
Crete Area Chamber of Commerce 1182 Main St PO Box 263; Web: www.cretechamber.com	Crete	IL	60417	708-672-9216	672-7640	139
Crete Carrier Corp 400 NW 56th St PO Box 81228; TF: 800-998-4095 ■ Web: cretecarrier.com	Lincoln	NE	68528	402-475-9521	479-2073	780
Crete Consulting Incorporated PC 108 S Washington St Ste 300; Web: creteconsulting.com	Seattle	WA	98104	253-797-6323		261
Crete-Monee School District No 201-U 1500 S Sangamon St; Web: www.cm201u.org	Crete	IL	60417	708-367-8300	672-2698	685
Creter Vault Corp 417 Rte 202; Web: www.cretervault.com	Flemington	NJ	08822	908-782-7771		183
Cretex Cos 311 Lowell Ave; TF: 800-328-4546 ■ Web: cretexcompanies.com	Elk River	MN	55330	763-441-2121		183
Creutzfeldt-Jakob Disease Foundation Inc 3610 W Market St Ste 110; *Fax Area Code: 234 ■ TF: 800-659-1991 ■ Web: www.cjdfoundation.org	Fairlawn	OH	44333	800-659-1991	466-7077*	48-17
Crew Energy Inc 250 5 St SW Ste 800; Web: www.crewenergy.com	Calgary	AB	T2P0R4	403-266-2088		536
Crew Engineers Inc 1250 NJ-23; Web: www.crewengineers.com	Butler	NJ	07405	973-492-3300		261
Crew Outfitters Inc 1001 Virginia Ave; TF: 888-345-5353 ■ Web: www.crewoutfitters.com	Atlanta	GA	30354	678-516-2067		156
Crew Software Inc 1030 E El Camino Real Ste 165; Web: www.crewsoft.com	Sunnyvale	CA	94087	408-523-9990		178-1
Crexendo Inc 1615 S 52nd St; OTC: CXDO ■ TF: 866-621-6111 ■ Web: www.crexendo.com	Tempe	AZ	85281	602-714-8500		39
CRF (Credit Research Foundation) 1812 Baltimore Blvd Ste H; Web: www.crfonline.org	Westminster	MD	21157	443-821-3000	821-3627	49-2
CRG (Council for Responsible Genetics) 5 Upland Rd Ste 3; Web: www.councilforresponsiblegenetics.org	Cambridge	MA	02140	617-868-0870	491-5344	49-19
CRG (Capital Review Group) 214 E Roosevelt St; TF: 877-666-5539 ■ Web: capitalreviewgroup.com	Phoenix	AZ	85004	877-666-5539		463
CRG Global Inc 3 Signal Ave Ste A; TF: 800-831-1718 ■ Web: www.crgglobalinc.com	Ormond Beach	FL	32174	386-677-5644		668
CRH Americas Inc 900 Ashwood Pkwy Ste 700; TF: 800-241-7074 ■ Web: www.crhamericasmaterials.com	Atlanta	GA	30338	770-522-5600	522-5608	188-4
CRH Medical Corp 999 Canada Pl Ste 522; TF: 800-660-2153 ■ Web: www.crhsystem.com	Vancouver	BC	V6C3E1	604-633-1440		476
CRI (Carpet & Rug Institute) 100 S Hamilton St PO Box 2048; Web: web.carpet-rug.org	Dalton	GA	30720	706-278-3176	278-8835	49-4
CRI 190 Godwin Ave; Web: www.cridps.com	Midland Park	NJ	07432	201-857-1267		627
Cricket Media Inc 1751 Pinnacle Dr Ste 600; *Fax Area Code: 703 ■ TF: 800-821-0115 ■ Web: cricketmedia.com	McLean	VA	22102	800-821-0115	885-3490*	457-6

Phone | Fax | Class

Crier Newspapers LLC
5064 Nandina Ln Ste C Dunwoody GA 30338 770-451-4147 451-4223 532-4
Web: www.thecrier.net
Crime Alert 690 Lenfest Rd San Jose CA 95133 800-367-1094 254-9813* 45
**Fax Area Code:* 408 ■ *TF:* 800-367-1094 ■ *Web:* www.crimealert.com
Crimetek Security Services
3448 N Golden State Blvd Turlock CA 95382 209-668-6208 693
Web: www.crimetek.com
Crimson Consulting Group
4970 El Camino Real Los Altos CA 94022 650-960-3600 195
Web: crimsonmarketing.com
Crimson Resource Management Corp
410 17th St Ste 1010 Denver CO 80202 303-892-9333 327-7660 536
Web: www.crimsonrm.com
Crippen Manufacturing Co
400 Woodside Dr Saint Louis MI 48880 989-681-4323 681-3818 273
TF: 800-872-2474 ■ *Web:* crippenmfg.com
Crisell & Assoc 2199 E Willow St Signal Hill CA 90755 562-595-0501 2
Web: www.crisellcpas.com
Crisp County 210 S Seventh St Cordele GA 31015 229-276-2672 276-2675 338
Web: www.crispcounty.com
Crisp County Power Commission Inc
202 S 7th St PO Box 1218 Cordele GA 31010 229-273-3811 273-3824 245
Web: crispcountypower.com
Crisp County Schools 201 Seventh St S Cordele GA 31015 229-276-3400 276-3406 685
Web: www.crispschools.org
Crispin Corp 600 Wade Ave Raleigh NC 27605 919-845-7744 225
Web: www.crispincorp.com
Crispin Porter & Bogusky LLC
6450 Gunpark Dr Boulder CO 80301 303-628-5100 5
Web: www.cpbgroup.com
Crisp-Ladew Fire & Life Safety Systems
5201 Saunders Rd Fort Worth TX 76119 817-572-3663 189-13
Web: crisp-ladew.com
Crissair Inc 28909 Ave Williams Valencia CA 91355 661-367-3300 790
Web: www.crissair.com
Crissey Field State Recreation Site
1655 Hwy 101 N Brookings OR 97415 541-469-2021 565
Web: stateparks.oregon.gov
Crist Charlie (Rep D - FL)
215 Cannon House Office Bldg Washington DC 20515 202-225-5961 225-9764 342-2
Web: crist.house.gov
Crist Engineers Inc
205 Executive Ct Little Rock AR 72207 501-664-1552 261
Web: cristengineers.com
Crist|Kolder Associates LLC
3250 Lacey Rd Ste 450 Downers Grove IL 60515 630-321-1110 321-1112 260
Web: www.cristkolder.com
CRISTA Ministries 19303 Fremont Ave N Seattle WA 98133 206-546-7200 48-5
TF: 888-236-6167 ■ *Web:* crista.org
Cristek Interconnects Inc
5395 E Hunter Ave Anaheim CA 92807 714-696-5200 696-5225 815
Web: www.cristek.com
Cristi Cleaning Service
77 Trinity Pl Hackensack NJ 07601 201-883-1717 883-1212 104
TF: 800-287-6173 ■ *Web:* www.cristicleaning.com
Cristo Rey Jesuit High School
1852 W 22nd Pl Chicago IL 60608 773-890-6800 890-6801 685
Web: www.cristorey.net
Cristobal & Co 10530 Venice Blvd Culver City CA 90232 424-361-5252 361-5253 734
TF: 800-899-6007 ■ *Web:* cristobalcpa.com
Criswell Automotive
503 Quince Orchard Rd Gaithersburg MD 20878 888-672-7559 57
TF: 888-672-7559 ■ *Web:* www.criswellauto.com
Criswell College 4010 Gaston Ave Dallas TX 75246 214-821-5433 166
Web: www.criswell.edu
Critchfield Mechanical Inc
1901 Junction Ave San Jose CA 95131 408-437-7000 437-7199 189-10
Web: www.cmihvac.com
Critchfield, Critchfield & Johnston Ltd
225 N Market St Wooster OH 44691 330-264-4444 428
TF: 800-686-0440 ■ *Web:* www.ccj.com
Criterion Laboratories Inc
400 Street Rd Ste 100 Bensalem PA 19020 215-244-1300 743
Web: www.criterionlabs.com
Criterion Machinery Inc
7655 Hub Pky Cleveland OH 44125 216-573-0311 573-0313 695
Web: criterionmachinery.com
Criterion Technologies Inc
101 Mcintosh Pkwy Thomaston GA 30286 706-647-5082 608
Web: ctioptics.com
Criterion Thread Company Inc
21744 98th Ave Queens Village NY 11429 718-464-4200 464-3594 594
TF: 800-695-0080 ■ *Web:* www.cthread.com
CRITFC (Columbia River Inter-Tribal Fish Commission)
700 NE Multnomah St Ste 1200 Portland OR 97232 503-238-0667 235-4228 48-13
Web: www.critfc.org
Critical Business Analysis Inc (CBA)
133 W Second St Perrysburg OH 43551 800-874-8080 463
TF: 800-874-8080 ■ *Web:* cbainc.com
Critical Care Services Inc
3010 Broadway St NE Minneapolis MN 55413 612-638-4900 30
Web: www.lifelinkiii.com
Critical Mass Inc
1011 Ninth Ave SE Ste 300 Calgary AB T2G0H7 403-262-3006 5
Web: www.criticalmass.com
Critical Mention Inc 521 Fifth Ave New York NY 10175 212-398-1141 225
TF: 855-306-2626 ■ *Web:* www.criticalmention.com
Criticom Monitoring Services
715 W State Rd 434 Longwood FL 32750 800-432-1429 818-1973 693
TF: 866-705-7705 ■ *Web:* www.criticominternational.com
Critigen LLC
7604 Technology Way Ste 300 Denver CO 80237 303-706-0990 463
Web: www.critigen.com
CritiTech Inc 1849 E 1450 Rd Lawrence KS 66044 785-841-7120 238
Web: crititech.com
Crittenden Publishing Company Inc
1010 State Hwy 77 Marion AR 72364 870-735-1010 735-1020 532-3
Web: theeveningtimes.com
Crittenton Children's Ctr
10918 Elm Ave Kansas City MO 64134 816-765-6600 374-1
Web: www.saintlukeskc.org
Critter Care Animal Clinic
2734 Calumet Dr Sheboygan WI 53083 920-458-3636 794
Web: crittercareanimalclinic.com
Critter Clips School of Dog Grooming
1865 Dublin Blvd Colorado Springs CO 80918 719-593-5880 593-2188 685
Web: www.critter-clipsgrooming.com
Critton, Luttier, & Coleman LLP
303 Banyan Blvd Ste 400 West Palm Beach FL 33401 561-842-2820 844-6929 41
Web: lawclc.com
Crivelli Chevrolet Buick
1520 Rt 31 Mount Pleasant PA 15666 724-620-4074 57
Web: www.crivellichev.com
Crivelli Ford Inc 2085 Brodhead Rd Aliquippa PA 15001 724-857-0400 57
Web: www.crivelliford.com
Crivello Carlson Sc
710 N Plankinton Ave Ste 500 Milwaukee WI 53203 414-271-7722 271-4438 428
Web: www.crivellocarlson.com
CRL Technologies Inc
9426 Ferry Landing Ct Alexandria VA 22309 703-297-9900 256
Web: www.crltechnologies.com
CRM 15800 S Avalon Blvd Rancho Dominguez CA 90220 310-538-2222 755
Web: www.crmrubber.com
CRM Dynamics
5800 Ambler Dr Unit 106 Mississauga ON L5W4J4 866-740-2424 196
TF: 866-740-2424 ■ *Web:* www.crmdynamics.com
CRM Innovation 8527 Bluejacket St Lenexa KS 66214 913-492-2764 177
Web: www.crminnovation.com
CRM Learning
11400 SE Eighth St Ste 210 Bellevue WA 98004 760-431-9800 513
TF: 800-421-0833 ■ *Web:* www.crmlearning.com
CRMC (Cheyenne Regional Medical Ctr)
214 E 23rd St Cheyenne WY 82001 307-634-2273 374-3
Web: www.cheyenneregional.org
CRMC (Cullman Regional Medical Ctr)
1912 Alabama Hwy 157 PO Box 1108 Cullman AL 35058 256-737-2000 374-3
Web: cullmanregional.com
CRMC (Capital Regional Medical Ctr)
2626 Capital Medical Blvd Tallahassee FL 32308 850-325-5000 374-3
Web: capitalregionalmedicalcenter.com
CRMC (Coffee Regional Medical Ctr)
1101 Ocilla Rd Douglas GA 31533 912-384-1900 374-3
TF: 800-555-4444 ■ *Web:* www.coffeeregional.org
CRMC (Colquitt Regional Medical Ctr)
3131 S Main St PO Box 40 Moultrie GA 31768 229-985-3420 374-3
TF: 888-262-2762 ■ *Web:* colquittregional.com
CRMC (Cape Regional Medical Center Inc)
2 Stone Harbor Blvd Cape May NJ 08210 609-463-2000 374-3
Web: www.caperegional.com
CRMC (Cookeville Regional Medical Ctr)
1 Medical Center Blvd Cookeville TN 38501 931-528-2541 374-3
TF: 800-897-1898 ■ *Web:* www.crmchealth.org
CRMPlus Consulting Inc
11531 Meridian Point Dr Tampa FL 33626 813-343-2173 827-9744* 463
**Fax Area Code:* 941 ■ *Web:* crmplusconsulting.com
CRMSE (Center for Research in Mathematics & Science Education)
San Diego State University 6505 Alvarado Rd
Ste 201 San Diego CA 92120 619-594-3977 668
Web: www.sci.sdsu.edu
CRN (Council for Responsible Nutrition)
1828 L St NW Ste 510 Washington DC 20036 202-204-7700 204-7701 49-6
Web: www.crnusa.org
CRN Digital Talk Radio
10487 Sunland Blvd Sunland CA 91040 818-352-7152 352-3229 740
Web: crntalk.com
CRN International Inc 1 Circular Ave Hamden CT 06514 203-288-2002 6
Web: www.crnradio.com
CRO Analytics LLC
6139 Stoney Hill Rd New Hope PA 18938 571-436-4835 463
Web: www.croanalytics.com
Croatian Fraternal Union of America (CFU)
100 Delaney Dr Pittsburgh PA 15235 412-843-0380 823-1594 48-14
Web: cfu.org
Croatian National Tourist Office
350 Fifth Ave Ste 4003 New York NY 10118 212-279-8672 279-8683 775
Web: www.croatia.hr
Crochet World Magazine 306 E Parr Rd Berne IN 46711 260-589-8741 457-14
Web: www.crochet-world.com
Crocker & Winsor Seafoods Inc
21 Highland Cir Needham MA 02494 617-269-3100 296-14
TF: 800-225-1597 ■ *Web:* www.crockerwinsor.com
Crocker Art Museum 216 'O' St Sacramento CA 95814 916-808-7000 808-7372 520
Web: www.crockerart.org
Crocker Law Firm 520 E Main Ave Bowling Green KY 42101 270-846-3100 846-3131 41
Web: crockerfirm.com
Crocker Park 189 Crocker Pk Blvd Westlake OH 44145 440-871-6880 871-6889 50-6
Web: www.crockerpark.com
Crockett County 1301 Avenue AA Ozona TX 76943 325-392-2721 392-2723 338
Web: crockett.agrilife.org
Crockett Hotel 320 Bonham St San Antonio TX 78205 210-225-6500 225-6251 379
Web: www.crocketthotel.com
Crocs Inc 7477 East Dry Creek Pkwy Niwot CO 80503 303-848-7000 301
NASDAQ: CROX ■ *TF:* 866-306-3179 ■ *Web:* www.crocs.com
Crocus Technology 2380 Walsh Ave Santa Clara CA 95051 408-732-0000 732-8250 180
Web: www.crocus-technology.com
Croda Inc 300 Columbus Cir Ste A Edison NJ 08837 732-417-0800 417-0804 145
Web: www.croda.com
Croft LLC 1800 N Clark Ave Magnolia MS 39652 601-684-6121 485
TF: 800-222-3195 ■ *Web:* croftllc.com
Croft State Natural Area
450 Croft State Park Rd Spartanburg SC 29302 864-585-1283 565
Web: southcarolinaparks.com
Crohn's & Colitis Foundation of America (CCFA)
733 Third Ave Ste 510 New York NY 10017 800-932-2423 679-3567* 48-17
**Fax Area Code:* 212 ■ *TF:* 800-932-2423 ■ *Web:* www.crohnscolitisfoundation.org

Name / Address	City	State	ZIP	Phone	Fax	Class
Croley Insurance						
3705 E Battlefield St	Springfield	MO	65809	417-881-3520		390
Web: croleyinsurance.com						
CROM LLC 250 SW 36th Terr	Gainesville	FL	32607	352-372-3436	372-6209	183
Web: www.cromcorp.com						
Croman Corp 801 Ave C	White City	OR	97503	541-826-4455		448
Web: www.croman.net						
Crombie REIT 115 King St	Stellarton	NS	B0K1S0	902-755-8100		655
Web: crombiereit.ca						
Cromer Material Handling Inc						
4701 Oakport St	Oakland	CA	94601	510-534-6566		770
TF: 800-974-5438 ■ *Web:* cromer.com						
Cromers Pnuts LLC 3030 N Main St	Columbia	SC	29201	800-322-7688		296-36
TF: 800-322-7688 ■ *Web:* cromers.com						
Crompco Corp						
1815 Gallagher Rd	Plymouth Meeting	PA	19462	610-278-7203		466
Web: www.crompco.com						
Cromwell Architect Engineers Inc						
1300 E 6th St	Little Rock	AR	72202	501-372-2900		261
Web: www.cromwell.com						
Cromwell Group Inc, The						
1824 Murfreesboro Rd	Nashville	TN	37217	615-361-7560	366-4313	647
Web: www.cromwellradio.com						
Cromwell Leather Grp						
147 Palmer Ave	Mamaroneck	NY	10543	914-381-0100	381-0046	432
Web: www.cromwellgroup.com						
Crone Lumber Company Inc						
501 N Park Ave PO Box 1171	Martinsville	IN	46151	765-342-2259		683
Web: www.cronelbr.com						
Croner Company Inc, The						
1028 Sir Francis Drake Blvd	Kentfield	CA	94904	415-485-5530		463
Web: www.croner.biz						
Cronin 50 Nye Rd	Glastonbury	CT	06033	860-659-0514	659-3455	7
Web: www.cronin-co.com						
Cronin & Cronin Law Firm PLLC						
200 Old Country Rd Ste 470	Mineola	NY	11501	516-747-2220		41
Web: cronintaxlaw.com						
Cronin Business Solutions						
11720 SW 37th Ct	Davie	FL	33330	954-243-3101	972-5002	180
Web: www.croninInc.com						
Cronin, Bisson & Zalinskly PC						
722 Chestnut St	Manchester	NH	03104	603-624-4333		41
Web: cbzlaw.com						
Cronland Lumber Co PO Box 574	Lincolnton	NC	28093	704-736-2691	735-8493	683
TF: 800-237-2428 ■ *Web:* www.cronlandlumber.com						
Cronomagic Canada Inc						
3333 Boul Graham Ste 700	Mont-Royal	QC	H3R3L5	514-341-1579	341-1766	180
TF: 800-427-6012 ■ *Web:* www.cronomagic.com						
Crook County						
300 NE Third St						
Crook County Courthouse Rm 23	Prineville	OR	97754	541-447-6553	416-2145	338
Web: www.co.crook.or.us						
Crook County						
309 Cleveland St PO Box 397	Sundance	WY	82729	307-283-1323	283-3038	338
Web: www.crookcounty.wy.gov						
Crook County Historical Society						
246 N Main St	Prineville	OR	97754	541-447-3715		637-2
Web: crookcountyhistorycenter.org						
Crook County School District 1						
122 Hwy 585 PO Box 830	Sundance	WY	82729	307-283-2299	283-1810	780
Web: www.crook1.com						
Crooked River State Park						
6222 Charlie Smith Sr Hwy	Saint Marys	GA	31558	912-882-5256		565
Web: gastateparks.org						
Crooker Construction LLC						
103 Lewiston Rd PO Box 5001	Topsham	ME	04086	207-729-3331	725-0926	189-5
Web: crooker.com						
Crookham Company Inc PO Box 520	Caldwell	ID	83606	208-459-7451		296-20
Web: www.crookham.com						
Crop Insurance Specialists Inc						
7509 N County Rd 200 E	Frankfort	IN	46041	765-258-3020		390
Web: ciscropins.com						
Crop Quest Inc 1204 W Frontview St	Dodge City	KS	67801	620-225-2233		192
Web: www.cropquest.com						
CropKing Inc 134 W Dr	Lodi	OH	44254	330-302-4203	302-4204	276
TF: 800-321-5656 ■ *Web:* www.cropking.com						
CropLife America 1156 15th St NW	Washington	DC	20005	202-296-1585	463-0474	48-2
TF: 800-266-9432 ■ *Web:* www.croplifeamerica.org						
Crosbie & Company Inc						
150 King St W Sun Life Financial Tower						
15th Fl	Toronto	ON	M5H1J9	416-362-7726		317
TF: 866-873-7002 ■ *Web:* www.crosbieco.com						
Crosbie Foundry Company Inc						
1600 Mishawaka St	Elkhart	IN	46514	574-262-1502	262-1503	308
TF: 800-419-0402 ■ *Web:* www.crosbiefoundry.com						
Crosby & Overton Inc						
1610 W 17th St	Long Beach	CA	90813	562-432-5445	436-7540	667
Web: www.crosbyoverton.com						
Crosby & Westbrock LLC						
91 Snelling Ave N Ste 120	Saint Paul	MN	55104	651-493-0097	318-3634	41
Web: crosbywestbrock.com						
Crosby ADR 1 Lakeside Dr Ste 201	Oakland	CA	94612	510-418-0040		445
Web: www.crosbyadr.com						
Crosby County 201 W Aspen St Ste 102	Crosbyton	TX	79322	806-675-2334	675-2980	338
Web: www.co.crosby.tx.us						
Crosby Group, The 2801 Dawson Rd	Tulsa	OK	74110	918-834-4611	832-0940	470
TF: 800-772-1500 ■ *Web:* www.thecrosbygroup.com						
Crosby Insurance Inc						
8181 E Kaiser Blvd PO Box 31150	Anaheim	CA	92809	714-221-5200	221-5210	390
Web: www.crosbyinsurance.com						
Crosby Marketing Communications Inc						
The Crosby Bldg 705 Melvin Ave Ste 200	Annapolis	MD	21401	410-626-0805		7
Web: www.crosbymarketing.com						
Crosby's Drugs Inc 2609 N High St	Columbus	OH	43202	614-263-9424	263-2929	237
TF: 888-991-1540 ■ *Web:* www.crosbysdrugs.com						
Crosby-Brownlie Inc 100 Nassau St	Rochester	NY	14605	585-325-1290	325-5543	610
TF: 877-252-8927 ■ *Web:* crosbybrownlie.com						
Crosbys Markets Inc 125 Canal St	Salem	MA	01970	978-745-4272		345
Web: www.crosbysmarkets.com						
Crosby-Wright 5907 N Rocking Rd	Scottsdale	AZ	85250	480-367-1112		7
Web: www.crosby-wright.com						
Crosman Corp 7629 Rt 5 & 20	Bloomfield	NY	14469	800-724-7486	657-5405*	284
**Fax Area Code:* 585 ■ *TF:* 800-724-7486 ■ *Web:* www.crosman.com						
Cross Atlantic Capital Partners						
150 N Radnor Chester Rd Ste A225	Radnor	PA	19087	610-995-2650		792
Web: www.xacp.com						
Cross Bros Inc 5255 Sheila St	Los Angeles	CA	90040	323-266-2000	266-2106	482
TF: 866-939-1057 ■ *Web:* www.crossbrothersinc.com						
Cross Check Inc 1440 N McDowell Blvd	Petaluma	CA	94954	707-665-2100	637-1884*	569
**Fax Area Code:* 800 ■ *Web:* www.cross-check.com						
Cross City Corrections Dept						
568 NE 255 St	Cross City	FL	32628	352-498-4444		213
Web: dc.state.fl.us						
Cross Co						
Automation 2001 Oak Pkwy	Belmont	NC	28012	704-523-2222	523-6500	246
Web: www.crossco.com						
Cross Country Automotive Services (CCAS)						
1 Cabot Rd	Medford	MA	02155	781-393-9300	395-6706	53
Web: www.agero.com						
Cross Country Healthcare Inc						
6551 Pk of Commerce Blvd	Boca Raton	FL	33487	561-998-2232	998-8533	721
NASDAQ: CCRN ■ *TF:* 800-347-2264 ■ *Web:* www.crosscountryhealthcare.com						
Cross Country Locums						
4775 Peachtree Industrial Blvd Ste 300	Berkeley Lake	GA	30092	800-780-3500	246-0882*	194
**Fax Area Code:* 770 ■ *TF:* 800-780-3500 ■ *Web:* www.crosscountrylocums.com						
Cross Country Medical Staffing Network						
6551 Park of Commerce Blvd	Boca Raton	FL	33487	800-676-8326	526-2856*	721
**Fax Area Code:* 866 ■ *TF:* 800-676-8326 ■ *Web:* www.crosscountrymsn.com						
Cross County 705 Union Ave E Ste 8	Wynne	AR	72396	870-238-5735	238-5739	338
Web: www.crosscountyar.org						
Cross County Shopping Ctr						
8000 Mall Walk	Yonkers	NY	10704	914-968-9570		460
Web: www.crosscountycenter.com						
Cross Creek Resort						
3815 Pennsylvania 8	Titusville	PA	16354	814-827-9611		379
TF: 800-461-3173 ■ *Web:* www.crosscreekresort.com						
Cross Financial Corp						
74 Gilman Rd PO Box 1388	Bangor	ME	04401	207-947-7345	941-0849	390
TF: 800-999-7345 ■ *Web:* www.crossagency.com						
Cross Group Inc, The 1962 S Van Ave	Houma	LA	70363	985-868-3906	868-3909	539
Web: www.thecrossgroup.com						
Cross Insurance Ctr 515 Main St	Bangor	ME	04401	207-561-8300		205
Web: www.crossinsurancecenter.com						
Cross Keys Village						
2990 Carlisle Pk	New Oxford	PA	17350	717-624-2161	624-5216	672
TF: 888-624-8242 ■ *Web:* www.crosskeysvillage.org						
Cross Manufacturing Inc						
11011 King St	Overland Park	KS	66210	785-625-2585	451-1235*	640
**Fax Area Code:* 913 ■ *Web:* crossmfg.com						
Cross Oil Refining & Marketing Inc						
484 E Sixth St	Smackover	AR	71762	870-881-8700	864-8656	580
TF: 800-725-3066 ■ *Web:* www.crossoil.com						
Cross Petroleum Inc 6920 Lockheed Dr	Redding	CA	96002	530-221-2588		581
TF: 800-655-4427 ■ *Web:* www.crosspetroleum.com						
Cross Timbers State Park 144 Hwy 105	Toronto	KS	66777	620-637-2213		565
Web: ksoutdoors.com						
Cross TV						
370 W Camino Gardens Blvd Ste 300	Boca Raton	FL	33432	561-367-7454		740
Web: www.crosstv.com						
Cross Valley Federal Credit Union						
640 Baltimore Dr	Wilkes-Barre	PA	18702	570-823-6836		219
Web: crossvalleyfcu.org						
Cross World Network 10 Van Winkle Rd	Hudson	NY	12534	518-851-6688		463
Web: www.crossworldnetwork.com						
Cross X. Platform LLC						
2570 Blvd of the Generals Ste X	Audubon	PA	19403	610-539-2297		194
Web: crossxplatform.com						
Crossbeam Capital						
6919 Portwest Dr Ste 160	Houston	TX	77024	713-439-1773		251
Web: www.crossbeamcapital.com						
Crosscheck Compliance LLC						
810 W Washington Blvd	Chicago	IL	60607	312-346-4600		194
Web: crosscheckcompliance.com						
CrossCircuit Networks Inc						
5655 Silver Creek Valley Rd Ste 545	San Jose	CA	95138	408-654-9637		225
Web: www.cross-circuit.com						
Crosscom National LLC						
900 Deerfield Pkwy	Buffalo Grove	IL	60089	847-520-9200		225
TF: 800-933-9203 ■ *Web:* www.crosscomnational.com						
CrossCountry Freight Solutions						
1841 Hancock Dr	Bismarck	ND	58502	701-222-8498	223-5963	546
TF: 800-521-0287 ■ *Web:* www.shipcc.com						
Crossed Sabres Ranch 829 N Fork Hwy	Cody	WY	82414	307-587-3750		239
Web: crossedsabresranch.com						
Crossett Inc 201 S Carver St	Warren	PA	16365	800-876-2778		780
TF: 800-876-2778 ■ *Web:* www.crossettinc.com						
Crossey Engineering Ltd						
2255 Sheppard Ave E Ste E-331	Toronto	ON	M2J4Y1	416-497-3111	497-7210	261
Web: www.cel.ca						
Crossfield Products Corp						
3000 E Harcourt St	Compton	CA	90221	310-886-9100	886-9119	605-2
Web: crossfieldproducts.com						
Crossfield Technology LLC						
3445 Executive Center Dr Ste 125	Austin	TX	78731	512-795-0220		696
Web: www.crossfieldtech.com						
Crossgates Baptist Church Inc						
8 Crosswoods Rd	Brandon	MS	39042	601-825-2562		48-20
Web: crossgates.org						
Crossgates Inc 3555 Washington Rd	McMurray	PA	15317	724-941-9240	941-4339	187
Web: crossgatesinc.com						
Crossgates Mall 1 Crossgates Mall Rd	Albany	NY	12203	518-869-3522		460
Web: www.shopcrossgates.com						
Crossgates Recreation Inc						
200 N Military Rd	Slidell	LA	70461	985-643-2557		354
Web: crossgatesclub.com						
CrossHarbor Capital Partners LLC						
1 Boston Pl Ste 2300	Boston	MA	02108	617-624-8300		401
TF: 855-701-9034 ■ *Web:* www.crossharborcapital.com						

Phone | Fax | Class

Crossings Community Church
14600 N Portland Ave Oklahoma City OK 73134 405-755-2227 48-20
Web: crossings.church

Crosslake Communications
35910 County Rd 66 PO Box 70 Crosslake MN 56442 218-692-2777 387
TF: 800-992-8220 ■ *Web:* www.crosslake.net

Crossland Construction
833 S East Ave PO Box 45 Columbus KS 66725 620-429-1414 429-1412 186
Web: www.crossland.com

Crossland Mechanical Inc
237 W 37th St Rm 400 New York NY 10018 212-213-2980 719-5366 610
Web: www.crosslandmech.com

Crosslink Capital
2 Embarcadero Ctr Ste 2200 San Francisco CA 94111 415-617-1800 792
Web: www.crosslinkcapital.com

CrossLink Professional Tax Solutions LLC
Petz Enterprises LLC
16916 S Harlan Rd Lathrop CA 95330 209-835-2720 835-0409 177
TF: 800-345-4337 ■ *Web:* www.crosslinktax.com

Crossman Post Production LLC
11083 Marjoram Ln South Jordan UT 84009 801-571-2575 512
Web: www.crossmanpost.com

Crossmark Graphics Inc
16100 W Overland Dr New Berlin WI 53151 262-821-1343 627
Web: www.crossmarkgraphicsinc.com

Crossmark Inc 5100 Legacy Dr Plano TX 75024 469-814-1000 195
TF: 877-699-6275 ■ *Web:* www.crossmark.com

Crosspoint Realty Services Inc
303 Sacramento St 3rd Fl San Francisco CA 94111 415-288-6888 288-6877 652
Web: www.crosspointrealty.com

Crosspoint Venture Partners
670 Woodside Rd Redwood City CA 94061 650-851-7600 792

CrossRealms Inc 20 W Kinzie 17th Fl Chicago IL 60654 312-278-4445 194
Web: www.crossrealms.com

Crossroad Engineers
3417 Sherman Dr Beech Grove IN 46107 317-780-1555 261
Web: www.crossroadengineers.com

Crossroad Farms Dairy
400 S Shortridge Rd Indianapolis IN 46219 317-229-7600 296-27

Crossroad Vintners 6429 Guion Rd Indianapolis IN 46268 317-471-1038 80-3
Web: crossroadvintners.com

Crossroads Audio Inc
2623 Myrtle Springs Ave Dallas TX 75220 214-358-2623 358-0185 52
TF: 800-287-0436 ■ *Web:* www.crossroadsaudio.com

Crossroads College
920 Mayowood Rd SW Rochester MN 55902 507-288-4563 288-9046 161
TF: 800-456-7651 ■ *Web:* www.crossroadscollege.edu

Crossroads Community Federal Credit Union
3031 William St Cheektowaga NY 14227 716-896-8084 219
Web: crcfcu.com

Crossroads For Youth
930 E Drahner PO Box 9 Oxford MI 48371 248-628-2561 48-6
Web: crossroadsforyouth.org

Crossroads Fuel Service Inc
1441 Fentress Rd Chesapeake VA 23322 757-482-2179 482-7849 579
Web: www.crossroadsfuel.com

Crossroads Juvenile Ctr
17 Bristol St Brooklyn NY 11212 718-495-8160 412
Web: www1.nyc.gov

Crossroads School For Arts & Sciences
1714 21st St Santa Monica CA 90404 310-829-7391 685
Web: www.xrds.org

Crossroads Systems Inc
11000 N Mopac Expy Austin TX 78759 252-227-7015 176
OTC: CRSS ■ *Web:* www.crossroads.com

Crossroads Veterinary Clinic
W5493 County Trunk KK Appleton WI 54915 920-749-9400 794
Web: crossroadsvet.org

CrossRoadsNews Inc 2346 Candler Rd Decatur GA 30032 404-284-1888 532-3
Web: www.crossroadsnews.com

Crosstex International Inc
10 Ranick Rd Hauppauge NY 11788 631-582-6777 228
Web: www.crosstex.com

Crossville Cumberland County Chamber of Commerce
34 S Main St Crossville TN 38555 931-484-8444 484-7511 139
TF: 877-465-3861 ■ *Web:* www.crossville-chamber.com

Crossville Porcelain Stone/USA
PO Box 1168 Crossville TN 38557 931-484-2110 751
TF: 800-221-9093 ■ *Web:* crossvilleinc.com

Crosswater Digital Media LLC
695 Delaware Ave Buffalo NY 14209 716-884-8486 514
Web: crosswater.net

Crossway Books 1300 Crescent St Wheaton IL 60187 630-682-4300 682-4785 637-2
TF: 800-543-1659 ■ *Web:* www.crossway.org

Crossway Community Church
13905 75th St Bristol WI 53104 262-857-4488 48-20
Web: cwc.church

Crosswhite, Limbrick & Sinclair LLP
25 Hooks Ln Ste 310 Baltimore MD 21208 410-653-6890 41
Web: crosswhitelimbricksinclair.com

Crossworld 306 Bala Ave Bala Cynwyd PA 19004 888-785-0087 48-20
TF: 888-785-0087 ■ *Web:* crossworld.org

Croswell Bus Lines Inc
975 W Main St Williamsburg OH 45176 513-724-2206 724-3261 107
TF: 800-782-8747 ■ *Web:* www.gocroswell.com

Crotched Mountain Foundation
1 Verney Dr Greenfield NH 03047 603-547-3311 547-3232 374-6
TF: 800-433-2900 ■ *Web:* crotchedmountain.org

Crouch Group Inc, The
300 N Carroll Blvd Ste 103 Denton TX 76201 940-383-1990 7
TF: 888-211-0273 ■ *Web:* thecrouchgroup.com

Crouch Industries Inc 1 Clark Rd Shelbyville IN 46176 317-398-8600 398-3223 454
TF: 800-245-7192 ■ *Web:* crouchindustries.com

Crounse Corp 400 Marine Way Paducah KY 42003 270-444-9611 314
Web: www.crounse.com

Crouse Hospital 736 Irving Ave Syracuse NY 13210 315-470-7111 374-3
Web: www.crouse.org

Crow Executive Air Inc
Toledo Metcalf Airport 28331 Lemoyne Rd Millbury OH 43447 567-200-0057 838-6911* 63
**Fax Area Code:* 419 ■ *TF:* 800-972-2769 ■ *Web:* www.crowair.com

Crow Holdings Capital Partners LLC
3819 Maple Ave Dallas TX 75219 214-661-8000 528
Web: www.crowholdingscapital.com

Crow Jason (Rep D - CO)
1229 Longworth House Office Bldg Washington DC 20515 202-225-7882 342-2
Web: www.crow.house.gov

Crow Wing Co-operative Power & Light Co
Hwy 371 N PO Box 507 Brainerd MN 56401 218-829-2827 825-2209 245
TF: 800-648-9401 ■ *Web:* www.cwpower.com

Crow Wing County 326 Laurel St Brainerd MN 56401 218-824-1067 824-1054 338
TF: 888-829-6680 ■ *Web:* crowwing.us

Crow Wing State Park
3124 State Park Rd Brainerd MN 56401 218-825-3075 825-3077 565
Web: www.dnr.state.mn.us

Crow Woods Publishing PO Box 7049 Evanston IL 60204 847-501-4533 637-2
Web: www.crowwoodspublishing.com

Crowded Ocean PO Box 82 Menlo Park CA 94026 408-355-0108 195
Web: www.crowdedocean.com

Crowder College 601 Laclede Ave Neosho MO 64850 417-451-3223 455-5731 162
TF: 866-238-7788 ■ *Web:* www.crowder.edu

Crowder Constructors Inc
6425 Brookshire Blvd Charlotte NC 28230 704-372-3541 376-3573 188-4
TF: 800-849-2966 ■ *Web:* www.crowderusa.com

Crowder State Park 76 Hwy 128 Trenton MO 64683 660-359-6473 565
Web: mostateparks.com

Crowders Mountain State Park
522 Pk Office Ln Kings Mountain NC 28086 704-853-5375 565
Web: www.ncparks.gov

CrowdGather Inc
20300 Ventura Blvd Ste 330 Woodland Hills CA 91364 818-435-2472 395
Web: www.crowdgather.com

CrowdSource Solutions Inc
33 Bronze Pointe Swansea IL 62226 877-642-7331 631
TF: 855-276-9376 ■ *Web:* www.crowdsource.com

CrowdStreet
621 SW Morrison St Ste 400 Portland OR 97205 888-432-7693 405
TF: 888-432-7693 ■ *Web:* www.crowdstreet.com

Crowe & Dunlevy
324 N Robinson Ave Ste 100 Oklahoma City OK 73102 405-235-7700 445
Web: www.crowedunlevy.com

Crowe Horwath Intl
488 Madison Ave 3rd Fl New York NY 10022 212-572-5500 572-5572 734
Web: www.crowe.com

Crowe-Innes & Associates LLC
1550G Tiburon Blvd Ste 221 Tiburon CA 94920 415-435-6211 435-6867 260
Web: www.croweinnes.com

Crowell State Bank 100 E Commerce St Crowell TX 79227 940-684-1531 70
Web: crowellstatebank.com

Crowell Weedon & Co
1 Wilshire Bldg 624 S Grand Ave 26th Fl Los Angeles CA 90017 213-244-9237 244-9388 690
TF: 800-227-0319 ■ *Web:* dadavidson.com

Crower Cams & Equipment
6180 Business Center Ct San Diego CA 92154 619-661-6477 661-6466 60
Web: www.crower.com

Crowes Mortuary & Chapel
118 US Hwy 74A Rutherfordton NC 28139 828-286-2304 286-2305 48-20
Web: crowemortuary.com

Crowl & Associates PLLC
2245 N Loop 336 W Ste G Conroe TX 77304 936-539-2133 539-6990 2
Web: crowl-associates.com

Crowley County 631 Main St Ste 102 Ordway CO 81063 719-267-5232 267-4608 338
Web: www.colorado.gov

Crowley Fleck PLLP
490 N 31st St Ste 500 Billings MT 59101 406-252-3441 256-8526 428
Web: crowleyfleck.com

Crowley Maritime Corp
9487 Regency Square Blvd Jacksonville FL 32225 904-727-2200 727-2501 312
TF: 800-276-9539 ■ *Web:* www.crowley.com

Crowley Museum & Nature Ctr
16405 Myakka Rd Sarasota FL 34240 941-322-1000 322-0369 520
Web: crowleyfl.org

Crowley Pipeline & Land Surveying LLC
117 W Archer St Jacksboro TX 76458 940-567-2234 727
Web: crowleysurveying.com

Crowley Ridge Regional Library
315 W Oak St Jonesboro AR 72401 870-935-5133 935-7987 434-3
Web: www.libraryinjonesboro.org

Crowley's Ridge College
100 College Dr Paragould AR 72450 870-236-6901 236-7748 162
TF: 800-264-1096 ■ *Web:* www.crc.edu

Crowley's Ridge State Park
2092 Hwy 168 N Paragould AR 72450 870-573-6751 565
Web: www.arkansasstateparks.com

Crown & Covenant Publications
7408 Penn Ave Pittsburgh PA 15208 412-241-0436 637-10
Web: www.crownandcovenant.com

Crown Advisors Inc
100 McKnight Park Dr Ste 110 Pittsburgh PA 15237 412-348-1540 193
Web: www.crownsearch.com

Crown American Hotels Co
Pasquerilla Plz Johnstown PA 15907 814-533-4600 379
TF: 800-245-9295 ■ *Web:* crownamericanassociates.com

Crown Asset Management LLC
3100 Breckinridge Blvd Ste 725 Duluth GA 30096 770-817-6700 463
TF: 866-696-4442 ■ *Web:* www.crownasset.com

Crown Audio Inc 1718 W Mishawaka Rd Elkhart IN 46517 574-294-8000 52
Web: www.crownaudio.com

Crown Auto Dealerships
6001 34th St N Saint Petersburg FL 33714 727-527-7151 57
Web: www.crowncars.com

Crown Automotive Sales Company Inc
83 Enterprise Dr Marshfield MA 02050 800-343-9666 54
Web: www.crownautomotive.net

Crown Battery Manufacturing Co
1445 Majestic Dr Fremont OH 43420 419-334-7181 334-7416 74
TF: 800-487-2879 ■ *Web:* www.crownbattery.com

Name / Address	City	State	ZIP	Phone	Fax	Class
Crown Castle 2000 Corporate Dr *TF:* 866-482-8890 ■ *Web:* www.crowncastle.com	Canonsburg	PA	15317	866-482-8890		745-8
Crown Castle USA Inc 2000 Corporate Dr *Web:* crowncastle.com	Canonsburg	PA	15317	724-416-2000		170
Crown Central Petroleum Corp 1 N Charles St *Web:* www.crowncentral.com	Baltimore	MD	21201	410-539-7400		580
Crown Coco Inc 1717 Broadway St NE	Minneapolis	MN	55413	612-378-9573		204
Crown College 8700 College View Dr *TF:* 800-346-9252 ■ *Web:* www.crown.edu	Saint Bonifacius	MN	55375	952-446-4100	446-4149	166
Crown Consulting Inc 1400 Key Blvd *Web:* www.crownci.com	Arlington	VA	22209	703-650-0663	243-1280	317
Crown Corr Inc 7100 W 21st Ave *Web:* www.crowncorr.com	Gary	IN	46406	219-949-8080	944-9922	189-12
Crown Crafts Inc 711 W Walnut St *Web:* www.crowncrafts.com	Compton	CA	90220	310-763-8100		64
Crown Distributing Company Inc 17117 59th Ave NE **Fax Area Code:* 360 ■ *Web:* www.crowndistributing.com	Arlington	WA	98223	425-252-4192	363-4319*	81-1
Crown Energy Co 1117 NW 24th St *TF:* 877-228-0801 ■ *Web:* www.crownec.com	Oklahoma City	OK	73106	405-526-0111	526-0112	536
Crown Enterprises Inc 145 Hutton Ranch Rd *Web:* www.sportsmanskihaus.com	Kalispell	MT	59901	406-755-6484	758-7425	711
Crown Equipment Corp 44 S Washington St *Web:* www.crown.com	New Bremen	OH	45869	419-629-2311	629-2900	470
Crown Extrusions Inc 122 Columbia Ct N *Web:* www.crownextrusions.com	Chaska	MN	55318	952-448-3533		492
Crown Financial Ministries 601 Broad St SE *TF:* 800-722-1976 ■ *Web:* www.crown.org	Gainesville	GA	30501	770-534-1000		401
Crown Group Inc, The 1564 W Algonquin Rd *Web:* crowngroup.com	Hoffman Estates	IL	60192	847-358-4455		652
Crown Hill National Cemetery 700 38th St **Fax Area Code:* 765 ■ *Web:* www.cem.va.gov	Indianapolis	IN	46208	317-925-3800	674-4521*	136
Crown Holdings Inc 1 Crown Way *NYSE: CCK* ■ *TF:* 800-523-3644 ■ *Web:* www.crowncork.com	Philadelphia	PA	19154	215-698-5100		124
Crown Industrial 213 Michelle Ct *Web:* www.crown-industrial.com	South San Francisco	CA	94080	650-952-5150		350
Crown Lift Trucks LLC 10685 Medallion Dr *Web:* www.crown.com	Cincinnati	OH	45241	513-874-2600	874-8755	111
Crown Machine Inc 2707 N Main St *Web:* www.crownmachineinc.com	Rockford	IL	61103	815-877-7700		567
Crown Management Services Inc 25 W Cedar St Ste 405 *TF:* 844-383-7500 ■ *Web:* www.crownlaundry.com	Pensacola	FL	32502	850-469-9909	438-9395	426
Crown Manufacturing Company Inc 8390 Wolf Lake Dr Ste 114 *Web:* www.crownmfg.com	Bartlett	TN	38133	901-371-8770	371-8761	207
Crown Metal Manufacturing Co 765 S SR 83 *Web:* www.crownmetal.com	Elmhurst	IL	60126	630-279-9800	279-9807	286
Crown Micro Inc 48351 Fremont Blvd *Web:* www.crownmicro.com	Fremont	CA	94538	510-490-8187		174
Crown Motors Ltd 196 Regent Blvd *TF:* 800-466-7000 ■ *Web:* www.crownmotors.com	Holland	MI	49423	616-396-5268		57
Crown Packaging Corp 17854 Chesterfld Airport Rd *TF:* 888-880-0852 ■ *Web:* crownpack.com	Chesterfield	MO	63005	314-731-4927		548
Crown Paint Co 1801 W Sheridan Ave *Web:* www.crownpaintok.com	Oklahoma City	OK	73106	405-232-8580		550
Crown Plastics Co 116 May Dr *TF:* 800-368-0238 ■ *Web:* crownplastics.com	Harrison	OH	45030	513-367-0238		600
Crown Plastics Inc 12615 16th Ave N *TF:* 800-423-2769 ■ *Web:* crownplasticsinc.com	Plymouth	MN	55441	763-557-6000	557-6638	603
Crown Point Press 20 Hawthorne St *Web:* crownpoint.com	San Francisco	CA	94105	415-974-6273	495-4220	520
Crown Point State Historic Site 21 Grandview Dr *Web:* parks.ny.gov	Crown Point	NY	12928	518-597-4666	597-3666	565
Crown Poly Inc 5700 Bickett St *Web:* www.crownpoly.com	Huntington Park	CA	90255	323-585-5522		66
Crown Polymers LLC 11111 Kiley Dr *TF:* 888-732-1270 ■ *Web:* www.crownpolymers.com	Huntley	IL	60142	847-659-0300	659-0310	390
Crown Products Company Inc 6390 Phillips Hwy *TF:* 800-683-7144 ■ *Web:* www.crownproductsco.com	Jacksonville	FL	32216	904-737-7144	737-3533	697
Crown Reef Resort 2913 S Ocean Blvd *TF:* 800-291-6598 ■ *Web:* www.crownreef.com	Myrtle Beach	SC	29577	843-626-8077	916-0735	379
Crown Roll Leaf Inc 91 Illinois Ave *TF:* 800-631-3831 ■ *Web:* www.crownrollleaf.com	Paterson	NJ	07503	973-742-4000	742-0219	295
Crown Steel Sales Inc 3355 W 31st St *Web:* www.crownsteel.com	Chicago	IL	60623	773-376-1700	376-8650	492
Crown Technology Inc 7513 E 96th St *Web:* www.crowntech.com	Indianapolis	IN	46256	317-845-0045	845-9086	145
Crown Technology LLC 35 Industrial Park Dr *TF:* 800-457-6267 ■ *Web:* www.crownthermo.com	Woodbury	GA	30293	706-553-9500	553-3958	605-2
Crown Title Corp 1 Sanford Ave *TF:* 800-841-4343 ■ *Web:* crowntitle.com	Baltimore	MD	21228	410-719-0200	719-0300	653
Crown Trophy 529 N State Rd *Web:* www.crowntrophy.com	Briarcliff Manor	NY	10510	914-941-0020		777
Crown Valley Imaging LLC 27401 Los Altos Ste 150 *Web:* www.crownvalleyimaging.com	Mission Viejo	CA	92691	949-367-1010		418
Crown Vision Ctr 406 E Broadway *Web:* www.crownvisioncenter.com	Alton	IL	62002	618-462-7611		543
Crown Xpress Transport 9931 Via De La Amistad *Web:* www.crownxt.com	San Diego	CA	92154	619-671-9611		770
Crowne Plaza Hotel St Louis-Clayton 7750 Carondelet Ave *Web:* www.cpclayton.com	Clayton	MO	63105	314-726-5400		378
Crowne Plaza Niagara Falls - Fallsview 5685 Falls Ave *TF:* 800-263-7135 ■ *Web:* www.niagarafallscrowneplazahotel.com	Niagara Falls	ON	L2E6W7	905-374-4447		378
Crowne Plaza Ravinia 4355 Ashford Dunwoody Rd *Web:* www.cpravinia.com	Atlanta	GA	30346	770-395-7700		378
Crowne Plaza Syracuse 701 E Genesee St *TF:* 866-305-4134 ■ *Web:* www.cpsyracuse.com	Syracuse	NY	13210	315-479-7000	472-2700	379
Crowned Grace Intl 4415 Nicole Dr Ste F *Web:* www.crownedgrace.com	Lanham	MD	20706	240-454-3624	842-1402	463
Crownline Boats Inc 11884 Country Club Rd *Web:* www.crownline.com	West Frankfort	IL	62896	618-937-6426		90
Crownover Lumber Company Inc 301 No Fairview Ava *Web:* www.crownoverlumber.com	McArthur	OH	45651	740-596-5229		683
CrownQuest Operating LLC 18 Desta Dr PO Box 53310 *Web:* crownquest.com	Midland	TX	79710	432-818-0300		540
Crozer-Chester Medical Ctr (CCMC) 1 Medical Center Blvd *TF:* 800-254-3258 ■ *Web:* www.crozerkeystone.org	Upland	PA	19013	610-447-2000		374-3
Crozier & Henderson Productions Inc 5151 Belt Line Rd Ste 101 *Web:* hotonhomes.com	Dallas	TX	75254	972-661-1975		653
CRP (Central Recovery Press) 3321 N Buffalo Dr Ste 275 *TF:* 888-855-7199 ■ *Web:* www.centralrecoverypress.com	Las Vegas	NV	89129	702-868-5830		637-2
CRP (COE Review Press) 1220 1st Ave NE *Web:* www.public.coe.edu	Cedar Rapids	IA	52402	319-399-8557		637-2
CRP 4X4 Truck OutFitters 2102 Ninth St *Web:* crp4x4.com	Greeley	CO	80631	970-351-8603		54
CRRG Inc PO Box 170904 *TF:* 800-687-9030 ■ *Web:* www.crrginc.com	Arlington	TX	76003	800-687-9030	592-8913	624
CRS (Catholic Relief Services) 228 W Lexington St *TF:* 800-235-2772 ■ *Web:* www.crs.org	Baltimore	MD	21201	410-625-2220	685-1635	48-5
CRS (Conference Recording Service Inc) 2317 Carquinez Ave *Web:* www.conferencerecording.com	El Cerrito	CA	94530	510-527-3600		637-10
CRS Inc 4851 White Bear Pkwy *TF:* 800-333-4949 ■ *Web:* www.crs-usa.com	Saint Paul	MN	55110	651-294-2700	294-2900	112
CRS Jet Spares Inc 6701 NW 12th Ave *TF:* 800-338-5387 ■ *Web:* crsjetspares.com	Fort Lauderdale	FL	33309	954-972-2807	972-2708	22
CRS Onesource 2803 Tamarack Rd PO Box 1984 *TF:* 800-264-0710 ■ *Web:* www.crsonesource.com	Owensboro	KY	42302	270-684-1469	685-5696	297-11
CRS Reprocessing LLC 9780 Ormsby Station Rd Ste 2500 *Web:* www.crs-reprocessing.com	Louisville	KY	40223	502-778-3600		579
CRSA Technologies 11831 Radium St *Web:* www.crsatech.com	San Antonio	TX	78216	210-366-4811		175
CRSI (Concrete Reinforcing Steel Institute) 933 N Plum Grove Rd *Web:* www.crsi.org	Schaumburg	IL	60173	847-517-1200	517-1206	49-3
CRST International Inc 3930 16th Ave SW PO Box 68 *TF:* 800-736-2778 ■ *Web:* www.crst.com	Cedar Rapids	IA	52406	800-736-2778		780
CR-T 629 E Quality Dr Ste 201 *Web:* www.cr-t.com	American Fork	UT	84003	801-222-0930		180
CRT Custom Products Inc 7532 Hickory Hills Ct *TF:* 800-453-2533 ■ *Web:* www.crtcustomproducts.com	Whites Creek	TN	37189	615-876-5490		761
CRU Acquisitions Group LLC 1000 SE Tech Center Dr Ste 160 *TF:* 800-260-9800 ■ *Web:* www.cru-inc.com	Vancouver	WA	98683	360-816-1800		173-8
Cru Cafe 18 Pinckney St *Web:* crucafe.com	Charleston	SC	29401	843-534-2434		671
Cru Solutions 1551 Towpath Rd Unit 1 *Web:* crusolutions.com	Broadview Heights	OH	44147	440-891-0330		175
Crucial Interactive Inc 21 Camden St 5th Fl *Web:* www.crucialinteractive.com	Toronto	ON	M5V1V2	416-645-0135		195
Crucial Technology 3475 E Commercial Ct *TF:* 800-336-8915 ■ *Web:* www.crucial.com	Meridian	ID	83642	208-363-5790	363-5501	625
Crucible Chemical Co PO Box 6786 *Web:* cruciblechemical.com	Greenville	SC	29606	864-277-1284	299-1192	151
Crucible Materials Corp 575 State Fair Blvd *TF:* 800-365-1180 ■ *Web:* www.crucible.com	Syracuse	NY	13209	315-487-4111	470-9358	723
Cruise America 11 W Hampton Ave *TF:* 800-671-8042 ■ *Web:* www.cruiseamerica.com	Mesa	AZ	85210	480-464-7300	464-7321	120
Cruise Brokers 2803 W Busch Blvd Ste 100 *TF:* 800-409-1919 ■ *Web:* www.cruisebrokers.com	Tampa	FL	33618	813-288-9597	932-9650	771
Cruise Bros, The 100 Boyd Ave *TF:* 800-827-7779 ■ *Web:* www.cruisebrothers.com	East Providence	RI	02914	401-941-3999		772
Cruise Concepts 1329 Eniswood Pkwy *TF:* 800-752-7963 ■ *Web:* www.cruiseconcepts.com	Palm Harbor	FL	34683	727-784-7245		771
Cruise Connection LLC 7932 N Oak Ste 210 *TF:* 800-572-0004 ■ *Web:* www.cruiseconnectionllc.com	Kansas City	MO	64118	816-420-8688	420-8667	771
Cruise Industry News 441 Lexington Ave Ste 809 *Web:* www.cruiseindustrynews.com	New York	NY	10017	212-986-1025	986-1033	531-13

Name / Address	Phone	Fax	Class
Cruise Lines International Assn (CLIA)			
1201 F St NW Ste 250 ... Washington DC 20004	202-759-9370		48-23
TF: 855-444-2542 ■ *Web:* cruising.org			
Cruise People Inc			
10191 W Sample Rd Ste 215 ... Coral Springs FL 33065	954-340-2016	340-1968	771
TF: 800-642-2469 ■ *Web:* www.cruisepeople.com			
Cruise Shop, The			
700 Pasquinelli Dr Ste C ... Westmont IL 60559	858-433-1506	321-1669*	771
**Fax Area Code:* 630 ■ *TF:* 800-622-6456 ■ *Web:* www.vikingtvl.com			
Cruise Specialists Inc			
221 First Ave W Ste 210 ... Seattle WA 98119	888-993-1318		771
TF: 888-993-1318 ■ *Web:* www.cruisespecialists.com			
Cruise Vacation Ctr			
2042 Central Park Ave ... Yonkers NY 10710	800-803-7245	337-8672*	771
**Fax Area Code:* 914 ■ *TF:* 800-803-7245 ■ *Web:* www.cruisevacationcenter.com			
Cruise Web Inc			
3901 Calverton Blvd Ste 350 ... Calverton MD 20705	800-377-9383		771
TF: 800-377-9383 ■ *Web:* www.cruiseweb.com			
CruiseCheap.com			
220 Congress Park Dr Ste 330 ... Delray Beach FL 33445	800-543-1915		772
TF: 800-543-1915 ■ *Web:* www.cruisecheap.com			
CruiseOne Inc			
1201 W Cypress Creek Rd Ste 100 ... Fort Lauderdale FL 33309	800-278-4731		772
TF: 800-278-4731 ■ *Web:* www.cruiseone.com			
Cruiser Rv LLC 7805 N State Rd 9 ... Howe IN 46746	260-562-3500	562-2373	120
TF: 866-277-5630 ■ *Web:* www.cruiserrv.com			
Cruises Inc			
1201 W Cypress Creek Rd Ste 100 ... Fort Lauderdale FL 33309	888-282-1249		771
TF: 888-282-1249 ■ *Web:* www.cruisesinc.com			
Cruisescom 100 Fordham Rd Bldg C ... Wilmington MA 01887	800-288-6006		773
TF: 800-288-6006 ■ *Web:* www.cruises.com			
Cruising Gide Publications Inc			
1130 Pinehurst Rd Ste B ... Dunedin FL 34698	727-733-5322		637-2
TF: 800-330-9542 ■ *Web:* www.cruisingguides.com			
Cruising World PO Box 6364 ... Harlan IA 51593	515-237-3697		530
TF: 866-436-2461 ■ *Web:* www.cruisingworld.com			
Crum & Forster Insurance Inc			
305 Madison Ave PO Box 1973 ... Morristown NJ 07962	973-490-6600		391-4
TF: 800-690-5520 ■ *Web:* www.cfins.com			
Crum & Forster Pet Insurance Group			
305 Madison Ave ... Morristown NJ 07962	844-592-4879		391-1
TF: 844-592-4879 ■ *Web:* www.cfpetinsurance.com			
Crum Electric Supply Co			
1165 W English Ave ... Casper WY 82601	307-266-1278	577-1312	246
TF: 800-726-2239 ■ *Web:* www.crum.com			
Crum Manufacturing Inc			
1265 Wtrville Monclova Rd ... Waterville OH 43566	419-878-9779	878-5793	757
Web: crummfg.com			
Crump Insurance Services			
105 Eisenhower Pkwy 4th Fl ... Roseland NJ 07068	973-461-2100		391-2
Web: www.crumplifeinsurance.com			
Crumpets 3920 Harry Wurzbach St ... San Antonio TX 78209	210-821-5600	821-5624	671
Web: www.crumpetsa.com			
Crumrine Manufacturing Jewelers			
145 Catron Dr ... Reno NV 89512	800-444-3575	786-8466*	409
**Fax Area Code:* 775 ■ *TF:* 800-444-3575 ■ *Web:* www.crumrineonline.com			
Crunch Fitness Intl 220 W 19th St ... New York NY 10011	212-993-0300		354
Web: www.crunch.com			
Crunchy Logistics			
379 W Michigan St Ste 206 ... Orlando FL 32806	407-476-2044	285-8304*	196
**Fax Area Code:* 321 ■ *Web:* crunchy.co			
Crus Oil Inc 2260 SW Temple ... Salt Lake City UT 84115	801-466-8783		316
Web: crusoil.com			
Crusader Paper Company Inc			
350 Holt Rd ... North Andover MA 01845	800-421-0007	794-1625*	554
**Fax Area Code:* 978 ■ *TF:* 800-421-0007 ■ *Web:* crusaderpaper.com			
Cruser & Mitchell LLP			
275 Scientific Dr ... Norcross GA 30092	404-881-2622		428
Web: cmlawfirm.com			
Crushproof Tubing Co 100 N St ... McComb OH 45858	419-293-2111	293-2609	676
TF: 800-654-6858 ■ *Web:* crushproof.com			
Crustacean 1475 Polk St Ste 6 ... San Francisco CA 94109	415-776-2722		671
Web: crustaceansf.com			
Crustacean Beverly Hills			
468 N Bedford Dr ... Beverly Hills CA 90210	310-205-8990		671
Web: www.houseofan.com			
Crutchfield Corp			
1 Crutchfield Pk ... Charlottesville VA 22911	434-817-1000		459
TF: 888-955-6000 ■ *Web:* www.crutchfield.com			
Cruxlab 12655 W Jefferson Blvd ... Los Angeles CA 90066	877-977-7996		180
TF: 877-977-7996 ■ *Web:* cruxlab.com			
Cruz Bay Publishing Inc			
2150 Grand Ave ... Des Moines IA 50312	800-311-3995		457-11
TF: 800-311-3995 ■ *Web:* www.cuisineathome.com			
Cruz Ted (Sen R - TX)			
127A Russell Senate Office Bldg ... Washington DC 20510	202-224-5922		342-2
Web: www.cruz.senate.gov			
Crw Engineering Group LLC			
3940 Arctic Blvd Ste 300 ... Anchorage AK 99503	907-562-3252		256
Web: www.crweng.com			
CRW Graphics Inc			
9100 Pennsauken Hwy ... Pennsauken Township NJ 08110	856-662-9111	665-1789	626
Web: www.crwgraphics.com			
Crw Parts Inc 1211 68th St ... Baltimore MD 21237	410-866-3300		61
TF: 800-638-5419 ■ *Web:* crwparts.com			
CRWI (Coalition for Responsible Waste Incineration)			
1615 L St NW Ste 1350 ... Washington DC 20036	202-452-1241		48-13
Web: www.crwi.org			
Crydom Inc			
2320 Paseo de las Americas Ste 201 ... San Diego CA 92154	619-210-1550		203
Web: www.crydom.com			
Crye-Leike Inc 6525 N Quail Hollow Rd ... Memphis TN 38120	866-310-3102	758-5641*	652
**Fax Area Code:* 901 ■ *TF:* 866-310-3102 ■ *Web:* www.crye-leike.com			
Cryobiology Inc			
4830D Knightsbridge Blvd ... Columbus OH 43214	614-451-4375	451-5284	545
TF: 800-359-4375 ■ *Web:* www.cryobio.com			
Cryogenic Experts Inc 531 Sandy Cir ... Oxnard CA 93036	805-981-4500		743
Web: www.cexi.com			

Name / Address	Phone	Fax	Class
Cryogenic Society of America Inc (CSA)			
218 Lake St ... Oak Park IL 60302	708-383-6220	383-9337	49-19
Web: www.cryogenicsociety.org			
Cryomagnetics Inc			
1006 Alvin Weinberg Dr ... Oak Ridge TN 37830	865-482-9551		295
Web: www.cryomagnetics.com			
Cryoquip Inc 25720 Jefferson Ave ... Murrieta CA 92562	951-677-2060		357
Web: www.cryoquip.com			
Crypsis Group, The 1410 Spring Hill Rd ... McLean VA 22102	855-875-4631		189-4
TF: 855-875-4631 ■ *Web:* www.crypsisgroup.com			
Cryptosystems Journal			
485 Middle Holland Rd ... Southampton PA 18966	215-579-9888		637-9
Web: www.glassblower.info			
Crysler Animal Hospital			
12440 E 40 Hwy ... Independence MO 64055	816-358-2857		794
Web: www.crysleranimalhospital.com			
Crystal Beach Suites & Health Club			
6985 Collins Ave ... Miami Beach FL 33141	305-865-9555		379
TF: 888-643-4630 ■ *Web:* www.crystalbeachsuites.com			
Crystal Blanc 225 Gap Way ... Erlanger KY 41018	877-681-6155		362
TF: 877-681-6155 ■ *Web:* www.jcharles.com			
Crystal Cabinet Works Inc			
1100 Crystal Dr ... Princeton MN 55371	763-389-4187	389-5846	115
Web: www.crystalcabinets.com			
Crystal Communications Ltd			
1525 Lakeville Dr Ste 230 ... Kingwood TX 77339	281-361-5199		196
TF: 888-949-6603 ■ *Web:* www.crystalcomltd.com			
Crystal Cove State Park			
8471 N Coast Hwy ... Laguna Beach CA 92651	949-494-3539		565
Web: www.parks.ca.gov			
Crystal Cruises Inc			
11755 Wilshire Blvd Ste 900 ... Los Angeles CA 90025	310-785-9300		220
TF: 888-722-0021 ■ *Web:* www.crystalcruises.com			
Crystal Engineering Solutions Inc			
645 Executive Dr ... Troy MI 48083	248-588-1390		261
Web: www.crystaleng.com			
Crystal Finishing Systems Inc			
2610 Ross Ave ... Schofield WI 54476	715-355-5351		481
Web: www.crystalfinishing.com			
Crystal Flash LP			
1754 Alpine Ave NW ... Grand Rapids MI 49504	616-363-4851		579
Web: www.crystalflash.com			
Crystal Fountain Publications (CFP)			
PO Box 4434 ... Diamond Bar CA 91765	909-396-1201	860-7803	637-10
Web: www.crystalfountain.org			
Crystal Group Inc 850 Kacena Rd ... Hiawatha IA 52233	319-378-1636	393-2338	176
TF: 877-279-7863 ■ *Web:* www.crystalrugged.com			
Crystal Hot Sauce			
2424 Edenborn Ave Ste 510 ... Metairie LA 70001	504-482-5761		296-20
Web: crystalhotsauce.com			
Crystal Inn			
185 S State St Ste 1300 ... Salt Lake City UT 84111	801-320-7200	320-7201	379
TF: 800-662-2525 ■ *Web:* www.crystalinns.com			
Crystal Inn Salt Lake City Downtown			
230 W 500 S ... Salt Lake City UT 84101	801-328-4466	320-7201	379
Web: www.crystalinnsaltlake.com			
Crystal Lake Chamber of Commerce			
427 W Virginia St ... Crystal Lake IL 60014	815-459-1300	459-0243	139
Web: www.clchamber.com			
Crystal Lake Public Library			
126 W Paddock St ... Crystal Lake IL 60014	815-459-1687		434-3
Web: www.clpl.org			
Crystal Lake State Park			
96 Bellwater Ave ... Barton VT 05822	802-525-6205		565
TF: 888-409-7579 ■ *Web:* www.vtstateparks.com			
Crystal McKenzie Inc 220 E 23rd St ... New York NY 10010	212-598-4567	598-4566	466
Web: www.cminyc.com			
Crystal Media Networks			
7200 Wisconsin Ave Ste 500 ... Bethesda MD 20814	240-223-0850		644
Web: www.crystalmedianetworks.com			
Crystal Meth Anonymous (CMA)			
4470 W Sunset Blvd Ste 107 PO Box 555 ... Los Angeles CA 90027	855-638-4373		48-21
TF: 877-262-6691 ■ *Web:* crystalmeth.org			
Crystal Mountain Inc			
33914 Crystal Mountain Blvd ... Enumclaw WA 98022	360-663-3050		378
Web: www.crystalmountainresort.com			
Crystal Mountain Resort			
12500 Crystal Mtn Dr ... Thompsonville MI 49683	231-378-2000		669
TF: 800-968-7686 ■ *Web:* www.crystalmountain.com			
Crystal River Archaeological State Park			
3400 N Museum Pointe ... Crystal River FL 34428	352-795-3817		565
Web: www.floridastateparks.org			
Crystal River Preserve State Park			
3266 N Sailboat Ave ... Crystal River FL 34428	352-228-6028		565
Web: www.floridastateparks.org			
Crystal Rock Holdings Inc			
1050 Buckingham St ... Watertown CT 06795	860-945-0661		80-2
NYSE: CRVP ■ *TF:* 800-525-0070 ■ *Web:* www.crystalrock.com			
Crystal Steel Fabricators Inc			
9317 Old Racetrack Rd ... Delmar DE 19940	302-846-0613	846-3223	186
Web: www.crystalsteel.com			
Crystal Technologies Group Inc			
1566 Mcdaniel Dr ... West Chester PA 19380	610-430-2005	430-7046	196
Web: crystaltechnologies.com			
Crystal Thai 4819 1st St N ... Arlington VA 22203	703-522-1311		671
Web: crystalthai.com			
Crystal Theatre Publishing			
12 June Ave ... Norwalk CT 06850	203-847-4850		226
Web: www.crystaltheatre.org			
Crystal Valley Coop			
721 W Humphrey PO Box 210 ... Lake Crystal MN 56055	507-726-6455	726-6901	276
TF: 800-622-2910 ■ *Web:* crystalvalley.coop			
Crystal Wealth Management System Ltd			
3385 Harvester Rd Ste 200 ... Burlington ON L7N3N2	905-332-4414		796
TF: 877-299-2854 ■ *Web:* crystalwealth.com			
Crystalcommerce Inc			
7116 220th St SW Ste A ... Mountlake Terrace WA 98043	866-213-4611		177
TF: 866-213-4611 ■ *Web:* crystalcommerce.com			

Phone | Fax | Class

Crystallex International Corp
8 King St E Ste 1201 . . . Toronto ON M5C1B5 416-203-2448 203-0099 502
TF: 800-738-1577 ■ *Web:* www.crystallex.com

Crystal-Like Plastics
21701 Plummer St . . . Chatsworth CA 91311 818-846-1818 846-0877 608
TF: 800-554-6091 ■ *Web:* www.crystal-likeplastics.com

Crystaltech Inc 1601 N 5th St . . . Duncan OK 73533 580-252-8893 696
Web: www.crystaltechinc.com

Crysteel Manufacturing Inc
52182 Ember Rd . . . Lake Crystal MN 56055 507-726-2728 726-2559 470
TF: 800-533-0494 ■ *Web:* www.crysteel.com

Crysteel Truck Equipment Inc
52248 Ember Rd . . . Lake Crystal MN 56055 800-722-0588 780
TF: 800-722-0588 ■ *Web:* www.crysteeltruckequipment.com

Crystek Crystals Corp
12730 Commonwealth Dr . . . Fort Myers FL 33913 239-561-3311 253
TF: 800-237-3061 ■ *Web:* www.crystek.com

Crystex Composites LLC
125 Clifton Blvd . . . Clifton NJ 07011 973-779-8866 779-2013 500
Web: crystexcompositesllc.com

CS (CenterSite LLC) PO Box 20709 . . . Columbus OH 43220 614-448-4055 637-10
Web: www.centersite.net

CS (Cornelius Systems Inc)
3966 Eleven Mile Rd . . . Berkley MI 48072 877-545-5558 545-0022 535
TF: 877-545-5558 ■ *Web:* www.mycornelius.com

CS (Clean Seal Inc)
20900 W Ireland Rd . . . South Bend IN 46614 574-299-1888 299-8044 676
TF: 800-366-3682 ■ *Web:* www.cleanseal.com

CS & P Technologies LP 18119 Telge Rd . . . Cypress TX 77429 713-467-0869 641
TF: 800-262-6103 ■ *Web:* csphouston.com

CS & S Computer Systems Inc
1440 W University Dr . . . Tempe AZ 85281 480-968-8585 196
Web: www.css-computers.com

CS Consulting Group LLC
11491 Raedene Way . . . San Diego CA 92131 858-530-8250 196
Web: www.csconsultinggroup.com

CS Controls Inc 101 Dickson Rd . . . Houma LA 70363 985-876-6040 876-0751 201
Web: www.cscontrols.com

CS Illumination Inc
1210 Kestone Way Ste A&B . . . Vista CA 92081 760-477-1244 362
Web: csillumination.com

CS Logistics Inc
11001 W Mitchell St . . . Milwaukee WI 53214 414-774-6322 546
Web: www.cslog.com

CS McCrossan Inc
7865 Jefferson Hwy . . . Maple Grove MN 55369 763-425-4167 425-1255 188-4
Web: www.mccrossan.com

CS Osborne & Company Inc
125 Jersey St . . . Harrison NJ 07029 973-483-3232 484-3621 758
Web: www.csosborne.com

CS Packaging Inc
155 Internationale Blvd . . . Glendale Heights IL 60139 630-690-1300 690-6109 88
Web: cspackaging.com

CS Solutions Inc 3440 Federal Dr Ste 100 . . . Eagan MN 55122 651-603-8288 177
Web: cssolutionsinc.com

CS Wo & Sons Ltd 702 S Beretania St . . . Honolulu HI 96813 808-543-5388 321
Web: www.cswo.com

CS2 Design Group LLC
837 Oakton St . . . Elk Grove Village IL 60007 847-981-1880 981-1885 261
Web: www.cs2designgroup.com

CS3 Technology 5272 S Lewis Ave Ste 100 . . . Tulsa OK 74105 918-496-1600 174
Web: cs3technology.com

CSA (Cryogenic Society of America Inc)
218 Lake St . . . Oak Park IL 60302 708-383-6220 383-9337 49-19
Web: www.cryogenicsociety.org

CSA Financial Corp
343 Commercial St Union Wharf Ste 109 . . . Boston MA 02109 617-357-1700 216
Web: csafinancial.com

CSA Group 178 Rexdale Blvd . . . Toronto ON M9W1R3 416-747-4000 317
TF: 800-463-6727 ■ *Web:* www.csagroup.org

CSA Inc
2110 Powers Ferry Rd SE Ste 202 . . . Atlanta GA 30339 770-955-3518 956-8748 178-5
Web: www.csaatl.com

CSA Research 100 Summit Dr . . . Burlington MA 01803 978-275-0500 256
Web: csa-research.com

Athletic Commission
2005 Evergreen St Ste 2010 . . . Sacramento CA 95815 916-263-2195 263-2197 712
TF: 800-326-2297 ■ *Web:* www.dca.ca.gov

CSAIL (Computer Science & Artificial Intelligence Laboratory)
32 Vassar St Bldg 32 . . . Cambridge MA 02139 617-253-5851 258-8682 668
Web: www.csail.mit.edu

CSBA 1667 K St NW Ste 900 . . . Washington DC 20006 202-331-7990 194
Web: csbaonline.org

CSBM (Charter School Business Management)
237 W 35th St Ste 301 . . . New York NY 10001 888-710-2726 393
TF: 888-710-2726 ■ *Web:* www.csbm.com

CSBS (Conference of State Bank Supervisors)
1129 20th St NW 9th Fl . . . Washington DC 20036 202-296-2840 296-1928 49-7
Web: www.csbs.org

CSC (Curtis Steel Co) 6504 Hurst St . . . Houston TX 77008 713-861-4621 861-9718 485
TF: 800-749-4621 ■ *Web:* www.curtissteelco.com

CSC (CSC Management LLC)
188 Broadway Ave . . . Woodcliff Lake NJ 07677 201-930-0533 681
Web: www.cscmgt.net

CSC Home & Hardware
1580 Earl L Core Rd . . . Morgantown WV 26505 304-292-1340 191-1
Web: www.wvcsc.com

CSC Inc 1109 Court St . . . Medford OR 97501 541-779-1970 492
TF: 800-547-5950 ■ *Web:* www.medfab.com

CSC Institute Inc 1111 Street Rd . . . Southampton PA 18966 215-396-7920 167-3
TF: 888-575-7555 ■ *Web:* www.baroudi-design.com

CSC Laboratories Inc
180 Westgate Dr . . . Watsonville CA 95076 831-763-6931 544
TF: 800-288-2721 ■ *Web:* www.csclabs.com

CSC Management LLC (CSC)
188 Broadway Ave . . . Woodcliff Lake NJ 07677 201-930-0533 681
Web: www.cscmgt.net

CSC ServiceWorks
303 Sunnyside Blvd Ste 70 . . . Plainview NY 11803 516-349-8555 426
TF: 877-264-6622 ■ *Web:* www.cscsw.com

CSCH (Centra Southside Community Hospital)
800 Oak St . . . Farmville VA 23901 434-392-8811 200-2994 374-3
TF: 800-400-7247 ■ *Web:* www.centrahealth.com

CSCOS (C & S Cos)
499 Col Eileen Collins Blvd . . . Syracuse NY 13212 315-455-2000 455-9667 261
Web: www.cscos.com

CSDG 2305 Kline Ave Ste 300 . . . Nashville TN 37211 615-248-9999 261
Web: csdgtn.com

CSDP (Customer Service Delivery Platform)
15615 Alton Pkwy Ste 310 . . . Irvine CA 92618 888-741-2737 177
TF: 888-741-2737 ■ *Web:* www.csdpcorp.com

CSE Corp 1001 Corporate Ln . . . Export PA 15632 412-856-9200 856-9203 678
TF: 800-245-2224 ■ *Web:* www.csecorporation.com

CSE Inc 5400 S Wridge Dr . . . New Berlin WI 53151 262-786-8400 5
Web: www.csepromo.com

CSE Insurance Group
2121 N California Blvd Ste 900 . . . Walnut Creek CA 94596 800-282-6848 391-4
TF: 800-282-6848 ■ *Web:* cseinsurance.com

CSF International Inc 1629 Barber Rd . . . Sarasota FL 34240 941-379-0881 371-5223 174
Web: www.csfi.com

CSG (Community Services Group)
320 Highland Dr PO Box 597 . . . Mountville PA 17554 717-285-7121 285-2658 353
TF: 877-907-7970 ■ *Web:* csgonline.org

CSG (Customer Solutions Group)
1355 S Colorado Blvd Ste 510 . . . Denver CO 80222 303-770-6381 770-6576 194
TF: 877-274-5221 ■ *Web:* insidesaleslab.com

CSG Direct 640 Maestro Dr Ste 100 . . . Reno NV 89511 775-852-9777 5
TF: 800-881-2150 ■ *Web:* www.csgdirect.com

CSG Government Solutions Inc
180 N Stetson Ave Ste 3200 . . . Chicago IL 60601 312-444-2760 938-2191 463
Web: www.csgdelivers.com

CSG Professional Services Inc
9755 SW Barnes Rd Ste 660 . . . Portland OR 97225 503-292-0859 177
Web: www.csgpro.com

CSG Systems Intl
6175 S Willow Dr 10th Fl . . . Greenwood Village CO 80111 303-200-2000 200-3333 178-10
NASDAQ: CSGS ■ *Web:* www.csgi.com

C-Sharp Technologies Inc
4700 Coolbrook Dr . . . Hilliard OH 43026 614-668-7182 177
Web: www.c-sharp.com

CSHL (Cold Spring Harbor Laboratory)
1 Bungtown Rd . . . Cold Spring NY 11724 516-367-8800 367-8455 668
Web: www.cshl.edu

CSI (Christian Schools Intl)
3350 E Paris Ave SE . . . Grand Rapids MI 49512 616-957-1070 957-5022 49-5
TF: 800-635-8288 ■ *Web:* www.csionline.org

CSI (Central States Indemnity Company of Omaha)
1212 N 96th St . . . Omaha NE 68114 402-997-8000 391-5
Web: www.csi omaha.com

CSI (Communications Systems Inc)
10900 Red Cir Dr . . . Minnetonka MN 55343 952-941-2322 735
NASDAQ: JCS ■ *Web:* www.commsystems.com

CSI 2916 Annandale Rd . . . Falls Church VA 22042 703-205-0000 92
Web: csi2.com

CSI - Computer Systems Inc
12975 Parkside Dr . . . Fishers IN 46038 317-913-4160 180
TF: 866-913-4160 ■ *Web:* computer-systems.com

CSI Aviation Services Inc
3700 Rio Grand Blvd NW . . . Albuquerque NM 87107 505-761-9000 13
Web: www.csiaviation.com

CSI Compressor Systems Inc
3809 S FM 1788 . . . Midland TX 79706 432-563-1170 172
Web: www.csicompressco.com

CSI Group Inc, The
160 Summit Ave Ste 200 . . . Montvale NJ 07645 201-587-1400 196
Web: www.thecsigroup.com

CSI Industries Inc 6910 W Ridge Rd . . . Fairview PA 16415 814-474-9353 474-5797 198
TF: 800-937-9033 ■ *Web:* www.flo-bin.com

CSI International Inc
8120 SR-138 . . . Williamsport OH 43164 740-420-5400 333-7335 178-12
TF: 800-795-4914 ■ *Web:* www.csi-international.com

CSI International Inc
6700 N Andrews Ave . . . Fort Lauderdale FL 33309 800-258-3330 152
TF: 800-258-3330 ■ *Web:* www.csiinternational.com

CSI Leasing Inc
9990 Old Olive St Rd . . . Saint Louis MO 63141 800-955-0960 264-1
TF: 800-955-0960 ■ *Web:* www.csileasing.com

Csi Recruiting 1905 Sherman St Ste 200 . . . Denver CO 80203 303-996-0400 260
Web: csirecruiting.com

CSI Technologies LLC
2202 Oil Center Ct . . . Houston TX 77073 281-784-7990 261
Web: www.csi-tech.net

CSI Worldwide Inc 40 Regency Plz . . . Glen Mills PA 19342 610-558-4500 184
TF: 800-523-7118 ■ *Web:* www.csiworldwide.net

CSJ Technologies Inc 7972 Tyler Blvd . . . Mentor OH 44060 440-269-8915 269-8928 175
Web: www.csjtech.com

CSL Group 759 Sq Victoria 6th Fl . . . Montreal QC H2Y2K3 514-982-3800 982-3801 313
Web: www.cslships.com

Csl Plasma Inc
1100 N Miami Blvd Ste 613 . . . Durham NC 27703 919-530-1388 530-1405 592
Web: www.cslplasma.com

CSM (Cambridge Street Metal Corp)
82 Stevens St . . . East Taunton MA 02718 508-822-2278 822-4667 492
TF: 800-254-7580 ■ *Web:* www.csmetal.net

CSM (Colonial Society of Massachusetts)
87 Mount Vernon St . . . Boston MA 02108 617-227-2782 48-13
Web: www.colonialsociety.org

CSM Capital Corp
625 Madison Ave 3rd Fl . . . New York NY 10022 212-400-9550 401
Web: www.csmcapitalcorp.com

CSM Group Inc
600 E Michigan Ave Ste A . . . Kalamazoo MI 49007 877-386-8214 186
TF: 877-386-8214 ■ *Web:* www.csmgroup.com

CSM Metal Fabricating & Engineering Inc
1800 S San Pedro St . . . Los Angeles CA 90015 213-748-7321 749-5106 482
TF: 800-272-4806 ■ *Web:* www.csmworks.com

	Phone	Fax	Class
CSM Worldwide Inc 269 Sheffield St . . . . Mountainside NJ 07092 *Web:* www.csmworldwide.com	908-233-2882	233-1064	18
CSMC (Cedars-Sinai Medical Ctr) 8700 Beverly Blvd. . . . . Los Angeles CA 90048 *TF:* 800-233-2771 ■ *Web:* www.cedars-sinai.org	310-423-3277		374-3
CSN Books PO Box 1450 . . . . Pine Valley CA 91962 *Web:* www.csnbooks.com	619-277-0068		637-2
CSN Intl PO Box 391 . . . . Twin Falls ID 83303 **Fax Area Code:* 208 ■ *TF:* 800-357-4226 ■ *Web:* www.csnradio.com	800-357-4226	736-1958*	647
CSO (Chattanooga Symphony & Opera) 701 Broad St. . . . . Chattanooga TN 37402 *Web:* chattanoogasymphony.org	423-267-8583	265-6520	573-3
CSO (Cheyenne Symphony Orchestra) 1904 Thomes Ave . . . . Cheyenne WY 82001 *Web:* www.cheyennesymphony.org	307-778-8561	634-7512	573-3
Cso Insights 36 Tamal Vista Blvd. . . . . Corte Madera CA 94925 *TF:* 877-506-2975 ■ *Web:* www.csoinsights.com	877-506-2975		194
C-Solutions Inc 1434 Spruce St Ste 100 . . . . Boulder CO 80302 *Web:* www.gmsworks.com	720-726-8080		178-10
CSP (Chicken Soup Press Inc) PO Box 164 . . . . Circleville NY 10919 *Web:* www.chickensouppress.com	845-692-6320	692-7574	637-2
CSP Associates Inc 55 Cambridge Pkwy Riverfront 2 . . . . Cambridge MA 02142 *Web:* www.cspassociates.com	617-225-2828		743
CSP Inc 43 Manning Rd . . . . Billerica MA 01821 *NASDAQ: CSPI* ■ *TF:* 800-325-3110 ■ *Web:* www.cspi.com	978-663-7598	663-0150	173-2
CSP Technologies 960 W Veterans Blvd. . . . . Auburn AL 36832 *TF:* 866-532-4277 ■ *Web:* www.csptechnologies.com	334-887-8300		601
CSPA (Columbia Scholastic Press Assn) Columbia University 90 Morningside Dr Ste B01 . . . . New York NY 10027 *Web:* cspa.columbia.edu	212-854-9400	854-9401	48-11
C-SPAN (Cable Satellite Public Affairs Network) 400 N Capitol St NW Ste 650 . . . . Washington DC 20001 *Web:* www.c-span.org	202-737-3220		740
CSR Enterprise Networks 155 Academy St . . . . Williamsport PA 17701 *Web:* www.csrinc.com	570-322-0590		180
CSR Professional Services Inc 830 NE Pop Tilton Pl . . . . Jensen Beach FL 34957 *TF:* 888-294-6971 ■ *Web:* csrps.com	888-294-6971		225
CSRC (UCLA Chicano Studies Research Ctr) 193 Haines Hall . . . . Los Angeles CA 90095 *Web:* www.chicano.ucla.edu	310-825-2363	206-1784	637-2
CSRM (Cascade Steel Rolling Mills Inc) 3200 N Hwy 99 W PO Box 687 . . . . McMinnville OR 97128 *TF:* 800-283-2776 ■ *Web:* www.cascadesteel.com	503-472-4181	434-5739	723
CSRwire LLC 36 West St. . . . . Springfield MA 01107 *Web:* csrwire.com	802-251-0110		530
CSS 10301 Democracy Ln Ste 300 . . . . Fairfax VA 22030 *TF:* 800-888-4612 ■ *Web:* www.css-inc.com	703-691-4612	691-4615	261
CSS (Computer Support Systems Inc) 3418 Hooper Ln . . . . Decatur AL 35602 *TF:* 800-925-9860 ■ *Web:* www.computersupportsystems.com	256-355-5973	340-0675	180
CSS Industries Inc 1845 Walnut St Ste 800 . . . . Philadelphia PA 19103 *NYSE: CSS* ■ *TF:* 800-327-0350 ■ *Web:* www.cssindustries.com	215-569-9900	569-9979	637-10
CSS International Inc 115 River Landing Dr Daniel Is. . . . . Charleston SC 29492 *TF:* 800-814-7705 ■ *Web:* cssus.com	800-814-7705		260
CSS Laboratories Inc 1641 McGaw Ave. . . . . Irvine CA 92614 *Web:* www.csslabs.com	949-852-8161		173-2
CSS Publications Inc PO Box 730 . . . . Mount Marion NY 12456 *Web:* www.arttimesjournal.com	845-246-6944		637-9
CSSA (Communications Supply Service Association CSSA) 5700 Murray St. . . . . Little Rock AR 72209 *TF:* 800-252-2772 ■ *Web:* www.cssa.net	501-562-7666	562-7616	49-20
CSSI Inc 400 Virginia Ave SW Ste 210 . . . . Washington DC 20024 *Web:* www.cssiinc.com	202-863-2175		180
CSSS du Lac des Deux-Montagnes 520 Boul Sauve . . . . Saint-Eustache QC J7R5B1 *Web:* www.moncsss.com	450-473-6811	473-6966	374-2
Cst Data 10725 John Price Rd . . . . Charlotte NC 28273 *TF:* 866-383-3282 ■ *Web:* cstdata.com	704-927-3282		225
CST Industries 903 East 104th St Ste 900 . . . . Kansas MO 64131 *Web:* www.cstindustries.com	913-621-3700	621-2145	49-13
CST Technologies Inc 55 Northern Blvd Ste 200 . . . . Great Neck NY 11021 *Web:* cstti.com	516-482-9001	482-0186	231
CST/Berger Corp 255 W Fleming St . . . . Watseka IL 60970 **Fax Area Code:* 800 ■ *TF:* 800-435-1859 ■ *Web:* www.cstberger.us	815-432-5237	913-0049*	544
CSTE (Council of State & Territorial Epidemiologists) 2872 Woodcock Blvd Ste 303 . . . . Atlanta GA 30341 *Web:* www.cste.org	770-458-3811	458-8516	49-7
CSU (Clayton State University) 2000 Clayton State Blvd . . . . Morrow GA 30260 *Web:* www.clayton.edu	678-466-4000	466-4149	166
Csubs 155 Chestnut Ridge Rd . . . . Montvale NJ 07645 *Web:* csubs.com	201-307-9900		96
CSV Midstream Solutions Corp Calgary Pl 2 355 Fourth Ave SW Ste 700 . . . . Calgary AB T2P0J1 *TF:* 844-808-4904 ■ *Web:* www.csvmidstream.com	587-316-6900	316-6901	539
Csw Stuber Stroeh Engineering Group Inc 1310 Redwood Way Ste 220 . . . . Petaluma CA 94954 *Web:* www.cswst2.com	707-795-4764		256
CSWD (Council on Size & Weight Discrimination) PO Box 305 . . . . Mount Marion NY 12456 *Web:* cswd.org	845-679-1209	679-1206	48-17
CSWE (Council on Social Work Education) 1701 Duke St Ste 200 . . . . Alexandria VA 22314 *Web:* cswe.org	703-683-8080	683-8099	49-5
CSX Corp 500 Water St 15th Fl . . . . Jacksonville FL 32202 *NASDAQ: CSX* ■ *TF:* 800-737-1663 ■ *Web:* www.csx.com	904-359-3200		185
CSZ (Congregation Sha'ar Zahav) 290 Dolores St . . . . San Francisco CA 94103 *Web:* www.shaarzahav.org	415-861-6932		48-20
CT (CalTel) 665 Main St . . . . Copperopolis CA 95228 *Web:* www.caltel.com	209-785-2211		224
CT Consultants Inc 8150 Sterling Ct . . . . Mentor OH 44060 *TF:* 800-925-0988 ■ *Web:* www.ctconsultants.com	440-951-9000	951-7487	261
Ct Gasket & Polymer Company Inc 12308 Cutten Rd. . . . . Houston TX 77066 *TF:* 800-299-1685 ■ *Web:* www.ctgasket.com	800-299-1685		326
CT River Valley Chamber of Commerce *Glastonbury Office* 2400 Main St. . . . . Glastonbury CT 06033 *Web:* www.crvchamber.org	860-659-3587	659-0102	139
CT Solutions Inc 12700 Fair Lakes Cir Ste 160 . . . . Fairfax VA 22033 *Web:* www.ctsols.com	703-289-1560		196
Ct. Wilson Construction Co PO Box 2011 . . . . Durham NC 27702 *Web:* www.ctwilson.com	919-383-2535		186
CTA (Chicago Transit Authority) 567 W Lake St . . . . Chicago IL 60661 *TF:* 888-578-7275 ■ *Web:* www.transitchicago.com	312-664-7200	681-5035	468
CTA (Carolina Training Associates) 3623 Latrobe Ste 120 . . . . Charlotte NC 28211 *TF:* 800-962-8815 ■ *Web:* www.carolinatraining.com	704-366-6309		423
CTA Acoustics Inc 25211 Dequindre Rd. . . . . Madison Heights MI 48071 *Web:* www.ctaacoustics.com	248-544-2580	544-2666	389
CTA Manufacturing Corp 263 Veterans Blvd. . . . . Carlstadt NJ 07072 *Web:* www.ctatools.com	201-896-1000	896-1378	758
CTAA (Community Transportation Association of America) 1341 G St NW 10th Fl. . . . . Washington DC 20005 **Fax Area Code:* 202 ■ *TF:* 800-891-0590 ■ *Web:* www.ctaa.org	800-891-0590	737-9197*	49-21
CTB Corp 26327 Fallbrook Ave. . . . . Wyoming MN 55092 *Web:* www.ctbcorp.com	651-462-3550		319-1
CTC (Central Texas Communications Inc) 1012 Reilly St. . . . . Goldthwaite TX 76844 *TF:* 877-212-2598 ■ *Web:* www.centex.net	325-648-2237		224
CTC (Community Telephone Company Inc) 10184 S Hwy 25E . . . . Windthorst TX 76389 *TF:* 800-794-6407 ■ *Web:* comcell.net	940-423-6201	423-2111	224
CTC (Cumberland Telephone Co) 121 Main St . . . . Cumberland IA 50843 *TF:* 888-774-2221 ■ *Web:* www.cumberlandtelephone.com	712-774-2221	774-2202	224
CTC (Cambridge Telephone Co) 611 Patterson St. . . . . Cambridge NE 69022 *TF:* 800-793-2788 ■ *Web:* www.pnpt.com	800-793-2788		224
CTC (Cambridge Telephone Company Inc) 130 N Superior . . . . Cambridge ID 83610 *Web:* www.ctcweb.net	208-257-3314	257-3310	224
CTC International Group 515 N Flagler Dr P 300 W. . . . . West Palm Beach FL 33401 *Web:* www.ctcintl.com	561-655-3111		693
CTC International Inc 11 York Ave. . . . . West Caldwell NJ 07006 *Web:* ctcint.com	973-228-2300		547
CTC Packaging 5264 Lake St PO Box 456 . . . . Sandy Lake PA 16145 *TF:* 800-241-0900 ■ *Web:* www.clinchtite.com	724-376-7315	376-2785	551
CTC Plastics 401 N Keowee St . . . . Dayton OH 45404 *Web:* www.ctcplastics.com	937-228-2880	228-9184	596
CTC Software 8101 4th Ave S Ste 100 . . . . Bloomington MN 55425 *TF:* 866-941-1181 ■ *Web:* ctcsoftware.com	866-941-1181		180
CTCG (Cambridge Technology Consulting Group Inc) 201 Wilshire Blvd Ste 41 . . . . Santa Monica CA 90401 *Web:* www.ctcg.com	310-229-8947		180
CTE Inc 30 Willow Springs Cir . . . . York PA 17406 *Web:* www.cte-inc.com	717-767-6636	764-2233	488
CTEC (Central Texas Electric Co-opeartive Inc) 386 Friendship Ln PO Box 553 . . . . Fredericksburg TX 78624 *TF:* 800-900-2832 ■ *Web:* www.ctec.coop	830-997-2126		245
CTF (Cottonwood Technology Funds) 422 Old Santa Fe Trail . . . . Santa Fe NM 87505 *Web:* cottonwoodtechnologyfund.com	505-412-8537		792
CTG (Computer Task Group Inc) 800 Delaware Ave . . . . Buffalo NY 14209 *OTC: CTG* ■ *TF:* 800-992-5350 ■ *Web:* www.ctg.com	716-882-8000	887-7464	180
CTG Development Co 7380 W Sandlake Rd Ste 500 . . . . Orlando FL 32819 *Web:* constructwo.com	407-295-9812		186
CTgov *State Board of Accountancy* 40B Jansen Ct . . . . Hartford CT 06106 *Web:* www.sots.ct.gov	860-509-6179		339-7
CTI (Cooling Technology Institute) 3845 Cypress Creek Pkwy Ste 420 . . . . Houston TX 77068 *Web:* www.coolingtechnology.org	281-583-4087	537-1721	48-12
CTI (Command Technology Inc) 404 Thames St . . . . Groton CT 06340 *Web:* www.commandtech.com	860-445-0156	446-2010	174
CTI & Associates Inc 28001 Cabot Dr Ste 250 . . . . Novi MI 48377 *Web:* cticompanies.com	248-486-5100	486-5050	256
CTI Consultants Inc 13500 E Boundary Rd. . . . . Midlothian VA 23112 *Web:* www.cti-consultants.com	804-622-8630		256
CTI Consulting 9711 Washingtonian Blvd Ste 550 . . . . Gaithersburg MD 20878 *Web:* www.countertech.com	301-528-8591		194
CTI Inc 11105 Norrth Casa Grande Hwy . . . . Rillito AZ 85654 *TF:* 800-362-4952 ■ *Web:* www.cti-az.com	520-624-2348	682-3509	780
CTI Property Services 5450 Old Wake Forest Rd . . . . Raleigh NC 27609 *Web:* ctipropertyservices.com	919-787-3789		776
CTI-SSi Food Services LLC 22303 Hwy 95 . . . . Wilder ID 83676 *Web:* www.ctifoods.com	208-482-7844	482-7457	296-26

	Phone	Fax	Class
CTJ (Citizens for Tax Justice) 1616 P St NW Ste 200 ... Washington DC 20036 *Web:* www.ctj.org	202-299-1066	299-1065	48-7
CTL (Cable Technology Laboratories Inc) 625 Jersey Ave Unit 14 ... New Brunswick NJ 08901 *Web:* www.cabtl.com	732-846-3133	846-5531	194
CTL Aerospace Inc 5616 Spellmire Dr ... Cincinnati OH 45246 *Web:* ctlaerospace.com	513-874-7900	874-2499	22
CTL Engineering Inc PO Box 44548 ... Columbus OH 43204 *Web:* www.ctleng.com	614-276-8123	276-6377	261
CTL Inc 375 Bridgeport Ave ... Shelton CT 06484 *Web:* www.ctlinc.com	203-925-4266		177
CTL/Thompson Inc 1971 W 12th Ave ... Denver CO 80204 *Web:* www.ctlthompson.com	303-825-0777	825-4252	261
CTLGroup 5400 Old Orchard Rd ... Skokie IL 60077 *TF:* 800-522-2285 ■ *Web:* www.ctlgroup.com	847-965-7500	965-6541	743
CTM Integration Inc 1318 Quaker Cir ... Salem OH 44460 *Web:* www.ctmlabelingsystems.com	330-332-1800	332-2144	547
CTM Media Group Inc 11 Largo Dr S ... Stamford CT 06907 *TF:* 800-888-2974 ■ *Web:* ctmmediagroup.com	203-323-5161		5
CTN (Christian Television Network Inc) 6922 142nd Ave N ... Largo FL 33771 *TF:* 800-716-7729 ■ *Web:* www.ctnonline.com	727-535-5622	531-2497	738
CTP (University of Washington) *Center for the Study of Teaching & Policy* University of Washington 100 Gerberding Hall PO Box 351265 ... Seattle WA 98195 *Web:* www.depts.washington.edu	206-543-6588		668
CTP Corp 3750 Shelby St ... Indianapolis IN 46227 *Web:* www.tubeproc.com	317-787-1322		490
CTPHC (Clifton T. Perkins Hospital Ctr) 1 Renaissance Blvd ... Oakbrook Terrace IL 60181 **Fax Area Code:* 630 ■ *TF:* 800-994-6610 ■ *Web:* health.maryland.gov	800-994-6610	792-5636*	374-5
CTR Automotive Service Ctr 3025 Woodlane Dr ... Janesville WI 53545 *Web:* www.ctrautomotive.com	608-373-9750	563-1583	230
CTR for LGBTQ Studies (CLAGS) CUNY Graduate Ctr 365 Fifth Ave Rm 7115 ... New York NY 10016 *Web:* www.clags.org	212-817-1955	817-1567	668
CTR Management Group 2751 Prosperity Dr Ste 540 ... Fairfax VA 22031 *Web:* www.ctrmg.com	703-638-1354	563-9284	48-9
CTrends Inc 27142 Burbank ... Foothill Ranch CA 92610 *TF:* 877-472-9050 ■ *Web:* www.ctrends.com	949-472-9050		179
Ctrpoint Medical Ctr 19600 E 39th St ... Independence MO 64057 *Web:* centerpointmedical.com	816-698-7000		374-3
CTS Computer Technology Solutions Inc 575 E Locust Ave Ste 120 ... Fresno CA 93720 *Web:* cts-technology.com	559-432-7007		180
CTS Corp 1142 W Beardsley Ave ... Elkhart IN 46514 *NYSE: CTS* ■ *Web:* www.ctscorp.com	574-523-3800		253
CTS Industries 408 S 2nd St ... Cedartown GA 30125 *TF:* 800-334-7117 ■ *Web:* ctsindustries.com	770-748-3497	748-5133	629
CTS Telecom Inc 13800 E Michigan Ave ... Galesburg MI 49053 *TF:* 800-627-5287 ■ *Web:* www.ctstelecom.com	269-746-4411		224
CTSI (Continental Traffic Service Inc) 5100 Poplar Ave 15th Fl ... Memphis TN 38137 *TF:* 888-836-5135 ■ *Web:* www.ctsi-global.com	901-766-1500	766-1520	311
CTT (Coil Tubing Technology Holding Inc) 3002 Farrell Rd ... Houston TX 77073 *Web:* www.coiltubingtechnology.com	281-651-0200		539
CTV 80 Patina Rise SW ... Calgary AB T3H2W4 *Web:* calgary.ctvnews.ca	403-240-5600		741-21
CTV Edmonton 18520 Stony Plain Rd ... Edmonton AB T5S1A8 *Web:* edmonton.ctvnews.ca	780-483-3311		740
CTV News Ottawa 87 George St ... Ottawa ON K1N9H7 *Web:* ottawa.ctvnews.ca	613-562-6725		741-96
CTV Regina No 1 Hwy E PO Box 2000 ... Regina SK S4P3E5 *Web:* www.regina.ctvnews.ca	306-569-2000	522-0090	647
CTV-TV Ch 5 (CTV) 345 Graham Ave Ste 400 ... Winnipeg MB R3C5S6 *TF:* 800-461-1542 ■ *Web:* winnipeg.ctvnews.ca	204-788-3300	788-3399	741-143
CTX Inc 14701 Harrison Rd ... Romulus MI 48174 **Fax Area Code:* 734 ■ *TF:* 800-447-5173 ■ *Web:* www.cxua.com	800-447-5173	955-2830*	311
CU (Communication Unlimited) 185 Shevelin Rd ... Novato CA 94948 *TF:* 800-563-1454 ■ *Web:* www.gordonburgett.com	415-884-2941	883-5707	637-2
CU (City Utilities of Springfield) 301 E Central St ... Springfield MO 65801 *TF:* 888-863-9001 ■ *Web:* www.cityutilities.net	417-831-8400		245
CU America Financial Services Inc 200 W 22nd St Ste 280 ... Lombard IL 60148 **Fax Area Code:* 224 ■ *TF:* 800-351-0449 ■ *Web:* www.cuamerica.com	630-620-5200	534-3327*	194
CU Conferences 8711 Watson Rd Ste 200 ... Saint Louis MO 63119 *TF:* 888-465-6010 ■ *Web:* www.cuconferences.com	888-465-6010		387
CU*Answers 6000 28th St SE Ste 100 ... Grand Rapids MI 49546 *TF:* 800-327-3478 ■ *Web:* www.cuanswers.com	616-285-5711		225
CUB (Concerned United Birthparents Inc) PO Box 503475 ... San Diego CA 92150 **Fax Area Code:* 858 ■ *TF:* 800-822-2777 ■ *Web:* www.cubirthparents.org	800-822-2777	712-3317*	48-21
CUB Energy Inc 5120 Woodway Dr Ste 10010 ... Houston TX 77056 *Web:* www.cubenergyinc.com	713-677-0439		536
CUB Foods Stores 421 S Third St ... Stillwater MN 55082 *Web:* www.cub.com	651-439-7200		345
Cuba City Telephone Exchange Co (CCTEC) 104 S Main St ... Cuba City WI 53807 *Web:* www.cubacity.org	608-744-2154		224
Cuba Free Press 501 E Washington ... Cuba MO 65453 *Web:* www.threeriverspublishing.com	573-885-7460	885-3803	532-2
Cuba Libre 2801 Pacific Ave ... Atlantic City NJ 08401 *Web:* www.cubalibrerestaurant.com	609-348-6700		671
Cuba Rushford Central School 5476 Rt 305 ... Cuba NY 14727 *Web:* www.crcs.wnyric.org	585-968-2650	968-2651	685
Cuban American National Council 1223 SW Fourth St ... Miami FL 33135 *Web:* www.cnc.org	305-642-3484	642-9122	48-14
Cuban Crafters Cigars 3604 NW 7th St ... Miami FL 33125 *TF:* 877-244-2701 ■ *Web:* www.cubancrafters.com	305-573-0222	573-0226	756
Cubby's Inc 9230 Mormon Bridge Rd ... Omaha NE 68152 *Web:* www.cubbys.com	402-453-2468	453-4513	345
Cubeit Portable Storage 100 Canadian Rd ... Scarborough ON M1R4Z5 *TF:* 844-897-3811 ■ *Web:* www.cubeit.ca	844-897-3811		111
Cubic Corp 9333 Balboa Ave ... San Diego CA 92123 *NYSE: CUB* ■ *Web:* www.cubic.com	858-277-6780	505-1523	703
Cubic Designs Inc 5487 S Westridge Dr ... New Berlin WI 53151 *TF:* 800-826-7061 ■ *Web:* www.cubicdesigns.com	262-789-1966		480
Cubicles Office Environments 6221-A Yarrow Dr ... Carlsbad CA 92011 *Web:* www.coeoffice.com	760-938-5572	597-0620	320
Cubist Media Group Ltd 234 Market St 3rd Fl ... Philadelphia PA 19106 *Web:* cubistmediagroup.com	267-765-7000	765-7002	514
Cubix Corp 2800 Lockheed Way ... Carson City NV 89706 *TF:* 800-829-0550 ■ *Web:* www.cubix.com	775-888-1000		176
Cubix Labs Inc 1875 K St NW ... Washington DC 20006 *TF:* 866-978-2220 ■ *Web:* www.socialcubix.com	866-978-2220		631
CUC (Commercial Utility Consultants Inc) 1556 McDaniel Dr ... West Chester PA 19380 **Fax Area Code:* 610 ■ *TF:* 800-296-2821 ■ *Web:* www.commercialutility.com	800-296-2821	431-1023*	393
Cucina Casalinga PO Box 7714 ... Wilton CT 06897 *Web:* www.cucinacasalinga.com	203-762-0768		167-3
Cucina Forte 768 S Eigth St ... Philadelphia PA 19147 *Web:* www.cucinaforte.com	215-238-0778		671
Cudahy Patrick Inc 1 Sweet Apple-Wood Ln ... Cudahy WI 53110 *TF:* 800-486-6900 ■ *Web:* www.patrickcudahy.com	414-744-2000	744-4213	473
Cudd Well Control 2828 Technology Forest Blvd ... The Woodlands TX 77381 *Web:* www.cuddwellcontrol.com	713-849-2769	849-3861	261
Cudner & O'Connor Co 4035 W Kinzie St ... Chicago IL 60624 *Web:* www.candocinks.com	773-826-0200		388
CUE Inc 11 Leonberg Rd ... Cranberry Township PA 16066 *TF:* 800-283-4621 ■ *Web:* www.cue-inc.com	724-772-5225	772-5280	600
Cuellar Henry (Rep D - TX) 2372 Rayburn House Office Bldg ... Washington DC 20515 *Web:* cuellar.house.gov	202-225-1640	225-1641	342-2
Cuenca & Associates Insurance Agency Inc 2990 Innsbruck Dr ... Redding CA 96003 *TF:* 800-345-4543 ■ *Web:* lifehelp.com	800-345-4543		390
CUES (Credit Union Executives Society) 5510 Research Pk Dr ... Madison WI 53711 *TF:* 800-252-2664 ■ *Web:* www.cues.org	608-271-2664	271-2303	49-2
CUES (Consolidated Utility & Equipment Service Inc) 53 Lebanon Rd N ... Franklin CT 06254 *TF:* 800-526-3916 ■ *Web:* www.cuesequip.com	860-886-7081	886-6546	385
CUES Inc 3600 Rio Vista Ave ... Orlando FL 32805 *TF:* 800-327-7791 ■ *Web:* www.cuesinc.com	407-849-0190		201
Cuesta College PO Box 8106 ... San Luis Obispo CA 93403 *TF:* 877-732-0436 ■ *Web:* www.cuesta.edu	805-546-3100	546-3975	162
Cufflinks.Com Holding Company LLC 4514 Cole Ave Ste 200 ... Dallas TX 75205 *Web:* cufflinks.com	214-780-0333		366
Cuisinart 1 Cummings Point Rd ... Stamford CT 06902 *TF:* 800-726-0190 ■ *Web:* www.cuisinart.com	203-975-4609	975-4660	37
Cuisine 670 Lothrop Rd ... Detroit MI 48202 *Web:* www.cuisinerestaurant.com	313-872-5110		671
Cuisine Solutions Corporate USA 22445 Sous Vide Ln Unit 100 ... Sterling VA 20166 *OTC: CUSI* ■ *TF:* 888-285-4679 ■ *Web:* www.cuisinesolutions.com	703-270-2900	270-2994	296-36
Cuivre River Electric Co-op 1112 E Cherry St ... Troy MO 63379 *TF:* 800-392-3709 ■ *Web:* www.cuivre.com	636-528-8261	528-7696	245
Cuivre River State Park 678 SR-147 ... Troy MO 63379 *Web:* mostateparks.com	636-528-7247		565
Culberson Construction Inc 4500 Colony Rd ... Granbury TX 76048 *Web:* ccincservices.com	817-573-3079	573-5349	536
Culberson County PO Box 158 ... Van Horn TX 79855 *Web:* www.co.culberson.tx.us	432-283-2058	283-9234	338
Culicidae Press LLC 922 5th St ... Ames IA 50010 *Web:* culicidaepress.com	515-462-0278		637-2
CulinAerie 1131 14th St NW ... Washington DC 20005 *TF:* 888-789-2665 ■ *Web:* www.culinaerie.com	202-587-5674	898-1088	167-3
Culinaire Intl 8303 Elmbrook Dr Ste 3100 ... Dallas TX 75247 *Web:* www.culinaireintl.com	214-754-1880	754-1891	299
Culinarte Marketting Group LLC 808 Packerland Dr ... Green Bay WI 54303 *Web:* www.bonewerksculinarte.com	920-498-3004		123
Culinary Arts Museum at Johnson & Wales University 315 Harborside Blvd ... Providence RI 02905 *Web:* culinaryartsmuseum.pastperfectonline.com	401-598-2805		520
Culinary Concepts AB 2041 Barracks Rd ... Charlottesville VA 22903 *Web:* www.culinaryconceptsab.com	434-617-4545		685
Culinary Depot Inc 2 Melnick Dr ... Monsey NY 10952 *TF:* 888-845-8200 ■ *Web:* www.culinarydepotinc.com	888-845-8200		406
Culinary Institute Alain & Marie LeNotre 7070 Allensby ... Houston TX 77022 *TF:* 888-536-6873 ■ *Web:* culinaryinstitute.edu	713-692-0077		163
Culinary Institute of America 1946 Campus Dr ... Hyde Park NY 12538 *TF:* 800-285-4627 ■ *Web:* www.ciachef.edu	845-452-9600	451-1068	163
Culinary School of Fort Worth 6550 Camp Bowie Blvd ... Fort Worth TX 76116 *Web:* www.csftw.edu	817-737-8427		685
Culinary Software Services Inc 1900 Folsom St Ste 210 ... Boulder CO 80302 *TF:* 800-447-1466 ■ *Web:* www.culinarysoftware.com	303-447-3334		177

	Phone	Fax	Class
Culinary Staffing Services 6363 Wilshire Blvd Ste 305 ... Los Angeles CA 90048 *Web:* culinarystaffing.com	323-965-7582		260
Culinary Trends 503 Vista Bella Ste 12 ... Oceanside CA 92057 *Web:* www.culinarytrends.net	760-721-2500		637-9
Cull Martin & Associates Inc 320 N Jensen Rd ... Vestal NY 13850 *Web:* www.cullmartin.com	607-722-3884	722-4264	317
Cullen/Frost Bankers Inc 100 W Houston St ... San Antonio TX 78205 *NYSE:* CFR ■ *TF:* 800-562-6732 ■ *Web:* www.frostbank.com	210-220-4011		360-2
Culligan International Co 9399 W Higgins Rd Ste 1100 ... Rosemont IL 60018 *TF:* 800-285-5442 ■ *Web:* culligan.com	847-430-2800		806
Cullinan Associates Inc 295 N Hubbards Ln 2nd Fl ... Louisville KY 40207 *TF:* 800-611-4841 ■ *Web:* www.cullinan.com	800-611-4841		401
Cullinan Properties Ltd 420 N Main St 2nd Fl ... Peoria IL 61614 *Web:* www.cullinanproperties.com	309-999-1700	999-1701	653
Cullman Area Chamber of Commerce 301 Second Ave SW ... Cullman AL 35055 *TF:* 800-313-5114 ■ *Web:* www.cullmanchamber.org	256-734-0454	737-7443	139
Cullman Cabinet & Supply Company Inc 1735 Childhaven Rd ... Cullman AL 35055 *Web:* www.cullmancabinet.com	256-734-1540	739-2682	115
Cullman Casting Corp 251 County Rd 490 ... Cullman AL 35055 *Web:* www.cullmancasting.com	256-735-0900	734-1626	492
Cullman City School 301 First St NE Ste 100 ... Cullman AL 35055 *TF:* 800-548-2547 ■ *Web:* www.cullmancats.net	256-734-2233		685
Cullman County 500 Second Ave SW ... Cullman AL 35055 *Web:* www.co.cullman.al.us	256-739-3530	775-4670	338
Cullman County Board of Education 402 Arnold St NE PO Box 1590 ... Cullman AL 35056 *Web:* www.ccboe.org	256-734-2933	736-2486	685
Cullman County Public Library System 200 Clark St NE ... Cullman AL 35055 *Web:* www.ccpls.com	256-734-1068	734-6902	434-3
Cullman Electric Coop 1749 Eva Rd NE ... Cullman AL 35055 *TF:* 800-242-1806 ■ *Web:* www.cullmanec.com	256-737-3201		245
Cullman Regional Medical Ctr (CRMC) 1912 Alabama Hwy 157 PO Box 1108 ... Cullman AL 35058 *Web:* cullmanregional.com	256-737-2000		374-3
Cullum Mechanical Construction Inc 3325 Pacific Ave ... North Charleston SC 29418 *Web:* www.culluminc.com	843-554-6645		189-10
Culp & Tanner Inc 55 Independence Cir Ste 201 ... Chico CA 95973 *Web:* culpandtanner.com	530-895-3518	895-3544	261
Culp Construction Co 2320 S Main St ... Salt Lake City UT 84115 *TF:* 888-555-4123 ■ *Web:* culpco.com	801-486-2064		186
Culp Inc 1823 Eastchester Dr ... High Point NC 27265 *NYSE:* CULP ■ *Web:* www.culp.com	336-889-5161		745-1
Culpeper Baptist Retirement Community 12425 Village Loop ... Culpeper VA 22701 *Web:* culpeperretirement.org	540-825-2411		672
Culpeper County Library 271 Southgate Shopping Ctr ... Culpeper VA 22701	540-825-8691		434-3
Culpeper Wood Preservers Inc 15487 Braggs Corner Rd PO Box 1148 ... Culpeper VA 22701 *TF:* 800-817-6215 ■ *Web:* culpeperwood.com	800-817-6215		818
Culpepper & Associates Security Services Inc 1810 Water Pl SE Ste 180 ... Atlanta GA 30339 *Web:* www.cassecurity.com	770-916-0060	916-0080	693
Culpepper & Terpening Inc 2980 S 25th St ... Fort Pierce FL 34981 *Web:* www.ct-eng.com	772-464-3537		186
Cultural Center for Language School (CCLS) 3191 Coral Way Ste 114 ... Miami FL 33145 *Web:* www.cclsmiami.edu	305-529-2257	443-8538	423
Cultural Survival Inc 215 Prospect St ... Cambridge MA 02139 *Web:* www.culturalsurvival.org	617-441-5400	441-5417	48-8
Cultural Tourism DC 1250 H St NW Ste 1000 ... Washington DC 20005 *Web:* www.culturaltourismdc.org	202-661-7581		772
Culturalink Inc 157 Technology Pkwy Ste 600 ... Norcross GA 30092 *Web:* theculturalink.com	888-844-1414		194
Culture Coop, The PO Box 463 ... Davis CA 95616 *Web:* www.cultureco-op.com	530-792-1334	753-8511	423
Culture Works 110 N Main St Ste 165 ... Dayton OH 45402 *Web:* cultureworks.org	937-222-2787		181
Culture22 935B N Plum Grove Rd ... Schaumburg IL 60173 *Web:* www.culture22.com	847-517-9022		195
Culver Academies 1300 Academy Rd ... Culver IN 46511 *TF:* 800-528-5837 ■ *Web:* www.culver.org	574-842-7000		622
Culver City Chamber of Commerce 6000 Sepulveda Blvd Ste 1260 ... Culver City CA 90230 *Web:* www.culvercitychamber.com	310-287-3850		139
Culver City Unified School District (CCUSD) 4034 Irving Pl ... Culver City CA 90232 *TF:* 855-446-2673 ■ *Web:* www.ccusd.org	310-842-4220	842-4205	685
Culver Duck Farms Inc 12215 CR 10 ... Middlebury IN 46540 *TF:* 800-825-9225 ■ *Web:* www.culverduck.com	574-825-9537		10-8
Culver Floor Covering Company Inc 2411 Ave X ... Brooklyn NY 11235 *Web:* www.culverfloors.org	718-332-3434	648-9286	131
Culver Franchising System Inc 1240 Water St ... Prairie du Sac WI 53578 *TF:* 833-224-7670 ■ *Web:* www.culvers.com	608-643-7980	643-7982	670
Culver Glass Co 2619 NW Industrial St ... Portland OR 97210 *Web:* culver-glass.com	503-226-2520	228-9155	330
Culver Studios 9336 W Washington Blvd ... Culver City CA 90232 *Web:* www.theculverstudios.com	310-202-1234		514
Culver Tool & Engineering Inc 1901 Walter Glaub Dr ... Plymouth IN 46563 *Web:* culvertool.com	574-935-9611	935-9612	393
Culwell & Son Inc 6319 Hillcrest Ave ... Dallas TX 75205 *Web:* www.culwell.com	214-522-7000		157-3
Cumberland Architectural Millwork Inc 603 Davidson St ... Nashville TN 37213 *Web:* cumberlandmillwork.com	615-254-1710		499
Cumberland Bank & Trust 2034 Wilma Rudolph Blvd ... Clarksville TN 37040 *Web:* bankatcbt.com	931-245-3068		70
Cumberland Bay State Park 152 Cumberland Head Rd ... Plattsburgh NY 12901 *Web:* parks.ny.gov	518-563-5240		565
Cumberland Chrysler Dodge Jeep Ram FIAT 1550 Interstate Dr ... Cookeville TN 38501 *Web:* www.cumberlandchryslercenter.com	931-263-0321		57
Cumberland County 164 W Broad St ... Bridgeton NJ 08302 *Web:* www.co.cumberland.nj.us	856-453-2125	451-0639	338
Cumberland County 601 Courthouse Sq PO Box 275 ... Burkesville KY 42717 *Web:* cumberlandcountyclerk.com	270-864-3726	864-5884	338
Cumberland County 117 Dick St PO Box 1829 ... Fayetteville NC 28302 *Web:* www.co.cumberland.nc.us	910-678-7659	678-7717	338
Cumberland County 142 Federal St ... Portland ME 04101 *Web:* www.cumberlandcounty.org	207-871-8380	871-8292	338
Cumberland County 140 Courthouse Sq PO Box 146 ... Toledo IL 62468 *Web:* cumberlandco.org	217-849-2631	849-2968	338
Cumberland County Library 800 E Commerce St ... Bridgeton NJ 08302 *Web:* www.clueslibs.org	856-453-2210		434-3
Cumberland Dairy Inc 899 Landis Ave ... Rosenhayn NJ 08352 **Fax Area Code:* 856 ■ *TF:* 800-257-8484 ■ *Web:* www.cumberlanddairy.com	800-257-8484	451-1332*	296-27
Cumberland Electric Membership Corp 1940 Madison St ... Clarksville TN 37043 *TF:* 800-987-2362 ■ *Web:* www.cemc.org	800-987-2362		245
Cumberland Emerging Technologies Inc 2525 W End Ave Ste 950 ... Nashville TN 37203 *Web:* www.cet-fund.com	615-255-0068	255-0094	582
Cumberland Falls State Resort Park 7351 Hwy 90 ... Corbin KY 40701 *TF:* 800-325-0063 ■ *Web:* parks.ky.gov	800-325-0063		565
Cumberland Furniture 321 Terminal St SW ... Grand Rapids MI 49548 *TF:* 800-401-7877 ■ *Web:* www.cumberlandfurniture.com	800-401-7877		321
Cumberland Industries Inc *Cumberland Steel Div* 4919 Grant Ave ... Cleveland OH 44125 *Web:* cumberlandind.com	216-441-1800		492
Cumberland Island National Seashore 101 Wheeler St ... Saint Marys GA 31558 *TF:* 877-860-6787 ■ *Web:* www.nps.gov	912-882-4336	673-7747	564
Cumberland Lumber & Manufacturing Co 202 Red Rd ... McMinnville TN 37110	931-473-9542		683
Cumberland Mall 1000 Cumberland Mall ... Atlanta GA 30339 *Web:* www.cumberlandmall.com	770-435-2206		460
Cumberland Medical Ctr (CMC) 421 S Main St ... Crossville TN 38555 *Web:* www.cmchealthcare.org	931-484-9511		374-3
Cumberland Mountain State Park 24 Office Dr ... Crossville TN 38555 *Web:* www.state.tn.us	931-484-6138		565
Cumberland Mutual Insurance 633 Shiloh Pk ... Bridgeton NJ 08302 **Fax Area Code:* 856 ■ *TF:* 800-232-6992 ■ *Web:* www.cumberlandmutual.com	800-232-6992	451-7564*	391-4
Cumberland Packing Corp 2 Cumberland St ... Brooklyn NY 11205 *Web:* www.sweetnlow.com	718-858-4200		296-38
Cumberland Private Wealth Management Inc 99 Yorkville Ave Ste 300 ... Toronto ON M5R3K5 *TF:* 800-929-8296 ■ *Web:* cumberlandprivate.com	416-929-1090		401
Cumberland Public Library 1464 Diamond Hill Rd ... Cumberland RI 02864 *Web:* www.cumberlandlibrary.org	401-333-2552	334-0578	434-3
Cumberland Telephone Co (CTC) 121 Main St ... Cumberland IA 50843 *TF:* 888-774-2221 ■ *Web:* www.cumberlandtelephone.com	712-774-2221	774-2202	224
Cumberland Times-News 19 Baltimore St ... Cumberland MD 21502 *Web:* www.times-news.com	301-722-4600	722-5270	532-2
Cumberland Tool & Die Inc 6 Brenneman Cir ... Mechanicsburg PA 17050 *Web:* www.cumberlandtool.com	717-691-1125	697-0628	488
Cumberland Trail State Park 220 Park Rd ... Caryville TN 37714 *Web:* tnstateparks.com	423-566-2229		565
Cumberland Truck Parts 15 Sylmar Rd ... Nottingham PA 19362 *TF:* 800-364-6995 ■ *Web:* www.cumberlandtruck.com	610-932-1152		54
Cumberland University 1 Cumberland Sq ... Lebanon TN 37087 *TF:* 800-467-0562 ■ *Web:* www.cumberland.edu	615-444-2562	444-2569	166
Cumberland Valley Electric Inc 6219 N US Hwy 25 E ... Gray KY 40734 *TF:* 800-513-2677 ■ *Web:* www.cumberlandvalley.coop	800-513-2677		245
Cumberland Wood Products Inc 275 Helenwood Detour Rd ... Helenwood TN 37755 *Web:* www.cwpinc.com	423-569-6363	569-9131	200
Cumberland-Perry Area Vocational Technical School 110 Old Willow Mill Rd ... Mechanicsburg PA 17050 *Web:* www.cpavts.org	717-697-0354		800
Cumbre Insurance Services LLC 3333 Concours Ste 5100 ... Ontario CA 91764 *TF:* 800-998-7986 ■ *Web:* www.cumbreinsurance.com	909-484-2456	484-2491	390

	Phone	Fax	Class
Cumby Telephone Cooperative Inc 200 Frisco St .... Cumby TX 75433 *TF:* 877-994-4440 ■ *Web:* www.cumbytel.com	903-994-2211	994-2200	224
Cuming County 200 S Lincoln St Rm 50 .... West Point NE 68788 *Web:* extension.unl.edu	402-372-6006		338
Cuming County Public Power District 500 S Main St .... West Point NE 68788 *TF:* 877-572-2463 ■ *Web:* ccppd.com	402-372-2463	372-5832	245
Cummer Museum of Art & Gardens 829 Riverside Ave .... Jacksonville FL 32204 *Web:* www.cummermuseum.org	904-356-6857	353-4101	520
Cumming Veterinary Clinic Pc 4110 Deputy Bill Cantrell Memorial Rd .... Cumming GA 30040 *Web:* cummingvetclinic.com	770-887-3119		794
Cumming-Forsyth County Chamber of Commerce 212 Kelly Mill Rd .... Cumming GA 30040 *Web:* www.focochamber.org	770-887-6461	781-8800	139
Cummings & Associates Inc 1 Houston St .... Mobile AL 36616 *Web:* cummingsassoc.com	251-476-6000		653
Cummings & Carroll PC 175 Great Neck Rd Ste 405 .... Great Neck NY 11021	516-482-3260		2
Cummings & Lockwood LLC 8000 Health Center Blvd Ste 300 .... Bonita Springs FL 34135 *Web:* www.cl-law.com	239-947-8811	947-8025	428
Cummings Properties LLC 200 W Cummings Pk .... Woburn MA 01801 *Web:* www.cummings.com	781-935-8000		652
Cummings Signs 15 Century Blvd Ste 200 .... Nashville TN 37214 *TF:* 800-489-7446 ■ *Web:* www.cummingssigns.com	800-489-7446		701
Cummings Transportation 19605 Broken Ct .... Shafter CA 93263 *Web:* www.cummings2.com	661-746-1786		539
Cummings Veneers Inc 601 E Fourth St .... New Albany IN 47150 *Web:* www.emcveneer.com	812-944-2269	944-0212	613
Cummings Violich Inc 7929 County Rd 9 .... Orland CA 95963	530-804-6404		10-10
Cummins & Bonestroo Law Office 1851 Buerkle Rd .... White Bear Lake MN 55110 *Web:* www.cblawoffices.com	651-328-8670		41
Cummins Aerospace 2200 E Orangethorpe Ave .... Anaheim CA 92806 *Web:* cumminsaerospace.com	714-879-2800	879-2991	529
Cummins Construction Company Inc 1420 W Chestnut Ave .... Enid OK 73702 *TF:* 800-375-6001 ■ *Web:* www.cumminsasphalt.com	580-233-6000		188-4
Cummins Facility Services 5202 Marion Waldo Rd .... Prospect OH 43342 *TF:* 800-451-5629 ■ *Web:* www.cumminsfs.com	740-726-9800		104
Cummins Filtration 26 Century Blvd .... Nashville TN 37214 **Fax Area Code:* 800 ■ *TF:* 800-777-7064 ■ *Web:* cumminsfiltration.com	615-367-0040	999-8664*	60
Cummins Inc 500 Jackson St PO Box 3005 .... Columbus IN 47201 *NYSE: CMI* ■ *TF:* 800-343-7357 ■ *Web:* www.cummins.com	812-377-5000	377-3334	262
Cummins Manufacturing Inc 301 Commerce Blvd .... Tipton IA 52772 *Web:* www.cummins-manufacturing.com	563-886-2255		454
Cummins Onan Elkhart 5125 Beck Dr .... Elkhart IN 46516 *TF:* 800-888-6626 ■ *Web:* www.cumminsonanelkhart.com	574-262-4611	389-0089	518
Cummins-Allison Corp 852 Feehanville Dr .... Mount Prospect IL 60056 *TF:* 800-786-5528 ■ *Web:* www.cumminsallison.com	847-299-9550		111
Cumsky & Levin LLP 6 University Rd .... Cambridge MA 02138 *Web:* cumskylevin.com	617-492-9700	492-9020	41
Cumulus Media 60 Monroe Ctr Ste 300 .... Grand Rapids MI 49503 *TF:* 800-882-9528 ■ *Web:* www.wlav.com	616-774-8461	451-3299	645-63
Cumulus Media Inc 3280 Peachtree Rd NW Ste 2200 .... Atlanta GA 30305 *Web:* www.cumulusmedia.com	404-949-0700	949-0740	645-5
CUNA Mutual Group 5910 Mineral Point Rd .... Madison WI 53705 *TF:* 800-356-2644 ■ *Web:* www.cunamutual.com	608-238-5851		360-4
Cunard Line Ltd 24303 Town Center Dr Ste 200 .... Valencia CA 91355 *TF:* 800-728-6273 ■ *Web:* www.cunard.com	661-753-1000		220
Cunetto House of Pasta 5453 Magnolia Ave .... Saint Louis MO 63139 *Web:* www.cunetto.com	314-781-1135		671
Cunningham Associates 180 Old Tappan Rd .... Old Tappan NJ 07675 *Web:* www.cunninghamassociates.com	201-767-4170	767-8065	7
Cunningham Distributing Inc 2015 E Mills Ave .... El Paso TX 79901	915-533-6993		38
Cunningham Falls State Park 14039 Catoctin Hollow Rd .... Thurmont MD 21788 *Web:* dnr.maryland.gov	301-271-7574		565
Cunningham Joe (Rep D - SC) 423 Cannon House Office Bldg .... Washington DC 20515 *Web:* www.cunningham.house.gov	202-225-3176		342-2
Cunningham Lindsey Group Ltd 3030 Rocky Point Dr Ste 530 .... Tampa FL 33607 *Web:* www.cunninghamlindsey.com	813-830-7100		390
Cunningham Manufacturing Co 318 S Webster St .... Seattle WA 98108 *TF:* 800-767-0038 ■ *Web:* www.cunninghamcylinders.com	206-767-3713	762-3457	223
Cunningham Memorial Library 510 N 6 1/2 St .... Terre Haute IN 47809 *TF:* 800-851-4279 ■ *Web:* library.indstate.edu	812-237-2580		434-6
Cunningham Pattern & Engineering Inc 4399 N US Hwy 31 PO Box 854 .... Columbus IN 47201 *Web:* cunninghamprecision.com	812-379-9571	379-9574	567
Cunningham-Limp 28970 Cabot Dr Ste 100 .... Novi MI 48377 *Web:* cunninghamlimp.com	248-489-2300		685
CUNY (City University of New York) 205 East 42nd St .... New York NY 10017 *TF:* 800-286-9937 ■ *Web:* www.cuny.edu	212-997-2869	794-5397	786

	Phone	Fax	Class
CUPA-HR (College & University Professional Association for Hum Res) 1811 Commons Pt Dr .... Knoxville TN 37932 *TF:* 877-287-2474 ■ *Web:* www.cupahr.org	865-637-7673	637-7674	49-5
Cupboard, The 1400 Union Ave .... Memphis TN 38104 *Web:* www.thecupboardrestaurant.com	901-276-8015	728-5518	671
Cupertino Chamber of Commerce 20455 Silverado Ave .... Cupertino CA 95014 *Web:* cupertino-chamber.org	408-252-7054		139
Cupertino Courier 4 N 2nd St 8th Fl .... San Jose CA 95113 *Web:* www.mercurynews.com	408-200-1039	200-1013	532-4
Cupertino Electric Inc 1132 N Seventh St .... San Jose CA 95112 *Web:* www.cei.com	408-808-8000	275-8575	189-4
Cupertino Inn 10889 N De Anza Blvd .... Cupertino CA 95014 *TF:* 800-222-4828 ■ *Web:* www.cupertino-hotel.com	408-996-7700		707
Cupid Foundations Inc 475 Park Ave S .... New York NY 10016 *TF:* 877-649-5283 ■ *Web:* www.cupidintimates.com	212-686-6224	481-9357	155-18
Cupini's 1809 Westport Rd .... Kansas City MO 64111 *Web:* www.cupinis.com	816-753-7662		671
Cupples' J & J Company Inc 1063 Whitehall St .... Jackson TN 38301 *Web:* www.cupplesjandj.com	731-424-3621	427-4620	697
Cura Hospitality Inc 2970 Corporate Ct Ste 5 .... Orefield PA 18069 *Web:* www.curahospitality.com	610-530-7300		196
CuraFlo 7436 Fraser Park Dr .... Burnaby BC V5J5B9 *Web:* curaflo.com	604-298-7278		481
Curate FoodService 100 Willow St Ste 2 .... North Andover MA 01845 *Web:* www.curatefoodservice.com	978-989-0012		345
Curatel LLC 1605 W Olympic Blvd Ste 800 .... Los Angeles CA 90015 *TF:* 866-287-2366 ■ *Web:* www.curatel.com	866-287-2366		387
Curb Records 48 Music Sq E .... Nashville TN 37203 *Web:* www.curb.com	615-321-5080		657
Curbell Inc 7 Cobham Dr .... Orchard Park NY 14127 *Web:* www.curbell.com	716-667-3377	667-3432	608
Curbside Lawn Care & Irrigation Inc 12469 Zinran Ave .... Savage MN 55378 *Web:* curbsidelandscape.com	952-403-9012		422
Curbstone Financial Management Corp 741 Chestnut St .... Manchester NH 03104 *Web:* curbstonefinancial.com	603-624-8462		194
Curcio Scrap Metal Inc 416 Lanza Ave .... Saddle Brook NJ 07663 *Web:* www.curcioscrapmetal.com	973-478-3133		686
Curd Enterprises Inc 476 Long Point Rd .... Mount Pleasant SC 29464 *TF:* 800-968-3091 ■ *Web:* curdbuoys.com	843-881-0323	881-0655	604
CureSearch for Children's Cancer 4600 East-West Hwy Ste 600 .... Bethesda MD 20814 *TF:* 800-458-6223 ■ *Web:* curesearch.org	301-718-0047		668
Curie Metropolitan High School 4959 S Archer Ave .... Chicago IL 60632 *Web:* www.curiehs.org	773-535-2100		685
Curiosities Greeting Cards 21 Ashwood Ct .... Lancaster NY 14086 *Web:* www.curiosities.com	716-681-2801		130
Curis Inc 4 Maguire Rd .... Lexington MA 02421 *NASDAQ: CRIS* ■ *Web:* www.curis.com	617-503-6500	503-6501	85
Curlew Lake State Park 62 State Park Rd .... Republic WA 99166 *Web:* www.parks.state.wa.us	509-775-3592		565
Curley & Rothman LLC 1100 E Hector St Ste 425 .... Conshohocken PA 19428 *Web:* curleyrothman.com	610-834-8819		41
Curly Girl Design 57 Chapel St Ste 100 .... Newton MA 02458 *Web:* www.curlygirldesign.com	617-916-9431	916-9415	241
Curra's Grill 614 E Oltorf St .... Austin TX 78704 *Web:* www.currasgrill.com	512-444-0012		671
Curran & Connors Inc 140 Adams Ave Ste 20 C .... Hauppauge NY 11788 *Web:* www.curran-connors.com	631-435-0400	435-0422	344
Curran Group Inc 286 Memorial Ct .... Crystal Lake IL 60014 *Web:* www.currangroup.com	815-455-5100	455-7894	188-4
Curran Investment Management 30 S Pearl St Omni Plz 9th Fl .... Albany NY 12207 *TF:* 866-432-1246 ■ *Web:* www.curranllc.com	518-391-4200	391-4242	401
Currence & Associates LLC 4853 Rosewood Ct .... Duluth GA 30096 *Web:* www.currenceassociates.com	770-447-2424		194
Current Designs PO Box 247 .... Winona MN 55987 *Web:* www.cdkayak.com	507-454-5430	454-5448	710
Current History Inc 4225 Main St .... Philadelphia PA 19127 *TF:* 800-726-4464 ■ *Web:* www.currenthistory.com	215-482-4464	482-9197	637-10
Current House Productions LLC *LW Marketing & Consulting LLC* 3860 Via Del Rey .... Bonita Springs FL 34134 *Web:* www.lwmarketing.com	239-405-8250		511
Current Inc 30 Tyler St PO Box 120183 .... East Haven CT 06512 *TF:* 877-436-6542 ■ *Web:* currentcomposites.com	203-469-1337	467-8435	599
Current Newspaper 6930 Carroll Ave Ste 350 .... Takoma Park MD 20912 *Web:* current.org	301-270-7240		532-3
Current USA Inc 1005 E Woodmen Rd .... Colorado Springs CO 80920 **Fax Area Code:* 800 ■ *TF:* 800-848-2848 ■ *Web:* www.currentcatalog.com	719-531-2097	993-3232*	459
Current360 1324 E Washington St .... Louisville KY 40206 *Web:* current360.com	502-589-3567		5
Curriculum Associates Inc 153 Rangeway Rd .... North Billerica MA 01862 *TF:* 800-225-0248 ■ *Web:* www.curriculumassociates.com	800-225-0248	366-1158	637-2
Curriculum Technology LLC 835 Fifth Ave Ste 205 .... San Diego CA 92101 *Web:* curriculumtechnology.com	619-255-0380	255-0386	387
Currie Management Consultants Inc 292 Lincoln St .... Worcester MA 01605 *Web:* curriemanagement.com	508-752-9229		463

Name / Address	City	State	ZIP	Phone	Fax	Class
Currier Construction Inc 36 N 56th St *Web:* www.currierinc.com	Phoenix	AZ	85034	602-274-4370	285-9295	188
Currier Museum of Art 150 Ash St *Web:* www.currier.org	Manchester	NH	03104	603-669-6144	669-7194	520
Currier Plastics Inc 101 Columbus St *Web:* www.currierplastics.com	Auburn	NY	13021	315-255-1779	252-6443	604
Curries Co 1502 12th St NW *Web:* www.curries.com	Mason City	IA	50401	641-423-1334	424-8305	234
Currin Compliance Services Inc 14 Main St Ste 200 *Web:* currincompliance.com	Greenwich	NY	12834	518-692-2494		41
Currituck County 153 Courthouse Rd Ste 204 *Web:* www.co.currituck.nc.us	Currituck	NC	27929	252-232-2075	232-3551	338
Currituck County Board of Education 2958 Caratoke Hwy *Web:* www.currituck.k12.nc.us	Currituck	NC	27929	252-232-2223	232-3655	685
Curry College 1071 Blue Hill Ave *TF:* 800-669-0686 ■ *Web:* www.curry.edu	Milton	MA	02186	617-333-2210	333-2114	166
Curry County 417 Gidding St Ste 100 *Web:* www.currycounty.org	Clovis	NM	88101	575-763-6016	763-3656	338
Curry County 94235 Moore St Ste 125 *Web:* www.co.curry.or.us	Gold Beach	OR	97444	541-247-3233	247-3436	338
Curry Printing Ltd 1109 Pamela Dr *Web:* curryprintinginc.com	Euless	TX	76040	817-545-7777	545-9065	627
Curt G. Joa Inc 100 Crocker Ave PO Box 903 *Web:* www.joa.com	Sheboygan Falls	WI	53085	920-467-6136	467-2924	556
Curt Manufacturing Inc 6208 Industrial Dr *Web:* www.curtmfg.com	Eau Claire	WI	54701	715-831-8713		567
Curt Pringle & Associates LLC 1801 E Katella Ave Ste 1002 *Web:* curtpringle.com	Anaheim	CA	92805	714-939-9070	939-9080	636
Curtain & Bath Outlet 1 Ann & Hope Way *TF:* 877-228-7824 ■ *Web:* www.curtainandbathoutlet.com	Cumberland	RI	02864	401-722-1000		229
Curtain Call Costumes 333 E Seventh Ave *TF:* 888-808-0801 ■ *Web:* www.curtaincallcostumes.com	York	PA	17404	800-677-7053	839-1039	155-6
Curtain Wall Design & Consulting Inc 8070 Park Ln Ste 400 *Web:* cdc-usa.com	Dallas	TX	75231	972-437-4200		261
Curtin & Heefner 250 N Pennsylvania *Web:* www.curtinheefner.com	Morrisville	PA	19067	215-736-2521		428
Curtin-Hebert Company Inc 11 Forest St *Web:* www.curtinhebert.com	Gloversville	NY	12078	518-725-7157	773-3805	695
Curtis 1105 Western Ave **Fax Area Code:* 800 ■ *Web:* www.curtisinc.com	Cincinnati	OH	45203	513-621-8895	733-2878*	514
Curtis & Lucero Law Firm 215 Central Ave NW Ste 300 *Web:* curtislawfirm.org	Albuquerque	NM	87102	505-633-7998		41
Curtis 1000 Inc 1725 Breckinridge Pkwy Ste 500 **Fax Area Code:* 800 ■ *TF:* 877-287-8715 ■ *Web:* www.curtis1000.com	Duluth	GA	30096	678-380-9095	944-8817*	263
Curtis Blakely & Company PC 2403 Judson Rd *Web:* cbandco.com	Longview	TX	75605	903-758-0734		2
Curtis Contracting Inc 7481 Theron Rd *Web:* www.curtiscontracting.net	West Point	VA	23181	804-843-4633		302
Curtis Dyna-Fog Ltd 525 Park St *Web:* www.dynafog.com	Westfield	IN	46074	317-896-2561	896-3788	172
Curtis Flower Farm Inc 5211 Snow Camp Rd *Web:* curtisflowerfarm.com	Graham	NC	27253	336-376-3598		293
Curtis Industries Inc 2400 S 43rd St PO Box 343925 *TF:* 800-657-0853 ■ *Web:* www.curtisind.com	Milwaukee	WI	53219	414-649-4200	649-4279	815
Curtis Industries LLC 70 Hartwell St *TF:* 800-343-7676 ■ *Web:* www.curtisindustries.net	West Boylston	MA	01583	508-853-2200	854-3377	516
Curtis Institute of Music 1726 Locust St *TF:* 800-640-4155 ■ *Web:* www.curtis.edu	Philadelphia	PA	19103	215-893-5252	893-9065	166
Curtis Instruments Inc 200 Kisco Ave *TF:* 800-777-3433 ■ *Web:* curtisinstruments.com	Mount Kisco	NY	10549	914-666-2971		248
Curtis John R (Rep R - UT) 125 Cannon House Office Bldg *Web:* curtis.house.gov	Washington	DC	20515	202-225-7751		342-2
Curtis Liquor Stores Inc 790 Chief Justice Cushing Hwy *Web:* www.curtisliquors.com	Cohasset	MA	02025	781-383-9800		443
Curtis Liquor Stores Inc 486 Columbian St *Web:* curtisliquors.com	South Weymouth	MA	02190	781-331-2345		443
Curtis M. Phillips Center for the Performing Arts 3201 Hull Rd PO Box 112750 *TF:* 800-905-2787 ■ *Web:* performingarts.ufl.edu	Gainesville	FL	32611	352-392-1900	392-3775	572
Curtis Machine Company Inc 2500 E Trl St *TF:* 800-835-9166 ■ *Web:* www.curtismachine.com	Dodge City	KS	67801	620-227-7164		709
Curtis Metal Finishing Co 6645 Sims Dr *Web:* www.curtismetal.com	Sterling Heights	MI	48313	586-939-2850		481
Curtis Miller Insurance Agency Inc 1800 Blizzard Dr *Web:* www.curtismillerins.com	Parkersburg	WV	26101	304-485-6431	485-8139	390
Curtis Packaging Corp 44 Berkshire Rd *Web:* www.curtispackaging.com	Sandy Hook	CT	06482	203-426-5861	426-2684	101
Curtis Packing Co 2416 Randolph Ave *TF:* 800-852-7890 ■ *Web:* www.curtispackingcompany.com	Greensboro	NC	27406	336-275-7684	275-1901	473
Curtis Products Inc 401 N Bendix Dr *Web:* www.curtisproducts.com	South Bend	IN	46628	574-289-4891	232-9589	595
Curtis Restaurant Supply & Equipment Co 6577 E 40th St *TF:* 800-766-2878 ■ *Web:* www.curtisequipment.com	Tulsa	OK	74145	918-622-7390	665-0990	300
Curtis Steel Co (CSC) 6504 Hurst St *TF:* 800-749-4621 ■ *Web:* www.curtissteelco.com	Houston	TX	77008	713-861-4621	861-9718	485
Curtis Stout 5110 Hollywood Ave *Web:* www.chstout.com	Shreveport	LA	71109	318-636-7777		518
Curtis Universal Joint Company Inc 4 Birnie Ave *Web:* www.curtisuniversal.com	Springfield	MA	01107	413-737-0281	737-8430	620
Curtis, Brinckerhoff & Barrett PC 666 Summer St *Web:* curtisbb.com	Stamford	CT	06901	203-324-6777		41
Curtis, The 1405 Curtis St *TF:* 800-525-6651 ■ *Web:* www.thecurtis.com	Denver	CO	80202	303-571-0300	825-4301	379
Curtis-Maruyasu America Inc 665 Metts Dr *Web:* www.curtismaruyasu.com	Lebanon	KY	40033	270-692-2109		60
Curtiss-Wright Corp 10 Waterview Blvd 2nd Fl *NYSE:* CW ■ *TF:* 855-449-0995 ■ *Web:* www.curtisswright.com	Parsippany	NJ	07054	973-541-3700	541-3699	22
Curtis-Toledo Inc 1905 Kienlen Ave *TF:* 800-925-5431 ■ *Web:* us.fscurtis.com	Saint Louis	MO	63133	314-383-1300		172
Curved Glass Distributors Inc 72 Chapel St *Web:* www.curvedglassdist.com	Derby	CT	06418	203-735-4665		54
Cusack Wholesale Meat Inc 301 SW 12th St *TF:* 800-241-6328 ■ *Web:* www.cusackmeats.com	Oklahoma City	OK	73109	405-232-2114	232-2127	297-9
Cushing 420 W Huron St *Web:* www.cushingco.com	Chicago	IL	60654	312-266-8228		627
Cushing & Dolan PC 375 Totten Pond Rd Ste 200 *TF:* 888-759-5109 ■ *Web:* cushingdolan.com	Waltham	MA	02451	617-523-1555	523-5653	41
Cushing Academy 39 School St PO Box 8000 *Web:* www.cushing.org	Ashburnham	MA	01430	978-827-7000	827-6253	622
Cushing Terrell *CTA Architects Engineers* 13 N 23rd St *TF:* 800-757-9522 ■ *Web:* www.cushingterrell.com	Billings	MT	59101	406-248-7455		261
Cushing-Malloy Inc 1350 N Main St *TF:* 888-295-7244 ■ *Web:* www.cushing-malloy.com	Ann Arbor	MI	48104	734-663-8554	663-5731	626
Cushman & Marden Inc 56 Pulaski St PO Box 3001 **Fax Area Code:* 208 ■ *Web:* www.cushmanandmarden.com	Peabody	MA	01960	978-532-1670	677-5250*	34
Cushman & Wakefield Inc 1290 Avenue of the Americas *Web:* www.cushmanwakefield.com	New York	NY	10104	212-841-7500		652
Cushman School - Elementary School 592 NE 60th St *Web:* www.cushmanschool.org	Miami	FL	33137	305-757-1966		685
CUSO (Champaign-Urbana Symphony Orchestra) 701 Devonshire Dr Ste C-24 *Web:* cusymphony.org	Champaign	IL	61820	217-351-9139		573-3
Cusp Dental Research Inc 381 Pearl St *Web:* cuspdental.com	Malden	MA	02148	781-388-0078		363
Cusseta-Chattahoochee County PO Box 120 *Web:* chattahoocheeclerkofcourt.com	Cusseta	GA	31805	706-989-3424	989-1508	338
Custer County PO Box 300 **Fax Area Code:* 580 ■ *Web:* custer.okcounties.org	Arapaho	OK	73620	405-522-0018	331-1131*	338
Custer County 431 S 10th *Web:* www.co.custer.ne.us	Broken Bow	NE	68822	308-872-5701		338
Custer County 801 E Main Ave PO Box 385 *Web:* www.co.custer.id.us	Challis	ID	83226	208-879-2360	879-5246	338
Custer County PO Box 150 *Web:* www.custercountygov.com	Westcliffe	CO	81252	719-783-2441	783-2885	338
Custer Public Power District 625 E South St PO Box 10 *TF:* 888-749-2453 ■ *Web:* www.custerpower.com	Broken Bow	NE	68822	308-872-2451	872-2378	245
Custer State Park 13329 US Hwy 16A *Web:* gfp.sd.gov	Custer	SD	57730	605-255-4515	255-4460	565
Cust-O-Fab Inc 8888 W 21st St *Web:* www.custofab.com	Sand Springs	OK	74063	918-245-6685		91
Custom Air 5338 Pinkney Ave *TF:* 888-856-4507 ■ *Web:* customairinc.com	Sarasota	FL	34233	888-856-4507		610
Custom Air Products & Services Inc 35 Southbelt Industrial Dr *Web:* customairproducts.com	Houston	TX	77047	713-460-9009		454
Custom Aircraft Interiors 3701 Industry Ave *Web:* customaircraftinteriors.com	Lakewood	CA	90712	562-426-5098	490-0213	689
Custom Aluminum Products Inc 540 Division St **Fax Area Code:* 847 ■ *TF:* 800-745-6333 ■ *Web:* www.custom-aluminum.com	South Elgin	IL	60177	800-745-6333	741-2266*	485
Custom Assembly Inc 1199 E Town Rd TT *Web:* www.customassemblyinc.com	Danbury	WI	54830	651-261-5131		735
Custom Automated Controls Inc 2019 Jefferson Terr *Web:* www.custautocont.com	New Iberia	LA	70560	337-369-1523		45
Custom Automated Services Inc 311 25th St NW *Web:* customautomatedservices.com	Fayette	AL	35555	205-932-7287	932-5101	253
Custom Benefits Insurance Group Inc 4204 Martin Rd Ste A *Web:* cbigi.com	Walled Lake	MI	48390	248-960-5100	960-5132	390
Custom Bilt Cabinet and Supply Inc 6000 Union Ave *Web:* www.custombiltcabinet.com	Shreveport	LA	71108	318-865-1412	865-1354	191-3
Custom Brackets 32 Alpha Pk *TF:* 800-530-2289 ■ *Web:* www.custombrackets.com	Cleveland	OH	44143	440-446-0819		454
Custom Builder Supply Company Inc PO Box 413 *Web:* www.custombuildersupply.com	Williamsburg	VA	23187	757-229-5150	253-7568	191-3

Company	City	State	ZIP	Phone	Fax	Class
Custom Building Products 13001 Seal Beach Blvd *TF:* 800-272-8786 ■ *Web:* www.custombuildingproducts.com	Seal Beach	CA	90740	562-598-8808		3
Custom Business Forms Inc 210 Edge Pl *Web:* www.cbfnet.com	Minneapolis	MN	55418	612-789-0002	789-6321	110
Custom Cable Corp 242 Butler St *TF:* 800-832-3600 ■ *Web:* www.customwireandcable.com	Westbury	NY	11590	516-334-3600		116
Custom Cable Industries Inc 3221 Cherry Palm Dr **Fax Area Code:* 813 ■ *TF:* 800-552-2232 ■ *Web:* customcable.com	Tampa	FL	33619	800-446-2232	626-9630*	189-4
Custom Canvas Prints 3030 S Main St Ste 400 *TF:* 877-220-9114 ■ *Web:* www.customcanvasprints.com	Salt Lake City	UT	84115	877-220-9114		627
Custom Chrome Inc 155 E Main Ave Ste 150 *TF:* 800-729-3332 ■ *Web:* www.customchrome.com	Morgan Hill	CA	95037	408-825-5000		61
Custom Coils Inc 4000 Industrial Way *Web:* www.ccoils.com	Benicia	CA	94510	707-752-8633	752-8637	482
Custom Communications Inc 1661 Greenview Dr SW *TF:* 855-288-5522 ■ *Web:* www.custom-alarm.com	Rochester	MN	55902	507-288-5522	287-0757	693
Custom Computer Specialists Inc (CCS) 70 Suffolk Ct *TF:* 800-598-8989 ■ *Web:* www.customonline.com	Hauppauge	NY	11788	800-598-8989	986-5518	180
Custom Computer Systems of Wisconsin Inc 6406 Odana Rd *Web:* www.iccnow.com	Madison	WI	53719	608-277-8000	276-6406	180
Custom Computing Corp 11135 Mill Valley Rd *Web:* ccccorp.com	Omaha	NE	68154	402-341-2197	341-8565	177
Custom Consulting Associates LLC 1112 SW 118th Pl *Web:* www.cca-llc.net	Oklahoma City	OK	73170	405-691-3417		180
Custom Control Manufacturer of Kansas Inc 5601 Merriam Dr *Web:* www.customcontrolmfr.com	Merriam	KS	66203	913-722-0343		201
Custom Control Sensors Inc 21111 Plummer St *Web:* www.ccsdualsnap.com	Chatsworth	CA	91311	818-341-4610	709-0426	201
Custom Control Solutions Inc 8500 Fowler Ave *Web:* www.ccsinc-florida.com	Pensacola	FL	32534	850-473-8704		729
Custom Controls Co 5712 Yale St *Web:* www.customcontrolsco.com	Houston	TX	77076	713-666-3258	666-2486	14
Custom Controls Technology Inc 2230 W 77th St *TF:* 888-693-4495 ■ *Web:* cct-inc.com	Hialeah	FL	33016	305-805-3700		261
Custom Coolers LLC 5609 Azle Ave **Fax Area Code:* 817 ■ *Web:* www.customcoolerstx.com	Fort Worth	TX	76114	800-627-0488	626-3737*	664
Custom Craft Controls Inc 1620 Triplett Blvd *Web:* www.customcraftcontrols.com	Akron	OH	44306	330-630-9599	630-3626	729
Custom Culinary 2505 S Finley Rd *TF:* 800-621-8827 ■ *Web:* www.customculinary.com	Lombard	IL	60148	800-621-8827		296-18
Custom Cylinders Inc 700 Industrial Dr Ste I *Web:* www.customcylinders.com	Cary	IL	60013	847-516-6467		641
Custom Cylinders International Inc 1220 Enterprise Dr *TF:* 800-779-5544 ■ *Web:* www.customcylindersintinc.com	Winchester	KY	40391	859-744-5618	744-5835	91
Custom Design of Troy LLC 7400 Triangle Dr Ste A *Web:* customdes.com	Sterling Heights	MI	48314	586-991-0930		261
Custom Direct Inc 715 E Irving Park Rd *Web:* www.customdirect.com	Roselle	IL	60172	630-529-1936		5
Custom Electric Manufacturing Co 48941 W Rd *Web:* custom-electric.com	Wixom	MI	48393	248-305-7700	305-7705	318
Custom Electronic Design & Installation Assn (CEDIA) 7150 Winton Dr Ste 300 *TF:* 800-669-5329 ■ *Web:* cedia.net	Indianapolis	IN	46268	317-328-4336	735-4012	49-19
Custom Electronics Co 7851 AirPark Rd *Web:* customelectronicsco.com	Gaithersburg	MD	20879	301-258-0811	948-0769	625
Custom Engineering Co 2800 Mc Clelland Ave *Web:* www.customeng.com	Erie	PA	16510	814-898-2800		480
Custom Engineering Inc 12760 E US Hwy 40 *Web:* www.customengr.com	Independence	MO	64055	816-350-1473		261
Custom Environmental Services Inc 8041 N I 70 Frontage Rd Unit 11 *TF:* 800-310-7445 ■ *Web:* www.customsvcs.com	Arvada	CO	80002	303-423-9949		667
Custom Equipment Design Inc 1057 Hwy 80 E *Web:* www.cedpackaging.net	Monroe	LA	71203	318-345-2222	343-0452	547
Custom Exhibits Corp 1830 N Indianwood Ave *TF:* 800-664-0309 ■ *Web:* www.customexhibits.com	Broken Arrow	OK	74012	918-250-2121		393
Custom Faberkin Inc 640 Fond Du Lac Ave *Web:* www.faberkin.com	Fond du Lac	WI	54935	920-921-5660	921-2840	67
Custom Fiberglass Manufacturing Corp *Snugtop* 1711 Harbor Ave PO Box 121 *TF:* 800-768-4867 ■ *Web:* www.snugtop.com	Long Beach	CA	90813	562-432-5454	435-2992	120
Custom Global Logistics LLC 317 W Lake St *TF:* 800-446-8336 ■ *Web:* www.customgl.com	Northlake	IL	60164	800-446-8336		314
Custom Helicopters Ltd 401 Helicopter Dr *Web:* www.customheli.com	Saint Andrews	MB	R1A3P7	204-338-7953		13
Custom Industries Inc 215 Aloe Rd	Greensboro	NC	27409	336-299-2885		744
Custom Laminations Inc 932 Market St *Web:* www.customlaminations.com	Paterson	NJ	07513	973-279-6916		745-2
Custom Learning Designs Inc 375 Concord Ave *Web:* www.cldinc.com	Belmont	MA	02478	617-489-1702		242
Custom Light & Sound Inc 2506 Guess Rd *Web:* customlightandsound.com	Durham	NC	27705	919-286-0011	286-1130	52
Custom Machine & Tool Inc 1723 Swepsonville Rd *Web:* custommachineandtool.com	Graham	NC	27253	336-226-1643	226-8464	454
Custom Machining Services Inc 326 N 400 E *Web:* www.customcrimp.com	Valparaiso	IN	46383	219-462-6128	464-2773	454
Custom Magnetics Inc 801 W Main St *Web:* www.custommag.com	North Manchester	IN	46962	260-982-8508	982-4942	767
Custom Management Group LLC 154 Hansen Rd *Web:* www.custommanagement.com	Charlottesville	VA	22911	434-971-4788	977-1856	47
Custom Metal Crafters Inc 815 N Mountain Rd *Web:* www.custom-metal.com	Newington	CT	06111	860-953-4210	953-1746	594
Custom Metal Fabricators Inc 7601 Whitepine Rd *TF:* 800-220-4084 ■ *Web:* custommetalfabricators.com	Richmond	VA	23237	800-220-4084		697
Custom Metalcraft Inc 2332 E Division St PO Box 10587 *Web:* custom-metalcraft.com	Springfield	MO	65808	417-612-7016		697
Custom Microwave Components Inc 44249 Old Warm Sprng Blvd *Web:* www.customwave.com	Fremont	CA	94538	510-651-3434	651-1054	253
Custom Millwork Inc 2298 N Second St *Web:* www.custommillworkinc.com	North Saint Paul	MN	55109	651-770-2356		499
Custom Mold Engineering Inc 9780 S Franklin Dr *TF:* 800-448-2005 ■ *Web:* www.custommold.com	Franklin	WI	53132	414-421-5444		757
Custom Molded Products LLC 92 Grant St *Web:* www.custommolded.com	Wilmington	OH	45177	937-382-1070		596
Custom Pack Inc 662 Exton Cmns *TF:* 800-722-7005 ■ *Web:* www.custompackinc.com	Exton	PA	19341	610-363-1900	321-2526	601
Custom Pack Inc 11661 Cardinal Cir *Web:* custompackincorporated.com	Garden Grove	CA	92843	714-534-5353		296-20
Custom Packaging Inc 1315 W Baddour Pkwy *Web:* www.hoodcontainer.com	Lebanon	TN	37087	615-444-6025		100
Custom Packing & Inspecting Inc 5232 Tod Ave SW *Web:* custompacking.com	Lordstown	OH	44481	330-399-8961	395-2990	393
Custom Pak Illinois Inc 361 Keyes Ave *Web:* www.cpillinois.com	Hampshire	IL	60140	847-683-3388	683-3110	393
Custom Paper Tubes 15900 Industrial Pkwy PO Box 35140 *TF:* 800-343-8823 ■ *Web:* www.custompapertubes.com	Cleveland	OH	44135	216-362-2964	362-2980	548
Custom Pipe & Coupling Inc 10560 Fern St PO Box 978 *TF:* 800-553-3058 ■ *Web:* www.custompipe.com	Stanton	CA	90680	714-761-8801	761-5794	595
Custom Plastic Developments Inc 2710 N John Young Pky *Web:* www.cpdfl.com	Kissimmee	FL	34741	407-847-3054	847-8687	604
Custom Plastics Inc 1940 Lunt Ave *Web:* www.customplasticsinc.com	Elk Grove Village	IL	60007	847-439-6770		596
Custom Poly Bag Inc 9465 Edison St NE *TF:* 800-715-1479 ■ *Web:* www.custompolybag.com	Alliance	OH	44601	330-935-2408	935-2400	345
Custom Processing Services Inc 2 Birchmont Dr *Web:* www.customprocessingservices.com	Reading	PA	19606	610-779-7001		225
Custom Products of Litchfield Inc 1715 S Sibley Ave *TF:* 800-222-5463 ■ *Web:* www.cpcabs.com	Litchfield	MN	55355	320-693-3221		273
Custom Profiles Inc 256 Benjamin H Hill Dr SE **Fax Area Code:* 229 ■ *TF:* 800-524-3053 ■ *Web:* www.customprofiles.com	Fitzgerald	GA	31750	800-524-3053	423-3724*	599
Custom Pultrusions Inc 1331 S Chillicothe Rd	Aurora	OH	44202	330-562-5201		599
Custom Resins Inc 1421 Hwy 136 W *Web:* customresins.com	Henderson	KY	42420	270-826-7641	827-8509	604
Custom Rollform Products Inc 3991 Green Park Rd *Web:* www.customrollformproducts.com	Saint Louis	MO	63125	314-894-3903		494
Custom Roto Mold Inc 555 22nd St S *Web:* customrotomold.com	Benson	MN	56215	320-842-3357		596
Custom Seafood Services Inc 3088 Kindred Ave *Web:* www.customseafoodservices.com	Tokeland	WA	98590	360-267-2666	267-2668	296-13
Custom Seating Inc 341 S 41st St *TF:* 800-223-7328 ■ *Web:* www.customseating.com	Muskogee	OK	74403	800-223-7328		91
Custom Sensors & Technology 531 Axminister Dr *Web:* www.customsensors.com	Fenton	MO	63026	636-305-0666		419
Custom Sensors Inc 30 York St *Web:* www.csensors.com	Auburn	NY	13021	315-252-3741	253-6910	173-1
Custom Service Plastics Inc 201 Sheridan Springs Rd *Web:* www.csplastics.com	Lake Geneva	WI	53147	262-248-9557	248-9603	604
Custom Staffing Inc 9995 Gate Pky N Ste 100 *TF:* 800-582-0828 ■ *Web:* thecsicompanies.com	Jacksonville	FL	32246	904-338-9515	338-9520	631
Custom Stamping Inc 4855 Hytech Dr *Web:* www.customstampinginc.com	Carson City	NV	89706	775-884-3003	884-1719	488
Custom Stone 2999 Teagarden St *Web:* www.customstoneusa.com	San Leandro	CA	94577	510-667-0099		189-2
Custom Stud Inc 8415 220th St W *Web:* www.customstud.com	Lakeville	MN	55044	952-985-7000		351
Custom Systems & Controls 30 Main St Ste 6 *Web:* custom-sys.com	Ashland	MA	01721	508-879-4390		180

	Phone	Fax	Class
Custom Toll Free 10940 Wilshire Blvd 17th Fl................Los Angeles CA 90024 *TF:* 800-287-8664 ■ *Web:* www.customtollfree.com	855-800-3030		387
Custom Tool and Die Co 7059 Red Arrow Hwy ....Stevensville MI 49127 *Web:* www.ctd1.com	269-465-9130	465-4077	757
Custom Transfer Inc 23512 230th St.........................Long Prairie MN 56347 *Web:* www.custom-transfer.com	320-732-3013	732-3016	780
Custom Ultrasonics Inc 144 Railroad Dr ....Ivyland PA 18974 *Web:* www.customultrasonics.com	215-364-1477	364-7674	425
Custom Window Systems Inc 1900 SW 44th Ave ....Ocala FL 34474 *Web:* www.cws.cc	352-368-6922		234
Custom Wire Industries Inc S83w18787 Saturn Dr ....Muskego WI 53150 *Web:* www.customwireind.com	262-679-9700		73
Customedialabs 460 E Swedesford Rd Ste 2020.................Wayne PA 19087 *Web:* www.customedialabs.com	610-225-0350		7
Customer Elation Inc 9065 Lyndale Ave S ....Bloomington MN 55420 *Web:* customerelation.com	952-653-0801		195
Customer Group, The 641 W Lake St Ste 304.......................Chicago IL 60661 *TF:* 844-802-7867 ■ *Web:* www.customergroup.com	844-802-7867		463
Customer Insight Group Inc 760 Bridger Pt ....LaFayette CO 80026 *Web:* www.customerinsightgroup.com	303-422-9758		449
Customer Magnetism 2697 International Pkwy 7 1st Fl...........Virginia Beach VA 23452 *Web:* www.customermagnetism.com	757-689-2875		7
Customer Paradigm Inc 5353 Manhattan Cir Ste 103...................Boulder CO 80303 *TF:* 888-772-0777 ■ *Web:* www.customerparadigm.com	303-499-9318		225
Customer Service Delivery Platform (CSDP) 15615 Alton Pkwy Ste 310......................Irvine CA 92618 *TF:* 888-741-2737 ■ *Web:* www.csdpcorp.com	888-741-2737		177
Customer Solutions Group (CSG) 1355 S Colorado Blvd Ste 510..................Denver CO 80222 *TF:* 877-274-5221 ■ *Web:* insidesaleslab.com	303-770-6381	770-6576	194
Customer Value Partners Inc 3701 Pender Dr Ste 200.......................Fairfax VA 22030 *Web:* www.cvpcorp.com	703-345-9100	991-5639	317
Customized Distribution Services Inc 20 Harry Shupe Blvd.........................Wharton NJ 07885 *Web:* www.cdslogistics.com	973-366-5090	537-8709	803-1
Customized Energy Solutions Ltd 1528 Walnut St 22nd Fl ....Philadelphia PA 19102 *Web:* ces-ltd.com	215-875-9440		196
Customized Performance Inc 780 Montague Expy Ste 201..................San Jose CA 95131 *Web:* custgroup.com	408-437-1720		104
Custom-Pak Inc 1131 Roosevelt St..............Clinton IA 52732 *Web:* www.custom-pak.com	563-242-1801	244-5362	199
Cut Bank Pioneer Press PO Box 847 517 E Main.....................Cut Bank MT 59427 *Web:* www.cutbankpioneerpress.com	406-873-2201	873-2443	189-6
Cut Flower Wholesale Inc 2122 Faulkner Rd NE ....Atlanta GA 30324 *Web:* www.cutflower.com	404-320-1619	634-7922	293
Cut to Size Technology Inc 345 S Fairbank St...........................Addison IL 60101 *Web:* www.cuttosizetech.com	630-543-8328		683
Cutco Corp 1116 E State St ....Olean NY 14760 *Web:* www.cutco.com	716-372-3111		222
Cutera Inc 3240 Bayshore Blvd .... Brisbane CA 94005 *NASDAQ: CUTR* ■ *TF:* 888-428-8372 ■ *Web:* www.cutera.com	415-657-5500	330-2444	476
Cuthbert Greenhouses Inc 4900 Hendron Rd ....Groveport OH 43125 *TF:* 800-321-1939 ■ *Web:* www.cuthbertgreenhouse.com	614-836-3866	836-3767	369
Cut-Heal Animal Care Products Inc 923 S Cedar Hill Rd .... Cedar Hill TX 75104 **Fax Area Code:* 240	972-293-9700	597-2157*	584
Cutlass Capital LLC 229 Marlborough St..........Boston MA 02116 *Web:* www.cutlasscapital.com	617-867-0820		792
Cutler Associates Inc 43 Harvard St...........Worcester MA 01609 *Web:* www.cutlerdb.com	508-757-7500		186
Cutler Group LP 101 Montgomery St Ste 700.............San Francisco CA 94104 *Web:* www.cutlergrouplp.com	415-645-6745		690
Cutler Group, The 201 Cajon St...............Redlands CA 92373 *TF:* 800-843-6054 ■ *Web:* churchwest.com	909-307-8500	307-1245	390
Cutler Investment Counsel LLC 525 Bigham Knoll........................Jacksonville OR 97530 *Web:* www.cutler.com	541-770-9000		401
Cutler Repaving Inc 921 E 27th St.............Lawrence KS 66046 *Web:* www.cutlerrepaving.com	785-843-1524	843-3942	188-4
Cutlery & More LLC 135 Prairie Lake Rd ....East Dundee IL 60118 *TF:* 800-650-9866 ■ *Web:* www.cutleryandmore.com	800-650-9866		362
Cutten Realty Inc 2120 Campton Rd Ste C .... Eureka CA 95503 *TF:* 800-776-4458 ■ *Web:* www.cuttenrealty.com	707-445-8811		652
Cutter & Buck Inc 701 N 34th St Ste 400 ....Seattle WA 98103 *TF:* 800-713-7810 ■ *Web:* cutterbuck.com	888-338-9944		155-1
Cutter Aviation 2802 E Old Tower Rd ....Phoenix AZ 85034 *TF:* 800-234-5382 ■ *Web:* cutteraviation.com	602-273-1237	275-4010	24
Cutter Consortium 37 Broadway Ste 1..........Arlington MA 02474 *Web:* www.cutter.com	781-648-8700	648-8707	531-3
Cutter Lumber Products 10 Rickenbacker Cir ....Livermore CA 94550 *Web:* cutterlumber.com	925-443-5959	443-0648	551
Cutter's Crabhouse 2001 Western Ave............Seattle WA 98121 *Web:* cutterscrabhouse.com	206-448-4884		671
Cutters Inc 515 N State St Ste 2500 ....Chicago IL 60654 *Web:* cutters.com	312-644-2500		512
Cutting Edge Countertops Inc 1300 Flagship Dr ....Perrysburg OH 43551 *TF:* 888-515-8677 ■ *Web:* www.cectops.com	419-873-9500		115
Cutting Edge Metal Fabrication Inc 220-A Tryon Rd .... Raleigh NC 27603 *Web:* cemfinc.com	919-865-1534		697
Cutting Edge Network Technologies 2211 Lee Rd Ste 207 ....Winter Park FL 32789 *Web:* cuttingedgenet.com	407-658-9009		177
Cutting Edge Networked Storage 435 W Bradley Ave Ste C ....El Cajon CA 92020 *TF:* 800-257-1666 ■ *Web:* www.cuttedge.com	619-258-7800		177
Cutting Edge Products LLC 350 Turk Hill Pk .... Fairport NY 14450 *TF:* 800-889-4184 ■ *Web:* www.celasers.com	800-889-4184		476
Cuyahoga Community College *Western* 11000 Pleasant Valley Rd .... Parma OH 44130 *TF:* 800-954-8742 ■ *Web:* www.tri-c.edu	216-987-2800	987-5071	162
Cuyahoga County 1219 Ontario St ....Cleveland OH 44113 *Web:* www.cuyahogacounty.us	216-443-7010	443-5091	338
Cuyahoga County Public Library 2111 Snow Rd .... Parma OH 44134 *TF:* 800-749-5560 ■ *Web:* cuyahogalibrary.org	216-398-1800		434-3
Cuyahoga Falls Chamber of Commerce (CFCC) 151 Portage Trl Ste 1 .... Cuyahoga Falls OH 44221 *TF:* 800-248-4040 ■ *Web:* www.cfchamber.com	330-929-6756	929-4278	139
Cuyahoga Molded Plastics Corp 1265 Babbitt Rd ....Cleveland OH 44132 *TF:* 800-805-9549 ■ *Web:* www.cuyahogaplastics.com	216-261-2744	261-3537	604
Cuyahoga Valley National Park 15610 Vaughn Rd..........................Brecksville OH 44141 **Fax Area Code:* 440 ■ *TF:* 800-445-9667 ■ *Web:* www.nps.gov	216-524-1497	546-5989*	564
Cuyamaca College 900 Rancho San Diego Pkwy ....El Cajon CA 92019 *Web:* cuyamaca.edu	619-660-4275	660-4575	162
Cuyuna Country State Recreation Area 307 3rd St.................................Ironton MN 56455 *Web:* www.dnr.state.mn.us	218-546-5926	546-7369	565
CV Ice Company Inc 83796 Date Ave.............. Indio CA 92201	760-347-3529		380
CVA (Connecticut Valley Arms) 1270 Progress Center Ave Ste 1............Lawrenceville GA 30043 *Web:* cva.com	770-449-4687		284
CVAC Systems Inc 26820 Hobie Cir Ste B ....Murrieta CA 92562 *TF:* 866-753-2822 ■ *Web:* cvacsystems.com	951-699-2086		250
CVC (Columbia Ventures Corp) 14301 SE 1st St Ste 201....................Vancouver WA 98684 *Web:* colventures.com	360-816-1840		405
CVD Diamond Corp 2061 Piper Ln .... London ON N5V3S5 *TF:* 877-457-9903 ■ *Web:* www.cvddiamond.com	519-457-9903		481
CVD Equipment Corp 1860 Smithtown Ave......................Ronkonkoma NY 11779 *Web:* www.cvdequipment.com	631-981-7081	981-7095	695
CVEA (Copper Valley Electric Association Inc) Mile 187 Glenn Hwy PO Box 45..............Glennallen AK 99588 *TF:* 866-835-2832 ■ *Web:* www.cvea.org	907-822-3211	822-5586	245
CVG International America Inc 7200 NW 19th St Ste 402....................... Miami FL 33126	305-470-8100		385
Cvikota Medical Business Services 2031 32nd St S............................ La Crosse WI 54601 *TF:* 800-657-5175 ■ *Web:* www.thebillingpros.com	608-788-8103	788-6613	396
C-Ville Weekly 308 E Main St............. Charlottesville VA 22902 *Web:* www.c-ville.com	434-817-2749	817-2758	532-5
CVMA (Canadian Veterinary Medical Assn) 339 Booth St................................. Ottawa ON K1R7K1 *TF:* 800-567-2862 ■ *Web:* www.canadianveterinarians.net	613-236-1162	236-9681	49-8
CVMC (Central Vermont Medical Ctr) 130 Fisher Rd...............................Berlin VT 05602 *Web:* www.cvmc.org	802-371-4100		374-3
CVS Health One CVS Dr....................Woonsocket RI 02895 *NYSE: CVS* ■ *TF:* 800-746-7287 ■ *Web:* www.cvshealth.com	401-765-1500		237
CVSP (Chuckawalla Valley State Prison) 19025 Wiley's Well Rd PO Box 2289 .... Blythe CA 92226 *Web:* cdcr.ca.gov	760-922-5300	922-6855	213
CW (College of Westchester) 325 Central Ave .... White Plains NY 10606 **Fax Area Code:* 914 ■ *TF:* 800-660-7093 ■ *Web:* www.cw.edu	800-660-7093	948-5441*	800
CW Brabender Instruments Inc 50 E Wesley St ....South Hackensack NJ 07606 *Web:* www.cwbrabender.com	201-343-8425		407
CW Brower Inc 413 S Riverside Dr .... Modesto CA 95354	209-523-5447		345
CW Cole & Company Inc 2560 Rosemead Blvd ....South El Monte CA 91733 *Web:* www.colelighting.com	626-443-2473	443-9253	439
CW Driver 468 N Rosemead Blvd ....Pasadena CA 91107 *TF:* 855-300-4774 ■ *Web:* www.cwdriver.com	626-351-8800	351-8880	186
CW Industries 130 James Way ....Southampton PA 18966 *Web:* www.cwind.com	215-355-7080	355-1088	729
CW Matthews Contracting Company Inc 1600 Kenview Dr ....Marietta GA 30061 *Web:* www.cwmatthews.com	770-422-7520		188-4
CW Network LLC, The 3300 W Olive Ave.........Burbank CA 91505 *Web:* www.cwtv.com	818-977-2500		738
CW Ohio Inc 1209 Maple Ave..................Conneaut OH 44030 *TF:* 800-677-5801 ■ *Web:* www.cwohio.com	440-593-5800	593-4545	499
CW Plumbing & Design Inc 41683 Date St...............................Murrieta CA 92562	951-894-7703		189-10
CW Stickley Inc 69 Middletown Rd............ Fairmont WV 26554 *Web:* www.cwstickley.com	304-363-0830		358
CW Wright Construction 11500 Iron Bridge Rd .... Chester VA 23831 *Web:* www.cwwright.com	804-768-1054	768-6057	188-10
CW11 Seattle - KSTW 2211 Elliott Ave Ste 200 .... Seattle WA 98121 *TF:* 866-313-5789 ■ *Web:* cwseattle.cbslocal.com	206-441-1111	861-8915	741
CWA (Communications Workers of America) 501 Third St NW.........................Washington DC 20001 *Web:* www.cwa union.org	202-434-1100		414

	Phone	Fax	Class
CWB (Central West Ballet Co) 5039 Pendecost Dr Ste B2 Modesto CA 95356 *Web:* cwballet.org	209-576-8957	576-1308	573-1
CWB (Cannon Wright Blount) 756 Ridge Lake Blvd Memphis TN 38120 *TF:* 888-681-9392 ■ *Web:* www.cannonwrightblount.com	901-685-7500	685-7569	2
CWB Maxium Financial 30 Vogell Rd Ste 1 Richmond Hill ON L4B3K6 *TF:* 800-379-5888 ■ *Web:* www.cwbmaxium.com	905-780-6150		569
CWB Property Management 5775 Perimeter Dr Ste 190 Dublin OH 43017 *Web:* cwbpm.com	614-793-2244	793-2328	652
CWC Energy Services Corp 205 - Fifth Ave SW Bow Valley Sq II Ste 610 Calgary AB T2P2V7 *TF:* 877-341-3933 ■ *Web:* www.cwcenergyservices.com	403-264-2177	264-2842	539
CWC Industries Inc 185 Foundry St Ste 2 Newark NJ 07105 *Web:* www.customfoilscompany.com	973-344-1434	589-1617	492
CWE 1561 E Orangethorpe Ave Ste 240 Fullerton CA 92831 *Web:* cwecorp.com	714-526-7500		261
CWF (Campaign for Working Families) PO Box 1222 Merrifield VA 22116 *Web:* www.cwfpac.com	703-671-8800		615
CWF (Canadian Wildlife Federation) 350 Michael Cowpland Dr Kanata ON K2M2W1 *TF:* 800-563-9453 ■ *Web:* www.cwf-fcf.org	613-599-9594	599-4428	48-13
CWF (California Wellness Foundation) 6320 Canoga Ave Ste 1700 Woodland Hills CA 91367 *Web:* www.calwellness.org	818-702-1900	702-1999	303
CWI Gifts & Crafts 77 Cypress St SW Reynoldsburg OH 43068 *TF:* 800-666-5858 ■ *Web:* www.shopcwi.com	740-964-6210	964-6212	44
CWISP (Community WISP Inc) 235 Bear Hill Rd Ste 102A Waltham MA 02451 **Fax Area Code:* 781 ■ *TF:* 866-863-1035 ■ *Web:* www.communitywisp.com	866-863-1035	658-2087*	224
CWLA (Child Welfare League of America) 727 15th St NW 12th Fl Washington DC 20005 *Web:* www.cwla.org	202-688-4200	833-1689	48-6
CWP (Clear Water Press) PO Box 62 Olathe KS 66051 **Fax Area Code:* 970 ■ *TF:* 800-401-4550 ■ *Web:* www.clearwaterpress.com	888-481-4550	692-2241*	637-2
CWPS Inc 14120 A Sullyfield Cir Chantilly VA 20151 *TF:* 877-297-7472 ■ *Web:* www.cwps.com	703-263-9539		180
CWR Manufacturing Corp 7000 Fly Rd East Syracuse NY 13057 *Web:* www.cwronline.com	315-437-1032	437-1493	697
CWRA (Canadian Water Resources Assn) 176 Gloucester St Ste 320 Ottawa ON K2P0A6 *Web:* www.cwra.org	613-237-9363	594-5190	48-13
CWS (Clean Water Systems Intl) 2322 Marina Dr Klamath Falls OR 97601 *Web:* www.cleanwatersysintl.com	541-882-9993	882-9994	806
Cws Insurance Agency Inc 435 E Kennedy St Spartanburg SC 29302 *Web:* cwsinsurance.com	864-583-1451		390
CWU (Church Women United) 475 Riverside Dr Ste 243 New York NY 10115 *TF:* 800-298-5551 ■ *Web:* www.churchwomenunited.net	212-870-2347	870-2338	48-20
CWV (Carleton-Willard Village) 100 Old Billerica Rd Bedford MA 01730 *Web:* www.cwvillage.org	781-275-8700	275-5787	672
cxLoyalty Group Inc 6 High Ridge Pk Stamford CT 06905 *TF:* 800-622-4863 ■ *Web:* www.cxloyalty.com	800-622-4863		196
CXM (Chicago Extruded Metals Co) 1601 S 54th Ave Cicero IL 60804 **Fax Area Code:* 708 ■ *TF:* 800-323-8102 ■ *Web:* www.cxm.com	800-323-8102	780-3479*	485
CXR Larus Corp 894 Faulstich Ct San Jose CA 95112 *Web:* www.cxr.com	909-942-3207		248
CXT Inc 3808 N Sullivan Rd Bldg 7 Spokane WA 99216 *TF:* 800-696-5700 ■ *Web:* www.cxtinc.com	509-921-0700		183
CXtec 5404 S Bay Rd Syracuse NY 13221 *TF:* 800-767-3282 ■ *Web:* www.cxtec.com	315-476-3000	455-1800	814
Cyan Worlds Inc 14617 N Newport Hwy Mead WA 99021 *Web:* cyan.com	509-468-0807	467-2209	178-6
Cyanotech Corp 73-4460 Queen Kaahumanu Hwy Ste 102 Kailua-Kona HI 96740 *NASDAQ: CYAN* ■ *TF:* 800-453-1187 ■ *Web:* www.cyanotech.com	808-326-1353	329-4533	479
Cyber 360 Inc 1600 Providence Hwy Walpole MA 02081 *Web:* www.cyber360solutions.com	781-438-4380		631
Cyber Acoustics LLC 3109 NE 109th Ave Vancouver WA 98682 *Web:* www.cyberacoustics.com	360-883-0333		173-5
Cyber City 224 W 30th St Rm 1100 New York NY 10001 *Web:* cybercity.nyc	212-633-0649		196
Cyber Digital Inc 400 Oser Ave Ste 1650 Hauppauge NY 11788 *OTC: CYBD* ■ *Web:* www.cyberdigitalinc.com	631-231-1200	231-1446	735
Cyber F/X Inc 2940 N Naomi St Burbank CA 91504 *Web:* www.cyberfx.com	818-246-2911	273-4963	180
Cyber Korp Inc 125 Fairfield Way Ste 380 Bloomingdale IL 60108 *Web:* www.cyberkorp.com	630-980-4416		180
Cyber Power Systems Inc 4241 12th Ave E Ste 400 Shakopee MN 55379 *TF:* 877-297-6937 ■ *Web:* www.cyberpowersystems.com	952-403-9500	403-0009	253
Cyber Press 3380 Viso Ct Santa Clara CA 95054 *Web:* www.cyberpress.net	408-970-9200		627
Cyber Pro Systems Inc 1 World Trade Ctr Ste 2400 Long Beach CA 90831	562-256-3800	256-3899	225
Cyber Sytes 19981 Panama Cty Bch Pkwy Panama City Beach FL 32413 *Web:* www.cysy.com	850-233-5514	234-2440	396
CyberAccess Inc 7290 Ober Ln Chagrin Falls OH 44023 *TF:* 877-524-5005 ■ *Web:* www.cyberacc.com	877-524-5005		224
Cyber-Ark Software Inc 60 Wells Ave Newton MA 02459 *TF:* 888-808-9005 ■ *Web:* www.cyberark.com	617-965-1544		177
CyberCare Health Network LLC 2401 PGA Blvd Ste 196 E Palm Beach Gardens FL 33410 *TF:* 866-771-3580 ■ *Web:* www.cybercarehn.com	866-771-3580		177
Cyberchrome Inc 3642 Main St Stone Ridge NY 12484 *Web:* www.cyberchromeusa.com	845-687-2671		177
CyberCoders Inc 6591 Irvine Center Dr Ste 200 Irvine CA 92618 *Web:* www.cybercoders.com	949-885-5151		193
CyberCore Technologies 6605 Business Pkwy Meadowridge Business Pk Elkridge MD 21075 *Web:* cybercoretech.com	410-560-7177		180
Cyberdata Corp 3 Justin Ct Monterey CA 93940 *TF:* 800-363-8010 ■ *Web:* www.cyberdata.net	831-373-2601	373-4193	176
CyberData Inc 20 Max Ave Hicksville NY 11801 *Web:* cyberdata.com	516-942-8000	942-0800	39
Cybereason Inc 200 Clarendon St 5th Fl Boston MA 02116 *TF:* 855-695-8200 ■ *Web:* www.cybereason.com	855-695-8200		387
Cybergrants LLC 300 Brickstone Sq Ste 601 Andover MA 01810 *Web:* impact.cybergrants.com	978-824-0300	824-0301	180
Cyberjaz Corp 2276 Todd Rd Aliquippa PA 15001 *Web:* www.cyberjaz.net	412-922-2000		180
Cyber-Logics Inc 512 Broadway Bayonne NJ 07002 *TF:* 877-246-4885 ■ *Web:* www.cyber-logics.com	201-437-3400	436-8684	224
CyberMark International Inc 18456 N 25th Ave Phoenix AZ 85023 *Web:* www.cybermark.com	623-889-3380		177
CyberNet Solutions Inc 3250 Old Farm Ln Ste 7 Commerce Charter Township MI 48390 *Web:* www.go-cybernet.com	248-960-1810		180
Cybernetics Inc 111 Cybernetics Way Yorktown VA 23693 *Web:* www.cybernetics.com	757-833-9100	833-9300	173-8
Cyberonic Internet Communications Inc 544 Pleasant St Worcester MA 01602 *Web:* cyberonic.com	508-753-4545	831-7325	225
CyberOptics Corp 5900 Golden Hills Dr Minneapolis MN 55416 *NASDAQ: CYBE* ■ *TF:* 800-746-6315 ■ *Web:* www.cyberoptics.com	763-542-5000	542-5100	248
Cyber-Rain Inc 5535 Balboa Blvd Ste 115 Encino CA 91316 *TF:* 877-888-1452 ■ *Web:* www.cyber-rain.com	877-888-1452		407
CyberScout LLC 7580 N Dobson Rd Ste 201 Scottsdale AZ 85256 *TF:* 888-682-5911 ■ *Web:* cyberscout.com	480-355-8500	355-8501	180
Cybersearch Ltd 800 E Northwest Hwy Ste 950 Palatine IL 60074 *Web:* cybsearch.com	847-357-0200		196
Cybersoft 1958 Butler Pk Ste 100 Conshohocken PA 19428 *Web:* www.cybersoft.com	610-825-6785		180
CyberSoft Inc 2016 E Muirwood Dr Phoenix AZ 85048 *TF:* 877-223-5459 ■ *Web:* www.nutribase.com	480-603-8359	878-7605	178-1
Cybersoft North America Inc 1500 S Dairy Ashford Ste 444 Houston TX 77077 *Web:* csnainc.com	281-752-0600	506-8083	177
Cybersoft Technologies Inc 4422 Cypress Creek Pkwy Ste 400 Houston TX 77068 *Web:* www.cybersoft.net	281-453-8500		180
CyberStaff America Ltd 3 E 28Th St 9Th Fl New York NY 10016	212-244-2300		721
CyberTech Systems and Software Inc 1301 W 22nd St Ste 308 Oak Brook IL 60523 **Fax Area Code:* 303 ■ *Web:* www.cybertech.com	630-472-3200	321-0689*	180
CyberThink Inc 1125 US Hwy 22 Ste 1 Bridgewater NJ 08807 *Web:* www.cyberthink.com	908-429-8008		177
Cybervillage Networkers 7773 Blueberry Hill Ln Ellicott City MD 21043 *Web:* www.cybernetworkers.com	410-579-1993		396
Cyberwolf Inc 1596 Pacheco St Ste 203 Santa Fe NM 87505 *Web:* www.cyberwolf.com	505-983-6463		177
Cyberwoven 1634 Main St Columbia SC 29201 *Web:* www.cyberwoven.com	803-376-8899		396
Cybex International Inc 10 Trotter Dr Medway MA 02053 *TF:* 888-462-9239 ■ *Web:* www.cybexintl.com	508-533-4300	533-5500	267
Cybra Corp 28 Wells Ave Yonkers NY 10701 **Fax Area Code:* 716 ■ *TF:* 800-292-7288 ■ *Web:* cybra.com	914-963-6600	712-0666*	177
Cybrary Inc 5801 University Research Ct Ste 150 College Park MD 20740 *Web:* www.cybrary.it	301-220-4526		177
Cybrix Group 710 Oakfield Dr Ste 266 Brandon FL 33511 *Web:* www.cybrixgroup.com	813-630-2744		180
Cycle World Magazine 1499 Monrovia Ave Newport Beach CA 92663 *Web:* www.cycleworld.com	949-720-5300		457-3
Cyclery USA Inc 415 Tennessee St Ste A Redlands CA 92373 *Web:* cycleryusa.com	909-792-2444		711
Cycle-safe Inc 5211 Cascade Rd SE Ste 210 Grand Rapids MI 49546 *TF:* 888-950-6531 ■ *Web:* cyclesafe.com	616-954-9977		711
Cycle-Tex Inc 702 S Thornton Ave Ste 101 Dalton GA 30720 *Web:* www.cycletex.com	706-226-1116		660
Cyclonaire Corp 2922 N Division Ave York NE 68467 *TF:* 800-445-0730 ■ *Web:* www.cyclonaire.com	402-362-2000	362-2001	207
Cyclone Drilling Inc PO Box 908 Gillette WY 82717 *Web:* www.cyclonedrilling.com	307-682-4161	682-3158	540
Cyclone Interactive Multimedia Group Inc 361 Newbury St 5th Fl Boston MA 02118 *Web:* www.cycloneinteractive.com	617-350-8834		344
Cyclone Land Development Company Inc 8097 Roswell Rd Atlanta GA 30350 *Web:* cycloneland.com	770-399-6006		653
Cyclone Software 5401 W 10th St Ste 100 Greeley CO 80634 *Web:* www.cyclonesoft.com	970-353-4555	353-3175	657
Cycom Canada Corp 31 Prince Andrew Pl North York ON M3C2H2 *TF:* 800-268-3171 ■ *Web:* www.cycom.com	416-494-5040	494-3946	196
Cyexx Inc 3050-G Business Park Dr Norcross GA 30071 *Web:* www.cyexx.com	678-532-9399		393
Cy-Fair Houston Chamber of Commerce 8711 Hwy 6 N Ste 120 Houston TX 77095 *TF:* 800-403-6120 ■ *Web:* cyfairchamber.com	281-373-1390	373-1394	139

Name / Address	City	State	Zip	Phone	Fax	Class
Cygan Hayes Ltd 20635 Abbey Woods Ct N *Web:* www.cyganhayes.com	Frankfort	IL	60423	815-534-5713	534-5523	2
Cygnus Corporation Inc 5640 Nicholson Ln Ste 227 *Web:* www.cygnusc.com	Rockville	MD	20852	301-231-7537	984-8527	196
Cygnus Inc 1701 Standish Ave *TF:* 888-760-8159 ■ *Web:* www.cygnusinc.net	Petoskey	MI	49770	231-347-5404		115
Cygnus Manufacturing Company LLC Victory Rd Business Pk 491 Chantler Dr *Web:* www.cmc-usa.com	Saxonburg	PA	16056	724-352-8000	352-8007	475
Cygnus Systems Inc 24700 Northwestern Hwy Ste 600 *TF:* 800-388-2280 ■ *Web:* www.cygnussystems.com	Southfield	MI	48075	248-557-4600		196
CYIOS Corp 1300 Pennsylvania Ave NW *Web:* www.cyios.com	Washington	DC	20004	202-204-3006		180
Cykic Software Inc PO Box 3098 *TF:* 800-438-7325 ■ *Web:* www.cykicsites.com	San Diego	CA	92163	619-459-8799		178-7
Cylix Inc 3045 Regal Dr **Fax Area Code:* 877 ■ *TF:* 888-978-4816 ■ *Web:* www.peepsquirrel.com	Alcoa	TN	37701	888-978-4816	978-4817*	111
Cyl-Tec Inc 971 W Industrial Dr *TF:* 888-429-5832 ■ *Web:* cyl-tec.com	Aurora	IL	60506	630-844-8800		743
Cyma Systems Inc 2330 W University Dr Ste 4 **Fax Area Code:* 480 ■ *TF:* 800-292-2962 ■ *Web:* www.cyma.com	Tempe	AZ	85281	800-292-2962	303-2969*	178-1
Cymbel Corp 154 Wells Ave *Web:* www.cymbel.com	Newton	MA	02459	617-581-6633		177
Cyn Environmental Services 100 Tosca Dr *TF:* 800-242-5818 ■ *Web:* www.cynenv.com	Stoughton	MA	02072	800-242-5818		667
Cynergy Solutions LLC 543 Country Club Dr Ste 538 *Web:* www.cynergysolutions.net	Simi Valley	CA	93065	805-416-1610		196
Cynergy Systems Inc 1851 Chespark Dr *Web:* cynergysystemsinc.com	Gastonia	NC	28052	704-864-2999		187
CynoSure Financial Inc 33490 Harper Ave *TF:* 800-711-4281 ■ *Web:* www.cynosurefinancial.com	Clinton Township	MI	48035	586-771-3334	771-4590	390
Cynosure Inc 5 Carlisle Rd *NASDAQ:* CYNO ■ *TF:* 800-886-2966 ■ *Web:* www.cynosure.com	Westford	MA	01886	978-256-4200		424
Cynthia Blumgart State Farm 2855 Telegraph Ave Ste 509 *Web:* cynthiablumgart.org	Berkeley	CA	94705	510-848-2132		390
Cynthia Publishing Co 11054 Ventura Blvd Ste 377 *Web:* www.cynthiapublishing.com	Studio City	CA	91604	323-876-7325	874-1591	637-2
Cynthia Rowley 394 Bleecker St *Web:* cynthiarowley.com	New York	NY	10014	212-242-3803		277
Cynthia Woods Mitchell Pavilion 2005 Lake Robbins Dr *Web:* www.woodlandscenter.org	The Woodlands	TX	77380	281-363-3300	364-3011	572
Cyon Research Corp 8220 Stone Trail Dr *Web:* www.cyonresearch.com	Bethesda	MD	20817	301-365-9085	365-4586	194
Cyphers Agency Inc, The 1682 Village Green *TF:* 888-412-7469 ■ *Web:* thecyphersagency.com	Crofton	MD	21114	888-412-7469		7
CypherWorX Inc 130 Andrews St *TF:* 888-685-4440 ■ *Web:* cypherworx.com	Rochester	NY	14604	888-685-4440		387
Cypremort Point State Park 306 Beach Ln *TF:* 888-867-4510 ■ *Web:* crt.state.la.us	Cypremort Point	LA	70538	337-867-4510		565
Cypress Asset Management Inc 4545 Post Oak Pl Dr Ste 205 *Web:* cypressasset.com	Houston	TX	77027	713-512-2100		690
Cypress Bayou Casino 832 Martin Luther King Rd *TF:* 800-284-4386 ■ *Web:* www.cypressbayou.casino	Charenton	LA	70523	800-284-4386		452
Cypress Capital Group Inc 251 Royal Palm Way Ste 500 *Web:* www.cypresstrust.com	Palm Beach Gardens	FL	33480	561-659-5889		401
Cypress Care Inc 2736 Meadow Church Rd Ste 300 *TF:* 800-419-7191 ■ *Web:* workcompauto.optum.com	Duluth	GA	30097	800-419-7191		367
Cypress Chamber of Commerce 5550 Cerritos Ave Ste D *Web:* cypresschamber.org	Cypress	CA	90630	714-484-5700		139
Cypress College 9200 Valley View St *Web:* www.cypresscollege.edu	Cypress	CA	90630	714-484-7000		162
Cypress Cove Publishing (CCP) PO Box 91195 *TF:* 888-606-3257 ■ *Web:* cypresscovepublishing.com	Lafayette	LA	70509	888-606-3257		637-2
Cypress Creek Hospital 17750 Cali Dr *Web:* www.cypresscreekhospital.com	Houston	TX	77090	281-586-5956		374-5
Cypress Environmental Partners LP 5727 S Lewis Ave Ste 300 *TF:* 855-990-0015 ■ *Web:* www.cypressenvironmental.biz	Tulsa	OK	74105	918-748-3900	748-3905	539
Cypress Food Distributors Inc 3111 N University Dr Ste 612 *Web:* www.cypressfood.com	Coral Springs	FL	33065	954-344-2900	344-3607	297-9
Cypress Gardens 3030 Cypress Gardens Rd *Web:* cypressgardens.berkeleycountysc.gov	Moncks Corner	SC	29461	843-553-0515	569-0644	50-5
Cypress Grill 4404 W William Cannon Ste L *Web:* cypressgrill.net	Austin	TX	78749	512-358-7474		671
Cypress Group LLC 437 Madison Ave 33rd Fl *Web:* www.cypressgp.com	New York	NY	10022	212-705-0150	705-0199	402
Cypress Health Institute 1119 Pacific Ave Ste 300 *Web:* www.cypresshealthinstitute.com	Santa Cruz	CA	95060	831-476-2115		167-3
Cypress Hills National Cemetery 625 Jamaica Ave *Web:* www.cem.va.gov	Brooklyn	NY	11208	631-454-4949	694-5422	136
Cypress Hills Resource Corp 602-11th Ave SW Ste 416 *Web:* www.cypresshillsresource.com	Calgary	AB	T2R1J8	403-265-7663		536
Cypress Networks 4125 Walker Ave *TF:* 866-625-3502 ■ *Web:* www.cypressnetworks.net	Greensboro	NC	27407	336-841-3030	217-8225	180
Cypress Operating Inc 330 Marshall St Ste 930 *Web:* www.cypressop.com	Shreveport	LA	71101	318-424-2031	425-8140	538
Cypress Regional Hospital 2004 Saskatchewan Dr *Web:* www.cypressrha.ca	Swift Current	SK	S9H5M8	306-778-9400		374-2
Cypress Security LLC 478 Tehama St *TF:* 866-345-1277	San Francisco	CA	94103	866-345-1277		693
Cypress Semiconductor Corp 198 Champion Ct *NASDAQ:* CY ■ *TF:* 800-541-4736 ■ *Web:* www.cypress.com	San Jose	CA	95134	408-943-2600	943-4730	696
Cypress Street Station 158 Cypress St *Web:* www.cypress-street.com	Abilene	TX	79601	325-676-3463	676-0715	671
Cypress, The 320 E Tennessee St *Web:* cypressrestaurant.com	Tallahassee	FL	32301	850-513-1100		671
Cypress-Fairbanks Independent School District PO Box 692003 *Web:* www.cfisd.net	Houston	TX	77269	281-897-4000		685
Cyprus *Embassy* 2211 R St NW *Web:* www.cyprusembassy.net	Washington	DC	20008	202-462-5772	483-6710	257
Cyprus Tourism Organization 13 E 40th St *Web:* www.visitcyprus.com	New York	NY	10016	212-683-5280	683-5282	775
Cyquent Inc 5410 Edson Ln Ste 210C *TF:* 866-509-0331 ■ *Web:* www.cyquent.com	Rockville	MD	20852	240-292-0230		180
Cyracom International Inc 5780 N Swan Rd *Web:* interpret.cyracom.com	Tucson	AZ	85718	520-745-9447		768
Cyril Bath Co 1610 Airport Rd *Web:* www.cyrilbath.com	Monroe	NC	28110	704-289-8531		456
Cyril J. Demeyere Ltd 261 Broadway *Web:* www.cjdleng.com	Tillsonburg	ON	N4G4H8	519-688-1000		261
Cyrus O'Leary's Pies 1528 S Hayford Rd *Web:* www.cyruspies.com	Airway Heights	WA	99001	509-624-5000		297-8
Cystic Fibrosis Foundation 6931 Arlington Rd Ste 200 *TF:* 800-344-4823 ■ *Web:* www.cff.org	Bethesda	MD	20814	301-951-4422	951-6378	48-17
Cystic Fibrosis Pharmacy Inc 3901 E Colonial Dr Ste D **Fax Area Code:* 407 ■ *TF:* 888-307-4427 ■ *Web:* hhcs.com	Orlando	FL	32803	888-307-4427	897-2108*	363
Cytak 6001 Shellmound St **Fax Area Code:* 800 ■ *TF:* 877-759-7464 ■ *Web:* cytak.com	Emeryville	CA	94608	877-759-7464	405-6445*	734
Cytec Engineered Materials Inc 2085 E Technology Cir Ste 102 *Web:* www.solvay.com	Tempe	AZ	85284	480-730-2000	730-2088	605-2
Cytokinetics Inc 280 E Grand Ave *NASDAQ:* CYTK ■ *Web:* cytokinetics.com	South San Francisco	CA	94080	650-624-3000	624-3010	85
Cytolab Pathology Services 6825 216th St SW Ste E	Lynnwood	WA	98036	425-712-8020		415
Cytori Therapeutics Inc 3020 Callan Rd *NASDAQ:* CYTX ■ *Web:* www.cytori.com	San Diego	CA	92121	858-458-0900		85
Cytosorbents Corp 7 Deer Park Dr Ste K *Web:* cytosorbents.com	Monmouth Junction	NJ	08852	732-329-8885	329-8650	250
CytoSport Inc 1340 Treat Blvd Ste 350 **Fax Area Code:* 707 ■ *TF:* 888-298-6629 ■ *Web:* www.musclemilk.com	Walnut Creek	CA	94597	888-298-6629	748-5732*	799
Cytovance Biologics 800 Research Pky Ste 200 *Web:* www.cytovance.com	Oklahoma City	OK	73104	405-319-8310		582
CytRx Corp 11726 San Vicente Blvd Ste 650 *NASDAQ:* CYTR ■ *Web:* www.cytrx.com	Los Angeles	CA	90049	310-826-5648	826-6139	85
Czech Airlines 147 W 35th St Ste 1505 **Fax Area Code:* 212 ■ *TF:* 855-359-2932 ■ *Web:* www.csa.cz	New York	NY	10001	855-359-2932	279-6602*	25
Czech Republic *Consulate General* 10990 Wilshire Blvd Ste 1100 *Web:* www.mzv.cz	Los Angeles	CA	90024	310-473-0889	473-9813	257
Consulate General 321 E 73rd St *Web:* www.mzv.cz	New York	NY	10021	646-422-3344	422-3311	257
Embassy 3900 Spring of Freedom St NW *Web:* www.mzv.cz	Washington	DC	20008	202-274-9100	966-8540	257
Czepiga Daly Pope & Perri LLC 15 Massirio Dr **Fax Area Code:* 866 ■ *Web:* www.czepigalaw.com	Berlin	CT	06037	860-259-1575	540-4616*	41
CZIP (Capital Z Partners) 142 W 57th St 3rd Fl *Web:* www.capitalz.com	New York	NY	10019	212-965-2400	965-2301	792
CZ-USA Inc PO Box 171073 *TF:* 800-955-4486 ■ *Web:* cz-usa.com	Kansas City	KS	66117	913-321-1811	321-2251	711

D

Name / Address	City	State	Zip	Phone	Fax	Class
D & A Building Services 321 Georgia Ave *Web:* www.dabuildingservices.com	Longwood	FL	32750	407-831-5388		41
D & B Industrial Group 21649 Cedar Creek Ave *Web:* www.dbindustrialgroup.com	Georgetown	DE	19947	302-855-0585		475
D & B Logistics 720 Washington St *Web:* www.dblinc.net	Hanover	MA	02339	781-829-4500		311

Name / Address	City	State	Zip	Phone	Fax	Class
D & B Machining Inc 53 John St *Web:* www.dbmachining.com	Cumberland	RI	02864	401-726-2347	727-3810	454
D & D Commodities Ltd PO Box 359 *TF:* 800-543-3308 ■ *Web:* www.ddcommodities.com	Stephen	MN	56757	800-543-3308		447
D & D Construction Services 2707 Rew Cir *Web:* ddcs.net	Ocoee	FL	34761	407-654-7545		186
D & D Distribution Services Inc 789 Kings Mill Rd *Web:* www.dd-dist.com	York	PA	17403	717-845-1646		803-1
D & D Elevator Maintenance Inc 38 Hayes St *Web:* www.ddelevator.com	Elmsford	NY	10523	914-347-4344		104
D & D Equipment Rental Inc 10936 Shoemaker Ave *Web:* www.ddrental.com	Santa Fe Springs	CA	90670	562-903-9333		264-3
D & D Foods Inc 9425 N 48th St *TF:* 800-208-0364 ■ *Web:* hy-vee.com	Omaha	NE	68152	402-571-4113		296-36
D & D Manufacturing Inc 500 Territorial Dr **Fax Area Code:* 630 ■ *TF:* 888-300-6869 ■ *Web:* www.danddmfg.wixsite.com	Bolingbrook	IL	60440	888-300-6869	759-0043*	757
D & D Sexton Inc PO Box 156 *TF:* 800-743-0265 ■ *Web:* ddsextoninc.com	Carthage	MO	64836	417-358-8727		780
D & E Machining LTD 150 Industrial Dr *Web:* www.demachining.com	Corry	PA	16407	814-664-3531		454
D & F Corp 42455 Merrill Rd *Web:* www.d-f.com	Sterling Heights	MI	48314	586-254-5300	254-5610	567
D & F Travel Inc 331 Alberta Dr Ste 103 *TF:* 800-335-1982 ■ *Web:* www.dfbuses.com	Amherst	NY	14226	716-835-9227		772
D & G Machine Products Inc 50 Eisenhower Dr *Web:* www.dgmachine.com	Westbrook	ME	04092	207-854-1500		454
D & H Distributing Company Inc 2525 N Seventh St *TF:* 800-877-1200 ■ *Web:* www.dandh.com	Harrisburg	PA	17110	800-340-1001		174
D & J Enterprises Inc 3495 Lee Rd 10 *Web:* www.djenterprises.net	Auburn	AL	36832	334-821-1249		188-4
D & J Oil Company Inc 4720 W Garriott *Web:* www.djoil.com	Enid	OK	73703	580-242-3636		539
D & L Entertainment Services Inc 4120 Main St *Web:* dandlentertainment.com	Dallas	TX	75226	214-634-0757		184
D & L Equipment 1 Maple St *Web:* www.dandlequipment.net	Kensett	IA	50448	641-845-2199		57
D & L Parts Company Inc 2100 Freedom Dr *Web:* www.dlpartsco.com	Charlotte	NC	28208	704-374-0705	377-6897	246
D & L Tooling and Plastics Inc 950 SE Loop 456 *Web:* www.dlplastics.com	Jacksonville	TX	75766	903-586-9894	586-8357	604
D & M Plastic Corp 150 French Rd PO Box 158 *Web:* www.dmplastics.com	Burlington	IL	60109	847-683-2054		604
D & P Custom Lights & Wiring Systems Inc 900 63rd Ave N *TF:* 800-251-2200 ■ *Web:* www.dandpcustomlights.com	Nashville	TN	37209	615-350-7800	350-8310	439
D & R International Ltd 1100 Wayne Ave Ste 700 *Web:* www.drintl.com	Silver Spring	MD	20910	301-588-9387		256
D & R Sports Center Inc 8178 W Main St *Web:* www.dandrsports.com	Kalamazoo	MI	49009	269-372-2277		711
D & S Cattle Co 2167 state Rd 66 PO Box 172	Zolfo Springs	FL	33890	863-735-1112		446
D & S Communications Inc 1355 N Mclean Blvd *TF:* 800-227-8403 ■ *Web:* www.dscomm.com	Elgin	IL	60123	800-227-8403		463
D & S Manufacturing Inc 301 E Main St *Web:* www.dsmfg.com	Black River Falls	WI	54615	715-284-5376	284-4084	482
D & S Marketing Systems Inc 1205 38th St *Web:* dsmarketing.com	Brooklyn	NY	11218	718-633-8383		194
D & S Mold & Tool Co 2417 Cleveland Ave *Web:* www.dsmold.com	Marinette	WI	54143	715-732-0504	732-4849	757
D & S Pump & Supply Company Inc 3784 Danbury Rd *Web:* dspumpco.com	Brewster	NY	10509	845-279-3785	279-5536	711
D & S Warehousing Inc 104 Alan Dr *Web:* www.wedistribute.com	Newark	DE	19711	302-731-7440		803-1
D & SR Inc 500 E Oregon Rd	Lancaster	PA	17606	717-569-3264	569-3403	627
D & T Fiberglass Inc 8900 Osage Ave D *Web:* www.dtfiberglass.com	Sacramento	CA	95828	916-383-9012	383-1851	604
D & W Fine Pack LLC 4162 Georgia Blvd *Web:* www.dwfinepack.com	San Bernardino	CA	92407	909-474-4200		596
D & W Inc 941 Oak St *TF:* 800-255-0829 ■ *Web:* www.dwincorp.com	Elkhart	IN	46514	574-264-9674		329
D + R Lathian LLC 745 Hope Rd 2nd Fl *Web:* www.drlathian.com	Eatontown	NJ	07724	732-460-2500	460-2640	5
D A Crowley & Associates Inc 3 Overlook Dr *Web:* www.dacrowley.com	Amherst	NH	03031	603-673-7050		195
D B Western Inc 95084 Larson Ln *Web:* www.dbwestern.com	North Bend	OR	97459	541-756-0533		595
D Canale Beverages Inc 45 W EH Crump Blvd	Memphis	TN	38106	901-948-4543		81-1
D Crupi & Sons Ltd 85 Passmore Ave Agincourt *Web:* www.crupigroup.com	Toronto	ON	M1V4S9	416-291-1986		261
D D Dunlap Companies Inc 16897 Algonquin St Ste A *Web:* dddunlap.com	Huntington Beach	CA	92649	714-840-6460		536
D Exposito & Partners LLC 875 Avenue of the Americas *Web:* newamericanagency.com	New York	NY	10001	646-747-8800		636
D F Richard Inc 124 Broadway *TF:* 800-649-6457 ■ *Web:* www.dfrichard.com	Dover	NH	03821	603-742-2020		316
D Hilton Associates Inc 9450 Grogans Mill Rd Ste 200 *TF:* 800-367-0433 ■ *Web:* www.dhilton.com	The Woodlands	TX	77380	281-292-5088	292-8893	194
D J Heating & Air Conditioning Inc 1409 Rt 9W	Marlboro	NY	12542	845-236-4436		189-10
D J Powers Company Inc 5000 Business Center Dr Ste 1000 *Web:* www.djpowers.com	Savannah	GA	31405	912-234-7241		311
D K Global 420 Missouri Ct *TF:* 866-375-2214 ■ *Web:* dkglobal.net	Redlands	CA	92373	909-747-0201		225
D L Evans Bank 375 N Overland PO Box 1188 *TF:* 888-873-9777 ■ *Web:* www.dlevans.com	Burley	ID	83318	208-678-2529	678-9093	70
D L S Electronic Systems Inc 1250 Peterson Dr *Web:* www.dlsemc.com	Wheeling	IL	60090	847-537-6400	537-6488	743
D M Bowman Inc 10228 Governor Ln Blvd Ste 3006 *TF:* 800-326-3274 ■ *Web:* www.dmbowman.com	Williamsport	MD	21795	800-326-3274		780
D M R International Inc 20 W 11th St Ste 203 *Web:* www.dmrinteractive.com	Covington	KY	41011	859-655-9200	655-3480	466
D M Sales Engineering Inc 1325 Sunday Dr *Web:* dmsales-eng.com	Indianapolis	IN	46217	317-783-5493		596
D Maldari & Sons Inc 557 3rd Ave *Web:* dmaldariandsons.com	Brooklyn	NY	11215	718-499-3555	499-6071	757
D Net Internet Service 189 E Palmer St *TF:* 877-601-3638 ■ *Web:* www.dnet.net	Franklin	NC	28734	828-349-3638		225
D P Brown of Saginaw Inc 2845 Universal Dr *TF:* 877-799-9400 ■ *Web:* www.dpbrowntech.com	Saginaw	MI	48603	989-799-9400		393
D Samuel Gottesman Library 1300 Morris Park Ave Forchheimer Bldg *Web:* library.einstein.yu.edu	Bronx	NY	10461	718-430-3108	430-8795	434-1
D Side Advisors 12601 Easton Dr *Web:* dside.com	Saratoga	CA	95070	408-255-4620		195
D V Brown & Associates Inc 567 Vickers St *Web:* dvbrown.com	Tonawanda	NY	14150	716-695-5533		610
D V O Enterprises Inc 620 Windsor Ct *Web:* www.dvo.com	Alpine	UT	84004	801-492-1290		39
D W Hammer & Company Inc 17480 Dallas Pkwy Ste 100 *Web:* www.dwhammerco.com	Dallas	TX	75287	972-250-2547		41
D W Smith Associates LLC 1450 SR-34 *Web:* www.dwsmith.com	Wall Township	NJ	07753	732-363-5850		727
D'Agostino Supermarkets Inc 1385 Boston Post Rd *Web:* www.dagnyc.com	Larchmont	NY	10538	914-833-4000		345
D'Agosto & Howe 738 Bridgeport Ave *TF:* 800-749-8616 ■ *Web:* dhctlaw.com	Shelton	CT	06484	203-712-0210	922-9911	41
D'Ambra Construction Company Inc 80 Ctr of New England Blvd *Web:* www.d-ambra.com	Coventry	RI	02816	401-737-1300		188-4
D'Angelo Sandwich Shops 600 Providence Hwy *TF:* 800-727-2446 ■ *Web:* www.dangelos.com	Dedham	MA	02026	800-727-2446		670
D'annunzio & Sons Inc 3730 Park Ave *Web:* dannunziooorp.com	South Plainfield	NJ	07080	732-574-1300	574-1244	100
D'Arcangelo & Co 510 Haight Ave *Web:* www.darcangelo.com	Poughkeepsie	NY	12603	845-473-7774		41
D'Arcy Lane Institute D'AL School of Equine Massage Therapy 627 Maitland St *TF:* 877-327-2952 ■ *Web:* www.darcylane.com	London	ON	N5Y2V7	519-673-4420		685
D'Arcy McGee's Irish Pub 199 Four Valley Dr *Web:* darcymcgees.com	Vaughan	ON	L4K0B8	613-230-4433		671
D'Arrigo Bros Company of California Inc PO Box 850 *TF:* 800-995-5939 ■ *Web:* www.andyboy.com	Salinas	CA	93902	831-455-4500	455-4445	10-11
D'Arrigo Bros Company of New York Inc 315 Hunts Pt Terminal Market *Web:* www.darrigony.com	Bronx	NY	10474	718-991-5900	960-0544	297-7
D'Artagnan LLC 600 Green Ln **Fax Area Code:* 973 ■ *TF:* 800-327-8246 ■ *Web:* www.dartagnan.com	Union	NJ	07083	800-327-8246	465-1870*	296-26
D'Classico 59-50 Ellison St	Paterson	NJ	07505	973-569-4300		671
D'Elia Gillooly Depalma LLC 700 State St *Web:* dgdlawct.com	New Haven	CT	06511	203-891-5310	891-6948	41
D'Huyvetter & Swichkow PC 519 Johnson Ferry Rd Bldg A Ste 100 *Web:* dspccpa.com	Marietta	GA	30068	404-231-3500	231-4086	2
D'Onofrio General Contractors Corp 202 28th St *Web:* donofrio.biz	Brooklyn	NY	11232	718-832-5700	832-5772	610
D'onofrio Kottke & Associates 7530 Wward Way *Web:* donofrio.cc	Madison	WI	53717	608-833-7530		261
D'Orsay Restaurant Pub 65 Rue de Buade *Web:* www.dorsayrestaurant.com	Quebec City	QC	G1R4A2	418-694-1582	694-1587	671
D'vontz 7208 E 38th St *TF:* 877-322-3600 ■ *Web:* dvontz.com	Tulsa	OK	74145	918-622-3600		610
D'Youville College 320 Porter Ave *TF:* 800-777-3921 ■ *Web:* www.dyc.edu	Buffalo	NY	14201	716-829-7600	829-7900	166
D+AC (Diliberto+Associates Consulting Inc) 3020 Bridgeway Ste 235 **Fax Area Code:* 800 ■ *TF:* 800-922-4750 ■ *Web:* www.dilibertoassoc.com	Sausalito	CA	94965	415-332-2227	257-7763*	192
D+H CollateralGuard RC 4126 Norland Ave Ste 200 *TF:* 866-873-9780 ■ *Web:* www.csrs.ca	Burnaby	BC	V5G3S8	604-637-4000	637-4001	635

Name / Address	City	State	ZIP	Phone	Fax	Class
D. A. G. Construction Company Inc 4924 Winton Rd *Web:* www.dag-cons.com	Cincinnati	OH	45232	513-542-8597		186
D. A. R. State Park 6750 VT Rt 17 W *Web:* www.vtstateparks.com	Addison	VT	05491	802-759-2354		565
D. F. Electronics Inc 200 Novner Dr *Web:* www.dfelectronics.com	Cincinnati	OH	45215	513-772-7792		696
D. Francis Murphy Insurance Agency Inc 50 Main St *Web:* dfmurphy.com	Hudson	MA	01749	978-568-8711		390
D. Lawless Wholesale 1707 E Main *Web:* www.dlawlesshardware.com	Olney	IL	62450	618-395-3945	395-3946	191-3
D. M. Reid Associates Ltd 50 Grove St Ste 227 *Web:* www.dmreid.com	Salem	MA	01970	978-744-3818		636
D. P. Curtis Trucking Inc 1450 S Hwy 118 *Fax Area Code:* 435 ■ *TF:* 800-257-9151 ■ *Web:* www.dpcurtis.com	Richfield	UT	84701	800-257-9151	896-6553*	780
D. Pagan Communications 20 Broadhollow Rd Ste 3008 *Web:* www.dpagan.com	Melville	NY	11747	631-659-2309		463
D. R. Payne & Associates Inc 119 N Robinson Ave Ste 400 *Web:* drpayne.com	Oklahoma City	OK	73102	405-272-0511		463
D.C. Industries Inc 200 Ida St *Web:* www.dcindustries.us	Waterloo	IA	50701	319-234-1075	234-3103	454
D.C. Lites Inc 10740 Goodnight Ln *Web:* www.dclites.net	Dallas	TX	75220	972-556-0260		493
D.D. Hamilton Company Inc 301 W Washington St *Web:* ddhamilton.net	Marshfield	MO	65706	417-859-2078	859-2020	653
D.D. Pagano Inc 4705 E Chapman Ave *Web:* asic.org	Orange	CA	92869	714-771-9200		261
D.E. Hokanson Inc 12840 NE 21st Pl *TF:* 800-999-8251 ■ *Web:* hokansonvascular.com	Bellevue	WA	98005	425-882-1689	881-1636	476
D.E. McNabb Flooring 31250 S Milford Rd *TF:* 800-544-2016 ■ *Web:* www.demcnabb.com	Milford	MI	48381	248-437-8146		290
D.J. Neff Enterprises Inc 6405 York Rd *Web:* neff-assoc.com	Parma Heights	OH	44130	440-884-3100		261
D.J. Parrone & Associates PC 349 W Commercial St Ste 3 *Web:* parroneeng.com	East Rochester	NY	14445	585-586-0200		261
D.L George & Sons Transportation 20 E 6th St *Web:* www.dl-george.com	Waynesboro	PA	17268	717-765-4700	765-4734	780
D.M. Manufacturing Inc 2750 Kennedy Dr *Web:* www.dmmfg.com	Beloit	WI	53511	608-362-2095	362-8740	91
D.P.C. General Contractors Inc 1860 NW 21 Terr *TF:* 800-488-0447 ■ *Web:* dpcgen.virb.com	Miami	FL	33142	305-325-0447		189-11
D.W. Morgan Company Inc 4185 Blackhawk Plaza Cir Ste 260 *Web:* www.dwmorgan.com	Danville	CA	94506	925-460-2700		311
D1 International Inc 95 E Main St *Web:* www.d1international.com	Huntington	NY	11743	631-673-6866	673-6893	246
D1 Sports Holdings LLC 7115 S Springs Dr *Web:* d1training.com	Franklin	TN	37067	615-224-8242		354
D2 (Development Dynamics LLC) 1001 Boardwalk Springs Pl Ste 50 *Web:* www.developmentdynamics.org	O Fallon	MO	63366	636-561-8602	561-8605	196
D2 Creative 28 World's Fair Dr *Web:* www.d2creative.com	Somerset	NJ	08873	732-539-2257		7
D2 Technologie 3814 Taschereau *TF:* 866-904-5888 ■ *Web:* d2technologie.com	Greenfield Park	QC	J4V2H9	450-671-0605		736
D2 Technologies Inc 104 W Anapamu St Ste J *Web:* d2nova.com	Santa Barbara	CA	93101	805-888-0388		261
D2M Inc 935 Benecia Ave *Web:* d2m-inc.com	Sunnyvale	CA	94085	650-567-9995		194
D3 Technologies 4600 W Kearney Ste 100 *Web:* www.teamd3.com	Springfield	MO	65803	417-831-7171		261
D3Logic Inc 89 Commercial Way *TF:* 844-385-5388 ■ *Web:* www.d3-inc.com	East Providence	RI	02914	401-435-4300		195
D4 Construction Services LLC 4121 Main St *Web:* d4constructionservices.com	Rowlett	TX	75088	972-463-0390		186
d50 Media 1330 Boylston St Ste 200 *TF:* 800-582-9606 ■ *Web:* www.d50media.com	Chestnut Hill	MA	02467	800-582-9606		195
DA (Debtors Anonymous) PO Box 920888 *TF:* 800-421-2383 ■ *Web:* www.debtorsanonymous.org	Needham	MA	02492	781-453-2743	453-2745	48-21
DA Camera of Houston 1427 Branard St *Web:* www.dacamera.com	Houston	TX	77006	713-524-7601	524-4148	573-3
DA Collins Construction Company Inc 269 Ballard Rd *Web:* www.dacollins.com	Wilton	NY	12831	518-664-9855	664-0925	188-4
DA Hoerr & Sons Inc 8020 N Shadetree Dr *Web:* www.hoerrnursery.com	Peoria	IL	61615	309-691-4561		323
DA Kreuter Associates Inc 2250 Hickory Rd Ste 400 *Web:* www.dakassociates.com	Plymouth Meeting	PA	19462	610-834-1100		194
DA Lubricant Co 1340 W 29th St *TF:* 800-645-5823 ■ *Web:* www.dalube.com	Indianapolis	IN	46208	317-923-5321	923-3884	541
Da Marco 1520 Westheimer Rd *Web:* www.damarcohouston.com	Houston	TX	77006	713-807-8857		671
Da Maurizio *Fine Dining* 1496 Lower Water St *Web:* damaurizio.ca	Halifax	NS	B3J1R7	902-423-0859		671
Da Mimmo Italian Cuisine 217 S High St *Web:* www.damimmo.com	Baltimore	MD	21202	410-727-6876	727-1927	671
Da Pope Inc 1160 Chess Dr Ste 11 *Web:* www.dapope.com	Foster City	CA	94404	650-349-5086		186
Da Vinci Discovery Center of Science & Technology 3145 Hamilton Blvd Bypass *Web:* www.davincisciencecenter.org	Allentown	PA	18103	484-664-1002		520
Da/Pro Rubber Inc 601 N Poplar Ave *Web:* www.daprorubber.com	Broken Arrow	OK	74012	918-258-9386	258-3286	677
DAA Draexlmaier Automotive of America LLC 1751 E Main St *Web:* www.us.draexlmaier.com	Duncan	SC	29334	864-433-8910		61
DAAD (German Academic Exchange Service) 871 United Nations Plz *Web:* www.daad.org	New York	NY	10017	212-758-3223	755-5780	48-11
Dabko Industries Inc 50 Emmett St *Web:* www.rgdtech.com	Bristol	CT	06010	860-589-0756	585-0874	621
Dabney S. Lancaster Community College 1000 Dabney Dr *Web:* dslcc.edu	Clifton Forge	VA	24422	540-863-2800		162
Dabora Inc 730 Madison St *Web:* www.saddlehorsereport.com	Shelbyville	TN	37162	931-684-8123	684-8196	532-2
DAC (Dougherty Arts Ctr, The) 1110 Barton Springs Rd *Web:* www.austintexas.gov	Austin	TX	78704	512-974-4000	974-4039	50-2
DAC International Inc 6702 McNeil Dr *TF:* 800-527-2531 ■ *Web:* dacint.com	Austin	TX	78729	512-331-5323	331-4516	770
Dac Products Inc 625 Montroyal Rd *TF:* 800-431-1982 ■ *Web:* www.dacproducts.com	Rural Hall	NC	27045	800-431-1982		499
DAC Systems 4 Armstrong Rd *Web:* www.dacsystems.com	Shelton	CT	06484	203-924-7000	944-1618	681
DAC Technologies 3630 W Miller Ste 350 *TF:* 800-800-1550 ■ *Web:* www.dactechnologies.com	Garland	TX	75041	972-677-2700	677-2800	542
Dacallc 6550 McDonough Dr *Web:* dacaspecialtyservices.com	Norcross	GA	30093	770-451-6433	451-8594	256
DACC (Dona Ana Community College) 2800 N Sonoma Ranch Blvd *TF:* 800-903-7503 ■ *Web:* dacc.nmsu.edu	Las Cruces	NM	88011	575-528-7000	528-7300	162
DAccord Shirts & Guayaberas Inc 7320 NW 12th St Ste 115 *Web:* daccordshirts.com	Miami	FL	33126	305-576-0926	436-0385	155-3
Dacey Insurance Agency Inc 631 Main St *Web:* daceyinsurance.com	East Greenwich	RI	02818	401-398-8020		390
Dacon Corp 16 Huron Dr *Web:* www.dacon1.com	Natick	MA	01760	508-651-3600		610
Dacotah Paper Co 3940 15th Ave N *TF:* 800-270-6352 ■ *Web:* store.dacotahpaper.com	Fargo	ND	58102	701-281-1730	281-9799	559
Dacro Industries Inc 9325-51 Ave *Web:* www.dacro.com	Edmonton	AB	T6E4W8	780-434-8900		106
Dadant & Sons Inc 51 S 2nd St *TF:* 888-922-1293 ■ *Web:* www.dadant.com	Hamilton	IL	62341	217-847-3324	847-3660	122
DADCO Inc 43850 Plymouth Oaks Blvd *TF:* 800-323-2687 ■ *Web:* www.dadco.net	Plymouth	MI	48170	734-207-1100	207-2222	641
Daddies Board Shop LLC 5909 NE 80th Ave *Web:* www.daddiesboardshop.com	Portland	OR	97218	503-281-5123		711
Daddy Don's Tax Service 8235 Santa Monica Blvd Ste 210 *Web:* www.daddydon.com	West Hollywood	CA	90046	323-656-7532		734
Dade Battlefield Historic State Park 3900 Commonwealth Blvd *Web:* www.floridastateparks.org	Tallahassee	FL	32399	352-793-4781		565
Dade County 71 Case Ave *Web:* www.dadecounty-ga.gov	Trenton	GA	30752	706-657-4625	657-8284	338
Dade Truss Company Inc 6401 NW 74th Ave *Web:* www.bcg.bz	Miami	FL	33166	305-592-8245		817
Dads Adventure Inc 15375 Barranca Pkwy Ste C107 *Web:* www.dadsadventure.com	Irvine	CA	92618	949-754-9067		48-6
DaEdoardo Foxtown Grille 2203 Woodward Ave *Web:* daedoardo.net	Detroit	MI	48201	313-471-3500	471-3499	671
Daemar Inc 861 Cranberry Ct *Web:* daemar.com	Oakville	ON	L6L6J7	905-847-6500		350
Daemen College 4380 Main St *TF:* 800-462-7652 ■ *Web:* www.daemen.edu	Amherst	NY	14226	716-839-8225		166
Daffodil Enterprises Inc 163 Pearl St Ste 1	Essex Junction	VT	05452	802-879-0212		157-6
Daft-Mccune-Walker Inc 501 Fairmount Ave Ste 300 *Web:* dmw.com	Towson	MD	21286	410-296-3333		261
DAG Media Inc 125-10 Queens Blvd Ste 14 *TF:* 800-261-2799 ■ *Web:* www.jewishyellow.com	Kew Gardens Hills	NY	11415	718-263-8454	793-2522	637-6
DAG Online Inc 23632 Calabasas Rd *Web:* www.dagonline.com	Calabasas	CA	91302	818-793-1000	793-1001	180
Dage-MTI Inc 701 N Roeske Ave *Web:* www.dagemti.com	Michigan City	IN	46360	219-872-5514	872-5559	647
Daggett County 95 N First W *TF:* 800-764-0844 ■ *Web:* www.daggettcounty.org	Manila	UT	84046	435-784-3154	784-3335	338
Daggett Truck Line Inc 32717 County Rd 10 *TF:* 800-262-9393 ■ *Web:* daggetttruck.com	Frazee	MN	56544	218-334-3711	334-2566	780
Dagny Johnson Key Largo Hammock Botanical State Park County Rd 905 Mile Marker 106 PO Box 370487 *Web:* www.floridastateparks.org	Key Largo	FL	33037	305-676-3777		565
Dagom Gaden Tensung-Ling Monastery 2150 E Dolan Rd *Web:* www.ganden.org	Bloomington	IN	47404	812-334-3456		50-1
Dagostino Electronic Services Inc 600 Mifflin Rd *TF:* 800-864-4166 ■ *Web:* descomm.com	Pittsburgh	PA	15207	412-531-4240		52
DAH Consulting Inc 303 Park Ave S Ste 1176 *Web:* www.dahcon.com	New York	NY	10010	212-514-6862		196
Dahab Associates Inc 423 S Country Rd *Web:* www.dahab.com	Bay Shore	NY	11706	631-665-6181	665-6813	401

	Phone	Fax	Class
Dahl Arts Ctr 713 Seventh St, Rapid City SD 57701 — TF: 800-487-3223 ■ Web: www.thedahl.org	605-394-4101	394-6121	50-2
Dahl Hatton Muir & Reese Ltd 217 S Birch Ave PO Box 698, Hallock MN 56728 — Web: www.dhmrcpa.com	218-843-2645	843-2880	2
Dahl Morrow Intl 11260 Roger Bacon St Ste 204, Reston VA 20190 — Web: www.dahl-morrowintl.com	703-787-8117		266
Dahl Plumbing 1000 Siler Park Ln, Santa Fe NM 87507 — Web: www.dahlplumbing.com	505-471-1811		612
Dahlak Paradise 4708 Baltimore Ave, Philadelphia PA 19143 — Web: www.dahlakrestaurant.com	215-726-6464		671
Dahle North America Inc 49 Vose Farm Rd, Peterborough NH 03458 — TF: 800-243-8145 ■ Web: www.dahle.com	603-924-0003	924-1616	534
Dahlgren Memorial Library Georgetown University Medical Ctr 3900 Reservoir R PO Box 571420, Washington DC 20057 — Web: dml.georgetown.edu	202-687-1448		434-1
Dahlonega Gold Museum State Historic Site 1 Public Sq, Dahlonega GA 30533 — Web: gastateparks.org	706-864-2257		565
Dahlsten Truck Line Inc 101 W Edgar PO Box 95, Clay Center NE 68933 — TF: 800-228-4313 ■ Web: www.dahlsten.com	402-762-3511	762-3592	780
Dahlstrom Display Inc 2875 S 25th Ave, Broadview IL 60155 — Web: www.dahlstromdisplay.com	708-410-4500		627
DAI (Development Alternatives Inc) 7600 Wisconsin Ave Ste 200, Bethesda MD 20814 — Web: www.dai.com	301-771-7600		463
DAI (Denali Advance Integration) 17735 NE 65th St Ste 130, Redmond WA 98052 — TF: 877-467-8008 ■ Web: www.denaliai.com	425-885-4000		180
Dai Ceramics Inc 38240 Airport Pkwy, Willoughby OH 44094 — Web: www.daiceramics.com	440-946-6964		751
Daido Corporation of America 1031 Fred White Blvd, Portland TN 37148 — Web: www.daidocorp.com	615-323-4020		620
Daidone Electric Inc 200 Raymond Blvd, Newark NJ 07105 — Web: daidoneelectric.com	973-690-5216	690-5710	189-4
Daifuku North American Holdings Co 6700 Tussing Rd, Reynoldsburg OH 43068 — Web: www.daifuku.com	614-863-1888		207
Daigle Oil Co PO Box 328, Fort Kent ME 04743 — TF: 800-654-1869 ■ Web: www.daigleoil.com	207-834-5027	834-5050	316
Daiichi Jitsugyo (America) Inc 939 AEC Dr, Wood Dale IL 60191 — Web: www.dja-global.com	630-875-0101		385
Daiichi Sankyo Inc 211 Mt Airy Rd, Basking Ridge NJ 07054 — *Fax Area Code: 973 ■ Web: www.dsi.com	908-992-6400	944-2645*	582
Dai-Ichi Seiko America Inc 41700 Gardenbrook Rd Ste 133, Novi MI 48375 — Web: www.daiichi-seiko.co.jp	248-308-2706	308-2707	757
Daikichi Sushi Japanese Bistro 1400 N Battlefield Blvd, Chesapeake VA 23320 — Web: www.welovesushi.net	757-549-0200		671
Daikin America Inc 20 Olympic Dr, Orangeburg NY 10962 — TF: 800-365-9570 ■ Web: daikin-america.com	800-365-9570		605-2
Dailey & Assn 8687 Melrose Ave, West Hollywood CA 90069 — Web: www.daileyla.com	310-360-3100		4
Dailey Marketing Group Inc 29829 Santa Margarita Pkwy Ste 100, Rancho Santa Margarita CA 92688 — Web: www.daileymarketing.com	949-454-0751		7
Daily Advertiser, The 1100 Bertrand Dr, LaFayette LA 70506 — TF: 800-259-8852 ■ Web: www.theadvertiser.com	337-289-6300		532-2
Daily American Republic 220 Poplar St, Poplar Bluff MO 63901 — TF: 888-276-2242 ■ Web: darnews.com	573-785-1414	785-2706	532-2
Daily Athenaeum 284 Prospect St, Morgantown WV 26505 — Web: www.thedaonline.com	304-293-4141	293-6857	532-2
Daily Breeze 21250 Hawthorne Blvd Ste 170, Torrance CA 90503 — Web: www.dailybreeze.com	310-540-5511		532-2
Daily Californian 2483 Hearst Ave, Berkeley CA 94709 — Web: www.dailycal.org	510-548-8300	849-2803	532-3
Daily Commercial 212 E Main St, Leesburg FL 34748 — Web: www.dailycommercial.com	352-365-8200		532-2
Daily Courier 1958 Commerce Center Cir, Prescott AZ 86301 — Web: www.dcourier.com	928-445-3333		532-2
Daily Courier 550 Doyle Ave, Kelowna BC V1Y7V1 — Web: www.kelownadailycourier.ca	250-762-4445		532-1
Daily Courier 409 SE Seventh St, Grants Pass OR 97526 — TF: 800-228-0457 ■ Web: www.thedailycourier.com	541-474-3700	474-3824	532-2
Daily Express Inc 1072 Harrisburg Pk, Carlisle PA 17013 — TF: 800-735-3136 ■ Web: www.dailyexp.com	717-243-5757	240-2103	780
Daily Freeman 79 Hurley Ave, Kingston NY 12401 — Web: www.dailyfreeman.com	845-331-5000	331-3557	532-2
Daily Gazette Co, The 2345 Maxon Rd Ext PO Box 1090, Schenectady NY 12301 — TF: 800-262-2211 ■ Web: dailygazette.com	518-374-4141	395-3072	532-2
Daily Globe 37 W Main St, Shelby OH 44875 — Web: www.sdgnewsgroup.com	419-342-4276		532-2
Daily Globe, The 118 E McLeod Ave PO Box 548, Ironwood MI 49938 — TF: 800-236-2887 ■ Web: www.yourdailyglobe.com	906-932-2211	932-4211	637-8
Daily Hampshire Gazette 115 Conz St, Northampton MA 01060 — Web: www.gazettenet.com	413-584-5000	585-5299	532-2
Daily Harvest 99 Hudson St 11th Fl, New York NY 10013 — TF: 888-302-0305 ■ Web: www.daily-harvest.com	888-302-0305		296-35
Daily Herald 1555 N Freedom Blvd, Provo UT 84604 — TF: 800-880-8075 ■ Web: www.heraldextra.com	801-373-5050		532-2
Daily Herald 155 E Algonquin Rd, Arlington Heights IL 60005 — TF: 888-903-4070 ■ Web: www.dailyherald.com	847-427-4300		532-2
Daily Instruments Inc 5700 Hartsdale Dr, Houston TX 77036 — Web: www.dailyinst.com	713-780-8600		639
Daily Inter Lake 727 E Idaho St, Kalispell MT 59901 — Web: www.dailyinterlake.com	406-755-7000	752-6114	532-2
Daily Item, The 110 Munroe St, Lynn MA 01901 — TF: 800-876-7060 ■ Web: www.itemlive.com	781-593-7700		532-2
Daily Item, The 200 Market St, Sunbury PA 17801 — TF: 800-326-9608 ■ Web: www.dailyitem.com	570-286-5671		532-3
Daily Journal 777 Walnut St, Franklin IN 46131 — TF: 888-736-7101 ■ Web: www.dailyjournal.net	317-736-2777		532-2
Daily Journal 1513 St Joe Dr PO Box A, Park Hills MO 63601 — TF: 800-660-8166 ■ Web: dailyjournalonline.com	573-431-2010	431-7640	532-2
Daily Journal 8 Dearborn Sq, Kankakee IL 60901 — TF: 866-299-9256 ■ Web: www.daily-journal.com	815-937-3300	937-3876	532-2
Daily Journal 891 E Oak Rd, Vineland NJ 08360 — TF: 800-222-0104 ■ Web: www.thedailyjournal.com	856-691-5000		532-2
Daily Journal 1242 S Green St, Tupelo MS 38804 — Web: www.djournal.com	662-842-2611		532-2
Daily Journal of Commerce 921 SW Washington St Ste 210, Portland OR 97205 — TF: 800-451-9998 ■ Web: djcoregon.com	503-226-1311	802-7239	532-2
Daily Juice Products 1 Daily Way, Verona PA 15147 — Web: www.dailyscocktails.com	412-828-9020		296-20
Daily Local News 250 N Bradford Ave, West Chester PA 19382 — TF: 800-568-7355 ■ Web: www.dailylocal.com	610-696-1775		532-2
Daily News 813 College St PO Box 90012, Bowling Green KY 42102 — Web: www.bgdailynews.com	270-781-1700		532-2
Daily News 724 Bell Fork Rd, Jacksonville NC 28540 — Web: www.jdnews.com	910-353-1171		532-2
Daily News 770 11th Ave PO Box 189, Longview WA 98632 — TF: 800-341-4745 ■ Web: tdn.com	360-577-2500		532-2
Daily News Broadcasting 804 College St, Bowling Green KY 42101 — TF: 888-847-9367 ■ Web: www.wdnsfm.com	270-781-2121		645-141
Daily News Journal 201 E Main St Ste 400, Murfreesboro TN 37130 — Web: www.dnj.com	615-893-5860		532-2
Daily News of Los Angeles 21060 Burbank Blvd Ste 200, Woodland Hills CA 91367 — Web: www.dailynews.com	818-222-3344		532-2
Daily News Publishing Co 193 Jefferson Ave, Memphis TN 38103 — Web: www.memphisdailynews.com	901-523-1561		532-3
Daily News-Record 231 S Liberty St, Harrisonburg VA 22801 — Web: www.dnronline.com	540-574-6200		532-2
Daily Nonpareil 535 W Broadway Ste 300, Council Bluffs IA 51503 — TF: 800-283-1882 ■ Web: www.nonpareilonline.com	712-328-1811	325-5776	532-2
Daily Planet Ltd 720 N Franklin St Ste 500, Chicago IL 60654 — Web: www.dailyplanetltd.com	312-640-7447		512
Daily Press 7505 Warwick Blvd, Newport News VA 23607 — Web: www.dailypress.com	757-247-4600		532-2
Daily Press 13891 Park Ave, Victorville CA 92393 — Web: www.vvdailypress.com	760-241-7744	241-7145	532-2
Daily Printing Inc 2333 Niagara Ln, Plymouth MN 55447 — Web: www.dailyprinting.com	763-475-2333		627
Daily Progress 685 W Rio Rd, Charlottesville VA 22901 — TF: 866-469-4866 ■ Web: www.dailyprogress.com	434-978-7200	978-7252	637-8
Daily Racing Form 100 Broadway 7th Fl, New York NY 10005 — TF: 800-306-3676 ■ Web: www.drf.com	212-366-7600		457-14
Daily Record 212 E Liberty St PO Box 918, Wooster OH 44691 — TF: 800-686-2958 ■ Web: www.the-daily-record.com	330-264-1125		532-2
Daily Record 16 W Main St, Rochester NY 14614 — Web: nydailyrecord.com	585-232-6920	232-2740	532-2
Daily Record Inc 6 Century Dr, Parsippany NJ 07054 — Web: www.dailyrecord.com	973-428-6200		637-8
Daily Record, The 200 St Paul Pl Ste 2480, Baltimore MD 21202 — Web: thedailyrecord.com	443-524-8100		637-8
Daily Republic 1250 Texas St, Fairfield CA 94533 — Web: www.dailyrepublic.com	707-425-4646	425-5924	532-2
Daily Sentinel 734 S 7th St, Grand Junction CO 81501 — Web: www.gjsentinel.com	970-242-5050	244-8578	532-2
Daily Sentinel 111 Ct St, Pomeroy OH 45769 — Web: www.mydailysentinel.com	740-992-2155	992-2157	532-2
Daily Sentinel 701 Veterans Dr, Scottsboro AL 35768 — TF: 877-985-9212 ■ Web: jcsentinel.com	256-259-1020	259-2709	532-2
Daily Star 5001 State Hwy 23 Ste 3-109, Oneonta NY 13820 — TF: 800-721-1000 ■ Web: www.thedailystar.com	607-432-1000	432-5707	532-2
Daily Sun 1100 Main St, The Villages FL 32159 — Web: www.thevillagesdailysun.com	352-753-1119		532-4
Daily Telegram, The 133 N Winter St, Adrian MI 49221 — Web: www.lenconnect.com	517-265-5111		532-2
Daily Telegraph 928 Bluefield Ave, Bluefield WV 24701 — TF: 800-763-2459 ■ Web: www.bdtonline.com	304-327-2811		532-2
Daily Times 618 Beam St, Salisbury MD 21801 — TF: 877-335-6278 ■ Web: www.delmarvanow.com	410-749-7171		532-2
Daily Times 307 E Harper St, Maryville TN 37804 — Web: www.thedailytimes.com	865-981-1100	981-1175	532-2
Daily Tribune 2142 First Ave, Hibbing MN 55746 — Web: www.hibbingmn.com	218-262-1011	262-4318	532-2
Daily World 315 S Michigan St, Aberdeen WA 98520 — Web: www.thedailyworld.com	360-532-4000	533-6039	532-2
Dailybreak Inc 46 Waltham St 4th Fl, Boston MA 02118 — Web: www.dailybreak.com	617-451-1790		387
DailyPay Inc 55 Broad St, New York NY 10004 — TF: 866-432-0472 ■ Web: www.dailypay.com	866-432-0472		39

Name / Address	City	State	Zip	Phone	Fax	Class
Daimler Vans Manufacturing LLC 8501 Palmetto Commerce Pkwy *Web:* www.daimler.com	Ladson	SC	29456	843-695-5000		58
DaimlerChrysler Corp *Jeep Div* PO Box 21-8004 *TF:* 800-992-1997 ■ *Web:* www.jeep.com	Auburn Hills	MI	48321	800-992-1997		59
Daines Insurance & Financial Services LLP 5806 Summerfield Dr *Web:* dainesinsurance.com	Texarkana	TX	75503	903-793-3034		390
Daines Steve (Sen R - MT) 320 Hart Senate Office Bldg *Web:* www.daines.senate.gov	Washington	DC	20510	202-224-2651		342-2
Daingerfield State Park 455 Park Rd 17 *Web:* tpwd.texas.gov	Daingerfield	TX	75638	903-645-2921		565
Daired's Salon & Spa Pangea 2400 W I-20 *Web:* daireds.com	Arlington	TX	76017	817-465-9797		77
Dairiconcepts LP 3253 E Chestnut Expy *TF:* 877-596-4374 ■ *Web:* www.dairiconcepts.com	Springfield	MO	65802	417-829-3400		296-5
Dairy Barn Stores Inc 544 Elwood Rd *Web:* www.dairybarn.com	East Northport	NY	11731	631-368-8050	266-2547	204
Dairy Center for the Arts 2590 Walnut St *Web:* www.thedairy.org	Boulder	CO	80302	303-440-7826		50-2
Dairy Conveyor Corp 38 Mt Ebo Dr S *Web:* www.dairyconveyor.com	Brewster	NY	10509	845-278-7878		207
Dairy Farmers of America Inc 10220 N Ambassador Dr *TF:* 888-332-6455 ■ *Web:* www.dfamilk.com	Kansas City	MO	64153	816-801-6455		296-5
Dairy Food USA Inc 2819 County Rd F *Web:* www.dairyfoodusa.com	Blue Mounds	WI	53517	608-437-5598		296-5
Dairy Fresh LLC 2221 Patterson Ave *Web:* www.dairyfoods.com	Winston-Salem	NC	27105	336-723-0311		296-27
Dairy Herd Management 8725 Rosehill Rd Ste 200 *TF:* 800-331-9310 ■ *Web:* www.dairyherd.com	Lenexa	KS	66215	913-438-8700		457-1
Dairy Management Inc (DMI) 10255 W Higgins Rd Ste 900 *TF:* 800-853-2479 ■ *Web:* www.usdairy.com	Rosemont	IL	60018	800-853-2479		48-2
Dairy One 730 Warren Rd *TF:* 800-344-2697 ■ *Web:* www.dairyone.com	Ithaca	NY	14850	607-257-1272	257-6808	11-2
Dairy Queen 7505 Metro Blvd *TF:* 800-883-4279 ■ *Web:* www.dairyqueen.com	Minneapolis	MN	55439	952-830-0200		381
Dairy Valley Distributing 1201 S 1st St *TF:* 800-682-7772 ■ *Web:* www.dairyvalleydist.com	Mount Vernon	WA	98273	360-424-7091	424-7092	297-4
Dairyamerica Inc 7815 N Palm Ave Ste 250 *TF:* 800-722-3110 ■ *Web:* www.dairyamerica.com	Fresno	CA	93711	559-251-0992	251-1078	49-18
Dairyland Laboratories Inc 217 E Main St *TF:* 800-658-2481 ■ *Web:* www.dairylandlabs.com	Arcadia	WI	54612	608-323-2123		743
Dairyland Power Co-op 3200 E Ave S *Web:* www.dairylandpower.com	La Crosse	WI	54601	608-788-4000		245
Dairyland USA Corp 240 Food Center Dr *Web:* www.chefswarehouse.com	Bronx	NY	10474	718-842-8700		297-9
Dairyman's Supply Co (DSC) 3114 State Rte 45 S *TF:* 800-626-3903 ■ *Web:* dairymanssupply.com	Mayfield	KY	42066	270-247-5641	247-0327	191-3
Dairymen's Feed & Supply Co 323 E Washington St	Petaluma	CA	94952	707-763-1585		447
Dairy-Mix Inc 3020 46th Ave N *TF:* 800-955-6101 ■ *Web:* www.dairymix.com	Saint Petersburg	FL	33714	727-525-6101	522-0769	296-25
Dais Analytic Corp 11552 Prosperous Dr *Web:* daisanalytic.com	Odessa	FL	33556	727-375-8484		14
Daishowa-Marubeni International Ltd 510 Burrard St Ste 700 *Web:* www.dmi.ca	Vancouver	BC	V6C3A8	604-684-4326		638
Daisy Blue Naturals 2610 Yh Hanson Ave Ste 108 *Web:* www.daisybluenaturals.com	Albert Lea	MN	56007	507-373-0229		231
Daisy Data Displays 2850 Lewisberry Rd *Web:* www.daisydata.com	York Haven	PA	17370	717-932-9999	932-8000	173-4
Daisy Farms 28355-M 152 *Web:* www.daisyfarms.net	Dowagiac	MI	49047	269-782-6321	782-7131	297-7
Daisy IT Supplies Sales & Service 8575 Red Oak Ave *TF:* 800-266-5585 ■ *Web:* daisyit.com	Rancho Cucamonga	CA	91730	909-989-5585		112
Daisy Outdoor Products 400 W Stribling Dr *TF:* 800-643-3458 ■ *Web:* www.daisy.com	Rogers	AR	72756	479-636-1200		710
Daisy Rock Guitars 16320 Roscoe Blvd Ste 100 *TF:* 877-693-2479 ■ *Web:* www.daisyrock.com	Van Nuys	CA	91410	855-417-8677		527
Daisy State Park 103 E Pk *Web:* www.arkansasstateparks.com	Kirby	AR	71950	870-398-4487		565
Daiwa Capital Markets America Inc Financial Sq 32 Old Slip *Web:* www.us.daiwacm.com	New York	NY	10005	212-612-7000		690
Daiwa Corp 11137 Warland Dr *TF:* 800-736-4653 ■ *Web:* www.daiwa.com	Cypress	CA	90630	562-375-6800		710
DAK Group, The 195 Rt 17 S *Web:* www.dakgroup.com	Rochelle Park	NJ	07662	201-712-9555		690
DAKE 724 Robbins Rd **Fax Area Code:* 616 ■ *TF:* 800-846-3253 ■ *Web:* www.dakecorp.com	Grand Haven	MI	49417	800-937-3253	842-0859*	351
Dakkota Integrated Systems 1875 Holloway Dr *Web:* dakkota.com	Holt	MI	48842	517-694-6500		247
Dakno 3101 Poplarwood Ct Ste 108 *Web:* www.dakno.com	Raleigh	NC	27604	919-877-8511		463
Dako Group, The 2966 Industrial Row *Web:* www.dakogroup.com	Troy	MI	48084	248-655-0100		260
Dakota Air Parts International Inc 1801 23rd Ave N Ste 119 *Web:* www.dakotaairparts.com	Fargo	ND	58102	701-297-9999	297-9991	21
Dakota Analytics Inc 205 5th Ave SW Ste 600 *Web:* dakotaanalytics.com	Calgary	AB	T2P2V7	403-264-6999		196
Dakota Brands International Inc 2121 13th St NE *TF:* 800-844-5073 ■ *Web:* www.dakotabrands.com	Jamestown	ND	58401	701-252-5073	251-1047	296-1
Dakota Central (DCT) 630 5th St N *TF:* 800-771-0974 ■ *Web:* www.daktel.com	Carrington	ND	58421	701-652-3184	674-8121	224
Dakota College at Bottineau 105 Simrall Blvd *TF:* 800-542-6866 ■ *Web:* dakotacollege.edu	Bottineau	ND	58318	701-228-2277	228-5499	162
Dakota Communications 800 Wilshire Blvd Ste 410 *Web:* dakcomm.com	Los Angeles	CA	90017	310-815-8444		636
Dakota Community Bank & Trust 1727 State St *Web:* www.dakotacommunitybank.com	Bismarck	ND	58501	701-255-9000	255-1510	70
Dakota County 1601 Broadway *Web:* dakotacountyne.org	Dakota City	NE	68731	402-987-2126	987-2186	338
Dakota County 1560 Hwy 55 *Web:* www.co.dakota.mn.us	Hastings	MN	55033	651-438-8100	438-4405	338
Dakota County Regional Chamber of Commerce 1121 Town Center Dr Ste 102 *Web:* www.dcrchamber.com	Eagan	MN	55123	651-452-9872	452-8978	139
Dakota County Technical College 1300 E 145th St *TF:* 877-937-3282 ■ *Web:* www.dctc.edu	Rosemount	MN	55068	651-423-8301	423-8775	800
Dakota Creek Industries Inc 820 Fourth St PO Box 218 *Web:* www.dakotacreek.com	Anacortes	WA	98221	360-293-9575	293-6432	698
Dakota Digital Inc 4510 W 61st St N *TF:* 800-593-4160 ■ *Web:* www.dakotadigital.com	Sioux Falls	SD	57107	605-332-6513		253
Dakota Drug Inc 28 Main St N *TF:* 800-437-2018 ■ *Web:* www.dakdrug.com	Minot	ND	58703	701-852-2141		238
Dakota Electric Assn 4300 220th St W *TF:* 800-874-3409 ■ *Web:* www.dakotaelectric.com	Farmington	MN	55024	651-463-6144		245
Dakota Energy Cooperative Inc PO Box 830 *TF:* 800-353-8591 ■ *Web:* dakotaenergy.coop	Huron	SD	57350	605-352-8591		245
Dakota Fabricating Inc 12111 W Northern Ave *TF:* 866-357-8433 ■ *Web:* www.dakotafab.com	Glendale	AZ	85307	623-935-7805		207
Dakota Granite Co 48391 150th St PO Box 1351 **Fax Area Code:* 605 ■ *TF:* 800-843-3333 ■ *Web:* dakotagranite.com	Milbank	SD	57252	800-843-3333	432-6155*	724
Dakota Homestead Title Insurance Co 315 S Phillips Ave *Web:* www.dakotahomestead.com	Sioux Falls	SD	57104	605-336-0388	996-3270	391-6
Dakota Jazz Club & Restaurant 1010 Nicollet Ave *Web:* www.dakotacooks.com	Minneapolis	MN	55403	612-332-1010		671
Dakota Line Inc PO Box 476 *TF:* 800-532-5682 ■ *Web:* www.dakotalines.com	Vermillion	SD	57069	605-624-5228	624-5338	780
Dakota Lions Sight & Health 4501 W 61st St N *TF:* 800-245-7846 ■ *Web:* www.dakotasight.org	Sioux Falls	SD	57107	605-373-1008	373-1261	269
Dakota Manufacturing Company Inc 1909 S Rowley St *TF:* 800-232-5682 ■ *Web:* traileze.com	Mitchell	SD	57301	605-996-5571	996-5572	779
Dakota Missouri Valley & Western Railroad (DMVW) 3501 E Rosser Ave *Web:* www.dmvwrr.com	Bismarck	ND	58501	701-223-9282	223-4147	649
Dakota Plains Co-op 151 Ninth Ave NW *Web:* www.chsdakotaplainsag.com	Valley City	ND	58072	701-845-0812		324
Dakota Refrigeration Inc 4322 15th Ave N *TF:* 800-433-1665 ■ *Web:* www.dakref.com	Fargo	ND	58102	701-235-9698		665
Dakota Riggers & Tool Supply Inc 704 E Benson Rd *TF:* 800-888-1612 ■ *Web:* www.dakotariggers.com	Sioux Falls	SD	57104	605-335-0041		492
Dakota Specialty Milling Inc 4014 15th Ave NW *TF:* 844-633-2746 ■ *Web:* www.dakotaspecialtymilling.com	Fargo	ND	58102	844-633-2746		296-16
Dakota State University 820 N Washington Ave *TF:* 888-378-9988 ■ *Web:* dsu.edu	Madison	SD	57042	605-256-5139	256-5020	166
Dakota Supply Group (DSG) 2601 3rd Ave N *TF:* 800-437-4702 ■ *Web:* www.dsgsupply.com	Fargo	ND	58102	701-237-9440	237-6504	246
Dakota Systems Inc 1057 Broadway Rd *Web:* www.dakotasystems.com	Dracut	MA	01826	978-275-0600	275-0606	696
Dakota Tube Inc 221 Airport Dr *Web:* www.dakotatube.com	Watertown	SD	57201	605-882-2156		454
Dakota Typewriter Exchange 1635 Deadwood Ave PO Box 2353 *Web:* dakotabusiness.com	Rapid City	SD	57702	605-342-8934		535
Dakota Valley Electric Co-op 7296 Hwy 281 *Web:* www.dakotavalley.com	Edgeley	ND	58433	701-493-2281		245
Dakota Vision Center LLC 5012 S Bur Oak Pl *Web:* www.dakotavisioncenter.com	Sioux Falls	SD	57108	605-361-1680	361-1590	543
Dakota Wesleyan University 1200 W University Ave *TF:* 800-333-8506 ■ *Web:* www.dwu.edu	Mitchell	SD	57301	605-995-2600	995-2699	166
Dakota Zoo 602 Riverside Park Rd *Web:* www.dakotazoo.org	Bismarck	ND	58504	701-223-7543	258-8350	823
Dakotacare 2600 W 49th St *TF:* 800-325-5598 ■ *Web:* www.dakotacare.com	Sioux Falls	SD	57105	605-334-4000	334-8717	391-3
Daktronics Inc 201 Daktronics Dr *NASDAQ: DAKT* ■ *TF:* 800-325-8766 ■ *Web:* www.daktronics.com	Brookings	SD	57006	605-692-0200	697-4700	173-4
DAL Inc 300 E Madison Ave *TF:* 800-355-9999 ■ *Web:* www.dalcollects.com	Clifton Heights	PA	19018	610-623-1400	623-1080	196

Phone | Fax | Class

Dal Poggetto & Company LLP
149 Stony Cir ... Santa Rosa CA 95401 707-545-3311 2
Web: www.dalpoggetto.com
Dalager Engineering Co
936 Railroad Ave PO Box 548 ... Bath SD 57427 605-229-2412 256
Web: www.dalagerengineering.com
Daland Corp 9313 Eat 34th St N Ste 100 ... Wichita KS 67226 316-681-1081 194
Web: www.dalandcorporation.com
DALB Inc 73 Industrial Blvd ... Kearneysville WV 25430 304-725-0300 627
Web: www.dalb.com
Dalbec Audio Lab 58 King St ... Troy NY 12180 518-272-7098 52
Web: www.Dalbec.com
Dalby, Wendland & Company PC
201 Centennial St Ste 300
PO Box 1150 ... Glenwood Springs CO 81602 970-945-8575 945-9236 196
Web: www.dalbycpa.com
Dalco Metals Inc 857 Walworth St ... Walworth WI 53184 262-275-6175 295
TF: 877-523-2526 ■ *Web:* www.dalcometals.com
Dale Barton Agency
1100 East 6600 South ... Salt Lake City UT 84121 801-288-1600 288-1944 390
TF: 866-288-1666 ■ *Web:* dalebarton.com
Dale Buchanan & Assn
1206 Pointe Center Dr Ste 110 ... Chattanooga TN 37421 800-945-4950 894-1821* 428
**Fax Area Code:* 423 ■ *TF:* 800-945-4950 ■ *Web:* dalebuchanan.com
Dale Carnegie & Associates Inc
290 Motor Pkwy ... Hauppauge NY 11788 800-231-5800 765
TF: 800-231-5800 ■ *Web:* www.dalecarnegie.com
Dale Corp 70 Limekiln Pke ... Glenside PA 19038 248-542-2400 737
Web: www.dalecorp.com
Dale County 202 Hwy 123 S Ste C ... Ozark AL 36360 334-774-6025 774-1841 338
Web: dalecountyal.org
Dale Earnhardt Inc
1675 Dale Earnhardt Hwy 3 ... Mooresville NC 28115 704-662-8000 642
Web: www.daleearnhardtinc.com
Dale Engineering & Son Inc
3 Alfred Cir ... Bedford MA 01730 781-541-6055 261
Web: daleengineering.com
Dale K. Ehrhart Inc
100 W Venice Ave Ste A & G ... Venice FL 34285 941-485-8220 488-8465 401
Web: www.dkeinc.com
Dale Laboratories 2960 Simms St ... Hollywood FL 33020 954-925-0103 922-3008 588
TF: 800-327-1776 ■ *Web:* www.dalelabs.com
Dale M. Krause Inc 1234 Enterprise Dr ... De Pere WI 54115 866-605-7437 41
TF: 866-605-7437 ■ *Web:* medicaidannuity.com
Dale Massey Insurance Agency Inc
4605 Roswell Rd NE ... Atlanta GA 30342 404-257-8880 390
Web: dalemassey.net
Dale Medical Products Inc
PO Box 1556 ... Plainville MA 02762 800-343-3980 695-6587* 476
**Fax Area Code:* 508 ■ *TF:* 800-343-3980 ■ *Web:* www.dalemed.com
Dale Meyer Trucking Co
2400 W Hillmont Rd ... Odessa TX 79764 432-366-3661 366-4585 780
Web: www.dalemeyertrucking.com
Dale Scott & Co
650 California St Ste 2050 ... San Francisco CA 94108 415-956-1030 401
Web: www.dalescott.com
Dale Tiffany Inc
14765 Firestone Blvd ... La Mirada CA 90638 714-739-2700 362
Web: www.daletiffany.com
Dale Willey Automotive 2840 Iowa St ... Lawrence KS 66046 785-727-1124 843-4903 57
Web: www.dalewilleyauto.com
Dalena & Bosch LLC 265 Main St Ste 2 ... Madison NJ 07940 973-377-2066 41
Web: dalenabosch.com
Daler-Rowney USA Ltd
7 Corporate Dr Ste 4 ... Cranbury NJ 08512 609-655-5252 655-5852 43
Web: www.daler-rowney.com
Dales Furniture LLC
705 W Kansas Ave ... Garden City KS 67846 620-275-6385 321
Web: dalesfurnituregc.com
Dalesio's of Little Italy
829 Eastern Ave ... Baltimore MD 21202 410-539-1965 671
Web: www.dalesios.com
Daley & Heft LLP
462 Stevens Ave Ste 201 ... Solana Beach CA 92075 858-755-5666 428
Web: daleyheft.com
Dalfen America Corp
Westmount 4444 Rue Sainte-Catherine W
Ste 100 ... Montreal QC H3Z1R2 514-938-1050 528
Web: www.dalfen.com
Dalhousie University
Health Law Institute
6061 University Ave PO Box 15000 ... Halifax NS B3H4R2 902-494-6881 494-6879 167-3
Web: www.dal.ca
Dalhousie University Faculty of Medicine
1459 Oxford St ... Halifax NS B3H4R2 902-494-1874 494-6369 167-2
TF: 866-327-8256 ■ *Web:* medicine.dal.ca
Dali Restaurant 415 Washington St ... Somerville MA 02143 617-661-3254 661-2813 671
Web: dalirestaurant.com
Daliah Plastics Corp
134 W Wainman Ave ... Asheboro NC 27203 336-629-0551 600
Web: www.daliahplastics.com
Dall Bay State Marine Park
400 Willoughby Ave PO Box 111020 ... Juneau AK 99801 907-465-3400 565
Web: www.dnr.alaska.gov
Dalla's Machine Inc
4410 Park View Dr ... Schnecksville PA 18078 610-799-2800 799-2844 488
Web: www.dallamachine.com
Dallago Corp 2411 E Aztec St ... Gallup NM 87301 505-722-6638 610
Dallam County PO Box 1352 ... Dalhart TX 79022 806-244-4751 338
Web: www.dallam.org
Dallas Airmotive Inc
900 Nolen Dr Ste 100 ... Grapevine TX 76051 214-956-3001 20
Web: www.dallasairmotive.com
Dallas Animal Clinic PC
135 SE Fir Villa Rd ... Dallas OR 97338 503-623-3943 794
Web: dallasanimalclinicpc.com
Dallas Arboretum & Botanical Garden
8525 Garland Rd ... Dallas TX 75218 214-515-6500 97
Web: www.dallasarboretum.org
Dallas Area Rapid Transit Authority (DART)
1401 Pacific Ave ... Dallas TX 75202 214-979-1111 468
Web: www.dart.org
Dallas Athletic Club
4111 Dallas Athletic Club Dr ... Dallas TX 75228 972-279-6517 120
Web: www.dallasathleticclub.org
Dallas Baptist University
3000 Mtn Creek Pkwy ... Dallas TX 75211 214-333-7100 333-5447 166
TF: 800-460-1328 ■ *Web:* www.dbu.edu
Dallas Bar Assn 2101 Ross Ave ... Dallas TX 75201 214-220-7400 220-7465 95
Web: www.dallasbar.org
Dallas Bias Fabrics Inc
1401 N Carroll Ave ... Dallas TX 75204 214-824-2036 34
Web: www.dallasbias.com
Dallas Black Dance Theatre
2700 Flora St ... Dallas TX 75201 214-871-2376 871-2842 573-1
Web: dbdt.com
Dallas Center - Grimes Community School District
1414 Walnut St Ste 200 ... Dallas Center IA 50063 515-992-3866 685
Web: dcgschools.com
Dallas Christian College
2700 Christian Pkwy ... Dallas TX 75234 972-241-3371 241-8021 161
TF: 800-688-1029 ■ *Web:* www.dallas.edu
Dallas City Hall 1500 Marilla St ... Dallas TX 75201 214-670-4538 670-3946 337
Web: www.dallascityhall.com
Dallas City Packing Inc
7455 Malabar Ln ... Dallas TX 75230 214-948-3901 473
Dallas Container Corp 8330 Endicott Ln ... Dallas TX 75227 214-381-7148 100
Web: www.dallascontainer.com
Dallas Contemporary 161 Glass St ... Dallas TX 75207 214-821-2522 821-9103 50-2
Web: www.dallascontemporary.org
Dallas Convention & Visitors Bureau
325 N St Paul St Ste 700 ... Dallas TX 75201 214-571-1000 206
TF: 800-232-5527 ■ *Web:* www.visitdallas.com
Dallas Convention Ctr 650 S Griffin St ... Dallas TX 75202 214-939-2700 205
TF: 877-850-2100 ■ *Web:* www.dallasconventioncenter.com
Dallas County 801 Ct St ... Adel IA 50003 515-993-5814 338
Web: www.dallascountyiowa.gov
Dallas County 411 Elm St ... Dallas TX 75202 214-653-7361 338
Web: www.dallascounty.org
Dallas County 105 Lauderdale ... Selma AL 36702 334-874-2553 874-2587 338
Web: www.dallascounty-al.org
Dallas County Hospital 610 Tenth St ... Perry IA 50220 515-465-3547 374-3
Web: www.dallascohospital.org
Dallas County Medical Society
140 E 12th St ... Dallas TX 75203 214-948-3622 533
Web: www.dallas-cms.org
Dallas Cowboys 1 Cowboys Pkwy ... Irving TX 75063 817-481-7277 715-3
Web: www.dallascowboys.com
Dallas Dating Co, The
14180 Dallas Pkwy Ste 110 ... Dallas TX 75254 972-332-5319 226
Web: www.thedallasdatingcompany.com
Dallas Desk Inc 15207 Midway Rd ... Addison TX 75001 972-788-1802 321
Web: www.dallasdesk.com
Dallas Digital Services LLC
5316 Bransford Rd ... Colleyville TX 76034 817-577-8794 180
Web: www.ddserv.com
Dallas Fan Fares Inc
5485 Beltline Rd Ste 270 ... Dallas TX 75254 972-239-9969 181
TF: 800-925-6979 ■ *Web:* www.fanfares.com
Dallas Firefighters Museum
3801 Parry Ave ... Dallas TX 75226 214-821-1500 520
Web: www.dallasfiremuseum.com
Dallas Galleria 13350 Dallas Pkwy ... Dallas TX 75240 972-661-1068 460
Web: www.galleriadallas.com
Dallas Heritage Village 1515 S Harwood ... Dallas TX 75215 214-421-5141 520
Web: www.dallasheritagevillage.org
Dallas Historical Society (DHS)
Hall of State at Fair Park 3939 Grand Ave ... Dallas TX 75210 214-421-4500 421-7500 48-13
Web: www.dallashistory.org
Dallas Holocaust & Human Rights Museum
300 N Houston ... Dallas TX 75202 214-741-7500 747-2270 520
Web: www.dhhrm.org
Dallas Independent School District
3700 Ross Ave ... Dallas TX 75204 972-925-3700 925-4201 685
TF: 866-796-3682 ■ *Web:* www.dallasisd.org
Dallas Institute of Funeral Service
3909 S Buckner Blvd ... Dallas TX 75227 214-388-5466 388-0316 800
TF: 800-235-5444 ■ *Web:* www.dallasinstitute.edu
Dallas International University
7500 W Camp Wisdom Rd ... Dallas TX 75236 972-708-7340 166
Web: www.diu.edu
Dallas Johnson Greenhouse Inc
2802 Twin City Dr ... Council Bluffs IA 51501 712-366-0407 369
TF: 800-445-4794 ■ *Web:* www.djgreenhouses.com
Dallas Love Field
8008 Cedar Springs Rd LB 16 ... Dallas TX 75235 214-670-5683 670-6051 27
Web: www.dallas-lovefield.com
Dallas Market Ctr
2100 Stemmons Fwy Ste 113 ... Dallas TX 75207 214-655-6100 749-5479 205
Web: www.dallasmarketcenter.com
Dallas Medical Ctr 7 Medical Pkwy ... Dallas TX 75234 972-888-7000 374-3
Web: www.dallasmedcenter.com
Dallas Morning News 1954 Commerce St ... Dallas TX 75202 214-977-8222 532-2
TF: 800-925-1500 ■ *Web:* www.dallasnews.com
Dallas Museum of Art 1717 N Harwood St ... Dallas TX 75201 214-922-1200 520
Web: dma.org
Dallas Northeast Chamber of Commerce
9543 Losa Dr Ste 118 ... Dallas TX 75218 214-328-4100 139
Web: www.eastdallaschamber.com
Dallas Observer
2501 Oak Lawn Ave Ste 700 PO Box 190289 ... Dallas TX 75219 214-757-9000 757-8590 532-5
Web: www.dallasobserver.com
Dallas Opera 2403 Flora St Ste 500 ... Dallas TX 75201 214-443-1043 443-1060 573-2
Web: dallasopera.org
Dallas Regional Chamber
500 N Akard St Ste 2600 ... Dallas TX 75201 214-746-6600 746-6799 139
Web: www.dallaschamber.org

Name / Address	City	State	Zip	Phone	Fax	Class
Dallas Regional Medical Ctr (DRMC) 1011 N Galloway Ave **Fax Area Code:* 972 ■ *Web:* www.dallasregionalmedicalcenter.com	Mesquite	TX	75149	214-320-7000	289-9468*	374-3
Dallas Strings Inc 20 E Mcdermott Dr *Web:* dallasstrings.com	Allen	TX	75002	469-675-0085		526
Dallas Symphony Orchestra 2301 Flora St *Web:* www.mydso.com	Dallas	TX	75201	214-849-4376		573-3
Dallas Theater Ctr (DTC) *Wyly Theatre* 2400 Flora St *Web:* www.dallastheatercenter.org	Dallas	TX	75201	214-526-8210	521-7666	749
Dallas Theological Seminary 3909 Swiss Ave *TF:* 800-992-0998 ■ *Web:* www.dts.edu	Dallas	TX	75204	800-387-9673		167-3
Dallas Waste Disposal & Recycling Inc 3303 Pluto St *Web:* www.dallasrecycling.net	Dallas	TX	75212	214-634-1831		660
Dallas Wholesalers 2141 Collins Rd Ste 1302 *Web:* www.dallaswholesalers.net	Denton	TX	76208	940-382-8110		523
Dallas World Aquarium 1801 N Griffin St *Web:* www.dwazoo.com	Dallas	TX	75202	214-720-2224		40
Dallas-Fort Worth International Airport (DFW) 2400 Aviation Dr PO Box 619428 *TF:* 800-252-7522 ■ *Web:* www.dfwairport.com	Dallas	TX	75261	972-973-3112		27
Dallastown Area School District 700 New School Ln *Web:* www.dallastown.net	Dallastown	PA	17313	717-244-4021		685
Dalmac Oilfield Services Inc 4934-89 St *Web:* www.dalmacenergy.com	Edmonton	AB	T6E5K1	780-988-8510		539
Dalmec Inc 469 Fox Ct *Web:* www.dalmec.com	Bloomingdale	IL	60108	630-307-8426		295
Dalo's Bakery Inc 1201 Freas Ave *Web:* dalosbakeryinc.com	Berwick	PA	18603	570-752-4519	752-7360	296-1
Dalrymple Gravel & Contracting Company Inc 2105 S Broadway *TF:* 800-957-3130 ■ *Web:* dalrymplecompanies.com	Pine City	NY	14871	607-737-6200	737-1056	46
Dalsin Industries Inc 9111 Grand Ave S *TF:* 800-258-2260 ■ *Web:* www.dalsinind.com	Bloomington	MN	55420	952-881-2260	881-2841	697
Dal-Tile International Inc 7834 Hawn Fwy *Web:* www.daltile.com	Dallas	TX	75217	214-398-1411		751
Dalton & Finegold L L P 34 Essex St *Web:* www.dfllp.com	Andover	MA	01810	978-470-8400		445
Dalton Agency, The 140 W Monroe St *Web:* www.daltonagency.com	Jacksonville	FL	32202	904-398-5222		4
Dalton Computer Services Inc 1612 Cleveland Hwy *Web:* www.daltoncomputer.com	Dalton	GA	30721	706-259-3327		175
Dalton Corp 310 Ellis St *Web:* www.daltoncorporation.com	Stryker	OH	43557	574-267-8111		203
Dalton Enterprises Inc 131 Willow St *TF:* 800-851-5606 ■ *Web:* latexite.com	Cheshire	CT	06410	203-272-3221	271-3396	46
Dalton Gear Co 212 Colfax Ave N *TF:* 800-328-7485 ■ *Web:* www.daltongear.com	Minneapolis	MN	55405	612-374-2150	374-2467	709
Dalton Greiner Hartman Maher & Company LLC 565 Fifth Ave Ste 2101 *TF:* 800-653-2839 ■ *Web:* dghm.com	New York	NY	10017	212-557-2445	557-4898	401
Dalton Investments LLC 1601 Cloverfield Blvd Ste 5050 N *Web:* www.daltoninvestments.com	Santa Monica	CA	90404	424-231-9100		401
Dalton Medical 4259 McEwen Rd **Fax Area Code:* 972 ■ *Web:* www.daltonmedical.com	Farmers Branch	TX	75244	469-329-5200	386-6615*	475
Dalton Public Schools 300 W Waugh St PO Box 1408 *Web:* www.daltonpublicschools.com	Dalton	GA	30722	706-876-4000	226-4583	685
Dalton Schools Inc 108 E 89th St *Web:* www.dalton.org	New York	NY	10128	212-423-5200		685
Dalton State College 650 N College Dr *TF:* 800-829-4436 ■ *Web:* www.daltonstate.edu	Dalton	GA	30720	706-272-4436		166
Dalton Utilities 1200 VD Parrot Jr Pky *Web:* www.dutil.com	Dalton	GA	30721	706-278-1313	281-1094	787
Dalton Watson Fine Books 1730 Christopher Dr *Web:* www.daltonwatson.com	Deerfield	IL	60015	847-274-5874		637-2
Dalton, Mowrer, and Chidister LLP 203 College Ave PO Box 529 *Web:* dmclawfirm.com	Kennett	MO	63857	573-888-4631		41
Dalton-Whitfield Chamber of Commerce 890 College Dr *Web:* daltonchamber.org	Dalton	GA	30720	706-278-7373	226-8739	139
Daly & Associates LLC 16 South St 2nd Fl *Web:* dalyfamilylaw.net	Morristown	NJ	07960	973-292-9222		41
Daly City Public Library 40 Wembley Dr *TF:* 888-227-7669 ■ *Web:* www.dalycity.org	Daly City	CA	94015	650-991-8025	991-8225	434-3
Daly City-Colma Chamber of Commerce 362 Gellert Blvd Ste 138 *Web:* dccchamber.org	Daly City	CA	94015	650-755-3900	755-5160	139
Daly Computers Inc 22521 Gateway Center Dr *TF:* 800-955-3259 ■ *Web:* www.daly.com	Clarksburg	MD	20871	301-670-0381	963-1516	176
Daly Insurance Brokerage Services LLC 231 Farmington Ave *Web:* dalybrokerage.com	Farmington	CT	06032	860-677-5707		390
Daly Seven Inc 4829 Riverside Dr *Web:* dalyseven.com	Danville	VA	24541	434-822-2161		379
Daman Consulting Inc 1250 S Capial of Texas Hw S Bldg One Ste 460 *Web:* damaninc.com	Austin	TX	78746	512-329-6646	329-0767	196
Daman Industrial Services Inc 754 Kittanning Hollow Rd PO Box 486 *Web:* damansuperior.com	East Brady	PA	16028	724-526-5714	526-5277	454
Daman Products Company Inc 1811 N Home St *TF:* 800-959-7841 ■ *Web:* www.daman.com	Mishawaka	IN	46545	574-259-7841	259-7665	790
Damar Machinery Co 3389 3 Mile Rd *Web:* damarmachinery.com	Walker	MI	49534	616-453-4655	453-2710	454
Damar Services Inc 6067 Decatur Blvd *Web:* www.damar.org	Indianapolis	IN	46241	317-856-5201		672
Damariscotta Lake State Park 8 State Park Rd *Web:* www.maine.gov	Jefferson	ME	04348	207-549-7600		565
Damascus Bakery Inc 56 Glod St *TF:* 800-367-7482 ■ *Web:* www.damascusbakery.com	Brooklyn	NY	11201	718-855-1456	403-0948	68
Damascus Steel Casting Co Blockhouse Rd Run Extn *TF:* 800-920-2210 ■ *Web:* www.damascussteel.com	New Brighton	PA	15066	724-846-2770		492
Dameron Alloy Foundries Inc 6330 Gateway Dr Ste B *TF:* 800-421-1985 ■ *Web:* www.dameron.net	Cypress	CA	90630	714-820-6699	820-6698	492
Dameron Hospital Assn (DHA) 525 W Acacia St *TF:* 866-735-2929 ■ *Web:* www.dameronhospital.org	Stockton	CA	95203	209-944-5550		374-3
Damian's Cucina Italiana 3011 Smith St *Web:* www.damians.com	Houston	TX	77006	713-522-0439	522-4408	671
Damick Enterprises 1801 Rochester Industrial Dr *Web:* damick.net	Rochester Hills	MI	48309	248-652-7500	652-1834	454
Damico Burchfield LLP 536 Atwells Ave *Web:* dblawri.com	Providence	RI	02909	401-454-1212		41
Damon Company of Salem Inc 2117 Salem Industrial Dr *Web:* www.damonco.com	Salem	VA	24153	540-389-8609	389-8556	488
Damon Industries Inc 12435 Rockhill Ave NE *TF:* 800-362-9850 ■ *Web:* www.damonq.com	Alliance	OH	44601	330-821-5310	821-6355	151
Damon's Steak House 317 N Brand Blvd *Web:* www.damonsglendale.com	Glendale	CA	91203	818-507-1510		671
Damsky Paper Co 3501 First Ave N *Web:* www.damskypaper.com	Birmingham	AL	35222	205-521-9840	521-9853	554
Damuth Trane 1100 Cavalier Blvd *Web:* www.damuth.com	Chesapeake	VA	23323	757-558-0200	558-9715	187
Dan Althoff Trucking Inc 4600 Waldo Industrial Dr *Web:* danalthofftrucking.com	High Ridge	MO	63049	636-677-7772		311
Dan Bailey Fly Shop 209 W Park St *TF:* 800-356-4052 ■ *Web:* dan-bailey.com	Livingston	MT	59047	406-222-9550		711
Dan Bieger PLC 565 Volunteer Pkwy *Web:* biegerlaw.com	Bristol	TN	37620	423-573-4440		41
Dan Dolan Printing 2301 E Hennepin Ave *Web:* dolanprinting.com	Minneapolis	MN	55413	612-379-2311	379-0934	627
Dan Gernatt Gravel Products Inc 13870 Taylor Hollow Rd *Web:* www.gernatt.com	Collins	NY	14034	716-532-3371		515
Dan K. Richardson - Entrepreneurship Development Institute (EDI) 3209 Virginia Ave *TF:* 888-283-1177 ■ *Web:* www.cctiirsc.com	Fort Pierce	FL	34981	888-283-1177		167-3
Dan Klores Communications Inc (DKC) 261 Fifth Ave *Web:* www.dkcnews.com	New York	NY	10016	212-685-4300	685-9024	636
Dan Post Boot Co 1751 Alpine Dr *Web:* www.danpostboots.com	Clarksville	TN	37040	931-645-4466		301
Dan Rinehart Taxidermy Studio & School 83 Artisan Dr *TF:* 866-296-2782 ■ *Web:* www.taxidermyarts.com	Edgerton	WI	53534	608-884-3047		685
Dan River Business Development Ctr 300 Ringgold Industrial Pky *Web:* www.drbdc.com	Danville	VA	24540	434-793-9100		393
Dan Schantz Farm & Greenhouses LLC 8025 Spinnerstown Rd *TF:* 800-451-3064 ■ *Web:* www.danschantz.com	Zionsville	PA	18092	610-967-2181		369
Dan Wood Plumbing Heating 40400 Grand River Ste F *Web:* www.danwoodplumbingheating.com	Novi	MI	48375	248-348-4242		189-10
Dan'l Webster Inn 149 Main St *TF:* 800-444-3566 ■ *Web:* www.danlwebsterinn.com	Sandwich	MA	02563	508-888-3622		379
Dan's Comp 1 Competition Way *TF:* 888-888-3267 ■ *Web:* www.danscomp.com	Mount Vernon	IN	47620	888-888-3267		711
Dan's Excavating Inc 12955 23 Mile Rd *Web:* www.dansexc.com	Shelby Township	MI	48315	586-254-2040		196
Dan's Supermarket 835 S Washington St *Web:* www.shopdanssupermarket.com	Bismarck	ND	58504	701-255-3517		345
Dana B. Kenyon Co 5772 Timuquana Rd *Web:* dbkenyon.com	Jacksonville	FL	32210	904-777-0833		652
Dana Communications Inc 2 E Broad St *Web:* www.danacommunications.com	Hopewell	NJ	08525	609-466-9187		4
Dana Distributors Inc 52 Hatfield Ln *Web:* www.danadistributors.com	Goshen	NY	10924	845-294-4100	294-4111	81-1
Dana Hall School 45 Dana Rd PO Box 9010 *Web:* www.danahall.org	Wellesley	MA	02482	781-235-3010		622
Dana Innovations 212 Avenida Fabricante *TF:* 800-582-7777 ■ *Web:* www.sonance.com	San Clemente	CA	92672	949-492-7777		52
Dana Kepner Company Inc 700 Alcott St *Web:* www.danakepner.com	Denver	CO	80204	303-623-6161		612
Dana Point *Chamber of Commerce* 34163 Pacific Coast Hwy Ste 100	Dana Point	CA	92629	949-496-1555	496-5321	139
Dana Safety Supply Inc 5221 W Market St *TF:* 800-845-0045 ■ *Web:* danasafetysupply.com	Greensboro	NC	27409	336-854-5536		791
Dana Transport Inc 210 Essex Ave E *TF:* 800-733-3262 ■ *Web:* www.danacompanies.com	Avenel	NJ	07001	732-750-9100	636-7441	780

Name / Address	City	State	ZIP	Phone	Fax	Class
Dana-Farber Cancer Institute 450 Brookline Ave. *TF:* 866-408-3324 ■ *Web:* www.dana-farber.org	Boston	MA	02115	617-632-3591		769
Danaher Attig & Plante Plc 41 Rye Cir PO Box 2166 *Web:* dapplc.com	South Burlington	VT	05407	802-383-0399		2
Danaher Corp 2200 Pennsylvania Ave NW Ste 800 *NYSE: DHR* ■ *Web:* www.danaher.com	Washington	DC	20037	202-828-0850	828-0860	472
Danamark Watercare Ltd 2-90 Walker Dr *TF:* 888-326-2627 ■ *Web:* danamark.com	Brampton	ON	L6T4H6	888-326-2627		610
Dana-Saad Co N 3808 Sullivan Rd Bldg 105 Spokane Ind Pk *Web:* www.dana-saad.com	Spokane	WA	99216	509-924-6711	924-3241	604
Dana-Thomas House (DTH) 301 E Lawrence Ave *Web:* www.dana-thomas.org	Springfield	IL	62703	217-782-6776		50-3
Danburg Management Corp 7700 Congress Ave Ste 3100 *Web:* www.danburg.com	Boca Raton	FL	33487	561-997-5777		509
Danbury Hospital (DH) 24 Hospital Ave *TF:* 800-516-3658 ■ *Web:* www.danburyhospital.org	Danbury	CT	06810	203-739-7000		374-3
Danbury Public Library 170 Main St *Web:* www.danburylibrary.org	Danbury	CT	06810	203-797-4505	796-1677	434-3
Danby Group LLP, The 3060-A Business Park Dr *Web:* www.danbygroup.com	Norcross	GA	30071	770-416-9044		535
Dancap Private Equity Inc 197 Sheppard Ave W *Web:* www.dancap.ca	Toronto	ON	M2N1M9	416-590-9444		528
Dance Bros Inc 825C Hammonds Ferry Rd *Web:* dancebrothers.com	Linthicum Heights	MD	21090	410-789-8200	636-3663	189-3
Dance Magazine 333 Seventh Ave 11th Fl *TF:* 800-331-1750 ■ *Web:* www.dancemagazine.com	New York	NY	10001	212-979-4800		457-9
Dance Theatre of Harlem Inc 466 W 152nd St *Web:* www.dancetheatreofharlem.org	New York	NY	10031	212-690-2800	690-8736	573-1
Dance/USA 1029 Vermont Ave NW Ste 400 *Web:* danceusa.org	Washington	DC	20005	202-833-1717	833-2686	48-4
Dancetime Publications 11212 Indian Trl *TF:* 888-854-5602 ■ *Web:* www.dancetimepublications.com	Dallas	TX	75229	972-247-9955	247-9959	637-10
Dancing Deer Baking Company Inc 65 Sprague St W A *Web:* www.dancingdeer.com	Boston	MA	02136	617-442-7300		68
Dancing Dragon 15 Yale Ct *TF:* 888-433-3588 ■ *Web:* www.ddfengshui.com	Branford	CT	06405	203-483-1966		194
Dancker 291 Evans Way *Web:* www.dancker.com	Somerville	NJ	08876	908-231-1600		320
Danco Inc 2727 Chemsearch Blvd *Web:* www.danco.com	Irving	TX	75062	800-523-5135		385
Danco Industrial Contractors Inc 1121 N Beverlye Rd *Web:* www.dancoindustrial.com	Dothan	AL	36303	334-792-3985		186
Danco Precision Inc 601 Wheatland St PO Box 448 *Web:* www.dancoprecision.com	Phoenixville	PA	19460	610-933-8981	935-2011	488
Dancor Inc 2155 Dublin Rd *Web:* dancorsolutions.com	Columbus	OH	43228	614-340-2155		627
Dandelion Cafe 725 E 2nd Ave *Web:* dandelioncafedurango.com	Durango	CO	81301	970-385-6884		671
Dandy Products Inc PO Box 1680 *TF:* 800-591-2284 ■ *Web:* www.dandyproducts.com	Powell	OH	43065	740-881-2790	397-1946	190
Dane County Regional Airport 4000 International Ln *Web:* www.msnairport.com	Madison	WI	53704	608-246-3380	246-3385	27
Dane Holdings Inc 13529 W Camino del Sol *Web:* www.daneholdings.com	Sun City West	AZ	85375	623-825-3173		463
Dane Media 170 NE 2nd St Ste 394 *TF:* 888-233-2863	Boca Raton	FL	33429	888-233-2863		195
Dane Street Congregational Church 10 Dane St *Web:* www.danestchurch.org	Beverly	MA	01915	978-922-4325	922-0472	48-20
Danecraft Inc 1 Baker St *Web:* www.danecraft.com	Providence	RI	02905	401-941-7700		409
Daner Law Firm, Aplc 4555 El Camino Real Unit J *Web:* danerlaw.com	Atascadero	CA	93422	805-464-5003		41
Danese/Corey 511 W 22nd St *Web:* www.danesecorey.com	New York	NY	10011	212-223-2227	605-1016	42
Danetracks Inc 7356 Santa Monica Blvd *Web:* www.danetracks.com	West Hollywood	CA	90046	323-512-8160		514
Danfords Hotel & Marina 25 E Broadway *TF:* 800-332-6367 ■ *Web:* www.danfords.com	Port Jefferson	NY	11777	800-332-6367		378
Danforth Art Museum 123 Union Ave *Web:* www.danforthmuseum.org	Framingham	MA	01702	508-620-0050	820-0258	520
Danforth Pewterers Ltd 52 Seymour St *Web:* www.danforthpewter.com	Middlebury	VT	05753	802-388-8666		411
Danfoss Scroll Technologies LLC 1 Scroll Dr *Web:* www.danfoss.com	Arkadelphia	AR	71923	870-246-0700		172
Danfoss Turbocor Compressors Inc 1769 E Paul Dirac Dr *Web:* www.turbocor.com	Tallahassee	FL	32310	850-504-4800	575-2126	172
Dangerous Goods Advisory Council (DGAC) 7501 Greenway Center Dr Ste 760 *Web:* www.dgac.org	Greenbelt	MD	20770	202-289-4550	289-4074	49-21
Dangerous Music Inc 231 Stevens Rd *Web:* dangerousmusic.com	Edmeston	NY	13335	845-202-5100		52
Danhauer Drug Company Inc 330 Frederica St *Web:* danhauerdrugs.com	Owensboro	KY	42301	270-684-2341	684-2396	237
DanHil Containers II Ltd 3715 Lucius McCelvey Dr *Web:* www.danhilcontainers.com	Temple	TX	76503	254-773-0704		100
Daniel 60 E 65th St *Web:* www.danielnyc.com	New York	NY	10065	212-288-0033		671
Daniel & Daniel Publishers Inc PO Box 2790 *TF:* 800-662-8351 ■ *Web:* www.danielpublishing.com	McKinleyville	CA	95519	707-839-3495		637-2
Daniel & Henry Co 1001 Highlands Plaza Dr W Ste 500 *TF:* 800-256-3462 ■ *Web:* danielandhenry.com	Saint Louis	MO	63110	314-421-1525	444-1990	390
Daniel & Stark Law Offices 100 W William Joel Bryan Pkwy *TF:* 800-474-1233 ■ *Web:* www.danielstarklaw.com	Bryan	TX	77803	979-846-8686		428
Daniel & Yeager (D&Y) 6767 Old Madison Pk Ste 690 *TF:* 800-955-1919 ■ *Web:* www.dystaffing.com	Huntsville	AL	35806	800-955-1919		266
Daniel B. Stephens & Associates Inc 6020 Academy NE Ste 100 *Web:* www.dbstephens.com	Albuquerque	NM	87109	505-822-9400	822-8877	743
Daniel Boone Regional Library 100 W Broadway *TF:* 800-324-4806 ■ *Web:* www.dbrl.org	Columbia	MO	65203	573-443-3161	443-3281	434-3
Daniel C. Tanney Inc 3268 Clive Ave *Web:* dctanney.com	Bensalem	PA	19020	215-639-3131	638-3333	482
Daniel Consultants Inc 8950 SR-108 229 *Web:* danielconsultants.com	Columbia	MD	21045	410-995-0090		261
Daniel Corp 505 20th St N Ste 1000 *Web:* www.danielcorp.com	Birmingham	AL	35203	205-443-4500		655
Daniel D. Stevens 7618 17th Ave *TF:* 800-647-7999 ■ *Web:* employeescreening.com	Brooklyn	NY	11214	718-234-0005		400
Daniel Defense Inc 101 War Fighter Way *TF:* 866-554-4867 ■ *Web:* www.danieldefense.com	Black Creek	GA	31308	912-851-3238	851-3248	807
Daniel Drake Ctr 151 W Galbraith Rd *TF:* 800-948-0003 ■ *Web:* www.uchealth.com	Cincinnati	OH	45216	513-418-2500		374-6
Daniel F. Young Inc 1235 Westlakes Dr Ste 255 *TF:* 866-407-0083 ■ *Web:* www.dfyoung.com	Berwyn	PA	19312	610-725-4000	725-0570	449
Daniel G Schuster LLC 3717 Crondall Ln Ste B *Web:* www.schusterconstruction.com	Owings Mills	MD	21117	410-363-9620		191-1
Daniel Gale Sotheby's International Realty 187 Park Ave *TF:* 800-942-5334 ■ *Web:* www.danielgale.com	Huntington	NY	11743	631-427-6600		652
Daniel George 2837 Culver Rd *Web:* www.danielgeorgerestaurant.com	Birmingham	AL	35223	205-871-3266		671
Daniel Group Ltd, The 400 Clarice Ave Ste 200 *TF:* 877-967-4242 ■ *Web:* thedanielgroup.com	Charlotte	NC	28204	877-967-4242		449
Daniel L. Jones & Assn 3510 Jeffco Blvd Ste 200 *TF:* 866-295-4173 ■ *Web:* djacpa.com	Arnold	MO	63010	636-464-1330	464-3076	2
Daniel Law Firm 145 Court Ave 2nd Fl *Web:* daniellawfirm.com	Memphis	TN	38103	901-525-5555		41
Daniel R. Bracciodieta & Assoc 312 Lake Ave *Web:* drbaccounting.com	Saint James	NY	11780	631-584-0004	584-2111	2
Daniel Smith Artist Materials 4150 First Ave S *Web:* www.danielsmithstores.com	Seattle	WA	98134	206-223-9599		459
Daniel Stowe Botanical Garden 6500 S New Hope Rd *Web:* www.dsbg.org	Belmont	NC	28012	704-825-4490	829-1240	97
Daniel Weaver Company Inc, The 1415 Weavertown Rd *Web:* www.weaverssnacks.com	Lebanon	PA	17046	717-274-6100	274-6103	296-26
Daniel Webster Birthplace 131 N Rd *Web:* www.nhstateparks.org	Franklin	NH	03235	603-934-5057		565
Daniele Inc PO Box 106 *TF:* 800-451-2535 ■ *Web:* www.danielefoods.com	Pascoag	RI	02859	401-568-6228	568-4788	296-26
Danielle House 160 Riverside Dr *Web:* www.daniellehouse.org	Binghamton	NY	13905	607-724-1540		372
Daniels & Roberts Inc 209 N Seacrest Blvd *TF:* 800-488-0066 ■ *Web:* danielsandroberts.com	Boynton Beach	FL	33435	561-241-0066	241-1198	7
Daniels Corp, The 20 Queen St W Ste 3400 *Web:* danielshomes.ca	Toronto	ON	M5H3R3	416-598-2129		186
Daniels County 120 Main St PO Box 91 *Web:* www.scobeymt.com	Scobey	MT	59263	406-487-2061		338
Daniels Home Ctr 255 S Euclid St *Web:* www.danielshomecenter.com	Anaheim	CA	92802	714-999-1285		321
Daniels Long Chevrolet 670 Automotive Dr *Web:* www.danielslong.com	Colorado Springs	CO	80905	719-387-1081		57
Daniels Manufacturing Corp 526 Thorpe Rd *Web:* www.dmctools.com	Orlando	FL	32859	407-855-6161	855-6884	758
Daniels Porco & Lusardi LLP 1 Memorial Ave *Web:* www.dpllawyers.com	Pawling	NY	12564	845-350-2837	855-5945	428
Danilo Black Inc 138 Madison Ave Ste 600	New York	NY	10016	212-683-1177		344
Danis Building Construction Co 3233 Newmark Dr *TF:* 800-326-4701 ■ *Web:* www.danis.com	Miamisburg	OH	45342	937-228-1225		186
Danisco US Inc *Genencor Div* 925 Page Mill Rd *Web:* biosciences.dupont.com	Palo Alto	CA	94304	650-846-7500		85
Danish-American Chamber of Commerce 885 Second Ave 18th Fl *Web:* www.daccny.com	New York	NY	10017	646-790-7169		138

Company / Address	City	State	ZIP	Phone	Fax	Class
Danisi Fuel Company Inc 3205 Rt 112 *Web:* danisienergy.com	Medford	NY	11763	631-732-6666		316
Danken Inc 9201 Roe St *Web:* www.dankeninc.com	Pensacola	FL	32514	850-484-3225	484-3228	293
Danlaw Inc 41131 Vincenti Ct *Web:* www.danlawinc.com	Novi	MI	48375	248-476-5571		256
Danly IEM 6779 Engle Rd Ste A-F **Fax Area Code:* 440 ■ *TF:* 800-652-6462 ■ *Web:* www.danly.com	Cleveland	OH	44130	800-652-6462	239-7605*	757
Dan-Mar Company Inc 200 Bluegrass Dr E *Web:* www.danmarco.com	Norwalk	OH	44857	419-660-8830	660-8833	696
Danmar Industries 2303 Oil Center Ct *Web:* www.danmarind.com	Houston	TX	77073	281-230-1000	230-1010	172
Danmark Energy L P 1907 E Old Hwy 80	White Oak	TX	75693	903-297-5136	297-5122	536
Dann, Dorfman, Herrell & Skillman PC 1601 Market St Ste 2400 *Web:* www.ddhs.com	Philadelphia	PA	19103	215-563-4100	563-4044	428
Dannemiller Inc 5711 NW Pkwy *TF:* 800-328-2308 ■ *Web:* www.dannemiller.com	San Antonio	TX	78249	800-328-2308		356
Dannenbaum Engineering Corp 3100 W Alabama *Web:* www.dannenbaum.com	Houston	TX	77098	713-520-9570	533-4111	261
Danner Corp 307 Oravetz Pl SE *Web:* www.danner.net	Auburn	WA	98092	253-833-5333		599
Danner Manufacturing Inc 160 Oval Dr *Web:* www.dannermfg.com	Islandia	NY	11749	631-234-5261		608
Danner Shoe Manufacturing Co 12021 NE Airport Way *TF:* 800-345-0430 ■ *Web:* www.danner.com	Portland	OR	97220	503-262-0103	251-1119	301
Dannible & McKee LLP 221 S Warren St *Web:* www.dmconsulting.com	Syracuse	NY	13202	315-472-9127		2
Dannon Co 100 Hillside Ave *Web:* www.dannon.com	White Plains	NY	10603	914-872-8400		296-27
Danny Byrd Inc 1416 Sandersville Sharon Rd *Web:* www.dannybyrdinc.com	Laurel	MS	39443	601-649-2524		480
Danny Herman Trucking Inc PO Box 55 *TF:* 800-251-7500 ■ *Web:* dannyherman.com	Mountain City	TN	37683	800-251-7500		449
Danson Decor Inc 3425 Douglas B Floreani *TF:* 800-363-1865 ■ *Web:* www.dansondecor.com	Saint-Laurent	QC	H4S1Y6	514-335-2435		292
DANSR Inc 818 W Evergreen Ave *Web:* www.dansr.com	Chicago	IL	60642	312-475-0464		194
Dant Clayton Corp 1500 Bernheim Ln *TF:* 800-626-2177 ■ *Web:* www.stadiumbleachers.com	Louisville	KY	40210	502-634-3626		697
Dante Consulting Inc 5328 Lee Hwy *Web:* www.danteinc.com	Arlington	VA	22207	703-807-0520		177
Dante's Creative Cuisine 1325 Eigth Ave N *Web:* dantesgreatfalls.com	Great Falls	MT	59401	406-453-9599		671
Danuser Machine Co 500 E Third St *Web:* www.danuser.com	Fulton	MO	65251	573-642-2246	642-2240	273
Danver 1 Grand St *TF:* 888-441-0537 ■ *Web:* danver.com	Wallingford	CT	06492	203-269-2300	265-6190	319-1
Danville Ambulance 740 A St *Web:* www.danvilleambulance.com	Danville	PA	17821	570-275-3031	275-6734	30
Danville Area Community College 2000 E Main St *TF:* 877-342-3042 ■ *Web:* dacc.edu	Danville	IL	61832	217-443-3222	443-8560	162
Danville Community College 1008 S Main St *TF:* 800-560-4291 ■ *Web:* danville.edu	Danville	VA	24541	434-797-2222	797-8541	162
Danville Correctional Ctr 3820 E Main St *Web:* www2.illinois.gov	Danville	IL	61834	217-446-0441		213
Danville (Independent City) 401 Patton St PO Box 3300 *Web:* www.danville-va.gov	Danville	VA	24543	434-799-5168	799-6502	338
Danville Metal Stamping Company Inc 20 Oakwood Ave *Web:* www.danvillemetal.com	Danville	IL	61832	217-446-0647		488
Danville National Cemetery 1900 E Main St *Web:* www.cem.va.gov	Danville	IL	61832	217-554-4550	554-4803	136
Danville Pittsylvania County Chamber of Commerce 8653 US Hwy 29 PO Box 99 *TF:* 800-826-2355 ■ *Web:* www.dpchamber.org	Blairs	VA	24527	434-836-6990	836-6955	139
Danville Public Library 511 Patton St *Web:* readdanvilleva.org	Danville	VA	24541	434-799-5195		434-3
Danville Public Library 319 N Vermilion St *Web:* danvillepubliclibrary.org	Danville	IL	61832	217-477-5220	477-5230	434-3
Danville Signal Processing Inc 38570 100th Ave *TF:* 877-230-5629 ■ *Web:* www.danvillesignal.com	Cannon Falls	MN	55009	507-263-5854		194
Danville State Hospital 200 State Hospital Dr *Web:* www.dhs.pa.gov	Danville	PA	17821	570-271-4500		374-5
Danville-Boyle County Chamber of Commerce 105 E Walnut St *TF:* 800-548-4229 ■ *Web:* www.developdanville.com	Danville	KY	40422	859-236-2361		139
DAP Products Inc 2400 Boston St Ste 200 **Fax Area Code:* 410 ■ *TF:* 800-543-3840 ■ *Web:* www.dap.com	Baltimore	MD	21224	888-327-8477	558-1068*	3
Dapco 2500 Bishop Cir E *Web:* dapcoind.com	Dexter	MI	48130	734-426-8900	426-2622	128
Daprato Rigali Studios Inc 6030 N NW Hwy *Web:* dapratorigali.com	Chicago	IL	60631	773-763-5511		724
Daq Electronics Inc 262B Old New Brunswick Rd *Web:* www.daq.net	Piscataway	NJ	08854	732-981-0050		625
DAR Industrial Products Inc 2 Union Hill Bldg 1 Union Hill Industrial Pk *Web:* www.darindustrial.com	West Conshohocken	PA	19428	610-825-4900	825-4901	326
DAR State Forest 78 Cape St Rt 112 *Web:* www.mass.gov	Goshen	MA	01032	413-268-7098		565
Dara Thai 14 S San Francisco St *Web:* darathaiflagstaff.com	Flagstaff	AZ	86001	928-774-0047		671
Daramic 11430 N Community House Rd Ste 350 *Web:* www.daramic.com	Charlotte	NC	28277	704-587-8599	587-8796	608
DaRan Inc 12280 -255th Ave NW *Web:* www.daraninc.com	Zimmerman	MN	55398	763-856-4000	856-4444	780
Darby Dan Farm 3225 Old Frankfort Pk *TF:* 888-321-0424 ■ *Web:* www.darbydan.com	Lexington	KY	40510	859-254-0424	281-6612	368
Darby Group Companies Inc 300 Jericho Quadrangle *TF:* 800-645-2310 ■ *Web:* www.darbydental.com	Jericho	NY	11753	800-645-2310		582
DarCars Ltd 12210 Cherry Hill Rd *TF:* 800-327-2277 ■ *Web:* www.darcars.com	Silver Spring	MD	20904	301-622-0300		57
Darco Products Inc 8406 Washington Pl NE *Web:* www.darcoproducts.com	Albuquerque	NM	87113	505-828-0498		454
Darco Southern Inc 253 Darco Dr *Web:* www.darcosouthern.com	Independence	VA	24348	276-773-2711	773-0208	326
DARD Products 912 Custer Ave *Web:* dardproducts.com	Evanston	IL	60202	847-328-5000		9
Darden Concepts Inc 1000 Darden Center Dr PO Box 695011 *Web:* www.darden.com	Orlando	FL	32837	407-245-4000		670
Dare 2 Share Ministries Intl PO Box 745323 *TF:* 800-462-8355 ■ *Web:* www.dare2share.org	Arvada	CO	80006	303-425-1606		48-20
Dare County 954 Marshall C Collins Dr PO Box 1000 *Web:* www.darenc.com	Manteo	NC	27954	252-475-5000		338
Dare Electronics Inc 3245 S County Rd 25a *Web:* www.dareelectronics.com	Troy	OH	45373	937-335-0031		253
Dare Enterprices Inc 700 River Ave Ste 215 *Web:* www.dareent.com	Pittsburgh	PA	15212	412-231-6100		256
Dare Foods Ltd 2481 Kingsway Dr *Web:* www.darefoods.com	Kitchener	ON	N2C1A6	519-893-5500		68
Dare Mighty Things Inc 1000 Market St Unit 1 *Web:* www.daremightythings.com	Portsmouth	NH	03801	603-431-4331		256
Dare Products Inc 860 Betterly Rd PO Box 157 *TF:* 800-922-3273 ■ *Web:* www.dareproducts.com	Battle Creek	MI	49015	269-965-2307	965-3261	279
Darex LLC 210 E Hersey St PO Box 730 *TF:* 800-597-6170 ■ *Web:* www.darex.com	Ashland	OR	97520	541-488-2224	488-2229	455
Daria Metal Fabricators 1507 W Park Ave *Web:* www.dariametalfabricators.com	Perkasie	PA	18944	215-453-2110		697
Daria Moraveck 4115 Blackhawk Plaza Cir Ste 220 *Web:* dariamoraveck.com	Danville	CA	94506	925-736-0204	736-0555	390
Darice Inc 13000 Darice Pkwy **Fax Area Code:* 440 ■ *TF:* 866-432-7423 ■ *Web:* www.darice.com	Strongsville	OH	44149	866-432-7423	238-1680*	44
Darien Lakes State Park 10475 Harlow Rd *Web:* parks.ny.gov	Darien Center	NY	14040	585-547-9242		565
Darien Nature Center Inc 120 Brookside Rd *Web:* dariennaturecenter.org	Darien	CT	06820	203-655-7459		50-5
Darien Sport Shop Inc, The 1127 Post Rd *Web:* dariensport.com	Darien	CT	06820	203-655-2575		711
Darigold 5601 Sixth Ave S Ste 300 *Web:* darigold.com	Seattle	WA	98108	206-216-4283		296-27
Dari-Mart Stores Inc 125 E 6th Ave *Web:* www.darimart.com	Junction City	OR	97448	541-998-2388		345
Dark Field Technologies Inc 70 Robinson Blvd *Web:* darkfield.com	Orange	CT	06477	203-298-0731		225
Dark Horse Comics LLC 10956 SE Main St *TF:* 800-862-0052 ■ *Web:* www.darkhorse.com	Milwaukie	OR	97222	503-652-8815	654-9440	637-5
Darke County 520 S Broadway St *Web:* www.co.darke.oh.us	Greenville	OH	45331	937-547-7300	547-7367	338
Darke County Chamber of Commerce 209 E Fourth St *TF:* 800-396-0787 ■ *Web:* darkecountyohio.com	Greenville	OH	45331	937-548-2102		139
Darkhorse Theater Ltd 4610 Charlotte Ave *Web:* darkhorsetheater.weebly.com	Nashville	TN	37209	615-297-7113		572
Darling & Risbrough LLP 19200 Von Karman Ste 750 *Web:* darlingrisbrough.com	Irvine	CA	92612	714-384-4250		41
Darling International Inc 251 O'Connor Ridge Blvd Ste 300 *NYSE: DAR* ■ *TF:* 800-800-4841 ■ *Web:* www.darlingii.com	Irving	TX	75038	972-717-0300		296-12
Darlington County 1 Public Sq *Web:* www.darcosc.com	Darlington	SC	29532	843-398-4100	393-8539	338
Darlington County Library 204 N Main St *Web:* www.darlington-lib.org	Darlington	SC	29532	843-398-4940	398-4942	434-3
Darlington Fabrics Corp 36 Beach St *Web:* www.darlingtonfabrics.com	Westerly	RI	02891	401-315-6279		745-4
Darlington Raceway 1301 Harry Bird Hwy **Fax Area Code:* 843 ■ *TF:* 866-459-7223 ■ *Web:* www.darlingtonraceway.com	Darlington	SC	29532	866-459-7223	395-8920*	515
Darlington School 1014 Cave Spring Rd *TF:* 800-368-4437 ■ *Web:* www.darlingtonschool.org	Rome	GA	30161	706-235-6051	232-3600	622
Darlington Veneer Company Inc 225 4th St *TF:* 800-845-2388 ■ *Web:* www.darlingtonveneer.com	Darlington	SC	29532	843-393-3861	393-8243	613

Name / Address	City	State	ZIP	Phone	Fax	Class
Darlingtonia State Natural Site 84505 Hwy 101 S *Web:* stateparks.oregon.gov	Florence	OR	97439	541-997-3851		565
Darmody, Merlino & Company LLP 75 Federal St 15th Fl *Web:* www.darmodymerlino.com	Boston	MA	02110	617-426-7300		2
Daroff Design Inc 2121 Market St *Web:* www.daroffdesign.com	Philadelphia	PA	19103	215-636-9900	636-9627	393
Daroga State Park 1 S Daroga Park Rd *Web:* www.parks.state.wa.us	Orondo	WA	98843	509-784-0229		565
Daron Worldwide Trading Inc 24 Stewart Pl Unit 4 *TF:* 800-776-2324 ■ *Web:* www.daronwwt.com	Fairfield	NJ	07004	973-882-0035		761
Daroth Capital Advisors LLC 130 E 59th St 12th Fl *Web:* www.daroth.com	New York	NY	10022	212-687-2500	687-3200	70
Darr & Collins LLC 1425 NW 150th St *Web:* www.darrcollins.com	Edmond	OK	73013	405-285-2400		261
Darr Feedlot Inc 42826 Rd 759 *Web:* www.darrfeedlot.com	Cozad	NE	69130	308-324-2363	324-2365	10-1
Dar-Ran Furniture Industries 2402 Shore St *TF:* 800-334-7891 ■ *Web:* www.darran.com	High Point	NC	27263	336-861-2400	861-6485	319-1
Darrell & King LLC 410 White Gables Ln *Web:* darrellandking.com	Charlottesville	VA	22903	434-977-7010		401
Darrell Andrews Trucking Inc 1365 Harold Andrews Rd *TF:* 800-334-2303 ■ *Web:* www.dandrewstrucking.com	Siler City	NC	27344	919-663-2142	663-4087	780
Darrell W. Cook & Associates, A Professional Corp 6688 N Central Expy Ste 1000 *Web:* attorneycook.com	Dallas	TX	75206	214-368-4686	593-5713	41
Darrell Walker Personnel Systems 1976 Gadsden Hwy Ste 210 *Web:* darrellwalkerworkforce.com	Birmingham	AL	35235	205-508-5511	508-5518	260
Darrow School 110 Darrow Rd *TF:* 877-432-7769 ■ *Web:* www.darrowschool.org	New Lebanon	NY	12125	518-794-6000	794-7065	622
Darroweverett LLP 1 Turks Head Pl Ste 1200 *Web:* darroweverett.com	Providence	RI	02903	401-453-1200	453-1201	41
Darryl L. Sink and Associates Inc (DSA) 1 Cielo Vista Pl *TF:* 800-650-7465 ■ *Web:* www.dsink.com	Monterey	CA	93940	831-649-8384	649-3914	194
Darryl's Wood Fired Grill 3300 City Gate Blvd *Web:* www.darryls.com	Greensboro	NC	27407	336-294-1781		671
DART (Dallas Area Rapid Transit Authority) 1401 Pacific Ave *Web:* www.dart.org	Dallas	TX	75202	214-979-1111		468
Dart Aerospace Ltd 1270 Aberdeen St *TF:* 800-556-4166 ■ *Web:* www.dartaerospace.com	Hawkesbury	ON	K6A1K7	613-632-3336		21
Dart Appraisalcom 2600 W Big Beaver Rd Ste 540 *TF:* 888-327-8123 ■ *Web:* dartappraisal.com	Troy	MI	48084	888-327-8123		652
Dart Container Corp 500 Hogsback Rd **Fax Area Code:* 517 ■ *TF:* 800-248-5960 ■ *Web:* www.dartcontainer.com	Mason	MI	48854	800-248-5960	676-3883*	601
Dart Entities 1430 S Eastman Ave *TF:* 800-285-0560 ■ *Web:* www.dartentities.com	Los Angeles	CA	90023	323-264-1011	264-6925	803-1
Dart Manufacturing Company Inc 3860 La Reunion Pkwy *Web:* www.dartpromo.com	Dallas	TX	75212	214-631-8024		534
Dart World Inc 140 Linwood St *TF:* 800-225-2558 ■ *Web:* www.dartworld.com	Lynn	MA	01905	781-581-6035		711
Dar-tech Inc 16485 Rockside Rd *TF:* 800-228-7347 ■ *Web:* dar-tech.com	Maple Heights	OH	44137	216-663-7600	663-8007	146
Dartmouth 6175 Robinson Hall *Web:* www.thedartmouth.com	Hanover	NH	03755	603-646-2600		532-2
Dartmouth College 6016 McNutt Hall *TF:* 800-490-7010 ■ *Web:* home.dartmouth.edu	Hanover	NH	03755	603-646-2875	646-1216	166
Dartmouth Company Inc, The 351 Newbury St *Web:* www.dartco.com	Boston	MA	02115	617-262-6620		652
Dartmouth General Hospital 325 Pleasant St *TF:* 800-461-5558 ■ *Web:* www.cdha.nshealth.ca	Dartmouth	NS	B2Y3S3	902-465-8300		374-2
Dartmouth Medical Equipment 19 Old Westport Rd *Web:* www.dmeinc.net	North Dartmouth	MA	02747	508-997-1241	997-7550	475
Dartmouth Public Libraries 732 Dartmouth St *Web:* www.town.dartmouth.ma.us	Dartmouth	MA	02748	508-999-0726		434-3
Dartmouth-Hitchcock Medical Ctr 1 Medical Center Dr *TF:* 800-543-1624 ■ *Web:* www.dartmouth-hitchcock.org	Lebanon	NH	03756	603-650-5000	650-8765	374-3
Darvin Furniture 15400 S La Grange Rd *Web:* www.darvin.com	Orland Park	IL	60462	708-460-4100		321
Darwill Inc 11900 Roosevelt Rd *Web:* www.darwill.com	Hillside	IL	60162	708-236-4900	236-5820	627
Darya Restaurant 3800 S Plaza Dr *Web:* daryasouthcoastplaza.com	Santa Ana	CA	92704	714-557-6600		671
Daryl Flood Inc 450 Airline Dr Ste 100 *TF:* 800-325-9340 ■ *Web:* www.darylflood.com	Coppell	TX	75019	972-471-1496		186
DAS Acquisition Company LLC 12140 Woodcrest Executive Dr Ste 150 *Web:* www.usa-mortgage.com	Saint Louis	MO	63141	314-628-2000		217
DAS Brot Inc 2441 Midway Rd *TF:* 800-522-7862 ■ *Web:* dasbrot.com	Carrollton	TX	75006	972-243-8443	484-9315	296-37
DAS Companies Inc 724 Lawn Rd **Fax Area Code:* 800 ■ *TF:* 800-706-0421 ■ *Web:* www.dasinc.com	Palmyra	PA	17078	717-964-3642	437-3659*	38
DAS Stein Haus 1436 Southridge Dr *Web:* www.dassteinhaus.info	Jefferson City	MO	65109	573-634-3869		671
DASAN Zhone Solutions Inc 7195 Oakport St *NASDAQ:* DZSI ■ *TF:* 877-946-6320 ■ *Web:* dasanzhone.com	Oakland	CA	94621	510-777-7000	777-7001	735
Dasaro Law Firm Pc 9 Leonardville Rd *Web:* dasarolaw.com	Middletown	NJ	07748	732-671-7007		41
Dascenzo Intellectual Property Law PC 1000 S W Broadway Ste 1555 *Web:* www.dgip.law	Portland	OR	97205	503-224-7529		428
DASCO Home Medical Equipment 375 NW St *Web:* www.godasco.com	Westerville	OH	43082	614-901-2226	901-2228	475
Dasco Insurance Agency Inc 628 Academy Dr *Web:* dascoins.com	Northbrook	IL	60062	847-291-0660		390
Dasco Pro Inc 340 Blackhawk Park Ave *TF:* 800-327-2690 ■ *Web:* dascopro.com	Rockford	IL	61104	815-962-3727		758
Dash Farrow LLP 39 E Main St *Web:* www.dashlawllp.com	Moorestown	NJ	08057	856-235-8300	235-2622	41
Dash Inc W176 N9830 Rivercrest Dr *Web:* dashdev.com	Germantown	WI	53022	262-345-5600	345-5604	225
Dash Point State Park 5700 SW Dash Pt Rd *Web:* parks.state.wa.us	Federal Way	WA	98023	253-661-4955		565
DashGo 1620 Broadway *Web:* dashgo.com	Santa Monica	CA	90404	310-997-0675		387
Dashiell Corp 12301 Kurland Dr 4th Fl *Web:* www.dashiell.com	Houston	TX	77034	713-558-6600	558-6694	189-4
Dashwood Industries Ltd 69323 Richmond St *TF:* 800-265-4284 ■ *Web:* www.dashwood.com	Centralia	ON	N0M1K0	519-228-6624		499
Dassault Falcon Jet Corp PO Box 2000 **Fax Area Code:* 302 ■ *TF:* 800-527-2463 ■ *Web:* www.dassaultfalcon.com	South Hackensack	NJ	07606	201-440-6700	322-7221*	20
Dassault Systemes 166 Valley St **Fax Area Code:* 401 ■ *Web:* www.3ds.com	Providence	RI	02909	781-810-3000	276-4408*	178-8
Dastmalchi Enterprises Inc 4490 Von Karman Ave Ste 150 *TF:* 888-358-0331 ■ *Web:* dastmalchi.com	Newport Beach	CA	92660	888-358-0331		217
Data & Mailing Resources Inc 4929 Blalock Rd *Web:* www.dmrhouston.com	Houston	TX	77041	713-426-1550		5
Data Access Corp 14000 SW 119th Ave *TF:* 800-451-3539 ■ *Web:* www.dataaccess.com	Miami	FL	33186	305-238-0012		178-2
Data Advantage Group Inc 145 Natoma St *Web:* www.dag.com	San Francisco	CA	94105	415-947-0400		177
Data Aire Inc 230 W BlueRidge Ave *TF:* 800-347-2473 ■ *Web:* www.dataaire.com	Orange	CA	92865	714-921-6000	921-6010	14
Data Business Equipment Inc 10513 Buena Vista Ct **Fax Area Code:* 515 ■ *TF:* 800-373-3000 ■ *Web:* databusinessequipment.com	Des Moines	IA	50322	800-373-3000	254-0299*	366
Data Cable Technologies Inc 1306 Enterprise Dr *Web:* datacabletech.com	Romeoville	IL	60446	630-226-5600		111
Data Cell Systems Inc 12 Mary Marr St	Winnsboro	LA	71295	318-435-5800		116
Data Center West Inc 739 Welch St *Web:* datacenterwest.com	Medford	OR	97501	541-326-4212		387
Data Clean Corp 1033 Graceland Ave **Fax Area Code:* 847 ■ *TF:* 800-328-2256 ■ *Web:* www.dataclean.com	Des Plaines	IL	60016	800-352-7282	296-6870*	104
Data Code Inc 80 Orville Dr Ste 100 *Web:* www.datacodeinc.com	Bohemia	NY	11716	631-218-4300		175
Data Communication Solutions Inc 10125 Crosstown Cir Ste 235 *Web:* www.dcs-is-edi.com	Eden Prairie	MN	55344	952-941-5466	681-2145	194
Data Communications Management Corp (DCM) 9195 Torbram Rd *TF:* 800-268-0128 ■ *Web:* www.datacm.com	Brampton	ON	L6S6H2	905-791-3151	791-3277	110
Data Computer Corporation of America 5310 Dorsey Hall Dr *Web:* www.dcca.com	Ellicott City	MD	21042	410-992-3760		180
Data Concepts LLC 4405 Cox Rd *Web:* www.dataconcepts-inc.com	Glen Allen	VA	23060	804-968-4700		196
Data Connectors LLC 500 Chesterfield Ctr Ste 320 *Web:* www.dataconnectors.com	Chesterfield	MO	63017	636-778-9495	778-9496	206
Data Consulting Group Inc 965 E Jefferson Ave *TF:* 800-258-4343 ■ *Web:* www.dcgroupinc.com	Detroit	MI	48207	313-963-7771		180
Data Conversion Laboratory Inc 61-18 190th St Ste 205 *TF:* 800-321-2816 ■ *Web:* www.dataconversionlaboratory.com	Fresh Meadows	NY	11365	718-357-8700		224
Data Dash Inc 4500 Telegraph Rd Ste 107 *TF:* 800-211-5988 ■ *Web:* datadash.com	Saint Louis	MO	63129	314-939-1430		225
Data Description Inc PO Box 4555 *Web:* datadescription.com	Ithaca	NY	14850	607-257-1000		178-5
Data Device Corp 105 Wilbur Pl **Fax Area Code:* 414 ■ *TF:* 800-332-5757 ■ *Web:* ddc-web.com	Bohemia	NY	11716	631-567-5600	259-0246*	253
Data Dimensions Corp 400 Midland Ct *TF:* 800-782-2907 ■ *Web:* www.datadimensions.com	Janesville	WI	53546	608-757-1100		225
Data Ductus Inc 201 Terry St Unit 2A *Web:* dataductus.com	Longmont	CO	80501	303-332-9806		177
Data Electronic Devices Inc 32 NW Dr *Web:* www.dataed.com	Salem	NH	03079	603-893-2047		518
Data Exchange Corp 3600 Via Pescador *TF:* 800-237-7911 ■ *Web:* www.dex.com	Camarillo	CA	93012	805-388-1711		175
Data Facts Inc 8520 Macon Rd Ste 2 *Web:* www.datafacts.com	Cordova	TN	38018	901-685-7599		218
Data Financial Inc 1100 Glen Oaks Ln *TF:* 800-334-8334 ■ *Web:* www.datafinancial.com	Mequon	WI	53092	262-243-5511		177
Data Flow Systems Inc 605 N John Rodes Blvd *Web:* dataflowsys.com	Melbourne	FL	32934	321-259-5009	259-4006	647
Data Fusion Corp 10190 Bannock St Ste 246 *Web:* www.datafusion.com	Northglenn	CO	80260	720-872-2145		256

	Phone	Fax	Class
Data Guardian 9136 Portage Industrial Dr ... Portage MI 49024 *Web:* www.kalamazooxray.com	269-327-6296		317
Data I/O Corp 6464 185th Ave NE Ste 101 ... Redmond WA 98052 *NASDAQ:* DAIO ■ *TF:* 800-426-1045 ■ *Web:* www.dataio.com	425-881-6444		695
Data Impressions 17418 Studebaker Rd ... Cerritos CA 90703 *TF:* 800-777-6488 ■ *Web:* www.dataimpressions.com	562-207-9050	207-9053	174
Data Inc 72 Summit Ave ... Montvale NJ 07645 *Web:* www.datainc.biz	201-802-9800	802-9808	177
Data Industries Ltd 1370 Broadway 5th Fl ... New York NY 10018 *Web:* www.dataind.com	646-902-1114		180
Data Innovations Inc 120 Kimball Ave Ste 100 ... South Burlington VT 05403 *Web:* www.datainnovations.com	802-658-2850	658-2782	180
Data Integrity Inc 228 Highland Ave ... West Newton MA 02465 *Web:* www.dii2000.com	617-964-1977		177
Data Lab 7333 N Oak Park Ave ... Niles IL 60714 *Web:* www.data-lab.com	847-647-6678		225
Data Label Inc 1000 Spruce St ... Terre Haute IN 47807 *TF:* 800-457-0676 ■ *Web:* www.data-label.com	812-232-0408	238-1847	413
Data Link Solutions (DLS) 350 Collins Rd NE ... Cedar Rapids IA 52498 *Web:* www.datalinksolutions.net	319-295-8144		21
Data Machine Inc 140 Brushcreek Rd ... Irwin PA 15642 *Web:* datamachinellc.com	724-864-4370	864-4372	454
Data Mail Inc 240 Hartford Ave ... Newington CT 06111 *Web:* www.data-mail.com	860-666-0399		5
Data Management Inc 537 New Britain Ave ... Farmington CT 06034 *TF:* 800-243-1969 ■ *Web:* www.datamanage.com	800-428-1951		86
Data Management Internationale Inc (DMI) 55 Lukens Dr ... New Castle DE 19720 *TF:* 800-364-4210 ■ *Web:* getwebdocs.com	302-656-1151	656-1169	658
Data Management Marketing 3225 Jordan Blvd ... Malabar FL 32950 *Web:* www.dmm-marketing.com	321-725-8081		177
Data Memory Systems Inc 24 Keewaydin Dr Ste 5 ... Salem NH 03079 *TF:* 800-662-7466 ■ *Web:* www.datamemorysystems.com	603-898-7750	898-6585	174
Data Panel 181 Cheshire Ln Ste 300 ... Plymouth MN 55441 *Web:* www.datapanel.com	952-941-3511	941-3931	246
Data Papers Inc 468 Industrial Park Rd ... Muncy PA 17756 **Fax Area Code:* 888 ■ *TF:* 800-233-3032 ■ *Web:* www.datapapers.com	800-233-3032	546-2366*	110
Data Paradigm Inc 2323 Bryan St Ste 2600 ... Dallas TX 75201 *Web:* dataparadigm.com	214-468-0200	722-1860	177
Data Partners 12857 Banyan Creek Dr ... Fort Myers FL 33908 *TF:* 866-423-1818 ■ *Web:* www.datapartners.com	866-423-1818		194
Data Path 318 McHenry Ave ... Modesto CA 95354 *TF:* 888-693-2827 ■ *Web:* www.mydatapath.com	209-521-0055		196
Data Perceptions Inc 174 Bridge St W ... Waterloo ON N2K1K9 *Web:* www.dataperceptions.com	519-749-9319		180
Data Physics Corp 2480 N First St Ste 100 ... San Jose CA 95131 *Web:* www.dataphysics.com	408-437-0100	456-0100	407
Data Pro Acctg Software Inc 111 Second Ave NE Ste 1200 ... Saint Petersburg FL 33701 *TF:* 800-237-6377 ■ *Web:* www.dpro.com	727-803-1500	803-1535	178-1
Data Pro Inc PO Box 457 ... Plainwell MI 49080 *Web:* www.data-pro.com	269-685-9214		178-1
Data Processing Services Inc 4 Center Green Ste 100 ... Carmel IN 46032 *TF:* 800-654-4689 ■ *Web:* dpslink.com	317-574-4300		225
Data Processing Solutions Inc 9160 Red Branch Rd Ste W1 ... Columbia MD 21045 *Web:* dpsolutions.com	410-720-3300		225
Data Records Management Services LLC 1400 Husband Rd PO Box 7256 ... Paducah KY 42002 *TF:* 800-443-1610 ■ *Web:* wp.drmsusa.com	270-443-1255		463
Data Reduction Systems Corp 1323 Burnet Ave ... Union NJ 07083 *Web:* www.drscorp.com	908-687-5636		225
Data Rx ManagementRxSense 99 High St Ste 2800 ... Boston MA 02110 *Web:* rxsense.com	903-465-0798	465-0799	237
Data Sales Company Inc 3450 W Burnsville Pkwy ... Burnsville MN 55337 *TF:* 800-328-2730 ■ *Web:* www.datasales.com	952-890-8838	895-3369	174
Data Science Automation Inc 375 Valleybrook Rd Ste 106 ... McMurray PA 15317 *Web:* dsautomation.com	724-942-6330		256
Data Sciences Intl 119 14th St NW Ste 100 ... Saint Paul MN 55112 *TF:* 800-262-9687 ■ *Web:* www.datasci.com	651-481-7400		668
Data Select Systems Inc 2829 Townsgate Rd Ste 300 ... Westlake Village CA 91361 *TF:* 800-535-9978 ■ *Web:* www.clcsiii.com	805-446-2090		177
Data Services Inc 31516 Winterplace Pkwy ... Salisbury MD 21804 *TF:* 800-432-4066 ■ *Web:* www.dataservicesinc.com	410-546-2206		225
Data Square LLC 396 Danbury Rd ... Wilton CT 06897 *TF:* 877-328-2738 ■ *Web:* www.datasquare.com	203-964-9733		809
Data Storage Systems Ctr (DSSC) *Carnegie Mellon University* 5000 Forbes Ave ... Pittsburgh PA 15213 *TF:* 800-864-8287 ■ *Web:* www.dssc.ece.cmu.edu	412-268-6600	268-3497	668
Data Stream Mobile Technologies 11531 Interchange Cir S ... Miramar FL 33025 *Web:* www.dswltech.net	954-271-1240		194
Data Systems Analysts Inc (DSA) Eigth Neshaminy Interplex Ste 209 ... Trevose PA 19053 *TF:* 877-422-4372 ■ *Web:* www.dsainc.com	215-245-4800	245-4375	180
Data Technique 3402 Airport Cir PO Box 1301 ... Pittsburg KS 66762 *Web:* www.datatechnique.com	620-235-1000		809
Data Trace Information Services LLC 200 Commerce ... Irvine CA 92602 *TF:* 800-221-2056 ■ *Web:* www.datatracetitle.com	800-221-2056		387
Data Transformation Corp 1 Penn Plz Ste 4515 ... New York NY 10119 *TF:* 800-228-3232 ■ *Web:* dtcss.com	212-563-7565	971-3178	697
Data Transmission Network Corp 9110 W Dodge Rd Ste 200 ... Omaha NE 68114 *TF:* 800-485-4000 ■ *Web:* www.dtn.com	402-390-2328		387
Data Ventures Inc 6101 Carnegie Blvd Ste 520 ... Charlotte NC 28209 *TF:* 888-431-2676 ■ *Web:* www.dataventures.com	704-887-1012	887-1082	177
Data Vista Inc 5198 US-130 Ste A ... Bordentown NJ 08505 *TF:* 800-797-3527 ■ *Web:* www.datavista.com	609-702-9300		175
Data Workers Po Box 25808 ... Santa Ana CA 92799 *Web:* www.dataworkers.com	714-546-5558		178-1
Data3 Corp 2448 E 81st St Ste 700 ... Tulsa OK 74137 *Web:* www.datathree.com	918-237-4400		177
DataBanque 5001 Baum Blvd Ste 435 ... Pittsburgh PA 15213 **Fax Area Code:* 866 ■ *TF:* 877-860-2702 ■ *Web:* www.databanque.com	877-860-2702	656-1900*	195
Database Access Systems Inc 1 Romaine Rd ... Mountain Lakes NJ 07046 *Web:* www.dbasinc.com	973-335-0800	335-1956	735
Databased Solutions Inc 1200 Rt 22 ... Bridgewater NJ 08807 *Web:* www.dbsiservices.com	908-314-0000		721
Databean LLC 550 Market St ... Saint Augustine FL 32095 *TF:* 844-664-3001 ■ *Web:* databean.com	844-664-3001		177
Databit Inc 200 Rt 17 ... Mahwah NJ 07430 *Web:* www.databitinc.com	201-529-8050		174
Databranch Inc 132 N Union St Ste 108 ... Olean NY 14760 *Web:* www.databranch.com	716-373-4467		180
Databricks 160 Spear St 13th Fl ... San Francisco CA 94105 *TF:* 866-330-0121 ■ *Web:* databricks.com	866-330-0121		657
DataCan Services Corp 7465 45 Ave Close ... Red Deer AB T4P4C2 *Web:* www.datacan.ca	403-352-2245		253
Dataccount Inc 299 Broadway Ste 1016 ... New York NY 10007 *Web:* www.dataccount.com	212-595-1044	595-0247	463
Dataclarity Corp 7200 Falls of Neuse Rd Ste 202 ... Raleigh NC 27615 *TF:* 800-963-5508 ■ *Web:* www.dataclaritycorp.com	919-256-6700		177
Datacolor 5 Princess Rd ... Lawrenceville NJ 08648 *Web:* www.datacolor.com	609-924-2189	895-7414	419
Datacom (DC) 100 Enterprise Blvd ... Lafayette LA 70506 *TF:* 877-559-1959 ■ *Web:* www.blackhawkdc.com	337-593-8700		681
Datacom Systems Inc 9 Adler Dr ... East Syracuse NY 13057 *Web:* www.datacomsystems.com	315-463-9541		203
DataComm Networks Inc 6801 N 54th St ... Tampa FL 33610 *TF:* 800-544-4627 ■ *Web:* www.datacomm.com	800-544-4627		180
Datacon Inc 60 Blanchard Rd ... Burlington MA 01803 *Web:* data-con.com	781-273-5800		625
Datacor Inc 25 Hanover Rd Bldg B Ste 300 ... Florham Park NJ 07932 *Web:* www.datacor.com	973-822-1551	822-3976	177
Datacore Consulting LLC 1300 E Granger Rd ... Brooklyn Heights OH 44131 *TF:* 800-244-4241 ■ *Web:* www.datacoreonline.com	216-398-8499		631
DataCore Software Corp 6300 NW Fifth Way Corporate Pk ... Fort Lauderdale FL 33309 *Web:* www.datacore.com	954-377-6000	938-7953	387
Datacorp 211 W 18th St ... Cheyenne WY 82001 *Web:* www.mjdatacorp.com	307-634-1808		396
DataDirect Networks 9351 Deering Ave ... Chatsworth CA 91311 *TF:* 800-837-2298 ■ *Web:* www.ddn.com	800-837-2298		173-8
Datadrill Communications 6701 Fairmount Dr SE ... Calgary AB T2H0X6 *Web:* datadrill.ca	403-269-7500	264-3292	387
Datafirst Corp 2700 Sumner Blvd ... Raleigh NC 27616 *TF:* 800-634-8504 ■ *Web:* www.datafirst.com	919-876-6650		177
Dataflo Consulting 2722 S 87th Ave ... Omaha NE 68124 *Web:* dataflo.com	402-861-9454		225
DataFlux 940 NW Cary Pkwy Ste 201 ... Cary NC 27513 *Web:* www.dataflux.com	919-674-2153		177
Dataforth Corp 3331 E Hemisphere Loop ... Tucson AZ 85706 *TF:* 800-444-7644 ■ *Web:* www.dataforth.com	520-741-1404	741-0762	173-3
Datagenic Tool & Die Inc 4280 Motor Ave ... Culver City CA 90232	310-253-9918		697
Data-Graphics Inc 240 Hartford Ave ... Newington CT 06111 *TF:* 800-639-4316 ■ *Web:* www.datagraphicsinc.com	800-639-4316		5
Dataiku 902 Broadway ... New York NY 10010 *Web:* dataiku.com	646-568-7477		225
Datalab Usa LLC 20261 Goldenrod Ln ... Germantown MD 20876 *TF:* 800-972-1430 ■ *Web:* datalabusa.com	301-972-1430		5
Data-Linc Group 1125 12th Ave NW Ste B-2 ... Issaquah WA 98027 *Web:* data-linc.com	425-882-2206	867-0865	173-3
Dataline LLC 6703 Albunda Dr PO Box 50816 ... Knoxville TN 37950 *TF:* 888-588-7740 ■ *Web:* www.datalinellc.com	865-588-7740	558-0942	261
Dataline Systems Inc 2709 Pemberton Dr ... Apopka FL 32703 *Web:* datalinesystems.info	407-298-1234		396
DataLink Interactive Inc 1120 Benfield Blvd Ste G ... Millersville MD 21108 *TF:* 888-565-3279 ■ *Web:* www.datalinktech.com	410-729-0440		180
Datalink Software Consultants Inc 4745 N Seventh St Ste 215 ... Phoenix AZ 85014 *Web:* www.datalinksc.com	602-279-7788		177
Datalogic Scanning 959 Terry St ... Eugene OR 97402 *TF:* 800-695-5700 ■ *Web:* www.datalogic.com	541-683-5700	345-7140	173-7
Datalogic Software 816 Manatee Ave E Ste 14 ... Bradenton FL 34208 *TF:* 800-766-6931 ■ *Web:* www.dmerc.com	941-714-0542		178-1
Datalogic Software Inc 1501 S 77 Sunshinestrip ... Harlingen TX 78550 *Web:* www.vesta.net	956-412-1424		177

Name / Address	City	State	Zip	Phone	Fax	Class
Datalogics Inc 101 N Wacker Dr Ste 1800 *Web:* www.datalogics.com	Chicago	IL	60606	312-853-8200	853-8282	178-1
Datalux Corp 155 Aviation Dr *TF:* 800-328-2589 ■ *Web:* www.datalux.com	Winchester	VA	22602	540-662-1500	662-1682	173-2
Dataman Group Inc 22594 Lemon Tree Ln *TF:* 800-771-3282 ■ *Web:* www.datamangroup.com	Boca Raton	FL	33428	561-451-9302		637-6
Datamann Inc 1994 Hartford Ave *TF:* 800-451-4263 ■ *Web:* www.datamann.com	Wilder	VT	05088	802-295-6600		178-11
DatamanUSA LLC 6890 S Tucson Way Ste 100 *Web:* www.datamanusa.com	Centennial	CO	80112	720-248-3121		631
Datamark Graphics Inc 603 W Bailey St *TF:* 888-629-6300 ■ *Web:* www.datamarkgraphics.com	Asheboro	NC	27203	888-629-6300		627
Datamark Inc 123 W Mills Ave Ste 400 *TF:* 800-477-1944 ■ *Web:* www.datamark.net	El Paso	TX	79901	800-477-1944		225
Datamatics Management Services Inc 3040 US-22 Ste 200 *TF:* 800-673-0366 ■ *Web:* www.datamaticsinc.com	Branchburg	NJ	08876	800-673-0366		178-1
Datamation Systems Inc 125 Louis St *Web:* pc-security.com	South Hackensack	NJ	07606	201-329-7200		697
Data-Matique 2110 Sherwin St *TF:* 866-706-0981 ■ *Web:* data-matique.com	Garland	TX	75041	972-272-3446		697
Datamatrix Systems Inc 505 Lincoln Hwy *Web:* www.getdatamatrix.com	East Mckeesport	PA	15035	412-825-3600		180
Datamax Corp 4501 Pkwy Commerce Blvd *Web:* www.datamaxcorp.com	Orlando	FL	32808	407-578-8007		173-6
Datamaxx Applied Technologies Inc 2001 Drayton Dr *Web:* www.datamaxx.com	Tallahassee	FL	32311	850-558-8000		174
Datamine Internet Marketing Solutions Inc 330 S Lake St *TF:* 877-328-2646 ■ *Web:* www.datamine.net	Gary	IN	46403	219-939-9987		7
Dataminr Inc 6 E 32nd St 2nd Fl *Web:* www.dataminr.com	New York	NY	10016	646-701-7826		387
DataMotion Inc 200 Park Ave *Fax Area Code: 973 ■ *TF:* 800-672-7233 ■ *Web:* www.datamotion.com	Florham Park	NJ	07932	800-672-7233	455-0750*	178-7
Datanational Corp 23382 Commerce Dr *Web:* datanat.com	Farmington Hills	MI	48335	248-426-0200		180
Datanomics 991 US Hwy 22 W Ste 301 *Web:* www.datanomics.com	Bridgewater	NJ	08807	908-707-8200		194
DataPath 2205 Northmont Pky *TF:* 866-855-3800 ■ *Web:* www.datapath.com	Duluth	GA	30096	678-597-0300		681
Datapay Inc 63 Cedar Ave Ste 8 *Web:* datapay.com	East Greenwich	RI	02818	401-886-4100		570
Dataprise Inc 9600 Blackwell Rd 4th Fl *Web:* www.dataprise.com	Rockville	MD	20850	301-945-0700		177
Datapro Inc 770 Ponce De Leon Blvd 2nd Fl *Web:* www.datapromiami.com	Coral Gables	FL	33134	305-374-0606		180
Datapro Solutions Inc 6336 E Utah Ave *TF:* 888-658-6881 ■ *Web:* datapronw.com	Spokane	WA	99212	509-532-3530		180
Dataprobe Inc 1B Pearl Ct *Web:* dataprobe.com	Allendale	NJ	07401	201-934-9944		174
Data-Quest Inc 4807 Jonestown Rd Ste 247 *Web:* www.dataquestinc.com	Harrisburg	PA	17109	717-545-2581	545-8117	180
Dataram Corp 777 Alexander Rd Ste 100 *NASDAQ: DRAM* ■ *TF:* 800-328-2726 ■ *Web:* www.dataram.com	Princeton	NJ	08540	609-799-0071	799-6734	625
Datarealm Internet Services Inc PO Box 1616 *TF:* 877-227-3783 ■ *Web:* www.datarealm.com	Hudson	WI	54016	877-227-3783		808
Datarobot Inc 1 International Pl 5th Fl *Web:* datarobot.com	Boston	MA	02110	617-765-4500		177
DataScan Field Services LLC 415 S Broad St *Web:* www.onedatascan.com	Alpharetta	GA	30009	770-754-6500		393
Datascan LP 2210 Hutton Dr Ste 100 *TF:* 866-441-4848 ■ *Web:* datascan.com	Carrollton	TX	75006	866-441-4848		196
Dataserv Corp 8625 F St *TF:* 888-901-8700 ■ *Web:* www.dataservcorp.com	Omaha	NE	68127	402-339-8700		175
Datashield LLC 1475 N Scottsdale Rd Ste 410 *TF:* 866-428-4567 ■ *Web:* www.datashieldprotect.com	Scottsdale	AZ	85257	866-428-4567		196
Dataskill Inc 2190 Carmel Valley Rd Ste D *TF:* 800-481-3282 ■ *Web:* www.dataskill.com	Del Mar	CA	92014	858-755-3800		180
Datasoft Inc 700 Plaza Dr *Web:* tradeblazer.com	Secaucus	NJ	07094	201-319-0494		225
DataSphere Technologies Inc 3350 161st Ave SE *TF:* 866-912-7090 ■ *Web:* www.secondspace.com	Bellevue	WA	98008	866-912-7090		5
Datassential 18 S Michigan 9th Fl *TF:* 888-556-3687 ■ *Web:* datassential.com	Chicago	IL	60603	312-655-0622		466
DataStarUSA Inc 5904 Stonecreek Dr Ste 120 *Fax Area Code: 214 ■ *TF:* 800-676-7826	The Colony	TX	75056	800-676-7826	291-0020*	260
Datastrait Networks Inc 3021 Harbor Ln N Ste 103 *Web:* www.datastrait.com	Minneapolis	MN	55447	763-746-4466		449
Datastrong LLC 8315 Lee Hwy Ste 600 *Web:* datastrong.com	Fairfax	VA	22031	703-992-9822		180
Datasyst Engineering & Testing Services Inc S14W33511 Hwy 18 *Web:* www.datasysttest.com	Delafield	WI	53018	262-968-4003		261
Datatech Depot Inc 4750 Ashley Dr *Web:* www.dtdi.com	Hamilton	OH	45011	513-860-5651		175
Datatech Labs 8000 E Quincy Ave *TF:* 888-288-3282 ■ *Web:* datatechlab.com	Denver	CO	80237	303-770-3282		624
Datatel Inc 4375 Fair Lakes Ct *TF:* 800-223-7036 ■ *Web:* www.ellucian.com	Fairfax	VA	22033	800-223-7036		178-10
Datatel Resources Corp 1729 Pennsylvania Ave *TF:* 800-245-2688 ■ *Web:* www.datatelcorp.com	Monaca	PA	15061	724-775-5300	775-0688	110
Datatel Solutions Inc 875 Laurel Dr *TF:* 888-224-8647 ■ *Web:* www.datatelsolutions.com	Roseville	CA	95678	888-224-8647		196
DataTicket Inc 4600 Campus Dr Ste 200 *Fax Area Code: 949 ■ *TF:* 888-752-0512 ■ *Web:* www.revenueexperts.com	Newport Beach	CA	92660	888-752-0512	752-6972*	160
Datatime Consulting 109 Forrest Ave *Web:* www.datatimeconsult.com	Narberth	PA	19072	610-668-9640		194
DataTrak Inc 5900 Landerbrook Dr Ste 170 *TF:* 888-677-3282 ■ *Web:* www.datatrak.com	Mayfield Heights	OH	44124	440-443-0082	442-3482	180
Datatrend Technologies Inc 121 Cheshire Ln Ste 700 *TF:* 800-367-7472 ■ *Web:* www.datatrend.com	Minnetonka	MN	55305	952-931-1203		180
DataTrends Publications Inc PO Box 3221 *Fax Area Code: 703 ■ *Web:* www.datatrendspublications.com	Leesburg	VA	20177	571-313-9916	771-9091*	637-9
Datatronic Distribution Inc 28151 Hwy 74 *Web:* www.datatronics.com	Menifee	CA	92585	951-928-7700	928-7701	767
Datavalet Technologies Inc 5275 Ch Queen-Mary *Web:* www.datavalet.com	Montreal	QC	H3W1Y3	514-385-4448		225
DataViz Inc 612 Wheelers Farms Rd *TF:* 800-733-0030 ■ *Web:* www.dataviz.com	Milford	CT	06460	203-874-0085	874-4345	178-12
Dataway Inc 5530 Lowell St *Web:* www.dataway.com	Oakland	CA	94608	415-882-8700		180
DataWorks Plus LLC 728 N Pleasantburg Dr *TF:* 866-632-2780 ■ *Web:* www.dataworksplus.com	Greenville	SC	29607	864-672-2780		177
Dataxport 10950 Pellicano Dr Ste C4 *Web:* www.dataxport.net	El Paso	TX	79935	915-771-9090		225
Datebook Publishing Inc 9322 W Lake Highlands Dr *Web:* www.datebook.com	Dallas	TX	75218	214-321-6759		637-2
Datel Systems Inc 4393 Viewridge Ave Ste C *Web:* datelsys.com	San Diego	CA	92123	858-571-3100	571-0452	179
Dates Weiser Furniture Corp 1700 Broadway St *TF:* 800-466-7037 ■ *Web:* www.datesweiser.com	Buffalo	NY	14212	716-891-1700		321
Datex Billing Services Inc 5520 Explorer Dr Ste 202 *TF:* 855-553-2839 ■ *Web:* www.datex.ca	Mississauga	ON	L4W5L1	855-553-2839		225
Datex Corp 10320 49th St N *TF:* 800-933-2839 ■ *Web:* www.datexcorp.com	Clearwater	FL	33762	727-571-4159	498-8635	177
Datonics LLC 37-18 Northern Blvd Ste 404 *Fax Area Code: 212 ■ *Web:* datonics.com	Long Island City	NY	11101	646-867-0647	504-8223*	387
Datotel LLC 710 N Tucker Ste 400 *Web:* www.datotel.com	Saint Louis	MO	63101	314-241-9101		387
Datrex Inc 13878 Hwy 165 *Web:* www.datrex.com	Kinder	LA	70648	337-738-4511	738-5675	296-37
Datron World Communications Inc 3030 Enterprise Ct *Web:* www.dtwc.com	Vista	CA	92081	760-597-1500	597-1510	647
Datroo Technologies 1292 N First St Ste 707 *Web:* www.datroo.com	Abilene	TX	79601	325-675-8880	202-3700	180
Datrose Inc 660 Basket Rd *TF:* 800-615-6144 ■ *Web:* www.datrose.com	Webster	NY	14580	585-265-1780	265-4016	225
DATTCO Inc 583 S St *TF:* 800-229-4879 ■ *Web:* www.dattco.com	New Britain	CT	06051	860-229-4878		107
Datum Engineers Inc 6516 Forest Park Rd *Web:* www.datumengineers.com	Dallas	TX	75235	214-358-0174		261
Datum Filing Systems Inc 89 Church Rd *TF:* 800-828-8018 ■ *Web:* bydatum.com	Emigsville	PA	17318	717-764-6350		286
Datum Inspection Services Inc 2350 W Shangri La Rd *Web:* datum-inspection.com	Phoenix	AZ	85027	602-997-1340		261
Dauber Company Inc 577 N 18th Rd *Web:* www.daubercompany.com	Tonica	IL	61370	815-442-3569	442-3669	696
Daubert Cromwell 12701 S Ridgeway Ave *TF:* 800-535-3535 ■ *Web:* www.daubertcromwell.com	Alsip	IL	60803	708-293-7750	293-7765	600
Daubert Law Firm LLC 1 Corporate Dr Ste 400 PO Box 1519 *TF:* 877-845-1805 ■ *Web:* daublaw.com	Wausau	WI	54401	715-845-1805	845-2624	41
Dauenhauer & Son Plumbing & Piping Company Inc 3416 Robards Ct *Web:* www.dauenhauerplumbing.com	Louisville	KY	40218	502-451-2233		189-10
Daugherty Systems Inc Three City Pl Ste 400 *Web:* www.daugherty.com	Saint Louis	MO	63141	314-432-8200		180
Daughters of Miriam Center/Gallen Institute 155 Hazel St *Web:* www.daughtersofmiriamcenter.org	Clifton	NJ	07011	973-772-3700		450
Daughters of Union Veterans of the Civil War 503 S Walnut St PO Box 211 *Web:* www.duvcw.org	Springfield	IL	62704	217-544-0616		520
Daum Commercial Real Estate Services 801 S Figueroa St Ste 600 *Web:* www.daumcommercial.com	Los Angeles	CA	90017	213-626-9101		652
Dauntless Industries 806 N Grand Ave *Web:* www.dauntlessmolds.com	Covina	CA	91724	626-966-4494	966-4062	697
Dauphin Capital Partners 108 Forest Ave *Web:* www.dauphincapital.com	Locust Valley	NY	11560	516-759-3339	759-3322	690
Dauphin County 2 S Second St 3rd Fl *TF:* 800-328-0058 ■ *Web:* www.dauphincounty.org	Harrisburg	PA	17101	717-780-6130	780-6468	338
Dauphin County Library System 101 Walnut St *Web:* dcls.org	Harrisburg	PA	17101	717-234-4961	234-7479	434-3
Dauphin Island Sea Lab Estuarium 101 Bienville Blvd *Web:* www.disl.org	Dauphin Island	AL	36528	251-861-2141	861-4646	40

	Phone	Fax	Class
Dauphin North America 300 Myrtle Ave .... Boonton NJ 07005 *Fax Area Code: 800 ■ TF: 800-631-1186 ■ Web: www.dauphin.com	973-263-1100	220-3844*	319-1
Dauphine Orleans Hotel 415 Dauphine St. .... New Orleans LA 70112 TF: 800-521-7111 ■ Web: www.dauphineorleans.com	504-586-1800		379
DAV (Disabled American Veterans) 3725 Alexandria Pk. .... Cold Spring KY 41076 TF: 877-426-2838 ■ Web: www.dav.org	859-441-7300	441-1416	48-19
Davalor Mold Corp 46480 Continental .... Chesterfield MI 48047 Web: www.davalor.com	586-598-0100		596
Davanac Inc 1936 St Regis .... Dorval QC H9P1H6 Web: davanac.com	514-421-0177	421-0188	770
Davanni's Inc 1100 Xenium Ln N .... Plymouth MN 55441 Web: www.davannis.com	952-927-2300		670
Davco Advertising Inc 89 N Kinzer Rd PO Box 288 .... Kinzers PA 17535 TF: 800-283-2826 ■ Web: www.davcoadvertising.com	717-442-4155		7
Davco Rest Home Resident 2526 W Tenth St. .... Owensboro KY 42301 Web: www.fernterrace.com	270-684-1705		371
Davco Technology LLC 1600 Woodland Dr PO Box 487 .... Saline MI 48176 TF: 800-328-2611 ■ Web: www.davcotec.com	734-429-5665	429-0741	60
Dave & Buster's 3000 Oakwood Blvd .... Hollywood FL 33020 TF: 888-300-1515 ■ Web: www.daveandbusters.com	954-923-5505		671
Dave Christian Construction Inc 2963 N Sunnyside Ave Ste 108 .... Fresno CA 93727 Web: davechristianconst.com	559-255-1222		41
Dave Droegkamp Heating Air Conditioning & Sheet Metal Inc 540 Norton Dr. .... Hartland WI 53029 Web: davedroegkamp.com	262-367-2820		189-10
Dave Evans Transports Inc 1122 Cedar Ave .... Superior WI 54880 Web: www.daveevanstransport.com	715-392-2211	392-5755	780
Dave Inc 1265 S Cochran Ave .... Los Angeles CA 90019 Web: www.dave.com	323-452-9807		70
Dave Meeker Auto Inc 24496 Eagle Rd. .... Purcell OK 73080 Web: davemeekerauto.com	405-527-9802	527-0013	62-5
Dave Phillips Music & Sound Inc 377 Irwin St .... Phillipsburg NJ 08865 Web: davephillipsmusicstore.com	908-454-3313		526
Dave Sinclair Ford Inc 7466 S Lindbergh Blvd. .... Saint Louis MO 63125 Web: www.davesinclairford.com	314-892-2600		57
Dave Steel Company Inc 40 Meadow Rd. .... Asheville NC 28803 Web: www.davesteel.com	828-252-2771		480
Dave Thomas Foundation for Adoption 716 Mt Airyshire Blvd Ste 100 .... Columbus OH 43235 TF: 800-275-3832 ■ Web: www.davethomasfoundation.org	800-275-3832		305
Dave White Chevrolet Inc 5880 Monroe St .... Sylvania OH 43560 Web: www.davewhitechevy.com	419-885-4444		57
Dave Wong's 2828 W March Ln. .... Stockton CA 95219 Web: www.davewongsrestaurant.com	209-951-4152		671
Dave's Place 210 Center St. .... Little Rock AR 72201 Web: www.davesplacerestaurant.com	501-372-3283		671
Daven Manufacturing LLC 55-B Dwight Pl .... Fairfield NJ 07004 TF: 800-834-8848 ■ Web: davenmfg.com	973-808-8848	808-8777	454
Davenport & Company LLC 901 E Cary St 1 James Ctr Ste 1100. .... Richmond VA 23219 TF: 800-846-6666 ■ Web: www.investdavenport.com	804-780-2000		690
Davenport College 275 Park St .... New Haven CT 06520 Web: www.davenport.yalecollege.yale.edu	203-432-0550		167-3
Davenport Cos, The 20 N Main St .... South Yarmouth MA 02664 TF: 800-822-3422 ■ Web: www.thedavenportcompanies.com	508-398-2293		186
Davenport Hotel, The 10 S Post St .... Spokane WA 99201 Web: www.davenporthotelcollection.com	509-455-8888	624-4455	379
Davenport House Museum 324 E State St. .... Savannah GA 31401 Web: www.davenporthousemuseum.org	912-236-8097	233-7938	520
Davenport Insulation 7400 Gateway Ct .... Manassas VA 20109 Web: www.truteam.com	703-631-7744		189-9
Davenport Public Library 321 Main St .... Davenport IA 52801 Web: www.davenportlibrary.com	563-326-7832	326-7809	434-3
Davenport Theatrical Enterprises 1501 Broadway Ste 1304 .... New York NY 10036 Web: www.davenporttheatrical.com	212-874-5348		514
Davenport University *Lansing* 220 E Kalamazoo St. .... Lansing MI 48933 TF: 800-686-1600 ■ Web: www.davenport.edu	517-484-2600	484-1132	166
Davenport, Evans, Hurwitz & Smith LLP 206 W 14th St. .... Sioux Falls SD 57101 Web: dehs.com	605-336-2880	335-3639	428
Davey Tree Expert Co 1500 N Mantua St. .... Kent OH 44240 Web: www.davey.com	330-673-9511	673-7089	776
Davey Tree Expert Co, The 1500 N Mantua St. .... Kent OH 44240 TF: 800-445-8733 ■ Web: www.davey.com	800-445-8733		776
David A. Bramble Inc 705 Morgnec Rd. .... Chestertown MD 21620 Web: www.davidabrambleinc.com	410-778-3023	778-3427	188-4
David A. Flanders CPA LLC 221 Maitland St .... Bel Air MD 21014 Web: flanderscpa.com	410-569-4506		2
David A. Noyes & Co 209 S LaSalle St. .... Chicago IL 60604 TF: 800-669-3732 ■ Web: danoyes.com	312-782-0400		41
David A. Smith Printing Inc 742 S 22nd St. .... Harrisburg PA 17104 TF: 800-564-3117 ■ Web: www.dasprint.com	717-564-3719		627
David A. Straz Jr Center for the Performing Arts 1010 N WC MacInnes Pl .... Tampa FL 33602 TF: 800-955-1045 ■ Web: www.strazcenter.org	813-222-1000	222-1057	572
David Adams Wealth Group LLC 2905 12 Ave S Ste 108. .... Nashville TN 37204 Web: davidadamsfinancialplanning.com	615-435-3644		390
David Allen Co 201 E Ojai Ave Ste 788 .... Ojai CA 93024 Web: gettingthingsdone.com	919-821-7100		194
David Aplin Group 700 Second St SW Scotia Ctr Ste 3850 .... Calgary AB T2P2W2 *Fax Area Code: 855 ■ Web: www.aplin.com	403-261-9000	273-7393*	260
David Berman Developments 340 Selby Ave. .... Ottawa ON K2A3X6 TF: 800-665-1809 ■ Web: davidberman.com	613-728-6777		344
David Black Agency 335 Adams St Ste 2707 .... Brooklyn NY 11201 Web: www.davidblackagency.com	718-852-5539		444
David Bohnett Foundation 245 S Beverly Dr. .... Beverly Hills CA 90212 Web: www.bohnettfoundation.org	310-276-0001	276-0007	305
David Boland Inc 219 Indian River Ave Ste 201 .... Titusville FL 32796 Web: www.dboland.com	321-269-1345	268-0577	189
David C. Conley PC 24 S Weber St Ste 300 .... Colorado Springs CO 80903 Web: davidconleylaw.com	719-633-3334		41
David C. Cook 4050 Lee Vance View .... Colorado Springs CO 80918 Web: davidccook.org	719-536-0100		637-9
David Chapman Agency Inc 5700 W Mt Hope Rd. .... Lansing MI 48917 Web: davidchapmanagency.com	517-321-4600	321-9443	390
David Clark Co 360 Franklin St. .... Worcester MA 01604 TF: 800-298-6235 ■ Web: www.davidclarkcompany.com	508-751-5800	753-5827	576
David Crockett State Park 1400 W Gaines .... Lawrenceburg TN 38464 Web: tnstateparks.com	931-762-9408		565
David Crumm Media LLC (DCM) 42807 Ford Rd Ste 234. .... Canton MI 48187 Web: www.readthespirit.com	734-751-7840		637-2
David Curtis School of Floral Design 209 N Main St .... Centerville OH 45459 TF: 800-437-7894 ■ Web: www.david-curtis-school.com	937-433-0566		685
David Dobbs Enterprises Inc 4600 US Hwy 1 N. .... Saint Augustine FL 32095 *Fax Area Code: 904 ■ TF: 800-889-6368 ■ Web: www.menudesigns.com	800-889-6368	826-3981*	92
David E. Quan Agency Insurance Brokers Inc 1767 16th St PO Box 3540. .... Oakland CA 94609 Web: quaninsurance.com	510-653-8880		390
David E. Wooster & Associates Inc 2 E Crafton Ave. .... Pittsburgh PA 15205 Web: dewooster.com	412-921-3303		261
David Evans & Associates Inc (DEA) 2100 SW River Pkwy .... Portland OR 97201 TF: 800-721-1916 ■ Web: www.deainc.com	503-223-6663	223-2701	261
David Firm, The 3415 S Sepulveda Blvd 11th Fl. .... Los Angeles CA 90034 Web: davidfirm.com	424-271-4570		41
David G. Cohen 1515 Lincoln Way .... Auburn CA 95603 Web: cohendefense.com	530-823-7700		41
David G. Denkhaus & Company PLLC 8163 Grand River Rd Ste 500. .... Brighton MI 48114 Web: denkhauscpa.com	810-844-1556		2
David Gooding Inc 173 Spark St. .... Brockton MA 02302 Web: www.goodingd.com	508-894-2000		612
David Grant US Air Force Medical Ctr 101 Bodin Cir. .... Fairfield CA 94535 Web: www.travis.af.mil	707-423-3000		374-4
David H. Fell & Company Inc 6009 Bandini Blvd .... Commerce CA 90040 TF: 800-822-1996 ■ Web: www.dhfco.com	323-722-9992	722-6567	407
David Hall Rare Coins PO Box 6220 .... Newport Beach CA 92658 TF: 800-759-7575 ■ Web: www.davidhall.com	949-567-1325	477-5874	411
David Hayman Jewellers Corp 18250 Imperial Hwy .... Yorba Linda CA 92886 Web: davidhaymanjewellers.com	714-996-9032		410
David Holden Consulting LLC 4146 S Birmingham Pl .... Tulsa OK 74105 Web: www.dwhweb.com	918-742-3985	948-9124	194
David Horowitz Freedom Ctr PO Box 55089 .... Sherman Oaks CA 91413 *Fax Area Code: 818 ■ TF: 800-752-6562 ■ Web: www.horowitzfreedomcenter.org	800-752-6562	849-3481*	196
David J. Frank Landscape Contracting Inc N120 W21350 Freistadt Rd. .... Germantown WI 53022 Web: www.davidjfrank.com	262-255-4888		776
David J. Joseph Co (DJJ) 300 Pike St .... Cincinnati OH 45202 Web: www.djj.com	513-419-6200		686
David King & Associates Inc 1011 Lake St Ste 313 .... Oak Park IL 60301 Web: dkacre.com	708-445-0505	445-1890	653
David Kucera Inc 42 Steves Ln. .... Gardiner NY 12525 Web: www.dkiconcrete.com	845-255-1044		183
David L. Adams Associates Inc 1536 Ogden St .... Denver CO 80218 Web: www.dlaa.com	303-455-1900		261
David L. Lawrence Convention Ctr 1000 Ft Duquesne Blvd .... Pittsburgh PA 15222 Web: www.pittsburghcc.com	412-565-6000	565-6008	205
David L. Wallace & Associates PA 542 Douglas Ave. .... Dunedin FL 34698 Web: dlwarchitects.com	727-736-6000		261
David Larson Financial & Insurance Services Inc 227 Main St S. .... Hutchinson MN 55350 TF: 855-892-2245 ■ Web: insuranceservicesminnesota.com	320-587-2245	587-0955	390
David M. Girardi, Od LLC 824 Franklin Park Dr. .... East Syracuse NY 13057 Web: seesharpeyewear.com	315-446-1288		543
David M. Peterson Pc 65 Broadway .... New York NY 10006 Web: lawpeterson.com	212-430-6352		41
David M. Siegel & Associates LLC 790 Chaddick Dr. .... Wheeling IL 60090 Web: davidmsiegel.com	847-520-8100		41

Name / Address	Phone	Fax	Class
David M. Wiseblood, Attorney 601 Montgomery St Ste 2000, San Francisco CA 94111 *Web:* wiseblodlaw.com	415-547-2703		41
David Mason & Assoc 800 S Vandeventer Ave, Saint Louis MO 63110 *Web:* www.davidmason.com	314-534-1030	534-1053	256
David Monn LLC 135 W 27th St Ste 2, New York NY 10001 *Web:* davidmonn.com	212-242-2009		232
David N, Rosen Counselor At Law Pc 400 Orange St, New Haven CT 06511 *Web:* davidrosenlaw.com	203-787-3513		41
David Nelson Construction Co 3483 Alternate 19, Palm Harbor FL 34683 *Web:* www.nelson-construction.com	727-784-7624		188-4
David Nolan Gallery 527 W 29th St, New York NY 10001 *Web:* www.davidnolangallery.com	212-925-6190	334-9139	42
David Peyser Sportswear Inc 90 Spence St, Bay Shore NY 11706	631-231-7788		155-12
David Plunkett Realty LLC 8832 Riverside Dr, Parker AZ 85344 *Web:* davidplunkettrealty.com	928-667-1699	667-1694	652
David Pomerantz & Associates LLC 1836 Metzerott Rd Ste Tc-1, Adelphi MD 20783 *Web:* acctdpa.com	301-445-6300		734
David R. Ramos CPA 4215 Old Rd 37, Lakeland FL 33813 *Web:* davidramoscpa.com	863-701-7885		2
David S. Palmer Arena 100 W Main St, Danville IL 61832 *Web:* palmerarena.com	217-431-2424	431-6444	720
David S. Sobotka, Esq 519 Walnut St, Reading PA 19601 *Web:* sobotkalaw.com	610-376-6018		41
David Saliba 4 Derne St, Boston MA 02114 *Web:* attyssaliba.com	617-227-8640		41
David Scott Insurance Agency Inc 8110 La Jolla Shores Dr, La Jolla CA 92037 *Web:* davescottins.com	858-459-4259		390
David Simpson Construction LLC 2342 Icewine Dr, Billings MT 59102 *Web:* www.davidsimpsonconstruction.com	406-855-9933		100
David Stires Associates LLC 678 US Hwy 202/206 N, Bridgewater NJ 08807 *Web:* www.dastires.com	908-252-7000	252-7090	261
David Suzuki Foundation 219-2211 W Fourth Ave, Vancouver BC V6K4S2 *TF:* 800-453-1533 ■ *Web:* davidsuzuki.org	604-732-4228		305
David Tate Insurance Agency Inc 1840 SW 22nd St 4th Fl, Miami FL 33145 *Web:* www.davidtateinsurance.com	727-210-2166		390
David Textiles Inc 1920 S Tubeway Ave, Commerce CA 90040 *Web:* davidtextilesinc.com	323-728-3231		258
David Traylor Zoo of Emporia 75 Soden Rd, Emporia KS 66801 *Web:* www.emporiazoo.org	620-341-4365		823
David Wade Correctional Ctr 670 Bell Hill Rd, Homer LA 71040 *Web:* www.doc.louisiana.gov	318-927-0400		213
David Weekley Homes Inc 1111 N Post Oak Rd, Houston TX 77055 *TF:* 800-390-6774 ■ *Web:* www.davidweekleyhomes.com	713-963-0500	963-0322	653
David William Hotel Condo Assn 700 Biltmore Way, Miami FL 33134 *Web:* davidwilliamcondo.com	305-903-1867		379
David Yurman Designs Inc 24 Vestry St, New York NY 10013 *TF:* 888-398-7626 ■ *Web:* www.davidyurman.com	888-398-7626		409
David Zwirner Gallery 525 W 19th St, New York NY 10011 *Web:* www.davidzwirner.com	212-727-2070	727-2072	42
David's Barbecue 5121 NW 39th Ave, Gainesville FL 32606 *Web:* davidsbbq.com	352-373-2002		671
David's Bridal Inc 1001 Washington St, Conshohocken PA 19428 *TF:* 844-400-3222 ■ *Web:* www.davidsbridal.com	610-943-5000		157-6
David's Furniture Ltd 5078 Jonestown Rd, Harrisburg PA 17112 *Web:* davidsfurniture.com	717-233-2955		321
Davidoff Associates Inc 10925 Royal Caribbean Cir, Boynton Beach FL 33437 **Fax Area Code: 772* ■ *TF:* 800-754-3170 ■ *Web:* www.davidoffassociates.com	561-742-3386	382-2707*	194
Davids Clarence & Co 22901 S Ridgeland Ave, Matteson IL 60443 *Web:* www.clarencedavids.com	708-720-4100	720-4200	422
Davids Sharice (Rep D - KS) 1541 Longworth House Office Bldg, Washington DC 20515 *Web:* www.davids.house.gov	202-225-2865		342-2
Davidson & Associates Insurance Agency Inc 610 Esther St Ste 101, Vancouver WA 98660 *Web:* davidsoninsurance.com	360-514-9550		390
Davidson & Bennett Real Estate Services Inc 1817 Jefferson St, Napa CA 94559 *Web:* davidsonandbennett.com	707-253-0220	253-0260	652
Davidson & Company LLP 1200 - 609 Granville St Pacific Centre, Vancouver BC V7Y1G6 *Web:* davidson-co.com	604-687-0947		734
Davidson & Jones Hotel Corp 1207 Front St Ste 100, Raleigh NC 27609	919-828-0880		379
Davidson College PO Box 7162, Davidson NC 28035 *TF:* 800-768-0380 ■ *Web:* www.davidson.edu	704-892-2000	894-2845	166
Davidson County 913 Greensboro St, Lexington NC 27292 *Web:* www.co.davidson.nc.us	336-242-2000	248-8440	338
Davidson County 205 Metro Courthouse, Nashville TN 37201 *Web:* www.nashville.gov	615-862-6770	862-6774	338
Davidson County Community College PO Box 1287, Lexington NC 27293 *Web:* www.davidsonccc.edu	336-249-8186	224-0240	162
Davidson Engineering LLC (DE) 606 NE 312th Ave, Washougal WA 98671 *Web:* tower-engineer.com	360-210-4032		261
Davidson Hotels & Resorts 1 Ravinia Dr Ste 1600, Atlanta GA 30346 *Web:* www.davidsonhotels.com	678-349-0909	349-0908	379
Davidson Institute for Talent Development 9665 Gateway Dr, Reno NV 89521 *Web:* www.davidsongifted.org	775-852-3483		196
Davidson Instruments Inc 9391 Grogan's Mill Rd, The Woodlands TX 77380 *Web:* www.davidson-instruments.com	281-362-4900		201
Davidson of Dundee Inc 28421 Hwy 27, Dundee FL 33838 *TF:* 800-654-0647 ■ *Web:* davidsonofdundee.com	863-439-2284	439-5049	297-3
Davidson Plyforms Inc 5505 33rd St SE, Grand Rapids MI 49512 *Web:* lpworkfurniture.com	616-956-0033	956-0041	820
Davidson Technologies Inc 530 Discovery Dr Cummings Research Pk, Huntsville AL 35806 *Web:* davidson-tech.com	256-922-0720	971-6861	21
Davidson Warren (Rep R - OH) 1107 Longworth House Office Bldg, Washington DC 20515 *Web:* www.davidson.house.gov	202-225-6205		342-2
Davidson's Inc 6100 Wilkinson Dr, Prescott AZ 86301 *Web:* www.galleryofguns.com	928-776-8055		690
Davidson, Davidson & Kappel LLC 589 Eighth Ave 16th Fl, New York NY 10018 *Web:* www.ddkpatent.com	212-736-1940		428
Davidson-Kennedy Co 800 Industrial Park Dr, Marietta GA 30062 *TF:* 800-733-3434 ■ *Web:* equipmentinnovators.com	770-427-9467		120
Davie County 123 S Main St, Mocksville NC 27028 *Web:* www.daviecountync.gov	336-753-6040	751-7408	338
Davie County Chamber of Commerce 371 N Main St, Mocksville NC 27028 *TF:* 877-800-2382 ■ *Web:* www.daviechamber.com	336-751-3304	751-5697	139
Davie County Schools 220 Cherry St, Mocksville NC 27028 *Web:* www.davie.k12.nc.us	336-751-5921	751-9013	685
Davie-Cooper City Chamber of Commerce 4185 Davie Rd, Davie FL 33314 *Web:* www.davie-coopercity.org	954-581-0790	581-9684	139
Davies 808 State St, Santa Barbara CA 93101 *Web:* www.daviespublicaffairs.com	805-963-5929		636
Davies Law Firm 126 E Jefferson St, Orlando FL 32801 *Web:* thedavieslawfirm.com	407-540-1010		41
Davies Manor House 9336 Davies Plantation Rd, Memphis TN 38133 *Web:* www.daviesmanorplantation.org	901-386-0715	388-4677	50-3
Davies Molding LLC 350 Kehoe Blvd, Carol Stream IL 60188 *TF:* 800-554-9208 ■ *Web:* www.daviesmolding.com	630-510-8188	510-9944	621
Davies Pearson PC 920 Fawcett Ave, Tacoma WA 98401 *TF:* 800-439-1112 ■ *Web:* www.dpearson.com	253-620-1500		428
Davies Publishing Inc 32 S Raymond Ave Ste 4 & 5, Pasadena CA 91105 *TF:* 877-792-0005 ■ *Web:* www.daviespublishing.com	626-792-3046	792-5308	637-10
Davies Ward Phillips & Vineberg LLP 155 Wellington St W, Toronto ON M5V3J7 *Web:* www.dwpv.com	416-863-0900		41
Davies-Imperial Coatings Inc 1275 State St, Hammond IN 46320 *Web:* www.daviesimperial.com	219-933-0877	932-4201	550
Daviess County 212 St Ann St, Owensboro KY 42303 *Web:* www.daviessky.org	270-685-8434		338
Daviess County 200 E Walnut St, Washington IN 47501 *Web:* www.daviess.org	812-254-1091		338
Daviess County Metal Sales Inc 9929 E US Hwy 60, Cannelburg IN 47519 *TF:* 800-279-4299 ■ *Web:* www.dcmetal.com	812-486-4299		697
Daviess County Public Library 2020 Frederica St, Owensboro KY 42301 *Web:* www.dcplibrary.org	270-684-0211		434-3
Daviess-Martin County REMC 12628 E 75 N PO Box 430, Loogootee IN 47553 *TF:* 800-762-7362 ■ *Web:* www.dmremc.com	812-295-4200	295-4216	245
Davila Pharmacy Inc 1423 Guadalupe St, San Antonio TX 78207 *Web:* www.davilapharmacy.com	210-226-5293	224-9257	237
Davinci Institute Inc 9191 Sheridan Blvd Ste 300, Westminster CO 80031 *Web:* www.davinciinstitute.com	303-666-4133		113
Davincimeetingrooms.com 2150 S 1300 E Ste 200, Salt Lake City UT 84106 **Fax Area Code: 888* ■ *TF:* 877-424-9767 ■ *Web:* www.davincimeetingrooms.com	801-990-8000	518-6665*	393
Davis & Associates CPA Firm 717 Cedar Bayou Rd Ste 100, Baytown TX 77520 *Web:* daviscpafirm.com	281-422-3087	837-9868	2
Davis & Associates Inc 2852 N Webster Ave, Indianapolis IN 46219 *Web:* davisassocindy.com	317-263-9947		186
Davis & Elkins College 100 Campus Dr, Elkins WV 26241 *TF:* 800-624-3157 ■ *Web:* www.dewv.edu	304-637-1900	637-1800	166
Davis & Floyd Inc 1319 Hwy 72 221 E, Greenwood SC 29649 *Web:* www.davisfloyd.com	864-229-5211	229-7844	261
Davis & Gilbert 1740 Broadway, New York NY 10019 *Web:* www.dglaw.com	212-468-4800		428
Davis & Langdale Company Inc 231 E 60th St, New York NY 10022 *Web:* www.davisandlangdale.com	212-838-0333	752-7764	42
Davis & Wright PC 5316 W Hwy 290 Ste 150, Austin TX 78735 *Web:* www.dwlaw.com	512-482-0614		428
Davis Aircraft Products Company Inc 1150 Walnut Ave, Bohemia NY 11716 *Web:* www.davisaircraftproducts.com	631-563-1500		22
Davis Amusement Cascadia Inc PO Box 1585, Clackamas OR 97015 *Web:* www.davisamusement.com	503-807-2154		239
Davis Applied Technology College 550 E 300 S, Kaysville UT 84037 *Web:* www.datc.edu	801-593-2500		167-3

Company / Address	City	State	ZIP	Phone	Fax	Class
Davis Automotive Group Inc 6135 Kruse Dr *Web:* www.davisautomotive.com	Solon	OH	44139	440-542-0600		57
Davis Bacon Material Handling Inc 5000 Valley Blvd *Fax Area Code: 323 ■ TF: 800-932-1921 ■ Web: www.davisbaconmh.com	Los Angeles	CA	90032	800-932-1921	227-1928*	286
Davis Bakery Inc 28700 Chagrin Blvd *Web:* www.davisbakery.net	Woodmere	OH	44122	216-464-5599	292-4588	297-2
Davis Brand Capital LLC 1180 Peachtree St Ste 2605 *Web:* davisbrandcapital.com	Atlanta	GA	30309	404-347-7778		195
Davis Capital Corp 200 S Wacker Dr 31st Fl *Web:* www.daviscapital.com	Chicago	IL	60606	312-623-4500		70
Davis Capital Partners LLC 3 Harbor Dr Ste 301 *Web:* www.daviscapitalpartners.com	Sausalito	CA	94965	415-362-3600		528
Davis Chamber of Commerce 604 Third St *Web:* www.davischamber.com	Davis	CA	95616	530-756-5160	756-5190	139
Davis Chamber of Commerce 450 Simmons Way Ste 220 *Web:* davischamberofcommerce.com	Kaysville	UT	84037	801-593-2200	593-2212	139
Davis College 400 Riverside Dr *TF:* 800-331-4137 ■ *Web:* www.davisny.edu	Johnson City	NY	13790	607-729-1581	729-2962	161
Davis College 4747 Monroe St *TF:* 800-477-7021 ■ *Web:* www.daviscollege.edu	Toledo	OH	43623	419-473-2700	473-2472	800
Davis Community Television 1623 5th St *Web:* www.davismedia.org	Davis	CA	95616	530-757-2419		647
Davis Contractors Ltd 5205 Fm 236	Cuero	TX	77954	361-275-5721		189-10
Davis Correctional Facility 6888 E 133rd Rd *TF:* 877-834-1550 ■ *Web:* cca.com	Holdenville	OK	74848	405-379-6400	379-6496	213
Davis Cos 325 Donald J Lynch Blvd *Fax Area Code: 508 ■ TF: 800-482-9494 ■ Web: www.daviscos.com	Marlborough	MA	01752	763-231-0700	481-8519*	721
Davis County Clerk of Courts 100 Courthouse Sq *Web:* www.daviscountyiowa.org	Bloomfield	IA	52537	641-664-2011	664-2041	338
Davis County Clipper Today 1370 S 500 W *Web:* davisclipper.com	Woods Cross	UT	84010	801-295-2251		532-3
Davis County Library 61 S Main St *Web:* www.co.davis.ut.us	Farmington	UT	84025	801-444-2300	451-3281	434-3
Davis Danny K (Rep D - IL) 2159 Rayburn House Office Bldg *Web:* davis.house.gov	Washington	DC	20515	202-225-5006	225-5641	342-2
Davis Demographics & Planning Inc 11850 Pierce St Ste 200 *TF:* 888-337-4471 ■ *Web:* www.davisdemographics.com	Riverside	CA	92505	951-270-5211		463
Davis Direct Inc 1241 Newell Pkwy *TF:* 877-277-0878 ■ *Web:* www.davisdirect.com	Montgomery	AL	36110	334-277-0878		627
Davis Elementary School 1050 Arlington Dr *Web:* davis.nmusd.us	Costa Mesa	CA	92626	714-424-7930		685
Davis Elen Adv 865 S Figueroa St Ste 1200 *Web:* www.daviselen.com	Los Angeles	CA	90017	213-688-7000		4
Davis Enterprise 315 G St *Web:* www.davisenterprise.com	Davis	CA	95616	530-756-0800	756-6707	532-2
Davis Ethical Pharmacy 124 N Long Beach Rd *Web:* www.davis-ethical-pharmacy.business.site	Rockville Centre	NY	11570	516-764-3200		237
Davis Express Inc PO Box 1276 *TF:* 800-874-4270 ■ *Web:* www.davis-express.com	Starke	FL	32091	800-874-4270		780
Davis Funds 2949 E Elvira Rd Ste 101 *TF:* 800-279-0279 ■ *Web:* www.davisfunds.com	Tucson	AZ	85756	800-279-0279		528
Davis Furniture Industries Inc 2401 S College Dr *Web:* www.davis-furniture.com	High Point	NC	27260	336-889-2009	889-0031	319-1
Davis Graham & Stubbs LLP 1550 17th St Ste 500 *Web:* www.dgslaw.com	Denver	CO	80202	303-892-9400	893-1379	428
Davis Hospital & Medical Ctr (DHMC) 1600 W Antelope Dr *TF:* 877-898-6080 ■ *Web:* www.davishospital.org	Layton	UT	84041	801-807-1000	807-7610	374-3
Davis Industries Inc 9920 Richmond Hwy *Web:* davisindustriesrecycling.com	Lorton	VA	22079	703-550-7402		686
Davis Instrument Corp 3465 Diablo Ave *TF:* 800-678-3669 ■ *Web:* www.davisinstruments.com	Hayward	CA	94545	510-732-9229		472
Davis Landscape Company Inc 78 Lisbon St *TF:* 800-675-4885 ■ *Web:* davislandscape.com	Lisbon	ME	04250	207-353-4848		422
Davis Law Firm 10500 Heitage Blvd Ste 102 *TF:* 800-770-0127 ■ *Web:* jeffdavislawfirm.com	San Antonio	TX	78216	210-444-4444		428
Davis Machine Works of Opelika Inc 1318 Lee Rd 42 *Web:* www.davismachineworks.com	Opelika	AL	36804	334-745-3548	705-0960	454
Davis Memorial Hospital 812 Gorman Ave *Web:* www.davishealthsystem.org	Elkins	WV	26241	304-636-3300		374-3
Davis Miles McGuire Gardner PLLC 40 E Rio Salado Pkwy Ste 425 *TF:* 844-366-4529 ■ *Web:* www.davismiles.com	Tempe	AZ	85281	480-733-6800	733-3748	445
Davis Mountains State Park State Hwy 118 *Web:* tpwd.texas.gov	Fort Davis	TX	79734	432-426-3337		565
Davis Oil Co 904 Jernigan St PO Box 1970 *TF:* 800-277-4355 ■ *Web:* www.davis-company.com	Perry	GA	31069	478-987-2443	987-3013	316
Davis Paint Company Inc 1311 Iron St *TF:* 800-821-2029 ■ *Web:* www.davispaint.com	North Kansas City	MO	64116	816-471-4447	471-1460	550
Davis Polk & Wardwell 450 Lexington Ave *Web:* www.davispolk.com	New York	NY	10017	212-450-4000	701-5800	428
Davis Powers Inc 640 N La Salle Dr Ste 565 *Web:* www.davispowers.com	Chicago	IL	60654	312-654-9239		177
Davis Professional Services Inc 820 Greenbrier Cir Ste 18 *Web:* www.davisproserv.com	Chesapeake	VA	23320	757-431-1344		104
Davis Regional Medical Ctr 218 Old Mocksville Rd PO Box 1823 *Web:* www.davisregional.com	Statesville	NC	28625	704-873-0281		374-3
Davis Reseland LLC 112 Westwood Pl Ste 365 *Web:* drwealthmgmt.com	Brentwood	TN	37027	615-309-8335		690
Davis Rodney (Rep R - IL) 1740 Longworth House Office Bldg *Web:* rodneydavis.house.gov	Washington	DC	20515	202-225-2371	226-0791	342-2
Davis Salvage Inc 3322 E Washington St *Web:* davissalvage.co	Phoenix	AZ	85034	602-267-7208		492
Davis Shapiro Lewit Grabel Leven Granderson & Blake LLP 414 W 14th St 5th Fl *Web:* davisshapiro.com	New York	NY	10014	212-230-5500		41
Davis Smith Accounting Associates PA 5582 Milford Harrington Hwy *Web:* www.davis-smithaccounting.com	Harrington	DE	19952	302-398-4020		2
Davis Steadman Ford & Mace LLC 167 N Main St *Web:* whiteriverlawyers.com	White River Junction	VT	05001	802-295-5631		41
Davis Susan (Rep D - CA) 1214 Longworth House Office Bldg *Web:* www.susandavis.house.gov	Washington	DC	20515	202-225-2040	225-2948	342-2
Davis Tool & Die Company Inc 888 Bolger Ct *Web:* www.davistool.com	Fenton	MO	63026	636-343-0828	343-0875	697
Davis Tool Inc 3740 NW Aloclek Pl *Web:* www.davistl.com	Hillsboro	OR	97124	503-648-0936		454
Davis Transfer Company Inc 520 Busha Rd *TF:* 800-736-4285 ■ *Web:* www.davistransfer.com	Carnesville	GA	30521	706-384-2030		780
Davis Transport Inc 216 Trade St *TF:* 800-548-3114 ■ *Web:* www.davistransport.com	Missoula	MT	59808	406-728-5510	728-5877	311
Davis Tuttle Venture Partners LP 110 W Seventh St Ste 1000 *Web:* www.davistuttle.com	Tulsa	OK	74103	918-584-7272	582-3404	792
Davis Vandenbossche Agency 51180 Bedford St PO Box 1060 *Web:* dvainsurance.com	New Baltimore	MI	48047	810-794-4907		390
Davis Vision Inc 711 Troy-Schenectady Rd *TF:* 800-999-5431 ■ *Web:* www.davisvision.com	Latham	NY	12110	800-999-5431		391-3
Davis Wire Corp 5555 Irwindale Ave *TF:* 800-350-7851 ■ *Web:* www.daviswire.com	Irwindale	CA	91706	626-969-7651	334-4780	490
Davis Wood Products Inc PO Box 604 *Web:* www.daviswoodproducts.com	Hudson	NC	28638	828-728-8444	728-4601	613
Davis Wright Tremaine LLP 1201 Third Ave Ste 2200 *Web:* www.dwt.com	Seattle	WA	98101	206-622-3150	757-7700	428
Davis, Goss & Williams PLLC 1441 Lakeover Rd *Web:* attorneyjacksonmississippi.com	Jackson	MS	39213	601-255-7225		41
Davis, Grass, Goldstein & Housouer 3105 Sedona Ct *Web:* davis-grass.com	Ontario	CA	91764	909-476-2662		41
Davisco International Inc 719 N Main St *TF:* 800-757-7611 ■ *Web:* www.daviscofoods.com	Le Sueur	MN	56058	507-665-8811	665-3701	296-10
Davis-Monthan Air Force Base 5275 E Granite St *Web:* www.dm.af.mil	Tucson	AZ	85707	520-228-3204		497-1
Davison & Mccarthy PC 645 Hamilton St Ste 510 *Web:* davisonmccarthy.com	Allentown	PA	18101	610-435-0450	435-3089	41
Davison County Auditor 200 East Fourth Ave *Web:* www.davisoncounty.org	Mitchell	SD	57301	605-995-8608	995-8618	338
Davison Fuels Inc 8450 Tanner Williams Rd *TF:* 800-737-4446 ■ *Web:* davisonoil.com	Mobile	AL	36608	251-633-4444	639-4755	579
Davissa Telephone Systems Inc 23800 Commerce Pk *Web:* www.davissa.com	Cleveland	OH	44122	216-464-6633		225
Davis-Ulmer Sprinkler Company Inc 1 Commerce Dr *TF:* 877-691-3200 ■ *Web:* www.davisulmer.com	Amherst	NY	14228	716-691-3200		386
Davisville Travel 420 2nd St *TF:* 800-255-4567 ■ *Web:* www.davisvilletravel.com	Davis	CA	95616	916-448-1951		771
DaVita Inc 1551 Wewatta St *NYSE: DVA ■ TF:* 800-310-4872 ■ *Web:* www.davita.com	Denver	CO	80202	303-405-2100		352
Davlan Engineering Inc 3644 Scarlet Oak Blvd *Web:* davlan.com	Saint Louis	MO	63122	636-225-5310	225-2713	454
Davroc 2051 Williams Pkwy Units 21 *Web:* www.davroc.com	Brampton	ON	L6S5T4	905-792-7792		261
Davy Crockett Birthplace State Park 1245 Davy Crockett Park Rd *Web:* www.state.tn.us	Limestone	TN	37681	423-257-2167		565
Daw & Frantz, CPA 1101 California Ave Ste 211 *Web:* www.dawfrantzcpas.com	Corona	CA	92881	951-582-9023		2
Daw Construction Group LLC 12552 South 125 West Ste 100 *TF:* 800-748-4778 ■ *Web:* www.dawcg.com	Draper	UT	84020	800-748-4778		186
Dawahares 1801 Alexandria Dr Ste 148 *TF:* 800-677-9108 ■ *Web:* www.dawahares.com	Lexington	KY	40504	859-278-0422	514-3299	157-2
Dawat 210 E 58th St *Web:* www.dawatny.com	New York	NY	10022	212-355-7555		671
Dawda, Mann, Mulcahy & Sadler PLC 39533 Woodward Ave Ste 200 *Web:* dawdamann.com	Bloomfield Hills	MI	48304	248-642-3700	642-7791	428
Dawe's Laboratories 3355 N Arlington Heights Rd *Web:* dawesnutrition.com	Arlington Heights	IL	60004	847-577-2020	577-1898	584
Dawes Arboretum 7770 Jacksontown Rd SE *Web:* dawesarb.org	Newark	OH	43056	740-323-2355	323-4058	97
Dawes County 451 Main St *Web:* dawes-county.com	Chadron	NE	69337	308-432-0100	432-5179	338

Name / Address	City	State	ZIP	Phone	Fax	Class
Dawes Rigging & Crane Rental Inc						
805 S 72nd St	Milwaukee	WI	53214	414-453-5335	453-2494	264-3
TF: 800-236-5335 ■ *Web:* www.allcrane.com						
Dawn Career Institute Inc						
3700 Lancaster Pke	Wilmington	DE	19805	302-633-9075		167-3
TF: 855-809-4202 ■ *Web:* www.dawncareerinstitute.edu						
Dawn Co 3340 S Lapeer Rd	Lake Orion	MI	48359	248-391-9200	391-9207	681
Web: www.dawnco.com						
Dawn Enterprises Inc						
9155 Sweet Valley Dr	Valley View	OH	44125	216-447-1777		596
TF: 800-548-4867 ■ *Web:* www.dawn-ent.com						
Dawn Fairbanks Insurance Services Inc						
12006 Broadway Ter	Oakland	CA	94611	510-339-1483		390
Web: fairbanks-ins.com						
Dawn Food Products Inc						
3333 Sargent Rd	Jackson	MI	49201	517-789-4400		296-16
TF: 800-292-1362 ■ *Web:* www.dawnfoods.com						
Dawn Horse Press, The PO Box 70	Lower Lake	CA	95457	707-928-6590		637-2
TF: 877-770-0772 ■ *Web:* www.dawnhorsepress.com						
Dawn Industries Inc 5055 W 58th Ave	Arvada	CO	80002	303-296-4041		604
Web: www.dawnindustries.com						
Dawn Sign Press 6130 Nancy Ridge Dr	San Diego	CA	92121	858-768-0428	625-2336	637-10
TF: 800-549-5350 ■ *Web:* www.dawnsign.com						
Dawnbreaker Inc 3161 Union St	North Chili	NY	14514	585-594-0025	594-8623	194
Web: www.dawnbreaker.com						
Dawson & Assoc 3250 Mary St	Coconut Grove	FL	33133	305-443-1500	444-3479	734
Web: www.flacpa.com						
Dawson Co 1681 W Second St	Pomona	CA	91766	626-797-9710		612
TF: 800-832-9766 ■ *Web:* www.dawsonco.com						
Dawson Community College						
300 College Dr	Glendive	MT	59330	406-377-3396		162
TF: 800-821-8320 ■ *Web:* www.dawson.edu						
Dawson Construction						
8401 Airport PO Box 35825	Juneau	AK	99801	907-780-1500	780-1501	186
Web: dawson.com						
Dawson County						
25 Justice Way Ste 2204	Dawsonville	GA	30534	706-344-3513	344-3514	338
Web: dawsoncounty.org						
Dawson County 207 W Bell St	Glendive	MT	59330	406-377-3058	687-3563	338
Web: www.dawsoncountymontana.com						
Dawson County PO Box 1268	Lamesa	TX	79331	806-872-3778	872-2473	338
Web: www.co.dawson.tx.us						
Dawson County 700 N Washington	Lexington	NE	68850	308-324-2127	324-9832	338
Web: dawsoncountyne.org						
Dawson County Board of Education, The						
28 Main St	Dawsonville	GA	30534	706-265-3246		685
Web: www.dawsoncountyschools.org						
Dawson Design Associates Inc						
315 Second Ave S 300	Seattle	WA	98104	206-932-3102		393
Web: www.dawsondesignassociates.com						
Dawson Food Products Inc						
251 W Euclid Ave	Jackson	MI	49203	517-788-9830	788-7852	296-37
Web: dawsonfoods.com						
Dawson Geophysical Co						
508 W Wall St Ste 800	Midland	TX	79701	432-684-3000	684-3030	538
NASDAQ: DWSN ■ *TF:* 800-332-9766 ■ *Web:* www.dawson3d.com						
Dawson Insurance 505 Broadway N Ste 100	Fargo	ND	58102	701-237-3311	232-4442	390
TF: 800-220-4514 ■ *Web:* dawsonins.com						
Dawson Logistics Inc 122 Eastgate Dr	Danville	IL	61834	618-205-8800		194
Web: dawsonlogistics.com						
Dawson Manufacturing Co						
1042 N Crystal Ave	Benton Harbor	MI	49022	269-925-0100	925-0997	676
Web: www.dawsonmfg.com						
Dawson Metal Company Inc						
825 Allen St	Jamestown	NY	14701	716-664-3815	664-3485	697
Web: www.dawsonmetal.com						
Dawson Public Power District						
75191 Rd 433	Lexington	NE	68850	308-324-2386		245
TF: 800-752-8305 ■ *Web:* dawsonpower.com						
Dawson School 199 N School Ave	Dawson	TX	76639	254-578-1031		393
Web: www.dawsonisd.net						
Dawson's Kitchen 3360 Brookdale Ave	Macon	GA	31204	478-742-9852		671
Web: www.dawsonskitchen.com						
Dawson, Smith, Purvis & Bassett PA						
15 Casco St	Portland	ME	04101	207-874-0355		2
Web: dspbcpa.com						
Dax Law Firm PC, The						
54 State St Ste 805	Albany	NY	12207	518-432-1002	432-1028	41
Web: daxlawfirm.com						
Dax Safety & Staffing Solutions LLC						
3219 NE 153rd Terr	Smithville	MO	64089	816-935-9137	734-0422	260
Web: daxsafety.com						
Daxor Corp 350 Fifth Ave Ste 4740	New York	NY	10118	212-330-8500	244-0806	419
NYSE: DXR ■ *Web:* www.daxor.com						
Day & Zimmermann Group Inc						
1500 Spring Garden St	Philadelphia	PA	19130	215-299-8000		727
TF: 877-319-0270 ■ *Web:* www.dayzim.com						
Day Automation Systems Inc						
7931 Rae Blvd	Victor	NY	14564	585-924-4630	924-4698	256
TF: 800-836-0969 ■ *Web:* dayautomation.com						
Day Lumber Co 70 Orange St	Chicopee	MA	01013	413-568-3511	536-5510	551
Web: www.daylumber.com						
Day Motor Sports LLC 6100 Hwy 69 N	Tyler	TX	75706	903-593-9815	593-8453	54
TF: 800-543-6238 ■ *Web:* www.daymotorsports.com						
Day Pitney LLP 242 Trumbull St	Hartford	CT	06103	860-275-0100	275-0343	428
Web: www.daypitney.com						
Day Publishing Co						
47 Eugene O'Neill Dr	New London	CT	06320	860-442-2200		637-8
TF: 800-542-3354 ■ *Web:* www.theday.com						
Day Robert & Morrison PC						
300 E 5th Ave Ste 365	Naperville	IL	60563	630-637-9811		41
Web: dayrobertmorrison.com						
Day Vision Marketing 2222 S 12th St	Allentown	PA	18103	610-403-3999		195
Web: www.dayvision.com						
Day Wireless Systems Inc						
4700 SE International Way	Milwaukie	OR	97222	503-659-1240	659-4723	480
TF: 800-503-3433 ■ *Web:* www.daywireless.com						
Daybreak Express Inc 500 Ave P	Newark	NJ	07105	973-589-5931		311
Web: www.daybreakexpress.com						
Daybreak Oil & Gas Inc 601 W Main Ave	Spokane	WA	99201	509-232-7674		539
Web: daybreakoilandgas.com						
Daybreak Star Ctr						
3801 W Government Way PO Box 99100	Seattle	WA	98199	206-285-4425	282-3640	50-2
TF: 800-321-4321 ■ *Web:* www.unitedindians.org						
Daybreak Venture LLC 9 Medical Dr	Denton	TX	76201	940-387-4388		371
TF: 800-345-5603 ■ *Web:* www.daybreakventure.com						
Dayco Inc 325 Circle of Progress	Pottstown	PA	19464	610-326-4500		60
TF: 800-438-4791 ■ *Web:* www.daycoinc.com						
Day-Glo Color Corp						
4515 St Clair Ave	Cleveland	OH	44103	216-391-7070	391-7751	550
Web: www.dayglo.com						
Dayhuff Group LLC, The						
740 Lakeview Plaza Blvd Ste 300	Worthington	OH	43085	614-854-9999		180
Web: www.dayhuffgroup.com						
Day-Lee Foods Inc						
13055 Molette St	Santa Fe Springs	CA	90670	562-903-3020		297-9
TF: 800-329-5331 ■ *Web:* www.day-lee.com						
Daylight Donut Flour Company LLC						
11707 E 11th St	Tulsa	OK	74128	918-438-0800		68
TF: 800-331-2245 ■ *Web:* www.daylightdonuts.com						
Daylight Transport						
1501 Hughes Way Ste 200	Long Beach	CA	90810	310-507-8200		780
TF: 800-468-9999 ■ *Web:* www.dylt.com						
Daymar College 3361 Buckland Sq	Owensboro	KY	42301	270-926-4040		800
Web: daymarcollege.edu						
Daymark Solutions Inc						
18 Hartwell Ave	Lexington	MA	02421	781-359-3000		174
Web: www.daymarksi.com						
Daymon Associates Inc						
333 Ludlow St 4th Fl	Stamford	CT	06902	203-352-7500		195
Web: www.daymon.com						
Dayner Hall Marketing & Advertising						
621 E Pine St	Orlando	FL	32801	407-428-5750		7
Web: daynerhall.com						
Days Chevrolet of Jasper 375 Hwy 515 S	Jasper	GA	30143	877-641-0949		57
TF: 877-641-0949 ■ *Web:* www.dayschevroletjasper.com						
Days Inn Hinton-Jasper Hotel						
358 Smith St	Hinton	AB	T7V2A1	780-817-1960		378
TF: 800-259-4827 ■ *Web:* www.daysinnhinton.com						
DaySpring Cards Inc						
21154 Hwy 16 E	Siloam Springs	AR	72761	877-751-4347		130
TF: 800-944-8000 ■ *Web:* www.dayspring.com						
Dayspring Restoration Inc						
5463 Trumpeter Way	Missoula	MT	59808	406-541-4911		104
Web: calldayspring.com						
Daystar Television Network						
3901 Hwy 121 PO Box 610546	Bedford	TX	76021	817-571-1229	571-7458	740
TF: 800-329-0029 ■ *Web:* www.daystar.com						
Daystarr Communications 307 N Ball St	Owosso	MI	48867	989-720-6000		224
TF: 866-655-5828 ■ *Web:* www.daystarr.net						
Dayton Area Board of Realtors						
1515 S Main St	Dayton	OH	45409	937-223-0900		653
Web: dabr.com						
Dayton Area Chamber of Commerce						
8 N Main St Ste 100	Dayton	OH	45402	937-226-1444	226-8254	139
Web: daytonchamber.org						
Dayton Art Institute 456 Belmonte Pk N	Dayton	OH	45405	937-223-5277	223-3140	520
Web: www.daytonartinstitute.org						
Dayton Aviation Heritage National Historical Park						
16 S Williams St	Dayton	OH	45402	937-225-7705		564
Web: www.nps.gov						
Dayton Barber College						
2741 C Lyons Rd	Miamisburg	OH	45342	937-222-9101	331-7166	167-3
Web: www.daytonbarbercollege.com						
Dayton Chronicle 100 E Main St	Dayton	WA	99328	509-382-2221		532-2
Web: www.historicdayton.com						
Dayton City Hall 101 W Third St	Dayton	OH	45401	937-333-3636	333-4297	337
Web: www.daytonohio.gov						
Dayton City Schools 115 S Ludlow St	Dayton	OH	45402	937-542-3000	542-3188	685
Web: www.dps.k12.oh.us						
Dayton Contemporary Dance Co						
840 Germantown St	Dayton	OH	45402	937-228-3232	223-6156	573-1
Web: www.dcdc.org						
Dayton Convention Ctr 22 E Fifth St	Dayton	OH	45402	937-333-4700	333-4711	205
Web: www.daytonconventioncenter.com						
Dayton Correctional Institution						
4104 Germantown St PO Box 17399	Dayton	OH	45417	937-263-0060	263-1322	213
Web: drc.ohio.gov						
Dayton Daily News 1611 S Main St	Dayton	OH	45409	937-225-7365	225-2489	532-2
TF: 888-397-6397 ■ *Web:* www.daytondailynews.com						
Dayton Door Sales Inc						
1112 Springfield St	Dayton	OH	45403	937-253-9181		191-3
TF: 800-783-9181 ■ *Web:* www.daytondoorsales.com						
Dayton Foundation 40 N Main St Ste 500	Dayton	OH	45423	937-222-0410	222-0636	303
TF: 877-222-0410 ■ *Web:* daytonfoundation.org						
Dayton Freight Lines Inc 6450 Poe Ave	Dayton	OH	45414	937-264-4060		314
Web: legacy.daytonfreight.com						
Dayton International Airport						
3600 Terminal Dr Ste 300	Vandalia	OH	45377	937-454-8200		27
Web: www.flydayton.com						
Dayton Machine Tool Co 1314 Webster St	Dayton	OH	45404	937-222-6444		455
Web: dmtnet.com						
Dayton Mall						
2700 Miamisburg Centerville Rd	Dayton	OH	45459	937-433-9834		460
Web: daytonmall.com						
Dayton Meat Products Inc						
102 Montezuma St	Malcom	IA	50157	641-528-3420	528-2043	296-26
Web: www.daytonmeatproducts.net						
Dayton Metro Library 215 E Third St	Dayton	OH	45402	937-463-2665		434-3
Web: www.daytonmetrolibrary.org						
Dayton Parts LLC						
3500 Industrial Rd PO Box 5795	Harrisburg	PA	17110	717-255-8500		60
TF: 800-225-2159 ■ *Web:* daytonparts.com						
Dayton Performing Arts Alliance						
126 N Main St Ste 210	Dayton	OH	45402	937-224-3521		573-3
Web: www.daytonperformingarts.org						
Dayton Power & Light Co PO Box 1247	Dayton	OH	45401	937-331-3900		787
Web: www.dpandl.com						

Name / Address	Phone	Fax	Class
Dayton Progress Corp 500 Progress Rd, Dayton OH 45449 *Web:* www.daytonprogress.com	937-859-5111	859-5353	757
Dayton Reliable Air Filter Inc 2294 N Moraine Dr, Dayton OH 45439 **Fax Area Code:* 937 ■ *TF:* 800-699-0747 ■ *Web:* www.reliablefilter.com	800-699-0747	293-3975*	17
Dayton Rogers Manufacturing Co 8401 W 35 W Service Dr, Minneapolis MN 55449 *TF:* 800-677-8881 ■ *Web:* daytonrogers.com	763-784-7714		488
Dayton Sayer Insurance Agency Inc 1166 Esplanade Ste 1, Chico CA 95926 *TF:* 800-432-9866 ■ *Web:* sayerins.com	530-345-5135		390
Dayton State Park 825 US Hwy 50 E, Dayton NV 89403 *Web:* parks.nv.gov	775-687-5678		565
Dayton Superior Corp 1125 Byers Rd, Miamisburg OH 45342 *TF:* 800-745-3700 ■ *Web:* www.daytonsuperior.com	937-866-0711		350
Dayton Systems Group Inc 3003 S Tech Blvd, Miamisburg OH 45342 *Web:* www.daytonsystemsgroup.com	937-885-5665		547
Dayton T. Brown Inc 1175 Church St, Bohemia NY 11716 *TF:* 800-232-6300 ■ *Web:* www.dtb.com	631-589-6300	589-3648	743
Dayton VA Medical Ctr 4100 W Third St, Dayton OH 45428 *TF:* 800-368-8262 ■ *Web:* dayton.va.gov	937-268-6511		374-8
Dayton/Montgomery County Convention & Visitors Bureau 1 Chamber Plz Ste A, Dayton OH 45402 *TF:* 800-221-8235 ■ *Web:* www.daytoncvb.com	937-226-8211	226-8294	206
Daytona Beach City Hall 301 S Ridgewood Ave Rm 210, Daytona Beach FL 32114 *Web:* www.codb.us	386-671-8000	671-8115	337
Daytona Beach Community College 1200 W International Speedway Blvd, Daytona Beach FL 32114 *TF:* 877-822-6669 ■ *Web:* www.daytonastate.edu	386-506-3000	506-3940	162
Daytona Beach International Airport 700 Catalina Dr Ste 300, Daytona Beach FL 32114 *Web:* www.flydaytonafirst.com	386-248-8030		27
Daytona Beach News-Journal 901 Sixth St, Daytona Beach FL 32117 *Web:* www.news-journalonline.com	386-252-1511		532-2
Daytona Beach Resort & Conference Ctr 2700 N Atlantic Ave, Daytona Beach FL 32118 *TF:* 800-654-6216 ■ *Web:* www.daytonabeachresort.com	386-672-3770		379
Daytona Beach Symphony Society PO Box 2, Daytona Beach FL 32115 *Web:* dbss.org	386-253-2901	253-5774	573-3
Daytona Inn Beach Resort 219 S Atlantic Ave, Daytona Beach FL 32118 *TF:* 800-874-1822 ■ *Web:* daytonainnbeachresort.com	386-252-3626	255-3680	379
Daytona International Speedway 1801 W International Speedway Blvd, Daytona Beach FL 32114 *Web:* www.daytonainternationalspeedway.com	386-254-2700		515
Dayton-Granger Inc 3299 SW Ninth Ave, Fort Lauderdale FL 33315 *Web:* www.daytongranger.com	954-463-3451	761-3172	647
Dayton-Phoenix Group Inc 1619 Kuntz Rd, Dayton OH 45404 *TF:* 800-657-0707 ■ *Web:* www.dayton-phoenix.com	937-496-3974		650
Daytronic Corp 2566 Kohnle Dr, Miamisburg OH 45342 *TF:* 800-668-4745 ■ *Web:* www.daytronic.com	937-293-2566	866-3327	201
DAZ Productions Inc 12637 S 265 W Ste 300, Draper UT 84020 *TF:* 800-267-5170 ■ *Web:* www.daz3d.com	801-495-1777		225
DAZ Systems Inc 880 Apollo St Ste 201, El Segundo CA 90245 *Web:* www.dazsi.com	310-640-1300		177
Dazeworks Inc 649 Mission St 5th Fl, San Francisco CA 94105 *Web:* dazeworks.com	415-818-8069	818-8068	180
Dazian LLC 18 Central Blvd, South Hackensack NJ 07606 *TF:* 877-232-9426 ■ *Web:* www.dazian.com	201-549-1000	641-2728	745-2
Dazor Lighting Solutions 430 Industrial Dr, Maryland Heights MO 63043 *TF:* 800-345-9103 ■ *Web:* www.dazor.com	314-652-2400	652-2069	439
DB (Dissident Books Ltd) PO Box 20547, New York NY 10021 *Web:* www.dissidentbooks.com	646-422-3100		637-2
DB (DeBois Textiles Inc) 1835 Washington Blvd, Baltimore MD 21230 *Web:* www.deboistextiles.com	410-837-8081	837-6459	594
DB & S Lumber Co 78 Accord Park Dr, Norwell MA 02061 *Web:* www.dbslumber.com	781-878-3345		190
DB Bistro Moderne 55 W 44th St, New York NY 10036 *Web:* www.dbbistro.com	212-391-2400		671
DB Consulting Group Inc 8403 Colesville Rd, Silver Spring MD 20910 *Web:* www.dbconsultinggroup.com	301-589-4020		193
DB Root & Company Inc 436 Seventh Ave Ste 2800, Pittsburgh PA 15219 *TF:* 888-227-0913 ■ *Web:* www.dbroot.com	412-227-2800	227-2805	194
DB Technologies Inc PO Box 280, Bloomfield NM 87413 *Web:* www.dbtechnm.com	505-632-7900		179
DB U.S. Holding Corp 120 White Plains Rd 4th Fl, Tarrytown NY 10591 *Web:* www.dbusholding.com	914-366-7200	366-8228	393
DBA Engineering Ltd 401 Hanlan Rd, Vaughan ON L4L3T1 *TF:* 800-819-8833 ■ *Web:* www.dbaeng.com	905-851-0090		256
DBADirect Inc 100 E Rivercenter Blvd Ste 900, Covington KY 41011 *Web:* www.dbadirect.com	859-283-2520	283-7860	194
DBC (Diagnostics Biochem Canada Inc) 384 Neptune Crescent, London ON N6M1A1 *Web:* dbc-labs.com	519-681-8731	681-8734	231
DBG Partners Inc 940 S Kimball Ave Ste 100, Southlake TX 76092	469-706-3318		631
DBI (Dee Brown Inc) 4101 S Shiloh Rd PO Box 570335, Dallas TX 75357 *Web:* www.deebrowncompanies.com	214-321-6443	328-1039	189-7
DBI Inc 912 E Michigan Ave, Lansing MI 48912 *TF:* 800-968 1324 ■ *Web:* www dhiyes.com	517-485-3200	485-3202	535
DBK Concepts Inc 12905 SW 129 Ave, Miami FL 33186 *TF:* 800-725-7226 ■ *Web:* www.dbk.com	305-596-7226	596-7222	175

Name / Address	Phone	Fax	Class
DBL (Dressman Benzinger LaVelle) 207 Thomas More Pkwy, Crestview Hills KY 41017 *Web:* www.dbllaw.com	859-341-1881		445
Dbnet Systems Inc 3602 Keenland Dr, Marietta GA 30062 *Web:* www.dbnetsystems.com	770-509-3638	828-0574	225
dBrn Associates Inc 189 Curtis Rd, Hewlett Neck NY 11598 *Web:* www.dbrnassociates.com	516-569-4557		194
DBS Bank Ltd 725 S Figueroa St, Los Angeles CA 90017 *TF:* 800-209-4555 ■ *Web:* www.dbs.com	213-627-0222		70
Dbs Inc 2017 S 28th St, Van Buren AR 72956 *Web:* www.dbs-electronics.com	479-471-8255	471-1866	625
DBS Productions LLC PO Box 94, Charlottesville VA 22902 **Fax Area Code:* 434 ■ *TF:* 800-745-1581 ■ *Web:* dbs-sar.com	800-745-1581	293-5502*	637-10
DBSA (Depression & Bipolar Support Alliance) 730 N Franklin St Ste 501, Chicago IL 60610 *TF:* 800-826-3632 ■ *Web:* secure2.convio.net	312-642-0049	642-7243	48-17
dbSpectra Inc 1590 E Hwy 121 Business Bldg A Ste 100, Lewisville TX 75056 *Web:* www.dbspectra.com	469-322-0080	322-0079	647
DBT Group Inc, The 10 S Riverside Plz Ste 1800, Chicago IL 60606 *Web:* www.dbtgroup.com	312-474-9200	747-9179	178-1
DC (Datacom) 100 Enterprise Blvd, Lafayette LA 70506 *TF:* 877-559-1959 ■ *Web:* www.blackhawkdc.com	337-593-8700		681
DC Connections 22650 Executive Dr Ste 125, Sterling VA 20166 *Web:* www.dcconnections.com	703-471-9757		116
DC Electronics 1870 Little Orchard St, San Jose CA 95125 *Web:* www.dcelectronics.com	408-947-4500		814
DC Engineering 440 E Corporate Dr, Meridian ID 83642 *Web:* www.dcengineering.net	208-288-2181	288-2182	261
DC Equipment Inc 57 Old Mill Rd, Geraldine AL 35974 *Web:* www.dcequipmentinc.com	256-659-4707		358
DC Group Inc 1977 W River Rd N, Minneapolis MN 55411 *TF:* 800-838-7927 ■ *Web:* www.dc-group.com	800-838-7927		767
DC Insurance Group 26333 Jefferson Ave Ste 103, Saint Clair Shores MI 48081 *Web:* dc-ins.com	586-774-6400		390
DC Morrison Company Inc 201 Johnson St, Covington KY 41011 *Web:* www.dcmorrison.com	859-581-7511		493
DC Taylor Co 312 29th St NE, Cedar Rapids IA 52402 *TF:* 800-876-6346 ■ *Web:* www.dctaylorco.com	319-363-2073	363-8311	189-12
DC United 2400 E Capitol St SE, Washington DC 20003 *Web:* www.dcunited.com	202-587-5000	587-5400	717
DCA (Diamond Council of America) 3212 W End Ave Ste 202, Nashville TN 37203 *TF:* 877-283-5669 ■ *Web:* diamondcouncil.org	615-385-5301	385-4955	49-4
DCA (Distribution Contractors Assn) 101 W Renner Rd Ste 460, Richardson TX 75082 *Web:* www.dcaweb.org	972-680-0261	680-0461	49-3
Dca Partners LLC 3721 Douglas Blvd Ste 350, Roseville CA 95661 *Web:* dcapartners.com	916-960-5350		360-3
DCAT (Drug Chemical & Associated Technologies Assn) 1 Washington Blvd Ste 7, Robbinsville NJ 08691 *TF:* 800-640-3228 ■ *Web:* www.dcat.org	609-448-1000		49-19
DCB (Denver Commercial Builders Inc) 909 E 62nd Ave, Denver CO 80216 *Web:* www.dcb1.com	303-287-5525	287-3697	186
DCBroadcasting Inc PO Box 1009, Jasper IN 47547 *Web:* www.dcbroadcasting.com	812-634-9232	482-3696	645-141
DCC Lee Enterprises 12276 San Jose Blvd Ste 601, Jacksonville FL 32223 *Web:* www.mcdjax.com	904-288-6750		194
DCCC (Democratic Congressional Campaign Committee) 430 S Capitol St SE, Washington DC 20003 *Web:* dccc.org	202-863-1500		48-7
DCCI (Dow Chemical Canada Inc) 450 1st St SW Ste 2100, Calgary AB T2P3L8 *TF:* 800-447-4369 ■ *Web:* www.dow.com	403-267-3527	267-3597	144
DCD (Diamond Comic Distributors Inc) 10150 York Rd Ste 300, Hunt Valley MD 21030 *TF:* 800-452-6642 ■ *Web:* www.diamondcomics.com	443-318-8001		637-5
DCEC (Delaware County Electric Co-op) 39 Elm St PO Box 471, Delhi NY 13753 *TF:* 866-436-1223 ■ *Web:* www.dce.coop	607-746-2341		245
DCG One 4401 E Marginal Way S, Seattle WA 98134 *Web:* www.dcgone.com	206-784-6892		7
DCG Precision Mfg 9 Trowbridge Dr, Bethel CT 06801 *Web:* www.dcgprecision.com	203-743-5525	791-1737	621
DCGS (Dutchess County Genealogical Society) PO Box 708, Poughkeepsie NY 12602 *Web:* www.dcgs-gen.org	845-462-4168		49-19
DCH (Doctors Community Hospital) 8118 Good Luck Rd, Lanham MD 20706 *Web:* www.dchweb.org	301-552-8118	552-8521	374-3
DCH Credit Union 1008 Veterans Memorial Pkwy, Tuscaloosa AL 35404 *Web:* dchcu.com	205-759-7317		219
DCH Health System 809 University Blvd E, Tuscaloosa AL 35401 *TF:* 800-266-4324 ■ *Web:* dchsystem.com	205-759-7111		353
DCH Honda of Nanuet 10 NY-304, Nanuet NY 10954 *TF:* 888-495-8660 ■ *Web:* www.dchhondaofnanuet.com	845-367-7050		57
DCHS (Delaware County Historical Society) 120 E Washington St, Muncie IN 47305 *Web:* www.delawarecountyhistory.org	765-282-1550		637-2
DCI (Dynamic Concepts Inc) 1730 17th St NE, Washington DC 20002 *Web:* www.dcihq.com	202-944-8787	526-7233	735
DCI (Drum Corps Intl) 110 W Washington St Ste C, Indianapolis IN 46204 *TF:* 800-495-7469 ■ *Web:* www.dci.org	317-275-1212	713-0690	48-4
DCI (Development Counsellors International Ltd) 215 Park Ave S 14th Fl, New York NY 10003 *Web:* aboutdci.com	212-725-0707	725-2254	230

Name / Address	Phone	Fax	Class
DCI (Discovery Center of Idaho) 131 Myrtle St ... Boise ID 83702 *Web:* www.dcidaho.org	208-343-9895		520
DCI Career Institute Beaver Valley Mall 366 Rt 18 ... Monaca PA 15061 *Web:* www.dci.edu	724-728-0260		167-3
DCI Consulting Group Inc 1920 I St NW ... Washington DC 20006 *Web:* dciconsult.com	202-828-6900		463
DCI Inc 600 N 54th Ave ... Saint Cloud MN 56303 *Web:* www.dciinc.com	320-252-8200	252-0866	91
DCI Intl 305 N Springbrook Rd ... Newberg OR 97132 *TF:* 800-624-2793 ■ *Web:* www.dcionline.com	503-538-8343	538-9302	228
DCI Marketing Inc 2727 W Good Hope Rd ... Milwaukee WI 53209 *Web:* www.dci-artform.com	414-228-7000		195
DCL (Door County Library) 107 S Fourth Ave ... Sturgeon Bay WI 54235 *Web:* www.doorcountylibrary.org	920-743-6578		434-3
DCL (Downey City Library) 11121 Brookshire Ave ... Downey CA 90241 *TF:* 877-846-3452 ■ *Web:* www.downeyca.org	562-904-7360	923-3763	434-3
DCL Corp 48641 Milmont Dr ... Fremont CA 94538 *Web:* dclcorp.com	510-651-5100		393
DCL Inc 8660 Ance Rd ... Charlevoix MI 49720 *Web:* www.dclinc.com	231-547-5600	547-5832	207
DCM (Data Communications Management Corp) 9195 Torbram Rd ... Brampton ON L6S6H2 *TF:* 800-268-0128 ■ *Web:* www.datacm.com	905-791-3151	791-3277	110
DCM (David Crumm Media LLC) 42807 Ford Rd Ste 234 ... Canton MI 48187 *Web:* www.readthespirit.com	734-751-7840		637-2
DCM Manufacturing Inc 4540 W 160th St ... Cleveland OH 44135 *Web:* www.dcm-mfg.com	216-265-8006		610
Dcm Tech Corp 4455 Theurer Blvd ... Winona MN 55987 *TF:* 800-533-5339 ■ *Web:* www.dcm-tech.com	507-452-4043	452-7970	454
DCM Ventures 2420 Sand Hill Rd Ste 200 ... Menlo Park CA 94025 *Web:* www.dcm.com	650-233-1400	854-9159	792
DCNA (District of Columbia Nurses Assn) 5100 Wisconsin Ave NW Ste 306 ... Washington DC 20016 *Web:* www.dcna.org	202-244-2705	362-8285	533
DCOR LLC 290 Maple Ct Ste 290 ... Ventura CA 93003 *Web:* dcorllc.com	805-535-2000		536
DCOTA (Design Center of the Americas) 1855 Griffin Rd ... Dania Beach FL 33004 *Web:* www.dcota.com	954-920-7997		460
DCP (Dick Clark Productions Inc) 2900 Olympic Blvd ... Santa Monica CA 90404 *Web:* www.dickclark.com	310-255-4600		514
DCP (Digital Communication Products Inc) 3720 S Calhoun St ... Fort Wayne IN 46807 *Web:* www.dcpfw.com	260-744-3365	745-1401	246
DCP Midstream Partners LP 370 17th St Ste 2775 ... Denver CO 80202 *NYSE:* DCP ■ *TF:* 888-204-1781 ■ *Web:* www.dcpmidstream.com	303-633-2900		325
DCPS (District of Columbia Public Schools) 1200 First St NE ... Washington DC 20002 *Web:* dcps.dc.gov	202-442-5885	442-5026	685
DCR Business Solutions Inc PO Box 297 ... Mulberry FL 33860 *Web:* www.dcrservices.com	863-904-1077	428-9027	188
DCR Workforce Inc 7795 NW Beacon Sq Blvd Ste 201 ... Boca Raton FL 33487 *Web:* www.dcrworkforce.com	561-998-3737		196
DCS (Detroit Community Schools) 12675 Burt Rd ... Detroit MI 48223 *Web:* www.detcomschools.org	313-537-3570	537-6904	685
Department of Children's Services UBS Twr 315 Deaderick 10th Fl ... Nashville TN 37243 *Web:* www.tn.gov	615-741-9701		339-43
DCS Corp 6909 Metro Park Dr Ste 500 ... Alexandria VA 22310 *Web:* www.dcscorp.com	571-227-6000		261
DCS Netlink 1800 Macauley Ave ... Rice Lake WI 54868 *TF:* 877-327-6385 ■ *Web:* www.dcsnetlink.com	715-236-7424		180
DCSE Inc 95 Argonaut Ste 260 ... Aliso Viejo CA 92656 *Web:* www.dcse.com	949-465-3400		180
DCT (Diversified Chemical Technologies Inc) 15477 Woodrow Wilson St ... Detroit MI 48238 *TF:* 800-243-1424 ■ *Web:* www.dchem.com	313-867-5444	867-3831	145
DCT (Digital Communications Technologies) 5835 Blue Lagoon Dr Ste 202 ... Miami FL 33126 *Web:* www.digitalcomtech.com	305-809-0638		472
DCT (Dakota Central) 630 5th St N ... Carrington ND 58421 *TF:* 800-771-0974 ■ *Web:* www.daktel.com	701-652-3184	674-8121	224
DCT Chambers Trucking Ltd 600 Waddington Dr ... Vernon BC V1T8T6 *TF:* 800-575-2355 ■ *Web:* www.chambersgroup.co	250-549-2157		478
DCU Ctr 50 Foster St ... Worcester MA 01608 *Web:* www.dcucenter.com	508-755-6800	929-0111	720
dcVAST Inc 1319 Butterfield Rd Ste 504 ... Downers Grove IL 60515 *TF:* 800-432-8278 ■ *Web:* dcvast.com	630-964-6060		196
Dcxcavation Inc 10641 Prospect Ave ... Santee CA 92071 *Web:* dcxcavation.com	619-312-1550		362
DCX-CHOL Enterprises Inc 12831 S Figueroa St ... Los Angeles CA 90061 *Web:* www.dcxchol.com	310-516-1692		625
DD & F Consulting Group 521 S Rock St ... Little Rock AR 72202 *Web:* www.ddfconsulting.com	501-374-2600		463
DD Bean & Sons Co 207 Peterborough St ... Jaffrey NH 03452 *TF:* 800-326-8311 ■ *Web:* www.ddbean.com	603-532-8311	532-6001	469
DD Studio 1817 Aston Ave Ste 101 ... Carlsbad CA 92008 *Web:* www.ddstudio.com	760-438-0243		393
DD Williamson & Company Inc 100 S Spring St ... Louisville KY 40206 *TF:* 800-227-2635 ■ *Web:* www.ddwcolor.com	502-895-2438		296-15
DDB Worldwide 437 Madison Ave ... New York NY 10022 *Web:* www.ddb.com	212-415-2000		4
DDC (DNA Diagnostics Ctr) 1 DDC Way ... Fairfield OH 45014 *TF:* 800-613-5768 ■ *Web:* dnacenter.com	513-881-7800	881-7803	417
DDC Group Inc, The 2 California Plz 350 S Grand Ave Ste 1670 ... Los Angeles CA 90071 *Web:* ddcgroup-inc.com	213-334-4565		396
DDCF (Doris Duke Charitable Foundation) 650 Fifth Ave 19th Fl ... New York NY 10019 *Web:* www.ddcf.org	212-974-7000	974-7590	305
DDC-I Inc 4600 E Shea Blvd Ste 102 ... Phoenix AZ 85028 *Web:* www.ddci.com	602-275-7172	252-6054	178-2
DDD USA Inc 6100 Center Dr Ste 1100 ... Los Angeles CA 90045	310-566-3340		174
DDF CPA Group 107A Edwards Rd ... Starke FL 32091 *TF:* 800-771-7404 ■ *Web:* www.ddfcpa.com	904-964-7404	964-6583	194
DDH Enterprise Inc 2220 Oak Ridge Way ... Vista CA 92081 *Web:* www.ddhent.com	760-599-0171	599-9397	815
DDI (Lyndale Plant Services) 301 W 92nd St ... Bloomington MN 55420 *Web:* www.lyndaleplants.com	952-345-8240		293
DDI Leasing Inc 221 Somerville Rd ... Bedminster NJ 07921 *Web:* ddicapitalinc.com	908-781-9300	781-7906	180
DDI System LLC 75 Glen Rd Ste 204 ... Sandy Hook CT 06482 *TF:* 877-599-4334 ■ *Web:* www.ddisystem.com	877-599-4334		179
dDirect 2707 Peachtree Sq ... Atlanta GA 30360 *Web:* ddirect.com	678-530-0034		195
DDJ Capital Management LLC 130 Turner St Bldg 3 Ste 600 ... Waltham MA 02453 *Web:* www.ddjcap.com	781-283-8500	419-9180	401
DDJ Myers Ltd 4455 E Camelback Rd Ste C138 ... Phoenix AZ 85018 *Web:* ddjmyers.com	602-840-9595		193
DDL Business Systems 190 Prosperity Dr Ste 2 ... Winchester VA 22602 *Web:* ddlbusiness.com	800-335-5159		535
DDL Inc 10200 Vly View Rd Ste 101 ... Eden Prairie MN 55344 *TF:* 800-229-4235 ■ *Web:* www.ddltesting.com	952-941-9226		743
DDLC Energy 410 Bank St ... New London CT 06320 *TF:* 888-225-5540 ■ *Web:* hopenergy.com	888-225-5540		316
DDM-Digital Imaging Data Processing & Mailing Services 1223 William St ... Buffalo NY 14206 *Web:* www.ddmdirect.com	716-893-8671		393
DDP (Dharma Drum Publications) Ch'an Meditation Ctr 90-56 Corona Ave ... Elmhurst NY 11373 *Web:* www.chancenter.org	718-592-6593		637-2
DDW LLC 480 Gate 5 Rd Ste 100 ... Sausalito CA 94965 *Web:* www.ddw.com	415-487-8520		344
DE 123 William St 26th Fl ... New York NY 10038 *Web:* digitalevolution.com	212-732-2722		627
DE (Davidson Engineering LLC) 606 NE 312th Ave ... Washougal WA 98671 *Web:* tower-engineer.com	360-210-4032		261
De Angelis Group Inc, The 16000 N 80th St Ste E ... Scottsdale AZ 85260 *Web:* www.orthospinesearch.com	480-999-7490		194
De Anza Veterinary Clinic 7325 Fallenleaf Ln ... Cupertino CA 95014 *Web:* deanzavet.com	408-996-1411		794
De Baufre Bakeries Inc 2900 Waterview Ave ... Baltimore MD 21230 *TF:* 800-398-2236 ■ *Web:* www.bergercookies.com	800-398-2236		296-9
De Beaubien Knight Simmons Mantzaris & Neal LLP 332 N Magnolia Ave ... Orlando FL 32801 *Web:* dsklawgroup.com	407-422-2454		445
De Bruin & Associates CPAs LLC 2100 Freedom Rd Ste A PO Box 207 ... Little Chute WI 54140 *Web:* debruinassociates.com	920-687-7200		2
De Cotiis Fitzpatrick Cole & Wisler LLP 500 Frank W Burr Blvd ... Teaneck NJ 07666 *Web:* www.decotiislaw.com	201-928-1100		428
De Dietrich Process Systems Inc 244 Sheffield St ... Mountainside NJ 07092 *Web:* www.ddpsinc.com	908-317-2585		454
De Forest Creative Group Ltd 300 W Lake St Ste 100A ... Elmhurst IL 60126 *Web:* www.deforestgroup.info	630-834-7200	279-8410	393
DE Harvey Builders Inc 3663 Briarpark Ste 101 ... Houston TX 77042 *Web:* www.harveybuilders.com	713-783-8710		186
De Jager Construction Inc 75-60th St SW ... Wyoming MI 49548 *Web:* www.dejagerconstruction.com	616-530-0060		186
De Jong Manufacturing Inc 1030 Hwy 146 ... New Sharon IA 50207 *Web:* www.dejongmfg.com	641-637-4455	637-4460	91
De Kadt Marketing & Research Inc 162 Danbury Rd ... Ridgefield CT 06877 *TF:* 800-243-2991 ■ *Web:* dekadt.com	203-431-1212		195
De Kalb Memorial Hospital Inc 1316 E Seventh St ... Auburn IN 46706 *Web:* www.dekalbhealth.com	260-925-4600		374-3
De la Cruz & Associates Puerto Rico Metro Office Park St 1 Ste 9 ... Guaynabo PR 00968 *Web:* www.delacruz.com	787-622-4141	622-4170	7
De La Housaye & Associates 1211 Newell Ave Ste 210 ... Walnut Creek CA 94596 *Web:* delahousayelaw.com	925-944-3300		428
De La Salle Collegiate (DLS) 14600 Common Rd ... Warren MI 48088 *Web:* www.delasallehs.com	586-778-2207	498-1628	166
De La Torre's 1606 Bardstown Rd ... Louisville KY 40205 *Web:* www.delatorres.com	502-456-4955		671
De Leon Enterprises 11934 Allegheny St ... Sun Valley CA 91352 *Web:* www.deleonenterprises.com	818-252-6690		625

Company	City	State	ZIP	Phone	Fax	Class
De Leon Springs State Park 601 Ponce De Leon Blvd *Web:* www.floridastateparks.org	De Leon Springs	FL	32130	386-985-4212		565
De Marque inc 400 Boul Jean-Lesage Bureau 540 *TF:* 888-458-9143 ■ *Web:* www.demarque.com	Quebec City	QC	G1K8W1	418-658-9143		174
de Maximis Data Management Solutions 60 Plato Blvd E Ste 150 *Web:* www.ddmsinc.com	Saint Paul	MN	55107	651-842-4224		180
De Maximis Inc 450 Montbrook Ln *Web:* www.demaximis.com	Knoxville	TN	37919	865-691-5052	691-6485	463
De Medici 815 Fifth Ave *Web:* www.demedicisandiego.com	San Diego	CA	92101	619-702-7228		671
De Nora Tech Inc 7590 Discovery Ln *Web:* www.denora.com	Painesville	OH	44077	440-710-5300	710-5301	145
De Rigo Rem 10941 La Tuna Canyon Rd *TF:* 800-423-3023 ■ *Web:* www.derigo.us	Sun Valley	CA	91352	818-504-3950	504-3966	237
De Ronde Tire Supply Inc 2010 Elmwood Ave *TF:* 800-227-4647 ■ *Web:* etrucktire.com	Buffalo	NY	14207	716-897-6690		755
De Ruijter int Usa 120 Harvest Dr *Web:* www.deruijterusa.com	Coldwater	OH	45828	419-678-3909		291
De Soto National Memorial 8300 Desoto Memorial Hwy *Web:* www.nps.gov	Bradenton	FL	34209	941-792-0458		564
De Soto Public School District 73 610 Vineland School Rd *Web:* www.desoto.k12.mo.us	De Soto	MO	63020	636-586-1000	586-1009	685
De Von's Jewelers Inc 1689 Arden Way *Web:* www.devonsjewelers.com	Sacramento	CA	95815	916-929-3991		410
De Wafelbakkers LLC 10000 Crystal Hill Rd PO Box 13570 *TF:* 800-924-3391 ■ *Web:* www.dewafelbakkers.net	North Little Rock	AR	72113	501-791-3320		296-1
De Well Group US 5553 Bandini Blvd Unit A *Web:* www.de-well.com	Bell	CA	90201	310-735-8600	735-8601	314
De'Vons Optics Inc 13243 Brookfield Dr *Web:* coppermax.com	Rancho Cucamonga	CA	91739	909-237-6660		542
DEA (Drug Enforcement Administration) 700 Army-Navy Dr *Web:* www.justice.gov	Arlington	VA	22202	202-307-3067		340-14
DEA (David Evans & Associates Inc) 2100 SW River Pkwy *TF:* 800-721-1916 ■ *Web:* www.deainc.com	Portland	OR	97201	503-223-6663	223-2701	261
DEA Specialties Company Ltd 5151 Castroville Rd *Web:* www.deaspecialties.com	San Antonio	TX	78227	210-523-1073	523-1544	300
Deacon Industrial Supply Company Inc 1510 Gehman Rd *Web:* deaconind.com	Harleysville	PA	19438	215-256-1715	256-1716	385
Deaconess Associations Inc 615 Elsinore Pl Ste 900 *Web:* www.deaconess-healthcare.com	Cincinnati	OH	45202	513-559-2111		48-5
Deaconess Hospital 600 Mary St *TF:* 800-677-3422 ■ *Web:* www.deaconess.com	Evansville	IN	47747	812-450-5000		374-3
Dead Horse Ranch State Park 675 Dead Horse Ranch Rd *Web:* azstateparks.com	Cottonwood	AZ	86326	928-634-5283		565
Deaf Hearing Communication Centre Inc 630 Fairview Rd Ste 100 *Web:* dhcc.org	Swarthmore	PA	19081	610-604-0450		768
Deaf Inter-link PO Box 510 Ste 206 *TF:* 800-330-7062 ■ *Web:* www.deafinterlink.com	Saint Louis	MO	63031	314-837-7757	837-0777	138
Deaf Smith County 140 E 3rd St *Web:* deafsmithcad.org	Hereford	TX	79045	806-364-0625	364-6895	338
Deal, The 14 Wall St 15th Fl *TF:* 888-667-3325 ■ *Web:* www.thedeal.com	New York	NY	10005	888-667-3325		637-9
Dealer Impact Systems LLC 7733 Douglas Ave *TF:* 800-247-2502 ■ *Web:* flickfusion.com	Urbandale	IA	50322	515-334-9638	253-0170	4
Dealer Media Group Inc 2435 N Central Expy Ste 100 *Web:* www.dealermediagroup.com	Richardson	TX	75080	469-930-6800		5
Dealer Tire LLC 7012 Euclid Ave *TF:* 800-933-2537 ■ *Web:* www.dealertire.com	Cleveland	OH	44103	216-432-0088	881-7923	755
Dealers Food Products Co 23800 Commerce Park Rd Ste D *Web:* www.dealersfoods.com	Cleveland	OH	44122	216-292-6666		523
Dealers Supply Co 2345 NW Nicolai St *Web:* www.dealerssupply.com	Portland	OR	97210	503-236-1195	236-4314	191-4
Dealers Truck Equipment Co 2460 Midway St *TF:* 800-259-7569 ■ *Web:* www.dealerstruck.com	Shreveport	LA	71108	318-635-7567	525-0903	516
DealersEdge PO Box 606 *TF:* 800-321-5312 ■ *Web:* dealersedge.com	Barnegat Light	NJ	08006	609-879-4456		531-13
Dealertrack CentralDispatch Inc 26387 Network Pl *Web:* www.centraldispatch.com	Chicago	IL	60673	858-259-6084		387
DealerTrack Holdings Inc 1111 Marcus Ave Ste M04 *NASDAQ: TRAK* ■ *TF:* 877-357-8725 ■ *Web:* us.dealertrack.com	Lake Success	NY	11042	516-734-3600		178-10
Dealey, Renton & Associates Insurance Brokers Inc 530 Water St 7th Fl *Web:* dealeyrenton.com	Oakland	CA	94607	510-465-3090		390
DealFlow Analytics Inc 131 Jericho Tpke *Web:* dealflow.com	Jericho	NY	11753	516-876-8006		387
DealNet Capital Corp 325 Milner Ave Ste 300 *TF:* 855-912-3444 ■ *Web:* www.dealnetcapital.com	Toronto	ON	M1B5N1	855-912-3444		463
Dealogic LLC 120 Broadway 8th Fl *Web:* www.dealogic.com	New York	NY	10271	212-577-4400		177
Deal-Rite Feeds Inc 109 Anna Dr *Web:* www.deal-ritefeeds.com	Statesville	NC	28625	704-873-8646	873-1060	447
Dealtaker Ranchero Rd *Web:* www.dealtaker.com	Plano	TX	75093	972-696-9377		387
Deam Lake State Recreation Area 1217 Deam Lake Rd *Web:* www.in.gov	Borden	IN	47106	812-246-5421		565
Dean & Co 8065 Leesburg Pk Ste 500 *Web:* www.dean.com	Vienna	VA	22182	703-506-3900	506-3905	194
Dean & DeLuca Brands Inc 560 Broadway *Web:* www.deandeluca.com	New York	NY	10012	212-226-6800		345
Dean Baldwin Painting LP 2395 Bulverde Rd Ste 105 *Web:* www.deanbaldwinpainting.com	Bulverde	TX	78163	830-438-5340		529
Dean Cluck Feedyard Inc 105 Dean Cluck Ave *Web:* www.deancluckfeedyard.com	Gruver	TX	79040	806-733-5021	733-2244	10-1
Dean College 99 Main St *TF:* 877-879-3326 ■ *Web:* www.dean.edu	Franklin	MA	02038	508-541-1508	541-8726	162
Dean Custom Air 120 Logan Rd *Web:* www.deancustomair.com	Bluffton	SC	29909	843-706-2850		189-10
Dean Foods 400 S Chamber Dr *Web:* www.deanfoods.com	Decatur	IN	46733	260-724-2136		296-25
Dean Greer & Assoc 2809 E Center St *Web:* deangreer.com	Kingsport	TN	37664	423-246-1988	378-4594	41
Dean Health Insurance Inc 1277 Deming Way **Fax Area Code:* 608 ■ *TF:* 800-279-1301 ■ *Web:* www.deancare.com	Madison	WI	53717	800-279-1301	827-4212*	391-3
Dean Kincaid Inc N2028 Hwy 106 *Web:* deankincaidinc.business.site	Palmyra	WI	53156	262-495-3000		10-11
Dean Kurtz Construction 1651 Rand Rd *Web:* www.deankurtzconstruction.com	Rapid City	SD	57702	605-343-6665		186
Dean Law Group, The 3990 Old Town Ave C-303 *Web:* thedeanlawgroup.com	San Diego	CA	92110	619-232-8377	238-8376	428
Dean Machinery International Inc 6855 Shiloh Rd E *Web:* www.deanmachinery.com	Alpharetta	GA	30005	678-947-8550	947-8554	385
Dean Madeleine (Rep D - PA) 129 Cannon House Office Bldg *Web:* www.dean.house.gov	Washington	DC	20515	202-225-4731		342-2
Dean Sausage Company Inc 3750 Pleasant Valley Rd PO Box 750 *Web:* deansausage.com	Attalla	AL	35954	256-538-6082		296-26
Dean Snyder Construction Co 913 N 14th St *Web:* www.deansnyder.com	Clear Lake	IA	50428	641-357-2283	357-2232	186
Dean Steel Buildings Inc 2929 Industrial Ave *TF:* 844-739-3326 ■ *Web:* www.deansteelbuildings.com	Fort Myers	FL	33901	239-334-1051	334-2432	105
Dean Team Automotive Group Inc 15121 Manchester Rd *TF:* 888-699-0663 ■ *Web:* www.deanteam.com	Ballwin	MO	63011	636-227-0100		57
Dean Transportation Inc 4812 Aurelius Rd *TF:* 800-282-3326 ■ *Web:* deantransportation.com	Lansing	MI	48910	517-319-8300		109
Dean Word Company Ltd 1245 River Rd *TF:* 800-683-3926 ■ *Web:* www.deanword.com	New Braunfels	TX	78130	830-625-2365	606-5008	188-4
Dean's Designs 3555 E Douglas Ave *TF:* 800-832-1411 ■ *Web:* www.deansdesignsflowers.com	Wichita	KS	67218	316-686-6674		293
Dean, Ringers, Morgan & Lawton PA 201 E Pine St Ste 1200 **Fax Area Code:* 904 ■ *Web:* drml-law.com	Orlando	FL	32801	407-422-4310	839-4089*	428
Deangelis - Diamond Construction Inc 6635 Willow Park Dr *Web:* www.deangelisdiamond.com	Naples	FL	34109	239-594-1994		186
Deanie's Seafood 1713 Lake Ave *Web:* www.deanies.com	Metairie	LA	70005	504-834-1225		671
Deans Knight Capital Management Ltd 999 W Hastings St Ste 1500 *Web:* www.deansknight.com	Vancouver	BC	V6C2W2	604-669-0212		401
Deans Mailing & List Services Inc 3015 W Weldon Ave *Web:* deansmailing.com	Phoenix	AZ	85017	602-272-2100		5
Deansteel Manufacturing Co 111 Merchant *TF:* 800-825-8271 ■ *Web:* www.deansteel.com	San Antonio	TX	78204	210-226-8271		234
DeAnza College 21250 Stevens Creek Blvd *Web:* www.deanza.edu	Cupertino	CA	95014	408-864-5678	864-8329	162
Dearborn Area Chamber of Commerce 22100 Michigan Ave *Web:* dearbornareachamber.org	Dearborn	MI	48124	313-584-6100	584-9818	139
Dearborn County 215 W High St *Web:* dearborncounty.org	Lawrenceburg	IN	47025	812-537-8877	532-2021	338
Dearborn County Chamber of Commerce 320 Walnut St *TF:* 800-322-8198 ■ *Web:* dearborncountychamber.org	Lawrenceburg	IN	47025	812-537-0814	537-0845	139
Dearborn Federal Credit Union 400 Town Center Dr *TF:* 888-336-2700 ■ *Web:* www.dfcufinancial.com	Dearborn	MI	48126	313-322-8209	336-2700	219
Dearborn Mid-West Conveyor Co (DMWCC) 20334 Superior Rd *Web:* www.dmwcc.com	Taylor	MI	48180	734-288-4400		207
Dearborn Partners LLC 200 W Madison St Ste 1950 *Web:* www.dearbornpartners.com	Chicago	IL	60606	312-795-1000		378
Dearborn Sausage Company Inc 2450 Wyoming Ave *TF:* 866-900-4426 ■ *Web:* dearbornbrand.com	Dearborn	MI	48120	313-842-2375		296-26
Dearborn Times-Herald 13730 Michigan Ave *TF:* 866-468-7630 ■ *Web:* downriversundaytimes.com	Dearborn	MI	48126	313-584-4000	584-1357	532-4
Deardorff 400 Market St Ste 800 *Web:* deardorffassociates.com	Philadelphia	PA	19106	215-982-1550		636
Dearing Compressor & Pump Co 3974 Simon Rd PO Box 6044 *TF:* 800-850-3440 ■ *Web:* www.dearingcomp.com	Youngstown	OH	44501	330-599-5720	599-5724	172

	Phone	Fax	Class
Dearth Chrysler Dodge Jeep Ram 520 Eigth St . . . . Monroe WI 53566 *TF:* 877-495-5321 ■ *Web:* www.dearthchryslerdodgejeepram.com	866-949-3653		57
Death Valley Natural History Assn (DVNHA) PO Box 188 . . . . Death Valley CA 92328 *TF:* 800-478-8564 ■ *Web:* dvnha.org	800-478-8564		637-2
Deaton Law Firm LLC 425 Red Bank Rd . . . . Goose Creek SC 29445 *Web:* deatonlaw.net	843-225-5723		41
Deauville Beach Resort 6701 Collins Ave . . . . Miami Beach FL 33141 *TF:* 800-327-6656 ■ *Web:* deauvillebeachresortmiami.com	305-865-8511		669
Deaver Industries Inc 3120 Morgan Rd. . . . . Bessemer AL 35022 *Web:* www.deaverind.com	205-426-4309	426-4364	439
DEB Inc 2815 Coliseum Centre Dr Ste 600 . . . . Charlotte NC 28217 *TF:* 800-248-7190 ■ *Web:* www.debgroup.com	704-263-4240	263-9601	214
Debbie's Staffing Services Inc 4431 N Cherry St Ste 50. . . . . Winston-Salem NC 27105 *Web:* www.debbiesstaffing.com	336-744-2393	776-1661	721
Deb-El Food Products LLC 2 Papetti Plz . . . . Elizabeth NJ 07206 *TF:* 800-421-3447 ■ *Web:* www.debelfoods.com	908-351-0330	351-0334	297-8
Debevoise & Plimpton LLP 919 Third Ave . . . . New York NY 10022 *Web:* www.debevoise.com	212-909-6000	909-6836	428
Deblasio & Gower LLC 2001 Midwest Rd Ste 100. . . . . Oak Brook IL 60523 *Web:* dgllc.net	630-560-1123		41
Debo's Diners Inc 7625 Hamilton Park Dr Ste 26 . . . . Chattanooga TN 37421 *Web:* www.debosdiners.com	423-855-4650		670
Deboer Transportation Inc PO Box 145 . . . . Blenker WI 54415 *Web:* www.deboertrans.com	715-652-2911		780
DeBois Textiles Inc (DB) 1835 Washington Blvd . . . . Baltimore MD 21230 *Web:* www.deboistextiles.com	410-837-8081	837-6459	594
Deborah Heart & Lung Ctr 200 Trenton Rd. . . . . Browns Mills NJ 08015 *TF:* 800-555-1990 ■ *Web:* demanddeborah.org	609-893-6611		374-7
DeBourgh Manufacturing 27505 Otero Ave. . . . . La Junta CO 81050 **Fax Area Code:* 719 ■ *TF:* 800-328-8829 ■ *Web:* www.debourgh.com	800-328-8829	384-7713*	286
DeBra-Kuempel 3976 S Ave . . . . Cincinnati OH 45227 *TF:* 800-395-5741 ■ *Web:* dkemcor.com	513-271-6500	271-4676	189-10
Debron Industrial Electronics Inc 591 Executive Dr. . . . . Troy MI 48083 *TF:* 888-891-1923 ■ *Web:* debron-electronics.com	248-588-7220	588-5236	253
Debruler Co 131 E Park Ave Ste 101 . . . . Libertyville IL 60048 *Web:* debrulerco.com	847-367-1111		653
Debtors Anonymous (DA) PO Box 920888. . . . . . . Needham MA 02492 *TF:* 800-421-2383 ■ *Web:* www.debtorsanonymous.org	781-453-2743	453-2745	48-21
Debus, Kazan & Westerhausen Ltd 1221 E Osborn Rd A-200. . . . . Phoenix AZ 85014 *Web:* debusandkazan.com	602-257-8900		41
DECA Aviation Engineering Ltd 7050 Telford Way . . . . Mississauga ON L5S1V7 *Web:* palaerospace.com	905-405-1371		194
DECA Inc 1908 Assn Dr . . . . Reston VA 20191 *Web:* www.deca.org	703-860-5000	860-4013	457-6
DECA Technologies Inc 7855 S River Pkwy Ste 111. . . . . Tempe AZ 85284 *Web:* thinkdeca.com	480-345-9895		696
Deca-Amr 850 Chastain Cor. . . . . Marietta GA 30066 *TF:* 800-783-3322 ■ *Web:* www.deca-amr.com	770-393-9056	393-9538	112
Decaprio CPA & Associates PC 500 E Main St. . . . . Branford CT 06405 *Web:* dfd-cpa.com	203-488-6374		2
DeCarolis Truck Rental Inc 333 Colfax St . . . . Rochester NY 14606 *TF:* 800-666-1169 ■ *Web:* www.decarolis.com	585-254-1169	458-4072	778
Decatur Area Convention & Visitors Bureau 202 E N St . . . . Decatur IL 62523 *TF:* 800-331-4479 ■ *Web:* www.decaturcvb.com	217-423-7000	423-7455	206
Decatur Computers Inc 1234 N Water St . . . . Decatur IL 62521 *Web:* decaturcomputers.com	217-475-0226	475-0231	175
Decatur Conference Center & Hotel 4191 W US Hwy 36 Wyckles Rd. . . . . Decatur IL 62522 *Web:* www.hoteldecatur.com	217-422-8800		378
Decatur Cooperative Assn 305 S York Ave. . . . . Oberlin KS 67749 *TF:* 800-886-2293 ■ *Web:* www.decaturcoop.net	785-475-2234		48-2
Decatur County 22 W Main St PO Box 488 . . . . Decaturville TN 38329 *TF:* 800-525-6834 ■ *Web:* www.decaturcountytn.org	731-852-2131		338
Decatur County 150 Courthouse Sq Ste 244 . . . . Greensburg IN 47240 *TF:* 800-622-4941 ■ *Web:* www.decaturcounty.in.gov	812-663-8223	662-6627	338
Decatur County 207 N Main St. . . . . Leon IA 50144 *Web:* www.decaturcountyiowa.org	641-446-4322	446-3616	338
Decatur County Bank 56 N Pleasant St. . . . . Decaturville TN 38329 *Web:* decaturcountybank.com	731-852-2821		70
Decatur County Rural Electric Membership Corp 1430 W Main St PO Box 46 . . . . Greensburg IN 47240 *TF:* 800-844-7362 ■ *Web:* www.dcremc.com	812-663-3391	663-8572	245
Decatur Daily 201 First Ave SE. . . . . Decatur AL 35601 *TF:* 888-353-4612 ■ *Web:* www.decaturdaily.com	256-353-4612	340-2392	532-2
Decatur Earthmover Credit Union 2600 Dividend Dr. . . . . Decatur IL 62526 *Web:* decu.com	217-875-2301		219
Decatur General Hospital 1201 Seventh St SE . . . . Decatur AL 35601 *Web:* decaturmorganhospital.net	256-341-2000		374-3
Decatur House Museum 1610 H St NW . . . . . . Washington DC 20006 *Web:* www.whitehousehistory.org	202-218-4337		520
Decatur Isd Education Foundation Inc 309 S Cates . . . . Decatur TX 76234 *Web:* www.decaturisd.us	940-393-7100		685
Decatur Memorial Hospital 2300 N Edward St. . . . . Decatur IL 62526 *TF:* 866-364-3600 ■ *Web:* www.dmhcares.com	217-876-8121	876-2615	374-3
Decatur Mold Tool & Engineering Inc 3330 N State Rd 7. . . . . North Vernon IN 47265 *Web:* www.decaturmold.com	812-346-5188	346-7357	757
Decatur Plastic Products Inc 3250 N State Hwy 7 . . . . North Vernon IN 47265 *Web:* www.decaturplastics.com	812-346-5159	346-5210	604
Decatur Public Library 130 N Franklin St . . . . Decatur IL 62523 *Web:* www.decaturlibrary.org	217-424-2900	233-4071	434-3
Decatur Public Schools 110 Cedar St. . . . . Decatur MI 49045 *Web:* raiderpride.org	269-423-6800	423-6849	685
Decatur Republican 121 S Phelps St. . . . . Decatur MI 49045 *Web:* www.decaturmi.org	269-423-2411		532-2
Decatur/Morgan County Convention & Visitors Bureau (DMCCVB) 719 Sixth Ave SE PO Box 2349 . . . . Decatur AL 35602 *Web:* www.decaturcvb.org	256-350-2028		206
Decatur-Morgan County Chamber of Commerce 515 Sixth Ave NE . . . . Decatur AL 35601 *TF:* 888-739-8662 ■ *Web:* www.dcc.org	256-353-5312	353-2384	139
Decca Design 476 S First St . . . . San Jose CA 95113 *Web:* www.decdesign.com	408-947-1411		194
Deccan Intl 9444 Waples St Ste 300 . . . . San Diego CA 92121 *Web:* deccanintl.com	858-764-8400		174
Decco Graphics Inc 24411 Frampton Ave. . . . . Harbor City CA 90710 *Web:* www.deccographics.com	310-534-2861	534-4529	488
Deccofelt Corp 555 S Vermont Ave. . . . . Glendora CA 91741 *TF:* 800-543-3226 ■ *Web:* www.deccofelt.com	626-963-8511		745-2
Decentrix Inc 1200 17th St Ste 770 . . . . Denver CO 80202 *Web:* www.decentrix.net	303-899-4000		225
Deception Pass State Park 41229 State Rte 20. . . . . Oak Harbor WA 98277 *Web:* www.parks.wa.gov	360-675-3767		565
Dechert Dynamics Corp 713 W Main St . . . . Palmyra PA 17078 *Web:* www.decherts.com	717-838-1326	838-1525	454
Dechert LLP 2929 Arch St Cira Ctr . . . . Philadelphia PA 19104 *Web:* www.dechert.com	215-994-4000	994-2222	428
Dechert-Hampe & Co (DHC) 33332 Valle Rd. . . . . San Juan Capistrano CA 92675 *Web:* www.dechert-hampe.com	949-429-1999		194
Decibel Hearing Services 2655 First St Ste 170 . . . . Simi Valley CA 93065 *Web:* www.decibelhearing.com	805-584-3327	584-3329	45
Decibels Inc 1551 Center St . . . . Tacoma WA 98409 *Web:* decibelsinc.com	253-473-5855		116
Decimal Engineering Inc 4300 Coral Ridge Dr. . . . . Coral Springs FL 33065 *Web:* www.decimal.net	954-975-7992		256
Decimal Technologies Inc 793 Jean-Paul-Vincent Blvd Ste 202 . . . . Longueuil QC J4G1R3 *Web:* www.decimal.ca	450-640-1222		463
Decipher Biosciences Inc 1038 Homer St. . . . . Vancouver BC V6B2W9 *TF:* 888-975-4540 ■ *Web:* genomedx.com	888-975-4540		743
Decision Academic Inc 1705 Tech Ave Ste 1. . . . . Mississauga ON L4W0A2 *TF:* 888-661-1933 ■ *Web:* www.decisionacademic.com	888-661-1933		174
Decision Analyst Inc 604 Ave H E. . . . . Arlington TX 76011 *Web:* www.decisionanalyst.com	817-640-6166	640-6567	466
Decision Counsel 4174 Park Blvd Ste C. . . . . Oakland CA 94602 *Web:* decisioncounsel.com	510-859-3605		195
Decision Diagnostics Corp 2660 Townsgate Rd Ste 300 . . . . Westlake Village CA 91361 *Web:* www.decisiondiagnostics.co	805-446-1973	446-1983	475
Decision Engineering Corp 112 Deer Path Ln . . . . Freehold NJ 07728 *Web:* deceng.net	908-309-1887		261
Decision Software Inc 10816 Town Center Blvd Ste 515 . . . . Dunkirk MD 20754 *Web:* www.dsimarketingservices.com	301-459-9000		690
DecisionHR Inc 100 Carillon Pkwy Ste 350. . . . . Saint Petersburg FL 33716 *Web:* decisionhr.com	727-572-7331		631
DecisionOne Corp 426 W Lancaster Ave. . . . . Devon PA 19333 *TF:* 800-767-2876 ■ *Web:* decisionone.com	610-296-6000	296-2910	175
DecisionPoint Systems Inc 8697 Research . . . . Irvine CA 92618 *OTC:* DPSI ■ *TF:* 800-336-3670 ■ *Web:* www.decisionpt.com	949-465-0065	215-9642	177
DecisionQuest Inc 21535 Hawthorne Blvd Ste 310 . . . . Torrance CA 90503 *TF:* 800-887-5696 ■ *Web:* www.decisionquest.com	310-618-9600	618-1122	445
Decisionwise Inc 815 W 450 S. . . . . Springville UT 84663 *TF:* 800-830-8086 ■ *Web:* www.decision-wise.com	801-515-6500		196
Decker Creative Marketing 99 Citizens Dr. . . . . Glastonbury CT 06033 *TF:* 800-777-3677 ■ *Web:* deckerct.com	860-659-1311		7
Decker Electric Company Inc 1282 Folsom St . . . . San Francisco CA 94103 *Web:* www.deckerelectric.com	415-552-1622		189-4
Decker Manufacturing Corp 703 N Clark St . . . . Albion MI 49224 *Web:* www.deckernut.com	517-629-3955		278
Decker Steel & Supply Inc 4500 Train Ave . . . . Cleveland OH 44102 *Web:* www.deckersteel.com	216-281-7900	281-1441	492
Decker Supply Company Inc 1115 O'Neill Ave. . . . . Madison WI 53704 **Fax Area Code:* 608 ■ *TF:* 800-274-5495 ■ *Web:* www.deckersupply.com	800-274-5495	242-5777*	9
Decker Tape Products Inc 2 Stewart Pl . . . . Fairfield NJ 07004 *TF:* 800-227-5252 ■ *Web:* www.deckertape.com	973-227-5350	808-9418	732

Company	Address	City	State	ZIP	Phone	Fax	Class	Details
Decker Truck Line Inc	4000 Fifth Ave S	Fort Dodge	IA	50501	515-576-4141		780	TF: 800-247-2537 ■ Web: www.deckertruckline.com
Decker Wright Corp	628 Shrewsbury Ave	Red Bank	NJ	07701	732-747-9373		177	Web: www.deckerwright.com
Deckers Brands	123 N Leroux St	Flagstaff	AZ	86001	928-779-5938		301	TF: 800-367-8382 ■ Web: www.teva.com
Deckers Outdoor Corp	495-A S Fairview Ave	Goleta	CA	93117	805-967-7611		301	NYSE: DECK ■ TF: 888-432-8530 ■ Web: www.deckers.com
Deckert & Van Loh PA	12912 63rd Ave N	Maple Grove	MN	55369	763-587-7100		41	Web: deckertvanloh.com
Decko Products Inc	2105 Superior St	Sandusky	OH	44870	419-626-5757	626-3135	296-8	Web: www.decko.com
Declara Inc	977 Commercial St	Palo Alto	CA	94303	877-216-0604		387	TF: 877-216-0604 ■ Web: declara.com
Declaration House	143 S Third St	Philadelphia	PA	19106	215-965-2305		50-3	Web: www.nps.gov
Declues, Burkett & Thompson, Apc	17011 Beach Blvd Ste 400	Huntington Beach	CA	92647	714-843-9444	843-9452	41	Web: dbtlaw.com
Deco Chem Inc	3502 N Home St	Mishawaka	IN	46545	574-259-3787		388	Web: www.decochem.com
Deco Designs Systems Furniture Inc	1435 Koll Cir Ste 106	San Jose	CA	95112	408-919-0234	496-0992	321	TF: 800-914-8622 ■ Web: decodesigns.com
DECO Inc	11140 Zealand Ave N	Champlin	MN	55316	800-968-9114		693	TF: 800-968-9114 ■ Web: www.deco-inc.com
Deco Products Co	506 Sanford St	Decorah	IA	52101	563-382-4264	382-9845	308	TF: 800-327-9751 ■ Web: www.decoprod.com
Deco Tools Inc	1541 Coining Dr	Toledo	OH	43612	419-476-9321	476-6669	172	Web: decotools.com
Deco West Inc	80 N Mojave Rd Ste 190	Las Vegas	NV	89101	702-644-8945		393	Web: www.decowest.com
DecoArt Inc	49 Cotton Ave	Stanford	KY	40484	606-365-3193		43	TF: 800-367-3047 ■ Web: www.decoart.com
Decor & You Inc	900 Main St S Bldg 2	Southbury	CT	06488	203-405-2126		310	Web: decorandyou.com
Decor Rest Furniture Ltd	222 S Main St	High Point	NC	27260	336-884-3420		321	Web: www.decor-rest.com
Decorating Den Systems Inc	8659 Commerce Dr	Easton	MD	21601	800-332-3367		393	TF: 800-332-3367 ■ Web: www.decoratingden.com
Decorating Elves	13670 Roosevelt Blvd	Clearwater	FL	33762	727-418-4127		393	TF: 800-695-4837 ■ Web: www.decoratingelves.com
Decorative Crafts Inc	50 Chestnut St	Greenwich	CT	06830	203-531-1500	531-1590	361	TF: 800-431-4455 ■ Web: decorativecrafts.com
Decorative Hardwoods Assn (DHA)	42777 Trade W Dr	Sterling	VA	20166	703-435-2900	435-2573	613	Web: www.decorativehardwoods.org
Decorator & Upholstery Supply Inc (DUS)	501 McNeilly Rd	Pittsburgh	PA	15226	412-561-3770	561-1105	238	TF: 800-242-0219 ■ Web: www.decoratorsupplyinc.com
Decore Hotels	10026 164 St NW	Edmonton	AB	T5P4Y3	780-481-7578		377	Web: decorehotels.com
Decore-ative Specialties Inc	2772 S Peck Rd	Monrovia	CA	91016	626-254-9191	254-1515	115	TF: 800-729-7277 ■ Web: www.decore.com
Decotech Systems Inc	1180 Mt Diablo Blvd Ste 200	Walnut Creek	CA	94596	925-954-1520	954-1521	180	Web: decotech.com
DeCoty Coffee Company Inc	1920 Austin St	San Angelo	TX	76903	800-588-8001	655-6837*	296-7	*Fax Area Code: 325 ■ TF: 800-588-8001 ■ Web: www.decoty.com
Dec-Tam Corp	50 Concord St	North Reading	MA	01864	978-470-2860		667	TF: 800-332-8261 ■ Web: www.dectam.com
Dectrader	275 E Hillcrest Dr Unit 160-184	Thousand Oaks	CA	91360	805-498-4848	480-1898	174	Web: www.dectrader.com
Dectro International Inc	1000 Blvd du Parc-Technologique	Quebec City	QC	G1P4S3	418-650-0303		475	TF: 800-463-5566 ■ Web: www.dectro.com
Dectron	5685 Rue Cypihot	Saint-Laurent	QC	H4S1R3	514-336-3330	337-3336	360-3	Web: www.dectron.com
Decurion Corp, The	120 N Robertson Blvd	Los Angeles	CA	90048	310-659-9432		748	Web: www.decurion.com
Decurtis Corp	3208 E Colonial Dr Ste C190	Orlando	FL	32803	407-522-8722		177	Web: www.decurtis.com
Decypher	200 Concord Plaza Dr Ste 780	San Antonio	TX	78216	210-735-9900		196	Web: www.decypherpsigov.com
Dedham Country Day School	90 Sandy Valley Rd	Dedham	MA	02026	781-329-0850		239	Web: www.dedhamcountryday.org
Dedham Historical Society (DHS)	612 High St	Dedham	MA	02026	781-326-1385		48-13	Web: dedhamhistorical.org
Dedham Institution For Savings	55 Elm St PO Box 9107	Dedham	MA	02026	781-329-6700		70	TF: 888-289-0342 ■ Web: www.dedhamsavings.com
Dedham Mall	300 Providence Hwy	Dedham	MA	02026	781-329-1210		460	Web: www.dedham-mall.com
Dedicated Computing	N26 W23880 Commerce Cir	Waukesha	WI	53188	262-951-7200	523-2222	173-2	TF: 877-333-4848 ■ Web: www.dedicatedcomputing.com
Dedicated Distribution Inc	640 Miami Ave	Kansas City	KS	66105	800-325-8367		475	TF: 800-325-8367 ■ Web: www.dedicateddistribution.com
Dedoes Industries Inc	1060 W Maple Rd	Walled Lake	MI	48390	248-624-7710		111	Web: www.dedoes.com
Dee Brown Inc (DBI)	4101 S Shiloh Rd PO Box 570335	Dallas	TX	75357	214-321-6443	328-1039	189-7	Web: www.deebrowncompanies.com
Dee Cramer Inc	4221 E Baldwin Rd	Holly	MI	48442	810-579-5000	579-2664	189-12	TF: 888-342-6995 ■ Web: www.deecramer.com
Dee Electronics Inc	2500 16th Ave SW	Cedar Rapids	IA	52404	319-365-7551	365-8506	246	TF: 800-747-3331 ■ Web: www.dee-inc.com
Dee Paper Box Company Inc	100 Broomall St	Chester	PA	19013	610-876-9285	876-7040	101	TF: 800-359-0041 ■ Web: www.deepkg.com
Dee Plumbing Inc	3828 W 128th Pl	Alsip	IL	60803	708-389-8075		189-10	Web: deeplumbing.com
Dee Zee Inc	1572 NE 58th Ave	Des Moines	IA	50313	515-265-7331		489	TF: 800-779-2102 ■ Web: www.deezee.com
Deegit	1900 E Golf Rd Ste 925	Schaumburg	IL	60173	847-330-1985		194	Web: www.deegit.com
Deeke Animal Hospital LLC	220 Catalpa Ave	Itasca	IL	60143	630-773-2040		794	Web: amcitasca.com
Deen Meats	PO Box 4155	Fort Worth	TX	76164	817-335-2257	338-9256	297-9	TF: 800-333-3953 ■ Web: deenmeat.com
Deep Blue Sea Inc	7206 NW 31 St	Miami	FL	33122	305-728-4789	594-4340	344	TF: 855-437-2583 ■ Web: deepbluesea.com
Deep Cleveland Press	PO Box 14248	Cleveland	OH	44114	440-891-2607		637-2	TF: 866-295-9755 ■ Web: www.deepcleveland.com
Deep Down Inc	18511 Beaumont Hwy	Houston	TX	77049	281-862-2201		539	Web: www.deepdowninc.com
Deep East Texas Electric Co-opeartive Inc	880 Texas Hwy 21 E PO Box 736	San Augustine	TX	75972	936-275-2314	275-2135	245	TF: 800-392-5986 ■ Web: www.deepeast.com
Deep Foods Inc	1090 Springfield Rd	Union	NJ	07083	908-810-7500		296-9	Web: www.deepfoods.com
Deep Imaging	990 Village Square Dr ste A	Tomball	TX	77375	281-290-0492		253	Web: www.deepimaging.com
Deep Meadow Correctional Ctr	3500 Woods Way	State Farm	VA	23160	804-598-5503		213	Web: vadoc.virginia.gov
Deep Mile Networks LLC	3100 Clarendon Blvd Ste 200	Arlington	VA	22201	703-635-7983		396	Web: www.deepmile.com
Deep River Dyeing & Finishing Company Inc	225 Poplar St PO Box 217	Randleman	NC	27317	336-498-4181	498-7252	745-7	Web: deepriverdyeing.com
Deep Sky Software Inc	12526 High Bluff Dr Ste 300	San Diego	CA	92130	858-794-6854	794-6864	179	Web: www.deepskysoftware.com
Deep South Crane & Rigging	15324 Airline Hwy	Baton Rouge	LA	70817	225-753-4371		190	TF: 877-490-4371 ■ Web: deepsouthcrane.com
Deep Sushi	2624 Elm St	Dallas	TX	75226	214-651-1177		671	Web: www.deepsushi.com
DeepFocus Productions Inc	3370 Glendale Blvd No 39548	Los Angeles	CA	90039	323-662-6577		511	Web: www.deepfocusproductions.com
Deepsea Technologies	7807 Fairview St	Houston	TX	77041	713-849-5555		261	Web: deepsea-tech.com
Deepwater Chemicals Inc	1210 Airpark Rd	Woodward	OK	73801	580-256-0500	256-0575	806	TF: 800-854-4064 ■ Web: www.deepwaterchemicals.com
Deepwell Services LLC	719 W New Castle St	Zelienople	PA	16063	724-473-0687		190	Web: deepwellservices.com
Deer Horn Aviation Limited Co	8818 W Hwy 80	Midland	TX	79706	432-561-9111		63	Web: www.deerhornaviation.com
Deer Mountain Campground	5309 N Main St	Pittsburg	NH	03592	603-538-6965		565	Web: www.nhstateparks.org
Deer Park Chamber of Commerce	110 Center St	Deer Park	TX	77536	281-479-1559	476-4041	139	Web: www.deerparkchamber.org
Deer Park Group Inc	21540 Inglenook Ln	Deer Park	IL	60010	847-387-8002		463	Web: www.deerparkinc.com
Deer Park Public Library	710 E San Augustine	Deer Park	TX	77536	281-478-7208	478-7212	434-3	Web: deerparktx.gov
Deer Path Industrial Technology Inc	14236 246th Pl SE	Issaquah	WA	98027	425-445-5434		385	Web: www.deerpathindustrial.com
Deer Path Inn	255 E Illinois Rd	Lake Forest	IL	60045	847-234-2280		379	Web: www.thedeerpathinn.com
Deer Valley Federal Credit Union	16215 N 28th Ave	Phoenix	AZ	85053	602-375-7300	375-7333	219	TF: 800-579-5051 ■ Web: deervalleycu.org
Deer Valley Homebuilders Inc	205 Carriage St	Guin	AL	35563	205-468-8400		505	Web: www.deervalleyhb.com
Deer Valley Petroglyph Preserve	3711 W Deer Valley Rd	Glendale	AZ	85308	480-965-2100		50-2	Web: www.shesc.asu.edu
Deer Valley Ranch	16825 County Rd 162	Nathrop	CO	81236	719-395-2353		239	Web: www.deervalleyranch.com
Deer Valley Resort Lodging	PO Box 889	Park City	UT	84060	435-645-6626	645-6538	669	TF: 800-558-3337 ■ Web: www.deervalley.com
Deerbrook Mall	20131 Hwy 59 N	Humble	TX	77338	281-540-1611		460	Web: www.shopdeerbrookmall.com
Deere & Co	1 John Deere Pl	Moline	IL	61265	309-765-8000		185	NYSE: DE ■ TF: 800-765-9588 ■ Web: www.deere.com
Deere-Hitachi Construction Machinery Corp	1000 Deere Hitachi Rd	Kernersville	NC	27284	336-996-8100	996-8200	190	Web: www.dhkernersville.com
Deerfield Academy	7 Boyden Ln	Deerfield	MA	01342	413-772-0241	772-1100	622	Web: deerfield.edu

	Phone	Fax	Class
Deerfield Bannockburn & Riverwoods Chamber of Commerce 405 Lake Cook Rd Ste A201 .... Deerfield IL 60015 *Web:* www.dbrchamber.com	847-945-4660	715-9129	139
Deerfield Communications Co 4241 Old US 27 S............................ Gaylord MI 49735 *Web:* www.deerfield.com	989-732-8856		178-7
Deerfield Construction Company Inc 8960 Glendale Milford Rd.................... Loveland OH 45140 *Web:* www.deerfieldconstruction.com	513-984-4096	984-4180	186
Deerfield Correctional Ctr 21360 Deerfield Dr...........................Capron VA 23829	434-658-4368		213
Deerfield Episcopal Retirement Community 1617 Hendersonville Rd...................... Asheville NC 28803 *TF:* 800-284-1531 ■ *Web:* www.deerfieldwnc.org	828-274-1531	274-0238	672
Deerfield Public Library Inc 920 Waukegan Rd........................... Deerfield IL 60015 *TF:* 800-829-4059 ■ *Web:* deerfieldlibrary.org	847-945-3311		435
Deerfield Spa 650 Resica Falls Rd ....East Stroudsburg PA 18302 *TF:* 800-852-4494 ■ *Web:* deerfieldspa.com	570-223-0160		706
Deerfoot Inn & Casino 1000 11500 35th St SE....................... Calgary AB T2Z3W4 *TF:* 877-236-5225 ■ *Web:* deerfootinn.com	403-236-7529		379
Deerhurst Resort 1235 Deerhurst Dr .... Huntsville ON P1H2E8 *TF:* 800-461-6522 ■ *Web:* deerhurstresort.com	800-461-4393		669
Deering Banjo Co 3733 Kenora Dr ....Spring Valley CA 91977 *TF:* 800-845-7791 ■ *Web:* www.deeringbanjos.com	619-464-8252		527
Deerwalk Inc 430 Bedford St..................Lexington MA 02420 *Web:* www.deerwalk.com	781-325-1775	498-2785	178-1
Deetken Group, The 1755 W Broadway Ste 501 .... Vancouver BC V6J4S5 *Web:* www.deetken.com	604-731-4424		463
Defabco Inc 3765 E Livingston Ave............ Columbus OH 43227 *Web:* www.defabco.com	614-231-2700		697
DeFazio Peter (Rep D - OR) 2134 Rayburn House Office Bldg .... Washington DC 20515 *Web:* defazio.house.gov	202-225-6416		342-2
DeFehr Furniture Ltd 125 Furniture Pk...........................Winnipeg MB R2G1B9 *TF:* 877-333-3471 ■ *Web:* www.defehr.com	204-988-5630	663-4458	319-2
Defence Construction Canada Constitution Sq 350 Albert St 19th Fl............. Ottawa ON K1A0K3 *TF:* 800-514-3555 ■ *Web:* dcc-cdc.gc.ca	613-998-9548	998-1061	463
Defender Association of Philadelphia 1441 Sansom St.........................Philadelphia PA 19102 *Web:* phillydefenders.org	215-568-3190		445
Defender Inc 3750 Priority Way S Dr....................Indianapolis IN 46240 *TF:* 800-860-0303 ■ *Web:* www.homedefenders.com	317-810-4720	810-4723	116
Defender Industries Inc 42 Great Neck Rd ....Waterford CT 06385 **Fax Area Code:* 860 ■ *TF:* 800-628-8225 ■ *Web:* www.defender.com	888-490-6844	701-3424*	770
Defender Services Inc 9031 Garners Ferry Rd.......................Hopkins SC 29061 *Web:* www.defenderservices.com	803-776-4220		104
Defenders of Wildlife 1130 17th St NW ....Washington DC 20036 *TF:* 800-385-9712 ■ *Web:* www.defenders.org	202-682-9400	682-1331	48-3
DefendX Software 119 Drum Hill Rd Ste 383.................. Chelmsford MA 01824 *TF:* 800-390-6937 ■ *Web:* info.defendx.com	603-622-4400	263-2220	178-12
Defense Commissary Agency 1300 E Ave .... Fort Lee VA 23801 *TF:* 877-332-2471 ■ *Web:* www.commissaries.com	804-734-8000		340-3
Defense Contract Audit Agency 8725 John J Kingman Rd Ste 2135 .... Fort Belvoir VA 22060 *TF:* 855-414-5892 ■ *Web:* www.dcaa.mil	703-767-3265		340-3
Defense Contract Management Agency 6350 Walker Ln Ste 300.................... Alexandria VA 22310 *TF:* 888-576-3262 ■ *Web:* www.dcma.mil	888-576-3262		340-3
Defense Finance & Accounting Service 8899 E 56th St ....Indianapolis IN 46249 *TF:* 888-332-7411 ■ *Web:* www.dfas.mil	888-332-7411		734
Defense Information Systems Agency 6910 Cooper Rd.......................... Fort Meade MD 20755 **Fax Area Code:* 301 ■ *Web:* www.disa.mil	703-607-6001	225-0535*	340-3
Defense Intelligence Agency 200 MacDill Blvd ....Washington DC 20340 **Fax Area Code:* 301 ■ *Web:* www.dia.mil	202-231-5554	394-5356*	340-3
Defense Logistics Agency (DLA) 8725 John J Kingman Rd.................... Fort Belvoir VA 22060 *TF:* 877-352-2255 ■ *Web:* www.dla.mil	877-352-2255		340-3
Defense Nuclear Facilities Safety Board 625 Indiana Ave NW Ste 700 ....Washington DC 20004 *TF:* 800-788-4016 ■ *Web:* www.dnfsb.gov	202-694-7000		340-20
Defense Office of Economic Adjustment The Office of Economic Adjustment Ste 520...... Arlington VA 22202 *Web:* www.oea.gov	703-697-2130	607-0170	340-3
Defense Research Institute (DRI) 55 W Monroe St Ste 20 ....Chicago IL 60603 *Web:* dri.org	312-795-1101	795-0749	49-10
Defense Software Corp 12587 Fair Lakes Cir Ste 335................... Fairfax VA 22033 *TF:* 888-999-5522 ■ *Web:* defensesoftware.com	888-999-5522		177
Defense Technical Information Ctr (DTIC) 8725 John J Kingman Rd Ste 0944 .... Fort Belvoir VA 22060 *TF:* 800-225-3842 ■ *Web:* discover.dtic.mil	800-225-3842		340-3
Defense Technology *Safariland Group* 1855 S Loop ....Casper WY 82601 *TF:* 877-248-3835 ■ *Web:* www.defense-technology.com	307-235-2136	473-2713	284
Defense Threat Reduction Agency 8725 John T Kingman Rd MS 6201.......... Fort Belvoir VA 22060 *TF:* 800-701-5096 ■ *Web:* www.dtra.mil	703-767-5870	767-4450	340-3
defi SOLUTIONS 1500 Solana Blvd Ste 6400 .... Westlake TX 76262 *TF:* 800-926-6750 ■ *Web:* defisolutions.com	800-926-6750		39
Defiance Area Chamber of Commerce 325 Clinton St ....Defiance OH 43512 *Web:* www.defiancechamber.com	419-782-7946	782-0111	139

	Phone	Fax	Class
Defiance College 701 N Clinton St..............Defiance OH 43512 *TF:* 800-520-4632 ■ *Web:* www.defiance.edu	419-784-4010	783-2468	166
Defiance County 500 Ct St..................Defiance OH 43512 *TF:* 800-675-3953 ■ *Web:* www.defiance-county.com	419-782-4761	782-8449	338
Defiance Metal Products 50 W Broad St Ste 1330.................... Columbus OH 43215 *TF:* 888-995-3195	419-784-5332	782-0148	488
Defiance Public Library 320 Ft St..............Defiance OH 43512 *Web:* www.defiancelibrary.org	419-782-1456	782-6235	434-3
Defiant Marine Inc 228 Redbud Ln .... Bostic NC 28018 *Web:* defiantmarine.net	828-245-2059	245-2079	90
Defibtech LLC 741 Boston Post Rd Ste 201...................Guilford CT 06437 *TF:* 866-333-4248 ■ *Web:* www.defibtech.com	203-453-4507		476
Defined Crowd 111 W John St................... Seattle WA 98119 *Web:* www.definedcrowd.com	425-615-3578		177
Defined Fitness 4930 Mcleod Rd NE .... Albuquerque NM 87109 *Web:* www.defined.com	505-888-7097		354
Defined Logic LLC 116 Chestnut St .... Red Bank NJ 07701 *Web:* definedlogic.com	732-222-4310		177
Definition 6 420 Plasters Ave.................... Atlanta GA 30324 *Web:* www.definition6.com	404-870-0323		7
Definition Press 141 Greene St................ New York NY 10012 *Web:* www.definitionpress.org	212-777-4490		139
Definity Partners 5474 Spellmire Dr .... West Chester OH 45246 *Web:* definitypartners.com	513-381-7200		463
Defino Law Associates PC 2541 S Broad St.........................Philadelphia PA 19148 *Web:* definolawyers.com	215-551-9099		41
Deflect-O Corp 7035 E 86th St ....Indianapolis IN 46250 *TF:* 800-428-4328 ■ *Web:* www.deflecto.com	800-428-4328		534
DeFoe Corp 800 S Columbus Ave .... Mount Vernon NY 10550 *Web:* www.defoecorp.com	914-699-7440	699-6734	194
Defta Partners 111 Pine St............... San Francisco CA 94111 *Web:* deftapartners.com	415-433-2262		792
Degan, Blanchard & Nash A Professional Law Corp 400 Poydras St Ste 2600 .... New Orleans LA 70130 *Web:* www.degan.com	504-529-3333		428
Degania Group, The 50 Pint St Ste 5Q..........Montclair NJ 07042 *TF:* 877-334-2642 ■ *Web:* www.thedeganiagroup.com	877-334-2642		194
Degenkolb 375 Beale St Ste 500 .... San Francisco CA 94105 *Web:* degenkolb.com	415-392-6952		261
Degesch America Inc PO Box 116.......... Weyers Cave VA 24486 *TF:* 800-330-2525 ■ *Web:* www.degeschamerica.com	540-234-9281		280
DeGette Diana (Rep D - CO) 2111 Rayburn House Office Bldg ....Washington DC 20515 *Web:* degette.house.gov	202-225-4431	225-5657	342-2
Degnon Associates Inc 6728 Old McLean Village Dr................... McLean VA 22101 *Web:* degnon.org	703-556-9222	556-8729	47
DeGol Organization 3229 Pleasant Valley Blvd..................... Altoona PA 16602 *TF:* 800-800-5881 ■ *Web:* www.degol.com	814-941-7777	941-5377	360-3
DeGraaf Nature Ctr 600 Graafschap Rd .... Holland MI 49423 *TF:* 888-535-5792 ■ *Web:* www.cityofholland.com	616-355-1057	355-1069	50-5
DeGrazia Gallery in the Sun 6300 N Swan Rd.............................Tucson AZ 85718 *TF:* 800-545-2185 ■ *Web:* www.degrazia.org	520-299-9191	299-1381	520
Degree Controls Inc 18 Meadowbrook Dr ....Milford NH 03055 *TF:* 877-334-7332 ■ *Web:* www.degreec.com	603-672-8900		256
Degreed 445 Bryant St .... San Francisco CA 94107 *TF:* 800-311-7061 ■ *Web:* degreed.com	800-311-7061		49-5
Dehart & Company Public Relations LLC 1375 Lenoir Rhyne Blvd SE Ste 109............. Hickory NC 28602 *Web:* www.dehartandcompany.com	828-325-4966	325-4968	636
Dehart Marine Electronics Inc 134 W Carolina Ave .... Memphis TN 38103 *Web:* www.marineelectronics.com	901-523-0945		179
Dehart Plumbing Heating & Air Inc 311 Bitritto Way .... Modesto CA 95356 *Web:* www.dehartinc.com	209-523-4578		189-10
DeHayes Consulting Group 2999 Douglas Blvd Ste 320 .... Roseville CA 95661 *Web:* dcgcorp.com	916-782-8321		194
Dehco Inc 3601 Charlotte Ave PO Box 638................. Elkhart IN 46517 *Web:* www.dehco.com	574-294-2684		3
Dehli Palace Cuisine of India 2500 S Woodlands Village Blvd Ste 8 ....Flagstaff AZ 86001 *Web:* www.delhipalaceflagstaff.com	928-556-0019		671
DeHoff Publications 749 NW Broad St ....Murfreesboro TN 37129 *TF:* 800-695-5385 ■ *Web:* www.dehoffpublications.com	615-893-8322		95
DeHumidification Technologies LP 6609 Ave U................................Houston TX 77011 *TF:* 866-736-8348 ■ *Web:* www.rentdh.com	713-939-1166	939-1186	14
DEI (Delta Engineering Group LLC) 111 W Jackson Blvd Ste 910 ....Chicago IL 60604 *Web:* www.deg-america.com	312-377-7700	427-6145	261
DEI (Directed Energy Inc) 1609 Oakridge Dr Ste 100 .... Fort Collins CO 80525 *Web:* ixyscolorado.com	970-493-1901	232-3025	253
DEI Holdings Inc 1 Viper Way .... Vista CA 92081 *OTC: DEI* ■ *TF:* 800-876-0800 ■ *Web:* www.deiholdings.com	760-598-6200	598-6400	52
DEI Inc 1550 Kemper Meadow Dr.............. Cincinnati OH 45240 *TF:* 866-749-6949 ■ *Web:* www.dei-corp.com	513-825-5800		186
Deig Bros Lumber & Construction Inc 2804 A St................................ Evansville IN 47712 *Web:* www.deigbros.com	812-423-4201	421-5058	186
Deighton Associates Ltd 223 Brock St N Unit 7.........................Whitby ON L1N4H6 *TF:* 888-219-6605 ■ *Web:* www.deighton.com	905-665-6605		261
Deister Electronics USA Inc 9817 Godwin Dr Ste 201 .... Manassas VA 20110 *Web:* www.deister.com	703-368-2739	368-9791	253
Deja View Video 417 S El Dorado St ....San Mateo CA 94402 *Web:* www.dejaview.com	650-343-8899		192

Name / Address	City	State	ZIP	Phone	Fax	Class
Dejana Industries Inc						
30 Sagamore Hill Dr	Port Washington	NY	11050	516-944-3103		776
Web: www.dejanaindustries.com						
Dejana Truck & Utility Equipment Company Inc						
490 Pulaski Rd	Kings Park	NY	11754	631-544-9000		780
TF: 877-335-2621 ■ *Web:* dejana.com						
Dejour Energy Inc 598-999 Canada Pl	Vancouver	BC	V6C3E1	604-638-5050		536
Web: www.dxienergy.com						
Dejuan Stroud Inc 348 W 36th St	New York	NY	10018	212-431-9099		292
Web: www.dejuanstroud.com						
DEKA Research & Development Corp						
340 Commercial St	Manchester	NH	03101	603-669-5139		668
Web: www.dekaresearch.com						
DeKalb Chamber of Commerce						
125 Clairemont Ave Ste 235	Tucker	GA	30084	404-378-8000	378-3397	139
Web: www.dekalbchamber.org						
DeKalb Chamber of Commerce						
164 E Lincoln Hwy	DeKalb	IL	60115	815-756-6306	756-5164	139
Web: www.dekalb.org						
DeKalb Convention & Visitors Bureau						
1957 Lakeside Pkwy Ste 510	Tucker	GA	30084	770-492-5000		206
TF: 866-633-5252 ■ *Web:* discoverdekalb.com						
DeKalb County						
109 W Main St PO Box 248	Maysville	MO	64469	816-449-5402	449-2440	338
Web: www.dekalbcountymo.com						
DeKalb County 215 Sycamore St	Decatur	GA	30030	404-371-2000		338
Web: www.dekalbcountyga.gov						
DeKalb County 732 S Congress Blvd	Smithville	TN	37166	615-597-5176		338
Web: www.dekalbtennessee.com						
DeKalb County 110 E Sycamore St	Sycamore	IL	60178	815-895-7149	895-7148	338
Web: www.dekalbcounty.org						
DeKalb County Alabama Commission						
111 Grand Ave SW Ste 200	Fort Payne	AL	35967	256-845-8500		338
Web: www.dekalbcountyal.us						
DeKalb County Public Library						
215 Sycamore St	Decatur	GA	30030	404-370-3070		434-3
Web: dekalblibrary.org						
Dekalb Farmers Market						
3000 E Ponce De Leon Ave	Decatur	GA	30030	404-377-6400		345
Web: www.dekalbfarmersmarket.com						
DeKalb Forge Co 1832 Pleasant St	DeKalb	IL	60115	815-758-6400		483
Web: www.forgeresourcesgroup.com						
DeKalb History Ctr (DHC)						
Old Courthouse on the Square 101 E Court Sq	Decatur	GA	30030	404-373-1088	373-8287	48-13
Web: www.dekalbhistory.org						
DeKalb Medical Center's School of Radiologic Technology						
2701 N Decatur Rd	Decatur	GA	30033	404-501-5307		685
Web: www.dekalbmedical.org						
DeKalb Public Library 309 Oak St	Dekalb	IL	60115	815-756-9568	756-7837	434-3
Web: dkpl.org						
DeKalb Regional Medical Ctr						
200 Medical Center Dr	Fort Payne	AL	35968	256-845-3150		374-3
Web: www.dekalbregional.com						
DeKalb Symphony Orchestra (DSO)						
PO Box 1313	Tucker	GA	30085	678-891-3565		573-3
Web: dekalbsymphony.org						
Dekker Bookbinding						
2941 Clydon Ave SW	Grand Rapids	MI	49519	616-538-5160	538-0720	92
Web: www.dekkerbook.com						
Dekko 2505 Dekko Dr	Garrett	IN	46738	260-357-3621	357-4293	815
TF: 800-829-3101 ■ *Web:* www.dekko.com						
Dekoron WIre & Cable						
1300 Industrial Blvd	Mount Pleasant	TX	75455	903-572-3475	572-6153	814
Web: www.dekoroncable.com						
DEKRA North America						
2932 Canton Rd NE Ste 100	Marietta	GA	30066	770-971-3788	971-5125	393
Web: www.dekra.us						
DEKRA Process Safety 113 Campus Dr	Princeton	NJ	08540	609-799-4449	799-5559	743
Web: www.dekra-process-safety.com						
Del Amo Hospital						
23700 Camino Del Sol	Torrance	CA	90505	310-530-1151		374-5
TF: 800-533-5266 ■ *Web:* www.delamohospital.com						
Del City Chamber of Commerce						
PO Box 15643	Del City	OK	73155	405-677-1910	672-5285	139
Web: www.delcitychamber.com						
Del Conte's Landscaping Inc						
41900 Boscell Rd	Fremont	CA	94538	510-353-6030		776
Web: visionrecycling.com						
Del E. Webb Memorial Library						
Loma Linda University 11072 Anderson St	Loma Linda	CA	92350	909-558-4550		434-1
Web: library.llu.edu						
Del Frisco's Double Eagle Steak House						
3925 Paradise Rd	Las Vegas	NV	89169	702-796-0063		671
Web: delfriscos.com						
Del Frisco's Restaurant Group Inc						
2900 Ranch Trail	Irving	TX	75063	203-682-8200		670
Web: www.dfrg.com						
Del Mar Avionics 11-B Marconi	Irvine	CA	92606	949-250-3200	261-0529	529
Web: www.dma.com						
Del Mar College						
East 101 Baldwin Blvd	Corpus Christi	TX	78404	361-698-1200	698-1595	162
TF: 800-652-3357 ■ *Web:* www.delmar.edu						
Del Mar Floral & Gifts						
12750 Carmel Country Rd Ste A-110	San Diego	CA	92130	858-755-0303		293
Web: delmarfloral.com						
Del Mar Food Products Corp						
1720 Beach Rd	Watsonville	CA	95076	831-722-3516	722-7690	296-21
Web: delmarfoods.com						
Del Mar Scientific Acquisition Ltd						
4951 Airport Pkwy Ste 803	Addison	TX	75001	972-661-5160		201
TF: 800-722-4270 ■ *Web:* www.delmarscientific.com						
Del Mar Seafoods 331 Ford St	Watsonville	CA	95076	831-763-3000		297-5
Web: delmarseafoods.com						
Del Mar Thoroughbred Club						
2260 Jimmy Durante Blvd	Del Mar	CA	92014	858-755-1141		642
TF: 800-467-7385 ■ *Web:* www.dmtc.com						
Del Mar Trade Shows Inc						
5724 La Jolla Hermosa Ave	La Jolla	CA	92037	858-459-1682		393
Web: www.mfgshow.com						
Del Mesa Carmel Community Association Inc						
500 Del Mesa Dr	Carmel By The Sea	CA	93923	831-624-1853		653
Web: delmesacarmel.org						
Del Monte Electric Company Inc						
6998 Sierra Ct	Dublin	CA	94568	925-829-6000	829-6033	189-4
Web: delmonteelectricco.com						
Del Monte Foods Co						
1 Maritime Plz	San Francisco	CA	94111	415-247-3000		296-20
TF: 800-543-3090 ■ *Web:* www.delmonte.com						
Del Monte Fresh PO Box 149222	Coral Gables	FL	33114	305-520-8400		297-7
TF: 800-950-3683 ■ *Web:* www.freshdelmonte.com						
Del Norte County						
981 H St Ste 200	Crescent City	CA	95531	707-464-7204		338
Web: www.co.del-norte.ca.us						
Del Packaging Ltd 18113 Telge Rd	Cypress	TX	77429	281-653-0099	653-0077	298
Web: www.delpackaging.com						
Del Paso Pipe & Steel Inc						
5519 Raley Blvd	Sacramento	CA	95838	916-992-6500	992-2828	492
TF: 800-233-1792 ■ *Web:* www.delpasopipeandsteel.com						
Del Posto 85 Tenth Ave	New York	NY	10011	212-497-8090		671
Web: delposto.com						
Del Real Foods LLC 11041 Inland Ave	Mira Loma	CA	91752	951-681-0395		345
Web: delrealfoods.com						
Del Rey Beverage Distributors						
4935 McConnell Ave Ste 14	Los Angeles	CA	90066	310-305-7387		81-1
Web: www.delreydistributors.com						
Del Rey Packing						
5287 S Del Rey Ave	Del Rey Oaks	CA	93616	559-888-2031	888-2715	315-5
Web: delreypacking.com						
Del Rio Chamber of Commerce (DRCOC)						
1915 Veterans Blvd	Del Rio	TX	78840	830-775-3551	774-1813	139
Web: www.drchamber.com						
Del Toro Loan Servicing Inc						
2300 Boswell Rd Ste 215	Chula Vista	CA	91914	619-474-5400		360-3
TF: 877-335-8676 ■ *Web:* deltoroloanservicing.com						
Dela Inc 175 Ward Hill Ave	Haverhill	MA	01835	978-372-7783		3
Web: www.delaquality.com						
Delaco Steel Corp 8111 Tireman Ave	Dearborn	MI	48126	313-491-1200		482
Web: thediezgroup.com						
Delafield Hambrecht Inc						
1301 2nd Ave Ste 2850	Seattle	WA	98101	206-254-4102		528
Web: www.delafieldhambrecht.com						
DelaGet LLC						
5320 W 23rd St Ste 140	Saint Louis Park	MN	55416	888-335-2438		196
TF: 888-335-2438 ■ *Web:* www.delaget.com						
Delaine James Inc 10508 Boyer Ste C	Austin	TX	78758	512-835-5333	999-5555*	87
**Fax Area Code:* 800						
Delamar Greenwich Harbor						
500 Steamboat Rd	Greenwich	CT	06830	203-661-9800		379
Web: delamar.com						
DeLand Area Chamber of Commerce						
336 N Woodland Blvd	DeLand	FL	32720	386-734-4331	734-4333	139
Web: www.delandchamber.org						
Deland Manufacturing Inc						
50674 Central Indus Dr	Shelby Township	MI	48315	586-323-2350	323-2353	454
Web: delandcorp.com						
Delaney Automotive Group 626 Water St	Indiana	PA	15701	888-868-0360		57
TF: 888-868-0360 ■ *Web:* www.delaneyauto.com						
Delaney Capital Management Ltd						
TD Bank Twr 4410-66 Wellington St W	Toronto	ON	M5K1H1	416-361-0688		528
TF: 800-268-2733 ■ *Web:* www.delaneycapital.com						
Delaney Computer Services Inc						
575 Corporate Dr Ste 400	Mahwah	NJ	07430	201-669-4300	575-4669	180
TF: 844-832-4437 ■ *Web:* www.dcsny.com						
Delaney Educational PO Box 656	Peotone	IL	60468	800-788-5557	660-2199	366
TF: 800-788-5557 ■ *Web:* www.deebooks.com						
Delaney House 3 Country Club Rd	Holyoke	MA	01040	413-532-1800		671
Web: www.delaneyhouse.com						
Delaney Meeting & Event Management						
46B Main St 4th Fl	Winooski	VT	05404	802-865-5202		195
Web: www.delaneymeetingevent.com						
Delaney, Wiles, Hayes, Gerety, Ellis & Young Inc						
1007 W Third Ave Ste 400	Anchorage	AK	99501	907-279-3581		428
Web: www.delaneywiles.com						
Delano Union School District						
1405 12th Ave	Delano	CA	93215	661-721-5000	725-2446	685
Web: www.duesd.org						
Delap LLP 5885 Meadows Rd Ste 200	Lake Oswego	OR	97035	503-697-4118		2
Web: www.delapcpa.com						
Delasoft Inc 92 Reads Way Ste 204	New Castle	DE	19720	302-533-7913		809
Web: www.delasoft.com						
DeLauro Rosa L (Rep D - CT)						
2413 Rayburn House Office Bldg	Washington	DC	20515	202-225-3661	225-4890	342-2
Web: delauro.house.gov						
Delavau 41 Suttons Ln	Piscataway	NJ	08854	855-671-3663		582
Web: www.delavaufood.com						
Delaware						
Administrative Office of the Courts						
The Renaissance Ctr 405 N King St Ste 507	Wilmington	DE	19801	302-255-0090	255-2217	339-8
Web: courts.delaware.gov						
Aging & Adults with Physical Disabilities Services						
1901 N DuPont Hwy	New Castle	DE	19720	800-223-9074		339-8
TF: 800-223-9074 ■ *Web:* www.dhss.delaware.gov						
Agriculture Dept 2320 S DuPont Hwy	Dover	DE	19901	302-698-4500		339-8
TF: 800-282-8685 ■ *Web:* agriculture.delaware.gov						
Arts Div 820 N French St 4th Fl	Wilmington	DE	19801	302-577-8278	577-6561	339-8
Web: arts.delaware.gov						
Attorney General 820 N French St	Wilmington	DE	19801	302-577-8400	577-6630	339-8
Web: attorneygeneral.delaware.gov						
Bank Commissioner						
555 E Loockerman St Ste 210	Dover	DE	19901	302-739-4235	739-3609	339-8
Web: banking.delaware.gov						
Child Support Enforcement Div (DCSE)						
84A Christiana Rd	New Castle	DE	19720	302-577-7171		339-8
Web: www.dhss.delaware.gov						
Consumer Protection Unit						
820 N French St 5th Fl	Wilmington	DE	19801	302-577-8600	577-6499	339-8
TF: 800-220-5424 ■ *Web:* attorneygeneral.delaware.gov						

Name / Address	City	State	Zip	Phone	Fax	Class
Correction Dept 245 McKee Rd *Web:* doc.delaware.gov	Dover	DE	19904	302-739-5601		339-8
Div of Motor Vehicles 303 Transportation Cir PO Box 698 *TF:* 800-232-5460 ■ *Web:* www.dmv.de.gov	Dover	DE	19903	302-744-2500		339-8
Economic Development Office 99 Kings Hwy *Web:* business.delaware.gov	Dover	DE	19901	302-739-4271	739-5749	339-8
Education Dept 1406 Forrest Ave Ste B *Web:* www.doe.state.de.us	Dover	DE	19901	302-735-4035	739-4654	339-8
Emergency Management Agency 165 Brick Store Landing Rd *TF:* 877-729-3362 ■ *Web:* dema.delaware.gov	Smyrna	DE	19977	302-659-3362	659-6855	339-8
Finance Dept 820 N French St 8th Fl *TF:* 800-338-6200 ■ *Web:* finance.delaware.gov	Wilmington	DE	19801	302-577-8987	577-8982	339-8
Fish & Wildlife Div 89 Kings Hwy *Web:* www.dnrec.delaware.gov	Dover	DE	19901	302-739-9910	739-6157	339-8
General Assembly 411 Legislative Ave *Web:* www.legis.delaware.gov	Dover	DE	19901	302-744-4114		339-8
Governor 150 Martin Luther King Jr Blvd S Tatnall Bldg *Web:* governor.delaware.gov	Dover	DE	19901	302-744-4101	739-2775	339-8
Historical & Cultural Affairs Div 21 The Green *Web:* history.delaware.gov	Dover	DE	19901	302-736-7400	739-5660	339-8
Housing Authority 18 The Green *TF:* 888-363-8808 ■ *Web:* delaware.gov	Dover	DE	19901	302-739-4263		339-8
Lieutenant Governor 28 Old Rudnick Ln 3rd Fl *Web:* ltgov.delaware.gov	Dover	DE	19901	302-744-4333		339-8
Natural Resources & Environmental Control Dept 89 Kings Hwy *Web:* www.dnrec.state.de.us	Dover	DE	19901	302-739-9400	739-3106	339-8
Parks & Recreation Div 89 Kings Hwy *TF:* 877-987-2757 ■ *Web:* www.destateparks.com	Dover	DE	19901	302-739-9220		339-8
Parole Board Carvel State Office Bldg 820 N French St 4th Fl *Web:* boardofparole.delaware.gov	Wilmington	DE	19801	302-577-5233	577-3501	339-8
Professional Regulation Div 861 Silver Lake Blvd Ste 203 *Web:* dpr.delaware.gov	Dover	DE	19904	302-744-4500	739-2711	339-8
Public Integrity Commission 410 Federal St Margaret O'Neill Bldg Ste 3 *Web:* depic.delaware.gov	Dover	DE	19901	302-739-2399		265
Revenue Div 820 N French St Carvel State Office Bldg *Web:* revenue.delaware.gov	Wilmington	DE	19801	302-577-8200	577-8202	339-8
Secretary of State 401 Federal St Ste 3 *Web:* sos.delaware.gov	Dover	DE	19901	302-739-4111	739-3811	339-8
Services for Children Youth & Their Families Dept 1825 Faulkland Rd *Web:* delaware.gov	Wilmington	DE	19805	302-633-2657		339-8
Technology & Information Dept 801 Silver Lake Blvd *Web:* dti.delaware.gov	Dover	DE	19904	302-739-9500	677-7043	339-8
Treasurer 820 Silver Lake Blvd Ste 100 *Web:* treasurer.delaware.gov	Dover	DE	19904	302-672-6700	739-5635	339-8
Veterans Affairs Commission 802 Silverlake Blvd Ste 100 *TF:* 800-344-9900 ■ *Web:* vets.delaware.gov	Dover	DE	19904	302-739-2792	739-2794	339-8
Vital Statistics Office PO Box 637 *Web:* www.dhss.delaware.gov	Dover	DE	19903	302-283-7130		339-8
Delaware & Raritan Canal State Park 145 Mapleton Rd *Web:* www.njparksandforests.org	Princeton	NJ	08540	609-924-5705		565
Delaware Agricultural Museum & Village 866 N DuPont Hwy *Web:* www.agriculturalmuseum.org	Dover	DE	19901	302-734-1618	734-0457	520
Delaware Alliance Federal Credit Union 2320 N Dupont Hwy *TF:* 800-822-9991 ■ *Web:* allyfed.org	New Castle	DE	19720	302-429-0404		219
Delaware Art Museum 2301 Kentmere Pkwy *TF:* 866-232-3714 ■ *Web:* www.delart.org	Wilmington	DE	19806	302-571-9590	571-0220	520
Delaware Association of Realtors 134 E Water St *Web:* www.delawarerealtor.com	Dover	DE	19901	302-734-4444	734-1341	656
Delaware Brick Co 1114 Centerville Rd *Web:* www.delawarebrick.com	Wilmington	DE	19804	302-994-0948	994-6359	191-1
Delaware Center for Horticulture 1810 N DuPont St *Web:* www.thedch.org	Wilmington	DE	19806	302-658-6262	658-6267	97
Delaware City School District 248 N Washington St *TF:* 844-723-3764 ■ *Web:* www.dcs.k12.oh.us	Delaware	OH	43015	740-833-1100	833-1149	685
Delaware College of Art & Design 600 N Market St *Web:* www.dcad.edu	Wilmington	DE	19801	302-622-8000	622-8870	164
Delaware Company Christian School 462 Malin Rd *Web:* www.dccs.org	Newtown Square	PA	19073	610-353-6522		685
Delaware Contemporary, The 200 S Madison St *Web:* www.decontemporary.org	Wilmington	DE	19801	302-656-6466		50-2
Delaware County 101 N Sandusky St *TF:* 800-277-2177 ■ *Web:* www.co.delaware.oh.us	Delaware	OH	43015	740-833-2000	833-2099	338
Delaware County PO Box 426 *Web:* www.co.delaware.ny.us	Delhi	NY	13753	607-746-2123		338
Delaware County 301 E Main St *TF:* 800-839-5005 ■ *Web:* www.co.delaware.ia.us	Manchester	IA	52057	800-839-5005		338
Delaware County 100 W Main St *Web:* www.co.delaware.in.us	Muncie	IN	47305	765-747-7730	747-7768	338
Delaware County Chamber of Commerce 1001 Baltimore Pk Ste 9LL *Web:* delawarepacoc.wliinc32.com	Springfield	PA	19064	610-565-3677		139
Delaware County Community College 901 Media Line Rd *Web:* www.dccc.edu	Media	PA	19063	610-359-5000	359-5343	162
Delaware County Daily Times 639 S Chester Rd *TF:* 888-799-6299 ■ *Web:* www.delcotimes.com	Swarthmore	PA	19081	610-622-8800		532-2
Delaware County District Library 84 E Winter St *Web:* www.delawarelibrary.org	Delaware	OH	43015	740-362-3861		434-3
Delaware County Electric Co-op (DCEC) 39 Elm St PO Box 471 *TF:* 866-436-1223 ■ *Web:* www.dce.coop	Delhi	NY	13753	607-746-2341		245
Delaware County Historical Society (DCHS) 120 E Washington St *Web:* www.delawarecountyhistory.org	Muncie	IN	47305	765-282-1550		637-2
Delaware County Intermediate Unit 200 Yale Ave *TF:* 800-441-3215 ■ *Web:* www.dciu.org	Morton	PA	19070	610-938-9000	938-9887	685
Delaware Democratic Party 19 E Commons Blvd 2nd Fl *TF:* 800-685-5544 ■ *Web:* www.deldems.org	New Castle	DE	19720	302-328-9036	328-9386	616-1
Delaware Diamond Knives Inc 3825 Lancaster Pke *TF:* 800-222-5143 ■ *Web:* www.ddk.com	Wilmington	DE	19805	302-999-7476	999-8320	222
Delaware Div of Libraries 497 S Red Haven Ln *Web:* lib.de.us	Dover	DE	19901	302-739-4748	739-6787	434-5
Delaware Dry Goods Co 1007 S Chapel St *TF:* 800-441-7300 ■ *Web:* www.delawaredg.com	Newark	DE	19702	302-731-0500	731-0573	594
Delaware Electric Co-opeartive Inc 14198 Sussex Hwy *TF:* 800-282-8595 ■ *Web:* www.delaware.coop	Greenwood	DE	19950	302-349-3147		245
Delaware History Museum 505 N Market St *Web:* dehistory.org	Wilmington	DE	19801	302-656-0637		520
Delaware Hospice Inc 1786 Wilmington-W Chester Pk Ste 200 A *TF:* 800-838-9800 ■ *Web:* www.delawarehospice.org	Glen Mills	PA	19342	302-478-5707		363
Delaware Hospital for the Chronically Ill 100 Sunnyside Rd *Web:* dhss.delaware.gov	Smyrna	DE	19977	302-223-1000		374-7
Delaware Machinery & Tool Company Inc 700 S Mulberry St *Web:* www.delawaredynamics.com	Muncie	IN	47302	765-284-3335	289-7185	757
Delaware Manufacturing Industries Corp 3776 Commerce Ct *TF:* 800-248-3642 ■ *Web:* www.dmic.com	Wheatfield	NY	14120	716-743-4360	743-4370	262
Delaware Medical Examiner 200 S Adam St *Web:* forensics.delaware.gov	Wilmington	DE	19801	302-577-3420	577-3416	339-8
Delaware Museum of Natural History 4840 Kennett Pk *Web:* www.delmnh.org	Wilmington	DE	19807	302-658-9111	658-2610	520
Delaware National Scenic River Delaware Water Gap National Recreation Area 1978 River Rd *TF:* 800-543-4295 ■ *Web:* www.nps.gov	Bushkill	PA	18324	570-426-2435		564
Delaware North Companies Inc 250 Delaware Ave *Web:* www.delawarenorth.com	Buffalo	NY	14202	716-858-5000		299
Delaware Nurses Assn (DNA) 4765 Ogletown-Stanton Rd Ste L10 *TF:* 800-626-4081 ■ *Web:* denurses.wildapricot.org	Newark	DE	19713	302-733-5880		533
Delaware Pharmacists Society 27 N Main St *Web:* www.dpsrx.org	Smyrna	DE	19977	302-659-3088		585
Delaware Racing Assn 777 Delaware Park Blvd **Fax Area Code:* 302 ■ *TF:* 888-850-8888 ■ *Web:* www.delawarepark.com	Wilmington	DE	19804	888-850-8888	994-3392*	642
Delaware River Port Authority 1 Port Ctr 2 Riverside Dr PO Box 1949 *Web:* www.drpa.org	Camden	NJ	08101	856-968-2000	968-2242	618
Delaware Seashore State Park 39415 Inlet Rd *Web:* destateparks.com	Rehoboth Beach	DE	19971	302-227-2800		565
Delaware Skills Ctr 500 Ship's Landing Way *Web:* deskillscenter.org	New Castle	DE	19720	302-654-5392		167-3
Delaware Sports Museum & Hall of Fame 801 Shipyard Dr *Web:* www.desports.org	Wilmington	DE	19801	302-425-3263	425-3713	522
Delaware State Bar Assn 405 N King St Ste 100 *Web:* www.dsba.org	Wilmington	DE	19801	302-658-5279	658-5212	72
Delaware State Chamber of Commerce 1201 N Orange St Ste 200 PO Box 671 *TF:* 800-292-9507 ■ *Web:* www.dscc.com	Wilmington	DE	19899	302-655-7221	654-0691	140
Delaware State Dental Society 200 Continental Dr Ste 111 *Web:* delawarestatedentalsociety.org	Newark	DE	19713	302-368-7634	368-7669	227
Delaware State Lottery 1575 McKee Rd Ste 102 *Web:* www.delottery.com	Dover	DE	19904	302-739-5291	739-7586	452
Delaware State News 110 Galaxy Dr *TF:* 800-282-8586 ■ *Web:* www.delawarestatenews.net	Dover	DE	19901	302-674-3600		532-2
Delaware State Park 5202 US Rt 23 N *TF:* 866-644-6727	Delaware	OH	43015	740-363-4561		565
Delaware State University 1200 N DuPont Hwy *TF:* 800-845-2544 ■ *Web:* www.desu.edu	Dover	DE	19901	302-857-6351	857-6352	166
Delaware Storage & Pipeline Co PO Box 313 *Web:* www.delawarespc.com	Dover	DE	19903	302-736-1774		539
Delaware Symphony Orchestra, The 818 N Market St *Web:* www.delawaresymphony.org	Wilmington	DE	19801	302-656-7442		573-3
Delaware Technical & Community College *Terry* 100 Campus Dr *Web:* www.dtcc.edu	Dover	DE	19904	302-857-1000		800

Name / Address	City	State	ZIP	Phone	Fax	Class
Delaware Theatre Co 200 Water St *Web:* www.delawaretheatre.org	Wilmington	DE	19801	302-594-1104	594-1107	749
Delaware Transit Corp 119 Lower Beach St *TF:* 800-652-3278 ■ *Web:* www.dartfirststate.com	Wilmington	DE	19805	800-652-3278		468
Delaware Valley Corp 500 Broadway *Web:* www.dvc500.com	Lawrence	MA	01841	978-688-6995	688-5825	131
Delaware Veterinary Medical Assn PO Box 9997 *Web:* www.devma.org	Newark	DE	19714	302-455-8387		795
DelBene Suzan (Rep D - WA) 2330 Rayburn House Office Bldg *Web:* www.delbene.house.gov	Washington	DC	20515	202-225-6311	226-1606	342-2
Delbridge Museum of Natural History 805 S Kiwanis Ave *Web:* greatzoo.org	Sioux Falls	SD	57104	605-367-7003		520
Delbridge Solutions 100 Four Valley Dr Unit B *TF:* 888-815-2996 ■ *Web:* www.delbridge.solutions	Vaughan	ON	L4K4T9	888-815-2996		317
Delcambre Telephone Company Inc 104 N Corner St *TF:* 800-352-8156 ■ *Web:* www.delcambre.net	Delcambre	LA	70528	337-685-2311		224
Delcath Systems Inc 1633 Broadway 22nd Fl Ste C *Web:* delcath.com	New York	NY	10019	212-489-2100	489-2102	476
Delco Automation Inc 3735 Thatcher Ave *Web:* www.delcoautomation.com	Saskatoon	SK	S7R1B8	306-244-6449	665-7500	256
Delco Diesel Services Inc 1100 S Agnew Ave *TF:* 800-256-0395 ■ *Web:* www.delcodiesel.com	Oklahoma City	OK	73108	405-232-3595		54
Delco Electric Inc 1 NW 132nd St *Web:* www.delcoelectric.com	Oklahoma City	OK	73114	405-302-0099		261
Delcoline Inc 4919 Lawrence St *Web:* delcoline.com	Hyattsville	MD	20781	301-864-4455		61
Delcom Group LP 2525B E SH 121 Ste 400 *TF:* 800-308-9228 ■ *Web:* www.delcomgroup.com	Lewisville	TX	75056	214-389-5500		196
Delcrest Medical Supplies 2670 Nottingham Way *Web:* delcrestmedical.net	Hamilton Township	NJ	08619	609-586-1679	586-1758	475
Delden Manufacturing Company Inc 3530 N Kimball Dr *TF:* 800-821-3708 ■ *Web:* www.deldenmfg.com	Kansas City	MO	64161	816-413-1600		499
Delectables Catering and Venue 427 E Limberlost Dr *Web:* www.delectables.com	Tucson	AZ	85705	520-884-9289		671
Delek Refining Ltd 425 McMurrey Dr *Web:* www.delekus.com	Tyler	TX	75702	903-579-3400		580
Del-engineering 51 Dawn Rd *Web:* www.del-engineering.com	Levittown	PA	19056	215-752-1619		192
DeLeon's Bromeliads Co 13745 SW 216th St *TF:* 800-448-8649 ■ *Web:* www.deleons4color.com	Miami	FL	33170	305-238-6028	235-2354	369
Delex Systems Inc 1953 Gallows Rd Ste 700 *Web:* www.delex.com	Vienna	VA	22182	703-734-8300	893-5338	261
Delfield Co 980 S Isabella Rd *TF:* 800-733-8821 ■ *Web:* www.delfield.com	Mount Pleasant	MI	48858	989-773-7981	773-3210	298
Delfin 15672 Producer Ln **Fax Area Code:* 800 ■ *TF:* 800-354-7919 ■ *Web:* www.delfinfs.com	Hurtington Beach	CA	92619	949-888-4644	385-4626*	362
Delfina 3621 18th St *Web:* www.delfinasf.com	San Francisco	CA	94110	415-552-4055		671
Delford Industries Inc 82 Washington St 84 *Web:* www.delfordind.com	Middletown	NY	10940	845-342-3901	342-3168	677
Delgado Antonio (Rep D - NY) 1007 Longworth House Office Bldg *Web:* www.delgado.house.gov	Washington	DC	20515	202-225-5614		342-2
Delgado Community College 615 City Park Ave *Web:* www.dcc.edu	New Orleans	LA	70119	504-671-5000		162
Delhi Palace 542 St Andrew Rd *Web:* www.delhipalacesc.net	Columbia	SC	29210	803-750-7760		671
Delhur Industries Inc 4410 S Airport Rd *Web:* delhur.com	Port Angeles	WA	98363	360-457-1133		358
Deli Express 16101 W 78th St *TF:* 800-328-8184 ■ *Web:* www.deliexpress.com	Eden Prairie	MN	55344	800-328-8184		296-36
Deli Management Inc 535 Dowlen Rd *Web:* www.jasonsdeli.com	Beaumont	TX	77706	409-838-1976		670
Deli Partners LLC 2217 Midtown Ln *Web:* www.jasonsdeli.com	Fort Worth	TX	76104	817-920-1880	920-1883	670
Delicious Living Magazine 1401 Pearl St *Web:* deliciousliving.com	Boulder	CO	80302	303-939-8440	998-9020	457-11
DeLine Box & Display 3700 Lima St *Web:* www.delinebox.com	Denver	CO	80239	303-373-1430		100
Delisa Pallet Corp 116 S Ave *Web:* www.delisapallet.com	Middlesex	NJ	08846	732-667-7070	667-7071	551
Delisi & Associates PC 217 S Pennsylvania Ave *Web:* www.delisiassociates.com	Greensburg	PA	15601	724-832-8585		2
Delisle Inc 80 Kimberly Dr *Web:* www.mtc62.com	South Windsor	CT	06074	860-289-8225	289-5970	743
Delius Restaurant 2951 Cherry Ave *Web:* www.deliusrestaurant.com	Signal Hill	CA	90755	562-426-0694		671
Deliverycom LLC 235 Park Ave S 5th Fl *TF:* 800-709-7191 ■ *Web:* www.delivery.com	New York	NY	10038	800-709-7191		387
Delkin Devices Inc 13350 Kirkham Way *TF:* 800-637-8087 ■ *Web:* www.delkin.com	Poway	CA	92064	858-391-1234		174
Delkor Systems Inc 4300 Round Lake Rd W *TF:* 800-328-5558 ■ *Web:* delkorsystems.com	Saint Paul	MN	55112	800-328-5558		547
Dell Inc 1 Dell Way *NASDAQ: DELL* ■ *TF:* 800-879-3355 ■ *Web:* www.dell.com	Round Rock	TX	78682	512-338 4400	283-6161	173-2
Dell Telephone Cooperative Inc (DTC) 610 S Main St *TF:* 800-245-2991 ■ *Web:* www.delltelephone.com	Dell City	TX	79837	915-964-2352		224
Dell'Arte International School of Physical Theatre PO Box 816 *Web:* www.dellarte.com	Blue Lake	CA	95525	707-668-5663		685
Dell'Oro Group Inc 230 Redwood Shores Pkwy *Web:* www.delloro.com	Redwood City	CA	94065	650-622-9400		668
Dellas Graphics Inc 344 S Warren St *Web:* www.dellasgraphics.com	Syracuse	NY	13202	315-474-4641		174
Dellenbach Motors 3111 S College Ave **Fax Area Code:* 970 ■ *TF:* 866-963-5689 ■ *Web:* www.dellenbach.com	Fort Collins	CO	80525	866-963-5689	226-0233*	57
Dellisart Lodging LLC 10800 Alpharetta Hwy Ste 208-776 **Fax Area Code:* 770 ■ *TF:* 877-606-0591 ■ *Web:* www.dellisart.com	Roswell	GA	30076	847-306-0954	558-4301*	377
Delmar Financial Co 1066 Executive Pky Ste 100 *TF:* 800-866-8734 ■ *Web:* www.delmarfinancial.com	Saint Louis	MO	63141	314-434-7000	222-0343	509
Delmar Gardens of Lenexa Inc 9701 Monrovia St *Web:* www.delmargardens.com	Lenexa	KS	66215	913-492-1130		672
Delmar International Inc 10636 Cote de Liesse *Web:* www.delmarcargo.com	Montreal	QC	H8T1A5	514-636-8800		314
Delmar Products Inc 400 Christian Ln *Web:* www.delmarproducts.com	Berlin	CT	06037	860-828-6501		596
Delmar Systems Inc 8114 W Hwy 90 *TF:* 800-489-1234 ■ *Web:* delmarsystems.com	Broussard	LA	70518	337-365-0180		536
Delmarva Collections Inc 820 E Main St *Web:* www.delmarvacollections.com	Salisbury	MD	21804	410-546-3005		160
Delmarva Foundation For Medical Care Inc (DFMC) 28464 Marlboro Ave *Web:* www.dfmc.org	Easton	MD	21601	410-822-0697	822-7971	474
Delmarva Power PO Box 231 *TF:* 800-898-8042 ■ *Web:* www.delmarva.com	Wilmington	DE	19899	800-898-8042		787
Delmonico's 56 Beaver St *Web:* www.delmonicosny.com	New York	NY	10004	212-509-1144		670
Delmonico's Italian Steakhouse Syracuse 2950 Erie Blvd E *Web:* delmonicositaliansteakhouse.com	Syracuse	NY	13224	315-445-1111	445-0257	671
Delmont Laboratories Inc 715 Harvard Ave PO Box 269 *TF:* 800-562-5541 ■ *Web:* delmontlabs.com	Swarthmore	PA	19081	610-543-2747	543-6298	584
DelMonte Hotel Group 909 Linden Ave *Web:* www.delmontehotels.com	Rochester	NY	14625	585-586-3121		379
Delnor-Wiggins Pass State Park 11135 Gulfshore Dr *Web:* www.floridastateparks.org	Naples	FL	34108	239-597-6196		565
Delo Screw Products 700 London Rd *Web:* deloscrew.com	Delaware	OH	43015	740-363-1971	363-0042	621
DeLoache Florist 2927 Millwood Ave *Web:* www.deloacheonlineflorist.com	Columbia	SC	29205	803-256-1681		292
Deloitte Digital 821 2nd Ave Ste 200 *Web:* www.deloittedigital.com	Seattle	WA	98104	206-633-1167		195
Deloitte LLP 30 Rockefeller Plz 41st Fl *Web:* www2.deloitte.com	New York	NY	10112	212-492-4000		2
Delon Hampton & Associates Chartered 900 Seventh St NW Ste 800 *Web:* www.delonhampton.com	Washington	DC	20001	202-898-1999	371-2073	261
Delong's Inc 301 Dix Rd *Web:* www.delongsinc.com	Jefferson City	MO	65109	573-635-6121	635-9101	480
Delos Research Group 333 W Maude Ave Ste 101 *Web:* www.delosresearch.com	Sunnyvale	CA	94085	408-733-8000		180
Delphi Body Works Inc 313 S Washington St PO Box 30 *Web:* www.delphibodyworks.com	Delphi	IN	46923	765-564-2212	564-4255	516
Delphi Business Properties Inc 7100 Hayvenhurst Ave Ste 211 *Web:* go2delphi.com	Van Nuys	CA	91406	818-780-7878	780-8152	652
Delphi Corp 5725 Delphi Dr *Web:* www.delphi.com	Troy	MI	48098	248-813-2334		60
Delphi Energy Corp 333 - 7 Ave SW Ste 2300 *TF:* 800-430-7207 ■ *Web:* www.delphienergy.ca	Calgary	AB	T2P2Z1	403-265-6171	265-6207	536
Delphi Engineering Group Inc 18006 Skypark Cir Ste 104 *Web:* www.delphieng.com	Irvine	CA	92614	949-537-7777		256
Delphi Financial Group Inc 1105 N Market St Ste 1230 *NYSE: DFG* ■ *Web:* www.delphifin.com	Wilmington	DE	19899	302-478-5142		360-4
Delphi Ventures 160 Bovet Rd Ste 408 *Web:* www.delphiventures.com	San Mateo	CA	94402	650-854-9650		792
Delphinus Engineering Inc 650 Baldwin Tower *Web:* www.delphinus.com	Eddystone	PA	19022	610-874-9160		261
Delphinus Medical Technologies LLC 45525 Grand River Ave *Web:* www.delphinusmt.com	Novi	MI	48374	248-522-9600		723
Delphos Herald Inc 405 N Main St *TF:* 800-589-6950 ■ *Web:* www.delphosherald.com	Delphos	OH	45833	419-695-0015		637-8
Delphus Inc 152 Speedwell Ave *Web:* www.delphus.com	Morristown	NJ	07960	973-267-9269		177
Delray Beach Library 100 W Atlantic Ave *Web:* www.delraylibrary.org	Delray Beach	FL	33444	561-266-0194		434-3
Delray Medical Ctr (DMC) 5352 Linton Blvd *Web:* www.delraymedicalctr.com	Delray Beach	FL	33484	561-498-4440	495-3103	374-3
Delreka Distributing 510 W Washington St *Web:* www.delrekadistributing.com	Eureka	CA	95501	707-442-1701		81-1
Delsey Luggage 6090 Dorsey Rd Ste C *TF:* 800-558-3344 ■ *Web:* www.delsey.com	Elkridge	MD	21075	410-796-5655		453

	Phone	Fax	Class
DelShah Capital LLC 114 E 13th St .... New York NY 10003 *Web:* www.delshah.com	212-677-4506		652
Delsys Inc 23 Strathmore Rd .... Natick MA 01760 *Web:* www.delsys.com	508-545-8200		250
Delta Air Lines Inc 1030 Delta Blvd .... Atlanta GA 30354 *NYSE: DAL* ■ *TF:* 800-221-1212 ■ *Web:* www.delta.com	404-715-2600	773-2108	25
Delta Air Lines Inc PO Box 20559 .... Atlanta GA 30320 **Fax Area Code: 404* ■ *TF:* 800-352-2737 ■ *Web:* www.deltacargo.com	800-352-2737	714-5022*	12
Delta Apparel Inc 2750 Premiere Pkwy Ste 100 .... Duluth GA 30097 *NYSE: DLA* ■ *TF:* 800-285-4456 ■ *Web:* www.deltaapparel.com	678-775-6900	775-6992	155-3
Delta Area Chamber of Commerce 301 Main St .... Delta CO 81416 *Web:* www.deltacolorado.org	970-874-8616	874-8618	139
Delta Area Hospice Care Ltd 2812 Oktibbeha St .... Greenville MS 38701	662-335-7040		371
Delta Bus Lines Inc 3107 Hwy 82E .... Greenville MS 38701 *Web:* deltabuslines.net	662-335-2633	335-2634	107
Delta Centrifugal Corp PO Box 1043 .... Temple TX 76503 *TF:* 888-433-3100 ■ *Web:* www.deltacentrifugal.com	254-773-9055		307
Delta Chamber of Commerce 6201 60th Ave .... Delta BC V4K4E2 *Web:* www.deltachamber.ca	604-946-4232	946-5285	137
Delta Chi Fraternity Inc 314 Church St .... Iowa City IA 52245 *Web:* www.deltachi.org	319-337-4811		48-16
Delta Children 114 W 26th St .... New York NY 10001 **Fax Area Code: 212* ■ *TF:* 800-377-3777 ■ *Web:* www.deltachildren.com	800-377-3777	736-7228*	64
Delta College 1961 Delta Rd .... University Center MI 48710 *Web:* www.delta.edu	989-686-9000	667-2202	162
Delta College of Arts & Technology 7380 Exchange Pl .... Baton Rouge LA 70806 *TF:* 800-858-0551 ■ *Web:* deltacollege.com	225-928-7770		162
Delta Companies Inc 114 S Silver Springs Rd .... Cape Girardeau MO 63703 *Web:* www.deltacos.com	573-334-5261	334-9576	188-4
Delta Compression & Equipment LLC 160 James Ln .... Krotz Springs LA 70750 *Web:* www.deltacompression.com	337-566-8888		530
Delta Concrete Products Inc 267.5 Mile Richardson Hwy PO Box 289 .... Delta Junction AK 99737 *Web:* www.deltaconcrete.us	907-895-4679	895-1001	182
Delta Controls Corp 585 Fortson St .... Shreveport LA 71107 *Web:* www.deltacnt.com	318-424-8471		246
Delta Controls Inc 17850 - 56th Ave .... Surrey BC V3S1C7 *Web:* www.deltacontrols.com	604-574-9444	574-7793	407
Delta Cooling Towers Inc PO Box 315 .... Rockaway NJ 07866 *TF:* 800-289-3358 ■ *Web:* deltacooling.com	973-586-2201	586-2243	472
Delta Corporate Services Inc 129 Littleton Rd .... Parsippany NJ 07054 *TF:* 800-335-8220 ■ *Web:* www.deltacorp.com	973-331-0144		180
Delta Correctional Ctr 11363 Lockhart Rd .... Delta CO 81416 *Web:* www.colorado.gov	970-874-7614	874-5810	213
Delta Corrugated Paper Products Corp W Ruby Ave .... Palisades Park NJ 07650 *Web:* www.deltacorrugated.com	201-941-1910	941-9399	100
Delta County 200 W Bonham St .... Cooper TX 75432 *Web:* www.deltacountytx.com	903-395-2146	395-2256	338
Delta County 501 Palmer St Ste 211 .... Delta CO 81416 *Web:* www.deltacounty.com	970-874-2150	874-2161	338
Delta County 310 Ludington St .... Escanaba MI 49829 *Web:* www.deltami.org	906-789-5105	789-5196	338
Delta County Federal Credit Union 100 Circle Dr .... Delta CO 81416 *Web:* deltacountyfcu.com	970-874-7674		219
Delta Dallas 15950 N Dallas Pkwy Ste 150 .... Dallas TX 75248 *Web:* www.deltadallas.com	972-788-2300		260
Delta Data 1500 6th Ave Ste 1 .... Columbus GA 31901 *TF:* 800-723-8274 ■ *Web:* www.deltadata.com	706-324-0855		177
Delta Delta Delta Fraternity 2331 Brookhollow Plaza Dr .... Arlington TX 76006 *TF:* 877-746-7333 ■ *Web:* www.tridelta.org	817-633-8001		48-16
Delta Democrat Times 988 N Broadway St .... Greenville MS 38701 *Web:* www.ddtonline.com	662-335-1155	335-2860	532-2
Delta Dental PO Box 2105 .... Mechanicsburg PA 17055 *TF:* 800-932-0783 ■ *Web:* www.deltadentalins.com	717-766-8500		227
Delta Dental of Arizona PO Box 43026 .... Phoenix AZ 85080 **Fax Area Code: 602* ■ *TF:* 800-352-6132 ■ *Web:* www.deltadentalaz.com	800-352-6132	588-3636*	391-3
Delta Dental of Arkansas 1513 Country Club Rd .... Sherwood AR 72120 **Fax Area Code: 877* ■ *TF:* 800-462-5410 ■ *Web:* www.deltadentalar.com	501-835-3400	992-1854*	391-3
Delta Dental of Colorado 4582 S Ulster St Ste 800 .... Denver CO 80237 *TF:* 800-233-0860 ■ *Web:* www.deltadentalco.com	303-741-9300	741-9338	391-3
Delta Dental of Idaho 555 E Parkcenter Blvd PO Box 2870 .... Boise ID 83706 *TF:* 800-356-7586 ■ *Web:* www.deltadentalid.com	208-489-3580	344-4649	391-3
Delta Dental of Iowa 9000 Northpark Dr .... Johnston IA 50131 *TF:* 800-544-0718 ■ *Web:* www.deltadentalia.com	515-331-4594	875-4163	391-3
Delta Dental of Kansas 1619 N Waterfront Pkwy PO Box 789769 .... Wichita KS 67278 *TF:* 800-234-3375 ■ *Web:* www.deltadentalks.com	316-264-4511	462-3392	391-3
Delta Dental of Kentucky 10100 Linn Station Rd Ste 700 .... Louisville KY 40223 *TF:* 800-955-2030 ■ *Web:* www.deltadentalky.com	800-955-2030		391-3
Delta Dental of Massachusetts 465 Medford St .... Boston MA 02129 **Fax Area Code: 617* ■ *TF:* 800-872-0500 ■ *Web:* www.deltadentalma.com	800-872-0500	886-1199*	391-3
Delta Dental of Minnesota PO Box 330 .... Minneapolis MN 55440 *TF:* 800-553-9536 ■ *Web:* www.deltadentalmn.org	651-406-5900		391-3
Delta Dental of Missouri 12399 Gravois Rd .... Saint Louis MO 63127 *TF:* 800-335-8266 ■ *Web:* www.deltadentalmo.com	314-656-3000	656-2900	391-3
Delta Dental of New Jersey 1639 SR-10 .... Parsippany NJ 07054 *TF:* 800-624-2633 ■ *Web:* www.deltadentalnj.com	973-285-4000	285-4141	391-3
Delta Dental of New Mexico 2500 Louisiana Blvd NE Ste 600 .... Albuquerque NM 87110 *TF:* 800-999-0963 ■ *Web:* www.deltadentalnm.com	505-883-4777	883-7444	391-3
Delta Dental of North Carolina 4242 Six Forks Rd Ste 970 .... Raleigh NC 27609 *TF:* 800-587-9514 ■ *Web:* www.deltadentalnc.com	800-662-8856		391-3
Delta Dental of Ohio PO Box 30416 .... Lansing MI 48909 *TF:* 800-524-0149 ■ *Web:* www.deltadentaloh.com	800-524-0149		391-3
Delta Dental of Oklahoma 16 NW 63rd St .... Oklahoma City OK 73116 *Web:* deltadentalok.org	405-607-2100	607-2190	391-3
Delta Dental of Rhode Island 10 Charles St .... Providence RI 02904 *TF:* 800-598-6684 ■ *Web:* www.deltadentalri.com	401-752-6000	752-6060	391-3
Delta Dental of South Dakota 720 N Euclid Ave PO Box 1157 .... Pierre SD 57501 **Fax Area Code: 605* ■ *TF:* 800-627-3961 ■ *Web:* www.southdakota.deltadental.com	877-841-1478	224-0909*	391-3
Delta Dental of Tennessee 240 Venture Cir .... Nashville TN 37228 **Fax Area Code: 615* ■ *TF:* 800-223-3104 ■ *Web:* www.tennessee.deltadental.com	800-223-3104	244-8108*	391-3
Delta Dental of Virginia 4818 Starkey Rd .... Roanoke VA 24018 *TF:* 800-237-6060 ■ *Web:* www.deltadentalva.com	540-989-8000		391-3
Delta Dental of Wisconsin 2801 Hoover Rd PO Box 828 .... Stevens Point WI 54481 *TF:* 800-236-3713 ■ *Web:* www.deltadentalwi.com	715-344-6087	344-9058	391-3
Delta Dental of Wyoming 6234 Yellowstone Rd PO Box 29 .... Cheyenne WY 82009 *TF:* 800-735-3379 ■ *Web:* www.deltadentalwy.org	307-632-3313	632-7309	391-3
Delta Downs Racetrack 2717 Delta Downs Dr .... Vinton LA 70668 *TF:* 800-589-7441 ■ *Web:* www.deltadowns.com	800-589-7441		642
Delta Education LLC 80 NW Blvd .... Nashua NH 03063 *TF:* 800-258-1302 ■ *Web:* www.deltaeducation.com	603-889-8899		243
Delta Electric Inc 911 Riverview Ave PO Box 1497 .... Logan WV 25601 *Web:* www.deltaelectricwv.com	304-752-4625	752-0948	358
Delta Electric Power Assn 1700 Hwy 82 W .... Greenwood MS 38930 *Web:* deltaepa.com	662-453-6352		245
Delta Electronics Inc 5730 General Wash Dr .... Alexandria VA 22312 *TF:* 800-833-5828 ■ *Web:* www.deltaelectronics.com	703-354-3350	354-0216	647
Delta Electronics Manufacturing Corp 416 Cabot St .... Beverly MA 01915 *Web:* www.deltarf.com	978-927-1060	922-6430	253
Delta Employees Credit Union 1025 Virginia Ave .... Atlanta GA 30354 *TF:* 800-544-3328 ■ *Web:* www.deltacommunitycu.com	404-715-4725		219
Delta Engineering Group LLC (DEI) 111 W Jackson Blvd Ste 910 .... Chicago IL 60604 *Web:* www.deg-america.com	312-377-7700	427-6145	261
Delta Fastener Corp 7122 Old Katy Rd .... Houston TX 77024 *Web:* www.deltafastener.com	713-868-2351		351
Delta Fine Arts Inc 2611 New Walkertown Rd .... Winston-Salem NC 27101 *Web:* deltaartscenter.org	336-722-2625		50-2
Delta Fire Sprinklers Inc 111 Tech Dr .... Sanford FL 32771 *Web:* www.delta-fire.com	407-328-3000		189-10
Delta Foremost Chemical Corp 3915 Air Park St .... Memphis TN 38118 *TF:* 800-238-5150 ■ *Web:* www.deltaforemost.com	800-238-5150		151
Delta Galil USA 1 Harmon Plz 5th Fl .... Secaucus NJ 07094 *Web:* www.deltagalil.com	201-902-0055	902-0070	155-18
Delta Gamma 3250 Riverside Dr Ste A-2 .... Columbus OH 43221 *TF:* 800-644-5414 ■ *Web:* www.deltagamma.org	614-481-8169		48-16
Delta Group Inc 4801 Lincoln Rd NE .... Albuquerque NM 87109 *Web:* www.deltagroupinc.com	505-883-7674		253
Delta Heritage Trail State Park 5539 Hwy 49 .... West Helena AR 72390 *Web:* www.arkansasstateparks.com	870-572-2352		565
Delta Hospital Foundation 5800 Mtn View Blvd .... Delta BC V4K3V6 *Web:* dhchfoundation.ca	604-940-9695	940-9670	374-2
Delta Industrial Services Inc 11501 Eagle St .... Minneapolis MN 55448 *Web:* www.deltamodtech.com	763-755-7744		186
Delta Industries 39 Bradley Park Rd .... East Granby CT 06026 *Web:* mbaerospace.com	860-653-5041		21
Delta Kappa Epsilon (DKE) 6921 Jackson Rd Ste 400 .... Ann Arbor MI 48103 *Web:* dke.org	734-302-4210		48-16
Delta King Riverboat Hotel 1000 Front St .... Sacramento CA 95814 *Web:* www.deltaking.com	916-444-5464		379
Delta Lake State Park 8797 SR- 46 .... Rome NY 13440 *Web:* parks.ny.gov	315-337-4670		565
Delta Life Insurance Co 4370 Peachtree Rd NE .... Atlanta GA 30319 *Web:* www.delta-life.com	404-231-2111	231-2220	796
Delta M Corp 1003 Larsen Dr .... Oak Ridge TN 37830 *TF:* 800-922-0083 ■ *Web:* www.deltamcorp.com	865-483-1569		407
Delta Machine & Ironworks Inc 5185 Adams Ave .... Baton Rouge LA 70806 *Web:* www.teamdeltausa.com	225-356-2000		454
Delta Machining Inc 2361 Reum Rd .... Niles MI 49120 *Web:* www.deltamach.com	269-683-7775		454
Delta Marine Industries Inc 1608 S 96th St .... Seattle WA 98108 *Web:* www.deltamarine.com	206-763-2383	762-2627	90
Delta Materials Handling Inc 4676 Clarke Rd .... Memphis TN 38141 *Web:* www.deltamat.com	901-795-7230		358

	City	State	Zip	Phone	Fax	Class
Delta Meadows 17645 State Hwy 160 *Web:* www.parks.ca.gov	Rio Vista	CA	94571	916-777-7701		565
Delta Medical Ctr (DMC) 3000 Getwell Rd *TF:* 877-627-4395 ■ *Web:* www.deltaspecialtyhospital.com	Memphis	TN	38118	877-627-4395		374-3
Delta Medical Systems Inc 3280 Gateway Rd Ste 200 *TF:* 800-798-7574 ■ *Web:* www.deltamedicalsystems.com	Brookfield	WI	53045	800-798-7574	323-9321	475
Delta Metals Company Inc 1388 N Seventh St *Web:* www.delta-metals.com	Memphis	TN	38107	901-575-3300	575-3322	492
Delta Mold Inc 9415 Stockport Pl *Web:* deltamold.com	Charlotte	NC	28273	704-588-6600		454
Delta Natural Gas Company Inc 3617 Lexington Rd *NASDAQ: DGAS* ■ *TF:* 800-262-2012 ■ *Web:* www.deltagas.com	Winchester	KY	40391	859-744-6171		787
Delta Oil & Gas Inc 710 N Post Oak Rd *Web:* www.deltaoilandgas.com	Houston	TX	77024	281-946-3582		536
Delta Pacific Products Inc 33170 Central Ave *Web:* www.deltapacificinc.com	Union City	CA	94587	510-487-4411		608
Delta Packing Co 6021 E Kettleman Ln *Web:* www.deltapacking.com	Lodi	CA	95240	209-334-1023	334-0811	11-1
Delta Pathology Group LLP 2915 Missouri Ave *Web:* deltapathology.com	Shreveport	LA	71109	318-621-8820		415
Delta Petroleum Company Inc 10352 River Rd	Saint Rose	LA	70087	504-467-1399	467-1398	541
Delta Phi Epsilon International Sorority 251 S Camac St *Web:* www.dphie.org	Philadelphia	PA	19107	215-732-5901		48-16
Delta Plastics 8801 Frazier Pke *TF:* 800-277-9172 ■ *Web:* www.deltaplastics.com	Little Rock	AR	72206	501-490-0395	217-0727	604
Delta Polymers Midwest Inc 6685 Sterling Dr N *TF:* 800-860-6848 ■ *Web:* www.deltapoly.com	Sterling Heights	MI	48312	586-795-2900		603
Delta Power Co 4484 Boeing Dr *Web:* www.delta-power.com	Rockford	IL	61109	815-397-6628	397-2526	790
Delta Process Equipment Inc 8275 Florida Blvd *TF:* 866-387-3871 ■ *Web:* www.deltaprocess.com	Denham Springs	LA	70726	225-665-1666	665-1855	385
Delta Products Corp 46101 Fremont Blvd *Web:* www.delta-americas.com	Fremont	CA	94538	510-668-5100	668-0680	253
Delta Publications Inc 606 Fremont St *Web:* www.deltapublications.com	Kiel	WI	53042	920-894-2828	894-2161	532-2
Delta Railroad Construction Inc 2648 W Prospect Rd *Web:* www.deltarr.com	Ashtabula	OH	44004	440-992-2997	992-1311	188-4
Delta Regional Medical Ctr (DRMC) 1400 E Union St *Web:* www.deltaregional.com	Greenville	MS	38703	662-378-3783		374-3
Delta Reporter, The 600 Ludington St *Web:* www.dailypress.net	Escanaba	MI	49829	906-786-2021		532-2
Delta Research Inc 996 Explorer Blvd *Web:* www.dr-inc.com	Huntsville	AL	35806	256-895-0881	837-5956	668
Delta Ridge Implement Inc 1150 Hwy 425 *TF:* 800-659-3337 ■ *Web:* www.deltaridgeimplement.com	Rayville	LA	71269	318-728-6423	728-6426	274
Delta Risk LLC 106 S St Mary's St Ste 601 *TF:* 888-763-3582 ■ *Web:* deltarisk.com	San Antonio	TX	78205	210-293-0707		196
Delta Sales Yard Inc 700 W Fifth St *Web:* www.deltasalesyard.com	Delta	CO	81416	970-874-4612	874-3087	446
Delta School of Business & Technology 517 Broad St *Web:* www.deltatech.edu	Lake Charles	LA	70601	337-439-5765		685
Delta Scientific Corp 40355 Delta Ln *Web:* deltascientific.com	Palmdale	CA	93551	661-575-1100	575-1109	678
Delta Sigma Phi Fraternity 2960 N Meridian St PO Box 88507 *Web:* www.deltasig.org	Indianapolis	IN	46208	317-634-1899		48-16
Delta Sigma Pi 330 S Campus Ave *Web:* www.deltasigmapi.org	Oxford	OH	45056	513-523-1907	523-7292	48-16
Delta Sigma Theta Sorority Inc 1707 New Hampshire Ave NW *TF:* 866-615-6464 ■ *Web:* www.deltasigmatheta.org	Washington	DC	20009	202-986-2400	986-2513	48-16
Delta Society 875 124th Ave NE Ste 101 *Web:* petpartners.org	Bellevue	WA	98005	425-679-5500		48-17
Delta Staffing LLC 5730 Bella Rosa Blvd Ste 300 *Web:* delta-staffing.com	Clarkston	MI	48348	248-394-3940		260
Delta Star Inc 270 Industrial Rd *TF:* 800-892-8673 ■ *Web:* www.deltastar.com	San Carlos	CA	94070	800-892-8673		767
Delta State Recreation Site PO Box 318 *Web:* www.dnr.alaska.gov	Delta Junction	AK	99737	907-895-2113	895-5043	565
Delta State University 1003 W Sunflower Rd *TF:* 800-468-6378 ■ *Web:* www.deltastate.edu	Cleveland	MS	38733	662-846-4020	846-4684	166
Delta Steel Inc 7355 Roundhouse Ln *TF:* 800-324-0220 ■ *Web:* www.deltasteel.com	Houston	TX	77078	713-635-1200	635-2060	492
Delta Steel Technologies 2204 Century Center Blvd *Web:* deltasteeltech.com	Irving	TX	75062	972-438-7150	579-0100	494
Delta SubSea LLC 550 Club Dr Ste 345 *TF:* 888-234-3684 ■ *Web:* www.deltasubsea-rov.com	Montgomery	TX	77316	936-582-7237		539
Delta Systems Inc 1734 Frost Rd *Web:* www.phoenixtechnologyit.com	Streetsboro	OH	44241	330-626-2811		729
Delta T Systems Inc 2171 HWY 175 *TF:* 800-733-4204 ■ *Web:* www.deltatsys.com	Richfield	WI	53076	262-628-0331		358
Delta Tao Software Inc 8032 Twin Oaks Ave *TF:* 800-827-9316 ■ *Web:* www.deltatao.com	Citrus Heights	CA	95610	800-827-9316		178-1
Delta Tau Data Systems Inc 21314 Lassen St *Web:* www.deltatau.com	Chatsworth	CA	91311	818-998-2095	998-7807	625
Delta Tau Delta Fraternity 10000 Allisonville Rd *Web:* www.delts.org	Fishers	IN	46038	317-284-0203	284-0214	48-16
Delta Technical College 6550D Interstate Blvd *TF:* 866-733-6652 ■ *Web:* www.deltatechnicalcollege.com	Horn Lake	MS	38637	662-280-1443		167-3
Delta Technology Corp 1223 Valentine Ave SE *Web:* www.hvacdelta.com	Pacific	WA	98047	253-863-8415		189-10
Delta Theta Phi 225 Hillsborough St Ste 432 *TF:* 800-783-2600 ■ *Web:* deltathetaphi.org	Raleigh	NC	27603	800-783-2600		48-16
Delta Tour & Travel Services Inc 3360 Flair Dr Ste 102 *Web:* deltatours.com	El Monte	CA	91731	626-300-0033		760
Delta Training Partners Inc 4020 Oleander Dr *Web:* deltatraining.com	Wilmington	NC	28403	910-790-1985		463
Delta Transformers Inc 1311-A Rue Ampere *Web:* www.delta.xfo.com	Boucherville	QC	J4B5Z5	450-449-9774		767
Delta Unit Arkansas Department of Corrections 880 E Gaines *TF:* 800-482-1127 ■ *Web:* adc.arkansas.gov	Dermott	AR	71638	870-538-2000	538-2027	213
Delta Upsilon International Fraternity 8705 Founders Rd *Web:* www.deltau.org	Indianapolis	IN	46268	317-875-8900	876-1629	48-16
Delta V Instruments Inc 1870 Firman Dr *Web:* www.delta-v.com	Richardson	TX	75081	972-644-6501		625
Delta Waterfowl PO Box 3128 *TF:* 888-987-3695 ■ *Web:* deltawaterfowl.org	Bismarck	ND	58502	701-222-8857		48-3
Delta Western Inc 420 L St Ste 101 *TF:* 800-478-2688 ■ *Web:* deltawestern.com	Anchorage	AK	99501	907-276-2688		316
Delta World Tire Co 203 Guilbeau Rd **Fax Area Code:* 504 ■ *Web:* www.deltaworldtire.com	LaFayette	LA	70506	337-984-3098	822-6966*	54
Delta Zeta Sorority 202 E Church St *Web:* www.deltazeta.org	Oxford	OH	45056	513-523-7597	523-1921	48-16
Deltagen Inc 1900 S Norfolk St Ste 105 *Web:* www.deltagen.com	San Mateo	CA	94403	650-345-7600		178-10
Delta-Montrose Electric Assn 11925 6300 Rd *TF:* 877-687-3632 ■ *Web:* www.dmea.com	Montrose	CO	81401	877-687-3632		245
DeltaOne Software Inc 2841-G Saturn St *Web:* d1sw.com	Brea	CA	92821	714-528-7226	528-7236	178-1
DeltaSoft Inc 624 Courtyard Dr *Web:* www.deltasoftinc.com	Hillsborough	NJ	08844	908-595-9777		177
Delta-T Inc 8323 Loch Lomond Dr *TF:* 800-928-5828 ■ *Web:* www.deltat.com	Pico Rivera	CA	90660	310-355-0355		612
DeltaTRAK Inc PO Box 398 *TF:* 800-962-6776 ■ *Web:* www.deltatrak.com	Pleasanton	CA	94566	925-249-2250	249-2251	202
Delta-Waseca 1400 2nd St SE *Web:* deltawaseca.com	Waseca	MN	56093	507-835-1172	835-1174	516
Deltawrx 21700 Oxnard St Ste 530 *Web:* www.deltawrx.com	Woodland Hills	CA	91367	818-227-9300		194
Deltec Asset Management LLC 623 Fifth Ave 28th Fl *Web:* www.deltec-ny.com	New York	NY	10022	212-546-6200		401
Deltec Homes Inc 69 Bingham Rd *TF:* 800-642-2508 ■ *Web:* www.deltechomes.com	Asheville	NC	28806	800-642-2508		186
Deltec Inc 4230 Grissom Dr *Web:* www.deltec-inc.com	Batavia	OH	45103	513-732-0800	732-0806	482
Del-Tec Packaging 4020 Pelham Ct PO Box 6879 *Web:* del-tec.com	Greenville	SC	29606	864-288-7390	288-7237	344
Deltech Corp 11911 Scenic Hwy *Web:* www.deltechcorp.com	Baton Rouge	LA	70807	225-775-0150	358-3149	605-1
Del-Ton Inc 330 Aviation Pkwy *Web:* www.del-ton.com	Elizabethtown	NC	28337	910-645-2172	645-2244	711
Deltona Corp 8014 SW 135th St Rd *Web:* www.deltona.com	Ocala	FL	34473	352-347-2322		653
Deltrol Corp 2740 S 20th St *Web:* deltrol.com	Milwaukee	WI	53215	414-671-6800		246
Deltrol Fluid Products 3001 Grant Ave *TF:* 800-477-9772 ■ *Web:* deltrolfluid.com	Bellwood	IL	60104	708-547-0500	547-6881	790
Del-tron Precision Inc 5 Trowbridge Dr *TF:* 800-245-5013 ■ *Web:* deltron.com	Bethel	CT	06801	203-778-2727		75
Deltronic Corp 3900 W Segerstrom Ave *TF:* 800-451-6922 ■ *Web:* www.deltronic.com	Santa Ana	CA	92704	714-545-5800	545-9548	493
Deltronic Crystal Industries Inc 64 Harding Ave *Web:* www.deltroniccrystal.com	Dover	NJ	07801	973-328-7000		544
Deluca's Restaurant 2006 W Willow St *Web:* delucaspizza.com	Lansing	MI	48917	517-487-6087		671
Delucchi Plus 1750 Pennsylvania Ave NW Ste 200 *Web:* www.delucchiplus.com	Washington	DC	20006	202-349-4000		5
Deluxe Building Systems Inc 499 W 3rd St *TF:* 800-843-7372 ■ *Web:* www.deluxemodular.com	Berwick	PA	18603	570-752-5914	752-1525	106
Deluxe Corp 3680 Victoria St N *NYSE: DLX* ■ *TF:* 800-328-0304 ■ *Web:* www.deluxe.com	Shoreview	MN	55126	651-483-7111		360-3
Deluxe Foods of Aptos Inc 783 Rio Del Mar Blvd Ste 39 *Web:* deluxefoodsofaptos.com	Aptos	CA	95003	831-688-7442		345
Deluxe Inn Odessa Hotel 1518 S Grant Ave *Web:* deluxeinnodessa.com	Odessa	TX	79761	432-333-1486		379
Deluxe Plastics Inc 220 Industrial Ave *Web:* www.deluxeplastics.com	Clintonville	WI	54929	715-823-4200		596
Deluxe Stitcher Company Inc 3747 Acorn Ln *TF:* 800-634-0810 ■ *Web:* deluxestitcher.com	Franklin Park	IL	60131	847-455-4400		757

Phone | Fax | Class

Delva Tool & Machine Corp
1603 Industrial Hwy .... Cinnaminson NJ 08077 856-786-8700 786-8708 757
Web: www.delvatool.com

Delve Group Inc, The
12 E 49th St 11th Fl .... New York NY 10017 212-255-3870 463
Web: sustenagroup.com

Delvinia Inc 370 King St W 5th Fl .... Toronto ON M5V1J9 416-364-1455 225
Web: www.delvinia.com

Delviom LLC 44790 Maynard Sq Ste 280 .... Ashburn VA 20147 703-953-2535 177
Web: delviom.com

Delware
State Police
1441 N DuPont Hwy PO Box 430 .... Dover DE 19903 302-739-5901 339-8
Web: dsp.delaware.gov

Delyse Inc 505 Reactor Way .... Reno NV 89502 775-857-1811 296-9
TF: 800-441-6887 ■ *Web:* delyse.com

Delzer Lithograph Co 510 S West Ave .... Waukesha WI 53186 262-522-2600 627
Web: www.rightbydelzer.com

DEMA (Diving Equipment & Marketing Assn)
3750 Convoy St Ste 310 .... San Diego CA 92111 858-616-6408 616-6495 49-4
TF: 800-862-3483 ■ *Web:* www.dema.org
Department of Emergency & Military Affairs, The
5636 E McDowell Rd .... Phoenix AZ 85008 602-267-2700 339-3
Web: dema.az.gov

Dema Engineering Co
10020 Big Bend Blvd .... Saint Louis MO 63122 314-966-3533 965-8319 789
TF: 800-325-3362 ■ *Web:* www.demaeng.com

Demae Japanese Restaurant
82 W Center St .... Provo UT 84601 801-374-0306 671
Web: www.demae-japanese.com

Demag Cranes & Components
29201 Aurora Rd .... Cleveland OH 44139 440-248-2400 248-3874 190
Web: www.demagcranes.com

Demakes Enterprises Inc 37 Waterhill St .... Lynn MA 01905 781-595-1557 595-7523 473
Web: oldneighborhoodfoods.com

Demanche Mcchristian LLC 49 W Main St .... Avon CT 06001 860-674-8230 41
Web: demc-law.com

Demand Metric 463 King St .... London ON N6B1S8 519-495-9619 400
TF: 866-947-7744 ■ *Web:* www.demandmetric.com

Demand Planning LLC
10g Roessler Rd Ste 508 .... Woburn MA 01801 781-995-0685 193
Web: demandplanning.net

Demar Direct Inc 1133 N Ridge Ave .... Lombard IL 60148 630-873-1000 873-1199 5
Web: demardirect.com

Demarest Lloyd State Park
115 Barneys Joy Rd .... Dartmouth MA 02748 508-636-3298 565
Web: www.mass.gov

DeMaria Building Company Inc
3031 W Grand Blvd Ste 624 .... Detroit MI 48202 313-870-2800 870-2810 186
Web: www.demariabuild.com

Demars Financial Group LLC
104 S Freya Ste 218 Lilac Flag .... Spokane WA 99202 509-536-9556 232-6604 690
TF: 800-846-8520 ■ *Web:* demarsfinancial.com

Dematic 507 Plymouth Ave NE .... Grand Rapids MI 49505 877-725-7500 913-7701* 470
**Fax Area Code:* 616 ■ *TF:* 877-725-7500 ■ *Web:* www.dematic.com

DeMatteo Research LLC
510 Madison Ave .... New York NY 10022 212-833-9900 690
Web: www.dmllc.com

DEMCO (Dixie Electric Membership Corp)
PO Box 15659 .... Baton Rouge LA 70895 225-261-1221 245
TF: 800-262-0221 ■ *Web:* demco.org

DEMCO (Dethmers Manufacturing Co)
4010 320th St .... Boyden IA 51234 712-725-2311 725-2380 763
TF: 800-543-3626 ■ *Web:* www.demco-products.com

Demco Electronics Inc
10516 Grevillea Ave .... Inglewood CA 90304 310-677-0801 674-5445 425
Web: www.demcoelectronics.com

Demco Inc 4010 Forest Run Rd .... Madison WI 53704 608-241-1201 241-1799 560
TF: 800-356-1200 ■ *Web:* www.demco.com

Demco Manufacturing Inc
1121 N Temple Dr .... Diboll TX 75941 936-829-4771 454
Web: www.demco-mfg.com

Demdaco 5000 W 134th St .... Leawood KS 66209 913-402-6800 362
TF: 888-336-3226 ■ *Web:* www.demdaco.com

Demello Mcauley Mcreynolds & Holland LLP
351 G St .... Eureka CA 95501 707-445-0871 445-3521 2
Web: www.dmmh-cpa.com

Dement Askew LLP
333 Fayetteville St Ste 1513 .... Raleigh NC 27601 919-833-5555 832-8287 41
Web: dementaskew.com

Dement Construction Co PO Box 1812 .... Jackson TN 38302 731-424-6306 424-5308 188-4
Web: www.dementconstruction.com

Demeo LLP 200 State St .... Boston MA 02109 617-263-2600 41
Web: demeollp.com

DeMesy & Company Ltd
4514 Cole Ave Ste 808 .... Dallas TX 75205 214-855-8777 871-6777 791
TF: 800-635-9006 ■ *Web:* www.demesy.com

Demeter Advisory Group LLC
220 Halleck St Ste 220 .... San Francisco CA 94129 415-632-4400 690
Web: demetergroup.net

Demetrio's 4410 S Tamiami Trl .... Sarasota FL 34231 941-922-1585 671
Web: www.demetriospizzeria.com

Demetrius J. Karos Ltd
1 Old Frankfort Way .... Frankfort IL 60423 815-806-9393 41
Web: karos-law.com

Deming Malone Livesay & Ostroff (DMLO)
9300 Shelbyville Rd Ste 1100 .... Louisville KY 40222 502-426-9660 425-0883 2
Web: www.dmlo.com

Demings Val (Rep D - FL)
217 Cannon House Office Bldg .... Washington DC 20515 202-225-2176 342-2
Web: demings.house.gov

Demiurge Studios 130 Prospect St .... Cambridge MA 02139 617-354-7772 354-7277 177
Web: demiurgestudios.com

Demler Egg Ranch 1455 N Warren Rd .... San Jacinto CA 92582 951-654-8166 10-8

Demmer Corp
1600 N Larch St PO Box 12030 .... Lansing MI 48906 517-321-3600 321-7449 757
Web: www.demmercorp.com

Demo's 2501 N St Mary's St .... San Antonio TX 78212 210-732-7777 671
Web: www.demosgreekfood.com

Democracy 21 1825 I St NW .... Washington DC 20006 202-429-2008 48-7
Web: www.democracy21.org

Democrat & Chronicle
55 Exchange Blvd .... Rochester NY 14614 585-232-7100 532-2
TF: 800-790-9565 ■ *Web:* www.democratandchronicle.com

Democrat Co, The 1226 Ave H .... Fort Madison IA 52627 319-372-6421 532-2
Web: www.dailydem.com

Democrat Printing & Lithographing Company Inc
6401 Lindsey Rd .... Little Rock AR 72206 800-622-2216 907-7953* 344
**Fax Area Code:* 501 ■ *TF:* 800-622-2216 ■ *Web:* democratprinting.com

Democratic Congressional Campaign Committee (DCCC)
430 S Capitol St SE .... Washington DC 20003 202-863-1500 48-7
Web: dccc.org

Democratic Governors Assn (DGA)
1225 Eye St NW Ste 1100 .... Washington DC 20005 202-772-5600 772-5602 48-7
Web: democraticgovernors.org

Democratic National Committee
430 S Capitol St SE .... Washington DC 20003 202-863-8000 616
Web: democrats.org

Democratic Party of Arkansas
1300 W Capitol Ave .... Little Rock AR 72201 501-374-2361 616-1
Web: www.arkdems.org

Democratic Party of Virginia
919 E Main St Ste 2050 .... Richmond VA 23219 804-644-1966 343-3642 616-1
Web: www.vademocrats.org

Democratic Party of Wisconsin, The
PO Box 1686 Ste 203 .... Madison WI 53703 608-255-5172 255-8919 616-1
Web: www.wisdems.org

Democratic Senatorial Campaign Committee (DSCC)
120 Maryland Ave NE .... Washington DC 20002 202-224-2447 969-0354 48-7
Web: www.dscc.org

Democratic Socialists of America
75 Maiden Ln Ste 702 .... New York NY 10038 212-727-8610 616
Web: www.dsausa.org

DeMolay Intl
10200 NW Ambassabor Dr .... Kansas City MO 64153 816-891-8333 891-9062 48-15
TF: 800-336-6529 ■ *Web:* demolay.org

DeMontrond 888 I- 45 S .... Conroe TX 77304 281-443-2500 57
TF: 888-843-6583 ■ *Web:* www.demontrond.com

Demos Medical Publishing Inc
11 W 42nd St 15th Fl .... New York NY 10036 212-683-0072 637-2
TF: 800-532-8663 ■ *Web:* www.demosmedical.com

Demott & Smith CPAS PC
100 White Spruce Blvd .... Rochester NY 14623 585-272-9880 2
Web: demottsmith.com

DeMoulas Super Markets Inc 875 E St .... Tewksbury MA 01876 978-851-8000 345
Web: www.shopmarketbasket.com

DeMoulin Bros & Company Inc
1025 S Fourth St .... Greenville IL 62246 618-664-2000 664-1647 155-19
TF: 800-228-8134 ■ *Web:* www.demoulin.com

Dempewolf Ford Inc 2530 Us 41 N .... Henderson KY 42420 270-827-3566 57
TF: 888-484-8803 ■ *Web:* www.hendersonfordky.com

Dempsey Corp 47 Davies Ave .... Toronto ON M4M2A9 416-461-0844 791
Web: www.dempseycorporation.com

Dempsey Insurance Agency Inc
145 Railroad Ave .... Norwood MA 02062 781-762-0042 769-7730 390
Web: www.demsure.com

Dempsey, Dempsey & Sheehan
387 Springfield Ave .... Summit NJ 07901 908-277-0388 41
Web: ddsnjlaw.com

Dempton Groupe Conseil
1255 University St Ste 450 .... Montreal QC H3B3B6 514-657-3517 631
Web: www.dempton.com

Demptos Napa Cooperage
1050 Soscol Ferry Rd .... Napa CA 94558 707-257-2628 200
Web: www.demptos.fr

Demsey Manufacturing Company Inc
78 New Wood Rd .... Watertown CT 06795 860-274-6209 274-0186 482
Web: www.demseymfg.com

Den Hartog Industries Inc
4010 Hospers Dr S PO Box 425 .... Hospers IA 51238 712-752-8432 752-8222 608
TF: 800-342-3408 ■ *Web:* www.denhartogindustries.com

Denali Advance Integration (DAI)
17735 NE 65th St Ste 130 .... Redmond WA 98052 425-885-4000 180
TF: 877-467-8008 ■ *Web:* www.denaliai.com

Denali Borough PO Box 480 .... Healy AK 99743 907-683-1330 683-1340 338
Web: www.denaliborough.org

Denali Commission 510 L St Ste 410 .... Anchorage AK 99501 907-271-1414 271-1415 340-20
TF: 888-480-4321 ■ *Web:* www.denali.gov

Denali Industrial Supply Inc
1499 Van Horn Rd .... Fairbanks AK 99701 907-452-4524 351
TF: 800-478-2658 ■ *Web:* denali-industrial.com

Denali National Park & Preserve
PO Box 9 .... Denali Park AK 99755 907-683-9532 564
Web: www.nps.gov

Denali State Park 7278 E Bogard Rd .... Wasilla AK 99654 907-745-3975 745-0938 565
Web: dnr.alaska.gov

Denark Construction Inc
1635 Western Ave .... Knoxville TN 37921 865-637-1925 186
Web: denark.com

Denbury Resources Inc 5320 Legacy Dr .... Plano TX 75024 972-673-2000 673-2430 536
NYSE: DNR ■ *TF:* 800-348-9030 ■ *Web:* www.denbury.com

Denco Manufacturing Inc
2300 S 179th St .... New Berlin WI 53146 262-782-2322 454
Web: www.dencomfg.com

DenCol 4630 Washington St .... Denver CO 80216 303-295-1683 295-1689 492
TF: 800-279-1683 ■ *Web:* www.dencol.com

Den-Con Tool Co 5354 S I-35 .... Oklahoma City OK 73129 405-670-5942 672-5884 358
Web: www.dencon.com

Dendreon Corp 1700 Saturn Way .... Seal Beach CA 90740 877-256-4545 85
OTC: DNDNQ ■ *TF:* 877-256-4545 ■ *Web:* www.dendreon.com

Denham Corp 567 W Shaw Ave Ste C1 .... Fresno CA 93704 559-222-5284 222-1321 260
Web: www.denham.net

Denham Springs Beauty School
923 Florida Ave SE .... Denham Springs LA 70726 225-665-6188 685
TF: 877-711-3501 ■ *Web:* www.dsbeautyschool.org

Denham-Blythe Company Inc
100 Trade St .... Lexington KY 40511 859-255-7405 256
Web: www.denhamblythe.com

Company / Address	City	State	Zip	Phone	Fax	Class
Denier Electric Company Inc 10891 SR- 128 *TF:* 800-676-3282 ■ *Web:* www.denier.com	Harrison	OH	45030	513-738-2641	738-5855	245
Denim Group Ltd 1354 N Loop 1604 E Ste 110 *TF:* 844-572-4400 ■ *Web:* www.denimgroup.com	San Antonio	TX	78232	844-572-4400		177
Deniro Marketing 6777 Embarcadero Dr Ste 3 *Web:* deniromarketing.com	Stockton	CA	95219	209-477-7676		195
Denis CIMAF Inc 211 Rue Notre-Dame *TF:* 877-279-2300 ■ *Web:* www.deniscimaf.com	Roxton Falls	QC	J0H1E0	450-548-7007	548-7008	190
Denise Granville 370 W San Bruno Ave Ste G *TF:* 800-952-1598 ■ *Web:* denisegranville.com	San Bruno	CA	94066	650-952-1599	952-2486	390
Denise Resnik & Associates Inc 717 E Maryland Ave Ste 110	Phoenix	AZ	85014	602-956-8834	957-3159	636
Denison Industries (DI) 22 Fielder Dr *Web:* denisonindustries.com	Denison	TX	75020	903-786-6500	786-6575	308
Denison Parking Inc 320 North Meridian Ste 700 *Web:* www.denisonparking.com	Indianapolis	IN	46204	317-633-4003	655-3101	562
Denison Public Library 300 W Gandy St *Web:* www.cityofdenison.com	Denison	TX	75020	903-465-1797		434-3
Denison University 100 W College St *TF:* 877-336-8648 ■ *Web:* denison.edu	Granville	OH	43023	740-587-6394	587-8321	166
Denison Yacht Sales 1535 SE 17th St Ste 119 *Web:* www.denisonyachtsales.com	Fort Lauderdale	FL	33316	954-763-3971		393
Denker & Butler PLLC 4700 NW 23rd Ste 112 *Web:* www.denkerzuhdi.com	Oklahoma City	OK	73127	405-563-7151		41
Denlea & Carton LLP 2 Westchester Park Dr Ste 410 *Web:* denleacarton.com	White Plains	NY	10604	914-331-0100		41
Denmar Services Inc 605 SW B Ave Ste 2 *Web:* denmarservices.com	Lawton	OK	73501	580-355-8900		463
Denmark 227 Sandy Springs Pl Ste 434 *Web:* www.denmarktheagency.com	Sandy Springs	GA	30328	404-256-3681		7
Embassy 3200 Whitehaven St NW *Web:* usa.um.dk	Washington	DC	20008	202-234-4300	328-1470	257
Denmark Technical College 1126 Solomon Blatt Blvd PO Box 327 *Web:* www.denmarktech.edu	Denmark	SC	29042	803-793-5176	793-5942	800
Den-Mat Corp 2727 Skyway Dr *TF:* 800-433-6628 ■ *Web:* www.denmat.com	Santa Maria	CA	93455	805-922-8491	922-6933	228
Dennen Steel Corp 3033 Fruit Ridge Ave NW *Web:* www.dennensteel.com	Grand Rapids	MI	49544	616-784-2000		480
Denney & Company Chtd 1096 N Eastland Dr Ste 200 *Web:* denneycpa.com	Twin Falls	ID	83301	208-733-3223	733-4200	2
Denning & Company LLC 333 Bush St Ste 2800 *Web:* www.denningandcompany.com	San Francisco	CA	94104	415-399-3939		401
Dennis A. Joiner & Associates 4975 Daru Way *Web:* www.joinertests.com	Fair Oaks	CA	95628	916-967-7795		311
Dennis Carpenter Ford Restoration Parts 4140 Concord Pkwy S *TF:* 800-476-9653 ■ *Web:* dennis-carpenter.com	Concord	NC	28027	704-786-8139	786-8180	247
Dennis Dillon Automotive 2495 S Orchard St *Web:* www.dennisdillon.com	Boise	ID	83705	208-639-0682		57
Dennis K. Burke Inc 284 Eastern Ave *TF:* 800-289-2875 ■ *Web:* www.burkeoil.com	Chelsea	MA	02150	617-884-7800	884-7638	449
Dennis P. Lee & Associates Pc 2433 S 130th Cir Ste 30 *Web:* leelawoffice.com	Omaha	NE	68144	402-334-8055		41
Dennis Paper Co 910 Acorn Dr *Web:* www.dennispaper.com	Nashville	TN	37210	615-883-9010	885-2969	553
Dennis PR Group 41 Crossroads *Web:* www.dennispr.com	West Hartford	CT	06117	860-778-3826		636
Dennis R. Jones Non Profit Management Consulting 868 Cherry Ln *Web:* www.jconsultants.net	Waterville	OH	43566	248-506-3030		463
Dennis Steel Inc 1105 Leander Dr *Web:* www.dennissteel.com	Leander	TX	78641	512-259-4001		492
Dennis Supply Co PO Box 3376 *TF:* 800-352-4618 ■ *Web:* www.dennissupply.com	Sioux City	IA	51102	712-255-7637	255-4913	665
Dennis Uniform Manufacturing Company Inc 135 SE Hawthorne Blvd *TF:* 800-854-6951 ■ *Web:* www.dennisuniform.com	Portland	OR	97214	800-854-6951		155-19
Dennis, Corry, Smith & Dixon LLP 900 Circle 75 Pkwy Ste 1400 *Web:* www.dcplaw.com	Atlanta	GA	30339	404-365-0102	365-0134	428
Dennis, Gartland & Niergarth Management PC 415 Munson Ave *Web:* dgncpa.com	Traverse City	MI	49685	231-946-1722		2
Dennis-Yarmouth Regional School District 296 Stn Ave *Web:* www.dy-regional.k12.ma.us	South Yarmouth	MA	02664	508-398-7600	398-7622	685
Denny's Corp 203 E Main St *NASDAQ: DENN* ■ *TF:* 800-733-6697 ■ *Web:* www.dennys.com	Spartanburg	SC	29319	864-597-8000		670
Denodo Technologies 530 Lytton Ave Ste 301 *Web:* www.denodo.com	Palo Alto	CA	94301	650-566-8833		177
Denooyer Chevrolet Inc 127 Wolf Rd *Web:* www.denooyerchevrolet.com	Albany	NY	12205	518-458-7700		57
DeNOVUS LLC PO Box 755 **Fax Area Code:* 972 ■ *Web:* www.denovus.com	Ennis	TX	75120	214-789-5725	875-3554*	386
Denso Air Systems Michigan Inc 300 Fritz Keiper Blvd *Web:* www.densocorp-na-asmi.com	Battle Creek	MI	49037	269-962-9676	962-4975	60
Denso International America Inc 24777 Denso Dr *Web:* www.denso.com	Southfield	MI	48033	248-350-7500		60
Denso North America Inc 9747 Whithorn Dr *TF:* 888-821-2300 ■ *Web:* www.densona.com	Houston	TX	77095	281-821-3355		146
Dent Clinic 6 711 48 Ave SE *Web:* www.dentclinic.com	Calgary	AB	T2G2A7	403-255-3111		62-4
Dent County 400 N Main St *Web:* www.salemmo.com	Salem	MO	65560	573-729-4144		338
Dent Instruments Inc 925 SW Emkay Dr *Web:* www.dentinstruments.com	Bend	OR	97702	541-388-4774		201
Dent Wizard Intl 4710 Earth City Expy *TF:* 800-336-8949 ■ *Web:* www.dentwizard.com	Bridgeton	MO	63044	800-336-8949		62-4
Dental Assistant Training Ctr 5701 NE Bothell Way Ste 2 *Web:* www.dentalassist.com	Kenmore	WA	98028	425-806-8816		167-3
Dental Care Alliance LLC 6240 Lake Osprey Dr *TF:* 888-876-4531 ■ *Web:* www.dentalcarealliance.net	Sarasota	FL	34240	941-955-3150	914-9684	463
Dental Care Plus Inc 100 Crowne Point Pl *TF:* 888-253-3279 ■ *Web:* www.mydentalcareplus.com	Cincinnati	OH	45241	513-554-1100		391-3
Dental Economics Magazine 1421 S Sheridan Rd *TF:* 800-331-4463 ■ *Web:* www.dentaleconomics.com	Tulsa	OK	74112	800-331-4463		457-16
Dental Health Service 3833 Atlantic Blvd *Web:* www.dentalhealthservices.com	Long Beach	CA	90807	562-595-6000		390
Dental Intelligence Inc 2100 W Pleasant Grove Blvd Ste 400 *TF:* 855-776-2673 ■ *Web:* www.dentalintel.com	Pleasant Grove	UT	84062	855-776-2673		178-1
Dental Lifeline Network 1800 15th St Ste 100 *TF:* 888-471-6334 ■ *Web:* dentallifeline.org	Denver	CO	80202	303-534-5360	534-5290	48-17
Dental Protection Plan Inc 7130 W Greenfield Ave *Web:* www.dentalprotectionplaninc.com	West Allis	WI	53214	414-259-9522		391-3
Dental Systems Inc PO Box 2009 **Fax Area Code:* 281 ■ *TF:* 800-683-2501 ■ *Web:* www.iaplus.com	Baytown	TX	77522	800-683-2501	943-8000*	180
Dental Trade Alliance (DTA) 4350 N Fairfax Dr Ste 220 *Web:* dentaltradealliance.org	Arlington	VA	22203	703-379-7755	931-9429	49-4
DEN-TAL-EZ Group Inc 2 W Liberty Blvd Ste 160 *TF:* 866-383-4636 ■ *Web:* www.dentalez.com	Malvern	PA	19355	610-725-8004	725-9898	228
DentaQuest 12121 N Corporate Pky *TF:* 800-417-7140 ■ *Web:* www.dentaquest.com	Mequon	WI	53092	262-241-7140	241-7401	391-3
DENTCA Inc 357 Van Ness Way Ste 250 *Web:* www.dentca.com	Torrance	CA	90501	424-558-8726	558-8738	228
DenTek Oral Care Inc 307 Excellence Way *TF:* 800-433-6835 ■ *Web:* www.dentek.com	Maryville	TN	37801	800-433-6835		228
Dentists Insurance Co, The 1201 K St 17th Fl **Fax Area Code:* 877 ■ *TF:* 800-733-0633 ■ *Web:* www.tdicinsurance.com	Sacramento	CA	95814	800-733-0633	498-6105*	391-5
Denton Chamber of Commerce 414 W Pkwy St *Web:* www.denton-chamber.org	Denton	TX	76201	940-382-9693	382-0040	139
Denton County 1450 E McKinney *TF:* 800-388-8477 ■ *Web:* dentoncounty.gov	Denton	TX	76209	940-349-2012		338
Denton Hill State Park c/o Lyman Run 454 Lyman Run Rd *Web:* www.dcnr.pa.gov	Galeton	PA	16922	814-435-2115		565
Denton Plastics Inc 18811 NE San Rafael St *TF:* 800-959-9945 ■ *Web:* www.dentonplastics.com	Portland	OR	97230	503-257-9945		596
Denton Record-Chronicle 314 E Hickory St *TF:* 800-275-1722 ■ *Web:* www.dentonrc.com	Denton	TX	76201	940-387-3811	566-6888	532-2
Denton, Navarro, Rocha and Bernal 700 E Harrison Ste 100 *Web:* www.rampage-rgv.com	Harlingen	TX	78550	956-421-4904		445
Dentons Cohen & Grigsby 625 Liberty Ave *Web:* www.cohenlaw.com	Pittsburgh	PA	15222	412-297-4900	209-0672	428
Dentsply International Inc *Tulsa Dental Div* 5100 E Skelly Dr Ste 300 *TF:* 800-662-1202 ■ *Web:* www.dentsplysirona.com	Tulsa	OK	74135	918-493-6598	493-6599	228
Dentsply Sirona 13320 Ballantyne Corporate Pl *TF:* 844-848-0137 ■ *Web:* www.dentsplysirona.com	Charlotte	NC	28277	844-848-0137		477
Dentsu Sports America Inc 32 Avenue of the Americas 24th Fl *Web:* dentsusports.com	New York	NY	10013	212-397-3333	261-4286	4
Dentt Inc 10450 S State St *Web:* www.hammondtoy.com	Sandy	UT	84070	801-561-3821		762
Denver Art Museum 100 W 14th Ave Pkwy *Web:* www.denverartmuseum.org	Denver	CO	80204	720-865-5000	913-0001	520
Denver Athletic Club 1325 Glenarm Pl *Web:* www.denverathleticclub.cc	Denver	CO	80204	303-534-1211		354
Denver Bookbinding Company Inc 1401 W 47th Ave *Web:* denverbook.com	Denver	CO	80211	303-455-5521	455-2677	86
Denver Botanic Gardens 1005 York St *Web:* www.botanicgardens.org	Denver	CO	80206	720-865-3500		97
Denver Broncos 13655 Broncos Pkwy *Web:* www.denverbroncos.com	Englewood	CO	80112	303-649-9000		715-3
Denver Center for the Performing Arts 1101 13th St *TF:* 800-641-1222 ■ *Web:* www.denvercenter.org	Denver	CO	80204	303-893-4000	595-9634	572
Denver City & County 201 W Colfax Ave 1st Fl *Web:* www.denvergov.org	Denver	CO	80202	720-865-8400		338
Denver Coliseum 4600 Humboldt St *Web:* www.denvercoliseum.com	Denver	CO	80216	720-865-2475		720
Denver Commercial Builders Inc (DCB) 909 E 62nd Ave *Web:* www.dcb1.com	Denver	CO	80216	303-287-5525	287-3697	186

Phone | Fax | Class

Denver Cyber Security
8100 E Union Ave Ste 2008 .... Denver CO 80237 303-997-5506 196
Web: www.denvercybersecurity.com

Denver Film Society 1510 York 3rd Fl .... Denver CO 80206 303-595-3456 282
Web: www.denverfilm.org

Denver Fire Department Federal Credit Union (DFDFCU)
12 Lakeside Ln .... Denver CO 80212 303-228-5300 228-5333 219
TF: 866-880-7770 ■ *Web:* www.dfdfcu.com

Denver Firefighters Museum
1326 Tremont Pl .... Denver CO 80204 303-892-1436 520
Web: www.denverfirefightersmuseum.org

Denver Gold Group Inc
1675 Larimer St Ste 680 .... Denver CO 80202 303-825-3368 410
Web: denvergold.org

Denver Health Medical Ctr (DHMC)
777 Bannock St .... Denver CO 80204 303-436-6000 374-3
Web: www.denverhealth.org

Denver Hospice, The
501 S Cherry St Ste 700 .... Denver CO 80246 303-321-2828 321-7171 371
Web: thedenverhospice.org

Denver International Airport
8500 Pena Blvd .... Denver CO 80249 303-342-2000 27
TF: 800-247-2336 ■ *Web:* www.flydenver.com

Denver Investment Advisors LLC
Republic Plaza 370 17th St Ste 5000 .... Denver CO 80202 303-312-5000 401
Web: denvest.com

Denver Metro Chamber of Commerce
1445 Market St .... Denver CO 80202 303-534-8500 534-3200 139
Web: denverchamber.org

Denver Metro Convention & Visitors Bureau
1555 California St Ste 300 .... Denver CO 80202 303-892-1112 206
TF: 800-480-2010 ■ *Web:* www.denver.org

Denver Museum of Miniatures Dolls & Toys
1880 Gaylord St .... Denver CO 80206 303-322-1053 520
Web: www.dmmdt.org

Denver Museum of Nature & Science
2001 Colorado Blvd .... Denver CO 80205 303-370-6000 520
Web: www.dmns.org

Denver Newspaper Agency
101 W Colfax Ave .... Denver CO 80202 303-954-1010 637-8
TF: 800-336-7678 ■ *Web:* www.denverpost.com

Denver Performing Arts Complex
1400 Curtis St .... Denver CO 80204 720-865-4220 865-4247 572
Web: www.artscomplex.com

Denver Public Library
10 W 14th Ave Pkwy .... Denver CO 80204 720-865-1111 434-3
Web: www.denverlibrary.org

Denver Public Schools 900 Grant St .... Denver CO 80203 720-423-3200 685
Web: www.dpsk12.org

Denver Rescue Mission 6100 Smith Rd .... Denver CO 80216 303-297-1815 295-1566 352
Web: www.denverrescuemission.org

Denver School of Nursing 1401 19th St .... Denver CO 80202 303-292-0015 974-0290* 685
**Fax Area Code:* 720 ■ *TF:* 888-479-5550 ■ *Web:* www.denvercollegeofnursing.edu

Denver Seminary 6399 S Santa Fe Dr .... Littleton CO 80120 303-761-2482 761-8060 167-3
TF: 800-922-3040 ■ *Web:* denverseminary.edu

Denver Veterans Affairs Medical Ctr
1055 Clermont St .... Denver CO 80220 303-399-8020 393-2861 374-8
TF: 888-336-8262 ■ *Web:* www.denver.va.gov

Denver Wholesale Florists Co
4800 Dahlia St .... Denver CO 80216 303-399-0970 376-3123 293
TF: 800-829-8280 ■ *Web:* www.dwfwholesale.com

Denver Women's Correctional Facility (DWCF)
3600 Havana St PO Box 392005 .... Denver CO 80239 303-371-4804 307-2514 213
Web: www.colorado.gov

Denver Zoo 2300 Steele St .... Denver CO 80205 720-337-1400 823
Web: denverzoo.org

Denver7 123 E Speer Blvd .... Denver CO 80203 303-832-7777 832-0119 741-39
TF: 800-824-3463 ■ *Web:* www.thedenverchannel.com

DEP (Detroit Engineered Products)
850 E Long Lake Rd .... Troy MI 48085 248-269-7130 180
Web: www.depusa.com

DePalma Hotel Corp
2000 E Lamar Blvd Ste 600 .... Arlington TX 76006 817-557-1811 557-4333 379
Web: www.depalmahotels.com

DePalma's Italian Cafe
2300 University Blvd .... Tuscaloosa AL 35401 205-759-1879 671
Web: depalmasdowntown.com

Department of Agriculture (USDA)
1400 Independence Ave SW .... Washington DC 20250 202-708-8177 340-1
TF: 844-433-2774 ■ *Web:* www.usda.gov

Department of Anthropology
211 Lafferty Hall .... Lexington KY 40506 859-257-2710 323-1968 520
Web: anthropology.as.uky.edu

Department of Commerce
1401 Constitution Ave NW Hoover Bldg .... Washington DC 20230 202-482-4883 482-5168 340-2
Web: www.commerce.gov

Department of Defense
1400 Defense Pentagon .... Washington DC 20301 703-571-3343 340-3
Web: www.defense.gov

Department of Education
Inspector General's Fraud & Abuse Hotline
400 Maryland Ave SW .... Washington DC 20202 800-647-8733 340-8
TF: 800-647-8733 ■ *Web:* www.ed.gov

Department of Education Regional Offices
Region 2
Financial Sq 32 Old Slip 25th Fl .... New York NY 10005 646-428-3906 340-8
Web: www.ed.gov
Region 3 100 Penn Sq E Ste 505 .... Philadelphia PA 19107 215-656-6010 656-6020 340-8
Web: www.ed.gov
Region 4 61 Forsyth St SW Ste 19T40 .... Atlanta GA 30303 404-974-9450 340-8
Web: www.ed.gov
Region 5 500 W Madison St Ste 1427 .... Chicago IL 60661 312-730-1700 730-1704 340-8
Web: www.ed.gov
Region 8
1244 Speer Blvd
Cesar E Chavez Memorial Bldg Ste 310 .... Denver CO 80204 303-844-3544 844-2524 340-8
Web: www.ed.gov

Department of Environmental Quality
Environmental Quality Dept
707 N Robinson .... Oklahoma City OK 73102 405-702-1000 702-1001 339-37
TF: 800-869-1400 ■ *Web:* www.deq.ok.gov

Department of Health & Human Services (HHS)
330 Independence Ave SW .... Washington DC 20201 202-619-0150 340-10
TF: 877-696-6775 ■ *Web:* www.hhs.gov

Department of Health & Human Services
Office on Women's Health
200 Independence Ave SW Rm 712E .... Washington DC 20201 202-690-7650 205-2631 340-10
Web: www.womenshealth.gov

Department of Health & Human Services Regional Offices
Region 2 26 Federal Plz Rm 4114 .... New York NY 10278 212-264-2890 264-4881 340-10
Web: www.acf.hhs.gov
Region 4 61 Forsyth St SW Ste 5M60 .... Atlanta GA 30303 404-562-7889 562-7899 340-10
Web: www.hhs.gov
Region 5 233 N Michigan Ave Ste 400 .... Chicago IL 60601 312-353-4237 353-2204 340-10
Web: www.acf.hhs.gov
Region 6 1301 Young St Ste 1124 .... Dallas TX 75202 214-767-3879 767-3209 340-10
Web: www.hhs.gov
Region 7 601 E 12th St .... Kansas City MO 64106 816-426-2821 426-2178 340-10
TF: 800-447-8477 ■ *Web:* www.hhs.gov

Department of Homeland Security (DHS)
245 Murray Ln SW .... Washington DC 20528 202-981-6100 235-0443* 340-11
**Fax Area Code:* 703 ■ *Web:* www.dhs.gov

Department of Homeland Security
Ready Campaign 500 C St SW .... Washington DC 20472 800-621-3362 340-11
TF: 800-621-3362 ■ *Web:* www.ready.gov

Department of Housing & Urban Development
Public Affairs Office
451 Seventh St SW .... Washington DC 20410 202-708-0980 340-12
Web: www.hud.gov

Department of Housing & Urban Development Regional Offices
Boston Regional Office
10 Causeway St Third Fl
Thomas P O'Neill Jr Federal Bldg .... Boston MA 02222 617-994-8200 565-6558 340-12
TF: 800-225-5342 ■ *Web:* www.hud.gov
Chicago Regional Office
77 W Jackson Blvd
Ralph Metcalfe Federal Bldg .... Chicago IL 60604 312-353-6236 913-8293 340-12
Web: www.hud.gov
Mid-Atlantic Region
100 Penn Sq E .... Philadelphia PA 19107 215-656-0500 656-3445 340-12
Web: www.hud.gov
New York City Regional Office
26 Federal Plz Ste 3541 .... New York NY 10278 212-264-8000 264-0246 340-12
TF: 800-496-4294 ■ *Web:* www.hud.gov
Rocky Mountain Region
1670 Broadway 25th Fl .... Denver CO 80202 303-672-5440 340-12
TF: 800-955-2232 ■ *Web:* www.hud.gov
Southeast/Caribbean Region
5 Points Plz 40 Marietta St 17th Fl .... Atlanta GA 30303 404-331-5136 730-2392 340-12
Web: www.hud.gov
Southwest Region
801 N Cherry St Unit 45 Ste 2500 .... Fort Worth TX 76102 817-978-5965 978-5569 340-12
Web: www.hud.gov

Department of Justice (DOJ)
950 Pennsylvania Ave NW .... Washington DC 20530 202-514-2007 514-5331 340-14
Web: www.justice.gov

Department of Justice
Community Relations Service
600 E St NW .... Washington DC 20004 202-514-3934 340-14
Web: www.justice.gov
Criminal Div 601 D St NW .... Washington DC 20530 202-616-2774 340-14
Web: www.justice.gov
Office of Information & Privacy
1425 New York Ave NW Ste 11050 .... Washington DC 20530 202-514-3642 514-1009 340-14
Web: www.justice.gov

Department of Justice Antitrust Div Regional Office
Atlanta Field Office
75 Ted Turner Dr SW Federal Bldg Ste 600 ...... Atlanta GA 30303 404-331-7100 331-7110 340-14
Web: www.justice.gov
Chicago Field Office
209 S LaSalle St Ste 600 .... Chicago IL 60604 312-984-7200 353-1046 340-14
Web: www.justice.gov
Cleveland Field Office
55 Erieview Plz Ste 700 .... Cleveland OH 44114 216-522-4070 522-8332 340-14
Web: www.justice.gov
Dallas Field Office
1601 Elm St Ste 4950 .... Dallas TX 75201 214-880-9401 353-8856* 340-14
**Fax Area Code:* 202 ■ *Web:* www.justice.gov
New York Field Office
26 Federal Plz Rm 3630 .... New York NY 10278 202-514-2000 264-0678* 340-14
**Fax Area Code:* 212 ■ *Web:* www.justice.gov
San Francisco Field Office
450 Golden Gate Ave Rm 10-0101
PO Box 36046 .... San Francisco CA 94102 415-436-6660 436-6687 340-14
Web: www.justice.gov

Department of Labor (DOL)
200 Constitution Ave NW .... Washington DC 20210 866-487-2365 340-15
TF: 866-487-2365 ■ *Web:* www.dol.gov
Job Corps
200 Constitution Ave NW Ste N4463 .... Washington DC 20210 202-693-3000 693-2767 340-15
TF: 800-733-5627 ■ *Web:* www.jobcorps.gov
Women's Bureau
200 Constitution Ave NW Rm S-3002 ...... Washington DC 20210 202-693-6710 850-4706* 340-15
**Fax Area Code:* 972 ■ *Web:* www.dol.gov

Department of Labor Regional Offices
Region 1 - Boston
JFK Federal Bldg Rm E-260 .... Boston MA 02203 857-264-4600 340-15
TF: 800-347-8029 ■ *Web:* www.dol.gov
Region 2 - New York
201 Varick St Rm 983 .... New York NY 10014 646-264-3650 340-15
Web: www.dol.gov
Region 3 - Philadelphia
170 S Independence Mall W Curtis Ctr
Ste 715 E .... Philadelphia PA 19106 215-861-4860 861-4867 340-15
Web: www.dol.gov

Name / Address	City	State	Zip	Phone	Fax	Class
Region 3 Atlanta						
400 W Bay St Rm 63A	Jacksonville	FL	32202	904-366-0100	351-0560	340-15
Web: www.dol.gov						
Region 6 Dallas						
525 S Griffin St Rm 407 Federal Bldg	Dallas	TX	75202	972-850-2409	850-2401	340-15
Web: www.dol.gov						
Region 8 - Denver						
1999 Broadway Ste 1620	Denver	CO	80202	303-844-1286	844-1283	340-15
TF: 800-827-5335 ■ *Web:* www.dol.gov						
Department of Management Services						
325 Conover Dr	Franklin	OH	45005	937-704-0357	704-0373	463
Web: www.supequipment.com						
Department of Natural Resources						
550 W Seventh Ave Ste 1360	Anchorage	AK	99501	907-269-8600	269-8904	565
Web: www.dnr.alaska.gov						
Department of Natural resources						
Donnelley/DePue State Fish & Wildlife Areas						
1001 W 4th St	DePue	IL	61322	815-447-2353		565
Web: www2.illinois.gov						
Department of State 2201 C St NW	Washington	DC	20520	202-647-4000		340-16
Web: www.state.gov						
Department of the Air Force						
1670 Air Force Pentagon	Washington	DC	20330	703-695-9664	693-9601	340-4
Web: www.af.mil						
Department of the Air Force						
North American Aerospace Defense Command						
250 Vandenberg St Ste B-016	Peterson AFB	CO	80914	719-554-6889	554-3165	340-4
Web: www.norad.mil						
Department of the Army						
1500 Army Pentagon	Washington	DC	20310	703-697-5131		340-5
Web: www.army.mil						
Department of the Army						
U.S. Army Center of Military History						
102 4th Ave Bldg 35	Fort McNair	DC	20319	202-685-2727	512-2104	340-5
Web: www.history.army.mil						
Department of the Interior (DOI)						
1849 C St NW	Washington	DC	20240	202-208-3100		340-13
Web: www.doi.gov						
Department of the Navy						
1000 Navy Pentagon	Washington	DC	20350	202-685-0412		340-6
Web: www.secnav.navy.mil						
Department of the Navy						
Bureau of Medicine & Surgery						
2300 E St NW	Washington	DC	20372	301-402-8878		340-6
Web: www.nlm.nih.gov						
Judge Advocate General's Corps						
1322 Patterson Ave Ste 3000	Washington Navy Yard	DC	20374	202-685-5275		340-6
Web: www.jag.navy.mil						
Office of Naval Intelligence						
4251 Suitland Rd	Washington	DC	20395	301-669-4002		340-6
Web: www.oni.navy.mil						
Department of Transportation (DOT)						
1200 New Jersey Ave SE	Washington	DC	20590	202-366-4000		340-17
TF: 800-877-8339 ■ *Web:* www.transportation.gov						
Department of Veterans Affairs (VA)						
810 Vermont Ave NW	Washington	DC	20420	202-461-7600		340-19
Web: www.va.gov						
Department of Veterans Affairs (PTSD)						
National Center for Post-Traumatic Stress Disorder						
215 N Main St	White River Junction	VT	05009	802-296-5132	296-5135	668
Web: www.ptsd.va.gov						
Depaul Industries						
4950 NE Martin Luther King Junior Blvd	Portland	OR	97211	503-281-1289		260
Web: www.depaulindustries.com						
DePaul University						
1 E Jackson Blvd Ste 9100	Chicago	IL	60604	312-362-8300	362-5749	166
Web: www.depaul.edu						
DePaul University College of Law						
25 E Jackson Blvd	Chicago	IL	60604	312-362-8701	362-5280	167-1
Web: www.law.depaul.edu						
DePaul University Library						
2350 N Kenmore Ave	Chicago	IL	60614	312-362-8433		434-6
Web: www.library.depaul.edu						
DePauw University						
204 E Seminary St	Greencastle	IN	46135	765-658-4006	658-4007	166
TF: 800-447-2495 ■ *Web:* www.depauw.edu						
DePelchin Children's Ctr						
4950 Memorial Dr	Houston	TX	77007	713-730-2335	802-3801	48-6
TF: 888-730-2335 ■ *Web:* www.depelchin.org						
Dependable Bagging Company Inc						
264 Hord St	New Orleans	LA	70123	504-733-8650	734-5762	183
TF: 800-224-4464 ■ *Web:* www.dependablebagging.com						
Dependable Cleaners 320 Quincy Ave	Quincy	MA	02169	617-471-1900		426
Web: www.dependablecleaners.com						
Dependable Highway Express Inc						
2440 S 48th Ave	Phoenix	AZ	85043	602-278-4401	278-4473	449
TF: 800-472-2037 ■ *Web:* www.godependable.com						
Dependable Nurses Inc (DNI)						
1121 N El Dorado Pl Ste 300	Tucson	AZ	85715	520-795-1290	886-9604	363
Web: www.dependablehealth.com						
Dependable Pattern Works Inc						
737 SE Market St	Portland	OR	97214	503-239-5464	239-8831	567
Web: www.dpwcorp.com						
Depersico Creative						
560 Grubbs Mill Rd	West Chester	PA	19380	484-454-3801		344
Web: depersico.com						
Depobook Reporting Services						
1600 G St Ste 101	Modesto	CA	95354	209-544-6466	544-6566	445
TF: 800-830-8885 ■ *Web:* www.depobook.com						
DepoMed Inc						
100 S Saunders Rd Ste 300	Lake Forest	IL	60045	224-419-7106		85
NASDAQ: DEPO ■ *Web:* www.assertiotx.com						
Deposition Sciences Inc						
3300 Coffey Ln	Santa Rosa	CA	95403	707-573-6700	573-6748	481
TF: 866-433-7724 ■ *Web:* www.depsci.com						
Depository Trust Co 55 Water St	New York	NY	10041	212-855-5181		401
Web: www.dtcc.com						

Name / Address	City	State	Zip	Phone	Fax	Class
Depot Law Office Plc						
222 W Apple St PO Box 248	Hastings	MI	49058	269-945-9557	945-2555	445
Web: www.depotlawoffice.com						
Depot Park Museum 270 1st St W	Sonoma	CA	95476	707-938-1762		637-2
Web: depotparkmuseum.org						
Depotstar Inc 6180 140th Ave NW	Ramsey	MN	55303	763-506-9990		261
Web: depotstar.com						
Depressed Anonymous PO Box 17414	Louisville	KY	40217	502-569-1989		48-21
Web: depressedanon.com						
Depression & Bipolar Support Alliance (DBSA)						
730 N Franklin St Ste 501	Chicago	IL	60610	312-642-0049	642-7243	48-17
TF: 800-826-3632 ■ *Web:* secure2.convio.net						
Deprince Race & Zollo Inc						
250 Park Ave S Ste 250	Winter Park	FL	32789	407-420-9903	841-8778	194
Web: drz-inc.com						
Deprospo, Petrizzo, Longo & Bartlett						
42 Park Pl	Goshen	NY	10924	845-294-3361		41
Web: www.petrizzolaw.com						
DEPTCOR 163 N Olden Ave	Trenton	NJ	08625	800-321-6524	633-2495*	630
**Fax Area Code:* 609 ■ *TF:* 800-321-6524 ■ *Web:* www.state.nj.us						
Deque Systems Inc						
2121 Cooperative Way Ste 210	Herndon	VA	20171	703-225-0380		177
Web: deque.com						
Der Rathskeller Restaurant						
1132 Auburn St	Rockford	IL	61103	815-963-2922		671
DeRaffele Manufacturing Company Inc						
2525 Palmer Ave	New Rochelle	NY	10801	914-636-6850		105
Derby Academy 56 Burditt Ave	Hingham	MA	02043	781-749-0746	740-2542	148
Web: www.derbyacademy.org						
Derby City Antique Mall						
3819 Bardstown Rd	Louisville	KY	40218	502-459-5151		460
Web: www.derbycityantiquemall.com						
Derby Industries LLC						
4451 Robards Ln	Louisville	KY	40218	502-451-7373	451-6330	803-1
TF: 800-569-4812 ■ *Web:* www.derbyllc.com						
Derby Molded Products Inc						
565 Jensen Rd	Neenah	WI	54956	920-725-1451		604
Web: www.derbymoldedproducts.com						
Derco Aerospace Inc						
8000 W Tower Ave	Milwaukee	WI	53223	414-355-3066		770
Web: www.dercoaerospace.com						
Derco Foods 2670 W Shaw Ln	Fresno	CA	93711	559-435-2664	435-8520	296-18
Web: www.dercofoods.com						
Dere Street						
41-B Eagle Rd Commerce Park	Danbury	CT	06810	203-797-9386		296-9
Web: www.derestreet.com						
Derecktor Shipyards Inc						
311 E Boston Post Rd	Mamaroneck	NY	10543	914-698-5020		698
Web: www.derecktor.com						
Derek C. Warner Insurance Agencies						
5241 Wilson Mills Rd Ste 3	Richmond Heights	OH	44143	216-486-8000		390
Web: derekwarnerinsurance.com						
Derek Engineering Inc						
2800 Constant Comment Pl	Louisville	KY	40299	502-266-0041		261
Web: derekengineering.com						
Derek Witham Insurance Agency Inc (DWIA)						
269 Broadway	Malden	MA	02148	781-322-2886	324-0105	390
Web: www.withaminsurance.com						
Derfner & Altman 575 King St Ste B	Charleston	SC	29403	843-723-9804	723-7446	445
Web: www.derfneraltman.com						
Derico of East Amherst Corp						
18 Limestone Dr Ste 4	Williamsville	NY	14221	716-810-0400		345
Deringer-Ney Inc						
616 Atrium Dr Ste 100	Vernon Hills	IL	60061	847-566-4100	367-6029	485
Web: www.deringerney.com						
Derita Precision Machine Company Inc						
605 Toddville Rd	Charlotte	NC	28214	704-392-7285	393-5430	488
Web: www.derita.com						
Dermatology Associates of Atlanta PC						
5555 Peachtree Dunwoody Rd NE Ste 190	Atlanta	GA	30342	404-256-4457	969-0683	374-7
TF: 800-233-0706 ■ *Web:* www.dermatlanta.com						
Dermody, Burke & Brown CPAs LLC						
443 N Franklin St	Syracuse	NY	13204	315-471-9171		2
Web: www.dbbllc.com						
Dero Bike Racks Inc						
504 Malcolm Ave SE Ste 100	Minneapolis	MN	55414	612-359-0689		61
TF: 888-337-6729 ■ *Web:* www.dero.com						
DeRoyal Industries Inc 200 DeBusk Ln	Powell	TN	37849	865-938-7828		477
TF: 800-251-9864 ■ *Web:* www.deroyal.com						
Derr & Gruenewald Construction Co (DGCC)						
PO Box 218	Henderson	CO	80640	303-287-3456		190
Web: dgccsteel.com						
Derr Flooring Company Inc						
525 Davisville Rd PO Box 912	Willow Grove	PA	19090	215-657-6300		361
TF: 800-523-3457 ■ *Web:* www.derrflooring.com						
Derrel's Mini Storage 3502 W San Jose	Fresno	CA	93711	559-277-1452		803-3
Web: www.derrels.com						
Derrick Equipment Co						
15630 Export Plaza Dr	Houston	TX	77032	281-590-3003		539
Web: derrick.com						
Derrick Publishing Co						
1510 W First St	Oil City	PA	16301	814-676-7444	677-8351	637-8
TF: 800-352-1002 ■ *Web:* www.thederrick.com						
Derry Public Library 64 E Broadway	Derry	NH	03038	603-432-6140	432-6128	434-3
Web: derrypl.org						
Derryfield Restaurant, The						
625 Mammoth Rd	Manchester	NH	03104	603-623-2880		671
Web: www.thederryfield.com						
Derse Exhibits Inc 3800 W Canal St	Milwaukee	WI	53208	414-257-2000		232
Web: derse.com						
Der-Tex Corp 1 Lehner Rd	Saco	ME	04072	800-669-0364		745-2
TF: 800-669-0364 ■ *Web:* www.dertexcorp.com						
DES (Draghi Environmental Services Inc)						
PO Box 601	Londonderry	NH	03053	603-437-1352	434-6485	192
TF: 866-867-2366 ■ *Web:* draghienvironmental.com						
Des Moines 100 Fourth St	Des Moines	IA	50309	515-288-3336		457-5
TF: 800-673-4763 ■ *Web:* businessrecord.com						

Name	City	State	Zip	Phone	Fax	Class
Des Moines Area Community College *Urban/Des Moines* 1100 Seventh St *TF:* 800-622-3334 ■ *Web:* www.dmacc.edu	Des Moines	IA	50314	515-244-4226	248-7253	162
Des Moines Art Ctr 4700 Grand Ave *Web:* www.desmoinesartcenter.org	Des Moines	IA	50312	515-277-4405		520
Des Moines Botanical Ctr 909 Robert D Ray Dr *Web:* www.dmbotanicalgarden.com	Des Moines	IA	50309	515-323-6290		97
Des Moines City Hall 400 Robert D Ray Dr *Web:* www.dmgov.org	Des Moines	IA	50309	515-283-4500		337
Des Moines County 513 N Main St *Web:* www.dmcounty.com	Burlington	IA	52601	319-753-8232	753-8729	338
Des Moines Golf & Country Club Educational Corp 1600 Jordan Creek Pkwy *Web:* www.dmgcc.org	West Des Moines	IA	50266	515-440-7500		226
Des Moines Independent School District 901 Walnut St *TF:* 800-452-1111 ■ *Web:* www.dmschools.org	Des Moines	IA	50309	515-242-7911	242-7579	685
Des Moines International Airport 5800 Fleur Dr *TF:* 877-686-0029 ■ *Web:* www.dsmairport.com	Des Moines	IA	50321	515-256-5050	256-5025	27
Des Moines Metro Credit Union 100 University Ave *TF:* 800-234-5354 ■ *Web:* dmmcu.org	Des Moines	IA	50314	515-283-4195	284-1652	219
Des Moines Metro Opera 106 W Boston Ave *Web:* desmoinesmetroopera.org	Indianola	IA	50125	515-961-6221	961-2994	573-2
Des Moines Public Library 1000 Grand Ave *Web:* dmpl.org	Des Moines	IA	50309	515-283-4152	237-1654	434-3
Des Moines Symphony 221 Walnut St *Web:* www.dmsymphony.org	Des Moines	IA	50309	515-280-4000	280-4005	573-3
Des Moines Trane 2220 NW 108th St *TF:* 800-798-0004 ■ *Web:* www.trane.com	Clive	IA	50325	515-270-0004		610
Des Moines Unviersity 3200 Grand Ave *Web:* www.dmu.edu	Des Moines	IA	50312	515-271-1400		800
Des Plaines Chamber of Commerce & Industry 1401 E Oakton St *TF:* 800-933-2412 ■ *Web:* www.dpchamber.com	Des Plaines	IL	60018	847-824-4200	824-7932	139
Des Plaines Park District 2222 Birch St *Web:* www.dpparks.org	Des Plaines	IL	60018	847-391-5700		31
Des Plaines Public Library 1501 Ellinwood Ave *Web:* dppl.org	Des Plaines	IL	60016	847-827-5551	827-7974	434-3
Des Plaines State Fish & Wildlife Area 24621 N River Rd *Web:* www2.illinois.gov	Wilmington	IL	60481	815-423-5326		565
DES Reprographics 3448 De La Cruz Blvd *TF:* 888-788-1898 ■ *Web:* desrepro.com	Santa Clara	CA	95054	408-970-8551		761
Desai Nasr Consulting Engineers Inc 6765 Daly Rd *Web:* desainasr.com	West Bloomfield	MI	48322	248-932-2010		261
Desai Systems Inc 199 Oakwood Ave *Web:* www.desai.com	West Hartford	CT	06119	860-233-0011		463
DeSales University 2755 Stn Ave *Web:* www.desales.edu	Center Valley	PA	18034	610-282-1100	282-0131	166
Desanctis Insurance Agency Inc 100 Unicorn Park Dr *Web:* desanctisins.com	Woburn	MA	01801	781-935-8480		390
DeSantis Breindel Inc 30 W 21 St *Web:* www.desantisbreindel.com	New York	NY	10010	212-994-7680		7
DeSantis Management Group 1950 Old Tustin Ave *Web:* www.desantisgroup.com	Santa Ana	CA	92705	714-550-9155		47
Desatnick Real Estate LLC 1001 Lafayette St *Web:* desatnickrealestate.com	Cape May	NJ	08204	609-884-1300		652
DeSaulnier Mark (Rep D - CA) 503 Cannon House Office Bldg *Web:* desaulnier.house.gov	Washington	DC	20515	202-225-2095	225-5609	342-2
Desbuild Inc 4744 Baltimore Ave *Web:* www.desbuild.com	Hyattsville	MD	20781	301-864-4095	864-3856	186
Descanso Gardens 1418 Descanso Dr *Web:* www.descansogardens.org	La Canada Flintridge	CA	91011	818-949-4200		97
Descartes Systems Group Inc 120 Randall Dr *TSE:* DSG ■ *TF:* 800-419-8495 ■ *Web:* www.descartes.com	Waterloo	ON	N2V1C6	519-746-8110	747-0082	178-12
Des-Case Corp 675 N Main St *Web:* www.descase.com	Goodlettsville	TN	37072	615-672-8800		54
DESCH Canada Ltd 240 Shearson Cres *TF:* 800-263-1866 ■ *Web:* www.desch.com	Cambridge	ON	N1T1J6	519-621-4560	623-1169	350
Deschutes County 1300 NW Wall St 2nd Fl *Web:* www.deschutes.org	Bend	OR	97701	541-388-6570	385-3202	338
Deschutes Public Library 507 NW Wall St *Web:* www.deschuteslibrary.org	Bend	OR	97701	541-312-1020	389-2982	434-3
Deschutes River State Recreation Area 89600 Biggs-Rufus Hwy *Web:* stateparks.oregon.gov	Wasco	OR	97065	541-739-2322		565
Desco Dental Systems LLC 5005 W Loomis Rd Ste 100 *TF:* 800-392-7610 ■ *Web:* www.descodental.com	Greenfield	WI	53220	414-281-9192		177
Desco Inc 1205 Lincolnton Rd *Web:* www.descoinc.com	Salisbury	NC	28147	704-633-6331	637-6966	246
Desco Inc 1240 Howard St *Web:* www.descodryers.com	Elk Grove Village	IL	60007	847-439-2130	439-0029	427
Desco Industries Inc 3651 Walnut Ave *Web:* desco.descoindustries.com	Chino	CA	91710	909-627-8178	627-7449	248
Desco Plumbing & Heating Supply Inc 39 Colborne St E *TF:* 800-564-5146 ■ *Web:* www.desco.ca	Lindsay	ON	K9V1K4	416-213-1555		612
Descor Builders 3164 Gold Camp Dr Ste 250 *Web:* www.descorbuilders.com	Rancho Cordova	CA	95670	916-463-0191		186
Deseret Book Co 45 W S Temple *TF:* 800-453-4532 ■ *Web:* deseretbook.com	Salt Lake City	UT	84101	801-534-1515	517-3126	637-3
Deseret Management Corp 55 N 300 W Ste 800 *Web:* www.deseretmanagement.com	Salt Lake City	UT	84101	801-538-0651	517-4600	185
Deseret Memorial Inc 36 E 700 S *Web:* www.memorialestates.com	Salt Lake City	UT	84111	801-364-6528		510
Deseret Mutual Benefit Administrators 150 Social Hall Ave Ste 170 *TF:* 800-777-3622 ■ *Web:* www.dmba.com	Salt Lake City	UT	84145	801-578-5600		391-3
Deseret News 55 N 300 W Ste 500 *TF:* 866-628-4677 ■ *Web:* www.deseret.com	Salt Lake City	UT	84101	801-204-6100		532-2
Desert Aire Corp N120 W18485 Freistadt Rd *Web:* www.desert-aire.com	Germantown	WI	53022	262-946-7400		14
Desert Botanical Garden 1201 N Galvin Pkwy *Web:* www.dbg.org	Phoenix	AZ	85008	480-941-1225	481-8124	97
Desert Edge Brewery 273 Trolley Sq *Web:* www.desertedgebrewery.com	Salt Lake City	UT	84102	801-521-8917		671
Desert Financial Credit Union 148 N 48th St *TF:* 800-456-9171 ■ *Web:* www.desertfinancial.com	Phoenix	AZ	85034	602-433-7000	634-2993	219
Desert Hot Springs Spa Hotel 10805 Palm Dr *Web:* www.dhsspa.com	Desert Hot Springs	CA	92240	760-329-6000		669
Desert Jade 3215 E Indian School Rd *Web:* www.desertjade68.com	Phoenix	AZ	85018	602-954-0048		671
Desert Mountain Properties LP 37700 Desert Mountain Pkwy *Web:* desertmountain.com	Scottsdale	AZ	85262	480-488-2998		653
Desert Paper & Envelope Company Inc 2700 Girard Blvd NE *Web:* www.desertenvelope.com	Albuquerque	NM	87107	505-884-0640		263
Desert Pipe & Supply 75200 Merle Dr *Web:* www.desertpipe.com	Palm Desert	CA	92211	760-340-6322		612
Desert Princess Country Club & HOA 28-555 Landau Blvd *Web:* www.desertprincesscc.com	Cathedral City	CA	92234	760-322-1655		671
Desert Regional Medical Ctr 47-111 Monroe St *Web:* www.desertcarenetwork.com	Indio	CA	92201	760-347-6191		374-3
Desert Research Institute 2215 Raggio Pkwy *Web:* www.dri.edu	Reno	NV	89512	775-673-7300	673-7397	668
Desert Ridge Marketplace 21001 N Tatum Blvd *Web:* shopdesertridge.com	Phoenix	AZ	85050	480-513-7586		50-6
Desert Riviera Hotel 610 E Palm Canyon Dr *Web:* desertrivierahotel.com	Palm Springs	CA	92264	760-327-5314		379
Desert Sands Charter High School 44130 20th St W *TF:* 877-360-5327 ■ *Web:* dschs.org	Lancaster	CA	93534	877-360-5327		685
Desert Sky Mall 7611 W Thomas Rd *Web:* www.desertskymall.com	Phoenix	AZ	85033	623-245-1400		460
Desert Springs Hospital Medical Ctr 2075 E Flamingo Rd *Web:* www.desertspringshospital.com	Las Vegas	NV	89119	702-733-8800		374-3
Desert Star Plastics 1336 N 22 Ave *TF:* 800-878-6144 ■ *Web:* www.desertstarplastics.com	Phoenix	AZ	85009	602-340-1236	340-0357	603
Desert Sun 750 N Gene Autry Trl *TF:* 800-233-3741 ■ *Web:* www.desertsun.com	Palm Springs	CA	92263	760-322-8889		532-2
Desert Sun Motors Inc 2600 N White Sands Blvd *Web:* www.desertsunmotors.com	Alamogordo	NM	88310	575-437-7530		57
Desert Veterinary Clinic PLC 995 S 5th Ave *Web:* desertvet.com	Yuma	AZ	85364	928-783-5010		794
Desha County 608 Robert S Moore Ave PO Box 188 *Web:* portal.arkansas.gov	Arkansas City	AR	71630	870-877-2426		338
DeShazo Group Inc 400 S Houston St Ste 330 *Web:* www.deshazogroup.com	Dallas	TX	75202	214-748-6740		261
Desiccare Inc 3400 Pomona Blvd *Web:* www.desiccare.com	Pomona	CA	91768	909-444-8272		77
Design & Molding Services Inc 25 Howard St *Fax Area Code: 815	Piscataway	NJ	08854	732-752-0300	667-4894*	604
Design & Production Inc 7110 Rainwater Pl *Web:* www.d-and-p.com	Lorton	VA	22079	703-550-8640	339-0296	232
Design 19 1165 Lincoln Ave Ste 8593 *TF:* 855-855-2040 ■ *Web:* www.design19.com	San Jose	CA	95155	855-855-2040		177
Design 3 Engineering Inc 1211 24th St W Ste 7 *Web:* www.design3eng.com	Billings	MT	59102	406-245-5599		261
Design 446 Inc 2411 Atlantic Ave *Web:* www.design446.com	Manasquan	NJ	08736	732-292-2400		4
Design Alliance Inc 520 N Washington St *Web:* www.designalliance.com	Alexandria	VA	22314	703-838-9894		344
Design Analysis Associates Inc 75 W 100 S *Web:* www.waterlog.com	Logan	UT	84321	435-753-2212	753-7669	201
Design Build Associates Inc 5655 Lindero Canyon Rd Ste 321 *Web:* dbuild.com	Westlake Village	CA	91362	818-889-0402		653
Design Center Inc 2040 St Clair Ave *TF:* 800-507-1443 ■ *Web:* www.designcenterideas.com	Saint Paul	MN	55105	651-333-4715		344
Design Center of the Americas (DCOTA) 1855 Griffin Rd *Web:* www.dcota.com	Dania Beach	FL	33004	954-920-7997		460

	Phone	Fax	Class
Design Compendium Inc, The 155 20th St .... Brooklyn NY 11232 *Web:* www.designcompendium.com	718-499-7722		195
Design Concepts Inc 1010 E Washington Ave Ste 210 .... Madison WI 53703 *Web:* www.delve.com	608-316-8400		261
Design Consultants Inc 120 Middlesex Ave Ste 20 .... Somerville MA 02145 *Web:* dci-ma.com	617-776-3350		261
Design Data Corp 1501 Old Cheney Rd PO Box 2 .... Lincoln NE 68512 *TF:* 800-443-0782 ■ *Web:* sds2.com	402-441-4000		177
Design Design Inc 19 La Grave SE .... Grand Rapids MI 49503 *TF:* 800-334-3348 ■ *Web:* www.designdesign.us	866-935-2648		130
Design Dimension Inc 112 North Church St .... Raleigh NC 27603 *Web:* www.designdimension.com	919-828-1485		463
Design Homes Inc 600 N Marquette Rd .... Prairie du Chien WI 53821 *TF:* 800-627-9443 ■ *Web:* www.designhomes.com	608-326-6041	326-4233	106
Design House Inc 7026 Old Katy Rd Ste 115 .... Houston TX 77024 *Web:* www.designhousetx.com	713-803-4949	803-4950	393
Design Hub 200 W Michigan Ave Ste C .... Saline MI 48176 *Web:* design-hub.com	734-944-8705	944-8735	177
Design Institute of San Diego 8555 Commerce Ave .... San Diego CA 92121 *TF:* 800-619-4337 ■ *Web:* www.disd.edu	858-566-1200	566-2711	166
Design Integrity Inc 1155 W Fulton Market .... Chicago IL 60607 *Web:* www.designintegrity.com	312-942-0602		261
Design It Yourself Gift Baskets LLC 7999 Hansen Rd Ste 204 .... Houston TX 77061 *TF:* 800-589-7553 ■ *Web:* www.designityourselfgiftbaskets.com	713-944-3440		129
Design Journal 23371 Mulholland Dr Ste 253 .... Woodland Hills CA 91364 *Web:* designjournalmag.com	310-394-4394		457-2
Design Management Institute (DMI) 38 Chauncy St Ste 800 .... Boston MA 02111 *Web:* www.dmi.org	617-338-6380	338-6570	48-4
Design Masonry Inc 20703 Santa Clara St .... Canyon Country CA 91351 *Web:* www.designmasonry.com	661-298-1013	298-0117	189-7
Design Molded Plastics 8220 Bavaria Dr E .... Macedonia OH 44056 *Web:* www.designmolded.com	330-963-4400	963-4300	596
Design Net Technical Products Inc 341 Washington Hwy .... Smithfield RI 02917 *Web:* designnettech.com	401-349-0695	349-0926	463
Design News 225 Wyman St .... Waltham MA 02451 *TF:* 800-869-6882 ■ *Web:* www.designnews.com	763-746-2792		457-21
Design Partners Inc 338 Main St .... Racine WI 53403 *Web:* design-partners.com	262-637-2233		344
Design Partnership LLP, The 949 Grant Ave .... San Francisco CA 94108 *Web:* www.dpsf.com	415-777-3737		186
Design Phase Inc 1771 S Lakeside Dr .... Waukegan IL 60085 *Web:* dphase.com	847-473-0077		393
Design Space Mdlar Bldings Inc 29336 Airport Rd .... Eugene OR 97402 *Web:* designspacemodular.com	541-461-9122		226
Design Specialties Inc 11100 W Heather Ave .... Milwaukee WI 53224 *Web:* glassfireplacedoors.com	414-371-1200		362
Design Systems Inc 38799 W 12 Mile Rd .... Farmington Hills MI 48331 *TF:* 800-660-4374 ■ *Web:* dsidsc.com	248-489-4300		261
Design Technologies & Manufacturing Co 2000 Corporate Dr .... Troy OH 45373 *Web:* www.destechmfg.com	937-335-1950	339-2961	494
Design Tool Inc 1607 Norfolk Pl SW .... Conover NC 28613 *TF:* 800-627-3674 ■ *Web:* designtoolinc.com	828-328-6414	328-4127	758
Design Toscano Inc 1400 Morse Ave .... Elk Grove Village IL 60007 *TF:* 800-525-5141 ■ *Web:* www.designtoscano.com	800-525-5141		459
Design Within Reach Inc 711 Canal St 3rd Fl .... Stamford CT 06902 *NASDAQ: DWRI* ■ *TF:* 800-944-2233 ■ *Web:* www.dwr.com	203-614-0600		362
Design Workshops 486 Lesser St .... Oakland CA 94601 *Web:* www.design-workshops.com	510-434-0727	434-0409	286
Design/Build Business Magazine 3030 Salt Creek Ln Ste 200 .... Arlington Heights IL 60005 *Web:* www.forresidentialpros.com	847-454-2714		457-2
Design/Craft Fabrics Corp 2230 Ridge Dr .... Glenview IL 60025 *Web:* www.design-craft.com	847-904-7000	904-7102	594
DesignAShirt.com 905 N Scottsdale Rd .... Tempe AZ 85281 *TF:* 800-594-1206 ■ *Web:* www.designashirt.com	480-966-3500		627
Designed Business Interiors of Topeka Inc 107 W 6th St .... Topeka KS 66603 *Web:* www.dbi-topeka.com	785-233-2078		321
Designed Stairs Inc 1480 E 6th St .... Sandwich IL 60548 *TF:* 877-478-2477 ■ *Web:* designedstairs.com	815-786-2021	786-6500	499
Designer Blinds 13815 Industrial Rd .... Omaha NE 68137 *Web:* designerblindsnshuttersomaha.com	402-964-2446		361
Designer Decal Inc 1120 E First Ave .... Spokane WA 99202 *TF:* 800-622-6333 ■ *Web:* www.designerdecal.com	509-535-0267	535-1476	687
Designer Diagnostics Inc 1930 Village Center Cir Ste 3-947 .... Las Vegas NV 89134 *Web:* www.designerdiagnostics.com	702-233-4804	233-4805	238
Designer Flower Ctr (DFC) 3450 W Gettysburg Ave .... Fresno CA 93722 *Web:* www.designerflowercenter.net	559-228-3300	228-3305	293
Designer Showroom of Texas 3841 Ranch Rd 620 S .... Austin TX 78738 *Web:* austin.abbeycarpet.com	512-520-0434	263-0990	290
Designers Choice Cabinetry Inc 100 TGK Cir .... Rockledge FL 32955 *Web:* dccabinetry.com	321-632-0772		115
Designers Midwest 9563 Montgomery Rd Ste 104 .... Cincinnati OH 45242 *Web:* www.designeers.com	513-793-6670		261
Designers' Press Inc 6305 Chancellor Dr .... Orlando FL 32809 *Web:* www.designerspressinc.com	407-843-3141		627
DesigneRx Pharmaceuticals Inc 4941 Allison Pkwy Ste B .... Vacaville CA 95688 *Web:* www.drxpharma.com	707-451-0441		231
Designhammer Media Group LLC 1912 E Nc Hwy 54 Ste 201 .... Durham NC 27713 *Web:* designhammer.com	919-544-0086		196
Designs for Tomorrow Inc 2290 Grissom Dr .... Saint Louis MO 63146 *Web:* designsfortomorrow.com	314-432-5566	432-6757	757
Designs for Vision Inc 760 Koehler Ave .... Ronkonkoma NY 11779 *Web:* www.designsforvision.com	631-585-3300		543
Designsensory Inc 1740 Commons Point Dr Centerpoint Commons Bldg 1 .... Knoxville TN 37932 *Web:* designsensory.com	865-690-2249		7
Designware Inc 54 Fieldstone-Bashan Dr .... East Haddam CT 06423 *Web:* www.designwareinc.com	860-873-8938	873-9993	566
DesignworksUSA Inc 2201 Corporate Center Dr .... Newbury Park CA 91320 *Web:* www.bmwgroupdesignworks.com	805-499-9590		261
DeSilva Gates Construction Inc 11555 Dublin Blvd .... Dublin CA 94568 *Web:* www.desilvagates.com	925-829-9220	803-4263	188-5
Desire2Learn Corp 151 Charles St W Ste 400 .... Kitchener ON N2G1H6 *TF:* 888-772-0325 ■ *Web:* www.d2l.com	519-772-0325	772-0324	174
Desjardins Securities Inc 1170 Peel St Ste 300 .... Montreal QC H3B0A9 *TF:* 866-985-7585 ■ *Web:* www.vmdconseil.ca	514-985-7585	987-9593	401
DesJarlais Scott (Rep R - TN) 2301 Rayburn House Office Bldg .... Washington DC 20515 *Web:* desjarlais.house.gov	202-225-6831	226-5172	342-2
Deskey 120 E Eighth St .... Cincinnati OH 45202 *Web:* www.deskey.com	513-721-6800		195
DeskFlex Inc 205 W Wacker Dr Ste 1320 .... Chicago IL 60606 *TF:* 877-253-2356 ■ *Web:* www.deskflex.com	847-359-3990		178-1
DeskNet Inc 30 Montgomery St .... Jersey City NJ 07302 *Web:* www.desknetinc.com	201-946-7080		178-1
Desks Incorporated Business Furniture 445 Bryant St Unit 8 .... Denver CO 80204 *Web:* desks-incorporated.com	303-777-7778		321
DeskTop Labels 7277 Boone Ave N .... Minneapolis MN 55428 *TF:* 800-241-9730 ■ *Web:* www.meyersdirect.com	800-241-9730		413
Desktop Publishing Supplies Inc 34 Raccio Park Rd Ste 9 .... Hamden CT 06514 *TF:* 800-443-3645 ■ *Web:* www.desktopsupplies.com	203-248-0003	248-0009	552-1
Desmond & Ahern Ltd 10827 S Western Ave .... Chicago IL 60643 *Web:* www.desmondcpa.com	773-779-4720	779-8310	2
Desmond Albany Hotel, The 660 Albany-Shaker Rd .... Albany NY 12211 *Web:* www.desmondhotelsalbany.com	518-869-8100		671
Desmond Nolan Livaich & Cunningham 1830 15th St .... Sacramento CA 95811 *Web:* dnlc.net	916-443-2051	443-2651	41
Desmos Inc 1488 Howard St .... San Francisco CA 94103 *Web:* www.desmos.com	415-636-8001	534-0941	387
DeSoto Chamber of Commerce 2010 N Hampton Rd Ste 200 .... DeSoto TX 75115 *Web:* www.desotochamber.org	972-224-3565		139
DeSoto Consulting LLC 9014 N 23rd Ave Ste 7 .... Phoenix AZ 85021 *Web:* www.desotollc.com	602-888-0341		151
Desoto Correctional Institution 13617 SE Hwy 70 .... Arcadia FL 34266 *Web:* dc.state.fl.us	863-494-3727		213
DeSoto County 201 E Oak St .... Arcadia FL 34266 *Web:* desotobocc.com	863-993-4800	993-4809	338
DeSoto County 365 Losher St DeSoto County Administration Bldg .... Hernando MS 38632 *Web:* www.desotocountyms.gov	662-469-8000		338
DeSoto County Chamber of Commerce 16 S Volusia Ave .... Arcadia FL 34266 *Web:* desotochamberflo.chambermaster.com	863-494-4033	494-3312	139
DeSoto County Library 125 N Hillsboro Ave .... Arcadia FL 34266 *TF:* 800-843-5678 ■ *Web:* myhlc.org	863-993-4851		434-3
DeSoto Memorial Hospital Inc 900 N Robert Ave .... Arcadia FL 34266 *Web:* www.dmh.org	863-494-3535	494-8400	374-3
DeSoto Parish 101 Texas St PO Box 1206 .... Mansfield LA 71052 *Web:* desotoparishclerk.org	318-872-3110	872-4202	338
DeSoto Parish Chamber of Commerce 115 N Washington Ave .... Mansfield LA 71052 *TF:* 800-844-4646 ■ *Web:* www.desotoparishchamber.net	318-872-1310	871-1875	139
DeSoto Parish Library 109 Crosby St .... Mansfield LA 71052 *Web:* desotoparishlibrary.org	318-872-6100	872-6120	434-3
Desoto Parish School District 201 Crosby St .... Mansfield LA 71052 *Web:* www.desotopsb.com	318-872-2836	872-1324	685
DeSoto Public Library 211 E Pleasant Run Rd .... DeSoto TX 75115 *TF:* 800-886-9008 ■ *Web:* www.ci.desoto.tx.us	972-230-9656	230-5797	434-3
Desoto Sales Inc 20945 Osborne St .... Canoga Park CA 91304 *TF:* 800-826-9779 ■ *Web:* www.desotosales.com	818-998-0853	998-7542	351
Despatch Industries Inc 8860 207th St W .... Lakeville MN 55044 *TF:* 800-726-0110 ■ *Web:* despatch.com	952-469-5424	469-4513	318

Name / Address	City	State	Zip	Phone	Fax	Class
Desroches & Company CPAS PC 200 Golden Oak Ct Ste 200 *Web:* desrochescpas.com	Virginia Beach	VA	23452	757-498-3000		2
Dessert Innovations Inc 25-B Enterprise Blvd. *TF:* 800-359-7351 ■ *Web:* dessertinnovations.com	Atlanta	GA	30336	404-691-5000	691-5001	296-2
Desso USA Inc 10 Corbin Dr 2nd Fl. **Fax Area Code:* 203 ■ *TF:* 888-337-7687 ■ *Web:* www.desso.com	Darien	CT	06820	888-337-7687	202-7647*	131
DESTACO 15 Corporate Dr. *Web:* www.destaco.com	Auburn Hills	MI	48326	248-836-6700		350
DESTACO 691 N Squirrel Rd Ste 250. *TF:* 888-337-8226 ■ *Web:* www.destaco.com	Auburn Hills	MI	48326	888-337-8226		335
Destin Area Chamber of Commerce 4484 Legendary Dr Ste A *Web:* www.destinchamber.com	Destin	FL	32541	850-837-6241	654-5612	139
Destin Paint Ctr 4014 Commons Dr W. *Web:* www.destinpaint.benmoorepaints.com	Destin	FL	32541	850-837-4141	837-4571	802
Destination America Inc 801 E Katella Ave *Web:* www.destamer.com	Anaheim	CA	92805	714-935-0040		48-20
Destination Canada 800 - 1045 Howe St *TF:* 822-733-7478 ■ *Web:* www.destinationcanada.com	Vancouver	BC	V6Z2A9	604-638-8300		774
Destination Cinema 3544 Lincoln Ave Ste C *TF:* 866-405-4629 ■ *Web:* destinationcinema.com	Ogden	UT	84401	801-392-5881	392-6703	514
Destination Gettysburg 571 W Middle St. **Fax Area Code:* 717 ■ *TF:* 800-337-5015 ■ *Web:* www.destinationgettysburg.com	Gettysburg	PA	17325	800-337-5015	334-1166*	206
Destination Hotels & Resorts Inc 10333 E Dry Creek Rd Ste 450 *TF:* 855-893-1011 ■ *Web:* www.destinationhotels.com	Englewood	CO	80112	303-799-3830		379
Destination Mansfield - Richland County 124 N Main St *TF:* 800-642-8282 ■ *Web:* www.destinationmansfield.com	Mansfield	OH	44902	419-525-1300	524-7722	206
Destination Maternity Corp 232 Strawbridge Dr. *NASDAQ: DEST* ■ *TF:* 800-466-6223 ■ *Web:* www.destinationmaternitycorp.com	Moorestown	NJ	08057	800-466-6223		157-6
Destination Resources 5435 Balboa Blvd Ste 106 *Web:* www.destinationresources.com	Encino	CA	91316	818-995-7915	990-6129	184
Destination toledo 401 Jefferson Ave *TF:* 800-243-4667 ■ *Web:* www.visittoledo.org	Toledo	OH	43604	419-321-6404		206
Destination Vacation 7 Executive Park Rd *Web:* destinationvacationhhi.com	Hilton Head Island	SC	29928	843-785-7774		653
Destinations Unlimited 419 First St SE *Web:* www.duagency.com	Cedar Rapids	IA	52401	319-393-1359		772
Destiny Capital Securities Corp 13922 Denver W Pkwy Ste 150. **Fax Area Code:* 720 ■ *Web:* destinycapital.com	Golden	CO	80401	303-277-9977	770-5404*	390
Destiny Corp 2075 Silas Deane Hwy *Web:* www.destinycorp.com	Rocky Hill	CT	06067	860-721-1684		631
Destiny House Publishing PO Box 19774. *TF:* 888-890-9455 ■ *Web:* www.destinyhousepublishing.com	Detroit	MI	48219	888-890-9455		637-2
Destiny Industries LLC 250 R W Bryant Rd *TF:* 866-782-6600 ■ *Web:* www.destinyhomebuilders.com	Moultrie	GA	31788	866-782-6600		505
Destiny Mfg 2974 Interstate Pkwy *Web:* www.destinymfg.com	Brunswick	OH	44212	330-273-9000		488
Destiny Solutions Inc 40 Holly St *TF:* 866-403-0500 ■ *Web:* destinysolutions.com	Toronto	ON	M4S3C3	416-480-0500		225
Destrehan Plantation 13034 River Rd. *Web:* www.destrehanplantation.org	Destrehan	LA	70047	985-764-9315	725-1929	50-3
Destron Fearing 2805 E 14th St *TF:* 800-328-0118 ■ *Web:* www.destronfearing.com	DFW Airport	TX	75261	800-328-0118		647
DET Distributing Co 301 Great Cir Rd. *Web:* www.detdist.com	Nashville	TN	37228	615-244-4113		81-1
Detail Drafting & Design Inc 1090 216th Ave. *Web:* ddd-services.com	East Bethel	MN	55011	763-434-2110		180
Detail Planners LLC 3822 W Cleveland St. *Web:* www.detailplanners.com	Tampa	FL	33609	813-991-1348		317
Detar Hospital Navarro 506 E San Antonio St *Web:* www.detar.com	Victoria	TX	77901	361-575-7441		374-3
DETC (Distance Education & Training Council) 1601 18th St NW Ste 2. *Web:* www.deac.org	Washington	DC	20009	202-234-5100	332-1386	48-1
Detco Industries Inc PO Box 430 *TF:* 800-282-2133 ■ *Web:* www.detco.com	Conway	AR	72033	501-329-6965		151
Detechtion Technologies 1100 Eighth Ave SW Ste 277 *TF:* 800-780-9798 ■ *Web:* detechtion.com	Calgary	AB	T2P3T8	403-250-9220		196
Detective Training Institute PO Box 909 **Fax Area Code:* 949 ■ *TF:* 888-425-9338 ■ *Web:* www.detectivetraining.com	San Juan Capistrano	CA	92693	888-425-9338	498-4751*	167-3
Detector Electronics Corp 6901 W 110th St. *Web:* www.det-tronics.com	Minneapolis	MN	55438	952-941-5665		692
Deteq Services 1771 Westborough Dr *Web:* www.deteqservices.com	Katy	TX	77449	281-828-3030	828-3003	261
Deterding's Market Inc 506 E Gibbsboro Rd *Web:* deterdingsmarket.com	Lindenwold	NJ	08021	856-783-1457		345
Detering Consulting Inc 306 Ferne Ave. *Web:* www.deteringconsulting.com	Palo Alto	CA	94306	650-576-4516		260
Detex Corp 302 Detex Dr *TF:* 800-729-3839 ■ *Web:* www.detex.com	New Braunfels	TX	78130	830-629-2900	620-6711	692
Dethmers Manufacturing Co (DEMCO) 4010 320th St. *TF:* 800-543-3626 ■ *Web:* www.demco-products.com	Boyden	IA	51234	712-725-2311	725-2380	763
Detmar Corp 2001 W Alexandrine Ave. *Web:* www.detmarcorp.com	Detroit	MI	48208	313-831-1155	831-0624	350
Detroit Athletic Club 241 Madison St *Web:* www.thedac.com	Detroit	MI	48226	313-963-9200	963-8891	354
Detroit Book Press 901 W Lafayette Blvd *Web:* www.rarebooklink.com	Detroit	MI	48226	313-961-0622	963-9138	637-2
Detroit Business Institute - Downriver 19100 Fort St *Web:* www.dbidownriver.edu	Riverview	MI	48193	734-479-0660	479-0738	167-3
Detroit Chassis LLC 6501 Lynch Rd *Web:* www.detroitchassis.com	Detroit	MI	48234	313-571-2100		59
Detroit City Hall 2 Woodward Ave Ste 200 *Web:* detroitmi.gov	Detroit	MI	48226	313-224-3270	224-1466	337
Detroit Community Schools (DCS) 12675 Burt Rd *Web:* www.detcomschools.org	Detroit	MI	48223	313-537-3570	537-6904	685
Detroit Diesel Corp 13400 Outer Dr. *Web:* demanddetroit.com	Detroit	MI	48239	313-592-5296		262
Detroit Edge Tool Co 6570 E Nevada St. *TF:* 800-404-2038 ■ *Web:* www.detroitedge.com	Detroit	MI	48234	313-366-4120	366-1890	493
Detroit Educational Television Foundation 1 Clover Ct *TF:* 800-859-9887 ■ *Web:* www.dptv.org	Wixom	MI	48393	248-305-3788		647
Detroit Elevator Co 2121 Burdette *Web:* detroitelevator.com	Ferndale	MI	48220	248-591-7484	591-7491	189-1
Detroit Engineered Products (DEP) 850 E Long Lake Rd *Web:* www.depusa.com	Troy	MI	48085	248-269-7130		180
Detroit Free Press 615 W Lafayette Blvd *TF:* 800-395-3300 ■ *Web:* www.freep.com	Detroit	MI	48226	313-222-6400	222-5981	532-2
Detroit Historical Museum 5401 Woodward Ave. *Web:* detroithistorical.org	Detroit	MI	48202	313-833-1805		520
Detroit Hoist Co 6650 Sterling Dr N *TF:* 800-521-9126 ■ *Web:* www.detroithoist.com	Sterling Heights	MI	48312	586-268-2600	268-0044	470
Detroit Institute of Arts 5200 Woodward Ave. *Web:* www.dia.org	Detroit	MI	48202	313-833-7900		520
Detroit Lake State Recreation Area PO Box 549 *Web:* stateparks.oregon.gov	Detroit	OR	97342	503-854-3346		565
Detroit Lakes Regional Chamber of Commerce 700 Summit Ave *TF:* 800-542-3992 ■ *Web:* www.visitdetroitlakes.com	Detroit Lakes	MN	56501	218-847-9202	847-9082	139
Detroit Legal News Co 1409 Allen Rd Ste B *TF:* 800-875-5275 ■ *Web:* www.legalnews.com	Troy	MI	48083	248-577-6100	577-6111	637-8
Detroit Lions 222 Republic Dr *Web:* www.detroitlions.com	Allen Park	MI	48101	313-216-4000		715-3
Detroit Medical Ctr (DMC) 4707 St Antoine *Web:* www.dmc.org	Detroit	MI	48201	313-745-6035		353
Detroit Metropolitan Airport 11050 Rogell Dr Ste 602 *Web:* www.metroairport.com	Detroit	MI	48242	734-942-3550		27
Detroit Metropolitan Convention & Visitors Bureau 211 W Fort St Ste 1000 *TF:* 877-424-5554 ■ *Web:* visitdetroit.com	Detroit	MI	48226	313-202-1800		206
Detroit Public Library 5201 Woodward Ave. *Web:* detroitpubliclibrary.org	Detroit	MI	48202	313-481-1300		434-3
Detroit Public Schools 3031 W Grand Blvd *Web:* www.detroitk12.org	Detroit	MI	48202	313-873-7927	873-4564	685
Detroit Pump & Manufacturing Co 450 Fair St Bldg D *TF:* 800-686-1662 ■ *Web:* www.detroitpump.com	Ferndale	MI	48220	248-544-4242	544-4141	385
Detroit Quality Brush Mfg 32165 Schoolcraft Rd *TF:* 800-722-3037 ■ *Web:* www.dqb.com	Livonia	MI	48150	734-525-5660	525-0437	103
Detroit Radiant Product Co 21400 Hoover Rd *TF:* 800-222-1100 ■ *Web:* www.reverberray.com	Warren	MI	48089	586-756-0950	756-2626	318
Detroit Regional Chamber 1 Woodward Ave Ste 1900 *TF:* 800-427-5100 ■ *Web:* www.detroitchamber.com	Detroit	MI	48226	313-596-0330	964-0183	139
Detroit Stoker Co 1510 E First St *TF:* 800-786-5374 ■ *Web:* www.detroitstoker.com	Monroe	MI	48161	734-241-9500	241-7126	318
Detroit Symphony Orchestra 3711 Woodward Ave. *TF:* 800-434-6340 ■ *Web:* www.dso.org	Detroit	MI	48201	313-576-5111	576-5109	573-3
Detroit Zoological Institute 8450 W Ten-Mile Rd. *Web:* detroitzoo.org	Royal Oak	MI	48067	248-541-5717		823
Detroit-Wayne County Port Authority 130 E Atwater St *Web:* www.portdetroit.com	Detroit	MI	48226	313-259-5091	259-5093	618
Detronic Industries Inc 35800 Beattie Dr. *Web:* www.detronic.com	Sterling Heights	MI	48312	586-977-5660	939-5340	697
Detrow & Underwood Inc 12 W Main St. *Web:* www.detrowunderwood.com	Ashland	OH	44805	419-289-0265		4
Detyens Shipyards Inc 1670 Drydock Ave Bldg 236 Ste 200 *Web:* www.detyens.com	North Charleston	SC	29405	843-308-8000	308-8059	698
Deublin Co 2050 Norman Dr W *Web:* www.deublin.com	Waukegan	IL	60085	847-689-8600	689-8690	620
Deuel County 718 3rd St *Web:* www.co.deuel.ne.us	Chappell	NE	69129	308-874-3308	874-3472	338
Deuel County 18028 SD-15. *TF:* 800-872-6190 ■ *Web:* www.deuelcountysd.com	Clear Lake	SD	57226	605-874-2312	874-1306	338
Deuel County Farmers Union Oil Co 375 Main Ave *Web:* www.deuelcountyfu.com	Toronto	SD	57268	605-794-4961		579
Deuster Co W140 N5940 Lilly Rd *TF:* 877-870-7829 ■ *Web:* www.deusterco.com	Menomonee Falls	WI	53051	262-703-4140	703-4141	300
Deutch Ted (Rep D - FL) 2447 Rayburn House Office Bldg *Web:* teddeutch.house.gov	Washington	DC	20515	202-225-3001	225-5974	342-2

Name / Address	City	State	ZIP	Phone	Fax	Class
Deutsch Inc 330 W 34th St *Web:* www.deutsch.com	New York	NY	10001	212-981-7600		4
Deutsch, Kerrigan & Stiles LLP 755 Magazine St *Web:* www.deutschkerrigan.com	New Orleans	LA	70130	504-581-5141		428
Deutsche Bank Americas Holding Corp 60 Wall St *Web:* www.db.com	New York	NY	10005	212-250-2500		360-4
Deutscher & Daughter Inc 10507 150th St *Web:* www.dddoors.com	Jamaica	NY	11435	718-291-5600		351
Dev Love Press 3342 Old Line Ave *Web:* devlovepress.com	Laurel	MD	20724	585-749-8467		637-2
DEVAR Inc 706 Bostwick Ave *Web:* www.devarinc.com	Bridgeport	CT	06605	203-368-6751		407
DeVaSys 98 Fiddlers Hollow *Web:* www.devasys.net	Penfield	NY	14526	585-377-9428		180
DeVaul Publishing Inc (DPI) 429 N Market Blvd *Web:* www.devaulpublishing.com	Chehalis	WA	98532	360-748-6848		637-9
Devault Foods 1 Fillippo Way *Web:* www.devaultfoods.com	Devault	PA	19432	800-426-2874		297-8
Devcare Solution Ltd 131 N High St Ste 640 *Web:* www.devcare.com	Columbus	OH	43215	614-221-2277		179
Devcon Construction Inc 690 Gibraltar Dr *Web:* www.devcon-const.com	Milpitas	CA	95035	408-942-8200		186
Develcon Inc 931 Progress Ave Units 11 *Web:* www.develcon.com	Toronto	ON	M1G3V5	416-385-1390	385-1610	736
Developing Solutions Inc 1801 W Louisiana St *Web:* developingsolutions.com	Mckinney	TX	75069	469-634-4200		180
Developing World Markets Finance LLP 750 Washington Blvd Ste 500 *Web:* www.dwmarkets.com	Stamford	CT	06901	203-655-5453		401
Development Alternatives Inc (DAI) 7600 Wisconsin Ave Ste 200 *Web:* www.dai.com	Bethesda	MD	20814	301-771-7600		463
Development Counsellors International Ltd (DCI) 215 Park Ave S 14th Fl *Web:* aboutdci.com	New York	NY	10003	212-725-0707	725-2254	230
Development Dimensions Intl 1225 Washington Pk *TF:* 800-933-4463 ■ *Web:* www.ddiworld.com	Bridgeville	PA	15017	412-257-0600	220-2942	193
Development Dynamics LLC (D2) 1001 Boardwalk Springs Pl Ste 50 *Web:* www.developmentdynamics.org	O Fallon	MO	63366	636-561-8602	561-8605	196
Development Planning & Financing Group Inc (DPFG) 27127 Calle Arroyo Ste 1910 *Web:* www.dpfg.com	San Juan Capistrano	CA	92675	949-388-9269	388-9272	652
Development Services of America 16100 N 71st St Ste 520 *Web:* www.developmentservicesofamerica.com	Scottsdale	AZ	85254	480-927-4892		653
Developmental Industries Inc 915 Hwy 45 *TF:* 888-343-0456 ■ *Web:* diroofseamers.com	Corinth	MS	38834	662-287-6626		456
Deveney Communication Consulting LLC 2406 Chartres St *Web:* deveney.com	New Orleans	LA	70117	504-949-3999		636
Devereux 1291 Stanley Rd NW PO Box 1688 *TF:* 800-342-3357 ■ *Web:* www.devereux.org	Kennesaw	GA	30156	678-303-5233		374-1
Devereux Glenholme School 81 Sabbaday Ln *Web:* www.theglenholmeschool.org	Washington Depot	CT	06793	860-868-7377	868-7894	622
Devex 1341 Connecticut Ave NW *Web:* www.devex.com	Washington	DC	20036	202-249-9222		194
DevFacto Technologies Inc 2250 Scotia Place Tower 1 10060 Jasper Ave *TF:* 877-323-3832 ■ *Web:* www.devfacto.com	Edmonton	AB	T5J3R8	877-323-3832		463
Device Engineering Inc 385 E Alamo Dr *Web:* www.deiaz.com	Chandler	AZ	85225	480-303-0822		261
Devicenet USA Inc 4000 Moorpark Ave Ste 116 *Web:* www.devicenet-usa.com	San Jose	CA	95117	408-557-0413	557-0414	177
Devicix LLC 7550 Meridian Cir N Ste 150 *TF:* 800-808-8281 ■ *Web:* www.devicix.com	Maple Grove	MN	55369	952-368-0073		41
Devier Enterprises LLC 22164 MCH Rd Ste E *Web:* www.devierway.com	Mandeville	LA	70471	985-893-0391	259-8799	186
deView Electronics 1420 Lakeside Pkwy Ste 110 *TF:* 877-433-8439	Lewisville	TX	75057	214-222-3332		692
Devil Dog Manufacturing Company Inc 400 E Gannon Ave	Zebulon	NC	27597	919-269-7485		155-4
Devil's Den State Park 11333 W Arkansas Hwy 74 *Web:* www.arkansasstateparks.com	West Fork	AR	72774	479-761-3325		565
Devil's Head Resort & Convention Ctr S 6330 Bluff Rd *TF:* 800-472-6670 ■ *Web:* www.devilsheadresort.com	Merrimac	WI	53561	608-493-2251	493-2176	669
Devil's Hole State Park c/o Niagara Frontier Reg PO Box 1132 *Web:* parks.ny.gov	Niagara Falls	NY	14303	716-284-5778		565
Devil's Hopyard State Park 366 Hopyard Rd *Web:* portal.ct.gov	East Haddam	CT	06423	860-424-3200		565
Devil's Lake State Park S5975 Park Rd *Web:* dnr.wi.gov	Baraboo	WI	53913	608-356-8301	356-4281	565
Devil's Millhopper Geological State Park 4732 Millhopper Rd *Web:* www.floridastateparks.org	Gainesville	FL	32653	352-955-2008		565
Devil's Sinkhole State Natural Area 101 N Sweeten St *Web:* tpwd.texas.gov	Rocksprings	TX	78880	830-683-3762		565
Devils Fork State Park 161 Holcombe Cir *Web:* southcarolinaparks.com	Salem	SC	29676	864-944-2639		565
Devils Postpile National Monument PO Box 3999 *Web:* www.nps.gov	Mammoth Lakes	CA	93546	760-934-2289		564
Devils River State Natural Area HC 01 PO Box 513 *Web:* tpwd.texas.gov	Del Rio	TX	78840	830-395-2133		565
Devils Tower National Monument Hwy 110 Bldg 170 PO Box 10 *Web:* www.nps.gov	Devils Tower	WY	82714	307-467-5283	467-5350	564
Devin International Inc 2545 SE Evangeline Thwy *Web:* www.nov.com	LaFayette	LA	70508	337-233-3846		539
DeVIncenzi Metal Products Inc 1809 Castenada Dr	Burlingame	CA	94010	650-692-5800	697-9031	610
Devine Bros Inc 38 Commerce St *Web:* devinebi.com	Norwalk	CT	06850	203-866-4421		182
Devine Intermodal 3870 Ch Dr *Web:* www.devineintermodal.com	West Sacramento	CA	95691	916-371-4430	371-0355	780
Devine Millimet 111 Amherst St *Web:* www.devinemillimet.com	Manchester	NH	03101	603-669-1000		445
Devlin Video International LLC 1501 Broadway	New York	NY	10036	212-391-1313		514
Devon Bank 6445 N Western Ave *Web:* www.devonbank.com	Chicago	IL	60645	773-465-2500		70
Devon Energy Corp 333 W Sheridan Ave *NYSE:* DVN ■ *TF:* 800-361-3377 ■ *Web:* www.devonenergy.com	Oklahoma City	OK	73102	405-235-3611		536
Devon International Group 1100 First Ave *TF:* 866-312-7164 ■ *Web:* www.devonintlgroup.com	King of Prussia	PA	19406	866-312-7164		177
Devon Precision Industries Inc 251 Munson Rd *Web:* www.devonprecision.com	Wolcott	CT	06716	203-879-1437	879-5556	621
Devon Self Storage Holdings LLC 2000 Powell St Ste 1240 *Web:* www.devonselfstorage.com	Emeryville	CA	94608	510-450-1300		803-3
Devore & Johnson Inc 176 Forest Pkwy *Web:* devoreandjohnson.com	Forest Park	GA	30297	404-366-4243		610
DeVore & Sons Inc 9020 E 35th St N *Web:* www.devoreandsons.com	Wichita	KS	67226	316-267-3211	267-1850	637-3
DeVos Place 303 Monroe Ave *Web:* devosplace.org	Grand Rapids	MI	49503	616-742-6500	742-6590	205
Devoted Health Inc 221 Crescent St Ste 202 *TF:* 800-338-6833 ■ *Web:* devoted.com	Waltham	MA	02453	800-338-6833		352
DeVries Global 909 Third Ave *Web:* www.devriesglobal.com	New York	NY	10022	212-546-8500		636
Devro Inc 785 Old Swamp Rd *Web:* www.devro.com	Columbia	SC	29211	803-796-9730	796-1636	473
DeVry University 8000 Jarvis Ave Ste 220 *Web:* www.devry.edu	Newark	CA	94560	510-574-1200		800
DevTech Systems Inc 1700 N Moore St Ste 1720 *Web:* devtechsys.com	Arlington	VA	22209	703-312-6038	312-6039	194
DEW Construction Corp 277 Blair Park Rd Ste 130 *Web:* dewconstruction.com	Williston	VT	05495	802-872-0505		186
Dew Distribution Services Inc 2201 Touhy Ave *TF:* 800-837-3391 ■ *Web:* www.dewdist.com	Elk Grove Village	IL	60007	800-837-3391		649
Dew Software Inc 983 Corporate Way *Web:* www.dewsoftware.com	Fremont	CA	94539	510-490-9995	743-4106	180
Dewalt Corp 1930 22nd St *Web:* dewaltcorp.com	Bakersfield	CA	93301	661-323-4600		261
Dewberry & Davis 8401 Arlington Blvd **Fax Area Code:* 703 ■ *Web:* www.dewberry.com	Fairfax	VA	22031	919-881-9939	849-0100*	261
Dewey County Clerk of Courts 710 C St *Web:* ujs.sd.gov	Timber Lake	SD	57656	605-865-3566	865-3641	338
Dewey Ford Inc 3055 SE Delaware Ave *TF:* 877-704-6793 ■ *Web:* www.deweyford.com	Ankeny	IA	50021	877-704-6793		126
Dewey Services Inc 939 E Union St **Fax Area Code:* 626 ■ *TF:* 877-339-3973 ■ *Web:* deweypest.com	Pasadena	CA	91106	877-339-3973	568-9204*	577
Dewied International Inc 5010 IH-10 E *TF:* 800-992-5600	San Antonio	TX	78219	210-661-6161	662-6112	296-26
DeWils Fine Cabinetry 6307 NE 127th Ave *Web:* dewils.com	Vancouver	WA	98682	360-892-0300		115
DeWitt County 201 W Washington St PO Box 439 *Web:* www.dewittcountyill.com	Clinton	IL	61727	217-935-7780	935-7789	338
DeWitt LLP 2 E Mifflin St Ste 600 *Web:* www.dewittllp.com	Madison	WI	53703	608-255-8891		428
Dewitt Products Co 5860 Plumer Ave *TF:* 800-962-8599 ■ *Web:* www.dewittproducts.com	Detroit	MI	48209	313-554-0575	554-2171	46
Dewolf Point State Park 45920 County Rt 191 *Web:* parks.ny.gov	Fineview	NY	13640	315-375-6371		565
DeWys Manufacturing Inc 15300 Eigth Ave *Web:* www.dewysmfg.com	Marne	MI	49435	616-677-5281		198
Dewz Restaurant 1505 J St *Web:* www.dineatdewz.com	Modesto	CA	95354	209-549-1101		671
DexCom Inc 6340 Sequence Dr *NASDAQ:* DXCM ■ *TF:* 888-738-3646 ■ *Web:* www.dexcom.com	San Diego	CA	92121	858-200-0200		85
Dexia 445 Park Ave 8th Fl *Web:* www.dexia.com	New York	NY	10022	212-515-7000		70
Dexisive Inc 21010 Southbank Ste 105 *Web:* www.secunetics.com	Sterling	VA	20165	703-935-0110		180
Dexmet Corp 22 Barnes Industrial Rd S *Web:* www.dexmet.com	Wallingford	CT	06492	203-294-4440		295
Dexta Corp 962 Kaiser Rd *TF:* 800-733-3902 ■ *Web:* www.dexta.com	Napa	CA	94558	707-255-2454		228

Phone | Fax | Class

Dexter Avenue King Memorial Baptist Church
454 Dexter Ave ... Montgomery AL 36104 334-263-3970 50-1
Web: www.dexterkingmemorial.org

Dexter Axle 2900 Industrial Pkwy ... Elkhart IN 46516 574-295-7888 60
Web: www.dexteraxle.com

Dexter Co 2211 W Grimes Ave ... Fairfield IA 52556 641-472-5131 427
Web: www.dexter.com

Dexter Fastener Technologies Inc
2110 Bishop Cir E ... Dexter MI 48130 734-426-5200 278
Web: www.dextech.net

Dexter Magnetic Technologies Inc
1050 Morse Ave ... Elk Grove Village IL 60007 847-956-1140 458
Web: www.dextermag.com

Dexter Research Center Inc
7300 Huron River Dr ... Dexter MI 48130 734-426-3921 201
Web: www.dexterresearch.com

Dexter State Recreation Site
725 Summer St NE Ste C ... Salem OR 97301 541-937-1173 565
Web: stateparks.oregon.gov

Dexter Wilson Engineering
2234 Faraday Ave ... Carlsbad CA 92008 760-438-4422 261
Web: www.dwilsoneng.com

Dexter-Russell Inc 44 River St ... Southbridge MA 01550 508-765-0201 764-2897 222
TF: 800-343-6042 ■ *Web:* www.dexter1818.com

Dey Mansion 199 Totowa Rd ... Wayne NJ 07470 973-706-6640 50-3
Web: www.deymansion.org

DeZurik Water Controls
250 Riverside Ave N ... Sartell MN 56377 320-259-2000 259-2227 789
Web: www.dezurik.com

DF (DiscountFavors.com) 7801 NW 67th St ... Miami FL 33166 786-838-4004 939-1934* 459
**Fax Area Code:* 800 ■ *TF:* 800-939-1980 ■ *Web:* www.discountfavors.com

DF Grafix 5131 Santa Fe St Ste C ... San Diego CA 92109 858-866-0858 866-0789 627
Web: www.dfgrafix.com

DFC (Designer Flower Ctr)
3450 W Gettysburg Ave ... Fresno CA 93722 559-228-3300 228-3305 293
Web: www.designerflowercenter.net

DFDFCU (Denver Fire Department Federal Credit Union)
12 Lakeside Ln ... Denver CO 80212 303-228-5300 228-5333 219
TF: 866-880-7770 ■ *Web:* www.dfdfcu.com

DFI 2404 51 Ave NW ... Edmonton AB T6P0E4 877-334-7453 536
TF: 877-334-7453 ■ *Web:* www.dfi.ca

DFJ (Draper Fisher Jurvetson)
2882 Sand Hill Rd Ste 150 ... Menlo Park CA 94025 650-233-9000 792
Web: www.dfj.com

DFMC (Delmarva Foundation For Medical Care Inc)
28464 Marlboro Ave ... Easton MD 21601 410-822-0697 822-7971 474
Web: www.dfmc.org

DFRC (U.S. Dairy Forage Research Ctr)
1925 Linden Dr W ... Madison WI 53706 608-890-0050 668
Web: www.ars.usda.gov

DFS 500 Main St ... Groton MA 01471 800-225-9528 110
TF: 800-225-9528 ■ *Web:* www.dfsonline.com

DFS (Diversified Fastening Systems Inc)
501 Richings St ... Charles City IA 50616 800-833-6417 228-6124* 351
**Fax Area Code:* 641 ■ *TF:* 800-833-6417 ■ *Web:* www.dfsusa.com

DFS Flooring Inc 15651 Saticoy St ... Van Nuys CA 91406 818-374-5200 779-1504 291
Web: www.dfsflooring.com

DFS Inc 167 W 1st St ... Newell IA 50568 712-299-8566 272-4258 447
Web: www.dfsfeed.com

DFT Communications 38 Temple St ... Fredonia NY 14063 716-673-3000 387
TF: 877-653-3100 ■ *Web:* www.dftcommunications.com

DFT Inc 140 Sheree Blvd ... Exton PA 19341 610-363-8903 524-9242 789
TF: 800-206-4013 ■ *Web:* www.dft-valves.com

DFW (Dallas-Fort Worth International Airport)
2400 Aviation Dr PO Box 619428 ... Dallas TX 75261 972-973-3112 27
TF: 800-252-7522 ■ *Web:* www.dfwairport.com

Dfw Consulting Group Inc
1616 Corporate Ct ... Irving TX 75038 972-929-1199 261
Web: dfwcgi.com

DG Capital Management Inc
800 Boylston St 16th Fl Ste 1600 ... Boston MA 02199 617-896-1500 453-6501* 194
**Fax Area Code:* 857 ■ *Web:* www.dgcap.com

DG Industries 226 Viking Ave ... Brea CA 92821 714-990-3787 990-6541 455
Web: www.dgindustries.com

DG Yuengling & Son Inc
310 Mill Creek Ave ... Pottsville PA 17901 570-622-4141 102
Web: www.yuengling.com

DG3 North America Inc
100 Burma Rd ... Jersey City NJ 07305 201-793-5000 627
Web: dg3.com

DGA (Democratic Governors Assn)
1225 Eye St NW Ste 1100 ... Washington DC 20005 202-772-5600 772-5602 48-7
Web: democraticgovernors.org

DGAC (Dangerous Goods Advisory Council)
7501 Greenway Center Dr Ste 760 ... Greenbelt MD 20770 202-289-4550 289-4074 49-21
Web: www.dgac.org

DGCC (Derr & Gruenewald Construction Co)
PO Box 218 ... Henderson CO 80640 303-287-3456 190
Web: dgccsteel.com

DGM Services Inc 1813 Greens Rd ... Houston TX 77032 281-821-0500 393
Web: www.dgm-usa.com

DGT (Dreyfus Global Trade LLC)
420 Lexington Ave Ste 2631 ... New York NY 10170 212-867-7700 867-7820 60
Web: www.dreyfusglobal.com

DGT Assoc 1071 Worcester Rd ... Framingham MA 01701 508-879-0030 261
TF: 800-696-2874 ■ *Web:* www.dgtassociates.com

DH (Danbury Hospital) 24 Hospital Ave ... Danbury CT 06810 203-739-7000 374-3
TF: 800-516-3658 ■ *Web:* www.danburyhospital.org

DH Bader Management Services Inc
14435 Cherry Ln Ct Ste 210 ... Laurel MD 20707 301-953-1955 652
Web: dhbader.nabrnetwork.com

DH Blattner & Sons Inc 392 County Rd 50 ... Avon MN 56310 320-356-7351 356-7392 188-4
Web: www.dhblattner.com

DH Capital LLC
810 Seventh Ave Ste 2005 ... New York NY 10019 212-774-3720 690
Web: www.dhcapital.com

DH Web Inc 11377 Robinwood Dr Ste D ... Hagerstown MD 21742 301-733-7672 177
TF: 877-567-6599 ■ *Web:* www.dhwebsites.com

DHA (Decorative Hardwoods Assn)
42777 Trade W Dr ... Sterling VA 20166 703-435-2900 435-2573 613
Web: www.decorativehardwoods.org

DHA (Dameron Hospital Assn)
525 W Acacia St ... Stockton CA 95203 209-944-5550 374-3
TF: 866-735-2929 ■ *Web:* www.dameronhospital.org

Dhaba 309 King St W ... Toronto ON M5V1J5 416-740-6622 740-4519 671
Web: www.dhaba.ca

Dharma Drum Publications (DDP)
Ch'an Meditation Ctr 90-56 Corona Ave ... Elmhurst NY 11373 718-592-6593 637-2
Web: www.chancenter.org

Dharma Publishing
35788 Hauser Bridge Rd ... Cazadero CA 95421 707-847-3717 637-2
TF: 800-873-4276 ■ *Web:* www.dharmapublishing.com

Dharma Sushi Restaurant
1576 Argyle St ... Halifax NS B3J2B3 902-425-7785 671
Web: dharmasushi.ca

Dharma Systems Inc
Brookline Business Ctr 55 Rte 13 ... Brookline NH 03033 603-732-4001 732-4003 178-1
Web: www.dharma.com

Dharma Trading Co 1604 Fourth St ... San Rafael CA 94901 415-456-1211 711
TF: 800-542-5227 ■ *Web:* dharmatrading.com

DHC (Dechert-Hampe & Co)
33332 Valle Rd ... San Juan Capistrano CA 92675 949-429-1999 194
Web: www.dechert-hampe.com

DHC (DeKalb History Ctr)
Old Courthouse on the Square 101 E Court Sq ... Decatur GA 30030 404-373-1088 373-8287 48-13
Web: www.dekalbhistory.org

DHC Communications Inc 607 Front St ... Nelson BC V1L4B6 250-352-0861 175
Web: www.dhc.bc.ca

DHI (Door & Hardware Institute)
14150 Newbrook Dr Ste 200 ... Chantilly VA 20151 703-222-2010 222-2410 49-3
Web: www.dhi.org

DHI Mortgage Company Ltd
10700 Pecan Park Blvd Ste 450 ... Austin TX 78750 512-502-0545 502-0031 217
TF: 800-315-8434 ■ *Web:* www.dhimortgage.com

DHL 570 Polaris Pkwy ... Westerville OH 43082 614-865-8500 449
Web: www.dhl.com

DHL Analytical
2300 Double Creek Dr ... Round Rock TX 78664 512-388-8222 388-8229 743
Web: dhlanalytical.com

DHM Adhesives Inc 509 S Wall St ... Calhoun GA 30703 706-629-7960 625-2819 711
Web: www.dhmadhesives.com

DHMC (Denver Health Medical Ctr)
777 Bannock St ... Denver CO 80204 303-436-6000 374-3
Web: www.denverhealth.org

DHMC (Davis Hospital & Medical Ctr)
1600 W Antelope Dr ... Layton UT 84041 801-807-1000 807-7610 374-3
TF: 877-898-6080 ■ *Web:* www.davishospital.org

DHR Intl 71 S Wacker Dr Ste 2700 ... Chicago IL 60606 312-782-1581 782-2096 266
Web: www.dhrinternational.com

DHS (Department of Homeland Security)
245 Murray Ln SW ... Washington DC 20528 202-981-6100 235-0443* 340-11
**Fax Area Code:* 703 ■ *Web:* www.dhs.gov

DHS (Dedham Historical Society)
612 High St ... Dedham MA 02026 781-326-1385 48-13
Web: dedhamhistorical.org

DHS (Dallas Historical Society)
Hall of State at Fair Park 3939 Grand Ave ... Dallas TX 75210 214-421-4500 421-7500 48-13
Web: www.dallashistory.org

DHS Consulting Inc
1820 E 1st St Ste 410 ... Santa Ana CA 92705 714-276-1135 261

DHX Advertising Inc
217 NE Eighth Ave ... Portland OR 97232 503-872-9616 7
Web: dhxadv.com

DI (Denison Industries) 22 Fielder Dr ... Denison TX 75020 903-786-6500 786-6575 308
Web: denisonindustries.com

Di Bari Engineering Pc 99 Main St ... Dobbs Ferry NY 10522 914-479-9705 261
Web: dibari.us

Di Highway Sign & Structure Corp
40 Greenman Ave ... New York NY 13417 315-736-8312 701
Web: www.dihighway.com

Di Paolo Restaurant
8560 Holcomb Bridge Rd ... Roswell GA 30075 770-587-1051 671
Web: www.dipaolorestaurant.com

Di Re' Hair Ltd 75 Third Ave ... Waltham MA 02451 781-895-4808 77
Web: direhair.com

Diabetes Research Institute
1450 NW Tenth Ave ... Miami FL 33136 954-964-4040 243-4404* 668
**Fax Area Code:* 305 ■ *TF:* 800-321-3437 ■ *Web:* www.diabetesresearch.org

Diabetic Care Services & Pharmacy
34099 Melinz Pkwy ... Eastlake OH 44095 800-633-7167 237
TF: 800-633-7167 ■ *Web:* www.diabeticexpress.com

Diablo Manufacturing Company Inc
900 Golden Gate Terr Ste B ... Grass Valley CA 95945 530-272-2241 272-2243 409
Web: www.diablosilver.com

Diablo Media LLC 2641 Walnut St ... Denver CO 80205 303-305-4052 4
Web: diablomedia.com

Diablo Valley College
321 Golf Club Rd ... Pleasant Hill CA 94523 925-685-1230 609-8085 162
TF: 800-227-1060 ■ *Web:* www.dvc.edu

Diacarb 2525 de Miniac St ... Saint-Laurent QC H4S1E5 514-331-4360 331-2694 358
Web: www.diacarb.com

Diageo North America 801 Main Ave ... Norwalk CT 06851 203-229-2100 80-1
Web: www.diageo.com

Diagnos Inc
7005 Taschereau Blvd Ste 340 ... Brossard QC J4Z1A7 450-678-8882 177
Web: www.diagnos.ca

Diagnostic Laboratory of Oklahoma LLC
225 N East 97th St ... Oklahoma City OK 73114 405-608-6100 415
TF: 800-891-2917 ■ *Web:* www.dlolab.com

Diagnostic Laboratory Services Inc
99-859 Iwaiwa St ... Aiea HI 96701 808-589-5100 415
Web: dlslab.com

Diagnostic Medical Group of Southern California
1129 S San Gabriel Blvd ... San Gabriel CA 91776 626-287-6746 287-8357 418
Web: www.dmg.net

Company / Address	City	State	Zip	Phone	Fax	Class
Diagnostic Pathology Medical Group Inc 3301 C St Ste 200e — *TF:* 800-464-0424 ■ *Web:* www.dpmginc.com	Sacramento	CA	95816	916-446-0424		415
Diagnostica Stago Inc 5 Century Dr — *TF:* 800-222-2624 ■ *Web:* www.stago-us.com	Parsippany	NJ	07054	973-631-1200	631-1618	476
Diagnostics Biochem Canada Inc (DBC) 384 Neptune Crescent — *Web:* dbc-labs.com	London	ON	N6M1A1	519-681-8731	681-8734	231
Diagraph 2538 Wisconsin Ave — *TF:* 800-626-3464 ■ *Web:* www.diagraph.com	Downers Grove	IL	60515	630-968-0646	968-7672	467
Diagrind Inc 10491 W 164th Pl — *Web:* www.diagrind.com	Orland Park	IL	60467	708-460-4333	460-8842	1
Dial Electric Supply Company Inc 2240 Kaluaopalena St — *Web:* www.dialelectricsupply.com	Honolulu	HI	96819	808-845-7811		361
Dial Machine Inc 2902 Eastrock Dr — *Web:* www.dialmachine.com	Rockford	IL	61109	815-397-6660	397-0562	454
Dial Precision Inc 17235 Darwin Ave — *Web:* www.dialprecision.com	Hesperia	CA	92345	760-947-3557	947-7746	454
Dial Security Inc 760 W Ventura Blvd — *Web:* www.dialcomm.com	Camarillo	CA	93010	805-389-6700	383-3401	693
Dial Tool Industries Inc 201 S Church St — *Web:* www.dialtool.com	Addison	IL	60101	630-543-3600		488
Dial800 10940 Wilshire Blvd 17th Fl — *TF:* 800-700-1987 ■ *Web:* www.dial800.com	Los Angeles	CA	90024	800-700-1987		224
DialAmerica Marketing Inc 960 MacArthur Blvd — *Web:* www.dialamerica.com	Mahwah	NJ	07495	201-327-0200		737
Dialight Corp 1501 SR 34 — *Web:* www.dialight.com	Farmingdale	NJ	07727	732-919-3119	751-5778	696
Dialink Corp 1660 S Amphlett Blvd Ste 340 — *TF:* 800-896-3425 ■ *Web:* www.dialink.com	San Mateo	CA	94402	800-896-3425	993-2987	387
Dialog Direct 13700 Oakland Ave Ste 400 — *TF:* 800-523-5867 ■ *Web:* www.dialog-direct.com	Troy	MI	48083	800-523-5867		317
Dialog One LLC 2380 Wycliff St Ste 200 — *TF:* 877-300-5326 ■ *Web:* dialog-one.com	Saint Paul	MN	55114	651-379-8600		768
Dialog Wireline Services LLC 3100 Maverick Dr — *TF:* 877-988-2311 ■ *Web:* www.dialogwireline.com	Kilgore	TX	75662	903-988-2311		539
Dialog, The PO Box 2030 — *Web:* thedialog.org	Wilmington	DE	19899	302-573-3109		532-4
Dialogic Inc 1504 Mccarthy Blvd — *TF:* 800-755-4444 ■ *Web:* www.dialogic.com	Milpitas	CA	95035	408-750-9400		180
Dialogue House Library 23400 Mercantile Rd Ste 2 — *TF:* 800-221-5844 ■ *Web:* www.intensivejournal.org	Beachwood	OH	44122	216-342-5170	342-5168	434-3
Dialup 4 Less.com 9586 Topanga Canyon Blvd — *Web:* www.dialup4less.com	Chatsworth	CA	91311	818-773-8023		681
Dialup USA Inc 4720 200th St SW Ste 103 — **Fax Area Code:* 866 ■ *TF:* 888-460-2286 ■ *Web:* www.dialupusa.net	Lynnwood	WA	98036	888-460-2286	627-8808*	224
Diamant Investment Corp 170 Mason St — *Web:* portfolioadvisor.com	Greenwich	CT	06830	203-661-6410		690
Diameters Inc 16700 W Ryerson Rd — *Web:* diameters-inc.com	New Berlin	WI	53151	262-785-8720	785-8724	454
Diamond & Huels PC 125 W Boeger Dr — *Web:* diamondandhuels.com	Arlington Heights	IL	60004	847-342-5920	342-5930	2
Diamond Aircraft Industries Inc 1560 Crumlin Sideroad — *TF:* 888-359-3220 ■ *Web:* www.diamondaircraft.com	London	ON	N5V1S2	519-457-4000		20
Diamond Antenna & Microwave Corp 59 Porter Rd — *Web:* www.diamondantenna.com	Littleton	MA	01460	978-486-0039		253
Diamond Attachments LLC 2801A S Mississippi — *TF:* 800-445-1917 ■ *Web:* diamondattachments.com	Atoka	OK	74525	580-889-6202		791
Diamond Avian 5300 NC Hwy 57 — **Fax Area Code:* 919 ■ *TF:* 800-353-2473 ■ *Web:* www.diamondavian.com	Hurdle Mills	NC	27541	800-353-2473	644-8511*	45
Diamond Bakery Co 756 Moowaa St — *Web:* www.diamondbakery.com	Honolulu	HI	96817	808-847-3551		297-3
Diamond Bar High School 21400 Pathfinder Rd — *Web:* dbhs.wvusd.k12.ca.us	Diamond Bar	CA	91765	909-594-1405		685
Diamond Brand Canvas Products 145 Cane Creek Industrial Park Rd Ste 1 — *Web:* www.diamondbrandgear.com	Fletcher	NC	28732	828-209-0322		733
Diamond Cellar Inc 6280 Sawmill Rd — *Web:* www.diamondcellar.com	Dublin	OH	43017	614-336-4545		410
Diamond Chain Co 402 Kentucky Ave — *TF:* 800-872-4246 ■ *Web:* www.diamondchain.com	Indianapolis	IN	46225	317-638-6431		620
Diamond Chemical Company Inc Union Ave & Dubois St — *Web:* www.diamondchem.com	East Rutherford	NJ	07073	201-935-4300	935-6997	151
Diamond Coach Corp 2300 W Fourth St — *TF:* 800-442-4645 ■ *Web:* www.diamondcoach.com	Oswego	KS	67356	620-795-2191		516
Diamond Comic Distributors Inc (DCD) 10150 York Rd Ste 300 — *TF:* 800-452-6642 ■ *Web:* www.diamondcomics.com	Hunt Valley	MD	21030	443-318-8001		637-5
Diamond Council of America (DCA) 3212 W End Ave Ste 202 — *TF:* 877-283-5669 ■ *Web:* diamondcouncil.org	Nashville	TN	37203	615-385-5301	385-4955	49-4
Diamond Creek Capital 28 N Vista De Catalina — *Web:* www.diamondcreekcap.com	Laguna Beach	CA	92651	949-429-7707		528
Diamond Cut Dog Grooming School 483 Medina Rd — *Web:* www.schoolfordoggrooming.com	Medina	OH	44256	330-239-1471	239-4744	685
Diamond D. General Engineering Inc 32500 State Hwy 16 — *Web:* www.ddge.net	Woodland	CA	95695	530-662-2042		256

Company / Address	City	State	Zip	Phone	Fax	Class
Diamond Die & Mold Co 35401 Groesbeck Hwy — *Web:* www.diamond-die.com	Clinton Township	MI	48035	586-791-0700	791-5419	757
Diamond Doctor 8127 Preston Rd — *Web:* diamondsdirect.com	Dallas	TX	75225	972-342-6663	490-9771	411
Diamond Drinks Inc 600 Railway St Unit 1 — *Web:* www.diamonddrinksinc.com	Williamsport	PA	17701	570-322-2422		98
Diamond Drugs Inc 645 Kolter Dr — *TF:* 800-882-6337 ■ *Web:* www.diamondpharmacy.com	Indiana	PA	15701	724-349-1111		231
Diamond Edge Inc 661 W State St Ste B — *Web:* www.diamondedge.com	Pleasant Grove	UT	84062	801-785-8473		178-2
Diamond Energy Services Inc 1521 N Service Rd W — *TF:* 800-567-1595 ■ *Web:* diamondenergy.ca	Swift Current	SK	S9H3S9	306-778-6682		317
Diamond Equipment Inc 1060 E Diamond Ave — *TF:* 800-258-4428 ■ *Web:* www.diamondequipment.com	Evansville	IN	47711	812-425-4428	421-1036	358
Diamond Foods LLC 1050 S Diamond St — *NASDAQ: DMND* ■ *Web:* www.diamondnuts.com	Stockton	CA	95205	209-467-6000		296-28
Diamond Fruit Growers Inc 3515 Chevron Dr — *Web:* www.diamondfruit.com	Hood River	OR	97031	541-354-5300	354-5394	11-1
Diamond Graphics Inc 14350 Azurite St NW — *Web:* www.dgiusa.net	Ramsey	MN	55303	763-235-4141	235-4144	627
Diamond H2O N1022 Quality Dr — *TF:* 800-236-8931 ■ *Web:* www.diamondh2o.com	Greenville	WI	54942	920-757-5440		104
Diamond Head Inn 605 Diamond St — *Web:* www.diamondheadinn.com	San Diego	CA	92109	858-273-1900	273-8532	379
Diamond Head State Monument PO Box 621 — *Web:* www.hawaii.gov	Honolulu	HI	96809	808-587-0404		565
Diamond Hill Nursing & Rehabilitation 100 New Tpke Rd — *Web:* www.news10.com	Troy	NY	12182	518-235-1410	426-4792	450
Diamond Light School of Massage & Healing Arts 100 Sacramento Ave PO Box 2110 — *Web:* www.diamondlight.net	San Anselmo	CA	94960	415-454-6651	459-4003	685
Diamond Manufacturing Co 243 W Eighth St PO Box 4174 — **Fax Area Code:* 570 ■ *TF:* 800-233-9601 ■ *Web:* www.diamondman.com	Wyoming	PA	18644	800-233-9601	693-3500*	488
Diamond Marketing Solutions Group Inc 900 Kimberly Dr — *Web:* www.dmsolutions.com	Carol Stream	IL	60188	630-597-9100		637-6
Diamond Materials 924 S Heald St — *Web:* www.diamondmaterials.com	Wilmington	DE	19801	302-658-6524		190
Diamond Mattress Company Inc 3112 Las Hermanas St E — *Web:* www.diamondmattress.com	Compton	CA	90221	310-638-0363	638-2005	471
Diamond Offshore Drilling Inc 15415 Katy Fwy — *NYSE: DO* ■ *TF:* 800-848-1980 ■ *Web:* www.diamondoffshore.com	Houston	TX	77094	281-492-5300	492-5316	540
Diamond Packaging Company Inc 111 Commerce Dr PO Box 23620 — *TF:* 800-333-4079 ■ *Web:* www.diamondpackaging.com	Rochester	NY	14692	585-334-8030	334-9141	101
Diamond Parking Inc 605 First Ave Ste 600 — *Web:* www.diamondparking.com	Seattle	WA	98104	206-284-3100		562
Diamond Perforated Metals Inc 7300 W Sunnyview Ave — *TF:* 800-642-4334 ■ *Web:* www.diamondperf.com	Visalia	CA	93291	559-651-1889	651-1815	488
Diamond Personnel 252 W 37th St — *Web:* diamondjob.com	New York	NY	10018	212-631-7520		260
Diamond Plastics Corp 1212 Johnstown Rd PO Box 1608 — *TF:* 800-782-7473 ■ *Web:* www.dpcpipe.com	Grand Island	NE	68802	308-384-4400		596
Diamond Products Inc 333 Prospect — *TF:* 800-321-5336 ■ *Web:* diamondproductsllc.com	Elyria	OH	44035	800-321-5336	634-4035	1
Diamond Saw Works Inc 12290 Olean Rd — *TF:* 800-828-1180 ■ *Web:* www.diamondsaw.com	Chaffee	NY	14030	716-496-7417		682
Diamond Services Co 4214 Oklahoma Ave — *Web:* diamond-services.com	Woodward	OK	73801	580-256-3385		539
Diamond Services Corp 503 S DeGravelle Rd — *TF:* 800-879-1162 ■ *Web:* www.dscgom.com	Amelia	LA	70340	985-631-2187	631-2442	539
Diamond Supply Co 447 N Fairfax Ave — *Web:* www.diamondsupplyco.com	Los Angeles	CA	90036	323-966-5970		459
Diamond Supply Inc 1901 N Davidson St — *Web:* www.diamondsupply.us	Charlotte	NC	28205	704-376-2125		604
Diamond Tech Inc 4347 Pacific St — *Web:* www.dtiinnovations.com	Rocklin	CA	95677	916-624-1118		759
Diamond Technologies Inc 221 W 9th St Ste 200 — *Web:* www.diamondtechnologies.com	Wilmington	DE	19801	302-656-6050		196
Diamond Technology Inc 567 Sutter St 3rd Fl — *Web:* www.diamondti.com	San Francisco	CA	94102	415-422-0074	727-3536	180
Diamond Tool & Die Inc 508 29th Ave — *TF:* 800-227-1084 ■ *Web:* www.dtdjobshop.com	Oakland	CA	94601	510-534-7050	534-0454	757
Diamond Tour 202 Lucas St Unit A — *TF:* 800-826-5340 ■ *Web:* www.diamondtour.com	Sycamore	IL	60178	815-787-2649	787-3720	711
Diamond Transportation System Inc 5021 21st St — *Web:* diamondtrans.net	Racine	WI	53406	262-554-5400		780
Diamond Truck Body Manufacturing Inc 1908 E Fremont St — *Web:* www.diamondtruckbody.com	Stockton	CA	95205	209-943-1655		60
Diamond V 2525 60th Ave SW PO Box 74570 — *TF:* 800-373-7234 ■ *Web:* www.diamondv.com	Cedar Rapids	IA	52404	319-366-0745	366-6333	447
Diamond Vogel 1110 Albany Pl SE PO Box 380 — *Web:* www.diamondvogel.com	Orange City	IA	51041	712-737-4993	737-4998	550

Phone Fax Class

Diamond Z 11299 Bass Ln ... Caldwell ID 83605 208-585-3031 585-2112 295
TF: 800-949-2383 ■ *Web:* www.diamondz.com

Diamond Z Engineering Inc
5670 State Rd ... Cleveland OH 44134 440-842-6501 261
Web: diamondzengineering.com

Diamondback Energy Inc
500 W Texas Ave Ste 1200 ... Midland TX 79701 432-221-7400 536
TF: 866-949-6476 ■ *Web:* www.diamondbackenergy.com

DiamondJacks Casino Resort
711 Diamond Jacks Blvd ... Bossier City LA 71111 318-678-7777 133
TF: 866-552-9629 ■ *Web:* www.diamondjacks.com

DiamondRock Hospitality Co (DRHC)
3 Bethesda Metro Ctr Ste 1500 ... Bethesda MD 20814 240-744-1150 744-1199 654
NYSE: DRH ■ *Web:* drhc.com

Dian Fossey Gorilla Fund Intl
800 Cherokee Ave SE ... Atlanta GA 30315 404-624-5881 48-3
TF: 800-851-0203 ■ *Web:* gorillafund.org

Diana L. Skaggs & Partners PLLC
623 W Main St ... Louisville KY 40202 502-562-0050 582-3523 41
Web: louisvilledivorce.com

Diana's Mexican Food Products Inc
16330 Pioneer Blvd ... Norwalk CA 90650 562-926-5802 123
Web: www.dianas.net

Diane Cleaners Inc
844 Beaver Grade Rd ... Moon Township PA 15108 412-264-5261 426
Web: drycleanersmoontwp.com

Diane K. Bross PC
2139 Chuckwagon Rd Ste 305 ... Colorado Springs CO 80919 719-634-7734 41
Web: dianebrosslaw.com

Diane M. Sternlieb, Attorney
111 College St ... Carrollton GA 30117 770-214-5933 41
Web: dsternlieblaw.com

Diane Von Furstenberg 440 W 14th St ... New York NY 10014 212-741-6607 277
TF: 888-472-2383 ■ *Web:* www.dvf.com

DIANON Systems Inc 1 Forest Pkwy ... Shelton CT 06484 203-926-7100 418
TF: 800-328-2666 ■ *Web:* www.dianon.com

Diario Las Americas
888 Brickell Ave 5th Fl ... Miami FL 33131 305-633-3341 532-2
Web: www.diariolasamericas.com

Dias, Clifford Pe PC 2 Wall St ... New York NY 10005 212-608-4811 261
Web: diaseng.com

DiaSorin Inc 1951 NW Ave ... Stillwater MN 55082 651-439-9710 231
TF: 855-677-0600 ■ *Web:* www.diasorin.com

DiaSorin Molecular LLC
11331 Vly View St ... Cypress CA 90630 562-240-6500 243-4703* 418
**Fax Area Code:* 714 ■ *TF:* 800-838-4548 ■ *Web:* www.focusdx.com

DIATHERIX Laboratories Inc
601 Genome Way Ste 2100 ... Huntsville AL 35806 256-327-0699 415
Web: eurofins-diatherix.com

Diaz Wholesale & Manufacturing Company Inc
5501 Fulton Industrial Blvd ... Atlanta GA 30336 404-344-5421 297-11
Web: www.diazfoods.com

Diaz-Balart Mario (Rep R - FL)
404 Cannon House Office Bldg ... Washington DC 20515 202-225-4211 225-8576 342-2
Web: mariodiazbalart.house.gov

DiAZiT Company Inc 8105 Diazit Dr ... Wake Forest NC 27587 919-556-5188 556-3757 701
TF: 800-334-6641 ■ *Web:* www.diazit.com

Diba Industries Inc 4 Precision Rd ... Danbury CT 06810 203-744-0773 419
Web: www.dibalnd.com

Dibble & Associates Consulting
7878 N 16th St Ste 200 ... Phoenix AZ 85020 602-957-1155 261
Web: www.dibblecorp.com

Dibble Institute, The PO Box 7881 ... Berkeley CA 94707 800-695-7975 423
TF: 800-695-7975 ■ *Web:* www.dibbleinstitute.org

Diboll Texas Independent School District
215 N Temple Dr ... Diboll TX 75941 936-829-4718 434-3
Web: www.dibollisd.com

Dibrina Suro Benefits Consulting Inc
62 Frood Rd Ste 302 ... Sudbury ON P3C4Z3 705-688-9393 688-9528 390
Web: www.dibrina.com

Dibuduo & Defendis
6873 N West Ave Ste 101 ... Fresno CA 93711 559-432-0222 390
Web: dibu.com

DIC Imaging Products USA Inc
7300 S 10th St ... Oak Creek WI 53154 414-764-5100 764-5032 388
Web: www.dic-global.com

Dicalite Management Group Inc
1 Belmont Ave Ste 500 ... Bala Cynwyd PA 19004 866-728-3303 668-1679* 500
**Fax Area Code:* 610 ■ *TF:* 866-728-3303 ■ *Web:* www.dicalite.com

DiCarlo Distributors Inc
1630 N Ocean Ave ... Holtsville NY 11742 631-758-6000 758-6096 297-8
TF: 800-342-2756 ■ *Web:* www.dicarlofood.com

Dice Inc 4101 NW Urbandale Dr ... Urbandale IA 50322 515-280-1144 280-1452 260
TF: 877-386-3323 ■ *Web:* www.dice.com

Dicentra 603-7 St Thomas St ... Toronto ON M5S2B7 416-361-3400 193
TF: 866-647-3279 ■ *Web:* dicentra.com

Dichello Distributors Inc
55 Marsh Hill Rd ... Orange CT 06477 203-891-2100 81-3
Web: www.dichello.com

Dick & Jenny's
4501 Tchoupitoulas St ... New Orleans LA 70115 504-894-9880 671
Web: www.dickandjennys.com

Dick Anderson Construction Inc
3424 Hwy 12 E ... Helena MT 59601 406-443-3225 443-1537 186
Web: daconstruction.com

Dick Blick Co PO Box 1267 ... Galesburg IL 61402 309-343-6181 45
TF: 800-447-8192 ■ *Web:* www.dickblick.com

Dick Brantmeier Ford Inc
3624 Kohler Memorial Dr ... Sheboygan WI 53082 920-458-6111 57
TF: 800-498-6111 ■ *Web:* www.dickbrantmeier.com

Dick Broadcasting Corp
192 East Lewis ... Greensboro NC 27406 336-274-8042 632
Web: www.dickbroadcasting.com

Dick Clark Productions Inc (DCP)
2900 Olympic Blvd ... Santa Monica CA 90404 310-255-4600 514
Web: www.dickclark.com

Dick Lavy Trucking Inc
8848 State Rt 121 ... Bradford OH 45308 937-448-2104 780
TF: 800-345-5289 ■ *Web:* dicklavytrucking.com

Dick Masheter Ford Inc
1090 S Hamilton Rd ... Columbus OH 43227 614-861-7150 57
TF: 888-839-9646 ■ *Web:* masheterford.net

Dick's Last Resort 2211 N Lambar St ... Dallas TX 75202 214-747-0001 670
Web: www.dickslastresort.com

Dick's Sporting Goods Inc
345 Court St ... Coraopolis PA 15108 877-846-9997 711
TF: 877-846-9997 ■ *Web:* www.dickssportinggoods.com

Dicke Safety Products
1201 Warren Ave ... Downers Grove IL 60515 630-969-0050 360-3
TF: 877-891-0050 ■ *Web:* www.dicketool.com

Dickel George A Co
1950 Cascade Hollow Rd ... Tullahoma TN 37388 931-857-4110 80-1
Web: www.georgedickel.com

Dickens County PO Box 120 ... Dickens TX 79229 806-623-5531 623-5240 338
Web: www.co.dickens.tx.us

Dickens Mitchener & Assn
2330 Randolph Rd ... Charlotte NC 28207 704-342-1000 652
Web: dickensmitchener.com

Dickenson County
293 Main St PO Box 1098 ... Clintwood VA 24228 276-926-1676 926-1649 338
Web: www.dickensonva.org

Dickenson County Public Schools
309 Volunteer Ave ... Clintwood VA 24228 276-926-4643 926-6374 685
Web: www.dickenson.k12.va.us

Dickerson Engineering Inc
3343 N Ridge Ave ... Arlington Heights IL 60004 847-966-0290 966-0294 256
Web: www.dei-pe.com

Dickerson Park Zoo
3043 North Fort ... Springfield MO 65803 417-833-1570 833-4459 823
Web: www.dickersonparkzoo.org

Dickerson Tool & Engineering LLC
1020 Mitchell Ave ... Chillicothe MO 64601 660-646-3378 646-1015 757
Web: www.dickersontool.com

Dickey County
205 15th St N PO Box 238 ... Ellendale ND 58436 701-349-4348 349-3277 338
Web: dickeynd.com

Dickey Transport 401 E Fourth St ... Packwood IA 52580 800-247-1081 579
TF: 800-247-1081 ■ *Web:* dickeytransport.com

DICKEY-John Corp 5200 Dickey-John Rd ... Auburn IL 62615 217-438-3371 639
Web: www.dickey-john.com

Dickie McCamey & Chilcote PC
2 Ppg Pl Ste 400 ... Pittsburgh PA 15222 412-281-7272 445
Web: dmclaw.com

Dickinson Area Partnership
600 S Stephenson Ave ... Iron Mountain MI 49801 906-774-2002 774-2004 139
Web: www.dickinsonchamber.com

Dickinson Brands Inc
31 E High St ... East Hampton CT 06424 888-860-2279 582
TF: 888-860-2279 ■ *Web:* www.dickinsonsusa.com

Dickinson Cameron Construction Company Inc
6184 Innovation Way ... Carlsbad CA 92009 760-438-9114 186
Web: dickinsoncameron.com

Dickinson College PO Box 1773 ... Carlisle PA 17013 717-243-5121 245-1442 166
TF: 800-644-1773 ■ *Web:* www.dickinson.edu

Dickinson Convention & Visitors Bureau
72 E Museum Dr ... Dickinson ND 58601 701-483-4988 206
TF: 800-279-7391 ■ *Web:* www.visitdickinson.com

Dickinson County 109 E First St ... Abilene KS 67410 785-263-3774 263-2045 338
Web: www.dkcoks.org

Dickinson County
705 S Stephenson Ave PO Box 609 ... Iron Mountain MI 49801 906-774-0988 774-4660 338
Web: www.dickinsoncountymi.gov

Dickinson County 1802 Hill Ave ... Spirit Lake IA 51360 712-336-3356 338
Web: dickinsoncountyiowa.org

Dickinson County Healthcare System
1721 S Stephenson Ave ... Iron Mountain MI 49801 906-774-1313 374-3
Web: www.dchs.org

Dickinson County Library
401 Iron Mtn St ... Iron Mountain MI 49801 906-774-1218 434-3
Web: www.dcl-lib.org

Dickinson Financial Corp
1111 Main St Ste 1600 ... Kansas City MO 64105 816-472-5244 360-2
Web: www.academybank.com

Dickinson Homes Inc
404 N Stephenson Ave/Hwy US-2 ... Iron Mountain MI 49801 906-774-2186 774-5207 106
TF: 800-438-4687 ■ *Web:* dickinsonhomes.com

Dickinson Roundell Inc 19 E 66th St ... New York NY 10065 212-772-8083 772-8186 42
Web: www.simondickinson.com

Dickinson State University
291 Campus Dr ... Dickinson ND 58601 701-483-2507 166
TF: 800-279-4295 ■ *Web:* www.dickinsonstate.edu

Dickinson Wright PLLC
1850 N Central Ave Ste 1400 ... Phoenix AZ 85004 602-285-5000 670-6009* 41
**Fax Area Code:* 844 ■ *Web:* www.dickinson-wright.com

Dickman Directories Inc
6145 Columbus Pk ... Lewis Center OH 43035 740-548-6130 637-6

Dickson Co 930 S Westwood Ave ... Addison IL 60101 630-543-3747 543-0498 201
TF: 800-757-3747 ■ *Web:* www.dicksondata.com

Dickson Consulting
351 Old Babcock Trl ... Gibsonia PA 15044 724-272-1527 463
Web: www.dicksonconsulting.biz

Dickson County 4 Court Sq ... Charlotte TN 37036 615-789-7003 789-6075 338
Web: dicksoncountytn.gov

Dickson County Chamber of Commerce
119 Hwy 70 E ... Dickson TN 37055 615-446-2349 441-3112 139
Web: www.dicksoncountychamber.com

Dickson Herald 104 Church St ... Dickson TN 37055 615-446-2811 532-4
Web: www.tennessean.com

Dickson Industries Inc
2425 Dean Ave ... Des Moines IA 50317 515-262-8061 262-1844 155-19
TF: 800-359-0325 ■ *Web:* www.dicksonindustries.com

Dickson, Gordner, & Hess
208 E Second St ... Berwick PA 18603 570-759-9814 41
Web: berwicklaw.com

Dicksons Inc 709 B Ave E ... Seymour IN 47274 812-522-1308 200
Web: www.dicksonsgifts.com

Company / Address	City	State	ZIP	Phone	Fax	Class
Dickstein Associates Agency LLC 4001 Asbury Ave 2nd Fl *Web:* dicksteininsurance.com	Tinton Falls	NJ	07753	732-578-0800		390
Dickten Masch Plastics LLC N44 W33341 Watertown Plank Rd *Web:* dicktenplastics.com	Nashotah	WI	53058	262-369-5555	367-5630	604
Diclaudio & Kramer LLC 5000 Waterdam Plaza Dr Ste 220 *Web:* www.dk-cpa.com	McMurray	PA	15317	412-220-7722		2
Dicom Inc 12412 Powerscourt Dr Ste 110 *Web:* www.dicominc.net	Saint Louis	MO	63131	314-403-7200		7
Dicon Connections Inc 33 Fowler Rd *Web:* www.diconconnections.com	North Branford	CT	06471	203-481-8080	481-8642	815
Dicon Fiberoptics Inc 1689 Regatta Blvd *Web:* diconfiber.com	Richmond	CA	94804	510-620-5000	620-4100	253
Didax Inc 395 Main St *TF:* 800-458-0024 ■ *Web:* www.didax.com	Rowley	MA	01969	800-458-0024	350-2345	243
Didi Burton Insurance Agency Inc 13860-7 Wellington Trace *Web:* didiburton.com	Wellington	FL	33414	561-333-6771		390
Didier Aaron Inc 32 E 67th St *Web:* www.didieraaron.com	New York	NY	10065	212-988-5248		42
Die Services Intl 45000 Van Born Rd *TF:* 800-555-1212 ■ *Web:* www.dieservicesinternational.com	Belleville	MI	48111	734-699-3400	699-4081	757
Diebold Nixdorf Inc 5995 Mayfair Rd *NYSE: DBD* ■ *TF:* 800-999-3600 ■ *Web:* www.dieboldnixdorf.com	North Canton	OH	44720	330-490-4000		801
Diecrafters 1349 55th Ct *Web:* www.diecrafters.com	Cicero	IL	60804	708-656-3336	656-3386	555
Diede Construction Inc 12393 N Hwy 99 W Frontage Rd *Web:* www.diedeconstruction.com	Lodi	CA	95240	209-369-8255	368-0600	186
Diederiks & Whitelaw Plc 13885 Hedgewood Dr Ste 317 *Web:* www.dwpatentlaw.com	Woodbridge	VA	22193	703-583-8300		428
Diedre Moire Corporation Inc 510 Horizon Ctr *Web:* www.diedremoire.com	Robbinsville	NJ	08691	609-584-9000		260
Dieffenbach's Potato Chips 51 Host Rd *Web:* www.dieffenbachs.com	Womelsdorf	PA	19567	610-589-2385		123
Diego & Son Printing Inc 2104 National Ave *Web:* www.diegoandson.com	San Diego	CA	92113	619-233-5373	233-4937	627
Diehl Automotive Group Inc 258 Pittsburgh Rd *TF:* 866-486-8795 ■ *Web:* www.diehlauto.com	Butler	PA	16002	724-282-8898		57
Diehl Woodworking Mach Inc 981 S Wabash St PO Box 465 *Web:* diehlmachines.com	Wabash	IN	46992	260-563-2102	563-0206	821
Diekema Hamann Engineering 612 S Park St *Web:* dhae.com	Kalamazoo	MI	49007	269-373-1108		261
Dielectric Communications Inc 22 Tower Rd *TF:* 800-341-9678 ■ *Web:* www.dielectric.com	Raymond	ME	04071	800-341-9678		647
Dielectric Corp W206N12865 Gateway Ct *Web:* dielectricmfg.com	Richfield	WI	53076	262-255-2600		596
Dielectric Laboratories Inc 2777 Rt 20 E *Web:* www.knowlescapacitors.com	Cazenovia	NY	13035	315-655-8710	655-0445	253
Dielectric Sciences Inc 88 Turnpike Rd *Web:* www.dielectricsciences.com	Chelmsford	MA	01824	978-250-1507		815
Dielectrics Industries Inc 300 Burnett Rd *TF:* 800-472-7286 ■ *Web:* www.dielectrics.com	Chicopee	MA	01020	413-594-8111	594-2343	600
Diemasters Manufacturing Inc 2100 Touhy Ave *Web:* www.thediemasters.com	Elk Grove Village	IL	60007	847-640-9900		757
Die-Matic Corp 201 Eastview Dr *Web:* www.die-matic.com	Brooklyn Heights	OH	44131	216-749-4656	749-1160	488
Die-Matic LLC 4309 Aldrich Ave SW *Web:* www.diematic.net	Grand Rapids	MI	49509	616-531-0060		456
Dierbergs Markets Inc 16690 Swingley Ridge Rd *Web:* www.dierbergs.com	Chesterfield	MO	63017	636-532-8884	532-8759	345
Dieringer Research Group Inc, The 200 Bishops Way *TF:* 888-432-5220 ■ *Web:* thedrg.com	Brookfield	WI	53005	888-432-5220		466
Diesel Dogs Fuel Service 2091 Energy Park Dr *Web:* www.dieseldogsfuelservice.com	Saint Paul	MN	55108	651-571-4242		579
Diesel Engine & Parts Co 8123 Hillsboro *Web:* www.depco.com	Houston	TX	77029	713-675-6100		358
Diesel Injection Service Company Inc 4710 Allmond Ave *TF:* 877-361-2531 ■ *Web:* www.dieselusa.com	Louisville	KY	40209	877-361-2531		247
Diesel Power Supply Co 2525 S University Park Dr *TF:* 800-234-1587 ■ *Web:* www.dieselpowersupply.com	Waco	TX	76706	254-753-1587	755-0100	62-7
Diesel Technology Forum Inc 5291 Corporate Dr Ste 102 *Web:* www.dieselforum.org	Frederick	MD	21703	301-668-7230	668-7234	533
Diesel Truck Driver Training School Inc 7190 Elder Ln *TF:* 800-332-7364 ■ *Web:* www.truck-school.com	Sun Prairie	WI	53590	608-837-7800	825-6554	685
Dieselpoint Inc 221 W Wisconsin st *Web:* dieselpoint.com	Chicago	IL	60614	773-528-1700		174
Dieste 1999 Bryan St Ste 2700 *Web:* dieste.com	Dallas	TX	75201	214-259-8000		4
Diestel Turkey Ranch 22200 Lyons Bald Mtn Rd *Web:* diestelturkey.com	Sonora	CA	95370	209-532-4950	532-5059	10-8
Die-Tech Inc 295 Sipe Rd *Web:* www.die-tech.com	York Haven	PA	17370	717-938-6771		488
Dietech Industries Inc 102 Automation Dr *Web:* www.1dietech.com	Carrollton	GA	30117	770-836-1042		350
Dieterich-Post Co 616 Monterey Pass Rd *TF:* 800-955-3729 ■ *Web:* www.dieterich-post.com	Monterey Park	CA	91754	800-955-3729	688-3729	112
Dietz & Watson Inc 5701 Tacony St *TF:* 800-333-1974 ■ *Web:* dietzandwatson.com	Philadelphia	PA	19135	215-831-9000		296-26
Diffenbaugh Inc 6865 Airport Dr *TF:* 800-394-5334 ■ *Web:* www.diffenbaugh.com	Riverside	CA	92504	951-351-6865	351-6880	186
Differentiation Strategies Inc 3950 River Ridge Dr NE Ste A	Cedar Rapids	IA	52402	319-365-3489		256
Diffraction International Inc 5810 Baker Rd Ste 225 *Web:* www.diffraction.com	Minnetonka	MN	55345	952-945-9912	400-8959	544
Diffraction Optics 4035 Transport St *Web:* www.diffractionoptics.com	Palo Alto	CA	94303	650-494-6414		544
Difilippo Flaherty & Steinhaus 305 Main St *Web:* dfslawyers.com	East Aurora	NY	14052	716-652-9600		41
DiFrancesco, Bateman, Coley, Yospin, Kunzman, Davis, Lehrer & Flaum PC 15 Mountain Blvd *Web:* newjerseylaw.net	Warren	NJ	07059	908-757-7800		428
Difusion Technologies Inc 111 Cooperative Way Ste 250 **Fax Area Code:* 512 ■ *Web:* www.difusiontech.com	Georgetown	TX	78626	800-274-8895	626-3084*	583
Dig Corp 1210 Activity Dr *TF:* 800-322-9146 ■ *Web:* www.digcorp.com	Vista	CA	92081	760-727-0914		273
Digalog Systems Inc 3180 S 166th St *Web:* www.digalogsystems.com	New Berlin	WI	53151	262-797-8000	797-8003	201
Digennaro Communications 18 W 21st St 6th Fl *Web:* digennaro-usa.com	New York	NY	10010	212-966-9525		636
Digerati Technologies Inc 3463 Magic Dr Ste 355 *OTC: DTGI* ■ *Web:* www.digerati-inc.com	San Antonio	TX	78229	210-614-7240		736
Digestive Care Inc 1120 Win Dr *TF:* 877-882-5950 ■ *Web:* www.digestivecare.com	Bethlehem	PA	18017	877-882-5950		231
Digett 4358 Lockhill Selma Ste 108 *Web:* digett.com	San Antonio	TX	78249	210-853-5808		180
Dighton Rock State Park 3rd Ave *Web:* www.mass.gov	Berkley	MA	02779	508-822-7537		565
Digi International Inc 11001 Bren Rd E *NASDAQ: DGII* ■ *TF:* 877-912-3444 ■ *Web:* www.digi.com	Minnetonka	MN	55343	952-912-3444	912-4991	176
Digicomm Systems 106 Metairie Lawn Dr 307 *Web:* www.digicommsystems.com	Metairie	LA	70001	504-212-6770	212-6772	396
DIGICON Corp 7361 Calhoun Pl Ste 430 *Web:* www.digicon.com	Rockville	MD	20855	301-721-6300		196
Digicorp Inc 3315 N 124th St Ste E *TF:* 800-253-3678 ■ *Web:* digicorp-inc.com	Brookfield	WI	53005	262-402-6100	402-6101	196
Digi-Key Corp 701 Brooks Ave S *TF:* 800-344-4539 ■ *Web:* www.digikey.com	Thief River Falls	MN	56701	218-681-6674	681-3380	246
Digilabs Inc 1017 Paradise Way Ste 245 *Web:* www.digilabstechnologies.com	Palo Alto	CA	94306	650-390-9749	390-9754	177
DigiLink Inc 840 S Pickett St *Web:* digilink-inc.com	Alexandria	VA	22304	703-340-1800		174
Digimap Data Services Inc 40 Kodiak Cres Unit 13 *TF:* 877-344-4627 ■ *Web:* www.digimap.com	Toronto	ON	M3J3G5	877-344-4627		226
Digimarc Corp 9405 SW Gemini Dr *NASDAQ: DMRC* ■ *TF:* 800-344-4627 ■ *Web:* www.digimarc.com	Beaverton	OR	97008	503-469-4800		178-12
Digineer 505 N Hwy 169 Ste 750 *Web:* digineer.com	Plymouth	MN	55441	763-210-2300	210-2301	178-10
DIGIOP 9340 Priority Way West Dr *TF:* 800-968-3606 ■ *Web:* www.digiop.com	Indianapolis	IN	46240	800-968-3606		693
Digipen Institute of Technology 9931 Willows Rd NE *TF:* 866-478-5236 ■ *Web:* www.digipen.edu	Redmond	WA	98052	425-558-0299		166
DigiPol Technologies 400 Morris Ave Ste 120 *Web:* www.digipoltechnologies.com	Denville	NJ	07834	973-227-0139	983-6290	419
Digirad Corp 13100 Gregg St Ste A *NASDAQ: DRAD* ■ *TF:* 800-947-6134 ■ *Web:* www.digirad.com	Poway	CA	92064	858-726-1600	726-1700	382
Digirati Networks 9255 E River Rd NW *Web:* digirati-networks.com	Coon Rapids	MN	55433	763-784-3500		175
Digiscribe International LLC 150 Clearbrook Rd Ste 125 *TF:* 800-686-7577 ■ *Web:* www.digiscribe.info	Elmsford	NY	10523	800-686-7577		226
Digistream Investigation 417 Mace Blvd *TF:* 800-747-4329 ■ *Web:* www.digistream.com	Davis	CA	95618	800-747-4329	866-9686	693
Digital Action Inc 8 E Germantown Pk *Web:* digital-action.com	Plymouth Meeting	PA	19462	610-941-0700		193
Digital Air Strike Co 6991 E Camelback Rd Ste B111 *TF:* 888-713-8958 ■ *Web:* digitalairstrike.com	Scottsdale	AZ	85251	888-713-8958		366
Digital Broadcast Inc 2731 NW 41 St Ste A *Web:* www.digitalbcast.com	Gainesville	FL	32606	352-377-8344		647
Digital Check Corp 10231 Trademark St *Web:* www.digitalcheck.com	Rancho Cucamonga	CA	91730	909-945-5106	948-3788	628
Digital ChoreoGraphics PO Box 8268 *TF:* 800-548-1969 ■ *Web:* www.dcgfx.com	Newport Beach	CA	92658	949-548-1969		177

	City	State	Zip	Phone	Fax	Class
Digital Communication Products Inc (DCP)						
3720 S Calhoun St	Fort Wayne	IN	46807	260-744-3365	745-1401	246
Web: www.dcpfw.com						
Digital Communications Technologies (DCT)						
5835 Blue Lagoon Dr Ste 202	Miami	FL	33126	305-809-0638		472
Web: www.digitalcomtech.com						
Digital Control Systems Inc						
7401 SW Capitol Hwy	Portland	OR	97219	503-246-8110	246-6747	203
TF: 877-468-6337 ■ *Web:* www.dcs-inc.net						
Digital Design Corp						
3820 Ventura Dr	Arlington Heights	IL	60004	847-359-3828		261
Web: digidescorp.com						
Digital Design Inc						
67 Sand Park Rd	Cedar Grove	NJ	07009	973-857-9500	857-7906	173-6
TF: 800-967-7746 ■ *Web:* evolutioninkjet.com						
Digital Dogs						
16416 N 92nd St Ste B-120	Scottsdale	AZ	85260	480-451-3647		177
Web: www.digitaldogs.com						
Digital Domain Productions Inc						
300 Rose Ave	Venice	CA	90291	310-314-2800		514
Web: www.digitaldomain.com						
Digital Dot Systems Inc 13213 F St	Omaha	NE	68137	402-408-0115		175
Web: www.ddsine.com						
Digital Employees' Federal Credit Union						
220 Donald Lynch Blvd	Marlborough	MA	01752	508-263-6700	263-6392	219
TF: 800-328-8797 ■ *Web:* www.dcu.org						
Digital Evidence Group Inc						
1730 M St NW Ste 812	Washington	DC	20036	202-232-0646		196
Web: digitalevidencegroup.com						
Digital Footprints International LLC						
2106 Pacific Ave Ste 600	Tacoma	WA	98402	253-590-4100		225
Digital Force Technologies						
6779 Mesa Ridge Rd Ste 150	San Diego	CA	92121	858-546-1244		256
Web: www.digitalforcetech.com						
Digital Formation Inc						
999 18th St Ste 2410	Denver	CO	80202	303-770-4235	770-0432	180
TF: 888-747-5372 ■ *Web:* digitalformation.com						
Digital Foundry Inc 1707 Tiburon Blvd	Tiburon	CA	94920	415-789-1600		180
Web: digitalfoundry.com						
Digital FX Inc						
6010 Perkins Rd Ste B	Baton Rouge	LA	70808	225-763-6010	763-6059	514
TF: 888-898-6010 ■ *Web:* www.digitalfx.tv						
Digital Harbor Inc						
1934 Old Gallows Rd Ste 350	Vienna	VA	22182	703-635-3477		178-10
TF: 888-368-1230 ■ *Web:* www.digitalharbor.com						
Digital Health Canada						
1100 - 151 Yonge St	Toronto	ON	M5C2W7	647-775-8555		138
TF: 844-220-3468 ■ *Web:* digitalhealthcanada.com						
Digital Hearts USA Inc						
3625 Del Amo Blvd Ste 130	Torrance	CA	90503	424-247-2800	247-2847	743
Web: digitalheartsusa.com						
Digital I/O						
7565 Siempre Viva Rd Ste A	San Diego	CA	92154	619-423-4433		177
TF: 866-423-4433 ■ *Web:* www.digitalio.com						
Digital Innovations						
3436 N Kennicott Ste 200	Arlington Heights	IL	60004	847-463-9000		52
Web: digitalinnovations.com						
Digital Innovations Inc						
PO Box 31725	Knoxville	TN	37930	865-691-6203		180
Web: www.globeserver.com						
Digital Inspections Inc						
804 NW Buchanan Ave	Corvallis	OR	97330	541-752-7233		365
Web: www.digitalinspections.com						
Digital Intelligence Systems Corp (DISYS)						
8270 Greensboro Dr Ste 1000	McLean	VA	22102	703-752-7900	854-7254*	177
**Fax Area Code:* 800 ■ *TF:* 855-765-8553 ■ *Web:* www.disys.com						
Digital Juice Inc						
18981 Us Hwy 441 Unit 354	Mount Dora	FL	32757	800-525-2203		366
TF: 800-525-2203 ■ *Web:* digitaljuice.com						
Digital Kitchen 1505 5th Ave Ste 600	Seattle	WA	98101	206-267-0400	267-0401	33
Web: www.thisisdk.com						
Digital Lagoon 9121 Bond St	Overland Park	KS	66214	913-888-3468		33
Web: lagoon.com						
Digital Light Innovations						
12317 Technology Blvd Ste 100	Austin	TX	78727	512-617-4700	599-8302	253
Web: www.dlinnovations.com						
Digital Lightbridge LLC						
11902 Little Rd	New Port Richey	FL	34654	727-863-7806		7
Web: digitallightbridge.com						
Digital Machining Systems LLC						
929 Ridge Rd	Duson	LA	70529	337-984-6013		454
TF: 800-530-8945 ■ *Web:* www.digitalmachining.com						
Digital Manga Inc						
1487 W 178th St Ste 300	Gardena	CA	90248	866-680-1589		95
Web: www.digitalmanga.com						
Digital Map Products						
18831 Von Karman Ave Ste 200	Irvine	CA	92612	949-333-5111		224
Web: www.digmap.com						
Digital Marketing Inc						
1305 W Main St Ste D	Greenwood	MO	64034	816-537-7950	537-7951	180
Web: digitalmarketinginc.net						
Digital Measures						
220 E Buffalo St 5th Fl	Milwaukee	WI	53202	866-348-5677		180
TF: 866-348-5677						
Digital Media Production Co						
907 Dimmocks Mill Rd	Hillsborough	NC	27278	919-732-3205		681
Web: www.digitalmp.com						
Digital Monitoring Products Inc						
2500 N Partnership Blvd	Springfield	MO	65803	417-831-9362		668
TF: 800-641-4282 ■ *Web:* dmp.com						
Digital Networks Group Inc						
100 Columbia Ste 100	Aliso Viejo	CA	92656	949-428-6333		224
Web: www.digitalnetworksgroup.com						
Digital Ocean Corp						
3701 Gillham Rd	Kansas City	MO	64111	816-522-5764		180
Web: www.digitaloceaninc.com						
Digital Operative Inc						
404 Camino del Rio S Ste 200	San Diego	CA	92108	619-795-0630		5
Web: www.digitaloperative.com						
Digital Outpost 2772 Loker Ave W	Carlsbad	CA	92010	760-431-3575		514
Web: www.digitaloutpost.com						
Digital Peach Web Design						
1109 Russell Pkwy	Warner Robins	GA	31088	478-922-1919		180
Web: www.digitalpeach.com						
Digital Peripheral Solutions Inc						
8015 E Crystal Dr	Anaheim	CA	92807	877-998-3440		173-8
TF: 877-998-3440 ■ *Web:* q-see.com						
Digital Photographer Magazine						
12121 Wilshire Blvd 12th Fl	Los Angeles	CA	90025	310-820-1500		457-14
TF: 800-537-4619 ■ *Web:* www.dpmag.com						
Digital Pictures 212 N Second St	Minneapolis	MN	55401	612-371-4515		177
Web: www.digitalpictures.com						
Digital Power Corp 41324 Christy St	Fremont	CA	94538	510-353-4023	657-2635	253
TF: 866-344-7697 ■ *Web:* www.digipwr.com						
Digital Printing Systems Inc						
777 N Georgia Ave	Azusa	CA	91702	626-334-1244	334-5663	627
Web: www.dpstickets.com						
Digital Pulp Inc						
220 E 23rd St Ste 900	New York	NY	10010	212-679-0676	679-6217	7
Web: www.digitalpulp.com						
Digital Realty Trust Inc						
4 Embarcadero Ctr Ste 3200	San Francisco	CA	94111	415-738-6500		654
NYSE: DLR-I ■ *Web:* www.digitalrealty.com						
Digital Reef Inc 1 Mill and Main Pl	Maynard	MA	01754	978-897-4004	689-1059*	387
**Fax Area Code:* 212 ■ *Web:* www.digitalreefinc.com						
Digital Rework Depot						
1500 Soldiers Field Rd	Brighton	MA	02135	617-562-1444		175
Web: digitalrework.com						
Digital River Inc 10380 Bren Rd W	Minnetonka	MN	55343	800-598-7450	253-8497*	39
NASDAQ: DRIV ■ **Fax Area Code:* 952 ■ *TF:* 800-598-7450 ■ *Web:* www.digitalriver.com						
Digital Room Inc 8000 Haskell Ave	Van Nuys	CA	91406	888-774-6889		627
TF: 866-266-5047 ■ *Web:* www.digitalroom.com						
Digital Security Controls (DSC)						
3301 Langstaff Rd	Concord	ON	L4K4L2	905-760-3000		692
TF: 888-888-7838 ■ *Web:* www.dsc.com						
Digital Storage Inc						
7611 Green Meadows Dr	Lewis Center	OH	43035	740-548-7179	803-8030*	174
**Fax Area Code:* 800 ■ *TF:* 800-232-3475 ■ *Web:* www.digitalstorage.com						
Digital Street Inc						
69550 Hwy 111 Ste 201	Rancho Mirage	CA	92270	866-464-5100		463
TF: 866-464-5100 ■ *Web:* www.digitalstreets.tv						
Digital Surgeons 470 James St Ste 1	New Haven	CT	06513	203-672-6201		809
Web: www.digitalsurgeons.com						
Digital Telecom Inc 6176 126th Ave	Largo	FL	33773	727-571-3300	571-1818	246
TF: 800-365-5957 ■ *Web:* www.digitaltele.com						
Digital Traffic Systems Inc						
11056 Air Park Rd	Ashland	VA	23005	804-381-5300		466
TF: 855-328-2487 ■ *Web:* www.digitaltrafficsystems.com						
Digital Video Group Inc						
8529 Meadowbridge Rd Ste 100	Mechanicsville	VA	23116	804-559-8850		647
Web: digitalvideogroup.com						
Digital Video Services						
401 Hall St SW Ste 489	Grand Rapids	MI	49503	616-975-9911		240
TF: 800-747-8273 ■ *Web:* www.dvs.com						
Digital Watchdog Inc 5436 W Crenshaw St	Tampa	FL	33634	813-888-9555		693
TF: 866-446-3595 ■ *Web:* digital-watchdog.com						
Digital West Media Inc						
15011 Highland Valley Rd	Escondido	CA	92025	760-740-1787		809
Web: www.dwmi.com						
Digital X-Ray Sales 2310 S Dock Str	Palmetto	FL	34221	941-870-3069	870-3905	743
Web: nationalxraycorp.com						
DigitalOptics Corp 3025 Orchard Pkwy	San Jose	CA	95134	408-473-2500		253
DigitalTown Inc						
10655 NE 4th St Ste 801	Bellevue	WA	98004	425-295-4564		395
Web: digitaltown.com						
DigitalWork Inc						
14300 N Northsight Blvd Ste 206	Scottsdale	AZ	85260	877-496-7571	272-6923*	39
**Fax Area Code:* 480 ■ *TF:* 877-496-7571 ■ *Web:* www.digitalwork.com						
Digite Inc						
82 Pioneer Way Ste 102	Mountain View	CA	94041	650-210-3900	210-3901	177
Web: www.digite.com						
Digitek Software Inc						
650 Radio Dr 43035	Lewis Center	OH	43035	888-764-8845		196
TF: 888-764-8845 ■ *Web:* www.digiteksoftware.com						
Digitell - Fiesta Mall 1445 W S Ave	Mesa	AZ	85202	480-835-0050		460
Digi-Trax 650 Heathrow Dr	Lincolnshire	IL	60069	847-613-2100	465-9055	351
TF: 800-356-6126 ■ *Web:* www.digi-trax.com						
Digiwaxx LLC 349 Fifth Ave	New York	NY	10016	212-665-8607		636
Web: www.digiwaxxmedia.com						
Dignity Health						
185 Berry St Ste 300	San Francisco	CA	94107	415-438-5500	438-5724	353
TF: 844-274-8497 ■ *Web:* www.dignityhealth.org						
DignityUSA Inc PO Box 376	Medford	MA	02155	202-861-0017	397-0584*	48-21
**Fax Area Code:* 781 ■ *TF:* 800-877-8797 ■ *Web:* www.dignityusa.org						
DiGrigoli School of Cosmetology						
1578 Riverdale St	West Springfield	MA	01089	413-827-0037	827-8026	685
Web: www.digrigoli.com						
DiHydro Services Inc						
40833 Brentwood Dr	Sterling Heights	MI	48310	586-978-0425	978-0370	806
TF: 888-344-9376 ■ *Web:* www.dihydro.com						
DII (Doucette Industries Inc) 20 Leigh Dr	York	PA	17406	717-845-8746	845-2864	14
TF: 800-445-7511 ■ *Web:* www.doucetteindustries.com						
Dii Computers Inc						
2425 Blair Mill Rd	Willow Grove	PA	19090	215-657-5055		246
Web: d2integratedsolutions.com						
Dijet Inc 45807 Helm St	Plymouth	MI	48170	734-454-9100	454-9395	493
Web: www.dijetusa.com						
Diji Integrated Press						
6704 Benjamin Rd Ste 100	Tampa	FL	33634	813-289-1660		5
Web: www.dijipress.com						
Dikar Tool Company Inc 22635 Heslip Dr	Novi	MI	48375	248-348-0010	348-1311	493
Web: www.dikartool.com						
Dileo Engineering LLC						
2241 W Larkspur Dr	Phoenix	AZ	85029	602-395-0756		256
Dileonardo International Inc						
2340 Post Rd	Warwick	RI	02886	401-732-2900		194
Web: www.dileonardo.com						

	Phone	Fax	Class
Diliberto+Associates Consulting Inc (D+AC) 3020 Bridgeway Ste 235 Sausalito CA 94965 *Fax Area Code: 800 ■ TF: 800-922-4750 ■ Web: www.dilibertoassoc.com	415-332-2227	257-7763*	192
Dillard Academy Charter School 504 W Elm St Goldsboro NC 27530 Web: www.dillardacademy.org	919-581-0166		685
Dillard Environmental Service 3120 Camino Diablo Rd Byron CA 94514 TF: 800-675-1066 ■ Web: dillardenv.com	925-634-6850	634-0874	780
Dillard Mill State Historic Site 142 Dillard Mill Rd Davisville MO 65456 Web: mostateparks.com	573-244-3120		565
Dillard University 2601 Gentilly Blvd New Orleans LA 70122 Web: www.dillard.edu	504-283-8822		95
Dillard's Inc 1600 Cantrell Rd Little Rock AR 72201 NYSE: DDS ■ TF: 800-643-8274 ■ Web: www.dillards.com	501-376-5200		229
Diller Telephone 318 Commercial St Diller NE 68342 TF: 877-668-9749 ■ Web: www.diodecom.net	402-793-5330		224
Dillingham & Murphy LLP 601 Montgomery St Ste 1900 San Francisco CA 94111 Web: dillinghammurphy.com	415-397-2700		41
Dillmeier Enterprises Inc 2903 Industrial Park Rd Van Buren AR 72956 Web: www.dillmeierglass.com	479-474-7733		321
Dillon Aero Inc 8009 E Dillons Way Scottsdale AZ 85260 TF: 800-881-4231 ■ Web: dillonaero.com	480-333-5450	948-6616	807
Dillon Bodley & Associates PC 63 Myron St West Springfield MA 01089 Web: bkdilloncpa.com	413-785-1150	734-0805	2
Dillon Chemical 705 General Washington Ave Ste 703 Jeffersonville PA 19403 TF: 800-998-3295 ■ Web: www.cleanitsupply.com	610-539-5202	539-5292	76
Dillon Clarence Public Library 2336 Lamington Rd Bedminster NJ 07921 Web: www.dillonlibrary.org	908-234-2325		434-3
Dillon County Library 600 E Main St Dillon SC 29536 Web: dillon.lib.sc.us	843-774-0330	774-0733	434-3
Dillon CPAS PLLC 23537 Kingsland Blvd Ste 100 Katy TX 77494 Web: dilloncpas.com	281-578-2002	578-2977	2
Dillon Manufacturing Inc 2115 Progress Dr Springfield OH 45505 *Fax Area Code: 800 ■ TF: 800-428-1133 ■ Web: dillonmfg.com	937-325-8482	634-6480*	493
Dillon Video & Film Productions Inc 1552 SW Seventh Rd PO Box 82 Ocala FL 34471 Web: www.dillonvideo.com	352-620-0686		514
Dillon Works! Inc 11775 Harbour Reach Dr Mukilteo WA 98275 Web: dillonworks.com	425-493-8309	493-8310	4
Dillon Yarn Inc 1019 Titan Rd Dillon SC 29536 Web: dillonyarn.com	843-774-7353		745-9
Dilmar Oil Company Inc 1951 W Darlington St PO Box 5629 Florence SC 29501 TF: 800-922-5823 ■ Web: www.dilmar.com	800-922-5823		780
Diloreto, Cosentino & Bolinger PC 330 Lincoln Way E Chambersburg PA 17201 Web: dcblaw.com	717-264-2096		41
Diman Regional Vocational Technical High School 251 Stonehaven Rd Fall River MA 02723 Web: www.dimanregional.org	508-678-2891	679-6423	800
Dimar Manufacturing Corp 10123 Main St Clarence NY 14031 Web: www.dimarmfg.com	716-759-0351	759-0389	697
DiMare Fresh Inc 4629 Diplomacy Rd Fort Worth TX 76155 Web: www.dimarefresh.com	817-385-3000		297-7
DiMare Homestead Inc PO Box 900460 Homestead FL 33090 Web: www.dimareinc.com	305-245-4211		297-7
DiMassimo Goldstein 220 E 23rd St 2nd Fl New York NY 10010 *Fax Area Code: 646 ■ Web: digobrands.com	212-253-7500	507-5850*	4
Dimatic Die and Tool Co 9520 N 48th St Omaha NE 68152 Web: dimatic.com	402-571-7300	571-0153	604
Dimation Inc 505 W Travelers Trl Burnsville MN 55337 Web: www.dimation.com	952-746-3030		253
Dimco Gray Corp 900 Dimco Way Centerville OH 45458 Web: dimcogray.com	937-433-7600		596
Dimco Steel Inc 3901 S Lamar St Dallas TX 75215 TF: 877-428-8336 ■ Web: www.dimcosteel.com	214-428-8336	428-1929	686
Dime Bank, The 820 Church St PO Box 509 Honesdale PA 18431 TF: 888-469-3463 ■ Web: www.thedimebank.com	570-253-1902	253-5845	70
Dime Community Bancshares Inc 209 Havemeyer St Brooklyn NY 11211 NASDAQ: DCOM ■ TF: 800-321-3463 ■ Web: www.dime.com	718-782-6200		360-2
Dimension Capital Management 800 Ponce de Leon Blvd 15th Fl Coral Gables FL 33134 Web: dimensioncapital.com	305-371-2776		194
Dimension Consulting Inc 501 W Broadway Ste 800 San Diego CA 92101 TF: 855-222-6444 ■ Web: www.dimcon.com	703-636-0933		196
Dimension Development Co 769 Hwy 494 Natchitoches LA 71457 Web: www.dimdev.com	318-352-8238	352-8276	379
Dimension Energy Services LLC 1 Fluor Daniel Dr Ste D1-7-50 Sugar Land TX 77478 Web: dimensionenergyservices.com	832-564-4500		256
Dimension Engineering LLC 5171 Hudson Dr Hudson OH 44236 Web: www.dimensionengineering.com	330-634-1430		261
Dimension Group I LP, The 10755 Sandhill Rd Dallas TX 75238 Web: dimensiongroup.com	214-343-9400		261
Dimension Health Inc 5881 NW 151st St Ste 201 Miami Lakes FL 33014 TF: 800-483-4992 ■ Web: www.dimensionhealth.com	305-823-7664	818-8814	391-3
Dimension One Spas 2070 Hacienda Dr Ste H Vista CA 92081 Web: www.d1spas.com	760-598-8922		375
Dimensional Control Systems Inc 580 Kirts Blvd Ste 309 Troy MI 48084 Web: www.3dcs.com	248-269-9777		256
Dimensional Insight Inc 60 Mall Rd Ste 210 Burlington MA 01803 Web: www.dimins.com	781-229-9111		387
Dimeo Construction Co 75 Chapman St Providence RI 02905 TF: 888-661-7388 ■ Web: www.dimeo.com	401-781-9800	461-4580	186
Dimeo Schneider & Associates LLC 500 W Madision St Ste 3855 Chicago IL 60661 TF: 800-392-9998 ■ Web: www.dimeoschneider.com	312-853-1000	853-3352	401
Dimerco Express (USA) Corp 955 Dillon Dr Wood Dale IL 60191 TF: 888-873-4637 ■ Web: dimerco.com	630-595-7310		311
Dimex LLC 28305 SR-7 Marietta OH 45750 TF: 800-334-3776 ■ Web: dimexcorp.com	740-374-3100	374-2700	596
DiMillo's on the Water 25 Long Wharf Portland ME 04101 Web: www.dimillos.com	207-772-2216	772-1081	671
Dimitri J. Ververelli Inc 211 N 13th St Philadelphia PA 19107 Web: www.djvinc.com	215-496-0000		261
Dimmit County 103 N Fifth St Carrizo Springs TX 78834 Web: www.dimmitcounty.org	830-876-2323		338
Di-Mo Manufacturing Inc 35 Harding St Middleboro MA 02346 Web: www.di-momfg.com	508-947-2200	947-8806	604
Dimon & Bacorn Inc 444 Commerce Rd Vestal NY 13850 TF: 800-828-1676 ■ Web: www.dimonandbacorn.com	607-798-0099	798-0117	780
Din Ho's Chinese BBQ 8557 Research Blvd Austin TX 78758 Web: www.dinhochinesebbq.com	512-832-8788		671
Dinah's Garden Hotel 4261 El Camino Real Palo Alto CA 94306 TF: 800-227-8220 ■ Web: www.dinahshotel.com	650-493-2844		379
Dine College Indian Rt 64 1 Circle Dr Tsaile AZ 86556 TF: 877-988-3463 ■ Web: www.dinecollege.edu	928-724-6600		167-3
Dineen Construction Corp 70 Disco Rd Ste 300 Toronto ON M9W1L9 Web: dineen.com	416-675-7676		186
Diners Club Intl 8430 W Bryn Mawr Ave Chicago IL 60631 TF: 800-234-6377 ■ Web: www.dinersclubus.com	773-380-5160	380-5337	215
Ding King Training Institute Inc, The 3100 Airway Ste 141 Costa Mesa CA 92626 TF: 800-304-3464 ■ Web: www.dingking.com	800-304-3464		167-3
Dingell Debbie (Rep D - MI) 116 Cannon House Office Bldg Washington DC 20515 Web: debbiedingell.house.gov	202-225-4071	226-0371	342-2
Dingle & Kane PA 356 E Main St Newark DE 19711 TF: 800-429-2028 ■ Web: dinglekane.com	302-731-5200		2
Dingmanlabowitz PC 526 King St Ste 423 Alexandria VA 22314 Web: dingmanlabowitz.com	703-519-0999		41
Dings Co 4740 W Electric Ave Milwaukee WI 53219 TF: 800-494-1918 ■ Web: www.dingsbrakes.com	414-672-7830		386
Dini Communications 340 Campus Dr Edison NJ 08837 TF: 877-825-3464 ■ Web: dini.net	732-225-4514		180
Dini Group, The 7469 Draper Ave La Jolla CA 92037 Web: www.dinigroup.com	858-454-3419		225
Dining Alliance 307 Waverley Oaks Rd Ste 401 Waltham MA 02452 *Fax Area Code: 585 ■ Web: www.diningalliance.com	617-275-8430	302-4447*	463
Dinkel R. A. & Associates Inc 4641 Willoughby Rd Holt MI 48842 Web: www.ideasideas.com	517-699-7000		4
Dinkel's Bakery 3329 N Lincoln Ave Chicago IL 60657 TF: 800-822-8817 ■ Web: www.dinkels.com	773-281-7300	281-6169	296-1
Dinkelspiel Rasmussen & Mink PLLC 1669 Kirby Pkwy Ste 106 Memphis TN 38120 Web: drmlawmemphis.com	901-754-7770	756-7772	41
Dinkes & Schwitzer 820 2nd Ave 10th FL New York NY 10017 TF: 800-933-1212 ■ Web: www.wsatlaw.com	212-683-3800		428
Dinklage Feedyards PO Box 274 Sidney NE 69162 TF: 888-343-5940 ■ Web: www.dinklagefeedyards.com	308-254-5940	254-6260	10-1
Dinn Brothers Inc 221 Interstate Dr West Springfield MA 01089 Web: www.dinntrophy.com	413-750-3466	733-4949	45
DI-NO Computers Inc 2817 E Foothill Blvd Pasadena CA 91107 Web: di-no.com	626-795-6674		179
Dino Software Corp PO Box 7105 Alexandria VA 22307 TF: 800-480-3466 ■ Web: dino-software.com	703-768-2610		177
Dino's 13 Lord St Worcester MA 01604 Web: www.dineatdinos.com	508-753-9978		671
Dino's Trucking Inc 9615 Continental Indus Dr Saint Louis MO 63123 TF: 800-771-7805 ■ Web: www.dinoslogistics.com	314-631-3001	638-3562	780
Dinosaur National Monument 4545 E Hwy 40 Dinosaur CO 81610 Web: www.nps.gov	970-374-3003		564
Dinosaur Securities LLC 470 Park Ave S 9th Fl New York NY 10016 Web: dinogroup.com	212-448-9944	448-9130	401
Dinosaur State Park 400 W St Rocky Hill CT 06067 Web: www.dinosaurstatepark.org	860-529-5816	257-7601	565
Dinova LLC 6455 E Johns Crossing Ste 220 Johns Creek GA 30097 TF: 888-346-6828 ■ Web: www.dinova.com	888-346-6828		393
Dinovite Inc 101 Miller Dr Crittenden KY 41030 Web: www.dinovite.com	859-428-1000		297-8
Dinstuhl's Fine Candy Company Inc 5280 Pleasant View Rd Memphis TN 38134 Web: www.dinstuhls.com	901-377-2639		123
Dinwiddie County Public Schools 14016 Boydton Plank Rd Dinwiddie VA 23841 Web: www.dinwiddie.k12.va.us	804-469-4190	469-4197	685

Name / Address	City	State	Zip	Phone	Fax	Class
Diocesan Telecommunications Corp 1200 Lantana St *Web:* goccn.org	Corpus Christi	TX	78407	361-289-6437	289-1420	741-99
Diocese of Allentown 4029 W Tilghman St PO Box F *Web:* www.allentowndiocese.org	Allentown	PA	18105	610-437-0755	433-7822	532-2
Diocese of Beaumont 703 Archie St *Web:* www.dioceseofbmt.org	Beaumont	TX	77701	409-924-4300	838-4511	48-20
Diocese of Davenport 780 W Central Park Ave *Web:* www.davenportdiocese.org	Davenport	IA	52804	563-324-1911		48-20
Diocese of Duluth 2830 E 4th St *Web:* www.dioceseduluth.org	Duluth	MN	55812	218-724-9111		48-20
Diocese of Greensburg 723 E Pittsburgh St *Web:* www.dioceseofgreensburg.org	Greensburg	PA	15601	724-837-0901	837-0857	48-20
Diocese of Harrisburg 4800 Union Deposit Rd *Web:* www.hbgdiocese.org	Harrisburg	PA	17111	717-657-4804		48-20
Diocese of Juneau 415 6th St Ste 300 *Web:* www.dioceseofjuneau.org	Juneau	AK	99801	907-463-3237		48-20
Diocese of La Crosse 3710 E Ave S *Web:* diolc.org	La Crosse	WI	54601	608-788-7700	788-8413	48-20
Diocese of Memphis 5825 Shelby Oaks Dr *Web:* www.cdom.org	Memphis	TN	38134	901-373-1200	373-1269	48-20
Diocese of Metuchen PO Box 191 *Web:* diometuchen.org	Metuchen	NJ	08840	732-562-1990		48-20
Diocese of Nashville 2400 21st Ave S *Web:* www.dioceseofnashville.com	Nashville	TN	37212	615-383-6393		48-20
Diocese of Owensboro 600 Locust St *Web:* www.owensborodiocese.org	Owensboro	KY	42301	270-683-1545	683-6883	48-20
Diocese of Phoenix 400 E Monroe St *Web:* dphx.org	Phoenix	AZ	85004	602-257-0030		48-20
Diocese of Rochester 1150 Buffalo Rd *TF:* 800-388-7177 ■ *Web:* www.dor.org	Rochester	NY	14624	585-328-3210		48-20
Diocese of Saint Cloud 305 7th Ave N *Web:* www.stcdio.org	Saint Cloud	MN	56302	320-251-3022	251-0424	48-20
Diocese of San Bernardino Education & Welfare Corp 1201 E Highland Ave *Web:* sbdiocese.org	San Bernardino	CA	92404	909-475-5300		48-20
Diocese of Springfield-Cape Girardeau The Catholic Ctr 601 S Jefferson Ave *Web:* dioscg.org	Springfield	MO	65806	417-866-0841	866-1140	48-20
Diocese of St Augustine Inc 11625 Old St Augustine *TF:* 800-775-4659 ■ *Web:* www.dosafl.com	Jacksonville	FL	32258	904-262-3200		48-20
Diocese of Steubenville Catholic Charities PO Box 969 *TF:* 800-339-7890 ■ *Web:* www.diosteub.org	Steubenville	OH	43952	740-282-3631	282-3327	637-8
Diodes Inc 15660 N Dallas Pkwy Ste 850 *NASDAQ: DIOD* ■ **Fax Area Code:* 805 ■ *Web:* www.diodes.com	Dallas	TX	75248	972-385-2810	446-4850*	696
Diopsys Inc 16 Chapin Rd Ste 911-912 PO Box 672 *Web:* diopsys.com	Pine Brook	NJ	07058	973-244-0622	244-0670	476
Diosynth RTP Inc 101 J Morris Commons Ln *Web:* www.fujifilmdiosynth.com	Morrisville	NC	27560	919-337-4477		479
Dip Seal Plastics Inc 2311 23rd Ave *TF:* 800-634-7821 ■ *Web:* www.dipseal.com	Rockford	IL	61104	815-398-3533	398-0353	605-2
Dipasa USA 6600 Fm 802 *TF:* 855-434-7272 ■ *Web:* dipasausa.com	Brownsville	TX	78526	956-831-4072	831-5893	297-8
Dipert Travel & Transportation Ltd PO Box 580 **Fax Area Code:* 817 ■ *TF:* 800-433-5335 ■ *Web:* www.dandipert.com	Arlington	TX	76004	800-433-5335	543-3728*	760
Dipietro & Thornton 9550 Prototype Ct Ste 101 *Web:* dipietro-thornton.com	Reno	NV	89521	775-825-1040		2
diPietro Todd Salon 177 Post St 2nd Fl *Web:* dipietrotodd.com	San Francisco	CA	94108	415-397-0177		77
Diplomat Specialty Pharmacy 4100 S Saginaw St **Fax Area Code:* 800 ■ *Web:* www.diplomatpharmacy.com	Flint	MI	48507	888-720-4450	550-6272*	237
Diplomatic Language Services LLC 1901 N Ft Myer Dr Ste 600 *Web:* dlsdc.com	Arlington	VA	22209	703-243-4855		423
Dircks Moving Services Inc 4340 W Mohave St *TF:* 800-523-5038 ■ *Web:* dircks.com	Phoenix	AZ	85043	602-267-9401	267-8188	780
Direct Answer Inc 6424 Bock Rd *Web:* www.directanswer.com	Oxon Hill	MD	20745	301-567-7999		5
Direct Book Service Inc 403 S Mission St *Web:* www.dogwise.com	Wenatchee	WA	98801	509-663-9115		637-2
Direct Business Connections Inc 715 S King St Ste 320 *Web:* dbcinc-usa.com	Honolulu	HI	96813	808-531-2771	536-3516	390
Direct Choice 480 E Swedesford Rd Ste 210 *Web:* www.directchoiceinc.com	Wayne	PA	19087	610-995-8201		7
Direct Connection Printing & Mailing 1968 Yeager Ave *TF:* 800-420-9937 ■ *Web:* www.directconnectionmail.com	La Verne	CA	91750	909-392-2334		627
Direct Dental Administrators LLC PO Box 497 *TF:* 855-844-0626 ■ *Web:* www.directdentalplans.com	Milwaukee	WI	53201	855-844-0626		352
Direct Dimensions Inc 10310 S Dolfield Rd *Web:* www.dirdim.com	Owings Mills	MD	21117	410-998-0880		419
Direct Edge Media 2900 E White Star Ave *TF:* 800-556-5576 ■ *Web:* directedgemedia.com	Anaheim	CA	92806	714-221-8686	221-8688	344
Direct Federal Credit Union 50 Cabot St PO Box 9123 *Web:* www.direct.com	Needham	MA	02494	781-455-6500	455-9922	219
Direct Holdings Americas Inc 8280 Willow Oaks Corporate Dr *TF:* 800-950-7887 ■ *Web:* timelife.com	Fairfax	VA	22031	800-950-7887		96
Direct Images Interactive Inc 1933 Davis St Ste 308 *Web:* www.directimages.com	San Leandro	CA	94577	510-613-8299		344
Direct Lines Inc 16472 E State Hwy 33 *TF:* 800-786-1630 ■ *Web:* www.directlinesinc.com	Effingham	IL	62401	217-857-6444	857-6040	780
Direct Link 10700 Montgomery Rd Ste 300 *TF:* 800-216-4196 ■ *Web:* www.homehelpershomecare.com	Cincinnati	OH	45242	800-216-4196		363
Direct Mail Processors Inc 1150 Conrad Ct *Web:* www.dmpinc.net	Hagerstown	MD	21740	301-714-4700		5
Direct Mail Systems 12450 Automobile Blvd *TF:* 800-683-6245 ■ *Web:* dmsmails.com	Clearwater	FL	33762	727-573-1985		194
Direct Marketing Association Inc (DMA) 1120 Avenue of the Americas *TF:* 855-422-0749 ■ *Web:* thedma.org	New York	NY	10036	212-768-7277	302-6714	49-18
Direct Office Furniture Outlet (DOFO) 2635 Paxton St *Web:* www.directofficefurnitureoutlet.com	Harrisburg	PA	17111	717-236-7200		320
Direct Online Marketing 4727 Jacob St *TF:* 800-979-3177 ■ *Web:* www.directom.com	Wheeling	WV	26003	304-214-4850		225
Direct Optical Research Co 8725 115th Ave *Web:* www.dorc.com	Largo	FL	33773	727-319-9000		544
Direct Relief Intl 6100 Wallace Becknell Rd *TF:* 800-676-1638 ■ *Web:* www.directrelief.org	Santa Barbara	CA	93117	805-964-4767	681-4838	48-5
Direct Resource Solutions LLC 6912 N 97th Cir *Web:* www.uaaclearinghouse.com	Omaha	NE	68122	402-312-5014		5
Direct Response Insurance Administrative Services (DRIASI) 7930 Century Blvd *TF:* 800-688-0760 ■ *Web:* www.driasi.com	Chanhassen	MN	55317	800-688-0760		390
Direct Sales Corp 2973 Castro Valley Blvd *Web:* dsfcarpetonecastrovalley.com	Castro Valley	CA	94546	510-962-9751		290
Direct Selling Assn (DSA) 1667 K St NW Ste 1100 *Web:* www.dsa.org	Washington	DC	20006	202-452-8866	452-9010	49-18
Direct Services Inc 14505 Commerce Way Ste 550 *Web:* www.directservices.com	Miami Lakes	FL	33016	954-433-9810	433-8950	180
Direct Source Inc 8176 Mallory Ct *TF:* 800-934-8055 ■ *Web:* directsource.com	Chanhassen	MN	55317	952-934-8000	934-8030	178-5
Direct Sports Inc 1720 Curve Rd *TF:* 800-456-0072 ■ *Web:* www.directsports.com	Pearisburg	VA	24134	800-456-0072		711
Direct Supply Inc 6767 N Industrial Rd *Web:* www.directsupply.com	Milwaukee	WI	53223	414-358-2805		192
Direct Systems Inc 7846 Forest Hill Ave *Web:* www.directsystems.com	Richmond	VA	23225	804-320-2040	330-4748	178-1
Direct Tire & Auto Service 126 Galen St *TF:* 800-847-3776 ■ *Web:* www.directtire.com	Watertown	MA	02472	617-923-1800	926-9514	57
Direct Travel 95 New Jersey 17 *TF:* 800-366-2496 ■ *Web:* www.dt.com	Paramus	NJ	07652	201-847-9000		771
DirectBuy Inc 8450 Broadway *TF:* 800-320-3462 ■ *Web:* www.directbuy.com	Merrillville	IN	46410	855-871-7788		310
Directec Corp 908 Lily Creek Rd Ste 101 *TF:* 800-588-7800 ■ *Web:* www.directec.com	Louisville	KY	40243	502-357-5000		196
Directed Energy Inc (DEI) 1609 Oakridge Dr Ste 100 *Web:* ixyscolorado.com	Fort Collins	CO	80525	970-493-1901	232-3025	253
Directed Media Inc (DMI) 1150 N Grover *Web:* www.directedmediainc.com	East Wenatchee	WA	98802	509-886-5759	884-3167	194
DirectEmployers Association Inc 7602 Woodland Dr Ste 200 *TF:* 866-268-6206 ■ *Web:* www.dejobs.org	Indianapolis	IN	46278	317-874-9000	874-9100	393
Directions in Design Inc 1849 Craig Rd *Web:* www.directionsindesign.com	Saint Louis	MO	63146	314-205-2010	205-0889	393
Directions Research Inc 401 E Court St Ste 200 *Web:* www.directionsrsch.com	Cincinnati	OH	45202	513-651-2990		466
Directly 333 Bryant St Ste 250 *TF:* 800-787-3176 ■ *Web:* www.directly.com	San Francisco	CA	94107	800-787-3176		177
DirectMail.com 5351 Ketch Rd *TF:* 866-284-5816 ■ *Web:* www.directmail.com	Prince Frederick	MD	20678	301-855-1700	494-0756	5
DirectNET Inc 2655 Crescent Dr Unit B *TF:* 800-638-2638 ■ *Web:* www.directnet.us	Lafayette	CO	80026	303-604-0727		300
Directory One Inc 9135 Katy Fwy Ste 204 *TF:* 800-477-1324 ■ *Web:* www.directoryone.com	Houston	TX	77024	713-465-0051		225
DIRECTV Inc 2230 E Imperial Hwy *TF:* 800-531-5000 ■ *Web:* www.directv.com	El Segundo	CA	90245	800-531-5000		116
DirectWest 355 Longman Crescent *TF:* 800-667-8201 ■ *Web:* directwest.com	Regina	SK	S4W1A1	306-777-0333	352-6514	225
Dirks Group, The 3802 Hummingbird Rd *TF:* 800-866-1486 ■ *Web:* www.dirksgroup.com	Wausau	WI	54401	715-848-9865		180
Dirks, Van Essen & Murray 119 E Marcy St Ste 100 *Web:* www.dirksvanessen.com	Santa Fe	NM	87501	505-820-2700	820-2900	463
Dirksen Screw Products Co 14490 23 Mile Rd *TF:* 800-732-5569 ■ *Web:* www.dirksenscrew.com	Shelby Township	MI	48315	586-247-5400	247-9507	621
DIRTT Environmental Solutions Ltd 7303-30th St SE *Web:* www.dirtt.net	Calgary	AB	T2C1N6	403-723-5000		236

Name / Address	City	State	ZIP	Phone	Fax	Class
Dirxion LLC 1859 Bowles Ave Ste 100 *TF:* 888-391-0202 ■ *Web:* www.dirxion.com	Fenton	MO	63026	888-391-0202		174
DIS Corp 1315 Cornwall Ave *TF:* 800-426-8870 ■ *Web:* www.discorp.com	Bellingham	WA	98225	360-647-6921		178-10
Disability Law Center Inc 205 North 400 West *TF:* 800-662-9080 ■ *Web:* disabilitylawcenter.org	Salt Lake City	UT	84103	801-363-1347		41
Disability Rights Center Inc 18 Low Ave *TF:* 800-834-1721 ■ *Web:* www.drcnh.org	Concord	NH	03301	603-228-0432	225-2077	48-17
Disabled & Alone/Life Services for the Handicapped 1440 Broadway 23rd Fl *TF:* 800-995-0066 ■ *Web:* www.disabledandalone.org	New York	NY	10018	212-532-6740		48-17
Disabled American Veterans (DAV) 3725 Alexandria Pk *TF:* 877-426-2838 ■ *Web:* www.dav.org	Cold Spring	KY	41076	859-441-7300	441-1416	48-19
Disabled Sports USA (DS/USA) 451 Hungerford Dr Ste 608 *TF:* 800-543-2754 ■ *Web:* www.moveunitedsport.org	Rockville	MD	20850	301-217-0960	217-0968	48-22
Disan Engineering Corp 101 Mohawk Dr *Web:* www.disancorp.com	Nowata	OK	74048	918-273-1636		22
Disandro & Malloy PC 1760 Market St Ste 1201 *Web:* disandromalloy.com	Philadelphia	PA	19103	215-587-9900		41
DiSanto Technology Inc 10 Constitution Blvd S *Web:* www.disanto.com	Shelton	CT	06484	203-712-1030		295
DISC (Document Imaging Systems Corp) 1523 Fenpark Dr *TF:* 800-710-3472 ■ *Web:* disccorporation.com	Fenton	MO	63026	800-710-3472		396
Disc Graphics Inc 10 Gilpin Ave *Web:* www.discgraphics.com	Hauppauge	NY	11788	631-234-1400	234-1460	627
Disc Makers 7905 N Rt 130 *TF:* 800-468-9353 ■ *Web:* www.discmakers.com	Pennsauken Township	NJ	08110	800-468-9353		173-8
Discalced Carmelite Friars 2131 Lincoln Rd NE *Web:* www.ocdwashprov.com	Washington	DC	20002	202-269-3792		48-20
Discflo Corp 10850 Hartley Rd *Web:* www.discflo.com	Santee	CA	92071	619-596-3181		641
Discharge Resource Group 400 Oyster Point Blvd Ste 434 *Web:* www.drgstaffing.com	South San Francisco	CA	94080	650-877-8111	877-8129	582
Disciplined Growth Investors Inc Fifth St Towers 150 S Fifth St Ste 2550 *Web:* www.dginv.com	Minneapolis	MN	55402	612-317-4100		401
DISCO International Inc 15 W 44th St 5th Fl *Web:* www.discointer.com	New York	NY	10036	212-382-0025		260
Discount Car & Truck Rentals Ltd 720 Arrow Rd *TF:* 866-742-5968 ■ *Web:* www.discountcar.com	North York	ON	M9M2M1	416-744-7942	744-8340	126
Discount Drug Mart Inc 211 Commerce Dr *TF:* 800-833-6278 ■ *Web:* discount-drugmart.com	Medina	OH	44256	330-725-2340	722-2990	237
Discount Labels Inc 4115 Profit Ct *TF:* 800-995-9500 ■ *Web:* www.discountlabels.com	New Albany	IN	47150	800-995-9500	995-9600	413
Discount Office Equipment 1991 Coolidge Hwy *Web:* www.discountoffice.com	Berkley	MI	48072	248-548-6900	548-6905	320
Discount RampsCom LLC 760 S Indiana Ave *TF:* 888-651-3431 ■ *Web:* www.discountramps.com	West Bend	WI	53095	888-651-3431		480
Discount School Supply PO Box 734309 *TF:* 800-919-5238 ■ *Web:* www.discountschoolsupply.com	Chicago	IL	60673	800-627-2829	919-5235	761
DiscountFavors.com (DF) 7801 NW 67th St **Fax Area Code:* 800 ■ *TF:* 800-939-1980 ■ *Web:* www.discountfavors.com	Miami	FL	33166	786-838-4004	939-1934*	459
DiscountMugs.com 12610 NW 115th Ave *TF:* 800-569-1980 ■ *Web:* www.discountmugs.com	Medley	FL	33178	800-569-1980		690
Discover 2500 Lake Cook Rd *Web:* www.discover.com	Riverwoods	IL	60015	224-405-3555		215
Discover Bank PO Box 30416 *TF:* 800-347-7000 ■ *Web:* www.discover.com	Salt Lake City	UT	84130	302-323-7810		70
Discover Bank PO Box 30943 *TF:* 800-347-2683 ■ *Web:* www.discover.com	Salt Lake City	UT	84130	800-347-2683		69
Discover Communications Inc 30 Victoria Cres *TF:* 888-456-8989 ■ *Web:* www.getconnected.ca	Brampton	ON	L6T1E4	905-455-5600		224
Discover Group Inc 2741 W 23rd St *TF:* 866-456-6555 ■ *Web:* www.discovergroup.net	Brooklyn	NY	11224	718-456-4500		535
Discover Jamestown North Dakota 404 Louis L'Amour Ln *TF:* 800-222-4766 ■ *Web:* discoverjamestownnd.com	Jamestown	ND	58401	701-251-9145	251-9146	206
Discover Klamath 205 Riverside Dr Ste B *TF:* 800-445-6728 ■ *Web:* discoverklamath.com	Klamath Falls	OR	97601	541-882-1501		206
Discover Mediaworks Inc 4801 Hayes Rd *Web:* discovermediaworks.com	Madison	WI	53704	608-442-5973		7
Discover Odessa 700 N Grant Ave Ste 200 *Web:* discoverodessa.org	Odessa	TX	79761	432-333-7871		206
Discover The Palm Beaches 1555 Palm Beach Lakes Blvd Ste 800 *TF:* 800-554-7256 ■ *Web:* www.thepalmbeaches.com	West Palm Beach	FL	33401	561-233-3000	233-3009	206
Discover Your Northwest 164 S Jackson St *TF:* 877-874-6775 ■ *Web:* www.discovernw.org	Seattle	WA	98104	206-220-4140		48-13
Discoverture Solutions LLC 16100 N 71st St Ste 250 *Web:* mindtree.com	Scottsdale	AZ	85254	480-269-8100		180
Discovery Care Centre Corp 601 N Tenth St *Web:* www.discoverycare.com	Hamilton	MT	59840	406-363-2273		107
Discovery Center Museum 711 N Main St *Web:* www.discoverycentermuseum.org	Rockford	IL	61103	815-963-6769		521
Discovery Center of Idaho (DCI) 131 Myrtle St *Web:* www.dcidaho.org	Boise	ID	83702	208-343-9895		520
Discovery Center of Springfield 438 E St Louis St *TF:* 888-636-4395 ■ *Web:* www.discoverycenter.org	Springfield	MO	65806	417-862-9910	862-6898	521
Discovery Center of the Southern Tier 60 Morgan Rd *Web:* www.thediscoverycenter.org	Binghamton	NY	13903	607-773-8661	773-8019	521
Discovery Communication Latin America 6505 Blue Lagoon Dr *Web:* corporate.discovery.com	Miami	FL	33126	786-273-4700		740
Discovery Cruises Bahamas Port Everglades Terminal 1 *Web:* discoverislandcruises.com	Fort Lauderdale	FL	33316	954-969-0069		220
Discovery Ctr 1944 N Winery Ave *TF:* 800-946-3039 ■ *Web:* www.fresnodiscoverycenter.org	Fresno	CA	93703	559-251-5533		521
Discovery Detective Academy 15230 N 75th St Ste 1005 *Web:* www.discoverycollege.education	Scottsdale	AZ	85260	480-951-6545		167-3
Discovery Gateway 444 West 100 South *Web:* www.discoverygateway.org	Salt Lake City	UT	84101	801-456-5437		521
Discovery Green Conservancy 1500 Mckinney St *Web:* www.discoverygreen.com	Houston	TX	77010	713-400-7336		652
Discovery Health Partners 2 Pierce Pl Ste 1900 *Web:* www.discoveryhealthpartners.com	Itasca	IL	60143	224-265-0400		178-1
Discovery Inc 1 Discovery Pl *Web:* www.corporate.discovery.com	Silver Spring	MD	20910	240-662-0000		615
Discovery Information Technologies Inc 904 North Hwy 69 *Web:* www.discoveryit.com	Nederland	TX	77627	409-727-7080		177
Discovery Inn Hotel 4701 Franklin Ave *Web:* www.discoveryinn.ca	Yellowknife	NT	X1A2N6	867-873-4151		378
Discovery Institute 208 Columbia St *Web:* www.discovery.org	Seattle	WA	98104	206-292-0401	682-5320	634
Discovery Museum & Planetarium 4450 Park Ave *Web:* www.discoverymuseum.org	Bridgeport	CT	06604	203-372-3521		520
Discovery Place 301 N Tryon St *TF:* 800-935-0553 ■ *Web:* www.discoveryplace.org	Charlotte	NC	28202	704-372-6261		521
Discovery Science Ctr 2500 N Main St *Web:* www.discoverycube.org	Santa Ana	CA	92705	714-542-2823		520
Discovery Theater PO Box 23293 *Web:* discoverytheater.org	Washington	DC	20026	202-633-8700	343-1073	572
Discovery World 500 N Harbor Dr *Web:* www.discoveryworld.org	Milwaukee	WI	53202	414-765-9966	765-0311	520
Discraft Inc 29592 Beck Rd *Web:* www.discraft.com	Wixom	MI	48393	248-624-2250	624-2310	596
Discretion Brewing LLC 2703 41st Ave Ste A *Web:* discretionbrewing.com	Soquel	CA	95073	831-316-0662		102
Disguise 12120 Kear Pl *Web:* www.disguise.com	Poway	CA	92064	858-391-3600	391-3601	155-6
DISH Network LLC 9601 S Meridian Blvd *NASDAQ: DISH* ■ *TF:* 800-823-4929 ■ *Web:* www.dish.com	Englewood	CO	80112	800-823-4929		116
Disk Doctor Labs Inc 106 Colony Park Dr Ste100 *TF:* 800-347-5377 ■ *Web:* www.diskdoctors.com	Cumming	GA	30040	770-441-0507		175
Disk Software Inc 205 Ridgestone Dr *Web:* www.disksoft.com	Murphy	TX	75094	972-423-7288		178-5
Dismas Distribution Services LLC 320-J Outerbelt St *Web:* dismas.net	Columbus	OH	43213	614-861-2525		631
Dismex Food Inc 12255 SW 133rd Ct *Web:* dismexfood.com	Miami	FL	33186	305-238-6146		297-8
Disney 1155 Long Island Ave **Fax Area Code:* 215 ■ *TF:* 855-553-4763 ■ *Web:* www.thewaltdisneycompany.com	Brentwood	NY	11717	855-553-4763	553-5402*	514
Disney Vacation Club 1390 Celebration Blvd *TF:* 800-500-3990 ■ *Web:* disneyvacationclub.disney.go.com	Celebration	FL	34747	407-566-3100		753
Disney/Little Blue State Park Hwy 28 E *TF:* 800-622-6317 ■ *Web:* www.travelok.com	Disney	OK	74340	918-435-8066	435-2101	565
Disneyland 1313 Disneyland Dr *Web:* disneyland.disney.go.com	Anaheim	CA	92802	714-781-4636		32
Dispatch 1401 W 94th St *Web:* www.dispatchit.com	Bloomington	MN	55431	952-444-5280		177
Dispatch Health 3455 Ringsby Ct Ste 102 *Web:* www.dispatchhealth.com	Denver	CO	80126	720-647-5329		48-17
Dispatch Publishing Company Inc, The 30 E First Ave *Web:* www.the-dispatch.com	Lexington	NC	27293	336-249-3981		532-3
Dispatch Technologies Inc 123 N Washington St 2nd Fl *Web:* dispatch.me	Boston	MA	02114	617-580-0607		463
Dispatch, The PO Box 248 *Web:* www.dispatchnews.com	Eatonville	WA	98328	360-832-4411		532-4
Dispenser Services Inc (DSI) 4273 Domino Ave *TF:* 800-742-2566 ■ *Web:* www.dispenserservices.com	Charleston	SC	29405	800-742-2566		300
Dispensers Optical Service Corp 1815 Plantside Dr	Louisville	KY	40299	502-491-3440		542
Dispensing Dynamics Intl 1020 Bixby Dr *TF:* 800-888-3698 ■ *Web:* dispensingdynamics.com	City of Industry	CA	91745	626-961-3691		610
Display Pack 650 West St *Web:* www.displaypack.com	Cedar Springs	MI	49319	616-451-3061	451-8907	88
Display Smart LLC 801 W 27th Terr *TF:* 888-843-1870 ■ *Web:* www.display-smart.com	Lawrence	KS	66046	785-843-1869		233
Display Technologies LLC 1111 Marcus Ave Ste M68 *TF:* 800-424-4220 ■ *Web:* www.display-technologies.com	Lake Success	NY	11042	800-424-4220		233
DisplayLink Corp 480 S California Ave Ste 305 *Web:* www.displaylink.com	Palo Alto	CA	94306	650-838-0481		668
Disposable Instrument Co 14248 Santa Fe Trl Dr *Web:* disposableinstrument.com	Shawnee Mission	KS	66215	913-492-6492		476

Name / Address	City	State	ZIP	Phone	Fax	Class
Dispute Resolution Management Inc						
770 E 9000 S Ste A2	Sandy	UT	84094	801-355-1444	568-2410	463
Web: www.drmworld.com						
Disqus Inc 301 Howard St Ste 300	San Francisco	CA	94105	415-738-8848		387
Web: disqus.com						
Disruptive Advertising						
384 S 400 W Ste 200	Lindon	UT	84042	877-956-7510		49-18
TF: 877-956-7510 ■ *Web:* www.disruptiveadvertising.com						
Dissident Books Ltd (DB) PO Box 20547	New York	NY	10021	646-422-3100		637-2
Web: www.dissidentbooks.com						
Dissolve Inc 425 78 Ave SW	Calgary	AB	T2V5K5	800-518-6748		224
TF: 800-518-6748 ■ *Web:* dissolve.com						
Disston Precision Inc						
6795 State Rd	Philadelphia	PA	19135	215-338-1200	338-7060	682
TF: 800-238-1007 ■ *Web:* www.disstonprecision.com						
Distance Education & Training Council (DETC)						
1601 18th St NW Ste 2	Washington	DC	20009	202-234-5100	332-1386	48-1
Web: www.deac.org						
Distant Focus Corp						
4114b Fieldstone Rd	Champaign	IL	61822	217-351-2655	351-2644	196
Web: distantfocus.com						
Distant Horizon PO Box 574	Frankfort	IL	60423	773-932-7483		177
Web: www.distanthorizon.com						
Distek Inc 121 N Center Dr	North Brunswick	NJ	08902	732-422-7585		111
Web: www.distekinc.com						
Distek Integration Inc						
6612 Chancellor Dr Ste 600	Cedar Falls	IA	50613	319-859-3600		177
Web: www.distek.com						
Distillata Co 1608 E 24th St	Cleveland	OH	44114	216-771-2900	771-1672	805
TF: 800-999-2906 ■ *Web:* distillata.com						
Distilled 120 W 2nd St	Lexington	KY	40507	859-255-0002		671
Web: distilledatgratzparkinn.com						
Distilled Spirits Council of the US Inc						
1250 'I' St NW Ste 400	Washington	DC	20005	202-628-3544	682-8888	49-6
Web: www.distilledspirits.org						
Distillery Restaurant Inc, The						
1142 Mt Hope Ave	Rochester	NY	14620	585-271-2044		360-3
Web: thedistillery.com						
Distinct Corp						
3315 Almaden Expy Ste 10	San Jose	CA	95118	408-445-3270	445-3274	178-12
Web: www.distinct.com						
Distinctive Dental Studio Limited Inc						
1504 Wall St	Naperville	IL	60563	800-552-7890		415
TF: 800-552-7890 ■ *Web:* www.ddsltdlab.com						
Distinctive Designs International Inc						
120 Sibley Dr	Russellville	AL	35654	800-243-4787		293
TF: 800-243-4787 ■ *Web:* www.distinctivedesigns.com						
Distinguished Programs Group LLC, The						
1180 Avenue of the Americas 16th Fl	New York	NY	10036	212-297-3100		390
TF: 888-355-4626 ■ *Web:* www.distinguished.com						
Dis-Tran Steel Fabrication LLC						
529 Cenla Dr	Pineville	LA	71360	318-448-0274	445-4454	480
Web: www.distransteel.com						
Distribution Contractors Assn (DCA)						
101 W Renner Rd Ste 460	Richardson	TX	75082	972-680-0261	680-0461	49-3
Web: www.dcaweb.org						
Distribution Management Systems Inc						
17002 Marcy St Ste 200	Omaha	NE	68118	402-330-6620		225
Web: dmsi.com						
Distribution Technology Inc						
1701 Continental Blvd	Charlotte	NC	28273	704-587-5587	587-5591	803-1
Web: www.distributiontechnology.com						
Distributor's Link Inc						
4297 Corporate Sq	Naples	FL	34104	239-643-2713	643-5220	637-9
TF: 800-356-1639 ■ *Web:* www.linkmagazine.com						
Distributors & Consolidators of America						
2240 Bernays Dr	York	PA	17404	888-519-9195		311
TF: 888-519-9195 ■ *Web:* www.dacacarriers.com						
Distributors Solutions LLC PO Box 4030	Golden	CO	80401	303-277-3359		196
Web: distributorssolutions.com						
Distributors Warehouse Inc						
1900 Tenth St	Paducah	KY	42001	270-442-8201	442-4914	61
Web: btbauto.com						
District 1199 C Training & Upgrade Fund						
100 S Broad St	Philadelphia	PA	19110	215-568-2220		507
Web: www.1199ctraining.org						
District Court of the Virgin Islands						
U.S. Virgin Islands						
3013 Estate Golden Rock Ste 219	Saint Croix	VI	00820	340-774-0640	775-8075	341-2
Web: www.vid.uscourts.gov						
District Creative Printing Inc						
6350 Fallard Dr	Upper Marlboro	MD	20772	301-868-8610	868-1015	627
Web: dcpprint.com						
District of Columbia						
Aging Office 500 K St NE	Washington	DC	20002	202-724-5626	724-2008	339-9
Web: dcoa.dc.gov						
Bill Status						
1350 Pennsylvania Ave NW	Washington	DC	20004	202-724-8026	724-8129	433
Web: dccouncil.us						
Commission on the Arts & Humanities						
200 I St SE	Washington	DC	20003	202-724-5613	727-4135	339-9
Web: www.dcarts.dc.gov						
Consumer & Regulatory Affairs Dept						
1100 4th St SW	Washington	DC	20024	202-442-4400	442-9445	339-9
Web: www.dcra.dc.gov						
Crime Victims Compensation Program						
515 Fifth St NW Court Bldg A Rm 109	Washington	DC	20001	202-879-4216	879-4230	339-9
Web: www.dccourts.gov						
Economic Development						
1350 Pennsylvania Ave NW Ste 317	Washington	DC	20004	202-727-6365	727-6703	339-9
Web: dmped.dc.gov						
Government Information						
920 Varnum St NE	Washington	DC	20017	202-269-7400		339-9
Web: dc.gov						
Historic Preservation Office (HPO)						
1100 Fourth St SW Ste E650	Washington	DC	20024	202-442-8800	442-7638	339-9
Web: planning.dc.gov						
Homeland Security & Emergency Management Agency						
2720 Martin Luther King Jr Ave SE	Washington	DC	20032	202-727-6161	715-7288	339-9
Web: hsema.dc.gov						
Housing Finance Agency						
815 Florida Ave NW	Washington	DC	20001	202-777-1600		339-9
Web: www.dchfa.org						
Human Services Dept						
64 New York Ave NE 6th Fl	Washington	DC	20002	202-671-4200	671-4326	339-9
Web: www.dhs.dc.gov						
Lottery & Charitable Games Co						
2235 Shannon Pl SE	Washington	DC	20020	202-645-8000		452
Web: www.dclottery.com						
Paternity & Child Support Enforcement Office						
441 Fourth St NW Ste 550N	Washington	DC	20001	202-442-9900		339-9
Web: cssd.dc.gov						
Public Service Commission						
1325 G St NW Ste 800	Washington	DC	20005	202-626-5100	393-1389	339-9
Web: www.dcpsc.org						
Rehabilitation Services Administration (RSA)						
250 E St SW	Washington	DC	20024	202-730-1700	730-1843	339-9
Web: dds.dc.gov						
Tuition Assistance Grant Program						
810 First St NE	Washington	DC	20001	202-727-2824		725
TF: 877-485-6751 ■ *Web:* osse.dc.gov						
Vital Records Div						
899 N Capitol St NE 1st Fl	Washington	DC	20002	202-442-5955	442-4795	339-9
Web: dchealth.dc.gov						
District of Columbia Academy of Veterinary Medicine						
PO Box 710477	Herndon	VA	20171	703-733-0556	742-8745	795
Web: www.dcavm.org						
District of Columbia Chamber of Commerce						
506 Ninth St NW	Washington	DC	20004	202-347-7201		140
Web: www.dcchamber.org						
District of Columbia Dental Society						
2025 M St NW Ste 800	Washington	DC	20036	202-367-1163		227
Web: www.dcdental.org						
District of Columbia Nurses Assn (DCNA)						
5100 Wisconsin Ave NW Ste 306	Washington	DC	20016	202-244-2705	362-8285	533
Web: www.dcna.org						
District of Columbia Public Schools (DCPS)						
1200 First St NE	Washington	DC	20002	202-442-5885	442-5026	685
Web: dcps.dc.gov						
District Petroleum Products Inc						
1814 River Rd Ste 100	Huron	OH	44839	419-433-8119		579
Web: hymiler.com						
District Photo Inc						
10501 Rhode Island Ave	Beltsville	MD	20705	301-937-5300		588
Web: www.districtphoto.com						
DISYS (Digital Intelligence Systems Corp)						
8270 Greensboro Dr Ste 1000	McLean	VA	22102	703-752-7900	854-7254*	177
**Fax Area Code:* 800 ■ *TF:* 855-765-8553 ■ *Web:* www.disys.com						
Ditch Witch Midwest						
124 N Schmale Rd	Carol Stream	IL	60188	630-665-5600	665-6484	358
TF: 800-243-1328 ■ *Web:* www.ditchwitchmidwest.com						
Ditch Witch of Houston 14565 N Fwy	Houston	TX	77090	713-462-8866	680-6966*	358
**Fax Area Code:* 832 ■ *TF:* 866-650-5013 ■ *Web:* www.dwhouston.com						
Ditch Witch Sales Inc						
1617 S Service Rd	Sullivan	MO	63080	573-468-8012	468-8016	385
TF: 800-392-3633 ■ *Web:* www.ditchwitchsales.com						
DIT-MCO International Corp						
5612 Brighton Terr	Kansas City	MO	64130	816-444-9700		248
TF: 800-821-3487 ■ *Web:* www.ditmco.com						
Dito LLC						
11710 Plaza America Dr Ste 2000	Reston	VA	20190	855-937-3486		180
TF: 855-937-3486 ■ *Web:* www.ditoweb.com						
Ditta Meat Co PO Box 5023	Pasadena	TX	77508	281-487-2010		297-9
Web: dittameat.com						
Dittman-Adams Co 4946 Rialto Rd	West Chester	OH	45069	513-870-7530	870-7535	756
TF: 800-686-0889 ■ *Web:* dittman-adams.com						
Ditto 1020 Ridge Ave	Pittsburgh	PA	15233	412-434-6666	434-7276	113
Web: www.dittohq.com						
Ditto Apparel of California Inc						
229 Webb Smith Dr	Colfax	LA	71417	318-627-3264		155-11
Ditto Sales Inc 2332 Cathy Ln	Jasper	IN	47546	812-482-3043	482-9318	487
Web: www.dittosales.com						
Dittoe Public Relations Inc						
5420 N College Ave Ste 200	Indianapolis	IN	46220	317-202-2280		636
Web: dittoepr.com						
Dittrich Specialties Inc						
2110 N Broadway St	New Ulm	MN	56073	507-359-2650	359-5413	393
Web: www.dittrichspecialties.com						
Div 15 Sales Inc 12026 Roberts Rd	La Vista	NE	68128	402-597-6353		641
Web: division-15.com						
Diva at the Met 645 Howe St	Vancouver	BC	V6C2Y9	604-602-7788		671
TF: 800-667-2300 ■ *Web:* www.metropolitan.com						
Divane Bros Electric Co						
2424 N 25th Ave	Franklin Park	IL	60131	847-455-7143		189-4
Web: www.divanebros.com						
Divaris Real Estate Inc						
4525 Main St Ste 900	Virginia Beach	VA	23462	757-497-2113	497-1338	652
Web: www.divaris.com						
DIVC O Inc 2806 N Sheridan Rd	Tulsa	OK	74115	918-836-9101	835-4801	385
TF: 800-874-1351 ■ *Web:* www.divcoinc.com						
Divcon Controls 14611 Burnet Rd Ste 109	Austin	TX	78728	214-821-6958		463
Web: www.divconcontrols.com						
DIVDAT (Diversified Data and Communications)						
10811 Northend Ave	Ferndale	MI	48220	800-356-8561		224
TF: 800-356-8561 ■ *Web:* www.divdat.com						
Dive N' Surf Inc 504 N Broadway	Redondo Beach	CA	90277	310-372-8423		711
Web: divensurf.com						
Divergent Energy Services						
1500 715 - Fifth Ave SW	Calgary	AB	T2P2X6	403-543-0060		539
Web: www.divergentenergyservices.com						
Divers Academy Intl 1500 Liberty Pl	Erial	NJ	08081	800-238-3483		800
TF: 800-238-3483 ■ *Web:* www.diversacademy.edu						
Divers Institute of Technology						
1341 N Northlake Way Ste 150	Seattle	WA	98103	800-634-8377	839-5099*	167-3
**Fax Area Code:* 206 ■ *TF:* 800-634-8377 ■ *Web:* www.diversinstitute.edu						

Company / Address	City	State	ZIP	Phone	Fax	Class
Divers Supply 5208 Mercer University Dr *TF:* 800-999-3483 ■ *Web:* www.divers-supply.com	Macon	GA	31210	478-474-6790		167-3
Divers Supply Indy Inc 104 S Post Rd *Web:* diverssupplyindy.com	Indianapolis	IN	46219	317-897-2822		711
Diversatech Plastics Group LLC 3830 Cowan Hwy *Web:* www.dpgllc.com	Winchester	TN	37398	931-967-7418		604
Diverse Optics Inc 10310 Regis Ct *Web:* www.diverseoptics.com	Rancho Cucamonga	CA	91730	909-593-9330	596-1452	544
Diverse Power Inc 1400 S Davis Rd *TF:* 800-845-8362 ■ *Web:* www.diversepower.com	LaGrange	GA	30241	706-845-2000		245
Diverse Staffing Inc 6325 Digital Way Ste 100 *Web:* www.diversestaffing.com	Indianapolis	IN	46278	317-813-8000		734
Diversegy LLC 520 Broad St **Fax Area Code:* 973 ■ *Web:* www.diversegy.com	Newark	NJ	07102	201-374-9641	438-1893*	393
Diversicare Healthcare Services Inc 1621 Galleria Blvd *Web:* dvcr.com	Brentwood	TN	37027	615-771-7575		194
Diversified 37 Market St *Web:* diversifiedus.com	Kenilworth	NJ	07033	908-245-4833		744
Diversified Adjustment Service Inc 600 Coon Rapids Blvd *TF:* 800-279-3733 ■ *Web:* www.diversifiedadjustment.com	Coon Rapids	MN	55433	763-783-2303	783-2390	160
Diversified Benefit Services Inc 1391 W Shaw Ave Ste A *TF:* 800-793-7133 ■ *Web:* dbs-ca.com	Fresno	CA	93711	559-226-7133	226-7354	390
Diversified Brokerage Services Inc 5501 Excelsior Blvd *Web:* www.dbs-lifemark.com	Minneapolis	MN	55416	952-697-5000		390
Diversified Business Communications 121 Free St *Web:* www.divcom.com	Portland	ME	04101	207-842-5500		637-9
Diversified Chemical Technologies Inc (DCT) 15477 Woodrow Wilson St *TF:* 800-243-1424 ■ *Web:* www.dchem.com	Detroit	MI	48238	313-867-5444	867-3831	145
Diversified Contractors Inc 15915 Highland Dr *Web:* www.diversifiedtn.com	Mckenzie	TN	38201	731-352-7996	352-7785	480
Diversified Data and Communications (DIVDAT) 10811 Northend Ave *TF:* 800-356-8561 ■ *Web:* www.divdat.com	Ferndale	MI	48220	800-356-8561		224
Diversified Distributors Inc 11921 Portland Ave S Ste A *Web:* ddicabinets.com	Burnsville	MN	55337	952-808-9646	808-9656	362
Diversified Electronics Company Inc PO Box 566 *TF:* 800-646-7278 ■ *Web:* www.diversifiedelectronics.com	Forest Park	GA	30298	404-361-4840	361-6327	246
Diversified Fastening Systems Inc (DFS) 501 Richings St **Fax Area Code:* 641 ■ *TF:* 800-833-6417 ■ *Web:* www.dfsusa.com	Charles City	IA	50616	800-833-6417	228-6124*	351
Diversified Foam Products Inc 121 High Hill Rd *TF:* 800-440-6008 ■ *Web:* www.diversifiedindustries.com	Swedesboro	NJ	08085	800-440-6008		328
Diversified Funding Services Inc 125 Habersham Dr 2nd Fl *TF:* 888-603-0055 ■ *Web:* www.divfunding.com	Fayetteville	GA	30214	770-603-0055		272
Diversified Health Management 3569 Refugee Rd Ste C *Web:* www.dhmcorp.net	Columbus	OH	43232	614-338-8888		363
Diversified Imports 556 Industrial Way W *TF:* 800-348-6663 ■ *Web:* www.diversifiedimports.com	Eatontown	NJ	07724	732-363-2333	905-7696	297-10
Diversified Labeling Solutions 1285 Hamilton Pkwy *TF:* 800-397-3013 ■ *Web:* teamdls.com	Itasca	IL	60143	630-625-1225		552-1
Diversified Laboratories Inc 4150 Lafayette Center Dr *Web:* www.diversifiedlaboratories.com	Chantilly	VA	20151	703-222-8700		668
Diversified Lenders Inc 5607 S Ave Q *TF:* 800-288-3024 ■ *Web:* diversifiedlenders.com	Lubbock	TX	79412	806-795-7782		194
Diversified Machining Inc 129 E Jarrettsville Rd *Web:* diversifiedmachining.com	Forest Hill	MD	21050	410-879-1400	879-3391	454
Diversified Maintenance Systems Inc 5110 Sunforest Dr Ste 250 *TF:* 800-351-1557 ■ *Web:* www.diversifiedm.com	Tampa	FL	33634	800-351-1557		152
Diversified Management Services 6919 Vista Dr W *Web:* www.assoc-mgmt.com	West Des Moines	IA	50266	515-282-8192	282-9117	47
Diversified Marketing Strategies Inc 1330 Arrowhead Ct *Web:* thinkdiversified.com	Crown Point	IN	46307	219-226-0300		653
Diversified Metal Fabricators Inc 665 Pylant St NE *Web:* dmfatlanta.com	Atlanta	GA	30306	404-875-1512	875-4835	650
Diversified Metal Products Inc 3710 N Yellowstone Hwy *Web:* www.diversifiedmetal.com	Idaho Falls	ID	83401	208-529-9655		295
Diversified Metals Inc 49 Main St *TF:* 800-628-3035 ■ *Web:* www.diversifiedmetals.com	Monson	MA	01057	413-267-5101	267-3151	492
Diversified Pattern & Engineering Company Inc 100 Progress Way *Web:* www.diversifiedpatternco.com	Avilla	IN	46710	260-897-3771	897-3687	567
Diversified Plastics Corp 120 W Mt Vernon St *Web:* www.dpcap.com	Nixa	MO	65714	417-725-2622		601
Diversified Precision Products Inc 6999 Spring Arbor Rd *TF:* 800-286-3797 ■ *Web:* diversifiedprecision.com	Spring Arbor	MI	49283	517-750-2310	750-9228	455
Diversified Production Services 1801 Willow Ave Ste 101 *Web:* www.dps-us.com	Weehawken	NJ	07086	646-386-2100		499
Diversified Search Cos 2005 Market St 33rd Fl *TF:* 800-423-3932 ■ *Web:* diversifiedsearch.com	Philadelphia	PA	19103	215-732-6666	568-8399	266
Diversified Technology Consultants Inc (DTC) 2321 Whitney Ave Ste 301 *Web:* www.teamdtc.com	Hamden	CT	06518	203-239-4200		261
Diversified Technology Inc 476 Highland Colony Pkwy *Web:* www.dtims.com	Ridgeland	MS	39157	601-856-4121		625
Diversified Transfer & Storage Inc (DTS) 1640 Monad Rd *TF:* 800-755-5855 ■ *Web:* www.dtsb.com	Billings	MT	59101	406-896-3443	896-3492	780
Diversified Vocational College 1670 Wilshire Blvd *Web:* www.dvcla.edu	Los Angeles	CA	90017	213-413-6714	413-6938	800
Diversitec LLC 14321 Sommerville Ct *TF:* 800-229-6772 ■ *Web:* www.diversitec.com	Midlothian	VA	23113	804-379-6772		317
DiversiTech Corp 6650 Sugarloaf Pkwy Ste 100 *TF:* 800-995-2222 ■ *Web:* www.diversitech.com	Duluth	GA	30097	678-542-3600	542-3700	14
Diversity Advertising Inc 11271 Ventura Blvd Ste 151 *Web:* www.hispanic-jobs.com	Studio City	CA	91604	818-530-4852		260
Divide County 200 N Main *Web:* www.ndaco.org	Crosby	ND	58730	701-965-6351		338
Divine Brothers Co 200 Seward Ave *Web:* www.divinebrothers.com	Utica	NY	13502	315-797-0470	797-0058	1
Divine Healthcare Network 856 Univerity Ave W *Web:* divinecorporation.com	Saint Paul	MN	55104	651-665-9795		363
Divine Providence Hospital 1100 Grampian Blvd *TF:* 800-433-0816 ■ *Web:* www.susquehannahealth.org	Williamsport	PA	17701	570-326-8000		374-3
Divine Redeemer PC 407 N Calaveras *Web:* www.divineredeemersa.org	San Antonio	TX	78207	210-433-9551		48-20
Divine Word College 102 Jacoby Dr SW *TF:* 800-553-3321 ■ *Web:* www.dwci.edu	Epworth	IA	52045	563-876-3353	876-3407	166
Diving Equipment & Marketing Assn (DEMA) 3750 Convoy St Ste 310 *TF:* 800-862-3483 ■ *Web:* www.dema.org	San Diego	CA	92111	858-616-6408	616-6495	49-4
Division Laundry & Cleaners Inc 6649 Old Hwy 90 W *Web:* divisionlaundry.com	San Antonio	TX	78227	210-674-5110	673-8510	426
Division Scolaire Franco-Manitobaine No 49 1263 Dawson Rd *TF:* 800-699-3736 ■ *Web:* www.dsfm.mb.ca	Lorette	MB	R0A0Y0	204-878-9399		685
Division Street News 108 Division St *Web:* www.timesjournalonline.com	Cobleskill	NY	12043	518-234-2515	234-7898	532-2
Divisions Maintenance Group 1 Riverfront Pl Ste 510 **Fax Area Code:* 859 ■ *TF:* 877-448-9730 ■ *Web:* mydivisions.com	Newport	KY	41071	877-448-9730	448-0124*	192
DIVSYS International LLC 8110 Zionsville Rd *Web:* www.divsys.com	Indianapolis	IN	46268	317-405-9427		625
Divvies LLC 700 Oakridge Common *Web:* divvies.com	South Salem	NY	10590	914-533-0333		297-8
Diw Group Inc 4845 International Blvd *Web:* www.specializedengineering.com	Frederick	MD	21703	301-607-4180		743
Dix & Eaton Inc 200 Public Sq Ste 3900 *Web:* www.dix-eaton.com	Cleveland	OH	44114	216-241-0405		636
Dix Industries Inc 5500 RL Ostos Rd *Web:* www.dixshipping.com	Brownsville	TX	78521	956-831-4228	831-2559	465
Dix Metals Inc 14801 Able Ln **Fax Area Code:* 714 ■ *TF:* 800-477-4349 ■ *Web:* www.dixmetals.com	Huntington Beach	CA	92647	800-477-4349	677-0800*	492
Dixie Aerospace Inc 416 Dividend Dr *TF:* 888-864-0462 ■ *Web:* www.dixieaerospace.com	Peachtree City	GA	30269	678-490-0140	490-0142	791
Dixie Building Products Inc 3342 Melrose Ave NW *Web:* www.dixieproducts.com	Roanoke	VA	24017	540-342-6787		361
Dixie Chemical Company Inc 10601 Bay Area Blvd *TF:* 866-266-6802 ■ *Web:* www.dixiechemical.com	Pasadena	TX	77507	281-474-3271		145
Dixie Clay Co 305 Dixie Clay Rd *Web:* www.vanderbiltminerals.com	Bath	SC	29816	803-593-2592		503-2
Dixie Construction Products Inc 970 Huff Rd NW *Web:* www.dixieconstruction.com	Atlanta	GA	30318	404-351-1100	350-2359	351
Dixie County 214 NE 351 Hwy PO Box 2600 *Web:* dixie.fl.gov	Cross City	FL	32628	352-498-1206	498-1207	338
Dixie Electric Co-op 9100 Atlanta Hwy *TF:* 888-349-4332 ■ *Web:* www.dixie.coop	Montgomery	AL	36117	334-288-1163		245
Dixie Electric Membership Corp (DEMCO) PO Box 15659 *TF:* 800-262-0221 ■ *Web:* demco.org	Baton Rouge	LA	70895	225-261-1221		245
Dixie Electric Power Assn 1863 US-184 PO Box 88 *TF:* 888-465-9209 ■ *Web:* www.dixieepa.com	Laurel	MS	39443	601-425-2535		245
Dixie Gas & Oil Corp 229 Lee Hwy PO Box 900 *TF:* 800-403-4943 ■ *Web:* www.dixiegas.com	Verona	VA	24482	540-248-6273	248-2524	204
Dixie Graphics Co 636 Grassmere Pk *Web:* www.dixiegraphics.com	Nashville	TN	37211	615-832-7000	832-7621	781
Dixie Group Inc 475 Reed Rd PO Box 2007 *NASDAQ: DXYN* ■ *TF:* 800-289-4811 ■ *Web:* www.thedixiegroup.com	Dalton	GA	30722	423-510-7000		131
Dixie Gun Works Inc 1412 W Reelfoot Ave *TF:* 800-238-6785 ■ *Web:* www.dixiegunworks.com	Union City	TN	38261	731-885-0561	885-0440	711
Dixie House Cafe 5401 S Hulen St *Web:* dixiehousecafes.com	Fort Worth	TX	76132	817-361-8500		671
Dixie Industries 3510 N Orchard Knob Ave *TF:* 800-933-4943 ■ *Web:* cmforge.com	Chattanooga	TN	37406	423-698-3323		350

Name / Address	City	State	ZIP	Phone	Fax	Class
Dixie Metal Products Inc 442 SW 54th Ct Web: www.dixiemetals.com	Ocala	FL	34474	352-873-2554		295
Dixie Outlet Mall 1250 S Service Rd Web: www.dixieoutletmall.com	Mississauga	ON	L5E1V4	905-278-8010	278-4283	460
Dixie Pipe Sales Inc 2407 Broiller TF: 800-733-3494 ■ Web: www.dixiepipe.com	Houston	TX	77054	713-796-2021	799-8628	490
Dixie Power 71 E Hwy 56 TF: 800-874-0904 ■ Web: www.dixiepower.com	Beryl	UT	84714	435-439-5311	439-5352	245
Dixie Restaurants Inc 1215 Rebsamen Park Rd Web: www.dixiecafe.com	Little Rock	AR	72202	501-666-3494		670
Dixie Southern Industrial Inc 1060 N Commonwealth Ave Web: www.dsisteel.com	Polk City	FL	33868	863-984-1900	984-1825	307
Dixie State University 225 S 700 E TF: 855-628-8140 ■ Web: dixie.edu	Saint George	UT	84770	435-652-7500		166
Dixie Store Fixtures & Sales Company Inc 2425 First Ave N TF: 800-323-4943 ■ Web: www.dixiestorefixtures.com	Birmingham	AL	35203	205-322-2442	322-2445	286
Dixieline Lumber Company Inc 3250 Sports Arena Blvd TF: 800-349-4354 ■ Web: www.dixieline.com	San Diego	CA	92110	619-224-4120	225-8192	364
Dixien 5286 Cir Dr Web: www.dixien.com	Lake City	GA	30260	404-366-7427		489
Dixie-Net PO Box 28 TF: 800-918-9023 ■ Web: www.dixie-net.com	Ripley	MS	38663	662-993-2000	993-2001	224
Dixon Associates Engineering LLC 335 E Jimmie Leeds Rd 2nd Fl Web: dixonassociates.com	Galloway	NJ	08205	609-652-7131	652-2613	261
Dixon Blind & Awning Service 1800 Sunset Ave	Rocky Mount	NC	27804	252-442-2145		87
Dixon Correctional Ctr 2600 N Brinton Ave Web: www2.illinois.gov	Dixon	IL	61021	815-288-5561	288-9713	213
Dixon Correctional Institute 5568 Hwy 68 Web: doc.louisiana.gov	Jackson	LA	70748	225-634-1200		213
Dixon Gallery & Gardens 4339 Park Ave Web: www.dixon.org	Memphis	TN	38117	901-761-5250	682-0943	520
Dixon Group Canada Ltd 2200 Logan Ave TF: 877-963-4966 ■ Web: www.canada.dixonvalve.com	Winnipeg	MB	R2R0J2	204-633-5650		358
Dixon Howell Westmoreland & Newman 1100 Glendon Ave 15th fl Web: dhwnlaw.com	Los Angeles	CA	90024	310-208-7723	208-8582	445
Dixon Hughes PLLC 6525 Morrison Blvd Ste 402 Web: www.dhg.com	Charlotte	NC	28211	704-367-7020	367-7760	2
Dixon Law Office 1415 W 55th St Ste 101 TF: 888-354-9880 ■ Web: attorneysmakingitright.com	LaGrange	IL	60525	888-354-9880		41
Dixon Mitchell Investment Counsel Inc 1055 W Hastings St Ste 1680 TF: 888-340-3136 ■ Web: www.dixonmitchell.com	Vancouver	BC	V6E2E9	604-669-3136		528
Dixon Public Library 230 N First St Web: www.dixonlibrary.com	Dixon	CA	95620	707-678-5447	678-3515	434-3
Dixon Schwabl Advertising 1595 Moseley Rd Web: dixonschwabl.com	Victor	NY	14564	585-383-0380		636
Dixon Ticonderoga Co 615 Crescent Executive Ct Ste 500 *Fax Area Code: 800 ■ TF: 800-824-9430 ■ Web: www.dixonticonderoga.com	Lake Mary	FL	32746	407-829-9000	232-9396*	571
Dixon Tool & Die Inc PO Box 188 Web: dixontool.net	Tyrone	PA	16686	814-684-0266	684-1550	757
Dixon Valve & Coupling Company Inc 800 High St Web: www.dixonvalve.com	Chestertown	MD	21620	410-778-2000		790
DIY Group Inc 2401 W 26th TF: 800-903-6610 ■ Web: diygroup.com	Muncie	IN	47302	800-903-6610		88
Dize Company Inc, The 1512 S Main St TF: 800-583-8243 ■ Web: www.dizecompany.com	Winston-Salem	NC	27127	336-722-5181	761-1334	350
DJ & A PC 3203 S Russell St TF: 800-398-3522 ■ Web: www.djanda.com	Missoula	MT	59801	406-721-4320		256
DJ Case & Associates Inc 317 E Jefferson Blvd Web: djcase.com	Mishawaka	IN	46545	574-258-0100		636
DJ Engineering Inc 219 W 6th Ave Web: www.djgrp.com	Augusta	KS	67010	316-775-1212	775-5993	22
DJ Jacobetti Home for Veterans 425 Fisher St TF: 800-433-6760 ■ Web: www.michigan.gov	Marquette	MI	49855	906-226-3576	226-2380	793
Djg Investigative Services North Carolina: 107 Commerce Centre Dr Ste 203 TF: 866-597-7457 ■ Web: djginvestigativeservices.com	Huntersville	NC	28078	704-536-8025	563-7433	693
DJJ (David J. Joseph Co) 300 Pike St Web: www.djj.com	Cincinnati	OH	45202	513-419-6200		686
DJL Construction Inc 1550 Ampere St Ste 200 Web: www.euroviaqc.ca	Boucherville	QC	J4B7L4	450-641-8000	655-1201	256
DJM Capital Partners Inc 60 S Market St Ste 1120 Web: www.djmcapital.com	San Jose	CA	95113	408-271-0366		652
DJM Real Estate 100 Crossways Park Dr W Ste 207 Web: www.gordonbrothers.com	Woodbury	NY	11797	516-682-4200	682-4201	652
DJS International Services Inc 4215 Gateway Dr Ste 100 Web: www.djsintl.com	Colleyville	TX	76034	972-929-8433		311
Djs Tree Service & Logging Inc 567 Depot Rd Web: djstree.com	Colchester	VT	05446	802-655-0264		752
DK Consulting LLC 10380 Old Columbia Rd Ste 100 Web: dkconsult.net	Columbia	MD	21046	443-552-5851	283-4010	194
DK Manufacturing Lancaster Inc 2118 Commerce St Web: dkmanufacturing.com	Lancaster	OH	43130	740-654-5566		608
DK Partners PC 1301 S Capitol of Texas Hwy Ste C200 Web: dktxcpa.com	Austin	TX	78746	512-258-6637		2
DK Realty Partners LLC 650 E Algonquin Rd Ste 201 *Fax Area Code: 847 ■ Web: www.dkrealty.com	Schaumburg	IL	60173	708-363-3900	397-8940*	652
DK Security 5160 Falcon View Ave SE TF: 800-535-0646 ■ Web: www.dksecurity.com	Grand Rapids	MI	49512	616-656-0123	656-4200	693
D-K Trading Corp PO Box E Web: www.dk-t.com	Clarks Summit	PA	18411	570-586-9662		559
DKA 5713 Corporate Way Ste 102 Web: www.dkawins.com	West Palm Beach	FL	33407	561-640-9171		463
DKC (Dan Klores Communications Inc) 261 Fifth Ave Web: www.dkcnews.com	New York	NY	10016	212-685-4300	685-9024	636
DKE (Delta Kappa Epsilon) 6921 Jackson Rd Ste 400 Web: dke.org	Ann Arbor	MI	48103	734-302-4210		48-16
DKM (Dyson-Kissner-Moran Corp) 2515 South Rd 5th Fl *Fax Area Code: 845 ■ Web: www.dkmcorp.com	Poughkeepsie	NY	12601	212-661-4600	463-3890*	185
DKN Hotels LLC 42 Corporate Pk Ste 200 *Fax Area Code: 949 ■ TF: 877-424-2449 ■ Web: www.dknhotels.com	Irvine	CA	92606	714-427-4320	337-4466*	378
Dky Inc 6009 Penn Ave S Web: dkyinc.com	Minneapolis	MN	55419	612-798-4070		7
DL Carlson Investment Group Inc 2 Capital Plz Ste 404 Web: www.carlsoninvest.com	Concord	NH	03301	603-224-5977		401
DL Geary Brewing Company Inc 38 Evergreen Dr Web: www.gearybrewing.com	Portland	ME	04103	207-878-2337	878-2388	102
DL Lee & Sons Inc 927 Hwy 32 E Web: www.dllee.com	Alma	GA	31510	912-632-4406	632-8298	473
DL Withers Construction 3220 E Harbour Dr Web: www.dlwithers.com	Phoenix	AZ	85034	602-438-9500	438-9600	186
DLA (Defense Logistics Agency) 8725 John J Kingman Rd TF: 877-352-2255 ■ Web: www.dla.mil	Fort Belvoir	VA	22060	877-352-2255		340-3
DLA Piper 203 N LaSalle St Ste 1900 Web: www.dlapiper.com	Chicago	IL	60601	312-368-4000		428
DLB Associates Consulting Engineers PC 265 Industrial Way W Web: www.dlbassociates.com	Eatontown	NJ	07724	732-774-2000		256
Dld Lawyers 150 Alhambra Cir Ph Web: www.dldlawyers.com	Coral Gables	FL	33134	305-443-4850		428
Dlg Engineering Inc 5825 Sunset Dr Ste 300 Web: dlgengineering.com	South Miami	FL	33143	305-665-9089		261
DLGL Technologies Corp 850 Blvd Michele Bohec Web: www.dlgl.com	Blainville	QC	J7C5E2	450-979-4646		178-1
DLH Holdings Corp 3565 Piedmont Rd NE Bldg 3 Ste 700 NASDAQ: DLHC ■ Web: www.dlhcorp.com	Atlanta	GA	30305	770-554-3545		721
DLite Press PO Box 824 Web: www.dlitepress.com	Yorktown Heights	NY	10598	845-270-5155		637-2
DLL 1111 Old Eagle School Rd TF: 800-873-2474 ■ Web: www.dllgroup.com	Wayne	PA	19087	610-386-5000		216
Dlm Inc 1215 Industrial Ln TF: 800-643-5423 ■ Web: www.dlminc.net	Malvern	AR	72104	501-332-5495		322
DLR Group Inc 6457 Frances Ste 200 Web: www.dlrgroup.com	Omaha	NE	68106	402-393-4100		261
DLS (Data Link Solutions) 350 Collins Rd NE Web: www.datalinksolutions.net	Cedar Rapids	IA	52498	319-295-8144		21
DLS (De La Salle Collegiate) 14600 Common Rd Web: www.delasallehs.com	Warren	MI	48088	586-778-2207	498-1628	166
DLS Engineering Assoc 5701 Cleveland St Ste 220 Web: dlsengineering.com	Virginia Beach	VA	23462	757-494-5151		261
DLT Manufacturing Inc 4081 Shilling Way TF: 800-833-3334 ■ Web: www.dltmanufacturing.com	Dallas	TX	75237	800-833-3334		454
DLT Solutions 13861 Sunrise Valley Dr Ste 400 TF: 800-262-4358 ■ Web: www.dlt.com	Herndon	VA	20171	703-709-7172	709-8450	174
DLZ Corp 6121 Huntley Rd Web: dlz.com	Columbus	OH	43229	614-888-0040		261
DM Camp & Sons 31798 Merced Ave TF: 800-826-0200 ■ Web: dmcamp.com	Bakersfield	CA	93308	661-399-5511		10-4
DM Contact Management 100-645 Tyee Rd Web: www.dmcontact.com	Victoria	BC	V9A6X5	250-383-8267		317
DM Figley Company Inc 10 Kelly Ct TF: 800-292-9919 ■ Web: www.dmfigley.com	Menlo Park	CA	94025	650-329-8700	329-0601	146
DM Kelly & Co 3900 Ingersoll Ave Ste 300 TF: 800-998-9773 ■ Web: www.dmkc.com	Des Moines	IA	50312	515-221-1133		690
DM Stamps & Specialties Inc 1101 N Riverfront Dr Web: www.dmstampsdiv.com	Mankato	MN	56001	507-387-4444	387-4447	467
DM Transportation Management Services Inc 740 Reading Ave TF: 888-399-0162 ■ Web: www.dmtrans.com	Boyertown	PA	19512	610-367-0162	369-0270	194
DMA (Direct Marketing Association Inc) 1120 Avenue of the Americas TF: 855-422-0749 ■ Web: thedma.org	New York	NY	10036	212-768-7277	302-6714	49-18
DMC (Delta Medical Ctr) 3000 Getwell Rd TF: 877-627-4395 ■ Web: www.deltaspecialtyhospital.com	Memphis	TN	38118	877-627-4395		374-3
DMC (Dominion Mechanical Contractors Inc) 5265 Port Royal Rd Ste 100 Web: dominionmc.com	Springfield	VA	22151	703-992-9588		610

Name / Address	Phone	Fax	Class
DMC (Dynamic Motion Control Inc) 2222 N Elston Ave Ste 200 ... Chicago IL 60614 *Web:* www.dmcinfo.com	312-255-8757		180
DMC (Delray Medical Ctr) 5352 Linton Blvd ... Delray Beach FL 33484 *Web:* www.delraymedicalctr.com	561-498-4440	495-3103	374-3
DMC (Detroit Medical Ctr) 4707 St Antoine ... Detroit MI 48201 *Web:* www.dmc.org	313-745-6035		353
DMC Corp 86 Northfield Ave Ste 130 ... Kearny NJ 08837 *Web:* www.dmc.com	973-589-0606	589-8931	745-9
DMC Technology Group Inc 7657 King's Pointe Rd ... Toledo OH 43617 *Web:* www.dmctechgroup.com	419-535-2900		180
DMCCVB (Decatur/Morgan County Convention & Visitors Bureau) 719 Sixth Ave SE PO Box 2349 ... Decatur AL 35602 *Web:* www.decaturcvb.org	256-350-2028		206
DME Co 29111 Stephenson Hwy ... Madison Heights MI 48071 **Fax Area Code:* 888 ■ *TF:* 800-626-6653 ■ *Web:* www.na.dmecompany.com	248-398-6000	808-4363*	695
DME-Direct Inc 28910 Ave Penn Ste 207 ... Valencia CA 91355 *TF:* 877-721-7701 ■ *Web:* www.dme-direct.com	877-742-8784		194
DMG Equipment Company Ltd 1575 Fm 1485 Rd ... Conroe TX 77301 *Web:* www.smithandcompany.net	936-756-6960	756-6903	188-4
DMG Events Inc 3 Stamford Landing 46 Southfield Ave Ste 400 ... Stamford CT 06902 *Web:* www.dmgt.com	203-973-2940		387
DMGS (Duane Morris Government Strategies LLC) 505 Ninth St NW Ste 1000 ... Washington DC 20004 *Web:* www.dmgs.com	202-776-7803	776-7801	393
DMI (Dairy Management Inc) 10255 W Higgins Rd Ste 900 ... Rosemont IL 60018 *TF:* 800-853-2479 ■ *Web:* www.usdairy.com	800-853-2479		48-2
DMI (Design Management Institute) 38 Chauncy St Ste 800 ... Boston MA 02111 *Web:* www.dmi.org	617-338-6380	338-6570	48-4
DMI (Data Management Internationale Inc) 55 Lukens Dr ... New Castle DE 19720 *TF:* 800-364-4210 ■ *Web:* getwebdocs.com	302-656-1151	656-1169	658
DMI (Directed Media Inc) 1150 N Grover ... East Wenatchee WA 98802 *Web:* www.directedmediainc.com	509-886-5759	884-3167	194
DMI Corp PO Box 53 ... Cedar Hill TX 75104 *Web:* www.deckermechanical.com	972-291-9907	299-6437	189-10
DMI Hotels 235 W Jefferson Ave ... Naperville IL 60540 *Web:* www.dmihotels.com	630-428-1000	428-1087	707
DMI Music & Media Solutions 35 W Dayton St ... Pasadena CA 91105 *Web:* www.dmimusic.com	626-795-0432		195
DMI Technology Group 406 Kays Dr ... Normal IL 61761 *Web:* www.dmitech.com	309-828-4439		177
DMI Wholesale Textiles Inc 8211 SW 29th St ... Oklahoma City OK 73179 **Fax Area Code:* 405 ■ *TF:* 800-238-9146 ■ *Web:* www.dmiscrubs.com	800-238-9146	745-2818*	157-4
DMIG Inc 2763 Marquis Dr ... Garland TX 75042 *Web:* www.gdmiinc.com	972-494-7477		214
DMK Associates Inc 421 Commercial Ct Ste C-D ... Venice FL 34292 *Web:* www.dmkassoc.com	941-412-1293	412-1043	261
DMLO (Deming Malone Livesay & Ostroff) 9300 Shelbyville Rd Ste 1100 ... Louisville KY 40222 *Web:* www.dmlo.com	502-426-9660	425-0883	2
DMR Consulting Inc 7946 Front Beach Rd ... Panama City Beach FL 32407 *Web:* www.dmrcinc.com	850-230-3767		196
DMS Facility Services 1040 Arroyo Dr ... South Pasadena CA 91030 *TF:* 800-443-8677 ■ *Web:* www.dmsfacilityservices.com	626-305-8500		104
Dms Inc 1120 Ensell Rd ... Lake Zurich IL 60047 *TF:* 800-655-7882 ■ *Web:* www.dmsdies.com	847-726-2828	726-9292	629
DMS INK 100 S Keowee St ... Dayton OH 45402 *Web:* dmsink.us	937-222-5056		5
DMS Laboratories Inc 2 Darts Mill Rd ... Flemington NJ 08822 *TF:* 800-567-4367 ■ *Web:* www.rapidvet.com	908-782-3353	782-0832	584
DMS Pharmaceutical Group Inc 810 Busse Hwy ... Park Ridge IL 60068 *TF:* 877-788-1100 ■ *Web:* www.dmspharma.com	847-518-1100		231
DMSI 2127 Ayrsley Town Blvd Ste 301 ... Charlotte NC 28273 *Web:* www.dmsi.net	704-587-3674		449
DMT Workholding Inc 210 Slinger Rd ... Slinger WI 53086 *Web:* www.dmtworkholding.com	262-644-5000		456
DMVW (Dakota Missouri Valley & Western Railroad) 3501 E Rosser Ave ... Bismarck ND 58501 *Web:* www.dmvwrr.com	701-223-9282	223-4147	649
DMW Worldwide LLC 701 Lee Rd Ste 103 ... Chesterbrook PA 19087 *Web:* www.dmwdirect.com	610-407-0407		5
DMWCC (Dearborn Mid-West Conveyor Co) 20334 Superior Rd ... Taylor MI 48180 *Web:* www.dmwcc.com	734-288-4400		207
DMX Transportation Inc 960 Berry Shoals Rd ... Duncan SC 29334 *Web:* www.dmxtransportation.com	864-877-7709	877-9228	780
DN Partners LLC 180 N LaSalle St Ste 3001 ... Chicago IL 60601 *Web:* www.dnpartners.com	312-332-7960		691
DN Tanks 351 Cypress Ln ... El Cajon CA 92020 *TF:* 855-368-2657 ■ *Web:* www.dntanks.com	619-440-8181		183
DNA (Delaware Nurses Assn) 4765 Ogletown-Stanton Rd Ste L10 ... Newark DE 19713 *TF:* 800-626-4081 ■ *Web:* denurses.wildapricot.org	302-733-5880		533
DNA Diagnostics Ctr (DDC) 1 DDC Way ... Fairfield OH 45014 *TF:* 800-613-5768 ■ *Web:* dnacenter.com	513-881-7800	881-7803	417
DNA Genotek Inc 3000 - 500 Palladium Dr ... Ottawa ON K2V1C2 *TF:* 866-813-6354 ■ *Web:* www.dnagenotek.com	613-723-5757	723-5057	477
DNA Labs Intl 260 SW Natura Ave 2nd Fl ... Deerfield Beach FL 33441 *Web:* dnalabsinternational.com	954-426-5163		415
DNA Model Management Inc 555 W 25th St ... New York NY 10001 *Web:* www.dnamodels.com	212-226-0080	226-7711	506
DNA Reference Lab Inc 5819 NW Loop 410 Ste 166 ... San Antonio TX 78238 *Web:* dnareferencelab.com	210-692-3800		418
DNA Specialty Inc 200 W Artesia Blvd ... Compton CA 90220 *Web:* www.dnaspecialty.com	310-767-4070		61
Dnastar Inc 3801 Regent St ... Madison WI 53705 *TF:* 800-182-4747 ■ *Web:* www.dnastar.com	608-258-7420	258-7439	178-1
DNB Engineering Inc 5969 Robinson Ave ... Riverside CA 92503 *Web:* www.dnbenginc.com	951-637-2630		256
DNF Controls 12843 Foothill Blvd Ste D ... Sylmar CA 91342 *Web:* www.dnfcontrols.com	818-898-3380		647
DNH Industries Inc 24100 Frampton Ave Bldg B ... Harbor City CA 90710 *Web:* www.dnhindustries.com	310-517-1769	517-0875	203
DNI (Dependable Nurses Inc) 1121 N El Dorado Pl Ste 300 ... Tucson AZ 85715 *Web:* www.dependablehealth.com	520-795-1290	886-9604	363
DNI (Dynamic Net Inc) 13 Cowpath ... Denver PA 17517 *TF:* 888-887-6727 ■ *Web:* www.dynamicnet.net	888-887-6727		225
DNP America LLC 335 Madison Ave 3rd Fl ... New York NY 10017 *Web:* www.dnpamerica.com	212-503-1060		360-3
Division of Natural Resources 324 Fourth Ave Bldg 74 ... South Charleston WV 25303 *Web:* www.wvdnr.gov	304-558-2754	558-2768	339-49
Do All Travel Company Inc 4620 18th Ave ... Brooklyn NY 11204 *Web:* doalltravel.com	718-972-6000		772
Do it Best Corp 6502 Nelson Ave PO Box 868 ... Fort Wayne IN 46803 *Web:* www.doitbest.com	260-748-5300		351
Do My Own Pest Control 4260 Communications Dr ... Norcross GA 30093 *TF:* 866-581-7378 ■ *Web:* www.domyown.com	866-581-7378		195
Do+Able Products Inc 5150 Edison Ave ... Chino CA 91710	909-465-0695		200
Doak House Museum Tusculum College Department of Museum Program & St PO Box 5026 ... Greeneville TN 37743 *Web:* doakhouse.tusculum.edu	423-636-8554		520
Doane College 1014 Boswell Ave ... Crete NE 68333 *TF:* 800-333-6263 ■ *Web:* www.doane.edu	402-826-2161	826-8600	166
DOAR Inc 1370 Broadway 15th Fl ... New York NY 10018 *TF:* 800-875-8705 ■ *Web:* www.doar.com	212-235-2700		445
Doba Inc 3401 N Thanksgiving Way Ste 150 ... Lehi UT 84043 *TF:* 877-321-3622 ■ *Web:* www.doba.com	801-765-6000		459
Dobama Theater 2340 Lee Rd ... Cleveland Heights OH 44118 *Web:* www.dobama.org	216-932-6838		572
Dobb Printing Inc 2431 S Harvey St ... Muskegon MI 49442 *TF:* 800-351-6625 ■ *Web:* dobbprinting.com	231-722-1060	722-1341	627
Dobbin House Inc 89 Steinwehr Ave ... Gettysburg PA 17325 *Web:* www.dobbinhouse.com	717-334-2100	334-6905	671
DOBER 11230 Katherine Crossing ... Woodridge IL 60517 *TF:* 800-323-4983 ■ *Web:* www.dober.com	630-410-7300	410-7444	145
Dobil Laboratories Inc 1661 E Sutter Rd ... Glenshaw PA 15116 *Web:* dobil.com	412-782-3399	781-2907	261
Doble Engineering Company Inc 85 Walnut St ... Watertown MA 02472 *TF:* 888-443-6253 ■ *Web:* www.doble.com	617-926-4900	926-0528	248
Dobson's 956 Broadway Cir ... San Diego CA 92101 *Web:* www.dobsonsrestaurant.com	619-231-6771		671
Doc 2 E-file Inc 4500 S Wayside Ste 102 ... Houston TX 77087 *TF:* 888-649-2006 ■ *Web:* www.doc2e-file.com	713-649-2006		225
Doc Chey's Noodle House 37 Biltmore Ave ... Asheville NC 28801 *Web:* www.doccheys.com	828-252-8220		671
DocASAP 560 Herndon Pkwy Ste 300 ... Herndon VA 20170 *TF:* 888-959-3654 ■ *Web:* www.docasap.com	888-959-3654		177
DocAuto Inc 5430 Metric Pl Ste 150 ... Norcross GA 30092 *Web:* www.docauto.com	770-242-6747		387
Dock at Crayton Cove 845 12th Ave S ... Naples FL 34102 *Web:* www.dockcraytoncove.com	239-263-9940		671
Dock's Oyster House 2405 Atlantic Ave ... Atlantic City NJ 08401 *Web:* www.docksoysterhouse.com	609-345-0092		671
Docken & Co 900-800 6 Ave SW ... Calgary AB T2P3G3 *TF:* 877-269-3612 ■ *Web:* docken.com	403-269-3612		428
Dockers Inn 3060 Green Mtn Dr ... Branson MO 65616 *Web:* www.dockersinnnranson.us	417-334-3600		379
Dockins Graphics Inc 1705 Ovrhd Bridge Rd NE ... Cleveland TN 37312 *Web:* www.dockinsgraphics.com	423-478-2540		627
Dockweiler State Beach 12000 Vista del Mar ... Playa del Rey CA 90293 *Web:* www.parks.ca.gov	424-526-7777		565
Doctor Genius 2121 Alton Pkwy Ste 150 ... Irvine CA 92606 *TF:* 877-477-2311 ■ *Web:* doctorgenius.com	877-477-2311		4
Doctor's Channel LLC, The 1133 Broadway 2nd Fl ... New York NY 10010 *Web:* www.thedoctorschannel.com	646-344-3013		387
Doctors Administrative Solutions LLC 1000 N Ashley Dr Ste 300 ... Tampa FL 33602 *Web:* dashealth.com	813-774-9800		463
Doctors Community Hospital (DCH) 8118 Good Luck Rd ... Lanham MD 20706 *Web:* www.dchweb.org	301-552-8118	552-8521	374-3
Doctors Hospital 3651 Wheeler Rd ... Augusta GA 30909 *TF:* 866-492-9082 ■ *Web:* doctors-hospital.net	706-651-3232		374-3
Doctors Hospital of Laredo 10700 McPherson Rd ... Laredo TX 78045 *TF:* 844-244-4074 ■ *Web:* www.doctorshosplaredo.com	956-523-2000	523-0444	374-3

Name / Address	City	State	ZIP	Phone	Fax	Class
Doctors Internet 800 Westchester Ave Ste 315N *TF:* 800-416-5235 ■ *Web:* doctorsinternet.com	Rye Brook	NY	10573	800-416-5235		788
Doctors Medical Ctr 1441 Florida Ave. *Web:* www.dmc-modesto.com	Modesto	CA	95350	209-578-1211		374-3
Doctors Pathology Services 1253 College Park Dr *Web:* www.dpspa.com	Dover	DE	19904	302-677-0000		418
Doctors Without Borders USA Inc 40 Rector St 16th Fl *TF:* 888-392-0392 ■ *Web:* www.doctorswithoutborders.org	New York	NY	10006	212-679-6800	679-7016	48-5
Doctors' Co, The 185 Greenwood Rd *TF:* 800-421-2368 ■ *Web:* www.thedoctors.com	Napa	CA	94558	707-226-0100		391-5
Documation Inc 4560 Lockhill Selma Ste 100 *TF:* 855-396-9301 ■ *Web:* www.mation.com	San Antonio	TX	78249	210-341-4431	341-5124	112
Documation LLC 1556 International Dr *Web:* www.documation.com	Eau Claire	WI	54701	715-839-8899		174
Document Destruction Company Inc 3885 W 41st St. *Web:* www.ddcshred.com	Chicago	IL	60632	773-890-5858	890-5757	393
Document Imaging Systems Corp (DISC) 1523 Fenpark Dr. *TF:* 800-710-3472 ■ *Web:* disccorporation.com	Fenton	MO	63026	800-710-3472		396
Document Security Systems Inc 200 Canal View Blvd Ste 300 *NYSE: DSS* ■ *Web:* www.dsssecure.com	Rochester	NY	14623	585-325-3610	325-2977	178-10
Document Storage Systems (DSS) 12575 US Hwy 1 Ste 200-A *TF:* 866-287-6962 ■ *Web:* www.dssinc.com	Juno Beach	FL	33408	561-284-7000	227-0208	177
Documentation Strategies Inc 15 Second Ave *Web:* www.docstrats.com	Rensselaer	NY	12144	518-432-1233		180
Docupak Inc 17515 Valley View Ave *Web:* www.docupakinc.com	Cerritos	CA	90703	714-670-7944	670-8449	86
Docuplex 630 N Pennsylvania Ave *Web:* www.docuplex.com	Wichita	KS	67214	316-262-2662	262-2805	627
Doc-U-Search Inc 63 Pleasant St *TF:* 800-332-3034 ■ *Web:* www.docusearchinc.com	Concord	NH	03301	603-224-2871		635
DocuSource of North Carolina LLC 2800 Slater Rd *Web:* www.docusourceofnc.com	Morrisville	NC	27560	919-459-5900		627
Dodd Camera 2077 E 30th St. *TF:* 855-544-1705 ■ *Web:* doddcamera.com	Cleveland	OH	44115	216-361-6800	361-6819	119
Dodd Creative Group Holding Company Inc 7263 Envoy Crt. *Web:* doddcreative.com	Dallas	TX	75247	214-821-6990		466
Dodd Technologies Inc 720 W Pioneer Trace Ste 200 *Web:* doddtechnologies.com	Pendleton	IN	46064	765-221-5010		8
Dodds & Eder 193 S St *Web:* doddsandeder.com	Oyster Bay	NY	11771	516-922-4412		293
Dodge & Cox 555 California St 40th Fl. *Web:* www.dodgeandcoxworldwide.com	San Francisco	CA	94104	415-981-1710		401
Dodge & Cox Funds 30 Dan Rd *TF:* 800-621-3979 ■ *Web:* www.dodgeandcox.com	Canton	MA	02021	800-621-3979		528
Dodge #4 State Park 4250 Pkwy Dr. *Web:* www.michigan.org	Waterford	MI	48327	248-682-7323		565
Dodge City Area Chamber of Commerce 311 W Spruce St. *Web:* www.dodgechamber.com	Dodge City	KS	67801	620-227-3119	227-2957	139
Dodge City Community College 2501 N 14th Ave. *TF:* 800-367-3222 ■ *Web:* www.dc3.edu	Dodge City	KS	67801	620-225-1321	227-9277	162
Dodge County PO Box 818 *Web:* www.dodgecountyga.com	Eastman	GA	31023	478-374-4361	374-8121	338
Dodge County 549 N Main St *TF:* 800-331-5666 ■ *Web:* dodgecounty.nebraska.gov	Fremont	NE	68025	402-727-2767	727-2764	338
Dodge County 22 Sixth St E Dept 91 *Web:* www.co.dodge.mn.us	Mantorville	MN	55955	507-635-6275	635-6323	338
Dodge County Convention & Visitors Bureau 1005 E 23rd St Ste 2. *TF:* 866-784-2329 ■ *Web:* www.fremontne.org	Fremont	NE	68025	402-753-6414		206
Dodge County Hospital 901 Griffin Ave. *Web:* www.dodgecountyhospital.com	Eastman	GA	31023	478-448-4000		374-3
Dodge County Schools 720 College St *Web:* www.dodge.k12.ga.us	Eastman	GA	31023	478-374-3783	374-6697	463
Dodge Nature Ctr 365 Marie Ave W *Web:* www.dodgenaturecenter.org	West Saint Paul	MN	55118	651-455-4531	455-2575	50-5
Dodger Industries 2075 Stultz Rd PO Box 711 *TF:* 800-436-3437 ■ *Web:* dodgerindustries.com	Martinsville	VA	24112	800-436-3437		155-1
Dodgeville Veterinary Service 105 County Rd Yz. *Web:* dodgevillevet.com	Dodgeville	WI	53533	608-935-2306	935-9367	794
Dodson Bros Exterminating Company Inc PO Box 10249 *Web:* www.dodsonbros.com	Lynchburg	VA	24501	434-847-9051		577
Dodson International Parts Inc 2155 Vermont Rd *Web:* www.dodson.com	Rantoul	KS	66079	785-878-8000		770
DOE (U.S. Department of Energy) 1000 Independence Ave SW. *Web:* www.energy.gov	Washington	DC	20585	202-586-8383	586-4403	340-9
Doe Anderson Inc 620 W Main St. *Web:* www.doeanderson.com	Louisville	KY	40202	502-589-1700		4
Doe Run Co, The 1801 Pk 270 Dr Ste 300 *TF:* 800-356-3786 ■ *Web:* doerun.com	Saint Louis	MO	63146	314-453-7100		485
Doe's Eat Place 1023 W Marckham St. *Web:* www.doeseatplace.com	Little Rock	AR	72201	501-376-1195		671
Doef's Greenhouses Ltd RR Site One Box 14 Ste 3 *Web:* www.doefsgreenhouses.com	Lacombe	AB	T4L2N3	403-782-2704	782-2702	192

Name / Address	City	State	ZIP	Phone	Fax	Class
Doepker Industries Ltd 300 Doepker Ave. *Web:* www.doepker.com	Annaheim	SK	S0K0G0	306-598-2171	598-2028	120
Doeren Mayhew 305 W Big Beaver Rd Ste 200. *TF:* 888-870-9873 ■ *Web:* doeren.com	Troy	MI	48084	248-244-3000		2
Doerfer Engineering Corp 1801 E Bremer Ave *Web:* www.doerfer.com	Waverly	IA	50677	877-483-4700		261
Doerr Assoc 31 Church St *Web:* mdoerr.com	Winchester	MA	01890	781-729-9020		636
DOF Subsea USA Inc 5355 W Sam Houston Pkwy N Ste 400. *Web:* www.dofsubsea.com	Houston	TX	77041	713-896-2500	726-5800	261
DOFO (Direct Office Furniture Outlet) 2635 Paxton St. *Web:* www.directofficefurnitureoutlet.com	Harrisburg	PA	17111	717-236-7200		320
Dog Face Equipment Sales 2094 Warm Springs Rd. *TF:* 866-908-5900 ■ *Web:* www.dogfaceequipment.com	Salt Lake City	UT	84116	801-908-5900	908-5902	358
Dog Soldier Press PO Box 1782 **Fax Area Code:* 866 ■ *Web:* www.dogsoldierpress.com	Ranchos de Taos	NM	87557	575-751-3781	319-2933*	637-10
Doggett Lloyd (Rep D - TX) 2307 Rayburn House Office Bldg *Web:* doggett.house.gov	Washington	DC	20515	202-225-4865		342-2
DogLeggs LLC 1155 Elm St *TF:* 800-313-1218 ■ *Web:* www.dogleggs.com	York	PA	17403	800-313-1218		475
DogTime Media Inc 545 Middlefield Rd Ste 210 *Web:* dogtime.com	Menlo Park	CA	94025	415-830-9300		5
Dogtown Artworks 704 N Main St Ste 102. *Web:* www.dogtownartworks.com	Tuscola	IL	61953	217-689-4575		637-2
Dogwood Productions Inc 757 Government St. *TF:* 800-254-9903 ■ *Web:* www.dogwoodproductions.com	Mobile	AL	36602	251-476-0858		7
Doheny Eye Institute 1355 San Pablo St *Web:* dohony.org	Los Angeles	CA	90033	323-342-7101		374-7
Doheny State Beach 25300 Dana Pt Harbor Dr *Web:* www.parks.ca.gov	Dana Point	CA	92629	949-496-6172		565
Doherty Enterprises Inc 7 Pearl Ct *Web:* www.dohertyinc.com	Allendale	NJ	07401	201-818-4669		194
Doherty Staffing Solutions Inc 7645 Metro Blvd Ste 1 *Web:* www.doherty.com	Edina	MN	55439	952-832-8300		260
Doherty Steel Inc 21110 W 311th St *Web:* dohertysteel.com	Paola	KS	66071	913-557-9200		492
Dohman, Akerlund & Eddy LLC 1117 12th St. *Web:* daecpa.com	Aurora	NE	68818	402-694-6404		2
Dohmen Research Inc PO Box 49-2433. *Web:* dohmencapital.com	Los Angeles	CA	90049	310-476-6933		531-9
Dohrn Transfer Co 625 Third Ave *TF:* 888-364-7621 ■ *Web:* www.dohrn.com	Rock Island	IL	61201	309-794-0723	794-1693	449
DOI (Department of the Interior) 1849 C St NW. *Web:* www.doi.gov	Washington	DC	20240	202-208-3100		340-13
Doing Good Works 12 Mauchly Bldg B. *Web:* ashburyimages.org	Irvine	CA	94107	949-354-0400		184
DOJ (Department of Justice) 950 Pennsylvania Ave NW *Web:* www.justice.gov	Washington	DC	20530	202-514-2007	514-5331	340-14
Dojindo Molecular Technologies Inc 30 W Gude Dr Ste 260 *TF:* 877-987-2667 ■ *Web:* www.dojindo.com	Rockville	MD	20850	301-987-2667	987-2687	668
Doka USA Ltd 214 Gates Rd. *TF:* 877-365-2872 ■ *Web:* www.doka.com	Little Ferry	NJ	07643	201-329-7839	641-6254	191-3
DOL (Department of Labor) 200 Constitution Ave NW *TF:* 866-487-2365 ■ *Web:* www.dol.gov	Washington	DC	20210	866-487-2365		340-15
Dolan Construction Inc 401 S 13th St. *Web:* www.dolanconstructioninc.com	Reading	PA	19602	610-372-4664		186
Dolbey Systems Inc 7280 Auburn Rd. *TF:* 800-878-7828 ■ *Web:* www.dolbey.com	Painesville	OH	44077	800-878-7828		178-1
Dolby Laboratories Inc 100 Potrero Ave *NYSE: DLB* ■ *Web:* www.dolby.com	San Francisco	CA	94103	415-558-0200	645-4000	52
Dolce Europa 7520 Fullerton Rd	Springfield	VA	22153	703-451-9501		297-8
Dolce Hayes Mansion 200 Edenvale Ave *TF:* 866-981-3300 ■ *Web:* www.hayesmansion.com	San Jose	CA	95136	408-226-3200		377
Dolce Printing Inc 29 Brook Ave *Web:* www.dolceprint.com	Maywood	NJ	07607	201-843-0400		627
Dolce Winery Inc PO Box 327 *Web:* www.dolcewine.com	Oakville	CA	94562	707-944-8868	944-2312	80-3
Dolcera 155 Bovet Rd Ste 302 *Web:* www.dolcera.com	San Mateo	CA	94402	650-425-6772		466
Dolden Wallace & Folick LLP 609 Granville St 18th Fl *TF:* 888-380-0130 ■ *Web:* www.dolden.com	Vancouver	BC	V7Y1G5	604-689-3222	689-3777	428
Dole Food Company Hawaii 802 Mapunapuna St *TF:* 800-697-9100 ■ *Web:* www.dolefruithawaii.com	Honolulu	HI	96819	808-861-8015	861-8020	297-7
Dole Food Company Inc 1 Dole Dr *NYSE: DOLE* ■ *TF:* 800-232-8888 ■ *Web:* www.dole.com	Westlake Village	CA	91362	818-879-6600		315-4
Dole Refrigerating Co 1420 Higgs Rd. *TF:* 800-251-8990 ■ *Web:* www.doleref.com	Lewisburg	TN	37091	931-359-6211	359-8664	664
Dolese Bros Co 20 NW 13th St *Web:* www.dolese.com	Oklahoma City	OK	73103	405-235-2311		183
Doling Chang Ashmore CPA Inc 430 Sherman Ave. *Web:* www.doling.com	Palo Alto	CA	94306	650-321-8744	321-8653	2
Dollamur LP 1734 E El Paso St *TF:* 800-520-7647 ■ *Web:* www.dollamur.com	Fort Worth	TX	76102	817-534-3344		711
Dollar Bank FSB 225 Forbes Ave *TF:* 800-828-5527 ■ *Web:* www.dollar.bank	Pittsburgh	PA	15222	800-828-5527		70

Name / Address	Phone	Fax	Class
Dollar Bill Copying 611 Church St .... Ann Arbor MI 48104 *TF:* 877-738-9200 ■ *Web:* www.dollarbillcopying.com	734-665-9200	930-2800	113
Dollar General Corp 100 Mission Rdg .... Goodlettsville TN 37072 *NYSE: DG* ■ *TF:* 800-678-9258 ■ *Web:* www.dollargeneral.com	615-855-4000	855-5899	791
Dollar Loan Center LLC 6122 W Sahara Ave......................... Las Vegas NV 89146 *TF:* 866-550-4352 ■ *Web:* www.dontbebroke.com	702-693-5626		217
Dollar Thrifty Automotive Group Inc 5330 E 31st St PO Box 35985 .... Tulsa OK 74135 *Web:* www.thrifty.com	918-660-7700		126
Dollar Tree Stores Inc 500 Volvo Pkwy .... Chesapeake VA 23320 *NASDAQ: DLTR* ■ *TF:* 877-530-8733 ■ *Web:* www.dollartree.com	877-530-8733		791
Dollar, Burns & Becker LC 1100 Main Ste 2600....................... Kansas City MO 64105 *Web:* dollar-law.com	816-876-2600		41
DollarDays International Inc 7575 E Redfield Rd Ste 201 .... Scottsdale AZ 85260 *TF:* 877-837-9569 ■ *Web:* www.dollardays.com	480-922-8155	922-3764	459
Dolliver Memorial State Park 2757 Dolliver Park Ave......................... Lehigh IA 50557 *Web:* www.iowadnr.gov	515-359-2539	359-2542	565
Dolly Packaging 320 N 4th St................. Tipp City OH 45371 *Web:* Www.dollypackaging.com	937-667-5414		64
Dollys Pizza 8197 Cooley Lake Rd ....Commerce Charter Township MI 48382 *Web:* www.dollyspizza.com	248-363-7770		670
Dollywood 2700 Dollywood Parks Blvd .... Pigeon Forge TN 37863 *TF:* 800-365-5996 ■ *Web:* www.dollywood.com	800-365-5996		32
Dolomite Group Inc 1260 Jefferson Rd.......................... Rochester NY 14623 *Web:* www.dolomitegroup.com	585-424-6040		182
Dolores County 409 N Main St .... Dove Creek CO 81324 *Web:* www.dolorescounty.org	970-677-2383	677-4144	338
Dolphin Aviation Inc 8191 N Tamiami Tr .... Sarasota FL 34243 *Web:* dolphinaviation.com	941-355-2902	351-7197	63
Dolphin Beach Resort 4900 Gulf Blvd .... Saint Pete Beach FL 33706 *TF:* 800-237-8916 ■ *Web:* www.dolphinbeach.com	727-360-7011	367-5909	379
Dolphin Carpet & Tile 3550 NW 77th Ct .... Miami FL 33122 *Web:* www.dolphincarpet.com	305-591-4141	378-1700	290
Dolphin Inc 440 N 51st Ave .... Phoenix AZ 85043 *Web:* dolphincasting.com	602-272-6747	233-9570	306
Dolphin Inn 1705 Atlantic Ave .... Virginia Beach VA 23451 *TF:* 800-749-0188 ■ *Web:* www.dolphininnhotel.com	757-491-1420		379
Dolphin Mall 11401 NW 12 St................... Miami FL 33172 *Web:* www.shopdolphinmall.com	305-365-7446	436-9000	460
Dolphin Press 21 Hyannis Cove .... San Rafael CA 94901 *Web:* www.dolphinpress.com	415-460-9910		344
Dolphin Shirt Co 757 Buckley Rd...................... San Luis Obispo CA 93401 *TF:* 800-377-3256 ■ *Web:* www.dolphinshirt.com	805-541-2566		627
Dolphin Swim School Inc 1530 El Camino Ave...................... Sacramento CA 95815 *TF:* 800-436-5744 ■ *Web:* www.dolphinscuba.com	916-929-8188		711
Dolphin Technology Inc 2025 Gateway Pl Ste 270 .... San Jose CA 95110 *Web:* www.dolphin-ic.com	408-392-0012		246
Dolphins Plus Inc 31 Corrine Pl .... Key Largo FL 33037 *TF:* 866-860-7946 ■ *Web:* www.dolphinsplus.com	305-451-0315		804
Domaille Engineering LLC 7100 Dresser Dr NE .... Rochester MN 55906 *Web:* www.domailleengineering.com	507-281-0275		697
Domain Associates LLC 1 Palmer Sq Ste 515......................... Princeton NJ 08542 *Web:* www.domainvc.com	609-683-5656	683-9789	792
Domain Systems Inc PO Box 175............ Farmington UT 84025 *Web:* www.domainsi.com	801-447-3777		463
Domain7 Solutions Inc 33820 S Fraser Way Unit 2A................ Abbotsford BC V2S2C5 *TF:* 866-367-0386 ■ *Web:* domain7.com	604-855-3772		387
Domaine Chandon Inc 1 California Dr .... Yountville CA 94599 *TF:* 888-242-6366 ■ *Web:* www.chandon.com	888-242-6366		80-3
Domaine Maizerets 2000 Montmorency Blvd .... Quebec City QC G1J5E7 *Web:* www.domainemaizerets.com	418-666-3331	666-8122	50-5
Domaine Select Wine & Spirits LLC (DSWS) 105 Madison Ave 13th Fl.................... New York NY 10016 *Web:* domaineselect.com	212-239-1275	279-0499	80-3
Domain-It! 9891 Montgomery Rd.............. Cincinnati OH 45242 *TF:* 866-269-2355 ■ *Web:* www.domainit.com	513-351-4222		396
DomainPeople Inc 550 Burrard St Ste 200 Bentall 5 .... Vancouver BC V6C2B5 *TF:* 877-734-3667 ■ *Web:* www.domainpeople.com	604-639-1680	688-9013	396
DomainRegistrycom Inc 2301 E Evesham Rd Ste 204................... Voorhees NJ 08043 *Web:* www.domainregistry.com	856-685-7427		396
Dome Printing 2031 Dome Ln................. McClellan CA 95652 *TF:* 800-343-3139 ■ *Web:* www.domeprinting.com	800-343-3139		627
DOmedia LLC 274 Marconi Blvd One Marconi Pl Ste 400...... Columbus OH 43215 *TF:* 866-939-3663 ■ *Web:* www.domedia.com	866-939-3663		225
Domengeaux Wright Roy & Edwards LLC 556 Jefferson St Ste 500...................... LaFayette LA 70501 *TF:* 800-375-6186 ■ *Web:* www.wrightroy.com	337-233-3033		428
Domenichelli & Associates Inc 1101 Investment Blvd Ste 115 .... El Dorado Hills CA 95762 *Web:* daengineering.net	916-933-1997	933-4778	261
Domenico's on the Wharf 50 Fisherman's Wharf Ste 1 .... Monterey CA 93940 *Web:* www.domenicosmonterey.com	831-372-3655	372-2073	671
Domer Law SC 3970 N Oakland Ste 201 .... Milwaukee WI 53211 *TF:* 888-353-8384 ■ *Web:* domerlaw.com	414-967-5656	967-5845	41
Domestic Linen Supply & Laundry Company Inc 30555 NW Hwy Ste 300............... Farmington Hills MI 48334 *Web:* www.domesticuniform.com	248-737-2000	737-5386	442
Dometek Inc 75 Sawyer Passway............... Fitchburg MA 01420 *Web:* www.dometek.net	978-345-8001		385
Dometic 1120 N Main St .... Elkhart IN 46514 *TF:* 800-546-8759 ■ *Web:* www.dometic.com	574-264-2131		60
Dom-Ex LLC 109 Grant St....................... Hibbing MN 55746 *Web:* www.h-eparts.com	218-262-6116		386
Domina Law Group Pc Llo 2425 S 144 St......... Omaha NE 68144 *Web:* dominalaw.com	402-493-4100		41
Dominant Systems Corp 3850 Varsity Dr........................... Ann Arbor MI 48108 *Web:* www.domsys.com	734-971-1210		180
Dominguez Law Firm PC 5801 W Roosevelt Rd .... Cicero IL 60804 *Web:* dominguezimmigrationlawfirm.com	708-222-0200		41
Dominguez State Jail 6535 Cagnon Rd......................... San Antonio TX 78252 *Web:* www.tdcj.texas.gov	210-675-6620		213
Domini Social Investments PO Box 9785 .... Providence RI 02940 *TF:* 800-582-6757 ■ *Web:* www.domini.com	212-217-1100		528
Dominic's 5101 Wilson Ave .... Saint Louis MO 63110 *Web:* www.dominicsrestaurant.com	314-771-1632		671
Dominic's 221 S Jefferson St .... Medina OH 44256 *Web:* www.dominicsitalianrestaurant.com	330-725-8424		671
Dominican College 470 Western Hwy .... Orangeburg NY 10962 *TF:* 866-432-4636 ■ *Web:* www.dc.edu	845-359-7800	365-3150	166
Dominican House of Studies 487 Michigan Ave NE..................... Washington DC 20017 *Web:* dhs.edu	202-495-3836		167-3
Dominican Republic *Consulate General* 1038 Brickell Ave............. Miami FL 33131 *Web:* www.domrep.org	305-358-3220	358-2318	257
Dominican Republic Tourist Board 136 E 57th St Ste 803....................... New York NY 10022 *Web:* www.un.int	212-588-1012		775
Dominican School of Philosophy & Theology 2301 Vine St............................... Berkeley CA 94708 *TF:* 888-450-3778 ■ *Web:* www.dspt.edu	510-849-2030		167-3
Dominican Sisters of Mission San Jos 43326 Mission Cir .... Fremont CA 94539 *Web:* www.msjdominicans.org	510-657-2468		162
Dominican University 7900 W Div St .... River Forest IL 60305 *TF:* 800-828-8475 ■ *Web:* www.dom.edu	708-366-2490	524-5990	166
Dominican University College 96 Empress Ave .... Ottawa ON K1R7G3 *Web:* www.udominicaine.ca	613-233-5696	233-6064	785
Dominick Abel Literary Agency Inc 146 W 82nd St Ste 1A .... New York NY 10024 *Web:* dalainc.com	212-877-0710		444
Dominick Feld Hyde PC 1130 22nd St S Ridge Pk Ste 4000........... Birmingham AL 35205 *Web:* www.dfhlaw.com	205-536-8888	271-9696	41
Dominion Aviation Services Inc 7511 Airfield Dr .... Richmond VA 23237 *TF:* 800-366-7793 ■ *Web:* www.dominionaviation.com	804-271-7793		579
Dominion Blue Reprographics 99 W Sixth Ave........................... Vancouver BC V5Y1K2 *Web:* dominionblue.com	604-681-7504		627
Dominion Chemical Co 2050 Puddledock Rd .... Petersburg VA 23803 *Web:* www.dominionchemical.com	804-733-7628	733-7698	146
Dominion Dental Services Inc 115 S Union St Ste 300 .... Alexandria VA 22314 *TF:* 888-681-5100 ■ *Web:* www.dominiondental.com	703-518-5000	518-8849	391-3
Dominion Diagnostics LLC 211 Circuit Dr....................... North Kingstown RI 02852 *Web:* www.dominiondiagnostics.com	401-667-0800		743
Dominion Diamond Mines 900 - 606 4 St SW .... Calgary AB T2P1T1 *Web:* www.ddmines.com	403-910-1933	910-1934	411
Dominion Due Diligence Group 201 Wylderose Dr Ste 200 .... Glen Allen VA 23060 *Web:* d3g.com	804-358-2020		104
Dominion Electric Supply Company Inc 5053 Lee Hwy............................. Arlington VA 22207 *TF:* 800-525-5006 ■ *Web:* www.dominionelectric.com	703-536-4400	741-0423	246
Dominion Energy Management 11250 Hopson Rd........................... Ashland VA 23005 *Web:* www.demiva.com	804-798-3189		610
Dominion Engineering Associates Inc 8511 Indian Hills Ct Ste 202.............. Fredericksburg VA 22407 *Web:* www.dea-inc.net	540-710-9339	710-7449	261
Dominion Homes Inc PO Box 23404 .... Chagrin Falls OH 44023 *Web:* dominionhomes.com	614-356-5000		653
Dominion Hospital 2960 Sleepy Hollow Rd .... Falls Church VA 22044 *Web:* dominionhospital.com	703-536-2000	533-9650	374-5
Dominion Lending Centres Inc 2215 Coquitlam Ave.................. Port Coquitlam BC V3B1J6 *TF:* 866-928-6810 ■ *Web:* dominionlending.ca	866-928-6810		509
Dominion Lodging Inc 658 Roanoke Rd.......... Daleville VA 24083 *Web:* dominionlodging.com	540-992-4077		379
Dominion Mechanical Contractors Inc (DMC) 5265 Port Royal Rd Ste 100 .... Springfield VA 22151 *Web:* dominionmc.com	703-992-9588		610
Dominion Post 1251 Earl L Core Rd .... Morgantown WV 26505 *TF:* 800-654-4676 ■ *Web:* www.dominionpost.com	304-292-6301	292-3704	532-2
Dominion Strategies LLC PO Box 26115 .... Alexandria VA 22301 *Web:* www.dominionstrategies.com	202-844-2020		194
Dominion Technologies Inc 15736 Sturgeon St .... Roseville MI 48066 *Web:* www.dominiontec.com	586-773-3303		757

Company	Address	City	State	ZIP	Phone	Fax	Class	Other
Dominion Ventures	1646 N California Blvd	Walnut Creek	CA	94596	925-280-6338		792	*Web:* www.dominion.com
Dominion Veterinary Laboratories Inc	1199 Sanford St	Winnipeg	MB	R3E3A1	204-589-7361	943-9612	584	*TF:* 800-465-7122 ■ *Web:* www.domvet.com
dominKnow Inc	183 Michael Cowpland Dr	Ottawa	ON	K2M0M3	613-800-8733		225	*Web:* www.dominknow.com
Domino Machine Inc	4040 98 St NW	Edmonton	AB	T6E3L3	780-462-1354		757	*Web:* www.dominomachine.com
Domino's Pizza Inc	30 Frank Lloyd Wright Dr	Ann Arbor	MI	48105	734-930-3296		670	*NYSE: DPZ* ■ *TF:* 800-253-8182 ■ *Web:* www.dominos.com
Doms Outdoor Outfitters	1870 First St	Livermore	CA	94550	925-447-9629		711	*TF:* 800-447-9629 ■ *Web:* www.domsoutdoor.com
Domtar Corp	395 de Maisonneuve W	Montreal	QC	H3A1L6	514-848-5555		683	*NYSE: UFS* ■ *Web:* www.domtar.com
Domtar Corp	234 Kingsley Park Dr	Fort Mill	SC	29715	803-802-7500		638	*TF:* 877-877-4685 ■ *Web:* www.domtar.com
Domtech Inc	40 E Davis St	Trenton	ON	K8V6S4	613-394-4884		492	*TF:* 888-278-8258 ■ *Web:* domtech.net
Domus Inc	123 Avenue of the Arts Ste 1980	Philadelphia	PA	19109	215-772-2805		194	*Web:* www.domusinc.com
Don Beyer Motors Inc	1231 W Broad St	Falls Church	VA	22046	855-844-0659		57	*TF:* 855-892-6528 ■ *Web:* www.fallschurchdonbeyervolvo.com
Don Bosco Technical Institute	1151 San Gabriel Blvd	Rosemead	CA	91770	626-940-2000	940-2001	167-3	*Web:* www.boscotech.edu
Don Buchwald & Assoc	5900 Wilshire Blvd 31st Fl	Los Angeles	CA	90036	323-655-7400		731	*Web:* www.buchwald.com
Don CeSar Beach Resort - A Loews Hotel	3400 Gulf Blvd	Saint Pete Beach	FL	33706	727-360-1881		669	*TF:* 888-430-4999 ■ *Web:* www.doncesar.com
Don Chalmers Ford Inc	2500 Rio Rancho Blvd	Rio Rancho	NM	87124	505-796-4500		57	*Web:* www.chalmersford.com
Don Chapin Company Inc, The	560 Crazy Horse Canyon Rd	Salinas	CA	93907	831-449-4273	449-0700	186	*Web:* www.donchapin.com
Don Chucho's Mexican Restaurant	5770 Milgen Rd	Columbus	GA	31907	706-561-3040		671	
Don Cohen - The Mathman	809 Stratford Dr	Champaign	IL	61821	800-356-4559		637-2	*TF:* 800-356-4559 ■ *Web:* www.mathman.biz
Don Congdon Associates Inc	110 William St Ste 2202	New York	NY	10038	212-645-1229	727-2688	444	*Web:* www.doncongdon.com
Don Dye Company Inc	PO Box 107	Kingman	KS	67068	620-532-3131	532-2141	620	*Web:* dondyeco.com
Don Farmer CPA PA	508 Mulberry St PO Box 1858	Lenoir	NC	28645	828-754-1613	754-1696	2	*Web:* donfarmercpa.com
Don Garlits Museums	13700 SW 16th Ave	Ocala	FL	34473	352-245-8661		522	*TF:* 877-271-3278 ■ *Web:* garlits.com
Don Hall's Guesthouse	1313 W Washington Center Rd	Fort Wayne	IN	46825	260-489-2524		379	*Web:* www.donhalls.com
Don Harrington Discovery Ctr	1200 Streit Dr	Amarillo	TX	79106	806-355-9547		521	*Web:* discoverycenteramarillo.org
Don Henefer Jewelers Inc	512 New Florissant Rd N	Florissant	MO	63031	314-921-3001		410	*Web:* donheneferjewelers.com
Don Herring Enterprises Ltd	4225 W Plano Pkwy	Plano	TX	75093	972-387-8600		57	*Web:* www.donherring.com
Don Hewlett Chevrolet Buick Inc	7601 S I-35	Georgetown	TX	78626	512-681-3000		57	*Web:* www.donhewlett.com
Don Hummer Trucking Corp	1486 Hwy 6 NW PO Box 310	Oxford	IA	52322	319-828-2000	828-2105	780	*Web:* www.donhummertrucking.com
Don Hutson Organization	516 Tennessee St Ste 219	Memphis	TN	38103	901-767-0000		765	*TF:* 800-647-9166 ■ *Web:* donhutson.com
Don Jagoda Associates Inc	100 Marcus Dr	Melville	NY	11747	631-454-1800	454-1834	384	*Web:* dja.com
Don Jerry X-Plo Inc	1080 Military Tpke	Plattsburgh	NY	12901	518-561-7810	563-0044	780	*TF:* 888-300-0012 ■ *Web:* x-plo.com
Don Jose Tequila's	351 Atwells Ave	Providence	RI	02903	401-454-8951		671	*Web:* donjosetequilas.com
Don Jose's	2052 E Northern Lights Blvd	Anchorage	AK	99508	907-279-5111	279-2053	671	*Web:* www.alaskadonjoses.com
Don Laughlin's Riverside Resort & Casino	1650 Casino Dr	Laughlin	NV	89029	702-298-2535		133	*TF:* 800-227-3849 ■ *Web:* www.riversideresort.com
Don Lee Farms	200 E Beach Ave	Inglewood	CA	90302	310-674-3180		296-2	*Web:* donleefarms.com
Don Luis	15 N 26th St	Billings	MT	59101	406-256-3355		671	*Web:* www.donluisrestaurantmt.com
Don Martin & Co	1035 N Alvarado	Los Angeles	CA	90026	213-413-3400		711	*Web:* donmartincompany.com
Don McGill Toyota Inc	11800 Katy Fwy	Houston	TX	77079	888-241-1642		57	*TF:* 866-938-0767 ■ *Web:* www.donmcgilltoyota.com
Don Pancho Authentic Mexican Foods Inc	3060 Industrial Way NE	Salem	OR	97301	503-370-9710		123	*Web:* donpancho.com
Don Park LP	842 York Mills Rd	North York	ON	M3B3A8	416-449-7275		401	*Web:* www.donpark.com
Don Pedro Island State Park	8450 Placida Rd PO Box 1150	Boca Grande	FL	33921	941-964-0375		565	*Web:* www.floridastateparks.org
Don Pepe Restaurant & Catering	844 McCarter Hwy	Newark	NJ	07102	973-623-4662		671	*Web:* www.donpeperestaurant.com
Don Quijote	362 Union St	Manchester	NH	03103	603-622-2246		671	*Web:* www.donquijoteunion.com
Don Quijote USA Company Ltd	801 Kaheka St	Honolulu	HI	96814	808-973-4800		345	*Web:* www.donquijotehawaii.com
Don R. Fruchey Inc	5608 Old Maumee Rd	Fort Wayne	IN	46803	260-749-8502	749-6337	189-1	*Web:* www.donrfruchey.com
Don Randon Real Estate Inc	825 Camp St	New Orleans	LA	70130	504-581-1111	581-1114	652	*Web:* www.donrandonrealestate.com
Don Rasmussen Co	720 NE Grand Ave	Portland	OR	97232	503-230-7700		57	*Web:* www.landroverportland.com
Don Ray George & Associates Inc	1604 Rio Grande St	Austin	TX	78701	512-476-1245		261	*Web:* drgainc.com
Don Roberto Jewelers	205 Avenida Fabricante	San Clemente	CA	92672	949-361-6700		410	*Web:* www.donrobertojewelers.com
Don Roberts School of Hair Design	152 E US Rte 30	Schererville	IN	46375	219-864-1600		685	*Web:* donrobertsschoolofhairdesign.edu
Don Shula's Hotel & Golf Club	6842 Main St	Miami Lakes	FL	33014	305-821-1150	820-8087	669	*Web:* www.donshulahotel.com
Don Small & Sons Oil Distributing Company Inc	112 Third St NW PO Box 626	Auburn	WA	98071	253-833-0430	854-0457	581	*TF:* 800-626-3213 ■ *Web:* www.smallandsonsoil.com
Don Stevens Inc	980 Discovery Rd	Eagan	MN	55121	651-452-0872	452-4189	665	*TF:* 800-444-2299
Don Young Co	8181 Ambassador Row	Dallas	TX	75247	214-630-0934	630-0406	480	*TF:* 800-367-0390 ■ *Web:* www.dycwindows.com
Don's Lighthouse Grille	8905 Lake Ave	Cleveland	OH	44102	216-961-6700		671	*Web:* www.donslighthouse.com
Don's Seafood & Steakhouse	301 E Vermilion St	LaFayette	LA	70501	337-235-3551		671	*Web:* www.donsdowntown.com
Dona Ana Community College (DACC)	2800 N Sonoma Ranch Blvd	Las Cruces	NM	88011	575-528-7000	528-7300	162	*TF:* 800-903-7503 ■ *Web:* dacc.nmsu.edu
Dona Ana County	845 N Motel Blvd	Las Cruces	NM	88007	575-647-7200	585-5538	338	*TF:* 800-477-3632 ■ *Web:* www.donaanacounty.org
Dona Lupe Cafe	2919 Pershing Dr	El Paso	TX	79903	915-566-9833		671	*Web:* www.donalupecafe.eatintakeout.net
Donadio & Olson Inc	121 W 27th St Ste 704	New York	NY	10001	212-691-8077		444	*Web:* www.donadio.com
Donahoe & Young LLP	25152 Springfield Ct Ste 345	Valencia	CA	91355	661-360-1211	461-1888*	41	**Fax Area Code:* 818 ■ *Web:* www.dywlaw.com
Donahoe Kearney LLP	1901 Pennsylvania Ave NW Ste 900	Washington	DC	20006	202-393-3320	393-3324	41	*Web:* donahoekearney.com
Donahue Paper Emporium (DPE)	7286 S Yosemite St	Centennial	CO	80112	303-741-3984		553	*Web:* www.donahuepaper.com
Donahue Schriber Realty Group Inc	200 E Baker St Ste 100	Costa Mesa	CA	92626	714-545-1400	545-4222	655	*Web:* www.donahueschriber.com
Donahuefavret Contractors Inc	3030 E Causeway Approach	Mandeville	LA	70448	985-626-4431		186	*TF:* 800-626-4431 ■ *Web:* donahuefavret.com
Donald C. Bowers Insurance Inc	1380 Dual Hwy	Hagerstown	MD	21740	301-791-7910		390	*TF:* 800-453-2105 ■ *Web:* bowersinsurance.com
Donald D. Hill County Administration Building, The	20 S 2nd St	Newark	OH	43055	740-670-5110	670-5119	338	*Web:* www.lcounty.com
Donald E. Graves CPA LLC	377 Main St Ste 1	Greenfield	MA	01301	413-774-6036	774-6037	2	*Web:* www.donaldegravescpa.com
Donald Harris Law Firm	158 Columbus Ave	Sandusky	OH	44870	419-621-9388		428	*Web:* donaldharrislawfirm.com
Donald R. Frey & Company Inc	40 N Grand Ave Ste 303	Fort Thomas	KY	41075	859-441-6566		177	*Web:* drfrey.com
Donald Smith & Company Inc	152 W 57th St 22nd Fl	New York	NY	10019	212-284-0990		401	*Web:* www.donaldsmithandco.com
Donald T. Ostop & Company PC	790 Farmington Ave Bldg 2	Farmington	CT	06032	860-677-0779		2	*Web:* dtoco.com
Donald W. Mcintosh Assoc	2200 N Park Ave	Winter Park	FL	32789	407-644-4068		261	*Web:* www.dwma.com
Donald W. Wyatt Detention Facility	950 High St	Central Falls	RI	02863	401-729-1190	729-1194	213	*TF:* 866-204-1603 ■ *Web:* www.wyattdetention.com
Donaldson Adoption Institute Inc, The	159 W 118th St 3F	New York	NY	10016	212-925-4089	796-6592*	48-6	**Fax Area Code:* 775
Donaldson Capital Management LLC	20 NW First St 5th Fl	Evansville	IN	47708	812-421-3211		401	*Web:* www.dcmol.com
Donaldson Company Inc	1400 W 94th St	Bloomington	MN	55431	952-887-3131		18	*NYSE: DCI* ■ *TF:* 800-365-1331 ■ *Web:* www.donaldson.com
Donaldsonville Chief	120 Railroad Ave	Donaldsonville	LA	70346	225-473-3101	473-4060	532-2	*Web:* www.donaldsonvillechief.com
Donan Engineering LLC	12450 Lk Sta Pl	Louisville	KY	40299	502-267-6936		400	*TF:* 800-482-5611 ■ *Web:* www.donan.com

Name / Address	City	State	Zip	Phone	Fax	Class
Donanelle's Bar & Grill 4321 U S Hwy 49	Hattiesburg	MS	39401	601-545-3860		671
Donart Electronics Inc 1005 Robinson Hwy *Web:* www.donartelectronics.com	McDonald	PA	15057	724-796-3021		248
Donatech Corp 2094 185th St Ste 110 *TF:* 800-328-2133 ■ *Web:* www.donatech.com	Fairfield	IA	52556	800-328-2133		177
Donatelle Plastics Inc 501 County Rd E2 Ext *Web:* www.donatellemedical.com	New Brighton	MN	55112	651-633-4200		596
Donatello, The 501 Post St *TF:* 800-258-2366 ■ *Web:* www.clubdonatello.org	San Francisco	CA	94102	415-441-7100		379
Donati Law Firm LLP 1545 Union Ave *Web:* www.donatilaw.com	Memphis	TN	38104	901-209-5500		428
Donatos Pizza 935 Taylor Stn Rd *TF:* 800-366-2867 ■ *Web:* www.donatos.com	Columbus	OH	43230	800-366-2867		670
Donco Recycling Solutions 737 N Michigan Ave Ste 1450 *Web:* www.doncosolutions.com	Chicago	IL	60611	312-337-7822	337-7891	638
Dondlinger & Sons Construction Company Inc 2656 S Sheridan *Web:* www.dondlinger.biz	Wichita	KS	67217	316-945-0555	945-9009	188-4
Donegal Group Inc 1195 River Rd *NASDAQ: DGICA* ■ *TF:* 800-877-0600 ■ *Web:* www.donegalgroup.com	Marietta	PA	17547	717-426-1931		360-4
Donegal School District 1051 Koser Rd *Web:* www.donegalsd.org	Mount Joy	PA	17552	717-653-1447		685
Doneger Group, The 463 Seventh Ave *Web:* www.doneger.com	New York	NY	10018	212-564-1266		195
Donelans Super Mkt 248 Great Rd *Web:* www.donelans.com	Acton	MA	01720	978-635-9893		345
Donelson-Hermitage Chamber of Commerce 2900 Lebanon Rd Ste 205 *Web:* www.donelsonhermitagechamber.com	Nashville	TN	37214	615-883-7896	391-4880	139
Doner Adv 25900 NW Hwy *Web:* doner.com	Southfield	MI	48075	248-354-9700		4
Doniphan County PO Box 278 *TF:* 800-232-0170 ■ *Web:* dpcountyks.com	Troy	KS	66087	785-985-3513	985-3723	338
Doniphan Electric Cooperative Association Inc 530 W Jones St *TF:* 800-699-0810 ■ *Web:* www.donrec.org	Troy	KS	66087	785-985-3523		245
Donjon Marine Company Inc 100 Central Ave *Web:* www.donjon.com	Hillside	NJ	07205	908-964-8812	964-7426	465
Donlen Corp 2315 Sanders Rd *TF:* 800-323-1483 ■ *Web:* www.donlen.com	Northbrook	IL	60062	847-714-1400		289
Donlevy Laboratories Inc 11165 Delaware Pkwy *Web:* www.donlevylab.com	Crown Point	IN	46307	219-226-0001	226-2050	418
Donley County Courthouse 300 S Sully St *TF:* 800-388-8075 ■ *Web:* www.co.donley.tx.us	Clarendon	TX	79226	806-874-3625	874-1181	338
Donna 11762 Marco Beach Dr Ste 6 *Web:* breastcancermarathon.com	Jacksonville	FL	32224	904-355-7465		48-5
Donna Karan Company Store LLC, The 200 Tanger Mall Dr Ste 907 *Web:* www.donnakaran.com	Riverhead	NY	11901	631-369-2820		155-21
Donna Law Firm 7601 France Ave S Ste 350 *Web:* donnalaw.com	Minneapolis	MN	55435	952-562-2460		41
Don-Nan 3427 E Garden City Hwy 158 *TF:* 800-348-7742 ■ *Web:* www.don-nan.com	Midland	TX	79706	800-348-7742		112
Donnell Systems Inc 130 S Main St Ste 375 *TF:* 800-232-3776 ■ *Web:* www.ocie.net	South Bend	IN	46601	574-232-3784		196
Donnelly College 608 N 18th St *Web:* www.donnelly.edu	Kansas City	KS	66102	913-621-8700	621-8734	162
Donnelly Custom Manufacturing Co 105 Donovan *Web:* www.donnmfg.com	Alexandria	MN	56308	651-698-8248		596
Donner Memorial State Park 12593 Donner Pass Rd *Web:* www.parks.ca.gov	Truckee	CA	96161	530-582-7892		565
Donner Plumbing & Heating Inc 107 Candelaria Rd NW *Web:* www.donnerplumbing.com	Albuquerque	NM	87107	505-884-1017		610
Donohoe & Stapleton LLC 2781 Zelda Rd *TF:* 800-365-6896 ■ *Web:* www.donohoeandstapletonlaw.com	Montgomery	AL	36106	334-269-3355		428
Donohoe Companies Inc 2101 Wisconsin Ave NW *Web:* www.donohoe.com	Washington	DC	20007	202-333-0880	342-3924	653
Donohue & Associates Inc 3311 Weeden Creek Rd *Web:* www.donohue-associates.com	Sheboygan	WI	53081	920-208-0296		256
Donohue Brown Mathewson & Smyth LLC 140 S Dearborn St Ste 800 *Web:* www.dbmslaw.com	Chicago	IL	60603	312-422-0900		428
Donor Alliance Inc 720 S Colorado Blvd Ste 800-N *TF:* 888-868-4747 ■ *Web:* www.donoralliance.org	Denver	CO	80246	303-329-4747	321-1183	545
Donor Network of Arizona 201 W Coolidge St *TF:* 800-447-9477 ■ *Web:* www.dnaz.org	Phoenix	AZ	85013	602-222-2200		269
Donor Network West 12667 Alcosta Blvd Ste 500 **Fax Area Code: 925* ■ *TF:* 888-570-9400 ■ *Web:* www.donornetworkwest.org	San Ramon	CA	94583	888-570-9400	480-3101*	545
Donordirect.Com Inc 2435 N Central Expy Ste 950 *Web:* donordirect.com	Richardson	TX	75080	972-744-9500		177
Donovan Advertising & Marketing Services 180 W Airport Rd *Web:* www.donovanadv.com	Lititz	PA	17543	717-560-1333	560-2034	7
Donovan Marine 10409 John Price Rd *Web:* batchgeo.com	Charlotte	NC	28273	501-562-5008		770
Donovan Marine Inc 6316 Humphreys St *TF:* 800-347-4464 ■ *Web:* www.donovanmarine.com	Harahan	LA	70123	504-488-5731		770
Donovan PC 5151 E US Hwy 36 *Web:* cpadonovan.com	Avon	IN	46123	317-745-6411		2
Donovan, Klimczak & Co 484 S Miller Rd *Web:* dkc-cpa.com	Fairlawn	OH	44333	330-836-9331	869-9991	2
Donsco Inc 124 N Front St *Web:* donsco.com	Wrightsville	PA	17368	717-252-1561		307
Dontech Inc 700 Airport Blvd *Web:* dontech.com	Doylestown	PA	18902	215-348-5010		596
Dontino's La Vita Gardens 555 E Cuyahoga Falls Ave *Web:* www.dontinos.com	Akron	OH	44310	330-928-9530		671
Donuts Inc 5808 Lake Washington Blvd NE Ste 300 *Web:* donuts.domains	Kirkland	WA	98033	425-298-2200		180
Doodad 7990 Second Flags Dr *TF:* 800-383-6973 ■ *Web:* www.doodad.com	Austell	GA	30168	770-732-0321		627
Doodles Campus Store 935 Main St *Web:* www.doodlesbooks.com	Montevallo	AL	35115	205-665-1719		95
Doody Enterprises Inc 1100 Lake St Ste LL25 *Web:* www.doody.com	Oak Park	IL	60301	312-239-6226		637-10
Doody Mechanical Inc 7450 Flying Cloud Dr *Web:* www.metromech.com	Eden Prairie	MN	55344	952-941-7010	941-9118	189-10
Dooley Electric Company Inc 4014 3rd Ave *TF:* 888-419-9408 ■ *Web:* www.dooleyelectric.com	Brooklyn	NY	11232	718-840-2200	840-2816	189-4
Dooley Enterprises Inc 1198 N Grove St Ste A *Web:* www.dooleyenterprises.com	Anaheim	CA	92806	714-630-6436	630-3910	350
Dooley's Petroleum Inc 304 Main Ave *TF:* 800-520-2466 ■ *Web:* www.dooleypetro.com	Murdock	MN	56271	320-235-5200		581
Dooly County 110 E Union St PO Box 308 *Web:* www.doolychamber.com	Vienna	GA	31092	229-268-8275	268-8200	338
Dooly State Prison 1412 Plunkett Rd *Web:* www.dcor.state.ga.us	Unadilla	GA	31091	478-627-2000	627-2140	213
Doonan Trailer Corp 36 NE Hwy 156 *TF:* 800-734-0608 ■ *Web:* www.doonan.com	Great Bend	KS	67530	620-792-6222	792-3308	779
Dooney & Bourke Inc 1 Regent St **Fax Area Code: 800* ■ *TF:* 800-347-5000 ■ *Web:* www.dooney.com	East Norwalk	CT	06855	203-853-7515	326-1496*	430
Door & Hardware Institute (DHI) 14150 Newbrook Dr Ste 200 *Web:* www.dhi.org	Chantilly	VA	20151	703-222-2010	222-2410	49-3
Door Components Inc 7980 Redwood Ave *TF:* 866-989-3667 ■ *Web:* www.dcihollowmetal.com	Fontana	CA	92336	866-989-3667		234
Door County 421 Nebraska St *Web:* www.co.door.wi.gov	Sturgeon Bay	WI	54235	920-746-2200	746-2330	338
Door County Library (DCL) 107 S Fourth Ave *Web:* www.doorcountylibrary.org	Sturgeon Bay	WI	54235	920-743-6578		434-3
Door Creek Church 6602 Dominion Dr *Web:* doorcreekchurch.org	Madison	WI	53718	608-222-8586		48-20
Door Engineering & Manufacturing LLC 400 Cherry St *TF:* 800-959-1352 ■ *Web:* www.doorengineering.com	Kasota	MN	56050	507-931-6910		350
Door Engineering Corp 1234 Ballentine Blvd *Web:* www.dooreng.com	Norfolk	VA	23504	757-622-5355		256
Door Systems Inc PO Box 511 *TF:* 800-545-3667 ■ *Web:* www.doorsys.com	Framingham	MA	01704	508-875-3508		191-3
Doormark Inc 430 Goolsby Blvd *TF:* 888-969-0124 ■ *Web:* www.doormark.com	Deerfield Beach	FL	33442	954-418-4700		115
Doorways, The 612 E Marshall St *Web:* www.thedoorways.org	Richmond	VA	23219	804-828-6901		372
Dopo 4293 Piedmont Ave *Web:* www.dopoadesso.com	Oakland	CA	94611	510-652-3676		671
Doppler Systems 37202 Bloody Basin *Web:* www.dopsys.com	Carefree	AZ	85377	480-488-9755	488-1295	529
Dora Hospitality Corp 9904 N by NE Blvd *Web:* www.dorahg.com	Fishers	IN	46037	317-577-8888	577-8466	377
Dora Hotel Company LLC 10734 Sky Prairie St *Web:* www.dorahotelco.com	Fishers	IN	46037	317-863-5700		379
Doral Steel Inc 1500 Coining Dr *Web:* www.samuel.com	Toledo	OH	43612	419-470-7070	470-7040	492
Doran Consulting LLC 2133 Upton Dr Ste 126-110 *Web:* doranconsulting.com	Virginia Beach	VA	23454	757-368-2208		463
Doran Independent Insurance 64 Center St PO Box 70 *Web:* doranindependentinsurance.com	Wolfeboro Falls	NH	03896	603-569-6464	569-8664	390
Doran Scales Inc 1315 Paramount Pkwy *Web:* doranscales.com	Batavia	IL	60510	630-879-1200		684
Dorchester Chamber of Commerce 528 Poplar St *Web:* dorchesterchamber.org	Cambridge	MD	21613	410-228-3575	228-6848	139
Dorchester County Council 501 Court Ln *Web:* www.dorchestercountymd.com	Cambridge	MD	21613	410-228-1700	228-9641	338
Dorchester County Library 506 N Parler Ave *Web:* dorchesterlibrarysc.org	Saint George	SC	29477	843-563-9189		434-3
Dorchester County Public Library 303 Gay St *Web:* www.dorchesterlibrary.org	Cambridge	MD	21613	410-228-7331	228-6313	434-3
Dorchester Minerals LP 3838 Oak Lawn Ave Ste 300 *NASDAQ: DMLP* ■ *TF:* 800-690-6903 ■ *Web:* www.dmlp.net	Dallas	TX	75219	214-559-0300	559-0301	536
Dorchester Real Estate Inc 1544 Dorchester Ave *Web:* century21cahill.com	Dorchester	MA	02122	617-265-1000		652
Dordick Law Corp 509 S Beverly Dr *Web:* www.dordicklaw.com	Beverly Hills	CA	90212	310-551-0949		445
Dordt College 498 Fourth Ave NE *TF:* 800-343-6738 ■ *Web:* www.dordt.edu	Sioux Center	IA	51250	712-722-6080		166
Dorel Industries Inc 1255 Greene Ave Ste 300 *TSX: DII.B* ■ *Web:* www.dorel.com	Montreal	QC	H3Z2A4	514-934-3034		319-2

Name / Address	City	State	Zip	Phone	Fax	Class
Dorel Juvenile USA 2525 State St *Web:* na.doreljuvenile.com	Columbus	IN	47201	812-372-0141		64
Doremus 200 Varick St *Web:* www.doremus.com	New York	NY	10014	212-366-3000		4
Doremus Financial Printing 228 E 45th St 10th Fl *Web:* www.doremusfp.com	New York	NY	10017	212-366-3800		627
Dorey Electric Co 894 Widgeon Rd PO Box 10158 *Web:* www.doreyelectric.com	Norfolk	VA	23513	757-855-3381		189-4
Dorf & Nelson LLP 555 Theodore Fremd Ave *Web:* dorflaw.com	Rye	NY	10580	914-381-7600		41
Dori Foods Inc 3410 Norfolk St *TF:* 800-776-6758 ■ *Web:* www.goodsource.com	Richmond	VA	23230	804-355-1600		805
Dorian Business Systems Inc 1985 Forest Ln *Web:* www.charmsoffice.com	Garland	TX	75042	972-485-1912	272-3927	177
Dorian Drake International Inc 2 Westchester Park Dr *Web:* www.doriandrake.com	White Plains	NY	10604	914-697-9800	697-9683	61
Dorian, Goldstein, Wisniewski, & Orchinik PC 2410 Bristol Rd *Web:* doriangoldstein.com	Bensalem	PA	19020	215-809-3882		41
Dorignac's Food Ctr 725 Focis St *Web:* dorignacs.com	Metairie	LA	70005	504-837-4650	832-8944	345
Doris Duke Charitable Foundation (DDCF) 650 Fifth Ave 19th Fl *Web:* www.ddcf.org	New York	NY	10019	212-974-7000	974-7590	305
Dorling Kindersley Ltd 375 Hudson St *TF:* 800-631-8571 ■ *Web:* www.dk.com	New York	NY	10014	646-674-4047		637-2
Dorman Products Inc 3400 E Walnut St *NASDAQ: DORM* ■ *TF:* 800-523-2492 ■ *Web:* www.rbinc.com	Colmar	PA	18915	215-997-1800	997-7969	60
Dormer Harpring LLC 3457 Ringsby Ct Ste 110 *Web:* denvertrial.com	Denver	CO	80216	303-747-4404		41
Dormify Inc 4999 Old Orchard Shopping Ctr *Web:* www.dormify.com	Skokie	IL	60077	413-922-6436		361
Dormont Manufacturing Co 6015 Enterprise Dr *TF:* 800-367-6668 ■ *Web:* www.watts.com	Export	PA	15632	800-367-6668		370
Dorn Color Inc 11555 Berea Rd *Web:* www.dorncolor.com	Cleveland	OH	44102	216-634-2252		561
Dornbracht Americas Inc 1700 Executive Dr S Ste 600 *TF:* 800-774-1181 ■ *Web:* www.dornbracht.com	Duluth	GA	30096	770-564-3599		610
Dornerworks Ltd 3445 Lake Eastbrook Blvd SE *Web:* dornerworks.com	Grand Rapids	MI	49546	616-245-8369	245-8372	696
Dorney Park & Wildwater Kingdom 3830 Dorney Park Rd *Web:* www.dorneypark.com	Allentown	PA	18104	610-395-3724		32
Dornier MedTech America Inc 1155 Roberts Blvd *Web:* www.dornier.com	Kennesaw	GA	30144	770-426-1315	514-6291	382
Doron Precision Systems Inc 150 Corporate Dr PO Box 400 *Web:* doronprecision.com	Binghamton	NY	13904	607-772-1610	772-6760	703
Doroshow Insurance Inc 2480 W Horizon Ridge Pkwy Ste 110 *Web:* doroshowinsurance.com	Henderson	NV	89052	702-369-1122		390
Dorothea Dix Hospital 820 S Boylan Ave	Raleigh	NC	27603	919-733-5540		374-5
Dorothy Bramlage Public Library Junction City 230 W Seventh St *TF:* 800-727-2785 ■ *Web:* www.jclib.org	Junction City	KS	66441	785-238-4311	238-7873	434-3
Dorothy Lane Market Inc 2710 Far Hills Ave *Web:* www.dorothylane.com	Dayton	OH	45419	937-299-3561		345
Dorr Street Cafe 5243 Dorr St *Web:* dorrstreetcafe.com	Toledo	OH	43615	419-531-4446		671
Dorris Lumber & Moulding Co, The 2601 Redding Ave *TF:* 800-827-5823 ■ *Web:* www.dorrismoulding.com	Sacramento	CA	95820	916-452-7531		499
Dorsett & Jackson Inc 3800 Noakes St *TF:* 800-871-8365 ■ *Web:* www.dorsettandjackson.com	Los Angeles	CA	90023	323-268-1815	268-9082	146
Dorsett Industries Inc 1304 May St PO Box 805 *TF:* 800-241-4035 ■ *Web:* www.dorsettind.com	Dalton	GA	30721	706-278-1961	217-1775	131
Dorsey & Semrau 714 Main St *Web:* dorseysemrau.com	Boonton	NJ	07005	973-334-1900	334-3408	41
Dorsey & Whitney LLP 50 S Sixth St Ste 1500 *Web:* www.dorsey.com	Minneapolis	MN	55402	612-340-2600	340-2868	428
Dorsey School 31450 Gratiot Ave *Web:* www.dorsey.edu	Roseville	MI	48066	586-296-3225		685
Dorson Vocational Training Institute 280 S Harrison St Ste 300 *Web:* www.dorsonvtischool.com	East Orange	NJ	07018	973-676-6300	766-1761	800
Dorst America Inc 64 S Commerce Way *Web:* www.dorst.de	Bethlehem	PA	18017	610-317-2000	317-6416	567
Dort Federal Credit Union Event Ctr 3501 Lapeer Rd *Web:* www.dorteventcenter.com	Flint	MI	48503	810-744-0580		720
Dortronics Systems Inc 1668 Sag Harbor Tpke *TF:* 800-906-0137 ■ *Web:* www.dortronics.com	Sag Harbor	NY	11963	800-906-0137		350
Dorvin D. Leis Company Inc 202 Lalo St *Web:* www.leisinc.com	Kahului	HI	96732	808-877-3902		189-10
Dos Locos 208 Rehoboth Ave *Web:* www.doslocos.com	Rehoboth Beach	DE	19971	302-227-3353		671
Dos Rios Consultants Inc (DRC) PO Box 1247 *Web:* bloodhound.tripod.com	Silver City	NM	88062	505-534-0035		192
Dos Rios Partners 205 Wild Basin Rd S Bldg 3 Ste 100 *Web:* dosriospartners.com	Austin	TX	78746	512-298-0801		528
Dosha Salon Spa 2281 NW Glisan St *Web:* dosha.org	Portland	OR	97210	503-228-8280		77
Dosoris Press PO Box 148 *Web:* www.dosoris.com	Glen Cove	NY	11542	516-671-0686		637-2
Dossett Big 4 Buick GMC Cadillac 628 S Gloster St *Web:* www.dossettbig4.com	Tupelo	MS	38801	662-269-4778		57
Dostal & Kirk Inc 120 S Sandusky *TF:* 877-562-6801 ■ *Web:* dostalkirk.com	Bucyrus	OH	44820	877-562-6801		390
Doster Construction Co 2100 International Pk Dr *Web:* www.dosterconstruction.com	Birmingham	AL	35243	205-443-3800	951-2612	186
DOT (Department of Transportation) 1200 New Jersey Ave SE *TF:* 800-877-8339 ■ *Web:* www.transportation.gov	Washington	DC	20590	202-366-4000		340-17
Dot Com Holdings of Buffalo Inc 1460 Military Rd *TF:* 877-636-3673 ■ *Web:* www.dchob.com	Buffalo	NY	14217	877-636-3673		80
Dot Foods Inc 1 Dot Way PO Box 192 *TF:* 800-366-3687 ■ *Web:* www.dotfoods.com	Mount Sterling	IL	62353	217-773-4411	773-3321	297-6
Dot Gibson Publications PO Box 117 *TF:* 800-336-8095 ■ *Web:* www.dotgibson.com	Waycross	GA	31502	912-285-2848		637-2
Dot Hill Systems Corp 1351 S Sunset St *NASDAQ: HILL* ■ *TF:* 800-872-2783 ■ *Web:* www.seagate.com	Longmont	CO	80501	303-845-3200	845-3655	176
Dot VN Inc 9449 Balboa Ave Ste 103 *Web:* www.dot.vn	San Diego	CA	92123	858-571-2007	571-8497	224
Dot Wo 10600 S Pennsylvania Ave *Web:* dotwofood.com	Oklahoma City	OK	73170	405-691-4888		671
DotCom Therapy 811 E Washington Ave Ste 500 *TF:* 844-536-8266 ■ *Web:* www.dotcomtherapy.com	Madison	WI	53703	844-536-8266		765
Dothan Area Botanical Gardens 5130 Headland Ave *Web:* www.dabg.com	Dothan	AL	36303	334-793-3224		97
Dothan Area Chamber of Commerce 102 Jamestown Blvd *TF:* 800-221-1027 ■ *Web:* www.dothan.com	Dothan	AL	36301	334-792-5138	794-4796	139
Dothan Chrysler-Dodge Inc 4074 Ross Clark Cir NW *TF:* 877-674-9574 ■ *Web:* www.dothanchryslerdodge.net	Dothan	AL	36303	334-794-0606		57
Dothan Eagle PO Box 1968 *TF:* 800-811-1771 ■ *Web:* www.dothaneagle.com	Dothan	AL	36302	334-792-3141	712-7979	532-2
Dot-Line Transportation PO Box 8739 *TF:* 800-423-3780 ■ *Web:* www.dotline.net	Fountain Valley	CA	92728	323-780-9010		188-5
DotLoop LLC 700 W Pete Rose Way Ste 446 *Web:* www.dotloop.com	Cincinnati	OH	45203	513-257-0550		387
DOTmedcom Inc 29 Broadway Ste 2500 *Web:* www.dotmed.com	New York	NY	10006	212-742-1200		387
dotPhoto PO Box 92 *Web:* www.dotphoto.com	Titusville	NJ	08560	609-608-0640		588
Dotronix Technology Inc 2420 Oakgreen Ave N *TF:* 800-720-7218 ■ *Web:* dotronix.com	West Lakeland Township	MN	55082	651-633-1742	633-1065	173-4
Dotson Iron Castings 200 W Rock St *Web:* www.dotson.com	Mankato	MN	56001	507-345-5018	345-1270	307
Dotster 8100 NE Pkwy Dr Ste 300 PO Box 821066 *TF:* 800-401-5250 ■ *Web:* www.dotster.com	Vancouver	WA	98682	360-449-5800	397-2699	396
Doty Group PS, The 1102 Broadway Ste 400 *Web:* dotygroupcpas.com	Tacoma	WA	98402	253-830-5450		2
Double Cola Company USA 537 Market St Ste 100 *Web:* www.doublecolacompany.com	Chattanooga	TN	37402	423-267-5691		80-2
Double Decker Press 4087 Silver Bar Rd *Web:* www.doubledeckerpress.com	Mariposa	CA	95338	209-966-3557		95
Double Diamond Co 5495 Belt Line Rd Ste 200 *TF:* 800-324-7438 ■ *Web:* ddresorts.com	Dallas	TX	75254	214-706-9801		653
Double Dragon 117 W Wayne St	Fort Wayne	IN	46802	260-431-8697		671
Double E. Co 319 Manley St *Web:* ee-co.com	West Bridgewater	MA	02379	508-588-8099	580-2915	556
Double Eagle Capital Management LP 1301 Solana Blvd 1st Bldg Ste 1480 *Web:* www.doubleeaglecapital.com	Westlake	TX	76262	972-869-6880		528
Double Eagle Distributing Inc 50 Lock Rd *Web:* www.doubleeagledist.com	Deerfield Beach	FL	33442	954-426-2970	427-6870	7
Double Eagle Hotel & Casino 442 E Bennett Ave *TF:* 800-711-7234 ■ *Web:* www.decasino.com	Cripple Creek	CO	80813	719-689-5000		133
Double Eagle Resort & Spa 5587 Hwy 158 *Web:* www.doubleeagle.com	June Lake	CA	93529	760-648-7004		669
Double Envelope Corp 7702 Plantation Rd *Web:* www.double-envelope.com	Roanoke	VA	24019	540-362-3311		263
Double H. Plastics Inc 50 W St Rd *TF:* 800-523-3932 ■ *Web:* www.doublehplastics.com	Warminster	PA	18974	800-523-3932		604
Double J. Saddlery Inc 2243 US Hwy 77A S *TF:* 800-669-2535 ■ *Web:* doublejsaddlery.com	Yoakum	TX	77995	361-293-6364		711
Double Quick Printing Services Inc 2233 S Monaco Pkwy *Web:* www.dqprint.com	Denver	CO	80222	303-759-9999	759-9900	627
Double R Productions 1621 Connecticut Ave NW Ste 400 *Web:* doublerproductions.com	Washington	DC	20009	202-797-7777		514
Double Trouble State Park 581 Pinewald Keswick Rd *Web:* www.state.nj.us	Bayville	NJ	08721	732-341-4098		565
Doublebees 111 Bill Foster Memorial Hwy *Web:* doublebees.com	Cabot	AR	72023	501-605-8989		297-8

Name / Address	Phone	Fax	Class
DoubleCheck LLC 101 Gilbraltar Dr........................Morris Plains NJ 07950 *TF:* 888-299-3980 ■ *Web:* www.doublechecksoftware.com	973-984-2229		177
Double-E Inc 1261 Profit Dr..................... Dallas TX 75247 *Web:* www.doubleeinc.com	214-631-2290	630-4712	537
Doublehorn Communications 1601 Rio Grande St 500....................... Austin TX 78701 *TF:* 855-618-6423 ■ *Web:* doublehorn.com	512-637-5200		224
Doubleknot LLC 20665 Fourth St Ste 103.................... Saratoga CA 95070 *Web:* www.doubleknot.com	408-971-9120	741-1000	463
DoublePositive 1111 Light St Ste 350 ....Baltimore MD 21230 *TF:* 888-376-7484 ■ *Web:* www.doublepositive.com	410-332-0464		7
DoubleStar Inc 1161 Mcdermott Dr Ste 200...............West Chester PA 19380 *TF:* 888-719-9311 ■ *Web:* www.doublestarinc.com	610-719-1900	719-8280	256
DoubleTree by Hilton Ann Arbor North 3600 Plymouth Rd .... Ann Arbor MI 48105 *Web:* doubletree3.hilton.com	734-769-9800		378
Doubletree by Hilton Hotel Tucson-Reid Park 445 S Alvernon Way..........................Tucson AZ 85711 *Web:* doubletree3.hilton.com	520-881-4200		378
DoubleVerify 233 Spring St...................New York NY 10013 *Web:* www.doubleverify.com	212-631-2002		387
Doucet & Associates Inc 7401B Hwy 71 W Ste 160...................... Austin TX 78735 *Web:* www.doucetengineers.com	512-583-2600		261
Doucette Industries Inc (DII) 20 Leigh Dr ....York PA 17406 *TF:* 800-445-7511 ■ *Web:* www.doucetteindustries.com	717-845-8746	845-2864	14
Doug Ashy Building Materials Inc 1801 Rees St .... Breaux Bridge LA 70517 *Web:* dougashy.com	337-332-5201	332-5226	364
Doug Butler Enterprises Inc 495 Table Rd.............................. Crawford NE 69339 *TF:* 800-728-3826 ■ *Web:* www.dougbutler.com	308-665-1510	665-1520	637-2
Doug Calcagni Associates Inc 330 S Main St............................. Cheshire CT 06410 *Web:* calcagni.com	203-272-1821		652
Doug Cornelius 864 Silliman Ave .... Erie PA 16511 *Web:* dougcornelius.net	814-899-1112	899-8343	390
Doug Fregolle Promotions 6351 Wilshire Blvd 2nd Fl ....Los Angeles CA 90048 *Web:* dfpromotions.com	323-939-0900		366
Doug Hansen & Associates Insurance 202 N Main St ....Thiensville WI 53092 *Web:* doughanseninsurance.com	262-643-4020		390
Doug Hollyhand Construction Co 527 Main Ave ....Northport AL 35476 *Web:* www.hollyhand.com	205-345-0955		186
Doug Menely Insurance 8606 SE 17th Ave...........................Portland OR 97202 *Web:* dougmenely.com	503-238-1903		390
Doug Mockett & Company Inc 1915 Abalone Ave...........................Torrance CA 90501 *Web:* www.mockett.com	310-318-2491		350
Doug Varone & Dancers 260 W Broadway Ste 4 ....New York NY 10013 *Web:* www.dovadance.org	212-279-3344		573-1
Doug's Hickory Pit Bar B Que 3313 S Georgia St ....Amarillo TX 79109	806-352-8471		671
Doug's Supermarket Inc 310 Main Ave NE ....Warroad MN 56763 *Web:* dougssupermarket.com	218-386-1246		345
Dougherty & Company LLC 90 S Seventh St Ste 4300.................Minneapolis MN 55402 *TF:* 800-328-4000 ■ *Web:* www.doughertymarkets.com	612-376-4000		690
Dougherty Arts Ctr, The (DAC) 1110 Barton Springs Rd....................... Austin TX 78704 *Web:* www.austintexas.gov	512-974-4000	974-4039	50-2
Dougherty County Public Library 300 N Pine Ave.............................Albany GA 31701 *Web:* www.docolib.org	229-420-3200		434-3
Dougherty Management Associates Inc 9 Meriam St Ste 4.........................Lexington MA 02420 *TF:* 800-814-7802 ■ *Web:* www.dmahealth.com	781-863-1519		463
Dougherty Sprague Environmental Inc 3902 Industrial St Ste A ....Rowlett TX 75088 *Web:* www.dsei.com	972-412-8666		256
Dougherty's Holdings Inc 16250 Dallas Pkwy Ste 102 .... Dallas TX 75248 *Web:* www.doughertys.com	214-373-5300		237
Dougherty, Leventhal & Price LLP 459 Wyoming Ave.......................... Kingston PA 18704 *Web:* dlplaw.com	570-288-1427	288-0799	41
Dough-to-Go Inc 3535 De La Cruz Blvd..................... Santa Clara CA 95054 *TF:* 800-220-2339 ■ *Web:* www.dough-to-go.com	408-727-4094		296-1
Douglas & London P C 59 Maiden Ln 6th Fl.........................New York NY 10038 *TF:* 800-963-4444 ■ *Web:* www.douglasandlondon.com	212-566-7500	566-7501	445
Douglas & Sturgess Inc 1023 Factory St .... Richmond CA 94801 *Web:* www.artstuf.com	510-235-8411	235-4211	45
Douglas Allred Co 11452 El Camino Real Ste 200............... San Diego CA 92130 *Web:* www.douglasallredco.com	858-793-0202	793-5363	655
Douglas Autotech Corp 300 Albers Rd ....Bronson MI 49028 *Web:* www.douglasautotech.com	517-369-2315	369-7217	60
Douglas Baldwin & Assoc PO Box 1249 .... La Canada Flintridge CA 91012 *Web:* www.baldwinpi.com	818-952-4433	790-4622	400
Douglas Battery Manufacturing Co 500 Battery Dr........................ Winston-Salem NC 27107 *TF:* 800-368-4527 ■ *Web:* www.douglasbattery.com	800-368-4527		74
Douglas Bros 423 Riverside Industrial Pkwy..................Portland ME 04103 *TF:* 800-341-0926 ■ *Web:* www.douglasbrothers.com	207-797-6771	797-8385	595
Douglas College 700 Royal Ave PO Box 2503............New Westminster BC V3M5Z5 *Web:* www.douglascollege.ca	604-527-5400	527-5095	167-3
Douglas Corp 9650 Valley View Rd ....Eden Prairie MN 55344 **Fax Area Code:* 952 ■ *TF:* 800-806-6113 ■ *Web:* www.douglascorp.com	800-806-6113	942-3125*	701
Douglas County 305 Eigth Ave W .... Alexandria MN 56308 *Web:* www.co.douglas.mn.us	320-762-3877		338
Douglas County 100 Third St .... Castle Rock CO 80104 *TF:* 800-654-2733 ■ *Web:* www.douglas.co.us	303-660-7401	688-1293	338
Douglas County 8700 Hospital Dr............Douglasville GA 30134 *Web:* www.celebratedouglascounty.com	770-949-2000		338
Douglas County 100 Massachusetts St.......... Lawrence KS 66044 *Web:* www.douglascountyks.org	785-832-5167		338
Douglas County 1616 8th St PO Box 218 .... Minden NV 89423 *Web:* cltr.douglasnv.us	775-782-9014	782-9017	338
Douglas County 1819 Farnam St.................Omaha NE 68183 *Web:* www.douglascounty-ne.gov	402-444-7025	444-6559	338
Douglas County 1036 SE Douglas St ....Roseburg OR 97470 *Web:* www.co.douglas.or.us	541-672-3311	440-4408	338
Douglas County 1313 Belknap St ....Superior WI 54880 *Web:* www.douglascountywi.org	715-395-1341	395-1421	338
Douglas County 401 S Center St PO Box 467................... Tuscola IL 61953 *Web:* www.douglascountyil.com	217-253-2411	253-2233	338
Douglas County *Board Of County Commissioners* 203 S Rainier St...........................Waterville WA 98858 *Web:* www.douglascountywa.net	509-745-8537	745-9045	338
Douglas County Board of Education 9030 Hwy 5 ....Douglasville GA 30134 *Web:* www.douglas.k12.ga.us	770-651-2000		685
Douglas County Chamber of Commerce 6658 Church St ....Douglasville GA 30134 *Web:* douglascountygeorgia.com	770-942-5022	942-5876	139
Douglas County Insurance Service 4348 Woodlands Blve Ste 229.............. Castle Rock CO 80104 *Web:* cowest.com	303-688-9597		390
Douglas County Libraries 100 S Wilcox .... Castle Rock CO 80104 *Web:* www.dcl.org	303-791-7323		434-3
Douglas County Library 720 Fillmore St........................... Alexandria MN 56308 *Web:* www.douglascountylibrary.org	320-762-3014		434-3
Douglas Cuddle Toys Company Inc 69 Krif Rd PO Box D...........................Keene NH 03431 *TF:* 800-992-9002 ■ *Web:* douglascuddletoy.com	603-352-3414	352-1248	762
Douglas Education Ctr 130 7th St............ Monessen PA 15062 *TF:* 800-413-6013 ■ *Web:* www.dec.edu	724-684-7463		167-3
Douglas Electric Cooperative Inc 400 Main Ave .... Armour SD 57313 *Web:* www.douglaselec.coop	605-724-2323		245
Douglas Elliman Property Management 675 Third Ave.............................New York NY 10017 *Web:* www.ellimanpm.com	212-370-9200		655
Douglas Industries Co 3441 S 11th Ave............................Eldridge IA 52748 *TF:* 800-553-8907 ■ *Web:* www.douglas-sports.com	563-285-4162	285-4163	710
Douglas J. Aveda Institute 333 Maynard St .... Ann Arbor MI 48104 *Web:* www.douglasj.edu	734-929-0453		166
Douglas Laboratories Inc 600 Boyce Rd............................ Pittsburgh PA 15205 *TF:* 800-245-4440 ■ *Web:* www.douglaslabs.com	800-245-4440		799
Douglas Lumber Corp 125 Douglas Pk .... Smithfield RI 02917 *Web:* douglaslumber.com	401-231-6800		351
Douglas Machine Inc 3404 Iowa St........... Alexandria MN 56308 *Web:* www.douglas-machine.com	320-763-6587	763-5754	547
Douglas Machines Corp 2101 Calumet St.......................... Clearwater FL 33765 *Web:* www.dougmac.com	727-461-3477		427
Douglas Orr Plumbing Inc 301 Flagler Dr.........................Miami Springs FL 33166 *Web:* www.orrplumbing.com	305-887-1687		610
Douglas Parking LLC 1721 Webster St........... Oakland CA 94612 *TF:* 800-877-9984 ■ *Web:* www.douglasparking.com	510-444-7412		562
Douglas Press Inc 2810 Madison St .... Bellwood IL 60104 *TF:* 800-323-0705 ■ *Web:* www.douglaspress.com	708-547-8400		322
Douglas State Forest 107 Wallum Lake Rd.........................Douglas MA 01516 *Web:* www.mass.gov	508-476-7872		565
Douglas Steel Fabricating Corp 1312 S Waverly Rd .... Lansing MI 48917 *Web:* www.douglassteel.com	517-322-2050	322-0050	307
Douglas Stewart Co, The 2402 Advance Rd .... Madison WI 53718 *TF:* 800-279-2795 ■ *Web:* www.dstewart.com	608-221-1155	221-5217	534
Douglas Udell Gallery 10332 124th St......... Edmonton AB T5N1R2 *Web:* www.udellxhibitions.com	780-488-4445	488-8335	42
Douglas Wilson Companies 1620 5th Ave Ste 400...................... San Diego CA 92101 *Web:* www.douglaswilson.com	619-641-1141		194
Douglas, Conroyd, Gibb & Pacheco PC 528 Cottage St NE .... Salem OR 97301 *Web:* dcm-law.com	503-364-7000		41
Douglas-Coffee County Chamber of Commerce 114 N Peterson Ave Ste 205..................Douglas GA 31533 *Web:* douglasga.org	912-384-1873	383-6304	139
Douglas-Guardian Services Corp 14800 St Mary's Ln..........................Houston TX 77079 *TF:* 800-255-0552 ■ *Web:* www.douglasguardian.com	281-531-0500		399
Douglass College 100 George St .... New Brunswick NJ 08901 *Web:* douglass.rutgers.edu	848-932-9500		166
Douglass Colony Group Inc 5901 E 58th Ave...................... Commerce City CO 80022 *TF:* 877-288-0650 ■ *Web:* www.douglasscolony.com	303-288-2635		189-12
Douglass Distributing Co 325 E Forest Ave........................... Sherman TX 75090 *TF:* 800-736-4316 ■ *Web:* www.douglassdist.com	903-893-1181		581

	Phone	Fax	Class
Douglass Industries Inc 412 Boston Ave PO Box 701............Egg Harbor City NJ 08215 *TF:* 800-950-3684 ■ *Web:* douglassfabric.com	609-965-6030		594
Douglass Theatre 355 ML King Jr Blvd...........Macon GA 31201 *Web:* www.douglasstheatre.org	478-742-2000		572
Douglass Truck Bodies Inc 231 21st St..............................Bakersfield CA 93301 *TF:* 800-635-7641 ■ *Web:* www.douglasstruckbodies.com	661-327-0258	327-3894	516
Douglasville Convention and Visitors Bureau 6694 E Broad St..........................Douglasville GA 30134 *TF:* 800-661-0013 ■ *Web:* www.visitdouglasville.com	770-947-5920		393
Douloi Automation Inc 3517 Ryder St........................... Santa Clara CA 95051 *Web:* www.douloiautomation.com	408-735-6942		178-1
Douthat State Park 14239 Douthat State Park Rd..................Millboro VA 24460 *Web:* www.dcr.virginia.gov	540-862-8100	862-8104	565
Douthitt Corp 245 Adair St.....................Detroit MI 48207 *TF:* 800-368-8448 ■ *Web:* www.douthittcorp.com	313-259-1565	259-6806	591
Dove Cleaners Inc 1560 Yonge St..............Toronto ON M4T2S9 *TF:* 866-999-3683 ■ *Web:* www.dovecleaners.com	416-413-7900		426
Dove Die & Stamping Co 15665 Brookpark Rd........................Cleveland OH 44142 *Web:* www.dovedie.com	216-267-3720		488
Dove Lewis Emergency Animal Hospital Inc 1945 NW Pettygrove St.......................Portland OR 97209 *Web:* www.dovelewis.org	503-228-7281		794
Dovel & Luner LLP 201 Santa Monica Blvd Ste 600............Santa Monica CA 90401 *Web:* dovel.com	310-656-7066		41
Dover Air Force Base 4304 Kirkwood Hwy.........Dover DE 19902 *Web:* www.dover.af.mil	302-677-3372	677-2901	497-1
Dover Behavioral Health System 725 Horsepond Rd............................Dover DE 19901 *TF:* 855-609-9711 ■ *Web:* www.doverbehavioral.com	302-741-0140		374-5
Dover Chemical Corp 3676 Davis Rd NW..........Dover OH 44622 *TF:* 800-321-8805 ■ *Web:* doverchem.com	330-343-7711		145
Dover City Hall 5 E Reed St......................Dover DE 19901 *Web:* www.cityofdover.com	302-736-7022		337
Dover Corp 3005 Highland Pkwy Ste 200............Downers Grove IL 60515 *NYSE: DOV* ■ *Web:* www.dovercorporation.com	630-541-1540	743-2671	185
Dover Downs Hotel & Casino 1131 N DuPont Hwy..........................Dover DE 19901 *NYSE: DDE* ■ *TF:* 800-711-5882 ■ *Web:* www.doverdowns.com	302-674-4600		642
Dover Federal Credit Union 1075 Silver Lake Blvd..........................Dover DE 19904 *Web:* www.doverfcu.com	302-678-8000		219
Dover Financial Research 208 Dover Rd............................Westwood MA 02090 *Web:* www.doverfr.com	781-461-0922		401
Dover High Performance Plastics Inc 140 Williams Dr.............................Dover OH 44622 *Web:* www.dhpp.net	330-343-3477	343-7642	605-2
Dover International Speedway 1131 N DuPont Hwy PO Box 843................Dover DE 19901 *TF:* 800-441-7223 ■ *Web:* www.doverspeedway.com	302-883-6500	672-0100	642
Dover Post 1196 S Little Creek Rd................Dover DE 19901 *TF:* 800-942-1616 ■ *Web:* www.doverpost.com	302-678-3616		532-4
Dover Public Library 73 Locust St...............Dover NH 03820 *Web:* www.dover.nh.gov	603-516-6050	516-6053	434-3
Dover Publications Inc 31 E Second St..........Mineola NY 11501 *Web:* store.doverpublications.com	516-294-7000		532-3
Dover Saddlery Inc 525 Great Rd...............Littleton MA 01460 *NASDAQ: DOVR* ■ *TF:* 800-406-8204 ■ *Web:* www.doversaddlery.com	978-952-8062		710
Dover Tank & Plate Co, The 5725 Crown Rd NW...........................Dover OH 44622 *Web:* www.dovertank.com	330-343-4443	364-3125	480
Doverco Inc 2111 32e Ave.......................Lachine QC H8T3J1 *TF:* 800-363-0697 ■ *Web:* www.doverco.ca	514-420-6060	420-6015	358
Dover-Phila Federal Credit Union 119 Fillmore Ave.............................Dover OH 44622 *TF:* 877-763-2162 ■ *Web:* dpfcu.org	330-364-8874	343-7270	219
Dovetail Communications Inc 30 E Beaver Creek Rd Ste 202............Richmond Hill ON L4B1J2 *Web:* dvtail.com	905-886-6640		224
Dovetail Internet Technologies LLC 40 Southbridge St Ste 210.................Worcester MA 01608 *TF:* 866-845-6465 ■ *Web:* www.dovetailinternet.com	508-845-6465		225
Dovetail Public Relations 15951 Los Gatos Blvd Ste 16................Los Gatos CA 95032 *Web:* www.dovetailpr.com	408-395-3600	395-8232	636
DOVICO Software Inc 236 St George St Ste 119....................Moncton NB E1C1W1 **Fax Area Code:* 506 ■ *TF:* 800-618-8463 ■ *Web:* www.dovico.com	800-618-8463	384-0727*	179
Dow AgroSciences LLC 9330 Zionsville Rd.......................Indianapolis IN 46268 **Fax Area Code:* 800 ■ *Web:* www.corteva.com	317-337-3000	905-7326*	280
Dow Chemical Canada Inc (DCCI) 450 1st St SW Ste 2100.......................Calgary AB T2P3L8 *TF:* 800-447-4369 ■ *Web:* www.dow.com	403-267-3527	267-3597	144
Dow Chemical Employees' Credit Union 600 E Lyon Rd..............................Midland MI 48640 *TF:* 800-835-7794 ■ *Web:* www.dcecu.org	989-835-7794	832-9283	219
Dow Cover Company Inc 373 Lexington Ave........................New Haven CT 06513 *TF:* 800-735-8877 ■ *Web:* www.dowcover.com	203-469-5394		349
Dow Electronics Inc 8603 E Adamo Dr...........Tampa FL 33619 *TF:* 800-627-2900 ■ *Web:* www.dowelectronics.com	813-626-5195	628-4990	246
Dow Event Ctr 303 Johnson St.................Saginaw MI 48607 *Web:* www.doweventcenter.com	989-759-1320	759-1322	572
Dow Gardens 1809 Eastman Ave................Midland MI 48640 *TF:* 800-362-4874 ■ *Web:* www.dowgardens.org	989-631-2677		97
Dow Hotel Company LLC, The 16400 Southcenter Pkwy Ste 405................Seattle WA 98188 *Web:* www.dowhotelco.com	206-575-3600	575-0600	378
Dow Hydraulic Systems Inc 1835 Wright Ave...........................La Verne CA 91750 *Web:* www.dowhydraulics.com	909-596-6602	596-6605	454
Dow Jones & Company Inc 1211 Avenue of the Americas.................New York NY 10036 **Fax Area Code:* 212 ■ *TF:* 800-369-0166 ■ *Web:* www.dowjones.com	800-369-0166	416-2658*	637-8
Dow Screw Products 3810 Paule Ave........Saint Louis MO 63125	314-638-5100		621
Dow Services Inc 2902 First Ave N................Fargo ND 58102 *Web:* dowservices.net	701-232-4336		104
Dow Theory Forecasts 7412 Calumet Ave......Hammond IN 46324 *TF:* 800-233-5922 ■ *Web:* www.dowtheory.com	800-233-5922		531-9
DOWA Cosmetics 230 Winston St Ste 2.....................Los Angeles CA 90013 *Web:* www.dowacosmetics.com	213-892-1098	892-1094	45
Dowding Industries Inc 502 Marilin Ave........................Eaton Rapids MI 48827 *Web:* www.dowdingindustries.com	517-663-5455		483
Dowdle Sports & Outdoors 981 N Germantown Pkwy.....................Cordova TN 38018 *Web:* www.dowdlesports.com	901-751-1499		711
Dowell & Dowell Pc 2560 Huntington Ave Ste 203................Alexandria VA 22303 *Web:* dowellpc.com	703-739-9888		41
Dow-Key Microwave Corp 4822 McGrath St...........................Ventura CA 93003 *TF:* 800-266-3695 ■ *Web:* www.dowkey.com	805-650-0260	650-1734	253
Dowl LLC 4041 B St............................Anchorage AK 99503 *TF:* 800-865-9847 ■ *Web:* www.dowl.com	907-562-2000		261
Dowley Security Systems Inc 10784 Kempwood Dr........................Houston TX 77043 *Web:* www.dowley.com	713-721-9732	456-2680	246
Dowling & Yahnke Inc 12340 El Camino Real.....................San Diego CA 92130 *Web:* www.dywealth.com	858-509-9500		690
Dowling Aaron Inc 8080 N Palm Ave 3rd Fl.......................Fresno CA 93711 *Web:* dowlingaaron.com	559-432-4500	432-4590	445
Dowling College 150 Idle Hour Blvd.............Oakdale NY 11769 *TF:* 800-369-5464 ■ *Web:* www.dowling.edu	631-244-3000		166
Dowling Graphics Inc 12920 Automobile Blvd...................Clearwater FL 33762 *TF:* 800-749-6933 ■ *Web:* www.dowlinggraphics.com	727-573-5997	572-9714	627
Down Beat Magazine 102 N Haven Rd..........Elmhurst IL 60126 **Fax Area Code:* 630 ■ *TF:* 877-904-5299 ■ *Web:* www.downbeat.com	651-251-9682	941-3210*	457-9
Down East 680 Commercial St.................Rockport ME 04856 *TF:* 800-766-1670 ■ *Web:* downeast.com	207-594-9544		457-22
Down Maine Veterinary Clinic PA 89 Country Club Rd.........................Sanford ME 04073 *Web:* downmainevets.com	207-324-4683	324-8629	794
Down the Shore Publishing Corp PO Box 100............................West Creek NJ 08092 *Web:* www.down-the-shore.com	609-812-5076	597-0422	637-2
Down to Earth 2525 S King St.................Honolulu HI 96826 *Web:* www.downtoearth.org	808-947-7678		479
Down To Earth Landscaping Inc 705 Wright-Debow Rd........................Jackson NJ 08527 *Web:* downtoearthlandscaping.com	732-833-7702		776
Down Under Bedding & Mattresses 5170 Dixie Rd Unit 3....................Mississauga ON L4W1E3 *TF:* 888-624-6484 ■ *Web:* downunderbedding.com	905-624-5854	624-7437	361
Downeast Correctional Facility 64 Base Rd............................Machiasport ME 04655 *Web:* www.maine.gov	207-255-1100		213
Downeast Energy Corp 18 Spring St..........Brunswick ME 04011 *Web:* www.downeastenergy.com	207-729-9921		612
Downeast Graphics & Printing Inc 477 Washington Jct Rd.....................Ellsworth ME 04605 *TF:* 800-427-5582 ■ *Web:* www.downeastgraphics.com	207-667-5582		627
Downeast Maritime Inc 145 Main St.........Thomaston ME 04861 *TF:* 888-693-0231 ■ *Web:* www.downeastmaritime.com	207-382-3037		167-3
Downeast School of Massage 99 Moose Meadow Ln PO Box 24............Waldoboro ME 04572 *Web:* www.downeastschoolofmassage.net	207-832-5531		685
Downers Grove Park District 2455 Warrenville Rd...................Downers Grove IL 60515 *Web:* www.dgparks.org	630-960-7500	960-7251	31
Downers Grove Public Library 1050 Curtiss St.......................Downers Grove IL 60515 *TF:* 800-227-0625 ■ *Web:* www.dglibrary.org	630-960-1200	960-9374	434-3
Downes Associates Inc 2129 Northwood Dr........................Salisbury MD 21801 *Web:* www.downesassociates.com	410-546-4422		261
Downey & Co 6565 Americas Pkwy Ste 750..............Albuquerque NM 87110 *Web:* downeyandco.com	505-881-0300		390
Downey Brand LLP 621 Capitol Mall 18th Fl...................Sacramento CA 95814 *Web:* www.downeybrand.com	916-444-1000	444-2100	428
Downey Chamber of Commerce 11131 Brookshire Ave........................Downey CA 90241 *Web:* www.downeychamber.org	562-923-2191	923-6388	139
Downey City Library (DCL) 11121 Brookshire Ave........................Downey CA 90241 *TF:* 877-846-3452 ■ *Web:* www.downeyca.org	562-904-7360	923-3763	434-3
Downey Federal Credit Union 8237 Third St...............................Downey CA 90241 *Web:* downeyfcu.org	562-862-8141		219
Downey Grinding Company Inc 12323 Bellflower Blvd........................Downey CA 90241 *Web:* downeygrinding.com	562-803-5556	803-3237	454
Downey High School 11040 Brookshire Ave........................Downey CA 90241 *Web:* www.dusd.net	562-869-7301		685
Downey Publishing Inc 2545 E Southlake Blvd......................Southlake TX 76092 *TF:* 800-343-8840 ■ *Web:* downeypublishing.com	817-416-6661		637-6
Downey Regional Medical Ctr 11500 Brookshire Ave........................Downey CA 90241 *TF:* 800-954-8000 ■ *Web:* www.pihhealth.org	562-904-5000		374-3
Downing Displays Inc 550 Techne Center Dr.........................Milford OH 45150 *TF:* 800-883-1800 ■ *Web:* www.downingdisplays.com	513-248-9800		232

Name / Address	City	State	ZIP	Phone	Fax	Class
Downing Heating & Air Conditioning Inc 31 Industrial Way *Web:* downinghvac.com	Greenbrae	CA	94904	415-485-1011		189-10
Downing Wellhead Equipment Inc 8528 S W 2nd St *Web:* downingusa.com	Oklahoma City	OK	73128	405-789-8182		539
Down-Lite International Inc 8153 Duke Blvd *TF:* 866-931-3696 ■ *Web:* www.downlite.com	Mason	OH	45040	866-931-3696		361
Downriver Grill 3315 W Northwest Blvd *Web:* www.downrivergrill.com	Spokane	WA	99205	509-323-1600		671
Downriver Refrigeration Supply Co 38170 N Executive Dr N *Web:* www.downriversupply.com	Westland	MI	48185	734-728-0795		665
Downs & Stanford PC 2001 Bryan St Ste 4000 *Web:* downsstanford.com	Dallas	TX	75201	214-748-7900		41
Downs Crane & Hoist Company Inc 8827 Juniper St *TF:* 800-748-5994 ■ *Web:* www.downscrane.com	Los Angeles	CA	90002	323-589-6061	589-6066	470
Downs Food Group 418 Benzel Ave SW *TF:* 800-967-2474 ■ *Web:* www.downsfoodgroup.com	Madelia	MN	56062	507-642-3203		345
Downstream 1624 NW Johnson St *Web:* www.downstream.com	Portland	OR	97209	503-226-1944		512
Downtown Aquarium 410 Bagby St & Memorial Dr *Web:* www.aquariumrestaurants.com	Houston	TX	77002	713-223-3474		40
Downtown at the Gardens 11701 Lake Victoria Gardens Ave *Web:* downtownatthegardens.com	Palm Beach Gardens	FL	33410	561-799-2407		50-6
Downtown Athletic Store Inc 1180 Seminole Trl Ste 210 *TF:* 800-348-2649 ■ *Web:* www.downtownathletic.com	Charlottesville	VA	22901	434-975-3696	975-2845	711
Downtown Austin Alliance 211 E Seventh St Ste 818 *Web:* downtownaustin.com	Austin	TX	78701	512-469-1766		138
Downtown Book Center Inc 247 SE 1st St *TF:* 800-599-8712 ■ *Web:* realpages.com	Miami	FL	33131	305-377-9939	371-5926	95
Downtown Cabaret Theatre 263 Golden Hill St *Web:* dtcab.com	Bridgeport	CT	06604	203-576-1636		573-4
Downtown Commons 660 J St *Web:* www.docosacramento.com	Sacramento	CA	95814	916-273-8124	442-3117	460
Downtown Community Improvement District of Columbia, The 11 S Tenth St Top Fl *Web:* www.discoverthedistrict.com	Columbia	MO	65201	573-442-6816		50-6
Downtown Erie Hotel 18 W 18th St *TF:* 800-832-9101 ■ *Web:* www.downtowneriehotel.com	Erie	PA	16501	814-456-2961	456-7067	379
Downtown Ford Sales Inc 525 N 16th St *Web:* www.dtfords.com	Sacramento	CA	95811	916-442-6931		57
Downtown Fun Zone, The 832 Hwy 101 *Web:* www.mydfz.com	Port Orford	OR	97465	541-332-6565		797
Downtown Grand Las Vegas 206 N 3rd St *Web:* www.downtowngrand.com	Las Vegas	NV	89101	855-384-7263		706
Downtown Grill 562 Mulberry St Ln *Web:* www.macondowntowngrill.com	Macon	GA	31201	478-742-5999	742-9708	671
Downtown Grill & Brewery 424 S Gay St *Web:* www.downtownbrewery.com	Knoxville	TN	37902	865-633-8111		671
Downtown Hyundai 1512 Broadway *TF:* 888-232-9902 ■ *Web:* www.downtownhyundainashville.com	Nashville	TN	37203	888-232-9902		57
Downtown Partners Chicago 200 E Randolph St Ste 3400 *Web:* www.downtownpartners.com	Chicago	IL	60601	312-552-5800		7
Downtown Safeway Tire & Car Care 4623 Superior Ave *Web:* www.safewaytire.net	Cleveland	OH	44103	216-881-1737	881-2808	755
Downtown Tempe Community 310 S Mill Ave Ste A-201 *Web:* www.downtowntempe.com	Tempe	AZ	85281	480-355-6060	968-7882	460
Downtown Wine & Spirit 225 Elm St *Web:* www.downtownwineandspirits.com	Somerville	MA	02144	617-625-7777	625-7773	81-1
Doxa Energy Ltd 777 Hornby St Ste 2080 *Web:* www.doxaenergy.com	Vancouver	BC	V6Z1S4	604-683-7361		536
Doyle & O'Donnell 901 F St *TF:* 800-632-5529 ■ *Web:* doinjurylaw.com	Sacramento	CA	95814	916-706-2616	922-0418	41
Doyle & Wachtstetter Inc 131 Commerce St *Web:* www.dw-surveyor.com	Clute	TX	77531	979-265-3622		727
Doyle Equipment Manufacturing Co 4001 Broadway St *Web:* www.doylemfg.com	Quincy	IL	62305	217-222-1592	223-3655	273
Doyle Michael (Rep D - PA) 306 Cannon House Office Bldg *Web:* www.doyle.house.gov	Washington	DC	20515	202-225-2135		342-2
Doyle New York 175 E 87th St *Web:* doyle.com	New York	NY	10128	212-427-2730	369-0892	520
Doyle Quane 571 Hartz Ave *Web:* www.familylawgroup.com	Danville	CA	94526	925-314-2320	855-4334	445
Doyle Security Systems Inc 792 Calkins Rd *TF:* 866-463-6953 ■ *Web:* www.godoyle.com	Rochester	NY	14623	585-244-3400		692
Doyle Signs Inc 232 W Interstate Rd *Web:* doylesigns.com	Addison	IL	60101	630-543-9490	543-9493	701
Doylestown Hospital 595 W State St *Web:* www.doylestownhealth.org	Doylestown	PA	18901	215-345-2200		374-3
Doyletech Corp 28 Thorncliff Pl Ste 201 *Web:* www.doyletechcorp.com	Ottawa	ON	K2H6L2	613-226-8900	226-7900	463
Doyon Drilling Inc 11500 C St Ste 200 *TF:* 800-478-9675 ■ *Web:* doyondrilling.com	Anchorage	AK	99515	907-563-5530	561-8986	540
Doyon Ltd 1 Doyon Pl Ste 300 *TF:* 888-478-4755 ■ *Web:* www.doyon.com	Fairbanks	AK	99701	907-459-2000		536
Dozens 2180 S Havana St *Web:* www.dozensrestaurant.com	Aurora	CO	80014	303-337-6627		671
Dozier, Miller, Pollard & Murphy LLP Cameron Brown Bldg 301 S McDowell St Ste 700 *Web:* doziermillerlaw.com	Charlotte	NC	28204	704-372-6373		428
DP & Company Inc 7743 SR 471 *Web:* www.dpciwholesale.com	Bushnell	FL	33513	352-678-3661	568-2232	351
DP Advanced Engineering Inc 3361 Walnut Blvd Ste 100 *Web:* advancedengineeringinc.com	Brentwood	CA	94513	925-516-3502		261
DP Guardian Inc 5837 S Gallup St *Web:* www.dpguardian.com	Littleton	CO	80120	303-783-0191		180
DP Murphy Company Inc 945 Grand Blvd *TF:* 800-424-8724 ■ *Web:* www.dpmurphy.com	Deer Park	NY	11729	631-673-9400		5
DP Products Inc 2015 Stone Ave *Web:* dpprod.com	San Jose	CA	95125	408-299-0190		454
DP Solutions Inc 1508 S First St *Web:* www.dpsol.com	Lufkin	TX	75901	936-637-7977		175
DP Technology Corp 1150 Avenida Acaso *TF:* 800-627-8479 ■ *Web:* www.espritcam.com	Camarillo	CA	93012	805-388-6000		178-5
D-Patrick Motoplex Inc 200 N Green River Rd *Web:* www.dpat.com	Evansville	IN	47715	812-473-6590		57
DPC DATA Inc 103 Eisenhower Pkwy Ste 300 *Web:* www.dpcdata.com	Roseland	NJ	07068	201-346-0701		174
DPE (Donahue Paper Emporium) 7286 S Yosemite St *Web:* www.donahuepaper.com	Centennial	CO	80112	303-741-3984		553
DPE Systems Inc 120 Lakeside Ave Ste 230 *TF:* 800-541-6566 ■ *Web:* www.dpes.com	Seattle	WA	98122	206-223-3737	223-0859	180
DPF Data Services 1345 Campus Pkw Unit A8 **Fax Area Code: 732 ■ TF:* 800-431-4416 ■ *Web:* www.dpfdata.com	Wall Township	NJ	07753	800-431-4416	370-1751*	225
DPFG (Development Planning & Financing Group Inc) 27127 Calle Arroyo Ste 1910 *Web:* www.dpfg.com	San Juan Capistrano	CA	92675	949-388-9269	388-9272	652
DPI (DeVaul Publishing Inc) 429 N Market Blvd *Web:* www.devaulpublishing.com	Chehalis	WA	98532	360-748-6848		637-9
Dpi Labs Inc 1350 Arrow Hwy *Web:* dpilabs.com	La Verne	CA	91750	909-392-5777		647
DPIS Engineering LLC 1600 E Huffsmith Rd *Web:* www.dpis.com	Tomball	TX	77375	281-351-0048		261
dpiX LLC 1635 Aeroplaza Dr *Web:* www.dpix.com	Colorado Springs	CO	80916	719-457-7700		407
DPL Inc 1065 Woodman Dr *TF:* 800-433-8500 ■ *Web:* www.dplinc.com	Dayton	OH	45432	800-433-8500		360-5
DPL Press Inc PO Box 2135 *TF:* 800-550-3502 ■ *Web:* www.debtproofliving.com	Paramount	CA	90723	562-630-6474	630-3433	637-2
DPL Wireless 53 Clark Rd *TF:* 800-561-8880 ■ *Web:* www.dplwireless.com	Rothesay	NB	E2E2K9	506-847-2347	847-2348	387
Dployit Inc 14673 Midway Rd Ste 108 *Web:* www.dployit.com	Addison	TX	75001	214-550-6124		260
DPM Consulting Services Inc 507 E Maple Rd *Web:* www.dpmcs.com	Troy	MI	48083	248-740-8735		196
DPNM (New Mexico Democratic Party) 8214 Second St NW Ste A *Web:* www.dpnm.net	Albuquerque	NM	87114	505-830-3650		616-1
DPR Construction Inc 1450 Veterans Blvd *Web:* www.dpr.com	Redwood City	CA	94063	650-474-1450	474-1451	186
DPRA Inc 10215 Technology Dr Ste 201 *Web:* www.dpra.com	Manhattan	KS	66502	865-777-3772		192
Department of Public Safety 5805 N Lamar Blvd PO Box 4087 *Web:* www.dmv.org	Austin	TX	78752	512-424-2000		693
DPS Management Consultants 2320 Gravel Dr *Web:* www.dpsconsultants.com	Fort Worth	TX	76118	817-284-7711	284-5656	194
DPS Printing Service Inc 3500 S Boulevard St 38c *Web:* www.dpsprinting.com	Edmond	OK	73013	405-340-0004		627
Dps Software Systems Inc 41 E Foothill Blvd Ste 105 *Web:* dpssoft.com	Arcadia	CA	91006	626-445-9190	445-9197	177
DPSI Inc 1801 Stanley Rd Ste 301 *TF:* 800-897-7233 ■ *Web:* www.dpsi.com	Greensboro	NC	27407	336-854-7700	854-7715	178-11
DPT Laboratories Ltd 318 McCullough *TF:* 866-225-5378 ■ *Web:* www.dptlabs.com	San Antonio	TX	78215	866-225-5378		582
Dr Arlene's Club 10940 Wilshire Blvd Ste 1600 *Web:* www.winwithoutcompeting.com	Los Angeles	CA	90024	310-443-4277		393
Dr Delphinium Designs & Events 5806 W Lovers Ln & Tollway *TF:* 800-783-8790 ■ *Web:* www.drdelphinium.com	Dallas	TX	75225	214-522-9911		292
Dr Edmund A Babler Memorial State Park 800 Guy Pk Dr *Web:* mostateparks.com	Wildwood	MO	63005	636-458-3813		565
Dr FirstCom Inc 9420 Key W Ave Ste 230 *Web:* www.drfirst.com	Rockville	MD	20850	301-231-9510		180
Dr Fresh Inc 6645 Caballero Blvd *TF:* 866-373-7371 ■ *Web:* www.drfreshdental.com	Buena Park	CA	90620	866-373-7371		475
Dr Georges L Dumont Regional Hospital 330 University Ave *Web:* www.vitalitenb.ca	Moncton	NB	E2A1A9	506-862-4000		374-2
DR Horton Inc 301 Commerce St Ste 500 *NYSE: DHI* ■ *TF:* 800-846-7866 ■ *Web:* www.drhorton.com	Fort Worth	TX	76102	817-390-8200		653
Dr Pepper Museum & Free Enterprise Institute, The 300 S Fifth St *Web:* drpeppermuseum.com	Waco	TX	76701	254-757-1025		522

Name / Address	City	State	ZIP	Phone	Fax	Class
Dr Reddy's Laboratories Inc 107 College Rd E *NYSE:* RDY ■ *Web:* www.drreddys.com	Bridgewater	NJ	08807	908-203-4900		582
Dr Revenue 1700 Mandeville Canyon Rd *Web:* www.drrevenue.com	Los Angeles	CA	90049	310-476-3355	471-7721	194
DR Sperry & Co 623 Rathbone Ave *TF:* 888-997-9297 ■ *Web:* www.drsperry.com	Aurora	IL	60506	630-892-4361	892-1664	456
Dr Sun Yat-Sen Classical Chinese Garden 578 Carrall St *Web:* www.vancouverchinesegarden.com	Vancouver	BC	V6B5K2	604-662-3207	682-4008	97
Dr Tavel Optical Group 2839 Lafayette Rd *Web:* www.drtavel.com	Indianapolis	IN	46222	317-924-1300		543
Dr Thomas Walker State Historic Site 4929 KY 459 *Web:* parks.ky.gov	Barbourville	KY	40906	606-546-4400		565
Dr Vinyl & Associates Ltd 1350 SE Hamblen Rd *TF:* 800-531-6600 ■ *Web:* www.drvinyl.com	Lee's Summit	MO	64081	816-525-6060		62-1
Dr Wilkinson's Hot Springs Resort 1507 Lincoln Ave *Web:* www.drwilkinson.com	Calistoga	CA	94515	707-942-4102	942-4412	669
Dr Willella Howe-Waffle House & Medical Museum 120 Civic Center Dr *Web:* www.santaanahistory.com	Santa Ana	CA	92701	714-547-9645		520
Dr Xie's Jing Tang Herbal Inc 9700 W Hwy 318 **Fax Area Code:* 866 ■ *TF:* 800-891-1986 ■ *Web:* store.tcvmherbal.com	Reddick	FL	32686	352-591-2141	700-8772*	76
Draeger Medical Inc 3135 Quarry Rd **Fax Area Code:* 215 ■ *TF:* 800-437-2437 ■ *Web:* www.draeger.com	Telford	PA	18969	800-437-2437	723-5935*	250
Draeger's Super Markets Inc 222 E Fourth Ave *Web:* www.draegers.com	San Mateo	CA	94401	650-685-3700		345
DraftKings Inc 222 Berkeley St 5th Fl *TF:* 800-522-4700 ■ *Web:* www.draftkings.com	Boston	MA	02116	800-522-4700		657
Drafto Corp 100 Pressler Ave *Web:* www.drafto.com	Cochranton	PA	16314	814-425-7445	425-8048	684
Draghi Environmental Services Inc (DES) PO Box 601 *TF:* 866-867-2366 ■ *Web:* draghienvironmental.com	Londonderry	NH	03053	603-437-1352	434-6485	192
Drago's 3232 N Arnoult Rd *Web:* www.dragosrestaurant.com	Metairie	LA	70002	504-888-9254		671
Dragon Door Publications Inc 5 E County Rd B Ste 3 *TF:* 800-899-5111 ■ *Web:* www.dragondoor.com	Little Canada	MN	55117	651-487-2180	487-3954	637-2
Dragon Press PO Box 78 *Web:* www.dragonpress.com	Pleasantville	NY	10570	914-769-5545		95
Dragon Products Co PO Box 1521	Portland	ME	04103	207-879-2328		135
Dragon Threads 490 Tucker Dr *Web:* www.dragonthreads.com	Worthington	OH	43085	614-841-9388		745-3
Dragonfly Capital Partners LLC The Packard Bldg 1310 S Tryon St Ste 109 *Web:* www.dragonflycapital.com	Charlotte	NC	28203	704-342-3491		401
Dragonfly Technologies 48 Wall St Ste 1100 *Web:* www.dragonflytech.com	New York	NY	10005	212-713-5250		113
Dragonhawk Publishing PO Box 10637 *Web:* www.dragonhawkpublishing.com	Jackson	TN	38308	731-987-3334	987-2484	637-2
Drais Pharmaceuticals Inc 520 US Hwy 22 Ste 201 *Web:* www.draispharma.com	Bridgewater	NJ	08807	908-895-1200		238
DRAIVER 9393 W 110th St Ste 500 *TF:* 844-366-6837 ■ *Web:* www.draiver.com	Overland Park	KS	66210	844-366-6837		224
Drake Capital Advisors LLC 1 Fawcett Pl Ste 140 *Web:* drakeadvisors.com	Greenwich	CT	06830	203-661-7500	861-2601	401
Drake Commercial Lp 19310 Stone Oak Pkwy Ste 201 *Web:* www.drakecommercial.com	San Antonio	TX	78258	210-402-6363		652
Drake Construction Co 1545 E 18th St *Web:* www.drakeconstructionco.com	Cleveland	OH	44114	216-664-6500	664-6565	186
Drake Hotel, The 140 E Walton Pl *TF:* 800-553-7253 ■ *Web:* www.thedrakehotel.com	Chicago	IL	60611	312-787-2200	787-1431	379
Drake Software 235 E Palmer St **Fax Area Code:* 828 ■ *TF:* 800-890-9500 ■ *Web:* www.drakesoftware.com	Franklin	NC	28734	800-890-9500	369-9928*	178-1
Drake University 2507 University Ave *TF:* 800-443-7253 ■ *Web:* www.drake.edu	Des Moines	IA	50311	515-271-3181	271-2831	166
Drake, Loeb, Heller, Kennedy, Gogerty, Gaba, Rodd PLLC 555 Hudson Vly Ave Ste 100 *Web:* www.drakeloeb.com	New Windsor	NY	12553	845-561-0550		428
Drake-Scruggs Equipment Inc 2000 S Dirksen Pkwy *TF:* 877-799-0398 ■ *Web:* www.drake-scruggs.com	Springfield	IL	62703	217-753-3871	753-2760	470
Drama Book Shop Inc 250 W 40th St *Web:* www.dramabookshop.com	New York	NY	10018	212-944-0595	730-8739	95
Dramatic Publishing 311 Washington St *Web:* www.dramaticpublishing.com	Woodstock	IL	60098	815-338-7170	338-8981	637-2
Dramatists Guild of America Inc 1501 Broadway Ste 701 *Web:* www.dramatistsguild.com	New York	NY	10036	212-398-9366	944-0420	48-4
Dramm & Echter Inc 1150 Quail Gardens Dr *TF:* 800-854-7021 ■ *Web:* www.drammechter.com	Encinitas	CA	92024	760-436-0188	436-2974	369
Dranetz-BMI 1000 New Durham Rd *TF:* 800-372-6832 ■ *Web:* www.dranetz.com	Edison	NJ	08818	732-287-3680	248-1834	248
Draper & Associates 5665 New Northside Dr Ste 100 *Web:* draperandassociates.com	Atlanta	GA	30328	404-256-3601	256-3922	361
Draper & Kramer Inc 55 E Monroe St Ste 3900 *Web:* draperandkramer.com	Chicago	IL	60603	312-346-8600		655
Draper & Mcginley PA 365 W Patrick St 1st Fl *Web:* www.drapermcginleypa.com	Frederick	MD	21701	301-694-7411	694-0954	2
Draper Aden Associates Inc 2206 S Main St *Web:* www.daa.com	Blacksburg	VA	24060	540-552-0444	552-0291	192
Draper Fisher Jurvetson (DFJ) 2882 Sand Hill Rd Ste 150 *Web:* www.dfj.com	Menlo Park	CA	94025	650-233-9000		792
Draper Knitting Co 28 Draper Ln *TF:* 800-808-7707 ■ *Web:* www.draperknitting.com	Canton	MA	02021	781-828-0029	828-3034	745-4
Draper Shade & Screen Co 411 S Pearl St *TF:* 800-238-7999 ■ *Web:* www.draperinc.com	Spiceland	IN	47385	765-987-7999		591
Draper Valley Farms 1500 E College Way PMB 449 Ste A *TF:* 800-682-1468 ■ *Web:* www.drapervalleyfarms.com	Mount Vernon	WA	98273	800-682-1468		619
DRAXIMAGE Inc 16751 Transcanada Hwy *TF:* 888-633-5343 ■ *Web:* www.draximage.com	Kirkland	QC	H9H4J4	514-630-7080		238
Drayton Group 2295 N Opdyke Rd Ste D *TF:* 888-655-4442 ■ *Web:* draytongroupinc.com	Auburn Hills	MI	48326	888-655-4442		104
Drayton, Drayton & Lamar Inc 616 Ponder Pl Dr Ste 2 *Web:* www.ddlinc.com	Evans	GA	30809	706-854-1145		180
Drazan, Henke & Associates PLLC 544 Bavaria Ln *Web:* dha-cpa.com	Chaska	MN	55318	952-448-2705		2
DRC (Dos Rios Consultants Inc) PO Box 1247 *Web:* bloodhound.tripod.com	Silver City	NM	88062	505-534-0035		192
DRCOC (Del Rio Chamber of Commerce) 1915 Veterans Blvd *Web:* www.drchamber.com	Del Rio	TX	78840	830-775-3551	774-1813	139
DRD Technology Corp 5506 S Lewis Ave *Web:* www.drd.com	Tulsa	OK	74105	918-743-3013	745-9037	178-1
DRE Inc 1800 Williamson Ct *Web:* www.dremed.com	Louisville	KY	40223	502-244-6333		475
Dream 210 W 55th St *Web:* www.dreamhotels.com	New York	NY	10019	212-247-2000		379
Dream Communications Inc PO Box 38 **Fax Area Code:* 781 ■ *TF:* 888-583-9200 ■ *Web:* dreamcom.com	Cohasset	MA	02025	888-583-9200	383-4000*	393
Dream Entertainment Inc 8489 W 3rd St Ste 1096 *Web:* www.hollywoodnetwork.com	Los Angeles	CA	90048	213-655-5501	655-5603	344
Dream Garden Press 268 S 200 E *Web:* www.dreamgardenpress.com	Salt Lake City	UT	84111	801-521-3819		637-2
Dream Local Digital 463 Main St *Web:* dreamlocal.com	Rockland	ME	04841	207-593-7665		5
Dream Publishing Co 1304 Devonshire Rd *Web:* www.dreampublish.com	Grosse Pointe Park	MI	48230	313-882-6603		637-2
Dream Vision International Studios 4100 W Charleston Blvd *Web:* www.dreamvisionstudios.us	Las Vegas	NV	89102	702-448-1600		514
Dreamentia Inc 453 S Spring St Ste 1101 *Web:* dreamentia.com	Los Angeles	CA	90013	213-347-6000		7
Dreamgear LLC 20001 S Western Ave *Web:* www.dreamgear.com	Torrance	CA	90501	310-222-5522	222-5577	52
DreamHost 417 Associated Rd *Web:* www.dreamhost.com	Brea	CA	92821	714-671-9098		225
DreamJobs 6545 W Central Ave Ste 102 *Web:* www.dreamjobsna.com	Toledo	OH	43617	567-455-5500		260
Dreamland Bar-B-que 1427 14th Ave S *TF:* 800-752-0544 ■ *Web:* www.dreamlandbbq.com	Birmingham	AL	35205	205-933-2133		671
Dreamline Manufacturing Inc 1514 S 2nd St PO Box 1250 *Web:* www.dreamlinebedding.com	Cabot	AR	72023	501-843-3585	843-2990	471
DreamMaker Bath & Kitchen by Worldwide 510 N Valley Mills Dr Ste 304 *TF:* 800-583-2133 ■ *Web:* www.dreammaker-remodel.com	Waco	TX	76710	800-583-2133		189-11
Dreamspan Product Innovation LLC 11645 N Cave Creek Rd *Web:* www.dreamspan.com	Phoenix	AZ	85020	602-354-7640		195
Dreamstime LLC 1616 Wgate Cir *Web:* www.dreamstime.com	Brentwood	TN	37027	615-771-5611		588
Dreamtime Inc 1500 S Lewis St **Fax Area Code:* 831 ■ *Web:* www.dreamtimeinc.com	Anaheim	CA	92805	714-490-7878	464-6703*	361
Dreamworks Animation LLC 1000 Flower St *Web:* www.dreamworks.com	Glendale	CA	91201	818-695-5000		514
Dreco Inc 7887 Root Rd *Web:* www.drecoinc.com	North Ridgeville	OH	44052	440-327-6021		608
Drees Co 211 Grandview Dr *TF:* 866-265-2980 ■ *Web:* www.dreeshomes.com	Fort Mitchell	KY	41017	859-578-4200		187
Dreher Island State Recreation Area 3677 State Park Rd *Web:* southcarolinaparks.com	Prosperity	SC	29127	803-364-4152		565
Dreher Tomkies LLP 2750 Huntington Ctr 41 S High St *Web:* www.dltlaw.com	Columbus	OH	43215	614-628-8000	628-1600	428
Dreisbach Wholesale Florists Inc 8021 Warwick Av *TF:* 800-928-2393 ■ *Web:* www.dreisbachs.com	Louisville	KY	40222	502-425-5842	813-2007	293
DREMC (Duck River Electric Membership Corp) 1411 Madison St *Web:* www.dremc.com	Shelbyville	TN	37160	931-909-1287	901-1318	245
Dremel Inc 4915 21st St *TF:* 800-437-3635 ■ *Web:* www.dremel.com	Racine	WI	53406	262-554-1390	554-7654	759
Drent Goebel North America Inc 2583 Chomedey Blvd *Web:* www.rdpmarathon.com	Laval	QC	H7T2R2	450-687-7262		628
Dresick Farms Inc PO Box 1260	Huron	CA	93234	559-945-2513		10-11
Dresner Partners 20 N Clark St Ste 3550 *Web:* www.dresnerpartners.com	Chicago	IL	60602	312-726-3600	726-7448	690
Dress for Success Worldwide 32 E 31st St 7th Fl *Web:* dressforsuccess.org	New York	NY	10016	212-532-1922		48-5

	Phone	Fax	Class
Dresser & Associates Inc 243 US Rt 1 . . . . Scarborough ME 04074 *TF:* 866-885-7212 ■ *Web:* www.dresserassociates.com	207-885-0809		463
Dressman Benzinger LaVelle (DBL) 207 Thomas More Pkwy . . . . Crestview Hills KY 41017 *Web:* www.dbllaw.com	859-341-1881		445
Dreumex USA 3445 Board Rd . . . . York PA 17406 *TF:* 800-233-9382 ■ *Web:* www.dreumex.com	717-767-6881		151
Drew & Rogers Inc 30 Plymouth St . . . . Fairfield NJ 07004 *TF:* 800-610-6210 ■ *Web:* www.drewandrogers.com	973-575-6210		627
Drew Eckl & Farnham LLP 303 Peachtree St NE Ste 3500 . . . . Atlanta GA 30308 *Web:* www.deflaw.com	404-885-1400	876-0992	445
Drew Foam Companies Inc 1093 Hwy 278 E . . . . Monticello AR 71655 *TF:* 800-643-1206 ■ *Web:* www.drewfoam.com	870-367-6245		601
Drew Marine Inc 100 S Jefferson Rd . . . . Whippany NJ 07981 *Web:* www.drew-marine.com	973-526-5700		261
Drew Scientific Inc/ M W I Inc 4230 Shilling Way . . . . Dallas TX 75237 *Web:* www.drew-scientific.com	214-210-4900		153
Drew Shoe Corp 252 Quarry Rd . . . . Lancaster OH 43130 *TF:* 800-837-3739 ■ *Web:* www.drewshoe.com	740-653-4271		301
Drew University 36 Madison Ave . . . . Madison NJ 07940 *Web:* www.drew.edu	973-408-3000	408-3068	166
Drew Wireless 459 Collindale NW . . . . Grand Rapids MI 49504 *Web:* www.drewwireless.com	616-453-7200		194
Drexel Agency Inc 101 State Rd . . . . Media PA 19063 *Web:* drexelagency.com	610-565-1730		390
Drexel Building Supply 227 W Main St . . . . Campbellsport WI 53010 *Web:* www.drexelteam.com	920-533-4412	533-4333	191-3
Drexel Chemical Co 1700 Ch Ave PO Box 13327 . . . . Memphis TN 38113 *Web:* www.drexchem.com	901-774-4370	774-4666	280
Drexel University 3141 Chestnut St . . . . Philadelphia PA 19104 *TF:* 866-358-1010 ■ *Web:* www.drexel.edu	215-571-4407	895-5939	166
Dreyco Inc 263 Veterans Blvd . . . . Carlstadt NJ 07072 *Web:* www.dreycoinc.com	201-896-9000		61
Dreyer's Grand Ice Cream Inc 5929 College Ave . . . . Oakland CA 94618 *Web:* www.dreyers.com	510-652-8187		296-25
Dreyfus Ashby & Co 630 Third Ave 15th Fl . . . . New York NY 10017 *Web:* www.dreyfusashby.com	212-818-0770	953-2366	80-3
Dreyfus Global Trade LLC (DGT) 420 Lexington Ave Ste 2631 . . . . New York NY 10170 *Web:* www.dreyfusglobal.com	212-867-7700	867-7820	60
Dreyfus-Cortney & Lowery Bros Rigging 4400 N Galvez St . . . . New Orleans LA 70117 *TF:* 800-228-7660 ■ *Web:* www.dcl-usa.com	504-944-3366	947-8557	770
Dreyfuss Williams & Associates Company LPA 1801 E Ninth St Ste 1110 . . . . Cleveland OH 44114 *TF:* 866-407-5497 ■ *Web:* dreyfuss.com	216-241-5300	241-2735	41
DRG International Inc 841 Mountain Ave . . . . Springfield NJ 07081 *Web:* drg-international.com	973-564-7555	564-7556	743
DRG News 214 W Pleasant Dr PO Box 1197 . . . . Pierre SD 57501 *TF:* 800-658-5439 ■ *Web:* www.drgnews.com	605-224-8686	224-8984	647
Drgreene.com 855 El Camino Real Ste 13A-230 . . . . Palo Alto CA 94301 *Web:* www.drgreene.com	925-964-1793		356
DRHC (DiamondRock Hospitality Co) 3 Bethesda Metro Ctr Ste 1500 . . . . Bethesda MD 20814 *NYSE:* DRH ■ *Web:* drhc.com	240-744-1150	744-1199	654
DRI (Defense Research Institute) 55 W Monroe St Ste 20 . . . . Chicago IL 60603 *Web:* dri.org	312-795-1101	795-0749	49-10
DRI Consulting Inc 2 Otter Ln . . . . Saint Paul MN 55127 *Web:* www.dric.com	651-415-1400		463
Dri Mark Products Inc 999 S Oyster Bay Rd Ste 312 . . . . Bethpage NY 11714 *TF:* 800-645-9662 ■ *Web:* www.drimark.com	516-484-6200		571
Dri-Air Industries Inc 16 Thompson Rd . . . . East Windsor CT 06088 *Web:* www.dri-air.com	860-627-5110	623-4477	318
DRIASI (Direct Response Insurance Administrative Services) 7930 Century Blvd . . . . Chanhassen MN 55317 *TF:* 800-688-0760 ■ *Web:* www.driasi.com	800-688-0760		390
Driehaus Capital Management Inc 25 E Erie St . . . . Chicago IL 60611 *TF:* 800-688-8819 ■ *Web:* www.driehaus.com	312-587-3800		401
Driessen Water Inc *Culligan* 1690 S Hwy 3 . . . . Northfield MN 55057 *Web:* www.culliganiswater.com	507-262-1960	645-6624	538
Driftwood Beach State Recreation Site 5580 S Coast Hwy . . . . Newport OR 97366 *Web:* stateparks.oregon.gov	541-867-7451		565
Driftwood Hospitality Management LLC 11770 US Hwy One Ste 202 . . . . North Palm Beach FL 33408 *Web:* driftwoodhospitality.com	561-207-2700		379
Driftwood Hotel 435 Willoughby Ave . . . . Juneau AK 99801 *TF:* 800-544-2239 ■ *Web:* www.dhalaska.com	907-586-2280	586-1034	379
Driftwood Shores Resort 88416 First Ave . . . . Florence OR 97439 *TF:* 800-422-5091 ■ *Web:* driftwoodshores.com	541-997-8263		379
Driggs 8700 Ashwood Dr . . . . Capitol Heights MD 20743 *Web:* www.driggs.net	301-350-4000		188-4
Driggs, Hogg, Daugherty & Del Zoppo Company LPA 38500 Chardon Rd . . . . Willoughby Hills OH 44094 *Web:* driggslaw.com	440-391-5100		41
Drillco National Group Inc 2432 44th St . . . . Astoria NY 11103 *TF:* 800-391-0052 ■ *Web:* www.drillcodevices.com	718-726-9801	956-3759	190
Drillers Service Inc 1792 Highland Ave NE . . . . Hickory NC 28601 *TF:* 800-334-2308 ■ *Web:* www.dsidsi.com	828-322-1100	322-7436	537
Drilling Structures Intl 2431 Kelly Ln . . . . Houston TX 77066 *Web:* www.drillingstructuresintl.com	281-880-8833		537
Drilltec Technologies Inc 10875 Kempwood Ste 2 . . . . Houston TX 77043 *Web:* www.drilltec.com	713-895-9852		539
Dril-Quip Inc 6401 N Eldridge Pkwy . . . . Houston TX 77041 *NYSE:* DRQ ■ *TF:* 877-316-2631 ■ *Web:* www.dril-quip.com	713-939-7711	939-8063	537
Drink More Water Store 7595-A Rickenbacker Dr . . . . Gaithersburg MD 20879 *TF:* 800-697-2070 ■ *Web:* www.drinkmorewater.com	800-697-2070		14
DRIP Investor 7412 Calumet Ave . . . . Hammond IN 46324 *Web:* www.dripinvestor.com	219-852-3220	931-6487	531-9
Dripping Springs State Park 16830 Dripping Springs Rd . . . . Okmulgee OK 74447 *Web:* www.travelok.com	918-756-5971	759-9933	565
Driptech Inc 2580 Wyandotte St Ste B . . . . Mountain View CA 94043 *Web:* www.driptech.com	415-793-6735		273
Dri-Rite Co 11600 S Ave O . . . . Chicago IL 60617 *Web:* www.dririte.com	773-409-4127	221-2909	500
Driscoll Children's Hospital 3533 S Alameda St . . . . Corpus Christi TX 78411 *TF:* 800-324-5683 ■ *Web:* www.driscollchildrens.org	361-694-5000		374-1
Driscoll Health Plan 615 N Upper Broadway Ste 1621 . . . . Corpus Christi TX 78401 *TF:* 877-324-7543 ■ *Web:* driscollhealthplan.com	877-324-7543		391-3
Driscoll Strawberry Associates Inc PO Box 50045 . . . . Watsonville CA 95077 *TF:* 800-871-3333 ■ *Web:* www.driscolls.com	800-871-3333		315-1
Driskill Hotel 604 Brazos St . . . . Austin TX 78701 *Web:* driskillhotel.com	512-439-1234	391-7057	379
DRISTEEM Corp 14949 Technology Dr . . . . Eden Prairie MN 55344 *TF:* 800-328-4447 ■ *Web:* www.dristeem.com	952-949-2415	229-3200	14
Drive Cleaning Inc 4837 Oakton St . . . . Skokie IL 60077 *Web:* drivecleaning.com	847-673-6400		426
Drive Products Income Fund 1665 Shawson Dr . . . . Mississauga ON L4W1T7 *Web:* www.driveproducts.com	905-564-5800		61
Drive Source International Inc 7900 Durand Ave Bldg 3 . . . . Sturtevant WI 53177 *TF:* 800-548-2169 ■ *Web:* dynamatic.com	262-554-7977	554-7041	620
Drive Train Industries Inc 5555 Joliet St . . . . Denver CO 80239 *TF:* 800-525-6177	303-292-5176	297-0473	61
Drivekore Inc 101 Wesley Dr . . . . Mechanicsburg PA 17055 *TF:* 800-382-1311 ■ *Web:* www.drivekore.com	717-766-7636		350
Driveline Holdings Inc 700 Freeport Pkwy Ste 100 . . . . Coppell TX 75019 *TF:* 888-824-7505 ■ *Web:* www.drivelineretail.com	888-824-7505		195
Driveline International Inc 143 E Business Hwy 83 . . . . Alamo TX 78516 **Fax Area Code:* 956 ■ *TF:* 800-487-7997 ■ *Web:* www.driveline.com	800-487-7997	787-7992*	780
Driven Brands Inc 440 S Church St Ste 700 . . . . Charlotte NC 28202 *Web:* www.drivenbrands.com	704-644-8101		360-3
DrivenBI LLC 221 E Walnut St Ste 229 . . . . Pasadena CA 91101 *Web:* www.drivenbi.com	626-795-2088		177
Drive-On-In Inc PO Box 96731 . . . . Las Vegas NV 89193 *Web:* kippsherer.com	702-885-4042	920-8513	791
Driver iQ 4500 S 129th E Ave Ste 127 . . . . Tulsa OK 74134 **Fax Area Code:* 918 ■ *TF:* 800-848-3397 ■ *Web:* www.driveriq.com	800-848-3397	591-2854*	387
Drivers License Guide Co 1492 Oddstad Dr . . . . Redwood City CA 94063 *TF:* 800-227-8827 ■ *Web:* www.driverslicenseguide.com	650-369-4849	364-8740	637-10
Drivers Village 5885 E Cir Dr . . . . Cicero NY 13039 *Web:* www.burdickdodgechryslerjeep.com	315-699-3846		57
DriveSavers Inc 400 Bel Marin Keys Blvd . . . . Novato CA 94949 *TF:* 800-440-1904 ■ *Web:* www.drivesaversdatarecovery.com	415-382-2000	883-0780	180
Drivescale Inc 1230 Midas Way Ste 210 . . . . Sunnyvale CA 94085 *Web:* drivescale.com	408-849-4651		180
Drivestaff 114 N Hale St Ste B . . . . Wheaton IL 60187 *Web:* www.drivestaff.com	630-941-3748		260
DriveTime Corp 4020 E Indian School Rd . . . . Phoenix AZ 85018 *TF:* 888-418-1212 ■ *Web:* www.drivetime.com	888-418-1212		57
Driving Force Inc, The 60 King Rd . . . . Inuvik NT X0E0T0 *Web:* www.drivingforce.ca	867-777-2346		126
Driving Records Facilities PO Box 1086 . . . . Glen Burnie MD 21061 *TF:* 800-772-5510 ■ *Web:* www.dr-rec-fac.com	800-772-5510		635
DrivingSales LLC 8871 S Sandy Pkwy Ste 250 . . . . Sandy UT 84070 *TF:* 866-943-8371 ■ *Web:* www.drivingsales.com	866-943-8371		387
Driv-Lok Inc 1140 Park Ave . . . . Sycamore IL 60178 *Web:* www.driv-lok.com	815-315-1004		350
Drivon Turner & Waters A Professional Law Corp 215 N San Joaquin St . . . . Stockton CA 95202 *Web:* drivonlaw.com	209-644-1234		41
Drizly 334 Boylston St . . . . Boston MA 02116 *Web:* drizly.com	774-234-1033		459
DRM Inc 5324 N 134th Ave . . . . Omaha NE 68164 *Web:* drmarbys.com	402-556-4098	573-0171	670
DRM LLC 520 Crews St . . . . Lawrenceburg TN 38464 *Web:* drmcontrols.com	931-766-4500	766-5314	610
DRMC (Delta Regional Medical Ctr) 1400 E Union St . . . . Greenville MS 38703 *Web:* www.deltaregional.com	662-378-3783		374-3
DRMC (Dallas Regional Medical Ctr) 1011 N Galloway Ave . . . . Mesquite TX 75149 **Fax Area Code:* 972 ■ *Web:* www.dallasregionalmedicalcenter.com	214-320-7000	289-9468*	374-3
DRMP (Dyer Riddle Mills & Precourt Inc) 941 Lake Baldwin Ln . . . . Orlando FL 32814 *TF:* 800-375-3767 ■ *Web:* www.drmp.com	407-896-0594	896-4836	261
DRO PROS 4992 Allison Pky Ste G . . . . Vacaville CA 95688 *TF:* 855-376-7767 ■ *Web:* www.dropros.com	707-452-8437	471-6575	385

Name / Address	City	State	ZIP	Phone	Fax	Class
Droege Computing Services Inc 20 W Colony Pl Ste 120 *Web:* droegecomputing.com	Durham	NC	27705	919-403-9459	403-8199	177
Droga5 LLC 120 Wall St 11th Fl *Web:* droga5.com	New York	NY	10005	917-237-8888		5
Dromar Inc PO Box 6720 *Web:* www.dromar.com	Ocean Isle	NC	28469	910-287-5411	287-5540	328
Droop Mountain Battlefield State Park 683 Droop Park Rd *Web:* wvstateparks.com	Hillsboro	WV	24946	304-653-4254		565
Dropbox Inc 801 Scott St PO Box 402 *TF:* 888-388-7768 ■ *Web:* www.dropboxinc.com	Worthington	KY	41183	740-532-7822		480
Dropkin & Matza LLP 424 Broadway *Web:* dropkinmatza.com	Somerville	MA	02145	617-623-4600		41
DropThought Inc 2755 Great America Way Ste 425 *TF:* 855-437-6776 ■ *Web:* www.dropthought.com	Santa Clara	CA	95054	855-437-6776		5
Droste Consultants 222 Merrimac St *Web:* www.drostesoftware.com	Newburyport	MA	01950	978-686-5775		177
Drowsy Water Ranch PO Box 147 *TF:* 800-845-2292 ■ *Web:* www.drowsywater.com	Granby	CO	80446	970-725-3456		239
DRR Partners LLC 4665 Cornell Rd Ste 160 *Web:* twpteam.com	Cincinnati	OH	45241	513-984-6696		691
DRS Technologies-Marlo Coil 6060 Hwy Pp *Web:* www.marlocoil.com	High Ridge	MO	63049	636-677-6600	677-1203	14
DRT Press PO Box 427 **Fax Area Code:* 866 ■ *Web:* www.drtpress.com	Pittsboro	NC	27312	919-360-7073	562-5040*	637-2
DRT Strategies Inc 4401 N Fairfax Dr Ste 800 **Fax Area Code:* 703 ■ *Web:* www.drtstrategies.com	Arlington	VA	22203	571-482-2500	528-4080*	196
Drug Chemical & Associated Technologies Assn (DCAT) 1 Washington Blvd Ste 7 *TF:* 800-640-3228 ■ *Web:* www.dcat.org	Robbinsville	NJ	08691	609-448-1000		49-19
Drug Detection Laboratories Inc 9700 Business Pk Dr Ste 407 *Web:* www.drugdetection.net	Sacramento	CA	95827	916-366-3113	366-3917	416
Drug Enforcement Administration 660 S Mesa Hills Ste 2000 *Web:* www.dea.gov	El Paso	TX	79912	915-832-6000		340-14
Drug Enforcement Administration (DEA) 700 Army-Navy Dr *Web:* www.justice.gov	Arlington	VA	22202	202-307-3067		340-14
Drug Enforcement Administration						
DEA Training Academy PO Box 1475 *Web:* www.justice.gov	Quantico	VA	22134	703-632-5000		340-14
El Paso Intelligence Ctr 11339 Simms St *Web:* www.justice.gov	El Paso	TX	79908	202-307-1000		340-14
Houston Div 1433 W Loop S Ste 600 *Web:* www.dea.gov	Houston	TX	77027	713-693-3000		340-14
Drug Enforcement Administration Museum & Visitors Ctr 700 Army Navy Dr *Web:* deamuseum.org	Arlington	VA	22202	202-307-3463	307-8956	520
Drug Enforcement Administration Regional Offices						
Atlanta Div 75 Spring St SW Rm 800 *Web:* www.dea.gov	Atlanta	GA	30303	404-893-7000		340-14
Boston Div 15 New Sudbury St Rm E400 *Web:* www.justice.gov	Boston	MA	02203	617-557-2100		340-14
Chicago Div 230 S Dearborn St Ste 1200 *Web:* www.dea.gov	Chicago	IL	60604	312-353-7875		340-14
Dallas Div 10160 Technology Blvd E *TF:* 800-882-9539 ■ *Web:* www.justice.gov	Dallas	TX	75220	214-366-6900		340-14
Detroit Div 431 Howard St *Web:* www.dea.gov	Detroit	MI	48226	313-234-4000		340-14
Los Angeles Div 255 E Temple St 17th Fl *Web:* www.justice.gov	Los Angeles	CA	90012	213-621-6700		340-14
New Orleans Div 3838 N Cswy Blvd Ste 1800 *Web:* www.justice.gov	Metairie	LA	70002	504-840-1100		340-14
New York Div 99 Tenth Ave *Web:* www.justice.gov	New York	NY	10011	212-337-3900		340-14
Philadelphia Div 600 Arch St Rm 10224 Federal Bldg *Web:* www.dea.gov	Philadelphia	PA	19106	215-861-3474		340-14
Phoenix Div 3010 N Second St Ste 301 *Web:* www.justice.gov	Phoenix	AZ	85012	602-664-5600		340-14
Saint Louis Div 317 S 16th St *Web:* www.justice.gov	Saint Louis	MO	63103	314-538-4600		340-14
San Diego Div 4560 Viewridge Ave *Web:* www.dea.gov	San Diego	CA	92123	858-616-4100		340-14
San Francisco Div 450 Golden Gate Ave *Web:* www.justice.gov	San Francisco	CA	94102	415-436-7900		340-14
Seattle Div 300 5th Ave Ste 1300 *Web:* www.dea.gov	Seattle	WA	98104	206-553-5443		340-14
Washington DC Div 800 K St NW Ste 500 *Web:* www.justice.gov	Washington	DC	20001	202-305-8500	514-1009	340-14
Drug Package Inc 901 Drug Package Ln *TF:* 800-325-6137 ■ *Web:* drugpackage.com	O'Fallon	MO	63366	800-325-6137		627
Drug Plastics & Glass Company Inc 1 Bottle Dr *Web:* www.drugplastics.com	Boyertown	PA	19512	610-367-5000	367-9800	98
Drug Policy Alliance 70 W 36th St 16th Fl *Web:* www.drugpolicy.org	New York	NY	10018	212-613-8020	613-8021	48-8
Drugco Discount Pharmacy 107 Smith Church Rd *TF:* 866-601-8434 ■ *Web:* www.drugcopharmacy.com	Roanoke Rapids	NC	27870	252-537-7010		237
Drugless Healthcare Solutions 2001 Crocker Rd Ste 100 **Fax Area Code:* 440 ■ *TF:* 888-922-5672 ■ *Web:* www.druglessdoctor.com	Westlake	OH	44145	888-922-5672	322-2502*	352

Name / Address	City	State	ZIP	Phone	Fax	Class
DrugLogic Inc 11490 Commerce Park Dr Ste 540 *Web:* www.druglogic.com	Reston	VA	20191	703-821-3200		194
DrugScan Inc 200 Precision Rd Ste 200 PO Box 347 *TF:* 800-235-4890 ■ *Web:* www.drugscan.com	Horsham	PA	19044	800-235-4890		416
Druide informatique Inc 1435 Rue Saint-Alexandre Bureau 1040 *TF:* 800-537-8433 ■ *Web:* www.druide.com	Montreal	QC	H3A2G4	514-484-4998		180
Druley Enterprises Inc 3305 N Anthony Blvd *Web:* www.belmontbev.com	Fort Wayne	IN	46805	260-424-4604	424-3301	443
Drum Corps Intl (DCI) 110 W Washington St Ste C *TF:* 800-495-7469 ■ *Web:* www.dci.org	Indianapolis	IN	46204	317-275-1212	713-0690	48-4
Drum Creative 35 Cessna Ct *Web:* drumcreative.com	Greenville	SC	29607	864-254-6096		344
Drum Filter Media Inc 901 W Fairfield Rd *Web:* dfmiusa.com	High Point	NC	27263	336-434-4195	434-4697	386
Drum-Line 2114 S Main St *Web:* www.drum-line.com	Stuttgart	AR	72160	870-673-2726	673-6312	627
Drummac Inc 251 Levy Rd *TF:* 800-780-0111 ■ *Web:* www.drummac.com	Atlantic Beach	FL	32233	904-241-4999	241-0640	393
Drummer Online & Wright County Journal Press 108 Central Ave PO Box 159 *TF:* 800-880-5047 ■ *Web:* www.thedrummer.com	Buffalo	MN	55313	763-682-1221	682-5458	532-3
Drummond 2472 Dennis St *Web:* rummond.com	Jacksonville	FL	32204	904-354-2818		627
Drummond Company Inc PO Box 10246 *TF:* 800-321-4015 ■ *Web:* www.drummondco.com	Birmingham	AL	35202	205-945-6300	849-1322	501
Drummond Wehle Yonge LLP 6987 E Fowler Ave *Web:* dwyfirm.com	Tampa	FL	33617	813-983-8000		41
Drummond Woodsum LLP 84 Marginal Way Ste 600 *TF:* 800-727-1941 ■ *Web:* www.dwmlaw.com	Portland	ME	04101	207-772-1941		428
Drumtech Inc 5200 Manchester Ave *Web:* www.drumtechus.com	Saint Louis	MO	63110	314-647-3464		198
Drury Capital Inc 47 Hulfish St Ste 340 *Web:* www.drurycapital.com	Princeton	NJ	08542	609-252-1230		791
Drury Design Dynamics Inc 49 W 27th St *Web:* www.drurydesign.com	New York	NY	10001	212-213-4600		514
Drury Hotels Company LLC 721 Emerson Rd Ste 400 *TF:* 800-378-7946 ■ *Web:* www.druryhotels.com	Saint Louis	MO	63141	314-429-2255	429-5166	379
Drury Supply Co 4072 State Hwy K	Cape Girardeau	MO	63701	573-334-8271		186
Drury University 900 N Benton Ave *TF:* 800-922-2274 ■ *Web:* www.drury.edu	Springfield	MO	65802	417-873-7879	866-3873	166
Drury's Inc 100 Main St PO Box 84 *TF:* 855-561-2010 ■ *Web:* drurysfurniture.com	Fountain	MN	55935	855-561-2010		321
Druva 150 Mathilda Pl Ste 450 *TF:* 844-303-7882 ■ *Web:* www.druva.com	Sunnyvale	CA	94086	650-241-3501		387
DRW Trading Group 540 W Madison St Ste 2500 *Web:* www.drw.com	Chicago	IL	60661	312-542-1000		690
Dry Cleaning Depot Inc 730 W Broward Blvd *Web:* www.drycleaningdepot.com	Fort Lauderdale	FL	33312	954-522-3660		426
Dry Creek Products Inc 51 Edward St PO Box 343	Arcade	NY	14009	585-492-2990		820
Dryclean USA Inc 290 NE 68th St *Web:* www.drycleanusa.com	Miami	FL	33138	305-754-9966	754-8010	426
Drycleaning & Laundry Institute 14700 Sweitzer Ln **Fax Area Code:* 240 ■ *TF:* 800-638-2627 ■ *Web:* www.dlionline.org	Laurel	MD	20707	301-622-1900	295-0685*	49-4
Dryden District Chamber of Commerce 284 Government St *Web:* www.dryden.ca	Dryden	ON	P8N2P3	807-223-2622		137
Dryden Municipal Telephone System 65 Princess St *Web:* www.dmts.biz	Dryden	ON	P8N1C8	807-223-1100		525
Dryg & Associates CPAS PC 2755 N Garfield Ave *Web:* drygcpas.com	Loveland	CO	80538	970-663-2020		2
Dryhead Ranch 1062 Rd 15 *Web:* cattledrivevacations.com	Lovell	WY	82431	307-548-6688		239
Drymalla Construction Company Ltd 608 Harbert St PO Box 698 *Web:* www.drymalla.com	Columbus	TX	78934	979-732-5731		186
Drysdales Inc 3220 S Memorial Dr *TF:* 800-444-6481 ■ *Web:* www.drysdales.com	Tulsa	OK	74145	918-664-6481		328
Dryvit Systems Inc 1 Energy Way *TF:* 800-556-7752 ■ *Web:* www.dryvit.com	West Warwick	RI	02893	401-822-4100	822-4510	389
Drywall Contractors Inc 2920 N Arlington Ave *Web:* drywallpartners.com	Indianapolis	IN	46218	317-546-6605		189-9
DS & B Ltd 222 S 9th St Ste 3000 *Web:* www.dsb-cpa.com	Minneapolis	MN	55402	612-359-9630		2
DS & O Rural Electric Cooperative Inc 129 W Main St PO Box 286 *TF:* 800-376-3533 ■ *Web:* www.dsoelectric.com	Solomon	KS	67480	785-655-2011	655-2805	245
DS Brown Co 300 E Cherry St *TF:* 800-848-1730 ■ *Web:* www.dsbrown.com	North Baltimore	OH	45872	419-257-3561	257-2200	191-2
DS Containers Inc 1789 Hubbard Ave *Web:* www.dscontainers.com	Batavia	IL	60510	630-406-9600		124
DS Distribution Inc 3500 Old Airport Rd *TF:* 800-752-5993 ■ *Web:* www.dsdistribution.com	Wooster	OH	44691	330-264-7400		237
DS Graphics Inc 120 Stedman St *Web:* www.dsgraphics.com	Lowell	MA	01851	978-970-1359		627
DS Mechanical LLC 61863 Rambling Way *TF:* 800-803-9202 ■ *Web:* www.dsmechanical.com	South Lyon	MI	48178	800-463-6599		194

Phone | Fax | Class

DS Pipe & Supply Company Inc
1301 Wicomico St Ste 3 .... Baltimore MD 21230 410-539-8000 612
TF: 800-368-8880 ■ *Web:* www.dspipe.com

DS Services of America Inc
5660 New Northside Dr Ste 500 .... Atlanta GA 30328 800-201-6218 805
TF: 800-201-6218 ■ *Web:* www.water.com

DS Smith 2366 Interstate Rd .... Riceboro GA 31323 912-884-3371 557
Web: www.dssmith.com

DS Smith 3475 Piedmont Rd Ste 1525 .... Atlanta GA 30305 470-645-1320 549
Web: www.dssmith.com

DS/USA (Disabled Sports USA)
451 Hungerford Dr Ste 608 .... Rockville MD 20850 301-217-0960 217-0968 48-22
TF: 800-543-2754 ■ *Web:* www.moveunitedsport.org

DSA (Data Systems Analysts Inc)
Eigth Neshaminy Interplex Ste 209 .... Trevose PA 19053 215-245-4800 245-4375 180
TF: 877-422-4372 ■ *Web:* www.dsainc.com

DSA (Direct Selling Assn)
1667 K St NW Ste 1100 .... Washington DC 20006 202-452-8866 452-9010 49-18
Web: www.dsa.org

DSA (Darryl L. Sink and Associates Inc)
1 Cielo Vista Pl .... Monterey CA 93940 831-649-8384 649-3914 194
TF: 800-650-7465 ■ *Web:* www.dsink.com

DSA Detection LLC
120 Water St Ste 211 .... North Andover MA 01845 978-975-3200 975-3201 693
TF: 866-372-3213 ■ *Web:* www.dsadetection.com

DSA Factors PO Box 577520 .... Chicago IL 60657 773-248-9000 248-9005 272
Web: www.dsafactors.com

DSC (Digital Security Controls)
3301 Langstaff Rd .... Concord ON L4K4L2 905-760-3000 692
TF: 888-888-7838 ■ *Web:* www.dsc.com

DSC (Dairyman's Supply Co)
3114 State Rte 45 S .... Mayfield KY 42066 270-247-5641 247-0327 191-3
TF: 800-626-3903 ■ *Web:* dairymanssupply.com

DSC Logistics 1750 S Wolf Rd .... Des Plaines IL 60018 800-372-1960 390-7276* 449
Fax Area Code: 847 ■ *TF:* 800-372-1960 ■ *Web:* www.dsclogistics.com

DSCC (Democratic Senatorial Campaign Committee)
120 Maryland Ave NE .... Washington DC 20002 202-224-2447 969-0354 48-7
Web: www.dscc.org

DSD Business Systems Inc
5120 Shoreham Pl Ste 280 .... San Diego CA 92122 858-550-5900 177
Web: www.dsdinc.com

DSG (Dakota Supply Group) 2601 3rd Ave N .... Fargo ND 58102 701-237-9440 237-6504 246
TF: 800-437-4702 ■ *Web:* www.dsgsupply.com

DSG Harmony 758 W Duval St .... Jacksonville FL 32202 888-354-3594 418
TF: 888-354-3594 ■ *Web:* www.dentalservices.net

DSG Systems Inc
56 Inverness Dr E Ste 260 .... Englewood CO 80112 303-790-0453 790-0866 177
Web: www.dsgsys.com

DSI (Dispenser Services Inc)
4273 Domino Ave .... Charleston SC 29405 800-742-2566 300
TF: 800-742-2566 ■ *Web:* www.dispenserservices.com

DSI (Dynamic Systems Inc)
104 Morrow Br .... Leicester NC 28748 828-683-3523 683-3511 471
TF: 844-270-6478 ■ *Web:* www.sunmatecushions.com

DSI Payroll Services 300 Atrium Dr .... Somerset NJ 08873 732-748-1700 570
Web: businessfinder.lehighvalleylive.com

DSI Real Estate Group Inc
100 River Pl Ste 1 .... Monona WI 53716 608-226-3060 653
Web: dsirealestate.com

DSI Underground Systems Inc
12427 S Pasture Rd Ste 201 .... Riverton UT 84096 385-557-5500 480
Web: www.dsiunderground.com

DSJ Printing Inc 3103 Pico Blvd .... Santa Monica CA 90405 310-828-8051 627
Web: www.dsjprinting.com

DSL Data Services LC
150 Creekside Ln .... Winchester VA 22602 540-667-4319 667-6538 177
Web: www.dsldata.com

DSL extreme 9221 Corbin Ave Ste 260 .... Northridge CA 91324 866-243-8638 206-0326* 398
Fax Area Code: 818 ■ *TF:* 866-243-8638 ■ *Web:* www.dslextreme.com

DSM 203 W Big Beaver Rd .... Troy MI 48084 812-435-7539 353
Web: www.dsm.com

DSN Group Inc 152 Lorraine Dr .... Lake Zurich IL 60047 888-445-2919 525
TF: 888-445-2919 ■ *Web:* dsngroup.net

DSO (DeKalb Symphony Orchestra)
PO Box 1313 .... Tucker GA 30085 678-891-3565 573-3
Web: dekalbsymphony.org

DSP Builders Inc
12000 E 47th Ave Ste 201 .... Denver CO 80239 303-289-0666 186
Web: www.dspbuilders.com

DSP Group Inc 2580 N First St Ste 460 .... San Jose CA 95131 408-240-6822 986-4323 696
NASDAQ: DSPG ■ *Web:* www.dspg.com

DSS (Document Storage Systems)
12575 US Hwy 1 Ste 200-A .... Juno Beach FL 33408 561-284-7000 227-0208 177
TF: 866-287-6962 ■ *Web:* www.dssinc.com

DSS ProDiesel Partners LLC
318 Fesslers Ln .... Nashville TN 37210 800-327-4373 242-8371* 385
Fax Area Code: 615 ■ *TF:* 800-327-4373 ■ *Web:* www.dssprodiesel.com

DSSC (Data Storage Systems Ctr)
Carnegie Mellon University
5000 Forbes Ave .... Pittsburgh PA 15213 412-268-6600 268-3497 668
TF: 800-864-8287 ■ *Web:* www.dssc.ece.cmu.edu

DST Controls 651 Stone Rd .... Benicia CA 94510 800-251-0773 203
TF: 800-251-0773 ■ *Web:* dstcontrols.com

DST Industries Inc 34364 Goddard Rd .... Romulus MI 48174 734-941-0300 60
Web: www.dstindustries.com

DSWS (Domaine Select Wine & Spirits LLC)
105 Madison Ave 13th Fl .... New York NY 10016 212-239-1275 279-0499 80-3
Web: domaineselect.com

DSX Access Systems Inc
10731 Rockwall Rd .... Dallas TX 75238 214-553-6140 553-6147 693
TF: 888-419-8353 ■ *Web:* www.dsxinc.com

DT Engineering 1107 Springfield Rd .... Lebanon MO 65536 417-532-2141 757
Web: www.dtengineering.com

DT Interpreting
140 Simmons Ave Ste 65 .... Pewaukee WI 53072 877-229-8119 563-0488* 768
Fax Area Code: 412 ■ *TF:* 877-304-0004 ■ *Web:* www.dtinterpreting.com

DT Transcription Consultants Inc
9 Fairway Ln .... Blythewood SC 29016 803-261-6307 744 1301* 478
Fax Area Code: 888 ■ *Web:* www.medi-grafix.com

DTA (Dental Trade Alliance)
4350 N Fairfax Dr Ste 220 .... Arlington VA 22203 703-379-7755 931-9429 49-4
Web: dentaltradealliance.org

D-Ta Systems Inc 2500 Lancaster Rd .... Ottawa ON K1B4S5 613-745-8713 177
TF: 877-382-3222 ■ *Web:* www.d-ta.com

DTC (Diversified Technology Consultants Inc)
2321 Whitney Ave Ste 301 .... Hamden CT 06518 203-239-4200 261
Web: www.teamdtc.com

DTC (DTC Communications Inc)
111 High St .... Alexandria TN 37012 615-529-2955 681
TF: 800-367-4274 ■ *Web:* www.dtccom.net

DTC (Dell Telephone Cooperative Inc)
610 S Main St .... Dell City TX 79837 915-964-2352 224
TF: 800-245-2991 ■ *Web:* www.delltelephone.com

DTC (Dallas Theater Ctr)
Wyly Theatre 2400 Flora St .... Dallas TX 75201 214-526-8210 521-7666 749
Web: www.dallastheatercenter.org

DTC Communications Inc (DTC)
111 High St .... Alexandria TN 37012 615-529-2955 681
TF: 800-367-4274 ■ *Web:* www.dtccom.net

DTE Energy Co 1 Energy Plz .... Detroit MI 48226 313-235-4000 360-5
NYSE: DTE ■ *TF:* 800-477-4747 ■ *Web:* www.newlook.dteenergy.com

DTE Energy Services
414 S Main St Ste 600 .... Ann Arbor MI 48104 734-302-4800 463
Web: dtepowerandindustrial.com

DTH (Dana-Thomas House)
301 E Lawrence Ave .... Springfield IL 62703 217-782-6776 50-3
Web: www.dana-thomas.org

DTI Associates Inc
DTI Associates Kratos Defense
30 M St SE Ste 700 .... Washington DC 20003 703-299-1600 449

DTI LLC 11210 Steeplecrest Dr Ste 107 .... Houston TX 77065 713-856-8735 112
Web: www.dtillc.com

DTIC (Defense Technical Information Ctr)
8725 John J Kingman Rd Ste 0944 .... Fort Belvoir VA 22060 800-225-3842 340-3
TF: 800-225-3842 ■ *Web:* discover.dtic.mil

DTLR 1300 Mercedes Dr .... Hanover MD 21076 844-788-4552 229
TF: 844-788-4552 ■ *Web:* www.dtlr.com

DTM Systems Inc
130-2323 Boundary Rd .... Vancouver BC V5K4R5 604-257-6700 179
Web: www.dtm.ca

DTrio Marketing Group
401 N Third St Ste 480 .... Minneapolis MN 55401 612-787-3333 195
Web: www.dtrio.com

DTRT Insurance Corp
12550 W Atlantic Blvd .... Coral Springs FL 33071 954-772-8232 390
TF: 855-329-3878 ■ *Web:* dtrtinsurance.com

DTS (Diversified Transfer & Storage Inc)
1640 Monad Rd .... Billings MT 59101 406-896-3443 896-3492 780
TF: 800-755-5855 ■ *Web:* www.dtsb.com

DTS (Dynamic Test Solutions Inc)
1762 Technology Dr Ste 201 .... San Jose CA 95110 408-264-8880 256
Web: www.dynamic-test.com

DTS (Dynamic Technology Systems Inc)
5285 Shawnee Rd 5285 Shawnee Rd Ste 500 .... Alexandria VA 22312 703-379-4800 379-4901 177
Web: www.dts-inc.com

DTS Financial Group
300 Spectrum Center Dr Ste 400 .... Irvine CA 92618 949-491-8227 528
Web: www.dtsfinancialgroup.com

DTS Group 3208 E Colonial Dr Ste 450 .... Orlando FL 32803 407-444-2770 194
Web: www.dtsg.com

DTS Inc 5220 Las Virgenes Rd .... Calabasas CA 91302 818-436-1000 52
NASDAQ: DTSI ■ *Web:* dts.com

DTS Software Inc
4350 Lassiter At North Hills Ave Ste 230 .... Raleigh NC 27609 919-833-8426 225
Web: dtssoftware.com

Du Hadaway Tool & Die Shop Inc
801 Dawson Dr .... Newark DE 19713 302-366-0113 757
Web: duhadawaytool.com

Du Page Airport Authority
2700 International Dr Ste 200 .... West Chicago IL 60185 630-584-2211 584-3022 27
TF: 800-208-5690 ■ *Web:* www.dupageairport.com

Du Quebec 1400 Blvd Guillaume-Couture .... Levis QC G6W8K7 418-838-5602 833-3871 403
TF: 800-749-3646 ■ *Web:* www.fadq.qc.ca

Dual Dynamics Inc 2241 Humphrey St .... Lincoln NE 68521 800-228-0394 128
TF: 800-228-0394 ■ *Web:* www.dualdynamics.com

Dual Print & Mail LLC
340 Nagel Dr .... Cheektowaga NY 14225 716-684-3825 684-3828 627
TF: 800-358-4348 ■ *Web:* dualprintandmail.com

Dualite Sales & Service Inc
1 Dualite Ln .... Williamsburg OH 45176 513-724-7100 701
TF: 800-543-7271 ■ *Web:* www.dualite.com

Dualtone Music Group Inc
801 Fifth Ave S Ste 206 .... Nashville TN 37203 615-320-0620 320-0692 657
Web: www.dualtone.com

Duane Hartness Insurance Agency Inc
1094 Historic Hwy 441 .... Demorest GA 30535 706-776-2246 390
Web: hartnessinsurance.com

Duane Livingston Trucking
169 Blankenship Rd .... Texarkana TX 75501 903-832-5373 832-1385 780
TF: 800-441-0697 ■ *Web:* www.livingstontrucking.com

Duane Morris Government Strategies LLC (DMGS)
505 Ninth St NW Ste 1000 .... Washington DC 20004 202-776-7803 776-7801 393
Web: www.dmgs.com

Duane Morris LLP 30 S 17th St .... Philadelphia PA 19103 215-979-1000 979-1020 428
Web: www.duanemorris.com

Duane Street Hotel 130 Duane St .... New York NY 10013 212-964-4600 964-4800 379
Web: www.duanestreethotel.com

Duarte Unified School District
1620 Huntington Dr .... Duarte CA 91010 626-599-5000 599-5069 685
TF: 888-225-7377 ■ *Web:* www.duarteusd.org

Duball LLC
11710 Plaza America Dr Ste 1100 .... Reston VA 20190 703-860-0901 653
Web: duball-llc.com

Dubhouse 404 SE 15th St .... Fort Lauderdale FL 33316 954-524-3658 522-1905 240
TF: 877-900-3827 ■ *Web:* www.thedubhouse.net

Dublin Building Systems Inc
6233 Avery Rd .... Dublin OH 43017 614-889-1445 889-5437 186
Web: www.dublinbuilding.com

Name / Address	City	State	ZIP	Phone	Fax	Class
Dublin Chamber of Commerce 7080 Donlon Way Ste 110 *Web:* www.dublinchamberofcommerce.org	Dublin	CA	94568	925-828-6200	828-4247	139
Dublin Construction Company Inc 305 S Washington St *Web:* www.dcc1945.com	Dublin	GA	31021	478-272-0721		182
Dublin Convention & Visitors Bureau 9 S High St *TF:* 800-245-8387 ■ *Web:* www.visitdublinohio.com	Dublin	OH	43017	614-792-7666		206
Dublin Pub 300 Wayne Ave *Web:* www.dubpub.com	Dayton	OH	45410	937-224-7822		671
Dublin School 18 Lehmann Way PO Box 522 *Web:* www.dublinschool.org	Dublin	NH	03444	603-563-8584		622
Dublin Unified School District 7471 Larkdale Ave *Web:* www.dublin.k12.ca.us	Dublin	CA	94568	925-828-2551	829-6532	685
Dublin Villager 7801 N Central Dr.	Lewis Center	OH	43035	614-841-1781		532-4
Dublin-Laurens County Chamber of Commerce 1200 Bellvue *Web:* www.dublin-georgia.com	Dublin	GA	31021	478-272-5546	275-0811	139
Dubois & King Inc 28 N Main St. *TF:* 866-783-7101 ■ *Web:* www.dubois-king.com	Randolph	VT	05060	802-728-3376		261
DuBois Area School District Inc 500 Liberty Blvd *Web:* www.dasd.k12.pa.us	DuBois	PA	15801	814-371-2700	371-2544	187
Dubois Chemicals 3630 E Kemper Rd *TF:* 800-438-2647 ■ *Web:* www.duboischemicals.com	Cincinnati	OH	45241	800-438-2647	543-1720	151
Dubois Rural Electric Co-opeartive Inc 1400 Energy Dr. *Web:* www.duboisrec.com	Jasper	IN	47547	812-482-5454		245
Dubois Wood Products Inc 707 E Sixth St. *Web:* www.duboiswood.com	Huntingburg	IN	47542	812-683-3613		499
DuBois, Sheehan, Hamilton, Levin & Weissman LLC 511 Cooper St *Web:* www.duboislaw.com	Camden	NJ	08102	856-365-7665		428
DuBose & Associates Insurance 2501 Parkview Dr Ste 610 **Fax Area Code:* 817 ■ *TF:* 800-390-2300 ■ *Web:* www.duboseandassociates.com	Fort Worth	TX	76102	800-390-2300	877-9184*	390
Dubose National Energy Services Inc 900 Industrial Dr. *Web:* www.dubosenes.com	Clinton	NC	28328	910-590-2151	590-3555	492
Dubose Strapping Inc 906 Industrial Dr. *TF:* 800-354-3020 ■ *Web:* www.dubosestrapping.com	Clinton	NC	28328	910-590-1020		567
Dubuque Advertiser Inc, The 2966 John F Kennedy Rd *Web:* www.dbqadvertiser.com	Dubuque	IA	52002	563-588-0162	582-0335	532-2
Dubuque Arboretum & Botanical Gardens 3800 Arboretum Dr. *Web:* www.dubuquearboretum.com	Dubuque	IA	52001	563-556-2100	556-2443	97
Dubuque Area Chamber of Commerce 300 Main St Ste 200 *TF:* 800-798-4748 ■ *Web:* www.dubuquechamber.com	Dubuque	IA	52001	563-557-9200	557-1591	139
Dubuque City Hall 50 W 13th St *Web:* www.cityofdubuque.org	Dubuque	IA	52001	563-589-4100	589-0890	337
Dubuque County 720 Central Ave *TF:* 800-637-0128 ■ *Web:* dubuquecounty.org	Dubuque	IA	52001	563-589-4432		338
Dubuque Fairgrounds Speedway 14569 Old Hwy Rd *Web:* www.dbqfair.com	Dubuque	IA	52002	563-588-1406		515
Dubuque Museum of Art 701 Locust St. *Web:* www.dbqart.org	Dubuque	IA	52001	563-557-1851		520
Dubuque Regional Airport 11000 Airport Rd *Web:* www.flydbq.com	Dubuque	IA	52003	563-589-4128		27
Dubuque Stamping & Manufacturing Inc 3190 Jackson St *Web:* www.dubuquestamping.com	Dubuque	IA	52001	563-583-5716	583-5718	488
Dubuque Symphony Orchestra 2728 Asbury Rd Ste 900 *TF:* 866-803-9280 ■ *Web:* www.dubuquesymphony.org	Dubuque	IA	52001	563-557-1677	557-9841	573-3
Duca Financial Services Credit Union Ltd 5290 Yonge St *TF:* 866-900-3822 ■ *Web:* www.duca.com	Toronto	ON	M2N5P9	416-223-8502		219
Ducci Electrical Contractors Inc 74 Scott Swamp Rd *Web:* duccielectrical.com	Farmington	CT	06032	860-489-9267	489-7980	189-4
DuCharme McMillen & Associates Inc 828 S Harrison St *TF:* 800-309-2110 ■ *Web:* www.dmainc.com	Fort Wayne	IN	46802	260-484-8631	482-8152	734
Duchesnay Inc 950 Boul Mich'Le-Bohec *TF:* 877-833-7734 ■ *Web:* www.duchesnay.com	Blainville	QC	J7C5E2	450-433-7734	433-2211	238
Duchesne County 734 N Center St PO Box 910 *Web:* www.duchesne.utah.gov	Duchesne	UT	84021	435-738-1100	738-5522	338
Duck Co 5601 Gray St. *TF:* 800-255-3565 ■ *Web:* www.duckco.com	Arvada	CO	80002	800-255-3565		687
Duck Flats Pharma 245 E Main St *Web:* www.dfpharma.com	Elbridge	NY	13060	315-689-3407	689-3409	463
Duck River Electric Membership Corp (DREMC) 1411 Madison St *Web:* www.dremc.com	Shelbyville	TN	37160	931-909-1287	901-1318	245
Duck River Textile 55 Talmadge Rd *Web:* www.duckrivertextile.com	Edison	NJ	08817	212-679-2980		258
Duck's Painting & Maintence 3010 Wilshire Blvd Ste 341 **Fax Area Code:* 310	Los Angeles	CA	90010	562-869-7005	478-0773*	33
Duckback 101 Prospect Ave. *TF:* 800-825-5382 ■ *Web:* www.superdeck.com	Cleveland	OH	44115	800-825-5382		550
Ducker Worldwide LLC 1250 Maplelawn Dr *TF:* 800-929-0086 ■ *Web:* www.ducker.com	Troy	MI	48084	248-644-0086	644-3128	463
Duckfat 43 Middle St *Web:* duckfat.com	Portland	ME	04101	207-774-8080		671
Ducks Unlimited Magazine 1 Waterfowl Way *TF:* 800-453-8257 ■ *Web:* www.ducks.org	Memphis	TN	38120	901-758-3825	758-3850	457-20
Duckworth Tammy (Sen D - IL) 524 Hart Senate Office Bldg *Web:* www.duckworth.senate.gov	Washington	DC	20510	202-224-2854		342-2
Ducky's Office Furniture 24 S Idaho St *Web:* www.duckys.com	Seattle	WA	98134	206-623-7777		321
Du-Co Ceramics Co 155 S Rebecca St PO Box 568 *Web:* www.du-co.com	Saxonburg	PA	16056	724-352-1511	352-1266	249
Ducommun Inc 23301 Wilmington Ave *NYSE:* DCO ■ *Web:* ducommun.com	Carson	CA	90745	310-513-7280	513-7279	203
Ducommun Inc 200 Sandpointe Ave Ste 700 *Web:* www.ducommun.com	Santa Ana	CA	92707	310-380-5390		22
Ducon Technologies Inc 19 Engineers Ln *Web:* www.ducon.com	Farmingdale	NY	11735	631-694-1700		18
DuCret School of Art 1030 Central Ave *Web:* www.ducret.edu	Plainfield	NJ	07060	908-757-7171	757-2626	685
Ductmate Industries Inc 210 Fifth St. *TF:* 800-990-8459 ■ *Web:* ductmate.com	Charleroi	PA	15022	724-258-0500	258-5494	198
Ductmedic 5200 N 57th St Ste 2 *Web:* ductmedic.com	Lincoln	NE	68507	402-435-3828		152
Duct-O-Wire Co 345 Adams Cir. *TF:* 800-752-6001 ■ *Web:* ductowire.com	Corona	CA	92882	951-735-8220	735-2372	203
Dude Girl *Paco's Bike and Ski* 12047 Donner Pass Rd *Web:* www.dudegirl.com	Truckee	CA	96161	530-587-5561	587-7635	772
Dude Rancher Lodge 415 N 29th St. *Web:* www.duderancherlodge.com	Billings	MT	59101	406-545-6331	259-0095	379
Dude Ranchers Assn 1122 12th St PO Box 2307 *TF:* 866-399-2339 ■ *Web:* duderanch.org	Cody	WY	82414	307-587-2339	587-2776	48-23
Dudek 605 Third St *Web:* dudek.com	Encinitas	CA	92024	760-942-5147		261
Dudek & Bock Spring Manufacturing Co 5100 W Roosevelt Rd *Web:* www.dudek-bock.com	Chicago	IL	60644	773-379-4100		719
Dudick Inc 1818 Miller Pkwy *Web:* www.dudick.com	Streetsboro	OH	44241	330-562-1970		596
Dudley & Smith PA 101 Fifth St E Ste 2602 *Web:* www.dudleyandsmith.com	Saint Paul	MN	55101	651-291-1717		428
Dudley Beauty College 2031 Rhode Island Ave NE *Web:* www.dudleybeautyschool-dc.com	Washington	DC	20018	202-269-3666		167-3
Dudley Farm Historic State Park 18730 W Newberry Rd *Web:* www.floridastateparks.org	Newberry	FL	32669	352-472-1142		565
Dudley Printing 931 Main St. *Web:* www.journalherald.com	Manson	IA	50563	712-469-2648		532-2
Dudley's 259 Westshort St *Web:* www.dudleysonshort.com	Lexington	KY	40507	859-252-1010	253-9383	671
Dudley's Bakery Inc 30218 Hwy 78 (Julian Rd) *Web:* www.dudleysbakery.com	Santa Ysabel	CA	92070	760-765-0488	765-1565	68
Dudnyk 5 Walnut Grove Dr Ste 300 *Web:* dudnyk.com	Horsham	PA	19044	215-443-9406		4
Due Amici 67 E Gay St *Web:* due-amici.com	Columbus	OH	43215	614-224-9373		671
Due North Consulting Inc 3112 Blue Lake Dr Ste 110 *TF:* 800-899-2676 ■ *Web:* duenorthmedia.com	Birmingham	AL	35243	205-989-9394		196
Dueck Auto Group 12100 Featherstone Way *Web:* www.dueckgm.com	Richmond	BC	V6W1K9	604-273-1311		57
Duff & Phelps Investment Management Co 200 S Wacker Dr Ste 500 *TF:* 800-338-8214 ■ *Web:* www.dpimc.com	Chicago	IL	60606	312-263-2610		401
Duff's Famous Wings 3651 Sheridan Dr *Web:* www.duffswings.com	Amherst	NY	14226	716-834-6234		671
Dufferin Gate Productions Inc 875 Bloor St W PO Box 6 *Web:* www.dufferingate.com	Toronto	ON	M8W3Z8	416-252-9998		514
Duffey Communications Inc 3379 Peachtree Rd NE Ste 740 *Web:* www.duffey.com	Atlanta	GA	30326	404-266-2600		636
Duffey Southeast Inc 7716 England St Ste A *Web:* duffeyse.com	Charlotte	NC	28273	704-527-3612		610
Duffield Adamson & Helenbolt PC 3430 E Sunrise Dr Ste 200 *Web:* duffieldlaw.com	Tucson	AZ	85718	520-792-1181		41
Duffield Aquatic 113 Metro Dr *TF:* 888-669-7551 ■ *Web:* www.duffieldaquatics.com	Anderson	SC	29625	864-226-5500		186
Duffield Associates Inc 5400 Limestone Rd. *TF:* 877-732-9633 ■ *Web:* duffnet.com	Wilmington	DE	19808	302-239-6634	239-8485	186
Duffin Manufacturing Co 316 Warden Ave *Web:* www.duffinmfg.com	Elyria	OH	44035	440-323-4681	420-4004	621
Duffner Engineering 50 W Summit Dr. *Web:* www.duffnerengineering.com	Emerald Hills	CA	94062	650-701-1055		261
Duffy & Partners 7900 Xerxes Ave S Ste 815 *Web:* duffy.com	Minneapolis	MN	55401	612-548-2333		195
Duffy & Shanley Inc 10 Charles St. *Web:* www.duffyshanley.com	Providence	RI	02904	401-274-0001		4
Duffy's Collectible Cars 1195 Boyson Rd. *Web:* www.duffys.com	Hiawatha	IA	52233	319-364-7000		520
Duffy's Steak & Lobster House 1007 Simonton St. *Web:* duffyskeywest.com	Key West	FL	33040	305-296-4900		671

Name / Address	City	State	ZIP	Phone	Fax	Class
DuffyGroup Inc 4727 E Union Hills Dr Ste 200 *Web:* duffygroup.com	Phoenix	AZ	85050	602-861-5840		193
Dufour Tax Group LLC 215 Commercial St. *Web:* dufourtax.com	Portland	ME	04101	207-329-4472		2
Dufresne Furniture Ltd 116 Nature Pk Way *Web:* dufresne.ca	Winnipeg	MB	R3P0X8	204-989-9898		321
Dufry 10300 NW 19th St Ste 114 *Web:* www.dufry.com	Doral	FL	33172	305-591-1763		443
Dugan & Meyers 11110 Kenwood Rd *Web:* dugan-meyers.com	Cincinnati	OH	45242	513-891-4300	891-0704	186
Dugan, Mckissick & Longmore LLC 22738 Maple Rd Ste 210 *Web:* paxlawyers.com	Lexington Park	MD	20653	301-862-3764	862-3789	41
Duggal Visual Solutions Inc 29 W 23th St. *Web:* duggal.com	New York	NY	10010	212-242-7000		344
Duggan Joiner & Company PA 334 NW Third Ave. *Web:* www.djcocpa.com	Ocala	FL	34475	352-732-0171	867-1370	2
Duggan Manufacturing 50150 Ryan Rd Ste 15 *Web:* www.dugganmfg.com	Shelby Township	MI	48317	586-254-7400	254-9833	697
Duhaney Home Health Care Inc 360 N Sepulveda Blvd Ste 2030 *Web:* www.duhaneyhomehealth.com	El Segundo	CA	90245	310-416-1160	416-1134	363
Duhig & Company Inc 5071 Telegraph Rd *Web:* www.duhig.com	Los Angeles	CA	90022	323-263-7161	263-3891	492
Duininck Inc 408 Sixth St PO Box 208 *TF:* 800-328-8949 ■ *Web:* www.duininckcompanies.com	Prinsburg	MN	56281	320-978-6011		188-4
Dukal Corp 2 Fleetwood Ct. *TF:* 800-243-0741 ■ *Web:* www.dukal.com	Ronkonkoma	NY	11779	631-656-3800	656-3810	475
Dukane 2900 Dukane Dr. *Web:* www.dukane.com	Saint Charles	IL	60174	630-584-2300		591
DuKane Precast Inc 1805 High Grove Ln *Web:* dukaneprecast.com	Naperville	IL	60540	630-355-8118		183
Duke Communications 1781 Jamestown Rd *Web:* www.dukecom.com	Williamsburg	VA	23185	757-253-9000		246
Duke Construction Inc 2600 Broad St Rd *Web:* www.dukeconstructioninc.net	Gum Spring	VA	23065	804-556-6992		390
Duke Endowment 800 E Morehead St. *Web:* www.dukeendowment.org	Charlotte	NC	28202	704-376-0291	376-9336	305
Duke Energy Corp 9700 David Taylor Dr *NYSE:* DUK ■ *TF:* 800-777-9898 ■ *Web:* www.duke-energy.com	Charlotte	NC	28202	800-777-9898		360-5
Duke Energy Ctr 525 Elm St *Web:* www.duke-energycenter.com	Cincinnati	OH	45202	513-419-7300	419-7327	205
Duke Farms 80 Rt 206 S *Web:* www.dukefarms.org	Hillsborough	NJ	08844	908-722-3700		97
Duke Graphics Inc 33212 Lakeland Blvd *TF:* 800-942-3853 ■ *Web:* dukeprint.com	Cleveland	OH	44102	440-946-0606	946-1627	627
Duke Health Raleigh Hospital 3400 Wake Forest Rd *Web:* www.dukehealth.org	Raleigh	NC	27609	919-954-3000		374-3
Duke Law 210 Science Dr PO Box 90362. *TF:* 888-529-2586 ■ *Web:* law.duke.edu	Durham	NC	27708	919-613-7006		167-1
Duke Manufacturing Co 2305 N Broadway *TF:* 800-735-3853 ■ *Web:* www.dukemfg.com	Saint Louis	MO	63102	314-231-1130	231-5074	298
Duke Memorial United Methodist Church 504 W Chapel Hill St *Web:* www.dukememorial.org	Durham	NC	27701	919-683-3467	682-3349	50-1
Duke Pediatric Blood & Marrow Transplant Program 1400 Morreene Rd PO Box 3350 *Web:* pediatrics.duke.edu	Durham	NC	27705	919-668-1100	668-1180	769
Duke Realty Corp 600 E 96th St Ste 100 *NYSE:* DRE ■ *TF:* 800-875-3366 ■ *Web:* www.dukerealty.com	Indianapolis	IN	46240	317-808-6000	808-6794	655
Duke Tower Residential Suites 807 W Trinity Ave	Durham	NC	27701	919-382-2000	683-1215	379
Duke University 2138 Campus Dr PO Box 90586. *TF:* 800-443-3853 ■ *Web:* www.duke.edu	Durham	NC	27708	919-684-3214	681-8941	166
Duke University Divinity School 407 Chapel Dr PO Box 90968. *TF:* 800-367-3853 ■ *Web:* divinity.duke.edu	Durham	NC	27708	919-660-3400	660-3473	167-3
Duke University Health System *Bone Marrow & Stem Cell Transplant Program* 2400 Pratt St *Web:* www.dukehealth.org	Durham	NC	27705	919-668-1002	668-1091	769
Duke University Medical Center Library 103 Seeley Mudd Bldg DUMC 3702. *Web:* mclibrary.duke.edu	Durham	NC	27710	919-660-1150	681-7599	434-1
Duke University Perkins Library 411 Chapel Dr *Web:* www.dukelibraries.contentdm.oclc.org	Durham	NC	27708	919-660-5870	660-5923	434-6
Duke University Press 905 W Main St Ste 18-B. **Fax Area Code:* 888 ■ *TF:* 888-651-0122 ■ *Web:* www.dukeupress.edu	Durham	NC	27701	919-687-3600	651-0124*	637-4
Duke University School of Medicine DUMC 3710 *Web:* medschool.duke.edu	Durham	NC	27710	919-684-2985		167-2
Duke University Talent Identification Program 300 Fuller St. *Web:* tip.duke.edu	Durham	NC	27701	919-668-9100	681-7921	304
Duke's 8th Avenue Hotel 630 W Eigth Ave *TF:* 800-478-4837 ■ *Web:* www.dukesalaskahotel.com	Anchorage	AK	99501	907-274-6213		379
Duke's Source for Sports 3876 Bloor St W *Web:* www.sourceforsports.com	Etobicoke	ON	M9B1L3	416-233-2011		711
Dukem 1100 Maryland Ave *Web:* www.dukemrestaurant.com	Baltimore	MD	21201	410-385-0318		671
Dukes Aerospace 9060 Winnetka Ave *Web:* www.dukesaerospace.com	Northridge	CA	91324	818-998-9811		22
Dukes Car Stereo Inc G4081 Miller Rd *Web:* www.dukescarstereo.com	Flint	MI	48507	810-230-9377		61
Dukes County PO Box 190. *TF:* 800-244-4630 ■ *Web:* www.dukescounty.org	Edgartown	MA	02539	508-696-3840	696-3841	338
Dukes Lumber Company Inc 28504 Dukes Lumber Rd *Web:* dukeslumber.com	Laurel	DE	19956	302-875-7551		364
Dukes, Ryan, Freed, Meents Ltd 146 N Vermilion St *Web:* dukesryanlaw.com	Danville	IL	61832	217-442-0384		41
Duley Hopkins & Associates Inc 1200 Mtn Creek Rd Ste 215 *Web:* www.dha-us.com	Chattanooga	TN	37405	423-877-1220		177
Duley Press Inc 2906 N Home St *Web:* duleypress.com	Mishawaka	IN	46545	574-259-5203	256-5935	627
Dulles Expo & Conference Ctr 4320 Chantilly Shopping Center Dr *Web:* www.dullesexpo.com	Chantilly	VA	20151	703-378-0910		232
Dultmeier Sales LLC 13808 Industrial Rd. *TF:* 888-677-5054 ■ *Web:* www.dultmeier.com	Omaha	NE	68137	402-333-1444		429
Duluth Area Chamber of Commerce 5 W First St Ste 101 *Web:* www.duluthchamber.com	Duluth	MN	55802	218-722-5501	722-3223	139
Duluth City Hall 411 W First St *Web:* www.duluthmn.gov	Duluth	MN	55802	218-730-5500	730-5923	337
Duluth Entertainment Convention Ctr 350 Harbor Dr. *TF:* 800-628-8385 ■ *Web:* decc.org	Duluth	MN	55802	218-722-5573	722-4247	205
Duluth International Airport 4701 Grinden Dr. *TF:* 855-787-2227 ■ *Web:* www.duluthairport.com	Duluth	MN	55811	218-727-2968	727-2960	27
Duluth News-Tribune 424 W First St *TF:* 800-456-8080 ■ *Web:* www.duluthnewstribune.com	Duluth	MN	55802	218-723-5281		532-2
Duluth Pack 365 Canal Park Dr *TF:* 800-777-4439 ■ *Web:* www.duluthpack.com	Duluth	MN	55802	800-777-4439		711
Duluth Playhouse 506 W Michigan St *Web:* www.duluthplayhouse.org	Duluth	MN	55802	218-733-7555		572
Duluth Public Library 520 W Superior St *Web:* www.duluthlibrary.org	Duluth	MN	55802	218-730-4200		434-3
Dumbarton House 2715 Q St NW *Web:* www.dumbartonhouse.org	Washington	DC	20007	202-337-2288	337-0348	50-3
Dumbarton Oaks 1703 32nd St NW *Web:* www.doaks.org	Washington	DC	20007	202-339-6400		520
Dumbarton Strategies LLC 3130 Dumbarton St NW *Web:* dumbartonstrategiesllc.com	Washington	DC	20007	202-337-3130		401
Dumbell Man Fitness Equipment, The 655 Hawaii Ave. *TF:* 800-432-6266 ■ *Web:* www.dumbellman.com	Torrance	CA	90503	310-381-2900		354
Dumdum Nelida 5925 N Sacramento Ave	Chicago	IL	60659	773-561-6776		361
Dummit, Buchholz & Trapp 11755 Wilshire Blvd 15th Fl *Web:* dbt.law	Los Angeles	CA	90025	310-479-0944		41
Dumont Center for Rehabilitation & Nursing Care 676 Pelham Rd *Web:* dumontcenter.com	New Rochelle	NY	10805	914-632-9600		450
Dumont Company LLC 289 Wells St. *TF:* 800-628-9648 ■ *Web:* www.dumont.com	Greenfield	MA	01301	413-773-3674	773-8430	493
DuMor Inc PO Box 142. *TF:* 800-598-4018 ■ *Web:* www.dumor.com	Mifflintown	PA	17059	717-436-2106	436-9839	319-4
Dumore Corp 1030 Veterans St *TF:* 888-467-8288 ■ *Web:* www.dumorecorp.com	Mauston	WI	53948	608-847-6420		518
Dumouchelle Art Gallery 409 E Jefferson Ave *Web:* www.dumoart.com	Detroit	MI	48226	313-963-6255	963-8199	44
Dun & Bradstreet Inc 103 JFK Pkwy *Web:* www.dnb.com	Short Hills	NJ	07078	973-921-5500		160
Dun Transportation & Stringing Inc 304 Reynolds Ln. *Web:* www.duntrans.com	Sherman	TX	75092	903-891-9660		780
Dunbar Barber Academy 325 W 2nd St. *Web:* www.dunbarbarberacademy.com	Tucson	AZ	85705	520-624-0131		167-3
Dunbar Cave State Natural Area 401 Dunbar Cave Rd. *Web:* tnstateparks.com	Clarksville	TN	37043	931-648-5526		565
Dunbar Goloboy LLP 197 Portland St 5th Fl. *Web:* dunbargoloboy.com	Boston	MA	02114	617-244-3550		41
Dunbar Mechanical Inc 2806 N Reynolds Rd. *TF:* 800-719-2201 ■ *Web:* www.dunbarmechanical.com	Toledo	OH	43615	419-537-1900	537-8840	189-10
Dunbarton Corp PO Box 8577. *TF:* 800-633-7553 ■ *Web:* dunbarton.com	Dothan	AL	36304	800-633-7553		234
Dunbarton Telephone Co 2 Stark Hwy S *TF:* 877-774-9911 ■ *Web:* dunbartontelephone.com	Dunbarton	NH	03046	603-774-9911		224
Duncan & Son Lines Inc 23860 W US Hwy 85 *TF:* 800-528-4283 ■ *Web:* duncanandson.com	Buckeye	AZ	85326	623-386-4511	386-3656	780
Duncan Aviation Inc 3701 Aviation Rd. *TF:* 800-228-4277 ■ *Web:* www.duncanaviation.aero	Lincoln	NE	68524	402-475-2611	475-5541	24
Duncan Cowichan Chamber of Commerce 2896 Drinkwater Rd *TF:* 888-303-3337 ■ *Web:* www.duncancc.bc.ca	Duncan	BC	V9L2C6	250-748-1111	746-8222	137
Duncan Disposal Co 1212 Harrison Ave	Arlington	TX	76011	817-317-2000	860-0330	804
Duncan Enterprises 5673 E Shields Ave *TF:* 800-438-6226 ■ *Web:* www.ilovetocreate.com	Fresno	CA	93727	559-291-4444		43
Duncan Jeff (Rep R - SC) 2229 Rayburn House Office Bldg *Web:* jeffduncan.house.gov	Washington	DC	20515	202-225-5301	225-3216	342-2

	Phone	Fax	Class
Duncan Machinery Movers Inc 2004 Duncan Machinery Dr . . . Lexington KY 40504 *Web:* www.dmmlex.com	859-233-7333	233-7365	780
Duncan Oil Company Inc 849 Factory Rd . . . Beavercreek OH 45434 *TF:* 800-527-2559 ■ *Web:* duncan-oil.com	800-527-2559		579
Duncan Printing Co 619 S Fremont Ave Ste A . . . Alhambra CA 91803 *Web:* www.duncanprinting.com	626-281-2016	281-6884	627
Duncan Regional Hospital 1407 Whisenant Dr . . . Duncan OK 73533 *Web:* www.duncanregional.com	580-252-5300	251-8829	374-3
Duncan Solutions Inc 633 W Wisconsin Ave Ste 1600 . . . Milwaukee WI 53203 *TF:* 888-993-8622 ■ *Web:* www.duncansolutions.com	888-993-8622		495
Duncan Supply Company Inc 910 N Illinois St . . . Indianapolis IN 46204 *TF:* 800-382-5528 ■ *Web:* www.duncansupply.com	317-634-1335	264-6689	612
Duncan Systems Inc 29391 Old US Hwy 33 . . . Elkhart IN 46516 *TF:* 800-551-9149 ■ *Web:* www.rvglass.com	800-551-9149		54
Duncan Valley Electric Co-opeartive Inc PO Box 440 . . . Duncan AZ 85534 *TF:* 800-669-2503 ■ *Web:* www.dvec.org	928-359-2503		245
Duncan-Parnell Inc 900 S McDowell St . . . Charlotte NC 28204 *TF:* 800-849-7708 ■ *Web:* www.duncan-parnell.com	704-372-7766	333-3845	113
Duncanville Chamber of Commerce 300 E Wheatland Rd . . . Duncanville TX 75116 *Web:* www.duncanvillechamber.org	972-780-4990	298-9370	139
Duncanville Public Library 201 James Collins Blvd . . . Duncanville TX 75116 *Web:* www.duncanville.com	972-780-5050	780-6426	434-3
Duncan-Williams Inc 6750 Poplar Ave Ste 300 . . . Memphis TN 38138 *Web:* www.duncanwilliams.com	901-260-6800		690
Duncaster 40 Loeffler Rd . . . Bloomfield CT 06002 *Web:* www.duncaster.org	860-380-5006		672
Dundalk Eagle PO Box 8936 . . . Dundalk MD 21222 *Web:* www.dundalkeagle.com	410-288-6060		532-4
Dundee Auction Service & Sale Barn Inc 3223 Dennison Rd . . . Dundee MI 48131 *Web:* www.markoberlyauctions.com	734-529-3800		446
Dundee Citrus Growers Assn 111 First St N . . . Dundee FL 33838 *Web:* www.dun-d.com	863-439-1574	439-1535	11-1
Dundee Corp 1 Adelaide St E Ste 2100 . . . Toronto ON M5C2V9 *Web:* www.dundeecorp.com	416-350-3388		360-3
Dundee Internet Service Inc 15000 Ostrander Rd . . . Dundee MI 48131 *TF:* 888-222-8485 ■ *Web:* dundee.net	734-529-5331		225
Dundick Corp 4616 W 20th St . . . Cicero IL 60804 *Web:* www.dundick.com	708-656-6363	656-2359	621
Dundy County PO Box 506 . . . Benkelman NE 69021 *Web:* dundycounty.nebraska.gov	308-423-2058		338
Dunedin Chamber of Commerce 301 Main St . . . Dunedin FL 34698 *Web:* www.dunedinfl.com	727-733-3197	734-8942	139
Dunes Learning Ctr 700 Howe Rd . . . Porter IN 46304 *Web:* duneslearningcenter.org	219-395-9555		242
Dunes Manor Hotel 2800 Baltimore Ave . . . Ocean City MD 21842 *TF:* 800-523-2888 ■ *Web:* www.dunesmanor.com	410-289-1100		379
Dungan & Lefevre Company LPA 210 W Main St . . . Troy OH 45373 *Web:* dunganattorney.com	937-339-0511		41
Dungan Engineering PA 1574 Hwy 98 E . . . Columbia MS 39429 *Web:* dunganeng.com	601-731-2600		256
Dunham Associates Inc 50 S 6th St Ste 1100 . . . Minneapolis MN 55402 *Web:* www.dunhameng.com	612-465-7550	465-7551	261
Dunham Machine Inc 1311 E Schaaf Rd Bldg A . . . Independence OH 44131 *Web:* www.dunhammachine.com	216-398-4500		454
Dunham Price Inc 210 Mike Hooks Rd PO Box 760 . . . Westlake LA 70669 *Web:* www.dunhamprice.com	337-433-3900	433-8895	182
Dunham Tavern Museum 6709 Euclid Ave . . . Cleveland OH 44103 *Web:* www.dunhamtavern.org	216-431-1060		520
Dunham's Sports 5000 Dixie Hwy . . . Waterford MI 48329 *TF:* 844-636-4109 ■ *Web:* www.dunhamssports.com	844-636-4109		157-5
Dunhill Hotel 237 N Tryon St . . . Charlotte NC 28202 *TF:* 800-354-4141 ■ *Web:* www.dunhillhotel.com	704-332-4141		379
Dunkiel Saunders Elliott Raubvogel & Hand 91 College St . . . Burlington VT 05401 *Web:* dunkielsaunders.com	802-860-1003		41
Dunkin' Brands Inc 130 Royall St . . . Canton MA 02021 *TF:* 800-859-5339 ■ *Web:* www.dunkindonuts.com	781-737-3000		381
Dunkin' Donuts Ctr 1 LaSalle Sq . . . Providence RI 02903 *Web:* www.dunkindonutscenter.com	401-331-0700		720
Dunkin's Diamonds Inc 897 Hebron Rd . . . Heath OH 43056 *TF:* 877-343-4883 ■ *Web:* www.dunkinsdiamonds.com	740-788-8611	788-8224	410
Dunkirk Aviation Sales & Service Inc 3389 Middle Rd . . . Dunkirk NY 14048 *Web:* dkkav.com	716-366-6938		63
Dunkirk Specialty Steel LLC 830 Brigham Rd . . . Dunkirk NY 14048 *Web:* www.dunkirkspecialtysteel.com	716-366-1000	366-0478	723
Dunkley International Inc 1910 Lake St . . . Kalamazoo MI 49001 *Web:* www.dunkleyinternational.net	269-343-5583	343-5614	298
Dunklin County 1175 Floyd St . . . Kennett MO 63857 *Web:* dunklincounty.org	573-888-2456	888-4120	338
Dunlap & Company Inc 6325 E 100 S . . . Columbus IN 47202 *Web:* dunlapinc.com	812-376-3021		186
Dunlap Industries Inc 297 Industrial Park Rd . . . Dunlap TN 37327 **Fax Area Code:* 423 ■ *TF:* 800-251-7214 ■ *Web:* www.dunlapworld.com	800-251-7214	949-3648*	594
Dunlap's 90 Buford Ave . . . Gettysburg PA 17325 *Web:* www.dunlapsrestaurant.com	717-334-4816	334-2053	671
Dunlop Manufacturing Inc 150 Industrial Way . . . Benicia CA 94510 *Web:* www.jimdunlop.com	707-745-2722		527
Dunlop Tires 200 Innovation Way . . . Akron OH 44316 *TF:* 800-522-7458 ■ *Web:* www.dunloptires.com	800-522-7458		754
Dunmore Corp 145 Wharton Rd . . . Bristol PA 19007 *TF:* 800-444-0242 ■ *Web:* www.dunmore.com	215-781-8895	781-9293	600
Dunn & Company Inc 75 Green St . . . Clinton MA 01510 *Web:* booktrauma.com	978-368-8505	368-7867	95
Dunn Capital Management LLC 309 SE Osceola St Dunn Bldg Ste 350 . . . Stuart FL 34994 *Web:* dunncapital.com	772-286-4777		401
Dunn Carney Allen Higgins & Tongue LLP 851 SW Sixth Ave Ste 1500 . . . Portland OR 97204 *Web:* www.dunncarney.com	503-224-6440		428
Dunn Construction 3905 Messer Airport Hwy . . . Birmingham AL 35222 *Web:* www.dunnconstruction.com	205-592-3866	592-4632	186
Dunn County 205 Owens St . . . Manning ND 58642 *Web:* www.dunncountynd.org	701-573-4448	573-4323	338
Dunn County 800 Wilson Ave . . . Menomonie WI 54751 *Web:* www.co.dunn.wi.us	715-232-1677	232-2534	338
Dunn Energy Co-op PO Box 220 . . . Menomonie WI 54751 *TF:* 800-924-0630 ■ *Web:* www.dunnenergy.com	715-232-6240		245
Dunn Engineers Inc 400 S Ruffner Rd . . . Charleston WV 25314 *Web:* dunnengineers.com	304-342-3436	342-7823	261
Dunn Group Inc, The 999 Riverview Dr Ste 386 . . . Totowa NJ 07512 *Web:* www.dunngrp.com	973-237-9500	237-9511	195
Dunn Hospitality Group LLC 300 SE Riverside Dr Ste 100 . . . Evansville IN 47713 *Web:* www.dunnhospitalitygroup.com	812-303-0050		379
Dunn Lambert LLC E 80 Rt 4 Ste 170 . . . Paramus NJ 07652 *Web:* www.njbizlawyer.com	201-957-0874	291-0140	428
Dunn Neal (Rep R - FL) 316 Cannon House Office Bldg . . . Washington DC 20515 *Web:* dunn.house.gov	202-225-5235	225-5615	342-2
Dunn Paper Inc 218 Riverview St . . . Port Huron MI 48060 *Web:* dunnpaper.com	810-984-5521		557
Dunn Roadbuilders LLC 411 W Oak St . . . Laurel MS 39440 *Web:* www.dunnroadbuilders.com	601-649-4111		188-4
Dunn School 2555 Hwy 154 PO Box 98 . . . Los Olivos CA 93441 *TF:* 800-287-9197 ■ *Web:* www.dunnschool.org	805-688-6471	686-9715	622
Dunn Sheehan LLP 3400 Carlisle St Ste 200 . . . Dallas TX 75204 *Web:* dunnsheehan.com	214-666-3338		41
Dunn Solutions Group Inc 5550 W Touhy Ave Ste 400 . . . Skokie IL 60077 *Web:* www.dunnsolutions.com	847-673-0900		177
Dunn State Park 289 Pearl St . . . Gardner MA 01440 *Web:* www.mass.gov	978-632-7897		565
Dunn-Edwards Corp 4885 E 52nd Pl . . . Los Angeles CA 90058 *TF:* 800-537-4098 ■ *Web:* www.dunnedwards.com	323-771-3330		550
Dunnellon chamber & Business Assn 20500 E Pennsylvania Ave . . . Dunnellon FL 34432 *Web:* www.dunnellonchamber.com	352-489-2320		139
Dunnhumby USA LLC 444 W Third St . . . Cincinnati OH 45202 *Web:* www.dunnhumby.com	513-632-1020		466
Dunning Motors Inc 3745 Jackson Rd . . . Ann Arbor MI 48103 *Web:* www.dunningtoyota.com	734-997-7600		57
Dunnington Bartholow & Miller LLP 250 Park Ave . . . New York NY 10177 *Web:* www.dunnington.com	212-682-8811		428
Dunrite Inc 3405 N Yager Rd . . . Fremont NE 68025 *TF:* 800-782-3061 ■ *Web:* www.dunriteinc.com	402-721-3061		76
Dunstan Press 681 Rte 1 Dunstan . . . Scarborough ME 04074 *Web:* www.dunstanpress.com	207-883-3108		637-2
Dunthorpe Marketing Group Inc 8825 SE 11th Ave . . . Portland OR 97202 *Web:* www.dunthorpemarketing.com	503-236-4242		463
Dunwoody College of Technology 818 Dunwoody Blvd . . . Minneapolis MN 55403 *TF:* 800-292-4625 ■ *Web:* dunwoody.edu	612-374-5800	374-4128	800
Dunwoody Village 3500 W Chester Pk . . . Newtown Square PA 19073 *Web:* www.dunwoody.org	610-359-4400		77
Duo Consulting Inc 641 W Lake St Ste 301 . . . Chicago IL 60661 *Web:* www.duoconsulting.com	312-529-3000		177
Duo Dogs Inc 10955 Linpage Pl . . . Saint Louis MO 63146 *Web:* duodogs.org	314-997-2325	997-7202	48-17
Duo-Fast Construction 155 Harlem Ave . . . Glenview IL 60025 **Fax Area Code:* 847 ■ *TF:* 877-489-2726 ■ *Web:* duo-fastconstruction.com	877-489-2726	619-8403*	758
Duo-Fast Northeast 22 Tolland St . . . East Hartford CT 06108 **Fax Area Code:* 860 ■ *TF:* 888-399-5712 ■ *Web:* www.nailersandstaplers.com	888-399-5712	291-8784*	351
Duoline Technologies 250 W Bluebird Rd . . . Gilmer TX 75645 *Web:* www.duoline.com	903-734-1371	734-1571	539
Duolingo 5900 Penn Ave . . . Pittsburgh PA 15206 *Web:* www.duolingo.com	412-567-6602		178-1
Duo-Safety Ladder Corp 513 W Ninth Ave . . . Oshkosh WI 54902 *TF:* 877-386-5377 ■ *Web:* www.duosafety.com	920-231-2740	231-2460	421
Dupaco Community Credit Union 3999 Pennsylvania Ave . . . Dubuque IA 52002 *TF:* 800-373-7600 ■ *Web:* www.dupaco.com	563-557-7600		219
DuPage Convention & Visitors Bureau 915 Harger Rd Ste 240 . . . Oak Brook IL 60523 *TF:* 800-232-0502 ■ *Web:* www.discoverdupage.com	630-575-8070	575-8078	206
DuPage County 421 N County Farm Rd . . . Wheaton IL 60187 *Web:* www.dupageco.org	630-407-5500	407-5501	338
DuPage Machine Products Inc 311 Longview Dr . . . Bloomingdale IL 60108 *Web:* www.dupagemachine.com	630-690-5400		621

Name / Address	City	State	ZIP	Phone	Fax	Class
Duplan Construction Inc 390 Industrial St *Web:* duplanconstruction.com	Campbell	CA	95008	408-866-6682	866-6043	186
Dupli Graphics Corp 6761 Thompson Rd N *TF:* 800-724-2477 ■ *Web:* www.duplionline.com	Syracuse	NY	13211	800-724-2477		627
Duplication Factory Inc 4275 Norex Dr	Chaska	MN	55318	952-448-9912		658
Duplicator Sales and Service Inc 839 E Broadway *Web:* derbycitylitho.com	Louisville	KY	40204	502-560-1440	560-0830	627
Duplin County 112 Duplin St *TF:* 800-685-8916 ■ *Web:* www.duplincountync.com	Kenansville	NC	28349	910-296-2150	296-2156	338
Duplin County Library 107 Bowdens Rd *Web:* duplincountync.com	Kenansville	NC	28349	910-296-2117		434-3
Dupli-Systems Inc 8260 Dow Cir *TF:* 800-321-1610 ■ *Web:* dupli-systems.com	Strongsville	OH	44136	440-234-9415	234-2350	110
DuPont 950 Stephenson Hwy PO Box 7013 *Web:* www.dupont.com	Troy	MI	48007	248-583-8000		550
DuPont Historical Museum 207 Barksdale Ave *Web:* www.dupontmuseum.com	Dupont	WA	98327	253-964-2399		520
Dupont Publishing Inc 3051 Tech Dr *Web:* www.dupontregistry.com	Saint Petersburg	FL	33716	727-573-9339		637-9
Dupps Co 548 N Cherry St *Web:* www.dupps.com	Germantown	OH	45327	937-855-6555	855-6554	298
Dupre 201 Energy Pkwy *TF:* 800-865-4039 ■ *Web:* www.duprelogistics.com	LaFayette	LA	70508	337-237-8471		311
Dupree Plumbing Company Inc 869 Worley Dr *Web:* www.dupreeplumbing.com	Marietta	GA	30066	770-766-9478		189-10
Duquesne Light Holdings Inc 411 Seventh Ave *TF:* 888-393-7000 ■ *Web:* duquesnelight.com	Pittsburgh	PA	15219	412-393-7000		360-5
Duquesne University 600 Forbes Ave *TF:* 800-456-0590 ■ *Web:* www.duq.edu	Pittsburgh	PA	15282	412-396-6000	396-5779	166
DuQuoin State Fair 655 Executive Dr *Web:* www2.illinois.gov	Du Quoin	IL	62832	618-542-1515	542-1541	642
DuQuoin Tourism Commission Inc 20 N Chestnut St PO Box 1037 *TF:* 800-455-9570 ■ *Web:* www.duquointourism.org	Du Quoin	IL	62832	618-542-8338		206
Dura Automotive Systems Inc 1780 Pond Run **Fax Area Code:* 442 ■ *Web:* www.duraauto.com	Auburn Hills	MI	48326	248-299-7500	211-7544*	60
Dura Coat Products Inc 5361 Via Ricardo *Web:* duracoatproducts.com	Riverside	CA	92509	951-341-6500		481
Dura Foam Inc 6302 59th Ave *Web:* www.trevanna.com	Flushing	NY	11378	718-894-2488	894-2493	601
Dura Medical Equipment Inc 7835 NW 148 St *Web:* www.bayshoreduramedical.com	Miami Lakes	FL	33016	305-821-1202	821-1297	475
Dura Plastics Products Inc 533 E Third St *Web:* www.duraplastics.com	Beaumont	CA	92223	951-845-3161		596
Dura Supreme Inc 300 Dura Dr *TF:* 800-242-3872 ■ *Web:* www.durasupreme.com	Howard Lake	MN	55349	320-543-3872		115
Dura Wax Co 4101 W Albany St **Fax Area Code:* 815 ■ *TF:* 800-435-5705 ■ *Web:* www.durawax.com	Mchenry	IL	60050	800-435-5705	344-8056*	151
Durabac Inc 22 ch Milton *Web:* www.durabac.net	Granby	QC	J2J0P2	450-378-1723		608
Dura-Bilt Products Inc PO Box 188 *Web:* www.durabilt.com	Wellsburg	NY	14894	570-596-2000		697
Durable Packaging International Inc 750 Northgate Pkwy *Web:* www.durablepackaging.com	Wheeling	IL	60090	847-541-4400	541-8360	295
Durable Products Inc PO Box 826 *TF:* 800-373-3502 ■ *Web:* www.durableproductsinc.com	Crossville	TN	38557	931-484-3502	456-7682	676
Dura-Bond Industries Inc 2658 Puckety Dr *Web:* www.dura-bond.com	Export	PA	15632	724-327-0782	387-2720	480
Duracell 14 Research Dr **Fax Area Code:* 866 ■ *TF:* 800-551-2355 ■ *Web:* www.duracell.in	Bethel	CT	06801	800-551-2355	889-7911*	74
Duraclean International Inc 220 Campus Dr **Fax Area Code:* 847 ■ *TF:* 800-251-7070 ■ *Web:* www.duraclean.com	Arlington Heights	IL	60004	800-251-7070	704-7101*	152
Duracote Corp 350 N Diamond St **Fax Area Code:* 330 ■ *TF:* 800-321-2252 ■ *Web:* www.duracote.com	Ravenna	OH	44266	800-321-2252	296-5102*	745-2
Duraflame Inc PO Box 1230 *Web:* www.duraflame.com	Stockton	CA	95201	209-461-6600		819
Dur-A-Flex Inc 95 Goodwin St *Web:* www.dur-a-flex.com	East Hartford	CT	06108	860-528-9838		683
DuraLine Imaging Inc 578 Upward Rd Ste 11 *TF:* 800-982-3872 ■ *Web:* www.duralineimaging.com	Flat Rock	NC	28731	828-692-1301		628
Duraloy Technologies Inc 120 Bridge St *Web:* duraloytechnologies.com	Scottdale	PA	15683	724-887-5100	887-5224	307
Duramax Marine LLC 17990 Great Lakes Pky **Fax Area Code:* 800 ■ *Web:* www.duramaxmarine.com	Hiram	OH	44234	440-834-5400	497-9283*	698
Dura-Mill Inc 16 Old Stonebreak Rd *TF:* 800-444-6455 ■ *Web:* www.duramill.com	Malta	NY	12020	518-899-2255	899-7869	493
Durand Chevrolet Inc 223 Washington St *TF:* 866-203-0921 ■ *Web:* www.durandchevrolet.com	Hudson	MA	01749	866-203-0921		57
Durand Hedden House & Garden Assn 523 Ridgewood Rd *Web:* www.durandhedden.org	Maplewood	NJ	07040	973-763-7712		50-3
Durango Area Tourism Office 828 Main Ave *TF:* 800-525-8855 ■ *Web:* www.durango.org	Durango	CO	81301	970-247-3500		206
Durango Arts Ctr 802 E Second Ave *Web:* durangoarts.org	Durango	CO	81301	970-259-2606	259-6571	50-2
Durango Herald 1275 Main Ave *TF:* 800-530-8318 ■ *Web:* durangoherald.com	Durango	CO	81301	970-247-3504		532-2
Durango's 2121 Richmond Rd	Lexington	KY	40502	859-268-0723		671
Durant Area Chamber of Commerce 215 N Fourth St *Web:* www.durantchamber.org	Durant	OK	74701	580-924-0848	924-0348	139
Durant's Restaurant 2611 N Central Ave *Web:* www.durantsaz.com	Phoenix	AZ	85004	602-264-5967		671
Dura-Stress Inc 11325 County Rd 44 *TF:* 800-342-9239 ■ *Web:* www.durastress.com	Leesburg	FL	34788	352-787-1422	787-0080	183
DuraTech Industries International Inc PO Box 1940 *TF:* 800-243-4601 ■ *Web:* www.duratechindustries.net	Jamestown	ND	58401	701-252-4601	252-0502	273
Duratrack Inc 950 Morse Ave *Web:* www.duratrack.com	Elk Grove Village	IL	60007	847-806-0202	806-1955	697
Dura-Vent Inc 877 Cotting Ct **Fax Area Code:* 707 ■ *TF:* 800-835-4429 ■ *Web:* www.duravent.com	Vacaville	CA	95688	800-835-4429	446-4740*	697
Duravit USA Inc 2205 Northmont Pkwy Ste 200 *TF:* 888-387-2848 ■ *Web:* www.duravit.us	Duluth	GA	30096	770-931-3575		612
Durawood Products Inc 18 Industrial Way *Web:* www.durawood.biz	Denver	PA	17517	717-336-0220		499
Durbin Richard J (Sen D - IL) 711 Hart Senate Office Bldg *Web:* www.durbin.senate.gov	Washington	DC	20510	202-224-2152	228-0400	342-2
Durcon Co 8464 Ronda Dr *Web:* www.durcon.com	Canton	MI	48187	734-455-4520		420
DURECT Corp 2 Results Way *NASDAQ: DRRX* ■ *Web:* www.durect.com	Cupertino	CA	95014	408-777-1417	777-3577	85
DureX Inc 5 Stahuber Ave *Web:* www.durexinc.com	Union	NJ	07083	908-688-0800		488
Durex Industries Inc 190 Detroit St *TF:* 866-712-5014 ■ *Web:* durexindustries.com	Cary	IL	60013	847-639-5600	639-2199	203
Durgin and Crowell Lumber Company Inc 231 Fisher Corner Rd *Web:* www.durginandcrowell.com	Springfield	NH	03284	603-763-2860	763-4498	683
Durham Academy Inc 3130 Pickett Rd *TF:* 888-904-9149 ■ *Web:* www.da.org	Durham	NC	27705	919-489-9118		685
Durham Christian Homes Hair Styling 200 Glen Hill Dr S *Web:* durhamchristianhomes.salonpages.ca	Whitby	ON	L1N8R4	905-430-1666		77
Durham City Hall 101 City Hall Plz *Web:* www.durhamnc.gov	Durham	NC	27701	919-560-1200	560-4835	337
Durham Co, The 722 Durham Rd *Web:* www.durhamusa.com	Lebanon	MO	65536	417-532-7121		816
Durham Convention & Visitors Bureau 212 W Main St Ste 101 *TF:* 800-446-8604 ■ *Web:* www.discoverdurham.com	Durham	NC	27701	919-687-0288	683-9555	206
Durham Correctional Ctr 3900 Guess Rd *Web:* department-of-corrections.org	Durham	NC	27705	919-477-2314	471-2257	213
Durham County 200 E Main St *Web:* www.dconc.gov	Durham	NC	27701	919-560-0000	560-0020	338
Durham County Library 300 N Roxboro St *Web:* durhamcountylibrary.org	Durham	NC	27701	919-560-0100		434-3
Durham Ellis Pecan Co 308 S Houston **Fax Area Code:* 325 ■ *TF:* 800-732-2629 ■ *Web:* www.durhams.com	Comanche	TX	76442	800-732-2629	356-3974*	296-28
Durham Exchange Club Industries Inc 1717 E Lawson St *Web:* www.deci.org	Durham	NC	27703	919-596-1341		721
Durham Furniture Inc 450 Lambton St W *Web:* durhamfurniture.com	Durham	ON	N0G1R0	519-369-2345	369-6515	319-2
Durham Jones & Pinegar 111 East Broadway Ste 2400 *Web:* www.djplaw.com	Salt Lake City	UT	84111	801-415-3000	415-3500	428
Durham Manufacturing Co 201 Main St *TF:* 800-243-3774 ■ *Web:* www.durhammfg.com	Durham	CT	06422	860-349-3427	349-8235	286
Durham Museum 801 S Tenth St *TF:* 888-444-1867 ■ *Web:* www.durhammuseum.org	Omaha	NE	68108	402-444-5071	444-5397	520
Durham Regional Association of Realtors Inc, The 4236 University Dr *Web:* durhamrealtors.org	Durham	NC	27707	919-403-2117		652
Durham Staffing Inc 6300 Transit Rd *Web:* www.durhamstaffing.com	Depew	NY	14043	716-684-3333	681-7408	721
Durham Symphony Orchestra PO Box 1993 *Web:* www.durhamsymphony.org	Durham	NC	27702	919-491-6576		573-3
Durham Technical Community College 1637 E Lawson St *Web:* www.durhamtech.edu	Durham	NC	27703	919-536-7200	686-3669	162
Durie Tangri LLP 217 Leidesdorff St *Web:* durietangri.com	San Francisco	CA	94111	415-362-6666		466
Durnin & James CPAS 401 E Thomas St *Web:* djcpa.com	Hammond	LA	70401	985-345-6262	345-9987	2
Duro Dyne Corp 81 Spence St *TF:* 800-899-3876 ■ *Web:* www.durodyne.com	Bay Shore	NY	11706	631-249-9000		14
Durocher Auto Sales Inc 4651 Rt 9 *TF:* 877-215-8954 ■ *Web:* www.durocherauto.com	Plattsburgh	NY	12901	518-563-3587		57
Duron Plastics 1792 Glasgow St *Web:* duronplastics.com	Kitchener	ON	N2N0A7	519-884-8011		608
Durra Print Inc 3044 W Tharpe St *Web:* www.durraprintpromotionals.com	Tallahassee	FL	32303	850-222-4768	224-3380	627
Durre Brothers Welding & Machine Shop Inc 405 S Chestnut *Web:* www.durrebros.com	Minonk	IL	61760	309-432-2512	432-2617	757
Durrin Productions Inc 4926 Sedgwick St Nw *Web:* www.durrinproductions.com	Washington	DC	20016	202-237-6700	237-6738	514
Durst Corporation Inc 129 Dermody St *TF:* 800-451-0234 ■ *Web:* www.durstcorp.com	Cranford	NJ	07016	908-653-1100	653-1166	612
Durst Image Technology US LLC 50 Methodist Hill Dr Ste 100 *Web:* durstus.com	Rochester	NY	14623	585-486-0340	486-0350	180
Dury's 1027 Murfreesboro Pk *TF:* 800-824-2379 ■ *Web:* durys.com	Nashville	TN	37217	615-255-3456		119
DUS (Decorator & Upholstery Supply Inc) 501 McNeilly Rd *TF:* 800-242-0219 ■ *Web:* www.decoratorsupplyinc.com	Pittsburgh	PA	15226	412-561-3770	561-1105	238

Name / Address	City	State	ZIP	Phone	Fax	Class
DuSable Museum of African American History 740 E 56th Pl *Web:* www.dusablemuseum.org	Chicago	IL	60637	773-947-0600		520
Dusini Drug Inc 315 E High Ave *Web:* dusini.medicineshoppe.com	New Philadelphia	OH	44663	330-364-5519		237
Dust Free LP 1112 Industrial Dr *TF:* 800-441-1107 ■ *Web:* www.dustfree.com	Royse City	TX	75189	972-635-9564	635-2713	18
Dustrol Inc 1201 E Main *Web:* dustrol.com	Towanda	KS	67144	316-536-2262	536-2789	189-16
Dutailier Group Inc 299 Rue Chaput *TF:* 800-363-9817 ■ *Web:* www.dutailier.com	Sainte-Pie	QC	J0H1W0	450-772-2403	772-5055	319-2
Dutch Gold Honey Inc 2220 Dutch Gold Dr *TF:* 800-846-2753 ■ *Web:* www.dutchgoldhoney.com	Lancaster	PA	17601	717-393-1716	393-8687	296-24
Dutch Group, The PO Box 2323 *Web:* www.thedutchgroup.net	Columbus	MS	39702	662-327-5202		579
Dutch Made Custom Cabinetry 10415 Roth Rd *Web:* www.dutchmade.com	Grabill	IN	46741	260-657-3311	657-5778	115
Dutch Maid Bakery Inc 50 Park St *Web:* www.dutchmaidbakery.com	Dorchester	MA	02122	617-265-5417		297-8
Dutch Quality Stone 18012 Dover Rd *TF:* 877-359-7866 ■ *Web:* www.dutchqualitystone.com	Mount Eaton	OH	44659	330-359-7866		724
Dutch Square Ctr 421 Bush River Rd *Web:* www.dutchsquare.com	Columbia	SC	29210	803-772-3864	750-0036	460
Dutch Valley Supply Company Inc (DVS) 970 Progress Center Ave *Web:* www.dutchvalley.com	Lawrenceville	GA	30043	770-513-0612	513-0716	770
Dutch Wonderland 2249 Lincoln Hwy E *TF:* 866-386-2839 ■ *Web:* www.dutchwonderland.com	Lancaster	PA	17602	717-291-1888		32
Dutchess Beer Distributors Inc 5 Laurel St *Web:* dutchessbeer.com	Poughkeepsie	NY	12601	845-452-0940	452-0958	81-1
Dutchess Community College 53 Pendell Rd *Web:* www.sunydutchess.edu	Poughkeepsie	NY	12601	845-431-8010	431-8605	162
Dutchess County 22 Market St *Web:* www.co.dutchess.ny.us	Poughkeepsie	NY	12601	845-486-2120		338
Dutchess County Genealogical Society (DCGS) PO Box 708 *Web:* www.dcgs-gen.org	Poughkeepsie	NY	12602	845-462-4168		49-19
Dutchess County Regional Chamber of Commerce 1 Civic Center Plz Ste 400 *TF:* 800-842-9710 ■ *Web:* www.dcrcoc.org	Poughkeepsie	NY	12601	845-454-1700	454-1702	139
Dutchland Inc PO Box 549 *Web:* www.dutchlandinc.com	Gap	PA	17527	717-442-8282	442-9330	183
Dutchland Plastics LLC 54 Enterprise Ct *Web:* www.dutchland.com	Oostburg	WI	53070	920-564-3633	564-3337	608
Dutchman Hospitality Group 4985 Walnut St PO Box 158 *Web:* www.dhgroup.com	Walnut Creek	OH	44687	330-893-2926	893-2637	670
Dutchman Tree Farms 9689 W Walker Rd *Web:* www.dutchmantreefarms.com	Manton	MI	49663	231-839-7901		752
Dutchmen Manufacturing Inc 2164 Caragana Ct PO Box 2164 *TF:* 866-425-4369 ■ *Web:* www.dutchmen.com	Goshen	IN	46527	574-537-0600		120
Dutile, Glines & Higgins Inc 146 Londonderry Tpke *Web:* dghcorp.com	Hooksett	NH	03106	603-622-0452	622-0487	201
Dutt & Wagner of Virginia Inc 1142 W Main St *TF:* 800-688-2116 ■ *Web:* duttandwagner.com	Abingdon	VA	24210	276-628-2116	628-4619	297-10
Dutton Family Theatre 3454 W 76 Country Blvd *Web:* www.theduttons.com	Branson	MO	65616	417-332-2772	339-4900	520
Dutton-Lainson Co 451 W Second St *Web:* www.dutton-lainson.com	Hastings	NE	68901	402-462-4141		612
Duty Free Americas Inc 6100 Hollywood Blvd Ste 700 *Web:* www.dutyfreeamericas.com	Hollywood	FL	33024	954-986-7700		241
Duval County 117 W Duval St *Web:* www.coj.net	Jacksonville	FL	32202	904-630-2489	630-2906	338
Duval County School System 1701 Prudential Dr *Web:* dcps.duvalschools.org	Jacksonville	FL	32207	904-390-2000	390-2586	685
Duval Paint and Decorating Inc 2855 St Johns Bluff Rd S *TF:* 800-457-1332 ■ *Web:* www.duvalpaint.com	Jacksonville	FL	32246	904-641-6664	641-6709	802
Duvall & Fall PC 4911 E 56th St *Web:* duvallfall.com	Indianapolis	IN	46220	317-634-9100		41
Duvall Drugs Inc 1616 E Main St *Web:* duvalldrugs.com	Humboldt	TN	38343	731-784-3610	784-9989	237
Duvinage Corp 60 W Oak Ridge Dr *TF:* 800-541-2645 ■ *Web:* www.duvinage.com	Hagerstown	MD	21740	301-733-8255	791-7240	491
DuVoice Corp 608 State St S *TF:* 800-888-1057 ■ *Web:* www.duvoice.com	Kirkland	WA	98033	425-889-9790		225
Duwest Tool & Die Inc 8400 Madison Ave *Web:* duwesttool.com	Cleveland	OH	44102	216-631-1060	631-4160	697
DV Die Cutting Inc 45 Prince St *TF:* 800-276-3364 ■ *Web:* www.dvdiecutting.com	Danvers	MA	01923	978-777-0300		326
dv01 915 Broadway 6th Fl *Web:* dv01.co	New York	NY	10010	646-854-5258		39
DVD Empire 2140 Woodland Rd *TF:* 888-383-1880 ■ *Web:* www.dvdempire.com	Warrendale	PA	15086	888-383-1880		797
DVFlora (DVWF) 520 Mantua Blvd N *TF:* 800-676-1212 ■ *Web:* www.dvflora.com	Sewell	NJ	08080	856-468-7000	464-2772	293
DVI Communications Inc 11 Park Pl Ste 906 *Web:* www.dvicomm.com	New York	NY	10007	212-267-2929		387
DVL Seigenthaler 700 12th Ave S *Web:* dvlseigenthaler.com	Nashville	TN	37203	615-244-1818		636
DVNHA (Death Valley Natural History Assn) PO Box 188 *TF:* 800-478-8564 ■ *Web:* dvnha.org	Death Valley	CA	92328	800-478-8564		637-2
Dvp Technologies LLC 123 Hillcrest Dr *Web:* www.dvptech.com	Southbury	CT	06488	203-262-6005		196
DVS (Dutch Valley Supply Company Inc) 970 Progress Center Ave *Web:* www.dutchvalley.com	Lawrenceville	GA	30043	770-513-0612	513-0716	770
DVWF (DVFlora) 520 Mantua Blvd N *TF:* 800-676-1212 ■ *Web:* www.dvflora.com	Sewell	NJ	08080	856-468-7000	464-2772	293
DW Clark Inc 692 N Bedford St *Web:* www.dwclark.com	East Bridgewater	MA	02333	508-378-4014		492
DW Green Co 8100 S Priest Dr *TF:* 800-253-7146 ■ *Web:* dwgreen.com	Tempe	AZ	85284	480-491-8483		4
DW Nicholson Corp 24747 Clawiter Rd *Web:* www.dwnicholson.com	Hayward	CA	94545	510-887-0900	783-9948	189-1
DWCF (Denver Women's Correctional Facility) 3600 Havana St PO Box 392005 *Web:* www.colorado.gov	Denver	CO	80239	303-371-4804	307-2514	213
Dwellworks LLC 1317 Euclid Ave *Web:* www.dwellworks.com	Cleveland	OH	44115	216-682-4200		393
Dwfritz Automation Inc 12100 SW Tualatin Rd *TF:* 800-763-4161 ■ *Web:* www.dwfritz.com	Wilsonville	OR	97070	503-598-9393		539
DWIA (Derek Witham Insurance Agency Inc) 269 Broadway *Web:* www.withaminsurance.com	Malden	MA	02148	781-322-2886	324-0105	390
Dwight D. Eisenhower Presidential Library & Museum 200 SE 4th St *TF:* 877-746-4453 ■ *Web:* www.eisenhowerlibrary.gov	Abilene	KS	67410	785-263-6700	263-6715	434-2
Dwight D. Eisenhower V A Medical Ctr 4101 S 4th St *TF:* 800-952-8387 ■ *Web:* www.leavenworth.va.gov	Leavenworth	KS	66048	913-682-2000		374-8
Dwight G. Lewis Lumber Company Inc 1895 Pennsylvania Rt 87 *Web:* www.lewislp.com	Hillsgrove	PA	18619	570-924-3507		683
Dwight L. Stewart, Jr. & Assoc 26 E Boyce Ct *Web:* dwightstewart.com	Manning	SC	29102	803-435-2301		653
Dwight Rudd & Company Inc 260 Franklin St Ste 900 *Web:* dwightrudd.com	Boston	MA	02110	617-542-1915	542-8501	390
Dwight's Bistro 1527 Penman Rd *Web:* www.dwightsbistro.com	Jacksonville Beach	FL	32250	904-241-4496		671
Dworken-Hillman-LaMorte & Sterczala 4 Corporate Dr Ste 488 *Web:* www.dhls.com	Shelton	CT	06484	203-929-3535		2
Dworshak State Park 9934 Freeman Creek *TF:* 888-922-6743 ■ *Web:* parksandrecreation.idaho.gov	Lenore	ID	83541	208-476-5994		565
DWS Inc 102 Kimball Ave Ste 2	South Burlington	VT	05403	802-862-6004		225
Dwyer Instruments Inc 102 Indiana Hwy 212 PO Box 373 **Fax Area Code:* 219 ■ *TF:* 800-872-9141 ■ *Web:* www.dwyer-inst.com	Michigan City	IN	46360	800-872-9141	872-9057*	201
Dxm Productions 472 S Shoreline Blvd *Web:* www.dxm.com	Mountain View	CA	94041	650-969-6580		180
DXO Communications Inc 1 Townline Cir *Web:* dxocom.com	Rochester	NY	14623	716-685-4395		5
DXP Enterprises Inc 7272 Pinemont Dr *NASDAQ:* DXPE ■ *TF:* 800-830-3973 ■ *Web:* www.dxpe.com	Houston	TX	77040	713-996-4700	996-4701	385
DXStormcom Inc 824 Winston Churchill Blvd *TF:* 877-397-8676 ■ *Web:* www.dxstorm.com	Oakville	ON	L6J7X2	905-842-8262		224
D&Y (Daniel & Yeager) 6767 Old Madison Pk Ste 690 *TF:* 800-955-1919 ■ *Web:* www.dystaffing.com	Huntsville	AL	35806	800-955-1919		266
Dyadic International Inc 140 Intracoastal Pointe Dr Ste 404 *OTC:* DYAI ■ *Web:* www.dyadic.com	Jupiter	FL	33477	561-743-8333	743-8343	85
DyAnsys Inc 300 N Bayshore Blvd *TF:* 888-950-4321 ■ *Web:* www.dyansys.com	San Mateo	CA	94401	888-950-4321		743
Dyatech 381 Highland Colony Pky *TF:* 866-651-4222 ■ *Web:* dyatech.com	Ridgeland	MS	39157	601-914-0533		390
Dyck Arboretum of the Plains 177 W Hickory St *Web:* dyckarboretum.org	Hesston	KS	67062	620-327-8127		97
Dyckman Farmhouse Museum 4881 Broadway at 204th St *Web:* www.dyckmanfarmhouse.org	New York	NY	10034	212-304-9422		520
Dyco Inc 50 Naus Way *TF:* 800-545-3926 ■ *Web:* www.dyco-inc.com	Bloomsburg	PA	17815	570-752-2757	752-7366	207
Dycom Industries Inc 11770 US Hwy 1 Ste 600 *NYSE:* DY ■ *Web:* www.dycomind.com	Palm Beach Gardens	FL	33408	561-627-7171		189-4
Dycor Technologies Ltd 1851 94 St *TF:* 800-663-9267 ■ *Web:* www.dycor.com	Edmonton	AB	T6N1E6	780-486-0091		668
Dydek Toxicology Consulting 5208 Ave H *Web:* www.tox-expert.com	Austin	TX	78751	512-280-5477		192
Dyer County 115 Market St PO Box 1360 *Web:* www.tn.gov	Dyersburg	TN	38025	731-286-7814		338
Dyer Engineering Consultants Inc 9160 Double Diamond Pkwy Ste A *Web:* dyerengineering.com	Reno	NV	89521	775-852-1440		261
Dyer Industries Inc 2013 Church Hollow Rd *Web:* www.dyerind.com	Bunola	PA	15020	724-258-3400	258-2640	322
Dyer Library/Saco Museum 371 Main St *Web:* www.sacomuseum.org	Saco	ME	04072	207-283-3861	283-0754	434-3
Dyer Quarry Inc Rock Hollow Rd *Web:* www.dyerquarry.com	Birdsboro	PA	19508	610-582-6010	582-2304	191-1
Dyer Riddle Mills & Precourt Inc (DRMP) 941 Lake Baldwin Ln *TF:* 800-375-3767 ■ *Web:* www.drmp.com	Orlando	FL	32814	407-896-0594	896-4836	261
Dyersburg Avionics of Caruthersville 2204 Airport Dr *Web:* www.dyersburgavionics.net	Caruthersville	MO	63830	573-333-4296	333-0674	63

Company / Address	City	State	ZIP	Phone	Fax	Class
Dyersburg Hospital Co 4000 Meridian Blvd *Web:* www.tennova.com	Franklin	TN	37067	731-285-2410		374-3
Dyersburg State Community College 1510 Lake Rd *Web:* www.dscc.edu	Dyersburg	TN	38024	731-286-3200	286-3325	162
Dyersburg/Dyer County Chamber of Commerce 2000 Commerce Ave. *Web:* dyerchamber.com	Dyersburg	TN	38024	731-285-3433	286-4926	139
Dykes Dairyman Supplier Inc 35504 Hwy 16 *Web:* dykesfeed.com	Montpelier	LA	70422	225-777-4346	777-4348	276
Dykes Library University of Kansas Medical Ctr 3901 Rainbow Blvd MS 1050 *Web:* library.kumc.edu	Kansas City	KS	66160	913-588-7166	588-8675	434-1
Dykes Lumber Company Inc 1218 Rte 34 *Web:* www.dykeslumber.com	Aberdeen	NJ	07747	732-290-9960	290-9963	364
Dykstra Agency Inc 4260 Plainfield Ave NE *Web:* dykstraagency.com	Grand Rapids	MI	49525	616-364-9421		390
Dylan Hotel NYC 52 E 41st St *Web:* www.dylanhotelnyc.com	New York	NY	10017	212-338-0500	338-0569	379
Dymax Corp 318 Industrial Ln *TF:* 877-396-2963 ■ *Web:* www.dymax.com	Torrington	CT	06790	860-482-1010	496-0608	3
Dymedix Diagnostics 5985 Rice Creek Pkwy *TF:* 888-212-1100 ■ *Web:* www.dymedix.com	Shoreview	MN	55126	763-789-8280	781-4120	476
Dymun & Co 200 1st Ave 4th Fl *Web:* www.dymun.com	Pittsburgh	PA	15222	412-281-2345		195
Dyn365Pros 2604-b El Camino Real Ste 251 *Web:* dyn365pros.com	Carlsbad	CA	92008	760-585-4250		196
Dyna Flex Ltd PO Box 99 *TF:* 800-489-4020 ■ *Web:* www.dynaflex.com	Saint Ann	MO	63074	314-426-4020		743
Dyna Lync Corp 44 E Beaver Creek Unit 16 *Web:* www.dynalync.ca	Richmond Hill	ON	L4B1G8	416-398-2000		463
Dyna Veyor Inc 10 Hudson St *TF:* 800-326-5009 ■ *Web:* www.dyna-veyor.com	Newark	NJ	07103	973-484-1119	484-7790	207
Dynabrade Inc 8989 Sheridan Dr *TF:* 800-828-7333 ■ *Web:* www.dynabrade.com	Clarence	NY	14031	716-631-0100	631-2073	759
Dynacast Inc 14045 Ballantyne Corporate Pl *Web:* www.dynacast.com	Charlotte	NC	28277	704-927-2790	927-2791	308
Dynaco Inc 7050 N Fresno St Ste 210	Fresno	CA	93720	559-485-8520		670
Dynacor Media 9314-60 Ave. *Web:* dynacormedia.com	Edmonton	AB	T6E0C1	780-448-0093		180
Dynacraft Co 650 Milwaukee Ave N. *Web:* dynacraftnet.com	Algona	WA	98001	253-333-3000	333-3041	370
Dynadot LLC PO Box 345 *Fax Area Code: 415 ■ *TF:* 866-652-2039 ■ *Web:* www.dynadot.com	San Mateo	CA	94401	650-585-1961	869-2893*	396
Dyna-Empire Inc 1075 Stewart Ave. *Web:* dyna-empire.com	Garden City	NY	11530	516-222-2700	222-1896	21
Dynaflair Corp 8147 Eagle Palm Dr. *TF:* 800-624-3667 ■ *Web:* www.dynaflair.com	Tampa	FL	33605	800-624-3667		234
Dynaflex Products 6466 Gayhart St *Web:* www.dynaflexproducts.com	Commerce	CA	90040	323-724-1555		567
Dynaflow Inc 10621-J Iron Bridge Rd *Fax Area Code: 301 ■ *Web:* www.dynaflow-inc.com	Jessup	MD	20794	207-604-3688	604-3689*	419
Dynagraphics Corp 4080 Norex Dr. *TF:* 800-959-0108 ■ *Web:* www.dyna-graphics.com	Chaska	MN	55318	800-959-0108		203
Dynalco 3690 NW 53rd St *TF:* 800-368-6666 ■ *Web:* www.dynalco.com	Fort Lauderdale	FL	33309	954-739-4300	484-3376	201
Dynalec Corp 87 W Main St. *Web:* www.dynalec.com	Sodus	NY	14551	315-483-6923	483-6656	529
Dynalectric Corp 4462 Corporate Center Dr. *Fax Area Code: 866 ■ *Web:* kdc-systems.com	Los Alamitos	CA	90720	714-828-7000	890-7794*	189-4
Dynalene Inc 5250 W Coplay Rd. *Fax Area Code: 610 ■ *TF:* 877-244-5525 ■ *Web:* www.dynalene.com	Whitehall	PA	18052	877-244-5525	262-7437*	194
DynaLifeDX Diagnostic Laboratory Services 10150 - 102 St Ste 200 *TF:* 800-661-9876 ■ *Web:* www.dynalife.ca	Edmonton	AB	T5J5E2	780-451-3702		415
Dynalloy Inc 14762 Bentley Cir *Web:* www.dynalloy.com	Tustin	CA	92780	714-436-1206	436-0511	253
Dynamation Research Inc 2301 Pontius Ave *TF:* 800-726-7997 ■ *Web:* www.dynamationresearch.com	Los Angeles	CA	90064	310-477-1224		350
Dynamet Inc 195 Museum Rd *TF:* 800-237-9655 ■ *Web:* www.carpentertechnology.com	Washington	PA	15301	724-229-4199	229-4195	485
DynaMetric Inc 717 S Myrtle Ave *TF:* 800-525-6925 ■ *Web:* www.dynametric.com	Monrovia	CA	91016	626-358-2559	359-5701	735
Dynamic Air Engineering Inc 620 E Dyer Rd. *Web:* www.dynamic-air.com	Santa Ana	CA	92705	714-540-1000	545-9145	18
Dynamic Air Inc 1125 Willow Lake Blvd *Web:* www.dynamicair.com	Saint Paul	MN	55110	651-484-2900	484-7015	207
Dynamic Automation 4525 Runway St. *Web:* dynamicautomation.com	Simi Valley	CA	93063	805-584-8476	584-8479	358
Dynamic Bracing Inc 511 S Pine St Ste A *Web:* dynamicbracing.com	Spokane	WA	99202	509-325-9144		363
Dynamic Business Solutions Inc 30100 Telegraph Rd Ste 322 *Web:* www.qualitech.net	Bingham Farms	MI	48025	248-646-0093		179
Dynamic Civil Solutions Inc 2210 Second Ave N *Web:* www.dcseng.com	Birmingham	AL	35203	205-358-7256		261
Dynamic Computer Corp 23400 Industrial Pk Ct *TF:* 866-257-2111 ■ *Web:* www.dccit.com	Farmington Hills	MI	48335	248-473-2200		174
Dynamic Computer Resources Inc 13089 Peyton Dr Ste C403 *Web:* www.cadcrew.com	Chino Hills	CA	91709	909-540-0465	344-8233	180
Dynamic Concepts Inc (DCI) 1730 17th St NE *Web:* www.dcihq.com	Washington	DC	20002	202-944-8787	526-7233	735
Dynamic Conveyor Corp 5980 Grand Haven Rd. *Web:* www.dynamicconveyor.com	Muskegon	MI	49441	231-798-9583		207
Dynamic Corporate Solutions Inc 1845 Town Center Blvd Ste 525 *Web:* www.dynamiccorp.com	Fleming Island	FL	32003	904-278-5383		463
Dynamic Design & Manufacturing Inc 6321 Monarch Park Pl *TF:* 877-815-8871 ■ *Web:* www.dycoinc.com	Niwot	CO	80503	303-652-0431	652-0413	488
Dynamic Design Solutions Inc 3565 Centre Cir *Web:* www.dynamicdesignsolutionsinc.com	Fort Mill	SC	29715	803-548-3609		256
Dynamic Designs Inc 2100 E Stan Schlueter Loop Ste F *Web:* www.dynamicdesignsinc.com	Killeen	TX	76542	254-628-8272		687
Dynamic Devices 8 Lewis Cir *Web:* dynamicdevices.com	Wilmington	DE	19804	302-994-2401	994-2409	463
Dynamic Digital Adv 1265 Industrial Blvd *Web:* www.zeroonezero.com	Southampton	PA	18966	215-355-6442		4
Dynamic Edge Inc 2245 S State St Ste 1200 *Web:* www.dynedge.com	Ann Arbor	MI	48104	734-975-0460	975-0461	180
Dynamic Engineering 221 Cessna St. *Web:* dynamicengineering.net	Watertown	SD	57201	605-886-5545		454
Dynamic Engineers Inc 2550 Gray Falls Dr Ste128 *Fax Area Code: 832 ■ *Web:* www.dynamiceng.com	Houston	TX	77077	281-870-8822	415-2776*	246
Dynamic Homes LLC 525 Roosevelt Ave *TF:* 800-492-4833 ■ *Web:* www.dynamichomes.com	Detroit Lakes	MN	56501	218-847-2611	847-2617	106
Dynamic It Solutions Inc 804 N Meadowbrook Dr Ste 136 *Web:* dynamicitsolutions.net	Olathe	KS	66062	913-488-7913		177
Dynamic Links International LLC 8286 Daleview Rd Ste 200 *Web:* www.dynamiclinksint.com	Cincinnati	OH	45247	513-385-2600		463
Dynamic Manufacturing Inc 1930 N Mannheim Rd. *Web:* www.dynamicmanufacturinginc.com	Melrose Park	IL	60160	708-343-8753	343-8768	386
Dynamic Medical Systems Inc 2811 E Ana St *TF:* 800-225-9080 ■ *Web:* www.godynamic.com	Compton	CA	90221	310-928-0251		475
Dynamic Motion Control Inc (DMC) 2222 N Elston Ave Ste 200 *Web:* www.dmcinfo.com	Chicago	IL	60614	312-255-8757		180
Dynamic Net Inc (DNI) 13 Cowpath *TF:* 888-887-6727 ■ *Web:* www.dynamicnet.net	Denver	PA	17517	888-887-6727		225
Dynamic Network Factory Inc 21353 Cabot Blvd. *TF:* 800-947-4742 ■ *Web:* www.dnfstorage.com	Hayward	CA	94545	510-265-1122		173-8
Dynamic Plastics Inc 29831 Commerce Blvd *Web:* www.dynamicplastics.com	Chesterfield	MI	48051	586-749-6100		608
Dynamic Research Inc 355 Van Ness Ave Ste 200 *Web:* www.dynres.com	Torrance	CA	90501	310-212-5211		261
Dynamic Robotic Solutions 1255 Harmon Rd *Web:* www.drsrobotics.com	Auburn Hills	MI	48326	248-829-2800	829-2750	386
Dynamic Sealing Technologies Inc 13829 Jay St NW *Web:* www.dsti.com	Andover	MN	55304	763-786-3758		454
Dynamic Security Concepts Inc 1037 Morningside Dr Ste 10 6090 Danenhauer Ln *Web:* www.dscinc.net	Mays Landing	NJ	08330	609-625-3942	625-7215	256
Dynamic Security Inc 1102 Woodward Ave. *Web:* www.dynamic.cc	Muscle Shoals	AL	35661	256-383-5798		693
Dynamic Source Manufacturing Inc 2765 - 48th Ave NE Unit 117 *Web:* dynamicsourcemfg.com	Calgary	AB	T3J5M9	403-516-1888		253
Dynamic Strategies Inc 259 Prospect Plains Rd Building K Ste 301 *TF:* 888-777-9733 ■ *Web:* www.ds-inc.com	Cranbury	NJ	08512	609-655-1707	655-1708	177
DYNAMIC SYSTEMS Inc 124 Maryland St. *Web:* www.dynamicsystemsinc.com	El Segundo	CA	90245	310-337-4400		174
Dynamic Systems Inc (DSI) 104 Morrow Br *TF:* 844-270-6478 ■ *Web:* www.sunmatecushions.com	Leicester	NC	28748	828-683-3523	683-3511	471
Dynamic Technology Systems Inc (DTS) 5285 Shawnee Rd 5285 Shawnee Rd Ste 500 *Web:* www.dts-inc.com	Alexandria	VA	22312	703-379-4800	379-4901	177
Dynamic Test Solutions Inc (DTS) 1762 Technology Dr Ste 201 *Web:* www.dynamic-test.com	San Jose	CA	95110	408-264-8880		256
Dynamic Tool & Design Inc W133 N5180 Campbell Dr *Web:* www.dyntool.com	Menomonee Falls	WI	53051	262-783-6340	783-6344	604
Dynamic Tool Company Inc 1421 Vanderbilt Dr *Web:* dynamictool.com	El Paso	TX	79935	915-598-2330	598-2486	697
DynamiCard Inc 215 S Hickory St Ste 220 *TF:* 800-928-7670 ■ *Web:* dynamicard.com	Escondido	CA	92025	800-928-7670	811-9248	5
Dynamics Edge Inc 2635 N First St Ste 148 *TF:* 800-453-5961 ■ *Web:* www.dynamicsedge.com	San Jose	CA	95134	800-453-5961		196
Dynamics Online 23811 Chagrin Blvd Ste 315 *Web:* www.dynamicsus.com	Beachwood	OH	44122	216-292-4410	292-4420	7
Dynamis Inc 3707 Henson Rd *Web:* www.dynamis-inc.com	Knoxville	TN	37921	865-588-5422	588-6857	196

Company / Address	City	State	ZIP	Phone	Fax	Class
Dynamix Engineering Ltd 855 Grandview Ave *Web:* www.veregy.com	Columbus	OH	43215	614-443-1178		261
Dynamo Technologies LLC 1775 Tysons Blvd 5th Fl **Fax Area Code:* 571 ■ *TF:* 844-730-3103 ■ *Web:* dynamotechnologies.com	McLean	VA	22102	844-730-3103	297-2227*	177
Dynamp LLC 3735 Gantz Rd *Web:* www.dynamp.com	Grove City	OH	43123	614-871-6900	871-6910	248
Dynan & Associates PS 2102 N Pearl St Bldg D Ste 400 *Web:* dynanassociates.com	Tacoma	WA	98406	253-752-1600		41
Dynanet Corp 8182 Lark Brown Rd Ste 300 *Web:* dynanetcorp.com	Elkridge	MD	21075	443-661-1403	661-1408	395
Dyna-Pak Corp 112 Helton Dr *TF:* 800-759-3962 ■ *Web:* www.dynapak.com	Lawrenceburg	TN	38464	931-762-4016	766-1814	557
Dynapar 1675 Delany Rd *TF:* 800-873-8731 ■ *Web:* www.dynapar.com	Gurnee	IL	60031	800-873-8731		801
Dynapoint Technologies Inc 475 Progress Rd *Web:* www.dynapointtech.com	Dayton	OH	45449	937-859-5193	859-4498	454
Dynapower Corp 85 Meadowland Dr *TF:* 800-332-1111 ■ *Web:* www.dynapower.com	South Burlington	VT	05403	802-860-7200		767
Dynaquip Controls 10 Harris Industrial Pk *TF:* 800-545-3636 ■ *Web:* www.dynaquip.com	Saint Clair	MO	63077	636-629-3700	629-5528	790
Dynarex Corp 10 Glenshaw St *TF:* 888-335-7500 ■ *Web:* www.dynarex.com	Orangeburg	NY	10962	845-365-8201		477
Dynaric Inc 5740 Bayside Rd *TF:* 800-526-0827 ■ *Web:* www.dynaric.com	Virginia Beach	VA	23455	800-526-0827		547
Dynasign Corp 44040 Fremont Blvd *Web:* www.dynasign.net	Fremont	CA	94538	510-405-5988	405-5999	701
Dynasil Corp 313 Washington St Ste 403 *Web:* www.dynasil.com	Newton	MA	02458	617-668-6855		332
Dynasplint Systems Inc 770 Ritchie Hwy Ste W21 **Fax Area Code:* 800 ■ *TF:* 800-638-6771 ■ *Web:* www.dynasplint.com	Severna Park	MD	21146	410-544-9530	380-3784*	264-4
Dynastar 530 Highland Dr *Web:* www.dynastar.com	Park City	UT	84098	435-252-3300	252-3301	710
Dynasty Chinese & Vietnamese Cuisine 5326 W 26th St *Web:* www.dynastychinesesf.com	Sioux Falls	SD	57106	605-361-7788		671
Dynasty Gallery 2765 16th St *TF:* 800-227-3344 ■ *Web:* www.dynastygallery.com	San Francisco	CA	94103	415-864-5084		787
Dynasty Schools 2373 S Hacienda Blvd *TF:* 800-888-8827 ■ *Web:* www.dynastyschool.com	Hacienda Heights	CA	91745	626-855-0455	608-2636	685
Dynasty Spas Inc 101 Dynasty Way *Web:* www.dynastyspas.com	Athens	TN	37303	423-745-1972		610
Dynasty Suites 1235 W Colton Ave *TF:* 800-874-8958 ■ *Web:* dynastysuites.com	Redlands	CA	92374	909-793-6648	792-5219	379
Dynatect Manufacturing Inc 2300 S Calhoun Rd *TF:* 800-298-2066 ■ *Web:* www.gortite.com	New Berlin	WI	53151	262-786-1500	786-3280	493
Dynatem Inc 23263 Madero Ste C *TF:* 800-543-3830 ■ *Web:* www.dynatem.com	Mission Viejo	CA	92691	949-855-3235	770-3481	625
DynaTen Corp 4375 Diplomacy Rd *Web:* dynaten.com	Fort Worth	TX	76155	817-616-2200	616-2201	261
Dynatronics Corp 7030 Pk Centre Dr *NASDAQ: DYNT* ■ *TF:* 800-874-6251 ■ *Web:* www.dynatronics.com	Salt Lake City	UT	84121	800-874-6251	221-1919	250
Dynavax Technologies Corp 2929 Seventh St Ste 100 *NASDAQ: DVAX* ■ *TF:* 877-848-5100 ■ *Web:* www.dynavax.com	Berkeley	CA	94710	510-848-5100	848-1327	582
Dynavox Electronics Inc 248 Puente Ave *Web:* www.dynavox.com	City of Industry	CA	91746	626-336-0516	336-3748	425
Dynaxys LLC 11911 Tech Rd *Web:* www.dynaccsys.com	Silver Spring	MD	20904	301-622-0900	622-5608	177
Dyne Systems Inc W209 N 17391 Industrial Dr *TF:* 800-657-0726 ■ *Web:* www.dynesystems.com	Jackson	WI	53037	800-657-0726		472
Dynetics 1002 Explorer Blvd *TF:* 800-964-4291 ■ *Web:* www.dynetics.com	Huntsville	AL	35806	256-964-4000		535
Dynetics Engineering Corp 515 Bond St *TF:* 800-888-8110 ■ *Web:* www.dyneticsengineering.com	Lincolnshire	IL	60069	847-541-7300	541-7488	111
Dynex Capital Inc 4991 Lake Brook Dr Ste 100 *NYSE: DX* ■ *Web:* www.dynexcapital.com	Glen Allen	VA	23060	804-217-5800		654
Dynex Rivett Inc 770 Capitol Dr *Web:* www.dynexhydraulics.com	Pewaukee	WI	53072	262-691-0300	691-0312	789
Dynisco LLC 38 Forge Pkwy *TF:* 800-396-4726 ■ *Web:* www.dynisco.com	Franklin	MA	02038	508-541-9400	541-6206	472
Dyno Nobel Inc 2795 E Cottonwood Pkwy Ste 500 *TF:* 800-473-2675 ■ *Web:* www.dynonobel.com	Salt Lake City	UT	84121	801-364-4800	328-6452	268
Dynolab 15927 20th Ave SW *Web:* www.dynolab.com	Burien	WA	98166	206-243-8877	246-7237	472
Dynomax Inc 1535 Abbott Dr *Web:* www.dynomaxinc.com	Wheeling	IL	60090	847-680-8833		454
DynTek Inc 4440 Von Karman Ste 200 *Web:* www.dyntek.com	Newport Beach	CA	92660	949-271-6700		178-10
Dyonyx LP 1235 N Loop W *TF:* 855-749-6758 ■ *Web:* dyopath.com	Houston	TX	77008	713-485-7000		180
Dyplast Products LLC 12501 NW 38th Ave *TF:* 800-433-5551 ■ *Web:* www.dyplastproducts.com	Opa Locka	FL	33054	800-433-5551		601
Dyslexia Discovery PO Box 170036 *Web:* www.dyslexiadiscovery.com	San Francisco	CA	94117	415-552-6330		637-2
Dyson-Kissner-Moran Corp (DKM) 2515 South Rd 5th Fl **Fax Area Code:* 845 ■ *Web:* www.dkmcorp.com	Poughkeepsie	NY	12601	212-661-4600	463-3890*	185
Dystel, Goderich & Bourret LLC 1 Union Sq W Ste 904 *Web:* www.dystel.com	New York	NY	10003	212-627-9100	627-9313	444
Dystonia Medical Research Foundation 1 E Wacker Dr Ste 2810 *TF:* 800-377-3978 ■ *Web:* www.dystonia-foundation.org	Chicago	IL	60601	312-755-0198	803-0138	48-17
Dytech Group 7201 Sandscove Ct Ste 4 *Web:* dytech.com	Winter Park	FL	32792	407-678-8300		180
Dywidag Systems Intl 320 Marmon Dr *TF:* 800-457-7633 ■ *Web:* www.dywidag-systems.com	Bolingbrook	IL	60440	630-739-1100	739-5517	189-3
Dzialo, Pickett & Allen PC 148 Broad St *Web:* dpapc.com	Middletown	CT	06457	860-316-2741	316-2747	41

E

Company / Address	City	State	ZIP	Phone	Fax	Class
E & A Consulting Group Inc 10909 Mill Valley Rd Ste 100 *Web:* eacg.com	Omaha	NE	68154	402-895-4700		256
E & A Industries Inc 101 W Ohio St Ste 1350 *Web:* ea-companies.com	Indianapolis	IN	46204	317-684-3150	681-5068	360-3
E & B Natural Resources Management Corp 1600 Norris Rd *Web:* www.ebresources.com	Bakersfield	CA	93308	661-679-1700		536
E & C Engineers & Consultants Inc 1010 Lamar Ste 650 *Web:* eceng.com	Houston	TX	77002	713-580-8800		261
E & E It Consulting Services Inc 5026 Arthur Ave *Web:* www.ene-it-consulting.com	Mechanicsburg	PA	17050	717-975-1664	975-1665	100
E & H Steel Corp 3635 Alabama 134 *Web:* www.ehsteel.com	Midland City	AL	36350	334-983-5636	983-6173	723
E & K Companies Inc 343 Carol Ln *Web:* e-kco.com	Elmhurst	IL	60126	630-530-9001		189-9
E & M Bindery Inc 11 Peekay Dr *Web:* www.embindery.com	Clifton	NJ	07014	973-777-9300		626
E & O Tool & Plastics Inc 19178 Industrial Blvd NW *Web:* www.avidims.com	Elk River	MN	55330	763-441-6100	441-6452	608
E & R Machine Inc 211 Grand St *Web:* www.er-machine.com	Lockport	NY	14094	716-434-6639	434-9857	454
E & R Sales 4800 Market Square Ln **Fax Area Code:* 804 ■ *TF:* 800-234-7474 ■ *Web:* www.ersales.com	Midlothian	VA	23112	800-234-7474	744-5125*	44
E & S International Enterprises Inc 7801 Hayvenhurst Ave *Web:* www.esintl.com	Van Nuys	CA	91406	818-887-0700		38
E & S Ring Management Corp 13900 Marquesas Wy *Web:* www.esring.com	Marina	CA	90292	310-337-5400		186
E & V Energy 5700 State Rte 34 *TF:* 800-455-6522 ■ *Web:* www.eandvenergy.com	Auburn	NY	13021	315-253-6522		581
E & V Restaurant 320 Chamberlain Ave *Web:* www.evrestaurant.com	Paterson	NJ	07502	973-942-4664		671
E Boineau & Co 128 Beaufain St *TF:* 800-579-2628 ■ *Web:* www.eboineauandco.com	Charleston	SC	29401	843-723-1462		636
E Boyd & Associates Inc PO Box 99189 *Web:* www.eboyd.com	Raleigh	NC	27624	919-846-8000	846-8197	360-3
E C Wise Inc 101 Glacier Pt Ste D *Web:* www.ecwise.com	San Rafael	CA	94901	415-578-9732		396
E Caligari & Son Inc 1333 Ingleside Rd *Web:* www.ecaligariandson.com	Norfolk	VA	23502	757-853-4511		189-8
E Commerce Partners 59 Franklin St *TF:* 866-431-6669 ■ *Web:* www.ecommercepartners.net	New York	NY	10013	212-334-3390		225
E Dillon & Co 2522 Swords Creek Rd PO Box 160 *TF:* 800-234-8970 ■ *Web:* www.edillon.com	Swords Creek	VA	24649	276-873-6816	873-4208	183
E E Wine Inc 9108 Centreville Rd *Web:* www.eewine.com	Manassas	VA	20110	703-368-6568		316
E G Ayers Distributing Inc 5819 S Broadway St *Web:* www.ayersdistributing.com	Eureka	CA	95503	707-445-2077	445-0283	297-8
E G Electro-graph Inc 1491 Poinsettia Ave Ste 138 *Web:* www.plansee.com	Vista	CA	92081	760-438-9090	438-3923	696
E Gluck Corp 60-15 Little Neck Pkwy *TF:* 800-840-2933 ■ *Web:* www.armitron.com	Little Neck	NY	11362	718-784-0700		153
E H Lynn Industries Inc 524 Anderson Dr *TF:* 800-633-2948 ■ *Web:* www.ehlynn.com	Romeoville	IL	60446	815-328-8800		790
E Hofmann Plastics Inc 51 Centennial Rd *TF:* 877-707-7245 ■ *Web:* www.hofmannplastics.com	Orangeville	ON	L9W3R1	519-943-5050	938-5349	603
E I Team Inc 2060 Sheridan Dr *Web:* www.eiteam.com	Buffalo	NY	14223	716-876-4669		256
E Ink Holdings Inc 733 Concord Ave *Web:* www.eink.com	Cambridge	MA	02138	617-499-6000		225
E J Davis Co, The 10 Dodge Ave *Web:* ejdavisinsulation.com	North Haven	CT	06473	203-239-5391	234-7724	389
E J Harrison & Sons PO Box 4009 *TF:* 800-418-7274 ■ *Web:* www.ejharrison.com	Ventura	CA	93007	805-647-1414	644-7751	804
E L Farmer & Co 3800 E 42nd St Ste 417 *Web:* www.elfarmer.com	Odessa	TX	79762	432-366-2010		539
E L Hamm Associates Inc 4801 Columbus St Ste 400 *Web:* www.elhamm.com	Virginia Beach	VA	23462	757-497-5000	497-5707	803-1
E M J D Corp 4590 S Windermere St *Web:* www.emjd.com	Englewood	CO	80110	303-761-5236		483
E Mitchell Inc 1580 Indiana St	San Francisco	CA	94107	415-826-2929		189-10

Company	City	State	ZIP	Phone	Fax	Class
E O W S Midland Co 1 Landmark Sq Ste 1100 *Web:* www.primeenergy.com	Stamford	CT	06901	203-358-5700	358-5786	540
E P Radiological Services Inc 8040 Remmet Ave *Web:* epradinc.com	Canoga Park	CA	91304	818-313-9729	313-8630	177
E P S 8845 Basil Western Rd *Web:* www.epsohio.com	Canal Winchester	OH	43110	614-834-9126		693
E R O Resources Corp 1842 Clarkson St *Web:* www.eroresources.com	Denver	CO	80218	303-830-1188		196
E S Investments LLC 14055 US Hwy 19 N *Web:* www.sunmicrostamping.com	Clearwater	FL	33764	727-536-8822		488
E S Robbins Corp 2802 Avalon Ave *TF:* 866-934-6018 ■ *Web:* www.esrobbins.com	Muscle Shoals	AL	35661	256-248-2400	248-2410	600
E Sam Jones Distributor Inc 4898 S Atlanta Rd *TF:* 800-624-9849 ■ *Web:* www.esamjones.com	Atlanta	GA	30339	404-351-3250	351-4140	246
E Sciences Inc 34 E Pine St *Web:* esciencesinc.com	Orlando	FL	32801	407-481-9006	481-9627	256
E T & F Fastening Systems Inc 29019 Solon Rd **Fax Area Code: 440* ■ *TF:* 800-248-2376 ■ *Web:* www.etf-fastening.com	Solon	OH	44139	800-248-2376	248-0423*	278
E T Marketing Solutions Ltd (ETMS) 207-3833 Henning Dr *Web:* etmarketingsolutions.com	Burnaby	BC	V5C6N5	604-801-6168	801-6165	7
E Tech Systems Inc 1900 E Golf Rd Ste 950 *Web:* www.etechsys.com	Schaumburg	IL	60173	847-352-4770		41
E W Scripps Co, The 312 Walnut St Ste 2800 *Web:* www.scripps.com	Cincinnati	OH	45202	513-977-3000		530
E Walker Consulting Inc 4902 Crosspoint Dr *Web:* www.ewalkerconsulting.com	Doylestown	PA	18901	215-806-3537		809
E! Entertainment Television 5750 Wilshire Blvd *Web:* www.eonline.com	Los Angeles	CA	90036	323-954-2400		740
E*Trade Bank 671 N Glebe Rd *TF:* 877-800-1208 ■ *Web:* www.etrade.com	Arlington	VA	22203	877-800-1208		70
E*Trade Financial Corp 1271 Avenue of the Americas 14th Fl *NASDAQ: ETFC* ■ *TF:* 800-387-2331 ■ *Web:* www.about.etrade.com	New York	NY	10020	866-789-0785		690
E+P (Eadie + Payne LLP) 3880 Lemon St Ste 300 *Web:* eadiepaynellp.com	Riverside	CA	92501	951-241-7800		2
E. Cohen and Company CPAS 1 Research Ct Ste 101 *Web:* ecohen.com	Rockville	MD	20850	301-917-6200	917-6220	2
E. D. Bullard Co 1898 Safety Way *TF:* 800-227-0423 ■ *Web:* apac.bullard.com	Cynthiana	KY	41031	859-234-6611	234-4352	576
E. F. Brannon Chattanooga Furniture Store 5245 Hwy 153 *Web:* chattanoogafurnitureshop.com	Hixson	TN	37343	423-877-1299		320
E. G. Mahler and Associates Inc (EGMA) 1202 Greystone Ln Ste 1A **Fax Area Code: 740* ■ *Web:* www.egma.com	Newark	DE	19711	302-250-2444	931-1554*	194
E. H. Perkins Construction Inc 560 Main St *Web:* www.ehperkins.com	Hudson	MA	01749	508-358-6161		191-1
E. L. Pruitt Co 3090 Colt Rd *Web:* www.elpruitt.com	Springfield	IL	62707	217-789-0966	789-2694	189-10
E. L. Robinson Engineering Co 5088 Washington St W *TF:* 800-856-6485 ■ *Web:* www.elrobinsonengineering.com	Charleston	WV	25313	304-776-7473		261
E. S. Kluft & Co 11096 Jersey Blvd *Web:* www.kluftmattress.com	Rancho Cucamonga	CA	91730	909-373-4211		321
E. V. M. Inc 1009 Madison St *Web:* www.evminc.com	Two Rivers	WI	54241	920-793-4467	793-1406	350
E.A. Morse & Company Inc 11-25 Harding St PO Box 728 *Web:* eamorse.com	Middletown	NY	10940	845-346-4700		366
E.C. Dicken Inc 1025 N Stemmons Fwy Ste 260 *Web:* www.ecdicken.com	Dallas	TX	75207	214-742-4801	651-7369	320
E.F. Heagen & Assoc 30448 Rancho Viejo Rd Ste 170 *TF:* 800-943-2436 ■ *Web:* efheagen.com	San Juan Capistrano	CA	92675	949-487-6711	487-6883	690
E.H. Wright Co 12125 Herbert Wayne Ct Ste 190 *TF:* 800-467-9801 ■ *Web:* www.ehwrightco.com	Huntersville	NC	28078	704-875-1001	875-8080	385
E.K. Machine Company Inc 671 S Main St *Web:* www.ekmachine.com	Fall River	WI	53932	920-484-3700	484-3709	480
E.N.R. General Machining Co 3725 W 49th St *Web:* www.enrmachine.com	Chicago	IL	60632	773-523-2944	523-4483	454
E.P. Ferris & Associates Inc 880 King Ave *Web:* epferris.com	Columbus	OH	43212	614-299-2999		261
E.P. Graphics Inc 169 S Jefferson St *TF:* 877-589-2145 ■ *Web:* www.epgraphics.com	Berne	IN	46711	260-589-2145	589-2810	627
E.R. Stuebner Construction Inc 227 Blair Ave *Web:* www.ersconstruction.com	Reading	PA	19601	610-376-6625		186
E.S. Boulos Co 45 Bradley Dr *Web:* www.esboulos.com	Westbrook	ME	04092	207-464-3706		189-4
E/The Environmental Magazine 28 Knight St PO Box 5098 *Web:* www.emagazine.com	Norwalk	CT	06851	203-854-5559	866-0602	457-19
E1 Asset Management Inc 185 Hudson St 25th Fl *TF:* 888-391-2670 ■ *Web:* www.e1am.com	Jersey City	NJ	07311	212-425-2670		690
E2 Consulting Engineers Inc 450 E 17th Ave Ste 200 *TF:* 866-550-5430 ■ *Web:* e2.com	Denver	CO	80203	303-232-9000		261
E3 Communications Inc 551 Franklin St *Web:* www.e3communications.com	Buffalo	NY	14202	716-854-8182	816-0900	445
E3 Consulting Inc 3333 S Bannock St Ste 500 *TF:* 877-788-6676 ■ *Web:* e3co.com	Englewood	CO	80110	303-762-7060	788-9725	261
E3 Partners Ministry 16787 Bernardo Center Dr Ste 7 *Web:* e3partners.org	San Diego	CA	92128	858-485-9904		48-20
e4Sciences 27 Glen Rd N Entrance *Web:* www.e4sciences.com	Sandy Hook	CT	06482	203-270-8100	364-0480	192
EA (Electronic Arts Inc) 209 Redwood Shores Pkwy *NASDAQ: EA* ■ *Web:* www.ea.com	Redwood City	CA	94065	650-628-1500		178-6
EA Consulting Inc 1024 Iron Point Rd *Web:* www.ea-inc.com	Folsom	CA	95630	916-357-6588	200-0368	180
EA Group 7118 Industrial Park Blvd *TF:* 800-875-3514 ■ *Web:* eagroupohio.com	Mentor	OH	44060	440-951-3514	951-3774	192
EA Patten Co 303 Wetherell St *Web:* www.camaerospace.com	Manchester	CT	06040	860-649-2851		790
EAA AirVenture Museum 3000 Poberezny Rd *TF:* 888-322-3229 ■ *Web:* www.eaa.org	Oshkosh	WI	54902	920-426-4800	426-6560	520
Eaa Environmental Abatement Associates Inc 239 Schuyler Ave Ste 125B *Web:* environmental-abatement.com	Kingston	PA	18704	570-283-0500	283-0577	192
eAcceleration Corp 1050 NE Hostmark St Ste 100-B *TF:* 800-803-4588 ■ *Web:* www.eacceleration.com	Poulsbo	WA	98370	360-779-6301	598-2450	178-7
Eaccess Solutions Inc 407 N Quentin Rd *Web:* eaccess.com	Palatine	IL	60067	847-991-7190		366
EAD Motors Inc 1 Progress Dr *Web:* www.electrocraft.com	Dover	NH	03820	603-742-3330		518
Eadie + Payne LLP (E+P) 3880 Lemon St Ste 300 *Web:* eadiepaynellp.com	Riverside	CA	92501	951-241-7800		2
EADS Group 1126 Eigth Ave *TF:* 800-626-0904 ■ *Web:* eadsgroup.com	Altoona	PA	16602	814-944-5035	944-4862	261
Eagan Convention & Visitors Bureau 1501 Central Pkwy *TF:* 866-324-2620 ■ *Web:* eaganmn.com	Eagan	MN	55121	651-675-5546		206
Eagan Insurance Agency Inc 2629 N Cswy Blvd *TF:* 888-882-9600 ■ *Web:* www.eaganins.com	Metairie	LA	70002	504-836-9600	836-9621	390
Eagle 96.9 5345 Madison Ave *Web:* eagle969.radio.com	Sacramento	CA	95841	916-766-9696		645-137
Eagle 98.1 929-B Government St *Web:* eagle981.com	Baton Rouge	LA	70802	225-388-9898		645-17
Eagle Applied Sciences LLC 1826 N Loop 1604 W Ste 350 *TF:* 877-726-4701 ■ *Web:* www.eagle-app-sci.com	San Antonio	TX	78248	210-477-9242	581-8609	177
Eagle Asset Management 880 Carillon Pkwy *TF:* 800-237-3101 ■ *Web:* www.raymondjames.com	Saint Petersburg	FL	33716	800-235-3898		401
Eagle Aviation Columbia Metropolitan Airport 2861 Aviation Way *TF:* 800-849-3245 ■ *Web:* www.eagle-aviation.com	West Columbia	SC	29170	803-822-5555	822-5529	63
Eagle Bancorp Inc 7815 Woodmont Ave *NASDAQ: EGBN* ■ *TF:* 800-364-8313 ■ *Web:* www.eaglebankcorp.com	Bethesda	MD	20814	301-986-1800	986-8529	360-2
Eagle Bank 2 S Franklin St *Web:* eaglebankmn.com	Glenwood	MN	56334	320-634-4545		70
Eagle Bend Manufacturing Inc 1000 Jd Yarnell Industrial Pkwy	Clinton	TN	37716	865-457-3800		247
Eagle Beverage Corp 1043 County Rt 25 *Web:* www.eaglebev.com	Oswego	NY	13126	315-343-5221		297-8
Eagle Brands Inc 3201 NW 72nd Ave *Web:* www.eaglebrands.com	Miami	FL	33122	305-599-2337		443
Eagle Bulk Shipping Inc 300 First Stamford Pl *Web:* www.eagleships.com	Stamford	CT	06902	212-785-2500		313
Eagle Button Company Inc 700 Broadway *Web:* www.eaglebutton.com	Westwood	NJ	07675	201-652-4063		594
Eagle Cleaning Service Inc 525 Belview St *TF:* 877-864-5696 ■ *Web:* www.eaglecleaningservice.com	Bessemer	AL	35020	205-424-5252		104
Eagle Communications Inc 2703 Hall St Ste 15 *TF:* 877-613-2453 ■ *Web:* eaglecom.net	Hays	KS	67601	785-625-5910		643
Eagle Compressors Inc 3003 Thurston Ave *Web:* www.eaglecompressors.com	Greensboro	NC	27406	336-398-8000	398-8001	172
Eagle Comtronics Inc 7665 Henry Clay Blvd *TF:* 800-448-7474 ■ *Web:* www.eaglecomtronics.com	Liverpool	NY	13088	315-622-3402	622-3800	647
Eagle Construction Services Inc 1624 Jacksonville Rd *Web:* eagle1construction.com	Burlington	NJ	08016	609-239-8000		463
Eagle Copters Ltd 823 Mctavish Rd NE *TF:* 800-564-6469 ■ *Web:* www.eaglecopters.com	Calgary	AB	T2E7G9	403-250-7370		359
Eagle Cornice Company Inc 89 Pettaconsett Ave *Web:* www.eaglecornice.com	Cranston	RI	02920	401-781-5978	781-6570	697
Eagle County 500 Broadway PO Box 850 *TF:* 800-225-6136 ■ *Web:* www.eaglecounty.us	Eagle	CO	81631	970-328-8600	328-8716	338
Eagle Creek Animal Clinic 7307 W 38th St *Web:* eaglecreekvet.com	Indianapolis	IN	46254	317-291-5830		794
Eagle Creek Publications PO Box 781166 *TF:* 866-870-9903 ■ *Web:* www.eaglecreekpubs.com	Indianapolis	IN	46278	317-870-9902	870-9904	637-2
Eagle Creek State Recreation Area 2341 Eagle Creek Rd *Web:* www.dnr.illinois.gov	Findlay	IL	62534	217-756-8260		565
Eagle Crusher Company Inc 525 S Market St *TF:* 800-253-2453 ■ *Web:* eaglecrusher.com	Galion	OH	44833	419-468-2288	468-2101	207

Company / Address	City	State	ZIP	Phone	Fax	Class
Eagle Direct 1 Printer's Dr TF: 800-675-7669 ■ Web: www.eagledirects.com	Hermon	ME	04401	207-735-4140	848-7400	69
Eagle Distributing Co 5463 Skylane Blvd Web: www.call4bud.com	Santa Rosa	CA	95403	707-575-3121	575-3178	81-3
Eagle Distributing Company Inc 310 Radford Pl Web: www.eagledistributing.com	Knoxville	TN	37917	865-637-3311	525-9530	81-1
Eagle Distributing of Nebraska 1100 S Bud Blvd Web: eagledistributing.beer	Fremont	NE	68025	402-721-9723		81-1
Eagle Elastomer Inc 70 Cuyhoga Fls Indus Pky Web: eagleelastomer.com	Peninsula	OH	44264	330-923-7070	923-4005	676
Eagle Energy Inc 500 4 Ave SW Ste 2710 TF: 855-531-1575 ■ Web: www.eagleenergytrust.com	Calgary	AB	T2P2V6	403-531-1575	508-9840	536
Eagle Engineering Inc 2013 Van Bruen Ave Web: eagleonline.net	Indian Trail	NC	28079	704-882-4222		261
Eagle Engineering Inc 2701 S 1st St Web: www.eagleengineeringinc.com	Eldridge	IA	52748	563-285-7515	285-9520	385
Eagle Environmental Inc 891 W Robinson Dr Ste 4 Web: www.eagleenvironmentalinc.com	North Salt Lake	UT	84054	801-936-1155		186
Eagle Express Lines Inc 925 W 175th St Web: www.eagleexpresslines.com	Homewood	IL	60430	708-333-8400	333-7302	780
Eagle Family Foods Group LLC 4020 Kinross Lakes Pkwy *Fax Area Code: 330 ■ TF: 888-550-9555 ■ Web: www.eaglebrand.com	Orrville	OH	44667	888-656-3245	684-6410*	296-27
Eagle Fire Protection Inc 1205 Crown Park Cir Web: www.eaglefirepro.com	Winter Garden	FL	34787	407-656-8387		189-10
Eagle Flexible Packaging 1100 Kingsland Dr Web: www.eagleflexible.com	Batavia	IL	60510	630-406-1760	406-9962	627
Eagle Ford Oil & Gas Corp 1110 Nasa Pkwy Ste 311	Houston	TX	77058	281-383-9468		536
Eagle Foundry 23123 SE Eagle Creek Rd Web: www.eaglefoundryco.com	Eagle Creek	OR	97022	503-637-3048	637-3091	307
Eagle Gate College 5588 S Green St TF: 866-284-8680 ■ Web: www.eaglegatecollege.edu	Murray	UT	84123	801-333-8100		167-3
Eagle Global Advisors LLC 5847 San Felipe Ste 930 Web: www.eagleglobal.com	Houston	TX	77057	713-952-3550		401
Eagle Graphics Inc 150 N Moyer St Web: eaglegraphic.com	Annville	PA	17003	717-867-5576		110
Eagle Grinding Wheel Corp 2519 W Fulton St Web: www.eaglegrindingwheel.com	Chicago	IL	60612	312-733-1770	733-5949	1
Eagle Grips Inc 460 Randy Rd TF: 800-323-6144 ■ Web: www.eaglegrips.com	Carol Stream	IL	60188	630-260-0400		711
Eagle Group Inc 100 Industrial Blvd *Fax Area Code: 302 ■ TF: 800-441-8440 ■ Web: www.eaglegrp.com	Clayton	DE	19938	800-441-8440	653-2065*	300
Eagle Harbor Book Co 157 Winslow Way E Web: www.eagleharborbooks.com	Bainbridge Island	WA	98110	206-842-5332		95
Eagle Haven Computers Inc 5860 Clearfield Woodland Hwy Web: eaglehaven.com	Clearfield	PA	16830	814-765-5779	765-8173	175
Eagle Herald Publishing 1809 Dunlap Ave Web: ehextra.com	Marinette	WI	54143	715-735-6611		532-3
Eagle Hill School 242 Old Petersham Rd PO Box 116 Web: www.eaglehill.school	Hardwick	MA	01037	413-477-6000	477-6837	622
Eagle Investment Systems LLC 65 LaSalle Rd Ste 305 Web: www.eagleinvsys.com	West Hartford	CT	06107	860-561-4602		401
Eagle Iron Works 129 E Holcomb Ave Web: www.eagleironworks.com	Des Moines	IA	50313	515-243-1123	243-8214	190
Eagle Island State Park 165 S Eagle Island Pkwy Web: www.visitidaho.org	Eagle	ID	83616	208-939-0696		565
Eagle Laboratories Inc 10201-A Trademark St Web: www.eaglelabs.com	Rancho Cucamonga	CA	91730	909-481-0011		475
Eagle Machine & Tool Corp 6060 Grand Haven Rd Web: www.eaglemachinetool.com	Norton Shores	MI	49441	231-798-8473		203
Eagle Manufacturing Company Inc 2400 Charles St Web: www.eagle-mfg.com	Wellsburg	WV	26070	304-737-3171	737-1752	124
Eagle Marine Industries Inc 1 Riverview Ave	Sauget	IL	62201	618-875-1153		465
Eagle Maritime Consultants Inc 1145 Fm 518 Rd Web: www.eaglemaritime.com	Houston	TX	77058	281-333-9880	333-9885	313
Eagle Marketing Inc *Perfume Originals Products Div* 150 W 1st St *Fax Area Code: 402 ■ TF: 800-233-7424 ■ Web: www.eimi.com	Cortland	NE	68331	800-233-7424	798-7002*	574
Eagle Microsystems Inc 366 Cir of Progress Dr Web: www.eaglemicrosystems.com	Pottstown	PA	19464	610-323-2250		362
Eagle Mountain Casino 681 S Reservation Rd PO Box 1659 *Fax Area Code: 559 ■ TF: 800-903-3353 ■ Web: www.eaglemtncasino.com	Porterville	CA	93257	800-903-3353	788-6223*	133
Eagle Mountain House 179 Carter Notch Rd PO Box 804 TF: 800-966-5779 ■ Web: www.eaglemt.com	Jackson	NH	03846	603-383-9111		379
Eagle Networks Inc 2738 W Bullard Ave Web: www.eaglenetworks.com	Fresno	CA	93711	559-448-8877		175
Eagle Newspapers Inc 4901 Indian School Rd NE PO Box 12008 Web: www.eaglenewspapers.com	Salem	OR	97305	503-393-1774		532-3
Eagle Parts & Products Inc 1411 Marvin Griffin Rd TF: 888-972-9911 ■ Web: www.eagleproducts.us	Augusta	GA	30906	706-790-6687	790-6066	61
Eagle Pass Chamber of Commerce 400 E Garrison St TF: 888-355-3224 ■ Web: eaglepasstexas.com	Eagle Pass	TX	78852	830-773-3224	773-8844	139
Eagle Pass Public Library 589 Main St Web: eaglepasspubliclibrary.org	Eagle Pass	TX	78852	830-773-7323		434-3
Eagle Point National Cemetery 2763 Riley Rd Web: www.cem.va.gov	Eagle Point	OR	97524	541-826-2511	826-2888	136
Eagle Point Software Corp 600 Star Brewery Dr Ste 200 TF: 800-678-6565 ■ Web: www.eaglepoint.com	Dubuque	IA	52001	800-678-6565		178-10
Eagle Pointe Golf Resort 2250 E Pt Rd Web: www.eaglepointe.com	Bloomington	IN	47401	812-824-4040		669
Eagle Power & Equipment Corp 953 Bethlehem Pk Web: www.eaglepowerandequipment.com	Montgomeryville	PA	18936	215-699-5871	699-6416	358
Eagle Professional Resources Inc 170 Laurier Ave W Ste 902 *Fax Area Code: 416 ■ TF: 800-281-2339 ■ Web: www.eagleonline.com	Ottawa	ON	K1P5V5	613-234-1810	861-8401*	721
Eagle Quest Golf Centers Inc 1001 United Blvd Web: eaglequestgolf.com	Coquitlam	BC	V3K4S8	604-523-6400		711
Eagle Raceway 617 S 238th St Web: eagleraceway.com	Eagle	NE	68347	402-238-2595	238-3768	515
Eagle Ridge Inn & Resort 444 Eagle Ridge Dr TF: 800-892-2269 ■ Web: www.eagleridge.com	Galena	IL	61036	815-777-2444	777-4502	669
Eagle River Homes LLC 21 S Groffdale Rd TF: 800-406-1062 ■ Web: www.eagleriverhomes.net	Leola	PA	17540	717-656-2381	656-0316	186
Eagle River Nature Ctr 32750 Eagle River Rd Web: www.ernc.org	Eagle River	AK	99577	907-694-2108	694-2119	50-5
Eagle Rock Baptist Church 1499 Colorado Blvd Web: www.erockchurch.com	Los Angeles	CA	90041	323-255-4611		48-20
Eagle Rock Chamber of Commerce PO Box 41354 Web: www.eaglerockchamberofcommerce.com	Eagle Rock	CA	90041	323-257-2197	257-4245	139
Eagle Rock Technologies Inc 1 Eagle Rock Dr Web: www.eaglerockonline.com	Bath	PA	18014	610-759-5200		757
Eagle Roofing Products 3546 N Riverside Ave TF: 888-845-3766 ■ Web: www.eagleroofing.com	Rialto	CA	92377	909-822-6000		191-4
Eagle Sales Company Inc 5100 Raleigh-Lagrange Rd TF: 800-264-1180 ■ Web: www.eaglesales.com	Memphis	TN	38134	901-458-6133	458-4144	246
Eagle Scaffolding Services Inc 67 Mill St Web: www.eaglescaffolding.com	Amityville	NY	11701	631-842-1700		358
Eagle Stainless Tube & Fabrication Inc 10 Discovery Way TF: 800-528-8650 ■ Web: www.eagletube.com	Franklin	MA	02038	508-528-8650	520-1954	492
Eagle Technologies Group 9850 Red Arrow Hwy Web: eagletechnologies.com	Bridgman	MI	49106	269-465-6986		494
Eagle Technology Inc 11019 N Towne Sq Rd TF: 800-388-3268 ■ Web: www.eaglecmms.com	Mequon	WI	53092	262-241-3845		177
Eagle Tool Co 101 Woodward Ave Web: eaglebroach.com	Iron Mountain	MI	49801	906-774-0284	774-0342	455
Eagle Transport Corp 300 S Wesleyan Blvd Ste 202 TF: 800-776-9937 ■ Web: www.eagletransportcorp.com	Rocky Mount	NC	27804	252-937-2464		780
Eagle Valley Enterprise 108 W Second St Web: www.vaildaily.com	Eagle	CO	81631	970-328-6656		532-4
Eagle Van Lines Inc 5041 Beech Pl TF: 800-476-4080 ■ Web: www.eaglevanlines.com	Temple Hills	MD	20748	301-899-2022		313
Eagle Video Productions 2201 Woodnell Dr Web: www.eaglevideo.com	Raleigh	NC	27603	919-779-7891		514
Eagle Vision Pharmaceutical Corp 175 Krauser Rd	Downingtown	PA	19335	610-458-2346		238
Eagle Well Servicing Corp 8113-49 Ave Close TF: 888-496-9995 ■ Web: www.wesc.ca	Red Deer	AB	T4P2V5	403-346-7789		540
Eagle Wings Industries Inc (EWI) 400 Shellhouse Dr Web: www.ewiusa.com	Rantoul	IL	61866	217-892-4322		60
Eagle's Crest Grill 5301 S Columbia Rd Web: eaglescrestgrill.com	Grand Forks	ND	58201	701-787-3491		671
Eagle's Flight, Creative Training Excellence Inc 489 Clair Rd W TF: 800-567-8079 ■ Web: www.eaglesflight.com	Guelph	ON	N1L0H7	519-767-1747		463
Eagle's Nest Foundation 43 Hart Rd TF: 800-951-7442 ■ Web: www.enf.org	Pisgah Forest	NC	28768	828-877-4349	884-2788	239
Eagle's Nest Resort 6103 Lavaque Rd Web: eaglesnestfishlake.com	Duluth	MN	55803	218-721-4147		669
Eagle:XM LLC 5105 E 41st Ave TF: 800-426-5376 ■ Web: www.eaglexm.com	Denver	CO	80216	303-320-5411		627
Eaglebrook School 271 Pine Nook Rd Web: www.eaglebrook.org	Deerfield	MA	01342	413-774-9111		622
Eagleburgmann Industries LP 10035 Brookriver Dr Web: www.eagleburgmann.us	Houston	TX	77040	713-939-9515		326
EagleClaw Midstream Services LLC 414 W Texas Ave Ste 315 Web: www.eagleclawmidstream.com	Midland	TX	79701	432-789-1333		539
EagleOne Case Management 745 McClintock Ste 360 Web: www.eagleonecms.com	Burr Ridge	IL	60527	630-655-0800		194

	Phone	Fax	Class
Eagle-Picher Minerals Inc 9785 Gateway Dr .... Reno NV 89521 *TF:* 800-228-3865 ■ *Web:* epminerals.com	775-824-7600	824-7601	500
Eagle-Record, The 5549 Memorial Blvd .... Saint George SC 29477 *Web:* www.theeaglerecord.com	843-563-3121	563-5355	532-2
Eaglerider Inc 11860 S La Cienga Blvd .... Hawthorne CA 90250 *Web:* www.eaglerider.com	310-536-6777	536-6776	239
Eagleton, Eagleton & Harrison Inc 320 S Boston Ave Ste 1700 .... Tulsa OK 74103 *Web:* www.eehlaw.com	918-584-0462		428
Eagle-Tribune 100 Tpke St .... North Andover MA 01845 *TF:* 800-927-9200 ■ *Web:* www.eagletribune.com	978-946-2000	687-6045	532-2
Eagleville Elementary Charter S101 W34511 Hwy .... Eagle WI 53119 *Web:* www.masd.k12.wi.us	262-363-6258	594-5495	685
Eagleville Hospital 100 Eagleville Rd .... Eagleville PA 19408 *TF:* 800-255-2019 ■ *Web:* www.eagleville.org	610-539-6000		726
Eaglewood Resort & Spa 1401 Nordic Rd .... Itasca IL 60143 *TF:* 877-285-6150 ■ *Web:* www.eaglewoodresort.com	630-773-1400		669
EAI (Education Associates Inc) PO Box 23308 .... Louisville KY 40223 **Fax Area Code:* 502 ■ *TF:* 800-626-2950 ■ *Web:* www.educationassociates.com	800-626-2950	244-9144*	423
EAI Incorporated Environmental Management Service 50 Prescott St .... Jersey City NJ 07304 *Web:* www.eaienviro.com	201-395-0010		194
Eakas Corp 6251 Rt 251 .... Peru IL 61354 *Web:* www.eakas.com	815-223-8811		247
Eakes Office Plus 617 W Third St .... Grand Island NE 68801 *TF:* 800-652-9396 ■ *Web:* www.eakes.com	308-382-8026	382-7401	535
Eakin Partners LLC 1201 Demonbreun St Ste 1400 .... Nashville TN 37203 *Web:* www.eakinpartners.com	615-250-1800	250-1805	652
EAL (Electrone Americas Limited Co) 129 NW 13th St Ste D-21 .... Boca Raton FL 33432 *Web:* www.electrone.com	561-395-3398	395-1678	173-1
EAM World 5502 NW 37th Ave .... Miami FL 33142 *Web:* eamworldwide.com	305-871-4050	637-8632	676
EANGUS (Enlisted Association of the National Guard of the US) 3133 Mt Vernon Ave .... Alexandria VA 22305 *TF:* 800-234-3264 ■ *Web:* eangus.org	703-519-3846	519-3849	48-19
EAP (Environmental Analysis and Permitting Inc) 299 Dr Martin Luther King Jr St N .... Saint Petersburg FL 33701 *Web:* www.eapermit.com	727-894-4643	822-2919	192
EAP Systems 500 W Cummings Pk .... Woburn MA 01801 *TF:* 800-535-4841 ■ *Web:* www.theeap.com	781-935-8850		462
EAPA (Employee Assistance Professionals Association Inc) 4350 N Fairfax Dr Ste 740 .... Arlington VA 22203 *TF:* 800-937-8461 ■ *Web:* www.eapassn.org	703-387-1000	522-4585	49-12
Earhart Petroleum Inc PO Box 39 .... Troy OH 45373 *TF:* 800-686-2928 ■ *Web:* www.earhartpetroleum.com	937-335-2928	339-5352	579
Earl & Brown Company Inc 5825 SW Arctic Dr .... Beaverton OR 97005 *TF:* 866-432-9237 ■ *Web:* www.earlbrown.com	503-670-1170		246
Earl Bacon Agency Inc 3131 Lonnbladh Rd .... Tallahassee FL 32308 *TF:* 800-369-0161 ■ *Web:* earlbacon.com	850-878-2121	878-2128	390
Earl F. Andersen Inc (EFA) 19740 Kenrick Ave .... Lakeville MN 55044 *TF:* 800-862-6026 ■ *Web:* www.efa-mn.com	952-884-7300		300
Earl K. Long Medical Ctr 5825 Airline Hwy .... Baton Rouge LA 70805 *Web:* legis.state.la.us	225-358-1000		374-3
Earl L. Henderson Trucking Inc 8118 Bunkum Rd .... Caseyville IL 62232 *TF:* 800-447-8084 ■ *Web:* www.hendersontrucking.com	618-623-0057		780
Earl May Seed & Nursery 208 N Elm St .... Shenandoah IA 51603 *TF:* 800-843-9608 ■ *Web:* www.earlmay.com	712-246-1020	246-2210	323
Earl W. Brydges Artpark State Park 450 S Fourth St .... Lewiston NY 14092 *Web:* parks.ny.gov	716-754-7766		565
Earl's Apparel Inc 908 S Fourth St .... Crockett TX 75835 *TF:* 800-527-3148 ■ *Web:* www.stanray.us	936-544-5521	544-7973	155-19
Earl's Auction Co 5199 Lafayette Rd .... Indianapolis IN 46254 *Web:* www.earlsauction.com	317-291-5843	291-5844	51
Earl's Rib Palace 6816 N Western Ave .... Oklahoma City OK 73116 *Web:* earlsribpalace.com	405-843-9922		671
Earlbeck Gases & Technologies 10792 Tucker St .... Beltsville MD 20705 *Web:* www.earlbeck.com	301-937-8884	937-1811	811
Earle Baum Center of The Blind 4539 Occidental Rd .... Santa Rosa CA 95401 *Web:* www.earlebaum.org	707-523-3222	230-6211	685
Earle Brown Heritage Ctr 6155 Earle Brown Dr .... Minneapolis MN 55430 *Web:* www.earlebrown.com	763-569-6300		205
Earle M. Jorgensen Co 10650 S Alameda St .... Lynwood CA 90262 *TF:* 800-336-5365 ■ *Web:* www.emjmetals.com	323-567-1122		490
Earle Press Inc 2140 Latimer Dr .... Muskegon MI 49442 *Web:* www.earlepress.com	231-773-2111	777-2743	627
Earle, The 121 W Washington St .... Ann Arbor MI 48104 *Web:* www.theearle.com	734-994-0211		671
Earlham College 801 National Rd W .... Richmond IN 47374 *TF:* 800-327-5426 ■ *Web:* www.earlham.edu	765-983-1600	983-1560	166
Earlham Savings Bank 7300 Lake Dr .... West Des Moines IA 50266 *TF:* 800-381-3326 ■ *Web:* earlhambank.com	515-223-4753	225-3298	70
Earlham School of Religion 228 College Ave .... Richmond IN 47374 *TF:* 800-432-1377 ■ *Web:* esr.earlham.edu	765-983-1423	983-1688	167-3
Earlimart School District 785 E Center Ave .... Earlimart CA 93219 *Web:* www.earlimart.org	661-849-3386	849-2352	685

	Phone	Fax	Class
Early Advantage LLC 426 Mine Hill Rd .... Fairfield CT 06824 *TF:* 888-999-4670 ■ *Web:* www.early-advantage.com	203-259-6480		5
Early Bird, The 8787 5312 Sebring Warner Rd .... Greenville OH 45331 *Web:* earlybirdpaper.com	937-548-3330		532-4
Early Childhood Learning Community 5490 Mills Creek Ln .... North Ridgeville OH 44039 *TF:* 877-644-6457 ■ *Web:* www.nrcs.net	440-353-1100		685
Early Cochran & Olson LLC 828 Interlaken Ln Ste 2510 .... Libertyville IL 60048 *Web:* www.ecollc.com	312-595-4200	595-4209	266
Early Construction Inc 435 Industrial Park Rd NE .... Cartersville GA 30121 **Fax Area Code:* 678 ■ *Web:* www.earlyconstruction.com	770-592-5585	669-2253*	187
Early County PO Box 693 .... Blakely GA 39823 *Web:* georgia.gov	229-723-4304	723-8684	338
Early County School District 11927 Columbia St .... Blakely GA 39823 *Web:* www.early.k12.ga.us	229-723-4337		685
Early Express Services Inc 1333 E Second St .... Dayton OH 45403 *Web:* www.earlyexpress.com	937-223-5801		5
Early Learning Coalition of Miami Dade & Monroe 2555 Ponce De Leon Blvd Ste 500 .... Coral Gables FL 33134 *TF:* 800-962-2873 ■ *Web:* www.elcmdm.org	305-646-7220		242
Early Sullivan Wright Gizer & Mc 6420 Wilshire Blvd 17th Fl .... Los Angeles CA 90048 *Web:* earlysullivan.com	323-301-4660		41
Earmark 1125 Dixwell Ave .... Hamden CT 06514 *Web:* www.earmark.com	203-777-2130	777-2886	647
Earnest C. Brooks Correctional Facility 2500 S Sheridan Dr .... Muskegon Heights MI 49444 *Web:* www.michigan.gov	231-773-9200		213
Earnest Machine 1250 Linda St .... Rocky River OH 44116 *Web:* www.earnestmachine.com	440-895-8400	356-2409	351
Earnest Partners LLC 1180 Peachtree St Ste 2300 .... Atlanta GA 30309 *TF:* 800-322-0068 ■ *Web:* www.earnestpartners.com	404-815-8772	815-8948	401
Earnhardt Auto Centers 7300 W Orchid Ln .... Chandler AZ 85226 *TF:* 888-378-7711 ■ *Web:* www.earnhardt.com	480-926-4000		57
Earnin 260 Sheridan Ave .... Palo Alto CA 94306 *TF:* 888-510-1119 ■ *Web:* earnin.com	888-510-1119		113
Earshot Jazz 3429 Fremont Pl N Ste 309 .... Seattle WA 98103 *Web:* www.earshot.org	206-547-6763		48-4
Earth Day Network (EDN) 1616 P St NW Ste 340 .... Washington DC 20036 *Web:* www.earthday.org	202-518-0044	518-8794	48-13
Earth Engineering Consultants LLC 4396 Greenfield Dr .... Windsor CO 80550 *Web:* earth-engineering.com	970-545-3908		261
Earth Island 9201 Owensmouth Ave .... Chatsworth CA 91311 *TF:* 888-394-3949 ■ *Web:* followyourheart.com	818-725-2820		296-33
Earth Island Institute 2150 Allston Wy Ste 460 .... Berkeley CA 94704 **Fax Area Code:* 415 ■ *Web:* www.earthisland.org	510-859-9100	788-7324*	48-13
Earth Networks Inc 12410 Milestone Center Dr Ste 300 .... Germantown MD 20876 *TF:* 800-544-4429 ■ *Web:* www.earthnetworks.com	301-250-4000		192
Earth Policy Institute 1350 Connecticut Ave NW Ste 403 .... Washington DC 20036 *Web:* www.earth-policy.org	202-496-9290	496-9325	634
Earth Resource Systems LLC 16285 Laconia Ln .... Alpharetta GA 30004 **Fax Area Code:* 770 ■ *Web:* www.earthresourcesystems.com	404-513-5429	592-1801*	192
Earth Science Systems LLC 11485 W I-70 Frontage Rd Unit B .... Wheat Ridge CO 80033 *Web:* earthsciencesystems.com	303-800-2000		261
Earth Share 7735 Old Georgetown Rd Ste 900 .... Bethesda MD 20814 *TF:* 800-875-3863 ■ *Web:* www.earthshare.org	240-333-0300	333-0301	48-13
Earth System Research Laboratory NOAA/ESRL 325 Broadway .... Boulder CO 80305 *Web:* www.esrl.noaa.gov	303-497-4091		668
Earth Systems Services Inc 720 Aerovista Pl Ste 102 .... San Luis Obispo CA 93401 *TF:* 866-781-0112 ■ *Web:* www.earthsystems.com	805-781-0112	781-0180	192
Earth Treks 7125 Columbia Gateway Dr Ste C .... Columbia MD 21046 *Web:* www.earthtreksclimbing.com	410-872-0060		711
Earth Waste & Metal 49 Wales St Ste 1 .... Rutland VT 05701 *Web:* www.earthwastesystems.com	802-775-7722	786-9070	686
Earth, Ocean & Atmospheric Sciences 2020 - 2207 Main Mall .... Vancouver BC V6T1Z4 *Web:* www.eoas.ubc.ca	604-822-2449		165
EarthBalance 2570 Commerce Pkwy .... North Port FL 34289 *Web:* www.earthbalance.com	941-426-7878	426-8778	196
Earthbound Farm 1721 San Juan Hwy .... San Juan Bautista CA 95045 *TF:* 800-690-3200 ■ *Web:* www.earthboundfarm.com	831-623-7880		10-11
EarthCam Inc 84 Kennedy St .... Hackensack NJ 07601 *Web:* www.earthcam.com	201-488-1111	488-1119	397
EarthColor 249 Pomeroy Rd .... Parsippany NJ 07054 *Web:* www.earthcolor.com	973-884-1300	952-8282	627
Earthcon Consultants Inc 1880 W Oak Pkwy Bldg 100 Ste 106 .... Marietta GA 30062 *TF:* 800-708-8525 ■ *Web:* www.earthcon.com	770-973-2100		192
EarthLink Inc 1170 Peachtree St Ste 900 .... Atlanta GA 30309 *NASDAQ: ELNK* ■ **Fax Area Code:* 404 ■ *TF:* 866-383-3080 ■ *Web:* www.earthlink.net	866-383-3080	795-1034*	398
EarthLinked Technologies Inc 4151 S Pipkin Rd .... Lakeland FL 33811 *TF:* 866-211-6102 ■ *Web:* earthlinked.com	863-701-0096		35
Earthplace 10 Woodside Ln .... Westport CT 06880 *Web:* www.earthplace.org	203-557-4400	227-8909	50-5
Earthquake Engineering Research Institute (EERI) 499 14th St Ste 320 .... Oakland CA 94612 *Web:* www.eeri.org	510-451-0905	451-5411	49-19

Name / Address	City	State	Zip	Phone	Fax	Class
EarthRes Group Inc 6912 Old Easton Rd PO Box 468 *TF:* 800-264-4553 ■ *Web:* www.earthres.com	Pipersville	PA	18947	215-766-1211		261
EarthRights Intl 1612 K St NW Ste 401 *Web:* earthrights.org	Washington	DC	20006	202-466-5188	466-5189	48-13
Earths Edge Inc 705 S Beacon Blvd *Web:* earthsedgeusa.com	Grand Haven	MI	49417	616-844-1724		711
Earthstone Energy Inc 633 17th St Ste 2320 *Web:* www.earthstoneenergy.com	Denver	CO	80202	303-296-3076		536
Earthwatch Institute 114 Western Ave *TF:* 800-776-0188 ■ *Web:* earthwatch.org	Boston	MA	02134	978-461-0081	461-2332	48-13
Earthwave Technologies Inc 710 E 64th St *Web:* www.earthwavetech.com	Indianapolis	IN	46220	317-257-8740		647
EarthWay Products Inc 1009 Maple St *TF:* 800-294-0671 ■ *Web:* www.earthway.com	Bristol	IN	46507	574-848-7491		429
EAS (Environmental Air Systems Inc) 250 Swathmore Ave *Web:* www.easinc.net	High Point	NC	27263	336-273-1975		14
EASA (Electrical Apparatus Service Assn) 1331 Baur Blvd *Web:* www.easa.com	Saint Louis	MO	63132	314-993-2220	993-1269	49-19
EASA (Eucharistic Adoration of San Antonio Inc) PO Box 691006 *Web:* www.adore24.org	San Antonio	TX	78269	210-558-8802		48-13
Ease 500 Treat Ave Ste 200 *TF:* 800-446-3273 ■ *Web:* www.ease.com	San Francisco	CA	94110	800-446-3273		788
EASI 7301 Pkwy Dr **Fax Area Code:* 780 ■ *TF:* 888-963-7740 ■ *Web:* easi.com	Hanover	MD	21076	410-567-8061	514-3381*	463
Easley Winery 205 N College Ave *Web:* www.easleywinery.com	Indianapolis	IN	46202	317-636-4516	974-0128	50-7
Easom Automation 32471 Industrial Dr *Web:* www.easomautomation.com	Madison Heights	MI	48071	248-307-0650	307-0701	386
East Air Corp 337 Second St *Web:* www.eastair.com	Hackensack	NJ	07601	201-487-6060	487-5938	770
East Alabama Chamber of Commerce 1107 Broad St *Web:* www.ealcc.com	Phenix City	AL	36867	334-298-3639		139
East Alabama Medical Ctr 2000 Pepperell Pkwy *Web:* www.eamc.org	Opelika	AL	36801	334-749-3411		250
East Arkansas Cable TV 4804 N Washington St *TF:* 800-903-0508 ■ *Web:* www.eastarkansasvideo.com	Forrest City	AR	72335	800-903-0508		647
East Arkansas Community College 1700 Newcastle Rd *TF:* 877-797-3222 ■ *Web:* www.eacc.edu	Forrest City	AR	72335	870-633-4480	633-3840	162
East Bank Club 500 N Kingsbury St *Web:* www.eastbankclub.com	Chicago	IL	60654	312-527-5800	644-3868	354
East Bank Community Theatre 630 Barksdale Blvd *Web:* www.bossierarts.org	Bossier City	LA	71111	318-741-8310		572
East Baton Rouge Parish 1755 Florida St *Web:* www.brla.gov	Baton Rouge	LA	70802	225-389-3129		338
East Baton Rouge Parish Library (EBRPL) 7711 Goodwood Blvd *Web:* www.ebrpl.com	Baton Rouge	LA	70806	225-231-3750		434-3
East Bay Chamber of Commerce 16 Cutler St *Web:* www.eastbaychamberri.org	Warren	RI	02885	401-245-0750	245-0110	139
East Bay Express 1335 Stanford Ave Ste 100 *Web:* www.eastbayexpress.com	Emeryville	CA	94608	510-879-3700	879-3794	532-5
East Bay Tire Co 2200 Huntington Dr Unit C *TF:* 800-831-8473 ■ *Web:* www.eastbaytire.com	Fairfield	CA	94533	707-437-4700	437-4800	755
East Beach 1 Burlingame State Pk *Web:* www.riparks.com	Charlestown	RI	02813	401-322-8910	322-3083	565
East Beach Veterinary Care & Housecalls LLC 3841 E Little Creek Rd Ste L *Web:* eastbeachvet.com	Norfolk	VA	23518	757-963-8387		794
East Bernard Isd 723 College St *Web:* www.ebisd.org	East Bernard	TX	77435	979-335-7519		685
East Bonner County Library District 1407 W Cedar St *Web:* ebonnerlibrary.org	Sandpoint	ID	83864	208-263-6930		434-3
East Boston Savings Bank 10 Meridian St *TF:* 800-657-3272 ■ *Web:* www.ebsb.com	East Boston	MA	02128	617-567-1500		70
East Brunswick Public Library 2 Jean Walling Civic Ctr *Web:* www.ebpl.org	East Brunswick	NJ	08816	732-390-6950	390-6869	434-3
East Buchanan Telephone Coop (EBTC) 214 3rd St N *TF:* 866-327-2748 ■ *Web:* www.eastbuchanan.com	Winthrop	IA	50682	319-935-3011	935-3010	224
East by Southwest 160 E College Dr *Web:* www.eastbysouthwest.com	Durango	CO	81301	970-247-5533		671
East Cafe Chinese Restaurant 15140 E Mississippi Ave *Web:* www.east-cafe.com	Aurora	CO	80012	303-369-6103		671
East Canyon Hotel & Spa 288 E Camino Monte Vista *Web:* www.eastcanyonps.com	Palm Springs	CA	92262	760-320-1928		379
East Carolina Radio Inc PO Box 1418 *Web:* www.ecri.net	Nags Head	NC	27959	252-441-1024	449-8354	645-141
East Carolina University E Fifth St *TF:* 800-328-0577 ■ *Web:* www.ecu.edu	Greenville	NC	27858	252-328-6131	328-6640	166
East Carroll Parish 400 First St *Web:* www.ecsheriff.com	Lake Providence	LA	71254	318-559-2800	559-3116	338
East Central College 1964 Prairie Dell Rd *TF:* 800-392-6848 ■ *Web:* www.eastcentral.edu	Union	MO	63084	636-583-5193	583-1897	162
East Central Community College 15738 Hwy 15 S PO Box 129 *TF:* 877-462-3222 ■ *Web:* www.eccc.edu	Decatur	MS	39327	601-635-2111	635-4011	162
East Central Energy PO Box 39 *TF:* 800-254-7944 ■ *Web:* www.eastcentralenergy.com	Braham	MN	55006	800-254-7944		245
East Central Oklahoma Electric Co-opeartive Inc 2001 S Wood Dr PO Box 1178 *Web:* www.ecoec.com	Okmulgee	OK	74447	918-756-0833		245
East Central Regional Hospital *Augusta* 3405 Mike Padgett Hwy *Web:* dbhdd.georgia.gov	Augusta	GA	30906	706-790-2011		374-5
East Central Regional Library 244 S Birch St *Web:* ecrlib.org	Cambridge	MN	55008	763-689-7390	689-7436	434-3
East Central University 1100 E 14th St *Web:* www.ecok.edu	Ada	OK	74820	580-332-8000		166
East Cheyenne County Library District (ECCLD) PO Box 939 *Web:* www.eccld.org	Cheyenne Wells	CO	80810	719-767-5138	767-5379	434-3
East Chicago Public Library (ECPL) 2401 E Columbus Dr *Web:* www.ecpl.org	East Chicago	IN	46312	219-397-2453		434-3
East Cleveland Board of Education 14305 Shaw Ave *Web:* www.east-cleveland.k12.oh.us	Cleveland	OH	44112	216-268-6600		685
East Coast Appliance Sales, Service & Parts Inc 2053 Laskin Rd *Web:* www.eastcoastappliance.com	Virginia Beach	VA	23454	757-425-2883		35
East Coast Datacom Inc 245 Gus Hipp Blvd Ste 3 *Web:* www.ecdata.com	Rockledge	FL	32955	321-637-9922	637-9980	225
East Coast Graphics 125 Wireless Blvd *Web:* www.ecoastgraphics.com	Hauppauge	NY	11788	631-231-9300		393
East Coast Lightning Equipment Inc 24 Lanson Dr *Web:* www.ecle.biz	Winsted	CT	06098	860-379-9072	379-2046	815
East Coast Lumber & Supply Co 308 Ave A *Web:* www.eastcoastlumber.com	Fort Pierce	FL	34950	772-461-5950		817
East Coast Metal Distributors Inc 1313 S Briggs Ave PO Box 570 *TF:* 844-227-9531 ■ *Web:* www.ecmdi.com	Durham	NC	27702	919-596-2136		612
East Coast Metals 171 Ruth Rd *TF:* 800-355-2060 ■ *Web:* eastcoastmetals.com	Harleysville	PA	19438	215-256-9550		492
East Coast Metals Inc 7905 W 20th Ave *TF:* 800-579-0944 ■ *Web:* www.eastcoast-metals.com	Hialeah	FL	33014	305-885-9991		491
East Coast Sales Company Inc 554 N State Rd *Web:* www.ecsceramics.com	Briarcliff Manor	NY	10510	914-923-5000		191-1
East Continental Gems Inc 580 Fifth Ave *TF:* 866-575-0944 ■ *Web:* www.eastcontinentalgems.com	New York	NY	10036	212-575-0944	944-6254	411
East Cooper Medical Ctr 2000 Hospital Dr *Web:* www.eastcoopermedctr.com	Mount Pleasant	SC	29464	843-881-0100		374-3
East End Computers LLC 50 Hilll St *Web:* www.eastendcomputers.com	Southampton	NY	11968	631-725-4000		179
East End Hospice 481 Westhampton-Riverhead Rd PO Box 1048 *Web:* www.eeh.org	Westhampton Beach	NY	11978	631-288-8400	288-8492	371
East Fairfield Coal Co (EFCC) 10900 S Ave PO Box 217 *Web:* efccfamily.com	North Lima	OH	44452	330-549-2165		501
East Feliciana Parish PO Box 427 *Web:* www.felicianatourism.org	Jackson	LA	70748	225-683-5145		338
East Georgia College 131 College Cir *TF:* 800-715-4255 ■ *Web:* www.ega.edu	Swainsboro	GA	30401	478-289-2017	289-2140	162
East Georgia Regional Medical Ctr (EGRMC) 1499 Fair Rd *TF:* 844-455-8708 ■ *Web:* www.eastgeorgiaregional.com	Statesboro	GA	30458	912-486-1000		374-3
East Goshen Veterinary Ctr 1506 Paoli Pk *Web:* www.eastgoshenvetcenter.com	West Chester	PA	19380	610-696-3303	696-3410	794
East Greenbush Community Library (EGCL) 10 Community Way *Web:* eastgreenbushlibrary.org	East Greenbush	NY	12061	518-477-7476	477-6692	434-3
East Hampton Star Inc, The 153 Main St PO Box 5002 *TF:* 844-324-0777 ■ *Web:* easthamptonstar.com	East Hampton	NY	11937	631-324-0002	324-7943	637-8
East Harbor State Park 1169 N Buck Rd *Web:* www.eastharborstatepark.org	Lakeside Marblehead	OH	43440	419-734-5857		565
East Harlem Tutorial Program 2050 Second Ave *Web:* ehtp.org	New York	NY	10029	212-831-0650		242
East Hartford Public Library 740 Main St *Web:* www.easthartfordct.gov	East Hartford	CT	06108	860-291-7100		434-3
East Hill Tire Inc 25239 104th Ave SE *Web:* www.easthilltire.com	Kent	WA	98030	253-852-3280		755
East India Co 349 York Ave *Web:* www.eastindiaco.com	Winnipeg	MB	R3C3S9	204-947-3097		671
East Iowa Plastics Inc 601 17th St Se *Web:* www.eastiowaplastics.com	Independence	IA	50644	319-334-2552		604
East Jefferson General Hospital (EJGH) 4200 Houma Blvd *TF:* 866-280-7737 ■ *Web:* ejgh.org	Metairie	LA	70006	504-454-4000		374-3
East Jersey State Prison 1100 Woodbridge Ave Lock Bag R *Web:* state.nj.us	Rahway	NJ	07065	732-499-5010	499-5022	213
East Jordan Plastics Inc PO Box 575 **Fax Area Code:* 231 ■ *TF:* 800-353-1190 ■ *Web:* www.eastjordanplastics.com	East Jordan	MI	49727	800-353-1190	536-7090*	602

Listing	Phone	Fax	Class
East Kansas Agri-Energy LLC 1304 S Main....Garnett KS 66032 *Web:* ekaellc.com	785-448-2888		580
East Kentucky Network LLC 101 Technology Trl....Ivel KY 41642 *Web:* www.appalachianwireless.com	606-438-2355		387
East Lansing Public Library 950 Abbott Rd....East Lansing MI 48823 *Web:* www.elpl.org	517-351-2420	351-9536	434-3
East Lee County Chamber of Commerce 25 Homestead Rd N Ste 41....Lehigh Acres FL 33936 *Web:* elccoc.org	239-369-3322	368-0500	139
East Liberty Quarter Chamber of Commerce 5907 Penn Ave Ste 314....Pittsburgh PA 15206 *Web:* www.eastlibertychamber.org	412-661-9660		139
East Lind Heat Treat Inc 32045 Dequindre Rd....Madison Heights MI 48071 *Web:* www.eastlind.com	248-585-1415	585-3045	484
East Lion Corp 318 Brea Canyon Rd....City of Industry CA 91789 *TF:* 877-939-1818 ■ *Web:* www.eastlioncorp.com	626-912-1818	935-5858	301
East Liverpool City Hospital (ELCH) 425 W Fifth St....East Liverpool OH 43920 *Web:* www.elch.org	330-385-7200		374-3
East Los Angeles Chamber of Commerce 4716 E Cesar Chavez Ave....Los Angeles CA 90022 *Web:* eastlachamber.com	323-263-2005		139
East Los Angeles College 1301 Avenida Cesar Chavez....Monterey Park CA 91754 *Web:* www.elac.edu	323-265-8650		162
East Louisiana State Hospital 4502 Hwy 951....Jackson LA 70748 *Web:* ldh.la.gov	225-634-0100		374-5
East Maine School District 63 (EMSD) 10150 Dee Rd....Des Plaines IL 60016 *Web:* www.emsd63.org	847-299-1900	299-9963	685
East Manufacturing Corp 1871 SR-44 PO Box 277....Randolph OH 44265 *TF:* 888-405-3278 ■ *Web:* www.eastmfg.com	330-325-9921	325-7851	779
East Meadow Public Library Front St & E Meadow Ave....East Meadow NY 11554 *Web:* eastmeadow.info	516-794-2570		434-3
East Mississippi Business Development Corp 1901 Front St PO Box 790....Meridian MS 39302 *Web:* www.embdc.org	601-693-1306	693-5638	139
East Mississippi Community College (EMCC) 1512 Kemper St....Scooba MS 39358 *Web:* www.eastms.edu	662-476-5000		162
East Mississippi Electric Power Assn (EMEPA) 2128 Hwy 39 N PO Box 5517....Meridian MS 39302 *Web:* emepa.com	601-581-8600	482-0701	245
East Moline Correctional Ctr 100 Hillcrest Rd....East Moline IL 61244 *Web:* www.illinois.gov	309-755-4511		213
East Mountain Insurors Inc 2395 Clower St....Snellville GA 30078 *Web:* eastmtnins.com	770-979-3215	978-7350	390
East Ocean City 27 Beach St....Boston MA 02111 *Web:* www.eastoceancity.com	617-542-2504		671
East Orange Campus of the VA New Jersey Health Care System (NJHCS) 385 Tremont Ave....East Orange NJ 07018 **Fax Area Code:* 202 ■ *TF:* 844-872-4681 ■ *Web:* www.usa.gov	844-872-4681	456-1414*	374-8
East Orange General Hospital 300 Central Ave....East Orange NJ 07018 *Web:* www.evh.org	973-672-8400		374-3
East Orange Public Library 21 S Arlington Ave....East Orange NJ 07018 *Web:* www.eopl.org	973-266-5600		434-3
East Penn Manufacturing Co 301 5th Ave SW Ste 3....Oelwein IA 50662 *Web:* www.eastpennmanufacturing.com	610-682-6361	682-4781	54
East Penn School District 800 Pine St....Emmaus PA 18049 *Web:* www.eastpennsd.org	610-966-8300	966-8349	685
East Perry Lumber Co 7029 Main St....Frohna MO 63748 *Web:* www.eastperrylumber.com	573-824-5272	824-5275	683
East Providence Chamber of Commerce 1011 Waterman Ave....East Providence RI 02914 *Web:* www.eastprovidenceareachamber.com	401-438-1212	435-4581	139
East Providence Public Library 41 Grove Ave....East Providence RI 02914 *Web:* www.eastprovidencelibrary.org	401-434-2453		434-3
East Ramapo Central School District 105 S Madison Ave....Spring Valley NY 10977 *Web:* www.ercsd.org	845-577-6000		685
East Ridge Printing 1249 Ridgeway Ave Ste Y....Rochester NY 14615 *Web:* eastridgeprint.com	585-266-4911	266-2721	627
East Ridge Retirement Village 9041 SW 214th St....Miami FL 33157 *Web:* eastridgeatcutlerbay.com	786-842-4596		672
East River Electric Power Coop 211 S Harth Ave....Madison SD 57042 *Web:* www.eastriver.coop	605-256-4536	256-8058	245
East River Energy Inc 401 Soundview Rd PO Box 388....Guilford CT 06437 *TF:* 800-336-3762 ■ *Web:* eastriverenergy.com	203-453-1200		579
East Rochester Public Library 317 Main St....East Rochester NY 14445 *Web:* www.libraryweb.org	585-586-8302		434-3
East Side Clinical Laboratory Inc 10 Risho Ave....East Providence RI 02914 *Web:* www.esclab.com	401-455-8400		415
East Side House Inc 337 Alexander Ave....Bronx NY 10454 *Web:* www.eastsidehouse.org	718-665-5250		242
East Side Plating Inc 8400 SE 26th Pl....Portland OR 97202 *TF:* 800-394-8554 ■ *Web:* www.eastsideplating.com	503-654-3774		481
East Side Union High School District 830 N Capitol Ave....San Jose CA 95133 *Web:* www.esuhsd.org	408-347-5000	347-5045	685
East Stroudsburg University 200 Prospect St....East Stroudsburg PA 18301 *TF:* 877-230-5547 ■ *Web:* www.esu.edu	570-422-3542	422-3933	166
East Teak Trading Group Inc 1106 Drake Rd....Donalds SC 29638 *TF:* 800-338-5636 ■ *Web:* www.eastteak.com	864-379-2111		350
East Tennessee Children's Hospital 2018 Clinch Ave PO Box 15010....Knoxville TN 37901 *Web:* www.etch.com	865-541-8000	541-8553	374-1
East Tennessee Historical Society 601 S Gay St PO Box 1629....Knoxville TN 37901 *Web:* www.easttnhistory.org	865-215-8824	215-8819	520
East Tennessee Human Resource Agency Inc (ETHRA) 9111 Cross Park Dr Ste D-100....Knoxville TN 37923 *Web:* www.ethra.org	865-691-2551	531-7216	195
East Tennessee Lions Eye Bank 1924 Alcoa Hwy U-26....Knoxville TN 37920 *Web:* lionseyebanktn.com	865-305-9625		269
East Tennessee Public Communications Corp 1611 E Magnolia Ave....Knoxville TN 37917 *Web:* www.easttennesseepbs.org	865-595-0220	595-0300	632
East Tennessee State University 1276 Gilbreath Dr PO Box 70300....Johnson City TN 37614 *Web:* www.etsu.edu	423-439-1000		167-3
East Texas Arboretum (ETABS) 1601 Patterson Rd....Athens TX 75751 *Web:* www.easttexasarboretum.org	903-675-5630		97
East Texas Baptist University 1209 N Grove St....Marshall TX 75670 *TF:* 800-804-3828 ■ *Web:* etbu.edu	903-935-7963	923-2001	166
East Texas Broadband Inc 2200 S Royall St....Palestine TX 75801 *Web:* www.etbroadband.net	903-723-3373	723-2858	681
East Texas Broadcasting Inc 1798 US Highway 67 W PO Box 990....Mount Pleasant TX 75455 *Web:* www.easttexasradio.com	903-572-8726	572-7232	647
East Town 718 E Wells St....Milwaukee WI 53202 *Web:* www.easttown.com	414-271-1416		50-6
East Towne Mall 89 E Towne Mall....Madison WI 53704 *Web:* www.shopeasttowne-mall.com	608-244-1387		460
East Valley Tribune 1620 W Fountainhead Pkwy Ste 219....Tempe AZ 85282 *Web:* www.eastvalleytribune.com	480-898-6500		532-2
East Valley Water District 3654 E Highland Ave Ste 18....Highland CA 92346 *Web:* www.eastvalley.org	909-889-9501		806
East View Information Services Inc 10601 Wayzata Blvd....Hopkins MN 55305 *TF:* 800-477-1005 ■ *Web:* www.eastview.com	952-252-1201	252-1202	387
East West Bank 135 N Los Robles Ave 7th Fl....Pasadena CA 91101 *NASDAQ: EWBC* ■ *TF:* 888-895-5650 ■ *Web:* www.eastwestbank.com	626-768-6000		360-2
East West Bookshop 324 Castro St....Mountain View CA 94041 *TF:* 800-909-6161 ■ *Web:* www.eastwestbooks.org	650-988-9800		95
East West Label Co 1000 E Hector St....Conshohocken PA 19428 *TF:* 800-441-7333 ■ *Web:* www.ewlabel.com	610-825-0410		413
Eastaboga Tackle Manufacturing Company Inc 261 Mudd St....Eastaboga AL 36260 *Web:* www.eastabogatackle.com	256-831-9682		710
Eastbay Home Health Services Inc 1710 Pennsylvania Ave Ste E....Fairfield CA 94533 *TF:* 888-440-1330 ■ *Web:* eastbayhomehealth.com	707-428-1473		363
East-Central Iowa Rural Electric Co-op 2400 Bing Miller Ln....Urbana IA 52345 *TF:* 877-850-4343 ■ *Web:* www.ecirec.com	319-443-4343		245
EastCoast Entertainment Inc 703 Southlake Blvd....Richmond VA 23236 *Web:* www.eastcoastentertainment.com	804-355-2178	353-3407	572
Eastconn 376 Hartford Tpke....Hampton CT 06247 *Web:* www.eastconn.org	860-455-0707		685
Eastech Flow Controls Inc 4250 S 76th East Ave....Tulsa OK 74145 *TF:* 800-226-3569 ■ *Web:* eastechflow.com	918-664-1212	664-8494	350
Easter & Stoney Ps 206 E 1st St....Aberdeen WA 98520	360-533-7272		2
Easter Owens Electric Co 6692 Fig St....Arvada CO 80004 *TF:* 866-204-3707 ■ *Web:* www.easter-owens.com	303-431-0111		203
Easter Seals 230 W Monroe St Ste 1800....Chicago IL 60606 *Web:* www.easterseals.com	312-726-6200	726-1494	48-17
Easterly + Assoc PO Box 541791....Houston TX 77254 *Web:* www.easterly.com	832-330-8120		4
Eastern Academy of Scuba Education 416 Miracle Mile Plz....Vero Beach FL 32960 *TF:* 800-732-9685 ■ *Web:* www.easedivepro.com	772-562-8338	562-3028	167-3
Eastern Acoustic Works (EAW) 1 Main St....Whitinsville MA 01588 *TF:* 800-992-5013 ■ *Web:* www.eaw.com	508-234-6158	234-8251	52
Eastern Adhesives Inc 904 Crosskeys Dr....Doylestown PA 18902 *TF:* 800-445-8049 ■ *Web:* easternadhesives.com	215-348-0119	348-3315	3
Eastern Alloys Inc 11 Henry Henning Dr PO Box 317....Maybrook NY 12543 *Web:* www.eazall.com	845-427-2151	427-5185	485
Eastern Analytical Inc 25 Chenell Dr....Concord NH 03301 *Web:* easternanalytical.com	603-228-0525		743
Eastern Arizona Academy of Cosmetology 1550 W Thatcher Blvd....Safford AZ 85546 *TF:* 800-949-8649 ■ *Web:* theacademy-cosmetology.com	928-348-8878	348-7714	167-3
Eastern Arizona College 615 N Stadium Ave....Thatcher AZ 85552 *TF:* 800-678-3808 ■ *Web:* www.eac.edu	928-428-8472	428-2578	162
Eastern Awning Systems Inc 843 Echo Lake Rd....Watertown CT 06795 *TF:* 800-445-4142 ■ *Web:* www.easternawning.com	800-445-4142		567

Name / Address	City	State	Zip	Phone	Fax	Class
Eastern Bank 1 Eastern Pl *TF:* 800-327-8376 ■ *Web:* www.easternbank.com	Lynn	MA	01901	781-599-2100	598-7697	70
Eastern Book Co (EBC) 7 Lincoln Ave *TF:* 800-937-0331 ■ *Web:* www.ebc.com	Scarborough	ME	04074	800-937-0331	214-3895	96
Eastern Business Forms Inc PO Box 10 *TF:* 800-387-2648 ■ *Web:* ebf-inc.com	Mauldin	SC	29662	800-387-2648		110
Eastern Carolina Nissan 3315 Hwy 70 E *TF:* 866-392-8286 ■ *Web:* www.ecnissan.com	New Bern	NC	28560	252-636-1000		57
Eastern Center for Arts & Technology 3075 Terwood Rd *Web:* www.eastech.org	Willow Grove	PA	19090	215-784-4800	784-4801	572
Eastern Co, The 112 Bridge St PO Box 460 *NASDAQ: EML* ■ *Web:* www.easterncompany.com	Naugatuck	CT	06770	203-729-2255	723-8653	350
Eastern College of Health Vocations 200 S University Ave. *Web:* www.easterncollege.edu	Little Rock	AR	72205	501-568-0211		167-3
Eastern Computer Exchange Inc 105 Cascade Blvd *Web:* www.ecei.com	Milford	CT	06460	203-877-4334		174
Eastern Connecticut State University 83 Windham St *TF:* 877-353-3278 ■ *Web:* www.easternct.edu	Willimantic	CT	06226	860-465-5000	465-5544	166
Eastern Connecticut Symphony Orchestra 289 State St *Web:* www.ectsymphony.com	New London	CT	06320	860-443-2876		573-3
Eastern Construction Company Ltd 505 Consumers Rd Ste 1100 *Web:* www.easternconstruction.com	Toronto	ON	M2J5G2	416-497-7110		186
Eastern Correctional Facility 30 Institution Rd PO Box 338 *Web:* www.doccs.ny.gov	Napanoch	NY	12458	845-647-7400		213
Eastern Correctional Institution 2821 Hwy 903 N PO Box 215 *Web:* www.ncdps.gov	Maury	NC	28554	252-747-8101	747-8260	213
Eastern Data Inc 4386 Park Dr *TF:* 866-327-8168 ■ *Web:* www.ediatlanta.com	Norcross	GA	30093	770-279-8888	279-1946	174
Eastern Design Services PO Box 17606 *TF:* 800-301-1763 ■ *Web:* www.easterndesign.com	Greenville	SC	29606	864-271-1228	232-3970	260
Eastern Exterior Wall Systems 3400 High Point Blvd *Web:* www.eews.com	Bethlehem	PA	18017	610-868-5522		106
Eastern Federal Corp 901 E Blvd *Web:* www.easternfederal.com	Charlotte	NC	28203	704-377-3495		748
Eastern Fisheries Inc 14 Hervey Tichon Ave *Web:* www.easternfisheries.com	New Bedford	MA	02740	508-993-5300	991-2226	296-14
Eastern Floral & Gift Shop 2836 Broadmoor Ave SE *TF:* 800-494-2202 ■ *Web:* www.easternfloral.com	Grand Rapids	MI	49504	616-949-2200		292
Eastern Florida State College 1519 Clearlake Rd *Web:* www.easternflorida.edu	Cocoa	FL	32909	321-632-1111		167-3
Eastern Gateway Community College 4000 Sunset Blvd *TF:* 800-682-6553 ■ *Web:* egcc.edu	Steubenville	OH	43952	740-264-5591		800
Eastern Illini Electric Co-op 330 W Ottawa PO Box 96 *TF:* 800-824-5102 ■ *Web:* www.eiec.org	Paxton	IL	60957	217-379-2131	379-2936	245
Eastern Illinois University 600 Lincoln Ave *TF:* 800-252-5711 ■ *Web:* www.eiu.edu	Charleston	IL	61920	217-581-2223	581-7060	166
Eastern Indiana Federal Credit Union 801 S Memorial Dr *Web:* easterninfcu.com	New Castle	IN	47362	765-529-6632		210
Eastern Iowa Airport, The 2515 Arthur Collins Pkwy SW *Web:* flycid.com	Cedar Rapids	IA	52404	319-362-8336	362-1670	27
Eastern Iowa Community Colleges 101 West Third St *TF:* 888-336-3907 ■ *Web:* www.eicc.edu	Davenport	IA	52801	888-336-3907		162
Eastern Iowa Light & Power Co-op 600 E 5th St PO Box 3003 *TF:* 800-728-1242 ■ *Web:* www.easterniowa.com	Wilton	IA	52778	563-732-2211		245
Eastern Kentucky Correctional Complex 200 Rd to Justice *Web:* www.corrections.ky.gov	West Liberty	KY	41472	606-743-2800	743-2811	213
Eastern Kentucky University 521 Lancaster Ave *TF:* 800-465-9191 ■ *Web:* www.eku.edu	Richmond	KY	40475	859-622-2106	622-8024	166
Eastern Lift Truck Company Inc 549 E Linwood Ave *TF:* 866-980-7175 ■ *Web:* www.easternlifttruck.com	Maple Shade	NJ	08052	856-779-8880	482-8804	385
Eastern Light Capital Inc 100 Pine St Ste 560 *OTC: ELCI* ■ *Web:* easternlight.capital	San Francisco	CA	94111	415-288-9575	288-9590	509
Eastern Long Island Hospital Assn, The 201 Manor Pl *Web:* elih.stonybrookmedicine.edu	Greenport	NY	11944	631-477-1000		374-3
Eastern Louisiana Mental Health System 628 N Fourth St PO Box 629 *Web:* ldh.la.gov	Baton Rouge	LA	70802	225-219-1917		374-5
Eastern Maine Community College 354 Hogan Rd *TF:* 800-286-9357 ■ *Web:* www.emcc.edu	Bangor	ME	04401	207-974-4600		800
Eastern Maine Electric Co-opeartive Inc 21 Union St *TF:* 800-696-7444 ■ *Web:* www.emec.com	Calais	ME	04619	207-454-7555		245
Eastern Maine Medical Ctr 489 State St *TF:* 877-366-3662 ■ *Web:* northernlighthealth.org	Bangor	ME	04401	207-973-7000		374-3
Eastern Maumee Bay Chamber of Commerce 2460 Navaree Ave *Web:* www.embchamber.org	Oregon	OH	43616	419-693-5580	693-9990	139
Eastern Mechanical Services Inc 3 Starr St *Web:* www.emsinc.us	Danbury	CT	06810	203-792-7668	748-0385	189-10
Eastern Mennonite University 1200 Park Rd *TF:* 800-368-2665 ■ *Web:* emu.edu	Harrisonburg	VA	22802	540-432-4118	432-4444	166
Eastern Metal Supply Inc 3600 23rd Ave S *TF:* 800-432-2204 ■ *Web:* www.easternmetal.com	Lake Worth	FL	33461	561-533-6061	588-4780	492
Eastern Metal/USA-SIGN 1430 Sullivan St *TF:* 800-872-7446 ■ *Web:* easternmetalsignsandsafety.com	Elmira	NY	14901	607-734-2295	734-8783	701
Eastern Mountain Sports 1 Vose Farm Rd *TF:* 888-463-6367 ■ *Web:* www.ems.com	Peterborough	NH	03458	203-379-2233		711
Eastern Museum of Motor Racing 100 Baltimore Rd *Web:* www.emmr.org	York Springs	PA	17372	717-528-8279		522
Eastern National 470 Maryland Dr Ste 1 *Web:* easternnational.org	Fort Washington	PA	19034	215-283-6900	283-6923	95
Eastern Nazarene College 23 E Elm Ave *TF:* 800-883-6288 ■ *Web:* enc.edu	Quincy	MA	02170	617-745-3000		166
Eastern Nc School for The Deaf 1311 US Hwy 301 N *Web:* www.encsd.net	Wilson	NC	27893	252-237-2450		685
Eastern Nebraska Veterans Home 12505 S 40th St *Web:* veterans.nebraska.gov	Bellevue	NE	68123	402-595-2180		793
Eastern New Mexico Medical Ctr 405 W Country Club Rd *Web:* www.enmmc.com	Roswell	NM	88201	575-622-8170		374-3
Eastern New Mexico University 1500 S Ave K *TF:* 800-367-3668 ■ *Web:* www.enmu.edu	Portales	NM	88130	575-562-1011		166
Eastern New Mexico University Roswell 52 University Blvd *TF:* 800-243-6687 ■ *Web:* www.roswell.enmu.edu	Roswell	NM	88203	575-624-7000		162
Eastern New Mexico University-ruidoso 700 Mechem Dr *TF:* 800-934-3668 ■ *Web:* www.ruidoso.enmu.edu	Ruidoso	NM	88345	575-257-2120		166
Eastern Oil Co 590 S Paddock St *Web:* www.easternoil.com	Pontiac	MI	48341	248-333-1333		579
Eastern Oklahoma Library System 14 E Shawnee *TF:* 888-291-8152 ■ *Web:* eols.org	Muskogee	OK	74403	918-682-6657	682-9466	434-3
Eastern Oklahoma State College 1301 W Main St *Web:* www.cosc.edu	Wilburton	OK	74578	918-465-2361	465-4417	162
Eastern Oregon University 1 University Blvd *TF:* 800-452-8639 ■ *Web:* www.eou.edu	La Grande	OR	97850	541-962-3393	962-3418	166
Eastern Oregon Youth Correctional Facility 1800 W Monroe St *Web:* www.oregon.gov	Burns	OR	97720	541-573-3133	573-3665	412
Eastern Oxygen and Medical Equipment Inc 818 Professional Pl W *Web:* www.easternoxygen.com	Chesapeake	VA	23320	757-547-8188	547-5936	476
Eastern Pennsylvania Supply Co 700 Scott St *TF:* 800-432-8075 ■ *Web:* www.easternpenn.com	Wilkes-Barre	PA	18705	570-823-1181	824-2514	612
Eastern Pierce County Chamber of Commerce 323 N Meridian PO Box 1298 *Web:* puyallupsumnerchamber.com	Puyallup	WA	98371	253-845-6755		139
Eastern Regional Research Ctr (ERRC) 600 E Mermaid Ln *Web:* www.ars.usda.gov	Wyndmoor	PA	19038	215-233-6400		668
Eastern Research Group Inc (ERG) c/o Dickran Babigian Director of Contracts 110 Hartwell Ave *Web:* www.erg.com	Lexington	MA	02421	781-674-7310	674-2851	196
Eastern Sanitation Ltd 17 Adam St *Web:* easternsanitation.com	Antigonish	NS	B2G2G1	902-863-1744		660
Eastern School of Acupuncture & Traditional Medicine 440 Franklin St 5th Fl *Web:* www.esatm.edu	Bloomfield	NJ	07003	973-755-2054	746-8714	685
Eastern Sheet Metal LLC 8959 Blue Ash Rd *TF:* 800-348-3440 ■ *Web:* www.easternsheetmetal.com	Blue Ash	OH	45242	800-348-3440		697
Eastern Shipbuilding Group Inc 2200 Nelson St *Web:* www.easternshipbuilding.com	Panama City	FL	32401	850-763-1900	763-7904	698
Eastern Shore Chamber of Commerce 29750 Larry Dee Cawyer Dr PO Box 310 *Web:* www.eschamber.com	Daphne	AL	36526	251-928-6387	621-8001	139
Eastern Shore Community College 29300 Lankford Hwy *Web:* www.es.vccs.edu	Melfa	VA	23410	757-789-1789	789-1737	162
Eastern Shore Ctr 30500 State Hwy 181 *Web:* easternshorecentre.com	Spanish Fort	AL	36527	251-625-0060	625-0039	460
Eastern Shore Foods LLC PO Box 38	Mappsville	VA	23407	757-987-6543		296-14
Eastern Shore Natural Gas Co 1110 Forest Ave Ste 201 *TF:* 877-650-1257 ■ *Web:* www.esng.com	Dover	DE	19904	302-734-6720		787
Eastern Shore of Virginia Chamber of Commerce 19056 Pkwy Rd *Web:* www.esvachamber.org	Melfa	VA	23410	757-787-2460	787-8687	139
Eastern Sierra Realty Inc 218 E Line St *Web:* mysierrahomes.com	Bishop	CA	93514	760-873-4161	873-4124	652
Eastern Skateboard Supply Inc 6612 Amsterdam Way *TF:* 800-358-7588 ■ *Web:* www.easternskatesupply.com	Wilmington	NC	28405	910-791-8240		711
Eastern Star Church 5750 E 30th St *Web:* www.easternstarchurch.org	Indianapolis	IN	46218	317-591-5050		48-20
Eastern State Hospital (ESH) 4601 Ironbound Rd *Web:* esh.dbhds.virginia.gov	Williamsburg	VA	23188	757-253-5161		374-5

Name / Address	City	State	ZIP	Phone	Fax	Class
Eastern State Penitentiary Historic Site 22nd St & Fairmount Ave *Web:* www.easternstate.org	Philadelphia	PA	19130	215-236-3300	236-5289	50-3
Eastern Steel Corp 1946 Pitkin Ave *Web:* www.easternsteel.com	Brooklyn	NY	11207	718-495-5300	498-5526	492
Eastern University 1300 Eagle Rd *TF:* 800-452-0996 ■ *Web:* www.eastern.edu	Wayne	PA	19087	610-341-5800	341-1723	166
Eastern Virginia Medical School (EVMS) PO Box 1980 *Web:* www.evms.edu	Norfolk	VA	23501	757-446-5244	446-5817	167-2
Eastern Washington University 102 Sutton Hall *TF:* 800-280-1256 ■ *Web:* www.ewu.edu	Cheney	WA	99004	509-359-2314	359-6692	166
Eastern West Virginia Community & Technical College 316 Eastern Dr *TF:* 877-982-2322 ■ *Web:* www.easternwv.edu	Moorefield	WV	26836	304-434-8000	434-7000	162
Eastern Wholesale Fence Company Inc 274 Middle Island Rd *TF:* 800-339-3362 ■ *Web:* easternfence.com	Medford	NY	11763	631-698-0900	698-6408	191-2
Eastern Winds 3740 Washington Blvd *Web:* easternwindsrestaurant.com	Ogden	UT	84403	801-627-2739		671
Eastern Wyoming College 3200 W 'C' St *TF:* 800-658-3195 ■ *Web:* ewc.wy.edu	Torrington	WY	82240	307-532-8200	532-8222	162
Eastex Environmental Laboratory Inc PO Box 631375	Nacogdoches	TX	75963	936-569-8879		196
Eastex Telephone Co-opeartive Inc PO Box 150 *TF:* 800-232-7839 ■ *Web:* www.eastex.com	Henderson	TX	75653	903-854-1000		736
Eastfield Mall 1655 Boston Rd *Web:* www.eastfieldmall.com	Springfield	MA	01129	413-543-8000		460
Eastgate Mall 4601 Eastgate Blvd *Web:* www.shopeastgate-mall.com	Cincinnati	OH	45245	513-752-2294		460
EastGroup Properties Inc 188 E Capitol St *NYSE: EGP* ■ *TF:* 800-695-1564 ■ *Web:* www.eastgroup.net	Jackson	MS	39201	601-354-3555	352-1441	655
Eastham, Watson, Dale & Forney LLP The Niels Esperson Bldg 808 Travis Ste 1300 *Web:* www.easthamlaw.com	Houston	TX	77002	713-225-0905		428
Eastland County 100 W Main St *Web:* www.eastlandcountytexas.com	Eastland	TX	76448	254-629-1583	629-8125	338
Eastland Ctr 18000 Vernier Rd *Web:* www.shopeastland.com	Harper Woods	MI	48225	313-371-1501		460
Eastland Food Corp 8305 Stayton Dr *TF:* 800-645-0769 ■ *Web:* www.eastlandfood.com	Jessup	MD	20794	301-621-8140		297-8
Eastland Mall 800 N Green River Rd *Web:* www.shopeastlandmall.com	Evansville	IN	47715	812-477-4848		460
Eastland Shoe Manufacturing Corp 4 Meeting House Rd *TF:* 888-988-1998 ■ *Web:* www.eastlandshoe.com	Freeport	ME	04032	207-865-6314	865-9261	301
Eastman & Beaudine Inc 7201 Bishop Rd Ste 220 *Web:* www.eastman-beaudine.com	Plano	TX	75024	972-312-1012		266
Eastman & Smith Ltd 1 Seagate 550 N Summit St 24th Fl *Web:* www.eastmansmith.com	Toledo	OH	43604	419-241-6000	247-1777	428
Eastman Chemical Co 200 S Wilcox Dr *NYSE: EMN* ■ *TF:* 800-327-8626 ■ *Web:* www.eastman.com	Kingsport	TN	37660	423-229-2000		144
Eastman Chemical Co 500 K Ave *Web:* www.eastman.com	Gaston	SC	29053	803-794-9200		145
Eastman Kodak Co 343 State St *NYSE: KODK* ■ *Web:* www.kodak.com	Rochester	NY	14650	585-477-5146		591
Eastman Machine Co 779 Washington St *TF:* 800-872-5571 ■ *Web:* www.eastmancuts.com	Buffalo	NY	14203	716-856-2200	856-1140	744
Eastman Theatre 26 Gibbs St *Web:* www.esm.rochester.edu	Rochester	NY	14604	585-274-1000		572
Eastman-Booth Inc 4101 W Commercial St *Web:* www.eastmanbooth.com	Harrison	AR	72601	870-741-1000	741-6978	488
Eastmont Towers 6315 O St *Web:* www.eastmontliving.com	Lincoln	NE	68510	402-489-6591		672
Eastmont Town Ctr 6450 Camden St	Oakland	CA	94605	510-632-1602		460
Easton Area School District Inc 1801 Bushkill Dr *Web:* www.eastonsd.org	Easton	PA	18040	610-250-2400		685
Easton Coach Co 1200 Conroy Pl *Web:* eastoncoach.com	Easton	PA	18040	610-253-4055		107
Easton Hospital 250 S 21st St *TF:* 866-800-3880 ■ *Web:* www.slhn.org	Easton	PA	18042	610-250-4000		374-3
Easton Telecom Services LLC PO Box 550 *TF:* 800-222-8122 ■ *Web:* www.eastontel.com	Richfield	OH	44286	330-659-6700	659-9379	196
Easton's Group of Hotels Inc 3100 Steeles Ave E Gateway Ctr Ste 601 *Web:* eastonsgroup.com	Markham	ON	L3R8T3	905-940-9409		378
Eastover Capital Management 5605 Carnegie Blvd Ste 375 *Web:* www.eastovercapital.com	Charlotte	NC	28209	704-336-6818	336-6824	401
Eastover Estate & Eco-Village 430 East St PO Box 2282 *TF:* 866-264-5139 ■ *Web:* www.eastover.com	Lenox	MA	01240	866-264-5139		378
Eastown Distributors Co 14400 Oakland Ave *Web:* www.eastown.com	Highland Park	MI	48203	313-867-6900		81-1
Eastpointe Memorial Library 15875 Oak St *Web:* www.cityofeastpointe.net	Eastpointe	MI	48021	586-445-5096		434-3
Eastpointe Rehabilitation & Skilled Care Ctr 255 Central Ave *Web:* www.eastpointerehab.com	Chelsea	MA	02150	617-884-5700		450
Eastport Liquors Inc 1007 Bay Ridge Ave *Web:* www.eastportliquors.com	Annapolis	MD	21403	410-263-4747		81-1
Eastport Port Authority 3 Madison St *Web:* www.portofeastport.org	Eastport	ME	04631	207-853-4614	853-9584	618
Eastridge Ctr 2200 Eastridge Loop Ste 2062 *Web:* www.eastridgecenter.com	San Jose	CA	95122	408-238-3600		460
Eastridge Workforce Solutions 2355 Northside Dr *TF:* 800-778-0197 ■ *Web:* www.eastridge.com	San Diego	CA	92108	619-260-2100		734
Eastside Animal Hospital LLC 1496 E Main St *Web:* eastsidespartanburg.com	Spartanburg	SC	29307	864-585-6404		794
Eastside Cafe 2113 Manor Rd *Web:* www.eastsidecafeaustin.com	Austin	TX	78722	512-476-5858		671
Eastside Chamber of Commerce 3501 E 106th St Lower Level *Web:* www.eastsidechamber.net	Chicago	IL	60617	773-721-7948	721-7446	139
Eastside Food Co-Op 2551 Central Ave NE *Web:* eastsidefood.coop	Minneapolis	MN	55418	612-788-0950		345
Eastside Union School District 45006 30th St E *Web:* www.eastsideusd.org	Lancaster	CA	93535	661-952-1200	952-1220	685
Eastview Mall 7979 Pittsford-Victor Rd *Web:* www.eastviewmall.com	Victor	NY	14564	585-223-4420		460
Eastway Supplies Inc 1561 Alum Creek Dr *Web:* eastwaysupplies.com	Columbus	OH	43209	614-252-0974		610
East-West Consulting Inc 1153 Bergen Pky Ste I-285 *Web:* www.east-westconsulting.com	Evergreen	CO	80439	303-279-1405	325-3525	401
EastWest Institute (EWI) 1 E 26th St 20th Fl *Web:* www.eastwest.ngo	New York	NY	10010	212-824-4100	824-4149	634
East-West University 816 S Michigan Ave *Web:* www.eastwest.edu	Chicago	IL	60605	312-939-0111	939-0083	166
Eastwick Colleges Inc 10 S Franklin Tpke *Web:* eastwick.edu	Ramsey	NJ	07446	201-327-8877		162
Eastwood Mall 5555 Youngstown-Warren Rd *Web:* www.eastwoodmall.com	Niles	OH	44446	330-652-6980	544-5929	460
Eastwood Towne Ctr 3003 Preyde Blvd *Web:* www.shopeastwoodtownecenter.com	Lansing	MI	48912	517-316-9209	316-9214	460
Easy Analytic Software Inc 101 Haag Ave *Web:* www.easidemographics.com	Bellmawr	NJ	08031	856-931-5780		387
Easy Automation Inc 102 Mill St *Web:* www.easy-automation.com	Welcome	MN	56181	507-728-8214		358
Easy Drive Stake 4111 Todd Ln	Austin	TX	78744	512-447-9879		279
Easy Dynamics Inc 2003 11th St NW *Web:* www.easydynamics.com	Washington	DC	20001	202-558-7275		225
Easy Grammar Systems PO Box 25970 *TF:* 800-641-6015 ■ *Web:* www.easygrammar.com	Scottsdale	AZ	85255	480-502-9454	991-5635	535
Easy Ice LLC 925 W Washington St Ste 100 *TF:* 866-327-9423 ■ *Web:* www.easyice.com	Marquette	MI	49855	866-327-9423		791
Easy Picker Golf Products Inc 415 Leonard Blvd N *TF:* 800-641-4653 ■ *Web:* www.easypicker.com	Lehigh Acres	FL	33971	239-368-6600	369-1579	711
Easy Rider Canoe & Kayak Co PO Box 88108 *Web:* www.easyriderkayaks.com	Seattle	WA	98138	425-228-3633	277-8778	710
Easy-Ad 155 S Harvard St *Web:* easyadhemet.com	Hemet	CA	92543	951-658-2244		532-3
easyDNS Technologies Inc 219 Dufferin St Ste 300A **Fax Area Code:* 647 ■ *TF:* 855-321-3279 ■ *Web:* easydns.com	Toronto	ON	M6K3J1	416-535-8672	438-6227*	396
EasyGrass 14181 SW 143rd Ct *TF:* 800-988-6156 ■ *Web:* www.easygrass.net	Miami	FL	33186	305-234-5800		293
Easypak LLC 24 Jytek Dr *Web:* www.easypak.com	Leominster	MA	01453	978-516-9155		344
EasyStreet 9705 SW Sunshine Ct *TF:* 800-207-0740 ■ *Web:* www.easystreet.com	Beaverton	OR	97005	503-646-8400		225
Easyturf 2750 La Mirada Dr *TF:* 866-353-3518 ■ *Web:* www.easyturf.com	Vista	CA	92081	866-327-9887		608
Eat With Us PO Box 1368 *TF:* 888-222-9550 ■ *Web:* eatwithusrestaurants.com	Columbus	MS	39703	662-327-6982	327-1672	671
Eat'n Park Hospitality Group 285 E Waterfront Dr *TF:* 800-947-4033 ■ *Web:* www.eatnpark.com	Homestead	PA	15120	412-461-2000	461-6000	670
Eatefan Enterprises Inc 420 Jefferson Ave *Web:* estefankitchenorlando.com	Miami Beach	FL	33139	305-695-7000		670
Eatek 19404 Business Ctr Dr *Web:* www.eatekelectronics.com	Northridge	CA	91324	818-709-7700	709-2475	625
Eatelcorp Llc 913 S Burnside Ave *TF:* 800-621-4211 ■ *Web:* www.eatel.com	Gonzales	LA	70737	225-621-4300		736
Eaton 1000 Eaton Blvd *TF:* 800-386-1911 ■ *Web:* www.eaton.com	Cleveland	OH	44122	800-386-1911		620
Eaton & Berube Insurance Agency Inc 11 Concord St *Web:* www.eatonberube.com	Milford	NH	03055	603-673-0500		390
Eaton & Torrenzano LLP 1662 Sheepshead Bay Rd *Web:* eatonandtorrenzano.com	Brooklyn	NY	11235	718-332-7766		41
Eaton Aerospace LLC 9650 Jeronimo Rd *Web:* www.eaton.com	Irvine	CA	92618	949-452-9500	452-9555	21
Eaton Clothing & Furniture 135 Washington St *Web:* www.eatoncounty.org	Charlotte	MI	48813	517-543-4334		321
Eaton Corp 1111 Superior Ave *TF:* 877-386-2273 ■ *Web:* www.eaton.com	Cleveland	OH	44114	877-386-2273		60
Eaton County 1045 Independence Blvd *Web:* eatoncounty.org	Charlotte	MI	48813	517-543-7500	541-0666	338
Eaton Fabricating CoInc 1009 McAlpin Ct *Web:* www.eatonfabricating.com	Grafton	OH	44044	440-926-3121		492
Eaton Family Credit Union 333 Babbitt Rd Ste 100 *Web:* eatonfamilycu.com	Euclid	OH	44123	216-920-2000		219
Eaton Farm Confectioners Inc 30 Durbank Rd	Sutton	MA	01590	508-865-5235		296-8

Company	City	State	Zip	Phone	Fax	Class
Eaton Hall Exhibitions 256 Columbia Tpke *TF:* 800-746-9646 ■ *Web:* www.eatonhall.com	Florham Park	NJ	07932	973-514-5900		637-9
Eaton Hydraulics 803 32nd Ave W *Web:* www.eaton.com	Spencer	IA	51301	712-264-3324		640
Eaton Incentives Inc 271 US Hwy 46	Fairfield	NJ	07004	973-882-7700		384
Eaton Metal Products Co 4803 York St *TF:* 800-208-2657 ■ *Web:* www.eatonsalesservice.com	Denver	CO	80216	303-296-4800		91
Eaton Office Supply Company Inc 180 John Glenn Dr *TF:* 800-365-3237 ■ *Web:* www.eatonofficesupply.com	Buffalo	NY	14228	716-691-6100	691-0074	534
Eaton Oil Tools Inc 118 Rue DuPain *TF:* 800-232-5317 ■ *Web:* www.eatonoiltools.com	Broussard	LA	70518	337-856-8820		539
Eaton Rapids Medical Ctr 1500 S Main St *Web:* www.eatonrapidsmedicalcenter.org	Eaton Rapids	MI	48827	517-663-2671		374-3
Eaton Realty LLC 14012 Spector Rd *Web:* eatonrealty.com	Lithia	FL	33547	813-672-8022		652
Eaton Steel Corp 10221 Capital Ave *TF:* 800-527-3851 ■ *Web:* www.eatonsteel.com	Oak Park	MI	48237	248-398-3434		492
Eaton Vance Mutual Funds 2 International Pl *TF:* 800-225-6265 ■ *Web:* www.eatonvance.com	Boston	MA	02110	800-836-2414		528
Eatonform 2280 Arbor Blvd *TF:* 800-338-2012 ■ *Web:* eatonformppg.com	Dayton	OH	45439	937-298-3406	298-3637	534
Eatons' Ranch 270 Eatons' Ranch Rd *TF:* 800-210-1049 ■ *Web:* eatonsranch.com	Wolf	WY	82844	307-655-9285		239
Eatonton Cooperative Feed Company Inc 504 S Jefferson Ave *Web:* eatonton.com	Eatonton	GA	31024	706-485-7701	485-6561	276
EatStreet Inc 316 Washington Ave Ste 725 *TF:* 866-654-8777 ■ *Web:* eatstreet.com	Madison	WI	53703	866-654-8777		387
EAU Claire Area Chamber of Commerce 101 N Farwell St Ste 101 *Web:* www.eauclairechamber.org	Eau Claire	WI	54703	715-834-1204	834-1956	139
Eau Claire County 721 Oxford Ave *Web:* co.eau-claire.wi.us	Eau Claire	WI	54703	715-839-4801	839-4854	338
Eau Claire Ford Lincoln Mercury 2909 Lorch Ave *Web:* www.eauclaireford.net	Eau Claire	WI	54701	715-852-1000		57
EAW (Eastern Acoustic Works) 1 Main St *TF:* 800-992-5013 ■ *Web:* www.eaw.com	Whitinsville	MA	01588	508-234-6158	234-8251	52
EB Computing 336 W 37th St Rm 450 *Web:* eb-computing.com	Ossining	NY	10562	914-523-8142		196
EBA Engineering Consultants Ltd 14940-123 Ave *Web:* www.tetratech.com	Edmonton	AB	T5V1B4	780-451-2121	454-5688	194
EBA Engineering Inc 4813 Seton Dr *Web:* ebaengineering.com	Baltimore	MD	21215	410-358-7171		261
EBAA (Eye Bank Association of America) 1015 18th St NW Ste 1010 *Web:* restoresight.org	Washington	DC	20036	202-775-4999	429-6036	49-8
Ebara Technologies Inc 51 Main Ave *TF:* 800-535-5376 ■ *Web:* www.ebaratech.com	Sacramento	CA	95838	916-920-5451		695
eBay Inc 2065 Hamilton Ave *NASDAQ: EBAY* ■ *TF:* 800-322-9266 ■ *Web:* www.ebay.com	San Jose	CA	95125	408-376-7400	376-7401	51
EBB Associates Inc 1064 W Ocean View Ave *Web:* www.ebbweb.com	Norfolk	VA	23503	757-588-3939		256
Ebbert's Field Seed Inc 6840 N State Rte 48 *TF:* 888-802-5715 ■ *Web:* www.ebbertsseeds.com	Covington	OH	45318	937-473-2521	473-3710	276
Ebbtide Corp 2545 Jones Creek Rd *Web:* www.ebbtideboats.com	White Bluff	TN	37187	615-797-3193	797-4889	90
EBC (Eastern Book Co) 7 Lincoln Ave *TF:* 800-937-0331 ■ *Web:* www.ebc.com	Scarborough	ME	04074	800-937-0331	214-3895	96
EBC Inc 1095 Valets St *Web:* ebcinc.com	L'Ancienne-Lorette	QC	G2E4M7	418-872-0600		186
EBC Industries 200 Martha St *Web:* www.stanleyengineeredfastening.com	Blairsville	PA	15717	814-456-4287		350
EBCO General Contractor Ltd 804 E First St *Web:* ebcogc.com	Cameron	TX	76520	254-697-8516	697-8656	186
Ebco Industries Ltd 7851 Alderbridge Way *Web:* www.ebco.com	Richmond	BC	V6X2A4	604-278-5578		454
Ebel Inc 8270 Arlington Expy *TF:* 866-752-6320 ■ *Web:* www.ebelinc.com	Jacksonville	FL	32211	866-752-6320		320
Ebenezer Baptist Church 407 Auburn Ave NE *Web:* ebenezeratl.org	Atlanta	GA	30312	404-688-7300	521-1129	50-1
Eberbach Corp 505 S Maple Rd *Web:* www.eberbachlabtools.com	Ann Arbor	MI	48103	734-665-8877		419
Eberhard Hardware Manufacturing Ltd 1523 Bellmill Rd *TF:* 800-567-3344 ■ *Web:* www.eberhard.com	Tillsonburg	ON	N4GOC9	519-688-3443		350
Eberhard Lumber Co 1445 Mcqueeney Rd *Web:* eberhardlumber.com	New Braunfels	TX	78130	830-625-4616		351
Eberhard Manufacturing Co 21944 Drake Rd *TF:* 800-334-6706 ■ *Web:* www.eberhard.com	Strongsville	OH	44149	440-238-9720	572-2732	350
Eberhart Accounting Services PC 496 W Boughton Rd *Web:* eataxes.com	Bolingbrook	IL	60440	630-759-5070	759-9101	2
Eberl Iron Works Inc 128 Sycamore St *TF:* 800-285-3056 ■ *Web:* www.eberliron.com	Buffalo	NY	14204	716-854-7633		480
Eberline Services Inc 4520 Montgomery Ave NE *Web:* www.eberlineservices.com	Albuquerque	NM	87109	505-508-1666		463
Eberly & Eberly 180 S Washington St *Web:* eberlylaw.com	Tiffin	OH	44883	419-448-0204		41
Eberly, Mcmahon LLC 2321 Kemper Ln Ste 100 *Web:* emclawyers.com	Cincinnati	OH	45206	513-533-9808		41
Eberspaecher North America Inc 29101 Haggerty Rd *Web:* www.eberspaecher.com	Novi	MI	48377	248-994-7010	994-7015	60
Ebert Construction 23350 County Rd 10 *Web:* www.ebertconstructionmn.com	Loretto	MN	55357	763-498-7844	498-9951	186
Ebert Machine Company Inc 2177 State Rd 19 *Web:* www.ebertmachine.com	Peru	IN	46970	765-473-3728	473-3804	621
Ebey's Landing National Historical Reserve 162 Cemetery Rd *Web:* www.nps.gov	Coupeville	WA	98239	360-678-6084		564
EBG (Employee Benefits Group Inc) 4405 E West Hwy Ste 202 *TF:* 800-225-3242 ■ *Web:* www.ebg.com	Bethesda	MD	20814	301-718-4637		196
EBG Consulting 419 Hudson Rd *Web:* www.ebgconsulting.com	Sudbury	MA	01776	978-261-5552		41
EBI (Editorial Bautista Independiente) 3417 Kenilworth Blvd *TF:* 800-398-7187 ■ *Web:* www.ebi-bmm.org	Sebring	FL	33870	863-382-6350	382-8650	48-20
EBI Consulting Inc 21 B St *TF:* 800-786-2346 ■ *Web:* www.ebiconsulting.com	Burlington	MA	01803	781-273-2500		196
Ebisu 1283 Ninth Ave *Web:* ebisusushi.com	San Francisco	CA	94122	415-566-1770		671
Ebix BPO 151 N Lyon Ave *TF:* 800-996-9964 ■ *Web:* www.certsonline.com	Hemet	CA	92543	951-658-4000		225
Ebix Inc 5 Concourse Pkwy Ste 3200 *NASDAQ: EBIX* ■ *TF:* 800-755-2326 ■ *Web:* ebix.com	Atlanta	GA	30328	678-281-2020	281-2019	178-11
eBizDocs 85 Broadway *Web:* ebizdocs.com	Menands	NY	12204	518-456-1011		363
eBlox Inc 404 W 30th St Ste A *Web:* eblox.com	Austin	TX	78705	512-867-1001		225
EBM-papst Inc 100 & 110 Hyde Rd *Web:* www.ebmpapst.in	Farmington	CT	06034	860-674-1515	674-8536	18
EBMS (Employee Benefit Management Services Inc) 2075 Overland Ave *TF:* 800-777-3575 ■ *Web:* www.ebms.com	Billings	MT	59102	406-245-3575	652-5380	390
Ebner and Sons Publishers 3714 48th Ave NE *Web:* www.ebnerandsons.com	Seattle	WA	98105	206-524-0930		637-2
Ebner Furnaces Inc 224 Quadral Dr *Web:* www.ebner.cc	Wadsworth	OH	44281	330-335-1600	335-1605	357
Ebonite International Inc PO Box 746 *TF:* 800-326-6483 ■ *Web:* www.ebonite.com	Hopkinsville	KY	42241	270-881-1200	881-1201	710
Ebony Magazine 200 S Michigan Ave 21st Fl *Web:* www.ebony.com	Chicago	IL	60604	312-322-9228	322-1099	457-11
EBQ 3000 S IH 35 Ste 320 *TF:* 800-566-3050 ■ *Web:* ebq.com	Austin	TX	78704	512-637-9696		195
EBR Systems Inc 480 Oakmead Pkwy *Web:* ebrsystemsinc.com	Sunnyvale	CA	94085	408-720-1906	720-1996	250
ebrary Inc 318 Cambridge Ave *Web:* www.ebrary.com	Palo Alto	CA	94306	650-475-8700	475-8881	225
EBRI (Employee Benefit Research Institute) 1100 13th St NW Ste 878 *Web:* www.ebri.org	Washington	DC	20005	202-659-0670	775-6312	634
Ebro Foods Inc 1330 W 43rd St *Web:* www.ebrofoods.com	Chicago	IL	60609	773-696-0150	696-0151	296-36
EBRPL (East Baton Rouge Parish Library) 7711 Goodwood Blvd *Web:* www.ebrpl.com	Baton Rouge	LA	70806	225-231-3750		434-3
EBS (Execu-Tech Business Systems Inc) 1829 Silver Star Rd *Web:* www.ebs-fl.com	Orlando	FL	32804	407-447-6800	447-6804	112
EBS Associates Inc 7150 SW Hampton St Ste 200 *TF:* 888-232-4758 ■ *Web:* ebsassociates.com	Tigard	OR	97223	503-885-0776		734
EBSCO Industries Inc 5724 Hwy 280 *Web:* www.ebscoind.com	Birmingham	AL	35242	205-991-6600		185
EBSCO Information Services 10 Estes St *TF:* 800-653-2726 ■ *Web:* www.ebsco.com	Ipswich	MA	01938	978-356-6500	356-6565	96
EBTC (East Buchanan Telephone Coop) 214 3rd St N *TF:* 866-327-2748 ■ *Web:* www.eastbuchanan.com	Winthrop	IA	50682	319-935-3011	935-3010	224
Ebtec Corp 120 Shoemaker Ln *Web:* ebtec.hanwhaaerospaceusa.com	Agawam	MA	01001	413-786-0393		454
E-Builder Inc 1800 NW 69 Ave Ste 201 *TF:* 800-580-9322 ■ *Web:* www.e-builder.net	Plantation	FL	33313	954-556-6701		39
Ebusiness Strategies LLC 18318 Fern Trl Ctr *Web:* askebiz.com	Houston	TX	77084	281-647-6183		463
eBusinessDesign 900 E Hamilton Ave Ste 100 *Web:* www.ebusinessdesign.com	Campbell	CA	95008	408-654-7900	654-7907	196
eBX LLC 101 Federal St Ste 1010 *TF:* 800-958-4813 ■ *Web:* www.levelats.com	Boston	MA	02110	617-350-1600	350-1699	690
Eby Co 4300 H St *TF:* 800-329-3430 ■ *Web:* www.ebycompany.com	Philadelphia	PA	19124	215-537-4700	537-4780	253
Eby-Brown Co 1415 W Diehl Rd Ste 300N *TF:* 800-553-8249 ■ *Web:* www.eby-brown.com	Naperville	IL	60563	630-778-2800	778-2830	756
EC Boston 1 Faneuil Hall Sq *Web:* www.ecenglish.com	Boston	MA	02109	617-247-3033	247-2959	423
EC Council University Inc 6330 Riverside Plaza Ln NW Ste 210 *Web:* www.eccouncil.org	Albuquerque	NM	87120	505-341-3228		95
EC Ernst Inc 132 Log Canoe Cir *TF:* 800-683-7770 ■ *Web:* www.ecernst.com	Stevensville	MD	21666	301-350-7770	499-0933	189-4
EC Infosystems Inc 333 Earle Ovington Blvd Ste 102 *Web:* ecinfosystems.com	Uniondale	NY	11553	516-874-8000		225
EC Power International Inc 1400 Preston Rd	Plano	TX	75093	713-626-8700		321
EC Shaw Co 1242 Mehring Way *TF:* 866-532-7429 ■ *Web:* ecshaw.com	Cincinnati	OH	45203	513-721-6334	721-6350	629

	Phone	Fax	Class
EC Source Services LLC 6644 E Thomas Rd .... Mesa AZ 85215 *Web:* ecsourceservices.com	480-245-7200		256
EC Suite LLC 2353 W University Dr .... Tempe AZ 85281 *Web:* www.ecsuite.com	480-449-8817		387
ECA (Engineering Contractors' Assn, The) 2190 S Towne Centre Pl .... Anaheim CA 92806 *Web:* ecasocal.org	714-937-5000	937-5030	49-19
ECA (Evangelical Church Alliance) 205 W Broadway St PO Box 9 .... Bradley IL 60915 *TF:* 888-855-6060 ■ *Web:* www.ecainternational.org	815-937-0720		48-20
ECA Edinburg Citrus Assn PO Box 428 .... Edinburg TX 78540 *TF:* 877-381-1322 ■ *Web:* www.txcitrus.com	956-383-2743		315-2
ECA Medical Instruments Inc 1107 Tourmaline Dr .... Newbury Park CA 91320 *Web:* www.ecamedical.com	805-376-2509		350
eCapital 600 Townpark Ln Ste 450 .... Kennesaw GA 30144 *TF:* 877-882-4229 ■ *Web:* ecapital.com	877-882-4229		272
eCapital Advisors LLC 7900 Xerxes Ave S Ste 1300 .... Bloomington MN 55431 *Web:* www.ecapitaladvisors.com	952-947-9300	947-9301	463
ECAT (Escambia County Area Transit) 1515 W Fairfield Dr .... Pensacola FL 32501 *Web:* goecat.com	850-595-3228	595-3222	468
ECC Capital Corp 2600 E Coast Hwy Ste 250 .... Corona Del Mar CA 92625 *OTC:* ECRO ■ *Web:* www.ecccapital.com	949-954-7052		654
ECCB (Erie 2-Chautauqua Cattaraugus Boces) 8685 Erie Rd .... Angola NY 14006 *TF:* 800-228-1184 ■ *Web:* www.e2ccb.org	716-549-4454		685
ECCLD (East Cheyenne County Library District) PO Box 939 .... Cheyenne Wells CO 80810 *Web:* www.eccld.org	719-767-5138	767-5379	434-3
Eccles Community Art Ctr 2580 Jefferson Ave .... Ogden UT 84401 *Web:* ogden4arts.org	801-392-6935		50-2
Ecclesia College 9653 Nations Dr .... Springdale AR 72762 *Web:* ecollege.edu	479-248-7236	248-1455	161
ECCO 833 W Diamond St .... Boise ID 83705 *TF:* 800-635-5900 ■ *Web:* www.eccolink.com	800-635-5900	688-3226	700
ECCO III Enterprises Inc 201 Saw Mill River Rd .... Yonkers NY 10701 *Web:* www.eccoiii.com	914-963-3600	476-8705	188-4
ECCO Select 4100 N Mulberry Dr Ste 105 .... Kansas City MO 64116 *TF:* 888-567-3226 ■ *Web:* www.eccoselect.com	816-960-3800		177
ECCS Nationwide Mobile Laboratories 2525 Advance Rd .... Madison WI 53718 *Web:* www.eccsmobilelab.com	608-221-8700		743
ECD Systems Inc 2415 W Erie Dr .... Tempe AZ 85282 *Web:* www.ecdsys.com	480-609-6300		177
ECDC (Ethiopian Community Development Council Inc) 901 S Highland St .... Arlington VA 22204 *Web:* www.ecdcus.org	703-685-0510	685-0529	48-5
EcElectric 2121 NW Thurman St .... Portland OR 97210 *TF:* 800-659-3511 ■ *Web:* ecpowerslife.com	503-224-3511		189-4
Ecendant Interactive Ltd 22970 Indian Creek Dr Ste 190 .... Sterling VA 20166 *Web:* www.ecendant.com	703-264-7437		178-1
Ecessa Corp 13755 First Ave N Ste 100 .... Plymouth MN 55441 *TF:* 800-669-6242 ■ *Web:* www.ecessa.com	763-694-9949		735
ECFA (Evangelical Council for Financial Accountability) 440 W Jubal Early Dr Ste 130 .... Winchester VA 22601 *TF:* 800-323-9473 ■ *Web:* www.ecfa.org	540-535-0103	535-0533	48-5
ECFC (Employers Council on Flexible Compensation) 1220 L St NW Ste 100-417 .... Washington DC 20005 *Web:* www.ecfc.org	202-659-4300	618-6060	49-12
ECG Consulting Group Inc 40 British American Blvd .... Latham NY 12110 *Web:* www.ecgconsulting.com	518-782-7500	782-7553	196
ECG Management Consultants 1111 Third Ave Ste 2500 .... Seattle WA 98101 *TF:* 800-729-7635 ■ *Web:* www.ecgmc.com	206-689-2200	689-2209	194
Echelbarger, Himebaugh, Tamm and Co 2301 E Paris Ave SE .... Grand Rapids MI 49546 *Web:* www.ehtc.com	616-575-3482	575-3481	2
Echo Associates Inc 933 Ridge Dr .... McLean VA 22101 *Web:* callecho.com	703-448-0633		177
Echo Canyon State Park HC 74 PO Box 295 ...... Pioche NV 89043 *Web:* www.parks.nv.gov	775-962-5103		565
Echo Communications Inc 59 Pleasant St .... New London NH 03257 *Web:* www.echocominc.com	603-526-6006	526-6062	627
Echo Design Group 10 E 40th St 16th Fl .... New York NY 10016 *TF:* 800-327-3896 ■ *Web:* echonewyork.com	212-686-8771		155-13
Echo Digital Audio Corp 6450 Via Real Ste 1 .... Carpinteria CA 93013 *Web:* echoaudio.com	805-684-4593		52
Echo Engineering & Production Supplies Inc 5406 W 78th St .... Indianapolis IN 46268 *Web:* www.echosupply.com	317-876-8848		791
Echo Global Logistics Inc 600 W Chicago Ave Ste 725 .... Chicago IL 60654 *TF:* 800-354-7993 ■ *Web:* www.echo.com	800-354-7993		194
Echo Group Inc, The 15 Washington St .... Conway NH 03818 *TF:* 800-635-8209 ■ *Web:* www.echobh.com	603-447-8600		177
Echo Inc 400 Oakwood Rd .... Lake Zurich IL 60047 *TF:* 800-673-1558 ■ *Web:* www.echo-usa.com	800-673-1558		429
Echo Industrial Inc 1615 Ritner Hwy .... Carlisle PA 17013 *Web:* www.echoindustrial.com	717-249-6319		454
Echo Lake Farm Produce Co PO Box 279 .... Burlington WI 53105 *TF:* 800-888-3447 ■ *Web:* www.echolakefoods.com	800-888-3447		10-8
Echo Media Group 2842 E Walnut Ave Ste A .... Tustin CA 92780 *Web:* www.echomediateam.com	714-573-0899		636
Echo Molding Inc 911 Springfield Rd Ste 1 .... Union NJ 07083 *Web:* www.echomolding.com	908-688-0099	688-0529	604
Echo Real Estate Services 560 Epsilon Dr .... Pittsburgh PA 15238 *Web:* echoretail.com	412-968-1660		652
Echo Rock Ventures 13620 Lincoln Way Ste 380 .... Auburn CA 95603	530-823-9600	823-9650	183
Echo Technology Solutions 44 Montgomery 3rd Fl PO Box 566 .... San Francisco CA 94104 *Web:* www.echots.com	415-857-3246		196
EchoData Services Inc 121 N Shirk Rd .... New Holland PA 17557 *TF:* 800-511-3870 ■ *Web:* www.echodata.com	800-511-3870		393
Echols County 110 General Beloach St .... Statenville GA 31648 *TF:* 877-854-0872 ■ *Web:* echolscountyga.com	229-559-6538	559-9436	338
Echometer Co 5001 Ditto Ln .... Wichita Falls TX 76302 *Web:* echometer.com	940-767-4334		639
EchoPoint Media 409 Massachusetts Ave .... Indianapolis IN 46204 *Web:* echopointmedia.com	317-264-8400	264-8016	5
Echota Fabrics Inc 1394 US 41 N .... Calhoun GA 30701 *TF:* 800-763-9750 ■ *Web:* www.echotafabrics.com	706-629-9750	629-5229	746
Echota Technologies Corp 3286 Northpark Blvd Ste A .... Alcoa TN 37701	865-273-1270		180
Echoworx Corp 4101 Yonge St Ste 708 .... Toronto ON M2P1N6 *TF:* 800-735-8916 ■ *Web:* www.echoworx.com	416-226-8600		179
ECI (Engine Components Inc) 9503 Middlex .... San Antonio TX 78217 *TF:* 800-324-2359	210-820-8100	820-8102	21
ECI (Effective Compensation Inc) 32045 Castle Ct Ste 103 .... Evergreen CO 80439 *TF:* 877-746-4324 ■ *Web:* www.effectivecompensation.com	303-854-1000	854-1030	194
ECI Telecom Ltd 5100 NW 33rd Ave Ste 150 .... Fort Lauderdale FL 33309 *Web:* www.ecitele.com	954-772-3070	351-4404	735
ECII (Engineered Controls International Inc) 100 Rego Dr PO Box 247 .... Elon NC 27244 *TF:* 800-650-0061 ■ *Web:* www.regoproducts.com	336-449-7707	449-6594	789
Ecity Interactive Inc 1608 Walnut St 12th Fl .... Philadelphia PA 19102 *Web:* www.ecityinteractive.com	215-557-0767		195
eCivis Inc 418 N Fair Oaks Ave Ste 301 .... Pasadena CA 91103 *TF:* 877-232-4847 ■ *Web:* www.ecivis.com	877-232-4847		69
ECK Industries Inc 1602 N Eigth St PO Box 967 .... Manitowoc WI 54221 *Web:* www.eckindustries.com	920-682-4618	682-9298	308
Eckards Home Improvement 2402 N Belt Hwy .... Saint Joseph MO 64506 *TF:* 800-264-2794 ■ *Web:* www.eckardsflooring.com	816-279-4522		290
Eckel Industries Inc 100 Groton Shirley Rd .... Ayer MA 01432 *Web:* eckelusa.com	978-772-0840		261
Eckel Manufacturing Company Inc 8035 N County Rd W .... Odessa TX 79764 *TF:* 800-654-4779 ■ *Web:* www.eckel.com	432-362-4336	362-1827	223
Eckell, Sparks, Levy, Auerbach, Monte, Sloane, Matthews & Auslander PC 344 W Front St .... Media PA 19063 *Web:* www.eckellsparks.com	610-565-3700		428
Eckenrod Ford Lincoln Mercury of Cullman Inc 5255 Alabama Hwy 157 .... Cullman AL 35058 *Web:* www.eckenrodford.com	256-734-3361		57
Eckerd College 4200 54th Ave S .... Saint Petersburg FL 33711 *TF:* 800-456-9009 ■ *Web:* www.eckerd.edu	727-867-1166	866-2304	166
Eckert & Ziegler Isotope Products Inc 24937 Ave Tibbitts .... Valencia CA 91355 **Fax Area Code:* 415 ■ *TF:* 800-871-3075 ■ *Web:* www.ezag.com	661-309-1010	461-8940*	419
Eckhardt & Company PC 1 Huntington Quadrangle Ste 4S14 .... Melville NY 11747 *Web:* eckhardtcompany.com	631-420-8100	420-8795	2
Eckhart & Company Inc 4011 W 54th St .... Indianapolis IN 46254 *TF:* 800-443-3791 ■ *Web:* www.eckhartandco.com	317-347-2665	347-2666	86
Eckhart Public Library 603 S Jackson St .... Auburn IN 46706 *Web:* www.epl.lib.in.us	260-925-2414		434-3
Eckhoff Accountancy Corp 145 N Redwood Dr .... San Rafael CA 94903 *Web:* www.eckhoff.com	415-499-9400		2
Eckler Ltd 110 Sheppard Ave E Ste 900 .... Toronto ON M2N7A3 *Web:* www.eckler.ca	416-429-3330		194
Ecklund-Harrison Technologies Inc 11000 Metro Pky Ste 40 .... Fort Myers FL 33966 *Web:* 0370869.netsolhost.com	239-936-6032	936-6327	472
Eck-mundy Associates Inc 450 E 11th St .... Jasper IN 47546 *Web:* eck-mundy.com	812-634-8001		180
Ecko Fin and Tooling Inc 221 Hopkins Ave .... Jamestown NY 14701 *Web:* www.eckofintooling.com	716-487-0200	487-0202	493
Eckoh 7172 Regional St Ste 431 .... Dublin CA 94568 **Fax Area Code:* 888 ■ *Web:* www.eckoh.com	925-208-2450	455-2285*	317
Eckroat Seed Co 1106 Martin Luther King Ave .... Oklahoma City OK 73117 *TF:* 800-331-7333 ■ *Web:* www.eckroatseed.com	405-427-2484		276
Eclectic Products Inc 1075 Arrowsmith St PO Box 2280 .... Eugene OR 97402 *TF:* 800-693-4667 ■ *Web:* eclecticproducts.com	800-693-4667		3
Eclectik Design LLC 161 N Clark St Ste 1600 .... Chicago IL 60601 **Fax Area Code:* 773 ■ *Web:* www.eclectik.com	312-690-3181	751-2075*	130
Eclipse Advertising Inc 1329 Scott Rd .... Burbank CA 91504 *Web:* eclipsead.com	818-238-9388		708
Eclipse Bistro 1020 N Union St .... Wilmington DE 19805 *Web:* www.platinumdininggroup.com	302-658-1588		671
Eclipse Capital Management Inc 7700 Bonhomme Ave Ste 500 .... Saint Louis MO 63105 *Web:* www.eclipsecap.com	314-725-2100	725-2116	401

Phone | Fax | Class

Eclipse Colour & Imaging Corp
875 Laurentian Dr ... Burlington ON L7N3W7 905-634-1900 627
TF: 800-668-6369 ■ Web: www.eclipseimaging.ca

Eclipse di Luna 764 Miami Cir ... Atlanta GA 30324 404-846-0449 671
Web: www.eclipsediluna.org

Eclipse Energy Systems Inc
2345 Anvil St N ... Saint Petersburg FL 33710 727-344-7300 196
Web: www.eclipsethinfilms.com

Eclipse Foundation 102 Centrepointe Dr ... Nepean ON K2G6B1 613-224-9461 303
Web: www.eclipse.org

Eclipse Inc 1665 Elmwood Rd ... Rockford IL 61103 815-877-3031 877-3336 318
TF: 888-826-3473 ■ Web: www.eclipsenet.com

Eclipse Marketing Services Inc
240 Cedar Knolls Rd Ste 100 ... Cedar Knolls NJ 07927 800-837-4648 195
TF: 800-837-4648 ■ Web: www.eclipsemarketingservices.com

Ecliptic Enterprises Corp
398 W Washington Blvd Ste 100 ... Pasadena CA 91103 626-798-2436 387
Web: www.eclipticenterprises.com

ECM (Eliza Coffee Memorial Hospital)
205 Marengo St ... Florence AL 35630 256-768-8323 374-3
Web: www.chgroup.org

ECM Consultants Inc
4409 Utica St Ste 200 ... Metairie LA 70006 504-885-4080 885-1439 256
Web: www.ecmconsultants.com

Ecm Intl 404 Executive Center Blvd ... El Paso TX 79902 915-351-1900 351-1908 261
Web: ecmintl.com

ECM Publishers Inc
4095 Coon Rapids Blvd ... Coon Rapids MN 55433 763-712-2400 637-8
Web: www.ecm-inc.com

ECMD Inc
2 Grandview St PO Box 130 ... North Wilkesboro NC 28659 336-667-5976 903-0000 690
TF: 800-745-5931 ■ Web: www.ecmd.com

Eco Canada 308 - 11th Ave SE Ste 200 ... Calgary AB T2G0Y2 403-233-0748 764
TF: 800-251-7773 ■ Web: www.eco.ca

Eco Engineering LLC
11815 Hwy Dr Ste 600 ... Cincinnati OH 45241 513-985-8300 985-9940 261
Web: ecoengineering.com

Eco Lips Inc
329 10th Ave SE Ste 213 ... Cedar Rapids IA 52401 319-364-2477 231
TF: 866-326-5477 ■ Web: ecolips.com

Eco Park Resort at Mt St Helens Inc
14000 Spirit Lake Hwy ... Toutle WA 98649 360-274-7007 760
Web: www.ecoparkresort.com

Eco Water Systems Inc
1890 Woodlane Dr ... Woodbury MN 55125 800-808-9899 427
TF: 800-808-9899 ■ Web: www.ecowater.com

Ecoair Corp 21 Overlook Dr ... Hamden CT 06514 203-230-3000 192
Web: ecoair.com

eCoast Marketing
35E Industrial Way Ste 201 ... Rochester NH 03867 603-516-7450 317
Web: www.ecoastmarketing.com

Ecodyne Ltd 4475 Corporate Dr ... Burlington ON L7L5T9 905-332-1404 332-6726 386
TF: 888-326-3963 ■ Web: ecodyne.com

Ecodyne MRM 8203 Market St ... Houston TX 77029 713-675-3511 675-7922 91
Web: www.ecodyne-heatexchangers.com

ECOF (Eye Centers of Florida)
4101 Evans Ave ... Fort Myers FL 33901 239-939-3456 936-8776 798
TF: 888-393-2455 ■ Web: www.ecof.com

Ecojustice Canada
131 Water St Ste 214 ... Vancouver BC V6B4M3 604-685-5618 685-7813 48-13
TF: 800-926-7744 ■ Web: www.ecojustice.ca

Ecola State Park
84318 Ecola State Park Rd ... Cannon Beach OR 97110 503-436-2844 565
Web: stateparks.oregon.gov

Ecolab Canada 5105 Tomken Rd ... Mississauga ON L4W2X5 800-268-0465 806
TF: 800-268-0465 ■ Web: www.ecolab.com

Ecole De La Cle-des-champs
3858 Rue Principale ... Dunham QC J0E1M0 450-295-2722 685
Web: cle-des-champs.csvdc.qc.ca

Ecole Nationale de Police du Quebec Centre de Documentation
350 rue Marguerite DYouville ... Nicolet QC J3T1X4 819-293-8631 293-8630 434-3
Web: www.enpq.qc.ca

Ecole Polytechnique de Montreal
2900 Boul Edouard-Montpetit ... Montreal QC H3T1J4 514-340-4711 162
Web: www.polymtl.ca

Ecolo Odor Control Technologies Inc
59 Penn Dr ... Toronto ON M9L2A6 416-740-3900 740-3800 104
TF: 800-667-6355 ■ Web: ecolo.com

Ecological Fibers 40 Pioneer Dr ... Lunenburg MA 01462 978-537-0003 537-2238 557
Web: www.ecofibers.com

Ecological Laboratories Inc
PO Box 184 ... Malverne NY 11565 516-823-3441 823-3440 145
TF: 800-645-2976 ■ Web: ecologicallabs.com

Ecological Resource Consultants Inc
35715 Us Hwy 40 Ste D204 ... Evergreen CO 80439 303-679-4820 261
Web: erccolorado.net

Ecological Restoration & Management Inc (ER&M)
10600 York Rd Ste 203 ... Cockeysville MD 21030 410-337-4899 583-5678 186
Web: www.er-m.com

Ecological Society of America (ESA)
1990 M St Ste 700 ... Washington DC 20036 202-833-8773 833-8775 49-19
Web: www.esa.org

Ecology & Environment Inc
368 Pleasant View Dr ... Lancaster NY 14086 716-684-8060 684-0844 192
NASDAQ: EEI ■ Web: www.ene.com

Ecology Action 5798 Ridgewood Rd ... Willits CA 95490 707-459-0150 459-5409 323
Web: www.growbiointensive.org

Ecom Engineering Inc
1796 Tribute Rd Ste 100 ... Sacramento CA 95815 916-641-5600 256
Web: www.ecomeng.com

Ecom Enterprises Inc
1230 Oakmead Pkwy Ste 318 ... Sunnyvale CA 94085 408-720-9194 180
Web: www.ecomenterprises.com

Ecom Solutions
7326 Yellowstone Blvd ... Forest Hills NY 11375 718-793-2828 732-4509 180
Web: www.ecomsolutions.net

Eco-Med Pharmaceuticals Inc
7050B Bramalea Rd Unit 58 ... Mississauga ON L5S1S9 905-405-1050 405-0775 582
Web: www.eco-med.com

E-Commerce Times (ECT)
16133 Ventura Blvd Ste 700 ... Encino CA 91436 818-461-9700 461-9710 457-5
TF: 877-328-5500 ■ Web: www.ectnews.com

Ecomuseum
21125 Ch Sainte-Marie ... Sainte-Anne-de-Bellevue QC H9X3Y7 514-457-9449 457-0769 823
Web: www.zooecomuseum.ca

Econcordia 1250 Guy ... Montreal QC H3H2T4 514-848-8770 165
Web: www.econcordia.com

Econoco Corp 300 Karin Ln ... Hicksville NY 11801 516-935-7700 505-8300* 286
*Fax Area Code: 800 ■ TF: 800-645-7032 ■ Web: www.econoco.com

Econ-o-copy Inc 4437 Trenton St Ste A ... Metairie LA 70006 504-457-0032 457-0114 535
TF: 877-256-0310 ■ Web: www.econ-o-copy.com

Econolite Control Products Inc
3360 E La Palma Av ... Anaheim CA 92806 714-630-3700 630-6349 700
TF: 800-225-6480 ■ Web: www.econolite.com

Econometric Society
New York Univ Dept of Economics 19 W Fourth St
Sixth Fl ... New York NY 10012 212-998-3820 995-4487 49-5
Web: www.econometricsociety.org

Economic Analysis Associates Inc
5 Glen Ct ... Greenwich CT 06830 203-869-9667 869-9549 466
Web: www.eaainc.com

Economic Consulting Services LLC
2001 L St NW ... Washington DC 20036 202-466-7720 466-2710 195
Web: www.economic-consulting.com

Economic Development Administration
1401 Constitution Ave NW ... Washington DC 20230 202-482-2900 340-2
Web: www.eda.gov

Economic Development Administration Regional Office
Atlanta 401 W Peachtree St NW Ste 1820 ... Atlanta GA 30308 404-730-3002 730-3025 340-2
Web: www.eda.gov
Austin 903 San Jacinto Ste 206 ... Austin TX 78701 512-381-8150 499-0478 340-2
Web: www.eda.gov
Chicago 230 S Dearborn St Ste 3280 ... Chicago IL 60606 312-353-8143 340-2
Web: www.eda.gov
Seattle 915 Second Ave Rm 1890 ... Seattle WA 98174 206-220-7660 220-7669 340-2
Web: www.eda.gov

Economic Development Alliance of Jefferson County
510 Main St ... Pine Bluff AR 71611 870-535-0110 196
Web: www.jeffersoncountyalliance.com

Economic Development in Orem
56 N State St Rm 101 ... Orem UT 84057 801-229-7172 139
Web: www.econdev.orem.org

Economic Opportunity Board of Clark County
330 W Washington Ave Ste 7 ... Las Vegas NV 89106 702-647-3307 647-3125 317
Web: www.eobcapsnv.org

Economic Policy Institute
1225 Eye St NW Ste 600 ... Washington DC 20005 202-775-8810 775-0819 634
TF: 800-374-4844 ■ Web: www.epi.org

Economic Progress Alliance of Crawford County
789 Bessemer St ... Meadville PA 16335 814-333-2299 653
Web: epacc.net

Economic Research Service (ERS)
US Dept of Agriculture 1400 Independence Ave SW MS 1800
... Washington DC 20250 202-694-5050 340-1
Web: www.ers.usda.gov

Economic Strategy Institute
3050 K St NW Ste 220 ... Washington DC 20007 202-965-9484 965-1104 634
Web: www.econstrat.org

Economic Systems Inc
3120 Frview Pk Dr Ste 500 ... Falls Church VA 22042 703-642-5225 463
Web: www.econsys.com

Economical Insurance
111 Westmount Rd S PO Box 2000 ... Waterloo ON N2J4S4 519-570-8200 570-8389 391-4
TF: 800-265-2180 ■ Web: www.economical.com

Economist Intelligence Unit
750 Third Ave 5th Fl ... New York NY 10017 212-698-9717 586-1181 637-9
Web: www.eiu.com

Economy Insurance Agency Inc
1691 Main St ... Springfield MA 01103 413-736-6785 390
Web: economyspringfield.com

Economy Linen & Towel Service Inc
80 Mead St ... Dayton OH 45402 937-222-4625 393
Web: www.economylinen.com

Economy Lumber 720 Camden Ave ... Campbell CA 95008 408-378-5231 378-0258 364
Web: www.economylumber.com

Economy Office Supply Co
1725 Gardena Ave ... Glendale CA 91204 818-548-1525 535
Web: www.economyofficesupply.com

Economy Shoe Shop Cafe & Bar
1663 Argyle St ... Halifax NS B3J2B5 902-423-8845 671
Web: www.economyshoeshop.ca

EcoPower Hybrid Systems Inc
9995 Ave de Catania Local G ... Brossard QC J4Z3V7 450-676-7755 676-7716 112
Web: ecopowerhs.com

eCornell 950 Danby Rd Ste 150 ... Ithaca NY 14850 607-330-3200 242
TF: 866-326-7635 ■ Web: www.ecornell.com

Ecorse Machinery Sales and Rebuilders Inc
4261 13th St ... Wyandotte MI 48192 313-383-2100 381-4464 456
Web: www.ecorse.com

Eco-Site Inc 240 Leigh Farm Rd Ste 415 ... Durham NC 27707 919-636-6810 647
Web: eco-site.com

Ecosmart 3315 N W 167th St ... Miami Gardens FL 33056 305-623-7900 36
TF: 877-474-6473 ■ Web: www.ecosmartus.com

Ecosphere Environmental Services Inc
776 E Second Ave ... Durango CO 81301 970-382-7256 382-7259 463
Web: www.ecosphere-services.com

EcoTarium 222 Harrington Way ... Worcester MA 01604 508-929-2700 929-2701 521
Web: www.ecotarium.org

EcoVadis Inc 205E 42nd St 20th Fl ... New York NY 10017 917-398-3333 196
Web: www.ecovadis.com

ECPA (Evangelical Christian Publishers Assn)
9633 S 48th St Ste 195 ... Phoenix AZ 85044 480-966-3998 966-1944 49-16
Web: www.ecpa.org

ECPI College of Technology
5555 Greenwich Rd ... Virginia Beach VA 23462 757-490-9090 507
Web: www.ecpi.edu

Name / Address	City	State	ZIP	Phone	Fax	Class
ECPL (East Chicago Public Library) 2401 E Columbus Dr *Web:* www.ecpl.org	East Chicago	IN	46312	219-397-2453		434-3
Ecra Group 1475 E Woodfield Rd 14th Fl *Web:* ecragroup.com	Schaumburg	IL	60173	847-318-0072	318-6751	242
eCreative Group Inc 1827 1st St W Ste B PO Box 66 *TF:* 877-334-5115 ■ *Web:* www.ecreativegroup.com	Independence	IA	50644	319-334-5115	334-3752	7
ECRI Institute 5200 Butler Pk *TF:* 866-247-3004 ■ *Web:* www.ecri.org	Plymouth Meeting	PA	19462	610-825-6000	834-1275	48-17
ECRM Inc 554 Clark Rd *Web:* www.ecrm.com	Tewksbury	MA	01876	978-851-0207	851-7016	111
ECS (Electronic Cash Systems Inc) 29883 Santa Margarita Pkwy *TF:* 888-327-2860 ■ *Web:* ecspayments.com	Rancho Santa Margarita	CA	92688	949-888-8580	888-8024	56
ECS (Education Commission of the States) 700 Broadway Ste 810 *Web:* www.ecs.org	Denver	CO	80203	303-299-3600	296-8332	49-5
ECS (Efficient Computer System) 530 US Hwy 70 SW *Web:* www.efficientcomputersystems.com	Hickory	NC	28602	828-328-2263	328-2264	177
ECS & R 3237 US Hwy 19 *TF:* 866-815-0016 ■ *Web:* www.ecsr.net	Cochranton	PA	16314	814-425-7773		196
ECS Composites Inc 3560 Rogue River Hwy *Web:* www.ecscomposites.com	Grants Pass	OR	97527	541-476-8871	474-2479	199
ECS Corporate Services LLC 14026 Thunderbolt Pl Ste 300 *Web:* www.ecslimited.com	Chantilly	VA	20151	571-299-6000		261
ECS Financial Services Inc 3400 Dundee Rd *TF:* 800-826-7070 ■ *Web:* www.ecsfinancial.com	Northbrook	IL	60062	847-291-1333		2
ECS Learning Systems Inc 2709 Bulverde Rd **Fax Area Code:* 877 ■ *TF:* 800-688-3224 ■ *Web:* ecslearningsystems.com	Bulverde	TX	78163	830-438-4262	688-3226*	637-2
ECSI International Inc 790 Bloomfield Ave Bldg C-1 *Web:* www.ecsiinternational.com	Clifton	NJ	07012	973-574-8555		693
ECT (E-Commerce Times) 16133 Ventura Blvd Ste 700 *TF:* 877-328-5500 ■ *Web:* www.ectnews.com	Encino	CA	91436	818-461-9700	461-9710	457-5
ECT (Electric Coating Technologies) 4407 Railroad Ave *Web:* www.materialsciencescorp.com	East Chicago	IN	46312	219-378-1930	378-1933	481
Ectaco Inc 31-21 31st St *TF:* 800-710-7920 ■ *Web:* www.ectaco.com	Long Island City	NY	11106	718-728-6110	728-4023	173-2
Ector County 300 N Grant Ave Rm 301 *Web:* www.co.ector.tx.us	Odessa	TX	79761	432-498-4130	498-4177	338
Ector County Library 321 W Fifth St *Web:* ector.lib.tx.us	Odessa	TX	79761	432-332-0633	337-6502	434-3
ECU (Educators Credit Union) 1400 N Newman Rd PO Box 081040 *TF:* 800-236-5898 ■ *Web:* www.ecu.com	Racine	WI	53406	262-886-5900	884-7233	219
ECUA (Emerald Coast Utilities Authority) 9255 Sturdevant St *Web:* www.ecua.fl.gov	Pensacola	FL	32514	850-476-0480		787
Ecuador						
Consulate General 1101 Brickell Ave Ste M102 *Web:* www.ecuador.org	Miami	FL	33131	305-373-8520	539-8313	257
Consulate General 8484 Wilshire Blvd Ste 500 *Web:* www.cancilleria.gob.ec	Beverly Hills	CA	90211	323-297-1150	297-1152	257
Ecuadorian-American Chamber of Commerce of Miami 1640 Town Center Cir Ste 210 *Web:* www.ecuachamber.org	Weston	FL	33326	954-659-1709		138
ECUATOURS PLANET Travel & Special Events 156 Giralda Ave *Web:* www.ecuatoursplanet.com	Coral Gables	FL	33134	305-446-3999		772
E-cubed Media Synthesis Ltd 3807 William St *TF:* 800-294-1556 ■ *Web:* e-cubed.com	Burnaby	BC	V5C3J1	604-294-1556		225
Ecumenical Theological Seminary (ETS) 2930 Woodward Ave *Web:* www.etseminary.org	Detroit	MI	48201	313-831-5200	831-1353	167-3
ECWA (Erie County Water Authority) 295 Main St Rm 350 *TF:* 855-748-1076 ■ *Web:* www.ecwa.org	Buffalo	NY	14203	716-849-8484	849-8467	787
e-Cycle 4105 Leap Rd Ste 250 *TF:* 877-215-5255 ■ *Web:* www.e-cycle.com	Hilliard	OH	43026	877-215-5255		518
ED Etnyre & Co 1333 S Daysville Rd *TF:* 800-995-2116 ■ *Web:* www.etnyre.com	Oregon	IL	61061	815-732-2116	732-7400	190
ED Fagan Inc 769 Susquehanna Ave *TF:* 800-335-6827 ■ *Web:* www.edfagan.com	Franklin Lakes	NJ	07417	201-891-4003	891-3207	492
Ed Grush, General Contractor Inc 3236 E Willow St *Web:* edgrush.com	Signal Hill	CA	90755	562-426-9526		186
Ed Levin Jewelry Inc 52 W Main St *Web:* www.edlevinjewelry.com	Cambridge	NY	12816	518-677-8595		410
Ed Martin Inc 3800 E 96th St *TF:* 800-211-5410 ■ *Web:* www.edmartinacura.com	Indianapolis	IN	46240	800-211-5410		57
Ed Miniat Inc (EMI) 16250 S Vincennes Ave *Web:* www.miniat.com	South Holland	IL	60473	708-589-2400	589-2525	297-9
Ed Napleton Honda 4780 N Service Rd *TF:* 888-840-9486 ■ *Web:* www.napletonhonda.com	Saint Peters	MO	63376	888-840-9486		57
Ed Robinson's Diving Adventures Inc 165 Halekuai St *Web:* www.mauiscuba.com	Kihei	HI	96753	808-879-3584		239
Ed Shults Chevrolet Inc 300 Fluvanna Ave *Web:* www.edshultschevrolet.com	Jamestown	NY	14701	716-720-9091		57
Ed Staub & Sons Petroleum Inc 1301 Esplanade Ave *TF:* 800-435-3835 ■ *Web:* www.edstaub.com	Klamath Falls	OR	97601	800-435-3835		316
Ed Taylor Construction South Inc 2713 N Falkenburg Rd *Web:* www.edtaylor.net	Tampa	FL	33619	813-623-3724	621-1439	186
Ed Thayer Inc 502 Main St *TF:* 800-341-0232 ■ *Web:* www.edthayer.com	Oxford	ME	04270	207-539-8241	539-8170	780
EDA (Equipment Dealers Assn) 165 N Meramec Ave Ste 430 *Web:* www.equipmentdealer.org	Saint Louis	MO	63105	636-349-5000	349-5443	49-18
EDA Engineers-Surveyors-Planners Inc 2404 NW 43rd St *Web:* edafl.com	Gainesville	FL	32606	352-373-3541	373-7249	261
EDA Staffing Inc 132 Central St Ste 206 *TF:* 800-886-9332 ■ *Web:* www.edastaffing.com	Foxborough	MA	02035	508-543-0333	698-0367	193
EDAC Systems Inc 10970 Pierson Dr *TF:* 888-610-3322 ■ *Web:* www.edacsystems.com	Fredericksburg	VA	22408	540-361-1580		174
Edaptive Systems 400 Red Brook Blvd Ste 120 *Web:* www.edaptivesys.com	Owings Mills	MD	21117	410-327-3366	327-0612	225
EDAX Inc 91 McKee Dr *Web:* www.edax.com	Mahwah	NJ	07430	201-529-4880	529-3156	419
EDC (Education Development Center Inc) 55 Chapel St *TF:* 800-225-4276 ■ *Web:* www.edc.org	Newton	MA	02458	617-969-7100	969-5979	48-11
EDC Inc 950 Old Winston Rd *Web:* www.edcinc.com	Kernersville	NC	27284	336-993-0468		625
Edco Disposal Corp 6670 Federal Blvd *Web:* www.edcodisposal.com	Lemon Grove	CA	91945	619-287-7555	287-4073	804
EDCO Products Inc 8700 Excelsior Blvd **Fax Area Code:* 763 ■ *TF:* 800-593-2680 ■ *Web:* www.edcoproducts.com	Hopkins	MN	55343	952-938-6313	241-4018*	697
Edcomm Group, The 1300 Virginia Dr Ste 220 *TF:* 888-433-2666 ■ *Web:* edcomm.com	Fort Washington	PA	19034	215-542-6900	542-6814	244
EDCON-PRJ Inc 6900 W Jefferson Ste 150 *Web:* edcon-prj.com	Denver	CO	80235	303-980-6556		536
Edcor Data Services Corp 3310 W Big Beaver Ste 305 *TF:* 888-222-9950 ■ *Web:* www.edcor.com	Troy	MI	48084	248-530-4200		225
Edcouch-Elsa Independent School District PO Box 127 *Web:* www.eeisd.org	Edcouch	TX	78538	956-262-6000	262-6032	685
Eddie Bauer LLC PO Box 7001 *TF:* 800-426-8020 ■ *Web:* www.eddiebauer.com	Groveport	OH	43125	800-426-8020		157-4
Eddie Brandt's Saturday Matinee 5006 Vineland Ave *Web:* www.ebsmvideo.com	North Hollywood	CA	91601	818-506-4242		511
Eddie Johnson Private Contractor 5005 Creston St	Hyattsville	MD	20781	301-772-0466		610
Eddie Lee's 4700 Nantucket Dr *Web:* www.eddielees.com	Toledo	OH	43623	419-882-0616		671
Eddie Merlot's 1502 Illinois Rd S *Web:* www.eddiemerlots.com	Fort Wayne	IN	46804	260-459-2222		671
Eddie's Tire Service 3077 Valley Rd *Web:* www.eddiestireservice.com	Berkeley Springs	WV	25411	304-258-1368	258-1777	755
Eddington Thread Manufacturing Co PO Box 446 *TF:* 800-220-8901 ■ *Web:* www.edthread.com	Bensalem	PA	19020	215-639-8900		745-9
Eddy County 101 W Greene St Ste 110 **Fax Area Code:* 575 ■ *Web:* www.co.eddy.nm.us	Carlsbad	NM	88220	505-887-9511	234-1835*	338
Eddy County 524 Central Ave *Web:* www.cityofnewrockford.com	New Rockford	ND	58356	701-947-2434	947-2279	338
Eddy Group Ltd 660 St Anne St *Web:* www.eddygroup.com	Bathurst	NB	E2A2N6	506-546-6631		652
Eddy Packing Company Inc 404 Airport Dr *TF:* 800-292-2361 ■ *Web:* www.eddypacking.com	Yoakum	TX	77995	361-293-2361	293-2254	473
Eddyline Kayaks 11977 Westar Ln *TF:* 800-635-5205 ■ *Web:* eddyline.com	Burlington	WA	98233	360-757-2300	757-2302	710
Edelbrock Corp 2700 California St *TF:* 800-739-3737 ■ *Web:* www.edelbrock.com	Torrance	CA	90503	310-781-2222	320-1187	60
Edelman Intelligence 1875 Eye St NW Ste 900 *Web:* www.edelmanintelligence.com	Washington	DC	20006	202-551-9840		463
Edelman Public Relations Worldwide 200 E Randolph Dr Ste 63 *Web:* www.edelman.com	Chicago	IL	60601	312-240-3000		636
Edelman Wealth Management Group Inc 1000 Floral Vale Ste 150 *Web:* edelmanwealthmanagement.com	Yardley	PA	19067	215-579-5601	579-5604	390
Edelson Technology Partners 300 Tice Blvd *Web:* www.edelsontech.com	Woodcliff Lake	NJ	07677	201-930-9898	930-8899	792
Edelweiss 34 E Ramona Ave *Web:* www.restauranteur.com	Colorado Springs	CO	80905	719-633-2220		671
Edelweiss German Restaurant 3801 SW Blvd A *Web:* edelweissgermanrestaurant.com	Fort Worth	TX	76116	817-738-5934		671
Eden Echo PO Box 1069 *Web:* www.edenecho.net	Eden	TX	76837	325-869-5717		532-2
Eden Foods Inc 701 Tecumseh Rd *TF:* 800-248-0320 ■ *Web:* www.edenfoods.com	Clinton	MI	49236	517-456-7424	456-6075	296-36
Eden Gardens State Park 181 Eden Gardens Rd *Web:* www.floridastateparks.org	Santa Rosa Beach	FL	32459	850-267-8320		565
Eden House 1015 Fleming St *TF:* 800-533-5397 ■ *Web:* edenhouse.com	Key West	FL	33040	305-296-6868		379
Eden I & R Inc 570 B St *TF:* 888-886-9660 ■ *Web:* edenir.org	Hayward	CA	94541	510-537-2710		138
Eden Labs LLC 309 S Cloverdale St *TF:* 888-626-3271 ■ *Web:* www.edenlabs.com	Seattle	WA	98108	888-626-3271		333
Eden Prairie Chamber of Commerce 11455 Viking Dr Ste 270 *TF:* 800-932-8677 ■ *Web:* epchamber.org	Eden Prairie	MN	55344	952-944-2830	944-0229	139
Eden Roc - A Renaissance Beach Resort & Spa 4525 Collins Ave *TF:* 855-433-3676 ■ *Web:* www.edenrochotelmiami.com	Miami Beach	FL	33140	305-531-0000	674-5555	669

	Phone	Fax	Class
Eden Stone Company Inc W4520 Lime Rd .... Eden WI 53019 *TF:* 800-472-2521 ■ *Web:* www.evstone.net	920-477-2521		503-6
Eden Theological Seminary 475 E Lockwood Ave. .... Saint Louis MO 63119 *TF:* 877-627-5652 ■ *Web:* www.eden.edu	314-961-3627		167-3
Edenbridge Inc 21771 Stevens Creek Blvd Ste 200-A ....Cupertino CA 95014 *Web:* edenbridgehomes.com	669-231-4242		652
Edens & Avant Realty Inc 1221 Main St Ste 1000......................Columbia SC 29201 **Fax Area Code:* 803	202-902-2600	765-0684*	460
Edenwald 800 Southerly Rd .... Towson MD 21286 *Web:* www.edenwald.org	410-339-6000	583-8786	672
Eder Flag Manufacturing Company Inc 1000 W Rawson Ave....................... Oak Creek WI 53154 *Web:* www.ederflagnews.com	414-764-3522		287
Edes Custom Meats LLC 6700 W Mccormick Rd.......................Amarillo TX 79118 *Web:* edesmeats.com	806-622-0205		345
EDF Ventures LLC 425 N Main St............. Ann Arbor MI 48104 *Web:* www.edfvc.com	734-663-3213	663-7358	792
EDG (Exhibits Development Group LLC) The Union Depot 214 E Fourth St Ste 170 ...... Saint Paul MN 55101 *Web:* exhibitsdevelopment.com	651-222-1121		184
EDG Inc 3900 N Causeway Blvd Ste 700........... Metairie LA 70002 *TF:* 888-334-9298 ■ *Web:* www.edg.net	504-455-0858		463
Edgar A. Weber & Co 549 Palwaukee Dr .... Wheeling IL 60090 *Web:* www.weberflavors.com	847-215-1980		296-15
Edgar Allan Poe Museum 1914-16 E Main St........................ Richmond VA 23223 *Web:* www.poemuseum.org	804-648-5523		520
Edgar Allan Poe National Historic Site 532 N Seventh St ....Philadelphia PA 19123 *Web:* www.nps.gov	215-597-8780		564
Edgar Boettcher Mason Contractors Inc 3803 N Euclid...............................Bay City MI 48706 *Web:* www.boettchermasonry.com	989-684-4807	684-4824	189-7
Edgar County 118 E Steidl Rd .... Paris IL 61944 *Web:* edgarcountyillinois.com	217-466-7433	466-7430	338
Edgar Dunn & Co 201 California St Ste 640 .... San Francisco CA 94111 *Web:* edgardunn.com	415-977-1870		195
Edgar Evins State Park 1630 Edgar Evins State Park Rd .... Silver Point TN 38582 *TF:* 800-250-8619 ■ *Web:* tnstateparks.com	931-858-2114		565
Edgar Fabrics Inc 50 Commerce Dr.......... Hauppauge NY 11788 *Web:* edgarfabrics.com	631-435-9116	435-9151	594
Edgar Lomax Co 6564 Loisdale Ct Ste 310...................Springfield VA 22150 *TF:* 866-205-0524 ■ *Web:* www.edgarlomax.com	703-719-0026		401
Edge Biosystems Inc 201 Perry Pkwy Ste 5.................... Gaithersburg MD 20877 **Fax Area Code:* 800 ■ *Web:* www.edgebio.com	301-990-2685	326-2685*	194
Edge Communications Inc 5419 Hollywood Blvd Ste 727 ....Los Angeles CA 90027 *Web:* www.edgecommunicationsinc.com	323-469-3397	645-7054	636
Edge Electronics Inc 75 Orville Dr .... Bohemia NY 11716 **Fax Area Code:* 631 ■ *TF:* 800-647-3343 ■ *Web:* www.edgeelectronics.com	800-647-3343	471-3405*	173-8
Edge Information Management Inc 1682 W Hibiscus Blvd ....Melbourne FL 32901 *TF:* 800-725-3343 ■ *Web:* edgeinformation.com	800-725-3343	780-3299	635
Edge Interactive Inc 67 Mowat Ave Ste 533 .... Toronto ON M6K3E3 *TF:* 800-211-5577 ■ *Web:* www.edgeip.com	416-494-3343		224
Edge of Texas Steakhouse 8690 Edge of Texas......................... El Paso TX 79934 *Web:* edgeoftexassteakhouse.com	915-822-3343		671
Edge Plastics Inc 449 Newman St.............Mansfield OH 44902 *Web:* edgeplasticsinc.com	419-522-6696		596
Edge Pro Inc PO Box 95 ....Hood River OR 97031 *Web:* www.edgeproinc.com	541-387-2222		455
Edge Products 1080 S Depot Dr................. Ogden UT 84404 *TF:* 888-360-3343 ■ *Web:* edgeproducts.com	801-476-3343	476-3348	247
Edge Systems LLC 3S721 W Ave Ste 200..................... Warrenville IL 60555 *TF:* 800-352-3343 ■ *Web:* www.edge.com	630-810-9669	810-9228	177
Edge Tech Corp 9101 Harlan St Unit 260...................Westminster CO 80031 *TF:* 800-259-6565 ■ *Web:* www.edgetechcorp.com	800-259-6565		625
Edge Technologies 12110 Sunset Hills Rd Ste 600..................Reston VA 20190 *TF:* 888-771-3343 ■ *Web:* www.edge-technologies.com	703-691-7900	691-4020	178-1
Edge Technology Services Inc 116 Washington Ave 2nd Fl ....North Haven CT 06473 *TF:* 866-334-3874 ■ *Web:* edgets.com	860-635-3342	632-8307	225
Edge Training Systems 11310 Business Center Dr ....North Chesterfield VA 23236 *Web:* www.edgetrainingsystems.com	804-272-1711	272-1683	195
Edge Velocity Corp 68 Stiles Rd Ste G............ Salem NH 03079 *Web:* edgevelocity.com	603-912-5618		647
Edgecombe County 201 St Andrew St PO Box 10 .... Tarboro NC 27886 *Web:* www.edgecombecountync.gov	252-641-7852		338
Edgecombe County Memorial Library 909 N Main St .... Tarboro NC 27886 *Web:* www.edgecombelibrary.libguides.com	252-823-1141		434-3
Edgecombe-Martin County Electric Membership Corp PO Box 188 .... Tarboro NC 27886 *TF:* 800-445-6486 ■ *Web:* www.ememc.com	800-445-6486		245
Edgefield County 129 Courthouse Sq PO Box 34................ Edgefield SC 29824 *Web:* www.edgefieldcounty.sc.gov	803-637-4080	637-4056	338
Edgeley Mail, The 215 6th Ave .... Edgeley ND 58433 *Web:* www.edgeley.com	701-493-2208		532-2
EdgeLink LLC 2525 SW First Ave Ste 110....................Portland OR 97201 *Web:* www.edgelink.com	503-246-3989		193
Edgemark Commercial Real Estate Services LLC 2215 York Rd Ste 503....................... Oak Brook IL 60523 *Web:* edgemarkllc.com	630-472-1010		652
Edgemark Partners 4510 Cox Rd Ste 305 .... Glen Allen VA 23060 *Web:* www.edgemarkpartners.com	804-967-2000		463
Edgemont Pharmaceuticals LLC 1250 Capital of Texas Hwy S Bldg 3 Bldg 3-400 W.............................Lake Hills TX 78746 **Fax Area Code:* 512 ■ *TF:* 888-594-4332	888-594-4332	329-2094*	231
Edgen Corp 18444 Highland Rd............. Baton Rouge LA 70809 *Web:* www.edgenmurray.com	225-756-9868		385
Edgenet 2948 Sidco Dr........................ Nashville TN 37204 *TF:* 877-334-3638 ■ *Web:* www.edgenet.com	877-334-3638		177
EdgePoint Capital Advisors LLC 2000 Auburn Dr Ste 330................... Beachwood OH 44122 *Web:* www.edgepoint.com	216-831-2430		690
Edger Enterprises of Elmira Inc 330 E 14th St ....Elmira Heights NY 14903 *Web:* www.edgerenterprises.com	607-733-9664		186
Edgerton & Edgerton 125 Wood St ....West Chicago IL 60185 *Web:* edgertonlawfirm.com	630-231-3000		41
Edgerton Contractors Inc 545 W Ryan Rd PO Box 901................. Oak Creek WI 53154 *Web:* edgerton.us	414-764-4443	764-9788	189-16
Edge-Sweets Co 2887 Three-Mile Rd NW..................Grand Rapids MI 49534 *Web:* www.edge-sweets.com	616-453-5458		601
EdgeTheory LLC 800 Woodlands Pkwy Ste 210 .... Ridgeland MS 39157 *Web:* edgetheory.com	650-830-5752		5
Edgewater Automation LLC 481 Renaissance Dr .... Saint Joseph MI 49085 *Web:* www.edgewaterautomation.com	269-983-1300		111
Edgewater Beach Hotel 1901 Gulf Shore Blvd N ....Naples FL 34102 *TF:* 866-624-1695 ■ *Web:* www.edgewaternaples.com	239-403-2000		379
Edgewater Beach Resort Management 11212 Front Beach Rd .... Panama City FL 32407 *Web:* www.resortcollection.com	850-235-4044		378
Edgewater Grill 861 W Harbor Dr............. San Diego CA 92101 *Web:* www.edgewatergrill.com	619-232-7581		671
Edgewater Hotel 2411 Alaskan Way.............. Seattle WA 98121 *TF:* 800-624-0670 ■ *Web:* www.edgewaterhotel.com	206-728-7000		379
Edgewater Hotel 1001 Wisconsin Pl .... Madison WI 53703 *Web:* isthmus.com	608-256-9071		671
Edgewater Hotel & Casino 2020 S Casino Dr.......................... Laughlin NV 89029 *TF:* 866-352-3553 ■ *Web:* www.edgewater-casino.com	702-298-2453	298-5606	133
Edgewater Networks Inc 2895 NW Pkwy.......................... Santa Clara CA 95051 *TF:* 844-405-3550 ■ *Web:* www.edgewaternetworks.com	408-351-7200	727-6430	225
EdgeWater Power Boats 211 Dale St .... Edgewater FL 32132 *Web:* www.ewboats.com	386-426-5457		90
Edgewater Resort 200 Edgewater Cir ....Hot Springs AR 71913 *TF:* 800-234-3687 ■ *Web:* www.ewresort.com	501-767-3311		379
Edgewater Resort & Waterpark 2400 London Rd............................. Duluth MN 55812 *TF:* 800-777-7925 ■ *Web:* www.duluthwaterpark.com	218-728-3601		379
Edgewater Resources LLC 518 Broad St Ste 200 .... Saint Joseph MI 49085 *Web:* edgewaterresources.com	269-932-4502		653
EdgeWave Inc 15333 Avenue of Science .... San Diego CA 92128 *TF:* 800-782-3762 ■ *Web:* www.edgewave.com	858-676-2277		177
Edgewood Building Supply Company Inc 1580 E Epler Ave...........................Indianapolis IN 46227 *Web:* www.edgewoodbuildingsupply.com	317-786-9208		350
Edgewood College 1000 Edgewood College Dr .... Madison WI 53711 *TF:* 800-444-4861 ■ *Web:* edgewood.edu	608-663-2294	663-2214	166
Edgewood Convalescent Home & Lincolnwood Assisted Living 513 S Bell St PO Box 39.................... Edgewood IA 52042 *Web:* www.edgewoodconvalescenthome.com	563-928-6461	928-6462	450
Edgewood Education Ctr 6601 Xylon Ave N.........................Minneapolis MN 55428 *Web:* www.district287.org	763-533-3821		685
Edgewood Management LLC 535 Madison Ave 15th Fl ....New York NY 10022 *Web:* www.edgewood.com	212-652-9100		194
Edgewood Vista 322 Demers Ave...........Grand Forks ND 58201 *Web:* www.edgewoodhealthcare.com	308-384-0717		371
EDI (Dan K. Richardson - Entrepreneurship Development Institute) 3209 Virginia Ave.........................Fort Pierce FL 34981 *TF:* 888-283-1177 ■ *Web:* www.cctiirsc.com	888-283-1177		167-3
EDI Specialists Inc 31 Bellows Rd............. Raynham MA 02767 **Fax Area Code:* 508 ■ *TF:* 800-821-4644 ■ *Web:* www.edistaffing.com	800-821-4644	822-7375*	193
Edible Arrangements LLC 95 Barnes Rd .... Wallingford CT 06492 **Fax Area Code:* 203 ■ *TF:* 877-363-7848 ■ *Web:* www.ediblearrangements.com	304-894-8901	774-0531*	310
Edibles Restaurant & Bar 704 University Ave ....Rochester NY 14607 *Web:* ediblesrochester.com	585-271-4910		671
EDIC College Inc Ave Rafael Cordero Urb #5 Cll Genova........... Caguas PR 00726 *Web:* www.juntedelmomento.com	787-744-8519		166
Ediciones Universal PO Box 450353............. Miami FL 33135 *Web:* www.ediciones.com	786-228-0974		95
Edifice Inc 4111 South Blvd.................. Charlotte NC 28209 *Web:* edificeinc.com	704-332-0900	332-0901	186
Edify Technologies Inc 2200 S Main St Ste 306 .... Lombard IL 60148 *Web:* www.edifytech.com	630-932-9310		196
EDI-Health Group Inc 17701 Cowan Ste 250 ....Irvine CA 92614 **Fax Area Code:* 800 ■ *TF:* 877-932-2567 ■ *Web:* www.dentalxchange.com	877-932-2567	866-0006*	178-1

Name / Address	City	State	Zip	Phone	Fax	Class
Edina Realty Inc 6800 France Ave S Ste 230 *Web:* www.edinarealty.com	Edina	MN	55435	952-463-5164		652
Edinboro University 219 Meadville St *TF:* 888-846-2676 ■ *Web:* www.edinboro.edu	Edinboro	PA	16444	814-732-2000		167-3
Edinburg Center Inc, The 205 Burlington Rd *Web:* www.edinburgcenter.org	Bedford	MA	01730	781-862-3600	275-7205	353
Edinburg Chamber of Commerce 602 W University Dr Ste A *TF:* 800-800-7214 ■ *Web:* edinburg.com	Edinburg	TX	78539	956-383-4974	383-6942	139
Edinburg Public Library Sekula Memorial Library 1906 S Closner Blvd *Web:* www.edinburg.lib.tx.us	Edinburg	TX	78539	956-383-6246		434-3
Edinburg Regional Medical Ctr (ERMC) 1102 W Trenton Rd *Web:* www.southtexashealthsystem.com	Edinburg	TX	78539	956-388-6000		374-3
eDirectory 7004 Little River Tpke Ste O *TF:* 800-630-4694 ■ *Web:* www.edirectory.com	Annandale	VA	22003	800-630-4694		530
Edison Carrier Solutions 2 Innovation Way 1st Fl *TF:* 800-634-7999 ■ *Web:* www.edisoncarriersolutions.com	Pomona	CA	91768	800-634-7999		387
Edison Chamber of Commerce 1028 Amboy Ave *Web:* www.edisonchamber.com	Edison	NJ	08837	732-738-9482	738-9485	139
Edison Chouest Offshore 16201 E Main St *TF:* 866-925-5161 ■ *Web:* www.chouest.com	Galliano	LA	70354	985-601-4444		465
Edison College *Charlotte* 26300 Airport Rd *TF:* 800-749-2322 ■ *Web:* www.fsw.edu	Punta Gorda	FL	33950	941-637-5629	637-3538	162
Edison Community College 1973 Edison Dr *Web:* www.edisonohio.edu	Piqua	OH	45356	937-778-8600	778-1920	162
Edison Credit Union 4200 E Front St *Web:* edisoncu.com	Kansas City	MO	64120	816-231-3380		219
Edison Electric Institute (EEI) 701 Pennsylvania Ave NW *TF:* 800-649-1202 ■ *Web:* www.eei.org	Washington	DC	20004	202-508-5000	508-5051	48-12
Edison Intl 2244 Walnut Grove Ave *NYSE: EIX* ■ *TF:* 800-655-4555 ■ *Web:* www.edison.com	Rosemead	CA	91770	626-302-1212		360-5
Edison Lithograph & Printing Corp 3725 Tonnelle Ave *Web:* edisonlitho.com	North Bergen	NJ	07047	201-902-9191		627
Edison National Bank 13000 S Cleveland Ave *TF:* 800-359-9034 ■ *Web:* edisonnationalbank.com	Fort Myers	FL	33907	239-466-1800		70
Edison Price Lighting Inc (EPL) 41-50 22nd St *Web:* www.epl.com	Long Island City	NY	11101	718-685-0700		439
Edison Properties LLC 100 Washington St *TF:* 888-727-5327 ■ *Web:* www.parkfast.com	Newark	NJ	07102	973-643-0895		562
Edison School Elementary School 246 S Fair Ave *Web:* edison.elmhurst205.org	Elmhurst	IL	60126	630-834-4272		685
Edison Township Free Public Library 340 Plainfield Ave *Web:* www.edisonpubliclibrary.net	Edison	NJ	08817	732-287-2298	819-9134	434-3
Edison Venture Fund 281 Witherspoon St *TF:* 800-899-3975 ■ *Web:* www.edisonpartners.com	Princeton	NJ	08540	609-896-1900		792
Edison Welding Institute (EWI) 1250 Arthur E Adams Dr *Web:* ewi.org	Columbus	OH	43221	614-688-5000	688-5001	49-13
EdisonLearning Inc 1 E Broward Blvd Ste 1111 *TF:* 877-890-7088 ■ *Web:* edisonlearning.com	Fort Lauderdale	FL	33301	201-630-2600		685
Edisto Beach State Park 8377 State Cabin Rd *Web:* southcarolinaparks.com	Edisto Island	SC	29438	843-869-2156		565
Edisto Electric Co-opeartive Inc 896 Calhoun St *TF:* 800-433-3292 ■ *Web:* edistoelectric.com	Bamberg	SC	29003	803-245-5141	245-0188	245
Edit Point Video 209 Oswego St Ste 8 *Web:* www.editpointvideo.com	Liverpool	NY	13088	315-472-3348		514
Edith Abbott Memorial Library 211 N Washington St *Web:* www.grand-island.com	Grand Island	NE	68801	308-385-5333	385-5339	434-3
Edith Macy Conference Ctr 550 Chappaqua Rd *TF:* 844-258-7212 ■ *Web:* www.edithmacy.com	Briarcliff Manor	NY	10510	914-945-8000		377
Edith Nourse Rogers Memorial Veterans Hospital 200 Springs Rd **Fax Area Code:* 415 ■ *Web:* www.bedford.va.gov	Bedford	MA	01730	781-687-2000	882-0495*	374-8
Editor & Publisher Magazine 17782 Cowan Ste C *TF:* 855-896-7433 ■ *Web:* www.editorandpublisher.com	Irvine	CA	92614	949-660-6150	660-6172	457-5
Editorial Bautista Independiente (EBI) 3417 Kenilworth Blvd *TF:* 800-398-7187 ■ *Web:* www.ebi-bmm.org	Sebring	FL	33870	863-382-6350	382-8650	48-20
Editorial Freelancers Assn (EFA) 71 W 23rd St 4th Fl *Web:* www.the-efa.org	New York	NY	10010	212-929-5400	929-5439	49-16
Editorial Projects in Education 6935 Arlington Rd Ste 100 *TF:* 800-346-1834 ■ *Web:* www.edweek.org	Bethesda	MD	20814	301-280-3100	280-3200	637-9
EDJ Associates Inc 13873 Park Center Rd Ste 301 *Web:* edjassociates.com	Herndon	VA	20191	703-738-9150		463
EDL Packaging Systems 1260 Parkview Rd *Web:* www.edlpackaging.com	Green Bay	WI	54304	920-336-7744		547
Edlund Company Inc 159 Industrial Pkwy *TF:* 800-772-2126 ■ *Web:* www.edlundco.com	Burlington	VT	05401	802-862-9661	862-4822	298
Edm Department Inc 1261 Humbracht Cir Ste A *Web:* www.edmdept.com	Bartlett	IL	60103	630-736-0531		358
EDM International Inc 4001 Automation Way *Web:* www.edmlink.com	Fort Collins	CO	80525	970-204-4001		256
Edm Services Inc 4100 Guardian St *Web:* edmsvc.com	Simi Valley	CA	93063	805-527-3300		261
EDM Zap Parts Inc 1108 Front St *Web:* www.edmzap.com	Lisle	IL	60532	630-852-1699		697
EDMC (Education Management Corp) 210 6th Ave 33rd Fl *NASDAQ: EDMC* ■ *TF:* 800-275-2440 ■ *Web:* www.edmc.edu	Pittsburgh	PA	15222	412-562-0900	562-0598	242
Edminster Hinshaw Russ & Associates Inc 10555 Woffice Dr *Web:* www.ehrainc.com	Houston	TX	77042	713-784-4500	784-4577	256
Edmo Distributors Inc 12830 E Mirabeau Pkwy *TF:* 800-235-3300 ■ *Web:* www.edmo.com	Spokane Valley	WA	99216	800-235-3300		770
Edmond A. Swad PC 38701 Seven Mile Rd *Web:* www.swadco.com	Livonia	MI	48152	734-462-9333		2
Edmond Area Chamber of Commerce 825 E Second St Ste 100 *TF:* 800-717-2601 ■ *Web:* www.edmondchamber.com	Edmond	OK	73034	405-341-2808	340-5512	139
Edmond Library 10 S Blvd *Web:* www.metrolibrary.org	Edmond	OK	73034	405-341-9282		434-3
Edmond Scientific Co 5680 King Center Dr Ste 600 *Web:* edmondsci.com	Alexandria	VA	22315	703-955-7722		261
Edmonds Community College 20000 68th Ave W *TF:* 866-886-4854 ■ *Web:* www.edcc.edu	Lynnwood	WA	98036	425-640-1459	640-1159	162
Edmonds Entertainment 1635 N Cahuenga Blvd *Web:* www.edmondsent.com	Los Angeles	CA	90028	323-860-1520		514
Edmonson County PO Box 830 *TF:* 800-368-8683 ■ *Web:* edmonsonclerk.com	Brownsville	KY	42210	270-597-2624	597-9714	338
Edmonton Chamber of Commerce 9990 Jasper Ave Ste 600 *Web:* www.edmontonchamber.com	Edmonton	AB	T5J1P7	780-426-4620	424-7946	137
Edmonton City Ctr 10025-102A Ave *Web:* edmontoncitycentre.com	Edmonton	AB	T5J2Z2	780-426-8444		460
Edmonton City Hall 1 Sir Winston Churchill Sq 3rd Fl *Web:* www.edmonton.ca	Edmonton	AB	T5J2R7	780-442-5311		337
Edmonton Eskimo Football Club, The 11000 Stadium Rd *Web:* www.esks.com	Edmonton	AB	T5H4E2	780-448-1525		713
Edmonton Exchanger Group of Cos 5545-89 St *Web:* www.edmontonexchanger.com	Edmonton	AB	T6E5W9	780-468-6722		295
Edmonton Folk Music Festival 10115 97a Ave NW *Web:* edmontonfolkfest.org	Edmonton	AB	T6E4T2	780-429-1899		138
Edmonton International Airport 1000 Airport Rd Edmonton International Airport Ste 1 *TF:* 800-268-7134 ■ *Web:* flyeia.com	Edmonton	AB	T9E0V3	780-890-8900	890-8329	63
Edmonton Journal 10006 - 101 St *TF:* 800-232-9486 ■ *Web:* www.edmontonjournal.com	Edmonton	AB	T5J0S1	780-429-5100		532-1
Edmonton Public Library Office MNP Tower 10235 101 St NW 7th Fl *Web:* www.epl.ca	Edmonton	AB	T5J3G1	780-496-7000		434
Edmonton Sun 10006 101 St *Web:* edmontonsun.com	Edmonton	AB	T5J0S1	780-468-0100		532-1
Edmonton Symphony Orchestra 9720 102nd Ave *TF:* 800-563-5081 ■ *Web:* www.winspearcentre.com	Edmonton	AB	T5J4B2	780-428-1108		573-3
Edmund A Allen Lumber Co 117 Industrial Dr *TF:* 800-892-1884 ■ *Web:* www.edmundallen.com	Momence	IL	60954	815-472-2471	472-3976	191-3
Edmund Optics Inc 101 E Gloucester Pk *TF:* 800-363-1992 ■ *Web:* www.edmundoptics.com	Barrington	NJ	08007	856-547-3488	573-6295	544
Edmunds Gages 45 Spring Ln *TF:* 800-878-1622 ■ *Web:* www.edmundsgages.com	Farmington	CT	06032	860-677-2813	677-4243	493
Edmunds GovTech 301 Tilton Rd *TF:* 888-336-6999 ■ *Web:* www.edmundsgovtech.com	Northfield	NJ	08225	609-645-7333	645-3111	5
EDN (Earth Day Network) 1616 P St NW Ste 340 *Web:* www.earthday.org	Washington	DC	20036	202-518-0044	518-8794	48-13
EDN Aviation Inc 6720 Valjean Ave *Web:* www.ednaviation.com	Van Nuys	CA	91406	818-988-8826	904-6799	790
Edna McConnell Clark Foundation, The 415 Madison Ave 10th Fl *Web:* www.emcf.org	New York	NY	10017	212-551-9100	421-9325	305
EDO 425 Spadina Rd *Web:* www.edorestaurants.com	Toronto	ON	M5P2W3	416-482-8973		671
Edo Japan International Inc 6807 Railway St SE Ste 310 *TF:* 888-336-9888 ■ *Web:* www.edojapan.com	Calgary	AB	T2B2S6	403-215-8800	215-8801	670
eDOC Communications 555 E Business Center Dr *Web:* www.edoccommunications.com	Mount Prospect	IL	60056	847-297-1443		627
Edom Laboratories Inc 100 E Jefryn Blvd Ste M *TF:* 800-723-3366 ■ *Web:* www.edomlaboratories.com	Deer Park	NY	11729	631-586-2266		799
Edon Controls Inc 2891 Industrial Row Dr *Web:* www.edoncontrols.com	Troy	MI	48084	248-280-0420	280-1730	207
Edon Farmers Cooperative Association Inc 205 S Michigan St PO Box 308 *TF:* 800-878-4093 ■ *Web:* www.edonfarmerscoop.com	Edon	OH	43518	419-272-2121		276
EDP Biotech Corp 6701 Baum Dr Ste 110 *Web:* edpbiotech.com	Knoxville	TN	37919	865-299-6250	247-4868	231
EDP University 560 Ave Ponce De Leon *Web:* edpuniversity.edu	Hato Rey	PR	00918	855-999-3378		165

	Phone	Fax	Class
EDPA (Exhibit Designers & Producers Assn) 19 Compo Rd S .... Westport CT 06880 *Web:* www.edpa.com	203-557-6321		49-18
EDR (Environmental Data Resources Inc) 6 Armstrong Rd 4th Fl .... Shelton CT 06484 *TF:* 800-352-0050 ■ *Web:* www.edrnet.com	800-352-0050	231-6802	387
EDR Electronics Inc 1504 E Algonquin Rd .... Arlington Heights IL 60005 *Web:* www.edrelectronics.com	847-640-6996	640-9717	203
Edro Corp 37 Commerce St .... East Berlin CT 06023 *Web:* edrocorp.com	860-828-0311	828-5984	427
Edro Engineering Inc 20500 Carrey Rd .... Walnut CA 91789 *TF:* 800-368-3376 ■ *Web:* www.edro.com	909-594-5751	598-2632	596
EDS Manufacturing Inc 765 N Target Range Rd .... Nogales AZ 85621 *Web:* www.edsmanufacturing.com	520-287-9711		814
Edsal Manufacturing Company Inc 4400 S Packers Ave .... Chicago IL 60609 *Web:* www.edsal.com	773-254-0600		286
Edsel & Eleanor Ford House 1100 Lake Shore Rd .... Grosse Pointe Shores MI 48236 *Web:* www.fordhouse.org	313-884-4222	884-5977	50-3
Edstrom Construction Inc 1305 S 12th W .... Rexburg ID 83440 *Web:* edstromconstruction.net	208-356-3577		261
EDT (Engineering Design Technologies Inc) 1705 Entp Way Ste 200 .... Marietta GA 30067 *Web:* www.edtinc.net	770-988-0400	988-0300	685
EDT Corp 1006-J NE 146th St .... Vancouver WA 98685 *TF:* 800-661-5568 ■ *Web:* www.edtcorp.com	360-574-7294		75
EDTA (Educational Theatre Assn) 2343 Auburn Ave .... Cincinnati OH 45219 *TF:* 800-848-2263 ■ *Web:* schooltheatre.org	513-421-3900	421-7077	48-4
Edtec Central LLC 10 S Main St Ste 101 .... Mount Clemens MI 48043 *Web:* www.edteccentral.net	248-582-8100	582-8101	196
EdTek Services Inc 30 Wascana Ave .... Toronto ON M5A1V5 **Fax Area Code:* 888 ■ *Web:* www.edtekservices.com	647-435-7133	827-1184*	177
Eduardo's Border Grill 1830 Westwood Blvd .... Los Angeles CA 90025 *Web:* www.eduardosbordergrill.com	310-475-2410		671
Educare Press PO Box 17222 .... Seattle WA 98127 *Web:* www.educarepress.com	206-706-4105		637-2
Education Associates Inc (EAI) PO Box 23308 .... Louisville KY 40223 **Fax Area Code:* 502 ■ *TF:* 800-626-2950 ■ *Web:* www.educationassociates.com	800-626-2950	244-9144*	423
Education Center Inc 101 Centreport Dr Ste 245 .... Greensboro NC 27403 *TF:* 800-334-0298 ■ *Web:* www.themailbox.com	800-334-0298		48-11
Education Commission of the States (ECS) 700 Broadway Ste 810 .... Denver CO 80203 *Web:* www.ecs.org	303-299-3600	296-8332	49-5
Education Development Center Inc (EDC) 55 Chapel St .... Newton MA 02458 *TF:* 800-225-4276 ■ *Web:* www.edc.org	617-969-7100	969-5979	48-11
Education Management Consulting LLC 49 Coryell St .... Lambertville NJ 08530 *Web:* education-expert.com	609-397-8989	397-1999	196
Education Management Corp (EDMC) 210 6th Ave 33rd Fl .... Pittsburgh PA 15222 *NASDAQ: EDMC* ■ *TF:* 800-275-2440 ■ *Web:* www.edmc.edu	412-562-0900	562-0598	242
Education Management Solutions Inc 436 Creamery Way Ste 300 .... Exton PA 19341 **Fax Area Code:* 484 ■ *TF:* 877-367-5050 ■ *Web:* www.simulationiq.com	610-701-7002	653-1070*	178-7
Education Management Systems Inc 4110 Shipyard Blvd .... Wilmington NC 28403 *TF:* 800-541-8999 ■ *Web:* www.mealsplus.com	910-799-0121		177
Education Personnel Federal Credit Union 1102 N Walnut .... Danville IL 61832 *Web:* educationpersonnelfcu.com	217-446-0777		219
Education Resources Information Ctr (ERIC) 655 15th St NW Ste 500 .... Washington DC 20005 *TF:* 800-538-3742 ■ *Web:* ncela.ed.gov	800-538-3742		197
Education Trust 1250 H St NW Ste 700 .... Washington DC 20005 *Web:* edtrust.org	202-293-1217	293-2605	48-11
Education Update Inc 17 Lexington Ave No A1207 .... New York NY 10010 *Web:* www.educationupdate.com	212-477-5600		532-2
Educational & Industrial Testing Service PO Box 7234 .... San Diego CA 92167 *TF:* 800-416-1666 ■ *Web:* www.edits.net	619-222-1666	226-1666	637-10
Educational Assessment Associates 5125 MacArthur Blvd NW Ste 16 .... Washington DC 20016 *Web:* www.eaadc.org	202-363-9805	363-9807	196
Educational Assessment Service Inc W6050 Apple Rd .... Watertown WI 53098 **Fax Area Code:* 920 ■ *TF:* 800-795-7466 ■ *Web:* www.sylviarimm.com	800-795-7466	261-6622*	192
Educational Coin Co 291 Upper North Rd .... Highland NY 12528 *Web:* www.educationalcoin.com	845-691-6100	691-4974	411
Educational Communications Inc PO Box 351419 .... Los Angeles CA 90035 *Web:* www.ecoprojects.org	310-559-9160		48-13
Educational Community Alliance Credit Union 3845 Angola Rd .... Toledo OH 43615 *TF:* 866-381-2323 ■ *Web:* educacu.com	419-381-2323		219
Educational Development Corp 5402 S 122nd E Ave .... Tulsa OK 74146 *NASDAQ: EDUC* ■ *TF:* 800-475-4522 ■ *Web:* www.edcpub.com	918-622-4522	665-7919	96
Educational Dividends PO Box 8646 .... Champaign IL 61826 *Web:* www.educationaldividends.com	217-359-9442		196
Educational Employees Credit Union PO Box 5242 .... Fresno CA 93755 *TF:* 800-538-3328 ■ *Web:* www.myeecu.org	559-437-7700	451-0198	219
Educational Furniture Ltd 620 E 18th St .... Muncie IN 47302 *TF:* 800-929-3375 ■ *Web:* edfurn.com	765-286-9041	286-8553	366

	Phone	Fax	Class
Educational Housing Services Inc 55 Clark St .... Brooklyn NY 11201 *TF:* 800-297-4694 ■ *Web:* www.studenthousing.org	800-297-4694		49-5
Educational Insights Inc 380 N Fairway Dr .... Vernon Hills IL 60061 *TF:* 800-995-4436 ■ *Web:* www.educationalinsights.com	847-968-3722		243
Educational Media Foundation 5700 W Oaks Blvd .... Rocklin CA 95765 *TF:* 800-525-5683 ■ *Web:* www.klove.com	916-251-1740		643
Educational Ministries Inc (EMI) 165 Plaza Dr .... Prescott AZ 86303 *TF:* 800-221-0910 ■ *Web:* www.educationalministries.com	800-221-0910		637-2
Educational Research Newsletter PO Box 2347 .... South Portland ME 04116 **Fax Area Code:* 815 ■ *TF:* 800-321-7471 ■ *Web:* www.ernweb.com	207-632-1954	461-5647*	531-4
Educational Testing Service Rosedale Rd .... Princeton NJ 08541 *Web:* www.ets.org	609-921-9000	734-5410	244
Educational Textbook Company Inc (ETC) PO Box 3597 .... Covina CA 91722 *Web:* www.etcbooks.com	626-339-7733	332-4744	637-2
Educational Theatre Assn (EDTA) 2343 Auburn Ave .... Cincinnati OH 45219 *TF:* 800-848-2263 ■ *Web:* schooltheatre.org	513-421-3900	421-7077	48-4
Educational Tours 1123 Sterling Rd .... Inverness FL 34450 *TF:* 800-343-9003 ■ *Web:* www.edtours-us.com	800-343-9003		760
Educational Travel Consultants (ETC) PO Box 1580 .... Hendersonville NC 28793 *TF:* 800-247-7969 ■ *Web:* educationaltravelconsultants.com	828-693-0412	692-1591	760
Educational Travel Tours Inc PO Box 9028 .... Trenton NJ 08650 *Web:* www.educationaltraveltours.com	609-587-1550		760
Educationcom Inc 333 S B St Unit 101 .... San Mateo CA 94401 *Web:* www.education.com	650-366-3380		387
Educationdynamics LLC 5 Marine View Plz Ste 212 .... Hoboken NJ 07030 *Web:* www.educationdynamics.com	201-377-3000		4
Educator's International Press Inc (EIP) 18 Colleen Rd .... Troy NY 12180 *Web:* www.edint.com	518-271-9886	266-9422	637-2
Educators Credit Union (ECU) 1400 N Newman Rd PO Box 081040 .... Racine WI 53406 *TF:* 800-236-5898 ■ *Web:* www.ecu.com	262-886-5900	884-7233	219
Educators of Beauty 211 E 3rd St .... Sterling IL 61081 *Web:* www.educatorsofbeauty.com	815-625-0247		167-3
Educators Publishing Service Inc (EPS) PO Box 9031 .... Cambridge MA 02139 *TF:* 800-225-5750 ■ *Web:* eps.schoolspecialty.com	800-225-5750		637-2
Educators Resource Inc 2575 Schillingers Rd .... Semmes AL 36575 *TF:* 800-868-2368 ■ *Web:* educatorsresource.com	800-868-1588	868-6212	243
Educause 1150 18th St NW Ste 1010 .... Washington DC 20036 *Web:* www.educause.edu	202-872-4200	872-4318	48-9
Edufficient Inc 6 Forest Ave 2nd Fl .... Paramus NJ 07652 *TF:* 888-648-1811 ■ *Web:* www.edufficient.com	201-881-0030		195
Eduplanet21 LLC 5020 Ritter Rd Ste 203 .... Mechanicsburg PA 17055 *Web:* www.eduplanet21.com	717-884-9900		387
Edushape Ltd 28 Brandywine Dr .... Deer Park NY 11729 *Web:* edushape.com	631-586-0900		761
Eduworks Corp 400 SW Fourth St Ste 110 .... Corvallis OR 97333 *Web:* eduworks.com	541-753-0844		196
EdVenture Children's Museum 211 Gervais St .... Columbia SC 29201 *Web:* www.edventure.org	803-779-3100	779-3144	521
Edvest College Savings Plan PO Box 55189 .... Boston MA 02205 *TF:* 888-338-3789 ■ *Web:* www.edvest.com	888-338-3789		725
Edward A. Kurmel Brokerage Ltd 180 Driggs Ave .... Brooklyn NY 11222 *Web:* kurmelinsurance.com	718-383-1481	383-0851	390
Edward Adams House Bed & Breakfast 729 S Water St .... Silverton OR 97381 *Web:* edwardadamshousebandb.com	503-873-8868		377
Edward B. Marks Music Co c/o Carlin America Inc 126 E 38th St .... New York NY 10016 *Web:* www.ebmarks.com	212-779-7977	779-7920	637-10
Edward B. O'reilly & Associates Inc 30 W Highland Ave .... Philadelphia PA 19118 *Web:* www.eboreilly.com	215-242-8100		610
Edward Ball Wakulla Springs State Park 465 Wakulla Park Dr .... Wakulla Springs FL 32327 *Web:* www.floridastateparks.org	850-561-7276		565
Edward C. Burt, Jr. PC 2583 Whitney Ave .... Hamden CT 06518 *Web:* burtlaw.us	203-248-2182		41
Edward C. Levy Co 9300 Dix Ave .... Dearborn MI 48120 *TF:* 877-938-0007 ■ *Web:* www.edwclevy.com	313-843-7200	849-9441	503-5
Edward D. Gompers & Company Ac The Wagner Bldg 2001 Main St Ste 401 .... Wheeling WV 26003 *Web:* gompersco.com	304-233-4272		2
Edward Don & Co 9801 Adam Don Pkw .... Woodridge IL 60517 *TF:* 800-777-4366 ■ *Web:* www.don.com	800-777-4366		300
Edward Fox Photography & Video 6133 N Northwest Hwy Ste A .... Chicago IL 60631 *Web:* edwardfox.com	773-736-0200		590
Edward Hines Jr Veterans Affairs Hospital 5000 S Fifth Ave .... Hines IL 60141 *Web:* www.hines.va.gov	708-202-8387		374-8
Edward Hospital 801 S Washington St .... Naperville IL 60540 *Web:* www.eehealth.org	630-527-3000		374-3
Edward J. Darby & Son Inc 2200 N Eigth St PO Box 50049 .... Philadelphia PA 19133 *TF:* 800-875-6374 ■ *Web:* www.darbywiremesh.com	215-236-2203		688
Edward J. Meloney Inc 22 Madison Ave .... Lansdowne PA 19050 *Web:* www.edward-j-meloney-inc.business.site	610-626-4900		189-10

Name / Address	City	State	ZIP	Phone	Fax	Class
Edward Jones 12555 Manchester Rd *TF:* 800-441-2357 ■ *Web:* www.edwardjones.com	Saint Louis	MO	63131	314-515-2000		690
Edward Joy Electric 905 Canal St *TF:* 800-724-0664 ■ *Web:* www.edwardjoyelectric.com	Syracuse	NY	13210	315-474-3361	479-8604	362
Edward King House 35 King St *Web:* www.edwardkinghouse.org	Newport	RI	02840	401-846-7426		50-3
Edward M. Bernstein & Assoc 500 S Fourth St *Web:* edbernstein.com	Las Vegas	NV	89101	702-471-5754		41
Edward P. Ryan 38 Eagle St *Web:* edryan.com	Albany	NY	12207	518-465-2488	465-6612	41
Edward R. Bacon Company Inc (ERBCO) 255 Fitzgerald St *Web:* www.erbacon.com	San Martin	CA	95046	408-846-1600		358
Edward R. Madigan State Fish & Wildlife Area 1366 1010th Ave *Web:* www2.illinois.gov	Lincoln	IL	62656	217-735-2424		565
Edward S. Babcock & Sons Inc 6100 Quail Vly Ct *Web:* www.babcocklabs.com	Riverside	CA	92507	951-653-3351		743
Edward Segal Inc 360 Reynolds Bridge Rd *Web:* www.edwardsegalinc.com	Thomaston	CT	06787	860-283-5821		454
Edward T. Lefever PA 1333 SE 25th Loop Ste 101 *Web:* lefeverlaw.com	Ocala	FL	34471	352-671-9266	671-9272	41
Edward Ted & Pat Jones- Confluence Point State Park 1000 Riverlands Way *Web:* mostateparks.com	West Alton	MO	63386	636-899-1135		565
Edward Thomas Cos, The 9950 Santa Monica Blvd	Beverly Hills	CA	90212	310-859-9366		707
Edward Tyler Nahem Fine Art LLC 37 W 57th St Frnt 2 *Web:* www.edwardtylernahemfineart.com	New York	NY	10019	212-517-2453		522
Edward W. Daniel LLC 46950 State Rte 18 W Ste B *TF:* 800-338-2658 ■ *Web:* www.ewdaniel.com	Wellington	OH	44090	440-647-1960	647-1970	350
Edwards & Co 140 Greene Ave *Web:* edwardsandco.net	Sayville	NY	11782	631-472-8400		390
Edwards Air Force Base 305 E Popson Ave *Web:* www.edwards.af.mil	Edwards	CA	93524	661-277-1110	277-2732	497-1
Edwards Construction Services Inc 85 SW 52nd Ave *Web:* www.edwardsconstruction.com	Ocala	FL	34474	352-854-6266	854-6280	186
Edwards County 915 IL-130 Ste 7 *Web:* www.sos.state.il.us	Albion	IL	62806	618-445-3265		338
Edwards County 721 Marsh Ave PO Box 161 *TF:* 877-464-3929 ■ *Web:* www.edwardscounty.org	Kinsley	KS	67547	620-659-2711	659-3613	338
Edwards County 400 Main St PO Box 348 *Web:* www.edwardscountytexas.us	Rocksprings	TX	78880	830-683-6122	683-6385	338
Edwards Freeman Nut Co 441 E Hector St *Web:* edwardsfreeman.com	Conshohocken	PA	19428	610-828-7440		296-32
Edwards Graphic Arts Inc 2700 Bell Ave *TF:* 800-280-9765 ■ *Web:* www.ega.com	Des Moines	IA	50321	515-280-9765		627
Edwards Industries LLC 6085 Marshalee Dr Ste 140 *Web:* edwps.com	Elkridge	MD	21075	443-561-0180	561-0199	196
Edwards Jet Ctr 1691 Aviation Pl *TF:* 866-353-8245 ■ *Web:* www.edwardsjetcenter.com	Billings	MT	59105	406-252-0508	245-9491	63
Edwards Jewelers Inc 1700 McHenry Ave Ste 22 *Web:* edwards-jewelers.com	Modesto	CA	95350	209-577-4626		411
Edwards Label 2277 Knoll Dr *Web:* www.edwardslabel.com	Ventura	CA	93003	805-658-2626		627
Edwards Lifesciences Corp 1 Edwards Way *NYSE: EW* ■ *TF:* 800-424-3278 ■ *Web:* www.edwards.com	Irvine	CA	92614	949-250-2500	250-2525	582
Edwards Lowell 8712 Wilshire Blvd *Web:* www.edwardslowell.com	Beverly Hills	CA	90211	310-360-0466		157-6
Edwards Manufacturing Co 1107 Sykes St *TF:* 800-373-8206 ■ *Web:* www.edwardsironworkers.com	Albert Lea	MN	56007	507-373-8206	373-9433	456
Edwards Publications Inc 125 Eagles Nest Dr St A *Web:* edwgroupinc.com	Seneca	SC	29678	864-882-3272		532-3
Edwards Steel Erectors Inc 1777 Mckinley Ave	Columbus	OH	43222	614-274-7015		492
Edwards Wood Products Inc 2215 Old Lawyers Rd PO Box 219 *Web:* www.ewpi.com	Marshville	NC	28103	704-624-5098	624-6812	551
Edwards, Kenny & Bray 1900 - 1040 W Georgia St *Web:* www.ekb.com	Vancouver	BC	V6E4H3	604-689-1811		428
Edwardsburg Public Schools 69410 Section St *Web:* www.edwardsburgpublicschools.org	Edwardsburg	MI	49112	269-663-1031	663-6485	685
Edwardsville Community School District 7 708 St Louis St *Web:* www.ecusd7.org	Edwardsville	IL	62025	618-656-1182	692-7423	685
Edwardsville Publishing Company Inc 117 N 2nd St *Web:* www.theintelligencer.com	Edwardsville	IL	62025	618-656-4700	656-7618	532-2
Edwin Gaynor Corp 200 Charles St *TF:* 800-342-9667 ■ *Web:* egaynor.com	Stratford	CT	06615	203-378-5545	381-9019	815
Edwin L. Heim Co 1918 Greenwood St *TF:* 800-692-7316 ■ *Web:* www.edwinlheim.com	Harrisburg	PA	17104	717-233-8711	233-8619	189-4
Edwin Mellen Press 240 Portage Rd *Web:* www.mellenpress.com	Lewiston	NY	14092	716-754-2266		637-2
Edwynn Houk Gallery 745 Fifth Ave 4th Fl *Web:* www.houkgallery.com	New York	NY	10151	212-750-7070	688-4848	42
EE Cruz & Company Inc 165 Ryan St The Cruz Bldg *Web:* eecruz.com	South Plainfield	NJ	07080	908-462-9600	462-9592	188-10
EE Reed Construction LP 333 Commerce Green Blvd *Web:* www.eereed.com	Sugar Land	TX	77478	281-933-4000	933-4852	186
EE Schenck Co 6000 N Cutter Cir *TF:* 800-433-0722 ■ *Web:* eeschenck.com	Portland	OR	97217	503-284-4124	288-4475	594
EECO Switch 1240 Pioneer St Ste A *TF:* 800-854-3808 ■ *Web:* www.eecoswitch.com	Brea	CA	92821	800-854-3808		815
EEDAR (Electronic Entertainment Design & Research) 2075 Corte Del Nogal *Web:* www.eedar.com	Carlsbad	CA	92011	760-579-7120		387
Eeea Inc 506 Palmetto Dr *Web:* www.eeea.com	Simpsonville	SC	29681	864-963-3651		625
Eegee's 3360 E Ajo Way *Web:* eegees.com	Tucson	AZ	85713	520-294-3333	889-4340	670
EEI (Edison Electric Institute) 701 Pennsylvania Ave NW *TF:* 800-649-1202 ■ *Web:* www.eei.org	Washington	DC	20004	202-508-5000	508-5051	48-12
EEI (Engineering Economics Inc) 780 Simms St Ste 210 *TF:* 800-869-6902 ■ *Web:* www.eeiengineers.com	Golden	CO	80401	800-869-6902		186
EEI (Environmental Enterprises Inc) 10163 Cincinnati-Dayton Rd *TF:* 800-722-2818 ■ *Web:* www.eeienv.com	Cincinnati	OH	45241	800-722-2818		667
EEL River Fuels Inc 3371 N State St *TF:* 800-343-8354 ■ *Web:* www.erenergy.com	Ukiah	CA	95482	707-462-5554		579
EEOC (Equal Employment Opportunity Commission) 1801 L St NW *Web:* www.eeoc.gov	Washington	DC	20507	202-663-4191		340-20
EERC (Energy & Environmental Research Ctr) University of N Dakota 15 N 23rd St S 9018 *Web:* undeerc.org	Grand Forks	ND	58202	701-777-5000	777-5181	668
EERI (Earthquake Engineering Research Institute) 499 14th St Ste 320 *Web:* www.eeri.org	Oakland	CA	94612	510-451-0905	451-5411	49-19
E-Escrows Inc 2501 N Sepulveda Blvd Ste 110 *Web:* e-escrows.com	Manhattan Beach	CA	90266	310-802-1888	802-1998	653
Eets Inc 6060 Sunrise Vista Dr Ste 3450 *Web:* eetsinc.com	Citrus Heights	CA	95610	916-339-9691		261
EF Ctr 2 Education Cir *TF:* 800-637-8222 ■ *Web:* www.eftours.com	Cambridge	MA	02141	800-665-5364		760
EF International Language Ctr 200 Lake St *Web:* www.ef.com	Brighton	MA	02135	617-746-1700		167-3
EF Precision Design Inc 2301 Computer Rd *TF:* 800-536-3900 ■ *Web:* www.efgroup.com	Willow Grove	PA	19090	215-784-0861		757
EFA (Editorial Freelancers Assn) 71 W 23rd St 4th Fl *Web:* www.the-efa.org	New York	NY	10010	212-929-5400	929-5439	49-16
EFA (Earl F. Andersen Inc) 19740 Kenrick Ave *TF:* 800-862-6026 ■ *Web:* www.efa-mn.com	Lakeville	MN	55044	952-884-7300		300
EFC (Evangelical Fellowship of Canada) 9821 Leslie St Ste 103 *TF:* 866-302-3362 ■ *Web:* www.evangelicalfellowship.ca	Richmond Hill	ON	L4B3Y4	905-479-5885	479-4742	48-20
EFC Systems Inc 9015 Overlook Blvd *Web:* www.efcsystems.com	Brentwood	TN	37027	615-864-8500		178-1
EFCC (East Fairfield Coal Co) 10900 S Ave PO Box 217 *Web:* efccfamily.com	North Lima	OH	44452	330-549-2165		501
EFCO Corp 1000 County Rd *TF:* 800-221-4169 ■ *Web:* www.efcocorp.com	Monett	MO	65708	417-235-3193	235-7313	234
Efco Products 136 Smith St *TF:* 800-284-3326 ■ *Web:* www.efcoproducts.com	Poughkeepsie	NY	12601	800-284-3326		123
EFD Induction Inc 31511 Dequindre Rd *Web:* www.efd-induction.com	Madison Heights	MI	48071	248-658-0700	658-0701	386
EFF (Electronic Frontier Foundation Inc) 454 Shotwell St *Web:* www.eff.org	San Francisco	CA	94110	415-436-9333	436-9993	48-9
Effective Compensation Inc (ECI) 32045 Castle Ct Ste 103 *TF:* 877-746-4324 ■ *Web:* www.effectivecompensation.com	Evergreen	CO	80439	303-854-1000	854-1030	194
Effective Data Inc 1515 E Wdfield Rd *TF:* 877-825-5233 ■ *Web:* www.effective-data.com	Schaumburg	IL	60173	847-969-9300		225
Effective Solar Products LLC 601 Crescent Ave *TF:* 888-824-0090 ■ *Web:* www.effectivesolar.com	Lockport	LA	70374	985-532-0800		610
Effective Training Inc 14143 Farmington Rd *TF:* 800-886-0909 ■ *Web:* www.etinews.com	Livonia	MI	48154	800-886-0909		194
Efficas Inc 7007 Winchester Cir Ste 120 *TF:* 866-446-0388 ■ *Web:* efficas.com	Boulder	CO	80301	303-381-2070		578
Efficient Computer System (ECS) 530 US Hwy 70 SW *Web:* www.efficientcomputersystems.com	Hickory	NC	28602	828-328-2263	328-2264	177
Efficient Forms 10394 W Chatfield Ave Bldg 3 Ste 109 *Web:* www.efficienthire.com	Littleton	CO	80127	303-785-8600		225
Efficient Machine Products 12133 Alameda Dr *Web:* www.efficientm.com	Strongsville	OH	44149	440-268-0205	268-0215	621
Effigy Mounds National Monument 151 Hwy 76 *Web:* www.nps.gov	Harpers Ferry	IA	52146	563-873-3491		564
Effingham Convention & Visitors Bureau 201 E Jefferson Ave *TF:* 800-772-0750 ■ *Web:* www.effinghamil.com	Effingham	IL	62401	217-342-5305	342-2746	206
Effingham County 601 N Laurel St *TF:* 800-338-6745 ■ *Web:* www.effinghamcounty.org	Springfield	GA	31329	912-754-2123	754-4157	338

Name / Address	City	State	Zip	Phone	Fax	Class
Effingham County Chamber of Commerce 520 W Third St. *Web:* www.effinghamcounty.com	Springfield	GA	31329	912-754-3301	754-1236	139
Effingham County Illinois 101 N Fourth St Effingham County Office Bldg PO Box 628. *Web:* www.co.effingham.il.us	Effingham	IL	62401	217-342-6535	342-3577	338
Effingham Equity Inc 201 W Roadway Ave. *TF:* 800-223-1337 ■ *Web:* theequity.com	Effingham	IL	62401	217-342-4101	347-7601	275
Effone Software Inc 4701 Patrick Henry Dr Bldg 16. *Web:* www.effone.com	Santa Clara	CA	95054	408-830-1010		177
Effort Foundry Inc 6980 Chrisphalt Dr. *Web:* www.effortfoundry.com	Bath	PA	18014	610-837-1837	837-0920	492
Effres & Associates, A Professional Law Corp 5115 Clareton Dr Ste 110. *Web:* effreslaw.com	Agoura Hills	CA	91301	818-696-4234		41
EFG Capital International Corp 701 Brickell Ave 9th Fl. *Web:* www.efgcapital.com	Miami	FL	33131	305-482-8000		690
E-Filliate Inc 11321 White Rock Rd. *TF:* 800-592-7031 ■ *Web:* www.efilliate.com	Rancho Cordova	CA	95742	916-858-1000		459
EFILM LLC 1146 N Las Palmas Ave. *Web:* www.efilm.com	Hollywood	CA	90038	323-463-7041		514
Efird Chrysler Jeep Dodge Inc 1711 W Lucas St. *TF:* 888-712-5860 ■ *Web:* www.efirdchryslerjeepdodge.com	Florence	SC	29501	888-712-5860		57
E-First Aid Supplies 3055 Brighton-Henrietta TL Rd. *Web:* www.e-firstaidsupplies.com	Rochester	NY	14623	585-427-2940		459
EFJohnson Technologies 1440 Corporate Dr. *TF:* 800-328-3911 ■ *Web:* www.efjohnson.com	Irving	TX	75038	972-819-0700	819-0639	647
EFK Group LLC 1027 S Clinton Ave. *TF:* 800-485-3188 ■ *Web:* www.efkgroup.com	Trenton	NJ	08611	609-393-5838		196
eFORMandFUNCTION 220 Woodland Rd. *Web:* www.eformandfunction.com	Stone Ridge	NY	12484	845-657-2875	657-2883	177
EFP Corp 223 Middleton Run Rd. *TF:* 800-205-8537 ■ *Web:* www.efpcorp.com	Elkhart	IN	46516	574-295-4690		604
EFR (Employee & Family Resources) 505 Fifth Ave Ste 600. *TF:* 800-327-4692 ■ *Web:* www.efr.org	Des Moines	IA	50309	515-288-9020		631
EFTEC North America LLC 20219 Northline Rd. **Fax Area Code:* 734 ■ *Web:* www.eftec.ch	Taylor	MI	48180	248-585-2200	374-2050*	3
EftiSoft Inc PO Box 52. *Web:* www.eftisoft.com	Danville	IL	61834	217-597-0828		178-1
eFulgent Datawarehousing Solutions 3404 W Cheryl Dr Ste A290. *Web:* www.efulgent.com	Phoenix	AZ	85051	602-439-5503		196
EFX Media 2300 S Ninth St Ste 136. *Web:* efxmedia.com	Arlington	VA	22204	703-486-2303		6
EG Capital Group LLC 39 W 54th St. *Web:* www.egcapitalgroup.com	New York	NY	10019	212-956-2600		77
EG Fisher Public Library 1289 Ingleside Ave. *Web:* fisherlibrary.org	Athens	TN	37303	423-745-7782	745-1763	434-3
EG Penner Building Centres 200 Park Rd W. *Web:* www.egpenner.com	Steinbach	MB	R5G1A1	204-326-1325		290
EG Systems LLC 6200 Village Pkwy. *TF:* 800-538-5124 ■ *Web:* www.electroglas.com	Dublin	CA	94568	408-528-3000	528-3562	695
EG Tax Service 2475 Niagara Falls Blvd. *TF:* 800-829-9998 ■ *Web:* www.egtax.com	Amherst	NY	14228	716-632-7886		734
EGA (Embroiderers Guild of America, The) 1205 E Washington St Ste 117. *Web:* egausa.org	Louisville	KY	40202	502-589-6956	584-7900	48-18
eGain Corp 1252 Borregas Ave. *NASDAQ: EGAN* ■ *TF:* 888-603-4246 ■ *Web:* www.egain.com	Sunnyvale	CA	94089	408-636-4500	636-4400	39
Egami & Ichikawa CPAS Inc 615 Piikoi St Ste 2001. *Web:* eicpas.com	Honolulu	HI	96814	808-591-2772		2
Egan Home Health and Hospice 1812 Main St. *Web:* www.eganhealthcare.com	Franklinton	LA	70438	985-795-0107	795-0109	363
Egan Printing Co 1245 Elati St. *Web:* eganprinting.com	Denver	CO	80204	303-534-0171	595-4796	627
Egan Visual Inc 300 Hanlan Rd. *TF:* 800-263-2387 ■ *Web:* www.egan.com	Woodbridge	ON	L4L3P6	905-851-2826		320
EGB Systems and Solutions Inc 1234 Summer St 6th Fl. **Fax Area Code:* 866 ■ *TF:* 877-342-7978 ■ *Web:* www.egbsystems.com	Stamford	CT	06905	203-653-2741	693-5396*	178-1
EGC Group Inc, The 1175 Walt Whitman Rd. *Web:* www.egcgroup.com	Melville	NY	11747	516-935-4944		5
EGCL (East Greenbush Community Library) 10 Community Way. *Web:* eastgreenbushlibrary.org	East Greenbush	NY	12061	518-477-7476	477-6692	434-3
EGE Seramik America Inc 1721 Oakbrook Dr Ste C. *Web:* www.egeseramik-usa.com	Norcross	GA	30093	678-291-0888		751
Egen Solutions Inc 40 Shuman Blvd Ste 302. *Web:* egen.solutions	Naperville	IL	60563	630-844-0440		196
Egenera Inc 80 Central St. *TF:* 866-301-3117 ■ *Web:* www.egenera.com	Boxborough	MA	01719	978-206-6300	206-6436	176
Egg Strategy 909 Walnut St Ste 200. *Web:* www.eggstrategy.com	Boulder	CO	80302	303-546-9311	546-9237	297-10
Egg, The PO Box 2065. *Web:* www.theegg.org	Albany	NY	12220	518-473-1845	473-1848	572
Egge Machine Company Inc 11707 Slauson Ave. *TF:* 800-866-3443 ■ *Web:* egge.com	Santa Fe Springs	CA	90670	562-945-3419		454
Eggelhof Inc 1999 Kolfahl St. *Web:* www.eggelhof.com	Houston	TX	77023	713-923-2101		358
EGGers Consulting Company Inc 11272 Elm St Eggers Plz. *TF:* 800-844-3480 ■ *Web:* www.eggersconsulting.com	Omaha	NE	68144	402-333-3480		193
Egging Co, The 12145 Rd 38. *Web:* www.egging.com	Gurley	NE	69141	308-884-2233		273
Eggleston & Eggleston PC 5115 Bernard Rd Ste 301. *Web:* egglestonandeggleston.com	Roanoke	VA	24018	540-345-3556		2
Eggleston Services 6431 Tidewater Dr. *Web:* www.egglestonservices.org	Norfolk	VA	23509	757-625-2311	858-8057	317
Egizii Electric 3009 Singer Ave. *Web:* www.egiziielectric.com	Springfield	IL	62703	217-528-4001	528-1677	189-4
EGL Holdings 3495 Piedmont Rd 11 Piedmont Ctr Ste 412	Atlanta	GA	30305	404-949-8300	949-8311	792
Egli Machine Company Inc 240 State Hwy 7. *Web:* www.eglimachine.com	Sidney	NY	13838	607-563-3663		608
Eglin Air Force Base Eglin Blvd. *Web:* www.eglin.af.mil	Eglin AFB	FL	32542	850-882-3931		497-1
Eglin Federal Credit Union 838 Eglin Pkwy NE. *TF:* 800-367-6159 ■ *Web:* www.eglinfcu.org	Fort Walton Beach	FL	32547	850-862-0111		219
EGM LLC 3748 Industrial Park Dr. *Web:* www.egm-llc.com	Mobile	AL	36693	251-662-1250		273
EGMA (E. G. Mahler and Associates Inc) 1202 Greystone Ln Ste 1A. **Fax Area Code:* 740 ■ *Web:* www.egma.com	Newark	DE	19711	302-250-2444	931-1554*	194
Egmont Associates 85 E India Row Ste 24F. *Web:* www.egmontassociates.com	Boston	MA	02110	857-449-0001	449-0011	194
Egmont Key State Park 3900 Commonwealth Blvd. *Web:* www.floridastateparks.org	Tallahassee	FL	32399	727-893-2627		565
Egon Zehnder International Inc 1 N Wacker Dr Ste 2300. *Web:* www.egonzehnder.com	Chicago	IL	60606	312-260-8800	782-2846	266
eGov Strategies LLC 101 W Ohio St Ste 2250. *TF:* 877-634-3468 ■ *Web:* www.egovstrategies.com	Indianapolis	IN	46204	877-634-3468		225
EGPI Firecreek Inc 6564 Smoke Tree Ln. *Web:* www.egpifirecreek.net	Paradise Valley	AZ	85253	480-948-9266		787
EGR Inc 601 N Miller Blvd. *Web:* www.egronline.com	Oklahoma City	OK	73107	405-943-0900		115
EGRMC (East Georgia Regional Medical Ctr) 1499 Fair Rd. *TF:* 844-455-8708 ■ *Web:* www.eastgeorgiaregional.com	Statesboro	GA	30458	912-486-1000		374-3
Egroup Inc 482 Wando Park Blvd. *TF:* 877-347-6871 ■ *Web:* www.egroup-us.com	Mount Pleasant	SC	29464	877-347-6871		195
eGumball Inc 7525 Irvine Center Dr Ste 100. **Fax Area Code:* 877 ■ *TF:* 800-890-8940 ■ *Web:* www.egumball.com	Irvine	CA	92618	800-890-8940	890-8940*	195
Egypt 90 Broad St Ste 501. *Web:* www.egyptembassy.net	New York	NY	10017	212-503-0300		784
Egypt *Consulate General* 500 N Michigan Ave Ste 1900. *TF:* 866-487-3279 ■ *Web:* egypt.embassy-online.net	Chicago	IL	60611	312-828-9162	828-9167	257
EgyptAir 90 Broad St Ste 501. *Web:* www.egyptair.com	New York	NY	10036	212-581-5600		25
Egyptian Electric Cooperative Assn PO Box 38. *TF:* 800-606-1505 ■ *Web:* eeca.coop	Steeleville	IL	62288	800-606-1505		245
Egyptian Tourist Authority 45 Rockefeller Plz. *Web:* www.egypt.travel	New York	NY	10111	212-332-2570		775
EH Ashley & Company Inc 1 White Squadron Rd. *TF:* 800-735-7424 ■ *Web:* ehashley.com	Riverside	RI	02915	401-431-0950		411
EH Hamilton Trucking 2612 W Morris St. *TF:* 800-347-1344 ■ *Web:* www.ehhtrucking.com	Indianapolis	IN	46221	800-347-1344		780
EH Krohl Consulting Inc 3704 Duxford Dr. *Web:* www.fdacompliance.com	Raleigh	NC	27614	919-676-4801		196
EH Media PO Box 989. *Web:* www.ehmedia.com	Framingham	MA	01701	508-663-1500	663-1599	637-9
EH Wachs Co 600 Knightsbridge Pkwy. *TF:* 800-323-8185 ■ *Web:* www.ehwachs.com	Lincolnshire	IL	60069	847-537-8800	520-1147	455
Eharmonycom Inc 10900 Wilshire Blvd Fl 17 Ste A200. *Web:* www.eharmony.com	Santa Monica	CA	90404	626-795-4814	585-4040	226
EHB Logistics Inc 40 Willow Springs Cir. *TF:* 800-233-9366 ■ *Web:* www.brotherstrucking.com	York	PA	17402	717-764-5800	764-0099	780
eHDL Inc 3106 Commerce Pkwy. *TF:* 800-338-1079 ■ *Web:* online271.ehdl.com	Miramar	FL	33025	800-338-1079		194
Ehealthcare Consulting Inc 12175 Visionary Way Ste 320. *TF:* 888-507-3036 ■ *Web:* ehealthcareconsulting.com	Fishers	IN	46038	317-759-3742		177
eHire LLC 3565 Piedmont Rd NE Ste 300. *Web:* www.ehire.com	Atlanta	GA	30305	404-477-2680		266
Ehlers & Associates Inc 3060 Centre Pointe Dr. *TF:* 800-552-1171 ■ *Web:* www.ehlers-inc.com	Roseville	MN	55113	651-697-8500		194
Ehob Inc 250 N Belmont Ave. *TF:* 800-899-5553 ■ *Web:* www.ehob.com	Indianapolis	IN	46222	317-972-4600	972-4601	477
EHP Inc PO Box 7777. *TF:* 888-498-9648 ■ *Web:* www.ehpservices.com	Lancaster	PA	17604	717-735-7760	399-1693	352
Ehresmann Engineering Inc 4400 W 31St St. *Web:* ehresmannengineering.com	Yankton	SD	57078	605-665-7532		480
Ehrhardt Engineered Solutions 25 Central Industrial Dr. *TF:* 877-386-7856 ■ *Web:* www.ehrhardtsolutions.com	Granite City	IL	62040	314-436-6900		757
Ehrhart Griffin & Associates Inc 300 N Dakota Ave Ste 114. *Web:* ehrhartgriffin.com	Sioux Falls	SD	57104	605-339-7215	339-7271	261

Name / Address	City	State	Zip	Phone	Fax	Class
EHS Support Inc 4885 McKnight Rd Ste 188 *Web:* www.ehs-support.com	Pittsburgh	PA	15237	412-449-9681	774-2990	192
Ehs-International Inc 1011 SW Klickitat Way Ste 104 *TF:* 800-666-2959 ■ *Web:* www.ehsintl.com	Seattle	WA	98134	206-381-1128	254-4279	192
Ehvert 200 Adelaide St W *Web:* ehvert.com	Toronto	ON	M5H1W7	416-868-1933		261
EI Electronics LLC 1800 Shames Dr *TF:* 877-346-3837 ■ *Web:* electroind.com	Westbury	NY	11590	516-334-0870	338-4741	37
EI Group Inc, The 2101 Gateway Centre Blvd Ste 200 *TF:* 800-717-3472 ■ *Web:* www.ei1.com	Morrisville	NC	27560	919-657-7500		186
EI Microcircuits Inc 1651 Pohl Rd *TF:* 800-713-4015 ■ *Web:* www.eimicro.com	Mankato	MN	56001	507-345-5786	345-7559	625
EIA (Environmental Information Assn) 6935 Wisconsin Ave Ste 306 *TF:* 888-343-4342 ■ *Web:* www.eia-usa.org	Chevy Chase	MD	20815	301-961-4999	961-3094	48-13
EIC Solutions Inc 700 Veterans Way Ste 200 **Fax Area Code:* 800 ■ *TF:* 800-497-4524 ■ *Web:* eicsolutions.com	Warminster	PA	18974	215-443-5190	726-7592*	14
Eichelberger Performing Arts Ctr 195 Stock St Ste 203 *Web:* www.theeich.org	Hanover	PA	17331	717-637-7086	637-4504	572
Eichelbergers Inc 107 Texaco Rd *TF:* 800-371-3313 ■ *Web:* www.eichelbergers.com	Mechanicsburg	PA	17050	717-766-4800		317
Eichen & Di Meglio 1 Dupont St *Web:* eanddcpa.com	Plainview	NY	11803	516-576-3333	576-3342	2
Eichhorn Printing Inc 10534 York Rd Ste 103 *Web:* eichhornprinting.com	Hunt Valley	MD	21030	410-584-7530	584-8154	627
Eichleay Engineers Incorporated of California 1390 Willow Pass Rd Ste 600 *Web:* www.eichleay.com	Concord	CA	94520	925-689-7000	689-7006	261
Eid-Co Homes 1701 32nd Ave S *Web:* www.eid-co.com	Fargo	ND	58103	701-237-0510		187
Eide Bailly LLP 4310 17th Ave S *Web:* www.eidebailly.com	Fargo	ND	58103	701-239-8500	239-8600	2
Eide Industries Inc 16215 Piuma Ave *TF:* 800-422-6827 ■ *Web:* www.eideindustries.com	Cerritos	CA	90703	562-402-8335	924-2233	733
Eidelman Virant Capital 8000 Maryland Ave Ste 380 *Web:* www.eidelmanvirant.com	Saint Louis	MO	63105	314-727-9686		401
Eiden & Hatfield LLC 392 Red Cedar St Ste 5 *Web:* eidenhatfield.com	Menomonie	WI	54751	715-953-4870		41
EIDOS (Everyone Is Doing Outrageous Sex) PO Box 96 *Web:* www.eidos.org	Boston	MA	02137	617-262-0096	364-0096	637-9
Eielson Air Force Base 354 Broadway St Unit 2B *TF:* 800-538-6647 ■ *Web:* www.eielson.af.mil	Eielson AFB	AK	99702	907-377-1110		497-1
Eifel Mold & Engineering 31071 Fraser Dr *Web:* www.eifel-inc.com	Fraser	MI	48026	586-296-9640		604
Eiffel Tower Restaurant 3655 Las Vegas Blvd S *Web:* eiffeltowerrestaurant.com	Las Vegas	NV	89109	702-948-6937		671
Eigen 13366 Grass Vly Ave *TF:* 888-924-2020 ■ *Web:* www.eigen.com	Grass Valley	CA	95945	530-274-1240		250
Eigenstate Consulting LLC PO Box 411607 *Web:* www.eigenstate.net	San Francisco	CA	94141	415-225-6703		180
Eileen Koch & Co 9350 Wilshire Blvd Ste 323 *Web:* www.eileenkoch.com	Beverly Hills	CA	90212	310-441-1000		636
Eimo Technologies Inc 14300 Portage Rd PO Box 156 *Web:* www.eimotech.com	Vicksburg	MI	49097	269-649-0545		608
Einhorn, Harris, Ascher, Barbarito & Frost PC 165 E Main St *Web:* www.einhornlawyers.com	Denville	NJ	07834	973-627-7300		428
Einstein at Elkins Park 60 E Township Line Rd *Web:* www.einstein.edu	Elkins Park	PA	19027	215-663-6000		374-3
Einstein HR Inc 3805 Crestwood Pkwy Ste 100 *TF:* 855-475-9044 ■ *Web:* www.einsteinhr.com	Duluth	GA	30096	770-962-1700		631
Einstein Noah Restaurant Group Inc 555 Zang St Ste 300 *Web:* www.einsteinbros.com	Lakewood	CO	80228	303-568-8000		670
EIP (Educator's International Press Inc) 18 Colleen Rd *Web:* www.edint.com	Troy	NY	12180	518-271-9886	266-9422	637-2
Eire Direct Marketing LLC 325 W Huron St Ste 200 *Web:* www.eiredirect.com	Chicago	IL	60654	312-640-4000		195
EIS Electro Imaging Systems 6553 Las Positas Rd *Web:* www.eisonline.net	Livermore	CA	94551	925-371-4100		535
Eisai Inc 100 Tice Blvd *TF:* 866-613-4724 ■ *Web:* www.eisai.com	Woodcliff Lake	NJ	07677	201-692-1100	692-1804	582
Eisenbach Consulting LLC 5759 Eagles Nest Blvd Ste 1 *TF:* 800-977-4020 ■ *Web:* www.eisenbachconsulting.com	Tyler	TX	75703	800-977-4020		463
Eisenberg & Spilman PLLC 600 S Adams Ste 100 *Web:* eisenbergspilman.com	Birmingham	MI	48009	248-358-8880		41
Eisenberg Group AC CPAs, The 2260 Avenida De La Playa *Web:* www.theeisenberggroup.com	La Jolla	CA	92037	858-551-5500		2
Eisenberg Law Offices SC 308 E Washington Ave *Web:* eisenberglaw.org	Madison	WI	53703	608-256-8356		41
Eisenhauer Manufacturing Co, The 409 Center St *Web:* www.eisenhauermfg.com	Van Wert	OH	45891	419-238-0081		488
Eisenhower Army Medical Ctr 300 E Hospital Rd *Web:* eisenhower.amedd.army.mil	Fort Gordon	GA	30905	706-787-5811		374-4
Eisenhower Birthplace State Historic Site 609 S Lamar Ave *Web:* www.thc.texas.gov	Denison	TX	75021	903-465-8908		565
Eisenhower Inn & Conference Ctr 2634 Emmitsburg Rd *Web:* www.eisenhower.com	Gettysburg	PA	17325	717-334-8121		379
Eisenhower Medical Ctr 39000 Bob Hope Dr *Web:* www.eisenhowerhealth.org	Rancho Mirage	CA	92270	760-340-3911		374-3
Eisenhower National Historic Site 1195 Baltimore Pk Ste 100 *Web:* www.nps.gov	Gettysburg	PA	17325	717-338-9114	338-0821	564
Eisenhower State Park 29810 S Fairlawn Rd *Web:* ksoutdoors.com	Osage City	KS	66523	785-528-4102		565
Eisenhower State Park 50 Park Rd 20 *Web:* tpwd.texas.gov	Denison	TX	75020	903-465-1956		565
Eisenmann Corp 150 E Dartmoor Dr *Web:* www.eisenmann.com	Crystal Lake	IL	60014	815-455-4100	455-1018	318
Eisenmenger, Robinson, Blaue & Peters PA 5450 Village Dr *Web:* ebplaw.com	Viera	FL	32955	321-504-0321	504-0320	41
Eisinger, Brown, Lewis, Frankel & Chaiet PA 4000 Hollywood Blvd Ste 265-S *Web:* eisingerlaw.com	Hollywood	FL	33021	954-894-8000	894-8015	41
Eisman & Russo Inc 6455 Powers Ave *Web:* eismanandrusso.com	Jacksonville	FL	32217	904-733-1478	636-8828	261
Eisner & Maglione CPAS LLC 66 Commack Rd Ste 201 *Web:* emcpallc.com	Commack	NY	11725	631-499-4039		2
Eisner LLP 750 Third Ave *Web:* www.eisneramper.com	New York	NY	10017	212-949-8700		2
EIT (Electronic Instrumentation & Technology Inc) 108 Carpenter Dr *Web:* www.eit.com	Sterling	VA	20164	703-478-0700	478-0291	253
E-IT Professionals Corp 42180 Ford Rd Ste 275 *Web:* www.eitprofessionals.com	Canton	MI	48187	734-416-0059		260
Eiteljorg Museum of American Indians & Western Art 500 W Washington St *Web:* www.eiteljorg.org	Indianapolis	IN	46204	317-636-9378	275-1400	520
EIZO Inc 5710 Warland Dr *TF:* 800-800-5202 ■ *Web:* www.eizoglobal.com	Cypress	CA	90630	562-431-5011	431-4811	173-4
EJ Basler Co 9511 Ainslie St *Web:* www.ejbasler.com	Schiller Park	IL	60176	847-678-8880	678-8896	621
E-J Electric Installation Co 46-41 Vernon Blvd *Web:* www.ej1899.com	Long Island City	NY	11101	718-786-9400	937-9120	189-4
EJ Group Inc 301 Spring St *TF:* 800-874-4100 ■ *Web:* www.ejco.com	East Jordan	MI	49727	231-536-2261	536-4486	307
EJ Welch Company Inc 13735 Lakefront Dr *Web:* www.ejwelch.com	Earth City	MO	63045	314-739-2273		361
EJA/Capacity Insurance Agency LLC 217 Rt 130 *TF:* 855-912-3537 ■ *Web:* ejainsurance.com	Bordentown	NJ	08505	609-291-9950		390
Ejcon Corp 5502 Shawland Rd *Web:* www.ejcon.com	Jacksonville	FL	32254	904-786-0622		480
Ejes Inc 12655 N Central Expy Ste 500 *Web:* ejesinc.com	Dallas	TX	75243	214-343-1210	343-3885	261
EJGH (East Jefferson General Hospital) 4200 Houma Blvd *TF:* 866-280-7737 ■ *Web:* ejgh.org	Metairie	LA	70006	504-454-4000		374-3
Ejh Construction Inc 30896 W 8 Mile Rd *TF:* 800-854-4534 ■ *Web:* ejhconstruction.com	Farmington Hills	MI	48336	800-854-4534		186
EJM Development Co 9061 Santa Monica Blvd *Web:* www.ejmdevelopment.com	Los Angeles	CA	90069	310-278-1830	278-2965	653
EJM Engineering Inc 411 S Wells St Ste 1000 *Web:* www.ejmengineering.com	Chicago	IL	60607	312-922-1700		261
EJQ Home Health Care Inc 800 Middle Ave *Web:* www.ejqhomehealthcare.com	Elyria	OH	44035	440-323-7004	322-4051	363
Ekahau 1925 Isaac Newton Sq E Ste 200 **Fax Area Code:* 703 ■ *TF:* 866-435-2428 ■ *Web:* www.ekahau.com	Reston	VA	20190	866-435-2428	860-2028*	387
Eki Environment & Water Inc 577 Airport Blvd Ste 500 *Web:* ekiconsult.com	Burlingame	CA	94010	650-292-9100		261
Eklind Tool Comany Inc 11040 King St *Web:* www.eklindtool.com	Franklin Park	IL	60131	847-994-8550		350
Eklund's Appliance & TV Co 1007 Central Ave W *Web:* www.eklundsappliance.com	Great Falls	MT	59404	406-761-3430		35
Eklunds Inc 2860 Market Loop *Web:* www.eklunds.com	Southlake	TX	76092	817-949-2030		186
Ekm Metering Inc 363 Berkeley Way *Web:* www.ekmmetering.com	Santa Cruz	CA	95062	831-425-7371		196
Ekmanian Tax & Accounting 404 E Branch St *Web:* ekmaniancpa.com	Arroyo Grande	CA	93420	805-556-4512	474-8593	2
E-Konomy Pool Service & Supplies 6020 E Speedway Blvd *Web:* e-konomy.com	Tucson	AZ	85712	520-325-6427		104
Ekornes Inc 615 Pierce St *Web:* www.stressless.com	Somerset	NJ	08873	732-302-0097		361
EKRiley Investments LLC 1420 Fifth Ave Ste 3300 *TF:* 800-809-9317 ■ *Web:* www.ekriley.com	Seattle	WA	98101	206-832-1520	832-1527	690
EKS Publishing Co 322 Castro St *TF:* 877-743-2739 ■ *Web:* www.ekspublishing.com	Oakland	CA	94607	510-251-9100	251-9102	96
EKSC Eagle 25740 College Blvd *Web:* www.eagle-audio.com	Olathe	KS	66061	913-780-4495		52

Company	Phone	Fax	Class
Ekuber Ventures Inc 8150 Leesburg Pke Ste 810 .... Tysons VA 22182 *Web:* www.ekuber.com	703-624-1473		180
El Al Israel Airlines Ltd 100 Wall St 4th Fl .... New York NY 10010 *TF:* 800-223-6700 ■ *Web:* www.elal.com	212-852-0600		25
El Aviso de Ocasion Inc 4850 E Gage Ave .... Bell CA 90201 *Web:* www.elaviso.com	323-586-9199	589-9395	532-2
El Basha 424 Belmont St .... Worcester MA 01604 *Web:* www.elbasharestaurant.com	508-797-0884		671
El Burrito 550 Piikoi St .... Honolulu HI 96814	808-596-8225		671
El Cajon Motors D/B/A El Cajon Ford 1595 E Main St .... El Cajon CA 92021 *Web:* www.elcajonmotors.com	619-312-4107		57
El Camino College 16007 Crenshaw Blvd .... Torrance CA 90506 *TF:* 866-352-2646 ■ *Web:* www.elcamino.edu	310-532-3670	660-3818	162
El Camino College *Compton Ctr* 1111 E Artesia Blvd .... Compton CA 90221 *Web:* www.compton.edu	310-900-1600		162
El Camino Hospital 2500 Grant Rd .... Mountain View CA 94040 *Web:* www.elcaminohealth.org	650-940-7000		475
El Camino Real 2500 W Sylvania Ave .... Toledo OH 43613 *Web:* www.elcaminorealtoledo.com	419-472-0700		671
El Camino Store, The 420 Athena Dr .... Athens GA 30601 *TF:* 888-685-5987 ■ *Web:* www.elcaminostore.com	888-685-5987		57
El Campo Independent School District 700 W Norris St .... El Campo TX 77437 *Web:* www.ecisd.org	979-543-6771		685
El Canelo 2709 W 12th St .... Erie PA 16505 *Web:* www.elcaneloerie.com	814-835-2290		671
El Capitan Fresh Mexican Grill 1800 S Milton Rd Ste 21 .... Flagstaff AZ 86001 *Web:* www.elcapitanmexicangrill.com	928-774-1083		671
El Caribe Resort 2125 S Atlantic Ave .... Daytona Beach FL 32118 *TF:* 800-445-9889 ■ *Web:* www.elcaribe.com	386-252-1558		707
El Centro Chamber of Commerce & Visitors Bureau 1095 S Fourth St .... El Centro CA 92243 *Web:* www.elcentrochamber.org	760-352-3681	352-3246	139
El Centro Elementary School District 1256 Broadway St .... El Centro CA 92243 *Web:* www.ecesd.org	760-352-5712		685
El Centro Public Library 539 State St .... El Centro CA 92243 *TF:* 877-482-5656 ■ *Web:* www.cityofelcentro.org	760-337-4565	352-1384	434-3
El Centro Regional Medical Ctr 1415 Ross Ave .... El Centro CA 92243 *Web:* www.ecrmc.org	760-339-7100		374-3
El Cerro Mexican Bar & Grill 108 S Kings Hwy .... Myrtle Beach SC 29577 *Web:* www.elcerromb.com	843-712-1844		671
El Charro Cafe 311 N Court Ave .... Tucson AZ 85701 *Web:* www.elcharrocafe.com	520-622-1922		671
El Chico 8409 I-30 .... Little Rock AR 72209 *TF:* 800-242-5353 ■ *Web:* www.elchico.com	501-562-3762		671
El Chorro Lodge 5550 E Lincoln Dr .... Paradise Valley AZ 85253 *Web:* www.elchorro.com	480-948-5170		671
El Comedor 1120 25th St S .... Great Falls MT 59405 *Web:* www.elcomedormexicanrestaurant.com	406-761-5500		671
El Conquistador Resort 1000 El Conquistador Ave .... Fajardo PR 00738 *Web:* www.elconresort.com	787-863-1000		669
El Corral 2201 E River Rd .... Tucson AZ 85718 *Web:* www.elcorraltucson.com	520-299-6092		671
El Cortez Hotel & Casino 600 E Fremont St .... Las Vegas NV 89101 *TF:* 800-634-6703 ■ *Web:* elcortezhotelcasino.com	702-385-5200		133
El Coyote 7404 State Rd .... Cincinnati OH 45230 *Web:* elcoyotecincy.com	513-232-5757		671
El Dorado And Wesson Railway Co 900 SW Ave .... El Dorado AR 71730	870-863-7100		648
El Dorado Correctional Facility 1737 SE Hwy 54 PO Box 311 .... El Dorado KS 67042 *Web:* www.doc.ks.gov	316-321-7284	322-2018	213
El Dorado County 360 Fair Ln .... Placerville CA 95667 *Web:* edcgov.us	530-621-5490	621-2147	338
El Dorado County Chamber of Commerce 542 Main St .... Placerville CA 95667 *TF:* 800-457-6279 ■ *Web:* www.eldoradocounty.org	530-621-5885	642-1624	139
El Dorado County Library 345 Fair Ln .... Placerville CA 95667 *Web:* www.eldoradolibrary.org	530-621-5540		434-3
El Dorado Engineering Inc 9089 S 1300 W Ste 150 .... West Jordan UT 84088 *Web:* www.eldoradoengineering.com	801-966-8288	966-8499	261
El Dorado Furniture Corp 4200 NW 167th St .... Miami FL 33054 *TF:* 888-451-7800 ■ *Web:* www.eldoradofurniture.com	305-624-2400		321
El Dorado Molds Inc 2691 Mercantile Dr .... Rancho Cordova CA 95742 *Web:* springboardmfg.com	916-635-4558	853-0711	697
El Dorado Nature Ctr 7550 E Spring St .... Long Beach CA 90815 *TF:* 800-662-8887 ■ *Web:* longbeach.gov	562-570-1745	570-8530	50-5
El Dorado Savings Bank 4040 El Dorado Rd .... Placerville CA 95667 *TF:* 800-874-9779 ■ *Web:* eldoradosavingsbank.com	530-622-1492		70
El Dorado State Park 618 NE Bluestem Rd .... El Dorado KS 67042 *Web:* www.ksoutdoors.com	316-321-7180		565
El Dorado Trading Group Inc 760 San Antonio Rd .... Palo Alto CA 94303 *Fax Area Code: 650 ■ *TF:* 800-227-8292 ■ *Web:* www.edtg.com	800-227-8292	494-1995*	112
El Encanto Inc 2001 Fourth St SW PO Box 293 .... Albuquerque NM 87103 *TF:* 800-888-7336 ■ *Web:* buenofoods.com	505-243-2722		296-36
El Farol 808 Canyon Rd .... Santa Fe NM 87501 *Web:* www.elfarolsantafe.com	505-983-9912		671
El Fenix Corp 1845 Woodall Rodgers Ste 1100 .... Dallas TX 75201 *TF:* 877-591-1918 ■ *Web:* www.elfenix.com	972-241-2171	241-3031	670
El Gallo Giro 1442 S Bristol St .... Santa Ana CA 92704 *Web:* gallogiro.com	714-549-2011		671
El Gaucho 2505 First Ave .... Seattle WA 98121 *Web:* elgaucho.com	206-728-1337		671
EL Harvey & Sons Inc 68 Hopkinton Rd .... Westborough MA 01581 *TF:* 800-321-3002 ■ *Web:* www.elharvey.com	508-836-3000	836-3040	804
El Huarache Azteca 3842 International Blvd .... Oakland CA 94601 *Web:* elhuaracheazteca.net	510-533-2395		671
El Loco Mexican Cafe 465 Madison Ave .... Albany NY 12210 *Web:* www.ellocomexicancafe.com	518-436-1855		671
El Loro Mexican Restaurant 801 Volvo Pkwy Ste 114 .... Chesapeake VA 23320 *Web:* elloromexican.com	757-436-3415	436-3181	671
El Maguey 3738 S Noland Rd .... Independence MO 64055	816-252-6868		671
El Malpais National Monument 123 E Roosevelt Ave .... Grants NM 87020 *Web:* www.nps.gov	505-285-4641	285-5661	564
El Mar Plastics Inc 833 E Walnut St .... Carson CA 90746	310-436-6444	327-0491	603
El Mariachi 144 Washington Ave .... Albany NY 12210 *Web:* elmariachisrestaurant.com	518-432-7580		671
El Matador 2564 Ogden Ave .... Ogden UT 84401 *Web:* www.elmatadorogden.com	801-393-3151		671
El Matador Foods Inc 7201 Bayway Dr .... Baytown TX 77520 *Web:* www.elmatadorfoods.com	281-424-4555	838-1375	345
El Metate Mercado 125 N Rancho Santiago Blvd .... Orange CA 92869 *Web:* www.elmetate.com	714-771-5527		345
El Mexicano 5801 Rue Ferrari .... San Jose CA 95138 *TF:* 800-858-1119 ■ *Web:* www.elmexicano.net	800-858-1119		532-2
El Mexicano Inn 1215 30th Ave .... Gulfport MS 39501	228-863-3691		671
El Mirasol Restaurants 140 E Palm Canyon Dr .... Palm Springs CA 92264 *Web:* www.cafeofloveny.com	760-323-0721		671
El Molino Gourmet Coffee Shop 2012 E 7th Ave .... Tampa FL 33605 *TF:* 800-531-9587 ■ *Web:* www.elmolinocoffee.com	800-531-9587		296-7
El Monte City School District 3540 Lexington Ave .... El Monte CA 91731 *Web:* www.emcsd.org	626-453-3700		685
El Monte Union High School District 3537 Johnson Ave .... El Monte CA 91731 *Web:* www.emuhsd.org	626-444-9005		685
El Monte/South El Monte Chamber of Commerce (EM/SEM) 1903 N Durfee Ave .... El Monte CA 91731 *Web:* www.emsem.biz	626-443-0180		139
El Morro National Monument HC 61 PO Box 43 .... Ramah NM 87321 *Web:* www.nps.gov	505-783-4226	783-4689	564
El Mundo 2345 Frankfort Ave .... Louisville KY 40206 *Web:* www.502elmundo.com	502-899-9930		671
El Museo Latino 4701 S 25th St .... Omaha NE 68107 *Web:* www.elmuseolatino.org	402-731-1137	733-7012	520
El Mustee & Sons Inc 5431 W 164th St .... Brook Park OH 44142 *Web:* mustee.com	216-267-3100		612
El Novillero 4216 Franklin Blvd .... Sacramento CA 95820 *Web:* www.elnov.com	916-456-4287	456-4149	671
El Novillo Restaurant 15450 New Barn Rd .... Miami Lakes FL 33014 *Web:* www.elnovillorestaurant.com	305-819-2755		671
El Nuevo Herald 3511 NW 91st Ave .... Doral FL 33172 *TF:* 866-949-6722 ■ *Web:* www.elnuevoherald.com	305-376-3535		532-2
El Observador Publications Inc 1042 W Hedding St Ste 250 .... San Jose CA 95126 *Web:* el-observador.com	408-938-1700	938-1705	532-3
El Paso Cafe 4235 N Pershing Dr .... Arlington VA 22203 *Web:* www.elpasocafeva.com	703-243-9811		671
El Paso City Hall 300 N Campbell .... El Paso TX 79901 *Web:* www.elpasotexas.gov	915-212-0000		337
El Paso Community College 10700 Gateway E .... El Paso TX 79927 *Web:* www.epcc.edu	915-831-7017		162
El Paso Convention & Performing Arts Ctr 1 Civic Center Plz .... El Paso TX 79901 *TF:* 800-351-6024 ■ *Web:* visitelpaso.com	915-534-0600	534-0687	205
El Paso County 200 S Cascade Ave .... Colorado Springs CO 80903 *Web:* www.elpasoco.com	719-520-6200		338
El Paso Electric Co 100 N Stanton Stanton Tower .... El Paso TX 79901 *NYSE: EE* ■ *TF:* 800-351-1621 ■ *Web:* www.epelectric.com	915-543-5711	521-4766	787
El Paso Health 1145 Westmoreland Dr .... El Paso TX 79925 *TF:* 877-532-3778 ■ *Web:* www.elpasohealth.com	915-532-3778	532-2877	48-17
El Paso Independent School District 6531 Boeing Dr .... El Paso TX 79925 *Web:* www.episd.org	915-779-3781	779-4280	685
El Paso International Airport 6701 Convair Rd .... El Paso TX 79925 *TF:* 800-288-1784 ■ *Web:* www.elpasointernationalairport.com	915-780-4749		27
El Paso Museum of Art 1 Art Festival Plz .... El Paso TX 79901 *Web:* epma.art	915-532-1707	532-1010	520
El Paso Museum of History 510 Santa Fe St .... El Paso TX 79901 *Web:* www.elpasotexas.gov	915-212-0320	351-4345	520
El Paso Public Library 501 N Oregon St .... El Paso TX 79901 *Web:* www.elpasolibrary.org	915-543-5433		435
El Paso Symphony Orchestra 1 Civic Center Plz .... El Paso TX 79901 *Web:* www.epso.org	915-532-3776	533-8162	573-3

Phone | Fax | Class

El Paso Times 300 N Campbell St. . . . . El Paso TX 79901 915-546-6300 546-6415 532-2
TF: 800-351-1677 ■ *Web:* www.elpasotimes.com
El Paso Zoo 4001 E Paisano Dr . . . . . El Paso TX 79905 915-212-0966 521-1857 823
Web: www.elpasozoo.org
El Patio Restaurant
37311 Fremont Blvd. . . . . Fremont CA 94536 510-796-1733 671
Web: elpatiooriginaldining.com
El Periodico USA Inc 801 E Fir Ave . . . . . Mcallen TX 78501 956-631-5628 631-0832 532-3
Web: www.elperiodicousa.com
El Pinto 10500 Fourth St NW . . . . . Albuquerque NM 87114 505-898-1771 890-0498 671
Web: www.elpinto.com
El Pollo Loco
3535 Harbor Blvd Ste 100 . . . . . Costa Mesa CA 92626 714-599-5000 670
TF: 877-375-4968 ■ *Web:* www.elpolloloco.com
El Puente PO Box 553 . . . . . Goshen IN 46527 219-533-9082 532-2
Web: www.webelpuente.com
El Ran Furniture Ltd
2751 Transcanada Hwy. . . . . Pointe-Claire QC H9R1B4 514-630-5656 319-2
TF: 800-361-6546 ■ *Web:* www.elran.com
El Rancho de las Golondrinas Museum
334 Los Pinos Rd. . . . . Santa Fe NM 87507 505-471-2261 520
Web: golondrinas.org
El Rancho Inc 2600 McCree Rd Ste 100 . . . . . Garland TX 75041 972-526-7300 345
Web: www.elranchoinc.com
El Rancho Inn-Steak & Lobster
1457 E Mariposa Rd. . . . . Stockton CA 95205 209-467-1529 671
Web: sites.google.com
El Rancho Mexican Restaurant
815 E Market St . . . . . Harrisonburg VA 22801 540-209-8936 671
Web: elranchomexican.com
El Rancho Supermercado
22291 Redwood Rd . . . . . Castro Valley CA 94546 510-728-1945 297-8
Web: www.elranchosupercv.com
El Rey Inn 1862 Cerillos Rd . . . . . Santa Fe NM 87505 505-982-1931 379
Web: www.elreycourt.com
El Rincon Community Clinic
3809 W Grand Ave . . . . . Chicago IL 60651 773-276-0200 726
Web: www.rinconfamilyservices.org
El Rincon Mexican Restaurant
720 S Main St. . . . . North Canton OH 44720 330-497-2229 671
Web: elrinconnorthcanton.com
El Rinconcito Restaurant
4013 Prescott St. . . . . Corpus Christi TX 78416 361-851-8020 671
El Rodeo 4659 Jonestown Rd. . . . . Harrisburg PA 17109 717-652-5340 671
Web: www.elrodeopa.com
El Rodeo 3404 Westgate Dr . . . . . Durham NC 27707 919-402-9190 671
Web: elrodeodurhamnc.com
El Rosal Mexican Restaurant
3718 S Mooney Blvd . . . . . Visalia CA 93277 559-733-7731 671
Web: elrosalrestaurant.com
El Salvador
Consulate General
3450 Wilshire Blvd Ste 250. . . . . Los Angeles CA 90010 213-234-9200 257
Web: www.elsalvador.org
El Sarape 4043 Martin Way E. . . . . Olympia WA 98506 360-459-5525 671
Web: www.elsarape.net
El Serrano 2151 Columbia Ave. . . . . Lancaster PA 17603 717-397-6191 671
Web: www.elserrano.com
El Sol 1448 Danforth Ave. . . . . Toronto ON M4J1N4 416-405-8074 671
Web: www.elsol.ca
El Sombrero 157 S Franklin St. . . . . Juneau AK 99801 907-586-6770 586-6772 671
El Taco de Mexico 714 Santa Fe Dr . . . . . Denver CO 80204 303-623-3926 671
Web: eltacodemexicodenver.com
El Tapatio Markets Inc
13635 Fwy Dr. . . . . Santa Fe Springs CA 90670 562-293-4200 297-8
Web: www.eltapatiomarkets.com
El Teatro Campesino
705 4th St. . . . . San Juan Bautista CA 95045 831-623-2444 514
Web: www.elteatrocampesino.com
El Tiempo Cantina 3130 Richmond Ave. . . . . Houston TX 77098 713-807-1600 671
Web: www.eltiempocantina.com
El Toreo Mexican Restaurants
3790 Peter's Creek . . . . . Roanoke VA 24018 540-342-7060 671
Web: eltoreoroanoke.com
El Torito Restaurants Inc
5995 Katella Ave. . . . . Cypress CA 90630 714-761-8155 670
Web: www.eltorito.com
El Toro 2600 S 48th St . . . . . Lincoln NE 68506 402-488-3939 671
El Toro Export LLC 96 E Fawcett Rd . . . . . Heber CA 92249 760-352-6312 352-1063 446
Web: www.eltoroexport.com
El Tovar Hotel 1 El Tovar Rd . . . . . Grand Canyon AZ 86023 928-638-2631 379
TF: 888-297-2757 ■ *Web:* www.grandcanyonlodges.com
El Vaquero 3230 Olentangy River Rd . . . . . Columbus OH 43221 614-486-4547 486-4050 671
Web: www.vaquerorestaurant.com
El Vez 121 S 13th St . . . . . Philadelphia PA 19107 215-928-9800 671
Web: elvezrestaurant.com
Ela Area Public Library District
275 Mohawk Trl . . . . . Lake Zurich IL 60047 847-438-3433 438-9290 434-3
TF: 800-436-0709 ■ *Web:* eapl.org
El-Ad US Holding Inc
575 Madison Ave 22nd Fl. . . . . New York NY 10022 212-213-8833 157-6
Web: www.eladgroup.com
Elaine Coyne Galleries Inc
PO Box 440666 . . . . . Kennesaw GA 30160 800-741-2523 332-1626* 411
**Fax Area Code:* 866 ■ *TF:* 800-741-2523 ■ *Web:* www.ecg.com
Elaine P. Nunez Community College
3710 Paris Rd. . . . . Chalmette LA 70043 504-278-7497 278-7480 162
TF: 800-256-3000 ■ *Web:* www.nunez.edu
Elam Chemical Company Inc PO Box 360 . . . . . Eureka MO 63025 636-938-4588 938-4766 151
Web: elamchemical.com
Elam Construction Inc
556 Struthers Ave. . . . . Grand Junction CO 81501 970-242-5370 188-4
TF: 800-675-4598 ■ *Web:* www.elamconstruction.com
Elan Chemical Co 268 Doremus Ave . . . . . Newark NJ 07105 973-344-8014 144
Web: www.elan-chemical.com
Elan Construction Ltd
3639-27 St NE Ste 100. . . . . Calgary AB T1Y5E4 403-291-1165 291-5396 187
Web: www.elanconstruction.com

Phone | Fax | Class

Elan Financial Services
4 E Station Square Dr Ste 620 . . . . . Pittsburgh PA 15219 800-343-7064 401
TF: 800-343-7064 ■ *Web:* www.elanfinancialservices.com
Elan Hotel 8435 Beverly Blvd. . . . . Los Angeles CA 90048 323-658-6663 658-6640 379
TF: 866-203-2212 ■ *Web:* www.elanhotel.com
Elan Technologies
400 E Royal Ln Ste 260 . . . . . Irving TX 75039 972-501-9021 196
Web: www.elantecs.com
Elan Technology 169 Elan Ct . . . . . Midway GA 31320 912-880-3526 332
Web: www.elantechnology.com
Elanco Animal Health
2500 Innovation Way . . . . . Greenfield IN 46140 877-352-6261 584
TF: 877-352-6261 ■ *Web:* www.elanco.com
Elangeni | SMART IT
115 Rt 46 W Bldg B Ste 13. . . . . Mountain Lakes NJ 07046 866-582-9800 180
TF: 866-582-9800 ■ *Web:* elangenismartit.com
Elantas PDG Inc 5200 N Second St. . . . . Saint Louis MO 63147 314-621-5700 436-1030 145
TF: 800-325-7492 ■ *Web:* www.elantas.com
ElanTech Inc 9250 Bendix Rd Ste 1030. . . . . Columbia MD 21045 301-486-0600 486-0619 177
Web: www.elantech-inc.com
Elara Systems
2880 Sunrise Blvd Ste 200. . . . . Rancho Cordova CA 95742 916-638-1658 180
Web: www.elarasystems.com
Elarbee, Thompson, Sapp & Wilson LLP
800 International Tower 229 Peachtree St NE . . . . . Atlanta GA 30303 404-659-6700 428
Web: elarbeethompson.com
Elastec 1309 W Main . . . . . Carmi IL 62821 618-382-2525 382-3610 539
Web: www.elastec.com
Elastic Fabrics of America
3112 Pleasant Garden Rd. . . . . Greensboro NC 27406 336-275-9401 745-4
Web: www.elasticfabrics.com
Elastic Therapy Inc
718 Industrial Park Ave. . . . . Asheboro NC 27205 336-625-0529 156
Web: www.elastictherapy.com
Elasticity LLC
1008 Locust Ave Ste 300 . . . . . Saint Louis MO 63101 314-561-8253 636
Web: goelastic.com
Elastomer Specialties Inc
2210 S Hwy 69. . . . . Wagoner OK 74467 918-485-0276 485-0253 604
TF: 866-786-4244 ■ *Web:* www.elastomer.com
Elavon 2 Concourse Pkwy Ste 800 . . . . . Atlanta GA 30328 678-731-5000 178-4
TF: 800-725-1243 ■ *Web:* www.elavon.com
eLaw Marketing
25 Robert Pitt Dr Ste 209G. . . . . Monsey NY 10952 866-833-6245 504-3773* 428
**Fax Area Code:* 718 ■ *TF:* 866-833-6245 ■ *Web:* www.elawmarketing.com
Elbar Duplicator Corp
105, 26 Jamaica Ave. . . . . Richmond Hill NY 11418 718-441-1123 113
TF: 800-540-1123 ■ *Web:* www.edcbizsolutions.com
Elbeco Inc 4418 Pottsville Pk. . . . . Reading PA 19605 610-921-0651 921-8651 155-19
TF: 800-468-4654 ■ *Web:* www.elbeco.com
Elbert County 215 Comanche St PO Box 7 . . . . . Kiowa CO 80117 303-621-2131 621-2343 338
Web: www.elbertcounty-co.gov
Elbert County Board of Education
50 Laurel Dr . . . . . Elberton GA 30635 706-213-4000 685
Web: www.elbert.k12.ga.us
Elbert County Chamber of Commerce
148 College Ave . . . . . Elberton GA 30635 706-283-5651 283-5722 338
Web: elbertchamber.com
Elberta Crate & Box Co
606 Dothan Hwy. . . . . Bainbridge GA 39818 229-246-2266 246-0387 200
Web: www.elbertacrate.com
Elbit Systems of America
4700 Marine Creek Pkwy . . . . . Fort Worth TX 76179 817-234-6600 24
Web: www.elbitsystems-us.com
Elbow River Casino (ERC) 218 18th Ave SE . . . . . Calgary AB T2G1L1 403-289-8880 379
Web: elbowrivercasino.com
Elbow River Marketing Ltd
1500 335 Eighth Ave SW . . . . . Calgary AB T2P1C9 403-232-6868 536
Web: www.elbowriver.com
Elbow Road Farm Inc 1400 Elbow Rd . . . . . Chesapeake VA 23320 757-547-3900 547-7364 660
Web: elbowroadfarm.com
Elburn Animal Hospital P C
403 E North St . . . . . Elburn IL 60119 630-365-9599 794
Web: elburnanimalhospital.net
ELC (English Language Ctr)
10850 Wilshire Blvd Ste 210 . . . . . Los Angeles CA 90024 310-470-3019 470-6733 423
Web: www.elc.edu
ELC Industries LLC
1439 Dave Lyle Blvd Ste 16-C . . . . . Rock Hill SC 29730 803-980-7600 980-7676 745-5
Web: www.ricebraid.com
ELCA (Evangelical Lutheran Church in America)
8765 W Higgins Rd . . . . . Chicago IL 60631 773-380-2700 380-1465 48-20
Web: www.elca.org
ELCH (East Liverpool City Hospital)
425 W Fifth St. . . . . East Liverpool OH 43920 330-385-7200 374-3
Web: www.elch.org
Elco Chevrolet Cadillac
15110 Manchester Rd. . . . . Ballwin MO 63011 636-232-0007 57
TF: 800-792-1275 ■ *Web:* www.elcochevrolet.com
Elco Corp 1000 Belt Line St . . . . . Cleveland OH 44109 216-749-2605 749-7462 541
TF: 800-321-0467 ■ *Web:* lubeperformanceadditives.com
Elco Laboratories Inc
2450 Horner Ave. . . . . University Park IL 60484 708-534-3000 151
Web: elcolabs.com
Elco Mutual Life & Annuity
916 Sherwood Dr . . . . . Lake Bluff IL 60044 800-321-3526 391-2
TF: 888-872-7954 ■ *Web:* www.elcomutual.com
Elcom Systems Ltd 300 Granite St . . . . . Braintree MA 02184 203-920-8054 178-1
OTC: ELCO ■ *Web:* www.elcom.com
ELCON (Electricity Consumers Resource Council)
1101 K St NW Ste 700 . . . . . Washington DC 20005 202-682-1390 289-6370 48-12
Web: elcon.org
Elcon Associates Inc
12670 NW Barnes Rd . . . . . Portland OR 97229 503-644-2490 256
Web: www.elcon.com
ELCON Inc 600 Twin Rail Dr . . . . . Minooka IL 60447 815-467-9500 203
Web: www.elconinc.net
ElDeCo Inc 5751 Augusta Rd . . . . . Greenville SC 29605 864-277-9088 277-2811 189-4
Web: www.eldecoinc.com

Entry	City	State	ZIP	Phone	Fax	Class
Elder Research Inc 300 W Main Ste 301 *Web:* www.elderresearch.com	Charlottesville	VA	22903	434-973-7673		466
Elderberry Press Inc 1393 Old Homestead Dr *Web:* www.elderberrypress.com	Oakland	OR	97462	541-459-6043		637-2
Eldercare Locator 1730 Rhode Island Ave NW Ste 1200 **Fax Area Code:* 202 ■ *TF:* 800-677-1116 ■ *Web:* www.eldercare.acl.gov	Washington	DC	20036	800-677-1116	872-0057*	197
Eldercaring LLC 10542 Metropolitan Ave *Web:* seniorhomecaremd.com	Kensington	MD	20895	301-949-0060		363
Elderhostel Inc 11 Ave de Lafayette **Fax Area Code:* 877 ■ *TF:* 800-454-5768 ■ *Web:* www.roadscholar.org	Boston	MA	02111	800-454-5768	426-2166*	48-23
Elder-Jones 1120 E 80th St Ste 211 *Web:* www.elderjones.com	Minneapolis	MN	55420	952-345-6030	854-2703	186
Elderkin Law Firm 150 E Eighth St *Web:* www.elderkinlaw.com	Erie	PA	16501	814-456-4000		428
Elderlee Inc 729 Cross Rd *TF:* 800-344-5917 ■ *Web:* www.elderlee.com	Oaks Corners	NY	14518	315-789-6670	789-4262	183
Elderly Instruments 1100 N Washington Ave *TF:* 888-473-5810 ■ *Web:* www.elderly.com	Lansing	MI	48906	517-372-7890	372-5155	526
ElderWood Senior Care 5271 Main St *TF:* 888-826-9663 ■ *Web:* www.elderwood.com	Williamsville	NY	14221	716-565-9663		451
Eldon Hazlet State Recreation Area 20100 Hazlet Park Rd *Web:* www2.illinois.gov	Carlyle	IL	62231	618-594-3015		565
Eldon James Corp 10325 E 47th Ave *Web:* www.eldonjames.com	Denver	CO	80238	970-667-2728	667-3204	601
Eldor Contracting Corp 30 Corporate Dr *Web:* www.eldor.com	Holtsville	NY	11742	631-218-0010		186
Eldorado Canyon State Park 9 Kneale Rd PO Box B *Web:* cpw.state.co.us	Eldorado Springs	CO	80025	303-494-3943	499-2729	565
Eldorado Gold Corp 550 Burrard St *NYSE:* ELD ■ *TF:* 888-353-8166 ■ *Web:* eldoradogold.com	Vancouver	BC	V6C2B5	604-687-4018	687-4026	502
Eldorado Grill 744 Williamson St *Web:* eldoradogrillmadison.com	Madison	WI	53703	608-280-9378		671
Eldorado Hotel 309 W San Francisco St *TF:* 800-955-4455 ■ *Web:* www.eldoradohotel.com	Santa Fe	NM	87501	505-988-4455		379
Eldorado Hotel Casino 345 N Virginia St *TF:* 800-879-8879 ■ *Web:* www.eldoradoreno.com	Reno	NV	89501	775-786-5700		379
Eldorado National 1655 Wall St *Web:* www.revgroup.com	Salina	KS	67401	785-827-1033		59
Eldorado Resort Casino Shreveport 451 Clyde Fant Pkwy *TF:* 877-602-0711 ■ *Web:* www.eldoradoshreveport.com	Shreveport	LA	71101	318-220-0711		133
Eldredge & Lumpkin Insurance Agency Inc 697 Main St *Web:* elinsurance.com	Chatham	MA	02633	508-945-0393		390
Eldridge Hotel 701 Massachusetts St *TF:* 800-527-0909 ■ *Web:* eldridgehotel.com	Lawrence	KS	66044	785-749-5011	749-4512	379
Eldridge Products Inc 465 Reservation Rd *TF:* 800-321-3569 ■ *Web:* www.epiflow.com	Marina	CA	93933	831-648-7777	648-7780	201
Eleanor Slater Hospital 14 Harrington Rd *TF:* 800-438-8477 ■ *Web:* www.bhddh.ri.gov	Cranston	RI	02920	401-462-2339	462-3204	374-7
eLease 550 First Ave N **Fax Area Code:* 800 ■ *TF:* 800-499-2577 ■ *Web:* elease.com	Saint Petersburg	FL	33701	727-209-1200	233-8303*	23
Elec Tron Inc 2050 Northern *Web:* www.elec-troninc.com	Wichita	KS	67216	316-522-3401		729
Elecraft Inc PO Box 69 *Web:* www.elecraft.com	Aptos	CA	95001	831-763-4211	763-4218	246
Elecsys Intl 846 N Mart-Way Ct *NASDAQ:* ESYS ■ *Web:* www.lindsay.com	Olathe	KS	66061	913-647-0158		360-3
Elec-Tec Inc 15656 Us Hwy 84 *Web:* www.elec-tec.com	Quitman	GA	31643	229-263-5755	263-5754	253
Election Impact Group 18 31st St **Fax Area Code:* 228 ■ *Web:* www.electionimpactgroup.com	Gulfport	MS	39507	662-832-8882	731-3178*	194
Election Services Corp 70 Trade Zone Ct *Web:* electionservicesco.com	Ronkonkoma	NY	11779	516-248-4200	248-4770	801
Election Systems & Software Inc 11208 John Galt Blvd *TF:* 877-377-8683 ■ *Web:* essvote.com	Omaha	NE	68137	402-593-0101	593-8107	801
Elections USA Inc 1927 E Saw Mill Rd *Web:* electionsusainc.com	Quakertown	PA	18951	215-538-0779	538-3283	801
Electra Bicycle Company LLC 3270 Corporate View Ste A *Web:* electra.trekbikes.com	Vista	CA	92081	760-607-2453		711
Electra Information Systems Inc 381 Park Ave S Rm 1413 *Web:* electrainfo.com	New York	NY	10016	212-696-1595	696-1599	177
Electralloy Corp 175 Main St *TF:* 800-458-7273 ■ *Web:* www.electralloy.com	Oil City	PA	16301	814-678-4100		723
Electra-med Corp 5332 Hill 23 Dr *Web:* www.electramed.com	Flint	MI	48507	810-232-4856		475
Electrex Inc 6 N Walnut St *TF:* 800-319-3676 ■ *Web:* www.electrexinc.com	Hutchinson	KS	67501	800-319-3676		253
Electric AI 408 Broadway 5th Fl *Web:* www.electric.ai	New York	NY	10013	617-648-9100		253
Electric Apparatus Co 409 Roosevelt St *Web:* www.elecapp.net	Howell	MI	48843	517-546-0520	546-0547	518
Electric Cable Compounds Inc 108 Rado Dr *Web:* www.electriccablecompounds.com	Naugatuck	CT	06770	203-723-2590		116
Electric City Trolley Station & Museum 300 Cliff St *TF:* 800-732-0999 ■ *Web:* www.ectma.org	Scranton	PA	18503	570-963-6590	963-6447	520
Electric Coating Technologies (ECT) 4407 Railroad Ave *Web:* www.materialsciencescorp.com	East Chicago	IN	46312	219-378-1930	378-1933	481
Electric Cooperatives of South Carolina Inc, The 808 Knox Abbott Dr *Web:* www.ecsc.org	Cayce	SC	29033	803-796-6060		138
Electric Easel Inc 2600 Behan Rd Ste G *Web:* electriceasel.com	Crystal Lake	IL	60014	815-444-9700		225
Electric Eel Manufacturing Company Inc 501 W Leffel Ln *Web:* www.electriceel.com	Springfield	OH	45506	937-323-4644	323-3767	758
Electric Equipment & Engineering Co 40 W 49th Ave *Web:* eeeusa.com	Denver	CO	80216	303-296-1476	296-1478	729
Electric Golf Car Co 6150 Auburn Blvd *Web:* www.electricgolfcarcompany.com	Citrus Heights	CA	95621	916-721-0507	721-0508	516
Electric Heater Co 45 Seymour St *TF:* 800-647-3165 ■ *Web:* www.hubbellheaters.com	Stratford	CT	06615	203-378-2659	378-3593	36
Electric Heating Equipment Co 1240 Oronoque Rd	Milford	CT	06461	800-958-9998		318
Electric Machinery Company Inc 800 Central Ave NE *Web:* www.electricmachinery.com	Minneapolis	MN	55413	612-378-8000	378-8050	518
Electric Materials Co 50 S Washington St *TF:* 800-356-2211 ■ *Web:* www.elecmat.com	North East	PA	16428	814-725-9621	725-3620	308
Electric Motor & Contracting Company Inc 3703 Cook Blvd *TF:* 800-655-1195 ■ *Web:* www.emc-co.com	Chesapeake	VA	23323	757-487-2121	487-5983	518
Electric Motor Repair (EMR) 9100 Yellow Brick Rd Ste H *TF:* 888-894-4810 ■ *Web:* www.emrco.com	Baltimore	MD	21237	410-467-8080	467-2512	300
Electric Motors & Specialties Inc 701 W King St PO Box 180 *TF:* 800-474-0520 ■ *Web:* emsmotors.com	Garrett	IN	46738	260-357-4141	357-3888	518
Electric Power Door 522 W 27th St *TF:* 800-346-5760 ■ *Web:* www.electricpowerdoor.com	Hibbing	MN	55746	218-263-8366		234
Electric Power Supply Assn (EPSA) 1401 New York Ave NW Ste 950 *Web:* epsa.org	Washington	DC	20005	202-628-8200	628-8260	48-12
Electric Power Systems Inc 3305 Arctic Blvd Ste 201 *Web:* epsinc.com	Anchorage	AK	99503	907-522-1953		261
Electric Pulp Inc 350 S Main Ave Ste 404 *Web:* www.electricpulp.com	Sioux Falls	SD	57104	605-988-0177		225
Electric Regulator Corp 6189 El Camino Real *TF:* 800-458-6566 ■ *Web:* www.electricregulator.com	Carlsbad	CA	92009	760-438-7873	438-0437	203
Electric Research & Manufacturing Co-opeartive Inc PO Box 1228 *TF:* 800-238-5587 ■ *Web:* www.ermco-eci.com	Dyersburg	TN	38025	731-285-9121		767
Electric Supply & Equipment Co 1812 E Wendover Ave *TF:* 800-632-0268 ■ *Web:* www.ese-co.com	Greensboro	NC	27405	336-272-4123	274-4632	246
Electric Supply Inc 4407 N Manhattan Ave *TF:* 800-678-1894 ■ *Web:* www.electricsupplyinc.com	Tampa	FL	33614	813-872-1894	874-1680	246
Electric Switchboard Solutions LLC 270 Park Ave *Web:* www.electricswitchboard.net	New Hyde Park	NY	11040	516-812-6950	812-6951	729
Electrical & Electronics 3881 Danbury Rd *Web:* www.eecontrols.com	Brewster	NY	10509	845-278-5777		203
Electrical & Mechanical Resources Inc 4640 International Trade Ct *TF:* 800-216-1616 ■ *Web:* emrva.com	Richmond	VA	23231	804-226-1600	222-2144	518
Electrical Apparatus Service Assn (EASA) 1331 Baur Blvd *Web:* www.easa.com	Saint Louis	MO	63132	314-993-2220	993-1269	49-19
Electrical Consultants Inc 3521 Gabel Rd *Web:* www.electricalconsultantsinc.com	Billings	MT	59102	406-259-9933		256
Electrical Contractors Inc 3510 Main St *Web:* www.ecincorporated.com	Hartford	CT	06120	860-549-2822	549-7948	189-4
Electrical Corporation of America 7320 Arlington Ave *Web:* www.ecahq.com	Raytown	MO	64133	816-737-3206		189-4
Electrical Distributing Inc 4600 NW St Helens Rd *TF:* 800-877-4229 ■ *Web:* edinw.com	Portland	OR	97210	503-226-4044	226-4040	38
Electrical Materials Co (EMC) 1236 First Ave S *TF:* 800-697-3137 ■ *Web:* emcfd.com	Fort Dodge	IA	50501	800-697-3137		612
Electricity Consumers Resource Council (ELCON) 1101 K St NW Ste 700 *Web:* elcon.org	Washington	DC	20005	202-682-1390	289-6370	48-12
Electri-Cord Manufacturing Company Inc 312 E Main St *Web:* www.electri-cord.com	Westfield	PA	16950	814-367-2265	367-2314	815
Electrified Discounters Inc 110 Webb St *TF:* 800-678-8585 ■ *Web:* www.electrified.com	Hamden	CT	06517	203-787-4246	777-7853	119
Electri-Flex Co 222 Central Ave *TF:* 800-323-6174 ■ *Web:* www.electriflex.com	Roselle	IL	60172	630-529-2920	529-0482	816
Electrix Inc 45 Spring St *Web:* www.electrixillumination.com	New Haven	CT	06519	203-776-5577	624-7545	439
Electro Adapter Inc 20640 Nordhoff St *Web:* www.electro-adapter.com	Chatsworth	CA	91311	818-998-1198	701-1389	815
Electro Arc Manufacturing Co 161 Enterprise Dr *Web:* www.electroarc.com	Ann Arbor	MI	48103	734-761-5400	761-5426	455
Electro Brand Inc 1127 S Mannheim Rd Ste 305 *TF:* 800-982-3954 ■ *Web:* www.electrobrand-usa.com	Westchester	IL	60154	800-982-3954		246
Electro Dynamics Crystal Corp 9075 Cody St *TF:* 800-332-9825 ■ *Web:* www.inficonedc.com	Overland Park	KS	66214	913-888-1750	888-1260	246

Company	City	State	ZIP	Phone	Fax	Class
Electro Enterprises Inc 3601 N I-35 Service Rd *TF:* 800-324-6591 ■ *Web:* www.electroenterprises.com	Oklahoma City	OK	73111	405-427-6591	424-0056	253
Electro Equipment Inc 3110 W 84th St Ste 4 *Web:* www.electroequipment.com	Hialeah	FL	33018	305-512-5707	512-5708	523
Electro Impulse Laboratory Inc 1805 Rte 33 PO Box 278 *Web:* www.electroimpulse.com	Neptune City	NJ	07753	732-776-5800	776-6793	14
Electro Industries Inc 2150 W River St *Web:* www.electromn.com	Monticello	MN	55362	763-295-4138		37
Electro Miniatures Corp 68 W Commercial Ave *Web:* electro-miniatures.com	Moonachie	NJ	07074	201-460-0510		518
Electro Optical Industries Inc 320 Storke Rd Ste 100 *Web:* www.electro-optical.com	Goleta	CA	93117	805-964-6701	967-8590	201
Electro Prime Group LLC 4510 Lint Ave Ste B *Web:* www.electroprime.com	Toledo	OH	43612	419-476-0100		295
Electro Products Inc 1710 S Hwy 29 *Web:* www.electro.bizland.com	Cantonment	FL	32533	850-968-4984	968-9100	201
Electro Rent Corp 6060 Sepulveda Blvd *NASDAQ: ELRC* ■ *TF:* 800-688-1111 ■ *Web:* www.electrorent.com	Van Nuys	CA	91411	818-787-2100	786-4354	264-1
Electro Scientific Industries Inc 13900 NW Science Pk Dr *NASDAQ: ESIO* ■ *TF:* 800-331-4708 ■ *Web:* esi.com	Portland	OR	97229	503-641-4141		425
Electro Standards Laboratories Inc 36 Western Industrial Dr *TF:* 877-943-1164 ■ *Web:* www.electrostandards.com	Cranston	RI	02921	401-943-1164		735
Electro Static Technology 31 Winterbrook Rd *TF:* 866-738-1857 ■ *Web:* www.est-static.com	Mechanic Falls	ME	04256	207-998-5140		639
Electro Steam Generator Corp 50 Indel Ave PO Box 438 *TF:* 866-617-0764 ■ *Web:* www.electrosteam.com	Rancocas	NJ	08073	609-288-9071	288-9078	262
Electro Technology 9811 Owensmouth Ave Ste 5 *Web:* www.electro-technology.com	Chatsworth	CA	91311	818-709-4506	709-4507	52
ElectroChem Inc 400 W Cummings Pk *Web:* fuelcell.com	Woburn	MA	01801	781-938-5300		194
Electrochemical Society 65 S Main St Bldg D *Web:* www.electrochem.org	Pennington	NJ	08534	609-737-1902	737-2743	49-19
Electrocube Inc 3366 Pomona Blvd *TF:* 800-515-1112 ■ *Web:* www.electrocube.com	Pomona	CA	91768	909-595-4037		253
Electrocut-Pacific 993 E San Carlos Ave *Web:* electrocutpacific.com	San Carlos	CA	94070	650-591-8718		358
Electrodata Inc 23020 Miles Rd *TF:* 800-441-6336 ■ *Web:* www.electrodata.com	Bedford Heights	OH	44128	216-663-3333	663-0507	248
Electrodes Inc 252 Depot Rd *Web:* www.electrodesinc.com	Milford	CT	06460	203-878-7408	882-5981	385
Electro-General Plastics Corporation of Columbus 6200 Enterprise Pkwy *Web:* www.electro-generalplastics.com	Grove City	OH	43123	614-871-2915		596
Electro-Hydraulic Automation Inc 1620 Blairs Ferry Rd NE *Web:* www.ehausa.com	Cedar Rapids	IA	52402	319-395-0005	395-0200	386
Electroid Co 45 Fadem Rd *Web:* www.electroid.com	Springfield	NJ	07081	973-467-8100	467-2606	203
Electroimpact Inc 4413 Chennault Beach Rd *Web:* www.electroimpact.com	Mukilteo	WA	98275	425-348-8090		21
Electrol Specialties Co 441 Clark St *Web:* www.esc4cip.com	South Beloit	IL	61080	815-389-2291	389-2294	254
Electroline Data Communications Inc N779 Communication Dr *TF:* 800-332-3553 ■ *Web:* www.edci.com	Appleton	WI	54912	920-733-0303		196
Electrolux Appliances PO Box 212237 *TF:* 877-435-3287 ■ *Web:* www.electroluxappliances.com	Augusta	GA	30907	877-435-3287		36
Electrolysis Training Institute Atrium Medical Ctr 1910 Rt 70 Ste 10 *Web:* www.electrolysistraininginstitute.com	Cherry Hill	NJ	08003	856-424-7333	424-7151	167-3
Electro-Magnetic Products Inc 355 Crider Ave *Web:* www.empmags.com	Moorestown	NJ	08057	856-235-3011	722-0566	757
Electro-Matic Products Co 2235 N Knox Ave *Web:* www.em-chicago.com	Chicago	IL	60639	773-235-4010	235-7317	203
Electro-Matic Products Inc 23409 Industrial Pk Ct *TF:* 888-879-1088 ■ *Web:* www.electro-matic.com	Farmington Hills	MI	48335	248-478-1182	478-1472	246
Electromech Technologies Inc 2600 S Custer *Web:* www.electromech.com	Wichita	KS	67217	316-941-0400		22
Electro-Mechanical Corp 1 Goodson St *Web:* www.electro-mechanical.com	Bristol	VA	24201	276-669-4084	669-1869	253
Electromek Diagnostic Systems Inc 412 W US Hwy 40 *TF:* 800-466-6761 ■ *Web:* www.electromek.com	Troy	IL	62294	618-667-6761		475
Electromet Corp 879 Commonwealth Ave *Web:* electromet.com	Hagerstown	MD	21740	301-797-5900		697
Electro-Methods Inc 330 Governors Hwy *Web:* electro-methods.com	South Windsor	CT	06074	860-289-8661		21
Electro-Metrics Corp 231 Enterprise Rd *Web:* electro-metrics.com	Johnstown	NY	12095	518-762-2600	762-2812	248
Electron Beam Technologies Inc 1275 Harvard Dr *Web:* www.electronbeam.com	Kankakee	IL	60901	815-935-2211		811

Company	City	State	ZIP	Phone	Fax	Class
Electron Energy Corp 924 Links Ave *TF:* 800-824-2735 ■ *Web:* www.electronenergy.com	Landisville	PA	17538	717-898-2294	898-0660	458
Electrone Americas Limited Co (EAL) 129 NW 13th St Ste D-21 *Web:* www.electrone.com	Boca Raton	FL	33432	561-395-3398	395-1678	173-1
Electronic Arts Inc (EA) 209 Redwood Shores Pkwy *NASDAQ: EA* ■ *Web:* www.ea.com	Redwood City	CA	94065	650-628-1500		178-6
Electronic Cabling & Assembly Inc 702 Charlton Ave *Web:* www.eclinc.com	Charlottesville	VA	22903	434-293-2593	293-9745	73
Electronic Cash Systems Inc (ECS) 29883 Santa Margarita Pkwy *TF:* 888-327-2860 ■ *Web:* ecspayments.com	Rancho Santa Margarita	CA	92688	949-888-8580	888-8024	56
Electronic Concepts & Engineering Inc 1465 Timberwolf Dr *Web:* eceinc.com	Holland	OH	43528	419-861-9000		180
Electronic Contracting Co 6501 N 70th St *TF:* 800-366-5320 ■ *Web:* eccoinc.com	Lincoln	NE	68507	402-466-8274	466-0819	189-4
Electronic Data Magnetics Inc 210 Old Thomasville Rd *TF:* 800-336-8115 ■ *Web:* www.electronicdata.com	High Point	NC	27260	336-882-8115	882-9644	627
Electronic Entertainment Design & Research (EEDAR) 2075 Corte Del Nogal *Web:* www.eedar.com	Carlsbad	CA	92011	760-579-7120		387
Electronic Environments Corp 410 Forest St *TF:* 800-342-5332 ■ *Web:* www.eecnet.com	Marlborough	MA	01752	508-229-1400	303-0579	174
Electronic Evolution Technologies Inc 9455 Double R Blvd *Web:* www.eetechinc.com	Reno	NV	89521	775-355-9191	853-4844	625
Electronic Expeditors Inc N15 W 22180 Watertown Rd *TF:* 800-201-1933 ■ *Web:* www.ee-usa.com	Waukesha	WI	53186	262-574-4400	574-4414	246
Electronic Frontier Foundation Inc (EFF) 454 Shotwell St *Web:* www.eff.org	San Francisco	CA	94110	415-436-9333	436-9993	48-9
Electronic Hardware Ltd 13257 Saticoy St *Web:* www.electronichardware.com	North Hollywood	CA	91605	818-982-6100	764-1889	246
Electronic Instrumentation & Technology Inc (EIT) 108 Carpenter Dr *Web:* www.eit.com	Sterling	VA	20164	703-478-0700	478-0291	253
Electronic Integration Inc 875 Pennsylvania Blvd Ste 4 *Web:* www.electronicii.com	Feasterville	PA	19053	215-364-3390	364-3394	625
Electronic Manufacturing of Texas 16300 IH-35 *Web:* www.electronicmanufacturingoftexas.com	Buda	TX	78610	512-295-5117		625
Electronic Metrology Laboratory (EML) 318 Seaboard Ln Ste 106 *Web:* www.eml1.com	Franklin	TN	37067	270-874-2233		393
Electronic Privacy Information Ctr (EPIC) 1718 Connecticut Ave NW Ste 200 *Web:* epic.org	Washington	DC	20009	202-483-1140	483-1248	48-9
Electronic Security Association Inc (ESA) 6333 N State Hwy 161 Ste 350 *TF:* 888-447-1689 ■ *Web:* esaweb.org	Irving	TX	75038	972-807-6800	807-6883	49-3
Electronic Security Integration Inc (ESI) 68-46 Selfridge St *Web:* www.esi-systems.com	Forest Hills	NY	11375	718-575-9493	268-4030	692
Electronic Service & Design Corp 2118 Church Rd *Web:* www.esdpcb.com	Hummelstown	PA	17036	717-561-1995	561-1980	625
Electronic Source Co 16032 Arminta St *Web:* www.electronic-source.com	Van Nuys	CA	91406	818-988-7696	988-7841	625
Electronic Surface Mounted Industries Inc 6731 Cobra Way *Web:* www.esmiinc.com	San Diego	CA	92121	858-455-1710	455-6745	625
Electronic Systems Packaging LLC (ESP) 1175 W Victoria St *Web:* www.espbus.com	Rancho Dominguez	CA	90220	310-639-2535	632-6666	815
Electronic Systems Technology Inc 415 N Quay Bldg B-1 *OTC: ELST* ■ *Web:* www.esteem.com	Kennewick	WA	99336	509-735-9092	783-5475	173-3
Electronic Technologies International Inc 1100 N Main St *Web:* www.etimfg.com	Fort Atkinson	WI	53538	920-563-0840	563-0859	253
Electronic Tele-Communications Inc 1915 MacArthur Rd *OTC: ETCIA* ■ *TF:* 888-746-4382 ■ *Web:* www.etcia.com	Waukesha	WI	53188	262-542-5600	542-1524	735
Electronic Theatre Controls Inc 3031 Pleasantview Rd *TF:* 800-688-4116 ■ *Web:* www.etcconnect.com	Middleton	WI	53562	608-831-4116	836-1736	203
Electronic Transactions Assn, The 1101 16th St NW Ste 402 *TF:* 800-695-5509 ■ *Web:* www.electran.org	Washington	DC	20036	202-828-2635		138
Electronic Warfare Associates Inc (EWA) 13873 Park Center Rd *Web:* www.ewa.com	Herndon	VA	20171	703-904-5700	904-5779	180
Electronics Assemblers Inc 616 Industrial Ave Ste 301 *Web:* www.eaiquality.com	Hood River	OR	97031	541-386-3227		253
Electronics for Imaging Inc 6750 Dumbarton Cir *Web:* www.efi.com	Fremont	CA	94555	650-357-3500	357-3907	176
Electronics Integration Technology Inc 10 Industrial Way E *Web:* www.eit-inc.com	Eatontown	NJ	07724	732-542-2292	542-2294	425
Electronics Representatives Assn (ERA) 1325 S Arlington Heights Rd Ste 204 *Web:* www.era.org	Elk Grove Village	IL	60007	312-419-1432	419-1660	49-18
Electronics Research 7777 Gardner Rd *Web:* www.eriinc.com	Chandler	IN	47610	812-925-6000		647

	City	State	ZIP	Phone	Fax	Class
Electronics Technicians Association Intl (ETA) 5 Depot St *TF:* 800-288-3824 ■ *Web:* www.eta-i.org	Greencastle	IN	46135	765-653-8262	653-4287	49-19
Electronika Inc 2041 W 139th St *Web:* www.electronika-inc.com	Gardena	CA	90249	310-527-8100	527-8101	767
Electronique Mercier Ltee 162 Rue Fraser *Web:* www.emercier.com	Riviere-du-Loup	QC	G5R1C8	418-862-7269		736
Electro-Petroleum Inc 8 Wistar Rd *Web:* electropetroleum.com	Villanova	PA	19085	484-380-3456		538
Electrosem LLC 2600 S Hardy Dr **Fax Area Code:* 480 ■ *Web:* www.electrosem.com	Tempe	AZ	85282	602-955-6566	921-9614*	253
Electro-Sensors Inc 6111 Blue Circle Dr *NASDAQ: ELSE* ■ *TF:* 800-328-6170 ■ *Web:* www.electro-sensors.com	Minnetonka	MN	55343	952-930-0100	930-0130	495
Electrosonics Inc 17150 15 Mile Rd *TF:* 800-858-8448 ■ *Web:* www.electrosonics.net	Fraser	MI	48026	586-415-5555		175
Electro-Space Fabricators Inc 300 W High St *Web:* www.esfinc.com	Topton	PA	19562	610-682-7181		697
Electro-spec Inc 1800 Commerce Pkwy *Web:* www.electro-spec.com	Franklin	IN	46131	317-738-9199	738-9491	481
Electrosteel USA LLC 270 Doug Baker Blvd *Web:* electrosteelusa.com	Birmingham	AL	35242	205-516-8154		492
Electroswitch Corp 180 King Ave *TF:* 800-572-0479 ■ *Web:* www.electroswitch.com	Weymouth	MA	02188	781-335-5200	335-4253	729
Electroswitch Electronic Products 2010 Yonkers Rd *TF:* 888-768-2797 ■ *Web:* www.electro-nc.com	Raleigh	NC	27604	919-833-0707	833-8016	815
Electrosynthesis Company Inc 72 Ward Rd *Web:* www.electrosynthesis.com	Lancaster	NY	14086	716-684-0513	684-0511	202
ElectroTech Inc 7101 Madison Ave W *TF:* 800-544-4288 ■ *Web:* www.electrotech-inc.com	Minneapolis	MN	55427	800-544-4288		246
Electro-Tech Machining 2000 W Gaylord St *Web:* www.etmgraphito.com	Long Beach	CA	90813	562-436-9281		454
Electro-Tech Products Inc 2001 E Gladstone St Blg A *Web:* www.etp-inc.com	Glendora	CA	91740	909-592-1434		253
Electroworld Security Systems Inc 3084 Bedford Ave	Brooklyn	NY	11210	718-338-5831		693
ElectSolve Technology Solutions & Services Inc 4300 Youree Dr Bldg 1 *TF:* 877-221-2055 ■ *Web:* www.electsolve.com	Shreveport	LA	71105	318-861-7700		179
Elegance Distributors 106 S Main St *TF:* 800-487-6157 ■ *Web:* www.elegancedistributors.com	Eaton Rapids	MI	48827	517-663-8152	663-8153	297-2
Elegance International School of Professional Makeup 1622 N Highland Ave *Web:* www.ei.edu	Los Angeles	CA	90028	323-871-8318	871-8367	685
Elegant Audio Solutions 8706 Blazyk *Web:* elegantaudiosolutions.com	Austin	TX	78737	512-288-7786		261
Elegant Illusions Inc 542 Lighthouse Ave Ste 5 *Web:* www.elegant-illusions.com	Pacific Grove	CA	93950	831-649-1814	649-1001	410
Elegant Voyages 1802 Keesling Ct *TF:* 800-555-3534 ■ *Web:* www.elegantvoyages.com	San Jose	CA	95125	408-239-0300	239-0304	771
Elektrisola Inc 126 High St *Web:* www.elektrisola.com	Boscawen	NH	03303	603-796-2114	796-2119	813
Elektro Assemblies 5140 Moundview Dr **Fax Area Code:* 651 ■ *TF:* 800-533-1558 ■ *Web:* www.elektroassemblies.com	Red Wing	MN	55066	800-533-1558	385-2292*	743
Elemco Software Integration Group Ltd 245 Atlantic St *Web:* www.elemcosoftware.com	Central Islip	NY	11722	631-234-3099		180
Element Federal Credit Union 3418 Maccorkle Ave SE *TF:* 888-588-1334 ■ *Web:* elementfcu.org	Charleston	WV	25304	304-721-4145	342-3147	219
Element Materials Technology 5405 E Schaaf Rd *TF:* 888-786-7555 ■ *Web:* www.element.com	Cleveland	OH	44131	216-524-1450	524-1459	743
Element Productions Inc 316 Stuart St 4th Fl *Web:* element.cc	Boston	MA	02116	617-779-8808		514
Elementis Specialties Inc 469 Old Trenton Rd **Fax Area Code:* 609 ■ *TF:* 800-866-6800 ■ *Web:* www.elementis.com	East Windsor	NJ	08512	800-866-6800	443-2422*	143
Elementum Solutions 3219 US 422 *Web:* elementumsolutions.com	New Castle	PA	16101	724-656-8837		175
Elen Consulting Inc 9150 Chesapeake Dr Ste 220 *Web:* elenconsulting.com	San Diego	CA	92123	619-550-1085		261
Elenbaas Co 421 Birch Bay Lynden Rd *Web:* www.elenbaasco.com	Lynden	WA	98264	360-354-3577		447
Elenco Electronics Inc 150 Carpenter Ave *TF:* 800-533-2441 ■ *Web:* www.elenco.com	Wheeling	IL	60090	847-541-3800		242
Eleni's 205 E 42nd St **Fax Area Code:* 800 ■ *TF:* 888-435-3647 ■ *Web:* www.elenis.com	New York	NY	10017	888-435-3647	306-2101*	68
Elephant & Castle/Delta Winnipeg Hotel 350 St Mary Ave *Web:* www.elephantcastle.com	Winnipeg	MB	R3C3J2	204-942-5555		671
Elephant Productions Inc 3404 Guadalupe St *Web:* elephantproductions.com	Austin	TX	78705	512-302-3130		514
Elephant Ventures LLC 21 W 46th St 10 Fl Ste 1003 **Fax Area Code:* 917 ■ *Web:* www.elephantventures.com	New York	NY	10036	212-730-6710	591-2809*	396
Elerick & Elerick PA 265 N Wymore Rd *Web:* www.elerickandelerick.com	Winter Park	FL	32789	407-629-9995	629-7059	2
Elevate Care Riverwoods 3705 Deerfield Rd *Web:* elevatecare.com	Riverwoods	IL	60015	847-947-9000	947-9200	450
Elevate Salon Institute 141 E Chubbuck Rd *Web:* www.esichubbuck.com	Chubbuck	ID	83202	208-232-9170		167-3
Elevating Boats LLC 201 Dean Ct *TF:* 800-843-2895 ■ *Web:* www.ebi-inc.com	Houma	LA	70363	985-868-9655	868-9656	698
Elevation 905 Bernina Ave *Web:* thisiselevation.com	Atlanta	GA	30307	404-221-1705		512
Elevation B2B Marketing 1955 S Val Vista Dr Ste 101	Mesa	AZ	85204	480-775-8880		4
Elevation Ltd 1027 33rd St NW Ste 260 *Web:* www.elevation-us.com	Washington	DC	20007	202-380-3230		738
Elevation Resources LLC 200 N Loraine Ste 1010 *Web:* elevationres.com	Midland	TX	79701	432-686-7500		536
Elevation Solar 2425 S Stearman Dr Ste 220 *TF:* 866-634-5291 ■ *Web:* www.elevationsolar.com	Chandler	AZ	85286	866-634-5291		4
Elevator Doors Inc 15 Jane St *Web:* www.edi-eci.com	Paterson	NJ	07522	973-790-9100		234
Elevator Equipment Corp 4035 Goodwin Ave *TF:* 888-577-3326 ■ *Web:* www.elevatorequipment.com	Los Angeles	CA	90039	323-245-0147	245-9771	256
Elevator Research & Manufacturing Corp 1417 Elwood St *Web:* www.elevatorresearch.com	Los Angeles	CA	90021	213-746-1914	749-1355	256
Eleven 315 SW 11th Ave *TF:* 866-435-3836 ■ *Web:* www.elevensoftware.com	Portland	OR	97205	503-222-4321	296-5607	174
Eleven Engineering Inc 10150 - 100 St Ste 800 *Web:* elevenengineering.com	Edmonton	AB	T5J0P6	780-425-6511	425-7006	256
Eleven Inc 445 Bush St *Web:* www.eleveninc.com	San Francisco	CA	94108	415-707-1111		7
Eleven Mile State Park 4229 County Rd 92 *Web:* cpw.state.co.us	Lake George	CO	80827	719-748-3401	748-3863	565
Eleven South 216 11th Ave S *Web:* www.elevensouth.com	Jacksonville Beach	FL	32250	904-241-1112		671
Eleven Twenty Ltd 3700 Fairway Dr *Web:* eleventwenty.com	Woodbury	MN	55125	651-797-3070	714-0524	403
Eleven Western Builders Inc 2862 Executive Pl *Web:* www.ewbinc.com	Escondido	CA	92029	760-796-6346	796-6360	186
Elexco Land Service Inc 505 W Henley St *Web:* elexco.com	Olean	NY	14760	716-372-0788		538
ELFA (Equipment Leasing & Finance Assn) 1825 K St NW Ste 900 *Web:* www.elfaonline.org	Washington	DC	20006	202-238-3400	238-3401	49-18
Elfenworks Foundation PO Box 608 *Web:* elffound.org	San Mateo	CA	94401	650-347-9700	347-9702	305
Elfreth's Alley Museum 126 Elfreth's Alley *Web:* www.elfrethsalley.org	Philadelphia	PA	19106	215-574-0560		520
ELG Metals Inc 369 River Rd *Web:* www.elg.de	McKeesport	PA	15132	412-672-9200	672-0824	686
Elge Inc 1000 Cole Ave *Web:* www.elgeinc.com	Rosenberg	TX	77471	281-342-8228		479
ELGI Compressors USA Inc 3335 Pelton St *Web:* www.elgi.us	Charlotte	NC	28217	704-943-7966		172
Elgiloy Specialty Metals Ltd 1565 Fleetwood Dr *TF:* 888-843-2350 ■ *Web:* www.elgiloy.com	Elgin	IL	60123	847-695-1900	695-0169	350
Elgin Academy 350 Park St *Web:* www.elginacademy.org	Elgin	IL	60120	847-695-0300		148
Elgin Area Chamber of Commerce 31 S Grove Ave *Web:* elginchamber.com	Elgin	IL	60120	847-741-5660	741-5677	139
Elgin Area Convention & Visitors Bureau 60 S Grove Ave *TF:* 800-217-5362 ■ *Web:* exploreelginarea.com	Elgin	IL	60120	847-695-7540	695-7668	206
Elgin Community College 1700 Spartan Dr *TF:* 855-850-2525 ■ *Web:* elgin.edu	Elgin	IL	60123	847-697-1000	608-5458	162
Elgin Fastener Group LLC 10217 Brecksville Rd Ste 101 *Web:* www.elginfasteners.com	Brecksville	OH	44141	812-689-8990		278
Elgin Industries Inc 1100 Jansen Farm Dr *TF:* 800-323-6764 ■ *Web:* www.elginind.com	Elgin	IL	60123	847-742-1720	742-2225	247
Elgin Molded Plastics 909 Grace St **Fax Area Code:* 800 ■ *TF:* 800-548-5483 ■ *Web:* www.elginmolded.com	Elgin	IL	60120	847-931-2455	524-0087*	604
Elgin National Industries Inc 2001 Butterfield Rd *Web:* www.elginindustries.com	Downers Grove	IL	60515	630-434-7200	434-7272	190
Elgin Paper Co 1025 N McLean Blvd *Web:* www.elginpaper.com	Elgin	IL	60123	847-741-0137	741-0293	553
Elgin Sweeper Co 1300 W Bartlett Rd *Web:* www.elginsweeper.com	Elgin	IL	60120	847-741-5370	742-3035	516
Elgin-Butler Brick Co 2601 McHale Crt *Web:* elginbutler.com	Austin	TX	78758	512-453-7366		150
ELI (Environmental Law Institute) 2000 L St NW Ste 620 *TF:* 800-433-5120 ■ *Web:* www.eli.org	Washington	DC	20036	202-939-3800	939-3868	49-10
ELI Inc 2675 Paces Ferry Rd SE Ste 470 *TF:* 800-497-7654 ■ *Web:* www.eliinc.com	Atlanta	GA	30339	770-319-7999		196
Eli Lilly & Co Lilly Corporate Ctr *NYSE: LLY* ■ *TF:* 800-545-5979 ■ *Web:* www.lilly.com	Indianapolis	IN	46285	317-276-2000		582
Eli Lilly Canada Inc 3650 Danforth Ave *TF:* 888-545-5972 ■ *Web:* www.lilly.ca	Toronto	ON	M1N2E8	416-694-3221		582
Eli Whitney Museum 915 Whitney Ave *Web:* www.eliwhitney.org	Hamden	CT	06517	203-777-1833	777-1229	520
Eli's Cheesecake Co 6701 W Forest Preserve Dr *TF:* 800-999-8300 ■ *Web:* www.elicheesecake.com	Chicago	IL	60634	773-736-3417	205-3801	296-2
Eli's Western Wear Inc 907 NW Park St *TF:* 800-226-3570 ■ *Web:* eliswesternwear.com	Okeechobee	FL	34972	800-226-3570		157-5
Elia Restaurant 1647 63rd St *Web:* eliarestaurant.com	Brooklyn	NY	11209	718-748-9891		671

	Phone	Fax	Class
Elias Industries Inc 605 Epsilon Dr . . . Pittsburgh PA 15238 *Web:* tapcogenuinepartscenter.com	412-782-4300		609
Elias Sports Bureau Inc 500 Fifth Ave. . . . New York NY 10110 *Web:* www.esb.com	212-869-1530		530
Elias Wilf Corp 10234 S Dolfield Rd . . . Owings Mills MD 21117 *Web:* www.eliaswilf.com	410-363-2400		290
Eliason Corp 9229 Shaver Rd . . . Portage MI 49024 *TF:* 800-828-3655 ■ *Web:* www.eliasoncorp.com	269-327-7003	327-7006	664
Eliassen Group LLC 55 Walkers Brook Dr 6th Fl. . . . Reading MA 01867 **Fax Area Code:* 781 ■ *TF:* 800-354-2773 ■ *Web:* www.eliassen.com	800-354-2773	245-6537*	260
Elide Building Corp 505 White Plains Rd . . . Eastchester NY 10709 *Web:* elide.com	914-961-8875		261
Elijah Clark State Park 2959 McCormick Hwy . . . Lincolnton GA 30817 *Web:* gastateparks.org	706-359-3458		565
Elim Christian School 13020 S Central Ave. . . . Palos Heights IL 60463 *Web:* www.elimcs.org	708-389-0555		685
Elim Park Place 140 Cook Hill Rd . . . Cheshire CT 06410 *TF:* 800-994-1776 ■ *Web:* www.elimpark.org	203-272-3547		672
Elimetal Inc 1515 Blvd Pitfield . . . Saint-Laurent QC H4S1G3 *Web:* elimetal.com	514-956-7400	956-8110	697
eLine Technology 9500 W 49th Ave Ste D106. . . . Wheat Ridge CO 80033 **Fax Area Code:* 561 ■ *TF:* 800-683-6835 ■ *Web:* elinetechnology.com	800-683-6835	288-5257*	693
Elinor Bedell State Park c/o Gull Pt State Pk 1500 Harpen St. . . . Milford IA 51351 *Web:* www.iowabeautiful.com	712-330-5192		565
Elinvar Corp 1804 Hillsborough St . . . Raleigh NC 27605 *Web:* www.elinvar.com	919-622-5141		721
Eliot Hotel, The 370 Commonwealth Ave . . . Boston MA 02215 *TF:* 800-443-5468 ■ *Web:* www.eliothotel.com	617-267-1607	536-9114	379
Eliot Inc 505 410th St. . . . Joice IA 50446 *Web:* eliotinc.com	641-588-3546	588-3596	456
Eliot Reiner A Professional Law Corp 701 Howe Ave Ste A-2 . . . Sacramento CA 95825 *Web:* reiner-law.com	916-778-3228		41
Eliot Rose Asset Management LLC 1000 Chapel View Blvd Ste 240 . . . Cranston RI 02920 *TF:* 866-585-5100 ■ *Web:* www.eliotrose.com	401-588-5100		401
Eliot Veterinary Hospital 1034 Goodwin Rd. . . . Eliot ME 03903 *Web:* eliotveterinaryhospital.com	207-748-1000		794
Eliot Werner Publications Inc (EWP) PO Box 268 . . . Clinton Corners NY 12514 *Web:* www.eliotwerner.com	845-266-4241	266-3317	637-2
Elisa Act Biotechnologies 109 Carpenter Dr Ste 100. . . . Sterling VA 20164 *TF:* 800-553-5472 ■ *Web:* www.elisaact.com	703-796-0400		415
Elisabeth Morrow School, The 435 Lydecker St . . . Englewood NJ 07631 *Web:* www.elisabethmorrow.org	201-568-5566		685
Elitch Gardens 2000 Elitch Cir . . . Denver CO 80204 *Web:* www.elitchgardens.com	303-595-4386	629-0740	32
Elite PO Box 9630. . . . Rancho Santa Fe CA 92067 *TF:* 800-204-3548 ■ *Web:* www.eliteworldwide.com	800-204-3548		765
Elite Aluminum Corp 4650 Lyons Technology Pkwy. . . . Coconut Creek FL 33073 *TF:* 800-535-4837 ■ *Web:* elitealuminum.com	954-949-3200	949-3201	596
Elite Coach 1685 W Main St . . . Ephrata PA 17522 *TF:* 800-722-6206 ■ *Web:* www.elitecoach.com	717-733-7710		107
Elite Comfort Senior Care LLC 401 Mobil Ave Ste 4. . . . Camarillo CA 93010 *Web:* elitecomfortcare.com	805-824-5291		363
Elite Electronic Engineering Inc 1516 Centre Cir . . . Downers Grove IL 60515 *Web:* www.elitetest.com	630-495-9770		261
Elite Floor Coverings Inc 3902 Auburn Way N . . . Auburn WA 98002 *Web:* www.elitefloorcoverings.com	253-735-2232		290
Elite Flooring 3480 Green Pointe Pky . . . Norcross GA 30092 *Web:* www.elitefloor.com	770-409-8228		189-2
Elite Home Cleaners LLC 733 Lakeview Plz Blvd Ste A. . . . Worthington OH 43085 *Web:* elitehomecleaners.com	614-854-9100		104
Elite Investigations Ltd 538 W 29th St. . . . New York NY 10001 *Web:* www.eliteinvestigation.com	212-629-3131		693
Elite Island Resorts Inc 1065 SW 30th Ave . . . Deerfield Beach FL 33442 *TF:* 800-771-4711 ■ *Web:* www.eliteislandresorts.com	954-481-8787		707
Elite Lighting Company Inc 412 S Cypress St . . . Mullins SC 29574 *TF:* 800-343-0764 ■ *Web:* www.elitelighting.com	800-343-0764		362
Elite Limousine Service Inc 1059 12th Ave Ste E. . . . Honolulu HI 96816 *TF:* 800-776-2098 ■ *Web:* www.elitelimohawaii.com	808-735-2431	735-5159	441
Elite Marketing Group 800 Bering Dr Ste 105 . . . Houston TX 77057 *Web:* www.elitemktg.net	713-507-1000		391-2
Elite Mold & Engineering Inc 51548 Filomena Dr. . . . Shelby Township MI 48315 *Web:* www.teameliteonline.com	586-314-4000		757
Elite Pharmaceuticals Inc 165 Ludlow Ave . . . Northvale NJ 07647 *OTC: ELTP* ■ *Web:* www.elitepharma.com	201-750-2646	750-2755	85
Elite Restaurant 141 E Capitol St. . . . Jackson MS 39201	601-352-5606		671
Elite Retails Services Inc PO Box 618 . . . Lake Jackson TX 77566 *Web:* www.elite-construction.com	979-285-0712		186
Elite Security & Staffing 2878 Camino Del Rio S Ste 260. . . . San Diego CA 92108 *TF:* 855-809-2047 ■ *Web:* www.elitesecuritystaffing.com	619-574-1589	574-1588	271
Elite Spice Inc 7151 Montevideo Rd. . . . Jessup MD 20794 *Web:* www.elitespice.com	410-796-1900	379-6933	123
Elite Sportswear LP 2136 N 13th St. . . . Reading PA 19604 *TF:* 800-345-4087 ■ *Web:* www.gkelite.com	610-921-1469		155-1
Elite Supply Partners Inc 2101 W 2nd St . . . Odessa TX 79763 *TF:* 844-307-4044 ■ *Web:* elitesupplypartners.com	432-332-1541		492
Elite Welding Academy 9740 Near Dr. . . . Cincinnati OH 45246 *TF:* 888-272-3809 ■ *Web:* www.eliteweldingacademy.com	513-874-1410	874-7473	167-3
Elitexpo Cargo Systems 845 Commerce Dr . . . South Elgin IL 60177 *TF:* 800-543-5484 ■ *Web:* elitexpo.com	800-543-5484		463
Elixir Industries Inc 24800 Chrisanta Dr Ste 210. . . . Mission Viejo CA 92691 *TF:* 800-421-1942 ■ *Web:* www.elixirind.com	949-860-5000	860-5011	234
Eliza Bryant Village 7201 Wade Park Ave. . . . Cleveland OH 44103 *Web:* www.elizabryant.org	216-361-6141		371
Eliza Coffee Memorial Hospital (ECM) 205 Marengo St . . . Florence AL 35630 *Web:* www.chgroup.org	256-768-8323		374-3
Elizabeth Arden Inc 880 SW 145th Ave Ste 200. . . . Pembroke Pines FL 33027 *NASDAQ: RDEN* ■ *TF:* 800-326-7337 ■ *Web:* www.elizabetharden.com	954-364-6900	364-6910	574
Elizabeth City Area Chamber of Commerce 502 E Ehringhaus St. . . . Elizabeth City NC 27909 *Web:* www.elizabethcitychamber.org	252-335-4365	335-5732	139
Elizabeth City State University 1704 Weeksville Rd . . . Elizabeth City NC 27909 *TF:* 800-347-3278 ■ *Web:* www.ecsu.edu	252-335-3400	335-3537	166
Elizabeth Companies, The 601 Linden St. . . . McKeesport PA 15132 *Web:* www.eliz.com	412-751-3000		454
Elizabeth Gamble Garden 1431 Waverley St . . . Palo Alto CA 94301 *Web:* www.gamblegarden.org	650-329-1356		97
Elizabeth Glaser Pediatric AIDS Foundation 1140 Connecticut Ave NW Ste 200. . . . Washington DC 20036 *TF:* 888-499-4673 ■ *Web:* www.pedaids.org	202-296-9165	296-9185	48-17
Elizabeth Grady Face First Inc 222 Boston Ave. . . . Medford MA 02155 *Web:* elizabethgrady.edu	978-475-2292		77
Elizabeth Hospice 500 La Terraza Blvd Ste 130. . . . Escondido CA 92025 *TF:* 800-797-2050 ■ *Web:* elizabethhospice.org	760-737-2050		371
Elizabeth on 37th 105 E 37th St. . . . Savannah GA 31401 *Web:* www.elizabethon37th.net	912-236-5547		671
Elizabeth Park Conservancy 1561 Asylum Ave . . . West Hartford CT 06117 *Web:* www.elizabethparkct.org	860-231-9443		97
Elizabeth Public Library 11 S Broad St. . . . Elizabeth NJ 07202 *Web:* www.elizpl.org	908-354-6060	354-5845	434-3
Elizabeth's 601 Gallier St. . . . New Orleans LA 70117 *Web:* www.elizabethsrestaurantnola.com	504-944-9272		671
Elizabethan Gardens 1411 National Pk Dr. . . . Manteo NC 27954 *Web:* elizabethangardens.org	252-473-3234	473-3244	97
Elizabethton/Carter County Chamber of Commerce 500 Veterans Memorial Pkwy Hwy 19E PO Box 190 . . . Elizabethton TN 37644 *Web:* elizabethtonchamber.com	423-547-3850	547-3854	139
Elizabethtown College 1 Alpha Dr . . . Elizabethtown PA 17022 *Web:* www.etown.edu	717-361-1000	361-1365	166
Elizabethtown Community & Technical College 600 College St Rd. . . . Elizabethtown KY 42701 *TF:* 877-246-2322 ■ *Web:* elizabethtown.kctcs.edu	270-769-2371	769-0736	162
Elizabethtown Gas Co 1 Elizabethtown Plz 1085 Morris Ave . . . Union NJ 07083 *TF:* 800-242-5830 ■ *Web:* www.elizabethtowngas.com	908-662-8452	289-1370	787
Elizabethtown-Hardin County Chamber of Commerce (HCCC) 111 W Dixie Ave . . . Elizabethtown KY 42701 *Web:* hardinchamber.com	270-765-4334	737-0690	139
Eljer Inc 1 Centennial Ave. . . . Piscataway NJ 08855 *TF:* 800-442-1902 ■ *Web:* www.eljer.com	800-442-1902		611
ELK Brand Manufacturing Co 1601 County Hospital Rd PO Box 281287 . . . Nashville TN 37228 *Web:* www.elkbrand.com	615-254-4300		155-11
ELK City State Park 4825 Squaw Creek Rd . . . Independence KS 67301 *Web:* www.ksoutdoors.com	620-331-6295		565
ELK County PO Box 606. . . . Howard KS 67349 *TF:* 877-504-2490 ■ *Web:* elkcountyks.org	620-374-2490	374-2771	338
ELK County 250 Main St PO Box 305. . . . Ridgway PA 15853 *Web:* www.co.elk.pa.us	814-772-5155	772-4411	338
ELK Environmental Services 1420 Clarion St . . . Reading PA 19601 *TF:* 800-851-7156 ■ *Web:* www.elkenv.com	610-372-4760		196
ELK Group Intl 12 Willow Ln . . . Nesquehoning PA 18240 **Fax Area Code:* 866 ■ *TF:* 800-613-3261 ■ *Web:* www.elklighting.com	800-613-3261	613-3264*	439
ELK Grove Citizen 8970 Elk Grove Blvd. . . . Elk Grove CA 95624 *Web:* www.egcitizen.com	916-685-3945		532-4
ELK Grove Graphics Inc 1200 Chase Ave . . . Elk Grove Village IL 60007 *Web:* www.elkgrovegraphics.com	847-439-7834		627
ELK Grove Toyota 9640 W Stockton Blvd . . . Elk Grove CA 95757 *Web:* www.elkgrovetoyota.com	916-405-8000		57
ELK Grove Village Public Library 1001 Wellington Ave. . . . Elk Grove Village IL 60007 *Web:* www.egvpl.org	847-439-0447	439-0475	434-3
ELK Lake Tool Co 203 EC Loomis Dr . . . Elk Rapids MI 49629 *Web:* www.elklaketool.com	231-264-5616	264-5927	493
ELK Mountain Ranch PO Box 910. . . . Buena Vista CO 81211 *TF:* 800-432-8812 ■ *Web:* elkmtn.com	800-432-8812		239

Name / Address	City	State	Zip	Phone	Fax	Class
ELK Neck State Park 4395 Turkey Pt Rd *Web:* www.dnr.maryland.gov	North East	MD	21901	410-287-5333		565
ELK Products Inc 3266 US 70 W *TF:* 800-797-9355 ■ *Web:* www.elkproducts.com	Hildebran	NC	28637	828-397-4200		692
ELK Public House 1931 W Pacific Ave *Web:* wedonthaveone.com	Spokane	WA	99204	509-363-1973		671
ELK River Systems Inc 22 S Central Ave PO Box 6934 **Fax Area Code:* 406 ■ *TF:* 888-771-0809 ■ *Web:* www.elkriversystems.com	Harlowton	MT	59036	855-798-0799	632-4781*	174
ELK Rock State Park 811 146th Ave *Web:* www.iowadnr.gov	Knoxville	IA	50138	641-842-6008		565
ELK State Park c/o Bendigo State Pk 533 State Pk Rd *Web:* www.dcnr.pa.gov	Johnsonburg	PA	15845	814-965-2646		565
ELK Valley Rancheria 2332 Howland Hill Rd *TF:* 866-464-4680 ■ *Web:* www.elk-valley.com	Crescent City	CA	95531	707-464-4680		708
Elkay Manufacturing Co 2222 Camden Ct *TF:* 800-476-4106 ■ *Web:* www.elkay.com	Oak Brook	IL	60523	630-574-8484	574-5012	609
Elkay Plastics Inc 6000 Sheila St *TF:* 800-631-6131 ■ *Web:* www.elkayplastics.com	Commerce	CA	90040	323-722-7073	869-3911	603
Elkco Corp 50 Dangelo Dr *Web:* www.elkco.com	Marlborough	MA	01752	508-842-2111	842-2222	177
Elkhart County 117 N 2nd St *Web:* www.elkhartcountyindiana.com	Goshen	IN	46526	574-534-3541		338
Elkhart County Convention & Visitors Bureau 3421 Cassopolis St *TF:* 800-262-8161 ■ *Web:* www.visitelkhartcounty.com	Elkhart	IN	46514	574-262-8161	262-3925	206
Elkhart Products Corp 1255 Oak St *Web:* www.elkhartproducts.com	Elkhart	IN	46514	574-264-3181	264-0103	595
Elkhartnet 401 E Colfax Ave Ste 303 *Web:* elkhart.net	South Bend	IN	46617	574-524-1000		225
Elkhorn Golf Club 1050 Elkhorn Dr *Web:* www.elkhorngc.com	Stockton	CA	95209	209-474-3900		669
Elkhorn Ranch Montana 33133 Gallatin Rd *Web:* www.elkhornranchmontana.com	Gallatin Gateway	MT	59730	406-995-4291		239
Elkhorn Rural Public Power District 206 N Fourth St *TF:* 800-675-2185 ■ *Web:* erppd.com	Battle Creek	NE	68715	402-675-2185	675-6275	245
Elkhorn State Park 1420 E 6thAve c/o Helena Area Resource Ofc PO Box 200701 *Web:* stateparks.mt.gov	Helena	MT	59620	406-495-3270		565
Elkins Retail Advertising Inc 6040 Hellyer Ave Ste 100 *Web:* elkinsadvertising.com	San Jose	CA	95138	408-249-1411		7
Elkins-Randolph County Chamber of Commerce 10 Eleventh St *Web:* www.ercc.com	Elkins	WV	26241	304-636-2717	637-4902	139
Elko Area Chamber of Commerce 1405 Idaho St *Web:* www.elkonevada.com	Elko	NV	89801	775-738-7135	738-7136	139
Elko Broadcasting Co 1800 Idaho St *Web:* www.elkoradio.com	Elko	NV	89801	775-738-1240	753-5556	647
Elko Convention & Visitors Authority 700 Moren Way *TF:* 800-248-3556 ■ *Web:* www.elkocva.com	Elko	NV	89801	775-738-4091	738-2420	205
Elko County 569 Ct St *Web:* www.elkocountynv.net	Elko	NV	89801	775-738-5398	753-8535	338
Elko County Fairgrounds PO Box 2067 *Web:* elkocountyfair.com	Elko	NV	89803	775-738-3616	778-3468	642
Elko Speedway 26350 France Ave *Web:* www.elkospeedway.com	Elko	MN	55020	952-461-7223		515
Elkon Gallery Inc 18 E 81st St Ste 2-A *Web:* www.elkongallery.com	New York	NY	10028	212-535-3940		42
Elkton Supply Company Inc 202 W Main St *Web:* www.elktonsupply.com	Elkton	MD	21921	410-398-1900		290
Ella Health 1 Lemoyne Sq Plz Ste 102 (On Camp Hill Bypass Rd) *Web:* ellahealthcom.wordpress.com	Lemoyne	PA	17043	717-695-9464		415
Elle K. Associates Inc 11900 Castlegate Ct *Web:* www.ellekassociates.com	Rockville	MD	20852	301-984-4494		226
Ellen Rose CPA MST CFP 15 S Main St *Web:* financialfocus.com	Ipswich	MA	01938	978-356-1008		2
Ellen Trout Zoo 402 Zoo Cir *Web:* www.cityoflufkin.com	Lufkin	TX	75904	936-633-0399	633-0311	823
Eller, Tonnsen, Bach 1306 S Church St *Web:* etblawfirm.com	Greenville	SC	29605	864-236-5013		41
Eller-ITO Stevedoring Company LLC 1007 N America Way *Web:* www.ellerito.com	Miami	FL	33132	305-379-3700	371-9969	465
Ellevest 48 W 25th St 6th Fl *TF:* 844-355-7100 ■ *Web:* www.ellevest.com	New York	NY	10010	844-355-7100		49-2
Ellicom Inc 905 Rue De Nemours *Web:* ellicom.com	Quebec City	QC	G1H6Z5	418-623-8804		261
Ellie Mae Inc 4155 Hopyard Rd Ste 200 *TF:* 800-848-4904 ■ *Web:* www.elliemae.com	Pleasanton	CA	94588	925-227-7000		177
Ellington Elementary School 1416 Maine St *Web:* www.qps.org	Quincy	IL	62301	217-222-5697	228-7149	685
Ellinwood Machado LLC 800 Lambert Dr NE Ste H *Web:* emstructural.com	Atlanta	GA	30324	404-262-0800		261
Elliot Companies, The 673 Blue Sky Pkwy *TF:* 888-768-2530 ■ *Web:* dhec.com	Lexington	KY	40509	859-263-5148	263-5486	189-4
Elliot Equipment Corp 1131 Country Club Rd *TF:* 800-823-7527 ■ *Web:* www.elliotequipment.com	Indianapolis	IN	46234	317-271-3065	271-3378	111

Name / Address	City	State	Zip	Phone	Fax	Class
Elliot Hospital 1 Elliot Way Ste 100 *TF:* 800-922-4999 ■ *Web:* www.elliothospital.org	Manchester	NH	03103	603-627-1669	624-2297	374-3
Elliot L. Bien 829 Las Pavadas Ave *Web:* biencounsel.com	San Rafael	CA	94903	415-472-1500		41
Elliot Tool Inc 4400 Gustine Ave *Web:* elliottoolinc.com	Saint Louis	MO	63116	314-652-6939	652-8511	454
Elliot Whittier Insurance Services LLC 75 Sylvan St Ste B202 *Web:* elliotwhittier.com	Danvers	MA	01923	978-977-4884		390
Elliott & Bradley Plumbing Inc 10030 Windisch Rd *Web:* elliottandbradley.com	West Chester	OH	45069	513-772-0050		189-10
Elliott & Frantz Inc 450 E Church Rd *TF:* 800-220-3025 ■ *Web:* elliottfrantz.com	King of Prussia	PA	19406	610-279-5200		358
Elliott & Stanek PC 943 Queen St PO Box 578 *Web:* southingtonchamber.com	Southington	CT	06489	860-628-5545		41
Elliott Aviation Inc 6601 74th Ave PO Box 100 *TF:* 800-447-6711 ■ *Web:* www.elliottaviation.com	Milan	IL	61264	309-799-3183	799-2014	24
Elliott Bay Book Co 1521 Tenth Ave *TF:* 800-962-5311 ■ *Web:* www.elliottbaybook.com	Seattle	WA	98122	206-624-6600	903-1601	95
Elliott Bay Design Group LLC 5305 Shilshole Ave NW Ste 100 *Web:* www.ebdg.com	Seattle	WA	98107	206-782-3082		698
Elliott Community, The 170 Metcalfe St *Web:* www.elliottcommunity.org	Guelph	ON	N1E4Y3	519-822-0491		371
Elliott Company of Indianapolis Inc 9200 Zionsville Rd *TF:* 800-545-1213 ■ *Web:* www.elliottfoam.com	Indianapolis	IN	46268	317-291-1213		601
Elliott County PO Box 710 *Web:* www.elliottcounty.ky.gov	Sandy Hook	KY	41171	606-738-5826	738-4509	338
Elliott Cove Capital Management 1000 Second Ave Ste 1440 *Web:* www.elliottcove.com	Seattle	WA	98104	206-267-2683		401
Elliott Davis LLC 629 Market St Ste 100 *Web:* www.elliottdavis.com	Chattanooga	TN	37402	423-756-7100		2
Elliott Electric Supply Co 2526 N Stallings Dr PO Box 630610 *TF:* 877-777-0242 ■ *Web:* www.elliottelectric.com	Nacogdoches	TX	75963	936-569-1184	569-1836	246
Elliott Group 901 N Fourth St *TF:* 888-352-7278 ■ *Web:* www.elliott-turbo.com	Jeannette	PA	15644	724-527-2811	600-8442	172
Elliott Homes 340 Palladio Pkwy Ste 521 *Web:* www.elliotthomes.com	Folsom	CA	95630	916-984-1300		653
Elliott Industries Inc 1509 Hamilton Rd *Web:* www.elliottindustries.com	Bossier City	LA	71111	318-746-3296	741-1127	729
Elliott Lawson & Minor PC 110 Piedmont Ave Ste 300 *TF:* 800-814-1892 ■ *Web:* elliottlawson.com	Bristol	VA	24201	276-466-8400	466-8161	41
Elliott Machine Works Inc 1351 Freese Works Pl *TF:* 800-299-0412 ■ *Web:* www.elliottmachine.com	Galion	OH	44833	419-468-4709		516
Elliott Manufacturing Company Inc 2664 Cherry Ave PO Box 11277 *Web:* www.elliottmfg.com	Fresno	CA	93772	559-233-6235	233-9833	547
Elliott Precision Products Inc 16309 E Latimer Pl *Web:* www.elliottprecision.com	Tulsa	OK	74116	918-234-4001	234-4012	454
Elliott Tape Inc 1882 Pond Run *Web:* www.egitape.com	Auburn Hills	MI	48326	248-475-2000	475-5893	386
Elliott Transport Inc 1612 Candler Rd *Web:* elliotttrans.com	Gainesville	GA	30507	770-530-0120		311
Elliott Wave Intl (EWI) PO Box 1618 *TF:* 800-336-1618 ■ *Web:* elliottwave.com	Gainesville	GA	30503	770-536-0309	536-2514	637-9
Elliott's Oyster House 1201 Alaskan Way Pier 56 *Web:* www.elliottsoysterhouse.com	Seattle	WA	98101	206-623-4340		671
Elliott, Ostrander & Preston PC Union Bank Tower 707 SW Washington St Ste 1500 *TF:* 866-716-3410 ■ *Web:* eoplaw.com	Portland	OR	97205	503-224-7112		428
Elliott-Lewis Corp 2900 Black Lake Pl *Web:* www.elliottlewis.com	Philadelphia	PA	19154	215-698-4400	698-4436	14
Ellipse Arts Ctr 3700 S Four Mile Run *Web:* arts.arlingtonva.us	Arlington	VA	22206	703-228-1850	228-0805	50-2
ElliptiGO Inc 722 Genevieve St Ste O *TF:* 888-796-8227 ■ *Web:* www.elliptigo.com	Solana Beach	CA	92075	858-876-8677		517
Elliquence 2455 Grand Ave *Web:* www.elliquence.com	Baldwin	NY	11510	516-277-9000		475
Ellis 1333 Corporate Dr Ste 266 **Fax Area Code:* 888 ■ *TF:* 888-988-3767 ■ *Web:* www.epmsonline.com	Irving	TX	75038	972-256-3767	988-9585*	196
Ellis & Associates CPAS PA 8336 Belair Rd *Web:* cpaellis.com	Baltimore	MD	21236	410-256-9298		2
Ellis & Associates Inc 5979 Vineland Rd Ste 105 *TF:* 800-742-8720 ■ *Web:* www.jellis.com	Orlando	FL	32819	407-401-7136		45
Ellis & Watts Inc 4400 Glen Willow Lake Ln *Web:* www.elliswatts.com	Batavia	OH	45103	513-752-9000	752-4983	14
Ellis Coffee Co 2835 Bridge St *TF:* 800-822-3984 ■ *Web:* www.elliscoffee.com	Philadelphia	PA	19137	800-822-3984		297-11
Ellis Corp 1400 W Bryn Mawr Ave *TF:* 800-611-6806 ■ *Web:* www.elliscorp.com	Itasca	IL	60143	630-250-9222	250-9241	427
Ellis County 101 W Main St *Web:* www.co.ellis.tx.us	Waxahachie	TX	75165	972-825-5000	825-5033	338
Ellis Hospital 1101 Nott St *Web:* www.ellismedicine.org	Schenectady	NY	12308	518-243-4000		374-3
Ellis Park Race Course LLC 3300 US 41 *Web:* ellisparkracing.com	Henderson	KY	42420	812-425-1456		642

Name / Address	City	State	ZIP	Phone	Fax	Class
Ellis Press PO Box 6	Granite Falls	MN	56241	612-564-2424	537-6815*	637-2
*Fax Area Code: 507 ■ Web: www.ellispress.com						
Ellis Stone Construction						
3201 Stanley St	Stevens Point	WI	54481	715-345-5000		186
Web: www.elliswi.com						
Ellis, Li & McKinstry PLLC						
Market Pl Tower 2025 First Ave Ph A	Seattle	WA	98121	206-682-0565		428
Web: www.elmlaw.com						
EllisDon Corp 2045 Oxford St	London	ON	N5V2Z7	519-455-6770		186
Web: www.ellisdon.com						
Ellis-harper Advertising Inc						
710 Stage Rd	Auburn	AL	36831	334-887-6536		463
Web: ellisharper.com						
Ellison Bakery 4108 W Ferguson Rd	Fort Wayne	IN	46809	800-711-8091		296-9
TF: 800-711-8091 ■ *Web:* www.ebakery.com						
Ellison Educational Equipment Inc						
25862 Commercentre Dr	Lake Forest	CA	92630	949-598-8822		358
TF: 800-253-2240 ■ *Web:* www.ellison.com						
Ellison Media Co						
16100 N Greenway Hayden Loop Ste 950	Scottsdale	AZ	85260	602-404-4000	404-1700	7
Web: www.ellisonmedia.com						
Ellison Medical Foundation						
104 E Ridgeville Blvd	Mount Airy	MD	21771	301-829-6410	657-1828	305
Web: www.ellisonfoundation.org						
Ellison Technologies						
9912 S Pioneer Blvd	Santa Fe Springs	CA	90670	562-949-8311	949-9091	385
Web: www.ellisontechnologies.com						
Ellison, Schneider, Harris & Donlan LLP						
2600 Capitol Ave Ste 400	Sacramento	CA	95816	916-447-2166	447-3512	428
Web: eslawfirm.com						
Ellkay 200 Riverfront Blvd	Elmwood Park	NJ	07407	201-791-0606	791-0605	177
Web: www.ellkay.com						
Ellsworth Adhesives						
W129 N10825 Washington Dr	Germantown	WI	53022	262-253-8600		146
TF: 877-454-9224 ■ *Web:* www.ellsworth.com						
Ellsworth Air Force Base						
1958 Scott Dr Ste 4	Ellsworth AFB	SD	57706	605-385-5056		497-1
Web: www.ellsworth.af.mil						
Ellsworth American Inc 30 Water St	Ellsworth	ME	04605	207-667-2576		532-3
Web: ellsworthamerican.com						
Ellsworth Area Chamber of Commerce						
163 High St	Ellsworth	ME	04605	207-667-5584	667-2617	139
Web: www.ellsworthchamber.org						
Ellsworth Builders Supply Inc						
261 State St	Ellsworth	ME	04605	207-667-7134		364
TF: 800-244-7134 ■ *Web:* www.ebsbuild.com						
Ellsworth Community College						
1100 College Ave	Iowa Falls	IA	50126	641-648-4611	648-3128	162
TF: 800-322-9235 ■ *Web:* ecc.iavalley.edu						
Ellsworth Cooperative Creamery						
232 N Wallace St PO Box 610	Ellsworth	WI	54011	715-273-4311	273-5318	296-5
Web: www.ellsworthcheese.com						
Ellsworth County 210 N Kansas St	Ellsworth	KS	67439	785-472-4161	472-3818	338
Web: www.ellsworthcounty.org						
Ellsworth Public Library (EPL)						
20 State St	Ellsworth	ME	04605	207-667-6363		434-3
Web: www.ellsworth.lib.me.us						
Ellumen Inc						
1401 Wilson Blvd Ste 1200	Arlington	VA	22209	703-253-5555	253-5554	196
Web: www.ellumen.com						
Ellwood City Forge						
800 Commercial Ave	Ellwood City	PA	16117	724-752-0055	752-3449	483
TF: 800-843-0166 ■ *Web:* www.ellwoodcityforge.com						
Ellwood Engineered Castings Co						
7158 Hubbard Masury Rd	Hubbard	OH	44425	330-534-8668		723
Web: ellwoodengineeredcastings.com						
ELLWOOD National Forge 441 E Main St	Corry	PA	16407	814-664-9664	664-9452	483
Web: www.ellwoodgroup.com						
Ellwood Thompson 4 N Thompson Ave	Richmond	VA	23221	804-359-7525		297-8
Web: ellwoodthompsons.com						
ELM Chevrolet Company Inc						
301 E Church St	Elmira	NY	14901	607-215-4556		57
Web: www.elmchevrolet.com						
ELM Consulting						
26741 Portola Pkwy Ste 1E 494	Foothill Ranch	CA	92610	678-200-5220		196
Web: www.elmgroup.com						
ELM Industries Inc						
380 Union St	West Springfield	MA	01089	413-734-7762	731-7709	604
Web: www.elmindustries-usa.com						
ELM Press 16 Tremco Dr	Terryville	CT	06786	860-583-3600	585-8518	627
Web: www.elmpress.com						
ELM Resources						
12950 Race Track Rd Ste 201	Tampa	FL	33626	866-524-8198		387
TF: 866-524-8198 ■ *Web:* www.elmresources.com						
ELM Street Oyster House 11 W Elm St	Greenwich	CT	06830	203-629-5795		671
Web: www.elmstreetoysterhouse.com						
ELM Street Technology PO Box 10768	Greensboro	NC	27404	888-378-3868		4
TF: 888-378-3868 ■ *Web:* elmstreettechnology.zendesk.com						
ELM Terrace Gardens 660 N Broad St	Lansdale	PA	19446	215-361-5600		672
Web: www.elmterracegardens.org						
Elma Electronic Inc						
44350 Grimmer Blvd	Fremont	CA	94538	510-656-3400	656-3783	253
Web: www.elma.com						
Elmar Worldwide Inc						
200 Gould Ave PO Box 245	Depew	NY	14043	716-681-5650		547
TF: 800-433-3562 ■ *Web:* www.elmarworldwide.com						
Elmbrook Home 1811 9th Ave	Ardmore	OK	73401	580-223-3303		610
Web: elmbrookhome.com						
Elmco Engineering Inc						
6107 Churchman Rd Bypass	Indianapolis	IN	46203	317-788-4114	788-0220	454
Web: www.elmco-press.com						
Elmech Inc 195 San Pedro Ave	Morgan Hill	CA	95037	408-782-2990		253
Web: www.elmechinc.com						
Elmer Candy Corp 401 N Fifth St	Ponchatoula	LA	70454	985-386-6166		296-8
TF: 800-843-9537 ■ *Web:* elmerchocolate.com						
Elmet Technologies Inc						
1560 Lisbon St	Lewiston	ME	04240	207-333-6100		485
TF: 800-343-8008 ■ *Web:* www.elmettechnologies.com						
Elmhirst Industries Inc						
7630 19 Mile Rd	Sterling Heights	MI	48314	586-731-8663		493
Web: www.elmhirst.net						
Elmhurst Art Museum						
150 S Cottage Hill Ave	Elmhurst	IL	60126	630-834-0202		522
Web: www.elmhurstartmuseum.org						
Elmhurst Chamber of Commerce & Industry						
300 A W Lake St Ste 201	Elmhurst	IL	60126	630-834-6060	834-6002	139
Web: www.elmhurstchamber.org						
Elmhurst College 190 Prospect Ave	Elmhurst	IL	60126	630-617-3400		166
TF: 800-697-1871 ■ *Web:* www.elmhurst.edu						
Elmhurst Group, The						
1 Bigelow Sq Ste 630	Pittsburgh	PA	15219	412-281-8731		528
Web: www.elmhurstgroup.com						
Elmhurst History Museum						
120 E Park Ave	Elmhurst	IL	60126	630-833-1457		637-2
Web: www.elmhursthistory.org						
Elmhurst Inn, The 40 Holland Ave	Bar Harbor	ME	04609	207-288-3044	288-2719	379
Web: www.theelmhurstinn.com						
Elmhurst Mutual Power & Light Co						
120 132nd St S	Tacoma	WA	98444	253-531-4646		245
TF: 855-841-2178 ■ *Web:* www.elmhurstmutual.org						
Elmhurst Public Library						
125 S Prospect Ave	Elmhurst	IL	60126	630-279-8696	279-0636	434-3
Web: elmhurstpubliclibrary.org						
Elmira Business Institute-elmira Campus						
303 N Main St	Elmira	NY	14901	607-733-7177		166
Web: ebi.edu						
Elmira College 1 Park Pl	Elmira	NY	14901	607-735-1724	735-1718	166
TF: 800-935-6472 ■ *Web:* elmira.edu						
Elmira Correctional Facility						
1879 Davis St	Elmira	NY	14901	607-734-3901		213
Web: www.doccs.ny.gov						
Elmira Psychiatric Ctr						
100 Washington St	Elmira	NY	14901	607-737-4711	737-9080	374-5
Web: omh.ny.gov						
Elmira Savings Bank 333 E Water St	Elmira	NY	14901	607-734-3374		70
NASDAQ: ESBK ■ *TF:* 888-372-9299 ■ *Web:* www.elmirasavingsbank.com						
Elmira Stamping & Manufacturing Corp						
1704 Cedar St	Elmira	NY	14904	607-734-2058	732-0573	488
Web: www.elmirastamping.com						
Elmont Union Free School District						
135 Elmont Rd	Elmont	NY	11003	516-326-5500	326-5574	685
Web: www.elmontschools.org						
Elmore County						
150 S Fourth E St Ste 5	Mountain Home	ID	83647	208-587-2129	587-2134	338
Web: www.elmorecounty.org						
Elmore County 100 E Commerce St	Wetumpka	AL	36092	334-567-1156		338
Web: www.elmoreco.org						
Elmore County Public School System						
100 H H Robison Dr	Wetumpka	AL	36092	334-567-1200	567-1405	685
Web: www.elmoreco.com						
Elmore State Park 856 VT Rt 12	Lake Elmore	VT	05657	802-888-2982		565
Web: www.vtstateparks.com						
ELMS College 291 Springfield St	Chicopee	MA	01013	413-592-3189		166
TF: 800-255-3567 ■ *Web:* www.elms.edu						
Elms Mansion & Gardens						
3029 St Charles Ave	New Orleans	LA	70115	504-895-9200		50-3
Web: www.elmsmansion.com						
Elmsford Sheet Metal Work Inc						
23 Arlo Ln	Cortlandt Manor	NY	10567	914-739-6300		189-12
Web: www.engiemep.com						
Elmwood Healthcare Center & Specialty Hospital (SFHCC)						
401 N Broadway	Green Springs	OH	44836	419-639-2626		374-7
Web: www.elmwoodcommunities.com						
Elmwood Inn, The 1256 Mt Hope Ave	Rochester	NY	14620	585-271-5195		671
Web: www.elmwoodinn.net						
Elmwood Park Zoo 1661 Harding Blvd	Norristown	PA	19401	610-277-3825	292-0332	823
TF: 800-652-4143 ■ *Web:* www.elmwoodparkzoo.org						
ELO Engineering Inc 7770 Ranchers Rd	Fridley	MN	55432	763-571-2820	571-0727	697
Web: www.elo1.com						
ELO TouchSystems Inc						
301 Constitution Dr	Menlo Park	CA	94025	650-361-4700	361-4747	173-1
TF: 800-557-1458 ■ *Web:* www.elotouch.com						
eLocal Listing LLC						
25240 Hancock Ave Ste 410	Murrieta	CA	92563	800-285-0484		5
TF: 800-285-0484 ■ *Web:* mylocally.com						
Elof Hansson Pulp Inc 565 Taxter Rd	Elmsford	NY	10523	914-345-8380		553
Web: www.elofhansson.com						
Elon University 100 Campus Dr	Elon	NC	27244	336-278-2000	278-7699	166
TF: 800-334-8448 ■ *Web:* www.elon.edu						
Elona Bio Technologies Inc						
1040 Sierra Dr Ste 1000	Greenwood	IN	46143	317-865-4770		582
Web: elonabiotech.wordpress.com						
Elos Medtech AB 1800 N Shelby Oaks Dr	Memphis	TN	38134	800-238-6981		475
TF: 800-238-6981 ■ *Web:* elosmedtech.com						
eLottery Inc						
46 Southfield Ave						
3 Stamford Landing Ste 310	Stamford	CT	06902	203-388-1808	388-1809	322
Web: www.elottery.com						
ElPaso Proud 801 N Oregon St	El Paso	TX	79902	915-532-5421	496-4590	741-43
Web: www.ktsm.com						
Elrod Pope Law Firm 212 E Black St	Rock Hill	SC	29731	803-599-3080		41
Web: elrodpope.com						
Elrod's Cost Plus- (2788)						
2025 Ft Worth Ave	Dallas	TX	75208	214-942-0161	942-3376	297-8
Web: www.elrodscostplus.com						
ELS Language Centers 7 Roszel Rd	Princeton	NJ	08540	609-759-5371		423
Web: www.els.edu						
ELS Marketing Inc 3133 Orlando Dr	Mississauga	ON	L4V1C5	905-612-1060		5
TF: 800-809-2512 ■ *Web:* corelogistics.net						
ELS Productions Inc 3298 Sanborn Dr	Riverton	UT	84065	801-676-0807		658
TF: 800-927-3472 ■ *Web:* www.elsproductions.com						
Elsa's 3618 Linden Ave	Dayton	OH	45410	937-252-9635		671
Web: elsas.net						
Elsa's on the Park						
833 N Jefferson St	Milwaukee	WI	53202	414-765-0615		671
Web: www.elsas.com						

Company	Phone	Fax	Class
ELSAG ALPR Global Software Development And Professional Services Ctr 7 Sutton Pl .... Brewster NY 10509 *Web:* www.leonardocompany-us.com	336-379-7135		253
ELSAL Inc 800 A St .... San Rafael CA 94901 *Web:* www2.elsal.com	415-472-8388	472-8389	309
Elsevier Science Ltd 360 Park Ave S .... New York NY 10010 *TF:* 888-437-4636 ■ *Web:* www.elsevier.com	212-989-5800	633-3990	637-9
Elsing Museum 7777 S Lewis Ave .... Tulsa OK 74171 *TF:* 800-678-8876 ■ *Web:* www.oru.edu	918-495-6262		520
Elsmar Home Health Care 2727 2nd Ave Ste 156 .... Detroit MI 48201 *TF:* 877-357-6275 ■ *Web:* www.elsmar-homehealth.com	313-961-5500		363
ElsnerHR 7904 E Chaparral Rd Ste A110-pmb 106 .... Scottsdale AZ 85250 *Web:* elsnerhr.com	602-266-5600		631
ElSohly Laboratories Inc 5 Industrial Pk Dr .... Oxford MS 38655 *Web:* www.elsohly.com	662-236-2609	234-0253	416
Elster American Meter Co 2221 Industrial Rd .... Nebraska City NE 68410 *TF:* 877-595-6254 ■ *Web:* www.elster-americanmeter.com	402-873-8200	873-7616	495
Elster Perfection Corp 436 N Eagle St .... Geneva OH 44041 *TF:* 800-544-6344 ■ *Web:* www.elster-perfection.com	440-415-1600		605-2
ELT Press 1412 Garland Dr .... Greensboro NC 27408 *Web:* www.eltpress.org	336-253-4074		637-2
Elte Carpets Ltd 80 Ronald Ave .... Toronto ON M6E5A2 *TF:* 888-276-3583 ■ *Web:* www.elte.com	416-785-7885		290
Eltec Instruments Inc 350 Fentress Blvd .... Daytona Beach FL 32114 *Web:* www.eltecinstruments.com	386-252-0411	258-3791	529
ELTEK USA Inc 80 Bridle Path Ln .... Mahwah NJ 07430 *Web:* www.eltekgroup.it	201-267-0305		393
Elton & Thompson PC 2615 Jenkintown Rd .... Glenside PA 19038 *Web:* etengr.com	215-576-6460		261
Elusys Therapeutics Inc 25 Riverside Dr .... Pine Brook NJ 07058 *Web:* www.elusys.com	973-808-0222		85
Elva Resa Publishing 8362 Tamarack Village Ste 119-106 .... Saint Paul MN 55125 **Fax Area Code:* 501 ■ *Web:* www.elvaresa.com	651-357-8770	641-0777*	637-2
Elvis Presley Birthplace & Museum 306 Elvis Presley Dr .... Tupelo MS 38801 *Web:* elvispresleybirthplace.com	662-841-1245		520
Elvis Unique Record Club 10933 E Elmwood St .... Mesa AZ 85207 *Web:* www.elvisunique.com	480-984-5026	984-5056	393
Elward Construction Co 680 Harlan St .... Lakewood CO 80214 *TF:* 800-933-5339 ■ *Web:* www.elward.com	800-933-5339		189-1
Elwood Corporation High Performance Motors Group 2701 N Green Bay Rd .... Racine WI 53404 **Fax Area Code:* 414 ■ *TF:* 800-558-9489 ■ *Web:* www.elwood.com	262-637-6591	764-4298*	518
Ely Company Inc, The 3046 Kashiwa St .... Torrance CA 90505 *Web:* www.elyco.com	310-539-5831	530-3569	454
Ely State Prison 4569 NV-90 .... Ely NV 89301 *Web:* doc.nv.gov	775-289-8800		213
Ely Times 515 Murry St PO Box 150820 .... Ely NV 89315 *Web:* www.elynews.com	775-289-4491	289-4566	532-4
Elyria Foundry Co 120 Filbert St .... Elyria OH 44036 *Web:* www.elyriafoundry.com	440-322-4657	323-1101	307
Elyria-Lorain Broadcasting Co 538 Broad St 4th Fl .... Elyria OH 44035 *Web:* elbc.northcoastnow.com	440-322-3761		645-11
Elyse Connolly Inc 23 W 16th St .... New York NY 10011 *Web:* www.elyseconnolly.com	212-255-0886		393
Elysian Brewing Company Inc 6010 Airport Way S .... Seattle WA 98108 *Web:* www.elysianbrewing.com	206-860-3977		102
Elysium Inc 3000 Town Ctr Ste 1330 .... Southfield MI 48075 *Web:* www.elysium-global.com	248-799-9800	281-0672	225
EM (EverMark LLC) 1050 Northbrook Pkwy .... Suwanee GA 30024 *Web:* www.evermark-lnl.com	678-455-5188	455-5190	236
EM Data Consultants Inc 42 Queen St S Ste 201 .... Mississauga ON L5M1K4 *Web:* www.emdci.com	905-858-8442	858-8408	180
EM Design 22661 Hwy 62 .... Shady Cove OR 97539 *Web:* www.em-design.com	541-878-3927	878-3937	253
EM Duggan Inc 140 Will Dr .... Canton MA 02021 *Web:* www.emduggan.com	781-828-2292	828-0991	189-10
EM Microelectronic-US Inc 5475 Mark Dabling Blvd Ste 200 .... Colorado Springs CO 80918 *Web:* www.emmicroelectronic.com	719-593-2883		246
EM Research Inc 1301 Corporate Blvd .... Reno NV 89502 *Web:* emresearch.com	775-345-2411	345-1030	256
EM Search Consulting 330 N Ashland Ave .... Chicago IL 60607 *TF:* 888-773-0268 ■ *Web:* www.emsc.com	888-773-0268		225
EM Technologies Inc 14755 Parvin Rd .... Prosper TX 75078 *Web:* www.lonestarelectronicsco.com	972-347-2041	347-2502	647
EM/SEM (El Monte/South El Monte Chamber of Commerce) 1903 N Durfee Ave .... El Monte CA 91731 *Web:* www.emsem.biz	626-443-0180		139
EMA (Envelope Manufacturers Assn) 700 S Washington St Ste 260 .... Alexandria VA 22314 *Web:* envelope.org	703-739-2200	739-2209	49-4
EMA (Entertainment Merchants Assn) 16530 Ventura Blvd Ste 400 .... Encino CA 91436 *Web:* www.entmerch.org	818-385-1500	933-0911	49-18
EMA (Engine Manufacturers Assn) 333 W Wacker Dr Ste 810 .... Chicago IL 60606 *Web:* www.truckandenginemanufacturers.org	312-929-1970	929-1975	49-13
EMA Design Automation Inc 225 Tech Park Dr .... Rochester NY 14623 *TF:* 877-362-3321 ■ *Web:* www.ema-eda.com	585-334-6001		180
EMAC Inc 2390 Emac Ln .... Carbondale IL 62902 *Web:* www.emacinc.com	618-529-4525	457-0110	177
EMAC Intl 1220 L St NW Ste 100-290 .... Washington DC 20005 **Fax Area Code:* 202 ■ *TF:* 800-963-3622 ■ *Web:* www.emacintl.com	800-963-3622	449-3794*	194
eMag Solutions LLC 1120 Sanctuary Pkwy Ste 275 .... Alpharetta GA 30009 *Web:* www.emagsolutions.com	404-995-6060		178-12
eMagin Inc 3006 Northup Way Ste 103 .... Bellevue WA 98004 *NYSE: EMAN* ■ *Web:* emagin.com	425-284-5200	284-5201	173-4
emagine 1082 Davol St .... Fall River MA 02720 *TF:* 877-530-7993 ■ *Web:* www.emagine.com	877-530-7993		180
Email Co, The 15 Kainona Ave .... Toronto ON M3H3H4 *TF:* 877-933-6245 ■ *Web:* www.theemailcompany.com	877-933-6245		366
EmailHosting.com LLC 795 Hammond Dr Ste 1801 .... Atlanta GA 30328 *TF:* 800-659-4268 ■ *Web:* www.emailhosting.com	800-659-4268		180
EmailLabs 4400 Bohannon Dr Ste 200 .... Menlo Park CA 94025 **Fax Area Code:* 650 ■ *TF:* 866-362-4522 ■ *Web:* email.uptilt.com	866-362-4522	388-3601*	178-1
Emaint Enterprises LLC 438 N Elmwood Rd .... Marlton NJ 08053 *Web:* www.emaint.com	856-810-2700		177
Emanate Health 1115 S Sunset Ave .... West Covina CA 91790 *Web:* www.emanatehealth.org	626-814-2572		374-3
Emanate Health Inter-Community Hospital 210 W San Bernardino Rd .... Covina CA 91723 *Web:* www.emanatehealth.org	626-331-7331		374-3
Emanio Inc 832 Bancroft Way .... Berkeley CA 94710 *Web:* www.emanio.com	510-849-9300	849-9302	178-1
Emanuel County 102 S Main St .... Swainsboro GA 30401 *Web:* www.emanuelchamber.org	478-237-6426	237-7460	338
Emanuel County Board of Education 201 N Main St PO Box 130 .... Swainsboro GA 30401 *Web:* www.emanuel.k12.ga.us	478-237-6674	419-1102	685
Emanuel Medical Ctr (EMC) 825 Delbon Ave .... Turlock CA 95382 *Web:* www.emanuelmedicalcenter.org	209-667-4200		374-3
eMarketer Inc (STN) 11 Times Sq .... New York NY 10036 *TF:* 800-405-0844 ■ *Web:* www.eMarketer.com	212-763-6010		194
E-Max Instruments Inc 13 Inverness Way S .... Englewood CO 80112 *Web:* www.e-maxinstruments.com	303-799-6640	790-2352	425
eMazzanti Technologies 701 Grand St .... Hoboken NJ 07030 *Web:* www.emazzanti.net	844-360-4400	360-4500	180
EMB Corp 1203 Hawkins Dr .... Elizabethtown KY 42701 *Web:* www.embcorp.com	270-737-1996	737-1909	247
Embarcadero Resort Hotel & Marina 1000 SE Bay Blvd .... Newport OR 97365 *Web:* www.embarcaderoresort.com	541-265-8521	265-7844	379
Embarcadero Technologies Inc 100 California St 12th Fl .... San Francisco CA 94111 *Web:* www.embarcadero.com	415-834-3131	434-1721	178-2
Embark 420 NW 5th St .... Oklahoma City OK 73102 *Web:* www.okladot.state.ok.us	405-235-7433	297-2111	468
Embark Corp 459 Broadway 4th Fl .... New York NY 10013 *Web:* www.embark.com	646-368-8394		387
Embark Tree & Landscape Services 2700 Palo Pinto Dr .... Houston TX 77080 *Web:* lmchouston.com	713-462-3261		776
Embassy and Consulates of Belgium 1430 K St NW Ste 101 .... Washington DC 20005 *Web:* unitedstates.diplomatie.belgium.be	202-333-6900		257
Embassy Hotel 610 Polk St .... San Francisco CA 94102 *Web:* www.theembassyhotelsf.com	415-673-1404		379
Embassy Hotel & Suites 25 Cartier St .... Ottawa ON K2P1J2 *TF:* 800-661-5495 ■ *Web:* www.ottawaembassy.com	613-237-2111	563-1353	379
Embassy Industries Inc 315 Oser Ave .... Hauppauge NY 11788 *Web:* www.embassyind.com	631-694-1800	694-1832	357
Embassy of Australia *Consulate General* 150 E 42nd St 34th Fl .... New York NY 10017 *Web:* usa.embassy.gov.au	212-351-6500	351-6501	257
Embassy of Belarus 1619 New Hampshire Ave NW .... Washington DC 20009 *Web:* www.belarusfacts.by	202-986-1606		257
Embassy of Brazil in Washington 3006 Massachusetts Ave NW .... Washington DC 20008 *Web:* washington.itamaraty.gov.br	202-238-2700		257
Embassy of Ethiopia 3506 International Dr NW .... Washington DC 20008 *Web:* www.ethiopianembassy.org	202-364-1200	587-0195	257
Embassy of Hungary 3910 Shoemaker St NW .... Washington DC 20008 *Web:* www.washington.mfa.gov.hu	202-362-6730	966-8135	257
Embassy of Japan in the USA 2520 Massachusetts Ave NW .... Washington DC 20008 *Web:* www.us.emb-japan.go.jp	202-238-6700	328-2187	257
Embassy of Malawi in the United States Library 2408 Massachusetts Ave NW .... Washington DC 20008 *Web:* www.malawiembassy-dc.org	202-721-0270	721-0288	434-3
Embassy of Malta 2017 Connecticut Ave NW .... Washington DC 20008 *Web:* foreignandeu.gov.mt	202-462-3611	387-5470	257
Embassy of Mauritania 2129 Leroy Pl NW .... Washington DC 20008 *Web:* www.mauritaniaembassy.com	202-232-5700	319-2623	257
Embassy of Papua New Guinea 1779 Massachusetts Ave NW Ste 805 .... Washington DC 20036 *Web:* www.pngembassy.org	202-745-3680	745-3679	257
Embassy of St Vincent & the Grenadines 1627 K St NW .... Washington DC 20016 *Web:* www.wa.embassy.gov.vc	784-457-1007		257
Embassy of the Commonwealth of Dominica 3216 New Mexico Ave NW .... Washington DC 20016 *Web:* www.dominicaembassy.com	202-364-6781	364-6791	257
Embassy of the Kingdom of Bahrain 3502 International Dr NW .... Washington DC 20008 *Web:* www.bahrainembassy.org	202-342-1111	362-2192	257
Embassy of the Republic of Azerbaijan to the United States of America 2741 34th St NW .... Washington DC 20008 *Web:* washington.mfa.gov.az	202-337-3500		257
Embassy of the Republic of Serbia 2134 Kalorama Rd NW .... Washington DC 20008 *Web:* www.washington.mfa.gov.rs	202-332-0333	332-3933	257

Name / Address	Phone	Fax	Class
Embassy of the Republic of the Union of Myanmar 2300 S St NW . . . Washington DC 20008 *Web:* www.mewashingtondc.com	202-332-3344	332-4351	257
EMBASSY Products & Logistics PO Box 8066 . . . Falls Church VA 22041 *Web:* www.embassy-usa.com	703-845-0800	820-9385	449
Embassy Suites Hotel & Casino-San Juan Puerto Rico 8000 Tartak St Isla Verde . . . Carolina PR 00979 *Web:* embassysuites3.hilton.com	787-791-0505		378
Embassy Theatre 125 W Jefferson Blvd . . . Fort Wayne IN 46802 *Web:* fwembassytheatre.org	260-424-6287		572
Embed Inc 410 Great Rd. . . . Littleton MA 01460 *Web:* embedinc.com	978-742-9014		261
Embedded Data Systems LLC 2019 Fortune Dr . . . Lawrenceburg KY 40342 *Web:* www.embeddeddatasystems.com	502-859-5490		177
Embedded Software Development Systems Inc (ESDS) 19925 Stevens Creek Blvd . . . Cupertino CA 95014 *Web:* esds.in	408-444-1456		178-1
Ember Industries Inc 321 Carlson Cir . . . San Marcos TX 78666 *Web:* www.emberindustries.com	512-396-1911	396-2329	253
Emberex Inc 220 E 11th Ave Ste 6. . . . Eugene OR 97401 *Web:* www.emberex.com	541-687-5778		177
Embience Inc 6450 Lusk Blvd E202203 . . . San Diego CA 92121 *Web:* www.embience.com	858-366-0415		196
EmblemHealth Co 55 Water St . . . New York NY 10041 *TF:* 800-447-8255 ■ *Web:* www.emblemhealth.com	646-447-5000		391-3
Embossed Graphics 1175 S Frontenac Rd . . . Aurora IL 60504 *TF:* 800-362-6773 ■ *Web:* www.embossedgraphics.com	800-362-6773		627
Embrace Care Management LLC 627 N Eighth St . . . Sheboygan WI 53081 *Web:* embracecaremanagement.com	920-451-6228		363
Embraer 276 SW 34th St . . . Fort Lauderdale FL 33315 *Web:* embraer.com	954-359-3700	359-3701	20
Embrey Partners Ltd 1020 NE Loop 410 Ste 700. . . . San Antonio TX 78209 *Web:* www.embreydc.com	210-824-6044	824-7656	653
Embroiderers Guild of America, The (EGA) 1205 E Washington St Ste 117. . . . Louisville KY 40202 *Web:* egausa.org	502-589-6956	584-7900	48-18
Embryotech Laboratories Inc 140 Hale St. . . . Haverhill MA 01830 *TF:* 800-673-7500 ■ *Web:* www.embryotech.com	978-373-7300		743
Embry-Riddle Aeronautical University 1 Aerospace Blvd . . . Daytona Beach FL 32114 *TF:* 800-222-3728 ■ *Web:* www.erau.edu	386-226-6000		167-3
Embrys Lansdowne Shoppes 3361 Tates Creek Rd . . . Lexington KY 40502 *Web:* embrys.com	859-269-3390		157-6
EMC (Carroll Electric Membership Corp) 155 N Hwy 113. . . . Carrollton GA 30117 *Web:* www.cemc.com	770-832-3552		245
EMC (Grady Electric Membership Corp) 1499 US Hwy 84 W . . . Cairo GA 39828 *TF:* 877-757-6060 ■ *Web:* gradyemc.com	229-377-4182		245
EMC (Equipment Manufacturing Corp) 14930 Marquardt Ave. . . . Santa Fe Springs CA 90670 *TF:* 888-833-9000 ■ *Web:* www.equipmentmanufacturing.com	562-623-9394		386
EMC (Emanuel Medical Ctr) 825 Delbon Ave. . . . Turlock CA 95382 *Web:* www.emanuelmedicalcenter.org	209-667-4200		374-3
EMC (Electrical Materials Co) 1236 First Ave S . . . Fort Dodge IA 50501 *TF:* 800-697-3137 ■ *Web:* emcfd.com	800-697-3137		612
EMC Creative 1444 N Main St Ste 440. . . . Walnut Creek CA 94596 *Web:* emccreative.com	925-837-9380		195
EMC Insurance Group Inc 717 Mulberry St . . . Des Moines IA 50309 *NASDAQ: EMCI* ■ *TF:* 800-447-2295 ■ *Web:* www.emcins.com	515-280-2511		360-4
EMC Outdoor 5074 W Chester Pk 2nd Fl . . . Newtown Square PA 19073 *Web:* www.emcoutdoor.com	610-353-9300		6
EMC Precision 145 Northrup St PO Box 479 . . . Elyria OH 44036 *TF:* 844-362-2378 ■ *Web:* www.emcprecision.com	440-365-4171	365-4000	111
EMC School 875 Montreal Way . . . Saint Paul MN 55102 **Fax Area Code:* 800 ■ *TF:* 800-328-1452 ■ *Web:* www.emcschool.com	651-290-2800	328-4564*	637-2
EMCC (East Mississippi Community College) 1512 Kemper St . . . Scooba MS 39358 *Web:* www.eastms.edu	662-476-5000		162
EMCO Chemical Distributors Inc 2100 Commonwealth Ave. . . . North Chicago IL 60064 *Web:* www.emcochem.com	847-689-2200		146
EMCO Corp 1108 Dundas St. . . . London ON N5W3A7 *Web:* emco.ca	519-453-9600	645-2465	612
EMCOR Construction Services Inc 1420 Spring Hill Rd Ste 500. . . . McLean VA 22102 **Fax Area Code:* 703 ■ *TF:* 866-890-7794 ■ *Web:* emcorgroup.com	866-890-7794	556-0890*	189-4
EMCOR Hyre Electric Co 2655 Garfield Ave. . . . Highland IN 46322 *Web:* emcorhyre.com	219-923-6100	838-3631	189-4
EMCOR Services Betlem 704 Clinton Ave S. . . . Rochester NY 14620 *TF:* 800-423-8536 ■ *Web:* www.emcorbetlem.com	800-423-8536		261
EMCORE Corp 10420 Research Rd SE . . . Albuquerque NM 87123 *Web:* emcore.com	505-332-5000		696
Emcure Pharmaceuticals USA INC 21/B Cotters Ln . . . East Brunswick NJ 08816 *Web:* www.emcureusa.com	732-238-7880	238-7881	231
EMD Millipore 480 S Democrat Rd . . . Gibbstown NJ 08027 *TF:* 800-222-0342 ■ *Web:* www.merckmillipore.com	800-222-0342	336-4422	144
EMD Serono Inc 1 Technology Pl . . . Rockland MA 02370 *TF:* 800-283-8088 ■ *Web:* www.emdserono.com	781-982-9000		85
Emeco 805 W Elm Ave . . . Hanover PA 17331 *TF:* 800-366-5951 ■ *Web:* www.emeco.net	717-637-5951	633-6018	319-1
eMedia Music Corp 664 NE Northlake Way . . . Seattle WA 98105 *TF:* 888-363-3424 ■ *Web:* www.emediamusic.com	206-329-5657		637-7
Emek Hebrew Academy 15365 Magnolia Blvd . . . Sherman Oaks CA 91403 *Web:* www.emek.org	818-783-3663	783-3739	685
Emelin Theater 153 Library Ln . . . Mamaroneck NY 10543 *Web:* emelin.org	914-698-0098	698-1404	572
EMEPA (East Mississippi Electric Power Assn) 2128 Hwy 39 N PO Box 5517. . . . Meridian MS 39302 *Web:* emepa.com	601-581-8600	482-0701	245
Emera Energy Inc 1223 Lower Water St PO Box 910. . . . Halifax NS B3J2W5 *TF:* 866-474-7800 ■ *Web:* www.emeraenergy.com	902-474-7800	428-6118	538
EmeraChem LLC 201 Perimeter Park Rd . . . Knoxville TN 37922 *TF:* 888-777-4538 ■ *Web:* www.emerachem.com	865-246-3000	246-3001	143
Emerald Bay Energy Inc 3 4015-1st St SE Ste 3A. . . . Calgary AB T2G4X7 *Web:* ebyinc.com	403-262-6000	263-6001	536
Emerald Bay State Park 138 Emerald Bay Rd . . . South Lake Tahoe CA 96150 *Web:* www.parks.ca.gov	530-541-3030		565
Emerald Chinese Seafood Restaurant 3709 Convoy St . . . San Diego CA 92111 *Web:* www.emeraldrestaurant.com	858-565-6888		671
Emerald City Graphics 23328 66th Ave S . . . Kent WA 98032 **Fax Area Code:* 253 ■ *TF:* 877-631-5178 ■ *Web:* www.emeraldcg.com	877-631-5178	520-2607*	627
Emerald Coast Convention and Visitors Bureau 1540 Miracle Strip Pky. . . . Fort Walton Beach FL 32548 *TF:* 800-322-3319 ■ *Web:* www.emeraldcoastfl.com	850-651-7131	651-7149	379
Emerald Coast Utilities Authority (ECUA) 9255 Sturdevant St. . . . Pensacola FL 32514 *Web:* www.ecua.fl.gov	850-476-0480		787
Emerald Correctional Management LLC 3800 N Central Ave Ste 460 . . . Phoenix AZ 85012	337-264-9777		652
Emerald Credit Union 13201 Granger Rd . . . Garfield Heights OH 44125 *Web:* emeraldgcu.com	216-581-5581	581-5590	219
Emerald Creek Garnet 59652 State Hwy 3 . . . Fernwood ID 83830 *Web:* optagroupllc.com	208-245-2096		1
Emerald Downs 2300 Emerald Downs Dr PO Box 617. . . . Auburn WA 98001 *TF:* 888-931-8400 ■ *Web:* emeralddowns.com	253-288-7000		133
EMERALD HEIGHTS 10901 17th Cir NE. . . . Redmond WA 98052 *Web:* www.emeraldheights.com	425-556-8100		672
Emerald Hospitality Associates Inc 2001 Crocker Rd Ste 300 . . . Westlake OH 44145 *Web:* www.emeraldhospitality.com	440-239-9848		195
Emerald Intarnational Corp 6895 Burlington Pk. . . . Florence KY 41042 *Web:* www.emeraldcoal.com	859-525-2522	525-4052	501
Emerald Kalama Chemical LLC 1296 Third St NW. . . . Kalama WA 98625 *TF:* 877-300-9545 ■ *Web:* www.emeraldmaterials.com	360-673-2550	673-3564	296-15
Emerald Lake State Park 65 Emerald Lake Ln . . . East Dorset VT 05253 *Web:* www.vtstateparks.com	802-362-1655		565
Emerald Packing 2823 N Orange Blossom Trl . . . Orlando FL 32804	407-420-9534		11-1
Emerald Queen Hotel & Casino 5700 Pacific Hwy E. . . . Fife WA 98424 *TF:* 888-831-7655 ■ *Web:* www.emeraldqueen.com	253-594-7777		379
Emerge Energy Services LP 1400 Civic Pl Ste 250. . . . Southlake TX 76092 *Web:* www.emergelp.com	817-488-7775		539
Emergency Ambulance Service Inc 1517 W Braden Ct Ste A. . . . Brea CA 92821 *TF:* 800-400-0689 ■ *Web:* emergencyambulance.com	714-990-1331	792-0464	30
Emergency Communications for SW British Columbia Inc 3301 E Pender St . . . Vancouver BC V5K5J3 *Web:* www.ecomm911.ca	604-215-5000		224
Emergency Nurses Assn (ENA) 915 Lee St . . . Des Plaines IL 60016 *TF:* 800-900-9659 ■ *Web:* ena.org	847-460-4000	460-4001	49-8
Emergency Physicians Medical Group Pc Inc 2000 Green Rd Ste 300. . . . Ann Arbor MI 48105 *Web:* www.epmgpc.com	734-995-3764	995-2913	374-3
EMERgency24 Inc 999 E Touhy . . . Des Plaines IL 60018 *TF:* 800-800-3624 ■ *Web:* www.emergency24.com	773-725-0222		693
Emergent Biosolutions Inc 2273 Research Blvd Ste 400. . . . Rockville MD 20850 *Web:* www.emergentbiosolutions.com	301-795-1800	795-1899	85
Emerging Markets Traders Assn (EMTA) 360 Madison Ave 18th Fl . . . New York NY 10017 *Web:* www.emta.org	212-313-1100	313-1016	49-2
Emerging Portfolio Fund Research Inc 80 Sherman St . . . Cambridge MA 02140 *Web:* www.epfr.com	617-864-4999		637-9
Emerging Power Inc 200 Holt St . . . Hackensack NJ 07601 *Web:* emergingpower.com	201-441-3590		253
Emerging Vision Inc 520 Eigth Ave . . . New York NY 10018 *Web:* emergingvision.com	646-737-1500		543
Emergycare Inc 1926 Peach St. . . . Erie PA 16502 *TF:* 800-814-1038 ■ *Web:* www.emergycare.org	814-870-1010		30
Emeril's 800 Tchoupitoulas St. . . . New Orleans LA 70130 *Web:* www.emerils.com	504-528-9393	558-3925	671
Emeril's New Orleans Fish House 3799 Las Vegas Blvd S. . . . Las Vegas NV 89109 *Web:* emerilsrestaurants.com	702-891-7374	891-7338	671
Emerson & Cuming Microwave Products Inc 28 York Ave. . . . Randolph MA 02368 *Web:* www.eccosorb.com	781-961-9600	961-2845	322
Emerson Climate Technologies 1675 Campbell Rd . . . Sidney OH 45365 *Web:* www.climate.emerson.com	937-498-3011	498-3334	14
Emerson College 120 Boylston St. . . . Boston MA 02116 *Web:* www.emerson.edu	617-824-8500		166

Phone | Fax | Class

Emerson Colonial Theatre
106 Boylston St .... Boston MA 02116 212-307-2166 572
Web: www.emersoncolonialtheatre.com
Emerson Electric Co
8000 West Florissant Ave PO Box 4100 .... Saint Louis MO 63136 314-553-2000 385
Web: www.emerson.com
Emerson Equity LLC
155 Bovet Rd Ste 725 .... San Mateo CA 94402 650-312-0200 690
Web: www.emersonequity.com
Emerson Group, The 407 E Lancaster Ave .... Wayne PA 19087 610-971-9600 971-9616 195
Web: www.emersongroup.com
Emerson Hardwood Co
2279 NW Front Ave .... Portland OR 97210 503-223-5667 227-2976 361
TF: 800-422-3040 ■ *Web:* www.emersonhardwood.com
Emerson Hospital
133 Old Rd To 9 Acre Corner .... Concord MA 01742 978-369-1400 374-3
TF: 800-439-0183 ■ *Web:* www.emersonhospital.org
Emerson Law Group
1055 Whitney Ranch Dr Ste 120 .... Henderson NV 89014 702-384-9444 41
Web: emersonlawgroup.com
Emerson Resort & Spa 5340 Rt 28 .... Mount Tremper NY 12457 845-688-2828 379
Web: emersonresort.com
Emerson Thomson & Bennett LLC
1914 Akron Peninsula Rd .... Akron OH 44313 330-434-9999 428
TF: 800-822-8113 ■ *Web:* www.etblaw.com
Emerson-Swan Inc 300 Pond St .... Randolph MA 02368 781-986-2000 986-2028 612
TF: 800-346-9219 ■ *Web:* www.emersonswan.com
Emery & Webb Inc 989 Main St .... Fishkill NY 12524 845-896-6727 390
TF: 800-942-5818 ■ *Web:* www.emerywebb.com
Emery Air Charter Inc 1 Airport Cir .... Rockford IL 61109 815-968-8287 186
TF: 800-435-8090 ■ *Web:* emeryair.net
Emery Corp PO Box 1104 .... Morganton NC 28680 828-433-1536 433-6809 456
TF: 800-255-0537 ■ *Web:* www.emerycorp.com
Emery County 75 E Main Rm 102 .... Castle Dale UT 84513 435-381-3530 381-3531 338
Web: www.emerycounty.com
Emery Distributors Inc 3800 Glover Rd .... Easton PA 18040 610-258-3651 44
TF: 800-221-6178 ■ *Web:* www.emerydistributors.com
Emery Reddy PLLC
600 Stewart St Ste 1100 .... Seattle WA 98101 206-442-9106 41
Web: emeryreddy.com
Emery Telcom 445 E Hwy 29 .... Orangeville UT 84537 435-748-2223 748-1050 224
TF: 888-749-1090 ■ *Web:* www.emerytelcom.net
Emery Winslow Scale Co 73 Cogwheel Ln ...... Seymour CT 06483 203-881-9333 881-9477 684
TF: 800-891-3952 ■ *Web:* www.emerywinslow.com
Emery-Pratt Co 1966 W M 21 .... Owosso MI 48867 989-723-5291 96
Web: www.emery-pratt.com
EMF (Engineering & Metal Fabrication)
124 Imperial St .... Merritt Island FL 32952 321-453-3670 452-4506 697
Web: www.emfinc.net
EMF Corp PO Box 389 .... Angola IN 46703 260-665-9541 253
TF: 800-847-2818 ■ *Web:* www.emfusa.com
EMF Inc 60 Foundry St .... Keene NH 03431 603-352-8400 175
TF: 800-992-3003 ■ *Web:* www.emfinc.com
Emfluence 106 W 11th St Ste 2220 .... Kansas City MO 64105 816-472-5643 177
Web: emfluence.com
EMG Corp
10461 Mill Run Cir Ste 1100 .... Owings Mills MD 21117 800-733-0660 785-6220* 656
*Fax Area Code: 410 ■ *TF:* 800-733-0660 ■ *Web:* emgcorp.com
Emgence Technologies Inc
11440 W Bernardo Ct .... San Diego CA 92127 858-753-1985 196
Web: www.emgence.com
EMH Inc 550 Crane Dr .... Valley City OH 44280 330-220-8600 220-0204 261
Web: emhcranes.com
EMHT (Evans Mechwart Hambleton & Tilton Inc)
5500 New Albany Rd .... New Albany OH 43054 614-775-4500 775-4800 261
TF: 888-775-3648 ■ *Web:* www.emht.com
EMI (Ed Miniat Inc)
16250 S Vincennes Ave .... South Holland IL 60473 708-589-2400 589-2525 297-9
Web: www.miniat.com
EMI (Educational Ministries Inc)
165 Plaza Dr .... Prescott AZ 86303 800-221-0910 637-2
TF: 800-221-0910 ■ *Web:* www.educationalministries.com
EMI Consulting 83 Columbia St Ste 400 .... Seattle WA 98104 206-621-1160 196
Web: emiconsulting.com
EMI Industries 1316 Tech Blvd .... Tampa FL 33619 813-626-3166 492
Web: www.emiindustries.com
EMI Network 9933 Alliance Rd .... Cincinnati OH 45242 513-407-9189 317
Web: www.eminetwork.com
EMI Services Inc 301 A St .... Idaho Falls ID 83402 208-522-1117 463
Web: www.emiservices.com
EMIDA Corp
27442 Portola Pkwy Ste 150 .... Foothill Ranch CA 92610 949-699-1401 69
Web: www.emida.net
Emil A. Schroth Inc
61 Yellowbrook Rd .... Farmingdale NJ 07727 732-938-5015 938-2363 492
Web: www.emilschroth.com
Emil Anderson Construction (EAC) Inc
907 Ethel St .... Kelowna BC V1Y2W1 250-762-9999 762-6171 652
TF: 800-667-5122 ■ *Web:* eac.bc.ca
Emil Finley 315 Hillcrest Dr .... Laurens SC 29360 864-984-3544 984-3545 645-141
Web: wlbg.com
Emile's 545 S Second St .... San Jose CA 95112 408-289-1960 671
Web: www.emilesrestaurant.com
Emily Fowler Central Library
502 Oakland St .... Denton TX 76201 940-349-8752 434-3
Web: library.cityofdenton.com
Emily Griffith Technical College
1860 Lincoln St .... Denver CO 80203 720-423-4700 167-3
Web: www.emilygriffith.edu
Emily Morgan Hotel
705 E Houston St .... San Antonio TX 78205 210-225-5100 225-7227 379
Web: www.emilymorganhotel.com
EMILY's List 1800 M St NW Ste 375N .... Washington DC 20036 202-326-1400 326-1415 48-7
Web: emilyslist.org
Eminence Speaker LLC
838 Mulberry Pk PO Box 360 .... Eminence KY 40019 502-845-5622 52
TF: 800-897-8373 ■ *Web:* www.eminence.com

Phone | Fax | Class

Emisare Inc 532 S Elm St Ste 200 .... Greensboro NC 27406 336-378-0510 7
Web: www.emisare.com
Emisphere Technologies Inc
240 Cedar Knolls Rd Ste 200 .... Cedar Knolls NJ 07927 973-532-8000 532-8115 85
Web: www.emisphere.com
Emissary 214 W 29th St 2nd Fl .... New York NY 10001 646-776-0501 657
Web: www.emissary.io
Emission Monitoring Service Inc
400 S Hwy 146 .... Baytown TX 77520 281-428-1114 196
Web: www.emsi-air.com
Emitations.com
6162 Mission Gorge Rd .... San Diego CA 92120 619-280-0550 791
EMJ Corp
2034 Hamilton Pl Blvd Ste 400 .... Chattanooga TN 37421 423-855-1550 855-6857 186
Web: www.emjcorp.com
Emjay Engineering & Construction Company Inc
1706 Whitehead Rd .... Baltimore MD 21207 410-298-2000 261
Web: www.emjaycons.com
Emka Inc 1961 Fulling Mill Rd .... Middletown PA 17057 717-986-1111 350
Web: www.emkausa.com
Emkay Inc 805 W Thorndale Ave .... Itasca IL 60143 630-250-7400 289
TF: 800-621-2001 ■ *Web:* www.emkay.com
EMKF (Ewing Marion Kauffman Foundation)
4801 Rockhill Rd .... Kansas City MO 64110 816-932-1000 305
Web: www.kauffman.org
EML (Electronic Metrology Laboratory)
318 Seaboard Ln Ste 106 .... Franklin TN 37067 270-874-2233 393
Web: www.eml1.com
Emma Willard School 285 Pawling Ave .... Troy NY 12180 518-833-1300 833-1805 622
Web: www.emmawillard.org
Emmanuel Bible College
100 Fergus Ave .... Kitchener ON N2A2H2 519-894-8900 894-5331 785
Web: www.emmanuelbiblecollege.ca
Emmanuel Books PO Box 321 .... New Castle DE 19720 302-325-9515 95
Web: emmanuelbooks.com
Emmanuel College 400 Fenway .... Boston MA 02115 617-735-9715 735-9801 166
Web: www.emmanuel.edu
Emmanuel College
181 Spring St .... Franklin Springs GA 30639 706-245-7226 245-2876 166
TF: 800-860-8800 ■ *Web:* www.ec.edu
Emmanuel Gospel Center Inc
2 San Juan St .... Boston MA 02118 617-262-4567 48-20
Web: www.egc.org
Emmart & Son Incorporated W H
305 Brick Kiln Rd .... Winchester VA 22603 540-662-3848 539
Emmaus Bible College 2570 Asbury Rd .... Dubuque IA 52001 563-588-8000 588-1216 161
TF: 800-397-2425 ■ *Web:* emmaus.edu
Emmaus Medical Inc
20725 S W Ave Ste 136 .... Torrance CA 90501 310-214-0065 214-0075 231
Web: emmausmedical.com
Emmaus Road Publishing Inc (ERP)
1468 Parkview Cir .... Steubenville OH 43952 740-283-2880 283-4011 637-2
Web: stpaulcenter.com
Emme Controls PO Box 2251 .... Bristol CT 06011 800-396-0523 407
TF: 800-396-0523 ■ *Web:* www.getemme.com
Emmer Group 2801 SW Archer Rd .... Gainesville FL 32608 352-376-2444 376-2260 653
Web: www.emmergroup.com
Emmer Tom (Rep R - MN)
315 Cannon House Office Bldg .... Washington DC 20515 202-225-2331 225-6475 342-2
Web: emmer.house.gov
Emmet County 609 First Ave N .... Estherville IA 51334 712-362-4261 362-7454 338
Web: www.emmetcountyia.com
Emmet County 200 Div St Ste 130 .... Petoskey MI 49770 231-348-1702 348-0602 338
TF: 866-731-1204 ■ *Web:* www.emmetcounty.org
Emmett O'Brien Technical High School
141 Prindle Ave .... Ansonia CT 06401 203-732-1800 685
Web: obrien.cttech.org
Emmis Communications Corp
40 Monument Cir 1 Emmis Plz Ste 700 .... Indianapolis IN 46204 317-266-0100 643
NASDAQ: EMMS ■ *Web:* www.emmis.com
Emmons County
100 NW Fourth St PO Box 272 .... Linton ND 58552 701-254-5410 338
Web: www.emmonsnd.com
Emmy Magazine
5220 Lankershim Blvd .... North Hollywood CA 91601 818-754-2800 457-9
Web: www.emmys.com
Emory & Henry College PO Box 947 .... Emory VA 24327 276-944-4121 166
Web: www.ehc.edu
Emory Conference Center Hotel
1615 Clifton Rd .... Atlanta GA 30329 404-712-6000 712-6025 377
TF: 800-933-6679 ■ *Web:* www.emoryconferencecenter.com
Emory Crawford Long Hospital
550 Peachtree St NE .... Atlanta GA 30308 404-686-4411 374-3
Web: www.emoryhealthcare.org
Emory L. Bennett Memorial Veterans' Nursing Home
1920 Mason Ave .... Daytona Beach FL 32117 386-274-3460 793
Web: www.floridavets.org
Emory University 201 Dowman Dr .... Atlanta GA 30322 404-727-6036 727-4303 166
TF: 800-727-6036 ■ *Web:* www.emory.edu
Emory University School of Law
1301 Clifton Rd .... Atlanta GA 30322 404-727-6816 727-6802 167-1
Web: law.emory.edu
Emoteq Corp
Allied Motion 10002 E 43rd St S .... Tulsa OK 74146 918-627-1845 518
Emotion Studios 85 Liberty Ship Way .... Sausalito CA 94965 415-331-6975 180
Web: emotionstudios.com
EMP (Engineered Machined Products Inc)
3111 N 28th St .... Escanaba MI 49829 906-789-7497 786-6635 128
Web: www.emp-corp.com
Empathy Logic Inc
15732 Los Gatos Blvd Ste 434 .... Los Gatos CA 95032 408-940-3951 225
Web: www.empathylogic.com
Emperor of China Restaurant
1010 E Brady St .... Milwaukee WI 53202 414-271-8889 671
Web: emperorofchinarestaurant.com
Emperor's Palace 7321 Martin Way E .... Olympia WA 98516 360-923-2323 671
Web: www.olychinese.com
Empire Ag Transport Inc
15374 County Line Rd .... Delano CA 93215 661-725-1406 311

Company	City	State	Zip	Phone	Fax	Class
Empire Airlines Inc 11559 N Atlas Rd *Web:* www.empireairlines.com	Hayden	ID	83835	208-292-3850	292-3851	12
Empire Architectural 409 N Main St *Web:* www.empirearchitecturalproducts.com	Freeport	NY	11520	516-377-8545		820
Empire Arts Ctr 415 DeMers Ave *Web:* www.empireartscenter.com	Grand Forks	ND	58201	701-746-5500	746-0500	572
Empire Bakery Equipment 171 Greenwich St *TF:* 800-878-4070 ■ *Web:* www.empirebake.com	Hempstead	NY	11550	516-538-1210		454
Empire Beauty School 456 High St *TF:* 877-327-6600 ■ *Web:* www.empirebeautyschools.com	Somersworth	NH	03878	603-692-1515		685
Empire Beauty School 396 St Clair Hwy *TF:* 800-964-1328 ■ *Web:* www.empire.edu	Pottsville	PA	17901	570-998-4149		685
Empire Blended Products Inc 250 Hickory Ln *Web:* empireblended.com	Bayville	NJ	08721	732-269-4949		183
Empire Building Materials Inc PO Box 220 **Fax Area Code:* 406 ■ *TF:* 800-548-8201 ■ *Web:* www.empireinc.com	Bozeman	MT	59771	800-548-8201	587-3144*	191-2
Empire Building Services 1570 E Edinger Ave *TF:* 888-296-2078 ■ *Web:* www.ebuildingservices.com	Santa Ana	CA	92705	714-836-7700		138
Empire Cheese Inc 4520 Haskell Rd *Web:* greatlakescheese.com	Cuba	NY	14727	585-968-1552	968-2660	296-5
Empire Cleaning Supply 12821 S Figueroa St **Fax Area Code:* 323 ■ *Web:* empirecleaningsupply.com	Los Angeles	CA	90061	310-527-0132	248-7770*	151
Empire College School of Business 3035 Cleveland Ave *TF:* 877-395-8535 ■ *Web:* www.empcol.edu	Santa Rosa	CA	95403	707-546-4000		685
Empire Comfort Systems Inc 918 Freeburg Ave *Web:* www.empirecomfort.com	Belleville	IL	62222	618-233-7420		357
Empire Company Ltd 115 King St *TSE:* EMP.A ■ *TF:* 800-387-0825 ■ *Web:* www.empireco.ca	Stellarton	NS	B0K1S0	902-755-4440	755-6477	185
Empire Diamond Corp 350 5th Ave Ste 4000 *TF:* 800-728-3425 ■ *Web:* www.empirediamond.com	New York	NY	10118	212-564-4777	564-4960	411
Empire Die Casting Company Inc 635 Highland Rd E *Web:* www.empiredie.com	Macedonia	OH	44056	330-467-0750	467-9118	308
Empire Discount 455 Tarrytown Rd *Web:* www.empirediscount.net	White Plains	NY	10607	914-684-1455	422-0506	44
Empire Electric Association Inc 801 N Broadway *TF:* 800-709-3726 ■ *Web:* www.eea.coop	Cortez	CO	81321	970-565-4444		245
Empire Energy Corporation Intl Level 3 65 Murray St Hobart Tasmania *Web:* www.empireenergy.com	Leawood	KS	66211	613-623-1933		536
Empire Express Inc 999 Channel Ave *TF:* 800-851-0152 ■ *Web:* www.empireexpress.com	Memphis	TN	38106	901-942-3300		780
Empire Financial Advisors Inc 3 Lear Jet Ln *Web:* empirefa.com	Latham	NY	12110	518-608-1100		390
Empire Food Brokers of Ohio Inc 11243 Cornell Pk Dr *Web:* empirefoods.com	Cincinnati	OH	45242	513-793-6241		297-8
Empire Industries Inc 180 Olcott St *TF:* 800-243-4844 ■ *Web:* www.empireindustries.com	Manchester	CT	06040	860-647-1431	647-1160	595
Empire Iron Works Ltd 21104 - 107 Ave *Web:* www.empireiron.com	Edmonton	AB	T5S1X2	780-447-4650		105
Empire Justice Ctr 1 W Main St Ste 200 *Web:* empirejustice.org	Rochester	NY	14614	585-454-4060	454-2518	428
Empire Kosher Poultry Inc 247 Empire Dr *Web:* www.empirekosher.com	Mifflintown	PA	17059	717-436-7055		619
Empire Level Manufacturing Corp 929 Empire Dr PO Box 800 **Fax Area Code:* 262 ■ *TF:* 800-558-0722 ■ *Web:* www.empirelevel.com	Mukwonago	WI	53149	800-558-0722	368-2127*	758
Empire Livestock Marketing LLC 5001 Brittonfield Pkwy *TF:* 800-462-8802 ■ *Web:* www.empirelivestock.com	East Syracuse	NY	13057	315-433-9129	433-0068	446
Empire Maintenance Company Inc 33 W 19th St *Web:* www.empiremaintenance.com	New York	NY	10011	212-537-5033	537-5173	104
Empire Media Services Inc 2050 E Continental Blvd *Web:* www.empiremedia.net	Southlake	TX	76092	469-855-5959		5
Empire Mine State Historic Park 10791 E Empire St *Web:* www.parks.ca.gov	Grass Valley	CA	95945	530-273-8522		565
Empire Office Inc 105 Madison Ave *Web:* www.empireoffice.com	New York	NY	10016	212-607-5500		320
Empire Optical Inc 3238 E 21st St *Web:* www.empireoptical.com	Tulsa	OK	74114	918-744-8005		543
Empire Paper Co 2708 Central Fwy E *TF:* 800-299-9626 ■ *Web:* www.empirepaper.com	Wichita Falls	TX	76301	940-766-3216	766-3867	559
Empire Pictures 595 Madison Ave 39th Fl *Web:* www.empirepicturesusa.com	New York	NY	10022	212-629-3629		514
Empire Plow Company Inc 3140 E 65th St *Web:* www.mckayempire.com	Cleveland	OH	44127	216-641-2290	441-4709	273
Empire Recycling Corp 64 N Genesee St *Web:* empirerecycling.com	Utica	NY	13502	315-724-7161		660
Empire Resorts Inc 204 Rt 17B *NASDAQ:* NYNY ■ *Web:* www.empireresorts.com	Monticello	NY	12701	845-807-0001		132
Empire Resources Inc 2115 Linwood Ave *NYSE:* ERS ■ *Web:* empireresources.com	Fort Lee	NJ	07024	201-944-2200	944-2226	485
Empire Safety & Supply Inc 10624 Industrial Ave **Fax Area Code:* 888 ■ *TF:* 800-995-1341 ■ *Web:* www.empiresafety.com	Roseville	CA	95678	800-995-1341	882-9060*	679
Empire School of Real Estate 123 W Main St *Web:* www.empirerealtycompany.com	Madison	WI	53703	608-257-4806	257-4809	685
Empire Screen Printing Inc N5206 Marco Rd PO Box 218 *Web:* www.empirescreen.com	Onalaska	WI	54650	608-783-3301	783-3306	687
Empire Southwest Co 1725 S Country Club Dr *TF:* 800-367-4731 ■ *Web:* www.empire-cat.com	Mesa	AZ	85210	480-633-4000		358
Empire Staple Co 200 E 55th Ave *TF:* 800-387-7140 ■ *Web:* www.empirestaple.com	Denver	CO	80216	303-433-6803		351
Empire State Aerosciences Museum 250 Rudy Chase Dr *Web:* www.esam.org	Glenville	NY	12302	518-377-2191	377-1959	520
Empire State Bank 68 N Plank Rd *Web:* www.esbna.com	Newburgh	NY	12550	845-561-0003		70
Empire State Bldg 350 Fifth Ave Ste 100 *TF:* 877-692-8439 ■ *Web:* www.esbnyc.com	New York	NY	10118	212-736-3100		50-4
Empire Telephone Corp 34 Main St PO Box 349 *TF:* 800-338-3300 ■ *Web:* www.empiretelephone.com	Prattsburgh	NY	14873	607-522-3712		736
Empire Travel Services The 20 Mall 2080 Western Ave *Web:* www.empiretravel.com	Guilderland	NY	12084	518-869-0738		772
Empire Turkish Grill 12448 Memorial Dr *Web:* www.empireturkishgrill.com	Houston	TX	77024	713-827-7475		671
Empire Visionworks 2921 Erie Blvd E	Syracuse	NY	13224	315-446-5120		543
Empire West Inc 9270 Graton Rd PO Box 511 *TF:* 800-521-4261 ■ *Web:* www.empirewest.com	Graton	CA	95444	707-823-1190	823-8531	602
Empire-Fulton Ferry State Park 1 Water St *Web:* www.brooklynbridgepark.org	Brooklyn	NY	11201	718-222-9939		565
EmpireWorks Inc 1940 Olivera Rd *TF:* 888-278-8200 ■ *Web:* empireworks.com	Concord	CA	94520	888-278-8200		260
Empirical Foods Inc 891 Two Rivers Dr *Web:* empiricalfoods.com	Dakota Dunes	SD	57049	605-217-8000		296-26
Empirical Testing Corp 4628 Northpark Dr *Web:* empiricaltech.com	Colorado Springs	CO	80918	719-264-9937	264-1926	743
Empirix Inc 600 Technology Park Dr Ste 100 *Web:* www.empirix.com	Billerica	MA	01821	978-313-7000	313-7001	178-12
Emplicity 9851 Irvine Center Dr *TF:* 877-476-2339 ■ *Web:* www.emplicity.com	Irvine	CA	92618	714-668-1388		260
Employco USA Inc 350 E Ogden Ave *Web:* www.employco.com	Westmont	IL	60559	630-920-0000	920-1675	260
Employee & Family Resources (EFR) 505 Fifth Ave Ste 600 *TF:* 800-327-4692 ■ *Web:* www.efr.org	Des Moines	IA	50309	515-288-9020		631
Employee Assistance Professionals Association Inc (EAPA) 4350 N Fairfax Dr Ste 740 *TF:* 800-937-8461 ■ *Web:* www.eapassn.org	Arlington	VA	22203	703-387-1000	522-4585	49-12
Employee Benefit Management Services Inc (EBMS) 2075 Overland Ave *TF:* 800-777-3575 ■ *Web:* www.ebms.com	Billings	MT	59102	406-245-3575	652-5380	390
Employee Benefit Research Institute (EBRI) 1100 13th St NW Ste 878 *Web:* www.ebri.org	Washington	DC	20005	202-659-0670	775-6312	634
Employee Benefits Corp 1350 Deming Way Ste 200 *TF:* 800-346-2126 ■ *Web:* www.ebcflex.com	Middleton	WI	53562	608-831-8445	831-4790	390
Employee Benefits Group Inc (EBG) 4405 E West Hwy Ste 202 *TF:* 800-225-3242 ■ *Web:* www.ebg.com	Bethesda	MD	20814	301-718-4637		196
Employee Development Systems Inc 7308 S Alton Way Ste 2J *TF:* 800-282-3374 ■ *Web:* www.employeedevelopmentsystems.com	Centennial	CO	80112	800-282-3374		179
Employee Involvement Assn 11 W Monument Ave Ste 510	Dayton	OH	45402	937-586-3724		49-12
Employee Leasing Solutions Inc 1401 Manatee Ave W Ste 600	Bradenton	FL	34205	941-746-6567		390
Employee Management Services 435 Elm St *TF:* 888-651-1536 ■ *Web:* www.emshro.com	Cincinnati	OH	45202	513-651-3244	381-2764	631
Employee Motivation and Performance Assessment Inc 210 Park St *Web:* surveysforbusiness.com	Chelsea	MI	48118	734-368-3348		194
Employee Owned Holdings Inc 5500 N Sam Houston Pkwy W Ste 100 *Web:* www.eoh-inc.com	Houston	TX	77086	281-569-7000		791
Employee Resource Systems Inc 29 E Madison St Ste 1600 *Web:* allonehealth.com	Chicago	IL	60602	312-780-6316		196
Employees Only Inc 3256 University Dr Ste 25 *Web:* www.employeesonly.net	Auburn Hills	MI	48326	248-276-0950		194
Employer Benefits Inc 31 Keystone Ave *Web:* ebi-nv.com	Reno	NV	89503	775-786-6381		390
Employer Flexible 7102 N Sam Houston Pkwy W Ste 200 *TF:* 866-501-4942 ■ *Web:* www.employerflexible.com	Houston	TX	77064	866-501-4942		631
Employer Plan Services Inc 2180 N Loop W Ste 400 *TF:* 800-447-6588 ■ *Web:* www.epsibenefitsinc.com	Houston	TX	77018	713-351-3500		193
Employers Assn, The 3020 W Arrowood Rd *Web:* www.employersassoc.com	Charlotte	NC	28273	704-522-8011		317
Employers Choice Solutions Inc 22476 Sacramento Ave *Web:* www.employerchoice.com	Port Charlotte	FL	33954	941-627-0777		631
Employers Council on Flexible Compensation (ECFC) 1220 L St NW Ste 100-417 *Web:* www.ecfc.org	Washington	DC	20005	202-659-4300	618-6060	49-12

	Phone	Fax	Class
Employers Group 400 N Continental Blvd Ste 300 . . . . El Segundo CA 90245 *TF:* 800-748-8484 ■ *Web:* www.employersgroup.com	800-748-8484		193
Employers Insurance Company of Nevada 10375 Professional Cir. . . . . Reno NV 89521 *TF:* 888-682-6671 ■ *Web:* www.employers.com	888-682-6671		390
Employers Resource Management Co 1301 S Vista Ave Ste 200 . . . . Boise ID 83705 *TF:* 800-574-4668 ■ *Web:* www.employersresource.com	208-376-3000		570
Employment & Training Administration (ETA) (ETA) *Region 4* 525 Griffin St Rm 317. . . . . Dallas TX 75202 *Web:* www.dol.gov	972-850-4600	850-4605	340-15
Region I - Boston 25 New Sudbury St Rm E-350. . . . . Boston MA 02203 *Web:* www.dol.gov	617-788-0170	788-0101	340-15
Region II-Philadelphia 170 S Independence Mall W Ste 825 E . . . . . Philadelphia PA 19106 *Web:* www.dol.gov	215-861-5200	861-5260	340-15
Employment & Training Administration Regional Offices *Region 5 - Chicago* 230 S Dearborn St 6th Fl . . . . Chicago IL 60604 *Web:* www.dol.gov	312-596-5400	596-5401	340-15
Employment Policies Institute 1090 Vermont Ave NW Ste 800. . . . . Washington DC 20005 *Web:* www.epionline.org	202-463-7650		634
Employment Screening Resources 7110 Redwood Blvd Ste C . . . . Novato CA 94945 **Fax Area Code:* 800 ■ *TF:* 888-999-4474 ■ *Web:* www.esrcheck.com	415-898-0044	399-5423*	631
Employment Screening Services Inc 627 E Sprague Ave Ste 100 . . . . Spokane WA 99202 **Fax Area Code:* 800 ■ *TF:* 800-473-7778 ■ *Web:* www.employscreen.com	509-624-3851	321-2905*	635
Emporia Area Chamber of Commerce 719 Commercial St. . . . . Emporia KS 66801 *Web:* www.emporiakschamber.org	620-342-1600	342-3223	139
Emporia State Federal Credit Union 310 W 12th Ave . . . . Emporia KS 66801 *Web:* esfcu.com	620-342-2336		219
Emporia State University 1200 Commercial St. . . . . Emporia KS 66801 *TF:* 877-468-6378 ■ *Web:* www.emporia.edu	620-341-5477	341-5599	166
Empower Financials Inc 305 E Eisenhower Ste 318 . . . . Ann Arbor MI 48108 *Web:* empowerfin.com	734-747-9393		177
Empower IT Inc 7101 Wisconsin Ave . . . . Bethesda MD 20814 *Web:* www.empowerit.com	301-718-7600	718-7652	194
Empower Rf Systems Inc 316 W Florence Ave . . . . Inglewood CA 90301 *Web:* www.empowerrf.com	310-412-8100	412-9232	647
Empowered Networks Inc 1315 Pickering Pkwy Ste 200. . . . . Pickering ON L1V7G5 *TF:* 877-325-1855 ■ *Web:* empowerednetworks.com	905-837-6585		463
Empowering People Inc PO Box 1926 . . . . Orem UT 84059 **Fax Area Code:* 801 ■ *TF:* 800-456-7770 ■ *Web:* www.empoweringpeople.com	800-456-7770	762-0022*	637-2
Empresas Berrios Management PO Box 674-Reyde Los. . . . . Cidra PR 00739	787-653-9393		321
Empress Hotel 7766 Fay Ave. . . . . La Jolla CA 92037 *Web:* www.empress-hotel.com	858-454-3001		379
Empress Software Inc 11785 Beltsville Dr. . . . . Beltsville MD 20705 *TF:* 866-626-8888 ■ *Web:* www.empress.com	301-572-1600	220-1997	178-2
Emprise Corp 3900 Kennesaw 75 Pkwy N W Ste 125. . . . . Kennesaw GA 30144 *TF:* 800-278-2119 ■ *Web:* www.emprise-usa.com	770-425-1420		261
Emprise Financial Corp 257 N Broadway St PO Box 2970. . . . . Wichita KS 67202 *TF:* 800-201-7118 ■ *Web:* www.emprisebank.com	316-383-4301		69
Emprico Publishing Inc 4700 Marshall Dr W . . . . Vestal NY 13850	607-772-0559		94
EmpXtrack 150 Motor Pkwy Ste 401 . . . . Hauppauge NY 11788 *TF:* 888-840-2682 ■ *Web:* empxtrack.com	888-840-2682		41
EMR (Electric Motor Repair) 9100 Yellow Brick Rd Ste H . . . . Baltimore MD 21237 *TF:* 888-894-4810 ■ *Web:* www.emrco.com	410-467-8080	467-2512	300
EMR Inc 2110 Delaware St Ste B . . . . Lawrence KS 66046 *Web:* www.emr-inc.com	785-842-9013		667
Emrico Technologies LLC 15001 Huntgate Ln. . . . . Dumfries VA 22025 *Web:* emrico.com	703-763-4985		261
EMS Energy Institute 201 Old Main . . . . University Park PA 16802 *Web:* www.energy.psu.edu	814-863-1333	863-7432	668
EMS Industrial Inc 802 Live Oak Dr. . . . . Chesapeake VA 23320	757-424-0134		698
EMS Software LLC 6465 Greenwood Plaza Blvd Ste 600 . . . . Centennial CO 80111 *TF:* 800-440-3994 ■ *Web:* www.emssoftware.com	303-771-0110	796-7429	178-1
EMSD (East Maine School District 63) 10150 Dee Rd. . . . . Des Plaines IL 60016 *Web:* www.emsd63.org	847-299-1900	299-9963	685
EMS-Tech Inc 699 Dundas St W . . . . Belleville ON K8N4Z2 *TF:* 844-450-8324 ■ *Web:* www.ems-tech.net	613-966-6611		256
EMT International Inc 780 Centerline Dr . . . . Hobart WI 54155 *Web:* www.emtinternational.com	920-468-5475	468-7991	100
EMTA (Emerging Markets Traders Assn) 360 Madison Ave 18th Fl . . . . New York NY 10017 *Web:* www.emta.org	212-313-1100	313-1016	49-2
EMTA (Erie Metropolitan Transit Authority) 127 E 14th St . . . . Erie PA 16503 *Web:* www.ride-the-e.com	814-452-3515		468
Emtec Consultants, Professional Engineers PLLC 3555 Veterans Memorial Hw. . . . . Ronkonkoma NY 11779 *Web:* emtec-engineers.com	631-981-3990		261
Emtech Laboratories Inc 7745 Garland Cir . . . . Roanoke VA 24019 *Web:* www.emtechlaboratories.com	540-265-9156	265-9164	477
Emtek Products Inc 15250 Stafford St . . . . City of Industry CA 91744 *TF:* 800-356-2741 ■ *Web:* emtek.com	626-961-0413		350
Emtex Inc 42 Cherry Hill Dr Ste B . . . . Danvers MA 01923 *TF:* 800-840-7035 ■ *Web:* emtexglobal.com	978-907-4500	907-4555	745-2
Emulso Corp 2750 Kenmore Ave . . . . Tonawanda NY 14150 *Web:* www.emulso.com	716-854-2889	854-2809	151
EMW Carpets & Furniture 2141 S Broadway . . . . Denver CO 80210 *Web:* www.emwcarpets.com	303-744-2754	744-9276	131
EMW Inc 10 W 2nd Ave . . . . Lititz PA 17543 *Web:* emwcorp.com	717-626-0248	626-0396	439
EMW Laser Inc 6840 114th Ave N. . . . . Largo FL 33773 *Web:* www.emwlaser.com	727-548-0452		494
EN Bisso & Son Inc 1 Walnut St . . . . New Orleans LA 70118 *Web:* enbisso.com	504-828-3296	831-6701	539
EN Engineering LLC 28100 Torch Pkwy Ste 400 . . . . Warrenville IL 60555 *Web:* www.enengineering.com	630-353-4000	353-7777	261
ENA (Emergency Nurses Assn) 915 Lee St . . . . Des Plaines IL 60016 *TF:* 800-900-9659 ■ *Web:* ena.org	847-460-4000	460-4001	49-8
Ena Meat Packing Inc 240 E 5th St. . . . . Paterson NJ 07524 *Web:* www.enameatpacking.com	973-742-4790		473
Enabling Technologies Corp 12226 Long Green Pk. . . . . Glen Arm MD 21057 *Web:* www.enablingtechcorp.com	443-625-5100		177
Enagic USA Inc 4115 Spencer St. . . . . Torrance CA 90503 *TF:* 833-579-7559 ■ *Web:* www.enagic.com	310-542-7700	542-1700	610
Enanta Pharmaceuticals Inc 500 Arsenal St . . . . Watertown MA 02472 *Web:* www.enanta.com	617-607-0800	607-0530	668
ENBALA Power Networks Ltd 360 Bay St Ste 401. . . . . Toronto ON M5H2V6 *Web:* www.enbala.com	416-623-2626		387
Enbase LLC 24 Greenway Plz Ste 1050 . . . . Houston TX 77046 *Web:* www.enbasesolutions.com	713-492-0008		538
Enbridge Energy Partners LP 1100 Louisiana Ste 3300 . . . . Houston TX 77002 *NYSE: EEP* ■ *TF:* 800-481-2804 ■ *Web:* www.enbridgepartners.com	713-821-2000		597
Encentus Federal Credit Union 1320 S Lewis Ave . . . . Tulsa OK 74104 *TF:* 800-290-1199 ■ *Web:* encentusfcu.org	918-430-3500	430-3510	219
Enchanted Garden Florist 225 N Main St . . . . Springhill LA 71075 *TF:* 800-417-4363 ■ *Web:* www.enchantedgardenfloristspringhill.net	318-539-5571		293
Enchanted Rock State Natural Area 16710 Ranch Rd 965 . . . . Fredericksburg TX 78624 *Web:* tpwd.texas.gov	830-685-3636		565
Enchantment Resort 525 Boynton Canyon Rd. . . . . Sedona AZ 86336 **Fax Area Code:* 928 ■ *TF:* 800-826-4180 ■ *Web:* www.enchantmentresort.com	844-244-9489	282-9249*	669
Encinitas Chamber of Commerce 527 Encinitas Blvd . . . . Encinitas CA 92024 *TF:* 800-953-6041 ■ *Web:* encinitaschamber.com	760-753-6041	753-6270	139
Encinitas Union School District 101 S Rancho Santa Fe Rd . . . . Encinitas CA 92024 *Web:* www.eusd.net	760-944-4300		685
Encino Chamber of Commerce 4933 Balboa Blvd . . . . Encino CA 91316 *Web:* encinochamber.org	818-789-4711	789-2485	139
EnCirca Inc 400 W Cummings Pk Ste 1725-307 . . . . Woburn MA 01801 *Web:* www.encirca.com	781-942-9975	823-8911	396
Encircle Publications PO Box 187 . . . . Farmington ME 04938 *Web:* www.encirclepub.com	207-778-0467		637-10
Encision Inc 6797 Winchester Cir . . . . Boulder CO 80301 *OTC: ECIA* ■ *TF:* 800-998-0986 ■ *Web:* www.encision.com	303-444-2600	444-2693	476
Enclave Suites of Orlando 6165 Carrier Dr. . . . . Orlando FL 32819 *TF:* 800-457-0077 ■ *Web:* www.enclavesuites.com	407-351-1155		379
Enclos Corp 2770 Blue Water Rd . . . . Eagan MN 55121 **Fax Area Code:* 651 ■ *TF:* 888-234-2966 ■ *Web:* www.enclos.com	888-234-2966	994-6360*	189-6
ENCO Laboratories Inc 10775 Central Port Dr. . . . . Orlando FL 32824 *Web:* encolabs.com	407-826-5314	850-6945	743
Encoder Products Co 464276 Hwy 95 S PO Box 249 . . . . Sagle ID 83860 *TF:* 800-366-5412 ■ *Web:* www.encoder.com	208-263-8541	263-0541	201
Encoll Corporation Inc 4576 Enterprise St . . . . Fremont CA 94538 *Web:* www.encoll.com	510-795-8581	795-7571	317
Encompass Financial Advisors Inc 11820 SW Pearson Ct . . . . Beaverton OR 97008	503-643-8075		401
Encompass Group LLC 615 Macon Rd . . . . McDonough GA 30253 *TF:* 800-284-4540 ■ *Web:* www.encompassgroup.com	770-957-1211		155-19
Encompass Health Corp 3660 Grandview Pkwy Ste 200. . . . . Birmingham AL 35243 *NYSE: EHC* ■ *TF:* 800-310-4919 ■ *Web:* www.encompasshealth.com	205-967-7116		374-6
Encompass Health Rehabilitation Hospital of Jonesboro 1201 Fleming Ave. . . . . Jonesboro AR 72401 **Fax Area Code:* 866 ■ *Web:* encompasshealth.com	870-932-0440	324-5444*	374-6
Encompass Iowa LLC 1420 1st Ave NE. . . . . Cedar Rapids IA 52402 *Web:* www.encompassiowa.com	319-862-0221		180
Encompass Media Inc 11-11 44th Dr. . . . . Long Island City NY 11101 *Web:* www.emgmediainc.com	212-993-9429		5
Encompass Niagara Federal Credit Union 2525 Military Rd. . . . . Niagara Falls NY 14304 *Web:* encompassniagara.com	716-236-7678		219
Encon Intl 7307 Remcon Cir 101 . . . . El Paso TX 79912 *Web:* www.enconinternational.com	915-833-3740		261
Encon Safety Products Co 6825 W Sam Houston Pkwy N PO Box 3826 . . . . . . Houston TX 77041 *TF:* 800-283-6266 ■ *Web:* www.enconsafety.com	713-466-1449	466-1703	678
Encore Capital Group Inc 3111 Camino Del Rio N Ste 1300. . . . . San Diego CA 92108 *NASDAQ: ECPG* ■ *TF:* 877-445-4581 ■ *Web:* www.encorecapital.com	858-560-2600		160
Encore Cbt Co 479 Lambourne Ave. . . . . Worthington OH 43085 *Web:* www.encorecbt.com	614-888-4179		463

Name / Address	City	State	ZIP	Phone	Fax	Class
Encore Consumer Capital 111 Pine St Ste 1825 *Web:* encoreconsumercapital.com	San Francisco	CA	94111	415-296-9850		194
Encore Creative Inc 410 S Madison Dr *Web:* www.encorecreative.com	Tempe	AZ	85281	480-736-2800		149
Encore Event Technologies 1 N Arlington 1500 W Shure Dr Ste 175 **Fax Area Code:* 847 ■ *TF:* 800-836-8361 ■ *Web:* www.encoreglobal.com	Arlington Heights	IL	60004	800-836-8361	358-3106*	52
Encore Health Network 8520 Allison Pointe Blvd Ste 200 *TF:* 888-574-8180 ■ *Web:* www.encoreconnect.com	Indianapolis	IN	46250	317-621-4250		390
Encore Hollywood 6344 Fountain Ave *Web:* www.encorepost.com	Los Angeles	CA	90028	323-466-7663		512
Encore Image Inc 303 W Main St *TF:* 800-791-1187 ■ *Web:* www.encoreimage.com	Ontario	CA	91762	909-986-4632	988-6376	5
Encore Manufacturing Company Inc 2415 Ashland Ave *TF:* 800-267-4255 ■ *Web:* www.encoreequipment.com	Beatrice	NE	68310	800-267-4255		429
Encore Networks Inc 3800 Concorde Pkwy Ste 1500 *Web:* www.encorenetworks.com	Chantilly	VA	20151	703-318-7750	787-4625	173-3
Encore Web Works Inc 1200 NW S Outer Rd Ste 319 *Web:* encorewebworks.com	Blue Springs	MO	64015	816-988-7299		177
Encore Wire Corp 1329 Millwood Rd *NASDAQ: WIRE* ■ *TF:* 800-962-9473 ■ *Web:* www.encorewire.com	McKinney	TX	75069	972-562-9473	562-3644	813
Encotech Engineering Cnsltnts 8500 Bluffstone Cv *Web:* www.encotechengineering.com	Austin	TX	78759	512-338-1101		261
Encounter Books 900 Broadway Ste 601 *TF:* 855-203-7220 ■ *Web:* www.encounterbooks.com	New York	NY	10003	212-871-6310		637-2
Encounter Video Inc 14825 NW Ash St *TF:* 800-677-7607 ■ *Web:* www.encountervideo.com	Portland	OR	97231	800-677-7607		514
Encur Inc 200 Division St *Web:* encur.com	Keyport	NJ	07735	732-264-2098		261
Encyclopaedia Britannica Inc 331 N La Salle St *TF:* 800-323-1229 ■ *Web:* www.britannica.com	Chicago	IL	60654	312-347-7159	294-2104	637-2
Encyclopedia.com 360 N Michigan Ave Ste 1900 *Web:* www.encyclopedia.com	Chicago	IL	60601	312-224-5000	224-5001	397
End Point Corp 304 Park Ave S Ste 214 *Web:* www.endpoint.com	New York	NY	10010	212-929-6923	929-6927	180
Endacea Inc 2 Davis Dr *Web:* www.endacea.com	Research Triangle Park	NC	27709	919-406-1888		668
Endagraph Inc 9000 Corporate Cir **Fax Area Code:* 724 ■ *TF:* 800-295-9384 ■ *Web:* www.endagraph.com	Export	PA	15632	800-295-9384	327-5289*	9
Endeavour Capital Inc 760 SW Ninth Ave Ste 2300 *Web:* endeavourcapital.com	Portland	OR	97205	503-223-2721		690
Enderle Group Inc 389 Photinia Ln *Web:* www.enderlegroup.com	San Jose	CA	95127	408-272-8560		463
Enders Island PO Box 399 *Web:* www.endersisland.org	Mystic	CT	06355	860-536-0565	572-7655	673
Enders Reservoir State Recreation Area 73122 338th Ave *Web:* outdoornebraska.gov	Enders	NE	69027	308-394-5118		565
Endevco Corp 30700 Rancho Viejo Rd *TF:* 800-982-6732 ■ *Web:* endevco.com	San Juan Capistrano	CA	92675	949-493-8181	661-7231	472
Endicott 57120 707th Rd *Web:* www.endicott.com	Endicott	NE	68350	402-729-3315		270
Endicott College 376 Hale St *TF:* 800-325-1114 ■ *Web:* www.endicott.edu	Beverly	MA	01915	978-927-0585	232-2520	166
Endicott Precision Inc 1328 Campville Rd *Web:* www.endicottprecision.com	Endicott	NY	13760	607-754-7076		697
Endicott Research Group Inc 2601 Wayne St *TF:* 800-215-5866 ■ *Web:* www.ergpower.com	Endicott	NY	13760	607-754-9187	754-9255	696
Endicott Rock State Historic Site 17 Endicott St *Web:* www.nhstateparks.org	Laconia	NH	03246	603-271-3556		565
Endive Software 2220 Meridian Blvd Ste TF616 *Web:* www.endivesoftware.com	Minden	NV	89423	941-312-2199		180
Endo Pharmaceuticals Inc 1400 Atwater Dr *TF:* 800-462-3636 ■ *Web:* www.endo.com	Malvern	PA	19355	484-216-0000		582
Endocrine Society 8401 Connecticut Ave Ste 900 *TF:* 888-363-6274 ■ *Web:* www.endocrine.org	Chevy Chase	MD	20815	301-941-0200	941-0259	49-8
Endologix Inc 11 Studebaker *NASDAQ: ELGX* ■ **Fax Area Code:* 877 ■ *TF:* 800-983-2284 ■ *Web:* endologix.com	Irvine	CA	92618	949-457-9546	843-1500*	476
Endomedix Inc 211 Warren St *Web:* endomedix.com	Newark	NJ	07103	848-248-1883		475
Endometriosis Assn 8585 N 76th Pl *TF:* 800-992-3636 ■ *Web:* endometriosisassn.org	Milwaukee	WI	53223	414-355-2200	355-6065	48-17
EndoShape Inc 5425 Airport Blvd Ste 101 *TF:* 844-870-5070 ■ *Web:* www.endoshape.com	Boulder	CO	80301	303-951-6898		475
Endot Industries Inc 60 Green Pond Rd *TF:* 800-443-6368 ■ *Web:* www.endot.com	Rockaway	NJ	07866	973-625-8500	625-4087	596
Endotec Inc 20 Valley St *Web:* www.endotec.com	South Orange	NJ	07079	973-762-0095		475
Endotronix Inc 815 Ogden Ave *Web:* endotronix.com	Lisle	IL	60532	630-473-3200		743
Endovac Animal Health 6080 Bass Ln **Fax Area Code:* 573 ■ *TF:* 800-944-7563 ■ *Web:* endovacanimalhealth.com	Columbia	MO	65201	800-944-7563	874-7108*	584
Endress+Hauser Inc 2350 Endress Pl *TF:* 888-363-7377 ■ *Web:* www.us.endress.com	Greenwood	IN	46143	317-535-7138	535-8498	201
Endries International Inc 714 W Ryan St PO Box 69 *TF:* 800-852-5821 ■ *Web:* www.endries.com	Brillion	WI	54110	920-756-5381	756-3772	385
Endsight 1440 Fourth St Ste D *Web:* www.endsight.net	Berkeley	CA	94710	510-280-2000		196
Endstream Communications LLC 401 E 34th St *Web:* www.endstream.com	New York	NY	10016	212-796-5502		387
Endtime Inc PO Box 940729 *TF:* 800-363-8463 ■ *Web:* www.endtime.com	Plano	TX	75074	800-363-8463		637-9
Endura Coatings LLC 42250 Yearego Dr *TF:* 800-336-3872 ■ *Web:* www.enduracoatings.com	Sterling Heights	MI	48314	586-739-0101	739-4040	481
Endura Plastics Inc 7955 Chardon Rd *TF:* 800-376-4466 ■ *Web:* endura.com	Kirtland	OH	44094	440-951-4466	256-3053	604
Endura Products Inc 8817 W Market St *TF:* 800-334-2006 ■ *Web:* www.enduraproducts.com	Colfax	NC	27235	800-334-2006		236
Endurance Carbide 4475 Marlea Dr *Web:* www.endurancecarbide.com	Saginaw	MI	48601	989-777-7950	777-8251	757
Endurance IT Services 295 Bendix Rd Ste 300 *Web:* www.endurance-it.com	Virginia Beach	VA	23452	757-379-8682	257-7173	196
Endurance Resources III LLC 15455 Dallas Pkwy Ste 1050 *Web:* www.enduranceresourcesllc.com	Addison	TX	75001	469-771-4524		536
Enduro Composites Inc 16602 Central Green Blvd *TF:* 800-231-7271 ■ *Web:* endurocomposites.com	Houston	TX	77032	713-358-4000	358-4100	601
Enduro Rubber Co 685 S Chestnut St *Web:* www.endurorubber.com	Ravenna	OH	44266	330-296-9603		676
Endview Plantation 362 Yorktown Rd *TF:* 888-493-7386 ■ *Web:* www.endview.org	Newport News	VA	23603	757-887-1862	888-3369	520
Endyn Manufacturing Inc 9615 Ball St *Web:* www.endyn.com	San Antonio	TX	78217	210-655-6046	655-6070	454
ENE Systems Inc 480 Neponset St Ste 11D *Web:* enesystems.com	Canton	MA	02021	781-828-6770		256
Eneflux Armtek Magnetics Inc 700 Hicksville Rd Ste 110 *TF:* 877-363-3589 ■ *Web:* www.eamagnetics.com	Bethpage	NY	11714	516-576-3434		458
Enel X One Marina Park Dr Ste 400 *NASDAQ: ENOC* ■ *Web:* www.enelx.com	Boston	MA	02110	617-224-9900	224-9910	463
Enerac Inc 67 Bond St *TF:* 800-695-3637 ■ *Web:* www.enerac.com	Westbury	NY	11590	516-997-2100		201
Enerbank USA Inc 1245 E Brickyard Rd Ste 600 *TF:* 888-390-1220 ■ *Web:* enerbank.com	Salt Lake City	UT	84106	888-390-1220		217
Enerco 750 3rd Ave 9th Fl *Web:* ener.co	New York	NY	10017	212-572-0784		610
EnerCom 410 17th St Ste 250 *Web:* www.enercominc.com	Denver	CO	80202	303-296-8834		539
Enercon Engineering Inc 201 Altorfer Ln *TF:* 800-218-8831 ■ *Web:* www.enercon-eng.com	East Peoria	IL	61611	309-694-1418	694-3703	203
Enercon Services Inc 5100 E Skelly Dr Ste 450 *Web:* www.enercon.com	Tulsa	OK	74135	918-665-7693	665-7232	261
Enerfab Inc 4955 Spring Grove Ave *TF:* 800-772-5066 ■ *Web:* www.enerfab.com	Cincinnati	OH	45232	513-641-0500		91
Enerflex Systems Ltd 1331 Macleod Trail SE Ste 904 *TF:* 800-242-3178 ■ *Web:* www.enerflex.com	Calgary	AB	T2G0K3	403-387-6377		386
Ener-G Foods Inc 5960 First Ave S PO Box 84487 *TF:* 800-331-5222 ■ *Web:* www.ener-g.com	Seattle	WA	98124	206-767-3928	764-3398	296-36
Energage Inc 397 Eagleview Blvd Ste 200 *Web:* www.energage.com	Exton	PA	19341	484-323-6300		463
Energetic Services Inc 13366 Thompkins Frontage Rd PO Box 6639 *Web:* energeticservices.com	Charlie Lake	BC	V1J4J1	250-785-4761	785-9980	478
Energetics International Inc PO Box 17056 *TF:* 866-815-0696 ■ *Web:* www.energems.com	Snowmass Village	CO	81615	970-923-0696		637-2
Energetiq Technology Inc 7 Constitution Way *Web:* www.energetiq.com	Woburn	MA	01801	781-939-0763		454
Energize Inc 5450 Wissahickon Ave *TF:* 800-395-9800 ■ *Web:* www.energizeinc.com	Philadelphia	PA	19144	215-438-8342	438-0434	423
Energy & Commerce, The *Energy & Commerce Committee* 2125 Rayburn Bldg *Web:* www.energycommerce.house.gov	Washington	DC	20515	202-225-2927		342-1
Energy & Environmental Building Alliance, The 6520 Edenvale Blvd Ste 112 *Web:* www.eeba.org	Eden Prairie	MN	55346	952-881-1098		242
Energy & Environmental Research Ctr (EERC) University of N Dakota 15 N 23rd St S 9018 *Web:* undeerc.org	Grand Forks	ND	58202	701-777-5000	777-5181	668
Energy & Resource Solutions Inc 120 Water St Ste 350 *Web:* www.ers-inc.com	North Andover	MA	01845	978-521-2550		194
Energy Air Inc 5401 Energy Air Ct *Web:* energyair.com	Orlando	FL	32810	407-708-9122	886-7580	610
Energy Alloys LLC 3 Waterway Square Pl Ste 600 *TF:* 866-448-9831 ■ *Web:* www.ealloys.com	The Woodlands	TX	77380	832-601-5800	601-5801	490
Energy Annex, The 1123 W Washington Blvd Fl 3 *Web:* www.energyannex.com	Chicago	IL	60607	312-733-2639	733-2551	271
Energy Authority Inc, The 301 W Bay St Ste 2600 *Web:* www3.teainc.org	Jacksonville	FL	32202	904-356-3900		463
Energy BBDO 225 N Michigan Ave *Web:* www.energybbdo.com	Chicago	IL	60601	312-337-7860		5
Energy Beam Sciences Inc 29 Kripes Rd *TF:* 800-992-9037 ■ *Web:* ebsciences.com	East Granby	CT	06026	860-653-0411		419
Energy Capital Solutions LP 2651 N Harwood Ste 410 *Web:* energycapitalsolutions.com	Dallas	TX	75201	214-219-8200		70

Name / Address	Phone	Fax	Class
Energy Concepts Inc 404 Washington Blvd ... Mundelein IL 60060 *TF:* 800-621-1247 ■ *Web:* www.eci-info.com	847-837-8191		703
Energy Control Systems Inc 2940 Cole Ct ... Norcross GA 30071 *TF:* 800-648-0970 ■ *Web:* energycontrolsystems.com	770-448-0651	446-1319	248
Energy Conversion Devices Inc 2956 Waterview Dr ... Rochester Hills MI 48309 *OTC: ENERQ*	248-293-0440	844-1214	253
Energy Conversion Technologies Inc 1271 Denison St Unit 56-59 ... Markham ON L3R4B5 *Web:* www.energyconversiontech.com	905-947-4300		203
Energy Conversions Inc 6411 Pacific Hwy E ... Tacoma WA 98424 *Web:* www.energyconversions.com	253-922-6670	922-2258	262
Energy Economics Inc 109 S St SE ... Dodge Center MN 55927 *TF:* 800-733-2557 ■ *Web:* www.eei.com	507-374-2557	374-2646	188-10
Energy Engineering Associates Inc 6615 Vaught Ranch Rd Ste 200 ... Austin TX 78730 *Web:* www.eeace.com	512-328-0082		261
Energy Enterprises Inc 10 Mill St ... Mount Morris NY 14510 *TF:* 800-724-9394 ■ *Web:* energyenterprisesinc.com	585-658-4820	658-4833	194
Energy Exchanger Co 1844 N Garnett Rd ... Tulsa OK 74116 *Web:* energyexchanger.com	918-437-3000	437-7144	91
Energy Focus Inc 32000 Aurora Rd ... Solon OH 44139 *OTC: EFOI* ■ *TF:* 800-327-7877 ■ *Web:* www.energyfocus.com	440-715-1300	715-1314	439
Energy Foundation, The 301 Battery St 5th Fl ... San Francisco CA 94111 *Web:* www.ef.org	415-561-6700		305
Energy Information Administration 1000 Independence Ave SW ... Washington DC 20585 *Web:* www.eia.gov	202-586-8800	586-0727	340-9
Energy Inspectors 2570 S Miller Ln ... Las Vegas NV 89117 *Web:* www.energyinspectors.com	702-365-8080		610
Energy Intelligence Group 5 E 37th St 5th Fl ... New York NY 10016 *Web:* www.energyintel.com	212-532-1112	532-4479	637-9
Energy Laboratories Inc 2393 Salt Creek Hwy ... Casper WY 82601 *TF:* 888-235-0515 ■ *Web:* www.energylab.com	307-235-0515	234-1639	743
Energy Labs Inc 9651 Airway Rd Ste E ... San Diego CA 92154 *Web:* www.energylabs.com	619-671-0100		14
Energy Management Solutions Inc 7935 Stone Creek Dr Ste 140 ... Chanhassen MN 55317 *Web:* www.emsenergy.com	952-767-7450		463
Energy Manufacturing Company Inc 204 Plastic Ln ... Monticello IA 52310 *Web:* www.energymfg.com	319-465-3537	465-5279	223
Energy Matters Inc 8045 Big Bend Blvd Ste 106 ... Saint Louis MO 63119 **Fax Area Code:* 877 ■ *Web:* www.energymat.com	314-918-7608	918-7607*	194
Energy Meter Systems 1161 S Main St ... Hennessey OK 73742 **Fax Area Code:* 405 ■ *TF:* 800-742-9376 ■ *Web:* www.energymetersystems.com	806-665-5700	853-4974*	201
Energy Northwest 76 N Power Plant Loop ... Richland WA 99354 *Web:* www.energy-northwest.com	509-372-5000		245
Energy Panel Structures Inc 603 N Van Gordon Ave ... Graettinger IA 51342 **Fax Area Code:* 712 ■ *TF:* 800-967-2130 ■ *Web:* www.epsbuildings.com	800-967-2130	859-3275*	106
Energy Petroleum Co 2130 Kienlen Ave ... Saint Louis MO 63121 *TF:* 800-536-6828 ■ *Web:* www.energypetroleum.com	314-383-3700		316
Energy Project, The 1 Larkin Plz 4th Fl ... Yonkers NY 10701 *Web:* theenergyproject.com	914-207-8800		463
Energy Recovery Council (ERC) 2200 Wilson Blvd Ste 310 ... Arlington VA 22201 *Web:* energyrecoverycouncil.org	202-467-6240		48-12
Energy Recovery Inc 1717 Doolittle Dr ... San Leandro CA 94577 *NASDAQ: ERII* ■ *Web:* www.energyrecovery.com	510-483-7370	483-7371	806
Energy Research & Generation Inc 964 Stanford Ave ... Oakland CA 94608 *Web:* ergaerospace.com	510-658-9785	658-7428	143
Energy Sciences Inc 42 Industrial Way ... Wilmington MA 01887 *Web:* www.ebeam.com	978-694-9000	694-9046	386
Energy Security Analysis Inc (ESAI) 401 Edgewater Pl Ste 640 ... Wakefield MA 01880 *Web:* www.esai.com	781-245-2036	245-8706	401
Energy Services Group International Inc (ESG) 3601 La Grange Pkwy ... Toano VA 23168 *Web:* www.esgi.net	757-741-4040	741-4045	721
Energy Spectrum Advisors Inc 5956 Sherry Ln Ste 900 ... Dallas TX 75225 *Web:* securities.bokfinancial.com	214-987-6100		690
Energy Steel & Supply Co 3123 John Conley Dr ... Lapeer MI 48446 *TF:* 866-261-3772 ■ *Web:* www.energysteel.com	810-538-4990		480
Energy Systems Design Inc 7135 E Camelback Rd Ste 275 ... Scottsdale AZ 85251 *Web:* www.esdengineers.com	480-481-4900	481-4903	261
Energy Transfer LP 3738 Oak Lawn Ave ... Dallas TX 75219 *NYSE: ETP* ■ *Web:* www.energytransfer.com	214-981-0700		316
Energy Transformation Systems Inc 43353 Osgood Rd ... Fremont CA 94539 *TF:* 800-752-8208 ■ *Web:* www.etslan.com	510-656-2012		767
Energy Ventures Analysis Inc 1901 N Moore St Ste 1200 ... Arlington VA 22209 *Web:* www.evainc.com	703-276-8900	276-9541	194
Energy Water Solutions LLC 9595 Six Pines Dr Ste 8210 ... The Woodlands TX 77380 *Web:* energywatersolutions.com	713-722-0408		536
Energy West Inc 1 First Ave S ... Great Falls MT 59401 *Web:* www.ewst.com	406-791-7500		787
Energy Worldnet 1210 S Bus Hwy 81/287 ... Decatur TX 76234 *Web:* www.energyworldnet.com	940-626-1941		192
ENERGYneering Solutions Inc 15820 Barclay Dr ... Sisters OR 97759 *Web:* energyneeringsolutions.com	541-549-8766		261
Energynetcom Inc 7201 I-40 W Ste 319 ... Amarillo TX 79106 *TF:* 877-351-4488 ■ *Web:* www.energynet.com	806-351-2953		690
EnergySolutions LLC 423 West Broadway Ste 200 ... Salt Lake City UT 84101 *Web:* www.energysolutions.com	801-649-2000	321-0453	804
EnergyUnited Electric Membership Corp PO Box 1831 ... Statesville NC 28687 *TF:* 800-522-3793 ■ *Web:* www.energyunited.com	704-873-5241		245
EnergyWorks Inc 71 Old Mill Bottom Rd N Ste 101 ... Annapolis MD 21409 *Web:* www.energyworks.com	410-349-2001	349-2063	463
EnerNex Corp 620 Mabry Hood Rd Ste 300 ... Knoxville TN 37932 *Web:* www.enernex.com	865-218-4600		192
Enerpac PO Box 3241 ... Milwaukee WI 53201 *TF:* 800-433-2766 ■ *Web:* www.enerpac.com	262-293-1600	781-1049	759
Enerplus Resources Fund 3000 Dome Tower 333 Seventh Ave SW Ste 3000 .. Calgary AB T2P2Z1 *TF:* 877-576-5636 ■ *Web:* www.enerplus.com	403-298-2200	298-2211	405
Enersul LP 7210 Blackfood Terr SE ... Calgary AB T2H1M5 *Web:* www.enersul.com	403-253-5969	259-2771	143
EnerSys 2366 Bernville Rd ... Reading PA 19605 *NYSE: ENS* ■ *TF:* 800-538-3627 ■ *Web:* www.enersys.com	610-208-1991	372-8457	74
EnerTech Capital 1 Tower Bridge 100 Front St Ste 1225 ... West Conshohocken PA 19428 *Web:* www.enertechcapital.com	484-539-1872	539-1870	792
Ener-Tel Services Inc 1911 S Bryant Blvd ... San Angelo TX 76903 *Web:* www.ener-tel.com	325-658-8375	653-2936	175
Enertopia Corp 1130 W Pender St Ste 950 ... Vancouver BC V6E4A4 *Web:* www.enertopia.com	604-602-1675		536
EnerVision Inc 4170 Ashford Dunwoody Rd Ste 550 ... Atlanta GA 30319 *TF:* 888-999-8840 ■ *Web:* www.enervision-inc.com	678-510-2900		194
Enesco LLC 225 Windsor Dr ... Itasca IL 60143 *TF:* 800-436-3726 ■ *Web:* www.enesco.com	630-875-5300		334
E-Net Corp 300 Valley St ... Sausalito CA 94965 *Web:* www.enet.com	415-332-6200	339-9592	178-12
Enetics Inc 830 Canning Pkwy ... Victor NY 14564 *Web:* www.enetics.com	585-924-5010	924-7271	246
eNcura Inc 715 N Pastoria Ave ... Sunnyvale CA 94085 *Web:* www.eneura.com	408-245-6400	245-6424	743
Enevate Corp 101 Theory Ste 200 ... Irvine CA 92617 *Web:* www.enevate.com	949-243-0399		253
En-fab Inc 3905 Jensen Dr ... Houston TX 77026 *Web:* www.en-fabinc.com	713-225-4913	224-7937	537
Enfield Correctional Institution 289 Shaker Rd PO Box 1500 ... Enfield CT 06082 *Web:* portal.ct.gov	860-814-4300		213
Enfield Public Library 104 Middle Rd ... Enfield CT 06082 *Web:* www.enfield-ct.gov	860-763-7510		434-3
Enfield Square 90 Elm St ... Enfield CT 06082 *Web:* www.shopenfieldmall.com	860-745-7000	745-3007	460
Enflite Inc 105 Cooperative Way ... Georgetown TX 78626 *Web:* lifeport.com	512-868-3399	868-3320	22
Enflo Corp 315 Lake Ave ... Bristol CT 06010 *TF:* 888-887-4093 ■ *Web:* www.enflo.com	860-589-0014	589-7179	600
Enfold Systems Inc 4617 Montrose Blvd ... Houston TX 77006 *Web:* www.enfoldsystems.com	713-942-2377		177
Enform 1538 25 Ave NE ... Calgary AB T2E8Y3 *Web:* www.energysafetycanada.com	403-250-9606		196
E-N-G Mobile Systems Inc 2245 Via De Mercados ... Concord CA 94520 *TF:* 800-662-4522 ■ *Web:* www.e-n-g.com	925-798-4060	798-0152	514
Engage Communications Inc 9565 Soquel Dr ... Aptos CA 95003 *Web:* www.engagecom.com	831-688-1021	688-1421	173-3
Engage Technologies Corp 7041 Boone Ave N ... Brooklyn Park MN 55428 *TF:* 800-877-5658 ■ *Web:* www.engagetechnologies.net	800-877-5658		388
Engage3 Inc 501 Second St ... Davis CA 95616 *Web:* www.engage3.com	530-231-5485	231-5325	393
EngagePoint 3901 Calverton Blvd Ste 110 ... Calverton MD 20705	301-388-7900		177
Engel Eliot (Rep D - NY) 2426 Rayburn House Office Bldg ... Washington DC 20515 *Web:* www.engel.house.gov	202-225-2464	225-5513	342-2
Engel Machinery Inc 3740 Board Rd ... York PA 17406 *Web:* www.engelglobal.com	717-764-6818		98
Engel Realty Company Inc 951 Eighteenth St S Ste 200 ... Birmingham AL 35201 *Web:* www.engelrealty.com	205-939-6800		652
Engelberg-Kristy Animal Hospital 181 Kings Hwy ... Fairfield CT 06825 *Web:* engelbergkristy.com	203-367-4475		794
Engelberth Construction Inc 463 Mtn View Dr Ste 200 2nd Fl ... Colchester VT 05446 *TF:* 800-639-9011 ■ *Web:* www.engelberth.com	802-655-0100		186
Engelman Accountancy Corp 177 Bovet Rd Ste 100 ... San Mateo CA 94402 *Web:* engelmanaccountancy.com	650-344-6525		2
Engelman Berger PC 3636 N Central Ave Ste 700 ... Phoenix AZ 85012 *Web:* www.eblawyers.com	602-271-9090		428
Engelson Assoc 3317 Mormon Coulee Rd ... La Crosse WI 54601 *Web:* cpas-4biz.com	608-788-2181	788-3162	2
EngenderHealth Inc 505 Ninth St NW Ste 601 ... Washington DC 20004 **Fax Area Code:* 212 ■ *TF:* 800-564-2872 ■ *Web:* www.engenderhealth.org	202-902-2000	561-8067*	48-17
Engenius Inc 31077 Schoolcraft Rd ... Livonia MI 48150 *Web:* www.engenius.com	734-522-2120		180

Company	Address	City	State	ZIP	Phone	Fax	Class
EnGenius Technologies Inc	1580 Scenic Ave *Web:* www.engeniustech.com	Costa Mesa	CA	92626	714-432-8668		246
Engent Inc	3140 Northwoods Pkwy Ste 300A *Web:* www.engentaat.com	Norcross	GA	30071	678-990-3320	990-3324	695
Engenuity Group Inc	1280 N Congress Ave Ste 101 *Web:* engenuitygroup.com	West Palm Beach	FL	33409	561-655-1151	832-9390	196
Engeo Inc	2010 Crow Canyon Pl Ste 250 *Web:* www.engeo.com	San Ramon	CA	94583	925-866-9000		261
Enghouse Interactive	2095 W Pinnacle Peak Rd Ste 110 *Web:* www.enghouseinteractive.com	Phoenix	AZ	85027	602-789-2800		178-1
Enghouse Systems Ltd	80 Tiverton Ct Ste 800 *TSX:* ENGH ■ *TF:* 866-233-4606 ■ *Web:* www.enghouse.com	Markham	ON	L3R0G4	905-946-3200	946-3201	178-10
Engine Company No 28	644 S Figueroa St *Web:* engineco.com	Los Angeles	CA	90017	213-624-6996		671
Engine Components Inc (ECI)	9503 Middlex *TF:* 800-324-2359	San Antonio	TX	78217	210-820-8100	820-8102	21
Engine Control & Monitoring	PO Box 40 *Web:* www.ecm-co.com	Los Altos	CA	94023	408-734-3433		317
Engine Interactive	1415 Tenth Ave 4 *Web:* www.enginei.com	Seattle	WA	98122	206-709-1955	709-1958	180
Engine Lab of Tampa Inc	201 S 78th St *Web:* www.enginelaboftampa.com	Tampa	FL	33619	813-605-5500		262
Engine Manufacturers Assn (EMA)	333 W Wacker Dr Ste 810 *Web:* www.truckandenginemanufacturers.org	Chicago	IL	60606	312-929-1970	929-1975	49-13
Engine Parts Warehouse	7301 Global Dr	Louisville	KY	40258	502-937-7258		247
Engine Power Components Inc	1333 Fulton St *Web:* www.engpwr.com	Grand Haven	MI	49417	616-846-0110	847-0500	60
Engine Power Source Inc	348 Bryant Blvd *TF:* 800-374-7522 ■ *Web:* enginepowersource.com	Rock Hill	SC	29732	704-944-1999		518
Engineer Sales Co	2500 25th Ave N *Web:* www.engineersales.com	Saint Petersburg	FL	33713	727-323-2100	323-1807	195
Engineered Building Products Inc	18 Southwood Dr *Web:* www.ebpfab.com	Bloomfield	CT	06002	860-243-1110		492
Engineered Controls International Inc (ECII)	100 Rego Dr PO Box 247 *TF:* 800-650-0061 ■ *Web:* www.regoproducts.com	Elon	NC	27244	336-449-7707	449-6594	789
Engineered Corrosion Solutions LLC	11336 Lackland Rd *Web:* ecscorrosion.com	Saint Louis	MO	63146	314-432-1377		261
Engineered Environments Inc	1620 Timocuan Way Ste 130 **Fax Area Code:* 561 ■ *Web:* www.eeigc.net	Longwood	FL	32750	407-831-6998	241-8409*	116
Engineered Inspection Services Inc	3259 Coral Ridge Rd *Web:* www.engineeredinspection.com	Brooks	KY	40109	502-955-9021	955-7589	248
Engineered Machined Products Inc (EMP)	3111 N 28th St *Web:* www.emp-corp.com	Escanaba	MI	49829	906-789-7497	786-6635	128
Engineered Materials Solutions Inc	39 Perry Ave *Web:* www.emsclad.com	Attleboro	MA	02703	508-342-2100		567
Engineered Medical Systems Inc	2055 Executive Dr *Web:* www.engmedsys.com	Indianapolis	IN	46241	317-246-5500		475
Engineered Mills Inc	888 E Belvidere Rd *Web:* emimills.com	Grayslake	IL	60030	847-548-0044	548-0099	455
Engineered Plastic Components Inc	1408 Zimmerman Dr S *Web:* www.epcmfg.com	Grinnell	IA	50112	641-236-3100		596
Engineered Plastic Systems (EPS)	885 Church Rd *TF:* 800-480-2327 ■ *Web:* www.epsplasticlumber.com	Elgin	IL	60123	847-289-8383	289-8382	603
Engineered Plastics Inc	211 Chase St *Web:* www.engplas.com	Gibsonville	NC	27249	336-449-4121		602
Engineered Polymer Solutions Inc	1400 N State St **Fax Area Code:* 815 ■ *TF:* 800-654-4242 ■ *Web:* www.epscca.com	Marengo	IL	60152	800-654-4242	568-4145*	605-2
Engineered Precision Casting Company Inc	952 Palmer Ave *Web:* www.epcast.com	Middletown	NJ	07748	732-671-2424	671-8615	306
Engineered Products Co (EPCO)	601 Kelso St PO Box 108 *TF:* 888-414-3726 ■ *Web:* www.epcohardware.com	Flint	MI	48506	810-767-2050	767-5084	350
Engineered Products Inc	500 Furman Hall Rd *TF:* 888-301-1421 ■ *Web:* www.engprod.com	Greenville	SC	29609	864-234-4868	234-4860	207
Engineered Products Inc (EPI)	200 Jones St *Web:* www.epimetal.com	Verona	PA	15147	412-423-4000	423-4002	234
Engineered Profiles LLC	2141 Fairwood Ave *Web:* www.engineeredprofiles.com	Columbus	OH	43207	614-754-3700		596
Engineered Protection Systems Inc	750 Front Ave NW *TF:* 800-966-9199 ■ *Web:* www.epssecurity.com	Grand Rapids	MI	49504	616-459-0281		189-4
Engineered Representation Inc	1320 N Lake St *Web:* engineeredrepinc.com	Neenah	WI	54956	920-751-3922	751-8816	261
Engineered Software	PO Box 408 *Web:* www.engsw.com	Grafton	MA	01519	336-299-4843		178-5
Engineered Software Products Inc	1075 Progress Cir *Web:* espatl.com	Lawrenceville	GA	30043	770-682-8259		177
Engineered Steel Products Inc	4977 Plainfield Rd *Web:* www.engineeredsteel.com	Sophia	NC	27350	336-438-9140		480
Engineered Systems & Products Inc	11438 Cronridge Dr Ste O *Web:* www.espcontrols.com	Owings Mills	MD	21117	410-998-9456	998-9467	729
Engineered Systems & Services	2950 Horizon Park Dr Ste B *Web:* essengineers.com	Suwanee	GA	30024	770-810-5700		261
Engineered With Layton PLC	1490 S Price Rd Ste 215 *Web:* engineeredwithlayton.com	Chandler	AZ	85286	480-244-3355		261
Engineering & Environmental Consultants Inc	4625 E Ft Lowell Rd *TF:* 800-887-2103 ■ *Web:* www.eec-info.com	Tucson	AZ	85712	520-321-4625	321-0333	261
Engineering & Equipment Company Inc	910 N Washington St *Web:* www.engineeringandequipmentcoalbany.com	Albany	GA	31701	229-518-3377		612
Engineering & Metal Fabrication (EMF)	124 Imperial St *Web:* www.emfinc.net	Merritt Island	FL	32952	321-453-3670	452-4506	697
Engineering Alliance Inc	194 Central St *Web:* engineeringalliance.net	Saugus	MA	01906	781-231-1349		261
Engineering and Technical Consultants Inc (ETC)	46040 Center Oak Plz Ste 100 *Web:* www.etc-web.com	Sterling	VA	20166	703-450-6220	444-2285	261
Engineering Associates Inc	1935 Eagle Pass *Web:* eaohio.com	Wooster	OH	44691	330-345-6556		261
Engineering Concepts Unlimited Inc	8950 Technology Dr *Web:* www.ecu-engine-controls.com	Fishers	IN	46038	317-849-8470	849-6475	203
Engineering Contractors' Assn, The (ECA)	2190 S Towne Centre Pl *Web:* ecasocal.org	Anaheim	CA	92806	714-937-5000	937-5030	49-19
Engineering Data Design Corp	105 Daventry Ln Ste 100 *TF:* 888-678-0683 ■ *Web:* ed2c.com	Louisville	KY	40223	502-412-4000		256
Engineering Design Industries Inc	9649 E Rush St *Web:* www.edimfg.com	South El Monte	CA	91733	626-443-7741	443-9651	454
Engineering Design Technologies Inc (EDT)	1705 Entp Way Ste 200 *Web:* www.edtinc.net	Marietta	GA	30067	770-988-0400	988-0300	685
Engineering Dynamics Inc	3925 S Kalamath St *Web:* www.engdynamics.com	Englewood	CO	80110	303-761-4367		743
Engineering Economics Inc (EEI)	780 Simms St Ste 210 *TF:* 800-869-6902 ■ *Web:* www.eeiengineers.com	Golden	CO	80401	800-869-6902		186
Engineering Management Concepts Inc	5051 Verdugo Way Ste 200 *Web:* www.emc-inc.com	Camarillo	CA	93012	805-484-9082	484-4607	463
Engineering Manufacturing Technologies LLC	101 Delaware Ave *Web:* emtmetals.com	Endicott	NY	13760	607-754-7111	754-2237	697
Engineering Mechanics Corporation of Columbus	3518 Riverside Dr Ste 202 *Web:* www.emc-sq.com	Columbus	OH	43221	614-459-3200		256
Engineering News-Record (ENR)	350 Fifth Ave Ste 6000 *TF:* 877-876-8208 ■ *Web:* www.enr.com	New York	NY	10118	646-849-7100		457-21
Engineering Planning & Management Inc	959 Concord St *Web:* www.epm-inc.com	Framingham	MA	01701	508-875-2121	879-3291	261
Engineering Plus Inc	1724-B 23rd Ave *Web:* engineeringplus.com	Meridian	MS	39301	601-693-4234		261
Engineering Research Center for Net Shape Mfg	1971 Neil Ave Rm 339 *Web:* ercnsm.osu.edu	Columbus	OH	43210	614-292-9267	292-7219	668
Engineering Services Network Inc (ESN)	2450 Crystal Dr Ste 1015 *Web:* www.esncc.com	Arlington	VA	22202	703-412-3640		193
Engineering Specialists Inc	21360 Gateway Ct *Web:* www.engspec.com	Brookfield	WI	53045	262-783-8000	783-8001	256
Engineering Technology Corp	2975 S 300 W *Web:* etcwinders.com	Salt Lake City	UT	84115	801-486-8721		49-13
Engineering Ventures Inc	208 Flynn Ave Ste 2A *Web:* engineeringventures.com	Burlington	VT	05401	802-863-6225		261
Engineering, Design & Development Inc	1001 W Jefferson St *Web:* www.engineeringdesignanddevelopment.biz	Morton	IL	61550	309-266-6298	263-2067	454
Engineering/Remediation Resources Group Inc (ERRG)	4585 Pacheco Blvd Ste 200 *Web:* www.errg.com	Martinez	CA	94553	925-969-0750	969-0751	261
Engineeringcom Inc	5285 Solar Dr Ste 101 *Web:* www.engineering.com	Mississauga	ON	L4W5B8	905-273-9991		387
Engineers Canada	180 Elgin St Ste 1100 *TF:* 877-408-9273 ■ *Web:* engineerscanada.ca	Ottawa	ON	K2P2K3	613-232-2474	230-5759	48-1
Enginetech Inc	1205 W Crosby Rd *TF:* 800-869-8711 ■ *Web:* enginetech.com	Carrollton	TX	75006	972-245-0110	245-2093	61
Enginuiti Inc	8321 Old Cthouse Rd *Web:* enginuiti.com	Vienna	VA	22182	703-620-2266		180
Enginuity Works Corp	2195 Defoor Hills Rd NW *Web:* enginuityworks.com	Atlanta	GA	30318	678-739-0001		256
Engis Corp	105 W Hintz Rd *TF:* 800-993-6447 ■ *Web:* www.engis.com	Wheeling	IL	60090	847-808-9400	808-9430	386
England & Company LLC	7201 Wisconsin Ave Ste 480 *Web:* englandco.com	Bethesda	MD	20814	202-386-6500	386-6599	691

Entry	City	State	ZIP	Phone	Fax	Class
England Logistics Inc 1325 South 4700 West *TF:* 800-848-7810 ■ *Web:* www.englandlogistics.com	Salt Lake City	UT	84104	801-656-4500		194
Englander Intl 1308 Teasley Ln Ste 183 *TF:* 800-489-9994 ■ *Web:* www.englander.com	Denton	TX	76205	888-909-0551		471
Englefield Oil Co 447 James Pkwy *TF:* 800-837-4458 ■ *Web:* englefieldoil.com	Heath	OH	43056	740-928-8215	928-1531	324
Engler Meier & Justus Inc 1030 Vandustrial Dr *Web:* www.westmontint.com	Westmont	IL	60559	630-852-4600	852-5029	191-1
Englert Inc 1200 Amboy Ave *TF:* 800-364-5378 ■ *Web:* www.englertinc.com	Perth Amboy	NJ	08861	732-826-8614		697
Engleside Inc 30 E Engleside Ave *Web:* engleside.com	Beach Haven	NJ	08008	609-492-1251		378
Englewood Cafe 10904 E Winner Rd *Web:* www.englewoodstation.com	Independence	MO	64052	816-461-9588		671
Englewood Chamber of Commerce PO Box 8161 *Web:* englewoodnjchamber.com	Englewood	NJ	07631	201-567-2381		139
Englewood Hospital & Medical Ctr 350 Engle St *TF:* 833-234-2234 ■ *Web:* www.englewoodhealth.org	Englewood	NJ	07631	201-894-3000	894-1473	374-3
Englewood Public Library 31 Engle St *Web:* www.englewoodlibrary.org	Englewood	NJ	07631	201-568-2215		434-3
Englewood Public Library 1000 Englewood Pkwy Englewood Civic Ctr 1st Fl *Web:* www.englewoodco.gov	Englewood	CO	80110	303-762-2560		434-3
Englewood-Cape Haze Area Chamber of Commerce 601 S Indiana Ave *Web:* www.englewoodchamber.com	Englewood	FL	34223	941-474-5511	475-9257	139
English American Tailoring Co 411 N Cranberry Rd *Web:* www.englishamericanco.com	Westminster	MD	21157	410-857-5774		155-12
English Construction Company Inc 615 Church St *Web:* www.englishconst.com	Lynchburg	VA	24504	434-845-0301	845-0306	188-4
English Ctr, The 1005 Atlantic Ave *Web:* www.englishcenter.edu	Alameda	CA	94501	510-836-6700	836-6900	167-3
English Inn, The 677 S Michigan Rd *TF:* 800-858-0598 ■ *Web:* englishinn.com	Eaton Rapids	MI	48827	517-663-2500	663-2643	671
English Language Ctr (ELC) 10850 Wilshire Blvd Ste 210 *Web:* www.elc.edu	Los Angeles	CA	90024	310-470-3019	470-6733	423
English Nanny & Governess School 37 S Franklin St *TF:* 800-733-1984 ■ *Web:* www.nanny-governess.com	Chagrin Falls	OH	44022	440-247-0600	247-0602	685
English Newsom Cellars 408 E Woodrow Rd *Web:* www.englishnewsom.com	Lubbock	TX	79423	806-863-2704		50-7
English Oaks Nursing & Rehabilitation Ctr 2633 W Rumble Rd *Web:* lifegen.net	Modesto	CA	95350	209-577-1001		450
English Village Manor Nursing Home 1515 Canterbury Blvd *Web:* englishvillagemanor.net	Altus	OK	73521	580-477-1133		371
English, Lucas, Priest & Owsley LLP 1101 College St *Web:* www.elpolaw.com	Bowling Green	KY	42102	270-781-6500	782-7782	428
English-Speaking Union of the US 144 E 39th St *Web:* www.esuus.org	New York	NY	10016	212-818-1200	867-4177	48-15
ENGlobal Corp 654 N Sam Houston Pkwy E Ste 400 *NASDAQ: ENG* ■ *Web:* www.englobal.com	Houston	TX	77060	281-878-1000	878-1010	173-2
Englund Marine & Industrial Supply Co 95 Hamburg Ave PO Box 296 *TF:* 800-228-7051 ■ *Web:* www.englundmarine.com	Astoria	OR	97103	503-325-4341	325-6421	221
Engman-Taylor Company Inc (ETCO) W142 N9351 Fountain Blvd *TF:* 800-236-1975 ■ *Web:* www.engman-taylor.com	Menomonee Falls	WI	53051	262-255-9300	255-6512	385
ENGworks Inc 1931 Newport Blvd Ste B *Web:* engworks.com	Costa Mesa	CA	92627	949-340-6924		256
Enhance Energy Inc 333 5 Ave SW Ste 900 *Web:* www.enhanceenergy.com	Calgary	AB	T2P3B6	403-984-0202		536
Enhanced Laser Products 10516 Katy Fwy *Web:* www.enhancedlaser.com	Houston	TX	77024	713-956-9481		112
Enhanced Retail Solutions Inc 214 W 39th St Rm 1202a *Web:* www.enhancedretailsolutions.com	New York	NY	10018	212-938-1991		129
Enhanced Software Products Inc 1811 N Hutchinson Rd *TF:* 800-456-5750 ■ *Web:* www.espsolution.net	Spokane	WA	99212	800-456-5750		225
Enhanced Telecommunication Inc 6065 Atlantic Blvd *TF:* 800-332-1078 ■ *Web:* etisoftware.com	Norcross	GA	30071	770-242-3620		180
enherent Corp 6800 Jericho Tpke Ste 116E *Web:* enherentcorp.com	Syosset	NY	11791	516-932-9080	932-3152	177
Enholm Law PLLC 2320 W Peoria Ave Ste A-108 *Web:* enholmlaw.com	Phoenix	AZ	85029	602-889-6273	889-6278	41
Eni Spa 1200 Smith St Ste 1707 *TF:* 800-922-9243 ■ *Web:* www.eni.com	Houston	TX	77002	713-393-6100	393-6328	536
Enid Beauty College 3905 S La Mesa Dr *Web:* www.enidokbeautycollege.com	Enid	OK	73703	580-237-6677		167-3
Enid News & Eagle 227 W Broadway PO Box 1192 *TF:* 800-299-6397 ■ *Web:* www.enidnews.com	Enid	OK	73701	580-233-6600	233-7645	532-2
Enidine Inc 7 Centre Dr *TF:* 800-852-8508 ■ *Web:* www.enidine.com	Orchard Park	NY	14127	716-662-1900	662-1909	472
Enigma Marketing Trvl Solutions 8463 Castlewood Dr *Web:* www.enigma-marketing.com	Indianapolis	IN	46250	317-585-0100		463
Enilon Group 945 Foch St *Web:* www.enilon.com	Fort Worth	TX	76107	817-632-3200		177
Enite Management LLC 101 W 13th St *Web:* enitegroup.com	Houston	TX	77008	713-298-6149		463
Enjet Inc 5373 W Alabama Ste 502 *Web:* www.enjet.com	Houston	TX	77056	713-552-1559		580
Enkeboll Designs 16506 Avalon Blvd *Web:* www.enkebolldesigns.com	Carson	CA	90746	310-532-1400		200
Enkei America Inc 1111 Executive Dr *Web:* www.enkei.com	Coppell	TX	75019	812-373-7000		247
Enlighten 711 N 4th Ave	Ann Arbor	MI	48104	734-668-6678	668-1883	180
Enlightened Inc 1101 Connecticut Ave NW Ste 800 *Web:* www.enlightened.com	Washington	DC	20036	202-728-7190	728-7198	177
Enlisted Association of the National Guard of the US (EANGUS) 3133 Mt Vernon Ave *TF:* 800-234-3264 ■ *Web:* eangus.org	Alexandria	VA	22305	703-519-3846	519-3849	48-19
Enlivant 330 N Wabash Ave Ste 3700 *Web:* www.enlivant.com	Chicago	IL	60611	312-725-7000		371
Enloe Medical Ctr 1531 Esplanade *TF:* 800-822-8102 ■ *Web:* www.enloe.org	Chico	CA	95926	530-332-7300		374-3
Enmark Tool & Gage Company Inc 18100 Cross Dr *Web:* www.enmarktool.com	Fraser	MI	48026	586-293-2797	293-1037	493
ENMAX Corp PO Box 2900 Station M *TF:* 877-571-7111 ■ *Web:* www.enmax.com	Calgary	AB	T2G4S7	403-245-7222		787
Ennead Architects 320 W 13 St *Web:* www.ennead.com	New York	NY	10014	212-807-7171		261
Ennis Inc 2441 Presidential Pkwy *TF:* 800-972-1069 ■ *Web:* www.ennis.com	Midlothian	TX	76065	972-775-9801		627
Ennis Independent School District 303 W Knox PO Box 1420 *Web:* www.ennis.k12.tx.us	Ennis	TX	75119	972-872-7000	875-8667	685
Ennis Pellum & Associates CPAS 5150 Belfort Rd S Bldg 600 *Web:* www.jaxcpa.com	Jacksonville	FL	32256	904-396-5965	399-4094	2
Ennis State Bank 815 W Ennis Ave *Web:* www.ennisstatebank.com	Ennis	TX	75119	972-875-9676		70
Ennis Steel Industries Inc 1801 S I-45 PO Box 1360 *Web:* ennissteel.com	Ennis	TX	75119	972-878-0400	878-0487	480
ENO Publishers PO Box 158 *Web:* www.enopublishers.org	Hillsborough	NC	27278	919-632-6893		637-10
ENO River State Park 6101 Cole Mill Rd *Web:* www.ncparks.gov	Durham	NC	27705	919-383-1686		565
ENO Vino Wine Bar & Bistro 601 Junction Rd *Web:* eno-vino.com	Madison	WI	53717	608-664-9565		671
Enoch Manufacturing Co 14242 SE 82nd Dr *TF:* 888-659-2660 ■ *Web:* enochmachining.com	Clackamas	OR	97015	503-659-2660		621
Enoch Pratt Free Library 400 Cathedral St *Web:* www.prattlibrary.org	Baltimore	MD	21201	410-396-5283	396-8134	434-3
ENOCHS Examining Room Furniture 14701 Cumberland Rd Ste 107 **Fax Area Code:* 317 ■ *TF:* 800-428-2305 ■ *Web:* www.enochsmed.com	Noblesville	IN	46060	800-428-2305	580-2944*	319-3
eNom Inc 5808 Lake Washington Blvd NE Ste 300 *Web:* www.enom.com	Kirkland	WA	98033	425-974-4689	974-4791	396
Enor Corp 246 S Dean St *Web:* enor.com	Englewood	NJ	07631	201-431-9110		608
Enos Home Oxygen Therapy Inc 35 Welby Rd *TF:* 800-473-4669 ■ *Web:* www.enoshomemedical.com	New Bedford	MA	02745	508-992-2146	998-1729	475
Enounce Inc 2666 E Bayshore Rd *Web:* www.enounce.com	Palo Alto	CA	94303	650-494-6200		177
Enovity Inc 100 Montgomery St *TF:* 888-900-9978 ■ *Web:* www.enovity.com	San Francisco	CA	94104	415-974-0390		261
Enphase Energy Inc 1420 N Mcdowell Blvd *TF:* 877-797-4743 ■ *Web:* investor.enphase.com	Petaluma	CA	94954	707-763-4784		696
Enplas USA Inc 1901 W Oak Cir *Web:* www.enplasusa.com	Marietta	GA	30062	770-795-1100	795-1190	757
Enpower Corp 2420 Camino Ramon Ste 101 *Web:* www.enpowercorp.com	San Ramon	CA	94583	925-244-1100		787
Enprecis Inc 60 Courtneypark Dr W Unit 3 *TF:* 877-476-9274 ■ *Web:* enprecis.com	Mississauga	ON	L5W0B3	905 565-5777		387
Enpro Inc 121 S Lombard Rd **Fax Area Code:* 630 ■ *TF:* 800-323-2416 ■ *Web:* www.enproinc.com	Addison	IL	60101	800-323-2416	629-3512*	385
EnPro Industries 5605 Carnegie Blvd Ste 500 *NYSE: NPO* ■ *Web:* www.enproindustries.com	Charlotte	NC	28209	704-731-1500		326
EnPro Industries Incorporated Fairbanks Morse Engine 701 White Ave *TF:* 800-356-6955 ■ *Web:* www.fairbanksmorse.com	Beloit	WI	53511	800-356-6955		262
Enprotech Corp 4259 E 49th St *Web:* www.enprotech.com	Cleveland	OH	44125	216-206-0081	206-0088	697
Enprotech Mechanical Services Inc 2200 Olds Ave *Web:* www.enpromech.com	Lansing	MI	48915	517-372-0950		697
ENR (Engineering News-Record) 350 Fifth Ave Ste 6000 *TF:* 877-876-8208 ■ *Web:* www.enr.com	New York	NY	10118	646-849-7100		457-21
ENRG Inc 155 Chandler St Ste 5	Buffalo	NY	14207	716-873-2939	873-3196	253
Enriching Spaces 1360 Kemper Meadow Dr *Web:* www.enrichingspaces.com	Cincinnati	OH	45240	513-851-0933	742-6415	320
Enroute Computer Solutions Inc 2511 Fire Rd Ste A4 *Web:* www.enroute-computer.com	Egg Harbor Township	NJ	08234	609-569-9255		261
ENSA North America 400 S West Ave *Web:* www.ensa-northamerica.com	Waukesha	WI	53186	262-787-8354		393
Ensave Energy Performance Inc 65 Millet St Ste 105 *TF:* 800-732-1399 ■ *Web:* www.ensave.com	Richmond	VT	05477	800-732-1399		463

Name / Address	City	State	ZIP	Phone	Fax	Class
En-Save Inc 18983 Wendover Ave *TF:* 800-247-4073 ■ *Web:* www.xlseedtreatment.com	Granger	IA	50109	800-247-4073		280
Enscicon Engineering & Construction 2420 W 26th Ave Ste 500 Bldg D *Web:* www.enscicon.com	Denver	CO	80211	303-980-8600		180
ENSCO Inc 3110 Fairview Pk Dr Ste 300 *TF:* 800-367-2682 ■ *Web:* www.ensco.com	Falls Church	VA	22042	703-321-9000		261
Ensearch Management Consultants 905 E Cotati Ave *TF:* 888-667-5627 ■ *Web:* ensearch.com	Cotati	CA	94931	888-667-5627		721
Ensemble Designs Inc 870 Gold Flat Rd *Web:* www.ensembledesigns.com	Nevada City	CA	95959	530-478-1832		647
Ensemble Theatre 3535 Main St *Web:* www.ensemblehouston.com	Houston	TX	77002	713-520-0055	520-1269	572
Ensemble Theatre Cincinnati 1127 Vine St *Web:* www.ensemblecincinnati.org	Cincinnati	OH	45202	513-421-3555	562-4104	573-4
Ensemble Travel 256 W 38th St 11th Fl *TF:* 800-576-2378 ■ *Web:* www.ensembletravel.com	New York	NY	10018	212-545-7460		772
Ensenada Mexican Restaurant Inc 2824 Virginia Beach Blvd	Virginia Beach	VA	23452	757-631-1090		671
Enseo Inc 1680 Prospect Dr Ste 100 *TF:* 866-717-3075 ■ *Web:* www.enseo.com	Richardson	TX	75081	972-234-2513		174
Enser Corp 1902 Taylor's Ln *Web:* enser.com	Cinnaminson	NJ	08077	856-829-5522		454
Ensign Corp 201 Ensign Rd **Fax Area Code:* 563 ■ *TF:* 888-797-8658 ■ *Web:* www.ensigncorp.com	Bellevue	IA	52031	630-628-9999	872-4575*	767
Ensign CPA Group Inc 3209 W Smith Valley Rd Ste 238 *Web:* ensigncpagroup.com	Greenwood	IN	46142	317-832-6794	534-3321	734
Ensign Emblem Ltd 1746 Keane Dr **Fax Area Code:* 888 ■ *TF:* 800-521-0575 ■ *Web:* www.ensignemblem.com	Traverse City	MI	49696	800-521-0575	946-7583*	258
Ensign Energy Services Inc 400 5th Ave SW Ste 1000 *TSE: ESI.TO* ■ *Web:* www.ensignenergy.com	Calgary	AB	T2P0L6	403-262-1361		540
Ensign Engineering p C 1111 Calhoun Ave *Web:* www.ensignengineering.com	Bronx	NY	10465	718-863-5590	863-6178	256
Ensign Group Inc, The 27101 Puerta Real Ste 450 *NASDAQ: ENSG* ■ *TF:* 866-256-0955 ■ *Web:* ensigngroup.net	Mission Viejo	CA	92691	949-487-9500		450
Ensign-Bickford Aerospace & Defense Co 640 Hopmeadow St PO Box 429 *Web:* www.ebad.com	Simsbury	CT	06070	860-843-2289	843-2621	268
Ensinger Inc 365 Meadowlands Blvd *TF:* 800-243-3221 ■ *Web:* www.ensinger-inc.com	Washington	PA	15301	724-746-6050	746-9209	605-2
Ensinger Putnam Precision Molding 11 Danco Rd *TF:* 800-752-7865 ■ *Web:* www.ensinger-pc.com	Putnam	CT	06260	860-928-7911	928-2229	604
ENSTAR Natural Gas Co 401 E International Airport Rd *TF:* 800-907-9767 ■ *Web:* www.enstarnaturalgas.com	Anchorage	AK	99518	907-277-5551		787
Enstar USA Inc 7035 Halcyon Pk Dr *NASDAQ: ESGR* ■ *Web:* www.enstargroup.com	Montgomery	AL	36117	334-834-5483		405
Enstoa 655 Third Ave *Web:* enstoa.com	New York	NY	10017	212-913-0870		205
Enstrom Helicopter Corporation USA 2209 22nd St *Web:* enstromhelicopter.com	Menominee	MI	49858	906-863-1200		20
EnSys Energy & Systems Inc 1775 Massachussets Ave *Web:* www.ensysenergy.com	Lexington	MA	02420	781-274-8454		195
Ensyte Energy Software Intl 770 S Post Oak Ln Ste 330 *Web:* ensyte.com	Houston	TX	77056	713-622-2875		177
Ent Federal Credit Union 7250 Campus Dr *TF:* 800-525-9623 ■ *Web:* www.ent.com	Colorado Springs	CO	80920	719-574-1100		219
Entact LLC 1 E Oak Hill Dr Ste 102 *TF:* 800-936-8228 ■ *Web:* entact.com	Westmont	IL	60559	800-255-2771		192
Entagon Inc 9805 Vly View Rd *Web:* www.entagon.com	Eden Prairie	MN	55344	952-941-5305		350
Entech Instruments Inc 2207 Agate Ct *TF:* 800-555-8034 ■ *Web:* www.entechinst.com	Simi Valley	CA	93065	805-527-5939		419
Entegee Inc 70 Blanchard Rd Ste 102 *TF:* 800-368-3433 ■ *Web:* www.entegee.com	Burlington	MA	01803	800-368-3433		721
EnteGreat Inc 1500 Urban Center Dr Ste 415 *Web:* www.entegreat.com	Vestavia Hills	AL	35242	205-968-3050		449
Entegrity Networks Inc 6220 Avanti Dr *Web:* entegritynetworks.com	Arlington	TX	76001	214-432-5418		45
Entek International LLC 250 Hansard Ave *Web:* www.entek.com	Lebanon	OR	97355	541-259-3901	259-3932	620
Entelechy Enterprises Inc 889 E Shore Dr *TF:* 800-376-8368 ■ *Web:* www.unlockit.com	Silver Lake	NH	03875	603-424-1237		463
Entellus Inc 3033 N 44th St Ste 250 *Web:* entellus.com	Phoenix	AZ	85018	602-244-2566		261
Enterasys Networks Inc 50 Minuteman Rd *Web:* www.extremenetworks.com	Andover	MA	01810	978-684-1000		176
Entercom Boston 83 Leo M Birmingham Pkwy *Web:* www.entercom.com	Brighton	MA	02135	833-277-7040		645
Enterey Inc 200 Spectrum Center Dr Ste 220 *Web:* www.enterey.com	Irvine	CA	92618	949-336-5200		463
Enterforce Inc 353 Forest Grove Dr Ste 100 *Web:* www.enterforce.com	Waukesha	WI	53188	262-542-2218		196
Entergy Arkansas Inc 425 W Capitol Ave *TF:* 800-368-3749 ■ *Web:* www.entergy-arkansas.com	Little Rock	AR	72201	501-377-3571		787
Entergy Corp 639 Loyola Ave *NYSE: ETR* ■ *Web:* www.entergy.com	New Orleans	LA	70113	504-576-4000		360-5
Enterprise Bancorp Inc 222 Merrimack St *NASDAQ: EBTC* ■ *Web:* www.enterprisebanking.com	Lowell	MA	01852	978-459-9000		360-2
Enterprise Bank of SC 13497 Broxton Bridge Rd PO Box 8 *Web:* ebsc.bank	Ehrhardt	SC	29081	803-267-3191	267-2316	70
Enterprise Community Partners Inc 10227 Wincopin Cir *TF:* 800-624-4298 ■ *Web:* www.enterprisecommunity.org	Columbia	MD	21044	410-964-1230	964-1918	48-5
Enterprise Computing Solutions Inc 26024 Acero *Web:* www.thinkecs.com	Mission Viejo	CA	92691	949-609-1980		177
Enterprise Ctr 1401 Clark Ave *Web:* www.enterprisecenter.com	Saint Louis	MO	63103	314-622-5400	622-5410	720
Enterprise Electric Co 4204 Shannon Dr *Web:* www.eecompany.com	Baltimore	MD	21213	410-488-8200	488-6639	189-4
Enterprise Financial Services Corp 150 N Meramec Ave *NASDAQ: EFSG* ■ *TF:* 800-396-8141 ■ *Web:* www.enterprisebank.com	Clayton	MO	63105	314-725-5500		360-2
Enterprise Inc PO Box 348 *Web:* www.theenterprise.net	Stuart	VA	24171	276-694-3101	694-5110	532-2
Enterprise Information Services Inc 1945 Old Gallows Rd Ste 500 *Web:* goeis.com	Vienna	VA	22182	703-749-0007		177
Enterprise Magazine 825 N 300 W Ste NE220 *Web:* www.slenterprise.com	Salt Lake City	UT	84103	801-533-0556	533-0684	457-5
Enterprise Precast Concrete Inc 13800 Giles Rd *Web:* www.enterpriseprecast.com	Omaha	NE	68138	402-895-3848		183
Enterprise Print Management So 1 Abbey Ln *TF:* 877-382-5380 ■ *Web:* entpms.com	Middleboro	MA	02346	877-382-5380		177
Enterprise Products Partners LP 1100 Louisiana St 10th Fl *NYSE: EPD* ■ *TF:* 866-230-0745 ■ *Web:* www.enterpriseproducts.com	Houston	TX	77002	713-381-6500		325
Enterprise Rent-A-Car 29 Hunter Ave *TF:* 800-307-6666 ■ *Web:* www.legacy.enterprise.com	Saint Louis	MO	63105	314-512-5000		126
Enterprise Roofing & Sheet Metal Co 1021 Irving St *Web:* www.enterpriserfg.com	Dayton	OH	45419	937-298-8664		189-12
Enterprise Sales Inc 540 SE 9th Ave *Web:* www.sharperbuilt.com	Ontario	OR	97914	541-889-5541		91
Enterprise State Community College (ESCC) 600 Plaza Dr *Web:* www.escc.edu	Enterprise	AL	36330	334-347-2623		162
Enterprise Welding & Fabricating Inc 6257 Heisley Rd *Web:* www.enterprisewelding.com	Mentor	OH	44060	440-354-4128	354-4431	697
Enterprise Wireless Alliance (EWA) 8484 Westpark Dr Ste 630 *TF:* 800-482-8282 ■ *Web:* www.enterprisewireless.org	McLean	VA	22102	703-528-5115	524-1074	49-20
EnterpriseWorks/VITA (EWV) 818 Connecticut Ave NW Ste 600 *Web:* www.enterpriseworks.org	Washington	DC	20006	202-639-8660	639-8664	48-5
Entertainment Fusion Group 6420 Wilshire Blvd Ste 620 *Web:* www.efgpr.com	Los Angeles	CA	90048	310-432-0020		636
Entertainment Merchants Assn (EMA) 16530 Ventura Blvd Ste 400 *Web:* www.entmerch.org	Encino	CA	91436	818-385-1500	933-0911	49-18
Entertainment Properties Trust 909 Walnut Ste 200 *NYSE: EPR* ■ *Web:* www.eprkc.com	Kansas City	MO	64106	816-472-1700		655
Entertainment Software Assn (ESA) 601 Massachusetts Ave NW Ste 300 *TF:* 800-949-3660 ■ *Web:* www.theesa.com	Washington	DC	20001	202-223-2400	223-2401	48-9
Entertainment Studios Inc 1925 Century Park E *Web:* entertainmentstudios.com	Los Angeles	CA	90067	310-277-3500	277-7298	514
Entertainment Weekly Magazine 225 Liberty St *TF:* 800-828-6882 ■ *Web:* ew.com	New York	NY	10281	800-828-6882		457-9
Entest Inc 15020 Beltway Dr *TF:* 800-955-0077 ■ *Web:* www.entestinc.com	Addison	TX	75001	972-980-9876		472
Enthalpy Analytical Inc 800-1 Capitola Dr *Web:* enthalpy.com	Durham	NC	27713	919-850-4392		743
Enthermics Inc W164 N9221 Water St *TF:* 800-862-9276 ■ *Web:* www.enthermics.com	Menomonee Falls	WI	53051	262-251-8356		475
Enthought Inc 515 Congress Ave Ste 2100 *Web:* www.enthought.com	Austin	TX	78701	512-536-1057		177
Enting Water Conditioning Inc 3211 Dryden Rd *Web:* www.enting.com	Dayton	OH	45439	937-294-5100		189-10
Entitle Direct Group Inc 1000 Gsk Dr Ste 210 *TF:* 877-936-8485 ■ *Web:* www.entitledirect.com	Coraopolis	PA	15108	877-936-8485	810-8531	391-6
Entium Technology Partners LLC 1288 Valley Forge Rd Ste 50 *Web:* entium.com	Valley Forge	PA	19482	610-415-7200		193
Entomological Society of America 10001 Derekwood Ln Ste 100 *TF:* 800-523-8635 ■ *Web:* www.entsoc.org	Lanham	MD	20706	301-731-4535	731-4538	49-19
Entravision Communications Corp 2425 Olympic Blvd Ste 6000 W *NYSE: EVC* ■ *Web:* www.entravision.com	Santa Monica	CA	90404	310-447-3870	447-3899	643
Entre Computer Solutions 8900 N Second St *Web:* www.entrerock.com	Machesney Park	IL	61115	815-399-5664		175
Entre Solutions 51 W Fairmont Ave *TF:* 877-352-1600 ■ *Web:* entresolutions.com	Savannah	GA	31406	912-352-1600		180
Entre Technology Service 1501 14th St W Ste 201 *Web:* www.entremt.com	Billings	MT	59102	406-256-5700		196

	Phone	Fax	Class
Entrepia Ventures 101 Eisenhower Pkwy Ste 300 . . . . Roseland NJ 07068 *TF:* 866-305-9610 ■ *Web:* www.entrepia.com	973-467-0880		792
Entrepreneur Media Inc 18061 Fitch . . . . Irvine CA 92614 *TF:* 800-779-5295 ■ *Web:* www.entrepreneur.com	949-261-2325	261-7729	637-9
Entrex Communication Services Inc 6600 Rockledge Dr Ste 550 . . . . Bethesda MD 20817 *Web:* entrex.com	202-408-0960		261
Entrust Datacard 5420 LBJ Fwy Ste 300 . . . . Dallas TX 75240 *TF:* 888-690-2424 ■ *Web:* www.entrustdatacard.com	888-690-2424		178-12
Entrust Manufacturing Technologies Inc N 58 W 14630 Shawn Cir . . . . Menomonee Falls WI 53051 *Web:* www.entrustmt.com	262-252-3802		455
Entrx Corp 800 Nicollet Mall Ste 2690. . . . . .Minneapolis MN 55402	612-333-0614		189-9
Entuity Inc 4 Mount Royal Ave. . . . . Marlborough MA 01752 *Web:* www.entuity.com	508-357-6344	357-6358	178-1
Entwistle Co *Dietzco Div* 6 Bigelow St . . . . Hudson MA 01749 *TF:* 800-445-8909 ■ *Web:* www.entwistleco.com	508-481-4000	481-4004	556
Enumclaw Area Chamber of Commerce 1421 Cole St. . . . . Enumclaw WA 98022 *Web:* www.enumclawchamber.com	360-825-7666	825-8369	139
ENV Insurance Agency LLC 7789 Oswego Rd . . . . Liverpool NY 13090 *TF:* 800-887-9146 ■ *Web:* insurewithenv.com	315-641-5848		390
Envar Services Inc 505 Milltown Rd. . . . . North Brunswick NJ 08902 *Web:* www.envarservices.com	732-296-9601	296-9602	261
ENVE Composites LLC 508 W Stockman Way . . . . . . Ogden UT 84401 **Fax Area Code:* 801 ■ *TF:* 877-358-2869 ■ *Web:* www.enve.com	877-358-2869	476-3393*	82
Envela Corp 13022 Preston Rd . . . . Dallas TX 75240 *NYSE: DGSE* ■ *Web:* envela.com	972-587-4049		410
Envelope Manufacturers Assn (EMA) 700 S Washington St Ste 260. . . . . Alexandria VA 22314 *Web:* onvolopo.org	703-739-2200	739-2209	49-4
Envelope Printery Inc, The 8979 Samuel Barton Dr . . . . Van Buren Township MI 48111 *Web:* envelopeprintery.com	734-398-7700	398-7924	263
Envelopes & Forms Inc 2505 Meadowbrook Pkwy. . . . . Duluth GA 30096 *Web:* www.efsurebill.com	770-623-5140		627
Envelopes Etcetera Inc 69-71 Townsend St. . . . . .Port Chester NY 10573 *Web:* www.envetc.com	914-937-6162	937-6365	627
Envelopes Only Inc 2000 S Park Ave . . . . .Streamwood IL 60107 *Web:* envelopesonly.net	630-213-2500		535
Enventure 15995 N Barkers Landing Ste 350 . . . . .Houston TX 77079 *Web:* www.enventuregt.com	281-552-2200		190
Enventys Partners LLC 520 Elliot St . . . . Charlotte NC 28202 *Web:* enventyspartners.com	704-333-5335		5
Envest private Equity 1206 Laskin Rd Ste 101 . . . . .Virginia Beach VA 23451 *Web:* envestcap.com	757-437-3000		792
Envestnet Inc 35 E Wacker Dr Ste 2400 . . . . .Chicago IL 60601 *Web:* www.envestnet.com	312-827-2800		690
Envieta LLC 7175 Columbia Gateway Dr Ste T. . . . . .Columbia MD 21046 *Web:* envieta.com	410-290-1136	290-1168	693
Enviro Clean Services LLC 11717 N Morgan Rd. . . . . Yukon OK 73099 *Web:* www.eccgrp.com	405-373-4545		192
Enviro Systems Inc 12037 N Hwy 99 . . . . Seminole OK 74868 *Web:* www.enviro-ok.com	405-382-0731	382-0737	22
Enviroapplications Inc 2831 Camino Del Rio S Ste 214. . . . . San Diego CA 92108 *Web:* www.enviroapplications.com	619-291-3636		196
EnviroCap 3401 W Cypress St Ste 201. . . . . Tampa FL 33607 *Web:* www.envirocap.com	813-341-3650		401
Envirocon Inc 101 International Dr . . . . Missoula MT 59808 *Web:* www.envirocon.com	406-523-1150		261
Envirodyne Systems Inc 75 Zimmerman Dr. . . . . Camp Hill PA 17011 *Web:* www.envirodynesystems.com	717-763-0500	763-9308	194
EnviroKinetics Inc 101 S Milliken Ave. . . . . .Ontario CA 91761 *Web:* www.envirokinetics.com	909-621-7599	621-7899	194
Envirologic Technologies Inc 2960 Interstate Pkwy. . . . . .Kalamazoo MI 49048 *TF:* 800-272-7802 ■ *Web:* www.envirologic.com	269-342-1100		463
EnviroLogix Inc 500 Riverside Industrial Pkwy. . . . . .Portland ME 04103 *TF:* 866-408-4597 ■ *Web:* www.envirologix.com	207-797-0300		743
Environamics Inc 13935 S Point Blvd . . . . Charlotte NC 28273 *TF:* 800-262-3613 ■ *Web:* www.environamics-inc.com	704-376-3613		186
Environics Analytics Group Ltd 33 Bloor St E Ste 400 . . . . Toronto ON M4W3H1 *TF:* 888-339-3304 ■ *Web:* www.environicsanalytics.com	416-969-2733		195
Environics Inc 69 Industrial Park Rd E . . . . .Tolland CT 06084 *Web:* www.environics.com	860-872-1111		419
Environment Associates Inc 9604 Variel Ave. . . . . Chatsworth CA 91311 *TF:* 800-395-7046 ■ *Web:* www.eatest.com	818-709-0568	709-8914	794
Environment Control 3430 N 1st Ave. . . . . .Tucson AZ 85719 *Web:* www.environmentcontrol.com	520-292-3992		256
Environment Ltd 10506 Kinghurst St . . . . .Houston TX 77099 *Web:* www.environmentmillwork.com	281-983-0100	983-0147	499
Environment One Corp 2773 Balltown Rd . . . . Niskayuna NY 12309 *Web:* eone.com	518-346-6161		641
Environmental & Safety Designs Inc 5724 Summer Trees Dr. . . . . Memphis TN 38134 *TF:* 800-588-7962 ■ *Web:* www.ensafe.com	901-372-7962	372-2454	192
Environmental Air Systems Inc (EAS) 250 Swathmore Ave . . . . High Point NC 27263 *Web:* www.easinc.net	336-273-1975		14
Environmental Analysis and Permitting Inc (EAP) 299 Dr Martin Luther King Jr St N . . . . Saint Petersburg FL 33701 *Web:* www.eapermit.com	727-894-4643	822-2919	192
Environmental Assessment & Remediation Management Inc 4097 Trl Creek Rd. . . . . Riverside CA 92505 *Web:* www.earmanagement.com	951-735-5575		256
Environmental Compliance Management Services 2377 Gold Meadow Way Ste 100 . . . . Gold River CA 95670 *Web:* www.ecms.com	916-988-0867	988-2139	192
Environmental Consultants Inc 207 Lakeside Dr Ste 203. . . . . .Southampton PA 18966 *Web:* www.eci-consulting.com	215-322-4040		302
Environmental Data Resources Inc (EDR) 6 Armstrong Rd 4th Fl . . . . Shelton CT 06484 *TF:* 800-352-0050 ■ *Web:* www.edrnet.com	800-352-0050	231-6802	387
Environmental Defense 257 Park Ave S . . . . New York NY 10010 *TF:* 800-505-0703 ■ *Web:* www.edf.org	212-616-1240	505-2100	48-13
Environmental Enterprises Inc (EEI) 10163 Cincinnati-Dayton Rd . . . . Cincinnati OH 45241 *TF:* 800-722-2818 ■ *Web:* www.eeienv.com	800-722-2818		667
Environmental Express Ltd 2345A Charleston Regional Pkwy. . . . . .Charleston SC 29492 *Web:* www.envexp.com	843-881-6560		419
Environmental Health & Engineering Inc 117 Fourth Ave. . . . . .Needham MA 02494 *TF:* 800-825-5343 ■ *Web:* eheinc.com	781-247-4300		256
Environmental Information Assn (EIA) 6935 Wisconsin Ave Ste 306 . . . . Chevy Chase MD 20815 *TF:* 888-343-4342 ■ *Web:* www.eia-usa.org	301-961-4999	961-3094	48-13
Environmental International Corp 161 Kimball Bridge Rd Ste 100. . . . . Alpharetta GA 30009 *Web:* eicusa.com	770-772-7100		261
Environmental Law Institute (ELI) 2000 L St NW Ste 620 . . . . .Washington DC 20036 *TF:* 800-433-5120 ■ *Web:* www.eli.org	202-939-3800	939-3868	49-10
Environmental Management Inc 5200 NE Hwy 33. . . . . .Guthrie OK 73044 *TF:* 800-510-8510 ■ *Web:* www.emiok.com	405-282-8510		668
Environmental Materials LLC 6300 E Stapleton Dr S . . . . .Denver CO 80216 *Web:* www.estoneworks.com	303-309-3040		724
Environmental Pneumatics Inc 215 Bowers Rd S . . . . Oakland TN 38060 *Web:* www.ep-corp.com	901-465-0211		697
Environmental Protection Agency (EPA) 1200 Pennsylvania Ave NW . . . . .Washington DC 20004 *TF:* 888-372-8255 ■ *Web:* www.epa.gov	202-564-4700		340-20
Environmental Protection Agency *U.S. National Response Team* 1200 Pennsylvania Ave NW. . . . . .Washington DC 20004 *TF:* 800-424-9346 ■ *Web:* nrt.org	202-267-2675		340-20
Environmental Protection Agency Regional Offices			
Region 1 1 Congress St Ste 1100 . . . . .Boston MA 02114 *TF:* 888-372-7341 ■ *Web:* www.epa.gov	617-918-1111	918-0101	340-20
Region 2 290 Broadway. New York NY 10007 *Web:* www.epa.gov	212-637-3000		340-20
Region 3 1650 Arch St. . . . . .Philadelphia PA 19103 *TF:* 800-438-2474 ■ *Web:* www.epa.gov	215-814-5000		340-20
Region 4 Sam Nunn Atlanta Federal Ctr 61 Forsyth St SW . . . . Atlanta GA 30303 *TF:* 800-241-1754 ■ *Web:* www.epa.gov	404-562-9900	562-8174	340-20
Region 5 77 W Jackson Blvd. . . . . .Chicago IL 60604 *TF:* 800-621-8431 ■ *Web:* www.epa.gov	312-353-2000		340-20
Region 6 1445 Ross Ave Ste 1200 . . . . Dallas TX 75202 *TF:* 800-887-6063 ■ *Web:* www.epa.gov	214-665-2200		340-20
Region 7 901 N Fifth St. . . . . Kansas City KS 66101 *TF:* 800-223-0425 ■ *Web:* www.epa.gov	913-551-7003		340-20
Region 8 1595 Wynkoop St. . . . . .Denver CO 80202 *TF:* 800-227-8917 ■ *Web:* www.epa.gov	303-312-6312		340-20
Region 9 75 Hawthorne St. . . . . San Francisco CA 94105 *TF:* 866-372-9378 ■ *Web:* www.epa.gov	415-947-8000		340-20
Region 10 1200 Sixth Ave Ste 900 . . . . Seattle WA 98101 *TF:* 800-424-4372 ■ *Web:* www.epa.gov	206-553-1200		340-20
Environmental Protection Information Ctr (EPIC) 145 G St Ste A . . . . Arcata CA 95521 *Web:* www.wildcalifornia.org	707-822-7711	822-7712	48-13
Environmental Resolutions Inc (ERI) 815 E Gate Dr Ste 103 . . . . .Mount Laurel NJ 08054 *Web:* www.erinj.com	856-235-7170		196
Environmental Resource Ctr 101 Center Pointe Dr . . . . .Cary NC 27513 *TF:* 800-537-2372 ■ *Web:* www.ercweb.com	919-469-1585	342-0807	167-3
Environmental Science Assoc 225 Bush St Ste 1700. . . . . San Francisco CA 94104 *Web:* www.esassoc.com	415-896-5900	896-0332	668
Environmental Service Partners 2531 Briarcliff Rd Ste 204. . . . . Atlanta GA 30329 *Web:* environmentalservicepartners.com	404-500-2488		104
Environmental Services Inc (ESI) 7220 Financial Way Ste 100. . . . . .Jacksonville FL 32256 *Web:* www.esinc.cc	904-470-2200	470-2112	192
Environmental Specialists Inc 3001 E 83rd St . . . . Kansas City MO 64132 *Web:* www.esicontractingcorp.com	816-523-5081	523-0183	189-11
Environmental Standards Inc 1140 Valley Forge Rd PO Box 810 . . . . .Valley Forge PA 19482 *Web:* www.envstd.com	610-935-5577		192
Environmental Systems Products Inc 7 Kripes Rd. . . . . East Granby CT 06026 *TF:* 800-446-4708 ■ *Web:* www.esp-global.com	860-392-2100		407
Environmental Systems Research Institute Inc 380 New York St. . . . . Redlands CA 92373 *TF:* 800-447-9778 ■ *Web:* www.esri.com	909-793-2853	793-5953	178-10
Environmental Technology Council (ETC) 1112 16th St Ste 420 . . . . .Washington DC 20036 *Web:* www.etc.org	202-783-0870		48-12

	Phone	Fax	Class
Environmental Tectonics Corp 125 James Way ... Southampton PA 18966 *OTC: ETCC* ■ *Web:* www.etcusa.com	215-355-9100	357-4000	703
Environmental Traveling Companions (ETC) 2 Marina Blvd Bldg C ... San Francisco CA 94123 *Web:* www.etctrips.org	415-474-7662	474-3919	48-23
Environmental Treatment & Technology Inc 3275 Walnut Ave ... Signal Hill CA 90755 *Web:* www.atlglobal.com	562-989-4045	989-4040	743
Enviroprobe Integrated Solutions Inc 630 Cross Lanes Dr ... Nitro WV 25143 *Web:* enviroprobeinc.com	304-776-6717		261
Enviro-Pro-Tech Inc 99 S Alcaniz St Ste A ... Pensacola FL 32507	850-458-5447		141
Envirosafe Services of Ohio Inc 876 Otter Creek Rd ... Oregon OH 43616 *Web:* envirosafeservices.com	419-698-3500		196
Enviro-Sciences (ESI) 781 Rt 15 S ... Lake Hopatcong NJ 07849 *Web:* www.enviro-sciences.com	973-398-8183	398-8037	261
Envirosearch Operations Inc 4166-15 Side Rd ... Rockwood ON N0B2K0 *Web:* www.envirosearchoperations.ca	905-854-4441		261
Envirosell Inc 907 Broadway ... New York NY 10010 *Web:* envirosell.com	212-673-9100		466
Envirosep Fluid & Heat Recovery Systems 31 Aviation Blvd ... Georgetown SC 29440 *Web:* www.envirosep.com	843-546-7400		196
EnviroServe JV 5502 Schaaf Rd ... Cleveland OH 44131 *Web:* enviroserve.com	216-642-1311		196
Enviro-Shred LLC 1045 Second Ave NW ... Hickory NC 28601 *Web:* www.enviroshrednc.com	828-328-9333		317
Envirospec Engineering 349 Northern Blvd Ste 3 ... Albany NY 12204 *Web:* envirospeceng.com	518-453-2203		261
Envirosure Solutions LLC 1979 E Broadway Rd ... Tempe AZ 85282 *Web:* envirosure.com	480-784-4621	784-2207	196
Envirosystems LLC 2555 N Coyote Dr Ste 118 ... Tucson AZ 85745 *TF:* 800-999-0501 ■ *Web:* www.envirosystemsllc.com	520-573-3064	572-3068	196
Enviro-Tote Inc 15 Industrial Dr ... Londonderry NH 03053 *TF:* 800-868-3224 ■ *Web:* www.enviro-tote.com	603-647-7171	647-0116	66
EnviroTrac Ltd 5 Old Dock Rd ... Yaphank NY 11980 *TF:* 800-652-5140 ■ *Web:* envirotrac.com	631-924-3001		192
EnviroVantage 629 Calef Hwy Rt 125 ... Epping NH 03042 *TF:* 800-640-5323 ■ *Web:* www.envirovantage.com	603-679-9682	679-9685	667
Envisa Inc 281 Pleasant St ... Framingham MA 01701 *Web:* www.envisa.com	508-405-1220	405-1219	194
Envision 1090 N Cole Rd ... Boise ID 83704 *TF:* 800-546-6889 ■ *Web:* www.envisionsight.org	208-338-5466	338-6543	269
Envision Capital Management Inc 2301 Rosecrans Ave Ste 4180 ... El Segundo CA 90245 *TF:* 800-400-0989 ■ *Web:* www.envisioncap.com	310-445-3252	445-3258	401
Envision Consulting 1425 Broadway Ste 36 ... Seattle WA 98122 *Web:* www.envisionconsult.com	206-306-3992	365-0542	194
Envision Creative Group 3400 Northland Dr ... Austin TX 78731 *Web:* www.envision-creative.com	512-292-1049		6
Envision Group 990 W 190th St Ste 220 ... Torrance CA 90502 *Web:* www.envisiongroup.com	310-523-2000		194
Envision Healthcare 1A Burton Hills Blvd ... Nashville TN 37215 *TF:* 877-235-3343 ■ *Web:* www.evhc.net	615-665-1283		360-3
Envision Inc 610 N Main St ... Wichita KS 67203 *TF:* 888-425-7072 ■ *Web:* www.envisionus.com	316-440-1500	440-1540	48-6
Envision Marketing Inc 26941 Cabot Rd Ste 121 ... Laguna Hills CA 92653 *Web:* www.envisionmarketing.net	949-367-7818	367-7822	195
Envision Media Inc 331 Soquel Ave Ste 100 ... Santa Cruz CA 95062 *Web:* www.envisionmedia.us	831-429-5400		344
Envision Online Media Inc 1150 Morrison Dr Ste 201 ... Ottawa ON K2H8S9 *Web:* www.envisiononline.ca	613-594-2804		225
Envision Payment Solutions Inc PO Box 157 ... Suwanee GA 30024 *TF:* 800-290-3957 ■ *Web:* envisionpayments.com	770-709-3007		179
Envision Radio Networks 3733 Pk E Dr Ste 222 ... Cleveland OH 44122 *Web:* www.envisionnetworks.com	216-831-3761		645-141
Envision Technology Advisors LLC 999 Main St ... Pawtucket RI 02860 *TF:* 855-679-2971 ■ *Web:* www.envisionsuccess.net	401-272-6688	272-0911	177
Envision Telephony Inc 901 Fifth Ave Ste 3300 ... Seattle WA 98164 *Web:* www.envisioninc.com	206-225-0800		178-10
Envisioneering Inc 5904 Richmond Hwy Ste 300 ... Alexandria VA 22303 *Web:* www.envisioneeringinc.com	571-483-4100		261
Envisionit Chicago LLC 130 E Randolph St Ste 1600 ... Chicago IL 60601 *Web:* envisionitagency.com	312-236-2000		344
EnvisionRxOptions 2181 E Aurora Rd Ste 201 ... Twinsburg OH 44087 **Fax Area Code:* 330 ■ *TF:* 800-361-4542 ■ *Web:* www.envisionrx.com	800-361-4542	405-8081*	390
Envisn Inc 233 Ayer Rd ... Harvard MA 01451 *Web:* envisn.com	978-779-0400		225
Enviva Lp 7200 Wisconsin Ave Ste 1100 ... Bethesda MD 20814 *Web:* www.envivabiomass.com	301-657-5560		820
Envoy Advisors 357 Commercial St Ste 817 ... Boston MA 02210 *Web:* www.envoyadvisors.com	617-292-7676		70
Envoy Inc 3317 N 107th St ... Omaha NE 68134 *Web:* www.envoyinc.com	402-558-0637		5
Envoy Plan Services Inc 901 Calle Amanecer Ste 200 ... San Clemente CA 92673 *TF:* 800-248-8858 ■ *Web:* envoyplanservices.com	949-366-5070		535
Envysion Inc 100 Superior Plaza Way Ste 260 ... Superior CO 80027 *TF:* 877-258-9441 ■ *Web:* www.envysion.com	303-590-2350	590-2351	177
Enwood Structures Inc 5724 McCrimmon Pkwy PO Box 2002 ... Morrisville NC 27560 *TF:* 800-777-8648 ■ *Web:* www.enwood.com	919-518-0464	469-2536	817
Enzi Michael B (Sen R - WY) 379A Russell Senate Office Bldg ... Washington DC 20510 *TF:* 888-250-1879 ■ *Web:* www.enzi.senate.gov	202-224-3424	228-0359	342-2
Enzo Biochem Inc 527 Madison Ave ... New York NY 10022 *NYSE: ENZ* ■ *TF:* 800-522-5052 ■ *Web:* www.enzo.com	212-583-0100	583-0150	231
Enzo Clinical Labs Inc 60 Executive Blvd ... Farmingdale NY 11735 *Web:* enzoclinicallabs.com	631-755-5500	715-3256	415
Enzo Life Sciences Inc 10 Executive Blvd ... Farmingdale NY 11735 *TF:* 800-942-0430 ■ *Web:* www.enzolifesciences.com	631-694-7070		231
Enzon Pharmaceuticals Inc 20 Kingsbridge Rd ... Piscataway NJ 08854 *NASDAQ: ENZN* ■ *Web:* www.enzon.com	732-980-4500		85
EO Media Group 211 SE Byers Ave ... Pendleton OR 97801 *Web:* www.eastoregonian.com	541-276-2211		532-3
EOA Inc 1410 Jackson St ... Oakland CA 94612 *Web:* eoainc.com	510-832-2852		261
EOG Resources Inc 1111 Bagby Sky Lobby 2 ... Houston TX 77002 *NYSE: EOG* ■ *TF:* 877-363-3647 ■ *Web:* www.eogresources.com	713-651-7000	651-6995	538
EOI Service Company Inc 1820 E 1st St Ste 400 ... Santa Ana CA 92705 *TF:* 800-229-4364 ■ *Web:* eoiservice.com	714-935-0503		390
Eola Hills Wine Cellars 501 S Pacific Hwy 99 W ... Rickreall OR 97371 *TF:* 800-291-6730 ■ *Web:* eolahillswinery.com	503-623-2405	623-0350	50-7
EON Reality Inc 39 Parker St Ste 100 ... Irvine CA 92618 *Web:* www.eonreality.com	949-460-2000		174
E-ONE Inc 1601 SW 37th Ave ... Ocala FL 34474 *Web:* www.e-one.com	352-237-1122	237-1151	516
EOR Energy Services Inc 3950 Braxton Ste 100 ... Houston TX 77063 *Web:* www.eorenergy.com	713-914-9300	914-9307	536
Eoriginal Inc 351 W Camden St Ste 800 ... Baltimore MD 21201 *TF:* 866-935-1776 ■ *Web:* www.eoriginal.com	866-935-1776		177
EOS Partners LP 320 Park Ave 14th Fl ... New York NY 10022 *Web:* www.eospartners.com	212-832-5800	832-5815	402
Eos Research Ltd 159 Walnut St ... Rochester NH 03867 *Web:* eosresearch.com	603-332-2099	332-2727	261
Eos Systems Inc 16 Franklin St Ste 102 ... Needham MA 02494 *TF:* 855-453-2600 ■ *Web:* www.eos-systems.com	781-453-2600		180
EOSPACE Inc 6222 185th Ave NE ... Redmond WA 98052 *Web:* www.eospace.com	425-869-8673		116
EP (Exceptional Parent) 38 River Edge Rd Ste B ... River Edge NJ 07661 *TF:* 800-372-7368 ■ *Web:* www.eparent.com	201-843-3274		637-9
EP "Tom" Sawyer State Park 3000 Freys Hill Rd ... Louisville KY 40241 *Web:* parks.ky.gov	502-429-7270	429-7273	565
EP Canada Film Services Inc 130 Bloor St W Ste 500 ... Toronto ON M5S1N5 *Web:* www.ep.com	416-923-9255		734
EP Foster Library 651 E Main St ... Ventura CA 93001 *Web:* www.vencolibrary.org	805-648-2716		434-3
EP Henry Corp 201 Park Ave ... Woodbury NJ 08096 **Fax Area Code:* 856 ■ *TF:* 800-444-3679 ■ *Web:* www.ephenry.com	800-444-3679	845-0023*	183
EP Wealth Advisors Inc 21515 Hawthorne Blvd Ste 1200 ... Torrance CA 90503 *TF:* 800-272-2328 ■ *Web:* www.epwealth.com	310-543-4559		194
EPA (Environmental Protection Agency) 1200 Pennsylvania Ave NW ... Washington DC 20004 *TF:* 888-372-8255 ■ *Web:* www.epa.gov	202-564-4700		340-20
Epac Software Technologies Inc 42 Ladd St ... East Greenwich RI 02818 *TF:* 888-336-3722 ■ *Web:* epacst.com	888-336-3722		177
E-Pak Machinery Inc 1535 S State Rd 39 ... La Porte IN 46350 *TF:* 800-328-0466 ■ *Web:* www.epakmachinery.com	219-393-5541	324-2884	547
EPC Consultants Inc 655 Davis St ... San Francisco CA 94111 *Web:* www.epcconsultants.com	415-675-7580		180
EPC Inc 2180 Bennett Rd ... Philadelphia PA 19116 *Web:* plastx.us	215-464-1440	464-1636	596
EPC IT Solutions Inc 1324 El Camino Real ... Belmont CA 94002 *TF:* 888-372-1233 ■ *Web:* www.epcservices.com	650-592-4372		175
EPCO (Engineered Products Co) 601 Kelso St PO Box 108 ... Flint MI 48506 *TF:* 888-414-3726 ■ *Web:* www.epcohardware.com	810-767-2050	767-5084	350
Epcon Communities Inc 500 Stonehenge Pkwy ... Dublin OH 43017 *TF:* 888-893-0590 ■ *Web:* www.epconcommunities.com	614-761-1010	761-1155	653
Epcon Industrial Systems LP 17777 I- 45 S ... Conroe TX 77385 *Web:* www.epconlp.com	936-273-3300		18
Epec LLC 174 Duchaine Blvd ... New Bedford MA 02745 *Web:* www.epectec.com	508-995-5171		625
ePerformax Contact Centers & BPO 100 Saddle Springs Blvd Ste 100 ... Thompsons Station TN 37179 *TF:* 888-384-7004 ■ *Web:* www.eperformax.com	888-384-7004		196
Epes Carriers Inc 3400 Edgefield Ct ... Greensboro NC 27409 *TF:* 800-869-3737 ■ *Web:* www.epestransport.com	336-668-3358		780
Ephesoft Inc 8707 Research Dr ... Irvine CA 92618 *Web:* ephesoft.com	949-335-5335		261
Ephibian Inc 3180 N Swan Rd ... Tucson AZ 85712 *Web:* www.ephibian.com	520-917-4747		177
Ephor Group LLC 24 E Greenway Plz Ste 440 ... Houston TX 77046 *TF:* 800-379-9330 ■ *Web:* www.ephorgroup.com	800-379-9330		463

Listing	Phone	Fax	Class
Ephox Corp 2100 Geng Rd . . . . Palo Alto CA 94303 *Web:* www.tiny.cloud	650-292-9659		177
Ephraim McDowell Regional Medical Ctr 217 S Third St . . . . Danville KY 40422 *Web:* www.emhealth.org	859-239-1000		374-3
EPI (Engineered Products Inc) 200 Jones St. . . . . Verona PA 15147 *Web:* www.epimetal.com	412-423-4000	423-4002	234
EPI Consultants 2828 Technology Forest Blvd . . . . The Woodlands TX 77381 *Web:* www.epiconsultants.com	281-820-2828		196
EPI labelers 1145 E Wellspring Rd . . . . New Freedom PA 17349 *Web:* www.epilabelers.com	717-235-8345		547
EPI Marketing Group 30262 Crown Vly Pkwy Ste B458 . . . . Laguna Niguel CA 92677 *Web:* epiinc.com	949-542-7743		463
EPI Marketing Services 5404 Wayne Rd. . . . . Battle Creek MI 49037 *TF:* 800-562-9733 ■ *Web:* www.epiinc.com	800-562-9733		627
EPIC (Environmental Protection Information Ctr) 145 G St Ste A . . . . Arcata CA 95521 *Web:* www.wildcalifornia.org	707-822-7711	822-7712	48-13
EPIC (Electronic Privacy Information Ctr) 1718 Connecticut Ave NW Ste 200. . . . Washington DC 20009 *Web:* epic.org	202-483-1140	483-1248	48-9
Epic AIR LLC 22590 Nelson Rd . . . . Bend OR 97701 *Web:* epicaircraft.com	541-318-8849	382-5125	20
Epic Aviation LLC 3871 Fairview Industrial Dr SE Ste 100 . . . . Salem OR 97302 *TF:* 866-501-3742 ■ *Web:* www.epicfuels.com	503-362-3633	566-2319	579
Epic Bible College & Graduate School 4330 Auburn Blvd. . . . . Sacramento CA 95842 *Web:* epic.edu	916-348-4689		166
Epic Design Studios 11641 Salinaz Ave . . . . Garden Grove CA 92843 *Web:* www.epicdesign.com	714-636-2554		344
Epic Engineering Group LLC 1531 Boettler Rd Ste B . . . . Uniontown OH 44685 *Web:* epic-eeg.com	330-899-4955		261
Epic Flight Academy New Smyrna Beach Municipal Airport 600 Skyline Dr . . . . New Smyrna Beach FL 32168 *TF:* 866-359-3742 ■ *Web:* www.epicflightacademy.com	386-409-5583		167-3
Epic Labs 95 Third St NE PO Box 7430 . . . . Waite Park MN 56387 **Fax Area Code: 800* ■ *TF:* 877-374-2522 ■ *Web:* epiclabsinc.com	877-374-2522	666-4513*	543
Epic Life Insurance Co 1717 W Broadway. . . . . Madison WI 53713 **Fax Area Code: 608* ■ *TF:* 800-520-5750 ■ *Web:* www.epiclife.com	800-520-5750	223-2159*	391-2
Epic Lift Systems LLC 14485 Hwy 377 S. . . . . Fort Worth TX 76126 *Web:* www.epiclift.com	817-443-3500		539
Epic Machine Inc 201 Industrial Way. . . . . Fenton MI 48430 *Web:* epicmachine.com	810-629-9400	629-1838	454
Epic Metals Corp 11 Talbot Ave . . . . Rankin PA 15104 *TF:* 877-696-3742 ■ *Web:* epicmetals.com	412-351-3913		697
Epic Research LLC 1105 N Market St Ste 1600. . . . . Wilmington DE 19801 *Web:* www.epicresearch.net	302-467-5445		195
Epic Systems Corp 1979 Milky Way. . . . . Verona WI 53593 *Web:* www.epic.com	608-271-9000	271-7237	180
Epic Ventures 15 W South Temple Ste 500 . . . . Salt Lake City UT 84101 *Web:* www.epicvc.com	801-524-8939		792
Epic! Creations Inc 702 Marshall St . . . . Redwood City CA 94003 *Web:* www.getepic.com	650-430-1658		434-2
Epicenter Network Inc *Epicenter Technologies LLC* 3400 188th St SW Ste 500 . . . . Lynnwood WA 98037	425-744-1450		7
Epicurean Inc 257 B Main St. . . . . Superior WI 54880 *TF:* 866-678-3500 ■ *Web:* www.epicureancs.com	218-740-3500		279
EPIEN Medical Inc 4225 White Bear Pkwy Ste 600. . . . . Saint Paul MN 55110 *Web:* www.epien.com	651-653-3380		668
Epi-Hab Phoenix Inc 2125 W Fillmore St. . . . . Phoenix AZ 85009 *Web:* www.epihab.org	602-254-7027	495-9316	393
Epilepsy Foundation 8301 Professional Pl Ste 200. . . . . Landover Hills MD 20785 *TF:* 800-332-1000 ■ *Web:* www.epilepsy.com	301-459-3700	577-2684	48-17
Epilog Corp 16371 Table Mtn Pkwy . . . . Golden CO 80403 *TF:* 888-437-4564 ■ *Web:* www.epiloglaser.com	303-277-1188		544
Epimed International Inc 141 Sal Landrio Dr . . . . Johnstown NY 12095 *Web:* www.epimed.com	518-725-0209		476
Epiomed Therapeutics Inc 34091 Formosa Dr . . . . Dana Point CA 92629	949-398-7357		231
Epiphany Biosciences Inc 1462 42nd Ave Ste 2800 . . . . San Francisco CA 94122	415-765-7193	765-7200	668
Epiphany Productions Inc 104 Hume Ave . . . . Alexandria VA 22301 *Web:* epiphanyproductions.com	703-683-7500		463
Epiq Systems Inc 10300 SW Allen Blvd . . . . Beaverton OR 97005 *Web:* www.epiqsystems.com	503-350-5800		41
EPIQ Technologies Inc 4711 Viewridge Ave Ste 230. . . . . San Diego CA 92123 *TF:* 866-316-3747 ■ *Web:* www.epiqtech.com	858-467-9961		225
EPIR Technologies Inc 590 Territorial Dr Unit B . . . . Bolingbrook IL 60440 *Web:* epirtech.com	630-771-0203	771-0207	246
Episcopal Church USA 815 Second Ave . . . . New York NY 10017 *TF:* 800-334-6946 ■ *Web:* www.episcopalchurch.org	212-716-6000	867-0395	48-20
Episcopal Diocese of West Texas 111 Torcido Dr . . . . San Antonio TX 78209 *TF:* 888-824-5387 ■ *Web:* www.dwtx.org	210-824-5387		48-20
Episcopal Divinity School 99 Brattle St . . . . Cambridge MA 02138 *Web:* www.eds.edu	617-864-5385		167-3
Episcopal Health Services Inc 327 Beach 19th St . . . . Far Rockaway NY 11691 *Web:* www.ehs.org	718-869-7000		363
Episcopal High School 1200 N Quaker Ln. . . . . Alexandria VA 22302 *TF:* 877-933-4347 ■ *Web:* www.episcopalhighschool.org	703-933-4062		622
Episcopal Relief & Development 815 Second Ave . . . . New York NY 10017 **Fax Area Code: 212* ■ *TF:* 800-334-7626 ■ *Web:* www.episcopalrelief.org	855-312-4325	687-5302*	48-5
Episode 11 Productions 2814 Bricker Dr . . . . Charlotte NC 28273 *Web:* episode11productions.com	704-998-3711		514
Epitec Inc 24800 Denso Dr Ste 150. . . . . Southfield MI 48033 **Fax Area Code: 800* ■ *Web:* epitec.com	248-353-6800	647-1898*	721
Epitome Networks LLC 1600 E Parham Rd . . . . Richmond VA 23228 *Web:* www.epitomenetworks.com	804-419-8300		196
Epitomione 4502 Chews Vineyard . . . . Ellicott City MD 21043 *Web:* www.epitomione.com	410-696-2772		180
Epix Films 23852 Pacific Coast Hwy Ste 379. . . . . Malibu CA 90265 *Web:* www.epixfilms.com	310-656-9100	656-9104	514
EPKO Industries Inc 1200 Arthur Ave . . . . Elk Grove Village IL 60007 *Web:* www.epko.com	847-437-4000		550
EPL (Edison Price Lighting Inc) 41-50 22nd St . . . . Long Island City NY 11101 *Web:* www.epl.com	718-685-0700		439
EPL (Ellsworth Public Library) 20 State St . . . . Ellsworth ME 04605 *Web:* www.ellsworth.lib.me.us	207-667-6363		434-3
EPL Bio Analytical Services 9095 W Harristown Blvd. . . . . Niantic IL 62551 *TF:* 866-963-2143 ■ *Web:* www.eplbas.com	217-963-2143		743
EPL Feed LLC 411 W Front St . . . . Sumas WA 98295 *TF:* 800-821-6288 ■ *Web:* w2c.eplfeed.com	360-988-5811	988-0411	447
EPLAN Software & Services LLC 37000 Grand River Ave Ste 380 . . . . Farmington Hills MI 48335 *Web:* www.eplan.de	248-945-9204		179
ePlus Inc 13595 Dulles Technology Dr. . . . . Herndon VA 20171 *NASDAQ: PLUS* ■ *TF:* 888-482-1122 ■ *Web:* www.eplus.com	703-984-8400	984-8600	39
Epoch 5 Public Relations 755 New York Ave. . . . . Huntington NY 11743 *Web:* epoch5.com	631-427-1713		636
Epoch Adv Agency Inc 888 E Brighton Ave. . . . . Syracuse NY 13205 *Web:* www.epoch-adv.com	315-492-3270		4
Epoch Design 17617 NE 65th St Ste 2. . . . . Redmond WA 98052 *TF:* 800-589-7990 ■ *Web:* www.epochbydesign.com	800-589-7990		321
Epoch Online 324 W Pershing Blvd Ste 11. . . . . North Little Rock AR 72114 *TF:* 877-312-7500 ■ *Web:* www.epochonline.com	501-907-7500	907-7501	180
Epoch Senior Living 51 Sawyer Rd Ste 500. . . . . Waltham MA 02453 *Web:* www.epochsl.com	781-891-0777		672
Epoch Software Systems Inc 913 Gulf Breeze Pkwy Ste 21A . . . . Gulf Breeze FL 32561 *TF:* 888-872-3762 ■ *Web:* epochsoftware.com	850-916-3201	916-3204	177
Epoch Times Atlanta PO Box 2041 . . . . Suwanee GA 30024 *Web:* www.epochtimes.com	678-485-0136		532-3
Epoque Hotels 2500 NE 135th St Ste 502 . . . . North Miami FL 33181 *Web:* www.epoquehotels.com	305-538-9697		379
Eportation LLC 401 S Second St Ste 305 . . . . Philadelphia PA 19147 *Web:* www.eportation.com	215-627-2651		177
E-Power Marketing Inc 111 N Main St Ste 405 . . . . Oshkosh WI 54901 *Web:* www.epower.com	920-303-1244		195
Eppendorf North America Inc 102 Motor Pkwy . . . . Hauppauge NY 11788 **Fax Area Code: 516* ■ *TF:* 800-645-3050 ■ *Web:* www.eppendorf.com	800-645-3050	334-7506*	419
Eppinger Manufacturing Co 6340 Schaefer Rd . . . . Dearborn MI 48126 *TF:* 888-771-8277 ■ *Web:* www.eppinger.net	313-582-3205		710
Eppley Airfield 4501 Abbott Dr Ste 2300 . . . . Omaha NE 68110 *Web:* www.flyoma.com	402-661-8000	661-8025	27
Eppley Laboratory Inc, The 12 Sheffield Ave . . . . Newport RI 02840 *Web:* www.eppleylab.com	401-847-1020	847-1031	472
Epps Aviation Inc DeKalb Peachtree Airport 1 Aviation Way . . . . Atlanta GA 30341 *TF:* 800-241-6807 ■ *Web:* www.eppsaviation.com	770-458-9851	458-0320	63
Epps, Holloway, Deloach & Hoipkemier LLC 1220 Langford Dr Bldg 200 Ste 101 . . . . Watkinsville GA 30677 *Web:* ehdhlaw.com	706-508-4000	842-6750	41
EPRI 3420 Hillview Ave . . . . Palo Alto CA 94304 *Web:* www.epri.com	650-855-2000		668
EPRO Tile Inc 10890 E CR 6 . . . . Bloomville OH 44818 *TF:* 866-818-3776 ■ *Web:* www.eprotile.com	866-818-3776	343-8453	751
ePromos Promotional Products LLC 113 5th Ave S Ste 1360 . . . . New York NY 10271 *TF:* 800-564-6216 ■ *Web:* www.epromos.com	212-286-8008		96
eProperty Innovations 3975 Fair Ridge Dr Ste 425 N. . . . . Fairfax VA 22033 *Web:* epropertyplus.com	703-460-9001		809
EPS (Educators Publishing Service Inc) PO Box 9031 . . . . Cambridge MA 02139 *TF:* 800-225-5750 ■ *Web:* eps.schoolspecialty.com	800-225-5750		637-2
EPS (Engineered Plastic Systems) 885 Church Rd . . . . Elgin IL 60123 *TF:* 800-480-2327 ■ *Web:* www.epsplasticlumber.com	847-289-8383	289-8382	603
EPS Group Incorporated Engineers, Planners & Surveyors 2045 S Vineyard Ste 101 . . . . Mesa AZ 85210 *Web:* www.epsgroupinc.com	480-503-2250		261

Name / Address	City	State	Zip	Phone	Fax	Class
EPSA (Electric Power Supply Assn) 1401 New York Ave NW Ste 950	Washington	DC	20005	202-628-8200	628-8260	48-12
Web: epsa.org						
EPSCO International & Companies Inc 717 Georgia Ave	Deer Park	TX	77536	281-476-8100		612
Web: eadsepsco.com						
Epsilon Fine Greek Restaurant 422 Tyler St	Monterey	CA	93940	831-655-8108		671
Web: www.epsilonrestaurant.com						
Epsilon Systems Solutions Inc 605 Commerce St	Portsmouth	VA	23707	619-702-1700	961-6281*	698
*Fax Area Code: 757 ■ *Web:* www.epsilonsystems.com						
Epsilonium Systems Inc 2111 E Baseline Rd Ste B7	Tempe	AZ	85283	480-219-2629	294-2371*	180
*Fax Area Code: 602 ■ *Web:* www.epsilonium.com						
ePsolutions Inc 6618 Sitio Del Rio Blvd	Austin	TX	78730	512-263-8765		178-1
Web: www.epsolutions.com						
Epson America Inc 3840 Kilroy Airport Way	Long Beach	CA	90806	800-463-7766		173-6
TF: 800-463-7766 ■ *Web:* www.epson.com						
Epson Electronics America Inc 214 Devcon Dr	San Jose	CA	95112	408-474-0500	922-0238	696
TF: 800-228-3964 ■ *Web:* global.epson.com						
Epson Portland Inc 3950 NW Aloclek Pl	Hillsboro	OR	97124	503-645-1118	690-5450	625
TF: 800-643-7766 ■ *Web:* epson.com						
Epstein Becker & Green PC 250 Park Ave	New York	NY	10177	212-351-4500	661-0989	428
Web: www.ebglaw.com						
Epstein Cole LLP 393 University Ave	Toronto	ON	M5G1E6	416-862-9888		428
Web: epsteincole.com						
epublicEye.com 1010 N Central Ave Ste 201	Glendale	CA	91202	818-547-0222		114
EPYGI Technologies Ltd 6900 Dallas Pkwy Ste 850	Plano	TX	75024	972-692-1166		111
Web: www.epygi.com						
EQ Inc 1235 Bay St Ste 401	Toronto	ON	M5R3K4	888-597-8889		5
TF: 888-597-8889 ■ *Web:* www.eqworks.com						
EQ School of Hair Design 536 W Broadway	Council Bluffs	IA	51503	712-328-2613		685
Web: www.eqschool.net						
EQT Corp 625 Liberty Ave Ste 1700	Pittsburgh	PA	15222	412-553-5700		787
NYSE: EQT ■ *Web:* www.eqt.com						
Equal Employment Opportunity Commission (EEOC) 1801 L St NW	Washington	DC	20507	202-663-4191		340-20
Web: www.eeoc.gov						
Equal Employment Opportunity Commission Regional Office						
Atlanta District 100 Alabama St SW Ste 4R30	Atlanta	GA	30303	800-669-6820	562-6909*	340-20
*Fax Area Code: 404 ■ *TF:* 800-669-6820 ■ *Web:* www.eeoc.gov						
Birmingham District 1130 22nd St S Ste 2000	Birmingham	AL	35205	205-212-2100	212-2105	340-20
Web: www.eeoc.gov						
Charlotte District 129 W Trade St Ste 400	Charlotte	NC	28202	704-344-6682	344-6734	340-20
Web: www.eeoc.gov						
Chicago District 500 W Madison St Ste 2000	Chicago	IL	60661	312-869-8084	869-8220	340-20
Web: www.eeoc.gov						
Dallas District 207 S Houston St 3rd Fl	Dallas	TX	75202	214-253-2700	253-2720	340-20
Web: www.eeoc.gov						
Indianapolis District 101 W Ohio St Ste 1900	Indianapolis	IN	46204	317-226-7212	226-7953	340-20
Web: www.eeoc.gov						
Los Angeles District 255 E Temple St 4th Fl	Los Angeles	CA	90012	800-669-4000	894-1118*	340-20
*Fax Area Code: 213 ■ *TF:* 800-669-4000 ■ *Web:* www.eeoc.gov						
Miami District 2 S Biscayne Blvd Ste 2700	Miami	FL	33131	305-808-1740	808-1834	340-20
Web: www.eeoc.gov						
New York District 33 Whitehall St 5th Fl	New York	NY	10004	212-336-3620	336-3790	340-20
TF: 866-408-8075 ■ *Web:* www.eeoc.gov						
Phoenix District 3300 N Central Ave Ste 690	Phoenix	AZ	85012	602-640-5000	640-5071	340-20
Web: www.eeoc.gov						
Saint Louis District 1222 Spruce St Rm 8100	Saint Louis	MO	63103	314-539-7800	539-7894	340-20
Web: www.eeoc.gov						
Equal Rights Advocates (ERA) 1170 Market St Ste 700	San Francisco	CA	94102	415-621-0672	621-6744	48-24
TF: 800-839-4372 ■ *Web:* www.equalrights.org						
Equal Vision Records 136 Fuller Rd	Albany	NY	12205	518-458-8250		226
Web: www.equalvision.com						
e-Quantum Inc 1380 Greg St Ste 230	Sparks	NV	89431	775-856-2800	856-2408	178-1
TF: 800-328-7804 ■ *Web:* www.e-quantum.com						
Equestrian Canada Equestre 2685 Queensview Dr	Ottawa	ON	K2B8K2	613-248-3484		652
TF: 866-282-8395 ■ *Web:* www.equestrian.ca						
Equi Tax Inc 17111 Rolling Creek Dr Ste 200	Houston	TX	77090	281-444-4866		317
Web: www.equitaxinc.com						
Equifax Credit Marketing Services 1550 Peachtree St NW	Atlanta	GA	30309	404-885-8913	885-8682	218
TF: 800-660-5125 ■ *Web:* www.equifax.com						
EquiLend Holdings LLC 225 Liberty St 10th Fl Ste 1020	New York	NY	10281	212-901-2200		360-3
Web: www.equilend.com						
Equilibar LLC 320 Rutledge Rd	Fletcher	NC	28732	828-650-6590		789
Web: www.equilibar.com						
Equilibrium Inc 100 Tamal Plz Ste 225	Corte Madera	CA	94925	415-332-4343	331-8374	178-8
Web: www.equilibrium.com						
Equine Medical Associates Inc 25200 Trabuco Rd	Lake Forest	CA	92630	949-588-6950		794
Web: equinemedicalassociates.net						
Equine Sports Massage 9791 NW 160th St	Reddick	FL	32686	352-591-6025	591-0988	167-3
Web: www.equinesportsmassage.com						
Equine Veterinary Dental Services 1333 Lundy's Lane Rd NW	Newark	OH	43055	740-587-3116		794
Web: equinevetdental.com						
Equinix Inc One Lagoon Dr	Redwood City	CA	94065	650-598-6000		654
NASDAQ: EQIX ■ *Web:* www.equinix.com						
Equinox 818 Connecticut Ave NW	Washington	DC	20006	202-331-8118		671
Web: www.equinoxrestaurant.com						
Equinox Engineering Ltd 940 Sixth Ave SW 4th Fl	Calgary	AB	T2P3T1	403-205-3833		256
Web: equinox-eng.com						
Equinox Gallery 2321 Granville St	Vancouver	BC	V6H3G4	604-736-2405	736-0464	42
Web: www.equinoxgallery.com						
Equinox Golf Resort & Spa 3567 Main St	Manchester Village	VT	05254	802-362-4700		707
Web: www.equinoxresort.com						
Equinox Ltd 1307 Park Ave	Williamsport	PA	17701	570-322-5900	322-0204	711
TF: 877-322-5909 ■ *Web:* www.equinoxltd.com						
Equinox Software Solutions Inc 12 Kingswood Ct	Marlton	NJ	08053	856-810-0244		180
Web: www.enox.com						
Equiom Inc 6947 Coal Creek Pkwy SE Ste 242	Bellevue	WA	98006	425-818-3043	650-6804	809
Web: www.equiom.com						
Equipment & Tool Institute (ETI) 134 W University Dr Ste 205	Rochester	MI	48307	248-656-5080	971-2375*	49-13
*Fax Area Code: 603 ■ *Web:* www.etools.org						
Equipment Corporation of America 1000 Sta St PO Box 306	Coraopolis	PA	15108	412-264-4480		23
Web: www.ecanet.com						
Equipment Dealers Assn (EDA) 165 N Meramec Ave Ste 430	Saint Louis	MO	63105	636-349-5000	349-5443	49-18
Web: www.equipmentdealer.org						
Equipment Depot Ltd 4100 S I-35	Waco	TX	76706	254-662-4322	252-1313*	358
*Fax Area Code: 512 ■ *Web:* www.eqdepot.com						
Equipment Development Company Inc 100 Thomas Johnson Dr	Frederick	MD	21702	800-638-3326		1
TF: 800-638-3326 ■ *Web:* www.edcoinc.com						
Equipment Fabricating Corp 729 45th Ave	Oakland	CA	94601	510-261-0343	261-0715	73
Web: www.equipmentfabricating.com						
Equipment Inc 2309 Hwy 80 W	Jackson	MS	39204	601-948-3272		190
TF: 888-836-5537 ■ *Web:* www.equipmentinc.com						
Equipment Insurance International 120 Westlake Rd Ste 7	Fayetteville	NC	28314	800-476-2379		390
TF: 800-476-2379 ■ *Web:* e-i-i.com						
Equipment Leasing & Finance Assn (ELFA) 1825 K St NW Ste 900	Washington	DC	20006	202-238-3400	238-3401	49-18
Web: www.elfaonline.org						
Equipment Manufacturing Corp (EMC) 14930 Marquardt Ave	Santa Fe Springs	CA	90670	562-623-9394		386
TF: 888-833-9000 ■ *Web:* www.equipmentmanufacturing.com						
Equipment Rental Co (ERC) 4788 1st Ave N	Duluth	MN	55803	218-728-4441	728-6816	23
TF: 800-925-8609 ■ *Web:* www.equipmentrentalco.com						
Equipment Share 5710 Bull Run Dr	Columbia	MO	65201	573-299-5222		190
Web: www.equipmentshare.com						
EquipmentWatch 6151 Powers Ferry Rd Ste 200	Atlanta	GA	30339	800-669-3282		387
TF: 800-669-3282 ■ *Web:* www.equipmentwatch.com						
EquipNet Inc 5 Dan Rd	Canton	MA	02021	781-821-3482		358
Web: www.equipnet.com						
Equipoise Dental Laboratory Inc 85 Portland Ave	Bergenfield	NJ	07621	201-385-4750	385-3280	418
TF: 800-999-4950 ■ *Web:* www.equipoisedental.com						
Equiptec Mechanical Inc PO Box 991	Capitola	CA	95010	831-462-9511		610
Web: www.equiptec.net						
EQUIPTO 225 Main St	Tatamy	PA	18085	610-253-2775	859-2121*	286
*Fax Area Code: 888 ■ *TF:* 800-323-0801 ■ *Web:* www.equipto.com						
Equipto Electronics Corp 351 Woodlawn Ave	Aurora	IL	60506	630-897-4691	897-5314	254
TF: 800-204-7225 ■ *Web:* www.equiptoelec.com						
EQUIS Hospitality Management LLC 1401 S Brentwood Blvd Ste 675	Saint Louis	MO	63144	314-932-3200	963-7598	194
Web: www.equishotels.com						
Equis Intl 90 South 400 West Ste 620	Salt Lake City	UT	84101	801-265-9996	265-3999	178-10
TF: 800-882-3040 ■ *Web:* www.metastock.com						
Equissage PO Box 447	Round Hill	VA	20142	540-338-1917	338-5569	167-3
TF: 800-843-0224 ■ *Web:* www.equissage.com						
Equitable Bank 113 N Locust St	Grand Island	NE	68801	308-382-3136		70
TF: 877-821-5783 ■ *Web:* equitableonline.com						
Equitable Life & Casualty Insurance Co 3 Triad Ctr	Salt Lake City	UT	84180	877-358-4060	579-3790*	391-2
*Fax Area Code: 801 ■ *TF:* 877-358-4060 ■ *Web:* www.equilife.com						
Equitec Group LLC 111 W Jackson Blvd 2nd Fl	Chicago	IL	60604	888-221-1353		690
Equitrust Financial Group Ltd 570 Lake Cook Rd Ste 101	Deerfield	IL	60015	847-317-0200		463
Web: www.equitrustfinancial.com						
Equity Bank 7701 E Kellogg Ste 100	Wichita	KS	67207	316-681-1776	681-2325	70
Web: www.equitybank.com						
Equity Communications 8025 Black Horse Pk Ste 100	West Atlantic City	NJ	08232	609-484-8444		647
Web: www.equitycommunications.net						
Equity Cooperative Livestock Sales Assn 401 Commerce Ave	Baraboo	WI	53913	608-356-8311	356-0117	446
TF: 800-362-3989 ■ *Web:* www.equitycoop.com						
Equity Exploration Consultants Ltd 1510-250 Howe St	VANCOUVER	BC	V6C3R8	604-688-9806	688-0235	256
Web: www.equityexploration.com						
Equity Funding 12505 Bel-Red Rd Ste 200	Bellevue	WA	98005	425-283-1040	283-1054	216
Web: www.equity-funding.com						
Equity Investment Corp 3007 Piedmont Rd Ste 200	Atlanta	GA	30305	404-239-0111		528
TF: 877-342-0111 ■ *Web:* www.eicatlanta.com						

Phone Fax Class

Equity Lifestyle Properties Inc
2 N Riverside Plz . . . . . Chicago IL 60606 312-279-1400 655
NYSE: ELS ■ *TF:* 800-274-7314 ■ *Web:* www.equitylifestyleproperties.com

Equity Methods LLC
15300 N 90th St Ste 400 . . . . . Scottsdale AZ 85260 480-428-3344 767-1374 196
Web: www.equitymethods.com

Equity Office Properties Trust
222 Riverside Plz Ste 2000 . . . . . Chicago IL 60606 312-466-3300 655
Web: www.eqoffice.com

Equity Residential
2 N Riverside Plz Ste 400 . . . . . Chicago IL 60606 312-474-1300 655
NYSE: EQR ■ *TF:* 800-733-5001 ■ *Web:* www.equityapartments.com

Equus 122 Sears Ave . . . . . Louisville KY 40207 502-897-9721 671
Web: www.equusrestaurant.com

Equus Computer Systems Inc
7725 Washington Ave S . . . . . Edina MN 55439 800-641-1475 173-2
TF: 866-378-8727 ■ *Web:* www.equuscs.com

Equus Magazine
656 Quince Orchard Rd Ste 600 . . . . . Gaithersburg MD 20878 301-977-3900 457-14
TF: 800-829-5910 ■ *Web:* equusmagazine.com

EQUUS Total Return Inc
700 Louisiana St 48th Fl . . . . . Houston TX 77002 888-323-4533 671-1534* 792
**Fax Area Code:* 212 ■ *TF:* 888-323-4533 ■ *Web:* www.equuscap.com

ER Jahna Industries Inc
202 E Stuart Ave . . . . . Lake Wales FL 33853 863-676-9431 676-5137 503-4
Web: www.jahna.com

ER Marketing 512 Delaware St . . . . . Kansas City MO 64105 816-471-1400 193
Web: www.ermarketing.net

ER Precision Optical Corp
805 W Central Blvd . . . . . Orlando FL 32805 407-292-5395 292-7984 542
Web: www.eroptics.com

ER Wagner Manufacturing Company Inc
W130 N8691 Old Orchard Rd . . . . . Menomonee Falls WI 53051 800-558-5596 350
TF: 800-558-5596 ■ *Web:* www.erwagner.com

ERA (Equal Rights Advocates)
1170 Market St Ste 700 . . . . . San Francisco CA 94102 415-621-0672 621-6744 48-24
TF: 800-839-4372 ■ *Web:* www.equalrights.org

ERA (Electronics Representatives Assn)
1325 S Arlington Heights Rd
Ste 204 . . . . . Elk Grove Village IL 60007 312-419-1432 419-1660 49-18
Web: www.era.org

ERA Grizzard Real Estate
1300 W N Blvd . . . . . Leesburg FL 34748 352-787-6966 652
Web: www.eragrizzard.com

ERA Helicopters LLC
600 Airport Service Rd PO Box 6550 . . . . . Lake Charles LA 70606 337-478-6131 474-3918 13
TF: 888-503-8172 ■ *Web:* www.erahelicopters.com

ERA Industries Inc
1800 Greenleaf Ave . . . . . Elk Grove Village IL 60007 847-678-6617 678-7829 454
Web: www.eraind.com

ERA Naper Realty Inc
865 N Columbia St . . . . . Naperville IL 60563 630-961-1776 652
Web: www.eranaper.com

ERA Teachers Inc 555 Grove St Ste 100 . . . . . Herndon VA 20170 703-742-6900 652
Web: era.com

ERA Wilder Realty Inc
120A Columbia Ave . . . . . Chapin SC 29036 803-345-6713 652
TF: 866-593-7653 ■ *Web:* www.era.com

eRad Inc 9 Pilgrim Rd . . . . . Greenville SC 29607 864-234-7430 177
Web: erad.com

Erasable.com PO Box 2761 . . . . . Abilene TX 79604 325-676-0844 459
TF: 800-541-4351 ■ *Web:* erasable.com

Erath County 100 W Washington . . . . . Stephenville TX 76401 254-965-1452 965-5732 338
Web: co.erath.tx.us

Erawan Thai Cuisine 42-31 Bell Blvd . . . . . Bayside NY 11361 718-428-2112 671
Web: www.erawanthaibayside.com

ERB & Roberts Inc 950 SE 21st Ave . . . . . Gainesville FL 32641 352-376-4888 678-6226 273
TF: 800-330-3402 ■ *Web:* www.terrariser.com

ERB Company Inc 1400 Seneca St . . . . . Buffalo NY 14210 716-825-1400 38
Web: erbco.com

ERB Equipment Company Inc
200 Erb Industrial Dr . . . . . Fenton MO 63026 636-349-0200 349-4426 358
TF: 800-634-9661 ■ *Web:* erbequipment.com

ERBCO (Edward R. Bacon Company Inc)
255 Fitzgerald St . . . . . San Martin CA 95046 408-846-1600 358
Web: www.erbacon.com

Erbsloeh Aluminum Solutions Inc
6565 S Sprinkle Rd . . . . . Portage MI 49002 269-323-2565 492
Web: www.wkw.de

ERC (Energy Recovery Council)
2200 Wilson Blvd Ste 310 . . . . . Arlington VA 22201 202-467-6240 48-12
Web: energyrecoverycouncil.org

ERC (Elbow River Casino) 218 18th Ave SE . . . . . Calgary AB T2G1L1 403-289-8880 379
Web: elbowrivercasino.com

ERC (Equipment Rental Co) 4788 1st Ave N . . . . . Duluth MN 55803 218-728-4441 728-6816 23
TF: 800-925-8609 ■ *Web:* www.equipmentrentalco.com

ERC Building Co
5102 S Pinnacle Hills Pkwy . . . . . Rogers AR 72758 479-452-9950 186
Web: erc.com

ERC Parts Inc 4001 Cobb Intl Blvd . . . . . Kennesaw GA 30152 800-241-6880 246
TF: 800-241-6880 ■ *Web:* www.erconline.com

Erchonia Corp 650 Atlantis Rd . . . . . Melbourne FL 32904 321-473-1251 473-1608 475
TF: 888-242-0571 ■ *Web:* www.erchonia.com

ERDC (U.S. Army Engineer Research & Development Ctr)
3909 Halls Ferry Rd . . . . . Vicksburg MS 39180 601-634-2502 668
Web: www.erdc.usace.army.mil

ERDCO Engineering Corp
721 Custer Ave . . . . . Evanston IL 60202 847-328-0550 328-3535 201
TF: 800-553-0550 ■ *Web:* erdco.com

Erdle Perforating Company Inc
100 Pixley Industrial Pkwy . . . . . Rochester NY 14624 585-247-4700 488
Web: www.erdle.com

ERDM (Ernan Roman Direct Marketing Corp)
3 Melrose Ln . . . . . Douglaston NY 11363 718-225-4151 463
Web: www.erdm.com

Erdman 1 Erdman Pl . . . . . Madison WI 53717 866 855-1001 186
TF: 866-855-1001 ■ *Web:* www.erdman.com

Erdman & Hockfield LLP
2300 E Seventh St Ste 100 . . . . . Charlotte NC 28204 704-333-7800 343-2886 41
Web: charlotte-nc-law.com

Erdman Anthony 145 Culver Rd Ste 200 . . . . . Rochester NY 14620 585-427-8888 261
Web: erdmananthony.com

Erdman Automation Corp
1603 14th St S . . . . . Princeton MN 55371 763-389-9475 454
Web: www.erdmanautomation.com

ERE (ERE Media Inc)
217 Thompson St Ste 202 . . . . . New York NY 10012 212-671-1181 631
Web: www.ere.net

ERE Media Inc (ERE)
217 Thompson St Ste 202 . . . . . New York NY 10012 212-671-1181 631
Web: www.ere.net

Erect-A-Tube Inc PO Box 100 . . . . . Harvard IL 60033 815-943-4091 943-4095 105
TF: 800-624-9219 ■ *Web:* www.erect-a-tube.com

ERG (Eastern Research Group Inc)
c/o Dickran Babigian Director of Contracts
110 Hartwell Ave . . . . . Lexington MA 02421 781-674-7310 674-2851 196
Web: www.erg.com

ERGO (Euthanasia Research & Guidance Organization)
24829 Norris Ln . . . . . Junction City OR 97448 541-998-1873 48-17
Web: www.finalexit.org

Ergo Resource Management Inc
801 N Huntington St Ste 7 PO Box 623 . . . . . Syracuse IN 46567 574-457-8020 457-8022 463
Web: www.ergo-syracuse.com

Ergodyne Corp
1021 Bandana Blvd E Ste 220 . . . . . Saint Paul MN 55108 651-642-9889 642-1882 477
TF: 800-225-8238 ■ *Web:* www.ergodyne.com

ErgoGenesis Workplace Solutions LLC
1 BodyBilt Pl . . . . . Navasota TX 77868 936-825-1700 825-1725 319-3
TF: 800-364-5299 ■ *Web:* www.bodybilt.com

Ergon Inc PO Box 1639 . . . . . Jackson MS 39215 601-933-3000 580
Web: www.ergon.com

Ergon Properties Inc PO Box 1639 . . . . . Jackson MS 39215 601-933-3174 653
Web: ergonproperties.com

Ergonomic Group Inc
609-3 Cantiague Rock Rd . . . . . Westbury NY 11590 516-746-7777 174
Web: www.ergogroup.com

Ergos Technology Partners Inc
3831 Golf Dr . . . . . Houston TX 77018 713-621-9220 196
Web: www.ergos.com

Ergotron Inc 1181 Trapp Rd . . . . . Saint Paul MN 55121 651-681-7600 681-7710 319-1
TF: 800-888-8458 ■ *Web:* www.ergotron.com

Erhard BMW of Bloomfield
1845 S Telegraph . . . . . Bloomfield Hills MI 48302 248-642-6565 57
TF: 888-481-4058 ■ *Web:* www.erhardbmw.com

ERHC Energy Inc
5444 Westheimer Rd Ste 1440 . . . . . Houston TX 77056 713-626-4700 536
Web: www.erhc.com

ERI (Evergreen Research Inc)
433 Park Point Dr . . . . . Golden CO 80401 303-526-7402 526-7416 177
Web: www.evergreenresearch.com

ERI (Environmental Resolutions Inc)
815 E Gate Dr Ste 103 . . . . . Mount Laurel NJ 08054 856-235-7170 196
Web: www.erinj.com

ERIC (Education Resources Information Ctr)
655 15th St NW Ste 500 . . . . . Washington DC 20005 800-538-3742 197
TF: 800-538-3742 ■ *Web:* ncela.ed.gov

Eric A. King 301 Grant St Ste 4300 . . . . . Pittsburgh PA 15219 281-667-4200 177
TF: 888-742-2454 ■ *Web:* the-modeling-agency.com

Eric Buchanan & Associates PLLC
414 Mccallie Ave . . . . . Chattanooga TN 37402 877-634-2506 445
TF: 877-634-2506 ■ *Web:* www.buchanandisability.com

Eric Javits 21-35 44th Rd . . . . . Long Island City NY 11101 800-374-1287 34
TF: 866-208-6200 ■ *Web:* www.ericjavits.com

Eric L. Hiser PLC
5080 N 40th St Ste 245 . . . . . Phoenix AZ 85018 480-505-3900 41
Web: jhjlawyers.com

Eric Mower & Assoc
211 W Jefferson St . . . . . Syracuse NY 13202 315-466-1000 4
Web: www.mower.com

Eric Scheffer Savoyasheville
641 Merrimon Ave . . . . . Asheville NC 28804 828-253-1077 671
Web: savoyasheville.com

Eric's San Jose Mexican Restaurant
4478 Rosewood Dr . . . . . Columbia SC 29209 803-783-6650 671
Web: ericssanjosemexicanrestaurant.business.site

Erica Lane Enterprises Inc
3226 Bob Wallace Ave SW Ste 114 . . . . . Huntsville AL 35805 256-536-7117 536-7133 261
Web: www.eleinc.com

Erick Nielsen Enterprises Inc
4453 County Rd Mm Ste 0 . . . . . Orland CA 95963 530-865-9409 196
TF: 800-844-9409 ■ *Web:* www.eneinc.com

Erickson & Sederstrom PC
10330 Regency Parkway Dr . . . . . Omaha NE 68114 402-397-2200 41
Web: eslaw.com

Erickson Consulting Engineers Inc
7201 Delainey Ct . . . . . Sarasota FL 34240 941-373-6460 261
Web: ericksonconsultingengineers.com

Erickson Inc
5550 SW Macadam Ave Ste 200 . . . . . Portland OR 97239 503-505-5800 20
NASDAQ: EAC ■ *TF:* 800-424-2413 ■ *Web:* ericksoninc.com

Erickson Metals Corp 25 Knotter Dr . . . . . Cheshire CT 06410 203-272-2918 492
Web: ericksonmetals.com

Erickson Transport Corp
2255 N Packer Rd . . . . . Springfield MO 65803 417-862-6741 780
Web: ericksontransport.net

Erickson's Flooring & Supply Company Inc
1013 Orchard St . . . . . Ferndale MI 48220 866-541-9663 361
TF: 866-541-9663 ■ *Web:* ericksonsfloors.com

ERICO Products Inc 34600 Solon Rd . . . . . Solon OH 44139 440-248-0100 248-0723 815
TF: 800-248-2677 ■ *Web:* www.erico.com

Ericson Elementary School
2309 Tulare St . . . . . Fresno CA 93721 559-253-6450 685
Web: www.fresnounified.org

Ericson Insurance Services LLC
92 Bee Brook Rd . . . . . Washington Depot CT 06794 860-868-7361 390
Web: ericsoninsurance.com

Name / Address	City	State	Zip	Phone	Fax	Class
Ericsson Inc 6300 Legacy Dr *TF:* 866-374-2272 ■ *Web:* www.ericsson.com	Plano	TX	75024	972-583-0000		735
Erie & Niagara Insurance Assn 8800 Sheridan Dr *Web:* www.enia.com	Williamsville	NY	14221	716-632-5433		391-2
Erie 2-Chautauqua Cattaraugus Boces (ECCB) 8685 Erie Rd *TF:* 800-228-1184 ■ *Web:* www.e2ccb.org	Angola	NY	14006	716-549-4454		685
Erie Art Museum 411 State St *Web:* erieartmuseum.org	Erie	PA	16501	814-459-5477	452-1744	520
Erie Canal Museum 318 Erie Blvd E *Web:* eriecanalmuseum.org	Syracuse	NY	13202	315-471-0593	471-7220	520
Erie City Hall 626 State St *Web:* cityof.erie.pa.us	Erie	PA	16501	814-870-1234	870-1296	337
Erie Community College 121 Ellicott St *Web:* www.ecc.edu	Buffalo	NY	14203	716-851-1189		162
Erie County 873 Abbott Rd *Web:* eriecountycremationservice.com	Buffalo	NY	14202	716-858-8785	858-6550	338
Erie County 140 W Sixth St *Web:* www.eriecountypa.gov	Erie	PA	16501	814-451-6344	451-6334	338
Erie County 2900 Columbus Ave **Fax Area Code:* 888 ■ *Web:* www.erie-county-ohio.net	Sandusky	OH	44870	419-627-7682	399-6065*	338
Erie County Chamber of Commerce 604 W Washington St *Web:* eriecountychamber.com	Sandusky	OH	44870	419-625-6421	625-7914	139
Erie County Medical Ctr 462 Grider St *Web:* www.ecmc.edu	Buffalo	NY	14215	716-895-4305	898-5178	374-3
Erie County Water Authority (ECWA) 295 Main St Rm 350 *TF:* 855-748-1076 ■ *Web:* www.ecwa.org	Buffalo	NY	14203	716-849-8484	849-8467	787
Erie Engineered Products Inc 3949 Walden Ave *Web:* erieengineered.com	Lancaster	NY	14086	716-206-0204	206-0206	198
Erie Foods International Inc 1201 S Main St PO Box 648 *Web:* www.eriefoods.com	Erie	IL	61250	309-659-2233	659-2822	296-10
Erie Forge & Steel Inc 1341 W 16th St *Web:* www.whemco.com	Erie	PA	16502	814-480-4509		483
Erie Institute of Technology 940 Millcreek Mall *TF:* 866-868-3743 ■ *Web:* www.erieit.edu	Erie	PA	16565	814-868-9900	868-9977	167-3
Erie International Airport 4411 W 12th St *Web:* www.erieairport.org	Erie	PA	16505	814-833-4258	833-0393	27
Erie Manufacturing Inc 1520 Centennial Blvd *Web:* www.eriemfgllc.com	Bartow	FL	33830	863-534-3743	533-7706	207
Erie Metro Federal Credit Union 3291 Lake Shore Rd *Web:* eriemetro.org	Blasdell	NY	14219	716-826-1976		219
Erie Metropolitan Transit Authority (EMTA) 127 E 14th St *Web:* www.ride-the-e.com	Erie	PA	16503	814-452-3515		468
Erie News Now 3514 State St *TF:* 866-571-4553 ■ *Web:* www.erienewsnow.com	Erie	PA	16508	814-454-5201	454-3753	532-2
Erie Philharmonic 609 Walnut St *Web:* www.eriephil.org	Erie	PA	16502	814-455-1375	455-1377	573-3
Erie Playhouse 13 W Tenth St *TF:* 800-305-0669 ■ *Web:* www.erieplayhouse.org	Erie	PA	16501	814-454-2852	454-0601	573-4
Erie Press Systems 1253 W 12th St PO Box 4061 *Web:* www.eriepress.com	Erie	PA	16512	814-455-3941		456
Erie Regional Chamber & Growth Partnership 208 E Bayfront Pkwy Ste 100 *Web:* www.eriepa.com	Erie	PA	16507	814-454-7191		139
Erie Specialty Products 645 W 11th St *Web:* www.eriespecialty.com	Erie	PA	16512	814-453-5611	452-4050	253
Erie Steel Treating Inc 5540 Jackman Rd *Web:* www.erie.com	Toledo	OH	43613	419-478-3743		492
Erie Strayer Co 1851 Rudolph Ave PO Box 1031 *TF:* 800-356-4848 ■ *Web:* eriestrayer.com	Erie	PA	16502	814-456-7001	452-3422	190
Erie Times-News 205 W 12th St *TF:* 800-352-0043 ■ *Web:* www.goerie.com	Erie	PA	16534	814-870-1600	870-1808	532-2
Erie VA Medical Ctr 135 E 38th St *TF:* 800-274-8387 ■ *Web:* www.erie.va.gov	Erie	PA	16504	814-868-8661		374-8
Erie Vehicle Co 60 E 51st St *TF:* 888-550-3743 ■ *Web:* erievehicle.com	Chicago	IL	60615	773-536-6300	536-5779	516
Erie Zoo 423 W 38th St *Web:* www.eriezoo.org	Erie	PA	16508	814-864-4091	864-1140	823
ErieTec Inc 1432 E 12th St *TF:* 800-777-6871 ■ *Web:* erietecinc.com	Erie	PA	16503	814-453-6871		385
Erie-Western Pennsylvania Port Authority 1 Holland St *Web:* www.porterie.org	Erie	PA	16507	814-455-7557	455-8070	618
Eriez Manufacturing Company Inc 2200 Asbury Rd *Web:* www.eriez.com	Erie	PA	16506	814-835-6000		207
Erik's Deli Cafe 365 Coral St *Web:* www.eriksdelicafe.com	Santa Cruz	CA	95060	831-458-1818	458-9797	670
Eriks Seals & Plastics Inc 15600 Trinity Blvd Ste 100 **Fax Area Code:* 817 ■ *Web:* www.eriksusa.com	Fort Worth	TX	76155	682-292-5060	571-4700*	326
Eris Exchange LLC 311 S Wacker Dr Ste 950 *TF:* 888-587-2699 ■ *Web:* www.erisfutures.com	Chicago	IL	60606	888-587-2699		691
Eritech Intl 1515 W Glenoaks Blvd *TF:* 888-808-6242 ■ *Web:* www.eritech.com	Glendale	CA	91201	818-244-6242	500-7699	174
Erlab Inc 388 Newburyport Tpke *TF:* 800-964-4434 ■ *Web:* www.erlab.com	Rowley	MA	01969	978-948-2216	948-3354	420
Erlander Home Museum 404 S Third St *Web:* www.swedishhistorical.org	Rockford	IL	61104	815-963-5559		520
Erlanger Health System 975 E Third St *TF:* 877-849-8338 ■ *Web:* www.erlanger.org	Chattanooga	TN	37403	423 778-7000		374-3
Erler Industries Inc 418 Stockwell St PO Box 219 *Web:* www.erler.com	North Vernon	IN	47265	812-346-4421	346-1892	481
Erling Jensen Restaurant 1044 S Yates Rd *Web:* www.ejensen.com	Memphis	TN	38119	901-763-3700	763-3800	671
ER&M (Ecological Restoration & Management Inc) 10600 York Rd Ste 203 *Web:* www.er-m.com	Cockeysville	MD	21030	410-337-4899	583-5678	186
ERMC (Edinburg Regional Medical Ctr) 1102 W Trenton Rd *Web:* www.southtexashealthsystem.com	Edinburg	TX	78539	956-388-6000		374-3
Ermco Inc 1625 W Thompson Rd *Web:* www.ermco.com	Indianapolis	IN	46217	317-780-2923	780-2853	189-4
Erminesoft 2443 Fillmore St *Web:* erminesoft.com	San Francisco	CA	94115	805-364-5433		180
Ernan Roman Direct Marketing Corp (ERDM) 3 Melrose Ln *Web:* www.erdm.com	Douglaston	NY	11363	718-225-4151		463
Ernest A. Buongiorno A Professional Law Corp 18425 Burbank Blvd Ste 600 *Web:* workerscompspecialistca.com	Tarzana	CA	91356	818-996-9800		41
Ernest F. Mariani Company Inc 573 West 2890 South **Fax Area Code:* 801 ■ *TF:* 800-453-2927 ■ *Web:* efmco.com	Salt Lake City	UT	84115	800-453-2927	531-9615*	665
Ernest Hemingway Home & Museum 907 Whitehead St *Web:* www.hemingwayhome.com	Key West	FL	33040	305-294-1136	294-2755	50-3
Ernest Maier Inc 4700 Annapolis Rd *TF:* 888-927-8303 ■ *Web:* www.emcoblock.com	Bladensburg	MD	20710	301-927-8300	779-8924	183
Ernest N. Morial Convention Ctr 900 Convention Center Blvd *Web:* www.mccno.com	New Orleans	LA	70130	504-582-3023	582-3088	205
Ernest Paper Products 5777 Smithway St *TF:* 800-233-7788 ■ *Web:* www.ernestpackaging.com	Commerce	CA	90040	800-233-7788		559
Ernest Ryan Investigators Inc 620 Washington Ave *TF:* 800-613-3832 ■ *Web:* www.ernestryaninvestigators.com	Rensselaer	NY	12144	518-477-0165	758-1362	693
Ernest's Orleans Restaurant & Cocktail Lounge 1601 Spring St S *Web:* www.ernestsorleans.com	Shreveport	LA	71101	318-226-1325	425-0900	671
Ernesto's Mexican Food 1901 16th St *Web:* ernestosmexicanfood.com	Sacramento	CA	95811	916-441-5850		671
Ernie Ball 151 Suburban Rd *TF:* 866-823-2255 ■ *Web:* www.ernieball.com	San Luis Obispo	CA	93401	800-543-2255		527
Ernie Morris Enterprises 232 N Main St *TF:* 800-457-2745 ■ *Web:* www.erniemorris.com	Bushnell	FL	33513	800-457-2745	457-2778	320
Ernie Saxton Communications Inc 1448 Hollywood Ave *Web:* www.saxtonsponsormarket.com	Langhorne	PA	19047	215-752-2392	752-1518	637-10
Ernie Williams Ltd 2613 Hwy 18 E	Algona	IA	50511	515-295-3561		274
Ernie's Cafe 1005 E Walnut St *Web:* www.erniescolumbia.com	Columbia	MO	65201	573-874-7804		671
Ernie's Texas Lunch 58 Chambersburg St *Web:* www.ernies-texas-lunch.com	Gettysburg	PA	17325	717-334-1970		671
Ernst & Young 5 Times Sq *Web:* www.ey.com	New York	NY	10036	212-773-3000	773-6350	2
Ernst Chevrolet Buick Gmc 615 E 23rd St *Web:* www.ernstgm.com	Columbus	NE	68601	402-835-4221		57
Ernst Enterprises Inc 3361 Successful Way *TF:* 800-353-1555 ■ *Web:* www.ernstconcrete.com	Dayton	OH	45414	937-233-5555		182
Ernst Joni (Sen R - IA) 730 Hart Senate Office Bldg *Web:* www.ernst.senate.gov	Washington	DC	20510	202-224-3254	224-9369	342-2
Ernst Publishing Company LLC 1 Commerce Plz 99 Washington Ave Ste 309 *TF:* 800-345-3822 ■ *Web:* marketing.ernstinfo.com	Albany	NY	12210	800-345-3822	252-0906	637-9
Ernst Swedean & Associates PC 4125 Gordon Dr *Web:* esacpaonline.com	Sioux City	IA	51106	712-274-6617		2
Ernst-Van Praag Inc 433 Plaza Real Ste 275 *Web:* evpconsulting.com	Boca Raton	FL	33432	561-447-0557		4
ERP (Emmaus Road Publishing Inc) 1468 Parkview Cir *Web:* stpaulcenter.com	Steubenville	OH	43952	740-283-2880	283-4011	637-2
ERP Group Inc 88 Farwell St	West Haven	CT	06516	203-931-0490		189-10
ERP International LLC 603 Seventh St Ste 203 *Web:* erpinternational.com	Laurel	MD	20707	301-490-0080		196
Errand Solutions LLC 118 S Clinton St Ste 760 *Web:* www.errandsolutions.com	Chicago	IL	60661	312-475-3800		113
ERRC (Eastern Regional Research Ctr) 600 E Mermaid Ln *Web:* www.ars.usda.gov	Wyndmoor	PA	19038	215-233-6400		668
ERRG (Engineering/Remediation Resources Group Inc) 4585 Pacheco Blvd Ste 200 *Web:* www.errg.com	Martinez	CA	94553	925-969-0750	969-0751	261
ERS (Economic Research Service) US Dept of Agriculture 1400 Independence Ave SW MS 1800 *Web:* www.ers.usda.gov	Washington	DC	20250	202-694-5050		340-1
ERS (Executive Reporting Service) 300 1st Ave S Suntrust Bldg Ste 402 *TF:* 800-621-9077 ■ *Web:* www.executivereporting.com	Saint Petersburg	FL	33701	727-823-4155	822-5458	478
ERS Industries Inc 1005 Indian Church Rd	West Seneca	NY	14224	716-675-2040	675-0300	770
Ershigs Inc 742 Marine Dr *Web:* www.ershigs.com	Bellingham	WA	98225	360-733-2620	733-2628	606
Erskine Academy 309 Windsor Rd *Web:* www.erskineacademy.org	South China	ME	04358	207-445-2962		148

Phone Fax Class

Erskine College 2 Washington St .... Due West SC 29639 888-359-4358 166
TF: 888-359-4358 ■ *Web:* www.erskine.edu

ERT 1818 Market St Ste 1000 .... Philadelphia PA 19103 215-972-0420 972-0414 178-10
NASDAQ: ERT ■ *TF:* 800-704-9698 ■ *Web:* www.ert.com

Erte Restaurant 323 13th Ave NE .... Minneapolis MN 55413 612-623-4211 671
Web: ertedining.com

Erthbound Entertainment Inc
PO Box 40011 .... Studio City CA 91614 818-884-3033 376-1042 514
Web: www.erthbound.com

Ervin & Smith Advertising & Public Relations Inc
16934 Frances St .... Omaha NE 68130 402-334-6969 7
Web: ervinandsmith.com

Ervin Cohen & Jessup
9401 Wilshire Blvd 9th Fl .... Beverly Hills CA 90212 310-273-6333 428
Web: www.ecjlaw.com

Ervin Equipment Inc 608 N Ohio St .... Toledo IL 62468 217-849-3125 449
TF: 877-873-6863 ■ *Web:* www.ervinusa.com

Ervin Industries Inc
3893 Research Pk Dr .... Ann Arbor MI 48108 734-769-4600 663-0136 1
TF: 800-748-0055 ■ *Web:* www.ervinindustries.com

Erving Paper Mills 97 E Main St .... Erving MA 01344 413-422-2700 558
Web: www.ervingpaper.com

Erwin & Co 6311 Ranch Dr.................. Little Rock AR 72223 501-868-7486 868-7750 2
Web: erwinco.com

Erwin Record 218 Gay St....................... Erwin TN 37650 423-743-4112 743-6125 532-2
Web: www.erwinrecord.net

Erwin Technical College
2010 E Hillsborough Ave .... Tampa FL 33610 813-769-5180 769-5181 167-3
Web: www.erwin.edu

Erwine Home Health & Hospice
270 Pierce St Ste 101....................... Kingston PA 18704 570-288-1013 371
Web: erwinehealthcare.com

Erwin-Keith Inc 1529 Hwy 193.................. Wynne AR 72396 888-535-7333 10-5
TF: 888-535-7333 ■ *Web:* www.progenyag.com

Erwin-Penland Inc
110 E Court St Ste 400..................... Greenville SC 29601 864-271-0500 636
Web: www.epandcompany.com

ES Components LLC (ESC)
100 Pratts Junction Rd .... Sterling MA 01564 978-422-7641 422-0011 246
Web: www.escomponents.com

ES Gallon & Assoc 2621 Dryden Rd............. Moraine OH 45439 937-586-3100 428
Web: esgallon.com

ES Originals Inc 440 Ninth Ave 7th Fl.......... New York NY 10001 212-736-8124 736-8366 301
TF: 800-677-6577 ■ *Web:* www.esoriginals.com

ES Thermal Inc 300 Ceran....................... Elyria OH 44035 440-323-3291 323-5734 357
Web: es-thermal.com

ES. Fox Ltd 9127 Montrose Rd............. Niagara Falls ON L2E7J9 905-354-3700 261
TF: 866-233-8933 ■ *Web:* esfox.com

ES3 Inc 1625 Star Batt Dr .... Rochester Hills MI 48309 248-537-0110 636
Web: www.es3.net

ESA (Ecological Society of America)
1990 M St Ste 700....................... Washington DC 20036 202-833-8773 833-8775 49-19
Web: www.esa.org

ESA (Evangelicals for Social Action)
PO Box 367 .... Wayne PA 19087 484-384-2988 48-7
TF: 800-650-6600 ■ *Web:* www.evangelicalsforsocialaction.org

ESA (Electronic Security Association Inc)
6333 N State Hwy 161 Ste 350.................. Irving TX 75038 972-807-6800 807-6883 49-3
TF: 888-447-1689 ■ *Web:* esaweb.org

ESA (Entertainment Software Assn)
601 Massachusetts Ave NW Ste 300 .... Washington DC 20001 202-223-2400 223-2401 48-9
TF: 800-949-3660 ■ *Web:* www.theesa.com

ESA Construction Inc
645 El Molino Blvd.......................... Las Cruces NM 88005 505-884-2171 888-3150 186
Web: esaconstruction.com

Esab Welding & Cutting Products
256 Midway Dr.............................. Union SC 29379 864-466-0921 664-4258* 811
**Fax Area Code:* 843 ■ *TF:* 800-372-2123 ■ *Web:* www.esabna.com

Esage Group LLC 605 First Ave Ste 510 .... Seattle WA 98104 206-342-9981 180
Web: www.esagegroup.com

ESAI (Energy Security Analysis Inc)
401 Edgewater Pl Ste 640.................... Wakefield MA 01880 781-245-2036 245-8706 401
Web: www.esai.com

Esalen Institute 55000 Hwy 1.................. Big Sur CA 93920 831-667-3000 667-2724 673
TF: 888-837-2536 ■ *Web:* www.esalen.org

Esbenshade Farms 220 Eby Chiques Rd .... Mount Joy PA 17552 717-653-8061 653-6922 10-8
Web: www.esbenshadefarmmill.com

ESC (ES Components LLC)
108 Pratts Junction Rd .... Sterling MA 01564 978-422-7641 422-0011 246
Web: www.escomponents.com

Escalade Inc 817 Maxwell Ave .... Evansville IN 47711 812-467-1200 710
NASDAQ: ESCA ■ *TF:* 800-426-1421 ■ *Web:* www.escaladesports.com

Escalante State Park
710 N Reservoir Rd......................... Escalante UT 84726 435-826-4466 565
Web: stateparks.utah.gov

Escalent 17430 College Pkwy .... Livonia MI 48152 734-542-7600 542-7620 466
TF: 800-420-9366 ■ *Web:* www.escalent.co

Escalera Inc
708 S Industrial Dr PO Box 1359.............. Yuba City CA 95993 530-673-6318 673-6376 470
TF: 800-622-1359 ■ *Web:* www.escalera.com

Escalon Medical Corp
435 Devon Pk Dr Bldg 100...................... Wayne PA 19087 610-688-6830 688-3641 476
OTC: ESMC ■ *Web:* www.escalonmedical.com

Escalon Premier Brands PO Box 424 .... Escalon CA 95320 209-838-7341 296-20
TF: 800-255-5750 ■ *Web:* www.escalon.net

Escambia County PO Box 848 .... Brewton AL 36427 251-867-0300 338
Web: www.co.escambia.al.us

Escambia County Area Transit (ECAT)
1515 W Fairfield Dr .... Pensacola FL 32501 850-595-3228 595-3222 468
Web: goecat.com

Escambia River Electric Co-opeartive Inc
3425 Florida 4 .... Jay FL 32565 850-675-4521 675-8415 245
TF: 800-235-3848 ■ *Web:* www.erec.com

Escambia Sun-Press Inc
605 S Old Corry Field Rd .... Pensacola FL 32507 850-456-3121 456-0103 532-2
Web: www.escambiasunpress.com

Escamilla & Poneck LLP
700 N St Mary's St Ste 850................. San Antonio TX 78205 210-225-0001 225-0041 428
TF: 888-700-7557 ■ *Web:* www.escamillaponeck.com

Phone Fax Class

Escanaba Public Library
400 Ludington St .... Escanaba MI 49829 906-789-7323 434-3
Web: www.uproc.lib.mi.us

Escape Enterprises Ltd
222 Neilston St........................... Columbus OH 43215 614-224-0300 224-6460 670
Web: www.steakescape.com

Escapees RV Club 100 Rainbow Dr .... Livingston TX 77351 888-757-2582 327-4388* 48-23
**Fax Area Code:* 936 ■ *TF:* 888-757-2582 ■ *Web:* www.escapees.com

ESCC (Enterprise State Community College)
600 Plaza Dr............................. Enterprise AL 36330 334-347-2623 162
Web: www.escc.edu

Eschenbach Optik of America Inc
22 Shelter Rock Ln .... Danbury CT 06810 800-487-5389 799-7200* 544
**Fax Area Code:* 888 ■ *TF:* 800-487-5389 ■ *Web:* www.eschenbach.com

eScholar LLC
222 Bloomingdale Rd Ste 107 .... White Plains NY 10605 914-989-2900 658
Web: www.escholar.com

Esco Corp 2141 NW 25th Ave................... Portland OR 97210 503-228-2141 226-8071 190
TF: 800-523-3795 ■ *Web:* www.escocorp.com

Esco Manufacturing Inc
2020 4th Ave Sw.......................... Watertown SD 57201 800-843-3726 886-5454* 9
**Fax Area Code:* 605 ■ *TF:* 800-843-3726 ■ *Web:* www.escomanufacturing.com

ESCO Technologies Inc
9900A Clayton Rd.......................... Saint Louis MO 63124 314-213-7277 213-7250 360-3
NYSE: ESE ■ *Web:* www.escotechnologies.com

Escobar Veronica (Rep D - TX)
1505 Longworth House Office Bldg .... Washington DC 20515 202-225-4831 342-2
Web: www.escobar.house.gov

Escondido Chamber of Commerce
720 N Broadway .... Escondido CA 92025 760-745-2125 745-1183 139
Web: escondidochamber.org

Escondido Public Library
239 S Kalmia St .... Escondido CA 92025 760-839-4683 434-3
Web: library.escondido.org

Escopazzo 1311 Washington Ave............ Miami Beach FL 33139 305-674-9450 671

Escort Inc 5440 W Chester Rd .... West Chester OH 45069 513-870-8500 942-8849 529
TF: 800-964-3138 ■ *Web:* www.escortradar.com

Escot Bus Lines Inc 6890 142nd Ave............. Largo FL 33771 727-545-2088 107
Web: www.escotbuslines.com

eScreen Inc
7500 W 110th St Ste 500 .... Overland Park KS 66210 800-881-0722 387
TF: 800-881-0722 ■ *Web:* www.escreen.com

Escrow Leaders
31601 Avenida Los Cerritos
Ste 200......................... San Juan Capistrano CA 92675 949-373-7000 276-8210 653
Web: escrowleaders.com

EscrowTech International Inc
3290 W Mayflower Way .... Lehi UT 84043 801-852-8202 393
Web: www.escrowtech.com

ESD (Etiwanda School District)
6061 E Ave .... Etiwanda CA 91739 909-899-2451 899-1235 685
Web: www.etiwanda.k12.ca.us

ESDS (Embedded Software Development Systems Inc)
19925 Stevens Creek Blvd .... Cupertino CA 95014 408-444-1456 178-1
Web: esds.in

Ese Partners LLC
19416 Park Row Ste 120 .... Houston TX 77084 281-501-6100 261
Web: esepartners.com

ESE Solutions LLC
11555 Heron Bay Blvd Ste 200............ Coral Springs FL 33076 954-603-7339 192
Web: www.esesolutions.com

ESEA A. California Corp
280 2nd St Ste 270.......................... Los Altos CA 94022 650-941-4175 941-1582 256
Web: esea.com

Eseco-Speedmaster 730 E Eseco Rd............ Cushing OK 74023 918-225-1266 225-1284 628
TF: 800-331-5904 ■ *Web:* www.eseco-speedmaster.com

eSecurity Solutions LLC
2280 University Dr Ste 104.............. Newport Beach CA 92660 949-261-5556 180
Web: www.esecuritysolutions.com

Eseeola Lodge, The
175 Linville Ave PO Box 99 .... Linville NC 28646 828-733-4311 669
TF: 800-742-6717 ■ *Web:* www.eseeola.com

eSentio Technologies
700 12th St NW Ste 700................... Washington DC 20005 202-628-6010 194
Web: www.esentio.com

ESG (Energy Services Group International Inc)
3601 La Grange Pkwy.......................... Toano VA 23168 757-741-4040 741-4045 721
Web: www.esgi.net

Esg of Baton Rouge LLC
711 Jefferson Hwy Ste 11................. Baton Rouge LA 70806 225-218-4397 218-6857 261
Web: esgbr.com

ESGR (National Committee for Employer Support of the Guard & Reserve)
1555 Wilson Blvd Ste 319 .... Arlington VA 22209 800-336-4590 48-19
TF: 800-336-4590 ■ *Web:* www.esgr.mil

ESH (Eastern State Hospital)
4601 Ironbound Rd...................... Williamsburg VA 23188 757-253-5161 374-5
Web: esh.dbhds.virginia.gov

Eshoo Anna G (Rep D - CA)
202 Cannon House Office Bldg............. Washington DC 20515 202-225-8104 225-8890 342-2
Web: eshoo.house.gov

ESI (Enviro-Sciences) 781 Rt 15 S........ Lake Hopatcong NJ 07849 973-398-8183 398-8037 261
Web: www.enviro-sciences.com

ESI (Environmental Services Inc)
7220 Financial Way Ste 100................ Jacksonville FL 32256 904-470-2200 470-2112 192
Web: www.esinc.cc

ESI (Electronic Security Integration Inc)
68-46 Selfridge St .... Forest Hills NY 11375 718-575-9493 268-4030 692
Web: www.esi-systems.com

ESI Electrical Contractors Inc
4696 Devitt Dr .... Cincinnati OH 45246 513-454-3741 454-0251 189-4
Web: www.esielectrical.com

ESI FME Engineers
1800 E 16th St Ste B......................... Santa Ana CA 92701 714-835-2800 256
Web: www.esifme.com

ESI Incorporated of Tennessee
1250 Roberts Blvd .... Kennesaw GA 30144 770-427-6200 261
Web: www.esitenn.com

Company / Address	City	State	ZIP	Phone	Fax	Class
ESI Software Inc 1465 Kelly Johnson Blvd Ste 305 *TF:* 877-638-7033 ■ *Web:* www.esisoft.us	Colorado Springs	CO	80920	719-638-7033		387
ESI Technologies 1550 Metcalfe St Ste 1100 *TF:* 800-260-3311 ■ *Web:* www.esitechnologies.com	Montreal	QC	H3A1X6	800-260-3311		196
Esignal 3955 Pt Eden Way *TF:* 800-815-8256 ■ *Web:* www.esignal.com	Hayward	CA	94545	510-266-6000	266-6100	178-1
ESIS Inc 7920 Arjons Dr Ste H *Web:* www.esisinc.com	San Diego	CA	92126	858-530-0060		387
Eskaton Inc 5105 Manzanita Ave *TF:* 800-729-2999 ■ *Web:* www.eskaton.org	Carmichael	CA	95608	916-334-0810	338-1248	672
Esker Inc 1212 Deming Way Ste 350 *TF:* 800-368-5283 ■ *Web:* www.esker.com	Madison	WI	53717	608-828-6000	828-6001	178-12
Eskimo North Inc PO Box 55816 *TF:* 800-246-6874 ■ *Web:* www.eskimo.com	Shoreline	WA	98155	206-812-0051	812-0054	177
Eskridge & Assocs 595 Round Rock W Dr Ste 406 *Web:* eskridgeassociates.com	Round Rock	TX	78681	512-244-7023		194
Eskridge Inc 1900 Kansas City Rd *Web:* www.eskridgeinc.com	Olathe	KS	66061	913-782-1238		620
ESL (Ethnic Studies Library) University of California 30 Stephens Hall Ste 2360 *Web:* eslibrary.berkeley.edu	Berkeley	CA	94720	510-643-1234	643-8433	637-2
Esma Inc 450 W Taft Dr *TF:* 800-276-2466 ■ *Web:* esmainc.com	South Holland	IL	60473	708-331-1855	331-8919	143
Esmark Steel Group 2500 Euclid Ave *TF:* 800-323-0340 ■ *Web:* www.esmark.com	Chicago Heights	IL	60411	708-756-0400		360-3
Esmeralda County PO Box 547 *TF:* 800-884-4072 ■ *Web:* www.accessesmeralda.com	Goldfield	NV	89013	775-485-6309	485-6376	338
ESN (Engineering Services Network Inc) 2450 Crystal Dr Ste 1015 *Web:* www.esncc.com	Arlington	VA	22202	703-412-3640		193
ESN Interactive 440 Seaton St Ste 301 *Web:* www.edusearch.com	Los Angeles	CA	90013	323-337-0600		195
eSnipe Inc 12819 SE 38th St *Web:* www.esnipe.com	Bellevue	WA	98006	425-260-5292		387
ESO Won Books 4327 Degnan Blvd *Web:* www.esowonbookstore.com	Los Angeles	CA	90008	323-290-1048		95
eSoftware Professionals 10450 SW Nimbus Ave Ste B *Web:* www.esopro.com	Portland	OR	97223	503-608-3601		631
Esolution Architects Inc 3325 Kessinger Dr *Web:* e-sainc.com	Montgomery	AL	36116	334-532-3663		180
ESOP Assn 1726 M St NW Ste 501 *TF:* 866-366-3832 ■ *Web:* www.esopassociation.org	Washington	DC	20036	202-293-2971	293-7568	49-12
ESP (Electronic Systems Packaging LLC) 1175 W Victoria St *Web:* www.espbus.com	Rancho Dominguez	CA	90220	310-639-2535	632-6666	815
ESP Solutions Group Inc 8627 N Mopac Ste 400 *Web:* www.espsolutionsgroup.com	Austin	TX	78759	512-879-5300	879-5399	387
Espaillat Adriano (Rep D - NY) 1630 Longworth House Office Bldg *Web:* www.espaillat.house.gov	Washington	DC	20515	202-225-4365	226-9731	342-2
Espanola Valley Chamber of Commerce 1 Calle de las Espanolas Ste F & G *Web:* www.espanolanmchamber.com	Espanola	NM	87532	505-753-2831	753-1252	139
ESPE Manufacturing Company Inc 9220 Ivanhoe St *TF:* 800-367-3773 ■ *Web:* www.espemfg.com	Schiller Park	IL	60176	847-678-8950	678-0253	350
ESPEC North America Inc 4141 Central Pky *TF:* 877-463-7732 ■ *Web:* www.espec.com	Hudsonville	MI	49426	616-896-6100	896-6150	202
Esperdyne Technologies LLC 245 Russell St Ste 23A *Web:* www.esperdyne.com	Hadley	MA	01035	413-376-8110		809
Espey Manufacturing & Electronics Corp 233 Ballston Ave *NYSE:* ESP ■ *Web:* www.espey.com	Saratoga Springs	NY	12866	518-245-4400	245-4421	253
Esplanade Tours 535 Boylston St Fl 5 Ste U-1A *TF:* 800-628-4893 ■ *Web:* esplanadetravel.com	Boston	MA	02116	617-266-7465	262-9829	760
ESPN 1170 AM 1229 Brady St *Web:* espn1170am.com	Davenport	IA	52803	563-326-2541		647
ESPN Digital Center 1 545 Middle St *Web:* www.espn.com	Bristol	CT	06010	860-766-5333		740
ESPN KCBF 820 Sports 529 5th Ave Ste 200 *Web:* www.820sports.com	Fairbanks	AK	99701	907-451-5910	451-5999	645-55
ESPN Radio 1410 10 Columbus Blvd *Web:* newsradio1410.iheart.com	Hartford	CT	06106	860-723-6000		645-69
Espo Engineering 855 Midway Dr *Web:* www.espocorp.com	Willowbrook	IL	60527	630-789-2525		256
Esprida Corp 5180 Orbitor Dr *Web:* esprida.com	Mississauga	ON	L4W5L9	905-629-0455		177
Esprit Miami 11475 NW 39th St *TF:* 800-327-2320 ■ *Web:* www.espritmiami.com	Miami	FL	33178	305-591-2244	591-2603	293
Espy Investigate Services 1264 Sapphire Ct *Web:* www.espyinvestigations.com	Ripon	CA	95366	209-609-2676		400
Espy Lumber Co 147 Arrow Rd *Web:* www.espylumber.com	Hilton Head Island	SC	29928	843-785-3821	842-9053	364
Esquire Deposition Solutions 2700 Centennial Tower 101 Marietta St *TF:* 800-211-3376 ■ *Web:* www.esquiresolutions.com	Atlanta	GA	30303	404-495-0777		445
Esquire Grill 1213 K St *Web:* www.paragarys.com	Sacramento	CA	95814	916-448-8900		671
Esquire Inc 21241 Bentura Blvd Ste 293 *Web:* www.esquiresearch.com	Woodland Hills	CA	91364	818-712-9700		260
Esquire Magazine 300 W 57th St 21st Fl *Web:* www.esquire.com	New York	NY	10019	212-649-4020		457-11
Esrey Energy Ltd 1075 Georgia St W Ste 250 *Web:* www.eseyresources.com	Vancouver	BC	V6E3C9	778-373-0103		538
ESRI Canada Ltd 12 Concorde Pl Ste 900 *TF:* 866-625-4577 ■ *Web:* www.esri.ca	Toronto	ON	M3C3R8	416-441-6035		174
Esrock Partners 14550 S 94th Ave *Web:* esrock.com	Orland Park	IL	60462	708-349-8400		7
ESS Data Recovery Inc 110 N Research Dr *Fax Area Code: 800 ■ *TF:* 800-237-4200 ■ *Web:* datarecovery.com	Edwardsville	IL	62025	618-307-0070	299-7815*	177
Ess Tec Inc 3347 128th Ave *Web:* www.ess-tec.com	Holland	MI	49424	616-394-0230		604
ESS Technology Inc 48401 Fremont Blvd *Web:* www.esstech.com	Fremont	CA	94538	510-492-1088		696
Esschem Inc 4000 Columbia Ave *TF:* 800-765-9637 ■ *Web:* www.esschem.com	Linwood	PA	19061	800-765-9637		605-2
Essco Inc 1933 Highland Rd *TF:* 800-321-2664 ■ *Web:* www.essco.net	Twinsburg	OH	44087	216-524-4141		605-2
Essco Inc 1991 Larsen Rd *TF:* 800-835-7134 ■ *Web:* esscoincorporated.com	Green Bay	WI	54303	920-499-6077	494-3483	556
Essdack 1500 E 11th Ave Ste 200 *Web:* www.essdack.org	Hutchinson	KS	67501	620-663-9566		196
Esseks Hefter & Angel 108 E Main St *Web:* www.ehalaw.com	Riverhead	NY	11901	631-369-1700		445
Essen Haus 514 E Wilson St *Web:* www.essen-haus.com	Madison	WI	53703	608-255-4674	258-8632	671
Essence Communications Inc 241 37th St 4th Fl *TF:* 800-274-9398 ■ *Web:* www.essence.com	Brooklyn	NY	11232	800-274-9398		637-9
Essence Printing Inc 270 Oyster Point Blvd *Web:* essenceprinting.com	South San Francisco	CA	94080	650-952-5072		627
Essendant Inc One Parkway North Blvd *TF:* 800-733-4000 ■ *Web:* www.essendant.com	Deerfield	IL	60015	847-627-7000		335
Essendant Printing and Imaging Essentials 13 Centre Dr *TF:* 800-888-8080 ■ *Web:* www.azerty.com	Orchard Park	NY	14127	800-888-8080		174
Essentia Health 502 E Second St *TF:* 855-469-6532 ■ *Web:* www.essentiahealth.org	Duluth	MN	55805	218-786-8376		374-3
Essential Baking Co, The 5601 First Ave S *Web:* essentialbaking.com	Seattle	WA	98108	206-545-3804	767-1176	345
Essential Dental Systems Inc 89 Leuning St Ste 8 *Web:* www.edsdental.com	South Hackensack	NJ	07606	201-487-9090		228
Essential Fire Protection Systems Inc 10920 Marconi Ln *Web:* essentialfire-ep.com	El Paso	TX	79935	915-592-5066	592-6771	390
Essential Management Solutions LLC 94 Brokhoff Rd *Web:* emsolutionsllc.net	Pottsville	PA	17901	570-621-9000	621-9080	463
Essential Network Technologies 924 Hemsath Rd *Web:* essentialnetworktech.com	Saint Charles	MO	63303	636-477-6301	477-6302	225
Essential Personnel Inc 1828 N Webb Rd Ste 1 *Web:* www.essentialpersonnel.com	Grand Island	NE	68803	308-381-4400	381-4401	193
Essential Sealing Products Inc 10145 Queens Way *TF:* 800-528-4368 ■ *Web:* www.espsealing.com	Chagrin Falls	OH	44023	800-528-4368	208-3102	326
Essential Technologies Inc 1107 Hazeltine Blvd Ste 477 *TF:* 844-375-7219 ■ *Web:* www.essentialtechinc.com	Chaska	MN	55318	952-368-9001	368-3334	175
Essentra PLC 7400 W Industrial Dr *Fax Area Code: 886 ■ *TF:* 800-847-0486 ■ *Web:* www.essentra.com	Forest Park	IL	60130	800-847-0486	561-6617*	154
Esser Hayes Insurance Group Inc 1811 High Grove *Web:* esserhayes.com	Naperville	IL	60540	630-355-2077	355-7996	390
Essex Boat Works Inc 9 Ferry St *Web:* www.essexboatworks.com	Essex	CT	06426	860-767-8276	767-1729	698
Essex County 465 Dr Martin Luther King Jr Blvd *Web:* essexcountynj.org	Newark	NJ	07102	973-621-4400	621-6343	338
Essex County 202 S Church Ln PO Box 1079 *TF:* 800-552-9745 ■ *Web:* www.essex-virginia.org	Tappahannock	VA	22560	804-443-4331	445-8023	338
Essex County College 303 University Ave *Web:* www.essex.edu	Newark	NJ	07102	973-877-3000	877-3446	162
Essex County Public Schools 109 Cross St PO Box 756 *Web:* www.essex.k12.va.us	Tappahannock	VA	22560	804-443-4366	443-4498	780
Essex County Teachers Federal Credit Union 125 Franklin St *Web:* ectcu.org	Bloomfield	NJ	07003	973-748-8847		219
Essex Electro Engineering Inc 2015 Mitchell Blvd *Web:* www.essexelectro.com	Schaumburg	IL	60193	847-891-4444	891-9111	111
Essex Experience 21 Essex Way Ste 107 *Web:* www.essexexperience.com	Essex	VT	05451	802-878-4200	879-5080	460
Essex Financial Services Inc 176 Westbrook Rd *TF:* 800-900-5972 ■ *Web:* www.essex.financial	Essex	CT	06426	860-767-4300		528
Essex Food Ingredients 9 Lee Blvd *Fax Area Code: 610 ■ *TF:* 800-441-1017 ■ *Web:* www.essexfoodingredients.com	Frazer	PA	19355	800-441-1017	647-4990*	297-11
Essex Industries Inc 7700 Gravois Rd *Web:* essexindustries.com	Saint Louis	MO	63123	314-832-4500	832-1633	807
Essex Investment Management Company LLC 125 High St 18th Fl *Web:* www.essexinvest.com	Boston	MA	02110	617-342-3200	342-3280	401
Essex Manufacturing Inc PO Box 92864 *TF:* 888-643-7739 ■ *Web:* www.essexmfg.com	Southlake	TX	76092	817-847-4555		155-5
Essex Meadows 30 Bokum Rd *TF:* 866-721-4838 ■ *Web:* www.essexmeadows.com	Essex	CT	06426	860-767-7201		672

Phone | Fax | Class

Essex North Shore Agricultural & Technical School
565 Maple St Hathorne MA 01937 978-304-4700 685
Web: essexnorthshore.org
Essex Oil Co 2174 Springfield Ave Vauxhall NJ 07088 973-372-7700 316
Web: essexoil.com
Essex PB & R Corp 8007 Chivvis Dr Saint Louis MO 63123 314-351-6116 576
Web: www.essexindustries.com
Essex Property Trust Inc
925 E Meadow Dr Palo Alto CA 94303 650-494-3700 494-8743 655
NYSE: ESS ■ *Web:* www.essexapartmenthomes.com
Essex Radez LLC
440 S LaSalle St Ste 1111 Chicago IL 60605 312-212-1815 194
Web: www.essexradez.com
Essex Savings Bank PO Box 950 Essex CT 06426 860-767-4414 70
TF: 877-377-3922 ■ *Web:* www.essexsavings.com
Essick Air Products Inc
5800 Murray St Little Rock AR 72209 501-562-1094 91
TF: 800-643-8341 ■ *Web:* www.essickair.com
Essig Research Inc 497 Cir Fwy Cincinnati OH 45246 513-942-7100 256
Web: www.essig.com
Essilor of America Inc 1355 N Steamons Dallas TX 75234 800-377-4567 542
TF: 800-377-4567 ■ *Web:* www.essilorusa.com
Essis & Sons Carpet One Floor & Home
6220 Carlisle Pk Mechanicsburg PA 17050 717-516-5169 290
Web: www.essisandsonscarpet1.com
Esskay Inc 111 Commerce St Smithfield VA 23430 855-411-7675 473
TF: 855-411-7675 ■ *Web:* www.esskaymeat.com
Essmueller Co 334 Ave A PO Box 1966 Laurel MS 39440 601-649-2400 649-4320 207
TF: 800-325-7175 ■ *Web:* www.essmueller.com
Essner Manufacturing LP
6651 Will Rogers Blvd Fort Worth TX 76140 817-551-5511 21
Web: www.essner.com
Esstech Inc 48 Powhatten Ave Essington PA 19029 800-245-3800 521-4600* 479
**Fax Area Code:* 610 ■ *TF:* 800-245-3800 ■ *Web:* www.esstechinc.com
EST Group LLC
1907 Ascension Blvd Ste 100 Arlington TX 76006 817-382-8000 180
Estabrook Capital Management LLC
900 Third Ave Ste 1004 New York NY 10022 212-605-5595 41
TF: 800-447-7443 ■ *Web:* www.estabrookcap.com
Estabrook Corp 700 W Bagley Rd Berea OH 44017 440-234-8566 234-3966 641
TF: 800-959-9161 ■ *Web:* www.estabrookcorp.com
Estabrook EZY CHEK Systems
1505 Woodside Ave Essexville MI 48732 989-891-9868 891-8737 201
TF: 877-368-7215 ■ *Web:* www.ezychek.com
Estancia Club 27998 N 99th Pl Scottsdale AZ 85262 480-473-4400 473-7705 354
Web: www.estanciaclub.com
Estates Pharmacy & Surgical
169-01 Hillside Ave Jamaica NY 11432 718-739-0311 237
Web: estatespharmacy.com
Estech Systems Inc 3701 E Plano Pkwy Plano TX 75074 972-422-9700 422-9705 246
Web: www.esi-estech.com
Estee Mold & Die Inc 1467 Stanley Ave Dayton OH 45404 937-224-7853 228-0257 757
Web: www.esteemold.com
Estep & Weber Capital Management Inc
432 W Spruce St Ste 102 Missoula MT 59802 406-830-3286 690
Web: estephopeweber.wfadv.com
Estep-Doctor & Company PC
3737 W Bethel Ave Muncie IN 47304 765-289-5366 2
Web: www.edcpa.com
Esterline & Sons Mfg
6508 Old Clifton Rd Springfield OH 45502 937-265-5278 757
Web: esterlineandsons.com
Esterline Defense Group
85901 Ave 53 Coachella CA 92236 760-398-0143 21
Web: www.armtecdefense.com
Estes Design & Manufacturing Inc
470 S Mitthoeffer Rd Indianapolis IN 46229 317-899-2203 898-2034 567
Web: www.estesdm.com
Estes Equipment Company Inc
2007 Polk St Chattanooga TN 37408 423-756-0090 358
TF: 800-933-7837 ■ *Web:* www.estes-equipment.com
Estes Express Lines
3901 W Broad St PO Box 25612 Richmond VA 23230 804-353-1900 780
Web: www.estes-express.com
Estes Mcclure & Associates Inc
328 S Broadway Ave Tyler TX 75703 903-581-2677 261
Web: emaengineer.com
Estes Park Trail-Gazette
251 Moraine Ave Estes Park CO 80517 970-586-3356 532-2
Web: www.eptrail.com
Estes Ron (Rep R - KS)
1524 Longworth House Office Bldg Washington DC 20515 202-225-6216 342-2
Web: estes.house.gov
Estes-Cox Corp 1295 H St Penrose CO 81240 719-372-6565 762
TF: 800-525-7561 ■ *Web:* www.estesrockets.com
Estex Manufacturing Company Inc
402 E Broad St PO Box 368 Fairburn GA 30213 800-749-1224 964-7534* 733
**Fax Area Code:* 770 ■ *TF:* 800-749-1224 ■ *Web:* www.estexmfg.com
Esther Myers Yoga Studio
390 Dupont St Ste 203 Toronto ON M5R1V9 416-944-0838 167-3
Web: www.estheryoga.com
Esther Pharmacy Inc 71 S Broadway Yonkers NY 10701 914-965-2661 965-2853 237
Web: www.estherpharmacy.com
Esther Price Candies Inc
1709 Wayne Ave Dayton OH 45410 937-253-2121 296-8
TF: 800-782-0326 ■ *Web:* www.estherprice.com
ESTI Consulting Services
302 2nd Ave N Saskatoon SK S7K2B9 306-242-2436 180
Web: www.esti.ca
Estiatorio Milos 125 W 55th St New York NY 10019 212-245-7400 671
Web: www.estiatoriomilos.com
Estill County 130 Main St Rm 202 Irvine KY 40336 606-723-7524 723-5471 338
Web: estillky.com
Estimating Edge, The
1301 N Congress Ave Ste 400 Boynton Beach FL 33426 561-276-9100 276-9492 809
TF: 844-334-3378 ■ *Web:* www.estimatingedge.com
Estis Compression LLC
545 Huey Lenard Loop West Monroe LA 71292 318-397-5557 172
Web: estiscompression.com

Estonia
Consulate General
305 E 47th St 3 Dag Hammarskjold Plz Ste 6B New York NY 10017 212-883-0636 883-0648 257
Web: newyork.mfa.ee
Embassy 2131 Massachusetts Ave NW Washington DC 20008 202-588-0101 588-0108 257
Web: www.estemb.org
Estrada Hinojosa & Company Inc
1717 Main St LB47 Dallas TX 75201 214-658-1670 401
TF: 800-676-5352 ■ *Web:* ehmuni.com
eStrategy Solutions Inc
6601 Vaught Ranch Rd Ste 100 Austin TX 78730 512-451-0100 637-1473 194
Web: www.esslearning.com
Estream Inc
22912 Mill Creek Dr Ste A Laguna Hills CA 92653 949-597-8555 177
Web: estream.com
Estrella Media Inc 1845 Empire Ave Burbank CA 91504 818-729-5300 741
Web: www.estrellamedia.com
Estrella Mountain Community College
3000 N Dysart Rd Avondale AZ 85392 623-935-8000 162
Web: www.estrellamountain.edu
Estron Chemicals Inc
807 N Main St Calvert City KY 42029 270-395-4195 395-5070 143
Web: www.estron.com
Estructure Inc 1144 65th St Ste A Oakland CA 94608 510-235-3116 261
Web: estruc.com
Estwing Manufacturing 2647 Eigth St Rockford IL 61109 815-397-9558 758
Web: www.estwing.com
Esty & Buckmir LLC 2340 Whitney Ave Hamden CT 06518 203-248-5678 41
Web: esty-buckmir.com
Esys Corp 1670 N Opdyke Rd Auburn Hills MI 48326 248-754-1900 256
Web: www.esysautomation.com
ET Lowe Publishing Co
220 Great Circle Rd Ste 122 Nashville TN 37228 615-254-8866 254-8867 781
Web: www.etlowe.com
ET Water Systems Inc
384 Bel Marin Keys Blvd Ste 145 Novato CA 94949 415-945-0303 178-11
Web: jainsusa.com
ETA (Evangelical Training Assn)
1551 Regency Ct Calumet City IL 60409 800-369-8291 48-20
TF: 800-369-8291 ■ *Web:* www.etaworld.org
ETA (Electronics Technicians Association Intl)
5 Depot St Greencastle IN 46135 765-653-8262 653-4287 49-19
TF: 800-288-3824 ■ *Web:* www.eta-i.org
ETA (Employment & Training Administration (ETA))
Region 4 525 Griffin St Rm 317 Dallas TX 75202 972-850-4600 850-4605 340-15
Web: www.dol.gov
E-T-A Circuit Breakers
1551 Bishop Ct Mount Prospect IL 60056 847-827-7600 827-7655 729
Web: www.e-t-a.com
Eta Sigma Gamma 2000 University Ave Muncie IN 47306 800-715-2559 285-3210* 48-16
**Fax Area Code:* 765 ■ *TF:* 800-715-2559 ■ *Web:* etasigmagamma.org
ETABS (East Texas Arboretum)
1601 Patterson Rd Athens TX 75751 903-675-5630 97
Web: www.easttexasarboretum.org
Etalex Inc 8501 Jarry St E Montreal QC H1J1H7 514-351-2000 819
TF: 800-351-3125 ■ *Web:* www.etalex.ca
ETC (Environmental Technology Council)
1112 16th St Ste 420 Washington DC 20036 202-783-0870 48-12
Web: www.etc.org
ETC (Educational Travel Consultants)
PO Box 1580 Hendersonville NC 28793 828-693-0412 692-1591 760
TF: 800-247-7969 ■ *Web:* educationaltravelconsultants.com
ETC (Environmental Traveling Companions)
2 Marina Blvd Bldg C San Francisco CA 94123 415-474-7662 474-3919 48-23
Web: www.etctrips.org
ETC (Engineering and Technical Consultants Inc)
46040 Center Oak Plz Ste 100 Sterling VA 20166 703-450-6220 444-2285 261
Web: www.etc-web.com
ETC (Educational Textbook Company Inc)
PO Box 3597 Covina CA 91722 626-339-7733 332-4744 637-2
Web: www.etcbooks.com
Etc Group Inc
1997 South 1100 East Salt Lake City UT 84106 801-278-1927 261
Web: etcgrp.com
ETCAI Products PO Box 1347 Collierville TN 38027 901-861-0232 861-0233 177
TF: 800-308-0154 ■ *Web:* www.etcai.com
Etchomatic Inc 179 Olde Canal Dr Lowell MA 01851 978-656-0011 656-9903 625
TF: 800-634-3006 ■ *Web:* www.etchomatic.com
ETCO (Engman-Taylor Company Inc)
W142 N9351 Fountain Blvd Menomonee Falls WI 53051 262-255-9300 255-6512 385
TF: 800-236-1975 ■ *Web:* www.engman-taylor.com
ETCO Inc 25 Bellows St Warwick RI 02888 401-467-2400 467-9230 815
TF: 800-689-3826 ■ *Web:* www.etco.com
ETCO Specialty Products Inc
621 W Saint John St Girard KS 66743 620-724-6463 724-8099 604
TF: 800-356-4540 ■ *Web:* etcoproducts.com
E-TechServices 5300 SW 91st Ter Gainesville FL 32608 800-785-5993 174
TF: 800-785-5993 ■ *Web:* www.e-techservices.com
Etegent Technologies Ltd
1775 Mentor Ave Cincinnati OH 45212 513-631-0579 261
Web: www.sdltd.com
Etek It Services Inc
830 E Higgins Rd Ste 102 Schaumburg IL 60173 847-969-0200 196
Web: etekit.com
Etelint Consulting Inc
1683 Moongate Cres Mississauga ON L5M4T2 905-826-3977 826-2934 196
Web: www.etelintconsulting.com
Etemco 1370 Arcadia Rd Lancaster PA 17601 717-393-9653 253
Web: www.etemco.net
Etera Solutions LLC
354 Turnpark St Ste 203 Canton MA 02021 888-536-6515 396
TF: 888-536-6515 ■ *Web:* eterasolutions.com
Eternabond 175 N Archer Ave Mundelein IL 60060 847-837-9400 837-9449 732
TF: 888-336-2663 ■ *Web:* www.eternabond.com
Eternity Healthcare Inc
8755 Ash St Ste 1 Vancouver BC V6P6T3 604-324-1113 476
TF: 855-324-1110 ■ *Web:* eternityhealthcare.com

Name / Address	City	State	ZIP	Phone	Fax	Class
Etex Telephone Co-opeartive Inc 1013 Hwy 155 N *TF:* 877-482-3839 ■ *Web:* www.etex.net	Gilmer	TX	75644	903-797-4357		736
Ethan Allen Homestead 1 Ethan Allen Homestead *Web:* www.ethanallenhomestead.org	Burlington	VT	05408	802-865-4556		50-3
Ethan Allen Hotel 21 Lake Ave Ext *TF:* 800-742-1776 ■ *Web:* www.ethanallenhotel.com	Danbury	CT	06811	203-744-1776		379
Ethan Allen Interiors Inc Ethan Allen Dr *NYSE: ETH* ■ *TF:* 888-324-3571 ■ *Web:* www.ethanallen.com	Danbury	CT	06811	888-324-3571		321
Ethan Allen Personnel Group Inc 59 Academy St *Web:* eaworkforce.com	Poughkeepsie	NY	12601	845-471-9667		260
Ethan Ellenberg Literary Agency 155 Suffolk St Ste 2R *Web:* ethanellenberg.com	New York	NY	10002	212-431-4554		637-2
Ethany Corp 19 Main St *Web:* ethany.com	Scottsville	NY	14546	585-889-2586		177
Ethel Walker School 230 Bushy Hill Rd *Web:* www.ethelwalker.org	Simsbury	CT	06070	860-408-4200		622
EtherCom Corp 1409 Fulton Pl *Web:* ethercom.com	Fremont	CA	94539	510-440-0242		174
Etheridge Printing 4434 Mcewen Rd	Dallas	TX	75244	214-827-8151		393
Ethex Corp 1 Corporate Woods Dr	Saint Louis	MO	63044	314-646-3750		583
Ethical Markets Media LLC PO Box 5190 *Web:* www.ethicalmarkets.com	Saint Augustine	FL	32085	904-829-3140	826-0325	463
Ethicon Endo-Surgery Inc 4545 Creek Rd *Web:* www.jnjmedicaldevices.com	Cincinnati	OH	45242	513-337-7000		476
Ethics & Public Policy Ctr 1730 M St NW Ste 910 *TF:* 800-935-0699 ■ *Web:* eppc.org	Washington	DC	20036	202-682-1200	408-0632	634
Ethics Resource Ctr 2345 Crystal Dr Ste 201 *Web:* www.ethics.org	Arlington	VA	22202	703-647-2185	647-2180	48-8
Ethier Assoc 736 6 Ave SW *Web:* www.ethier.ca	Calgary	AB	T2P3T7	403-234-8960		449
Ethiopian Community Development Council Inc (ECDC) 901 S Highland St *Web:* www.ecdcus.org	Arlington	VA	22204	703-685-0510	685-0529	48-5
Ethis Communications Inc 44 Church St Ste 200 *Web:* ethisinc.com	White Plains	NY	10601	212-791-1440		194
Ethnic Dance Theatre 3507 Clinton Ave S *Web:* www.ethnicdancetheatre.com	Minneapolis	MN	55408	651-341-5312		573-1
Ethnic Heritage Museum 1129 S Main St *Web:* ethnicheritagemuseum.org	Rockford	IL	61101	815-962-7402		520
Ethnic Studies Library (ESL) University of California 30 Stephens Hall Ste 2360 *Web:* eslibrary.berkeley.edu	Berkeley	CA	94720	510-643-1234	643-8433	637-2
Ethnos360 Bible Institute 915 N Hartwell Ave *Web:* www.ntbi.org	Waukesha	WI	53186	262-542-9411	542-3578	167-3
Ethnoscope Film and Video PO Box 92353 *Web:* www.docfilm.com	Rochester	NY	14692	585-442-5274		514
Ethos 17 Ash St *Web:* www.ethos-marketing.com	Westbrook	ME	04092	207-856-2610		195
Ethos Risk Services Inc 300 First Ave S Ste 300 *TF:* 866-783-0525 ■ *Web:* ethosrs.com	Saint Petersburg	FL	33701	866-783-0525	695-9645	463
EthosIQ LLC 17121 W Rd 201 *Web:* ethosiq.com	Houston	TX	77095	281-616-5711		177
ETHRA (East Tennessee Human Resource Agency Inc) 9111 Cross Park Dr Ste D-100 *Web:* www.ethra.org	Knoxville	TN	37923	865-691-2551	531-7216	195
Ethyl Corp 330 S Fourth St *Web:* www.ethyl.com	Richmond	VA	23219	804-788-5000		580
ETI (Equipment & Tool Institute) 134 W University Dr Ste 205 **Fax Area Code:* 603 ■ *Web:* www.etools.org	Rochester	MI	48307	248-656-5080	971-2375*	49-13
ETI Converting 525 Jean-Paul-Vincent *Web:* www.eticonverting.com	Longueuil	QC	J4G1R3	450-641-7900		628
ETI School of Skilled Trades 500 Joliet Rd Ste 100 N *TF:* 888-572-9937 ■ *Web:* eticampus.edu	Willowbrook	IL	60527	888-572-9937		685
ETI Technical College of Niles 2076 Youngstown-Warren Rd *Web:* eticollege.edu	Niles	OH	44446	330-652-9919	652-4399	800
Etic Engineering 2285 Morello Ave *Web:* eticeng.com	Pleasant Hill	CA	94523	925-602-4710		256
Eti-Net 505 Maisonneuve W Ste 400 *Web:* etinet.com	Montreal	QC	H3A3C2	514-395-1200		177
Etiwanda School District (ESD) 6061 E Ave *Web:* www.etiwanda.k12.ca.us	Etiwanda	CA	91739	909-899-2451	899-1235	685
Etkin Equities LLC 200 Franklin Ctr 29100 NW Hwy *Web:* etkinllc.com	Southfield	MI	48034	248-358-0800		652
Etko Machine Inc 2796 Barber Rd *Web:* www.etko.com	Norton	OH	44203	330-745-4033	745-5780	454
Etm Electromatic Inc 35451 Dumbarton Ct *Web:* www.etm-inc.com	Newark	CA	94560	510-797-1100	797-4358	647
ETMS (E T Marketing Solutions Ltd) 207-3833 Henning Dr *Web:* etmarketingsolutions.com	Burnaby	BC	V5C6N5	604-801-6168	801-6165	7
ETNA Supply 4901 Clay Ave SW *TF:* 855-839-8011 ■ *Web:* www.etnasupply.com	Grand Rapids	MI	49548	616-245-4373	241-4786	612
Etobicoke Ironworks Ltd 141 Rivalda Rd *TF:* 866-274-6971 ■ *Web:* www.eiw.ca	Weston	ON	M9M2M6	416 742-7111		480
Etonien LLC 222 N Sepulveda Blvd Ste 1507 *Web:* etonien.com	El Segundo	CA	90245	310-321-5800		734
Etopolos Design PO Box 751603 *Web:* www.etopolos.com	Petaluma	CA	94975	415-845-8897		393
Etowah County 800 Forrest Ave *Web:* www.etowahcounty.org	Gadsden	AL	35901	256-549-5300	549-5400	338
Etowah Indian Mounds State Historic Site 813 Indian Mounds Rd SW *Web:* gastateparks.org	Cartersville	GA	30120	770-387-3747		565
EtQ Management Consultants Inc 399 Conklin St Ste 208 *TF:* 800-354-4476 ■ *Web:* www.etq.com	Farmingdale	NY	11735	516-293-0949		195
Etrafficers Inc 881 S Orem Blvd Ste 1 *Web:* www.etrafficers.com	Orem	UT	84058	801-221-9400		180
Etruscan Press 84 W South St *Web:* www.etruscanpress.org	Wilkes-Barre	PA	18766	570-408-4546		637-2
ETS (Ecumenical Theological Seminary) 2930 Woodward Ave *Web:* www.etseminary.org	Detroit	MI	48201	313-831-5200	831-1353	167-3
ETS-Lindgren LP 1301 Arrow Pt Dr *Web:* www.ets-lindgren.com	Cedar Park	TX	78613	512-531-6400		420
Etsy 117 Adams St *NASDAQ: ETSY* ■ *TF:* 844-659-3879 ■ *Web:* www.etsy.com	Brooklyn	NY	11201	844-659-3879		459
ettain group Inc 127 W Worthington Ave Ste 100 *Web:* www.ettaingroup.com	Charlotte	NC	28203	704-525-5499		260
Ettika LLC 714 S Hill St Ste 405 *Web:* www.ettika.com	Los Angeles	CA	90014	213-817-5510		411
Ettl Engineers & Consultants Inc 1717 E Erwin St *Web:* www.ettlinc.com	Tyler	TX	75702	903-595-4421		743
Ettore Products Co 2100 N Loop Rd *TF:* 800-438-8673 ■ *Web:* www.ettore.com	Alameda	CA	94502	510-748-4130	748-4146	508
ETV Endowment of South Carolina Inc 401 E Kennedy St Ste B-1 *TF:* 877-253-2092 ■ *Web:* www.etvendowment.org	Spartanburg	SC	29302	864-591-0046	573-7792	741-99
Etymotic Research Inc 61 Martin Ln *Web:* www.etymotic.com	Elk Grove Village	IL	60007	847-228-0006	228-6836	466
ETZEL Agency 9640 SW Sunshine Ct Ste 400 *Web:* www.etzelagency.com	Beaverton	OR	97005	503-721-7477		711
Eubanks Engineering Co 3022 Inland Empire Blvd *TF:* 800-729-4208 ■ *Web:* www.eubanks.com	Ontario	CA	91764	909-483-2456	483-2498	813
Eubel Brady & Suttman Asset Management Inc 10100 Innovation Dr Ste 410 *TF:* 800-391-1223 ■ *Web:* www.ebs-asset.com	Miamisburg	OH	45342	937-291-1223		194
Eucharistic Adoration of San Antonio Inc (EASA) PO Box 691006 *Web:* www.adore24.org	San Antonio	TX	78269	210-558-8802		48-13
Euclid Chamber of Commerce 22639 Euclid Ave PO Box 32611 *Web:* www.euclidchamber.com	Euclid	OH	44117	216-731-9322		139
Euclid Chemical Co 19218 Redwood Rd *TF:* 800-321-7628 ■ *Web:* www.euclidchemical.com	Cleveland	OH	44110	216-531-9222	531-9596	3
Euclid Heat Treating Co 1340 E 222nd St *TF:* 800-962-2909 ■ *Web:* www.euclidheattreating.com	Euclid	OH	44117	216-481-8444		484
Euclid Industries Inc 1655 Tech Dr *Web:* www.euclidindustries.com	Bay City	MI	48706	989-686-8920		757
Euclid Public Library 631 E 222nd St *Web:* www.euclidlibrary.org	Euclid	OH	44123	216-261-5300		434-3
Euclid Spiral Paper Tube Corp 339 Mill St	Apple Creek	OH	44606	330-698-4711		124
Euclid SR Partners 45 Rockefeller Plz Ste 3240	New York	NY	10111	212-218-6880		792
Eudora Welty Library, The 300 N State St *Web:* jhlibrary.org	Jackson	MS	39201	601-968-5811		434-3
Eudy's Cabinet Shop Inc 12303 Renee Ford Rd *Web:* www.eudyscabinets.com	Stanfield	NC	28163	704-888-4454		321
EUE/Screen Gems Studios 603 Greenwich St *Web:* euescreengems.com	New York	NY	10014	212-450-1600		514
Eufaula/Barbour County Chamber of Commerce 333 E Broad St *TF:* 800-524-7529 ■ *Web:* eufaulachamber.com	Eufaula	AL	36027	334-687-6664		139
Eufloria Flowers 885 Mesa Rd *TF:* 866-929-4683 ■ *Web:* eufloriaflowers.com	Nipomo	CA	93444	805-929-4683	929-1843	292
Eugene Airport 28801 Douglas Dr *TF:* 800-741-5097 ■ *Web:* www.eugene-or.gov	Eugene	OR	97402	541-682-5430	682-6838	27
Eugene Burger Management Corp 6600 Hunter Dr *TF:* 800-788-0233 ■ *Web:* www.ebmc.com	Rohnert Park	CA	94928	707-584-5123	584-5124	655
Eugene Cascades Coast 754 Olive St *TF:* 800-547-5445 ■ *Web:* www.eugenecascadescoast.org	Eugene	OR	97440	541-484-5307	343-6335	206
Eugene Chamber of Commerce 1401 Willamette St *Web:* www.eugenechamber.com	Eugene	OR	97401	541-484-1314	484-4942	139
Eugene F. Sarkey Ins Agy Inc 9467 Joliet St *Web:* genesarkeyins.com	Saint John	IN	46373	219-365-3550		390
Eugene O'Neill National Historic Site 1000 Kuss Rd *Web:* www.nps.gov	Danville	CA	94526	925-838-0249		564
Eugene Public Library 100 W Tenth Ave *Web:* www.eugene-or.gov	Eugene	OR	97401	541-682-5450	682-5898	434-3
Eugene Sand & Gravel Inc 3000 Delta Hwy N *Web:* rbmaterials.com	Eugene	OR	97408	541-347-4615		182
Eugene School District 4J 200 N Monroe St *Web:* www.4j.lane.edu	Eugene	OR	97402	541-790-7700	790-7711	685
Eugene Symphony 115 W Eigth Ave Ste 115 *Web:* www.eugenesymphony.org	Eugene	OR	97401	541-687-9487	687-0527	573-3

Name / Address	City	State	Zip	Phone	Fax	Class
Eugene T. Mahoney State Park 28500 W Pk Hwy *Web:* www.nebraskastateparks.reserveamerica.com	Ashland	NE	68003	402-944-2523		565
Eugene Weekly 1251 Lincoln St *Web:* eugeneweekly.com	Eugene	OR	97401	541-484-0519	484-4044	532-5
Euler Hermes ACI 800 Red Brook Blvd *TF:* 877-883-3224 ■ *Web:* www.eulerhermes.com	Owings Mills	MD	21117	410-753-0753		391-5
Euless Public Library 201 N Ector Dr *Web:* eulesstx.gov	Euless	TX	76039	817-685-1480		434-3
Eunice Kennedy Shriver Ctr 200 Trapelo Rd *Web:* umassmed.edu	Waltham	MA	02452	774-455-6562		668
Euphemia Haye 5540 Gulf of Mexico Dr *Web:* www.euphemiahaye.com	Longboat Key	FL	34228	941-383-3633		671
Eureka Broadcasting Comapny Inc 1101 Marsh Rd *Web:* www.eurekaradio.com	Eureka	CA	95501	707-442-5744		647
Eureka Casino Hotel 275 Mesa Blvd *Web:* www.eurekamesquite.com	Mesquite	NV	89027	702-346-4600		443
Eureka College 300 E College Ave *TF:* 888-438-7352 ■ *Web:* www.eureka.edu	Eureka	IL	61530	309-467-6350	467-6576	166
Eureka County 10 S Main St *Web:* www.co.eureka.nv.us	Eureka	NV	89316	775-237-5262	237-6015	338
Eureka Electrical Products Inc 79 Clay St	North East	PA	16428	814-725-9638		815
Eureka Equity Partners LP 1717 Arch St 34th Fl *Web:* www.eurekaequity.com	Philadelphia	PA	19103	267-238-4200	238-4201	405
Eureka Foundry Co 1601 Carter St *Web:* www.eurekafoundryco.com	Chattanooga	TN	37402	423-267-3328	756-2607	307
Eureka Homestead 1922 Veterans Memorial Blvd *TF:* 855-858-5179 ■ *Web:* www.eurekahomestead.com	Metairie	LA	70005	504-834-0242		69
Eureka Lighting 225 De Li ge ouest Ste 200 *Web:* www.eurekalighting.com	Montreal	QC	H2P1H4	514-385-3515		393
Eureka Resources LLC 419 Second St *Web:* eureka-resources.com	Williamsport	PA	17701	570-323-2535		192
Eureka Software Solutions Inc 3305 Northland Dr Ste 305 *TF:* 866-936-9292 ■ *Web:* eurekasoft.com	Austin	TX	78731	512-459-9292		177
Eureka Technocrats Inc 1985 W Big Beaver Rd *TF:* 888-387-3521 ■ *Web:* www.eurekatek.com	Troy	MI	48084	248-816-1617		177
Eureka Union School District 5455 Eureka Rd *Web:* www.eurekausd.org	Granite Bay	CA	95746	916-791-4939	791-5527	685
Eureka Welding Alloys Inc 2000 E Avis Dr *TF:* 800-962-8560 ■ *Web:* www.eurekaweldingalloys.com	Madison Heights	MI	48071	248-588-0001	585-7711	811
Euro Lloyd Travel Inc 1640 Hempstead Tpke *Web:* www.eurolloyd.com	East Meadow	NY	11554	516-228-4970	228-8258	771
Euro Pacific Capital Inc 88 Post Rd W 2nd Fl *TF:* 800-727-7922 ■ *Web:* www.europac.com	Westport	CT	06880	203-662-9700		70
Eurofase Inc 33 W Beaver Creek Rd *TF:* 800-660-5391 ■ *Web:* www.eurofase.com	Richmond Hill	ON	L4B1L8	905-695-2055		41
Eurofins Scientific Inc 2200 Rittenhouse St Ste 150 *Web:* www.eurofinsus.com	Des Moines	IA	50321	515-265-1461	266-5453	417
Eurogentec 3347 Industrial Ct Ste A *Web:* www.eurogentec.com	San Diego	CA	92121	858-793-2661		190
Eurokera North America Inc 140 Southchase Blvd *Web:* eurokera.com	Fountain Inn	SC	29644	864-963-8082		362
Euromarket Designs Inc 1250 Techny Rd **Fax Area Code:* 630 ■ *TF:* 800-967-6696 ■ *Web:* www.crateandbarrel.com	Northbrook	IL	60062	847-272-2888	527-1448*	362
Euromoney Institutional Investor PLC 225 Park Ave S *TF:* 800-715-9197 ■ *Web:* www.institutionalinvestor.com	New York	NY	10003	212-224-3300		637-9
Euronet Worldwide Inc 3500 College Blvd *NASDAQ:* EEFT ■ *TF:* 877-282-1168 ■ *Web:* www.euronetworldwide.com	Leawood	KS	66211	913-327-4200	327-1921	255
Europa Bistro 2515 N Proctor St *Web:* www.europabistro.net	Tacoma	WA	98406	253-761-5660		671
Europa Market Company Inc, The 8100 Water St *Web:* www.europa-market.com	Saint Louis	MO	63111	314-631-7288		297-8
Europa! 323 E 55th St *Web:* www.cafeeuropakc.com	Kansas City	MO	64113	816-523-1212		671
European School of Esthetics 1580 Sparkman Dr Ste 207 *TF:* 800-584-7290 ■ *Web:* www.european-school-of-esthetics.com	Huntsville	AL	35816	256-722-9008		685
European-American Business Council 919 18th St NW Ste 220 *Web:* transatlanticbusiness.org	Washington	DC	20006	202-828-9104		138
Euro-Pharm International Canada Inc 9400 Boul Langelier *TF:* 888-929-0835 ■ *Web:* www.euro-pharm.com	Montreal	QC	H1P3H8	514-323-8757	323-6325	231
EuroPharma Inc 955 Challenger Dr *TF:* 866-598-5487 ■ *Web:* www.europharmausa.com	Green Bay	WI	54311	920-406-6500		345
Europlay Capital Advisors LLC 15260 Ventura Blvd 20th Fl *Web:* www.europlaycapital.com	Sherman Oaks	CA	91403	818-444-4400		401
Euro-Suites Hotel University Centre 501 Chestnut Ridge Rd *TF:* 800-678-4837 ■ *Web:* www.euro-suites.com	Morgantown	WV	26505	800-678-4837		379
Eurotainer Inc 5810 Wilson Rd Ste 200 *Web:* www.eurotainer.com	Humble	TX	77396	832-300-5001	300-5050	264-5
Eurotherm USA 44621 Guilford Dr Ste 100 *Web:* www.eurotherm.com	Ashburn	VA	20147	703-724-7300	724-7301	202
Eurotire Inc 200 S Biscayne Blvd 55th Fl *Web:* www.eurotire.net	Miami	FL	33131	212-262-2251		755
Eustis Company Inc 12407b Mukilteo Speedway *Web:* www.eustispyrocom.com	Lynnwood	WA	98087	425-423-9996	423-7966	472
Eutaw Construction 109 1/2 W Commerce St *Web:* eutaw.com	Aberdeen	MS	39730	662-369-8868	369-7770	186
Eutectic Corp N94 W14355 Garwin Mace Dr *TF:* 800-558-8524 ■ *Web:* www.castolin.com	Menomonee Falls	WI	53051	262-532-4677	255-5542	811
Euthanasia Research & Guidance Organization (ERGO) 24829 Norris Ln *Web:* www.finalexit.org	Junction City	OR	97448	541-998-1873		48-17
Euthenics Inc 1213 Arlington Ave *Web:* www.euthenics.com	Saint Petersburg	FL	33705	727-471-0600	471-0610	393
EV Connect Inc 615 N Nash St Ste 203 *TF:* 866-790-3155 ■ *Web:* www.evconnect.com	El Segundo	CA	90245	866-790-3155		393
EV Construction 86 E 6th St *Web:* ev.construction	Holland	MI	49423	616-392-2383	392-3752	685
EVA Airways 200 N Sepulveda Blvd Ste 1600 *TF:* 800-695-1188 ■ *Web:* www.evaair.com	El Segundo	CA	90245	310-362-6600	362-6660	25
Evaheart Inc 6655 Travis St Ste 590 *Web:* www.evaheart-usa.com	Houston	TX	77030	713-520-7979		475
Evan K. Thalenberg Law Offices 216 E Lexington St *TF:* 800-778-1181 ■ *Web:* ektlaw.com	Baltimore	MD	21202	410-625-9100		428
Evana Automation 5825 Old Boonville Hwy *TF:* 800-468-6774 ■ *Web:* www.preh-ima.us	Evansville	IN	47715	812-485-5500		207
Evangel Cathedral 13901 Central Ave *Web:* evangelcathedral.net	Upper Marlboro	MD	20774	301-249-9400	249-0200	95
Evangel University 1111 N Glenstone Ave *TF:* 800-382-6435 ■ *Web:* www.evangel.edu	Springfield	MO	65802	417-865-2815	865-9599	166
Evangelical Christian Credit Union 955 W Imperial Hwy Ste 100 *TF:* 800-634-3228 ■ *Web:* eccu.org	Brea	CA	92821	714-671-5700	671-5775	219
Evangelical Christian Publishers Assn (ECPA) 9633 S 48th St Ste 195 *Web:* www.ecpa.org	Phoenix	AZ	85044	480-966-3998	966-1944	49-16
Evangelical Church Alliance (ECA) 205 W Broadway St PO Box 9 *TF:* 888-855-6060 ■ *Web:* www.ecainternational.org	Bradley	IL	60915	815-937-0720		48-20
Evangelical Community Hospital 1 Hospital Dr *Web:* www.evanhospital.com	Lewisburg	PA	17837	570-522-2000		374-3
Evangelical Council for Financial Accountability (ECFA) 440 W Jubal Early Dr Ste 130 *TF:* 800-323-9473 ■ *Web:* www.ecfa.org	Winchester	VA	22601	540-535-0103	535-0533	48-5
Evangelical Fellowship of Canada (EFC) 9821 Leslie St Ste 103 *TF:* 866-302-3362 ■ *Web:* www.evangelicalfellowship.ca	Richmond Hill	ON	L4B3Y4	905-479-5885	479-4742	48-20
Evangelical Free Church of America, The 901 E 78th St *TF:* 800-745-2202 ■ *Web:* www.efca.org	Minneapolis	MN	55420	952-854-1300		48-20
Evangelical Lutheran Church in America (ELCA) 8765 W Higgins Rd *Web:* www.elca.org	Chicago	IL	60631	773-380-2700	380-1465	48-20
Evangelical Lutheran Good Samaritan Foundation, The 4800 W 57th St *TF:* 800-928-1635 ■ *Web:* www.good-sam.com	Sioux Falls	SD	57108	605-362-3100		305
Evangelical Presbyterian Church of Plant City 1107 Charlie Griffin Rd *Web:* www.gracepointpc.org	Plant City	FL	33566	813-759-9383		48-20
Evangelical School of Theology 121 S College St *TF:* 800-532-5775 ■ *Web:* evangelical.edu	Myerstown	PA	17067	717-866-5775	866-4667	167-3
Evangelical Training Assn (ETA) 1551 Regency Ct *TF:* 800-369-8291 ■ *Web:* www.etaworld.org	Calumet City	IL	60409	800-369-8291		48-20
Evangelicals for Social Action (ESA) PO Box 367 *TF:* 800-650-6600 ■ *Web:* www.evangelicalsforsocialaction.org	Wayne	PA	19087	484-384-2988		48-7
Evangeline Bank & Trust Co, The 497 W Main St *Web:* www.therealbank.com	Ville Platte	LA	70586	337-363-5541	363-0678	70
Evangeline Parish 200 Ct St Ste 104 *Web:* www.evangelineparishclerkofcourt.com	Ville Platte	LA	70586	337-363-5671	363-5780	338
Evangeline Parish Library 242 W Main St *Web:* evangelinelibrary.org	Ville Platte	LA	70586	337-363-1369	363-2353	434-3
Evangeline's 1653 McFarland Blvd *Web:* evangelinestuscaloosa.com	Tuscaloosa	AL	35406	205-752-0830		671
Evangola State Park 10191 Old Lake Shore Rd *Web:* parks.ny.gov	Irving	NY	14081	716-549-1802		565
Evan-Moor Educational Publishers Inc 18 Lower Ragsdale Dr *TF:* 800-777-4362 ■ *Web:* www.evan-moor.com	Monterey	CA	93940	831-649-5901	649-6256	243
Evanov Radio Group 5312 Dundas St W *Web:* www.evanovradio.com	Etobicoke	ON	M9B1B3	416-213-1035		360-2
Evans & Associates Construction Company Inc 3320 N 14th St *TF:* 800-324-6693 ■ *Web:* evans-assoc.com	Ponca City	OK	74601	580-765-6693		188-4
Evans & Sutherland Computer Corp 770 Komas Dr *OTC:* ESCC ■ *TF:* 800-327-5707 ■ *Web:* es.com	Salt Lake City	UT	84108	801-588-1000		703
Evans Analytical Group Inc 810 Kifer Rd *Web:* www.eag.com	Sunnyvale	CA	94086	408-530-3500	530-3501	743
Evans and Associates 1 E State St *Web:* evansandassociates.net	Sharon	PA	16146	724-346-0150		196

Phone | Fax | Class

Evans Army Community Hospital
1650 Cochran Cir . . . Fort Carson CO 80913 719-526-7000 374-4
Web: evans.amedd.army.mil
Evans Bancorp Inc 1 Grimsby Dr . . . Hamburg NY 14075 716-926-2000 926-2005 360-2
NYSE: EVBN ■ *TF:* 866-310-0763 ■ *Web:* evansbank.com
Evans Cabinet Corp 1321 N Franklin St . . . Dublin GA 31021 478-272-2530 115
Web: www.evanscabinet.com
Evans Carpet Corp 511 Branchway Rd . . . Richmond VA 23236 804-794-9025 290
Web: flooring-professionals.com
Evans Caseload Inc 1915 Danforth Ave . . . Toronto ON M4C1J5 416-762-0236 177
Web: www.caseload.com
Evans Colbaugh & Associates Inc
1565 Creek St Ste 107 . . . San Marcos CA 92069 760-510-9686 261
Web: eca-geo.com
Evans Concrete LLC
518 E Smith St PO Box 128 . . . Claxton GA 30417 912-739-3733 183
Web: www.evansconcrete.com
Evans Consulting Group LLC
2300 Computer Ave Ste K-59 . . . Willow Grove PA 19090 215-830-0304 830-0351 194
Web: theevansconsultinggroup.com
Evans Correctional Institution
610 Hwy 9 W . . . Bennettsville SC 29512 843-479-4181 213
Web: doc.sc.gov
Evans County 3 Freeman St . . . Claxton GA 30417 912-739-1141 739-0111 338
Web: evanscounty.org
Evans Data Corp 340 Soquel Ave . . . Santa Cruz CA 95062 831-425-8451 668
TF: 800-831-3080 ■ *Web:* evansdata.com
Evans Delivery Company Inc
PO Box 268 . . . Pottsville PA 17901 570-385-9048 311
TF: 800-666-7885 ■ *Web:* www.evansdelivery.com
Evans Distribution Systems
18765 Seaway Dr . . . Melvindale MI 48122 313-388-3200 388-0136 803-1
Web: www.evansdist.com
Evans Dwight (Rep D - PA)
1105 Longworth House Office Bldg . . . Washington DC 20515 202-225-4001 225-5392 342-2
Web: evans.house.gov
Evans Engineering Inc
2793 Old Post Rd Ste 100 . . . Harrisburg PA 17110 717-541-1580 541-1583 261
Web: evanseng.com
Evans Enterprises Inc
1536 S Western Ave . . . Oklahoma City OK 73109 405-631-1344 246
TF: 800-423-8267 ■ *Web:* www.goevans.com
Evans Equipment Inc
7800 Bristol Pike . . . Levittown PA 19057 215-547-7200 780
Web: www.evanstruck.com
Evans Ewan & Brady Insurance Agency Inc
2404 Williams Dr . . . Georgetown TX 78628 512-869-1511 390
Web: www.eebins.com
Evans Food Group Ltd
4118 S Halsted St . . . Chicago IL 60609 773-254-7400 254-7791 296-35
TF: 888-643-8267 ■ *Web:* www.evansfood.com
Evans Fruit Farm
200 Cowiche City Rd PO Box 70 . . . Cowiche WA 98923 509-678-4127 678-5450 315-3
Web: www.evansfruitco.com
Evans Hairstyling College
169 North 100 West . . . Cedar City UT 84720 435-586-4486 167-3
Web: www.evanscollege.com
Evans Hardy & Young Inc
829 De La Vina St . . . Santa Barbara CA 93101 805-963-5841 4
Web: www.ehy.com
Evans Hydro 18128 S Santa Fe Ave . . . Compton CA 90221 310-608-5801 608-0685 641
Web: www.hydroinc.com
Evans Investment Advisors LLC
6713 Perkins Rd . . . Baton Rouge LA 70808 225-761-7870 761-8581 690
Web: www.evansinvestmentadvisors.com
Evans Latham & Campisi
1 Post St Ste 600 . . . San Francisco CA 94104 415-421-0288 421-0464 428
Web: www.elc-law.com
Evans Limestone Co 1201 Limestone Dr . . . Bedford IN 47421 812-279-9744 275-2408 724
Web: evanslimestone.com
Evans Mactavish Agricraft Inc
5123 Ivy Ct . . . Wilson NC 27893 252-243-4006 273
Web: www.evansmactavish.com
Evans Mechwart Hambleton & Tilton Inc (EMHT)
5500 New Albany Rd . . . New Albany OH 43054 614-775-4500 775-4800 261
TF: 888-775-3648 ■ *Web:* www.emht.com
Evans Oil Company LLC
8450 Millhaven Rd . . . Monroe LA 71203 318-345-1502 579
Evans Publications Inc 314 SW 2nd St . . . Perkins OK 74059 918-695-2992 637-2
Web: www.readonoklahoma.com
Evans Tire & Service Centers Inc
510 N Broadway . . . Escondido CA 92025 877-338-2678 62-5
TF: 877-338-2678 ■ *Web:* evanstire.com
Evans Tool & Die Inc
157 N Salem Rd NE . . . Conyers GA 30013 770-922-3480 483-7570 488
Web: evanstd.com
Evans, Craven & Lackie PS
818 W Riverside Ste 250 . . . Spokane WA 99201 509-455-5200 41
Web: ecl-law.com
Evans, Rowe & Holbrook PC
10101 Reunion Pl Ste 900 . . . San Antonio TX 78216 210-340-6555 340-6664 41
Web: evans-rowe.com
Evansburg State Park
851 May Hall Rd . . . Collegeville PA 19426 610-409-1150 565
Web: www.dcnr.pa.gov
Evans-Mason Inc
1021 S Grand Ave E . . . Springfield IL 62703 217-522-3396 522-3190 189-7
Web: evans-mason.com
Evanston Chamber of Commerce
1609 Sherman Ave Ste 205 . . . Evanston IL 60201 847-328-1500 328-1510 139
Web: www.evchamber.com
Evanston Hospital 2650 Ridge Ave . . . Evanston IL 60201 847-570-2000 374-3
TF: 888-364-6400 ■ *Web:* www.northshore.org
Evanston Lumber Co 1001 Sherman Ave . . . Evanston IL 60202 847-864-7700 864-3618 364
Web: evanstonlumber.com
Evanston Public Library
1703 Orrington Ave . . . Evanston IL 60201 847-448-8600 866-0313 434-3
TF: 888-253-7003 ■ *Web:* www.epl.org

Phone | Fax | Class

Evanston/Skokie School District 65
1500 McDaniel Ave . . . Evanston IL 60201 847-859-8000 859-8707 685
Web: www.district65.net
Evansville City Hall
1 NW ML King Jr Blvd
Civic Center Complex Rm 310 . . . Evansville IN 47708 812-436-4992 436-4999 337
Web: www.evansvillegov.org
Evansville Civic Theatre
717 N Fulton St . . . Evansville IN 47710 812-425-2800 572
Web: www.evansvillecivictheatre.org
Evansville Convention & Visitors Bureau
401 SE Riverside Dr . . . Evansville IN 47713 812-421-2200 421-2207 206
TF: 800-433-3025 ■ *Web:* www.visitevansville.com
Evansville Courier & Press
300 E Walnut St . . . Evansville IN 47713 844-900-7104 532-2
TF: 844-900-7104 ■ *Web:* www.courierpress.com
Evansville Museum of Arts History & Science
411 SE Riverside Dr . . . Evansville IN 47713 812-425-2406 421-7509 520
Web: emuseum.org
Evansville Philharmonic Orchestra
401 SE 6th St Ste 105 . . . Evansville IN 47713 812-425-5050 426-7008 573-3
Web: evansvillephilharmonic.org
Evansville Regional Airport
7801 Bussing Dr . . . Evansville IN 47725 812-421-4401 421-4412 27
Web: flyevv.com
Evansville Sheet Metal Works Inc
1901 W Maryland St . . . Evansville IN 47712 812-423-7871 697
Web: www.esmw.com
Evansville Teachers Federal Credit Union
PO Box 5129 . . . Evansville IN 47716 812-477-9271 473-9704 219
TF: 800-800-9271 ■ *Web:* etfcu.org
Evansville Vanderburgh Public Library
200 SE ML King Jr Blvd . . . Evansville IN 47713 812-428-8200 428-8397 434-3
Web: www.evpl.org
Evansville's Classic Rock Station
1162 Mt Auburn Rd . . . Evansville IN 47720 812-424-8284 426-7928 645-54
Web: www.wabx.net
Evansville-Vanderburgh School Corp
951 Walnut St . . . Evansville IN 47713 812-435-8453 685
Web: district.evscschools.com
Evapco Inc 5151 Allendale Ln . . . Taneytown MD 21787 410-756-2600 756-6450 14
Web: www.evapco.com
Evaporated Coatings Inc
2365 Maryland Rd . . . Willow Grove PA 19090 215-659-3080 659-1275 481
Web: www.evaporatedcoatings.com
EVC Group Inc
125 Half Mile Rd Ste 200 . . . Red Bank NJ 07701 732-933-2755 401
Web: evcgroup.com
Evco Plastics
100 W North St PO Box 497 . . . De Forest WI 53532 800-507-6000 251-0822 604
TF: 800-507-6000 ■ *Web:* www.evcoplastics.com
Evelinecharles Salons-spas
3625 Shaganappi Trail NW . . . Calgary AB T2J3V1 403-571-5666 77
Web: www.evelinecharles.com
Evelyn & Walter Haas Jr Fund
114 Sansome St Ste 600 . . . San Francisco CA 94104 415-856-1400 856-1500 305
Web: www.haasjr.org
Evelyn Hill Inc 1 Liberty Is . . . New York NY 10004 212-363-3180 327
Web: thestatueofliberty.com
Even Responsible Finance Inc
1440 Broadway . . . Oakland CA 94612 510-350-7678 178-1
Web: even.com
Evenflo Company Inc 1801 Commerce Dr . . . Piqua OH 45356 800-233-5921 64
TF: 800-233-5921 ■ *Web:* www.evenflo.com
Evenglow Lodge Inc
215 E Washington St . . . Pontiac IL 61764 815-844-6131 450
Web: evenglowlodge.org
Evenhouse & Company PC
1S660 Midwest Rd Ste 250 . . . Oakbrook Terrace IL 60181 630-832-3225 832-5520 2
Web: evenhousecpa.com
Evening Call Publishing Co, The
75 Main St . . . Woonsocket RI 02895 401-762-3000 767-8509 532-2
Web: www.woonsocketcall.com
Evening Observer
8-10 E Second St PO Box 391 . . . Dunkirk NY 14048 716-366-3000 366-3005 532-2
TF: 800-836-0931 ■ *Web:* www.observertoday.com
Evening Star Cafe
2000 Mt Vernon Ave . . . Alexandria VA 22301 703-549-5051 671
Web: eveningstarcafe.net
Evensky & Katz LLC
4000 Ponce de Leon Blvd Ste 850 . . . Coral Gables FL 33146 305-448-8882 448-1326 194
TF: 800-448-5435 ■ *Web:* evensky.com
Event 360 Inc
55 E Jackson Blvd Ste 1010 . . . Chicago IL 60604 773-247-5360 194
Web: www.event360.com
eVent Medical 60 Empire Dr . . . Lake Forest CA 92630 949-900-1917 900-1905 475
Web: event-medical.com
Event Producers Inc
5724 Salmen St . . . New Orleans LA 70123 504-466-4066 514
Web: www.eventproducers.com
Event Solutions International Inc
1757 Larchwood Dr . . . Troy MI 48083 248-307-9400 393
Eventech 1833 Alford Ave . . . Los Altos CA 94024 650-961-7845 463
Web: www.eventech.com
E-Ventexe
8780 Auburn Folsom Blvd Ste 3 . . . Granite Bay CA 95746 916-458-5820 789-0188 260
Web: e-ventexe.com
Eventide Inc 1 Alsan Way . . . Little Ferry NJ 07643 201-641-1200 647
Web: www.eventide.com
Eventnet Usa 1129 SE 4th Ave . . . Fort Lauderdale FL 33316 954-467-9898 175
Web: www.eventnetusa.com
EventPro Strategies LLC
Scottsdale Rd Ste B120 . . . Scottsdale AZ 85253 480-449-4100 283-1190 721
Web: www.eventprostrategies.com
EventRebels com Inc
10013 Fox Den Rd . . . Ellicott City MD 21042 877-883-1786 5
TF: 877-883-1706 ■ *Web:* www.eventrebels.com

Company / Address	Phone	Fax	Class
Events Forum Inc 2 Oxford Crossing Ste 4 .... New Hartford NY 13413 *Web:* eventsforum.net	315-792-7600	724-4460	196
Events.Com Inc 12255 El Camino Real Ste 210 .... San Diego CA 92130 *Web:* events.com	858-257-2300		180
Eventsful Inc 305 E 40th St Apt 6f .... New York NY 10016 *Web:* www.eventsful.com	212-682-8405		195
Eventure Interactive Inc 3420 Bristol St 6th Fl .... Costa Mesa CA 92626 **Fax Area Code:* 949 ■ *TF:* 855-986-5669 ■ *Web:* www.eventure.com	855-986-5669	209-1920*	395
Eventus Solutions Group 9777 Pyramid Crt Ste 160 .... Englewood CO 80112 *TF:* 888-990-9982 ■ *Web:* www.eventusg.com	303-376-6161	376-6164	180
Eventwristbands.com 1369 Spring St NW .... Atlanta GA 30309 *TF:* 877-725-4881 ■ *Web:* www.eventwristbands.com	404-897-2389		45
Ever Roll Specialties Co 3988 Lawrenceville Dr .... Springfield OH 45504 *Web:* www.ever-roll.com	937-964-1302		595
Ever Win International Corp 17579 Railroad St .... City of Industry CA 91748 *Web:* www.everwin.com	626-810-8218	810-6628	735
Everbloom Growers Inc 20450 SW 248th St .... Homestead FL 33031 *TF:* 800-889-8919 ■ *Web:* www.everbloomgrowers.com	305-248-1478	248-1449	292
Ever-Bloom Inc 4701 Foothill Rd .... Carpinteria CA 93013 *TF:* 800-388-8112 ■ *Web:* www.ever-bloom.com	805-684-5566		369
Everbridge Inc 500 N Brand Blvd Ste 1000 .... Glendale CA 91203 *TF:* 888-366-4911 ■ *Web:* www.everbridge.com	818-230-9700		224
Everbrite Electronics Inc 720 W Cherry St .... Chanute KS 66720 *TF:* 800-431-7383 ■ *Web:* www.evertron.net	800-431-7383		767
Everbrite Inc 4949 S 110th St PO Box 20020 .... Greenfield WI 53220 *TF:* 800-558-3888 ■ *Web:* www.everbrite.com	414-529-3500	529-7191	701
Evercoat 6600 Cornell Rd .... Cincinnati OH 45242 *Web:* www.evercoat.com	513-489-7600	489-9229	60
Evercore Partners Inc 55 E 52nd St .... New York NY 10055 *Web:* www.evercore.com	212-857-3100		401
Eveready Drugs LLC 1229 Third Ave .... New York NY 10021 *Web:* evereadydrug.com	212-249-1050		237
Eveready Printing Inc 20700 Miles Pkwy .... Cleveland OH 44128 *Web:* evereadyprint.com	216-587-2379	587-2260	627
Everest 440 S LaSalle St 40th Fl .... Chicago IL 60605 *Web:* www.everestrestaurant.com	312-663-8920		671
Everest 9902 Carver Rd Sycamore Office Pk Ste 105 .... Cincinnati OH 45242 *Web:* www.everestrealestate.com	513-769-2500	769-2512	690
Everest Consulting Group Inc 3840 Park Ave Ste 203 .... Edison NJ 08820 *Web:* www.everestconsulting.net	732-548-2700	548-6200	177
Everest International Consultants Inc 444 W Ocean Blvd Ste 1104 .... Long Beach CA 90802 *Web:* everestconsultants.com	562-435-9305	435-9310	261
Everest on Grand 1278 Grand Ave .... Saint Paul MN 55105 *Web:* www.everestongrand.com	651-696-1666		671
Everest Re Group Ltd 477 Martinsville Rd PO Box 830 .... Liberty Corner NJ 07938 *TF:* 800-269-6660 ■ *Web:* www.everestre.com	908-604-3000	604-3322	360-4
Everett & Jones BBQ 126 Broadway .... Oakland CA 94607 *Web:* eandjbbq.com	510-663-2350	663-8856	671
Everett Carpet & Flooring 318 Ashman St .... Midland MI 48640 *Web:* www.everettcarpetandflooring.com	989-835-7191	835-7621	290
Everett Cash Mutual Insurance Co 10591 Lincoln Hwy .... Everett PA 15537 *Web:* www.everettcash.com	814-652-6111		390
Everett Chamber of Commerce 467 Broadway .... Everett MA 02149 *Web:* www.everettmachamber.com	617-387-9100	389-6655	139
Everett Charles Technologies *Test Equipment Div* 700 E Harrison Ave .... Pomona CA 91767 *Web:* ect-cpg.com	909-625-5551		248
Everett Community College 2000 Tower St .... Everett WA 98201 *TF:* 866-575-9027 ■ *Web:* www.everettcc.edu	425-388-9100	388-9129	162
Everett Griffith Jr & Associates Inc 408 N 3rd St .... Lufkin TX 75901 *Web:* everettgriffith.com	936-634-5528		261
Everett J. Prescott Inc 32 Prescott St .... Gardiner ME 04345 *TF:* 800-357-2447 ■ *Web:* www.ejprescott.com	207-582-1851	582-5637	612
Everett Public Library 2702 Hoyt Ave .... Everett WA 98201 *Web:* www.epls.org	425-257-8010		434-3
Everfast Inc 203 Gale Ln .... Kennett Square PA 19348 *TF:* 800-213-6366 ■ *Web:* www.calicocorners.com	610-444-9700	444-1221	270
Evergage Inc 212 Elm St Ste 402 .... Somerville MA 02144 *TF:* 888-310-0589 ■ *Web:* evergage.com	888-310-0589		177
eVerge Group 4965 Preston Pk Blvd Ste 700 .... Plano TX 75093 *TF:* 888-548-1973 ■ *Web:* www.evergegroup.com	972-608-1803	608-1893	180
Everglades Alligator Farm 40351 SW 192nd Ave .... Homestead FL 33034 *Web:* www.everglades.com	305-247-2628	248-9711	823
Everglades Boats 544 Air Park Rd .... Edgewater FL 32132 *TF:* 800-368-5647 ■ *Web:* www.evergladesboats.com	386-409-2202	409-7939	90
Everglades Holiday Park 21940 Griffin Rd .... Fort Lauderdale FL 33332 *Web:* www.evergladesholidaypark.com	954-434-8111		50-5
Everglades National Park 40001 SR-9336 .... Homestead FL 33034 *TF:* 800-788-0511 ■ *Web:* www.nps.gov	305-242-7700		564
Everglades Safari Park 26700 SW Eighth St .... Miami FL 33194 *Web:* www.evergladessafaripark.com	305-226-6923	554-5666	823
Everglades Steel Corp 5901 NW 74th Ave .... Miami FL 33166 *Web:* evergladessteel.com	305 591-9460		492

Company / Address	Phone	Fax	Class
Everglades Technologies 1 Union Sq W 3rd Fl .... New York NY 10003 *Web:* www.etny.net	212-741-0000		196
Everglades University 5002 T-Rex Ave Ste 100 .... Boca Raton FL 33431 *TF:* 888-772-6077 ■ *Web:* www.evergladesuniversity.edu	561-912-1211	912-1191	786
EverGlow NA Inc 1122 Industrial Dr .... Matthews NC 28105 *Web:* www.everglow.us	704-841-2580		45
Evergreen Advisors LLC 9256 Bendix Rd Ste 300 .... Columbia MD 21045 *Web:* evergreenadvisorsllc.com	410-997-6000		401
Evergreen Beauty College 14045 NE 20th St Ste B .... Bellevue WA 98007 *Web:* www.evergreenbeauty.edu	425-336-5123		167-3
Evergreen Business Capital 13925 Interurban Ave S Ste 100 .... Seattle WA 98168 *TF:* 800-878-6613 ■ *Web:* www.evergreen504.com	206-622-3731		393
Evergreen Capital Management LLC 10500 N E 8th Ste 950 .... Bellevue WA 98004 *Web:* www.evergreengavekal.com	425-467-4600		401
Evergreen Construction Managem 30941 Suneagle Dr .... Mount Dora FL 32757 *Web:* evergreencm.net	352-227-1460		261
Evergreen Engineering Portland LLC 1740 Willow Creek Cir .... Eugene OR 97402 *TF:* 888-484-4771 ■ *Web:* www.evergreenengineering.com	888-484-4771		186
Evergreen Enterprises Inc 5915 Midlothian Tpke .... Richmond VA 23225 *TF:* 800-774-3837 ■ *Web:* www.myevergreen.com	800-774-3837		320
Evergreen FS Inc 402 N Hershey Rd .... Bloomington IL 61704 **Fax Area Code:* 309 ■ *TF:* 877-963-2392 ■ *Web:* www.evergreen-fs.com	877-963-2392	663-0494*	276
Evergreen Hospice Services 12822 124th Ln NE .... Kirkland WA 98034 *Web:* www.evergreenhealth.com	425-899-1070	899-1033	371
Evergreen Lodge 250 S Frontage Rd W .... Vail CO 81657 *TF:* 800-284-8245 ■ *Web:* www.evergreenvail.com	970-476-7810	476-4504	379
Evergreen Lumber & Truss Inc 84 Central Industrial Row .... Purvis MS 39475 *Web:* evergreentruss.com	601-794-8404		364
Evergreen Mortuary & Cemetery 3015 N Oracle Rd .... Tucson AZ 85705 *TF:* 800-852-0269 ■ *Web:* evergreenmortuary-cemetery.com	520-257-4831		510
Evergreen North American Co 2525 Cherry Ave Ste 105 .... Signal Hill CA 90755 *TF:* 877-267-2840 ■ *Web:* www.enais.com	562-595-7075		668
Evergreen Park Chamber of Commerce 9449 S Kedzie Ave Ste 196 .... Evergreen Park IL 60805 *Web:* www.evergreenparkchamber.org	708-423-1118		139
Evergreen Plastics Inc 202 Watertower Dr .... Clyde OH 43410 *Web:* www.evergreenplastics.com	419-547-1400		601
Evergreen Printing Company Inc 101 Haag Ave .... Bellmawr NJ 08031 *Web:* www.egpp.com	856-933-0222		532-3
Evergreen Public Schools 13501 NE 28th St PO Box 8910 .... Vancouver WA 98668 *Web:* sites.google.com	360-604-4000	892 5307	685
Evergreen Regional Library 55 1st Ave PO Box 1140 .... Gimli MB R0C1B0 *Web:* erlibrary.ca	204-642-7912	642-8319	436
Evergreen Research Inc (ERI) 433 Park Point Dr .... Golden CO 80401 *Web:* www.evergreenresearch.com	303-526-7402	526-7416	177
Evergreen Resort 7880 Mackinaw Trl .... Cadillac MI 49601 *TF:* 800-634-7302 ■ *Web:* www.evergreenresortmi.com	800-634-7302		669
Evergreen Shipping Agency (America) Corp 1 Evertrust Plz .... Jersey City NJ 07302 *Web:* www.evergreen-line.com	201-761-3000	761-3011	360-3
Evergreen Slate Company Inc 2027 County Rte 23 .... Middle Granville NY 12849 *Web:* www.evergreenslate.com	518-642-2530	642-9313	724
Evergreen Speedway 14405 179th Ave SE .... Monroe WA 98272 *Web:* evergreenspeedway.com	360-805-6100	805-6110	515
Evergreen State College, The 2700 Evergreen Pkwy .... Olympia WA 98505 *TF:* 888-492-9480 ■ *Web:* www.evergreen.edu	360-867-6000	867-5114	166
Evergreen Valley College 3095 Yerba Buena Rd .... San Jose CA 95135 *Web:* www.evc.edu	408-274-7900	223-9351	162
Evergreen Veterinary Clinic Pa 1611 E Capitol Expy .... San Jose CA 95121 *Web:* evergreenvetclinic.com	408-238-0690		794
Evergreen Woods 88 Notch Hill Rd .... North Branford CT 06471 *TF:* 866-413-6378 ■ *Web:* evergreen-woods.com	203-488-8000		672
Everhard Products Inc 1016 Ninth St SW .... Canton OH 44707 *TF:* 800-225-0984 ■ *Web:* everhard.com	330-453-7786		758
Everhart Museum 1901 Mulberry St .... Scranton PA 18510 *Web:* everhart-museum.org	570-346-7186	346-0652	520
Everi Holdings Inc (EVRI) 7250 S Tenaya Way Ste 100 .... Las Vegas NV 89113 *NYSE:* EVRI ■ *TF:* 800-833-7110 ■ *Web:* www.everi.com	702-855-3000		56
Everidge 15600 37th Ave N Ste 100 .... Plymouth MN 55446 *TF:* 888-227-1629 ■ *Web:* www.everidge.com	888-227-1629		664
Everingham & Kerr Inc 1300 Rt 73 Ste 103 .... Mount Laurel NJ 08054 *Web:* www.everkerr.com	856-546-6655		708
Everist Genomics Inc 709 W Ellsworth Rd .... Ann Arbor MI 48108 *TF:* 855-383-7478 ■ *Web:* www.everisthealth.com	855-383-7478		743
Everite Machine Products 1555 Rte 73 S .... Pennsauken Township NJ 08110 **Fax Area Code:* 215 ■ *Web:* www.everite.com	856-330-6700	426-7768*	455
Everkrisp Vegetables Inc 9202 W Harrison St .... Tolleson AZ 85353 *Web:* everkrispvegetables.com	623-936-3321		10-11
Everlast Plastic Lumber Inc 800 W Market St PO Box 367 .... Auburn PA 17922 *Web:* plasticlumber.org	570-754-7440		661

	City	State	Zip	Phone	Fax	Class
Everlaw 2020 Milvia St	Berkeley	CA	94704	844-383-7529		387
TF: 844-383-7529 ■ *Web:* www.everlaw.com						
Ever-Lite Company Inc						
1717 N Bayshore Dr	Miami	FL	33132	305-577-0819		9
Web: www.ever-lite.com						
Everlube Products						
100 Cooper Cir	Peachtree City	GA	30269	770-261-4800		481
TF: 800-428-7802 ■ *Web:* www.everlubeproducts.com						
Everlywell Inc						
800 W Cesar Chavez St Ste B101	Austin	TX	78701	512-309-5588		477
Web: www.everlywell.com						
EverMark LLC (EM) 1050 Northbrook Pkwy	Suwanee	GA	30024	678-455-5188	455-5190	236
Web: www.evermark-lnl.com						
Evers & Company CPAS LLC						
520 Dix Rd	Jefferson City	MO	65109	573-635-0227	634-3764	2
Web: everscpas.com						
Everson Cordage Works Inc						
7180 Everson-Goshen Rd	Everson	WA	98247	800-966-0203		208
TF: 800-966-0203 ■ *Web:* www.eversoncordage.com						
Everson Museum of Art						
401 Harrison St	Syracuse	NY	13202	315-474-6064		520
Web: www.everson.org						
Everson Tesla Inc 615 Daniel's Rd	Nazareth	PA	18064	610-746-1520	746-1530	518
Web: www.eversontesla.com						
Eversource 800 Boylston St	Boston	MA	02199	800-592-2000		360-5
NYSE: NST ■ *TF:* 800-592-2000 ■ *Web:* www.eversource.com						
EverStaff LLC						
6150 Oak Tree Blvd Ste 175	Cleveland	OH	44131	877-392-6151		260
TF: 877-392-6151 ■ *Web:* www.everstaff.com						
EverTrue LLC 330 Congress St 2nd Fl	Boston	MA	02210	855-387-8783		387
TF: 855-387-8783 ■ *Web:* www.evertrue.com						
Everwise Corp 1178 Broadway 4th Fl	New York	NY	10001	888-734-0011		387
TF: 888-734-0011 ■ *Web:* www.geteverwise.com						
Every Promotional Product						
30851 Agoura Rd Ste 110	Agoura Hills	CA	91301	818-597-9900		184
Web: www.everypromotionalproduct.com						
Everybody Fights 15 Channel Center St	Boston	MA	02210	857-250-4140		354
Web: everybodyfights.com						
Everyday Health Inc						
345 Hudson St 16th Fl	New York	NY	10014	646-728-9500	728-9501	637-10
TF: 888-795-4719 ■ *Web:* www.everydayhealth.com						
Everyday Technologies Inc						
2005 Campbell Rd	Sidney	OH	45365	937-492-4171		358
Web: www.everydaytech.com						
EveryLife Foundation for Rare Diseases						
PO Box 77210	Washington	DC	20013	202-697-7273		305
Web: everylifefoundation.org						
Everyman Theatre 315 W Fayette St	Baltimore	MD	21201	410-752-2208	615-7053*	572
**Fax Area Code:* 443 ■ *Web:* everymantheatre.org						
Everyone Is Doing Outrageous Sex (EIDOS)						
PO Box 96	Boston	MA	02137	617-262-0096	364-0096	637-9
Web: www.eidos.org						
EveryScape Inc 65 Chapel St	Newton	MA	02458	781-250-4800		387
Web: www.everyscape.com						
Evesham Township Board of Education						
25 S Maple Ave	Marlton	NJ	08053	856-983-1800		685
Web: www.evesham.k12.nj.us						
EVH Manufacturing Co 4895 Red Bluff Rd	Loris	SC	29569	843-756-2555	756-4436	273
Web: hardeebyevh.com						
Evident Point Software Corp						
160-3751 Shell Rd	Richmond	BC	V6X2W2	604-241-2711		179
Web: www.evidentpoint.com						
Eview 360 Corp						
39255 Country Club Dr Ste B-1	Farmington Hills	MI	48331	248-306-5191	306-5195	195
Web: www.eview360.com						
Evil Eye Pictures LLC						
665 Third St Ste 503	San Francisco	CA	94107	415-777-0666		514
Web: evileyepictures.com						
Evins Communications Ltd						
830 Third Ave	New York	NY	10022	212-688-8200	935-6730	7
Web: www.evins.com						
Evins Personnel Consultants Inc						
2013 W Anderson Ln	Austin	TX	78757	512-454-9561	483-9191	260
Web: www.evinspersonnelconsultants.com						
Evins Regional Juvenile Ctr						
3801 E Monte Cristo Rd	Edinburg	TX	78542	956-289-5500		412
eVision LLC 179 E Main St	Branford	CT	06405	203-481-8005		5
Web: www.evisionsem.com						
Evite LLC 600 Wilshire Blvd 4th Fl	Los Angeles	CA	90017	213-699-5005		387
Web: www.evite.com						
EVMS (Eastern Virginia Medical School)						
PO Box 1980	Norfolk	VA	23501	757-446-5244	446-5817	167-2
Web: www.evms.edu						
Evo Exhibits 399 Wegner Dr	West Chicago	IL	60185	630-520-0710		7
TF: 888-404-4224 ■ *Web:* evoexhibits.com						
Evogen Inc						
9393 W 110th St Ste 500	Overland Park	KS	66210	913-948-5640		743
Web: www.evogen.com						
Evok Advertising Inc						
1485 International Pkwy Ste 3001	Heathrow	FL	32746	407-302-4416		7
TF: 855-292-3865 ■ *Web:* www.evokad.com						
Evoke Health						
101 Avenue of the Americas 13th Fl	New York	NY	10013	212-228-7200		5
Web: www.evokegroup.com						
Evoke Kyne 252 W 37th St Ste 500E	New York	NY	10018	212-594-5500		5
Web: www.evokekyne.com						
Evoke Research & Consulting LLC						
1000 Wilson Blvd Ste 2500	Arlington	VA	22209	703-415-1007		196
Web: evokeconsulting.com						
Evoke Technologies 7106 Corporate Way	Dayton	OH	45459	937-202-4161		196
Web: www.evoketechnologies.com						
Evola Music Center Inc						
12745 23 Mile Rd	Shelby Township	MI	48315	586-726-6570		526
Web: www.evola.com						
Evolution Computing						
7000 N 16th St Ste 120 514	Phoenix	AZ	85020	800-874-4028		178-5
TF: 800-874-4028 ■ *Web:* www.fastcad.com						
Evolution Petroleum Corp						
1155 Dairy Ashford St Ste 425	Houston	TX	77079	713-935-0122	935-0199	580
Web: evolutionpetroleum.com						
Evolve IP LLC						
989 Old Eagle School Rd Ste 815	Wayne	PA	19087	877-459-4347		737
TF: 877-459-4347 ■ *Web:* www.evolveip.net						
Evolve Media 39 Mesa St Ste 101	San Francisco	CA	94129	415-324-5002		7
Web: www.evolvemedia.tv						
Evolve Payment Systems						
2974 Rice St	Saint Paul	MN	55113	651-628-4000		180
Web: evolve-systems.com						
Evonik Corp 299 Jefferson Rd	Parsippany	NJ	07054	973-929-8000		146
Web: corporate.evonik.com						
Evonik Corp 2 Turner Pl	Piscataway	NJ	08855	732-981-5000	981-5033	434-3
Web: www.corporate.evonik.com						
EVOO Cannon Beach Cooking School						
188 S Hemlock St PO Box 1368	Cannon Beach	OR	97110	503-436-8555	436-8999	685
TF: 877-436-3866 ■ *Web:* www.evoo.biz						
EVRI (Everi Holdings Inc)						
7250 S Tenaya Way Ste 100	Las Vegas	NV	89113	702-855-3000		56
NYSE: EVRI ■ *TF:* 800-833-7110 ■ *Web:* www.everi.com						
EVS Ltd 3702 W Sample St	South Bend	IN	46619	574-233-5707		320
TF: 800-364-3218 ■ *Web:* www.evsltd.com						
EVS Metal Inc 1 Kenner Ct	Riverdale	NJ	07457	973-839-4432		697
Web: www.evsmetal.com						
Evviva Brands LLC						
237 Kearny St No 112	San Francisco	CA	94108	415-997-8482		195
Web: www.evvivabrands.com						
EVY of California Inc						
810A S Flower St	Los Angeles	CA	90017	213-746-4647	746-9788	277
Web: www.evy.com						
EW Brandt & Sons Inc (EWB) 561 Ragan Rd	Wapato	WA	98951	509-877-3193		315-3
Web: rembrandtfruit.com						
EW James & Sons Inc						
1308-14 Nailling Dr	Union City	TN	38261	731-885-0601		345
Web: www.ewjamesandsons.com						
EW Tompkins Company Inc						
126 Sheridan Ave	Albany	NY	12210	518-462-6577	462-6570	189-10
Web: www.thetompkinsgroup.com						
EW Wylie Corp 1520 Second Ave NW	West Fargo	ND	58078	800-437-4132		780
TF: 800-437-4132 ■ *Web:* www.wylietrucking.com						
EWA (Electronic Warfare Associates Inc)						
13873 Park Center Rd	Herndon	VA	20171	703-904-5700	904-5779	180
Web: www.ewa.com						
EWA (Enterprise Wireless Alliance)						
8484 Westpark Dr Ste 630	McLean	VA	22102	703-528-5115	524-1074	49-20
TF: 800-482-8282 ■ *Web:* www.enterprisewireless.org						
Ewald Consulting Group Inc						
1000 Westgate Dr Ste 252	Saint Paul	MN	55114	651-290-6260	290-2266	47
Web: www.ewald.com						
Ewald's Hartford Ford						
5788 State Hwy 60	Hartford	WI	53027	262-228-8435		57
Web: www.ewaldshartfordford.com						
eWareness Inc						
1900 S Harbor City Blvd Ste 122	Melbourne	FL	32901	321-953-2435		809
TF: 800-517-4130 ■ *Web:* www.ewarenessinc.com						
Ewart-Ohlson Machine Company Inc, The						
1435 Main St PO Box 359	Cuyahoga Falls	OH	44222	330-928-2171		757
Web: www.ewart-ohlson.com						
EWASTE+ 7318 Victor Mendon Rd	Victor	NY	14564	888-563-1340	924-3841*	179
**Fax Area Code:* 585 ■ *TF:* 888-563-1340 ■ *Web:* www.ewaste.com						
EWB (EW Brandt & Sons Inc) 561 Ragan Rd	Wapato	WA	98951	509-877-3193		315-3
Web: rembrandtfruit.com						
EWI (EastWest Institute)						
1 E 26th St 20th Fl	New York	NY	10010	212-824-4100	824-4149	634
Web: www.eastwest.ngo						
EWI (Edison Welding Institute)						
1250 Arthur E Adams Dr	Columbus	OH	43221	614-688-5000	688-5001	49-13
Web: ewi.org						
EWI (Executive Women Intl)						
3860 S 2300 E Ste 211	Salt Lake City	UT	84109	801-355-2800		49-12
TF: 877-439-4669 ■ *Web:* ewirichmond.org						
EWI (Eagle Wings Industries Inc)						
400 Shellhouse Dr	Rantoul	IL	61866	217-892-4322		60
Web: www.ewiusa.com						
EWI (Elliott Wave Intl) PO Box 1618	Gainesville	GA	30503	770-536-0309	536-2514	637-9
TF: 800-336-1618 ■ *Web:* elliottwave.com						
EWI RE Inc						
5430 LBJ Fwy Three Lincoln Ctr Ste 1600	Dallas	TX	75240	972-866-6815	866-6801	390
Web: www.ewirisk.com						
EWI Worldwide Inc 13211 Merriman Rd	Livonia	MI	48150	734-525-9010		5
Web: www.ewiworldwide.com						
EWIE Company Inc						
1099 Highland Dr Ste D	Ann Arbor	MI	48108	734-971-6265		393
Web: www.ewie.com						
Ewing Cole 100 N Sixth St	Philadelphia	PA	19106	215-923-2020		261
Web: ewingcole.com						
Ewing Group						
2820 S Padre Island Dr Ste 211	Corpus Christi	TX	78415	361-502-7664		186
Web: www.ewinggcc.com						
Ewing Marion Kauffman Foundation (EMKF)						
4801 Rockhill Rd	Kansas City	MO	64110	816-932-1000		305
Web: www.kauffman.org						
Ewing Morris & Company Investment Partners						
1407 Yonge St Ste 500	Toronto	ON	M4T1Y7	416-640-2791		528
Web: www.ewingmorris.com						
Ewing-Foley Inc						
10061 Bubb Rd Ste 1000	Cupertino	CA	95014	408-342-1200		246
TF: 800-399-3319 ■ *Web:* ewingfoley.com						
Ewm Group PC						
3635 Peachtree Industrial Blvd Ste 200	Duluth	GA	30096	678-584-0222		2
Web: gtcowners.com						
eWomenNetwork						
14900 Landmark Blvd Ste 540	Dallas	TX	75254	972-620-9995		225
Web: www.ewomennetwork.com						
EWP (Eliot Werner Publications Inc)						
PO Box 268	Clinton Corners	NY	12514	845-266-4241	266-3317	637-2
Web: www.eliotwerner.com						

Name / Address	City	State	ZIP	Phone	Fax	Class
EWR Weather Radar 336 Leffingwell Ave. *Web:* ewradar.com	Saint Louis	MO	63122	314-821-1022		529
EWV (EnterpriseWorks/VITA) 818 Connecticut Ave NW Ste 600 *Web:* www.enterpriseworks.org	Washington	DC	20006	202-639-8660	639-8664	48-5
Exacom Inc 99 Airport Rd *TF:* 800-757-8184 ■ *Web:* www.exacom.com	Concord	NH	03301	603-228-0706	228-0254	735
Exact Cutting Service Inc 6892 W Snwvlle Rd *Web:* exactcut.com	Brecksville	OH	44141	440-546-1319	546-1322	393
Exact Eye Care 431 Pierce St *Web:* www.exacteyecare.com	Sioux City	IA	51101	712-252-4691		543
Exact Inc 5285 Ramona Blvd *Web:* exactinc.com	Jacksonville	FL	32205	904-783-6640		697
Exact Metrology 11575 Goldcoast Dr. *TF:* 866-722-2600 ■ *Web:* www.exactmetrology.com	Cincinnati	OH	45249	513-831-6620		358
Exact Sciences 101 Galveston Dr. *NASDAQ: GHDX* ■ *TF:* 866-662-6897 ■ *Web:* www.exactsciences.com	Redwood City	CA	94063	650-556-9300	556-1132	85
Exacta Corp 10437 Innovation Dr *TF:* 800-258-2070 ■ *Web:* exactacorp.com	Wauwatosa	WI	53226	262-796-0000		180
Exactax Inc 2301 W Lincoln Ave Ste 100 *TF:* 844-327-6740 ■ *Web:* www.exactax.com	Anaheim	CA	92801	714-284-4802		734
Exactearth Ltd 60 Struck Ct *Web:* www.exactearth.com	Cambridge	ON	N1R8L2	519-622-4445		387
Exactech Inc 2320 NW 66th Ct *NASDAQ: EXAC* ■ *TF:* 800-392-2832 ■ *Web:* www.exac.com	Gainesville	FL	32653	352-377-1140	378-2617	477
Exacto Spring Corp 1201 Hickory St *Web:* exacto.com	Grafton	WI	53024	262-377-3970	377-3854	719
Exact-Tool & Die Inc 5425 W 140th St. *Web:* exact-tool.com	Brook Park	OH	44142	216-676-9140	676-0091	489
ExaDigm Inc 2871 Pullman St *Web:* exadigm.com	Santa Ana	CA	92705	949-486-0320		194
ExaGrid Systems Inc 2000 W Park Dr *TF:* 800-868-6985 ■ *Web:* www.exagrid.com	Westborough	MA	01581	508-898-2872	898-2401	180
Exair Corp 11510 Goldcoast Dr *TF:* 800-903-9247 ■ *Web:* www.exair.com	Cincinnati	OH	45249	513-671-3322	671-3363	567
Exal Corp 1 Performance Pl *Web:* www.exal.com	Youngstown	OH	44502	330-744-2267		124
Exalpha Biologicals Inc 2 Shaker Rd Unit B101 *Web:* www.exalpha.com	Shirley	MA	01464	978-425-1370		231
Exalt Integrated Technologies 3000 Northwoods Pkwy Ste 350 *Web:* www.exaltit.com	Norcross	GA	30071	678-920-3019		196
Examination Management Services Inc 3050 Regent Blvd Ste 100 **Fax Area Code:* 214 ■ *TF:* 800-872-3674 ■ *Web:* www.emsinet.com	Irving	TX	75063	800-872-3674	689-3644*	225
Examiner, The 410 S Liberty St *Web:* www.examiner.net	Independence	MO	64050	816-254-8600	836-3805	532-2
ExamWorks Inc 3280 Peachtree Rd Ste 2625 *Web:* examworks.com	Atlanta	GA	30305	404-952-2400	846-1554	415
Exane Inc 640 Fifth Ave 15th Fl *Web:* www.exane.com	New York	NY	10019	212-634-4990		690
Exantas Capital Corp 717 Fifth Ave 15th Fl *NYSE: XAN* ■ *Web:* www.exantas.com	New York	NY	10022	212-621-3210		654
Exatron Inc 2842 Aiello Dr. *Web:* www.exatron.com	San Jose	CA	95111	408-629-7600		253
Excalibre Engineering 9201 Irvine Blvd *TF:* 877-922-5427 ■ *Web:* www.excaliburengineering.com	Irvine	CA	92618	949-454-6603		743
Excalibur Associates Inc 8687 W 108th Ave *TF:* 800-218-8846 ■ *Web:* www.excaliburassociates.com	Westminster	CO	80021	800-218-8846		463
Excalibur Cutlery and Gifts Inc 174 Wallis St *TF:* 800-366-7405 ■ *Web:* www.excaliburcutlery.com	Eugene	OR	97404	541-232-5454		222
Excalibur Data Recovery Inc 13 Branch St Ste 207B *TF:* 800-466-0893 ■ *Web:* www.excaliburdatarecovery.com	Methuen	MA	01844	978-681-1200	681-1203	177
Excalibur Data Systems 115 Sagamore Hill Rd. *Web:* www.excaliburdata.com	Pittsburgh	PA	15239	724-387-1331		175
Excalibur Engineering Services Inc 962 E 2100 N	North Logan	UT	84341	435-787-2085		256
Excalibur Equipment LLC *Gregory Industrial Trucks* 285 Eldridge Rd. *Web:* www.exequipment.com	Fairfield	NJ	07004	973-808-8399	808-8398	470
Excalibur Hotel & Casino 3850 S Las Vegas Blvd *TF:* 877-750-5464 ■ *Web:* excalibur.mgmresorts.com	Las Vegas	NV	89109	702-597-7777	597-7009	133
Excalibur Technology Corp 700 Fox Glen Lowr Level *Web:* www.excaltech.com	Barrington	IL	60010	847-842-9570		196
Exceed Consulting 2488 84th St SW *Web:* www.exceed-corp.com	Byron Center	MI	49315	616-878-0000		180
Exceed Resources Inc 294 New Rd *Web:* exceedresourcesinc.com	Monmouth Junction	NJ	08852	732-329-2742		193
Exceed Staffing 363 N Sam Houston Pkwy E Ste 1100 **Fax Area Code:* 713 ■ *TF:* 866-609-2884	Houston	TX	77060	866-609-2884	455-7419*	193
Exceed Technologies Inc 2605 Cleda Dr *Web:* exceedtech.net	Columbus	MS	39701	662-328-8333		225
Excel Bridge Manufacturing Co 12001 Shoemaker Ave *TF:* 800-548-0054 ■ *Web:* www.excelbridge.com	Santa Fe Springs	CA	90670	562-944-0701		480
Excel Decorators Inc 3748 Kentucky Ave. *Web:* www.exceldecorators.com	Indianapolis	IN	46221	317-856-1300	856-1301	184
Excel Diagnostic Imaging Clinics 9701 Richmond Ave Ste 122 *Web:* www.exceldiagnostics.com	Houston	TX	77042	713-781-6200		383
Excel Engineering Inc 5267 Program Ave *Web:* exceleng.net	Saint Paul	MN	55112	763-571-5008		261
Excel Federal Credit Union 5070 Peachtree Industrial Blvd *TF:* 888-441-9235 ■ *Web:* excelfcu.org	Norcross	GA	30071	770-416-2166		219
Excel Home Care LLC 1102 S Lebanon St *Web:* excelhomehealthcare.com	Lebanon	IN	46052	765-482-6680		363
Excel Homes Inc 10642 S Susquehanna Trl. *TF:* 844-875-9160 ■ *Web:* www.excelhomes.com	Liverpool	PA	17045	844-875-9160		187
Excel Injection Molding Inc 977 Sullivan Dr. *Web:* www.excelinjection.com	Hattiesburg	MS	39401	601-544-6133	544-7133	604
Excel Machine & Fabrication Inc 1230 Ridgely St *Web:* www.excelmachine-fab.com	Baltimore	MD	21230	410-576-9480		697
Excel Machinery Ltd 12100 I-40 E *TF:* 800-858-4002 ■ *Web:* www.excelmach.com	Amarillo	TX	79120	806-335-1553		757
Excel Management Systems Inc 691 N High St 2nd Fl *TF:* 800-886-4925 ■ *Web:* www.emsi.com	Columbus	OH	43215	614-224-4007	224-4995	196
Excel Manufacturing Inc 1705 E Fourth St. *Web:* www.excelmanufacturinginc.com	Seymour	IN	47274	812-523-6764		454
Excel Partners Inc 1177 Summer St *Web:* www.excel-partners.com	Stamford	CT	06905	203-978-6200		260
Excel Personnel 10111 Inverness Main St *Web:* www.excelpersonnel.com	Englewood	CO	80112	303-805-2300	805-2400	260
Excel Precision Co 3255 Scott Blvd 1-101 *Web:* www.excelprecision.com	Santa Clara	CA	95054	408-727-4260	727-1026	248
Excel Printing & Mailing 924 E 162nd St. *Web:* www.excelprintmail.com	South Holland	IL	60473	708-333-0773		627
Excel Program Inventions 375 Redondo Ave *Web:* www.epi-software.com	Long Beach	CA	90814	562-366-0350		178-1
Excel Railcar Corp 28367 Davis Pkwy Ste 300 *Web:* excelrailcar.com	Warrenville	IL	60555	630-657-1100		23
Excel Screen Printing & Embroidery Inc 10507 Delta Pkwy *Web:* www.excelscreenprinting.com	Schiller Park	IL	60176	847-801-5200	801-5205	687
Excel Services Corp 11921 Rockville Pk Ste 100 *Web:* excelservices.com	Rockville	MD	20852	301-984-4400		256
Excel Software 515 N Racetrack Rd *Web:* www.excelsoftware.com	Henderson	NV	89015	702-445-7645	445-7814	178-1
Ex-Cel Solutions Inc 14618 Grover St *Web:* www.excels.com	Omaha	NE	68144	402-333-6541		175
Excel Sports Boulder 2045 32nd St. *TF:* 800-627-6664 ■ *Web:* www.excelsports.com	Boulder	CO	80301	303-444-6737		711
Excel Staffing 2100 Osuna Rd NE Ste 100 *TF:* 888-607-1695 ■ *Web:* www.excelstaff.com	Albuquerque	NM	87113	505-262-1871		193
Excel Technologies LLC 3701 Pender Dr *TF:* 866-392-3583 ■ *Web:* excel-technologies.com	Fairfax	VA	22030	703-246-9002		180
Excel Telecommunications 433 Las Colinas Blvd Ste 400 *TF:* 877-668-0808 ■ *Web:* www.excel.com	Irving	TX	75039	972-910-1900		736
Excel Tool Inc 2020 First Ave *Web:* www.exceleti.com	Seymour	IN	47274	812-522-6880	522-6524	757
Excel Transportation Inc 333 Ongman Rd *TF:* 888-567-6977 ■ *Web:* exceltransportation.ca	Prince George	BC	V2K4K9	250-563-7356		311
Exceletech Coating & Applications LLC 221 N Hwy 27 Ste I *Web:* www.excelcoatings.com	Clermont	FL	34711	352-394-2155		261
Excell Communications Inc 6247 Amber Hills Rd *Web:* www.excellcommunications.com	Trussville	AL	35173	205-956-0198		116
Excell Machine Company Inc 602 S 4th Ave *Web:* www.excellmachine.com	Mansfield	TX	76063	817-473-6121	473-6170	454
Excell Marketing L C 5501 Park Ave *Web:* www.excellmktg.com	Des Moines	IA	50321	515-244-0300		195
Ex-Cell Metal Products Inc 11240 Melrose St. *TF:* 800-392-3557 ■ *Web:* www.ex-cell.com	Franklin Park	IL	60131	847-451-0451	261-9448	286
Excella Co 2300 Wilson Blvd Ste 600 *Web:* www.excella.com	Arlington	VA	22201	703-840-8600		180
Excellance Inc 453 Lanier Rd *TF:* 800-882-9799 ■ *Web:* excellance.com	Madison	AL	35758	256-772-9321	772-8792	30
Excellence in Communications Inc 9507 74th St. *Web:* www.excellence-in-communications.com	Kenosha	WI	53142	262-694-0446	694-8329	192
Excellent Coffee Co 259 E Ave **Fax Area Code:* 401 ■ *TF:* 800-345-2007 ■ *Web:* www.downeastcoffee.com	Pawtucket	RI	02860	800-345-2007	724-0560*	296-7
Excelleris Technologies Inc 200-3500 Gilmore Way *TF:* 866-728-4777 ■ *Web:* www.excelleris.com	Burnaby	BC	V5C2W7	604-658-2111	291-6837	45
Excello Circuits & Manufacturing Corp 1924 Nancita Cr *Web:* www.excello.com	Placentia	CA	92870	714-993-0560		625
Excellon Automation Inc 20001 S Rancho Way *TF:* 800-392-3556 ■ *Web:* www.excellon.com	Rancho Dominguez	CA	90220	310-668-7700	668-7800	470
Excelltech Inc PO Box 839 *Web:* www.excelltech.net	Yankton	SD	57078	605-665-5811		178-1
Excellus BlueCross BlueShield of Central New York 333 Butternut Dr *TF:* 800-633-6066 ■ *Web:* www.excellusbcbs.com	Syracuse	NY	13214	315-671-6400		391-3
Excelsior College 7 Columbia Cir *TF:* 888-647-2388 ■ *Web:* www.excelsior.edu	Albany	NY	12203	518-464-8500	464-8833	166
Excelsior Defense Inc 2232 Central Ave *TF:* 877-955-4636 ■ *Web:* www.excelsiordefense.com	Saint Petersburg	FL	33712	727-527-9600		693

Phone | Fax | Class

Excelsior Electric Membership Corp
986 SE Broad St . . . . . Metter GA 30439 912-685-2115 685-5782 245
Web: www.excelsioremc.com

Excelsior Inc 4982 27th Ave . . . . . Rockford IL 61109 815-987-2900 962-5466 326
Web: www.excelsiorinc.com

Excelsior Marking Products
888 W Waterloo Rd. . . . . . Akron OH 44314 330-745-2300 745-2333 467
TF: 800-433-3615 ■ *Web:* www.excelsiormarking.com

Excelsior Medical Corp
1933 Heck Ave . . . . . Neptune City NJ 07753 732-776-7525 776-7600 596
TF: 800-487-4276 ■ *Web:* excelsiormedical.com

Excelsior Springs Standard
417 S Thompson Ave . . . . . Excelsior Springs MO 64024 816-637-6155 637-8411 532-2
Web: www.excelsiorspringsstandard.com

Excelsys 3230 N Braeswood Blvd. . . . . . Houston TX 77025 713-662-0172 662-0173 768
Web: excelsys.org

Excelta Corp 60 Easy St. . . . . . Buellton CA 93427 805-686-4686 351
Web: www.excelta.com

Exceptional Home Care LLP
1510 E Grande Blvd . . . . . Tyler TX 75703 903-533-0290 363
Web: exceptionalhc.com

Exceptional Parent (EP)
38 River Edge Rd Ste B. . . . . . River Edge NJ 07661 201-843-3274 637-9
TF: 800-372-7368 ■ *Web:* www.eparent.com

Excet 6225 Brandon Ave Ste 360 . . . . . Springfield VA 22150 703-635-7089 624
Web: www.excetinc.com

Exchange Bank & Trust Co
700 Front St . . . . . Natchitoches LA 71457 318-352-8141 70
Web: exchange-bank.com

Exchange Conference Ctr
212 Northern Ave . . . . . Boston MA 02210 617-790-1900 205
Web: exchangeconferencecenter.com

Exchange Enterprises Inc
919-7 Stratford Ave. . . . . . Stratford CT 06615 203-386-9466 386-9913 393
Web: www.exchangeenterprises.com

Exchange Publishing Corp
19401 Industrial Dr. . . . . . New Paris IN 46553 574-831-2138 831-2131 532-2
Web: www.farmers-exchange.net

Exchange State Bank
3992 Chandler St PO Box 68 . . . . . Carsonville MI 48419 810-657-9333 70
TF: 888-488-9300 ■ *Web:* www.exchangestatebank.com

Exchange, The
3911 S Walton Walker Blvd . . . . . Dallas TX 75236 800-527-2345 446-0163 791
TF: 800-527-2345 ■ *Web:* www.shopmyexchange.com

Excipio Consulting LLC
1216 E Kenosha St . . . . . Broken Arrow OK 74012 918-357-5507 401
Web: www.excipio.net

Exclaim Inc 220 N Smith St. . . . . . Palatine IL 60067 847-392-0008 4
Web: www.exclaim-inc.com

Exclaimit Inc 3825 Misty Landing Dr . . . . . Valrico FL 33594 813-731-8718 195
Web: exclaimit.com

Exclusive Transportation for Industry
2202 26th SW St . . . . . Allentown PA 18103 610-798-0300 798-7416 780
TF: 800-355-3355 ■ *Web:* www.eticompany.com

EXCO Resources Inc
12377 Merit Dr Ste 1700 . . . . . Dallas TX 75251 214-368-2084 368-2087 538
OTC: XCO ■ *TF:* 888-788-9449 ■ *Web:* www.excoresources.com

Exec Air Montana Inc 2430 Airport Rd . . . . . Helena MT 59601 406-442-2190 442-2199 13
TF: 800-513-2190 ■ *Web:* www.execairmontana.com

ExecSuite 702 3 Ave SW . . . . . Calgary AB T2P3B4 403-294-5800 294-5959 210
TF: 800-667-4980 ■ *Web:* www.execsuite.ca

Execu/Tech Systems Inc
537 Harrison Ave . . . . . Panama City FL 32401 850-747-0581 177
TF: 800-232-1626 ■ *Web:* www.execu-tech.com

Execu|Search Group, The
707 Summer St 4th Fl. . . . . . Stamford CT 06901 203-653-4700 653-4701 631
Web: www.execu-search.com

Execulink Telecom 1127 Ridgeway Rd. . . . . . Woodstock ON N4V1E3 519-602-9878 224
Web: execulink.com

ExecUNet Inc 295 Westport Ave . . . . . Norwalk CT 06851 800-637-3126 260
TF: 800-637-3126 ■ *Web:* www.execunet.com

Execupharm Inc
610 Freedom Business Center Dr
Ste 200 . . . . . King of Prussia PA 19406 610-272-8771 272-8056 721
Web: www.execupharm.com

Execushield Inc 4104 24th St. . . . . . San Francisco CA 94114 415-508-0825 693
Web: www.execushield.com

Execusys Inc 6767 N Wickham Rd . . . . . Melbourne FL 32940 321-253-0077 177
TF: 800-454-3081 ■ *Web:* www.execusys.com

Executech 4000 Genesee Pl Ste 213 . . . . . Woodbridge VA 22192 571-285-3331 285-3360 179
Web: www.esc-techsolutions.com

Execu-Tech Business Systems Inc (EBS)
1829 Silver Star Rd. . . . . . Orlando FL 32804 407-447-6800 447-6804 112
Web: www.ebs-fl.com

Executive Administration Inc
85 W Algonquin Rd Ste 550 . . . . . Arlington Heights IL 60005 847-427-9600 47
Web: www.execadmin.com

Executive Air
Austin Straubel International Airport 2131 Airport Dr
. . . . . Green Bay WI 54313 920-498-4880 498-4890 63
Web: executiveair.com

Executive Arrangements
2460 Fairmount Blvd Ste 205. . . . . . Cleveland OH 44106 216-231-9311 184
Web: www.executivearrangements.com

Executive Business Media Inc
825 Old Country Rd . . . . . Westbury NY 11590 516-334-3030 334-3059 463
Web: www.ebmpubs.com

Executive Cabinetry
2838 Grandview Dr. . . . . . Simpsonville SC 29680 800-654-6120 115
TF: 800-654-6120 ■ *Web:* www.executivecabinetry.com

Executive Car Leasing Inc
7807 Santa Monica Blvd. . . . . . Los Angeles CA 90046 323-654-5000 848-9015 289
TF: 800-994-2277 ■ *Web:* www.executivecarleasing.com

Executive Coach Builders Inc
4400 W Production St . . . . . Springfield MO 65803 417-831-3535 59
Web: ecbbus.com

Executive Director Inc
555 E Wells St Ste 1100. . . . . . Milwaukee WI 53202 414-276-6445 276-3349 47
Web: www.execinc.com

Executive Diversity Services Inc
1700 Seventh Ave Ste 2100 . . . . . Seattle WA 98101 206-224-9293 224-9303 463
Web: www.executivediversity.com

Executive Flyers Aviation Inc - KBED
Civil Air Terminal Hanscom Field . . . . . Bedford MA 01730 781-274-7227 274-6719 167-3
Web: www.executiveflyers.com

Executive Flyers Inc
6151 Freeport Blvd Ste 151 . . . . . Sacramento CA 95822 916-427-1888 427-1881 167-3
Web: www.learntoflysacramento.com

Executive Hotel Vintage Court
650 Bush St . . . . . San Francisco CA 94108 415-392-4666 433-4065 379
TF: 888-388-3932 ■ *Web:* www.executivehotels.net

Executive Impact Inc
1776 Old Spring House Ln Ste 100 . . . . . Dunwoody GA 30338 678-547-0072 631
Web: www.executivecareerconsultant.com

Executive Insurance Brokerage Financial Services
515 Johnson Ave . . . . . Bohemia NY 11716 631-563-8433 390
Web: eifsonline.info

Executive Jet 4556 Airport Rd. . . . . . Cincinnati OH 45226 513-979-6600 13
TF: 877-356-5387 ■ *Web:* executivejetmanagement.com

Executive Management Assoc
210 N Glenoaks Blvd Ste C. . . . . . Burbank CA 91502 818-843-5660 843-7423 47
Web: www.emaoffice.com

Executive Office for Immigration Review
5107 Leesburg Pk. . . . . . Falls Church VA 22041 703-305-0289 605-0365 340-14
Web: www.justice.gov

Executive Protection Institute
16 Penn Plz Ste 1570. . . . . . New York NY 10001 212-268-4555 766
TF: 800-947-5827 ■ *Web:* www.personalprotection.com

Executive Reporting Service (ERS)
300 1st Ave S Suntrust Bldg Ste 402 . . . . . Saint Petersburg FL 33701 727-823-4155 822-5458 478
TF: 800-621-9077 ■ *Web:* www.executivereporting.com

Executive Resources International LLC
63 Atlantic Ave . . . . . Boston MA 02110 617-742-8970 193
Web: erisearch.net

Executive Security Intl
715 Horizon Dr Ste 301 . . . . . Grand Junction CO 81506 800-874-0888 167-3
TF: 800-874-0888 ■ *Web:* www.esibodyguardschool.com

Executive Self Storage Associates Inc
5353 W Dartmouth Ave Ste 401 . . . . . Denver CO 80227 303-703-1289 803-3
Web: www.executiveselfstorage.com

Executive Sounding Board Associates Inc
3959 Welsh Rd Ste 354 . . . . . Willow Grove PA 19090 215-568-5788 463
Web: www.esba.com

Executive Speakers Bureau
3012 Ctr Oak Way Ste 102 . . . . . Germantown TN 38138 901-754-9404 756-4237 708
TF: 800-754-9404 ■ *Web:* www.executivespeakers.com

Executive Surf Club
309 N Water St . . . . . Corpus Christi TX 78401 361-884-7873 671
Web: www.waterstmarketcc.com

Executive Technologies Corp
8731 Northpark Blvd Ste B . . . . . Charleston SC 29406 843-824-5906 693
Web: etcfirst.com

Executive Transportation Inc
1810 Monmouth St. . . . . . Newport KY 41071 859-261-8841 107
Web: executivetransportation.org

Executive Travel Consultants Ltd
345 118th Ave SE Ste 130 . . . . . Bellevue WA 98005 425-453-8200 772
Web: www.etctravel.com

Executive Travel Inc 1212 O St . . . . . Lincoln NE 68508 402-435-8888 435-2735 772
Web: executivetravel.com

Executive Visions Inc
7000 Miller Ct E . . . . . Norcross GA 30071 770-416-6100 181
Web: executivevisions.com

Executive Women Intl (EWI)
3860 S 2300 E Ste 211. . . . . . Salt Lake City UT 84109 801-355-2800 49-12
TF: 877-439-4669 ■ *Web:* ewirichmond.org

Executrade 9917 112 St NW . . . . . Edmonton AB T5K1L6 780-944-1122 260
Web: www.executrade.com

Exedy America Corp
2121 Holston Bend Dr PO Box 8 . . . . . Mascot TN 37806 865-932-3700 247
Web: eac.exedy.com

Exelate Inc 7 W 22nd St 9th Fl . . . . . New York NY 10010 646-380-4400 466
Web: exelate.com

Exelixis Inc
210 E Grand Ave. . . . . . South San Francisco CA 94080 650-837-7000 837-8300 85
NASDAQ: EXEL ■ *Web:* www.exelixis.com

Exelon Corp 10 S Dearborn St . . . . . Chicago IL 60603 800-483-3220 245
NASDAQ: EXC ■ *TF:* 800-483-3220 ■ *Web:* www.exeloncorp.com

Exeltech Consulting Inc
8729 Commerce Place Dr NE . . . . . Lacey WA 98516 360-357-8289 261
Web: xltech.com

Ex-Eltronics Inc 137 Express St . . . . . Plainview NY 11803 516-622-1430 622-1431 22
Web: www.exelgroup.com

Exergame Fitness
1595 Brummel Ave. . . . . . Elk Grove Village IL 60007 877-668-4664 963-8966* 177
**Fax Area Code:* 847 ■ *TF:* 877-668-4664 ■ *Web:* www.exergamefitness.com

Exergen Corp 400 Pleasant St . . . . . Watertown MA 02472 617-923-9900 923-9911 419
TF: 800-422-3006 ■ *Web:* www.exergen.com

Exergonix Inc 101 SE 30th St . . . . . Lee's Summit MO 64082 816-875-4790 262
Web: www.exergonix.com

Exergy LLC 320 Endo Blvd . . . . . Garden City NY 11530 516-832-9300 832-9304 480
TF: 800-832-9375 ■ *Web:* www.exergyllc.com

Exerplay Inc 12001 State Hwy 14 N. . . . . . Cedar Crest NM 87008 505-281-0151 711
TF: 800-457-5444 ■ *Web:* www.exerplay.com

Exerve Inc 2909 Langford Rd Ste 400B . . . . . Norcross GA 30071 770-447-1566 734
TF: 800-364-0637 ■ *Web:* www.exerve.com

Exeter Hospital 5 Alumni Dr. . . . . . Exeter NH 03833 603-580-6668 374-3
Web: www.exeterhospital.com

Exeter Software PO Box 521 . . . . . Setauket NY 11733 631-689-7838 422-2361* 178-1
**Fax Area Code:* 713 ■ *TF:* 888-695-0285 ■ *Web:* www.exetersoftware.com

Exeter Unified School District
215 N Crespi Ave . . . . . Exeter CA 93221 559-592-9421 685
Web: www.exeter.k12.ca.us

EXFO Inc 400 Godin Ave. . . . . . Quebec City QC G1M2K2 418-683-0211 683-2170 248
NASDAQ: EXFO ■ *TF:* 800-663-3936 ■ *Web:* www.exfo.com

Exhibit Concepts Inc
700 Crossroads Ct . . . . . Vandalia OH 45377 800-324-5063 184
TF: 800-324-5063 ■ *Web:* www.exhibitconcepts.com

Name / Address	City	State	Zip	Phone	Fax	Class
Exhibit Designers & Producers Assn (EDPA) 19 Compo Rd S *Web:* www.edpa.com	Westport	CT	06880	203-557-6321		49-18
Exhibit Source Inc, The 145 Wells Ave. *TF:* 866-949-6113 ■ *Web:* theexhibitsource.com	Newton Center	MA	02459	781-449-1600		393
Exhibitor Media Group 310 S Broadway Ste 101 *TF:* 888-235-6155 ■ *Web:* www.exhibitoronline.com	Rochester	MN	55904	507-289-6556	289-5253	637-9
Exhibits & More 7843 Goguen Dr. *Web:* www.exhibitsandmore.com	Liverpool	NY	13090	315-652-0383		232
Exhibits Development Group LLC (EDG) The Union Depot 214 E Fourth St Ste 170 *Web:* exhibitsdevelopment.com	Saint Paul	MN	55101	651-222-1121		184
Ex-IBM Corp 2713 Foxboro Dr. *Web:* www.ibmalumni.com	Garland	TX	75044	214-557-6969		225
exida.com LLC 64 N Main St. *Web:* www.exida.com	Sellersville	PA	18960	215-453-1720		256
Exide Technologies 13000 Deerfield Pkwy Bldg 200 *NASDAQ: XIDE* ■ *TF:* 888-563-6300 ■ *Web:* www.exide.com	Milton	GA	30004	678-566-9000	566-9188	74
Exigo Office Inc 8130 John W Carpenter Fwy. *Web:* exigo.com	Dallas	TX	75247	214-367-9999		225
Exiss Aluminum Trailers Inc 900 E Trailer Blvd *TF:* 800-256-6668 ■ *Web:* www.exiss.com	El Reno	OK	73036	877-553-9477		120
EXIT Theatre 156 Eddy St *Web:* www.theexit.org	San Francisco	CA	94102	415-931-1094	931-2699	572
ExitCertified 8950 Cal Center Dr Bldg 1 Ste 110. *TF:* 800-803-3948 ■ *Web:* www.exitcertified.com	Sacramento	CA	95826	916-669-3970	669-3977	179
Exl Media Corp 803 Tahoe Blvd Ste 7 *Web:* exlmedia.com	Incline Village	NV	89451	775-832-0202		7
EXMAR Offshore Co 3700 W Sam Houston Pky S Ste 300 *Web:* www.exmaroffshore.com	Houston	TX	77042	281-679-3900	497-3370	261
Exocor Inc 271 Ridley Rd. *TF:* 888-317-2209 ■ *Web:* exocor.com	Saint Catharines	ON	L2R6P7	905-704-0603		111
Exodyne Inc 8433 N Black Canyon Hwy. *Web:* www.exodyne.com	Phoenix	AZ	85021	602-995-3700	995-4091	261
ExOne Co 127 Industry Blvd *Web:* www.exone.com	North Huntingdon	PA	15642	724-863-9663		628
Exopolis Inc 3000 E Cesar Chavez.	Austin	TX	78702	512-708-1113	480-9860	5
Exordium Group Inc, The 1288 Echo Valley Dr. *Web:* www.exordiumgroup.com	San Jose	CA	95120	650-935-2308		344
Exotic Automation & Supply Inc 34700 Grand River Ave. *Web:* www.exoticautomation.com	Farmington Hills	MI	48335	248-477-2122	477-0427	608
Exotic Metals Forming Company LLC 5411 S 226th St *Web:* www.exoticmetals.com	Kent	WA	98032	253-395-3710		22
Exoxemis Inc PO Box 7570 *Web:* exoxemis.com	Little Rock	AR	72217	402-884-2316		231
Expanded Rubber Products Inc 41 Industrial Ave. *Web:* www.expandedrubberproducts.com	Sanford	ME	04073	207-324-8226	324-4778	676
Expanding Light 14618 Tyler Foote Rd *TF:* 800-346-5350 ■ *Web:* www.expandinglight.org	Nevada City	CA	95959	530-478-7518	478-7519	673
Expanko Resilient Flooring 180 Gordon Dr Ste 107. **Fax Area Code:* 610 ■ *TF:* 800-345-6202 ■ *Web:* www.expanko.com	Exton	PA	19341	800-345-6202	363-0735*	291
Expansion Management Magazine 1300 E Ninth St *TF:* 866-505-7173 ■ *Web:* www.industryweek.com	Cleveland	OH	44114	216-696-7000		457-5
Expanxion 860 Hampshire Rd Ste I *Web:* expanxion.com	Westlake Village	CA	91361	650-261-0211		260
Expedient Communications 810 Parish St *TF:* 877-570-7827 ■ *Web:* www.expedient.com	Pittsburgh	PA	15220	877-570-7827		398
Expedition Tripscom 5932 California Ave SW *TF:* 877-412-8527 ■ *Web:* www.expeditiontrips.com	Seattle	WA	98136	206-547-0700		772
Expeditor Systems Inc 4090 Nine McFarland Dr *TF:* 800-843-9651 ■ *Web:* www.expeditor.com	Alpharetta	GA	30004	800-843-9651		475
Expeditors International of Washington Inc 1015 Third Ave 12th Fl. *NASDAQ: EXPD* ■ *Web:* www.expeditors.com	Seattle	WA	98104	206-674-3400		449
Expel 12950 Worldgate Dr Ste 200 *TF:* 844-397-3524 ■ *Web:* expel.io	Herndon	VA	20170	844-397-3524		113
Expense Reduction Analysts Inc 16415 Addison Rd Ste 410. *TF:* 877-299-7801 ■ *Web:* us.expensereduction.com	Addison	TX	75001	469-310-2970		463
ExpenseVisor 910 Kenyon Ct Ste 110. *TF:* 877-219-5448 ■ *Web:* www.expensevisor.com	Charlotte	NC	28210	704-644-0019		809
Experian Information Solutions Inc 475 Anton Blvd. *Web:* www.experian.com	Costa Mesa	CA	92626	714-830-7000		218
Experience Bryan College Station (BCS) 715 University Dr E. *TF:* 800-777-8292 ■ *Web:* www.experiencebcs.com	College Station	TX	77840	979-260-9898	260-9800	206
ExpERIEnce Children's Museum 420 French St. *Web:* www.eriechildrensmuseum.org	Erie	PA	16507	814-453-3743		521
Experience Columbia SC 1101 Lincoln St *TF:* 800-264-4884 ■ *Web:* www.experiencecolumbiasc.com	Columbia	SC	29201	803-545-0000	545-0102	206
Experience Jackson 134 W Michigan Ave. *Web:* www.experiencejackson.com	Jackson	MI	49201	517-764-4440		760
Experience Works Inc 4401 Wilson Blvd Ste 1100 *TF:* 866-397-9757 ■ *Web:* www.experienceworks.org	Arlington	VA	22203	703-522-7272	522-0141	48-6
Experient Inc 2500 E Enterprise Pkwy *TF:* 800-935-8333 ■ *Web:* www.experient-inc.com	Twinsburg	OH	44087	330-425-8333		184
Experiential Wealth Inc 8460 Tyco Rd Ste E. *Web:* experientialwealth.com	Vienna	VA	22182	703-847-4380		194
Experi-Metal Inc 28101 Schoolcraft Rd **Fax Area Code:* 586 ■ *Web:* www.qmc-emi.com	Livonia	MI	48150	734-261-6700	977-6981*	697
Experis Data Centers Inc 7811 Montrose Rd Ste 360. *TF:* 877-689-3282 ■ *Web:* experisdatacenters.com	Potomac	MD	20854	877-689-3282		387
Experity Health 8777 Velocity Dr. *TF:* 866-995-9863 ■ *Web:* www.experityhealth.com	Machesney Park	IL	61115	866-995-9863		180
ExperShare LLC 205 N Mt Shasta Blvd Ste 500 *Web:* expershare.com	Mount Shasta	CA	96067	530-926-0300	926-0381	194
Expert Choice Inc 2111 Wilson Blvd Ste 700 *Web:* expertchoice.com	Arlington	VA	22201	703-243-5595	243-5587	178-12
Expert Communications Inc 394 Pacific Ave. *Web:* www.eciww.com	San Francisco	CA	94111	415-981-9900		7
Expert Crane Inc 5755 Grant Ave **Fax Area Code:* 216 ■ *TF:* 800-860-6680 ■ *Web:* www.expertcrane.com	Cleveland	OH	44105	800-860-6680	451-9904*	385
ExPert E & P Consultants LLC 101 Ashland Way *TF:* 888-231-8639 ■ *Web:* www.expertep.com	Madisonville	LA	70447	844-522-7900		539
Expert Industries Inc 848 E 43rd St. *Web:* www.rubiconhx.com	Brooklyn	NY	11210	718-434-6060		770
Expert Laser Service 62 Pleasant St PO Box 744. *TF:* 800-622-3535 ■ *Web:* expertlaserservices.com	Southbridge	MA	01550	800-622-3535		175
Expert Recruiters 883 Helmcken St *TF:* 888-407-7799 ■ *Web:* www.expertrecruiters.com	Vancouver	BC	V6Z1B1	604-689-3600		260
Expert Semiconductor Technology Inc 10 Victor Sq Ste 100. *Web:* www.exper-tech.com	Scotts Valley	CA	95066	831-439-9300	439-8139	695
Expert System Applications Inc 2681 Ashley Rd *Web:* www.expert-system.com	Shaker Heights	OH	44122	440-668-8184		180
Expert System Usa Inc 908 King St Ste 201 *Web:* expertsystem.us	Alexandria	VA	22314	703-567-2255	647-9924	180
Expertise Cosmetology Institute 1911 N Stella Lake St *Web:* www.expertisebeauty.com	Las Vegas	NV	89106	702-636-8686	636-0367	167-3
Experts Exchange LLC PO Box 1062 *Web:* www.experts-exchange.com	San Luis Obispo	CA	93406	805-787-0603		177
Experts in Growth Leadership Consulting LLC 9016 Taylorsville Rd. *Web:* vivianblade.com	Louisville	KY	40299	502-419-2433		194
Explora 1701 Mtn Rd NW *Web:* www.explora.us	Albuquerque	NM	87104	505-224-8300	224-8325	520
Exploration Place 300 N McLean Blvd. *Web:* exploration.org	Wichita	KS	67203	316-660-0600	660-0670	521
Exploratorium, The Pier 15 The Embarcadero *Web:* www.exploratorium.edu	San Francisco	CA	94111	415-528-4444	561-0370	520
Explore & More Hands-On Children's Museum 20 E High St *Web:* www.exploreandmore.com	Gettysburg	PA	17325	717-337-9151		521
Explore & More-A Children's Museum 300 Gleed Ave. *Web:* www.exploreandmore.org	East Aurora	NY	14052	716-655-5131		521
Explore Communications Inc 3213 Zuni St. *Web:* www.explorehq.com	Denver	CO	80211	303-393-0567		4
Explore Information Services LLC 2750 Blue Water Rd Ste 200. **Fax Area Code:* 651 ■ *TF:* 800-531-9125 ■ *Web:* exploredata.com	Eagan	MN	55121	800-531-9125	681-4476*	635
Explore Saint Louis *Executive Conference Ctr* 701 Convention Plz *Web:* www.explorestlouis.com	Saint Louis	MO	63101	314-421-1023	421-0039	205
Exploreco International LLC 11930 S Sam Houston Pkwy E **Fax Area Code:* 281 ■ *Web:* www.exploreco.com	Houston	TX	77089	713-796-6000	922-7363*	492
Explorer's Guide Maritime Academy 2217 W Spencer St. *TF:* 800-487-6029 ■ *Web:* www.explorersguidellc.com	Appleton	WI	54914	920-733-5500		196
Explorica Inc 145 Tremont St *TF:* 888-310-7120 ■ *Web:* www.explorica.com	Boston	MA	02111	888-310-7120	310-7088	760
Exploris 401 Hillsborough St *Web:* www.exploris.org	Raleigh	NC	27603	919-715-3690	715-2042	685
Explorium of Lexington 440 W Short St. *Web:* www.explorium.com	Lexington	KY	40507	859-258-3253		521
Expo Chemical Company Inc 506 Honea Egypt *Web:* expochem.com	Magnolia	TX	77354	281-895-9200	895-9201	146
Expo Group, The 5931 W Campus Cir Dr *TF:* 800-736-7775 ■ *Web:* www.theexpogroup.com	Irving	TX	75063	972-580-9000	550-7877	184
Expo Square 4145 East 21st St *Web:* www.exposquare.com	Tulsa	OK	74114	918-744-1113	744-8725	205
ExpoMarketing LLC 2741 Dow Ave *TF:* 800-867-3976 ■ *Web:* www.expomarketing.com	Tustin	CA	92780	800-867-3976		184
Expon Exhibits 909 Fee Dr *TF:* 800-783-9766 ■ *Web:* www.exponexhibits.com	Sacramento	CA	95815	916-924-1600		232
Exponent Inc 149 Commonwealth Dr *NASDAQ: EXPO* ■ *TF:* 888-656-3976 ■ *Web:* www.exponent.com	Menlo Park	CA	94025	650-326-9400	326-8072	668
Exponential Engineering Co 2950 E Harmony Rd Ste 265. *Web:* www.exponentialengineering.com	Fort Collins	CO	80528	970-207-9648	207-9657	261
ExpoPlus 1055 Research Ctr Atlanta Dr SW. *Web:* www.expoplus.com	Atlanta	GA	30331	404-699-0650		7

Company	Phone	Fax	Class
Export Corp 6060 Whitmore Lake Rd . . . Brighton MI 48116 *Web:* exportcorporation.com	810-227-6153		549
Export-Import Bank of the US 811 Vermont Ave NW . . . Washington DC 20571 *TF:* 800-565-3946 ■ *Web:* www.exim.gov	202-565-3946		340-20
Exporting Commodities International Inc 12000 Lincoln Dr W Ste 108 . . . Marlton NJ 08053 *Web:* eci-coal.com	856-797-2004		791
Expoships LLLP 27598 Riverview Center Blvd . . . Bonita Springs FL 34134	239-949-5411		387
Exposition Gardens 1601 W Northmoor Rd . . . Peoria IL 61614 *Web:* www.expogardensinc.com	309-691-6332	691-2372	205
Expositions Inc PO Box 550 . . . Cleveland OH 44107 *Web:* expoinc.com	216-529-1300	529-0311	393
Exposito School of Hair Design 3710 Mockingbird Ln . . . Amarillo TX 79109 *TF:* 800-627-5875 ■ *Web:* www.expositoschoolofhair.com	806-355-9111		685
Expositor, The 195 Henry St Bldg 4 . . . Brantford ON N3S5C9 *Web:* www.brantfordexpositor.ca	519-756-2020	756-3285	532-1
Expotel Hospitality Services LLC 401 Veterans Memorial Blvd Ste 102 . . . Metairie LA 70005 *Web:* www.expotelhospitality.com	504-212-1492		463
Express 1 Limited Pkwy . . . Columbus OH 43230 *NYSE: EXPR* ■ *TF:* 888-397-1980 ■ *Web:* www.express.com	888-397-1980		157-6
Express Cargo USA LLC 1790 Yardley-Langhorne Rd Carriage House 202 . . . Yardley PA 19067 **Fax Area Code:* 215 ■ *TF:* 888-505-7361 ■ *Web:* expresscargousa.com	201-603-9155	493-4430*	465
Express Computer Distributors 10773 NW 58th St Ste 98 . . . Miami FL 33178 *Web:* www.expcd.com	305-599-1584	395-4011	174
Express Diagnostics Int'l Inc 1550 Industrial Dr . . . Blue Earth MN 56013 *Web:* drugcheck.com	507-526-3951		415
Express Employment Professionals 9701 Boardwalk Blvd . . . Oklahoma City OK 73162 *TF:* 800-222-4057 ■ *Web:* www.expresspros.com	405-840-5000		721
Express Envelopes Unlimited LLP 1745 Suburban Dr . . . De Pere WI 54115 *Web:* expressenvelopesunlimited.com	920-997-0182		627
Express Image Inc 2942 Rice St . . . Little Canada MN 55113 *TF:* 866-482-8602 ■ *Web:* expressimage.com	866-482-8602		687
Express Logic 11423 W Bernardo Ct . . . San Diego CA 92127 *Web:* rtos.com	858-613-6640		179
Express Manufacturing Inc 3519 W Warner Ave . . . Santa Ana CA 92704 *Web:* www.eminc.com	714-979-2228	556-0575	454
Express Marine Inc PO Box 329 . . . Pennsauken Township NJ 08110 *Web:* www.expressmarine.com	856-541-4600	541-0338	312
Express Oil Change & Tire Engineers 1880 S Pk Dr . . . Hoover AL 35244 *TF:* 888-945-1771 ■ *Web:* www.expressoil.com	844-268-3972		62-5
Express Packaging of Ohio Inc 301 Enterprise Dr . . . Newcomerstown OH 43832 *Web:* expk.co	740-498-4700		393
Express Printing & Graphics Inc 1205 Alderwood Ave . . . Sunnyvale CA 94089 *Web:* sunnyvale-ca.minutemanpress.com	408-400-0223		627
Express Scale Parts Inc 14560 W 99th St . . . Lenexa KS 66215 *TF:* 866-411-4787 ■ *Web:* www.espmfg.com	913-441-4787	745-1361	273
Express Systems & Parts Networks 325 Harris Dr . . . Aurora OH 44202 *Web:* express-systems.net	330-995-4350		366
Express Tire 1148 Industrial Ave . . . Escondido CA 92029 *Web:* www.firestonecompleteautocare.com	760-741-4044		62-5
Expressall 260 Dean Rd . . . Brookline MA 02445 *TF:* 800-944-6190 ■ *Web:* www.expressall.com	800-944-6190		393
expresscopy.com 6623 NE 59th Pl . . . Portland OR 97218 *TF:* 800-260-5887 ■ *Web:* www.expresscopy.com	800-260-5887		627
Expression Home Gallery 100 East 15th St Ste 200 . . . Fort Worth TX 76102 **Fax Area Code:* 817 ■ *TF:* 844-842-0841 ■ *Web:* www.expressionshomegallery.com	844-842-0841	877-4942*	321
Expression Pathology Inc 9600 Medical Center Dr Ste 300 . . . Rockville MD 20850 *Web:* www.expressionpathology.com	301-977-3654		668
ExpressJet Airlines Inc 990 Toffie Terr . . . Atlanta GA 30354 *Web:* www.expressjet.com	404-856-1000		25
Express-News Corp PO Box 2171 . . . San Antonio TX 78297 *TF:* 800-555-1551 ■ *Web:* www.mysanantonio.com	210-250-3000		637-8
Express-Times 30 N Fourth St . . . Easton PA 18042 *Web:* www.lehighvalleylive.com	610-258-7171	258-7130	532-2
Expressway Hotels 4303 17th Ave S . . . Fargo ND 58103 *TF:* 877-239-4303 ■ *Web:* expresswaysuitesfargo.com	701-239-4303		379
Expressworks Intl 2410 Camino Ramon Ste 167 . . . San Ramon CA 94583 *Web:* www.expressworks.com	925-244-0900		256
ExRxnet LLC 9 E Ottawa St . . . Paola KS 66071 *Web:* exrx.net	816-728-3979		690
EXSIF Worldwide Inc 2700 Westchester Ave Ste 400 . . . Purchase NY 10577 *Web:* www.exsif.com	914-848-4200	848-4201	264-5
EXSL/Ultra Labs Inc 30921 Wiegman Rd . . . Hayward CA 94544 *Web:* exsl.net	510-324-4567	324-8881	406
Extended Care Hospital Westminster 206 Hospital Cir . . . Westminster CA 92683 *TF:* 800-236-9747 ■ *Web:* westminsterec.com	714-891-2769	895-9069	450
Extended Family Care 1251 S Cedar Crest Blvd Ste 102B . . . Allentown PA 18103 *Web:* extendedfamilycare.com	610-200-6097	432-6737	363
Extended Home Care 2617 E 16th St Ste 2 . . . Brooklyn NY 11235 *TF:* 866-217-5881 ■ *Web:* extendedhc.net	212-356-4200		363
Extended Presence 3570 E 12th Ave Ste 200 . . . Denver CO 80206 *TF:* 800-398-8957 ■ *Web:* extendedpresence.com	303-325-8600		317
Extended Stay Hotels *Extended Stay America* 11525 N Community House Rd Ste 100 . . . Charlotte NC 28277 *Web:* www.extendedstayamerica.com	980-345-1600		379
Extendicare Inc 3000 Steeles Ave E . . . Markham ON L3R9W2 *TSE: EXE* ■ *Web:* www.extendicare.com	905-470-4000	470-5588	451
ExteNet Systems Inc 3030 Warrenville Rd . . . Lisle IL 60532 *TF:* 866-892-5327 ■ *Web:* www.extenetsystems.com	630-505-3800	577-1332	681
Extensis 1800 SW First Ave Ste 500 . . . Portland OR 97201 *TF:* 800-796-9798 ■ *Web:* www.extensis.com	503-274-2020	274-0530	177
Exterior Wood Inc 2685 Index St . . . Washougal WA 98671 *Web:* www.exteriorwood.com	360-835-8561		818
ExterNetworks Inc 10 Corporate Pl S . . . Piscataway NJ 08854 *TF:* 800-238-6360 ■ *Web:* www.externetworks.com	732-465-0001		177
Exterran 16666 Northchase Dr . . . Houston TX 77060 *Web:* www.exterran.com	281-836-7000		385
Exterro Inc 4145 SW Watson Ave Ste 400 . . . Beaverton OR 97005 *Web:* exterro.com	503-501-5100		177
Extol of Ohio Inc 208 Republic St . . . Norwalk OH 44857 *TF:* 800-486-9865 ■ *Web:* extolohio.com	419-668-2072	663-1992	389
Extole Inc 350 Sansome St Ste 700 . . . San Francisco CA 94104 *Web:* www.extole.com	415-625-0411		195
Exton Region Chamber of Commerce 185 Exton Square Mall . . . Exton PA 19341 *TF:* 800-666-0191 ■ *Web:* www.ercc.net	610-363-7746		139
Extra Help Inc 3911 W Ernestine Dr . . . Marion IL 62959 *Web:* hirelevel.com	618-993-9675		141
Extra Mile Marketing Inc 12600 SE 38th St Ste 205 . . . Bellevue WA 98006 *TF:* 866-907-1753 ■ *Web:* www.extramilemarketing.com	425-746-1572		194
Extraco Technology PO Box 2299 . . . Waco TX 76703 *TF:* 866-428-9070 ■ *Web:* www.extraco.tech	866-428-9070		509
Extraordinary Events 13425 Ventura Blvd Ste 300 . . . Sherman Oaks CA 91423 *Web:* extraordinaryevents.com	818-783-6112	783-8957	149
ExtraView Corp 269 Mt Hermon Rd Ste 207 . . . Scotts Valley CA 95066 *Web:* www.extraview.com	831-461-7100		174
Extrel CMS LLC 575 Epsilon Dr . . . Pittsburgh PA 15238 *Web:* www.extrel.com	412-963-7530		246
Extreme Engineering Solutions Inc 3225 Deming Way Ste 120 . . . Middleton WI 53562 *Web:* www.xes-inc.com	608-833-1155		261
Extreme Packing Solutions 5 Dodge St . . . Beverly MA 01915 *TF:* 855-297-9278 ■ *Web:* extremepackingsolutions.com	978-232-9190	232-9196	549
Extreme Reach Crew Services 3601 W Olive Ave Ste 500 . . . Burbank CA 91505 *TF:* 800-301-1992 ■ *Web:* extremereachcrewservices.com	818-729-0080	295-3886	631
Extreme Reach Inc 75 Second Ave Ste 720 . . . Needham MA 02494 *TF:* 877-769-9382 ■ *Web:* extremereach.com	800-324-5672		511
Extreme Technologies Inc 1411 Ave A . . . Katy TX 77493 *Web:* www.extreme-technologies.com	281-293-7800		194
Extrication.Com LLC 19 Baldwin Cir . . . Plymouth MA 02360 *TF:* 888-971-5724 ■ *Web:* www.extrication.com	508-747-0860		196
Extron Electronics 1230 S Lewis St . . . Anaheim CA 92805 *TF:* 800-633-9876 ■ *Web:* www.extron.com	714-491-1500	491-1517	52
Extron Logistics LLC 496 S Abbott Ave . . . Milpitas CA 95035 *Web:* www.extroninc.com	510-353-0177		449
Extrude Hone LLC 235 Industry Blvd . . . Irwin PA 15642 *TF:* 800-835-3668 ■ *Web:* extrudehone.com	724-863-5900	863-8759	455
Extruded Aluminum Corp 7200 Industrial Dr . . . Belding MI 48809 *Web:* www.extrudedaluminum.com	616-794-0300		492
Extrudex Aluminum Ltd 411 Chrislea Rd . . . Woodbridge ON L4L8N4 *TF:* 800-668-7210 ■ *Web:* www.extrudex.com	416-745-4444		492
Extrutech Plastics Inc 5902 W Custer St . . . Manitowoc WI 54220 *TF:* 888-818-0118 ■ *Web:* www.epiplastics.com	888-818-0118		596
Exvere 1301 Fifth Ave Ste 3300 . . . Seattle WA 98101 *Web:* www.exvere.com	206-728-1800		401
Exxact Corp 45445 Warm Springs Blvd . . . Fremont CA 94539 *Web:* www.exxactcorp.com	510-226-7366		174
EXXCEL Project Management Inc 328 S Civic Center Dr . . . Columbus OH 43215 *Web:* www.exxcel.com	614-621-4500		186
Exxel Engineering Inc 5252 Clyde Park Ave SW . . . Grand Rapids MI 49509 *Web:* exxelengineering.com	616-531-3660		261
Exxon Mobil Corp 5959 Las Colinas Blvd . . . Irving TX 75039 *NYSE: XOM* ■ *TF:* 800-252-1800 ■ *Web:* corporate.exxonmobil.com	972-444-1000		536
ExxonMobil Pipeline Co 211 E 7th St Ste 620 . . . Austin TX 78701 *Web:* www.exxonmobilpipeline.com	713-656-3636	656-9586	597
EY Laboratories Inc 107 N Amphlett Blvd . . . San Mateo CA 94401 *TF:* 800-821-0044 ■ *Web:* www.eylabs.com	650-342-3296	342-2648	668
Eyak Corp, The 360 W Benson Blvd Ste 210 . . . Anchorage AK 99503 *TF:* 800-478-7161 ■ *Web:* eyakcorporation.com	907-334-6971		360-3
Eyak Technology LLC 615 E 82nd Ave Ste 300 . . . Anchorage AK 99518 *Web:* www.eyaktek.com	907-276-0420		196
Eyde Co 300 S Washington Sq Ste 400 . . . Lansing MI 48933 *TF:* 800-422-3933 ■ *Web:* www.eyde.com	517-351-2480	484-5695	187
Eye Bank Association of America (EBAA) 1015 18th St NW Ste 1010 . . . Washington DC 20036 *Web:* restoresight.org	202-775-4999	429-6036	49-8
Eye Bank for Sight Restoration Inc 120 Wall St 3rd Fl . . . New York NY 10005 *TF:* 866-287-3937 ■ *Web:* www.eyedonation.org	212-742-9000	269-3139	269
Eye Bank of British Columbia 855 W 12th Ave JPPN - B205 . . . Vancouver BC V5Z1M9 *TF:* 800-667-2060 ■ *Web:* eyebankofbc.ca	604-875-4567	875-5316	269

	Phone	Fax	Class
Eye Candy Cinema 31 Fells Rd . . . Wellesley MA 02482 *Web:* www.eyecandycinema.com	617-827-3808		514
Eye Care for Animals 372 S Milwaukee Ave . . . Wheeling IL 60090 *Web:* www.eyecareforanimals.com	847-215-3933		237
Eye Center Surgeons & Associates Ll 401 Meridian St N Ste 200 . . . Huntsville AL 35801 *TF:* 800-233-9083 ■ *Web:* www.eyecentersurgeons.com	256-705-3937		237
Eye Centers of Florida (ECOF) 4101 Evans Ave . . . Fort Myers FL 33901 *TF:* 888-393-2455 ■ *Web:* www.ecof.com	239-939-3456	936-8776	798
Eye Glass World Inc 2435 Commerce Ave Bldg 2200 . . . Duluth GA 30096 *TF:* 800-637-3597 ■ *Web:* www.eyeglassworld.com	800-637-3597		543
Eye Lighting International NA 9150 Hendricks Rd . . . Mentor OH 44060 *TF:* 888-665-2677 ■ *Web:* www.eyelighting.com	440-354-2938	350-7001	437
Eye Marker Systems Inc 886 Chestnut Ridge Rd . . . Morgantown WV 26505	304-282-0419		743
Eye To Eye Vision Ctr 2255 Sewell Mill Rd Ste 310 . . . Marietta GA 30062 *Web:* eyetoeyevisioncenter.com	770-578-1900		543
Eyebeam Atelier 540 W 21st St . . . New York NY 10011 *Web:* www.eyebeam.org	212-937-6580		720
Eyecon Marketing Group 6738 Jamestown Dr . . . Alpharetta GA 30005 *Web:* www.eyeconmktg.com	770-752-0043		7
Eyedro Green Solutions Inc 130 Weber St W Ste 201 . . . Kitchener ON N2H4A2 **Fax Area Code:* 416 ■ *TF:* 888-440-7610 ■ *Web:* eyedro.com	226-499-0944	850-5710*	180
Eyefinity Inc 10875 International Dr Ste 200 . . . Rancho Cordova CA 95670 *TF:* 877-448-0707 ■ *Web:* www.eyefinity.com	877-448-0707		177
Eye-Kraft Optical Inc 8 McLeland Rd . . . Saint Cloud MN 56303 **Fax Area Code:* 800 ■ *TF:* 888-455-2022 ■ *Web:* www.eyekraft.com	888-455-2022	950-7070*	542
Eyelet Crafters Inc 2712 S Main St PO Box 2542 . . . Waterbury CT 06723 *Web:* www.eyeletcrafters.com	203-757-9221	757-2205	483
Eyeline Golf 2990 W 29th St Ste 7 . . . Greeley CO 80631 *Web:* eyelinegolf.com	719-481-4915		711
Eyelit Inc 5685 Whittle Rd . . . Mississauga ON L4Z3P8 *TF:* 877-579-9629 ■ *Web:* www.eyelit.com	905-502-6184		179
Eye-Mart Express Inc 13800 Senlac Dr Ste 200 . . . Farmers Branch TX 75234 *TF:* 888-372-2763 ■ *Web:* www.eyemartexpress.com	972-488-2016		543
Eye-Mate Inc 77 N Centre Ave Ste 204 . . . Rockville Centre NY 11570	516-678-9613		543
EyeMed Vision Care 4000 Luxottica Pl . . . Mason OH 45040 *TF:* 866-939-3633 ■ *Web:* eyemed.com	866-939-3633		391-3
EyePoint Pharmaceuticals 400 Pleasant St . . . Watertown MA 02472 *NASDAQ: PSDV* ■ *Web:* eyepointpharma.com	617-926-5000	926-5050	85
Eyereturn Marketing 110 Eglinton Ave E Ste 701 . . . Toronto ON M4P2Y1 *Web:* eyereturnmarketing.com	416-929-4834	929-6046	5
EyeSee360 Inc 300 Fleet St Ste 250 . . . Pittsburgh PA 15220 *Web:* www.eyesee360.com	412-922-6002		179
Eyetique Corp 2242 Murray Ave . . . Pittsburgh PA 15217 *Web:* eyetique.com	412-422-5300		543
Eye-To-Eye Communications Inc 2624 W Canyon Ave . . . San Diego CA 92123 *Web:* eyetoeyepr.com	858-565-9800		41
Eyexam of California Inc PO Box 2756 . . . Mission Viejo CA 92690 *TF:* 888-439-3392 ■ *Web:* www.eyexamofca.com	949-364-1289		391-3
EYP Inc 201 Fuller Rd 5th Fl . . . Albany NY 12203 *Web:* www.eypae.com	518-795-3800		261
Eyre Bus Service Inc 13600 Triadelphia Rd PO Box 239 . . . Glenelg MD 21737 *TF:* 800-321-3973 ■ *Web:* www.eyre.com	410-442-1330	442-0010	107
E-Z Burr Tool Co 41180 Joy Rd . . . Plymouth MI 48170 **Fax Area Code:* 734 ■ *TF:* 800-783-2877 ■ *Web:* www.ezburr.com	800-783-2877	459-2427*	493
EZ Electric Inc 1250 Birchwood Dr . . . Sunnyvale CA 94089 *Web:* www.ez-electric.com	408-734-4282		439
E-Z Form Cable Corp 285 Welton St . . . Hamden CT 06517 *Web:* www.ezform.com	203-785-8215		116
EZ Grip Inc 224 E 12th St N Hwy 83 . . . White River SD 57579 *Web:* www.ezgrip.com	605-259-3056	259-3452	60
EZ Loader Boat Trailers Inc 717 N Hamilton St . . . Spokane WA 99202 *TF:* 800-398-5623 ■ *Web:* www.ezloader.com	509-489-0181		763
EZ Micro Solutions Inc 2670 Lehigh St . . . Whitehall PA 18052 *Web:* www.ezmicro.com	610-264-1232		180
E-Z Mix Inc 11450 Tuxford St . . . Sun Valley CA 91352 *Web:* www.ezmixinc.com	818-768-0568		191-1
E-Z Movers Inc 3400 Oakton St . . . Skokie IL 60076 *TF:* 866-452-7801 ■ *Web:* www.e-zmovers.com	847-568-9380		311
EZ Systemscom 3400 W MacArthur Blvd . . . Santa Ana CA 92704 *Web:* www.ezsystems.com	714-815-4968	662-6859	175
EZ Trail Inc 1050 E Columbia St PO Box 168 . . . Arthur IL 61911 *TF:* 800-677-2802 ■ *Web:* e-ztrail.com	217-543-3471	543-3473	273
E-Z Trench Manufacturing Inc 2315 Hwy 701 S . . . Loris SC 29569 *Web:* www.eztrench.com	843-756-6444		190
EZ Way Inc 710 E Main St . . . Clarinda IA 51632 *TF:* 800-627-8940 ■ *Web:* www.ezlifts.com	712-542-5102	542-1899	763
EZ8 Motels Inc 1010 Outer Rd . . . San Diego CA 92108 *Web:* www.ez8motels.com	619-291-4824		707
ezCater Inc 40 Water St 5th Fl . . . Boston MA 02109 *TF:* 800-488-1803 ■ *Web:* www.ezcater.com	800-488-1803		387
eZCom Software Inc 25 Rockwood Pl Ste 420 . . . Englewood NJ 07631 *Web:* www.ezcomsoftware.com	201-731-1800	731-1776	174
EZCORP Inc 1901 Capital Pkwy . . . Austin TX 78746 *NASDAQ: EZPW* ■ *TF:* 800-873-7296 ■ *Web:* www.ezcorp.com	512-314-3405		569
Eze Castle Integration Inc 260 Franklin St 12th Fl . . . Boston MA 02110 *TF:* 800-752-1382 ■ *Web:* www.eci.com	617-217-3000	217-3001	195
Eze Lap Diamond Products 3572 Arrowhead Dr . . . Carson City NV 89706 *TF:* 800-843-4815 ■ *Web:* eze-lap.com	775-888-9500		697
Ezenia! Inc 14 Celina Ave Ste 17 . . . Nashua NH 03063 *TF:* 800-966-2301 ■ *Web:* www.ezenia.com	253-509-7850		176
Ez-Flo International Inc 2750 E Mission Blvd . . . Ontario CA 91761 **Fax Area Code:* 866 ■ *TF:* 800-486-5256 ■ *Web:* www.ez-flo.net	800-486-5256	827-3012*	610
EZG Manufacturing 1833 N Riverview Rd . . . Malta OH 43758 *TF:* 800-417-9272 ■ *Web:* ezgmfg.com	800-417-9272		135
E-Z-GO 1451 Marvin Griffin Rd . . . Augusta GA 30906 *TF:* 800-241-5855 ■ *Web:* ezgo.txtsv.com	800-241-5855		516
Ezoic 6023 Innovation Way 2nd Fl . . . Carlsbad CA 92009 *Web:* www.ezoic.com	760-550-9689		178-8
E-Zoil Products Inc 234 Fillmore Ave . . . Tonawanda NY 14150 *Web:* ezoil.com	716-213-0106	213-0447	362
Ezra Sutton Law Offices 900 US Hwy 9 N Ste 201 . . . Woodbridge NJ 07095 *Web:* ezrasutton.com	732-634-3520		428
EZSigma Group 200 Town Centre Blvd Ste 402 . . . Markham ON L3R8G5 *Web:* www.ezsigmagroup.com	905-947-8562		196
EZSolution Corp 111 Centerville Rd . . . Lancaster PA 17601 *Web:* www.ezsolution.com	717-291-4689		809
EZZI Net 85 Tenth Ave 7th Fl . . . New York NY 10011 *TF:* 877-399-4638 ■ *Web:* www.ezzi.net	646-375-3390		387

F

	Phone	Fax	Class
F & A Federal Credit Union 2625 Corporate Pl . . . Monterey Park CA 91754 *TF:* 800-222-1226 ■ *Web:* fafcu.org	323-268-1226		219
F & B Communications 103 Main St N . . . Wheatland IA 52777 *Web:* www.fbc.bz	563-374-1236	374-1930	224
F & E Sportswear Corp 1230 Newell Pkwy . . . Montgomery AL 36110 *TF:* 800-523-7762 ■ *Web:* www.fandesportswear.com	334-244-6477		687
F & F Productions LLC 14333 Myerlake Cir . . . Clearwater FL 33760 *Web:* www.fandfhd.tv	727-530-5000	535-6547	514
F & G Mechanical Corp 348 New County Rd . . . Secaucus NJ 07094 *Web:* www.fgmech.com	201-864-3580		610
F & H Construction 1115 E Lockeford St . . . Lodi CA 95240 *Web:* www.f-hconst.com	209-931-3738	931-4427	186
F & H Food Equipment Co 1526 S Enterprise . . . Springfield MO 65804 *Web:* www.fhfoodequipment.com	417-881-6114		358
F & H Ribbon Company Inc 3010 S Pipeline Rd . . . Euless TX 76040 *TF:* 800-877-5775 ■ *Web:* www.fhribbon.com	800-877-5775		777
F & H Solutions Group 1300 19th St NW Ste 420 . . . Washington DC 20036 *Web:* www.fhsolutionsgroup.com	202-719-2083	719-2088	195
F & M Bank 50 Franklin St . . . Clarksville TN 37040 *TF:* 800-645-4199 ■ *Web:* www.myfmbank.com	931-906-0005		70
F & M Bank & Trust Co 505 Broadway . . . Hannibal MO 63401 *TF:* 877-221-6424 ■ *Web:* www.bankfm.com	573-221-6424	221-1366	360-2
F & M Hat Company Inc 103 Walnut St PO Box 40 . . . Denver PA 17517 *TF:* 800-953-4287 ■ *Web:* www.fmhat.com	717-336-5505	336-0501	155-9
F & M Mafco Inc PO Box 11013 . . . Cincinnati OH 45211 *TF:* 800-333-2151 ■ *Web:* www.fmmafco.com	513-367-2151	367-0363	190
F & ME Consultants 1825 Blanding St . . . Columbia SC 29205 *Web:* fmeconsultants.com	803-254-4540		261
F & P America Manufacturing Inc 2101 Corporate Dr . . . Troy OH 45373 *Web:* www.fandp.com	937-339-0212		59
F & P Georgia Manufacturing Inc 88 Enterprise Dr SE . . . Rome GA 30161 *Web:* www.fandpgeorgia.com	706-291-7550		247
F & S Engraving Inc 1620 W Central Rd . . . Mount Prospect IL 60056 *Web:* fandsstamps.com	847-870-8400	870-8414	298
F & W Equipment 164 Boston Post Rd . . . Orange CT 06477 *Web:* www.fwequip.com	203-795-0591		358
F & W Forestry Services Inc 1310 W Oakridge Dr PO Box 3610 . . . Albany GA 31707 *Web:* www.fwforestry.com	229-883-0505	883-0515	302
F C Kerbeck & Sons 100 Rt 73 N . . . Palmyra NJ 08065 *TF:* 855-846-1500 ■ *Web:* www.fckerbeck.com	855-581-5700		57
F D Rich Co 222 Summer St . . . Stamford CT 06901 *Web:* fdrich.com	203-359-2900	328-7980	187
F D Thomas Inc 217 Bateman Dr . . . Central Point OR 97502 *TF:* 800-554-3010 ■ *Web:* www.fdthomas.com	541-664-3010	664-1105	189-8
F G Quality Supply Inc 41 N Hillside Ave . . . Hillside IL 60162	708-449-0300		366
F Gilbert Hills State Forest 45 Mill St . . . Foxborough MA 02035 *Web:* www.mass.gov	508-543-9084		565
F H Paschen S N Nielsen Inc 5515 N East River Rd . . . Chicago IL 60656 *Web:* www.fhpaschen.com	773-444-3474	693-0064	188-4
F H Video Inc 6137 Geary Blvd 2nd Fl . . . San Francisco CA 94121 *Web:* www.fhvideo.com	415-221-6128	221-8819	647

Phone | Fax | Class

F Korbel & Bros Inc
13250 River Rd Guerneville CA 95446 707-824-7313 80-3
Web: www.korbel.com

F M Brush Manufacturing Co
7002 72nd Pl Glendale NY 11385 718-821-5939 362
Web: www.fmbrush.com

F M C of Plymouth Ohio Inc
500 Donnenwirth Dr PO Box 45 Plymouth OH 44865 419-687-8237 492
Web: www.fetzermfg.com

F Mcconnell & Sons Inc
11102 Lincoln Hwy E New Haven IN 46774 260-493-6607 749-6116 297-8
TF: 800-552-0835 ■ *Web:* www.fmcconnell.com

F S Prestress LLC 190 Prestress Rd Princeton LA 71067 318-949-2444 949-2446 183
Web: www.fsprestress.com

F+W Media 1140 Broadway 14th Fl New York NY 10001 212-447-1400 658
Web: www.fwmedia.com

F. D. Hurka Co 4731 Stockholm Ct Charlotte NC 28273 704-552-0008 553-8772 385
Web: www.fdhurka.com

F. M. Howell & Co 79 Pennsylvania Ave Elmira NY 14904 607-734-6291 734-8667 101
Web: howellpkg.com

F.B.P. Insurance Services LLC
130 Theory Ste 200 Irvine CA 92617 949-955-1430 390
Web: www.preceptgroup.com

F.D.S. Manufacturing Co
2200 S Reservoir St Pomona CA 91766 909-591-1733 591-1571 554
Web: www.fdsmfg.com

F.I.L.M. Archives Inc
35 W 35th St Ste 504 New York NY 10001 212-696-2616 514
Web: www.filmarchivesonline.com

F.Tech R & D North America Inc
1191 Horizon W Ct Troy OH 45373 937-339-2777 339-4742 60
Web: www.ftech.co.jp

F.W. Lombard Co 34 S Pleasant St Ashburnham MA 01430 978-827-5333 827-6553 319-2
Web: www.fwlombard.com

F.W. Winter Incorporated & Co
550 Delaware Ave Camden NJ 08102 856-963-7490 963-7463 492
Web: fwwinter.com

F-11 Photo the print refinery
5 W Mendenhall St Ste 202 Bozeman MT 59715 406-586-3281 119
Web: f11photo.com

F5 Networks Inc 401 Elliott Ave W Seattle WA 98119 206-272-5555 272-5556 176
NASDAQ: FFIV ■ *TF:* 888-882-4447 ■ *Web:* f5.com

FA (Food Addicts In Recovery Anonymous)
400 W Cummings Pk Ste 1700 Woburn MA 01801 781-932-6300 48-21
Web: www.foodaddicts.org

FA Bartlett Tree Expert Co
1290 E Main St Stamford CT 06902 203-323-1131 776
TF: 877-227-8538 ■ *Web:* www.bartlett.com

FA Davis Co 1915 Arch St Philadelphia PA 19103 215-568-2270 568-5065 637-2
TF: 800-323-3555 ■ *Web:* www.fadavis.com

FA Wilhelm Construction Company Inc
3914 Prospect St Indianapolis IN 46203 317-359-5411 186
Web: www.fawilhelm.com

FAA (Federal Aviation Administration Regional Offices)
Alaskan Region
222 W Seventh Ave Ste 14 Anchorage AK 99513 907-271-5438 271-2851 340-17
Web: www.faa.gov

FAA Federal Credit Union
3920 Whitebrook Dr Memphis TN 38118 901-366-0066 219
TF: 800-346-0069 ■ *Web:* www.faafcu.org

FAAC Inc 1229 Oak Valley Dr Ann Arbor MI 48108 734-761-5836 761-5368 703
TF: 877-322-2387 ■ *Web:* www.faac.com

FAAN (Food Allergy & Anaphylaxis Network)
11781 Lee Jackson Hwy Ste 160 Fairfax VA 22033 703-691-3179 691-2713 48-17
Web: www.foodallergy.org

Fab Masters Company Inc 51787 M 40 Marcellus MI 49067 269-646-5315 646-3378 454
Web: www.fabmasters.net

FabArc Steel Supply Inc 111 Meadow Ln Oxford AL 36203 256-831-8770 492
Web: www.fabarc.com

Fabbri Sausage Manufacturing Co
166 N Aberdeen St Chicago IL 60607 312-829-6363 829-0396 296-26
Web: www.fabbrisausage.com

Fabco Industries Inc 2985 E Pearl Odessa TX 79761 432-367-4988 367-4980 516
TF: 800-767-4988 ■ *Web:* www.fabcoindustries.net

Fabco Steel Fabrication Inc
14688 San Bernardino Ave Fontana CA 92335 909-350-1535 480
Web: www.fabcosteel.com

Fabco-Air Inc 3716 NE 49th Ave Gainesville FL 32609 352-373-3578 375-8024 223
Web: www.fabco-air.com

Fabcon Precast 6111 Hwy 13 W Savage MN 55378 952-890-4444 890-6657 183
Web: fabconprecast.com

Fabcon Precast 3400 Jackson Pk Grove City OH 43123 614-875-8601 821-5371* 183
**Fax Area Code:* 866 ■ *TF:* 800-727-4444 ■ *Web:* www.fabconprecast.com

FabCorp Inc 6951 W Little York Houston TX 77040 713-466-3962 466-3470 595
TF: 888-830-3962 ■ *Web:* www.fabcorp.com

Faber Enterprises Inc
14800 S Figueroa St Gardena CA 90248 818-999-1300 712-0512 790
Web: www.faberent.com

Fabgroups Technologies Inc
1100 St Amour Saint-Laurent QC H4S1J2 514-331-3712 111
TF: 800-561-8910 ■ *Web:* www.fabgroups.com

Fabian Oil Inc 20 Oak St PO Box 99 Oakland ME 04963 207-465-2000 324
Web: www.fabianoil.com

Fabiano Brothers Inc 1885 Bevanda Ct Bay City MI 48706 989-509-0200 509-0300 81-1
Web: www.fabianobrothers.com

Fabick Inc 4118 Robertson Rd Madison WI 53714 608-242-1100 605-2
Web: www.fabick.com

FABNexus Inc 660 Arboleda Dr Los Altos CA 94024 650-383-0587 276-7456 178-1
Web: fabnexus.com

Fabral Inc 3449 Hempland Rd Lancaster PA 17601 800-477-2741 397-1040* 480
**Fax Area Code:* 717 ■ *TF:* 800-477-2741 ■ *Web:* www.fabral.com

Fabre Engineering Inc
119 Gregory Sq Pensacola FL 32502 850-433-6438 261
Web: fabreinc.com

Fabreeka International Inc
1023 Tpke St Stoughton MA 02072 781-341-3655 341-3983 677
TF: 800-322-7352 ■ *Web:* www.fabreeka.com

Fabre-Kramer Pharmaceuticals Inc
5847 San Felipe Ste 2000 Houston TX 77057 713-975-6900 977-1574 238
Web: www.fabrekramer.com

Fabric Finders Inc PO Box 999 Florence AL 35631 256-767-7615 767-8366 594
Web: www.fabricfindersinc.com

Fabric Images Inc 325 Corporate Dr Elgin IL 60123 847-488-9877 791
Web: www.fabricimages.com

Fabric Workshop & Museum
1214 Arch St Philadelphia PA 19107 215-561-8888 561-8887 520
Web: www.fabricworkshopandmuseum.org

Fabrica International Inc
3201 S Susan St Santa Ana CA 92704 949-261-7181 364
Web: www.fabrica.com

Fabricated Components Inc
PO Box 431 Stroudsburg PA 18360 570-421-4110 421-2553 482
TF: 800-233-8163 ■ *Web:* www.fabricatedcomponents.com

Fabricated Extrusion Company LLC
2331 Hoover Ave Modesto CA 95354 209-529-9200 608
Web: fabexco.com

Fabricated Metals LLC
6300 Kenjoy Dr Louisville KY 40214 502-363-2625 363-3827 198
Web: fabricatedmetals.com

Fabrication Concepts Corp
1800 E St Andrew Pl Santa Ana CA 92705 714-881-2000 697
Web: www.fabcon.com

Fabrication Designs Inc
7463 New Ridge Rd Ste A Hanover MD 21076 410-850-0042 234
TF: 800-366-7725 ■ *Web:* www.febr-fdi.com

Fabrication JR Tardif Inc
62 Blvd Cartier Riviere-du-Loup QC G5R6B2 418-862-7273 862-7390 273
TF: 877-962-7273 ■ *Web:* www.jrtardif.com

Fabrication Products Inc
4201 NE Minnehaha St Vancouver WA 98661 360-696-1324 480
Web: www.fabproducts.com

Fabrication Technologies Industries Inc
2200 Haffley Ave National City CA 91950 619-477-4141 54
Web: www.ftisd.com

Fabricators & Manufacturers Association Intl (FMA)
833 Featherstone Rd Rockford IL 61107 815-399-8700 49-13
TF: 888-394-4362 ■ *Web:* connect.fmanet.org

Fabricon Products
1721 W Pleasant Ave River Rouge MI 48218 313-841-8200 841-4819 554
Web: www.fabriconproducts.com

Fabricut Inc 9303 E 46th St Tulsa OK 74145 918-622-7700 664-8919 361
TF: 800-999-8200 ■ *Web:* www.fabricut.com

Fabriform Plastics Inc
3300 Airport Way S Seattle WA 98134 206-587-5303 604
Web: www.fabriform.com

Fabrik Molded Plastics
5213 Prime Pkwy Mchenry IL 60050 815-385-9480 385-9614 596
Web: www.fabrikind.com

Fabri-Kal Corp 600 Plastics Pl Kalamazoo MI 49001 269-385-5050 385-0197 602
TF: 800-888-5054 ■ *Web:* www.fabri-kal.com

Fabri-Quilt Inc
901 E 14th Ave North Kansas City MO 64116 816-421-2000 471-2853 258
TF: 800-279-0622 ■ *Web:* www.fabri-quilt.com

Fabritech Inc 5740 Salmen St New Orleans LA 70123 504-733-5009 745-8
TF: 888-733-5009 ■ *Web:* www.fabritechonline.com

Fabrizio, McLaughlin & Assn
2624 NE 15th St Fort Lauderdale FL 33304 703-684-4510 463
Web: fabriziolee.com

Fabtrol Systems Inc
1025 Willamette St Ste 300 Eugene OR 97401 541-345-1494 177
Web: www.fabtrol.com

Fabulous Fox, The
527 N Grand Blvd Saint Louis MO 63103 314-534-1678 572
TF: 800-293-5949 ■ *Web:* www.fabulousfox.com

Fabulous Specialties Inc
600 Livingston Ave Ste 208 Livingston NJ 07039 973-535-6300 366

FAC (Fargo Assembly Co)
3300 Seventh Ave N PO Box 2340 Fargo ND 58102 701-298-3803 298-3806 814
Web: www.facnd.com

FAC (Fac Farmers Coop) 12543 190th St Arcadia IA 51430 712-689-2296 689-2327 276
TF: 800-779-4000 ■ *Web:* www.faccooperative.com

Fac Farmers Coop (FAC) 12543 190th St Arcadia IA 51430 712-689-2296 689-2327 276
TF: 800-779-4000 ■ *Web:* www.faccooperative.com

FACC (French-American Chamber of Commerce of Chicago)
205 N Michigan Ave 37th fl Chicago IL 60601 312-578-0444 578-0445 138
Web: www.facc-chicago.com

FACC (French-American Chamber of Commerce of Florida)
100 N Biscayne Blvd Ste 1105 Miami FL 33132 305-374-5000 358-8203 138
Web: www.faccmiami.com

FACC (French-American Chamber of Commerce of Philadelphia)
1617 John F Kennedy Blvd Ste 555 Philadelphia PA 19103 215-716-1996 138
Web: www.faccphila.org

FACC (Franklin Area Chamber of Commerce)
1327 Liberty St Franklin PA 16323 814-432-5823 437-2453 139
Web: www.franklinareachamber.org

FACCPNW (French-American Chamber of Commerce of the Pacific Northwest)
2200 Alaskan Way Ste 490 Seattle WA 98121 206-443-4703 448-4218 138
Web: www.faccpnw.org

Face Stockholm Ltd 324 Joslen Blvd Hudson NY 12534 518-828-6600 231
TF: 888-334-3223 ■ *Web:* www.facestockholm.com

Facekey Corp
900 NE Loop 410 Ste D401 San Antonio TX 78209 210-826-8811 569
Web: www.facekey.com

Facet Computers 2103 Court St Pekin IL 61554 309-353-4727 353-4730 175
Web: facettech.com

Facets Multimedia Inc
1517 W Fullerton Ave Chicago IL 60614 773-281-9075 511
TF: 800-331-6197 ■ *Web:* www.facets.org

Facey Medical Group & Foundation
11211 Sepulveda Blvd Mission Hills CA 91345 818-365-9531 305
Web: www.facey.com

Facilitator4hire 646 Seed Farm Rd Westminster SC 29693 864-324-3005 194
Web: www.facilitator4hire.com

Facilite Informatique Canada Inc
1045-5 Pl Ville-Marie Montreal QC H3B2G2 514-284-5636 284-9529 180
Web: www.facilite.com

Name / Address	City	State	ZIP	Phone	Fax	Class
Facilitech Inc 1111 Vly View Ln *Web:* www.businessinteriors.com	Irving	TX	75061	817-858-2000		320
Facilities Management and Maintenance Inc 25 Beach St 3R *Web:* www.fmm-inc.com	Dorchester	MA	02122	617-561-7003		194
Facility Construction Services Inc 8200 Lovett Ave *Web:* www.fcsdallas.com	Dallas	TX	75227	214-381-0101		186
Facility Dynamics Engineering 6760 Alexander Bell Dr *Web:* www.facilitydynamics.com	Columbia	MD	21046	410-290-0900		261
Facility Gateway Corp 4916 E Broadway *TF:* 866-432-1711 ■ *Web:* www.facilitygateway.com	Madison	WI	53716	608-838-6060		180
Facility Group Inc 2233 Lake Pk Dr *Web:* fdgatlanta.com	Smyrna	GA	30080	770-437-2700		186
Facility Masters Inc 1604 Kerley Dr *Web:* www.facilitymasters.com	San Jose	CA	95112	408-436-9090		256
Facility Programming & Consulting Inc 100 W Houston St Ste 1100 *Web:* www.facilityprogramming.com	San Antonio	TX	78205	210-228-9600		196
Facility Solutions Group (FSG) 4401 Westgate Blvd Ste 310 *TF:* 800-854-6465 ■ *Web:* www1.fsgi.com	Austin	TX	78745	512-440-7985	440-0399	246
Facing History & Ourselves 16 Hurd Rd *TF:* 800-856-9039 ■ *Web:* www.facinghistory.org	Brookline	MA	02445	617-232-1595	232-0281	48-11
Factor Gas Liquids Inc 240 Vidal St N *Web:* www.factorgas.com	Sarnia	ON	N7T5Y3	519-332-8978		316
Factor Sales 676 N Archibald St	San Luis	AZ	85349	928-627-8033		345
Factory at Franklin 230 Franklin Rd *Web:* factoryatfranklin.com	Franklin	TN	37064	615-791-1777	591-2511	460
Factory Direct Appliance Inc 14105 Marshall Dr *Web:* www.kcfda.com	Lenexa	KS	66215	913-888-8028		38
Factory Direct Furniture 5411 S Blvd	Charlotte	NC	28217	704-527-8788		321
Factory Steel & Metal Supply Co 14020 Oakland *Web:* www.factorysteel.com	Detroit	MI	48203	313-883-6300	883-4883	402
FactSet Research Systems Inc 601 Merritt 7 *NYSE: FDS* ■ *TF:* 877-322-8738 ■ *Web:* www.factset.com	Norwalk	CT	06851	203-810-1000		404
Factual Data 5100 Hahns Peak Dr. **Fax Area Code:* 866 ■ *TF:* 877-237-8317 ■ *Web:* www.factualdata.com	Loveland	CO	80538	800-216-3463	516-3502*	218
Faculty of Education University of British Columbia 2125 Main Mall *Web:* educ.ubc.ca	Vancouver	BC	V6T1Z4	604-822-5242		162
FACVB (Fayetteville Area Convention & Visitors Bureau) 245 Person St *TF:* 800-255-8217 ■ *Web:* www.visitfayettevillenc.com	Fayetteville	NC	28301	910-483-5311	484-6632	206
Faddis Concrete Products 2206 Horseshoe Pk *Web:* www.faddis.com	Honey Brook	PA	19344	610-269-4685	942-2629	135
Faded Banner Publications PO Box 101 *TF:* 888-799-3787 ■ *Web:* www.fadedbanner.com	Bryan	OH	43506	419-636-3807		637-2
Fader Agencies 83 Shore Rd *Web:* www.faderagencies.ca	Dartmouth	NS	B3A1A5	902-466-2333		518
FADER Inc, The 71 W 23 St 1st Fl *Web:* www.thefader.com	New York	NY	10010	212-741-7100		530
Fadi's Mediterranean Grill 3001 Knox St *Web:* www.fadiscuisine.com	Dallas	TX	75205	214-528-1800		671
Fado's Irish Pub 214 W 4th St *Web:* fadoirishpub.com	Austin	TX	78701	512-457-0172		671
FAE (Foundation for Acctg Education) 14 Wall St 19th Fl *TF:* 800-537-3635 ■ *Web:* www.nysscpa.org	New York	NY	10005	212-719-8300	719-3365	49-1
Faegre Drinker Biddle & Reath LLP 1 Logan Sq Ste 2000 *Web:* www.faegredrinker.com	Philadelphia	PA	19103	215-988-2700	988-2757	428
FAES (Foundation for Advanced Education in the Sciences) 10 Center Dr Rm 1N241 - MSC 1115 *Web:* www.faes.org	Bethesda	MD	20892	301-594-8985	402-0174	49-19
FAF (Form-A-Feed Inc) 740 Bowman St *TF:* 800-422-3649 ■ *Web:* formafeed.com	Stewart	MN	55385	320-562-2413		447
FAF 26 Lark Industrial Pkwy *TF:* 800-949-3311 ■ *Web:* www.faf.com	Greenville	RI	02828	800-949-3311		411
Fafco Inc 435 Otterson Dr *TF:* 800-994-7652 ■ *Web:* fafco.com	Chico	CA	95928	530-332-2100	332-2109	91
Fafinski Mark & Johnson PA 775 Prairie Center Dr Ste 400 *TF:* 855-806-1525 ■ *Web:* www.fmjlaw.com	Eden Prairie	MN	55344	952-995-9500		428
FAFP (Florida Academy of Family Physicians) 13241 Bartram Pk Blvd Ste 1321 *TF:* 800-223-3237 ■ *Web:* www.fafp.org	Jacksonville	FL	32258	904-726-0944	726-0923	78
Fagan Co 3125 Brinkerhoff Rd PO Box 15238 *Web:* faganco.com	Kansas City	KS	66115	913-621-4444	621-1735	189-10
Fagen Inc 501 W Hwy 212 PO Box 159 *Web:* www.fageninc.com	Granite Falls	MN	56241	320-564-3324		194
Fager's Island Restaurant 201 60th St *TF:* 855-432-4377 ■ *Web:* www.fagers.com	Ocean City	MD	21842	410-524-5500		671
Fagor Automation Corp 2250 Estes Ave *Web:* www.fagorautomation.com	Elk Grove Village	IL	60007	847-981-1500		188
Fagundes Agribusiness 8700 Fargo Ave *Web:* fagundes.net	Hanford	CA	93230	559-582-2000	582-0683	315-3
Fahlgren Mortine 4030 Easton Stn Ste 300 *TF:* 800-731-8927 ■ *Web:* fahlgrenmortine.com	Columbus	OH	43219	614-383-1500	383-1501	4
Fahr Beverage 1369 Martin Rd *Web:* www.fahrbeverage.com	Waterloo	IA	50701	319-234-2605	234-5644	81-1
Fahrenheit 2417 Professor Ave *Web:* www.chefroccowhalen.com	Cleveland	OH	44113	216-781-8858		671
Fahrenheit Advisors 1700 Bayberry Ct Ste 201 *Web:* fahrenheitadvisors.com	Richmond	VA	23226	804-955-4440		260
Faidley's Seafood 203 N Paca St *Web:* www.faidleyscrabcakes.com	Baltimore	MD	21201	410-727-4898		671
Failsafe Controls LLC 2712 SW Dr *Web:* failsafecontrols.com	New Iberia	LA	70560	337-365-2493		539
Faimon Publications LLC 324 Hudson *Web:* www.coffeycountyonline.com	Burlington	KS	66839	620-364-5325		532-2
Fain Anderson Vanderhoef Rosendahl O'Halloran Spillane PLLC 701 Fifth Ave Ste 4750 *Web:* favros.com	Seattle	WA	98104	206-749-0094	749-0194	41
FAIR (Federation for American Immigration Reform) 25 Massachusetts Ave NW Ste 330 *TF:* 877-627-3247 ■ *Web:* www.fairus.org	Washington	DC	20001	202-328-7004	387-3447	48-7
Fair & Yeager Insurance Agency Inc 10 Main St *TF:* 800-660-3131 ■ *Web:* fyins.com	Natick	MA	01760	508-653-3131	651-0129	390
Fair Anderson & Langeman 3065 S Jones Blvd Ste 100 *Web:* www.falcpa.com	Las Vegas	NV	89146	702-870-7999		2
Fair Grounds Race Course 1751 Gentilly Blvd *TF:* 800-262-7983 ■ *Web:* www.fairgroundsracecourse.com	New Orleans	LA	70119	504-944-5515	948-1160	642
Fair Haven Beach State Park 14985 State Park Rd *Web:* parks.ny.gov	Sterling	NY	13156	315-947-5205		565
Fair Hills Resort 24270 County Hwy 20 *TF:* 800-323-2849 ■ *Web:* fairhillsresort.com	Detroit Lakes	MN	56501	218-847-7638		669
Fair Isaac Corp 2665 Long Lake Rd Bldg C *NYSE: FICO* ■ *TF:* 888-342-6336 ■ *Web:* www.fico.com	Roseville	MN	55113	612-758-5200	758-5201	225
Fair Labor Assn (FLA) 1111 19th St NW Ste 401 *Web:* www.fairlabor.org	Washington	DC	20036	202-898-1000	898-9050	48-5
Fair Lawn Chamber of Commerce 12-45 River Rd *TF:* 800-474-1299 ■ *Web:* www.fairlawnchamber.org	Fair Lawn	NJ	07410	201-796-7050	475-0619	139
Fair Manufacturing Inc 2900 Alumax Rd *Web:* www.fairmfg.com	Yankton	SD	57070	005-653-3247		429
Fair Oaks Farms Inc 7600 95th St *Web:* www.fairoaksfarms.com	Pleasant Prairie	WI	53158	262-947-0320	947-0348	473
Fair Oaks Ford Inc 2055 Wodgen Ave *Web:* www.fairoaksford.com	Naperville	IL	60540	630-250-5750		57
Fair Oaks Mall 11750 Lee Jackson Hwy *Web:* www.shopfairoaksmall.com	Fairfax	VA	22033	703-359-8300		460
Fair Square Financial Services LLC 1000 N W St *TF:* 844-937-6556 ■ *Web:* ollocard.com	Wilmington	DE	19801	844-937-6556		113
Fair View Nursing Home 1714 W 16th St	Sedalia	MO	65301	660-827-1594		371
Fair Wind Air Charter 2525 SE Witham Field Hangar 7 **Fax Area Code:* 772 ■ *TF:* 800-989-9665 ■ *Web:* flyfairwind.com	Stuart	FL	34996	800-989-9665	288-4230*	13
Fairbanks Animal Clinic 7151 Fairbanks N Houston Rd *Web:* fairbanks.vetstreet.com	Houston	TX	77040	713-937-7274	937-1194	794
Fairbanks Chamber of Commerce 100 Cushman St Ste 102 *Web:* www.fairbankschamber.org	Fairbanks	AK	99701	907-452-1105	456-6968	139
Fairbanks City Hall 800 Cushman St *Web:* www.fairbanksalaska.us	Fairbanks	AK	99701	907-459-6715	452-5913	337
Fairbanks Co, The 202 Division St **Fax Area Code:* 800 ■ *TF:* 800-831-0022 ■ *Web:* www.fairbankscasters.com	Rome	GA	30162	706-234-6701	576-2239*	351
Fairbanks Convention & Visitors Bureau 101 Dunkel St Ste 111 *TF:* 800-327-5774 ■ *Web:* www.explorefairbanks.com	Fairbanks	AK	99701	907-456-5774	459-3757	206
Fairbanks Correctional Ctr 1931 Eagan Ave *Web:* doc.alaska.gov	Fairbanks	AK	99701	907-458-6700	458-6751	213
Fairbanks Daily News Miner 200 N Cushman St *Web:* www.newsminer.com	Fairbanks	AK	99707	907-456-6661	452-7917	532-2
Fairbanks Hospital 3910 Lima Rd *TF:* 800-225-4673 ■ *Web:* www.fairbankscd.org	Indianapolis	IN	46256	317-849-8222		726
Fairbanks International Airport 6450 Airport Way *Web:* www.dot.state.ak.us	Fairbanks	AK	99709	907-474-2500		27
Fairbanks Memorial Hospital 1650 Cowles St *Web:* www.foundationhealth.org	Fairbanks	AK	99701	907-452-8181		374-3
Fairbanks Museum & Planetarium 1302 Main St *Web:* www.fairbanksmuseum.org	Saint Johnsbury	VT	05819	802-748-2372	748-1893	520
Fairbanks North Star Borough 809 Pioneer Rd *TF:* 800-331-6158 ■ *Web:* www.fnsb.us	Fairbanks	AK	99701	907-459-1000	459-1224	338
Fairbanks North Star Borough Public Library 1215 Cowles St *Web:* fnsblibrary.org	Fairbanks	AK	99701	907-459-1020		434-3
Fairbanks Princess Riverside Lodge 4477 Pikes Landing Rd *TF:* 800-426-0500 ■ *Web:* www.princesslodges.com	Fairbanks	AK	99709	907-455-4477	455-4476	379
Fairbanks Scales Inc 821 Locust St *TF:* 800-451-4107 ■ *Web:* www.fairbanks.com	Kansas City	MO	64106	800-451-4107		684
Fairbanks Symphony Orchestra 312 Tanana Dr *Web:* fairbankssymphony.org	Fairbanks	AK	99775	907-474-5733		573-3
Fairbanks Youth Facility 1502 Wilbur St *Web:* www.dhss.alaska.gov	Fairbanks	AK	99701	907-451-2150		412
Fairborn Area Chamber of Commerce 12 N Central Ave *Web:* fairbornchamber.com	Fairborn	OH	45324	937-878-3191	878-3197	139
FairBridge Inns LLC 211 S Division St *Web:* www.fairbridgeinns.com	Spokane	WA	99202	509-838-6630		378
Fairbury Winnelson Co 2525 K St *Web:* www.fairbury.com	Fairbury	NE	68352	402-729-2215		612

Name / Address	City	State	Zip	Phone	Fax	Class
Fairchild Air Force Base 100 W Ent St Ste 155 *Web:* www.fairchild.af.mil	Fairchild AFB	WA	99011	509-484-1130		497-1
Fairchild Auto-mated Parts Inc 10 White St *TF:* 800-927-2545 ■ *Web:* www.fairchildparts.com	Winsted	CT	06098	860-379-2725	379-5340	621
Fairchild Imaging Inc 1801 McCarthy Blvd *TF:* 800-325-6975 ■ *Web:* www.fairchildimaging.com	Milpitas	CA	95035	408-433-2500	435-7352	696
Fairchild Industrial Products Co 3920 Westpoint Blvd. *TF:* 800-334-8422 ■ *Web:* fairchildproducts.com	Winston-Salem	NC	27103	336-659-3400	659-9323	201
Fairchild Lebel & Rice PC 5123 W St Joseph *Web:* www.flrcpas.com	Lansing	MI	48917	517-321-5990	321-9439	2
Fairchild Tropical Botanic Garden 10901 Old Cutler Rd *Web:* www.fairchildgarden.org	Coral Gables	FL	33156	305-667-1651	661-8953	97
Faire 300 California St *TF:* 800-208-8926 ■ *Web:* www.faire.com	San Francisco	CA	94104	800-208-8926		788
Fairell Law Firm, The 3469 Lawrenceville Hwy Ste 102 *Web:* fairellfirm.com	Tucker	GA	30084	678-973-2803		41
Fairfax County 12000 Government Center Pkwy *Web:* www.fairfaxcounty.gov	Fairfax	VA	22035	703-324-2531	324-3956	338
Fairfax County Chamber of Commerce (FCCC) 8230 Old Courthouse Rd Ste 350 *TF:* 800-628-6011 ■ *Web:* www.novachamber.org	Vienna	VA	22182	703-749-0400	749-9075	139
Fairfax County Convention & Visitors Bureau (FXVA) 3702 Pender Dr Ste 420 *TF:* 800-732-4732 ■ *Web:* www.fxva.com	Fairfax	VA	22030	703-790-0643		206
Fairfax Financial Holdings Ltd 95 Wellington St W Ste 800 *Web:* www.fairfax.ca	Toronto	ON	M5J2N7	416-367-4941	367-4946	360-4
Fairfax Forum, The 119 Main St *Web:* farmerpublishing.com	Fairfax	MO	64446	606-686-2741		532-2
Fairfax Hospital *Fairfax Behavioral Health* 10200 NE 132nd St *Web:* www.fairfaxhospital.com	Kirkland	WA	98034	425-821-2000		374-5
Fairfax (Independent City) 10455 Armstrong St *Web:* www.fairfaxcounty.gov	Fairfax	VA	22030	703-324-7329		338
Fairfax Inn 8660 S Fairfax Rd *Web:* www.thefairfaxinn.com	Bloomington	IN	47401	812-824-8552		671
Fairfax PET Imaging Ctr 8503 Arlington Blvd Ste LL-120 *Web:* www.fairfaxradiology.com	Fairfax	VA	22031	703-698-4441	698-5930	769
Fairfax Symphony Orchestra 2667 Prosperity Ave *Web:* www.fairfaxsymphony.org	Fairfax	VA	22031	703-563-1990		573-3
Fairfield Chair Co 1331 Harper Ave SW *TF:* 800-841-6279 ■ *Web:* www.fairfieldchair.com	Lenoir	NC	28645	828-758-5571	758-0211	319-2
Fairfield Chamber of Commerce 1597 Post Rd *Web:* fairfieldctchamber.com	Fairfield	CT	06824	203-255-1011	256-9990	139
Fairfield Chamber of Commerce 670 Wessel Dr *Web:* fairfieldchamber.com	Fairfield	OH	45014	513-881-5500	881-5503	139
Fairfield County 210 E Main St *TF:* 800-450-8845 ■ *Web:* www.co.fairfield.oh.us	Lancaster	OH	43130	740-652-7075	687-6048	338
Fairfield County Bank 150 Danbury Rd *Web:* www.fairfieldcountybank.com	Ridgefield	CT	06877	203-438-6518		70
Fairfield County District Library 219 N Broad St *Web:* www.fcdlibrary.org	Lancaster	OH	43130	740-653-2745		434-3
Fairfield Judicial District 1061 Main St *Web:* jud.ct.gov	Bridgeport	CT	06604	203-579-6527		338
Fairfield Lake State Park 123 State Park Rd 64 *Web:* tpwd.texas.gov	Fairfield	TX	75840	903-389-4514		565
Fairfield Machine Co 1143 Lower Elkton Rd PO Box 27 *Web:* www.fairfieldmachine.com	Columbiana	OH	44408	330-482-3388	482-5052	674
Fairfield Manufacturing Company Inc 2309 Concord Rd *Web:* www.oerlikon.com	LaFayette	IN	47909	765-772-4000	772-4001	709
Fairfield Medical Ctr (FMC) 401 N Ewing St *TF:* 800-548-2627 ■ *Web:* www.fmchealth.org	Lancaster	OH	43130	740-687-8000		374-3
Fairfield Museum & History Ctr 370 Beach Rd *Web:* www.fairfieldhistory.org	Fairfield	CT	06824	203-259-1598	255-2716	520
Fairfield Nursing & Rehabilitation 420 Moody St *Web:* www.fairfieldnursingandrehab.com	Fairfield	TX	75840	903-389-1236		450
Fairfield Processing Corp 88 Rose Hill Ave *TF:* 800-980-8000 ■ *Web:* www.fairfieldworld.com	Danbury	CT	06810	203-744-2090		605-1
Fairfield Public Library 1080 Old Post Rd *Web:* fairfieldpubliclibrary.org	Fairfield	CT	06824	203-256-3155		434-3
Fairfield Research Corp 65 Locust Ave *Web:* www.fairfieldbush.com	New Canaan	CT	06840	203-777-5900	972-0875	401
Fairfield Theatre Co 70 Sanford St *Web:* fairfieldtheatre.org	Fairfield	CT	06824	203-259-1036		748
Fairfield University 1073 N Benson Rd *Web:* www.fairfield.edu	Fairfield	CT	06824	203-254-4000	254-4199	166
Fairfield-Suisun Chamber of Commerce 1111 Webster St *Web:* fairfieldsuisunchamber.com	Fairfield	CA	94533	707-425-4625	425-0826	139
Fairhaven 7200 Third Ave *Web:* www.fairhavenccrc.org	Sykesville	MD	21784	410-795-8801		672
Fairhaven 435 W Starin Rd *TF:* 877-624-2298 ■ *Web:* www.fairhaven.org	Whitewater	WI	53190	262-473-2140	473-5468	672
Fairhill School & Diagnostic 16150 Preston Rd *Web:* fairhill.org	Dallas	TX	75248	972-233-1026	233-8205	685
FairHope Hospice & Palliative Care Inc 282 Sells Rd *TF:* 800-994-7077 ■ *Web:* fairhopehospice.org	Lancaster	OH	43130	740-654-7077	654-6321	371
Fairlane Town Ctr 18900 Michigan Ave *TF:* 800-992-9500 ■ *Web:* www.shopfairlane.com	Dearborn	MI	48126	800-992-9500		460
Fairleigh Dickinson University 285 Madison Ave *TF:* 800-338-8803 ■ *Web:* www.fdu.edu	Madison	NJ	07940	973-443-8500	443-8088	166
Fairly Painless Advertising Inc 44 E Eighth St *Web:* fairlypainless.com	Holland	MI	49423	616-394-5900		7
FairMarket Life Settlements Corp 600 S Hwy 169 Ste 690 *TF:* 866-326-3757 ■ *Web:* fairmarket.life	Saint Louis Park	MN	55426	952-405-7000		390
Fairmont Capital Inc 3350 E Birch St Ste 206 *Web:* www.fairmontcapital.com	Brea	CA	92821	714-524-4770	524-4775	405
Fairmont Convention & Visitors Bureau 323 E Blue Earth Ave *TF:* 800-657-3280 ■ *Web:* visitfairmontmn.com	Fairmont	MN	56031	507-235-8585		206
Fairmont General Hospital (FGH) 1325 Locust Ave *Web:* www.frmcwv.com	Fairmont	WV	26554	304-367-7500	367-7577	374-3
Fairmont Homes Inc 502 S Oakland Ave *Web:* www.fairmonthomes.com	Nappanee	IN	46550	574-773-7941		505
Fairmont Hot Springs Resort 1500 Fairmont Rd *TF:* 800-332-3272 ■ *Web:* www.fairmontmontana.com	Fairmont	MT	59711	406-797-3241	797-3337	669
Fairmont Hotels & Resorts Inc 100 Wellington St W PO Box 40 *TF:* 866-840-8077 ■ *Web:* www.frhi.com	Toronto	ON	M5K1B7	416-874-2600		379
Fairmont Insurance Brokers Ltd 1600 60th St *Web:* fairmontins.com	Brooklyn	NY	11204	718-232-3300		390
Fairmont Olympic Hotel Seattle, The 411 University St *Web:* www.seattleskal.org	Seattle	WA	98101	206-621-1700		378
Fairmont Sign Company Inc 3750 E Outer Dr *Web:* www.fairmontsign.com	Detroit	MI	48234	313-368-4000		701
Fairmont State University 1201 Locust Ave *TF:* 800-641-5678 ■ *Web:* www.fairmontstate.edu	Fairmont	WV	26554	304-367-4892	367-4789	166
Fairmont Supply Co 437 Jefferson Ave *TF:* 800-245-9900 ■ *Web:* www.fairmontsupply.com	Washington	PA	15301	800-245-9900		385
Fairmount Adult Theater 33 Main St	New Haven	CT	06512	203-467-3832		572
Fairmount Behavioral Health System 561 Fairthorne Ave *TF:* 800-235-0200 ■ *Web:* fairmountbhs.com	Philadelphia	PA	19128	215-487-4000		374-5
Fairmount Foundry Inc 25 Second Ave *Web:* fairmountfdry.com	Woonsocket	RI	02895	401-769-1585	769-0616	492
Fairmount Hotel, The 401 S Alamo St *TF:* 877-229-8808 ■ *Web:* www.fairmountsa.com	San Antonio	TX	78205	210-224-8800	475-0082	379
Fairmount Park 9301 Collinsville Rd **Fax Area Code:* 314 ■ *Web:* www.fairmountpark.com	Collinsville	IL	62234	618-345-4300	436-1516*	642
Fairmount Partners LP 100 Four Falls Corporate Ctr Ste 660 *Web:* www.fairmountpartners.com	West Conshohocken	PA	19428	610-260-6200		690
Fairmount Ventures Inc 2 Penn Ctr 1500 JFK Blvd Ste 1150 *Web:* fairmountinc.com	Philadelphia	PA	19102	215-717-2299		194
Fairplay Inc 4640 S Halsted St *Web:* www.fairplayfoods.com	Chicago	IL	60609	773-247-3077		345
FairPoint Communications Inc 521 E Morehead St Ste 250 *NASDAQ: FRP* ■ *TF:* 866-984-2001 ■ *Web:* www.fairpoint.com	Charlotte	NC	28202	704-344-8150		736
Fair-Rite Products Corp 1 Commerical Row PO Box J *TF:* 888-324-7748 ■ *Web:* www.fair-rite.com	Wallkill	NY	12589	845-895-2055	895-2629	249
Fairview Advisors LLC 3838 Tamiami Trl N Ste 416 *Web:* www.fairviewadvisors.com	Naples	FL	34103	239-213-1107	213-9213	194
Fairview Capital Partners Inc 75 Isham Rd Ste 200 *Web:* www.fairviewcapital.com	West Hartford	CT	06107	860-674-8066	678-5108	405
Fairview Commons Nursing & Rehabilitation Ctr 151 Christian Hill Rd *Web:* fairviewcommons.org	Great Barrington	MA	01230	413-528-4560		450
Fairview Elementary School 300 Salem Dr *Web:* www.plymouth.k12.wi.us	Plymouth	WI	53073	920-892-2621	892-5071	685
Fairview Farms 5911 Heuermann Rd *Web:* www.fairview-farm.com	Peoria	IL	61607	309-697-4111		671
Fairview Fellowship Home For Senior Citizens Inc 605 E State Rd *Web:* www.fellowshiphome.com	Fairview	OK	73737	580-227-3783		371
Fairview Health Services 2450 Riverside Ave *TF:* 800-824-1953 ■ *Web:* fairview.org	Minneapolis	MN	55454	612-672-2020		353
Fairview Park Hospital 200 Industrial Blvd *Web:* fairviewparkhospital.com	Dublin	GA	31021	478-275-2000		374-3
Fairview-Riverside State Park 119 Fairview Dr *TF:* 888-677-3247 ■ *Web:* crt.state.la.us	Madisonville	LA	70447	985-845-3318		565
Fairway Consulting Group 300 Merrick Rd Ste 404 *Web:* fcgsearch.com	Lynbrook	NY	11563	516-596-2800		194

Phone | Fax | Class

Fairway Ford Henderson Inc
301 Hwy 79 S ... Henderson TX 75654 903-657-2566 57
Web: www.fairwayfordhenderson.net

Fairway Golf Inc 5040 Convoy St ... San Diego CA 92111 858-268-1702 711
TF: 877-509-0830 ■ *Web:* www.fairwaygolfusa.com

Fairway Injection Molding Systems
20109 Paseo Del Prado ... Walnut CA 91789 909-595-2201 596
Web: www.fairwaymolds.com

Fairway Outdoor Advertising Inc
814 Duncan-Reidville Rd ... Duncan SC 29334 864-485-1899 8
Web: fairwayoutdoor.com

Fairway Packing Inc 1313 Erskine St ... Detroit MI 48207 313-832-2710 832-1649 297-9
Web: www.fairwaypacking.com

Fairway Partners 5944 Luther Ln Ste 307 ... Dallas TX 75225 214-265-7044 390
Web: fairway-partners.com

Fairweather LLC 301 E 83rd Ave ... Anchorage AK 99518 907-346-3247 349-1920 539
Web: www.fairweather.com

Fairwind Sunglasses Trading Company Inc
8301 Biscayne Blvd ... Miami FL 33138 305-758-0057 777-4987* 542
**Fax Area Code:* 800 ■ *Web:* www.fairwindsunglasses.com

Fairwinds Federal Credit Union
3087 N Alafaya Trl ... Orlando FL 32826 407-277-5045 658-7937 219
TF: 800-443-6887 ■ *Web:* www.fairwinds.org

Fairwinds International Inc
128 Northpark Blvd ... Covington LA 70433 985-809-3808 261
Web: www.fairwindsintl.com

Fairy Stone State Park
967 Fairystone Lake Dr ... Stuart VA 24171 276-930-2424 565
Web: www.dcr.virginia.gov

Fairygodboss 15 W 38th St ... New York NY 10018 631-513-2404 178-8
Web: fairygodboss.com

Faith & Reason Institute
1730 Rhode Island Ave NW Ste 212 ... Washington DC 20036 202-289-8775 634
Web: frinstitute.org

Faith Alive Christian Resources
1700 28th St SE ... Grand Rapids MI 49508 616-224-0728 642-8606* 637-2
**Fax Area Code:* 888 ■ *TF:* 800-333-8300 ■ *Web:* www.faithaliveresources.org

Faith Baptist Bible College
1900 NW Fourth St ... Ankeny IA 50023 515-964-0601 964-1638 161
Web: www.faith.edu

Faith Enterprises Inc
129 S Corona St ... Colorado Springs CO 80903 719-578-8281 186
Web: www.faithenterprisesinc.com

Faith Furniture 302 E Poyntz Ave ... Manhattan KS 66502 785-776-6755 321
Web: faithfurnitureinc.net

Faith Group Company Inc
195 Rt 9 Ste 205 ... Manalapan NJ 07726 732-431-1326 431-1673 603
Web: www.faith-group.com

Faith Library Publications Inc
PO Box 50126 ... Tulsa OK 74150 918-258-1588 872-7710 637-2
TF: 888-258-0999 ■ *Web:* www.rhema.org

Faith Manufacturing Company Inc
406 Atascocita Rd ... Humble TX 77396 281-441-9595 441-9555 539
Web: www.faithmfg.com

Faith Popcorn's BrainReserve
55 E 59th St Ste 1700 ... New York NY 10022 212-772-7778 772-7787 195
Web: www.faithpopcorn.com

Faith Regional Health Services
2700 W Norfolk Ave ... Norfolk NE 68701 402-371-4880 374-3
Web: www.frhs.org

Faith Tabernacle Pentecostal Church of Montgomery County
121 W 4th St M/a 608 Maple St ... Montgomery City MO 63361 573-564-3700 48-20

Faithbridge United Methodist Church
18000 Stuebner Airline Rd ... Spring TX 77379 281-320-7588 48-20
Web: www.faithbridgeumc.org

FaithTalk 570 & 910 WTBN
5211 W Laurel St ... Tampa FL 33607 813-639-1903 639-1272 645-160
TF: 800-576-3771 ■ *Web:* letstalkfaith.com

FaithTrust Institute
2400 N 45th St Ste 101 ... Seattle WA 98103 206-634-1903 634-0115 48-17
Web: www.faithtrustinstitute.org

Fakahatchee Strand Preserve State Park
137 Coastland Dr ... Copeland FL 34137 239-695-4593 565
Web: www.floridastateparks.org

Fakouri Electrical Engineering Inc
30001 Comercio ... Rancho Santa Margarita CA 92688 800-669-8862 261
TF: 800-669-8862 ■ *Web:* www.fee-ups.com

Fala Technologies Inc
430 Old Neighborhood Rd ... Kingston NY 12401 845-336-4000 336-4030 256
Web: www.falatech.com

Falafel King Restaurant
5461 Wern Ave Unit B ... Boulder CO 80301 303-449-9321 671
Web: falafelkingfoods.com

Falasca Mechanical Inc
3329 N Mill Rd ... Vineland NJ 08360 856-794-2010 610
Web: www.falascamechanical.com

Falcon Carpet Services Inc
2766 Elliott Ave ... Troy MI 48083 248-585-8780 290
Web: falconcarpetservices.com

Falcon Creek Publishing Co (FCP)
13504 Francisquito Ave Ste E ... Baldwin Park CA 91706 626-657-0377 637-2
Web: www.falconcreekbooks.com

Falcon Crest Aviation Supply Inc
8318 Braniff ... Houston TX 77061 713-644-2290 256
TF: 800-833-8229 ■ *Web:* www.falconcrestaviation.com

Falcon Executive Aviation Inc
4766 E Falcon Dr ... Mesa AZ 85215 480-832-0704 358
TF: 800-237-2359 ■ *Web:* www.falconaviation.com

Falcon Express Inc
2250 E Church St ... Philadelphia PA 19124 215-992-3140 992-3150 780
TF: 800-544-6566 ■ *Web:* www.falconexp.com

Falcon Express Transportation Inc
12200 Indian Creek Ct ... Beltsville MD 20705 240-264-1215 314
TF: 800-296-9696 ■ *Web:* www.fxtran.com

Falcon Foundry Co 96 Sixth St ... Lowellville OH 44436 330-536-6221 536-6371 308
Web: www.falconfoundry.com

Falcon Fuels Inc
7300 Alondra Blvd Ste 204 ... Paramount CA 90723 562-272-4226 579
Web: falconfuelsinc.com

Falcon Industries Inc 371 Campus Dr ... Somerset NJ 08873 732-563-9889 697
Web: www.falcon-industries.com

Falcon Natural Gas Corp
2500 City W Blvd Ste 300 ... Houston TX 77042 713-267-2240 456-2581 538

Falcon Plastics Inc
1313 Western Ave ... Brookings SD 57006 605-696-2500 696-2585 604
Web: falconplastics.com

Falcon Safety Products Inc
25 Imclone Dr ... Branchburg NJ 08876 908-707-4900 707-8855 151
TF: 800-332-5266 ■ *Web:* falconsafety.com

Falcon Seaboard
109 N Post Oak Ln Ste 540 ... Houston TX 77024 713-622-0055 622-0045 540
Web: www.falconseaboard.com

Falcon State Park PO Box 2 ... Falcon Heights TX 78545 956-848-5327 565
Web: tpwd.texas.gov

Falcon Technologies Inc
2631 Metro Blvd ... Maryland Heights MO 63043 314-994-9066 994-7554 246
TF: 866-958-4499 ■ *Web:* www.falcontech.com

Falcon Transport Inc PO Box 11415 ... Lancaster PA 17605 717-735-0561 735-0592 780
Web: www.falcon-transport.com

Falconer Electronics Inc
421 W Everett St ... Falconer NY 14733 716-665-4176 665-2017 625
Web: www.falconerelectronics.net

FalconStor Software Inc
2 Huntington Quad Ste 2S01 ... Melville NY 11747 631-777-5188 501-7633 178-12
OTC: FALC ■ *TF:* 800-886-1071 ■ *Web:* falconstor.com

Falconwood Inc
1011 Camino Del Rio S Ste 610 ... San Diego CA 92108 619-297-9080 175
Web: www.falconwood.biz

Falk and Hamblin Attorneys at Law
15991 Red Hill Ave Ste 101 ... Tustin CA 92780 714-647-9444 647-9001 41
Web: falkandhamblin.com

Falk Harrison Creative Inc
1300 Baur Blvd ... Saint Louis MO 63132 314-531-1410 344
Web: falkharrison.com

Falk Legal Group LLC
740 N Plankinton Ave Ste 800 ... Milwaukee WI 53203 414-316-2120 316-2137 41
Web: falklegal.com

Falk Library of the Health Sciences
200 Scaife Hall 3550 Terrace St ... Pittsburgh PA 15261 412-648-8866 648-9020 637-10
Web: www.hsls.pitt.edu

Falk Marques Group LLC
9 Meriam St Ste 21 ... Lexington MA 02420 781-652-0900 463
Web: falkmarquesgroup.com

Falk Plumbing Supply Co
223 3rd St ... Hot Springs AR 71913 501-321-1231 321-4015 612
TF: 800-844-3255 ■ *Web:* www.falksupply.com

Falkenberg Capital Corp
501 S Cherry St Ste 670 ... Denver CO 80246 303-320-4800 401
Web: falkenbergcapital.com

Falkenberg Ives LLP
30 N Lasalle St Ste 4020 ... Chicago IL 60602 312-566-4803 41
Web: ffilaw.com

Fall Consulting PO Box 2034 ... Parker CO 80134 800-691-5214 194
TF: 800-691-5214 ■ *Web:* www.fallconsulting.com

Fall Creek Engineering Inc
1525 Seabright Ave ... Santa Cruz CA 95062 831-426-9054 261
Web: fallcreekengineering.com

Fall Creek Falls State Park
2009 Village Camp Rd ... Spencer TN 38585 423-881-5298 565
Web: www.state.tn.us

Fall River Area Chamber of Commerce and Industry Inc
200 Pocasset St ... Fall River MA 02721 508-676-8226 675-5932 139
Web: bristolcountychamber.org

Fall River Feedyard LLC
27962 Angostura Rd ... Hot Springs SD 57747 605-745-4109 10-1

Fall River Group 670 S Main ... Fall River WI 53932 920-484-3311 308
Web: www.fallriverfoundry.com

Fall River Heritage State Park
Davol St ... Fall River MA 02720 508-675-5759 565
Web: www.mass.gov

Fall River Rural Electric Co-opeartive Inc
1150 N 3400 E ... Ashton ID 83420 208-652-7431 652-7825 245
TF: 800-632-5726 ■ *Web:* www.fallriverelectric.com

Fallbrook Chamber of Commerce
111 S Main Ave ... Fallbrook CA 92028 760-728-5845 728-4031 139
Web: www.fallbrookchamberofcommerce.org

Fallbrook Printing Corp
504 E Alvarado St ... Fallbrook CA 92028 760-731-2020 728-2857 627
Web: www.fallbrookprinting.com

Faller Davis & Associates Inc
4200 W Cypress St ... Tampa FL 33607 813-261-5136 302
Web: www.fallerdavis.com

Falling Colors Technology
125 Lincoln Ave ... Santa Fe NM 87501 505-428-0838 177
Web: fallingcolors.com

Falling Waters State Park
1130 State Park Rd ... Chipley FL 32428 850-638-6130 565
Web: www.floridastateparks.org

Fallingwater 1491 Mill Run Rd ... Mill Run PA 15464 724-329-8501 50-3
Web: waterlandlife.org

Fallon 901 Marquette Ave Ste 2400 ... Minneapolis MN 55402 612-758-2345 4
Web: www.fallon.com

Fallon Chamber of Commerce
85 N Taylor St ... Fallon NV 89406 775-423-2544 423-0540 139
TF: 800-242-0478 ■ *Web:* www.fallonchamber.com

Fallon Community Health Plan Inc
10 Chestnut St ... Worcester MA 01608 508-799-2100 391-3
TF: 800-333-2535 ■ *Web:* www.fchp.org

Fallon County 10 W Fallon St PO Box 1061 ... Baker MT 59313 406-778-3152 338
Web: www.falloncounty.net

Fallon Wellness Pharmacy LLC
1057 Troy Schenectady Rd ... Latham NY 12110 800-890-1137 237
TF: 800-890-1137 ■ *Web:* fallonpharmacy.com

Falls Catholic Credit Union
33 Graham Rd ... Cuyahoga Falls OH 44223 330-929-7341 219
Web: fallsccu.org

				Phone	Fax	Class
Falls Church News Press (FCNP) 200 Little Falls St Ste 508 *Web:* www.fcnp.com	Falls Church	VA	22046	703-532-3267	342-0352	532-2
Falls County 520 Lawrence St *Web:* texasfile.com	Corpus Christi	TX	78401	254-883-1408		338
Falls Lake State Recreation Area 13304 Creedmoor Rd *Web:* www.ncparks.gov	Wake Forest	NC	27587	919-676-1027		565
Falls Landing 200 E 8th St *Web:* www.falls-landing.com	Sioux Falls	SD	57103	605-336-2290		671
Falls of the Ohio State Park 201 W Riverside Dr *Web:* www.in.gov	Clarksville	IN	47129	812-280-9970	280-7110	565
Falls Park on the Reedy 601 S Main St *Web:* www.greenvillesc.gov	Greenville	SC	29601	864-467-4350		50-5
Falls River Group LLC 599 Ninth St N Ste 101 *Web:* fallsrivergroup.com	Naples	FL	34102	239-649-4222		401
Falls Terrace 106 Deschutes Way SW *Web:* www.fallsterrace.com	Tumwater	WA	98501	360-943-7830		671
Fallsview Casino Resort 6380 Fallsview Blvd *TF:* 888-325-5788 ■ *Web:* www.fallsviewcasinoresort.com	Niagara Falls	ON	L2G7X5	888-325-5788		669
Falmouth Chamber of Commerce 20 Academy Ln *TF:* 800-526-8532 ■ *Web:* www.falmouthchamber.com	Falmouth	MA	02540	508-548-8500	548-8521	139
Falmouth Inn 824 Main St *Web:* www.falmouthinn.com	Falmouth	MA	02540	508-540-2500		379
Falmouth Lumber Inc 670 Teaticket Hwy *Web:* www.falmouthlumber.com	East Falmouth	MA	02536	508-548-6868		191-3
Falmouth Public Library 300 Main St *Web:* www.falmouthpubliclibrary.org	Falmouth	MA	02540	508-457-2555		434-3
Falmouth Scientific Inc 1400 Rt 28A *Web:* www.falmouth.com	Cataumet	MA	02534	508-564-7640		757
False Cape State Park 4001 Sandpiper Rd *TF:* 800-933-7275 ■ *Web:* www.dcr.virginia.gov	Virginia Beach	VA	23456	757-426-7128	426-0055	565
Falstrom Co 147 Falstrom Ct *Web:* www.falstromcompany.com	Passaic	NJ	07055	973-777-0013		697
FAM (Fresno Art Museum) 2233 N First St *Web:* www.fresnoartmuseum.org	Fresno	CA	93703	559-441-4221	441-4227	520
Fam Funds 384 N Grand St PO Box 310 *TF:* 800-721-5391 ■ *Web:* www.famfunds.com	Cobleskill	NY	12043	518-234-4393	234-4473	317
FAM International Logistics Inc 5400 S University Dr Ste 402 *TF:* 888-326-0070 ■ *Web:* www.faminternational.com	Fort Lauderdale	FL	33328	954-252-0166	252-8308	693
Fama PR Inc Liberty Wharf 250 Northern Ave Ste 300 *Web:* www.famapr.com	Boston	MA	02210	617-986-5002		636
Famcor Oil Inc 7887 San Felipe Ste 250	Houston	TX	77063	713-974-0002		536
Finance Authority of Maine 5 Community Dr PO Box 949 *TF:* 800-228-3734 ■ *Web:* www.famemaine.com	Augusta	ME	04332	207-623-3263	623-0095	725
Families Against Mandatory Minimums (FAMM) 1612 K St NW Ste 700 *Web:* famm.org	Washington	DC	20006	202-822-6700	822-6704	48-8
Families USA 1201 New York Ave NW Ste 1100 *Web:* familiesusa.org	Washington	DC	20005	202-628-3030	347-2417	48-7
Familiprix Inc 6000 Rue Armand-Viau *TF:* 800-463-5160 ■ *Web:* www.familiprix.com	Quebec City	QC	G2C2C5	418-847-3311		238
Family Arena 2002 Arena Pkwy *Web:* familyarena.com	Saint Charles	MO	63303	636-896-4242	896-4205	720
Family Behavioral Resources 4900 Perry Hwy Bldg 2 Ste 200 *Web:* www.familybehavioralresources.com	Pittsburgh	PA	15229	724-850-8118		726
Family Broadcasting Corp 61300 S Ironwood Rd *TF:* 800-365-3732 ■ *Web:* familybroadcastingcorporation.com	South Bend	IN	46614	574-291-8200	291-9043	738
Family Business Institute Inc, The 4050 Wake Forest Rd Ste 110 *TF:* 877-326-2493 ■ *Web:* www.familybusinessinstitute.com	Raleigh	NC	27609	877-326-2493		463
Family Business USA 107 Glenhaven Dr *TF:* 877-609-1918 ■ *Web:* www.familybusinessusa.com	Chapel Hill	NC	27516	919-741-1943		196
Family Campers & RVers (FCRV) 4804 Transit Rd Bldg 2 *TF:* 800-245-9755 ■ *Web:* www.fcrv.org	Depew	NY	14043	800-245-9755		48-23
Family Career & Community Leaders of America (FCCLA) 1910 Assn Dr *Web:* www.fcclainc.org	Reston	VA	20191	703-476-4900	439-2662	48-11
Family Caregiver Alliance (FCA) 101 Montgomery St Ste 2150 *TF:* 800-445-8106 ■ *Web:* www.caregiver.org	San Francisco	CA	94104	415-434-3388	434-3508	48-17
Family Centre, The 9912-106 St NW Ste 20 *Web:* www.familycentre.org	Edmonton	AB	T5K1C5	780-423-2831		393
Family Circle Tennis Ctr 161 Seven Farms Dr *TF:* 800-677-2293 ■ *Web:* www.familycircletenniscenter.com	Daniel Island	SC	29492	843-856-7900		463
Family Credit Management 111 N Wabash Ave Ste 1410 *TF:* 877-322-8319 ■ *Web:* www.familycredit.org	Chicago	IL	60602	800-994-3328		41
Family Credit Union, The 1530 W 53rd St *TF:* 800-437-0415 ■ *Web:* familycu.com	Davenport	IA	52806	563-388-8328		219
Family Dollar Stores Inc PO Box 1017 *TF:* 866-377-6420 ■ *Web:* www.familydollar.com	Charlotte	NC	28201	844-636-7687		791
Family Entertainment Group LLC 1265 Hamilton Pky *Web:* fegllc.com	Itasca	IL	60143	847-842-6310	842-6311	748
Family Fare 212 Bay St *Web:* www.shopfamilyfare.com	Chippewa Falls	WI	54729	715-726-2500		345
Family Firm Institute (FFI) 200 Lincoln St Ste 201 *Web:* www.ffi.org	Boston	MA	02111	617-482-3045	482-3049	49-12
Family First Credit Union 3604 Atlanta Ave Ste 110 *Web:* ffcuga.org	Hapeville	GA	30354	404-768-4980	768-5496	219
Family Formation Law Offices 3685 Mt Diablo Blvd Ste 203 *TF:* 800-877-1880 ■ *Web:* familyformation.com	LaFayette	CA	94549	925-945-1880		41
Family Friends Veterinary Hospital & Kennel 864 Massachusetts Ave *Web:* www.familyfriendsvetandkennel.com	Boxborough	MA	01719	978-263-3412		794
Family Guidance Center of Warren County Inc 492 Rt 57 W *Web:* www.fgcwc.org	Washington	NJ	07882	908-689-1000		726
Family Handyman Magazine 2915 Commers Dr Ste 700 *TF:* 800-285-4961 ■ *Web:* www.familyhandyman.com	Eagan	MN	55121	800-285-4961		457-14
Family Health Care Services Inc *Home Health Care Service* 8655 S E Ave	Las Vegas	NV	89102	702-614-0575		371
Family Healthcare Network 305 E Center Ave *Web:* www.fhcn.org	Visalia	CA	93291	559-737-4700		374-3
Family Home Medical Inc 50 S Oak St *TF:* 877-339-4049 ■ *Web:* familyhomemedical.net	Mount Carmel	PA	17851	570-339-4049	339-1643	475
Family Horizons Credit Union 6665 E 21st St *TF:* 888-716-3009 ■ *Web:* familyhorizons.com	Indianapolis	IN	46219	317-352-0423	352-0524	219
Family Hospice & Palliative Care 50 Moffett St *TF:* 800-513-2148 ■ *Web:* www.familyhospicepa.org	Pittsburgh	PA	15243	412-572-8800	572-8827	371
Family Hospice of Belleville Area 5110 W Main St *Web:* familyhospice.org	Belleville	IL	62226	618-277-1800	277-1074	371
Family House Inc 1339 E Nebraska Ave *Web:* www.familyhousepeoria.org	Peoria	IL	61603	309-685-5300	685-8122	372
Family Housing Network 7050 S G St *TF:* 800-372-3697 ■ *Web:* www.ccsww.org	Tacoma	WA	98408	253-471-5340		656
Family Kingdom Amusement Park & Oceanfront Water Park 300 S Ocean Blvd *Web:* www.familykingdomfun.com	Myrtle Beach	SC	29577	843-626-3447		32
Family Life Communications Inc PO Box 35300 *TF:* 800-776-1070 ■ *Web:* www.myflr.org	Tucson	AZ	85740	800-776-1070		644
Family Life Publishing 87 Rebecca Rd *TF:* 800-633-1357 ■ *Web:* www.rmwainwright.com	Scituate	MA	02066	781-363-3813		637-2
Family Life Worship Center World wide Ministries Inc 1517 Joyner Pond Rd	Aiken	SC	29801	803-641-0218		48-20
Family Means 1875 NW Ave S *TF:* 800-327-3203 ■ *Web:* www.familymeans.org	Stillwater	MN	55082	651-439-4840	439-4894	810
Family Motor Coach Assn 8291 Clough Pk *TF:* 800-543-3622 ■ *Web:* site.fmca.com	Cincinnati	OH	45244	513-474-3622	474-2332	457-22
Family of the Americas Foundation 5929 Talbot Rd *TF:* 800-443-3395 ■ *Web:* familyplanning.net	Lothian	MD	20711	301-627-3346		48-17
Family Pet Animal Hospital 1401 W Webster Ave *Web:* familypetanimalhospital.com	Chicago	IL	60614	773-935-2311		794
Family Radio 290 Hegenberger Rd *TF:* 800-543-1495 ■ *Web:* www.familyradio.org	Oakland	CA	94621	800-543-1495		643
Family Research Council (FRC) 801 G St NW *Web:* www.frc.org	Washington	DC	20001	202-393-2100	393-2134	48-6
Family Service Foundation Inc 5301 76th Ave *Web:* www.fsfinc.org	Landover Hills	MD	20784	301-459-2121	459-0675	303
Family Tree Magazine 4700 E Galbraith Rd *TF:* 855-278-0408 ■ *Web:* www.familytreemagazine.com	Cincinnati	OH	45236	855-278-0408		457-14
Family Video 2500 Lehigh Ave *TF:* 888-332-6843 ■ *Web:* www.familyvideo.com	Glenview	IL	60026	847-904-9000		797
FamilySearch 35 N W Temple St *TF:* 866-406-1830 ■ *Web:* www.familysearch.org	Salt Lake City	UT	84150	866-406-1830		387
FamilyTime LLC 101 Merritt Blvd Ste 102 *Web:* www.familytime.com	Trumbull	CT	06611	203-610-8270		387
FAMM (Families Against Mandatory Minimums) 1612 K St NW Ste 700 *Web:* famm.org	Washington	DC	20006	202-822-6700	822-6704	48-8
Famous Bonanza Casino 107 Main St *Web:* www.famousbonanza.com	Central City	CO	80427	303-582-5914		133
Famous Dave's of America Inc 12701 Whitewater Dr Ste 200 *NASDAQ: DAVE* ■ *TF:* 800-929-4040 ■ *Web:* www.famousdaves.com	Minnetonka	MN	55343	952-294-1300		670
Famous Footwear 247 Junction Rd *TF:* 800-888-7198 ■ *Web:* www.famousfootwear.com	Madison	WI	53717	608-841-4071		301
Famous Mart Inc 6600 N Tryon St *Web:* www.famousmart.com	Charlotte	NC	28213	704-596-3132		155-3
Famous Natchitoches LA Meat Pies Inc 1414 Industrial Dr **Fax Area Code: 318* ■ *TF:* 800-955-4610 ■ *Web:* www.natchitochesmeatpies.com	Coushatta	LA	71019	800-955-4610	932-3471*	296-37
Famous Supply 2620 Ridgewood Rd *Web:* famous-supply.com	Akron	OH	44313	330-762-9621	762-8722	14
Famous Tate Electric Co 8317 N Armenia Ave *Web:* www.famoustate.com	Tampa	FL	33604	813-935-3151		321
Fan Asylum 1250 Folsom St *Web:* www.fanasylum.com	San Francisco	CA	94103	415-575-6600		393
Fancort Industries Inc 31 Fairfield Pl *Web:* www.fancort.com	West Caldwell	NJ	07006	973-575-0610	575-9234	757
Fancy Foods Inc Bldg B-12 Hunts Point Cooperative Market *Web:* www.fancyfoodsinc.com	Bronx	NY	10474	718-617-3000		345

	Phone	Fax	Class
Fandango Inc 12200 W Olympic Blvd Ste 400 .... Los Angeles CA 90064 *TF:* 855-646-2580 ■ *Web:* www.fandango.com	855-646-2580		116
Fandango Productions Inc 1050 S Paca St .... Baltimore MD 21230	410-539-7236		226
Fandel Retail Group 650 5th St Ste 405 .... San Francisco CA 94107 *Web:* www.fandelretail.com	415-538-8355		463
Fandor Homes 68 Romina Dr. .... Vaughan ON L4K4Z7 *TF:* 800-844-9936 ■ *Web:* www.fandorhomes.com	905-669-5820	738-7203	187
Fanello Industries Inc 50 E Main St .... Lavonia GA 30553 *Web:* fanello-industries.com	706-356-5359		488
Faneuil Hall Marketplace 4 S Market Bldg .... Boston MA 02109 *Web:* faneuilhallmarketplace.com	617-523-1300	523-1779	50-6
Faneuil Inc 2 Eaton St Ste 1002 .... Hampton VA 23669 *Web:* faneuil.com	757-722-3235		196
Fanfare Sports & Entertainment 4415 S Westnedge Ave .... Kalamazoo MI 49008 *Web:* www.fanfare-se.com	269-349-8866		95
Fanlight Productions c/o Icarus Films 32 Court St. .... Brooklyn NY 11201 *TF:* 800-876-1710 ■ *Web:* www.fanlight.com	718-488-8900	488-8642	511
Fannie & John Hertz Foundation 2300 First St Ste 250 .... Livermore CA 94550 *Web:* www.hertzfoundation.org	925-373-1642		305
Fannie Mae 3900 Wisconsin Ave NW .... Washington DC 20016 *OTC:* FNMA ■ *TF:* 800-732-6643 ■ *Web:* www.fanniemae.com	800-232-6643		509
Fannin Battleground State Historic Site 734 FM 2506 .... Fannin TX 77960 *Web:* www.thc.texas.gov	512-463-7948		565
Fannin County 400 W Main St. .... Blue Ridge GA 30513 *Web:* www.fannincountyga.com	706-632-2203	632-2507	338
Fannin County 800 E Second St .... Bonham TX 75418 *Web:* www.co.fannin.tx.us	903-583-7448	583-7682	338
Fannin County Board of Education 2290 E First St .... Blue Ridge GA 30513 *TF:* 800-308-2145 ■ *Web:* www.fannin.k12.ga.us	706-632-3771		685
Fannin County Electric Co-opeartive Inc 1530 Silo Rd. .... Bonham TX 75418 *TF:* 800-695-9020 ■ *Web:* www.fcec.coop	903-583-2117	583-7384	245
Fanning Springs State Park 18020 NW Hwy 19 .... Fanning Springs FL 32693 *Web:* www.floridastateparks.org	352-463-3420		565
Fanning/Howey Associates Inc 540 E Market St .... Celina OH 45822 *Web:* www.fhai.com	419-586-7771		261
Fannon Petroleum Services Inc 7755 Progress Ct .... Gainesville VA 20155 *Web:* www.fannonpetroleum.com	703-468-2060	754-2590	579
Fanshawe College 1001 Fanshawe College Blvd .... London ON N5Y5R6 *TF:* 800-717-4412 ■ *Web:* www.fanshawec.on.ca	519-452-4430		165
Fansteel Inc 1746 Commerce Rd .... Creston IA 50801 *Web:* www.fansteel.com	641-782-8521	782-4844	483
FANTA Equipment Co 6521 Storer Ave. .... Cleveland OH 44102 *Web:* www.fantaequip.com	216-281-1515	281-7755	494
Fanta Insurance 1023 Garfield Ave. .... Parkersburg WV 26102 *TF:* 888-677-0277 ■ *Web:* watersinsurance.com	304-485-5569	485-3372	390
Fantagraphics Books 7563 Lake City Way NE. .... Seattle WA 98115 *TF:* 800-657-1100 ■ *Web:* www.fantagraphics.com	206-524-1967	524-2104	637-5
Fantastic Indoor Swapmeet 1717 S Decatur Blvd. .... Las Vegas NV 89102 *Web:* fantasticindoorswapmeet.net	702-877-0087		460
Fantastic Sams Inc 500 Cummings Ctr Ste 1100 .... Beverly MA 01915 *Web:* www.fantasticsams.com	651-770-1449		77
Fantastic Tours & Travel 6143 Jericho Tpke .... Commack NY 11725 *TF:* 800-552-6262 ■ *Web:* www.fantastictours.com	631-462-6262	462-2311	760
Fantasy Cookie Co 12800 Arroyo St .... Sylmar CA 91342	818-361-6901		805
Fantasy Diamond Corp 1550 W Carrol Ave .... Chicago IL 60607 *TF:* 800-621-4445 ■ *Web:* endlessdiamond.com	312-583-3200	583-3434	410
Fantasy Gifts 440 Nepperhan Ave .... Yonkers NY 10701 *Web:* www.fantasy-gift.com	914-375-6100		241
Fantasy Springs Resort Casino 84-245 Indio Springs Pkwy .... Indio CA 92203 *Web:* www.fantasyspringsresort.com	760-342-5000		133
Fanthorp Inn State Historic Site 579 Main St .... Anderson TX 77830 *Web:* tpwd.texas.gov	936-873-2633		565
Fantini Baking Company Inc 375 Washington St .... Haverhill MA 01832 **Fax Area Code:* 978 ■ *TF:* 800-223-9037 ■ *Web:* www.fantinibakery.com	800-223-9037	373-6250*	296-1
Fantus Paper Products PS. Greetings Inc 5730 N Tripp Ave .... Chicago IL 60646 **Fax Area Code:* 773 ■ *TF:* 800-621-8823 ■ *Web:* psgreetings.com	800-334-2141	267-6055*	130
FANUC America Corp 3900 W Hamlin Rd .... Rochester Hills MI 48309 *TF:* 800-477-6268 ■ *Web:* www.fanucamerica.com	248-377-7000		386
Fapco Inc 216 Post Rd. .... Buchanan MI 49107 *TF:* 800-782-0167 ■ *Web:* www.fapcoinc.com	800-782-0167		549
FAPRI (Food & Agricultural Policy Research Institute) Iowa State University 578 Heady Hall .... Ames IA 50011 *Web:* www.fapri.iastate.edu	515-294-1183	294-6336	634
FAPS Inc 371 Craneway St .... Newark NJ 07114 *Web:* www.fapsinc.com	973-589-5656		62-7
Far Bank Enterprises Inc 8500 NE Day Rd .... Bainbridge Island WA 98110 *Web:* www.farbank.com	206-780-8767	842-6830	787
Far Best Foods Inc 4689 S 400 W PO Box 480 .... Huntingburg IN 47542 *Web:* farbestfoods.com	812-683-4200	683-4226	619
Far Chemical 2210 Wilhelmina Ct NE .... Palm Bay FL 32905 *Web:* far-chemical.com	321-723-6160	723-8753	583
Far East Broadcasting Company Inc 15700 Imperial Hwy PO Box 1 .... La Mirada CA 90638 *TF:* 800-523-3480 ■ *Web:* www.febc.org	800-523-3480		643
Far East Energy Corp 400 N Sam Houston Pkwy Ste 205 .... Houston TX 77060 *Web:* www.fareastenergy.com	832-598-0470	598-0479	536
Far Hills Group LLC 747 Third Ave 30th Fl .... New York NY 10017 *Web:* farhills.com	212-840-7779		194
Far Horizons Montessori School 264 N Main St .... Orange CA 92868 *Web:* fhmschool.org	714-997-8333		685
Far Niente Winery Inc 1350 Acacia Dr .... Oakville CA 94562 *Web:* farniente.com	707-944-2861	944-2312	10-11
Farabee Publishing 400 N Coronado St Ste 1135 .... Chandler AZ 85244 *Web:* www.farabeepublishing.com	602-616-9866		637-2
Faradyne Motors Inc 2077 Division St .... Palmyra NY 14522 *Web:* www.faradynemotors.com	315-502-0125		518
Farallon 450 Post St. .... San Francisco CA 94102 *Web:* www.farallonrestaurant.com	415-956-6969	834-1234	671
Farallones Marine Sanctuary Assn PO Box 29386 .... San Francisco CA 94129 *Web:* farallones.org	415-561-6625		41
Farber Group 150 York St Ste 1600 .... Toronto ON M5H3S5 *TF:* 855-775-8777 ■ *Web:* farbergroup.com	416-497-0150		401
Farber Specialty Vehicle Inc 7052 Americana Pkwy .... Reynoldsburg OH 43068 *TF:* 800-331-3188 ■ *Web:* www.farberspecialty.com	614-863-6470	759-2098	59
Farcountry Press 2222 Washington St. .... Helena MT 59602 *Web:* www.farcountrypress.com	406-422-1263	443-5480	637-2
Fard Engineers Inc 309 Lennon Ln Ste 200 .... Walnut Creek CA 94598 *Web:* www.fard.com	925-932-5505		256
Farewell Bend State Recreation Area 23751 Old Hwy 30 .... Huntington OR 97907 *Web:* stateparks.oregon.gov	541-869-2365		565
Farfalla Trattoria 1978 Hillhurst Ave .... Los Angeles CA 90027 *Web:* trattoriafarfalla.com	323-661-7365	661-5956	671
Fargo Air Museum 1609 19th Ave N. .... Fargo ND 58102 *Web:* www.fargoairmuseum.org	701-293-8043		520
Fargo Assembly Co (FAC) 3300 Seventh Ave N PO Box 2340 .... Fargo ND 58102 *Web:* www.facnd.com	701-298-3803	298-3806	814
Fargo Assembly of Pennsylvania Inc 800 W Washington St PO Box 550 .... Norristown PA 19404 *Web:* www.fargopa.com	610-272-6850	272-6858	247
Fargo Automation Inc 969 34th St N. .... Fargo ND 58102 *Web:* www.fargoautomation.com	701-232-1780		111
Fargo City Hall 200 N Third St .... Fargo ND 58102 *Web:* fargond.gov	701-241-1310	476-4136	337
Fargo Glass & Paint Company Inc 1801 Seventh Ave N .... Fargo ND 58102 *Web:* www.fargoglass.com	701-235-4441		191-2
Fargo Jet Center Inc 3802 20th St N. .... Fargo ND 58102 *TF:* 800-770-0538 ■ *Web:* www.fargojet.com	701-235-3600		63
Fargo Public Schools Federal Credit Union 1609 32nd Ave S .... Fargo ND 58103 *Web:* fpsfcu.com	701-241-4770		219
Fargo Theatre 314 Broadway N. .... Fargo ND 58102 *Web:* www.fargotheatre.org	701-239-8385		572
FargoDome 1800 N University Dr. .... Fargo ND 58102 *TF:* 855-694-6367 ■ *Web:* www.fargodome.com	701-241-9100	237-0987	720
Fargo-Moorhead Community Theatre 333 Fourth St S .... Fargo ND 58103 *Web:* www.fmct.org	701-235-6778		573-4
Fargo-Moorhead Convention & Visitors Bureau 2001 44th St S .... Fargo ND 58103 *TF:* 800-235-7654 ■ *Web:* www.fargomoorhead.org	701-282-3653	282-4366	206
Fargo-Moorhead Opera Co 3100 25th St S Ste A .... Fargo ND 58103 *Web:* www.fmopera.org	701-239-4558		573-2
Farhang & Medcoff PLLC 4801 E Broadway Blvd Ste 311 .... Tucson AZ 85711 *Web:* farhangmedcoff.com	520-790-5433		41
Faria Beede Instruments 88 Village St .... Penacook NH 03303 *Web:* www.fariabeede.com	603-753-6362		248
Faribault Foods Inc 222 S 9th St Ste 3380 .... Minneapolis MN 55402 *Web:* www.faribaultfoods.com	612-333-6461		296-20
Faribault Woolen MillCo 1500 NW Second Ave .... Faribault MN 55021 *Web:* www.faribaultmill.com	507-412-5510		745-1
Faribo Insurance Agency Inc 1404 Seventh St NW .... Faribault MN 55021 *TF:* 888-923-0430 ■ *Web:* insuranceagencymn.com	507-334-3929		390
Faris Machinery Co 5770 E 77th Ave .... Commerce City CO 80022 *Web:* www.farismachinery.com	303-289-5743		358
Faris Mailing Inc 701 N Holt Rd Ste 3 .... Indianapolis IN 46222 *Web:* www.farismailing.net	317-246-3315	246-3330	5
Farley's 3499 Foothills Rd .... Las Cruces NM 88011 *Web:* www.farleyspub.com	575-522-0466		671
Farm and Ranch Guide 707 E Front Ave .... Bismarck ND 58504 *Web:* www.agupdate.com	701-255-4905	255-2312	532-2
Farm Antiques, The 294 Mildram Rd. .... Wells ME 04090 *Web:* thefarmantiques.com	207-985-2656		321
Farm Boy Meats of Evansville Inc 2761 N Kentucky Ave .... Evansville IN 47711 *TF:* 800-852-3976 ■ *Web:* farmboyfoodservice.com	812-425-5231		473
Farm Bureau Bank 2165 Green Vista Dr Ste 204 .... Sparks NV 89431 **Fax Area Code:* 866 ■ *TF:* 800-492-3276 ■ *Web:* farmbureaubank.com	775-673-4566	913-5087*	70
Farm Bureau Life Insurance Co 5400 University Ave .... West Des Moines IA 50266 *TF:* 800-247-4170 ■ *Web:* www.fbfs.com	515-225-5400		391-2

	Phone	Fax	Class
Farm Bureau Life Insurance Company of Michigan 7373 W Saginaw Hwy ... Lansing MI 48909 *TF:* 800-292-2680 ■ *Web:* www.farmbureauinsurance-mi.com	517-323-7000		796
Farm Bureau Press 10720 Kanis Rd ... Little Rock AR 72211 *Web:* www.arfb.com	501-228-1300		457-1
Farm Business Consultants Inc 150 3015 Fifth Ave NE ... Calgary AB T2A6T8 *TF:* 800-265-1002 ■ *Web:* www.fbc.ca	403-735-6105		734
Farm Credit Administration 1501 Farm Credit Dr ... McLean VA 22102 *Web:* fca.gov	703-883-4000	734-5784	340-20
Farm Credit Administration Regional Offices			
Dallas Field Office 511 E Carpenter Fwy Ste 650 ... Irving TX 75062 *Web:* fca.gov	972-869-0550		340-20
Denver Field Office 3131 S Vaughn Way Ste 250 ... Aurora CO 80014 *Web:* fca.gov	303-696-9737		340-20
Sacramento Field Office 2180 Harvard St Ste 300 ... Sacramento CA 95815 *Web:* fca.gov	916-648-1118		340-20
Farm Credit Council 50 F St NW Ste 900 ... Washington DC 20001 *Web:* farmcredit.com	202-626-8710	626-8718	49-2
Farm Credit East 4363 Federal Dr ... Batavia NY 14020 *TF:* 800-929-1350 ■ *Web:* www.farmcrediteast.com	585-815-1900		196
Farm Credit Leasing (FCL) 600 Hwy 169 S Ste 300 ... Minneapolis MN 55426 *TF:* 800-444-2929 ■ *Web:* www.cobank.com	952-417-7800		216
Farm Credit of Central Florida Aca 115 S Missouri Ave Ste 400 ... Lakeland FL 33815 *TF:* 800-533-2773 ■ *Web:* www.farmcreditcfl.com	863-682-4117	688-9364	216
Farm Credit of Northwest Florida Aca 5052 Hwy 90 ... Marianna FL 32446 *TF:* 800-527-0647 ■ *Web:* www.farmcredit-fl.com	850-526-4910	482-6597	216
Farm Credit of The Virginias Aca 106 Sangers Ln ... Staunton VA 24401 *TF:* 800-559-1016 ■ *Web:* www.farmcreditofvirginias.com	540-886-3435		217
Farm Credit West 3755 Atherton Rd ... Rocklin CA 95765 *Web:* www.farmcreditwest.com	916-780-1166	780-1820	217
Farm Equipment Manufacturers Assn (FEMA) 1000 Executive Pkwy Ste 100 ... Saint Louis MO 63141 *Web:* www.farmequip.org	314-878-2304	732-1480	48-2
Farm Financial Strategies 2029 400th St ... Osage IA 50461 *Web:* www.farmestate.com	641-732-3839		734
Farm First Dairy Co-op 4001 Nakoosa Trl Ste 100 ... Madison WI 53714 *TF:* 800-525-7704 ■ *Web:* www.farmfirstdairycooperative.com	608-244-3373		393
Farm For Profit Inc 4345 Hwy 21 ... Embarrass MN 55732 *TF:* 800-232-7693 ■ *Web:* www.farmforprofit.com	218-984-3757	984-3212	192
Farm Implement & Supply Company Inc 1200 S Washington Hwy 183 ... Plainville KS 67663 *TF:* 888-589-6029 ■ *Web:* www.farmimp.com	785-434-4824	434-7390	274
Farm Industry News 7900 International Dr Ste 300 ... Minneapolis MN 55425 *Web:* www.farmprogress.com	630-524-4749		457-1
Farm Island Recreation Area 1301 Farm Island Rd ... Pierre SD 57501 *Web:* gfp.sd.gov	605-773-2885		565
Farm Journal 8725 Rosehill Rd Ste 200 ... Lenexa KS 66215 *Web:* www.farmjournal.com	847-268-3297		457-1
Farm Journal Agricultural Foundation 30 S 15th Ste 900 ... Philadelphia PA 19102 *Web:* www.agweb.com	215-557-8757		457-1
Farm Service Agency 1400 Independence Ave SW ... Washington DC 20228 *Web:* www.fsa.usda.gov	202-720-3865	690-2828	340-1
Farm Service Co-op 2308 Pine St ... Harlan IA 51537 *TF:* 800-452-4372 ■ *Web:* www.fscoop.com	712-755-3185	755-7098	276
Farm Show Magazine 20088 Kenwood Trial ... Lakeville MN 55044 **Fax Area Code:* 952 ■ *TF:* 800-834-9665 ■ *Web:* www.farmshow.com	800-834-9665	469-5575*	457-1
Farm Stores Corp 16777 Old Cutler Rd ... Palmetto Bay FL 33157 *TF:* 800-726-3276 ■ *Web:* www.farmstores.com	305-879-2941		297-8
Farm, The 5321 S Sheridan Ste 27 ... Tulsa OK 74145 *Web:* www.farmshoppingcenter.com	918-622-3860	622-4675	460
Farmdale Creamery Inc 1049 W Baseline St ... San Bernardino CA 92411 *TF:* 800-346-7306 ■ *Web:* farmdale.net	909-889-3002		296-5
Farmer & Irwin Corp 3300 Ave K ... Riviera Beach FL 33404 *Web:* fandicorp.com	561-842-5316	842-5999	189-10
Farmer Boy Ag 50 W Stoever Ave ... Myerstown PA 17067 **Fax Area Code:* 717 ■ *TF:* 800-845-3374 ■ *Web:* www.farmerboyag.com	800-845-3374	866-6233*	274
Farmer Bros Co 20333 S Normandie Ave ... Torrance CA 90502 *NASDAQ: FARM* ■ *TF:* 800-735-2878 ■ *Web:* www.farmerbros.com	310-787-5200		296-7
Farmer's Cooperative Assn 110 S Keokuk Wash Rd ... Keota IA 52248 *TF:* 877-843-4893 ■ *Web:* www.keotafarmerscoop.com	641-636-3748		48-2
Farmer's State Bank 555 S Commercial ... Harrisburg IL 62946 *Web:* www.farmersstatebank.com	618-252-2600		186
Farmer, Lumpe & Mcclelland Advertising Agency Ltd 500 W Wilson Bridge Rd Ste 316 ... Worthington OH 43085 *Web:* flmharvest.com	614-601-5195		5
Farmers & Merchants Bank 112 E Ladiga St ... Piedmont AL 36272 *Web:* www.fandm.bank	256-447-9041	447-9143	70
Farmers Alliance Mutual Insurance Co 1122 N Main PO Box 1401 ... McPherson KS 67460 *TF:* 800-362-1075 ■ *Web:* www.fami.com	620-241-2200	241-5482	391-4
Farmers and Merchants Mutual Telephone Co 210 W Main St ... Wayland IA 52654 *TF:* 800-822-2736 ■ *Web:* www.farmtel.net	319-256-2736		224
Farmers Bank & Savings Company Inc 211 W Second St ... Pomeroy OH 45769 *Web:* www.fbsc.com	740-992-2136	667-3162	70
Farmers Bank & Trust 101 S Fourth St PO Box 279 ... Atwood KS 67730 *TF:* 877-226-2351 ■ *Web:* farmersbank-trust.com	785-626-3233		70
Farmers Bank, The 9 E Clinton St PO Box 129 ... Frankfort IN 46041 *TF:* 800-992-3808 ■ *Web:* www.thefarmersbank.com	765-654-8731	654-8738	70
Farmers Branch Chamber of Commerce 2815 Valley View Ln Ste 118 ... Farmers Branch TX 75234 *Web:* farmersbranchchamber.org	972-243-8966		139
Farmers Building & Savings Bank 290 W Park St ... Rochester PA 15074	724-774-4970		70
Farmers Co-op 208 W Depot ... Dorchester NE 68343 *Web:* www.farmersco-operative.com	402-946-2211		275
Farmers Co-op 2105 Industrial Park Rd ... Van Buren AR 72956 *Web:* www.farmercoop.com	479-474-6622	474-4787	48-2
Farmers Coop 112 E Main ... Carmen OK 73726 *Web:* www.carmencoop.com	580-987-2234		276
Farmers Co-opeartive Society 317 Third St NW ... Sioux Center IA 51250 *Web:* www.farmerscoopsociety.com	712-722-2671		48-2
Farmers Cooperative Assn 402 E Country Rd ... Columbus KS 66725 *Web:* www.farmersco-op.coop	620-429-1296		276
Farmers Co-operative Elevator Co 177 W Main St ... Cottonwood MN 56229 *Web:* www.farmerscoopelevator.com	507-423-5412	423-5551	447
Farmers Co-operative Elevator Co 109 Isabella St PO Box 200 ... Radcliffe IA 50230 *Web:* www.radcliffecoop.com	515-899-2101	899-2105	447
Farmers Electric Co-opeartive Inc 1959 Yoder Ave SW ... Kalona IA 52247 *Web:* www.feckalona.net	319-683-2510		245
Farmers Electric Co-opeartive Inc 2000 E I-30 ... Greenville TX 75402 *TF:* 800-541-2662 ■ *Web:* www.farmerselectric.coop	903-455-1715	455-8125	245
Farmers Electric Co-opeartive Inc 3701 Thornton PO Box 550 ... Clovis NM 88101 *TF:* 800-445-8541 ■ *Web:* fecnm.org	575-762-4466		245
Farmers Feed & Grain Company Inc 306 Birch St PO Box 291 ... Riceville IA 50466 *Web:* www.ffgcoinc.com	641-985-2147	985-4000	276
Farmers Fire Insurance Co 2875 Eastern Blvd ... York PA 17402 *TF:* 800-537-0928 ■ *Web:* www.farmersfire.com	717-751-4435		390
Farmers Insurance Group of Cos 6301 Owensmouth Ave ... Woodland Hills CA 91367 *TF:* 888-327-6335 ■ *Web:* www.farmers.com	888-327-6335		2
Farmers Livestock Auction Incorporated of Springdale 1581 E Emma Ave ... Springdale AR 72764	479-751-5727		446
Farmers Market Garden Ctr 4110 N Elston Ave ... Chicago IL 60618 *Web:* www.gardenchicago.com	773-539-1200		323
Farmers Merchants Bank & Trust Co 100 S Main St PO Box 910 ... Breaux Bridge LA 70517 *Web:* www.fmbanking.com	337-332-2115	332-5089	70
Farmers Mutual Hail Insurance Company of Iowa 6785 Westown Pkwy ... West Des Moines IA 50266 **Fax Area Code:* 515 ■ *TF:* 800-247-5248 ■ *Web:* www.fmh.com	800-247-5248	282-1220*	391-4
Farmers Mutual Insurance Company of Nebraska 501 S 13th St ... Lincoln NE 68508 *TF:* 800-742-7433 ■ *Web:* www.fmne.com	402-434-8300		391-4
Farmers Mutual Telephone Co (FMTC) 410 Broad Ave ... Stanton IA 51573 *TF:* 800-469-2111 ■ *Web:* www.myfmtc.com	712-829-2111		224
Farmers Mutual Telephone Co (FMTC) N012 County Rd 17D ... Okolona OH 43550 *TF:* 888-659-0014 ■ *Web:* www.fmtc.cc	419-758-3322	758-3100	224
Farmers Mutual Telephone Co (FMT) 541 Young St ... Jesup IA 50648 *Web:* www.heartlandtechnology.com	319-827-1151	827-1110	224
Farmers National Bank of Buhl 914 Main St PO Box 392 ... Buhl ID 83316 *Web:* www.farmersbankidaho.com	208-543-4351		70
Farmers National Bank of Emlenton 612 Main St ... Emlenton PA 16373 *TF:* 844-767-2311 ■ *Web:* farmersnb.com	844-767-2311		70
Farmers National Bank of Prophetstown, The 114 W Third St ... Prophetstown IL 61277 *Web:* www.farmersnationalbank.bank	815-537-2348		70
Farmers National Co 11516 Nicholas St Ste 100 ... Omaha NE 68154 *TF:* 800-346-2650 ■ *Web:* www.farmersnational.com	402-496-3276		390
Farmers Rice Co-op PO Box 15223 ... Sacramento CA 95851 *TF:* 800-326-2799 ■ *Web:* www.farmersrice.com	916-923-5100	920-3321	296-23
Farmers Rice Milling Co 3211 Hwy 397 S ... Lake Charles LA 70615 *Web:* frmco.com	337-433-5205	433-1735	296-23
Farmers Rural Electric Co-opeartive Corp 504 S Broadway St ... Glasgow KY 42141 *TF:* 800-253-2191 ■ *Web:* www.farmersrecc.com	270-651-2191	651-7332	245
Farmers Savings Bank 205 W Main St ... Marshalltown IA 50158 *Web:* fsb-iowa.com	641-752-2525	752-0853	70
Farmers Select LLC 7321 N Loop Rd ... El Paso TX 79915	915-772-2736		296-27
Farmers State Bancshares Inc 100 W Main St PO Box 9 ... Mountain City TN 37683 *Web:* www.fsbankmctn.com	423-727-8121	727-5382	70
Farmers State Bank 115 Shelbyville ... Center TX 75935 *Web:* fsbctx.bank	936-598-3311		70
Farmers State Bank 110 W State St ... Phillipsburg KS 67661 *TF:* 888-879-2183 ■ *Web:* fsbphillipsburg.com	785-543-5199	543-3137	70
Farmers State Bank & Trust Co, The 200 W State St ... Jacksonville IL 62650 *Web:* www.fsbtco.com	217-479-4000		70
Farmers State Bank of Canton 220 E Fifth St ... Canton SD 57013 *Web:* cantonfarmersstatebank.com	605-987-2671		70

Name / Address	City	State	Zip	Phone	Fax	Class
Farmers State Bank of Underwood 110 Main St *Web:* farmersstbank.com	Underwood	MN	56586	218-826-6112	826-6124	70
Farmers Telecommunications Co-op (FTC) 144 McCurdy Ave N PO Box 217 *TF:* 866-638-2144 ■ *Web:* farmerstel.com	Rainsville	AL	35986	256-638-2144	638-4830	736
Farmers Telephone Company Inc (FTC) 615 Iowa St *TF:* 800-628-5989 ■ *Web:* www.heartland.net	Coin	IA	51636	712-379-3001	379-4000	224
Farmers Telephone Co-opeartive Inc 1101 E Main St **Fax Area Code:* 843 ■ *TF:* 888-218-5050 ■ *Web:* www.ftc.net	Kingstree	SC	29556	888-218-5050	382-2333*	736
Farmers Trust Co 42 McClurg Rd *TF:* 877-228-1643 ■ *Web:* www.farmerstrustco.com	Youngstown	OH	44512	330-743-7000		401
Farmers Union Co-op 1913 County Road B32 *TF:* 888-211-8910 ■ *Web:* www.farmerunion.net	Ossian	IA	52161	563-532-9381		447
Farmers Union Oil Company of Southern Valley (FUOSV) 204 S Front St *Web:* www.fuosv.com	Fairmount	ND	58030	701-474-5440		316
Farmers Win Coop (FFC) 110 N Jefferson *TF:* 800-562-8389 ■ *Web:* www.farmerswincoop.agricharts.com	Fredericksburg	IA	50630	563-237-5324	237-6123	10-4
Farmers' Electric Co-op 201 W Business 36 PO Box 680 *TF:* 800-279-0496 ■ *Web:* www.fec-co.com	Chillicothe	MO	64601	660-646-4281	646-3569	245
Farmers-Merchants Bank of Illinois 101 W Main St *Web:* www.fmbankil.com	Joy	IL	61260	309-584-4146	431-4309	360-2
Farmhouse Restaurant 119 W Main St *Web:* www.farmhouserestaurantbranson.com	Branson	MO	65616	417-334-9701		671
Farmingdale State University of New York 2350 Broadhollow Rd *TF:* 800-557-7392 ■ *Web:* www.farmingdale.edu	Farmingdale	NY	11735	631-420-2482	420-2633	166
Farmington Capital Partners PO Box 1461 *Web:* www.farmingtoncapital.com	Hartford	CT	06144	860-284-1096		691
Farmington Center Salem on Oregon LP 960 Boone Rd SE *Web:* www.farmingtonsquare-salem.com	Salem	OR	97306	503-715-0727		77
Farmington Chamber of Commerce 100 W Broadway *Web:* www.gofarmington.com	Farmington	NM	87401	505-325-0279	327-7556	139
Farmington Convention & Visitors Bureau 3041 E Main St *TF:* 800-448-1240 ■ *Web:* farmingtonnm.org	Farmington	NM	87402	505-326-7602		206
Farmington Correctional Ctr 1012 W Columbia St *TF:* 800-844-6591 ■ *Web:* www.mo.gov	Farmington	MO	63640	573-218-7100		213
Farmington Daily Times 203 W Main *TF:* 877-599-3331 ■ *Web:* www.daily-times.com	Farmington	NM	87401	505-325-4545	564-4630	532-2
Farmington Displays Inc 21 Hyde Rd *Web:* www.fdi-group.com	Farmington	CT	06032	860-677-2497	677-1418	286
Farmington Foods Inc 7419 W Franklin St *Web:* www.farmingtonfoods.com	Forest Park	IL	60130	708-771-3600		296-26
Farmington Historic Plantation 3033 Bardstown Rd *Web:* farmingtonhistoricplantation.org	Louisville	KY	40205	502-452-9920		520
Farmington Public Library 2101 Farmington Ave *Web:* farm.ent.sirsi.net	Farmington	NM	87401	505-599-1270	599-1257	434-3
Farmington School District R-7 1022 St Genevieve Ave *Web:* www.fsdknights.com	Farmington	MO	63640	573-701-1300	701-1309	187
Farmland Dairies LLC 520 Main Ave *TF:* 866-648-5252 ■ *Web:* farmlandmilk.com	Wallington	NJ	07057	866-648-5252		296-27
Farmland Management Services 301 E Main St *Web:* www.hancockagriculture.com	Turlock	CA	95380	209-669-0742		10-10
FarmLink Marketing Solutions Inc 93 Lombard Ave Ste 110 *TF:* 877-376-5465 ■ *Web:* www.farmlinksolutions.ca	Winnipeg	MB	R3B3B1	877-376-5465		195
FarmTek 1395 John Fitch Blvd *TF:* 800-327-6835 ■ *Web:* www.farmtek.com	South Windsor	CT	06074	860-528-1119		10-4
Farner, Barley & Associates Inc 4450 NE 83rd Rd *Web:* www.farnerbarley.com	Wildwood	FL	34785	352-748-3126	748-0823	261
Farner-Bocken Co 1751 US Hwy 30 E PO Box 368 *TF:* 800-274-8692 ■ *Web:* www.farner-bocken.com	Carroll	IA	51401	712-792-3503		297-8
Farnsworth Art Museum 16 Museum St *Web:* www.farnsworthmuseum.org	Rockland	ME	04841	207-596-6457		520
Farnsworth Engineering 313 Smith St *Web:* www.farnsworthengineering.com	East Liverpool	OH	43920	330-385-1745	385-1443	454
Farnsworth Group Inc 2709 McGraw Dr *Web:* www.f-w.com	Bloomington	IL	61704	309-663-8435		261
Farnsworth House Inn 401 Baltimore St *Web:* www.farnsworthhouseinn.com	Gettysburg	PA	17325	717-334-8838		671
Farouk Systems Inc 250 Pennbright Dr *TF:* 800-237-9175 ■ *Web:* farouk.com	Houston	TX	77090	281-876-2000		214
Farr Johnen & Associates Insurance Services LLC 996 S Seaward Ave *TF:* 800-350-2611 ■ *Web:* fjinsure.com	Ventura	CA	93001	805-644-3500	644-7868	390
Farr Regional Library 1939 61st Ave *TF:* 888-861-7323 ■ *Web:* www.mylibrary.us	Greeley	CO	80634	888-861-7323		434-3
Farr's Ice Cream - SLC 2575 S 300 W *TF:* 877-553-2777 ■ *Web:* www.farrsicecream.com	Salt Lake City	UT	84115	801-484-8724	484-8768	296-25
Farr, Farr, Emerich, Hackett & Carr PA 99 Nesbit St Earl D Farr Bldg *TF:* 855-327-7529 ■ *Web:* farr.com	Punta Gorda	FL	33950	941-639-1158		428
Farragut Folklife Museum 11408 Municipal Center Dr *Web:* www.townoffarragut.org	Farragut	TN	37934	865-966-7057	675-2096	520
Farragut Press 11863 Kingston Pk *Web:* www.farragutpress.com	Knoxville	TN	37934	865-675-6397	675-1675	532-4
Farragut State Park 13550 E Hwy 54 *Web:* visitidaho.org	Athol	ID	83801	208-683-2425		565
Farrar Corp 142 W Burns Ave *TF:* 800-536-2215 ■ *Web:* farrarusa.com	Norwich	KS	67118	620-478-2212	478-2200	307
Farrar Pump & Machinery Company Inc 1701 S Big Bend Blvd *TF:* 800-752-1050 ■ *Web:* farrarpump.com	Saint Louis	MO	63117	314-644-1050	644-2855	366
Farrar Scientific LLC 30765 SR-7 *Web:* www.farrarscientific.com	Marietta	OH	45750	740-374-8300		194
Farrel Corp 25 Main St *TF:* 800-800-7290 ■ *Web:* www.farrel-pomini.com	Ansonia	CT	06401	203-736-5500	736-5580	386
Farrell Distributing 19 Delaware Ave *Web:* www.farrelldistributing.com	Endicott	NY	13760	607-754-0707		290
Farrell Fritz 400 RXR Plz *Web:* www.farrellfritz.com	Uniondale	NY	11556	516-227-0700		428
Farrell-Calhoun Inc 221 E Carolina Ave *TF:* 888-832-7735 ■ *Web:* www.farrellcalhoun.com	Memphis	TN	38126	901-526-2211	774-4213	550
Farrey's Wholesale Hardware Company Inc 1850 NE 146th St *TF:* 888-854-5483 ■ *Web:* www.farreys.com	North Miami	FL	33181	305-947-5451		361
Farris Evans Insurance Agency Inc 1568 Union Ave *TF:* 800-395-8207 ■ *Web:* www.farrisevans.com	Memphis	TN	38104	901-274-5424		390
Farris Vaughan Wills & Murphy 700 W Georgia St Pacific Centre S 25th Fl PO Box 10026 *TF:* 877-684-9151 ■ *Web:* www.farris.com	Vancouver	BC	V7Y1B3	604-684-9151		41
Farris, Cooke & Assoc 118 S Colonial Ave Ste 200 *Web:* farriscooke.com	Charlotte	NC	28207	704-372-9406		2
Farris, Riley & Pitt LLP 505 20th St N Ste 1700 *Web:* www.frplegal.com	Birmingham	AL	35203	205-324-1212		428
Farrish Johnson Law Office, Chtd 1907 Excel Dr *Web:* farrishlaw.com	Mankato	MN	56001	507-625-2525		41
Farroh Roof Truss Company Inc 5 27th St NE *Web:* www.trussmasters.com	Minot	ND	58703	701-852-1717		817
Farruggio's Express 1 Biondi St *Web:* www.farruggio.com	Cliffwood	NJ	07721	732-583-2900	583-2997	780
FarSounder Inc 43 Jefferson Blvd *Web:* www.farsounder.com	Warwick	RI	02888	401-784-6700		459
Farstad Oil Inc 100 NE 27th St *TF:* 800-735-5788 ■ *Web:* www.farstadoil.com	Minot	ND	58703	701-852-1194		580
Farstone Technology Inc 1758 N Shoreline Blvd Ste B **Fax Area Code:* 650 ■ *Web:* farstone.com	Mountain View	CA	94043	562-373-5370	969-4567*	658
Faruki Ireland & Cox PLL 110 N Main St Ste 1600 *Web:* www.ficlaw.com	Dayton	OH	45402	937-227-3700		428
Farwest Corrosion Control Co 1480 W Artesia Blvd *TF:* 888-532-7937 ■ *Web:* www.farwestcorrosion.com	Gardena	CA	90248	310-532-9524	532-3934	261
Farwest Freight Systems Inc 4504 E Vly Hwy E	Sumner	WA	98390	253-826-4565		685
Farwest Sports Inc 4602 20th St E *TF:* 800-859-4694 ■ *Web:* www.sportco.com	Fife	WA	98424	253-922-2222	922-4914	711
Farwest Steel Corp 2000 Henderson Ave *TF:* 800-269-8720 ■ *Web:* www.farweststeel.com	Eugene	OR	97403	541-686-2000	681-7250	492
Farzad Family Law Apc 1851 E 1st St Ste 1150 *Web:* farzadlaw.com	Santa Ana	CA	92705	714-937-1193	937-1192	41
FAS (Federation of American Scientists) 1725 DeSales St NW Ste 600 *Web:* fas.org	Washington	DC	20036	202-546-3300		49-19
FASB (Financial Acctg Standards Board) 401 Merritt 7 PO Box 5116 *TF:* 800-748-0659 ■ *Web:* www.fasb.org	Norwalk	CT	06856	203-847-0700	849-9714	49-1
Fascet LLC 224 W 30 St Ste 203 *TF:* 888-327-2381 ■ *Web:* marketing.fascet.com	New York	NY	10001	212-448-9830		528
FASCore LLC 8515 E Orchard Rd **Fax Area Code:* 303 ■ *TF:* 800-537-2033 ■ *Web:* www.fascore.com	Greenwood Village	CO	80111	800-537-2033	801-6063*	535
FASEB (Federation of American Societies for Experimental Biology) 9650 Rockville Pk *TF:* 800-433-2732 ■ *Web:* www.faseb.org	Bethesda	MD	20814	301-634-7000	634-7001	49-19
Fashion Architectural Designs 4005 Carnegie Ave *TF:* 800-362-9930 ■ *Web:* www.fashionadco.com	Cleveland	OH	44103	216-904-1380	432-0800	802
Fashion Cabinet Manufacturing Inc 5440 Axel Park Rd *Web:* fashioncabinet.com	West Jordan	UT	84081	801-280-0646	280-8934	115
Fashion Focus Hair Academy 2184 Gulf Gate Dr *Web:* www.fashionfocusacad.com	Sarasota	FL	34231	941-921-4877	924-2850	167-3
Fashion Glass & Mirrors 585 S I-35 E *Web:* www.fashionglass.com	DeSoto	TX	75115	972-223-8936		362
Fashion Group International Inc (FGI) 8 W 40th St 7th Fl *Web:* www.fgi.org	New York	NY	10018	212-302-5511	302-5533	49-4
Fashion Inc 1019 N St *TF:* 800-255-1009 ■ *Web:* fashioninc.com	Ottawa	KS	66067	785-242-8111	242-2022	697
Fashion Institute of Design & Merchandising 350 Tenth Ave *TF:* 800-243-3436 ■ *Web:* fidm.edu	San Diego	CA	92101	619-235-2049	232-4322	164
Fashion Institute of Technology 227 W 27th St *Web:* www.fitnyc.edu	New York	NY	10001	212-217-7999		164
Fashion Island Shopping Ctr 401 Newport Center Dr *TF:* 855-658-8527 ■ *Web:* www.fashionisland.com	Newport Beach	CA	92660	949-721-2000	720-3350	460
Fashion Jewelry for Everyone LLC 16905 39th Ave N *Web:* www.fashionjewelryforeveryone.com	Minneapolis	MN	55446	763-540-0955		410

Name / Address	City	State	ZIP	Phone	Fax	Class
Fashion Place 6191 S State St Web: www.fashionplace.com	Murray	UT	84107	801-262-9447		460
Fashion Show Mall 3200 Las Vegas Blvd S Ste 600 Web: www.thefashionshow.com	Las Vegas	NV	89109	702-369-0704		460
Fashion Snoops Inc 39W 38th St Web: www.fashionsnoops.com	New York	NY	10018	212-768-8804		466
Fashions Inc PO Box 604 Web: www.fashionsinc.net	Jackson	MS	39205	601-353-4490	352-2010	156
Fasig-Tipton Company Inc 2400 Newtown Pk TF: 877-945-2020 ■ Web: www.fasigtipton.com	Lexington	KY	40511	859-255-1555	254-0794	51
Faske Lay & Co 3508 Far W Blvd 300 Web: www.faskelay.com	Austin	TX	78731	512-346-9623	346-8109	2
Fasken Martineau DuMoulin LLP 333 Bay St Bay Adelaide Ctr Ste 2400 PO Box 20 TF: 800-268-8424 ■ Web: www.fasken.com	Toronto	ON	M5H2T6	416-366-8381		41
Fasny Museum of Firefighting 117 Harry Howard Ave Web: www.fasnyfiremuseum.com	Hudson	NY	12534	518-822-1875		520
Fassberg Construction Co 17000 Ventura Blvd Ste 200 TF: 800-795-1747 ■ Web: www.fassbergcc.com	Encino	CA	91316	818-386-1800	784-5600	186
Fast Company Magazine 7 World Trade Ctr TF: 800-542-6029 ■ Web: www.fastcompany.com	New York	NY	10007	800-501-9571		457-5
Fast Fastfurnishings 340 S Lemon Ave Ste 6043 *Fax Area Code: 866 ■ TF: 877-404-6072 ■ Web: www.fastfurnishings.com	Walnut	CA	91789	443-371-3278	720-0126*	321
Fast Global Solutions Inc 20631 State Hwy 55 Web: www.waspinc.com	Glenwood	MN	56334	320-634-5126	634-5881	470
Fast Heat Inc 776 Oaklawn Ave TF: 877-747-8575 ■ Web: www.fastheat.com	Elmhurst	IL	60126	630-359-6300	833-2040	318
Fast Horse 240 Ninth Ave N Web: www.fasthorseinc.com	Minneapolis	MN	55401	612-746-4610		195
Fast Slow Motion 2120 16th Ave S Ste 310 TF: 866-917-8833 ■ Web: fastslowmotion.com	Birmingham	AL	35205	866-917-8833		177
Fast Undercar Inc 4277 Transport St Web: www.fastundercar.com	Ventura	CA	93003	805-676-3410	676-1571	61
Fastbolt Corp 200 Louis St TF: 800-631-1980 ■ Web: www.fastboltcorp.com	South Hackensack	NJ	07606	201-440-9100		350
Fastco Industries Inc PO Box 141427 Web: fastcoindustries.com	Grand Rapids	MI	49514	616-453-5428	453-0728	278
Fastec Industrial 112 Sherlake Rd TF: 800-837-2505 ■ Web: www.fastecindustrial.com	Knoxville	TN	37922	800-837-2505		351
Fastek International Ltd 1425 60th St NE Web: www.fastekintl.com	Cedar Rapids	IA	52402	319-294-6664	294-6672	261
Fastenal Co 2001 Theurer Blvd NASDAQ: FAST ■ TF: 877-507-7555 ■ Web: www.fastenal.com	Winona	MN	55987	507-454-5374	453-8049	351
Fastener Supply Co PO Box 7369 Web: www.fastenersupply.com	Charlotte	NC	28241	704-596-7634	598-0116	487
Faster Solutions 10 E Superior St Ste 200 TF: 877-204-7890 ■ Web: fastersolutions.com	Duluth	MN	55802	218-733-3936		396
Fast-Fix Jewelry & Watch Repairs 451 Altamonte Ave TF: 800-359-0407 ■ Web: fastfix.com	Altamonte Springs	FL	32701	407-261-1595		310
Fastframe USA Inc 212 Marine St Ste 100 TF: 800-631-4964 ■ Web: fastframe.com	Santa Monica	CA	90405	800-631-4964		45
Fast-Impact Consulting Inc 5605 Riggins CT Ste 200	Reno	NV	89502	775-284-3704		463
Fastline Publications LLC 4900 Fox Run Rd Web: www.fastline.com	Buckner	KY	40010	502-222-0146	222-0615	637-9
Fastly 475 Brannan St Ste 300 Web: www.fastly.com	San Francisco	CA	94107	415-604-5348		225
FasTracKids International Ltd 6900 E Belleview Ave Ste 100 TF: 888-576-6888 ■ Web: www.fastrackids.com	Greenwood Village	CO	80111	303-224-0200	224-0222	310
Fastron Co, The 2040 Janice Ave Web: www.fastron.com	Melrose Park	IL	60160	630-766-5000	766-6251	815
Fastserv Supply 200 Brooklyn Ave Web: www.fastservsupply.com	San Antonio	TX	78215	210-226-0244		351
FASTSIGNS International Inc 2542 Highlander Way TF: 800-327-8744 ■ Web: www.fastsigns.com	Carrollton	TX	75006	214-346-5600		701
FastWeb Inc 444 N Michigan Ave Ste 600 Web: www.fastweb.com	Chicago	IL	60611	444-536-1212		725
Fat Bob's Smokehouse 41 Virginia Pl Web: www.fatbobs.com	Buffalo	NY	14202	716-887-2971		671
Fat Brain Toys LLC 20516 Nicholas Cir TF: 800-590-5987 ■ Web: www.fatbraintoys.com	Elkhorn	NE	68022	402-779-3181	779-3253	761
Fat Canary 410 W Duke of Gloucester St Web: www.fatcanarywilliamsburg.com	Williamsburg	VA	23185	757-229-3333		671
Fat Cats 2061 W Tenth St Web: coolplacestoeat.com	Cleveland	OH	44113	216-579-0200		671
Fat Dawgs 7 1590 Alluvial Ave	Clovis	CA	93611	559-325-1819		647
Fat Matt's Rib Shack 1811 Piedmont Ave Web: www.fatmattsribshack.com	Atlanta	GA	30324	404-607-1622		671
Fat Willy's 2416 W Schubert Ave Web: www.fatwillys.com	Chicago	IL	60647	773-782-1800		671
FATA Automation Inc 6050 Nineteen Mile Rd Web: www.fatainc.com	Sterling Heights	MI	48314	586-323-4075		207
Fata Inc 3701 Malden Ave TF: 800-934-1620 ■ Web: fataonline.com	Baltimore	MD	21211	410-578-3600	578-0550	6
Fatburger North America Inc 9720 Wilshire Blvd Stc 500 Web: www.fatburger.com	Beverly Hills	CA	90212	310-319-1850	319-1863	670
Fate Therapeutics Inc 3535 General Atomics Ct Ste 200 TF: 866-875-1833 ■ Web: fatetherapeutics.com	San Diego	CA	92121	858-875-1800		85
Fath Properties LLC 255 E 5th St Ste 2300 Web: www.fathproperties.com	Cincinnati	OH	45202	513-721-4070	721-4098	652
Father Hennepin State Park 41294 Father Hennepin Park Rd PO Box 397 Web: www.dnr.state.mn.us	Isle	MN	56342	320-676-8763	676-3748	565
Father's Table LLC, The 2100 Country Club Rd Web: www.thefatherstable.com	Sanford	FL	32771	407-324-1200	324-1228	345
Fathers Press 590 NW 1921 St Rd Web: www.fatherspress.com	Kingsville	MO	64061	816-566-0654		637-2
Fathom 4 LLC 672 Marina Dr Ste 202 Web: fathom4.com	Charleston	SC	29492	843-352-2463		261
Fathom Five National Marine Park PO Box 189 Web: www.pc.gc.ca	Tobermory	ON	N0H2R0	519-596-2233	596-2298	563
Fathom Publishing Co PO Box 200448 Web: www.fathompublishing.com	Anchorage	AK	99520	907-272-3305		637-2
FatTail Inc 20969 Ventura Blvd Ste 209 Web: www.fattail.com	Woodland Hills	CA	91364	818-615-0380		179
Fattmerchant 618 E S St Ste 510 Web: www.fattmerchant.com	Orlando	FL	32801	407-982-1782		113
Fatz Cafe 4324 Wade Hampton Blvd Web: www.fatz.com	Taylors	SC	29687	864-322-1331	322-1332	670
Faubion Associates Inc 1000 Forest Ave Web: www.faubionassoc.com	Dallas	TX	75215	469-607-7086		499
Faulk & Winkler LLC 6811 Jefferson Hwy TF: 800-927-6811 ■ Web: www.fw-cpa.com	Baton Rouge	LA	70806	225-927-6811		194
Faulkner Animal Hospital 739 Lancaster Bypass E Web: faulkneranimalhospital.com	Lancaster	SC	29720	803-286-8131	289-1993	794
Faulkner County 801 Locust St Web: www.faulknercounty.org	Conway	AR	72034	501-450-4909	450-4938	338
Faulkner Hospital 1153 Centre St Web: www.brighamandwomensfaulkner.org	Jamaica Plain	MA	02130	617-983-7000		374-3
Faulkner Information Services 7905 Browning Rd TF: 800-843-0460 ■ Web: www.faulkner.com	Pennsauken Township	NJ	08109	856-662-2070	662-0905	637-11
Faulkner Pontiac Buick Gmc Truck Inc 705 Autopark Blvd Web: www.faulknerauto.com	West Chester	PA	19382	610-436-5600		390
Faulkner University 5345 Atlanta Hwy TF: 800-879-9816 ■ Web: www.faulkner.edu	Montgomery	AL	36109	334-272-5820		166
Faultless Linen 330 W 19th Terr Web: faultlesslinen.com	Kansas City	MO	64108	816-421-2373		442
Fauquier Bank, The (TFB) 10 Courthouse Sq TF: 800-638-3798 ■ Web: www.tfb.bank	Warrenton	VA	20186	540-347-2700		70
Fauquier County 10 Hotel St Ste 204 Web: www.fauquiercounty.gov	Warrenton	VA	20186	540-422-8001	422-8022	338
Fauquier County Chamber of Commerce 98 Alexandria Pk Web: www.fauquierchamber.org	Warrenton	VA	20186	540-347-4414	347-7510	139
Fauquier County Public Schools 320 Hospital Dr Ste 40 Web: www.fcps1.org	Warrenton	VA	20186	540-422-7000	422-7057	780
Fauquier Hospital 500 Hospital Dr Web: www.fauquierhealth.org	Warrenton	VA	20186	540-316-5000		374-3
Fauquier Times-Democrat 39 Culpeper St Web: www.fauquier.com	Warrenton	VA	20186	540-347-4222	349-8676	532-4
Fauser Energy Resources Inc 106 Center St PO Box 163 TF: 800-328-7371	Elgin	IA	52141	563-426-5811		579
Fauske & Associates LLC 16w070 83rd St TF: 877-328-7531 ■ Web: www.fauske.com	Burr Ridge	IL	60527	630-323-8750		192
Faust & Assoc 200 Third St Web: www.faustcpa.com	Mccomb	MS	39648	601-684-6382		2
Faust Institute of Cosmetology 1290 N Lake Ave Web: www.faustinstitute.com	Storm Lake	IA	50588	712-732-6570		167-3
Faustel Inc W 194 N 11301 McCormick Dr Web: www.faustel.com	Germantown	WI	53022	262-253-3333	253-3334	556
Fausto's Bistro 530 Veterans Memorial Blvd Web: www.faustosbistro.com	Metairie	LA	70005	504-833-7121		671
Fausto's Fried Chicken Inc 851 Arthur Irwin Rd	Dequincy	LA	70633	337-786-7264		670
Faux Pas Prints Inc 620 Papworth Ave Web: www.fauxpasprints.com	Metairie	LA	70005	504-834-8342		687
Faux Press c/o Jack Kimball Editor 24 Dale Web: www.fauxpress.com	Newton	MA	02460	617-803-2009		637-2
Favelle Favco Cranes (USA) Inc 26360 FM 106 Port of Harlingen Web: www.favellefavco.com	Harlingen	TX	78550	956-428-7488	428-7749	190
Faver-Dykes State Park 1000 Faver Dykes Rd *Fax Area Code: 386 ■ Web: www.floridastateparks.org	Saint Augustine	FL	32086	904-794-0997	446-6781*	565
Favori 3502 W First St Web: www.favorirestaurant.com	Santa Ana	CA	92703	714-531-6838		671
Favorite Office Automation 2011 W State St TF: 800-466-8338 ■ Web: www.favorite1.com	New Castle	PA	16101	724-658-8300		116
Favorite Plastics 1465 Utica Ave	Brooklyn	NY	11234	718-253-7000		596
Fawn Industries Inc 225 International Cir Ste 200 Web: fawnplastics.com	Hunt Valley	MD	21030	410-308-9200	308-9202	604
Faxaway 417 Second Ave W TF: 800-906-4329 ■ Web: www.faxaway.com	Seattle	WA	98119	206-479-7000	301-7500	736

Name / Address	Phone	Fax	Class
FaxBack Inc 7007 SW Cardinal Ln Ste 105 .... Portland OR 97224 *TF:* 800-329-2225 ■ *Web:* www.faxback.com	503-597-5350	597-5399	736
Faxon Machining Inc 11101 Adwood Dr. .... Cincinnati OH 45240 *Web:* faxon-machining.com	513-851-4644	851-4444	454
Faxton Saint Luke's Healthcare *Saint Luke's Campus* 1656 Champlin Ave .... Utica NY 13413 *Web:* mvhealthsystem.org	315-624-6000		374-3
Faxts Telysis Inc 2628 175th Ave NE .... Redmond WA 98052 *Web:* www.faxbroadcasters.com	425-647-0974	702-8758	681
Fay Bainbridge State Park 15446 Sunrise Dr NE .... Bainbridge Island WA 98110 *Web:* biparks.org	206-842-3931		565
Fay Block Materials Inc 130 Builders Blvd .... Fayetteville NC 28302 *TF:* 800-326-9198 ■ *Web:* www.fayblock.com	800-326-9198		191-1
Fay Industries Inc 17200 Foltz Pkwy .... Strongsville OH 44149 *Web:* www.fayindustries.com	440-572-5030		492
Fay School 48 Main St .... Southborough MA 01772 *Web:* www.fayschool.org	508-485-0100	481-7872	622
Fay Sharpe LLP 1228 Euclid Ave The Halle Bldg Fifth Fl .... Cleveland OH 44115 *Web:* www.faysharpe.com	216-363-9000	363-9001	445
Fayette Chamber of Commerce 65 W Main St .... Uniontown PA 15401 *Web:* www.fayettechamber.com	724-437-4571	438-3304	139
Fayette County 103 First Ave NW Ste 4 .... Fayette AL 35555 *Web:* sos.alabama.gov	205-932-5432		338
Fayette County 140 Stonewall Ave W Ste 100 .... Fayetteville GA 30214 *Web:* www.fayettecountyga.gov	770-460-5730		338
Fayette County 310 Oyler Ave .... Oak Hill WV 25901 *Web:* fayettecounty.com	304-465-5617		338
Fayette County 246 W Colorado St .... LaGrange TX 78945 *Web:* www.co.fayette.tx.us	979-968-3251	968-8531	338
Fayette County Fayette County Courthouse 221 S Seventh St ...... Vandalia IL 62471 *Web:* www.fayettecountyillinois.org	618-283-5000	283-5004	338
Fayette County 703 State Rte 41 SW .... Washington Court House OH 43160 *Web:* www.fayette-co-oh.com	740-313-7220		338
Fayette County 114 N Vine St .... West Union IA 52175 *Web:* fayettecountyiowa.org	563-422-3552	422-3137	338
Fayette County Board of Education 210 Stonewall Ave .... Fayetteville GA 30214 *Web:* www.fcboe.org	770-460-3535	460-8191	685
Fayette County Chamber of Commerce 600 W Lanier Ave Ste 250 .... Fayetteville GA 30214 *Web:* www.fayettechamber.org	770-461-9983	461-9622	139
Fayette County Chamber of Commerce 206 E East St .... Washington Court House OH 43160 *Web:* fayettecountyohio.com	740-335-0761		139
Fayette County Clerk 162 E Main St .... Lexington KY 40507 *Web:* local.dmv.org	859-253-3344	231-9619	338
Fayette County Library 216 W Market St .... Somerville TN 38068 *TF:* 866-465-3591 ■ *Web:* fayettetn.us	901-465-5248	465-5271	434-3
Fayette County Public Library 531 Summit St .... Oak Hill WV 25901 *TF:* 855-275-5737 ■ *Web:* fayette.lib.wv.us	304-465-0121	465-5306	434-3
Fayette County Public Library 828 N Grand Ave .... Connersville IN 47331 *TF:* 844-829-3746 ■ *Web:* www.fcplibrary.lib.in.us	765-827-0883		434-3
Fayette County Public Schools 701 E Main St .... Lexington KY 40502 *Web:* www.fcps.net	859-381-4100	381-4271	685
Fayette County Union Inc 119 S Vine St .... West Union IA 52175 *Web:* www.westunionfayettecountyunion.com	563-422-3888	422-3488	532-2
Fayette Electric Co-opeartive Inc 357 N Washington St .... LaGrange TX 78945 *TF:* 800-874-8290 ■ *Web:* www.fayette.coop	979-968-3181		245
Fayette Institute of Commerce & Technology Inc 45 W Kerr St PO Box 136 .... Uniontown PA 15401 *Web:* www.fict.com	724-438-4568		166
Fayette Mall 3401 Nicholasville Rd .... Lexington KY 40503 *Web:* www.shopfayette-mall.com	859-272-3493		460
Fayette Regional Health System (FRHS) 1941 Virginia Ave .... Connersville IN 47331 *Web:* www.fayetteregional.org	765-825-5131		374-3
Fayetteville Area Convention & Visitors Bureau (FACVB) 245 Person St .... Fayetteville NC 28301 *TF:* 800-255-8217 ■ *Web:* www.visitfayettevillenc.com	910-483-5311	484-6632	206
Fayetteville Athletic Club 2920 E Zion Rd .... Fayetteville AR 72703 *Web:* www.fayac.com	479-587-0500		354
Fayetteville Chamber of Commerce 113 West Mountain St .... Fayetteville AR 72701 *TF:* 877-715-5535 ■ *Web:* www.fayettevillear.com	479-521-1710	521-1791	139
Fayetteville Free Library Inc 300 Orchard St .... Fayetteville NY 13066 *Web:* www.fflib.org	315-637-6374		434-3
Fayetteville National Cemetery 700 Government Ave .... Fayetteville AR 72701 *Web:* www.cem.va.gov	479-442-2566	442-3046	136
Fayetteville Observer 458 Whitfield St .... Fayetteville NC 28306 *TF:* 800-345-9895 ■ *Web:* www.fayobserver.com	910-323-4848	486-3545	532-2
Fayetteville Public Utilities 408 W College St .... Fayetteville TN 37334 *TF:* 800-379-2534 ■ *Web:* www.fpu-tn.com	931-433-1522	433-0646	245
Fayetteville State University 1200 Murchison Rd .... Fayetteville NC 28301 *TF:* 800-222-2594 ■ *Web:* www.uncfsu.edu	910-672-1371	672-1414	166
Fayetteville Technical Community College 2201 Hull Rd .... Fayetteville NC 28303 *Web:* www.faytechcc.edu	910-678-8473	678-0085	162
Fayetteville-Lincoln County Chamber of Commerce 208 S Elk Ave .... Fayetteville TN 37334 *TF:* 888-433-1238 ■ *Web:* www.fayettevillelincolncountychamber.com	931-433-6154	433-9087	139
Fayez Sarofim & Co 909 Fannin St Ste 2907 .... Houston TX 77010 *Web:* www.sarofim.com	713-654-4484		401
Faygo Beverages Inc 3579 Gratiot Ave .... Detroit MI 48207 *TF:* 800-347-6591 ■ *Web:* www.faygo.com	313-925-1600		80-2
Faz Restaurants Inc 5121 Hopyard Rd .... Pleasanton CA 94588 *Web:* www.fazrestaurants.com	925-460-0444	469-1604	670
FB (Fishbait Marketing LLC) 1968 Long Creek Rd .... Wadmalaw Island SC 29487 *Web:* fishbaitmarketing.com	843-557-0535	557-0536	463
FB (Fearless Books) PO Box 4199 .... Napa CA 94558 *Web:* www.fearlessbooks.com	707-266-1322		637-2
FB Johnston Group 300 E Boundary St .... Chapin SC 29036	803-345-5481		627
FB Washburn Candy Corp 137 Perkins Ave .... Brockton MA 02302 *Web:* www.fbwashburncandy.com	508-588-0820	588-2205	296-8
FB Wright Company Inc 9999 Mercier Ave PO Box 770 .... Dearborn MI 48121 *Web:* www.fbwright.com	313-843-8250		326
FBA (Fibre Box Assn) 25 NW Pt Blvd Ste 510 .... Elk Grove Village IL 60007 *Web:* www.fibrebox.org	847-364-9600	364-9639	49-13
FBC (Florida Brick & Clay Company Inc) 1708 Turkey Creek Rd .... Plant City FL 33567 *Web:* www.floridabrickandclay.com	813-754-1521	754-5469	291
FBC Industries Inc 110 E Ave H .... Rochelle IL 61068 *Web:* www.fbcindustries.com	815-562-8169		345
FBG Service Corp 407 S 27th Ave .... Omaha NE 68131 *TF:* 800-777-8326 ■ *Web:* www.fbgservices.com	800-777-8326		104
FBI (Federal Bureau of Investigation) 935 Pennsylvania Ave NW .... Washington DC 20535 *Web:* www.fbi.gov	202-324-3000		340-14
FBI Buildings Inc 3823 W 1800 S .... Remington IN 47977 *TF:* 800-552-2981 ■ *Web:* www.fbibuildings.com	800-552-2981		186
FBJ (Flowers By Jerri Inc) 616 W Kimberly Rd .... Davenport IA 52806 *TF:* 800-368-5374 ■ *Web:* www.flowersbyjerri.com	563-391-6290		293
FBLA-PBL (Future Business Leaders of America-Phi Beta Lambda Inc) 1912 Assn Dr .... Reston VA 20191 **Fax Area Code:* 866 ■ *TF:* 800-325-2946 ■ *Web:* www.fbla-pbl.org	800-325-2946	500-5610*	48-11
FBN Metal Products 5020 S Nathaniel Lyon St .... Battlefield MO 65619 *TF:* 800-538-2830 ■ *Web:* fbnmetal.com	417-882-2830		295
FBS (Fullerton Building Systems) 34620 250th St PO Box 308 .... Worthington MN 56187 *TF:* 800-450-9782 ■ *Web:* www.fullertonbuildingsystems.com	507-376-3128	376-9530	817
FBS (Franchise Business Systems Inc) 2319 N Andrews Ave .... Fort Lauderdale FL 33311 *TF:* 800-382-1040 ■ *Web:* www.franchiseaccounting.com	800-382-1040		194
FC & E Engineering LLC 917 Marquett Rd .... Brandon MS 39042 *Web:* fce-engineering.com	601-824-1860		261
FC Dallas 9200 World Cup Way Ste 202 .... Frisco TX 75034 *Web:* www.fcdallas.com	214-705-6700	705-6799	717
FC Haab Company Inc 2314 Market St .... Philadelphia PA 19103 *TF:* 800-486-5663 ■ *Web:* www.fchaab.com	215-563-0800	563-9448	316
FC Phillips Inc 471 Washington St .... Stoughton MA 02072 *Web:* www.fcphillips.com	781-344-9400		621
FC Publishing LLC PO Box 5675 .... Huntsville AL 35816 *Web:* www.fcpublishing.com	256-479-2611		637-2
FC Tucker Company Inc 9201 N Meridian St Ste 100 .... Indianapolis IN 46260 *Web:* www.talktotucker.com	317-566-2399		652
FCA (Family Caregiver Alliance) 101 Montgomery St Ste 2150 .... San Francisco CA 94104 *TF:* 800-445-8106 ■ *Web:* www.caregiver.org	415-434-3388	434-3508	48-17
FCA (Fellowship of Christian Athletes) 8701 Leeds Rd .... Kansas City MO 64129 *TF:* 800-289-0909 ■ *Web:* www.fca.org	816-921-0909	921-8755	48-22
FCA (First Cooperative Assn) 960 Riverview Dr PO Box 60 .... Cherokee IA 51012 *TF:* 877-753-5400 ■ *Web:* www.firstcoop.com	712-225-5400	225-5493	447
FCA Corp 791 Town & Country Blvd Ste 250 .... Houston TX 77024 *Web:* fcacorp.com	713-781-2856		401
FCA LLC 7601 John Deere Pkwy PO Box 758 .... Moline IL 61266 *Web:* fcapackaging.com	309-792-3444		111
FCB (Florida Community Bank) 1400 N 15th St .... Immokalee FL 34142 *TF:* 866-764-0006 ■ *Web:* www.floridacommunitybank.net	239-657-3171		70
FCC (First Community Corp) 5455 Sunset Blvd .... Lexington SC 29072 *NASDAQ: FCCO* ■ *TF:* 800-829-6372 ■ *Web:* www.firstcommunitysc.com	803-951-0555		360-2
FCC (Federal Communications Commission) 445 12th St SW .... Washington DC 20554 **Fax Area Code:* 202 ■ *TF:* 888-225-5322 ■ *Web:* www.fcc.gov	888-225-5322	418-0232*	340-20
FCC (Fremont Contract Carriers Inc) 865 S Bud Blvd .... Fremont NE 68025 **Fax Area Code:* 402 ■ *TF:* 800-228-9842 ■ *Web:* www.fcc-inc.com	800-228-9842	727-8712*	449
FCC Commercial Furniture Inc 8452 Old Hwy 99 N .... Roseburg OR 97470 *TF:* 800-322-7328 ■ *Web:* fcc-create.com	800-322-7328		321
FCC Services 7951 E Maplewood Ave Ste 225 .... Greenwood Village CO 80111 *Web:* www.fccservices.com	303-721-3200		463
FCCC (Fairfax County Chamber of Commerce) 8230 Old Courthouse Rd Ste 350 .... Vienna VA 22182 *TF:* 800-628-6011 ■ *Web:* www.novachamber.org	703-749-0400	749-9075	139
FCCI Insurance Group 6300 University Pkwy .... Sarasota FL 34240 *TF:* 800-226-3224 ■ *Web:* www.fcci-group.com	941-907-3224		391-4
FCCLA (Family Career & Community Leaders of America) 1910 Assn Dr .... Reston VA 20191 *Web:* www.fcclainc.org	703-476-4900	439-2662	48-11

Phone | Fax | Class

FCCU (First Community Credit Union)
17151 Chesterfield Airport Rd
PO Box 1030 Chesterfield MO 63005 636-728-3333 219
TF: 800-767-8880 ■ Web: www.firstcommunity.com

FCF (Fremont Correctional Facility)
E US Hwy 50 Evans Blvd PO Box 999 Canon City CO 81215 719-269-5002 269-5020 213
TF: 800-886-7683 ■ Web: www.colorado.gov

FCG (Florida City Gas) 955 E 25th St Hialeah FL 33013 800-993-7546 787
TF: 800-993-7546 ■ Web: floridacitygas.com

FCG Advisors LLC 1 Main St Ste 202 Chatham NJ 07928 973-635-7374 194
Web: www.fcgadvisors.com

FCI (Fluid Controls Institute)
1300 Sumner Ave Cleveland OH 44115 216-241-7333 241-0105 49-13
Web: www.fluidcontrolsinstitute.org

FCI (Federal Correctional Institution)
Bastrop 1341 Hwy 95 N PO Box 730 Bastrop TX 78602 512-321-3903 304-0117 212
TF: 800-995-6429 ■ Web: www.bop.gov

FCI Constructors Inc
3070 I-70 Business Loop Ste A Grand Junction CO 81504 970-434-9093 434-7583 188-4
Web: www.fciol.com

FCI Enterprises LLC
14170 Newbrook Dr Ste 100 Chantilly VA 20151 703-961-1818 177

FCI Industrial
Industrial Parts Mfg 4661 Giles Rd Cleveland OH 44135 216-251-2000 621
Web: www.fci-usa.com

FCI Lender Services Inc
8180 E Kaiser Blvd Anaheim Hills CA 92808 714-282-2424 282-2429 393
TF: 800-931-2424 ■ Web: www.trustfci.com

FCIS LLC 206 Mapeat Ln New Castle PA 16101 724-652-8828 78
Web: www.fcisllc.com

FCL (Farm Credit Leasing)
600 Hwy 169 S Ste 300 Minneapolis MN 55426 952-417-7800 216
TF: 800-444-2929 ■ Web: www.cobank.com

FCL (Florida Classics Library)
11300 SE Dixie Hwy Hobe Sound FL 33455 772-546-9380 637-2
Web: floridaclassicslibrary.com

FCL Builders 1150 Spring Lake Dr Itasca IL 60143 630-773-0050 773-4030 186
Web: fclbuilders.com

FCL Graphics Inc
4600 N Olcott Ave Harwood Heights IL 60706 708-867-5500 627
TF: 800-274-3380 ■ Web: www.fclgraphics.com

FCM Investments
2200 Ross Ave Ste 4600 W Dallas TX 75201 214-665-6900 665-6940 401

FCNL (Friends Committee on National Legislation)
245 Second St NE Washington DC 20002 202-547-6000 547-6019 615
TF: 800-630-1330 ■ Web: www.fcnl.org

FCNP (Falls Church News Press)
200 Little Falls St Ste 508 Falls Church VA 22046 703-532-3267 342-0352 532-2
Web: www.fcnp.com

FCP (Falcon Creek Publishing Co)
13504 Francisquito Ave Ste E Baldwin Park CA 91706 626-657-0377 637-2
Web: www.falconcreekbooks.com

FCPL (Frankfort Community Public Library)
208 W Clinton St Frankfort IN 46041 765-654-8746 654-8747 434-3
Web: myfcpl.org

FCPL (Frederick County Public Libraries)
110 E Patrick St Frederick MD 21701 301-600-1630 434-3
Web: www.fcpl.org

FCRV (Family Campers & RVers)
4804 Transit Rd Bldg 2 Depew NY 14043 800-245-9755 48-23
TF: 800-245-9755 ■ Web: www.fcrv.org

FCS GROUP
Redmond Town Ctr 7525 166th Ave NE Ste D-215 Redmond WA 98052 425-867-1802 867-1937 401
Web: www.fcsgroup.com

FCT Solder 1309 N 17th Ave Greeley CO 80631 970-346-8002 407
Web: fctsolder.com

FCWGS (Four Corners Welding and Gas Supply)
606 E Hwy 66 Gallup NM 87301 505-722-3845 722-2645 492
Web: www.fourcornerswelding.com

FCX Systems Inc 400 Fcx Ln Morgantown WV 26501 304-983-0400 256
Web: www.fcxinc.com

FD Gallery LLC 26 E 80th St New York NY 10075 212-772-2440 410
Web: fd-gallery.com

FD Lawrence Electric Co
3450 Beekman St Cincinnati OH 45223 513-542-1100 542-2422 246
TF: 800-582-4490 ■ Web: www.fdlawrence.com

FD Roosevelt State Park
2970 GA Hwy 190 Pine Mountain GA 31822 706-663-4858 663-8906 565
Web: gastateparks.org

FDA (First District Assn)
101 S Swift Ave Litchfield MN 55355 320-693-3236 296-5
Web: www.firstdistrict.com

FDA (Food & Drug Administration)
5600 Fishers Ln Rockville MD 20857 301-443-1726 443-3100 340-10
TF: 888-463-6332 ■ Web: www.fda.gov

FDB (First DataBank Inc)
701 Gateway Blvd Ste 600 South San Francisco CA 94080 800-633-3453 178-10
TF: 800-633-3453 ■ Web: www.fdbhealth.com

FDC (Federal Detention Ctr)
Honolulu 351 Elliot St Honolulu HI 96820 808-838-4200 212
Web: www.bop.gov

FDC Graphics Films Inc
3820 William Richardson Dr South Bend IN 46628 574-273-4400 514
TF: 800-634-7523 ■ Web: www.fdcfilms.com

FDF Energy Services 240 Jasmine Rd Crowley LA 70526 337-783-8685 146
TF: 800-252-3104 ■ Web: fdfenergy.com

FDH Infrastructure Services
6521 Meridien Dr Raleigh NC 27616 919-755-1012 755-1031 261
Web: www.fdhvelocitel.com

FDI Group 39500 High Pointe Blvd Ste 400 Novi MI 48375 800-828-0759 390
TF: 800-828-0759 ■ Web: fdigroup.com

FDI Planning Consultants Inc
505 N Brand Blvd Ste 815 Glendale CA 91203 855-334-7526 311
TF: 855-334-7526 ■ Web: www.fdiplan.com

FDLI (Food & Drug Law Institute)
1155 15th St NW Ste 910 Washington DC 20005 202-371-1420 371-0649 49-10
TF: 800-956-6293 ■ Web: www.fdli.org

FDM (Fred Del Marva) 21666 N 58th Ave Glendale AZ 85308 623-566-5300 566-5354 196
Web: www.freddelmarva.com

FDM Software
113 949 W 3 St Ste 113 North Vancouver BC V7P3P7 604-986-9941 179
Web: www.fdmsoft.com

FDR & CP Services LLC PO Box 3930 Bryan TX 77805 979-778-0333 778-4444 196
TF: 800-337-5325 ■ Web: fdrservices.com

FDR Services Corporation of New Jersey Inc
44 Newmans Ct Hempstead NY 11550 516-483-6111 442
Web: fdrcorp.com

FDRA (Footwear Distributors & Retailers of America)
1319 F St NW Ste 700 Washington DC 20004 202-737-5660 645-0789 49-4
Web: www.fdra.org

FDS (FloraDec Sales Inc)
373 N Nimitz Hwy Honolulu HI 96817 808-537-6194 528-1854 293
Web: www.floradec.com

FDSI Logistics Inc
27680 Avenue Mentry 2nd Fl Valencia CA 91355 818-971-3300 314
TF: 800-444-3374 ■ Web: www.fdsi.com

FDUSA (Fukuda Denshi USA Inc)
17725 NE 65th St Redmond WA 98052 425-881-7737 869-2018 476
TF: 800-365-6668 ■ Web: www.fukuda.com

FE Moran 2265 Carlson Dr Northbrook IL 60062 847-498-4800 498-9091 189-10
Web: www.femoran.com

FE Moran Security Solutions
201 W University Ave Champaign IL 61820 217-403-6444 693
Web: www.femoransecurity.com

FEA Industries Inc 1 N Morton Ave Morton PA 19070 800-327-2002 955-7770 542
TF: 800-327-2002 ■ Web: www.feaind.com

Fearing's 2121 McKinney Ave Dallas TX 75201 214-922-4848 671
Web: fearingsrestaurant.com

Fearless Books (FB) PO Box 4199 Napa CA 94558 707-266-1322 637-2
Web: www.fearlessbooks.com

Fearless Records
11783 Cardinal Cir Garden Grove CA 92843 714-638-7090 317
Web: www.fearlessrecords.com

Fearrington House
2000 Fearrington Village Ctr Pittsboro NC 27312 919-542-2121 379
TF: 800-277-0130 ■ Web: www.fearrington.com

Feast 3719 E Speedway Tucson AZ 85712 520-326-9363 326-9245 671
Web: www.eatatfeast.com

Feather Publishing Company Inc
287 Lawrence St Quincy CA 95971 530-283-0800 283-3952 637-8
Web: www.plumasnews.com

Feather River College
570 Golden Eagle Ave Quincy CA 95971 530-283-0202 283-9961 162
TF: 800-442-9799 ■ Web: www.frc.edu

Featherlite Building Products Corp
508 McNeil St PO Box 425 Round Rock TX 78681 512-255-2573 255-2572 183
TF: 800-792-1234 ■ Web: featherlitetexas.com

Featherlite Trailers
Hwy 63 & 9 PO Box 320 Cresco IA 52136 563-547-6000 547-6100 779
TF: 800-800-1230 ■ Web: fthr.com

Featherstonhaugh, Wiley & Clyne LLP
111 Washington Ave Ste 501 Albany NY 12210 518-436-0786 427-0452 41
Web: fwc-law.com

Fechheimer Bros Company Inc
4545 Malsbary Rd Cincinnati OH 45242 513-793-5400 793-7819 155-19
TF: 800-543-1939 ■ Web: www.fechheimer.com

Fedchoice Federal Credit Union
10001 Willowdale Rd Lanham MD 20706 301-699-6100 219
TF: 800-969-6151 ■ Web: www.fedchoice.org

Fedco Manufacturing Inc 11585 Rt 993 Larimer PA 15647 724-863-2252 567
Web: www.fedcomfg.com

Fedco Steel Corp 785 Harrison Ave Harrison NJ 07029 973-481-1424 492
Web: www.fedcosteel.com

Fedder & Janofsky LLC
2650 Quarry Lake Dr Ste 100 Baltimore MD 21209 410-415-0080 41
Web: mdcounsel.com

Fedele & Murray PC 17 Walpole St Norwood MA 02062 781-551-5900 41
Web: fedeleandmurray.com

Federal Acctg Standards Advisory Board
441 G St NW Ste 1155 Washington DC 20548 202-512-7350 512-7366 340-20
Web: www.fasab.gov

Federal Assembly Inc 115 S Hall St Princeton IN 47670 812-386-7062 386
Web: www.federalassembly.com

Federal Aviation Administration
FAA Academy
Bldg 12 Rm 129 PO Box 25082 Oklahoma City OK 73125 405-954-6900 954-3018 340-17
Web: www.faa.gov
Great Lakes Region
2300 E Devon Ave Des Plaines IL 60018 847-294-7272 294-7036 340-17
Web: www.faa.gov
Mike Monroney Aeronautical Ctr
6500 S MacArthur Blvd Oklahoma City OK 73125 405-954-4821 340-17
Web: www.faa.gov
William J Hughes Technical Ctr
Atlantic City International Airport
Bldg 300 Fourth Fl G34 Atlantic City NJ 08405 609-485-6675 485-4667 340-17
Web: www.faa.gov

Federal Aviation Administration Northwest Mountain Region
1601 Lind Ave SW Renton WA 98057 425-227-2001 340-17
TF: 800-220-5715 ■ Web: www.faa.gov

Federal Aviation Administration Regional Offices (FAA)
Alaskan Region
222 W Seventh Ave Ste 14 Anchorage AK 99513 907-271-5438 271-2851 340-17
Web: www.faa.gov
Central Region
901 Locust St Federal Bldg Kansas City MO 64106 816-329-3050 340-17
Web: www.faa.gov
Eastern Region 159-30 Rockaway Blvd Jamaica NY 11434 718-553-3001 340-17
Web: www.faa.gov
New England Region
12 New England Executive Pk Burlington MA 01803 781-238-7020 238-7608 340-17
Web: www.faa.gov
Western Pacific Region
15000 Aviation Blvd Lawndale CA 90261 310-725-7800 340-17
Web: www.faa.gov

Federal Aviation Administration Southern Region
1701 Columbia Ave College Park GA 30337 404-305-5250 340-17
Web: www.faa.gov

Phone | Fax | Class

Federal Bar Council
123 Main St Ste 505 New York NY 10038 646-736-6163 571-0604 138
Web: www.federalbarcouncil.org
Federal Block Corp 247 Walsh Ave New Windsor NY 12553 845-561-4108 561-5344 183
TF: 800-724-1999 ■ *Web:* www.montfortgroup.com
Federal Bureau of Investigation (FBI)
935 Pennsylvania Ave NW Washington DC 20535 202-324-3000 340-14
Web: www.fbi.gov
Federal Bureau of Investigation
Criminal Justice Information Services
1000 Custer Hollow Rd Clarksburg WV 26306 304-625-4995 340-14
Web: www.fbi.gov
FBI Laboratory 1970 E Parham Rd Richmond VA 23228 804-261-1044 340-14
Web: www.fbi.gov
Federal Bureau of Prisons
Management & Specialty Training Ctr
791 Chambers Rd Aurora CO 80011 303-340-7800 340-14
Web: www.bop.gov
Mid-Atlantic Region
302 Sentinel Dr Ste 200 Annapolis Junction MD 20701 301-317-3100 317-3119 340-14
Web: www.bop.gov
National Institute of Corrections
320 First St NW Washington DC 20534 202-307-3106 340-14
Web: nicic.gov
National Institute of Corrections Information Ctr
11900 E Cornell Ave Unit C Aurora CO 80014 800-877-1461 340-14
TF: 800-877-1461 ■ *Web:* nicic.gov
Phoenix 37900 N 45th Ave Phoenix AZ 85086 623-465-9757 465-5199 212
Web: www.bop.gov
Federal Bureau of Prisons Regional Offices
North Central Region
400 State Ave Ste 800 Kansas City KS 66101 913-551-1061 551-1175 340-14
Web: www.bop.gov
Northeast Region
200 Chestnut St 7th Fl Philadelphia PA 19106 215-521-7301 340-14
Web: www.bop.gov
South Central Region
4211 Cedar Springs Rd Dallas TX 75219 214-224-3389 340-14
Web: www.bop.gov
Southeast Region
3800 Camp Creek Pk SW Bldg 2000 Atlanta GA 30331 678-686-1200 340-14
Web: www.bop.gov
Federal Cartridge Co 900 Ehlen Dr Anoka MN 55303 800-379-1732 323-2506* 284
**Fax Area Code:* 763 ■ *TF:* 800-379-1732 ■ *Web:* www.federalpremium.com
Federal Communications Commission (FCC)
445 12th St SW Washington DC 20554 888-225-5322 418-0232* 340-20
**Fax Area Code:* 202 ■ *TF:* 888-225-5322 ■ *Web:* www.fcc.gov
Federal Computer Week Magazine
3141 Fairview Pk Dr Ste 777 Falls Church VA 22042 703-876-5100 457-7
TF: 877-534-2208 ■ *Web:* www.fcw.com
Federal Correctional Complex
Beaumont 5830 Knauth Rd Beaumont TX 77705 409-727-0101 720-5000 212
Web: www.bop.gov
Coleman 846 NE 54th Terr Coleman FL 33521 352-689-5000 689-5027 212
Web: www.bop.gov
Federal Correctional Institution (FCI)
Bastrop 1341 Hwy 95 N PO Box 730 Bastrop TX 78602 512-321-3903 304-0117 212
TF: 800-995-6429 ■ *Web:* www.bop.gov
Big Spring 1900 Simler Ave Big Spring TX 79720 432-466-2300 466-2576 212
Web: www.bop.gov
Butner Old NC Hwy 75 PO Box 1000 Butner NC 27509 919-575-4541 575-5023 212
Web: www.bop.gov
Cumberland 14601 Burbridge Rd SE Cumberland MD 21502 301-784-1000 784-1008 212
Web: www.bop.gov
Edgefield
501 Gary Hill Rd PO Box 723 Edgefield SC 29824 803-637-1500 637-9840 212
Web: www.bop.gov
El Reno 4205 Hwy 66 W El Reno OK 73036 405-262-4875 319-7626 212
Web: www.bop.gov
Englewood 9595 W Quincy Ave Littleton CO 80123 303-763-4300 763-2553 212
Web: www.bop.gov
Fairton
655 Fairton-Millville Rd PO Box 280 Fairton NJ 08320 856-453-1177 453-4015 212
Web: www.bop.gov
Florence 5880 State Hwy 67 S Florence CO 81226 703-740-4001 212
Web: www.usmarshals.gov
Forrest City
1400 Dale Bumpers Rd Forrest City AR 72335 870-630-6000 494-4496 212
TF: 877-623-8426 ■ *Web:* www.bop.gov
Jesup 2600 Hwy 301 S Jesup GA 31599 912-427-0870 427-1125 212
Web: www.bop.gov
Loretto 772 St Joseph St Loretto PA 15940 814-472-4140 472-6046 212
Web: www.bop.gov
Manchester 805 Fox Hollow Rd Manchester KY 40962 606-598-1900 599-4115 212
Web: www.bop.gov
McKean FCI 6975 Rt 59 Lewis Run PA 16738 814-362-8900 363-6821 212
Web: www.bop.gov
Milan 4004 Arkona Rd Milan MI 48160 734-439-1511 439-0949 212
Web: www.bop.gov
Morgantown 446 Greenbag Rd Morgantown WV 26501 304-296-4416 284-3613 212
Web: www.bop.gov
Oxford PO Box 500 Oxford WI 53952 608-584-5511 584-6371 212
Web: www.bop.gov
Pekin 2600 S Second St Pekin IL 61554 309-346-8588 477-4685 212
Web: www.bop.gov
Ray Brook
128 Ray Brook Rd PO Box 300 Ray Brook NY 12977 518-897-4000 897-4216 212
Web: www.bop.gov
Safford 1529 W Hwy 366 Safford AZ 85546 928-428-6600 348-1331 212
Web: www.bop.gov
Talladega 565 E Renfroe Rd Talladega AL 35160 256-315-4100 315-4495 212
Web: www.bop.gov
Tallahassee 501 Capital Cir NE Tallahassee FL 32301 850-878-2173 671-6105 212
TF: 888-966-8655 ■ *Web:* www.bop.gov
Terminal Island 1299 Seaside Ave San Pedro CA 90731 310-831-8961 732-5335 212
Web: www.bop.gov
Yazoo City
2225 Haley Barbour Pkwy PO Box 5050 Yazoo City MS 39194 662-751-4800 751-4958 212
Web: www.bop.gov

Federal Deposit Insurance Corp
550 17th St NW Washington DC 20429 877-275-3342 340-20
TF: 877-275-3342 ■ *Web:* www.fdic.gov
Federal Deposit Insurance Corporation Regional Offices
Atlanta Regional Office
10 Tenth St NW Ste 800 Atlanta GA 30309 678-916-2200 340-20
TF: 800-765-3342 ■ *Web:* www.fdic.gov
Boston Area Office
15 Braintree Hill Office Pk Ste 300 Braintree MA 02184 781-794-5500 340-20
TF: 866-728-9953 ■ *Web:* www.fdic.gov
Chicago Area Office
300 S Riverside Plz Ste 1700 Chicago IL 60606 312-382-6000 340-20
TF: 800-944-5343 ■ *Web:* www.fdic.gov
Dallas Area Office 1601 Bryan St Dallas TX 75201 214-754-0098 340-20
TF: 800-568-9161 ■ *Web:* www.fdic.gov
Kansas City Area Office
2345 Grand Blvd Ste 1200 Kansas City MO 64108 816-234-8000 340-20
TF: 800-209-7459 ■ *Web:* www.fdic.gov
Memphis Area Office
5100 Poplar Ave Ste 1900 Memphis TN 38137 901-685-1603 340-20
TF: 800-210-6354 ■ *Web:* www.fdic.gov
New York Area Office
350 Fifth Ave Ste 1200 New York NY 10118 917-320-2500 340-20
TF: 800-334-9593 ■ *Web:* www.fdic.gov
San Francisco Area Office
25 Jessie St at Ecker Sq Ste 2300 San Francisco CA 94105 415-546-0160 340-20
TF: 800-756-3558 ■ *Web:* www.fdic.gov
Federal Detention Ctr (FDC)
Honolulu 351 Elliot St Honolulu HI 96820 808-838-4200 212
Web: www.bop.gov
Oakdale PO Box 5060 Oakdale LA 71463 318-335-4466 215-2046 212
Web: www.bop.gov
Philadelphia PO Box 572 Philadelphia PA 19106 215-521-4000 521-7220 212
Web: www.bop.gov
SeaTac 2425 S 200th St Seattle WA 98198 206-870-5700 870-5717 212
Web: www.bop.gov
Federal Direct
150 Clove Rd 5th Fl Little Falls NJ 07424 973-667-9800 110
TF: 800-927-5123 ■ *Web:* www.feddirect.com
Federal Direct Tax Services
11905 Pendleton Pk Indianapolis IN 46236 866-357-2052 734
TF: 866-357-2052 ■ *Web:* federaldirecttax.com
Federal Education Assn
1201 16th St NW Ste 117 Washington DC 20036 202-822-7850 414
Web: www.feaonline.org
Federal Election Commission
999 E St NW Washington DC 20463 202-694-1100 265
TF: 800-424-9530 ■ *Web:* www.fec.gov
Federal Electronics Inc
75 Stamp Farm Rd Cranston RI 02921 401-944-6200 625
Web: federalelec.com
Federal Emergency Management Agency
National Flood Insurance Program
500 C St SW Washington DC 20472 800-427-4661 340-11
TF: 800-427-4661 ■ *Web:* www.floodsmart.gov
U.S. Fire Administration
16825 S Seton Ave Emmitsburg MD 21727 301-447-1000 340-11
TF: 888-382-3827 ■ *Web:* www.usfa.fema.gov
Region 3
1 Independence Mall 615 Chestnut St
Sixth Fl Philadelphia PA 19106 215-931-5500 931-5621 340-11
Web: www.fema.gov
Federal Emergency Management Agency Regional Office (FEMA)
Region 1 99 High St Boston MA 02110 877-336-2734 340-11
TF: 877-336-2734 ■ *Web:* www.fema.gov
Region 4 3003 Chamblee-Tucker Rd Atlanta GA 30341 770-220-5200 220-5230 340-11
Web: www.fema.gov
Region 5 536 S Clark St 6th Fl Chicago IL 60605 312-408-5500 340-11
TF: 877-336-2627 ■ *Web:* www.fema.gov
Region 2 1 World Trade Ctr New York NY 10007 212-680-3600 340-11
Web: www.fema.gov
Region 6 800 N Loop 288 Denton TX 76209 940-898-5399 898-5325 340-11
TF: 800-426-5460 ■ *Web:* www.fema.gov
Region 7 11224 Holmes Rd Kansas City MO 64114 816-283-7061 340-11
Web: www.fema.gov
Region 8
Denver Federal Ctr Bldg 710 PO Box 25267 Denver CO 80225 303-235-4800 235-4976 340-11
Web: www.fema.gov
Region 9 1111 Broadway Ste 1200 Oakland CA 94607 510-627-7100 340-11
Web: www.fema.gov
Region 10
Federal Regional Ctr 130 228th St SW Bothell WA 98021 425-487-4600 340-11
Web: www.fema.gov
Federal Energy Regulatory Commission
888 First St NE Washington DC 20426 202-502-8200 208-2106 340-9
TF: 866-208-3372 ■ *Web:* ferc.gov
Federal Energy Regulatory Commission Regional Offices
Chicago 230 S Dearborn St Rm 3130 Chicago IL 60604 312-596-4437 340-9
Web: ferc.gov
New York 19 W 34th St Ste 400 New York NY 10001 844-434-0053 631-8124* 340-9
**Fax Area Code:* 212 ■ *TF:* 844-434-0053 ■ *Web:* ferc.gov
Portland
805 SW Broadway Fox Tower Ste 550 Portland OR 97205 503-552-2715 552-2799 340-9
Web: ferc.gov
San Francisco
100 First St Ste 2300 San Francisco CA 94105 415-369-3300 369-3322 340-9
Web: www.ferc.gov
Federal Envelope Co
608 Country Club Dr Bensenville IL 60106 630-595-2000 263
Web: www.federalenvelope.com
Federal Equipment Co 5298 River Rd Cincinnati OH 45233 513-621-5260 621-0524 172
TF: 877-435-4723 ■ *Web:* www.federalequipment.com
Federal Farm Credit Banks Funding Corp
10 Exchange Pl Ste 1401 Jersey City NJ 07302 201-200-8131 200-8109 402
Web: www.farmcreditfunding.com
Federal Financing Bank (FFB)
US Department of the Treasury 1500 Pennsylvania Ave NW
Washington DC 20220 202-622-2470 340-20
Web: ffb.treasury.gov

Phone | Fax | Class

Federal Flange 4014 Pinemont St. Houston TX 77018 713-681-0606 681-3005 483
TF: 800-231-0150 ■ *Web:* www.federalflange.com

Federal Foam Technologies Inc
600 Wisconsin Dr. New Richmond WI 54017 715-246-9500 246-9599 601
TF: 800-898-9559 ■ *Web:* www.federalfoam.com

Federal Gateway 400 7th St SW. Washington DC 20590 202-366-0660 340-17
Web: www.fedgate.org

Federal Hall National Memorial
26 Wall St. New York NY 10005 212-825-6990 668-2899 564
Web: www.nps.gov

Federal Hearings & Appeals Services Inc
117 W Main St. Plymouth PA 18651 570-779-5122 533
TF: 800-664-7177 ■ *Web:* fhas.com

Federal Heath Sign Co 4602 N Ave. Oceanside CA 92056 760-941-0715 941-0719 701
Web: www.federalheath.com

Federal Highway Administration
National Highway Institute
4600 Fairfax Dr Ste 800. Arlington VA 22203 703-235-0500 235-0593 340-17
TF: 877-558-6873 ■ *Web:* www.nhi.fhwa.dot.gov

Federal Home Loan Bank of Indianapolis
8250 Woodfield Crossing Blvd. Indianapolis IN 46240 317-465-0200 434-3
Web: www.fhlbi.com

Federal House Bar & Grille
22 Market Spc. Annapolis MD 21401 410-268-2576 280-0195 671
Web: federalhouse.com

Federal Housing Finance Board
400 Seventh St SW. Washington DC 20024 202-649-3800 649-1071 340-20
Web: www.fhfa.gov

Federal Industries Div Standex Corp
215 Federal Ave. Belleville WI 53508 800-356-4206 424-3234* 664
*Fax Area Code: 608 ■ *TF:* 800-356-4206 ■ *Web:* www.federalind.com

Federal International Inc
7935 Clayton Rd. Saint Louis MO 63117 314-721-3377 660
Web: www.federalinternational.com

Federal Judicial Ctr
1 Columbus Cir NE. Washington DC 20002 202-502-4000 341
Web: www.fjc.gov

Federal Labor Relations Authority Regional Offices
Atlanta Region 225 Peachtree St NE. Atlanta GA 30303 404-331-5300 331-5280 340-20
Web: www.flra.gov
Boston Region
10 Causeway St
Thomas P O'Neill Jr Federal Bldg Ste 472. Boston MA 02222 617-565-5100 565-6262 340-20
Web: www.flra.gov
Chicago Region
224 S Michigan Ave Ste 445. Chicago IL 60604 312-886-3465 886-5977 340-20
Web: www.flra.gov
Dallas Region
525 S Griffin St Ste 926 LB-107. Dallas TX 75202 214-767-6266 767-0156 340-20
Web: www.flra.gov
Denver Region 1391 Speer Blvd Ste 300. Denver CO 80204 303-844-5224 844-2774 340-20
Web: www.flra.gov
San Francisco Region
901 Market St Ste 470. San Francisco CA 94103 415-356-5000 356-5017 340-20
Web: www.flra.gov
Washington (DC) Region
1400 K St NW 2nd Fl. Washington DC 20424 202-357-6029 482-6724 340-20
Web: www.flra.gov

Federal Laboratory Consortium for Technology Transfer
950 Kings Hwy N Ste 208. Cherry Hill NJ 08034 856-667-7727 667-8009 340-20
Web: www.federallabs.org

Federal Law Enforcement Officers Assn (FLEOA)
1100 Connecticut Ave NW Ste 900. Washington DC 20036 202-293-1550 49-7
Web: www.fleoa.org

Federal Law Enforcement Training Ctr
1131 Chapel Crossing Rd. Glynco GA 31524 912-267-2100 340-11
TF: 800-743-5382 ■ *Web:* www.fletc.gov

Federal Life Insurance Co
3750 W Deerfield Rd. Riverwoods IL 60015 847-520-1900 391-2
TF: 800-233-3750 ■ *Web:* www.federallife.com

Federal Management Systems Inc
462 K St NW. Washington DC 20001 202-842-3003 829-4470 2
Web: www.fmshq.com

Federal Managers Assn (FMA)
1641 Prince St. Alexandria VA 22314 703-683-8700 683-8707 49-7
Web: www.fedmanagers.org

Federal Maritime Commission
800 N Capitol St NW. Washington DC 20573 202-523-5725 523-0014 340-20
Web: www.fmc.gov

Federal Maritime Commission Regional Offices
New Orleans Area 1515 Poydras St. New Orleans LA 70112 504-589-6662 340-20
Web: www.fmc.gov
South Florida Area PO Box 813609. Hollywood FL 33081 954-963-5362 340-20
Web: www.fmc.gov

Federal Materials Concrete
2425 Wayne Sullivan Dr. Paducah KY 42003 270-442-5496 443-6484 182
Web: www.fmc1.com

Federal Mediation & Conciliation Service
1300 Godward St Ste 3950. Minneapolis MN 55413 612-331-6006 340-20
Web: www.fmcs.gov

Federal Mediation & Conciliation Service
2100 K St NW. Washington DC 20427 202-606-8100 606-4251 340-20
Web: www.fmcs.gov

Federal Mediation & Conciliation Service Regional Offices
Eastern Region
6161 Oak Tree Blvd Ste 120. Independence OH 44131 216-520-4800 340-20
Web: www.fmcs.gov

Federal Medical Ctr
Butner Old N Carolina Hwy 75. Butner NC 27509 919-575-3900 575-4801 212
Web: www.bop.gov
Lexington 3301 Leestown Rd. Lexington KY 40511 859-255-6812 253-8821 212
Web: www.bop.gov

Federal Mine Safety & Health Review Commission
1331 Pennsylvania Ave NW Ste 520N. Washington DC 20004 202-434-9900 434-9944 340-20
Web: www.fmshrc.gov

Federal Motor Carrier Safety Administration (FMCSA)
1200 New Jersey Ave SE. Washington DC 20590 800-832-5660 340-17
TF: 800-832-5660 ■ *Web:* www.fmcsa.dot.gov

Phone | Fax | Class

Federal Network Inc (FEDNET)
122 C St NW Ste 520. Washington DC 20001 202-393-7300 530
Web: www.fednet.net

Federal Plastics Manufacturing Ltd
Fedplast 5100 Fisher St. Montreal QC H4T1J5 514-342-5411 342-3744 601
Web: www.fedplast.com

Federal Prison Camp
Duluth 6902 Airport Rd PO Box 1400. Duluth MN 55814 218-722-8634 733-4701 212
Web: www.bop.gov
Montgomery Maxwell AFB. Montgomery AL 36112 334-293-2100 293-2326 212
Web: www.bop.gov

Federal Prison Industries Inc
320 First St NW. Washington DC 20534 800-827-3168 630
TF: 800-827-3168 ■ *Web:* www.unicor.gov

Federal Protection Inc
2500 N Airport Commerce Ave. Springfield MO 65803 800-299-5400 693
TF: 800-299-5400 ■ *Web:* www.federalprotection.com

Federal Railroad Administration Regional Offices (FRA)
Region 1 55 Broadway Rm 1077. Cambridge MA 02142 617-494-2302 494-2967 340-17
TF: 800-724-5991 ■ *Web:* railroads.dot.gov
Region 3 61 Forsyth St SW Ste 16T20. Atlanta GA 30303 404-562-3800 562-3830 340-17
TF: 800-724-5993 ■ *Web:* railroads.dot.gov
Region 4 200 W Adams St. Chicago IL 60606 312-353-6203 886-9634 340-17
TF: 800-724-5040 ■ *Web:* railroads.dot.gov
Region 5
4100 International Plz Ste 450. Fort Worth TX 76109 817-862-2200 862-2204 340-17
Web: railroads.dot.gov
Region 6 901 Locust St Ste 464. Kansas City MO 64106 816-329-3840 329-3867 340-17
TF: 800-724-5996 ■ *Web:* railroads.dot.gov
Region 7 801 'I' St Ste 466. Sacramento CA 95814 916-498-6540 498-6546 340-17
Web: railroads.dot.gov

Federal Realty Investment Trust
1626 E Jefferson St. Rockville MD 20852 301-998-8100 998-3700 655
NYSE: FRT ■ *TF:* 800-658-8980 ■ *Web:* www.federalrealty.com

Federal Reserve Bank of Atlanta
1000 Peachtree St NE. Atlanta GA 30309 404-498-8500 71
TF: 888-500-7390 ■ *Web:* www.frbatlanta.org

Federal Reserve Bank of Atlanta
Jacksonville Branch 800 Water St. Jacksonville FL 32204 904-632-1000 71
Web: www.federalreserve.gov

Federal Reserve Bank of Boston
600 Atlantic Ave. Boston MA 02210 617-973-3000 71
Web: www.bostonfed.org

Federal Reserve Bank of Chicago
Detroit Branch 1600 E Warren Ave. Detroit MI 48207 313-961-6880 71
Web: www.chicagofed.org

Federal Reserve Bank of Cleveland
1455 E Sixth St PO Box 6387. Cleveland OH 44101 216-579-2000 71
TF: 877-372-2457 ■ *Web:* clevelandfed.org

Federal Reserve Bank of Dallas
Houston Branch 1801 Allen Pkwy. Houston TX 77019 713-483-3000 71
Web: www.dallasfed.org

Federal Reserve Bank of Kansas City
1 Memorial Dr PO Box 1200. Kansas City MO 64198 816-881-2000 881-2704 71
TF: 800-333-1010 ■ *Web:* www.kansascityfed.org

Federal Reserve Bank of Minneapolis
90 Hennepin Ave. Minneapolis MN 55401 612-204-5000 204-5905 71
TF: 800-553-9656 ■ *Web:* minneapolisfed.org

Federal Reserve Bank of Minneapolis
Helena Branch 100 Neill Ave. Helena MT 59601 406-447-3800 71
Web: www.federalreserve.gov

Federal Reserve Bank of Philadelphia
10 Independence Mall. Philadelphia PA 19106 215-574-6000 71
TF: 866-574-3727 ■ *Web:* philadelphiafed.org

Federal Reserve Bank of Richmond
Baltimore Branch 502 S Sharp St. Baltimore MD 21201 410-576-3300 71
TF: 800-446-7045 ■ *Web:* www.richmondfed.org

Federal Reserve Bank of Saint Louis
Broadway & Locust St 1 Federal Reserve Bank Plz
Saint Louis MO 63102 314-444-8444 71
TF: 800-333-0810 ■ *Web:* www.stlouisfed.org

Federal Reserve Bank of Saint Louis
Louisville Branch
101 S Fifth St Ste 1920. Louisville KY 40202 502-568-9200 71
Web: frbservices.org

Federal Reserve Bank of San Francisco
Salt Lake City Branch
101 Market St. San Francisco CA 94105 415-974-3171 974-2168 71
TF: 800-227-4133 ■ *Web:* www.frbsf.org

Federal Reserve System
20th Street and Constitution Ave NW. Washington DC 20551 202-452-3000 212
Web: www.federalreserve.gov

Federal Retirement Thrift Investment Board
77 K St NE Ste 1000. Washington DC 20002 202-942-1600 340-20
TF: 866-817-5023 ■ *Web:* www.frtib.gov

Federal Screw Works 34846 Goddard Rd. Romulus MI 48174 734-941-4211 621
OTC: FSCR ■ *Web:* federalscrewworks.com

Federal Signal Corp
1415 W 22nd St Ste 1100. Oak Brook IL 60523 630-954-2000 954-2030 185
NYSE: FSS ■ *TF:* 855-533-0494 ■ *Web:* www.federalsignal.com

Federal Signal Corp
Emergency Products Div
2645 Federal Signal Dr. University Park IL 60466 708-534-3400 700
TF: 800-264-3578 ■ *Web:* www.fedsig.com

Federal Staffing Resources LLC
2200 Somerville Rd Ste 300. Annapolis MD 21401 410-990-0795 260
TF: 866-886-2300 ■ *Web:* www.fsrpeople.com

Federal Steel Supply Inc
747 Goddard Ave PO Box 840. Chesterfield MO 63005 636-537-2393 492
Web: fedsteel.com

Federal Street Press
25-13 Old Kings Hwy N Ste 277. Darien CT 06820 203-852-1280 852-1389 637-9
TF: 877-886-2830 ■ *Web:* www.federalstreetpress.com

Federal Technology Solutions Inc
1828 Railroad St. Corona CA 92880 951-808-9660 180
Web: www.federalsales.com

Name / Address	Phone	Fax	Class
Federal Trade Commission Regional Offices			
East Central Region 1111 Superior Ave Ste 200 ....Cleveland OH 44114 *Web:* www.ftc.gov	216-263-3455	263-3426	340-20
Midwest Region 55 W Monroe St Ste 1825.......Chicago IL 60603 *Web:* www.ftc.gov	202-326-2222		340-20
Northeast Region 1 Bowling Green ....New York NY 10004 *Web:* www.ftc.gov	212-607-2829	607-2822	340-20
Northwest Region 915 Second Ave Rm 2896 ....Seattle WA 98174 *Web:* www.ftc.gov	206-220-6350		340-20
Southwest Region 1999 Bryan St Ste 2150........ Dallas TX 75201 *Web:* www.ftc.gov	214-979-9350		340-20
Western Region 901 Market St Ste 570................San Francisco CA 94103 **Fax Area Code:* 310 ■ *TF:* 877-382-4357 ■ *Web:* www.ftc.gov	877-382-4357	824-4380*	340-20
Federal Transit Administration Regional Offices			
Region 1 55 Broadway Ste 920 ....Cambridge MA 02142 *Web:* www.transit.dot.gov	617-494-2055	494-2865	340-17
Region 2 1 Bowling Green Rm 429 ....New York NY 10004 *Web:* www.transit.dot.gov	212-668-2170	668-2136	340-17
Region 3 1760 Market St Ste 500 ....Philadelphia PA 19103 *Web:* www.transit.dot.gov	215-656-7100	656-7260	340-17
Region 6 819 Taylor St Rm 8A36.............Fort Worth TX 76102 *Web:* www.transit.dot.gov	817-978-0550	978-0575	340-17
Region 7 901 Locust St Ste 404 ....Kansas City MO 64106 *Web:* www.transit.dot.gov	816-329-3920	329-3921	340-17
Region 8 1961 Stout St Ste 13 301 ....Denver CO 80202 *Web:* www.transit.dot.gov	303-362-2400	362-2424	340-17
Region 9 201 Mission St Ste 1650 .... San Francisco CA 94105 *Web:* www.transit.dot.gov	415-744-3133	744-2726	340-17
Region 10 915 Second Ave Ste 3142 .... Seattle WA 98174 *Web:* www.transit.dot.gov	206-220-7954	220-7518	340-17
Federal Wage & Labor Institute 7001 W 43rd St ....Houston TX 77092 *TF:* 800-767-9243 ■ *Web:* www.fwlli.com	713-690-5676		752
Federal Warehouse Co 200 National Rd ....East Peoria IL 61611 *TF:* 800-747-4100 ■ *Web:* www.federalcos.com	309-694-4500		803-1
Federal White Cement Ltd PO Box 1609 ....Woodstock ON N4S0A8 *TF:* 800-265-1806 ■ *Web:* www.federalwhitecement.com	519-485-5410	485-5892	135
Federalist Society for Law & Public Policy Studies 1015 18th St NW Ste 425..................Washington DC 20036 *Web:* fedsoc.org	202-822-8138	296-8061	49-10
Federally Employed Women (FEW) 455 Massachusetts Ave NW Ste 306 ....Washington DC 20001 *Web:* www.few.org	202-898-0994		49-7
Federal-Mogul Corp 27300 W 11 Mile Rd....................... Southfield MI 48034 *TF:* 800-325-8886 ■ *Web:* www.federalmogul.com	248-354-7700		60
Federated Adjustment Company Inc 7929 N Port Washington Rd.................Milwaukee WI 53217 *Web:* www.facpaid.com	414-228-0900		160
Federated Co-opeartives Inc 502 S 2nd St Ste 2 ....Princeton MN 55371 *TF:* 800-638-8228 ■ *Web:* federatedcoops.com	763-389-2582		579
Federated Co-operatives Ltd 401 22nd St E PO Box 1050................. Saskatoon SK S7K0H2 *TF:* 800-848-6347 ■ *Web:* www.coopconnection.ca	306-244-3311	244-3403	275
Federated Group Inc 3025 W Salt Creek Ln.................Arlington Heights IL 60005 *Web:* www.fedgroup.com	847-577-1200	632-8302	345
Federated Insurance Cos 121 E Pk Sq.........Owatonna MN 55060 *TF:* 800-533-0472 ■ *Web:* federatedinsurance.com	507-455-5200		360-4
Federated Investors 1001 Liberty Ave Federated Investors Twr...... Pittsburgh PA 15222 *NYSE:* FII ■ *TF:* 800-245-0242 ■ *Web:* www.federatedinvestors.com	412-288-1000		401
Federated Media 245 Edison Rd Ste 250.....................Mishawaka IN 46545 *TF:* 888-333-6133 ■ *Web:* www.federatedmedia.com	888-333-6133		645-11
Federated Rural Electric Assn 77100 US Hwy 71 PO Box 69..................Jackson MN 56143 *TF:* 800-321-3520 ■ *Web:* www.federatedrea.coop	507-847-3520	728-8366	245
Federation for American Immigration Reform (FAIR) 25 Massachusetts Ave NW Ste 330 ....Washington DC 20001 *TF:* 877-627-3247 ■ *Web:* www.fairus.org	202-328-7004	387-3447	48-7
Federation Forest State Park 49201 SE Enumclaw Chinook Pass Rd......... Enumclaw WA 98022 *Web:* www.parks.wa.gov	360-663-2207		565
Federation of American Hospitals 750 Ninth St NW Ste 600..................Washington DC 20001 *Web:* fah.org	202-624-1500		49-8
Federation of American Scientists (FAS) 1725 DeSales St NW Ste 600...............Washington DC 20036 *Web:* fas.org	202-546-3300		49-19
Federation of American Societies for Experimental Biology (FASEB) 9650 Rockville Pk..........................Bethesda MD 20814 *TF:* 800-433-2732 ■ *Web:* www.faseb.org	301-634-7000	634-7001	49-19
Federation of Quebec Chambers of Commerce 555 Boul Rene-Levesque W Ste 1100........... Montreal QC H2Z1B1 *TF:* 800-361-5019 ■ *Web:* www.fccq.ca	514-844-9571	844-0226	137
Federation of State Medical Boards of the US Inc (FSMB) 400 Fuller Wiser Rd Ste 300................... Euless TX 76039 *TF:* 800-793-7939 ■ *Web:* www.fsmb.org	817-868-4000	868-4098	49-8
Federation of Tax Administrators (FTA) 444 N Capitol St NW Ste 348.................Washington DC 20001 *TF:* 800-829-9188 ■ *Web:* www.taxadmin.org	202-624-5890	624-7888	49-7
Federico Beauty Institute 1515 Sports Dr...........................Sacramento CA 95834 *Web:* www.federico.edu	916-929-4242		167-3
Federico College of Fresno 5660 N Blackstone Ave.........................Fresno CA 93710 *Web:* www.gofederico.com	559-540-7188		167-3
Federico Consulting Inc 333 W Shaw Ave Ste 104 ....Fresno CA 93704 *Web:* www.federico.net	559-224-5922		225
FedEx Corp 3610 Hacks Cross Rd ....Memphis TN 38125 *NYSE:* FDX ■ *TF:* 800-463-3339 ■ *Web:* www.fedex.com	901-818-7500		360-3
FedEx Field 1600 FedEx Way..............Landover Hills MD 20785 *Web:* www.redskins.com	301-276-6000	276-6001	720
Fedmet Resources Corp PO Box 278 .... Montreal QC H3Z2T2 *TF:* 800-609-5711 ■ *Web:* www.fedmet.com	514-931-5711	931-8378	663
Fednav Ltd 1000 Rue de la GauchetiFre O Bureau 3500...... Montreal QC H3B4W5 *TF:* 800-678-4842 ■ *Web:* www.fednav.com	514-878-6500	878-6642	313
FEDNET (Federal Network Inc) 122 C St NW Ste 520.....................Washington DC 20001 *Web:* www.fednet.net	202-393-7300		530
Fedstar Federal Credit Union 5005 Melrose Ave NW ....Roanoke VA 24017 *Web:* fedstar.org	540-986-0652		219
Fedtech Inc 4763 Mustang Cir ....Mounds View MN 55112 *Web:* www.fedtech.com	763-784-4600		454
FedTek Inc 12700 Black Forest Ln Ste 202..............Woodbridge VA 22192 *Web:* www.fedtek.com	703-551-4718		180
Fedtrust Federal Credit Union 167 N Main St Ste 102 ....Memphis TN 38103 *TF:* 877-523-3110 ■ *Web:* fedtrustfcu.com	901-526-6771	526-8667	219
Feduke Ford 2200 Vestal Pkwy E..................Vestal NY 13850 *Web:* www.fedukeford.com	607-754-5533		57
Fedway Associates Inc 505 Westgate Dr.......................Basking Ridge NJ 07920 *Web:* www.fedway.com	973-624-6444		81-3
FEE (Foundation for Economic Education) 1819 Peachtree Rd NE Ste 300..................Atlanta GA 30309 *TF:* 800-960-4333 ■ *Web:* fee.org	404-554-9980	393-3142	634
Fee Bros Inc 453 Portland Ave ....Rochester NY 14605 *Web:* www.feebrothers.com	585-544-9530		296-40
Fee Smith Sharp & Vitullo L L P 3 Galleria Tower 13155 Noel Rd Ste 1000 .... Dallas TX 75240 *Web:* www.feesmith.com	972-934-9100		445
Feeco International Inc 3913 Algoma Rd.......................... Green Bay WI 54311 **Fax Area Code:* 920 ■ *TF:* 800-373-9347 ■ *Web:* www.feeco.com	800-373-9347	469-5110*	207
Feed Products North Inc 1300 Mcknight Rd N...................... Maplewood MN 55119 **Fax Area Code:* 651 ■ *TF:* 800-625-6079 ■ *Web:* originationo2d.com	800-625-6079	777-8939*	582
Feed the Children (FTC) PO Box 36 ....Oklahoma City OK 73101 *TF:* 800-627-4556 ■ *Web:* www.feedthechildren.org	405-942-0228		48-5
Feeley Bonaventura & Hyzy CPAsPc 5695 Main St .... Williamsville NY 14221 *Web:* fbhcpa.com	716-632-0606	632-3544	2
Feenaughty Machinery Co 4800 NE Columbia Blvd......................Portland OR 97218 *Web:* www.feenaughty.com	503-282-2566	282-1755	358
Feesers Inc 5561 Grayson Rd ....Harrisburg PA 17111 *TF:* 800-326-2828 ■ *Web:* www.feesers.com	717-564-4636		297-8
Fegley Oil Company Inc 551 W Penn Pke....... Tamaqua PA 18252 *TF:* 800-572-4925 ■ *Web:* www.fegleyoil.com	570-386-4151	386-4179	579
Feheley Fine Arts 65 George St................ Toronto ON M5A4L8 *Web:* feheleyfinearts.com	416-323-1373		42
Fehr Bros Industries Inc 895 Kings Hwy.......................... Saugerties NY 12477 *Web:* www.endurancehardware.com	845-246-9525		492
Fehr-Graham & Associates LLC 221 E Main St Ste 200 ....Freeport IL 61032 *Web:* fehr-graham.com	815-235-7643		261
FEI (Financial Executives Intl) 1250 Headquarters Plz W Twr 7th Fl.......... Morristown NJ 07960 *Web:* financialexecutives.org	973-765-1000	765-1018	49-2
FEI Behavioral Health 648 N Plankinton Ave Ste 425 ....Milwaukee WI 53203 **Fax Area Code:* 414 ■ *TF:* 800-987-4368 ■ *Web:* www.feinet.com	800-987-4368	359-1973*	462
FEI Co 5350 NE Dawson Creek Dr............... Hillsboro OR 97124 *NASDAQ:* FEIC ■ *TF:* 866-693-3426 ■ *Web:* www.fei.com	503-726-7500	726-2570	419
FEI Zyfer Inc 7321 Lincoln Way.............Garden Grove CA 92841 *Web:* www.fei-zyfer.com	714-933-4000	933-4001	647
Feibleman & Case PC 1815 Commercial St SE .... Salem OR 97302 *Web:* feiblemancase.com	503-399-9218	589-0159	41
Feighner Insurance Inc 959 E 4th St.............Marion IN 46952 *Web:* insmgt.com	765-664-2333		390
Feiltd 37 Arnold'S Valley Rd.............Natural Bridge Station VA 24579	540-291-3398		480
Feinberg Consulting Inc 7125 Orchard Lake Rd .... West Bloomfield MI 48322 *TF:* 877-538-5425 ■ *Web:* feinbergconsulting.com	877-538-5425		363
Feinberg Real Estate Advisors LLC 1390 Ridgeview Dr Ste 301 ....Allentown PA 18104 *Web:* feinbergrea.com	610-360-9733	398-4057	652
Feiner & Lavy Pc 325 Broadway Ste 401 .... New York NY 10007 *Web:* drimmigration.com	212-571-9200		41
Feingold & Feingold Insurance Agency Inc 22 Elm St .... Worcester MA 01608 *Web:* www.feingoldco.com	508-831-9500		390
Feingold Association of the US 11849 Suncatcher Dr ....Fishers IN 46037 *TF:* 800-321-3287 ■ *Web:* feingold.org	631-369-9340		48-17
Feinstein Dianne (Sen D - CA) 331 Hart Senate Office Bldg ....Washington DC 20510 *Web:* www.feinstein.senate.gov	202-224-3841	228-3954	342-2
Feinstein Doyle Payne & Kravec LLC 429 Fourth Ave Ste 1300 .... Pittsburgh PA 15219 *TF:* 888-355-1735 ■ *Web:* fdpklaw.com	412-281-8400	281-1007	41
Feith Systems & Software Inc 425 Maryland Dr..................... Fort Washington PA 19034 *Web:* www.feith.com	215-646-8000		180
Feizy Import & Export Company Ltd 1949 Stemmons Fwy .... Dallas TX 75207 *TF:* 800-779-0877 ■ *Web:* www.feizy.com	214-747-6000	760-0521	290
Felbro Food Products Inc 5700 W Adams Blvd......................Los Angeles CA 90016 *Web:* felbro.com	323-936-5266		297-8
Felbro Inc 3666 E Olympic Blvd..............Los Angeles CA 90023 *Web:* www.felbrodisplays.com	323-263-8686	263-8874	233

Name	Address	City	State	ZIP	Phone	Fax	Class
Feld Entertainment Inc	8607 Westwood Center Dr TF: 800-844-3545 ■ Web: www.feldentertainment.com	Vienna	VA	22182	703-448-4000		149
Feld Law Firm PC, The	150 Broadway Ste 1703 Web: feldlawfirm.com	New York	NY	10038	212-964-4100	964-4295	41
Felder Communications Group	1593 Galbraith Ave SE Ste 200 Web: www.felder.com	Grand Rapids	MI	49546	616-459-1200		195
Feldesman Tucker Leifer Fidell LLP	1129 20th St NW Ste 400 Web: www.feldesmantucker.com	Washington	DC	20036	202-466-8960		428
Feldheim Publishers	208 Airport Executive Pk TF: 800-237-7149 ■ Web: www.feldheim.com	Nanuet	NY	10954	845-356-2282	425-1908	637-2
Feldman Bros Electrical Supply Co	26 Maryland Ave Web: www.feldmanbros.com	Paterson	NJ	07503	973-742-7329	742-2220	246
Feldman Financial Advisors Inc	1001 Connecticut Ave NW Ste 840 Web: www.feldmanfinancial.com	Washington	DC	20036	202-467-6862		734
Feldman, Kramer & Monaco PC	330 Vanderbilt Motor Pkwy TF: 800-292-8063 ■ Web: www.fkmlaw.com	Hauppauge	NY	11788	631-231-1450	231-4732	428
Feldmeier Equipment Inc	6800 Townline Rd TF: 800-258-0118 ■ Web: feldmeier.com	Syracuse	NY	13211	315-454-8608	454-3701	298
Felicia Oil Co	78 Commercial St	Gloucester	MA	01930	978-283-3808		316
Felician College	*Rutherford* 223 Montross Ave Web: www.felician.edu	Rutherford	NJ	07070	201-559-3559	559-3578	166
Felician Sisters CSSF	1600 W Oklahoma Ave	Milwaukee	WI	53215	414-645-5329		48-20
Felicita Resort	550 Lakewood Dr Web: www.felicitaresort.com	Harrisburg	PA	17112	717-599-5301		669
Felicity HC Fang CPA PA	3250 NE 1st Ave Ste 209 Web: ffangcpa.com	Miami	FL	33137	305-728-2484		2
Felidia	243 E 58th St Web: www.felidia-nyc.com	New York	NY	10022	212-758-1479		671
Felins USA Inc	8306 W Parkland Ct Web: www.felins.com	Milwaukee	WI	53223	414-355-7747		111
Felipe's	2241 N Woodlawn Web: www.felipeswichita.com	Wichita	KS	67220	316-652-0027		671
Felix Neck Wildlife Sanctuary	100 Felix Neck Dr TF: 866-627-2267 ■ Web: www.massaudubon.org	Edgartown	MA	02539	508-627-4850	627-6052	823
Felix Schoeller North America Inc	179 County Rt 2A Web: www.felix-schoeller.com	Pulaski	NY	13142	315-298-5133		552-1
Felix Storch Inc	770 Garrison Ave TF: 800-932-4267 ■ Web: www.summitappliance.com	Bronx	NY	10474	718-893-3900		38
Felix Valle House State Historic Site	198 Merchant St PO Box 89 Web: mostateparks.com	Sainte Genevieve	MO	63670	573-883-7102		565
Felker Bros Corp	22 N Chestnut Ave TF: 800-826-2304 ■ Web: www.felkerbrothers.com	Marshfield	WI	54449	715-384-3121	387-6837	490
Felle & Associates S C	7001 Washington Ave Web: rightcpa.com	Racine	WI	53406	262-886-9640		2
Fellheimer Law Firm	210 N Main St Web: fellheimerlawfirm.com	Pontiac	IL	61764	815-842-3858		41
Fellini's	3910 Colley Ave Web: www.fellinisva.com	Norfolk	VA	23508	757-625-3000		671
Fellowes Inc	1789 Norwood Ave TF: 800-945-4545 ■ Web: www.fellowes.com	Itasca	IL	60143	630-893-1600		111
Fellowship Community	3000 Fellowship Dr Web: www.fellowshipcommunity.com	Whitehall	PA	18052	610-799-3000		48-20
Fellowship Hall Inc	5140 Dunstan Rd TF: 800-659-3381 ■ Web: www.fellowshiphall.com	Greensboro	NC	27405	800-659-3381		726
Fellowship of Christian Athletes (FCA)	8701 Leeds Rd TF: 800-289-0909 ■ Web: www.fca.org	Kansas City	MO	64129	816-921-0909	921-8755	48-22
Fellowship Senior Living	8000 Fellowship Rd TF: 877-824-4909 ■ Web: fellowshipseniorliving.org	Basking Ridge	NJ	07920	877-343-6059		48-20
Felly's Flowers Inc	205 E Broadway TF: 800-993-7673 ■ Web: www.fellys.net	Madison	WI	53716	608-221-4200		292
Felsburg Holt & Ullevig Inc	6300 S Syracuse Way Ste 600 Web: www.fhueng.com	Centennial	CO	80111	303-721-1440		256
Feltl & Company Inc	2100 LaSalle Plz 800 LaSalle Ave Web: feltl.com	Minneapolis	MN	55402	612-492-8800		401
Felton Brush Inc	7 Burton Dr TF: 800-258-9702 ■ Web: www.feltoninc.com	Londonderry	NH	03053	603-425-0200		103
Felts Field Aviation Inc	6205 E Rutter Ave TF: 800-676-5538 ■ Web: www.feltsfield.com	Spokane	WA	99212	509-535-9011	535-9014	63
Felts Lock & Alarm Company Inc	4000 E Indiana St Web: www.feltsonline.com	Evansville	IN	47715	812-473-4000		692
FEM Electric Association Inc	PO Box 468 TF: 800-587-5880 ■ Web: www.femelectric.coop	Ipswich	SD	57451	605-426-6891	426-6791	245
FEMA (Farm Equipment Manufacturers Assn)	1000 Executive Pkwy Ste 100 Web: www.farmequip.org	Saint Louis	MO	63141	314-878-2304	732-1480	48-2
FEMA (Federal Emergency Management Agency Regional Office)	*Region 1* 99 High St TF: 877-336-2734 ■ Web: www.fema.gov	Boston	MA	02110	877-336-2734		340-11
Female Health Co	515 N State St Ste 2225 Web: fc2femalecondom.com	Chicago	IL	60654	312-595-9123		477
Femco Machine Co	754 S Main St Ext TF: 800-458-3445 ■ Web: www.femcomachine.com	Punxsutawney	PA	15767	814-938-9763	938-8332	454
Feminist Majority Foundation-East Coast (FMF)	1600 Wilson Blvd Ste 801 Web: www.feminist.org	Arlington	VA	22209	703-522-2214	522-2219	48-24
Feminist Press at the City University of New York	365 Fifth Ave Ste 5406 Web: www.feministpress.org	New York	NY	10016	212-817-7915		637-2
Femme Pharma Consumer Healthcare	175 Strafford Ave Bldg 4 Web: femmepharma.com	Wayne	PA	19087	610-995-0801		194
Femto Tech Inc	25 Eagle Ct Web: www.femto-tech.com	Carlisle	OH	45005	937-746-4427	746-9134	250
Fencecrete America Inc	15089 Tradesman Dr *Fax Area Code: 281 ■ TF: 800-229-7811 ■ Web: www.fencecrete.com	San Antonio	TX	78249	210-492-7911	438-1451*	183
Fender Musical Instruments Corp	17600 N Perimeter Dr Ste 100 TF: 800-488-1818 ■ Web: www.fender.com	Scottsdale	AZ	85255	480-596-9690	596-1384	527
Fendt Builders Supply Inc	22005 Gill Rd PO Box 418 Web: www.fendtproducts.com	Farmington Hills	MI	48335	248-474-3211		183
Fene-Tech Inc	264 St-Benoit E Blvd Web: www.fene-tech.com	Amqui	QC	G5L2C5	418-629-4675	629-3982	236
Fengate Capital Management Ltd	77 King St W Ste 4230 Web: fengate.com	Toronto	ON	M5K1H1	416-488-4184		528
Fenimore Manufacturing Inc	900 N 18th St Web: www.fenimoremfg.com	Chickasha	OK	73018	405-224-2637	224-2648	629
Fenix Constructors Inc	215 Drew St SW Web: www.fenixci.com	Ardmore	OK	73401	580-223-4313	223-4315	780
Fenix Insurance Inc	903 E St SE Web: fenixinsurance.com	Auburn	WA	98002	253-735-3355		390
Fennebresque & Company LLC	5960 Fairview Rd Ste 359 Web: fennebresque.com	Charlotte	NC	28202	704-295-8900		41
Fennell Spring LLC	295 Hemlock St Web: www.fennellspring.com	Horseheads	NY	14845	607-739-3541		719
Fennemore Craig PC	2394 E Camelback Rd Ste 600 Web: www.fclaw.com	Phoenix	AZ	85016	602-916-5000	916-5999	428
Fenner Drives	311 W Stiegel St TF: 800-243-3374 ■ Web: www.fennerdrives.com	Manheim	PA	17545	717-665-2421	664-8214	370
Fenster & Fenster	1514 S D St Web: fensterandfenster.com	San Bernardino	CA	92408	909-889-0288		2
Fenton	1010 Vermont Ave NW Ste 1100 Web: fenton.com	Washington	DC	20005	202-822-5200		514
Fenton Art Glass Co	700 Elizabeth St TF: 800-933-6766 ■ Web: www.fentonartglass.com	Williamstown	WV	26187	304-375-6122	375-6459	334
Fenton Lake State Park	455 Fenton Lk Web: www.stateparks.com	Jemez Springs	NM	87025	575-829-3630		565
Fenton Rigging & Contracting Inc	2150 Langdon Farm Rd Web: fenton1898.com	Cincinnati	OH	45237	513-631-5500		189-14
Fentress Bradburn Architects Ltd	421 Broadway Web: fentressarchitects.com	Denver	CO	80203	303-722-5000		261
Fentress County	114 Central Ave W PO Box 1294 Web: www.jamestowntn.org	Jamestown	TN	38556	931-879-9948	879-6767	338
Fentress Inc	945 Sunset Vly Dr TF: 888-329-0040 ■ Web: www.fentress.com	Sykesville	MD	21784	888-329-0040		196
Fenway Health	1340 Boylston St Web: fenwayhealth.org	Boston	MA	02215	617-267-0900	425-5713	743
Fenwick Inn	13801 Coastal Hwy Web: www.fenwickinn.com	Ocean City	MD	21842	410-250-1100	250-0087	379
Feral House	1240 W Sims Way Ste 124 Web: www.feralhouse.com	Port Townsend	WA	98368	323-666-3311	297-4331	637-2
Feralloy Corp	8755 W Higgins Rd Ste 970 TF: 844-450-6400 ■ Web: www.feralloy.com	Chicago	IL	60631	773-380-1500		492
Ferber Sheet Metal Works Inc	4121 Evergreen Ave Web: www.ferbersmw.com	Jacksonville	FL	32206	904-356-3042	354-3219	189-12
Ferche Millwork Inc	400 Division St TF: 800-328-7867 ■ Web: www.ferche.com	Rice	MN	56367	320-393-5700	393-5800	499
Fergus & Associates PA	200 SE 18th Ct Web: fergusandassociates.com	Fort Lauderdale	FL	33316	954-468-0008		41
Fergus County	712 W Main St Web: www.co.fergus.mt.us	Lewistown	MT	59457	406-535-5026	535-6076	338
Fergus Electric Co-opeartive Inc	84423 US Hwy 87 Web: www.ferguselectric.coop	Lewistown	MT	59457	406-538-3465	323-1602	245
Fergus Partnership Consulting Inc	1325 Avenue Of Americas Web: www.ferguslex.com	New York	NY	10019	212-767-1775		266
Ferguson & Redelsperger PC	1026 Main St	Duncan	OK	73533	580-255-2190		2
Ferguson A. Drew (Rep R - GA)	1032 Longworth House Office Bldg Web: ferguson.house.gov	Washington	DC	20515	202-225-5901		342-2
Ferguson Buick Gmc	1015 N I- Dr Web: www.fergusonchallenge.com	Norman	OK	73069	405-253-0918		57
Ferguson Construction Co	400 Canal St Web: ferguson-construction.com	Sidney	OH	45365	937-498-2381	498-2243	186
Ferguson Enterprises Inc	12500 Jefferson Ave TF: 800-721-2590 ■ Web: www.ferguson.com	Newport News	VA	23602	757-874-7795	989-2501	612
Ferguson Library	1 Public Library Plz Web: fergusonlibrary.org	Stamford	CT	06904	203-964-1000	357-9098	434-3
Ferguson Manufacturing Company Inc	590 Madison Ave Web: www.fergusonmfgco.com	Suffolk	VA	23434	757-539-3409	934-3612	273

Company	Address	City	State	ZIP	Phone	Fax	Class
Ferguson Perforating & Wire Co	130 Ernest St	Providence	RI	02905	401-941-8876		483
TF: 800-341-9800 ■ Web: www.fergusonperf.com							
Ferguson Production Inc	2130 Industrial Dr	Mcpherson	KS	67460	620-241-2400	241-2084	596
Web: www.fergusonproduction.com							
Ferguson Schetelich & Ballew PA	100 S Charles St Ste 1401	Baltimore	MD	21201	410-837-2200	837-1188	41
Web: fsb-law.com							
Ferguson Supply & Box Manufacturing Co	10820 Quality Dr	Charlotte	NC	28278	704-597-0310	597-5623	100
TF: 800-821-1023 ■ Web: www.fergusonbox.com							
Ferguson Tools Inc	103 Industrial Dr	Edgerton	OH	43517	419-298-2327	298-2455	493
Web: www.fergusontools.com							
Ferguson Wellman Capital Management Inc	888 S W Fifth Ave	Portland	OR	97204	503-226-1444		528
TF: 800-327-5765 ■ Web: www.fergusonwellman.com							
Ferma Corp	1265 Montecito Ave	Mountain View	CA	94043	650-961-2742		189-16
Web: www.fermacorp.com							
Fermi National Accelerator Laboratory	PO Box 500	Batavia	IL	60510	630-840-3000	840-4343	668
Web: www.fnal.gov							
Fernandes Steak House	158 Fleming Ave	Newark	NJ	07105	973-589-4344		671
Web: www.fernandessteakhouse.com							
Fernbank Museum of Natural History	767 Clifton Rd NE	Atlanta	GA	30307	404-929-6300		522
Web: www.fernbankmuseum.org							
Fernbank Science Ctr	156 Heaton Pk Dr	Atlanta	GA	30307	678-874-7102	874-7110	520
Web: fernbank.edu							
Fernco Inc	300 S Dayton St	Davison	MI	48423	810-653-9626	653-8714	596
TF: 800-521-1283 ■ Web: www.fernco.com							
Ferndale Chamber of Commerce	1938 Burdette St Ste 112	Ferndale	MI	48220	248-542-2160		139
TF: 800-495-5464 ■ Web: www.ferndaleareachamber.com							
Ferndale Electric Company Inc	915 E Drayton Ave	Ferndale	MI	48220	248-545-4404	545-8140	189-4
TF: 800-258-0423 ■ Web: www.ferndale-electric.com							
Ferndale Enterprise Inc	207 Francis St	Ferndale	CA	95536	707-786-3068	786-4311	532-2
Web: www.ferndaleenterprise.us							
Ferndale Public Library	222 E Nine-Mile Rd	Ferndale	MI	48220	248-546-2504	545-5840	434-3
Web: www.ferndalepubliclibrary.org							
Ferndale Record Inc	PO Box 38	Ferndale	WA	98248	360-384-1411	384-1417	532-2
Web: www.ferndalerecord.com							
Ferndale School District 502	6041 Vista Dr PO Box 698	Ferndale	WA	98248	360-383-9200	383-9201	685
Web: www.ferndalesd.org							
Ferne Clyffe State Park	PO Box 10	Goreville	IL	62939	618-995-2411		565
Web: www.dnr.illinois.gov							
Fernley & Fernley Inc	100 N 20th St 4th Fl	Philadelphia	PA	19103	215-564-3484		47
Web: www.fernley.com							
Ferno-Washington Inc	70 Weil Way	Wilmington	OH	45177	937-382-1451	382-1191	477
TF: 800-733-3766 ■ Web: www.ferno.com							
Fernwood Botanical Gardens & Nature Preserve	13988 Range Line Rd	Niles	MI	49120	269-695-6491		97
Web: www.fernwoodbotanical.org							
Feroleto Steel Company Inc	300 Scofield Ave	Bridgeport	CT	06605	203-366-3263	366-8058	723
TF: 800-243-2839 ■ Web: www.feroletosteel.com							
Ferragon Corp	11103 Memphis Ave	Cleveland	OH	44144	216-671-6161	671-4078	295
Web: ferragon.com							
Ferragon Corp	38 County Rd 370	Iuka	MS	38852	662-424-0115		295
Web: www.ferrousmetalprocessing.com							
Ferran Services & Contracting	530 Grand St	Orlando	FL	32805	407-422-3551	648-0961	189-10
Web: www.ferran-services.com							
Ferrandino & Son Inc	71 Carolyn Blvd	Farmingdale	NY	11735	866-571-4609		610
TF: 866-571-4609 ■ Web: www.ferrandinoandson.com							
Ferrara & Buckworth	60 Pompton Ave	Verona	NJ	07044	973-857-8800		2
Ferrara Candy Co	1 Tower Ln Ste 2700	Oakbrook Terrace	IL	60181	800-323-1768		296-6
TF: 800-323-1768 ■ Web: www.ferrarausa.com							
Ferrara Fiorenza Larrison Barrett & Reitz PC	5010 Campuswood Dr	East Syracuse	NY	13057	315-437-7600		428
TF: 800-777-4742 ■ Web: www.ferrarafirm.com							
Ferrara Fire Apparatus Inc	PO Box 249	Holden	LA	70744	225-567-7100	567-5260	59
TF: 800-443-9006 ■ Web: www.ferrarafire.com							
Ferrari North America Inc	250 Sylvan Ave	Englewood Cliffs	NJ	07632	201-816-2600		59
Web: www.ferrari.com							
Ferraro Foods Inc	287 S Randolphville Rd	Piscataway	NJ	08854	732-424-3400		805
Web: www.ferrarofoods.com							
Ferraro's	4480 Paradise Rd	Las Vegas	NV	89169	702-364-5300		671
Web: www.ferraroslasvegas.com							
Ferreira Cafe	1446 Peel St	Montreal	QC	H3A1S8	514-848-0988		671
Web: www.ferreiracafe.com							
Ferrell Capital Management Inc	4 Greenwich Office Pk	Greenwich	CT	06831	203-862-9500	862-8515	194
Web: www.ferrellcapital.com							
Ferrell Wealth Management Inc	1400 W Fairbanks Ave	Winter Park	FL	32789	407-629-7008		2
Web: ferrellwm.com							
Ferrellgas Partners LP	1 Liberty Plz	Liberty	MO	64068	816-792-1600		316
NYSE: FGP ■ TF: 888-337-7355 ■ Web: www.ferrellgas.com							
Ferrell-Ross Roll Manufacturing Inc	102 FM 2856 (Holly Sugar Rd)	Hereford	TX	79045	806-364-9051		295
Web: www.ferrellross.com							
Ferrer Freeman & Company LLC	10 Glenville St	Greenwich	CT	06831	203-532-8011	532-8016	792
Web: www.ffandco.com							
Ferrero USA Inc	600 Cottontail Ln	Somerset	NJ	08873	732-764-9300		296-8
TF: 800-688-3552 ■ Web: www.ferreronorthamerica.com							
Ferrilli	41 S Haddon Ave Ste 7	Haddonfield	NJ	08033	888-864-3282		463
TF: 888-864-3282 ■ Web: www.ferrilli.com							
Ferring Pharmaceuticals Inc	100 Interpace Pkwy	Parsippany	NJ	07054	973-796-1600		238
TF: 888-337-7464 ■ Web: www.ferringusa.com							
Ferriot Inc	1000 Arlington Cir	Akron	OH	44306	330-786-3000	786-3001	757
Web: www.ferriot.com							
Ferris Manufacturing Corp	16W300 83rd St	Burr Ridge	IL	60527	630-887-9797		558
Web: www.polymem.com							
Ferris School	959 Centre Rd	Wilmington	DE	19805	302-993-3800	993-3820	412
TF: 800-292-9582 ■ Web: kids.delaware.gov							
Ferris State University	1201 S State St	Big Rapids	MI	49307	231-591-2000	591-3944	166
TF: 800-433-7747 ■ Web: ferris.edu							
FerriShield Inc	12420 Race Track Rd	Tampa	FL	33626	813-855-6921	855-3291	253
TF: 866-832-4364 ■ Web: www.ferrishield.com							
Ferriter & Ferriter LLC	1669 Northampton St	Holyoke	MA	01040	413-535-4200		41
Web: ferriter.com							
Ferro Corp							
Electronic Materials Div	4150 E 56th St	Cleveland	OH	44105	216-641-8580		143
Web: www.ferro.com							
Ferro Labella & Zucker LLC	27 Warren St Ste 201	Hackensack	NJ	07601	201-489-9110		41
Web: ferrolabella.com							
Ferro Solutions Inc	5 Constitution Way	Woburn	MA	01801	781-995-3893		639
Web: www.ferrosi.com							
Ferronics Inc	45 O'Connor Rd	Fairport	NY	14450	585-388-1020	388-0036	249
Web: www.ferronics.com							
Ferrotherm Corp	4758 Warner Rd	Cleveland	OH	44125	216-883-9350		262
Web: www.ferrotherm.com							
Ferrous Processing & Trading	3400 E Lafayette	Detroit	MI	48207	313-567-9710		822
Web: www.fptscrap.com							
Ferrum College	215 Ferrum Mtn Rd	Ferrum	VA	24088	540-365-2121	365-4266	166
TF: 800-868-9797 ■ Web: www.ferrum.edu							
Ferruzzo & Ferruzzo	3737 Birch St Ste 400	Newport Beach	CA	92660	949-608-6900		41
Web: ferruzzo.com							
Ferry Beach State Park	95 Bayview Rd	Saco	ME	04072	207-283-0067		565
Web: www.maine.gov							
Ferry County	771 S Keller St PO Box 1117	Republic	WA	99166	509-775-5229	775-5230	338
Web: www.ferry-county.com							
Ferry Industries Inc	4445 Allen Rd	Stow	OH	44224	330-920-9200	920-4200	454
Web: www.ferryindustries.com							
Ferry Plaza Wine Merchant	1 Ferry Bldg Shop 23	San Francisco	CA	94111	415-391-9400		443
Web: fpwm.com							
Ferry Transportation Inc	672 Paulding Rd	Ellisville	MS	39437	601-425-5542		685
Fertilizer Institute, The (TFI)	425 Third St SW Ste 950	Washington	DC	20024	202-962-0490	962-0577	48-2
Web: www.tfi.org							
Fertizona	2850 S Peart Rd	Casa Grande	AZ	85293	520-836-7477		791
Web: www.fertizona.com							
FESCO Agencies NA Inc	1000 Second Ave Ste 1310	Seattle	WA	98104	206-583-0860	583-0889	311
TF: 800-275-3372 ■ Web: www.fesco-na.com							
FESCO Ltd	1000 Fesco Ave	Alice	TX	78332	361-661-7000	661-7004	539
Web: www.fescoinc.com							
Fessenden School	250 Waltham St	West Newton	MA	02465	617-630-2300	630-2303	622
Web: www.fessenden.org							
Festiva Resorts	One Vance Gap Rd	Asheville	NC	28805	828-254-3378		753
TF: 866-933-7848 ■ Web: www.festiva.com							
Festival Ballet Theatre							
Fountain Valley	9527 Garfield Ave	Fountain Valley	CA	92708	714-962-5440	309-1280	573-1
Web: www.festivalballet.org							
Festival Co, The	5901 W Century Blvd Ste 700	Los Angeles	CA	90045	310-665-9600	665-9009	655
Web: festivalcos.com							
Festival Flea Market Mall	2900 W Sample Rd	Pompano Beach	FL	33073	877-554-1777		460
TF: 800-353-2627 ■ Web: shopfestival.com							
Festival Inn, The	1144 Ontario St	Stratford	ON	N5A6Z3	519-273-1150		707
TF: 800-463-3581 ■ Web: www.festivalinnstratford.com							
Festival Plaza	101 Crockett St	Shreveport	LA	71101	318-673-5100	673-5105	205
Web: www.shreveportla.gov							
Festive Holidays Inc	5501 New Jersey Ave	Wildwood Crest	NJ	08260	609-522-6316	729-8606	760
TF: 800-257-8920 ■ Web: www.festiveholidays.com							
Festo Corp	395 Moreland Dr	Hauppauge	NY	11788	800-993-3786		454
TF: 800-993-3786 ■ Web: www.festo.com							
Fet Engineering Inc	903 Nutter Dr	Bardstown	KY	40004	502-348-2130	348-7040	596
Web: www.fetusa.com							
Feta Med Inc	530D S Henderson Rd	King of Prussia	PA	19406	866-834-1202	205-0011*	475
*Fax Area Code: 610 ■ TF: 866-834-1202 ■ Web: www.fetamed.com							
Fetch Logistics Inc	25 Northpointe Pkwy Ste 200	Amherst	NY	14228	716-689-4556	689-0676	311
TF: 800-964-4940 ■ Web: www.fetchlogistics.com							
Fetch Recruiting Inc	21143 Hawthorne Blvd Ste 322	Torrance	CA	90503	310-379-9965		260
Web: fetchrecruiting.com							
Fetco	600 Rose Rd	Lake Zurich	IL	60047	847-719-3000		296
Web: www.fetco.com							
Feuerborn Associates Engineering PA	357 W Ctr Ste 216	Pocatello	ID	83204	208-904-3170		261
Web: faengr.com							
Feussner'S Ford Inc	200 E South St	Freeland	PA	18224	570-636-3920		57
Web: www.feussnersford.com							
Feutz Contractors Inc	1120 N Main St PO Box 130	Paris	IL	61944	217-465-8402	463-2256	189-5
Web: www.feutzcontractors.com							
FEV Inc	4554 Glenmeade Ln	Auburn Hills	MI	48326	248-373-6000	373-8084	261
Web: www.fev.com							

	Phone	Fax	Class
FEW (Federally Employed Women) 455 Massachusetts Ave NW Ste 306 . . . . Washington DC 20001 *Web:* www.few.org	202-898-0994		49-7
Fey Industries Inc 200 4th Ave N . . . . Edgerton MN 56128 *TF:* 800-533-5340 ■ *Web:* fey-line.com	507-442-4311	442-3686	86
FEY Printing Co 910 29th Ave N . . . . Wisconsin Rapids WI 54495 *Web:* feyprinting.com	715-423-2400	423-3818	627
FF Soucy Inc 191 Delage . . . . Riviere-du-Loup QC G5R3Z1 *Web:* www.ffsoucy.com	418-862-6941		557
FF Thompson Hospital 350 Parrish St. . . . . Canandaigua NY 14424 *Web:* www.thompsonhealth.com	585-396-6000		374-3
FFB (First Financial Bancorp) 255 E Fifth St Ste 700. . . . . Cincinnati OH 45202 *NASDAQ: FFBC* ■ *TF:* 877-322-9530 ■ *Web:* www.bankatfirst.com	877-322-9530		360-2
FFB (Federal Financing Bank) US Department of the Treasury 1500 Pennsylvania Ave NW . . . . Washington DC 20220 *Web:* ffb.treasury.gov	202-622-2470		340-20
FFC (Farmers Win Coop) 110 N Jefferson . . . . Fredericksburg IA 50630 *TF:* 800-562-8389 ■ *Web:* www.farmerswincoop.agricharts.com	563-237-5324	237-6123	10-4
FFC Inc 4010 Pilot Dr Ste 103 . . . . Memphis TN 38118 *Web:* www.ffcfuelcells.com	901-842-7110		22
FFE Transportation Inc 1145 Empire Central Pl. . . . . Dallas TX 75247 *TF:* 800-569-9200 ■ *Web:* www.ffeinc.com	214-630-8090	819-5625	780
FFF (Freedom From Fear) 308 Seaview Ave. . . . . Staten Island NY 10305 *Web:* www.freedomfromfear.org	718-351-1717		48-17
FFF Enterprises Inc 44000 Winchester Rd . . . . Temecula CA 92591 *TF:* 800-843-7477 ■ *Web:* www.fffenterprises.com	951-296-2500		582
FFHSJ (Fried Frank Harris Shriver & Jacobson LLP) 1 New York Plz . . . . New York NY 10004 *Web:* www.friedfrank.com	212-859-8000	859-4000	428
FFI (Family Firm Institute) 200 Lincoln St Ste 201 . . . . Boston MA 02111 *Web:* www.ffi.org	617-482-3045	482-3049	49-12
FFL Partners LLC 1 Maritime Plz Ste 2200 . . . . San Francisco CA 94111 *Web:* www.fflpartners.com	415-402-2100	402-2111	792
FFP (Food for the Poor Inc) 6401 Lyons Rd . . . . Coconut Creek FL 33073 *TF:* 800-427-9104 ■ *Web:* www.foodforthepoor.org	954-427-2222		48-5
FFW Corp 1205 N Cass St . . . . Wabash IN 46992 *OTC: FFWC* ■ *Web:* www.crossroadsbanking.com	260-563-3185	563-4841	360-2
FG (Fontana Group Inc, The) 3509 N Campbell Ave. . . . . Tucson AZ 85719 *Web:* www.fontanagroup.com	520-325-9800		194
FG Wilson Inc 10431 N Commerce Pkwy . . . . Miramar FL 33025 *Web:* www.fgwilsonmiami.com	954-433-2212	433-4431	191-1
FGH (Fairmont General Hospital) 1325 Locust Ave. . . . . Fairmont WV 26554 *Web:* www.frmcwv.com	304-367-7500	367-7577	374-3
FGI (Fashion Group International Inc) 8 W 40th St 7th Fl. . . . . New York NY 10018 *Web:* www.fgi.org	212-302-5511	302-5533	49-4
FGI (FOIA Group Inc) 1250 Connecticut Ave NW Ste 200. . . . . Washington DC 20036 **Fax Area Code:* 202 ■ *TF:* 888-461-7951 ■ *Web:* www.foia.com	716-608-0800	347-8419*	387
FGMK LLC 2801 Lakeside Dr 3rd Fl . . . . Bannockburn IL 60015 *Web:* www.fgmk.com	847-374-0400		734
FGS (Freedom Graphic Systems Inc) 1101 S Janesville St. . . . . Milton WI 53563 *TF:* 800-334-3540 ■ *Web:* fgs.com	800-334-3540		110
FGS Inc 815 W Van Buren St Ste 302 . . . . Chicago IL 60607 *Web:* fgs-inc.com	312-421-3060		671
FGX International Inc 500 George Washington Hwy . . . . Smithfield RI 02917 *Web:* fgxi.com	401-231-3800	232-7235	408
FH Bonn Co 338 W Columbus Rd. . . . . South Charleston OH 45368 *TF:* 800-323-0143 ■ *Web:* fhbonn.com	937-323-7024	323-0388	745-3
FH Martin Constructors 28740 Mound Rd . . . . Warren MI 48092 *Web:* www.fhmartin.com	586-558-2100	558-2921	187
FH Peterson Machine Corp 143 S St . . . . Stoughton MA 02072 **Fax Area Code:* 781 ■ *TF:* 800-567-0080 ■ *Web:* www.fhpetersonmachine.com	800-567-0080	341-6022*	456
FHA (Frankenmuth Historical Assn) Frankenmuth Historical Museum 613 S Main St. . . . . Frankenmuth MI 48734 *Web:* www.frankenmuthmuseum.org	989-652-9701		637-2
FHG Inc 6809 Orchard Ridge Rd . . . . Charlotte NC 28227 *TF:* 800-333-6115 ■ *Web:* www.fhg-inc.com	704-567-9548		536
FHL Capital Corp 1926 4th Ave N . . . . Birmingham AL 35203 *Web:* fhlcapital.com	205-328-3098	323-0001	401
FHM Insurance Co 4601 Touchton Rd E Bldg 300 Ste 3150. . . . . . . Jacksonville FL 32246 **Fax Area Code:* 407 ■ *Web:* www.fhmic.com	904-724-9890	926-9419*	391-4
FHN Memorial Hospital 1045 W Stephenson St. . . . . Freeport IL 61032 *TF:* 800-747-4131 ■ *Web:* fhn.org	815-599-6000		374-3
FIA (Futures Industry Assn) 2001 Pennsylvania Ave NW Ste 600. . . . . Washington DC 20006 *Web:* fia.org	202-466-5460	296-3184	49-2
FIA (Forging Industry Assn) 1111 Superior Ave Ste 615. . . . . Cleveland OH 44114 *Web:* www.forging.org	216-781-6260	781-0102	49-13
FIAAH (Foundation for Indigenous Americans of Anasazi Heritage) Greenbrier Pkwy Ste 201 . . . . Atlanta GA 30331 *TF:* 877-571-9788 ■ *Web:* www.fiaah.org	828-293-1363		48-13
FIAF (French Institute Alliance Francaise) 22 E 60th St . . . . New York NY 10022 *Web:* www.fiaf.org	212-355-6100	935-4119	48-14
Fiba Technologies Inc 1535 Grafton Rd PO Box 360 . . . . Millbury MA 01527 *Web:* www.fibatech.com	508-887-7100	754-2254	198
Fibar Group LLC, The 80 Business Park Dr Ste 300 . . . . Armonk NY 10504 *TF:* 800-342-2721 ■ *Web:* www.fibar.com	914-273-8770		711
Fiber Art Inc 120 Industrial Dr. Cibolo TX 78108	210-658-8866		22
Fiber Bond Corp 110 Menke Rd . . . . Michigan City IN 46360 *Web:* www.fiberbond.net	219-879-4541	874-7502	745-6
Fiber Conversion Inc 15 E Elm St . . . . Broadalbin NY 12025 *Web:* fiberconversion.net	518-883-3431		745-8
Fiber Instruments Sales Inc 161 Clear Rd. . . . . Oriskany NY 13424 *TF:* 800-500-0347 ■ *Web:* www.fiberinstrumentsales.com	315-736-2206	736-2285	472
Fiber Materials Inc 5 Morin St . . . . Biddeford ME 04005 *Web:* fibermaterialsinc.com	207-282-5911	282-7529	127
Fiber Optic Center New Trust 23 Centre St . . . . New Bedford MA 02740 *TF:* 800-473-4237 ■ *Web:* focenter.com	508-992-6464		246
Fiber Pad Inc 2201 N 170th E Ave. . . . . Tulsa OK 74116 *Web:* www.fiberpad.com	918-438-7430	438-4513	608
Fiber SenSys LLC 2925 NW Aloclek Dr Ste 120 . . . . Hillsboro OR 97124 *TF:* 800-641-8150 ■ *Web:* www.fibersensys.com	503-692-4430		692
Fibercel Packaging LLC 46 Brooklyn St . . . . Portville NY 14770 *Web:* www.fibercel.com	716-933-8703		548
Fibercomm Lc 1605 Ninth St. . . . . Sioux City IA 51101 *TF:* 800-836-2472 ■ *Web:* www.fibercomm.net	712-224-2020		116
Fibercorp Mills Inc 670 17th St NW . . . . Massillon OH 44646 *Web:* fibercorr.com	330-837-5151		125
Fiberesin Industries Inc 37031 E Wisconsin Ave PO Box 88 . . . . Oconomowoc WI 53066 *TF:* 800-450-0051 ■ *Web:* www.fiberesin.com	262-567-4427	567-4814	599
Fiberglass Fabricators Inc 964 Douglas Pke . . . . Smithfield RI 02917 *Web:* www.fibfab.com	401-231-3552		91
Fiberglass Hawaii Inc 1377 Colburn St. . . . . Honolulu HI 96817 *TF:* 800-566-2653 ■ *Web:* www.fiberglasshawaii.com	808-847-3951	841-2108	603
Fiberglass Specialties Inc PO Box 1340 . . . . Henderson TX 75653 *TF:* 800-527-1459 ■ *Web:* www.fsiweb.com	903-657-6522	657-2318	608
Fibergrate Composite Structures Inc 5151 Beltline Rd Ste 700 . . . . Dallas TX 75254 *TF:* 800-527-4043 ■ *Web:* www.fibergrate.com	972-250-1633	250-1530	606
Fiberlay Inc 24 S Idaho St. . . . . Seattle WA 98134 **Fax Area Code:* 206 ■ *TF:* 800-942-0660 ■ *Web:* www.fiberlay.com	800-942-0660	782-0662*	191-4
Fiberlight LLC 11700 Great Oaks Way Ste 100 . . . . Alpharetta GA 30022 *TF:* 800-672-0181 ■ *Web:* www.fiberlight.com	678-366-0027	366-0411	188-10
FiberMark North America Inc 161 Wellington Rd . . . . Brattleboro VT 05302 *TF:* 800-784-8558 ■ *Web:* www.fibermark.com	800-843-1243		561
Fibernetics Corp 605 Boxwood Dr . . . . Cambridge ON N3E1A5 *TF:* 866-973-4237 ■ *Web:* www.fibernetics.ca	519-489-6700		224
Fiberoptics Technology Inc 1 Quassett Rd . . . . Pomfret CT 06258 *TF:* 800-433-5248 ■ *Web:* www.fiberopticstech.com	860-928-0443	928-7664	330
FiberPlus Inc 8240 Preston Ct Ste C. . . . . Jessup MD 20794 *TF:* 800-394-3301 ■ *Web:* www.fiberplusinc.com	301-317-3300		180
Fiber-Tech Industries Inc 2000 Kenskill Ave. . . . . Washington Court House OH 43160 *TF:* 800-879-4377 ■ *Web:* www.fiber-tech.net	740-335-9400	335-4843	613
Fibertek Inc 13605 Dulles Technology Dr. . . . . Herndon VA 20171 *Web:* fibertek.com	703-471-7671	471-5806	256
Fibertex Nonwovens LLC 27981 W Concrete Dr . . . . Ingleside IL 60041 *Web:* www.fibertex.com	815-349-3200	344-2165	745-6
Fiberutilities Group 222 3rd Ave SE Ste 500 . . . . Cedar Rapids IA 52401 *Web:* www.networkbetter.com	319-364-3200	364-8100	256
Fiberwave Inc 140 58th St Bldg B Unit 6E. . . . . Brooklyn NY 11220 *TF:* 800-280-9011 ■ *Web:* www.fiberwave.com	718-802-9011	802-0116	813
Fibre Box Assn (FBA) 25 NW Pt Blvd Ste 510. . . . . Elk Grove Village IL 60007 *Web:* www.fibrebox.org	847-364-9600	364-9639	49-13
Fibre Converters Inc PO Box 130 . . . . Constantine MI 49042 *Web:* www.fibreconverters.com	269-279-1700		548
Fibre Noire Internet Inc 550 Ave Beaumont Ste 320. . . . . Montreal QC H3N1V1 *TF:* 877-907-3002 ■ *Web:* www.fibrenoire.ca	877-907-3002		224
Fibrebond Corp 1300 Davenport Dr. . . . . Minden LA 71055 *TF:* 800-824-2614 ■ *Web:* www.fibrebond.com	318-377-1030		183
Fibreflex Packing & Manufacturing Company Inc 5101 Umbria St . . . . Philadelphia PA 19128 *Web:* www.fibreflex.com	215-482-1490		326
Fibre-Metal 2000 Plainfield Pk . . . . Cranston RI 02921 *TF:* 800-430-4110 ■ *Web:* www.honeywellsafety.com	800-430-4110	572-6346	576
Fibres International Inc 2600 94th St SW Ste 100. . . . . Everett WA 98204 *Web:* www.fibres.net	425-405-1700		686
Fibrex Corp 401 Sharon Ave PO Box 428 . . . . Burlington WA 98233 *Web:* www.fibrex.com	361-572-4040		596
FibroGen Inc 409 Illinois St. . . . . San Francisco CA 94158 *Web:* www.fibrogen.com	415-978-1200	978-1902	231
FIC Capital Inc 260 Madison Ave Ste 8035. . . . . New York NY 10016 *Web:* www.ficcapital.com	212-679-2100		401
FIC Corp 12216 Parklawn Dr. . . . . Rockville MD 20852 *Web:* www.ficcorp.com	301-881-8124		729
FICOA (Film Instruction Company of America) 5928 W Michigan St. . . . . Wauwatosa WI 53213 *Web:* www.ficoa.biz	414-258-6492		637-2
Fidalgo Networking Inc 1725 Continental Pl Ste D . . . . Mount Vernon WA 98273 *Web:* www.home.fidalgo.net	360-542-9660	416-0471	681

Phone | Fax | Class

Fidelco Guide Dog Foundation Inc
103 Vision Way............Bloomfield CT 06002 860-243-5200 693
TF: 800-225-7566 ■ Web: www.fidelco.org

Fidelifacts
114 Old Country Rd Ste 652............New York NY 10004 212-425-1520 248-5619 635
TF: 800-678-0007 ■ Web: www.fidelifacts.com

Fidelio Insurance Co
2826 Mt Carmel Ave............Glenside PA 19038 215-885-2443 576-5849 390
TF: 800-262-4949 ■ Web: www.fideliodental.com

Fidelis Consultants LLC
1350 Jackie Rd SE Ste 105............Rio Rancho NM 87124 505-389-4305 390
TF: 855-872-6565 ■ Web: fidelisins.com

Fidelitone Inc 1260 Karl Ct............Wauconda IL 60084 847-487-3300 246
TF: 800-475-0917 ■ Web: www.fidelitone.com

Fidelity ActionsXchange Inc
200 Seaport Blvd............Boston MA 02210 617-392-2900 387
Web: www.actionsxchange.com

Fidelity Associates Inc
PO Box 550968............Gastonia NC 28055 704-864-3766 864-2165 637-2
TF: 800-626-3766 ■ Web: fidelityassociates.com

Fidelity Bancshares NC Inc
PO Box 8............Fuquay-Varina NC 27526 919-552-2242 70
TF: 800-816-9608 ■ Web: www.fidelitybanknc.com

Fidelity Bank 100 E English St............Wichita KS 67201 800-658-1637 268-7383* 70
*Fax Area Code: 316 ■ TF: 800-658-1637 ■ Web: www.fidelitybank.com

Fidelity Bank & Trust
208 Second St SE PO Box 277............Dyersville IA 52040 563-875-7157 70
TF: 800-403-8333 ■ Web: www.bankfidelity.bank

Fidelity Building Services Group
25 Loveton Cir PO Box 2500............Sparks MD 21152 410-771-9400 14
TF: 800-787-6000 ■ Web: fidelitybsg.com

Fidelity Capital Holdings Inc
Fidelity Creditor Service Inc
PO Box 3963............Glendale CA 91221 818-502-1981 160
Web: www.olddebts.com

Fidelity Claims Inc 4832 Nashwood Ln............Dallas TX 75244 469-443-0433 242-2089* 390
*Fax Area Code: 214 ■ Web: www.fidelityclaimsinc.com

Fidelity Communications Company Inc
64 N Clark St............Sullivan MO 63080 573-468-8081 116
TF: 800-392-8070 ■ Web: www.fidelitycommunications.com

Fidelity Federal Bancorp
18 NW Fourth St............Evansville IN 47708 812-424-0921 360-2
OTC: FDLB ■ TF: 800-280-8280 ■ Web: unitedfidelity.com

Fidelity Investment Funds
PO Box 770001............Cincinnati OH 45277 800-343-3548 528
TF: 800-343-3548 ■ Web: www.fidelity.com

Fidelity Investments
483 Bay St Ste 200............Toronto ON M5G2N7 416-307-5200 528
TF: 800-263-4077 ■ Web: www.fidelity.ca

Fidelity Investments Charitable Gift Fund
PO Box 770001............Cincinnati OH 45277 800-262-6039 665-4274* 405
*Fax Area Code: 877 ■ TF: 800-262-6039 ■ Web: www.fidelitycharitable.org

Fidelity National Title Group Inc
601 Riverside Ave............Jacksonville FL 32204 904-854-8100 391-6
Web: www.fntg.com

Fidelity National Title Insurance Company of Oregon
1433 SW Sixth Ave............Portland OR 97201 503-372-0644 606-4194* 391-6
*Fax Area Code: 866 ■ Web: www.fntic.com

Fidelity Security Life Insurance Co
3130 Broadway............Kansas City MO 64111 800-648-8624 968-0580* 796
*Fax Area Code: 816 ■ TF: 800-648-8624 ■ Web: www.fslins.com

Fidelity State Bank & Trust Co
600 S Kansas Ave............Topeka KS 66603 785-295-2100 233-7571 70
Web: www.fidelitytopeka.com

Fidelity Technologies Corp
2501 Kutztown Rd............Reading PA 19605 610-929-3330 929-1969 647
Web: www.fidelitytech.com

Fidelity Tool & Mold Ltd
1885 Suncast Ln............Batavia IL 60510 630-879-2300 757
Web: www.fidelitytool.com

Fidessa Financial Corp
17 State St 42nd Fl............New York NY 10004 212-269-9000 943-0353 178-1
Web: www.fidessa.com

Fido Solutions Inc
800 De La Gauchetiere St W Ste 4000............Montreal QC H5A1K3 514-933-3436 736
Web: www.fido.ca

Fiducial 10100 Old Columbia Rd............Columbia MD 21046 410-910-5902 734
TF: 800-323-9000 ■ Web: www.fiducial.com

Fiduciary Management Incorporated of Milwaukee
100 E Wisconsin Ave Ste 2200............Milwaukee WI 53202 414-226-4545 226-4522 401
TF: 800-264-7684 ■ Web: www.fmimgt.com

Fidus Partners LLC
227 W Trade St Ste 1910............Charlotte NC 28202 704-334-2222 334-2202 690
Web: www.fiduspartners.com

Fiedor Van Epps & Assoc
964 Fifth Ave............San Diego CA 92101 619-544-1422 463
Web: fiedorvanepps.com

Fieger Law 19390 W 10-Mile Rd............Southfield MI 48075 248-558-2315 428
TF: 800-294-6637 ■ Web: www.fiegerlaw.com

Field & Stream Licenses Company LLC
18 Kings Hwy N............Westport CT 06880 203-221-0050 360-3

Field Aviation Company Inc
2450 Derry Rd E Flngr 2............Mississauga ON L5S1B2 905-676-1540 21
Web: www.fieldav.com

Field Controls LLC 2630 Airport Rd............Kinston NC 28504 252-522-3031 522-0214 17
Web: www.fieldcontrols.com

Field Fresh Foods Inc
14805 S San Pedro St............Gardena CA 90248 800-411-0588 345
TF: 800-411-0588 ■ Web: www.fieldfresh.com

Field House Museum 634 S Broadway............Saint Louis MO 63102 314-421-4689 588-9468 520
Web: fieldhousemuseum.org

Field Law 10175 101 St NW Ste 2500............Edmonton AB T5JOH3 780-423-3003 428-9329 428
Web: www.fieldlaw.com

Field Museum 1400 S Lake Shore Dr............Chicago IL 60605 312-922-9410 520
TF: 800-438-9644 ■ Web: fieldmuseum.org

Field Nation LLC
901 Marquette Ave Ste 2300............Minneapolis MN 55402 877-573-4353 317
TF: 877-573-4353 ■ Web: www.fieldnation.com

Field Paper Co 3950 D St............Omaha NE 68107 800-969-3435 553
TF: 800-969-3435 ■ Web: www.fieldpaper.com

Field Precision LLC PO Box 13595............Albuquerque NM 87192 505-220-3975 752-9077* 178-1
*Fax Area Code: 617 ■ Web: www.fieldp.com

Field Trip Factory
2211 N Elston Ave Ste 304............Chicago IL 60614 800-987-6409 297-8
TF: 800-987-6409 ■ Web: www.fieldtripfactory.com

Field Works PO Box 9897............Washington DC 20016 202-667-4400 318-8225 194
Web: www.fieldworks.com

Field, The 544 Fifth Ave............San Diego CA 92101 619-232-9840 232-9842 671
Web: www.thefield.com

Fieldale Farms Corp PO Box 558............Baldwin GA 30511 800-241-5400 619
TF: 800-241-5400 ■ Web: www.fieldale.com

Fielder House Museum
1616 W Abram St............Arlington TX 76013 817-460-4001 520
Web: historicalarlington.org

Fieldman Rolapp & Assoc
19900 Macarthur Blvd............Irvine CA 92612 949-660-7300 474-8773 463
Web: www.fieldman.com

FieldPoint Petroleum Corp
609 Castle Ridge Rd Ste 335............Austin TX 78746 512-579-3560 536
OTC: FPPP ■ Web: fppcorp.com

Fieldpoint Private Bank & Trust
100 Field Pt Rd............Greenwich CT 06830 203-413-9300 690
Web: www.fieldpointprivate.com

Fields Company LLC 2240 Taylor Way............Tacoma WA 98421 800-627-4098 383-2181* 46
*Fax Area Code: 253 ■ TF: 800-627-4098 ■ Web: www.fieldscorp.com

Fields Spring State Park 992 Park Rd............Anatone WA 99401 509-256-3332 565
Web: www.parks.wa.gov

Fieldstone Consulting Inc
293 N Dyer Neck Rd............Newcastle ME 04553 207-586-5001 194
Web: www.fieldstoneconsulting.com

Fieldstone Credit Union
395 N Kinzie Ave............Bradley IL 60915 815-929-1870 219
Web: fieldstonecu.com

Fieldstone Homes
12896 S Pony Express Rd Ste 400............Draper UT 84020 801-233-8300 653
Web: www.fieldstone-homes.com

Fieldstone Partners
1800 Bering Dr Ste 430............Houston TX 77057 713-850-0080 850-0085 690
Web: fieldstone.com

Fieldtech Avionics & Instruments Inc
4151 N Main St............Fort Worth TX 76106 817-625-2719 770
Web: www.ftav.com

Fieldwire 459 Geary St Ste 200............San Francisco CA 94102 855-222-4959 178-8
TF: 855-222-4959 ■ Web: www.fieldwire.com

FieldWorker Products Ltd
88 Queens Quay W Ste 200............Toronto ON M5J0B8 905-944-0863 470-9434 177
TF: 800-220-0779 ■ Web: www.fieldworker.com

Fiera Foods Co 50 Marmora St............Toronto ON M9M2X5 416-746-1010 68
Web: www.fierafoods.com

Fierst Bloomberg Ohm LLP
64 Gothic St............Northampton MA 01060 413-584-8067 41
Web: www.fierstbloomberg.com

Fiesta Cafe 216 S First St............Champaign IL 61820 217-352-5902 671
Web: www.fiestacafe.com

Fiesta Cafe Bar 1645 N Broadway............Rochester MN 55906 507-288-1116 671
Web: www.fiestacafebar.com

Fiesta Canning Company Inc
1480 E Bethany Home Ste 110............Phoenix AZ 85014 520-642-3366 274-7233* 296-36
*Fax Area Code: 602

Fiesta Fresh Mexican Grill
51 New Orleans Rd Ste 4............Hilton Head Island SC 29928 843-785-4788 671
Web: www.fiestafreshmexicangrill.com

Fiesta Henderson
777 W Lake Mead Pkwy............Henderson NV 89015 702-558-7000 379
TF: 888-899-7770 ■ Web: www.fiestacasinohenderson.com

Fiesta Mart Inc 5235 Katy Fwy............Houston TX 77007 713-869-5060 345
Web: www.fiestamart.com

Fiesta Rancho Hotel & Casino
2400 N Rancho Dr............Las Vegas NV 89130 702-631-7000 133
TF: 800-678-2846 ■ Web: fiestacasinorancho.com

Fiesta San Antonio Commission
2611 Broadway............San Antonio TX 78215 210-227-5191 720
Web: fiestasanantonio.org

Fiffik Law Group PC
661 Andersen Dr............Pittsburgh PA 15219 412-391-1014 428
Web: www.fiffiklaw.com

Fifield Land Co 4307 Fifield Rd............Brawley CA 92227 760-344-6391 344-6394 276
TF: 800-536-6395 ■ Web: www.kfseeds.com

Fifs LLC 199 Telford Pk PO Box 438............Telford PA 18969 267-384-5300 390
Web: fifs.com

Fifteen Beacon Hotel 15 Beacon St............Boston MA 02108 617-670-1500 670-6925 379
Web: xvbeacon.com

Fifth Baptist Church
3736 Natural Bridge Ave............Saint Louis MO 63107 314-531-2602 48-20

Fifth Business Inc
24 Greenway Plz Ste 1200............Houston TX 77046 713-622-5423 180
Web: www.fifthbusiness.com

Fifth inc, The
221 Richmond St W Ste 501............Toronto ON M5V1W2 416-979-0055 671
Web: www.thefifth.com

Fifth Street Public Market
296 E Fifth Ave............Eugene OR 97401 541-484-0383 686-1220 50-6
TF: 800-553-0135 ■ Web: www.5stmarket.com

Fifth Sun Inc 495 Ryan Ave............Chico CA 95973 530-343-8725 393
Web: www.5sun.com

Fifth Third Bank Central Ohio
21 E State St............Columbus OH 43215 800-972-3030 70
TF: 866-671-5353 ■ Web: www.53.com

Fig Garden Swim & Racquet Club
4722 N Maroa Ave............Fresno CA 93704 559-222-4816 354
Web: www.fig-garden.com

Fig Garden Village 790 W Shaw Ave............Fresno CA 93704 559-412-5296 460
Web: www.shopfiggardenvillage.com

FIG restaurant 232 Meeting St............Charleston SC 29401 843-805-5900 671
Web: eatatfig.com

Fig Tree 515 Villita............San Antonio TX 78205 210-224-1976 271-9180 671
Web: figtreerestaurant.com

Name / Address	City	State	ZIP	Phone	Fax	Class
Figaretti's 1035 Mt de Chantel Rd	Wheeling	WV	26003	304-243-5625		671
Web: www.figarettis.net						
Figaro's Italian Pizza Inc 1500 Liberty St SE Ste 160	Salem	OR	97302	503-371-9318	363-5364	670
TF: 888-344-2767 ■ *Web:* figaros.com						
Figg Engineering Group 424 N Calhoun St	Tallahassee	FL	32301	850-224-7400		256
Web: www.figgbridge.com						
Figge Art Museum 225 W Second St	Davenport	IA	52801	563-326-7804	326-7876	520
Web: www.figgeartmuseum.org						
Figma 116 New Montgomery St Ste 700	San Francisco	CA	94105	415-890-5404		657
Web: www.figma.com						
Figo Pasta Italian Restaurants 1170 Collier Rd NW	Atlanta	GA	30318	404-351-9667		671
Web: www.figopasta.com						
Figueroa Hotel 939 S Figueroa St	Los Angeles	CA	90015	213-627-8971		379
Web: www.hotelfigueroa.com						
Figures 5 Castle Hill Ave	Great Barrington	MA	01230	413-528-2552		637-2
Web: www.geoffreyyoung.com						
FII (Financial Information Inc) 1 Cragwood Rd 2nd Fl	South Plainfield	NJ	07080	908-222-5300	344-3292*	637-10
**Fax Area Code:* 800 ■ *TF:* 800-367-3441 ■ *Web:* fiinet.com						
Fiji Airways Ltd 5777 W Century Blvd Ste 1610	Los Angeles	CA	90045	800-227-4446		12
TF: 800-227-4446 ■ *Web:* www.fijiairways.com						
Fiji Embassy 1707 L St NW Ste 200	Washington	DC	20036	202-466-8320	466-8325	257
TF: 800-932-3454 ■ *Web:* www.fijiembassydc.com						
Fiji Visitors Bureau 5777 W Century Blvd Ste 220	Los Angeles	CA	90045	310-568-1616	670-2318	775
Web: www.fiji.travel						
Fiji Water 11444 W Olympic Blvd 2nd Fl	Los Angeles	CA	90064	310-312-2850	312-2828	80-2
TF: 888-426-3454 ■ *Web:* www.fijiwater.com						
Fike Corp 704 SW Tenth St	Blue Springs	MO	64015	816-229-3405		283
TF: 877-342-3453 ■ *Web:* www.fike.com						
File Keepers LLC 6277 E Slauson Ave	Los Angeles	CA	90040	323-728-3133	728-0867	463
Web: filekeepers.com						
FileCatalyst Inc 1725 St Laurent Blvd Ste 205	Ottawa	ON	K1G3V4	613-667-2439		177
TF: 877-327-9387 ■ *Web:* filecatalyst.com						
File-Ez Folder Inc 4111 E Mission Ave	Spokane	WA	99210	509-534-1044	534-8969	552-2
Web: file-ez.com						
FileHeads PO Box 691	Decatur	GA	30031	404-231-6172		393
Web: www.fileheads.net						
FileStream Inc 240 Glen Head Rd Ste 93	Glen Head	NY	11545	516-759-4100	759-3011	178-12
Web: www.filestream.com						
FileTrail Inc 1990 The Alameda	San Jose	CA	95126	408-289-1300	293-5357	177
TF: 800-310-0299 ■ *Web:* www.filetrail.com						
Filibuster Press 5 Kim Ct	Elkhart	IN	46514	574-266-6622		637-2
Web: www.filibusterpress.com						
Filippo's 6915 W Lincoln Ave	Milwaukee	WI	53219	414-321-4040		671
Web: www.filippositalian.com						
Fill n Foods 10554 Scott Hwy	Helenwood	TN	37755	423-663-2749		297-8
Fillauer Inc PO Box 5189	Chattanooga	TN	37406	423-624-0946	629-7936	477
TF: 800-251-6398 ■ *Web:* fillauer.com						
Fillion Associates Inc PO Box 14518	East Providence	RI	02914	800-776-7665	438-6599*	189-11
**Fax Area Code:* 401 ■ *TF:* 800-776-7665 ■ *Web:* www.fillionassociates.com						
Fillmore County 900 G St	Geneva	NE	68361	402-759-4931	759-4307	338
Web: fillmorecounty.org						
Fillmore County 101 Fillmore St	Preston	MN	55965	507-765-3356		338
Web: www.co.fillmore.mn.us						
Fillmore Detroit, The 2115 Woodward Ave	Detroit	MI	48201	313-961-5451		572
Web: www.thefillmoredetroit.com						
Fillmore Glen State Park 1686 St Rt 38	Moravia	NY	13118	315-497-0130		565
Web: parks.ny.gov						
Fillmore Group Inc, The 8501 La Salle Rd Ste 318	Towson	MD	21286	410-465-6335		177
Web: www.thefillmoregroup.com						
Fillmore-Piru Citrus Assn (FPCA) 357 N Main St PO Box 350	Piru	CA	93040	805-521-1781	521-0990	11-1
Web: www.fillmorepirucitrus.com						
Film Actors Workshop 2050 S Bundy Dr Ste 100	Los Angeles	CA	90025	310-442-9488		167-3
Web: www.filmactorsworkshop.com						
Film at Lincoln Ctr 70 Lincoln Center Plz	New York	NY	10023	212-875-5610		457-9
TF: 888-313-6085 ■ *Web:* filmlinc.org						
Film Instruction Company of America (FICOA) 5928 W Michigan St	Wauwatosa	WI	53213	414-258-6492		637-2
Web: www.ficoa.biz						
Film Workers Club 1006 17th Ave S	Nashville	TN	37212	615-322-9337		514
Web: www.filmworkers.com						
Filmfax Magazine Inc PO Box 1900	Evanston	IL	60204	847-866-7155		637-9
Web: www.filmfax.com						
Film-Pak Inc 201 S Magnolia	Crowley	TX	76036	817-297-2231		596
Web: www.film-pak.com						
Filmtech Corp 2121 31st St SW	Allentown	PA	18103	610-709-9999	709-9990	601
Web: www.filmtech-corp.com						
Filnor Inc 227 N Freedom Ave PO Box 2328	Alliance	OH	44601	330-821-7667	829-3175	253
Web: www.filnor.com						
Filoli 86 Canada Rd	Woodside	CA	94062	650-364-8300	366-7836	97
Web: filoli.org						
Filomena Ristorante 1063 Wisconsin Ave NW	Washington	DC	20007	202-338-8800		671
Web: www.filomena.com						
Filson Historical Society 1310 S Third St	Louisville	KY	40208	502-635-5083	635-5086	520
TF: 800-928-7000 ■ *Web:* www.filsonhistorical.org						
Filtek Inc 2334 W Frontage Rd	Tubac	AZ	85646	520-398-2856		253
Web: www.filtek.com						
Filter Factory Inc, The 19105 S Ave B	Somerton	AZ	85350	928-627-5500	627-5505	386
Web: www.filterfact.com						
Filter LLC 1425 Fourth Ave Ste 1000	Seattle	WA	98101	800-336-0809		260
TF: 800-336-0809 ■ *Web:* www.filterdigital.com						
FilterBoxx Water & Environmental Corp 200 Rivercrest Dr SE Ste 160	Calgary	AB	T2C2X5	403-203-4747	203-4774	192
TF: 877-868-4747 ■ *Web:* filterboxx.com						
Filtertech Inc 113 Fairgrounds Dr PO Box 527	Manlius	NY	13104	315-682-8815	682-8825	18
Web: www.filtertech.com						
Filtertek Inc 11411 Price Rd	Hebron	IL	60034	815-648-1001	648-2929	604
TF: 800-248-2461 ■ *Web:* www.filtertek.com						
Filtra-Systems Co 23900 Haggerty Rd	Farmington Hills	MI	48335	248-427-9090	427-9895	806
Web: www.filtrasystems.com						
Filtration Group Inc 912 E Washington St	Joliet	IL	60433	815-726-4600	518-1162*	18
**Fax Area Code:* 800 ■ *TF:* 877-603-1003 ■ *Web:* www.filtrationgroup.com						
Filtrine Manufacturing Co 15 Kit St	Keene	NH	03431	603-352-5500	352-0330	14
TF: 800-930-3367 ■ *Web:* www.filtrine.com						
Filtronetics Inc 6010 Parretta Dr	Kansas City	MO	64120	816-231-7375	241-0368	246
Web: www.filtro.net						
Fimbel Architectural Door Specialties PO Box 96	Whitehouse Station	NJ	08889	908-534-1732		234
Web: www.fimbelads.com						
Fimc Commercial Realty 1619 Tyler	Amarillo	TX	79102	806-358-7151		652
TF: 800-658-2616 ■ *Web:* www.fimcrealty.com						
FIN (Financial Information Network Inc) 6656 Valjean Ave	Van Nuys	CA	91409	818-782-0331		177
Web: www.fingps.com						
Fin & Feather Resort Inc 445889 Hwy 10-A	Gore	OK	74435	918-487-5148		669
Web: finandfeatherresort.com						
Fin Pan Inc 3255 Symmes Rd	Hamilton	OH	45015	513-870-9200	870-9606	183
TF: 800-833-6444 ■ *Web:* finpan.com						
Finagle-a-Bagel Inc 77 Rowe St	Auburndale	MA	02466	617-726-1111		345
Web: www.finagleabagel.com						
FinAid Page LLC PO Box 2056	Cranberry Township	PA	16066	724-538-4500	538-4502	725
TF: 800-433-3243 ■ *Web:* www.finaid.org						
Final Draft Inc 26707 W Agoura Rd Ste 205	Calabasas	CA	91302	818-995-8995	995-4422	178-10
TF: 800-231-4055 ■ *Web:* www.finaldraft.com						
Final Filtration LLC 139 Columbia Dr	Williamsville	NY	14221	716-568-8080	568-8079	189-11
Web: www.cleanerpools.net						
Finance & Commerce 730 Second Ave S US Trust Bldg Ste 100	Minneapolis	MN	55402	617-249-2600	333-3243*	457-5
**Fax Area Code:* 612 ■ *Web:* finance-commerce.com						
Finance Center Federal Credit Union PO Box 26501	Indianapolis	IN	46226	317-916-7700	543-5869	219
Web: www.fcfcu.com						
Finance Factors Ltd 1164 Bishop St	Honolulu	HI	96813	808-548-4940	548-5148	217
TF: 800-648-7136 ■ *Web:* www.financefactors.com						
Finance of America Mortgage 300 Welsh Rd Bldg 5	Horsham	PA	19044	800-355-5626		217
TF: 800-355-5626 ■ *Web:* www.foamortgage.com						
Financial & Realty Services LLC 1110 Bonifant St Ste 301	Silver Spring	MD	20910	301-650-9112		271
TF: 800-650-9714 ■ *Web:* frsllc.com						
Financial Accounting Services Inc 41635 Enterprise Cir N Ste A	Temecula	CA	92590	951-719-1515		2
Web: taxmanfred.com						
Financial Acctg Standards Board (FASB) 401 Merritt 7 PO Box 5116	Norwalk	CT	06856	203-847-0700	849-9714	49-1
TF: 800-748-0659 ■ *Web:* www.fasb.org						
Financial Advantage Federal Credit Union 300 E Eighth Ave	Homestead	PA	15120	412-461-5100		219
Web: financialadvantagecu.com						
Financial Advisory Service Inc 4747 W 135th St	Leawood	KS	66224	913-239-2300		194
Web: www.faskc.com						
Financial America Securities Inc 26600 Detroit Rd	Cleveland	OH	44115	440-899-9591		690
Financial American Life Insurance Co PO Box 41255	Jacksonville	FL	32203	844-882-1948		796
TF: 844-882-1948 ■ *Web:* www.famli.com						
Financial Benefits Inc 8280 Ymca Plaza Dr No 4	Baton Rouge	LA	70810	225-763-7010	763-7040	390
TF: 800-942-2777 ■ *Web:* shobe.com						
Financial Builders Federal Credit Union 2828 S Lafountain St	Kokomo	IN	46902	765-455-0500	453-2461	219
TF: 800-858-8874 ■ *Web:* financialbuilders.org						
Financial Courier Service Inc 2496 Ayrshire CV	Memphis	TN	38119	901-761-4555		546
Financial Crimes Enforcement Network 2070 Chain Bridge Rd	Vienna	VA	22182	703-905-3591	354-6411*	340-18
**Fax Area Code:* 202 ■ *Web:* www.fincen.gov						
Financial Designs Ltd 1775 Sherman St Ste 1800	Denver	CO	80203	303-832-6100	832-7100	390
Web: fdltd.com						
Financial Dimensions Group Inc 3900 Northwoods Dr Ste 125	Arden Hills	MN	55112	651-481-6280	481-6289	401
Web: www.fdg-advisors.com						
Financial Directions Group Inc 5001 Weston Pkwy Ste 200	Cary	NC	27513	919-678-0007	678-0065	390
Web: financialdirections.com						
Financial Engines Inc 1804 Embarcadero Rd	Palo Alto	CA	94303	408-498-6000	565-4905*	178-10
NASDAQ: FNGN ■ **Fax Area Code:* 650 ■ *TF:* 888-443-8577 ■ *Web:* financialengines.com						
Financial Executives Intl (FEI) 1250 Headquarters Plz W Twr 7th Fl	Morristown	NJ	07960	973-765-1000	765-1018	49-2
Web: financialexecutives.org						
Financial Federal 1715 Aaron Brenner Dr Ste 100	Memphis	TN	38120	901-756-2848		509
Web: www.finfedmem.com						
Financial Guaranty Insurance Co 463 Seventh Ave	New York	NY	10018	212-312-3000	312-3093	391-5
TF: 800-352-0001 ■ *Web:* www.fgic.com						

Name / Address	City	State	Zip	Phone	Fax	Class
Financial Industry Regulatory Authority (FINRA) 9509 Key W Ave TF: 800-321-6273 ■ Web: www.finra.org	Rockville	MD	20850	301-590-6500		49-2
Financial Information Inc (FII) 1 Cragwood Rd 2nd Fl *Fax Area Code: 800 ■ TF: 800-367-3441 ■ Web: fiinet.com	South Plainfield	NJ	07080	908-222-5300	344-3292*	637-10
Financial Information Network Inc (FIN) 6656 Valjean Ave Web: www.fingps.com	Van Nuys	CA	91409	818-782-0331		177
Financial Institutions Inc 220 Liberty St NASDAQ: FISI ■ TF: 866-296-3743 ■ Web: www.snl.com	Warsaw	NY	14569	585-786-1100		360-2
Financial Intelligence LLC PO Box 2094 Web: www.financial-intelligence.com	Saratoga	CA	95070	650-946-1720		734
Financial Management Association Intl (FMA) 4202 E Fowler Ave Web: www.fma.org	Tampa	FL	33620	813-974-2084		49-2
Financial Management Professionals Inc 6034 W Courtyard Dr Ste 380 Web: www.fmpwa.com	Austin	TX	78730	512-329-5174		194
Financial Managers Society (FMS) 100 W Monroe St Ste 810 TF: 800-275-4367 ■ Web: www.fmsinc.org	Chicago	IL	60603	312-578-1300	578-1308	49-2
Financial Pacific Leasing Inc 3455 S 344th Way Ste 300 *Fax Area Code: 800 ■ TF: 800-447-7107 ■ Web: www.finpac.com	Federal Way	WA	98001	253-568-6000	447-7106*	216
Financial Partners Credit Union PO Box 7005 TF: 800-950-7328 ■ Web: fpcu.org	Downey	CA	90241	562-923-0311		219
Financial Planning Assn 1290 Broadway Ste 1625 TF: 800-322-4237 ■ Web: www.financialplanningassociation.org	Denver	CO	80203	303-759-4900	759-0749	457-5
Financial Plans & Strategies Inc 375 N Madison Ave Web: www.finplans.com	Greenwood	IN	46142	317-882-5981		401
Financial Resources Group Inc 3063 Center Point Rd NE Web: frginvest.com	Cedar Rapids	IA	52402	319-298-1260		690
Financial Retirement Solutions LLC 100 Great Meadow Rd Ste 502 Web: johnsonbrunetti.com	Wethersfield	CT	06109	860-372-4800		390
Financial Security Bank 1011 Atlantic Ave Web: financialsecuritybank.com	Kerkhoven	MN	56252	320-264-2161	264-1306	70
Financial Sense Wealth Management PO Box 503147 Web: www.financialsense.com	San Diego	CA	92150	888-486-3939		401
Financial Service Centers of America Inc (FISCA) 21 Main St 1st Fl *Fax Area Code: 201 ■ Web: www.fisca.org	Hackensack	NJ	07602	202-719-2388	487-3954*	49-2
Financial Technology Laboratories Inc 727 W Beebe Capps Expy TF: 866-375-6731 ■ Web: www.ftlabs.com	Searcy	AR	72143	321-248-4248		178-1
Financial Technology Partners LP 601 California St 22nd Fl Web: www.ftpartners.com	San Francisco	CA	94108	415-512-8700		401
Financial Transmission Network Inc 13220 Birch Dr Ste 120 Web: www.ftni.com	Omaha	NE	68164	402-502-8777		251
FinancialCAD Corp 13450 102nd Ave Ste 1750 TF: 800-304-0702 ■ Web: www.fincad.com	Surrey	BC	V3T5X3	604-957-1200	957-1201	39
FINCA (Foundation for International Community Assistance) 1201 15th St NW 8th Fl TF: 855-903-4622 ■ Web: www.finca.org	Washington	DC	20005	202-682-1510	682-1535	48-5
Fincannon & Associates Inc 2013 Olde Regent Way Web: www.fincannoncasting.com	Leland	NC	28451	910-251-1500	251-9325	512
Fincantieri Marine Systems North America Inc 800-C Principal Ct TF: 877-436-7643 ■ Web: fincantierimarinesystems.com	Chesapeake	VA	23320	757-548-6000		690
Finch Paper LLC 1 Glen St TF: 800-833-9983 ■ Web: www.finchpaper.com	Glens Falls	NY	12801	518-793-2541		557
Fincher Engineering LLC 12402 Slide Rd Ste 403 Web: finchereng.com	Lubbock	TX	79424	806-701-5109		261
Finchey Corporation of California 800 S Brand Blvd Web: www.pacificbmw.com	Glendale	CA	91204	818-246-5600		57
Finck & Perras Insurance Agency Inc 6 Campus Ln Web: insuringyourway.com	Easthampton	MA	01027	413-527-3000		390
Finck Cigar Co 414 Vera Cruz St TF: 800-221-0638 ■ Web: www.finckcigarcompany.com	San Antonio	TX	78207	210-226-4191	226-2825	756
Find it Quick.com Inc 1817 Saunders Settlement Rd	Niagara Falls	NY	14304	716-297-5292		225
Find the Children 2656 29th St Ste 203 TF: 888-477-6721 ■ Web: www.findthechildren.com	Santa Monica	CA	90405	310-314-3213		48-6
Find Your Dreams Inc 636 Plank Rd Ste 205 *Fax Area Code: 866 ■ Web: www.internetmarketingninjas.com	Clifton Park	NY	12065	518-631-6227	303-8266*	631
FindLaw 610 Opperman Dr *Fax Area Code: 800 ■ TF: 800-455-4565 ■ Web: www.findlaw.com	Eagan	MN	55123	651-687-7000	392-6206*	397
Findlay Automobile Club 1550 Tiffin Ave Web: www.findlay.aaa.com	Findlay	OH	45840	419-422-4961	422-5620	53
Findlay Automotive Group 310 N Gibson Rd TF: 888-474-1660 ■ Web: www.findlayauto.com	Henderson	NV	89014	702-982-4100		57
Findlay Country Club Pro Shop 1500 Country Club Dr Web: www.findlaycc.com	Findlay	OH	45840	419-422-9263		354
Findlay Hancock County District Public Library 206 Broadway Web: www.findlaylibrary.org	Findlay	OH	45840	419-422-1712	422-0638	434-3
Findlay Inn & Conference Ctr 200 E Main Cross St TF: 800-825-1455 ■ Web: www.findlayinn.com	Findlay	OH	45840	419-422-5682		379
Findlay Market PO Box 14727 Web: www.findlaymarket.org	Cincinnati	OH	45250	513-665-4839		50-6
Findlay-Hancock County Chamber of Commerce 123 E Main Cross St Web: findlayhancockchamber.com	Findlay	OH	45840	419-422-3313	422-9508	139
Findley Davies 1 Seagate Ste 2050 TF: 800-456-1360 ■ Web: findley.com	Toledo	OH	43604	419-255-1360	259-5685	193
Findley State Park 25381 SR-58 Web: ohiodnr.gov	Wellington	OH	44090	440-647-5749		565
Findleys Pharmacy Inc 136 W Main St Web: www.findleyspharmacy.com	Somerset	PA	15501	814-445-7939		237
Findorff JH & Son Inc 300 S Bedford St Web: www.findorff.com	Madison	WI	53703	608-257-5321		186
FindPromos.com PO Box 20687 Web: www.findpromos.com	Huntington Station	NY	11746	631-421-8301		328
Findspace 197 Spadina Ave Ste 402 Web: www.findspace.com	Toronto	ON	M5T2C8	416-800-0405		387
Findwell 920 Dexter Ave N Web: www.findwell.com	Seattle	WA	98109	206-462-6200	462-6300	652
Fine Arts Assn, The 38660 Mentor Ave Web: www.fineartsassociation.org	Willoughby	OH	44094	440-951-7500	975-4592	138
Fine Arts Museums of San Francisco 50 Hagiwara Tea Garden Dr Web: deyoung.famsf.org	San Francisco	CA	94118	415-750-3600		397
Fine Book Club of Claifornia 312 Sutter St Ste 500 Web: www.bccbooks.org	San Francisco	CA	94108	415-781-7532		533
FINE Design Group Inc 3450 Sansome St Web: www.wearefine.com	San Francisco	CA	94118	415-552-9300		506
Fine Furniture Inc 305 S Hamilton St Web: www.ffdm.com	High Point	NC	27260	336-883-9918		194
Fine Homebuilding Magazine 63 S Main St PO Box 5506 TF: 800-309-8955 ■ Web: www.finehomebuilding.com	Newtown	CT	06470	203-426-8171	426-3434	457-21
Fine Hospitality Group LLC 545 W Lambert Rd Ste D Web: www.finehospitality.com	Brea	CA	92821	714-990-8800		226
Fine Laboratories Inc 100 Ashley Park Dr Web: www.finelabs.com	Piedmont	MO	63957	573-223-2388		247
Fine Line Production 2221 Regal Pkwy TF: 800-887-5625 ■ Web: finelineproduction.com	Euless	TX	76040	817-267-6750		483
FINE Mortuary College LLC 150 Kerry Pl Web: www.fine-ne.com	Norwood	MA	02062	781-762-1211	762-7177	800
Fine Organics Corp 420 Kuller Rd PO Box 2277 TF: 800-526-7480 ■ Web: www.fineorganicscorp.com	Clifton	NJ	07015	973-478-1000	478-6120	151
Fine Print Graphics Inc 5229 N 125th St Web: www.fineprintgraphics.com	Butler	WI	53007	262-781-2255	781-4455	627
Fine Technology Solutions 7936 Grado El Tupelo Web: fineonline.com	Carlsbad	CA	92009	760-274-2370		177
Fineberg Companies, The 1 Washington St Ste 400 Web: finebergcompanies.com	Wellesley	MA	02481	781-239-1480	239-1493	656
Fineline Circuits & Technology Inc 594 Apollo Web: www.finelinecircuits.com	Brea	CA	92821	714-529-2942	255-8313	625
Fineline Graphics & Design Inc 1820 Bellomy St Web: finelinegd.com	Santa Clara	CA	95050	408-261-7676		344
Fineline Imprints Inc 516 State St TF: 800-669-0045 ■ Web: finelineimprints.com	Zanesville	OH	43701	740-453-1083	452-3550	45
Fineline Printing Group 8081 Zionsville Rd TF: 877-334-7687 ■ Web: finelineprintinggroup.com	Indianapolis	IN	46268	317-872-4490		627
Fineline Technologies Inc 3145 Medlock Bridge Rd TF: 800-500-8687 ■ Web: www.finelinetech.com	Norcross	GA	30071	678-969-0835	969-9201	196
Finelite Inc 30500 Whipple Rd Web: www.finelite.com	Union City	CA	94587	510-441-1100		4
Finesse Tax Accounting 1600 Wilson Blvd Ste 720 Web: finessetax.com	Arlington	VA	22209	703-812-4750		2
Fin-Feather-Fur Outfitters 652 US Hwy 250 E Web: www.finfeatherfur.com	Ashland	OH	44805	419-281-2557		711
Finfrock Industries Inc 2400 Apopka Blvd Web: finfrock.com	Apopka	FL	32703	407-293-4000	297-0512	183
Finger & Finger A Professional Corp 158 Grand St Web: www.fingerandfinger.com	White Plains	NY	10601	914-949-0308		41
Finger Lake State Recreation Area 7278 E Bogard Rd Web: www.dnr.alaska.gov	Wasilla	AK	99654	907-745-8950		565
Finger Lakes Community College 3325 Marvin Sands Dr Web: www.fingerlakes.edu	Canandaigua	NY	14424	585-394-3500	394-5005	162
Finger Lakes Gaming & Race Track 5857 Rt 96 TF: 877-846-7369 ■ Web: fingerlakesgaming.com	Farmington	NY	14425	585-924-3232	924-3967	642
Finger Lakes Library System 1300 Dryden Rd TF: 800-909-3557 ■ Web: www.flls.org	Ithaca	NY	14850	607-273-4074	273-3618	434-3
Finger Lakes Livestock Exchange Inc Geneva Tpke 3865 Rts 5 & 20 Web: www.fingerlakeslivestockex.com	Canandaigua	NY	14424	585-394-1515	394-9151	446

	Phone	Fax	Class
Finger Lakes Partners LLC 62 Reed St. . . . . Geneva NY 14456 *Web:* fingerlakesinsurance.com	315-789-0700	789-8577	390
Finger Lakes State Park 1505 E Peabody Rd . . . . Columbia MO 65202 *Web:* mostateparks.com	573-443-5315		565
Finger Lakes Stone Company Inc 33 Quarry Rd . . . . Ithaca NY 14850 *Web:* fingerlakesstone.com	607-273-4646	273-4692	724
Finger Lakes Times 218 Genesse St . . . . Geneva NY 14456 *TF:* 800-388-6652 ■ *Web:* www.fltimes.com	315-789-3333	789-4077	637-8
Finger Lakes Tire 40 York St . . . . Auburn NY 13021 *Web:* www.fingerlakestire.net	315-252-5858		755
Finger Lakes Visitors Connection 25 Gorham St . . . . Canandaigua NY 14424 *TF:* 877-386-4669 ■ *Web:* www.visitfingerlakes.com	585-394-3915		206
Fingerhut 6250 Ridgewood Dr . . . . Saint Cloud MN 56303 *TF:* 800-208-2500 ■ *Web:* www.fingerhut.com	800-208-2500		459
Fingerpaint Marketing Inc 395 Broadway . . . . Saratoga Springs NY 12866 *Web:* www.fingerpaint.com	518-693-6960		194
Finial Co, The 4030 La Reunion Pkwy. . . . . Dallas TX 75212 *TF:* 800-392-4341 ■ *Web:* www.thefinialcompany.com	214-678-0805		361
Finish Line Inc, The 3308 N Mitthoeffer Rd . . . . Indianapolis IN 46235 *NASDAQ: FINL* ■ *TF:* 888-777-3949 ■ *Web:* www.finishline.com	317-899-1022		301
Finishes Unlimited Inc 482 Wheeler Rd . . . . Sugar Grove IL 60554 *Web:* www.uvcompositecoatings.com	630-466-4881	466-1064	550
Finishing Line Press PO Box 1626 . . . . Georgetown KY 40324 *Web:* www.finishinglinepress.com	859-514-8966		637-2
FinishMaster Inc 115 W Washington St 700 S. . . . . Indianapolis IN 46204 *TF:* 888-311-3678 ■ *Web:* www.finishmaster.com	317-237-3678	237-2150	550
Finity Inc 1200 NW Natio Pkwy Ste 220. . . . . Portland OR 97209 *TF:* 800-509-1346 ■ *Web:* www.finity.com	503-808-9240		195
Finkelstein & Partners LLP 1279 Rt 300 . . . . Newburgh NY 12551 *TF:* 800-529-2676 ■ *Web:* www.lawampm.com	845-562-0203		428
Finken Plumbing Heating & Cooling 628 19th Ave NE. . . . . Saint Joseph MN 56374 *TF:* 877-346-5367 ■ *Web:* finkens.com	320-258-2005	258-2006	610
Finkenauer Abby (Rep D - IA) 124 Cannon House Office Bldg. . . . . Washington DC 20515 *Web:* www.finkenauer.house.gov	202-225-2911		342-2
Finkler & Company CPAS Inc 16600 W Sprague Rd Ste 285. . . . . Middleburg Heights OH 44130 *Web:* www.hwco.com	440-826-1550	826-1552	2
Finks Jewelry Inc 3545 Electric Rd . . . . Roanoke VA 24018 *Web:* www.finks.com	540-342-2991		410
Finlandia Sauna Products Inc 14010 SW 72nd Ave Ste B . . . . Portland OR 97224 *TF:* 800-354-3342 ■ *Web:* www.finlandiasauna.com	503-684-8289	684-1120	711
Finlandia University 601 Quincy St. . . . . Hancock MI 49930 *TF:* 800-682-7604 ■ *Web:* www.finlandia.edu	906-482-5300	487-7383	166
Finley 699 Walnut St Ste 1700 . . . . Des Moines IA 50309 *Web:* www.finleylaw.com	515-288-0145		428
Finley Engineering Company Inc 104 E 11th St . . . . Lamar MO 64759 *TF:* 800-225-9716 ■ *Web:* finleyusa.com	417-682-5531	682-3220	256
Finley Fire Equipment Company Inc 5255 N SR-60 NW . . . . Mcconnelsville OH 43756 *Web:* finleyfire.com	740-962-4328		406
Finley Point / Flathead Lake State Park 8600 MT Hwy 35 . . . . Bigfork MT 59911 *Web:* www.stateparks.mt.gov	406-887-2715		565
Finley Resources Inc 1308 Lake St. . . . . Fort Worth TX 76102 *Web:* finleyresources.com	817-336-1924	336-1709	581
Finn & Porter 5000 Seminary Rd. . . . . Alexandria VA 22311 *Web:* www.finnandporteralexandria.com	703-379-2346		671
Finn Corp 9281 Le St Dr. . . . . Fairfield OH 45014 *TF:* 800-543-7166 ■ *Web:* www.finncorp.com	513-874-2818	874-2914	273
Finney & Turnipseed Transportation & Civil Engineering 610 SW Tenth St Ste 200 . . . . Topeka KS 66612 *Web:* finturn.com	785-235-2394		261
Finney County 311 N Ninth St. . . . . Garden City KS 67846 *Web:* www.finneycounty.org	620-272-3500	272-3599	338
Finney County Public Library Garden City 605 E Walnut St . . . . Garden City KS 67846 *Web:* finneylibrary.org	620-272-3680	272-3682	434-3
Finney Law Firm LLC 4270 Ivy Pointe Blvd Ste 225 . . . . Cincinnati OH 45245 *Web:* finneylawfirm.com	513-943-6650		41
Finnish American Chamber of Commerce Inc 2 Park Ave. . . . . New York NY 10016 *Web:* facc-ny.com	917-622-7076		138
Finnleo Sauna 575 Cokato St E. . . . . Cokato MN 55321 *TF:* 800-346-6536 ■ *Web:* www.finnleo.com	800-346-6536		319-2
Fino Consulting LLC 20 W 37th St 12th Fl. . . . . New York NY 10018 *Web:* www.finoconsulting.com	212-532-0020		463
Finotex USA Corp 6942 NW 50th St . . . . Miami FL 33166 *Web:* www.finotex.com	305-470-2400		693
FINRA (Financial Industry Regulatory Authority) 9509 Key W Ave . . . . Rockville MD 20850 *TF:* 800-321-6273 ■ *Web:* www.finra.org	301-590-6500		49-2
FinSer Corp 9601 McAllister Fwy Ste 301 . . . . San Antonio TX 78216 *Web:* www.finser.com	210-224-5492		194
Finsoft Consultants Inc 545 8th Ave Ste 4 . . . . New York NY 10018 *Web:* www.finsoftus.com	212-239-9191		180
FinTrack Systems 194 Calyer St. . . . . Brooklyn NY 11222 *Web:* www.fintrack.com	212-742-1800		317
FintronX LED LLC 5995 Chapel Hill Rd Ste 119 . . . . Raleigh NC 27607 *TF:* 800-541-9082 ■ *Web:* fintronxled.com	919-324-3960		77
Finz & Finz PC 410 E Jericho Tpke . . . . Mineola NY 11501 *Web:* finzfirm.com	516-433-3000	433-3001	41
Finzer Roller Co 129 Rawls Rd . . . . Des Plaines IL 60018 *TF:* 888-486-1900 ■ *Web:* www.finzerroller.com	847-390-6200	390-6201	677
Fior D'Italia 2237 Mason St. . . . . San Francisco CA 94133 *Web:* www.fior.com	415-986-1886		671
Fiore Industries Inc 8601 Washington St NE Ste B . . . . Albuquerque NM 87113 *Web:* fiore-ind.com	505-255-9797		261
Fiorella's Jack Stack Barbecue 9520 Metcalf Ave . . . . Overland Park KS 66212 *Web:* www.jackstackbbq.com	913-385-7427		671
Fiorucci Foods Inc 1800 Ruffin Mill Rd . . . . Colonial Heights VA 23834 *Web:* www.fioruccifoods.com	804-520-7775		297-8
FIP Construction Inc 1536 New Britain Ave . . . . Farmington CT 06032 *Web:* www.fipconstruction.com	860-470-1800		186
Fire & Life Safety America 3017 Vernon Rd . . . . Richmond VA 23228 *TF:* 800-252-5069 ■ *Web:* flsamerica.com	919-524-5740		283
Fire & Rain 1 N 3rd Ave. Evansville IN 47710 *Web:* www.fireandrain.com	812-464-5244		4
Fire 2 Wire 5462 Pirrone Rd . . . . Salida CA 95368 *TF:* 888-905-3473 ■ *Web:* www.fire2wire.com	209-543-1800	545-1469	637-10
Fire and Building Code Services Inc 10 E Merrick Rd Ste 308. . . . . Valley Stream NY 11580 *Web:* firecodeservices.com	516-256-7780	256-7783	261
Fire Brick Engineers Co 2400 S 43rd St. . . . . Milwaukee WI 53219 *Web:* www.firebrickengineers.com	414-383-6000		191-4
Fire Creek Resources Ltd 206-11th Ave. . . . . Calgary AB T2G0X8 *Web:* www.fcrl.ca	403-234-9309		539
Fire Engine Red 700 Locust St Apt A4 . . . . Philadelphia PA 19106 *Web:* fire-engine-red.com	215-829-1850		177
Fire Equipment Inc 20 Hall St . . . . Medford MA 02155 *TF:* 888-296-1381 ■ *Web:* www.firefire.com	888-296-1381	296-1384	76
Fire Fighter Sales & Service Co 791 Commonwealth Dr. Warrendale PA 15086 *Web:* www.firefighter-pgh.com	724-720-6000		610
Fire Fighters Credit Union 9200 E 41st St . . . . Tulsa OK 74145 *TF:* 800-786-3328 ■ *Web:* firefighterscu.org	918-582-1191	583-3609	219
Fire Fighters Equipment Co 3053 Rt 10 E. . . . . Denville NJ 07834 *TF:* 800-523-7222 ■ *Web:* www.firefightersequipment.com	973-366-4466		679
Fire Food & Drink 13220 Shaker Sq. . . . . Cleveland OH 44120 *Web:* firefoodanddrink.com	216-921-3473		671
Fire Hall Theatre 412 Second Ave N . . . . Grand Forks ND 58203 *Web:* www.ggfct.com	701-746-0847		572
Fire Island National Seashore 120 Laurel St . . . . Patchogue NY 11772 *Web:* www.nps.gov	631-687-4750	289-4898	564
Fire Mountain Gems Inc 1 Fire Mountain Way. . . . . Grants Pass OR 97526 *TF:* 800-355-2137 ■ *Web:* www.firemountaingems.com	800-355-2137		411
Fire Museum of Maryland 1301 York Rd . . . . Lutherville Timonium MD 21093 *Web:* www.firemuseummd.org	410-321-7500		520
Fire Museum of Memphis 118 Adams Ave . . . . . . Memphis TN 38103 *Web:* www.firemuseum.com	901-320-5650	529-8422	520
Fire Protection Service Inc 8050 Harrisburg Blvd . . . . Houston TX 77012 *Web:* www.fps-usa.com	713-924-9600	923-6272	679
Fire Protection Systems Inc 22 Industrial Pk Dr . . . . Hendersonville TN 37075 *Web:* www.fireprotectionsys.com	615-822-3600	822-3427	189-13
Fire Rock Products LLC 3620 Ave C . . . . Birmingham AL 35218 *Web:* www.firerock.us	205-639-5000		364
Fire Systems West Inc 206 Frontage Rd N Ste C . . . . Pacific WA 98047 *Web:* www.firesystemswest.com	253-833-1248	735-0113	283
Fireapps Inc 8777 N Gainey Center Dr Ste 201. . . . . Scottsdale AZ 85258 *TF:* 866-928-3473 ■ *Web:* www.fireapps.com	480-443-7333		177
Firecom Inc 39-27 59th St. Woodside NY 11377 *Web:* firecominc.com	718-899-6100	899-1932	283
Fire-End & Croker Corp 7 Westchester Plz . . . . Elmsford NY 10523 *TF:* 800-759-3473 ■ *Web:* www.fire-end.com	914-592-3640	592-3892	576
Firefighters Bookstore 16821 Knott Ave. . . . . La Mirada CA 90638 *TF:* 800-727-3327 ■ *Web:* www.firebooks.com	800-727-3327		95
Firefighters Community Credit Union Inc 2300 St Clair Ave NE . . . . Cleveland OH 44114 *TF:* 800-621-4644 ■ *Web:* www.ffcommunity.com	216-621-4644	694-3600	219
Firefighters' Museum 226 W Washington Blvd. Fort Wayne IN 46802 *TF:* 800-767-7752 ■ *Web:* fortwaynefiremuseum.com	260-426-0051		520
Firefly 4288 24th St . . . . San Francisco CA 94114 *Web:* www.fireflyrestaurant.com	415-821-7652		671
FireFly Balloons 850 Meacham Rd. . . . . Statesville NC 28677 *Web:* www.fireflyballoons.net	704-878-9501	878-9505	28
Firefly Milward Brown 401 Merritt 7 3rd Fl . . . . Norwalk CT 06851 *Web:* www.millwardbrown.com	203-221-0411	221-0791	466
Firefly Press 119 Braintree St No 202 . . . . Boston MA 02134 *Web:* www.fireflyletterpress.com	617-987-0599		637-2
Firehouse Brewing Co 610 Main St. . . . . Rapid City SD 57701 *Web:* firehousebrewing.com	605-348-1915		671
Firehouse Image Ctr 2000 N Illinois St . . . . Indianapolis IN 46202 *TF:* 800-382-9179 ■ *Web:* onyx.fire-house.net	317-236-1747		627
Firehouse Museum 1572 Columbia St. . . . . San Diego CA 92101 *Web:* sandiegofirehousemuseum.com	619-232-3473		520
Firehouse Restaurant 627 W Walnut St. . . . . Johnson City TN 37604 *Web:* www.thefirehousc.com	423-929-7377		671

Name	Address	City	State	Zip	Phone	Fax	Class	Other
Firehouse Restaurant Group Inc	12735 Gran Bay Pkwy Ste 150	Jacksonville	FL	32258	904-886-8300		310	*TF:* 800-388-3473 ■ *Web:* www.firehousesubs.com
Firehouse, The	1112 Second St	Sacramento	CA	95814	916-442-4772	442-6617	671	*Web:* www.firehouseoldsac.com
FireKeepers	*Nottawaseppi Huron Band of the Potawatomi* 11177 E Michigan Ave	Battle Creek	MI	49014	877-352-8777		292	*TF:* 800-270-7117 ■ *Web:* www.firekeeperscasino.com
FireKing Security Group	101 Security Pkwy	New Albany	IN	47150	812-948-8400		692	*TF:* 800-457-2424 ■ *Web:* www.fireking.com
Firelands Electric Co-opeartive Inc	1 Energy Pl PO Box 32	New London	OH	44851	419-929-1571	929-8550	245	*TF:* 800-533-8658 ■ *Web:* www.firelandsec.com
Firelands Regional Medical Ctr	1111 Hayes Ave	Sandusky	OH	44870	419-557-7400	557-6977	374-3	*TF:* 800-342-1177 ■ *Web:* www.firelands.com
FireMon	8400 W 110th St Ste 500	Overland Park	KS	66210	913-948-9570	948-9571	809	*Web:* www.firemon.com
Fireplace	1634 Beacon St	Brookline	MA	02446	617-975-1900		671	*Web:* www.fireplacerest.com
Fireplace & Bar-B-Q Center Inc	10470 Metcalf Ave	Overland Park	KS	66212	913-383-2286		362	*Web:* fireplacecenterkc.com
Firepoint Technologies Inc	27-180 Wilkinson Rd	Brampton	ON	L6T4W0	905-874-9400		261	*Web:* www.firepoint.ca
Fire-Safe Protection Services	1815 Sherwood Forest St	Houston	TX	77043	713-722-7800		283	*Web:* www.fire-safe.net
Fireship Press	PO Box 68412	Tucson	AZ	85737	520-360-6228		637-2	*Web:* www.fireshippress.com
Fireside Guard	123 N Allen St	Centralia	MO	65240	573-682-3361		532-2	*Web:* firesideguard.com
Fireside Hearth & Home	7571 215th St W	Lakeville	MN	55044	651-452-3399		111	*Web:* www.fireside.com
Fireside Inn & Suites	25 Airport Rd	West Lebanon	NH	03784	603-298-5900	298-0340	379	*TF:* 877-258-5900 ■ *Web:* www.firesideinnwestlebanon.com
Fireside Office Solutions	1713 E Bismarck Expy	Bismarck	ND	58504	701-258-8586	223-9598	112	*Web:* www.firesideos.com
Fireside Restaurant	810 Woodward Ave	New Haven	CT	06512	203-466-1919		671	*Web:* www.firesideeasthaven.com
Firestone & Parson	30 Newbury St	Boston	MA	02116	617-266-1858		410	*Web:* www.firestoneandparson.com
Firestone Fibers & Textiles Co	100 Firestone Ln PO Box 1369	Kings Mountain	NC	28086	704-734-2132	734-2104	745-3	*TF:* 800-441-1336 ■ *Web:* www.firestonefibers.com
Firestone Industrial Products Co	250 W 96th St	Indianapolis	IN	46260	800-247-4337	818-8645*	60	**Fax Area Code:* 317 ■ *TF:* 800-888-0650 ■ *Web:* www.firestoneip.com
Firestone Metal Products	1001 Lund Blvd	Anoka	MN	55303	800-426-7737	576-9596*	189-12	**Fax Area Code:* 763 ■ *TF:* 800-426-7737 ■ *Web:* firestonebpco.com
Firestone Tube Co	2700 E Main St	Russellville	AR	72802	479-968-1443		754	*Web:* www.firestonetubes.com
Firestorm Wildland Fire Suppression Inc	1100 Fortress St Ste 2	Chico	CA	95973	530-898-8153		302	*Web:* firestormfire.com
Firetrol Protection Systems Inc	3696 West 900 South Ste A	Salt Lake City	UT	84104	801-485-6900	485-6902	189-13	*Web:* www.firetrol.net
Fireworks	3307 Utah Ave S	Seattle	WA	98134	206-682-8707	467-6366	520	*TF:* 800-505-8882 ■ *Web:* www.fireworksgallery.net
Fireworks By Grucci	20 Pinehurst Dr	Bellport	NY	11713	631-286-0088	286-9036	145	*Web:* www.grucci.com
Fireworks Supermarket	3010 S Ingram Dr	Springfield	MO	65803	417-862-1931	862-9250	45	*TF:* 800-345-3957 ■ *Web:* www.fireworkssupermarket.com
Fireye Inc	3 Manchester Rd	Derry	NH	03038	603-432-4100		407	*Web:* www.fireye.com
Firezat Inc	5173 Waring Rd Ste 158	San Diego	CA	92120	619-324-9025		302	*Web:* www.firezat.com
Firm Consulting Group	2107 W Cass St Ste B	Tampa	FL	33606	877-636-9525		463	*TF:* 877-636-9525 ■ *Web:* www.firmconsultinggrp.com
FIRMA Foreign Exchange Corp	10205 101 St NW Ste 400	Edmonton	AB	T5J4H5	780-426-5971	426-5920	691	*TF:* 866-426-2605 ■ *Web:* firmafx.ca
Firmenich Inc	250 Plainsvoro	Plainsboro	NJ	08536	609-452-1000		296-15	*Web:* www.firmenich.com
Firmwater	20 Maud St Ste 405	Toronto	ON	M5V2M5	416-815-1496		180	*TF:* 877-347-6928 ■ *Web:* www.firmwater.com
FIRST	200 Bedford St	Manchester	NH	03101	603-666-3906	666-3907	48-11	*TF:* 800-871-8326 ■ *Web:* www.firstinspires.org
First - Call Medical Inc	574 Boston Rd Unit 11	Billerica	MA	01821	800-274-5399	670-5457*	415	**Fax Area Code:* 978 ■ *TF:* 800-274-5399 ■ *Web:* www.fcminc.com
First & Last Tavern	939 Maple Ave	Hartford	CT	06114	860-956-6000		671	*Web:* www.firstandlasttavern.com
First Act Inc	745 Boylston St	Boston	MA	02116	617-226-7888		526	*TF:* 888-551-1115 ■ *Web:* www.firstact.com
First Action Security Security Team Inc	525 Northern Ave PO Box 2070	Hagerstown	MD	21742	301-797-2124		692	*TF:* 800-372-7447 ■ *Web:* www.firstactionteam.com
First Affirmative Financial Network LLC	5475 Mark Dabling Blvd Ste 108	Colorado Springs	CO	80918	719-636-1045		401	*Web:* www.firstaffirmative.com
First Alarm Security & Patrol Inc	1111 Estates Dr	Aptos	CA	95003	831-476-1111		693	*TF:* 800-684-1111 ■ *Web:* firstalarm.com
First Allied Securities Inc	655 W Broadway 12th Fl	San Diego	CA	92101	800-336-8842		690	*TF:* 800-336-8842 ■ *Web:* www.firstallied.com

Name	Address	City	State	Zip	Phone	Fax	Class	Other
First American Bank	1650 Louis Ave PO Box 0794	Elk Grove Village	IL	60009	847-952-3700		360-2	*TF:* 866-449-1150 ■ *Web:* www.firstambank.com
First American Bank & Trust	2785 Hwy 20 W PO Box 550	Vacherie	LA	70090	225-265-2265	265-7339	70	*TF:* 800-738-2265 ■ *Web:* www.fabt.com
First American Corp	1 First American Way	Santa Ana	CA	92707	714-250-3000		391-6	*NYSE: FAF* ■ *TF:* 800-854-3643 ■ *Web:* www.firstam.com
First American Funds	PO Box 701	Milwaukee	WI	53201	800-677-3863		528	*TF:* 800-677-3863 ■ *Web:* www.firstamericanfunds.com
First Analysis Corp	1 S Wacker Dr Ste 3900	Chicago	IL	60606	312-258-1400		792	*Web:* firstanalysis.com
First Arizona Title Agency LLC	6263 N Scottsdale Rd Ste 190	Scottsdale	AZ	85250	480-385-6500		653	*Web:* firstaztitle.com
First Arkansas Bank & Trust	600 W Main St	Jacksonville	AR	72076	501-982-4511		70	*TF:* 800-982-4511 ■ *Web:* www.fabandt.bank
First Assembly of God	1701 N E Ave	Panama City	FL	32405	850-769-3558		48-20	*Web:* firstassemblypc.org
First Atlantic Capital Ltd	477 Madison Ave Ste 330	New York	NY	10022	212-207-0300	207-8842	401	*Web:* www.firstatlanticcapital.com
First Aviation Services Inc	15 Riverside Ave	Westport	CT	06880	203-291-3300	291-3330	770	*Web:* www.firstaviation.com
First BanCorp	PO Box 9146	San Juan	PR	00908	787-725-2511		360-2	*NYSE: FBP* ■ *TF:* 866-695-2511 ■ *Web:* www.1firstbank.com
First Bancorp	341 N Main St	Troy	NC	27371	910-576-6171	576-1070	360-2	*NASDAQ: FBNC* ■ *TF:* 800-548-9377 ■ *Web:* localfirstbank.com
First Bancorp of Indiana Inc	5001 Davis Lant Dr PO Box 1111	Evansville	IN	47706	812-492-8100		360-2	*OTC: FBPI*
First Bank Blue Earth	300 S Main St	Blue Earth	MN	56013	507-526-3241		70	*Web:* firstbankblueearth.com
First Bank of Highland Park	1835 First St	Highland Park	IL	60035	847-432-7800	433-2156	685	*TF:* 877-651-7800 ■ *Web:* www.firstbankhp.com
First Bank of Muleshoe	202 S 1st PO Box 565	Muleshoe	TX	79347	806-272-4515	272-4436	70	*TF:* 888-653-9558 ■ *Web:* fbmuleshoe.com
First Bank of Okarche, The	203 W Oklahoma Ave	Okarche	OK	73762	405-263-7215		70	*Web:* firstbankokarche.com
First Bank Southwest	2401 S Georgia	Amarillo	TX	79109	800-944-9561	355-9661*	70	**Fax Area Code:* 806 ■ *TF:* 800-944-9561 ■ *Web:* www.fbsw.com
First Bankers Trust Company NA	1201 Broadway PO Box 3566	Quincy	IL	62305	217-228-8000	228-8091	70	*TF:* 888-509-4619 ■ *Web:* www.firstbankers.com
First Banks Inc	135 N Meramec Ave	Clayton	MO	63105	314-854-4600		360-2	*Web:* www.firstbanks.com
First Baptist Church Dallas	1707 San Jacinto St	Dallas	TX	75201	214-969-0111		48-20	*Web:* www.firstdallas.org
First Baptist Church of Orlando Inc, The	3000 S John Young Pkwy	Orlando	FL	32805	407-425-2555		48-20	*Web:* www.firstorlando.com
First Bethany Bank & Trust	6500 NW 39th Expy	Bethany	OK	73008	405-789-1110	616-3300	70	*Web:* www.firstbethany.com
First Book	1319 F St NW Ste 1000	Washington	DC	20004	202-393-1222		48-5	*Web:* firstbook.org
First Busey Corp	100 W University Ave	Champaign	IL	61820	217-365-4516		360-2	*NASDAQ: BUSE* ■ *TF:* 800-672-8739 ■ *Web:* www.busey.com
First Business Financial Services Inc	401 Charmany Dr	Madison	WI	53719	608-238-8008		70	*NASDAQ: FBIZ* ■ *TF:* 866-281-5746 ■ *Web:* firstbusiness.com
First Calgary Savings	510 16th Ave NE	Calgary	AB	T2E1K4	866-923-4778	276-5299*	70	**Fax Area Code:* 403 ■ *TF:* 866-923-4778 ■ *Web:* www.firstcalgary.com
First California Press Inc	1075 Folsom St	San Francisco	CA	94103	415-626-8965	626-2632	627	*Web:* www.firstcalpress.com
First Call Computer Solutions Inc	500 N Higgins Ave Ste 201	Missoula	MT	59802	406-721-6462		179	*Web:* firstsolution.com
First Call International Inc	6329 Airport Fwy	Fort Worth	TX	76117	817-831-2220		22	*Web:* www.firstcallintl.com
First Call Nursing Services Inc	1313 N Milpitas Blvd Ste 210	Milpitas	CA	95035	408-262-1533		260	*Web:* www.firstcallnursingservices.com
First Candle	49 Locust Ave Ste 104	New Canaan	CT	06840	203-966-1300		48-17	*TF:* 800-221-7437 ■ *Web:* firstcandle.org
First Carolina Management Inc	300 N Winstead Ave	Rocky Mount	NC	27804	252-937-8111		463	*Web:* www.1stcarolina.net
First Choice Community Credit Union Inc	804 Warren Ave	Niles	OH	44446	330-652-3887	652-2681	219	*Web:* fcccu.com
First Choice Credit Union	1614 E Fourth St	Marshfield	WI	54449	715-387-8405	389-1007	219	*Web:* firstchoicecreditunion.com
First Choice Health Plan	600 University St Ste 1400	Seattle	WA	98101	800-467-5281	667-8062*	391-3	**Fax Area Code:* 206 ■ *TF:* 800-467-5281 ■ *Web:* www.fchn.com
First Choice Home Care Inc	506 Carthage St	Sanford	NC	27330	919-775-3306		363	*TF:* 877-223-3662 ■ *Web:* www.firstchoicehomecare.com
First Choice Home Health Inc	4745 NW Seventh Ct	Boynton Beach	FL	33426	561-296-2770	296-2771	363	*Web:* firstchoicehh.com
First Choice Lending Services	9821 Cogdill Rd Ste 2	Knoxville	TN	37932	855-392-4141		217	*TF:* 855-392-4141 ■ *Web:* fcls.com

Name / Address	Phone	Fax	Class
First Choice of the Midwest Inc PO Box 5078 Sioux Falls SD 57104 *TF:* 888-246-9949 ■ *Web:* www.1choicem.com	605-332-5955	332-5953	393
First Choice Packaging Solutions 1501 W State St Fremont OH 43420 *TF:* 866-700-7225 ■ *Web:* firstchoicepackaging.com	419-333-4100	333-4101	596
First Choice Senior Care Inc 10 Corporate Hill Dr Ste Little Rock AR 72205 *Web:* firstchoiceseniorcare.com	501-916-9307		363
First Choice Software LLC PO Box 490 Pocono Lake PA 18347 *Web:* www.fcs-software.com	610-436-6825	436-6829	734
First Christian Church 531 Fifth St Columbus IN 47201 *Web:* fccoc.org	812-379-4491		48-20
First Church of Christ in New Haven, The *Center Church on-the-Green* 311 Temple St New Haven CT 06511 *Web:* centerchurchonthegreen.org	203-787-0121	787-2187	50-4
First Church of Christ Scientist 210 Massachusetts Ave Boston MA 02115 *TF:* 800-288-7155 ■ *Web:* www.christianscience.com	617-450-2000		48-20
First Citizens Bancorp Inc 1230 Main St Columbia SC 29201 *OTC: FCBN* ■ *Web:* www.firstcitizens.com	803-733-2025		360-2
First Citizens National Bank Charitable Foundation PO Box 1708 Mason City IA 50402 *TF:* 800-423-1602 ■ *Web:* www.myfcb.bank	641-423-1600	423-4600	360-2
First City Bank 1885 Northwest Blvd Columbus OH 43212 *Web:* www.myfirstcitybank.com	614-487-1010		70
First City Bank of Florida 135 Perry Ave SE Fort Walton Beach FL 32548 *Web:* firstcitybank.com	850-244-5151		70
First Class Air Repair 8508 Justice Pl Ste G Groveland FL 34736 *Web:* fcar.co	352-241-7684		529
First Class Federal Credit Union 510 Business Park Ln Allentown PA 18109 *TF:* 888-458-7332 ■ *Web:* firstclass.org	610-439-4102	439-1323	219
First Class Foods Inc 12500 Inglewood Ave Hawthorne CA 90250 *Web:* firstclassfoods.com	310-676-2500		473
First Class Services Inc 9355 US Hwy 60 E Lewisport KY 42351 *TF:* 800-467-8684 ■ *Web:* www.firstclassservices.com	270-295-3746		780
First Class Solutions Inc 11426 Dorsett Rd Maryland Heights MO 63043 *Web:* www.firstclasssolutions.com	314-209-7800	209-1911	225
First Class Title Inc 1803 Research Blvd Ste 512 Rockville MD 20850 *Web:* firstclasstitle.net	301-770-4107		41
First Clinical Research LLC 2249 Sutter St San Francisco CA 94115 *Web:* www.firstclinical.com	650-465-0119		194
First Coast Energy LLP 7014 A C Skinner Pkwy Ste 290 Jacksonville FL 32256 *Web:* firstcoastenergy.com	904-596-3283		345
First Coast Hearing Clinic Inc 1835 US Hwy 1 S Ste 121 Saint Augustine FL 32084 *Web:* www.firstcoasthearing.com	904-824-6007		475
First Coast Hosting PO Box 2944 Ponte Vedra Beach FL 32004 *Web:* www.firstcoasthosting.com	904-853-6207		225
First Coast Logistics Services Inc 11460 Boote Blvd Ste 1 Jacksonville FL 32256 *Web:* www.firstcoast.net	904-757-6008	751-6244	311
First Coast No More Homeless Pets Inc 6817 Norwood Ave Jacksonville FL 32208 *Web:* fcnmhp.org	904-520-7912		794
First Colony Mall 16535 SW Fwy Sugar Land TX 77479 *Web:* www.firstcolonymall.com	281-265-6123		460
First Colorado National Bank 133 Grand Ave Paonia CO 81428 *Web:* firstcoloradobank.com	970-527-4141		70
First Command Financial Services Inc 1 Firstcomm Plz Fort Worth TX 76109 *TF:* 800-443-2104 ■ *Web:* www.firstcommand.com	817-731-8621		194
First Commercial Real Estate Services LLC 3550 Liberty Rd S Ste 290 Salem OR 97302 *Web:* firstcommercialoregon.com	503-364-7400		652
First Commonwealth Financial Corp 601 Philadelphia St Indiana PA 15701 *NYSE: FCF* ■ *TF:* 800-711-2265 ■ *Web:* www.fcbanking.com	724-463-8555		360-2
First Community Bank 420 Second Ave SW Cullman AL 35055 *Web:* www.fcbcullman.com	256-734-4863	737-8900	360-2
First Community Bank 119 S Fulton PO Box 295 Newell IA 50568 *Web:* fcb4u.com	712-272-3321		70
First Community Bank 500 Central Ave Lester Prairie MN 55354 *Web:* fcblpsl.com	320-395-2515	395-2160	70
First Community Bank 165 S Randall Rd Elgin IL 60123 *Web:* elginstatebank.com	847-622-8800		70
First Community Bank of The Ozarks 121 S Commercial Branson MO 65616 *TF:* 866-235-3122 ■ *Web:* fcboz.com	417-336-6310		70
First Community Corp (FCC) 5455 Sunset Blvd Lexington SC 29072 *NASDAQ: FCCO* ■ *TF:* 800-829-6372 ■ *Web:* www.firstcommunitysc.com	803-951-0555		360-2
First Community Credit Union (FCCU) 17151 Chesterfield Airport Rd PO Box 1030 Chesterfield MO 63005 *TF:* 800-767-8880 ■ *Web:* www.firstcommunity.com	636-728-3333		219
First Community Village 1800 Riverside Dr Columbus OH 43212 *TF:* 877-364-2570 ■ *Web:* www.nationalchurchresidences.org	614-324-4455		672
First Congregational Church 62 Centre St Nantucket MA 02554 *Web:* nantucketfcc.org	508-228-0950		50-1
First Cooperative Assn (FCA) 960 Riverview Dr PO Box 60 Cherokee IA 51012 *TF:* 877-753-5400 ■ *Web:* www.firstcoop.com	712-225-5400	225-5493	447
First Corporate Sedans Inc 60 E 42nd St Ste 2424 New York NY 10165 *Web:* www.fcsny.com	212-972-2282	286-9130	316
First County Bank Inc, The 117 Prospect St Stamford CT 06901 *Web:* www.firstcountybank.com	203-462-4407	462-4420	70
First Credit Union of Scranton 605 Davis St Scranton PA 18505 *TF:* 888-347-7818 ■ *Web:* firstcu.org	570-961-8953	961-5010	219
First Dallas Securities 2905 Maple Ave Dallas TX 75201 *Web:* firstdallas.com	214-954-1177	954-1281	690
First DataBank Inc (FDB) 701 Gateway Blvd Ste 600 South San Francisco CA 94080 *TF:* 800-633-3453 ■ *Web:* www.fdbhealth.com	800-633-3453		178-10
First Defiance Financial Corp 601 Clinton St Defiance OH 43512 *NASDAQ: FDEF* ■ *TF:* 800-472-6292 ■ *Web:* www.fdef.com	419-782-5015		360-2
First Dental Health 5771 Copley Dr Ste 101 San Diego CA 92111 *TF:* 800-334-7244 ■ *Web:* www.firstdentalhealth.com	800-334-7244		415
First District Assn (FDA) 101 S Swift Ave Litchfield MN 55355 *Web:* www.firstdistrict.com	320-693-3236		296-5
First Eagle Federal Credit Union 600 Red Brook Blvd Rm 350 Owings Mills MD 21117 *TF:* 888-231-2022 ■ *Web:* www.firsteaglefcu.com	443-548-8008	548-8030	219
First Eagle Investment Management LLC 1345 Ave of the Americas 48th Fl New York NY 10105 *Web:* www.feim.com	212-698-3300		401
First Electric Co-opeartive Corp 1000 S JP Wright Loop Rd Jacksonville AR 72076 *TF:* 800-489-7405 ■ *Web:* www.firstelectric.coop	501-982-4545		245
First Environment Inc 91 Fulton St Boonton NJ 07005 *Web:* www.firstenvironment.com	973-334-0003	334-0928	192
First Equipment Co 4851 Keller Springs Rd Ste 100 Addison TX 75001 *Web:* www.firstequipment.com	972-380-2300		264-1
First Equity Mortgage Bankers 9300 S Dadeland Blvd Ste 500 Miami FL 33156 *TF:* 800-973-3654 ■ *Web:* www.fembi.com	305-666-3333	666-3181	509
First Evangelical Free Church of st Louis County 1375 Carman Rd Manchester MO 63021 *Web:* www.efree.org	636-227-0125		48-20
First Farmers & Merchants National Bank 816 S Garden St PO Box 1148 Columbia TN 38401 *OTC: FFMH* ■ *TF:* 800-882-8378 ■ *Web:* www.myfirstfarmers.com	931-388-3145		685
First Federal Bank Fsb 6900 N Executive Dr Kansas City MO 64120 *TF:* 888-651-4759 ■ *Web:* www.ffbkc.com	816-241-7800		70
First Federal Bank of Ohio 1660 W Market St Ste A Tiffin OH 44883 *Web:* www.firstfederalbankofohio.com	419-468-1518		70
First Federal Lakewood 14806 Detroit Ave Lakewood OH 44107 *TF:* 800-966-7300 ■ *Web:* www.ffl.net	216-529-2700		70
First Federal Savings Bank of Frankfort 216 W Main St PO Box 535 Frankfort KY 40602 *TF:* 888-818-3372 ■ *Web:* ffsbky.bank	502-223-1638	223-7136	360-2
First Federal Savings Bank of Mascoutah 101 W Main St Mascoutah IL 62258 *Web:* firstfederalmascoutah.com	618-566-2343		70
First Fidelity Brokerage Inc 1140 Avenue of the Americas 9th Fl New York NY 10036 *Web:* ffbinsurance.com	212-933-9050		390
First Fidelity Capital Markets Inc 10463 Stonebridge Blvd Boca Raton FL 33498 *TF:* 800-485-3670 ■ *Web:* www.ffidelity.com	561-558-0730		401
First Fidelity Funding & Mortgage Corp 6000 Lake Forrest Dr Ste 290 Atlanta GA 30328 *Web:* firstfidelityfunding.com	404-943-1533		141
First Financial Bancorp (FFB) 255 E Fifth St Ste 700 Cincinnati OH 45202 *NASDAQ: FFBC* ■ *TF:* 877-322-9530 ■ *Web:* www.bankatfirst.com	877-322-9530		360-2
First Financial Bank PO Box 2122 Terre Haute IN 47802 *TF:* 800-511-0045 ■ *Web:* www.first-online.bank	812-238-6000		70
First Financial Bank 301 W Beauregard San Angelo TX 76903 *Web:* www.ffin.com	325-659-5900		70
First Financial Bank In Winnebago 1 Main St S Winnebago MN 56098 *Web:* 1stbago.com	507-893-3155		70
First Financial Equity Corp 7373 N Scottsdale Rd Ste D-120 Scottsdale AZ 85253 *TF:* 800-687-3800 ■ *Web:* www.ffec.com	480-951-0079		194
First Financial Network Inc 9211 Lake Hefner Pky Ste 200 Oklahoma City OK 73120 *Web:* www.ffncorp.com	405-748-4100		401
First Flight Insurance Group Inc 4112 N Croatan Hwy Kitty Hawk NC 27949 *Web:* firstflightinsurance.com	252-261-1903		390
First Flight Island Restaurant & Brewery 301 Whitehead St Key West FL 33040 *TF:* 800-507-9955 ■ *Web:* firstflightkw.com	305-293-8484	296-0047	671
First Florida Credit Union 500 W First St Jacksonville FL 32202 *Web:* www.firstflorida.org	904-359-6800		219
First Foundation Bank 18101 Von Karman Ave Ste 750 Irvine CA 92612 *TF:* 800-224-7931 ■ *Web:* firstfoundationinc.com	949-202-4100		70
First FSB 633 La Salle St Ottawa IL 61350 *Web:* www.ffsbweb.com	815-434-3500		71
First General Bank 1744 S Nogales St Rowland Heights CA 91748 *Web:* www.fgbusa.com	626-820-1234		70

Company	Phone	Fax	Class
First Generation Productions 410 Allentown Dr, Allentown PA 18109 *Web:* www.firstgencom.com	610-437-4300		514
First Gold Hotel 270 Main St, Deadwood SD 57732 *TF:* 800-274-1876 ■ *Web:* firstgold.com	605-578-9777	578-3979	379
First Hartford Corp 149 Colonial Rd, Manchester CT 06042 *OTC:* FHRT ■ *Web:* www.firsthartford.com	860-646-6555		653
First Hawaiian Bank 999 Bishop St, Honolulu HI 96813 *TF:* 888-844-4444 ■ *Web:* www.fhb.com	808-525-6340		70
First Health Group Corp *Coventry* 3200 Highland Ave, Downers Grove IL 60515 *TF:* 800-247-2898 ■ *Web:* firsthealth.com	630-737-7900		463
First Heartland Capital Inc 1839 Lake St Louis Blvd, Lake Saint Louis MO 63367 *Web:* www.joinfhc.com	636-625-0900		690
First Heritage Federal Credit Union 110 Village Sq Ste 101, Painted Post NY 14870 *Web:* fhfcu.org	607-936-4667		219
First Horizon Bank 165 Madison Ave, Memphis TN 38103 *TF:* 800-382-5465 ■ *Web:* www.firsthorizon.com	901-523-4883		70
First Industrial Realty Trust Inc 311 S Wacker Dr Ste 4200, Chicago IL 60606 *NYSE:* FR ■ *Web:* www.firstindustrial.com	312-344-4300	922-6320	655
First Infrastructure LLC 15 Wendover Rd, Montclair NJ 07042 *Web:* www.1stinfrastructure.com	973-783-0088		463
First Insight Corp 6723 NE Bennett St Ste 200, Hillsboro OR 97124 **Fax Area Code:* 503 ■ *TF:* 800-920-1940 ■ *Web:* www.first-insight.com	800-920-1940	707-8188*	177
First Institute Inc 790 S Mchenry Ave, Crystal Lake IL 60014 *Web:* firstinstitute.edu	815-459-3500		570
First Insurance Agency 20 E State St, Mason City IA 50401 *TF:* 800-247-0713 ■ *Web:* 1stinsurance.com	641-421-8000	421-1940	390
First Insurance Company of Hawaii Ltd 1100 Ward Ave PO Box 2866, Honolulu HI 96803 *TF:* 800-272-5202 ■ *Web:* www.ficoh.com	808-527-7777		391-4
First Insurance Funding Corp 450 Skokie Blvd Ste 1000, Northbrook IL 60062 *TF:* 800-837-3707 ■ *Web:* www.firstinsurancefunding.com	800-837-3707	837-3709	217
First Intercontinental Bank, The 5593 Buford Hwy, Doraville GA 30340 *Web:* www.firsticbank.com	770-451-7200		70
First International Health Foods Ltd 7 Hoover Ave, Haverstraw NY 10927 *Web:* www.bradsorganic.com	845-429-9080		805
First Interstate Bancsystem Inc 401 N 31st St, Billings MT 59101 *NASDAQ:* FIBK ■ *TF:* 888-752-3341 ■ *Web:* www.firstinterstatebank.com	406-255-5000		360-2
First Investors Financial Services Group Inc 380 Interstate North Pkwy 3rd Fl, Atlanta GA 30339 *Web:* www.fifsg.com	770-956-3800		390
First Jackson Bank 43243 US Hwy 72, Stevenson AL 35772 *TF:* 888-950-2265 ■ *Web:* firstjacksonbank.com	256-437-2107		70
First Keystone Community Bank 111 W Front St, Berwick PA 18603 *TF:* 888-759-2266 ■ *Web:* www.fkc.bank	570-752-3671		70
First Ladies National Historic Site 205 Market Ave S, Canton OH 44702 *Web:* www.nps.gov	330-452-0876	456-3414	564
First Lease Inc 1 Walnut Grove Dr Ste 300, Horsham PA 19044 **Fax Area Code:* 215 ■ *TF:* 866-493-4778 ■ *Web:* www.firstleaseonline.com	866-493-4778	283-9870*	264-4
First Madison Valley Bank 213 E Main St, Ennis MT 59729 *Web:* bankingonthofuturo.com	406-682-4215		70
First Manhattan Co 399 Park Ave, New York NY 10022 *Web:* firstmanhattan.com	212-756-3300	223-4175	690
First Manhattan Consulting Group 90 Park Ave 18th Fl, New York NY 10016 *Web:* www.fmcgdirect.com	212-557-0500	338-9296	194
First Mercantile Trust Co 57 Germantown Ct 4th Fl, Cordova TN 38018 *TF:* 800-753-3682 ■ *Web:* www.firstmerc.com	901-753-9080		70
First Metro Bank 406 Avalon Ave, Muscle Shoals AL 35661 *Web:* www.firstmetro.com	256-386-0600	386-0651	70
First Mid-Illinois Bank & Trust 1515 Charleston Ave, Mattoon IL 61938 *NASDAQ:* FMBH ■ *TF:* 866-258-0686 ■ *Web:* www.firstmid.com	217-234-7454	258-0426	70
First Midwest Bancorp Inc 1 Pierce Pl Ste 1500, Itasca IL 60143 *NASDAQ:* FMBI ■ *TF:* 800-322-3623 ■ *Web:* www.firstmidwest.com	630-875-7450		360-2
First National Bank PO Box 578, Fort Collins CO 80521 *TF:* 800-883-8773 ■ *Web:* www.fnbo.com	970-495-9450		70
First National Bank 316 E Bremer Ave PO Box 837, Waverly IA 50677 *Web:* www.firstiowa.bank	319-352-1340	352-6323	70
First National Bank Alaska 101 W 36 Ave PO Box 100720, Anchorage AK 99510 *OTC:* FBAK ■ *TF:* 800-856-4362 ■ *Web:* www.fnbalaska.com	907-777-4362		70
First National Bank Creston PO Box 445, Creston IA 50801 *TF:* 877-782-2195 ■ *Web:* www.fnbcreston.com	641-782-2195		70
First National Bank In Alamogordo 414 Tenth St PO Box 9, Alamogordo NM 88311 *Web:* www.fnb4u.com	575-437-4880	437-1631	70
First National Bank In Amboy 220 E Main St PO Box 80, Amboy IL 61310 *TF:* 888-586-8327 ■ *Web:* fnbamboy.com	815-857-3625	857-2341	70
First National Bank In Frankfort 124 N Kansas, Frankfort KS 66427 *Web:* fnbfrankfortks.com	785-292-4433		70
First National Bank In Olney 101 E Main St, Olney IL 62450 *Web:* fnbolney.com	618-395-8541		70
First National Bank In Tremont 134 S Sampson St PO Box 23, Tremont IL 61568 *Web:* www.tremontbank.com	309-925-2121	925-5448	70
First National Bank Jasper 301 E Houston St, Jasper TX 75951 *TF:* 800-340-7167 ■ *Web:* www.fnbjasper.com	409-384-3486		70
First National Bank of Carrollton 604 Highland Ave, Carrollton KY 41008 *Web:* fnbkentucky.com	502-732-4406		70
First National Bank of Dennison, Ohio 105 Grant St, Dennison OH 44621 *Web:* fnbdennison.com	740-922-2532		70
First National Bank of Granbury 101 E Bridge St, Granbury TX 76048 *Web:* fnbgranbury.com	817-573-2655		70
First National Bank of Grayson 200 S Carol Malone Blvd, Grayson KY 41143 *TF:* 800-880-6621 ■ *Web:* fnbgrayson.com	606-474-5139	474-6626	70
First National Bank of Hebbronville, The 305 N Smith Ave, Hebbronville TX 78361 *TF:* 800-268-1312 ■ *Web:* fnbhebb.com	361-527-3221	527-5451	70
First National Bank of Illinois Inc 3256 Ridge Rd, Lansing IL 60438 *Web:* www.fnbiweb.com	708-474-1300		70
First National Bank of Lacon 111 S Broad St PO Box 308, Lacon IL 61540 *Web:* fnblacon.com	309-246-2415		70
First National Bank of Manchester 100 W High St, Manchester TN 37355 *Web:* www.fnbmbank.com	931-728-3518		70
First National Bank of Muscatine 300 E Second St, Muscatine IA 52761 *Web:* www.fnbmusc.com	563-263-4221		70
First National Bank of Omaha 134 S 13th St Ste 100, Omaha NE 68197 *TF:* 800-462-5266 ■ *Web:* firstnational.locatorsearch.com	402-602-3022		70
First National Bank of Oneida, The 18418 Alberta St PO Box 4699, Oneida TN 37841 *Web:* www.fnboneida.com	423-569-8586	569-9826	70
First National Bank of Paragould 200 W Ct St, Paragould AR 72450 *Web:* www.fnbank.net	870-215-4000		70
First National Bank of Santa Fe PO Box 609, Santa Fe NM 87504 *TF:* 888-912-2265 ■ *Web:* www.firstnational1870.com	505-992-2000		70
First National Bank of South Miami 5750 Sunset Dr, Miami FL 33143 *Web:* www.fnbsm.com	305-667-5511		70
First National Bank of Suffield, The 30 Bridge St, Suffield CT 06078 *Web:* location.bankatpeoples.com	860-668-3950		70
First National Bank of Syracuse 509 N Main PO Box 719, Johnson KS 67855 *Web:* fnb-windmill.com	620-492-1754	276-3495	70
First National Bank of Tennessee 214 E Main St, Livingston TN 38570 *Web:* www.fnbotn.com	931-823-1261	520-6875	360-2
First National Bank of Winnsboro 315 N Main St, Winnsboro TX 75494 *Web:* fnbwinnsboro.com	903-342-5275		70
First National Bank South 423 W 12th St, Alma GA 31510 *Web:* fnbsouth.net	912-632-7262	632-7865	70
First National Bankers Bankshares Inc (FNBB) 7813 Office Pk Blvd, Baton Rouge LA 70809 *TF:* 800-421-6182 ■ *Web:* www.bankers-bank.com	225-924-8015	952-0899	70
First National of Nebraska Inc 1620 Dodge St, Omaha NE 68197 *TF:* 800-688-7070 ■ *Web:* www.fnni.com	402-341-0500	938-5302	360-2
First Nations Bank 7757 W Devon Ave, Chicago IL 60631 *Web:* fnbwbank.com	773-594-5900		70
First Nations Development Institute 2217 Princess Anne St Ste 111-1, Fredericksburg VA 22401 *Web:* firstnations.org	540-371-5615		48-14
First Nations University of Canada *Prince Albert Campus* 1301 Central Ave, Prince Albert SK S6V4W1 *Web:* www.fnuniv.ca	306-765-3333	765-3330	785
Saskatoon 229 Fourth Ave S, Saskatoon SK S7K4K3 *TF:* 800-267-6303 ■ *Web:* fnuniv.ca	306-931-1800	931-1849	785
First New Mexico Financial Corp 300 S Gold Ave, Deming NM 88030 *Web:* firstnewmexicobank.com	575-546-2691		70
First Niles Financial Inc 55 N Main St, Niles OH 44446 *NYSE:* FNFI ■ *Web:* www.homefedniles.com	330-652-2539		360-2
First of Long Island Corp 10 Glen Head Ave, Glen Head NY 11545 *NASDAQ:* FLIC ■ *Web:* www.fnbli.com	516-671-4900	676-7900	360-2
First Oklahoma Federal Credit Union 1419 S Denver Ave, Tulsa OK 74119 *TF:* 800-843-9661 ■ *Web:* firstokfcu.org	918-582-1965	592-7721	219
First Operations LP 8273 Moberly Ln, Dallas TX 75227 *Web:* www.firstco.com	214-388-5751	388-2255	14
First Options of Chicago Inc 135 S LaSalle St Ste 4000, Chicago IL 60603 *Web:* firstoptions.com	312-933-5884		690
First Pacific Advisors Inc 11601 Wilshire Blvd Ste 1200, Los Angeles CA 90025 *TF:* 800-982-4372 ■ *Web:* fpa.com	310-473-0225	996-5450	401
First Palmetto Bank PO Box 430, Camden SC 29021 *TF:* 800-922-7411 ■ *Web:* www.firstpalmetto.com	803-432-2265		70
First Peak Visitor Ctr 20 E Mills St PO Box 308, Columbus NC 28722 *TF:* 800-440-7848 ■ *Web:* firstpeaknc.com	828-894-2324		206
First Peoples Bank 105 Chipley St, Pine Mountain GA 31822 *Web:* firstpeoplesbank.com	706-663-2700		70
First Peoples Buffalo Jump State Park 342 Ulm Vaughn Rd, Ulm MT 59485 *Web:* www.fwp.mt.gov	406-866-2217		565
First Personal Bank 14701 Ravinia Ave, Orland Park IL 60462 *Web:* www.firstpersonalbank.net	708-226-2727		70

				Phone	Fax	Class
First Piedmont Corp 108 S Main St *Web:* www.relyonred.com	Chatham	VA	24531	434-432-0211		525
First Plastics Corp 22 Jytek Rd *Web:* firstplastics.com	Leominster	MA	01453	978-537-0367	840-6908	604
First Port City Bank 400 W Shotwell St *TF:* 866-323-3664 ■ *Web:* firstportcity.com	Bainbridge	GA	39818	229-246-6200	248-2709	70
First Priority Inc 1590 Todd Farm Dr *TF:* 800-650-4899 ■ *Web:* www.prioritycare.com	Elgin	IL	60123	847-289-1600		582
First Pryority Bank 310 E Graham *Web:* www.firstpryoritybank.com	Pryor	OK	74361	918-825-2121		70
First Quality Enterprises Inc 80 Cuttermill Rd Ste 500 *Web:* www.firstquality.com	Great Neck	NY	11021	516-829-3030	829-4949	548
First Quality Products Inc 121 N Rd *Web:* www.firstquality.com	Mcelhattan	PA	17748	570-769-6900		476
First Quality Tissue 904 Woods Ave *Web:* www.firstquality.com	Lock Haven	PA	17745	570-748-1200		557
First Quantum Minerals Ltd 543 Granville St 14th Fl *TSX:* FM ■ *TF:* 888-688-6577 ■ *Web:* www.first-quantum.com	Vancouver	BC	V6C1X8	604-688-6577	688-3818	502
First Rapha Home Health Inc 4402 Broadway Blvd Ste 15 *Web:* www.firstraphahhi.com	Garland	TX	75043	972-240-5300	240-5332	363
First Rate Staffing 1920 W Camelback Rd Ste 102 *TF:* 800-357-6242 ■ *Web:* www.first-ratestaffing.com	Phoenix	AZ	85015	602-442-5277		260
First Real Estate Investment Trust of New Jersey 505 Main St *Web:* freitnj.com	Hackensack	NJ	07601	201-488-6400	487-1798	655
First Realty Management Corp 151 Tremont St PH 1 *Web:* www.firstrealtymgt.com	Boston	MA	02111	617-423-7000		655
First Recruiting LLC 33 N LaSalle St Ste 2250 *Web:* firstassoc.com	Chicago	IL	60602	312-253-4000		260
First Regional Library 370 W Commerce St *Web:* firstregional.org	Hernando	MS	38632	662-429-4439	429-8853	434-3
First Reliance Bank 2170 W Palmetto St *TF:* 888-543-5510 ■ *Web:* www.firstreliance.com	Florence	SC	29501	843-656-5000		70
First Republic Bank 111 Pine St *NYSE:* FRC ■ *TF:* 800-392-1400 ■ *Web:* www.firstrepublic.com	San Francisco	CA	94111	415-392-1400	392-1413	70
First Resource Bank 7449 Village Dr *Web:* myfrbank.com	Lino Lakes	MN	55014	651-785-9320		70
First Resource Computer Inc 590 Reservoir Ave *Web:* www.frcomputers.com	Cranston	RI	02910	401-941-2500	941-9544	175
First Run Features 630 Ninth Ave Ste 1213 *TF:* 800-229-8575 ■ *Web:* www.firstrunfeatures.com	New York	NY	10036	212-243-0600	989-7649	511
First Savings Bank 2804 N Telshor Blvd *TF:* 800-555-6895 ■ *Web:* www.firstsavingsbanks.bank	Las Cruces	NM	88011	575-521-7931		70
First Security Bank of Missoula 1704 Dearborn PO Box 4506 *TF:* 888-782-3115 ■ *Web:* www.fsbmsla.com	Missoula	MT	59801	406-728-3115		70
First Security Bank of Sleepy Eye 100 Main St E PO Box 469 *Web:* www.firstsecuritybanks.com	Sleepy Eye	MN	56085	507-794-3911	794-5140	70
First Security Company Inc 212 Third Ave NW *Web:* firstsecuritycompany.com	Hickory	NC	28601	828-322-4171		390
First Security Mortgage Home Loans Inc 11839 Sorrento Valley Rd Ste 903 *Web:* www.1stsecuritymortgage.com	San Diego	CA	92121	858-565-4466		509
First Sentinel Bank 315 Railroad Ave *Web:* www.firstsentinelbank.com	Richlands	VA	24641	276-963-0836		70
First Service (FS) 737 Southpoint Blvd Ste D **Fax Area Code:* 707 ■ *TF:* 800-227-1742 ■ *Web:* store.clubstuff.com	Petaluma	CA	94954	800-227-1742	781-1970*	711
First Shore Federal 106-108 S Div St PO Box 4248 *TF:* 800-634-6309 ■ *Web:* www.firstshorefederal.com	Salisbury	MD	21803	410-546-1101	546-9590	71
First Signal LLC 2150 NW Pkwy SE Ste P *Web:* www.firstsignal.com	Marietta	GA	30067	770-988-8744		647
First South Insurance Agency Inc 107 Brookside Pkwy *TF:* 800-354-0303 ■ *Web:* fsia.net	Lexington	SC	29072	803-356-0303		390
First Southern Bank 301 S Ct St *TF:* 800-625-7131 ■ *Web:* www.firstsouthern.com	Florence	AL	35630	256-718-4200	718-4296	360-2
First Southwest Bancorp 720 Main St *Web:* www.fswb.bank	Alamosa	CO	81101	719-587-4200		70
First State Ballet Theatre 818 N Market St *Web:* firststateballet.org	Wilmington	DE	19801	302-658-7897		573-1
First State Bank 730 Harry Sauner Rd *TF:* 800-987-2566 ■ *Web:* www.fsb4me.com	Hillsboro	OH	45133	937-393-9170		360-2
First State Bank 708 Azalea Dr PO Box 506 **Fax Area Code:* 601 ■ *TF:* 866-408-3582 ■ *Web:* www.firststatebnk.bank	Waynesboro	MS	39367	866-408-3582	735-0231*	70
First State Bank 206 N Penn Ave *Web:* fsbnesscity.com	Ness City	KS	67560	785-798-3347		70
First State Bank 105 W Main St *Web:* firstatebank.com	Norton	KS	67654	785-877-3341		70
First State Bank & Trust Co 1005 E 23rd St *TF:* 888-674-4344 ■ *Web:* www.firststatebankandtrust.com	Fremont	NE	68025	402-721-2500		70
First State Bank of Brownsboro 14225 Hwy 31 E *Web:* fsbbrownsboro.com	Brownsboro	TX	75756	903-852-6911		70
First State Bank of Burnet 136 E Washington PO Box 10 *Web:* fsbburnet.com	Burnet	TX	78611	512-756-2191		70
First State Bank of De Queen 402 W Collin Raye Dr *Web:* firststatebankdequeen.com	De Queen	AR	71832	870-642-4423		70
First State Bank of Kansas City 650 Kansas Ave *TF:* 800-883-1242 ■ *Web:* www.cfbkc.com	Kansas City	KS	66105	913-371-1242	371-7516	70
First State Heritage Park 102 S State St *Web:* www.destateparks.com	Dover	DE	19901	302-739-9194	739-6264	565
First Street for Boomers & Beyond Inc 1998 Ruffin Mill Rd *TF:* 800-958-8324 ■ *Web:* www.firststreetonline.com	Colonial Heights	VA	23834	804-524-9888		195
First Sun EAP 2700 Middleburg Dr Ste 208 *TF:* 800-968-8143 ■ *Web:* www.firstsuneap.com	Columbia	SC	29204	803-376-2668		463
First Supply LLC 6800 Gisholt Dr *Web:* www.firstsupply.com	Madison	WI	53713	608-222-7799	223-6664	612
First Surgical Partners Inc 411 First St *Web:* www.firstsurgicalpartners.com	Bellaire	TX	77401	713-665-1111	665-4146	787
First Texas Bank 501 E 3rd St *TF:* 866-220-1598 ■ *Web:* www.firstexbank.com	Lampasas	TX	76550	512-556-3691	556-6104	70
First to The Finish Inc 1325 N Broad St *TF:* 800-747-9013 ■ *Web:* www.firsttothefinish.com	Carlinville	IL	62626	800-747-9013		711
First Tool Corp 612 Linden Ave *Web:* www.firsttoolcorp.com	Dayton	OH	45403	937-254-6197	254-0625	757
First Trinity Financial Corp 7633 E 63rd Pl Ste 230 *TF:* 888-883-1499 ■ *Web:* www.firsttrinityfinancial.com	Tulsa	OK	74133	888-883-1499		360-2
First Truck Centre Inc 11313 170 St *TF:* 888-882-8530 ■ *Web:* www.firsttruck.ca	Edmonton	AB	T5M3P5	780-413-8800		57
First Tryon Securities LLC 1355 Greenwood Cliff Ste 401 *Web:* www.firsttryon.com	Charlotte	NC	28204	704-372-6118		690
First Unitarian Church of Philadelphia 2125 Chestnut St *Web:* www.philauu.org	Philadelphia	PA	19103	215-563-3980	563-4209	50-1
First United Bank 1400 W Main St *TF:* 800-924-4427 ■ *Web:* www.firstunitedbank.com	Durant	OK	74701	580-924-2211	916-3287	70
First United Bank 503 Briggs Ave S *Web:* firstunitedonline.com	Park River	ND	58270	701-284-7244		70
First United Bank & Trust 19 S Second St *NASDAQ:* FUNC ■ **Fax Area Code:* 301 ■ *TF:* 888-692-2654 ■ *Web:* www.mybank.com	Oakland	MD	21550	888-692-2654	334-5784*	360-2
First UNUM Life Insurance Co 2211 Congress St *TF:* 800-633-7491 ■ *Web:* www.unum.com	Portland	ME	04122	207-575-2211		391-2
First Utah BanCorp 3826 South 2300 East *Web:* www.firstutahbank.com	Salt Lake City	UT	84109	801-272-9454		70
First West Inc 1905 Stadium Dr *Web:* 1stwestinsurance.com	Bozeman	MT	59715	406-587-5111		390
First Western Advisors 3165 E Millrock Dr Ste 340 *TF:* 800-937-3500 ■ *Web:* www.raymondjames.com	Holladay	UT	84121	801-930-6500	930-6501	463
First Western Bank & Trust PO Box 1090 *TF:* 800-688-2584 ■ *Web:* www.firstwestern.bank	Minot	ND	58702	701-852-3711	857-7195	70
First Whitney Bank & Trust 223 Chestnut St *Web:* www.firstwhitneybank.com	Atlantic	IA	50022	712-243-3195		70
Firstbank of Nebraska 201 E Fifth St *TF:* 888-667-2865 ■ *Web:* firstbankne.com	Wahoo	NE	68066	402-443-4117	443-5093	70
Firstbase Business Services 1500 W Georgia 13 Fl *TF:* 800-758-2922 ■ *Web:* www.firstbase.ca	Abbotsford	BC	V2S2E1	604-850-5334		344
FirstCare 1901 W Loop 289 Ste 9 *TF:* 800-884-4901 ■ *Web:* www.firstcare.com	Lubbock	TX	79407	806-784-4300		391-2
FirstCash Inc 1600 W 7th St *NASDAQ:* FCFS ■ *TF:* 800-290-4598 ■ *Web:* www.firstcash.com	Fort Worth	TX	76102	817-335-1100	461-7019	569
FirstCom Music 1325 Capital Pkwy Ste 109 *TF:* 800-858-8880 ■ *Web:* www.firstcom.com	Carrollton	TX	75006	972-389-2800	242-6526	525
Firstech Environmental Inc 1433 Hwy 34 Ste A6 *TF:* 800-997-2820 ■ *Web:* www.askusfirst.com	Farmingdale	NJ	07727	732-751-1640		192
FirstEnergy Corp 76 S Main St *NYSE:* FE ■ *TF:* 800-633-4766 ■ *Web:* www.firstenergycorp.com	Akron	OH	44308	800-633-4766		360-5
Firstenergy Family Credit Union Inc 575 White Pond Dr Ste E *Web:* fefcu.com	Akron	OH	44320	330-535-3611		219
Firstexpress Inc 1137 Freightliner Dr **Fax Area Code:* 615 ■ *TF:* 800-848-9203 ■ *Web:* www.firstexpress.com	Nashville	TN	37210	800-848-9203	244-1448*	780
FirstFed Bancorp Inc 1630 Fourth Ave N PO Box 340 *TF:* 800-436-5112 ■ *Web:* www.firstfedbessemer.com	Bessemer	AL	35020	205-428-8472	428-8652	360-2
FirstGiving Inc 100 Cambridge Park Dr *TF:* 800-687-8505 ■ *Web:* www.firstgiving.com	Cambridge	MA	02140	800-687-8505		387
Firsthand Capital Management Inc 150 Almaden Blvd Ste 1250 *Web:* firsthandcapital.com	San Jose	CA	95113	408-886-7096		401
FirstHealth Hospice 5 Aviemore Dr *Web:* www.firsthealth.org	Pinehurst	NC	28374	910-715-6000		371
FirsTier Bank (Kimball NE) 115 S Walnut *Web:* www.firstierbanks.com	Kimball	NE	69145	308-235-4633	235-3499	70
Firstline Business Systems Inc 6108 Northeast Hwy 99 Ste 104 *Web:* firstline-online.com	Vancouver	WA	98660	360-695-3138		535
Firstoption Workforce Solutions 8918 Tesoro Dr Ste 500 *Web:* www.firstoptionws.com	San Antonio	TX	78217	210-733-3700	733-3711	260
FirstPoint Inc 225 Commerce Pl *TF:* 800 288 7408 ■ *Web:* www.firstpointresources.com	Greensboro	NC	27401	336-378-6310		393

Phone | Fax | Class

Firstrust Savings Bank
15 E Ridge Pk 4th Fl . . . . . Conshohocken PA 19428 610-238-5000 941-5544 70
TF: 800-220-2265 ■ *Web:* www.firstrust.com

FirstService Corp
1140 Bay St 1st Service Bldg Ste 4000 . . . . . Toronto ON M5S2B4 416-960-9500 185
TSE: FSV ■ *Web:* www.firstservice.com

Firstsight Vision Services Inc
1202 Monte Vista Ave Ste 17 . . . . . Upland CA 91786 800-841-2790 698-7773* 391-3
**Fax Area Code:* 866 ■ *TF:* 800-841-2790 ■ *Web:* www.firstsightvision.net

Firstwave Technologies Inc
99 MedTech Dr . . . . . Batavia NY 14020 877-784-0269 178-11
TF: 877-784-0269 ■ *Web:* firstwavetechnologies.com

Fisc Investment Services Corp
1849 Clairmont Rd . . . . . Decatur GA 30033 404-321-1212 690
TF: 800-241-3203 ■ *Web:* www.palmeragency.com

FISCA (Financial Service Centers of America Inc)
21 Main St 1st Fl . . . . . Hackensack NJ 07602 202-719-2388 487-3954* 49-2
**Fax Area Code:* 201 ■ *Web:* www.fisca.org

Fiscal Doctor Inc 812 Hallbrook Ln . . . . . Alpharetta GA 30004 678-319-4739 194
Web: www.fiscaldoctor.com

Fiscal Note
1201 Pennsylvania Ave NW . . . . . Washington DC 20004 202-793-5300 177
Web: www.fiscalnote.com

Fischbach Gallery 210 11th Ave . . . . . New York NY 10001 212-759-2345 42
Web: www.fischbachgallery.com

Fischbein Co 151 Walker Rd . . . . . Statesville NC 28625 704-871-1159 872-3303 547
TF: 800-927-4674 ■ *Web:* www.hamer-fischbein.com

Fischer Cunnane & Associates Ltd
11 Turner Ln . . . . . West Chester PA 19380 610-431-1003 2
Web: www.fischercunnane.com

Fischer Custom Communications Inc
20603 Earl St . . . . . Torrance CA 90503 310-303-3300 248
Web: www.fischercc.com

Fischer Deb (Sen R - NE)
454 Russell Senate Office Bldg . . . . . Washington DC 20510 202-224-6551 228-1325 342-2
Web: www.fischer.senate.gov

Fischer Environmental Service Inc
1980 Surgi Dr . . . . . Mandeville LA 70448 800-391-2565 577
TF: 800-391-2565 ■ *Web:* www.fischerenv.com

Fischer International Systems Corp
9045 Strada Stell Ct Ste 201 . . . . . Naples FL 34109 239-643-1500 643-3772 178-1
TF: 800-776-7258 ■ *Web:* www.fisc.com

Fischer Meats 85 Front St N . . . . . Issaquah WA 98027 425-392-3131 392-0168 296-26
Web: www.fischermeatsnw.com

Fischer Tool & Die Corp
7155 Industrial Dr . . . . . Temperance MI 48182 734-847-4788 757
Web: www.fischertool.com

Fischer, Brown, Bartlett & Gunn PC
1319 E Prospect Rd . . . . . Fort Collins CO 80525 970-407-9000 407-1055 41
Web: fbbglaw.com

Fischler Diamonds Inc
580 Fifth Ave Ste 3100 . . . . . New York NY 10036 212-921-8196 410
Web: fischlerdiamonds.be

Fiserv Inc 255 Fiserv Dr PO Box 979 . . . . . Brookfield WI 53008 262-879-5000 69
NASDAQ: FISV ■ *TF:* 800-872-7882 ■ *Web:* www.fiserv.com

Fisgard Capital Corp 3378 Douglas St . . . . . Victoria BC V8Z3L3 250-382-9255 690
TF: 866-382-9255 ■ *Web:* fisgard.com

Fish & Richardson One Marina Park Dr . . . . . Boston MA 02110 617-542-5070 428
Web: www.fr.com

Fish City Grill 445 Coneflower Dr . . . . . Garland TX 75040 972-675-1600 671
Web: fishcitygrill.com

Fish Enterprises 905 S Fair Oaks Ave . . . . . Pasadena CA 91105 626-773-8800 773-8820 187
Web: www.fishenterprises.com

Fish House, The 4919 N University St . . . . . Peoria IL 61614 309-691-9358 671
Web: www.fishhousepeoria.com

Fish Market 105 King St . . . . . Alexandria VA 22314 703-836-5676 671
Web: www.fishmarketva.com

Fish Oven & Equipment Corp
120 W Kent Ave PO Box 875 . . . . . Wauconda IL 60084 847-526-8686 526-7447 298
TF: 877-526-8720 ■ *Web:* www.fishoven.com

Fish Window Cleaning Services Inc
200 Enchanted Pkwy . . . . . Manchester MO 63021 636-779-1500 530-7856 310
TF: 877-707-3474 ■ *Web:* www.fishwindowcleaning.com

Fishbait Marketing LLC (FB)
1968 Long Creek Rd . . . . . Wadmalaw Island SC 29487 843-557-0535 557-0536 463
Web: fishbaitmarketing.com

Fishbeck Inc
1515 Arboretum Dr SE . . . . . Grand Rapids MI 49546 616-575-3824 261
TF: 800-456-3824 ■ *Web:* fishbeck.com

FISHBIO 180 E Fourth St Ste 160 . . . . . Chico CA 95928 530-892-9686 192
Web: fishbio.com

Fishbowl Brew Pub & Cafe
515 Jefferson St SE . . . . . Olympia WA 98501 360-943-3650 671
Web: www.fishbrewing.com

Fisher & Arnold Inc
9180 Crestwyn Hills Dr . . . . . Memphis TN 38125 901-748-1811 194
TF: 888-583-9724 ■ *Web:* www.fisherarnold.com

Fisher & Ludlow Nucor Grating Inc
2000 Corporate Dr PO Box 1238 . . . . . Wexford PA 15090 724-934-5320 491
TF: 800-334-2047 ■ *Web:* www.nucorgrating.com

Fisher & Paykel Appliances Inc
5900 Skylab Rd . . . . . Huntington Beach CA 92647 888-936-7872 547-1971* 36
**Fax Area Code:* 800 ■ *TF:* 888-936-7872 ■ *Web:* www.fisherpaykel.com

Fisher & Paykel Healthcare Inc
173 Technology Dr Ste 100 . . . . . Irvine CA 92618 949-453-4000 453-4001 250
TF: 800-446-3908 ■ *Web:* www.fphcare.com

Fisher & Son Company Inc 110 Summit Dr . . . . . Exton PA 19341 610-363-5225 363-0563 276
TF: 800-262-2127 ■ *Web:* www.fisherandson.com

Fisher Air Heating & Air Conditioning Services
239 Viking Ave . . . . . Brea CA 92821 714-529-9600 189-10
Web: fisherair.com

Fisher Athletic Equipment Inc
2060 Cauble Rd . . . . . Salisbury NC 28144 800-438-6028 711
TF: 800-438-6028 ■ *Web:* www.fisherathletic.com

Fisher Auction Company Inc
2112 E Atlantic Blvd . . . . . Pompano Beach FL 33062 954-942-0917 782-8143 655
TF: 800-331-6620 ■ *Web:* www.fisherauction.com

Fisher Auto Parts
512 Greenville Ave PO Box 2246 . . . . . Staunton VA 24401 540-885-8901 61
Web: www.fisherautoparts.com

Fisher Bag Company Inc 7121 S 188th St . . . . . Kent WA 98032 206-575-4888 575-9861 66
Web: www.fisherbag.com

Fisher Canvas Products Inc
415 St Mary St . . . . . Burlington NJ 08016 800-892-6688 733
TF: 800-892-6688 ■ *Web:* www.fishercanvas.com

Fisher College 118 Beacon St . . . . . Boston MA 02116 617-236-8800 236-5473 162
TF: 866-266-6007 ■ *Web:* www.fisher.edu

Fisher Container Corp
1111 Busch Pkwy . . . . . Buffalo Grove IL 60089 847-541-0000 541-0075 548
TF: 800-837-2247 ■ *Web:* ppcflex.com

Fisher Corp 1625 W Maple Rd . . . . . Troy MI 48084 248-280-0808 489
Web: www.fisherco.com

Fisher County PO Box 368 . . . . . Roby TX 79543 325-776-2401 776-3274 338
Web: www.fishercounty.org

Fisher Dachs Assoc
22 W 19th St 6th Fl . . . . . New York NY 10011 212-691-3020 633-1644 722
Web: www.fda-online.com

Fisher Development Inc
601 California St Ste 300 . . . . . San Francisco CA 94108 415-228-3060 186
Web: www.fisherinc.com

Fisher Electric Technology
2801 72nd St N . . . . . Saint Petersburg FL 33710 727-345-9122 247
Web: www.fisherelectric.com

Fisher Engineering 50 Gordon Dr . . . . . Rockland ME 04841 207-701-4200 516
Web: www.fisherplows.com

Fisher Foods Marketing Inc
5215 Fulton Dr NW . . . . . Canton OH 44718 330-497-3179 297-8
Web: www.fishersfoods.com

Fisher Group Inc 4517 W 1730 S . . . . . Salt Lake City UT 84104 801-262-6451 261-5658 393
Web: www.fishergroupinc.com

Fisher Grove State Park
17290 Fishers Ln . . . . . Frankfort SD 57440 605-472-1212 565
Web: gfp.sd.gov

Fisher Hawaii 950 Mapunapuna St . . . . . Honolulu HI 06810 808-524-8770 535
Web: www.fisherhawaii.net

Fisher Home Furnishings 2175 N Main St . . . . . Logan UT 84341 435-753-1018 321
Web: www.fisherhf.com

Fisher House Inc
7323 Hwy 90 W Ste 107 . . . . . San Antonio TX 78227 210-673-7500 372
Web: fisherhouseinc.org

Fisher International Inc 50 Water St . . . . . Norwalk CT 06854 203-854-5390 854-5070 194
Web: www.fisheri.com

Fisher Investments
13100 Skyline Blvd . . . . . Woodside CA 94062 800-587-5512 401
TF: 800-550-1071 ■ *Web:* www.fisherinvestments.com

Fisher Island Club & Resort
1 Fisher Island Dr . . . . . Miami FL 33109 305-535-6000 535-6003 669
TF: 800-537-3708 ■ *Web:* www.fisherislandclub.com

Fisher Law Firm LLC
7 Wakeley St 2nd Fl . . . . . Danbury CT 06810 203-828-6191 828-6193 41
Web: kfisherlaw.com

Fisher Lynch Capital
2929 Campus Dr Ste 420 . . . . . San Mateo CA 94403 650-287-2700 287-2701 792
Web: www.fisherlynch.com

Fisher Manufacturing Co PO Box 60 . . . . . Tulare CA 93275 800-421-6162 832-8238 609
TF: 800-421-6162 ■ *Web:* www.fisher-mfg.com

Fisher Printing Inc
8640 S Oketo Ave . . . . . Bridgeview IL 60455 708-598-1500 687
TF: 800-366-0006 ■ *Web:* gofisher.net

Fisher Products LLC 1320 W 22nd Pl . . . . . Tulsa OK 74107 918-582-2204 757
Web: www.fisherproductsllc.com

Fisher Research Laboratory Inc
1120 Alza Dr . . . . . El Paso TX 79907 915-225-0333 225-0336 472
TF: 800-685-5050 ■ *Web:* www.fisherlab.com

Fisher Sand & Gravel Co
3020 Energy Dr PO Box 1034 . . . . . Dickinson ND 58602 701-456-9184 503-4
TF: 800-932-8740 ■ *Web:* www.fisherind.com

Fisher Science Education
4500 Turnberry Dr . . . . . Hanover Park IL 60133 800-766-7000 955-0740 243
TF: 800-955-1177 ■ *Web:* www.fishersci.com

Fisher Scientific Company Inc
112 Colonnade Rd . . . . . Ottawa ON K2E7L6 800-234-7437 419
TF: 800-234-7437 ■ *Web:* www.fishersci.ca

Fisher Space Pen Co 711 Yucca St . . . . . Boulder City NV 89005 702-293-3011 293-6616 571
TF: 800-102-7366 ■ *Web:* www.spacepen.com

Fisher Tank Co 3131 W Fourth St . . . . . Chester PA 19013 610-494-7200 91
Web: www.fishertank.com

Fisher Textiles Inc
139 Business Pk Dr . . . . . Indian Trail NC 28079 704-821-8870 821-8880 745-6
TF: 800-554-8886 ■ *Web:* www.fishertextiles.com

Fisher Theatre 3011 W Grand Blvd . . . . . Detroit MI 48202 313-872-1000 572
Web: www.broadwayindetroit.com

Fisher Vista LLC
911 Center St Ste D . . . . . Santa Cruz CA 95060 831-685-9700 5

Fisher, Bren & Sheridan LLP
920 Second Ave S Ste 975 . . . . . Minneapolis MN 55402 612-332-0100 41
Web: fisherbren.com

Fisher, Patterson, Sayler & Smith LLP
3550 SW Fifth St . . . . . Topeka KS 66606 785-232-7761 41
Web: fisherpatterson.com

Fisher-Barton Inc 201 Frederick St . . . . . Watertown WI 53094 920-261-0131 484

Fisheries Museum of the Atlantic
68 Bluenose Dr PO Box 1363 . . . . . Lunenburg NS B0J2C0 902-634-4794 634-8990 520
TF: 866-579-4909 ■ *Web:* fisheriesmuseum.novascotia.ca

Fisheries Supply Co
1900 N Northlake Way . . . . . Seattle WA 98103 206-632-4462 634-4600 770
TF: 800-426-6930 ■ *Web:* www.fisheriessupply.com

Fisherman's Island State Park
16480 Bells Bay Rd PO Box 456 . . . . . Charlevoix MI 49720 231-547-6641 565
Web: michigandnr.com

Fisherman's Market 830 W Seventh Ave . . . . . Eugene OR 97402 541-484-2722 671
Web: eugenefishmarket.com

Fisherman's Market & Grill
235 S Indian Canyon Dr . . . . . Palm Springs CA 92262 760-327-1766 671
Web: www.fishermans.com

Name / Address	City	State	ZIP	Phone	Fax	Class
Fisherman's Wharf Inn 22 Commercial St *Web:* fishermanswharfinn.com	Boothbay Harbor	ME	04538	207-633-5090	633-5092	379
Fisherman, The 14 Ramsey Rd *TF:* 866-347-4836 ■ *Web:* www.thefisherman.com	Shirley	NY	11967	631-345-5200		637-9
Fishermen's Memorial State Park 1011 Point Judith Rd *Web:* www.riparks.com	Narragansett	RI	02882	401-789-8374		565
Fishermen's Pride Processors 4510 S Alameda St *Web:* www.neptunefoods.com	Vernon	CA	90058	323-232-8300	232-8833	296-14
Fisher-Price Inc 636 Girard Ave *TF:* 800-432-5437 ■ *Web:* corporate.mattel.com	East Aurora	NY	14052	716-687-3000		762
Fisher-Titus Medical Ctr (FTMC) 272 Benedict Ave *TF:* 800-589-3862 ■ *Web:* www.fishertitus.org	Norwalk	OH	44857	419-668-8101		374-3
Fishing Holdings LLC PO Box 179 *TF:* 800-373-2628 ■ *Web:* www.rangerboats.com	Flippin	AR	72634	870-453-2222		90
Fishman's Fabrics Inc 1101 S Des Plaines St *Web:* www.fishmansfabrics.com	Chicago	IL	60607	312-922-7250	922-7402	270
Fishman, Carp, Bescheinen & Van Berkom Ltd 10405 Sixth Ave N Ste 115 *Web:* fcblawfirm.com	Minneapolis	MN	55441	952-546-6000		41
Fishmonger's Seafood 1915 N Central Expy *Web:* fishmongersplano.com	Plano	TX	75075	972-423-3699		671
Fishmonger's Seafood Restaurant 806 W Main St	Durham	NC	27701	919-682-0128		671
Fishtech 5802 W Dempster St *Web:* www.fishtechmg.com	Morton Grove	IL	60053	847-966-5900		711
Fishtrap Lake State Park 2204 Fishtrap Rd *Web:* www.stateparks.com	Shelbiana	KY	41562	502-564-2172		565
Fisk Alloy Wire Inc 10 Thomas Rd N *Web:* www.fiskalloy.com	Hawthorne	NJ	07506	973-427-7550	825-8501	73
Fisk Electric Co 10855 Westview Dr *Web:* www.fiskcorp.com	Houston	TX	77043	713-868-6111	865-9420	189-4
Fisk University 1000 17th Ave N *TF:* 888-702-0022 ■ *Web:* fisk.edu	Nashville	TN	37208	615-329-8500	329-8774	166
Fiskars Brands Inc 7800 Discovery Dr *Web:* www.fiskars.com	Middleton	WI	53562	608-259-1649		222
Fiske Bros Refining Co 129 Lockwood St *TF:* 800-733-4755 ■ *Web:* www.lubriplate.com	Newark	NJ	07105	973-589-9150	589-4432	541
FIT (Forest Industries Telecommunications) 1565 Oak St *Web:* www.fcclicense.org	Eugene	OR	97401	541-485-8441	485-7556	49-20
Fit & Fresh Inc 295 Promenade St *TF:* 800-858-8840 ■ *Web:* www.fit-fresh.com	Providence	RI	02908	800-858-8840		300
Fit Properties Inc 814 Morena Blvd Ste 310 *Web:* fitproperties.com	San Diego	CA	92110	619-800-1542		652
Fit Small Business 355 Lexington Ave 18th Fl *Web:* fitsmallbusiness.com	New York	NY	10017	718-407-0724		568
Fit Zone For Women 2455 E Sunrise Blvd Ste 1204 *TF:* 800-988-4712 ■ *Web:* fitzoneforwomen.com	Fort Lauderdale	FL	33304	800-988-4712		354
Fitch & Assoc 2901 Williamsburg Ter Ste G PO Box 170 *Web:* fitchassoc.com	Platte City	MO	64079	816-431-2600		463
Fitch Co 2201 Russell St *TF:* 800-933-4824 ■ *Web:* www.fitchco.com	Baltimore	MD	21230	410-539-1953	727-2244	406
Fitch Co, The 631 Hammond St *Web:* fitchcompany.com	Bangor	ME	04401	207-947-3932		261
Fitch Inc 585 S Front St Ste 300 *Web:* www.fitch.com	Columbus	OH	43215	614-885-3453		195
Fitch Ratings Inc 33 Whitehall St *TF:* 800-753-4824 ■ *Web:* www.fitchratings.com	New York	NY	10004	212-908-0500		218
Fitchburg Hardware Co 692 N Main St *Web:* fhcindustrial.com	Leominster	MA	01453	978-534-4956		351
Fitchburg Public Library 610 Main St *Web:* www.fitchburgpubliclibrary.org	Fitchburg	MA	01420	978-829-1780	345-9632	434-3
Fite Building Company Inc 3116 Sexton Rd Ste A *Web:* www.fitebuilding.com	Decatur	AL	35603	256-353-5759		186
Fitger's Brewery Complex 600 E Superior St *Web:* www.fitgers.com	Duluth	MN	55802	218-722-8826		671
Fitness Club Warehouse Inc 2210 S Sepulveda Blvd *TF:* 800-348-4537 ■ *Web:* www.fitnessblowout.com	Los Angeles	CA	90064	310-235-2040		711
Fitness Ctr 1914 Round Barn Rd *Web:* www.fitcen.com	Champaign	IL	61821	217-356-1616		354
Fitness Depot 1808 Lower Roswell Rd *TF:* 800-974-6828 ■ *Web:* www.thefitnessdepot.com	Marietta	GA	30068	800-974-6828		354
Fitness Expo Inc 4124 Vetarnes Blvd *TF:* 800-323-1831 ■ *Web:* www.fitnessexpostores.com	Metairie	LA	70002	504-887-0880		711
Fitness Formula Ltd 619 W Jackson *Web:* ffc.com	Chicago	IL	60661	312-648-4666		354
Fitness Zone 3439 Colonnade Pkwy Se 800 *TF:* 800-875-9145 ■ *Web:* www.fitnesszone.com	Birmingham	AL	35243	800-875-9145		711
Fitocracy Inc 51 E 12th St 4th Fl *Web:* www.fitocracy.com	New York	NY	10003	646-450-3029		387
FitOrbit Inc 11611 San Vicente Blvd Ste 515 *Web:* www.fitorbit.com	Los Angeles	CA	90049	424-652-9650	652-9659	387
Fitt Telecommunications Inc 1740 W Sam Houston Pkwy N *Web:* fittcom.com	Houston	TX	77043	281-497-8181		196
Fitts Roberts Kolkhorst & Company PC 5718 Westheimer Rd Ste 800 *Web:* www.frkpc.com	Houston	TX	77057	713-260-5230	260-5240	2
Fitz Chem Corp 450 E Devon Ave Ste 175 *Web:* www.fitzchem.com	Itasca	IL	60143	630-467-8383	467-1183	146
Fitzgerald & Co 3333 Piedmont Rd 11th Fl *Web:* www.fitzco.com	Atlanta	GA	30305	404-504-6900		4
Fitzgerald & Company CPAS PC 8150 Leesburg Pk Ste 500 *Web:* fcocpas.com	Vienna	VA	22182	703-847-4600		2
Fitzgerald & Halliday Inc 416 Asylum St *TF:* 888-579-6643 ■ *Web:* www.fhiplan.com	Hartford	CT	06103	860-247-7200	247-7206	256
Fitzgerald & Mcgroarty PA 747 Shore Rd *TF:* 800-465-1307 ■ *Web:* fmlpa.com	Linwood	NJ	08221	609-365-0036	926-3104	41
Fitzgerald Attorneys At Law PC 46 Center Sq *Web:* fitzgeraldatlaw.com	East Longmeadow	MA	01028	413-486-1110	486-1120	41
Fitzgerald Auto Mall Inc 114 Baughmans Ln *Web:* www.fitzmall.com	Frederick	MD	21702	301-696-9200		57
FitzGerald Contractors LLC 7103 St Vincent Ave *Web:* www.fitzgeraldcontractors.com	Shreveport	LA	71106	318-869-3262	865-9640	189-10
Fitzgerald Electro-mechanical Co 6 S Linden Ave Ste 4 *TF:* 800-448-9832 ■ *Web:* www.fitzgeraldemco.com	South San Francisco	CA	94080	650-589-9935		610
Fitzgerald Formliners Inc 1500 E Chestnut Ave *Web:* formliners.com	Santa Ana	CA	92701	714-547-6710		183
Fitzgerald Hotel 620 Post St *Web:* www.fitzgeraldhotel.com	San Francisco	CA	94109	415-775-8100		379
Fitzgerald Industries International Inc 30 Sudbury Rd Ste 1A N *TF:* 800-370-2222 ■ *Web:* www.fitzgerald-fii.com	Acton	MA	01720	978-371-6446	371-2266	231
Fitzgerald Theater 10 E Exchange St *Web:* thefitzgeraldtheater.com	Saint Paul	MN	55101	651-290-1200		572
Fitzgerald,Schorr,Barmettler & Brenna Pc, Llo 10050 Regency Cir Ste 200 *Web:* fitzlaw.com	Omaha	NE	68114	402-342-1000		41
Fitzgeralds Casino & Hotel Tunica 711 Lucky Ln *TF:* 888-766-5825 ■ *Web:* www.fitzgeraldstunica.com	Robinsonville	MS	38664	662-363-5825		133
Fitzmartin Inc 2917 Central Ave Ste 211 *Web:* fitzmartin.com	Homewood	AL	35209	205-322-1010		4
Fitzpatrick & Weller Inc 12 Mill St PO Box 490 *Web:* www.fitzweller.com	Ellicottville	NY	14731	716-699-2393	699-2893	683
Fitzpatrick Brian (Rep R - PA) 1722 Longworth House Office Bldg *Web:* fitzpatrick.house.gov	Washington	DC	20515	202-225-4276	225-9511	342-2
Fitzpatrick Engineering Group PLLC 19520 W Catawba Ave Ste 311 *Web:* www.fegstructural.com	Cornelius	NC	28031	704-987-9114		261
Fitzpatrick Manhattan Hotel 687 Lexington Ave *TF:* 800-367-7701 ■ *Web:* www.fitzpatrickhotels.com	New York	NY	10022	212-355-0100	355-1371	379
Fitzsimmons Abrams LLP 7600 Jericho Tpke Ste 403 *Web:* fallpcpa.com	Woodbury	NY	11797	516-682-0100		2
Fitzsimmons Law Firm PLLC 1609 Warwood Ave *TF:* 888-492-4303 ■ *Web:* fitzsimmonsfirm.com	Wheeling	WV	26003	304-716-4575		41
Fitz-Thors Engineering Inc 3094 Morgan Rd *TF:* 888-470-1652 ■ *Web:* fitz-thors.com	Bessemer	AL	35022	205-383-4430		261
FIU (Florida International University) 11200 SW Eigth St *Web:* www.fiu.edu	Miami	FL	33199	305-348-2000		166
Fiumara & Milligan Law Pc 182 Farmers Ln Ste 100 A *Web:* fiumara.com	Santa Rosa	CA	95405	707-571-8600		41
Five Below Inc 1818 Market St *TF:* 844-452-3569 ■ *Web:* www.fivebelow.com	Philadelphia	PA	19103	215-546-7909	546-8099	762
Five Branches University: Graduate School of Traditional Chinese Medicine 1885 Lundy Ave Ste 108 *Web:* www.fivebranches.edu	San Jose	CA	95131	408-260-0208		685
Five Civilized Tribes Museum 1101 Honor Heights Dr *Web:* www.fivetribes.org	Muskogee	OK	74401	918-683-1701	683-3070	520
Five Corners Strategies 3109 M St NW Ste 200 *Web:* fivecornersstrategies.com	Washington	DC	20007	202-244-1596		194
Five Fingers Press PO Box 4 *TF:* 800-869-7553 ■ *Web:* www.fivefingersreview.org	San Leandro	CA	94577	800-869-7553		637-2
Five Fishermen Restaurant & Grill, The 1740 Argyle St *Web:* www.fivefishermen.com	Halifax	NS	B3J2B6	902-422-4421		671
Five K TEchnologies Inc 104 S 6th Ave *Web:* fivek.com	Yakima	WA	98902	509-575-3600		177
Five Mile Pet Clinic Ps 6825 N Country Homes Blvd *Web:* 5milepetclinic.com	Spokane	WA	99208	509-326-3465		794
Five Nines Technology Group 5617 Thompson Creek Blvd *Web:* www.gonines.com	Lincoln	NE	68516	402-817-2630		196
Five Sails Restaurant 999 Canada Pl Ste 410 *Web:* www.fivesails.ca	Vancouver	BC	V6C3E1	604-844-2855	682-6321	671
Five Star Bank 55 N Main St *TF:* 877-226-5578 ■ *Web:* www.five-starbank.com	Warsaw	NY	14569	877-226-5578		70
Five Star Computing Inc 6316 St Andrews Rd Ste C *Web:* ncsetoff.org	Columbia	SC	29212	803-561-0056		396
Five Star Distributing Inc 4055 E Parl 30 Dr *Web:* www.fivestardistributing.net	Columbia City	IN	46725	260-244-3775		81-1
Five Star Dodge 3068 Riverside Dr *Web:* www.fivestarcdjr.com	Macon	GA	31210	478-474-3700		57

Company	Phone	Fax	Class
Five Star Electric of Houston Inc 19424 Pk Row Dr Ste 100 Houston TX 77084 *TF:* 888-492-7090 ■ *Web:* vfd.com	281-492-7090		518
Five Star Food Service Inc 6005 Century Oaks Dr Ste 100 Chattanooga TN 37416 *Web:* fivestarfoodservice.com	423-643-2600		299
Five Star International LLC 6100 Wattsburg Rd Erie PA 16509 *TF:* 800-243-7241 ■ *Web:* www.fivestarinternational.com	800-243-7241		57
Five Star Productions 430 S Congress Ave Ste 2 Delray Beach FL 33445 *Web:* www.vstar.com	561-279-7827		742
Five Star Professional Maids 8714 N 52nd Ave Omaha NE 68152	402-502-3100		256
Five Star Publishing Inc 1200 3rd Ave NW Fort Dodge IA 50501 *TF:* 800-622-8836 ■ *Web:* www.fivestarpublishing.com	800-622-8836		637-9
Five Star Quality Care Inc 400 Centre St Newton MA 02458 *NYSE: FVE* ■ *TF:* 866-230-1286 ■ *Web:* www.fivestarseniorliving.com	617-796-8387	796-8385	451
Five Star Trucking Inc 4380 Glenbrook Rd Willoughby OH 44094 *TF:* 800-321-3658 ■ *Web:* www.fivestartrucking.com	440-953-9300		780
Five Stone Tax Advisers LLC 11211 Taylor Draper Ln Ste 300 Austin TX 78759 *TF:* 855-770-5829 ■ *Web:* fivestonetax.com	512-833-5829		734
Five Towns College 305 N Service Rd Dix Hills NY 11746 *Web:* www.ftc.edu	631-656-2110	656-2172	166
Fives Bronx Inc 8817 Pleasantwood Ave NW North Canton OH 44720 *Web:* www.fivesgroup.com	330-277-1366	244-1961	674
FiveStars Loyalty Inc 340 Bryant St Ste 300 San Francisco CA 94107 *Web:* www.fivestars.com	860-578-2770		195
FIX Flyer LLC 105 Stone Cliff Cir Ste 812 New York NY 10018 *TF:* 888-349-3593 ■ *Web:* fixflyer.com	888-349-3593		251
Fixation Marketing Inc 4340 E-W Hwy Ste 200 Bethesda MD 20814 *Web:* www.fixation.com	240-207-2009		195
Fixtureworks LLC 33792 Doreka Fraser MI 48026 *TF:* 888-794-8687 ■ *Web:* www.fixtureworks.net	586-294-1188		454
Fizer Inc 731 Werne Dr Lexington KY 40504 *Web:* www.fizerinc.com	859-253-2220		454
Fizzano Bros Concrete Products Inc 1776 Chester Pk Crum Lynne PA 19022 *Web:* fizzano.com	610-833-1100	833-5347	183
FJ McLain State Park 18350 Hwy M-203 Hancock MI 49930 *Web:* www.michigan.org	906-482-0278		565
FJC 520 Eighth Ave 20th Fl New York NY 10018 *Web:* www.fjc.org	212-714-0001	714-0303	305
FJH Music Company Inc, The 2525 Davie Rd Ste 360 Davie FL 33317 *TF:* 800-262-8744 ■ *Web:* www.fjhmusic.com	954-382-6061		95
FK Instrument Company Inc (FKI) 2134 Sunnydale Blvd Clearwater FL 33765 *Web:* www.fk-instrument.com	727-461-6060	447-5166	454
FKG Oil Co 721 W Main Belleville IL 62220 *TF:* 800-873-3546 ■ *Web:* www.mymotomart.com	618-233-6754		204
FKI (FK Instrument Company Inc) 2134 Sunnydale Blvd Clearwater FL 33765 *Web:* www.fk-instrument.com	727-461-6060	447-5166	454
FL Crane & Sons Inc 508 S Spring St PO Box 428 Fulton MS 38843 *TF:* 800-748-9523 ■ *Web:* flcrane.com	662-862-2172	862-2649	189-9
FL Emmert Company Inc 2007 Dunlap St Cincinnati OH 45214 *TF:* 800-441-3343 ■ *Web:* emmert.com	513-721-5808	721-6087	447
FL Roberts & Company Inc 93 W Broad St Springfield MA 01105 *Web:* www.flroberts.com	413-781-7444	781-0601	324
FL Smidth Inc 2040 Ave C Bethlehem PA 18017 *TF:* 800-523-9482 ■ *Web:* www.flsmidth.com	610-264-6011	264-6170	470
FLA (Fair Labor Assn) 1111 19th St NW Ste 401 Washington DC 20036 *Web:* www.fairlabor.org	202-898-1000	898-9050	48-5
FLA (Forest Landowners Assn) 950 Glenn Dr Ste 150 Folsom CA 95630 *Web:* www.forestlandowners.org	404-325-2954	325-2955	48-13
Flack Broadcasting Group LLC, The 7606 N State St Lowville NY 13367 *Web:* www.themoose.net	315-376-7500	376-8549	632
Flad & Assoc 644 Science Dr Madison WI 53711 *Web:* www.flad.com	608-238-2661	238-6727	261
Flagel Huber Flagel & Co 3400 S Dixie Dr Dayton OH 45439 *Web:* fhf-cpa.com	937-299-3400		2
Flagler College 74 King St Saint Augustine FL 32084 *TF:* 800-304-4208 ■ *Web:* www.flagler.edu	904-829-6481		166
Flagler County 1769 E Moody Blvd Bldg 2 Bunnell FL 32110 *Web:* www.flaglercounty.org	386-313-4000		338
Flagler County Chamber of Commerce 20 Airport Rd Ste C Palm Coast FL 32164 *Web:* www.flaglerchamber.org	386-437-0106	437-5700	139
Flagpole PO Box 1027 Athens GA 30603 *Web:* flagpole.com	706-549-9523	548-8981	532-5
Flagship All Suites Resort 60 N Maine Ave Atlantic City NJ 08401 *TF:* 800-647-7890 ■ *Web:* www.fantasearesorts.com	609-343-7447		379
Flagship Bank 29750 Us Hwy 19 N Clearwater FL 33761 *Web:* flagshipbank.com	727-451-2020	451-3400	70
Flagship Converters Inc 205 Shelter Rock Rd Danbury CT 06810 *Web:* flagshipconverters.com	203-792-0034		608
Flagship Facility Services Inc 1050 N 5th St San Jose CA 95112 *TF:* 877-352-4668 ■ *Web:* www.flagshipinc.com	408-977-0155	977-0165	104
Flagship Fire Inc 1500 15th Ave Dr E Palmetto FL 34221 *TF:* 866-242-3307 ■ *Web:* flagshipfire.com	866-242-3307		138
Flagship Pioneering 55 Cambridge Pkwy Ste 800E Cambridge MA 02142 *Web:* flagshippioneering.com	617-868-1888	868-1115	792
Flagship Press Inc 150 Flagship Dr North Andover MA 01845 *TF:* 800-733-1520 ■ *Web:* www.flagshippress.com	978-975-3100	975-0635	627
Flagship Properties Corp 1 Greenway Plz Houston TX 77046 *Web:* flagshipco.com	713-623-6000		653
Flagstaff Central.com Inc 2532 N 4th St Flagstaff AZ 86004 *Web:* www.reliablewebdesigns.com	928-526-6991		180
Flagstaff Chamber of Commerce 101 W Rt 66 Flagstaff AZ 86001 *TF:* 888-693-3769 ■ *Web:* www.flagstaffchamber.com	928-774-4505	779-1209	139
Flagstaff City Hall 211 W Aspen Ave Flagstaff AZ 86001 *Web:* www.flagstaff.az.gov	928-774-5281	779-7696	337
Flagstaff City-Coconino County Public Library System 300 W Aspen Ave Flagstaff AZ 86001 *Web:* www.flagstaffpubliclibrary.org	928-213-2330		434-3
Flagstaff Convention & Visitors Bureau 323 W Aspen Ave Flagstaff AZ 86001 *TF:* 800-217-2367 ■ *Web:* www.flagstaffarizona.org	928-779-7611	556-1305	206
Flagstaff House 1138 Flagstaff Rd Boulder CO 80302 *Web:* flagstaffhouse.com	303-442-4640		671
Flagstaff Medical Ctr 1200 N Beaver St Flagstaff AZ 86001 *Web:* www.nahealth.com	928-779-3366		374-3
Flagstaff Pulliam Airport 6200 S Pulliam Dr Flagstaff AZ 86001 *TF:* 800-463-1389 ■ *Web:* www.flagstaff.az.gov	928-213-2930	556-1288	27
Flagstaff Symphony Orchestra PO Box 122 Flagstaff AZ 86002 *TF:* 888-520-7214 ■ *Web:* www.flagstaffsymphony.org	928-774-5107	774-5109	573-3
Flagstar Bank FSB 5151 Corporate Dr Troy MI 48098 *TF:* 800-945-7700 ■ *Web:* www.flagstar.com	248-312-5400		70
Flagstop Corp 11031 Ironbridge Rd Chester VA 23831 *Web:* flagstopcarwash.com	804-768-0090		62-1
FlagZone LLC 105A Industrial Dr Gilbertsville PA 19525 *TF:* 800-976-4201 ■ *Web:* www.theflagzone.com	800-976-4201		258
Flaherty & Collins Properties Inc 1 Indiana Sq Ste 3000 Indianapolis IN 46240 *TF:* 888-684-0338 ■ *Web:* flco.com	317-816-9300		656
Flair Beauty College 23754 Valencia Blvd Valencia CA 91355 **Fax Area Code: 407* ■ *Web:* www.flairbeautycollege.com	202-729-3516	886-4900*	167-3
FLAIR Flexible Packaging Corp 4100 72 Ave SE Calgary AB T2C2C1 *Web:* www.flairpackaging.com	403-207-3226		358
Flair Molded Plastics Inc 2521 Lynch Rd Evansville IN 47711 *Web:* www.flairplastics.com	812-425-6155	425-6168	604
FLAIRS (Florida Alliance of Information and Referral Services) 2-1-1 Big Bend Tallahassee FL 32302 *TF:* 866-728-8445 ■ *Web:* www.flairs.org	866-728-8445		48-13
Flakeboard America Ltd 515 River Crossing Dr Ste 110 Fort Mill SC 29715 *Web:* www.arauco.cl	803-431-2100	431-2091	820
Flambeau Inc 15981 Valplast Rd Middlefield OH 44062 *TF:* 800-457-5252 ■ *Web:* www.flambeau.com	440-632-1631	632-1581	604
Flambeau River State Forest W1613 County Rd Winter WI 54896 *Web:* dnr.wi.gov	715-332-5271		565
Flamboro Downs 967 Hwy Ste 5 W Dundas ON L9H5E2 *Web:* www.flamborodowns.com	905-627-3561	627-0480	642
Flamborough Chamber of Commerce 7 Innovation Dr Ste 227 Flamborough ON L9H7H9 *Web:* flamboroughchamber.ca	905-689-7650	689-1313	137
Flame Control Coatings LLC 4120 Hyde Park Blvd Niagara Falls NY 14305 *Web:* www.flamecontrol.com	716-282-1399	285-6303	481
Flame Enterprises Inc 21500 Gledhill St Chatsworth CA 91311 *TF:* 800-854-2255 ■ *Web:* www.flamecorp.com	818-700-2905	700-9168	246
Flame Metals Processing Corp 12450 Ironwood Cir Rogers MN 55374 *Web:* flamemetals.com	763-428-2596	428-3689	484
Flame Spray Inc 4674 Alvarado Canyon Rd San Diego CA 92120 *Web:* flamesprayinc.com	619-283-2007	283-5467	567
Flame Treating Systems Inc 715 E Geer St Durham NC 27701 *Web:* flametreatingsystems.com	919-956-5208	956-5057	318
Flamenco Vivo Carlota Santana 4 W 43rd St Ste 608 New York NY 10036 *Web:* flamenco-vivo.org	212-736-4499		573-1
Flamer's Grill 1515 International Pkwy Ste 2013 Heathrow FL 32746 *TF:* 866-749-4889 ■ *Web:* www.flamersgrill.com	407-574-8363		670
Flamingo 2777 Fourth St Santa Rosa CA 95405 *TF:* 800-848-8300 ■ *Web:* www.flamingoresort.com	707-545-8530	528-1404	378
Flamingo Gardens 3750 S Flamingo Rd Davie FL 33330 *Web:* www.flamingogardens.org	954-473-2955	473-1738	97
Flamingo Grille 7050 N Kings Hwy Myrtle Beach SC 29572 *Web:* flamingogrill.com	843-449-5388		671
Flamingo Seismic Solutions 4815 S Harvard Ste 401 Tulsa OK 74135 *Web:* flamingoseismic.com	918-492-3773		538
Flanagan Industries 81 National Dr Glastonbury CT 06033 *Web:* www.flanaganindustries.com	860-633-9474	659-3936	22
Flanagan's Restaurant & Pub 6525 Covington Rd Fort Wayne IN 46804 *Web:* eatatflanagans.com	260-432-6666		671
Flanary Group 701 Decatur Ave N 205B Golden Valley MN 55427	763-545-4564		390

Name / Address	Phone	Fax	Class
Flanders Group Inc, The 2850 Clover St Pittsford NY 14534 *TF:* 800-462-6435 ■ *Web:* flandersgroup.com	585-381-8070		390
FLANDERS Inc 8101 Baumgart Rd Evansville IN 47725 *TF:* 855-875-5888 ■ *Web:* www.flandersinc.com	812-867-7421		518
Flanders Provision Company LLC 1104 Gilmore St Waycross GA 31501 *Web:* www.flandersprovision.com	912-283-5191		297-9
Flandrau Science Center & Planetarium 1601 E University Blvd Tucson AZ 85721 *Web:* flandrau.org	520-621-4516		520
Flandrau State Park 1300 Summit Ave New Ulm MN 56073 *Web:* www.dnr.state.mn.us	507-233-1260		565
Flanigan Firm, The 555 University Ave Ste 280 Sacramento CA 95825 *Web:* flaniganfirm.net	916-443-0381		41
Flanigan's 5059 NE 18th Ave Fort Lauderdale FL 33334 *NYSE: BDL* ■ *TF:* 800-833-5239 ■ *Web:* www.flanigans.net	954-377-1961		670
Flannery Machine and Tool Inc 8420 Hwy US 131 Mancelona MI 49659 *Web:* www.flannerymachine.com	231-587-5075	587-0441	757
Flans & Weiner Inc 16200 Ventura Blvd Ste 417 Encino CA 91436 *Web:* flansweiner.com	818-501-4888	783-7875	652
FLARVC (Florida Association of RV Parks and Campgrounds) 1340 Vickers Rd Tallahassee FL 32303 *Web:* www.campflorida.com	850-562-7151		637-2
Flash Code Solutions LLC 2130 Geer Rd Ste E Turlock CA 95382 **Fax Area Code: 209* ■ *TF:* 800-711-7873 ■ *Web:* www.flashcode.com	800-711-7873	669-0282*	178-1
Flash Foods Inc 215 Pendleton St Waycross GA 31501 *TF:* 877-362-0959 ■ *Web:* www.flashfoods.com	912-285-4011		297-8
Flash Technology Corp 332 Nichol Mill Ln Franklin TN 37067 *Web:* www.spx.com	615-261-2000		529
Flash Telecommunications Inc PO Box 20415 Castro Valley CA 94546 **Fax Area Code: 708* ■ *Web:* flashtelecommunications.net	510-537-6500	298-6030*	224
Flashbanc LLC 185 NW Spanish River Blvd Boca Raton FL 33431 *TF:* 800-808-1622 ■ *Web:* flashbanc.com	561-278-8888		138
Flasher Ltd 246 W Josephine St San Antonio TX 78212 *Web:* www.flasherequipment.com	210-736-4251	736-2084	393
Flashes Publishers Inc 595 Jenner Dr Allegan MI 49010 *Web:* www.flashespublishers.com	269-673-1658	673-4761	637-8
Flashlight Press 527 Empire Blvd Brooklyn NY 11225 *Web:* www.flashlightpress.com	718-288-8300	972-6307	637-2
Flashman Studios LLC 4280 26th St San Francisco CA 94131 *Web:* www.flashmanstudios.com	415-826-7654		195
FlashStarts 50 Public Sq Ste 200 Cleveland OH 44113 *Web:* flashstarts.com	216-220-0200		196
Flaster Greenberg 1810 Chapel Ave W Cherry Hill NJ 08002 *Web:* www.flastergreenberg.com	856-661-1900		428
Flat Branch Pub & Brewing Co 115 S Fifth St Columbia MO 65201 *Web:* www.flatbranch.com	573-499-0400		671
Flat Rock Metal Inc (FRM) 26601 W Huron River Dr PO Box 1090 Flat Rock MI 48134 *Web:* www.frm.com	734-782-4454	782-5640	485
Flat Rock Playhouse 2661 Greenville Hwy Flat Rock NC 28731 *TF:* 866-732-8008 ■ *Web:* www.flatrockplayhouse.org	828-693-0731		572
Flathead Convention & Visitors Bureau PO Box 2164 Bigfork MT 59911 *TF:* 800-543-3105 ■ *Web:* www.fcvb.org	406-756-9091		206
Flathead County 800 S Main St Kalispell MT 59901 *Web:* flathead.mt.gov	406-758-5503	758-5861	338
Flathead Electric Co-opeartive Inc 2510 US Hwy 2 E Kalispell MT 59901 *TF:* 800-735-8489 ■ *Web:* www.flatheadelectric.com	406-751-4483		245
Flathead Lake Lodge & Ranch 150 Flathead Lodge Rd Bigfork MT 59911 *Web:* www.flatheadlakelodge.com	406-837-4391		760
Flathead Travel Service 500 Main St Kalispell MT 59901 *Web:* www.flatheadtravel.com	406-752-8700		772
Flathead Valley Community College 777 Grandview Dr Kalispell MT 59901 *TF:* 800-313-3822 ■ *Web:* www.fvcc.edu	406-756-3822	756-3815	162
Flatiron Constructors Corp 385 Interlocken Crescent Ste 900 Broomfield CO 80021 *Web:* www.flatironcorp.com	303-485-4050	485-3922	188-4
FlatIron Crossing 1 W FlatIron Crossing Dr Broomfield CO 80021 *Web:* www.flatironcrossing.com	303-256-2184		50-6
Flatley Co, The 35 Braintree Hill Office Pk Braintree MA 02184 *Web:* www.flatleyco.com	781-848-2000		655
Flatness International Inc 104 Stony Mtn Rd Tunkhannock PA 18657 *Web:* www.flatnessintl.com	570-836-3527	836-1549	11-2
Flatout Inc PO Box 51370 Saline MI 48176 *TF:* 888-254-5480 ■ *Web:* www.flatoutbread.com	888-254-5480		296
Flats Cat Boats 1565 Patton Rd Rosenberg TX 77471 *Web:* www.flatscat.com	281-342-3940		90
Flatter & Associates Inc 10707 Spotsylvania Ave Ste 102 Fredericksburg VA 22408 *Web:* flatterinc.com	540-658-1922		261
Flavine North America Inc 10 Reuten Dr Closter NJ 07624 *Web:* www.flavine.com	201-768-4190	768-2854	479
Flavor Dynamics Inc 640 Montrose Ave South Plainfield NJ 07080 *TF:* 888-271-8424 ■ *Web:* www.flavordynamics.com	908-822-8855		297-8
Flavorchem Corp 1525 Brook Dr Downers Grove IL 60515 *Web:* www.flavorchem.com	630-932-8100		297-8
FLAVORx Inc 9475 Gerwig Ln Columbia MD 21046 **Fax Area Code: 240* ■ *TF:* 800-884-5771 ■ *Web:* www.flavorx.com	800-884-5771	223-1099*	238
Flavurence Corp 1916 Tubeway Ave Commerce CA 90040	323-727-1957		296-37
Flax Art & Design Fort Mason Ctr 2 Marina Blvd Bldg D San Francisco CA 94123 *TF:* 844-352-9278 ■ *Web:* flaxart.com	415-530-3510		45
Fleet Advantage LLC 401 E Las Olas Blvd 17th Fl Fort Lauderdale FL 33301 *Web:* www.fleetadvantage.com	954-615-4400		177
Fleet Brake Parts & Service Ltd 7707 54 St SE Calgary AB T2C4R7 *Web:* www.fleetbrake.com	403-279-8661		61
Fleet Engineers Inc 1800 E Keating Ave Muskegon MI 49442 *TF:* 800-333-7890 ■ *Web:* www.fleetengineers.com	231-777-2537	777-2720	516
Fleet Equipment Corp 567 Commerce St Franklin Lakes NJ 07417 *TF:* 800-631-0873 ■ *Web:* www.fectrucks.com	201-337-3294		516
Fleet Feet 310 E Main St Carrboro NC 27510 *TF:* 855-588-2786 ■ *Web:* www.fleetfeet.com	919-942-3102		366
Fleet Landing Retirement Community 1 Fleet Landing Blvd Atlantic Beach FL 32233 *TF:* 877-591-6547 ■ *Web:* fleetlanding.com	904-246-9900		672
Fleet Management Solutions Inc 3426 Empresa Dr Ste 100 San Luis Obispo CA 93401 *Web:* www.fleetmanagementsolutions.com	805-787-0508		681
Fleet Products LLC 6510 Golden Groves Ln Tampa FL 33610 *Web:* www.fleetproductsfl.com	813-621-1734		61
Fleet Reserve Assn (FRA) 125 NW St Alexandria VA 22314 *TF:* 800-372-1924 ■ *Web:* www.fra.org	703-683-1400	549-6610	48-19
Fleet Safety Equipment Inc 1100 Hemlock St North Little Rock AR 72114 *Web:* www.fleetsafety.com	501-370-9500		647
FleetBoss Global Positioning Solutions Inc 241 O'Brien Rd Fern Park FL 32730 *TF:* 877-265-9559 ■ *Web:* www.fleetboss.com	407-265-9559	265-0365	735
FLEETBridge 7056B Farrell Rd SE Calgary AB T2H0T2 *TF:* 877-885-6254 ■ *Web:* fleetbridge.com	403-253-3651		387
Fleet-Fisher Engineering Inc 4250 E Camelback Rd Ste 410K Phoenix AZ 85018 *Web:* www.ffeng.com	602-264-3335		261
Fleetpride 269 State St North Haven CT 06473 *TF:* 800-967-6206 ■ *Web:* fleetpride.com	203-281-0111		61
Fleetwash Inc 26 Law Dr Fairfield NJ 07004 *TF:* 800-847-3735 ■ *Web:* www.fleetwash.com	800-847-3735		62-1
Fleetway Inc 84 Chain Lake Dr Ste 200 Halifax NS B3S1A2 *Web:* www.fleetway.ca	902-450-2200	450-2292	261
Fleetwing Corp 742 S Combee Rd Lakeland FL 33801 *TF:* 800-282-5678 ■ *Web:* www.fleetwingoil.com	863-665-7557		579
Fleetwood Group Inc 11832 James St Holland MI 49424 *TF:* 800-257-6390 ■ *Web:* www.fleetwoodgroup.com	800-257-6390		319-3
Fleetwood Homes 7007 Jurupa Ave Riverside CA 92504 *TF:* 888-568-2080 ■ *Web:* fleetwoodhomes.com	888-568-2080		106
Fleetwood Homes of Idaho Inc 2611 E Comstock Ave Nampa ID 83687 *TF:* 800-334-8958 ■ *Web:* www.fleetwoodhomes.com	208-466-2438		505
Fleetwood Windows & Doors 395 Smitty Way Corona CA 92879 *Web:* www.fleetwoodusa.com	951-279-1070		362
Fleetwood-Fibre Packaging & Graphicsinc 15250 Don Julian Rd City of Industry CA 91745 *Web:* www.fleetwood-fibre.com	626-968-8503		548
Fleetwood-Signode 3624 W Lake Ave Glenview IL 60026 *TF:* 800-862-7997 ■ *Web:* www.fleetsig.com	847-657-5111	657-5116	559
Flegels Home Furnishings 870 Santa Cruz Ave Menlo Park CA 94025 *Web:* www.flegels.com	650-326-9661		321
Fleischmann Chuck (Rep R - TN) 2410 Rayburn House Office Bldg Washington DC 20515 *Web:* fleischmann.house.gov	202-225-3271	225-3494	342-2
Fleishman-Hillard Inc 200 N Broadway Saint Louis MO 63102 *Web:* www.fleishmanhillard.com	314-982-1700		636
Fleming & Associates Calibration Inc 1060 N Capitol Ave E100 Indianapolis IN 46204 *Web:* flemingairflow.com	317-631-4605	631-4611	472
Fleming & Van Metre Advertising 600 W Germantown Pk Plymouth Meeting PA 19462 *Web:* www.thinkfvm.com	610-941-0395		4
Fleming College 200 Albert St S Lindsay ON K9V5E6 *TF:* 866-353-6464 ■ *Web:* flemingcollege.ca	705-324-9144		162
Fleming Door Products Ltd 101 Ashbridge Cir Woodbridge ON L4L3R5 *TF:* 800-263-7515 ■ *Web:* www.flemingdoor.com	800-263-7515		234
Fleming Law Group PA, The 2701 Fifth Ave N Saint Petersburg FL 33713 *Web:* fleminglawgroup.com	727-202-4858		41
Fleming Mason Energy Co-op 1449 Elizaville Rd PO Box 328 Flemingsburg KY 41041 *TF:* 800-464-3144 ■ *Web:* www.fme.coop	606-845-2661	845-1008	245
Fleming Outdoors 5480 State Hwy 94 Ramer AL 36069 **Fax Area Code: 334* ■ *TF:* 800-624-4493 ■ *Web:* www.flemingoutdoors.com	800-624-4493	562-9000*	276
Fleming's Prime Steakhouse & Wine Bar 2202 NW Shore Blvd Tampa FL 33607 *Web:* www.flemingssteakhouse.com	949-222-2223		671
Fleming-Lee Shue Inc 158 W 29th St 9th Fl New York NY 10001 *Web:* flemingleeshue.com	212-675-3225	675-3224	196
Flemington Furs 8 Spring St Flemington NJ 08822 *Web:* www.flemingtonfurs.com	908-782-2212		157-6
Flemington Veterinary Hospital PC 54 Voorhees Corner Rd Flemington NJ 08822 *Web:* flemingtonvethospital.com	908-782-5731		794
FLEOA (Federal Law Enforcement Officers Assn) 1100 Connecticut Ave NW Ste 900 Washington DC 20036 *Web:* www.fleoa.org	202-293-1550		49-7
Fleschner Stark Tanoos & Newlin 201 Ohio St Terre Haute IN 47807 *TF:* 800-477-7315 ■ *Web:* fleschnerlaw.com	812-232-2000		41

Phone Fax Class

Flesh Co 2118 59th St Saint Louis MO 63110 314-781-4400 110
TF: 800-869-3330 ■ *Web:* www.fleshco.com
Flesher & Associates Inc
445 S San Antonio Rd Ste 103 Los Altos CA 94022 650-917-9900 917-9903 260
Web: www.flesher.com
Flesher Schaff & Schroeder Inc
2202 Plaza Dr Rocklin CA 95765 916-672-6558 41
Web: fsslawfirm.com
FletchAir Inc 103 Turkey Run Ln Comfort TX 78013 830-995-5900 995-5903 22
TF: 800-329-4647 ■ *Web:* www.fletchair.com
Fletcher & Associates PC
424 E Jackson St Thomasville GA 31792 229-226-2241 226-2295 2
Web: www.fletchcpa.com
Fletcher Construction Company Inc
3311 Short Cut Rd Pascagoula MS 39581 228-762-5792 186
Web: www.fletcherconst.com
Fletcher Csi LLC 237 Commerce St Williston VT 05495 802-660-9636 463
Web: fletchercsi.com
Fletcher Farm School for the Arts & Crafts
611 Rt 103 S Ludlow VT 05149 802-228-8770 228-7402 685
Web: www.fletcherfarm.org
Fletcher Free Public Library
235 College St Burlington VT 05401 802-863-3403 434-3
Web: www.fletcherfree.org
Fletcher Granite 535 Groton Rd Westford MA 01886 978-320-4129 692-1325 503-6
Web: fletchergranite.com
Fletcher Jones Imports
7300 W Sahara Ave Las Vegas NV 89117 702-364-2700 57
Web: www.fjimports.com
Fletcher Lizzie (Rep D - TX)
1429 Longworth House Office Bldg Washington DC 20515 202-225-2571 342-2
Web: www.fletcher.house.gov
Fletcher Music Centers Inc
3966 Airway Cir Clearwater FL 33762 727-456-7134 526
TF: 800-258-1088 ■ *Web:* www.fletchermusic.com
Fletcher Oil Co 521 Shirley Ave Douglas GA 31533 912-384-1246 579
Web: www.fletcheroil.com
Fletcher Spaght Inc 500 Boylston St Boston MA 02116 617-247-6700 792
Web: www.fletcherspaght.com
Fletcher Technical Community College
1407 Hwy 311 Schriever LA 70395 985-876-8900 446-3308 162
Web: www.fletcher.edu
Fletcher'S Medical Supplies Inc
6851 S Distribution Ave Jacksonville FL 32256 904-387-4481 363
TF: 855-541-7809 ■ *Web:* www.fletchermedical.com
Fletcher, Heald & Hildreth PLC
1300 N 17th St 11th Fl Arlington VA 22209 703-812-0400 428
Web: www.fhhlaw.com
Fletcher-Thompson Inc 200 Main St Ansonia CT 06401 203-225-6500 261
Web: www.fletcherthompson.com
Fleur De Lis Federal Credit Union
433 Metairie Rd Ste 114 Metairie LA 70005 504-838-5456 838-5463 219
TF: 800-256-9072 ■ *Web:* fdlfcu.com
Fleur de Lis Publishing Inc
c/o American Journal of Transportation 116 Court St
Ste 5 Plymouth MA 02360 508-927-4188 637-9
TF: 800-599-6358 ■ *Web:* ajot.com
Flex Checks Inc PO Box 141215 Grand Rapids MI 49514 616-791-7900 791-7901 2
TF: 866-791-7900 ■ *Web:* www.flexchecks.com
Flex Foam 617 N 21st Ave Phoenix AZ 85009 602-252-5819 131
TF: 800-266-3626 ■ *Web:* www.flexfoam.net
Flex Hr
10700 Medlock Bridge Rd Ste 206 Johns Creek GA 30097 770-814-4225 814-4123 354
TF: 877-735-3947 ■ *Web:* www.flexhr.com
Flex Technologies 5479 Gundy Dr Midvale OH 44653 740-922-5992 625
Web: www.flextechnologies.com
Flexan Corp 6626 W Dakin St Chicago IL 60634 773-685-6446 677
Web: www.flexan.com
Flexaust Co 1510 Armstrong Rd Warsaw IN 46580 574-267-7909 382-8464* 370
**Fax Area Code:* 800 ■ *TF:* 800-343-0428 ■ *Web:* www.flexaust.com
Flexbar Machine Corp 250 Gibbs Rd Islandia NY 11749 631-582-8440 697
TF: 800-879-7575 ■ *Web:* www.flexbar.com
Flex-Cable Inc 5822 N Henkel Rd Howard City MI 49329 231-937-8000 937-8091 816
TF: 800-245-3539 ■ *Web:* www.flexcable.com
Flexcell International Corp
437 Dimmocks Mill Rd Ste 28 Hillsborough NC 27278 919-732-1591 596
Web: www.flexcellint.com
Flexco Inc 6855 Suva St Bell Gardens CA 90201 562-927-2525 927-2528 22
Web: www.flexcoinc.com
Flexco Products Inc 2415 Bryant St Elkhart IN 46516 574-294-2502 294-1734 697
Web: www.flexcoproducts.com
FLEXcon Company Inc
1 Flexcon Industrial Pk Spencer MA 01562 508-885-8200 885-8400 600
Web: www.flexcon.com
FlexEnergy Inc
30 New Hampshire Ave Portsmouth NH 03801 877-477-6937 194
TF: 877-477-6937 ■ *Web:* www.flexenergy.com
Flexfab LLC 1699 W M-43 Hwy Hastings MI 49058 800-311-0003 945-4802* 370
**Fax Area Code:* 269 ■ *TF:* 800-331-0003 ■ *Web:* flexfab.com
Flexfirm Products Inc
2300 N Chico Ave South El Monte CA 91733 626-448-7627 579-5116 745-2
Web: www.flexfirmproducts.com
Flexial Corp 1483 Gould Dr Cookeville TN 38506 931-432-1853 432-1889 401
Web: www.flexial.com
Flexible Automation Inc
3387 E Bristol Rd Burton MI 48529 810-742-8540 386
Web: www.flexautoinc.com
Flexible Benefit Service Corp
8700 W Bryn Mawr Ave Ste 1010S Chicago IL 60631 847-699-6900 699-6906 390
TF: 888-353-9178 ■ *Web:* flexiblebenefit.com
Flexible Business Systems
380 Oser Ave Hauppauge NY 11788 631-756-0404 180
Web: www.flexiblesystems.com
Flexible Concepts 1620 Middlebury St Elkhart IN 46516 574-296-0941 75
Web: www.flexibleconcepts.com
Flexible Lifeline Systems Inc
14325 W Hardy Rd Houston TX 77060 800-353-9425 477
TF: 800-353-9425 ■ *Web:* fall-arrest.com

Phone Fax Class

Flexible Materials Inc
1202 Port Rd Jeffersonville IN 47130 812-280-7000 280-7001 613
TF: 800-244-6492 ■ *Web:* www.flexwood.com
Flexible Packaging Assn (FPA)
971 Corporate Blvd Ste 403 Linthicum Heights MD 21090 410-694-0800 694-0900 49-13
Web: www.flexpack.org
Flexible Plan Investments Ltd
3883 Telegraph Rd Ste 100 Bloomfield Hills MI 48302 248-642-6640 642-6741 401
TF: 800-347-3539 ■ *Web:* www.flexibleplan.com
Flexible Resources Inc
78 Harvard Ave Ste 200 Stamford CT 06902 203-351-1180 260
Web: www.flexibleresources.com
Flexible Steel Lacing Co
2525 Wisconsin Ave Downers Grove IL 60515 630-971-0150 207
TF: 800-323-3444 ■ *Web:* www.flexco.com
Flexible Technologies Inc
528 Carwellyn Rd Abbeville SC 29620 864-366-5441 370
Web: www.flexibletechnologies.com
Flexicell Inc 10463 Wilden Dr Ashland VA 23005 804-550-7300 55
Web: www.flexicell.com
Flexicon Corp 2400 Emrick Blvd Bethlehem PA 18020 610-814-2400 547
TF: 888-353-9426 ■ *Web:* www.flexicon.com
Flexicore of Texas 8634 McHard Rd Houston TX 77053 281-437-5700 437-8913 183
Web: www.flexicoreoftexas.com
FlexiInternational Software Inc
2 Enterprise Dr Shelton CT 06484 203-925-3040 178-1
OTC: FLXI ■ *TF:* 800-353-9492 ■ *Web:* www.flexi.com
Flexitallic Ltd 6915 Hwy 225 Deer Park TX 77536 281-604-2400 326
Web: www.flexitallic.com
Flexi-Van Leasing Inc
251 Monroe Ave Kenilworth NJ 07033 908-276-8000 276-7666 264-5
TF: 866-965-9288 ■ *Web:* www.flexivan.com
Flexlink Systems Inc
6580 Snowdrift Rd Ste 200 Allentown PA 18106 610-973-8200 973-8345 385
Web: www.flexlink.com
Flexmag Industries Inc
107 Industry Rd Marietta OH 45750 740-374-0024 374-5060 458
TF: 800-543-4426 ■ *Web:* www.arnoldmagnetics.com
Flexo Impressions Inc
8647 Eagle Creek Pkwy Savage MN 55378 952-884-9442 627
TF: 800-752-2357 ■ *Web:* www.flexoimpressions.com
Flexo Transparent Inc 28 Wasson St Buffalo NY 14210 716-825-7710 825-0139 815
Web: www.flexotransparent.com
Flexographic Technical Assn (FTA)
3920 Veterans Memorial Hwy Ste 9 Bohemia NY 11716 631-737-6020 737-6813 49-16
Web: www.flexography.org
Flexospan Steel Buildings Inc
253 Railroad St Sandy Lake PA 16145 800-245-0396 106
TF: 800-245-0396 ■ *Web:* www.flexospan.com
Flexoveyor Industries Inc
3795 Paris St Denver CO 80239 303-375-0200 373-5149 207
TF: 800-466-1232 ■ *Web:* www.flexoveyor.com
Flexpak Corp 3720 W Washington St Phoenix AZ 85009 602-269-7648 269-7640 601
Web: www.nelipak.com
Flexpak Inc 1894 W 2425 S Woods Cross UT 84087 801-956-0696 96
Web: flexpak.net
Flexport 760 Market St 8th Fl San Francisco CA 94102 415-231-5252 311
Web: flexport.com
FlexPrint Inc 2845 N Omaha St Mesa AZ 85215 888-353-9774 589
TF: 888-353-9774 ■ *Web:* www.flexprintinc.com
FlexSim Software Products Inc
Canyon Park Technology Ctr 1577 N Technology Way
Bldg A Ste 2300 Orem UT 84097 801-224-6914 224-6984 177
Web: www.flexsim.com
FLEXSTAR Packaging Inc
13320 River Rd Richmond BC V6V1W7 604-273-9277 601
TF: 800-663-1177 ■ *Web:* www.flexstar.ca
Flexsystems USA Inc 727 W Main St El Cajon CA 92020 619-401-1858 401-1848 599
Web: www.flexsystems.com
Flextech Inc 7300 W 27th St Saint Louis Park MN 55426 952-345-0012 601
Web: www.flextechfoam.com
Flextron Industries Inc 720 Mt Rd Aston PA 19014 610-459-4600 459-5379 548
TF: 800-633-2181 ■ *Web:* flextronindustries.com
Flexy Foam 12315 Colony Ave Chino CA 91710 909-465-5555 344
Flicker, Kerin, Kruger & Bissada LLP
120 B Santa Margarita Ave Menlo Park CA 94025 650-289-1400 428
Web: www.fkkblaw.com
Flickinger Center for Performing Arts
1110 New York Ave Alamogordo NM 88310 575-437-2202 572
Web: flickingercenter.com
Fliers Underground Sprinkler Systems Inc
7425 Clyde Pk SW Byron Center MI 49315 616-583-9040 422
Web: fliersprinkling.com
Flight 93 National Memorial
National Park Service PO Box 911 Shanksville PA 15560 814-893-6322 443-2180 564
Web: www.nps.gov
Flight Deck Restaurant & Lounge
2680 Aerial Way Salem OR 97302 503-581-5721 671
Web: flightdeckrestaurant.com
Flight Deck Specialists Inc
1288 Belmont Dr Mcminnville TN 37110 931-668-6761 22
Web: www.flightdeckspecialists.com
Flight Light Inc 2708 47th Ave Sacramento CA 95822 800-806-3548 63
TF: 800-806-3548 ■ *Web:* flightlight.com
Flight Safety Foundation
801 N Fairfax St Ste 400 Alexandria VA 22314 703-739-6700 739-6708 49-21
Web: flightsafety.org
Flight School of Gwinnett Inc
800 Airport Rd Ste 101 Lawrenceville GA 30046 770-513-0000 685
Web: www.theflightschool.com
Flight Systems Inc
505 Fishing Creek Rd Lewisberry PA 17339 717-932-9900 247
TF: 800-403-3728 ■ *Web:* www.flightsystems.com
Flight Test & Mechanical Solutions Inc
2401 Triana Blvd SW Huntsville AL 35805 256-724-7340 261
Web: fmsaero.com
Flight Trak Inc PO Box 430 Palisade CO 81526 970-464-7242 196
TF: 888-354-8725 ■ *Web:* www.flighttrak.com

Name	Address	City	State	Zip	Phone	Fax	Class
FlightAware	Eleven Greenway Plz Ste 2900	Houston	TX	77046	713-877-9010	877-9020	19
TF: 800-713-8570 ■ *Web:* www.uk.flightaware.com							
Flightline Group Inc	3256 Capital Cir SW	Tallahassee	FL	32310	850-574-4444	576-4210	63
Web: www.flightlinegroup.com							
Flightpath Inc	118-35 Queens Blvd 15th Fl	New York	NY	10010	212-674-5600		225
Web: www.flightpath.com							
Flightsafety Services Corp	10770 E Briarwood Ave Ste 100	Centennial	CO	80112	303-783-1023		21
Web: www.flightsafety.com							
Flightstar Corp	Willard Airport 7 Airport Rd	Savoy	IL	61874	217-351-7700	351-9843	13
TF: 800-747-4777 ■ *Web:* www.flightstar.com							
FLIK Conference Centers & Hotels	2 International Dr 2nd Fl	Rye Brook	NY	10573	914-629-0542		271
TF: 855-832-3545 ■ *Web:* www.flikccm.compass-usa.com							
Flinchbaugh Engineering Inc	4387 Run Way	York	PA	17406	717-755-1900		487
Web: www.flinchbaughengineering.com							
Flinn Broadcasting Corp	6080 Mt Moriah Rd Ext	Memphis	TN	38115	901-375-9324	375-5889	643
Web: www.flinn.com							
Flinn Foundation, The	1802 N Central Ave	Phoenix	AZ	85004	602-744-6800		305
Web: www.flinn.org							
Flint & Walling Inc	95 N Oak St	Kendallville	IN	46755	800-345-9422		641
TF: 800-345-9422 ■ *Web:* www.flintandwalling.com							
Flint Children's Museum	1602 W University Ave	Flint	MI	48504	810-767-5437	767-4936	521
Web: flintchildrensmuseum.org							
Flint Cliffs Manufacturing Co	1600 Bluff Rd	Burlington	IA	52601	319-752-2781		273
Web: www.flintcliffs.com							
Flint Community Schools	923 E Kearsley St	Flint	MI	48503	810-760-1000		685
Web: www.flintschools.org							
Flint Cultural Center Corp	1310 E Kearsley St	Flint	MI	48503	810-237-7330		50-2
Web: www.flintculturalcenter.com							
Flint Energies	3 S Macon St	Reynolds	GA	31076	478-847-3415		245
TF: 800-342-3616 ■ *Web:* www.flintenergies.com							
Flint Equipment Company - West Columbia	3464 Sunset Blvd	West Columbia	SC	29169	803-794-9340		190
Web: www.flintequipco.com							
Flint Group	101 10th St N Ste 100	Grand Forks	ND	58201	701-746-4573		7
Web: flint-group.com							
Flint Hills Resources LP	4111 E 37th St N	Wichita	KS	67220	316-828-3477	828-9536	579
TF: 800-577-2703 ■ *Web:* www.fhr.com							
Flint Hills Rural Electric Cooperative Association Inc	1564 S 1000 Rd	Council Grove	KS	66846	620-767-5144		245
Web: www.flinthillsrec.com							
Flint Hydrostatics Inc	4084 E Shelby Dr	Memphis	TN	38118	901-794-2462	366-4905	640
TF: 800-238-0155 ■ *Web:* www.flinthydrostatics.com							
Flint Institute of Arts	1120 E Kearsley St	Flint	MI	48503	810-234-1695	234-1692	520
TF: 800-222-7270 ■ *Web:* flintarts.org							
Flint Machine Tools Inc	3710 Hewatt Ct	Snellville	GA	30039	770-985-2626		358
TF: 800-984-2620 ■ *Web:* flintmachine.com							
Flint Public Library	1026 E Kearsley St	Flint	MI	48502	810-232-7111	249-2635	434-3
Web: fpl.info							
Flint River Mills Inc	1100 Dothan Rd	Bainbridge	GA	39817	800-841-8502	288-4376	447
TF: 800-841-8502 ■ *Web:* frmfeeds.com							
Flint River Regional Library	800 Memorial Dr	Griffin	GA	30223	770-412-4770		434-3
Web: www.frrls.net							
Flint Surveying & Engineering Company Inc	5370 Miller Rd	Swartz Creek	MI	48473	810-230-1333		261
TF: 800-624-6089 ■ *Web:* www.fseinc.us							
Flintco LLC	1624 W 21st St	Tulsa	OK	74107	918-587-8451	582-7506	186
TF: 800-947-2828 ■ *Web:* www.flintco.com							
Flintridge Operating Foundation	236 W Mountain St Ste 106	Pasadena	CA	91103	626-449-0839		305
Web: www.flintridge.org							
Flintridge Sacred Heart Academy	440 St Katherine Dr	La Canada Flintridge	CA	91011	626-685-8300		622
Web: www.fsha.org							
Flip Publicity & Promotions	500 Bloor St W	Toronto	ON	M5S1Y3	416-533-7710		6
Web: www.flip-publicity.com							
Flippen Group, The	1199 Haywood Dr	College Station	TX	77845	979-693-7660		463
TF: 800-316-4311 ■ *Web:* flippengroup.com							
Flippo Lumber Corp	PO Box 38	Doswell	VA	23047	804-798-6616		683
Flipside Media Inc	1050 Saxonburg Blvd	Glenshaw	PA	15116	412-492-9448	492-8750	225
TF: 800-982-0473 ■ *Web:* www.flipsidemedia.com							
FLIR Systems Inc	27700-A SW Pkwy Ave	Wilsonville	OR	97070	503-498-3547	498-3904	529
NASDAQ: FLIR ■ *TF:* 877-773-3547 ■ *Web:* www.flir.com							
Flite Hockey Inc	3400 Ridgeway Dr Unit 2	Mississauga	ON	L5L0A2	905-828-6030		711
Web: www.flitehockey.com							
Floating Island International Inc	10052 Floating Island Way	Shepherd	MT	59079	406-373-5200		188
Web: www.floatingislandinternational.com							
Floating Word Press LLC	1017 SW Morrison St Ste 215	Portland	OR	97205	503-243-1072	973-5433	637-2
TF: 877-356-9673 ■ *Web:* www.floatingwordpress.com							
Flodraulic Group Inc	3539 N 700 W	Greenfield	IN	46140	317-890-3700		358
Web: www.flodraulic.com							
Floe International Inc	48473 State Hwy 65	Mcgregor	MN	55760	800-336-6337		779
TF: 800-336-6337 ■ *Web:* floeintl.com							
Flo-Form Industries Ltd	125 Hamelin St	Winnipeg	MB	R3T3Z1	204-474-2334		115
Web: floform.com							
Flomatic Corp	15 Pruyn's Island Dr	Glens Falls	NY	12801	518-761-9797	761-9798	145
TF: 800-833-2040 ■ *Web:* www.flomatic.net							
Flood & Peterson	2000 S Colorado Blvd Twr 1 4000	Denver	CO	80222	970-356-0123		390
TF: 800-356-2295 ■ *Web:* floodpeterson.com							
Flooid	4270 Glendale Milford Rd	Cincinnati	OH	45246	844-200-7267		177
Web: www.flooid.com							
Floor Concepts Inc	4315 Kirkwood Hwy	Wilmington	DE	19808	302-994-5002		290
Web: wilmington.abbeycarpet.com							
Floor Coverings Intl	5250 Triangle Pwy Ste 100	Norcross	GA	30092	770-874-7600		290
TF: 800-955-4324 ■ *Web:* floorcoveringsinternational.com							
Floor King Inc	10961 Research Blvd	Austin	TX	78759	512-346-7034		290
Web: www.floorking.net							
Floor Seal Technology Inc	1005 Ames Ave	Milpitas	CA	95035	408-436-8181		291
TF: 800-572-2344 ■ *Web:* www.floorseal.com							
Flooring Sales Group	1251 First Ave S	Seattle	WA	98134	206-624-7800	622-8407	290
TF: 877-478-3577 ■ *Web:* www.greatfloors.com							
Floors Northwest Inc	5780 Main St NE	Minneapolis	MN	55432	763-586-7070	586-7074	361
TF: 800-284-3595 ■ *Web:* www.floorsnw.com							
Floppydisk.com	26439 Rancho Parkway S Ste 155	Lake Forest	CA	92630	714-669-8301	669-8305	459
TF: 800-397-7890 ■ *Web:* www.floppydisk.com							
Flora Family Foundation, The	2121 Sand Hill Rd Ste 123	Menlo Park	CA	94025	650-233-1335		305
Web: www.florafamily.org							
Flora Manufacturing & Distributing Ltd	7400 Fraser Park Dr	Burnaby	BC	V5J5B9	604-436-6000		479
Web: www.florahealth.com							
Florabundance Inc	1296 Cravens Ln	Carpinteria	CA	93013	805-566-6607	566-9728	293
TF: 800-201-3597 ■ *Web:* www.florabundance.com							
FloraDec Sales Inc (FDS)	373 N Nimitz Hwy	Honolulu	HI	96817	808-537-6194	528-1854	293
Web: www.floradec.com							
Floral Design Institute Inc	1138 NW 17th Ave	Portland	OR	97209	503-223-8089		167-3
TF: 800-819-8089 ■ *Web:* www.floraldesigninstitute.com							
Floral Merchandising Systems Inc (FMS)	12209 Nicollet Ave S	Burnsville	MN	55337	952-854-8751	854-1324	293
Web: www.floralmerchandising.com							
Floral Plant Growers LLC	PO Box 790	Denmark	WI	54208	920-863-2107		77
Web: www.natbeauty.com							
Floralawn Inc	734 S Combee Rd	Lakeland	FL	33801	863-668-0494	668-0495	776
Web: floralawn.com							
Florance & Associates Consulting	1011 Hampshire Ln Ste 200	Richardson	TX	75080	972-690-1909		196
Web: floranceandassociates.com							
Floreant Press	6195 Anderson Rd	Forestville	CA	95436	707-887-7868		637-2
Web: www.floreantpress.com							
Florence Area Chamber of Commerce	290 Hwy 101	Florence	OR	97439	541-997-3128	997-4101	139
Web: florencechamber.com							
Florence Career Ctr	126 E Howe Springs Rd	Florence	SC	29505	843-664-8465	413-4688	167-3
Web: www.fsd1.org							
Florence Concrete Products Inc	PO Box 5506	Florence	SC	29502	843-662-2549	667-0729	183
Web: www.florenceconcreteproducts.com							
Florence Convention & Visitors Bureau	3290 W Radio Dr	Florence	SC	29501	843-664-0330		206
TF: 800-325-9005 ■ *Web:* visitflo.com							
Florence County	180 N Irby St	Florence	SC	29501	843-665-3035	665-3070	338
TF: 800-523-3577 ■ *Web:* www.florenceco.org							
Florence County	501 Lake Ave	Florence	WI	54121	715-528-3201	528-4762	338
Web: www.florencecountywi.com							
Florence County Library	509 S Dargan St	Florence	SC	29506	843-662-8424		434-3
Web: florencelibrary.org							
Florence Eiseman company LLC	1966 S Fourth St	Milwaukee	WI	53204	800-558-9013		155-4
TF: 800-558-9013 ■ *Web:* www.florenceeiseman.com							
Florence Events Ctr	715 Quince St	Florence	OR	97439	541-902-2183	902-0991	205
Web: www.ci.florence.or.us							
Florence Motor Speedway	836 E Smith St	Timmonsville	SC	29161	843-346-7711		515
Web: www.florencemotorspeedway.com							
Florence National Cemetery	803 E National Cemetery Rd	Florence	SC	29506	843-669-8783	662-8318	136
Web: www.cem.va.gov							
Florence Savings Bank	85 Main St PO Box 60700	Florence	MA	01062	413-586-1300		70
Web: www.florencebank.com							
Florence-Darlington Technical College	2715 W Lucas St	Florence	SC	29502	843-661-8324		800
TF: 800-228-5745 ■ *Web:* www.fdtc.edu							
Florence-Lauderdale Public Library (FLPL)	350 N Wood Ave	Florence	AL	35630	256-764-6564		434-3
Web: flpl.org							
Florentine Opera Co	700 N Water St Ste 950	Milwaukee	WI	53202	414-291-5700	291-5706	573-2
TF: 800-326-7372 ■ *Web:* www.florentineopera.org							
Flores Bill (Rep R - TX)	2228 Rayburn House Office Bldg	Washington	DC	20515	202-225-6105	225-0350	342-2
Web: flores.house.gov							
Flores Financial Services	314 Sage St Ste 100	Lake Geneva	WI	53147	262-248-2771		251
Web: rflores.com							
Flores, Sternick, Poosikian LLC	220 Goffle Rd	Hawthorne	NJ	07506	973-423-2888	423-3088	41
Web: floressternick.com							

Name / Address	City	State	ZIP	Phone	Fax	Class
Florestone Products Company Inc						
2851 Falcon Dr.	Madera	CA	93637	559-661-4171	661-2070	610
TF: 800-446-8827 ■ *Web:* www.florestone.com						
Floresville Independent School District						
908 10th St.	Floresville	TX	78114	830-393-5300		685
Web: www.fisd.us						
Florexpo LLC 1960 Kellogg Ave	Carlsbad	CA	92008	800-830-3567		708
TF: 800-830-3567 ■ *Web:* www.florexpo.co						
Florida						
Attorney General						
State Capitol PL-01	Tallahassee	FL	32399	850-245-0140		339-10
TF: 866-966-7226 ■ *Web:* myfloridalegal.com						
Business & Professional Regulation Dept						
2601 Blair Stone Rd.	Tallahassee	FL	32399	850-487-1395		339-10
TF: 866-532-1440 ■ *Web:* www.myfloridalicense.com						
Citrus Dept 605 E Main St PO Box 9010	Bartow	FL	33830	863-272-8180		339-10
Web: www.floridacitrus.org						
Corrections Dept 501 S Calhoun St.	Tallahassee	FL	32399	850-488-5021		339-10
Web: www.dc.state.fl.us						
Cultural Affairs Div						
329 N Meridian St	Tallahassee	FL	32301	850-891-3900	245-6454	339-10
Web: dos.myflorida.com						
Education Dept						
325 W Gaines St Ste 1514	Tallahassee	FL	32399	850-245-0505	245-9667	339-10
TF: 800-445-6739 ■ *Web:* www.fldoe.org						
Elder Affairs Dept						
4040 Esplanade Way	Tallahassee	FL	32399	850-414-2000	414-2004	339-10
Web: www.elderaffairs.state.fl.us						
Ethics Commission						
325 John Knox Rd Bldg E Ste 200	Tallahassee	FL	32303	850-488-7864	488-3077	265
Web: www.ethics.state.fl.us						
Financial Services Dept						
200 E Gaines St	Tallahassee	FL	32399	850-413-3149		339-10
Web: myfloridacfo.com						
Fish & Wildlife Conservation Commission						
620 S Meridian St	Tallahassee	FL	32399	850-488-4676		339-10
Web: myfwc.com						
Florida Department of Environmental Protection						
3900 Commonwealth Blvd.	Tallahassee	FL	32399	850-245-2118	245-2128	339-10
Web: floridadep.gov						
Historical Resources Div						
500 S Bronough St Ste 305	Tallahassee	FL	32399	850-245-6300	245-6435	339-10
Web: www.dos.myflorida.com						
Housing Finance Corp						
227 N Bronough St Ste 5000	Tallahassee	FL	32301	850-488-4197	488-9809	339-10
Web: www.floridahousing.org						
Information Technology Services						
1721 W Paul Dirac Dr	Tallahassee	FL	32310	850-644-2525		339-10
Web: its.fsu.edu						
Legislature 111 W Madison St.	Tallahassee	FL	32399	850-488-4371		339-10
Web: www.leg.state.fl.us						
Lieutenant Governor						
400 S Monroe St	Tallahassee	FL	32399	850-488-7146	921-6114	339-10
Web: www.flgov.com						
Lottery Dept 250 Marriott Dr	Tallahassee	FL	32301	850-487-7787	488-8049	452
Web: www.flalottery.com						
Medical Quality Assurance Div						
4052 Bald Cypress Way	Tallahassee	FL	32399	850-488-0595	245-4791	339-10
Web: www.floridahealth.gov						
Military Affairs Dept						
82 Marine St	Saint Augustine	FL	32084	904-823-0364		339-10
Web: dma.myflorida.com						
Parole Commission						
4070 Esplanade Way	Tallahassee	FL	32399	850-488-3417		339-10
TF: 800-335-3396 ■ *Web:* www.fcor.state.fl.us						
Prepaid College Board PO Box 6567	Tallahassee	FL	32314	800-552-4723	309-1766*	725
**Fax Area Code:* 850 ■ *TF:* 800-552-4723 ■ *Web:* www.myfloridaprepaid.com						
Public Service Commission						
2540 Shumard Oak Blvd	Tallahassee	FL	32399	850-413-6042		339-10
TF: 800-342-3552 ■ *Web:* www.floridapsc.com						
Recreation & Parks Div						
3900 Commonwealth Blvd.	Tallahassee	FL	32399	850-245-2157		339-10
TF: 800-326-3521 ■ *Web:* www.floridastateparks.org						
Student Financial Assistance Office						
1940 N Monroe St Ste 70	Tallahassee	FL	32303	850-410-5200	488-3612	725
Web: www.floridastudentfinancialaid.org						
Supreme Court 500 S Duval St	Tallahassee	FL	32399	850-922-5081		339-10
Web: www.flcourts.org						
Transportation Dept						
605 Suwannee St.	Tallahassee	FL	32399	850-414-4111		339-10
TF: 866-374-3368 ■ *Web:* www.fdot.gov						
Vital Records Bureau						
1217 N Pearl St	Jacksonville	FL	32202	904-359-6900		339-10
Web: www.floridahealth.gov						
Vocational Rehabilitation Services Div						
4070 Esplanade Way	Tallahassee	FL	32399	850-245-3399		339-10
TF: 800-451-4327 ■ *Web:* www.rehabworks.org						
Florida A & M University Federal Credit Union						
1610 S Monroe St	Tallahassee	FL	32301	850-222-4541		219
Web: famufcu.com						
Florida Academy 4387 Colonial Blvd	Fort Myers	FL	33966	239-489-2282		167-3
TF: 800-324-9543 ■ *Web:* www.florida academy.edu						
Florida Academy of Family Physicians (FAFP)						
13241 Bartram Pk Blvd Ste 1321	Jacksonville	FL	32258	904-726-0944	726-0923	78
TF: 800-223-3237 ■ *Web:* www.fafp.org						
Florida Agricultural & Mechanical University						
1601 S Martin L King Jr Blvd	Tallahassee	FL	32307	850-599-3000		167-3
Web: www.famu.edu						
Florida Agricultural Museum						
7900 Old Kings Rd	Palm Coast	FL	32137	386-446-7630		520
Web: www.floridaagmuseum.org						
Florida Alliance of Information and Referral Services (FLAIRS)						
2-1-1 Big Bend	Tallahassee	FL	32302	866-728-8445		48-13
TF: 866-728-8445 ■ *Web:* www.flairs.org						
Florida Aquarium 701 Channelside Dr	Tampa	FL	33602	813-273-4000		40
TF: 800-353-4741 ■ *Web:* www.flaquarium.org						
Florida Aquastore & Utility Construction Inc						
4722 NW Boca Raton Blvd Ste C-102	Boca Raton	FL	33431	561-994-2400		358
Web: www.florida-aquastore.com						
Florida Association of Counties						
100 S Monroe St	Tallahassee	FL	32301	850-922-4300		138
Web: www.fl-counties.com						
Florida Association of Realtors						
7025 Augusta National Dr.	Orlando	FL	32822	407-438-1400	438-1411	656
TF: 800-669-4327 ■ *Web:* www.floridarealtors.org						
Florida Association of RV Parks and Campgrounds (FLARVC)						
1340 Vickers Rd	Tallahassee	FL	32303	850-562-7151		637-2
Web: www.campflorida.com						
Florida Auctioneer Academy						
8930 S US Hwy 1	Port Saint Lucie	FL	34952	407-886-4900		167-3
TF: 800-422-9155 ■ *Web:* www.f-a-a.com						
Florida Bar 651 E Jefferson St	Tallahassee	FL	32399	850-561-5600		72
TF: 800-342-8060 ■ *Web:* www.floridabar.org						
Florida Botanical Gardens						
12520 Ulmerton Rd	Largo	FL	33774	727-582-2100		97
Web: www.flbg.org						
Florida Brick & Clay Company Inc (FBC)						
1708 Turkey Creek Rd.	Plant City	FL	33567	813-754-1521	754-5469	291
Web: www.floridabrickandclay.com						
Florida Business Bank						
340 N Harbor City Blvd.	Melbourne	FL	32935	321-253-1555		70
TF: 800-237-8990 ■ *Web:* floridabusinessbank.com						
Florida Career College						
3750 W 18th Ave	Hialeah	FL	33012	786-475-5900		166
TF: 888-852-7272 ■ *Web:* www.floridacareercollege.edu						
Florida Caverns State Park						
3345 Caverns Rd	Marianna	FL	32446	850-482-1228		565
Web: www.floridastateparks.org						
Florida Center for Addictions & Dual Disorders						
100 W College Dr.	Avon Park	FL	33825	863-452-3858	452-3863	726
Web: tchsonline.org						
Florida Chamber of Commerce						
136 S Bronough St PO Box 11309	Tallahassee	FL	32301	850-521-1200		140
Web: www.flchamber.com						
Florida City Gas (FCG) 955 E 25th St.	Hialeah	FL	33013	800-993-7546		787
TF: 800-993-7546 ■ *Web:* floridacitygas.com						
Florida Classics Library (FCL)						
11300 SE Dixie Hwy	Hobe Sound	FL	33455	772-546-9380		637-2
Web: floridaclassicslibrary.com						
Florida Coast Equipment						
357 Pike Rd	West Palm Beach	FL	33411	561-209-2705	369-1282	264
TF: 877-697-8347 ■ *Web:* floridacoasteq.com						
Florida Coastal School of Law						
8787 Bay Pine Rd.	Jacksonville	FL	32256	904-680-7700	680-7692	167-1
TF: 877-210-2591 ■ *Web:* www.fcsl.edu						
Florida College						
119 N Glen Arven Ave.	Temple Terrace	FL	33617	813-988-5131	899-6772	166
TF: 800-326-7655 ■ *Web:* www.floridacollege.edu						
Florida College of Integrative Medicine						
7100 Lake Ellenor Dr	Orlando	FL	32809	407-888-8689	888-8211	166
Web: www.fcim.edu						
Florida Community Bank (FCB)						
1400 N 15th St.	Immokalee	FL	34142	239-657-3171		70
TF: 866-764-0006 ■ *Web:* www.floridacommunitybank.net						
Florida Council Against Sexual Violence Inc						
1820 E Park Ave Ste 100	Tallahassee	FL	32301	850-297-2000		41
TF: 888-956-7273 ■ *Web:* www.fcasv.org						
Florida Crystals Corp						
1 N Clematis St Ste 200	West Palm Beach	FL	33401	561-366-5100	366-5158	296-38
Web: www.floridacrystals.com						
Florida Custom Mold Inc 1806 Gunn Hwy	Odessa	FL	33556	813-343-5080	343-5085	604
Web: www.fla-mold.com						
Florida Democratic Party						
214 S Bronough St.	Tallahassee	FL	32301	850-222-3411		616-1
Web: www.floridadems.org						
Florida Dental Assn						
1111 E Tennessee St.	Tallahassee	FL	32308	850-681-3629	561-0504	227
TF: 800-877-9922 ■ *Web:* www.floridadental.org						
Florida Department of Agriculture and Consumer Services						
Agriculture & Consumer Services Dept						
400 S Monroe St Plz Level 10 The Capitol	Tallahassee	FL	32399	850-488-3022		339-10
Web: www.fdacs.gov						
Consumer Services Div						
2005 Apalachee Pkwy	Tallahassee	FL	32399	800-435-7352	245-1330*	339-10
**Fax Area Code:* 850 ■ *TF:* 800-435-7352 ■ *Web:* www.fdacs.gov						
Florida Department of Juvenile Justice						
2737 Centerview Dr Knight Bldg.	Tallahassee	FL	32399	850-488-1850	922-2992	340
Web: www.djj.state.fl.us						
Florida Department of Transportation Credit Union						
640 E Gaines St	Tallahassee	FL	32301	850-414-4400	414-5223	219
TF: 877-884-0112 ■ *Web:* fldotcu.com						
Florida Design Group LLC, The						
2269 S Universiy Dr Ste 275	Davie	FL	33324	954-745-9585		180
Web: www.thefloridadesigngroup.com						
Florida Detroit Diesel-Allison Inc						
5040 University Blvd W	Jacksonville	FL	32216	904-737-7330	733-5871	385
Web: www.fdda.com						
Florida Distributing Source						
14038 63rd Way N	Clearwater	FL	33760	727-531-0899	531-2906	300
TF: 800-741-4970 ■ *Web:* www.eaton-marketing.com						
Florida Diving Institute Inc						
3465 Edgewater Dr	Orlando	FL	32804	407-843-3483	849-1427	167-3
Web: www.divestation.com						
Florida Family Insurance						
27599 Riverview Center Blvd Ste 100	Bonita Springs	FL	34134	888-486-4663	948-7381*	391-4
**Fax Area Code:* 239 ■ *TF:* 888-850-4663 ■ *Web:* www.floridafamily.com						
Florida Farm Bureau						
5700 SW 34th St	Gainesville	FL	32608	352-378-1321	374-1577	391-4
Web: www.floridafarmbureau.org						
Florida Fertilizer Company Inc						
PO Box 1087	Wauchula	FL	33873	863-773-4159		276
Web: www.sfbfp.ifas.ufl.edu						
Florida Gateway College						
149 SE College Pl.	Lake City	FL	32025	386-752-1822	754-4594	162
Web: www.fgc.edu						
Florida Grand Opera 8390 NW 25th St.	Miami	FL	33122	305-854-1643	856-1042	573-2
TF: 800-741-1010 ■ *Web:* www.fgo.org						

	Phone	Fax	Class
Florida Graphic Printing Inc 503 Mason Ave. . . . . Daytona Beach FL 32117 *TF:* 877-203-6907 ■ *Web:* floridagraphicprinting.com	386-253-4532	253-1787	627
Florida Heritage Museum 167 San Marco Ave. . . . . Saint Augustine FL 32084 *Web:* www.amtrakvacations.com	904-829-9729		520
Florida Holocaust Museum 55 Fifth St S . . . . . Saint Petersburg FL 33701 *Web:* www.flholocaustmuseum.org	727-820-0100	821-8435	520
Florida Homecare Specialists of Citrus LLC 6216 W Gulf To Lake Hwy. . . . . Crystal River FL 34429 *Web:* floridahomecarespecialists.com	352-794-6097		363
Florida Industrial Products Inc 1602 N 39th St . . . . . Tampa FL 33605 *Web:* www.fiponline.com	813-247-5356		610
Florida Institute of Technology 150 W University Blvd . . . . . Melbourne FL 32901 *TF:* 800-888-4348 ■ *Web:* fit.edu	321-674-8000	674-8004	166
Florida Instructional Materials Ctr 4210 W Bay Villa Ave . . . . . Tampa FL 33611 *Web:* www.fimcvi.org	813-837-7826	837-7979	95
Florida International Museum 244 Second Ave N St Petersburg College Downtown Ctr . . . . . Saint Petersburg FL 33701 *Web:* www.floridamuseum.org	727-341-7900	341-7908	520
Florida International University (FIU) 11200 SW Eigth St . . . . . Miami FL 33199 *Web:* www.fiu.edu	305-348-2000		166
Florida Keys Community College 5901 College Rd. . . . . Key West FL 33040 *TF:* 866-567-2665 ■ *Web:* www.fkcc.edu	305-296-9081	292-5155	162
Florida Keys Electric Cooperative Assn 91630 Overseas Hwy . . . . . Tavernier FL 33070 *TF:* 800-858-8845 ■ *Web:* www.fkec.com	305-852-2431	853-5381	245
Florida Keys Media 93351 Overseas Hwy . . . . . Tavernier FL 33070 *Web:* radiopeople.com	305-852-9085		658
Florida Logos Inc 3764 New Tampa Hwy . . . . . Lakeland FL 33815 *TF:* 888-608-0833 ■ *Web:* www.interstatelogos.com	863-686-5261	284-2622	9
Florida Mariner PO Box 8070. . . . . North Port FL 34290 *TF:* 800-615-5089 ■ *Web:* www.floridamariner.com	941-488-9307	488-9309	637-9
Florida Mechanical LLC 3615 Fiscal Ct . . . . . Riviera Beach FL 33404 *Web:* flamech.com	561-863-3606	863-3642	610
Florida Memorial University 15800 NW 42nd Ave. . . . . Miami Gardens FL 33054 *TF:* 800-822-1362 ■ *Web:* www.fmuniv.edu	305-626-3600		166
Florida Mobility & Medical Products 8451 S John Young Pky. . . . . Orlando FL 32819 *TF:* 866-363-3535 ■ *Web:* www.floridamobilityproducts.com	407-363-3535	363-4475	475
Florida Museum of Natural History 3215 Hull Rd . . . . . Gainesville FL 32611 *TF:* 800-595-7760 ■ *Web:* www.floridamuseum.ufl.edu	352-392-1721	392-8783	520
Florida National Cemetery 6502 SW 102nd Ave. . . . . Bushnell FL 33513 *Web:* www.cem.va.gov	352-793-7740	793-9560	136
Florida Newsclips LLC PO Box 2190. . . . . Palm Harbor FL 34682 **Fax Area Code:* 727 ■ *TF:* 800-442-0332 ■ *Web:* rocketreach.co	800-442-0332	736-5005*	624
Florida Nurses Assn (FNA) 1235 E Concord St PO Box 536985 . . . . . Orlando FL 32803 *Web:* floridanurse.org	407-896-3261	896-9042	533
Florida Osteopathic Medical Association District 3 Inc 7855 Argyle Forest Blvd Ste 601 . . . . . Jacksonville FL 32244 *Web:* www.fomadistrict2.com	904-406-3026	619-1080	533
Florida Panhandle Technical College 757 Hoyt St. . . . . Chipley FL 32428 *TF:* 855-345-9482 ■ *Web:* www.washingtonholmestechcenter.schoolinsites.com	850-638-1180		167-3
Florida Pest Control & Chemical Company Inc 116 NW 16th Ave . . . . . Gainesville FL 32601 *Web:* www.flapest.com	352-376-2661	376-2791	577
Florida Pharmacy Assn 610 N Adams St . . . . . Tallahassee FL 32301 *Web:* www.floridapharmacy.org	850-222-2400	561-6758	585
Florida Pneumatic Manufacturing Corp 851 Jupiter Pk Ln . . . . . Jupiter FL 33458 *Web:* www.florida-pneumatic.com	561-744-9500	575-9134	759
Florida Power & Light Co (FPL) 700 Universe Blvd . . . . . Juno Beach FL 33408 *TF:* 800-226-3545 ■ *Web:* www.fpl.com	561-691-7574		787
Florida Presbyterian Homes 16 Lake Hunter Dr. . . . . Lakeland FL 33803 *TF:* 866-294-3352 ■ *Web:* www.fphi.org	863-688-5521		672
Florida Public Interest Research Group 3110 First Ave N Ste 2H . . . . . Saint Petersburg FL 33713 *Web:* floridapirg.org	727-431-9686		633
Florida Public Utilities Co (FPUC) 401 S Dixie Hwy. . . . . West Palm Beach FL 33401 *TF:* 800-427-7712 ■ *Web:* www.fpuc.com	800-427-7712		787
Florida Regional Minority Supplier Development Inc (FSMSDC) 9499 NE Second Ave Ste 201. . . . . Miami FL 33138 *Web:* www.sfmsdc.org	305-762-6151	762-6158	78
Florida Repertory Theatre Inc 2267 Bay St . . . . . Fort Myers FL 33901 *TF:* 877-787-8053 ■ *Web:* www.floridarep.org	239-332-4665		720
Florida Resources & Environmental Analysis Ctr *Florida State University* Florida State University UC6140 University Ctr . . . . . Tallahassee FL 32306 *Web:* www.freac.fsu.edu	850-644-2007	644-7360	668
Florida Retail Federation Services Inc 227 S Adams St . . . . . Tallahassee FL 32301 *Web:* www.frf.org	850-222-4082		138
Florida Rock and Tank Lines Inc 200 W Forsyth St 7th Fl . . . . . Jacksonville FL 32202 *Web:* www.floridarockandtanklines.com	904-396-5733	353-3210	780
Florida School of the Arts 5001 St Johns Ave . . . . . Palatka FL 32177 *Web:* floarts.org	386-312-4300		164

	Phone	Fax	Class
Florida Solar Energy Ctr 1679 Clearlake Rd . . . . . Cocoa FL 32922 *Web:* www.fsec.ucf.edu	321-638-1000	638-1010	668
Florida Southern College 111 Lake Hollingsworth Dr. . . . . Lakeland FL 33801 *TF:* 800-274-4131 ■ *Web:* www.flsouthern.edu	863-680-4131	680-4120	166
Florida Sportsman Magazine 2700 S Kanner Hwy . . . . . Stuart FL 34994 *Web:* www.floridasportsman.com	772-219-7400		457-20
Florida State College at Jacksonville *South* 11901 Beach Blvd. . . . . Jacksonville FL 32246 *TF:* 800-700-2795 ■ *Web:* www.fccj.org	904-646-2111		162
Florida State Conference Ctr 555 W Pensacola St . . . . . Tallahassee FL 32306 *Web:* learningforlife.fsu.edu	850-644-3801		205
Florida State Hospital Library Services PO Box 1000 . . . . . Chattahoochee FL 32324 *Web:* www.fllibraries.org	850-663-7671	663-2442	434-3
Florida State Prison 23916 NW 83rd Ave PO Box 800 . . . . . Raiford FL 32083 *Web:* dc.state.fl.us	904-368-2500	368-2732	213
Florida State University College of Law 425 W Jefferson St . . . . . Tallahassee FL 32306 *Web:* www.law.fsu.edu	850-644-3400	644-5487	167-1
Florida State University College of Medicine 1115 W Call St . . . . . Tallahassee FL 32306 *Web:* www.med.fsu.edu	850-644-1855	645-2846	167-2
Florida State University Museum of Fine Arts 530 W Call St 250 Fine Arts Bldg. . . . . Tallahassee FL 32306 *Web:* mofa.fsu.edu	850-644-6836		520
Florida State University Strozier Library 116 Honors Way Rm 314 . . . . . Tallahassee FL 32306 *Web:* www.lib.fsu.edu	850-644-2706	644-5016	434-6
Florida State University, The 600 W College Ave. . . . . Tallahassee FL 32306 *Web:* www.fsu.edu	850-644-4357		166
Florida Surplus Lines Service Office 1441 Maclay Commerce Dr . . . . . Tallahassee FL 32312 *TF:* 800-562-4496 ■ *Web:* www.fslso.com	850-224-7676		41
Florida Technical College 12900 Challenger Pkwy . . . . . Orlando FL 32826 *Web:* www.ftccollege.edu	407-447-7300	447-7301	800
Florida Theatre 128 E Forsyth St Ste 300 . . . . . Jacksonville FL 32202 *Web:* floridatheatre.com	904-355-5661	358-1874	572
Florida Tile Industries Inc 998 Governors Ln Ste 300 . . . . . Lexington KY 40513 *TF:* 800-352-8453 ■ *Web:* www.floridatile.com	859-219-5200		751
Florida Times-Union 1 Riverside Ave. . . . . Jacksonville FL 32202 *TF:* 800-472-6397 ■ *Web:* www.jacksonville.com	904-359-4111	359-4478	532-2
Florida Venture Forum Inc, The 707 W Azeele St . . . . . Tampa FL 33606 *TF:* 888-375-7136 ■ *Web:* flventure.org	813-335-8116		138
Florida Webcrafters Inc 2030 Shadow Pine Dr. . . . . Brandon FL 33511 **Fax Area Code:* 727 ■ *Web:* www.floridawebcrafters.com	480-624-2500	495-0122*	225
Florida West Coast Credit Union 1225 Millennium Pkwy. . . . . Brandon FL 33511 *TF:* 800-554-8969 ■ *Web:* fwccu.com	813-643-5572	685-5202	219
Floridagriculture Magazine PO Box 147030 . . . . . Gainesville FL 32614 **Fax Area Code:* 352 ■ *TF:* 866-275-7322 ■ *Web:* www.floridagriculture.org	866-275-7322	374-1530*	457-1
FloridaWest 3 W Garden St Ste 618 . . . . . Pensacola FL 32502 *Web:* www.floridawesteda.com	850-898-2201		393
Florissant Fossil Beds National Monument PO Box 185 . . . . . Florissant CO 80816 *Web:* www.nps.gov	719-748-3253	748-3164	564
Florist Distributing Inc 2403 Bell Ave. . . . . Des Moines IA 50321 *TF:* 800-373-3741 ■ *Web:* www.fdionline.net	515-243-5228	282-9241	293
Florsheim Inc 333 W Estabrook Blvd. . . . . Glendale WI 53212 **Fax Area Code:* 414 ■ *TF:* 866-454-0449 ■ *Web:* www.florsheim.com	866-454-0449	908-1601*	301
Flory Industries 4737 Toomes Rd. . . . . Salida CA 95368 *Web:* www.floryindustries.com	209-545-1167	543-7646	273
Flotech Inc 3330 Evergreen Ave . . . . . Jacksonville FL 32206 *Web:* www.flotechinc.com	904-358-1849		595
Floturn Inc 4236 Thunderbird Ln. . . . . Fairfield OH 45014 *Web:* www.floturn.com	513-860-8040	860-8044	697
Flourish Inc 1001 Huron Rd E Ste 102 . . . . . Cleveland OH 44115 *Web:* flourishagency.com	216-696-9116		7
Flournoy Development Co 900 Brookstone Center Pkwy . . . . . Columbus GA 31904 *TF:* 888-801-3404 ■ *Web:* flournoycompanies.com	706-324-4000	324-4150	653
Flow Construction Company Inc 3628 Trousdale Dr Ste E. . . . . Nashville TN 37204 *Web:* www.flowconstruction.com	615-832-0707		186
Flow Consulting Inc 10340 SE 138th Pl Rd . . . . . Summerfield FL 34491 *Web:* flowconsulting.com	386-208-6146		449
Flow Dry Technology Inc 379 Albert Rd PO Box 190 . . . . . Brookville OH 45309 *TF:* 800-533-0077 ■ *Web:* flowdry.com	937-833-2161	833-3208	326
Flow Dynamics & Automation Inc 1024 11th Ct W . . . . . Birmingham AL 35204 *Web:* www.flowdynamics.net	205-581-1200	581-1222	358
Flow International Corp 23500 64th Ave S. . . . . Kent WA 98032 *NASDAQ: FLOW* ■ *TF:* 800-446-3569 ■ *Web:* www.flowwaterjet.com	253-850-3500		455
Flow Solutions Inc 2500 Central Pkwy Ste P . . . . . Houston TX 77092 *Web:* flowsolutionsinc.com	713-939-7000	939-7999	358
Flowell Electric Association Inc 495 N 3200 W . . . . . Fillmore UT 84631 *Web:* www.flowellelectric.com	435-743-6214		245
Flower City Communications LLC 1848 Lyell Ave . . . . . Rochester NY 14606 *Web:* flowercitycommunications.com	585-458-5350		292

Phone | Fax | Class

Flower City Printing Inc
1725 Mount Read Blvd .... Rochester NY 14606 585-663-9000 663-4908 101
TF: 800-444-4832 ■ *Web:* flowercityprinting.com

Flower City Tissue Mills Co
700 Driving Park Ave PO Box 14397 .... Rochester NY 14613 800-595-2030 548
TF: 800-595-2030 ■ *Web:* www.flowercitytissue.com

Flower Hospital 5200 Harroun Rd .... Sylvania OH 43560 419-824-1444 374-3
Web: www.promedica.org

Flower Memorial Library
229 Washington St .... Watertown NY 13601 315-785-7705 788-2584 434-3
Web: www.flowermemoriallibrary.org

Flower Mound Chamber of Commerce
700 Parker Sq Ste 100 .... Flower Mound TX 75028 972-539-0500 539-4307 139
Web: www.flowermoundchamber.com

Flower Patch Inc 4370 S 300 W .... Murray UT 84107 801-747-2824 263-7896 292
TF: 888-865-6858 ■ *Web:* www.flowerpatch.com

Flower Pentecostal Heritage Ctr (FPHC)
1445 N Boonville Ave .... Springfield MO 65802 417-862-1447 862-6203 434-3
TF: 877-840-5200 ■ *Web:* ifphc.org

Flower Pot Florists
2314 N Broadway St .... Knoxville TN 37917 865-523-5121 292
TF: 800-824-7792 ■ *Web:* www.knoxvilleflowerpot.com

Flower Shop Network Inc
103 Monroe Rd .... Paragould AR 72450 800-858-9925 292
TF: 800-858-9925 ■ *Web:* flowershopnetwork.com

Flower Valley Press Inc
PO Box 83925 .... Gaithersburg MD 20883 301-841-7020 637-2
Web: www.flowervalleypress.com

Flowerbud.com PO Box 761 .... Lake Oswego OR 97034 877-524-5400 292
TF: 877-524-5400 ■ *Web:* www.flowerbud.com

Flowers & Fancies-greenlea
11404 Cronridge Dr .... Owings Mills MD 21117 410-653-0600 292
Web: www.flowersandfancies.com

Flowers Auto Parts Co 935 Hwy 70 SE .... Hickory NC 28602 828-322-5414 61
TF: 800-538-6272 ■ *Web:* www.napaonline.com

Flowers by Anthony Inc
3300 SW Ninth St Ste 1 .... Des Moines IA 50315 515-288-6789 292
TF: 800-618-9609 ■ *Web:* flowersbyanthony.com

Flowers By Burton Inc
426 Old Walt Whitman Rd .... Melville NY 11747 631-424-3377 292
Web: flowersbyburton.com

Flowers By Jerri Inc (FBJ)
616 W Kimberly Rd .... Davenport IA 52806 563-391-6290 293
TF: 800-368-5374 ■ *Web:* www.flowersbyjerri.com

Flowers By Josie 212 Michigan Ave .... Grayling MI 49738 989-348-4006 292
Web: www.flowersbyjosie.com

Flowers By Lucille 122 S Main St .... Springhill LA 71075 318-539-3634 293
TF: 800-447-3590 ■ *Web:* www.flowersbylucille.com

Flowers by Sleeman for All Seasons & Reasons Ltd
1201 Memorial Rd .... Houghton MI 49931 906-482-4023 292
TF: 800-400-4023 ■ *Web:* www.flowersbysleeman.com

Flowers Chemical Laboratories Inc
481 Newburyport Ave .... Altamonte Springs FL 32701 407-339-5984 260-6110 292
Web: www.flowerslabs.com

Flowers Davis PLLC
1021 E Southeast Loop 323 Ste .... Tyler TX 75701 903-534-8063 41
Web: flowersdavis.com

Flowers Foods Inc
1919 Flowers Cir .... Thomasville GA 31757 229-226-9110 296-1
NYSE: FLO ■ *Web:* www.flowersfoods.com

Flowers Hospital 4370 W Main St .... Dothan AL 36305 334-793-5000 374-3
Web: www.flowershospital.com

FlowerSchool New York LLC
213 W 14th St .... New York NY 10011 212-661-8074 685
Web: www.flowerschoolny.com

Flow-Eze Co 3209 Auburn St .... Rockford IL 61101 815-965-1062 965-1329 687
TF: 800-435-4873 ■ *Web:* www.flow-eze.com

Flowing Tide Pub 10580 N McCarran Blvd .... Reno NV 89503 775-747-7707 671
Web: www.flowingtidepub.com

Flowline Inc 10500 Humbolt St .... Los Alamitos CA 90720 562-598-3015 431-8507 472
Web: www.flowline.com

Flowmetrics Inc
9201 Independence Ave .... Chatsworth CA 91311 818-407-3420 700-1961 250
TF: 800-356-6387 ■ *Web:* flowmetrics.com

Flowroute Inc 1218 Third Ave 600th Fl .... Seattle WA 98101 855-356-9768 387
TF: 855-356-9768 ■ *Web:* flowroute.com

Flowserve Corp
5215 N O'Connor Blvd Ste 2300 .... Irving TX 75039 972-443-6500 443-6800 641
NYSE: FLS ■ *TF:* 800-543-3927 ■ *Web:* www.flowserve.com

Floyd Bell Inc 720 Dearborn Park Ln .... Columbus OH 43085 614-294-4000 291-0823 246
Web: www.floydbell.com

Floyd Blinsky Trucking Inc 210 Keys Rd .... Yakima WA 98901 509-457-3484 685
Web: blinsky.com

Floyd County 101 S Main St .... Charles City IA 50616 641-228-7777 228-7772 338
Web: www.floydcoia.org

Floyd County PO Box 218 .... Floyd VA 24091 540-745-9300 745-9305 338
Web: floydcova.org

Floyd County
313 Westminster St Ste 210 .... Prestonsburg KY 41653 606-886-0364 889-6574 338
Web: www.floydcountykentucky.com

Floyd County 2526 New Calhoun Hwy .... Rome GA 30161 706-291-4111 233-0021 338
Web: www.romefloyd.com

Floyd County Board of Education
600 Riverside Pkwy NE .... Rome GA 30161 706-234-1031 236-1824 685
Web: www.floydboe.net

Floyd E. Tut Fann State Veterans Home
2701 Meridian St .... Huntsville AL 35811 256-851-2807 851-2967 793
TF: 855-212-8028 ■ *Web:* hmrveteranservices.com

Floyd Medical Ctr 304 Turner McCall Blvd .... Rome GA 30165 706-509-5000 374-3
TF: 866-874-2772 ■ *Web:* www.floyd.org

Floyd Memorial Hospital
1850 State St .... New Albany IN 47150 812-944-7701 374-3
Web: floydmemorial.com

FLP (Foreign Language Publications)
The Ohio State University 198 Hagerty Hall
1775 S College Rd .... Columbus OH 43210 614-292-3838 637-2
TF: 800-678-6999 ■ *Web:* www.flpubs.osu.edu

FLPL (Florence-Lauderdale Public Library)
350 N Wood Ave .... Florence AL 35630 256-764-6564 434-3
Web: flpl.org

FLRCC (Fort Lee Regional Chamber of Commerce)
210 Whiteman St .... Fort Lee NJ 07024 201-944-7575 944-5168 139
Web: www.fortleechamber.com

Fluent 7319 104 St NW .... Edmonton AB T6E4B9 855-238-4826 693
TF: 855-238-4826 ■ *Web:* www.fluenthome.com

Fluetsch & Busby Insurance
725 W 18th St .... Merced CA 95340 209-722-1541 390
Web: fandb1912.com

Fluid Components Intl
1755 La Costa Meadows Dr .... San Marcos CA 92078 760-744-6950 736-6250 201
TF: 800-863-8703 ■ *Web:* www.fluidcomponents.com

Fluid Conditioning Products Inc
Kleine & Warwick Sts .... Lititz PA 17543 717-627-1550 610
Web: www.fcp-filters.com

Fluid Controls Institute (FCI)
1300 Sumner Ave .... Cleveland OH 44115 216-241-7333 241-0105 49-13
Web: www.fluidcontrolsinstitute.org

Fluid Delivery Solutions LLC
6795 Corporation Pkwy Ste 200 .... Fort Worth TX 76126 817-730-9761 539
Web: www.fdsllc.com

Fluid Engineering Div 1432 Walnut St .... Erie PA 16502 814-453-5014 256
Web: www.fluideng.com

Fluid Equipment Development Company LLC
800 Ternes Dr .... Monroe MI 48162 734-241-3935 641
Web: fedco-usa.com

Fluid Flow Products Inc
2108 Crown View Dr .... Charlotte NC 28227 704-847-4464 789
Web: fluidflow.com

Fluid Imaging Technologies Inc
200 Enterprise Dr .... Scarborough ME 04074 207-289-3200 289-3101 419
Web: www.fluidimaging.com

Fluid Line Products Inc
38273 W Pkwy .... Willoughby OH 44094 440-946-9470 790
Web: www.fluidlineproducts.com

Fluid Management Inc
1023 S Wheeling Rd .... Wheeling IL 60090 847-537-0880 386
TF: 800-462-2466 ■ *Web:* www.fluidman.com

Fluid Metering Inc
5 Aerial Way Ste 500 .... Syosset NY 11791 516-922-6050 624-8261 640
TF: 800-223-3388 ■ *Web:* fluidmetering.com

Fluid Power Distributors Assn (FPDA)
PO Box 1420 .... Cherry Hill NJ 08034 856-424-8998 424-9248 49-13
Web: www.fpda.org

Fluid Power Equipment Inc
6305 Cunningham Rd .... Houston TX 77041 713-466-8088 466-3338 641
Web: www.fluidpowerequipment.com

Fluid System Components Inc
1700 Suburban Dr .... De Pere WI 54115 920-337-0234 337-0577 385
Web: www.fscinc.com

Fluid Systems Inc
16619 Aldine Westfield Rd .... Houston TX 77032 832-467-9898 467-9897 539
TF: 800-232-1804 ■ *Web:* www.fluidsystems.com

Fluidmaster Inc
30800 Rancho Viejo Rd .... San Juan Capistrano CA 92675 949-728-2000 728-2205 609
TF: 800-631-2011 ■ *Web:* www.fluidmaster.com

Fluke Corp 6920 Seaway Blvd .... Everett WA 98203 425-446-6100 446-5116 248
TF: 877-355-3225 ■ *Web:* www.fluke.com

Fluor Constructors International Inc
352 Halton Rd .... Greenville SC 29607 864-234-7335 186
Web: www.fluorconstructors.com

Fluor Corp 6700 Las Colinas Blvd .... Irving TX 75039 469-398-7000 398-7255 194
Web: www.fluor.com

Fluoresco Lighting & Sign Corp
5505 S Nogales Hwy .... Tucson AZ 85706 520-623-7953 884-0161 261
Web: www.fluoresco.com

Fluorolite Plastics Inc
2 Central St .... Framingham MA 01701 508-788-1200 783-4374* 604
*Fax Area Code: 800 ■ *TF:* 800-858-1201 ■ *Web:* www.Fluorolite.com

Fluortek Inc 12 Mcfadden Rd .... Easton PA 18045 610-559-9000 559-1919 604
Web: www.fluortek.com

Flushing Bank 260E RXR Plaza .... Uniondale NY 11556 516-327-0028 70
Web: www.flushingbank.com

Flushing Hospital Medical Ctr
4500 Parsons Blvd .... Flushing NY 11355 718-670-5000 374-3
Web: www.flushinghospital.org

Flutes Inc 5252 E 65th St .... Indianapolis IN 46268 317-870-6010 100
Web: www.flutesinc.com

Fluvanna County 132 Main St .... Palmyra VA 22963 434-591-1910 591-1911 338
TF: 800-814-5339 ■ *Web:* www.fluvannacounty.org

Fluxdata Inc
176 Anderson Ave Ste F304 .... Rochester NY 14607 800-425-0176 52
TF: 800-425-0176 ■ *Web:* www.oceaninsight.com

Flw Intl 1147 W Ohio St .... Chicago IL 60642 312-239-2174 225
Web: www.flwint.net

Fly Exclusive 2860 Jetport Rd .... Kinston NC 28504 800-544-2165 12
TF: 800-544-2165 ■ *Web:* www.flyexclusive.com

Fly Fishing Shop E 67296 Hwy 26 .... Welches OR 97067 503-622-4607 622-5490 711
TF: 800-266-3971 ■ *Web:* flyfishusa.com

FlyData Inc
1043 N Shoreline Blvd Ste 200 .... Mountain View CA 94043 855-427-9787 624
TF: 855-427-9787 ■ *Web:* www.flydata.com

FlyerCom 201 Kelsey Ln .... Tampa FL 33619 800-995-4433 637-10
TF: 800-995-4433 ■ *Web:* www.theflyer.com

Flying Aces Technology Inc
1 S Wacker Ste 200 .... Chicago IL 60606 847-299-7815 39
Web: www.flying-aces.com

Flying Biscuit Cafe 1655 McLendon Ave .... Atlanta GA 30307 404-687-8888 671
TF: 833-322-2330 ■ *Web:* www.flyingbiscuit.com

Flying Bridge Technologies
2709 Water Ridge Pkwy Ste 480 .... Charlotte NC 28217 704-357-8011 4
Web: flyingbridge.net

Flying Dog Brewery LLC
4607 Wedgewood Blvd .... Frederick MD 21703 301-694-7899 102
Web: www.flyingdog.com

Flying Dog Press PO Box 105 .... Saint Johnsville NY 13452 518-568-3325 637-2
TF: 800-735-9364 ■ *Web:* www.suzanneclothier.com

	Phone	Fax	Class
Flying E. Ranch 2801 W Wickenburg Way ... Wickenburg AZ 85390 *TF:* 888-684-2650 ■ *Web:* flyingeranch.com	928-684-2690	684-5304	239
Flying Fig 2523 Market St ... Cleveland OH 44113 *Web:* www.theflyingfig.com	216-241-4243		671
Flying Fish 300 Westlake Ave N ... Seattle WA 98109 *Web:* www.flyingfishseattle.com	206-728-8595	728-1551	671
Flying Fish & Grill 211 San Mateo Rd ... Half Moon Bay CA 94019 *Web:* www.flyingfishgrill.net	831-625-1962	620-1287	671
Flying Hippo Investments L L C 130 E Third St Ste 103 ... Des Moines IA 50309 *Web:* www.flyinghippo.com	515-288-5316		525
Flying Leatherneck Aviation Museum Mcas Miramar Anderson Ave ... San Diego CA 92145 *Web:* www.flyingleathernecks.org	858-693-1723		520
Flying Rhino Cafe 278 Shrewsbury St ... Worcester MA 01604 *Web:* www.flyingrhinocafe.com	508-757-1450	754-8102	671
Flying W Ranch 3330 Chuckwagon Rd ... Colorado Springs CO 80919 *Web:* www.flyingw.com	719-598-4000		671
Flynn Burner Corp 425 Fifth Ave ... New Rochelle NY 10801 *Web:* flynnburner.com	914-636-1320		612
Flynn Center for the Performing Arts 153 Main St ... Burlington VT 05401 *Web:* www.flynncenter.org	802-863-5966	863-8788	572
Flynn Enterprises Inc 2203 Walnut St ... Hopkinsville KY 42240	270-886-0223		155-11
Flynn Systems Corp 74 Northeastern Blvd ... Nashua NH 03062 *Web:* flynn.com	603-598-4444	598-4111	225
Flynn's Tire & Auto Service 718 Hope Hollow Rd ... Carnegie PA 15106 **Fax Area Code:* 724 ■ *Web:* www.flynnstire.com	412-276-2141	906-8160*	54
Flywheel Communications Inc 164 Townsend St Ste 7 ... San Francisco CA 94107	415-401-7290		387
FM 99 WNOR 870 Greenbrier Cir Ste 399 ... Chesapeake VA 23320 *Web:* fm99.com	757-366-9900	366-0022	645
FM Brown's Sons Inc 205 Woodrow Ave PO Box 2116 ... Sinking Spring PA 19608 **Fax Area Code:* 610 ■ *TF:* 800-334-8816 ■ *Web:* www.fmbrown.com	800-334-8816	678-7023*	447
FM Communications Inc 1914 Colvin Blvd ... Tonawanda NY 14150 *Web:* fmcommunications.com	716-832-2026		179
FM Corp 3535 Hudson Rd ... Rogers AR 72756 *Web:* www.fmcorp.com	479-636-3540		601
FM Global 270 Central Ave PO Box 7500 ... Johnston RI 02919 *TF:* 800-343-7722 ■ *Web:* www.fmglobal.com	401-275-3000	275-3029	391-4
FM Industries Inc 221 Warren Ave ... Fremont CA 94539 *Web:* www.fmindustries.com	510-668-1900	668-1920	454
FM Machine Co 1114 Triplett Blvd ... Akron OH 44306 *Web:* www.fmmachine.com	330-773-8237	773-4085	454
FM NEWS 101 KXL 1211 SW Fifth Ave Ste 6 ... Portland OR 97204 *Web:* www.kxl.com	503-517-6000		645-126
FM3 Systems Inc 16602 N 23rd Ave Ste 110 ... Phoenix AZ 85023 *Web:* fm3systems.com	602-288-1416		177
FMA (Federal Managers Assn) 1641 Prince St ... Alexandria VA 22314 *Web:* www.fedmanagers.org	703-683-8700	683-8707	49-7
FMA (Financial Management Association Intl) 4202 E Fowler Ave ... Tampa FL 33620 *Web:* www.fma.org	813-974-2084		49-2
FMA (Fabricators & Manufacturers Association Intl) 833 Featherstone Rd ... Rockford IL 61107 *TF:* 888-394-4362 ■ *Web:* connect.fmanet.org	815-399-8700		49-13
FMA Advisory Inc 1631 N Front St ... Harrisburg PA 17102 *Web:* fma-advisory.com	717-232-8850		691
FMA Alliance Ltd 12339 Cutten Rd ... Houston TX 77066 *TF:* 800-955-5598 ■ *Web:* www.fmaalliance.com	281-931-5050		160
FMA Realty Inc 1248 O St Ste 550 ... Lincoln NE 68508 *Web:* naifmarealty.com	402-441-5808		652
FMC (Fairfield Medical Ctr) 401 N Ewing St ... Lancaster OH 43130 *TF:* 800-548-2627 ■ *Web:* www.fmchealth.org	740-687-8000		374-3
FMC Corp 2929 Walnut St ... Philadelphia PA 19104 *NYSE:* FMC ■ *TF:* 888-548-4486 ■ *Web:* www.fmc.com	215-299-6000	299-5998	143
FMC Ice Sports 100 Schoosett St Bldg 3 ... Pembroke MA 02359 *TF:* 888-747-5283 ■ *Web:* fmcicesports.com	781-826-3085		717
FMC Transport 1 Coastal Dr ... Willow Springs MO 65793 *Web:* www.coastal-fmc.com	417-469-2777	469-2294	316
FMCSA (Federal Motor Carrier Safety Administration) 1200 New Jersey Ave SE ... Washington DC 20590 *TF:* 800-832-5660 ■ *Web:* www.fmcsa.dot.gov	800-832-5660		340-17
FMF (Feminist Majority Foundation-East Coast) 1600 Wilson Blvd Ste 801 ... Arlington VA 22209 *Web:* www.feminist.org	703-522-2214	522-2219	48-24
FMF Financial Services 8050 Spring Arbor Rd ... Spring Arbor MI 49283 *TF:* 800-325-8975 ■ *Web:* fmffinancial.org	517-750-2727		305
FMG Enterprises Inc 1125 Memorex Dr ... Santa Clara CA 95050 *TF:* 800-327-6177 ■ *Web:* www.fmgvacpump.com	408-982-0110		641
FMG Financial Services 228 Park Ave ... Worcester MA 01609 *Web:* fmgfinancialservices.com	508-757-5675		390
FMG Inc 3700 Sturgis Rd ... Rapid City SD 57702 *Web:* fmgengineering.com	605-342-4105	342-4222	261
FMG Suite LLC 12395 World Trade Dr Ste 200 ... San Diego CA 92128 *Web:* fmgsuite.com	858-251-2420		177
FMI (Food Marketing Institute) 2345 Crystal Dr Ste 800 ... Arlington VA 22202 *TF:* 800-732-2639 ■ *Web:* www.fmi.org	202-452-8444	429-4519	49-18
FMI Corp 5171 Glenwood Ave Ste 200 ... Raleigh NC 27612 *Web:* www.fminet.com	919-787-8400	785-9320	194
FMI Inc 2100 kubach Rd ... Philadelphia PA 19116 *Web:* www.fmidm.com	215-464-0111		5
FMOLHS (Franciscan Missionaries of Our Lady Health System) 4200 Essen Ln ... Baton Rouge LA 70809 *Web:* www.fmolhs.org	225-923-2701	926-4846	353
FMP (Frank Murken Products Inc) 2125 Technology Dr ... Schenectady NY 12308 *TF:* 800-321-6488 ■ *Web:* www.fmproducts.com	518-381-4270	381-4351	326
FMS (Financial Managers Society) 100 W Monroe St Ste 810 ... Chicago IL 60603 *TF:* 800-275-4367 ■ *Web:* www.fmsinc.org	312-578-1300	578-1308	49-2
FMS (Floral Merchandising Systems Inc) 12209 Nicollet Ave S ... Burnsville MN 55337 *Web:* www.floralmerchandising.com	952-854-8751	854-1324	293
FMS Bank 520 Sherman St ... Fort Morgan CO 80701 *Web:* fmsbank.com	970-867-3319		70
FMS Inc 8150 Leesburg Pk Ste 600 ... Vienna VA 22182 *TF:* 866-367-7801 ■ *Web:* www.fmsinc.com	703-356-4700	448-3861	178-2
FMT (Farmers Mutual Telephone Co) 541 Young St ... Jesup IA 50648 *Web:* www.heartlandtechnology.com	319-827-1151	827-1110	224
FMTC (Farmers Mutual Telephone Co) 410 Broad Ave ... Stanton IA 51573 *TF:* 800-469-2111 ■ *Web:* www.myfmtc.com	712-829-2111		224
FMTC (Farmers Mutual Telephone Co) N012 County Rd 17D ... Okolona OH 43550 *TF:* 888-659-0014 ■ *Web:* www.fmtc.cc	419-758-3322	758-3100	224
FN America LLC PO Box 9424 ... McLean VA 22102 *TF:* 800-619-4703 ■ *Web:* fnamerica.com	703-288-3500	288-4507	807
FNA (Florida Nurses Assn) 1235 E Concord St PO Box 536985 ... Orlando FL 32803 *Web:* floridanurse.org	407-896-3261	896-9042	533
FNB of Central Alabama 2323 Paul W Bryant Dr ... Tuscaloosa AL 35401 *TF:* 800-240-8796 ■ *Web:* fnbca.com	205-469-1700	373-6262	70
FNBB (First National Bankers Bankshares Inc) 7813 Office Pk Blvd ... Baton Rouge LA 70809 *TF:* 800-421-6182 ■ *Web:* www.bankers-bank.com	225-924-8015	952-0899	70
FNF Construction Inc 115 S 48th St ... Tempe AZ 85281 *Web:* www.fnfinc.com	480-784-2910	829-8607	188-4
FNNB 100 N 2nd Ave W ... Newton IA 50208 *Web:* fnnbbank.com	641-792-3010		70
FNS (Food & Nutrition Service Regional Offices) *Mid-Atlantic Regional Office* 300 Corporate Blvd ... Robbinsville NJ 08691 *Web:* www.fns.usda.gov	609-259-5025	259-5185	340-1
Saskatoon 229 Fourth Ave S ... Saskatoon SK S7K4K3 *TF:* 800-267-6303 ■ *Web:* fnuniv.ca	306-931-1800	931-1849	785
FNY Capital Management LP 90 Park Ave 5th Fl ... New York NY 10016 *Web:* www.firstny.com	212-848-0600		690
FOA (Friends of Animals Inc) 777 Post Rd Ste 205 ... Darien CT 06820 *TF:* 800-321-7387 ■ *Web:* friendsofanimals.org	203-656-1522	656-0267	48-3
Foam Concepts Inc 44 Rivulet St ... Uxbridge MA 01569 *Web:* www.foamconcepts.com	508-278-7255	278-3623	601
Foam Fabricators Inc 950 Progress Blvd ... New Albany IN 47150 *TF:* 800-626-1197 ■ *Web:* www.foamfabricatorsinc.com	812-948-1696	948-2450	601
Foam Molders & Specialty Corp 20004 State Rd ... Cerritos CA 90703 *TF:* 800-378-8987 ■ *Web:* www.foammolders.com	800-378-8987		601
Foam Products Corp 350 Beamer Rd ... Calhoun GA 30701 *TF:* 800-526-3626 ■ *Web:* www.foamproducts.com	706-629-1256	625-0855	601
Foamcraft Inc 800 Industrial Pkwy ... Elkhart IN 46516 *Web:* foamcraftinc.com	574-293-8569		601
Foard County 101 S Main St PO Box 660 ... Crowell TX 79227 *Web:* www.foardcountytexas.us	940-684-1424	684-1426	338
Focal Point Energy Inc 2880 Zanker Rd ... San Jose CA 95134 *Web:* focalpointenergy.com	408-923-1541		14
Focal Point LLC, The 501 14th St Ste 200 ... Oakland CA 94612 *Web:* www.thefocalpoint.com	510-208-1760		344
FocalPoint Partners LLC 11150 Santa Monica Blvd Ste 1550 ... Los Angeles CA 90025 *Web:* www.focalpointllc.com	310-405-7000	405-7077	792
Focus 603 Park Point Dr Ste 200 ... Golden CO 80401 *Web:* www.focus.org	303-962-5750		48-20
Focus 360 Inc 27721 La Paz Rd ... Laguna Niguel CA 92677 *Web:* www.focus360.com	949-234-0008		177
Focus Camera Inc 905 McDonald Ave ... Brooklyn NY 11218 *TF:* 800-221-0828 ■ *Web:* www.focuscamera.com	800-221-0828		119
Focus Center of Pittsburgh 102 Broadway St Ste 302 ... Carnegie PA 15220 *Web:* fcpresearch.com	412-279-5900		463
Focus Daily News 1337 Marilyn Ave ... DeSoto TX 75115 *Web:* www.focusdailynews.com	972-223-2998		532-2
Focus Features 100 Universal City Plz Bldg 2160 Ste 7C ... Universal City CA 91608 **Fax Area Code:* 818 ■ *Web:* www.focusfeatures.com	424-214-6360	866-4577*	514
Focus Forward LLC 950 W Valley Rd Ste 2700 ... Wayne PA 19087 *Web:* www.focusfwd.com	215-367-4000		668
Focus Hope Machinist Training Institute 1200 Oakman Blvd ... Detroit MI 48238 *Web:* www.focushope.edu	313-494-4300		167-3
Focus Industrial Workforces 8651 Hauser Ct ... Lenexa KS 66215 *Web:* focusjobs.com	913-268-1222		260
Focus Logistics Inc 1311 Howard Dr ... West Chicago IL 60185 *TF:* 877-924-3600 ■ *Web:* www.focuslogisticsinc.com	630-231-8200		314
Focus Management Group USA Inc 5001 W Lemon St ... Tampa FL 33609 *Web:* www.focusmg.com	813-281-0062		463
Focus Media Inc 10 Matthews St ... Goshen NY 10924 *Web:* www.focusmediausa.com	845-291-3342		636

Phone | Fax | Class

Focus Mfg 38127 Willoughby Pkwy. Willoughby OH 44094 440-946-8766 567
Web: focusmanufacturing.com

Focus on the Family
8605 Explorer Dr Colorado Springs CO 80920 719-531-3400 531-3424 48-6
TF: 800-232-6459 ■ *Web:* www.focusonthefamily.com

Focus Realty Services Inc
3675 Mount Diablo Blvd Ste 350 Lafayette CA 94549 925-283-8470 194
Web: descoplaza.com

Focus Strategic Communications Inc
2474 Waterford St. Oakville ON L6L5E6 905-825-8757 94
Web: focussc.com

Focus Technology Solutions Inc
99 High st Ste 3110 Boston MA 02110 617-938-6200 180
Web: www.focustsi.com

Focus Ventures Inc 1 1st St Ste 7 Los Altos CA 94022 650-325-7400 325-8400 792
Web: www.focusventures.com

Focus Vision 7 River Park Pl E Ste 110 Fresno CA 93720 559-436-6940 668
Web: www.focusvision.com

FocusCFO
1010 Jackson Hole Dr Ste 202 Blacklick OH 43004 855-236-0600 463
TF: 855-236-0600 ■ *Web:* focuscfo.com

Focused Management Inc
6354 Walker Ln Ste 101 Franconia VA 22310 703-922-9600 180
Web: www.focusedmgmtinc.com

Fodera 68 34th St Ste 3 Brooklyn NY 11232 718-832-3455 832-3458 526
Web: www.fodera.com

Foegley Landscape Inc
52215 Lilac Rd South Bend IN 46628 574-277-2424 422
Web: foegleylandscape.com

Foellinger-Freimann Botanical Conservatory
1100 S Calhoun St Fort Wayne IN 46802 260-427-6440 427-6450 97
Web: www.botanicalconservatory.org

Foerster Instruments Inc
140 Industry Dr. Pittsburgh PA 15275 412-788-8976 788-8984 813
Web: www.foerstergroup.com

Fogarty Creek State Recreation Area
US Hwy 101 Depoe Bay OR 97341 541-265-4560 565
Web: stateparks.oregon.gov

Fogel Capital Management Inc
453 Riverside Dr. Stuart FL 34994 772-223-9686 401
Web: fogelcapital.com

Fogel International Inc
5110 N 32nd St Ste 206 Phoenix AZ 85018 602-508-0728 690
Web: www.fogelinternational.com

Fogelman Executive Conference Center & Hotel
330 Innovation Dr Ste 206 Memphis TN 38152 901-678-2021 678-5329 377
Web: bf.memphis.edu

Fogg Filler Co
3455 John F Donnelly Dr Holland MI 49424 616-786-3644 111
Web: www.foggfiller.com

Fogo de Chao 14881 Quorum Dr Ste 750 Dallas TX 75254 972-503-7300 670
Web: fogodechao.com

Fogo de Chao
5908 Headquarters Dr Ste K200 Plano TX 75024 412-312-5001 379
Web: www.fogodechao.com

FOI Services Inc
704 Quince Orchard Rd Ste 275 Gaithersburg MD 20878 301-975-9400 975-0702 387
TF: 800-654-1147 ■ *Web:* www.foiservices.com

FOIA Group Inc (FGI)
1250 Connecticut Ave NW Ste 200 Washington DC 20036 716-608-0800 347-8419* 387
**Fax Area Code:* 202 ■ *TF:* 888-461-7951 ■ *Web:* www.foia.com

Foit-Albert Assoc 295 Main St. Buffalo NY 14203 716-856-3933 856-3961 261
Web: www.foit-albert.com

Folbot Inc 4209 Pace St. Charleston SC 29405 843-744-3483 710

Folder Factory Inc
5421 Main St Ste 300 Mount Jackson VA 22842 540-477-3852 477-9677 627
TF: 800-296-4321 ■ *Web:* business-folders.com

Folderwave 238 Littleton Rd Westford MA 01886 978-392-2055 177
Web: folderwave.com

Foley & Foley PC 495 Palmer Ave Ste 3 Falmouth MA 02540 508-548-4888 41
Web: foleyworkplacelaw.com

Foley & Lardner LLP
777 E Wisconsin Ave Milwaukee WI 53202 414-271-2400 297-4900 428
Web: www.foley.com

Foley Bezek Behle & Curtis LLP
15 W Carrillo St Santa Barbara CA 93101 805-962-9495 610-4600* 41
**Fax Area Code:* 415 ■ *Web:* foleybezek.com

Foley Carrier Services LLC
140 Huyshope Ave Hartford CT 06106 800-253-5506 463
TF: 800-253-5506 ■ *Web:* www.foleyservices.com

Foley Equipment 1550 SW St. Wichita KS 67213 877-761-9027 943-0896* 358
**Fax Area Code:* 316 ■ *TF:* 877-761-9027 ■ *Web:* www.foleyeq.com

Foley Group, The
1661 Front St Ste 3 Yorktown Heights NY 10598 914-245-3625 245-8587 627
Web: www.tfgny.com

Foley High School 1 Pride Pl Foley AL 36535 320-968-7246 685
Web: www.foley.k12.mn.us

Foley House Inn 14 W Hull St. Savannah GA 31401 800-647-3708 379
TF: 800-647-3708 ■ *Web:* www.foleyinn.com

Foley Inc 855 Centennial Ave. Piscataway NJ 08854 732-885-5555 62-7
TF: 888-417-6464 ■ *Web:* www.foleyinc.com

Foley Pattern Company Inc
500 W 11th St. Auburn IN 46706 260-925-4113 567

Folger Levin LLP
199 Fremont St 20th Fl. San Francisco CA 94105 415-625-1050 41
Web: www.folgerlevin.com

Folger Shakespeare Library
201 E Capitol St SE Washington DC 20003 202-544-4600 544-4623 434-4
Web: folger.edu

Folgergraphics Inc 2339 Davis Ave Hayward CA 94545 510-887-5656 174
Web: www.folgergraphics.com

Folio Weekly 45 W Bay St Ste 103 Jacksonville FL 32202 904-260-9770 260-9773 532-5
Web: www.folioweekly.com

Folk Alliance Intl
509 Delaware St Ste 101 Kansas City MO 64105 816-221-3655 48-4
Web: www.folk.org

Folk Art Ctr PO Box 9545 Asheville NC 28815 828-298-7928 298-7962 520
TF: 888-672-7717 ■ *Web:* www.southernhighlandguild.org

Phone | Fax | Class

Folk's Folly Prime Steak House
551 S Mendenhall Rd Memphis TN 38117 901-762-8200 671
Web: www.folksfolly.com

Folkman Law Offices PC
1949 Berlin Rd Ste 100 Cherry Hill NJ 08003 856-354-9444 41
Web: folkmanlaw.com

Folks Creative Printers Inc
101 E George St Marion OH 43302 740-383-6326 382-5628 627
Web: folksprinting.com

Folks Southern Kitchen
180 Pkwy 575 Ste 100 Woodstock GA 30188 770-904-6595 904-6805 670
Web: www.folkskitchen.com

Follett Corp 1340 Ridgeview Dr. McHenry IL 60050 815-759-1700 759-9831 96
TF: 877-899-8550 ■ *Web:* www.follettlearning.com

Follett Corp
3 Westbrook Corporate Ctr Ste 200 Westchester IL 60154 708-884-0000 96
TF: 800-365-5388 ■ *Web:* follett.com

Follett Corp 801 Church Ln. Easton PA 18040 610-252-7301 250-0169 664
TF: 800-523-9361 ■ *Web:* www.follettice.com

Follow Up Sales Systems
400 S Summit St Arkansas City KS 67005 620-442-2460 449
Web: www.fussinc.com

Folly Theater
300 W 12th St PO Box 26505 Kansas City MO 64105 816-474-4444 842-8709 572
Web: follytheater.org

Folsom Buick Gmc 12640 Auto Mall Cir Folsom CA 95630 916-358-8963 57
Web: www.folsombuickgmc.com

Folsom Chamber of Commerce 200 Wool St. Folsom CA 95630 916-985-2698 985-4117 139
Web: www.folsomchamber.com

Folsom Lake Ford 12755 Folsom Blvd. Folsom CA 95630 916-353-2000 57
Web: www.folsomlakeford.com

Folsom Powerhouse State Historic Park
9980 Greenback Ln. Folsom CA 95630 916-985-4843 565
Web: www.parks.ca.gov

Folsom Ready Mix Inc
3401 Fitzgerald Rd Rancho Cordova CA 95742 916-851-8300 135
Web: folsomreadymix.com

Folsom State Prison 300 Prison Rd. Represa CA 95671 916-985-2561 213
Web: cdcr.ca.gov

Foltz Concrete Pipe Company LLC
11875 N NC Hwy 150 Winston-Salem NC 27127 800-229-8525 183
TF: 800-229-8525 ■ *Web:* www.foltzconcretepipe.com

Foltz Machine LLC 2030 Allen Ave SE Canton OH 44707 330-453-9235 454
Web: www.foltzmachine.com

Foltz Manufacturing & Supply Co
63 E Washington St Hagerstown MD 21740 301-739-1076 454
Web: www.foltzcompany.com

Foltz Trucking Inc
19097 Frontage Rd Detroit Lakes MN 56501 218-847-4451 847-8424 780
TF: 800-346-3950 ■ *Web:* www.foltztrucking.com

Fona International Inc 1900 Averill Rd Geneva IL 60134 630-578-8600 123
Web: www.fona.com

Fonar Corp 110 Marcus Dr. Melville NY 11747 631-694-2929 390-7766 382
NASDAQ: FONR ■ *Web:* www.fonar.com

Fond du Lac Band of Lake Superior Chippewa
1720 Big Lake Rd Cloquet MN 55720 218-879-4593 878-7169 132
TF: 888-888-6007 ■ *Web:* fdlrez.com

Fond du Lac Convention & Visitors Bureau
171 S Pioneer Rd Fond du Lac WI 54935 920-923-3010 929-6846 206
TF: 800-937-9123 ■ *Web:* www.fdl.com

Fond du Lac County 160 S Macy St Fond du Lac WI 54935 920-929-3000 929-3293 338
Web: www.fdlco.wi.gov

Fond Du Lac Lutheran Home Inc
244 N Macy St Fond Du Lac WI 54935 920-921-9520 371
Web: www.lutheranhomesfonddulac.org

Fond du Lac Public Library
32 Sheboygan St Fond du Lac WI 54935 920-929-7080 929-7082 434-3
Web: fdlpl.org

Fond du Lac Tribal & Community College
2101 14th St. Cloquet MN 55720 218-879-0800 879-0814 165
TF: 800-657-3712 ■ *Web:* www.fdltcc.edu

Fonda San Miguel 2330 W N Loop Blvd. Austin TX 78756 512-459-4121 671
Web: www.fondasanmiguel.com

Fondaction
Bureau 501 125 Boul Charest Est Montreal QC H2K4S3 514-525-5505 528
TF: 800-253-6665 ■ *Web:* fondaction.com

Fonds Capital Culture Quebec
905 Ave De Lorimier 4e etage Montreal QC H2K3V9 514-940-6820 528
Web: capitalculture.ca

Fonds de solidarite FTQ
545 Cremazie Blvd E Ofc 200 Montreal QC H2M2W4 800-567-3663 528
TF: 800-567-3663 ■ *Web:* www.fondsftq.com

FONEX Data Systems Inc
5400 Ch St-Francois Saint-Laurent QC H4S1P6 514-333-6639 333-6635 224
TF: 800-363-6639 ■ *Web:* www.fonex.com

Fong Brothers Printing Inc
320 Valley Dr Brisbane CA 94005 415-467-1050 467-0653 627
Web: www.fbp.com

Fonkoze USA Inc
1718 Connecticut Ave NW Ste 201 Washington DC 20009 202-628-9033 463
Web: www.fonkoze.org

Fonner Park
700 E Stolley Park Rd Grand Island NE 68801 308-382-4515 384-2753 642
Web: www.fonnerpark.com

Fontaine Fifth Wheel
3520 Industrial Pkwy Jasper AL 35501 205-847-3250 445-6130* 60
**Fax Area Code:* 800 ■ *TF:* 800-874-9780 ■ *Web:* www.fifthwheel.com

Fontaine Modification
9827 Mt Holly Rd Charlotte NC 28214 704-391-1355 409-1607 516
TF: 800-366-8246 ■ *Web:* www.fontainemodification.com

Fontaine Trailer Co 150 S Perry St Montgomery AL 36104 205-486-5251 779
TF: 800-821-6535 ■ *Web:* fontainetrailer.com

Fontaine Truck Equipment Co
7574 Commerce Cir Trussville AL 35173 205-661-4900 655-9982 516
Web: www.fontaine.com

Fontainebleau Miami Beach
4441 Collins Ave Miami Beach FL 33140 800-548-8886 669
TF: 800-548-8886 ■ *Web:* fontainebleau.com

Name / Address	City	State	ZIP	Phone	Fax	Class
Fontainebleau State Park 67825 US Hwy 190 *TF:* 888-677-3668 ■ *Web:* crt.state.la.us	Mandeville	LA	70448	985-624-4443		565
Fontana & Fontana Inc 8600 Crown Crescent Ct *TF:* 866-774-2453 ■ *Web:* www.fontanaltd.com	Charlotte	NC	28227	866-774-2453		156
Fontana Chamber of Commerce 8491 Sierra Ave *Web:* www.fontanachamber.org	Fontana	CA	92335	909-822-4433	822-6238	139
Fontana CPAs Pa 2519 N Mcmullen Booth Rd Ste 5 *Web:* www.fontanacpas.com	Clearwater	FL	33761	727-799-9533		2
Fontana Group Inc, The (FG) 3509 N Campbell Ave *Web:* www.fontanagroup.com	Tucson	AZ	85719	520-325-9800		194
Fontana Paper Mills Inc 13733 Valley Blvd *TF:* 800-634-8915 ■ *Web:* www.fontanaroof.com	Fontana	CA	92335	909-823-4100	823-6063	557
Fontana Regional Library 33 Fryemont Rd *Web:* www.fontanalib.org	Bryson City	NC	28713	828-488-2382	488-9857	434-3
Fontana Village Resort 300 Woods Rd PO Box 68 *TF:* 800-849-2258 ■ *Web:* www.fontanavillage.com	Fontana Dam	NC	28733	828-498-2211		669
FontHaus 2232 S Main St Ste 388 *Web:* www.fonthaus.com	Ann Arbor	MI	48103	734-332-6291		178-1
Foo Dog Feng Shui 373 W Windowmaker Rd *Web:* foodogfengshui.byregion.net	Tucson	AZ	85737	520-400-7206		194
Food & Agricultural Policy Research Institute (FAPRI) Iowa State University 578 Heady Hall *Web:* www.fapri.iastate.edu	Ames	IA	50011	515-294-1183	294-6336	634
Food & Drug Administration (FDA) 5600 Fishers Ln *TF:* 888-463-6332 ■ *Web:* www.fda.gov	Rockville	MD	20857	301-443-1726	443-3100	340-10
Food & Drug Administration						
Center for Devices & Radiological Health (CDRH) 10903 New Hampshire Ave *TF:* 800-638-2041 ■ *Web:* www.fda.gov	Silver Spring	MD	20993	301-796-7100	847-8149	340-10
Center for Veterinary Medicine 7519 Standish Pl *Web:* www.fda.gov	Rockville	MD	20855	240-402-7001		340-10
CFSAN 5100 Paint Branch Pkwy *TF:* 888-723-3366 ■ *Web:* www.fda.gov	College Park	MD	20740	888-723-3366		340-10
National Center for Toxicological Research 3900 N Center Rd *Web:* www.fda.gov	Jefferson	AR	72079	870-543-7391	543-7576	340-10
Vaccines, Blood & Biologics 1401 Rockville Pk Ste 200N MS HFM-4 *Web:* www.fda.gov	Rockville	MD	20852	301-827-3844		340-10
Northeast Region 158-15 Liberty Ave *Web:* www.fda.gov	Jamaica	NY	11433	718-662-5416	662-5434	340-10
Food & Drug Law Institute (FDLI) 1155 15th St NW Ste 910 *TF:* 800-956-6293 ■ *Web:* www.fdli.org	Washington	DC	20005	202-371-1420	371-0649	49-10
Food & Nutrition Service						
Western Regional Office 90 Seventh St Ste 10-100 *Web:* www.fns.usda.gov	San Francisco	CA	94103	415-705-1310		340-1
Food & Nutrition Service Regional Offices (FNS)						
Mid-Atlantic Regional Office 300 Corporate Blvd *Web:* www.fns.usda.gov	Robbinsville	NJ	08691	609-259-5025	259-5185	340-1
Midwest Region 77 W Jackson Blvd 20th Fl *Web:* www.fns.usda.gov	Chicago	IL	60604	312-353-6664		340-1
Mountain Plains Region 1244 Speer Blvd Ste 903 *Web:* www.fns.usda.gov	Denver	CO	80204	303-844-0300	844-2160	340-1
Northeast Region 10 Cswy St Rm 501 *Web:* www.fns.usda.gov	Boston	MA	02222	617-565-6370	565-6473	340-1
Southeast Region 61 Forsyth St SW *Web:* www.fns.usda.gov	Atlanta	GA	30303	404-562-1801	562-1807	340-1
Southwest Region 1100 Commerce St Rm 555 *Web:* www.fns.usda.gov	Dallas	TX	75242	214-290-9800		340-1
Food & Water Watch 1616 P St NW Ste 300 *TF:* 855-340-8083 ■ *Web:* www.foodandwaterwatch.org	Washington	DC	20036	202-683-2500		305
Food 4 Less 678 N Wilson Way *Web:* www.food4less.com	Stockton	CA	95205	209-466-2751		297-8
Food Addicts In Recovery Anonymous (FA) 400 W Cummings Pk Ste 1700 *Web:* www.foodaddicts.org	Woburn	MA	01801	781-932-6300		48-21
Food Allergy & Anaphylaxis Network (FAAN) 11781 Lee Jackson Hwy Ste 160 *Web:* www.foodallergy.org	Fairfax	VA	22033	703-691-3179	691-2713	48-17
Food Bank For New York City 39 Broadway 10th Fl *Web:* www.foodbanknyc.org	New York	NY	10006	212-566-7855	566-1463	299
Food City 1005 N Arizona Ave *Web:* www.myfoodcity.com	Chandler	AZ	85224	480-857-2198		345
Food Concepts Inc 2551 Parmenter St *TF:* 800-419-9324 ■ *Web:* www.foodconcepts.com	Middleton	WI	53562	608-831-5006		463
Food Consulting Co, The 13724 Recuerdo Dr *TF:* 800-793-2844 ■ *Web:* www.foodlabels.com	Del Mar	CA	92014	858-793-4658		473
Food Corps 1140 SE Seventh Ave Ste 110 *Web:* foodcorps.org	Portland	OR	97214	212-596-7045		305
Food Country USA 532 East Main St *Web:* foodcountryusainc.com	Abingdon	VA	24210	276-628-3332		345
Food Fight Restaurant 5111 Monona Dr *Web:* foodfightinc.com	Monona	WI	53716	608-246-2719		671
Food for the Poor Inc (FFP) 6401 Lyons Rd *TF:* 800-427-9104 ■ *Web:* www.foodforthepoor.org	Coconut Creek	FL	33073	954-427-2222		48-5
Food for Thought Inc 7738 N Long Lake Rd *TF:* 888-935-2748 ■ *Web:* foodforthought.net	Traverse City	MI	49685	231-326-5444		345
Food Giant Supermarkets 120 Industrial Dr *Web:* www.foodgiant.com	Sikeston	MO	63801	573-471-3500		345
Food Management Associates Inc 22349 La Palma Ave Ste 115 *Web:* www.foodmgt.com	Yorba Linda	CA	92887	714-694-2828		194
Food Marketing Institute (FMI) 2345 Crystal Dr Ste 800 *TF:* 800-732-2639 ■ *Web:* www.fmi.org	Arlington	VA	22202	202-452-8444	429-4519	49-18
Food Perspectives Inc 13755 First Ave N Ste 500 *Web:* www.foodperspectives.com	Plymouth	MN	55441	763-553-7787		743
Food Research & Action Ctr (FRAC) 1875 Connecticut Ave NW Ste 540 *Web:* www.frac.org	Washington	DC	20009	202-986-2200	986-2525	48-6
Food Research Institute University of Wisconsin Madison 1550 Linden Dr *Web:* fri.wisc.edu	Madison	WI	53706	608-263-7777	263-1114	668
Food Safety & Inspection Service 1400 Independence Ave SW *TF:* 877-374-7435 ■ *Web:* www.fsis.usda.gov	Washington	DC	20228	202-720-7025	205-0158	340-1
Food Service Technologies Inc 5256 Eisenhower Ave *Web:* www.mytech24.com	Alexandria	VA	22304	703-354-3835		610
Food Warming Equipment Company Inc 7900 S IL Rt 31 Ste A *TF:* 800-222-4393 ■ *Web:* www.fwe.com	Crystal Lake	IL	60014	815-459-7500	459-7989	298
Foodbank of Southeastern Virginia & the Eastern Shore 800 Tidewater Dr *TF:* 877-486-4379 ■ *Web:* foodbankonline.org	Norfolk	VA	23504	757-627-6599	627-8588	299
Foodbuy LLC 1105 Lakewood Pkwy *Web:* www.foodbuy.com	Alpharetta	GA	30009	678-256-8000		194
FoodChain ID 504 N 4th St *Web:* www.global-id-group.com	Fairfield	IA	52556	641-472-9979		743
FoodChek Systems Inc 1414 8 St SW Ste 450 *TF:* 877-298-0208 ■ *Web:* www.foodcheksystems.com	Calgary	AB	T2R1J6	403-269-9424		407
Foodjets Inc 4370 Auburn Blvd *Web:* foodjets.com	Sacramento	CA	95841	916-649-3663		178-1
Foodland Super Market Ltd 3536 Harding Ave *Web:* www.foodland.com	Honolulu	HI	96816	808-732-0791	737-6952	345
FoodLink Online LLC 475 Alberto Way Ste 100 *Web:* www.itradenetwork.com	Los Gatos	CA	95032	925-660-1100		387
Foods of All Nations 2121 Ivy Rd *Web:* www.foodsofallnations.com	Charlottesville	VA	22903	434-296-6131		345
Foodsby 733 S Marquette Ave S *Web:* www.foodsby.com	Minneapolis	MN	55402	612-354-3956		113
Foodscience Corp 20 New England Dr Ste 10 *TF:* 800-451-5190 ■ *Web:* www.foodsciencecorp.com	Essex Junction	VT	05452	802-878-5508	878-0549	799
Foodservice & Packaging Institute (FPI) 7700 Leesburg Pk Ste 421 *Web:* www.fpi.org	Falls Church	VA	22043	703-592-9889	592-9864	49-13
FoodSpot 1025 S Moorland Rd Ste 400 *Web:* www.foodspot.com	Brookfield	WI	53005	262-522-8400	522-8405	671
Foodtools Inc 315 Laguna St *TF:* 877-836-6386 ■ *Web:* www.foodtools.com	Santa Barbara	CA	93101	805-962-8383	966-3614	298
Fool Hollow Lake Recreation Area 1500 N Fool Hollow Lake Rd *Web:* azstateparks.com	Show Low	AZ	85901	928-537-3680		565
Foot Locker Inc 112 W 34th St *NYSE: FL* ■ *Web:* www.footlocker-inc.com	New York	NY	10120	212-720-3700		301
Foot of the Mountain Motel 200 W Arapahoe Ave *TF:* 866-773-5489 ■ *Web:* www.footofthemountainmotel.com	Boulder	CO	80302	303-442-5688	442-5719	379
Foot Solutions 4101 Roswell Rd *TF:* 866-338-2597 ■ *Web:* www.footsolutions.com	Marietta	GA	30062	866-338-2597		310
Foothill College 12345 El Monte Rd *TF:* 800-234-1597 ■ *Web:* foothill.edu	Los Altos	CA	94022	650-949-7777	949-7048	162
Foothill Federal Credit Union 30 S First Ave *TF:* 866-995-3328 ■ *Web:* foothillcu.org	Arcadia	CA	91006	626-445-0950	445-6763	219
Foothill Ready Mix Inc 11415 State Hwy 99W *Web:* www.foothillreadymix.com	Red Bluff	CA	96080	530-527-2565		191-1
Foothill Village 1400 S Foothill Dr *Web:* www.foothillvillage.com	Salt Lake City	UT	84108	801-487-6670		460
Foothill.Net Inc 24388 Main St *Web:* www.foothill.net	Foresthill	CA	95631	530-820-1031	367-4140	393
Foothills Asset Management Ltd 8767 E Via de Ventura Ste 175 *TF:* 800-663-9870 ■ *Web:* www.faml.net	Scottsdale	AZ	85258	480-777-9870		401
Foothills Correctional Institution 5150 Western Ave *Web:* www.ncdps.gov	Morganton	NC	28655	828-438-5585	438-5598	412
Foothills Inn 1625 N La Crosse St *TF:* 877-428-5666 ■ *Web:* www.thefoothillsinn.com	Rapid City	SD	57701	605-348-5640	348-0073	379
Foothills Mall 7401 N La Cholla Blvd *Web:* www.shopfoothillsmall.com	Tucson	AZ	85741	520-219-0650		460
Foothills Mall Inc 197 Foothills Mall *Web:* www.foothillsmall.com	Maryville	TN	37801	865-982-3613		655
Foothill-Sierra Pest Control Inc 11072A Mountain Brow Rd *TF:* 800-464-3772 ■ *Web:* foothillpest.com	Sonora	CA	95370	209-532-7378	532-3389	104
Foothold Technology 36 E 12th St 5th Fl **Fax Area Code:* 646 ■ *Web:* www.footholdtechnology.com	New York	NY	10003	212-780-1450	365-3066*	178-1
Footlockercom Inc 112 W 34th St *TF:* 800-863-8932 ■ *Web:* www.footaction.com	New York	NY	10120	715-261-9719		301
Footwear Distributors & Retailers of America (FDRA) 1319 F St NW Ste 700 *Web:* www.fdra.org	Washington	DC	20004	202-737-5660	645-0789	49-4

	Phone	Fax	Class
FOP (Fraternal Order of Police) 701 Marriott Dr. Nashville TN 37214 *TF:* 800-451-2711 ■ *Web:* fop.net	615-399-0900	399-0400	48-15
Foppiano Wine Co 12707 Old Redwood Hwy Healdsburg CA 95448 *Web:* foppiano.com	707-433-7272		443
For Eyes 3601 SW 160th Ave Ste 400. Hialeah FL 33014 *TF:* 800-367-3937 ■ *Web:* www.foreyes.com	800-367-3937		543
For Leadership Growth Inc 4369 Woodland Western Springs IL 60558 *Web:* www.forleadershipgrowth.com	708-784-1600	784-1616	194
For the Bride Magazine 222 W 37th St. New York NY 10018	212-967-0750		457-11
For-A-Corporation of America 11155 Knott Ave Ste H Cypress CA 90630 *Web:* www.for-a.com	714-894-3311	894-5399	300
Forager Press LLC, The 23 Bridge St Cleveland NY 13042 *Web:* theforagerpress.com	315-675-9704		637-2
Foranne Manufacturing Inc 83 Steam Whistle Dr. Ivyland PA 18974 *Web:* foranne.com	215-357-4650	357-4631	454
Forbes Capretto 470 Cayuga Rd. Cheektowaga NY 14225 *Web:* www.forbescapretto.com	716-688-5597	688-6674	187
Forbes Energy Services LLC 3000 S Business Hwy 28 Alice TX 78333 *Web:* www.forbesenergyservices.com	361-664-5020	396-0564	536
Forbes Library 20 West St. Northampton MA 01060 *Web:* forbeslibrary.org	413-587-1012	587-1015	434-3
Forbes Media LLC 499 Washington Blvd Jersey City NJ 07310 *TF:* 800-295-0893 ■ *Web:* www.forbes.com	800-295-0893		531-11
Forbes Road Career & Technology Ctr 607 Beatty Rd Monroeville PA 15146 *Web:* www.forbesroad.org	412-373-8100		800
Forbes Seed & Grain Inc 94904 Hwy 99 E Junction City OR 97448 *TF:* 800-547-8004 ■ *Web:* www.forbesseed.com	541-998-8086	998-1091	276
Forbes Snyder Tristate Cash 54 Northampton St Easthampton MA 01027 *TF:* 800-222-4064 ■ *Web:* www.forbes-snyder.com	413-529-2950		253
Forbo Siegling LLC 12201 Vanstory Huntersville NC 28078 *Web:* www.forbo.com	704-948-0800		207
Force 3 Inc 2151 Priest Bridge Dr Crofton MD 21114 **Fax Area Code:* 410 ■ *TF:* 800-391-0204 ■ *Web:* www.force3.com	800-391-0204	721-5624*	180
FORCE America Inc 501 E Cliff Rd Burnsville MN 55337 *TF:* 800-328-2732 ■ *Web:* www.forceamerica.com	952-707-1300		358
Force Capital Management LLC 767 Fifth Ave 12th Fl New York NY 10153 *Web:* www.forcecapital.com	212-451-9150		690
Force Construction Company Inc 990 N National Rd Columbus IN 47201 *Web:* www.forceco.com	812-372-8441	372-5424	264-3
Force Control Industries Inc 3660 Dixie Hwy Fairfield OH 45014 *TF:* 800-829-3244 ■ *Web:* www.forcecontrol.com	513-868-0900	868-2105	620
Force Flow Inc 2430 Stanwell Dr Concord CA 94520 *TF:* 800-893-6723 ■ *Web:* www.forceflowscales.com	800-893-6723		362
Force Management LLC 10815 Sikes Pl Ste 200 Charlotte NC 28277 *Web:* www.forcemanagement.com	704-246-2400		463
Force Mass Acceleration 20 W 22nd St Ste 601. New York NY 10010 *Web:* www.fmaonline.com	212-691-5000	691-5066	637-10
Force10 Networks Inc 1415 N McDowell Blvd Petaluma CA 94954 *TF:* 866-600-5100 ■ *Web:* www.force10networks.com	707-665-4400		681
Forced Exposure 219 Medford St. Malden MA 02148 *Web:* www.forcedexposure.com	781-321-0320	321-0321	637-9
Forcum Lannom Contractors LLC 350 US Hwy 51 Bypass S Dyersburg TN 38024 *Web:* www.forcumlannom.com	731-287-4700	287-4701	188-7
Ford & Garland Inc 1304 Locust St Des Moines IA 50309 *Web:* www.fordandgarland.com	515-288-6324		54
Ford & Harrison LLP 271 17th St NW Ste 1900. Atlanta GA 30363 *Web:* www.fordharrison.com	404-888-3800		428
Ford Audio-Video Systems Inc 8349 East 51st St Oklahoma City OK 73128 *TF:* 800-654-6744 ■ *Web:* www.fordav.com	405-946-9966	946-9991	52
Ford Bacon & Davis 12021 Lakeland Pk Blvd. Baton Rouge LA 70809 *Web:* www.fbd.com	225-292-0050		261
Ford Broadcasting Inc PO Box 1388. Kannapolis NC 28082 *Web:* www.fordbroadcasting.com	704-857-1101		645-141
Ford Construction Co 1311 E Court St Dyersburg TN 38024 *Web:* www.bid-best.com	731-285-5185	286-1528	188-4
Ford County 100 Gunsmoke St Dodge City KS 67801 *Web:* www.fordcounty.net	620-227-4670	227-4699	338
Ford County Feed Yard Inc PO Box 1489 Junction City KS 66441 *Web:* www.kansascattlemen.com	785-238-1483	238-1518	10-1
Ford Development Corp 11148 Woodward Ln. Cincinnati OH 45241 *Web:* www.forddevelopment.com	513-772-1521		186
Ford Engineering Inc 10927 Wye Dr Ste 104 San Antonio TX 78217 *Web:* fordengineering.com	210-590-4777		261
Ford Equity Research Inc 11722 Sorrento Valley Rd Ste I. San Diego CA 92121 *TF:* 800-842-0207 ■ *Web:* www.fordequity.com	858-755-1327		401
Ford Family Foundation 1600 NW Stewart Pkwy. Roseburg OR 97471 *TF:* 877-864-2872 ■ *Web:* www.tfff.org	541-957-5574		305
Ford Fasteners Inc 110 S Newman St Hackensack NJ 07601 *TF:* 800-272-3673 ■ *Web:* www.fordfasteners.com	201-487-3151	487-1919	278
Ford Foundation 1440 Broadway New York NY 10017 *Web:* www.fordfoundation.org	212-573-5000		305
Ford Gum & Machine Company Inc 18 Newton Ave Akron NY 14001 *Web:* fordgum.com	716-542-4561	542-4610	296-6
Ford Hotel Supply Company Inc 2204 N Broadway Saint Louis MO 63102 *TF:* 800-472-3673 ■ *Web:* fordstl.com	314-231-8400		707
Ford Insurance Agency Inc 2 Harold Dow Hwy Eliot ME 03903 *Web:* fordinsurance.com	207-439-2500		390
Ford Meter Box Company Inc, The 775 Manchester Ave PO Box 443 Wabash IN 46992 *Web:* www.fordmeterbox.com	260-563-3171	563-0167	192
Ford Models Inc 11 E 26th St 14th Fl New York NY 10010 *Web:* www.fordmodels.com	212-219-6500		506
Ford Motor Co PO Box 6248 Dearborn MI 48126 *NYSE:* F ■ *TF:* 800-392-3673 ■ *Web:* www.ford.com	800-555-5259		59
Ford Nassen & Baldwin, A Professional Corp 8080 N Central Expy Ste 1600 Dallas TX 75206 *Web:* www.fordnassen.com	214-523-5100		428
Ford of Montebello Inc 2747 Via Campo Montebello CA 90640 *TF:* 888-313-2305 ■ *Web:* www.fordofmontebello.com	888-313-2305		57
Ford of Ocala Inc 2816 NW Pine Ave Ocala FL 34475 *TF:* 888-255-1788 ■ *Web:* www.fordofocala.com	352-732-4800		516
Ford Steel Company Inc 2475 Rock Island Blvd Maryland Heights MO 63043 *TF:* 800-325-4012 ■ *Web:* www.fordsteel.com	314-567-4680	567-5762	492
Ford Theaters PO Box 1951 Hollywood CA 90078 *Web:* www.fordtheatres.org	323-850-2000	871-5904	572
Ford Tool & Machining Inc 2205 Range Rd Loves Park IL 61131 *Web:* www.fordtool.com	815-633-5727	633-5752	757
Ford Tool Steels Inc 5051 Pattison Ave. Saint Louis MO 63110 *TF:* 800-325-9093 ■ *Web:* fordtoolsteels.com	314-772-3322	772-1919	492
Ford's Theatre National Historic Site 511 Tenth St NW Washington DC 20004 *Web:* www.fords.org	202-347-4833	638-1001	564
FordDirect 1740 US Hwy 60 PO Box 700. Republic MO 65738 *TF:* 888-578-8478 ■ *Web:* www.republicford.com	417-732-2626		57
Fordham Auto Sales Inc 236 W Fordham Rd Bronx NY 10468 *TF:* 800-407-1153 ■ *Web:* www.fordhamtoyota.com	800-407-1153		57
Fordham Financial Management Inc 14 Wall St. New York NY 10005 *TF:* 877-436-3673 ■ *Web:* www.fordhamfinancial.com	212-732-8500	349-2550	690
Fordham Plastics 1204 Village Market Pl Ste 262 Morrisville NC 27560 *TF:* 866-467-0708 ■ *Web:* www.fordhamplastics.com	919-467-0708		319-3
Fordham University 441 E Fordham Rd Bronx NY 10458 *TF:* 800-367-3426 ■ *Web:* www.fordham.edu	718-817-3240		166
Fordia Inc 2745 de Miniac Ville Saint-Laurent QC H4S1E5 *TF:* 800-768-7274 ■ *Web:* www.fordia.com	514-336-9211		358
Fordyce Picture Frame Company Inc 2926 N Hwy 167 Fordyce AR 71742 *TF:* 877-443-7263 ■ *Web:* www.fordyceonline.com	870-352-2115	352-2606	820
Fore Street 288 Fore St Portland ME 04101 *Web:* www.forestreet.biz	207-775-2717		671
Forecast Intl 22 Commerce Rd Newtown CT 06470 *TF:* 800-451-4975 ■ *Web:* forecastinternational.com	203-426-0800	426-1964	637-10
Forecaster, The 5 Fundy Rd Falmouth ME 04105 *Web:* www.pressherald.com	207-781-3661	781-2060	532-4
Forefront Analytics LLC 1 Tower Bridge 100 Front St Ste 1111 West Conshohocken PA 19428 *Web:* forefrontanalytics.com	610-341-3900	341-9455	401
Forefront Technology Solutions Corp 2201 Cooperative Way Ste 600. Herndon VA 20171 *Web:* forefrontnow.com	571-210-5443		261
Foreign Affairs 58 E 68th St New York NY 10065 *TF:* 800-829-5539 ■ *Web:* www.foreignaffairs.com	212-434-9527		457-17
Foreign Agricultural Service 1400 Independence Ave SW Washington DC 20228 *Web:* www.fas.usda.gov	202-720-7115		340-1
Foreign Candy Company Inc 1 Foreign Candy Dr Hull IA 51239 *TF:* 800-831-8541 ■ *Web:* www.foreigncandy.com	712-439-1496		297-3
Foreign Cinema 2534 Mission St San Francisco CA 94110 *Web:* foreigncinema.com	415-648-7600		671
Foreign Claims Settlement Commission of the US 600 E St NW Ste 10300 Washington DC 20004 *Web:* www.justice.gov	202-616-6975	616-6993	340-14
Foreign Language Publications (FLP) The Ohio State University 198 Hagerty Hall 1775 S College Rd Columbus OH 43210 *TF:* 800-678-6999 ■ *Web:* www.flpubs.osu.edu	614-292-3838		637-2
Foreign Policy Assn (FPA) 470 Park Ave S. New York NY 10016 *TF:* 800-628-5754 ■ *Web:* fpa.org	212-481-8100	481-9275	48-7
Foreign Policy Institute 1740 Massachusetts Ave Washington DC 20036 *Web:* www.fpi.sais-jhu.edu	202-663-5600	663-5769	634
Foreign Policy Research Institute (FPRI) 1528 Walnut St Ste 610 Philadelphia PA 19102 *Web:* www.fpri.org	215-732-3774	732-4401	634
Foreign Service Institute 4000 Arlington Blvd Rt 50 Arlington VA 22204 *Web:* www.state.gov	703-302-6703		340-16
Foreign Service Network *Honorary Consulate General* 913 E Franklin Ave Ste 101 Minnetonka MN 55343 *Web:* foreignservice.network	612-332-3338	332-1386	257
Foreign Tire Sales Inc 2204 Morris Ave Union NJ 07083 *TF:* 800-634-8335 ■ *Web:* www.foreigntire.com	908-687-0559	687-0231	755
Foreign Trade Export Packing Co 1350 Lathrop St Houston TX 77020 *Web:* www.ftep.com	713-672-8211		311
Forell-Elsesser Engineers Inc 160 Pine St Ste 600 San Francisco CA 94111 *Web:* www.forell.com	415-837-0700		261

Phone | Fax | Class

Foreman Tool & Mold Corp
3850 Swenson Ave ..... Saint Charles IL 60174 630-377-6389 604
Web: www.foremantool.com

Foremost Farms USA E10889A Penny Ln ..... Baraboo WI 53913 608-355-8700 355-8699 296-10
TF: 800-362-9196 ■ *Web:* www.foremostfarms.com

Foremost Industries Inc
2375 Buchanan Trl W ..... Greencastle PA 17225 717-597-7166 106
Web: www.foremost.ca

Foremost Insurance Co
5600 Beech Tree Ln ..... Caledonia MI 49316 800-532-4221 391-4
TF: 800-532-4221 ■ *Web:* www.foremost.com

Foremost Machine Builders Inc
23 Spielman Rd ..... Fairfield NJ 07004 973-227-0700 111
Web: foremostmachine.com

Foremost Manufacturing Company Inc
941 Ball Ave ..... Union NJ 07083 908-687-4646 483
Web: foremostmfg.com

Foremost Media 1337 Excalibur Dr ..... Janesville WI 53546 608-758-4841 177
Web: www.foremostmedia.com

Foremostco Inc 8457 NW 66th St ..... Miami FL 33166 305-592-8986 426-1362* 694
**Fax Area Code:* 800 ■ *TF:* 800-421-8986 ■ *Web:* www.foremostco.com

Forensic Fluids Laboratories Inc
225 Parsons St ..... Kalamazoo MI 49007 269-492-7700 743
Web: www.forensicfluids.com

Forensic It 57 E Southcrest Cir ..... Edwardsville IL 62025 314-677-3950 743
TF: 877-483-3284 ■ *Web:* forensicit.com

Forenta LP
2300 W Andrew Johnson Hwy Ste A ..... Morristown TN 37814 423-586-5370 586-3470 427
Web: www.forentausa.com

Forepaugh's 276 S Exchange St ..... Saint Paul MN 55102 651-224-5606 671
Web: www.forepaughs.com

Foresight Financial Group Inc
3106 N Rockton Ave ..... Rockford IL 61103 815-847-7500 70
Web: www.foresightfg.com

Foresight Group Inc 2822 N Mlk Blvd ..... Lansing MI 48906 517-485-5700 485-0202 687
Web: www.foresightgroup.net

Foresite Group Inc
3740 Davinci Ct Ste 100 ..... Peachtree Corners GA 30092 770-368-1399 368-1944 261
Web: www.foresitegroup.net

Foresite Software LLC
S2756A County Rd T ..... Baraboo WI 53913 608-393-1019 525
Web: www.foresitesoftware.com

Forest at Duke 2701 Pickett Rd ..... Durham NC 27705 800-474-0258 672
TF: 800-474-0258 ■ *Web:* forestduke.org

Forest Capital Museum State Park
204 Forest Pk Dr ..... Perry FL 32348 850-584-3227 565
Web: www.floridastateparks.org

Forest City Technologies Inc
299 Clay St ..... Wellington OH 44090 440-647-2115 647-2644 326
Web: www.forestcitytech.com

Forest City Trading Group LLC
10250 SW Greenburg Rd Ste 300 ..... Portland OR 97223 503-246-8500 246-1116 191-3
TF: 800-767-3284 ■ *Web:* www.fctg.com

Forest County 200 E Madison St ..... Crandon WI 54520 715-478-3475 478-3815 338
Web: www.forestcountywi.com

Forest County 526 Elm St Ste 3 ..... Tionesta PA 16353 814-755-3537 755-8837 338
Web: www.co.forest.pa.us

Forest County Potawatomi Cultural Center Library & Museum
5416 Everybody's Rd ..... Crandon WI 54520 715-478-7200 434-3
TF: 800-960-5479 ■ *Web:* www.fcpotawatomi.com

Forest Electric Corp 1375 Broadway ..... New York NY 10018 212-318-1500 318-1518 189-4
Web: forestelectric.net

Forest Haven Nursing & Rehabilitation Center LLC
171 Thrasher Dr ..... Jonesboro LA 71251 318-259-2729 371
Web: www.foresthavennursingandrehab.com

Forest Hills Local School
7550 Forest Rd ..... Cincinnati OH 45255 513-231-3600 685
Web: www.foresthills.edu

Forest Hills Public Schools
6590 Cascade Rd SE ..... Grand Rapids MI 49546 616-493-8800 493-8519 532-4
Web: www.fhps.net

Forest History Society
701 William Vickers Ave ..... Durham NC 27701 919-682-9319 682-2349 48-13
Web: foresthistory.org

Forest Industries Telecommunications (FIT)
1565 Oak St ..... Eugene OR 97401 541-485-8441 485-7556 49-20
Web: www.fcclicense.org

Forest Insurance
7310 W Madison St ..... Forest Park IL 60130 708-383-9000 205-4100* 390
**Fax Area Code:* 847 ■ *TF:* 800-421-6208 ■ *Web:* forestinsured.com

Forest Investment Assoc
15 Piedmont Ctr Ste 1250 ..... Atlanta GA 30305 404-261-9575 261-9574 401
Web: www.forestinvest.com

Forest Lake Area Chamber of Commerce
PO Box 474 ..... Forest Lake MN 55025 651-464-3200 464-3201 139
Web: forestlakechamber.org

Forest Lake Area Schools
6100 N 210th St ..... Forest Lake MN 55025 651-982-8100 982-8137 685
Web: www.flaschools.org

Forest Lake State Park
397 Forest Lake Rd ..... Dalton NH 03598 603-466-3860 565
Web: www.nhstateparks.org

Forest Landowners Assn (FLA)
950 Glenn Dr Ste 150 ..... Folsom CA 95630 404-325-2954 325-2955 48-13
Web: www.forestlandowners.org

Forest Lawn Memorial-Parks & Mortuaries
1712 S Glendale Ave ..... Glendale CA 91205 323-254-3131 510
TF: 800-204-3131 ■ *Web:* forestlawn.com

Forest of Nisene Marks State Park
Aptos Creek Rd ..... Aptos CA 95003 831-763-7063 565
Web: www.parks.ca.gov

Forest Park National Bank
7348 Madison St ..... Forest Park IL 60130 708-222-2800 70
Web: forestparkbank.com

Forest Park Nature Ctr
5809 Forest Pk Dr ..... Peoria IL 61616 309-686-3360 50-5
Web: peoriaparks.org

Forest Preserve Dist of Dupage County
1717 31st St ..... Oak Brook IL 60523 630-616-8424 226
TF: 800-526-0857 ■ *Web:* www.dupageforest.org

Forest Press 80 E Corydon St ..... Bradford PA 16701 800-473-9370 368-9370* 637-2
**Fax Area Code:* 814 ■ *TF:* 800-473-9370 ■ *Web:* visitanf.com

Forest Products Group Inc, The
1033 Dublin Rd ..... Columbus OH 43215 614-488-9743 191-3
TF: 855-239-2310 ■ *Web:* forestproductsgroup.com

Forest Products Manufacturing Company Inc
PO Box 606 ..... Jasper IN 47547 812-482-5625 482-9148 683
Web: forestp.com

Forest Resources Association Inc
600 Jefferson Plz Ste 350 ..... Rockville MD 20852 301-838-9385 49-3
Web: www.forestresources.org

Forest River Inc 58277 SR 19 S ..... Elkhart IN 46517 574-296-7700 120
Web: www.forestriverinc.com

Forest Service
1400 Independence Ave SW ..... Washington DC 20228 202-205-8333 340-1
TF: 800-832-1355 ■ *Web:* www.fs.usda.gov

Forest Service Employees for Environmental Ethics (FSEEE)
PO Box 11615 ..... Eugene OR 97440 541-484-2692 484-3004 49-7
Web: www.fseee.org

Forest Service Regional Offices
Northern Region-Regional Office
26 Fort Missoula Rd ..... Missoula MT 59804 406-329-3511 329-3347 340-1
Web: www.fs.usda.gov
US Forest Service Rocky Mountain Region
740 Simms St ..... Golden CO 80401 303-275-5350 340-1
Web: www.fs.usda.gov
Region 3 (Southwestern Region)
333 Broadway Blvd SE ..... Albuquerque NM 87102 505-842-3292 340-1
Web: www.fs.usda.gov
Region 5 (Pacific Southwest Region)
1323 Club Dr ..... Vallejo CA 94592 707-562-8737 562-9130 340-1
Web: www.fs.usda.gov
Region 6 (Pacific Northwest Region)
333 SW 1st Ave PO Box 3623 ..... Portland OR 97208 503-808-2468 808-2469 340-1
Web: www.fs.usda.gov
Region 8 (Southern Region)
1720 Peachtree Rd NW ..... Atlanta GA 30309 404-347-2784 340-1
TF: 877-372-7248 ■ *Web:* www.fs.usda.gov
Region 9 (Eastern Region)
626 E Wisconsin Ave ..... Milwaukee WI 53202 414-297-3600 297-3808 340-1
Web: www.fs.usda.gov

Forest Travel
2440 NE Miami Gardens Dr Ste 107 ..... Miami FL 33180 305-932-5560 772
TF: 800-432-2132 ■ *Web:* foresttravel.com

Forest Valley Veterinary Clinic
2555 Mosby Creek Rd ..... Cottage Grove OR 97424 541-942-9132 794
Web: www.fvvet.com

Foresters Financial Services Inc
PO Box 7836 ..... Edison NJ 08818 800-832-7783 796
TF: 800-832-7783 ■ *Web:* www.firstinvestors.com

Forestiere Underground Gardens
5021 W Shaw Ave ..... Fresno CA 93722 559-271-0734 97
Web: www.undergroundgardens.com

Forestry Management Consultants
PO Box 351 ..... Lawai HI 96765 808-332-5200 196
Web: www.forestryhawaii.com

Forestry Suppliers Inc
205 W Rankin St ..... Jackson MS 39201 601-354-3565 292-0165 459
TF: 800-752-8460 ■ *Web:* www.forestry-suppliers.com

Forestville/Mystery Cave State Park
21071 County 118 ..... Preston MN 55965 507-352-5111 352-5113 565
Web: www.dnr.state.mn.us

Foretravel Motorcoach Inc
1221 NW Stallings Dr ..... Nacogdoches TX 75964 936-564-8367 120
TF: 800-955-6226 ■ *Web:* www.foretravel.com

Forever 21 Inc
3880 N Mission Rd Ste 3030 ..... Los Angeles CA 90058 213-741-5100 157-6
TF: 800-966-1355 ■ *Web:* www.forever21.com

Forever Living Products International Inc
7501 E McCormick Pkwy ..... Scottsdale AZ 85258 480-998-8888 905-8451 214
TF: 888-440-2563 ■ *Web:* www.foreverliving.com

Forever Media 1 Forever Dr ..... Hollidaysburg PA 16648 814-941-9800 643
Web: www.forevermediainc.com

Forever Media Inc 275 Radio Rd ..... Hanover PA 17331 717-637-3831 632
Web: www.foreveryork.com

Forever Spring
2629 E Craig Rd Ste E ..... North Las Vegas NV 89030 310-657-5910 238
TF: 800-523-4334 ■ *Web:* www.foreverspring.com

Forge Energy
15727 Anthem Pkwy Ste 501 ..... San Antonio TX 78249 210-478-5950 536
Web: www.forgenergy.com

Forge Industries Inc
4450 Market St ..... Youngstown OH 44512 330-782-8301 360-3

Forge Precision Co
31800 W 8 Mile Rd ..... Farmington Hills MI 48336 248-477-0020 477-0128 454
Web: www.forgeprecision.com

Forged Components Inc 14527 Smith Rd ..... Humble TX 77396 281-441-4088 441-8899 483
Web: forgedcomponents.com

Forged Metals Inc 10685 Beech Ave ..... Fontana CA 92337 909-349-6604 21

Forged Products Inc (FPI)
6505 N Houston Rosslyn Rd ..... Houston TX 77091 713-462-3416 460-9404 483
TF: 800-876-3416 ■ *Web:* www.fpitx.com

Forging Industry Assn (FIA)
1111 Superior Ave Ste 615 ..... Cleveland OH 44114 216-781-6260 781-0102 49-13
Web: www.forging.org

Forgy Process Instruments Inc
1879 Craig Rd ..... Saint Louis MO 63146 314-439-9149 385
TF: 800-229-8258 ■ *Web:* www.forgyprocess.com

Fori Automation Inc
13231 23 Mile Rd ..... Shelby Township MI 48315 586-247-2336 247-3126 493
TF: 888-220-3674 ■ *Web:* foriauto.com

Foria International Inc
18689 Arenth Ave ..... City of Industry CA 91748 626-912-6100 156
Web: www.foria.com

Forino 555 Mtn Home Rd ..... Sinking Spring PA 19608 610 670 2200 670-2608 186
Web: www.forino.com

Company	City	State	ZIP	Phone	Fax	Class
Fork Restaurant 306 Market St *Web:* forkrestaurant.com	Philadelphia	PA	19106	215-625-9425		671
Forkardt 2155 Traverse Field Dr *TF:* 800-544-3823 ■ *Web:* www.forkardt.com	Traverse City	MI	49686	231-995-8300	995-8361	493
Forked Deer Electric Co-op PO Box 67 *TF:* 844-333-2729 ■ *Web:* www.forkeddeer.com	Halls	TN	38040	731-836-7508		245
Forked Run State Park 63300 SR-124 *Web:* www.stateparks.com	Reedsville	OH	45772	740-378-6206		565
Forklifts and Tires 14503 Sommermeyer St *TF:* 800-687-3884 ■ *Web:* www.forkliftsandtires.com	Houston	TX	77041	713-460-8197	460-5941	755
Forklifts of Minnesota Inc 2201 W 94th St *TF:* 800-752-4300 ■ *Web:* forkliftsofmn.com	Bloomington	MN	55431	952-887-5400		385
Forklifts of St Louis Inc 4720 Laguardia Dr *TF:* 888-317-4293 ■ *Web:* forkliftsofstlouis.com	Saint Louis	MO	63134	314-426-4040	427-5490	385
Forks of Cheat Winery 2811 Stewart Town Rd *Web:* www.wvwines.com	Morgantown	WV	26508	304-598-2019		50-7
Forks Outfitters 950 S Forks Ave *Web:* www.forksthriftway.com	Forks	WA	98331	360-374-6161	374-2095	345
Form Cut Industries Inc 197 Mt Pleasant Ave *Web:* formcut.com	Newark	NJ	07104	973-483-5154	483-4512	621
Form Grind Corp 30062 Aventura *Web:* www.formgrind.com	Rancho Santa Margarita	CA	92688	949-858-7000		481
Form Plastics Co 3825 Stern Ave *Web:* www.formplastics.com	Saint Charles	IL	60174	630-443-1400		608
Form-A-Feed Inc (FAF) 740 Bowman St *TF:* 800-422-3649 ■ *Web:* formafeed.com	Stewart	MN	55385	320-562-2413		447
Formaggio Kitchen on Line LLC 244 Huron Ave *TF:* 888-212-3224 ■ *Web:* www.formaggiokitchen.com	Cambridge	MA	02138	617-354-4750		292
Formall Inc 3908 Fountain Vly Dr *TF:* 800-643-3676 ■ *Web:* www.formall.com	Knoxville	TN	37918	865-259-6298	922-3941	602
Forman Holt Eliades & Ravin LLC 66 Rte 17 N *Web:* www.formanlaw.com	Paramus	NJ	07652	201-845-1000		445
Forman Mills 1070 Thomas Busch Memorial Hwy *TF:* 800-784-1077 ■ *Web:* formanmills.com	Pennsauken Township	NJ	08110	856-486-1447		157-2
Forman School 12 Norfolk Rd PO Box 80 *Web:* www.formanschool.org	Litchfield	CT	06759	860-567-8712	567-3501	622
For-Mar Nature Preserve & Arboretum 2142 N Genesee Rd *TF:* 800-648-7275 ■ *Web:* www.geneseecountyparks.org	Burton	MI	48509	810-789-8567		823
Formatech It Services 3263 Claremont Way Ste B *Web:* www.formatech-it.com	Napa	CA	94558	707-258-1492	258-1331	196
Formation Development Group LLC 178 S Main St Ste 375 *Web:* fs-partners.com	Alpharetta	GA	30009	770-777-9898		653
Formax Manufacturing Corp 168 Wealthy St SW *TF:* 800-242-2833 ■ *Web:* formaxmfg.com	Grand Rapids	MI	49503	616-456-5458	456-7507	1
Formco Metal Products Inc 556 Clayton Ct *Web:* www.formcometal.com	Wood Dale	IL	60191	630-766-4441	766-4517	295
Formed Fiber Technologies Inc 125 Allied Rd PO Box 1300 *Web:* www.formedfiber.com	Auburn	ME	04211	207-784-1118	784-1137	606
Formers by Ernie Inc 7905 Almeda Genoa Rd Ste B *Web:* www.formersbyernie.net	Houston	TX	77075	713-991-3455		358
Formetco Inc 2963 Pleasant Hill Rd *TF:* 800-367-6382 ■ *Web:* www.formetco.com	Duluth	GA	30096	800-367-6382		701
Formex Manufacturing Inc 601 Hurricane Shoals Rd NW *TF:* 800-310-3867 ■ *Web:* www.formex.com	Lawrenceville	GA	30046	770-962-9816		596
Formex Metal Industries Inc N2b-221 Riverbend Dr *Web:* www.formexmetal.com	Kitchener	ON	N2B2E8	519-745-2260		757
FormFactor Inc 7005 Southfront Rd *NASDAQ: FORM* ■ *TF:* 800-665-7301 ■ *Web:* www.formfactor.com	Livermore	CA	94551	925-290-4000	290-4010	695
Formflex Inc PO Box 218 *TF:* 800-255-7659 ■ *Web:* www.formflexproducts.com	Bloomingdale	IN	47832	800-255-7659		86
Formica & Dobkin PC 1309 Berlin Tpke *Web:* formicadobkin.com	Berlin	CT	06037	860-828-5329	828-8001	2
Formica Corp 10155 Reading Rd *TF:* 800-367-6422 ■ *Web:* www.formica.com	Cincinnati	OH	45241	513-786-3400		599
Formosa Garden 1011 NE Loop 410 *Web:* formosagardensa.com	San Antonio	TX	78209	210-828-9988		671
Formosa Plastics Corporation USA 9 Peach Tree Hill Rd *TF:* 888-664-4040 ■ *Web:* www.fpcusa.com	Livingston	NJ	07039	973-992-2090		605-2
Formosa Restaurant 913 E Broadway *Web:* www.formosatogo.com	Columbia	MO	65201	573-449-3339		671
Formosa's II - Augusta 3830 Washington Rd A-36 *Web:* www.formosas2.com	Augusta	GA	30907	706-855-8998		671
Formost Graphic Communications Inc 19209 Chennault Way Ste A *TF:* 800-777-4242 ■ *Web:* www.formostgc.com	Gaithersburg	MD	20879	301-424-4242	424-7489	534
Formotus Inc 10400 NE Fourth St Ste 500 *Web:* www.formotus.com	Bellevue	WA	98004	206-973-5060		177
Forms & Surfaces Inc 30 Pine St *Web:* www.forms-surfaces.com	Pittsburgh	PA	15223	412-781-9003		701
Formsprag Clutch Inc 23601 Hoover Rd *TF:* 800-348-0881 ■ *Web:* www.formsprag.com	Warren	MI	48089	800-348-0881		770
Formtek Metal Forming Inc 4899 Commerce Pkwy *TF:* 800-631-0520 ■ *Web:* formtekgroup.com	Cleveland	OH	44128	216-292-4460		674
Formula Consultants Inc 222 S Harbor Blvd Ste 650 *Web:* www.formula.com	Anaheim	CA	92805	714-778-0123	778-6364	180
Formula Ford Inc 265 River St *TF:* 866-787-2199 ■ *Web:* www.formulatruckland.com	Montpelier	VT	05602	802-223-5201		57
Formula G Intl 6444 E Spring St Ste 159 *Web:* www.g-site.com	Long Beach	CA	90815	562-596-1472		180
Formula Growth Ltd 1010 Sherbrooke St W Ste 2300 *Web:* www.formulagrowth.com	Montreal	QC	H3A2R7	514-288-5136		401
Forney Corp 16479 N Dallas Pkwy Ste 600 *TF:* 800-356-7740 ■ *Web:* www.forneycorp.com	Addison	TX	75001	972-458-6100		201
Forney Independent School District (Inc) 600 S Bois D ARC St *Web:* www.forneyisd.net	Forney	TX	75126	972-564-4055		685
Forney Industries Inc 1830 LaPorte Ave *TF:* 800-521-6038 ■ *Web:* www.forneyind.com	Fort Collins	CO	80521	800-521-6038		811
Forney LLC 2050 Jackson's Pointe Ct *TF:* 800-367-6397 ■ *Web:* forneyonline.com	Zelienople	PA	16063	724-346-7400		419
Forney Museum of Transportation 4303 Brighton Blvd *Web:* www.forneymuseum.org	Denver	CO	80216	303-297-1113		520
Fornos of Spain 47 Ferry St *Web:* www.fornosrestaurant.com	Newark	NJ	07105	973-589-4767		671
Forrest Avenue Animal Hospital PA 3156 Forrest Ave *Web:* faah.vetstreet.com	Dover	DE	19904	302-736-3000	736-9816	794
Forrest College 601 E River St *Web:* www.forrestcollege.edu	Anderson	SC	29624	864-225-7653		167-3
Forrest General Hospital 6051 US Hwy 49 *TF:* 800-503-5980 ■ *Web:* www.forresthealth.org	Hattiesburg	MS	39402	601-288-7000	288-4180	374-3
Forrest Hills Mountain Resort & Conference Ctr 135 Forrest Hills Rd *TF:* 800-654-6313 ■ *Web:* forresthillsresort.com	Dahlonega	GA	30533	706-864-6456		669
Forrest Machining Inc 27756 Ave Mentry *Web:* www.forrestmachining.com	Valencia	CA	91355	661-257-0231		529
Forry Ullman Ullman & Forry 540 Court St *Web:* forryullman.com	Reading	PA	19601	610-777-5700		41
ForSaleByOwnercom LLC 701 Griswold *TF:* 888-367-7253 ■ *Web:* www.forsalebyowner.com	Detroit	MI	48226	888-367-7253		387
Forsberg & Umlauf PS 901 Fifth Ave Ste 1400 *Web:* foum.law	Seattle	WA	98164	206-689-8500	689-8501	41
Forsberg Real Estate Co 2422 Jolly Rd Ste 200 *Web:* lansingrealestate.com	Okemos	MI	48864	517-349-9330	349-7131	653
Forsbergs Inc 1210 Pennington Ave PO Box 510 *TF:* 800-654-1927 ■ *Web:* www.forsbergs.com	Thief River Falls	MN	56701	218-681-1927	681-2037	273
Forshaw Industries Inc PO Box 327 *Web:* forshaw.com	Charlotte	NC	28208	704-372-6790		690
Forshey & Prostok LLP 777 Main St Ste 1290 *Web:* forsheyprostok.com	Fort Worth	TX	76102	817-877-8855		41
Forster Electrical Engineering Inc 550 N Burr Oak Ave *Web:* www.forstereng.com	Oregon	WI	53575	608-835-9009		256
Forsyth Animal Hospital 2619 Atlanta Hwy *Web:* forsythanimalhospital.com	Cumming	GA	30041	770-887-8099		794
Forsyth County 110 E Main St *Web:* www.forsythco.com	Cumming	GA	30040	770-781-2120		338
Forsyth County Board of Education 1120 Dahlonega Hwy *Web:* www.forsyth.k12.ga.us	Cumming	GA	30040	770-887-2461	781-6632	685
Forsyth County Public Library 201 N Chestnut St *TF:* 866-345-1884 ■ *Web:* www.forsyth.cc	Winston-Salem	NC	27101	336-703-2665	727-2549	434-3
Forsyth Technical Community College 2100 Silas Creek Pkwy *Web:* www.forsythtech.edu	Winston-Salem	NC	27103	336-723-0371	761-2399	800
Forsythe & Long Inc 4560 Helton dr	Florence	AL	35630	256-760-0000	766-7113	261
Fort Abercrombie State Historic Site 35 miles S of Fargo County Hwy-22 *Web:* history.nd.gov	Abercrombie	ND	58001	701-553-8513		565
Fort Abraham Lincoln State Park 4480 Ft Lincoln Rd *Web:* www.parkrec.nd.gov	Mandan	ND	58554	701-667-6340		565
Fort Adams State Park Harrison Ave *Web:* www.riparks.com	Newport	RI	02840	401-847-2400		565
Fort AP Hill 18436 Fourth St *Web:* www.army.mil	Fort AP Hill	VA	22427	804-633-8120		497-2
Fort Atkinson Memorial Hospital 611 Sherman Ave E *TF:* 800-844-5575 ■ *Web:* www.forthealthcare.com	Fort Atkinson	WI	53538	920-568-5000		374-3
Fort Atkinson State Historical Park 201 S Seventh St *Web:* www.fortatkinsononline.org	Fort Calhoun	NE	68023	402-468-5611		565
Fort Atkinson State Preserve 303 Second St NW *Web:* www.iowadnr.gov	Fort Atkinson	IA	52144	563-425-4161		565
Fort Belknap Electric Co-opeartive Inc 1302 W Main PO Box 486 *TF:* 844-834-4453 ■ *Web:* www.fortbelknapec.com	Olney	TX	76374	940-564-2343	564-3247	245
Fort Bend Chamber of Commerce 445 Commerce Green Blvd *Web:* www.fortbendchamber.com	Sugar Land	TX	77478	281-491-0800	491-0112	139
Fort Bend County 301 Jackson St 1st Fl *Web:* www.fortbendcountytx.gov	Richmond	TX	77469	281-342-3411	341-8669	338
Fort Bend Herald 1902 S Fourth St *Web:* www.fbherald.com	Rosenberg	TX	77471	281-342-4474		532-2
Fort Bend Museum 500 Houston St *Web:* www.fortbendmuseum.org	Richmond	TX	77469	281-342-6478		520

				Phone	Fax	Class
Fort Bliss National Cemetery 5200 Fred Wilson Rd PO Box 6342 *Web:* www.cem.va.gov	El Paso	TX	79906	915-564-0201	564-3746	136
Fort Boonesborough State Park 4375 Boonesborough Rd *Web:* parks.ky.gov	Richmond	KY	40475	859-527-3131		565
Fort Bragg Unified School District 312 S Lincoln St *Web:* www.fbusd.us	Fort Bragg	CA	95437	707-961-2850	964-5002	685
Fort Bridger State Historic Site PO Box 35 *Web:* www.travelwyoming.com	Fort Bridger	WY	82933	307-782-3842		565
Fort Buford State Historic Site 15349 39th Ln NW *Web:* www.history.nd.gov	Williston	ND	58801	701-572-9034		565
Fort Caroline National Memorial 12713 Ft Caroline Rd *Web:* www.nps.gov	Jacksonville	FL	32225	904-641-7155	641-3798	564
Fort Casey State Park 1280 S Engle Rd *TF:* 888-226-7688 ■ *Web:* www.parks.state.wa.us	Coupeville	WA	98239	360-678-4519		565
Fort Caspar Museum 4001 Fort Caspar Rd *TF:* 800-877-7353 ■ *Web:* www.casperwy.gov	Casper	WY	82604	307-235-8462		520
Fort Churchill State Historic Park 10000 Hwy 95A *Web:* www.parks.nv.gov	Silver Springs	NV	89429	775-577-2345		565
Fort Clinch State Park 2601 Atlantic Ave *Web:* www.floridastateparks.org	Fernandina Beach	FL	32034	904-277-7274	277-7225	565
Fort Cobb Lake State Park 27022 Copperhead Rd *Web:* www.travelok.com	Fort Cobb	OK	73038	405-643-2249		565
Fort Collins Area Chamber of Commerce 225 S Meldrum St *TF:* 877-652-8607 ■ *Web:* fortcollinschamber.com	Fort Collins	CO	80521	970-482-3746	482-3774	139
Fort Collins City Hall 300 Laporte Ave *Web:* www.fcgov.com	Fort Collins	CO	80521	970-221-6505	224-6107	337
Fort Collins Coloradoan 1300 Riverside Ave *TF:* 877-424-0063 ■ *Web:* www.coloradoan.com	Fort Collins	CO	80524	970-493-6397		532-2
Fort Collins Convention & Visitors Bureau 19 Old Town Sq Ste 137 *TF:* 800-274-3678 ■ *Web:* www.visitftcollins.com	Fort Collins	CO	80524	970-232-3840	232-3841	206
Fort Collins Museum of Discovery 408 Mason Ct *Web:* www.fcmdsc.org	Fort Collins	CO	80524	970-221-6738		520
Fort Collins Symphony 214 S College Ave *Web:* www.fcsymphony.org	Fort Collins	CO	80524	970-482-4823		573-3
Fort Columbia State Park Fort Columbia State Pk *Web:* parks.state.wa.us	Chinook	WA	98614	360-777-8221		565
Fort Cooper State Park 3100 S Old Floral City Rd *Web:* www.floridastateparks.org	Inverness	FL	34450	352-726-0315		565
Fort Custer National Cemetery 15501 Dickman Rd *Web:* www.cem.va.gov	Augusta	MI	49012	269-731-4164	731-2428	136
Fort Custer Recreation Area 5163 Ft Custer Dr *Web:* www.michigan.org	Augusta	MI	49012	269-731-4200		565
Fort Davidson State Historic Site 118 E Maple *Web:* mostateparks.com	Pilot Knob	MO	63663	573-546-3454		565
Fort Davis National Historic Site PO Box 1379 *Web:* www.nps.gov	Fort Davis	TX	79734	432-426-3224	426-3122	564
Fort Dearborn Co 6035 W Gross Pt Rd *Web:* www.fortdearborn.com	Niles	IL	60714	773-774-4321	774-9105	627
Fort Defiance State Park 3642 174th St *Web:* www.iowadnr.gov	Estherville	IA	51334	712-337-3211		565
Fort Detrick 810 Schreider St *TF:* 800-256-7621 ■ *Web:* www.detrick.army.mil	Frederick	MD	21702	301-619-7613		497-2
Fort Docs 533 Pacific Ave *Web:* www.ftdocs.com	Santa Rosa	CA	95407	707-571-8313		317
Fort Dodge Correctional Facility 1550 L St *Web:* doc.iowa.gov	Fort Dodge	IA	50501	515-574-4700		213
Fort Dodge Public Library 424 Central Ave *Web:* www.fortdodgeiowa.org	Fort Dodge	IA	50501	515-573-8167	573-5422	434-3
Fort Donelson National Battlefield PO Box 434 *Web:* www.nps.gov	Dover	TN	37058	931-232-5706	232-4085	564
Fort Dummer State Park 517 Old Guilford Rd *Web:* www.vtstateparks.com	Brattleboro	VT	05301	802-254-2610		565
Fort Duncan Regional Medical Ctr 3333 N Foster Maldonado Blvd *Web:* www.fortduncanmedicalcenter.com	Eagle Pass	TX	78852	830-773-5321	872-2549	374-3
Fort DuPont State Park 45 Clinton St *Web:* www.destateparks.com	Delaware City	DE	19706	302-834-7941		565
Fort East Martello Museum 3501 S Roosevelt Blvd *Web:* www.kwahs.org	Key West	FL	33040	305-296-3913		520
Fort Ebey State Park 400 Hill Vly Dr **Fax Area Code:* 888 ■ *Web:* www.parks.state.wa.us	Coupeville	WA	98239	360-678-4636	226-7688*	565
Fort Edgecomb State Historic Site 66 Ft Rd *Web:* www.maine.gov	Edgecomb	ME	04556	207-882-7777		565
Fort Edward Express Company Inc 1402 Rt 9 *TF:* 800-342-1233 ■ *Web:* www.bulktransporter.com	Fort Edward	NY	12828	518-792-6571		780
Fort Erie Race Track 230 Catherine St PO Box 1130 *TF:* 800-295-3770 ■ *Web:* www.forterieracing.com	Fort Erie	ON	L2A5N9	905-871-3200		642
Fort Fetterman State Historic Site 752 Hwy 93 *Web:* wyoparks.wyo.gov	Douglas	WY	82633	307-358-2864		565
Fort Fisher State Recreation Area 1000 Loggerhead Rd *Web:* www.ncparks.gov	Kure Beach	NC	28449	910-458-5798		565
Fort Flagler State Park 10541 Flagler Rd *Web:* parks.state.wa.us	Nordland	WA	98358	360-385-1259		565
Fort Frederica National Monument 6515 Frederica Rd *Web:* www.nps.gov	Saint Simons Island	GA	31522	912-638-3639		564
Fort Frederick State Park 11100 Ft Frederick Rd *Web:* www.dnr.maryland.gov	Big Pool	MD	21711	301-842-2155		565
Fort Gaines Historic Site 51 Bienville Blvd *Web:* www.dauphinisland.org	Dauphin Island	AL	36528	251-861-6992		50-3
Fort Garry, The 222 Broadway *TF:* 800-665-8088 ■ *Web:* www.fortgarryhotel.com	Winnipeg	MB	R3C0R3	204-942-8251	956-2351	379
Fort Gibson National Cemetery 1423 Cemetery Rd *Web:* www.cem.va.gov	Fort Gibson	OK	74434	918-478-2334	478-2661	136
Fort Griffin State Park & Historic Site 1701 N US Hwy 283 *Web:* www.thc.texas.gov	Albany	TX	76430	325-762-3592		565
Fort Group 100 Challenger Rd 7th Fl *Web:* fortgroupinc.com	Ridgefield Park	NJ	07660	201-445-0202	445-0626	738
Fort Halifax State on the Kennebec 201 US Hwy *Web:* www.maine.gov	Winslow	ME	04901	207-872-2776		565
Fort Hamilton Hospital 630 Eaton Ave *Web:* www.ketteringhealth.org	Hamilton	OH	45013	513-867-2133	867-2881	374-3
Fort Harrison State Park 5753 Glenn Rd *Web:* www.in.gov	Indianapolis	IN	46216	317-591-0904		565
Fort Hartsuff State Historical Park 82034 Fort Ave *Web:* outdoornebraska.gov	Burwell	NE	68823	308-346-4715		565
Fort Hays State University 600 Park St *TF:* 800-628-3478 ■ *Web:* fhsu.edu	Hays	KS	67601	785-628-4293		166
Fort Henry National Historic Site PO Box 213 *TF:* 800-437-2233 ■ *Web:* www.forthenry.com	Kingston	ON	K7L4V8	613-542-7388	542-3054	520
Fort Hill Construction Inc 8118 Hollywood Blvd *Web:* www.forthill.com	Los Angeles	CA	90069	323-656-7425		186
Fort Hood 1001 761st Tank Battalion Ave Bldg 1001 Rm W105 *Web:* www.militarybases.us	Fort Hood	TX	76544	254-286-5139		497-2
Fort Huachuca 15423 Fort Huachuca Bldg 50010 *Web:* www.army.mil	Sierra Vista	AZ	85613	520-533-2330	533-3778	497-2
Fort Humboldt State Historic Park 3431 Fort Ave *Web:* www.parks.ca.gov	Eureka	CA	95503	707-445-6567		565
Fort Hunter Mansion & Park 5300 N Front St *Web:* forthunter.org	Harrisburg	PA	17110	717-599-5751	599-5838	50-3
Fort Jesup State Historic Site 32 Geoghagan Rd *TF:* 888-677-5378 ■ *Web:* crt.state.la.us	Many	LA	71449	877-226-7652		565
Fort Kearny State Recreation Area 1020 V Rd 1020 'V' Rd *Web:* www.nps.gov	Kearney	NE	68845	308-865-5305		565
Fort Kent State Historic Site 87 State Park Rd *Web:* www.maine.gov	Presque Isle	ME	04769	207-768-8341		565
Fort Knox 125 6th Ave Bldg 1110B 2nd Fl *Web:* www.fkgoldstandard.com	Fort Knox	KY	40121	502-624-4985	624-2096	497-2
Fort Knox State Historic Site 711 Ft Knox Rd *Web:* www.maine.gov	Prospect	ME	04981	207-469-7719		565
Fort Lancaster State Historic Site 629 Fort Lancaster Rd *Web:* www.thc.texas.gov	Sheffield	TX	79781	432-836-4391		565
Fort Langley National Historic Site 23433 Mavis Ave PO Box 129 *Web:* www.pc.gc.ca	Fort Langley	BC	V1M2R5	604-513-4777	513-4798	563
Fort Laramie National Historic Site 965 Grey Rocks Rd *Web:* www.nps.gov	Fort Laramie	WY	82212	307-837-2221		564
Fort Larned National Historic Site 1767 Kansas Hwy 156 *Web:* www.nps.gov	Larned	KS	67550	620-285-6911		564
Fort Lauderdale Antique Car Museum 1527 SW 1st Ave *Web:* www.antiquecarmuseum.net	Fort Lauderdale	FL	33315	954-779-7300		520
Fort Lauderdale Behavioral Health Ctr 5757 N Dixie Hwy *TF:* 888-616-3089 ■ *Web:* ftlauderdalebehavioral.com	Oakland Park	FL	33334	954-734-2000		374-5
Fort Lauderdale City Hall 100 N Andrews Ave 5th Fl *Web:* www.fortlauderdale.gov	Fort Lauderdale	FL	33301	954-828-5000		337
Fort Lauderdale Executive Airport 5101 NW 21st Ave *Web:* www.fortlauderdale.gov	Fort Lauderdale	FL	33309	954-828-4955	938-4974	27
Fort Lauderdale Historical Society 219 SW 2nd Ave *Web:* historyfortlauderdale.org	Fort Lauderdale	FL	33312	954-463-4431		520
Fort Lauderdale Museum of Art 1 E Las Olas Blvd *Web:* nsuartmuseum.org	Fort Lauderdale	FL	33301	954-525-5500		520

Name / Address	City	State	ZIP	Phone	Fax	Class
Fort Leaton State Historic Site PO Box 2349 *Web:* tpwd.texas.gov	Presidio	TX	79845	432-229-3613		565
Fort Leavenworth 881 Mcclellan Ave *Web:* usacac.army.mil	Fort Leavenworth	KS	66027	913-684-4986		497-2
Fort Leavenworth National Cemetery 395 Biddle Blvd *Web:* www.cem.va.gov	Fort Leavenworth	KS	66027	913-727-1376	758-4136	136
Fort Lee 500 Lee Ave *Web:* www.lee.army.mil	Fort Lee	VA	23801	804-765-3000		497-2
Fort Lee Regional Chamber of Commerce (FLRCC) 210 Whiteman St *Web:* www.fortleechamber.com	Fort Lee	NJ	07024	201-944-7575	944-5168	139
Fort Lewis College 1000 Rim Dr *TF:* 877-352-2656 ■ *Web:* fortlewis.edu	Durango	CO	81301	970-247-7010	247-7179	166
Fort Loudoun State Historic Park 338 Ft Loudoun Rd *Web:* tnstateparks.com	Vonore	TN	37885	423-884-6217		565
Fort Lyon National Cemetery 15700 County Rd HH *Web:* www.cem.va.gov	Las Animas	CO	81054	303-761-0117	781-9378	136
Fort MacArthur Museum 3601 S Gaffey St *Web:* www.ftmac.org	San Pedro	CA	90731	310-548-2631		520
Fort Madison 3440 Avenue L *Web:* www.fortmadison.com	Fort Madison	IA	52627	319-372-5471	372-6404	206
Fort Malden National Historic Site 100 Laird Ave *Web:* www.pc.gc.ca	Amherstburg	ON	N9V2Z2	519-736-5416	736-6603	563
Fort Massac State Park 1308 E Fifth St *Web:* www.dnr.illinois.gov	Metropolis	IL	62960	618-524-4712		565
Fort Matanzas National Monument 8635 A1A S *Web:* www.nps.gov	Saint Augustine	FL	32080	904-471-0116		564
Fort McAllister State Historic Park 3894 Ft McAllister Rd *Web:* gastateparks.org	Richmond Hill	GA	31324	912-727-2339	727-3614	565
Fort McClary State Historic Site 28 Oldsfields Rd *Web:* www.maine.gov	South Berwick	ME	03908	207-384-5160		565
Fort McDowell Casino 10424 N Ft McDowell Rd *TF:* 800-843-3678 ■ *Web:* www.fortmcdowellcasino.com	Fort Mcdowell	AZ	85264	800-843-3678		133
Fort McHenry National Monument & Historic Shrine 2400 E Fort Ave *Web:* www.nps.gov	Baltimore	MD	21230	410-962-4290		520
Fort McKavett State Historic Site 7066 FM 864 Rd *Web:* www.thc.texas.gov	Fort McKavett	TX	76841	325-396-2358		565
Fort McMurray Chamber of Commerce 9912 Franklin Ave Ste 105 *Web:* www.fortmcmurraychamber.ca	Fort McMurray	AB	T9H2K5	780-743-3100	790-9757	137
Fort McNab National Historic Site c/o Halifax Citadel National Historic Site PO Box 9080 Sta A *Web:* www.pc.gc.ca	Halifax	NS	B3K5M7	902-426-5080		563
Fort Meade Museum PO Box 164 *Web:* www.fortmeademuseum.org	Fort Meade	SD	57741	605-347-9822		520
Fort Meigs State Memorial 29100 W River Rd *TF:* 800-283-8916 ■ *Web:* www.fortmeigs.org	Perrysburg	OH	43551	419-874-4121	874-9446	50-3
Fort Miller Company Inc, The 688 Wilbur Ave *Web:* www.fortmiller.com	Greenwich	NY	12834	518-695-5000	695-4970	183
Fort Mitchell National Cemetery 553 Hwy 165 *Web:* www.cem.va.gov	Fort Mitchell	AL	36856	334-855-4731	855-4740	136
Fort Mojave Tribal Council 500 Merriman Ave *Web:* www.fortmojaveindiantribe.com	Needles	CA	92363	760-629-4591		132
Fort Montgomery State Historic Site 690 Rt 9W PO Box 213 *Web:* parks.ny.gov	Fort Montgomery	NY	10922	845-446-2134		565
Fort Morgan Area Chamber of Commerce 300 Main St *TF:* 800-354-8660 ■ *Web:* www.fortmorganchamber.com	Fort Morgan	CO	80701	970-867-6702		139
Fort Morris State Historic Site 2559 Ft Morris Rd *Web:* gastateparks.org	Midway	GA	31320	912-884-5999		565
Fort Mose Historic State Park 15 Ft Mose Trl *Web:* www.floridastateparks.org	Saint Augustine	FL	32084	904-823-2232		565
Fort Mott State Park 454 Ft Mott Rd *Web:* www.njparksandforests.org	Pennsville	NJ	08070	856-935-3218		565
Fort Mountain State Park 181 Ft Mtn Park Rd *Web:* gastateparks.org	Chatsworth	GA	30705	706-422-1932		565
Fort Myer Construction Corp 2237 33rd St NE *Web:* www.fortmyer.com	Washington	DC	20018	202-636-9535	526-8572	186
Fort Myers Beach Chamber of Commerce 1054 Fifth St *Web:* www.fortmyersbeach.org	Fort Myers Beach	FL	33931	239-454-7500	454-7910	139
Fort Necessity National Battlefield 1 Washington Pkwy *Web:* www.nps.gov	Farmington	PA	15437	724-329-5512		564
Fort Niagara State Park 1 Scott Ave *Web:* parks.ny.gov	Youngstown	NY	14174	716-745-7273		565
Fort Ontario State Historic Site 1 E Fourth St *Web:* parks.ny.gov	Oswego	NY	13126	315-343-4711		565
Fort Orange Press Inc 11 Sand Creek Rd *Web:* www.fortorangepress.com	Albany	NY	12205	518-489-3233		627
Fort Owen State Park PO Box 995 *Web:* stateparks.mt.gov	Lolo	MT	59847	406-273-4253		565
Fort Parker State Park 194 Park Rd 28 *Web:* tpwd.texas.gov	Mexia	TX	76667	254-562-5751		565
Fort Peck Community College PO Box 398 *Web:* www.fpcc.edu	Poplar	MT	59255	406-768-6300	768-6301	165
Fort Phil Kearny State Historic Site 528 Wagon Box Rd *Web:* www.fortphilkearny.com	Banner	WY	82832	307-684-7629		565
Fort Phoenix State Reservation Green St *Web:* www.mass.gov	Fairhaven	MA	02719	508-992-4524		565
Fort Pierce Inlet State Park 905 Shorewinds Dr *Web:* www.floridastateparks.org	Fort Pierce	FL	34949	772-468-3985		565
Fort Pillow State Historic Park 3122 Park Rd *Web:* www.state.tn.us	Henning	TN	38041	731-738-5581		565
Fort Pitt Capital Group Inc 680 Andersen Dr Foster Plz Ten *TF:* 800-471-5827 ■ *Web:* www.fortpittcapital.com	Pittsburgh	PA	15220	412-921-1822		528
Fort Pitt Museum 601 Commonwealth Pl Bldg C *Web:* www.fortpittblockhouse.com	Pittsburgh	PA	15222	412-471-1764		520
Fort Point Capital Partners LLC 275 Sacramento St 8th Fl *Web:* www.fortpointcap.com	San Francisco	CA	94111	415-625-0909		401
Fort Point National Historic Site Fort Mason Bldg 201 *Web:* www.nps.gov	San Francisco	CA	94123	415-556-1693		564
Fort Point State Park *Bureau of Parks & Lands* 22 State House Stn 18 Elkins Ln *Web:* www.maine.gov	Augusta	ME	04333	207-287-3200	287-6170	565
Fort Popham State Historic Site 10 Perkins Farm Ln *Web:* www.maine.gov	Phippsburg	ME	04562	207-389-1335		565
Fort Pulaski National Monument PO Box 30757 *Web:* www.nps.gov	Savannah	GA	31410	912-786-8182	786-6023	564
Fort Ransom State Park 5981 Walt Hjelle Pkwy *Web:* www.parkrec.nd.gov	Fort Ransom	ND	58033	701-973-4331		565
Fort Recovery Industries Inc 2440 Ohio 49 *Web:* www.fortrecoveryindustries.com	Fort Recovery	OH	45846	419-375-4121	375-4194	199
Fort Richardson State Park Historic Site & Lost Creek Reservoir State Trailway 228 State Park Rd 61 *Web:* tpwd.texas.gov	Jacksboro	TX	76458	940-567-3506		565
Fort Ridgely State Park 72158 County Rd 30 *Web:* www.dnr.state.mn.us	Fairfax	MN	55332	507-426-7840	426-7112	565
Fort Robinson State Park PO Box 392 *Web:* www.stateparks.com	Crawford	NE	69339	308-665-2900		565
Fort Rock State Natural Area 725 Summer St NE Ste C *TF:* 800-551-6949 ■ *Web:* stateparks.oregon.gov	Salem	OR	97301	800-551-6949		565
Fort Rodd Hill National Historic Site 603 Ft Rodd Hill Rd *Web:* www.pc.gc.ca	Victoria	BC	V9C2W8	250-478-5849	478-2816	563
Fort Roofing & Sheet Metal Works Inc 14 W Oakland Ave *Web:* www.fortroofing.com	Sumter	SC	29150	803-773-9391	773-7711	189-12
Fort Rosecrans National Cemetery 1700 Cabrillo Memorial Dr *Web:* www.cem.va.gov	San Diego	CA	92106	858-658-7360	658-7397	136
Fort Ross State Historic Park 19005 Coast Hwy 1 *Web:* www.parks.ca.gov	Jenner	CA	95450	707-847-3286		565
Fort Saint Jean Baptiste State Historic Site 155 Jefferson St *TF:* 888-677-7853 ■ *Web:* crt.state.la.us	Natchitoches	LA	71457	318-357-3101		565
Fort Saint John & District Chamber of Commerce 104 - 9907 99th Ave *Web:* fsjchamber.com	Fort Saint John	BC	V1J4N4	250-785-6037	785-6050	137
Fort Sam Houston 3630 Stanley Rd *Web:* www.cs.amedd.army.mil	Fort Sam Houston	TX	78234	210-221-8580		497-2
Fort Sam Houston National Cemetery 1520 Harry Wurzbach Rd *Web:* www.cem.va.gov	San Antonio	TX	78209	210-820-3891	820-3445	136
Fort Sanders Regional Medical Ctr 1901 Clinch Ave *Web:* www.fsregional.com	Knoxville	TN	37916	865-541-1111		374-3
Fort Scott Community College 2108 S Horton St *TF:* 800-874-3722 ■ *Web:* www.fortscott.edu	Fort Scott	KS	66701	620-223-2700	223-6530	162
Fort Scott Livestock Market Inc Old 54 Hwy W *Web:* www.fslivestock.com	Fort Scott	KS	66701	620-223-4600	223-4785	446
Fort Scott National Cemetery 900 E National Ave *Web:* www.cem.va.gov	Fort Scott	KS	66701	620-223-2840	223-2505	136
Fort Scott National Historic Site PO Box 918 *Web:* www.nps.gov	Fort Scott	KS	66701	620-223-0310	223-0188	564
Fort Simcoe State Park 5150 Ft Simcoe Rd *Web:* parks.state.wa.us	White Swan	WA	98952	509-874-2372		565
Fort Sisseton State Historical Park 11907 434th Ave *Web:* gfp.sd.gov	Lake City	SD	57247	605-448-5474		565
Fort Smith Convention & Visitors Bureau 2 N B St *TF:* 800-637-1477 ■ *Web:* www.fortsmith.org	Fort Smith	AR	72901	479-783-8888	784-2421	206
Fort Smith Dixie Cup Federal Credit Union 4411 Midland Blvd *Web:* dixiecupfcu.com	Fort Smith	AR	72904	479-782-3133		219
Fort Smith Little Theatre 401 N Sixth St *Web:* www.fslt.org	Fort Smith	AR	72913	479-783-2966		573-4

Name / Address	City	State	ZIP	Phone	Fax	Class
Fort Smith Museum of History 320 Rogers Ave *Web:* www.fortsmithmuseum.org	Fort Smith	AR	72903	479-783-7841		520
Fort Smith National Cemetery 522 Garland Ave *Web:* www.cem.va.gov	Fort Smith	AR	72901	479-783-5345	785-4189	136
Fort Smith National Historic Site 301 Parker Ave *Web:* www.nps.gov	Fort Smith	AR	72901	479-783-3961	783-5307	564
Fort Smith Paper Co 5721 B S Zero St *Web:* www.fortsmithpaper.com	Fort Smith	AR	72903	479-646-6171	646-0425	559
Fort Smith Public Library 3201 Rogers Ave *Web:* fortsmithlibrary.org	Fort Smith	AR	72903	479-783-0229	782-8571	434-3
Fort Smith Radio Group 323 N Greenwood Ave *Web:* www.sportshog1031.com	Fort Smith	AR	72901	479-288-1047	785-2638	647
Fort Smith Regional Airport 6700 McKennon Blvd Ste 200 *TF:* 800-992-7433 ■ *Web:* flyfsm.com	Fort Smith	AR	72903	479-452-7000	452-7008	27
Fort Smith Regional Chamber of Commerce 612 Garrison Ave *Web:* www.fortsmithchamber.org	Fort Smith	AR	72901	479-783-3111	783-6110	139
Fort Smith Trolley Museum 100 S Fourth St *Web:* www.fstm.org	Fort Smith	AR	72901	479-783-0205		520
Fort Snelling National Cemetery 7601 34th Ave *Web:* www.cem.va.gov	Minneapolis	MN	55450	612-726-1127		136
Fort Snelling State Park 101 Snelling Lake Rd *Web:* www.dnr.state.mn.us	Saint Paul	MN	55111	612-279-3550	725-2391	565
Fort Stevens State Park 100 Peter Iredale Rd *Web:* stateparks.oregon.gov	Hammond	OR	97121	503-861-1671		565
Fort Stevenson State Park 1252A 41st St NW *Web:* www.parkrec.nd.gov	Garrison	ND	58540	701-337-5576		565
Fort Stockton Pioneer 210 N Nelson St *Web:* www.fortstocktonpioneer.com	Fort Stockton	TX	79735	915-336-2281		532-2
Fort Sumter National Monument 1214 Middle St *Web:* www.nps.gov	Sullivans Island	SC	29482	843-883-3123	883-3910	564
Fort Tejon State Historic Park PO Box 895 *Web:* www.parks.ca.gov	Lebec	CA	93243	661-248-6692	248-8373	565
Fort Totten State Historic Site PO Box 224 *Web:* www.history.nd.gov	Fort Totten	ND	58335	701-766-4441		565
Fort Transfer 225 S Maple St *TF:* 800-262-1190 ■ *Web:* www.forttransfer.com	Morton	IL	61550	800-262-1190		780
Fort Trumbull State Park 90 Walbach St *Web:* portal.ct.gov	New London	CT	06320	860-444-7591		565
Fort Union National Monument PO Box 127 *Web:* www.nps.gov	Watrous	NM	87753	505-425-8025		564
Fort Union Trading Post National Historic Site 15550 Hwy 1804 *Web:* www.nps.gov	Williston	ND	58801	701-572-9083		564
Fort Valley State University 1005 State University Dr *TF:* 877-462-3878 ■ *Web:* www.fvsu.edu	Fort Valley	GA	31030	478-825-6211		166
Fort Vancouver National Historic Site 612 E Reserve St *Web:* www.nps.gov	Vancouver	WA	98661	360-816-6230		564
Fort Vancouver Regional Library 1007 E Mill Plain Blvd *Web:* www.fvrl.org	Vancouver	WA	98663	360-906-5000		434-3
Fort Walton Beach Medical Ctr (FWBMC) 1000 Mar-Walt Dr *Web:* fwbmc.com	Fort Walton Beach	FL	32547	850-862-1111		374-3
Fort Walton Machining Inc 43 Jet Dr NW *TF:* 800-223-0881 ■ *Web:* www.fwmachining.com	Fort Walton Beach	FL	32548	850-244-9095	244-4874	454
Fort Ward Museum & Historic Site 4301 W Braddock Rd *Web:* www.alexandriava.gov	Alexandria	VA	22304	703-838-4848	671-7350	520
Fort Washington State Park 500 Bethlehem Pk *Web:* www.dcnr.pa.gov	Fort Washington	PA	19034	215-591-5250		565
Fort Wayne Ballet Inc 300 E Main St *Web:* www.fortwayneballet.org	Fort Wayne	IN	46802	260-484-9646	484-9647	573-1
Fort Wayne Children's Zoo 3411 Sherman Blvd *Web:* kidszoo.org	Fort Wayne	IN	46808	260-427-6800	427-6820	823
Fort Wayne City Hall 1 Main St *Web:* www.cityoffortwayne.org	Fort Wayne	IN	46802	260-427-1221		337
Fort Wayne Civic Theater 303 E Main St *Web:* www.fwcivic.org	Fort Wayne	IN	46802	260-422-8641		573-4
Fort Wayne Community Schools (FWCS) 1200 S Clinton St *Web:* www.fwcs.k12.in.us	Fort Wayne	IN	46802	260-467-2005		685
Fort Wayne Dance Collective 437 E Berry St *Web:* www.fwdc.org	Fort Wayne	IN	46802	260-424-6574		573-1
Fort Wayne International Airport 3801 W Ferguson Rd Ste 209 *Web:* fwairport.com	Fort Wayne	IN	46809	260-747-4146	747-1762	27
Fort Wayne Metals Inc 9609 Ardmore Ave *Web:* fwmetals.com	Fort Wayne	IN	46809	260-747-4154	747-0398	295
Fort Wayne Mold & Engineering Inc 4501 Earth Dr *Web:* fortwaynemold.com	Fort Wayne	IN	46809	260-747-9168	747-3601	757
Fort Wayne Museum of Art 311 E Main St *Web:* www.fwmoa.org	Fort Wayne	IN	46802	260-422-6467	422-1374	520
Fort Wayne Newspapers Inc 600 W Main St *TF:* 800-444-3303 ■ *Web:* www.fortwayne.com	Fort Wayne	IN	46802	260-461-8843		637-8
Fort Wayne Public Transportation Corp 801 Leesburg Rd *Web:* www.fwcitilink.com	Fort Wayne	IN	46808	260-432-4546	436-7729	468
Fort Wayne Wire Die Inc 2424 American Way *Web:* www.fwwd.com	Fort Wayne	IN	46809	260-747-1681	747-4269	757
Fort Wayne/Allen County Convention & Visitors Bureau 927 S Harrison St *Web:* www.visitfortwayne.com	Fort Wayne	IN	46802	260-424-3700	424-3914	206
Fort Wellington National Historic Site 370 Vankoughnet St *Web:* www.pc.gc.ca	Prescott	ON	K0E1T0	613-925-2896	925-1536	563
Fort Wilkins State Park 15223 US Hwy 41 *Web:* www.michigan.gov	Copper Harbor	MI	49918	906-289-4215		565
Fort William Henry Corp, The 48 Canada St *TF:* 800-234-0267 ■ *Web:* www.fortwilliamhenry.com	Lake George	NY	12845	518-668-3081		378
Fort Worden 200 Battery Way *Web:* fortworden.org	Port Townsend	WA	98368	360-344-4400		565
Fort Worth Botanic Garden 3220 Botanic Garden Blvd *Web:* www.fwbg.org	Fort Worth	TX	76107	817-392-5510		97
Fort Worth Chamber of Commerce 777 Taylor St Ste 900 *TF:* 800-433-5747 ■ *Web:* www.fortworthchamber.com	Fort Worth	TX	76102	817-336-2491	877-4034	139
Fort Worth City Credit Union PO Box 100099 *TF:* 888-732-3085 ■ *Web:* www.fwccu.org	Fort Worth	TX	76185	817-732-2803	377-7966	219
Fort Worth City Hall 200 Texas St *Web:* fortworthtexas.gov	Fort Worth	TX	76102	817-392-2255		337
Fort Worth Community Credit Union 1905 Forest Ridge Dr PO Box 210848 *TF:* 800-817-8234 ■ *Web:* www.ffwccu.org	Bedford	TX	76021	817-835-5000	835-5235	219
Fort Worth Convention & Visitors Bureau 111 W Fourth St Ste 200 *Web:* www.fortworth.com	Fort Worth	TX	76102	817-336-8791	698-7823	206
Fort Worth Convention Ctr 200 Texas St *TF:* 866-630-2588 ■ *Web:* www.fortworth.com	Fort Worth	TX	76102	817-392-7894	392-2756	205
Fort Worth F & D Head Co 3040 E Peden Rd *TF:* 800-451-2684 ■ *Web:* www.fwfdhead.com	Fort Worth	TX	76179	817-236-8773	236-1061	723
Fort Worth Independent School District 100 N University Dr *Web:* www.fwisd.org	Fort Worth	TX	76107	817-814-2875		685
Fort Worth Lumber Co 9101 S Fwy *TF:* 800-372-6467 ■ *Web:* www.fortworthlumber.com	Fort Worth	TX	76140	817-293-5211	293-3487	191-3
Fort Worth Museum of Science & History 1600 Gendy St *TF:* 888-255-9300 ■ *Web:* www.fwmuseum.org	Fort Worth	TX	76107	817-255-9300	732-7635	520
Fort Worth Opera 1300 Gendy St *TF:* 877-396-7372 ■ *Web:* fwopera.org	Fort Worth	TX	76107	817-731-0833	731-0835	573-2
Fort Worth Star-Telegram 808 Throckmorton St *TF:* 800-776-7827 ■ *Web:* www.star-telegram.com	Fort Worth	TX	76102	800-776-7827		532-2
Fort Worth Stockyards National Historic District PO Box 64203 *Web:* www.fortworthstockyards.org	Fort Worth	TX	76164	817-626-7921	740-8635	50-6
Fort Worth Stockyards Station 130 E Exchange Ave *Web:* www.fortworthstockyards.com	Fort Worth	TX	76164	817-625-9715		50-6
Fort Worth Symphony Orchestra Assn 330 E Fourth St Ste 200 *Web:* www.fwsymphony.org	Fort Worth	TX	76102	817-665-6500	665-6600	573-3
Fort Worth Weekly 3311 Hamilton Ave *Web:* www.fwweekly.com	Fort Worth	TX	76107	817-321-9700	321-9733	532-5
Fort Yargo State Park 210 S Broad St *Web:* gastateparks.org	Winder	GA	30680	770-867-3489		565
Fortbrand Services Inc 50 Fairchild Ct *Web:* www.fortbrand.com	Plainview	NY	11803	516-576-3200		641
Forte & Tablada Inc 9107 Interline Ave *Web:* forteandtablada.com	Baton Rouge	LA	70809	225-927-9321		261
Forte Data Systems Inc 3330 Paddock Pkwy *TF:* 800-571-8702 ■ *Web:* www.fortedata.com	Johns Creek	GA	30024	678-208-0206		225
Forte Holdings 5137 Golden Foothill Pky Ste 110 *TF:* 800-456-2622 ■ *Web:* www.fortesystemsinc.com	El Dorado Hills	CA	95762	916-673-4850		180
Forte Information Resources LLC 2000 S Colorado Blvd Twr II Ste 400 *Web:* www.forteinformation.com	Denver	CO	80222	303-321-3888		463
Forte Payment Systems 500 W Bethany Dr Ste 200 *TF:* 866-290-5400 ■ *Web:* www.achdirect.com	Allen	TX	75013	866-290-5400		569
Forte Systems Inc 1501 N Broadway Ste 360 *Web:* forte-systems.com	Walnut Creek	CA	94596	510-525-3000		180
FORTECH Inc 2124 Wilkinson Blvd *Web:* www.fortech-inc.com	Charlotte	NC	28208	704-333-0621	333-2820	203
Fortegra 10151 Deerwood Pk Blvd Bldg 100 Ste 330 *TF:* 800-888-2738 ■ *Web:* www.fortegra.com	Jacksonville	FL	32256	866-961-9529		391-5
Fortemedia Inc 4051 Burton Dr *Web:* www.fortemedia.com	Santa Clara	CA	95054	408-861-8088		256
Fortenberry Jeff (Rep R - NE) 1514 Longworth House Office Bldg *Web:* www.fortenberry.house.gov	Washington	DC	20515	202-225-4806	225-5686	342-2
Forth Inc 6080 Center Dr Ste 600 *TF:* 800-553-6784 ■ *Web:* www.forth.com	Los Angeles	CA	90045	310-999-6784	943-3806	178-2

Company / Address	City	State	ZIP	Phone	Fax	Class
Forthea Interactive Marketing 2727 Allen Pkwy Ste 1200 *Web:* www.forthea.com	Houston	TX	77019	713-568-2763		5
Forti's Mexican Elder 321 Chelsea St *Web:* fortisrestaurant.com	El Paso	TX	79905	915-772-0066		671
Fortifiber Building Systems Group 300 Industrial Dr *TF:* 800-773-4777 ■ *Web:* fortifiberflooring.com	Fernley	NV	89408	775-333-6400		552-1
Fortified Provider Network Inc 8712 E Via De Commercio Ste 2 **Fax Area Code:* 602 ■ *Web:* www.fortifiedprovider.com	Scottsdale	AZ	85258	480-607-0222	607-2199*	390
Fortifire Inc 46560 Fremont Blvd Ste 119 *Web:* www.fortifire.com	Fremont	CA	94538	510-651-7770		177
Fortify Group Inc 209 S Tenth St PO Box 424 *Web:* fortifygroup.net	Geneva	NE	68361	402-759-3300		390
Fortin Consulting Inc 215 Hamel Rd *TF:* 844-273-3117 ■ *Web:* fortinconsulting.com	Hamel	MN	55340	763-478-3606		196
Fortis College 653 Enterprise Pky *TF:* 855-436-7847 ■ *Web:* www.fortis.edu	Ravenna	OH	44266	330-297-7319		166
Fortis Construction Inc 1705 SW Taylor St Ste 200 *Web:* fortisconstruction.com	Portland	OR	97205	503-459-4477	459-4478	261
Fortistar LLC 1 N Lexington Ave *Web:* www.fortistar.com	White Plains	NY	10601	914-421-4900	421-0052	196
Fortney & Weygandt Inc 31269 Bradley Rd *Web:* www.fortneyweygandt.com	North Olmsted	OH	44070	440-716-4000		186
Fortney Scott LLC 1750 K St NW Ste 325 *Web:* www.fortneyscott.com	Washington	DC	20006	202-689-1200		428
Fortrad Eye Instruments 8 Franklin Rd *Web:* www.fortrad.com	Mendham	NJ	07945	973-543-2371	543-5446	475
Fortrend Engineering 2220 O'Toole Ave *TF:* 888-937-3637 ■ *Web:* www.fortrend.com	San Jose	CA	95131	408-734-9311	734-4299	695
Fortress Computer Pros 11305 Rancho Bernardo Rd Ste 116 *Web:* www.fortresscomputerpros.com	San Diego	CA	92127	858-451-7020		175
Fortress Integrated Technologies 5805 State Bridge Rd Ste G332 *Web:* accessfortress.com	Johns Creek	GA	30097	678-474-0705		808
Fortress Technology Inc 51 Grand Marshall Dr *TF:* 888-220-8737 ■ *Web:* www.fortresstechnology.com	Toronto	ON	M1B5N6	416-754-2898		692
Fortun Insurance 365 Palermo Ave *TF:* 877-643-2055 ■ *Web:* www.fortuninsurance.com	Coral Gables	FL	33134	305-445-3535		390
Fortunato Group Inc 5011 Falls of Neuse Rd Ste A *Web:* geico.com	Raleigh	NC	27609	919-862-1300		390
Fortune Bay Resort & Casino 1430 Bois Forte Rd *TF:* 800-992-7529 ■ *Web:* fortunebay.com	Tower	MN	55790	218-753-6400		452
Fortune Brands Inc 520 Lake Cook Rd *NYSE:* FBHS ■ *TF:* 800-225-2719 ■ *Web:* www.fbhs.com	Deerfield	IL	60015	847-484-4400		185
Fortune Cookie 7006 University Ave *Web:* www.fortunecookietx.com	Lubbock	TX	79413	806-745-2205		671
Fortune Cookie Supply 1108 W Valley Blvd Ste 6119 **Fax Area Code:* 818 ■ *TF:* 888-592-4248 ■ *Web:* www.fortunecookiesupply.com	Alhambra	CA	91803	888-592-4248	743-7731*	297-3
Fortune Fabrics Inc 315 Simpson St	Swoyersville	PA	18704	570-288-3666	283-2124	745-1
Fortune House All Suites Hotel 185 SE 14th Terr *Web:* www.fortunehousehotel.com	Miami	FL	33131	305-349-5200		132
Fortune Metals Inc 330 Hwy 7 E Ste 201 *Web:* www.fortunemetals.com	Richmond Hill	ON	L4B3P8	905-707-0786		791
Fortune Practice Management 1265 El Camino Real Ste 205 *TF:* 800-628-1052 ■ *Web:* fortunemgmt.com	Santa Clara	CA	95050	800-628-1052		463
Fortune Title Agency Inc 39 Woodland Rd *Web:* fortunetitle.com	Roseland	NJ	07068	973-226-6555		390
FortuNet Inc 3901 Graphic Dr *Web:* www.fortunet.com	Las Vegas	NV	89118	702-796-9090		322
Fortville Feeders Inc 750 E Broadway St *Web:* www.fortvillefeeders.com	Fortville	IN	46040	317-485-5195	485-6182	454
Forty 1 North 351 Thames St *Web:* www.41north.com	Newport	RI	02840	401-846-8018		671
Forum Communications Co 101 Fifth St N *Web:* www.forumcomm.com	Fargo	ND	58102	701-235-7311		637-8
Forum Credit Union PO Box 50738 *TF:* 800-845-8887 ■ *Web:* www.forumcu.com	Indianapolis	IN	46250	317-558-6000		219
Forum Energy Technologies Inc 831 Industrial Blvd *Web:* www.dynacon.com	Bryan	TX	77803	979-823-2690		470
Forum Gallery 475 Park Ave 57th St *Web:* forumgallery.com	New York	NY	10022	212-355-4545	355-4547	42
Forum Inc 100 Chapel Harbor Dr *Web:* www.forumlighting.com	Pittsburgh	PA	15238	412-781-5970		439
Forum Manufacturing Inc 77 Brown St *Web:* www.forummfg.com	Milford Center	OH	43045	937-349-8685		321
Forum Motor Inn 800-814 Atlantic Ave PO Box 448 *Web:* theforuminoc.homestead.com	Ocean City	NJ	08226	609-399-8700		379
Forum One Communications Corp 2200 Mt Vernon Ave *Web:* forumone.com	Alexandria	VA	22301	703-548-1855		809
Forum Publishing Co 383 E Main St *TF:* 800-635-7654 ■ *Web:* www.forum123.com	Centerport	NY	11721	631-754-5000		637-9
Forward 180 Sutter St *TF:* 833-334-6393 ■ *Web:* goforward.com	San Francisco	CA	94104	833-334-6393		49-8
Forward Air Corp 1915 Snapps Ferry Rd Bldg N *NASDAQ:* FWRD ■ *TF:* 800-726-6654 ■ *Web:* www.forwardair.com	Greeneville	TN	37745	423-636-3300	703-9019	700
Forward Analytics 3234 Eastmont Ave *Web:* www.forwardanalytics.com	Pittsburgh	PA	15216	412-207-2114		466
Forward Branding & Identity 34 May St *Web:* www.forwardbranding.com	Webster	NY	14580	585-872-9222		195
Forward Concepts Co 1462 E Grandview St *Web:* www.fwdconcepts.com	Mesa	AZ	85203	480-284-7486		637-10
Forward Corp 219 N Front St *TF:* 800-664-4501 ■ *Web:* www.forwardcorp.com	Standish	MI	48658	989-846-4501		324
Forward Edge LLC 2724 E Kemper Rd *Web:* www.forward-edge.net	Sharonville	OH	45241	513-761-3343		260
Forward Financing 53 State St 20th Fl *TF:* 888-244-9099 ■ *Web:* www.forwardfinancing.com	Boston	MA	02109	888-244-9099		49-2
Forward Industries 477 S Rosemary Ave Ste 219 *Web:* www.forwardindustries.com	West Palm Beach	FL	33401	561-465-0030		453
Forward Publishing 45 East 33rd St *Web:* forward.com	New York	NY	10038	212-889-8200		637-8
Forward Technology Inc 260 Jenks Ave *TF:* 800-307-6040 ■ *Web:* www.forwardtech.com	Cokato	MN	55321	320-286-2578	286-2467	386
Forward Thinking Systems 105 Rt 101A Ste 21 *Web:* forwardthinkingsys.com	Amherst	NH	03031	603-882-8465		180
Forward Ventures 4747 Executive Dr Ste 700 *Web:* www.forwardventures.com	San Diego	CA	92121	858-677-6077		792
Forza Silicon Corp 2947 Bradley St Ste 130 *Web:* www.forzasilicon.com	Pasadena	CA	91107	626-796-1182		256
Fosdick & Hilmer Inc 525 Vine St *Web:* www.fosdickandhilmer.com	Cincinnati	OH	45202	513-241-5640		261
Fosdick Fulfillment Corp 26 Barnes Industrial Park Rd *TF:* 800-759-5558 ■ *Web:* www.fosdickfulfillment.com	Wallingford	CT	06492	800-759-5558		366
Foseco Inc 20200 Sheldon Rd *Web:* www.foseco.com	Cleveland	OH	44142	440-826-4548	243-7658	145
Foshay Electric 7676 Engineer Rd *Web:* www.foshayelectric.com	San Diego	CA	92154	858-277-7676	277-2629	189-4
Foss Maritime Co 1151 Fairview Ave N *TF:* 800-426-2885 ■ *Web:* www.foss.com	Seattle	WA	98109	206-281-3800		465
Foss National Leasing 125 Commerce Valley Dr W Ste 801 *TF:* 800-461-3677 ■ *Web:* www.fossnational.com	Markham	ON	L3T7W4	905-886-4244		126
Foss Performance Materials 11 Merrill Industrial Dr *Web:* www.fosspm.com	Hampton	NH	03842	603-929-6000		745-6
Foss State Park 10252 Hwy 44 *Web:* www.travelok.com	Foss	OK	73647	580-592-4433	592-4701	565
Foss Waterway Seaport 705 Dock St *Web:* www.fosswaterwayseaport.org	Tacoma	WA	98402	253-272-2750		520
Fossil Butte National Monument PO Box 592 *Web:* www.nps.gov	Kemmerer	WY	83101	307-877-4455		564
Fossil Creek Nursery Inc 7029 S College Ave *Web:* www.fossilcreeknursery.com	Fort Collins	CO	80525	970-226-4924		292
Fossil Creek Resources LLC 1521 N Cooper St Ste 650	Arlington	TX	76011	817-701-4970	701-4984	539
Fossil Energy Research Corp 23342 S Pointe Dr Ste C *Web:* www.ferco.com	Laguna Hills	CA	92653	949-859-4466	859-7916	41
Fossil Power Systems Inc 10 Mosher Dr Burnside Industrial Pk *Web:* www.fossil.ca	Dartmouth	AB	B3B1N5	902-468-2743		407
Fossil Rim Wildlife Ctr 2299 County Rd 2008 *Web:* fossilrim.org	Glen Rose	TX	76043	254-897-2960		823
Fosta-Tek Optics Inc 320 Hamilton St *Web:* www.fosta-tek.com	Leominster	MA	01453	978-534-6511	537-2168	544
Foster & Motley Inc 7755 Montgomery Rd Ste 100 *TF:* 800-532-2962 ■ *Web:* www.fosterandmotley.com	Cincinnati	OH	45236	513-561-6640		401
Foster & Sear LLP 817 Greenview Dr *TF:* 800-631-5908 ■ *Web:* fostersear.com	Grand Prairie	TX	75050	817-633-3355		41
Foster & Wolkind PC 80 Fifth Ave Ste 1401 *Web:* foster-wolkind.com	New York	NY	10011	212-691-2313		41
Foster Animal Hospital PA 730 Concord Pkwy N *Web:* fosteranimalhospital.com	Concord	NC	28027	704-786-0104		794
Foster Bill (Rep D - IL) 2366 Rayburn House Office Bldg *Web:* foster.house.gov	Washington	DC	20515	202-225-3515	225-9420	342-2
Foster Blue Water Oil LLC 36065 Water St *TF:* 800-426-3800 ■ *Web:* www.fosteroil.com	Richmond	MI	48062	586-727-3996	727-3466	579
Foster Botanical Garden 50 N Vineyard Blvd *Web:* www.honolulu.gov	Honolulu	HI	96817	808-522-7066	522-7050	97
Foster City *Chamber of Commerce* 1064F Shell Blvd *Web:* fostercitychamber.com	Foster City	CA	94404	650-573-7600		139
Foster Construction Products Inc 1105 S Frontenac Rd *TF:* 800-231-9541 ■ *Web:* www.fosterproducts.com	Aurora	IL	60504	800-231-9541	942-6856	3
Foster County PO Box 79 *Web:* fostercounty.com	Carrington	ND	58421	701-652-1001	652-1075	338
Foster Electric America 1420 Campbell Ave *Web:* www.fosterelectric.com	Lynchburg	VA	24501	434-528-4100		52
Foster Farms Inc PO Box 306 *TF:* 800-255-7227 ■ *Web:* www.fosterfarms.com	Livingston	CA	95334	800-255-7227		10-8
Foster Fuels Inc 16720 Brookneal Hwy *TF:* 800-344-6457 ■ *Web:* fosterfuels.com	Brookneal	VA	24528	434-376-2322		579

Name / Address	City	State	Zip	Phone	Fax	Class
Foster Lake & Pond Management Inc 9020 White Oak Rd PO Box 1294 *Web:* fosterlake.com	Garner	NC	27529	919-772-8548		463
Foster Marketing LLC 3909-F Ambassador Caffery *Web:* fostermarketing.com	LaFayette	LA	70503	337-235-1848	237-7246	7
Foster Murphy Altman & Nickel PC 1150 18th St NW Ste 775 *Web:* fostermurphy.com	Washington	DC	20036	202-822-4100		41
Foster Pepper PLLC 1111 Third Ave Ste 3400 *Web:* www.foster.com	Seattle	WA	98101	206-447-4400	447-9700	428
Foster Swift Collins & Smith 313 S Washington Sq *Web:* www.fosterswift.com	Lansing	MI	48933	517-371-8100		428
Foster Thomas Inc 1788 Forest Dr *TF:* 800-372-3626 ■ *Web:* fosterthomas.com	Annapolis	MD	21401	800-372-3626		391-3
Foster Townsend LLP 150 Dufferin Ave *TF:* 888-354-0448 ■ *Web:* fostertownsend.com	London	ON	N6A5N6	519-672-5272		428
Fostermation Inc 200 Valleyview Dr *TF:* 888-227-8074 ■ *Web:* fostermation.com	Meadville	PA	16335	814-336-6211	333-1297	621
Foster-Miller Inc 350 Second Ave *Web:* www.qinetiq-na.com	Waltham	MA	02451	781-684-4000		256
Fosters 11 Main St *Web:* www.fosters.com	Dover	NH	03820	603-742-4455		637-8
Fosters Freeze International LLC 400 E 18th St *Web:* www.fostersfreeze.com	Antioch	CA	94509	909-529-1324		670
Fostoria Area *Chamber of Commerce* 121 N Main St *Web:* www.fostoriaohio.org	Fostoria	OH	44830	419-435-0486	435-0936	139
Fothergill Segale & Valley PC 143 Barre St *Web:* fsv-cpas.com	Montpelier	VT	05602	802-223-6261	223-1550	2
Foto News 807 E First St *Web:* www.merrillfotonews.com	Merrill	WI	54452	715-536-7121		532-4
Foto Source Canada Inc 2333 Wyecroft Rd *Web:* www.fotosource.com	Oakville	ON	L6L6L4	905-465-2759	465-0470	119
Foto-Care Ltd 41-43 W 22nd St *Web:* www.fotocare.com	New York	NY	10010	212-741-2990	741-3217	628
Fotofabrication Corp 3758 W Belmont Ave *Web:* www.fotofab.com	Chicago	IL	60618	773-463-6211	463-3387	492
Fotofest Inc 1113 Vine St Ste 101 *Web:* www.fotofest.org	Houston	TX	77002	713-223-5522		184
FotoKem Industries Inc 2801 W Alameda Ave *Web:* fotokem.com	Burbank	CA	91505	818-846-3101		225
Fotoprint 975 Pandora Ave *TF:* 888-382-8211 ■ *Web:* www.fotoprint.ca	Victoria	BC	V8V3P4	250-382-8218		627
Fotorecord Print Ctr 45 E Pittsburgh St *Web:* fotorecord.com	Greensburg	PA	15601	724-837-0530		627
Fought & Company Inc 14255 SW 72nd Ave *Web:* www.foughtsteel.com	Tigard	OR	97224	503-639-3141		189-14
Foulk Bros Plumbing & Heating Co 322 W 7th St *Web:* www.foulkbrothers.com	Sioux City	IA	51103	712-258-3388		189-10
Foulkeways at Gwynedd 1120 Meetinghouse Rd *Web:* www.foulkeways.org	Gwynedd	PA	19436	215-643-2200	646-2917	672
Foulston & Siefkin LLP 1551 N Waterfront Pkwy Ste 100 *Web:* www.foulston.com	Wichita	KS	67206	316-267-6371	267-6345	428
Foundation Capital 250 Middlefield Rd *Web:* foundationcapital.com	Menlo Park	CA	94025	650-614-0500		792
Foundation Constructors Inc 81 Big Break Rd *TF:* 800-841-8740 ■ *Web:* www.foundationpiledriving.com	Oakley	CA	94561	925-754-6633		189-5
Foundation Engineering Inc 820 NW Cornell Ave *Web:* foundationengr.com	Corvallis	OR	97330	541-757-7645		261
Foundation Fighting Blindness 11435 Cron Hill Dr *TF:* 800-683-5555 ■ *Web:* www.fightingblindness.org	Owings Mills	MD	21117	410-568-0150		48-17
Foundation for Acctg Education (FAE) 14 Wall St 19th Fl *TF:* 800-537-3635 ■ *Web:* www.nysscpa.org	New York	NY	10005	212-719-8300	719-3365	49-1
Foundation for Advanced Education in the Sciences (FAES) 10 Center Dr Rm 1N241 - MSC 1115 *Web:* www.faes.org	Bethesda	MD	20892	301-594-8985	402-0174	49-19
Foundation For Affordable Housing Vi Inc 384 Forest Ave Ste 14 *Web:* ffah.org	Laguna Beach	CA	92651	949-443-9101	443-9133	653
Foundation for Economic Education (FEE) 1819 Peachtree Rd NE Ste 300 *TF:* 800-960-4333 ■ *Web:* fee.org	Atlanta	GA	30309	404-554-9980	393-3142	634
Foundation for Indigenous Americans of Anasazi Heritage (FIAAH) Greenbrier Pkwy Ste 201 *TF:* 877-571-9788 ■ *Web:* www.fiaah.org	Atlanta	GA	30331	828-293-1363		48-13
Foundation for International Community Assistance (FINCA) 1201 15th St NW 8th Fl *TF:* 855-903-4622 ■ *Web:* www.finca.org	Washington	DC	20005	202-682-1510	682-1535	48-5
Foundation for Montessori Education 291B Jane St *Web:* montessori-ami.ca	Toronto	ON	M6S3Z3	416-769-7457		166
Foundation for Moral Law PO Box 4086 *Web:* morallaw.org	Montgomery	AL	36103	334-262-1245	262-1708	48-7
Foundation for the Carolinas 217 S Tryon St *TF:* 800-973-7244 ■ *Web:* www.fftc.org	Charlotte	NC	28202	704-973-4500	973-4599	303
Foundation Laboratory 1716 W Holt Ave *TF:* 800-843-7190 ■ *Web:* foundationlaboratory.com	Pomona	CA	91768	909-623-9301		415
Foundation on Economic Trends 4520 E W Hwy Ste 600 *Web:* www.foet.org	Bethesda	MD	20814	301-656-6272	654-0208	49-12
Foundation Publications Inc 900 S Euclid St *TF:* 800-257-6272 ■ *Web:* www.foundationpublications.com	La Habra	CA	90631	714-879-2286		637-2
Foundation Source Inc 55 Walls Dr *TF:* 800-839-0054 ■ *Web:* www.foundationsource.com	Fairfield	CT	06824	800-839-0054	839-1754	463
Foundation Technologies Inc 1400 Progress Industrial Blvd *TF:* 800-773-2368 ■ *Web:* www.foundationtechnologies.com	Lawrenceville	GA	30043	678-407-4640		191-1
Founders Equity Inc 711 5th Ave 5th Fl *Web:* www.fequity.com	New York	NY	10022	212-829-0900	829-0901	690
Founders Financial Inc 1020 Cromwell Bridge Rd *TF:* 800-288-3035 ■ *Web:* www.foundersfinancial.com	Towson	MD	21286	410-308-9988		796
Founders Garden 2450 Milledge Ave *Web:* gardenclub.uga.edu	Athens	GA	30602	706-227-5369	227-5370	97
Founders Inn and Spa, The 5641 Indian River Rd *TF:* 800-926-4466 ■ *Web:* tapestrycollection3.hilton.com	Virginia Beach	VA	23464	757-424-5511		377
Foundry Solutions & Design LLC 316 Maxwell Rd Ste 500 *Web:* foundrysd.com	Alpharetta	GA	30004	770-667-4545	667-4544	261
Fountain Circle Care & Rehabilitation Ctr 200 Glenway Rd *Web:* fountaincirclecare.com	Winchester	KY	40391	859-744-1800		450
Fountain Construction Co 5655 Hwy 18 W *Web:* www.fountainconstruction.com	Jackson	MS	39209	601-373-4162	373-4300	189-10
Fountain County 301 Fourth St *TF:* 800-800-5556 ■ *Web:* www.fountaincounty.net	Covington	IN	47932	765-793-2411		338
Fountain House Inc 425 W 47th St *Web:* www.fountainhouse.org	New York	NY	10036	718-742-9884		726
Fountain Industries Co 922 E 14th St *TF:* 800-328-3594 ■ *Web:* www.fountainindustries.com	Albert Lea	MN	56007	507-373-2351		111
Fountain People Inc 4600 Hwy 123 *Web:* fountainpeople.com	San Marcos	TX	78666	512-392-1155	392-1154	183
Fountain Spa, The 1100 SR-17 *Web:* www.thefountainspa.com	Ramsey	NJ	07446	201-327-5155		77
Fountain Valley Chamber of Commerce 10055 Slater Ave Ste 250 *Web:* www.fvchamber.com	Fountain Valley	CA	92708	714-962-3822		139
Fountain Valley Regional Hospital & Medical Ctr 17100 Euclid St *TF:* 866-904-6871 ■ *Web:* www.fountainvalleyhospital.com	Fountain Valley	CA	92708	714-966-7200		374-3
Fountain Valley School of Colorado 6155 Fountain Vly School Rd *Web:* www.fvs.edu	Colorado Springs	CO	80911	719-390-7035		622
Fountaindale Public Library 300 W Briarcliff Rd *Web:* www.fountaindale.org	Bolingbrook	IL	60440	630-759-2102		434-3
Fountainhead Group Inc 23 Garden St *TF:* 800-311-9903 ■ *Web:* www.thefountainheadgroup.com	New York	NY	13417	315-736-0037	768-4220	172
Fountainhead Hotels 1501 Queens Way *TF:* 800-528-4916 ■ *Web:* www.fountainheadhotels.com	Fairbanks	AK	99701	907-456-3642		379
Fountains at Millbrook, The 79 Flint Rd *Web:* www.watermarkcommunities.com	Millbrook	NY	12545	845-605-4457		672
Four C's Holdings Ltd 330 Mackenzie Blvd *Web:* casman.ca	Fort McMurray	AB	T9H4C4	780-791-9283		499
Four Cedars Accounting Group LLC 411 First Ave S Ste 505 *Web:* fourcedarsgroup.com	Seattle	WA	98104	206-451-7105		2
Four Colour Print Group 2410 Frankfort Ave *Web:* fourcolour.com	Louisville	KY	40206	502-896-9644	896-9594	627
Four Corners Welding and Gas Supply (FCWGS) 606 E Hwy 66 *Web:* www.fourcornerswelding.com	Gallup	NM	87301	505-722-3845	722-2645	492
Four County Electric Membership Corp 1822 NC Hwy 53 W PO Box 667 *TF:* 888-368-7289 ■ *Web:* www.fourcty.org	Burgaw	NC	28425	910-259-2171	259-1860	245
Four County Library System 304 Clubhouse Rd *Web:* www.4cls.org	Vestal	NY	13850	607-723-8236	723-1722	434-3
Four Health Inc 1075 E 14 St *Web:* fourhealthinc.com	Hialeah	FL	33002	305-805-4151		476
Four Mile Creek State Park 1055 Lake Rd *Web:* parks.ny.gov	Youngstown	NY	14174	716-745-3802		565
Four Queens Hotel & Casino 202 Fremont St *TF:* 800-634-6045 ■ *Web:* www.fourqueens.com	Las Vegas	NV	89101	702-385-4011	387-5158	379
Four Rivers Career Ctr 1978 Image Dr *Web:* www.frcc-sdow-mo.schoolloop.com	Washington	MO	63090	636-231-2100	239-0791	167-3
Four Roses Distillery LLC 1224 Bonds Mill Rd *Web:* fourrosesbourbon.com	Lawrenceburg	KY	40342	502-839-3436	839-8338	80-1
Four Sails Resort Hotel 3301 Atlantic Ave *TF:* 800-227-4213 ■ *Web:* www.foursails.com	Virginia Beach	VA	23451	757-491-8100	491-0573	379
Four Seasons General Merchandise (4SGM) 2801 E Vernon *Web:* www.4sgm.com	Los Angeles	CA	90058	323-582-4444	582-9630	812
Four Seasons Hospice & Palliative Care 571 S Allen Rd *TF:* 866-466-9734 ■ *Web:* fourseasons.teleioscn.org	Flat Rock	NC	28731	828-692-6178	233-0351	371
Four Seasons Hotels Inc 1165 Leslie St *TF:* 800-332-3442 ■ *Web:* www.fourseasons.com	Toronto	ON	M3C2K8	416-449-1750	441-4374	379
Four Seasons Inc 1801 Waters Ridge Dr *Web:* www.4s.com	Lewisville	TX	75057	972-316-8100		612
Four Seasons Retirement Ctr 1901 Taylor Rd *Web:* www.fourseasonsretirement.com	Columbus	IN	47203	812-372-8481		672

Name / Address	City	State	ZIP	Phone	Fax	Class
Four Seasons Solar Products LLC 5005 Veterans Memorial Hwy *TF:* 800-368-7732 ■ *Web:* www.fourseassonsunrooms.com	Holbrook	NY	11741	631-325-4042	563-4010	105
Four Seasons Town Ctr 410 Four Seasons Town Centre *Web:* www.shopfourseasons.com	Greensboro	NC	27407	336-292-0171		460
Four Star Plastics 6733 Mid Cities Ave *TF:* 888-595-4626 ■ *Web:* www.fourstarplastics.com	Beltsville	MD	20705	301-595-4626		603
Four States Livestock Sales 501 E First St *Web:* www.fourstateslivestocksales.com	Hagerstown	MD	21740	301-733-8120	733-7318	446
Four Ways West Publications 14618 Valley View Ave *Web:* fourwayswest.com	La Mirada	CA	90638	714-521-4259		637-2
Four Wheel Campers 1460 Churchill Downs Ave *TF:* 800-242-1442 ■ *Web:* fourwheelcampers.com	Woodland	CA	95776	530-666-1442		120
Four Winds Casino Resort 11111 Wilson Rd *TF:* 866-494-6371 ■ *Web:* www.fourwindscasino.com	New Buffalo	MI	49117	866-494-6371		132
Four Winds Hospital 800 Cross River Rd *TF:* 800-528-6624 ■ *Web:* www.fourwindshospital.com	Katonah	NY	10536	914-763-8151		374-5
Four Winds Manufacturing LLC 251 Mayfield Dr *Web:* www.fourwindsspas.com	Smyrna	TN	37167	615-220-8879		596
Four Winns Inc 925 Frisbie St *Web:* www.fourwinns.com	Cadillac	MI	49601	231-775-1343	779-2345	90
Fourandhalf Inc 22320 Foothill Blvd Ste 620 *Web:* fourandhalf.com	Hayward	CA	94541	510-889-9921		195
FourFront Design Inc 517 Seventh St *Web:* fourfrontdesign.com	Rapid City	SD	57701	605-342-9470		256
Fournitures De Bureau Denis Inc 2990 Boul Le Corbusier *TF:* 800-338-5567 ■ *Web:* www.denis.ca	Laval	QC	H7L3M2	800-338-5567		320
Foursome Inc 3570 Vicksveurg Ln N Ste 100 *TF:* 888-368-7766 ■ *Web:* www.thefoursome.com	Plymouth	MN	55447	763-473-4667	504-5555	157-2
Fourteen Company Ltd 18271 W McDurmott St Ste F *Web:* www.fourteengolf.com	Irvine	CA	92614	949-852-8811		711
Fourteen Hills Dept of Creative Writing 1600 Holloway Ave *Web:* www.14hills.net	San Francisco	CA	94132	510-524-1668		637-9
Fourth Avenue 434 E Ninth St *Web:* www.fourthavenue.org	Tucson	AZ	85705	520-624-5004		50-6
Fourth Presbyterian Church 3016 Preston Hwy *Web:* www.fourthpc.org	Louisville	KY	40217	502-634-8021		48-20
Fourth Street Bowl 1441 N Fourth St *Web:* www.4thstreetbowl.com	San Jose	CA	95112	408-453-5555		99
Four-Way Tool and Die Inc 239 Indusco Ct *Web:* www.4waytool.com	Troy	MI	48083	248-585-8255	585-3846	757
Fourwinds Resort & Marina 9301 Fairfax Rd *Web:* www.bestinboating.com	Bloomington	IN	47401	812-824-2628		669
Foushee & Associates Inc 3260 118th Ave SE *Web:* www.foushee.com	Bellevue	WA	98005	425-746-1000	746-3737	186
Fowler Bell PLLC 300 W Vine St Ste 600 *Web:* fowlerlaw.com	Lexington	KY	40507	859-252-6700	255-3735	41
Fowler Engineering LLC 1989 Oak Tree Cv Ste A *Web:* fowlereng.com	Hernando	MS	38632	662-469-9571		261
Fowler Equity Exchange Inc 302 S Main St *Web:* www.fowlerequity.com	Fowler	KS	67844	620-646-5284		276
Fowler Financial Services 14205 SE 36th St Ste 100 *Web:* fowlerfinancial.com	Bellevue	WA	98006	425-453-1585		390
Fowler Foods Inc 139 SW Dr	Jonesboro	AR	72401	870-935-6032		345
Fowler General Construction Inc 2161 Henderson Loop *Web:* fowlergc.com	Richland	WA	99354	509-375-3331		261
Fowler Holding Company Inc 2721 NW 36th Ave *Web:* fowlerholding.com	Norman	OK	73072	405-573-9909		57
Fowler Museum at UCLA 308 Charles E Young Dr N PO Box 951549 *Web:* www.fowler.ucla.edu	Los Angeles	CA	90095	310-825-4361	206-7007	520
Fowler Packing Company Inc 8570 S Cedar Ave *Web:* fowlerpacking.com	Fresno	CA	93725	559-834-5911	834-5272	315-3
Fowler State Bank 300 E 5th St PO Box 511 *TF:* 800-439-3951 ■ *Web:* www.fowlerstatebank.com	Fowler	IN	47944	765-884-1200		70
Fowler's Chocolate Co 100 River Rock Dr Ste 102 *TF:* 800-824-2263 ■ *Web:* www.fowlerschocolates.com	Buffalo	NY	14207	716-877-9983		296-8
Fownes Bros & Company Inc 16 E 34th St **Fax Area Code: 212* ■ *TF:* 800-345-6837 ■ *Web:* www.fownesbrothers.com	New York	NY	10016	800-345-6837	683-2832*	155-8
Fox & Company Inc 1 Gilbert Hill Rd *Web:* www.foxandcompany.com	Chester	CT	06412	860-526-2286	526-9974	194
FOX - WRSR, The 4511 Miller Rd *Web:* classicfox.com	Flint	MI	48507	810-720-9510	720-9513	645-58
FOX 102.3 1900 Pineview Rd *Web:* www.fox1023.com	Columbia	SC	29209	803-696-8600		645-38
FOX 11 1999 S Bundy Dr *Web:* www.foxla.com	Los Angeles	CA	90025	310-584-2000		741-76
FOX 2 / KPLR 11 2250 Ball Dr *Web:* fox2now.com	Saint Louis	MO	63146	314-213-7831		647
FOX 29 WFLXCOM 4119 W Blue Heron Blvd *Web:* www.wflx.com	West Palm Beach	FL	33404	561-845-2929		741-140
FOX 42 KPTM 4625 Farnam St *Web:* fox42kptm.com	Omaha	NE	68132	402-554-4282	554-4290	741-94
FOX 68 MY43 1000 James St *Web:* www.foxsyracuse.com	Syracuse	NY	13203	315-472-6800		741-131
FOX 7 Austin 119 E Tenth St *Web:* www.fox7austin.com	Austin	TX	78701	512-495-7757	495-7001	741-9
Fox Chapel Area School District 611 Field Club Rd *Web:* www.fcasd.edu	Pittsburgh	PA	15238	412-963-9600		685
Fox Chase Cancer Ctr 333 Cottman Ave *TF:* 888-369-2427 ■ *Web:* www.foxchase.org	Philadelphia	PA	19111	215-728-6900		374-7
Fox Cities Chamber of Commerce & Industry 125 N Superior St *Web:* foxcitieschamber.com	Appleton	WI	54911	920-734-7101	734-7161	139
Fox Cities Convention & Visitors Bureau 3433 W College Ave *TF:* 800-236-6673 ■ *Web:* www.foxcities.org	Appleton	WI	54914	920-734-3358	734-1080	206
Fox Cities Performing Arts Ctr 400 W College Ave *TF:* 800-216-7469 ■ *Web:* foxcitiespac.com	Appleton	WI	54911	800-216-7469		522
Fox College 6640 S Cicero Ave *Web:* www.foxcollege.edu	Bedford Park	IL	60638	708-444-4500		167-3
Fox Communities Credit Union 3401 E Calumet St *Web:* foxcu.org	Appleton	WI	54915	920-993-9000		219
Fox Company Inc, The 11000 W Becher St *Web:* www.thefoxco.com	Milwaukee	WI	53227	414-321-4700		627
Fox Contractors Corp 5430 W Ferguson Rd *Web:* www.foxcontractors.com	Fort Wayne	IN	46809	260-747-7461		188-4
Fox Converting Inc 1250 Cornell Rd *Web:* www.foxconverting.com	Green Bay	WI	54313	920-434-5272		638
Fox CPA Group Ltd 204 E Cherry St	Watcoka	IL	60070	815 432 3126		2
Fox Creek Leather Inc 2029 Elk Creek Pkwy *TF:* 800-766-4165 ■ *Web:* www.foxcreekleather.com	Independence	VA	24348	800-766-4165		711
Fox Electric Ltd 1104 Colorado Ln *Web:* www.foxelectric.com	Arlington	TX	76015	817-461-2571	261-7311	189-4
Fox Engineering Associates Inc 414 S 17th St Ste 107 *TF:* 800-433-3469 ■ *Web:* www.foxeng.com	Ames	IA	50010	515-233-0000		261
Fox Harb'r Resort & Spa 1337 Fox Harbour Rd *TF:* 866-257-1801 ■ *Web:* www.foxharbr.com	Wallace	NS	B0K1Y0	902-257-1801		707
Fox Hill Village 10 Longwood Dr *Web:* www.foxhillvillage.com	Westwood	MA	02090	781-329-4433	461-2464	672
Fox Hills Resort & Convention Ctr 250 W Church St *Web:* www.foxhillsresort.com	Mishicot	WI	54228	920-755-2376		669
Fox Industries Inc 3100 Falls Cliff Rd *TF:* 888-760-0369 ■ *Web:* www.thefoxbuilding.com	Baltimore	MD	21211	410-646-8405		3
Fox IV Technologies 6011 Enterprise Dr *TF:* 877-436-2434 ■ *Web:* foxiv.com	Export	PA	15632	724-387-3500		547
Fox Lake Correctional Institution PO Box 147 *Web:* www.doc.wi.gov	Fox Lake	WI	53933	920-928-3151	928-6929	213
Fox Lite Inc 8300 Dayton Rd *Web:* www.foxlite.com	Fairborn	OH	45324	937-864-1966	864-7010	608
Fox Lumber Sales Inc PO Box 1000 *Web:* www.foxlumber.com	Hamilton	MT	59840	406-363-5140	363-6774	820
Fox News Ch 1211 Avenue of the Americas *Web:* www.foxnews.com	New York	NY	10036	212-301-3000		740
Fox Packaging Co 2200 Fox Dr *Web:* www.foxbag.com	McAllen	TX	78504	956-682-6176	682-5768	67
Fox Plaza 2121 Avenue of the Stars Ste LL20 *Web:* thechirofusion.com	Los Angeles	CA	90067	310-467-5218		741
Fox Pool Corp 3490 Board Rd *TF:* 800-723-1011 ■ *Web:* www.foxpool.com	York	PA	17406	800-723-1011		728
Fox Richmond 1925 Westmoreland St *Web:* www.foxrichmond.com	Richmond	VA	23230	804-358-3535	358-1495	741-108
Fox Ridge State Park 18175 State Park Rd *Web:* www2.illinois.gov	Charleston	IL	61920	217-345-6416		565
Fox River Mall 4301 W Wisconsin Ave *Web:* www.foxrivermall.com	Appleton	WI	54913	920-739-4100		460
Fox Rothschild LLP 2000 Market St 10th Fl *TF:* 800-580-9136 ■ *Web:* www.foxrothschild.com	Philadelphia	PA	19103	215-299-2000	299-2150	428
Fox Run Vineyards 670 SR-14 *TF:* 800-636-9786 ■ *Web:* foxrunvineyards.com	Penn Yan	NY	14527	315-536-4616		443
Fox Service Co 4300 S Congress Ave *Web:* www.foxservice.com	Austin	TX	78745	512-975-3102		189-10
Fox Smith LLC 1 S Memorial Dr 12th Fl *Web:* foxsmithlaw.com	Saint Louis	MO	63102	314-588-7000		428
Fox Sports 1070 The Game 2651 S Fish Hatchery Rd *Web:* 1070thegame.iheart.com	Madison	WI	53711	608-274-5450		645-92
Fox Sports Interactive Media LLC 10201 W Pico Blvd *Web:* www.foxsports.com	Los Angeles	CA	90035	310-369-7069	969-5660	740
Fox Sports Radio 1400 316 Greystone Blvd *Web:* foxsportsradio1400.iheart.com	Columbia	SC	29210	803-343-1100		645-38
Fox Sports Radio AM 1 Boston Store Pl *Web:* www.sportsradio1330.com	Erie	PA	16501	814-461-1000		645-53
Fox Studios Lot 10201 W Pico Blvd *Web:* www.foxstudiolot.com	Los Angeles	CA	90064	310-369-1000		512
Fox Television Stations Inc (FTS) 1999 S Bundy Dr *Web:* www.myfoxla.com	Los Angeles	CA	90025	310-584-2025		741-99

Name / Address	City	State	Zip	Phone	Fax	Class
Fox Theatre 660 Peachtree St NE	Atlanta	GA	30308	404-881-2100	872-2972	572
TF: 855-285-8499 ■ *Web:* www.foxtheatre.org						
Fox Valley Buick-GMC Inc 1421 E Main St	Saint Charles	IL	60174	630-524-2758		57
Web: www.foxvalleybuickgmc.com						
Fox Valley Credit Union 575 N Broadway	Aurora	IL	60505	630-859-2276	859-2472	219
Web: foxvalleycu.com						
Fox Valley Fire & Safety Company Inc 2730 Pinnacle Dr	Elgin	IL	60124	847-695-5990	695-3699	189-4
Web: www.foxvalleyfire.com						
Fox Valley Spring Company Inc N915 Craftsmen Dr	Greenville	WI	54942	920-757-7777		492
TF: 800-776-2645 ■ *Web:* www.foxvalleyspring.com						
Fox Valley Technical College 1825 N Bluemound Dr PO Box 2277	Appleton	WI	54912	920-735-5600	735-2484	800
TF: 800-735-3882 ■ *Web:* www.fvtc.edu						
Fox World Travel School 2150 S Washburn St	Oshkosh	WI	54904	920-236-8022		685
TF: 800-236-8475 ■ *Web:* www.foxworldtravel.com						
Fox's 80 Main St	Mineola	NY	11501	516-294-8321		157-6
Web: foxs.com						
Fox's Pizza Den Inc 4425 Willaim Penn Hwy	Murrysville	PA	15668	724-733-7888		670
Web: www.foxspizza.com						
FOX21 560 Wooten Rd	Colorado Springs	CO	80915	719-596-2100	591-4180	741-32
Web: www.fox21news.com						
FOX35 35 Skyline Dr	Lake Mary	FL	32746	407-644-3535		647
Web: www.fox35orlando.com						
Foxboro Industries Inc 603 W Flottmann Rd	Gerald	MO	63037	573-764-4224		454
Web: www.foxboroindustries.com						
Foxcom Inc 136 Main St Ste 300b	Princeton	NJ	08540	609-228-8104		246
Web: www.foxcom.com						
Foxcroft School 22407 Foxhound Ln PO Box 5555	Middleburg	VA	20118	540-687-5555	687-3675	622
Web: www.foxcroft.org						
Foxdale Village 500 E Marylyn Ave	State College	PA	16801	814-238-3322	238-2920	672
TF: 800-253-4951 ■ *Web:* www.foxdalevillage.org						
Foxes Music Co 416 S Washington St	Falls Church	VA	22046	703-533-7393	536-2171	526
TF: 800-446-4414 ■ *Web:* foxesmusic.com						
FoxGuard Solutions Inc 2285 Prospect Dr	Christiansburg	VA	24073	877-446-4732		180
TF: 877-446-4732 ■ *Web:* www.foxguardsolutions.com						
Foxlink International Inc 3010 Saturn St Ste 200	Brea	CA	92821	714-256-1777		253
Web: www.foxlink.com						
FoxNet Solutions Inc 92 Erb St E	Waterloo	ON	N2J1L6	519-886-8895		180
Web: www.foxnetsolutions.com						
Foxwoods Resort Casino 350 Trolley Line Blvd	Mashantucket	CT	06338	860-312-3000		379
TF: 866-436-9562 ■ *Web:* www.foxwoods.com						
Foxworth-Galbraith Lumber Co 4965 Preston Pk Blvd Ste 400	Plano	TX	75093	972-665-2400		191-3
TF: 800-688-8082 ■ *Web:* www.foxgal.com						
Foxx Equipment Co 421 SW Blvd	Kansas City	MO	64108	816-421-3600		358
TF: 800-821-2254 ■ *Web:* foxxequipment.com						
Foxx Virginia (Rep R - NC) 2462 Rayburn House Office Bldg	Washington	DC	20515	202-225-2071	225-2995	342-2
TF: 866-677-8968 ■ *Web:* foxx.house.gov						
Foyer, The 3655 Perkins Rd	Baton Rouge	LA	70808	225-343-3655		460
Web: www.thefoyerbr.com						
FP Horak Co 401 Saginaw St	Bay City	MI	48708	989-892-6505		627
Web: www.fphorak.com						
FP Mailing Solutions 140 N Mitchell Ct	Addison	IL	60101	800-341-6052		112
TF: 800-341-6052 ■ *Web:* www.fp-usa.com						
FPA (Foreign Policy Assn) 470 Park Ave S	New York	NY	10016	212-481-8100	481-9275	48-7
TF: 800-628-5754 ■ *Web:* fpa.org						
FPA (Flexible Packaging Assn) 971 Corporate Blvd Ste 403	Linthicum Heights	MD	21090	410-694-0800	694-0900	49-13
Web: www.flexpack.org						
FPC (Frank Phillips College) 1301 W Roosevelt	Borger	TX	79007	806-457-4200		162
Web: fpctx.edu						
FPC Flexible Packaging Corp 1891 Eglinton Ave E	Toronto	ON	M1L2L7	416-288-3060	288-0808	548
TF: 888-288-7386 ■ *Web:* www.fpcflexible.com						
FPCA (Fillmore-Piru Citrus Assn) 357 N Main St PO Box 350	Piru	CA	93040	805-521-1781	521-0990	11-1
Web: www.fillmorepirucitrus.com						
FPDA (Fluid Power Distributors Assn) PO Box 1420	Cherry Hill	NJ	08034	856-424-8998	424-9248	49-13
Web: www.fpda.org						
FPHC (Flower Pentecostal Heritage Ctr) 1445 N Boonville Ave	Springfield	MO	65802	417-862-1447	862-6203	434-3
TF: 877-840-5200 ■ *Web:* ifphc.org						
FPI (Forged Products Inc) 6505 N Houston Rosslyn Rd	Houston	TX	77091	713-462-3416	460-9404	483
TF: 800-876-3416 ■ *Web:* www.fpitx.com						
FPI (Franklin Precision Industry Inc) 3220 Bowling Green Rd	Franklin	KY	42134	270-598-4300		60
Web: www.fpik.com						
FPI (Foodservice & Packaging Institute) 7700 Leesburg Pk Ste 421	Falls Church	VA	22043	703-592-9889	592-9864	49-13
Web: www.fpi.org						
FPI Management Inc 800 Iron Pt Rd	Folsom	CA	95630	916-357-5300		652
Web: fpimgt.com						
FPIS Inc 2095 Premier Row	Ocoee	FL	34761	407-656-8818		7
TF: 800-346-5977 ■ *Web:* www.fpis.com						
FPL (Florida Power & Light Co) 700 Universe Blvd	Juno Beach	FL	33408	561-691-7574		787
TF: 800-226-3545 ■ *Web:* www.fpl.com						
Fpl Food LLC 1301 New Savannah Rd	Augusta	GA	30901	706-722-2694		473
Web: www.fplfood.net						
FPL Group Inc *NextEra Energy Inc* 700 Universe Blvd	Juno Beach	FL	33408	561-694-4000	694-4620	360-5
NYSE: NEE ■ *TF:* 888-218-4392 ■ *Web:* www.nexteraenergy.com						
Fpm Group Ltd 909 Marconi Ave	Ronkonkoma	NY	11779	631-737-6200		261
Web: www.fpm-group.com						
FPM LLC 1501 S Lively Blvd	Elk Grove Village	IL	60007	847-228-2525	228-5912	484
TF: 877-437-6432 ■ *Web:* www.fpmht.com						
FPMI Solutions Inc 1033 N Fairfax St Ste 200	Alexandria	VA	22314	888-644-3764		193
TF: 888-644-3764 ■ *Web:* www.fednews-online.com						
FPRI (Foreign Policy Research Institute) 1528 Walnut St Ste 610	Philadelphia	PA	19102	215-732-3774	732-4401	634
Web: www.fpri.org						
FPSA 1451 Dolley Madison Blvd Ste 101	McLean	VA	22101	703-761-2600	761-4334	49-13
Web: www.fpsa.org						
FPT USA Corp 801 E Campbell Rd Ste 525	Richardson	TX	75081	214-253-2662	253-2988	196
Web: www.fpt-software.com						
FPUC (Florida Public Utilities Co) 401 S Dixie Hwy	West Palm Beach	FL	33401	800-427-7712		787
TF: 800-427-7712 ■ *Web:* www.fpuc.com						
FRA (Fleet Reserve Assn) 125 NW St	Alexandria	VA	22314	703-683-1400	549-6610	48-19
TF: 800-372-1924 ■ *Web:* www.fra.org						
FRA (Federal Railroad Administration Regional Offices) *Region 1* 55 Broadway Rm 1077	Cambridge	MA	02142	617-494-2302	494-2967	340-17
TF: 800-724-5991 ■ *Web:* railroads.dot.gov						
FRAC (Food Research & Action Ctr) 1875 Connecticut Ave NW Ste 540	Washington	DC	20009	202-986-2200	986-2525	48-6
Web: www.frac.org						
Fractal Analytics Ltd 951 Mariners Island St Ste 307	San Mateo	CA	94404	650-378-1284		225
Web: fractal.ai						
Fraen Corp 324 New Boston St	Woburn	MA	01801	781-205-5400	205-5472	621
Web: www.fraen.com						
Fragomen, Del Rey, Bernsen, & Loewy LLP 1101 15th St NW Ste 700	Washington	DC	20005	202-223-5515	371-2898	41
Web: www.fragomen.com						
Fragrance Foundation 60 E 56th St 5TH FL	New York	NY	10022	212-725-2755		49-4
Web: fragrance.org						
Fraim & Fiorella PC 150 Boush St Ste 601	Norfolk	VA	23510	757-227-5900	227-5901	428
Web: fraimandfiorella.com						
Frain Industries 245 E North Ave	Carol Stream	IL	60188	630-629-9900	629-6575	23
Web: www.fraingroup.com						
Frakco Inc 606 E Dodge St	Luverne	MN	56156	507-283-4416	283-4417	612
TF: 800-967-1762 ■ *Web:* www.frakco.com						
Frakes Engineering Inc 7950 Castleway Dr Ste 160	Indianapolis	IN	46250	317-577-3000		256
Web: www.frakesengineering.com						
Fraley and Schilling Inc 1920 S State Rd 3	Rushville	IN	46173	800-428-6640	932-5594*	780
**Fax Area Code:* 765 ■ *TF:* 800-428-6640 ■ *Web:* www.gofands.com						
Fralinger Engineering PA 629 Shiloh Pk	Bridgeton	NJ	08302	856-451-2990		261
Web: www.fralinger.com						
FRAM (Frederic Remington Art Museum) 303 Washington St	Ogdensburg	NY	13669	315-393-2425		637-2
Web: www.fredericremington.org						
Fram Trak Industries Inc 205 Hallock Ave	Middlesex	NJ	08846	732-424-8400	424-8811	604
Web: framtrak.com						
Frame.io 22 Cortlandt St 31st Fl	New York	NY	10007	212-620-0818		39
Web: frame.io						
Framed on Madison Inc 740 Madison Ave	New York	NY	10021	212-734-4680		362
Web: www.framedonmadison.com						
Framingham Heart Study 73 Mt Wayte Ave Ste 2	Framingham	MA	01702	508-935-3418	626-1262	668
TF: 800-854-7582 ■ *Web:* www.framinghamheartstudy.org						
Framingham State College 100 State St PO Box 9101	Framingham	MA	01701	508-620-1220	626-4017	166
TF: 866-361-8970 ■ *Web:* framingham.edu						
Frampton Mailing Systems 450 Horton St E	London	ON	N6B1M3	519-680-6245		5
Web: fms.ca						
France						
Consulate General 10390 Santa Monica Blvd Ste 410	Los Angeles	CA	90025	310-235-3200	479-4813	257
Web: losangeles.consulfrance.org						
Consulate General 1340 Poydras St Ste 1710	New Orleans	LA	70112	504-569-2870	569-2871	257
Web: nouvelleorleans.consulfrance.org						
Consulate General 1395 Brickell Ave Ste 1050	Miami	FL	33131	305-403-4185	403-4187	257
TF: 877-624-8737 ■ *Web:* miami.consulfrance.org						
Consulate General 205 N Michigan Ave Ste 3700	Chicago	IL	60601	312-327-5200	327-5201	257
TF: 866-858-4430 ■ *Web:* chicago.consulfrance.org						
Consulate General 777 Post Oak Blvd Ste 600	Houston	TX	77056	713-572-2799	572-2911	257
TF: 888-902-5322 ■ *Web:* houston.consulfrance.org						
Consulate General 934 Fifth Ave	New York	NY	10021	212-606-3600	606-3614	257
Web: newyork.consulfrance.org						
Consulate General 540 Bush St	San Francisco	CA	94108	415-397-4330	433-8357	257
TF: 800-553-4133 ■ *Web:* sanfrancisco.consulfrance.org						
Consulate General 31 St James Ave Ste 750	Boston	MA	02116	617-832-4400		257
Web: boston.consulfrance.org						
Embassy 4101 Reservoir Rd NW	Washington	DC	20007	202-944-6000	944-6175	257
TF: 800-622-6232 ■ *Web:* franceintheus.org						
Frances Collin Literary Agent PO Box 33	Wayne	PA	19087	610-254-0555	254-5029	444
Web: www.francescollin.com						
Frances Slocum State Park 565 Mt Olivet Rd	Wyoming	PA	18644	570-696-3525		565
Web: www.dcnr.pa.gov						

				Phone	Fax	Class
Francesca's on Taylor 1400 W Taylor St *Web:* www.miafrancesca.com	Chicago	IL	60607	312-829-2828		671
Franchise Business Systems Inc (FBS) 2319 N Andrews Ave. *TF:* 800-382-1040 ■ *Web:* www.franchiseaccounting.com	Fort Lauderdale	FL	33311	800-382-1040		194
Franchise Capital Advisors Inc 9903 E Bell Rd Ste 130 *Web:* franchisecapitaladvisors.com	Scottsdale	AZ	85260	480-355-4399		70
Franchise Co, The (TFC) 14502 N Dale Mabry Ste 200 *TF:* 800-294-5591 ■ *Web:* www.fsvbrands.com	Tampa	FL	33618	800-294-5591		463
Franchise Direct USA Inc 750 Hammond Dr Bldg 16 Ste 350 *TF:* 844-294-6258 ■ *Web:* www.franchisedirect.com	Atlanta	GA	30328	404-500-5635		393
Franchise Handbook 5555 N Port Washington Rd Ste 305 *TF:* 800-272-0246 ■ *Web:* www.franchisehandbook.com	Milwaukee	WI	53217	800-272-0246		457-11
Franchise Information Services Inc 4075 Wilson Blvd Ste 410 *TF:* 800-485-9570 ■ *Web:* www.frandata.com	Arlington	VA	22203	800-485-9570		387
Franchoice Inc 7500 Flying Cloud Dr Ste 600 *TF:* 888-307-1371 ■ *Web:* www.franchoice.com	Eden Prairie	MN	55344	888-307-1371		194
Francis A. Countway Library of Medicine, The 10 Shattuck St *Web:* www.countway.harvard.edu	Boston	MA	02115	617-432-2136	432-4739	434-1
Francis Cheney Family Place 2825 E Barnett Rd *Web:* www.asante.org	Medford	OR	97504	541-789-5876		372
Francis Coppola Winery LLC 300 Via Archimedes *Web:* www.francisfordcoppolawinery.com	Geyserville	CA	95441	707-857-1471		81-3
Francis Investment Counsel LLC 19435 W Capitol Dr *TF:* 866-232-6457 ■ *Web:* www.francisinvco.com	Brookfield	WI	53045	866-232-6457		796
Francis Land House 3131 Virginia Beach Blvd *Web:* www.museumsvb.org	Virginia Beach	VA	23452	757-385-5100		50-3
Francis Manufacturing Co 500 E Main St PO Box 400 *Web:* www.francismanufacturing.com	Russia	OH	45363	937-526-4551	526-5508	492
Francis Marion Hotel, The 387 King St *TF:* 877-756-2121 ■ *Web:* www.francismarionhotel.com	Charleston	SC	29403	843-722-0600		379
Francis Marion University PO Box 100547 *TF:* 800-368-7551 ■ *Web:* www.fmarion.edu	Florence	SC	29501	843-661-1231	661-4635	166
Francis Martino Insurance Services 10 Township Line Rd *Web:* francismartinoinsurance.com	Elkins Park	PA	19027	215-379-2400		390
Francis O. Day Construction Company Inc 850 E Gude Dr *Web:* www.foday.com	Rockville	MD	20850	301-652-2400	340-6592	188-4
Francis Scott Key Family Resort 12806 Ocean Gateway *TF:* 800-213-0088 ■ *Web:* fskfamily.com	Ocean City	MD	21842	410-213-0088	213-2854	669
Francis Tuttle Technology Center School District 21 12777 N Rockwell Ave *Web:* www.francistuttle.edu	Oklahoma City	OK	73142	405-717-7799		186
Franciscan ACO Inc 700 E Southport Rd *TF:* 855-268-9086 ■ *Web:* www.franciscanhealth.org	Indianapolis	IN	46227	855-268-9086		374-3
Franciscan Estates 1178 Galleron Rd *Web:* www.franciscan.com	Saint Helena	CA	94574	707-967-3830		80-3
Franciscan Hospital for Children 30 Warren St *Web:* franciscanchildrens.org	Boston	MA	02135	617-254-3800		374-1
Franciscan Missionaries of Our Lady Health System (FMOLHS) 4200 Essen Ln *Web:* www.fmolhs.org	Baton Rouge	LA	70809	225-923-2701	926-4846	353
Franciscan Missionaries of Our Lady University *Our Lady of the Lake College* 5414 Brittany Dr. *TF:* 877-242-3509 ■ *Web:* www.franu.edu	Baton Rouge	LA	70808	225-768-1700	768-1726	166
Franciscan Monastery of the Holly Land 1400 Quincy St NE *Web:* myfranciscan.org	Washington	DC	20017	202-526-6800		50-1
Franciscan School of Theology 1712 Euclid Ave *TF:* 855-355-1550 ■ *Web:* www.fst.edu	Berkeley	CA	94709	760-547-1800		167-3
Franciscan Sisters of Chicago Inc 11500 Theresa Dr *TF:* 800-524-6126 ■ *Web:* www.franciscanministries.org	Lemont	IL	60439	800-524-6126		48-20
Franciscan Spirituality Ctr 920 Market St *Web:* www.fscenter.org	La Crosse	WI	54601	608-791-5295		673
Franciscan University of Steubenville (FUS) 1235 University Blvd *TF:* 800-783-6220 ■ *Web:* www.franciscan.edu	Steubenville	OH	43952	740-283-3771		166
Franciscan Villa 3601 S Chicago Ave *Web:* www.homeishere.org	South Milwaukee	WI	53172	414-764-4100		450
Francisco Grande Hotel & Golf Resort 26000 Gila Bend Hwy *TF:* 800-237-4238 ■ *Web:* www.franciscogrande.com	Casa Grande	AZ	85222	520-836-6444		669
Franck's Pharmacy 7548 Soquel Dr. *Web:* www.franksrx.com	Aptos	CA	95003	831-685-1100	685-1132	238
Franco Manufacturing Company Inc 555 Prospect St *Web:* www.franco-mfg.com	Metuchen	NJ	08840	732-494-0500	494-8270	746
Franco's 6200 N Military Hwy *Web:* www.francositalian.restaurantwebexpert.com	Norfolk	VA	23518	757-853-0177		671
Franco's Ristorante Italiano 824 E Fifth St *Web:* www.francos-italiano.com	Dayton	OH	45402	937-222-0204	222-1380	671
Franconia Notch State Park 9 Franconia Notch Pkwy *Web:* www.nhstateparks.org	Franconia	NH	03580	603-745-8391		565
Francorp Inc 20200 Governors Dr *TF:* 800-372-6244 ■ *Web:* francorp.com	Olympia Fields	IL	60461	708-481-2900		463
Franczek Sullivan Pc 300 S Wacker Dr Ste 3400 *Web:* www.franczek.com	Chicago	IL	60606	312-786-6119		428
Franden, Farris, Quillin, Goodnight & Roberts 2 W Second St Ste 900 *Web:* tulsalawyer.com	Tulsa	OK	74103	918-583-7129		41
Frandsen Bank & Trust 501 Chestnut St W *Web:* www.frandsenbank.com	Virginia	MN	55792	507-744-2361		71
Frank A. Bruno Plc 807 Howard Ave *Web:* fabruno.com	New Orleans	LA	70113	504-523-3593		41
Frank B. Fuhrer Wholesale Co 3100 E Carson St *TF:* 800-837-2212 ■ *Web:* www.fuhrerwholesale.com	Pittsburgh	PA	15203	412-488-8844	488-0195	81-1
Frank B. Ross Company Inc 970-H New Brunswick Ave *TF:* 800-541-6752 ■ *Web:* www.frankbross.com	Rahway	NJ	07065	732-669-0810	669-0814	151
Frank Bryan Inc 1107 Thompson Ave *Web:* bryanmaterialsgroup.com	McKees Rocks	PA	15136	412-331-1630		182
Frank C. Alegre Trucking Inc PO Box 1508 *TF:* 800-769-2440 ■ *Web:* www.alegretrucking.com	Lodi	CA	95241	209-334-2112	367-0572	780
Frank Capurro & Son LLC 2250 Salinas Rd	Moss Landing	CA	95039	831-786-0731		10-11
Frank Edmunds & Co 6111 S Sayre *TF:* 800-447-3516 ■ *Web:* www.frankedmunds.com	Chicago	IL	60638	773-586-2772	586-2783	820
Frank Edwards Co 3075 Windriver Dr *Web:* feco.net	Layton	UT	84040	801-736-8000		61
Frank Erwin Ctr 1701 Red River PO Box 2929 *Web:* www.uterwincenter.com	Austin	TX	78701	512-471-7744	471-9652	720
Frank Family Vineyards LLC 1091 Larkmead Ln *Web:* www.frankfamilyvineyards.com	Calistoga	CA	94515	707-942-0859		443
Frank Grisanti's 1022 S Shady Grove Rd *Web:* frankgrisanti.com	Memphis	TN	38120	901-761-9462		671
Frank H. McClung Museum University of Tennessee 1327 Cir Pk Dr *Web:* mcclungmuseum.utk.edu	Knoxville	TN	37996	865-974-2144	974-3827	520
Frank H. Reis Inc 475 Washington Ave *TF:* 800-285-6724 ■ *Web:* reisinsurance.com	Kingston	NY	12401	800-285-6724		390
Frank Holten State Recreation Area 4500 Pocket Rd *Web:* www2.illinois.gov	East Saint Louis	IL	62205	618-874-7920		565
Frank J. Zamboni & Company Inc 15714 Colorado Ave *Web:* zamboni.com	Paramount	CA	90723	562-633-0751	633-9365	516
Frank Jackson State Park 100 Jerry Adams Dr *Web:* www.alapark.com	Opp	AL	36467	334-493-6988	493-2478	565
Frank Kent Cadillac Inc 3500 W Loop 820 S *TF:* 877-558-5468 ■ *Web:* www.frankkentcadillac.com	Fort Worth	TX	76116	877-558-5468		57
Frank L. Blum Construction Co 830 E 25th St *Web:* www.flblum.com	Winston-Salem	NC	27105	336-724-5528	722-2104	186
Frank Levy Inc 451 E 58th Ave Ste 4482 *TF:* 800-295-2286 ■ *Web:* www.frank-levy-outerwear.com	Denver	CO	80216	303-295-2286	295-6595	155-14
Frank Lill & Son Inc 785 Old Dutch Rd *Web:* www.franklillandson.com	Victor	NY	14564	585-265-0490	265-1842	189-10
Frank Lloyd Wright Home & Studio 951 Chicago Ave *Web:* flwright.org	Oak Park	IL	60302	708-848-1976		520
Frank Lloyd Wright House in Ebbsworth Park 120 N Ballas Rd *Web:* ebsworthpark.org	Kirkwood	MO	63122	314-822-8359		50-3
Frank Lloyd Wright's Martin House Complex 125 Jewett Pkwy *TF:* 877-377-3858 ■ *Web:* www.martinhouse.org	Buffalo	NY	14214	716-856-3858	856-4009	50-3
Frank Lynn & Associates Inc 500 Park Blvd Ste 785 *TF:* 800-245-5966 ■ *Web:* www.franklynn.com	Itasca	IL	60143	312-263-7888		196
Frank M. Booth Inc 222 Third St *Web:* www.frankbooth.com	Marysville	CA	95901	530-742-7134	742-8109	189-10
Frank Mayer & Associates Inc 1975 Wisconsin Ave **Fax Area Code:* 262 ■ *TF:* 855-294-2875 ■ *Web:* www.frankmayer.com	Grafton	WI	53024	855-294-2875	377-3449*	233
Frank Miller Lumber Company Inc 1690 Frank Miller Rd *TF:* 800-345-2643 ■ *Web:* frankmiller.com	Union City	IN	47390	765-964-3196		191-3
Frank Millman Distributors Inc 8 Progress St *TF:* 800-526-0910 ■ *Web:* www.millmans.com	Edison	NJ	08820	908-561-7300		54
Frank Murken Products Inc (FMP) 2125 Technology Dr *TF:* 800-321-6488 ■ *Web:* www.fmproducts.com	Schenectady	NY	12308	518-381-4270	381-4351	326
Frank Novak & Sons Inc 23940 Miles Rd *Web:* www.franknovak.com	Cleveland	OH	44128	216-475-5440		189-2
Frank O. Waterman & Assoc 2 Wisteria Way *Web:* h2omanassociates.com	Canton	MA	02021	781-401-0711		261
Frank Paxton Lumber Co 7455 Dawson Rd **Fax Area Code:* 513 ■ *TF:* 800-325-9800 ■ *Web:* paxtonwood.com	Cincinnati	OH	45243	888-826-5580	984-9060*	191-3
Frank Penney Injury Lawyers Pc 1544 Eureka Rd Ste 120 *Web:* penneylaw.com	Roseville	CA	95661	916-788-1960		41
Frank Phillips College (FPC) 1301 W Roosevelt *Web:* fpctx.edu	Borger	TX	79007	806-457-4200		162

	Phone	Fax	Class
Frank Rewold & Son Inc 333 E Second St ... Rochester MI 48307 *Web:* www.frankrewold.com	248-651-7242		186
Frank Rimerman & Company LLP 1801 Page Mill Rd ... Palo Alto CA 94304 *Web:* www.frankrimerman.com	650-845-8100	494-1975	2
Frank Roberts & Sons Inc 1130 Robertsville Rd ... Punxsutawney PA 15767 *TF:* 800-262-8955 ■ *Web:* www.frankrobertsandsons.com	814-938-5000		191-4
Frank Roth Company Inc 1795 Stratford Ave ... Stratford CT 06615 *Web:* www.frankroth.com	203-377-2155		454
Frank Sterles Slovenian Restaurant 1401 E 55th St ... Cleveland OH 44103 *Web:* www.sterlescountryhouse.com	216-881-4181		671
Frank Strategic Marketing Inc 8775 Centre Park Dr Ste 211 ... Columbia MD 21045 *Web:* www.frankbiz.com	410-203-1228		232
Frank Trygar Inc 2117 General Booth Blvd ... Virginia Beach VA 23454 *Web:* bhhstownerealty.com	757-821-1130		652
Frank W. Diver Inc 2101 Pennsylvania Ave ... Wilmington DE 19806 *Web:* www.diverchev.com	302-575-0161		57
Frank W. Mayborn Civic & Convention Ctr 3303 N Third St ... Temple TX 76501 *Web:* ci.temple.tx.us	254-298-5720	298-5388	205
Frank's Great Outdoors 1212 N Huron Rd ... Linwood MI 48634 *Web:* www.franksgreatoutdoors.com	989-697-5341		711
Frank, Hirsch, Subelsky & Freedman PC 30600 Northwestern Hwy Ste 305 ... Farmington Hills MI 48334 *Web:* fhsfcpa.com	248-855-6616		2
Franke Kindred Canada Ltd 1000 Kindred Rd ... Midland ON L4R4K9 **Fax Area Code:* 866 ■ *Web:* www.franke.com	705-526-5427	227-3035*	480
Frankel Lois (Rep D - FL) 2305 Rayburn House Office Bldg ... Washington DC 20515 *TF:* 866-264-0957 ■ *Web:* frankel.house.gov	202-225-9890		342-2
Frankel PLLC 1707 L St NW Ste 500 ... Washington DC 20036 *Web:* frankelpllc.com	202-293-6841		41
Frankenmuth Convention & Visitors Bureau 635 S Main St ... Frankenmuth MI 48734 *TF:* 800-386-8696 ■ *Web:* www.frankenmuth.org	989-652-6106	652-3841	206
Frankenmuth Historical Assn (FHA) Frankenmuth Historical Museum 613 S Main St ... Frankenmuth MI 48734 *Web:* www.frankenmuthmuseum.org	989-652-9701		637-2
Frankenmuth Insurance 1 Mutual Ave ... Frankenmuth MI 48787 *TF:* 800-234-4433 ■ *Web:* www.fmins.com	989-652-6121		391-4
Frankferd Farms 717 Saxonburg Blvd ... Saxonburg PA 16056 *Web:* www.frankferd.com	724-352-9500	352-9510	297-2
Frankford Candy & Chocolate Company Inc 9300 Ashton Rd ... Philadelphia PA 19114 *Web:* www.frankfordcandy.com	215-735-5200		296-8
Frankfort Area Chamber of Commerce 229 W Main St Ste 102 ... Frankfort KY 40601 *Web:* www.frankfortky.info	502-223-8261	223-5942	139
Frankfort City Hall 315 W Second St PO Box 697 ... Frankfort KY 40601 *Web:* www.frankfort.ky.gov	502-875-8500		337
Frankfort Community Public Library (FCPL) 208 W Clinton St ... Frankfort IN 46041 *Web:* myfcpl.org	765-654-8746	654-8747	434-3
Frankfort Regional Medical Ctr 299 King's Daughters Dr ... Frankfort KY 40601 *TF:* 888-696-4505 ■ *Web:* frankfortregional.com	502-875-5240	226-7936	374-3
Frankfort/Franklin County Tourist & Convention Commission 300 Saint Clair St Ste 102 ... Frankfort KY 40601 *TF:* 800-960-7200 ■ *Web:* www.visitfrankfort.com	502-875-8687		206
Frankfurt Kurnit Klein & Selz Pc 488 Madison Ave 10th Fl ... New York NY 10022 *Web:* fkks.com	212-980-0120	593-9175	428
Frankie Rowland's Steakhouse 104 Jefferson St ... Roanoke VA 24011 *Web:* frankierowlandssteakhouse.com	540-527-2333		671
Frankie's BBQ 1583-1691 W Washington St ... South Bend IN 46628	574-287-8993		671
Frankies 457 Court Street Spuntino 457 Ct St ... Brooklyn NY 11231 *Web:* frankiesspuntino.com	718-403-0033		671
Frankl & Thomas Inc 111 Smith Hines Rd ... Greenville SC 29616 *TF:* 800-832-7746 ■ *Web:* www.frankl-thomas.com	864-288-5050	234-7544	385
Franklin - Oil Region Credit Union 25 E First St ... Oil City PA 16301 *Web:* for-cu.com	814-676-4504		219
Franklin & Prokopik A Professional Corp The B & O Bldg 2 N Charles St Ste 600 ... Baltimore MD 21201 *Web:* www.fandpnet.com	410-752-8700		428
Franklin American Mortgage Co 6100 Tower Cir Ste 600 ... Franklin TN 37067 *TF:* 800-295-1020 ■ *Web:* www.franklinamerican.com	615-778-1000		217
Franklin Area Chamber of Commerce (FACC) 1327 Liberty St ... Franklin PA 16323 *Web:* www.franklinareachamber.org	814-432-5823	437-2453	139
Franklin Art Glass Studios Inc 222 E Sycamore St ... Columbus OH 43206 *TF:* 800-848-7683 ■ *Web:* www.franklinartglass.com	800-848-7683		189-6
Franklin Banner-Tribune 115 Wilson St ... Franklin LA 70538 *Web:* www.banner-tribune.com	337-828-3706	828-2874	532-2
Franklin Cafe 278 Shawmut Ave ... Boston MA 02118 *Web:* www.franklincafe.com	617-350-0010		671
Franklin College 101 Branigin Blvd ... Franklin IN 46131 **Fax Area Code:* 317 ■ *TF:* 800-852-0232 ■ *Web:* www.franklincollege.edu	800-852-0232	738-8274*	166
Franklin Corp 600 Franklin Dr ... Houston MS 38851 *Web:* franklincorp.com	662-456-4286		319-2
Franklin Correctional Ctr 5918 NC 39 Hwy S PO Box 155 ... Bunn NC 27508 *Web:* www.ncdps.gov	919-496-6119	496-6032	213
Franklin Correctional Facility 62 Bare Hill Rd ... Malone NY 12953 *Web:* www.doccs.ny.gov	518-483-6040		213
Franklin County 33 Market St Ste 203 ... Apalachicola FL 32320 *Web:* www.franklincountyflorida.com	850-653-8861	653-8279	338
Franklin County PO Box 607 ... Benton IL 62812 *Web:* www.franklincountyil.gov	618-438-3221	435-3405	338
Franklin County 459 Main St ... Brookville IN 47012 *Web:* franklincounty.in.gov	765-647-5111	647-3224	338
Franklin County 211 Athens St PO Box 313 ... Carnesville GA 30521 *Web:* franklincountyga.gov	706-384-4390	384-3506	338
Franklin County 14 N Main St ... Chambersburg PA 17201 *Web:* www.franklincountypa.gov	717-264-4125	267-3438	338
Franklin County 373 S High St ... Columbus OH 43215 *Web:* clerk.franklincountyohio.gov	614-525-3600		338
Franklin County 615 Wilton Rd ... Farmington ME 04938 *Web:* www.franklincountymaine.org	207-778-4215	778-2438	338
Franklin County 321 W Main St ... Frankfort KY 40601 *Web:* franklincounty.ky.gov	502-875-8751	875-8755	338
Franklin County 405 15th Ave ... Franklin NE 68939 *Web:* co.franklin.ne.us	308-425-6202	425-6093	338
Franklin County 12 First Ave NW Ste 203 ... Hampton IA 50441 *Web:* www.co.franklin.ia.us	641-456-4375	456-5628	338
Franklin County 113 Market St ... Louisburg NC 27549 *Web:* www.franklincountync.us	919-496-5994	496-2683	338
Franklin County 355 W Main St ... Malone NY 12953 *TF:* 800-397-8686 ■ *Web:* www.franklincony.org	518-481-1681	483-0141	338
Franklin County PO Box 267 ... Meadville MS 39653 *Web:* franklin.msghn.org	601-384-2320		338
Franklin County 200 N Kaufman St ... Mount Vernon TX 75457 *Web:* www.co.franklin.tx.us	903-537-2342		338
Franklin County 315 S Main St ... Ottawa KS 66067 *Web:* www.franklincoks.org	785-229-3485	229-3419	338
Franklin County 211 W Commercial St ... Ozark AR 72949 **Fax Area Code:* 501	479-667-0075	609-9887*	338
Franklin County 1016 N Fourth Ave ... Pasco WA 99301 *Web:* www.co.franklin.wa.us	509-545-3535	545-3573	338
Franklin County 39 W Oneida St ... Preston ID 83263 *Web:* www.franklincountyidaho.org	208-852-1090	852-1094	338
Franklin County 1255 Franklin St ... Rocky Mount VA 24151 *Web:* www.franklincountyva.gov	540-483-3030		338
Franklin County 405 N Jackson Ave PO Box 1028 ... Russellville AL 35653 *Web:* www.franklincountyal.org	256-332-8850		338
Franklin County 2 N Main St ... Saint Albans VT 05478 *Web:* www.fcrccvt.com	802-524-2444		338
Franklin County 400 E Locust ... Union MO 63084 *Web:* www.franklinmo.org	636-583-6355	583-7320	338
Franklin County 855 Dinah Shore Blvd Ste 3 ... Winchester TN 37398 *Web:* www.franklincotn.us	931-967-2905		338
Franklin County Chamber of Commerce 395 Main St ... Greenfield MA 01301 *Web:* franklincc.org	413-773-5463	773-7008	139
Franklin County Chamber of Commerce 103 N Jackson Ave ... Russellville AL 35653 *Web:* franklincountychamber.org	256-332-1760	332-1740	139
Franklin County Chamber of Commerce 44 Chamber Way PO Box 280 ... Winchester TN 37398 *Web:* www.franklincountychamber.com	931-967-6788		139
Franklin County Library 105 S Porter St ... Winchester TN 37398 *Web:* www.franklincountylibrary.org	931-967-3706	962-1477	434-3
Franklin County Library 355 Franklin St ... Rocky Mount VA 24151 *Web:* library.franklincountyva.gov	540-483-3098	483-6652	434-3
Franklin County Veterans Memorial 300 W Broad St ... Columbus OH 43215 *Web:* www.fcvm.com	614-221-5938		205
Franklin Covey Co 2200 W Parkway Blvd ... Salt Lake City UT 84119 *NYSE:* FC ■ *TF:* 800-827-1776 ■ *Web:* www.franklincovey.com	801-817-1776		765
Franklin Crates Inc 311 NE Bay 6th Ave ... Micanopy FL 32667	352-466-3141		200
Franklin Credit Management Corp 101 Hudson St ... Jersey City NJ 07302 **Fax Area Code:* 201 ■ *TF:* 800-255-5897 ■ *Web:* www.franklincredit.com	800-255-5897	839-4512*	217
Franklin Creek State Natural Area 1872 Twist Rd ... Franklin Grove IL 61031 *Web:* www2.illinois.gov	815-456-2878		565
Franklin D. Roosevelt Presidential Library & Museum 4079 Albany Post Rd ... Hyde Park NY 12538 *TF:* 800-337-8474 ■ *Web:* fdrlibrary.org	845-486-7770	486-1147	434-2
Franklin D. Roosevelt State Park 2957 Crompond Rd ... Yorktown Heights NY 10598 *Web:* parks.ny.gov	914-245-4434		565
Franklin Display Group Inc 910 E Lincoln Ave ... Belvidere IL 61008 *Web:* www.franklindisplay.com	815-544-6676	547-5356	73
Franklin Electric Co 10 Twosome Dr ... Moorestown NJ 08057 *Web:* www.franklinelectric.net	856-963-0541		186
Franklin Electric Company Inc 9255 Coverdale Rd ... Fort Wayne IN 46809 *NASDAQ:* FELE ■ *TF:* 800-962-3787 ■ *Web:* franklin-electric.com	260-824-2900	824-2909	518
Franklin Empire 8421 Darnley Rd ... Montreal QC H4T2B2 *TF:* 800-361-5044 ■ *Web:* www.feinc.com	514-341-3720	341-3907	253
Franklin Feed & Supply Co 1977 Philadelphia Ave ... Chambersburg PA 17201 *Web:* franklinhardwareandpetcenter.com	717-264-6148	264-7865	447
Franklin Fibre-Lamitex Corp 903 E 13th St ... Wilmington DE 19802 *TF:* 800-233-9739 ■ *Web:* www.franklinfibre.com	302-652-3621	571-9754	599

	City	State	ZIP	Phone	Fax	Class
Franklin Financial Group Inc 755 Maidstone Ct *Web:* www.franklinfinancialgroup.com	Cincinnati	OH	45230	513-231-4927	231-5094	509
Franklin G. Burroughs-Simeon B Chapin Art Museum 3100 S Ocean Blvd *Web:* www.myrtlebeachartmuseum.org	Myrtle Beach	SC	29577	843-238-2510		520
Franklin Homes Inc 10655 Hwy 43 **Fax Area Code:* 256 ■ *TF:* 800-332-4511 ■ *Web:* www.franklinhomesusa.com	Russellville	AL	35653	800-332-4511	331-2203*	505
Franklin Imaging LLC 500 Schrock Rd *TF:* 877-885-6894 ■ *Web:* www.franklinimaging.com	Columbus	OH	43229	614-885-6894		627
Franklin (Independent City) 1020 Pretlow St *Web:* www.courts.state.va.us	Franklin	VA	23851	757-562-8550	562-1156	338
Franklin Institute 4745 Hwy 6 N *Web:* www.franklininstitute.net	Houston	TX	77084	832-683-4792		685
Franklin Institute, The 222 N 20th St *Web:* www.fi.edu	Philadelphia	PA	19103	215-448-1200	448-1235	520
Franklin Interiors Inc 2740 Smallman St Ste 600 *Web:* franklininteriors.com	Pittsburgh	PA	15222	412-261-2525		321
Franklin Intl 2020 Bruck St *TF:* 800-877-4583 ■ *Web:* www.franklininternational.com	Columbus	OH	43207	614-443-0241		3
Franklin Iron and Metal Corp 1939 E 1st St *Web:* www.franklin-iron.com	Dayton	OH	45403	937-253-8184		686
Franklin Journal 187 Wilton Rd *Web:* www.thefranklinjournal.com	Farmington	ME	04938	207-778-2075	778-6970	637-9
Franklin Karibjanian & Law PLLC 1101 17th St NW Ste 820 *Web:* fkl-law.com	Washington	DC	20036	202-857-3434		41
Franklin Local School District 4000 Millers Ln *TF:* 800-846-4976 ■ *Web:* www.franklinlocalschools.org	Duncan Falls	OH	43734	740-674-5203		685
Franklin Mutual Insurance Co 5 Broad St *TF:* 800-842-0551 ■ *Web:* www.fmiweb.com	Branchville	NJ	07826	973-948-3120	948-7190	391-4
Franklin Park Associates LLC 251 St Asaphs Rd Three Bala Plz Ste 500 W *Web:* franklinparkllc.com	Bala Cynwyd	PA	19004	610-822-0500		401
Franklin Park Conservatory & Botanical Gardens 1777 E Broad St *Web:* www.fpconservatory.org	Columbus	OH	43203	614-715-8000	715-8199	97
Franklin Park Zoo 1 Franklin Park Rd *Web:* www.zoonewengland.org	Boston	MA	02121	617-541-5466	989-2025	823
Franklin Pierce University *Rindge* 40 University Dr *TF:* 800-437-0048 ■ *Web:* www.franklinpierce.edu	Rindge	NH	03461	603-899-4000	899-4394	166
Franklin Precision Industry Inc (FPI) 3220 Bowling Green Rd *Web:* www.fpik.com	Franklin	KY	42134	270-598-4300		60
Franklin Press Inc 1391 Highland Rd *TF:* 800-375-0504 ■ *Web:* gofranklingo.com	Baton Rouge	LA	70802	225-387-0504	344-5024	5
Franklin Real Estate Services & Abstracting Company Inc 458 E King St *Web:* franklinrealestateinc.com	Chambersburg	PA	17201	717-264-3290		653
Franklin Resources Inc 1 Franklin Pkwy Bldg 970 First Fl *NYSE: BEN* ■ **Fax Area Code:* 650 ■ *TF:* 800-632-2301 ■ *Web:* www.franklintempleton.com	San Mateo	CA	94403	800-223-2141	525-7141*	401
Franklin Rural Electric Co-op 1560 Hwy 65 PO Box 437 *TF:* 800-750-3557 ■ *Web:* www.franklinrec.coop	Hampton	IA	50441	641-456-2557	456-5183	245
Franklin Southampton Economic Development 601 N Mechanic St Ste 300 *Web:* www.franklinsouthamptonva.com	Franklin	VA	23851	757-562-1958		393
Franklin Special School District 507 New Hwy 96 W *Web:* fssd.org	Franklin	TN	37064	615-794-6624	790-4716	685
Franklin Sports Inc 17 Campanelli Pkwy *TF:* 800-225-8649 ■ *Web:* franklinsports.com	Stoughton	MA	02072	781-344-1111	341-0333	710
Franklin Square Public Library, The 19 Lincoln Rd *Web:* www.franklinsquarepl.org	Franklin Square	NY	11010	516-488-3444		434-3
Franklin Street Properties Corp (FSP) 401 Edgewater Pl *NYSE: FSP* ■ *TF:* 877-686-9496 ■ *Web:* www.fspreit.com	Wakefield	MA	01880	800-950-6288		654
Franklin Supply Inc 75 Lee St *Web:* franklinsupplyinc.com	Franklin	LA	70538	337-828-3208		297-8
Franklin Team Inc, The 5205 S Mason Rd Ste 190 *Web:* thefranklinteaminc.com	Katy	TX	77450	281-347-2200		652
Franklin Technology Ctr MSSU Campus 3950 E Newman Rd *Web:* joplinftc.ss11.sharpschool.com	Joplin	MO	64801	417-659-4400		167-3
Franklin Township Chamber of Commerce 675 Franklin Blvd *Web:* www.franklinchambernj.org	Somerset	NJ	08873	732-545-7044		139
Franklin Township Public Library 485 DeMott Ln *Web:* www.franklintwp.org	Somerset	NJ	08873	732-873-8700	873-0746	434-3
Franklin Truck Parts Inc 6925 Bandini Blvd *Web:* www.franklintruckparts.com	Commerce	CA	90040	323-726-1034		770
Franklin University 201 S Grant Ave *TF:* 877-341-6300 ■ *Web:* www.franklin.edu	Columbus	OH	43215	614-797-4700		166
Franklin W. Olin College of Engineering 1000 Olin Way *Web:* www.olin.edu	Needham	MA	02492	781-292-2300	292-2210	166
Franklin, The 164 E 87th St *TF:* 800-607-4009 ■ *Web:* www.franklinhotel.com	New York	NY	10128	212-369-1000	369-8000	379
Franklin/Kerr Press LLC 349-L Copperfield Blvd Ste 502 *Web:* www.franklinkerr.com	Concord	NC	28025	704-659-3915		637-2
Franklin-Pierce Schools 315 129th St S *Web:* fpschools.org	Tacoma	WA	98444	253-298-3000		685
Franklin-Southampton Area Chamber of Commerce 108 W Third Ave *Web:* fsachamber.com	Franklin	VA	23851	757-562-4900	562-6138	139
Frankly Media LLC 50 W 17th St *Web:* www.franklymedia.com	New York	NY	10011	212-931-1200		658
Franks Bike Shop 553 Grand St *Web:* www.franksbikes.com	New York	NY	10002	212-533-6332		711
Franks International Services Inc 10260 Westheimer Rd Ste 700 *Web:* franksinternational.com	Houston	TX	77042	281-966-7300		45
Franks Koenig & Neuwelt LLC 8371 N Military Trail Ste 101 *Web:* franksandkoenig.com	Palm Beach Gardens	FL	33410	561-616-3800		41
Franks Supply Company Inc 3311 Stanford Dr NE *TF:* 800-432-5254 ■ *Web:* www.franks-supply.com	Albuquerque	NM	87107	505-884-0000	884-1787	358
Frankston Packaging 699 N Frankston Hwy *TF:* 800-881-1495 ■ *Web:* frankstonpackaging.com	Frankston	TX	75763	903-876-2550		557
FranNet LLC 10302 Brookridge Village Blvd Ste 201 *Web:* www.frannet.com	Louisville	KY	40291	502-753-2380		196
Fransmart Inc 105 Oronoco St Ste 200 *Web:* www.fransmart.com	Alexandria	VA	22314	703-537-5396	543-0750	195
Fran-TEC Computer PO Box 261 *Web:* www.fran-tec.com	Somerset	MA	02726	508-675-3950	677-3258	35
Frantic Films 220 Portage Ave Ste 1300 *Web:* franticfilms.com	Winnipeg	MB	R3C0A5	204-949-0070	949-0050	514
Frantz Group Inc, The 1245 Cheyenne Ave *TF:* 800-707-0064 ■ *Web:* www.thefrantzgroup.com	Grafton	WI	53024	262-204-6000		195
Frantz McConnell & Seymour LLP 550 Main Ave Ste 500 *Web:* www.fmsllp.com	Knoxville	TN	37902	865-546-9321	637-5249	445
Frantz Wholesale Nursery LLC 12161 Delaware Rd *Web:* www.frantznursery.com	Hickman	CA	95323	209-874-1760		202
Franz Family Bakeries 340 NE 11th St *Web:* franzbakery.com	Portland	OR	97232	541-772-5816		296-1
Franz Jevne State Park State Hwy 11 *Web:* www.dnr.state.mn.us	Birchdale	MN	56629	218-647-8592		565
Franzen & Franzen LLP 125 E De La Guerra St Ste 201 *Web:* franzencpa.com	Santa Barbara	CA	93101	805-563-0821		2
Franzen Graphics Inc 5300 WI-42 *Web:* franzengraphics.com	Sheboygan	WI	53083	920-565-4656		627
Frasca International Inc 906 E Airport Rd *Web:* www.frasca.com	Urbana	IL	61802	217-344-9200	344-9207	703
Frascati 1901 Hyde St *Web:* www.frascatisf.com	San Francisco	CA	94109	415-928-1406		671
Frasco Investigative Services 215 W Alameda Ave *TF:* 877-372-7261 ■ *Web:* frasco.com	Burbank	CA	91502	877-372-7261	734-6478	400
Fraser Direct Distribution Services Ltd 8300 Lawson Rd *Web:* www.fraserdirect.ca	Milton	ON	L9T0A4	905-877-4411		314
Fraser Forbes Real Estate services 6862 Elm St Ste 820 *Web:* fraserforbes.com	McLean	VA	22101	703-790-9400		652
Fraser Health Authority Central City Tower 13450 - 102nd Ave Ste 400 *TF:* 877-935-5669 ■ *Web:* www.fraserhealth.ca	Surrey	BC	V3T0H1	604-587-4600	587-4666	353
Fraser Optical 32925 Groesbeck Hwy *Web:* www.fraseroptical.com	Fraser	MI	48026	586-293-8888	859-0233	544
Fraser Shipyards Inc 1 Clough Ave *Web:* www.frasershipyards.com	Superior	WI	54880	715-394-7787	394-2807	698
Fraser Stryker PC LLO 500 Energy Plz 409 S 17th St *TF:* 800-544-6041 ■ *Web:* www.fraserstryker.com	Omaha	NE	68102	402-341-6000		428
Fraser Trebilcock Davis & Dunlap PC 124 W Allegan St Ste 1000 *Web:* www.fraserlawfirm.com	Lansing	MI	48933	517-482-5800		428
Fraser Watson Croutch LLP (FWC) 100 W Broadway Ste 650 *Web:* www.fwclawyers.com	Glendale	CA	91210	818-543-1380	543-1389	445
Fraser Yachts Florida Inc 1800 Southeast Tenth Ave Ste 400 *Web:* www.fraseryachts.com	Fort Lauderdale	FL	33316	954-463-0600		41
Fratelli 499 Terry Fox Dr *Web:* www.fratelli.ca	Ottawa	ON	K2T1H7	613-592-0225		671
Fratelli 124 N Nevada Ave *Web:* fratelliristorante.com	Colorado Springs	CO	80903	719-575-9571		671
Fratelli Beretta USA Inc 750 Clark Dr *Web:* www.fratelliberettausa.com	Mount Olive	NJ	07828	201-438-0723		296-26
Fratello's Ristorante Italiano 155 Dow St *Web:* fratellos.com	Manchester	NH	03101	603-624-2022		671
Fraternal Order of Alaska State Troopers Museum 245 W 5th Ave *TF:* 800-770-5050 ■ *Web:* foast.org	Anchorage	AK	99501	907-279-5050	279-5054	520
Fraternal Order of Eagles 1623 Gateway Cir S *Web:* www.foe.com	Grove City	OH	43123	614-883-2200	883-2201	457-10
Fraternal Order of Police (FOP) 701 Marriott Dr *TF:* 800-451-2711 ■ *Web:* fop.net	Nashville	TN	37214	615-399-0900	399-0400	48-15
Fraternal Order of Police 11630 Caroline Rd *Web:* fop5.org	Philadelphia	PA	19154	215-629-3600		414
Fraternity of Alpha Kappa Lambda 354 Gradle Dr *Web:* akl.org	Carmel	IN	46032	317-564-8003		48-16
Fratus Law Group LLC 566 Baltimore Annapolis Blvd *TF:* 844-240-1557 ■ *Web:* fratuslaw.com	Severna Park	MD	21146	410-205-7100		41

	Phone	Fax	Class
Fraulob * Brown 2207 J St, Sacramento CA 95816 *Web:* rivercityattorneys.com	916-442-5835		41
Fravert Services Inc 133 W Park Dr, Birmingham AL 35211 *Web:* www.fravert.com	205-940-7180		9
Fraze Pavilion 695 Lincoln Pk Blvd, Dayton OH 45429 *Web:* www.fraze.com	937-296-3300	296-3302	572
Frazer & Feldman LLP 1415 Kellum Pl, Garden City NY 11530 *Web:* frazerfeldman.com	516-742-7777	742-7868	41
Frazer Lanier Company Inc 300 Water St, Montgomery AL 36104 *TF:* 800-223-2631 ■ *Web:* www.frazerlanier.com	334-265-8483	265-8524	690
Frazier & Deeter LLC 1230 Peachtree St NE Ste 1500, Atlanta GA 30309 *Web:* www.frazierdeeter.com	404-253-7500	573-4201	194
Frazier & Frazier Industries Inc 817 S First St PO Box 279, Coolidge TX 76635 *Web:* www.ffcastings.com	254-786-2293	786-2284	307
Frazier Healthcare 601 Union St 2 Union Sq Ste 3200, Seattle WA 98101 *Web:* www.frazierhealthcare.com	206-621-7200		792
Frazier History Museum 829 W Main St, Louisville KY 40202 *Web:* fraziermuseum.org	502-753-5663		520
Frazier Industrial Co 91 Fairview Ave, Long Valley NJ 07853 *TF:* 800-859-1342 ■ *Web:* www.frazier.com	908-876-3001	876-3615	286
Frazier Precision Instrument Company Inc 925 Sweeney Dr, Hagerstown MD 21740 *Web:* frazierinstrument.com	301-790-2585	790-2589	472
Frazier Rehabilitation Institute 220 Abraham Flexner Way, Louisville KY 40202 *TF:* 800-333-2230 ■ *Web:* www.uoflhealthnetwork.org	502-582-7400	582-7477	374-6
FRC (Family Research Council) 801 G St NW, Washington DC 20001 *Web:* www.frc.org	202-393-2100	393-2134	48-6
FRC Component Products Inc 1511 S Benjamin Ave, Mason City IA 50401 *Web:* www.frccorp.com	641-424-0370	424-1945	253
FRCC (Front Range Community College) *Boulder County* 2190 Miller Dr, Longmont CO 80501 *TF:* 888-800-9198 ■ *Web:* www.frontrange.edu	303-678-3722	678-3699	162
Frecom 435 W Baltimore Pk, West Grove PA 19390 *Web:* www.frecominc.com	610-869-3307		196
Fred B. Goldberg Pc 10440 Little Patuxent Pkwy Ste 900, Columbia MD 21044 *Web:* fredbgoldberg.com	410-844-5221		41
Fred Barton Company Inc 565 E Milwaukee St, Detroit MI 48202 *Web:* www.fredbartonco.com	313-872-9440		189-10
Fred C. ChurchInc 41 Wellman St, Lowell MA 01851 *TF:* 800-225-1865 ■ *Web:* www.fredcchurch.com	978-458-1865	454-1865	390
Fred Christen & Sons Co 714 George St, Toledo OH 43608 *Web:* www.toledochamber.com	419-243-4161	243-1292	697
Fred D. Pfening Co 1075 W Fifth Ave, Columbus OH 43212 *Web:* www.pfening.com	614-294-5361		207
Fred Daniel & Sons Inc 5727 S Lewis Ave Ste 420, Tulsa OK 74105 *Web:* fdands.com	918-582-8206		390
Fred Del Marva (FDM) 21666 N 58th Ave, Glendale AZ 85308 *Web:* www.freddelmarva.com	623-566-5300	566-5354	196
Fred Gannon Rocky Bayou State Park 4281 E Hwy 20, Niceville FL 32578 *Web:* www.floridastateparks.org	850-833-9144		565
Fred Garrison Oil Co 1107 Walter Griffin St PO Box 100, Plainview TX 79073 *Web:* www.allstarfuel.com	806-296-6353	296-9270	579
Fred Heroman's Florist 6868 Florida Blvd, Baton Rouge LA 70806 *Web:* www.flowerlandflowers.com	225-927-6070		292
Fred Hutchinson Cancer Research Ctr 1100 Fairview Ave N PO Box 19024, Seattle WA 98109 *Web:* www.fredhutch.org	206-667-5000	667-4051	668
Fred Jones Enterprises LLC 6200 SW 29th St Ste A, Oklahoma City OK 73179 **Fax Area Code:* 405 ■ *TF:* 800-927-7845 ■ *Web:* www.fred-jones.com	800-927-7845	231-3233*	60
Fred Knapp Engraving Company Inc 5102 Douglas Ave, Racine WI 53402 *TF:* 800-558-5950 ■ *Web:* air-logic.com	262-639-9035	639-5996	201
Fred Loya Insurance 1800 Lee Trevino Ste 201, El Paso TX 79936 *TF:* 800-554-0595 ■ *Web:* www.fredloya.com	915-590-5692		390
Fred M. Schildwachter & Sons Inc 1400 Ferris Pl, Bronx NY 10461 *TF:* 800-642-3646 ■ *Web:* schildwachteroil.com	718-828-2500	828-3661	316
Fred Netterville Lumber Co 3975 Buffalo Rd, Woodville MS 39669 *TF:* 800-343-4577 ■ *Web:* www.nettervillelumber.com	601-888-4343	888-6469	683
Fred Oberlender & Associates Inc 10421 Sanden Dr, Dallas TX 75238 *Web:* oberlender.com	214-343-1946		261
Fred Olivieri Construction Company Inc 6315 Promway Ave NW, North Canton OH 44720 *TF:* 800-847-5085 ■ *Web:* www.fredolivieri.com	330-494-1007		186
Fred Peet 55 Patchen Rd, South Burlington VT 05403 *Web:* peetlaw.com	802-860-4767		41
Fred Porter & Associates Inc 1200 21st St, Bakersfield CA 93301 *Web:* www.portercivil.com	661-327-0362	327-1065	261
Fred Pryor Seminars 9757 Metcalf Ave, Overland Park KS 66212 **Fax Area Code:* 913 ■ *TF:* 800-780-8476 ■ *Web:* www.pryor.com	800-780-8476	967-8842*	765
Fred Rau Dairy 10255 W Manning Ave, Fresno CA 93706	559-237-3393		10-3
Fred Safford Forestry Consultant LLC 4175 W Highland Pky, Buffalo NY 14219 *Web:* www.fsforestry.com	716-574-6432		196
Fred Usinger Inc 1030 N Old World 3rd St, Milwaukee WI 53203 *TF:* 800-558-9998 ■ *Web:* www.usinger.com	414-276-9100	291-5277	296-26
Fred Weber Inc 2320 Creve Coeur Mill Rd, Maryland Heights MO 63043 *TF:* 866-739-8855 ■ *Web:* www.fredweberinc.com	314-344-0070	344-0970	188-4
Fred Wilson & Associates Inc 3970 Hendricks Ave, Jacksonville FL 32207 *Web:* www.fredwilson.com	904-398-8636		261
Fred's Leather Shop & Shoe Repair 309 N Marion Ave Ste 1, Lake City FL 32055 *Web:* www.fredsleathershopandshoerepair.com	386-752-0083		430
Fredd J. Haas Law Offices PC 5001 SW Ninth St, Des Moines IA 50315 *Web:* freddhaas.com	515-256-6301		41
Freddie Georges Production Group 15362 Graham St, Huntington Beach CA 92649 *Web:* freddiegeorges.com	714-367-9260	367-9261	184
Freddie Mac *Southeast/Southwest Region* 2300 Windy Ridge Pkwy SE Ste 200 N Twr, Atlanta GA 30339 *TF:* 800-373-3343 ■ *Web:* www.freddiemac.com	770-857-8800		509
Freddie Villacci Insurance Agency Inc 2241 W Irving Park Rd, Chicago IL 60618 *Web:* freddiev.com	773-463-7733		390
Freddie's Beach Bar & Restaurant 555 23rd St S, Arlington VA 22202 *Web:* freddiesbeachbar.com	703-685-0555		671
Frederic Dorwart Lawyers 124 E 4th St, Tulsa OK 74103 *Web:* www.fdlaw.com	918-583-9922		428
Frederic Printing Co 14701 E 38th Ave, Aurora CO 80011 *Web:* www.fredericprinting.com	303-371-7990		627
Frederic Remington Art Museum (FRAM) 303 Washington St, Ogdensburg NY 13669 *Web:* www.fredericremington.org	315-393-2425		637-2
Frederic W. Cook & Company Inc 685 Third Ave 28th Fl, New York NY 10017 *Web:* www.fwcook.com	212-986-6330		193
Frederick & Hagle 129 W Main, Urbana IL 61801 *Web:* frederickandhagle.com	217-367-6092		41
Frederick Community College 7932 Opossumtown Pk, Frederick MD 21702 *Web:* www.frederick.edu	301-846-2400		162
Frederick County 107 N Kent St, Winchester VA 22601 *Web:* www.fcva.us	540-665-5600	667-0370	338
Frederick County Chamber of Commerce 118 N Market St Ste 200, Frederick MD 21701 *Web:* www.frederickchamber.org	301-662-4164	846-4427	139
Frederick County Public Libraries (FCPL) 110 E Patrick St, Frederick MD 21701 *Web:* www.fcpl.org	301-600-1630		434-3
Frederick Douglass National Historic Site 1900 Anacostia Dr SE, Washington DC 20020 *Web:* www.nps.gov	202-426-5961	426-0880	564
Frederick Goldman Inc 154 W 14th St, New York NY 10011 *TF:* 800-221-3232 ■ *Web:* www.b2b.fgoldman.com	800-221-3232		411
Frederick Health 400 W 7th St, Frederick MD 21701 *Web:* www.frederickhealth.org	240-566-3300		374-3
Frederick J. Tansill & Associates LLC 6723 Whittier Ave Ste 104, McLean VA 22101 *Web:* fredtansill.com	703-847-1359	847-1357	41
Frederick L. Ehrman Medical Library *New York University Medical Ctr School of Medicine* 550 First Ave Medical Science Bldg Ground Fl, New York NY 10016 *Web:* hsl.med.nyu.edu	212-263-7238	263-6534	434-1
Frederick Law Olmsted National Historic Site 99 Warren St, Brookline MA 02445 *Web:* www.nps.gov	617-566-1689	232-4073	564
Frederick Motor Co, The 1 Waverley Dr, Frederick MD 21702 *TF:* 800-734-9118 ■ *Web:* www.fredmotorco.com	800-734-9118		57
Frederick News Post 351 Ballenger Center Dr, Frederick MD 21703 *TF:* 800-486-1177 ■ *Web:* www.fredericknewspost.com	301-662-1177		532-2
Frederick Quinn Corp 103 S Church St, Addison IL 60101 *Web:* www.fquinncorp.com	630-628-8500	628-8595	186
Frederick Steel LLC 630 Glendale Milford Rd, Cincinnati OH 45215 *TF:* 800-949-1340 ■ *Web:* www.fredericksteel.com	513-475-3200		492
Frederick Taylor University 2050 W Chapman Ave Ste 108, Orange CA 92868 *TF:* 888-370-7589 ■ *Web:* ftu.edu	714-949-2304	602-7243	507
Frederick Ward Associates (FWA) 5 S Main St, Bel Air MD 21014 *Web:* www.frederickward.com	410-838-7900		192
Frederick Wildman & Sons Ltd 111 Broadway Ste 1102, New York NY 10006 *TF:* 800-733-9463 ■ *Web:* www.frederickwildman.com	212-355-0700	355-4719	81-3
Frederick's Machine & Tool Shop Inc 3903 2nd St Acadiana Regional Airport, New Iberia LA 70560 *TF:* 800-326-6130 ■ *Web:* fredmach.com	337-367-9943	367-9959	537
Frederick's of Hollywood 6255 Sunset Blvd 6th Fl, Los Angeles CA 90028 *Web:* www.fredericks.com	323-466-5151		157-6
Fredericks Co, The 2400 Philmont Ave, Huntingdon Valley PA 19006 *TF:* 800-367-2919 ■ *Web:* www.frederickscompany.com	215-947-2500	947-7464	332
Fredericks Michael & Co 430 Park Ave, New York NY 10022 *Web:* fm-co.com	212-732-1600		401
Fredericksburg & Spotsylvania National Military Park 120 Chatham Ln, Fredericksburg VA 22405 *Web:* www.nps.gov	540-693-3200	371-1907	564
Fredericksburg Chamber of Commerce 302 E Austin St, Fredericksburg TX 78624 *Web:* www.fredericksburg-texas.com	830-997-6523	997-8588	206
Fredericksburg City Public Schools 817 Princess Anne St, Fredericksburg VA 22401 *Web:* www.cityschools.com	540-372-1130	372-1111	685
Fredericksburg (Independent City) 715 Princess Ann St Rm 217, Fredericksburg VA 22401 *Web:* www.fredericksburgva.gov	540-372-1028	372-1201	338

Name / Address	City	State	ZIP	Phone	Fax	Class
Fredericksburg Regional Chamber of Commerce 2300 Fall Hill Ave Ste 240 *TF:* 888-338-0252 ■ *Web:* www.fredericksburgchamber.org	Fredericksburg	VA	22401	540-373-9400	373-9570	139
Fredericksburg Standard-Radio Post 712 W Main St *Web:* www.fredericksburgstandard.com	Fredericksburg	TX	78624	830-997-2155		532-2
Fredericton Chamber of Commerce 364 York St Ste 200 *Web:* www.frederictonchamber.ca	Fredericton	NB	E3B3P7	506-458-8006	451-1119	137
Fredericton Tourism 11 Carleton St *Web:* www.fredericton.ca	Fredericton	NB	E3B4Y7	506-460-2041		772
Frederik Meijer Gardens & Sculpture Park 1000 E Beltline Ave NE *TF:* 877-975-3171 ■ *Web:* www.meijergardens.org	Grand Rapids	MI	49525	616-957-1580	957-5792	97
Fredonia State University of New York 280 Central Ave *TF:* 800-642-4272 ■ *Web:* www.fredonia.edu	Fredonia	NY	14063	716-673-3111		166
Fredrick, Fredrick & Heller Engineers Inc 672 E Royalton Rd *Web:* www.ffhengineers.com	Broadview Heights	OH	44147	440-546-9696		261
Fredrickson, Mazeika & Grant LLP 5720 Oberlin Dr *TF:* 800-231-8440 ■ *Web:* fmglegal.com	San Diego	CA	92121	858-642-2002		428
Fredson Travel Inc 11077 Biscayne Blvd Ste 401	Miami	FL	33161	305-577-8422		772
Free Flite Inc 2949 Canton Rd Ste 1000 *Web:* freeflite.com	Marietta	GA	30066	770-422-5237		711
Free Lance Star 616 Amelia St *TF:* 800-877-0500 ■ *Web:* www.fredericksburg.com	Fredericksburg	VA	22401	540-374-5000	373-8455	532-2
Free Library of Philadelphia 1901 Vine St *Web:* www.freelibrary.org	Philadelphia	PA	19103	215-686-5322		434-3
Free Press 418 S Second St *TF:* 800-657-4662 ■ *Web:* www.mankatofreepress.com	Mankato	MN	56001	507-625-4451	388-4355	532-2
Free Press Standard, The 43 E Main St *Web:* freepressstandard.com	Carrollton	OH	44615	330-627-5591		532-3
Free Service Tire Company Inc 183 Lynn Rd *TF:* 855-646-1423 ■ *Web:* freeservicetire.com	Johnson City	TN	37602	423-979-2250	979-2262	755
Free Sons of Israel, The PO Box 10485 *Web:* freesons.org	Westbury	NY	11590	516-775-4919		48-13
Free Speech TV (FSTV) PO Box 44099 *TF:* 877-378-8669 ■ *Web:* freespeech.org	Denver	CO	80201	303-542-4813		740
Free Spirit Publishing Inc 217 Fifth Ave N Ste 200 *TF:* 800-735-7323 ■ *Web:* www.freespirit.com	Minneapolis	MN	55401	612-338-2068		637-2
Free State Growers Inc 12819 198th St *Web:* www.armasson.com	Linwood	KS	66052	913-301-3281	301-3288	369
Free State Veterinary Hospital LLC 1825 Wakarusa Dr *Web:* wakavet.com	Lawrence	KS	66047	785-843-5577		794
Freebord Manufacturing Inc 455 Irwin St Unit 104 *Web:* freebord.com	San Francisco	CA	94107	415-285-2673		711
Freeborn & Peters 311 S Wacker Dr Ste 3000 *Web:* www.freeborn.com	Chicago	IL	60606	312-360-6000	360-6520	428
Freeborn Tool Company Inc 3304 E Ferry Ave *TF:* 800-523-8988 ■ *Web:* freeborntool.com	Spokane	WA	99202	509-484-3033		350
Freeborn-Mower Co-opeartive Services 2501 E Main St *TF:* 800-734-6421 ■ *Web:* www.fmcs.coop	Albert Lea	MN	56007	507-373-6421	369-0259	245
Freed Advertising LP 1650 Hwy 6 Ste 400 *Web:* www.freedad.com	Sugar Land	TX	77478	281-240-4949		7
Freed Associates Inc 412 Yale Ave *Web:* www.freedassociates.com	Berkeley	CA	94708	510-525-1853	525-6453	196
Freed Maxick & Battaglia CPAs 800 Liberty Bldg *Web:* www.freedmaxick.com	Buffalo	NY	14202	716-847-2651		2
Freed Photography Inc 4931 Cordell Ave *Web:* freedphoto.com	Bethesda	MD	20814	301-652-5452		590
Freed's Bakery LLC 299 Pepsi Rd	Manchester	NH	03109	603-627-7746		68
Freed'S Super Markets Inc 2024 Swamp Pk *Web:* www.freedsmarket.com	Gilbertsville	PA	19525	610-326-4189		345
Freeda Wigs 779 E New York Ave *Web:* www.freeda.com	Brooklyn	NY	11203	718-771-2000		348
Freed-Hardeman University 158 E Main St **Fax Area Code:* 731 ■ *TF:* 800-348-3481 ■ *Web:* www.fhu.edu	Henderson	TN	38340	800-348-3481	989-6047*	166
Freedman & Goldberg CPAS PC 31150 Northwestern Hwy Ste 200 *Web:* freedmangoldberg.com	Farmington Hills	MI	48334	248-626-2400		2
Freedman Boyd Et Al 20 First Plz Ste 700 *Web:* fbdlaw.com	Albuquerque	NM	87102	505-842-9960		41
Freedman Financial Associates Inc 41 Cross St 2nd Fl *Web:* www.freedmanfinancial.com	Peabody	MA	01960	978-531-8108	532-2666	251
Freedman Seating Co 4545 W Augusta Blvd *TF:* 800-443-4540 ■ *Web:* www.freedmanseating.com	Chicago	IL	60651	773-524-2440	252-7450	689
Freedom 95 Radio 645 Industrial Dr *Web:* www.freedom95.us	Franklin	IN	46131	317-736-4040	736-4781	645
Freedom Alliance 22570 Markey Ct Ste 240 *TF:* 800-475-6620 ■ *Web:* freedomalliance.org	Sterling	VA	20166	703-444-7940		615
Freedom Arms Inc 314 Wyoming 239 *Web:* www.freedomarms.com	Freedom	WY	83120	307-883-2468	883-2005	284
Freedom Aviation 310 Hangar Rd *Web:* www.flyfreedom.com	Lynchburg	VA	24502	434-237-8420		167-3
Freedom Cad Services Inc 20 Cotton Rd Ste 201 *Web:* www.freedomcad.com	Nashua	NH	03063	603-864-1300	864-1301	41
Freedom Consulting Group Inc 9881 Broken Land Pkwy Ste 300 *Web:* freedomconsultinggroup.com	Columbia	MD	21046	410-290-9035		225
Freedom Designs Inc 2241 N Madera Rd *TF:* 800-331-8551 ■ *Web:* www.freedomdesigns.com	Simi Valley	CA	93065	805-582-0077		475
Freedom Finanical Bank 1255 Jordan Creek Pkwy *Web:* freedomfinancialbank.com	West Des Moines	IA	50266	515-223-1113		70
Freedom Fire Pro LLC 811 Lester Ln *Web:* www.freefirepro.com	Rogers	AR	72756	479-631-6363		610
Freedom Forum 555 Pennsylvania Ave NW *Web:* www.freedomforuminstitute.org	Washington	DC	20001	202-639-0537		48-7
Freedom From Fear (FFF) 308 Seaview Ave *Web:* www.freedomfromfear.org	Staten Island	NY	10305	718-351-1717		48-17
Freedom from Hunger 1460 Drew Ave Ste 300 *TF:* 800-708-2555 ■ *Web:* www.freedomfromhunger.org	Davis	CA	95618	530-758-6200	758-6241	48-5
Freedom Graphic Systems Inc (FGS) 1101 S Janesville St *TF:* 800-334-3540 ■ *Web:* fgs.com	Milton	WI	53563	800-334-3540		110
Freedom Greeting Card Company Inc 774 American Dr *Web:* www.freedomgreetings.com	Bensalem	PA	19020	215-604-0300		130
Freedom House Inc 120 Wall St 26th Fl *Web:* freedomhouse.org	New York	NY	10005	212-514-8040		194
Freedom Investments Inc 375 Raritan Center Pkwy *TF:* 800-944-4033 ■ *Web:* www.freedominvestments.com	Edison	NJ	08837	800-944-4033	830-1855	690
Freedom Medical Inc 219 Welsh Pool Rd *TF:* 800-784-8849 ■ *Web:* www.freedommedical.com	Exton	PA	19341	610-903-0200	903-0180	264-4
Freedom Meditech Inc 5090 Shoreham Pl Ste 109 *Web:* www.freedom-meditech.com	San Diego	CA	92122	858-638-1433		743
Freedom Middle School 3016 Ridgeland Ave *Web:* www.bsd100.org	Berwyn	IL	60402	708-795-5800		685
Freedom of Mind Resource Ctr 716 Beacon St Ste 590443 *Web:* www.freedomofmind.com	Newton	MA	02459	617-396-4638	628-8153	139
Freedom Oil Co 814 W Chestnut St *Web:* www.freedomoil.com	Bloomington	IL	61701	309-828-7750		324
Freedom Scientific Inc 11800 31st Ct N *TF:* 800-444-4443 ■ *Web:* www.freedomscientific.com	Saint Petersburg	FL	33716	727-803-8000		177
Freedom Technologies Inc 1100 Wilson Blvd Ste 1200 *Web:* freedomtechnologiesinc.com	Arlington	VA	22209	703-516-3020		463
Freedom Technology Solutions Inc 920 Hartford Ave *TF:* 800-940-0040 ■ *Web:* ftssupport.com	Johnston	RI	02919	800-940-0040		225
Freedom Trail 99 Chauncy St Ste 401 *Web:* www.thefreedomtrail.org	Boston	MA	02111	617-357-8300	357-8303	50-3
Freedom Village 23442 El Toro Rd *TF:* 800-584-8084 ■ *Web:* www.freedomvillageorangecounty.org	Lake Forest	CA	92630	949-472-4700		672
Freedom Voices Publications PO Box 423115 *Web:* www.freedomvoices.org	San Francisco	CA	94142	415-558-8759		637-2
FreedomWorks 400 N Capitol St NW Ste 765 *TF:* 888-564-6273 ■ *Web:* www.freedomworks.org	Washington	DC	20001	202-783-3870	942-7649	48-7
Freedonia Group Inc, The 767 Beta Dr *Web:* www.freedoniagroup.com	Cleveland	OH	44143	440-684-9600	646-0484	466
FreeFlight Systems Inc 8080 Tristar Ste 100 *Web:* www.freeflightsystems.com	Irving	TX	75063	254-662-0000	662-9450	57
Freehand Miami 2727 Indian Creek Dr *Web:* freehandhotels.com	Miami Beach	FL	33140	305-531-2727	531-5651	379
Freehold Raceway 130 Park Ave *Web:* www.freeholdraceway.com	Freehold	NJ	07728	732-462-3800	462-2920	642
Freelancers Union 408 Jay St 2nd Fl *TF:* 888-447-9883 ■ *Web:* www.freelancersunion.org	Brooklyn	NY	11201	718-532-1515		414
Freeland Contracting 6689 Kilby Rd	Lucasville	OH	45648	740-981-2819		610
Freeland Cooper & Foreman LLP 150 Spear St Ste 1800 *Web:* www.freelandlaw.com	San Francisco	CA	94105	415-541-0200		428
Freelin-Wade Co 1730 NE Miller St *TF:* 888-373-9233 ■ *Web:* www.freelin-wade.com	McMinnville	OR	97128	503-434-5561	472-1989	370
Freeman 1600 Viceroy Dr Ste 100 *TF:* 800-453-9228 ■ *Web:* www.freeman.com	Dallas	TX	75235	214-445-1000		184
Freeman & Mills Inc 350 S Figueroa St Ste 900 *Web:* freemanmills.com	Los Angeles	CA	90071	213-576-1829		463
Freeman & Supran PA 600 Northlake Blvd *Web:* freemansupran.com	North Palm Beach	FL	33408	561-655-6025		41
Freeman Coliseum 3201 E Houston St *Web:* www.freemancoliseum.com	San Antonio	TX	78219	210-226-1177	226-5081	720
Freeman Corp, The 415 Magnolia St PO Box 96 *Web:* www.freemancorp.com	Winchester	KY	40392	859-744-4311	744-4363	613
Freeman Freeman & Smiley LLP 1888 Century Pk E Ste 1900 *Web:* www.ffslaw.com	Los Angeles	CA	90067	310-255-6100	255-6200	428
Freeman Gas Inc 113 Peake Rd *TF:* 800-277-5730 ■ *Web:* www.freemangas.com	Roebuck	SC	29376	864-582-5475		357
Freeman Health System 1102 W 32nd St *TF:* 800-297-3337 ■ *Web:* www.freemanhealth.com	Joplin	MO	64804	417-347-1111		374-3
Freeman Howard PC 441 E Allen St PO Box 1328 *Web:* freemanhoward.com	Hudson	NY	12534	518-828-2021		41

Name / Address	Phone	Fax	Class
Freeman Industries Inc 2061 State Rte 193 . . . . . Dorset OH 44032 *Web:* www.freemanindustriesinc.com	440-858-2600	858-2006	189-11
Freeman Injury Law PA 5 Harvard Cir Ste 110. . . . . West Palm Beach FL 33409 *TF:* 800-561-7777 ■ *Web:* lawofficesofdeanhfreeman.com	561-272-1504	689-4310	41
Freeman Manufacturing & Supply Co 1101 Moore Rd. . . . . Avon OH 44011 *TF:* 800-321-8511 ■ *Web:* www.freemansupply.com	440-934-1902	934-7200	567
Freeman Manufacturing Co 900 W Chicago Rd . . . . . Sturgis MI 49091 *TF:* 800-253-2091 ■ *Web:* www.freemanmfg.com	269-651-2371	651-8248	477
Freeman Marcus Jewelers 76 Merchants Row . . . . . Rutland VT 05701 *TF:* 800-451-4167 ■ *Web:* rutlanddowntown.com	802-773-2792		410
Freeman Spogli & Co 299 Park Ave 20th Fl . . . . . New York NY 10171 *Web:* www.freemanspogli.com	212-758-2555	758-7499	792
Freeman Webb Co 3810 Bedford Ave Ste 300 . . . . . Nashville TN 37215 *Web:* www.freemanwebb.com	615-271-2700		652
Freeman's Flowers & Event Consultants 2934 Duniven Cir . . . . . Amarillo TX 79109 *TF:* 800-846-3104 ■ *Web:* www.freemansflowers.com	806-355-4451		292
Freeman/Fine Arts of Philadelphia 1808 Chestnut St . . . . . Philadelphia PA 19103 *Web:* www.freemansauction.com	215-563-9275	563-8236	51
Freemason Abbey 209 W Freemason St. . . . . Norfolk VA 23510 *Web:* www.freemasonabbey.com	757-622-3966	622-3592	671
FreeMind Group LLC 423 Brookline Ave Ste 124 . . . . . Boston MA 02215 *Web:* www.freemindconsultants.com	617-648-0340	904-1767	466
Freemire & Associates Inc 1215 Old Dorsey Rd . . . . . Harmans MD 21077 *Web:* freemire.com	410-768-8500		653
Freeport Center Assoc PO Box 160466 . . . . . Clearfield UT 84016 *Web:* www.freeportcenter.com	801-825-9741	825-3587	655
Freeport Marine Supply 47 W Merrick Rd. . . . . Freeport NY 11520 *TF:* 800-645-2565 ■ *Web:* www.freeportmarine.com	516-379-2610	379-2909	770
Freeport Press Inc 121 Main St. . . . . Freeport OH 43973 *Web:* freeportpress.com	740-658-4000		627
Freeport Public Library 100 E Douglas St . . . . . Freeport IL 61032 *Web:* www.freeportpubliclibrary.org	815-233-3000	297-8236	434-3
Freeport Welding and Fabricating Inc 200 N Navigation Blvd . . . . . Freeport TX 77541 *TF:* 800-560-0121 ■ *Web:* www.freeweld.com	979-233-0121	233-0349	91
Freeport West Self Storage Freeport W Industrial Pk Bldg E-4 . . . . . Clearfield UT 84016 *Web:* www.freeportwestselfstorage.com	801-773-7867	825-3819	803-1
Freeport-McMoRan Inc 333 N Central Ave. . . . . Phoenix AZ 85004 *NYSE: FCX* ■ *Web:* www.fcx.com	602-366-8100		501
Freer Gallery of Art / Arthur M Sackler Gallery 1050 Independence Ave SW PO Box 37012 MRC 707 . . . . . Washington DC 20013 *Web:* asia.si.edu	202-633-1000	357-4911	520
Freese & Nichols Inc 4055 International Plz Ste 200 . . . . . Fort Worth TX 76109 *Web:* www.freese.com	817-735-7300	735-7491	261
Freeservers 1253 N Research Way Ste Q-2500 . . . . . Orem UT 84097 *TF:* 800-396-1999 ■ *Web:* www.freeservers.com	800-396-1999		808
FreeState Electric Cooperative Inc 1100 SW Auburn Rd. . . . . Topeka KS 66615 *TF:* 800-794-2011 ■ *Web:* www.kve.coop	785-478-3444		245
Freestone County 103 E Main PO Box 1010. . . . . Fairfield TX 75840 *Web:* www.co.freestone.tx.us	903-389-2635	389-3839	338
Freestone Inn at Wilson Ranch 31 Early Winters Dr. . . . . Mazama WA 98833 *TF:* 800-639-3809 ■ *Web:* www.freestoneinn.com	509-996-3906		669
Freestone Resources Inc 101 W Ave D . . . . . Ennis TX 75119 *Web:* www.freestoneresources.com	972-875-8427		539
Freestyle Photo Biz 5124 Sunset Blvd. . . . . Hollywood CA 90027 *TF:* 800-292-6137 ■ *Web:* www.freestylephoto.biz	800-292-6137		590
Freetech Plastics Inc 2211 Warm Springs Ct . . . . . Fremont CA 94539 *Web:* www.freetechplastics.com	510-651-9996	651-9917	608
Freetown Village Living History Museum PO Box 1041 . . . . . Indianapolis IN 46206 *Web:* www.freetown.org	317-631-1870	631-0224	520
Freetown-Fall River State Forest 110 Slab Bridge Rd. . . . . Assonet MA 02702 *Web:* www.mass.gov	508-644-5522		565
FreeWave Technologies Inc 5395 Pearl Pkwy. . . . . Boulder CO 80301 *TF:* 866-923-6168 ■ *Web:* www.freewave.com	303-381-9200	786-9948	173-3
Freeway Corp 9301 Allen Dr . . . . . Cleveland OH 44125 *Web:* www.freewaycorp.com	216-524-9700	524-7396	75
Freeway Ford Truck Sales Inc 8445 W 45th St. . . . . Lyons IL 60534 *TF:* 888-435-1323 ■ *Web:* www.freewaytruck.com	708-442-9000		57
Freezetone Products Inc 7986 NW 14th St . . . . . Doral FL 33126 *Web:* www.freezetone-usa.com	305-640-0414		145
Freight All Kinds Inc 10885 E 51st Ave . . . . . Denver CO 80239 *TF:* 800-321-7182 ■ *Web:* www.fakinc.com	303-289-5433	289-1940	780
Freight Handlers Inc 310 N Judd Pkwy NE . . . . . Fuquay-Varina NC 27526 *Web:* www.fhiworks.com	919-552-3157		314
Freight Logistics Inc PO Box 1712 . . . . . Medford OR 97501 *TF:* 800-866-7882 ■ *Web:* www.shipfli.com	541-734-5617		311
Freight Transportation Research Associates Inc 1720 N Kinser Pk . . . . . Bloomington IN 47404 **Fax Area Code:* 877 ■ *TF:* 888-988-1699 ■ *Web:* ftrintel.com	812-988-1699	222-9060*	463
FreightCar America Inc 17 Johns St. . . . . Johnstown PA 15901 *NASDAQ: RAIL* ■ **Fax Area Code:* 814 ■ *TF:* 800-458-2235 ■ *Web:* www.freightcaramerica.com	800-458-2235	533-5010*	650
Freightliner Custom Chassis Corp 552 Hyatt St . . . . . Gaffney SC 29341 *TF:* 855-253-0421 ■ *Web:* www.freightlinerchassis.com	864-487-1700		247
Freightliner Northwest 277 Stewart Rd SW. . . . . Pacific WA 98047 **Fax Area Code:* 253 ■ *TF:* 800-523-8014 ■ *Web:* www.freightlinernorthwest.com	800-523-8014	863-6473*	57
Freightliner of Hartford Inc 222 Roberts St . . . . . East Hartford CT 06108 *TF:* 800-453-6967 ■ *Web:* www.freightlinerofhartford.com	800-453-6967		57
Freightliner Specialty Vehicles Inc 2300 S 13th St . . . . . Clinton OK 73601 *TF:* 800-358-7624 ■ *Web:* www.sportchassis.com	580-323-4100	323-4111	59
FreightPros 3307 Northland Dr Ste 360. . . . . Austin TX 78731 *TF:* 888-297-6968 ■ *Web:* www.freightpros.com	888-297-6968		478
Freightquote 901 W Carondelet Dr . . . . . Kansas City MO 64114 *TF:* 800-323-5441 ■ *Web:* www.freightquote.com	800-323-5441		312
FreightWaves 405 Cherry St. . . . . Chattanooga TN 37402 *Web:* www.freightwaves.com	423-205-3050		568
Freimark & Associates Inc 7056 Corporate Way. . . . . Dayton OH 45459 *TF:* 800-942-4576 ■ *Web:* loantrackusa.com	937-435-0012	435-0146	390
Freitag Weinhardt Inc 5900 N 13th St. . . . . Terre Haute IN 47805 *Web:* www.freitaginc.com	812-466-9861		610
Freitas Law Group PLLC 544 29th Ave . . . . . Seattle WA 98122 *Web:* vfreitaslaw.com	206-328-7362		41
Freixenet USA 967 Broadway . . . . . Sonoma CA 95476 *Web:* www.freixenetusa.com	707-996-7256		80-3
Fremada Gold Inc 2 W 45th St Ste 1605. . . . . New York NY 10036 *Web:* www.fremadaspecials.com	212-921-8829		411
Fremont Area Community Foundation 4424 W 48th St. . . . . Fremont MI 49412 *Web:* facommunityfoundation.org	231-924-5350		305
Fremont Bank 39150 Fremont Blvd. . . . . Fremont CA 94538 *Web:* www.fremontbank.com	510-505-5222	795-5758	70
Fremont Beef Co 960 S Schneider St . . . . . Fremont NE 68025 *Web:* www.fremontbeef.com	402-727-7200		296-26
Fremont Broadcasting Inc 1530 Main St. . . . . Lander WY 82520 *Web:* www.wyo10.com	307-332-4567		647
Fremont Chamber of Commerce 39488 Stevenson Pl Ste 100. . . . . Fremont CA 94539 *TF:* 888-236-5031 ■ *Web:* www.fremontbusiness.com	510-795-2244	795-2240	139
Fremont City Hall PO Box 5006 . . . . . Fremont CA 94537 *TF:* 800-462-3271 ■ *Web:* fremont.gov	510-284-4000	284-4001	337
Fremont Co, The 802 N Front St. . . . . Fremont OH 43420 *Web:* www.fremontcompany.com	419-334-8995	334-8120	296-20
Fremont College 18000 Studebaker Rd Ste 900A . . . . . Cerritos CA 90703 *TF:* 800-373-6668 ■ *Web:* www.fremont.edu	800-373-6668		167-3
Fremont Contract Carriers Inc (FCC) 865 S Bud Blvd. . . . . Fremont NE 68025 **Fax Area Code:* 402 ■ *TF:* 800-228-9842 ■ *Web:* www.fcc-inc.com	800-228-9842	727-8712*	449
Fremont Correctional Facility (FCF) E US Hwy 50 Evans Blvd PO Box 999. . . . . Canon City CO 81215 *TF:* 800-886-7683 ■ *Web:* www.colorado.gov	719-269-5002	269-5020	213
Fremont County 615 Macon Ave Rm 102 . . . . . Canon City CO 81212 *Web:* fremontco.com	719-276-7330	276-7338	338
Fremont County 450 N 2nd St. . . . . Lander WY 82520 *TF:* 800-967-2297 ■ *Web:* fremontcountywy.org	307-332-2405		338
Fremont County 151 W First N St . . . . . Saint Anthony ID 83445 *Web:* www.co.fremont.id.us	208-624-7332	624-7335	338
Fremont County 506 Filmore St PO Box 299 . . . . . Sidney IA 51652 *Web:* www.co.fremont.ia.us	712-374-2122	374-6202	338
Fremont County Library System 451 N 2nd St . . . . . Lander WY 82520 *Web:* www.fclsonline.org	307-332-5194	332-3909	434-3
Fremont Floor Covering Outlet Ltd 218 N Front St . . . . . Fremont OH 43420 *Web:* fremontfloorcovering.com	419-355-8480		290
Fremont Group 199 Fremont St. . . . . San Francisco CA 94105 *Web:* www.fremontgroup.com	415-284-8500		405
Fremont Health 450 E 23rd St. . . . . Fremont NE 68025 *Web:* www.fremonthealth.com	402-721-1610	727-3656	374-3
Fremont Hotel & Casino 200 Fremont St. . . . . Las Vegas NV 89101 *TF:* 800-634-6460 ■ *Web:* www.fremontcasino.com	702-385-3232		133
Fremont Indian State Park & Museum 3820 W Clear Creek Canyon Rd . . . . . Sevier UT 84766 *Web:* stateparks.utah.gov	435-527-4631		565
Fremont Lakes State Recreation Area 4349 W State Lakes Rd. . . . . Fremont NE 68025 *Web:* outdoornebraska.gov	402-727-2922		565
Fremont Main Library 2400 Stevenson Blvd . . . . . Fremont CA 94538 *TF:* 800-434-0222 ■ *Web:* www.aclibrary.org	510-745-1400	797-6557	434-3
Fremont Market Broiler 43406 Christy St. . . . . Fremont CA 94538 *Web:* www.marketbroiler.com	510-791-8675		671
Fremont Public Schools 450 E Pine . . . . . Fremont MI 49412 *Web:* www.fremont.net	231-924-2350	924-5264	685
Fremont Unified School District 4210 Technology Dr . . . . . Fremont CA 94538 *TF:* 800-544-5248 ■ *Web:* fusd-ca.schoolloop.com	510-657-2350	770-9851	685
French and English Communication Services 3104 E Camelback Rd Ste 124 . . . . . Phoenix AZ 85016 *Web:* www.FrenchAndEnglish.com	602-870-1000		393
French Broad Electric Membership Corp 3043 Nc 213 Hwy. . . . . Marshall NC 28753 *TF:* 800-222-6190 ■ *Web:* www.frenchbroademc.com	828-649-2051	649-2989	245
French Country Waterways Ltd 24 Bay Rd . . . . . Duxbury MA 02332 *TF:* 800-222-1236 ■ *Web:* www.fcwl.com	800-222-1236		221
French Creek Outfitters Inc 270 Schuylkill Rd . . . . . Phoenixville PA 19460 *Web:* www.frenchcreekoutfitters.com	610-933-7200		711

Name / Address	City	State	ZIP	Phone	Fax	Class
French Creek State Park 843 Park Rd *Web:* www.dcnr.pa.gov	Elverson	PA	19520	610-582-9680		565
French Culinary Institute 462 Broadway *TF:* 888-324-2433 ■ *Web:* www.internationalculinarycenter.com	New York	NY	10013	888-324-2433		163
French Hen 7143 S Yale Ave *Web:* www.frenchhentulsa.net	Tulsa	OK	74136	918-492-2596		671
French Institute Alliance Francaise (FIAF) 22 E 60th St *Web:* www.fiaf.org	New York	NY	10022	212-355-6100	935-4119	48-14
French Legation Museum 802 San Marcos St *Web:* www.frenchlegationmuseum.org	Austin	TX	78702	512-472-8180		520
French Lick Resort 8670 W State Rd 56 *TF:* 888-936-9360 ■ *Web:* www.frenchlick.com	French Lick	IN	47432	812-936-9300	936-2100	669
French Market Grille 425 Highland Ave *Web:* www.thefrenchmarketgrille.com	Augusta	GA	30909	706-737-4865		671
French Oil Mill Machinery Co 1035 W Greene St *Web:* www.frenchoil.com	Piqua	OH	45356	937-773-3420	773-3424	386
French Paper Co 100 French St *Web:* www.frenchpaper.com	Niles	MI	49120	269-683-1100		552-1
French Park Care Ctr 600 E Washington Ave *Web:* www.frenchparkcarecenter.com	Santa Ana	CA	92701	714-973-1656	836-4349	450
French Pastry School 226 W Jackson Blvd *Web:* www.frenchpastryschool.com	Chicago	IL	60606	312-726-2419	726-2446	685
French Quarter Suites Hotel 1119 N Rampart St *TF:* 800-457-2253 ■ *Web:* www.frenchquartersuites.com	New Orleans	LA	70116	504-524-7725	522-9716	379
French Trucking Inc 53 Elliott Power Dr *Web:* www.frenchtrucking.com	Lexington	TN	38351	731-968-5391		780
French West Vaughan 112 E Hargett St *Web:* fwv-us.com	Raleigh	NC	27601	919-832-6300		636
French-American Chamber of Commerce in New York 1350 Broadway Ste 2101 *TF:* 800-821-2241 ■ *Web:* www.faccnyc.org	New York	NY	10018	212-867-0123	867-9050	138
French-American Chamber of Commerce of Atlanta 3399 Peachtree Rd NE Ste 500 *Web:* www.facc-atlanta.com	Atlanta	GA	30326	404-997-6800		138
French-American Chamber of Commerce of Chicago (FACC) 205 N Michigan Ave 37th fl *Web:* www.facc-chicago.com	Chicago	IL	60601	312-578-0444	578-0445	138
French-American Chamber of Commerce of Florida (FACC) 100 N Biscayne Blvd Ste 1105 *Web:* www.faccmiami.com	Miami	FL	33132	305-374-5000	358-8203	138
French-American Chamber of Commerce of Houston 1301 Fannin St Ste 2440 *Web:* www.facchouston.org	Houston	TX	77002	713-449-9445		138
French-American Chamber of Commerce of Philadelphia (FACC) 1617 John F Kennedy Blvd Ste 555 *Web:* www.faccphila.org	Philadelphia	PA	19103	215-716-1996		138
French-American Chamber of Commerce of San Francisco 26 O'Farrell St Ste 500 *Web:* www.faccsf.com	San Francisco	CA	94108	415-442-4717	442-4621	138
French-American Chamber of Commerce of the Pacific Northwest (FACCPNW) 2200 Alaskan Way Ste 490 *Web:* www.faccpnw.org	Seattle	WA	98121	206-443-4703	448-4218	138
Frenchie's 1041 Nasa Pkwy *Web:* frenchiesvillacapri.com	Houston	TX	77058	281-486-7144	486-3952	671
Frenchman Valley Farmers Co-opeartive Exchange 202 Broadway *TF:* 800-538-2667 ■ *Web:* www.fvcoop.com	Imperial	NE	69033	308-882-3200	882-3242	276
French-Reneker-Associates Inc 1501 S Main St PO Box 135 *Web:* french-reneker.com	Fairfield	IA	52556	641-472-5145	472-2653	261
Frentzel Products Inc W227n6370 Sussex Rd **Fax Area Code: 262* ■ *Web:* www.frentzelproducts.com	Sussex	WI	53089	414-962-2448	372-4996*	454
Frequency Electronics Inc 55 Charles Lindbergh Blvd *NASDAQ: FEIM* ■ *Web:* www.freqelec.com	Uniondale	NY	11553	516-794-4500	794-4340	248
Freres Lumber Company Inc PO Box 276 *Web:* frereslumber.com	Lyons	OR	97358	503-859-2121		613
Fresca Mexican Foods Inc 2009 Smeed Pkwy *Web:* frescamex.com	Caldwell	ID	83605	208-376-6922		123
Fresco Ristorante 514 S Brand Blvd *Web:* www.frescoristorante.com	Glendale	CA	91204	818-247-5541	247-1964	671
Fresenius Medical Care 920 Winter St *TF:* 800-662-1237 ■ *Web:* fmcna.com	Waltham	MA	02451	781-699-9000		475
Fresh Air Educators Inc 203-1568 Carling Ave *TF:* 866-495-4868 ■ *Web:* www.freshaireducators.com	Ottawa	ON	K1Z7M4	866-495-4868		244
Fresh Air Fund 633 Third Ave 14th Fl *TF:* 800-367-0003 ■ *Web:* www.freshair.org	New York	NY	10017	800-367-0003		239
Fresh Air Media PO Box 6078 *Web:* freshairmedia.com	Auburn	CA	95604	530-888-7676		514
Fresh Ale Pubs LLC 1317 W N Lights Blvd *Web:* www.tooth-merch.myshopify.com	Anchorage	AK	99503	907-222-1560		102
Fresh Baby 523 E Mitchell St *TF:* 866-403-7374 ■ *Web:* www.freshbaby.com	Petoskey	MI	49770	231-348-2706		328
Fresh Consulting LLC 14725 SE 36th St Ste 300 *Web:* www.freshconsulting.com	Bellevue	WA	98006	425-201-3713		195
Fresh Cut Lawn Maintenance Inc 47147 Ryan Rd *Web:* freshcutlandscape.com	Shelby Township	MI	48317	586-739-6646		422
Fresh Encounter Inc 317 W Main Cross St *Web:* www.freshencounter.com	Findlay	OH	45840	419-422-8090		345
Fresh Express Inc PO Box 00599 *TF:* 800-242-5472 ■ *Web:* www.freshexpress.com	Salinas	CA	93912	800-242-5472		11-1
Fresh Ideas Group 3350 Frontier Ave Unit A2 *Web:* freshideasgroup.com	Boulder	CO	80301	303-449-2108		636
Fresh Lime 3300 Ashton Blvd Ste 210 *Web:* www.freshlime.com	Lehi	UT	84043	801-653-5600		195
Fresh Mark-Massillon 1888 Southway St SE *Web:* www.freshmark.com	Massillon	OH	44646	330-832-7491		473
Fresh Meadow Mechanical Corp 65-01 Fresh Meadow Ln *Web:* www.fmmcorp.com	Fresh Meadows	NY	11365	718-961-6634	358-4378	610
Fresh Start Janitorial & Property Services Inc 806 E 9th St *Web:* www.freshstartjanitorial.com	South Sioux City	NE	68776	402-494-9980		104
Fresh Start Produce Sales Inc 5353 W Atlantic Ave Executive Square Ste 403 *Web:* www.freshstartproducesales.com	Delray Beach	FL	33484	561-496-7250		297-7
FreshAddress Inc 36 Crafts St *TF:* 800-321-3009 ■ *Web:* www.freshaddress.com	Newton	MA	02458	800-321-3009		196
FreshDirect Inc 23-30 Borden Ave *TF:* 866-511-1240 ■ *Web:* www.freshdirect.com	Long Island City	NY	11101	718-928-1000		345
Freshens Quality Brands 1750 The Exchange *Web:* www.freshens.com	Atlanta	GA	30339	678-627-5400		381
FreshGrade Inc 301-1447 Ellis St *TF:* 877-957-7757 ■ *Web:* www.freshgrade.com	Kelowna	BC	V1Y2A3	877-957-7757		224
Freshly 115 E 23rd St *TF:* 844-373-7459 ■ *Web:* freshly.com	New York	NY	10010	844-373-7459		546
FreshPoint Inc 1390 Enclave Pkwy *TF:* 800-367-5690 ■ *Web:* www.freshpoint.com	Houston	TX	77077	800-367-5690		297-7
Freshwater Farm Products LLC 4554 State Hwy 12 E PO Box 850 *Web:* www.freshwatercatfish.com	Belzoni	MS	39038	662-247-4205	247-4442	296-14
Freshwater Fish Marketing Corp 1199 Plessis Rd *Web:* www.freshwaterfish.com	Winnipeg	MB	R2C3L4	204-983-6601		297-9
Freshwater Society 2500 Shadywood Rd *TF:* 888-471-9773 ■ *Web:* freshwater.org	Excelsior	MN	55331	952-471-9773	471-7685	48-13
Freshway Foods 601 Stolle Ave *Web:* www.freshwayfoods.com	Sidney	OH	45365	937-498-4664	498-4124	297-7
Freshworks 2950 S Delaware St Ste 201 *TF:* 866-832-3090 ■ *Web:* www.freshworks.com	San Mateo	CA	94403	866-832-3090		178-8
Freskeeto Frozen Foods Inc 8019 Rt 209 *TF:* 800-356-3663 ■ *Web:* www.freskeeto.com	Ellenville	NY	12428	845-647-5111		296-18
Fresno & Clovis Convention & Visitors Bureau 1550 E Shaw Ave Ste 101 *TF:* 800-788-0836 ■ *Web:* www.visitfresnocounty.org	Fresno	CA	93710	559-981-5500	445-0122	206
Fresno Area Express 2223 G St *Web:* www.fresno.gov	Fresno	CA	93706	559-621-7433	488-1065	468
Fresno Art Museum (FAM) 2233 N First St *Web:* www.fresnoartmuseum.org	Fresno	CA	93703	559-441-4221	441-4227	520
Fresno Bee 1626 E St *TF:* 800-877-3400 ■ *Web:* www.fresnobee.com	Fresno	CA	93786	559-441-6111		532-2
Fresno Chaffee Zoo 894 W Belmont Ave *Web:* www.fresnochaffeezoo.org	Fresno	CA	93728	559-498-5910		823
Fresno Chamber of Commerce 2331 Fresno St *Web:* www.fresnochamber.com	Fresno	CA	93721	559-495-4800	495-4811	139
Fresno City College 1101 E University Ave *Web:* www.fresnocitycollege.edu	Fresno	CA	93741	559-442-4600		162
Fresno Convention & Entertainment Ctr 848 M St 2nd Fl *Web:* www.fresnoconventioncenter.com	Fresno	CA	93721	559-445-8100		205
Fresno County 1100 Van Ness Ave *TF:* 800-742-1011 ■ *Web:* www.co.fresno.ca.us	Fresno	CA	93721	559-488-1710		338
Fresno County Public Library 2420 Mariposa St *Web:* www.fresnolibrary.org	Fresno	CA	93721	559-600-7323		434-3
Fresno Distributing Company Inc 2055 E McKinley Ave *TF:* 800-655-2542 ■ *Web:* www.fresnod.com	Fresno	CA	93703	559-442-8800	264-3809	612
Fresno Philharmonic 7170 N Financial Dr Ste 135 *Web:* www.fresnophil.org	Fresno	CA	93720	559-261-0600	261-0700	573-3
Fresno Valves & Castings Inc 7736 E Springfield Ave PO Box 40 *TF:* 800-333-1658 ■ *Web:* www.fresnovalves.com	Selma	CA	93662	559-834-2511	834-2017	790
Fresno Yosemite International Airport 4995 E Clinton Way *TF:* 800-244-2359 ■ *Web:* www.flyfresno.com	Fresno	CA	93727	559-621-4500	251-4825	27
FRETTE Inc 850 Third Ave 10th Fl *Web:* www.frette.com	New York	NY	10022	212-299-0400		442
Fretwater Press 1000 Grand Canyon Ave *Web:* www.fretwater.com	Flagstaff	AZ	86001	928-774-8853		637-2
Freud America Inc 210 Feld Ave *TF:* 800-334-4107 ■ *Web:* www.freudtools.com	High Point	NC	27263	336-434-3171		350
Freudenberg-NOK General Partnership 47690 E Anchor Ct *Web:* www.fst.com	Plymouth	MI	48170	734-451-0020	451-0043	326
Freund, Freeze & Arnold, A Legal Professional Assn 1 S Main St Fifth Third Ctr Ste 1800 *Web:* www.ffalaw.com	Dayton	OH	45402	937-222-2424		428
Freundlich Supply Company Inc 2200 Arthur Kill Rd *TF:* 800-221-0260 ■ *Web:* www.fresupco.com	Staten Island	NY	10309	718-356-1500	356-3661	770
Frew Mill Die Crafts Inc 311 W Grant St *Web:* www.frewmilldiecrafts.com	New Castle	PA	16101	724-658-9026	658-9029	757
Frey Vineyards Winery 14000 Tomki Rd *Web:* www.freywine.com	Redwood Valley	CA	95470	707-485-5177		443

	Phone	Fax	Class
Freyer & Laureta Inc 144 N San Mateo Dr........................San Mateo CA 94401 *Web:* www.freyerlaureta.com	650-344-9901	344-9920	261
Freyssinet Inc 44880 Falcon Pl Ste 100 ....Sterling VA 20166 *TF:* 800-423-6587 ■ *Web:* www.freyssinetusa.com	703-378-2500		261
FRHS (Fayette Regional Health System) 1941 Virginia Ave........................Connersville IN 47331 *Web:* www.fayetteregional.org	765-825-5131		374-3
Friars Club 57 E 55th St......................New York NY 10022 *Web:* www.friarsclub.com	212-751-7272		48-15
Friary of Lakeview Ctr, The 4400 Hickory Shores Blvd ....Gulf Breeze FL 32563 *TF:* 800-332-2271 ■ *Web:* www.elakeviewcenter.org	850-932-9375	934-1281	726
Frick Art & Historical Ctr 7227 Reynolds St..........................Pittsburgh PA 15208 *Web:* thefrickpittsburgh.org	412-371-0600		520
Frick Collection 10 E 71st St.................New York NY 10021 *Web:* www.frick.org	212-288-0700	628-4417	520
Frick Hospital 508 S Church St...........Mount Pleasant PA 15666 *TF:* 877-771-1234 ■ *Web:* www.excelahealth.org	724-547-1500		374-3
Frick Services Inc 570 E Boundary Rd...........Portage IN 46368 *Web:* www.frickservices.com	219-787-8548	787-8101	275
Frick Tri-County Federal Credit Union 235 Pittsburgh St.........................Uniontown PA 15401 *TF:* 800-991-4961 ■ *Web:* fricktricountyfcu.org	724-438-5123		219
Frick's Meat Products Inc 360 M E Frick Dr ....Washington MO 63090 *TF:* 800-241-2209 ■ *Web:* frickmeats.com	636-239-2200	239-7003	296-26
Fricke-Parks Press Inc 33250 Transit Ave.........................Union City CA 94587 *Web:* www.fricke-parks.com	510-489-6543		627
Friday Milner Lambert Turner 3401 Glenview Ave...........................Austin TX 78703 *Web:* fmltlaw.com	512-420-0555		41
Friday, Eldredge & Clark LLP 400 W Capitol Ave Ste 2000................Little Rock AR 72201 *Web:* www.fridayfirm.com	501-376-2011		428
Fridgedoor Inc 21 Dixwell Ave ....Quincy MA 02169 *TF:* 800-955-3741 ■ *Web:* www.fridgedoor.com	617-770-7913	801-8026	328
Fridrich & Clark Realty Llc Brentwood 5200 Maryland Way Ste 101.................Brentwood TN 37027 *Web:* fridrichandclark.com	615-263-4800		652
Fried Frank Harris Shriver & Jacobson LLP (FFHSJ) 1 New York Plz ....New York NY 10004 *Web:* www.friedfrank.com	212-859-8000	859-4000	428
Frieda's Inc 4465 Corporate Center Dr.................Los Alamitos CA 90720 *Web:* www.friedas.com	714-826-6100		297-7
Friedemann Goldberg LLP 420 Aviation Blvd Ste 201 ....Santa Rosa CA 95403 *Web:* www.frigolaw.com	707-543-4900		428
Friedman & Feiger LLP 5301 Spring Valley Rd Ste 200..................Dallas TX 75254 *Web:* www.fflawoffice.com	972-788-1400		428
Friedman & Friedman LLP 409 Washington Ave Ste 900 ....Towson MD 21204 *Web:* friedmanandfriedmanlaw.com	410-494-0100		41
Friedman & Huey Associates LLP 1313 W 175th St.........................Homewood IL 60430 *Web:* fhassoc.com	708-799-6800	799-5134	2
Friedman & Martin LLP 114 Barnard St Ste 2A ....Savannah GA 31401 *Web:* savinjurylaw.com	912-232-8500	238-1764	41
Friedman Bros Decorative Arts 9015 NW 105th Way..........................Medley FL 33178 *TF:* 800-327-1065 ■ *Web:* www.friedmanmirrors.com	305-887-3170	885-5331	334
Friedman Electric 1321 Wyoming Ave.............Exeter PA 18643 *TF:* 800-545-5517 ■ *Web:* www.friedmanelectric.com	570-654-3371	655-6194	246
Friedman Group, The 11065 Hauser St...........Lenexa KS 66210 *Web:* thefriedmangroup.com	209-813-5492		196
Friedman Law Firm PC 9401 Courthouse Rd Ste A.................Chesterfield VA 23832 *Web:* friedmandivorce.com	804-717-1969		41
Friedman Law Group Ltd 1700 W Irving Park Rd Ste 305A ....Chicago IL 60613 *Web:* marketing-law.com	773-248-9455		41
Friedman LLP 1700 Broadway.................New York NY 10019 *Web:* www.friedmanllp.com	212-842-7000	842-7001	2
Friedman Michael G Atty 56 E Main St Ste 301 ....Somerville NJ 08876 *Web:* www.centraljerseylaw.com	908-526-0707		428
Friedman Recycling Co 3640 W Lincoln St ....Phoenix AZ 85009 *Web:* www.friedmanrecycling.com	602-269-9324		660
Friedman, James & Buchsbaum LLP 132 Nassau St Ste 900......................New York NY 10038 *Web:* friedmanjames.com	212-233-9385		41
Friedrich 10001 Reunion Pl Ste 500 ....San Antonio TX 78216 *TF:* 800-541-6645 ■ *Web:* www.friedrich.com	210-546-0500	357-4480	14
Friedrich Petzel Gallery Inc 456 W 18th St.............................New York NY 10011 *Web:* petzel.com	212-680-9467	680-9473	42
Friend Tire Co 11 Industrial Dr ....Monett MO 65708 *TF:* 800-950-8473 ■ *Web:* www.friendtire.com	800-950-8473		755
Friend's of Pruyn House 207 Old Niskayuna Rd PO Box 1254 ....Latham NY 12110 *Web:* www.pruynhouse.org	518-783-1435		50-3
Friend's Professional Stationery Inc 1535 Lewis Ave................................Zion IL 60099 *TF:* 800-323-4394 ■ *Web:* www.friendsstationery.com	800-323-4394	323-1535	535
Friendemic 1165 E Wilmington Ave Ste 290............Salt Lake City UT 84106 *Web:* www.friendemic.com	801-415-9314		5
Friendfinder Network Inc 1615 S Congress Ave Ste 103 ....Delray Beach FL 33445 *TSE:* FFN ■ *TF:* 888-575-8383 ■ *Web:* www.ffn.com	561-912-7000		226
Friendly Cruises 3081 S Sycamore Village Dr........Superstition Mountain AZ 85118 *TF:* 800-842-1786 ■ *Web:* www.friendlycruises.com	480-358-1496		771
Friendly Excursions Inc PO Box 69.............Sunland CA 91041 *TF:* 800-775-5018 ■ *Web:* friendlyexcursions.net	818-353-7726	353-3903	760
Friendly Express # 14 507 City Blvd ....Waycross GA 31503 *Web:* friendlyexpress.com	912-285-7703		345
Friendly Gift Shop Inc 1812 Marsh Rd..........................Wilmington DE 19810	302-475-6560		327
Friendly Ice Cream Corp 1855 Boston Rd ....Wilbraham MA 01095 *TF:* 800-966-9970 ■ *Web:* www.friendlys.com	800-966-9970		670
Friendly Oaks Publications 227 Bunker Hill...........................Pleasanton TX 78064 *TF:* 800-659-6628 ■ *Web:* www.friendlyoakspublications.com	830-569-3586	281-2617	637-2
Friendly Solutions Corp 3837 N Panama Ave ....Chicago IL 60634 *Web:* friendlysol.com	773-957-7800		180
Friends Committee on National Legislation (FCNL) 245 Second St NE.........................Washington DC 20002 *TF:* 800-630-1330 ■ *Web:* www.fcnl.org	202-547-6000	547-6019	615
Friends Cove Mutual Insurance Co 500 E Pitt St ....Bedford PA 15522 *Web:* friendscove.com	814-623-1100		390
Friends General Conference 1216 Arch St Ste 2B......................Philadelphia PA 19107 *Web:* www.fgcquaker.org	215-561-1700		48-20
Friends Hospital 4641 Roosevelt Blvd......................Philadelphia PA 19124 *TF:* 800-889-0548 ■ *Web:* friendshospital.com	215-831-4600		374-5
Friends of Animals Inc (FOA) 777 Post Rd Ste 205............................Darien CT 06820 *TF:* 800-321-7387 ■ *Web:* friendsofanimals.org	203-656-1522	656-0267	48-3
Friends of Castlewood Canyon State Park 2989 S Hwy 83..........................Franktown CO 80116 *Web:* cpw.state.co.us	303-688-5242		565
Friends of Jockey's Ridge State Park PO Box 358 ....Nags Head NC 27959 *Web:* friendsofjockeysridge.org	252-441-7132		565
Friends of K-State Libraries 1117 Mid-Campus Dr N....................Manhattan KS 66506 *Web:* www.lib.ksu.edu	785-532-3014		434-3
Friends of Navajo State Park Po Box 1897...............................Arboles CO 81121 *Web:* cpw.state.co.us	970-883-2208		565
Friends of Roseville Public Library, The 35 Kingsbury Crt ....Roseville CA 95678 *Web:* library.roseville.ca.us	916-774-5221		434-3
Friends of The Earth 1101 15th St NW 11th Fl ....Washington DC 20005 *TF:* 866-217-8499 ■ *Web:* foe.org	202-222-0722	783-0444	302
Friends of the Everglades 11767 S Dixie Hwy Ste 232 ....Miami FL 33156 *Web:* www.everglades.org	305-669-0858		48-13
Friends of the River 1418 20th St Ste 100 ....Sacramento CA 95811 *TF:* 888-464-2477 ■ *Web:* www.friendsoftheriver.org	916-442-3155	442-3396	48-13
Friends of the Topiary Park 480 E Town St............................Columbus OH 43215 *Web:* www.topiarygarden.org	614-645-0197		97
Friends Research Institute Inc *Social Research Ctr* 1040 Park Ave Ste 103....................Baltimore MD 21201 *TF:* 800-705-7757 ■ *Web:* friendsresearch.org	410-837-3977	752-4218	668
Friends School of Wilmington Inc 350 Peiffer Ave..........................Wilmington NC 28409 *Web:* www.fsow.org	910-792-1811		685
Friends United Press (FUP) 101 Quaker Hill Dr ....Richmond IN 47374 *TF:* 800-537-8839 ■ *Web:* shop.fum.org	765-962-7573	966-1293	637-2
Friends University 2100 W University Ave.......................Wichita KS 67213 *TF:* 800-794-6945 ■ *Web:* www.friends.edu	316-295-5000		166
Friendship Automotive Inc 1855 Volunteer Pkwy ....Bristol TN 37620 *Web:* friendshipford.com	423-652-6200		57
Friendship Hill National Historic Site 223 New Geneva Rd ....Point Marion PA 15474 *Web:* www.nps.gov	724-725-9190		564
Friendship Hospital for Animals 4105 Brandywine St NW...................Washington DC 20016 *Web:* www.friendshiphospital.com	202-363-7300		794
Friendship House PO Box 3778 ....Scranton PA 18505 *Web:* www.friendshiphousepa.org	570-342-8305		685
Friendship Manor 1209 21st Ave............Rock Island IL 61201 *Web:* www.friendshipmanor.org	309-786-9667	794-9141	672
Friendship Village 600 Pk Ln.................Waterloo IA 50702 *Web:* www.friendshipvillageiowa.com	319-291-8100		672
Friendship Village Kalamazoo 1400 N Drake Rd ....Kalamazoo MI 49006 *TF:* 800-613-3984 ■ *Web:* friendshipvillagemi.com	269-381-0560		672
Friendship Village of columbus 5800 Forest Hills Blvd ....Columbus OH 43231 *Web:* www.fvcolumbus.org	614-890-8282		672
Friendship Village of South County 12563 Village Cir Dr.....................Sunset Hills MO 63127 *Web:* www.friendshipvillagestl.com	314-842-6840		672
Friendship Village of Tempe 2645 E Southern Ave ....Tempe AZ 85282 *Web:* www.friendshipvillageaz.com	480-831-5000		672
Friendsview Retirement Community 1301 E Fulton St..........................Newberg OR 97132 *TF:* 866-307-4371 ■ *Web:* friendsview.org	503-538-3144		672
Friendswood Chamber of Commerce 1100 S Friendswood Dr ....Friendswood TX 77546 *Web:* friendswoodchamber.com	281-482-3329		139
Friendswood Development Co 11506 Island Manor St......................Pearland TX 77584 *Web:* www.friendswooddevelopment.com	713-436-6951		653

	City	State	ZIP	Phone	Fax	Class
Friendswood Public Library 416 S Friendswood Dr *Web:* www.friendswood.lib.tx.us	Friendswood	TX	77546	281-482-7135		434-3
Friesen's Inc 1389 Cormorant Ave *Web:* www.friesensinc.com	Detroit Lakes	MN	56501	218-844-4437	844-0358	695
Friesens Corp 1 Printers Way *Web:* www.friesens.com	Altona	MB	R0G0B0	204-324-6401	324-1333	626
Frigel North America Inc 150 Prairie Lake Rd *Web:* www.frigel.com	East Dundee	IL	60118	847-540-0160		610
Frigid Fluid Co 11631 W Grand Ave *TF:* 800-621-4719 ■ *Web:* frigidfluid.com	Northlake	IL	60164	708-836-1215	836-1247	144
Frigoscandia Inc 400 Highpoint Dr *TF:* 888-362-3628 ■ *Web:* www.jbtcorporation.com	Chalfont	PA	18914	215-822-4600	822-4553	537
Friman Home Health Services PLLC 42000 Koppernick Rd Ste A-7 *TF:* 800-821-1937 ■ *Web:* www.frimanhomehealth.com	Canton	MI	48187	734-254-0092	254-0180	363
Fringe Benefits Management Co PO Box 1878 *TF:* 800-872-0345 ■ *Web:* www.fbmc.com	Tallahassee	FL	32302	850-425-6200	425-6220	390
Fringe Theatre Adventures Society 10330 84 Ave NW *Web:* www.fringetheatre.ca	Edmonton	AB	T6E2G9	780-448-9000		749
Frio County 500 E San Antonio St *Web:* www.co.frio.tx.us	Pearsall	TX	78061	830-334-2154	334-0010	338
Friona Industries 500 S Taylor St Ste 601 *TF:* 800-658-6014 ■ *Web:* www.frionaindustries.com	Amarillo	TX	79101	806-374-1811	374-3003	10-1
Frisbie Memorial Hospital 11 Whitehall Rd *Web:* www.frisbiehospital.com	Rochester	NH	03867	603-332-5211		374-3
Frisch's Restaurants Inc 2800 Gilbert Ave *NYSE: FRS* ■ *TF:* 800-873-3633 ■ *Web:* www.frischs.com	Cincinnati	OH	45206	513-961-2660	559-5160	670
Frisco Baking Company Inc 621 W Ave 26 *Web:* www.friscobakingcompany.com	Los Angeles	CA	90065	323-225-6111	225-3554	296-1
Frishmuth Consulting Services LLC PO Box 690626 *Web:* www.appliedmechanics.com	Houston	TX	77269	281-807-0203	807-9134	192
Fristam Pumps USA LP 2410 Parview Rd *TF:* 800-841-5001 ■ *Web:* www.fristam.com	Middleton	WI	53562	608-831-5001		641
Frit Car Inc 2012 US Hwy 17 N *Web:* www.fritcar.com	Brewton	AL	36426	251-867-7752		650
Frit Industries Inc 1792 Jodie Parker Rd *TF:* 800-633-7685 ■ *Web:* www.fritind.com	Ozark	AL	36360	334-774-2515	774-9306	280
Frite Alors! 1562 Laurier St E *Web:* fritealors.com	Montreal	QC	H2J1H9	514-524-6336		671
Frith Anderson & Peake Pc 29 Franklin Rd SW *TF:* 888-529-9696 ■ *Web:* faplawfirm.com	Roanoke	VA	24011	540-772-4600		41
Frito-Lay North America 7701 Legacy Dr *TF:* 800-352-4477 ■ *Web:* www.fritolay.com	Plano	TX	75024	800-352-4477		296-35
Frittl 309 N Highland Ave *Web:* frittiatl.com	Atlanta	GA	30307	404-880-9559		671
Fritz & Alfredo's 1007 S McCord Rd *Web:* www.arturosfritzandalfredos.com	Holland	OH	43528	419-729-9775		671
Fritz Enterprises Inc 1650 W Jefferson Ave *Web:* www.fritzinc.com	Trenton	MI	48183	734-362-3200		660
Fritz Pet Products 500 N Sam Houston Rd *TF:* 800-955-1323 ■ *Web:* www.fritzind.com	Mesquite	TX	75149	972-329-8800		751
Frize Corp 16605 E Gale Ave *TF:* 800-834-2127 ■ *Web:* www.frizecorp.com	City of Industry	CA	91745	800-834-2127		186
FRL Furniture 460 Grand Blvd *TF:* 800-529-4375 ■ *Web:* www.frlalternatives.com	Westbury	NY	11590	516-333-4400	333-4759	664
FRM (Flat Rock Metal Inc) 26601 W Huron River Dr PO Box 1090 *Web:* www.frm.com	Flat Rock	MI	48134	734-782-4454	782-5640	485
FRMC (Frye Regional Medical Ctr) 420 N Center St *Web:* www.fryemedctr.com	Hickory	NC	28601	828-315-5000		374-3
Froehling & Robertson Inc 3015 Dumbarton Rd *Web:* www.fandr.com	Richmond	VA	23228	804-264-2701	264-1202	743
Frog Street Press Inc 800 Industrial Blvd Ste 100 *TF:* 800-884-3764 ■ *Web:* www.frogstreet.com	Grapevine	TX	76051	800-884-3764	759-3828	243
Frog Switch & Manufacturing Co 600 E High St *TF:* 800-233-7194 ■ *Web:* www.frogswitch.com	Carlisle	PA	17013	717-243-2454		307
Frogco Amphibious Equipment Inc 2280 Coteau Rd *Web:* www.gcseservices.com	Houma	LA	70364	985-853-2200		567
Frogdesign Inc 660 Third St 4th Fl *Web:* www.frogdesign.com	San Francisco	CA	94107	415-442-4804	442-4803	4
Frohm Kelley Butler & Ryan PC 333 Ft St *Web:* www.fkbrpc.com	Port Huron	MI	48060	810-987-2727		2
From Tao to Earth 107 Boulder View Ln **Fax Area Code: 303* ■ *TF:* 800-800-3139 ■ *Web:* www.taotoearthpmpubs.com	Boulder	CO	80304	800-800-3139	415-4161*	637-2
Fromm Electric Supply 2101 Centre Ave PO Box 15147 *TF:* 800-360-4441 ■ *Web:* www.frommelectric.com	Reading	PA	19605	610-374-4441	374-8756	246
Fromm Packaging Systems Inc 85 Fulton St Unit 4 *TF:* 877-248-1645 ■ *Web:* www.airpadusa.com	Boonton	NJ	07005	973-334-5777	334-2111	547
Fromm, Smith & Gadow PC 4722 N 24th St Ste 460 *Web:* frommsmithandgadow.com	Phoenix	AZ	85016	602-955-1515		41
Fronk Oil Company Inc PO Box F *Web:* www.fronkoil.com	Booker	TX	79005	806-658-4565		579

	City	State	ZIP	Phone	Fax	Class
Front App Inc 525 Brannan St Ste 300 *TF:* 877-331-5984 ■ *Web:* frontapp.com	San Francisco	CA	94107	877-331-5984		39
Front End Audio 130 Hunter Village Dr Ste D *TF:* 888-228-4530 ■ *Web:* www.frontendaudio.com	Irmo	SC	29063	803-748-0914		526
Front Porch Communities & Services 800 N Brand Blvd 19th Fl **Fax Area Code: 818* ■ *TF:* 800-233-3709 ■ *Web:* frontporch.net	Glendale	CA	91203	800-233-3709	254-4101*	450
Front Range Community College (FRCC) *Boulder County* 2190 Miller Dr *TF:* 888-800-9198 ■ *Web:* www.frontrange.edu	Longmont	CO	80501	303-678-3722	678-3699	162
Front Range Energy LLC 31375 Great Western Dr *Web:* www.frontrangeenergy.com	Windsor	CO	80550	970-674-2910		143
Front Row Motorsports 2670 Peachtree Rd *Web:* www.teamfrm.com	Statesville	NC	28625	704-873-6445		717
Front Row USA Entertainment 900 N Federal Hwy *TF:* 800-277-8499 ■ *Web:* www.frontrowusa.com	Hallandale Beach	FL	33009	800-277-8499		750
Front Royal-Warren County Chamber of Commerce 201 E Second St *Web:* www.frontroyalchamber.com	Front Royal	VA	22630	540-635-3185	635-9758	139
Front Runner Consulting LLC 6850 O'Bannon Bluff *TF:* 877-328-3360 ■ *Web:* frontrunnerconsulting.com	Loveland	OH	45140	513-697-6850		194
Front Street Restaurant 230 Commercial St *Web:* www.frontstreetrestaurant.com	Provincetown	MA	02657	508-487-9715		671
Frontage Laboratories LLC 700 Pennsylvania Dr *Web:* www.frontagelab.com	Exton	PA	19341	610-232-0100		743
Frontenac Co 1 S Wacker Ste 2980 *Web:* www.frontenac.com	Chicago	IL	60606	312-368-0044	368-9520	792
Frontenac State Park 29223 County 28 Blvd *Web:* www.dnr.state.mn.us	Frontenac	MN	55026	651-345-3401	345-3694	565
Frontend Graphics 1951 Old Cuthbert Rd Ste 414 *Web:* www.frontendgraphics.com	Cherry Hill	NJ	08034	856-547-1600	547-3837	627
Frontera Grill 445 N Clark St *Web:* www.rickbayless.com	Chicago	IL	60654	312-661-1434	661-1830	671
Frontier Adjusters of America Inc 4745 N Seventh St Ste 320 *TF:* 800-426-7228 ■ *Web:* www.frontieradjusters.com	Phoenix	AZ	85014	800-426-7228	553-4799	390
Frontier Airlines Inc Frontier Airlines 4545 Airport Way *TF:* 800-265-5505 ■ *Web:* www.flyfrontier.com	Denver	CO	80249	720-374-4200		360-1
Frontier Asset Management LLC 50 E Loucks Ste 201 *Web:* frontierasset.com	Sheridan	WY	82801	307-673-5675	673-5963	401
Frontier Central School District 5120 Orchard Ave *Web:* www.frontiercsd.org	Hamburg	NY	14075	716-926-1700		685
Frontier City Theme Park 11501 N I-35 Service Rd *Web:* www.frontiercity.com	Oklahoma City	OK	73131	405-478-2140	478-2118	32
Frontier Communications Corp 3 High Ridge Pk *NASDAQ: FTR* ■ *TF:* 800-877-4390 ■ *Web:* frontier.com	Stamford	CT	06905	203-614-5600	614-4602	736
Frontier Computer Corp 1275 Business Pk Dr *TF:* 866-226-6344 ■ *Web:* www.frontiercomputercorp.com	Traverse City	MI	49686	231-929-1386		180
Frontier Consulting Inc 7107 Sage Walk Ln *Web:* frontier-consulting.com	Sugar Land	TX	77479	713-778-0799	778-0989	180
Frontier Co-op 211 S Lincoln PO Box 37 *TF:* 800-869-0379 ■ *Web:* www.frontiercooperative.com	Brainard	NE	68626	402-545-2811	545-2821	275
Frontier Co-op 3021 78th St PO Box 299 *TF:* 800-669-3275 ■ *Web:* www.frontiercoop.com	Norway	IA	52318	800-669-3275		805
Frontier County 1 Wellington St *Web:* www.co.frontier.ne.us	Stockville	NE	69042	308-367-8641	367-8730	338
Frontier Electronic Systems Corp 4500 W Sixth Ave *TF:* 800-677-1769 ■ *Web:* www.fescorp.com	Stillwater	OK	74074	405-624-1769		529
Frontier Energy Inc 2695 Bingley Rd PO Box 641 *Web:* frontierenergy.com	Cazenovia	NY	13035	315-655-1063		194
Frontier Enterprises 8520 Crownhill Blvd *Web:* www.frontier-enterprises.com	San Antonio	TX	78209	210-828-1493		187
Frontier Fasteners Inc 12710 Market St *Web:* www.frontierfasteners.com	Houston	TX	77015	713-451-4242	451-6565	278
Frontier Ford 3701 Stevens Creek Blvd *TF:* 844-480-0574 ■ *Web:* www.frontierford.com	Santa Clara	CA	95051	844-877-9039		57
Frontier Health PO Box 9054 *TF:* 877-928-9062 ■ *Web:* www.frontierhealth.org	Gray	TN	37615	423-467-3600		462
Frontier Home Medical 304 W Eighth St *Web:* frontierhomemedical.com	Cozad	NE	69130	308-784-3040		363
Frontier Industries Inc 1911 Commercial Ave *Web:* www.fbs.us	Anacortes	WA	98221	360-293-4588		683
Frontier Investment Management Co 8401 N Central Expy Ste 300 *Web:* frontierinvest.com	Dallas	TX	75225	972-934-2590		401
Frontier Logistic Services 1700 N Alameda St *Web:* www.frontier-logistics.com	Compton	CA	90222	310-604-8208		449
Frontier Logistics LP 1806 S 16th St **Fax Area Code: 281* ■ *TF:* 800-610-6808 ■ *Web:* www.frontierlogistics.com	La Porte	TX	77571	800-610-6808	307-2399*	311
Frontier Mechanical Inc 2771 W Mansfield Ave *Web:* www.frontiermech.net	Englewood	CO	80110	303-806-5400		610

Name / Address	City	State	Zip	Phone	Fax	Class
Frontier Metal Stamping 3764 Puritan Way *Fax Area Code: 303 ■ TF: 888-316-1266 ■ Web: www.frontiermetal.com	Frederick	CO	80516	877-549-5955	458-1521*	483
Frontier Networks Inc 530 Kipling Ave TF: 866-833-2323 ■ Web: www.frontiernetworks.ca	Toronto	ON	M8Z5E3	416-847-5240		387
Frontier Power Co 770 S Second St PO Box 280 TF: 800-624-8050 ■ Web: www.frontier-power.com	Coshocton	OH	43812	740-622-6755	622-0711	245
Frontier Publications Inc PO Box 527 Web: bingobugle.com	Vashon	WA	98070	206-463-5656		532-2
Frontier Supply Inc 981 Van Horn Rd TF: 800-478-7867 ■ Web: www.frontiersupply.com	Fairbanks	AK	99701	907-374-3500	374-3570	612
Frontier-Kemper Constructors Inc 1695 Allen Rd TF: 877-554-8600 ■ Web: www.frontierkemper.com	Evansville	IN	47710	812-426-2741	428-0337	188-10
Frontiers 600 Warrendale Rd TF: 800-245-1950 ■ Web: www.frontierstravel.com	Gibsonia	PA	15044	724-935-1577	935-5388	760
Frontiers of Flight Museum 6911 Lemon Ave TF: 800-568-8924 ■ Web: www.flightmuseum.com	Dallas	TX	75209	214-350-1651		520
Frontline Communications PO Box 98 *Fax Area Code: 845 ■ TF: 888-376-6854 ■ Web: www.frontlinelite.com	Orangeburg	NY	10962	888-376-6854	680-6541*	398
Frontline Group of Texas LLC 15021 Katy Fwy Ste 575 TF: 800-285-5512 ■ Web: www.frontline-group.com	Houston	TX	77094	281-453-6000		765
Frontline Logistics Inc 10315 Grand River Ste 300 TF: 800-245-6632 ■ Web: www.frontlinelogistics.com	Brighton	MI	48116	734-449-9474		314
Frontline Software Technology Inc 6400 E Grant Rd Ste 110 *Fax Area Code: 520 ■ TF: 800-483-7668 ■ Web: www.gofrontline.com	Tucson	AZ	85715	800-483-7668	298-6705*	178-1
Frontline Systems Inc PO Box 4288 TF: 888-831-0333 ■ Web: www.solver.com	Incline Village	NV	89450	775-831-0300	831-0314	809
Frontpoint 1310 W 233 N Ste 101 Web: www.frontpoint-it.com	Centerville	UT	84014	801-312-9400		393
Frontwave Credit Union 1278 Rocky Point Dr *Fax Area Code: 877 ■ TF: 800-736-4500 ■ Web: www.frontwavecu.com	Oceanside	CA	92056	760-631-8700	789-7628*	219
Frosch International Travel Inc 1 Greenway Plz Ste 800 TF: 800-866-1623 ■ Web: www.froschtravel.com	Houston	TX	77046	800-866-1623		772
Frost & Sullivan 7550 IH 10 W Ste 400 *Fax Area Code: 888 ■ TF: 877-463-7678 ■ Web: ww2.frost.com	San Antonio	TX	78229	210-348-1000	690-3329*	531-12
Frost Art Museum at Florida International University 10975 SW 17th St Web: frost.fiu.edu	Miami	FL	33199	305-348-2890	348-2762	520
Frost Brown Todd 3300 Great American Tower 301 E Fourth St Ste 3300 Web: www.frostbrowntodd.com	Cincinnati	OH	45202	513-651-6800	651-6981	428
Frost Cutlery Company LLC 6861 Mtn View Rd Web: www.frostcutlery.com	Ooltewah	TN	37363	423-894-6079		351
Frost Hardwood Lumber Co 6565 Miramar Rd Web: www.frosthardwood.com	San Diego	CA	92121	858-455-9060	455-0455	191-3
Frost PLLC 425 W Capitol Ave Ste 3300 Web: frostpllc.com	Little Rock	AR	72201	501-376-9241	374-5520	2
Frost Roofing Inc 2 Broadway St Web: www.frost-roofing.com	Wapakoneta	OH	45895	419-739-2700		697
Frost Valley Ymca 2000 Frost Valley Rd Web: frostvalley.org	Claryville	NY	12725	845-985-2291		379
Frostburg State University 101 Braddock Rd Web: www.frostburg.edu	Frostburg	MD	21532	301-687-4000	687-7074	166
Frozen Fire Films Inc 325 N St Paul St Web: frozenfire.com	Dallas	TX	75201	214-745-3456		5
Frozen Head State Natural Area 964 Flat Fork Rd Web: www.state.tn.us	Wartburg	TN	37887	423-346-3318		565
Frozen Specialties Inc 8600 S Wilkinson Wy Ste G Web: www.frozenspecialties.com	Perrysburg	OH	43551	419-867-2005		296-36
Fruhauf Uniforms Inc 800 E Gilbert St TF: 800-858-8050 ■ Web: fruhauf.com	Wichita	KS	67211	316-263-7500	263-5550	155-5
Fruit & Spice Park 24801 SW 187th Ave Web: www.floridaplants.com	Homestead	FL	33031	305-247-5727	245-3369	97
Fruit Basket Flowerland 765 28th St SW Web: www.myflowerland.com	Wyoming	MI	49509	616-532-7404	531-7858	323
Fruit Co, The 2900 Van Horn Dr TF: 800-387-3100 ■ Web: www.thefruitcompany.com	Hood River	OR	97031	541-387-3100		292
Fruit Growers Laboratory Inc 853 Corporation St TF: 800-440-7821 ■ Web: www.fglinc.com	Santa Paula	CA	93060	805-392-2000		743
Fruit Growers Supply Company Inc 27770 N Entertainment Dr *Fax Area Code: 818 ■ TF: 888-997-4855 ■ Web: fruitgrowers.com	Valencia	CA	91355	888-997-4855	783-1941*	274
Fruit of The Earth Inc 3325 W Trinity Blvd Web: www.fote.com	Grand Prairie	TX	75050	817-510-1600		214
Fruit of the Loom Inc 1 Fruit of the Loom Dr PO Box 90015 TF: 888-378-4829 ■ Web: www.fruitactivewear.com	Bowling Green	KY	42102	270-781-6400	781-1754	155-3
Fruit Yard, The 7948 Yosemite Blvd Web: www.thefruityard.com	Modesto	CA	95357	209-577-3093	577-0600	671
Fruitful Yield Inc 229 W Roosevelt Rd TF: 800-469-5552 ■ Web: www.fruitfulyield.com	Lombard	IL	60148	800-469-5552		799
Fruition.net 201 Filmore St Ste 200 Web: fruition.net	Denver	CO	80206	303-395-1880		180
Fruitridge Printing & Lithograph Inc 3258 Stockton Blvd TF: 800-835-4846 ■ Web: www.fruitridge.com	Sacramento	CA	95820	916-452-9213		627
Fruth Pharmacy Inc 4016 Ohio River Rd TF: 800-438-5390 ■ Web: www.fruthpharmacy.com	Point Pleasant	WV	25550	304-675-1612		237
FRWD 120 First Ave N Ste 300 Web: www.frwd.com	Minneapolis	MN	55401	612-235-5030		5
FRX Polymers Inc 200 Turnpike Rd Web: www.frxpolymers.com	Chelmsford	MA	01824	978-244-9500		601
Fry Communications Inc 800 W Church Rd TF: 800-334-1429 ■ Web: www.frycomm.com	Mechanicsburg	PA	17055	800-334-1429		627
Fry Fastening Systems 1740 Carillon Blvd Web: www.frysys.com	Cincinnati	OH	45240	513-851-2233	742-6332	351
Fry Steel Company Inc 13325 Molette St TF: 800-423-6651 ■ Web: www.frysteel.com	Santa Fe Springs	CA	90670	562-802-2721	802-1553	492
Fry's Electronics 600 E Brokaw Rd Web: www.frys.com	San Jose	CA	95112	408-487-1000	487-4700	35
Fry's Food Stores of Arizona Inc 500 S 99th Ave TF: 866-221-4141 ■ Web: www.frysfood.com	Tolleson	AZ	85353	623-936-2100		345
Frye Properties 300 W Freemason St Web: www.fryeproperties.com	Norfolk	VA	23510	757-627-1980		652
Frye Regional Medical Ctr (FRMC) 420 N Center St Web: www.fryemedctr.com	Hickory	NC	28601	828-315-5000		374-3
Fryeburg Academy 745 Main St Web: www.fryeburgacademy.org	Fryeburg	ME	04037	207-935-2001	935-5013	622
Fryer-Knowles Inc 205 S Dawson St TF: 800-544-6052 ■ Web: www.fryerk.com	Seattle	WA	98108	206-767-7710		291
Frymaster LLC 8700 Line Ave TF: 800-221-4583 ■ Web: www.frymaster.com	Shreveport	LA	71106	318-865-1711		298
Frymire Home Services 2818 Satsuma Dr Web: www.frymire.com	Dallas	TX	75229	972-620-3600		261
Fry-Wagner Moving & Storage Co 3700 Rider Trl S TF: 800-899-4035 ■ Web: www.fry-wagner.com	Earth City	MO	63045	314-291-4100		780
FS (First Service) 737 Southpoint Blvd Ste D *Fax Area Code: 707 ■ TF: 800-227-1742 ■ Web: store.clubstuff.com	Petaluma	CA	94954	800-227-1742	781-1970*	711
FS Precision Tech Company LLC 3025 E Victoria St Web: fs-precision.com	Compton	CA	90221	424-241-3778		306
FS S Inc 5202 Moundview Dr TF: 800-657-0811 ■ Web: www.foodservicespecialties.com	Red Wing	MN	55066	800-657-0811		296-19
FS Tool Corp 71 Hobbs Gate TF: 800-387-9723 ■ Web: www.fstoolcorp.com	Markham	ON	L3R9T9	905-475-1999		697
FSB (1st Security Bank of Washington) 19002 33rd Ave W TF: 800-683-0973 ■ Web: www.fsbwa.com	Lynnwood	WA	98036	425-774-5536		70
FSB Premier Wealth Management Inc 131 Tower Park Dr Ste 115 Web: www.fsbfs.com	Waterloo	IA	50701	319-235-6561		690
FSC Securities Corp 2300 Windy Ridge Pkwy Ste 750 TF: 800-372-5646 ■ Web: www.fscsecurities.com	Atlanta	GA	30339	800-547-2382		690
FSEEE (Forest Service Employees for Environmental Ethics) PO Box 11615 Web: www.fseee.org	Eugene	OR	97440	541-484-2692	484-3004	49-7
FS-Elliott Company LLC 5710 Mellon Rd TF: 800-943-0459 ■ Web: www.fs-elliott.com	Export	PA	15632	724-387-3200		172
FSG (Facility Solutions Group) 4401 Westgate Blvd Ste 310 TF: 800-854-6465 ■ Web: www1.fsgi.com	Austin	TX	78745	512-440-7985	440-0399	246
FSI International Inc 3455 Lyman Blvd Web: www.tel.com	Chaska	MN	55318	952-448-5440	448-2825	695
FSI Technologies Inc 668 E Western Ave TF: 800-468-6009 ■ Web: www.fsinet.com	Lombard	IL	60148	630-932-9380	932-0016	203
FSMB (Federation of State Medical Boards of the US Inc) 400 Fuller Wiser Rd Ste 300 TF: 800-793-7939 ■ Web: www.fsmb.org	Euless	TX	76039	817-868-4000	868-4098	49-8
FSMSDC (Florida Regional Minority Supplier Development Inc) 9499 NE Second Ave Ste 201 Web: www.sfmsdc.org	Miami	FL	33138	305-762-6151	762-6158	78
FSO Onsite Outsourcing 19 W 44th St 9th Fl Web: www.forrestsolutions.com	New York	NY	10036	212-204-1193		260
FSP (Franklin Street Properties Corp) 401 Edgewater Pl NYSE: FSP ■ TF: 877-686-9496 ■ Web: www.fspreit.com	Wakefield	MA	01880	800-950-6288		654
FSP (Fugue State Press) PO Box 80 Cooper Station *Fax Area Code: 208 ■ Web: www.fuguestatepress.com	New York	NY	10276	917-806-1648	693-6152*	637-2
Fsr Inc 244 Bergen Blvd Web: fsrinc.com	Woodland Park	NJ	07424	973-998-2300		127
FST Logistics Inc 2040 Atlas St Web: fstlogistics.com	Columbus	OH	43228	614-529-7900		194
FSTV (Free Speech TV) PO Box 44099 TF: 877-378-8669 ■ Web: freespeech.org	Denver	CO	80201	303-542-4813		740
Ft. Walton Radiator Auto Air & Repair 39 Perry Ave Web: www.fwrad.mechanicnet.com	Fort Walton Beach	FL	32548	850-243-6788	243-5287	62-5
FTA (Federation of Tax Administrators) 444 N Capitol St NW Ste 348 TF: 800-829-9188 ■ Web: www.taxadmin.org	Washington	DC	20001	202-624-5890	624-7888	49-7
FTA (Flexographic Technical Assn) 3920 Veterans Memorial Hwy Ste 9 Web: www.flexography.org	Bohemia	NY	11716	631-737-6020	737-6813	49-16
FTC (Farmers Telecommunications Co-op) 144 McCurdy Ave N PO Box 217 TF: 866-638-2144 ■ Web: farmerstel.com	Rainsville	AL	35986	256-638-2144	638-4830	736
FTC (Feed the Children) PO Box 36 TF: 800-627-4556 ■ Web: www.feedthechildren.org	Oklahoma City	OK	73101	405-942-0228		48-5
FTC (Farmers Telephone Company Inc) 615 Iowa St TF: 800-628-5989 ■ Web: www.heartland.net	Coin	IA	51636	712-379-3001	379-4000	224

Phone | Fax | Class

FTC (Fulton Telephone Company Inc)
402 W Beene St .... Fulton MS 38843 662-862-2196 224
Web: www.fultontelephone.com

FTD Inc 3113 Woodcreek Dr .... Downers Grove IL 60515 800-736-3383 292
TF: 800-736-3383 ■ *Web:* www.ftd.com

FTF Engineering Inc
1916 Mcallister St .... San Francisco CA 94115 415-931-8460 261
Web: www.ftfengineering.com

FTG Circuits Inc 20750 Marilla St. .... Chatsworth CA 91311 818-407-4024 625
Web: www.ftgcorp.com

FTG Inc 725 Marshall Phelps Rd. .... Windsor CT 06095 860-610-6000 610-6001 246

FTG Texas 7300 N Gessner. .... Houston TX 77040 713-856-2000 535
Web: www.ftg-texas.com

FTI Consulting
16701 Melford Blvd Ste 200. .... Annapolis MD 21401 800-334-5701 224-9740* 445
NYSE: FCN ■ **Fax Area Code:* 410 ■ *TF:* 800-334-5701 ■ *Web:* www.fticonsulting.com

FTI Flow Technology Inc
8930 S Beck Ave Ste 107 .... Tempe AZ 85284 480-240-3400 201
Web: ftimeters.com

FTJ FundChoice LLC
2300 Litton Ln Ste 102 .... Hebron KY 41048 800-379-2513 387
TF: 800-379-2513 ■ *Web:* portalcontent.ftjfundchoice.com

FTMC (Fisher-Titus Medical Ctr)
272 Benedict Ave .... Norwalk OH 44857 419-668-8101 374-3
TF: 800-589-3862 ■ *Web:* www.fishertitus.org

FTS (Fox Television Stations Inc)
1999 S Bundy Dr .... Los Angeles CA 90025 310-584-2025 741-99
Web: www.myfoxla.com

FTS International Express Inc
840 Mark St .... Elk Grove Village IL 60007 630-694-0644 694-0778 311
Web: www.fts.com

FTZ Industries Inc
515 Palmetto Dr .... Simpsonville SC 29681 864-963-5000 963-5352 815
Web: www.ftzind.com

Fu Lin Chinese Restaurant
200 N Bowman Rd .... Little Rock AR 72211 501-225-8989 671
Web: www.fulinlr.com

Fuchs Lubricants Canada Ltd
405 Dobbie Dr .... Cambridge ON N1T1S9 519-622-2040 541
Web: www.fuchs.com

Fuchs North America
3800 Hampstead Mexico Rd. .... Hampstead MD 21074 410-363-1700 363-6619 296-37
TF: 800-365-3229 ■ *Web:* www.fuchsna.com

Fudge Hut, The 933 Front St. .... Leavenworth WA 98826 509-548-0466 296-8
Web: www.fudgehut.com

Fudge Marcia L (Rep D - OH)
2344 Rayburn House Office Bldg .... Washington DC 20515 202-225-7032 225-1339 342-2
Web: www.fudge.house.gov

FUEL Digital Marketing & Branding
25 E Court St Ste 100. .... Greenville SC 29601 864-627-1676 5
Web: fuelforbrands.com

Fuel Education LLC
2300 Corporate Park Dr .... Herndon VA 20171 866-912-8588 178-3
TF: 866-912-8588 ■ *Web:* www.fueleducation.com

Fuel Masters LLC 133 Caddo Dr. .... Abilene TX 79602 325-676-3835 579
TF: 866-455-3835 ■ *Web:* www.fuelmasters.com

Fuel Tech Inc
27601 Bella Vista Pkwy .... Warrenville IL 60555 630-845-4500 845-4502 18
NASDAQ: FTEK ■ *TF:* 800-666-9688 ■ *Web:* www.ftek.com

FuelCell Energy Inc
3 Great Pasture Rd .... Danbury CT 06810 203-825-6000 253
NASDAQ: FCEL ■ *Web:* www.fuelcellenergy.com

FuelFX LLC 1811 Bering Dr .... Houston TX 77057 855-472-7316 195
TF: 855-472-7316 ■ *Web:* www.fuelfx.com

Fuga Salon & Spa 3853 N Southport Ave .... Chicago IL 60613 773-880-1280 77
Web: www.salonfuga.com

Fugato 325 Alcazar Ave. .... Coral Gables FL 33134 786-420-2910 671
Web: www.fugatorestaurant.com

Fugro Consultants LP
6100 Hillcroft Ave. .... Houston TX 77081 713-369-5400 261
Web: www.fugro.com

Fugue State Press (FSP)
PO Box 80 Cooper Station .... New York NY 10276 917-806-1648 693-6152* 637-2
**Fax Area Code:* 208 ■ *Web:* www.fuguestatepress.com

Fuji Chemical Industries USA
3 Terri Ln Unit 12 .... Burlington NJ 08016 609-386-3030 386-3033 297-8
TF: 877-385-4777 ■ *Web:* www.fujihealthscience.com

Fuji Machine America
171 Corporate Woods Pky .... Vernon Hills IL 60061 847-821-7137 821-7815 695
Web: www.fujimachine.com

Fuji Sushi Bar 8226 E 71st St .... Tulsa OK 74133 918-250-1821 671
Web: fujitulsa.com

Fuji Trading (America) Inc
8515 Kelso Dr Ste A&B .... Baltimore MD 21221 410-238-7985 238-7989 559
Web: www.fujitrading.us

Fuji Vegetable Oil Inc
1 Barker Ave .... White Plains NY 10601 912-966-5900 296-30
Web: www.fujioilusa.com

FUJIFILM Holdings America Corp
200 Summit Lake Dr. .... Valhalla NY 10595 914-789-8100 658
TF: 800-755-3854 ■ *Web:* www.fujifilm.com

Fujii Farms Inc
2511 S Troutdale Rd PO Box 188 .... Troutdale OR 97060 503-665-6659 661-2799 315-1
Web: fujiifarms.com

Fujikin of America Inc 454 Kato Ter .... Fremont CA 94539 408-980-8269 980-0572 612
Web: www.fujikin.com

Fujimi Corp 11200 SW Leveton Dr. .... Tualatin OR 97062 503-682-7822 612-9721 1
Web: www.fujimiam.com

Fujisankei Communications International Inc
150 E 52nd St 34th Fl. .... New York NY 10022 212-753-8100 514
Web: www.fujisankei.com

Fujita Research PO Box 55545. .... Valencia CA 91385 818-981-2657 981-0829 174
Web: www.fujitaresearch.com

Fujitec America Inc 7258 Innovation Way. .... Mason OH 45040 513-932-8000 256
Web: www.fujitecamerica.com

Fujitsu General America Inc
353 Rt 46 W .... Fairfield NJ 07004 973-575-0380 610
TF: 888-888-3424 ■ *Web:* www.fujitsugeneral.com

Fuji-Ya 600 W Lake St. .... Minneapolis MN 55408 612-871-4055 671
Web: fujiyasushi.com

Fujiyama Steakhouse of Japanese
5149 Victory Dr .... Indianapolis IN 46203 317-787-7900 671
Web: www.fujiyamaindy.com

Fukken Wax
175 Liza Ln. .... Commerce Charter Township MI 48382 877-385-5361 723-9710* 151
**Fax Area Code:* 800 ■ *TF:* 877-385-5361 ■ *Web:* www.FukkenWax.com

Fukuda Denshi USA Inc (FDUSA)
17725 NE 65th St .... Redmond WA 98052 425-881-7737 869-2018 476
TF: 800-365-6668 ■ *Web:* www.fukuda.com

Fukuvi USA Inc 7631 Progress Ct .... Huber Heights OH 45424 937-236-7288 596
Web: www.fukuvi-usa.com

Fulbright & Fulbright CPA PA
5302 NC Hwy 55 Ste 104 PO Box 13156 .... Durham NC 27713 919-544-0398 544-8719 2
Web: moneyful.com

Fulcher Russ (Rep R - ID)
1520 Longworth House Office Bldg .... Washington DC 20515 202-225-6611 342-2
Web: www.fulcher.house.gov

Fulcher's Point Pride Seafood Inc
101 S Ave .... Oriental NC 28571 252-249-0123 249-2337 296-14
Web: www.fulchers.com

Fulco Fulfillment Inc 26 Richboynton Rd .... Dover NJ 07801 973-361-1700 317
Web: www.fulcofulfillment.com

Fulcrum Analytics Inc
70 W 40th St 10th Fl. .... New York NY 10018 212-651-7000 195
Web: www.fulcrumanalytics.com

Fulcrum ConsultingWorks Inc
17204 Dorchester Dr .... Cleveland OH 44119 216-486-9570 194
Web: www.fulcrumcwi.com

Fulcrum Container LLC
3180 Spruce St. .... Saint Paul MN 55117 651-481-8601 481-8726 98
Web: www.fulcruminc.com

Fulcrum Financial Inquiry LLP
888 S Figueroa St Ste 2000 .... Los Angeles CA 90017 213-787-4100 463
Web: www.fulcrum.com

Fulcrum Group Inc, The
5751 Kroger Dr Ste 279 .... Fort Worth TX 76244 817 337 0300 180
Web: www.fulcrum.pro

Fulcrum International Ltd
164 Mason St .... Greenwich CT 06830 203-869-8181 194
Web: www.thefulcrumintl.com

Fulcrum Publishing
4690 Table Mountain Dr Ste 100 .... Golden CO 80403 303-277-1623 726-7112* 637-2
**Fax Area Code:* 800 ■ *TF:* 800-992-2908 ■ *Web:* www.fulcrum-books.com

Fulcrum Technologies Inc
712 Aurora Ave N .... Seattle WA 98109 206-336-5656 177
TF: 855-336-5160 ■ *Web:* www.fulcrum.net

Fuld & Company Inc 131 Oliver St 3rd Fl. .... Boston MA 02110 617-492-5900 463
Web: www.fuld.com

Fulenwider Enterprises Inc
104 Mull St. .... Morganton NC 28655 828-437-8000 194
Web: www.fulenwider.net

Fulfillment Concepts Inc
2200 Ampere Dr .... Jeffersontown KY 40299 800-910-5306 5
TF: 800-910-5306 ■ *Web:* www.fulfillmentconcepts.com

Fulflex Inc 32 Justin Holden Dr .... Brattleboro VT 05301 802-257-5256 257-5602 745-5
TF: 800-283-2500 ■ *Web:* www.fulflex.com

Fulghum Industries 317 S Main St. .... Wadley GA 30477 478-252-5223 683
Web: www.fulghum.com

Fulghum Macindoe & Associates Inc
10330 Hardin Valley Rd Ste 201 .... Knoxville TN 37932 865-690-6419 261
Web: www.fulghummacindoe.com

Fulham & Company Inc
593 Washington St .... Wellesley MA 02482 781-235-2266 528
Web: www.fulhamco.com

Fulkerson Services Inc 111 Parce Rd .... Fairport NY 14450 585-223-2541 321
Web: fulkersonservices.com

Full Access Brokerage
1240 Charnelton St. .... Eugene OR 97401 541-284-5070 690
TF: 866-890-5743 ■ *Web:* fullaccess.org

Full Cir Bookstore 1900 NW Expy .... Oklahoma City OK 73118 405-842-2900 842-2894 95
Web: fullcirclebooks.com

Full Circle Health Services
1460 Morris Ave Ste 2A .... Union NJ 07083 908-624-1005 624-1010 363
Web: www.fullcirclehealthservices.com

Full Employment Council Inc
1740 Paseo Blvd. .... Kansas City MO 64108 816-471-2330 260
Web: www.feckc.org

Full Frame Documentary Film Festival
201 Foster St .... Durham NC 27701 919-687-4100 282
Web: www.fullframefest.org

Full House Resorts Inc
4670 S Fort Apache Rd Ste 190 .... Las Vegas NV 89147 702-221-7800 221-8101 132
NASDAQ: FLL ■ *TF:* 800-209-9436 ■ *Web:* www.fullhouseresorts.com

Full Sail University
3300 University Blvd .... Winter Park FL 32792 407-679-6333 800
TF: 800-226-7625 ■ *Web:* www.fullsail.edu

Full Spectrum Laser LLC
6216 S Sandhill Rd. .... Las Vegas NV 89120 702-802-3100 987-0150 177
Web: fslaser.com

Full Spectrum Software
225 Tpke Rd .... Southborough MA 01772 508 620 6400 177
Web: www.fullspectrumsoftware.com

Full Swing Golf Inc
10890 Thornmint Rd. .... San Diego CA 92127 858-675-1100 253
TF: 800-798-9094 ■ *Web:* www.fullswinggolf.com

Fullen Dock & Warehouse Inc
382 Klinke Rd .... Memphis TN 38127 901-358-9544 191-1
TF: 800-467-7104 ■ *Web:* www.fullendock.com

Fullen School of Hair Design
1909 Broadway St. .... Scottsbluff NE 69361 308-632-3731 632-4793 685
Web: www.fullenschoolofhairdesign.com

Fuller Box Co
150 Chestnut St PO Box 9 .... North Attleboro MA 02760 508-695-2525 695-2187 488
Web: www.fullerbox.com

Fuller Brush Co
1 Fuller Way PO Box 729 .... Great Bend KS 67530 620-792-1711 103
TF: 800-522-0499 ■ *Web:* fuller.com

Phone Fax Class

Fuller Craft Museum 455 Oak St .... Brockton MA 02301 508-588-6000 587-6191 520
TF: 800-639-4808 ■ *Web:* fullercraft.org

Fuller Engineering Co 4135 W 99th St .... Carmel IN 46032 317-228-5800 228-5810 186
Web: fullerengr.com

Fuller Industrial 65 Nelson Rd .... Lively ON P3Y1P4 705-682-2777 682-4777 595
TF: 888-524-3777 ■ *Web:* www.fullerindustrial.com

Fuller Landau SENCRL
1010 De La Gauchetiere St W Pl du Canada
Ste 200 .... Montreal QC H3B2S1 514-875-2865 2
Web: www.fullerlandau.com

Fuller Manufacturing Inc
130 Ridge Rd .... Sutter Creek CA 95685 209-267-5071 267-9338 425
Web: www.fullermfg.com

Fuller Supply Co
1958 Turner Ave NW .... Grand Rapids MI 49504 616-364-8455 364-4817 385
TF: 800-292-8768 ■ *Web:* www.fullersupplycompany.com

Fuller Theological Seminary
135 N Oakland Ave .... Pasadena CA 91182 626-584-5200 167-3
TF: 800-235-2222 ■ *Web:* www.fuller.edu

Fullerton & Knowles PC
12644 Chapel Rd Ste 206 .... Clifton VA 20124 703-818-2600 428
Web: www.fullertonlaw.com

Fullerton Arboretum
1900 Associated Rd .... Fullerton CA 92831 657-278-3407 278-7066 97
Web: www.fullertonarboretum.org

Fullerton Building Systems (FBS)
34620 250th St PO Box 308 .... Worthington MN 56187 507-376-3128 376-9530 817
TF: 800-450-9782 ■ *Web:* www.fullertonbuildingsystems.com

Fullerton Chamber of Commerce
444 N Harbor Blvd Ste 200 .... Fullerton CA 92832 714-871-3100 871-2871 139
Web: www.nocchamber.com

Fullerton College 321 E Chapman Ave .... Fullerton CA 92832 714-992-7000 162
Web: www.fullcoll.edu

Fullerton Public Library
353 W Commonwealth Ave .... Fullerton CA 92832 714-738-6333 447-3280 434-3
Web: www.cityoffullerton.com

Fullerton Tool Company Inc
121 Perry St .... Saginaw MI 48602 989-799-4550 792-3335 493
TF: 855-722-7243 ■ *Web:* www.fullertontool.com

Fullsteam Brewery LLC 726 Rigsbee Ave .... Durham NC 27701 919-682-2337 102
Web: fullsteam.ag

FullStory 1745 Peachtree Rd NW Ste G .... Atlanta GA 30309 678-337-1868 39
Web: www.fullstory.com

Fully Promoted
2121 Vista Pkwy .... West Palm Beach FL 33411 561-640-7367 310
TF: 877-877-0234 ■ *Web:* fullypromoted.com

Fulmer Co 122 Gayoso Ave .... Memphis TN 38103 901-525-5711 517
Web: www.fulmerlogistics.com

Fulton 58
Fulton Missouri 2 Hornet Dr .... Fulton MO 65251 573-590-8000 590-8090 685
TF: 800-456-2634 ■ *Web:* www.fulton58.org

Fulton Breakefield Broenniman LLC
4520 E W Hwy Ste 450 .... Bethesda MD 20814 301-657-8870 657-0866 401
TF: 800-966-6554 ■ *Web:* www.fbbcapitalpartners.com

Fulton Corp 303 Eighth Ave .... Fulton IL 61252 800-252-0002 589-4433* 350
**Fax Area Code:* 815 ■ *TF:* 800-252-0002 ■ *Web:* www.fultoncorp.com

Fulton Cos 972 Centerville Rd .... Pulaski NY 13142 315-298-5121 298-6390 357
Web: www.fulton.com

Fulton County 141 Pryor St .... Atlanta GA 30303 404-612-4000 338
Web: www.fultoncountytaxes.org

Fulton County 2216 Myron Cory Dr Ste 1 .... Hickman KY 42050 270-236-2594 236-7904 338
Web: www.fultoncounty.ky.gov

Fulton County 100 N Main St .... Lewistown IL 61542 309-547-3041 547-3674 338
Web: www.fultonco.org

Fulton County
122 W Market St Ste 202 .... McConnellsburg PA 17233 717-485-6862 485-9411 338
Web: co.fulton.pa.us

Fulton County 815 Main St .... Rochester IN 46975 574-223-4339 224-4340 338
Web: www.co.fulton.in.us

Fulton County 152 S Fulton St .... Wauseon OH 43567 419-337-9255 337-9285 338
Web: www.fultoncountyoh.com

Fulton County Rural Electric Membership Corp
1448 W State Rd 14 PO Box 230 .... Rochester IN 46975 574-223-3156 245
Web: www.faqs.org

Fulton Five 5 Fulton St .... Charleston SC 29401 843-853-5555 671
Web: www.fultonfivecharleston.com

Fulton Homes Corp
9140 S Kyrene Rd Ste 202 .... Tempe AZ 85284 480-753-6789 753-5554 187
Web: www.fultonhomes.com

Fulton Industries Inc
135 E Linfoot St .... Wauseon OH 43567 419-335-3015 335-3215 439
TF: 800-537-5012 ■ *Web:* www.fultonindoh.com

Fulton Iron & Manufacturing LLC
3844 Walsh St .... Saint Louis MO 63116 314-752-2400 298
Web: www.fultoniron.net

Fulton Montgomery Regional Chamber of Commerce
2 North Main St .... Gloversville NY 12078 518-725-0641 47
Web: www.fultonmontgomeryny.org

Fulton Precision Industries Inc
300 Success Dr .... McConnellsburg PA 17233 717-485-5158 14
Web: www.fultonprecision.com

Fulton State Hospital 600 E Fifth St .... Fulton MO 65251 573-592-4100 592-3000 374-5
Web: dmh.mo.gov

Fulton Telephone Company Inc (FTC)
402 W Beene St .... Fulton MS 38843 662-862-2196 224
Web: www.fultontelephone.com

Fulton Theatre
12 N Prince St PO Box 1865 .... Lancaster PA 17608 717-394-7133 397-3780 572
Web: thefulton.org

Fulton-Denver Co 3500 Wynkoop St .... Denver CO 80216 303-294-9292 67
TF: 800-521-1414 ■ *Web:* fultonpacific.com

Fulton-Montgomery Community College
2805 State Hwy 67 .... Johnstown NY 12095 518-762-4651 762-4334 162
Web: www.fmcc.edu

Fultz Maddox Dickens PLC
101 S Fifth St 27th Fl .... Louisville KY 40202 502-588-2000 588-2020 428
Web: fmdlegal.com

Fumoto Engineering of America Inc
3330 Industrial Dr .... Santa Rosa CA 95403 707-545-7020 546-1910 61
TF: 800-918-3406 ■ *Web:* www.fumotousa.com

Fun 101.3 FM 1996 Auction Rd .... Manheim PA 17545 717-653-0800 653-0122 645
TF: 800-655-4101 ■ *Web:* www.fun1013.com

Fun Beverage Inc
175 School House Loop .... Kalispell MT 59901 406-752-1455 752-5678 81-1
Web: www.funbeverage.com

Fun Express PO Box 2389 .... Omaha NE 68103 800-228-0122 228-1002 44
TF: 800-228-0122 ■ *Web:* www.funexpress.com

Fun Media Group Inc
981 N Brindlee Mountain Pkwy .... Arab AL 35016 256-586-9300 645-141
Web: www.fun927.com

Fun Town Splash Town USA Inc
US Rt 1 774 Portland Rd .... Saco ME 04072 207-284-5139 283-4716 32
Web: www.funtownsplashtownusa.com

Funagain Games of Ashland
149 E Main St .... Ashland OR 97520 541-708-6788 761
Web: www.funagain.com

Funai Corp 201 Rt 17 N Ste 903 .... Rutherford NJ 07070 614-497-2689 52
Web: www.funai.us

Function Engineering Inc
163 Everett Ave .... Palo Alto CA 94301 650-326-8834 261
Web: www.function.com

Function Junction Inc
2450 Grand Blvd .... Kansas City MO 64108 816-283-3033 362
Web: www.functionjunction.com

Function Point Productivity Software Inc
2034 11th Ave W Ste 140 .... Vancouver BC V6J2C9 877-731-2522 809
TF: 877-731-2522 ■ *Web:* functionpoint.com

Functional Products Inc
8282 Bavaria Dr E .... Macedonia OH 44056 330-963-3060 963-3322 541
Web: functionalproducts.com

Fund for American Studies, The
1706 New Hampshire Ave NW .... Washington DC 20009 202-986-0384 986-0390 242
Web: tfas.org

Fund for Peace, The
1101 14th St NW Ste 1020 .... Washington DC 20005 202-223-7940 48-5
Web: global.fundforpeace.org

Fundamental Broadcasting Network
520 Roberts Rd .... Newport NC 28570 252-223-4600 223-2201 647
TF: 800-245-9685 ■ *Web:* www.fbnradio.com

Fundcraft Publishing Inc
410 Hwy 72 W .... Collierville TN 38027 901-853-7070 853-6196 627
TF: 800-259-2592 ■ *Web:* www.fundcraft.com

Funder America Inc 200 Funder Dr .... Mocksville NC 27028 336-751-3501 751-5623 819
Web: funderamerica.com

Fundera 123 William St 21st Fl .... New York NY 10038 800-386-3372 49-2
TF: 800-386-3372 ■ *Web:* www.fundera.com

Fundrise 11 Dupont Cir NW 9th Fl .... Washington DC 20036 202-584-0550 178-1
Web: fundrise.com

FundThrough Inc
260 Spadina Ave Ste 400 .... Toronto ON M5T2E4 800-766-0460 224
TF: 800-766-0460 ■ *Web:* www.fundthrough.com

Funeral Consumers Alliance
33 Patchen Rd .... South Burlington VT 05403 802-865-8300 865-2626 48-10
TF: 800-765-0107 ■ *Web:* funerals.org

Funeral Service Insider
3349 Hwy 138 Bldg D Ste B .... Wall NJ 07719 800-500-4585 531-13
TF: 800-500-4585 ■ *Web:* kates-boylston.com

Fung's Kitchen Catering Inc
7320 SW Fwy Ste 115 .... Houston TX 77074 713-779-2288 271-2288 671
Web: eatatfungs.com

FUNimation Entertainment Ltd
1200 Lakeside Pkwy Bldg 1 .... Flower Mound TX 75028 972-355-7300 514
Web: www.funimation.com

Funter Bay State Marine Park
400 Willoughby Ave 5th Fl PO Box 111071 .... Juneau AK 99811 907-465-2495 465-3886 565
Web: www.dnr.alaska.gov

Funville Mobile Carnival
415 Plainview Heights Cir .... Greeneville TN 37745 423-638-9818 366
Web: www.funvilleisfun.com

FUOSV (Farmers Union Oil Company of Southern Valley)
204 S Front St .... Fairmount ND 58030 701-474-5440 316
Web: www.fuosv.com

FUP (Friends United Press)
101 Quaker Hill Dr .... Richmond IN 47374 765-962-7573 966-1293 637-2
TF: 800-537-8839 ■ *Web:* shop.fum.org

Fuqua Development, Lp
3575 Piedmont Rd .... Atlanta GA 30305 404-907-1709 653
Web: fuquadevelopment.com

Fuqua Homes Inc
4621 S Cooper St Ste 131 .... Arlington TX 76017 817-465-3211 505

Fuquay-Varina Area Chamber of Commerce
1000 N Main St Ste 102 .... Fuquay-Varina NC 27526 919-552-4947 552-1029 139
Web: fuquay-varina.com

Furino & Son Inc 66 Columbia Rd .... Branchburg NJ 08876 908-756-7736 186
Web: www.furinoandsons.com

Furiwa Restaurant
15111 Beach Blvd .... Westminster CA 92683 714-534-3996 671
Web: www.furiwa.com

Furman 1690 Corporate Cir .... Petaluma CA 94954 707-763-1010 763-1310 52
TF: 877-486-4738 ■ *Web:* www.furmanpower.com

Furman Roth Advertising
801 2nd Ave Rm 1400 .... New York NY 10017 212-687-2300 7
Web: www.furmanroth.com

Furman University
3300 Poinsett Hwy .... Greenville SC 29613 864-294-2000 294-2018 166
Web: www.furman.edu

Furmano Foods Inc
770 Cannery Rd .... Northumberland PA 17857 570-473-3516 473-7367 296-20
TF: 877-877-6032 ■ *Web:* www.furmanos.com

Furnace Improvements Services Inc
1600 Hwy 6 Ste 480 .... Sugar Land TX 77478 281-980-0325 261
Web: heatflux.com

Furnel Inc 350 S Stewart Ave .... Addison IL 60101 630-543-0885 604
Web: www.furnel.com

Company	Address	City	State	Zip	Phone	Fax	Class
Furniture Buy Consignment Inc	1348 W Main St *Web:* www.furniturebuyconsignment.com	Lewisville	TX	75067	972-436-4389		321
Furniture Connection Inc	1891 Ft Campbell Blvd *Web:* furnitureconnectionclarksville.com	Clarksville	TN	37042	931-645-1340		321
Furniture Fair	7200 Dixie Hwy *Web:* furniturefair.net	Fairfield	OH	45014	513-874-5553		321
Furniture Institute of Massachusetts, The	116 Water St *Web:* www.furnituremakingclasses.com	Beverly	MA	01915	978-922-0615		167-3
Furniture Mall of Kansas	1901 SW Wanamaker Rd *Web:* www.furnituremallofkansas.com	Topeka	KS	66604	785-271-0684		321
Furniture Medic	2183 Monroe Ave *TF:* 888-611-7320 ■ *Web:* www.furnituremedic.com	Memphis	TN	38104	901-597-8727		310
Furniture Outlets USA Inc	140 E Hinks Ln *TF:* 877-395-8998 ■ *Web:* www.thefurnituremart.com	Sioux Falls	SD	57104	605-336-5000		290
Furniture Values International LLC	601 N 75th Ave *Web:* www.aspenhome.net	Phoenix	AZ	85043	602-442-5600		319-2
Furniture/Today Magazine	7025 Albert Pick Rd Ste 200 *Web:* www.furnituretoday.com	Greensboro	NC	27409	336-605-0121	605-1143	457-21
FurnitureDealernet Inc	507 E Travelers Trl *Web:* www.furnituredealer.net	Burnsville	MN	55337	952-345-7171		530
Furnitureland South Inc	5635 Riverdale Rd *Web:* www.furniturelandsouth.com	Jamestown	NC	27282	336-822-3000		321
Furry Inc	2005 E Voorhees St *Web:* www.furryinc.net	Danville	IL	61834	217-446-0084	446-0085	454
Furst-McNess Co	120 E Clark St *TF:* 800-435-5100 ■ *Web:* www.mcness.com	Freeport	IL	61032	815-232-9705		447
Further	1750 Yankee Doodle Rd *TF:* 800-859-2144 ■ *Web:* hellofurther.com	Eagan	MN	55121	651-662-5065	662-7247	463
Furuno USA Inc	4400 NW Pacific Rim Blvd *Web:* www.furuno.com	Camas	WA	98607	360-834-9300		770
Furusato	10012 82nd Ave *Web:* www.furusatoedmonton.com	Edmonton	AB	T6E1Y9	780-439-1335		671
Fury Duarte PS	1606 148th Ave SE Ste 102 *Web:* furyduarte.com	Bellevue	WA	98007	425-643-1606		41
FUS (Franciscan University of Steubenville)	1235 University Blvd *TF:* 800-783-6220 ■ *Web:* www.franciscan.edu	Steubenville	OH	43952	740-283-3771		166
Fusato CPA Inc	1748 Wili Pa Loop *Web:* fusatocpa.com	Wailuku	HI	96793	808-242-9100		2
Fusco Corp	555 Long Wharf Dr Long Wharf Maritime Ctr Ste 14 *Web:* www.fusco.com	New Haven	CT	06511	203-777-7451		186
Fuscoe Engineering Inc	16795 Von Karman Ave Ste 100 *Web:* www.fuscoe.com	Irvine	CA	92606	949-474-1960		256
Fuse Inc	802 N First St *Web:* www.fuseadvertising.com	Saint Louis	MO	63102	314-421-4040		7
FuseGlobal Partners	1000 Brannan St Ste 503 *Web:* www.fuseglobal.com	San Francisco	CA	94103	415-869-8669	680-2476	194
Fuseproject LLC	1401 16th St *Web:* fuseproject.com	San Francisco	CA	94103	415-908-1492	908-1491	196
Fusibond Piping Systems Inc	2615 Curtiss St *Web:* www.fusibond.com	Downers Grove	IL	60515	630-969-4488	969-2355	596
Fusicology LLC	2658 Griffith Park Blvd Ste 128 *TF:* 800-980-3873 ■ *Web:* fusicology.com	Los Angeles	CA	90039	323-988-2424		393
FUSION b2b Inc	1548 Bond St Ste 114 *Web:* www.fusionb2b.com	Naperville	IL	60563	630-579-8300		7
Fusion Ceramics Inc	PO Box 127 *Web:* fusionceramics.com	Carrollton	OH	44615	330-627-2191	627-2082	145
Fusion Design	440 N Central Ave *Web:* www.fusiondesigninc.com	Campbell	CA	95008	408-378-9980		256
Fusion Grill	550 Academy Rd *Web:* www.fusiongrill.mb.ca	Winnipeg	MB	R3N0E3	204-489-6963		671
Fusion Imaging inc	601 Boro St *TF:* 800-943-5200 ■ *Web:* www.fusionimaging.com	Kaysville	UT	84037	801-546-4567		5
Fusion Inc	4658 E 355th St *Web:* www.fusion-inc.com	Willoughby	OH	44094	440-946-3300	942-9083	386
Fusion Optix Inc	19 Wheeling Ave *Web:* www.fusionoptix.com	Woburn	MA	01801	781-995-0805		608
Fusion Packaging Solutions Inc	3333 Welborn St - Ste 400 *Web:* fusionpkg.com	Dallas	TX	75219	214-747-2004		393
Fusion Risk Management Inc	3601 W Algonquin Rd Ste 500 *Web:* www.fusionrm.com	Rolling Meadows	IL	60008	847-632-1002		195
Fusion Solutions Inc	5000 Legacy Dr Ste 220 *TF:* 888-817-1951 ■ *Web:* www.fusionsolutionsinc.com	Plano	TX	75024	972-764-1708	732-1733	194
Fusion Tech	218 20th Ave *Web:* ftiinc.org	Roseville	IL	61473	309-774-4275		791
Fusion Telecommunications International Inc	420 Lexington Ave Ste 1718 *NASDAQ: FSNN* ■ *TF:* 888-301-1721 ■ *Web:* www.fusionconnect.com	New York	NY	10170	212-201-2400	972-7884	736
Fusionapps LLC	110 Meadowlands Pkwy *Web:* fusionapps.com	Secaucus	NJ	07094	201-751-9988		180
Fusionary Media	220 Grandville SW *Web:* www.fusionary.com	Grand Rapids	MI	49503	616-454-2357		7
Fusionbox Inc	2031 Curtis St *Web:* www.fusionbox.com	Denver	CO	80205	303-952-7490		178-11
Fusionist LLC	438 Amapola Ave Ste 225 *Web:* www.fusionist.com	Torrance	CA	90501	310-787-7877	787-7871	410
FusionOne Inc	11 N Roselle Rd **Fax Area Code:* 630 ■ *TF:* 877-387-6300 ■ *Web:* www.fusiononeinc.com	Roselle	IL	60172	877-387-6300	307-7147*	177
Fusionworks Inc	120 Condado Ave Pico Ctr Ste 102 *Web:* fwpr.com	San Juan	PR	00907	787-721-1039		180
Fuss & O'Neill Consulting Engineers Inc	146 Hartford Rd **Fax Area Code:* 860 ■ *TF:* 800-286-2469 ■ *Web:* www.fando.com	Manchester	CT	06040	800-286-2469	533-5143*	261
Fust Charles Chambers LLP	5786 Widewaters Pkwy *Web:* www.fcc-cpa.com	Syracuse	NY	13214	315-446-3600		2
Fuston, Petway & French LLP	600 Luckie Dr Ste 300 *Web:* fpflaw.com	Birmingham	AL	35223	205-977-9798		41
Futaba Corporation of America	711 E State Pkwy *Web:* www.futaba.com	Schaumburg	IL	60173	847-884-1444	884-1635	173-4
Futaba Industrial Texas Corp	1 Lone Star Pass Bldg 34 *Web:* www.futabasangyo.com	San Antonio	TX	78264	210-927-2288	927-4500	61
FUTEK Advanced Sensor Technology Inc	10 Thomas *TF:* 800-233-8835 ■ *Web:* www.futek.com	Irvine	CA	92618	949-465-0900		256
Futrend Technology Inc	8605 Westwood Center Dr Ste 502 *Web:* www.futrend.com	Vienna	VA	22182	703-556-0016	556-0199	177
Futrex Inc	130 Western Maryland Pkwy *Web:* www.futrex.com	Hagerstown	MD	21740	301-791-9220		250
Futuramic Tool & Engineering Co	24680 Gibson Dr *Web:* www.futuramic.com	Warren	MI	48089	586-758-2200	758-0641	757
Future Acquisition Company LLC	9990 Richmond Ave Ste 202s *TF:* 855-849-2056 ■ *Web:* www.futureacq.com	Houston	TX	77042	832-831-3700	831-3719	536
Future Business Leaders of America-Phi Beta Lambda Inc (FBLA-PBL)	1912 Assn Dr **Fax Area Code:* 866 ■ *TF:* 800-325-2946 ■ *Web:* www.fbla-pbl.org	Reston	VA	20191	800-325-2946	500-5610*	48-11
Future Chevrolet of Sacramento	4811 Madison Ave *Web:* www.futurechevyofsac.com	Sacramento	CA	95841	916-331-6777		516
Future Com Ltd	3600 William D Tate Ave Ste 300 *TF:* 888-710-5250 ■ *Web:* www.myfuturecom.com	Grapevine	TX	76051	817-510-1100	510-1159	180
Future Computing Solutions Inc	23800 Via Del Rio *Web:* www.fcsinet.com	Yorba Linda	CA	92887	714-692-9120	692-9420	177
Future Cure Inc	2 W Mountain Rd **Fax Area Code:* 203 ■ *TF:* 800-673-2493 ■ *Web:* www.futurecure.com	Ridgefield	CT	06877	800-673-2493	438-6017*	695
Future Electronics	237 Hymus Blvd *TF:* 800-675-1619 ■ *Web:* www.futureelectronics.com	Pointe-Claire	QC	H9R5C7	514-694-7710	695-3707	246
Future Financial Planners Inc	847 Broadway *Web:* www.ffpinc.com	Bayonne	NJ	07002	201-823-1030		463
Future Foam Inc	1610 Avenue North *TF:* 800-733-8061 ■ *Web:* www.futurefoam.com	Council Bluffs	IA	51501	712-323-9122		601
Future Force Inc	15800 NW 57th Ave *TF:* 800-683-0681 ■ *Web:* www.futureforcepersonnel.com	Miami Lakes	FL	33014	305-557-4900		260
Future Harvest Development Ltd	725 Evans Crt *Web:* www.futureharvest.com	Kelowna	BC	V1X6G4	250-491-0255		429
Future Home Technology Inc	33 Ralph St *TF:* 800-342-8650 ■ *Web:* www.modulartoday.com	Port Jervis	NY	12771	800-342-8650		364
Future Horizons Inc	721 W Abram St *TF:* 800-489-0727 ■ *Web:* www.fhautism.com	Arlington	TX	76013	817-277-0727	277-2270	637-2
Future Image Inc	520 S El Camino Real Ste 206a *Web:* www.futureimage.com	San Mateo	CA	94402	650-579-0493	579-0566	668
Future Inns	30 Fairfax Dr *Web:* www.futureinns.co.uk	Halifax	NS	B3S1P1	902-443-4200		379
Future Media Concepts Inc	299 Broadway Ste 1510 *TF:* 877-362-8724 ■ *Web:* www.fmctraining.com	New York	NY	10007	212-233-3500	233-3517	772
Future Path Medical Holding Company LLC	7757 Auburn Rd Ste 21 *Web:* future-path.net	Painesville	OH	44077	440-354-4044	210-6502	743
Future Pipe Industries Inc	11811-11812 Proctor Rd *Web:* www.futurepipe.com	Houston	TX	77038	281-847-2987		595
Future PLC	11 W 42nd St 15th Fl *Web:* www.futureplc.com	New York	NY	10036	212-378-0465		457-11
Future Pro Inc	200 N Main St **Fax Area Code:* 620 ■ *TF:* 800-328-4625 ■ *Web:* www.futureproinc.com	Inman	KS	67546	800-328-4625	585-6799*	711
Future Products Corp	885 Rochester Rd S *Web:* future-products.com	Troy	MI	48083	248-588-1060	588-7303	757
Future Research Corp	675 Discovery Dr Bldg 2 Ste 102 *Web:* www.future-research.com	Huntsville	AL	35806	256-430-4304		261
Future Tech	6500 Spid *Web:* www.futuretechsolutions.com	Corpus Christi	TX	78415	361-991-8669		175
Future Tech Enterprise Inc	101-8 Colin Dr *Web:* www.ftei.com	Holbrook	NY	11741	631-472-5500	472-6599	177
Future Technologies Inc	12600 Fair Lakes Cir Ste 200 *Web:* www.ftechi.com	Fairfax	VA	22033	703-278-0199	385-0886	261
Future Test Inc	24430 N 20th Dr *Web:* www.futuretest.com	Phoenix	AZ	85085	623-580-0162	516-4934	256
Future Visions	PO Box 591 *Web:* futurevisions.com	Taylorsville	KY	40071	502-419-1087		177
Futurebiotics LLC	70 Commerce Dr *TF:* 800-645-1721 ■ *Web:* www.bronsonvitamins.com	Hauppauge	NY	11788	800-645-1721		799
FutureCare Canton Harbor	1300 S Ellwood Ave *Web:* futurecare.com	Baltimore	MD	21224	410-342-6644		450

Phone | Fax | Class

Futurecom Systems Group Inc
3277 Langstaff Rd Concord ON L4K5P8 905-660-5548 246
TF: 800-701-9180 ■ *Web:* www.futurecom.com

Futuredontics Inc
6060 Center Dr 7th Fl Los Angeles CA 90045 310-215-6400 195
Web: www.futuredontics.com

FutureFuel Corp
8235 Forsyth Blvd 4th Fl Clayton MO 63105 805-565-9800 146
NYSE: FF ■ *Web:* futurefuelcorporation.com

Futureguard Building Products Inc
101 Merrow Rd Auburn ME 04211 800-858-5818 256
TF: 800-858-5818 ■ *Web:* www.futureguard.net

FutureNet Group Inc 12801 Auburn St Detroit MI 48223 313-544-7117 186
Web: www.futurenetgroup.com

Futureproof LLC
2374 St Claude Ave New Orleans LA 70119 504-822-8995 196
Web: www.futureproofsustainability.com

Futures Industry Assn (FIA)
2001 Pennsylvania Ave NW Ste 600 Washington DC 20006 202-466-5460 296-3184 49-2
Web: fia.org

Futures Magazine
222 S Riverside Plz Ste 620 Chicago IL 60606 312-846-4600 457-5
Web: www.futuresmag.com

FutureSoft Inc 1660 Townhurst Dr Ste E Houston TX 77043 281-496-9400 496-1090 178-7
TF: 800-989-8908 ■ *Web:* www.futuresoft.com

Futurewise 816 Second Ave Ste 200 Seattle WA 98104 206-343-0681 415
Web: futurewise.org

Futurex Inc 864 Old Boerne Rd Bulverde TX 78163 830-980-9782 438-8782 176
TF: 800-251-5112 ■ *Web:* www.futurex.com

Fuze Fit for a Kid
15405 Los Gatos Blvd Los Gatos CA 95032 408-358-7529 810
Web: www.fuzefit.com

Fuzio Universal Pasta
1020 Tenth St Ste 100 Modesto CA 95354 209-557-9711 671
Web: www.fuzio.com

FVB Energy Inc 3901 Hwy 7 Ste 300 Vaughan ON L4L8L5 905-265-9777 256
Web: www.fvbenergy.com

FW Gartner Thermal Spraying Ltd
25 Southbelt Industrial Dr Houston TX 77047 713-225-0010 481
TF: 888-439-4872 ■ *Web:* www.fwgts.com

FW Webb Co 160 Middlesex Tpke Bedford MA 01730 781-272-6600 275-3354 385
TF: 800-343-7555 ■ *Web:* www.fwwebb.com

FWA (Frederick Ward Associates)
5 S Main St Bel Air MD 21014 410-838-7900 192
Web: www.frederickward.com

FWBMC (Fort Walton Beach Medical Ctr)
1000 Mar-Walt Dr Fort Walton Beach FL 32547 850-862-1111 374-3
Web: fwbmc.com

FWC (Fraser Watson Croutch LLP)
100 W Broadway Ste 650 Glendale CA 91210 818-543-1380 543-1389 445
Web: www.fwclawyers.com

FWCS (Fort Wayne Community Schools)
1200 S Clinton St Fort Wayne IN 46802 260-467-2005 685
Web: www.fwcs.k12.in.us

FWT LLC 5750 E I-20 Fort Worth TX 76119 817-255-3060 480
TF: 800-433-1816 ■ *Web:* fwtllc.com

FX. Matt Brewing Co 811 Edward St Utica NY 13502 315-624-2400 102
Web: www.saranac.com

FXC Corp 3050 Red Hill Ave Costa Mesa CA 92626 714-556-7400 641-5093 203
Web: www.pia.com

FXCM Inc 32 Old Slip New York NY 10005 212-897-7660 229-0004* 178-10
OTC: GLBR ■ **Fax Area Code: 877* ■ *TF:* 888-503-6739 ■ *Web:* www.fxcm.com

FXI 1400 N Providence Rd Media PA 19063 610-744-2300 601
TF: 800-355-3626 ■ *Web:* fxi.com

FXVA (Fairfax County Convention & Visitors Bureau)
3702 Pender Dr Ste 420 Fairfax VA 22030 703-790-0643 206
TF: 800-732-4732 ■ *Web:* www.fxva.com

Fyda Freightliner Youngstown Inc
5260 76th Dr Youngstown OH 44515 330-797-0224 797-0230 62-5
TF: 800-837-3932 ■ *Web:* www.fydafreightliner.com

Fyffes Inc
999 Ponce de Leon Blvd Ste 900 Coral Gables FL 33134 305-529-1276 443-8908 297-7
Web: www.fyffes.com

FYI Systems Inc 35 Waterview Blvd Parsippany NJ 07054 973-331-9050 331-9055 180
Web: www.fyisolutions.com

FYZICAL 5922 Cattlemen Ln Ste 100 Sarasota FL 34232 941-378-8977 354
Web: www.fyzical.com

FZE Manufacturing Solutions LLC
528 Harrison Ct North Fond Du Lac WI 54937 920-921-4084 454
Web: fzemanufacturing.com

G

Phone | Fax | Class

G & A Label Inc 1601 Wyoming Ave El Paso TX 79902 915-544-1766 627
Web: www.gna30.com

G & B Oil Company Inc 667 N Bridge St Elkin NC 28621 336-835-3607 581
Web: gbenergy.com

G & C Equipment Corp
1875 W Redondo Beach Blvd Ste 102 Gardena CA 90247 310-515-6715 515-5046 264-3
TF: 800-559-5529 ■ *Web:* www.gandccorp.com

G & D Integrated 50 Commerce Dr Morton IL 61550 800-451-6680 186
TF: 800-451-6680 ■ *Web:* gdintegrated.com

G & F Industries
709 Main St Rte 20 Sturbridge MA 01566 508-347-9132 596
Web: gandfprecision.com

G & G Fitness Equipment Inc
7350 Transit Rd Williamsville NY 14221 716-633-2527 354
TF: 800-537-0516 ■ *Web:* livefit.com

G & G Mfg 4432 Mckinley Omaha NE 68112 402-453-9595 453-1740 620
TF: 800-442-6000 ■ *Web:* www.ggmfg.com

G & G Oil Company of Indiana Inc
220 E Centennial Ave Muncie IN 47303 765-288-7795 579
Web: www.ggoil.com

G & G Outfitters Inc 4901 Forbes Blvd Lanham MD 20706 301-731-2099 258
Web: www.ggoutfitters.com

G & G Publishers Inc
2 Americana Blvd Hopewell Junction NY 12533 845-221-8638 221-8559 637-2
Web: www.ggpublishers.com

G & G Steel
15825 Hwy 243 Industrial Pk PO Box 179 Russellville AL 35653 256-332-6652 697
TF: 800-332-6652 ■ *Web:* www.ggsteel.com

G & G Technologies Inc
1517 Old Apex Rd Ste 100 Cary NC 27513 919-461-9848 809
Web: www.gandgtech.com

G & H Decoys Inc PO Box 1208 Henryetta OK 74437 918-652-3314 710
TF: 800-443-3269 ■ *Web:* www.ghdecoys.com

G & H Financial Insurance Services Inc
5503 Fourth St Katy TX 77493 281-395-5497 390
Web: gandhfinancial.com

G & H Towing Company Inc
PO Drawer 2270 Galveston TX 77553 409-744-6311 465
Web: www.gandhtowing.com

G & H Wire Company Inc
2165 Earlywood Dr Franklin IN 46131 317-346-6655 228
TF: 800-526-1026 ■ *Web:* www.ghorthodontics.com

G & J Land & Marine Food Distributors Inc
506 Front St Morgan City LA 70380 985-385-2620 385-3614 345
TF: 800-256-9187 ■ *Web:* www.gjfood.com

G & J Seiberlich & Company LLP
3264 Villa Ln Napa CA 94558 707-224-7948 224-7940 734
Web: www.gjscollp.com

G & J Steel & Tubing Inc
406 Roycefield Rd Hillsborough NJ 08844 908-526-4445 526-9487 595
TF: 800-322-8823 ■ *Web:* www.gjsteel.com

G & L Manufacturing Inc
1975 Fisk Rd Cookeville TN 38506 931-528-1732 492
Web: www.glmanufacturing.com

G & M Compliance Inc 154 S Cypress St Orange CA 92866 714-628-1020 764
Web: www.gmcompliance.com

G & M Electrical Contractors Co
1746 N Richmond St Chicago IL 60647 773-278-8200 278-8038 189-4
Web: www.gm-electric.com

G & N Aircraft Inc 1701 E Main St Griffith IN 46319 219-924-7110 924-1059 770
TF: 800-348-6504 ■ *Web:* gnaircraft.com

G & O Thermal Supply Co
5435 N Northwest Hwy Chicago IL 60630 773-763-1300 111
TF: 800-621-4997 ■ *Web:* www.gothermal.com

G & R Foods Inc 321 Wengel Dr Reedsburg WI 53959 608-524-3776 524-1752 10-3
Web: grfoodsinc.com

G & R Labs Inc
2395 De La Cruz Blvd Santa Clara CA 95050 408-986-0377 986-0416 743
Web: www.grlabs.com

G & S Metal Products Company Inc
3330 E 79th St Cleveland OH 44127 216-441-0700 441-0736 486
Web: www.gsmetal.com

G & S Packing 16600 Florida 25 Weirsdale FL 32195 352-821-2251 315-2
Web: gsfruitpackers.com

G & S Structural Engineers PA
505 Lindsay Blvd Idaho Falls ID 83402 208-523-6918 523-6922 261
Web: gsengineers.net

G & S Super Abrasives Inc
1601 Wohlert St Angola IN 46703 260-665-5562 665-8266 493
Web: www.gssuperabrasives.com

G & T Industries Inc
1001 76th St SW Byron Center MI 49315 616-452-8611 583-1524 601
TF: 800-968-6035 ■ *Web:* gtindustries.com

G & W Commercial Flooring Inc
6407 S 211th St Kent WA 98032 253-479-1760 479-1764 290
Web: gwcfloor.com

G & W Engineering Corp
138 Weldon Pkwy Maryland Heights MO 63043 314-469-3737 261
Web: www.gandwengineering.com

G & W Foods Inc
2041 Railroad Dr Willow Springs MO 65793 417-469-4000 345
Web: www.gwfoodsinc.com

G & W Laboratories Inc
111 Coolidge St South Plainfield NJ 07080 800-922-1038 582
TF: 800-922-1038 ■ *Web:* www.gwlabs.com

G & Z Industries Inc 541 Chaddick Dr Wheeling IL 60090 847-215-2300 215-2579 488
Web: www.gzind.com

G and F Trucking Leasing Inc
7640 W 15th Ave Gary IN 46406 219-944-8695 944-8756 780
TF: 800-975-8699 ■ *Web:* www.gf-trucking.com

G Bar M Ranch
821 Brackett Creek Rd PO Box 143 Clyde Park MT 59018 406-686-4425 239
Web: www.gbarm.com

G Brands Ltd 4302 Broadway Grove City OH 43123 614-707-4445 104
Web: gbrands.biz

G D C Inc 815 Logan St Goshen IN 46528 574-533-3128 601
Web: www.gdc-corp.com

G D G Environment Group Ltd
430 Rue St-Laurent Trois-Rivieres QC G8T6H3 888-567-8567 192
TF: 888-567-8567 ■ *Web:* www.gdg.ca

G Dc Home 695 Coleman Blvd Mount Pleasant SC 29464 843-849-0711 393
Web: www.gdchome.com

G E Tignall & Company Inc
14 Mccann Ave Cockeysville MD 21030 410-666-3000 666-3775 189-10
Web: getignall.com

G F Studio Inc 540 Ravine Ct Wyckoff NJ 07481 201-445-1002 592
Web: gfstudio.net

G G Schmitt & Sons Inc
2821 Old Tree Dr Lancaster PA 17603 717-394-3701 291-9739 350
TF: 866-724-6488 ■ *Web:* www.ggschmitt.com

G Greene Construction Company Inc
240 Lincoln St PO Box 160 Allston MA 02134 617-782-1100 782-6857 186
Web: www.ggreene.com

G L Wilson Building Co
190 Wilson Park Rd Statesville NC 28625 704-872-2411 186
Web: www.glwilson.com

Name / Address	City	State	Zip	Phone	Fax	Class
G Michael's Bistro 595 S Third St	Columbus	OH	43215	614-464-0575		671
Web: gmichaelsbistroandbar.com						
G P Aviation Services 95 Round Hill Rd	Armonk	NY	10504	914-273-0123		23
Web: www.gpaviation.com						
G R Manufacturing Inc						
4800 Commerce Dr	Trussville	AL	35173	205-655-8001		297-8
TF: 800-841-8001 ■ *Web:* www.grtractors.com						
G Robert Cotton Correctional Facility						
3500 N Elm Rd	Jackson	MI	49201	517-780-5000	780-5100	213
Web: www.michigan.gov						
G Stephens Inc 133 N Summit St	Akron	OH	44304	330-762-1386		196
Web: www.gstephensinc.com						
G Systems LP						
1240 Campbell Rd Ste 100	Richardson	TX	75081	972-234-6000	234-6018	261
Web: www.gsystems.com						
G. & M. Die Consulting Company Inc						
284 Richert Rd	Wood Dale	IL	60191	630-595-2340		358
Web: www.gmdiecasting.com						
G. A. Bove & Sons Inc						
76 Railroad St	Mechanicville	NY	12118	518-664-5111		316
Web: bovefuels.com						
G. A. Fleet Associates Inc						
55 Calvert St	Harrison	NY	10528	914-835-4000	835-1331	385
Web: www.gafleet.com						
G. H. Tool & Mold LLC						
28 Chamber Dr	Washington	MO	63090	636-390-2424	390-2626	757
Web: www.ghtool.com						
G. I. A. Publications Inc						
7404 S Mason Ave	Chicago	IL	60638	708-496-3800	496-3828	637-10
TF: 800-442-1358 ■ *Web:* giamusic.com						
G. J. Builders Hardware Inc						
1500 E Eldorado St	Decatur	IL	62521	217-428-6671		351
Web: gjbuildershardware.com						
G. Q. F. Manufacturing Company Inc						
2343 Louisville Rd	Savannah	GA	31415	912-236-0651		273
Web: www.gqfmfg.com						
G. R. Stucker & Associates Inc						
14661 S Harrell's Ferry Rd	Baton Rouge	LA	70816	225-291-9988		261
Web: grsaeng.com						
G. S. Proctor & Associates Inc						
14408 Old Mill Rd Ste 201	Upper Marlboro	MD	20772	301-952-8885		463
Web: www.gsproctor.com						
G. Todd Houck, Attorney At Law LC						
105 Guyandotte Ave	Mullens	WV	25882	304-294-8055		41
Web: beckleyattorney.com						
G. V. (Sonny) Montgomery VA Medical Ctr						
1500 E Woodrow Wilson Dr	Jackson	MS	39216	601-362-4471		374-8
Web: www.jackson.va.gov						
G.A.I.M. Plastics Inc 789 Golf Ln	Bensenville	IL	60106	630-350-9500	350-9555	604
Web: www.gaimplasticsinc.com						
G.A.P. Federal Credit Union						
111 Franklin St Rm 224	Johnstown	PA	15901	814-535-4165	535-2175	219
TF: 800-228-9180 ■ *Web:* gapfcu.org						
G.A.S. Global 14100 SW Fwy Ste 320	Sugar Land	TX	77478	281-295-5600	295-5699	256
Web: www.gasunlim.com						
G.B.T. Inc 17358 Railroad St	City of Industry	CA	91748	626-854-9338	854-9339	173-1
Web: www.gigabyte.us						
G.L. Barron Construction Inc						
6221 SW Blvd Ste 100	Fort Worth	TX	76132	877-909-6104	231-8144*	186
**Fax Area Code: 817* ■ *TF:* 877-909-6104 ■ *Web:* thebarroncompanies.com						
G.M. Crisalli Associates Inc						
843 Hiawatha Blvd W	Syracuse	NY	13204	315-454-0000		186
Web: gmca.com						
G.N.W. Machine Inc						
2289 E Cedar St Ste 106	Lino Lakes	MN	55038	651-426-8708	426-9429	454
Web: www.gnwmachine.com						
G.Page Wholesale Flowers						
120 W 28th St	New York	NY	10001	212-741-8928	741-2868	293
Web: www.gpage.com						
G.R. Rush & Company PLLC						
5720 Skurlock Rd 6500 Ste 8400	Chattanooga	TN	37411	423-899-5162		2
Web: www.rushcpa.com						
G.S.W. Manufacturing Inc						
1801 Production Dr	Findlay	OH	45839	419-423-7111		60
Web: www.gswiring.com						
G.W. Smith Lumber Co						
720 W Center St	Lexington	NC	27292	336-249-4941	249-4913	364
Web: www.gwsmithlumber.com						
G2 Crowd 100 S Wacker Dr Ste 600	Chicago	IL	60606	847-748-7559		177
Web: www.g2.com						
G2 Insurance Services LLC						
140 New Montgomery St 21St Fl	San Francisco	CA	94105	415-426-6600		390
Web: g2insurance.com						
G2 Intelligence						
c/o Plain Language Media LLLP PO Box 509	New London	CT	06320	604-210-4580	649-1623*	637-9
**Fax Area Code: 855* ■ *TF:* 888-729-2315 ■ *Web:* www.g2intelligence.com						
G2 Secure Staff LLC						
400 E Las Colians Blvd Ste 750	Irving	TX	75039	972-915-6979	915-1299	393
TF: 800-845-4388 ■ *Web:* www.g2securestaff.com						
G2 Software Systems Inc						
4025 Hancock St Ste 105	San Diego	CA	92110	619-222-8025		177
Web: g2ss.com						
G2 Solutions LLC						
1475 Powell St Ste 202	Emeryville	CA	94608	425-789-0200		653
Web: g2globalsolutions.com						
G2 USA 636 11th Ave	New York	NY	10036	212-537-3700		5
Web: www.geometry.com						
G3 Communications						
777 Terrace Ave Ste 202	Hasbrouck Heights	NJ	07604	888-603-3626		195
TF: 888-603-3626 ■ *Web:* www.gthreecom.com						
G3 Enterprises Inc 502 E Whitmore Ave	Modesto	CA	95358	800-321-8747		124
TF: 800-321-8747 ■ *Web:* www.g3enterprises.com						
G3 Technologies Inc						
10280 Old Columbia Rd Ste 260	Columbia	MD	21046	410-290-8110		224
Web: www.g3ti.net						
G3 Telecom Inc 1039 McNicoll Ave	Toronto	ON	M1W3W6	416-499-2121		387
TF: 855-323-4343 ■ *Web:* www.g3telecom.com						
G4S Chicago						
701 Willowbrook Centre Pkwy	Willowbrook	IL	60527	630-920-4432		693
TF: 800-275-8319 ■ *Web:* www.g4s.com						
G4S PLC 1395 University Blvd	Jupiter	FL	33458	561-691-6669		631
TF: 800-275-8305 ■ *Web:* www.g4s.com						
G-51 Capital Management LLC						
3939 Bee Caves Rd Ste C100	West Lake Hills	TX	78746	512-929-5151	732-0886	792
Web: www.g51-amplify.com						
G6 Hospitality LLC						
Motel 6 4001 International Pkwy	Carrollton	TX	75007	972-360-9000		379
TF: 800-466-8356 ■ *Web:* www.motel6.com						
GA (Gamblers Anonymous) PO Box 17173	Los Angeles	CA	90017	626-960-3500	960-3501	48-21
Web: www.gamblersanonymous.org						
GA Braun Inc 79 General Irwin Blvd	Syracuse	NY	13212	315-475-3123	475-4130	427
TF: 800-432-7286 ■ *Web:* www.gabraun.com						
GA Industries Inc						
9025 Marshall Rd	Cranberry Township	PA	16066	724-776-1020	776-1254	789
Web: www.gaindustries.com						
GA Repple & Co 101 Normandy Rd	Casselberry	FL	32707	407-339-9090		194
Web: www.garepple.com						
GA Telesis LLC						
1850 NW 49th St	Fort Lauderdale	FL	33309	954-676-3111	676-9998	21
Web: www.gatelesis.com						
GA Wintzer & Son Co						
204 W Auglaize St	Wapakoneta	OH	45895	419-739-4900		296-12
TF: 800-331-1801 ■ *Web:* www.gawintzer.com						
Gabbard Tulsi (Rep D - HI)						
1433 Longworth House Office Bldg	Washington	DC	20515	202-225-4906	225-4987	342-2
Web: gabbard.house.gov						
Gabberts Inc 3501 Galleria	Minneapolis	MN	55435	952-927-1500		321
Web: www.gabberts.com						
Gabi Insurance						
106 Lincoln Blvd Ste 106	San Francisco	CA	94129	415-842-2411		391-2
Web: www.gabi.com						
Gabler Trucking Inc						
5195 Technology Ave	Chambersburg	PA	17201	717-261-1492		780
Web: www.hcgabler.com						
Gables Engineering Inc						
247 Greco Ave	Coral Gables	FL	33146	305-774-4400	774-4465	529
Web: www.gableseng.com						
Gables Residential Trust						
3399 Peachtree Rd NE Ste 600	Atlanta	GA	30326	404-923-5500		654
Web: www.gables.com						
GableSigns Inc 7440 Ft Smallwood Rd	Baltimore	MD	21226	410-255-6400	437-5336	701
TF: 800-854-0568 ■ *Web:* gablecompany.com						
GableStage						
1200 Anastasia Ave Biltmore Hotel	Coral Gables	FL	33134	305-446-1116	445-8645	573-4
Web: www.gablestage.org						
Gabriel and Associates CPAs PA (GACPAS)						
10117 Old St Augustine Rd Ste 100	Jacksonville	FL	32257	904-260-3820	260-9725	194
Web: gacpas.org						
Gabriel Communications Co						
PO Box 201483	Nashville	TN	37221	615-673-2846	673-2848	514
Web: www.gabrielcommunications.com						
Gabriel Container Co						
8844 S Millergrove Dr	Santa Fe Springs	CA	90670	562-699-1051		557
Web: gabrielcontainer.com						
Gabriel E. Senor PC						
90 N Central Ave	Hartsdale	NY	10530	914-422-0070		727
Web: www.gabrielesenorpc.com						
Gabriel Roeder Smith & Co (GRS)						
1 Towne Sq Ste 800	Southfield	MI	48076	248-799-9000	799-9020	193
TF: 800-521-0498 ■ *Web:* www.grsconsulting.com						
Gabriel Venture Partners						
999 Baker Way Ste 400	San Mateo	CA	94404	650-551-5000	551-5001	792
Web: www.gabrielvp.com						
Gabriel, Burger & Else CPA PC						
135 N Fifth St	Seward	NE	68434	402-643-4557		2
Web: gbecpa.com						
Gabriele & Marano LLP						
100 Quentin Roosevelt Blvd PO Box 8022	Garden City	NY	11530	516-542-1000	542-1226	41
Web: gabrielemarano.com						
Gabriella 3907 Jonestown Rd	Harrisburg	PA	17109	717-540-0040		671
Web: gabriellaristorante.com						
Gabrielli Truck Sales Ltd						
153-20 S Conduit Ave	Jamaica	NY	11434	718-977-7348		57
Web: www.gabriellitruck.com						
Gabriels Technology Solutions Inc						
9 E 40th St 2nd Fl	New York	NY	10016	212-741-0700		224
Web: www.gabriels.net						
GACCPHL (German-American Chamber of Commerce Inc - Philadelphia)						
1635 Market St Ste 1600	Philadelphia	PA	19103	215-501-7102	968-0973	138
Web: www.gaccphiladelphia.com						
Gachina Landscape Management Inc						
1130 O'Brien Dr	Menlo Park	CA	94025	650-853-0400		776
TF: 866-848-4634 ■ *Web:* www.gachina.com						
Gachman Metals & Recycling Company Inc						
2600 Shamrock Ave	Fort Worth	TX	76107	817-334-0211	877-1528	686
TF: 800-749-0423 ■ *Web:* www.gachman.com						
Gaco Western Inc						
200 W Mercer St Ste 202	Seattle	WA	98119	800-331-0196	575-0587*	601
**Fax Area Code: 206* ■ *TF:* 800-456-4226 ■ *Web:* gaco.com						
GACPAS (Gabriel and Associates CPAs PA)						
10117 Old St Augustine Rd Ste 100	Jacksonville	FL	32257	904-260-3820	260-9725	194
Web: gacpas.org						
Gadabout Inc 3501 E Kleindale Rd	Tucson	AZ	85716	520-325-0000		77
TF: 800-600-3662 ■ *Web:* www.gadabout.com						
Gadabout Vacations						
1801 E Tahquitz Canyon Way Ste 100	Palm Springs	CA	92262	760-325-5556		760
Web: www.gadaboutvacations.com						
GadellNet Consulting Services LLC						
1520 S Vandeventer	Saint Louis	MO	63110	314-431-0358		180
Web: gadellnet.com						
Gadsby's Tavern Museum Society						
134 N Royal St	Alexandria	VA	22314	703-746-4242		520
Web: www.gadsbystavernmuseum.us						
Gadsden & Etowah County Chamber						
1 Commerce Sq	Gadsden	AL	35901	256-543-3472	543-9887	139
TF: 800-659-2955 ■ *Web:* www.etowahchamber.org						

				Phone	Fax	Class
Gadsden County 9 E Jefferson St PO Box 1799 *Web:* www.gadsdencountyfl.gov	Quincy	FL	32353	850-875-8650	875-8655	338
Gadsden County Chamber of Commerce 208 N Adams St *Web:* www.gadsdencc.com	Quincy	FL	32351	850-627-9231	875-3299	139
Gadsden County Public Library 732 Pat Thomas Pkwy *Web:* www2.youseemore.com	Quincy	FL	32351	850-627-7106		434-3
Gadsden Public Library 254 College St *Web:* gadsdenlibrary.org	Gadsden	AL	35901	256-549-4699		434-3
Gadsden Regional Medical Ctr 1007 Goodyear Ave *Web:* www.gadsdenregional.com	Gadsden	AL	35903	256-494-4000	494-4474	374-3
Gadsden State Community College 1001 George Wallace Dr PO Box 227 *TF:* 800-226-5563 ■ *Web:* www.gadsdenstate.edu	Gadsden	AL	35902	256-549-8200	549-8205	162
Gadsden Times 401 Locust St *Web:* www.gadsdentimes.com	Gadsden	AL	35901	256-549-2033	549-2105	532-2
Gaebler Ventures 12301 Whitewater Dr *Web:* www.gaebler.com	Minnetonka	MN	55343	952-936-9333	936-9755	457-20
Gaetz Matt (Rep R - FL) 1721 Longworth House Office Bldg *Web:* gaetz.house.gov	Washington	DC	20515	202-225-4136		342-2
GAF 1361 Alps Rd *Web:* www.gaf.com	Wayne	NJ	07470	973-628-3000		46
Gaffney-Kroese Supply Corp 60 Kingsbridge Rd *Web:* www.gaffney-kroese.com	Piscataway	NJ	08854	732-885-9000		385
Gaffoglio Family Metalcrafters Inc 11161 Slater Ave *Web:* www.metalcrafters.com	Fountain Valley	CA	92708	714-444-2000		489
Gafford Technology 848 N Rainbow Blvd Ste 2628 *Web:* gaffordtech.wordpress.com	Las Vegas	NV	89107	702-736-8660	541-9509	180
Gage 10000 Hwy 55 *Web:* www.gage.com	Minneapolis	MN	55441	763-595-3800		737
Gage Brothers Concrete Products Inc 4301 W 12th St *Web:* gagebrothers.com	Sioux Falls	SD	57106	605-336-1180		183
Gage County District Clerk 612 Grant St PO Box 429 *Web:* gagecountynebraska.us	Beatrice	NE	68310	402-223-1300	223-1371	338
Gage Pattern & Model Inc 32070 Townley *Web:* www.gagepattern.com	Madison Heights	MI	48071	248-585-2476	585-9234	547
Gage Team, The 601 S Phillips Ave *Web:* thegageteam.com	Sioux Falls	SD	57104	605-332-1242		225
Gagemaker LP 712 Southmore Ave *Web:* gagemaker.com	Pasadena	TX	77502	713-472-7360		639
Gagen, McCoy, McMahon, Koss, Markowitz & Raines A Professional Corp 630 San Ramon Valley Blvd Ste 100 *Web:* www.gagenmccoy.com	Danville	CA	94526	925-837-0585	838-5985	428
Gaggle Net 2205 E Empire St Ste B PO Box 1352 *TF:* 800-288-7750 ■ *Web:* www.gaggle.net	Bloomington	IL	61704	309-665-0572	665-0171	225
Gaglione, Dolan and Kaplan 11377 W Olympic Blvd *Web:* www.gaglionedolan.com	Los Angeles	CA	90064	310-231-1600	231-1610	41
Gahanna Area Chamber of Commerce 81 Mill St Ste 300 *Web:* gahannaareachamber.com	Gahanna	OH	43230	614-471-0451	471-5122	139
Gahr Machine Co 26470 Lakeland Blvd *Web:* www.gahrmachine.com	Euclid	OH	44132	216-732-3035		385
Gai Allen Insurance Agency Inc 9400 Livingston Rd Ste 125 *Web:* gaiallen.com	Fort Washington	MD	20744	301-248-4505		390
GAI Consultants Inc 385 E Waterfront Dr *Web:* gaiconsultants.com	Homestead	PA	15120	412-476-2000		261
Gaiam Inc 833 W S Boulder Rd Bldg G *NASDAQ:* GAIA ■ *TF:* 877-989-6321 ■ *Web:* www.gaiam.com	Louisville	CO	80027	303-222-3600		459
Gail Rosen CPA PC 2032 Washington Valley Rd *Web:* gailrosencpa.com	Martinsville	NJ	08836	732-469-4202	469-6291	2
Gaillard Municipal Auditorium 95 Calhoun St *Web:* gaillardcenter.org	Charleston	SC	29401	843-724-5212		572
Gaines County 101 S Main St PO Box 847 *Web:* co.gaines.tx.us	Seminole	TX	79360	432-758-5411		338
Gaines Motor Lines Inc 2349 13th Ave SW PO Box 1549 *TF:* 800-438-7311 ■ *Web:* www.gainesml.com	Hickory	NC	28603	828-322-2000	324-7026	186
Gainescraft Inc 203 N Hannah St *Web:* www.moormannbros.com	Rushville	IN	46173	765-932-3590	932-3594	201
Gainesville Area Chamber of Commerce 300 E University Ave *Web:* gainesvillechamber.com	Gainesville	FL	32601	352-334-7100	334-7141	139
Gainesville Carpet & Flooring 6510 NW 13th St *Web:* gainesvillecarpetsplus.com	Gainesville	FL	32653	352-378-2627		290
Gainesville City Schools 508 Oak St *TF:* 800-533-0682 ■ *Web:* www.gcssk12.net	Gainesville	GA	30501	770-536-5275	287-2019	685
Gainesville Correctional Institution 2845 NE 39th Ave *Web:* www.dc.state.fl.us	Gainesville	FL	32609	352-955-2001	334-1675	213
Gainesville Hearing Services Inc 250 John W Morrow Jr Pky Ste 113 *Web:* www.gainesvillehearing.com	Gainesville	GA	30501	770-532-5092		415
Gainesville Raceway 11211 N County Rd 225 *Web:* gainesvilleraceway.com	Gainesville	FL	32609	352-377-0046	371-4212	515
Gainesville State College University of N Georgia Gainesville Campus 3820 Mundy Mill Rd *Web:* ung.edu	Oakwood	GA	30566	678-717-3639		162
Gainesville State School 1379 FM 678 *Web:* www.tjjd.texas.gov	Gainesville	TX	76240	940-665-0701	665-0469	412
Gainesville Sun, The 2700 SW 13th St *Web:* www.gainesville.com	Gainesville	FL	32608	352-378-1411		532-2
Gainesville Times 345 Green St NW *TF:* 800-395-5005 ■ *Web:* www.gainesvilletimes.com	Gainesville	GA	30501	770-532-1234	532-0457	532-2
Gainesway Farm 3750 Paris Pk *Web:* gainesway.com	Lexington	KY	40511	859-293-2676	299-9371	368
Gainsburgh, Benjamin, David, Meunier & Warshauer 1100 Poydras St 2800 Energy *TF:* 800-489-2304 ■ *Web:* gainsburghbenjamin.com	New Orleans	LA	70163	504-522-2304	528-9973	41
Gainshare Inc 3110 N Central Ave Ste 160 *TF:* 800-264-9029 ■ *Web:* www.interfacett.com	Phoenix	AZ	85012	602-266-8500		764
GAINSystems Inc 1200 N Ashland Ave Ste 300 *Web:* www.gainsystems.com	Chicago	IL	60622	872-206-8500		178-1
Gaio Trucking Inc 200 Erie St *Fax Area Code:* 909 ■ *TF:* 800-662-2371 ■ *Web:* lexmardistribution.com	Pomona	CA	91768	800-662-2371	620-8001*	311
Gaithersburg-Germantown Chamber of Commerce 910 Clopper Rd Ste 205N *Fax Area Code:* 240 ■ *Web:* www.ggchamber.org	Gaithersburg	MD	20878	301-840-1400	261-6395*	139
Galahad Publishing PO Box 5451 *Web:* www.galahadpublishing.com	North Hollywood	CA	91616	818-761-5198	766-8645	637-2
Galanga 1129 Broadway *Web:* www.galangathai.com	Tacoma	WA	98402	253-272-3393		671
Galapagos Partners LP 55 Waugh Dr Ste 1130 *Web:* www.gplp.com	Houston	TX	77007	713-803-4326		610
Galasso's Bakery 10820 San Sevaine Way *TF:* 800-339-7494 ■ *Web:* galassos.com	Mira Loma	CA	91752	951-360-1211		68
Galatea Associates LLC 20 Holland St Ste 405 *Web:* www.galatea-associates.com	Somerville	MA	02144	617-623-5466	623-4012	390
Galatoire's Restaurant 209 Bourbon St *Web:* www.galatoires.com	New Orleans	LA	70130	504-525-2021	525-5900	671
Galaxie Coffee Services 110 Sea Ln *TF:* 800-564-9104 ■ *Web:* galaxiecoffee.com	Farmingdale	NY	11735	631-694-2688		113
Galaxie Defense Marketing Services 5330 Napa St *TF:* 888-711-3427 ■ *Web:* www.galaxiemgmt.com	San Diego	CA	92110	619-299-9950		186
Galaxy Builders Ltd 4729 College Pk *Web:* www.galaxybuilders.com	San Antonio	TX	78249	210-493-0550		187
Galaxy Electronics Associates Inc 9885 Washington Blvd *Web:* www.galaxyelectronics.com	Laurel	MD	20723	301-362-3100	362-1055	625
Galaxy Hotel Systems LLC 5 Peters Canyon Ste 375 *TF:* 800-624-2953 ■ *Web:* www.galaxylightspeed.com	Irvine	CA	92606	714-258-5800	258-5880	178-11
Galaxy Integrated Technologies 100 Leo M Birmingham Pkwy *TF:* 877-313-0883 ■ *Web:* galaxyintegrated.com	Brighton	MA	02135	617-202-6388	202-6389	693
Galaxy Media 235 Walton St *Web:* galaxymediapartners.com	Syracuse	NY	13202	315-472-9111	472-1888	643
Galaxy Nutritional Foods Inc 66 Whitecap Dr *TF:* 800-441-9419 ■ *Web:* www.goveggiefoods.com	North Kingstown	RI	02852	401-667-5000		296-5
Galaxy Software Solutions Inc 5820 N Lilley Rd Ste 8 *TF:* 877-269-4774 ■ *Web:* galaxy-soft.com	Canton	MI	48187	877-269-4774		260
Galaxy Technologies Inc 1111 Industrial Blvd *Web:* www.galaxytool.com	Winfield	KS	67156	620-221-6262	221-0913	494
Galbraith Laboratories Inc 2323 Sycamore Dr *Web:* galbraith.com	Knoxville	TN	37921	865-546-1335		743
Galco Industrial Electronics Inc 26010 Pinehurst Dr *TF:* 888-783-4611 ■ *Web:* www.galco.com	Madison Heights	MI	48071	248-542-9090	542-8031	246
Galderma Laboratories Inc 14501 N Fwy *TF:* 866-735-4137 ■ *Web:* galderma.com	Fort Worth	TX	76177	817-961-5000		582
Gale Associates Inc 163 Libbey Pky *TF:* 800-659-4753 ■ *Web:* www.gainc.com	Weymouth	MA	02189	781-335-6465	335-6467	196
Gale Cengage Learning 27500 Drake Rd *Fax Area Code:* 877 ■ *TF:* 800-877-4253 ■ *Web:* www.gale.com	Farmington Hills	MI	48331	800-877-4253	363-4253*	637-2
Gale Credit Union 631 N Henderson St *Web:* galecu.net	Galesburg	IL	61401	309-343-1777		219
Galecki Financial Management Inc 7743 W Jefferson Blvd *Web:* galecki.com	Fort Wayne	IN	46804	260-436-8525		528
Galectin Therapeutics 4960 Peachtree Industrial Blvd Ste 240 *Fax Area Code:* 770 ■ *Web:* www.galectintherapeutics.com	Norcross	GA	30071	678-620-3186	864-1327*	85
Galen College of Nursing 7411 John Smith Ste 300 *Web:* www.galencollege.edu	San Antonio	TX	78229	210-733-3056	485-2222	167-3
Galen Films 110 Daggett Ave *Web:* www.galenfilms.com	Vineyard Haven	MA	02568	508-693-0752	696-7649	514
Galen Press Ltd PO Box 64400 *TF:* 800-442-5369 ■ *Web:* www.galenpress.com	Tucson	AZ	85728	520-577-8363	529-6459	637-2
Galena Gazette 716 S Bench St *TF:* 800-373-6397 ■ *Web:* www.galenagazette.com	Galena	IL	61036	815-777-0019	777-3809	532-4
Galena Interior Learning Academy PO Box 359 *Web:* www.galenaalaska.org	Galena	AK	99741	907-656-2053	656-4589	685
Galena Veterinary Hospital 9475 Double R Blvd Ste 20 *Web:* galenavet.net	Reno	NV	89521	775-853-4003	853-3617	794

Name / Address	City	State	ZIP	Phone	Fax	Class
Galera Therapeutics Inc 2 W Liberty Blvd Ste 110 *Web:* www.galeratx.com	Malvern	PA	19355	610-725-1500		231
Galerie Lelong 528 W 26th St *Web:* www.galerie-lelong.com	New York	NY	10001	212-315-0470		42
Galerie Matisse Ltd 830 W Main St *Web:* galeriematisse.com	Lake Geneva	WI	53147	262-248-9264		42
Galerie St Etienne 24 W 57th St *Web:* www.gseart.com	New York	NY	10019	212-245-6734	765-8493	42
Galerie Valentin 1490 Sherbrooke Quest Ste 200 *Web:* www.galerievalentin.com	Montreal	QC	H3G1L3	514-939-0500	939-0413	42
Galesburg Area Chamber of Commerce 200 E Main St *Web:* www.galesburg.org	Galesburg	IL	61401	309-343-1194	343-1195	139
Galesburg Castings Inc 940 Ave C St *Web:* www.galesburgcastings.com	Galesburg	IL	61401	309-343-6178		492
Galesburg Cottage Hospital (GCH) 695 N Kellogg St *Web:* www.cottagehospital.com	Galesburg	IL	61401	309-343-8131		374-3
Galesburg Printing & Publishing Co 140 S Prairie St *Web:* www.galesburg.com	Galesburg	IL	61401	309-343-7181	343-2382	637-8
Galesburg Public Library 40 E Simmons St *Web:* galesburglibrary.org	Galesburg	IL	61401	309-343-6118	343-4877	434-3
Galfand Berger LLP 1835 Market St Ste 2710 *TF:* 800-222-8792 ■ *Web:* galfandberger.com	Philadelphia	PA	19103	215-665-1600		41
Galileo Global Advisors LLC 10 Rockefeller Plz Ste 1001 *Web:* www.galileoglobalgroup.com	New York	NY	10020	212-332-6055		690
Galion Inc 515 NE St *Web:* www.galionllc.com	Galion	OH	44833	419-468-5214	468-1661	60
Galison Publishing LLC 28 W 44th St Ste 1411 *TF:* 800-670-7441 ■ *Web:* www.galison.com	New York	NY	10036	212-354-8840		130
Gallade Chemical Inc 1230 E St Gertrude Pl *TF:* 888-830-9092 ■ *Web:* www.galladechem.com	Santa Ana	CA	92707	714-546-9901	546-2501	146
Gallagher 6967 S River Gate Dr Ste 200 *TF:* 800-924-1404 ■ *Web:* locations.ajg.com	Midvale	UT	84047	801-924-1400	924-1441	194
Gallagher 1052 Yonge St *TF:* 866-969-8588 ■ *Web:* ajgcanada.com	Toronto	ON	M4W2L1	416-969-8588		463
Gallagher & Burk Inc 344 High St *Web:* www.gallagherandburk.com	Oakland	CA	94601	925-361-1645		188-4
Gallagher Asphalt Corp 18100 S Indiana Ave **Fax Area Code: 708* ■ *TF:* 800-536-7160 ■ *Web:* www.gallagherasphalt.com	Thornton	IL	60476	800-536-7160	877-5222*	188-4
Gallagher Corp 3908 Morrison Dr *TF:* 800-524-8597 ■ *Web:* gallaghercorp.com	Gurnee	IL	60031	847-249-3440		605-2
Gallagher Flynn & Company LLP 55 Community Dr *Web:* www.gfc.com	South Burlington	VT	05403	802-863-1331	651-7305	2
Gallagher Mike (Rep R - WI) 1230 Longworth House Office Bldg *Web:* www.gallagher.house.gov	Washington	DC	20515	202-225-5665		342-2
Gallagher Systems Group Inc 2502 N Clark St *Web:* www.gallaghersystems.ca	Chicago	IL	60614	773-348-5400		177
Gallagher, Gams, Pryor, Tallan & Littrell LLP 471 E Broad St 19th Fl *TF:* 866-378-1624 ■ *Web:* www.ggtbl.com	Columbus	OH	43215	614-228-5151		428
Gallagher-Kaiser Corp 13710 Mt Elliott St *Web:* www.gkcorp.com	Detroit	MI	48212	313-368-3100	368-3109	550
Galland Henning Nopak Inc 10179 S 57th St *Web:* www.nopak.com	Franklin	WI	53132	414-645-6000	645-6048	223
Gallant & Wein Corp 11-20 43rd Rd *Web:* galwein.com	Long Island City	NY	11101	718-784-5210	937-6426	814
Gallant Greetings Corp 4300 United Pkwy *TF:* 800-621-4279 ■ *Web:* www.gallantgreetings.com	Schiller Park	IL	60176	847-671-6500		130
Gallant Insurance Agency Inc 199 Great Rd *Web:* gallantins.com	Acton	MA	01720	978-263-3500		390
Gallatin County 311 W Main St *Web:* gallatincomt.virtualtownhall.net	Bozeman	MT	59715	406-582-3050	582-3068	338
Gallatin County 200 Washington St PO Box 144 *Web:* www.gallatincounty.ky.gov	Warsaw	KY	41095	859-567-5691	567-4764	338
Gallaudet University 800 Florida Ave NE *TF:* 800-995-0550 ■ *Web:* www.gallaudet.edu	Washington	DC	20002	202-651-5000	651-5744	166
Gallea Transfer & Storage Inc 4500 N County Rd 45 *Web:* galleatransfer.com	Owatonna	MN	55060	507-451-4318		311
Gallego Ruben (Rep D - AZ) 1131 Longworth House Office Bldg *Web:* rubengallego.house.gov	Washington	DC	20515	202-225-4065		342-2
Gallegos Corp PO Box 821 *TF:* 800-425-5346 ■ *Web:* www.gallegoscorp.com	Vail	CO	81658	970-926-3737	926-3727	189-7
Gallegos United 300 Pacific Coast Hwy Ste 200 *Web:* www.gallegosunited.com	Huntington Beach	CA	92648	714-794-6400		7
Galleher Corp 9303 Greenleaf Ave *Web:* galleher.com	Santa Fe Springs	CA	90670	562-944-8885		361
Gallen Insurance Inc 2237 Lancaster Pk PO Box 100 *Web:* galleninsurance.com	Shillington	PA	19607	610-777-4123	777-9957	390
Galleon Resort & Marina 617 Front St *TF:* 800-544-3030 ■ *Web:* www.galleonresort.com	Key West	FL	33040	305-296-7711	296-0821	669
Galleria at Fort Lauderdale 2414 E Sunrise Blvd *Web:* www.galleriamall-fl.com	Fort Lauderdale	FL	33304	954-564-1015	566-9976	460
Galleria at Pittsburgh Mills 590 Pittsburgh Mills Cir *Web:* www.pittsburghmills.com	Tarentum	PA	15084	724-904-9010		460
Galleria at Sunset 1300 W Sunset Rd *Web:* www.galleriaatsunset.com	Henderson	NV	89014	702-434-2409		460
Galleria at Tyler 1299 Galleria at Tyler St *Web:* www.galleriatyler.com	Riverside	CA	92503	951-351-3112		460
Galleria at White Plains 100 Main St *Web:* galleriaatwhiteplains.com	White Plains	NY	10601	914-682-0111		460
Gallerie 454 15105 Kercheval Ave *TF:* 800-914-3538 ■ *Web:* www.gallerie454.com	Grosse Pointe Park	MI	48230	313-822-4454	822-3768	520
Galleries of Syracuse, The 441 S Salina St *Web:* galleries-of-syracuse.business.site	Syracuse	NY	13202	315-475-5351		460
Gallery 78 Inc 796 Queen St *TF:* 888-883-8322 ■ *Web:* www.gallery78.com	Fredericton	NB	E3B1C6	506-454-5192		42
Gallery Model Homes Inc 6006 N Fwy *Web:* www.galleryfurniture.com	Houston	TX	77076	713-694-5570		321
Gallery Moos Ltd 305-722 College St *Web:* www.gallerymoos.com	Toronto	ON	M6G1C4	416-504-5445	504-5446	42
Gallery of History Inc 3601 W Sahara Ave *TF:* 800-425-5379 ■ *Web:* www.galleryofhistory.com	Las Vegas	NV	89102	702-364-1000	364-1285	51
Gallery Paule Anglim 14 Geary St *Web:* www.gallerypauleanglim.com	San Francisco	CA	94108	415-433-2710		42
Gallery, The 200 E Pratt St *Web:* www.thegalleryatharborplace.com	Baltimore	MD	21202	410-332-4192		50-6
Galletto Ristorante 1101 J St *Web:* www.galletto.biz	Modesto	CA	95354	209-523-4500		671
Gallia County Chamber of Commerce 16 State St PO Box 465 *Web:* galliacounty.org	Gallipolis	OH	45631	740-446-0596		338
Galliard Capital Management Inc 800 La Salle Ave Ste 1100 *TF:* 800-717-1617 ■ *Web:* www.galliard.com	Minneapolis	MN	55402	612-667-3220		402
Gallier House Museum 1132 Royal St *Web:* www.hgghh.org	New Orleans	LA	70116	504-525-5661		520
Galliker Dairy Company Inc 143 Donald Ln *TF:* 800-477-6455 ■ *Web:* www.gallikers.com	Johnstown	PA	15907	814-266-8702		296-27
Gallo & Iacovangelo LLP 180 Canal View Blvd Ste 100 *Web:* gallolaw.com	Rochester	NY	14623	585-454-7145		41
Gallo Equipment Company Inc 11835 S Ave O *Web:* www.galloequipment.com	Chicago	IL	60617	773-374-5515		54
Gallo Moving & Storage LLC 120 Quarry Dr *Web:* gallomoving.com	Milford	MA	01757	508-422-4400		311
Gallo Salame 2411 Baumann Ave *TF:* 800-988-6464 ■ *Web:* gallosalame.com	San Lorenzo	CA	94580	800-988-6464		296-26
Gallon Takacs Boissoneault & Schaffer Company LPA 3516 Granite Cir *Web:* www.gallonlaw.com	Toledo	OH	43617	419-843-2001		428
Galloup 3838 Clay Ave SW *TF:* 888-755-3110 ■ *Web:* www.galloup.com	Wyoming	MI	49548	269-965-4005	965-3263	191-2
Galloway Company Inc 601 S Commercial St *Web:* www.gallowaycompany.com	Neenah	WI	54956	920-722-7741		296-10
Galloway Research Service 4751 Hamilton-Wolfe *Web:* www.gallowayresearch.com	San Antonio	TX	78229	210-734-4346	732-4500	466
Galloway, Lucchese, Everson & Picchi A Professional 2300 Contra Costa Blvd Ste 350 *Web:* www.glattys.com	Pleasant Hill	CA	94523	925-930-9090	930-9035	428
Galls Inc 2680 Palumbo Dr *TF:* 800-477-7766 ■ *Web:* www.galls.com	Lexington	KY	40509	859-266-7227		576
Gallun Snow 1920 Market St Ste 201 *TF:* 866-846-7514 ■ *Web:* gallunsnow.com	Denver	CO	80202	303-433-9500		393
Gallup Inc 1001 Gallup Dr *TF:* 888-500-8282 ■ *Web:* www.gallup.com	Omaha	NE	68102	402-951-2003		466
Gallup Independent 500 N Ninth St *Web:* www.gallupindependent.com	Gallup	NM	87301	505-863-6811		532-2
Gallup Indian Medical Ctr 516 E Nizhoni Blvd *Web:* www.ihs.gov	Gallup	NM	87301	505-722-1000		374-3
Gallup Inter-Tribal Indian Ceremonial Assn 206 W Coal Ave *Web:* gallupceremonial.com	Gallup	NM	87301	505-863-3896		637-2
Gally Public Affairs Inc 68 State Cir Ste 6 *Web:* www.gallypublicaffairs.com	Annapolis	MD	21401	410-990-0069		636
Galman Group, The 261 Old York Rd Ofc *Web:* www.galmangroup.com	Jenkintown	PA	19046	215-886-2000		652
Galpin Motors Inc 15505 Roscoe Blvd *Web:* www.galpin.com	North Hills	CA	91343	818-351-5027		57
Galsterer Abramowitz PA 2000 NE 45th St *TF:* 833-332-1333 ■ *Web:* flinjuryfirm.com	Fort Lauderdale	FL	33308	954-951-0000	951-1000	41
Galt House Hotel 140 N Fourth St *TF:* 800-843-4258 ■ *Web:* www.galthouse.com	Louisville	KY	40202	502-589-5200		379
Galt Toys 900 N Michigan Ave *Web:* galtbaby.com	Chicago	IL	60611	773-327-9980		761
Galtere 25887 County Road 12 *Web:* www.galtere.com	Preston	MN	55965	212-598-1837		194
Galvan Industries Inc 7320 Millbrook Rd *TF:* 800-277-5678 ■ *Web:* galvan-ize.com	Harrisburg	NC	28075	704-455-5102	455-5215	481
Galvanic Applied Sciences USA Inc 41 Wellman St *TF:* 866-252-8470 ■ *Web:* www.galvanic.com	Lowell	MA	01851	978-848-2701		201

	Phone	Fax	Class
Galveston Central Appraisal District 9850 Emmett F Lowry Expy Ste A . . . . Texas City TX 77591 *TF:* 866-277-4725 ■ *Web:* www.galvestoncad.org	409-935-1980		317
Galveston College 4015 Ave Q. . . . . .Galveston TX 77550 *TF:* 866-483-4242 ■ *Web:* gc.edu	409-944-4242	944-1501	162
Galveston Computer Solutions LLC 523 24th St Ste 5 . . . . .Galveston TX 77550 *Web:* galvcs.com	409-762-4326		379
Galveston County 722 Moody Ave . . . . Galveston TX 77550 *Web:* www.galvestoncountytx.gov	409-766-2200		338
Galveston County Daily News 8522 Teichman Rd PO Box 628 . . . . .Galveston TX 77553 *TF:* 800-561-3611 ■ *Web:* www.galvnews.com	409-683-5200	740-3421	532-2
Galveston Independent School District (GISD) 3904 Ave T PO Box 660 .Galveston TX 77550 *Web:* www.gisd.org	409-766-5100		685
Galveston Island State Park 14901 Termini San Luis Pass Rd . . . . .Galveston TX 77554 *Web:* tpwd.texas.gov	409-737-1222		565
Galvestonian Condominium Assn 1401 E Beach Dr. . . . . .Galveston TX 77550 *TF:* 888-526-6161 ■ *Web:* www.galvestonian.com	409-765-6161		707
Galvin Flying Services 7001 Perimeter Rd . . . . Seattle WA 98108 *Web:* galvinflying.com	206-763-0350		63
Galway Bay Irish Pub 63 Maryland Ave. . . . . Annapolis MD 21401 *Web:* www.galwaybaymd.com	410-263-8333		671
Galway Group LLC 3009 Post Oak Blvd Ste 950. . . . . .Houston TX 77056 *Web:* www.galwaygroup.com	713-952-0186		70
GAMA (General Aviation Manufacturers Assn) 1400 K St NW Ste 801 . . . . Washington DC 20005 *TF:* 866-427-3287 ■ *Web:* www.gama.aero	202-393-1500	842-4063	49-21
Gama Aviation Signature 2 Corporate Dr Ste 1050. . . . . Shelton CT 06484 *TF:* 800-468-1110 ■ *Web:* www.gamasignature.com	203-337-4600		21
GAMA Intl 3112 Fairview Park Dr. . . . . Falls Church VA 22042 *TF:* 800-345-2687 ■ *Web:* gamaweb.com	800-345-2687		49-9
Gam-Anon International Service Office Inc PO Box 157 . . . . .Whitestone NY 11357 *Web:* www.gam-anon.org	718-352-1671	746-2571	48-21
Gamber-Johnson Inc 3001 Borham Ave . . . . .Stevens Point WI 54481 *Web:* www.gamberjohnson.com	715-344-3482		295
Gambia Embassy DC 5630 16th St NW . . . . Washington DC 20011 *Web:* www.gambiaembassydc.us	202-785-1399		257
Gambit Weekly 3923 Bienville St . . . . New Orleans LA 70119 *Web:* www.nola.com	504-486-5900	483-3116	532-5
Gamble Parts-Dart Inc 2816 Mt Olive Rd . . . . .Mount Olive AL 35117 *Web:* www.partsdart.com	205-631-4705		780
Gamble Plantation Historic State Park 3708 Patten Ave . . . . .Ellenton FL 34222 *Web:* www.floridastateparks.org	941-723-4536		565
Gamblers Anonymous (GA) PO Box 17173 . . . .Los Angeles CA 90017 *Web:* www.gamblersanonymous.org	626-960-3500	960-3501	48-21
Gamblers General Store Inc (GGS) 800 S Main St. . . . . Las Vegas NV 89101 *Web:* www.gamblersgeneralstore.com	702-382-9903		761
Gambone Bros Development Co 1030 W Germantown Pk . . . . East Norriton PA 19403 *Web:* www.gambone.com	610-539-4700	539-4701	653
Gambone Steel Company Inc 545 Foundry Rd . . . . .Norristown PA 19403 *Web:* www.gambonesteelcompany.com	610-539-6505	631-1127	480
Gambrill State Park 8602 Gambrill Park Rd . . . . Frederick MD 21702 *TF:* 800-830-3974 ■ *Web:* www.dnr.maryland.gov	301-473-8417		565
Gambrinus Co, The 14800 San Pedro 3rd Fl . . . . .San Antonio TX 78232 *Web:* www.gambrinus.com	210-490-9128	490-9984	81-1
Gambro BCT 10811 W Collins Ave. . . . . Lakewood CO 80215 *TF:* 877-339-4228 ■ *Web:* www.terumobct.com	303-231-4357		419
GAMCO Investors Inc 1 Corporate Ctr . . . . Rye NY 10580 *NYSE: GBL* ■ *TF:* 800-422-3554 ■ *Web:* www.gabelli.com	914-921-5100	921-5118	528
Game & Parks Commission 301 E State Farm Rd . . . . North Platte NE 69101 *Web:* www.outdoornebraska.gov	308-535-8025		565
Game Country USA 2403 Commerce Ln . . . . Albany GA 31707 *Web:* www.gamecountryusa.com	229-883-4706	883-4766	710
Game Creek Video LLC 23 Executive Dr. . . . . Hudson NH 03051 *Web:* www.gamecreekvideo.com	603-882-5222		514
Game Informer 724 N First St 3rd Fl . . . . .Minneapolis MN 55401 *Web:* www.gameinformer.com	612-486-6100		761
GameChanger Products LLC 2207 Harbor Bay Pkwy . . . . .Alameda CA 94502 *Web:* www.gamechanger.net	510-521-7985	521-8254	196
GameFly Inc 3000 Ocean Pk Blvd . . . . .Santa Monica CA 90405 *Web:* www.gamefly.com	310-664-6400		93
Games Unlimited 2115 Murray Ave . . . . Pittsburgh PA 15217 *Web:* www.bgamers.com	412-421-8807		44
GameStop Corp 625 Westport Pkwy . . . . Grapevine TX 76051 *NYSE: GME* ■ *TF:* 800-883-8895 ■ *Web:* www.gamestop.com	817-424-2000		179
Gamewell FCI 12 Clintonville Rd. . . . . .Northford CT 06472 *TF:* 800-606-1983 ■ *Web:* www.gamewell-fci.com	203-484-7161	484-7118	283
Gaming Laboratories International Inc 600 Airport Rd . . . . Lakewood NJ 08701 *Web:* www.gaminglabs.com	732-942-3999	942-0043	193
Gaming Partners International Inc 3945 W Cheyenne Ave Ste 208. . . . . North Las Vegas NV 89032 *NASDAQ: GPIC* ■ *TF:* 800-728-5766 ■ *Web:* gpigaming.com	702-384-2425	384-1965	322
Gamma Aerospace LLC 601 Airport Dr . . . . .Mansfield TX 76063 *Web:* www.gammaaero.com	817-477-2193		256
Gamma Beta Phi Society 5204 Kingston Pk Ste 31-33. . . . . Knoxville TN 37919 *TF:* 800-628-9920 ■ *Web:* www.gammabetaphi.org	865-483-6212		48-16
Gamma Construction Co 2808 Joanel St. . . . . .Houston TX 77027 *Web:* www.gammaconst.com	713-963-0086	963-0961	186
Gamma Dynacare Medical Laboratories Inc 115 Midair Ct . . . . .Brampton ON L6T5M3 *TF:* 800-668-2714 ■ *Web:* www.dynacare.ca	800-668-2714		415
Gamma High Voltage Research Inc 1096 N US Hwy 1 Ste 109 . . . . .Ormond Beach FL 32174 *Web:* gammahighvoltage.com	386-677-7070	677-3039	425
Gamma Phi Beta International Sorority (GPB) 12737 E Euclid Dr. . . . . Centennial CO 80111 *Web:* www.gammaphibeta.org	303-799-1874	799-1876	48-16
Gamma Products Inc 7730 W 114th Pl. . . . . Palos Hills IL 60465 *Web:* gammaproducts.com	708-974-4100	974-0071	472
Gamma Sports 200 Waterfront Dr . . . . Pittsburgh PA 15222 *TF:* 800-333-0337 ■ *Web:* gammasports.com	412-323-0335	323-0317	710
Gamma Vacuum LLC 2915 133rd St W. . . . . .Shakopee MN 55379 *Web:* www.gammavacuum.com	952-445-4841		419
Gammon Technical Products Inc 2300 Hwy 34 . . . . Manasquan NJ 08736 *Web:* www.gammontech.com	732-223-4600		358
GAMS Communications LLC 308 W Erie St Ste 400. . . . . .Chicago IL 60654 *Web:* www.gamscom.com	312-280-2740		195
GAMS Development Corp 1217 Potomac St NW . . . . .Washington DC 20007 *Web:* www.gams.com	202-342-0180	342-0181	178-1
Gamse Lithographing Company Inc 7413 Pulaski Hwy. . . . . .Baltimore MD 21237 *Web:* www.gamse.com	410-866-4700		174
Gamut Music Inc 1600 London Rd. . . . . Duluth MN 55812 *TF:* 888-724-8099 ■ *Web:* www.gamutmusic.com	888-724-8099		637-10
GaN Corp 11247 S Memorial Pkwy. . . . . Huntsville AL 35803 *Web:* www.geeksandnerds.com	256-489-2471		261
Ganahl Lumber Co 1220 E Ball Rd . . . . Anaheim CA 92805 *Web:* www.ganahllumber.com	714-772-5444	772-0639	364
Ganan & Shapiro PC 120 N Lasalle St Ste1750 . . . . .Chicago IL 60602 *Web:* ganan-shapiro.com	312-822-0040	321-1114	41
Ganaraska Region Conservation 2216 28 Hwy . . . . Port Hope ON L1A3V8 *Web:* www.grca.on.ca	905-885-8173		192
GANCOM Reprographics Services 207-209 Senate Ave . . . . Camp Hill PA 17011 *Web:* www.gancom.com	717-763-7387	763-8150	344
Gandee & Associates Inc 642 Brooksedge Blvd . . . . .Westerville OH 43081 *Web:* gandee.net	614-942-6040		261
Gander & Area Chamber of Commerce 109 Trans Canada Hwy. . . . . .Gander NL A1V1P6 *Web:* www.ganderchamber.nf.ca	709-256-7110	256-4080	137
Gander Mountain Co 180 Fifth St E Ste 1300. . . . . Saint Paul MN 55101 *TF:* 888-542-6337 ■ *Web:* www.ganderoutdoors.com	888-542-6337		711
Gandhi Cuisine of India 150 W Ft Lowell Rd . . . . .Tucson AZ 85705 *Web:* gandhicuisineofindia.com	520-292-1738		671
Gandhi India's Cuisine 4080 Paradise Rd . . . . Las Vegas NV 89169 *Web:* gandhiindianscuisine.com	702-734-0094		671
Gandy Co 528 Gandrud Rd .Owatonna MN 55060 *TF:* 800-443-2476 ■ *Web:* www.gandy.net	507-451-5430	451-2857	273
Gandy Printers Inc 1800 S Monroe St . . . . Tallahassee FL 32301 *Web:* www.gandyprinters.com	850-222-5847		627
Gandy's Dairies LLC 201 University Ave . . . . .Lubbock TX 79415	806-765-8833		296-25
Ganek PC 197 14th St NW Ste 300. . . . . Atlanta GA 30318 *Web:* www.ganekpc.com	404-892-7300		41
Ganesh Machinery 20869 Plummer St. . . . . Chatsworth CA 91311 *TF:* 888-542-6374 ■ *Web:* ganeshmachinery.com	818-349-9166		385
Gangloff Industries Inc 1040 W County Rd 250 S . . . . Logansport IN 46947 *Web:* www.gangloffind.com	574-722-3888	722-3893	780
Ganna Walska Lotusland 695 Ashley Rd . . . . Santa Barbara CA 93108 *Web:* www.lotusland.org	805-969-3767	969-4423	97
Ganneston Construction Corp 3025 N Belfast Ave . . . . .Augusta ME 04332 *Web:* www.gannestonconstruction.com	207-621-8505	621-8508	186
Gannett Company Inc 7950 Jones Branch Dr . . . . McLean VA 22102 *NYSE: GCI* ■ *TF:* 800-778-3299 ■ *Web:* www.gannett.com	703-854-6000		738
Gannett Fleming 207-209 Senate Ave . . . . Camp Hill PA 17011 *TF:* 800-233-1055 ■ *Web:* www.gannettfleming.com	717-763-7211	763-8150	261
Gannett Welsh & Kotler LLC 222 Berkeley St. . . . . .Boston MA 02116 *TF:* 800-225-4236 ■ *Web:* www.gwkinvest.com	617-236-8900	236-1815	401
Gannon University 109 University Sq. . . . . Erie PA 16541 *TF:* 800-426-6668 ■ *Web:* www.gannon.edu	814-871-7000	871-5803	166
Ganondagan State Historic Site SR-444 Victor-Bloomfield Rd .Victor NY 14564 *Web:* parks.ny.gov	585-924-5848		565
Ganong Bros Ltd 1 Chocolate Dr. . . . . Saint Stephen NB E3L2X5 *TF:* 888-598-8811 ■ *Web:* ganong.com	506-465-5600	465-5610	296-8
Gans Ink & Supply Company Inc 1441 Boyd St . . . . .Los Angeles CA 90033 **Fax Area Code:* 323 ■ *TF:* 800-421-6167 ■ *Web:* www.gansink.com	800-421-6167	264-2916*	388
Gant Travel Management 400 W Seventh St Ste 233 . . . . Bloomington IN 47404 *TF:* 800-742-4198 ■ *Web:* www.ganttravel.com	630-227-3800		771
Gantec Corp 1111 Plaza Dr Ste 310. . . . . Schaumburg IL 60173 *Web:* www.gantecusa.com	847-885-7655	885-7988	196
Gantec Publishing Solutions LLC 1827 Walden Office Sq Ste 260 . . . . Schaumburg IL 60173 *Web:* www.gantecpublishing.com	847-598-1144		530
Ganther Construction & Architecture Inc 4825 County Rd A . . . . Oshkosh WI 54901 *Web:* www.ganther.com	920-426-4774	426-4788	186

Name	Address	City	State	ZIP	Phone	Fax	Class	Other
Gantry Plaza State Park	4-09 47th Rd	Long Island City	NY	11101	718-786-6385		565	*Web:* parks.ny.gov
GAO (Government Accountability Office)	441 G St NW	Washington	DC	20548	202-512-4800		342	*Web:* www.gao.gov
Gap Engineering Inc	21703 Kingsland Blvd Ste 103	Katy	TX	77450	281-578-0500		261	*Web:* gap-eng.com
Gap Inc	2 Folsom St	San Francisco	CA	94105	800-333-7899		157-4	*NYSE:* GPS ■ *TF:* 800-333-7899 ■ *Web:* www.gapinc.com
Gap International Inc	700 Old Marple Rd	Springfield	PA	19064	610-328-0308	328-1092	463	*TF:* 855-328-0308 ■ *Web:* www.gapinternational.com
Gap Solutions Inc	205 Van Buren St Ste 205	Herndon	VA	20170	703-707-2090		317	*TF:* 800-503-5125 ■ *Web:* www.gapsi.com
Gapco Inc	2151 Centennial Dr	Gainesville	GA	30504	770-534-7928		811	*TF:* 866-534-7928 ■ *Web:* gapcoinc.com
GAR Enterprises	418 E Live Oak Ave	Arcadia	CA	91006	626-574-1175		174	*Web:* www.kgselectronics.com
GAR Foundation	Andrew Jackson House 277 E Mill St	Akron	OH	44308	330-576-2926		305	*Web:* garfoundation.org
GAR Wood Securities LLC	440 S LaSalle St Ste 2201	Chicago	IL	60605	312-566-0740		690	*TF:* 866-694-2757 ■ *Web:* garwoodsecurities.net
Garaga Inc	8500 25th Ave	Saint-Georges	QC	G6A1K5	418-227-2828	227-6282	480	*TF:* 800-464-2724 ■ *Web:* www.garaga.com
Garagiste Inc	707 S Lander St	Seattle	WA	98134	888-264-0053		443	*TF:* 888-264-0053 ■ *Web:* www.garagiste.com
Garamendi John (Rep D - CA)	2368 Rayburn House Office Bldg	Washington	DC	20515	202-225-1880	225-5914	342-2	*Web:* garamendi.house.gov
Garan Lucow Miller PC	1000 Woodbridge St	Detroit	MI	48207	313-446-1530		428	*TF:* 800-875-1530 ■ *Web:* www.garanlucow.com
Garantice Su Futuro Limited Liability Co	3710 Kennedy Blvd	Union	NJ	07087	201-867-2222		390	*Web:* garanticesufuturo.com
Garavi Gujarat Publications	2020 Beaver Ruin Rd	Norcross	GA	30071	770-263-7728		532-3	*Web:* www.amg.biz
GARBC (General Association of Regular Baptist Churches)	1300 N Meacham Rd	Schaumburg	IL	60173	888-588-1600		48-20	*TF:* 888-588-1600 ■ *Web:* www.garbcinternational.org
Garbe Industries Inc	4137 S 72nd E Ave	Tulsa	OK	74145	918-627-0284		351	*TF:* 800-735-2241 ■ *Web:* garbes.com
Garbe Iron Works Inc	456 N Broadway St	Aurora	IL	60505	630-897-5100	897-4090	480	*Web:* www.giwinc.com
Garber Atlas Fries & Assoc. Inc	3070 Lawson Blvd	Oceanside	NY	11572	516-837-1100		390	*Web:* gafinsurance.com
Garber Chevrolet Saginaw	8800 Gratiot Rd	Saginaw	MI	48609	989-607-0584		516	*Web:* www.garberchevroletsaginaw.net
Garbett, Allen & Roza PA	80 SW Eighth St Ste 3100	Miami	FL	33130	305-579-0012		41	*Web:* gsarlaw.com
Garcia & Associates Inc	1 Saunders Ave	San Anselmo	CA	94960	415-458-5803	458-5829	194	*Web:* www.garciaandassociates.com
Garcia & Garcia Attorneys At Law PLLC	308 E Rundberg	Austin	TX	78753	512-828-7956		41	*Web:* garciagarcialaw.com
Garcia Foods Inc	1802 Jackson Keller Rd	San Antonio	TX	78213	210-349-6262		296-26	*Web:* garciafoods.com
Garcia Galuska & De Sousa Inc	375 Faunce Corner Rd Ste D	Dartmouth	MA	02747	508-998-5700		261	*Web:* g-g-d.com
Garcia Hamilton & Associates LP	5 Houston Ctr 1401 McKinney Ste 1600	Houston	TX	77010	713-853-2322	853-2300	401	*Web:* garciahamiltonassociates.com
Garcia Jesus (Rep D - IL)	530 Cannon House Office Bldg	Washington	DC	20515	202-225-8203		342-2	*Web:* www.chuygarcia.house.gov
Garcia Sylvia (Rep D - TX)	1620 Longworth House Office Bldg	Washington	DC	20515	202-225-1688		342-2	*Web:* www.sylviagarcia.house.gov
Garcia's Seafood Grille & Fish Marke	398 NW N River Dr	Miami	FL	33128	305-375-0765		671	*Web:* garciasmiami.com
Garco Building Systems	2714 S Garfield Rd	Airway Heights	WA	99001	509-244-5611	244-2850	105	*TF:* 800-941-2291 ■ *Web:* www.garcobuildings.com
Garco Construction Inc	4114 E Broadway	Spokane	WA	99202	509-535-4688		186	*Web:* www.garco.com
Garcon French Restaurant	1101 Valencia St	San Francisco	CA	94110	415-401-8959		671	*Web:* www.garconsf.com
Gard Analytics Inc	1334 N Walnut Ave	Arlington Heights	IL	60004	847-698-5686		196	*Web:* www.gard.com
Gard Communications	1140 SW 11th Ave Ste 300	Portland	OR	97205	503-221-0100		636	*TF:* 800-800-7132 ■ *Web:* gardcommunications.com
Garde Arts Ctr	325 State St	New London	CT	06320	860-444-7373	701-0189	572	*Web:* www.gardearts.org
Garden Bar	NE Hassalo St 1061 NE 9th Ave	Portland	OR	97232	503-206-5655		670	*Web:* www.gardenbarpdx.com
Garden Center Solutions LLC	649 S Ave Ste 5	Secane	PA	19018	610-690-7345		532-3	*Web:* gardencentersolutions.com
Garden City Area Chamber of Commerce	1509 E Fulton Terr	Garden City	KS	67846	620-275-1900		139	*Web:* www.gardencitychamber.net
Garden City Community College	801 N Campus Dr	Garden City	KS	67846	620-276-7611	276-9573	162	*TF:* 800-658-1696 ■ *Web:* www.gcccks.edu
Garden City Ctr	100 Midway Rd Ste 14	Cranston	RI	02920	401-942-2800		460	*Web:* www.gardencitycenter.com
Garden City Feed Yard	1805 W Annie Scheer	Garden City	KS	67846	620-275-4191		10-1	
Garden City Hospital (GCH)	6245 Inkster Rd	Garden City	MI	48135	734-458-3300		374-3	*Web:* www.gch.org
Garden City Hotel	45 Seventh St	Garden City	NY	11530	516-747-3000		379	*TF:* 877-549-0400 ■ *Web:* www.gardencityhotel.com
Garden City Plumbing & Heating Inc	3955 Flynn Ln	Missoula	MT	59808	406-728-5550		610	*Web:* gardencityplumbing.com
Garden City Public Library	31735 Maplewood St	Garden City	MI	48135	734-793-1830	793-1831	434-3	*Web:* www.gardencitylib.org
Garden County	611 Main St PO Box 350	Oshkosh	NE	69154	308-772-3924	772-9926	338	*Web:* www.gardencountyne.org
Garden Court Hotel	520 Cowper St	Palo Alto	CA	94301	650-322-9000		379	*TF:* 800-824-9028 ■ *Web:* www.gardencourt.com
Garden District Animal Hospital, The	1302 Perkins Rd	Baton Rouge	LA	70806	225-381-9661		794	*Web:* www.gardendistrictanimalhospital.com
Garden Grove Animal Hospital PA	3033 Cypress Gardens Rd	Winter Haven	FL	33884	863-324-0623	324-7849	794	*Web:* ggahvet.com
Garden Grove Chamber of Commerce	12866 Main St Ste 102	Garden Grove	CA	92840	714-638-7950	636-6672	139	*TF:* 800-959-5560 ■ *Web:* www.gardengrovechamber.com
Garden Grove City Hall	11222 Acacia Pkwy	Garden Grove	CA	92840	714-741-5000	741-5044	337	*Web:* ggcity.org
Garden Grove Hospital & Medical Ctr	12601 Garden Grove Blvd	Garden Grove	CA	92843	714-537-5160		374-3	*Web:* www.gardengrovehospital.com
Garden Grove Regional	11200 Stanford Ave	Garden Grove	CA	92840	714-530-0711		434-3	*Web:* www.ocsd.org
Garden Grove Unified School District	10331 Stanford Ave	Garden Grove	CA	92840	714-663-6000	663-6100	685	*Web:* www.ggusd.us
Garden of Life Inc	4200 Northcrop Pkwy Ste 200	Palm Beach Gardens	FL	33410	561-748-2477	472-9298	799	*TF:* 866-465-0051 ■ *Web:* www.gardenoflife.com
Garden Spa at MacArthur Place	29 E MacArthur St	Sonoma	CA	95476	707-933-3193		707	*TF:* 800-722-1866 ■ *Web:* www.macarthurplace.com
Garden Spot Foods	191 Commerce Dr	New Holland	PA	17557	800-829-5100		297-11	*TF:* 800-829-5100 ■ *Web:* www.gardenspotfoods.com
Garden State Engine & Equipment	3509 Rt 22 E	Somerville	NJ	08876	908-534-5444	534-5623	358	*TF:* 800-479-3857 ■ *Web:* gseecrane.com
Garden State Fireworks Inc	PO Box 403	Millington	NJ	07946	908-647-1086	647-6258	145	*TF:* 800-999-0912 ■ *Web:* www.gardenstatefireworks.com
Garden State Growers	99 Locust Grove Rd	Pittstown	NJ	08867	908-730-8888	730-6676	369	*TF:* 800-288-8484 ■ *Web:* www.gardenstategrowers.com
Garden State Lumber Products	22 Muller Rd	Oakland	NJ	07436	201-651-1600	651-1666	186	*TF:* 800-526-4708 ■ *Web:* www.gardenstatelumber.com
Garden State Mltple Lsting Services	1719 SR- 10 Ste 223	Parsippany	NJ	07054	973-898-1900		652	*Web:* www.gsmls.com
Garden State Orthopaedic Assoc	28-04 Broadway	Fair Lawn	NJ	07410	201-791-4434	791-9377	238	*Web:* www.gardenstateortho.com
Garden State Precast	1630 Wyckoff Rd	Wall	NJ	07727	732-938-4436	938-7096	183	*Web:* www.gardenstateprecast.com
Garden State Tile	1324 Wyckoff Rd	Wall Township	NJ	07753	732-938-6675	938-7485	191-1	*Web:* www.gstile.com
Garden Valley Telephone Co	201 Ross Ave	Erskine	MN	56535	218-687-5251	687-2454	224	*TF:* 800-448-8260 ■ *Web:* www.gvtel.com
Garden Vietnamese Restaurant	304 Reily St	Harrisburg	PA	17102	717-238-9310		671	*Web:* www.gardenvn.net
Gardena Recycling Center Inc	1538 W 134th St	Gardena	CA	90249	877-464-5255		686	*TF:* 877-464-5255 ■ *Web:* www.gardenarecyclingcenter.com
Gardena Valley Chamber of Commerce	1204 W Gardena Blvd Ste E	Gardena	CA	90247	310-532-9905	329-7307	139	*Web:* www.gardenachamber.org
Gardena Valley News	15005 S Vermont Ave	Gardena	CA	90247	310-329-6351	329-7501	532-4	*Web:* gardenavalleynews.org
Gardener's Supply Co	128 Intervale Rd	Burlington	VT	05401	802-660-3505		323	*TF:* 888-833-1412 ■ *Web:* www.gardeners.com
Gardeners' Guild Inc	2780 Goodrick Ave	Richmond	CA	94801	415-457-0400		776	*Web:* www.gardenersguild.com
Gardens Alive Inc	5100 Schenley Pl	Lawrenceburg	IN	47025	513-354-1482	354-1484	459	*Web:* www.gardensalive.com
Gardens Hotel	526 Angela St	Key West	FL	33040	305-294-2661		379	*TF:* 800-526-2664 ■ *Web:* www.gardenshotel.com
Gardens Mall, The	3101 PGA Blvd	Palm Beach Gardens	FL	33410	561-622-2115	694-9380	460	*Web:* www.thegardensmall.com
Gardens of Salonica	19 Fifth St NE	Minneapolis	MN	55413	612-378-0611		671	*Web:* gardensofsalonica.com
Gardens Veterinary Hospital Inc	9087 Marshall Rd	Cranberry Township	PA	16066	724-772-1870		794	*Web:* gardensvet.com

Phone | Fax | Class

Gardenside Ltd 808 Anthony St Berkeley CA 94710 415-455-4500 455-4505 319-4
TF: 888-999-8325 ■ *Web:* www.gardenside.com
Gardenswartz & Dodds PC
600 17th St Ste 1800 N Denver CO 80202 303-534-6770 2
Gardien Services USA Inc
3700 24th Ave Bldg A Forest Grove OR 97116 503-430-8980 393
Web: na.gardien.com
Gardiner Museum 111 Queen's Pk Toronto ON M5S2C7 416-586-8080 586-8085 520
Web: www.gardinermuseum.on.ca
Gardner Cory (Sen R - CO)
354 Russell Senate Office Bldg Washington DC 20510 202-224-5941 224-6524 342-2
Web: www.gardner.senate.gov
Gardner Cryogenics
2136 City Line Rd Bethlehem PA 18017 610-264-4523 763
Web: www.gardnercryo.com
Gardner Denver Inc 1800 Gardner Expy Quincy IL 62305 217-222-5400 172
NYSE: GDI ■ *Web:* www.gardnerdenver.com
Gardner Glass Products Inc
301 Elkin Hwy PO Box 1570 North Wilkesboro NC 28659 800-334-7267 334
TF: 800-334-7267 ■ *Web:* www.gardnerglass.com
Gardner Hotel 311 E Franklin Ave El Paso TX 79901 915-532-3661 379
Web: www.gardnerhotel.com
Gardner Inc 3641 Interchange Rd Columbus OH 43204 614-456-4000 456-4001 274
TF: 800-848-8946 ■ *Web:* www.gardnerinc.com
Gardner Industries Inc
12 Commerce Rd Fairfield NJ 07004 973-887-3700 290
Web: gardnerindustries.com
Gardner James Nakken Hugo & Nolan
429 First St Woodland CA 95695 530-662-7367 428
Web: yololaw.com
Gardner Linn Burkhart & Ondersma LLP
2851 Charlevoix Dr SE Ste 207 Grand Rapids MI 49546 616-975-5500 975-5505 445
Web: www.gardner-linn.com
Gardner Manufacturing Inc
1201 W Lake St Horicon WI 53032 800-558-8890 198
TF: 800-558-8890 ■ *Web:* www.gardnermfg.com
Gardner Mattress Corp 254 Canal St Salem MA 01970 978-341-4780 321
Web: www.gardnermattress.com
Gardner Publications Inc
6915 Valley Ave Cincinnati OH 45244 513-527-8800 527-8801 637-9
TF: 800-950-8020 ■ *Web:* www.gardnerweb.com
Gardner Trabolsi & Associates PLLC
2200 Sixth Ave Ste 600 Seattle WA 98121 206-256-6309 256-6318 41
Web: gandtlawfirm.com
Gardner Village 1100 W 7800 S West Jordan UT 84088 801-566-8903 460
Web: www.gardnervillage.com
Gardner White Furniture Company Inc
4445 N Atlantic Blvd Auburn Hills MI 48326 248-481-2108 321
Web: www.gardner-white.com
Gardner's Seafood & Pasta
111 Thurston Ave NW Olympia WA 98501 360-786-8466 671
Web: gardnersrestaurant.com
Gardner, Weiss & Rosenblum LLP
270 Madison Ave 13th Fl New York NY 10016 212-907-0600 41
Web: gardnerweiss.com
Gardner-Gibson PO Box 5449 Tampa FL 33675 813-248-2101 248-6768 46
TF: 800-237-1155 ■ *Web:* gardner-gibson.com
Gardners Candies Inc
2600 Adams Ave PO Box E Tyrone PA 16686 814-684-3925 684-3928 123
TF: 800-242-2639 ■ *Web:* www.gardnerscandies.com
Gardner-Webb University
110 S Main St PO Box 997 Boiling Springs NC 28017 704-406-4000 406-4488 166
TF: 800-253-6472 ■ *Web:* www.gardner-webb.edu
Gardner-Zemke Company Inc
6821 Academy Pkwy NE Albuquerque NM 87109 505-881-0555 884-2191 189-4
Web: www.gardnerzemke.com
Garduno's 10031 Coors Blvd NW Albuquerque NM 87114 505-890-7000 670
Web: gardunosrestaurants.com
Gare Inc 165 Rosemont St Haverhill MA 01832 978-373-9131 292-0885* 43
**Fax Area Code: 800* ■ *TF:* 888-289-4273 ■ *Web:* store.gareceramics.com
Gared Sports Inc
707 N 2nd St Ste 220 Saint Louis MO 63102 314-421-0044 421-6014 710
TF: 800-325-2682 ■ *Web:* www.garedsports.com
Garelick Manufacturing Co
644 Second St Saint Paul Park MN 55071 651-459-9795 459-8269 350
Web: www.garelick.com
Garfield County 114 W Broadway Rm 106 Enid OK 73701 580-237-0220 249-5989 338
Web: www.garfieldok.com
Garfield County
2933 Grand Ave Glenwood Springs CO 81601 970-945-1377 945-7785 338
Web: www.garfield-county.com
Garfield County PO Box 370 Jordan MT 59337 406-557-6178 338
Web: www.garfieldcounty.com
Garfield County 375 N 700 W Panguitch UT 84759 435-676-2678 338
Web: gcutsheriff.com
Garfield County 789 Main St PO Box 915 Pomeroy WA 99347 509-843-3731 338
Web: co.garfield.wa.us
Garfield Elementary School
1514 S Ninth Ave Maywood IL 60153 708-450-2009 344-0593 685
Web: garfield.maywood89.org
Garfield Industries 62 Clinton Rd Fairfield NJ 07004 973-575-8800 575-6840 1
Web: www.garfieldbuff.com
Garfield Medical Ctr
525 N Garfield Ave Monterey Park CA 91754 626-573-2222 571-8972 374-3
Web: www.garfieldmedicalcenter.com
Garfield Park Conservatory
300 N Central Park Ave Chicago IL 60624 312-746-5100 97
Web: garfieldconservatory.org
Garfield Park Library
705 Woodrow Ave Santa Cruz CA 95060 831-427-7713 434-3
Web: www.santacruzpl.org
Garfield Refining Co
810 E Cayuga St Philadelphia PA 19124 800-523-0968 410
TF: 800-523-0968 ■ *Web:* www.garfieldrefining.com
Garfunkel Wild & Travis PC
111 Great Neck Rd Ste 503 Great Neck NY 11021 516-393-2200 428
Web: garfunkelwild.com
Garganese, Weiss, D'Agresta & Salzman PA
111 N Orange Ave Ste 2000 Orlando FL 32801 407-425-9566 425-9596 428
Web: www.orlandolaw.net
Garganigo, Goldsmith & Weiss
14 Penn Plz Ste 1020 New York NY 10122 212-643-6400 643-6549 428
Web: www.ggw.com
Gargiula Construction Inc
12611 Panasoffkee Dr North Fort Myers FL 33903 239-597-3131 194
Web: www.gargiulaconstruction.com
Gargoyles Inc
500 George Washington Hwy Smithfield RI 02917 800-426-6396 542
TF: 866-807-0195 ■ *Web:* gargoyleseyewear.com
Gari Melchers Home & Studio
224 Washington St Fredericksburg VA 22405 540-654-1015 654-1785 97
Web: www.garimelchers.org
Garibaldi Cafe 315 W Congress St Savannah GA 31401 912-232-7118 671
Web: garibaldisavannah.com
Garibaldi's Italian Kitchen
307 N Carson St Carson City NV 89701 775-884-4574 671
Web: garibaldisitaliankitchen.com
Garibaldis 347 Presidio Ave San Francisco CA 94118 415-563-8841 671
Web: www.garibaldisrestaurant.com
Garick Corp 13600 Broadway Ave Cleveland OH 44125 800-242-7425 820
TF: 800-242-7425 ■ *Web:* www.garick.com
Garing Taylor & Associates Inc
141 S Elm St Arroyo Grande CA 93420 805-489-1321 261
Web: www.garingtaylor.com
Garkane Energy Co-op
120 W 300 S PO Box 465 Loa UT 84747 800-747-5403 245
TF: 800-747-5403 ■ *Web:* www.garkaneenergy.com
Gar-Kenyon Technologies
106 Evansville Ave Meriden CT 06451 203-729-4900 729-4950 790
Web: garkenyon.com
Garland & Mason LLC
Manalapan Corporate Plz 195 Rt 9 S Manalapan NJ 07726 732-358-2028 358-2029 428
Web: www.kmrslaw.com
Garland Chamber of Commerce
520 N Glenbrook Dr Garland TX 75040 972-272-7551 276-9261 139
Web: www.garlandchamber.com
Garland City
200 N 5th St PO Box 469002 Garland TX 75040 972-205-2000 337
Web: www.garlandtx.gov
Garland Civic Theatre
2703 National Pl Garland TX 75040 972-485-8884 573-4
Web: www.garlandcivic.org
Garland Commercial Industries
185 S St Freeland PA 18224 570-636-1000 624-0218* 298
**Fax Area Code: 800* ■ *TF:* 800-424-2411 ■ *Web:* www.garland-group.com
Garland Company Inc 3800 E 91st St Cleveland OH 44105 216-641-7500 641-0633 46
TF: 800-321-9336 ■ *Web:* www.garlandco.com
Garland County 501 Ouachita Ave Hot Springs AR 71901 501-622-3610 624-0665 338
TF: 800-482-5964 ■ *Web:* www.garlandcounty.org
Garland County Historical Society Archives
PO Box 21335 Hot Springs AR 71903 501-321-2159 434-3
Web: www.garlandcountyhistoricalsociety.com
Garland F. Fulcher Seafood Company Inc
301 Hodges St Oriental NC 28571 252-249-1341 297-5
Web: www.townoforiental.com
Garland Independent School District (GISD)
501 S Jupiter PO Box 469026 Garland TX 75042 972-494-8201 685
Web: www.garlandisd.net
Garland Landmark Museum
200 Museum Plaza Dr Garland TX 75040 972-205-2749 520
Web: garlandhistorical.org
Garland Light & Power Co 755 Hwy 14A Powell WY 82435 307-754-2881 245
Web: garlandpower.org
Garland Manufacturing Co PO Box 538 Saco ME 04072 207-283-3693 283-4834 758
TF: 800-727-1900 ■ *Web:* www.garlandmfg.com
Garland Power & Light PO Box 469002 Garland TX 75046 972-205-2650 41
Web: www.gpltexas.org
Garland Resort 4700 N Red Oak Rd Lewiston MI 49756 877-442-7526 669
TF: 877-442-7526 ■ *Web:* www.garlandusa.com
Garland Sales Inc 1800 Antioch Rd Dalton GA 30720 706-278-7880 131
TF: 800-524-0361 ■ *Web:* www.garlandrug.com
Garland, The
4222 Vineland Ave North Hollywood CA 91602 818-980-8000 766-0112 379
TF: 800-238-3759 ■ *Web:* www.thegarland.com
Garlic Bros 6629 Embarcadero Dr Stockton CA 95219 209-474-6585 671
Web: www.garlicbrothersonline.com
Garlich Printing Co 525 Rudder Rd Fenton MO 63026 844-449-4752 626
TF: 844-449-4752 ■ *Web:* www.garlich.com
Garlick Swift & Garry LLP
5150 Tamiami Trail N Ste 501 Naples FL 34103 239-597-7088 41
Web: garlaw.com
Garling Construction Inc
1120 11th St Belle Plaine IA 52208 319-444-3409 444-2437 186
Web: www.garlingconstruction.com
Garlinghouse Co, The
2121 Boundary St Ste 208 Beaufort SC 29902 843-271-6107 454-9101* 459
**Fax Area Code: 866* ■ *TF:* 800-482-0464 ■ *Web:* www.familyhomeplans.com
Garlington Landeweer Marine Inc
3370 SE Slater St Stuart FL 34997 772-283-7124 90
Web: www.garlingtonyachts.com
Garlington Lohn Robinson PLLP
350 Ryman St Missoula MT 59802 406-523-2500 523-2595 445
Web: www.garlington.com
Garlin-Neumann Leathers Company Inc
66-D River Rd Hudson NH 03051 603-595-6319 881-9431 431
Web: www.leatherusa.com
Garlock Equipment Co
2601 Niagara Ln N Plymouth MN 55447 800-328-5914 190
TF: 800-328-5914 ■ *Web:* garlockequip.com
Garlock Printing & Converting Corp
164 Fredette St Gardner MA 01440 978-630-1028 627
TF: 800-473-1328 ■ *Web:* www.garlockprinting.com
Garlow Petroleum Inc 707 Kakoi St Honolulu HI 96819 808-836-1957 833-5825 579
Web: www.garlowpetroleum.com
Garment District Inc 200 Broadway Cambridge MA 02139 617-876-5230 426-5509 157-3
TF: 888-482-1632 ■ *Web:* www.garment-district.com

	Phone	Fax	Class
Garment Graphics LLC 220 W Ft Lowell Rd ... Tucson AZ 85705 *Web:* garmentgraphics.net	520-544-0529		687
Garmin Ltd 1200 E 151st St ... Olathe KS 66062 *NASDAQ: GRMN* ■ *TF:* 888-442-7646 ■ *Web:* www.garmin.com	913-397-8200	397-8282	529
Garner 825 E Cooley Ave ... San Bernardino CA 92408 *Web:* www.garnerholt.com	909-799-3030		385
Garner Correctional Institution 50 Nunnawauk Rd ... Newtown CT 06470 *Web:* portal.ct.gov	203-270-2800		213
Garner Environmental Services Inc 1717 W 13th St ... Deer Park TX 77536 *TF:* 800-424-1716 ■ *Web:* garner-es.com	281-930-1200		667
Garner Industries Inc 7201 N 98th St PO Box 29709 ... Lincoln NE 68507 *TF:* 800-228-0275 ■ *Web:* www.garnerindustries.com	402-434-9100	434-9133	608
Garnet A. Wilson Public Library of Pike County 207 N Market St ... Waverly OH 45690 *Web:* www.pikecountylibrary.org	740-947-4921	947-2918	434-3
Garnet Career Ctr 422 Dickinson St ... Charleston WV 25301 *Web:* www.garnet.edu	304-348-6195	348-6198	167-3
Garnet Hill Inc 231 Main St ... Franconia NH 03580 **Fax Area Code:* 888 ■ *TF:* 800-870-3513 ■ *Web:* www.garnethill.com	603-823-5545	842-9696*	745-1
Garnet River LLC 60 Railroad Pl Ste 501 ... Saratoga Springs NY 12866 *Web:* garnetriver.com	518-275-4800		180
Garnett State Savings Bank 106 E Fifth St ... Garnett KS 66032 *TF:* 877-477-2301 ■ *Web:* www.gssb.us.com	785-448-3111		70
Garney Construction 1333 NW Vivion Rd ... Kansas City MO 64118 *TF:* 800-832-1517 ■ *Web:* www.garney.com	816-741-4600	741-4488	188-10
Garozzo's 526 Harrison St ... Kansas City MO 64106 *Web:* garozzos.com	816-221-2455		671
GARP Research 406 Main St ... Reisterstown MD 21136 *Web:* www.garpresearch.com	410-318-5020		401
Garr Tool Co 7800 N Alger Rd ... Alma MI 48801 *TF:* 800-248-9003 ■ *Web:* garrtool.com	989-463-6171	463-3600	403
Garrard Central Record 106 Richmond St ... Lancaster KY 40444 *Web:* garrardcentralrecord.com	859-792-2831	792-3448	637-9
Garrard County 15 Public Sq ... Lancaster KY 40444 *Web:* garrardcounty.us	859-792-3531	792-2010	338
Garratt-Callahan Co 50 Ingold Rd ... Burlingame CA 94010 *Web:* garrattcallahan.com	650-466-7912	692-6098	145
Garrett & Tully A Professional Corp 225 S Lake Ave Ste 1400 ... Pasadena CA 91101 *Web:* www.garrett-tully.com	626-577-9500		428
Garrett College 687 Mosser Rd ... McHenry MD 21541 *TF:* 866-554-2773 ■ *Web:* www.garrettcollege.edu	301-387-3000	387-3038	162
Garrett County 203 S Fourth St Rm 207 ... Oakland MD 21550 *Web:* www.garrettcounty.org	301-334-8970	334-5000	338
Garrett County Chamber of Commerce 15 Visitors Center Dr ... McHenry MD 21541 *TF:* 866-351-1119 ■ *Web:* www.visitdeepcreek.com	301-387-4386	387-2080	139
Garrett Metal Detectors 1881 W State St ... Garland TX 75042 *TF:* 800-234-6151 ■ *Web:* garrett.com	972-494-6151	494-1881	472
Garrett Nagle & Company Inc 300 Unicorn Park Dr 3rd Fl ... Woburn MA 01801 *Web:* www.garrettnagle.com	617-737-9090		528
Garrett Printing & Graphics Inc 331 Riverside Ave ... Bristol CT 06010 *Web:* www.garrettprinting.us	860-589-6710		627
Garrett State Forest 1431 Potomac Camp Rd ... Oakland MD 21550 *Web:* www.dnr.maryland.gov	301-334-2038		565
Garrett's Cafe 1631 N Bell School Rd ... Rockford IL 61107 *Web:* www.garrettsrestaurantbar.com	815-484-9473		671
GarrettCom Inc 47823 Westinghouse Dr ... Fremont CA 94539 *Web:* www.garrettcom.com	510-438-9071	438-9072	173-1
Garrigan Lyman Group Inc, The 1524 Fifth Ave Ste 400 ... Seattle WA 98101 *Web:* www.glg.com	206-223-5548		7
Garrison Forest School 300 Garrison Forest Rd ... Owings Mills MD 21117 *Web:* www.gfs.org	410-363-1500		622
Garrison Investment Group LP 1290 Avenue of the Americas Ste 914 ... New York NY 10104 *Web:* www.garrisoninv.com	212-372-9500		401
Garrison Printing Co 7155 Airport Hwy ... Pennsauken NJ 08109 *Web:* www.gogarrison.com	856-488-1900	488-6191	627
Garrison-Ross Agency Inc 602 W Flint St ... Davison MI 48423 *Web:* www.garrisonross.com	810-653-2101		390
Garrod Hydraulics Inc 1050 Locust Point Rd ... York PA 17406 *TF:* 866-442-7763 ■ *Web:* www.garrod.com	866-442-7763		223
Garrott Bros Continous Mix Inc PO Box 419 ... Gallatin TN 37066 *Web:* www.garrottbros.com	615-452-2385		182
Garroutte Products PO Box 2930 ... Ponca City OK 74602 **Fax Area Code:* 580 ■ *TF:* 800-870-8207 ■ *Web:* www.circlegbrand.com	800-870-8207	767-1750*	431
Garruto & Calabria, Attorneys At Law 609 Franklin Ave ... Nutley NJ 07110 *Web:* garrutolaw.com	973-661-4455		41
Garry Packing Inc 11272 E Central Ave ... Del Rey Oaks CA 93616 *TF:* 800-248-2126 ■ *Web:* www.garryscountrystore.com	559-888-2126		296-18
Garsite LLC 539 S 10th St ... Kansas City KS 66105 *TF:* 888-427-7483 ■ *Web:* garsite.com	913-342-5600	342-0638	21
Garston Sign & Screen Printing 570 Tolland St ... East Hartford CT 06108 *Web:* garston.com	860-289-3040		492
Gart Companies, The 299 Milwaukee St Ste 500 ... Denver CO 80206 *Web:* www.gartcompanies.com	303-333-1933	333-1905	652
Gartech Enterprises Inc 3037 W State Rd 256 ... Austin IN 47102 *Web:* gartechenterprises.com	812-794-4796		256
Gartenhaus Furs 7101 Wisconsin Ave ... Bethesda MD 20814 *Web:* www.fursbygartenhaus.com	301-656-2800		157-6
Garth Fagan Dance 50 Chestnut St ... Rochester NY 14604 *Web:* www.garthfagandance.org	585-454-3260		573-1
Gartland & Mellina Group Corp 1385 Broadway Ste 912 ... New York NY 10018 *Web:* gartlandandmellina.com	212-418-4780		463
Gartland Foundry Company Inc 330 Grant St ... Terre Haute IN 47802 *Web:* www.gartlandfoundry.com	812-232-0226		307
Gartner & Bloom Pc 801 Second Ave ... New York NY 10017 *Web:* gartnerbloom.com	212-759-5800	759-5842	41
Gartner Inc 56 Top Gallant Rd ... Stamford CT 06902 *NYSE: IT* ■ *TF:* 866-471-2526 ■ *Web:* www.gartner.com	203-964-0096		466
Gartner Refrigeration Inc 2331 W Superior St ... Duluth MN 55806 *Web:* www.gartner1.com	218-722-4439		189-10
Gartner Studios 220 Myrtle St E ... Stillwater MN 55082 *TF:* 888-235-0484 ■ *Web:* www.gartnerstudios.com	888-235-0484		590
Garton Tractor Inc 2400 N Golden State Blvd PO Box 1849 ... Turlock CA 95382 *Web:* gartontractor.com	209-632-3931	632-8006	274
Garvan Woodland Gardens 550 Arkridge Rd PO Box 22240 ... Hot Springs AR 71903 *TF:* 800-366-4664 ■ *Web:* www.garvangardens.org	501-262-9300	262-9301	97
Garver Engineers 4701 Northshore Dr ... North Little Rock AR 72118 *Web:* www.garverusa.com	501-376-3633		261
Garvey Corp 208 S Rt 73 ... Blue Anchor NJ 08037 *TF:* 800-257-8581 ■ *Web:* www.garvey.com	609-561-2450	561-2328	207
Garvey Wholesale Beverage Inc 2542 San Gabriel Blvd ... Rosemead CA 91770 *TF:* 800-287-2075 ■ *Web:* www.garveywholesalebeverage.com	626-280-5244		80-3
Garvin & Hickey LLC 181 E Livingston Ave ... Columbus OH 43215 *Web:* garvin-hickey.com	614-225-9000		428
Garvin County 201 W Grant St 2nd Fl ... Pauls Valley OK 73075 *Web:* okcountyrecords.com	405-238-2772		338
Garvin Industries Inc 3700 Sandra St ... Franklin Park IL 60131 *Web:* www.garvinindustries.com	847-455-0188		488
Garvin-Allen Solutions Ltd 155 Chain Lake Dr Unit 12 ... Halifax NS B3S1B3 *TF:* 877-325-9062 ■ *Web:* www.garvin-allen.com	902-453-3554		180
Gary & Leos Inc 730 First St ... Havre MT 59501 *Web:* www.garyandleos.com	406-265-1404		345
Gary Area Career Ctr 1988 Polk ... Saint Gary IN 46407 *Web:* www.garycsc.k12.in.us	219-963-2901	962-6269	167-3
Gary Bergman Associates Inc 14 Hickory Ln ... North Brunswick NJ 08902 *TF:* 800-603-3114 ■ *Web:* www.debugcics.com	732-247-2727	846-3515	180
Gary Chamber of Commerce One Buffington Harbor Dr ... Gary IN 46406 *Web:* www.garychamber.com	219-885-7407		139
Gary Comer Inc 20875 Crossroads Cir Ste 100 ... Waukesha WI 53186 *Web:* gcionline.com	262-798-5080		360-3
Gary D. Mccallister & Associates LLC 120 N La Salle St Ste 2800 ... Chicago IL 60602 *Web:* mccallisterlawgroup.com	312-345-0611		428
Gary Drug Co 59 Charles St ... Boston MA 02114 *Web:* www.garydrug.com	617-227-0023	227-2879	237
Gary Jet Center Inc 5401 Industrial Hwy ... Gary IN 46406 *Web:* garyjetcenter.com	219-944-1210		316
Gary K. Walch 23801 Calabasas Rd Ste 1019 ... Calabasas CA 91302 *Web:* www.walchlaw.com	818-222-3400		428
Gary Lee Partners (GLP) 833 N Orleans St Ste 400 ... Chicago IL 60610 *Web:* www.garyleepartners.com	312-640-8300		393
Gary Linarducci, Attorney-At-Law PA 910 W Basin Rd Ste 100 ... New Castle DE 19720 *Web:* delawaredisability.com	302-613-0707		41
Gary M.Perkiss PC 801 Old York Rd Ste 313 ... Jenkintown PA 19046 *Web:* perkiss.com	215-885-7100	572-8470	41
Gary Manuel Aveda Institute 1514 10th Ave ... Seattle WA 98122 *Web:* www.gmaveda.com	206-329-9933		167-3
Gary Mathews Motors Inc 1100 Ashland City Rd ... Clarksville TN 37040 *TF:* 866-705-1380 ■ *Web:* www.garymathewsmotors.com	931-552-7100		516
Gary Merlino Construction Co 9125 10th Ave S ... Seattle WA 98108	206-623-1414	763-4178	183
Gary Olszewski & Company PC 94 N Elm St Ste 209 ... Westfield MA 01085 *Web:* qualitycpa.com	413-562-5709		2
Gary Plastic Packaging Corp 1340 Viele Ave ... Bronx NY 10474 *TF:* 800-221-8150 ■ *Web:* www.plasticboxes.com	718-893-2200	378-2141	600
Gary Pools Inc 438 Sandau Rd ... San Antonio TX 78216 *Web:* www.garypools.com	210-341-5153	341-5154	728
Gary Public Library 220 W Fifth Ave ... Gary IN 46402 *Web:* www.garypubliclibrary.org	219-886-2484	886-6829	434-3
Gary Public Transportation Corp 2101 W 35th Ave ... Gary IN 46408 *Web:* www.gptcbus.com	219-884-6100		108
Gary Soren Smith Center for the Fine & Performing Arts *Ohlone College* 43600 Mission Blvd ... Fremont CA 94539 *TF:* 800-309-2131 ■ *Web:* www.ohlone.edu	510-659-6031	659-6188	572
Gary Stock Co 7 Sutton Pl ... Brewster NY 10509 *Web:* www.gstockco.com	914-276-2700		7
Gary's Wine & Marketplace 121 Main St ... Madison NJ 07940 *Web:* www.garyswine.com	973-822-0200		443

Phone | Fax | Class

Garza County PO Box 366 .... Post TX 79356 806-495-4430 495-4431 338
TF: 866-549-1010 ■ *Web:* www.garzacounty.net

Garza Creative Group PO Box 190595 .... Dallas TX 75219 214-720-3888 4
Web: www.garzacreative.com

GAS (Glass Art Society)
6512 23rd Ave NW Ste 329 .... Seattle WA 98117 206-382-1305 382-2630 48-4
Web: www.glassart.org

Gas & Electrical Equipment Co (GE)
300 NE 34th St .... Oklahoma City OK 73105 405-528-3551 557-1172 38
Web: www.geeco-inc.com

Gas 'n' Shop Inc
701 Marina Bay Pl PO Box 81463 .... Lincoln NE 68528 402-475-1101 475-0976 324
Web: gitnsplit.com

Gas Daily 1200 G St NW Ste 1000 .... Washington DC 20005 202-942-8788 383-2024 531-5
Web: www.spglobal.com

Gas Depot Oil Company Inc
8700 N Waukegan Rd Ste 200 .... Morton Grove IL 60053 847-581-0303 581-0309 324
Web: www.gasdepot.com

Gas Equipment Company Inc
11616 Harry Hines Blvd .... Dallas TX 75229 972-241-2333 620-1403 385
TF: 800-821-1829 ■ *Web:* www.gasequipment.com

Gas Field Specialists Inc
2107 SR- 44 S .... Shinglehouse PA 16748 814-698-2122 698-2124 539
Web: www.gfsinc.net

Gas Inc 103 Durham St .... Dallas GA 30132 770-502-8800 316
Web: www.gasinc.com

Gas Liquids Engineering Ltd
2749-39th Ave NE Ste 300 .... Calgary AB T1Y4T8 403-250-2950 539
Web: www.gasliquids.com

Gas Technology Energy Concepts LLC
401 William L Gaiter Pkwy Ste 4 .... Buffalo NY 14215 800-451-8294 172
TF: 800-451-8294 ■ *Web:* www.gas-tec.com

Gas Technology Institute (GTI)
1700 S Mt Prospect Rd .... Des Plaines IL 60018 847-768-0500 768-0501 668
Web: www.gti.energy

Gas Turbine Controls Corp
6 Skyline Dr .... Hawthorne NY 10532 914-693-0830 693-3824 362
TF: 844-482-3278 ■ *Web:* gasturbinecontrols.com

Gasbarre Products Inc 590 Division St .... Dubois PA 15801 814-371-3015 236-3651 697
Web: www.gasbarre.com

Gasch Printing LLC 1780 Crossroads Dr .... Odenton MD 21113 301-362-0700 627
Web: gaschprinting.com

Gasconade County 119 E First St Rm 23 .... Hermann MO 65041 573-486-3100 486-3693 338
Web: www.gasconadecountyassessor.com

Gascosage Electric Co-op
803 S Hwy 28 PO Box G .... Dixon MO 65459 573-759-7146 759-6020 245
TF: 866-568-8243 ■ *Web:* gascosage.coop

Gas-Fired Products Inc
305 Doggett St .... Charlotte NC 28203 704-372-3485 332-5843 318
TF: 800-830-3983 ■ *Web:* gasfiredproducts.com

Gaska-Tape Inc 1810 W Lusher Ave .... Elkhart IN 46517 574-294-5431 293-4504 732
TF: 800-423-1571 ■ *Web:* www.gaska.com

Gasket & Seal Fabricators Inc
1640 Sauget Industrial Pkwy .... Sauget IL 62206 618-332-0425 326
Web: www.gasketandseal.com

Gasket Engineering Company Inc
4500 E 75th Terr .... Kansas City MO 64132 816-363-8333 363-3558 326
Web: www.gasketeng.com

Gasket Manufacturing Co 18001 Main St .... Gardena CA 90248 310-217-5600 217-5608 326
TF: 800-442-7538 ■ *Web:* www.gasketmfg.com

Gaskets Inc 301 W Hwy 16 .... Rio WI 53960 920-992-3137 992-3124 326
TF: 800-558-1833 ■ *Web:* www.gasketsinc.com

Gaskins Surveying Company Inc
1266 Powder Springs Rd .... Marietta GA 30064 770-424-7168 261
Web: www.gscsurvey.com

Gaslamp Plaza Suites 520 E St .... San Diego CA 92101 619-232-9500 379
Web: www.gaslampplaza.com

Gaslamp Quarter Assn
614 Fifth Ave Ste E .... San Diego CA 92101 619-233-5227 233-4693 50-6
Web: www.gaslamp.org

Gaslight Media 120 E Lake St .... Petoskey MI 49770 231-487-0692 487-0313 180
Web: www.gaslightmedia.com

Gasoline Alley
870 N Cleveland Massillon Rd .... Akron OH 44333 330-666-2670 671
Web: www.gasolinealleyinbath.com

Gaspard Inc 200 N Janacek Rd .... Brookfield WI 53045 262-784-6800 784-7567 155-14
TF: 800-784-6868 ■ *Web:* www.gaspardinc.com

Gass Horse Supply 476 Main St .... Orono ME 04473 207-866-8593 156
Web: www.gasshorsesupply.com

Gassaway Mansion 106 Dupont Dr .... Greenville SC 29607 864-271-0188 242-9935 50-3
TF: 888-912-7469 ■ *Web:* www.gassawaymansion.com

Gassco Inc PO Box 9866 .... Bakersfield CA 93389 661-832-7406 832-9795 579
TF: 800-390-7837 ■ *Web:* gasscoinc.com

Gasser & Sons Inc 440 Moreland Rd .... Commack NY 11725 631-543-6600 543-6649 488
Web: www.gasser.com

Gasser Chair Company Inc
4136 Logan Way .... Youngstown OH 44505 800-323-2234 759-9844* 319-3
**Fax Area Code:* 330 ■ *TF:* 800-323-2234 ■ *Web:* www.gasserchair.com

Gast Johnson & Muffly Pc
323 S College Ave Ste 1 .... Fort Collins CO 80524 970-482-4846 41
Web: gjmlawfirm.com

Gast Manufacturing Inc
2300 M-139 Hwy PO Box 97 .... Benton Harbor MI 49023 269-926-6171 925-8288 172
Web: www.gastmfg.com

Gastar Exploration Ltd
1331 Lamar St Ste 1080 .... Houston TX 77010 713-739-1800 739-0458 536
NYSE: GST ■ *Web:* www.gastar.com

Gaston Chamber of Commerce
601 W Franklin Blvd .... Gastonia NC 28052 704-864-2621 854-8723 139
Web: www.gastonchamber.com

Gaston College 201 Hwy 321-S .... Dallas NC 28034 704-922-6200 922-2344 162
Web: www.gaston.edu

Gaston Correctional Ctr 520 Justice Ct .... Dallas NC 28034 704-922-3861 922-1491 213
Web: www.ncdps.gov

Gaston County
128 W Main Ave PO Box 1578 .... Gastonia NC 28053 704-866-3111 866-3147 338
Web: www.gastongov.com

Gaston County Dyeing Machine Co
PO Box 308 .... Stanley NC 28164 704-822-5000 822-0753 744
Web: www.gaston-county.com

Gaston County Family Ymca
3210 Union Rd .... Gastonia NC 28056 704-865-2193 354
Web: www.gastonymca.org

Gaston County Public Library
1555 E Garrison Blvd .... Gastonia NC 28054 704-868-2164 853-0609 434-3
Web: gastonlibrary.org

Gaston County School 943 Osceola St .... Gastonia NC 28054 704-866-6100 685
Web: www.gaston.k12.nc.us

Gaston County Travel & Tourism
620 N Main St .... Belmont NC 28012 704-825-4044 206
Web: www.gogastonnc.org

Gaston Gazette 1893 Remount Rd .... Gastonia NC 28054 704-869-1700 869-1708 532-2
Web: www.gastongazette.com

Gaston Systems Inc 200 S Main St .... Stanley NC 28164 704-263-6000 263-0954 552-1
Web: gastonsystems.com

Gaston's White River Resort
1777 River Rd .... Lakeview AR 72642 870-431-5202 669
Web: www.gastons.com

Gastonian, The 220 E Gaston St .... Savannah GA 31401 912-232-2869 232-0710 379
TF: 800-322-6603 ■ *Web:* www.gastonian.com

Gastronomy Inc
48 W Market St Ste 250 .... Salt Lake City UT 84101 801-322-4668 363-5275 670
Web: marketstreetgrill.com

Gatan Inc 5794 W Las Positas Blvd .... Pleasanton CA 94588 925-463-0200 419
TF: 888-887-3377 ■ *Web:* www.gatan.com

Gatco Inc 1550 Factor Ave .... San Leandro CA 94577 510-352-8770 787
TF: 800-227-5640 ■ *Web:* www.gatco-inc.com

Gate Petroleum Co
9540 San Jose Blvd PO Box 23627 .... Jacksonville FL 32241 904-737-7220 732-7660 324
TF: 866-571-1982 ■ *Web:* www.gatepetro.com

Gate6 Inc 16624 N 90th Ste 111 .... Scottsdale AZ 85260 623-572-7725 5
Web: www.gate6.com

Gatehouse Group Inc, The
120 Forbes Blvd Ste 180 .... Mansfield MA 02048 508-337-2500 653
Web: www.gatehousemgt.com

GateHouse Media LLC
5300 Crosswind Dr .... Columbus OH 43228 740-888-6000 532-4
Web: www.thisweeknews.com

Gatekeeper Systems Inc 8 Studebaker .... Irvine CA 92618 949-453-1940 453-8148 199
TF: 888-808-9433 ■ *Web:* www.gatekeepersystems.com

Gately Communication Co
501 Industry Dr .... Hampton VA 23661 757-455-5151 246
Web: www.gately.com

Gater Industries Inc
4400 Dell Range Blvd .... Cheyenne WY 82009 307-635-4166 350
Web: www.gaterindustries.com

Gates Albert Inc 3434 Union St .... North Chili NY 14514 585-594-9401 594-4305 621
Web: www.gatesalbert.com

Gates Bar-B-Q 1026 State Ave .... Kansas City KS 66102 913-621-1134 671
Web: gatesbbq.com

Gates Capital Management Inc
1177 Avenue of the Americas between 45th & 46th Sts
46th Fl .... New York NY 10036 212-626-1421 401
Web: www.gatescap.com

Gates Corp 1551 Wewatta St .... Denver CO 80202 303-744-1911 744-4000 370
TF: 800-709-6001 ■ *Web:* www.gates.com

Gates County 200 Court St .... Gatesville NC 27938 252-357-2411 357-0073 338
Web: gatescounty.govoffice2.com

Gates Family Foundation
1390 Lawrence St .... Denver CO 80204 303-722-1881 316-3038 305
TF: 866-590-4377 ■ *Web:* www.gatesfamilyfoundation.org

Gates Public Library
902 Elmgrove Rd .... Rochester NY 14624 585-247-6446 426-5733 434-3
Web: www.gateslibrary.org

Gates, Gonter, Guy,Proudfoot & Muench LLP
15373 Innovation Dr Ste 170 .... San Diego CA 92128 858-676-8600 676-8601 428
Web: g3pmlaw.com

Gatestone & Company International Inc
455 N 3rd St Ste 260 .... Phoenix AZ 85004 602-443-2920 160

Gatesworth 1 Mcknight Pl .... Saint Louis MO 63124 314-993-0111 371
Web: www.thegatesworth.com

Gateway Arch
50 S Leonor K Sullivan Blvd .... Saint Louis MO 63102 877-982-1410 50-4
TF: 877-982-1410 ■ *Web:* www.gatewayarch.com

Gateway Clipper Fleet
350 W Stn Sq Dr .... Pittsburgh PA 15219 412-355-7980 355-7987 221
Web: www.gatewayclipper.com

Gateway Community & Technical College (GCTC)
500 Technology Wy .... Florence KY 41042 859-441-4500 800
TF: 855-346-4282 ■ *Web:* gateway.kctcs.edu

GateWay Community College
108 N 40th St .... Phoenix AZ 85034 602-286-8000 286-8072 162
TF: 888-994-4433 ■ *Web:* www.gatewaycc.edu

Gateway Community College
20 Church St .... New Haven CT 06510 203-285-2000 285-2260 162
TF: 800-390-7723 ■ *Web:* www.gatewayct.edu

Gateway Concrete Forming Services Inc
PO Box 130 State Rte 128 .... Miamitown OH 45041 513-353-2000 353-2002 189-3
Web: gatewayconcreteforming.com

Gateway Credit Union
100 Otis Smith Dr .... Clarksville TN 37043 931-551-8271 551-3357 219
Web: gatewaycreditunion.com

Gateway Ctr 1 Gateway Dr .... Collinsville IL 62234 618-345-8998 345-9024 205
TF: 800-289-2388 ■ *Web:* www.gatewaycenter.com

Gateway Design Inc
4299 San Felipe St Ste 100 .... Houston TX 77027 713-572-9600 572-0777 7

Gateway Distribution Inc
11755 Lebanon Rd .... Cincinnati OH 45241 513-891-4477 891-5224 780
Web: www.gatewaydistribution.net

Gateway Energy Services Corp
400 Rella Blvd Ste 300 .... Montebello NY 10901 800-805-8586 316
TF: 800-805-8586 ■ *Web:* www.gesc.com

GateWay Fax Systems Inc
11032 Merganser Ter .... Chesterfield VA 23838 804-796-1900 796-1116 735
TF: 877-951-9800 ■ *Web:* www.gwfs.com

Name / Address	City	State	ZIP	Phone	Fax	Class
Gateway Foundation Inc 1080 E Park St *TF:* 877-505-4673 ■ *Web:* www.gatewayfoundation.org	Carbondale	IL	62901	877-377-2027		726
Gateway Group One Inc 604-608 Market St *Web:* www.gatewaygroupone.com	Newark	NJ	07105	973-465-8006	465-9389	692
Gateway Inc 7565 Irvine Center Dr *TF:* 800-846-2000 ■ *Web:* www.gateway.com	Irvine	CA	92618	949-471-7040		173-2
Gateway Insurance Services Inc 1416 Buckeye Ave. *Web:* gisiowa.com	Ames	IA	50010	515-232-6001		390
Gateway Limousines 1550 Gilbreth Rd *TF:* 800-486-7077 ■ *Web:* gatewayglobalsf.com	Burlingame	CA	94010	650-697-5548		441
Gateway Logistics Group Inc, The 18201 Viscount Rd *TF:* 800-338-8017 ■ *Web:* gateway-group.com	Houston	TX	77032	281-443-7447		311
Gateway Mastering Studios Inc 428 Cumberland Ave *Web:* www.gatewaymastering.com	Portland	ME	04101	207-828-9400		658
Gateway Mortgage Group LLC 244 S Gateway Pl PO Box 974 *TF:* 877-764-9319 ■ *Web:* www.gatewayloan.com	Jenks	OK	74037	877-406-8109		217
Gateway National Recreation Area 210 New York Ave. *Web:* www.nps.gov	Staten Island	NY	10305	718-354-4606		564
Gateway Newspapers 610 Beatty Rd *Web:* triblive.com	Monroeville	PA	15146	412-856-7400		637-8
Gateway Newstands 240 Chrislea Rd *TF:* 800-942-5351 ■ *Web:* gatewaynewstands.com	Woodbridge	ON	L4L8V1	905-851-9652		530
Gateway Pacific Contractors Inc 8055 Freeport Blvd *Web:* www.gatewaypacific.com	Sacramento	CA	95832	916-665-4100		610
Gateway Plastics Inc 5650 W County Line Rd *Web:* www.gatewayplastics.com	Mequon	WI	53092	262-242-2020		596
Gateway Printing Company Inc 925 Pacific Ave *Web:* www.gatewayprint.com	Bremen	GA	30110	770-537-4329	537-2241	627
Gateway Products Inc 301 S Main St **Fax Area Code:* 888 ■ *TF:* 800-421-2828 ■ *Web:* www.su-per.com	Holly	CO	81047	800-421-2828	473-2954*	447
Gateway Products Recycling Inc 4223 E 49th St *Web:* gatewayrecycle.com	Cleveland	OH	44125	216-341-8777		638
Gateway Real Estate Inc 7720 Old Canton Rd Ste C-1 *Web:* bhhsgatewayrealestate.com	Madison	MS	39110	601-624-6827		652
Gateway Regional Chamber of Commerce 135 Jefferson Ave *Web:* www.gatewaychamber.com	Elizabeth	NJ	07201	908-352-0900	352-0865	139
Gateway Regional Medical Ctr (GRMC) 2100 Madison Ave *Web:* www.gatewayregional.net	Granite City	IL	62040	618-798-3000		374-3
Gateway Supply Company Inc 1312 Hamrick St *TF:* 800-922-5312 ■ *Web:* www.gatewaysupply.net	Columbia	SC	29201	803-771-7160		612
Gateway Technical College 3520 - 30th Ave *TF:* 800-247-7122 ■ *Web:* www.gtc.edu	Kenosha	WI	53144	262-564-2200		800
Gateway to Care 3611 Ennis St *Web:* www.guidestar.org	Houston	TX	77004	713-783-4616		363
Gateway Travel Service Inc 28470 W 13 Mile Rd Ste 200 *TF:* 800-423-4898 ■ *Web:* www.gatewaytrvl.com	Farmington Hills	MI	48334	248-432-8600		772
Gateway Truck & Refrigeration 921 Fournie Ln *TF:* 800-449-2131 ■ *Web:* www.gipower.com	Collinsville	IL	62234	618-345-0123	242-8420	57
Gateway, The 18 N Rio Grande St *Web:* shopthegateway.com	Salt Lake City	UT	84101	801-456-0000	456-0005	50-6
Gateways Books and Tapes PO Box 370 *TF:* 800-869-0658 ■ *Web:* www.gatewaysbooksandtapes.com	Nevada City	CA	95959	530-271-2239	272-0184	637-2
Gateways Inn & Restaurant 51 Walker St *Web:* www.gatewaysinn.com	Lenox	MA	01240	413-637-2532	637-1432	379
Gator of Florida Inc 5002 N Howard Ave *Web:* gatorofflorida.com	Tampa	FL	33603	813-877-8267		155-21
Gator Park 24050 SW Eigth St *TF:* 800-559-2205 ■ *Web:* gatorpark.com	Miami	FL	33194	305-559-2255		823
Gatorade Sports Science Institute 617 W Main St *TF:* 800-616-4774 ■ *Web:* www.gssiweb.org	Barrington	IL	60010	800-616-4774		668
Gatorland 14501 S Orange Blossom Trl *TF:* 800-393-5297 ■ *Web:* www.gatorland.com	Orlando	FL	32837	407-855-5496		823
Gatorland Toyota-scion 2985 N Main St *Web:* www.gatorlandtoyota.com	Gainesville	FL	32609	352-376-3262		57
GATRA 2 Oak St *TF:* 800-483-2500 ■ *Web:* www.gatra.org	Taunton	MA	02780	508-823-8828		108
Gatterdam Industrial Services (GIS) 4615 Bittersweet Rd *Web:* www.gatterdam.com	Louisville	KY	40218	502-776-3937	776-9929	454
Gatti, Keltner, Bienvenu & Montesi 219 Adams Ave *Web:* gkbm.com	Memphis	TN	38103	901-526-2126		41
Gatto's Tires & Auto Service 15 W Hibiscus Blvd *Web:* gattos.com	Melbourne	FL	32901	321-727-3322		54
GATX Rail Canada 1801 Magill College Ave *Web:* www.cgtx.com	Montreal	QC	H3A2N4	514-931-7343		264-5
Gaucho's Churrascaria 62 Lowell St *Web:* www.gauchosbraziliansteakhouse.com	Manchester	NH	03101	603-669-9460		671
Gaudenzia 106 W Main St *Web:* www.gaudenzia.org	Norristown	PA	19401	610-239-9600	239-9195	726
Gaudette Insurance Agency Inc 1 Plummers Corner *TF:* 800-922-8381 ■ *Web:* gaudette-insurance.com	Whitinsville	MA	01588	508-266-6469		390
Gauger + Assoc 360 Post St Ste 701 *Web:* www.gauger-associates.com	San Francisco	CA	94108	415-434-0303		7
Gauging Systems Inc 910 Industrial Blvd Ste A *Web:* www.gaugingsystemsinc.com	Sugar Land	TX	77478	281-980-3999	980-6929	493
Gault Energy & Home Solutions 11 Ferry Ln W *Web:* www.gaultenergy.com	Westport	CT	06880	203-227-5181		539
Gaum Inc 1080 Us Hwy 130 *Web:* www.gauminc.com	Robbinsville	NJ	08691	609-586-0132	586-9748	454
Gauntlett & Assoc 18400 Von Karman Ave Ste 300 *Web:* www.gauntlettlaw.com	Irvine	CA	92612	949-553-1010		428
Gausman & Moore Assoc 1700 Hwy 36 W *Web:* www.gausman.com	Roseville	MN	55113	651-639-9606	639-9618	256
Gaussian Inc 340 Quinnipiac St Bldg 40 *Web:* gaussian.com	Wallingford	CT	06492	203-284-2501	284-2521	261
Gauthier & Macmartin PLLC 123 Elm St *Web:* gauthierandmacmartin.com	Milford	NH	03055	603-673-7220		41
Gauthier Biomedical Inc 2221 Washington St *TF:* 866-546-0010 ■ *Web:* www.gauthierbiomedical.com	Grafton	WI	53024	262-546-0010	546-0011	476
Gauthier Industries Inc 3105 22nd St NW *Web:* www.gauthind.com	Rochester	MN	55901	507-289-0731		697
Gauthier Real Estate 408 Vincent Rd *Web:* homesforsaleinlafayette.com	LaFayette	LA	70508	337-856-0056		653
Gavant Software Inc 216 River St Ste 200 *Web:* gavant.com	Troy	NY	12180	518-273-2880		177
Gavco Plastics 9840 S 219th E Ave *Web:* www.gavcoplastics.com	Broken Arrow	OK	74014	918-455-7888		608
Gavel International Corp 935 Lakeview Pkwy Ste 190 *TF:* 800-544-2835 ■ *Web:* www.gavelintl.com	Vernon Hills	IL	60061	800-544-2835		184
Gavial Holdings Inc 1435 W McCoy Ln *Web:* www.gavialholdings.com	Santa Maria	CA	93455	805-614-0060		253
Gavilan College 5055 Santa Teresa Blvd *Web:* www.gavilan.edu	Gilroy	CA	95020	408-848-4800	846-4940	162
Gavin C. Roberts Insurance Agency Inc 2645 Frederica St Ste 100 *Web:* kyfb.com	Owensboro	KY	42301	270-926-9600		390
Gavin de Becker & Associates 350 N Glendale Ave Ste 517 *Web:* gdba.com	Glendale	CA	91206	818-760-4213	506-0426	194
Gavis Pharmaceuticals LLC 400 Campus Dr *Web:* www.empr.com	Somerset	NJ	08873	908-603-6080		238
Gawfco Enterprises Inc 1790 Ygnacio Valley Rd *Web:* www.gawfco.com	Walnut Creek	CA	94596	925-979-0560		324
Gawryl & Macallister Attorneys At Law 41 E Pearl St *Web:* gmac-law.com	Nashua	NH	03061	603-821-4237		41
Gawthrop Greenwood PC 17 E Gay St Ste 100 *Web:* gawthrop.com	West Chester	PA	19381	610-696-8225		428
Gay & Chacker 1731 Spring Garden St *Web:* gayandchacker.com	Philadelphia	PA	19130	215-567-7955		41
Gay & Robinson Inc PO Box 156	Kaumakani	HI	96747	808-335-3133		10-9
Gay Ad Network 1628 NE 17th Way *Web:* www.gayadnetwork.com	Fort Lauderdale	FL	33305	954-485-9910		7
Gay Men's Health Crisis (GMHC) 119 W 24th St *TF:* 800-243-7692 ■ *Web:* www.gmhc.org	New York	NY	10011	212-367-1000		48-17
Gay WW Mechanical Contractor Inc 524 Stockton St *Web:* wwgmc.com	Jacksonville	FL	32204	904-388-2696		189-10
Gayellow Pages PO Box 533 *Web:* www.gayellowpages.com	New York	NY	10014	646-213-0263		637-2
Gayla Industries Inc PO Box 920800 **Fax Area Code:* 713 ■ *TF:* 800-231-7508 ■ *Web:* www.gaylainc.com	Houston	TX	77292	800-231-7508	682-1357*	762
Gayle Manufacturing Company Inc 1455 E Kentucky Ave *Web:* gaylemfg.com	Woodland	CA	95776	530-662-0284		480
Gayle's Chocolates 417 S Washington Ave *Web:* www.gayleschocolates.com	Royal Oak	MI	48067	248-398-0001		296-8
Gaylor Electric 5750 Castle Creek Pkwy N Dr Ste 400 *TF:* 800-878-0577 ■ *Web:* www.gaylor.com	Indianapolis	IN	46250	317-843-0577	848-0364	189-4
Gaylord Bros 7282 William Barry Blvd *TF:* 800-345-5330 ■ *Web:* www.gaylord.com	Syracuse	NY	13212	800-448-6160	272-3412	319-3
Gaylord Hospital Gaylord Farms Rd PO Box 400 *TF:* 866-429-5673 ■ *Web:* www.gaylord.org	Wallingford	CT	06492	203-284-2800	294-8705	374-6
Gaylord Hub, The 234 4th St N *Web:* gaylordhub.digitaltown.com	Gaylord	MN	55334	507-237-2476		532-2
Gaylord Industries Inc 10900 SW Avery St *TF:* 800-547-9696 ■ *Web:* www.gaylordventilation.com	Tualatin	OR	97062	503-691-2010	692-6048	18
Gaylord Manufacturing Co 1088 Montclaire Dr *TF:* 800-375-0091 ■ *Web:* www.gaylordmfg.com	Ceres	CA	95307	209-538-3313		816
Gaylord Nelson Insurance Agency Inc 8516 S Pulaski Rd *Web:* gaylordnelson.net	Chicago	IL	60652	773-581-0844		390
Gaymar Industries Inc 10 Centre Dr *TF:* 800-828-7341 ■ *Web:* www.stryker.com	Orchard Park	NY	14127	800-327-0770		476
Gazelle Sports 3930 20th St SE *Web:* gazellesports.com	Grand Rapids	MI	49512	616-940-9888		711

Name / Address	Phone	Fax	Class
Gazelle Transportation Inc 34915 Gazelle Ct, Bakersfield CA 93308 *Web:* gazelletrans.com	661-322-8868		311
Gazelles Publishing Inc 21246 Dubois Ct, Ashburn VA 20147 *Web:* gazelles.com	703-858-2400		449
Gazette Library, The 1010 Catherine St W., Montreal QC H3B5L1 *Web:* www.montrealgazette.com	514-987-2222	987-2399	434-3
Gazette Publishing Inc 1114 Broadway, Wheaton MN 56296 *Web:* mnnews.com	320-563-8146		627
Gazette, The 885 W Liberty St., Medina OH 44256 *TF:* 800-633-4623 ■ *Web:* www.medina-gazette.com	330-725-4299		532-2
Gazette, The 501 Second Ave SE, Cedar Rapids IA 52401 *TF:* 800-397-8333 ■ *Web:* www.thegazette.com	319-398-8333		532-2
Gazette-Virginian, The 3201 Halifax Rd, South Boston VA 24592 *Web:* www.yourgv.com	434-572-3945	572-1173	532-2
GazetteXtra *Janesville Gazette* 1 S Parker Dr PO Box 5001, Janesville WI 53547 *TF:* 800-362-6712 ■ *Web:* www.gazettextra.com	608-755-8250	755-8349	532-2
GB Collects LLC 145 Bradford Dr, West Berlin NJ 08091 *Web:* www.gbcollects.com	856-768-9995		160
GB Manufacturing Co 1120 E Main St., Delta OH 43515 *Web:* www.gbmfg.com	419-822-5323		483
GB Tubulars Inc 950 Threadneedle St Ste 130, Houston TX 77079 *TF:* 888-245-3848 ■ *Web:* www.gbtubulars.com	713-465-3585		492
GBCA (Greater Bergen Community Action) 392 Main St, Hackensack NJ 07601 *Web:* www.greaterbergen.org	201-968-0200		379
GBCVB (Greater Boston Convention & Visitors Bureau) 2 Copley Pl Ste 105, Boston MA 02116 *TF:* 888-733-2678 ■ *Web:* www.bostonusa.com	617-536-4100	424-7664	206
GBF Enterpnrises Inc 2709 Halladay St, Santa Ana CA 92705 *Web:* www.gbfenterprises.com	714-979-7131		454
GBF Inc 2427 Penny Rd, High Point NC 27265 *TF:* 800-338-4168 ■ *Web:* www.gbf-inc.com	336-665-0205		627
GBG (Greenleaf Book Group LLC) PO Box 91869, Austin TX 78709 *Web:* www.greenleafbookgroup.com	512-891-6100	891-6150	637-2
GBI (Grand Beach Inn) 198 E Grand Ave., Old Orchard Beach ME 04064 *Web:* grandbeachinnmaine.com	207-934-4621		379
GBI Tile & Stone Inc 5900 Skylab Rd Ste 150, Huntington Beach CA 92647 *Web:* www.gbitile.com	949-567-1880		361
GBMC (Greater Baltimore Medical Ctr) 6701 N Charles St, Baltimore MD 21204 *Web:* www.gbmc.org	443-849-2000	849-6889	374-3
GBQ Partners LLC 230 W St Ste 700., Columbus OH 43215 *Web:* gbq.com	614-221-1120		2
GBRA (Guadalupe-Blanco River Authority) 933 E Ct St, Seguin TX 78155 *Web:* www.gbra.org	830-379-5822	379-9718	245
GBS (Greater Bridgeport Symphony) 446 University Ave, Bridgeport CT 06604 *Web:* www.gbs.org	203-576-0263		573-3
GBS Financial Corp 558 B St, Santa Rosa CA 95401 *Web:* www.gbsfinancial.com	707-568-2400		690
GBT Realty Corp 9010 Overlook Blvd, Brentwood TN 37027 *Web:* gbtrealty.com	615-373-3111		653
GBTA (Global Business Travel Assn, The) 123 N Pitt St., Alexandria VA 22314 *TF:* 888-574-6447 ■ *Web:* www.gbta.org	703-684-0836	684-0263	48-23
GC America Inc 3737 W 127th St, Alsip IL 60803 *TF:* 800-323-7063 ■ *Web:* www.gcamerica.com	708-597-0900	371-5103	228
GC Broach Co 7667 E 46th Pl, Tulsa OK 74145 *Web:* www.broach.com	918-664-7420	627-4083	318
GC Controls Inc 3926 Pine Cir, North Olmsted OH 44070 *Web:* www.gccontrols.net	440-779-4777	779-9097	203
GC Engineering Inc 10010 Indian School Rd NE, Albuquerque NM 87112 *Web:* www.gc-engineering.com	505-275-0022		256
GC Marketing Services 10 E 23rd St Ste 300., New York NY 10010 *Web:* www.gcmarketingservices.com	212-780-5200		195
GC Packaging 204 E Bethany Dr, Allen TX 75002 *Web:* www.gcpackaging.com	630-758-4100	833-1058	554
GC Partners Inc 3816 Forrestgate Dr, Winston-Salem NC 27103 *Web:* www.gcpartners.com	336-767-1600		299
GC Services LP 6330 Gulfton St, Houston TX 77081 *TF:* 800-756-6524 ■ *Web:* www.gcserv.com	713-777-4441		160
GCA (Greeting Card Assn) 1444 I St NW Ste 700., Washington DC 20005 *Web:* www.greetingcard.org	202-216-9627	216-9646	49-16
GCA Law Partners LLP 2570 W El Camino Real Ste 400., Mountain View CA 94040 *Web:* www.gcalaw.com	650-428-3900	428-3901	428
Gcas Inc 1531 Grand Ave, San Marcos CA 92078 *TF:* 888-300-4227 ■ *Web:* gcas.net	760-591-4227	471-9538	180
GCC (Geneva Construction Co) 1350 Aurora Ave., Aurora IL 60507 *Web:* www.genevaconstruction.net	630-892-4357	892-7738	186
GCC Printers USA 209 Burlington Rd, Bedford MA 01730 *Web:* www.gccprinters.de	781-275-1115		173-6
GCCA 600 S Cherry St Cherry Creek Plz 1 10th Fl, Glendale CO 80246 *Web:* www.gcc.com	303-739-5900	739-5938	135
GCEC (Grayson-Collin Electric Coop) 14568 FM 121 PO Box 548, Van Alstyne TX 75495 *TF:* 800-967-5235 ■ *Web:* gcec.net	903-482-7100		245
GCF (General Credit Forms Inc) 3595 Rider Trl S, Saint Louis MO 63045 *TF:* 800-325-1158 ■ *Web:* www.gcfinc.com	314-216-8600	216-8570	110

Name / Address	Phone	Fax	Class
GCFB (Granite City Food & Brewery Ltd) 1636 42nd St SW, Fargo ND 58103 *Web:* www.gcfb.com	701-293-3000		671
GCG Marketing 2421 W Seventh St Ste 400, Fort Worth TX 76107 *Web:* www.gcgmarketing.com	817-332-4600		466
GCH (Garden City Hospital) 6245 Inkster Rd, Garden City MI 48135 *Web:* www.gch.org	734-458-3300		374-3
GCH (Galesburg Cottage Hospital) 695 N Kellogg St, Galesburg IL 61401 *Web:* www.cottagehospital.com	309-343-8131		374-3
GCH (Grinders Clearing House Inc) 13301 E 8 Mile Rd, Warren MI 48089 *Web:* www.gchmachinery.com	586-771-1500	771-5958	385
GCHA (Grand County Historical Assn) PO Box 165, Hot Sulphur Springs CO 80451 *Web:* grandcountyhistory.org	970-725-3939		48-13
GCHGS (Gratiot County Historical and Genealogical Society) 129 W Center St, Ithaca MI 48847 *Web:* gchgs.org	989-875-6232		49-19
GCHS (Gloucester County Historical Society) 17 Hunter St, Woodbury NJ 08096 *Web:* www.gchsnj.org	856-845-4771		48-13
GCI Holdings Inc 2550 Denali St Ste 1000., Anchorage AK 99503 **Fax Area Code:* 907 ■ *TF:* 800-770-7886 ■ *Web:* www.gci.com	800-770-7886	265-5676*	224
GCI Outdoor Inc 66 Killingworth Rd, Higganum CT 06441 *TF:* 800-956-7328 ■ *Web:* www.gcioutdoor.com	860-345-9595		321
GCI Technologies Inc 1301 Precision Dr, Plano TX 75074 *Web:* www.gcitechnologies.com	972-423-8411		256
GCMC (Gulf Coast Medical Ctr) 10141 US 59 Rd, Wharton TX 77488 *Web:* www.gulfcoastmedical.com	979-532-2500		374-3
Gcom Software Inc 24 Madison Ave Ext, Albany NY 12203 *Web:* www.gcomsoft.com	518-869-1671		177
GCR Inc 2021 Lakeshore Dr Ste 500, New Orleans LA 70122 *Web:* gcrincorporated.com	504-304-2500		463
GCS (Georgia Cancer Specialists Pc) 1835 Savoy Dr, Atlanta GA 30341 *TF:* 800-491-5991 ■ *Web:* www.gacancer.com	770-496-9400	496-9490	374-7
GCS (Georgia Cycle Sport) 1029 Baxter St, Athens GA 30606 *Web:* www.georgiacyclesport.com	706-549-2453		711
GCS Inc 7640 Omnitech Pl, Victor NY 14564 *Web:* www.globalcoms.com	585-742-9100		647
GCSAA (Golf Course Superintendents Association of America) 1421 Research Pk Dr, Lawrence KS 66049 *TF:* 800-472-7878 ■ *Web:* www.gcsaa.org	785-841-2240		48-2
GCT (Gold Coast Transit) 1901 Auto Center Dr, Oxnard CA 93036 *Web:* www.goldcoasttransit.org	805-487-4222	487-0925	468
GCT Semiconductor Inc 2121 Ringwood Ave, San Jose CA 95131 *Web:* www.gctsemi.com	408-434-6040	434-6050	696
GCTC (Gateway Community & Technical College) 500 Technology Wy, Florence KY 41042 *TF:* 855-346-4282 ■ *Web:* gateway.kctcs.edu	859-441-4500		800
GCTC (Griswold Cooperative Telephone Co) 607 Main St, Griswold IA 51535 *Web:* www.griswoldtelco.com	712-778-2121	778-2500	224
GCU Trucking Inc 7819 Crane Rd, Oakdale CA 95361 *Web:* gcutrucking.com	209-845-2117	845-2153	311
GCube Insurance Services Inc 3101 Wcoast Hwy Ste 100, Newport Beach CA 92663 *TF:* 877-903-4777 ■ *Web:* www.gcube-insurance.com	949-515-9981		390
GDB International Inc 1 Home News Row, New Brunswick NJ 08901 *Web:* www.gdbinternational.com	732-246-3001	246-3004	313
GDC (Ginsburg Development Companies LLC) 100 Summit Lake Dr, Valhalla NY 10595 *Web:* gdchomes.com	914-747-3600		653
GDEB (General Dynamics Electric Boat Corp) 75 E Pt Rd., Groton CT 06340 *TF:* 800-742-9692 ■ *Web:* gdeb.com	860-433-3000	433-1400	698
GDH Consulting 4200 E Skelly Dr Ste 650., Tulsa OK 74135 *TF:* 888-392-1434 ■ *Web:* www.gdhconsulting.com	918-392-1600	491-0800	180
GDI Infotech Inc 3775 Varsity Dr, Ann Arbor MI 48108 *Web:* www.gdii.com	734-477-6900		177
GDI Integrated Facility Services 4952 W 128th Pl., Alsip IL 60803 *Web:* gdi.com	708-385-3575		256
GDKN Corp 9700 Stirling Rd Ste 110-B., Cooper City FL 33024 *Web:* www.gdkn.com	954-985-6650		387
GDP Technologies 1180 Eisenhower Pkwy, Macon GA 31206 *TF:* 800-239-3025 ■ *Web:* southeast.xeroxbusinesssolutions.com	478-781-8991	788-5459	317
GDS Associates Inc 1850 Pkwy Pl Ste 800., Marietta GA 30067 *Web:* www.gdsassociates.com	770-425-8100		261
GDS Publishing Ltd 55 Water St Ste 32001 32nd Fl., New York NY 10005 *Web:* gdsgroup.com	212-796-2000	796-7010	387
GE (Gas & Electrical Equipment Co) 300 NE 34th St, Oklahoma City OK 73105 *Web:* www.geeco-inc.com	405-528-3551	557-1172	38
GE Aircraft Engines 1 Neumann Way, Cincinnati OH 45215 *Web:* www.geaviation.com	513-243-2000		21
GE Analytical Instruments Inc 6060 Spine Rd, Boulder CO 80301 *TF:* 800-255-6964 ■ *Web:* www.geinstruments.com	303-444-2009		692
GE Capital Aviation Services 901 Main Ave, Norwalk CT 06851 *Web:* www.gecapital.com	203-842-5200		23
GE Foodland Inc 1105 E Beltline Rd, Carrollton TX 75006 *Web:* elrodscostplus.com	972-245-0470		345
GE Healthcare 8200 W Tower Ave, Milwaukee WI 53223 *TF:* 800-558-5102 ■ *Web:* www.gehealthcare.com	414-355-5000		250

Name / Address	City	State	ZIP	Phone	Fax	Class
GE Healthcare Financail Services						
500 W Monroe	Chicago	IL	60661	312-697-3999		216
Web: www.gehcfinance.com						
GE Johnson Construction Co						
25 N Cascade Ave Ste 400	Colorado Springs	CO	80903	719-473-5321		186
Web: gejohnson.com						
GE Mathis Co 6100 S Oak Park Ave	Chicago	IL	60638	773-586-3800	586-0070	697
Web: www.gemathis.com						
GE Richards Graphic Supplies Company Inc						
928 Links Ave	Landisville	PA	17538	717-898-3151		627
TF: 800-233-0410 ■ *Web:* www.gerichards.com						
GE Walker Inc 4420 E Adamo Dr Ste 206	Tampa	FL	33605	800-749-2483	621-4291*	475
**Fax Area Code:* 813 ■ *TF:* 800-749-2483 ■ *Web:* www.gewalker.com						
Geaghan's Restaurant & Pub 570 Main St	Bangor	ME	04401	207-945-3730	941-6758	671
Web: www.geaghans.com						
Gear Energy Ltd						
240 - Fourth Ave SW Ste 2600	Calgary	AB	T2P2V6	403-538-8435	705-2660	536
TF: 877-494-3430 ■ *Web:* www.gearenergy.com						
Gear for Sports Inc 9700 Commerce Pkwy	Lenexa	KS	66219	913-693-3200		155-1
TF: 800-255-1065 ■ *Web:* www.gearforsports.com						
Gear Source Inc						
3101 Fairlane Farms Rd Ste 4	Wellington	FL	33414	561-296-9555	792-0602	246
TF: 866-669-4327 ■ *Web:* www.gearsource.com						
Gearbox Software LLC						
101 E Park Blvd Ste 1200	Plano	TX	75074	972-312-8202		174
Web: www.gearboxsoftware.com						
Gearhart By the Sea						
1157 N Marion Ave	Gearhart	OR	97138	503-738-8331	738-0881	669
TF: 800-547-0115 ■ *Web:* www.gearhartresort.com						
Gearn Inc 3375 Us Hwy 60	Hereford	TX	79045	806-357-2222		273
Web: www.gearn.com						
Geartronics Inc						
100 Chelmsford Rd	North Billerica	MA	01862	978-663-6566	667-3130	709
Web: www.geartronics.com						
Geary County 200 E 8th	Junction City	KS	66441	785-238-3912	238-5419	338
Web: www.gearycounty.org						
Geary Pacific Corp						
1908 N Enterprise St	Orange	CA	92865	714-279-2950		690
TF: 800-444-3279 ■ *Web:* www.gearypacific.com						
Geary Whiting's Equine Massage School						
PO Box 1836	Big Sur	CA	93920	530-410-5270		685
Web: www.howtomassageahorse.com						
GEARYS Beverly Hills						
351 N Beverly Dr	Beverly Hills	CA	90210	800-793-6670		362
TF: 800-793-6670 ■ *Web:* www.gearys.com						
Geater Machining and Manufacturing Co						
901 12th St Ne	Independence	IA	50644	319-334-6026	334-6450	697
Web: www.geater.com						
Geauga County 470 Center St Bldg 8	Chardon	OH	44024	440-285-2222	285-7761	338
Web: www.co.geauga.oh.us						
Geauga County Public Library						
110 East Park St	Chardon	OH	44024	440-285-7601		434-3
Web: www.divi.geaugalibrary.net						
Geauga County Transit						
12555 Merritt Rd	Chardon	OH	44024	440-279-2150	285-9476	108
TF: 888-287-7190 ■ *Web:* www.geaugatransit.org						
GeBBS Healthcare Solutions Inc						
600 Corporate Pointe Ste 1250	Culver City	CA	90230	888-539-4282	604-8717*	177
**Fax Area Code:* 866 ■ *TF:* 888-539-4282 ■ *Web:* gebbs.com						
Gebco Insurance						
5430 Campbell Blvd Ste 215	White Marsh	MD	21162	410-668-3100	882-2872	390
TF: 800-464-3226 ■ *Web:* www.gogebco.com						
Gebhard Woods State Park						
401 Ottawa St PO Box 272	Morris	IL	60450	815-942-0796		565
Web: www2.illinois.gov						
GEC (Golden Educational Ctr)						
857 Lake Blvd	Redding	CA	96003	530-244-0101		637-10
TF: 800-800-1791 ■ *Web:* www.goldened.com						
GEC Inc 8282 Goodwood Blvd	Baton Rouge	LA	70806	225-612-3000		256
TF: 800-883-5588 ■ *Web:* www.gecinc.com						
Gecko Grill 855 N 13th St	San Jose	CA	95112	408-971-1826		671
Ged Lawyers LLP 7171 N Federal Hwy	Boca Raton	FL	33487	561-995-1966		428
TF: 844-443-3529 ■ *Web:* www.gedlawyers.com						
Geddy's Pub 19 Main St PO Box 955	Bar Harbor	ME	04609	207-288-5077	288-9927	671
Web: geddys.com						
Gedeon Grc Consulting						
6901 Jericho Tpke Ste 216	Syosset	NY	11791	516-873-7010	687-1489*	256
**Fax Area Code:* 518 ■ *Web:* gedeongrc.com						
Gedney M. Howe, III PA						
8 Chalmers St	Charleston	SC	29401	843-722-8048	722-2140	41
Web: gedneyhowe.com						
Gee Group 184 Shuman Blvd Ste 420	Naperville	IL	60563	630-954-0400	954-0447	721
NYSE: JOB ■ *Web:* www.geegroup.com						
Geehan Group 40 N Main St Ste 1570	Dayton	OH	45423	937-226-1622		463
Web: www.geehangroup.com						
Geeks On Call						
7100 E Pleasant Valley Rd Ste 300	Independence	OH	44131	800-905-4335		264-1
TF: 800-905-4335 ■ *Web:* www.geeksoncall.com						
Geekscom 43195 Business Park Dr	Temecula	CA	92590	951-694-4335		179
Web: geeks.com						
Geerpres Inc 1780 Harvey St	Muskegon	MI	49442	231-773-3211	773-8263	806
TF: 800-253-0373 ■ *Web:* www.geerpres.com						
Geetingsville Telephone Company Inc						
9155 N County Rd 200 E	Frankfort	IN	46041	765-258-3111	258-3365	224
Web: www.geetel.net						
Geezeo 35 Braintree Hill Office Pk	Braintree	MA	02186	866-876-3654		387
Web: www.geezeo.com						
GEFCO (GEFCO Inc) 2215 S Van Buren	Enid	OK	73703	580-234-4141		537
TF: 800-759-7441 ■ *Web:* www.gefco.com						
GEFCO Inc (GEFCO) 2215 S Van Buren	Enid	OK	73703	580-234-4141		537
TF: 800-759-7441 ■ *Web:* www.gefco.com						
Geffen Mesher & Co						
888 SW Fifth Ave Ste 800	Portland	OR	97204	503-221-0141		466
Web: gmco.com						
Geffen Playhouse						
10886 Le Conte Ave	Los Angeles	CA	90024	310-208-5454	208-8383	749
Web: www.geffenplayhouse.org						
Gefinor Capital						
2700 Westchester Ave Ste 303	Purchase	NY	10577	212-308-1111	308-1182	401
Web: www.gefinorcapital.com						
Gefran ISI Inc 8 Lowell Ave	Winchester	MA	01890	781-729-5249		201
TF: 888-888-4474 ■ *Web:* www.gefran.com						
Gehan Homes						
15725 N Dallas Pkwy Ste 300	Addison	TX	75001	972-383-4300	383-4399	653
Web: www.gehanhomes.com						
Gehi & Assoc						
118-21 Queens Blvd Ste 409	Forest Hills	NY	11375	718-263-5999		41
Web: immigrationquestion.com						
Gehl Foods						
N116 W15970 Main St PO Box 1004	Germantown	WI	53022	262-251-8572	250-6847	296-10
TF: 800-521-2873 ■ *Web:* www.gehls.com						
Gehr Industries						
7400 E Slauson Ave	Los Angeles	CA	90040	323-728-5558	728-1983	813
TF: 800-688-6606 ■ *Web:* www.gehrindustries.com						
Gehring LP & Gehring Diato LP						
24800 Drake Rd	Farmington Hills	MI	48335	248-427-3901		393
TF: 888-923-9760 ■ *Web:* www.gehring-group.com						
Gehring Tricot Corp						
1225 Franklin Ave Ste 300	Garden City	NY	11530	516-747-4555	747-8885	745-4
Web: www.gehring-tricot.com						
GEI (Gilmore Enterprises Inc)						
3514-A Drawbridge Pky	Greensboro	NC	27410	336-282-5550		393
Web: www.gilmoreshows.com						
GEI Consultants Inc 400 Unicorn Pk Dr	Woburn	MA	01801	781-721-4000		261
Web: www.geiconsultants.com						
GEICO 5260 Western Ave	Chevy Chase	MD	20076	800-841-3000		391-4
TF: 800-841-3000 ■ *Web:* www.geico.com						
Geier, Homar, & Roy LLP						
635 Water St	Sauk City	WI	53583	608-370-7175		41
Web: wislaw.net						
Geiger 70 Mt Hope Ave	Lewiston	ME	04240	888-953-9340	755-2422*	9
**Fax Area Code:* 207 ■ *TF:* 888-953-9340 ■ *Web:* www.geiger.com						
Geiger & Peters Inc						
761 S Sherman Dr PO Box 33807	Indianapolis	IN	46203	317-359-9521	359-9525	91
Web: www.gpsteel.com						
Geiger Inc 660 W Sunset Dr	Waukesha	WI	53189	262-542-4856	542-2539	222
TF: 800-306-8024 ■ *Web:* www.geigerawards.com						
Geiger International Inc						
6095 Fulton Industrial Blvd SW	Atlanta	GA	30336	404-344-1100	836-7519	319-1
TF: 800-456-6452 ■ *Web:* www.geigerfurniture.com						
Geiger Manufacturing Inc						
1110 E Scotts Ave	Stockton	CA	95205	209-464-7746	464-0536	454
Web: www.geigermfg.com						
Geiger Ready Mix Company Inc						
PO Box 50	Leavenworth	KS	66048	913-281-0111	772-8661	182
Web: geigerreadymix.com						
Geile/Leon Marketing Communications						
130S Bemiston Ste 800	Saint Louis	MO	63105	314-727-5850		4
Web: www.geileon.com						
Geis Co 10020 Aurora Hudson Rd	Streetsboro	OH	44241	330-528-3500		186
Web: www.geiscompanies.com						
Geisinger Health System						
100 N Academy Ave	Scranton	PA	18510	570-703-8000		374-3
TF: 800-230-4565 ■ *Web:* www.geisinger.org						
Geisz Agency						
2812 S Brentwood Blvd	Saint Louis	MO	63144	314-968-0575		4
Web: www.geiszagency.com						
Geja's Cafe 340 W Armitage Ave	Chicago	IL	60614	773-281-9101		671
Web: gejascafe.com						
Gekkeikan Sake USA Inc 1136 Sibley St	Folsom	CA	95630	916-985-3111	985-2221	80-1
Web: www.gekkeikan-sake.com						
Gekko Engineering Inc 1210 E 223rd St	Carson	CA	90745	310-513-0000		261
Web: gekkoeng.com						
GEL Group Inc, The 2040 Savage Rd	Charleston	SC	29407	843-556-8171		256
Web: www.gel.com						
Gelb & Gelb LLP						
900 Cummings Ctr Ste 207-V	Beverly	MA	01915	617-345-0010		41
Web: gelbgelb.com						
Gelb & Gelb PC 1634 Eye St Ste 350	Washington	DC	20006	202-331-7227		41
Web: gelbandgelb.com						
Gelber Schachter & Greenberg PA						
1221 Brickell Ave Ste 2010	Miami	FL	33131	305-728-0950	728-0951	41
Web: gsgpa.com						
Gelch & Associates Pa						
8751 W Broward Blvd Ste 305	Plantation	FL	33324	954-424-6100		41
Web: gelchlaw.com						
Gelfand Rennert & Feldman LLP						
1880 Century Pk E Ste 1600	Los Angeles	CA	90067	310-553-1707		2
Web: www.grfllp.com						
Gelia, Wells & Mohr Inc						
390 S Youngs Rd	Williamsville	NY	14221	716-629-3146	629-3299	636
TF: 888-711-4884 ■ *Web:* www.gelia.com						
Gelita USA Inc						
2445 Port Neal Industrial Rd	Sergeant Bluff	IA	51054	712-943-5516	943-3372	296-22
TF: 800-223-9244 ■ *Web:* www.gelita.com						
Gellert, Klein & Macleod LLP						
80 Washington St Ste 301	Poughkeepsie	NY	12601	845-454-3250	359-0237	41
Web: gkmlaw.us						
Gelmart International Industries						
48 W 38th St 10th Fl	New York	NY	10010	212 743 6900		155-18
Web: www.gelmart.com						
GELPAK 31398 Huntwood Ave	Hayward	CA	94544	510-576-2220	576-2282	696
TF: 888-621-4147 ■ *Web:* www.gelpak.com						
Gelson's Markets						
16400 Ventura Blvd Ste 240	Encino	CA	91436	310-638-2842	788-4018*	345
**Fax Area Code:* 818 ■ *Web:* gelsons.com						
GEM (Grand Encampment Museum)						
807 Barnett	Encampment	WY	82325	307-327-5308		520
Web: www.gemuseum.com						
Gem City College 700 State St	Quincy	IL	62301	217-222-0391	222-1557	800
Web: www.gemcitycollege.com						
Gem City Engineering & Manufacturing Co, The						
401 Leo St	Dayton	OH	45404	937-223-5544		695
Web: gemcity.com						
Gem County 415 E Main St	Emmett	ID	83617	208-365-4561	365-7795	338
Web: www.gemcounty.org						

Name / Address	City	State	ZIP	Phone	Fax	Class
Gem Dandy Inc 200 W Academy St *TF:* 800-334-5101 ■ *Web:* www.gem-dandy.com	Madison	NC	27025	336-548-9624		155-2
Gem East Corp 8639 Pacific Ave **Fax Area Code: 253* ■ *Web:* www.gemeast.com	Tacoma	WA	98444	206-441-1700	531-8237*	409
Gem Edwards Inc 5640 Hudson Industrial Pkwy PO Box 429 *TF:* 800-733-7976 ■ *Web:* www.gemcomedical.com	Hudson	OH	44236	800-733-7976		476
Gem Engineering Inc 485 N Aviation Way *Web:* gemeng.com	Cedar City	UT	84721	502-493-7100		261
Gem Equipment of Oregon Inc 2150 Progress Wy PO Box 359 *Web:* www.gemequipment.com	Woodburn	OR	97071	503-982-9902	981-6316	298
Gem Group 9 International Way *TF:* 800-800-3200 ■ *Web:* www.gemline.com	Lawrence	MA	01843	978-691-2000	691-2085	67
Gem Health Care Services Inc-services De Sant Gem Inc 304-383 Parkdale Ave *Web:* gemhealthcare.com	Ottawa	ON	K1Y4R4	613-761-7474		363
Gem Instrument Co 2832 Nationwide Pky *Web:* www.gem-instrument.com	Brunswick	OH	44212	330-273-6117	273-4949	350
Gem Jewelers 12 E Broadway Rte 102 *Web:* www.gem-jewelers.com	Derry	NH	03038	603-432-1920		411
Gem Manufacturing Company Inc 78 Brookside Rd *Web:* www.gemmfg.com	Waterbury	CT	06708	203-574-1466		488
Gem State Distributors Inc (GSD) 350 Industrial Ln *TF:* 800-234-1525 ■ *Web:* www.gemstatedist.com	Pocatello	ID	83201	208-237-5151	237-0802	393
Gem State Paper & Supply Co 1801 Highland Ave E *TF:* 800-727-2737 ■ *Web:* www.gemstatepaper.com	Twin Falls	ID	83303	208-733-6081		559
Gem Systems Inc 135 Spy Ct *Web:* www.gemsys.ca	Markham	ON	L3R5H6	905-752-2202		639
Gem Technologies Inc 2033 Castaic Ln *Web:* www.gemtechnologiesinc.com	Knoxville	TN	37932	865-560-9434		610
Gem Technology International Corp 2665 S Bayshore Dr Ste M103-5 *Web:* gemtechnology.com	Miami	FL	33133	305-447-1344	447-3830	652
Gem Theatre & Century Grille 333 Madison Ave *Web:* gemcolonyevents.com	Detroit	MI	48226	313-963-9800	963-0873	572
Gem Transportation LLC 11774 Missouri Bottom Rd *Web:* gemtransportation.com	Hazelwood	MO	63042	314-731-1707		107
GEMCH (Greater El Monte Community Hospital) 1701 Santa Anita Ave *Web:* www.greaterelmonte.com	South El Monte	CA	91733	626-579-7777	350-0368	374-3
GemChem Inc 53 N Cedar St *TF:* 800-976-8111 ■ *Web:* www.gemchemsolutions.com	Lititz	PA	17543	717-626-3900	626-3909	660
Gemco Manufacturing Company Inc 555 W Queen St *Web:* www.gemcomfg.com	Southington	CT	06489	860-378-8926	628-9120	488
Gemco of Port Lavaca Inc 6611 Lone Tree Rd *Web:* www.gemcodies.com	Victoria	TX	77905	361-570-6611	570-6612	757
Gemco Valve Co 301 Smalley Ave *TF:* 800-654-3626 ■ *Web:* www.gemcovalve.com	Middlesex	NJ	08846	732-733-1143	733-1168	695
Gem-Craft Inc 1420 Elmwood Ave	Cranston	RI	02910	401-854-1200		408
Gemeinhardt Company LLC 3302 Nappanee St *TF:* 800-348-7461 ■ *Web:* www.gemeinhardt.com	Elkhart	IN	46517	574-295-5280		527
Gemel Precision Tool Inc 31 Industrial Dr *Web:* www.gemel.com	Ivyland	PA	18974	215-355-9396	355-9274	488
Gemex Systems Inc 6040 W Executive Dr Ste A *TF:* 866-694-3639 ■ *Web:* gemex.com	Mequon	WI	53092	262-242-1111		411
Gemi Trucking Inc 42 Artley Rd *Web:* www.gemitrucking.com	Savannah	GA	31408	912-963-0023		780
Gemini 2000 Penncraft Ct *TF:* 800-317-9929 ■ *Web:* www.geminichildrensmusic.com	Ann Arbor	MI	48103	734-665-0165	786-4007	572
Gemini Coatings Inc 421 SE 27th St *TF:* 800-262-5710 ■ *Web:* www.gemini-coatings.com	El Reno	OK	73036	800-262-5710		550
Gemini Computer Systems 1645 Temple Ln *Web:* www.geminicomputersystems.com	Rockford	IL	61112	815-227-5800	227-5606	180
Gemini Inc 103 Mensing Way *TF:* 800-538-8377 ■ *Web:* www.geminisignproducts.com	Cannon Falls	MN	55009	507-263-3957	263-4887	701
Gemini Industries Inc 200 Wheeler Rd N Tower *Web:* www.gemini-ind.com	Burlington	MA	01803	781-203-0100		610
Gemini Investors LLC 20 William St Ste 250 *Web:* www.gemini-investors.com	Wellesley	MA	02481	781-237-7001	237-7233	402
Gemini Pharmaceuticals Inc 87 Modular Ave *Web:* geminipharm.com	Commack	NY	11725	631-543-3334		479
Gemini Publishing Co 3102 W Bay Area Blvd Ste 707 *Web:* www.getgirls.com	Friendswood	TX	77546	281-316-1024		637-2
Gemini Valve 2 Otter Ct *TF:* 800-370-0936 ■ *Web:* geminivalve.com	Raymond	NH	03077	603-895-4761	895-6785	789
Gemma Power Systems LLC 769 Hebron Ave *Web:* www.gemmapower.com	Glastonbury	CT	06033	860-659-0509		256
Gemmy Industries Corp 117 Wrangler Dr *TF:* 800-231-6789 ■ *Web:* www.gemmy.com	Coppell	TX	75019	800-231-6789		364
Gemological Institute of America (GIA) 5345 Armada Dr *TF:* 800-421-7250 ■ *Web:* www.gia.edu	Carlsbad	CA	92008	760-603-4000	603-4003	49-4
Gems Sensors Inc 1 Cowles Rd **Fax Area Code: 860* ■ *TF:* 800-378-1600 ■ *Web:* www.gemssensors.com	Plainville	CT	06062	855-877-9666	747-4244*	201
Gemstone Systems Inc 1260 NW Waterhouse Ave Ste 200 *Web:* www.gemstonesystems.net	Beaverton	OR	97006	503-533-3000	533-3198	178-1
Gemtex Abrasives 234 Belfield Rd *TF:* 800 387 5100 ■ *Web:* gemtexabrasives.com	Toronto	ON	M9W1H3	416-245-5605	245-3723	1
Gemtor Inc 1 Johnson Ave *TF:* 800-405-9048 ■ *Web:* www.gemtor.com	Matawan	NJ	07747	732-583-6200	290-9391	678
Gemu Valves Inc 3800 Camp Creek Pkwy SW **Fax Area Code: 404* ■ *Web:* www.gemu-group.com	Atlanta	GA	30331	678-553-3400	344-9350*	789
Gemveto Company Inc 18 E 48th St Ste 502 *Web:* www.gemlok.com	New York	NY	10017	212-755-2522	755-2027	409
Genability 221 Main St Ste 400 *Web:* www.genability.com	San Francisco	CA	94105	415-371-0136		387
Genalco Inc 333 Reservoir St **Fax Area Code: 800* ■ *TF:* 877-436-2526 ■ *Web:* www.genalco.com	Needham	MA	02494	781-444-9500	653-6068*	385
Genatt Associates Inc 3333 New Hyde Park Rd Ste 400 *Web:* www.genatt.com	New Hyde Park	NY	11042	516-869-8666		390
GenBio 15222 Avenue of Science Ste A *TF:* 800-288-4368 ■ *Web:* www.genbio.com	San Diego	CA	92128	858-592-9300		231
Genco Energy Services Inc 1701 W Hwy 107 *TF:* 877-922-3710 ■ *Web:* www.genco.us	Mcallen	TX	78504	956-380-3710		539
Genco Shipping & Trading Ltd 299 Park Ave 12th Fl *NYSE: GNK* ■ *Web:* www.gencoshipping.com	New York	NY	10171	646-443-8550		313
Genco Stamping & Manufacturing Co 2001 Genco Dr *Web:* www.gencostamping.com	Cookeville	TN	38506	931-528-5574	528-8379	489
Genco Systems Inc 13800 Coppermine Rd Ste 300 *Web:* gencosystems.com	Herndon	VA	20171	703-234-2200	234-1211	261
Gencor Industries Inc 5201 N Orange Blossom Trl *NASDAQ: GENC* ■ *TF:* 888-887-1266 ■ *Web:* www.gencor.com	Orlando	FL	32810	407-290-6000	578-0577	190
Gene & Georgetti 500 N Franklin St *Web:* geneandgeorgetti.com	Chicago	IL	60654	312-527-3718	527-2039	671
Gene B. Glick Company Inc 8801 River Crossing Blvd Ste 200 *Web:* www.genebglick.com	Indianapolis	IN	46240	317-469-0400		655
Gene By Gene LTD 1445 N Loop W 820 *Web:* www.genebygene.com	Houston	TX	77008	713-474-2401		415
Gene Codes Corp 775 Technology Dr *TF:* 800-497-4939 ■ *Web:* www.genecodes.com	Ann Arbor	MI	48108	734-769-7249		177
Gene Gaffney Insurance Services Inc 75 Main St *Web:* gaffneyins.com	Occidental	CA	95465	707-874-2666	874-1233	390
Gene Haynes 8316 Medical Plaza Dr Ste A *Web:* genehaynes.com	Charlotte	NC	28262	704-549-1515		390
Gene Langley Ford Inc 3500 E End Dr *Web:* www.genelangleyford.com	Humboldt	TN	38343	731-784-9311		57
Gene Lilly Surety Bonds Inc 735 S 56th St *TF:* 800-659-4445 ■ *Web:* glsbinc.com	Lincoln	NE	68510	402-475-7700		390
Genealogy.com 360 W 4800 N *TF:* 800-262-3787 ■ *Web:* www.genealogy.com	Provo	UT	84604	800-262-3787		397
GeneChem 1 Westmount Sq Ste 800 *Web:* www.genechem.com	Montreal	QC	H3Z2P9	514-849-7696	849-5191	792
Gen-El-Mec Associates Inc 2 Fox Hollow Rd *Web:* www.gen-el-mec.com	Oxford	CT	06478	203-828-6566	881-9367	454
Genemed Biotechnologies Inc 458 Carlton Ct *TF:* 877-436-3633 ■ *Web:* www.genemed.com	South San Francisco	CA	94080	650-952-0110		668
Geneos Wealth Management Inc 9055 E Mineral Cir Ste 200 *TF:* 888-812-5043 ■ *Web:* www.geneoswealth.com	Centennial	CO	80112	303-785-8470		690
GenePharm Inc 1237 Midas Way *Web:* www.genepharminc.com	Sunnyvale	CA	94085	408-773-0106	773-1018	668
Gener8 Inc 500 Mercury Dr *Web:* www.gener8.net	Sunnyvale	CA	94085	650-940-9898		506
Generac Power Systems Inc PO Box 8 *TF:* 888-436-3722 ■ *Web:* www.generac.com	Waukesha	WI	53187	262-544-4811	544-4851	518
General Air Products Inc 118 Summit Dr *TF:* 888-863-7389 ■ *Web:* www.generalairproducts.com	Exton	PA	19341	888-863-7389		172
General Air Service & Supply Company Inc 1105 Zuni St *TF:* 877-782-8434 ■ *Web:* www.generalair.com	Denver	CO	80204	303-892-7003		146
General Asphalt Company Inc 4850 NW 72nd Ave *Web:* generalasphalt.com	Miami	FL	33166	305-592-3480		46
General Association of Regular Baptist Churches (GARBC) 1300 N Meacham Rd *TF:* 888-588-1600 ■ *Web:* www.garbcinternational.org	Schaumburg	IL	60173	888-588-1600		48-20
General Atlantic LLC 600 Steamboat Rd Ste 105 *Web:* www.generalatlantic.com	Greenwich	CT	06830	203-629-8600	622-8818	792
General Atomics 3550 General Atomics Ct PO Box 85608 *Web:* www.ga.com	San Diego	CA	92121	858-455-3000	455-3621	668
General Atomics Aeronautical 16761 Via Del Campo Ct *Web:* www.ga-asi.com	San Diego	CA	92127	858-762-6700	762-6952	21
General Automatic Transfer Co 100 Larkin Williams Industrial Ct *Web:* www.gat-systems.com	Fenton	MO	63026	636-343-6370		207
General Aviation Industries Inc 415 Jones Rd *Web:* www.gaiinc.net	Weatherford	TX	76088	817-598-4848	598-4844	22
General Aviation Manufacturers Assn (GAMA) 1400 K St NW Ste 801 *TF:* 866-427-3287 ■ *Web:* www.gama.aero	Washington	DC	20005	202-393-1500	842-4063	49-21
General Aviation Services LLC 1155 E Ensell Rd *Web:* www.genav.com	Lake Zurich	IL	60047	847-726-5000	726-7668	770
General Baptist Nursing Home 17108 US Hwy 62 *Web:* www.generalbaptisthealthcare.com	Campbell	MO	63933	573-246-2155		672
General Bearing Corp 44 High St *TF:* 800-431-1766 ■ *Web:* www.generalbearing.com	West Nyack	NY	10994	845-358-6000	358-6277	75

Company	City	State	ZIP	Phone	Fax	Class
General Beer Distributors 6169 McKee Rd *Web:* www.visitmadison.com	Fitchburg	WI	53719	608-271-1234		81-3
General Biodiesel Inc 6333 First Ave S *Web:* www.gbdnw.com	Seattle	WA	98108	206-932-1600		580
General Broach Co 307 Salisbury St *TF:* 800-889-7555 ■ *Web:* www.generalbroach.com	Morenci	MI	49256	517-458-7555		493
General Burnside Island State Park 8801 S Hwy 27 *Web:* parks.ky.gov	Burnside	KY	42519	606-561-4104		565
General Butler State Resort Park 1608 US Hwy 227 *TF:* 866-462-8853 ■ *Web:* parks.ky.gov	Carrollton	KY	41008	502-732-4384		669
General Cable Corp 4 Tesseneer Dr *NYSE:* BGC ■ *TF:* 800-572-8000 ■ *Web:* generalcable.com	Highland Heights	KY	41076	859-572-8000		814
General Carbide Corp 1151 Garden St **Fax Area Code:* 724 ■ *TF:* 800-245-2465 ■ *Web:* www.generalcarbide.com	Greensburg	PA	15601	800-245-2465	836-6274*	757
General Code 781 Elmgrove Rd *TF:* 800-836-8834 ■ *Web:* www.generalcode.com	Rochester	NY	14624	585-328-1810	328-8189	428
General Coffee State Park 46 John Coffee Rd *Web:* gastateparks.org	Nicholls	GA	31554	912-384-7082		565
General Collection Company inc 402 W Third St *TF:* 888-603-1423 ■ *Web:* www.generalcollection.com	Grand Island	NE	68802	308-381-1423	381-0219	160
General Container 5450 Dodds Ave *Web:* www.gcc-pkg.com	Buena Park	CA	90621	714-562-8700		100
General Credit Forms Inc (GCF) 3595 Rider Trl S *TF:* 800-325-1158 ■ *Web:* www.gcfinc.com	Saint Louis	MO	63045	314-216-8600	216-8570	110
General Crook House Museum 5730 N 30th St Ste 11B *Web:* www.douglascohistory.org	Omaha	NE	68111	402-455-9990		50-3
General Cutting Tools 6440 Ridgeway Ave *Web:* www.generalcuttingtools.com	Lincolnwood	IL	60712	847-677-8770		493
General Daniel Bissell House 10225 Bellefontaine Rd *Web:* stlouisco.com	Saint Louis	MO	63137	314-615-8800		50-3
General Data Company Inc 4354 Ferguson Dr *TF:* 800-733-5252 ■ *Web:* www.general-data.com	Cincinnati	OH	45245	513-752-7978	752-6947	174
General DataComm Inc 6 Rubber Ave *Web:* www.gdc.com	Naugatuck	CT	06770	203-729-0271	723-2883	176
General Devices Company Inc 1410 S Post Rd *TF:* 800-821-3520 ■ *Web:* www.generaldevices.com	Indianapolis	IN	46239	317-897-7000		201
General Die Casters Inc 2150 Highland Rd *Web:* generaldie.com	Twinsburg	OH	44087	330-657-2300		308
General Digital Corp 8 Nutmeg Rd S *TF:* 800-952-2535 ■ *Web:* www.generaldigital.com	South Windsor	CT	06074	860-282-2900	282-2244	173-4
General Distributing Co 430 17th Ave NE *Web:* www.gendco.com	Great Falls	MT	59404	406-454-1351	454-0835	385
General Doors Corp 1 Monroe St PO Box 205 *Web:* www.general-doors.com	Bristol	PA	19007	215-788-9277	788-9450	236
General Dynamics Advanced Information Systems 12450 Fair Lakes Cir *TF:* 877-449-0600 ■ *Web:* gdmissionsystems.com	Fairfax	VA	22033	877-449-0600		529
General Dynamics Corp 2941 Fairview Pk Dr Ste 100 *NYSE:* GD ■ *Web:* www.gd.com	Falls Church	VA	22042	703-876-3000	876-3125	807
General Dynamics Electric Boat Corp (GDEB) 75 E Pt Rd *TF:* 800-742-9692 ■ *Web:* gdeb.com	Groton	CT	06340	860-433-3000	433-1400	698
General Dynamics Information Technology 3211 Jermantown Rd *TF:* 800-242-0230 ■ *Web:* gdit.com	Fairfax	VA	22030	703-995-8700		180
General Dynamics NASSCO 2798 E Harbor Dr *Web:* www.nassco.com	San Diego	CA	92113	619-544-3400	544-3541	698
General Dynamics Ordnance & Tactical Systems Inc 11399 16th Ct N Ste 200 *Web:* www.gd-ots.com	Saint Petersburg	FL	33716	727-578-8100		268
General Ecology Inc 151 Sheree Blvd *Web:* generalecology.com	Exton	PA	19341	610-363-7900		427
General Educational Development Testing Service *American Council on Education* 1 Dupont Cir NW *TF:* 866-205-6267 ■ *Web:* www.acenet.edu	Washington	DC	20036	202-939-9300		244
General Electrodynamics Corporation Inc 8000 Calendar Rd *TF:* 800-551-6038 ■ *Web:* www.gecscales.com	Arlington	TX	76001	817-572-0366		22
General Energy Services 29-19 39th Ave *Web:* www.genergy.com	Long Island City	NY	11101	212-664-7600		194
General Engineering Co 26485 Hillman Hwy *Web:* generalengr.com	Abingdon	VA	24212	276-628-6068	628-4311	223
General Engineering Works 1515 W Wrightwood Ct *Web:* www.gewinc.com	Addison	IL	60101	630-543-8000	543-8005	621
General Equipment & Supplies Inc 4300 Main Ave *TF:* 800-437-2924 ■ *Web:* www.genequip.com	Fargo	ND	58103	701-282-2662	364-2190	358
General Equipment Co 620 Alexander Dr SW PO Box 334 *TF:* 800-533-0524 ■ *Web:* www.generalequip.com	Owatonna	MN	55060	507-451-5510	451-5511	386
General Extrusions Inc 4040 Lake Park Rd *Web:* www.genext.com	Youngstown	OH	44512	330-783-0270	788-1250	485
General Fasteners Co 37584 Amrhein Rd **Fax Area Code:* 734 ■ *TF:* 800-945-2658 ■ *Web:* www.genfast.com	Livonia	MI	48150	800-945-2658	452-2257*	351
General Federation of Women's Clubs (GFWC) 1734 N St NW *TF:* 800-443-4392 ■ *Web:* www.gfwc.org	Washington	DC	20036	202-347-3168	835-0246	48-24
General Films Inc 645 S High St *TF:* 888-436-3456 ■ *Web:* www.generalfilms.com	Covington	OH	45318	888-436-3456		600
General Filters Inc 43800 Grand River Ave **Fax Area Code:* 248 ■ *TF:* 866-476-5101 ■ *Web:* www.generalfilters.com	Novi	MI	48375	866-476-5101	349-2366*	18
General Financial Supply Inc 1235 N Ave *TF:* 800-759-4374 ■ *Web:* www.generalfinancialsupply.com	Nevada	IA	50201	515-382-3549		627
General Floor Industries Inc 190 Benigno Blvd *Web:* www.generalfloor.com	Bellmawr	NJ	08031	856-931-0012		361
General Formulations Inc 309 S Union St *TF:* 800-253-3664 ■ *Web:* www.generalformulations.com	Sparta	MI	49345	616-887-7387	887-0537	600
General Glass Equipment Co 900 W Leeds Ave *Web:* www.generalglassequipment.com	Absecon	NJ	08201	609-345-7500	652-5700	385
General Grand Chapter Order of the Eastern Star 1618 New Hampshire Ave NW *Web:* www.easternstar.org	Washington	DC	20009	202-667-4737	462-5162	48-15
General Grant National Memorial Riverside Dr & W 122nd St *Web:* www.nps.gov	New York	NY	10027	646-670-7251		564
General Graphics 1608 Leishman Ave *TF:* 800-887-5894 ■ *Web:* ggbarcode.com	Arnold	PA	15068	724-337-1470	337-6589	344
General Grind & Machine 2103 Se 5th St *Web:* www.generalgrind.com	Aledo	IL	61231	309-582-5959		454
General Healthcare Resources Inc 2250 Hickory Rd Ste 240 *TF:* 800-879-4471 ■ *Web:* www.ghresources.com	Plymouth Meeting	PA	19462	610-834-1122	834-7525	363
General Hearing Corp 175 Brookhollow Esplanade *TF:* 800-824-3021 ■ *Web:* generalhearing.com	Harahan	LA	70123	504-733-3767		237
General Hotels Corp 2501 S High School Rd *Web:* www.genhotels.com	Indianapolis	IN	46241	317-556-1500	243-1077	707
General Hydronics Inc 1001 Zuni Dr *Web:* www.generalhydronicsplumbing.com	Alamogordo	NM	88310	575-437-6512		189-10
General Industries Inc 3048 Thoroughfare Rd *Web:* www.gitank.com	Goldsboro	NC	27534	919-751-1791	751-8186	91
General Inspection LLC 10585 Enterprise Dr *Web:* www.generalinspection.com	Davisburg	MI	48350	248-625-0529	625-0789	425
General Insulation Company Inc 278 Mystic Ave Ste 209 *TF:* 800-229-9148 ■ *Web:* www.generalinsulation.com	Medford	MA	02155	781-391-2070	391-3094	191-4
General John J Pershing Boyhood Home State Historic Site 1100 Pershing Dr *Web:* mostateparks.com	Laclede	MO	64651	660-963-2525		565
General Kinematics Corp 5050 Rickert Rd *Web:* generalkinematics.com	Crystal Lake	IL	60014	815-455-3222	455-2285	207
General Kinetics Engineering Corp 110 E Dr *Web:* www.generalkinetics.com	Brampton	ON	L6T1C1	905-458-0888		21
General Loose Leaf Bindery Co 3811 Hawthorn Ct *TF:* 800-621-0493 ■ *Web:* www.looseleaf.com	Waukegan	IL	60087	847-244-9700	244-9741	86
General Machine Products Company Inc 3111 Old Lincoln Hwy *TF:* 800-345-6009 ■ *Web:* www.gmptools.com	Trevose	PA	19053	215-357-5500	357-6216	758
General Machine Service Inc 494 E Morley Dr *Web:* www.genmachine.com	Saginaw	MI	48601	989-752-5161	752-5168	454
General Machine Shop Inc 6000 Columbia Park Rd *Web:* generalmachine.com	Landover	MD	20785	301-773-5050	341-9761	454
General Machine-Diecron Inc 3131 Hwy 41 **Fax Area Code:* 770 ■ *Web:* gmdiecron.com	Griffin	GA	30224	478-474-1645	228-6299*	454
General Machinery Company Inc (GM) 921 1st Ave N *TF:* 800-821-5937 ■ *Web:* www.generalmachinery.com	Birmingham	AL	35203	205-251-9243	252-9723	385
General Magnaplate Corp 1331 Us Rt 1 *TF:* 800-441-6173 ■ *Web:* www.magnaplate.com	Linden	NJ	07036	908-862-6200		487
General Materials Inc 2995 Brooklyn Rd *TF:* 800-968-3191 ■ *Web:* www.generalmaterials.com	Jackson	MI	49203	800-968-3191		191-3
General Metal Finishing Company Inc (GMF) 42 Frank Mossberg Dr *Web:* www.pepgenmetal.com	Attleboro	MA	02703	508-226-5606		481
General Microcircuits Inc 1133 N Main St PO Box 748 *Web:* www.gmimfg.com	Mooresville	NC	28115	704-663-5975	663-6569	253
General Microsystems Inc (GMI) 3220 118th Ave SE *Web:* www.gmi.com	Bellevue	WA	98005	425-644-2233		174
General Mills Inc 1 General Mills Blvd *NYSE:* GIS ■ **Fax Area Code:* 763 ■ *TF:* 800-248-7310 ■ *Web:* www.generalmills.com	Minneapolis	MN	55426	800-248-7310	764-8330*	299
General Mitchell International Airport 5300 S Howell Ave *Web:* www.mitchellairport.com	Milwaukee	WI	53207	414-747-5300		27
General Moly Inc 1726 Cole Blvd Ste 115 *Web:* www.generalmoly.com	Lakewood	CO	80401	303-928-8599		502
General Monitors Inc 26806 Vista Ter *Web:* us.msasafety.com	Lake Forest	CA	92630	949-581-4464	581-1151	392
General Morgan Inn 111 N Main St *Web:* www.generalmorganinn.com	Greeneville	TN	37743	423-787-1000		379
General Motors 300 Renaissance Ctr *Web:* www.gm.com	Detroit	MI	48243	313-665-4699		518

Name / Address	Phone	Fax	Class
General Motors Acceptance Corp (GMAC) 8375 Dix Ellis Tr Ste 200 ...... Detroit MI 48265 *Fax Area Code: 800 ■ TF: 877-320-2559 ■ Web: www.ally.com	877-320-2559	428-4622*	217
General Music Corp 605 Country Club Dr ...... Bensenville IL 60106	630-766-8230		527
General Networks Corp 3524 Ocean View Blvd ...... Glendale CA 91208 TF: 833-436-6381 ■ Web: gennet.com	818-249-1962		174
General Nuclear Corp 3519 Wheeler St ...... New Stanton PA 15672 Web: www.generalnuclearcorp.com	724-925-3565		454
General Office Interiors (GOI) 50 Cardinal Dr ...... Westfield NJ 07090 Web: www.generalofficeinteriors.com	908-688-9400	688-6894	320
General Office Products Co 4521 Hwy 7 ...... Minneapolis MN 55416 Web: www.gopco.com	952-925-7500		320
General Oil Equipment Company Inc 60 John Glenn Dr ...... Amherst NY 14228 Web: www.goe-amhfab.com	716-691-7012	691-7990	358
General Partitions Manufacturing Corp 1702 Peninsula Dr PO Box 8370 ...... Erie PA 16505 Web: www.generalpartitions.com	814-833-1154	838-3473	286
General Parts LLC 11311 Hampshire Ave S ...... Bloomington MN 55438 TF: 888-498-1238 ■ Web: generalparts.com	952-944-5800		300
General Pattern Co 3075 84th Ln NE ...... Blaine MN 55449 Web: www.generalpattern.com	763-780-3518		567
General Pencil Company Inc 3160 Bay Rd PO Box 5311 ...... Redwood City CA 94063 Web: www.generalpencil.com	650-369-4889	369-7169	571
General Pet Supply Inc 7711 N 81st St ...... Milwaukee WI 53223 TF: 800-433-9786 ■ Web: www.generalpet.com	414-365-3400		96
General Petroleum Inc 7404 Disalle Blvd ...... Fort Wayne IN 46825 Web: www.genpet.com	260-489-8504		579
General Pickett's Buffet 571 Steinwehr Ave ...... Gettysburg PA 17325 Web: www.generalpickettsbuffets.com	717-334-7580		671
General Plastex Inc 35 Stuver Pl ...... Barberton OH 44203 TF: 800-777-4719 ■ Web: generalplastex.com	330-745-7775	745-6939	278
General Plastic Extrusions Inc 1238 Kasson Dr ...... Prescott WI 54021 TF: 800-532-3888 ■ Web: www.generalplastic.com	715-262-3806	262-3836	548
General Plastics & Composites Lp 5727 Ledbetter ...... Houston TX 77087 Web: www.genplastics.com	713-644-1449	644-6530	599
General Plastics Manufacturing Co 4910 Burlington Way ...... Tacoma WA 98409 TF: 800-806-6051 ■ Web: www.generalplastics.com	253-473-5000	473-5104	601
General Plumbing Supply Company Inc 1530 San Luis Rd PO Box 4666 ...... Walnut Creek CA 94597 Web: www.generalplumbingsupply.com	925-939-4622	939-1548	612
General Press Corp 110 Allegheny Dr ...... Natrona Heights PA 15065 Web: www.generalpress.com	724-224-3500		627
General Produce Co 1330 N 'B' St ...... Sacramento CA 95811 TF: 800-366-4991 ■ Web: www.generalproduce.com	916-441-6431	441-2483	297-7
General Produce Inc 16 Forest Pky Bldg M State Farmers Market ...... Forest Park GA 30297 TF: 800-391-8222 ■ Web: www.generalproducellc.com	404-366-8367	366-1967	297-7
General Revenue Corp 4660 Duke Dr Ste 300 ...... Mason OH 45040 TF: 800-234-6258 ■ Web: www.generalrevenue.com	800-234-6258		160
General Sealants Inc 300 Turnbull Canyon Rd ...... City of Industry CA 91745 TF: 800-762-1144 ■ Web: generalsealants.com	626-961-0211	968-5140	3
General Security Services Corp 9110 Meadowview Rd ...... Minneapolis MN 55425 Web: gssc.net	952-858-5000		693
General Service Bureau 5807 N 102nd St ...... Omaha NE 68134 Web: eosgsb.com	402-255-5025		160
General Services Administration (GSA) 1275 F St NE ...... Washington DC 20417 Web: www.gsa.gov	202-501-0800		340-20
Regulatory Information Service Ctr 1800 F St NW ...... Washington DC 20405 Web: www.gsa.gov	202-482-7340		340-20
Region 1 - New England 10 Cswy St Thomas P O'Neill Federal Bldg Rm 900 ...... Boston MA 02222 TF: 866-734-1727 ■ Web: www.gsa.gov	866-734-1727		340-20
Region 2 - Northeast & Caribbean 26 Federal Plz ...... New York NY 10278 Web: www.gsa.gov	212-264-2600		340-20
Region 3 - Mid-Atlantic 20 N Eighth St Strawbridge Bldg ...... Philadelphia PA 19107 Web: www.gsa.gov	215-446-5100		340-20
Region 7 - Greater Southwest 819 Taylor St ...... Fort Worth TX 76102 Web: www.gsa.gov	817-978-2321		340-20
Region 8 - Rocky Mountain Denver Federal Ctr Bldg 41 ...... Denver CO 80225 TF: 888-999-4777 ■ Web: www.gsa.gov	303-236-7329		340-20
General Services Administration Regional Offices			
Pacific Rim Region 9 450 Golden Gate Ave PO Box 36038 ...... San Francisco CA 94102 Web: www.gsa.gov	415-436-7940		340-20
Region 10 - Northwest/Arctic 400 15th St SW ...... Auburn WA 98001 Web: www.gsa.gov	253-931-7000		340-20
Region 11 - National Capital Region 301 Seventh St SW ...... Washington DC 20407 Web: www.gsa.gov	202-708-9100		340-20
General Shale Products LLC 3015 Bristol Hwy ...... Johnson City TN 37601 TF: 800-414-4661 ■ Web: generalshale.com	423-282-4661	952-4104	150
General Sheet Metal Company LLC 2330 Louisiana Ave N ...... Minneapolis MN 55427 Web: www.gsm-hvac.com	763-544-8747	544-6580	189-10
General Shelters of Texas Ltd 1639 State Hwy 87 N ...... Center TX 75935 Web: www.generalshelters.com	936-598-3389	598-1432	106
General Ship Repair Corp, The 1449 Key Hwy ...... Baltimore MD 21230 Web: generalshiprepair.com	410-752-7620		698
General Star National Insurance Co 120 Long Ridge Rd PO Box 10354 ...... Stamford CT 06902 TF: 800-624-5237 ■ Web: www.generalstar.com	203-328-5000		391-4
General Steamship Agencies Inc 575 Redwood Hwy Ste 200 ...... Mill Valley CA 94941 Web: www.gensteam.com	415-389-5200	389-9020	465
General Steel Drum LLC 4500 S Blvd ...... Charlotte NC 28209 TF: 800-796-4226 ■ Web: generalsteeldrum.com	704-525-7160		198
General Steel Warehouse Inc 3314 Clovis Rd ...... Lubbock TX 79415 TF: 800-658-2636 ■ Web: www.general-steel.com	806-763-7327	741-1812	723
General Systemantics Press 7027 S Walker Bay Rd NW ...... Walker MN 56484 Web: www.generalsystemantics.com	218-547-0095	547-0195	637-2
General Theming Contractors LLC 3750 Courtright Ct ...... Columbus OH 43227	614-252-6342		344
General Theological Seminary 440 W 21st St ...... New York NY 10011 TF: 888-487-5649 ■ Web: gts.edu	212-243-5150	727-3907	167-3
General Tool & Supply Company Inc 2705 NW Nicolai St ...... Portland OR 97210 TF: 800-526-9328 ■ Web: www.motionindustries.com	503-226-3411		385
General Tool Co 101 Landy Ln ...... Cincinnati OH 45215 *Fax Area Code: 513 ■ TF: 800-314-9817 ■ Web: gentool.com	800-314-9817	733-5604*	757
General Tool Inc 2025 Alton Pkwy ...... Irvine CA 92606 TF: 877-266-2322 ■ Web: www.gtdiamond.com	877-266-2322		190
General Tools Manufacturing Company LLC 80 White St ...... New York NY 10013 TF: 800-697-8665 ■ Web: www.generaltools.com	212-431-6100	431-6499	758
General Tours 53 Summer St ...... Keene NH 03431 *Fax Area Code: 603 ■ TF: 800-221-2216 ■ Web: www.alexanderroberts.com	800-221-2216	357-4548*	760
General Transport Inc 1100 Jenkins Blvd ...... Akron OH 44306 TF: 800-678-6055 ■ Web: www.generaltransport.com	330-786-3400	786-3401	780
General Truck Body 7110 Jensen Dr ...... Houston TX 77093 TF: 800-395-8585 ■ Web: www.generalbody.com	713-692-5177		516
General Truck Parts & Equipment Co 4040 W 40th St ...... Chicago IL 60632 TF: 800-621-3914 ■ Web: www.generaltruckparts.com	773-247-6900	247-2632	61
General Utilities Inc 100 Fairchild Ave ...... Plainview NY 11803 TF: 800-290-9202 ■ Web: www.generalutilities.com	516-349-8989		580
General Vision Services LLC 520 Eigth Ave 9th Fl ...... New York NY 10018 *Fax Area Code: 212 ■ TF: 855-653-0586 ■ Web: www.generalvision.com	855-653-0586	967-4781*	543
General Wax & Candle Co 6863 Beck Ave PO Box 9398 ...... North Hollywood CA 91605 TF: 800-929-7867 ■ Web: www.generalwax.com	818-765-5800	765-0555	122
General Wayne A Downing Peoria International Airport 6100 W Everett McKinley Dirksen Pkwy ...... Peoria IL 61607 Web: www.flypia.com	309-697-8272	697-8132	27
General Wire Spring Co 1101 Thompson Ave ...... McKees Rocks PA 15136 TF: 800-245-6200 ■ Web: www.generalwirespring.com	412-771-6300	771-6317	718
Generali Global Assistance 4330 East-West Hwy Ste 1000 ...... Bethesda MD 20814 Web: us.generaliglobalassistance.com	240-330-1000		775
Generations at Regency 6631 N Milwaukee Ave ...... Niles IL 60714 Web: generationsregency.com	847-647-7444		450
Generations Credit Union 5618 Harrison Ave ...... Rockford IL 61108 Web: generationscu.org	815-316-2900		219
Generations Restaurant & Pub 338 National Rd ...... Wheeling WV 26003 Web: www.generationswhg.com	304-232-7917		671
Generations United (GU) 1333 H St NW Ste 500-W ...... Washington DC 20005 Web: www.gu.org	202-289-3979	289-3952	48-6
Generex Biotechnology Corp 4145 N Service Rd Ste 200 ...... Burlington ON L7L6A3 OTC: GNBT ■ TF: 800-391-6755 ■ Web: www.generex.com	800-391-6755		85
Generic Theater 215 St Paul's Blvd ...... Norfolk VA 23510 Web: www.generictheater.org	757-441-2160		573-4
Genesco Inc 1415 Murfreesboro Rd ...... Nashville TN 37217 NYSE: GCO ■ *Fax Area Code: 615 ■ TF: 877-441-2998 ■ Web: www.genesco.com	877-441-2998	367-8579*	301
Genesee & Wyoming Inc 20 West Ave ...... Darien CT 06820 Web: www.gwrr.com	203-202-8900		648
Genesee Community College 1 College Rd ...... Batavia NY 14020 TF: 866-225-5422 ■ Web: genesee.edu	585-343-0055	345-6810	162
Genesee Country Village & Museum 1410 Flint Hill Rd ...... Mumford NY 14511 Web: www.gcv.org	585-538-6822	538-6927	520
Genesee County 15 Main St Ste 1 ...... Batavia NY 14020 Web: www.co.genesee.ny.us	585-344-2550	344-8582	338
Genesee County 900 S Saginaw St ...... Flint MI 48502 Web: www.co.genesee.mi.us	810-424-4355		338
Genesee County Chamber of Commerce 8276 Park Rd ...... Batavia NY 14020 Web: www.geneseeny.com	585-343-7440	343-7487	139
Genesee County Parks & Recreation 5045 Stanley Rd ...... Flint MI 48506 Web: www.geneseecountyparks.org	810-736-7100	736-7220	50-5
Genesee District Library			
Flint Township-McCarty Library 2071 Graham Rd ...... Flint MI 48532 TF: 866-732-1120 ■ Web: www.thegdl.org	810-732-9150	732-0878	434-3
Genesee Group Inc 1470 Ave T ...... Grand Prairie TX 75050 Web: www.gabtn.com	972-623-2004	623-0404	488

	Phone	Fax	Class
Genesee Packaging Inc 2010 Dort Hwy . . . . Flint MI 48506 *Web:* genpackaging.com	810-235-6120		88
Genesee Regional Chamber of Commerce 519 S Saginaw St Ste 200 . . . . Flint MI 48502 *Web:* www.flintandgenesee.org	810-600-1404	600-1461	139
Genesee Reserve Supply Inc 200 Jefferson Rd. . . . . Rochester NY 14623 *TF:* 800-724-1000 ■ *Web:* www.geneseereserve.com	585-292-7040	292-7046	191-3
Genesee Theatre 203 N Genesee St. . . . . Waukegan IL 60085 *Web:* www.geneseetheatre.com	847-782-2366	782-2355	749
Genesee Valley Ctr 3341 S Linden Rd. . . . . Flint MI 48507 *TF:* 866-236-1128 ■ *Web:* www.geneseemall.com	810-732-4000	732-4343	460
Genesee Valley Penny Saver Inc 391 Rochester Rd . . . . Avon NY 14414 *Web:* www.gvpennysaver.com	585-226-8111		532-3
Geneseo Community Unit School District 228 648 N Chicago St . . . . Geneseo IL 61254 *Web:* www.dist228.org	309-945-0450	945-0445	685
Geneseo Telephone Co 111 E First St . . . . Geneseo IL 61254 *TF:* 800-852-3611 ■ *Web:* www.geneseo.com	309-944-2103	944-4406	224
Genesic Semiconductor Inc 43670 Trade Center Pl . . . . Sterling VA 20166 *Web:* www.genesicsemi.com	703-996-8200	665-2347	696
Genesis 10 950 3rd Ave 2nd Fl . . . . New York NY 10022 *TF:* 800-261-1776 ■ *Web:* www.genesis10.com	212-688-5522	421-6292	180
Genesis Advisors LLC 4550 New Linden Hill Rd Ste 120. . . . . Wilmington DE 19808 *Web:* genesisadv.net	302-504-8782		690
Genesis AEC 1 Sentry Pkwy Ste 100 . . . . Blue Bell PA 19422 *Web:* www.genesisaec.com	610-592-0280	592-0286	261
Genesis Associates Inc 217 Middlesex Tpke . . . . Burlington MA 01803 *Web:* www.genesisa.com	781-270-9540		253
Genesis Attachments LLC 1000 Genesis Dr Main St . . . . Superior WI 54880 *Web:* www.genesisattachments.com	715-395-5252		190
Genesis Automation Inc 3480 Swenson Ave . . . . Saint Charles IL 60174 *Web:* www.genesisautomation.com	630-587-0444		358
Genesis Bicycles 126 Bushkill St. . . . . Easton PA 18042 *Web:* genesisbicycles.com	610-253-1140		711
Genesis Biosystems Inc 1500 Eagle Ct Ste 75057 . . . . Lewisville TX 75057 *TF:* 888-577-7335 ■ *Web:* www.genesisbiosystems.com	972-315-7888		77
Genesis Capital LLC 3414 Peachtree Rd NE Ste 700. . . . . Atlanta GA 30326 *Web:* www.genesis-capital.com	404-816-7540		70
Genesis Career College 1315 Abutment Rd . . . . Dalton GA 30721 *Web:* www.genesiscareer.edu	706-278-1300	260-2857	167-3
Genesis Career College - Cookeville 880-A E 10th St . . . . Cookeville TN 38501 *TF:* 800-639-7284 ■ *Web:* www.genesiscareer.educookeville-tn	931-526-8735	372-8798	167-3
Genesis Chevrolet 21800 Gratiot Ave. . . . . Eastpointe MI 48021 *Web:* www.genesischevrolet.com	586-775-8300		57
Genesis Communications Network 190 Cobblestone Ln . . . . Burnsville MN 55337 *TF:* 877-996-4327 ■ *Web:* www.gcnlive.com	877-996-4327		647
Genesis Computer Consultants Inc 32 Morris Rd . . . . Tappan NY 10983 *Web:* genesiscc.com	917-359-1273		177
Genesis Concepts & Consultants LLC 1777 NE Loop 410 Ste 1009. . . . . San Antonio TX 78217 *Web:* www.genconcepts.com	210-451-5100		177
Genesis Diamonds Cool Springs LLC 3742 Hillsboro Pk. . . . . Nashville TN 37215 *Web:* www.genesisdiamonds.net	615-269-6996		411
Genesis Direct 8514 Sunstate St. . . . . Tampa FL 33634 *Web:* www.genesisdirect.com	813-855-4274		5
Genesis Energy LP 919 Milam Ste 2100. . . . . Houston TX 77002 *NYSE: GEL* ■ *TF:* 800-284-3365 ■ *Web:* www.genesisenergy.com	713-860-2500	860-2640	597
Genesis Global Group Inc 28 Highland Rd. . . . . Westport CT 06880 *Web:* www.g3global.com	203-222-1795		193
Genesis Health System 1227 E Rusholme St. . . . . Davenport IA 52803 *Web:* www.genesishealth.com	563-421-1000		353
Genesis HealthCare Corp 101 E State St. . . . . Kennett Square PA 19348 *TF:* 800-944-7776 ■ *Web:* www.genesishcc.com	610-444-6350	925-4000	451
Genesis Home Care Inc 116 E Heritage Dr . . . . Tyler TX 75703 *TF:* 800-947-0273 ■ *Web:* genesishomecare.net	903-509-3374		363
Genesis Inc 301 W Central Ave . . . . Roselle IL 60172 **Fax Area Code:* 847 ■ *Web:* genesisincorporated.com	630-894-6634	894-6669*	697
Genesis Industries Inc 601 Pro Ject Dr. . . . . Elmwood WI 54740 *TF:* 800-826-3301 ■ *Web:* www.genesisindustriesinc.com	715-639-2435	639-2739	596
Genesis International Inc 1040 Fox Chase Industrial Dr. . . . . Arnold MO 63010 *Web:* www.genesis-international.com	636-282-0011		203
Genesis Plastics Welding Inc 720 E Broadway . . . . Fortville IN 46040 *Web:* genesisplasticswelding.com	317-485-7887		393
Genesis Products Inc 2608 Almac Ct . . . . Elkhart IN 46514 *Web:* genesisproductsinc.com	574-266-8292		492
Genesis Publisher Services 3310 Eagle Pk Dr NE Ste 200. . . . . Grand Rapids MI 49525	616-831-2800	831-0831	637-6
Genesis Spiritual Life Ctr 53 Mill St . . . . Westfield MA 01085 *Web:* genesisspiritualcenter.org	413-562-3627		673
Genesis Telecommunications 2009 Tillman Rd. . . . . Fort Wayne IN 46816 *Web:* www.gentec1.com	260-447-6349	447-2467	681
Genesis Vocational Institute 12861 SW 42nd St . . . . Miami FL 33175 *Web:* www.genesisvocationalinstitute.com	305-223-0506	223-0509	800
Genesisfour Corp 7747 Ten Acre Rd. . . . . Andrews SC 29510 **Fax Area Code:* 855 ■ *TF:* 800-937-4364 ■ *Web:* www.genesisfour.com	843-461-4117	937-4364*	177
GenesisXD Inc 500 Queens Quay W Ste 103e . . . . Toronto ON M5V3K8 *Web:* www.genesisxd.com	416-595-9823		344
Genesys Consulting Services Inc 1 Marcus Blvd Ste 102 . . . . Albany NY 12205 *Web:* genesysonline.com	518-459-9500		177
Genesys Engineering PC 629 Fifth Ave Bldg 3. . . . . Pelham NY 10803 *TF:* 888-265-8522 ■ *Web:* www.genesysengineering.net	914-633-6490	633-6951	196
Genesys Partners Inc 126 5th Ave. . . . . New York NY 10011 *Web:* www.genesyspartners.com	212-686-2828	686-5155	792
Genesys Telecommunications Laboratories Inc 2001 Junipero Serra Blvd. . . . . Daly City CA 94014 **Fax Area Code:* 650 ■ *TF:* 888-436-3797 ■ *Web:* www.genesys.com	888-436-3797	466-1260*	735
Genesys Venture Inc 4-1250 Waverley St . . . . Winnipeg MB R3T6C6 *Web:* www.genesysventure.com	204-487-2328		194
Genet Property Group Inc 5701 N Pine Island Rd Ste 370. . . . . Tamarac FL 33321 *Web:* genetgroup.com	954-572-9159		653
Genetec Inc 2280 Alfred-Nobel Blvd Ste 400. . . . . Montreal QC H4S2A4 *TF:* 866-684-8006 ■ *Web:* www.genetec.com	514-332-4000		225
GeneThera Inc 7577 W 103rd Ave Ste 212. . . . . Westminster CO 80021 *Web:* www.genethera.net	303-439-2085		85
Genetic Alliance Inc 4301 Connecticut Ave NW Ste 404. . . . . Washington DC 20008 *TF:* 800-860-8747 ■ *Web:* www.geneticalliance.org	202-966-5557	966-8553	48-17
Genetic Assays Inc 4711 Trousdale Dr Ste 209. . . . . Nashville TN 37220 *TF:* 800-390-5280 ■ *Web:* www.geneticassays.com	800-390-5280		415
Genetic Engineering News 140 Huguenot St 3rd Fl . . . . New Rochelle NY 10801 *TF:* 888-211-4235 ■ *Web:* www.genengnews.com	914-740-2100	740-2101	531-12
Genetic Profiles Corp 10675 Treena St Ste 103. . . . . San Diego CA 92131 *TF:* 800-551-7763 ■ *Web:* www.geneticprofiles.com	800-551-7763		417
Genetics & IVF Institute Inc 3015 Williams Dr . . . . Fairfax VA 22031 *TF:* 800-552-4363 ■ *Web:* www.givf.com	703-698-7355	991-8030	415
Genetics Associates Inc 1916 Patterson St Ste 400 . . . . Nashville TN 37203 *TF:* 800-331-4363 ■ *Web:* geneticsassociates.com	615-327-4532		415
Genetrack Biolabs Inc 401-1508 Broadway W. . . . . Vancouver BC V6J1W8 *TF:* 888-828-1899 ■ *Web:* www.genetrack.com	604-325-7282		418
Genetti Hospitality Inc 77 E Market St . . . . Wilkes-Barre PA 18701 *Web:* www.genetti.com	570-823-6152		377
Geneva Area Chamber of Commerce 866 E Main St PO Box 84. . . . . Geneva OH 44041 *Web:* www.genevachamber.org	440-466-8694	466-0823	139
Geneva Capital LLC 522 Broadway St Ste 4 . . . . Alexandria MN 56308 *TF:* 800-408-9352 ■ *Web:* www.gogc.com	800-408-9352		194
Geneva College 3200 College Ave . . . . Beaver Falls PA 15010 *TF:* 800-847-8255 ■ *Web:* www.geneva.edu	724-847-6500	847-6776	166
Geneva Construction Co (GCC) 1350 Aurora Ave. . . . . Aurora IL 60507 *Web:* www.genevaconstruction.net	630-892-4357	892-7738	186
Geneva Consulting Group Inc 14 Vanderventer Ave Ste 250 . . . . Port Washington NY 11050 **Fax Area Code:* 516 ■ *Web:* www.genevaconsulting.com	212-244-9595	944-2356*	194
Geneva County 200 N Commerce St. . . . . Geneva AL 36340 *Web:* www.genevacountyal.gov	334-684-5660		338
Geneva County Board of Education PO Box 250 . . . . Geneva AL 36340 *Web:* www.genevacountyschools.com	334-684-5690	248-6355	685
Geneva General Hospital 196 N St. . . . . Geneva NY 14456 *Web:* www.flhealth.org	315-787-4000		374-3
Geneva Laboratories Inc 1001 Proctor Dr . . . . Elkhorn WI 53121 *Web:* www.genevalabs.com	262-723-5669	723-4015	743
Geneva on the Lake 1001 Lochland Rd . . . . Geneva NY 14456 *Web:* www.genevaonthelake.com	315-789-7190	789-0332	379
Geneva Pipe Inc 1465 W 400 N . . . . Orem UT 84057 *Web:* www.genevapipe.com	801-225-2416	225-2467	183
Geneva Rock Products Inc 302 W 5400 S Ste 200 . . . . Murray UT 84107 *Web:* genevarock.com	801-281-7900		182
Geneva Trading 190 S Lasalle St Ste 1800. . . . . Chicago IL 60603 *Web:* www.geneva-trading.com	312-471-6100		691
Geneva Woods Pharmacy Inc 501 W International Airport Rd Ste 1A . . . . Anchorage AK 99518 *TF:* 800-478-0005 ■ *Web:* www.genevawoods.com	907-565-6100		237
Genex Co-opeartive Inc PO Box 469. . . . . Shawano WI 54166 *TF:* 888-333-1783 ■ *Web:* genex.coop	715-526-2141		11-2
Genex Services Inc 440 E Swedesford Rd Ste 1000. . . . . Wayne PA 19087 *TF:* 888-464-3639 ■ *Web:* www.genexservices.com	610-964-5100	964-1919	194
GeneXus Inc 1143 W Rundell PL Ste 200 . . . . Chicago IL 60607 *Web:* www.genexus.com	312-836-9152	836-9153	178-1
Genghis Cohen 740 N Fairfax Ave . . . . Los Angeles CA 90046 *Web:* www.genghiscohen.com	323-653-0640		671
Genghis Grill 8200 Springwood Dr Ste 230. . . . . Irving TX 75063 *TF:* 888-436-4447 ■ *Web:* www.genghisgrill.com	888-436-4447		671
Genie Co 1 Door Dr PO Box 67. . . . . Mount Hope OH 44660 *TF:* 800-354-3643 ■ *Web:* www.geniecompany.com	800-354-3643		350
Genie Electronics Company Inc 1087 Valley View Rd. . . . . York PA 17406 *Web:* www.genieelectronics.com	717-840-6999	757-0194	625
Genie Industries Inc 18340 NE 76th St . . . . Redmond WA 98052 *TF:* 800-536-1800 ■ *Web:* genielift.com	425-881-1800	883-3475	470
Genie Manufacturing Corp 999 Rush Henrietta Townli . . . . Rush NY 14543 *Web:* www.geniemfg.com	585-359-4100	359-2627	88

Company	City	State	Zip	Phone	Fax	Class
Genie Repros Inc 2211 Hamilton Ave *TF:* 877-496-6611 ■ *Web:* www.genierepros.com	Cleveland	OH	44114	216-696-6677		627
Genieco Inc 200 N Laflin St *TF:* 800-223-8217 ■ *Web:* gonesh.com	Chicago	IL	60607	312-421-2383		145
Genius Jones Inc 170 NE 40th St 101 PO Box 370188 *TF:* 866-436-4875 ■ *Web:* www.geniusjones.com	Miami	FL	33137	866-436-4875		174
Genius SIS Inc 150 S Pine Island Rd Ste 420 *Web:* www.geniussis.com	Plantation	FL	33324	954-667-7747		387
Genki Sushi Hawaii 677 Ala Moana Blvd Ste 612 *Web:* www.genkisushiusa.com	Honolulu	HI	96813	808-523-3315	523-3316	671
Genmab Inc 902 Carnegie Ctr Ste 301 *Web:* www.genmab.com	Princeton	NJ	08540	609-430-2481		743
Genmark Automation Inc 46723 Lakeview Blvd *Web:* www.genmarkautomation.com	Fremont	CA	94538	510-897-3400		386
Gennaro Inc 1725 Pontiac Ave *Web:* www.gennaroinc.com	Cranston	RI	02920	401-632-4100		411
Gennaro's Ristorante 1109 N Brand Blvd *Web:* www.gennarosristorante.com	Glendale	CA	91202	818-243-6231		671
Gennett Lumber Co 284 Lyman St *Web:* www.gennettlumber.com	Asheville	NC	28801	828-253-3626		364
GenNext Publishing PO Box 670 *Web:* gennextpublishing.homestead.com	Anderson	SC	29622	928-437-4578		637-2
Genoa Business Forms Inc 445 Park Ave **Fax Area Code:* 815 ■ *TF:* 800-383-2801 ■ *Web:* www.genoabusforms.com	Sycamore	IL	60178	800-383-2801	895-8206*	110
Genocea Biosciences Inc 100 Acorn Park Dr *Web:* www.genocea.com	Cambridge	MA	02140	617-876-8191	876-8192	668
Genova Diagnostics 63 Zillicoa St *TF:* 800-522-4762 ■ *Web:* www.gdx.net	Asheville	NC	28801	828-253-0621	252-9303	418
Genova Products Inc 7034 E Court St *TF:* 800-521-7488 ■ *Web:* www.genovaproducts.com	Davison	MI	48423	800-521-7488		608
Genova Technologies Inc 4250 River Center Ct NE Ste A *Web:* www.genovatech.com	Cedar Rapids	IA	52402	319-378-8455		177
Genpak Carthage 505 E Cotton St *TF:* 800-626-6695 ■ *Web:* www.genpak.com	Carthage	TX	75633	903-693-7151		300
GenPore 1136 Morgantown Rd PO Box 380 *TF:* 800-654-4391 ■ *Web:* www.genpore.com	Reading	PA	19607	610-374-5171	374-4990	608
Gen-Probe Inc 10210 Genetic Center Dr *TF:* 800-523-5001 ■ *Web:* www.hologic.com	San Diego	CA	92121	858-410-8000		231
GenQuest DNA Analysis Laboratory 133 Coney Island Dr *TF:* 877-362-5227 ■ *Web:* genquestdnalab.com	Sparks	NV	89431	775-358-0652		417
Genscape Inc 1140 Garvin Pl *TF:* 866-292-8060 ■ *Web:* www.genscape.com	Louisville	KY	40203	502-583-3435	583-3464	463
Gensco Equipment (1990) Inc 53 Carlaw Ave *Web:* www.genscoequip.com	Toronto	ON	M4M2R6	416-465-7521		258
Gensco Inc 4402 20th St E *TF:* 877-620-8203 ■ *Web:* gensco.com	Tacoma	WA	98424	253-620-8203		612
GenServe Inc 100 Newtown Rd *TF:* 800-247-7215 ■ *Web:* www.genserveinc.com	Plainview	NY	11803	631-435-0437		111
Gensler 2 Harrison St Ste 400 *Web:* www.gensler.com	San Francisco	CA	94105	415-433-3700	836-4599	261
Gentec Inc 2625 Dalton *TF:* 800-463-4480 ■ *Web:* gentec.ca	Quebec City	QC	G1P3S9	418-651-8000		203
Gentech Systems Management LLC PO Box 3426 *TF:* 800-399-4876 ■ *Web:* www.gentech.com	Trenton	NJ	08619	609-890-2522	890-2277	196
Gentek Building Products Inc 11 Craigwood Rd *TF:* 800-489-1144 ■ *Web:* www.gentekinc.com	Avenel	NJ	07001	732-381-0900		697
Gentell Corp 2701 Bartram Rd *Web:* www.gentell.com	Bristol	PA	19007	215-788-2700	788-2715	238
Gentex Corp 600 N Centennial St *NASDAQ: GNTX* ■ *Web:* www.gentex.com	Zeeland	MI	49464	616-772-1800	772-7348	329
GENTEX Corp 324 Main St *TF:* 888-894-1755 ■ *Web:* www.gentexcorp.com	Simpson	PA	18407	570-282-3550	282-8555	542
Gentile Pismeny & Brengel LLP 1581 Franklin Ave PO Box 149 *Web:* www.gpb.net	Great Neck	NY	11021	516-487-4110		2
Gentle Dental 22 Alpine Ln *Web:* www.gentledental.com	Chelmsford	MA	01824	978-256-7581		390
Gentle Revolution Press, The 8801 Stenton Ave *TF:* 866-895-5437 ■ *Web:* www.gentlerevolution.com	Wyndmoor	PA	19038	215-233-2050		637-2
Gentry County 200 W Clay St *Web:* www.gentrycounty.net	Albany	MO	64402	660-726-3525		338
Gentry Homes Ltd 733 Bishop St Ste 1400 *Web:* www.gentryhawaii.com	Honolulu	HI	96813	808-685-0811	689-5840	653
Gentry Locke Rakes & Moore LLP 10 Franklin Rd S E Ste 900 *TF:* 866-983-0866 ■ *Web:* www.gentrylocke.com	Roanoke	VA	24011	540-983-9300		428
Gentry Trucking LLC 8125 W 70th St *Web:* www.gentrytrucking.com	Greenwood	LA	71033	318-938-5396	938-7475	780
Genuine Parts Co (GPC) 2999 Wildwood Pkwy *NYSE: GPC* ■ *Web:* www.genpt.com	Atlanta	GA	30339	678-934-5000		61
Genuitec LLC 2221 Justin Rd Ste 119-340 *Web:* www.genuitec.com	Flower Mound	TX	75028	214-224-0461		180
Genuity Concepts Inc 507 N Church St *Web:* www.genuityconcepts.com	Greensboro	NC	27401	336-379-1850		184
Genus Capital Management Inc 860 980 Howe St 6th Fl *Web:* genuscap.com	Vancouver	BC	V6C1E5	604-683-4554		401
Genus Oncology LLC 650 Albany St **Fax Area Code:* 617 ■ *Web:* www.genusoncology.com	Boston	MA	02118	847 549 6500	638 0364*	231
Genus Technologies LLC 520 Nicollet Mall Ste 900 *Web:* www.genusllc.com	Minneapolis	MN	55402	612-361-8400		387
Genwealth Group Inc, The 6 Inwood Pl *Web:* thegenwealthgroup.com	Maplewood	NJ	07040	973-761-0400		690
Genwest Systems Inc PO Box 397 *Web:* www.genwest.com	Edmonds	WA	98020	425-771-2700	672-8471	180
Genx Corp 2911 Emerald Dr *Web:* www.genxcomparators.com	Kalamazoo	MI	49001	269-341-4242		544
Genzyme Corp 500 Kendall St *TF:* 800-745-4447 ■ *Web:* www.sanofigenzyme.com	Cambridge	MA	02142	617-252-7500		85
Genzyme Genetics 3400 Computer Dr *TF:* 800-255-7357 ■ *Web:* www.labcorp.com	Westborough	MA	01581	508-898-9001		417
GEO Drilling Fluids Inc 1431 Union Ave *TF:* 800-438-7436 ■ *Web:* geodf.com	Bakersfield	CA	93305	661-325-5919	325-5648	540
Geo Environmental Resources Inc 2712 Southern Blvd Ste 101 *Web:* geronline.com	Virginia Beach	VA	23452	757-463-3200		261
Geo Group Corp, The 6 Odana Ct *TF:* 800-993-2262 ■ *Web:* www.thegeogroup.com	Madison	WI	53719	608-230-1000	230-1010	768
GEO Group Inc, The 4955 Technology Way *Web:* www.geogroup.com	Boca Raton	FL	33431	561-893-0101		49-15
Geo Heiser Body Company Inc 11210 Tukwila International Blvd *Web:* www.heiserbody.com	Seattle	WA	98168	206-622-7985	622-7135	516
Geo M. Robinson & Co 1461 Atteberry Ln	San Jose	CA	95131	408-432-6264		189-13
Geo Owl LLC 1904 Eastwood Rd *Web:* www.geoowl.com	Wilmington	NC	28403	910-239-9207		657
Geo Products LLC 12626 N Houston Rosslyn Rd *Web:* www.geoproducts.org	Houston	TX	77086	281-820-5493		819
GEO Specialty Chemicals Inc 401 S Earl Ave *TF:* 888-519-3883 ■ *Web:* www.geosc.com	LaFayette	IN	47904	765-448-9412		145
Geo Strata Environmental Consultants Inc 4718 College Pk Condo 205	San Antonio	TX	78249	210-492-7282		256
Geocal Inc 7290 S Fraser St *Web:* geocal.us	Centennial	CO	80112	303-337-0338		256
Geocel Corp 2504 Marina Dr *TF:* 800-348-7615 ■ *Web:* www.geocelusa.com	Elkhart	IN	46514	800-348-7615	348-7009	3
Geo-Cleanse International Inc 400 SR-34 Ste B *Web:* www.geocleanse.com	Matawan	NJ	07747	732-970-6696	970-6697	145
Geocom Inc 366 Madison Ave 10th Fl *Web:* www.geocom-inc.com	New York	NY	10017	212-949-0712		194
Geo-Comm Inc 601 W St Germain St *TF:* 888-436-2666 ■ *Web:* www.geo-comm.com	Saint Cloud	MN	56301	888-436-2666		196
Geocomp Corp 1145 Massachusetts Ave *TF:* 800-822-2669 ■ *Web:* www.geocomp.com	Boxborough	MA	01719	978-635-0012	635-0266	178-5
Geoconcepts Engineering 19955 Highland Vista Dr *TF:* 877-813-4617 ■ *Web:* www.geoconcepts-eng.com	Ashburn	VA	20147	703-726-8030	726-8032	261
Geode State Park 3333 Racine Ave *Web:* www.iowadnr.gov	Danville	IA	52623	319-392-4601		565
Geodetic Designs 2300 N Grand River Ave *Web:* geodeticdesigns.com	Lansing	MI	48906	517-908-0008		727
GeoDigital 140 - 1 Antares Dr *Web:* www.geodigital.com	Ottawa	ON	K2E8C4	613-820-4545	820-9772	407
Geodis Wilson Canada Ltd 6285 Northam Dr *Web:* www.geodis.com	Mississauga	ON	L4V1R4	905-677-5266	677-5819	311
Geoenergy Inc 3100 Wilcrest Dr Ste 220 *Web:* geoenergycorp.com	Houston	TX	77042	713-339-9024	339-3876	261
GeoEngineers Inc 8410 154th Ave NE *Web:* www.geoengineers.com	Redmond	WA	98052	425-861-6000	861-6050	261
Geofields Inc Bank of America Plz 600 Peachtree St Ste 440 *Web:* www.geofields.com	Atlanta	GA	30308	404-253-1000	875-2442	178-10
Geoforce Inc 5830 Granite Prkwy Ste 1200 *TF:* 888-574-3878 ■ *Web:* www.geoforce.com	Coppell	TX	75024	972-546-3878		536
GeoGlobal Resources Inc (GGR) 625 Fourth Ave SW *OTC: GGLR* ■ *Web:* geoglobal.com	Calgary	AB	T2P0K2	403-777-9250		538
Geographia Map Co 75 Moore St *TF:* 800-416-4331 ■ *Web:* www.geographiamaps.com	Hackensack	NJ	07601	201-488-4411	488-4401	637-10
Geographic Expeditions 1008 General Kennedy Ave *TF:* 888-570-7108 ■ *Web:* www.geoex.com	San Francisco	CA	94129	415-922-0448	346-5535	760
Geographics 108 Main St 3rd Fl **Fax Area Code:* 866 ■ *TF:* 800-436-4919 ■ *Web:* www.geographics.com	Norwalk	CT	06851	800-436-4919	520-1955*	552-2
Geo-instruments Inc 24 Celestial Dr *TF:* 800-477-2506 ■ *Web:* www.geo-instruments.com	Narragansett	RI	02882	800-477-2506		463
Geokon Inc 48 Spencer St *Web:* www.geokon.com	Lebanon	NH	03766	603-448-1562	448-3216	472
Geolo Capital The Embarcadero Ste 102 *Web:* www.geolo.com	San Francisco	CA	94111	415-694-5802		528
Geologic Data Systems 5994 S Prince St Ste 203 *Web:* geologicdata.com	Littleton	CO	80120	303-837-1699	837-1698	536
Geological Society of America, The (GSA) 3300 Penrose Pl PO Box 9140 *TF:* 800-472-1988 ■ *Web:* geosociety.org	Boulder	CO	80301	303-357-1000	357-1070	49-19
GeoLogics Corp 5285 Shawnee Rd Ste 300 *TF:* 800-684-3455 ■ *Web:* geologics.com	Alexandria	VA	22312	703-750-4000	750-4010	180
Geomagic Inc 430 Davis Dr Ste 300 *TF:* 800-691-1839 ■ *Web:* www.geomagic.com	Morrisville	NC	27560	800-691-1839		180
GeoMark Research Ltd 218 Higgins St *Web:* geomarkresearch.com	Humble	TX	77338	832-644-1184		536

Name / Address	City	State	ZIP	Phone	Fax	Class
Geomat Inc 915 Malta Ave *Web:* geomatengineering.com	Farmington	NM	87401	505-327-7928		261
Geomedia Inc 4242 Medical Dr Ste 4200 *Web:* geomedia.com	San Antonio	TX	78229	210-614-5900		514
Geometric Americas Inc 50 Kirts Blvd Ste A *Web:* geometricglobal.com	Troy	MI	48084	248-404-3500		261
Geometrica Inc 12300 Dundee Ct Ste 200 *Web:* www.geometrica.com	Cypress	TX	77429	832-220-1200		198
Geometrics Inc 2190 Fortune Dr *Web:* www.geometrics.com	San Jose	CA	95131	408-954-0522	954-0902	472
Geonautics Manufacturing Inc 506 Merrimac St *Web:* www.geonauticsmfg.com	Newburyport	MA	01950	978-462-7161		608
Geopath 271 Madison Ave Ste 1504 *Web:* geopath.org	New York	NY	10016	212-972-8075		49-18
Geopentech 101 Academy Dr Ste 100 *Web:* geopentech.com	Irvine	CA	92617	714-796-9100		261
Geophysical Fluid Dynamics Laboratory NOAA/OAR/GFDL 201 Forrestal Rd *Web:* www.gfdl.noaa.gov	Princeton	NJ	08540	609-452-6500	987-5063	668
Geophysical Pursuit Inc 3501 Allen Pkwy *Web:* www.geopursuit.com	Houston	TX	77019	713-529-3000		539
Geophysical Survey Systems Inc 40 Simon St *TF:* 800-524-3011 ■ *Web:* geophysical.com	Nashua	NH	03060	603-893-1109	889-3984	529
Geophysics GPR International Inc 100 - 2545 Delorimier St **Fax Area Code:* 514 ■ *TF:* 800-672-4774 ■ *Web:* www.geophysicsgpr.com	Longueuil	QC	J4K3P7	450-679-2400	521-4128*	727
Geoprofessional Business Assn 15800 Crabbs Branch Way Ste 300 *Web:* www.geoprofessional.org	Rockville	MD	20855	301-565-2733	589-2017	49-19
Georesults Inc 309 Pirkle Ferry Rd *Web:* www.georesults.com	Cumming	GA	30040	770-205-8111		463
Georgaklis & Mallas PLLC 9118 Fifth Ave *Web:* gmlawny.com	Brooklyn	NY	11209	718-238-2400	238-2116	41
George 111C Queen St E *Web:* www.georgeonqueen.com	Toronto	ON	M5C1S2	416-863-6006	368-6093	671
George & Associates, Consulting Engineers Inc 1967 Commonwealth Ln Ste 200 *Web:* gaceng.net	Tallahassee	FL	32303	850-521-0344		261
George & Lynch Inc 150 Lafferty Ln *Web:* www.geolyn.com	Dover	DE	19901	302-736-3031		188-4
George & Sons 11291 E Via Linda *Web:* georgeandsonsasiancuisine.com	Scottsdale	AZ	85259	480-661-6336		671
George B. Woodcock and Co 9667 Canoga Ave *TF:* 800-358-2786 ■ *Web:* www.gbwoodcock.com	Chatsworth	CA	91311	818-998-3774	882-0652	559
George Bagley & Company LLC 1315 W 22nd St Ste 305 *Web:* www.bagleycpa.com	Oak Brook	IL	60523	630-990-0355	990-0374	2
George Borchardt Inc 136 E 57th St *Web:* gbagency.com	New York	NY	10022	212-753-5785		444
George Braziller Inc 277 Broadway Ste 708 *Web:* www.georgebraziller.com	New York	NY	10007	212-260-9256	267-3165	637-2
George Brown College PO Box 1015 Sta B *TF:* 800-265-2002 ■ *Web:* www.georgebrown.ca	Toronto	ON	M5T2T9	416-415-2000		167-3
George Bush Presidential Library and Museum 1000 George Bush Dr W *Web:* bush41.org	College Station	TX	77845	979-691-4000	691-4050	434-3
George Butler Associates Inc 9801 Renner Blvd *Web:* gbateam.com	Lenexa	KS	66219	913-492-0400		261
George C. Marshall Foundation VMI Parade *Web:* www.marshallfoundation.org	Lexington	VA	24450	540-463-7103	464-5229	520
George C. Page Museum at La Brea Tar Pits 5801 Wilshire Blvd *Web:* tarpits.org	Los Angeles	CA	90036	323-857-6300		520
George C. Patrick & Associates PC 706 Merrillville Rd *Web:* georgepatrick.com	Crown Point	IN	46307	219-662-7959		41
George County Times 5133 Main St *Web:* www.gctimesonline.com	Lucedale	MS	39452	601-947-2967	947-6828	637-9
George Darling Consulting Group Inc Towle Office Bldg 260 Merrimac St *Web:* www.darlingconsulting.com	Newburyport	MA	01950	978-463-0400		463
George Dolan 706 Brookline Blvd *Web:* www.partycakeshop.com	Pittsburgh	PA	15226	412-531-5322	531-3240	68
George E. DeLallo Company Inc 6390 Rt 30 *TF:* 877-335-2556 ■ *Web:* www.delallo.com	Jeannette	PA	15644	724-523-6577		297-8
George E. Masker Inc 887 71st Ave *Web:* www.maskerpainting.com	Oakland	CA	94621	510-568-1206	638-2530	189-8
George E. Warren Corp 3001 Ocean Dr Ste 203 *Web:* www.gewarren.com	Vero Beach	FL	32963	772-778-7100	778-7171	579
George Eastman Museum 900 E Ave *Web:* www.eastman.org	Rochester	NY	14607	585-327-4800		520
George F. Lang Co 1001 N Union St *Web:* langcarpet.com	Wilmington	DE	19805	302-655-1533		290
George Fox University 414 N Meridian St *TF:* 800-765-4369 ■ *Web:* www.georgefox.edu	Newberg	OR	97132	503-538-8383	554-3110	166
George G. Sharp Inc 160 Broadway 8th Fl *Web:* www.georgesharp.com	New York	NY	10038	212-732-2800	732-2809	261
George H Ratchford Inc PO Box 640 *Web:* www.ratchfordinc.com	Wadley	GA	30477	478-252-5524		780
George H. Swatek Inc 1095 Edgewater Ave *Web:* www.ghswatek.com	Ridgefield	NJ	07657	201-941-2400	941-8681	559
George H. Wilson Inc 250 Harvey W Blvd *Web:* www.geohwilson.com	Santa Cruz	CA	95060	831-423-9522	423-9903	189-10
George Harms Construction Company Inc PO Box 817 *Web:* ghcci.com	Farmingdale	NJ	07727	732-938-4004	938-2782	188-4
George Harte Nissan Inc 426 Derby Ave *TF:* 866-860-4383 ■ *Web:* www.georgehartenissan.com	West Haven	CT	06516	866-860-4383		57
George Heinl & Co 201 Church St *TF:* 800-387-7858 ■ *Web:* georgeheinl.com	Toronto	ON	M5B1Y7	416-363-0093		527
George Henry George Partners 9524 Linden St *Web:* www.ghgpec.com	Bethesda	MD	20814	301-897-3841		196
George Industries Inc 1 S Page St *Web:* georgeindustries.com	Endicott	NY	13760	607-748-3371		492
George J Falter Company Inc 3501 Benson Ave *TF:* 800-322-3491 ■ *Web:* www.georgejfalter.com	Baltimore	MD	21227	410-644-6414	646-3745	756
George J. Igel & Company Inc 2040 Alum Creek Dr *Web:* www.buildwithigel.com	Columbus	OH	43207	614-445-8421	445-8205	189-5
George J. Shaw Construction Co 1601 Bellefontaine Ave *Web:* www.georgeshawconstruction.com	Kansas City	MO	64127	816-231-8200		186
George K's Catering & Banquet Hall 2108 Cedar Fork Dr *Web:* gkcatering.net	Greensboro	NC	27407	336-854-0008		671
George K. Baum & Co 4801 Main St Ste 500 *TF:* 800-821-7195 ■ *Web:* www.gkbaum.com	Kansas City	MO	64112	816-474-1100	283-5180	690
George Kaiser Family Foundation 7030 S Yale Ave Ste 600 *Web:* www.gkff.org	Tulsa	OK	74136	918-392-1612		305
George Kelk Corp 48 Lesmill Rd *Web:* kelk.com	Toronto	ON	M3B2T5	416-445-5850		407
George Koch Sons LLC 10 S 11th Ave *TF:* 888-873-5624 ■ *Web:* www.kochllc.com	Evansville	IN	47712	812-465-9600		386
George L. Smith State Park 8 George L Smith State Park Rd *Web:* gastateparks.org	Twin City	GA	30471	478-763-2759		565
George L. Throop Co 444 N Fair Oaks Ave *Web:* www.throop.com	Pasadena	CA	91103	626-796-0285		183
George Mason Mortgage Corp 4100 Monu Crnr Dr Ste 100 *TF:* 800-867-6859 ■ *Web:* www.gmmllc.com	Fairfax	VA	22030	703-273-2600	934-9122	509
George Mason University 4400 University Dr *TF:* 888-627-6612 ■ *Web:* www2.gmu.edu	Fairfax	VA	22030	703-993-1000		166
George Mason University's Center for the Arts George Mason University 4400 University Dr MS 2F5 *Web:* cfa.gmu.edu	Fairfax	VA	22030	703-993-8888	993-8650	572
George Mcelroy & Associates Inc (GMA) 1412 Main St Ste 1500 *Web:* www.gmainc.com	Dallas	TX	75202	214-905-3700	905-3777	463
George Memorial Library 1001 Golfview Dr *Web:* www.fortbend.lib.tx.us	Richmond	TX	77469	281-342-4455	341-2689	434-3
George Nutting Company Inc 1907 Dothan Rd *Web:* georgenutting.com	Bainbridge	GA	39817	229-246-0002	246-0082	454
George Ohsawa Macrobiotic Foundation 1277 Marian Ave *TF:* 800-232-2372 ■ *Web:* www.ohsawamacrobiotics.com	Chico	CA	95928	530-566-9765	566-9768	48-6
George P. Johnson Co 3600 Giddings Rd *Web:* www.gpj.com	Auburn Hills	MI	48326	248-475-2500		195
George Pappas' Liberty Lanes 2501 S York Rd *Web:* www.georgepappaslibertylanes.com	Gastonia	NC	28052	704-868-2695		99
George R. Brown Convention Ctr 1001 Avenida de Las Americas *TF:* 800-427-4697 ■ *Web:* www.grbhouston.com	Houston	TX	77010	713-853-8000	853-8090	205
George R. Peters Associates Inc PO Box 850 *TF:* 800-929-5972 ■ *Web:* www.grpeters.com	Troy	MI	48099	248-524-2211	524-1758	246
George Ranch Historical Park 10215 FM 762 *Web:* www.georgeranch.org	Richmond	TX	77469	281-343-0218		520
George Reed Inc 140 Empire Ave *TF:* 877-823-2305 ■ *Web:* www.georgereed.com	Modesto	CA	95354	877-823-2305		261
George Regional Hospital 859 Winter St *Web:* www.georgeregional.com	Lucedale	MS	39452	601-947-3161		374-3
George Risk Industries Inc 802 S Elm St *OTC:* RSKIA ■ *TF:* 800-523-1227 ■ *Web:* www.grisk.com	Kimball	NE	69145	308-235-4645	235-2609	692
George Rogers Clark National Historical Park 401 S Second St *Web:* www.nps.gov	Vincennes	IN	47591	812-882-1776	882-7270	564
George S. & Dolores Dore Eccles Foundation 79 S Main St 14th Fl *Web:* www.gsecclesfoundation.org	Salt Lake City	UT	84111	801-246-5340	350-3510	305
George S. Coyne Chemical Co 3015 State Rd *TF:* 800-523-1230 ■ *Web:* www.coynechemical.com	Croydon	PA	19021	215-785-3000	785-1585	146
George S. Mickelson Trail 11361 Nevada Gulch Rd *TF:* 800-888-1798 ■ *Web:* gfp.sd.gov	Lead	SD	57754	605-584-3896		565
George Schmitt & Company Inc 251 Boston Post Rd *Web:* www.georgeschmitt.com	Guilford	CT	06437	203-453-4334		627
George School 1690 Newtown-Langhorne Rd *Web:* www.georgeschool.org	Newtown	PA	18940	215-579-6547	579-6549	622

	Phone	Fax	Class
George Schroeder Trucking Inc 8855 Mchenry St . . . . Burlington WI 53105 *Web:* safer.fmcsa.dot.gov	262-539-3525		311
George Shumway Publisher Inc 3900 Deep Run Rd . . . . York PA 17406 *Web:* www.shumwaypublisher.com	717-755-1196		637-2
George Sintsirmas, Esq. LLC 2226 Enterprise Pkwy . . . . Twinsburg OH 44087 *Web:* smimmigrationattorneys.com	330-423-0899		41
George Sollitt Construction 790 N Central Ave . . . . Wood Dale IL 60191 *Web:* www.sollitt.com	630-860-7333	860-7347	186
George Stone Technical Ctr 2400 Longleaf Dr . . . . Pensacola FL 32526 *Web:* www.georgestonecenter.com	850-941-6200		167-3
George Street Photo & Video LLC 230 W Huron St Ste 3W . . . . Chicago IL 60654 *TF:* 866-831-4103 ■ *Web:* www.georgestreetphoto.com	866-831-4103		590
George Street Playhouse 9 Livingston Ave . . . . New Brunswick NJ 08901 *Web:* georgestreetplayhouse.org	732-246-7717	247-9151	749
George T. Bagby State Park & Lodge 330 Bagby Pkwy . . . . Fort Gaines GA 39851 *TF:* 877-591-5575 ■ *Web:* gastateparks.org	229-768-2571		565
George T. Sanders Co (GTS) 10201 W 49th Ave . . . . Wheat Ridge CO 80033 *Web:* www.gtsanders.com	303-940-5290		612
George Uhe Company Inc 219 River Dr . . . . Garfield NJ 07026 *TF:* 800-850-4075 ■ *Web:* www.uhe.com	201-843-4000	843-7517	479
George W. Auch Co 735 S Paddock St . . . . Pontiac MI 48341 *Web:* www.auchconstruction.com	248-334-2000		189-1
George W. Radebaugh & Sons 120 Burke Ave . . . . Towson MD 21286 *Web:* radebaugh.com	410-825-4341		292
George Washington Birthplace National Monument 1732 Popes Creek Rd . . . . Colonial Beach VA 22443 *Web:* www.nps.gov	804-224-1732	224-2142	564
George Washington Carver Museum & Cultural Ctr 1165 Angelina St . . . . Austin TX 78702 *Web:* www.austintexas.gov	512-974-4926	974-3699	520
George Washington Carver National Monument 5646 Carver Rd . . . . Diamond MO 64840 *Web:* www.nps.gov	417-325-4151		564
George Washington Masonic National Memorial 101 Callahan Dr . . . . Alexandria VA 22301 *Web:* gwmemorial.org	703-683-2007	519-9270	50-4
George Washington Memorial Parkway Turkey Run Pk . . . . McLean VA 22101 *Web:* www.nps.gov	703-285-2223	289-2598	564
George Washington University *Gelman Library* 2130 H St NW . . . . Washington DC 20052 *Web:* library.gwu.edu	202-994-6558		434-6
George Washington University Hospital 900 23rd St NW . . . . Washington DC 20037 *TF:* 888-449-3627 ■ *Web:* www.gwhospital.com	202-715-4000		374-3
George Washington University Law School 2000 H St NW . . . . Washington DC 20052 *Web:* www.law.gwu.edu	202-994-6261	994-7230	167-1
George Washington University School of Medicine & Health Sciences 2300 Eye St NW Ross Hall . . . . Washington DC 20037 *TF:* 866-846-1107 ■ *Web:* smhs.gwu.edu	202-994-3506	994-1753	167-2
George Washington University, The 1918 F St NW . . . . Washington DC 20052 *Web:* www.gwu.edu	202-994-1000		167-3
George Washington's Grist Mill 5513 Mt Vernon Memorial Hwy . . . . Alexandria VA 22309 *Web:* www.mountvernon.org	703-780-3383		565
George Weston Ltd 22 St Clair Ave E . . . . Toronto ON M4T2S7 *TSE:* WN ■ *Web:* www.weston.ca	416-922-2500	922-4395	360-3
George Wyth State Park 3659 Wyth Rd . . . . Waterloo IA 50703 *Web:* www.iowadnr.gov	319-232-5505		565
George's Greek Cafe 5316 E Second St . . . . Long Beach CA 90803 *Web:* www.georgesgreekcafe.com	562-433-1755		671
George, Miles & Buhr LLC 206 W Main St . . . . Salisbury MD 21801 *TF:* 800-789-4462 ■ *Web:* www.gmbnet.com	410-742-3115		261
Georges Inc 402 W Robinson Ave . . . . Springdale AR 72764 *TF:* 800-800-2449 ■ *Web:* georgesinc.com	479-927-7000		619
Georges Music Inc 912 Third St S . . . . Jacksonville Beach FL 32250 *TF:* 800-544-7625 ■ *Web:* www.georgesmusic.com	904-270-2220	270-2215	526
Georgeson Securities Corp 480 Washington Blvd . . . . Jersey City NJ 07310 *TF:* 800-428-0717 ■ *Web:* www.georgeson.com	800-428-0717		690
Georgetown Animal Clinic PC 5155 Sheridan Dr . . . . Williamsville NY 14221 *Web:* georgetownanimalclinic.com	716-633-7123		794
Georgetown Chamber of Commerce 1 Chamber Wy . . . . Georgetown TX 78626 *Web:* georgetownchamber.org	512-930-3535	930-3587	139
Georgetown College 400 E College St . . . . Georgetown KY 40324 *TF:* 800-788-9985 ■ *Web:* www.georgetowncollege.edu	502-863-8000		166
Georgetown Convention & Visitors Bureau 1101 N College St . . . . Georgetown TX 78626 *TF:* 800-436-8696 ■ *Web:* www.georgetown.org	512-930-3545		206
Georgetown County 129 Screven St PO Box 421270 . . . . Georgetown SC 29442 *TF:* 800-868-2284 ■ *Web:* www.georgetowncountysc.org	843-545-3063	545-3292	338
Georgetown County Chamber of Commerce 531 Front St . . . . Georgetown SC 29440 *TF:* 800-777-7705 ■ *Web:* www.visitgeorge.com	843-546-8436	520-4876	139
Georgetown Heritage Society (GHS) 811 S Main St . . . . Georgetown TX 78626 *Web:* georgetownheritagesociety.org	512-869-8597		637-2
Georgetown Inn 1310 Wisconsin Ave . . . . Washington DC 20007 *Web:* www.georgetowninn.com	202-333-8900	333-8308	379
Georgetown Preparatory School 10900 Rockville Pk . . . . North Bethesda MD 20852 *Web:* www.gprep.org	301-493-5000		622
Georgetown Rail Equipment Co 111 Cooperative Way Ste 100 . . . . Georgetown TX 78626 *Web:* georgetownrail.com	512-869-1542	863-0405	770
Georgetown Times 615 Front St . . . . Georgetown SC 29440 *Web:* www.georgetowntimesprinting.com	843-546-4148	264-5511	532-4
Georgetown Township Library 1525 Baldwin St . . . . Jenison MI 49428 *Web:* www.georgetown-mi.gov	616-457-9620	457-3670	434-3
Georgetown University 37th & 'O' Sts NW . . . . Washington DC 20057 *Web:* www.georgetown.edu	202-687-0100	687-5084	166
Georgetown University Hotel & Conference Ctr 3800 Reservoir Rd NW . . . . Washington DC 20057 *Web:* www.acc-guhotelandconferencecenter.com	202-687-3200	687-3297	377
Georgetown University Law Ctr 600 New Jersey Ave NW . . . . Washington DC 20001 *Web:* www.law.georgetown.edu	202-662-9000	662-9439	167-1
Georgetown-Scott County Chamber of Commerce 160 E Main St . . . . Georgetown KY 40324 *Web:* gtown.org	502-863-5424	863-5756	139
Georgia			
Aging Services Div 2 Peachtree St NW 33rd Fl . . . . Atlanta GA 30303 *TF:* 866-552-4464 ■ *Web:* aging.georgia.gov	404-657-5258	657-5285	339-11
Agriculture Dept 5450 Lemoyne Dr SW . . . . Atlanta GA 30334 *Web:* www.agr.state.ga.us	404-656-3627		339-11
Attorney General 40 Capitol Sq SW . . . . Atlanta GA 30334 *Web:* georgia.gov	404-656-3300	657-8733	339-11
Bill Status 309 State Capitol . . . . Atlanta GA 30334 *Web:* www.house.ga.gov	404-656-5015		433
Community Affairs Dept 60 Executive Pk S NE . . . . Atlanta GA 30329 *TF:* 800-359-4663 ■ *Web:* www.dca.ga.gov	404-679-4940		339-11
Composite Medical Board 2 Peachtree St NW 36th Fl . . . . Atlanta GA 30303 *Web:* medicalboard.georgia.gov	404-656-3913	656-9723	339-11
Corrections Dept 300 Patrol Rd . . . . Forsyth GA 31029 *TF:* 888-343-5627 ■ *Web:* www.dcor.state.ga.us	404-656-4661		339-11
Department of Behavioural Health & Developmental Disabilities 2 Peachtree St NW 24th Fl . . . . Atlanta GA 30303 *Web:* dbhdd.georgia.gov	404-657-2252		339-11
Department of Driver Services 2206 E View Pkwy . . . . Conyers GA 30013 *Web:* dds.georgia.gov	678-413-8400		339-11
Department of Labor 148 Andrew Young International Blvd NE . . . . Atlanta GA 30303 *Web:* dol.georgia.gov	404-232-3515		259
Division of Child Support Services 2 Peachtree St NW 20th Fl . . . . Atlanta GA 30303 *TF:* 844-694-2347 ■ *Web:* childsupport.georgia.gov	844-694-2347		339-11
Economic Development Dept 75 Fifth St NW Ste 845 . . . . Atlanta GA 30308 *TF:* 800-255-0056 ■ *Web:* www.georgia.org	404-962-4005		339-11
Environmental Protection Div 2 Martin Luther King Jr Dr Ste 1456 E Tower . . . . Atlanta GA 30334 *TF:* 888-373-5947 ■ *Web:* epd.georgia.gov	404-657-5947		339-11
Family & Children Services Div 2 Peachtree St NW 19 Fl . . . . Atlanta GA 30303 *Web:* dfcs.georgia.gov	404-657-8409	657-5105	339-11
Governor 203 State Capitol 206 Washington St . . . . Atlanta GA 30334 *Web:* gov.georgia.gov	404-657-7332		339-11
Governor's Office of Consumer Protection 2 ML King Jr Dr Ste 356 . . . . Atlanta GA 30334 **Fax Area Code:* 404 ■ *TF:* 800-869-1123 ■ *Web:* consumer.georgia.gov	800-869-1123	651-9018*	339-11
Historic Preservation Div 2610 GA Hwy 155 SW . . . . Atlanta GA 30329 *Web:* georgiashpo.org	404-656-2840		339-11
Human Resources Dept 2 Peachtree St NW Ste 27 . . . . Atlanta GA 30303 *Web:* dhs.georgia.gov	404-656-6750	651-8669	339-11
Insurance Commissioner 2 Martin Luther King Jr Dr W Tower Ste 704 . . . . Atlanta GA 30334 *TF:* 800-656-2298 ■ *Web:* www.oci.ga.gov	404-656-2070		339-11
Labor Dept 148 Andrew Young International Blvd NE . . . . Atlanta GA 30303 *Web:* www.dol.state.ga.us	404-232-7300		339-11
Lieutenant Governor 240 State Capitol . . . . Atlanta GA 30334 *Web:* ltgov.georgia.gov	404-656-5030	656-6739	339-11
Natural Resources Dept 2 ML King Jr Dr SE Ste 1252E . . . . Atlanta GA 30334 *TF:* 800-366-2661 ■ *Web:* gadnr.org	404-656-3500	656-0770	339-11
Ports Authority 2 Main St . . . . Savannah GA 31402 *TF:* 800-342-8012 ■ *Web:* www.gaports.com	912-964-3811		618
Professional Licensing Boards Div 237 Coliseum Dr . . . . Macon GA 31217 *Web:* www.sos.ga.gov	478-207-2440		339-11
Public Health Div 2 Peachtree St NW 15th Fl . . . . Atlanta GA 30303 *Web:* dph.georgia.gov	404-657-2700		339-11
Rehabilitation Services Div 1718 Peachtree St NW Ste 376 S . . . . Atlanta GA 30309 *TF:* 844-367-4872 ■ *Web:* gvs.georgia.gov	404-206-6000		339-11
Revenue Dept PO Box 105006 . . . . Atlanta GA 30345 *TF:* 877-423-6711 ■ *Web:* www.etax.dor.ga.gov	404-417-6760		339-11
Secretary of State 214 State Capitol . . . . Atlanta GA 30334 *Web:* georgia.gov	470-240-5060		339-11
Securities & Business Regulation Div 2 Martin Luther King Jr Dr SE W Tower Ste 820 . . . . Atlanta GA 30334 *TF:* 844-753-7825 ■ *Web:* sos.ga.gov	844-753-7825		339-11
State Government Information 7 Martin Luther King Jr Dr Ste 643 . . . . Atlanta GA 30334 *Web:* georgia.gov	404-656-6996		339-11
State Patrol PO Box 1456 . . . . Atlanta GA 30371 *TF:* 888-409-2001 ■ *Web:* dps.georgia.gov	404-624-7000		339-11

				Phone	Fax	Class
udent Finance Commission 2082 E Exchange Pl TF: 800-505-4732 ■ Web: gsfc.georgia.gov	Tucker	GA	30084	770-724-9000		725
preme Court 244 Washington St SW Rm 572 Web: www.gasupreme.us	Atlanta	GA	30334	404-656-3470	656-2253	339-11
ansparency & Campaign Finance Commission 200 Piedmont Ave SE Ste 1416 W Tower TF: 866-589-7327 ■ Web: ethics.ga.gov	Atlanta	GA	30334	404-463-1980	463-1988	265
eterans Service Dept Floyd Veterans Memorial Bldg Ste 970E Web: veterans.georgia.gov	Atlanta	GA	30334	404-656-2300	657-9738	339-11
ital Records Office 2600 Skyland Dr NE Web: dph.georgia.gov	Atlanta	GA	30319	404-679-4702		339-11
Wildlife Resources Div 2070 US Hwy 278 SE Web: georgiawildlife.com	Social Circle	GA	30025	770-918-6400		339-11
Workers' Compensation Board 270 Peachtree St NW Web: sbwc.georgia.gov	Atlanta	GA	30303	404-656-2048		339-11
orgia Aquarium 225 Baker St Web: www.georgiaaquarium.org	Atlanta	GA	30313	404-581-4000		40
orgia Association of Realtors 5065 Barfield Rd TF: 866-280-0576 ■ Web: www.garealtor.com	Atlanta	GA	30328	770-451-1831	458-6992	656
orgia Avenue Rock Creek East Family Support Collaborative 1104 Allison St NW Web: gafsc-dc.org	Washington	DC	20011	202-722-1815		533
eorgia Ballet 1255 Field Pkwy Web: www.georgiaballet.org	Marietta	GA	30066	770-528-0881		573-1
eorgia Boot Inc 39 E Canal St TF: 866-442-4908 ■ Web: www.georgiaboot.com	Nelsonville	OH	45764	866-442-4908		301
eorgia Cancer Specialists Pc (GCS) 1835 Savoy Dr TF: 800-491-5991 ■ Web: www.gacancer.com	Atlanta	GA	30341	770-496-9400	496-9490	374-7
eorgia Career Institute 900 Flat Shoals Rd SE TF: 877-222-6306 ■ Web: www.gci.edu	Conyers	GA	30094	770-922-7653		167-3
eorgia Chamber of Commerce 270 Peachtree St NW TF: 800-241-2286 ■ Web: www.gachamber.com	Atlanta	GA	30303	404-223-2264	223-2290	140
eorgia College & State University 231 W Hancock St TF: 800-342-0471 ■ Web: www.gcsu.edu	Milledgeville	GA	31061	478-445-5004	445-3653	166
Georgia Correctional Industries 2984 Clifton Springs Rd TF: 800-282-7130 ■ Web: www.gci-ga.com	Decatur	GA	30034	404-244-5100	244-5141	630
Georgia Crown Distributing Co 100 Georgia Crown Dr TF: 800-342-2350 ■ Web: www.georgiacrown.com	McDonough	GA	30253	770-302-3000		81-3
Georgia Cu Affiliates 6705 Sugarloaf Pkwy Ste 200 TF: 800-768-4282 ■ Web: gcua.org	Duluth	GA	30097	770-476-9625		219
Georgia Cycle Sport (GCS) 1029 Baxter St Web: www.georgiacyclesport.com	Athens	GA	30606	706-549-2453		711
Georgia Dental Assn 7000 Peachtree Dnwdy Rd NE Ste 200 Bldg 17 TF: 800-432-4357 ■ Web: www.gadental.org	Atlanta	GA	30328	404-636-7553	633-3943	227
Georgia Department of Education *Education Dept* 205 Jesse Hill Jr Dr SE TF: 800-311-3627 ■ Web: www.gadoe.org	Atlanta	GA	30334	404-656-2800	651-8737	339-11
Georgia department of natural resources *Fort King George State Historic Site Darien* 302 McIntosh Rd SE Web: www.gastateparks.org	Darien	GA	31305	912-437-4770		565
Georgia Emergency Management 935 E Confederate Ave SE PO Box 18055 TF: 800-879-4362 ■ Web: gema.georgia.gov	Atlanta	GA	30316	404-635-7000		339-11
Georgia Farm Bureau News 1620 Bass Rd TF: 800-342-1192 ■ Web: www.gfb.org	Macon	GA	31210	478-474-8411		457-1
Georgia Federation of Teachers 4 Executive Pk East NE Ste 120 Web: aft.org	Atlanta	GA	30329	404-315-0222		414
Georgia Flooring Outlet 1660 Hwy 155 S Web: www.georgiaflooringoutlet.com	Mcdonough	GA	30253	770-474-9270		361
Georgia Grille 2290 Peachtree Rd Web: www.georgiagrille.com	Atlanta	GA	30309	404-352-3517		671
Georgia Hardy Tours 20 Eglinton Ave E TF: 800-813-4509 ■ Web: www.ghardytours.com	Toronto	ON	M4R1K8	416-483-7533		772
Georgia Highlands College *Floyd* 3175 Cedartown Hwy TF: 800-332-2406 ■ Web: www.highlands.edu	Rome	GA	30161	706-802-5000	295-6341	162
Georgia Institute of Technology 225 N Ave NW Web: www.gatech.edu	Atlanta	GA	30332	404-894-7412	894-9511	166
Georgia Institute of Technology Library 266 Fourth St NW TF: 888-225-7804 ■ Web: www.library.gatech.edu	Atlanta	GA	30332	404-894-4500	894-0399	434-6
Georgia International Convention Ctr 2000 Convention Ctr Concourse Web: www.gicc.com	College Park	GA	30337	770-997-3566	994-8559	205
Georgia Lottery Corp 250 Williams St NW Ste 3000 TF: 800-425-8259 ■ Web: www.galottery.com	Atlanta	GA	30303	404-215-5000		452
Georgia McBride Media Group 4208 6 Forks Rd Ste 1000 Web: www.georgiamcbride.com	Raleigh	NC	27609	919-645-5786		637-2
Georgia Military College 201 E Green St TF: 800-342-0413 ■ Web: www.gmc.edu	Milledgeville	GA	31061	478-387-4900	445-6520	162
Georgia Mountains Ctr 301 Main St SW PO Box 2496 Web: www.gainesville.org	Gainesville	GA	30501	770-534-8420		205
Georgia Municipal Assn 201 Pryor St SW TF: 888-488-4462 ■ Web: www.gacitics.com	Atlanta	GA	30303	404-688-0472		533
Georgia Museum of Art 90 Carlton St Web: georgiamuseum.org	Athens	GA	30602	706-542-4662		520
Georgia Northwestern Technical College Foundation Inc 1 Maurice Culberson Dr SW TF: 866-983-4682 ■ Web: www.gntc.edu	Rome	GA	30161	706-295-6842		305
Georgia Nurses Assn (GNA) 3032 Briarcliff Rd NE TF: 800-324-0462 ■ Web: georgianurses.nursingnetwork.com	Atlanta	GA	30329	404-325-5536	325-0407	533
Georgia O'Keeffe Museum 217 Johnson St Web: www.okeeffemuseum.org	Santa Fe	NM	87501	505-946-1000		520
Georgia Perimeter College *Dunwoody Campus* 2101 Womack Rd Web: perimeter.gsu.edu	Dunwoody	GA	30338	770-274-5000		162
Georgia Pharmacy Assn (GPHA) 50 Lenox Pointe NE TF: 888-871-5590 ■ Web: www.gpha.org	Atlanta	GA	30324	404-231-5074	237-8435	585
Georgia Piedmont Technical College 495 N Indian Creek Dr Web: www.gptc.edu	Clarkston	GA	30021	404-297-9522	298-3617	167-3
Georgia Poultry Improvement Assn 3235 Abit Massey Way Web: www.gapoultrylab.org	Gainesville	GA	30501	770-766-6810		138
Georgia Press Assn (GPA) 3066 Mercer University Dr Ste 200 Web: www.gapress.org	Atlanta	GA	30341	770-454-6776	454-6778	139
Georgia Printco 90 S Oak St TF: 866-572-0146 ■ Web: www.georgiaprintco.com	Lakeland	GA	31635	866-572-0146		627
Georgia Public Broadcasting (GPB) 260 14th St NW TF: 800-222-6006 ■ Web: www.gpb.org	Atlanta	GA	30318	800-222-6006		632
Georgia Public Interest Research Group (PIRG) 108 E Ponce de Leon Ave Ste 210 Web: www.georgiapirg.org	Decatur	GA	30030	404-370-1762		633
Georgia Public Library 1800 Century Pl NE Ste 150 TF: 800-248-6701 ■ Web: www.georgialibraries.org	Atlanta	GA	30345	404-235-7200		31
Georgia Public Service Commission 244 Washington St SW TF: 800-282-5813 ■ Web: psc.ga.gov	Atlanta	GA	30334	404-656-4501	656-2341	339-11
Georgia Regional Hospital at Atlanta 3073 Panthersville Rd Web: dbhdd.georgia.gov	Decatur	GA	30034	404-243-2100		374-5
Georgia Regional Hospital at Savannah 1915 Eisenhower Dr Web: www.dbhdd.georgia.gov	Savannah	GA	31406	912-356-2011	356-2691	374-5
Georgia Republican Party 3110 Maple Dr Web: gagop.org	Atlanta	GA	30305	404-257-5559	257-0779	616-2
Georgia Review, The The University of Georgia 706A Main Library 320 S Jackson St TF: 800-542-3481 ■ Web: thegeorgiareview.com	Athens	GA	30602	706-542-3481	542-0047	637-9
Georgia Society of CPAS 6 Concourse Pkwy Ste 800 TF: 800-330-8889 ■ Web: www.gscpa.org	Atlanta	GA	30328	404-231-8676		138
Georgia Southern University 11935 Abercorn St Web: www.georgiasouthern.edu	Savannah	GA	31419	912-344-2576		166
Georgia Southwestern State University 800 Gsw State University Dr TF: 800-338-0082 ■ Web: www.gsw.edu	Americus	GA	31709	229-928-1273	931-2983	166
Georgia Sports Hall of Fame 301 Cherry St PO Box 4644 Web: www.georgiasportshalloffame.com	Macon	GA	31201	478-752-1585	752-1587	522
Georgia State Parks & Historic Sites 2600 Hwy 155 SW TF: 800-864-7275 ■ Web: www.gastateparks.org	Stockbridge	GA	30281	800-864-7275		565
Georgia State Prison 1978 Georgia Hwy 147 Web: www.dcor.state.ga.us	Reidsville	GA	30453	912-557-7771	557-7163	213
Georgia State University College of Law 140 Decatur St Web: law.gsu.edu	Atlanta	GA	30303	404-413-9155		167-1
Georgia Straight 1701 W Broadway Web: www.straight.com	Vancouver	BC	V6J1Y3	604-730-7000	730-7010	532-5
Georgia Tech *Information Technology Office* 177 North Ave Web: www.oit.gatech.edu	Atlanta	GA	30332	404-894-7173		339-11
Georgia Tech Fusion Research Ctr Boggs Bldg Rm 3-15 Web: frc.gatech.edu	Atlanta	GA	30332	404-894-3714		668
Georgia Tech Research Institute (GTRI) *Georgia Institute of Technology* 250 14th St NW Web: gtri.gatech.edu	Atlanta	GA	30318	404-407-7400		668
Georgia Timberlands Inc 3250 Waterville Rd Web: gatimberlands.com	Macon	GA	31206	478-788-4660		302
Georgia Trust, The 1516 Peachtree St NW Web: www.georgiatrust.org	Atlanta	GA	30309	404-881-9980	875-2205	50-3
Georgia Veterans State Park 2459 US 280 W Web: gastateparks.org	Cordele	GA	31015	229-276-2371		565
Georgia Veterinary Medical Assn 2200 Century Pkwy Ste 725 TF: 800-853-1625 ■ Web: www.gvma.net	Atlanta	GA	30345	678-309-9800	309-3361	795
Georgia Winery, The 6469 Battlefield Pkwy Web: www.georgiawines.com	Ringgold	GA	30736	706-937-9463	937-9860	50-7
Georgia World Congress Ctr 285 Andrew Young International Blvd NW Web: www.gwcca.org	Atlanta	GA	30313	404-223-4200	223-4211	205
Georgia's Greek Cuisine 3550 Rosecrans St Web: www.georgiasgreekcuisine.com	San Diego	CA	92110	619-523-1007	523-2455	671

Phone | Fax | Class

Georgia's Own Credit Union
1155 Peachtree St NE Ste 600 — Atlanta GA 30309 — 800-533-2062 — 881-2950* — 219
*Fax Area Code: 404 ■ TF: 800-533-2062 ■ Web: www.georgiasown.org

Georgia-Carolina Radiocasting Companies LLC
233 Big A Rd — Toccoa GA 30577 — 706-297-7264 — 643
Web: www.gacaradio.com

Georgian College 1 Georgian Dr — Barrie ON L4M3X9 — 705-728-1968 — 179
Web: www.georgiancollege.ca

Georgian Court Hotel 773 Beatty St — Vancouver BC V6B2M4 — 604-682-5555 — 682-8830 — 379
TF: 800-663-1155 ■ Web: www.georgiancourthotelvancouver.com

Georgian Court University
900 Lakewood Ave — Lakewood NJ 08701 — 800-458-8422 — 987-2000* — 166
*Fax Area Code: 732 ■ TF: 800-458-8422 ■ Web: georgian.edu

Georgian Hotel, The
1415 Ocean Ave — Santa Monica CA 90401 — 800-538-8147 — 379
TF: 800-538-8147 ■ Web: www.georgianhotel.com

Georgian Partners
2 St Clair Ave W Ste 1400 — Toronto ON M4V1L5 — 416-868-9696 — 401
Web: georgianpartners.com

Georgian Resort 384 Canada St — Lake George NY 12845 — 518-668-5401 — 668-5870 — 379
TF: 800-525-3436 ■ Web: www.georgianresort.com

Georgian Terrace Hotel
659 Peachtree St NE — Atlanta GA 30308 — 404-897-1991 — 379
TF: 800-651-2316 ■ Web: www.thegeorgianterrace.com

Georgia-Pacific Corp
133 Peachtree St NE — Atlanta GA 30303 — 404-652-4000 — 558
Web: www.gp.com

Georgia-Pacific LLC
2 Jericho Plz Ste 110 — Jericho NY 11753 — 516-997-3400 — 661
Web: www.gapacrecycling.com

Georgie's Ceramic & Clay Company Inc
756 NE Lombard St — Portland OR 97211 — 503-283-1353 — 283-1387 — 43
TF: 800-999-2529 ■ Web: www.georgies.com

Georgio's Cafe Intl 426 N Superior St — Toledo OH 43604 — 419-242-2424 — 671
Web: www.georgiostoledo.com

Georgio's Fine Food & Spirits
2971 Apalachee Pkwy — Tallahassee FL 32301 — 850-877-3211 — 671
Web: georgiostallahassee.com

Geoscience Publications (GP)
227 Howe-Russell Bldg — Baton Rouge LA 70893 — 225-578-5942 — 578-4420 — 637-2
Web: ga.lsu.edu

Geo-slope International Ltd
633 6 Ave SW Ste 1400 — Calgary AB T2P2Y5 — 403-269-2002 — 261
Web: www.geoslope.com

Geo-Solutions 1250 Fifth Ave — New Kensington PA 15068 — 412-856-7700 — 373-3357 — 189-5
TF: 800-544-6235 ■ Web: www.geo-solutions.com

Geospan Corp
6901 E Fish Lake Rd Ste 156 — Minneapolis MN 55369 — 763-493-9320 — 424-6633 — 225
TF: 800-436-7726 ■ Web: www.geospan.com

Geospatial Information & Technology Assn (GITA)
14456 E Evans Ave — Aurora CO 80014 — 303-337-0513 — 49-19
Web: www.gita.org

Geostruct Engineers Inc
2910 Austin Bluffs Pkwy — Colorado Springs CO 80918 — 719-548-0600 — 261
Web: rmg-engineers.com

GeoSyntec Consultants Inc
900 Broken Sound Pkwy NW Ste 200 — Boca Raton FL 33487 — 561-995-0900 — 995-0925 — 261
TF: 866-676-1101 ■ Web: www.geosyntec.com

Geo-Synthetics Inc (GSI)
2401 Pewaukee Rd — Waukesha WI 53188 — 262-524-7979 — 524-7961 — 192
TF: 800-444-5523 ■ Web: www.geo-synthetics.com

GEOSYS Inc 3030 Harbor Ln — Plymouth MN 55447 — 866-782-4661 — 194
TF: 866-782-4661 ■ Web: www.urthecast.com

Geotab Inc 1081 S Service Rd W — Oakville ON L6L6K3 — 416-434-4309 — 387
TF: 877-436-8221 ■ Web: www.geotab.com

Geotech Environmental Equipment Inc
2650 E 40th Ave — Denver CO 80205 — 303-320-4764 — 322-7242 — 201
TF: 800-833-7958 ■ Web: www.geotechenv.com

Geotech Ltd 245 Industrial Pkwy N — Aurora ON L4G4C4 — 905-841-5004 — 727
Web: geotech.ca

Geotechnologies Inc
3200 Wellington Ct Ste 108 — Raleigh NC 27615 — 919-954-1514 — 954-1428 — 261
Web: www.geotechpa.com

Geotek Engineering & Testing Services Inc
909 E 50th St N — Sioux Falls SD 57104 — 605-335-5512 — 256
TF: 800-354-5512 ■ Web: www.geotekeng.com

Geotest - Marvin Test Systems Inc
1770 Kettering — Irvine CA 92614 — 949-263-2222 — 201
Web: marvintest.com

Geotest Engineering Inc
5600 Bintliff Dr — Houston TX 77036 — 713-266-0588 — 266-2977 — 261
Web: geotesteng.com

GeoTrust Inc 350 Ellis St Bldg J — Mountain View CA 94043 — 650-426-5010 — 237-8871 — 178-7
TF: 866-511-4141 ■ Web: www.geotrust.com

GeoVax Inc 1900 Lake Park Dr Ste 380 — Smyrna GA 30080 — 678-384-7220 — 384-7281 — 85
Web: www.geovax.com

GeoVera Holdings Inc 1455 Oliver Rd — Fairfield CA 94534 — 707-863-3700 — 391-6
Web: www.geoveraholdingsinc.com

GEP (Gifted Education Press)
10201 Yuma Ct — Manassas VA 20108 — 703-369-5017 — 637-2
Web: www.giftededpress.com

Gerace Construction Company Inc
4055 S Saginaw Rd — Midland MI 48640 — 989-496-2440 — 496-2465 — 186
Web: www.geraceconstruction.com

Geraghty & Bonnano LLC
38 Granite St — New London CT 06320 — 860-447-8077 — 41
Web: geraghtybonnano.com

Geragos & Geragos PC
644 S Figueroa St — Los Angeles CA 90017 — 213-625-3900 — 625-1600 — 428
Web: www.geragos.com

Gerald A. Teel Co
974 Campbell Rd Ste 204 — Houston TX 77024 — 713-467-5858 — 467-0704 — 652
Web: www.valbridge.com

Gerald H. Phipps
5995 Greenwood Florida Plaza Blvd
Ste 100 — Greenwood Village CO 80111 — 303-571-5377 — 629-7467 — 186
TF: 877-574-4777 ■ Web: ghphipps.com

Phone | Fax | Cl.

Gerald M. Yaroslow
1875 Century Pk E Ste 1600 — Los Angeles CA 90067 — 424-274-2977 — 551-8189* — 41
*Fax Area Code: 310 ■ Web: geraldyaroslowlaw.com

Gerald Peters Gallery
1005 Paseo de Peralta — Santa Fe NM 87501 — 505-954-5700 — 954-5754 — 637-
Web: www.gpgallery.com

Gerald Printing Service Inc
105 Hunter Ct — Bowling Green KY 42103 — 270-781-4770 — 627
Web: www.geraldprinting.com

Gerald R. Ford Conservation Ctr
1326 S 32nd St — Omaha NE 68105 — 402-595-1180 — 595-1178 — 50-2
TF: 800-634-6932 ■ Web: history.nebraska.gov

Gerald R. Ford International Airport
5500 44th St SE — Grand Rapids MI 49512 — 616-233-6000 — 233-6025 — 27
Web: www.grr.org

Gerald R. Ford Museum
303 Pearl St NW — Grand Rapids MI 49504 — 616-254-0400 — 254-0386 — 520
TF: 800-888-9487 ■ Web: www.fordlibrarymuseum.gov

Gerald R. Ford Presidential Library & Museum
1000 Beal Ave — Ann Arbor MI 48109 — 734-205-0555 — 434-3
Web: www.fordlibrarymuseum.gov

Geraldine R. Dodge Foundation
14 Maple Ave — Morristown NJ 07962 — 973-540-8442 — 540-1211 — 305
Web: www.grdodge.org

Geralds of Northville Inc
41012 Five Mile Rd — Plymouth MI 48170 — 734-420-0111 — 77
Web: geraldssalon.com

Gerard Daniel Worldwide
34 Barnhart Dr — Hanover PA 17331 — 717-637-5901 — 633-7095 — 688
TF: 800-232-3332 ■ Web: www.gerarddaniel.com

Gerard Design
28371 Davis Pkwy Ste 100 — Warrenville IL 60555 — 630-355-0775 — 355-0776 — 344
Web: www.gerardagency.com

Gerardi Construction Inc 1604 N 19th St — Tampa FL 33605 — 813-248-4341 — 248-4991 — 186
Web: www.gerardiconstruction.com

Gerardi Insurance Services Inc
16 Pomfret St — Putnam CT 06260 — 860-928-7771 — 390
Web: gerardionline.com

Gerber Akron Beauty School
1915 W Market St — Akron OH 44313 — 330-867-6200 — 867-9933 — 685
Web: www.akronbeautyschool.com

Gerber Childrenswear Inc
7005 Pelham Rd Ste D — Greenville SC 29615 — 877-313-2114 — 987-5264* — 155-4
*Fax Area Code: 864 ■ TF: 800-642-4452 ■ Web: www.gerberchildrenswear.com

Gerber Collision & Glass
400 W Grand Ave — Elmhurst IL 60126 — 847-679-0510 — 679-0549 — 62-4
TF: 877-743-7237 ■ Web: www.gerbercollision.com

Gerber Legendary Blades Inc
14200 SW 72nd Ave — Portland OR 97224 — 800-950-6161 — 222
TF: 800-950-6161 ■ Web: www.gerbergear.com

Gerber Life Insurance Co
1311 Mamaroneck Ave — White Plains NY 10605 — 914-272-4000 — 391-2
TF: 800-704-2180 ■ Web: www.gerberlife.com

Gerber Metal Supply Co
2 Boundary Rd — Somerville NJ 08876 — 908-823-9150 — 492
Web: www.gerbermetal.com

Gerber Plumbing Fixtures LLC
2500 International Pkwy — Woodridge IL 60517 — 630-679-1420 — 611
Web: www.gerberonline.com

Gerber Products Co 445 State St — Fremont MI 49413 — 800-284-9488 — 296-36
TF: 800-284-9488 ■ Web: www.gerber.com

Gerber Technology Inc
24 Industrial Park Rd W — Tolland CT 06084 — 860-871-8082 — 744
TF: 800-826-3243 ■ Web: www.gerbertechnology.com

Gerber Tours Inc
100 Crossways Park Dr W Ste 400 — Woodbury NY 11797 — 516-826-5000 — 760
TF: 800-645-9145 ■ Web: www.gerbertours.com

Gerber/Hart Library & Archives
6500 N Clark St — Chicago IL 60626 — 773-381-8030 — 434-3
Web: www.gerberhart.org

Gerdau 4221 W Boy Scout Blvd Ste 600 — Tampa FL 33607 — 813-286-8383 — 723
TF: 800-876-7833 ■ Web: www2.gerdau.com

Gerflor Group 595 Supreme Dr — Bensenville IL 60106 — 877-437-3567 — 751
TF: 877-437-3567 ■ Web: www.gerflorusa.com

Gerhart Systems & Controls Corp
754 Roble Rd Ste 140 — Allentown PA 18109 — 610-264-2800 — 639
TF: 888-437-4278 ■ Web: www.gerhart.com

Geriatric Medical and Surgical Inc
28 Torrice Dr — Woburn MA 01801 — 800-442-1205 — 829-0506* — 475
*Fax Area Code: 866 ■ TF: 800-442-1205 ■ Web: www.geriatricmedical.com

Gerken Capital Assoc
110 Tiburon Blvd Ste 5 — Mill Valley CA 94941 — 415-383-1464 — 383-1253 — 194
Web: gerkencapital.com

Gerling & Associates Inc
138 Stelzer Ct — Sunbury OH 43074 — 740-965-2888 — 779
Web: www.gerlinggroup.com

Gerlinger Foundry & Machine Works Inc
1527 Sacramento St — Redding CA 96001 — 530-243-1053 — 480
Web: gerlinger.com

Gerloff Company Inc
14955 Bulverde Rd — San Antonio TX 78247 — 210-490-2777 — 494-0610 — 186
TF: 800-486-3621 ■ Web: www.gerloffinc.com

Germain Motor Co
Mercedes-Benz of Easton
4300 Morse Crossing — Columbus OH 43219 — 855-217-5986 — 57
TF: 855-217-5986 ■ Web: www.germain.com

German Academic Exchange Service (DAAD)
871 United Nations Plz — New York NY 10017 — 212-758-3223 — 755-5780 — 48-11
Web: www.daad.org

German American Bancorp 711 Main St — Jasper IN 47546 — 812-482-1314 — 482-0758 — 360-2
NASDAQ: GABC ■ TF: 800-482-1314 ■ Web: www.germanamerican.com

German Flatts Veterinary Clinic PC
2717 SR-51 — Ilion NY 13357 — 315-894-9923 — 794
Web: germanflattsveterinaryclinic.com

German Gallagher & Murtagh PC
200 S Broad St Ste 500 — Philadelphia PA 19102 — 215-545-7700 — 41
Web: ggmfirm.com

				Phone	Fax	Class
an Language Services LLC						
52 41st Ave SW Ste B	Seattle	WA	98116	206-938-3600	938-8308	768
b: germanlanguageservices.com						
an Language Video Ctr						
25 Pendleton Pke	Indianapolis	IN	46226	317-547-1257	547-1263	525
eb: www.germanvideo.com						
an Marshall Fund of the United States						
44 R St NW	Washington	DC	20009	202-745-3950	265-1662	784
eb: www.gmfus.org						
man May Pc 1201 Walnut Ste 2000	Kansas City	MO	64106	816-471-7700	471-2221	41
F: 888-471-2221 ■ Web: gmlawpc.com						
man National Tourist Office						
22 E 42nd St Ste 2000	New York	NY	10168	212-661-7200		775
eb: www.germany.travel						
rman Village 588 S Third St	Columbus	OH	43215	614-221-8888	222-4747	50-3
Web: germanvillage.com						
man-American Chamber of Commerce Inc						
0 Pine St 24th Fl	New York	NY	10005	212-974-8830	974-8867	138
Web: www.gaccny.com						
rman-American Chamber of Commerce Inc - Philadelphia (GACCPHL)						
1635 Market St Ste 1600	Philadelphia	PA	19103	215-501-7102	968-0973	138
Web: www.gaccphiladelphia.com						
rman-American Chamber of Commerce of the Midwest Inc						
321 N Clark St Ste 1425	Chicago	IL	60654	312-644-2662	644-0738	138
Web: www.gaccmidwest.org						
erman-American Chamber of Commerce of the Southern US Inc						
1170 Howell Mill Rd Ste 300	Atlanta	GA	30318	404-586-6800	586-6820	138
Web: www.gaccsouth.com						
erman-American National Congress						
4740 N W Ave Ste 206	Chicago	IL	60625	312-263-0472	275-4010*	48-14
*Fax Area Code: 773 ■ Web: www.dank.org						
erman-Bliss Equipment Inc						
624 W Spring St	Princeville	IL	61559	309-385-4316	385-2540	274
TF: 800-728-4734 ■ Web: www.germanbliss.com						
ermanDeli.com						
7561 Center Ave Ste 49a	Huntington Beach	CA	92647	817-410-9955		345
TF: 877-437-6269 ■ Web: germandeli.com						
ermania Farm Mutual Insurance Assn						
507 Hwy 290 E	Brenham	TX	77833	979-836-5224	836-1977	391-4
TF: 800-392-2202 ■ Web: www.germaniainsurance.com						
Germanna Community College						
Fredericksburg						
10000 Germanna Pt Dr	Fredericksburg	VA	22408	540-891-3000	710-2092	162
Web: www.germanna.edu						
Germantown Area Chamber of Commerce						
2195 S Germantown Rd	Germantown	TN	38138	901-755-1200	755-9168	139
Web: www.germantownchamber.com						
Germantown Community Library						
N112 W16957 Mequon Rd	Germantown	WI	53022	262-253-7760	253-7763	434-3
Web: germantownlibrarywi.org						
Germantown Performing Arts Ctr (GPAC)						
1801 Exeter Rd	Germantown	TN	38138	901-751-7500		572
Web: www.gpacweb.com						
Germantown Trust and Savings Bank						
601 Main St	Germantown	IL	62245	618-523-4202	526-8202	70
Web: www.gtsb.com						
Germany						
Consulate General						
100 Biscayne Blvd Ste 2200	Miami	FL	33132	305-358-0290		257
Web: www.germany.info						
Consulate General						
1330 Post Oak Blvd Ste 1850	Houston	TX	77056	713-627-7770	627-0506	257
Web: www.germany.info						
Consulate General						
1960 Jackson St	San Francisco	CA	94109	415-775-1061	775-0187	257
Web: www.germany.info						
Consulate General						
676 N Michigan Ave Ste 3200	Chicago	IL	60611	312-202-0480	202-0466	257
Web: www.germany.info						
Consulate General						
285 Peachtree Center Ave NE Ste 901	Atlanta	GA	30303	404-659-4760	659-1280	257
Web: www.germany.info						
Consulate General						
6222 Wilshire Blvd Ste 500	Los Angeles	CA	90048	323-930-2703	930-2805	257
Web: germany.info						
Consulate General 871 UN Plz	New York	NY	10017	212-610-9700	610-9702	257
Web: www.germany.info						
Embassy 4645 Reservoir Rd NW	Washington	DC	20007	202-298-4000		257
Web: www.germany.info						
Germer Gertz LLP 550 Fannin Ste 400	Beaumont	TX	77701	409-654-6700		428
Web: www.germer.com						
Germfree Laboratories Inc						
11 Aviator Way	Ormond Beach	FL	32174	800-888-5357	677-1114*	476
*Fax Area Code: 386 ■ TF: 800-888-5357 ■ Web: www.germfree.com						
Germiphene Corp 1379 Colborne St E	Brantford	ON	N3T5M1	800-265-9931	759-1625*	582
*Fax Area Code: 519 ■ TF: 800-265-9931 ■ Web: germiphene.com						
Gerome Manufacturing Company Inc						
80 Laurel View Dr	Smithfield	PA	15478	724-438-8544	437-5608	697
Web: www.geromemfg.com						
Geron Corp 149 Commonwealth Dr	Menlo Park	CA	94025	650-473-7700	473-7750	85
NASDAQ: GERN ■ Web: www.geron.com						
Geronimo 724 Canyon Rd	Santa Fe	NM	87501	505-982-1500		671
Web: www.geronimorestaurant.com						
Gerontological Society of America, The						
1220 L St NW Ste 901	Washington	DC	20005	202-842-1275		49-5
Web: www.geron.org						
Gerotech Inc 29220 Commerce Dr	Flat Rock	MI	48134	734-379-7788	379-2244	385
Web: gerotech.com						
Gerref Industries 206 N York St	Belding	MI	48809	616-794-3110		697
Web: www.gerref.com						
Gerresheimer Glass Inc						
537 Crystal Ave	Vineland	NJ	08360	856-692-3600		333
Web: www.gerresheimer.com						
Gerretsen Building Supply Co						
1900 NE Airport Rd	Roseburg	OR	97470	541-672-2636		191-3
Web: gerretsen.com						
Gerrish McCreary Smith PC						
700 Colonial Rd Ste 200	Memphis	TN	38117	901-767-0900	684-2339	428
Web: www.gerrish.com						
Gerrity Stone Inc 225 Merrimac St	Woburn	MA	01801	781-938-1820		191-1
Web: www.gerritystone.com						
Gerrity's Supermarket Inc						
100 Old Lackawanna Trl	Clarks Summit	PA	18411	570-587-3800		345
Web: gerritys.com						
Gerrus Maintenance Inc						
95 Northfield Ave	Edison	NJ	08837	732-225-0662	225-0807	104
Web: www.gerrus.com						
Gerry Abbott Incorporated Realtors						
43 N Main St	Mansfield	MA	02048	508-339-6336		652
Web: gerryabbott.com						
Gerry Cosby & Company Inc						
11 Pennsylvania Plz	New York	NY	10001	877-563-6464	967-0876*	711
*Fax Area Code: 212 ■ TF: 877-563-6464 ■ Web: www.cosbysports.com						
Gerry's Frankly Speaking Inc						
PO Box 2225	Salem	OR	97308	503-585-8411	585-1076	637-2
TF: 800-692-2665 ■ Web: newyorkcityguidebook.net						
Gersh Agency 9465 Wilshire Blvd	Beverly Hills	CA	90212	310-274-6611		731
Web: www.gersh.com						
Gershman, Brickner & Bratton Inc						
8550 Arlington Blvd Ste 304	Fairfax	VA	22031	703-573-5800		192
TF: 800-573-5801 ■ Web: gbbinc.com						
Gershow Recycling Corp						
71 Peconic Ave PO Box 526	Medford	NY	11763	631-289-6188	289-6368	686
Web: www.gershow.com						
Gerson Co 1450 S Lone Elm Rd	Olathe	KS	66061	913-262-7400	535-7592	411
TF: 800-444-8172 ■ Web: www.gersoncompany.com						
Gerspacher Real Estate Group						
5164 Normandy Park Dr Ste 285	Medina	OH	44256	330-722-5002	723-6330	652
Web: gerspachergroup.com						
Gerstein Science Information Ctr						
University of Toronto						
9 King's College Cir	Toronto	ON	M5S1A5	416-978-2280		434-1
Web: gerstein.library.utoronto.ca						
Gerstenblatt Law Offices Ltd						
100 Jefferson Blvd Ste 315	Warwick	RI	02888	401-738-3600		41
Web: jkglawri.com						
Gertrude Hawk Chocolates Inc						
9 Keystone Pk	Dunmore	PA	18512	570-342-7556		296-8
TF: 866-932-4295 ■ Web: www.gertrudehawkchocolates.com						
Gertrude Herbert Institute of Art						
506 Telfair St	Augusta	GA	30901	706-722-5495	722-3670	520
Web: ghia.org						
Gertrude's 10 Art Museum Dr	Baltimore	MD	21218	410-889-3399		671
Web: gertrudesbaltimore.com						
Gervais & Vine 620-A Gervais St	Columbia	SC	29201	803-799-8463		671
Web: www.gervaisandvine.com						
Gerzeny's Rv Nokomis						
2110 N Tamiami Trl	Nokomis	FL	34275	941-966-2182		57
TF: 800-262-2182 ■ Web: www.gerzenysrvworld.com						
GES 7000 Lindell Rd	Las Vegas	NV	89118	702-515-5500	515-5765	184
TF: 800-443-9767 ■ Web: www.ges.com						
GES (Groundwater & Environmental Services Inc)						
1599 Rte 34 Ste 1	Wall Township	NJ	07727	800-220-3068		192
TF: 800-220-3068 ■ Web: www.gesonline.com						
GES Global Energy Services Inc						
3220 Cypress Creek Pkwy	Houston	TX	77068	888-523-6797		190
TF: 888-523-6797 ■ Web: global-energy.ca						
Gesa Credit Union						
51 Gage Blvd PO Box 500	Richland	WA	99352	888-946-4372		219
TF: 888-946-4372 ■ Web: www.gesa.com						
Gessner Products Company Inc						
241 N Main St PO Box 389	Ambler	PA	19002	215-646-7667		608
TF: 800-874-7808 ■ Web: gessnerproducts.com						
Gestalt Therapy Page, The						
The Gestalt Journal Press PO Box 990	Highland	NY	12528	775-599-3950		637-9
Web: www.gestalt.org						
Get & Go Market 10950 Beech Daly Rd	Taylor	MI	48180	313-295-3434		297-8
GET Engineering Corp 9350 Bond Ave	El Cajon	CA	92021	619-443-8295	443-8613	203
TF: 877-494-1820 ■ Web: gethdio.com						
Get Found First LLC 45 N Broadway	Blackfoot	ID	83440	208-991-3463		5
Web: getfoundfirst.com						
Get Graphics Now 1223 N Cameron St	Harrisburg	PA	17103	717-233-2457	213-0621	344
TF: 866-213-4333 ■ Web: www.getgraphicsnow.com						
Get In Shape For Women						
1201 Highland Ave	Needham	MA	02494	781-444-4810		354
Web: www.getinshapeforwomen.com						
Get It LLC 128 N Pitt St Ste 2	Alexandria	VA	22314	877-285-7861		387
TF: 877-285-7861 ■ Web: get.it						
Get Noticed Promotions Inc						
233 Fillmore Ste 16	Tonawanda	NY	14225	716-688-8152		129
Web: getnoticedpromotions.com						
Get Real Health						
51 Monroe St Ste 1700	Rockville	MD	20850	301-309-0058	309-0037	177
Web: getrealhealth.com						
Getboards.com						
40905 Big Bear Blvd	Big Bear Lake	CA	92315	909-878-3155		711
Web: www.getboards.com						
Getchell Brothers Inc 1 Union St	Brewer	ME	04412	207-989-7335	989-7810	380
TF: 800-949-4423 ■ Web: www.getchellbros.com						
Getconnect 14114 Dallas Pkwy Ste 430	Dallas	TX	75254	888-200-1831		366
TF: 888-200-1831 ■ Web: www.getconnect.com						
Getinge USA Inc 1777 E Henrietta Rd	Rochester	NY	14623	800-475-9040		477
TF: 800-475-9040 ■ Web: www.getinge.com						
GetMeFriends 7801 Broadway St	San Antonio	TX	78209	888-663-9143		631
TF: 888-663-9143 ■ Web: www.getmefriends.com						
Gett Industries Ltd 7307 50th St	Milan	IL	61264	309-799-5131	799-5773	454
Web: gettindustries.com						
Gettel Automotive Group						
5959 E SR 64	Bradenton	FL	34208	941-417-5269		57
Web: www.gettel.com						
Getty Realty Corp						
2 Jericho Plz Ste 110	Jericho	NY	11753	516-478-5400		324
NYSE: GTY ■ Web: www.gettyrealty.com						
Gettysburg Battle Theatre						
778 Baltimore St	Gettysburg	PA	17325	717-334-6100		520
Web: www.gettysburgbattlefieldtours.com						

Name / Address	Phone	Fax	Class
Gettysburg College 300 N Washington St, Gettysburg PA 17325 *Fax Area Code: 717 ■ TF: 800-431-0803 ■ Web: www.gettysburg.edu	800-431-0803	337-6145*	166
Gettysburg Heritage Ctr 297 Steinwehr Ave, Gettysburg PA 17325 Web: www.gettysburgmuseum.com	717-334-6245		520
Gettysburg Hospital 147 Gettys St PO Box 3786, Gettysburg PA 17325 Web: wellspan.org	717-334-2121	334-1302	374-3
Gettysburg Hotel 1 Lincoln Sq, Gettysburg PA 17325 TF: 866-378-1797 ■ Web: www.hotelgettysburg.com	717-337-2000	337-2075	671
Gettysburg Times, The 1570 Fairfield Rd, Gettysburg PA 17325 Web: www.gettysburgtimes.com	717-334-1131	334-4243	532-2
Gettysburg-Adams Chamber of Commerce 1382 Biglerville Rd, Gettysburg PA 17325 Web: www.gettysburg-chamber.org	717-334-8151	334-3368	139
GetWell StayWell, America! PO Box 558, Concrete WA 98237 Web: www.getwellstaywellamerica.com	360-853-7048		637-2
GetWireless LLC 10901 Red Cir Dr, Minnetonka MN 55343 Web: www.getwirelessllc.com	952-890-6669		736
Getzel Schiff & Pesce 100 Crossways Pk W Ste 403, Woodbury NY 11797 Web: gspcpa.com	516-692-8500		2
Getzen Company Inc 530 S Cty Hwy H PO Box 440, Elkhorn WI 53121 TF: 800-366-5584 ■ Web: www.getzen.com	262-723-4221	723-4245	527
Getzschman Heating LLC 1700 E 23rd St, Fremont NE 68025 Web: www.getzschman.com	402-721-6301		189-10
Geum Services Inc PO Box 35, Richland MI 49083 Web: www.prairiesmoke.com	269-370-0984		196
Geutebruck USA Inc 537 N US Hwy 301 S, Tampa FL 33619 Web: www.geutebruckusa.com	813-586-1000	586-2000	693
Geva Theatre Ctr 75 Woodbury Blvd, Rochester NY 14607 Web: www.gevatheatre.org	585-232-4382	232-4031	573-4
Gevity Consulting Inc 375 Water St Ste 350, Vancouver BC V6B5C6 TF: 800-785-3303 ■ Web: gevityinc.com	604-608-1779		177
Gexco 3460 Vine St, Norco CA 92860 Web: gexcoenterprises.com	951-735-4951		710
Geygan & Geygan Ltd 8050 Hosbrook Rd Ste 107, Cincinnati OH 45236 Web: geygan.net	513-791-1673	791-1683	428
GF Goodman & Son Inc 2 Ivybrook Blvd, Ivyland PA 18974 TF: 800-458-8000 ■ Web: gfgoodman.com	215-672-8810	441-8949	455
GF Health Products Inc 2935 NE Pkwy, Atlanta GA 30360 *Fax Area Code: 800 ■ TF: 800-347-5678 ■ Web: www.grahamfield.com	770-447-1609	726-0601*	477
GF Machining Solutions 560 Bond St, Lincolnshire IL 60069 TF: 800-282-1336 ■ Web: www.gfms.com	847-913-5300	913-5340	455
GF Management Inc 1628 John F Kennedy Blvd 8 Penn Ctr 23rd Fl, Philadelphia PA 19103 Web: www.gfhotels.com	215-972-2222	972-2259	378
GF Piping Systems 3401 Aero Jet Ave, El Monte CA 91731 Web: www.gfps.com	626-571-2770	573-2057	201
GF Private Equity Group LLC 14929 Hwy 172 Ste 302, Ignacio CO 81137 TF: 866-304-0016 ■ Web: www.gfprivateequity.com	970-563-5000		670
GFG Instrumentation Inc 1194 Oak Vly Dr Ste 20, Ann Arbor MI 48108 TF: 800-959-0329 ■ Web: www.gfg-inc.com	734-769-0573		201
GFI Energy Ventures LLC 333 S Grand Ave 28 Fl, Los Angeles CA 90071 Web: www.oaktreecapital.com	213-830-6300	830-6293	792
GFI Genfare 800 Arthur Ave, Elk Grove Village IL 60007 Web: www.genfare.com	847-871-1231	593-1824	472
GFI Group Inc 55 Water St, New York NY 10041 Web: www.gfigroup.com	212-968-4100		690
GFJ (Goldfather's Jewelry Inc) 3230 E Flamingo Rd Ste 8-354, Las Vegas NV 89121 TF: 800-642-2545 ■ Web: www.goldfathers.com	702-891-8836	891-8837	411
GFK Custom Research Inc 8401 Golden Valley Rd, Minneapolis MN 55427 Web: www.gfk.com	763-542-0800		466
GFK Flight Support 2403 Air Cargo Dr, Grand Forks ND 58203 Web: www.flygfk.com	701-772-5504	772-8917	167-3
GFMCO (Goldens' Foundry & Machine Co) 600 12th St, Columbus GA 31902 Web: www.gfmco.com	706-323-0471		307
GFMD Ltd 22650 Heslip, Novi MI 48375 Web: gfmd.com	248-305-6113		668
GFOA (Government Finance Officers Assn) 203 N LaSalle St Ste 2700, Chicago IL 60601 Web: www.gfoa.org	312-977-9700	977-4806	49-7
G-Force Protective Services & Training Academy Inc 13800 SW 144 Ave Rd, Miami FL 33186 Web: www.gforcemiami.com	305-380-1212		260
GFP (Grail Foundation Press) 14318 Shirley Bohn Rd, Mount Airy MD 21771 TF: 800-427-9217 ■ Web: shop-grail.com	607-723-5163		637-2
GFRC Cladding Systems LLC 118 N Shiloh Rd, Garland TX 75042 Web: gfrccladding.com	972-494-9000	494-1900	183
GFS Building Maintenance Inc 20 Blaine St, Manchester NH 03102 Web: gfsservices.com	603-668-6612		104
GFWC (General Federation of Women's Clubs) 1734 N St NW, Washington DC 20036 TF: 800-443-4392 ■ Web: www.gfwc.org	202-347-3168	835-0246	48-24
GFX International Inc 333 Barron Blvd, Grayslake IL 60030 TF: 800-274-3225 ■ Web: www.gfxi.com	847-543-4600		687
GG Barnett Transport Inc W7530 County S, Juneau WI 53039 TF: 800-336-7249 ■ Web: www.ggbarnett.com	800-336-7249		700
GGB Industries Inc PO Box 10958, Naples FL 34101 Web: www.ggb.com	239-643-4400	643-4403	248
GGB North America 700 Mid Atlantic Pkwy PO Box 189, Thorofare NJ 08086 Web: www.ggbearings.com	856-848-3200	848-5115	620
GGBTS (Golden Gate Baptist Theological Seminary) 201 Seminary Dr, Mill Valley CA 94941 Web: gsapps.org	415-380-1300	380-1302	167-3
GGC Wholesale Flooring LLC 1962 E Main St, Columbus OH 43205 Web: ggcflooring.com	614-253-9300		290
Ggi Worldwide Inc 552 Forest Crest, Lake Saint Louis MO 63367 Web: www.ggiww.com	636-561-4900		711
GGLO LLC 1301 First Ave Ste 301, Seattle WA 98101 Web: www.gglo.com	206-467-5828		393
GGLS (GoalsGuy Learning Systems Inc) 36181 E Lake Rd Ste 139, Palm Harbor FL 34685 TF: 877-462-5748 ■ Web: www.goalsguy.com	877-462-5748		192
GGMC Parking LLC 1651 Third Ave, New York NY 10128 Web: www.ggmcparking.com	212-996-6363		562
GGP Publishing Inc PO Box 635, Larchmont NY 10538 Web: ggppublishing.com	914-834-8896	834-7566	94
GGR (GeoGlobal Resources Inc) 625 Fourth Ave SW, Calgary AB T2P0K2 OTC: GGLR ■ Web: geoglobal.com	403-777-9250		538
GGS (Gamblers General Store Inc) 800 S Main St, Las Vegas NV 89101 Web: www.gamblersgeneralstore.com	702-382-9903		761
GGS Technical Publications Services 3265 Farmtrail Rd, York PA 17406 TF: 800-927-4474 ■ Web: www.ggsinc.com	717-764-2222		781
GH Berlin Windward 1064 Goffs Falls Rd, Manchester NH 03103 TF: 800-426-7754 ■ Web: www.ghberlinwindward.com	603-222-2900		579
GH Metal Solutions Inc 2890 Airport Rd NW, Fort Payne AL 35968 Web: www.ghmetalsolutions.com	256-845-5411		295
GH Package Product & Testing Consulting Inc 4090 Thunderbird Ln, Fairfield OH 45014 Web: ghtesting.com	513-870-0080	870-0017	196
GH Printing Company Inc 5207 Walnut Ave, Downers Grove IL 60515 Web: www.ghprinting.com	630-960-4115	960-5313	627
GHA design studios 1100 Ave des Canadiens-de-Montreal Ste 130, Montreal QC H3B2S2 Web: www.ghadesign.com	514-843-5812		393
Ghafari Associates Inc 17101 Michigan Ave, Dearborn MI 48126 TF: 800-289-7822 ■ Web: ghafari.com	313-441-3000		261
Ghana			
Consulate General 19 E 47th St, New York NY 10017 Web: ghanaconsulatenewyork.org	212-832-1300	751-6743	257
Embassy 3512 International Dr NW, Washington DC 20008 Web: www.ghanaembassydc.org	202-686-4520	686-4527	257
GHBLP (Grand Haven Board of Lightand & Power) 1700 Eaton Dr, Grand Haven MI 49417 Web: ghblp.org	616-846-6250	846-3114	245
GHC Mechanical Inc 990 Pauly Dr, Elk Grove Village IL 60007 Web: www.ghcmech.com	847-593-0123		14
GHD 1240 N Mountain Rd, Harrisburg PA 17112 Web: www.ghd.com	717-541-0622		261
Ghekko Networks Inc 11800 31st Ct N, Saint Petersburg FL 33716 Web: www.ghekkonetworks.com	727-576-5001		246
Ghent Manufacturing Inc 2999 Henkle Dr, Lebanon OH 45036 TF: 800-543-0550 ■ Web: ghent.com	513-932-3445	932-9252	243
GHG Corp 960 Clear Lake City Blvd, Webster TX 77598 TF: 866-380-4146 ■ Web: www.ghgcorp.com	281-488-8806	488-1838	178-10
Ghiorsi & Sorrenti Inc (GSI) 255 Madison Ave, Wyckoff NJ 07481 Web: www.gsiphilanthropy.com	201-307-1970	307-5632	194
Ghiotto & Associates Inc 2426 Phillips Hwy, Jacksonville FL 32207 TF: 844-304-7262 ■ Web: ghiotto.com	904-886-0071	886-7174	655
Ghirardelli Chocolate Co 1111 139th Ave, San Leandro CA 94578 TF: 800-877-9338 ■ Web: www.ghirardelli.com	800-877-9338		296-8
Ghirardelli Square 900 N Pt St Ste E-100, San Francisco CA 94109 Web: www.ghirardellisq.com	415-775-5500	775-0912	50-6
Ghirardo CPA 7200 Redwood Blvd Ste 403, Novato CA 94945 Web: ghirardocpa.com	415-897-5678		2
GHJ&M (Goldner Hawn) 90 S 7th St 3700 Wells Fargo Ctr, Minneapolis MN 55402 Web: goldnerhawn.com	612-338-5912		403
GHNH Inc 520 Friendship St, New Castle PA 16101 Web: goldenhill.com	724-654-7791		371
GHO Ventures LLC 92 Nassau St 2nd Fl, Princeton NJ 08542 Web: www.ghoventures.com	609-497-6333		696
Ghost Armor LLC 70 S Val Vista Dr Unit A3-281, Gilbert AZ 85295 Web: www.ghost-armor.com	480-264-1052		791
Ghost Town Museum 400 S 21st St, Colorado Springs CO 80904 Web: www.ghosttownmuseum.com	719-634-0696		520
GHR Engineers & Associates Inc 1615 S Neil St, Champaign IL 61820 Web: www.ghrinc.com	217-356-0536		261
GHR Management LLC 4730 Wistar Rd, Richmond VA 23228 Web: www.worldclassag.com	804-308-1877		57
GHS (Greenville Hospital System) 701 Grove Rd, Greenville SC 29605 Web: www.ghs.org	864-455-8976		353
GHS (Georgetown Heritage Society) 811 S Main St, Georgetown TX 78626 Web: georgetownheritagesociety.org	512-869-8597		637-2

	Phone	Fax	Class
Corp 2813 Wilber Ave .... Battle Creek MI 49037 TF: 800-388-4447 ■ Web: www.ghsstrings.com	800-388-4447	860-6913	527
Holdings Inc 251 Greenwood Ave .... Bethel CT 06801	203-748-5242		360-3
P Co 1250 S Beechtree St............... Grand Haven MI 49417 Web: www.ghsp.com	616-842-5500	842-2730	489
(Global Health Care Exchange LLC) 315 W Century Dr......................... Louisville CO 80027 TF: 800-968-7449 ■ Web: www.ghx.com	720-887-7000	887-7200	225
Plastek Corp 5 Wickers Dr .... Wolfeboro NH 03894 Web: www.giplastek.com	603-569-5100		604
(Gemological Institute of America) 5345 Armada Dr.................................. Carlsbad CA 92008 TF: 800-421-7250 ■ Web: www.gia.edu	760-603-4000	603-4003	49-4
acona Container Co 121 Industrial Ave....................... New Orleans LA 70121 TF: 800-299-4332 ■ Web: giacona.com	504-835-5465	835-5581	559
act Systems Inc 700 Central Expy S............. Allen TX 75013 TF: 866-918-2409 ■ Web: www.giact.com	214-644-0450		225
anforte Greg (Rep R - MT) 1222 Longworth House Office Bldg .... Washington DC 20515 Web: www.gianforte.house.gov	202-225-3211	225-5687	342-2
annini Garden Ornaments Inc 225 Shaw Rd .... South San Francisco CA 94080 Web: www.gianninigarden.com	650-873-4493	873-4934	183
iant Bicycle USA 3587 Old Conejo Rd.................... Newbury Park CA 91320 Web: www.giant-bicycles.com	805-267-4600		82
iant City State Park 235 Giant City Rd.......................... Makanda IL 62958 Web: www2.illinois.gov	618-529-4110		565
iant Communications Inc 418 W 5th St Ste C........................... Holton KS 66436 TF: 800-346-9084 ■ Web: support.giantcomm.net	785-362-9331		116
Giant Crab 9597 N Kings Hwy .... Myrtle Beach SC 29572 Web: giantcrab.com	843-449-1097		671
Giant Eagle Inc 101 Kappa Dr................ Pittsburgh PA 15238 TF: 800-553-2324 ■ Web: www.gianteagle.com	412-963-6200		345
Giant Food Inc 8301 Professional Pl Ste 115............. Landover Hills MD 20785 *Fax Area Code: 301 ■ TF: 888-469-4426 ■ Web: giantfood.com	888-469-4426	618-4998*	345
Giant Food Stores LLC 1149 Harrisburg Pk .... Carlisle PA 17013 TF: 888-814-4268 ■ Web: www.giantfoodstores.com	717-249-4000	249-1553	345
Giant Oil Inc 1806 N Franklin St .... Tampa FL 33602 TF: 877-807-2677 ■ Web: www.giantoil.com	813-740-0422		579
Giant Resource Recovery - Harleyville Inc (GRR) 654 Judge St PO Box 352.................... Harleyville SC 29448 *Fax Area Code: 803 ■ TF: 800-786-0477 ■ Web: www.grr-giant.com	800-786-0477	496-2200*	192
Giantbank.Com 6300 NE First Ave...................... Fort Lauderdale FL 33334 *Fax Area Code: 954 ■ TF: 877-446-4200 ■ Web: www.giantbank.com	877-446-4200	493-8969*	70
Giardoni Foods Inc 44 W Jefryn Blvd Ste R...................... Deer Park NY 11729 Web: www.giardonifoods.com	631-586-2331		297-8
Gibbes Museum of Art 135 Meeting St........................... Charleston SC 29401 Web: www.gibbesmuseum.org	843-722-2706	720-1682	520
Gibbon Conservation Ctr 19100 Esguerra Rd...................... Santa Clarita CA 91390 Web: www.gibboncenter.org	661-296-2737		823
Gibbons & Conley 3480 Buskirk Ave Ste 200................. Pleasant Hill CA 94523 Web: www.gibbons-conley.com	925-932-3600	932-1623	445
Gibbons PC 1 Gateway Ctr .... Newark NJ 07102 Web: www.gibbonslaw.com	973-596-4500		428
Gibbs 369 Community Dr .... Henderson KY 42420 Web: www.gibbsdc.com	270-827-1801		308
Gibbs & Heinle LLP 57 River St Ste 204.......................... Wellesley MA 02481 Web: gibbsheinle.com	781-371-4940		41
Gibbs & Soell Inc 60 E 42nd St 4th Fl .... New York NY 10165 Web: www.gscommunications.com	212-697-2600		636
Gibbs Bob (Rep R - OH) 2446 Rayburn House Office Bldg .... Washington DC 20515 Web: www.gibbs.house.gov	202-225-6265	225-3394	342-2
Gibbs Construction LLC 5736 Citrus Blvd Ste 200 .... New Orleans LA 70123 Web: gibbsconstruction.com	504-733-4336		186
Gibbs Flying Service Inc 3717 John J Montgomery Dr .... San Diego CA 92123 Web: www.gibbsflyingservice.com	858-277-0310	277-0678	63
Gibbs Museum of Pioneer & Dakotah Life 2097 W Larpenteur Ave.................... Saint Paul MN 55113 Web: www.rchs.com	651-646-8629		520
Gibbs Wire & Steel Company Inc Metals Dr PO Box 520 .... Southington CT 06489 TF: 800-800-4422 ■ Web: www.gibbswire.com	860-621-0121	628-7780	492
GIBCO Products International Inc PO Box 880 .... Langley OK 74350 TF: 800-822-0802 ■ Web: www.gibco-usa.com	918-782-4000	782-4002	182
Gibgot Willenbacher & Co 310 E Shore Rd........................... Great Neck NY 11023 Web: gw-cpa.com	516-482-3660		2
Gibraltar 488 Royer Dr....................... Lancaster PA 17601 Web: gibraltargrille.com	717-397-2790		671
Gibraltar Industries Inc 3556 Lakeshore Rd.......................... Buffalo NY 14219 NASDAQ: ROCK ■ Web: www.gibraltar1.com	716-826-6500	826-1589	723
Gibraltar Savings Bank 1039 S Orange Ave.......................... Newark NJ 07106 Web: www.gibraltarbanknj.com	973-372-1221		70
Gibson 309 Plus Pk Blvd...................... Nashville TN 37217 TF: 800-444-2766 ■ Web: www.gibson.com	615-871-4500	889-5509	527
Gibson & Barnes 1900 Weld Blvd Ste 140...................... El Cajon CA 92020 *Fax Area Code: 800 ■ TF: 800-748-6693 ■ Web: www.gibson-barnes.com	619-440-6977	748-6694*	155-19
Gibson & Tuttle Inc 100 Estates Dr .... Roseville CA 95678 Web: gibsontuttlelaw.com	916-782-4402		41
Gibson Arnold & Assoc 5433 Westheimer Rd Ste 1016................. Houston TX 77056 TF: 800-879-2007 ■ Web: gibsonarnold.com	713-572-3000		721
Gibson Corrugated PO Box 380 .... Tupelo MS 38802 Web: www.gibsoncorrugated.com	662-842-1862	842-2895	100
Gibson County 101 N Main................... Princeton IN 47670 Web: www.gibsoncounty-in.gov	812-385-4885	385-3089	338
Gibson Dunn & Crutcher LLP 333 S Grand Ave......................... Los Angeles CA 90071 Web: www.gibsondunn.com	213-229-7000	229-7520	428
Gibson Electric Company Inc 3100 Woodcreek Dr .... Downers Grove IL 60515 Web: gibsonelec.com	630-288-3800	743-2100	189-4
Gibson Electric Membership Corp 1207 S College St PO Box 47.................. Trenton TN 38382 TF: 800-977-4076 ■ Web: www.gibsonemc.com	731-855-4740		245
Gibson Energy Inc 440 - Second Ave SW Ste 1700 .... Calgary AB T2P5E9 Web: www.gibsonenergy.com	403-206-4000		536
Gibson Engineering Company Inc 90 Broadway.............................. Norwood MA 02062 Web: www.gibsonengineering.com	781-769-3600		256
Gibson General Hospital 1808 Sherman Dr.......................... Princeton IN 47670 Web: www.gibsongeneral.com	812-385-3401		374-3
Gibson House Museum 137 Beacon St .... Boston MA 02116 Web: www.thegibsonhouse.org	617-267-6338		520
Gibson Insurance Agency Inc 130 S Main St Ste 400.................... South Bend IN 46601 Web: www.gibsonins.com	574-245-3500		390
Gibson Laboratories Inc 1040 Manchester St........................ Lexington KY 40508 TF: 800-477-4763 ■ Web: www.gibsonbioscience.com	859-254-9500	253-1476	231
Gibson Performance Exhaust 1270 Webb Cir.............................. Corona CA 92879 TF: 800-528-3044 ■ Web: gibsonperformance.com	951-372-1220		247
Gibson-Myers & Assoc 2876 S Arlington Rd........................... Akron OH 44312 TF: 800-671-7665 ■ Web: auiinfo.com	330-645-6338		390
Gibsons Steakhouse 1028 N Rush St............ Chicago IL 60611 Web: www.gibsonssteakhouse.com	312-266-8999	266-3327	671
Gibson-Thomas Engineering Company Inc 1004 Ligonier St............................ Latrobe PA 15650 Web: gibson-thomas.com	724-539-8562		261
GIC Group Inc, The 1434 Duke St............. Alexandria VA 22314 Web: gicgroup.com	703-684-1366		463
Giddings Independent Schl Dst 2337 N Main St .... Giddings TX 78942 Web: www.giddingsisd.net	979-542-2854	542-9264	685
Giddings Manufacturing Company Inc 1426 Us Rt 7............................... Pittsford VT 05763 Web: giddingsvt.com	802-483-2292		817
Giddings State School 2261 James Turman Rd PO Box 600 .... Giddings TX 78942 Web: www.tjjd.texas.gov	979-542-4500	542-0177	412
Gideon Hixon Fund 2476 Lillie Ave.......... Summerland CA 93067 Web: www.gideonhixon.com	805-963-2277	565-0929	792
GIDEON Informatics Inc 8721 Santa Monica Blvd Ste 234 .... Los Angeles CA 90069 Web: www.gideononline.com	323-934-0000		177
Gideon Putnam Resort & Spa 24 Gideon Putnam Rd................ Saratoga Springs NY 12866 TF: 800-452-7275 ■ Web: www.gideonputnam.com	518-584-3000		379
Gieger Laborde & Laperouse L L C 701 Poydras St Ste 4800 .... New Orleans LA 70139 Web: www.glllaw.com	504-561-0400	561-1011	445
Gielowski Federice & Caligiuri 135 Delaware Ave Ste 405 .... Buffalo NY 14202 Web: workerscomp-buffalo.com	716-854-3455		41
Giering Metal Finishing Inc 2655 State St .... Hamden CT 06517 Web: gieringmetalfinishing.com	203-248-5583		481
Giesecke & Devrient America Inc 45925 Horseshoe Dr......................... Sterling VA 20166 Web: www.gi-de.com	703-480-2000		596
Giesecke Devrient Cardtech Inc 2020 Enterprise Pkwy...................... Twinsburg OH 44087	330-425-1515		596
Gif Services Inc 2525 Brunswick Ave Ste 204 .... Linden NJ 07036 Web: www.gifservices.com	908-474-1270		311
Giffels-Webster Engineers Inc 28 W Adams Ste 1200 .... Detroit MI 48226 TF: 866-271-9663 ■ Web: www.giffelswebster.com	866-271-9663		261
Giffin Inc 1900 Brown Rd.................. Auburn Hills MI 48326 Web: www.giffininc.com	248-494-9600		695
Giffin Interior & Fixture Inc 500 Scotti Dr .... Bridgeville PA 15017 Web: www.giffininterior.com	412-221-1166	221-3745	499
Gifford Arboretum University of Miami 1301 Memorial Dr....... Coral Gables FL 33146 Web: biology.as.miami.edu	305-284-5364	284-3039	97
Gifford Pinchot State Park 2200 Rosstown Rd .... Lewisberry PA 17339 Web: www.dcnr.pa.gov	717-432-5011		565
Gifford Woods State Park 34 Gifford Woods.......................... Killington VT 05751 Web: www.vtstateparks.com	802-775-5354		565
Gifford-Heiden Insurance Inc 111 E Venice Ave .... Venice FL 34285 Web: giffordheidenins.com	941-484-0681		390
Gift Card Partners Inc 47 Pine Plain Rd.......................... Wellesley MA 02482 TF: 800-413-9101 ■ Web: www.giftcardpartners.com	800-413-9101		7
Gift Card Systems Inc 218 Cedar St .... Abilene TX 79601 *Fax Area Code: 972 ■ TF: 888-745-4112 ■ Web: www.worldgiftcard.com	888-745-4112	769-5746*	196
Gift of Hope Organ & Tissue Donor Network 425 Spring Lake Dr........................... Itasca IL 60143 TF: 877-577-3747 ■ Web: www.giftofhope.org	630-758-2600		545

Name / Address	City	State	ZIP	Phone	Fax	Class
Gift of Life Bone Marrow Foundation 800 Yamato Rd Ste 101 *TF:* 800-962-7769 ■ *Web:* www.giftoflife.org	Boca Raton	FL	33431	561-982-2900		48-17
Gift of Life Donor Program 401 N Third St *TF:* 800-543-6391 ■ *Web:* www.donors1.org	Philadelphia	PA	19123	215-557-8090		545
Gift of Life Michigan 3861 Research Park Dr *TF:* 866-500-5801 ■ *Web:* www.giftoflifemichigan.org	Ann Arbor	MI	48108	866-500-5801		292
Gift of Life Transplant House 705 Second St SW *TF:* 800-479-7824 ■ *Web:* gift-of-life.org	Rochester	MN	55902	507-288-7470		372
Gift Wrap Co 338 Industrial Blvd *TF:* 800-443-4429 ■ *Web:* www.giftwrapcompany.com	Midway	GA	31320	800-443-4429		548
GiftCertificates.com 11510 Blondo St *TF:* 800-773-7368 ■ *Web:* www.giftcertificates.com	Omaha	NE	68164	877-737-0200		327
Gifted Education Press (GEP) 10201 Yuma Ct *Web:* www.giftededpress.com	Manassas	VA	20108	703-369-5017		637-2
GiftsForYouNow.com 10305 Argonne Dr *TF:* 866-443-8748 ■ *Web:* www.giftsforyounow.com	Woodridge	IL	60517	866-443-8748		292
Giftwares Co 436 First Ave *Web:* www.giftwaresco.com	Royersford	PA	19468	610-948-1111		292
GIG (Gluten Intolerance Group) 31214 124th Ave SE *Web:* www.gluten.org	Auburn	WA	98092	253-833-6655	833-6675	48-17
Gig Harbor Chamber of Commerce 3125 Judson St *Web:* www.gigharborchamber.net	Gig Harbor	WA	98335	253-851-6865	851-6881	139
GigaCrete Inc 6775 Speedway Blvd Ste M105 *Web:* gigacrete.com	Las Vegas	NV	89115	702-643-6363		225
Gigante Vaz Partners Inc 915 Broadway Ste 1208 *Web:* www.gigantevaz.com	New York	NY	10010	212-343-0004		4
Gigaram Inc 9 Spectrum Pointe Dr *TF:* 866-444-2726 ■ *Web:* www.gigaram.com	Lake Forest	CA	92630	949-461-9999	461-9251	173-8
Gigasonic 260 E Gish Rd *TF:* 888-246-4442 ■ *Web:* www.gigasonic.com	San Jose	CA	95112	408-573-1400		526
Giga-Tronics Inc 4650 Norris Canyon Rd *OTC: GIGA* ■ *TF:* 800-726-4442 ■ *Web:* go-asg.gigatronics.com	San Ramon	CA	94583	925-328-4650	328-4700	248
Giggledoon 1812 Front St *Web:* www.giggledoon.com	Scotch Plains	NJ	07076	908-322-8961		637-2
Giglio Distributing Co 155 S Martin Luther King Jr Pky *Web:* gigliodistributing.com	Beaumont	TX	77701	409-838-1654	838-4018	81-1
GIH (Grantmakers in Health) 1100 Connecticut Ave NW Ste 1200 *Web:* www.gih.org	Washington	DC	20036	202-452-8331	452-8340	48-5
GII Solutions Inc 201 Bank St *TF:* 800-948-5478 ■ *Web:* www.giisolutions.com	Central	SC	29630	864-639-6605	639-4056	493
G-III Apparel Group Ltd 512 Seventh Ave *NASDAQ: GIII* ■ *Web:* www.giii.com	New York	NY	10018	212-403-0500	403-0551	155-5
Giken America Corp 5770 Hoffner Ave Ste 101 *Web:* www.giken.com	Orlando	FL	32822	407-380-3232	380-9411	189-3
Gil Haugan Construction Inc 200 E 60th St N *Web:* www.gilhaugan.com	Sioux Falls	SD	57104	605-336-6082	336-0051	186
Gil Tours Travel Inc 1511 Walnut St 2nd Fl *TF:* 800-223-3855 ■ *Web:* www.giltravel.com	Philadelphia	PA	19102	215-568-6655	568-0696	771
Gila Cliff Dwellings National Monument HC 68 PO Box 100 *Web:* www.nps.gov	Silver City	NM	88061	575-536-9461	536-9344	564
Gila Regional Medical Ctr 1313 E 32nd St *Web:* www.grmc.org	Silver City	NM	88061	575-538-4000		374-3
Gila River Arena 9400 W Maryland Ave *Web:* www.gilariverarena.com	Glendale	AZ	85305	623-772-3800		720
Gila River Telecommunications Inc 7065 W Allison Rd PO Box 5015 *Web:* www.gilarivertel.com	Chandler	AZ	85226	520-796-3333	796-7534	196
Gilardi's 820 E Walnut St *Web:* gilardisonwalnut.com	Springfield	MO	65806	417-862-6400		671
Gilbane Building Co 7 Jackson Walkway *TF:* 800-445-2263 ■ *Web:* www.gilbaneco.com	Providence	RI	02903	401-456-5800		188-7
Gilbane Report, The 763 Massachusetts Ave *Web:* gilbane.com	Cambridge	MA	02139	617-497-9443		395
Gilbarco Inc 7300 W Friendly Ave *Web:* www.gilbarco.com	Greensboro	NC	27420	336-547-5000	547-5890	639
Gilbert & Barnhill PA 503 Belle Hall Pkwy Unit 101 *Web:* gilbertbarnhill.publishpath.com	Mount Pleasant	SC	29464	843-856-9227		445
Gilbert & Calabrese LLC 181 Rt 206 *Web:* www.gcllc-cpa.com	Flanders	NJ	07836	973-448-1099		2
Gilbert Associates Inc 2880 Gateway Oaks Dr Ste 100 *Web:* gilbertcpa.com	Sacramento	CA	95833	916-646-6464		2
Gilbert Chamber of Commerce 119 N Gilbert Rd Ste 101 PO Box 527 *Web:* www.gilbertaz.com	Gilbert	AZ	85299	480-892-0056		139
Gilbert Displays Inc 110 Spagnoli Rd *TF:* 855-577-1100 ■ *Web:* gilbertexperience.com	Melville	NY	11747	631-577-1100		232
Gilbert Electric Company Inc 1760 E Pace Ct *Web:* www.gilbertelectric.com	Tucson	AZ	85719	520-884-8020	884-8546	189-4
Gilbert Global Equity Partners 767 Fifth Ave 15th Fl *Web:* www.gilbertglobal.com	New York	NY	10153	212-584-6200	584-6211	690
Gilbert Industries Inc 5611 Krueger Dr *TF:* 800-643-0400 ■ *Web:* www.gilbertinc.com	Jonesboro	AR	72401	870-932-6070		577
Gilbert Lake State Park 18 CCC Rd *Web:* parks.ny.gov	Laurens	NY	13796	607-432-2114		565
Gilbert Mechanical Contractors Inc 5251 W 74th St *Web:* www.gilbertmech.com	Edina	MN	55439	952-835-3810	835-4765	697
Gilbert Metzger & Madigan LLP 6029 Park Dr PO Box 677 *Web:* gmmcpa.com	Charleston	IL	61920	217-345-2128		2
Gilbert Plumbing LLC 1 Bridlepath Rd	West Simsbury	CT	06092	860-658-4653		610
Gilbert's Chowder House 92 Commercial St *Web:* www.gilbertschowderhouse.com	Portland	ME	04101	207-871-5636		671
Gilbride, Tusa, Last & Spillane 31 Brookside Dr *Web:* www.gtlslaw.com	Greenwich	CT	06830	203-622-9360	622-9392	428
Gilchrist 11311 McCormick Rd Ste 350 *TF:* 888-823-8880 ■ *Web:* www.gilchristcares.org	Hunt Valley	MD	21031	888-823-8880		371
Gilchrist County 112 S Main St *Web:* gilchrist.fl.us	Trenton	FL	32693	352-463-3170	463-3166	338
Gilchrist Metal Fabricating Company Inc 18 Park Ave *Web:* www.gmfco.com	Hudson	NH	03051	603-889-2600	889-2489	492
Gilcrease Museum 1400 N Gilcrease Museum Rd *TF:* 888-655-2278 ■ *Web:* gilcrease.org	Tulsa	OK	74127	918-596-2700	596-2770	520
Gilded Magic Publishing 1985 King Ave *Web:* www.gildedmagic.com	Kings Mills	OH	45034	513-898-1676		637-2
Gilead Group LLC 12444 Powerscourt Dr Ste 375 *Web:* www.gileadgroup.net	Saint Louis	MO	63131	314-821-2500	821-2501	10-11
Gilead Sciences Inc 333 Lakeside Dr *NASDAQ: GILD* ■ *TF:* 800-445-3235 ■ *Web:* www.gilead.com	Foster City	CA	94404	650-574-3000	578-9264	85
Giles & Kendall Inc 3470 Maysville Rd NE PO Box 188 *TF:* 800-225-6738 ■ *Web:* cedarsafe.com	Huntsville	AL	35804	256-776-2978		817
Giles & Lambert PC 1 E Main St **Fax Area Code:* 540 ■ *Web:* www.gileslambert.com	Martinsville	VA	24112	276-632-7000	981-9327*	428
Giles Chemical Corp 102 Commerce St *Web:* www.gileschemical.com	Waynesville	NC	28786	828-452-4784	452-4786	143
Giles Communications 2875 Rte 35 Ste 6N 300 *Web:* giles.com	Katonah	NY	10536	914-644-3500		636
Giles County 315 N Main St *Web:* virginiasmtnplayground.com	Pearisburg	VA	24134	540-921-1722	921-3825	338
Giles County Chamber of Commerce 110 N Second St *Web:* gilescountychamber.com	Pulaski	TN	38478	931-363-3789	363-7279	139
Giles County Public Library 122 S Second St *Web:* www.gilescountylibrary.org	Pulaski	TN	38478	931-363-2720		434-3
Giles Craig Communications Inc 504 Snidow St *Web:* www.pemtel.com	Pembroke	VA	24136	540-544-2288		224
Giles Engineering Associates Inc N8 W22350 Johnson Dr *TF:* 800-782-0610 ■ *Web:* www.gilesengr.com	Waukesha	WI	53186	262-544-0118		256
Giles Foodservice Equipment 2750 Gunter Park Dr W *Web:* www.gfse.com	Montgomery	AL	36109	334-272-1457		123
Giles Industries Inc 405 S Broad St *Web:* www.gilesindustries.com	New Tazewell	TN	37825	423-626-7243		505
Gilford Corp 4600 Powder Mill Rd Ste 350 *Web:* www.gilfordcorp.com	Beltsville	MD	20705	301-931-3900	931-9152	186
Gilford Johnson Flooring 1874 Defoor Ave NW **Fax Area Code:* 404 ■ *TF:* 877-722-5545 ■ *Web:* gilfordjohnson.com	Atlanta	GA	30325	800-282-0154	352-1560*	131
Gilkey Window Company Inc 3625 Hauck Rd *Web:* www.gilkey.com	Cincinnati	OH	45241	513-769-4527		596
Gill Athletics Inc 2808 Gemini Ct *TF:* 800-637-3090 ■ *Web:* www.gillathletics.com	Champaign	IL	61822	217-367-8438	367-8440	710
Gill Devine PC 100 Grandview Rd Ste 405 *Web:* gilldevine.com	Braintree	MA	02184	781-843-8300		41
Gill Elrod Ragon Owen & Sherman PA 425 W Capitol Ave Ste 3800 *Web:* www.gill-law.com	Little Rock	AR	72201	501-376-3800		428
Gill Foundation Inc 1550 Wewatta St *TF:* 888-530-4455 ■ *Web:* gillfoundation.org	Denver	CO	80202	303-292-4455	292-2155	303
Gill Industries Inc 5271 Plainfield Ave NE *Web:* www.gill-industries.com	Grand Rapids	MI	49525	616-559-2700		689
Gill Manufacturing Ltd 9 Kenview Blvd *Web:* www.gillmanufacturing.com	Brampton	ON	L6T5G5	905-792-0999		454
Gill Ranch Storage LLC 220 NW 2nd Ave *TF:* 866-537-9245 ■ *Web:* gillranchstorage.com	Portland	OR	97209	866-537-9245		325
Gill Studios Inc 10800 Lackman Rd *Web:* gill-line.com	Lenexa	KS	66219	913-888-4422		687
Gilleland Chevrolet Inc 3019 W Division St *TF:* 866-246-5236 ■ *Web:* www.gillelandchevrolet.com	Saint Cloud	MN	56301	320-281-4290		57
Gillespie County 101 W Main St *Web:* www.gillespiecounty.org	Fredericksburg	TX	78624	830-997-6515	997-9958	338
Gillespie County Fair & Festivals Assn 530 Fair Dr PO Box 526 *Web:* www.gillespiefair.net	Fredericksburg	TX	78624	830-997-2359	997-4923	642
Gillespie Graphics 27676 SW Pkwy Ave *TF:* 800-547-6841 ■ *Web:* www.gillespie-graphics.com	Wilsonville	OR	97070	503-682-1122		687
Gillespie, Prudhon & Associates Inc 16111 SE 106th Ave Ste 100 *TF:* 800-595-2145 ■ *Web:* www.gpatelecom.com	Clackamas	OR	97015	503-657-0424		261

Name / Address	City	State	ZIP	Phone	Fax	Class
ette Air Conditioning Company Inc 215 San Francisco Veb: www.gillette-ac.com	San Antonio	TX	78201	210-735-9235	736-1932	189-10
lette Castle State Park 7 River Rd Veb: portal.ct.gov	East Haddam	CT	06423	860-526-2336		565
lette Children's Specialty Healthcare 200 E University Ave TF: 800-719-4040 ■ Web: www.gillettechildrens.org	Saint Paul	MN	55101	651-291-2848		374-1
lette Generators Inc 2921 Thorne Dr TF: 800-777-9639 ■ Web: www.gillettegenerators.com	Elkhart	IN	46514	574-264-9639		518
lette Stadium 1 Patriots Pl Web: www.gillettestadium.com	Foxborough	MA	02035	508-543-8200		720
liam & Sons Inc 9831 Rosedale Hwy Web: www.gilliamandsons.com	Bakersfield	CA	93312	661-589-0913	589-6334	539
lliam Youth Services Ctr 2844 Downing St Web: www.colorado.gov	Denver	CO	80205	303-291-8951		412
illibrand Kirsten E (Sen D - NY) 478 Russell Senate Office Bldg Web: www.gillibrand.senate.gov	Washington	DC	20510	202-224-4451	228-0282	342-2
illick, Gillick & Wicht SC 6300 W Bluemound Rd TF: 800-942-2880 ■ Web: gillickwicht.com	Milwaukee	WI	53213	414-257-2667	257-9297	41
illies & Prittie Inc 151 Pleaseant Hill Rd Web: www.gilliesandprittie.com	Scarborough	ME	04074	207-883-7815		752
Gillig Corp 25800 Clawiter Rd TF: 800-735-1500 ■ Web: www.gillig.com	Hayward	CA	94545	510-785-1500	785-6819	516
Gilligan, Gooding, Franjola & Batsel PA 1531 SE 36th Ave Web: ocalalaw.com	Ocala	FL	34471	352-867-7707		41
Gillis Gilkerson 150 W Market St Ste 200 Riverview Commons Web: ggibuilds.com	Salisbury	MD	21801	410-749-4821		186
Gillis Insurance Agency Inc 290 High St Web: gillisinsuranceagency.com	Holyoke	MA	01040	413-536-1294		390
Gillispie & Ogilbee Pc 4400 N Meridian Ave Web: www.gocpas.com	Oklahoma City	OK	73112	405-947-3030	942-0017	2
Gillmore Security Systems Inc 26165 Broadway Ave TF: 800-899-8995 ■ Web: www.gillmoresecurity.com	Cleveland	OH	44146	440-232-1000		693
Gilman Brothers Co, The Gilman Rd Web: gilmanbrothers.com	Gilman	CT	06336	860-889-8444		596
Gilman USA 1230 Cheyenne Ave PO Box 5 TF: 800-445-6267 ■ Web: www.gilmanprecision.com	Grafton	WI	53024	262-377-2434	377-9438	493
Gil-Mar Manufacturing Company Inc 7925 Ronda Dr Web: gil-mar.com	Canton	MI	48187	734-459-4803		358
Gilmer Area Chamber of Commerce 106 Buffalo St Web: www.gilmerareachamber.com	Gilmer	TX	75644	903-843-2413	843-3759	139
Gilmer Chamber 696 First Ave PO Box 505 Web: www.gilmerchamber.com	East Ellijay	GA	30540	706-635-7400	635-7410	338
Gilmer County 10 Howard St Web: www.courtswv.gov	Glenville	WV	26351	304-462-7241	462-7038	338
Gilmer Mirror Co PO Box 250 Web: www.gilmermirror.com	Gilmer	TX	75644	903-843-2503		637-8
Gilmore Enterprises Inc (GEI) 3514-A Drawbridge Pky Web: www.gilmoreshows.com	Greensboro	NC	27410	336-282-5550		393
Gilmore Jasion & Mahler Ltd 1715 Indianwood Cir Ste 100 Web: gjmltd.com	Maumee	OH	43537	419-794-2000		2
Gilmore Magness Janisse, Apc 7789 N Ingram Ave Ste 105 Web: gmlegal.net	Fresno	CA	93711	559-448-9800		41
Gilmore Services Inc 31 E Fairfield Dr TF: 888-439-7458 ■ Web: www.gilmoreservices.com	Pensacola	FL	32501	850-434-1054	434-1056	358
Gilmore Solutions Inc 115 S Broadway Ave Ste B TF: 866-978-3600 ■ Web: gilmoresolutions.com	Sterling	KS	67579	620-278-3600		180
Gilmore, Rees & Carlson PC 1000 Franklin Village Dr Web: grcpc.com	Franklin	MA	02038	508-520-2200		41
Gilmour 7800 Discovery Dr TF: 866-348-5661 ■ Web: gilmour.com	Middleton	WI	53562	866-348-5661		429
Gilmour Academy 34001 Cedar Rd TF: 800-533-5140 ■ Web: www.gilmour.org	Gates Mills	OH	44040	440-442-1104	473-8010	622
Gilmour Craves 455 Irwin St Ste 201 Web: www.gilmourcraves.com	San Francisco	CA	94107	415-431-9955		4
Gilpin Casino, The 111 Main St PO Box 50 Web: thegilpincasino.com	Black Hawk	CO	80422	303-582-1133		133
Gilpin County 203 Eureka St Web: www.co.gilpin.co.us	Central City	CO	80427	303-582-5321	582-3086	338
Gilroy Chamber of Commerce 7471 Monterey St Web: www.gilroy.org	Gilroy	CA	95020	408-842-6437	842-6010	139
Gilroy Chevrolet 6720 Auto Mall Dr TF: 800-237-6318 ■ Web: www.gilroychevy.com	Gilroy	CA	95020	408-427-3708		57
Gilroy Gardens Family Theme Park 3050 Hecker Pass Hwy Web: www.gilroygardens.org	Gilroy	CA	95020	408-840-7100		97
Gilroy Unified School District 7810 Arroyo Cir Web: www.gilroyunified.org	Gilroy	CA	95020	408-847-2700	842-1158	685
Gilsanz, Murray, Steficek LLP 129 W 27th St 5th Fl Web: www.gmsllp.com	New York	NY	10001	212-254-0030		261
Gilsbar 2100 Covington Ctr TF: 800-445-7227 ■ Web: www.gilsbar.com	Covington	LA	70433	985-892-3520	898-1500	462
Gilson Inc 3000 Parmenter St TF: 800-445-7661 ■ Web: www.gilson.com	Middleton	WI	53562	608-836-1551	831-4451	419
Gilson Screen Inc 8-810 K 2 Rd Web: www.gilsonscreen.com	Malinta	OH	43535	419-256-7711	256-7005	697
Gilster-Mary Lee Corp 1037 State St PO Box 227 Web: www.gilstermarylee.com	Chester	IL	62233	618-826-2361	826-2973	296-16
Gilton Solid Waste Management 755 S Yosemite Ave Web: www.gilton.com	Oakdale	CA	95361	209-527-3781		804
Gimbel, Reilly, Guerin & Brown LLP 330 E Kilbourn Ave Ste 1170 Web: grgblaw.com	Milwaukee	WI	53202	414-271-1440		41
Gimmal LLC 24 Greenway Plz Ste 1000 TF: 877-944-6625 ■ Web: www.gimmal.com	Houston	TX	77046	713-586-6500		178-1
Gina B & Company Inc 23811 Aliso Creek Rd Ste 136 Web: www.ginab.com	Laguna Niguel	CA	92677	949-643-1430		361
Gina B Designs Inc 12700 Industrial Pk Blvd Ste 40 *Fax Area Code: 763 ■ TF: 800-228-4856 ■ Web: www.ginabdesigns.com	Plymouth	MN	55441	800-228-4856	559-3899*	130
Giner Inc 89 Rumford Ave Web: www.ginerinc.com	Newton	MA	02466	781-529-0500		668
Ginger Bay Salon Group Ltd 437 S Kirkwood Rd Web: www.gingerbay.com	Kirkwood	MO	63122	314-966-0655		77
Ginger Cove 4000 River Crescent Dr TF: 800-299-2683 ■ Web: www.gingercove.com	Annapolis	MD	21401	410-266-7300		672
Ginger Elizabeth Chocolates 1801 L St Ste 60 Web: www.gingerelizabeth.com	Sacramento	CA	95811	916-706-1738		123
Ginger T. Levinson CPA PA 1101 S Lombard St Web: gingerlevinsoncpa.com	Clayton	NC	27520	919-553-3437		734
Gingko Press Inc 1321 5th St Web: www.gingkopress.com	Berkeley	CA	94710	510-898-1195	898-1196	637-10
Gingrich, Smith, Klingensmith & Dolan 222 S Market St Ste 201 Web: gskdlaw.com	Elizabethtown	PA	17022	717-367-1370	367-3219	41
Ginkgo Intl 8102 Lemont Rd Ste 1100 Web: www.ginkgoint.com	Woodridge	IL	60517	630-910-5244		362
Ginkgo Petrified Forest State Park 4511 Huntzinger Rd Web: www.parks.state.wa.us	Vantage	WA	98950	509-856-2700		565
Ginkgo Residential LLC 1023 W Morehead St Ste 301 Web: ginkgores.com	Charlotte	NC	28208	704-944-0100		655
Ginn Group Inc, The 200 Westpark Dr Ste 100 Web: www.theginngroup.com	Peachtree City	GA	30269	404-669-9214		256
Ginnos Kitchen & Appliance Systems Inc 2505 Zanella Way Web: ginnos.com	Chico	CA	95928	530-342-2182		35
Ginny's Printing 8410-B Tuscany Way Web: www.ginnysprinting.com	Austin	TX	78754	512-454-6874	453-2178	627
Gino Morena Enterprises LLC 111 Starlite St TF: 800-227-6905	South San Francisco	CA	94080	800-227-6905		77
Gino's 4542 Bennington Ave Web: www.ginosrestaurant.com	Baton Rouge	LA	70808	225-927-7156		671
Ginsberg's Foods Inc 29 Ginsberg Ln PO Box 17 TF: 800-999-6006 ■ Web: ginsbergs.com	Hudson	NY	12534	518-828-4004		355
Ginsburg & Associates PC 2112 Walnut St Web: ginsburg-law.com	Philadelphia	PA	19103	215-564-4400		41
Ginsburg & Leshin LLC 1 Hollis St Ste 423 Web: glmediation.com	Wellesley	MA	02482	781-235-3332		41
Ginsburg & Misk Attys 21548 Jamaica Ave Web: www.gmlawyers.net	Queens Village	NY	11428	718-468-0500		428
Ginsburg Development Companies LLC (GDC) 100 Summit Lake Dr Web: gdchomes.com	Valhalla	NY	10595	914-747-3600		653
Ginsu Brands 118 E Douglas Rd *Fax Area Code: 870 ■ TF: 800-982-5233 ■ Web: ginsu.com	Walnut Ridge	AR	72476	800-982-5233	886-2911*	222
Gioffre Companies Inc 6262 Eiterman Rd Web: www.gioffreco.com	Dublin	OH	43016	614-764-0032	764-1620	187
Giordano Construction Company Inc 1155 Main St Web: www.giordanoconstruction.com	Branford	CT	06405	203-488-7264		186
Giordano S. Solid Waste Removal 110 N Mill Rd TF: 800-636-8625 ■ Web: www.giordanosrecycling.com	Vineland	NJ	08360	856-696-2068		660
Giordano, Halleran & Ciesla PC 125 Half Mile Rd Web: www.ghclaw.com	Middletown	NJ	07748	732-741-3900	224-6599	428
Giorgio Foods Inc PO Box 96 TF: 800-220-2139 ■ Web: www.giorgiofresh.com	Temple	PA	19560	610-926-2139	926-7012	296-20
Giorgio's 1131 NW Hoyt St Web: www.giorgiospdx.com	Portland	OR	97209	503-221-1888		671
Giovanni's 362 Preston St Web: giovannis-restaurant.com	Ottawa	ON	K1S4M7	613-234-3156		671
Giovanni's Restaurant & Convention Ctr 610 N Bell School Rd TF: 877-926-8300 ■ Web: giodine.com	Rockford	IL	61107	815-398-6411		671
Giovanni's Ristorante 330 S Oakwood Blvd Web: www.giovannisristorante.com	Detroit	MI	48217	313-841-0122		671
Giovatto Advertising & Consulting Inc 95 New Jersey 17 Web: giovatto.com	Paramus	NJ	07652	201-226-9700		7
Gipe Associates Inc 8719 Brooks Dr Web: gipe.net	Easton	MD	21601	410-822-8688		261
Giphy Inc 416 W 13th St Web: giphy.com	New York	NY	10014	917-693-1910		225

Phone | Fax | Class

Gipson Hoffman & Pancione
1901 Avenue of The Stars 11th Fl ... Los Angeles CA 90067 310-556-4660 428
Web: www.ghplaw.com

Girard College
2101 S College Ave ... Philadelphia PA 19121 215-787-2600 622
Web: www.girardcollege.edu

Girard Equipment Inc
70 Royal Palm Pointe ... Vero Beach FL 32960 908-862-6300 789
Web: www.girardequip.com

Girard Machine Company Inc 700 Dot St ... Girard OH 44420 330-545-9731 545-6164 492
Web: www.girardmachine.com

Girard Wood Products Inc 802 E Main ... Puyallup WA 98372 253-845-0505 845-5463 551
Web: www.girardwoodproducts.com

Girardin Blue Bird
4000 Girardin St ... Drummondville QC J2E0A1 819-477-3222 108
TF: 800-567-1467 ■ *Web:* www.girardinbluebird.com

Girardin Moulding Inc
567 Halfway House Rd ... Windsor Locks CT 06096 860-623-4486 627-6716 604
Web: girardinmoulding.com

Girasole Ristorante & Lounge
3108 Pacific Ave ... Atlantic City NJ 08401 609-345-5554 671
Web: mygirasole.com

Girl Scouts of the USA 420 Fifth Ave ... New York NY 10018 212-852-8000 48-15
TF: 800-478-7248 ■ *Web:* www.girlscouts.org

Girls Inc 120 Wall St 18th Fl ... New York NY 10005 212-509-2000 509-8708 48-24
TF: 800-374-4475 ■ *Web:* girlsinc.org

Girls Incorporated of Alameda County
510 16th St ... Oakland CA 94612 510-357-5515 533
Web: girlsinc-alameda.org

Girls Nation
American Legion Auxiliary
8945 N Meridian St ... Indianapolis IN 46260 317-569-4500 569-4502 48-7
TF: 800-504-4098 ■ *Web:* www.alaforveterans.org

Girls' Life Acquisition Co
3 S Frederick St Ste 806 ... Baltimore MD 21202 410-426-9600 457-6
TF: 800-931-2237 ■ *Web:* www.girlslife.com

Giroux Glass Inc
850 W Washington Blvd ... Los Angeles CA 90015 213-747-7406 747-8778 189-6
TF: 800-684-5277 ■ *Web:* girouxglass.com

Girtz Industries Inc
5262 N E Shafer Dr ... Monticello IN 47960 574-278-7510 278-6221 697
Web: www.girtzindustries.com

Girvin Inc 121 Stewart St Ste 212 ... Seattle WA 98101 206-674-7808 674-7909 344
Web: girvin.com

GIS (Gatterdam Industrial Services)
4615 Bittersweet Rd ... Louisville KY 40218 502-776-3937 776-9929 454
Web: www.gatterdam.com

GIS Planning Inc
1 Hallidie Plz Ste 760 ... San Francisco CA 94102 415-294-4775 294-4770 196
TF: 866-646-4447 ■ *Web:* www.gisplanning.com

Gis Workshop LLC 4949 NW 1st St Ste 1 ... Lincoln NE 68521 402-436-2150 180
Web: www.gworks.com

GISD (Garland Independent School District)
501 S Jupiter PO Box 469026 ... Garland TX 75042 972-494-8201 685
Web: www.garlandisd.net

GISD (Galveston Independent School District)
3904 Ave T PO Box 660 ... Galveston TX 77550 409-766-5100 685
Web: www.gisd.org

Giselle's Travel Inc
1300 Ethan Way Ste 100 ... Sacramento CA 95825 916-922-5500 679-3090 771
TF: 800-782-5545 ■ *Web:* www.globaltrav.com

Gislason & Hunter LLP 2700 S Broadway ... New Ulm MN 56073 507-354-3111 428
TF: 800-469-0234 ■ *Web:* www.gislason.com

Gistics Inc 92 Templar Pl ... Oakland CA 94618 510-450-9999 224
Web: gistics.com

GITA (Geospatial Information & Technology Assn)
14456 E Evans Ave ... Aurora CO 80014 303-337-0513 49-19
Web: www.gita.org
Government Information Technology Agency
100 N 15th Ave Ste 440 ... Phoenix AZ 85007 602-771-2800 364-4799 339-3
Web: www.azdfi.gov

Gita Sporting Goods Ltd
12500 Steele Creek Rd ... Charlotte NC 28273 800-366-4482 588-4322* 711
**Fax Area Code:* 704 ■ *TF:* 800-729-4482 ■ *Web:* www.gitabike.com

GitHub
88 Colin P Kelly Junior St ... San Francisco CA 94107 877-448-4820 520-5597* 387
**Fax Area Code:* 415 ■ *TF:* 877-448-4820 ■ *Web:* github.com

GitLab 268 Bush St Ste 350 ... San Francisco CA 94104 415-829-2854 178-1
Web: about.gitlab.com

Gitman Bros 2309 Chestnut St ... Ashland PA 17921 800-526-3929 972-3854 155-12
TF: 800-526-3929 ■ *Web:* www.gitman.com

Gitomer & Berenholz PC
445 Shady Ln ... Huntingdon Valley PA 19006 215-379-3500 379-3593 2
Web: www.gbm-cpa.com

Gits Manufacturing Co 4601 121st St ... Urbandale IA 50323 800-323-3238 903-2120* 247
**Fax Area Code:* 641 ■ *TF:* 800-323-3238 ■ *Web:* www.gitsmfg.com

Giuffre Bros Cranes Inc
6635 S 13th St ... Milwaukee WI 53221 414-764-9200 764-8180 358
TF: 877-321-3710 ■ *Web:* giuffre.com

Giuffrida Associates Inc
204 E St NE ... Washington DC 20002 202-547-6340 47
Web: www.thegateam.com

Giunta's Meat Farms
1067 Rt 112 ... Port Jefferson NY 11776 631-474-3910 345
Web: giuntasmeatfarms.com

Giuseppe's 17937 SE Stark St ... Portland OR 97233 503-669-8767 671
Web: giuseppespdx.com

Giuseppe's Italian Kitchen
2824 E Indian School Rd ... Phoenix AZ 85016 602-381-1237 671
Web: giuseppeson28th.com

Givaudan Flavors Corp
1199 Edison Dr ... Cincinnati OH 45216 513-948-8000 296-15
Web: www.givaudan.com

Giveanythingcom LLC
307 Fifth Ave 4th Fl ... New York NY 10016 212-689-1200 387
Web: www.giveanything.com

Givenhansco Inc 848 Morrison Rd ... Columbus OH 43231 614-310-0060 177
Web: www.givenhansco.com

Givens Transportation Inc
1724 S Military Hwy ... Chesapeake VA 23320 757-233-4300 780
Web: www.givens.com

Giventer Software Systems
215 N Cayuga St ... Ithaca NY 14850 607-272-2602 178-1
Web: www.lightlink.com

Givhans Ferry State Park
746 Givhans Ferry Rd ... Ridgeville SC 29472 843-873-0692 565
Web: southcarolinaparks.com

Giving Greetings PO Box 456 ... Sudbury MA 01776 866-544-9540 288-7734* 130
**Fax Area Code:* 857 ■ *TF:* 866-544-9540 ■ *Web:* www.givinggreetings.com

Giving Institute
225 W Wacker Dr Ste 650 ... Chicago IL 60606 312-981-6794 265-2908 48-5
Web: www.givinginstitute.org

GivingTrax 7921 S Hosmer Ste A ... Tacoma WA 98408 206-486-0185 387
Web: www.givingtrax.com

Givinity Press 3374 Maplewood Ct ... Fargo ND 58103 701-235-4241 280-2016 45
TF: 866-221-5860 ■ *Web:* www.givinity.com

GIW Industries Inc
5000 Wrightsboro Rd ... Grovetown GA 30813 706-863-1011 860-5897 641
TF: 888-832-4449 ■ *Web:* www.ksb.com

Gizmo Art Production Inc
PO Box 411372 ... San Francisco CA 94141 415-222-6181 279
Web: gizmosf.com

GJ Chemical Co 40 Veronica Ave ... Somerset NJ 08873 973-589-1450 249-0082* 146
**Fax Area Code:* 732 ■ *Web:* www.gjchemical.com

GJ Grewe Inc 9109 Watson Rd ... Saint Louis MO 63126 314-962-6300 653
Web: gjgrewe.com

GJ Littlewood & Son Inc
4045 Main St ... Philadelphia PA 19127 215-483-3970 483-6129 745-7
Web: www.littlewooddyers.com

GJ Nikolas & Company Inc
2800 Washington Blvd ... Bellwood IL 60104 708-544-0320 544-9722 549
Web: www.finish1.com

GJ Sales Co 64 Hope Ave ... Hope RI 02831 401-826-2650 826-3304 385
Web: www.gjsalesco.com

GK (Grand-Kahn Electric)
2455 W Grand Ave ... Chicago IL 60612 312-298-1500 298-1501 189-4
Web: www.grandkahn.com

GK Industries Ltd 50 Precidio Ct ... Brampton ON L6S6E3 905-799-1972 799-0852 61
TF: 800-463-8889 ■ *Web:* gkindustries.com

GK Partners Inc 401 E 74th St ... New York NY 10021 212-535-5617 452-1168 193
Web: gk-partners.com

GKCCF (Greater Kansas City Community Foundation & Affiliated Trusts)
1055 Broadway Blvd Ste 130 ... Kansas City MO 64105 816-842-0944 842-8079 303
Web: www.growyourgiving.org

GKG (Global Knowledge Group Inc)
302 N Bryan Ave ... Bryan TX 77803 866-776-7584 808
TF: 866-776-7584 ■ *Web:* www.gkg.net

GKN Aerospace Chem-tronics Inc
1160 W Bradley Ave PO Box 1504 ... El Cajon CA 92020 619-448-2320 258-5270 22
Web: www.gkn.com

GKV 1500 Whetstone Way 4th Fl ... Baltimore MD 21230 410-539-5400 4
Web: www.gkv.com

GL Communications Inc
818 W Diamond Ave 3rd Fl ... Gaithersburg MD 20878 301-670-4784 177
Web: www.gl.com

GL Homes of Florida Corp
1600 Sawgrass Corporate Pkwy Ste 400 ... Sunrise FL 33323 954-753-1730 653
Web: www.glhomes.com

GL Seaman & Co
4201 International Pkwy ... Carrollton TX 75007 214-764-6400 764-6420 320
Web: www.glsc.com

G-L Veneer Company Inc
2224 E Slauson Ave ... Huntington Park CA 90255 323-582-5203 582-9681 613
TF: 800-588-5003 ■ *Web:* www.glveneer.com

GLA (Grassfed Livestock Alliance)
525 N Lamar Blvd ... Austin TX 78703 830-562-2333 473
Web: www.grassfedlivestockalliance.com

Glacial Energy
2701 N Dallas Pkwy Ste 120 ... Plano TX 75093 469-467-8332 192
Web: glacialenergy.com

Glacial Lakes Energy LLC
301 20th Ave SE PO Box 933 ... Watertown SD 57201 605-882-8480 579
TF: 866-934-2676 ■ *Web:* www.glaciallakesenergy.com

Glacial Ridge Hospital Foundation Inc
10 Fourth Ave SE ... Glenwood MN 56334 320-634-4521 374-3
TF: 866-667-4747 ■ *Web:* glacialridge.org

Glacial Waters Spa at Grand View Lodge
23521 Nokomis Ave ... Nisswa MN 56468 866-801-2951 707
TF: 866-801-2951 ■ *Web:* www.grandviewlodge.com

Glacier Aviation
Olympia Airport 7645 Old Hwy 99 SW ... Olympia WA 98501 360-705-3214 753-0083 27
Web: www.helicopterflightschool.com

Glacier Bancorp Inc PO Box 27 ... Kalispell MT 59903 406-756-4200 360-2
NASDAQ: GBCI ■ *TF:* 800-735-4371 ■ *Web:* www.glacierbank.com

Glacier Bay Country Inn 35 Tong Rd ... Gustavus AK 99826 907-697-2288 379
Web: www.glacierbayalaska.com

Glacier Brew House 737 W Fifth Ave ... Anchorage AK 99501 907-274-2739 671
Web: www.glacierbrewhouse.com

Glacier Clear Enterprises Inc
3291 Thomas St ... Innisfil ON L9S3W3 705-436-6363 436-4949 805
TF: 800-668-5118 ■ *Web:* www.glacierclear.com

Glacier County 512 E Main St ... Cut Bank MT 59427 406-873-2711 338
Web: www.glaciercountygov.com

Glacier Creek Publishing PO Box 2662 ... Seattle WA 98111 866-517-2001 453-5511 637-2
TF: 866-517-2001 ■ *Web:* www.glaciercreekpublishing.com

Glacier Electric Co-opeartive Inc
410 E Main St ... Cut Bank MT 59427 406-873-5566 245
TF: 844-834-4457 ■ *Web:* www.glacierelectric.com

Glacier Gardens Rainforest Adventure
7600 Glacier Hwy ... Juneau AK 99801 907-790-3377 790-3907 97
Web: www.glaciergardens.com

Glacier Hills 1200 Earhart Rd ... Ann Arbor MI 48105 734-769-6410 672
Web: www.glacierhills.org

Glacier National Park PO Box 128 ... West Glacier MT 59936 406-888-7800 888-7808 564
Web: www.nps.gov

Glacier Park Inc PO Box 2025 ... Columbia Falls MT 59912 406-892-2525 892-1375 669
TF: 844-868-7474 ■ *Web:* www.glacierparkcollection.com

	City	State	Zip	Phone	Fax	Class
cier Real Estate Finance Inc 800 156th Ave Ste 210 Web: www.glacier.com	Bellevue	WA	98007	425-746-6446		652
cier Technologies LLC 200 Golden Key Cir Ste 400 Web: www.glacier-tech.com	El Paso	TX	79925	915-751-6014		261
AD (Greater Los Angeles Agency on Deafness Inc) 2222 Laverna Ave Web: www.gladinc.org	Los Angeles	CA	90041	323-478-8000		637-2
ad Music Co 14340 Torrey Chase Blvd Ste 380 Web: www.gladmusicco.com	Houston	TX	77014	281-397-7300		637-9
ad Works Inc 545 Pawtucket Ave Studio C208 Web: www.gladworks.com	Pawtucket	RI	02860	401-724-4523		344
adding Braided Products LLC 110 Country Rd Web: gladdingbraid.com	South Otselic	NY	13155	315-653-7211	653-4492	208
adding-Hearn Shipbuilding 1 Riverside Ave PO Box 300 Web: gladding-hearn.com	Somerset	MA	02726	508-676-8596	672-1873	698
lade & Grove Supply 305 CR 17A W *Fax Area Code: 561 ■ TF: 800-433-4451 ■ Web: www.gladeandgroveused.com	Avon Park	FL	33825	877-513-8182	996-2048*	274
lade Springs Resort 255 Resort Dr TF: 866-562-8054 ■ Web: www.gladesprings.com	Daniels	WV	25832	304-763-2000		669
lades County 500 Ave K PO Box 1527 Web: www.myglades.com	Moore Haven	FL	33471	863-946-6000	946-2860	338
ladowsky & Gladowsky 18 Manor Rd Web: gladowskygroup.com	Smithtown	NY	11787	631-360-0902	361-7200	2
ladstein Neandross & Associates LLC 2525 Ocean Park Blvd Ste 200 Web: www.gladstein.org	Santa Monica	CA	90405	310-314-1934	314-9196	196
Gladstone Area Chamber of Commerce 7001 N Oak Trfwy Web: www.gladstonechamber.com	Gladstone	MO	64118	816-436-4523	436-4352	139
Gladstone Care & Rehabilitation Ctr 435 E Gladstone St Web: www.gladstonecare.com	Glendora	CA	91740	626-963-5955	963-8683	450
Gladstone Dodge Chrysler Jeep RAM 5610 N Oak Trafficway TF: 866-695-2043 ■ Web: www.kcpowerhouse.com	Gladstone	MO	64118	816-656-3589		57
Gladstone Media Corp 214 Clarks Tract TF: 800-834-4177 ■ Web: gladstonemedia.shop.musictoday.com	Keswick	VA	22947	434-293-8471	293-1117	95
Gladstone School District 115 17789 Webster Rd Web: gladstone.k12.or.us	Gladstone	OR	97027	503-655-2777	655-5201	685
Gladwin County 401 W Cedar Ave Web: gladwincounty-mi.gov	Gladwin	MI	48624	989-426-7351	426-6917	338
Gladys Porter Zoo 500 Ringgold St Web: www.gpz.org	Brownsville	TX	78520	956-546-7187		823
Glamorise Foundations Inc 135 Madison Ave Web: glamorise.com	New York	NY	10016	212-684-5025		155-18
Glamos Wire Products Company Inc 5561 N 152nd St TF: 800-328-5062 ■ Web: www.glamoswire.com	Hugo	MN	55038	651-429-5386	429-7733	73
Glance Networks Inc 1167 Massachusetts Ave TF: 877-452-6236 ■ Web: ww2.glance.net	Arlington	MA	02476	781-646-8505		225
Glancy Prongay & Murray LLP 1801 Avenue of the Stars Web: www.glancylaw.com	Los Angeles	CA	90067	310-201-9150		428
Glanstein LLP 711 3rd Ave 17th Fl Web: glansteinllp.com	New York	NY	10017	212-370-5100	697-6299	41
Glascock County PO Box 66 Web: www.glascockcountyga.com	Gibson	GA	30810	706-598-2671	598-0124	338
Glas-Col LLC 711 Hulman St TF: 800-452-7265 ■ Web: www.glascol.com	Terre Haute	IN	47802	812-235-6167	234-6975	14
Glaser & Associates 1740 Craigmont TF: 800-980-0321 ■ Web: www.theglasers.com	Eugene	OR	97405	541-343-7575	343-1706	423
Glaser Weil Fink Jacobs Howard Avchen & Shapiro LLP 10250 Constellation Blvd 19th Fl Web: www.glaserweil.com	Los Angeles	CA	90067	310-553-3000	556-2920	428
Glasfloss Industries Inc PO Box 789 *Fax Area Code: 800 ■ Web: www.glasfloss.com	Dallas	TX	75373	214-741-7056	435-8377*	18
Glasford Telephone Co 209 E Main St Web: www.glastel.net	Glasford	IL	61533	309-389-2111		224
Glasgow Inc 104 Willow Grove Ave TF: 877-222-5514 ■ Web: www.glasgowinc.com	Glenside	PA	19038	215-884-8800	884-1465	188-4
Glasgow Spray-Dry Inc 1117 Cleveland Ave *Fax Area Code: 502 ■ TF: 800-794-4840 ■ Web: www.bluegrassdairy.com	Glasgow	KY	42141	800-794-4840	651-8844*	296-10
Glasgow-Barren County Chamber of Commerce 118 E Public Sq TF: 800-264-3161 ■ Web: www.glasgowbarrenchamber.com	Glasgow	KY	42141	270-651-3161	651-3122	139
Glass & Company CPA PC 500 W Fifth St Ste 1210 Web: www.glasscpa.com	Austin	TX	78701	512-480-8182	480-9465	2
Glass Art Society (GAS) 6512 23rd Ave NW Ste 329 Web: www.glassart.org	Seattle	WA	98117	206-382-1305	382-2630	48-4
Glass Cap Federal Credit Union 241 N Pittsburgh St Web: glasscapfcu.com	Connellsville	PA	15425	724-628-2424		219
Glass City Federal Credit Union 1340 Arrowhead Dr Web: glasscityfcu.com	Maumee	OH	43537	419-887-1000		219
Glass House Inn 3202 W 26th St TF: 800-956-7222 ■ Web: www.glasshouseinn.com	Erie	PA	16506	814-833-7751	833-4222	379
Glass Jacobson Financial Group 10711 Red Run Blvd Ste 101 TF: 800-356-7666 ■ Web: www.glassjacobson.com	Owings Mills	MD	21117	410-356-1000	356-2892	2
Glass Magazine 1945 Old Gallows Rd Ste 750 Web: glassmagazine.com	Vienna	VA	22182	703-442-4890		457-21
Glass Packaging Institute (GPI) 1220 N Fillmore St Ste 400 Web: www.gpi.org	Arlington	VA	22201	703-684-6359	546-0588	49-13
Glasscock County 117 E Currie St Web: www.co.glasscock.tx.us	Garden City	TX	79739	432-354-2371		338
GlassCraft Door Co 2002 Brittmoore Rd TF: 800-766-2196 ■ Web: www.glasscraft.com	Houston	TX	77043	713-690-8282		234
Glassfab Tempering Services Inc 1448 Mariani Ct TF: 800-535-2133 ■ Web: www.glassfabusa.com	Tracy	CA	95376	209-229-1060		329
Glassline Corp PO Box 147 Web: www.glassline.com	Perrysburg	OH	43552	419-666-5942	666-1549	493
Glassmere Fuel Service Inc 1967 Saxonburg Blvd TF: 800-235-9054 ■ Web: www.glassmerefuel.com	Tarentum	PA	15084	800-235-9054		316
GlassPoint Solar Inc 47669 Fremont Blvd Web: www.glasspoint.com	Fremont	CA	94538	415-778-2800	762-1966	14
GlassRatner Advisory & Capital Group LLC 3445 Peachtree Rd Ste 1225 Web: www.glassratner.com	Atlanta	GA	30326	678-904-1990		796
Glasstech Inc 995 4th St Web: www.glasstech.com	Perrysburg	OH	43551	419-661-9500	661-9616	330
Glassybaby LLC 3406 E Union St Web: www.glassybaby.com	Seattle	WA	98122	206-518-9071		362
Glast Phillips & Murray 14801 Quorum Dr Ste 500 Web: www.glastphillips.com	Dallas	TX	75254	972-419-8300		445
Glastender Inc 5400 N Michigan Rd TF: 800-748-0423 ■ Web: www.glastender.com	Saginaw	MI	48604	989-752-4275	752-4444	386
Glastonbury Citizen Inc PO Box 373 Web: www.glcitizen.com	Glastonbury	CT	06033	860-633-4691	657-3258	637-8
Glastonbury Southern Gage 46 Industrial Park Rd TF: 800-251-4243 ■ Web: www.gsgage.com	Erin	TN	37061	800-251-4243		493
Glastron 925 Frisbie St TF: 800-354-3141 ■ Web: www.glastron.com	Cadillac	MI	49601	800-354-3141		90
Glatfelter 96 S George St Ste 500 Web: www.glatfelter.com	York	PA	17401	717-225-4711	846-7208	557
Glatt Air Techniques Inc 20 Spear Rd Web: www.glatt.com	Ramsey	NJ	07446	201-825-8700	825-0389	385
Glauber Equipment Corp 1600 Commerce Pkwy TF: 888-452-8237 ■ Web: www.glauber.com	Lancaster	NY	14086	716-681-1234		358
Glaucoma Foundation 80 Maiden Ln Ste 700 Web: www.glaucomafoundation.org	New York	NY	10038	212-285-0080	651-1888	48-17
Glaucoma Research Foundation 251 Post St Ste 600 TF: 800-826-6693 ■ Web: www.glaucoma.org	San Francisco	CA	94108	415-986-3162	986-3763	48-17
Glaval Bus 914 County Rd 1 TF: 800-445-2825 ■ Web: www.glavalbus.com	Elkhart	IN	46514	574-262-2212		59
GlaxoSmithKline Inc 7333 Mississauga Rd N TF: 800-387-7374 ■ Web: ca.gsk.com	Mississauga	ON	L5N6L4	905-819-3000	819-3099	582
Glaze Tool and Engineering Inc 1610 Summit St Web: www.glazetool.com	New Haven	IN	46774	260-493-4557	493-3489	757
Glaz-Tech Industries Inc 2207 E Elvira Rd TF: 800-755-8062 ■ Web: www.glaztech.com	Tucson	AZ	85756	520-629-0268	629-8811	329
Glb Insurance Group of Nevada 4455 S Pecos Rd TF: 888-735-9333 ■ Web: glb.aleragroup.com	Las Vegas	NV	89121	702-735-9333	735-6129	390
GLBC (Greater Lansing Ballet Co) 15643 S US Hwy 27 Web: greaterlansingballet.com	Lansing	MI	48912	517-575-6854		573-1
GLC (God's Learning Ch) PO Box 61000 TF: 800-707-0420 ■ Web: glc.us.com	Midland	TX	79711	432-563-0420	563-1736	740
GLE Associates Inc 5405 Cypress Center Dr Ste 110 TF: 888-453-4531 ■ Web: www.gleassociates.com	Tampa	FL	33609	813-241-8350		192
Gleaner's Food Bank of Indianapolis 3737 Waldemere Ave TF: 800-944-9166 ■ Web: www.gleaners.org	Indianapolis	IN	46241	317-925-0191		305
Gleason Corp 1000 University Ave Web: www.gleason.com	Rochester	NY	14607	585-473-1000	461-4348	455
Gleason Industrial Products Inc 8575 Forest Home Ave Ste 100 Web: www.milwaukeehandtrucks.com	Greenfield	WI	53228	414-529-8357	529-3491	554
Gleason Law Offices PC 163 Merrimack St Web: www.gleasonlawoffices.com	Haverhill	MA	01830	978-521-4044		428
Gleason Printing Inc 3325 Republic Ave Web: www.gleasonprinting.com	Minneapolis	MN	55426	952-925-1345	925-2273	627
Gleason Public Library (GPL) 22 Bedford Rd Web: www.gleasonlibrary.org	Carlisle	MA	01741	978-369-4898		434-3
Gleason Research Associates Inc 5030 Bradford Dr NW Bldg One Ste 220 Web: www.grainc.net	Huntsville	AL	35805	256-883-7000		261
Gleim Publications Inc 4201 NW 95th Blvd Web: www.gleim.com	Gainesville	FL	32606	352-375-0772		532-3
Gleim The Jeweler 540 University Ave Web: www.gleimjewelers.com	Palo Alto	CA	94301	650-323-1331	323-3804	410
Glen Canyon National Recreation Area 691 Scenic View Dr PO Box 1507 Web: www.nps.gov	Page	AZ	86040	928-608-6200	608-6259	564
Glen Cove Mansion Hotel & Conference Ctr 200 Dosoris Ln TF: 877-782-9426 ■ Web: www.glencovemansion.com	Glen Cove	NY	11542	516-671-6400		377
Glen Dow Academy of Hair Design 309 W Riverside Web: www.glendow.com	Spokane	WA	99201	509-624-3244	624-3351	167-3
Glen Eagles 3700 N Carson St Web: www.gleneaglesrestaurant.com	Carson City	NV	89706	775-884-4414		671
Glen Eden Corp 25999 Glen Eden Rd TF: 800-843-6833 ■ Web: gleneden.com	Corona	CA	92883	951-277-4650		121

Name / Address	City	State	ZIP	Phone	Fax	Class
Glen Elder State Park 2131 180 Rd *Web:* www.ksoutdoors.com	Glen Elder	KS	67446	785-545-3345		565
Glen Ellyn Chamber of Commerce 800 Roosevelt Rd Bldg D Ste 108 *Web:* www.glenellynchamber.com	Glen Ellyn	IL	60137	630-469-0907	469-0426	139
Glen Ellyn Public Library 400 Duane St *Web:* gepl.org	Glen Ellyn	IL	60137	630-469-0879		435
Glen Ellyn School District 41 793 N Main St *Web:* www.d41.org	Glen Ellyn	IL	60137	630-790-6400	790-1867	685
Glen Foerd on the Delaware 5001 Grant Ave *Web:* www.glenfoerd.org	Philadelphia	PA	19114	215-632-5330		50-3
Glen Grove Elementary School 3900 Glenview Rd *Web:* www.glenview34.org	Glenview	IL	60025	847-998-5030		685
Glen Grove Suites 208 - 50 Oxton Ave *TF:* 800-565-3024 ■ *Web:* www.glengrove.com	Toronto	ON	M4N2J6	416-489-8441	440-3065	379
Glen Magnetics Inc 1165 3rd Ave *Web:* www.glenmagnetics.com	Alpha	NJ	08865	908-454-3717		767
Glen Mills Inc 220 Delawanna Ave *Web:* www.glenmills.com	Clifton	NJ	07014	973-777-0777	777-0070	393
Glen Mills Schools PO Box 5001 *TF:* 800-441-2064 ■ *Web:* www.glenmillsschool.org	Concordville	PA	19331	610-459-8100	558-1493	623
Glen Oak Park 2320 N Prospect Rd *Web:* www.peoriazoo.org	Peoria	IL	61603	309-686-3365	685-6240	823
Glen Oaks Community College 62249 Shimmel Rd *TF:* 888-994-7818 ■ *Web:* www.glenoaks.edu	Centreville	MI	49032	269-467-9945	467-9068	162
Glen Raven Inc 1831 N Park Ave *Web:* www.glenraven.com	Burlington	NC	27217	336-227-6211	226-8133	745-1
Glen Research Corp 22825 Davis Dr *TF:* 800-327-4536 ■ *Web:* www.glenresearch.com	Sterling	VA	20164	703-437-6191		668
Glen Ridge Pharmacy and Surgical 855 Bloomfield Ave *Web:* www.glenridgepharmacy.com	Glen Ridge	NJ	07028	973-743-5900		237
Glenair Inc 1211 Air Way *TF:* 888-465-4094 ■ *Web:* www.glenair.com	Glendale	CA	91201	818-247-6000	500-9912	815
Glenbeigh 2863 SR 45 *TF:* 800-234-1001 ■ *Web:* www.glenbeigh.com	Rock Creek	OH	44084	440-563-3400	563-9619	726
Glenbow Museum 130-9 Ave SE *Web:* www.glenbow.org	Calgary	AB	T2G0P3	403-268-4100	265-9769	520
Glenbrook Square 4201 Coldwater Rd *Web:* www.glenbrooksquare.com	Fort Wayne	IN	46805	260-483-2119		460
Glencannon Press PO Box 1428 *Web:* www.glencannon.com	El Cerrito	CA	94530	510-455-9027		637-2
Glencoe/McGraw-Hill 8787 Orion Pl *TF:* 800-848-1567 ■ *Web:* www.glencoe.com	Columbus	OH	43240	800-848-1567		637-2
Glencom Systems Inc 25 E Price St *Web:* www.glen.com	Linden	NJ	07036	908-486-0420		180
Glencrest Farm 1576 Moores Mill Rd PO Box 4468 *TF:* 800-903-0136 ■ *Web:* www.glencrest.com	Midway	KY	40347	859-233-7032	233-9404	368
Glencroft 8611 N 67th Ave *Web:* www.glencroft.com	Glendale	AZ	85302	623-939-9475		672
Glendale (CA) City Hall 613 E Broadway Rm 110 *Web:* www.glendaleca.gov	Glendale	CA	91206	818-548-2090	241-5386	337
Glendale Career College 240 N Brand Blvd Lower Level *Web:* www.glendalecareer.com	Glendale	CA	91203	818-696-0101		167-3
Glendale Centre Theatre 324 N Orange St *Web:* www.glendalecentretheatre.com	Glendale	CA	91203	818-244-8481	244-5042	572
Glendale Chamber of Commerce 5800 W Glenn Dr Ste 275 *Web:* www.glendaleazchamber.org	Glendale	CA	91205	818-240-7870	240-2872	139
Glendale Civic Ctr 5750 W Glenn Dr *Web:* www.glendaleciviccenter.com	Glendale	AZ	85301	623-930-4300	930-4319	205
Glendale Community College 6000 W Olive Ave *Web:* www.gccaz.edu	Glendale	AZ	85302	623-845-3000		162
Glendale Community College 1500 N Verdugo Rd *TF:* 866-251-1977 ■ *Web:* www.glendale.edu	Glendale	CA	91208	818-240-1000	551-5255	162
Glendale Federal Credit Union 500 E Wilson Ave *TF:* 866-444-6714 ■ *Web:* glendalefcu.org	Glendale	CA	91206	818-548-3976	545-7826	219
Glendale Galleria 100 W Broadway *Web:* www.glendalegalleria.com	Glendale	CA	91210	818-246-6737		460
Glendale Infiniti 812 S Brand Blvd *Web:* www.glendaleinfiniti.com	Glendale	CA	91204	818-201-2637		57
Glendale Public Library 2465 Montrose Ave *Web:* www.glendaleca.gov	Glendale	CA	91205	818-548-2030	548-7225	434-3
Glendale Securities Inc 15233 Ventura Blvd Ste 712 *Web:* glendalesecurities.com	Sherman Oaks	CA	91403	818-907-1505	907-1506	690
Glendale Star 7122 N 59th Ave *Web:* www.glendalestar.com	Glendale	AZ	85301	623-842-6000		532-3
Glendalough State Park 24869 Whitetail Ln *Web:* www.dnr.state.mn.us	Battle Lake	MN	56515	218-864-0110	864-0587	565
Glendinning Marine Products 740 Century Cir *TF:* 800-500-2380 ■ *Web:* www.glendinningprods.com	Conway	SC	29526	843-399-6146	399-5005	203
Glendo Corp PO Box 1153 *TF:* 800-835-3519 ■ *Web:* glendo.com	Emporia	KS	66801	620-343-1084		295
Glendo State Park 397 Glendo Park Rd *Web:* wyoparks.wyo.gov	Glendo	WY	82213	307-735-4433		565
Glendon College 2275 Bayview Ave *Web:* www.glendon.yorku.ca	Toronto	ON	M4N3M6	416-487-6710		167-3
Glendora Chamber of Commerce 131 E Foothill Blvd *Web:* glendora-chamber.org	Glendora	CA	91741	626-963-4128	914-4822	139
Glendorn 1000 Glendorn Dr *TF:* 800-843-8568 ■ *Web:* www.glendorn.com	Bradford	PA	16701	814-362-6511		379
Glenerin Inn, The 1695 The Collegeway *TF:* 877-991-9971 ■ *Web:* www.glenerininn.com	Mississauga	ON	L5L3S7	905-828-6103		379
Glen-Gery Corp 1166 Spring St PO Box 7001 *Web:* www.glengery.com	Wyomissing	PA	19610	610-374-4011	374-1622	150
Glenmede Funds 1650 Market St Ste 1200 *TF:* 800-966-3200 ■ *Web:* www.glenmede.com	Philadelphia	PA	19103	215-419-6000		528
Glenmoor Country Club 4191 Glenmoor Rd *Web:* www.glenmoorcc.com	Canton	OH	44718	330-966-3600	966-3611	669
Glenmoore Veterinary Hospital LLP 3 Andover Rd *Web:* glenmooreveterinaryhospital.com	Glenmoore	PA	19343	610-942-4404		794
Glenmore Inn 1000 Glenmore Ct SE *TF:* 800-661-3163 ■ *Web:* www.glenmoreinn.com	Calgary	AB	T2C2E6	403-279-8611	236-8035	379
Glenmount Global Solutions 5960 Southport Rd *Web:* www.glenmountglobal.com	Portage	IN	46368	219-762-0700	762-1636	261
Glenn County 526 W Sycamore St Ste B1 *Web:* www.countyofglenn.net	Willows	CA	95988	530-934-6400	934-6419	338
Glenn H. Johnson Construction 1776 Winthrop Dr *Web:* www.ghjohnson.com	Des Plaines	IL	60018	847-297-4700		186
Glenn Insurance Inc 500 E Absecon Blvd *Web:* glenninsurance.com	Absecon	NJ	08201	609-641-3000	641-2355	390
Glenn M. Gelman & Associates CPA 1940 E 17th St *Web:* www.gelmanllp.com	Santa Ana	CA	92705	714-667-2600		2
Glenn Machine Works Inc 734 Hwy 45 S *TF:* 888-868-4611 ■ *Web:* www.glennmachineworks.com	Columbus	MS	39701	662-328-4611	328-4638	23
Glenn Miller Insurance Agency Inc 404 E N Ave *Web:* glennmilleragency.com	Northlake	IL	60164	708-562-3404		390
Glenn O. Hawbaker Inc 1952 Waddle Rd Ste 203 *TF:* 800-221-1355 ■ *Web:* www.goh-inc.com	State College	PA	16803	814-237-1444		46
Glenn Research Ctr 21000 Brookpark Rd *Web:* www.nasa.gov	Cleveland	OH	44135	216-433-4000	433-8000	668
Glenn's Optiques 10611 Garland Rd Ste 216 *Web:* www.glennsoptiques.com	Dallas	TX	75218	214-321-6753	320-1015	542
Glenndale Flight Training Ctr 3637 S 400 W *Web:* www.flighttrainingcenters.com	Kokomo	IN	46902	765-319-3295		167-3
Glenner Memory Care Centers 3702 4th Ave *Web:* www.glenner.org	San Diego	CA	92103	619-543-4700		167-3
Glennville Bank 102 E Barnard St *Web:* gbbankgroup.com	Glennville	GA	30427	912-654-3471		70
Glenora Wine Cellars Inc 5435 State Rte 14 *TF:* 800-243-5513 ■ *Web:* www.glenora.com	Dundee	NY	14837	607-243-9500		80-3
Glenro Inc 39 McBride Ave *TF:* 888-453-6761 ■ *Web:* www.glenro.com	Paterson	NJ	07501	973-279-5900	279-9103	318
Glenrock International Inc 985 E Linden Ave **Fax Area Code:* 908 ■ *TF:* 800-453-6762 ■ *Web:* www.glenrock.com	Linden	NJ	07036	800-453-6762	862-0430*	724
Glens Falls City School District 15 Quade St *Web:* www.gfsd.org	Glens Falls	NY	12801	518-792-1212	792-1538	685
Glens Falls Hospital 100 Park St *Web:* www.glensfallshospital.org	Glens Falls	NY	12801	518-926-1000		374-3
Glentek Inc 208 Standard St *Web:* www.glentek.com	El Segundo	CA	90245	310-322-3026	322-7709	518
Glenview Chamber of Commerce 2320 Glenview Rd *TF:* 800-459-4250 ■ *Web:* www.glenviewchamber.com	Glenview	IL	60025	847-724-0900		139
Glenview Public Library 1930 Glenview Rd *Web:* www.glenviewpl.org	Glenview	IL	60025	847-729-7500	729-7558	434-3
Glenview State Bank 800 Waukegan Rd *Web:* www.gsb.com	Glenview	IL	60025	847-729-1900		70
Glenville State College 200 High St *TF:* 800-924-2010 ■ *Web:* www.glenville.edu	Glenville	WV	26351	304-462-7361	462-8619	166
Glenwood LLC 111 Cedar Ln *TF:* 800-542-0772 ■ *Web:* www.glenwood-llc.com	Englewood	NJ	07631	201-569-0050		583
Glenwood Park Retirement Village 1924 Glenwood Park Rd *Web:* gwpinc.org	Princeton	WV	24739	304-425-8128		450
Glenwood Regional Medical Ctr 503 McMillan Rd *Web:* www.glenwoodregional.org	West Monroe	LA	71291	318-329-4200	329-4710	374-3
Glenwood Resource Ctr 711 S Vine St *Web:* dhs.iowa.gov	Glenwood	IA	51534	712-527-4811		230
Glenwood State Bank 5 E Minnesota Ave PO Box 197 *TF:* 800-207-7333 ■ *Web:* www.glenwoodstate.bank	Glenwood	MN	56334	320-634-5111	634-5114	70
GLERL (Great Lakes Environmental Research Laboratory) 4840 S State St *Web:* www.glerl.noaa.gov	Ann Arbor	MI	48108	734-741-2235	741-2055	668
Glessner & Associates PLLC 2084 National Rd *Web:* www.theglessnergroup.com	Wheeling	WV	26003	304-243-9071		2
Glessner House Museum 1800 S Prairie Ave *Web:* www.glessnerhouse.org	Chicago	IL	60616	312-326-1480		520
Glex Inc 12900 Fm 529 Rd *Web:* www.glexinc.com	Houston	TX	77041	713-849-4985	849-2113	261
Glhn Architects & Engineers Inc 2939 E Broadway Blvd *Web:* glhn.com	Tucson	AZ	85716	520-881-4546		261
Glickman, Sugarman, Kneeland & Gribouski 11 Harvard St *Web:* gskandg.com	Worcester	MA	01609	508-756-6206		41
Glidden House 1901 Ford Dr *TF:* 866-812-4537 ■ *Web:* www.gliddenhouse.com	Cleveland	OH	44106	216-231-8900	231-2130	379

Name / Address	City	St	ZIP	Phone	Fax	Class
ldepath Power Solutions 132 N York St Ste 3L *Web:* glidepath.net	Elmhurst	IL	60126	630-501-0162		173-8
ldewell Laboratories Inc 4141 MacArthur Blvd *TF:* 800-854-7256 ■ *Web:* glidewelldental.com	Newport Beach	CA	92660	800-854-7256		743
lidewell Specialties Foundry Company Inc 600 Foundry Rd *Web:* www.glidewell-foundry.com	Calera	AL	35040	205-668-1881	668-1972	492
liers Meats Inc 533 Goetta Pl *TF:* 800-446-3882 ■ *Web:* www.goetta.com	Covington	KY	41011	859-291-1800		296-26
lik Co 3248 Nameoki Rd *TF:* 800-454-5181 ■ *Web:* www.gliks.com	Granite City	IL	62040	800-454-5181		229
limmerglass Festival 7300 State Hwy 80 PO Box 191 *Web:* glimmerglass.org	Cooperstown	NY	13326	607-547-0700		573-2
limmerglass State Park 1527 County Hwy 31 *Web:* parks.ny.gov	Cooperstown	NY	13326	607-547-8662		565
lines & Rhodes Inc 189 E St *TF:* 800-343-1196 ■ *Web:* www.glinesandrhodes.com	Attleboro	MA	02703	508-226-2000	226-7136	485
linsmann & Glinsmann, Chartered 12 Russell Ave *Web:* mygreencardlawyer.com	Gaithersburg	MD	20877	301-987-0030		428
Glint Inc 1100 Island Dr Ste 101 *Web:* www.glintinc.com	Redwood City	CA	94063	650-817-7240		224
Glissen Chemical Company Inc 1321 58th St *Web:* www.glissenchemical.com	Brooklyn	NY	11219	718-436-4200		151
Glitterex Corp 7 Commerce Dr *Web:* www.glitterex.com	Cranford	NJ	07016	908-272-9121		761
GLK Foods LLC 158 E Northland Ave *TF:* 855-572-8800 ■ *Web:* www.glkfoods.com	Appleton	WI	54911	855-572-8800		296-19
GLM Industries LP 1508 - Eighth St *TF:* 800-661-9828 ■ *Web:* www.glmindustries.com	Nisku	AB	T9E7S6	780-955-2233		480
GLM Transport Inc 7887 Hwy 27 S *TF:* 800-957-5442 ■ *Web:* glmtransport.com	Berne	IN	46711	800-957-5442		780
GLMV Chamber of Commerce 1123 S Milwaukee Ave *Web:* www.glmvchamber.org	Libertyville	IL	60048	847-680-0750	680-0760	139
GLNX Corp 2201 Timberloch Pl Ste 125 *TF:* 866-457-4649 ■ *Web:* www.glnx.com	The Woodlands	TX	77380	281-363-0185	363-7060	264-5
GlobaFone Inc 1950 Lafayette Rd Ste 207 *TF:* 800-826-6152 ■ *Web:* globafone.com	Portsmouth	NH	03801	603-433-7232		387
Global 1 Federal Credit Union 7512 Maple Ave *Web:* global1fcu.com	Pennsauken Township	NJ	08109	856-320-4706		219
Global Access 9815 S Monroe St Ste 510 *TF:* 877-811-8108 ■ *Web:* www.globalaccess.com	Sandy	UT	84070	877-811-8108		311
Global Air Response 5919 Approach Rd **Fax Area Code:* 941 ■ *TF:* 800-631-6565 ■ *Web:* www.airresponse.net	Sarasota	FL	34238	800-631-6565	926-7690*	30
Global Aquaculture Alliance 2 International Dr Ste 105 *Web:* www.aquaculturealliance.org	Portsmouth	NH	03801	603-317-5000		474
Global Bakeries Inc 13336 Paxton St *Web:* www.globalbakeriesinc.com	Pacoima	CA	91331	747-245-5901		805
Global Benefits Group Inc 26000 Towne Centre Dr Ste 100 *Web:* www.gbg.com	Foothill Ranch	CA	92610	949-470-2100		391-2
Global Body & Equipment Co 2061 Sylvan Rd *Web:* www.cncmetalproducts.com	Wooster	OH	44691	330-264-6640		454
Global Brass & Copper Inc 475 N Martingale Rd Ste 1050 *Web:* gbcholdings.com	Schaumburg	IL	60173	847-240-4700		492
Global Building Services Inc 25129 The Old Rd Ste 102 *TF:* 800-675-6643 ■ *Web:* www.globalbuildingservices.com	Stevenson Ranch	CA	91381	800-675-6643	914-2485	393
Global Business Travel Assn, The (GBTA) 123 N Pitt St *TF:* 888-574-6447 ■ *Web:* www.gbta.org	Alexandria	VA	22314	703-684-0836	684-0263	48-23
Global Cash Card 7 Corporate Pk Ste 130 *TF:* 888-220-4477 ■ *Web:* www.globalcashcard.com	Irvine	CA	92606	949-751-0360		401
Global Center for Economic Enabling Environments 273 24th Ave *Web:* gceee.com	San Francisco	CA	94121	206-877-2460		463
Global Change Assoc 2576 Broadway *Web:* www.global-change.com	New York	NY	10025	212-316-0223		194
Global Citizen Year Inc 1625 Clay St Ste 400 *Web:* www.globalcitizenyear.org	Oakland	CA	94612	415-963-9293		305
Global Cloud 30 W Third St Unit 2 *TF:* 866-244-0450 ■ *Web:* www.globalcloud.net	Cincinnati	OH	45202	866-244-0450		196
Global Commercial Credit 30200 Telegraph Rd Ste 450 *Web:* gccrisk.com	Bingham Farms	MI	48025	248-646-9400	646-0525	390
Global Communication Semiconductors Inc 23155 Kashiwa Ct *Web:* www.gcsincorp.com	Torrance	CA	90505	310-530-7274	517-8200	695
Global Computer Supplies Inc 11 Harbor Pk Dr *TF:* 888-381-2868 ■ *Web:* www.globalindustrial.com	Port Washington	NY	11050	888-381-2868		174
Global Concepts Enterprise Inc 785 Waverly Ct *Web:* www.globalconcepts.com	Holland	MI	49423	616-355-7657	355-7662	757
Global Consultants Inc 110 Allen Rd *TF:* 877-264-6424 ■ *Web:* www.collabera.com	Basking Ridge	NJ	07960	973-889-5200	292-1643	180
Global Contact Services LLC 118 S Main St *TF:* 844-324-5427 ■ *Web:* www.gcsagents.com	Salisbury	NC	28144	704-647-9621		393
Global Convergence Inc 700 Brooker Creek Blvd Ste 1000 *TF:* 877-818-8597 ■ *Web:* www.globalconvergence.com	Oldsmar	FL	34677	813-818-8597	818-9659	176
Global Credit Advisers LLC 101 Park Ave 26th Fl *Web:* www.globalcreditadvisers.com	New York	NY	10178	212-949-1860		401
Global Custom Security Inc 755 Lakefield Rd Ste B *TF:* 800-771-9991 ■ *Web:* globalcustom.com	Westlake Village	CA	91361	818-889-6900		366
Global Data Consultants LLC 1144 Kennebec Dr *TF:* 866-966-4562 ■ *Web:* gdcitsolutions.com	Chambersburg	PA	17201	717-262-2080		225
Global Domains International Inc 701 Palomar Airport Rd Ste 300 *Web:* www.worldsite.ws	Carlsbad	CA	92011	760-602-3000	602-3099	736
Global Dynamic Consulting Inc 11111 Houze Rd Ste 200 *Web:* www.gdcus.com	Roswell	GA	30076	678-292-5017	704-3339	194
Global Education New York 519 8th Ave 2nd Fl **Fax Area Code:* 212 ■ *Web:* www.genyusa.com	New York	NY	10018	646-794-8333	564-9358*	167-3
Global Educational Tours 7216 Madison Ave Ste U *Web:* www.globaledtours.com	Indianapolis	IN	46227	317-787-2787	787-2765	760
Global Elite Group 825 E Gate Blvd Ste 301 *TF:* 877-425-0999 ■ *Web:* globaleliteinc.com	Garden City	NY	11530	877-425-0999		693
Global Endowment Management LP 550 S Tryon St Ste 3500 *Web:* www.globalendowment.com	Charlotte	NC	28202	704-333-8282		303
Global Energy Services USA Inc 3220 Cypress Creek Pkwy Unit A3 *Web:* www.global-energy.ca	Houston	TX	77068	281-866-8544	770-0149	538
Global Entertainment Corp 6751 N Sunset Blvd Ste 200 *OTC:* GNTP	Glendale	AZ	85305	480-994-0772		360-3
Global Environment & Technology Foundation 2900 S Quincy St Ste 375 *Web:* www.getf.org	Arlington	VA	22206	703-379-2713	820-1815	196
Global Environmental Engineering Inc 363 S Airport *TF:* 800-423-2043 ■ *Web:* globaleei.com	Traverse City	MI	49686	231-264-3000		261
Global Equipment Services Corp 5215 Hellyer Ave Ste 130 *Web:* www.geservs.com	San Jose	CA	95138	669-234-1110		696
Global Exchange 901 Mission St Ste 306 *Web:* globalexchange.org	San Francisco	CA	94110	415-255-7296	255-7498	48-7
Global Experiences Inc 14 Annapolis St *TF:* 877-432-2762 ■ *Web:* www.globalexperiences.com	Annapolis	MD	21401	410-267-7306		194
Global Fastener Inc 10634 Control Pl *TF:* 800-553-7998 ■ *Web:* www.globalfasteners.com	Dallas	TX	75238	214-340-6068	340-3618	351
Global Filtration Inc 9207 Emmott St *TF:* 888-717-0888 ■ *Web:* www.globalfiltration.com	Houston	TX	77040	713-856-9800		21
Global Finance Magazine E 20th St *Web:* www.gfmag.com	New York	NY	10003	212-447-7900		457-5
Global Fitness Center Inc 215 Hamilton St *Web:* globalfitnesscenter.com	Leominster	MA	01453	978-537-2100		354
Global Franchise Group LLC 5555 Glenridge Connector Ste 850 *TF:* 800-524-6444 ■ *Web:* www.globalfranchise.com	Atlanta	GA	30342	770-514-4500	514-4903	792
Global Fulfillment 4 S Idaho St *Web:* www.gloful.com	Seattle	WA	98134	206-405-3350		781
Global Gaming Solutions LLC 1921 Cradduck Ste 200 *Web:* www.globalgamingsol.com	Ada	OK	74820	580-559-0886		642
Global Gear & Machining LLC 2500 Curtiss St *Web:* www.globalgearllc.com	Downers Grove	IL	60515	630-969-9400		295
Global Geophysical Services Inc 13927 S Gessner Rd *NYSE:* GGS ■ *Web:* www.globalgeophysical.com	Missouri City	TX	77489	713-972-9200	972-1008	225
Global Graphics Software Inc 5996 Clark Center Ave Ste 315 *Web:* www.globalgraphics.com	Sarasota	FL	34238	978-849-0011		225
Global Ground Support LLC 540 Old Hwy 56 *TF:* 888-780-0303 ■ *Web:* globalgroundsupport.com	Olathe	KS	66061	913-780-0300	780-0829	22
Global Health Care Exchange LLC (GHX) 1315 W Century Dr *TF:* 800-968-7449 ■ *Web:* www.ghx.com	Louisville	CO	80027	720-887-7000	887-7200	225
Global Help Desk Services Inc 2080 Silas Deane Hwy *TF:* 800-770-1075 ■ *Web:* www.ghdsi.com	Rocky Hill	CT	06067	800-770-1075		180
Global Hope Network 934 N Magnolia Ave Ste 310 *Web:* www.globalhopenetwork.org	Orlando	FL	32803	407-207-3256		138
Global HR Research LLC 24201 Walden Center Dr Ste 206 *TF:* 800-790-1205 ■ *Web:* www.ghrr.com	Bonita Springs	FL	34134	239-274-0048		260
Global Imaging Inc 2011 Cherry St Ste 116 *TF:* 800-787-9801 ■ *Web:* www.globalimaginginc.com	Louisville	CO	80027	303-673-9773		41
Global Immigration Associates PC 230 W Monroe Ste 2800 *Web:* giafirm.com	Chicago	IL	60606	312-722-6300		41
Global Inc 160 Cannery Rd *Web:* www.globalsfc.com	Somerset	PA	15501	814-445-9671	443-1453	454
Global Indemnity Group 3 Bala Plz E Ste 300 *Web:* www.global-indemnity.com	Bala Cynwyd	PA	19004	610-664-1500		403
Global Industries Inc 17 W Stow Rd *TF:* 800-220-1900 ■ *Web:* www.globalfurnituregroup.com	Marlton	NJ	08053	856-596-3390	596-5684	319-1
Global Inflight Products 8918 152nd Ave NE *Web:* www.gipusa.com	Redmond	WA	98052	425-558-2778		196
Global Infotek Inc 1920 Association Dr Ste 100 *Web:* globalinfotek.com	Reston	VA	20191	703-652-1600	652-1697	180
Global Inventures Inc 2400 Camino Ramon Ste 375 *Web:* www.inventures.com	San Ramon	CA	94583	925-275-6690		194

Company / Address	City	State	Zip	Phone	Fax	Class
Global IT Communications Inc 6720 Bright Ave *TF:* 877-822-5565 ■ *Web:* globalit.com	Whittier	CA	90601	562-698-2500		196
Global IT Inc 1300 W Walnut Hill Ln Ste 153 **Fax Area Code:* 214 ■ *Web:* www.globalitinc.com	Irving	TX	75038	972-536-6063	614-4954*	180
Global Knowledge Group Inc (GKG) 302 N Bryan Ave *TF:* 866-776-7584 ■ *Web:* www.gkg.net	Bryan	TX	77803	866-776-7584		808
Global Knowledge Training LLC 9000 Regency Pkwy Ste 400 *TF:* 877-200-8866 ■ *Web:* www.globalknowledge.com	Cary	NC	27518	919-461-8600	461-8646	764
Global Learning Partners (GLP) PO Box 301 *TF:* 888-432-2763 ■ *Web:* www.globalearning.com	Montpelier	VT	05601	207-926-6183		196
Global Learning Resources Inc 46330 Sentinel Dr *Web:* www.glresources.com	Fremont	CA	94539	510-659-0179		194
Global Linguist Solutions LLC 1155 Herndon Pkwy Falls Church Ste 100 **Fax Area Code:* 866 ■ *TF:* 800-349-9142 ■ *Web:* www.gls-corp.com	Herndon	VA	20170	800-349-9142	452-7591*	393
Global Link Productions Inc 16315 Vineyard Blvd Ste B *Web:* www.globalinktv.com	Morgan Hill	CA	95037	408-465-2787		681
Global Logistics 99 W Hawthorne Ave L-12 *Web:* www.globallog.com	Valley Stream	NY	11580	516-825-2922	825-1143	449
Global LT Inc 1871 Woodslee Dr *TF:* 888-645-5881 ■ *Web:* global-lt.com	Troy	MI	48083	248-786-0999	786-0985	260
Global Management Systems Inc (GMSI) 2201 Wisconsin Ave NW Ste 300 *Web:* gmsi.com	Washington	DC	20007	202-471-4674		180
Global Market Development Ctr (GMDC) 1275 Lake Plaza Dr *Web:* www.gmdc.org	Colorado Springs	CO	80906	719-576-4260	576-2661	49-18
Global Marketing Group Worldwide LLC 704 Executive Blvd Ste I *Web:* www.gmgww.com	Valley Cottage	NY	10989	201-475-7755		194
Global Material Technologies 750 W Lake Cook Rd Ste 480 *Web:* www.gmt-inc.com	Buffalo Grove	IL	60089	847-202-7000	215-4838	1
Global Maxfin Investments Inc 100 Mural St Ste 201 *TF:* 866-666-5266 ■ *Web:* www.globalmaxfin.ca	Richmond Hill	ON	L4B1J3	416-741-1544		690
Global Medical Imaging LLC 222 Rampart St *TF:* 800-958-9986 ■ *Web:* gmi3.com	Charlotte	NC	28203	800-958-9986		475
Global Medical LLC 8332 Bristol Ct *TF:* 800-528-1001 ■ *Web:* www.joerns.com	Jessup	MD	20794	800-528-1001		475
Global Medical Solutions LLC 1750 S Brentwood Blvd Ste 300 **Fax Area Code:* 888 ■ *TF:* 877-346-0909 ■ *Web:* www.global-medical-solutions.com	Saint Louis	MO	63144	877-346-0909	950-3461*	475
Global Medical Solutions Ltd 14140 Ventura Blvd *Web:* www.globalmedicalsolutions.com	Sherman Oaks	CA	91423	818-783-2915	783-2942	363
Global MetalForm LP 733 Davis St *Web:* www.markreuther.com	Scranton	PA	18505	570-346-3871	346-1612	254
Global Micro Solutions Inc 21250 Hawthorne Blvd Ste 540 *Web:* www.gmsnet.com	Torrance	CA	90503	310-218-5678		177
Global Mrv Inc 385 Cleveland Dr Ste 202 *Web:* globalmrv.com	Buffalo	NY	14215	716-893-5800		104
Global Nest LLC 281 SR-79 N Ste 208 *TF:* 866-850-5872 ■ *Web:* www.globalnest.com	Morganville	NJ	07751	732-333-5848		177
Global Neuro-Diagnostics LP 2670 Firewheel Dr Ste B *TF:* 866-848-2522 ■ *Web:* globalneuro.natus.com	Flower Mound	TX	75028	866-848-2522		418
Global New Beginnings Inc 4042 W 82nd Ct *Web:* www.gnbiusa.com	Merrillville	IN	46410	219-738-3600	738-3610	463
Global Nursing Home Health Inc 7105 SW 8th St Ste 401 *Web:* www.globalnursinghomehealth.com	Miami	FL	33157	305-646-8220	646-8213	363
Global Offset & Countertrade Assn (GOCA) 818 Connecticut Ave NW 12th Fl *Web:* www.globaloffset.org	Washington	DC	20006	202-887-9011		49-18
Global Organization & Planning Services LLC PO Box 3091 *Web:* www.globalorganizationplanning.com	Newark	NJ	07103	973-374-6637		193
Global Outsourcing Services Inc 40 Fleetwood Ct Ste 2 *Web:* www.gostechnicalservices.com	Ronkonkoma	NY	11779	631-471-6798		180
Global Pacific Financial Services Ltd 10430 144 St *TF:* 800-561-1177 ■ *Web:* www.globalpacific.com	Surrey	BC	V3T4V5	800-561-1177		317
Global Parts Distributors LLC 3279 Avondale Mill Rd *TF:* 800-722-5089 ■ *Web:* www.globalpartsdist.com	Macon	GA	31216	478-781-9854	781-6006	61
Global Parts Support Inc 2550 NW 4th Ct *Web:* www.globalpartssupport.com	Fort Lauderdale	FL	33023	954-989-5988		770
Global Payment Technologies Inc 170 Wilbur Pl *OTC:* GPTX ■ *Web:* www.gpta.com.au	Bohemia	NY	11716	631-563-2500		111
Global Payments Inc 3550 Lenox Rd Ste 3000 *NYSE:* GPN ■ *TF:* 800-560-2960 ■ *Web:* www.globalpaymentsinc.com	Atlanta	GA	30326	770-829-8000		255
Global Polymer Industries Inc 1001 SE 12th St *Web:* www.globalpolymer.com	Madison	SD	57042	605-256-3150	256-3154	604
Global Power Equipment Group Inc 400 E Las Colinas Blvd Ste 400 *NASDAQ:* GLPW	Irving	TX	75039	214-574-2700	853-4744	697
Global Precast Inc 2101 Teston Rd *Web:* www.globalprecast.com	Maple	ON	L6A1R3	905-832-4307		106
Global Productivity Solutions LLC 19176 Hall Rd Ste 250 *Web:* globalproductivitysolutions.com	Clinton Township	MI	48038	586-412-9609	314-0203	196
Global Public Affairs Inc 50 O'Connor St Ste 901 *Web:* www.globalpublicaffairs.ca	Ottawa	ON	K1P6L2	613-782-2336		194
Global Pump Company LLC 10162 E Coldwater Rd *TF:* 866-360-7867 ■ *Web:* www.globalpump.com	Davison	MI	48423	810-653-4828		641
Global Quality Assurance Inc 6900 Tavistock Lakes Blvd Ste 400 **Fax Area Code:* 800 ■ *TF:* 888-322-3330 ■ *Web:* globalqualityassurance.com	Orlando	FL	32827	888-322-3330	308-6217*	463
Global Reach Internet Productions LLC 2321 N Loop Dr Ste 101 *TF:* 877-254-9828 ■ *Web:* www.globalreach.com	Ames	IA	50010	515-996-0996		177
Global Relay Communications Inc 220 Cambie St *TF:* 866-484-6630 ■ *Web:* www.globalrelay.com	Vancouver	BC	V6B2M9	604-484-6630		224
Global Resources International Inc 4142 Industry Way *Web:* www.gri-usa.com	Flowery Branch	GA	30542	678-866-0550	866-0551	475
Global Results Communications 201 E Sandpointe Ave Ste 650 *Web:* www.globalresultspr.com	Santa Ana	CA	92707	949-608-0276		636
Global SATCOM Technology Inc 9141 Arbuckle Dr *Web:* www.globalsatcom.com	Gaithersburg	MD	20877	301-963-0088		194
Global Science & Technology Inc 7855 Walker Dr Ste 200 **Fax Area Code:* 240 ■ *Web:* www.gst.com	Greenbelt	MD	20770	301-474-9696	366-5743*	387
Global Search Network Inc 118 S Fremont Ave *TF:* 800-254-3398 ■ *Web:* www.globalsearchnetwork.com	Tampa	FL	33606	813-832-8300		193
Global Security Glazing 616 Selfield Rd *TF:* 800-633-2513 ■ *Web:* www.security-glazing.com	Selma	AL	36703	334-875-1900		329
Global Security Intl 8757 Rand Ave Ste B *Web:* gsii.net	Daphne	AL	36526	251-621-0770	621-0760	692
Global Security Management Agency Inc 1781 Vineyard Dr *Web:* www.gsmasecurity.com	Antioch	CA	94509	925-262-4181		692
Global Shop Solutions Inc 975 Evergreen Cir *TF:* 800-364-5958 ■ *Web:* www.globalshopsolutions.com	The Woodlands	TX	77380	281-681-1959	681-2663	178-1
Global Solar Energy Inc 8500 S Rita Rd *Web:* www.globalsolar.com	Tucson	AZ	85747	520-546-6313	546-6318	696
Global Solutions Network Inc 121 Congressional Ln Ste 302 *Web:* www.gsnhome.com	Rockville	MD	20852	301-881-7012		177
Global Specialty Products Ltd 2480 Chaska Blvd *Web:* globalspecialtyproducts.net	Chaska	MN	55318	952-448-6566		553
Global Sports & Entertainment Inc 2121 Rosecrans Ave Ste 4320 *Web:* globalsports-ent.com	El Segundo	CA	90245	310-414-2690	414-9740	717
Global Steering Systems LLC 156 Park Rd *Web:* www.globalsteering.com	Watertown	CT	06795	860-945-5400		247
Global Stock Trends Corp 1 Park Pl 621 NW 53rd St Ste 240 *Web:* www.globalstocktrends.com	Boca Raton	FL	33487	401-885-4606	886-5678	194
Global Strategy Group LLC 215 Park Ave S 5th Fl *Web:* www.globalstrategygroup.com	New York	NY	10003	212-260-8813		194
Global Systems Technologies Inc 109 Floral Vale Blvd *Web:* gstpa.com	Yardley	PA	19067	215-579-8200		256
Global Tax Network US LLC 7950 Main St N Ste 200 *TF:* 888-486-2695 ■ *Web:* www.gtn.com	Maple Grove	MN	55369	763-746-4556	252-0304	734
Global Telecom Group Inc 43488 White Birch Way *Web:* www.globaltelecomgroup.com	Ashburn	VA	20147	678-896-2468		224
Global Tissue Group 870 Express Dr S *Web:* www.gtgtissue.com	Medford	NY	11763	631-419-1300		548
Global Titanium Inc (GTI) 19300 Filer Ave **Fax Area Code:* 313 ■ *TF:* 800-762-7602 ■ *Web:* www.globaltitanium.com	Detroit	MI	48234	800-762-7602	366-5305*	723
Global Touchpoints Inc 3005 Douglas Blvd Ste 108 *Web:* touchpointsinc.com	Roseville	CA	95661	916-878-5940	878-5951	177
Global Trading & Sourcing Corp 1587 College Park Business Center Rd *Web:* www.gtsco.com	Orlando	FL	32804	407-532-7600		360-3
Global Travel Intl 1060 Maitland Center Commons Ste 305 *TF:* 800-715-4440 ■ *Web:* www.globaltravel.com	Maitland	FL	32751	407-660-7800	875-0711	772
Global Trim Sales Inc 22835 Savi Ranch Pkwy Ste A *Web:* www.globaltrim.com	Yorba Linda	CA	92887	714-998-4400	998-4884	627
Global TV Concepts Ltd 676 S Military Trl *Web:* www.globaltvconcepts.com	Deerfield Beach	FL	33442	954-570-9999	570-9990	7
Global University 1211 S Glenstone Ave *TF:* 800-443-1083 ■ *Web:* www.globaluniversity.edu	Springfield	MO	65804	417-862-9533	865-7167	766
Global Ventures Inc 4721 354th Ave SE *Web:* www.globalventuresinc.com	Fall City	WA	98024	206-292-1428	292-1426	194
Global Village English Centres 888 Cambie St *Web:* gvenglish.com	Vancouver	BC	V6B2P6	604-684-1118		423
Global Village Marketing & Data Services Inc 2710 Thomes Ave *Web:* www.globalvillagemktg.com	Cheyenne	WY	82001	307-222-4135		7
Global Voyages Group LLC 10400 NE 4th St Ste 500 *Web:* globalvoyagesgroup.com	Bellevue	WA	98004	425-637-8558		463

Phone | Fax | Class

obal Wildlife Ctr 26389 Hwy 40 Folsom LA 70437 985-796-3585 796-9487 823
Web: www.globalwildlife.com
obal Window Solutions
128 Industrial Park Rd Richibucto NB E4W4A4 506-523-4900 499
Web: globalwindows.ca
obal Winds Harvest 103 Front St Schenectady NY 12305 518-280-2927 245
Web: www.globalwinds.com
lobalDie 1130 Minot Ave PO Box 1120 Auburn ME 04211 207-514-7252 514-7202 757
TF: 800-910-3747 ■ *Web:* www.globaldie.com
lobalFluency Inc 1494 Hamilton Way San Jose CA 95125 408-677-5300 677-5301 194
Web: www.globalfluency.com
lobalfoundries Inc
2600 Great America Way Santa Clara CA 95054 408-462-3900 308
Web: www.globalfoundries.com
lobalGiving Foundation Inc
1110 Vermont Ave NW Ste 550 Washington DC 20005 202-232-5784 305
Web: www.globalgiving.org
lobalMedia Group LLC
15020 N 74th St Scottsdale AZ 85260 480-922-0044 922-1090 52
Web: www.globalmed.com
GlobalMeet
2300 Lakeview Pkwy Ste 300 Alpharetta GA 30009 866-962-8400 176
TF: 866-962-8400 ■ *Web:* www.pgi.com
GlobalParts.aero 901 Industrial Rd Augusta KS 67010 316-733-9240 22
TF: 855-398-4252 ■ *Web:* www.globalparts.aero
GlobalPhone Corp
137 N Washington St Falls Church VA 22046 703-533-2122 194
TF: 800-705-5033 ■ *Web:* www.gphone.com
Globalscale Technologies Inc
1200 N Van Buren St Ste D Anaheim CA 92807 714-632-9239 632-7550 787
Web: globalscaletechnologies.com
Globalspec Inc 350 Jordan Rd Troy NY 12180 518-880-0200 880-0250 180
TF: 800-261-2052 ■ *Web:* www.globalspec.com
Globalstar 300 Holiday Square Blvd Covington LA 70433 877-452-5782 933-4100* 681
**Fax Area Code:* 408 ■ *TF:* 877-728-7466 ■ *Web:* www.globalstar.com
Globalstor Data Corp
9960 Congoga Ave Unit D9 Chatsworth CA 91311 818-701-7771 761
Web: globalstor.com
GlobalTranz Inc 5415 E High St Phoenix AZ 85054 866-275-1407 311
TF: 866-275-1407 ■ *Web:* www.globaltranz.com
GlobalWorks Group LLC 220 5th Ave New York NY 10001 212-252-8800 4
Global-Z International Inc
395 Shields Dr Bennington VT 05201 802-445-1011 196
Web: globalz.com
Globat LLC
11684 Ventrura Blvd Ste 825 Studio City CA 91604 323-874-9000 225
Web: www.globat.com
Globe & Mail Inc, The
351 King St East Ste 1600 Toronto ON M5A0N1 416-585-5420 531-2
Web: www.theglobeandmail.com
Globe Consultants Inc
3112 Porter St Ste D Soquel CA 95073 800-208-0663 193
TF: 800-208-0663 ■ *Web:* www.globeconsultants.com
Globe Die-Cutting Products Inc
76 Liberty St Metuchen NJ 08840 732-494-7744 561
Web: www.globediecutting.com
Globe Electronic Hardware Inc
34-24 56th St Woodside NY 11377 718-457-0303 457-7493 203
TF: 800-221-1505 ■ *Web:* www.globelectronics.com
Globe Energy Services LLC
3204 W Hwy 180 Snyder TX 79549 325-573-1310 592-4809* 539
**Fax Area Code:* 806 ■ *TF:* 888-580-7747 ■ *Web:* gravityoilfieldservices.com
Globe Engineering Company Inc
1539 S St Paul St PO Box 12407 Wichita KS 67213 316-943-1266 943-3089 22
Web: www.globeeng.com
Globe Food Equipment Co 2153 Dryden Rd Dayton OH 45439 937-299-5493 299-8623 298
TF: 800 347 5423 ■ *Web:* globefoodequip.com
Globe Institute of Recording & Production
351 9th St Ste 202 San Francisco CA 94103 415-777-2486 250
Web: globe-recording.com
Globe Iron Foundry Inc
5649 E Randolph St Commerce CA 90040 323-723-8983 888-9664 492
Web: www.globeiron.com
Globe Life PO Box 8080 McKinney TX 75070 405-755-8282 194
Web: www.globelifeinsurance.com
Globe Machine Manufacturing Company Inc
701 E D St Tacoma WA 98421 253-383-2584 572-9672 190
Web: www.globemachine.com
Globe Midwest/Adjusters Intl
25800 NW Hwy Ste 885 Southfield MI 48075 248-352-2100 354-0193 194
TF: 800-445-1554 ■ *Web:* www.globemw-ai.com
Globe Motors 2275 Stanley Ave Dayton OH 45404 937-228-3171 229-8531 518
Web: www.globe-motors.com
Globe Photos LLC
6445 S Tenaya Way Ste B130 Las Vegas NV 89113 631-661-3131 442-2747* 588
**Fax Area Code:* 702 ■ *Web:* www.globephotos.com
Globe Products Inc 5051 Kitridge Rd Dayton OH 45424 937-233-0233 233-5290 386
Web: www.globe-usa.com
Globe Tax Services Inc
1 New York Plz 34th Fl New York NY 10004 212-747-9100 194
Web: www.globetax.com
Globe Ticket 350 Randy Rd Ste 1 Carol Stream IL 60188 800-523-5968 627
TF: 800-523-5968 ■ *Web:* www.globeticket.com
Globe Turbocharger Specialties Inc
201 Edison Way Reno NV 89502 775-856-7337 262
Web: www.globeturbocharger.com
Globecomm Systems Inc 45 Oser Ave Hauppauge NY 11788 631-231-9800 231-1557 647
NASDAQ: GCOM ■ *TF:* 866-499-0223 ■ *Web:* www.globecomm.com
Globe-Gazette 300 N Washington Mason City IA 50402 641-421-0500 421-7108 532-2
TF: 800-421-0546 ■ *Web:* globegazette.com
Globenet International Corp
4995 NW 72nd Ave Ste 303 Miami FL 33166 305-513-0323 180
Web: globenetcorp.com
GlobeRanger Corp
1130 E Arapaho Rd Ste 600 Richardson TX 75081 972-744-9977 744-9988 177
TF: 877-744-9977 ■ *Web:* www.globeranger.com
Globespan Capital Partners
1 Boston Pl Ste 2810 Boston MA 02108 617-305-2300 792
Web: www.globespancapital.com

Globetrotter Services Inc (GSI)
PO Box 154801 Waco TX 76715 254-799-9556 192
Web: www.mwradio.com
Globetrotters Engineering Corp
300 S Wacker Dr Ste 400 Chicago IL 60606 312-922-6400 261
Web: www.gec-group.com
Globex Corp 3620 Stutz Dr Canfield OH 44406 330-533-0030 256
TF: 800-533-8610 ■ *Web:* www.globexcorp.com
Globex International Inc
570 Lexington Ave 15th Fl New York NY 10022 212-308-2300 308-0202 196
Web: www.globexusa.com
Globitech Inc 200 Fm 1417 W Sherman TX 75092 903-957-1999 186
Web: www.globitech.com
Glock Inc 6000 Highlands Pkwy Smyrna GA 30082 770-432-1202 433-8719 284
Web: us.glock.com
Glo-Quartz Electric Heater Company Inc
7084 Maple St Mentor OH 44060 440-255-9701 255-7852 318
TF: 800-321-3574 ■ *Web:* www.gloquartz.com
Gloretta H. Hall PA 1115 SE Ocean Blvd Stuart FL 34996 772-324-8166 41
Web: glorettahhallpa.com
Gloria Ferrer Caves & Vineyards
23555 Hwy 121 Sonoma CA 95476 707-933-1917 226
TF: 866-845-6742 ■ *Web:* www.gloriaferrer.com
Gloria Francis School of Make-Up Artistry Ltd
2 Nelson Ave Hicksville NY 11801 516-822-5546 685
TF: 877-277-2434 ■ *Web:* www.gloriafrancis.com
Gloria K. School
1979 Marcus Ave Ste C100 Lake Success NY 11042 516-487-7200 487-4891 685
Web: www.gloriak.net
Glorietta Bay Inn
1630 Glorietta Blvd Coronado CA 92118 619-435-3101 435-6182 379
TF: 800-283-9383 ■ *Web:* www.gloriettabayinn.com
Glory Foods Inc 901 Oak St Columbus OH 43205 614-252-2042 297-8
Web: www.gloryfoods.com
Glorybee Foods Inc 29548 B Airport Rd Eugene OR 97402 800-456-7923 689-9692* 296-24
**Fax Area Code:* 541 ■ *TF:* 800-456-7923 ■ *Web:* glorybee.com
Glotech Inc
1801 Research Blvd Ste 605 Rockville MD 20850 757-499-3650 180
Web: glotech.net
Gloto Corp 8171 Maple Lawn Blvd Ste 250 Fulton MD 20759 301-317-9800 177
Web: www.gloto.com
Gloucester County 6467 Main St Gloucester VA 23061 804-693-4042 693-6004 338
Web: gloucesterva.info
Gloucester County
2 S Broad St PO Box 337 Woodbury NJ 08096 856-853-3237 853-3327 338
Web: gloucestercountynj.gov
Gloucester County Historical Society (GCHS)
17 Hunter St Woodbury NJ 08096 856-845-4771 48-13
Web: www.gchsnj.org
Gloucester County Library System
389 Wolfert Stn Rd Mullica Hill NJ 08062 856-223-6000 223-6039 434-3
Web: gcls.org
Gloves Inc 1950 Collins Blvd Austell GA 30106 770-944-9186 944-0012 155-8
TF: 800-476-4568 ■ *Web:* www.glovesinc.com
Gloyer'S Pharmacy Inc 1010 W Main St Tomball TX 77375 281-351-5454 237
Web: www.gloyers.com
GLP (Gary Lee Partners)
833 N Orleans St Ste 400 Chicago IL 60610 312-640-8300 393
Web: www.garyleepartners.com
GLP (Graham Lundberg & Peschel)
2153 Bethel Rd SE Port Orchard WA 98366 360-876-5005 428
Web: www.glpattorneys.com
GLP (Global Learning Partners)
PO Box 301 Montpelier VT 05601 207-926-6183 196
TF: 888-432-2763 ■ *Web:* www.globalearning.com
GLS (Golden Lab Software Inc)
1735 Buford Hwy Ste 215-144 Cumming GA 30041 770-886-8947 180
Web: www.goldenlabsoftware.com
GLS (Government Liaison Services Inc)
200 N Glebe Rd Ste 321 Arlington VA 22203 703-524-8200 525-8451 635
TF: 800-642-6564 ■ *Web:* www.trademarkinfo.com
GLS Associates Inc PO Box 7174 Alexandria VA 22307 703-549-8800 549-8803 681
Web: www.gls.net
GLS Companies Inc
6845 Winnetka Cir Brooklyn Park MN 55428 763-535-7277 195
TF: 888-646-7277 ■ *Web:* glsprecisionmarketing.com
Gls Group Inc 27850 Detroit Rd Westlake OH 44145 800-955-9435 184
TF: 800-955-9435 ■ *Web:* www.glsgroup.com
Glu Mobile Inc
500 Howard St Ste 300 San Francisco CA 94105 415-800-6100 800-6087 177
Web: www.glu.com
Glumac Inc 150 California St San Francisco CA 94111 415-398-7667 256
Web: www.glumac.com
Glunt Industries Inc 319 N River Rd NW Warren OH 44483 330-399-7585 393-0387 386
Web: www.glunt.com
Glunz & Jensen K & F Inc
12633 Industrial Dr Granger IN 46530 574-272-9950 628
Web: www.glunz-jensen.com
Gluten Intolerance Group (GIG)
31214 124th Ave SE Auburn WA 98092 253-833-6655 833-6675 48-17
Web: www.gluten.org
Glynn & Finley LLP
100 Pringle Ave Ste 500 Walnut Creek CA 94596 925-210-2800 945-1975 428
Web: www.glynnfinley.com
Glynn County 701 G St Brunswick GA 31520 912-554-7400 554-7596 338
Web: www.glynncounty.org
Glynndevins Adv & Mktg
8880 Ward Pkwy Ste 400 Kansas City MO 64114 913-491-0600 4
Web: www.glynndevins.com
Glyph Language Services Inc
16201 E Indiana Ave Ste 4500 Spokane WA 99216 866-274-3218 390-9651* 768
**Fax Area Code:* 877 ■ *TF:* 866-274-3218 ■ *Web:* www.glyphservices.com
Glytec LLC 10 Patewood Dr Greenville SC 29615 864-370-3297 743
Web: www.glytecsystems.com
Gly-Tech Services Inc 2054 Paxton St Harvey LA 70058 504-348-8566 348-8261 539
Web: www.glytech.com
GM (General Machinery Company Inc)
921 1st Ave N Birmingham AL 35203 205-251-9243 252-9723 385
TF: 800-821-5937 ■ *Web:* www.generalmachinery.com

Phone | Fax | Class

GM Cable Contractors Inc
9232 Joor Rd . . . Baton Rouge LA 70818 225-261-9800 261-9884 116
TF: 800-460-8070 ■ *Web:* gmcable.com

Gm Financial Consultants Corp
191 Presidental Blvd Ste W-1 . . . Bala Cynwyd PA 19004 610-664-4088 390
Web: www.gmfinan.com

GM Nameplate Inc 2040 15th Ave W . . . Seattle WA 98119 206-284-2200 284-3705 481
TF: 800-366-7668 ■ *Web:* www.gmnameplate.com

GMA (Gospel Music Assn)
4012 Granny White Pk . . . Nashville TN 37204 615-242-0303 254-9755 48-4
Web: www.gospelmusic.org

GMA (George Mcelroy & Associates Inc)
1412 Main St Ste 1500 . . . Dallas TX 75202 214-905-3700 905-3777 463
Web: www.gmainc.com

GMAC (General Motors Acceptance Corp)
8375 Dix Ellis Tr Ste 200 . . . Detroit MI 48265 877-320-2559 428-4622* 217
**Fax Area Code:* 800 ■ *TF:* 877-320-2559 ■ *Web:* www.ally.com

GMAC (Graduate Management Admission Council)
11921 Freedom Dr Ste 300 . . . Reston VA 20190 703-668-9600 668-9601 48-11
TF: 866-505-6559 ■ *Web:* www.gmac.com

GMarie Group Inc, The
5621 W Beverly Ln . . . Glendale AZ 85306 602-864-1385 196
Web: www.gmariegroup.com

Gmb Plastics Inc 4490 Alicia Ln . . . Cumming GA 30028 770-887-8008 605-2
Web: www.gmbplastics.com

GMBHA (Greater Miami & The Beaches Hotel Assn)
1688 Meridian Ave Ste 500 . . . Miami Beach FL 33139 305-531-3553 531-8954 376
Web: www.gmbha.com

GMDC (Global Market Development Ctr)
1275 Lake Plaza Dr . . . Colorado Springs CO 80906 719-576-4260 576-2661 49-18
Web: www.gmdc.org

GMF (General Metal Finishing Company Inc)
42 Frank Mossberg Dr . . . Attleboro MA 02703 508-226-5606 481
Web: www.pepgenmetal.com

GMF (Gross Mortgage Finance Inc)
3325 S University Dr Ste 200 . . . Davie FL 33328 954-475-7784 688-2522 509
Web: www.grossmortgage.com

GMFSI (Green Mountain Florist Supply Inc)
45 Swift St . . . South Burlington VT 05403 802-865-4447 863-8330 293
TF: 800-639-7077 ■ *Web:* www.gmfsi.com

GMHC (Gay Men's Health Crisis)
119 W 24th St . . . New York NY 10011 212-367-1000 48-17
TF: 800-243-7692 ■ *Web:* www.gmhc.org

GMI (Grace Management Inc)
6900 Wedgwood Rd N Ste 300 . . . Minneapolis MN 55422 763-544-9934 194
Web: www.gracemanagement.com

GMI (General Microsystems Inc)
3220 118th Ave SE . . . Bellevue WA 98005 425-644-2233 174
Web: www.gmi.com

GMI Building Services Inc
8001 Vickers St . . . San Diego CA 92111 866-803-4464 256
TF: 866-803-4464 ■ *Web:* www.gmiweb.com

Gmi Inc 4822 E 355th St . . . Willoughby OH 44094 440-953-8811 326
Web: www.gmiincusa.com

GMO LLC 40 Rowes Wharf . . . Boston MA 02110 617-330-7500 528
Web: www.gmo.com

GMP Laboratories of America Inc
2931 E La Jolla St . . . Anaheim CA 92806 714-630-2467 237-1374 582
Web: gmplabs.com

GMP Metal Products Inc
3883 Delor St . . . Saint Louis MO 63116 314-481-0300 481-1379 273
TF: 800-325-9808 ■ *Web:* www.gmpmetal.com

Gmp Networks LLC
4729 E Sunrise Dr Ste 121 . . . Tucson AZ 85718 480-719-0540 180
Web: www.gmpnet.net

GMP Scientific Inc
41 University Dr Ste 400 . . . Newtown PA 18940 267-334-5722 192
Web: www.gmpscientific.com

GMR Marketing LLC 5000 S Towne Dr . . . New Berlin WI 53151 262-786-5600 636
TF: 800-447-8560 ■ *Web:* www.gmrmarketing.com

GMS Group LLC, The
5 N Regent St Ste 513 . . . Livingston NJ 07039 973-535-5000 690
Web: www.gmsgroup.com

GMSI (Global Management Systems Inc)
2201 Wisconsin Ave NW Ste 300 . . . Washington DC 20007 202-471-4674 180
Web: gmsi.com

GMW Associates Inc
955 Industrial Rd . . . San Carlos CA 94070 650-802-8292 802-8298 358
Web: www.gmw.com

GN Bank 4619 S King Dr . . . Chicago IL 60653 773-624-2000 70
Web: www.gnbank.net

GN Diamond LLC 800 Chestnut St . . . Philadelphia PA 19107 800-724-8810 410
TF: 800-724-8810 ■ *Web:* www.gndiamond.com

GN Hearing 8001 E Bloomington Fwy . . . Bloomington MN 55420 888-735-4327 250
TF: 888-735-4327 ■ *Web:* www.resound.com

GN Plastics Company Ltd
345 Old Trunk 3 . . . Chester NS B0J1J0 902-275-3571 358
Web: www.gnplastics.com

GNA (Georgia Nurses Assn)
3032 Briarcliff Rd NE . . . Atlanta GA 30329 404-325-5536 325-0407 533
TF: 800-324-0462 ■ *Web:* georgianurses.nursingnetwork.com

Gnarus Advisors LLC
4350 N Fairfax Dr Ste 830 . . . Arlington VA 22203 571-279-8853 463
Web: gnarusllc.com

Gnc Community Federal Credit Union
201 S Jefferson St . . . New Castle PA 16101 724-652-5783 652-9864 219
TF: 800-790-5250 ■ *Web:* gncfcu.com

GNC Consulting Inc
21195 S LaGrange Rd . . . Frankfort IL 60423 815-469-7255 196
Web: www.gnc-consulting.com

GNC Inc 300 Sixth Ave . . . Pittsburgh PA 15222 412-288-4600 355
NYSE: GNC ■ *TF:* 877-462-4700 ■ *Web:* www.gnc.com

GNCB Consulting Engineers PC
130 Elm St PO Box 802 . . . Old Saybrook CT 06475 860-388-1224 261
Web: gncbengineers.com

GNFCC (Greater North Fulton Chamber of Commerce)
11605 Haynes Bridge Rd Ste 100 . . . Alpharetta GA 30009 770-993-8806 594-1059 139
Web: www.gnfcc.com

Gnomon School of Visual Effects
1015 N Cahuenga Blvd . . . Hollywood CA 90038 323-466-6663 466-6710 685
Web: www.gnomonschool.com

Gnutti Carlo USA Inc
1310 Francis St W . . . Jacksonville AL 36265 256-435-2200 768-5470* 60
**Fax Area Code:* 201 ■ *Web:* gnutticarlo.com

Go 2 Group 138 N Hickory Ave . . . Bel Air MD 21014 877-442-4669 177
TF: 877-442-4669 ■ *Web:* www.go2group.com

Go 963 420 N Fifth St Ste 150 . . . Minneapolis MN 55401 612-659-4848 645
Web: goradiomn.com

Go Edit Inc 5542 Satsuma Ave . . . North Hollywood CA 91601 818-284-6260 301-3262 512
Web: goedit.tv

Go Industries Inc 420 N Grove Rd . . . Richardson TX 75081 972-783-7444 54
Web: goindustriesinc.com

Go Native Yacht Charters
1900 Purdy Ave . . . Miami Beach FL 33139 305-534-5522 148
Web: www.gnyc.com

Go Next 8000 W 78th St Ste 345 . . . Minneapolis MN 55439 952-918-8950 918-8975 760
TF: 800-842-9023 ■ *Web:* www.gonext.com

Go Pro Management Inc 22 Cynthia Rd . . . Needham MA 02494 781-444-5753 196
Web: www.gopromanagement.com

Go Transit 20 Bay St Ste 600 . . . Toronto ON M5J2W3 416-869-3200 869-3525 468
Web: www.gotransit.com

Go Travel Inc 2811 W SR 434 . . . Longwood FL 32779 800-848-3005 775
TF: 800-848-3005 ■ *Web:* www.gotravel.com

Go West Adventures Inc
PO Box 882319 . . . Los Angeles CA 90009 310-216-2522 760
Web: www.gowestadventures.com

Go West Tours Inc
790 Eddy St at Van Ness . . . San Francisco CA 94109 415-837-0154 775
Web: www.gowesttours.com

Go. With Jo! Tours & Travels
121 W Tyler . . . Harlingen TX 78550 956-423-1446 760
TF: 800-999-1446 ■ *Web:* www.gowithjo.com

Go2 Communications Inc 8 Cedar St . . . Woburn MA 01801 781-376-2100 371-0369* 5
**Fax Area Code:* 815 ■ *Web:* go2communications.com

Go2 Media Design Inc
40 Oakridge Pkwy . . . Peekskill NY 10566 914-734-1430 631
Web: www.go2mediadesign.com

GOA Regional Business Assn
1200 N Arlington Heights Rd Ste 240 . . . Itasca IL 60143 630-773-2944 139
Web: www.thegoa.com

Goal Sporting Goods Inc
37 Industrial Park Rd PO Box 236 . . . Essex CT 06426 860-767-9112 767-9121 710
TF: 800-334-4625 ■ *Web:* www.goalsports.com

GoalBusters LLC 555 N Pinecliff Dr . . . Flagstaff AZ 86001 888-883-2690 194
TF: 888-883-2690 ■ *Web:* www.goalbusters.net

GoalLine Solutions
3115 Harvester Rd Ste 200 . . . Burlington ON L7N3H8 866-788-4625 399-3099 195
TF: 866-788-4625 ■ *Web:* www.goallinesolutions.com

Goals & Poles 7575 Jefferson Hwy . . . Baton Rouge LA 70806 225-923-0622 710
TF: 800-275-0317 ■ *Web:* www.goalsandpoles.com

Goalsetter Systems Inc
1041 Cordova Ave . . . Lynnville IA 50153 800-362-4625 594-3343* 710
**Fax Area Code:* 641 ■ *TF:* 800-362-4625 ■ *Web:* www.goalsetter.com

GoalsGuy Learning Systems Inc (GGLS)
36181 E Lake Rd Ste 139 . . . Palm Harbor FL 34685 877-462-5748 192
TF: 877-462-5748 ■ *Web:* www.goalsguy.com

Gobbell Hays Partners Inc
12015 E 46th Ave Ste 450 . . . Denver CO 80239 303-574-0082 463
Web: ghp1.com

Gobin's Inc 615 N Santa Fe Ave . . . Pueblo CO 81003 719-544-2324 544-2378 535
TF: 800-425-2324 ■ *Web:* www.gobins.com

Goblin Valley State Park
PO Box 637 . . . Green River UT 84525 435-275-4584 565
Web: utah.com

GOCA (Global Offset & Countertrade Assn)
818 Connecticut Ave NW 12th Fl . . . Washington DC 20006 202-887-9011 49-18
Web: www.globaloffset.org

God Owns This Company Inc
777 Hill Ave . . . Muskegon MI 49442 231-727-3333 48-20
Web: godownsthiscompany.com

God's Bible School & College
1810 Young St . . . Cincinnati OH 45202 513-721-7944 161
Web: www.gbs.edu

God's Learning Ch (GLC) PO Box 61000 . . . Midland TX 79711 432-563-0420 563-1736 740
TF: 800-707-0420 ■ *Web:* glc.us.com

GoDaddy East LLC 14455 N Hayden Rd . . . Scottsdale AZ 85260 480-505-8800 387
Web: www.godaddy.com

Godbersen-Smith Construction Company Inc
5784 State Hwy 175 . . . Ida Grove IA 51445 712-364-3388 188-4
Web: www.godbersensmith.com

Godbersen-Smith Construction Company Inc
121 E State Hwy 175 . . . Ida Grove IA 51445 712-364-3347 364-3986 190
Web: www.gomaco.com

Goddard College 123 Pitkin Rd . . . Plainfield VT 05667 802-454-8311 454-1029 166
TF: 800-468-4888 ■ *Web:* www.goddard.edu

Goddard Institute for Space Studies
2880 Broadway . . . New York NY 10025 212-678-5500 678-5552 668
Web: www.giss.nasa.gov

Goddard Memorial State Park
1095 Ives Rd . . . Warwick RI 02818 401-884-2010 885-7720 565
Web: riparks.com

Goddard Space Flight Ctr
8800 Greenbelt Rd . . . Greenbelt MD 20771 301-286-8981 286-1707 668
Web: www.nasa.gov

Goddard Systems Inc
1016 W Ninth Ave . . . King of Prussia PA 19406 877-256-7046 310
TF: 800-463-3273 ■ *Web:* www.goddardschool.com

Godfathers Pizza Inc 2808 N 108th St . . . Omaha NE 68164 402-391-1452 670
Web: godfathers.com

Godfrey & Kahn SC
833 E Michigan St Ste 1800 . . . Milwaukee WI 53202 414-273-3500 428
Web: www.gklaw.com

Godfrey & Wing Inc 220 Campus Dr . . . Aurora OH 44202 330-562-1440 308
Web: www.godfreywing.com

Godfrey Adv Inc 40 N Christian St . . . Lancaster PA 17602 717-393-3831 4
Web: www.godfrey.com

Phone | Fax | Class

Godfrey Johnson PC
9557 S Kingston Ct . . . Englewood CO 80112 303-228-0700 41
Web: gojolaw.com

Godfrey Memorial Library
134 Newfield St . . . Middletown CT 06457 860-346-4375 347-9874 434-3
Web: www.godfrey.org

Godfrey Trucking Inc
6173 W 2100 S . . . West Valley City UT 84128 801-972-0660 972-0709 780
TF: 800-444-7669 ■ *Web:* www.godfreytrucking.com

Godfrey, Leibsle, Blackbourn & Howarth SC
354 Seymour Ct . . . Elkhorn WI 53121 262-422-6607 723-7538 41
Web: godfreylaw.com

Godosky & Gentile PC
61 Broadway Ste 2010 . . . New York NY 10006 212-742-9700 41
Web: godoskygentile.com

Godshall Recruiting PO Box 1984 . . . Greenville SC 29602 864-242-3491 721
Web: www.godshall.com

Godwin Plumbing Inc
3703 Division Ave . . . Grand Rapids MI 49548 616-243-3131 189-10
Web: godwinplumbing.com

Godwin, Morris, Laurenzi & Bloomfield PC
50 N Front St Ste 800 . . . Memphis TN 38103 901-528-1702 528-0246 41
TF: 800-582-6213 ■ *Web:* gmlblaw.com

Goebel Fixture Co 528 Dale St . . . Hutchinson MN 55350 320-587-2112 286
Web: www.gf.com

Goede, Adamczyk, Deboest & Cross PLLC
8950 Fontana Del Sol Way Ste 101 . . . Naples FL 34109 239-331-5100 41
Web: gadclaw.com

Goehring, Rutter & Boehm
437 Grant St 14th Fl . . . Pittsburgh PA 15219 412-281-0587 281-2971 428
TF: 866-677-5970 ■ *Web:* www.grblaw.com

Goelzer Investment Management Inc
111 Monument Cir Ste 500 . . . Indianapolis IN 46204 317-264-2600 264-2601 401
Web: www.goelzerinc.com

Goes Lithographing Company Inc
111 Hallberg St . . . Delavan WI 53115 800-348-6700 728-5679* 627
*Fax Area Code: 262 ■ *TF:* 800-348-6700 ■ *Web:* www.goesproducts.com

Goethe Institut Atlanta/German Cultural Ctr
1197 Peachtree St NE . . . Atlanta GA 30361 404-892-2388 892-3832 520
Web: www.goethe.de

Goethel Engelhardt PLLC
3049 Miller Rd . . . Ann Arbor MI 48103 734-769-6838 41
Web: cmtjustice.com

Goetsch's Welding & Machine Inc
9480 S County Rd K . . . Merrill WI 54452 715-536-2658 454
Web: www.goetschs.com

Goetting Rowe Engineering LLC
130 Regents Pk . . . San Antonio TX 78216 210-530-7800 256
Web: www.goettingrowe.com

Goettl Air Conditioning Inc
1845 W 1st St Ste 108 . . . Tempe AZ 85281 602-386-2728 14
Web: www.goettl.com

Goettsch Partners Inc (GP)
224 S Michigan Ave 1st Fl . . . Chicago IL 60604 312-356-0600 356-0601 261
Web: www.gpchicago.com

Goetz Energy Corp 1319 Military Rd . . . Tonawanda NY 14217 716-876-4324 579
TF: 800-866-4324 ■ *Web:* www.goetzenergy.com

Goetz Insurors Inc 227 Main St . . . Fort Morgan CO 80701 970-867-8246 867-4408 390
TF: 800-233-0428 ■ *Web:* goetzinsurors.com

Goetz Printing Co, The
7939 Angus Ct . . . Springfield VA 22153 703-569-8232 627
TF: 866-245-0977 ■ *Web:* www.goetzprinting.com

Goetz Schenker Blee & Wiederhorn LLP
2 Rector St 2nd Fl . . . New York NY 10006 212-363-6900 363-1090 506
Web: www.gsbwlaw.com

Goetze Dental 3939 NE 33 Terr . . . Kansas City MO 64117 816-413-1200 475
TF: 800-692-0804 ■ *Web:* www.goetzedental.com

Goetze's Candy Company Inc
3900 E Monument St . . . Baltimore MD 21205 410-342-2010 522-7681 296-8
TF: 800-295-8058 ■ *Web:* www.goetzecandy.com

GOFCC (Greater Oswego-Fulton Chamber of Commerce)
44 E Bridge St . . . Oswego NY 13126 315-343-7681 342-0831 139
Web: www.oswegofultonchamber.com

Gofen and Glossberg LLC
455 N Cityfront Plz Ste 3000 . . . Chicago IL 60611 312-828-1100 828-9685 401
Web: www.gofen.com

Goff Backa Alfera & Company LLC
3325 Saw Mill Run Blvd . . . Pittsburgh PA 15227 412-885-5045 885-4870 734
Web: www.gbaco.com

Goff Inc 12216 Ns 3520 . . . Seminole OK 74868 405-278-6200 382-7013 386
TF: 800-654-4633 ■ *Web:* www.goff-inc.com

Goffa Intl
200 Murray Hill Pkwy Ste 1 . . . East Rutherford NJ 07073 201-528-8999 528-8133 762
Web: www.goffausa.com

GOG (Gynecologic Oncology Group)
1600 JFK Blvd Ste 1020 . . . Philadelphia PA 19103 215-854-0770 854-0716 49-8
TF: 800-225-3053 ■ *Web:* www.gog.org

Gogebic Community College
E 4946 Jackson Rd . . . Ironwood MI 49938 906-932-4231 932-0868 162
TF: 800-682-5910 ■ *Web:* www.gogebic.cc.mi.us

Gogebic County 200 N Moore St . . . Bessemer MI 49911 906-663-4518 663-4660 338
Web: www.gogebiccountymi.gov

Gogebic Medical Care Facility
402 N St . . . Wakefield MI 49968 906-224-9811 371
Web: www.gogebicmedicalcare.com

Gogo Inc
1250 N Arlington Heights Rd Ste 500 . . . Itasca IL 60143 630-647-1400 387
Web: www.gogoair.com

GOGO WorldWide Vacations
69 Spring St . . . Montvale NJ 07645 800-254-3477 771
TF: 800-254-3477 ■ *Web:* www.gogowwv.com

Gohmann Asphalt & Construction Inc
PO Box 2428 . . . Clarksville IN 47131 812-282-1349 188-4
Web: www.gohmannasphalt.com

Gohmert Louie (Rep R - TX)
2267 Rayburn House Office Bldg . . . Washington DC 20515 202-225-3035 226-1230 342-2
TF: 866-535-6302 ■ *Web:* gohmert.house.gov

GOI (General Office Interiors)
50 Cardinal Dr . . . Westfield NJ 07090 908-688-9400 688-6894 320
Web: www.generalofficeinteriors.com

Goidosik, Morse & Associates PLC
5900 Portage Rd . . . Kalamazoo MI 49002 269-344-5566 41
Web: gmdisabilitylaw.com

Going Bonkers Inc 229 N 48th St . . . Quincy IL 62305 217-223-6331 31
Web: www.goingbonkers.com

Going Global Inc 258 College Ln . . . Mobile AL 36608 251-342-9811 432-7676 78
Web: www.goinglobal.com

Goizueta Foundation
4401 Northside Pkwy Ste 400 . . . Atlanta GA 30327 404-239-0390 239-0018 305
Web: www.goizuetafoundation.org

GOJO Industries Inc 1 Gojo Plz Ste 500 . . . Akron OH 44311 330-255-6000 329-4656* 214
*Fax Area Code: 800 ■ *TF:* 800-321-9647 ■ *Web:* www.gojo.com

Gokeyless 3646 Cargo Rd . . . Vandalia OH 45377 937-890-2333 41
TF: 877-439-5377 ■ *Web:* www.gokeyless.com

Golan Christie Taglia LLP
70 W Madison St Ste 1500 . . . Chicago IL 60602 312-263-2300 263-0939 445
Web: gct.law

Golars LLC 15755 N Point Blvd . . . Noblesville IN 46060 317-500-0000 261
Web: golars.com

Golberg Companies Inc
4179 County Rd 40 NW . . . Garfield MN 56332 320-834-2211 295
Web: www.gcilift.com

Gold & Rosenblatt LLC
840 Grand Concourse Ste 1B . . . Bronx NY 10451 718-585-2511 41
Web: bronxlandlordlaw.com

Gold & Silver Exchange
6101 Menaul Blvd NE . . . Albuquerque NM 87110 505-884-9230 411
Web: goldandsilverexchangenm.com

Gold Bond Inc 5485 Hixson Pk . . . Hixson TN 37343 800-438-5757 9
TF: 800-438-5757 ■ *Web:* www.goldbondinc.com

Gold Canyon Golf Resort
6100 S Kings Ranch Rd . . . Gold Canyon AZ 85118 480-982-9090 830-5211 669
TF: 800-827-5281 ■ *Web:* www.gcgr.com

Gold Capital LLC
3566 Olivet Church Rd . . . Paducah KY 42001 270-408-4653 442-4750 106
TF: 877-281-3656 ■ *Web:* www.goldcapitalky.com

Gold Coast Animal Hospital
225 W Division St . . . Chicago IL 60610 312-337-7387 337-1032 794
Web: goldcoastah.com

Gold Coast Broadcasting
2284 Victoria Ave Ste 2-G . . . Ventura CA 93003 805-289-1400 647
Web: www.goldcoastbroadcasting.com

Gold Coast Executive Transportation
PO Box 6345 . . . Santa Barbara CA 93455 805-966-5466 441
Web: goldcoastlimos.com

Gold Coast Hotel & Casino
4000 W Flamingo Rd . . . Las Vegas NV 89103 702-367-7111 133
TF: 800-331-5334 ■ *Web:* www.goldcoastcasino.com

Gold Coast Ingredients Inc
2429 Yates Ave . . . Commerce CA 90040 323-724-8935 297-8
TF: 800-352-8673 ■ *Web:* goldcoastinc.com

Gold Coast Jazz Society
1350 E Sunrise Blvd . . . Fort Lauderdale FL 33304 954-524-0805 525-7880 48-4
Web: www.goldcoastjazz.org

Gold Coast Marine Distributor Inc
640 SW Flagler Ave . . . Fort Lauderdale FL 33301 954-463-8281 462-8412 770
Web: www.goldcoastmarine.com

Gold Coast Tours 105 Gemini Ave . . . Brea CA 92821 714-449-6888 107
TF: 800-638-6427 ■ *Web:* www.goldcoasttours.com

Gold Coast Transit (GCT)
1901 Auto Center Dr . . . Oxnard CA 93036 805-487-4222 487-0925 468
Web: www.goldcoasttransit.org

Gold Dust West Carson City
2171 E William St . . . Carson City NV 89701 775-885-9000 888-8018 133
TF: 877-519-5567 ■ *Web:* www.gdwcasino.com

Gold Eagle Co 4400 S Kildare Ave . . . Chicago IL 60632 800-367-3245 376-5749* 145
*Fax Area Code: 773 ■ *TF:* 800-367-3245 ■ *Web:* www.goldeagle.com

Gold Key Resorts Phr Career Ctr
313 Laskin Rd Ste 103 . . . Virginia Beach VA 23451 757-213-4344 707
Web: www.goldkeyphr.com

Gold Key Technology Solutions
4212 S Fifth St . . . Temple TX 76501 254-774-9035 180
TF: 866-321-1531 ■ *Web:* goldkeytechnology.com

Gold Line Connector Inc
PO Box 500 . . . West Redding CT 06896 203-938-2588 938-8740 248
Web: www.gold-line.com

Gold Mechanical Inc
4735 W Division St . . . Springfield MO 65802 417-873-9770 189-10
TF: 877-873-9770 ■ *Web:* www.goldmechanical.com

Gold Medal Bakery Inc 1397 Bay St . . . Fall River MA 02724 508-674-5766 674-6090 68
TF: 800-642-7568 ■ *Web:* www.goldmedalbakery.com

Gold Medal Products Co
10700 Medallion Dr . . . Cincinnati OH 45241 513-769-7676 298
Web: www.gmpopcorn.com

Gold Meltzer Plasky & Wise PA
505 Pleasant Vly Ave . . . Moorestown NJ 08057 856-727-0100 2
Web: www.gmpw.com

Gold Miners Daughter 10160 Hwy 210 E . . . Alta UT 84092 801-742-2300 378
Web: goldminersdaughterlodge.com

Gold Newsletter PO Box 84900 . . . Phoenix AZ 85071 800-877-8847 531-9
TF: 800-877-8847 ■ *Web:* jeffersoncompanies.com

Gold Point Lodging & Realty Inc
75 Snowflake Dr . . . Breckenridge CO 80424 970-453-4440 653
Web: www.grandtimber.com

Gold Pure Food Products LLC
1 Brooklyn Rd . . . Hempstead NY 11550 516-483-5600 296-19
TF: 800-422-4681 ■ *Web:* www.goldshorseradish.com

Gold Ranch Casino & RV Resort
350 Gold Ranch Rd . . . Verdi NV 89439 775-345-6789 133
Web: www.goldranchrvcasino.com

Gold Reserve Inc
926 W Sprague Ave Ste 200 . . . Spokane WA 99201 509-623-1500 623-1634 502
OTC: GDRZF ■ *TF:* 800-625-9550 ■ *Web:* www.goldreserveinc.com

Gold Shield Fiberglass of Ind
2004 Patterson St . . . Decatur IN 46733 260-728-2476 596
Web: www.goldshield.com

Name / Address	City	State	Zip	Phone	Fax	Class
Gold Spike 217 Las Vegas Blvd N *Web:* goldspike.com	Las Vegas	NV	89101	702-476-1082		133
Gold Standard Baking Inc 3700 S Kedzie Ave Ste A *Web:* goldstandardbaking.com	Chicago	IL	60632	773-523-2333		345
Gold Standard Enterprises Inc 5100 W Dempster St *TF:* 888-942-9463 ■ *Web:* www.binnys.com	Skokie	IL	60077	847-674-4200		443
Gold Standard Productions 12952 Miriam Pl *Web:* www.goldstandardproductions.com	Santa Ana	CA	92705	714-544-7000		514
Gold Star Chili 650 Lunken Pk Dr *TF:* 800-643-0465 ■ *Web:* www.goldstarchili.com	Cincinnati	OH	45226	513-231-4541	624-4415	670
Gold Star FS Inc PO Box 135 *TF:* 800-443-8497 ■ *Web:* www.goldstarfs.com	Cambridge	IL	61238	309-937-3369	937-5465	276
Gold Stars Speakers Bureau 7478 N La Cholla Blvd *Web:* www.goldstars.com	Tucson	AZ	85741	520-742-4384		195
Gold Strike Casino Resort 1010 Casino Center Dr *TF:* 888-245-7829 ■ *Web:* goldstrike.mgmresorts.com	Tunica Resorts	MS	38664	662-357-1111		133
Gold Tip LLC 584 E 1100 S Ste 5 *TF:* 800-551-0541 ■ *Web:* www.goldtip.com	American Fork	UT	84003	800-551-0541		711
Goldak Inc 15835 Monte St Ste 104 *Web:* www.goldak.com	Sylmar	CA	91342	818-367-0149		529
Goldbelt Hotel Juneau 51 Egan Dr *TF:* 800-770-5866 ■ *Web:* www.goldbelt.com	Juneau	AK	99801	907-790-4990	463-3567	379
Goldberg & Noone LLC 1533 Hendry St Ste 200 *Web:* goldberg-law.com	Fort Myers	FL	33901	239-461-5508		41
Goldberg & Osborne 4423 E Thomas Rd Ste 3 *TF:* 800-843-3245 ■ *Web:* 1800theeagle.com	Phoenix	AZ	85018	602-808-6200		445
Goldberg Bros Inc 8000 E 40th Ave *Web:* goldbergbrothers.com	Denver	CO	80207	303-321-1099		697
Goldberg Harder Adelstein & Co 132 Lincoln St	Boston	MA	02111	617-426-3350		2
Goldberg Law Group 100 Passaic Ave Ste 303 *Web:* njelc.com	Fairfield	NJ	07004	973-228-1795		41
Goldberg Realty Assoc 33 Clinton Rd *Web:* goldberg-realty.com	West Caldwell	NJ	07006	973-808-7170		652
Goldberg, Persky & White PC 1030 Fifth Ave *TF:* 800-471-3980 ■ *Web:* www.gpwlaw.com	Pittsburgh	PA	15219	412-471-3980	471-8308	428
Goldbug Inc 511 16th St Ste 400 *TF:* 800-942-9442 ■ *Web:* goldbuginc.com	Denver	CO	80202	303-371-2535		157-1
Goldcrest Wallcoverings PO Box 245 *TF:* 800-535-9513 ■ *Web:* www.wallcovering.com	Slingerlands	NY	12159	518-478-7214	478-7216	802
Gold-Eagle Co-op PO Box 280 *TF:* 800-825-3331 ■ *Web:* www.goldeaglecoop.com	Goldfield	IA	50542	800-825-3331		10-4
Goldec Hamm's Manufacturing Ltd 6760 65 Ave *TF:* 800-661-1665 ■ *Web:* www.goldec.com	Red Deer	AB	T4P1A5	403-343-6607		393
Golden Acres 2525 Centerville Rd *Web:* goldenacresliving.com	Dallas	TX	75228	214-327-4503		371
Golden Alaska Seafoods LLC 2200 Alaskan Way Ste 420 *Web:* www.goldenalaska.com	Seattle	WA	98121	206-441-1990		296-14
Golden Aluminum Inc 1405 14th St *TF:* 800-838-1004 ■ *Web:* goldenaluminum.com	Fort Lupton	CO	80621	800-838-1004		492
Golden Anchor Travel 1909 Southwood St *TF:* 800-299-1125 ■ *Web:* www.goldenanchortravel.com	Sarasota	FL	34231	941-922-4070		775
Golden Artists Colors Inc 4785 SR-31 *TF:* 800-959-6543 ■ *Web:* www.goldenpaints.com	New Berlin	NY	13411	607-847-6154	847-6767	43
Golden Aura Publishing 201 W Evergreen Ave Ste 503 *Web:* www.mrbasketball.net	Philadelphia	PA	19118	215-247-4459		637-2
Golden Bridge International Inc 9700 Harbour Pl Ste 129 *Web:* gbi-inc.com	Mukilteo	WA	98275	425-493-1801		231
Golden Chair Inc 958 Washington Rd *Web:* www.goldenchair.com	Houlka	MS	38850	662-568-7830		321
Golden Chopsticks 329 N York St *Web:* www.goldenchopstickswheeling.com	Wheeling	WV	26003	304-232-2888		671
Golden Communications Inc 3420 Irvine Ave *Web:* goldencomm.com	Newport Beach	CA	92660	949-574-5500		225
Golden Corral Corp 5151 Glenwood Ave *Web:* www.goldencorral.com	Raleigh	NC	27612	919-781-9310		670
Golden Dental Plans Inc 29377 Hoover Rd *TF:* 800-451-5918 ■ *Web:* www.goldendentalplans.com	Warren	MI	48093	586-573-8118	573-8720	391-3
Golden Door 777 Deer Springs Rd *TF:* 866-420-6414 ■ *Web:* www.goldendoor.com	San Marcos	CA	92069	760-744-5777	471-2393	706
Golden Eagle Extrusions Inc 1762 SR-131 *Web:* www.goldeneagleextrusions.com	Milford	OH	45150	513-248-8292		603
Golden Eagle Insurance 9145 Miller Rd *TF:* 800-461-9224 ■ *Web:* www.goldeneagle-insurance.com	Johnstown	OH	43031	800-461-9224		391-4
Golden Eagle of Arkansas Inc 1900 E 15th St *Web:* www.donations-goldeneagleofark.com	Little Rock	AR	72202	501-372-2800		81-1
Golden Eagle Resort 511 Mountain Rd *TF:* 866-970-0786 ■ *Web:* www.goldeneagleresort.com	Stowe	VT	05672	802-253-4811	253-2561	379
Golden Eagle Syrup Company Inc 205 First Ave SE *Web:* www.goldeneaglesyrup.com	Fayette	AL	35555	205-932-5294		296-39
Golden Educational Ctr (GEC) 857 Lake Blvd *TF:* 800-800-1791 ■ *Web:* www.goldened.com	Redding	CA	96003	530-244-0101		637-10
Golden Empire Transit District 1830 Golden State Ave *Web:* www.getbus.org	Bakersfield	CA	93301	661-324-9874	869-6394	468
Golden Equipment Co 721 Candelaria NE *Web:* www.goldenequipment.com	Albuquerque	NM	87107	505-876-9127	345-0401	358
Golden Flower 205 W 5th St	Reno	NV	89503	775-323-1628		671
Golden Flowers 2600 NW 79th Ave *TF:* 800-333-9929 ■ *Web:* goldenflowers.com	Doral	FL	33122	305-599-0193	477-0616	292
Golden Franchising Corp 1131 Rockingham Ste 250 *Web:* www.goldenchick.com	Richardson	TX	75080	972-831-0911	831-0401	670
Golden Gate Baptist Theological Seminary (GGBTS) 201 Seminary Dr *Web:* gsapps.org	Mill Valley	CA	94941	415-380-1300	380-1302	167-3
Golden Gate Bridge Golden Gate Bridge Toll Plz Presidio Stn PO Box 9000 *TF:* 877-229-8655 ■ *Web:* www.goldengate.org	San Francisco	CA	94129	415-921-5858	956-1663	50-4
Golden Gate Canyon State Park 92 Crawford Gulch Rd *Web:* cpw.state.co.us	Golden	CO	80403	303-582-3707		565
Golden Gate Capital 1 Embarcadero Ctr 3rd Fl *Web:* www.goldengatecap.com	San Francisco	CA	94111	415-983-2700	983-2701	405
Golden Gate Chinese Restaurant 2640 W Baseline Rd *Web:* www.goldengatechinese.biz	Mesa	AZ	85202	480-897-1335		671
Golden Gate Fields 1100 Eastshore Hwy *Web:* www.goldengatefields.com	Berkeley	CA	94710	510-559-7300		642
Golden Gate National Cemetery 1300 Sneath Ln *Web:* www.cem.va.gov	San Bruno	CA	94066	650-589-7737	873-6578	136
Golden Gate National Parks Conservancy 201 Fort Mason *Web:* www.parksconservancy.org	San Francisco	CA	94123	415-561-3000	561-3003	48-13
Golden Gate National Recreation Area Fort Mason Bldg 201 *Web:* www.nps.gov	San Francisco	CA	94123	415-561-4700		564
Golden Gate Park 970 47th Ave *Web:* goldengateparkgolf.com	San Francisco	CA	94121	415-751-8987		50-5
Golden Gate Rehabilitation & Health Care Ctr 191 Bradley Ave *Web:* goldengaterehab.com	Staten Island	NY	10314	718-698-8800		450
Golden Gate University *Roseville* 3000 Mission College Blvd *TF:* 800-448-4968 ■ *Web:* www.ggu.edu	Santa Clara	CA	95054	415-442-7800		800
Golden Gate University School of Law 536 Mission St *Web:* law.ggu.edu	San Francisco	CA	94105	415-442-6600	442-6609	167-1
Golden Gates Casino 300 Main St *Web:* www.goldenmardigras.com	Black Hawk	CO	80422	303-582-5600		133
Golden Glow Investigative & Protective Services 147 Belmont Blvd *Web:* goldenglowsecurity.com	Elmont	NY	11003	516-437-7486		693
Golden Grain Energy LLC 1822 43rd St SW *TF:* 888-443-2676 ■ *Web:* www.ggecorn.com	Mason City	IA	50401	641-423-8525		10-5
Golden Green Press PO Box 1058 *Web:* www.dontgetthin-gethealthy.com	Fair Oaks	CA	95628	916-966-3453		637-2
Golden Health Services 2100 Scattergood St *Web:* www.goldenhealthservices.com	Philadelphia	PA	19124	215-289-9005	289-9024	363
Golden Hill State Park 9691 Lower Lake Rd *Web:* parks.ny.gov	Barker	NY	14012	716-795-3885		565
Golden Hind Press, The 532 Washington St *Web:* www.projecthindsight.com	Cumberland	MD	21502	301-724-4463	724-3003	637-2
Golden Hotel, The 800 Eleventh St *TF:* 800-233-7214 ■ *Web:* www.thegoldenhotel.com	Golden	CO	80401	303-279-0100	279-9353	379
Golden India 2097 Madison Ave *Web:* www.goldenindiamem.com	Memphis	TN	38104	901-728-5111		671
Golden Ink Litho & Design 7602 Vickers St *Web:* www.goldeninklitho.com	San Diego	CA	92111	858-541-2259		627
Golden Jared (Rep D - ME) 1223 Longworth House Office Bldg *Web:* www.golden.house.gov	Washington	DC	20515	202-225-6306		342-2
Golden Krust Carribean Bakery & Grill 3958 Park Ave *Web:* www.goldenkrust.com	Bronx	NY	10457	718-655-7878	583-1883	310
Golden Lab Software Inc (GLS) 1735 Buford Hwy Ste 215-144 *Web:* www.goldenlabsoftware.com	Cumming	GA	30041	770-886-8947		180
Golden Light Cafe 2906 SW 6th Ave *Web:* goldenlightcafe.com	Amarillo	TX	79106	806-374-9237		671
Golden LivingCenters 1000 fianna way *TF:* 877-823-8375 ■ *Web:* www.goldenlivingcenters.com	FORT SMITH	AR	72919	877-823-8375		353
Golden Memorial State Park 2104 Damascus Rd *Web:* www.mdwfp.com	Walnut Grove	MS	39189	601-253-2237		565
Golden Moon 4527 Miller Rd *Web:* goldenmoonflint.com	Flint	MI	48507	810-733-7030		671
Golden Nugget Hotel 129 E Fremont St *TF:* 800-634-3454 ■ *Web:* www.goldennugget.com	Las Vegas	NV	89101	702-385-7111		669
Golden Oak Books 605 Michigan St *Web:* www.secondamendmentinfo.com	Ontonagon	MI	49953	906-884-2961		637-2
Golden Oaks Village 5801 N Oakwood Rd *TF:* 800-259-0914 ■ *Web:* www.goldenoaks.com	Enid	OK	73703	580-249-2600		672
Golden Omega USA LLC 65 Enterprise *Web:* www.goldenomega.cl	Aliso Viejo	CA	92656	949-330-7030	330-7031	296-13
Golden Palace 2195 Carling Ave *Web:* www.goldenpalacerestaurant.ca	Ottawa	ON	K2B7E8	613-820-8444		671
Golden Peanut Company LLC 100 N Pt Ctr E Ste 400 *Web:* www.goldenpeanut.com	Alpharetta	GA	30022	770-752-8160		11-1

Company / Address	City	State	Zip	Phone	Fax	Class
Golden Pheasant Foods 6931 S 234th St *Web:* www.goldenpheasantfoods.com	Kent	WA	98032	253-520-7747		123
Golden Phoenix 2421 W Main St *Web:* www.goldenphoenixrc.com	Rapid City	SD	57702	605-348-4195		671
Golden Platter Foods 37 Tompkins Point Rd *Web:* goldenplatter.com	Newark	NJ	07114	973-344-8770		297-8
Golden Ring Trucking Inc 1728 N 1st Ave *TF:* 800-328-3629 ■ *Web:* www.goldenringtrucking.com	Fergus Falls	MN	56537	800-328-3629		780
Golden Sands General Contractors Inc 2500 NW 39 St *Web:* www.goldensandsgc.com	Miami	FL	33142	305-633-3336	634-8000	186
Golden Specialty Foods LLC 14605 Best Ave *Web:* goldenspecialtyfoods.com	Norwalk	CA	90650	562-802-2537		296-37
Golden Spike Event Ctr 1000 N 1200 W *Web:* www.goldenspikeeventcenter.com	Ogden	UT	84404	801-399-8798		205
Golden Spike National Historic Site PO Box 897 *Web:* www.nps.gov	Brigham City	UT	84302	435-471-2209	471-2341	564
Golden Sports Tours 301 W Parker Rd Ste 206 *TF:* 800-966-8258 ■ *Web:* www.goldensports.com	Plano	TX	75023	800-966-8258		771
Golden Star Inc 4770 N Belleview Ave Ste 209 *TF:* 800-821-2792 ■ *Web:* www.goldenstar.com	Kansas City	MO	64116	816-842-0233	842-1129	508
Golden Star Resources Ltd 150 King St W Ste 1200 *NYSE: GSS* ■ *Web:* www.gsr.com	Toronto	ON	M5H1J9	416-583-3800		502
Golden State Engineering Inc 15338 Garfield Ave *TF:* 800-292-2838 ■ *Web:* www.goldenstateeng.com	Paramount	CA	90723	562-634-3125	630-1408	454
Golden State Foods 18301 Von Karman Ave Ste 1100 *Web:* www.goldenstatefoods.com	Irvine	CA	92612	949-247-8000		473
Golden State Health Centers Inc 13347 Ventura Blvd *Web:* www.goldenstatehealth.com	Sherman Oaks	CA	91423	818-385-3200		371
Golden State Medical Supply Inc 5187 Camino Ruiz *TF:* 800-284-8633 ■ *Web:* gsms.us	Camarillo	CA	93012	805-477-9866	477-9869	231
Golden Sufi Ctr (GSC) PO Box 456 *Web:* www.goldensufi.org	Point Reyes Station	CA	94956	415-663-0100	663-0103	48-20
Golden Technologies Inc 401 Bridge St *TF:* 800-624-6374 ■ *Web:* www.goldentech.com	Old Forge	PA	18518	800-624-6374		475
Golden Thai 105 Church St *Web:* goldenthai.ca	Toronto	ON	M5C2G3	416-868-6668		671
Golden Times 73 Buffalo St *Web:* www.mpnnow.com	Canandaigua	NY	14424	585-394-0770		532-2
Golden Valley Bank 190 Cohasset Rd Ste 170 *Web:* www.goldenvalley.bank	Chico	CA	95926	530-894-1000	894-4938	70
Golden Valley County 150 First Ave SE PO Box 67 *Web:* www.goldenvalleycounty.org	Beach	ND	58621	701-872-3713	872-4383	338
Golden Valley County 107 Kemp St PO Box 10 *Web:* www.co.golden-valley.mt.us	Ryegate	MT	59074	406-568-2231	568-2428	338
Golden Valley Electrical Association Inc 758 Illinois St *TF:* 800-770-4832 ■ *Web:* www.gvea.com	Fairbanks	AK	99701	907-452-1151	458-6365	245
Golden Valley Memorial Hospital 1000 N Second St *Web:* www.gvmh.org	Clinton	MO	64735	660-885-5511		374-3
Golden West Casino 1001 S Union Ave *Web:* goldenwestcasino.com	Bakersfield	CA	93307	661-324-6936		133
Golden West College 15744 Golden West St PO Box 2748 *Web:* www.goldenwestcollege.edu	Huntington Beach	CA	92647	714-892-7711	895-8960	162
Golden West Industrial Supply Corp 2180 Agate Ct *Web:* goldenwestindustrialsupply.com	Simi Valley	CA	93065	805-522-1000		350
Golden West Intl 757 Bryant St *TF:* 800-722-7020 ■ *Web:* www.golden-west-wine.com	San Francisco	CA	94107	415-931-2300		81-3
Golden West Technology 1180 E Valencia Dr *Web:* www.goldenwesttech.com	Fullerton	CA	92831	714-738-3775	738-7727	625
Golden West Telecommunications 415 Crown St PO Box 411 *TF:* 866-279-2161 ■ *Web:* www.goldenwest.com	Wall	SD	57790	605-279-2161	279-2727	736
Golden Wok 8822 Wurzbach Rd *Web:* www.goldenwoksa.com	San Antonio	TX	78240	210-615-8282		671
Golden, Rothschild, Spagnola, Lundell, Boylan & Garubo PC 1011 Rt 22 W Ste 300 *Web:* grsl.com	Bridgewater	NJ	08807	908-722-6300		41
Goldenarea Furniture LLC 207 Wickham Ave Rte 211 E *Web:* goldenarea.net	Middletown	NY	10940	845-342-1880		321
Goldenberg Group Inc, The 630 Sentry Pkwy Ste 300 *Web:* www.goldenberggroup.com	Blue Bell	PA	19422	610-260-9600		653
Goldendale Observatory State Park 1602 Observatory Dr *Web:* parks.state.wa.us	Goldendale	WA	98620	509-773-3141		565
Goldener Hirsch Inn 7570 Royal St E *TF:* 800-252-3373 ■ *Web:* www.goldenerhirschinn.com	Park City	UT	84060	435-649-7770		379
Goldens' Foundry & Machine Co (GFMCO) 600 12th St *Web:* www.gfmco.com	Columbus	GA	31902	706-323-0471		307
Goldense Group Inc 1346 South St *Web:* www.goldensegroupinc.com	Needham	MA	02492	781-444-5400		195
GoldenSource Corp 22 Cortlandt St *Web:* www.thegoldensource.com	New York	NY	10007	212-798-7100	798-7238	178-10
Golden-Tech International Inc 13555 SE 36th St Ste 330 *TF:* 800-311-8090 ■ *Web:* www.gtiinc.com	Bellevue	WA	98006	425-869-1461	867-1368	297-5
Goldenwest Diamond Corp 15732 Tustin Village Way *TF:* 800-441-0715 ■ *Web:* www.jewelryexchange.com	Tustin	CA	92780	714-542-9000	542-9226	410
Goldenwest Electric Co-opeartive Inc PO Box 177 *Web:* www.uppermo.com	Wibaux	MT	59353	406-796-2423		245
Golder Associates Inc 3730 Chamblee Tucker Rd *Web:* www.golder.com	Atlanta	GA	30341	770-496-1893	934-9476	261
Goldey Beacom College 4701 Limestone Rd *TF:* 800-833-4877 ■ *Web:* www.gbc.edu	Wilmington	DE	19808	302-998-8814	996-5408	166
Goldfarb & Lipman LLP 1300 Clay St 11th Fl *Web:* goldfarblipman.com	Oakland	CA	94612	510-836-6336	836-1035	428
Goldfather's Jewelry Inc (GFJ) 3230 E Flamingo Rd Ste 8-354 *TF:* 800-642-2545 ■ *Web:* www.goldfathers.com	Las Vegas	NV	89121	702-891-8836	891-8837	411
Goldfield Corp 1684 W Hibiscus Blvd *NYSE: GV* ■ *Web:* www.goldfieldcorp.com	Melbourne	FL	32901	321-724-1700		189-4
Goldfield Ghost Town & Mine 4650 N Mammoth Mine Rd *Web:* www.goldfieldghosttown.com	Apache Junction	AZ	85119	480-983-0333		50-3
Goldin Associates LLC 350 Fifth Ave The Empire State Bldg *Web:* www.goldinassociates.com	New York	NY	10118	212-593-2255		194
Goldin Metals Inc 12440 Seaway Rd *Web:* www.goldinmetals.com	Gulfport	MS	39503	228-896-6216	896-4873	697
Goldline International Equipment Manufacturing LLC 110 N Shaver St *Web:* goldlinesafewalk.com	Pasadena	TX	77506	713-475-1201		480
Goldline International Inc 1601 Cloverfield Blvd 100 S Tower *TF:* 877-376-2646 ■ *Web:* www.goldline.com	Santa Monica	CA	90404	310-587-1423	319-0265	491
Goldman & Ehrlich 20 S Clark St Ste 500 *Web:* goldmanandehrlich.com	Chicago	IL	60603	312-332-6733	372-7076	41
Goldman Antonetti & Cordova 250 Munoz Rivera Ave Ste 1400 *TF:* 888-614-1507 ■ *Web:* www.gaclaw.com	San Juan	PR	00918	787-759-8000		428
Goldman Sachs 200 W St *NYSE: GS* ■ *TF:* 800-526-7384 ■ *Web:* www.goldmansachs.com	New York	NY	10282	212-902-1000		528
Goldman Sloan Nash & Haber LLP 480 University Ave Ste 1600 *Web:* www.gsnh.com	Toronto	ON	M5G1V2	416-597-9922		41
Goldner Hawn (GHJ&M) 90 S 7th St 3700 Wells Fargo Ctr *Web:* goldnerhawn.com	Minneapolis	MN	55402	612-338-5912		403
Goldrich & Kest Industries 5150 Overland Ave *Web:* www.goldrichkest.com	Culver City	CA	90230	310-204-2050		653
Goldring Gulf Distributing Co 8245 Opportunity Dr *Web:* www.goldringgulf.com	Milton	FL	32583	850-432-9883	432-5509	81-3
Goldsboro Milling Co 938 Millers Chapel Rd *Web:* cals.ncsu.edu	Goldsboro	NC	27534	919-778-3130		447
Goldsboro News-Argus 310 N Berkeley Blvd *Web:* www.newsargus.com	Goldsboro	NC	27534	919-778-2211	778-5408	637-8
Goldsmith & Eggleton Inc 300 First St *TF:* 800-321-0954 ■ *Web:* www.goldsmith-eggleton.com	Wadsworth	OH	44281	330-336-6616	334-4709	605-2
Goldsmith & Ogrodowski LLC 247 Fort Pitt Blvd 5th Fl *TF:* 877-404-6529 ■ *Web:* golawllc.com	Pittsburgh	PA	15222	412-281-4340	281-4347	41
Goldsmith Gallery Jewelers Inc 903 Shiloh Crossing Blvd *Web:* goldsmithgalleryjewelers.com	Billings	MT	59102	406-252-3662		410
Goldsmith Molis & Gray PLLC 32 Orange St *Web:* gmg-cpa.com	Asheville	NC	28801	828-281-3161		2
Goldsmith New York at Studio 350 601 W 26th St Ste 350 *Web:* www.goldsmith-inc.com	New York	NY	10001	212-366-9040		464
Goldsmith, The 31 Lewis St *Web:* thegoldsmith.com	Binghamton	NY	13901	607-723-0001		410
Goldstein & Goldstein LLP 1 Civic Center Plz Ste 541 *Web:* goldsteinlawfirm.com	Poughkeepsie	NY	12601	845-473-5100		41
Goldstein Law Group PA 100 NE Third Ave Ste 700 *Web:* mydefenselawyers.com	Fort Lauderdale	FL	33301	954-767-8393		41
Goldwater Dube 3500 De Maisonneuve Blvd W Ste 2310 *Web:* www.goldwaterdube.com	Montreal	QC	H3Z3C1	514-861-4367	861-7601	428
Goldwater Institute 500 E Coronado Rd *Web:* goldwaterinstitute.org	Phoenix	AZ	85004	602-462-5000	256-7045	634
Goldwin America Inc 3713 Highland Ave Ste 6 *Web:* www.goldwin.co.jp	Manhattan Beach	CA	90266	310-545-2110	545-2119	710
Goleta Union School District 401 N Fairview Ave *Web:* www.goleta.k12.ca.us	Goleta	CA	93117	805-681-1200		685
Goleta Valley Chamber of Commerce 5662 Calle Real Ste 204 *Web:* goletachamber.com	Goleta	CA	93117	805-967-2500		139
Goleta Water District 4699 Hollister Ave *Web:* www.goletawater.com	Goleta	CA	93110	805-964-6761		787
Golf & Ski Warehouse Inc 290 Plainfield Rd *Web:* golfskiwarehouse.com	West Lebanon	NH	03784	603-298-8282	298-8754	711
Golf Academy Hawaii Kaneohe Klipper Golf Course *Web:* www.golfacademyhawaii.com	Kaneohe Bay	HI	96863	808-386-3500		167-3

Name / Address	Phone	Fax	Class
Golf Course Superintendents Association of America (GCSAA) 1421 Research Pk Dr . . . . Lawrence KS 66049 *TF:* 800-472-7878 ■ *Web:* www.gcsaa.org	785-841-2240		48-2
Golf Creations 18250 Beck Rd . . . . Marengo IL 60152 *Web:* golfcreations.com	815-923-3400		188
Golf Etc Granbury 2461 E Hwy 377 . . . . Granbury TX 76049 *Web:* golfetcgranbury.com	817-579-5400		711
Golf Instruments Co 3210 Production Ave Unit A . . . . Oceanside CA 92058 *Web:* www.golfinstruments.com	760-722-1129		710
Golf Mill Shopping Ctr 239 Golf Mill Ctr. . . . . . . Niles IL 60714 *Web:* www.golfmill.com	847-699-1070		460
Golf Shack Inc 1631 N Bell School Rd . . . . Rockford IL 61107 *Web:* www.golfshack.com	815-397-3709		711
Golf Shoe Centers of America 1530 Hwy 17 S . . . . North Myrtle Beach SC 29582 *Web:* www.golfshoesonly.com	843-497-0507		711
Golf Stix 6752 Shady Oak Rd . . . . Eden Prairie MN 55344 *TF:* 800-555-1234 ■ *Web:* golfstixvalueguide.com	612-216-5205		711
Golf Visions LLC 344 E Lyndale Ave . . . . Northlake IL 60164 *Web:* golfvisions.net	708-562-5247		188-3
Golf Works Inc 3660 Stone Ridge Rd . . . . Austin TX 78746	512-327-8089		188-3
Golfballs.com Inc 126 Arnould Blvd . . . . LaFayette LA 70506 *Web:* www.golfballs.com	337-210-4653		711
GolfBC Holdings Inc 1800-1030 W Georgia St . . . . Vancouver BC V6E2Y3 *TF:* 800-446-5322 ■ *Web:* www.golfbc.com	800-446-5322		787
Golfland Entertainment Centers Inc 155 W Hampton Ave. . . . . . . Mesa AZ 85210 *Web:* www.golfland.com	480-834-8319		31
Golflogix Inc 15685 N Greenway-Hayden Loop Ste 100A . . . . . Scottsdale AZ 85260 *TF:* 877-977-0162 ■ *Web:* www.golflogix.com	877-977-0162		148
Golfsmith International Inc 11000 N IH-35 . . . . Austin TX 78753 *Web:* www.golfgalaxy.com	512-821-4037	837-1019	711
GolfWorks, The 4820 Jacksontown Rd PO Box 3008. . . . . . . Newark OH 43058 *TF:* 800-848-8358 ■ *Web:* www.golfworks.com	740-328-4193	323-0311	710
Goliad County PO Box 50 . . . . Goliad TX 77963 *Web:* www.co.goliad.tx.us	361-645-3294		338
Goliad Independent School District 161 N Welch St. . . . . . . Goliad TX 77963 *Web:* www.goliadisd.org	361-645-3259		685
Goliad State Park 108 Park Rd 6 . . . . Goliad TX 77963 *Web:* tpwd.texas.gov	361-645-3405		565
Gollob Morgan Peddy & Company CPA 1001 Ese Loop 323 Ste 300 . . . . Tyler TX 75701 *Web:* www.gmpcpa.com	903-534-0088		401
Golomb & Honik PC 1835 Market St Ste 2900 . . . . Philadelphia PA 19102 *Web:* golombhonik.com	215-985-9177		41
Golub Corp 461 Nott St. . . . . . . Schenectady NY 12308 *TF:* 800-666-7667 ■ *Web:* www.pricechopper.com	800-666-7667		345
Go-Mart Inc 915 Riverside Dr . . . . Gassaway WV 26624 *Web:* gomart.com	304-364-8000	364-4690	204
Gomembers Inc 1155 Perimeter Ctr W . . . . Atlanta GA 30338 *TF:* 855-411-2783 ■ *Web:* www.aptean.com	855-411-2783		178-10
Gomers of Kansas LLC 12740 W 87th St Pkwy . . . . Lenexa KS 66215 *Web:* gomersofkansas.com	913-894-0600		443
Gomez & Associates Company LLC 3216 Industry Dr Ste D. . . . . . . North Charleston SC 29418 *Web:* gomezandassociate.net	843-552-4552	552-4532	697
Gomez & Sullivan PC 288 Genesee St . . . . Utica NY 13502 *Web:* www.gomezandsullivan.com	315-724-4860	724-4862	261
Gomez Construction Co 7100 SW 44th St. . . . . . . Miami FL 33155 *Web:* www.gomezconstruction.com	305-661-7660	661-0504	186
Gomez Jimmy (Rep D - CA) 1530 Longworth House Office Bldg . . . . Washington DC 20515 *Web:* www.gomez.house.gov	202-225-6235		342-2
GoMotion Inc 10 Kendrick Rd Unit 3. . . . . . . Wareham MA 02571 *TF:* 866-446-1069 ■ *Web:* gomotiongear.com	508-322-7695	503-9993	253
Gompers 6601 N 27th Ave . . . . Phoenix AZ 85017 *Web:* gompers.org	602-336-0061		256
Gompers & Associates PLLC 117 Edgington Ln. . . . . . . Wheeling WV 26003 *TF:* 844-805-9844 ■ *Web:* www.gomperscpa.com	304-242-9300		2
Gonella Realty Inc 701 W Olive Ave. . . . . . . Merced CA 95348 *Web:* gonellarentals.com	209-383-6277		652
Gongos Research Inc 2365 Pontiac Rd. . . . . . . Auburn Hills MI 48326 *TF:* 800-899-9590 ■ *Web:* gongos.com	248-239-2300		668
Gonnella Baking Co 1117 E Wiley Rd . . . . Schaumburg IL 60173 **Fax Area Code:* 312 ■ *TF:* 800-322-8829 ■ *Web:* www.gonnella.com	800-322-8829	733-7056*	68
Gonser Gerber 1776 Legacy Cir Ste 100 . . . . Naperville IL 60563 *Web:* www.gonsergerber.com	630-505-1433		317
Gonzaga University 502 E Boone Ave. . . . . . . Spokane WA 99258 *TF:* 800-986-9585 ■ *Web:* www.gonzaga.edu	509-313-6572		166
Gonzales Computer Services Inc 1928 E Main St. . . . . . . Farmington NM 87402 *Web:* gcs-inc.biz	505-325-0029		179
Gonzales County 427 St George Ste 200 . . . . Gonzales TX 78629 *Web:* www.co.gonzales.tx.us	830-672-2801	672-2636	338
Gonzales Inquirer, The 622 St Paul PO Box 616. . . . . . . Gonzales TX 78629 *Web:* www.gonzalesinquirer.com	830-672-2861	672-7029	789
Gonzales Weekly 231 W Cornerview St . . . . Gonzales LA 70737 *Web:* www.weeklycitizen.com	225-644-6397	644-2069	532-2
Gonzalez Anthony (Rep R - OH) 1023 Longworth House Office Bldg . . . . Washington DC 20515 *Web:* www.anthonygonzalez.house.gov	202-225-3876		342-2
Gonzalez Design Group 29401 Stevenson Hwy . . . . Madison Heights MI 48071 *Web:* www.gonzalez-group.com	248-548-6010	548-3160	261

Name / Address	Phone	Fax	Class
Gonzalez Strength & Assoc 2176 Pkwy Lake Dr. . . . . . . Hoover AL 35244 *Web:* www.gonzalez-strength.com	205-942-2486	942-3033	261
Gonzalez Vicente (Rep D - TX) 113 Cannon House Office Bldg. . . . . . . Washington DC 20515 *TF:* 888-217-0261 ■ *Web:* gonzalez.house.gov	202-225-2531		342-2
Gonzalez-Colon Jenniffer (Rep R - PR) 1609 Longworth House Office Bldg . . . . Washington DC 20515 *Web:* www.gonzalez-colon.house.gov	202-225-2615		342-2
Gooch & Housego (Ohio) LLC 676 Alpha Dr . . . . Cleveland OH 44143 *Web:* goochandhousego.com	216-486-6100		544
Goochland County 1800 Sandy Hook Rd . . . . Goochland VA 23063 *Web:* www.goochlandva.us	804-556-5800	556-4617	338
Good Co 65 Centennial Loop Ste B. . . . . . . Eugene OR 97401 *Web:* www.goodcompany.com	541-341-4663		192
Good Company Players 928 E Olive Ave . . . . Fresno CA 93728 *TF:* 800-371-4747 ■ *Web:* gcplayers.com	559-266-0660	266-1342	572
Good Day Pharmacy 2033 Boise Ave . . . . Loveland CO 80538 *Web:* www.gooddaypharmacy.com	970-669-7500	667-1095	237
Good Design LLC 450 Industrial Park Rd . . . . Deep River CT 06417 *Web:* gooddesignusa.com	860-526-1600		177
Good Dog Design 21 Corte Madera Ave Ste 2. . . . . . . Mill Valley CA 94941 *Web:* gooddogdesign.com	415-383-0110		180
Good Earth Lighting Inc 5260 Capitol Dr . . . . Wheeling IL 60090 *Web:* www.goodearthlighting.com	847-808-1133	808-0838	439
Good Earth Teas Inc 5901 W Side Ave 4th Fl . . . . North Bergen NJ 07047 *TF:* 888-625-8227 ■ *Web:* www.goodearth.com	888-625-8227		296-7
Good Earth Tools Inc 4 Industrial Dr. . . . . . . Crystal City MO 63019 *Web:* www.goodearthtools.com	636-937-3330	937-3386	190
Good Food Inc 4960 Horseshoe Pk . . . . Honey Brook PA 19344 *TF:* 800-327-4406 ■ *Web:* www.goldenbarrel.com	610-273-3776	273-2087	805
Good Friends 507 E Lincolnway. . . . . . . Cheyenne WY 82001	307-778-7088		671
Good From the Woods 667 County Rd 4060 . . . . Salem MO 65560 *Web:* www.pinenut.com	573-247-2689		200
Good Ground Press 1884 Randolph Ave. . . . . . . Saint Paul MN 55105 *TF:* 800-232-5533 ■ *Web:* www.goodgroundpress.com	651-690-7010	690-7039	637-2
Good Hope Lutheran Church 129 W Charles St . . . . Bucyrus OH 44820 *Web:* www.goodhopelutheran.com	330-859-2480		48-20
Good Hospitality Services Inc 1351 Silhavy Rd Ste 100 . . . . Valparaiso IN 46383 *Web:* www.goodhsi.com	219-462-6265	462-7699	379
Good Hotel 112 Seventh St. . . . . . . San Francisco CA 94103 *TF:* 800-444-5819 ■ *Web:* www.haiyi-hotels.com	415-621-7001	626-3974	379
Good Jobs Inc, The 2120 E Jarvis St . . . . Milwaukee WI 53211 *Web:* www.thegoodjobs.com	414-949-5627		260
Good Lad Apparel 431 E Tioga St. . . . . . . Philadelphia PA 19134 *Web:* www.goodlad.com	215-739-0200		155-4
Good Law PC 3430 E Sunrise Dr Ste 270. . . . . . . Tucson AZ 85718 *Web:* goodlaw.net	520-628-8221		41
Good Leads 224 Main St Unit 2B. . . . . . . Salem NH 03079 *TF:* 866-894-5323 ■ *Web:* www.goodleads.com	603-894-5323		393
Good Lite Co 1155 Jansen Farm Dr. . . . . . . Elgin IL 60123 *TF:* 800-362-3860 ■ *Web:* www.good-lite.com	847-841-1145	841-1149	246
Good Metals Co 440 32nd St SW . . . . Wyoming MI 49548 *TF:* 800-543-4630 ■ *Web:* www.goodmetals.com	616-241-4425	241-0996	307
Good Neighbor Pharmacy 1300 Morris Dr. . . . . . . Chesterbrook PA 19087 *Web:* www.mygnp.com	610-727-7000		587
Good Old Boat Magazine 1300 Evergreen Dr NW. . . . . . . Jamestown ND 58401 *Web:* www.goodoldboat.com	701-952-9433	952-9434	457-4
Good Printers Inc 213 Dry River Rd . . . . Bridgewater VA 22812 *TF:* 800-296-3731 ■ *Web:* www.goodprinters.com	540-828-4663		174
Good Sam Club PO Box 6888 . . . . Englewood CO 80155 *TF:* 800-234-3450 ■ *Web:* www.goodsam.com	800-234-3450		48-23
Good Samaritan Hospice 2408 Electric Rd . . . . Roanoke VA 24018 *TF:* 888-466-7809 ■ *Web:* goodsamhospice.com	540-776-0198		371
Good Samaritan Hospital 255 Lafayette Ave . . . . Suffern NY 10901 *Web:* www.goodsamhosp.org	845-368-5000		374-3
Good Samaritan Hospital 520 S Seventh St . . . . Vincennes IN 47591 *Web:* www.gshvin.org	812-882-5220		374-3
Good Samaritan Hospital 1225 Wilshire Blvd. . . . . . . Los Angeles CA 90017 *Web:* www.goodsam.org	213-977-2121		374-3
Good Samaritan Regional Medical Ctr 3600 NW Samaritan Dr. . . . . . . Corvallis OR 97330 *TF:* 800-640-5339 ■ *Web:* www.samhealth.org	541-768-5111	768-5100	374-3
Good Search LLC, The 4 Valley Rd. . . . . . . Westport CT 06880 *Web:* tgsus.com	203-539-0847		260
Good Shepherd Hospice 4350 Will Rogers Pkwy Ste 400 . . . . Oklahoma City OK 73108 *TF:* 855-527-9354 ■ *Web:* goodshepherdhospice.com	405-943-0903		371
Good Shepherd Hospice 4747-20 Nesconset Hwy. . . . . . . Port Jefferson NY 11777 *Web:* goodshepherdhospice.chsli.org	631-642-4200		371
Good Shepherd Rehabilitation & Nursing Ctr 20 Plantation Dr . . . . Jaffrey NH 03452 *Web:* www.cc-nh.org	603-532-8762		450
Good Shepherd Rehabilitation Hospital 850 S Fifth St . . . . Allentown PA 18103 *Web:* www.goodshepherdrehab.org	610-776-3586		374-6
Good Sports Outdoor Outfitters 12730 W I-10 Ste 300 . . . . San Antonio TX 78230 *TF:* 877-443-1951 ■ *Web:* www.goodsports.com	210-694-0881	694-4137	711
Good Time Tours 455 Corday St . . . . Pensacola FL 32503 *TF:* 800-446-0886 ■ *Web:* www.goodtimetours.com	850-476-0046	476-7637	760

	Phone	Fax	Class
Good Times Restaurants Inc 141 Union Blvd Ste 400 .... Lakewood CO 80228 *NASDAQ: GTIM* ■ *TF:* 877-605-5911 ■ *Web:* goodtimesburgers.com	303-384-1400		670
Good Times Travel Inc 17132 Magnolia St.................... Fountain Valley CA 92708 *TF:* 888-488-2287 ■ *Web:* www.goodtimestravel.com	714-848-1255	848-2855	760
Good Water Warehouse Inc 1700 E Walnut Ave .... Fullerton CA 92831 *TF:* 800-749-0252 ■ *Web:* www.goodwaterwarehouse.com	714-441-2893	441-0525	328
Good Wildman, Attorneys at Law 19000 MacArthur Blvd Ste 575.................... Irvine CA 92612 *Web:* www.goodwildman.com	949-955-1100		445
Good Will Publishers Inc PO Box 269.......... Gastonia NC 28052 *TF:* 800-219-4663 ■ *Web:* www.goodwillpublishers.com	704-865-1256		637-2
Good's Store 1338 Main St .... East Earl PA 17519 *Web:* goodsstores.com	717-354-4026	355-2230	229
Goodale & Barbieri Co 818 W Riverside Ave Ste 300 .... Spokane WA 99201 *TF:* 800-572-9181 ■ *Web:* www.g-b.com	509-459-6109	344-4939	655
Goodale State Park 650 Park Rd .... Camden SC 29020 *Web:* southcarolinaparks.com	803-432-2772		565
Goodby Silverstein & Partners 720 California St....................... San Francisco CA 94108 *Web:* goodbysilverstein.com	415-392-0669		4
Goodcity 5049 W Harrison St.................... Chicago IL 60644 *Web:* www.goodcitychicago.org	773-473-4790	378-8928	305
Goode Casseb Jones Riklin Choate & Watson A Professional 2122 N Main Ave .... San Antonio TX 78212 *Web:* goodelaw.com	210-733-6030		428
Goode Company BBQ Hall of Flame LLC 13843 N Promenade Blvd Ste 900 .... Stafford TX 77477 *TF:* 800-627-3502 ■ *Web:* www.goodecompany.com	800-627-3502		671
Goodell Devries Leech & Dann LLP 1 South St 20th Fl.......................... Baltimore MD 21202 *TF:* 888-229-4354 ■ *Web:* www.gdldlaw.com	410-783-4000	783-4040	428
Gooden Lance (Rep R - TX) 425 Cannon House Office Bldg.............. Washington DC 20515 *Web:* www.gooden.house.gov	202-225-3484		342-2
Goodfellow Air Force Base 351 Kearney Blvd .... Goodfellow AFB TX 76908 *Web:* www.goodfellow.af.mil	325-654-3877		497-1
Goodfellow Inc 225 Goodfellow St .... Delson QC J5B1V5 *TF:* 800-361-6503 ■ *Web:* www.goodfellowinc.com	450-635-6511	635-3729	817
Goodgame Company Inc 2311 Third Ave S .... Pell City AL 35128 *Web:* www.goodgamecompany.com	205-338-2551		261
GoodGuide Inc 98 Battery St Ste 400 .... San Francisco CA 94111 *Web:* www.goodguide.com	415-732-7722		387
Goodhart National Gorman Agency Inc 598 Tuckahoe Rd PO Box 159 .... Yonkers NY 10710 *TF:* 800-734-5578 ■ *Web:* goodhartinsurance.com	914-779-0500	779-0515	390
Goodhart Sons Inc 2515 Horseshoe Rd .... Lancaster PA 17605 *Web:* www.goodhartsons.com	717-656-2404	656-3301	91
Goodheart-Willcox Publisher 18604 W Creek Dr .... Tinley Park IL 60477 **Fax Area Code:* 888 ■ *TF:* 800-323-0440 ■ *Web:* www.g-w.com	708-687-5000	409-3900*	637-2
Goodhue County 454 W Sixth St............... Red Wing MN 55066 *Web:* www.co.goodhue.mn.us	651-267-4800		338
Goodhue County Cooperative Electric Assn 1410 Northstar Dr.......................... Zumbrota MN 55992 *TF:* 800-927-6864 ■ *Web:* www.gccea.com	507-732-5117	732-5110	245
Goodin Co 2700 N 2nd St................... Minneapolis MN 55411 *TF:* 800-328-8433 ■ *Web:* www.goodinco.com	612-588-7811	588-7820	612
Gooding County 624 Main St .... Gooding ID 83330 *Web:* www.goodingcounty.org	208-934-4841	934-5085	338
Gooding, Simpson & Mackes Inc 345 S Reading Rd........................... Ephrata PA 17522 *TF:* 800-532-7663 ■ *Web:* www.gsmroofing.com	800-532-7663		189-12
Goodland Star-News 1205 Main St .... Goodland KS 67735 *Web:* www.nwkansas.com	785-899-2338	899-6186	532-2
Goodman Allen & Filetti PLLC 4501 Highwoods Pkwy Ste 210 .... Glen Allen VA 23060 *Web:* www.goodmanallen.com	804-346-0600		428
Goodman Capital Finance 3010 LBJ Fwy Ste 140 .... Dallas TX 75234 *TF:* 877-446-6362 ■ *Web:* www.goodmancapitalfinance.com	972-241-3297	243-6285	272
Goodman Correctional Institution 4556 Broad River Rd........................ Columbia SC 29210 *TF:* 866-230-7761 ■ *Web:* doc.sc.gov	803-896-8565	896-1671	213
Goodman Couture 224 W 30th St Ste 402 .... New York NY 10001	212-244-7422		155-7
Goodman Decorating Co 3400 Atlanta Industrial Pkwy NW .... Atlanta GA 30331 *Web:* www.goodman-decorating.com	404-965-3626		189-8
Goodman Manufacturing Company LP 5151 San Felipe St Ste 500 .... Houston TX 77056 *Web:* www.goodmanmfg.com	713-861-2500		15
Goodman Real Estate Inc 2801 Alaskan Way Ste 310...................... Seattle WA 98121 *Web:* goodmanre.com	206-448-0259		656
Goodman Solutions 2801 Network Blvd Ste 300 .... Frisco TX 75034 *Web:* www.goodmansolutions.com	972-406-9692		194
Goodman Theatre 170 N Dearborn St............ Chicago IL 60601 *Web:* www.goodmantheatre.org	312-443-3811	443-3821	572
Goodmanagement 739 Thimble Shoals Blvd Ste 304 PO Box 12967 .... Newport News VA 23606 *Web:* goodmanagement.com	757-349-7076	596-7273	379
Goodmans LLP 333 Bay St Ste 3400 .... Toronto ON M5H2S7 *Web:* www.goodmans.ca	416-979-2211		41
GoodMedia Press 25 Highland Park Village 100-810 .... Dallas TX 75205 *Web:* goodmediapress.com	214-240-4503		637-2
Goodness & Daigle Pc 393 Totten Pond Rd Ste 403.................. Waltham MA 02451 *Web:* goodnesscpa.com	781-290-4750		2
Good-Nite Inn Fremont 4135 Cushing Pkwy .... Fremont CA 94538 *TF:* 800-648-3466 ■ *Web:* www.goodnite.com	510-656-9307	656-9110	379
Goodrich Petroleum Corp 801 Louisiana Ste 700 .... Houston TX 77002 *NYSE: GDP* ■ *Web:* www.goodrichpetroleum.com	713-780-9494	780-9254	539
GoodRx 233 Wilshire Blvd Ste 990 .... Santa Monica CA 90401 *TF:* 888-799-2553 ■ *Web:* www.goodrx.com	888-799-2553		582
Goods Insurance Agency Inc 20 Trinity Dr Ste 100........................... Leola PA 17540 *Web:* goodsinsuranceagency.com	717-661-6100		390
Goodsill Anderson Quinn & Stifel 1099 Alakea St Ste 1800..................... Honolulu HI 96813 *Web:* www.goodsill.com	808-547-5600		428
Goodsmith Gregg & Unruh LLP 150 S Wacker Dr Ste 3150 .... Chicago IL 60606 *Web:* ggulaw.com	312-322-1981		41
Goodsons' Supermarkets Inc 18616 Coal Heritage Rd .... Welch WV 24801 *Web:* www.shopgoodsons.com	304-436-8481		345
Goodspeed Musicals PO Box A............ East Haddam CT 06423 *Web:* www.goodspeed.org	860-873-8664	873-2329	749
Goodtime Medical 25 Cooperative Way .... Wright City MO 63390 *TF:* 888-386-8225 ■ *Web:* www.examtables.com	888-386-8225		319-3
Goodway Print & Copy Inc 15121 Ventura Blvd .... Sherman Oaks CA 91403 *Web:* www.goodwayprintcopy.com	818-783-5172		627
Goodwill 714 S 27th St......................... Tacoma WA 98409 *Web:* www.goodwillwa.org	253-573-6500		260
Goodwill Easter Seals of Gulf Coast 2440 Gordon Smith Dr .... Mobile AL 36617 *Web:* www.gesgc.org	251-471-1581		242
Goodwill Ind of Fort Worth 4005 Campus Dr .... Fort Worth TX 76119 *Web:* www.goodwillfortworth.org	817-332-7866		104
Goodwill Industries International Inc 15810 Indianola Dr.......................... Rockville MD 20855 *TF:* 800-741-0197 ■ *Web:* www.goodwill.org	800-466-3945		48-5
Goodwill Industries of Akron Ohio Inc, The 570 E Waterloo Rd .... Akron OH 44319 *TF:* 800-989-8428 ■ *Web:* www.goodwillakron.org	330-724-6995		193
Goodwill Industries of Central Texas 1015 Norwood Park Blvd .... Austin TX 78753 *TF:* 800-735-2989 ■ *Web:* www.goodwillcentraltexas.org	512-637-7106	637-7400	48-15
Goodwill Keystone Area Inc 1150 Goodwill Dr......................... Harrisburg PA 17101 *Web:* www.yourgoodwill.org	717-232-1831		260
Goodwill Northern Michigan 2279 S Airport Rd W..................... Traverse City MI 49684 *Web:* www.goodwillnmi.org	231-922-4805		415
Goodwill of the East Bay 1301 30th Ave.............................. Oakland CA 94601 *Web:* eastbaygoodwill.org	510-698-7200		256
Goodwin Biotechnology Inc 1850 NW 69th Ave .... Plantation FL 33313 *TF:* 800-814-8600 ■ *Web:* www.goodwinbiotechnology.com	954-327-9656	587-6378	231
Goodwin College 1 Riverside Dr............ East Hartford CT 06118 *TF:* 800-889-3282 ■ *Web:* www.goodwin.edu	860-528-4111		167-3
Goodwin Company Inc, The 12102 Industry St...................... Garden Grove CA 92841 *Web:* www.goodwininc.com	714-894-0531	894-6293	151
Goodwin House 4800 Fillmore Ave .... Alexandria VA 22311 *Web:* www.goodwinhouse.org	703-578-1000		672
Goodwin Procter LLP 100 Northern Ave........... Boston MA 02210 *Web:* www.goodwinlaw.com	617-570-1000	523-1231	428
Goodwin-Lasiter-Strong 1609 S Chestnut St Ste 202 .... Lufkin TX 75901 *Web:* www.goodwinlasiterstrong.com	936-637-4900		256
Goodwood Museum & Gardens 1600 Miccosukee Rd .... Tallahassee FL 32308 *Web:* www.goodwoodmuseum.org	850-877-4202	877-3090	520
Goodyear Canada Inc 450 Kipling.............. Toronto ON M8Z5E1 *TF:* 800-387-3288 ■ *Web:* www.goodyear.ca	416-201-4300		755
Goodyear Tire & Rubber Co 200 Innovation Way .... Akron OH 44316 *NASDAQ: GT* ■ *TF:* 800-321-2136 ■ *Web:* www.goodyear.com	330-796-2121	796-2222	754
Goody-Goody Liquors Inc 10301 Harry Hines Blvd .... Dallas TX 75220 *Web:* www.goodygoody.com	214-459-9962		443
Google Inc 1600 Amphitheatre Pkwy .... Mountain View CA 94043 *NASDAQ: GOOGL* ■ *Web:* www.google.com	650-253-0000	253-0001	397
GoogLife 45 31 Skyline Dr................... Lake Mary FL 32746 *Web:* tv45.org	407-215-6745	215-6789	741
Goomzee Corp 4852 Kendrick Pl Ste 101 .... Missoula MT 59808 *Web:* www.goomzee.com	406-542-9955		387
Goose Creek State Park 2190 Camp Leach Rd..................... Washington NC 27889 *TF:* 877-722-6762 ■ *Web:* www.ncparks.gov	252-923-2191		565
Goose Island State Park 202 S Palmetto St.......................... Rockport TX 78382 *Web:* tpwd.texas.gov	361-729-2858		565
Goose Lake Prairie State Natural Area 5010 N Jugtown Rd .... Morris IL 60450 *Web:* gooselakeprairie.org	815-942-2899		565
Gooseberry Falls State Park 3206 Hwy 61 .... Two Harbors MN 55616 *Web:* www.dnr.state.mn.us	218-595-7100	834-3787	565
Goosebottom Books LLC 543 Trinidad Ln.......................... Foster City CA 94404 **Fax Area Code:* 888 ■ *TF:* 800-788-3123 ■ *Web:* www.goosebottombooks.com	800-788-3123	407-5286*	637-2
Gooseneck Trailer Manufacturing Co 4400 E Hwy 21 PO Box 832 .... Bryan TX 77808 *TF:* 800-688-5490 ■ *Web:* www.gooseneck.net	979-778-0034	778-0615	763
Goosenecks State Park c/o Edge of the Cedars State Park Museum 660 W 400 N .... Blanding UT 84511 *Web:* stateparks.utah.gov	435-678-2238	678-3348	565

Name / Address	City	State	ZIP	Phone	Fax	Class
Goostree Law Group PC 555 S Randall Rd Ste 200 *Web:* familydivorcelaw.com	Saint Charles	IL	60174	630-584-4800		41
Gootee Construction Inc 2400 N Arnoult Rd *Web:* gootee.com	Metairie	LA	70001	504-831-1909		186
GOPAC 2300 Clarendon Blvd Ste 1305 *Web:* www.gopac.org	Arlington	VA	22201	703-566-0376		615
Gopher Electronics Company Inc 222 Little Canada Rd *TF:* 800-592-9519 ■ *Web:* www.gopherelectronics.com	Saint Paul	MN	55117	651-490-4900		179
Gopher Sign Co 1310 Randolph Ave *TF:* 800-383-3156 ■ *Web:* www.gophersign.com	Saint Paul	MN	55105	651-698-5095	699-3727	701
Gopro Inc 300 Freehill Rd *Web:* www.goproinc.com	Hendersonville	TN	37077	615-824-4800		425
Gorant Candies 8301 Market St *TF:* 800-572-4139 ■ *Web:* gorant.com	Youngstown	OH	44512	330-726-8821	726-0325	123
Gorat's Steakhouse 4917 Center St *Web:* www.goratsomaha.com	Omaha	NE	68106	402-551-3733		671
Gorayeb & Associates PC 100 William St Ste 1900 *Web:* gorayeb.com	New York	NY	10038	212-267-9222		41
Gordee, Nowicki & Blakeney LLP 100 Spectrum Center Dr Ste 870 *Web:* gna-law.com	Irvine	CA	92618	949-567-9923		41
Gordley Group 2540 N Tucson Blvd *Web:* www.gordleygroup.com	Tucson	AZ	85716	520-327-6077	327-4687	344
Gordon & Betty Moore Foundation PO Box 29910 *Web:* www.moore.org	San Francisco	CA	94129	650-213-3000		305
Gordon Aluminum Industries Inc 1000 Mason St *Web:* www.gordonaluminum.com	Schofield	WI	54476	715-359-6101		492
Gordon Associates Insurance Services Inc 20 El Camino Real *TF:* 877-877-7755 ■ *Web:* gordoninsurance.com	Redwood City	CA	94062	650-654-5555	654-5550	390
Gordon Brush Manufacturing Company Inc 3737 Capitol Ave *TF:* 800-950-7950 ■ *Web:* www.gordonbrush.com	City of Industry	CA	90601	323-724-7777	724-1111	103
Gordon C. James Public Relations Inc 4715 N 32nd St Ste 104 *Web:* www.gcjpr.com	Phoenix	AZ	85018	602-274-1988		636
Gordon Center for Performing Arts 3506 Gwynnbrook Ave *Web:* www.jcc.org	Owings Mills	MD	21117	410-356-7469	356-7605	572
Gordon College 255 Grapevine Rd *TF:* 800-343-1379 ■ *Web:* www.gordon.edu	Wenham	MA	01984	978-927-2300	867-4682	166
Gordon Companies, The 50 State St 6th Fl *Web:* gordoncompanies.net	Albany	NY	12207	518-462-7411	462-8586	377
Gordon County 201 N Wall St *Web:* www.gordoncounty.org	Calhoun	GA	30701	706-629-3795	629-9516	338
Gordon County Board of Education 205 Warrior Path PO Box 12001 *Web:* www.gcbe.org	Calhoun	GA	30703	706-629-7366		685
Gordon County Chamber of Commerce 300 S Wall St *Web:* www.gordoncountychamber.com	Calhoun	GA	30701	706-625-3200	625-5062	139
Gordon Feinblatt LLC 233 E Redwood St *Web:* www.gfrlaw.com	Baltimore	MD	21202	410-576-4156	576-4246	428
Gordon Flesch Company Inc 2675 Research Pk Dr *TF:* 800-333-5905 ■ *Web:* www.gflesch.com	Madison	WI	53711	800-677-7877		264-2
Gordon Glass Co 5116 Warrensville Center Rd **Fax Area Code:* 216 ■ *TF:* 888-663-9830 ■ *Web:* www.gordonglassusa.com	Maple Heights	OH	44137	888-663-9830	663-9831*	330
Gordon L. Seaman Inc 29 Old Dock Rd *Web:* gordonlseaman.com	Yaphank	NY	11980	631-567-8000		194
Gordon Paper Company Inc PO Box 1806 *TF:* 800-457-7366 ■ *Web:* www.gordonpaper.com	Norfolk	VA	23501	757-464-3581	363-9355	552-2
Gordon Rees Scully Mansukhani LLP 275 Battery St Ste 2000 *Web:* www.grsm.com	San Francisco	CA	94111	415-986-5900		41
Gordon Rubber and Packing Company Inc 12 Cemetery Ave *TF:* 888-480-2477 ■ *Web:* www.gordonrubber.com	Derby	CT	06418	203-735-7441	734-7152	677
Gordon Schanzlin New Vision Institute 8910 University Center Ln Ste 800 *Web:* www.gwsvision.com	San Diego	CA	92122	858-455-6800		798
Gordon Sevig Trucking Co 1100 Commercial Dr *Web:* www.gstcinc.com	Walford	IA	52351	319-846-5555	846-5557	685
Gordon Sign 2930 W Ninth Ave *Web:* www.gordonsign.com	Denver	CO	80204	303-629-6121		701
Gordon State College 419 College Dr *TF:* 800-282-6504 ■ *Web:* www.gordonstate.edu	Barnesville	GA	30204	770-358-5021		167-3
Gordon Stockman & Waugh PC 8726 Industrial Rd *Web:* www.gswcpa.com	Peoria	IL	61615	309-692-4030	692-4159	2
Gordon Terminal Service Co 1000 Ella St *Web:* www.gtscofpa.com	McKees Rocks	PA	15136	412-331-9410		541
Gordon Thomas Honeywell LLP 1201 Pacific Ave Ste 2100 *Web:* www.gth-law.com	Tacoma	WA	98402	253-620-6500	620-6565	428
Gordon Tilden Thomas & Cordell LLP 1001 Fourth Ave Ste 4000 *Web:* gordontilden.com	Seattle	WA	98154	206-467-6477		41
Gordon's Photo Service 5067 S McCarran Blvd *Web:* www.gordonsphotoservice.com	Reno	NV	89502	775-826-6488		628
Gordon, Chodak & Chapin CPAS PC 40 Office Park Way *Web:* gcc-cpa.com	Pittsford	NY	14534	585-586-6210		2
Gordon, Fournaris & Mammarella PA 1925 Lovering Ave *Web:* www.gfmlaw.com	Wilmington	DE	19806	302-652-2900		428
Gordon-Conwell Theological Seminary 130 Essex St *TF:* 800-428-7329 ■ *Web:* www.gordonconwell.edu	South Hamilton	MA	01982	978-468-7111	468-6691	167-3
Gordon-Darby Inc 2410 Ampere Dr *Web:* gordon-darby.com	Louisville	KY	40299	502-266-5797		407
Gordon-Lee Mansion 217 Cove Rd *Web:* leeandgordonsmills.com	Chickamauga	GA	30707	706-375-4728		50-3
Gordons Specialties Inc 720 W Wintergreen Rd *Web:* www.gsihighway.com	Hutchins	TX	75141	972-225-1660	225-6662	697
Gore Design Completions Ltd 2060 Eagle Pkwy *Web:* www.gdctechnics.com	Fort Worth	TX	76177	210-496-5614		22
Gore Drug 305 N Main St *Web:* goredrug.com	Gore	OK	74435	918-489-5558		237
Gore Propane LLC PO BOX 76 *Web:* gorepropanegas.com	Wallisville	TX	77597	409-389-2242		316
Gorelick & Wolfert LLP 200 Frank H Ogawa Plz *Web:* bpgcomp.com	Oakland	CA	94612	510-272-0300		41
Gores Technology Group 9800 Wilshire Blvd *Web:* www.gores.com	Beverly Hills	CA	90212	310-209-3010	209-3310	405
Goreville Gazette 205 S Broadway *Web:* gorevillegazette.com	Goreville	IL	62939	618-995-9445		532-2
Gorfaine/Schwartz Agency Inc 4111 W Alameda Ave Ste 509 *Web:* www.gsamusic.com	Burbank	CA	91505	818-260-8500		731
Gorfine Schiller & Gardyn PA 10045 Red Run Blvd Ste 250 *Web:* www.gsg-cpa.com	Owings Mills	MD	21117	410-356-5900		2
Gorges State Park 976 Grassy Ridge Rd *Web:* www.ncparks.gov	Sapphire	NC	28774	828-966-9099		565
Gorham Savings Bank 64 Main St *TF:* 800-492-8120 ■ *Web:* www.gorhamsavings.bank	Gorham	ME	04038	207-839-4450	839-4790	70
Gorilla Capital Inc 1342 High St *Web:* gorillacapital.com	Eugene	OR	97401	541-344-7867		652
Gorilla Circuits 1445 Oakland Rd *Web:* www.gorillacircuits.com	San Jose	CA	95112	408-294-9897	297-1540	625
Gorilla Marketing 4100 Flat Rock Dr Ste A *Web:* www.gorillamarketing.net	Riverside	CA	92505	951-353-8133		195
Gorman & Associates PC Certified 1825 Franklin St Ste B *Web:* www.gaapc.com	Northampton	PA	18067	610-262-1280		2
Gorman Milling Company Inc 502 E Lubbock *TF:* 800-588-2252 ■ *Web:* www.redchainfeeds.com	Gorman	TX	76454	254-734-2252	734-2375	447
Gorman's 29145 Telegraph Rd *Web:* www.gormans.com	Southfield	MI	48034	248-353-9880		321
Gorman-Rupp Co PO Box 1217 *NYSE:* GRC ■ *Web:* www.gormanrupp.com	Mansfield	OH	44901	419-755-1011		641
Gorman-Rupp Industries 180 Hines Ave *Web:* gripumps.com	Bellville	OH	44813	419-886-3001	886-2338	641
Gorrie 2770 Matheson Blvd E *Web:* gorrie.com	Mississauga	ON	L4W4M5	416-760-9100	760-7924	7
Gort & Kraker PC 4475 Wilson Ave SW Ste 7 *Web:* gkpccpa.com	Grandville	MI	49418	616-530-2929	530-2339	2
Gorton Studios 4640 Nicols Rd Ste 205 *Web:* gortonstudios.com	Eagan	MN	55122	651-365-7891		177
Gorton's Inc 128 Rogers St *TF:* 800-222-6846 ■ *Web:* www.gortons.com	Gloucester	MA	01930	978-283-3000		296-14
Gosa Toys 1002 E Chestnut Ave *Web:* pinatasorangecounty.com	Santa Ana	CA	92701	714-361-9898		44
Gosar Paul A (Rep R - AZ) 2057 Rayburn House Office Bldg *Web:* gosar.house.gov	Washington	DC	20515	202-225-2315		342-2
Goschie Farms Inc 7365 Meridian Rd NE *Web:* goschiefarms.com	Silverton	OR	97381	503-873-5638		10-6
Goshen Chamber of Commerce 232 S Main St *TF:* 800-307-4204 ■ *Web:* www.goshen.org	Goshen	IN	46526	574-533-2102	533-2103	139
Goshen College 1700 S Main St *TF:* 800-348-7422 ■ *Web:* www.goshen.edu	Goshen	IN	46526	574-535-7000	535-7609	166
Goshen County 626 W 25th Ave *Web:* www.goshencounty.org	Torrington	WY	82240	307-532-4051	532-7375	338
Goshen County School District 1 626 W 25th Ave *TF:* 844-996-7233 ■ *Web:* www.goshen.k12.wy.us	Torrington	WY	82240	307-532-2171	532-7085	685
Goshen Historic Track Inc 44 Pk Pl *Web:* goshenhistorictrack.com	Goshen	NY	10924	845-294-5333	294-3998	642
Goshen News 114 S Main St PO Box 569 *TF:* 800-487-2151 ■ *Web:* www.goshennews.com	Goshen	IN	46527	574-533-2151	534-8830	532-2
Goshen Veterinary Clinic Inc 4548 Us Hwy 26/85 *Web:* goshenvetclinic.com	Torrington	WY	82240	307-532-4195		794
Gosiger Inc 108 McDonough St *TF:* 877-288-1538 ■ *Web:* www.gosiger.com	Dayton	OH	45402	937-228-5174	228-5189	385
Gosline Murchie Agency 10 Old Brunswick Rd *Web:* gosline-murchie.com	Gardiner	ME	04345	207-582-4120		390
Gosling Czubak Engineering Sciences Inc 1280 Business Park Dr *TF:* 800-968-1062 ■ *Web:* goslingczubak.com	Traverse City	MI	49686	231-946-9191		261
GoSolo 5410 Mariner St Ste 175 *TF:* 866-246-7656 ■ *Web:* login.gosolo.com	Tampa	FL	33609	866-246-7656		617
Gospel Advocate Co 1006 Elm Hill Pke *TF:* 800-251-8446 ■ *Web:* www.gospeladvocate.com	Nashville	TN	37210	615-254-8781	254-7411	95
Gospel Music Assn (GMA) 4012 Granny White Pk *Web:* www.gospelmusic.org	Nashville	TN	37204	615-242-0303	254-9755	48-4
Gospel Opportunities Inc 130 Carmen Dr *TF:* 800-359-9673 ■ *Web:* www.whwl.net	Marquette	MI	49855	906-249-1423		647

Name / Address	Phone	Fax	Class
Gospel Projects Press 6331 Chestnut St . . . . Milton FL 32572 *Web:* www.childrensbibleclub.com	850-623-4015		637-2
Gospel Publishers 100 S Ave C . . . . Moundridge KS 67107 *Web:* www.gospelpublishers.com	620-345-2532	345-2582	637-2
Gospel Services Inc PO Box 262302 . . . . Houston TX 77207 *TF:* 800-231-9641 ■ *Web:* gospelservices.com	800-231-9641		514
Gosper County *Nebraska* 507 Smith Ave E . . . . Elwood NE 68937 *Web:* www.co.gosper.ne.us	308-785-2611	785-2300	338
Goss & Deleeuw Parts Co, The 44 Washington Ave Ste 16 . . . . Kensington CT 06037 *Web:* goss-deleeuw.com	860-828-4121		493
Goss & Mclain Insurance Agency Inc 1767 Northampton St . . . . Holyoke MA 01040 *Web:* gossmclain.com	413-534-7355	536-9286	390
Goss Inc 1511 William Flynn Hwy . . . . Glenshaw PA 15116 *TF:* 800-367-4677 ■ *Web:* www.gossonline.com	412-486-6100	486-6844	811
Goss Intl 121 Technology Dr . . . . Durham NH 03824 *Web:* www.gossinternational.com	603-750-6600	750-6860	629
Gossamer Bio 3013 Science Park Rd . . . . San Diego CA 92121 *Web:* www.gossamerbio.com	858-684-1300		764
Gossner Foods Inc 1051 N 1000 W . . . . Logan UT 84321 *TF:* 800-944-0454 ■ *Web:* www.gossner.com	435-227-2500	227-2550	296-5
Gostanian Law Group 1201 Dove St Ste 475 . . . . Newport Beach CA 92660 *TF:* 866-330-0578 ■ *Web:* www.aglawpc.com	949-250-7800	250-7407	41
Gotech Inc 8383 Bluebonnet Blvd . . . . Baton Rouge LA 70810 *Web:* www.gotech-inc.com	225-766-5358	766-5879	256
Gotelli Plumbing Co 21 Lovell Ave . . . . San Rafael CA 94901 *Web:* www.gotelliplumbing.com	415-457-1145	456-1744	610
Goten 1719 W End Ave Ste 101W . . . . Nashville TN 37203 *Web:* www.gotennashville.com	615-321-4537		671
Gotham Bar & Grill 12 E 12th St . . . . New York NY 10003 *Web:* gothambarandgrill.com	212-620-4020		671
Gotham Brokerage Company Inc 75 Maiden Ln Ste 804 . . . . New York NY 10038 *Web:* gothambrokerage.com	212-406-7300	571-0690	390
Gotham Distributing Corp 60 Portland Rd . . . . Conshohocken PA 19428 *TF:* 800-446-8426 ■ *Web:* oldies.com	610-649-7565	649-0315	523
Gotham Growth Group 301 Tory Turn . . . . Wayne PA 19087 *Web:* www.gothamgrowth.com	484-433-9806		42
Gotham Sales Co 302 Main St . . . . Millburn NJ 07041 *Web:* gothamsales.com	973-912-8412		38
Gotham Steakhouse & Cocktail Bar 615 Seymour St . . . . Vancouver BC V6B3K3 *Web:* www.gothamsteakhouse.com	604-605-8282		671
Gotham Technology Group LLC 1 Paragon Dr Ste 200 . . . . Montvale NJ 07645 *Web:* www.gothamtg.com	201-474-4200		174
Gothic Cabinet Craft Inc 5877 57th St . . . . Maspeth NY 11378 *Web:* www.gothiccabinetcraft.com	347-881-1458		321
GOTHS (Green Oak Township Historical Society) 10789 Silver Lake Rd . . . . South Lyon MI 48178 *Web:* www.greenoaktownshiphistoricalsociety.org	248-342-0978		637-2
GoToConnect 1275 W 1600 N Ste 100 . . . . Orem UT 84057 *TF:* 866-768-5429 ■ *Web:* www.goto.com	866-768-5429		179
GotPrint 7651 N San Fernando Rd . . . . Burbank CA 91505 *TF:* 877-922-7374 ■ *Web:* www.gotprint.com	818-252-3000		781
Gottheimer Josh (Rep D - NJ) 213 Cannon House Office Bldg . . . . Washington DC 20515 *Web:* www.gottheimer.house.gov	202-225-4465	225-9048	342-2
Gottlieb & Janey LLP 111 Broadway Ste 701 . . . . New York NY 10006 *Web:* gottliebjaney.com	212-566-7766	374-1506	41
Gottlieb Bros Inc 55 E Washington St Ste 709 . . . . Chicago IL 60602	312-609-2222		411
Gottlieb Martin & Associates Inc 4932 Sunbeam Rd . . . . Jacksonville FL 32257 *TF:* 800-833-9986 ■ *Web:* www.gottlieb.com	904-346-3088		463
Gottlieb Memorial Hospital 701 W North Ave . . . . Melrose Park IL 60160 *TF:* 800-424-4840 ■ *Web:* www.gottliebhospital.org	708-681-3200		374-3
Gottlieb, Siegel & Schwartz LLP Mezzanine Level 207 E 94th St . . . . New York NY 10128 *Web:* gsslawllp.com	646-449-8141		41
Gottsch Cattle Co 3303 West 12th St . . . . Hastings NE 68901 *Web:* www.gottschcattlecompany.com	402-463-6215	463-6715	473
Gottsch Feeding Corp 20507 Nicholas Cir Ste 100 . . . . Elkhorn NE 68022 *Web:* gottschcattlecompany.com	402-289-4421		10-1
Gottscho Printing Systems Inc 601 Davisville Rd Ste 200 . . . . Willow Grove PA 19090 *Web:* gottscho.com	267-387-3005	387-3015	547
Goucher College 1021 Dulaney Valley Rd . . . . Towson MD 21204 *TF:* 800-468-2437 ■ *Web:* www.goucher.edu	410-337-6000	337-6354	166
Gough Financial Group Inc 9415 E Harry St Ste 602 . . . . Wichita KS 67207 *Web:* www.gfgks.com	316-683-8400		251
Gould & Bass Company Inc 1431 W 2nd St . . . . . . Pomona CA 91766 *Web:* gould-bass.net	909-623-6793	629-1467	248
Gould & Goodrich Leather Inc 709 E McNeill St . . . . Lillington NC 27546 *TF:* 800-277-0732 ■ *Web:* www.gouldusa.com	910-893-2071	893-4742	431
Gould & Ratner 222 N LaSalle Ste 800 . . . . Chicago IL 60601 *Web:* www.gouldratner.com	312-236-3003	236-3241	41
Gould Academy 39 Church St PO Box 860 . . . . Bethel ME 04217 *Web:* gouldacademy.org	207-824-7700	824-7711	622
Gould Asset Management LLC 341 W First St Ste 200 . . . . Claremont CA 91711 *Web:* gouldasset.com	909-445-1291		401
Gould Evans Intl 4041 Mill St . . . . Kansas City MO 64111 *Web:* www.gouldevans.com	816-931-6655		261
Gould Paper South LLC 10400 NW 21st Ste 104 . . . . Doral FL 33172 *Web:* www.gouldpaper.com	305-470-0003	470-0088	559

Name / Address	Phone	Fax	Class
Gould Technology LLC 1121 Benfield Blvd Stes J-P . . . . Millersville MD 21108 *TF:* 800-544-6853 ■ *Web:* gouldfo.com	410-987-5600		544
Gould's Discount Medical 3901 Dutchmans Ln Ste 100 . . . . Louisville KY 40207 *TF:* 800-876-6846 ■ *Web:* www.gouldsdiscountmedical.com	502-491-2000	495-2476	264-4
Gould's Salon Spa 766 S White Station Rd Ste 3 . . . . Memphis TN 38117 *Web:* gouldsalonspa.com	901-842-1444		77
Goulds Pumps Incorporated Goulds Water Technologies Group 240 Fall St . . . . Seneca Falls NY 13148 *TF:* 800-327-7700 ■ *Web:* www.gouldspumps.com	315-568-2811	568-2418	789
Goulston & Storrs 400 Atlantic Ave . . . . Boston MA 02110 *Web:* www.goulstonstorrs.com	617-482-1776		428
Goulston Technologies Inc 700 N Johnson St . . . . Monroe NC 28110 *Web:* www.goulston.com	704-289-6464	296-6400	145
Gourdie-Fraser Inc 123 W Front St . . . . Traverse City MI 49684 *Web:* gfa.tc	231-946-5874		261
Gourmet Settings 245 W Beaver Creek Rd Ste 10 . . . . Richmond Hill ON L4B1L1 *TF:* 800-551-2649 ■ *Web:* www.gourmetsettings.com	800-551-2649		361
Gouveia Engineering Inc 456 Sixth St . . . . Gustine CA 95322 *Web:* gouveiaengineering.com	209-854-3300		261
Gouvernement du Quebec 95 Avenue de la Verdure . . . . Chateauguay QC J6K0E8 *Web:* www.santemonteregie.qc.ca	450-699-3333		353
Gouverneur Correctional Facility 112 Scotch Settlement Rd PO Box 370 . . . . Gouverneur NY 13642 *Web:* www.doccs.ny.gov	315-287-7351		213
Gouverneur Hotel Montreal (Place-Dupuis) 1000 Sherbrooke St W Ste 2300 . . . . Montreal QC H3A3R3 *TF:* 888-910-1111 ■ *Web:* www.gouverneur.com	888-910-1111		379
Gouverneur Tribune-Press Inc 74 Trinty Ave . . . . Gouverneur NY 13642 *Web:* gouvernourtribuncprcss.com	315-287-2100		532-2
Govconnection Inc 7503 Standish Pl . . . . Rockville MD 20855 *Fax Area Code: 603 ■ *TF:* 800-998-0009 ■ *Web:* www.govconnection.com	800-998-0009	423-6192*	179
Gove County 520 Washington St Ste 105 PO Box 128 . . . . Gove KS 67736 *Web:* govecountyks.org	785-754-3341	938-4486	338
Gove Group Inc Gove Business Ctr 226 Paul St . . . . Pittsburgh PA 15211 *Web:* www.gove.org	412-431-5087	431-5214	194
Gove Group Real Estate LLC 70 Portsmouth Ave . . . . Stratham NH 03885 *Web:* www.thegovegroup.com	603-778-6400	772-4786	652
Gover & Perry LLC 2411 N Front St . . . . Harrisburg PA 17110 *Web:* pswzlawfirm.com	717-232-9900		41
Governair Corp 4841 N Sewell Ave . . . . Oklahoma City OK 73118 *Web:* www.nortekair.com	405-525-6546		14
Governing Magazine 1100 Connecticut Ave NW Ste 1300 . . . . Washington DC 20036 *TF:* 800-940-6039 ■ *Web:* www.governing.com	202-862-8802		457-12
Government Accountability Office (GAO) 441 G St NW . . . . Washington DC 20548 *Web:* www.gao.gov	202-512-4800		342
Government Accountability Office			
Atlanta Office 2635 Century Pkwy Ste 700 . . . . Atlanta GA 30345 *Web:* www.gao.gov	404-679-2008		342
Boston Office 10 Causeway St Rm 575 . . . . Boston MA 02222 *Web:* www.gao.gov	617-565-6795		342
Dallas Office 1999 Bryan St Ste 2200 . . . . Dallas TX 75201 *Web:* www.gao.gov	214-777-5600		342
Dayton Office 2196 D St Area B Bldg 39 . . . . Wright-Patterson AFB OH 45433 *Web:* www.gao.gov	937-258-7900		342
Denver Office 1244 Speer Blvd Ste 800 . . . . Denver CO 80204 *Web:* www.gao.gov	303-572-7306		342
Huntsville Office 7027 Old Madison Pk Ste 106 . . . . Huntsville AL 35806 *Web:* www.gao.gov	202-512-7600		342
Los Angeles Office 350 S Figueroa St Ste 1010 . . . . Los Angeles CA 90071 *Web:* www.gao.gov	213-688-3813		342
Norfolk Office 5029 Corporate Woods Dr Ste 300 . . . . . . Virginia Beach VA 23462 *Web:* www.gao.gov	757-552-8100		342
San Francisco Office 301 Howard St Ste 1200 . . . . San Francisco CA 94105 *Web:* www.gao.gov	202-512-8000		342
Seattle Office 701 Fifth Ave Ste 3700 . . . . Seattle WA 98104 *Web:* www.gao.gov	206-287-4800		342
Government Canyon State Natural Area 12861 Galm Rd . . . . San Antonio TX 78254 *Web:* tpwd.texas.gov	210-688-9055		565
Government Contracting Resources Inc 315 Page Rd PO Box 7 . . . . Pinehurst NC 28374 *Web:* www.gcrinc.net	910-215-1900		549
Government Finance Officers Assn (GFOA) 203 N LaSalle St Ste 2700 . . . . Chicago IL 60601 *Web:* www.gfoa.org	312-977-9700	977-4806	49-7
Government Island State Recreation Area 7005 NE Marine Dr . . . . Portland OR 97218 *Web:* www.oregonstateparks.org	503-281-0944		565
Government Liaison Services Inc (GLS) 200 N Glebe Rd Ste 321 . . . . Arlington VA 22203 *TF:* 800-642-6564 ■ *Web:* www.trademarkinfo.com	703-524-8200	525-8451	635
Government National Mortgage Assn 451 Seventh St SW Rm B-133 . . . . Washington DC 20410 *TF:* 800-234-4662 ■ *Web:* www.ginniemae.gov	202-708-1535		509
Government of Quebec 41 Boul Comtois . . . . Louiseville QC J5V2H8 *TF:* 888-693-3506 ■ *Web:* www.csssm.qc.ca	819-228-2731		374-2

	Phone	Fax	Class
Government Personnel Mutual Life Insurance Co PO Box 659567 .... San Antonio TX 78265 *TF:* 800-938-4765 ■ *Web:* www.gpmlife.com	800-938-4765		796
Government Research Service 1516 SW Boswell Ave. .... Topeka KS 66604 *TF:* 800-346-6898 ■ *Web:* statelegislativesourcebook.com	785-232-7720	232-1615	637-2
Government Retirement & Benefits Inc 333 John Carlyle St Ste 600 .... Alexandria VA 22314 *Web:* grbinc.com	703-461-9100		180
Governor Control Systems Inc 3101 SW Third Ave. .... Fort Lauderdale FL 33315 *TF:* 877-659-6328 ■ *Web:* www.govconsys.com	954-462-7404	761-8768	407
Governor Daniel Dunklin's Grave State Historic Site 104 Dunklin Dr .... Herculaneum MO 63048 *Web:* mostateparks.com	636-464-2976		565
Governor Dodge State Park 4175 State Hwy 23 N .... Dodgeville WI 53533 *Web:* dnr.wi.gov	608-935-2315		565
Governor Dummer Academy 1 Elm St. .... Byfield MA 01922 *Web:* www.thegovernorsacademy.org	978-499-3120	462-1278	622
Governor Henry Lippitt House Museum 199 Hope St .... Providence RI 02906 *Web:* www.preserveri.org	401-453-0688		520
Governor Knowles State Forest 325 SR 70 .... Grantsburg WI 54840 *Web:* dnr.wi.gov	715-463-2898		565
Governor Nelson State Park 5140 County Hwy M .... Waunakee WI 53597 *Web:* dnr.wi.gov	608-831-3005		565
Governor Thompson State Park N10008 Paust Ln .... Crivitz WI 54114 *Web:* dnr.wi.gov	715-757-3979		565
Governor's Avenue Animal Hospital 1008 S Governor's Ave .... Dover DE 19904 *Web:* www.governorsavenueanimalhospital.com	302-734-5588		794
Governor's Inn 700 W Sioux Ave .... Pierre SD 57501 *TF:* 877-523-0080 ■ *Web:* www.govinn.com	605-224-4200		379
Governor's Inn 210 Richards Blvd .... Sacramento CA 95811 *TF:* 800-999-6689 ■ *Web:* www.governorsinnhotel.com	916-448-7224	448-7382	379
Governor's Mansion State Historic Park 1526 H St .... Sacramento CA 95814 *Web:* www.parks.ca.gov	916-323-3047		565
Governor's Square 1500 Apalachee Pkwy .... Tallahassee FL 32301 *Web:* www.governorssquare.com	850-877-8106		460
Governors America Corp 720 Silver St .... Agawam MA 01001 *Web:* www.governors-america.com	413-233-1888	789-7736	203
Governors Inn 209 S Adams St .... Tallahassee FL 32301 *Web:* govinntallahassee.com	850-681-6855	222-3105	379
Governors State University 1 University Pkwy .... University Park IL 60484 *TF:* 800-478-8478 ■ *Web:* www.govst.edu	708-534-5000	534-1640	166
Govier, Katskee, Suing & Maxell 10404 Essex Ct Ste 100 .... Omaha NE 68114 *Web:* gksmlaw.com	402-391-1697		41
Govind Development LLC 9359 IH 37 Ste A .... Corpus Christi TX 78409 *Web:* www.govinddevelopment.com	361-241-2777		256
GovQA 900 S Frontage Rd Ste 110 .... Woodridge IL 60517 *Web:* webqa.com	630-985-1300		174
Gow School 2491 Emery Rd PO Box 85 .... South Wales NY 14139 *Web:* www.gow.org	716-652-3450	652-3457	622
Gowan Company LLC PO Box 5569 .... Yuma AZ 85366 *TF:* 800-883-1844 ■ *Web:* www.gowanco.com	928-783-8844		276
Gowan Construction Inc PO Box 228 .... Oslo MN 56744 *Web:* gowanconstruction.com	701-699-5171	699-3400	188-4
Gowan Inc 5550 Airline Dr .... Houston TX 77076 *Web:* gowaninc.com	713-696-5400	695-1726	189-10
Gowanda Correctional Facility S Rd PO Box 350 .... Gowanda NY 14070 *Web:* www.doccs.ny.gov	716-532-0177		213
Gowans-Knight Company Inc 49 Knight St .... Watertown CT 06795 *TF:* 800-352-4871 ■ *Web:* www.gowansknight.com	860-274-8801	274-7937	516
Goway Travel Ltd 3284 Yonge St Ste 300 .... Toronto ON M4N3M7 *TF:* 800-665-4432 ■ *Web:* www.goway.com	416-322-1034		772
Gowling WLG 100 King St W 1 First Canadian Pl Ste 1600 .... Toronto ON M5X1G5 *Web:* www.gowlingwlg.com	416-862-7525	862-7661	41
Goyette & Associates Inc 2366 Gold Meadow Way Ste 200 .... Gold River CA 95670 *TF:* 888-993-1600 ■ *Web:* goyetteassociates.com	916-851-1900		428
Goyette Machine Associates Inc 23 Carrington St .... Lincoln RI 02865 *Web:* www.goyettemachine.com	401-724-7772	723-1680	454
Goyette Mechanical Inc 3842 Gorey Ave PO Box 33 .... Flint MI 48506 *Web:* goyettemechanical.com	810-742-8530	743-9090	189-10
GP (Goettsch Partners Inc) 224 S Michigan Ave 1st Fl .... Chicago IL 60604 *Web:* www.gpchicago.com	312-356-0600	356-0601	261
GP (Geoscience Publications) 227 Howe-Russell Bldg .... Baton Rouge LA 70893 *Web:* ga.lsu.edu	225-578-5942	578-4420	637-2
GP Strategies Corp 11000 Broken Land Pkwy Ste 200 .... Columbia MD 21044 *TF:* 888-843-4784 ■ *Web:* www.gpstrategies.com	443-367-9600		180
GPA (GPA Midstream Assn) 6060 American Plz Ste 700 .... Tulsa OK 74135 *Web:* gpamidstream.org	918-493-3872		48-12
GPA (Georgia Press Assn) 3066 Mercer University Dr Ste 200 .... Atlanta GA 30341 *Web:* www.gapress.org	770-454-6776	454-6778	139
GPA Corp 8740 W 47th St Ste A .... McCook IL 60525 **Fax Area Code:* 800 ■ *TF:* 800-395-9000 ■ *Web:* www.askgpa.com	773-650-2020	395-3581*	553
GPA Midstream Assn (GPA) 6060 American Plz Ste 700 .... Tulsa OK 74135 *Web:* gpamidstream.org	918-493-3872		48-12
GPA Technologies Inc 2368 Eastman Ave Ste 8 .... Ventura CA 93003 *Web:* www.gpatech.com	805-643-7878	643-7474	256
GPAC (Germantown Performing Arts Ctr) 1801 Exeter Rd .... Germantown TN 38138 *Web:* www.gpacweb.com	901-751-7500		572
GPB (Georgia Public Broadcasting) 260 14th St NW .... Atlanta GA 30318 *TF:* 800-222-6006 ■ *Web:* www.gpb.org	800-222-6006		632
GPB (Gamma Phi Beta International Sorority) 12737 E Euclid Dr .... Centennial CO 80111 *Web:* www.gammaphibeta.org	303-799-1874	799-1876	48-16
GPC (Genuine Parts Co) 2999 Wildwood Pkwy .... Atlanta GA 30339 *NYSE:* GPC ■ *Web:* www.genpt.com	678-934-5000		61
GPCCVB (Greenville-Pitt County Convention & Visitors Bureau) 417 Cotanche St Ste 100 .... Greenville NC 27858 *TF:* 800-537-5564 ■ *Web:* visitgreenvillenc.com	252-329-4200	329-4205	206
GPD Global Inc 611 Hollingsworth St .... Grand Junction CO 81505 *TF:* 800-742-5473 ■ *Web:* www.gpd-global.com	970-245-0408	245-9674	201
GPD Group 520 S Main St Ste 2531 .... Akron OH 44311 *Web:* gpdgroup.com	330-572-2100	572-2101	261
GPD PC 524 First Ave S .... Great Falls MT 59401 *Web:* gpdpc.com	406-452-9558		261
GPHA (Georgia Pharmacy Assn) 50 Lenox Pointe NE .... Atlanta GA 30324 *TF:* 888-871-5590 ■ *Web:* www.gpha.org	404-231-5074	237-8435	585
GPI (Glass Packaging Institute) 1220 N Fillmore St Ste 400 .... Arlington VA 22201 *Web:* www.gpi.org	703-684-6359	546-0588	49-13
GPI Anatomicals 940 N Shore Dr .... Lake Bluff IL 60044 *Web:* www.gpianatomicals.com	847-615-8900		477
GPK Luxury Real Estate 1177 California St Ste A .... San Francisco CA 94108 *Web:* gpk-sf.com	415-775-7272		652
GPK Products Inc 1601 43rd St NW .... Fargo ND 58102 *TF:* 800-437-4670 ■ *Web:* www.gpk-fargo.com	701-277-3225	277-9286	608
GPL (Gleason Public Library) 22 Bedford Rd .... Carlisle MA 01741 *Web:* www.gleasonlibrary.org	978-369-4898		434-3
GPM Inc 4432 Venture Ave .... Duluth MN 55811 *Web:* www.gpmco.com	218-722-9904		358
GPM Investments LLC 8565 Magellan Pkwy Ste 400 .... Richmond VA 23227 *Web:* gpminvestments.com	804-730-1568		345
GPO (U.S. Government Printing Office Bookstore) 732 N Capitol St NW .... Washington DC 20401 *TF:* 866-512-1800 ■ *Web:* bookstore.gpo.gov	202-512-1800	512-2104	342
GPP (Great Plains Processing) 301 S Walnut Ave .... Luverne MN 56156 *Web:* www.gpp-co.com	507-283-4421		159
GPS (Great Plains Stainless) 1004 N 129th E Ave .... Tulsa OK 74116 *TF:* 800-345-5757 ■ *Web:* www.gpss.com	918-437-5400	437-5440	492
GPS Insight LLC 7201 E Henkel Way Ste 400 .... Scottsdale AZ 85255 **Fax Area Code:* 480 ■ *TF:* 866-477-4321 ■ *Web:* www.gpsinsight.com	866-477-4321	513-1694*	177
GPT 4990 Iris St .... Wheat Ridge CO 80033 *Web:* www.gptindustries.com	303-988-1242	988-1922	326
GPX Inc 60 Progress Ave .... Cranberry Township PA 16066 *Web:* www.gpxinc.com	724-779-9000	779-9025	188-3
GR Publishing PO Box 371 .... Felton CA 95018 *TF:* 877-477-6732 ■ *Web:* www.grandmarose.com	831-335-5366	335-5333	637-2
GR Sponaugle & Sons Inc 4391 Chambers Hill Rd .... Harrisburg PA 17111 *TF:* 800-868-9353 ■ *Web:* www.grsponaugle.com	717-564-1515	564-3675	189-10
GRA Inc 115 W Ave Ste 201 .... Jenkintown PA 19046 *Web:* gra-inc.com	215-884-7500	884-1385	449
GRAA (Greater Rockford Auto Auction Inc) 5937 Sandy Hollow Rd .... Rockford IL 61109 *TF:* 800-830-4722 ■ *Web:* www.graa.net	815-874-7800	874-1325	51
Grabber Construction Products Inc 20 W Main St Ct Ste 200 .... Alpine UT 84004 *Web:* www.grabberman.com	925-680-0777		350
Grabber School of Hair Design 9833 Watson Rd .... Saint Louis MO 63126 *Web:* www.grabberschool.edu	314-966-8888	287-6208	685
Graber Animal Hospital Inc 3311 Laskey Rd .... Toledo OH 43623 *Web:* grabersanimalhospital.com	419-475-3456		794
Graber Olive House Inc 315 E Fourth St .... Ontario CA 91764 **Fax Area Code:* 909 ■ *TF:* 800-996-5483 ■ *Web:* www.graberolives.com	800-996-5483	984-2180*	336
Grabill Cabinet Company Inc 13844 Sawmill Dr .... Grabill IN 46741 *TF:* 877-472-2782 ■ *Web:* www.grabillcabinets.com	260-376-1500		115
Grace A. Dow Memorial Library 1710 W St Andrews Rd .... Midland MI 48640 *TF:* 800-422-5245 ■ *Web:* cityofmidlandmi.gov	989-837-3430	837-3468	434-3
Grace Acres Press PO Box 22 .... Larkspur CO 80118 *TF:* 888-700-4722 ■ *Web:* www.graceacrespress.com	303-681-9995	681-9996	637-2
Grace Christian University 1011 Aldon St SW PO Box 910 .... Grand Rapids MI 49509 *TF:* 800-968-1887 ■ *Web:* gracechristian.edu	616-538-2330	538-0599	161
Grace College 200 Seminary Dr .... Winona Lake IN 46590 *TF:* 800-544-7223 ■ *Web:* www.grace.edu	574-372-5100	372-5120	166
Grace Communion Intl PO Box 5005 .... Glendora CA 91740 *Web:* www.gci.org	980-495-3977		637-9
Grace Creek Media Inc 100 Cathedral St Ste 9 .... Annapolis MD 21401 *Web:* www.gracecreek.com	410-280-8528		514
Grace Episcopal Church 33 Church St .... White Plains NY 10601 *Web:* www.gracewhiteplains.org	914-949-2874		48-20
Grace General Hospital 300 Booth Dr .... Winnipeg MB R3J3M7 *Web:* www.gracehospital.ca	204-837-0111	831-0029	374-2
Grace Hospice 6400 S Lewis Ave Ste 1000 .... Tulsa OK 74136 *TF:* 800-659-0307 ■ *Web:* www.gracehospice.com	918-744-7223		371

	Phone	Fax	Class
Grace Management Inc (GMI) 6900 Wedgwood Rd N Ste 300 .... Minneapolis MN 55422 *Web:* www.gracemanagement.com	763-544-9934		194
Grace Manufacturing Inc 614 SR 247 .... Russellville AR 72802 *TF:* 866-968-6665 ■ *Web:* www.gracemfg.com	866-968-6665		295
Grace Marketing Co 6120 Parkland Blvd Ste 225 .... Mayfield Village OH 44124 *Web:* gracemarketingco.com	440-442-7000	442-7005	195
Grace Museum 102 Cypress St .... Abilene TX 79601 *Web:* www.thegracemuseum.org	325-673-4587	675-5993	520
Grace Park Animal Hospital PLLC 11010 Lake Grove Blvd Ste 104 .... Morrisville NC 27560 *Web:* graceparkanimalhospital.com	919-462-1212		794
Grace Place Wellness Ministries 10733 Sunset Office Dr Ste 263 .... Saint Louis MO 63127 *Web:* www.graceplacewellness.org	314-842-3077	842-3099	48-20
Grace To You 28001 Harrison Pkwy .... Valencia CA 91355 *Web:* www.gty.org	661-295-5777	295-5871	116
Grace University 1311 S Ninth St .... Omaha NE 68108 *TF:* 800-383-1422 ■ *Web:* www.graceuniversity.edu	402-449-2800		161
Graceland (Elvis Presley Mansion) 3734 Elvis Presley Blvd .... Memphis TN 38116 *TF:* 800-238-2000 ■ *Web:* www.graceland.com	901-332-3322		520
Graceland Fruit Inc 1123 Main St .... Frankfort MI 49635 *TF:* 800-352-7181 ■ *Web:* www.gracelandfruit.com	231-352-7181	352-4711	296-18
Graceland University 1 University Pl .... Lamoni IA 50140 *TF:* 800-859-1215 ■ *Web:* www.graceland.edu	641-784-5000	784-5480	166
Graceworks Church Inc 16131 Hwy 44 .... Prairieville LA 70769	225-622-7805		48-20
Graceworks Lutheran Services 6430 Inner Mission Way .... Dayton OH 45459 *Web:* graceworks.org	937-433-2140		371
Gracey - Backer Inc 275 George Bush Blvd .... Delray Beach FL 33444 *TF:* 800-272-6055 ■ *Web:* graceybacker.com	561-276-6055	265-0034	390
Gracie Films 10201 W Pico Blvd Bldg 41/42 .... Los Angeles CA 90064 *Web:* www.graciefilms.com	310-369-7222		514
Gracious Home 1210 3rd Ave .... New York NY 10021 *TF:* 800-338-7809 ■ *Web:* gracioushome.com	212-517-6300		362
Gracious Living Corp 7200 Martin Grove Rd .... Woodbridge ON L4L9J3 *TF:* 800-465-5660 ■ *Web:* www.graciousliving.com	905-264-5660		321
Gracious Living Innovations Inc 151 Courtney Park Dr W .... Mississauga ON L5W1Y5 *Web:* www.glinnov.com	905-795-5505	795 5523	601
Graco Inc 88 11th Ave NE PO Box 1441 .... Minneapolis MN 55413 *NYSE:* GGG ■ *TF:* 800-328-0211 ■ *Web:* www.graco.com	612-623-6000	623-6777	641
Graco Supply Co 1001 Miller Ave .... Fort Worth TX 76105 *TF:* 866-629-8252 ■ *Web:* www.gracosupply.com	817-535-3200		21
Gradall Industries Inc 406 Mill Ave SW .... New Philadelphia OH 44663 *TF:* 800-445-4752 ■ *Web:* www.gradall.com	330-339-2211	339-8468	190
Gradcast.com LLC 203 Main St Ste 100 .... Lake Dallas TX 75065 *TF:* 800-396-4822 ■ *Web:* www.myopenjobs.com	800-396-4822	446-9634	260
Grade A 9 Slack Rd Ste 200 .... Ottawa ON K2G0B7 *Web:* www.gradea.ca	613-721-3331		196
Grade Finders Inc PO Box 944 .... Exton PA 19341 *Web:* www.gradefinders.com	610-269-7070	269-7077	637-2
Gradient Analytics LLC 8700 E Via de Ventura Blvd Ste 150 .... Scottsdale AZ 85258 *Web:* www.gradientanalytics.com	480-998-8585	998-4747	466
Gradient Corp 20 University Rd .... Cambridge MA 02138 *Web:* gradientcorp.com	617-395-5000	395-5001	194
Gradiva Publications PO Box 831 .... Stony Brook NY 11790 *Web:* www.italianstudies.org	631-632-7448	632-9612	637-2
Gradkell Systems Inc 4910 University Sq Ste 5 .... Huntsville AL 35816 *TF:* 866-472-3535 ■ *Web:* gradkell.com	866-472-3535		177
Graduate Management Admission Council (GMAC) 11921 Freedom Dr Ste 300 .... Reston VA 20190 *TF:* 866-505-6559 ■ *Web:* www.gmac.com	703-668-9600	668-9601	48-11
Graduate Providence 11 Dorrance St .... Providence RI 02903 *Web:* www.graduatehotels.com	401-421-0700		379
Graduate State College 125 S Atherton St .... State College PA 16801 *Web:* www.graduatehotels.com	814-231-2100		671
Graduate Storrs 855 Bolton Rd .... Storrs CT 06268 *Web:* www.graduatehotels.com	860-427-7888	427-7850	379
Graduate Theological Union 2400 Ridge Rd .... Berkeley CA 94709 *TF:* 800-826-4488 ■ *Web:* www.gtu.edu	510-649-2400	649-1730	167-3
Grady Brothers Inc 915 S Somerset Ave .... Indianapolis IN 46241 *Web:* www.gradybros.com	317-244-3343	240-5958	188-4
Grady Consulting LLC 71 Evergreen St Ste 1 .... Kingston MA 02364 *Web:* www.gradyconsulting.com	781-585-2300	585-2378	261
Grady County 250 N Broad St .... Cairo GA 39828 *Web:* www.gradycountyga.gov	229-377-1512	377-1039	338
Grady County 326 Choctaw St .... Chickasha OK 73018 *Web:* www.gradycountyok.com	405-224-7388	222-4506	338
Grady Electric Membership Corp (EMC) 1499 US Hwy 84 W .... Cairo GA 39828 *TF:* 877-757-6060 ■ *Web:* gradyemc.com	229-377-4182		245
Grady Gammage Memorial Auditorium 1200 S Forest Ave .... Tempe AZ 85281 *Web:* www.asugammage.com	480-965-3434	965-3583	572
Grady Health System 80 Jesse Hill Jr Dr SE .... Atlanta GA 30303 *Web:* www.gradyhealth.org	404-616-1000		374-3
Grady Management Inc 8630 Fenton St Ste 625 .... Silver Spring MD 20910 *Web:* www.gradymgt.com	301-587-3330		655
Grady Memorial Hospital 2220 Iowa Ave .... Chickasha OK 73018 *TF:* 800-299-9665 ■ *Web:* www.gradymem.org	405-224-2300	779-2413	374-3
Grady-White Boats Inc 5121 Martin Luther King Jr Hwy .... Greenville NC 27834 *Web:* www.gradywhite.com	252-752-2111		90
Grae-Con Construction Inc 880 Kingsdale Rd .... Steubenville OH 43952 *Web:* www.graecon.com	740-282-6830		186
GRAEF-USA Inc 125 S 84th St Ste 401 .... Milwaukee WI 53214 *Web:* www.graef-usa.com	414-259-1500	259-0037	261
Graeter's Inc 2145 Reading Rd .... Cincinnati OH 45202 *TF:* 800-721-3323 ■ *Web:* www.graeters.com	513-721-3323		296-25
Graf & Sons 4050 S Clark St .... Mexico MO 65265 *TF:* 800-531-2666 ■ *Web:* www.grafs.com	573-581-2266		711
Graf Creamery Inc N4051 Creamery St .... Bonduel WI 54107 **Fax Area Code:* 715 ■ *Web:* www.grafcreamery.com	920-822-5877	758-8020*	296-3
Graffiti's Italian Restaurant 7811 Cantrell Rd .... Little Rock AR 72227 *Web:* littlerockgraffitis.net	501-224-9079		671
Grafico Inc 15320 Cornet Ave .... Santa Fe Springs CA 90670 *Web:* www.grafico.com	562-404-4976		627
Grafik Marketing Communications Ltd 625 N Washington St Ste 302 .... Alexandria VA 22314 *TF:* 800-750-9772 ■ *Web:* grafik.agency	703-299-4500		7
Grafika Commercial Printing Inc 710 Johnston St .... Sinking Spring PA 19608 *Web:* www.grafikaprint.com	610-678-8630		627
GrafTech International Holdings Inc 12900 Snow Rd .... Parma OH 44130 *NYSE:* GTI ■ *Web:* www.graftech.com	216-676-2000		127
Graftek Imaging Inc 8900 Shoal Creek Blvd 300 B .... Austin TX 78757 *Web:* www.graftek.biz	512-416-1099		180
Grafton City Hospital 1 Hospital Plz .... Grafton WV 26354 *Web:* www.graftonhospital.com	304-265-0400		374-3
Grafton County 3855 Dartmouth College Hwy PO Box 4 .... North Haverhill NH 03774 *Web:* www.nhdeeds.com	603-787-6921	787-2363	338
Grafton Law Office PC LLO 1125 12th St .... Aurora NE 68818 *Web:* graftonlawoffice.com	402-694-5414		41
Grafton National Cemetery 431 Walnut St .... Grafton WV 26354 *Web:* www.cem.va.gov	304-265-2044	265-4336	136
Grafton Notch State Park 1941 Bear River Rd .... Newry ME 04261 *Web:* www.maine.gov	207-824-2912		565
Grafton on Sunset 8462 W Sunset Blvd .... West Hollywood CA 90069 **Fax Area Code:* 323 ■ *TF:* 800-821-3660 ■ *Web:* www.graftononsunset.com	800-821-3660	654-5918*	379
Grafton Transit Inc 5001 G Hwy G .... West Bend WI 53095 *Web:* www.graftontransit.com	262-306-9195		780
Gragg Advertising Inc 450 E Fourth St Ste 100 .... Kansas City MO 64106 *Web:* graggadv.com	816-931-0050		7
Grahall LLC 50 Fairlee Rd .... Waban MA 02468 *Web:* www.grahall.com	917-453-4341		260
Graham & Assoc 2100 Riverchase Ctr Ste 412 .... Birmingham AL 35244 *Web:* grahammktres.com	205-443-5399	443-5389	466
Graham & Company PC 1295 S Broadway Ste B .... Boulder CO 80305 *Web:* grahamcpas.com	303-253-7900		2
Graham Architectural Products Corp 1551 Mt Rose Ave .... York PA 17403 *TF:* 800-755-6274 ■ *Web:* www.grahamwindows.com	717-849-8100		234
Graham Cadillac 1515 W Fourth St .... Mansfield OH 44906 *Web:* www.grahamchevycadillac.com	419-989-4012		516
Graham Co, The 1 Penn Sq W 25th Fl .... Philadelphia PA 19102 *TF:* 888-472-4262 ■ *Web:* www.grahamco.com	215-567-6300		390
Graham Communications 516 Princeton Blvd .... Wenonah NJ 08090 *Web:* www.graham.marketing	617-328-0069		7
Graham Corp 20 Florence Ave .... Batavia NY 14020 *NYSE:* GHM ■ *TF:* 800-828-8150 ■ *Web:* www.graham-mfg.com	585-343-2216	343-1097	386
Graham Correctional Ctr 12078 Illinois Rt 185 PO Box 499 .... Hillsboro IL 62049 *Web:* www2.illinois.gov	217-532-6961	532-6799	213
Graham Cos 6843 Main St .... Miami Lakes FL 33014 *Web:* www.miamilakes.com	305-821-1130	557-0313	655
Graham County 34 Wall St Ste 407 .... Asheville NC 28801 *TF:* 866-962-6246 ■ *Web:* www.main.nc.us	828-255-0182	254-2286	338
Graham County 921 W Thatcher Blvd .... Safford AZ 85546 *TF:* 888-428-3252 ■ *Web:* www.graham.az.gov	928-428-3250	428-5951	338
Graham County Chamber of Commerce 1051 W Thatcher Blvd .... Safford AZ 85546 *TF:* 888-837-1841 ■ *Web:* www.grahamchamber.org	928-428-2511	428-0744	139
Graham County Electric Inc 9 W Center St .... Pima AZ 85543 *TF:* 800-577-9266 ■ *Web:* www.gce.coop	928-485-2451	485-9491	245
Graham Engineering Corp 1203 Eden Rd .... York PA 17402 *Web:* www.grahamengineering.com	717-848-3755	846-1931	480
Graham Enterprise Inc 628 N Lake St .... Mundelein IL 60060 *Web:* www.grahamei.com	847-837-0777	837-0778	324
Graham Group Inc 505 5th Ave Ste 200 .... Des Moines IA 50309 *TF:* 800-798-2656 ■ *Web:* www.thegrahamgroupinc.com	800-798-2656		653
Graham Group Inc, The 2014 W Pinhook Rd Ste 210 .... LaFayette LA 70508 *Web:* www.graham-group.com	337-232-8214		4
Graham Hospital 210 W Walnut St .... Canton IL 61520 *Web:* www.grahamhealthsystem.org	309-647-5240		374-3
Graham Law Group 11 E Kansas St .... Liberty MO 64068 *Web:* www.grahamlg.com	816-792-0500	781-6843	428
Graham Lindsey (Sen R - SC) 290 Russell Senate Office Bldg .... Washington DC 20510 *Web:* www.lgraham.senate.gov	202-224-5972	224-3808	342-2

	Phone	Fax	Class
Graham Lundberg & Peschei (GLP) 2153 Bethel Rd SE .... Port Orchard WA 98366 *Web:* www.glpattorneys.com	360-876-5005		428
Graham Media Group Inc 1408 N St Mary's St .... San Antonio TX 78215 *Web:* www.grahammedia.com	210-351-1200		647
Graham Medical Products 2273 Larsen Rd .... Green Bay WI 54303 *TF:* 800-558-6765 ■ *Web:* www.grahammedical.com	800-558-6765		576
Graham Newspapers Inc PO Box 600 .... Graham TX 76450 *Web:* www.grahamleader.com	940-549-7800	549-4364	532-2
Graham Oleson 525 Communication Cir .... Colorado Springs CO 80905 **Fax Area Code:* 719 ■ *TF:* 800-776-7336 ■ *Web:* grahamoleson.com	800-776-7336	635-1143*	5
Graham Packaging Co 2401 Pleasant Valley Rd .... York PA 17402 *TF:* 800-777-0065 ■ *Web:* grahampackaging.com	717-849-8500	854-4269	98
Graham Personnel Services 2100 W Cornwallis Dr .... Greensboro NC 27408 *Web:* www.grahamjobs.com	336-288-9330		260
Graham Real Estate Inc 198 E Main St .... Harbor Springs MI 49740 *Web:* grahamre.com	231-526-6251		652
Graham Research Inc 13305 Industrial Park Blvd .... Plymouth MN 55441 *Web:* grahamresearch.com	763-553-1339	553-9228	454
Graham Trucking Inc (GTI) 722 S Chicago .... Seattle WA 98108 *Web:* www.grahamtrucking.com	206-763-9734		780
Graham Webb Academy 1621 N Kent St Ste 1617 .... Arlington VA 22209 *TF:* 800-869-9322 ■ *Web:* www.grahamwebbacademy.edu	703-243-9322	525-4356	167-3
Graham, The 1075 Thomas Jefferson St NW .... Washington DC 20007 *Web:* www.thegrahamgeorgetown.com	202-337-0900	333-6526	379
Grahamgolden Technologies LLC 1020 W 11th Ave .... Denver CO 80204 *Web:* grahamgoldentech.com	303-722-7668		180
Graham-Pelton Consulting Inc 39 Beechwood Rd .... Summit NJ 07901 *Web:* grahampelton.com	908-608-1388		463
Grail Foundation Press (GFP) 14318 Shirley Bohn Rd .... Mount Airy MD 21771 *TF:* 800-427-9217 ■ *Web:* shop-grail.com	607-723-5163		637-2
Grail Insights 1970 Broadway Ste 1140 .... Oakland CA 94612 *Web:* www.grailinsights.com	510-834-1910		194
Grain Belt Supply Company Inc PO Box 615 .... Salina KS 67402 *TF:* 800-447-0522 ■ *Web:* www.grainbeltsupply.com	785-827-4491	827-4494	480
Grain Inspection Packers & Stockyards Administration 1400 Independence Ave SW .... Washington DC 20228 *Web:* www.gipsa.usda.gov	202-720-0219		340-1
Grain Processing Corp 1600 Oregon St .... Muscatine IA 52761 *Web:* www.grainprocessing.com	563-264-4265	264-4289	296-23
Grainger County Chamber of Commerce 460 Water St .... Rutledge TN 37861 *Web:* graingercochamber.com	865-828-4222		338
Grainger Terry Inc 8 S Michigan Ave 35th Fl .... Chicago IL 60603 *Web:* www.graingerterry.com	312-541-1600		194
Gram Lumber Co 985 NW Second St .... Kalama WA 98625 *Web:* www.rsgfp.com	360-673-5231	673-5558	683
Grambling State University 403 Main St .... Grambling LA 71245 *TF:* 800-569-4714 ■ *Web:* www.gram.edu	318-247-3811		166
Gramercy Advisors LLC 20 Dayton Ave .... Greenwich CT 06830 *Web:* www.gramercyadvisors.com	203-552-1900		401
Gramercy Park Hotel 2 Lexington Ave .... New York NY 10010 *TF:* 866-784-1300 ■ *Web:* www.gramercyparkhotel.com	212-920-3300	673-5890	379
Gramercy Tavern 42 E 20th St .... New York NY 10003 *Web:* www.gramercytavern.com	212-477-0777		671
Grammy Museum Foundation Inc 800 W Olympic Blvd Ste A245 .... Los Angeles CA 90015 *Web:* www.grammymuseum.org	213-765-6800		522
Gran Tierra Energy Inc 200 150 13th Ave SW .... Calgary AB T2R0V2 *Web:* www.grantierra.com	403-265-3221		536
Granada Hills Chamber of Commerce 17723 Chatsworth St .... Granada Hills CA 91344 *Web:* www.granadachamber.com	818-368-3235		139
Granahan Investment Management Inc 404 Wyman St Ste 460 .... Waltham MA 02451 *Web:* www.granahan.com	781-890-4412		401
Gran-Aire Inc 9305 W Appleton Ave .... Milwaukee WI 53225 *Web:* springcityaviation.com	414-461-3222	461-8207	167-3
Granary Books Inc 168 Mercer St 2nd Fl .... New York NY 10012 *Web:* www.granarybooks.com	212-337-9979	337-9774	637-2
Grand 1894 Opera House 2020 Postoffice St .... Galveston TX 77550 *TF:* 800-821-1894 ■ *Web:* www.thegrand.com	409-765-1894	763-1068	572
Grand Aire Express Inc 11777 W Airport Service Rd .... Swanton OH 43558 **Fax Area Code:* 419 ■ *TF:* 800-704-7263 ■ *Web:* www.grandaire.com	800-704-7263	865-2965*	63
Grand America Hotel 555 S Main St .... Salt Lake City UT 84111 *TF:* 800-304-8696 ■ *Web:* grandamerica.com	801-258-6000	258-6911	379
Grand Avenue 752 Grand Ave Ste 1 .... Saint Paul MN 55105 *Web:* grandave.com	651-699-0029		460
Grand Avenue Veterinary Clinic PA 5503 Grand Ave .... Duluth MN 55807 *Web:* grandavevetclinic.com	218-628-0301		794
Grand Banks Yachts Ltd 450 SW Salerno Rd .... Stuart FL 34997 *Web:* grandbanks.com	206-352-0116		90
Grand Beach Inn (GBI) 198 E Grand Ave .... Old Orchard Beach ME 04064 *Web:* grandbeachinnmaine.com	207-934-4621		379
Grand Blanc Cement Products 10709 Center Rd .... Grand Blanc MI 48439 *TF:* 800-875-7500 ■ *Web:* www.grandblanccementproducts.com	810-694-7500	694-2995	183
Grand Blanc Chamber of Commerce 512 E Grand Blanc Rd .... Grand Blanc MI 48439 *Web:* grandblancchamber.com	810-695-4222		139
Grand Cafe Key West 314 Duval St .... Key West FL 33040 *Web:* www.grandcafekeywest.com	305-292-4740		671
Grand Canyon National Park PO Box 129 .... Grand Canyon AZ 86023 *Web:* www.nps.gov	928-638-7888		564
Grand Canyon Railway Inc 1201 W Rt 66 Ste 200 .... Flagstaff AZ 86001 *TF:* 800-843-8724 ■ *Web:* www.thetrain.com	928-773-1976		649
Grand Canyon Trust 2601 N Fort Valley Rd .... Flagstaff AZ 86001 *TF:* 800-827-5722 ■ *Web:* www.grandcanyontrust.org	928-774-7488	774-7570	48-13
Grand Canyon University 3300 W Camelback Rd .... Phoenix AZ 85017 *TF:* 800-800-9776 ■ *Web:* gcu.edu	602-639-7500		166
Grand Casino Hinckley 777 Lady Luck Dr .... Hinckley MN 55037 *TF:* 800-472-6321 ■ *Web:* grandcasinomn.com	800-472-6321		133
Grand Casino Mille Lacs & Hinckley 777 Grand Ave .... Onamia MN 56359 *TF:* 800-626-5825 ■ *Web:* www.grandcasinomn.com	800-626-5825		379
Grand China 658 Kirkwood Mall .... Bismarck ND 58504 *Web:* www.grandchinabismarck.com	701-222-1518		671
Grand China Restaurant 2905 Peachtree Rd NE .... Atlanta GA 30305 *Web:* grandchinaatl.com	404-231-8690		671
Grand Concourse 100 W Stn Sq Dr .... Pittsburgh PA 15219 *Web:* www.grandconcourserestaurant.com	412-261-1717	261-6041	671
Grand Country Inn Grand Country Sq 1945 W 76 Country Blvd .... Branson MO 65616 *TF:* 888-505-4096 ■ *Web:* www.grandcountry.com	888-505-4096		379
Grand County 308 Byers Ave PO Box 264 .... Hot Sulphur Springs CO 80451 *Web:* www.co.grand.co.us	970-725-3347	725-0100	338
Grand County 125 E Center St .... Moab UT 84532 *Web:* www.grandcountyutah.net	435-259-1321	259-2959	338
Grand County Historical Assn (GCHA) PO Box 165 .... Hot Sulphur Springs CO 80451 *Web:* grandcountyhistory.org	970-725-3939		48-13
Grand Electric Co-opeartive Inc 801 Coleman Ave PO Box 39 .... Bison SD 57620 *TF:* 800-592-1803 ■ *Web:* www.grandelectric.coop	605-244-5211		245
Grand Encampment Museum (GEM) 807 Barnett .... Encampment WY 82325 *Web:* www.gemuseum.com	307-327-5308		520
Grand European Tours 6000 Meadows Rd Ste 520 .... Lake Oswego OR 97035 *TF:* 877-622-9109 ■ *Web:* www.getours.com	503-635-9627	718-5198	760
Grand Finale Cleaning 2001 Button Ln Ste D .... LaGrange KY 40031 *Web:* gfcleaning.com	502-222-0736		104
Grand Food Ctr 606 Green Bay Rd .... Winnetka IL 60093 *Web:* grandfoodcenter.com	847-446-6707	446-9050	345
Grand Forks Air Force Base Grand Forks AFB 344 Tuskegee Airmen Blvd .... Grand Forks ND 58205 *Web:* www.grandforks.af.mil	701-747-3316		497-1
Grand Forks Chamber of Commerce 202 N Third St .... Grand Forks ND 58203 *Web:* www.gochamber.org	701-772-7271	772-9238	139
Grand Forks City Hall 255 N Fourth St .... Grand Forks ND 58203 *Web:* www.grandforksgov.com	701-746-4636	787-3740	337
Grand Forks County 124 S Fourth St .... Grand Forks ND 58206 *Web:* www.gfcounty.nd.gov	701-787-2730		338
Grand Forks Herald 375 Second Ave N .... Grand Forks ND 58203 *Web:* www.grandforksherald.com	701-780-1100	780-1123	532-2
Grand Forks Human Nutrition Research Ctr USDA/ARS 2420 Second Ave N .... Grand Forks ND 58203 *Web:* www.ars.usda.gov	701-795-8291	795-8395	668
Grand Furniture Discount Store 836 E Little Creek Rd .... Norfolk VA 23518 *Web:* www.grandfurniture.com	757-588-1331		321
Grand Gateway Hotel 1721 N LaCrosse St .... Rapid City SD 57701 *TF:* 866-742-1300 ■ *Web:* www.grandgatewayhotel.com	866-742-1300		379
Grand Geneva Resort & Spa 7036 Grand Geneva Way .... Lake Geneva WI 53147 *Web:* www.grandgeneva.com	262-248-8811		669
Grand Harbor Resort & Waterpark 350 Bell St .... Dubuque IA 52001 *TF:* 866-690-4006 ■ *Web:* www.grandharborresort.com	563-690-4000		669
Grand Haven Board of Lightand & Power (GHBLP) 1700 Eaton Dr .... Grand Haven MI 49417 *Web:* ghblp.org	616-846-6250	846-3114	245
Grand Haven Gasket Co 1701 Eaton Dr .... Grand Haven MI 49417 *TF:* 800-688-8181 ■ *Web:* www.ghgc.com	616-842-7682	842-7694	326
Grand Haven Plastics Inc 1425 Aerial View Dr .... Grand Haven MI 49417 *Web:* www.wmmolding.com	616-846-4950		596
Grand Haven State Park 1001 S Harbor Ave .... Grand Haven MI 49417 *Web:* www.michigan.org	616-847-1309		565
Grand Home Furnishings 4235 Electric Rd SW .... Roanoke VA 24018 *TF:* 888-555-7463 ■ *Web:* www.grandhomefurnishings.com	540-776-7000		321
Grand Homes Inc 15455 Dallas Pkwy Ste 1000 .... Addison TX 75001 *Web:* www.grandhomes.com	214-750-6528	750-6849	653

Name / Address	City	State	ZIP	Phone	Fax	Class
Grand Hotel & Suites Toronto 225 Jarvis St *Web:* grandhoteltoronto.com	Toronto	ON	M5B2C1	416-863-9000		379
Grand Hotel of Cape May Beach Ave *TF:* 800-257-8550 ■ *Web:* www.grandhotelcapemay.com	Cape May	NJ	08204	609-884-5611		379
Grand Hotel, The 149 SR-64 *TF:* 888-634-7263 ■ *Web:* www.grandcanyongrandhotel.com	Grand Canyon	AZ	86023	928-638-3333		379
Grand Image Inc 560 Main St *Fax Area Code: 978 ■ *TF:* 888-973-2622 ■ *Web:* grandimageinc.com	Hudson	MA	01749	888-973-2622	567-9410*	8
Grand Island Area Chamber of Commerce 309 W Second St *Web:* www.gichamber.com	Grand Island	NE	68802	308-382-9210	382-1154	139
Grand Island Independent 422 W First St *TF:* 800-658-3160 ■ *Web:* www.theindependent.com	Grand Island	NE	68801	308-382-1000	382-8129	532-2
Grand Island Veterans' Home 2300 W Capital Ave *TF:* 800-358-8802 ■ *Web:* www.dhhs.ne.gov	Grand Island	NE	68803	308-385-6252		793
Grand Isle County 9 Hyde Rd PO Box 49 *Web:* www.grandislevt.org	Grand Isle	VT	05458	802-372-8830	372-8815	338
Grand Isle State Park Admiral Craik Dr *TF:* 888-787-2559 ■ *Web:* crt.state.la.us	Grand Isle	LA	70358	985-787-2559		565
Grand Isle State Park 36 E Shore S *Web:* vtstateparks.com	Grand Isle	VT	05458	802-372-4300		565
Grand Junction Area Chamber of Commerce 360 Grand Ave *TF:* 800-352-5286 ■ *Web:* gjchamber.org	Grand Junction	CO	81501	970-242-3214	242-3694	139
Grand Junction Concrete Pipe Co PO Box 1849 *Web:* www.gjpipe.com	Grand Junction	CO	81501	970-243-4604		135
Grand Junction Convention Ctr, The 159 Main St *Web:* www.grandjunctionconventioncenter.com	Grand Junction	CO	81501	970-263-5700	263-5720	205
Grand Junction Real Estate Group 120 W Park Dr Ste 200 *Web:* thekimbroughteam.com	Grand Junction	CO	81505	970 263 7355		652
Grand Junction VA Medical Ctr 2121 N Ave *Web:* www.grandjunction.va.gov	Grand Junction	CO	81501	970-242-0731		374-8
Grand Junction Visitors & Convention Bureau 740 Horizon Dr *TF:* 800-962-2547 ■ *Web:* www.visitgrandjunction.com	Grand Junction	CO	81506	970-244-1480	243-7393	206
Grand Lake Casino 24701 S 655 Rd *Web:* grandlakecasino.com	Grove	OK	74344	918-786-8528		452
Grand Lake Mental Health Center Inc 114 W Delaware *TF:* 800-722-3611 ■ *Web:* www.glmhc.net	Nowata	OK	74048	918-273-1841		726
Grand Mesa Youth Sevices Ctr 360 28th Rd *Web:* www.colorado.gov	Grand Junction	CO	81501	970-242-1521	242-8127	412
Grand Oaks Hotel 2315 Green Mountain Dr *TF:* 800-553-6423 ■ *Web:* www.grandoakshotel.net	Branson	MO	65616	800-553-6423		379
Grand Ole Opry 2804 Opryland Dr *TF:* 800-733-6779 ■ *Web:* www.opry.com	Nashville	TN	37214	615-871-6779		572
Grand Opera House 651 Mulberry St *Web:* www.thegrandmacon.com	Macon	GA	31201	478-301-5470		572
Grand Pacific Palisades Resort & Hotel 5805 Armada Dr *TF:* 800-725-4723 ■ *Web:* www.grandpacificpalisades.com	Carlsbad	CA	92008	760-827-3200		669
Grand Pacific Resorts Inc Grand Pacific Plz 5900 Pasteur Ct Ste 200 *Web:* grandpacificresorts.com	Carlsbad	CA	92008	760-431-8500		378
Grand Palms Hotel & Golf Resort 110 Grand Palms Dr *TF:* 800-327-9246 ■ *Web:* www.grandpalmsresort.com	Pembroke Pines	FL	33027	954-431-8800	435-5988	669
Grand Peaks Properties Inc 4582 S Ulster St Ste 1200 *Web:* grandpeaks.com	Denver	CO	80237	720-889-9200		656
Grand Portage Lodge & Casino PO Box 233 *TF:* 800-543-1384 ■ *Web:* www.grandportage.com	Grand Portage	MN	55605	218-475-2401	475-2309	669
Grand Portage National Monument PO Box 426 *Web:* www.nps.gov	Grand Portage	MN	55605	218-475-0123		564
Grand Portage State Park 9393 E Hwy 61 *Web:* www.dnr.state.mn.us	Grand Portage	MN	55605	218-475-2360	475-2365	565
Grand Prairie Credit Union 209 N Center St *TF:* 888-268-4728 ■ *Web:* gpcreditunion.org	Grand Prairie	TX	75050	972-262-7935	263-5265	219
Grand Premier Tire & Custom Wheel 591 Columbia Tpke *TF:* 800-287-4753 ■ *Web:* www.grandpremiertire.com	East Greenbush	NY	12061	800-287-4753		755
Grand Prix of Long Beach 3000 Pacific Ave *TF:* 888-827-7333 ■ *Web:* gplb.com	Long Beach	CA	90806	562-981-2600		642
Grand Rapids Area Chamber of Commerce 1 NW Third St *TF:* 800-472-6366 ■ *Web:* www.grandmn.com	Grand Rapids	MN	55744	218-326-6619	326-4825	139
Grand Rapids Area Chamber of Commerce 111 Pearl St NW *Web:* www.grandrapids.org	Grand Rapids	MI	49503	616-771-0300	771-0318	139
Grand Rapids Art Museum 101 Monroe Center St NW *Web:* www.artmuseumgr.org	Grand Rapids	MI	49503	616-831-1000	831-1001	520
Grand Rapids Ballet Co 341 Ellsworth Ave SW *Web:* www.grballet.com	Grand Rapids	MI	49503	616-454-4771	454-0672	573-1
Grand Rapids Bar Assn (GRBA) 161 Ottawa Ave NW Ste 203-B *Web:* www.grbar.org	Grand Rapids	MI	49503	616-454-5550	454-7707	49-19
Grand Rapids Business Journal (GRBJ) 549 Ottawa Ave NW Ste 201 *Web:* www.grbj.com	Grand Rapids	MI	49503	616-459-4545		457-5
Grand Rapids Children's Museum 11 Sheldon Ave NE *Web:* www.grcm.org	Grand Rapids	MI	49503	616-235-4726	235-4728	521
Grand Rapids City Hall 300 Monroe Ave NW *TF:* 800-860-8610 ■ *Web:* www.grandrapidsmi.gov	Grand Rapids	MI	49503	616-456-3010	456-4607	337
Grand Rapids Civic Theatre 30 N Division Ave *Web:* www.grct.org	Grand Rapids	MI	49503	616-222-6650		572
Grand Rapids Community College 143 Bostwick Ave NE *Web:* grcc.edu	Grand Rapids	MI	49503	616-234-4000	234-4107	162
Grand Rapids Controls 825 Northland Dr NE *Web:* www.grcontrols.com	Rockford	MI	49341	616-884-7100		247
Grand Rapids Gravel Co 2700 28th St Sw *Web:* www.grgravel.com	Wyoming	MI	49519	616-538-9000		182
Grand Rapids Label Co 2351 Oak Industrial Dr NE *TF:* 800-552-5215 ■ *Web:* www.grlabel.com	Grand Rapids	MI	49505	616-459-8134	459-4543	413
Grand Rapids Public Library 111 Library St NE *Web:* www.grpl.org	Grand Rapids	MI	49503	616-988-5400		434-3
Grand Rapids Public Schools (GRPS) 1331 Franklin St SE PO Box 117 *Web:* www.grps.org	Grand Rapids	MI	49506	616-819-2000	819-2104	685
Grand Rapids Scale Company Inc 4215 Stafford Ave SW *TF:* 800-348-5701 ■ *Web:* www.grmetrology.com	Grand Rapids	MI	49548	800-348-5701		362
Grand Rapids Symphony 300 Ottawa Ave NW Ste 100 *Web:* www.grsymphony.org	Grand Rapids	MI	49503	616-454-9451	454-7477	573-3
Grand Rapids Transport Inc 2278 Port Sheldon St *Fax Area Code: 616 ■ *TF:* 800-333-3694 ■ *Web:* www.grandrapidstransport.com	Jenison	MI	49428	800-333-3694	669-9193*	780
Grand Rapids/Kent County Convention & Visitors Bureau 171 Monroe Ave NW Ste 545 *TF:* 800-678-9859 ■ *Web:* www.experiencegr.com	Grand Rapids	MI	49503	616-258-7388		206
Grand River Academy 3042 College St *Web:* www.grandriver.org	Austinburg	OH	44010	440-275-2811	275-1825	622
Grand River Agricultural Society 7445 Wellington County Rd 21 RR 2 *TF:* 800-898-7792 ■ *Web:* grandriveragsociety.com	Elora	ON	N0B1S0	519-846-5455	846-1980	642
Grand River Hospital Kitchener-Waterloo Health Ctr 835 King St W PO Box 9056 *Web:* www.grhosp.on.ca	Kitchener	ON	N2G1G3	519-749-4300		374-2
Grand River Mutual (GRM) 1001 Kentucky St *TF:* 800-451-2301 ■ *Web:* www.grm.net	Princeton	MO	64673	660-748-3231		224
Grand River Rubber & Plastics Co 2029 Aetna Rd *Web:* www.grandriverrubber.com	Ashtabula	OH	44004	440-998-2900		677
Grand Rounds Inc 360 3rd St *TF:* 800-929-0926 ■ *Web:* www.grandrounds.com	San Francisco	CA	94107	800-929-0926		352
Grand Savings Bank 1022 S Main St *Web:* grandsavingsbank.com	Grove	OK	74344	918-786-2203		70
Grand Seas Resort Partners 2424 N Atlantic Ave *Web:* www.grandseas.com	Daytona Beach	FL	32118	386-677-7880		378
Grand Sierra Resort & Casino 2500 E Second St *TF:* 800-501-2651 ■ *Web:* www.grandsierraresort.com	Reno	NV	89595	775-789-2000		669
Grand Strand Airport 2800 Terminal St *Web:* www.beachaviationservices.com	North Myrtle Beach	SC	29582	843-848-7400		63
Grand Strand Medical Ctr 809 82nd Pkwy *TF:* 866-492-9084 ■ *Web:* mygrandstrandhealth.com	Myrtle Beach	SC	29572	843-692-1000		374-3
Grand Strand Sandwich Co 8910 Hwy 90 *Web:* www.grandstrandsandwichcompany.com	Longs	SC	29568	843-399-2999	399-0547	297-2
Grand Street Cafe 4740 Grand Ave *Web:* grandstreetkc.com	Kansas City	MO	64112	816-561-8000		671
Grand Street Theater 325 N Park Ave *Web:* www.grandstreettheatre.com	Helena	MT	59601	406-442-4270	447-1573	572
Grand Summit Hotel 570 Springfield Ave *TF:* 800-346-0773 ■ *Web:* www.grandsummit.com	Summit	NJ	07901	908-273-3000	273-4228	379
Grand Targhee Resort 3300 E Ski Hill Rd *TF:* 800-827-4433 ■ *Web:* www.grandtarghee.com	Alta	WY	83414	307-353-2300	353-8148	669
Grand Telephone Company Inc (GTC) 226 S 4th St *TF:* 888-400-5587 ■ *Web:* www.grand.net	Jay	OK	74346	918-253-4231	253-3400	224
Grand Terrace Healthcare Ctr 12000 Mt Vernon Ave *Web:* www.grandterracecare.com	Grand Terrace	CA	92313	909-825-5221	783-4811	450
Grand Teton Lodge Company & Jackson Lake Lodge 101 Jackson Lake Lodge Rd *TF:* 800-628-9988 ■ *Web:* www.gtlc.com	Moran	WY	83013	307-543-2811	543-3143	669
Grand Teton National Park PO Box 170 *Web:* www.nps.gov	Moose	WY	83012	307-739-3399	739-3438	564
Grand Times Hotel 6515 Wilfrid-Hamel Blvd *TF:* 888-902-4444 ■ *Web:* www.grandtimeshotel.com	Quebec City	QC	G2E5W3	418-877-7788	877-3333	379
Grand Transformers Inc 1500 Marion Ave *TF:* 844-383-8644 ■ *Web:* www.grandpowersystems.com	Grand Haven	MI	49417	616-842-5430		767
Grand Traverse Continuous Inc 1661 Park Dr *Fax Area Code: 800 ■ *TF:* 800-227-0010 ■ *Web:* gtcontinuous.com	Traverse City	MI	49686	231-941-5400	777-2357*	110
Grand Traverse County 400 Boardman Ave *Web:* www.co.grand-traverse.mi.us	Traverse City	MI	49684	231-922-4700		338
Grand Traverse Machine (GTM) 1247 Boon St *Web:* www.gtmachine.com	Traverse City	MI	49686	231-946-8006		621
Grand Traverse Resort & Spa 100 Grand Traverse Blvd PO Box 404 *TF:* 800-236-1577 ■ *Web:* www.grandtraverseresort.com	Acme	MI	49610	231-534-6000		669

				Phone	Fax	Class
Grand Valley Health Plan 2680 Leonard St NE *Web:* gvfhc.com	Grand Rapids	MI	49525	616-949-2410		352
Grand Valley Manufacturing Co (GVM) 701 E Spring St Bldg 52 *Web:* grandvalleymfg.com	Titusville	PA	16354	814-827-2707	827-4349	454
Grand Valley Public Radio Inc 1310 Ute Ave *Web:* www.kafmradio.org	Grand Junction	CO	81501	970-241-8801		645-141
Grand Valley Rural Power Lines Inc 845 22 Rd PO Box 190 *TF:* 877-760-7435 ■ *Web:* www.gvp.org	Grand Junction	CO	81505	970-242-0040		245
Grand Valley State University 1 Campus Dr *TF:* 800-748-0246 ■ *Web:* www.gvsu.edu	Allendale	MI	49401	616-331-5000	331-2000	166
Grand View Health 700 Lawn Ave *Web:* www.gvh.org	Sellersville	PA	18960	215-453-4000		374-3
Grand View Research Inc 201 Spear St Ste 1100 *Web:* www.grandviewresearch.com	San Francisco	CA	94105	415-349-0058		225
Grand View University 1200 Grandview Ave *TF:* 800-444-6083 ■ *Web:* www.gvc.edu	Des Moines	IA	50316	515-263-2800	263-2974	166
Grand Wailea Resort & Spa 3850 Wailea Alanui Dr *TF:* 800-888-6100 ■ *Web:* www.grandwailea.com	Wailea	HI	96753	808-875-1234	879-4077	669
Grand Wayne Convention Ctr 120 W Jefferson Blvd *Web:* www.grandwayne.com	Fort Wayne	IN	46802	260-426-4100	420-9080	205
GrandBanks Capital 75 2nd Ave Ste 360 *Web:* www.grandbankscapital.com	Needham	MA	02481	781-997-4300	997-4301	792
Grandbridge Real Estate Capital LLC 271 17th St NW Ste 750 *Web:* www.grandbridge.com	Atlanta	GA	30363	704-332-4454		216
Grande Cheese Co 301 E Main St **Fax Area Code:* 920 ■ *TF:* 800-772-3210 ■ *Web:* www.grandecig.com	Lomira	WI	53048	800-772-3210	269-1445*	296-5
Grande Colonial 910 Prospect St **Fax Area Code:* 858 ■ *TF:* 888-828-5498 ■ *Web:* thegrandecolonial.com	La Jolla	CA	92037	888-828-5498	454-5679*	379
Grande Communications Networks LLC 401 Carlson Cir *TF:* 844-357-0942 ■ *Web:* mygrande.com	San Marcos	TX	78666	512-878-4000		194
Grande Prairie & District *Chamber of Commerce* 11330 106th St Ctr 2000 Ste 127 *Web:* www.grandeprairiechamber.com	Grande Prairie	AB	T8V7X9	780-532-5340	532-2926	137
Grande Prairie Public Library 3479 W 183rd St *TF:* 800-321-9511 ■ *Web:* www.grandeprairie.org	Hazel Crest	IL	60429	708-798-5563	798-5874	434-3
Grande Prairie Regional College 10726 106 Ave *TF:* 888-539-4772 ■ *Web:* www.gprc.ab.ca	Grande Prairie	AB	T8V4C4	780-539-2911		165
Grandite Inc PO Box 47133 *TF:* 866-808-3932 ■ *Web:* www.grandite.com	Quebec City	QC	G1S4X1	581-318-2018	703-0924	178-1
Grand-Kahn Electric (GK) 2455 W Grand Ave *Web:* www.grandkahn.com	Chicago	IL	60612	312-298-1500	298-1501	189-4
Grandma Brown's Beans Inc 5837 Scenic Ave *Web:* ontarioorchards.com	Mexico	NY	13114	315-963-7221		296-36
Grandma's Bakery Inc 1765 Buerkle Rd *Web:* www.grandmasbakery.com	White Bear Lake	MN	55110	651-779-0707		345
Grandma's Sports Garden 425 S Lake Ave *Web:* www.thesportsgarden.com	Duluth	MN	55802	218-722-4724		671
Grandmother's Buttons Museum 9814 Royal St *Web:* www.grandmothersbuttons.com	Saint Francisville	LA	70775	225-635-4107	635-6067	520
Grandover Resort & Conference Ctr 1000 Club Rd *TF:* 800-472-6301 ■ *Web:* grandover.com	Greensboro	NC	27407	336-294-1800	856-9991	377
Grandparents Rights Organization (GRO) 1760 S Telegraph Rd Ste 300 *Web:* www.grandparentsrights.org	Bloomfield Hills	MI	48302	248-646-7177		48-6
Grandstand Publishing LLC 990 Grove St Ste 400 *Web:* baseballdigest.com	Evanston	IL	60201	847-491-6440	491-0459	637-9
Grandview Cabinetry 1601 Superior Dr *TF:* 800-247-9105 ■ *Web:* grandviewcabinetry.com	Parsons	KS	67357	620-421-6950	421-4211	115
Grandview Heights School 1587 W 3rd Ave *Web:* www.ghschools.org	Columbus	OH	43212	614-481-3600		685
Grandview Heights/Marble Cliff Historical Society 1685 W 1st Ave *Web:* www.ghmchs.org	Columbus	OH	43212	614-488-0425		520
Grandview Medical Ctr 405 W Grand Ave *Web:* www.ketteringhealth.org	Dayton	OH	45405	937-723-3200	395-8327	374-3
Grandview Pharmacy 474 Southpoint Cir *TF:* 866-827-7575 ■ *Web:* grandrx.com	Brownsburg	IN	46112	866-827-7575		237
Grandview Speedway 43 Passmore Rd *Web:* www.grandviewspeedway.com	Bechtelsville	PA	19505	610-754-7688		515
Grandville Printing Company Inc 4719 Ivanrest Ave SW *TF:* 800-748-0248 ■ *Web:* www.gpco.com	Grandville	MI	49418	800-748-0248		627
Grandvue Medical Care Facility 1728 S Peninsula Rd *Web:* grandvue.org	East Jordan	MI	49727	231-536-2286	536-2476	371
Grandwell Industries Inc 6109 S NC Hwy 55 *TF:* 800-338-6554 ■ *Web:* www.grandwell.com	Fuquay-Varina	NC	27526	919-557-1221	552-9830	701
Grane Transportation Lines Ltd 1001 S Laramie Ave *Web:* www.gograne.com	Chicago	IL	60644	773-379-9711	854-2266	780
Grange Cooperative Supply Assn 2833 N Pacific Hwy *TF:* 800-888-6317 ■ *Web:* www.grangecoop.com	Medford	OR	97501	541-773-7087	664-1246	45
Grange Insurance 671 S High St *TF:* 800-422-0550 ■ *Web:* www.grangeinsurance.com	Columbus	OH	43206	800-422-0550		391-2
Granger & Mueller PC 605 W 10th St *Web:* grangerandmueller.com	Austin	TX	78701	512-474-9999		41
Granger Construction 6267 Aurelius Rd *Web:* www.grangerconstruction.com	Lansing	MI	48911	517-393-1670	393-1382	186
Granger House Victorian Museum, The 970 10th St *Web:* grangerhouse.org	Marion	IA	52302	319-377-6672		520
Granger Kay (Rep R - TX) 1026 Longworth House Office Bldg *Web:* kaygranger.house.gov	Washington	DC	20515	202-225-5071	225-5683	342-2
Granger Plastics Co, The 1600 Made Industrial Dr *TF:* 866-510-9701 ■ *Web:* www.grangerplastics.com	Middletown	OH	45044	513-424-1955	424-4799	596
Grangetto's Farm & Garden Supply Co 1105 W Mission Ave *TF:* 800-536-4671 ■ *Web:* www.grangettos.com	Escondido	CA	92025	760-745-4671		276
Granite Broadcasting LLC 767 3rd Ave Ste 34	New York	NY	10017	212-826-2530	826-2858	738
Granite City Electric Supply Co 19 Quincy Ave *TF:* 800-850-9400 ■ *Web:* www.granitecityelectric.com	Quincy	MA	02169	617-472-6500	472-8661	362
Granite City Food & Brewery Ltd (GCFB) 1636 42nd St SW *Web:* www.gcfb.com	Fargo	ND	58103	701-293-3000		671
Granite Construction Inc 585 W Beach St *NYSE: GVA* ■ *Web:* www.graniteconstruction.com	Watsonville	CA	95076	831-724-1011	722-9657	188-4
Granite County 220 N Sansome St PO Box 925 *Web:* www.co.granite.mt.us	Philipsburg	MT	59858	406-859-3771	859-3817	338
Granite Falls Energy LLC 15045 Hwy 23 SE *Web:* www.granitefallsenergy.com	Granite Falls	MN	56241	320-564-3100		297-8
Granite Group Wholesalers LLC 6 Storrs St *TF:* 800-258-3690 ■ *Web:* www.thegranitegroup.com	Concord	NH	03301	603-545-3345	224-4125	612
Granite Industries Inc 595 E Lugbill Rd *Web:* www.graniteind.com	Archbold	OH	43502	419-445-4733		492
Granite Industries of Vermont Inc PO Box 537 *TF:* 800-451-3236 ■ *Web:* www.granitevermont.com	Barre	VT	05641	800-451-3236		724
Granite Information Systems 1490 Union Lake Rd *Web:* graniteinfosys.com	White Lake	MI	48386	248-360-8400		180
Granite Links Golf Club 100 Quarry Hills Dr *Web:* www.granitelinks.com	Quincy	MA	02169	617-689-1900		42
Granite Mortgage Inc 2614 Navajo Rd *TF:* 888-201-2050 ■ *Web:* www.granitemortgage.net	El Cajon	CA	92020	619-718-9999	718-9998	509
Granite Point Capital Management LP 109 State St 5th Fl *Web:* www.granitepoint.com	Boston	MA	02109	617-587-7500	587-7501	401
Granite Quill Publishing PO Box 1190 *TF:* 800-281-2859 ■ *Web:* www.granitequill.com	Hillsborough	NH	03244	603-464-3388	464-4106	532-2
Granite Seed Co 1697 W 2100 N *Web:* www.graniteseed.com	Lehi	UT	84043	801-768-4422	768-3967	276
Granite State College 8 Old Suncook Rd *TF:* 888-228-3000 ■ *Web:* www.granite.edu	Concord	NH	03301	603-228-3000	513-1389	166
Granite State Independent Living Foundation 21 Chenell Dr *TF:* 800-826-3700 ■ *Web:* www.gsil.org	Concord	NH	03301	603-228-9680		305
Granite State Manufacturing Co 124 Joliette St *TF:* 800-464-7646 ■ *Web:* gogsmgo.com	Manchester	NH	03102	800-464-7646		454
Granite Telecommunications LLC 100 Newport Ave Ext **Fax Area Code:* 617 ■ *TF:* 866-847-1500 ■ *Web:* www.granitenet.com	Quincy	MA	02171	866-847-5500	328-0312*	736
Graniterock Co 350 Technology Dr PO Box 50001 *Web:* www.graniterock.com	Watsonville	CA	95077	831-768-2000	768-2201	191-1
Granite-Tops Inc 1480 Prairie Dr *TF:* 866-685-3005 ■ *Web:* stonecountertopoutlet.com	Cold Spring	MN	56320	320-685-3005		115
Granitize Products Inc 11022 Vulcan St *Web:* www.granitize.com	South Gate	CA	90280	562-923-5438	861-3475	151
Grant & Weber Inc 26610 Agoura Rd Ste 209 *Web:* www.grantweber.com	Calabasas	CA	91302	818-871-7700		393
Grant Advisor, The 248 Marilyn Cir *Web:* www.grantadvisor.com	Cary	NC	27513	919-461-1649	882-9465	637-10
Grant Assembly Technologies 90 Silliman Ave *TF:* 800-227-2150 ■ *Web:* www.grantriveters.com	Bridgeport	CT	06605	203-366-4557	366-0370	456
Grant Bennett Accountants 1375 Exposition Blvd Ste 230 *TF:* 888-763-7323 ■ *Web:* www.gbacpa.com	Sacramento	CA	95815	916-922-5109		2
Grant Career Ctr 718 W Plane St *Web:* www.grantcareer.com	Bethel	OH	45106	513-734-6222		685
Grant Cottage State Historic Site 1000 Mt McGregor Rd *Web:* parks.ny.gov	Wilton	NY	12831	518-587-8277		565
Grant County 301 W Main St *TF:* 800-769-5664 ■ *Web:* www.gcoregonlive.com	John Day	OR	97845	541-575-0547		338
Grant County 106 2nd Ave NE *Web:* www.grantcountynd.com	Carson	ND	58529	701-622-3615	622-3717	338
Grant County 10 Second St NE *Web:* www.co.grant.mn.us	Elbow Lake	MN	56531	218-685-4825	685-5349	338
Grant County 35 C St NW PO Box 37 *TF:* 800-572-0119 ■ *Web:* www.grantcountywa.gov	Ephrata	WA	98823	509-754-2011	765-2160	338
Grant County 105 E Harrison St **Fax Area Code:* 402 ■ *Web:* www.nrrs.ne.gov	Hyannis	NE	69350	308-458-2422	471-4020*	338
Grant County 1800 Bronson Blvd *TF:* 866-472-6894 ■ *Web:* www.grantcounty.org	Fennimore	WI	53809	608-822-3501		338
Grant County 101 E Fourth St *Web:* www.grantcounty.net	Marion	IN	46952	765-668-8121	668-6541	338

Name / Address	City	State	ZIP	Phone	Fax	Class
Grant County 112 E Guthrie St Rm 105 *Web:* grantcountyok.com	Medford	OK	73759	580-395-2284		338
Grant County 47789 151st St *Web:* grantcounty.sd.gov	Milbank	SD	57252	605-432-6711	432-9004	338
Grant County 5 Highland Ave *Web:* www.grantcountywv.org	Petersburg	WV	26847	304-257-4422	257-9645	338
Grant County 1400 Hwy 180 *Web:* www.grantcountynm.com	Silver City	NM	88061	575-574-0000	574-0073	338
Grant County 108 S Glenn St *Web:* www.grantcoks.org	Ulysses	KS	67880	620-356-1335	356-3081	338
Grant County 105 Baton Rouge Rd *Web:* grantcounty.ky.gov	Williamstown	KY	41097	859-824-3321		338
Grant County Courthouse 101 W Center St *Web:* grantcountyar.com	Sheridan	AR	72150	870-942-2631	942-3564	338
Grant County Herald 35 Central Ave N *TF:* 877-852-2796 ■ *Web:* grantcountyherald.com	Elbow Lake	MN	56531	218-685-5326		532-3
Grant County Journal 29 Alder St SW PO Box 998	Ephrata	WA	98823	509-754-4636		637-8
Grant County Public Library 207 E Park Ave *Web:* www.grantcountylibrary.com	Milbank	SD	57252	605-432-6543		434-3
Grant County Veterinary Clinic 490 Helton Rd *Web:* grantcountyvet.com	Williamstown	KY	41097	859-824-4012	824-4796	794
Grant Industries Inc 33415 Groesbeck Hwy *Web:* www.grantgrp.com	Fraser	MI	48026	586-293-9200		489
Grant Milleret CPA 10801 W Charleston Blvd *Web:* www.mbcpa-lv.com	Las Vegas	NV	89135	702-367-0341	367-6107	2
Grant Parish 512 Main St PO Box 208 *Web:* www.gpsb.org	Colfax	LA	71417	318-627-3274	627-2842	338
Grant Park Orchestra 205 E Randolph St *Web:* www.grantparkmusicfestival.com	Chicago	IL	60601	312-742-7638	742-7662	573-3
Grant Park Packing Company Inc 842 W Lake St *Web:* www.grantparkpacking.com	Chicago	IL	60607	312-421-4096	421-1484	297-9
Grant Piston Rings 1360 Jefferson St *Web:* www.grantpistonrings.com	Anaheim	CA	92807	714-996-0050		128
Grant Plaza Hotel 465 Grant Ave *TF:* 800-472-6899 ■ *Web:* www.grantplaza.com	San Francisco	CA	94108	415-434-3883	434-3886	379
Grant Street Group Inc 339 Sixth Ave Ste 1400 *TF:* 800-410-3445 ■ *Web:* www.grantstreet.com	Pittsburgh	PA	15222	412-391-5555		225
Grant Thornton 1400 Computer Dr *Web:* www.grantthornton.com	Westborough	MA	01581	508-926-2200		2
Grant W. Kehres PA 2000 Glades Rd Ste302 *Web:* bocaclosings.com	Boca Raton	FL	33431	561-392-5200	392-6180	41
Grant's 977 Farmington Ave *Web:* billygrant.com	West Hartford	CT	06107	860-236-1930		671
Grant, Herrmann, Schwartz & Klinger 675 Third Ave *Web:* www.ghsklaw.com	New York	NY	10017	212-682-1800		428
Grant, Konvalinka & Harrison PC Republic Ctr 633 Chestnut St 9th Fl *TF:* 888-463-8117 ■ *Web:* www.gkhpc.com	Chattanooga	TN	37450	423-933-2731	756-6518	428
Grantek Systems Integration Inc 4480 Harvester Rd *TF:* 866-936-9509 ■ *Web:* grantek.com	Burlington	ON	L7L4X2	866-936-9509		180
Grantham Poole CPAs 1062 Highland Colony Pkwy Ste 201 *Web:* www.granthampoole.com	Ridgeland	MS	39157	601-499-2400	499-2401	2
Grantham University Inc 7200 NW 86th St *Web:* www.grantham.edu	Kansas City	MO	64153	816-595-5759		166
Grant-Kohrs Ranch National Historic Site 266 Warren Ln *Web:* www.nps.gov	Deer Lodge	MT	59722	406-846-2070	846-3962	564
Grantmakers in Health (GIH) 1100 Connecticut Ave NW Ste 1200 *Web:* www.gih.org	Washington	DC	20036	202-452-8331	452-8340	48-5
Grants Pass Chamber of Commerce 1995 NW Vine St *TF:* 800-547-5927 ■ *Web:* www.grantspasschamber.org	Grants Pass	OR	97526	541-476-7717	476-9574	139
Grants/Cibola County Chamber of Commerce 100 N Iron Ave *TF:* 866-270-5110 ■ *Web:* www.grants.org	Grants	NM	87020	505-287-4802	287-8224	139
Grantsgov *U.S. Department of Health & Human Services* 200 Independence Ave SW *TF:* 800-518-4726 ■ *Web:* www.hhs.gov	Washington	DC	20201	800-518-4726		197
Granutech-Saturn Systems Corp 201 E Shady Grove *TF:* 877-582-7800 ■ *Web:* www.granutech.com	Grand Prairie	TX	75050	877-582-7800		494
Granville Central School District 58 Quaker St *Web:* www.granvillecsd.org	Granville	NY	12832	518-642-1051	642-2491	685
Granville County 141 Williamsboro St PO Box 1286 *Web:* www.granvillecounty.org	Oxford	NC	27565	919-693-4761		338
Granville County Chamber of Commerce 124 Hillsboro St *Web:* granville-chamber.com	Oxford	NC	27565	919-693-6125	693-6126	139
Granville Island Hotel 1253 Johnston St *TF:* 800-663-1840 ■ *Web:* www.granvilleislandhotel.com	Vancouver	BC	V6H3R9	604-683-7373	683-3061	379
Granville Milling Co 400 S Main St *Web:* granvillemilling.net	Granville	OH	43023	740-587-0221	587-3401	45
Granville State Forest 323 W Hartland Rd *Web:* www.mass.gov	Granville	MA	01034	413-357-6611		565
Grape Wine Company of San Antonio Inc, The 1747 Citadel Plz *Web:* www.grapewineco.blogspot.com	San Antonio	TX	78209	210-828-2222		443
Grapeland Elementary School PO Box 249 *Web:* www.grapelandisd.net	Grapeland	TX	75844	936-687-2317		685
Grapevine Chamber of Commerce 200 Vine St *Web:* www.grapevinechamber.org	Grapevine	TX	76051	817-481-1522	424-5208	139
Grapevine Communications International Inc 5201 Paylor Ln *Web:* www.grapeinc.com	Sarasota	FL	34240	941-351-0024		7
Grapevine Convention & Visitor Bureau 636 S Main St *TF:* 800-457-6338 ■ *Web:* www.grapevinetexasusa.com	Grapevine	TX	76051	800-457-6338		80-3
Grapevine Executive Recruiters Inc 269 Richmond St W *Web:* www.grapevinerecruiters.com	Toronto	ON	M5V1X1	416-581-1445		260
Grapevine Media & Marketing 1055 E Colorado Blvd 5th Fl *Web:* www.gmmla.com	Pasadena	CA	91106	626-240-4667	240-4668	7
Grapevine Public Library 1201 Municipal Way *Web:* grapevinetexas.gov	Grapevine	TX	76051	817-410-3400		434-3
Grapevine Video 4021 W San Juan Ave *Web:* www.grapevinevideo.com	Phoenix	AZ	85019	602-973-3661	973-2973	511
Graphcom Inc 1219 Chambersburg Rd *Web:* graphcom.com	Gettysburg	PA	17325	717-334-3107		627
Graphel Corp 6115 Centre Pk Dr *TF:* 800-255-1104 ■ *Web:* graphel.com	West Chester	OH	45069	513-779-6166		500
Graphic Artists Guild 31 W 34th St 8th Fl *Web:* www.graphicartistsguild.org	New York	NY	10001	212-791-3400	791-0333	414
Graphic Arts Assn 1210 Northbrook Dr Ste 200 *TF:* 800-475-6708 ■ *Web:* www.graphicartsassociation.org	Trevose	PA	19053	215-396-2300		138
Graphic Connections Group LLC 174 Chesterfield Industrial Blvd *Web:* www.gcfrog.com	Chesterfield	MO	63005	636-519-8320		174
Graphic Controls LLC 400 Exchange St *TF:* 800-669-1535 ■ *Web:* dr.graphiccontrols.com	Buffalo	NY	14204	800-669-1535	347-2420	628
Graphic Creations Inc 213 E Fourth Ave *Web:* graphiccreations.com	Knoxville	TN	37916	865-522-6221	522-0309	184
Graphic Design Inc 315 Second St E *Web:* www.gd-inc.com	Hastings	MN	55033	651-437-6459		627
Graphic Equipment Corp 55 Wester Ave *Web:* www.gecorp.com	Metuchen	NJ	08840	732-494-5350	494-4596	454
Graphic Finishing Services Inc 11490 Xeon St NW Coon Rapids *Web:* www.gfsmn.com	Minneapolis	MN	55448	763-767-3026	767-3027	92
Graphic Innovators Inc 855 Morse Ave *Web:* www.graphicinnovators.com	Elk Grove Village	IL	60007	847-718-1516	718-1517	629
Graphic Management Specialty Products Inc 139 Evergreen Rd PO Box 408 *TF:* 800-421-0039 ■ *Web:* www.gmsp.com	Oconto	WI	54153	800-421-0039		174
Graphic Packaging Intl 1500 Riveredge Pkwy NW Ste 100 *NYSE:* GPK ■ *Web:* www.graphicpkg.com	Atlanta	GA	30328	770-240-7200		101
Graphic Partners Inc 4300 IL Rte 173 *Web:* www.graphicpartners.com	Zion	IL	60099	847-872-9445		174
Graphic Products Inc PO Box 4030 *TF:* 888-326-9244 ■ *Web:* www.graphicproducts.com	Beaverton	OR	97076	503-644-5572	646-0183	174
Graphic Resources Inc 1911 Vernon St *Web:* www.gribusinessforms.com	Kansas City	MO	64116	816-221-3555		110
Graphic Response Inc 4460 Commerce Cir Sw *Web:* www.graphicresponse.com	Atlanta	GA	30336	404-696-9000		627
Graphic Solutions Group Inc 8575 Cobb Intl Blvd NW *Web:* www.gsghome.com	Kennesaw	GA	30152	770-424-2300		781
Graphic Specialties Inc 3110 Washington Ave N *TF:* 800-486-4605 ■ *Web:* www.signsbygsi.com	Minneapolis	MN	55411	612-522-5287		701
Graphic Systems Inc 2632 26th Ave S *Web:* www.graphicsystems.com	Minneapolis	MN	55406	612-721-6100		588
Graphic Systems Inc (GSI) 7200 Goodlet Farms Pky Ste 102 *Web:* www.yesgsi.com	Cordova	TN	38016	901-937-5500	937-5555	534
Graphic Trends Inc 7301 Adams St *Web:* www.graphictrends.net	Paramount	CA	90723	562-531-2339		687
Graphic World Inc 11687 Adie Rd *Web:* graphicworldmedia.com	Maryland Heights	MO	63043	314-567-9854	567-7178	781
Graphicast Inc 36 Knight St *Web:* www.graphicast.com	Jaffrey	NH	03452	603-532-4481	532-4261	492
Graphics Group 2800 Taylor St *Web:* www.graphicsgroup.com	Dallas	TX	75226	214-749-2222		781
Graphics Press LLC PO Box 430 *TF:* 800-822-2454 ■ *Web:* www.edwardtufte.com	Cheshire	CT	06410	203-272-9187	272-8600	637-2
Graphics Type & Color Enterprises Inc 2300 NW Seventh Ave *TF:* 800-433-9298 ■ *Web:* www.clubflyers.com	Miami	FL	33127	305-591-7600		627
GraphicWorks Inc 5611 Silverado Way Ste D *Web:* graphicworks.net	Anchorage	AK	99518	907-272-7400		627
Graphik Dimensions Ltd 2103 Brentwood St *Web:* www.pictureframes.com	High Point	NC	27263	336-887-3500		200
Graphique De France 9 State St *TF:* 800-444-1464 ■ *Web:* www.graphiquedefrance.com	Woburn	MA	01801	781-935-3405		130
Graphiques M & H 87 Rue Prince Bureau 310 *Web:* mh.ca	Montreal	QC	H3C2M7	514-866-6736		627
Graphite Machining Inc 240 N Main St *Web:* www.graphitemachininginc.com	Topton	PA	19562	610-682-0080		127
Graphite Metallizing Corp 1050 Nepperhan Ave *Web:* www.graphalloy.com	Yonkers	NY	10703	914-968-8400	968-8468	500

Name	Address	City	State	ZIP	Phone	Fax	Class	Other
Graphite Sales Inc	16710 W Pk Cir Dr	Chagrin Falls	OH	44023	440-543-8221		500	*TF:* 800-321-4147 ■ *Web:* www.graphitesales.com
Graphnet	40 Fultron St 28th Fl	New York	NY	10038	212-584-1000		736	*Web:* www.graphnet.com
Graphpad Software Inc	7825 Fay Ave Ste 230	La Jolla	CA	92037	858-454-5577		177	*Web:* graphpad.com
Graph-Pak Corp	11250 Addison Ave	Franklin Park	IL	60131	847-451-7400		100	*Web:* www.graphpakcustompackaging.com
Graphtech	1310 Crooked Hill Rd	Harrisburg	PA	17110	717-238-5751		627	*Web:* thinkgraphtech.com
Grapnel Tech Services LLC	2175 NW 86th St Ste 14A	Des Moines	IA	50325	515-953-5767	309-9715	177	*Web:* www.grapneltech.com
Grappa Restaurant	690 The Queensway	Etobicoke	ON	M8Y1K8	416-535-3337		671	*Web:* www.grapparestaurant.ca
Grasan Equipment Co	440 S Illinois Ave	Mansfield	OH	44907	419-526-4440		207	*TF:* 800-526-4602 ■ *Web:* www.grasan.com
Grasing's	PO Box 2906	Carmel By The Sea	CA	93923	831-624-6562	624-7431	671	*Web:* grasings.com
Grask Peterbilt	9201 Sixth St SW	Cedar Rapids	IA	52404	888-434-2511	848-4302*	780	*Fax Area Code: 319 ■ *TF:* 888-434-2511 ■ *Web:* www.graskpeterbilt.com
Grass America Inc	1202 NC Hwy 66 S	Kernersville	NC	27284	800-334-3512		350	*TF:* 800-334-3512 ■ *Web:* www.grassusa.com
Grass Point State Park	42247 Grassy Pt Rd	Alexandria Bay	NY	13607	315-686-4472		565	*Web:* parks.ny.gov
Grass Roots Software LLC	7577 Central Parke Blvd Ste 319	Mason	OH	45040	513-910-3973		177	*Web:* grassrootsoftware.com
Grass Valley Inc	3499 Douglas-B-Floreani	Montreal	QC	H4S2C6	514-333-1772	333-9828	52	*Web:* www.grassvalley.com
Grassfed Livestock Alliance (GLA)	525 N Lamar Blvd	Austin	TX	78703	830-562-2333		473	*Web:* www.grassfedlivestockalliance.com
Grasshopper Co, The	105 Old US Hwy 81 PO Box 637	Moundridge	KS	67107	620-345-8621	345-2301	429	*Web:* www.grasshoppermower.com
Grassi & Co	488 Madison Ave	New York	NY	10022	212-661-6166		2	*Web:* www.grassicpas.com
Grassi Investment Management LLC	2350 Mission College Blvd Ste 190	Santa Clara	CA	95054	650-934-0770		401	*Web:* www.grassiinvest.com
Grassland Dairy Products Company Inc	N 8790 Fairgrounds Ave	Greenwood	WI	54437	800-428-8837	267-6044*	296-3	*Fax Area Code: 715 ■ *TF:* 800-428-8837 ■ *Web:* www.grassland.com
Grassland Equipment & Irrigation Corp	892-898 Troy Schenectady Rd	Latham	NY	12110	518-785-5841	785-5740	429	*TF:* 800-564-5587 ■ *Web:* www.grasslandcorp.com
Grasslands Federal Credit Union	PO Box 79	Circle	MT	59215	406-485-2288		219	*Web:* mcconecu.com
Grassley Chuck (Sen R - IA)	135 Hart Senate Office Bldg	Washington	DC	20510	202-224-3744	224-6020	342-2	*Web:* www.grassley.senate.gov
Grassley Group, The	600 State St Ste A	Cedar Falls	IA	50613	866-619-5580	342-0411*	47	*Fax Area Code: 703 ■ *TF:* 866-619-5580 ■ *Web:* www.grassleygroup.com
Grasso Southeastern Technical High School	189 Fort Hill Rd	Groton	CT	06340	860-448-0220		685	*Web:* grasso.cttech.org
Grassroots Cannabis	344 N Ogden Ave	Chicago	IL	60607	312-521-2787		582	*Web:* grassrootscannabis.com
Grassroots Motorsports Magazine	915 Ridgewood Ave	Holly Hill	FL	32117	386-239-0523	239-0573	457-3	*TF:* 800-520-8292 ■ *Web:* www.grassrootsmotorsports.com
Grassroots Targeting LLC	707 Prince St	Alexandria	VA	22314	703-535-7590		194	*Web:* www.grassrootstargeting.com
Grate Signs Inc	4044 W McDonough St	Joliet	IL	60431	815-729-9700	729-3355	9	*TF:* 800-458-8669 ■ *Web:* gratesigns.com
Gratiot Area Chamber of Commerce	110 W Superior St PO Box 516	Alma	MI	48801	989-463-5525	463-6588	139	*Web:* gratiot.org
Gratiot County	County Courthouse 214 E Center St	Ithaca	MI	48847	989-875-5215	875-5254	338	*Web:* www.gratiotmi.com
Gratiot County Historical and Genealogical Society (GCHGS)	129 W Center St	Ithaca	MI	48847	989-875-6232		49-19	*Web:* gchgs.org
Gratiot-Isabella Regional Education Service District	1131 E Center St PO Box 310	Ithaca	MI	48847	989-875-5101	875-2858	685	*Web:* www.giresd.net
Gratz College	7605 Old York Rd	Melrose Park	PA	19027	215-635-7300		166	*TF:* 800-475-4635 ■ *Web:* www.gratz.edu
Grauls Market Inc	7713 Bellona Ave	Ruxton	MD	21204	410-823-6077		345	*Web:* graulsmarket.com
Gravel & Shea	76 St Paul St PO Box 369	Burlington	VT	05402	802-658-0220		428	*Web:* www.gravelshea.com
Gravely & Pearson LLP	425 Soledad St Ste 600	San Antonio	TX	78205	210-472-1111		428	*Web:* www.gplawfirm.com
Graver Technologies LLC	200 Lake Dr	Newark	DE	19702	302-731-1700	731-1707	806	*TF:* 800-249-1990 ■ *Web:* www.gravertech.com
Graver Water Systems LLC	675 Central Ave Ste 3	New Providence	NJ	07974	908-516-1400	516-1401	806	*Web:* www.graver.com
Graves & Company PC	20550 Vernier Rd	Harper Woods	MI	48225	313-886-8892		2	*Web:* gravescpa.com
Graves Bros Co	2770 Indian River Blvd Ste 201	Vero Beach	FL	32960	772-562-3886	562-3565	315-2	*Web:* gravesbrotherscompany.com
Graves County	101 E S St	Mayfield	KY	42066	270-247-3626	247-1274	338	*Web:* www.gravescounty.ky.gov
Graves Engineering Inc	100 Grove St	Worcester	MA	01605	508-856-0321		261	*Web:* gravesengineering.com
Graves Food	913 Big Horn Dr	Jefferson City	MO	65109	573-893-3000	893-2172	297-7	*Web:* gravesfoods.com
Graves Garret (Rep R - LA)	2402 Rayburn House Office Bldg	Washington	DC	20515	202-225-3901	225-7313	342-2	*Web:* garretgraves.house.gov
Graves Lumber Co	1315 S Cleveland-Massillon Rd	Copley	OH	44321	330-666-1115	666-1377	499	*TF:* 877-500-5515 ■ *Web:* www.graveslumber.com
Graves Metal Products Inc	220 Commerce St	Jackson	TN	38301	731-422-1925		492	*Web:* www.gravesmetal.com
Graves Piano & Organ Company Inc	5798 Karl Rd	Columbus	OH	43229	614-847-4322		526	*TF:* 800-686-4322 ■ *Web:* gravespianos.com
Graves Sam (Rep R - MO)	1135 Longworth House Office Bldg	Washington	DC	20515	202-225-7041	225-8221	342-2	*Web:* www.graves.house.gov
Graves Tom (Rep R - GA)	2078 Rayburn House Office Bldg	Washington	DC	20515	202-225-5211	225-8272	342-2	*Web:* tomgraves.house.gov
Gravina Smith & Matte Inc	12474 Brantley Commons Ct	Fort Myers	FL	33907	239-275-5758		636	*Web:* gsma.pro
Gravitec Systems Inc	21291 Urdahl Rd NW	Poulsbo	WA	98370	206-780-2898	780-2893	261	*TF:* 800-755-8455 ■ *Web:* www.gravitec.com
Gravity Group	107 E Water St	Harrisonburg	VA	22801	540-433-3071		195	*Web:* www.gravitygroup.com
Gravity Switch Inc	89 Market St	Northampton	MA	01060	413-586-9596		344	*Web:* www.gravityswitch.com
Gravograph-New Hermes Inc	2200 Northmont Pkwy	Duluth	GA	30096	770-623-0331		629	*TF:* 800-843-7637 ■ *Web:* www.gravograph.com
Gravy Train Express LLC	65 Gravy Train Ln	Lewistown	PA	17044	717-242-8515		311	*Web:* gravytrainllc.com
Gray & Associates LLP	2677 Tritt Springs Trce NE	Marietta	GA	30062	770-633-4201		7	*Web:* www.grayassoc.net
Gray & Co	3325 W Polk Rd	Hart	MI	49420	503-248-4729		296-20	*Web:* www.cherryman.com
Gray & Osborne Inc	1130 Rainier Ave S Ste 300	Seattle	WA	98144	206-284-0860	283-3206	256	*Web:* grayandosborne.net
Gray & Sons Inc	430 W Padonia Rd	Timonium	MD	21093	410-771-4311	771-8125	188-4	*Web:* www.graynson.com
Gray Blodgett & Company PLLC	629 24th Ave SW	Norman	OK	73069	405-360-5533	364-3771	2	*Web:* www.cpagray.com
Gray Callison & Company PA	3813 Forrestgate Dr	Winston-Salem	NC	27103	336-760-3210	765-1049	2	*Web:* www.graycallison.com
Gray Chevrolet Cadillac	1245 N Ninth St	Stroudsburg	PA	18360	866-505-3058		57	*TF:* 866-505-3058 ■ *Web:* www.graychevrolet.com
Gray Construction	10 Quality St	Lexington	KY	40507	859-281-5000	252-5300	186	*TF:* 800-814-8468 ■ *Web:* www.gray.com
Gray County	300 S Main St	Cimarron	KS	67835	620-855-3486	872-3380	10-1	*Web:* www.grayco.org
Gray County	PO Box 1902	Pampa	TX	79066	806-669-8004		338	*Web:* www.co.gray.tx.us
Gray Glass Co	217-44 98th Ave	Queens Village	NY	11429	718-217-2943	217-0280	329	*TF:* 800-523-3320 ■ *Web:* www.grayglass.net
Gray Hunter Stenn LLP	500 Maine St	Quincy	IL	62301	217-222-0304	222-1691	2	*Web:* www.gray-hunter-stenn.com
Gray Line Corporation Inc	1900 16th St Ste 210	Denver	CO	80202	303-539-8502		760	*TF:* 800-472-9546 ■ *Web:* www.grayline.com
Gray Lumber & Hardware Inc	16204 Market St	Channelview	TX	77530	281-452-7101		351	*Web:* truevalue.com
Gray Manufacturing Company Inc	3501 S Leonard Rd	Saint Joseph	MO	64503	816-233-6121	233-7251	386	*TF:* 800-821-7320 ■ *Web:* grayusa.com
Gray Manufacturing Industries	6258 Icehouse Rd PO Box 126	Hornell	NY	14843	607-281-1325	281-1327	650	*Web:* gmihornell.com
Gray Matter Group	88 Vilcom Center Dr Ste 180	Chapel Hill	NC	27514	919-932-6150		180	*TF:* 877-970-4747 ■ *Web:* www.isisit.com
Gray Metal Products Inc	495 Rochester St	Avon	NY	14414	585-226-8660		295	*Web:* www.graymetal.com
Gray Robinson PA	301 E Pine St Ste 1400	Orlando	FL	32801	407-843-8880	244-5690	41	*Web:* www.gray-robinson.com
Gray Rust St Amand Moffett & Brieske LLP	950 E Paces Ferry Rd NE	Atlanta	GA	30326	404-870-7373		41	*Web:* www.grsmb.com
Gray Television Inc	4370 Peachtree Rd NE	Atlanta	GA	30319	404-266-8333		738	*NYSE: GTN* ■ *Web:* gray.tv
Gray Television Inc	126 N Washington St	Albany	GA	31701	877-571-0774		647	*TF:* 877-571-0774 ■ *Web:* www.gray.tv
Gray Tools Canada Inc	299 Orenda Rd	Brampton	ON	L6T1E8	905-457-3014	457-1050	350	*Web:* graytools.com
Gray Transportation Inc	2459 GT Dr	Waterloo	IA	50703	319-234-3930	234-8841	685	*TF:* 800-234-3930 ■ *Web:* www.graytran.com
Gray, Ackerman & Haines PA	125 NE First Ave Ste 1	Ocala	FL	34470	352-732-8121		41	*Web:* gah-law.com
Gray, Layton, Kersh, Solomon, Sigmon, Furr & Smith PA	516 S New Hope Rd	Gastonia	NC	28054	704-865-4400		428	*Web:* www.gastonlegal.com

Name	Address	City	State	ZIP	Phone	Fax	Class	Other
Gray, Ritter & Graham PC	701 Market St Ste 800	Saint Louis	MO	63101	314-241-5620		41	*Web:* grgpc.com
Graybar Electric Company Inc	34 N Meramec Ave	Saint Louis	MO	63105	314-573-9200		246	*TF:* 800-472-9227 ■ *Web:* www.graybar.com
Graybill Bartz & Thompson	135 S Cottage Hill	Elmhurst	IL	60126	630-941-9460	832-3491	401	*Web:* www.graybillbartz.com
Graybill Machines Inc	221 W Lexington Rd	Lititz	PA	17543	717-626-5221	626-1886	296	*Web:* www.graybillmachines.com
Grayd-A Metal Fabricators	13233 Florence Ave	Santa Fe Springs	CA	90670	562-944-8951		697	*Web:* www.grayd-a.com
Grayhawk General Agency Inc	2816 E Cullumber Ct	Gilbert	AZ	85234	480-245-5995		390	*TF:* 888-442-1121 ■ *Web:* ggagency.com
Grayhawk LLC	2424 Merchant St	Lexington	KY	40511	859-255-2754	259-0957	189-9	*Web:* www.grayhawk-ky.com
Grayhill Inc	561 W Hillgrove Ave	LaGrange	IL	60525	708-354-1040	354-2820	729	*TF:* 800-683-0366 ■ *Web:* www.grayhill.com
Graylyn International Conference Center Inc	1900 Reynolda Rd	Winston-Salem	NC	27106	336-758-2600		184	*TF:* 800-472-9596 ■ *Web:* graylyn.com
Graymills Corp	3705 N Lincoln Ave	Chicago	IL	60613	773-477-4100	477-4133	641	*TF:* 877-465-7867 ■ *Web:* www.graymills.com
Graymont Ltd	10991 Shellbridge Way Ste 200	Richmond	BC	V6X3C6	604-276-9331	276-9337	440	*TF:* 866-207-4292 ■ *Web:* www.graymont.com
Grayrose Culinary Innovation Group	9631 NE Colfax St	Portland	OR	97220	503-281-1922		195	*Web:* www.grayrose.com
Grays Harbor Chamber of Commerce	506 Duffy St	Aberdeen	WA	98520	360-532-1924	533-7945	139	*TF:* 800-321-1924 ■ *Web:* www.graysharbor.org
Grays Harbor College	1620 Edward P Smith Dr	Aberdeen	WA	98520	360-532-9020	538-4293	162	*TF:* 800-562-4830 ■ *Web:* www.ghc.edu
Grays Harbor Community Hospital	915 Anderson Dr	Aberdeen	WA	98520	360-532-8330		374-3	*Web:* www.ghcares.org
Grays Harbor County	100 W Broadway	Montesano	WA	98563	360-249-3842		338	*Web:* www.co.grays-harbor.wa.us
Grays Harbor Raceway	32 Elma McCleary Rd PO Box 911	Elma	WA	98541	360-482-4374	892-6582	642	*Web:* www.graysharborraceway.com
Grays Harbor Tourism	PO Box 1229	Elma	WA	98541	360-482-2651		206	*TF:* 800-621-9625 ■ *Web:* www.visitgraysharbor.com
Grayson College	6101 Grayson Dr	Denison	TX	75020	903-465-6030	463-5284	162	*Web:* www.grayson.edu
Grayson Collin Communications	555 N Henry Hynds Expy	Van Alstyne	TX	75495	903-482-7000		224	*TF:* 800-867-2887 ■ *Web:* graysoncollin.com
Grayson County	100 W Houston St	Sherman	TX	75090	903-813-4207		338	*Web:* www.co.grayson.tx.us
Grayson County Chamber of Commerce	425 S Main St	Leitchfield	KY	42754	270-259-5587	230-0615	338	*Web:* www.graysoncountychamber.com
Grayson Lake State Park	314 Grayson Lake Park Rd	Olive Hill	KY	41164	606-474-9727		565	*Web:* parks.ky.gov
Grayson Rural Electric Co-opeartive Corp	109 Bagby Park St	Grayson	KY	41143	606-474-5136	474-5862	245	*TF:* 800-562-3532 ■ *Web:* www.graysonrecc.com
Grayson-Collin Electric Coop (GCEC)	14568 FM 121 PO Box 548	Van Alstyne	TX	75495	903-482-7100		245	*TF:* 800-967-5235 ■ *Web:* gcec.net
Graystone Group Advertising	55 Merritt Blvd	Bridgeport	CT	06604	203-549-0060	549-0061	7	*TF:* 800-544-0005 ■ *Web:* www.graystoneadv.com
Grayton Beach State Park	357 Main Park Rd	Santa Rosa Beach	FL	32459	850-267-8300		565	*Web:* www.floridastateparks.org
Graytor Printing Company Inc	149 Park Ave	Lyndhurst	NJ	07071	201-933-0100		627	
Graywolf Press Inc	250 3rd Ave N Ste 600	Minneapolis	MN	55401	651-641-0077	641-0036	637-2	*Web:* www.graywolfpress.org
GrayWolf Sensing Solutions LLC	6 Research Dr	Shelton	CT	06484	203-402-0477		419	*TF:* 800-218-7997 ■ *Web:* graywolfsensing.com
Graziano's	9227 SW 40th St	Miami	FL	33165	305-225-0008		671	*Web:* www.grazianosgroup.com
Grazie Italiano	106 W Sixth St	Bloomington	IN	47401	812-323-0303		671	*Web:* www.grazieitaliano.com
Grazies Italian Grill	2851 S Oneida St	Green Bay	WI	54304	920-499-6365		671	*Web:* graziesitaliangrill.com
Grb Entertainment Inc	13400 Riverside Dr Ste 300	Sherman Oaks	CA	91423	818-728-7600	728-7601	514	*Web:* www.grbtv.com
GRBA (Grand Rapids Bar Assn)	161 Ottawa Ave NW Ste 203-B	Grand Rapids	MI	49503	616-454-5550	454-7707	49-19	*Web:* www.grbar.org
GRBJ (Grand Rapids Business Journal)	549 Ottawa Ave NW Ste 201	Grand Rapids	MI	49503	616-459-4545		457-5	*Web:* www.grbj.com
Grbm Insurance	2022 Rt 22	Brewster	NY	10509	845-878-9293		390	*Web:* grbminc.com
GRC Enterprises	5311 33rd Ave S	Seattle	WA	98118	206-725-5537		603	*Web:* www.staticbags.com
GRE America Inc	425 Harbor Blvd	Belmont	CA	94002	650-591-1400		173-3	*TF:* 800-233-5973 ■ *Web:* www.greamerica.com
Grease Monkey Intl	5575 DTC Pkwy Ste 100	Greenwood Village	CO	80111	303-308-1660	308-5908	62-5	*TF:* 800-822-7706 ■ *Web:* www.greasemonkeyauto.com
Great American Bancorp Inc	1311 S Neil St	Champaign	IL	61820	217-356-2265	356-2502	360-2	*OTC: GTPS* ■ *Web:* www.greatamericanbancorp.com
Great American Casino	10117 S Tacoma Way	Lakewood	WA	98499	253-396-0500		133	*Web:* www.greatamericancasino.com
Great American Cookie Company Inc	3300 Chambers Rd	Horseheads	NY	14845	607-739-7403		68	*Web:* www.greatamericancookies.com
Great American Custom Insurance Services Inc	725 S Figueroa St	Los Angeles	CA	90017	213-430-4300		390	*Web:* www.gamcustom.com
Great American Farms Inc	1255 W Atlantic Blvd Ste 218	Pompano Beach	FL	33069	954-785-9400		10-4	
Great American Group Inc	21860 Burbank Blvd Ste 300	Woodland Hills	CA	91367	818-884-3737	884-2976	655	*OTC: GAMR* ■ *Web:* www.greatamerican.com
Great American Home Store	5295 Pepper Chase Dr	Southaven	MS	38671	662-996-1000		321	*TF:* 800-260-4898 ■ *Web:* www.greatamericanhomestore.com
Great American Products	1661 S Seguin Ave	New Braunfels	TX	78130	830-620-4400	620-8430	702	*Web:* www.gap1.com
Great Arrow Graphics	2495 Main St Ste 457	Buffalo	NY	14214	716-836-0408	836-0702	130	*TF:* 800-835-0490 ■ *Web:* www.greatarrow.com
Great Basin College	1500 College Pkwy	Elko	NV	89801	775-738-8493	753-2311	166	*TF:* 888-590-6726 ■ *Web:* www.gbcnv.edu
Great Basin Internet Services	PO Box 17520	Reno	NV	89511	775-348-7299		338	*TF:* 888-477-7299 ■ *Web:* www.greatbasin.net
Great Basin National Park	100 Great Basin National Pk	Baker	NV	89311	775-234-7331	234-7269	564	*Web:* www.nps.gov
Great Basin Scientific Inc	2441 S 3850 W Ste 520	Salt Lake City	UT	84120	801-307-4881	206-3006	476	*TF:* 888-320-7636 ■ *Web:* www.gbscience.com
Great Bay Distributors Inc	2750 Eagle Ave N	Saint Petersburg	FL	33716	727-584-8626	585-9425	81-1	*Web:* www.greatbaybud.com
Great Bend Industries	8701 Sixth St	Great Bend	KS	67530	620-792-4368	792-3935	223	*Web:* www.greatbendindustries.com
Great Books Foundation	35 E Wacker Dr Ste 400	Chicago	IL	60601	312-332-5870		48-11	*TF:* 800-222-5870 ■ *Web:* www.greatbooks.org
Great Britain Tile Inc	9533 Land O Lakes Blvd	Land O' Lakes	FL	34638	813-235-9775	235-9779	290	*TF:* 877-895-9775 ■ *Web:* greatbritaintile.com
Great Brook Farm State Park	165 N Rd	Carlisle	MA	01741	978-369-6312		565	*Web:* www.mass.gov
Great Central Steel Co	9801 S 76th Ave	Bridgeview	IL	60455	708-599-8090	599-8763	492	*Web:* www.greatcentralsteel.us
Great Circle Media	1117 West Rt 66	Flagstaff	AZ	86001	928-774-5231		531-11	*Web:* www.gcmaz.com
Great Clips Inc	4400 W 78th St Ste 700	Minneapolis	MN	55435	800-947-1143		77	*TF:* 800-999-5959 ■ *Web:* www.greatclips.com
Great Country Broadcasting Inc	PO Box 757	Bishop	CA	93515	760-872-2639		741-99	*Web:* www.kibskbov.com
Great Dane Trailers Inc	602 E Lathrop Ave	Savannah	GA	31415	912-644-2100		779	*Web:* www.greatdane.com
Great Day Improvements LLC	700 E Highland Rd	Macedonia	OH	44056	330-468-0700		236	*TF:* 800-230-8301 ■ *Web:* www.greatdayimprovements.com
Great Eastern Energy LLC	1515 Sheephead Bay Rd	Brooklyn	NY	11235	646-832-4433		316	*TF:* 888-651-4121 ■ *Web:* www.greateasternenergy.com
Great Eastern Sun Trading Company Inc	92 Mcintosh Rd	Asheville	NC	28806	828-665-7790		805	*TF:* 800-334-5809 ■ *Web:* great-eastern-sun.com
Great Ecology	379 W Broadway 5th Fl	New York	NY	10012	212-579-6800		192	*Web:* greatecology.com
Great Erie Federal Credit Union	4000 N Buffalo St	Orchard Park	NY	14127	716-662-1311		219	*Web:* greateriefcu.com
Great Explorations Children's Museum	1925 Fourth St N	Saint Petersburg	FL	33704	727-821-8992	823-7287	521	*Web:* greatex.org
Great Falls Area Chamber of Commerce	100 1st Ave N	Great Falls	MT	59401	406-761-4434	761-6129	139	*Web:* www.greatfallschamber.org
Great Falls Historic District Cultural Ctr	65 McBride Ave Ext	Paterson	NJ	07501	973-279-9587	279-0587	50-2	*Web:* www.patersonnj.gov
Great Falls International Airport	2800 Terminal Dr	Great Falls	MT	59404	406-727-3404	727-6929	27	*Web:* www.flygtf.com
Great Falls Marketing LLC	121 Mill St	Auburn	ME	04210	800-221-8895		195	*TF:* 800-221-8895 ■ *Web:* greatfallsmarketing.com
Great Falls Public Library	301 Second Ave N	Great Falls	MT	59401	406-453-0349	453-0181	434-3	*Web:* www.greatfallslibrary.org
Great Falls Region Chamber of Commerce	5 Westminster St	Bellows Falls	VT	05101	802-463-4280		139	*Web:* www.gfrcc.org
Great Falls Regional Federal Credit Union	34 Bates St	Lewiston	ME	04240	207-782-7192		219	*TF:* 800-472-3272 ■ *Web:* greatfallsfcu.com
Great Falls Tribune	205 River Dr S	Great Falls	MT	59405	406-791-1444	791-1431	532-2	*TF:* 800-438-6600 ■ *Web:* www.greatfallstribune.com
Great Fidelity Life Insurance Co	PO Box 9510	Wichita	KS	67277	316-794-2200	794-8470	796	*Web:* www.iai-online.com

Name / Address	City	State	Zip	Phone	Fax	Class
Great GetAways Inc 313 Cambridge St Web: www.ggatravel.com	Boston	MA	02114	617-720-6100		772
Great Harvest Bread Co 28 S Montana St TF: 800-442-0424 ■ Web: www.greatharvest.com	Dillon	MT	59725	406-683-6842	683-5537	68
Great Hill Partners LLC 1 Liberty Sq Web: www.greathillpartners.com	Boston	MA	02109	617-790-9400	790-9401	792
Great Ideas for Teaching Inc PO Box 444 TF: 800-839-8498 ■ Web: www.greatideasforteaching.com	Wrightsville Beach	NC	28480	910-256-4494	256-4493	637-2
Great Lake Woods Inc 3303 John F Donnelly Dr Web: www.greatlakewoods.com	Holland	MI	49424	616-399-3300		550
Great Lakes Aquarium 353 Harbor Dr Web: glaquarium.org	Duluth	MN	55802	218-740-3474	740-2020	40
Great Lakes Aviation Ltd 1022 Airport Pkwy OTC: GLUX ■ TF: 800-554-5111 ■ Web: www.greatlakesav.com	Cheyenne	WY	82001	307-432-7000		25
Great Lakes Case & Cabinet Company Inc 4193 Rt 6N Web: www.werackyourworld.com	Edinboro	PA	16412	814-734-7303		567
Great Lakes Castings LLC 800 N Washington Ave Web: www.greatlakescastings.com	Ludington	MI	49431	231-843-2501	845-1534	307
Great Lakes Cheese Company Inc 17825 Great Lakes Pkwy Web: www.greatlakescheese.com	Hiram	OH	44234	440-834-2500	834-1002	296-5
Great Lakes Christian College 6211 W Willow Hwy TF: 800-937-4522 ■ Web: www.glcc.edu	Lansing	MI	48917	517-321-0242	321-5902	161
Great Lakes Community Partnership 127 S Front St PO Box 590 TF: 800-775-9767 ■ Web: www.glcap.org	Fremont	OH	43420	419-334-8911		8
Great Lakes Construction Co 2608 Great Lakes Way Web: greatlakesway.com	Hinckley	OH	44233	330-220-3900	220-7670	188-4
Great Lakes Crossing Outlets 4000 Baldwin Rd TF: 877-746-7452 ■ Web: www.greatlakescrossingoutlets.com	Auburn Hills	MI	48326	248-454-5000		50-6
Great Lakes Cruise Co 3270 Washtenaw Ave *Fax Area Code: 734 ■ TF: 888-891-0203 ■ Web: www.greatlakescruising.com	Ann Arbor	MI	48104	888-891-0203	677-1428*	220
Great Lakes Dart Manufacturing Inc S84 W19093 Enterprise Dr TF: 800-225-7593 ■ Web: www.gldproducts.com	Muskego	WI	53150	262-679-8730		761
Great Lakes Dental Technologies 200 Cooper Ave TF: 800-828-7626 ■ Web: www.greatlakesdentaltech.com	Tonawanda	NY	14150	800-828-7626		228
Great Lakes Dredge & Dock Co 2122 York Rd NASDAQ: GLDD ■ Web: www.gldd.com	Oak Brook	IL	60523	630-574-3000	574-2909	188-5
Great Lakes Energy Co-op 1323 Boyne Ave TF: 888-485-2537 ■ Web: www.gtlakes.com	Boyne City	MI	49712	231-487-1327	582-6213	245
Great Lakes Environmental Research Laboratory (GLERL) 4840 S State St Web: www.glerl.noaa.gov	Ann Arbor	MI	48108	734-741-2235	741-2055	668
Great Lakes Filters 301 Arch Ave TF: 800-521-8565 ■ Web: greatlakesfilters.com	Hillsdale	MI	49242	800-521-8565		18
Great Lakes Foods 1230 48th Ave TF: 800-800-7492 ■ Web: www.greatlakesfoods.com	Menominee	MI	49858	906-863-5503		186
Great Lakes Forge Inc 2465 N Aero Park Ct *Fax Area Code: 231 ■ TF: 800-748-0271 ■ Web: www.glforge.com	Traverse City	MI	49686	800-748-0271	947-5836*	483
Great Lakes Gypsum & Supply 33900 Concord Rd Web: www.lwsupply.com	Livonia	MI	48150	734-421-1170		191-3
Great Lakes Industry Inc 1927 Wildwood Ave Web: www.greatlakesind.com	Jackson	MI	49202	517-784-3153	784-3154	620
Great Lakes Institute of Technology Toni & Guy Hair 5100 Peach St TF: 800-394-4548 ■ Web: www.glit.edu	Erie	PA	16509	814-864-6666		166
Great Lakes International Inc 1905 Kearney Ave Web: www.greatlakesintl.com	Racine	WI	53403	262-634-2386		427
Great Lakes Outdoor Supply Inc 14855 N State Ave Web: greatlakesoutdoorsupply.com	Middlefield	OH	44062	440-632-9151		711
Great Lakes Packaging Corp W 190 N 11393 Carnegie Dr TF: 800-261-4572 ■ Web: www.glpc.com	Germantown	WI	53022	262-255-2100	255-7290	100
Great Lakes Packers Inc 400 Great Lakes Pkwy	Bellevue	OH	44811	419-483-2956		11-1
Great Lakes Packing Co 1535 W 43rd St Web: glpacking.com	Chicago	IL	60609	773-927-6660	927-8587	296-26
Great Lakes Plumbing & Heating Company Inc 4521 W Diversey Ave Web: www.glph.com	Chicago	IL	60639	773-489-0400	489-1492	14
Great Lakes Power Products Inc 7455 Tyler Blvd TF: 800-325-6880 ■ Web: www.glpower.com	Mentor	OH	44060	440-951-5111	953-1052	350
Great Lakes Publishing Co 1422 Euclid Ave Ste 730 Web: www.clevelandmagazine.com	Cleveland	OH	44115	216-771-2833		637-8
Great Lakes Rubber Company Inc 30573 Beck Rd TF: 800-893-3645 ■ Web: greatlakesrubberco.com	Wixom	MI	48393	248-624-5710	624-4770	789
Great Lakes Science Ctr 601 Erieside Ave Web: www.greatscience.com	Cleveland	OH	44114	216-694-2000		520
Great Lakes Theater Festival 1501 Euclid Ave Ste 300 Web: www.greatlakestheater.org	Cleveland	OH	44115	216-241-5490	241-6315	749
Great Lakes Towing Co 4500 Div Ave TF: 800-321-3663 ■ Web: www.thegreatlakesgroup.com	Cleveland	OH	44102	216-621-4854	621-7616	465
Great Lakes Veneer Inc 222 S Parkview Ave PO Box 497 Web: www.greatlakesveneer.com	Marion	WI	54950	715-754-2501	754-2582	613
Great Lakes Window Inc 30499 Tracy Rd TF: 844-247-6226 ■ Web: greatlakeswindow.com	Walbridge	OH	43465	844-247-6226		234
Great Lakes Woodworking Co 11345 Mound Rd Web: www.g-l-w.com	Detroit	MI	48212	313-892-8500		499
Great Meetings! Inc PO Box 3883 TF: 888-374-6010 ■ Web: www.greatmeetingsinc.com	Portland	ME	04104	207-772-2680		637-2
Great Migrations LLC 565 Metro Pl S Ste 300 Web: www.greatmigrations.com	Dublin	OH	43017	614-389-0361	389-0381	177
Great Neck Saw Manufacturing Inc 165 E Second St *Fax Area Code: 516 ■ TF: 800-457-0600 ■ Web: www.greatnecksaw.com	Mineola	NY	11501	800-457-0600	746-5358*	682
Great North Artists Management 350 Dupont St Web: www.tamac.ca	Toronto	ON	M5R1V9	416-925-2051	925-3904	731
Great Northern Corp 395 Stroebe Rd TF: 800-236-3671 ■ Web: www.greatnortherncorp.com	Appleton	WI	54914	800-236-3671		100
Great Northern Equipment Inc 20195 S Diamond Lake Rd Ste 100 TF: 800-822-0295 ■ Web: www.gnedi.com	Rogers	MN	55374	763-428-2237	428-4821	385
Great Northern Lumber 2200 W 127th St *Fax Area Code: 708 ■ TF: 800-288-2202 ■ Web: www.greatnorthernlumber.com	Blue Island	IL	60406	800-288-2202	388-0887*	191-3
Great Northern Products Ltd 2700 Plainfield Pk Web: www.northernproducts.com	Cranston	RI	02921	401-490-4590	490-5595	296-14
Great Pacific Fixed Income Securities Inc 151 Kalmus Dr Ste H-8 TF: 800-284-4804 ■ Web: greatpac.com	Costa Mesa	CA	92626	714-619-3000	619-3018	690
Great Plains Annuity Marketing Inc 10901 W 84th Ter Ste 125 TF: 800-710-1115 ■ Web: brokersedgeal.com	Lenexa	KS	66214	913-492-9994	492-9998	390
Great Plains Coca-Cola Bottling Company Inc 600 N May Ave TF: 800-753-2653 ■ Web: www.greatplainscocacola.com	Oklahoma City	OK	73107	405-280-2000		80-2
Great Plains Communications Inc 1600 Great Plains Ctr TF: 888-343-8014 ■ Web: www.gpcom.com	Blair	NE	68008	402-426-9511		224
Great Plains Health Alliance Inc 625 Third St TF: 800-432-2779 ■ Web: www.gpha.com	Phillipsburg	KS	67661	785-543-2111		353
Great Plains Industries Inc 5252 E 36th St N TF: 888-996-3837 ■ Web: gpimeters.net	Wichita	KS	67220	316-219-1106	686-6746	639
Great Plains Laboratory Inc 11813 W 77th St TF: 800-288-0383 ■ Web: www.greatplainslaboratory.com	Lenexa	KS	66214	913-341-8949		418
Great Plains Nature Ctr 6232 E 29th St N Web: www.gpnc.org	Wichita	KS	67220	316-683-5499	688-9555	50-5
Great Plains Processing (GPP) 301 S Walnut Ave Web: www.gpp-co.com	Luverne	MN	56156	507-283-4421		159
Great Plains Stainless (GPS) 1004 N 129th E Ave TF: 800-345-5757 ■ Web: www.gpss.com	Tulsa	OK	74116	918-437-5400	437-5440	492
Great Plains State Park 22487 E 1566 Rd Web: www.travelok.com	Mountain Park	OK	73559	580-569-2032	569-2375	565
Great Plains Transportation Museum 700 E Douglas St Web: www.gptm.us	Wichita	KS	67202	316-263-0944		520
Great Plains Tribal Chairmen's Health Board 711 Odde Pl TF: 800-745-3466 ■ Web: www.aatchb.org	Rapid City	SD	57701	605-721-1922		194
Great Planes Model Distributors PO Box 9021 TF: 800-637-7660 ■ Web: www.gpmd.com	Champaign	IL	61826	217-398-3630	398-1104	762
Great Point Investors LLC 98 N Washington St Ste 501 Web: www.gpinvestors.com	Boston	MA	02114	617-526-8800		401
Great Point Partners LLC 165 Mason St 3rd Fl Web: gppfunds.com	Greenwich	CT	06830	203-971-3300		194
Great River Energy 12300 Elm Creek Blvd Web: greatriverenergy.com	Maple Grove	MN	55369	763-445-5000	445-5050	245
Great River Health System 1221 S Gear Ave Web: www.greatriverhealth.org	West Burlington	IA	52655	319-768-1000		374-3
Great River Office Products 115 S Wabasha St Web: greatriverofficeproducts.com	Saint Paul	MN	55107	651-293-1135		535
Great River Regional Library 1300 W St Germain St Web: griver.org	Saint Cloud	MN	56301	320-650-2500		434-3
Great Road Veterinary Hospital 272 Great Rd Web: greatroadvet.com	Acton	MA	01720	978-263-0553	263-0383	794
Great Salt Lake Book Festival Utah Humanities Council 202 W 300 N TF: 877-786-7598 ■ Web: www.utahhumanities.org	Salt Lake City	UT	84103	801-359-9670	531-7869	281
Great Salt Plains State Park 23280 S Spillway Dr Web: www.travelok.com	Jet	OK	73749	580-626-4731	626-4730	565
Great Sand Dunes National Park & Preserve 11500 Hwy 150 Web: www.nps.gov	Mosca	CO	81146	719-378-6300	378-6310	564
Great Seats Inc 5010 Sunnyside Ave Ste 108A Web: greatseatsusa.com	Beltsville	MD	20705	301-985-6250		750
Great Skate Hockey Supl Co 3395 Sheridan Dr Web: www.greatskate.com	Buffalo	NY	14226	716-838-5100		711
Great Smoky Mountains National Park 107 Park Headquarters Rd Web: www.nps.gov	Gatlinburg	TN	37738	865-436-1200		564

Name / Address	City	State	ZIP	Phone	Fax	Class
Great Source Education Group 181 Ballardvale St. *TF:* 800-289-4490 ■ *Web:* www.hmhco.com	Wilmington	MA	01887	800-289-4490	289-3994	243
Great Southern Bank (GSB) 1451 E Battlefield St *TF:* 800-749-7113 ■ *Web:* www.greatsouthernbank.com	Springfield	MO	65804	417-887-4400		70
Great Southern Restaurants 226 South Palafox St Ste 1100 *Web:* www.greatsouthernrestaurants.com	Pensacola	FL	32502	850-470-0003	470-0694	670
Great Southern Wood Preserving 1050 N Main St *Web:* www.yellawood.com	Rocky Mount	VA	24151	540-483-5264		818
Great Southwest Paper Co 5707 Harvey Wilson Dr. *Web:* www.gswpaper.com	Houston	TX	77020	713-223-5050	223-3030	554
Great Southwest Sales 3313 81st St. *Web:* gswtx.com	Lubbock	TX	79423	806-792-9981	792-9983	297-8
Great Valley Management Corp 75 Commerce Dr *Web:* greatvalleyconsultants.com	Wyomissing	PA	19610	610-375-8822		261
Great Wall 410 N Hillside Ave *Web:* greatwallwichita.com	Wichita	KS	67214	316-688-0881		671
Great West Casualty Co 1100 W 29th St PO Box 277 *TF:* 800-228-8602 ■ *Web:* info.gwccnet.com	South Sioux City	NE	68776	402-494-2411		391-4
Great Western Bank 6001 NW Radial Hwy *TF:* 800-952-2043 ■ *Web:* www.greatwesternbank.com	Omaha	NE	68104	402-552-1200		70
Great Western Drilling Company Inc 700 W Louisiana St PO Box 1659 *Web:* www.gwdc.com	Midland	TX	79701	432-682-5241		536
Great Western Ink Inc 2100 NW 22nd Ave. *Web:* www.gw-inks.com	Portland	OR	97210	503-226-3595		388
Great Western Malting Co 1701 NW Harborside Dr *Web:* www.greatwesternmalting.com	Vancouver	WA	98660	360-693-3661		461
Great Western Manufacturing Company Inc 2017 S Fourth St PO Box 149. *TF:* 800-682-3121 ■ *Web:* www.gwmfg.com	Leavenworth	KS	66048	913-682-2291	682-1431	298
Great Western Recycling Industries Inc 521 Barge Channel Rd	Saint Paul	MN	55107	651-224-4877		492
Great Western Supply Inc 2626 Industrial Dr. *TF:* 866-776-8289 ■ *Web:* www.gwsupply.com	Ogden	UT	84401	866-776-8289		612
Great Wolf Lodge of Sandusky LLC 4600 Milan Rd US 250 *TF:* 800-641-9653 ■ *Web:* www.greatwolf.com	Sandusky	OH	44870	800-641-9653		378
Great Works Internet (GWI) 43 Landry St. *TF:* 866-494-2020 ■ *Web:* www.gwi.net	Biddeford	ME	04005	207-494-2000		608
Great Wraps 17 Executive Park Dr NE Ste 150 *TF:* 888-489-7277 ■ *Web:* greatwraps.com	Atlanta	GA	30329	404-248-9900		670
Greater Aiken Chamber of Commerce 121 Richland Ave E PO Box 892 *TF:* 800-251-7234 ■ *Web:* www.aikenchamber.net	Aiken	SC	29802	803-641-1111	641-4174	139
Greater Akron Chamber 1 Cascade Plz 17th Fl *Web:* www.greaterakronchamber.org	Akron	OH	44308	330-376-5550	379-3164	139
Greater Albuquerque Association of Realtors Inc 1635 University Blvd NE *Web:* gaar.com	Albuquerque	NM	87102	505-842-1433		653
Greater Altoona Career & Technology Ctr 1500 4th Ave. *Web:* www.gactc.edu	Altoona	PA	16602	814-946-8450		167-3
Greater Atlanta Christian 1575 Indian Trl Lilburn Rd *TF:* 800-450-1327 ■ *Web:* www.greateratlantachristian.org	Norcross	GA	30093	770-243-2000		48-20
Greater Atlantic City Chamber 12 S Virginia Ave *Web:* acchamber.com	Atlantic City	NJ	08401	609-345-4524	345-1666	139
Greater Augusta Regional Chamber of Commerce 30 Ladd Rd PO Box 1107 *TF:* 866-922-2514 ■ *Web:* www.augustava.com	Fishersville	VA	22939	540-324-1133	324-1136	139
Greater Austin Performing Arts Center Inc 701 W Riverside Dr. *Web:* thelongcenter.org	Austin	TX	78704	512-457-5100		720
Greater Bakersfield Chamber of Commerce 1725 Eye St *TF:* 800-500-5376 ■ *Web:* bakochamber.com	Bakersfield	CA	93301	661-327-4421	327-8751	139
Greater Bakersfield Convention & Visitors Bureau 515 Truxtun Ave *TF:* 866-425-7353 ■ *Web:* www.visitbakersfield.com	Bakersfield	CA	93301	661-852-7282	325-7074	206
Greater Baltimore Medical Ctr (GBMC) 6701 N Charles St *Web:* www.gbmc.org	Baltimore	MD	21204	443-849-2000	849-6889	374-3
Greater Bangor Convention & Visitors Bureau 40 Harlow St. *TF:* 800-916-6673 ■ *Web:* www.visitbangormaine.com	Bangor	ME	04401	207-947-5205		206
Greater Baton Rouge Chamber of Commerce 564 Laurel St *Web:* www.brac.org	Baton Rouge	LA	70801	225-381-7125		139
Greater Beauregard Chamber of Commerce 111 N Washington St *Web:* www.beauchamber.org	DeRidder	LA	70634	337-463-5533	463-2244	139
Greater Beloit Chamber of Commerce 500 Public Ave *TF:* 866-981-5969 ■ *Web:* greaterbeloitchamber.org	Beloit	WI	53511	608-365-8835	365-6850	139
Greater Bentonville Area Chamber of Commerce 200 E Central St PO Box 330 *Web:* greaterbentonville.com	Bentonville	AR	72712	479-273-2841	273-2180	139
Greater Bergen Community Action (GBCA) 392 Main St *Web:* www.greaterbergen.org	Hackensack	NJ	07601	201-968-0200		379
Greater Berryville Area *Chamber of Commerce* 506 S Main St *Web:* www.berryvillechamber.com	Berryville	AR	72616	870-423-3704	423-2330	139
Greater Bethesda Chamber of Commerce, The 7910 Woodmont Ave Ste 1204 *Web:* bethesdachevychasemdcoc.wliinc28.com	Bethesda	MD	20814	301-652-4900	657-1973	139
Greater Binghamton Chamber of Commerce 5 S College Dr Ste 101 **Fax Area Code:* 607 ■ *Web:* greaterbinghamtonchamber.com	Binghamton	NY	13905	800-836-6740	722-4513*	139
Greater Binghamton Health Ctr 425 Robinson St. *Web:* omh.ny.gov	Binghamton	NY	13904	607-724-1391	773-4387	374-5
Greater Birmingham Convention & Visitors Bureau 1819 Morris Ave *TF:* 800-458-8085 ■ *Web:* www.birminghamal.org	Birmingham	AL	35203	205-458-8000	458-8086	206
Greater Bloomington Chamber of Commerce 400 W Seventh St Ste 102 *TF:* 888-644-7744 ■ *Web:* www.chamberbloomington.org	Bloomington	IN	47404	812-336-6381	336-0651	139
Greater Boca Raton Chamber of Commerce 1800 N Dixie Hwy *Web:* www.bocaratonchamber.com	Boca Raton	FL	33432	561-395-4433	392-3780	139
Greater Boston Chamber of Commerce 265 Franklin St *TF:* 800-476-3094 ■ *Web:* www.bostonchamber.com	Boston	MA	02110	617-227-4500	227-7505	139
Greater Boston Convention & Visitors Bureau (GBCVB) 2 Copley Pl Ste 105 *TF:* 888-733-2678 ■ *Web:* www.bostonusa.com	Boston	MA	02116	617-536-4100	424-7664	206
Greater Bowie Chamber of Commerce 1525 Pointer Ridge Pl Ste 117 *Web:* www.bowiechamber.org	Bowie	MD	20715	301-262-0920	262-0921	139
Greater Boynton Beach Chamber of Commerce 1880 N Congress Ave Ste 214 *Web:* www.boyntonbeach.org	Boynton Beach	FL	33426	561-732-9501	734-4304	139
Greater Brandon Chamber of Commerce 330 Pauls Dr Ste 100 *Web:* www.brandonchamber.com	Brandon	FL	33511	813-689-1221	689-9440	139
Greater Bridgeport Conference & Vistors Ctr 164 W Main St *TF:* 800-368-4324 ■ *Web:* www.greater-bridgeport.com	Bridgeport	WV	26330	304-842-7272		206
Greater Bridgeport Symphony (GBS) 446 University Ave *Web:* www.gbs.org	Bridgeport	CT	06604	203-576-0263		573-3
Greater Brighton Area Chamber of Commerce 218 E Grand Riv *Web:* www.brightoncoc.org	Brighton	MI	48116	810-227-5086	227-5940	139
Greater Bristol Chamber of Commerce 440 N Main St *Web:* www.centralctchambers.org	Bristol	CT	06010	860-584-4718	584-4722	139
Greater Brookfield Chamber of Commerce 17100 W Bluemound Rd Ste 202 *Web:* www.brookfieldchamber.com	Brookfield	WI	53005	262-786-1886	786-1959	139
Greater Capital Area Association of Realtors 15201 Diamondback Dr Ste 100 *Web:* gcaar.com	Rockville	MD	20850	301-590-2000		656
Greater Cayce West Columbia Chamber of Commerce 1006 12th St. *TF:* 866-720-5400 ■ *Web:* www.cwcchamber.com	Cayce	SC	29033	803-794-6504	794-6505	139
Greater Central Texas Federal Cr 3305 E Elms Rd *Web:* gctfcu.net	Killeen	TX	76542	254-690-2274		219
Greater Chambersburg Chamber of Commerce 100 Lincoln Way E Ste A *TF:* 800-840-9081 ■ *Web:* www.chambersburg.org	Chambersburg	PA	17201	717-264-7101	267-0399	139
Greater Charlottetown Area Chamber of Commerce PO Box 67 *TF:* 866-746-5282 ■ *Web:* charlottetownchamber.com	Charlottetown	PE	C1A7K2	902-628-2000	368-3570	137
Greater Cheyenne Chamber of Commerce 121 W 15th St Ste 204 *Web:* www.cheyennechamber.org	Cheyenne	WY	82001	307-638-3388	778-1407	139
Greater Cincinnati Convention & Visitors Bureau 525 Vine St Ste 1200 *TF:* 800-543-2613 ■ *Web:* www.cincyusa.com	Cincinnati	OH	45202	513-621-2142	621-5020	206
Greater Cincinnati Foundation 200 W Fourth St *TF:* 800-742-6253 ■ *Web:* www.gcfdn.org	Cincinnati	OH	45202	513-241-2880		303
Greater Cleveland Partnership 1240 Huron Rd E Ste 300 *TF:* 888-304-4769 ■ *Web:* www.gcpartnership.com	Cleveland	OH	44115	216-621-3300	621-6013	139
Greater Cleveland Regional Transit Authority (RTA) 1240 W Sixth St *Web:* www.riderta.com	Cleveland	OH	44113	216-621-9500	781-4484	468
Greater Columbia Chamber of Commerce 930 Richland St *Web:* www.columbiachamber.com	Columbia	SC	29201	803-733-1110	733-1149	139
Greater Columbus Chamber of Commerce 1200 Sixth Ave PO Box 1200 *TF:* 800-360-8552 ■ *Web:* www.columbusgachamber.com	Columbus	GA	31902	706-327-1566	327-7512	139
Greater Columbus Convention & Visitors Bureau 277 W Nationwide Blvd Ste 125 *TF:* 866-397-2657 ■ *Web:* www.experiencecolumbus.com	Columbus	OH	43215	614-221-6623	221-5618	206
Greater Columbus Convention Ctr 400 N High St *TF:* 800-626-0241 ■ *Web:* columbusconventions.com	Columbus	OH	43215	614-827-2500	221-7239	205
Greater Concord Chamber of Commerce 2280 Diamond Blvd Ste 200 *TF:* 800-427-8686 ■ *Web:* www.concordchamber.com	Concord	CA	94520	925-685-1181	685-5623	139
Greater Concord Chamber of Commerce 49 S Main St Ste 104 *TF:* 800-360-4839 ■ *Web:* www.concordnhchamber.com	Concord	NH	03301	603-224-2508	224-8128	139
Greater Corner Brook Board of Trade 11 Confederation Dr PO Box 475 *Web:* www.gcbbt.com	Corner Brook	NL	A2H6E6	709-634-5831	639-9710	137
Greater Crofton Chamber of Commerce 2126 Espey Ct Ste A **Fax Area Code:* 443 ■ *Web:* croftonchamber.com	Crofton	MD	21114	410-721-9131	274-6060*	139
Greater Danbury Chamber of Commerce 39 West St *TF:* 800-722-2936 ■ *Web:* www.danburychamber.com	Danbury	CT	06810	203-743-5565	794-1439	139
Greater Data & Mailing Inc 551 Acorn St. *Web:* greaterdata.com	Deer Park	NY	11729	631-667-1450	667-1443	5

Name / Address	City	State	Zip	Phone	Fax	Class
Greater Decatur Chamber of Commerce 101 S Main St Ste 102 *Web:* www.decaturchamber.com	Decatur	IL	62523	217-422-2200	422-4576	139
Greater Deerfield Beach Chamber of Commerce 1601 E Hillsboro Blvd. *TF:* 866-551-9805 ■ *Web:* www.deerfieldchamber.com	Deerfield Beach	FL	33441	954-427-1050	427-1056	139
Greater Delray Beach Chamber of Commerce 140 NE First St *Web:* delraybeach.com	Delray Beach	FL	33444	561-278-0424	278-6012	139
Greater Derry Chamber of Commerce 29 West Broadway *Web:* www.gdlchamber.org	Derry	NH	03038	603-432-8205		139
Greater Des Moines Convention & Visitors Bureau 400 Locust St Ste 265 *TF:* 800-451-2625 ■ *Web:* www.catchdesmoines.com	Des Moines	IA	50309	515-286-4960	244-9757	206
Greater Des Moines Partnership 700 Locust St Ste 100 *Web:* www.dsmpartnership.com	Des Moines	IA	50309	515-286-4950	286-4902	139
Greater Detroit Landscape Co 21000 Fairfield Ave. *Web:* greaterdetroitlandscape.com	Warren	MI	48089	586-777-2000		422
Greater Dover Chamber of Commerce 550 Central Ave *Web:* www.dovernh.org	Dover	NH	03820	603-742-2218	749-6317	139
Greater Durham Chamber of Commerce 300 W Morgan St Ste 1400 PO Box 3829 *Web:* www.durhamchamber.org	Durham	NC	27702	919-328-8700	688-8351	139
Greater Easley Chamber of Commerce 2001 E Main St PO Box 241 *Web:* www.easleychamber.net	Easley	SC	29641	864-859-2693	859-1941	139
Greater East Aurora Chamber of Commerce 652 Main St *Web:* www.eanycc.com	East Aurora	NY	14052	716-652-8444	652-8384	139
Greater Edmonds Chamber of Commerce 121 5th Ave N. *Web:* edmondschamber.com	Edmonds	WA	98020	425-670-1496	712-1808	139
Greater El Monte Community Hospital (GEMCH) 1701 Santa Anita Ave *Web:* www.greaterelmonte.com	South El Monte	CA	91733	626-579-7777	350-0368	374-3
Greater El Paso Chamber of Commerce 10 Civic Center Plz. *Web:* www.elpaso.org	El Paso	TX	79901	915-534-0500	534-0510	139
Greater Elkhart Chamber of Commerce 418 S Main St. *Web:* www.elkhart.org	Elkhart	IN	46516	574-293-1531	294-1859	139
Greater Englewood Chamber of Commerce 3501 S Broadway 2nd Fl. *Web:* myenglewoodchamber.com	Englewood	CO	80113	303-789-4473	789-0098	139
Greater Enid Chamber of Commerce PO Box 907 *Web:* www.enidchamber.com	Enid	OK	73702	580-237-2494	237-2497	139
Greater Eureka Chamber of Commerce, The 2112 Broadway. *Web:* www.eurekachamber.com	Eureka	CA	95501	707-442-3738	442-0079	139
Greater Fayetteville Chamber 159 Maxwell St. *Web:* www.faybiz.com	Fayetteville	NC	28301	910-483-8133	483-0263	139
Greater Federal Way Chamber of Commerce 31919 1st Ave S Ste 202 *Web:* federalwaychamber.com	Federal Way	WA	98003	253-838-2605	661-9050	139
Greater Fort Lauderdale Chamber of Commerce 512 NE Third Ave *Web:* www.ftlchamber.com	Fort Lauderdale	FL	33301	954-462-6000	527-8766	139
Greater Fort Lauderdale Convention & Visitors Bureau 101 NE Third Ave Ste 100. *TF:* 800-227-8669 ■ *Web:* www.sunny.org	Fort Lauderdale	FL	33301	954-765-4466		206
Greater Fort Lauderdale-Broward County Convention Ctr 1950 Eisenhower Blvd *TF:* 800-327-1390 ■ *Web:* www.ftlauderdalecc.com	Fort Lauderdale	FL	33316	954-765-5900		205
Greater Fort Myers Chamber of Commerce 2310 Edwards Dr *TF:* 800-366-3622 ■ *Web:* fortmyers.org	Fort Myers	FL	33901	239-332-3624	332-7276	139
Greater Fort Walton Beach Chamber of Commerce 34 Miracle Strip Pkwy SE *TF:* 800-225-5797 ■ *Web:* www.fwbchamber.org	Fort Walton Beach	FL	32548	850-244-8191	244-1935	139
Greater Fort Wayne Chamber of Commerce 826 Ewing St *Web:* www.fwchamber.org	Fort Wayne	IN	46802	260-424-1435	426-7232	139
Greater Fort Worth Association of Realtors Inc 2650 Parkview Dr. *Web:* www.gfwar.org	Fort Worth	TX	76102	817-336-5165		652
Greater Franklin County Chamber of Commerce, The 112 E Nash St PO Box 62. *Web:* www.franklin-chamber.org	Louisburg	NC	27549	919-496-3056	496-0422	139
Greater Gardner Chamber of Commerce 29 Parker St PO Box 1381 *Web:* gardnerma.com	Gardner	MA	01440	978-632-1780	630-1767	139
Greater Gibson County Area Chamber of Commerce 309 S College St. *Web:* www.gibsoncountytn.com	Trenton	TN	38382	731-855-2013	855-1091	139
Greater Giving Inc 1920 N W Amberglen Pkwy Ste 140. *TF:* 800-276-5992 ■ *Web:* www.greatergiving.com	Beaverton	OR	97006	800-276-5992		317
Greater Golden Chamber of Commerce 1010 Washington Ave. *Web:* goldenchamber.org	Golden	CO	80401	303-279-3113		139
Greater Grand Forks Convention & Visitors Bureau 4251 Gateway Dr *TF:* 800-866-4566 ■ *Web:* visitgrandforks.com	Grand Forks	ND	58203	701-746-0444	746-0775	206
Greater Green Bay Chamber 300 N Broadway Ste 3A *Web:* www.greatergbc.org	Green Bay	WI	54303	920-437-8704		139
Greater Green Bay Convention & Visitors Bureau 1901 S Oneida St. *TF:* 888-867-3342 ■ *Web:* www.greenbay.com	Green Bay	WI	54304	920-494-9507	405-1271	206
Greater Greenbrier Chamber of Commerce 200 W Washington St Ste C *TF:* 855-453-4858 ■ *Web:* www.greenbrierwvchamber.org	Lewisburg	WV	24901	855-453-4858		139
Greater Greencastle Chamber of Commerce 2 S Jackson St PO Box 389 *Web:* goputco.com	Greencastle	IN	46135	765-653-4517		139
Greater Greenville Chamber of Commerce 24 Cleveland St *TF:* 866-485-5262 ■ *Web:* www.greenvillechamber.org	Greenville	SC	29601	864-242-1050	282-8509	139
Greater Greenville Convention & Visitors Bureau 148 River St Ste 222. *TF:* 800-351-7180 ■ *Web:* www.visitgreenvillesc.com	Greenville	SC	29601	864-421-0000		206
Greater Hackensack Chamber of Commerce 5 University Plaza Dr *Web:* www.hackensackchamber.org	Hackensack	NJ	07601	201-489-3700	489-1741	139
Greater Hall Chamber of Commerce 230 EE Butler Pkwy. *Web:* www.ghcc.com	Gainesville	GA	30501	770-532-6206	535-8419	139
Greater Hamilton Chamber of Commerce 201 Dayton St. *Web:* www.hamilton-ohio.com	Hamilton	OH	45011	513-844-1500	844-1999	139
Greater Hammonton Chamber of Commerce, The 10 S Egg Harbor Rd PO Box 554 *Web:* www.hammontonnj.us	Hammonton	NJ	08037	609-561-9080		139
Greater Hartford Police Federal Credit Union 253 High St *Web:* ghpfcu.org	Hartford	CT	06103	860-522-0899		219
Greater Hartsville Chamber of Commerce 214 N Fifth St. *Web:* www.hartsvillechamber.org	Hartsville	SC	29550	843-332-6401	332-8017	139
Greater Haverhill Chamber of Commerce 80 Merrimack St. *Web:* haverhillchamber.com	Haverhill	MA	01830	978-373-5663	373-8060	139
Greater Heights Area Chamber of Commerce 2050 N Loop W Ste 203 *Web:* heightschamber.org	Houston	TX	77018	713-861-6735	861-9310	139
Greater Hernando County Chamber of Commerce 15588 Aviation Loop Dr *Web:* www.hernandochamber.com	Brooksville	FL	34604	352-796-0697	796-3704	139
Greater Hollywood Chamber of Commerce 330 N Federal Hwy *Web:* hollywoodchamber.org	Hollywood	FL	33020	954-923-4000		139
Greater Holy Temple Christian Academy 5575 N 76th St. *Web:* greaterholy.org	Milwaukee	WI	53218	414-265-4131		148
Greater Holyoke Chamber of Commerce 177 High St *Web:* www.holycham.com	Holyoke	MA	01040	413-534-3376		139
Greater Hot Springs Chamber of Commerce 659 Ouachita Ave *TF:* 866-820-0132 ■ *Web:* www.hotspringschamber.com	Hot Springs	AR	71901	501-321-1700		139
Greater Houston Convention & Visitors Bureau 701 Avenida de las Americas Ste 200. *TF:* 800-446-8786 ■ *Web:* www.visithoustontexas.com	Houston	TX	77010	800-446-8786		206
Greater Houston Partnership 1200 Smith St Ste 700 *Web:* www.houston.org	Houston	TX	77002	713-844-3600	844-0200	139
Greater Huntington Park Area Chamber of Commerce 6330 Pacific Blvd Ste 208. *Web:* www.hpchamber.org	Huntington Park	CA	90255	323-585-1155	585-2176	139
Greater Iberia Chamber of Commerce 111 W Main St *Web:* iberiachamber.org	New Iberia	LA	70560	337-364-1836	367-7405	139
Greater Illinois Title Co 120 N La Salle St Ste 900. *Web:* www.gitc.com	Chicago	IL	60602	312-236-7300	236-0284	391-6
Greater Indianapolis Chamber of Commerce 111 Monument Cir Ste 1950 *Web:* indychamber.com	Indianapolis	IN	46204	317-464-2200		139
Greater Irvine Chamber 2485 McCabe Way Ste 150 *Web:* www.greaterirvinechamber.com	Irvine	CA	92614	949-660-9112	660-0829	139
Greater Issaquah Chamber of Commerce 155 NW Gilman Blvd *Web:* www.issaquahchamber.com	Issaquah	WA	98027	425-392-7024	392-8101	139
Greater Jackson Chamber of Commerce 141 S Jackson St *Web:* www.jacksonchamber.org	Jackson	MI	49201	517-782-8221	780-3688	139
Greater Jackson Chamber Partnership PO Box 22548 *Web:* www.greaterjacksonpartnership.com	Jackson	MS	39225	601-948-7575	352-5539	139
Greater Jackson County Chamber of Commerce, The 407 E Willow St *TF:* 800-259-5508 ■ *Web:* www.discoverjacksoncountyalabama.com	Scottsboro	AL	35768	256-259-5500	259-4447	139
Greater Johnstown Career & Technology Ctr 445 Schoolhouse Rd *TF:* 888-434-4436 ■ *Web:* www.gjctc.org	Johnstown	PA	15904	814-266-6073	269-4586	800
Greater Johnstown/Cambria County Chamber of Commerce 245 Market St Ste 100 *TF:* 800-790-4522 ■ *Web:* www.crchamber.com	Johnstown	PA	15901	814-536-5107	539-5800	139
Greater Johnstown/Cambria County Convention & Visitors Bureau 111 Roosevelt Blvd Ste A *TF:* 800-237-8590 ■ *Web:* www.visitjohnstownpa.com	Johnstown	PA	15906	814-536-7993		206
Greater Kalamazoo Association of Realtors Inc 5830 Venture Park Dr *Web:* gkar.com	Kalamazoo	MI	49009	269-382-1597	382-3462	653
Greater Kansas City Chamber of Commerce 911 Main St Ste 2600. *Web:* www.kcchamber.com	Kansas City	MO	64105	816-221-2424	221-7440	139
Greater Kansas City Community Foundation & Affiliated Trusts (GKCCF) 1055 Broadway Blvd Ste 130 *Web:* www.growyourgiving.org	Kansas City	MO	64105	816-842-0944	842-8079	303
Greater Keene Chamber of Commerce 48 Central Sq *Web:* www.keenechamber.com	Keene	NH	03431	603-352-1303	358-5341	139
Greater Killeen Chamber of Commerce 1 Santa Fe Plz. *TF:* 866-790-4769 ■ *Web:* www.killeenchamber.com	Killeen	TX	76540	254-526-9551	526-6090	139
Greater Kingston Chamber of Commerce 67 Brock St. *TF:* 800-558-4696 ■ *Web:* www.kingstonchamber.ca	Kingston	ON	K7L1R8	613-548-4453	548-4743	137

				Phone	Fax	Class
Greater Kirkland Chamber of Commerce 440 Central Way *TF:* 800-501-7772 ■ *Web:* kirklandchamber.org	Kirkland	WA	98033	425-822-7066	827-4878	139
Greater Lafayette Commerce 337 Columbia St *Web:* www.greaterlafayettecommerce.com	LaFayette	IN	47901	765-742-4044	742-6276	139
Greater Lafourche Port Commission PO Box 490 *Web:* portfourchon.com	Galliano	LA	70354	985-632-6701	632-6703	618
Greater Lake Placid Chamber of Commerce 18 N Oak Ave *Web:* www.lpfla.com	Lake Placid	FL	33852	863-465-4331	465-2588	139
Greater Lansing Ballet Co (GLBC) 15643 S US Hwy 27 *Web:* greaterlansingballet.com	Lansing	MI	48912	517-575-6854		573-1
Greater Lansing Convention & Visitors Bureau 500 E Michigan Ave Ste 180 *TF:* 888-252-6746 ■ *Web:* www.lansing.org	Lansing	MI	48912	517-487-0077	487-5151	206
Greater Las Cruces Chamber of Commerce 760 W Picacho Ave *Web:* www.lascruces.org	Las Cruces	NM	88005	575-524-1968	527-5546	139
Greater Lawrence Township Chamber of Commerce 9120 Otis Ave Ste 100 *Web:* www.greaterlawrencechamber.org	Indianapolis	IN	46216	317-541-9876		139
Greater Lehigh Valley Chamber of Commerce 1 E Broad St *Web:* www.lehighvalleychamber.org	Bethlehem	PA	18018	610-419-1535		139
Greater Lexington Chamber of Commerce Inc 330 E Main St Ste 100 *TF:* 800-848-1224 ■ *Web:* www.commercelexington.com	Lexington	KY	40507	859-254-4447	233-3304	139
Greater Limestone County Chamber of Commerce 101 S Beaty St *TF:* 866-953-6565 ■ *Web:* www.tourathens.com	Athens	AL	35611	256-232-2600	232-2609	139
Greater Lincoln Lakes Region Chamber of Commerce 256 W Broadway *Web:* lincolnmechamber.org	Lincoln	ME	04457	207-794-8065		139
Greater Liverpool Chamber of Commerce 314 Second St *Web:* liverpoolchamber.com	Liverpool	NY	13088	315-457-3895	234-3226	139
Greater Long Branch Chamber of Commerce 228 Broadway PO Box 628 *Web:* www.longbranchchamber.org	Long Branch	NJ	07740	732-222-0400		139
Greater Los Angeles Agency on Deafness Inc (GLAD) 2222 Laverna Ave *Web:* www.gladinc.org	Los Angeles	CA	90041	323-478-8000		637-2
Greater Louisville Inc 614 W Main St *Web:* www.greaterlouisville.com	Louisville	KY	40202	502-625-0000	625-0010	139
Greater Lowell Chamber of Commerce 131 Merrimack St *Web:* greaterlowellcc.org	Lowell	MA	01852	978-459-8154	452-4145	139
Greater Lynn Chamber of Commerce 583 Chestnut St Ste 8 *Web:* greaterlynnchamber.com	Lynn	MA	01904	781-592-2900	592-2903	139
Greater Macon Chamber of Commerce 305 Coliseum Dr *Web:* maconchamber.com	Macon	GA	31217	478-621-2000	621-2021	139
Greater Madison Chamber of Commerce PO Box 71 *TF:* 800-750-5437 ■ *Web:* madisonbiz.com	Madison	WI	53701	608-256-8348	256-0333	139
Greater Mahopacs-Carmel Chamber of Commerce 953 S Lake Blvd *Web:* www.mahopaccarmelonline.com	Mahopac	NY	10541	845-628-5553	628-5962	139
Greater Manchester Chamber of Commerce 20 Hartford Rd *Web:* www.manchesterchamber.com	Manchester	CT	06040	860-646-2223	646-5871	139
Greater Mankato Growth 1961 Premier Dr *TF:* 800-697-0652 ■ *Web:* greatermankato.com	Mankato	MN	56001	507-385-6640	345-4451	206
Greater Maple Valley-Black Diamond Chamber of Commerce 23745 225th Way SE Ste 205 *Web:* www.maplevalleychamber.org	Maple Valley	WA	98038	425-432-0222		139
Greater Marathon Chamber of Commerce 12222 Overseas Hwy *TF:* 800-262-7284 ■ *Web:* www.floridakeysmarathon.com	Marathon	FL	33050	305-743-5417	289-0183	139
Greater Marion Area Chamber of Commerce 2305 W Main St *Web:* www.marionillinois.com	Marion	IL	62959	618-997-6311	233-8765	139
Greater Marshall Chamber of Commerce 213 W Austin St *Web:* www.marshall-chamber.com	Marshall	TX	75670	903-935-7868		139
Greater Media Inc 35 Braintree Hill Pk Ste 300	Braintree	MA	02184	781-348-8600		637-8
Greater Memphis Chamber 22 N Front St Ste 200 *Web:* www.memphischamber.com	Memphis	TN	38103	901-543-3500	543-3510	139
Greater Menomonie Area Chamber of Commerce 342 E Main St *TF:* 800-283-1862 ■ *Web:* www.menomoniechamber.org	Menomonie	WI	54751	715-235-9087	235-2824	139
Greater Merced County Multi-Cultural Chamber of Commerce, The 1131 Martin Luther King Way *Web:* merced-chamber.com	Merced	CA	95340	209-384-7092	384-8472	139
Greater Meriden Chamber of Commerce 3 Colony St Ste 301 *TF:* 877-283-8158 ■ *Web:* www.midstatechamber.com	Meriden	CT	06451	203-235-7901	686-0172	139
Greater Merrimack Valley Convention & Visitors Bureau 61 Market St Unit 1C *Web:* merrimackvalley.org	Lowell	MA	01852	978-459-6150		206
Greater Miami & The Beaches Hotel Assn (GMBHA) 1688 Meridian Ave Ste 500 *Web:* www.gmbha.com	Miami Beach	FL	33139	305-531-3553	531-8954	376
Greater Miami Chamber of Commerce 1601 Biscayne Blvd *Web:* www.miamichamber.com	Miami	FL	33132	305-350-7700	374-6902	139
Greater Miami Convention & Visitors Bureau 701 Brickell Ave Ste 2700 *TF:* 800-933-8448 ■ *Web:* www.miamiandbeaches.com	Miami	FL	33131	305-539-3000	530-5859	206
Greater Milwaukee Association of Realtors Inc 12300 W Center St *Web:* www.gmar.com	Milwaukee	WI	53222	414-778-4929	778-4920	652
Greater Milwaukee Convention & Visitors Bureau 648 N Plankinton Ave Ste 220 *TF:* 800-554-1448 ■ *Web:* www.visitmilwaukee.org	Milwaukee	WI	53203	414-273-7222	273-5596	206
Greater Milwaukee Foundation 101 W Pleasant St Ste 210 *Web:* www.greatermilwaukeefoundation.org	Milwaukee	WI	53212	414-272-5805	272-6235	303
Greater Missouri Builders Inc 1551 Wall St Ste 220 *Web:* greatermissouribuilders.com	Saint Charles	MO	63303	636-946-1341	949-9992	653
Greater Moncton Chamber of Commerce 1273 Main St Ste 200 *Web:* gmcc-nb.chambermaster.com	Moncton	NB	E1C0P4	506-857-2883	857-9209	137
Greater Monmouth Chamber of Commerce 10 E Main St Ste 1A *Web:* www.monmouthregionalchamber.com	Freehold	NJ	07728	732-462-3030		139
Greater Monticello Chamber of Commerce 116 N Main St *TF:* 800-541-7906 ■ *Web:* www.monticelloin.com	Monticello	IN	47960	574-583-7220	583-3399	139
Greater Mount Airy Chamber of Commerce 200 N Main St *TF:* 800-948-0949 ■ *Web:* www.mtairyncchamber.org	Mount Airy	NC	27030	336-786-6116	786-1488	139
Greater Muskogee Area Chamber of Commerce PO Box 797 *TF:* 866-381-6543 ■ *Web:* www.visitmuskogee.com	Muskogee	OK	74402	918-682-2401	682-2403	139
Greater Mystic Chamber of Commerce 62 Greenmanville Ave PO Box 143 *Web:* www.mysticchamber.org	Mystic	CT	06355	860-572-9578	572-9273	139
Greater Nanaimo Chamber of Commerce 2133 Bowen Rd *Web:* nanaimochamber.bc.ca	Nanaimo	BC	V9S1H8	250-756-1191	756-1584	137
Greater Naples Chamber of Commerce, The 2390 Tamiami Trl N Ste 210 *Web:* www.napleschamber.org	Naples	FL	34103	239-262-6376	262-8374	139
Greater Naples Marco Island Everglades Convention & Visitors Bureau 2800 Horseshoe Dr *TF:* 800-688-3600 ■ *Web:* www.paradisecoast.com	Naples	FL	34104	239-252-2384	252-2404	206
Greater Nashua Chamber of Commerce 142 Main St *Web:* www.nashuachamber.com	Nashua	NH	03060	603-881-8333	881-7323	139
Greater New Braunfels Chamber of Commerce Inc, The 390 S Seguin Ave **Fax Area Code:* 830 ■ *TF:* 800-572-2626 ■ *Web:* www.playinnewbraunfels.com	New Braunfels	TX	78130	800-572-2626	625-7918*	206
Greater New Britain Chamber of Commerce 1 Court St 4th Fl *Web:* greaternewbritainchamber.com	New Britain	CT	06051	860-229-1665	223-8341	139
Greater New Haven Chamber of Commerce 900 Chapel St 10th Fl *TF:* 800-953-4467 ■ *Web:* www.gnhcc.com	New Haven	CT	06510	203-787-6735	782-4329	139
Greater New Milford Chamber of Commerce 11 Railroad St *TF:* 800-998-2984 ■ *Web:* www.newmilford-chamber.com	New Milford	CT	06776	860-354-6080		139
Greater New Orleans Hotel & Lodging Assn 2020 St Charles Ave 5th Fl *TF:* 866-366-1121 ■ *Web:* www.gnohla.com	New Orleans	LA	70130	504-525-2264	210-0356	376
Greater New York Chamber of Commerce 20 W 44th St 4th Fl *TF:* 800-344-6088 ■ *Web:* www.chamber.nyc	New York	NY	10036	212-686-7220	686-7232	139
Greater New York Dental Meeting 200 W 41st St Ste 800 *TF:* 844-797-7469 ■ *Web:* www.gnydm.com	New York	NY	10036	212-398-6922	398-6934	194
Greater Newport Chamber of Commerce 555 SW Coast Hwy *TF:* 800-262-7844 ■ *Web:* newportchamber.org	Newport	OR	97365	541-265-8801	265-5589	139
Greater Niagara Federal Credit Union 2901 Military Rd *TF:* 800-299-9842 ■ *Web:* greaterniagarafcu.com	Niagara Falls	NY	14304	716-297-5944	297-6074	219
Greater Niagara General Hospital 5546 Portage Rd *Web:* www.niagarahealth.on.ca	Niagara Falls	ON	L2E6X2	905-378-4647		374-2
Greater North County Chamber of Commerce 420 W Washington St *Web:* greaternorthcountychamber.com	Florissant	MO	63031	314-831-3500	831-9682	139
Greater North Fulton Chamber of Commerce (GNFCC) 11605 Haynes Bridge Rd Ste 100 *Web:* www.gnfcc.com	Alpharetta	GA	30009	770-993-8806	594-1059	139
Greater North Miami Chamber of Commerce 13100 W Dixie Hwy *TF:* 800-939-3848 ■ *Web:* northmiamichamber.com	North Miami	FL	33161	305-891-7811	893-8522	139
Greater Northampton Chamber of Commerce 99 Pleasant St *Web:* www.northamptonchamber.com	Northampton	MA	01060	413-584-1900	584-1934	139
Greater Northeast Philadelphia Chamber of Commerce 8025 Roosevelt Blvd Ste 200 *Web:* www.nephilachamber.com	Philadelphia	PA	19152	215-332-3400	332-6050	139
Greater Norwalk Chamber of Commerce 101 E Ave *Web:* www.norwalkchamberofcommerce.com	Norwalk	CT	06851	203-866-2521	852-0583	139
Greater Ocean City Chamber of Commerce 12320 Ocean Gateway *TF:* 888-626-3386 ■ *Web:* oceancity.org	Ocean City	MD	21842	410-213-0552	213-7521	139
Greater Oklahoma City Chamber of Commerce 6701 W Wilshire Blvd *TF:* 800-225-5652 ■ *Web:* www.okcchamber.com	Oklahoma City	OK	73102	405-297-8900	297-8916	139
Greater Olean Area Chamber of Commerce 120 N Union St *Web:* www.oleanny.com	Olean	NY	14760	716-372-4433	372-7912	139
Greater Omaha Chamber of Commerce 808 Conagra Dr Ste 400 *TF:* 800-852-2622 ■ *Web:* www.omahachamber.org	Omaha	NE	68102	402-346-5000	346-7050	139
Greater Omaha Convention & Visitors Bureau 1001 Farnam St *TF:* 866-937-6624 ■ *Web:* www.visitomaha.com	Omaha	NE	68102	402-444-4660	444-4511	206
Greater Omaha Packing Company Inc 3001 L St *TF:* 800-747-5400 ■ *Web:* www.greateromaha.com	Omaha	NE	68107	402-731-1700		473

Name / Address	City	State	ZIP	Phone	Fax	Class
Greater Orange Area Chamber of Commerce 1012 Green Ave *Web:* www.orangetexaschamber.org	Orange	TX	77630	409-883-3536		139
Greater Oshawa Chamber of Commerce 44 Richmond St W Ste 100 *Web:* www.oshawachamber.com	Oshawa	ON	L1G1C7	905-728-1683	432-1259	137
Greater Oswego-Fulton Chamber of Commerce (GOFCC) 44 E Bridge St *Web:* www.oswegofultonchamber.com	Oswego	NY	13126	315-343-7681	342-0831	139
Greater Owensboro Chamber of Commerce 200 E Third St *Web:* chamber.owensboro.com	Owensboro	KY	42302	270-926-1860	926-3364	139
Greater Palm Harbor Area Chamber of Commerce 1151 Nebraska Ave *Web:* palmharborchamber.com	Palm Harbor	FL	34683	727-784-4287	786-2336	139
Greater Paramus Chamber of Commerce Neptune Plz 332 Rt 4 E S Lbby 2nd Fl PO Box 325 *Web:* paramuschamber.org	Paramus	NJ	07652	201-261-3344	261-3346	139
Greater Parkersburg Convention & Visitors Bureau 350 Seventh St *TF:* 800-752-4982 ■ *Web:* www.greaterparkersburg.com	Parkersburg	WV	26101	304-428-1130	428-8117	206
Greater Paterson Chamber of Commerce 100 Hamilton Plz Ste 1201 *TF:* 800-220-2892 ■ *Web:* www.greaterpatersoncc.org	Paterson	NJ	07505	973-881-7300		139
Greater Peoria Mass Transit District 407 SW Adams St *Web:* www.ridecitylink.org	Peoria	IL	61602	309-676-4040		468
Greater Peterborough Chamber of Commerce 175 George St N *TF:* 877-640-4037 ■ *Web:* www.peterboroughchamber.ca	Peterborough	ON	K9J3G6	705-748-9771	743-2331	137
Greater Pflugerville Chamber of Commerce 101 S Third St PO Box 483 *Web:* www.pfchamber.com	Pflugerville	TX	78691	512-251-7799	251-7802	139
Greater Philadelphia Chamber of Commerce 200 S Broad St Ste 700 *Web:* chamberphl.com	Philadelphia	PA	19102	215-545-1234	790-3600	139
Greater Phoenix Chamber of Commerce 201 N Central Ave Ste 2700 *Web:* www.phoenixchamber.com	Phoenix	AZ	85004	602-254-5521	495-8913	139
Greater Phoenix Convention & Visitors Bureau 400 E Van Buren St Ste 600 *TF:* 877-225-5749 ■ *Web:* www.visitphoenix.com	Phoenix	AZ	85004	602-254-6500	253-4415	206
Greater Pittsburgh Chamber of Commerce 11 Stanwix St 17th Fl *Web:* www.greaterpittsburghchamberofcommerce.com	Pittsburgh	PA	15222	412-281-1890		139
Greater Pittsburgh Convention & Visitors Bureau 120 Fifth Ave Fifth Avenue Pl Ste 2800 *TF:* 800-359-0758 ■ *Web:* www.visitpittsburgh.com	Pittsburgh	PA	15222	412-281-7711	644-5512	206
Greater Pittsburgh Police Federal Credit Union 1338 Chartiers Ave *Web:* pittsburghpolicefcu.com	Pittsburgh	PA	15220	412-922-4800		219
Greater Plant City Chamber of Commerce 106 N Evers St *Web:* www.plantcity.org	Plant City	FL	33563	813-754-3707	752-8793	139
Greater Plantation Chamber of Commerce 7401 NW Fourth St *Web:* plantationchamber.org	Plantation	FL	33317	954-587-1410	587-1886	139
Greater Pocatello Chamber of Commerce 324 S Main St *TF:* 800-632-0905 ■ *Web:* www.pocatelloidaho.com	Pocatello	ID	83204	208-233-1525	233-1527	139
Greater Pompano Beach Chamber of Commerce 2200 E Atlantic Blvd *TF:* 888-939-5711 ■ *Web:* www.pompanobeachchamber.com	Pompano Beach	FL	33062	954-941-2940	785-8358	139
Greater Port Arthur Chamber of Commerce 4749 Twin City Hwy Ste 300 *Web:* www.portarthurtexas.com	Port Arthur	TX	77642	409-963-1107	962-1997	139
Greater Portage Chamber of Commerce 2642 Eleanor St *Web:* portageinchamber.com	Portage	IN	46368	219-762-3300	983-8080	139
Greater Portland Convention & Visitors Bureau 94 Commercial St Ste 300 *Web:* www.visitportland.com	Portland	ME	04101	207-772-4994	874-9043	206
Greater Portland Metro 114 Valley St *Web:* gpmetro.org	Portland	ME	04102	207-774-0351		468
Greater Providence Chamber of Commerce 30 Exchange Terr *Web:* www.providencechamber.com	Providence	RI	02903	401-521-5000	621-6109	139
Greater Pueblo Chamber of Commerce 302 N Santa Fe Ave *TF:* 800-233-3446 ■ *Web:* pueblochamber.org	Pueblo	CO	81003	719-542-1704	542-1624	139
Greater Raleigh Chamber of Commerce PO Box 2978 *TF:* 888-456-8535 ■ *Web:* www.raleighchamber.org	Raleigh	NC	27602	919-664-7000	664-7097	139
Greater Raleigh Convention & Visitors Bureau 421 Fayetteville St Ste 1505 *TF:* 800-849-8499 ■ *Web:* www.visitraleigh.com	Raleigh	NC	27601	919-834-5900	831-2887	206
Greater Reading Chamber of Commerce & Industry 201 Penn St *Web:* greaterreading.org	Reading	PA	19601	610-376-6766	376-4135	139
Greater Redding Chamber of Commerce 747 Auditorium Dr *Web:* www.reddingchamber.com	Redding	CA	96001	530-225-4433	225-4398	139
Greater Renton Chamber of Commerce 625 S Fourth St *TF:* 877-467-3686 ■ *Web:* www.gorenton.com	Renton	WA	98057	425-226-4560		139
Greater Reston Chamber of Commerce 1886 Metro Center Dr *Web:* www.restonchamber.org	Reston	VA	20190	703-707-9045		139
Greater Richmond Convention Ctr 403 N Third St *Web:* www.richmondcenter.com	Richmond	VA	23219	804-783-7300		205
Greater Riverside Chambers of Commerce 3985 University Ave *Web:* www.riverside-chamber.com	Riverside	CA	92501	951-683-7100	683-2670	139
Greater Riverview Chamber of Commerce 10011 Water Works Ln *Web:* www.riverviewchamber.com	Riverview	FL	33578	813-234-5944	234-5945	139
Greater Rochester Chamber of Commerce 18 S Main St *Web:* www.rochesternh.org	Rochester	NH	03867	603-332-5080	332-5216	139
Greater Rochester International Airport 1200 Brooks Ave *Web:* www.monroecounty.gov	Rochester	NY	14624	585-753-7020	753-7008	27
Greater Rockford Airport 60 Airport Dr *Web:* flyrfd.com	Rockford	IL	61109	815-969-4000	969-4001	27
Greater Rockford Auto Auction Inc (GRAA) 5937 Sandy Hollow Rd *TF:* 800-830-4722 ■ *Web:* www.graa.net	Rockford	IL	61109	815-874-7800	874-1325	51
Greater Rome Chamber of Commerce 1 Riverside Pkwy *Web:* www.romega.com	Rome	GA	30161	706-291-7663	232-5755	139
Greater Rome Convention & Visitors Bureau 402 Civics Center Dr *TF:* 800-444-1834 ■ *Web:* romegeorgia.org	Rome	GA	30161	706-295-5576		206
Greater Saint Charles Convention & Visitors Bureau 230 S Main St *TF:* 800-366-2427 ■ *Web:* www.discoverstcharles.com	Saint Charles	MO	63301	636-946-7776	949-3217	206
Greater Salem Chamber of Commerce 81 Main St *Web:* www.gschamber.com	Salem	NH	03079	603-893-3177	894-5158	139
Greater San Antonio Chamber of Commerce 602 E Commerce St *TF:* 888-828-8680 ■ *Web:* www.sachamber.org	San Antonio	TX	78205	210-229-2100	229-1600	139
Greater Sarasota Chamber of Commerce 1945 Fruitville Rd *Web:* www.sarasotachamber.com	Sarasota	FL	34236	941-955-8187	366-5621	139
Greater Saskatoon Chamber of Commerce 104-202 Fourth Ave N *Web:* www.saskatoonchamber.com	Saskatoon	SK	S7K0K1	306-244-2151	244-8366	137
Greater Scranton Chamber of Commerce 222 Mulberry St *Web:* www.scrantonchamber.com	Scranton	PA	18503	570-342-7711	347-6262	139
Greater Seattle Chamber of Commerce 1301 Fifth Ave Ste 1500 *TF:* 866-978-2997 ■ *Web:* seattlechamber.com	Seattle	WA	98101	206-389-7200		139
Greater Sebring Chamber of Commerce 227 US 27 N *Web:* sebring.org	Sebring	FL	33870	863-385-8448	385-8810	139
Greater Seminole Area Chamber of Commerce SC Bldg 9200 113th St *Web:* www.myseminolechamber.com	Seminole	FL	33772	727-392-3245	397-7753	139
Greater Severna Park Chamber of Commerce 1 Holly Ave *Web:* www.gspacc.com	Severna Park	MD	21146	410-647-3900	647-3999	139
Greater Shelby County Chamber of Commerce 1301 County Services Dr *Web:* shelbychamber.org	Pelham	AL	35124	205-663-4542	663-4524	139
Greater Sherman Oaks Chamber of Commerce 14241 Ventura Blvd Ste 207 *Web:* www.shermanoakschamber.org	Sherman Oaks	CA	91403	818-906-1951		139
Greater Shreveport Chamber of Commerce 400 Edwards St *Web:* www.shreveportchamber.org	Shreveport	LA	71101	318-677-2500	677-2541	139
Greater Silver Spring Chamber of Commerce 8601 Georgia Ave Ste 203 *Web:* www.gsscc.org	Silver Spring	MD	20910	301-565-3777	565-3377	139
Greater Southington Chamber of Commerce 31 Liberty St Ste 210 *Web:* www.southingtonchamber.com	Southington	CT	06489	860-628-8036		139
Greater Spokane Inc 801 W Riverside Ave Ste 100 *Web:* greaterspokane.org	Spokane	WA	99201	509-624-1393	747-0077	139
Greater Springfield Chamber of Commerce 6434 Brandon Ave Ste 208 *Web:* www.springfieldchamber.org	Springfield	VA	22150	703-866-3500		139
Greater Springfield Chamber of Commerce, The 1011 S Second St *Web:* www.gscc.org	Springfield	IL	62701	217-525-1173	525-8768	139
Greater Springfield Convention & Visitors Bureau 1441 Main St *TF:* 800-723-1548 ■ *Web:* explorewesternmass.com	Springfield	MA	01103	413-787-1548	781-4607	206
Greater Springfield Convention & Visitors Bureau 20 S Limestone St Ste 100 *TF:* 800-803-1553 ■ *Web:* www.greaterspringfield.com	Springfield	OH	45502	937-325-7621	325-8765	206
Greater St Charles County Chamber of Commerce 2201 First Capitol Dr *Web:* www.gstccc.com	Saint Charles	MO	63301	636-946-0633		139
Greater Starkville Development Partnership 200 E Main St *TF:* 800-649-8687 ■ *Web:* www.starkville.org	Starkville	MS	39759	662-323-3322	323-5815	139
Greater Stillwater Chamber of Commerce 200 Chestnut St E Ste 204 *Web:* greaterstillwaterchamber.com	Stillwater	MN	55082	651-439-4001	439-4035	139
Greater Stockton Chamber of Commerce 445 W Weber Ave Ste 220 *Web:* stocktonchamber.org	Stockton	CA	95203	209-547-2770	466-5271	139
Greater Sudbury Chamber of Commerce 100-40 Elm St *Web:* sudburychamber.ca	Sudbury	ON	P3C1S8	705-673-7133	673-1951	137
Greater Summerville-Dorchester County Chamber of Commerce 402 N Main St *Web:* www.greatersummerville.org	Summerville	SC	29483	843-873-2931	875-4464	139
Greater Sumter Chamber of Commerce 32 E Calhoun St *Web:* www.sumterchamber.com	Sumter	SC	29150	803-775-1231	775-0915	139
Greater Susquehanna Valley Chamber of Commerce 2859 N Susquehanna Trl PO Box 10 *TF:* 800-410-2880 ■ *Web:* www.gsvcc.org	Shamokin Dam	PA	17876	570-743-4100	743-1221	139
Greater Tacoma Convention & Trade Ctr 1500 Broadway *Web:* tacomaconventioncenter.org	Tacoma	WA	98402	253-830-6601	573-2363	205
Greater Talladega Area Chamber of Commerce 210 E St S *Web:* www.talladegalincolnchamber.com	Talladega	AL	35160	256-362-9075	362-9093	139

Phone | Fax | Class

Greater Tallahassee Chamber of Commerce
300 E Park Ave ... Tallahassee FL 32301 850-224-8116 561-3860 139
Web: www.talchamber.com

Greater Tampa Chamber of Commerce
201 N Franklin St Ste 201 PO Box 420 ... Tampa FL 33602 813-228-7777 223-7899 139
Web: www.tampabaychamber.com

Greater Tehachapi Chamber of Commerce
209 E Tehachapi Blvd PO Box 401 ... Tehachapi CA 93581 661-822-4180 822-9036 139
Web: www.tehachapi.com

Greater Texas Federal Credit Union
6411 N Lamar Blvd ... Austin TX 78752 512-458-2558 219
TF: 800-749-9732 ■ *Web:* www.gtfcu.org

Greater Texas Foundation
6100 Foundation Pl Dr ... Bryan TX 77807 979-779-6100 779-6699 305
TF: 866-914-7268 ■ *Web:* www.greatertexasfoundation.org

Greater Toms River Chamber of Commerce
1027 Hooper Ave Ste 5 Bldg 1 Second Fl ... Toms River NJ 08753 732-349-0220 139
Web: tomsriverchamber.com

Greater Topeka Chamber of Commerce
719 S Kansas Ave Ste 110 ... Topeka KS 66603 785-234-2644 234-8656 139
Web: government-affairs.topekapartnership.com

Greater Toronto Airports Authority
Toronto Pearson International Airport 3111 Convair
PO Box 6031 ... Toronto ON L5P1B2 416-776-3000 63
Web: www.torontopearson.com

Greater Tulare Chamber of Commerce
220 E Tulare Ave ... Tulare CA 93274 559-686-1547 686-4915 139
Web: www.tularechamber.org

Greater Valley Area Chamber of Commerce
2918 20th Ave ... Valley AL 36854 334-642-1411 642-1410 139
TF: 800-245-2244 ■ *Web:* www.greatervalleyarea.com

Greater Valley Chamber of Commerce
10 Progress Dr 2nd Fl ... Shelton CT 06484 203-925-4981 925-4984 139
Web: greatervalleychamber.com

Greater Vancouver Chamber of Commerce
1101 Broadway Ste 100 ... Vancouver WA 98660 360-694-2588 693-8279 139
Web: www.vancouverusa.com

Greater Vancouver Convention & Visitors Bureau
200 Burrard St ... Vancouver BC V6C3L6 604-682-2222 682-1717 206
Web: www.tourismvancouver.com

Greater Vernon Chamber of Commerce
PO Box 1228 ... Leesville LA 71496 337-238-0349 238-0340 139
Web: www.chambervernonparish.com

Greater Vernon Chamber of Commerce
2901 32nd St Ste 102 ... Vernon BC V1T5M2 250-545-0771 545-3114 137
Web: www.vernonchamber.ca

Greater Victoria Chamber of Commerce
852 Ft St Ste 100 ... Victoria BC V8W1H8 250-383-7191 385-3552 137
Web: www.victoriachamber.ca

Greater Vineland Chamber of Commerce
2115 S Delsea Dr ... Vineland NJ 08360 856-691-7400 691-2113 139
Web: www.vinelandchamber.org

Greater Waco Chamber of Commerce
101 S Third St ... Waco TX 76701 254-757-5600 752-6618 139
Web: wacochamber.com

Greater Washington Community Foundation
1325 G St NW Ste 480 ... Washington DC 20005 202-955-5890 955-8084 303
Web: www.thecommunityfoundation.org

Greater Washington Publishing Inc
1800 Alexander Bell Dr Ste 120 ... Reston VA 20191 703-992-1100 893-8356 637-9

Greater Watertown Federal Credit Union
48 Woodruff Ave ... Watertown CT 06795 860-945-0611 274-6389 219
Web: greaterwatertown.com

Greater Watertown-North Country Chamber of Commerce
1241 Coffeen St ... Watertown NY 13601 315-788-4400 788-3369 139
Web: www.watertownny.com

Greater Waynesboro Chamber of Commerce
118 Walnut St Ste 111 ... Waynesboro PA 17268 717-762-7123 762-7124 139
Web: www.waynesboro.org

Greater West Chester Chamber of Commerce
119 N High St ... West Chester PA 19380 610-696-4046 696-9110 139
TF: 800-210-8008 ■ *Web:* greaterwestchester.com

Greater Westfield Chamber of Commerce
16 N Elm St ... Westfield MA 01085 413-568-1618 139
Web: www.westfieldbiz.org

Greater Westside Board of Trade
2372 Dobbin Rd ... Westbank BC V4T2H9 250-768-3378 768-3465 137
Web: www.gwboardoftrade.com

Greater Wilkes-Barre Chamber of Business & Industry
2 Public Sq PO Box 5340 ... Wilkes-Barre PA 18710 570-823-2101 822-5951 139
Web: www.wilkes-barre.org

Greater Williamsburg Chamber & Tourism Alliance
421 N Boundary St ... Williamsburg VA 23185 757-229-6511 229-2047 139
TF: 800-368-6511 ■ *Web:* www.williamsburgcc.com

Greater Wilmington Chamber of Commerce
1 Estell Lee Pl ... Wilmington NC 28401 910-762-2611 762-9765 139
Web: wilmingtonchamber.org

Greater Wilmington Convention & Visitors Bureau
100 W Tenth St Ste 20 ... Wilmington DE 19801 800-489-6664 652-4726* 206
*Fax Area Code: 302 ■ *TF:* 800-489-6664 ■ *Web:* www.visitwilmingtonde.com

Greater Winston-Salem Chamber of Commerce
411 W Fourth St Ste 211 ... Winston-Salem NC 27101 336-728-9200 721-2209 139
Web: www.winstonsalem.com

Greater Winter Haven Area Chamber of Commerce
401 Ave 'B' NW ... Winter Haven FL 33881 863-293-2138 297-5818 139
TF: 800-260-9220 ■ *Web:* www.winterhavenchamber.com

Greater Woodfield Convention & Visitors Bureau
1375 E Woodfield Rd Ste 120 ... Schaumburg IL 60173 847-490-1010 490-1212 206
TF: 800-847-4849 ■ *Web:* chicagonorthwest.com

Greater Yakima Chamber of Commerce
10 N 9th St PO Box 1490 ... Yakima WA 98901 509-248-2021 248-0601 139
Web: www.yakima.org

Greater Yellowstone Coalition (GYC)
215 S Wallace Ave ... Bozeman MT 59715 406-586-1593 556-2839 48-13
TF: 800-775-1834 ■ *Web:* greateryellowstone.org

Greatlookz 4635 N Black Canyon Hwy ... Phoenix AZ 85015 602-218-5976 791
Web: greatlookz.com

Phone | Fax | Class

Great-West Life & Annuity Insurance Co
8515 E Orchard Rd ... Greenwood Village CO 80111 303-737-3000 391-2
Web: www.greatwest.com

Greaves Company Inc 107 N 2nd St ... La Conner WA 98257 360-466-1600 466-1212 201
Web: www.greavesco.com

Grebe's Inc 703 N 3rd Ave ... Wausau WI 54401 715-675-2341 351
Web: grebesonline.com

Grecian Delight Foods
1201 Tonne Rd ... Elk Grove Village IL 60007 800-621-4387 296-1
TF: 800-621-4387 ■ *Web:* greciandelight.com

Greddy Performance Products Incorporated Mnmt
9 Vanderbilt ... Irvine CA 92618 949-588-8300 588-6318 61
Web: www.greddy.com

Greece
Consulate General
12424 Wilshire Blvd Ste 1170 ... Los Angeles CA 90025 310-826-5555 826-8670 257
Web: www.mfa.gr
Consulate General 650 N St Clair St ... Chicago IL 60611 312-335-3915 335-3958 257
Web: www.mfa.gr
Consulate General 86 Beacon St ... Boston MA 02108 617-523-0100 523-0511 257
Web: www.mfa.gr
Consulate General 69 E 79th St ... New York NY 10075 212-988-5500 734-8492 257
Web: www.mfa.gr
Consulate General 2441 Gough St ... San Francisco CA 94123 415-775-2102 776-6815 257
Web: www.mfa.gr
Embassy 2217 Massachusetts Ave NW ... Washington DC 20008 202-939-1300 939-1324 257
Web: www.mfa.gr

Greece Public Library
2 Vince Tofany Blvd ... Greece NY 14612 585-225-8951 434-3
Web: www.greecepubliclibrary.org

Greek Catholic Union of the USA
5400 Tuscarawas Rd ... Beaver PA 15009 724-495-3400 391-2
TF: 800-722-4428 ■ *Web:* gcuusa.com

Greek Islands 3821 Center St ... Omaha NE 68105 402-346-1528 345-7428 671
Web: greekislandsomaha.com

Greek Islands Restaurant
906 S Meridian St ... Indianapolis IN 46225 317-636-0700 671
Web: www.greekislandsrestaurant.com

Greek Islands Taverna
3300 N Ocean Blvd ... Fort Lauderdale FL 33308 954-565-5505 671
Web: greekislandstaverna.com

Greek Isles Grille & Taverna
3309 N Central Expy Ste 370 ... Plano TX 75023 972-423-7778 671
Web: greekislesgrille.com

Greek National Tourism Organization
800 Third Ave 23rd Fl ... New York NY 10022 212-421-5777 826-6940 775
Web: www.visitgreece.gr

Greek Palace
8878 Clairmont Mesa Blvd ... San Diego CA 92123 858-573-0155 573-9645 671
Web: www.greekpalace.com

Greek Peak Mountain Resort
2000 NYS Rt 392 ... Cortland NY 13045 855-677-7927 194
TF: 855-677-7927 ■ *Web:* greekpeak.net

Greek Theatre, The
2700 N Vermont Ave ... Los Angeles CA 90027 323-665-5857 666-8202 572
Web: www.lagreektheatre.com

Greektown Superholdings Inc
555 E Lafayette ... Detroit MI 48226 313-223-2999 133
Web: www.greektowncasino.com

Greekworks.com 307 W 89th St ... New York NY 10024 646-505-5291 505-5292 637-2
Web: www.greekworks.com

Greeley & Hansen
100 S Wacker Dr Ste 1400 ... Chicago IL 60606 312-558-9000 558-1006 261
TF: 800-837-9779 ■ *Web:* www.greeley-hansen.com

Greeley Chamber of Commerce
902 Seventh Ave ... Greeley CO 80631 970-352-3566 352-3572 206
TF: 800-449-3866 ■ *Web:* greeleychamber.com

Greeley County 510 Broadway PO Box 656 ... Tribune KS 67879 620-376-2548 376-2549 338
Web: www.greeleycounty.org

Greeley Tribune 501 Eigth Ave ... Greeley CO 80631 970-352-0211 356-5780 532-2
TF: 800-275-0321 ■ *Web:* www.greeleytribune.com

Green & Gross Pc
1087 Broad St Ste 401 ... Bridgeport CT 06604 203-335-5141 41
Web: gglaw.net

Green & Halliburton 521 Barret Ave ... Louisville KY 40204 502-583-4412 390
Web: greenhalliburton.com

Green Acres Baptist Church
16163 N Peninsula Rd ... Whitehouse TX 75791 903-566-2515 48-20
Web: www.gabc.org

Green Acres Contracting Company Inc
703 Pennsylvania Ave ... Scottdale PA 15683 724-887-8096 186
Web: www.greenacrescontracting.com

Green Acres Mall
2062 Green Acres Mall ... Valley Stream NY 11581 516-561-1157 460
Web: www.greenacresmallonline.com

Green Al (Rep D - TX)
2347 Rayburn House Office Bldg ... Washington DC 20515 202-225-7508 225-2947 342-2
Web: algreen.house.gov

Green Alley Strategies PO Box 180122 ... Chicago IL 60618 510-612-8733 194
Web: greenalleystrategies.com

Green Bay Austin Straubel International Airport
2077 Airport Dr Ste 18 ... Green Bay WI 54313 920-498-4800 498-8799 27
Web: www.flygrb.com

Green Bay Botanical Garden
2600 Larsen Rd ... Green Bay WI 54303 920-490-9457 490-9461 97
Web: gbbg.org

Green Bay City Hall
100 N Jefferson St ... Green Bay WI 54301 920-448-3000 448-3016 337
Web: greenbaywi.gov

Green Bay Correctional Institution
2833 Riverside Dr ... Green Bay WI 54307 920-432-4877 448-6545 213
Web: www.doc.wi.gov

Green Bay Drop Forge 1341 State St ... Green Bay WI 54304 920-432-6401 432-0859 483
TF: 800-824-4896 ■ *Web:* www.greenbaydropforge.com

Green Bay Packaging Inc
1700 Webster Ct ... Green Bay WI 54302 920-433-5111 548
TF: 800-236-8400 ■ *Web:* www.gbp.com

Name / Address	City	State	ZIP	Phone	Fax	Class
Green Bay Packers 1265 Lombardi Ave PO Box 10628 *Web:* www.packers.com	Green Bay	WI	54304	920-569-7500	569-7301	715-3
Green Bay Plastics Inc 1028 N Ashland Ave *Web:* www.greenbayplastics.com	Green Bay	WI	54303	920-435-3957		604
Green Bay Press-Gazette Media PO Box 3249 *Web:* www.greenbaypressgazette.com	Milwaukee	WI	53201	920-431-8400		532-2
Green Belt Bank & Trust 616 Washington Ave *Web:* www.greenbeltbank.bank	Iowa Falls	IA	50126	641-648-2544		70
Green Bits 75 E Santa Clara St *TF:* 877-420-7628 ■ *Web:* www.greenbits.com	San Jose	CA	95113	877-420-7628		788
Green Brick Partners Inc 2805 Dallas Pkwy Ste 400 *TF:* 800-374-0137 ■ *Web:* greenbrickpartners.com	Plano	TX	75093	469-573-6755		787
Green Bros. Jewelers Inc 2121 Ave G *Web:* greenbrothersjewelers.com	Bay City	TX	77414	979-245-2598		410
Green Building Consulting 1401 Main St *Web:* www.greenbldgconsulting.com	Cincinnati	OH	45202	513-381-1470	381-2080	196
Green Bulk 170 N Arrowhead Ave Ste D *TF:* 800-764-1238 ■ *Web:* www.greenbulk.com	Rialto	CA	92376	909-877-5587		459
Green Circle Growers Inc 51051 US Hwy 20 *TF:* 800-368-4759 ■ *Web:* www.greencirclegrowers.com	Oberlin	OH	44074	440-775-1411	774-1465	369
Green County 980 Hwy 88 *Web:* www.greencounty.ky.gov	Greensburg	KY	42743	270-932-4024	932-3635	338
Green County 1016 16th Ave *Web:* www.co.green.wi.gov	Monroe	WI	53566	608-328-9430	328-2835	338
Green Crow Corp 727 E Eigth St PO Box 2469 *Web:* greencrow.com	Port Angeles	WA	98362	360-452-3325		448
Green Depot Inc 1 Ivy Hill Rd *TF:* 800-238-5008 ■ *Web:* www.greendepot.com	Brooklyn	NY	11211	718-782-2991		429
Green Diamond Resource Co 1301 Fifth Ave Ste 2700 *Web:* greendiamond.com	Seattle	WA	98101	206-224-5800		302
Green Door 198 Main St *Web:* www.thegreendoor.ca	Ottawa	ON	K1S1C6	613-234-9597		671
Green Dot Corp 3465 E Foothill Blvd *TF:* 866-795-7597 ■ *Web:* www.greendot.com	Pasadena	CA	91107	866-795-7597		215
Green Earth Cleaning 51 W 135th St *TF:* 877-926-0895 ■ *Web:* www.greenearthcleaning.com	Kansas City	MO	64145	816-926-0895		116
Green Field Churrascaria 5305 E Pacific Coast Hwy *Web:* www.greenfieldlongbeach.com	Long Beach	CA	90804	562-597-0906		671
Green Field Paper Co 7196 Clairemont Mesa Blvd *TF:* 888-402-9979 ■ *Web:* www.greenfieldpaper.com	San Diego	CA	92111	858-565-2585		557
Green Foods Corp 4083 E Airport Dr Ste B *Web:* greenfoods.com	Ontario	CA	91761	909-218-5988		296-25
Green Ford 2211 W Pioneer Pkwy *Web:* www.greenfordstore.com	Peoria	IL	61615	309-693-2525		57
Green Frog Productions Ltd 189 Waterbury Way *TF:* 800-227-1336 ■ *Web:* www.greenfrog.com	Douglasville	GA	30134	770-977-3555	949-3727	514
Green Gateau 330 S Tenth St *Web:* www.greengateau.com	Lincoln	NE	68508	402-477-0330		671
Green Grass Golf Corp 282 Newbridge Rd *Web:* www.greengrassgolf.com	Hicksville	NY	11801	516-935-6722	935-7064	710
Green Harbor Resort 182 Baxter Ave *Web:* redjacketresorts.com	West Yarmouth	MA	02673	508-771-1126		379
Green Haven Correctional Facility 594 Rt 216 *Web:* www.doccs.ny.gov	Stormville	NY	12582	845-221-2711		213
Green Hills Software Inc 30 W Sola St *TF:* 800-765-4733 ■ *Web:* www.ghs.com	Santa Barbara	CA	93101	805-965-6044	965-6343	178-2
Green Idea 950 Page St *Web:* www.greenidea.com	San Francisco	CA	94117	415-863-2157	437-1764	225
Green Lake Conference Ctr W2511 State Rd 23 *Web:* www.glcc.org	Green Lake	WI	54941	920-294-3323	294-3686	205
Green Lake County 492 Hill St *TF:* 800-664-3588 ■ *Web:* www.co.green-lake.wi.us	Green Lake	WI	54941	920-294-4005	294-4009	338
Green Lake Jewelry Works 550 NE Northgate Way *TF:* 888-339-1709 ■ *Web:* www.greenlakejewelry.com	Seattle	WA	98125	206-527-1108		410
Green Lakes State Park 7900 Green Lakes Rd *Web:* parks.ny.gov	Fayetteville	NY	13066	315-637-6111		565
Green Lantern Press 2337 N Milwaukee Ave *Web:* www.sector2337.com	Chicago	IL	60647	773-687-8481		637-2
Green Lawn Fertilizing Inc 1004 Saunders Ln *TF:* 888-581-5296 ■ *Web:* www.greenlawnfertilizing.com	West Chester	PA	19380	888-581-5296		577
Green Leads Holdings LLC 183 Rockingham Rd *Web:* www.green-leads.com	Windham	NH	03087	978-633-3233		195
Green Leaf Press PO Box 880 **Fax Area Code:* 323 ■ *Web:* www.gogreenleaf.com	Alhambra	CA	91802	626-281-7221	221-4334*	637-2
Green Line Hose & Fittings (BC.) Ltd 1477 Derwent Way *TF:* 800-665-5444 ■ *Web:* www.greenlinehose.com	Delta	BC	V3M6N3	604-525-6700		358
Green Lines Transportation Inc 7089 Alliance Rd *TF:* 800-321-6461 ■ *Web:* www.greenlines.net	Malvern	OH	44644	330-863-2111	863-1558	780
Green Mark (Rep R - TN) 533 Cannon House Office Bldg *Web:* www.markgreen.house.gov	Washington	DC	20515	202-225-2811		342-2
Green Mechanical Construction Inc 322 W Main St *TF:* 800-264-6048 ■ *Web:* gmci.com	Glasgow	KY	42141	800-264-6048		189-10
Green Mill Restaurant & Bar 1342 Grand Ave *Web:* www.greenmill.com	Saint Paul	MN	55105	651-203-3101		671
Green Moon Solutions LLC 6841 Elm St Ste 1211 *Web:* www.greenmoonsolutions.com	McLean	VA	22101	703-869-4459	852-7036	225
Green Mountain at Fox Run 262 Fox Ln *TF:* 800-448-8106 ■ *Web:* www.fitwoman.com	Ludlow	VT	05149	802-228-8885	228-8887	706
Green Mountain Credit Union 4 Laurel Hill Dr *Web:* greenmountaincu.com	South Burlington	VT	05403	802-864-6892		219
Green Mountain Energy Co PO Box 25211 *Web:* www.greenmountainenergy.com	Lehigh Valley	PA	18002	512-691-6100		787
Green Mountain Florist Supply Inc (GMFSI) 45 Swift St *TF:* 800-639-7077 ■ *Web:* www.gmfsi.com	South Burlington	VT	05403	802-865-4447	863-8330	293
Green Mountain Inn 18 Main St PO Box 60 *TF:* 800-253-7302 ■ *Web:* greenmountaininn.com	Stowe	VT	05672	802-253-7301	253-5096	379
Green Mountain Post Films PO Box 229 *Web:* www.gmpfilms.com	Turners Falls	MA	01376	413-863-4754		514
Green Mountain Power Corp 163 Acorn Ln *TF:* 888-835-4672 ■ *Web:* greenmountainpower.com	Colchester	VT	05446	888-835-4672		787
Green Mountain Rifle Barrel Co 153 W Main St PO Box 2670 *Web:* www.gmriflebarrel.com	Conway	NH	03818	603-447-1095	447-1099	284
Green Oak Tire Inc 7480 Kensington Rd *Web:* www.greenoaktire.com	Brighton	MI	48116	248-437-1753	437-2038	54
Green Oak Township Historical Society (GOTHS) 10789 Silver Lake Rd *Web:* www.greenoaktownshiphistoricalsociety.org	South Lyon	MI	48178	248-342-0978		637-2
Green Papaya 256 Preston St *Web:* www.greenpapaya.ca	Ottawa	ON	K1R7R5	613-231-8424		671
Green Papaya 3211 Oak Lawn Ave Ste B *Web:* greenpapayavietnamesecuisine.com	Dallas	TX	75219	214-521-4811		671
Green Park Inn 9239 Valley Blvd *Web:* www.greenparkinn.com	Blowing Rock	NC	28605	828-414-9230		379
Green Pastures 811 W Live Oak St *Web:* www.mattiesaustin.com	Austin	TX	78704	512-444-1888		671
Green Pharmaceuticals Inc 591 Constitution Ave Ste A *TF:* 877-766-7378 ■ *Web:* snorestop.com	Camarillo	CA	93012	877-766-7378		231
Green Plains Renewable Energy Inc 450 Regency Pkwy Ste 400 *NASDAQ: GPRE* ■ *Web:* www.gpreinc.com	Omaha	NE	68114	402-884-8700	884-8776	143
Green Pond Animal Care Ctr 165 Green Pond Rd *Web:* greenpondanimalcare.com	Rockaway	NJ	07866	973-784-4640		794
Green Public Affairs and Campaigns 8581 Santa Monica Blvd Ste 304 *Web:* www.greenpaac.com	West Hollywood	CA	90069	310-659-9450		194
Green Ridge State Forest 28700 Headquarters Dr NE *Web:* www.dnr.maryland.gov	Flintstone	MD	21530	301-478-3124		565
Green River Community College 12401 SE 320th St *Web:* www.greenriver.edu	Auburn	WA	98092	253-833-9111	288-3454	162
Green River Correctional Complex 1200 River Rd *Web:* www.corrections.ky.gov	Central City	KY	42330	270-754-5415		213
Green River Lake State Park 179 Pk Office Rd *Web:* parks.ky.gov	Campbellsville	KY	42718	270-465-8255		565
Green River Reservoir State Park 1394 Green River Dam Rd *Web:* www.vtstateparks.com	Hyde Park	VT	05655	802-888-1349		565
Green River State Park PO Box 637 *Web:* utah.com	Green River	UT	84525	435-564-3633		565
Green River State Wildlife Area 375 Game Rd *Web:* www2.illinois.gov	Harmon	IL	61042	815-379-2324		565
Green Room at the Hotel duPont 42 W 11th St *TF:* 800-441-9019 ■ *Web:* www.hoteldupont.com	Wilmington	DE	19801	302-594-3154	594-3108	671
Green Seal 1001 Connecticut Ave NW Ste 827 *Web:* www.greenseal.org	Washington	DC	20036	202-872-6400	872-4324	48-10
Green Seal Environmental Inc 114 State Rd Bldg B *Web:* www.gseenv.com	Sagamore Beach	MA	02562	508-888-6034	888-1506	192
Green Spring Gardens Park 4603 Green Spring Rd *Web:* www.fairfaxcounty.gov	Alexandria	VA	22312	703-642-5173	642-8095	97
Green Tangerine Spa & Salon 238 Patriot Pl *Web:* www.greentangerinespa.com	Foxborough	MA	02035	508-203-9414		77
Green Tape LLC 14143 Denver W Pkwy Ste 100 *Web:* greentape.com	Golden	CO	80401	303-221-1306	484-7980	463
Green Team of San Jose 1333 Oakland Rd *Web:* www.greenteam.com	San Jose	CA	95112	408-282-4400	283-8509	660
Green Technology Group LLC, The 10619 Canterberry Rd *Web:* www.tgtgllc.com	Fairfax Station	VA	22039	202-285-4748		180
Green Thumb Industries 325 W Huron St Ste 412 *Web:* www.gtigrows.com	Chicago	IL	60654	312-471-6720		475
Green Tokai Company Ltd 55 Robert Wright Dr *Web:* www.greentokai.com	Brookville	OH	45309	937-833-5444		604

Name / Address	City	State	ZIP	Phone	Fax	Class
Green Top Sporting Goods Corp PO Box 1015 *Web:* www.greentophuntfish.com	Glen Allen	VA	23060	804-550-2188		711
Green Tortoise Adventure Travel & Hostels 494 Broadway *TF:* 800-867-8647 ■ *Web:* greentortoise.com	San Francisco	CA	94133	415-956-7500	956-4900	760
Green Transfer & Storage Co 10099 N Portland Rd *Web:* greentransfer.com	Portland	OR	97203	503-286-0673		780
Green Tree Event Consultants 35 Storer St *Web:* www.nemadeshows.com	Saco	ME	04072	207-781-2982		149
Green Tree Packing Co 65 Central Ave *Web:* www.greentreepacking.com	Passaic	NJ	07055	973-473-1305		296-26
Green Turtle Bay Inc 263 Green Turtle Bay Dr *Web:* www.greenturtlebay.com	Grand Rivers	KY	42045	270-362-8364		378
Green Valley Consulting Engineers 335 Tesconi Cir. *Web:* www.gvalley.com	Santa Rosa	CA	95401	707-579-0388		256
Green Valley Corp 777 N 1st St 5th Fl *Web:* www.barryswensonbuilder.com	San Jose	CA	95112	408-287-0246	998-1737	187
Green Valley Floral Co 24999 Potter Rd *Web:* greenvalleyfloral.us	Salinas	CA	93908	831-424-7691	424-4473	369
Green Valley Grill 622 Green Valley Rd *Web:* www.greenvalleygrill.com	Greensboro	NC	27408	336-854-2015		671
Green Valley Manufacturing 100 Green Valley Dr *Web:* www.greenvalleyinc.com	Mount Zion	IL	62549	217-864-4125		695
Green Valley Pecan Co 1625 E Sahuarita Rd *TF:* 800-533-5269 ■ *Web:* www.greenvalleypecan.com	Sahuarita	AZ	85629	520-791-2852	791-2853	10-10
Green Valley Ranch Resort Casino & Spa 2300 Paseo Verde Pkwy *Web:* greenvalleyranch.sclv.com	Henderson	NV	89052	702-617-7777		379
Green Valley Recreation Inc 921 W Via Rio Fuerte *TF:* 844-693-2116 ■ *Web:* www.gvrec.org	Green Valley	AZ	85614	520-393-0360		354
Green Valley Seed 7472 Akron Canfield Rd *TF:* 800-535-7882 ■ *Web:* www.greenvalleyseed.com	Canfield	OH	44406	330-533-4353	533-0618	276
Green Valley State Park 1480 130th St *Web:* www.iowadnr.gov	Creston	IA	50801	641-782-5131		565
Green Wave Consulting LLC 4440 Ash Grove Ste A *Web:* greenwavecon.com	Springfield	IL	62711	217-726-7569		261
Greenan, Peffer, Sallander & Lally LLP 2000 Crow Canyon Pl Ste 380 *Web:* www.gpsllp.com	San Ramon	CA	94583	925-866-1000	830-8787	428
Greenbank Mill Associates Inc 500 Greenbank Rd *Web:* www.greenbankmill.org	Wilmington	DE	19808	302-999-9001		50-3
Greenbaum Rowe Smith & Davis LLP 99 Wood Ave S *Web:* www.greenbaumlaw.com	Iselin	NJ	08830	732-549-5600	549-1881	428
Greenbelt Electric Co-opeartive Inc PO Box 948 *TF:* 800-527-3082 ■ *Web:* www.greenbeltelectric.coop	Wellington	TX	79095	806-447-2536		245
Greenbelt Federal Credit Union 112 Centerway *Web:* greenbeltfcu.com	Greenbelt	MD	20770	301-474-5900		219
Greenbelt Park 6565 Greenbelt Rd *Web:* www.nps.gov	Greenbelt	MD	20770	301-344-3948		564
Greenberg & Lieberman LLC 1775 Eye St NW Ste 1150 *Web:* aplegal.com	Washington	DC	20006	202-625-7000	625-7001	445
Greenberg Farrow 44 W 28th St *Web:* www.greenbergfarrow.com	New York	NY	10001	212-725-9530		261
Greenberg Glusker Fields Claman & Machtinger LLP 1900 Avenue of the Stars 21st Fl *Web:* www.greenbergglusker.com	Los Angeles	CA	90067	310-553-3610		428
Greenberg Rosenblatt Kull & Bitsoli PC The Day Bldg 306 Main St Ste 400 *Web:* www.grkb.com	Worcester	MA	01615	508-791-0901	799-2059	2
Greenberg Smoked Turkeys Inc 221 Mcmurrey Dr *Web:* www.gobblegobble.com	Tyler	TX	75702	903-595-0725		619
Greenberry Industrial 2273 NW Professional Dr *Web:* greenberry.com	Corvallis	OR	97330	541-757-8458		610
Greenblatt & Laube Pc 200 N Eighth St *Web:* greenblattlaube.com	Vineland	NJ	08360	856-691-0424	696-1010	445
Greenbriar Animal Hospital 1004 State Rd 13 *Web:* greenbriarah.com	Jacksonville	FL	32259	904-287-5570		794
Greenbriar Animal Hospital LLC 4307 N Green River Rd *Web:* greenbrieranimalhospital.com	Evansville	IN	47715	812-479-0867		794
Greenbriar Inn, The 8735 N Foothills Hwy *TF:* 800-253-1474 ■ *Web:* www.greenbriarinn.com	Boulder	CO	80302	303-440-7979	449-2054	671
Greenbriar Mall 2841 Greenbriar Pkwy SW *Web:* shopgreenbriar.com	Atlanta	GA	30331	404-344-6611		460
Greenbrier Co 1 Centerpointe Dr Ste 200 *NYSE:* GBX ■ *TF:* 800-343-7188 ■ *Web:* www.gbrx.com	Lake Oswego	OR	97035	503-684-7000	684-7553	650
Greenbrier County 200 W Washington St *TF:* 800-833-2068 ■ *Web:* greenbrierwv.com	Lewisburg	WV	24901	304-647-6602		338
Greenbrier Farms Inc 225 Sign Pine Rd *TF:* 800-829-2141 ■ *Web:* www.historicgreenbrierfarms.com	Chesapeake	VA	23322	757-421-2141		323
Greenbrier State Park 21843 National Pk *Web:* www.dnr.maryland.gov	Boonsboro	MD	21713	301-791-4767		565
Greenbrier Valley Medical Ctr 202 Maplewood Ave *Web:* www.gvmc.com	Ronceverte	WV	24970	304-647-4411	647-6010	374-3
Greenbrier, The 300 W Main St *TF:* 800-453-4858 ■ *Web:* www.greenbrier.com	White Sulphur Springs	WV	24986	304-536-1110	536-7854	669
Greenbusch Group Inc 1900 W Nickerson St Ste 201 *TF:* 855-476-2874 ■ *Web:* www.greenbusch.com	Seattle	WA	98119	206-378-0569		196
Greencastle Associates Consulting LLC 627 Swedesford Rd. *Web:* www.greencastleconsulting.com	Malvern	PA	19355	610-640-9958	640-9259	463
GreenChem Industries LLC 222 Clematis St Ste 207 *Web:* www.greenchemindustries.com	West Palm Beach	FL	33401	561-659-2236	659-2237	690
GREENCREST Marketing Inc 120 Northwoods Blvd *Web:* greencrest.com	Columbus	OH	43235	614-885-7921		4
Greencroft Retirement Communities Inc 1721 Greencroft Blvd *Web:* www.greencroft.org	Goshen	IN	46527	574-537-4000		672
Greene & Bradford Inc 3501 Constitution Dr *Web:* www.gnbil.com	Springfield	IL	62711	217-793-8844	793-6227	727
Greene & Roberts LLP 455 Capitol Mall Ste 405 *Web:* greeneroberts.com	Sacramento	CA	95814	916-753-1300	753-1333	41
Greene Consulting Associates LLC Waterstone Bldg 4751 Best Rd Ste 450 *Web:* www.greeneconsults.com	Atlanta	GA	30337	404-324-4600	324-4610	196
Greene Correctional Facility 165 Plank Rd PO Box 8 *Web:* www.doccs.ny.gov	Coxsackie	NY	12051	518-731-2741		213
Greene Correctional Institution 2699 Hwy 903 N PO Box 39 *Web:* www.ncdps.gov	Maury	NC	28554	252-747-3676	747-4432	213
Greene County 411 Main St *TF:* 800-355-2287 ■ *Web:* www.greenegovernment.com	Catskill	NY	12414	518-719-3270	719-3793	338
Greene County 204 N Cutler St *TF:* 800-232-5454 ■ *Web:* www.greenecountytngov.com	Greeneville	TN	37745	423-798-1766		338
Greene County 1034 Silver Dr. *TF:* 800-248-7689 ■ *Web:* www.greenecountyga.gov	Greensboro	GA	30642	706-453-7716	453-9555	338
Greene County 114 N Chestnut St. *Web:* www.co.greene.ia.us	Jefferson	IA	50129	515-386-2516	386-2321	338
Greene County 229 Kingold Blvd *Web:* www.greenecountync.gov	Snow Hill	NC	28580	252-747-3446		338
Greene County 940 N Boonville Ave *Web:* greenecountymo.gov	Springfield	MO	65802	417-868-4055	868-4170	338
Greene County 40 Celt Rd. *Web:* www.greenecountyva.gov	Stanardsville	VA	22973	434-985-5208	985-6723	338
Greene County 35 Green St. *Web:* www.co.greene.oh.us	Xenia	OH	45385	937-562-5006	562-5331	338
Greene County Chamber of Commerce 327 Main St PO Box 248 *TF:* 800-888-3586 ■ *Web:* greenecountychamber.com	Catskill	NY	12414	518-943-4222	943-1700	139
Greene County Convention & Visitors Bureau 1221 Meadowbridge Dr *TF:* 800-733-9109 ■ *Web:* www.greenecountyohio.org	Beavercreek	OH	45434	937-429-9100	429-7726	206
Greene County General Hospital 1185 N 1000 W *TF:* 800-847-9496 ■ *Web:* greenecountyhospital.com	Linton	IN	47441	812-847-9496		363
Greene County Partnership & Chamber of Commerce 115 Academy St *Web:* www.greenecountypartnership.com	Greeneville	TN	37743	423-638-4111	638-5345	139
Greene County Public Library 76 E Market St PO Box 520 *Web:* greenelibrary.info	Xenia	OH	45385	937-352-4000	372-4673	434-3
Greene Espel Law Firm 222 S Ninth St Ste 2200 *Web:* www.greeneespel.com	Minneapolis	MN	55402	612-373-0830	373-0929	445
Greene Hamrick Quinlan & Schermer PA 601 12th St W *Web:* www.manateelegal.com	Bradenton	FL	34205	941-747-1071	745-2800	445
Greene Infuso LLP 3030 S Jones Blvd Ste 101 *Web:* greeneinfusolaw.com	Las Vegas	NV	89146	702-570-6000		41
Greene Law PC 11 Talcott Notch Rd *Web:* greenelawpc.com	Farmington	CT	06032	860-676-1336		41
Greene Lyon Group Inc 100 Cummings Ctr Ste 207P *Web:* www.greenelyon.com	Beverly	MA	01915	978-496-3455	496-3454	192
Greene Memorial Hospital 1141 N Monroe Dr *Web:* ketteringhealth.org	Xenia	OH	45385	937-352-2000		374-3
Greene Metal Products Inc 24500 Capital Blvd	Clinton Township	MI	48036	586-465-6800		697
Greene Prairie Press 516 N Main St *Web:* www.greeneprairiepress.com	Carrollton	IL	62016	217-942-9100		532-2
Greene Realty Group LLC 1722 Harrison Ave NW Ste A *Web:* greenerealty.com	Olympia	WA	98502	360-528-4167		652
Greene Resources 6601 Six Forks Rd *TF:* 800-784-9619 ■ *Web:* www.greeneresources.com	Raleigh	NC	27615	919-862-8602		260
Greene Rubber Company Inc 20 Cross St *Web:* www.greenerubber.com	Woburn	MA	01801	781-937-9909		385
Greene Tweed & Co 2075 Detwiler Rd *Web:* www.gtweed.com	Kulpsville	PA	19443	215-256-9521	256-0189	326
Greenefficient Inc 4602 Deepdale Dr Ste 210 *TF:* 855-713-2973 ■ *Web:* greenefficient.net	Corpus Christi	TX	78413	281-227-5732		104
Greene-Niesen Insurance Agency Inc 6810 University Ave *Web:* greeneniesen.com	Middleton	WI	53562	608-831-3168		390
Greener Cleaner 5312 N Broadway St. *TF:* 855-938-2532 ■ *Web:* www.greenercleaner.net	Chicago	IL	60640	773-271-8350		426
Greenerd Press & Machine Company Inc 41 Crown St PO Box 886 *TF:* 800-877-9110 ■ *Web:* www.greenerd.com	Nashua	NH	03061	603-889-4101	889-7601	456

				Phone	Fax	Class
GreenerU Inc 480 Pleasant St Ste C300 *Web:* www.greeneru.com	Watertown	MA	02472	781-891-3750		192
Greenery Speciality Care 2200 Hill Church-Houston Rd *Web:* greenerycenter.com	Canonsburg	PA	15317	724-745-8000		450
Greeneville Light & Power System PO Box 1690 *TF:* 866-466-1438 ■ *Web:* www.glps.net	Greeneville	TN	37744	423-636-6200		245
Greeneville Sun 121 W Summer St *Web:* www.greenevillesun.com	Greeneville	TN	37743	423-638-4181	638-7348	532-2
Greenfield Area Chamber of Commerce One Courthouse Plz *Web:* www.thegreenfieldchamber.com	Greenfield	IN	46140	414-327-8500		139
Greenfield Banking Co 1920 N State St *Web:* www.gbcbank.com	Greenfield	IN	46140	317-462-1431		70
Greenfield Community College 1 College Dr *Web:* www.gcc.mass.edu	Greenfield	MA	01301	413-775-1837	775-1827	162
Greenfield Public Library 5310 W Layton Ave *Web:* www.greenfieldlibrary.org	Greenfield	WI	53220	414-321-9595	321-8595	434-3
Greenfield Research Inc 347 Edgewood Ave *Web:* www.greenfield-research.com	Greenfield	OH	45123	937-981-7763		34
Greenfield Savings Bank 400 Main St PO Box 1537 *TF:* 888-324-3191 ■ *Web:* www.greenfieldsavings.com	Greenfield	MA	01302	413-774-3191		70
Greenfield Stein & Senior LLP 600 Third Ave *Web:* gss-law.com	New York	NY	10016	212-818-9600	818-1264	41
Greenfield Union School District 1624 Fairview Rd *Web:* www.gfusd.net	Bakersfield	CA	93307	661-837-6000	832-2873	685
Greenfield Village 20900 Oakwood Blvd *TF:* 800-835-5237 ■ *Web:* www.thehenryford.org	Dearborn	MI	48124	313-271-1620	982-6225	520
Greengate Power Corp 237 Eighth Ave SE Ste 350 *Web:* greengatepower.com	Calgary	AB	T2G5C3	403-930-1300	514-0567	612
GreenGeeks LLC 5739 Kanan Rd Ste 300 *TF:* 877-326-7483 ■ *Web:* www.greengeeks.com	Agoura Hills	CA	91301	310-496-8946		225
Greenhaus Inc 2660 1st Ave *Web:* www.greenhaus.agency	San Diego	CA	92103	619-744-4024		7
Greenheart Exchange 746 N La Salle Dr *TF:* 866-224-0061 ■ *Web:* greenheartexchange.org	Chicago	IL	60654	312-944-2544		194
Greenheart Farms Inc 902 Zenon Way *TF:* 800-549-5531 ■ *Web:* www.greenheartfarms.com	Arroyo Grande	CA	93420	805-481-2234	481-7374	10-11
Greenheck Fan Corp 1100 Greenheck Dr PO Box 410 *TF:* 800-355-5354 ■ *Web:* www.greenheck.com	Schofield	WI	54476	715-359-6171	355-2399	18
Greenhill & Company Inc 300 Park Ave 23rd Fl *NYSE: GHL* ■ *Web:* www.greenhill.com	New York	NY	10022	212-389-1500	389-1700	401
Greenhorn Creek Guest Ranch 2116 Greenhorn Ranch Rd *TF:* 800-334-6939 ■ *Web:* www.greenhornranch.com	Quincy	CA	95971	530-283-0930		239
Greenhorn Creek Resort 711 McCauley Ranch Rd *Web:* www.greenhorncreek.com	Angels Camp	CA	95222	209-729-8111		669
Greenhouse Software 18 W 18th St 11th Fl *Web:* www.greenhouse.io	New York	NY	10011	917-780-4130		39
Greenhurst Nursing Ctr 226 Skyler Dr *Web:* greenhurst.net	Charleston	AR	72933	479-965-7373		371
Greening of Detroit 13000 W McNichols *Web:* greeningofdetroit.com	Detroit	MI	48235	313-237-8733	237-8737	196
Greeninglaw PC 12900 Preston Rd Ste 600 *Web:* greeninglaw.com	Dallas	TX	75230	972-934-8900	934-1119	41
GreenLancer.com 615 Griswold St Ste 1020 *TF:* 866-436-1440 ■ *Web:* www.greenlancer.com	Detroit	MI	48226	866-436-1440		256
Greenland (America) Inc 1905 Woodstock Rd Ste 2200 *Web:* www.greenlandamerica.com	Roswell	GA	30075	770-435-1100	435-1200	690
Greenland International Consulting Ltd 120 Hume St *Web:* www.grnland.com	Collingwood	ON	L9Y1V5	705-444-8805		192
Greenleaf Apothecary LLC 10154 Brooks School Rd *Web:* mygreenleafrx.com	Fishers	IN	46037	317-436-8328		237
Greenleaf Book Group LLC (GBG) PO Box 91869 *Web:* www.greenleafbookgroup.com	Austin	TX	78709	512-891-6100	891-6150	637-2
Greenleaf Ctr 2209 Pineview Dr *Web:* www.greenleafhospital.com	Valdosta	GA	31602	229-671-6700		726
Greenleaf Inc 588 San Ramon Valley Blvd *Web:* www.greenleafsf.com	San Francisco	CA	94124	415-647-2991		345
Greenleaf Media 1917 Winnebago St *Web:* greenleafmedia.com	Madison	WI	53704	608-240-9611	240-9612	177
Greenleaf Nursery Co 28406 Hwy 82 **Fax Area Code: 800* ■ *TF:* 800-331-2982 ■ *Web:* www.greenleafnursery.com	Park Hill	OK	74451	918-457-5172	407-5550*	369
Greenleaf State Park Hwy 10 S *Web:* www.travelok.com	Braggs	OK	74423	918-487-5196	487-5406	565
Greenlee County 223 Fifth St PO Box 908 *Web:* www.co.greenlee.az.us	Clifton	AZ	85533	928-865-3872	865-5358	338
Greenlee Textron 1390 Aspen Way *TF:* 800-642-2155 ■ *Web:* www.greenlee.com	Vista	CA	92081	760-598-8900		253
Greenline Emeritus Consulting 29 S Lasalle St Ste 333 *Web:* www.greenlineemeritus.com	Chicago	IL	60603	312-436-1883	277-2550	463
Greenline Equipment 14750 S Pony Express Rd *TF:* 888-201-5500 ■ *Web:* www.stotzequipment.com	Bluffdale	UT	84065	801-966-4231	966-4313	274
GreenLine Foods Inc 4575 W Main St PO Box 727 *Web:* www.greenlinefoods.com	Guadalupe	CA	93434	419-353-2326		345
GreenLine Paper Company Inc 631 S Pine St *TF:* 800-641-1117 ■ *Web:* greenlinepaper.com	York	PA	17403	717-845-8697	846-3806	553
Greenlining Institute, The 360 14th St 2nd Fl *Web:* greenlining.org	Oakland	CA	94612	510-926-4001	926-4010	765
GreenMan Technologies Inc 7 Kimball Ln Bldg A *TF:* 866-994-7697 ■ *Web:* www.americanpowergroupinc.com	Lynnfield	MA	01940	781-224-2411		660
Greenman-Pedersen Inc 325 W Main St *Web:* www.gpinet.com	Babylon	NY	11702	631-587-5060	587-5029	261
Greenpages Inc 33 Badgers Island W *TF:* 888-687-4876 ■ *Web:* www.greenpages.com	Kittery	ME	03904	207-439-7310	439-7334	180
Greenpath Inc 36500 Corporate Dr *TF:* 800-550-1961 ■ *Web:* www.greenpath.com	Farmington Hills	MI	48331	248-553-5400		810
Greenpeace Canada 33 Cecil St *TF:* 800-320-7183 ■ *Web:* www.greenpeace.org	Toronto	ON	M5T1N1	416-597-8408		48-13
Greenpoint Metals Inc 301 Shotwell Dr *Web:* www.greenpointmetals.com	Franklin	OH	45005	937-743-4075		492
GreenPointe Holdings LLC 7807 Baymeadows Rd E Ste 205 *Web:* www.greenpointellc.com	Jacksonville	FL	32256	904-996-2485		360-3
Greenray Industries Inc 840 W Church Rd *Web:* www.greenrayindustries.com	Mechanicsburg	PA	17055	717-766-0223	790-9509	248
Greens Fort Mason Ctr Bldg A *Web:* greensrestaurant.com	San Francisco	CA	94123	415-771-6222		671
Greensboro Area Convention & Visitors Bureau 2200 Pinecroft Rd Ste 200 *TF:* 800-344-2282 ■ *Web:* visitgreensboronc.com	Greensboro	NC	27407	336-274-2282	230-1183	206
Greensboro Area Health Education Ctr 1200 N Elm St *Web:* www.gahec.org	Greensboro	NC	27401	336-832-8025		196
Greensboro Children's Museum 220 N Church St *Web:* www.gcmuseum.com	Greensboro	NC	27401	336-574-2898	574-3810	521
Greensboro City Hall 300 W Washington St PO Box 3136 *Web:* www.greensboro-nc.gov	Greensboro	NC	27401	336-373-2489		337
Greensboro Coliseum Complex 1921 W Lee St *Web:* www.greensborocoliseum.com	Greensboro	NC	27403	336-373-7400	373-2170	572
Greensboro College 815 W Market St *TF:* 800-346-8226 ■ *Web:* greensboro.edu	Greensboro	NC	27401	336-272-7102	378-0154	166
Greensboro Public Library 219 N Church St *Web:* www.greensboro-nc.gov	Greensboro	NC	27401	336-373-2471		434-3
Greensboro Science Ctr 4301 Lawndale Dr *Web:* www.greensboroscience.org	Greensboro	NC	27455	336-288-3769	288-2531	520
Greensboro Symphony Orchestra 200 N Davie St Ste 301 *Web:* www.greensborosymphony.org	Greensboro	NC	27401	336-335-5456	335-5580	573-3
Greenscape Pump Services Inc 1425 Whitlock Ln Ste 108 *TF:* 877-401-4774 ■ *Web:* greenscapepump.com	Carrollton	TX	75006	972-446-0037		612
Greenscapes Home & Garden Products Inc 200 Union Grove Rd SE *Web:* greenscapesinc.net	Calhoun	GA	30701	706-602-9042		429
GreenSeed Contract Packaging 1025 Paramount Pkwy *Web:* greenseedcp.com	Batavia	IL	60510	630-761-8544		393
Greensfelder, Hemker & Gale PC 10 S Broadway St Ste 2000 *Web:* www.greensfelder.com	Saint Louis	MO	63102	314-241-9090	241-8624	41
GreenSky Trade Credit LLC 1797 NE Expy *TF:* 866-936-0602	Atlanta	GA	30329	866-936-0602		224
GreensLedge Group LLC, The 399 Park Ave 37th Fl *Web:* www.greensledge.com	New York	NY	10022	212-792-5270		70
Greenspan Humphrey Lavine Barristers 15 Bedford Rd *Web:* www.15bedford.com	Toronto	ON	M5R2J7	416-868-1755		445
Greenspoint Mall 12300 IH-45 N Fwy *Web:* www.greenspointmall.com	Houston	TX	77060	281-875-4201		460
Greenspring Associates Inc 100 Painters Mill Rd Ste 700 *Web:* www.greenspringassociates.com	Owings Mills	MD	21117	410-363-2725		792
Greenspring Center for Lifelong Learning 10807 Tony Dr *Web:* www.marylandmontessori.org	Lutherville Timonium	MD	21093	410-321-8555		167-3
Greenspun Media Group 2275 Corporate Cir Ste 300 *Web:* gmgvegas.com	Henderson	NV	89074	702-990-2550		532-3
Greenstar Environmental Solutions LLC 6 Gellatly Dr *Web:* www.greenstarsolutions.com	Wappingers Falls	NY	12590	845-223-9944		196
Greenstein Delorme & Luchs PC 1620 L St NW Ste 900 *Web:* gdllaw.com	Washington	DC	20036	202-452-1400	452-1410	41
Greenstein Rogoff Olsen & Company LLP 39159 Paseo Padre Pkwy Ste 315 *Web:* www.groco.com	Fremont	CA	94538	510-797-8661		2
Greenstone Farm Credit Services Aca 3515 West Rd *TF:* 800-444-3276 ■ *Web:* www.greenstonefcs.com	East Lansing	MI	48823	800-968-0061		216
Greensville Correctional Ctr 901 Corrections Way *Web:* vadoc.virginia.gov	Jarratt	VA	23870	434-535-7000		213

Name / Address	City	State	ZIP	Phone	Fax	Class
Greensville County 201 Uriah Branch Way *Web:* www.greensvillecountyva.gov	Emporia	VA	23847	434-348-4215	348-4020	338
Greentec 95 Struck Ct *TF:* 888-858-1515 ■ *Web:* www.greentec.com	Cambridge	ON	N1R8L2	519-624-3300		660
Green-Tek Inc 3708 Enterprise Dr *TF:* 800-747-6440 ■ *Web:* green-tek.com	Janesville	WI	53546	608-754-7336		601
GreenTree Financial Group Inc 7951 SW Sixth St Ste 216 *Web:* gtfinancial.com	Plantation	FL	33324	954-424-2345		463
Greentree Group Inc, The 1360 Technology Ct Ste 100 *Web:* www.greentreegroup.com	Dayton	OH	45430	937-490-5500		463
Greenup County 301 Main St *Web:* greenupcountyclerk.com	Greenup	KY	41144	606-473-7394	473-5354	338
Greenview Data Inc 8178 Jackson Rd *TF:* 800-458-3348 ■ *Web:* www.greenviewdata.com	Ann Arbor	MI	48103	734-426-7500		196
Greenville Advocate, The PO Box 507 *Web:* www.greenvilleadvocate.com	Greenville	AL	36037	334-382-3111	382-7104	532-4
Greenville Area Chamber of Commerce 1 Depot Sq *Web:* www.greenvillealchamber.com	Greenville	AL	36037	334-382-3251		139
Greenville Business Magazine 303 Haywood Rd *Web:* www.greenvillebusinessmag.com	Greenville	SC	29607	864-271-1105		457-5
Greenville City Hall 206 S Main St *TF:* 800-829-4477 ■ *Web:* www.greenvillesc.gov	Greenville	SC	29601	864-232-2273		337
Greenville College 315 E College Ave *TF:* 800-345-4440 ■ *Web:* www.greenville.edu	Greenville	IL	62246	618-664-7100	664-9841	166
Greenville County 305 E N St *Web:* www.greenvillecounty.org	Greenville	SC	29601	864-467-8551	467-8540	338
Greenville County Library System 25 Heritage Green Pl *Web:* www.greenvillelibrary.org	Greenville	SC	29601	864-242-5000	235-8375	434-3
Greenville County Museum of Art 420 College St *Web:* www.gcma.org	Greenville	SC	29601	864-271-7570		520
Greenville Financial Consultants Inc 269 Main St *TF:* 800-808-7091 ■ *Web:* securewithgfc.com	Greenville	PA	16125	800-808-7091		390
Greenville Hospital System (GHS) 701 Grove Rd *Web:* www.ghs.org	Greenville	SC	29605	864-455-8976		353
Greenville Library 1 Lou Finney Ln *Web:* www.ci.greenville.tx.us	Greenville	TX	75401	903-457-2992	457-2961	434-3
Greenville Little Theatre 444 College St *Web:* www.greenvilletheatre.org	Greenville	SC	29601	864-233-6238		572
Greenville Museum of Art 802 S Evans St *Web:* www.gmoa.org	Greenville	NC	27834	252-758-1946	758-7989	520
Greenville News 305 S Main St *TF:* 800-800-5116 ■ *Web:* www.greenvilleonline.com	Greenville	SC	29601	864-298-4100	298-4395	532-2
Greenville Symphony Orchestra 200 S Main St *Web:* www.greenvillesymphony.org	Greenville	SC	29601	864-232-0344	467-3113	573-3
Greenville Technical College *Brashier* 1830 W Georgia Rd *Web:* www.gvltec.edu	Simpsonville	SC	29680	864-250-7950		162
Greenville Tool & Die Co 1215 S Lafayette St *Web:* www.gtd.com	Greenville	MI	48838	616-754-5693	754-5500	757
Greenville Transformer Co 1807 Church St *Web:* greenvilletransformer.com	Greenville	TX	75401	903-455-1610		767
Greenville Zoo 150 Cleveland Pk Dr *Web:* www.greenvillezoo.com	Greenville	SC	29601	864-467-4300	467-4314	823
Greenville-Muhlenberg Chamber of Commerce 100 E Main Cross *Web:* www.greatermuhlenberg.com	Greenville	KY	42345	270-338-5422		139
Greenville-Pitt County Chamber of Commerce 302 S Greene St *Web:* www.greenvillenc.org	Greenville	NC	27834	252-752-4101	752-5934	139
Greenville-Pitt County Convention & Visitors Bureau (GPCCVB) 417 Cotanche St Ste 100 *TF:* 800-537-5564 ■ *Web:* visitgreenvillenc.com	Greenville	NC	27858	252-329-4200	329-4205	206
Greenville-Spartanburg Airport (GSP) 2000 GSP Dr Ste 1 *TF:* 800-331-1212 ■ *Web:* gspairport.com	Greer	SC	29651	864-877-7426	848-6225	27
Greenvity Communications Inc 2150 Trade Zone Blvd Ste 203 *Web:* www.greenvity.com	San Jose	CA	95131	408-935-9370	273-6597	201
Greenwald Industries 212 Middlesex Ave *TF:* 800-221-0982 ■ *Web:* greenwaldindustries.com	Chester	CT	06412	860-526-0800	526-4205	495
Greenway Enterprises Inc PO Box 5553 *Web:* greenwayent.com	Helena	MT	59604	406-458-9411	458-6516	186
Greenway Ford Inc 9001 E Colonial Dr *TF:* 888-832-6125 ■ *Web:* www.greenwayford.com	Orlando	FL	32817	407-275-3200		57
Greenway Print Solutions 5425 E Bell Rd Ste 120 *Web:* www.greenwayprintsolutions.com	Scottsdale	AZ	85254	602-482-1100	482-1127	627
Greenway Station 1650 Deming Way *Web:* www.reddevelopment.com	Middleton	WI	53562	608-824-9111		460
Greenwell Chisholm Printing Co 420 E Parrish Ave *TF:* 800-844-1876 ■ *Web:* gc1919.com	Owensboro	KY	42303	270-684-3267		627
Greenwell Foundation Inc 25450 Rosedale Manor Ln PO Box 198 *Web:* greenwellfoundation.org	Hollywood	MD	20636	301-373-9775		565
Greenwich Associates LLC 6 High Ridge Pk *TF:* 800-704-1027 ■ *Web:* www.greenwich.com	Stamford	CT	06905	203-629-1200	629-1229	194
Greenwich Chamber of Commerce 45 E Putnam Ave Ste 121 *Web:* www.greenwichchamber.com	Greenwich	CT	06830	203-869-3500	869-3502	139
Greenwich Historical Society 47 Strickland Rd *Web:* www.hstg.org	Cos Cob	CT	06807	203-869-6899	861-9720	50-3
Greenwich Hospital 5 Perryridge Rd *TF:* 800-657-8355 ■ *Web:* www.greenwichhospital.org	Greenwich	CT	06830	203-863-3000	863-3845	374-3
Greenwich Hotel, The 377 Greenwich St *Web:* www.thegreenwichhotel.com	New York	NY	10013	212-941-8900		378
Greenwich Symphony Orchestra PO Box 35 *Web:* www.greenwichsymphony.org	Greenwich	CT	06836	203-869-2664		573-3
Greenwood Chamber of Commerce 110 Phoenix St *Web:* www.greenwoodscchamber.org	Greenwood	SC	29646	864-223-8431	229-9785	139
Greenwood Communities & Resorts Inc 104 Maxwell Ave *Web:* www.greenwoodcr.com	Greenwood	SC	29646	864-941-4044		653
Greenwood Consulting Group 1150 Junonia St *Web:* www.g-jgreenwood.com	Sanibel	FL	33957	239-395-9446		393
Greenwood County 311 N Main St *Web:* www.greenwoodcounty.org	Eureka	KS	67045	620-583-8121	583-8124	338
Greenwood County 600 Monument St *Web:* www.greenwoodsc.gov	Greenwood	SC	29646	864-942-8500	942-8566	338
Greenwood Cultural Ctr 322 N Greenwood Ave *Web:* www.greenwoodculturalcenter.com	Tulsa	OK	74120	918-596-1020		50-2
Greenwood Furnace State Park 15795 Greenwood Rd *Web:* www.dcnr.pa.gov	Huntingdon	PA	16652	814-667-1800		565
Greenwood House 53 Walter St *Web:* www.greenwoodhouse.org	Ewing	NJ	08628	609-883-5391		371
GreenWood Inc 160 Milestone Way Ste A *Web:* www.gwood.com	Greenville	SC	29615	864-244-9669	244-4718	186
Greenwood King Properties 2 Inc 1616 S Voss Rd Ste 900 *Web:* www.greenwoodking.com	Houston	TX	77057	713-784-0888		196
Greenwood Leflore Hospital 1401 River Rd *Web:* glh.org	Greenwood	MS	38930	662-459-7000		374-3
Greenwood Mills Inc 300 Morgan Ave *Web:* www.greenwoodmills.com	Greenwood	SC	29646	864-227-2121		745-1
Greenwood Municipal Federal Credit Union 617 Durst Ave E *Web:* gm-fcu.org	Greenwood	SC	29649	864-229-6177		219
Greenwood Plantation 6838 Highland Rd *Web:* www.greenwoodplantation.com	Saint Francisville	LA	70775	225-655-4475		50-3
Greenwood Racing Inc 3001 St Rd *TF:* 888-238-2946 ■ *Web:* www.parxracing.com	Bensalem	PA	19020	215-639-9000		360-2
Greenwood School 14 Greenwood Ln *Web:* www.greenwood.org	Putney	VT	05346	802-387-4545		622
Greenwood School District 50 1855 Calhoun Rd *TF:* 888-260-9430 ■ *Web:* www.gwd50.org	Greenwood	SC	29648	864-941-5400	941-5427	685
Greenwood Village South 295 Village Ln *Web:* www.greenwoodvillagesouth.com	Greenwood	IN	46143	317-881-2591		672
Greenwood-Leflore County Chamber of Commerce 402 Hwy 82 *Web:* www.greenwoodms.com	Greenwood	MS	38930	662-453-4152		139
Greenwood-Leflore Public Library 405 W Washington St *Web:* glpls.com	Greenwood	MS	38930	662-453-3634		434-3
Greer & Associates Inc 1271 No Stuart Place Rd *Web:* greerins.com	Harlingen	TX	78552	956-425-7776	425-7778	390
Greer Capital Advisors LLC 4 Office Park Cir Ste 316 *Web:* www.greercap.com	Birmingham	AL	35209	205-445-1011	445-1013	792
Greer County 129 N Pennsylvania Ave	Mangum	OK	73554	580-782-2329	782-3803	338
Greer Galloway Group Inc, The 973 Crawford Dr *Web:* greergalloway.com	Peterborough	ON	K9J3X1	705-743-5780	743-9592	256
Greer Group Inc, The 3109 Charles B Root Wynd *Web:* www.thegreergroup.com	Raleigh	NC	27612	919-571-0051	571-7450	260
Greer Herz & Adams LLP 2525 S Shore Blvd Ste 203 *Web:* www.greerherz.com	League City	TX	77573	281-480-5278		428
Greer Industries Inc 2521 E Loop 820 N *Web:* www.greerindustriesinc.com	Fort Worth	TX	76117	817-222-1414	222-1075	757
Greer Steel Co 624 Blvd **Fax Area Code:* 330 ■ *TF:* 800-388-2868 ■ *Web:* www.greersteel.com	Dover	OH	44622	800-388-2868	343-1700*	723
Greer Tank Inc 2921 International Airport Rd *TF:* 800-770-8265 ■ *Web:* www.greertank.com	Anchorage	AK	99502	907-243-2455		480
Greeters of Hawaii Ltd 300 Rodgers Blvd *TF:* 800-366-8559 ■ *Web:* www.greetersofhawaii.com	Honolulu	HI	96819	808-836-0161		292
Greeting Card Assn (GCA) 1444 I St NW Ste 700 *Web:* www.greetingcard.org	Washington	DC	20005	202-216-9627	216-9646	49-16
Grefe & Sidney PLC 500 E Ct Ave Ste 200 *Web:* www.grefesidney.com	Des Moines	IA	50309	515-245-4300	245-4452	445
Greg Kofford Books PO Box 1362 *Web:* gregkofford.com	Draper	UT	84020	801-572-7417		637-2
Greg Norman Collection 134 W 37th St 4th Fl *Web:* gregnormancollection.com	New York	NY	10018	646-840-5200		155-12
Greg'S Heating & Air Cond Inc 2474 SW Ferry St *Web:* gregsheating.com	Albany	OR	97322	541-926-8950		189-10
Gregath Publishing Co PO Box 505 *TF:* 800-955-5232 ■ *Web:* www.gregathcompany.com	Wyandotte	OK	74370	918-542-4148		637-2

Name / Address	City	State	ZIP	Phone	Fax	Class
Gregg Bruce Auto and Performance 601 High St *Web:* www.greggbruceauto.com	Baldwin City	KS	66006	785-594-4088		62-7
Gregg County 101 E Methvin Ste 559 *Web:* www.greggcountytexas.us	Longview	TX	75601	903-236-8400	753-3560	338
Gregg Distributors Ltd 16215-118 Ave *TF:* 800-545-9379 ■ *Web:* www.greggdistributors.ca	Edmonton	AB	T5V1C7	780-447-3447		652
Gregg Engineering Inc 403 Julie Rivers Dr *Web:* www.greggeng.com	Sugar Land	TX	77478	281-494-8100		177
Gregg Industrial Insulators Inc 201 Estes Dr *Web:* www.greggindustrialinsulators.com	Longview	TX	75602	903-757-5754	757-8864	155-5
Gregg Investigations Inc 500 E Milwaukee St *TF:* 800-866-1976 ■ *Web:* gregginvestigations.com	Janesville	WI	53545	800-866-1976		400
Gregg Ruth & Co 22809 Pacific Coast Hwy *Web:* www.greggruth.com	Malibu	CA	90265	310-456-1888		410
Gregg's Greenlake Cycle 7007 Woodlawn Ave NE *Web:* www.greggscycles.com	Seattle	WA	98115	206-523-1822		711
Gregor Jonsson Inc 13822 W Laurel Dr *Web:* jonsson.com	Lake Forest	IL	60045	847-247-4200	247-4272	298
Gregor Technologies LLC 529 Technology Park Dr *Web:* www.gregortech.com	Torrington	CT	06790	860-482-2569	482-4523	454
Gregory & Associates PLLC 14 E Tabb St *Web:* www.gregory-cpas.com	Petersburg	VA	23803	804-733-4511	733-0098	2
Gregory & Swapp PLLC 9980 S 300 W Ste 400 *Web:* craigswapp.com	Sandy	UT	84070	801-990-1919		41
Gregory Electric Company Inc 2124 College St *TF:* 877-432-4968 ■ *Web:* www.gregoryelectric.com	Columbia	SC	29205	803-748-1122	748-1102	189-4
Gregory J. Cannata & Associates LLP 60 E 42nd St Ste 932 *Web:* cannatalaw.com	New York	NY	10165	212-553-9205		41
Gregory Logistics Inc 2844 Fair St	Poplar Bluff	MO	63901	573-785-1088		57
Gregory Poole Equipment Co 4807 Beryl Rd PO Box 469 *TF:* 800-451-7278 ■ *Web:* www.gregorypoole.com	Raleigh	NC	27606	919-828-0641		386
Gregory Welteroth Advertising Inc 356 Laurens Rd *TF:* 866-294-5765 ■ *Web:* www.gwa-inc.com	Montoursville	PA	17754	570-433-3366		5
Gregory Wood Products Inc 2800 Woodtech Dr	Newton	NC	28658	704-462-0001		683
Gregory's Foods Inc 1301 Trapp Rd *Web:* www.gregorysfoods.com	Eagan	MN	55121	651-454-0277	454-2254	297-11
Gregory, Sharer & Stuart PA 100 Second Ave S Ste 600 *Web:* gsscpa.com	Saint Petersburg	FL	33701	727-821-6161		2
Gregs Japanese Auto Parts & Service 8301 S 216th St *Web:* www.gregs.com	Federal Way	WA	98003	253-815-1500		57
Gregstrom Corp 64 Holton St *Web:* www.gregstrom.com	Woburn	MA	01801	781-935-6600	935-4905	602
Greibo Entertainment 8 Market Pl Ste 200 *Web:* www.greibo.com	Baltimore	MD	21202	410-244-8861	244-8862	514
Greif Inc 425 Winter Rd *NYSE:* GEF ■ *TF:* 877-781-9797 ■ *Web:* www.greif.com	Delaware	OH	43015	877-781-9797		198
Greiner Construction Inc 121 S 8th St Ste 1200 *Web:* www.greinerconstruction.com	Minneapolis	MN	55402	612-338-1696	338-1892	186
Gremada Industries Inc 825 28th St SW Unit E *Web:* www.gremada.com	Fargo	ND	58103	701-356-0814		757
Gremarco Industries Inc 131 E Main St *Web:* www.gremarco.com	West Brookfield	MA	01585	508-867-5244	867-5747	18
Grenada *Embassy* 1701 New Hampshire Ave NW *Web:* www.grenadaembassyusa.org	Washington	DC	20009	202-265-2561	265-2468	257
Grenada Career & Technical Ctr 2035 Jackson Ave *Web:* www.gsd.k12.ms.us	Grenada	MS	38901	662-226-5969		242
Grenald Waldron Associates 260 Haverford Ave *Web:* www.gwalighting.com	Narberth	PA	19072	610-667-6330		393
Grenelefe Golf & Tennis Resort 3271 Camelot Dr *Web:* www.thelefe.com	Haines City	FL	33844	863-422-7511		669
Greno Industries Inc 2820 Amsterdam Rd *TF:* 800-721-5833 ■ *Web:* www.greno.com	Scotia	NY	12302	518-393-4195		454
Grenzebach Corp 10 Herring Rd *Web:* www.grenzebach.com	Newnan	GA	30265	770-253-4980	253-5189	386
Grenzebach Glier & Associates Inc 401 N Michigan Ave Ste 2800 *TF:* 800-222-9233 ■ *Web:* www.grenzebachglier.com	Chicago	IL	60611	312-372-4040	589-6358	317
Gresham Area Chamber of Commerce 701 NE Hood Ave *TF:* 800-572-0011 ■ *Web:* www.greshamchamber.org	Gresham	OR	97030	503-665-1131	666-1041	139
Gresham Driving Aids Inc 30800 Wixom Rd *TF:* 800-521-8930 ■ *Web:* greshamdrivingaids.com	Wixom	MI	48393	248-624-1533	624-6358	477
Gresham Petroleum Co 415 Pershing Ave PO Box 690 *TF:* 800-748-8934 ■ *Web:* www.greshampetroleum.com	Indianola	MS	38751	662-884-5000		581
Gresham Smith & Partners 511 Union St Ste 1400 *Web:* www.greshamsmith.com	Nashville	TN	37201	615-770-8100		261
Gresham Transfer Inc 24001 NE Sandy Blvd *TF:* 888-444-7902 ■ *Web:* www.greshamtransfer.com	Wood Village	OR	97060	503-255-7900	255-9245	780
Gressco Ltd 328 Moravian Valley Rd *TF:* 800-345-3480 ■ *Web:* gresscoltd.com	Waunakee	WI	53597	608-849-6300		321
Gresslin Information Ctr 1899 Reddington Rd *Web:* gresslin.xenia.us	Newark	OH	43055	740-522-3793		167-3
Grey Bruce Health Services 1800 Eigth St E PO Box 1800 *Web:* www.gbhs.on.ca	Owen Sound	ON	N4K6M9	519-376-2121		374-2
Grey Group 200 Fifth Ave *Web:* www.grey.com	New York	NY	10010	212-546-2000	546-1495	4
Grey House Publishing 4919 Rt 22 PO Box 56 *TF:* 800-562-2139 ■ *Web:* greyhouse.com	Amenia	NY	12501	518-789-8700	789-0556	637-2
Grey Law of Ventura County Inc 3585 Maple St Ste 126 *Web:* www.greylaw.us	Ventura	CA	93003	805-658-2266		428
Grey Matter Group Inc 131 Division Ave S Ste 300 *Web:* greymattergroup.com	Grand Rapids	MI	49503	616-458-8750		7
Grey Moss Inn 19010 Scenic Loop Rd *Web:* www.grey-moss-inn.com	Helotes	TX	78023	210-695-8301	695-3237	671
Greybrook Capital Inc 890 Yonge St 7th Fl *Web:* www.greybrook.com	Toronto	ON	M4W3P4	416-322-9700		528
GreyCastle Security LLC 500 Federal St Ste 540 *TF:* 800-403-8350 ■ *Web:* www.greycastlesecurity.com	Troy	NY	12180	518-274-7233		196
Greycliff Prairie Dog Town State Park 2300 Lake Elmo Dr *Web:* stateparks.mt.gov	Billings	MT	59105	406-247-2940		565
Greycroft Partners LLC 292 Madison Ave *Web:* www.greycroft.com	New York	NY	10017	212-756-3508	832-0117	401
Greyfield Inn 4 N Second St Ste 300 *TF:* 866-401-8581 ■ *Web:* greyfieldinn.com	Fernandina Beach	FL	32034	904-261-6408		379
GREYHAWK 2000 Midlantic Dr Ste 210 *TF:* 888-280-4295 ■ *Web:* www.greyhawk.com	Mount Laurel	NJ	08054	516-921-1900	921-5649	194
Greyhound Canada Transportation Corp 1111 International Blvd Ste 700 *TF:* 800-661-8747 ■ *Web:* www.greyhound.ca	Burlington	ON	L7L6W1	800-661-8747		107
Greyhound Friends Inc 167 Saddle Hill Rd *Web:* www.greyhoundfds.org	Hopkinton	MA	01748	508-435-5969		48-3
Greyhound Hall of Fame 407 S Buckeye Ave *TF:* 800-932-7881 ■ *Web:* greyhoundhalloffame.com	Abilene	KS	67410	785-263-3000		522
Greylock Federal Credit Union 150 W St *TF:* 800-207-5555 ■ *Web:* www.greylock.org	Pittsfield	MA	01201	413-236-4000	443-0292	219
Greystar Development & Construction LP 750 Bering Dr Ste 300 *Web:* www.greystar.com	Houston	TX	77057	713-535-9512	966-5065	225
Greystar Electronics Inc 215 N Central Ave *Web:* www.greystarelectronics.com	Duluth	MN	55807	218-624-0617	624-8012	22
Greyston Bakery Inc 104 Alexander St *TF:* 800-289-2253 ■ *Web:* greyston.org	Yonkers	NY	10701	914-375-1510	375-1514	296-1
Greystone Construction Co 500 S Marschall Rd Ste 300 *TF:* 888-742-6837 ■ *Web:* www.greystoneconstruction.com	Shakopee	MN	55379	952-496-2227		186
Greystone Healthcare Network 4042 Park Oaks Blvd Ste 300 *Web:* greystonehealth.com	Tampa	FL	33610	813-635-9500		196
Greystone of Lincoln Inc 7 Wellington Rd *TF:* 800-446-1761 ■ *Web:* greyst.com	Lincoln	RI	02865	401-333-0444	334-5745	621
Greystone Park Psychiatric Hospital 59 Koch Ave *Web:* www.nj.gov	Morris Plains	NJ	07950	973-538-1800		374-5
Greystone Power Corp 4040 Bankhead Hwy *TF:* 866-473-9786 ■ *Web:* www.greystonepower.com	Douglasville	GA	30134	770-942-6576	489-0940	245
Greystone Steakhouse 658 Fifth Ave *Web:* www.greystonesteakhouse.com	San Diego	CA	92101	619-232-0225	233-3606	671
GRFI Ltd 400 E Randolph St Ste 700 *TF:* 888-856-5161 ■ *Web:* www.grfiltd.com	Chicago	IL	60601	888-856-5161		466
Grid Dynamics Consulting Services Inc 5000 Executive Pkwy Ste 520 *Web:* www.griddynamics.com	San Ramon	CA	94583	650-523-5000		225
Grid One Solutions LLC 700 Turner Way Ste 205 *TF:* 800-606-7981 ■ *Web:* www.gridonesolutions.com	Aston	PA	19014	800-606-7981		393
Grid4 Communications Inc 2107 Crooks Rd *Web:* www.grid4.com	Troy	MI	48084	248-244-8100		387
Gridley Country Ford-mercury 1709 State Hwy 99 *Web:* gridleycountryford.com	Gridley	CA	95948	530-846-4724		57
Gridley Ward & Hamilton PC 635 25th St *Web:* yourinjuryattorneys.net	Ogden	UT	84401	801-621-3317		532-3
GridPoint Inc 2801 Clarendon Blvd Ste 100 *Web:* www.gridpoint.com	Arlington	VA	22201	703-667-7000	667-7001	787
Grier School 2522 Grier Rd PO Box 308 *Web:* www.grier.org	Tyrone	PA	16686	814-684-3000	684-2275	622
Grier-Musser Museum 403 S Bonnie Brae St *Web:* griermussermuseum.org	Los Angeles	CA	90057	213-413-1814		520
Gries Financial LLC 1801 E Ninth St Ste 1600 *Web:* gries.com	Cleveland	OH	44114	216-861-1148		194
Gries Seed Farms Inc 2348 N 5th St *TF:* 800-472-4797 ■ *Web:* seedtoday.com	Fremont	OH	43420	419-332-5571		694
Grieve Corp, The 500 Hart Rd *Web:* www.grievecorp.com	Round Lake	IL	60073	847-546-8225		591
Griffel Dorshow & Johnson Chartered Attorneys at Law 2000 Plymouth Rd Ste 222 *Web:* www.612law3333.com	Minnetonka	MN	55305	612-529-3333		428

Name	Address	City	State	ZIP	Phone	Fax	Class	Notes
Griffin & Assn	119 Dartmouth Dr SE	Albuquerque	NM	87106	505-764-4444	764-8636	636	Web: sunny505.com
Griffin Care LLC	80 Manheim Ave	Bridgeton	NJ	08302	856-455-6870		475	TF: 800-366-6870 ■ Web: www.griffincare.com
Griffin Communitcations Group	3101 Nasa Pkwy Ste L	Seabrook	TX	77586	281-335-0200		463	Web: www.griffincg.com
Griffin Consulting	1625 Glenwood Ave	Raleigh	NC	27608	919-291-0019		179	Web: www.phillipgriffin.com
Griffin Filters	106 Metropolitan Park Dr	Liverpool	NY	13088	315-451-5300	451-2338	18	Web: www.griffinfilters.com
Griffin Frey PLLC	900 W Ave Ste 201	Austin	TX	78701	512-271-3800		41	Web: griffinfrey.com
Griffin Gear Inc	131 Railroad St	Roebuck	SC	29376	864-576-6495		744	Web: www.griffingear.com
Griffin Group LLC	4 Rebelo Ln Ste D	Novato	CA	94947	415-892-4569	898-1973	463	Web: www.tgg.us.com
Griffin Hospital	130 Div St	Derby	CT	06418	203-735-7421	732-7569	374-3	Web: www.griffinhealth.org
Griffin Lumber Co	1284 Charity Hwy	Woolwine	VA	24185	276-930-2727		683	Web: www.griffithlumber.net
Griffin Memorial Hospital	900 E Main St	Norman	OK	73071	405-573-6623		374-5	TF: 800-955-3468 ■ Web: ok.gov
Griffin Pipe Products Company LLC	1011 Warrenville Rd	Lisle	IL	60532	630-719-6500		595	Web: uspipe.com
Griffin Publishing Group	18022 Cowan	Irvine	CA	92614	949-263-3733		626	
Griffin Ranches Inc	9490 W County 19th St	Somerton	AZ	85350	928-627-8809		10-11	
Griffin Thermal Products	100 Hurricane Creek Rd	Piedmont	SC	29673	800-722-3723	845-5001*	60	*Fax Area Code: 864 ■ TF: 800-722-3723 ■ Web: www.griffinrad.com
Griffin Transport Services	5360 Capital Ct	Reno	NV	89502	775-331-8010		449	TF: 800-361-5028 ■ Web: legacyscs.com
Griffin-Spalding Chamber of Commerce	143 N Hill St	Griffin	GA	30223	770-228-8200		139	Web: www.griffinchamber.com
Griffith ID Inc	735 S Market St	Wilmington	DE	19801	302-656-8253	656-8268	189-10	Web: www.idgriffith.com
Griffith Morgan (Rep R - VA)	2202 Rayburn House Office Bldg	Washington	DC	20515	202-225-3861	225-0076	342-2	Web: morgangriffith.house.gov
Griffith Observatory	2800 E Observatory Rd	Los Angeles	CA	90027	213-473-0800		393	Web: www.griffithobs.org
Griffith Rubber Mills	2625 NW Industrial St	Portland	OR	97210	503-226-6971	226-6976	677	TF: 800-321-9677 ■ Web: www.griffithrubber.com
Griffith, Freeman & Liipfert LLC	600 Monson St	Beaufort	SC	29902	843-521-4242		41	Web: griffithfreeman.com
Griffiths Corp	2717 Niagara Ln N	Minneapolis	MN	55447	763-557-8935		488	Web: www.griffithscorp.com
Griffiths Law Pc	10375 Park Meadows Dr Ste 520	Lone Tree	CO	80124	303-858-8090	858-8181	41	Web: griffithslawpc.com
Griffon Aerospace	106 Commerce Cir	Madison	AL	35758	256-258-0035		256	Web: www.griffonaerospace.com
Griffon Corp	712 Fifth Ave 18th Fl	New York	NY	10019	212-957-5000	957-5040	185	NYSE: GFF ■ TF: 800-378-1475 ■ Web: www.griffon.com
Grifols USA LLC	2410 Lillyvale Ave	Los Angeles	CA	90032	888-474-3657		85	TF: 888-474-3657 ■ Web: www.grifols.com
Grigg Graphic Services Inc	20982 Bridge St	Southfield	MI	48033	248-356-5005		627	Web: www.grigg.com
Griggs County	808 Rollin Ave SW	Cooperstown	ND	58425	701-797-3613		338	Web: www.cooperstownnd.com
Griggs Steel Company Inc	1200 Souter Dr	Troy	MI	48083	248-298-0540		492	Web: www.griggssteel.com
Grignard Company LLC	505 Capobianco Plz	Rahway	NJ	07065	732-340-1111	340-0111	146	Web: www.grignard.com
Grijalva Raul (Rep D - AZ)	1511 Longworth House Office Bldg	Washington	DC	20515	202-225-2435	225-1541	342-2	Web: grijalva.house.gov
Grill 225	225 E Bay St	Charleston	SC	29401	843-266-4222	723-4320	671	TF: 877-440-2250 ■ Web: www.marketpavilion.com
Grill 23 & Bar	161 Berkeley St	Boston	MA	02116	617-542-2255	542-5114	671	Web: grill23.com
Grill at Hacienda del Sol	5501 N Hacienda del Sol Rd	Tucson	AZ	85718	520-529-3500		671	TF: 800-728-6514 ■ Web: www.haciendadelsol.com
Grill Concepts Inc	6300 Canoga Ave Ste 600	Woodland Hills	CA	91367	818-251-7000		670	NASDAQ: GLLC ■ Web: www.dailygrill.com
Grill of India	354 Ludlow Ave	Cincinnati	OH	45220	513-961-3600		671	Web: www.grillofindiaoh.com
Grill on The Alley, The	172 S Market St	San Jose	CA	95113	408-294-2244	294-2255	671	Web: www.thegrill.com
Grillfish	1444 Collins Ave	Miami Beach	FL	33139	305-538-9908		671	Web: www.grillfish.com
Grimaldi & Yeung LLP	9201 Fourth Ave 6th Fl	Brooklyn	NY	11209	718-238-6960		41	Web: gylawny.com
Grimaud Farms of California Inc	1320-A S Aurora St	Stockton	CA	95206	209-466-3200		619	Web: www.grimaudfarms.com
Grimbleby Coleman CPAS Inc	200 W Roseburg Ave	Modesto	CA	95350	209-527-4220	527-4247	2	Web: www.grimbleby-coleman.com
Grimco Inc	1585 Fencorp Dr	Fenton	MO	63026	800-542-9941		350	TF: 800-542-9941 ■ Web: www.grimco.com
Grimes Legal	8264 Louisville Rd	Bowling Green	KY	42101	270-782-3820		260	TF: 800-875-3820 ■ Web: grimeslegal.com
Grimmway Farms Inc	PO Box 81498	Bakersfield	CA	93380	800-301-3101		10-11	TF: 800-301-3101 ■ Web: www.grimmway.com
Grimstad	S84w18887 Enterprise Dr	Muskego	WI	53150	414-422-2300		358	TF: 877-474-6782 ■ Web: www.grimstad.com
Grind Lap Services Inc	1045 W National Ave	Addison	IL	60101	630-458-1111	458-0787	393	Web: www.grindlap.com
Grindal Co	1551 E Industrial Dr	Itasca	IL	60143	630-250-8950	250-7082	455	Web: grindal.com
Grindco Inc	288 W 1050 N	Chesterton	IN	46304	219-763-6130	763-6231	454	Web: www.hecomach.com
Grinders	417 E 18th St	Kansas City	MO	64108	816-472-5454		671	Web: grinderspizza.com
Grinders Clearing House Inc (GCH)	13301 E 8 Mile Rd	Warren	MI	48089	586-771-1500	771-5958	385	Web: www.gchmachinery.com
Grinders Inc	9002 Cotter St	Lewis Center	OH	43035	614-766-2313	766-4030	670	Web: www.wggrinders.com
Grinding & Dicing Services Inc	925 Berryessa Rd	San Jose	CA	95133	408-451-2000		696	Web: www.wafergrind.com
Grinding Products Company Inc	11084 E 9 Mile Rd	Warren	MI	48089	586-757-2118	757-5243	757	Web: grindingproducts.net
Grindstaff's Interior Inc	1007 W Main St	Forest City	NC	28043	828-245-4263	245-7758	321	Web: www.grindstaffs.com
Griner Engineering Inc	2500 N Curry Pk	Bloomington	IN	47404	812-332-2220	332-2229	621	Web: www.griner.com
Grinnell College	1115 Eighth Ave	Grinnell	IA	50112	641-269-3600	269-4800	166	TF: 800-247-0113 ■ Web: www.grinnell.edu
Grinnell Mutual Reinsurance Co	4215 Hwy 146 PO Box 790	Grinnell	IA	50112	641-269-8000		391-4	TF: 800-362-2041 ■ Web: grinnellmutual.com
Grinnell State Bank	814 4th Ave	Grinnell	IA	50112	641-236-3174	236-4329	70	Web: www.grinnellbank.com
Grinnen-Barrett Publishing Co	PO Box 1883	Brookline	MA	02446	617-787-1331		637-2	Web: www.morningsickness.net
Grinner's Food Systems Ltd	105 Walker St	Truro	NS	B2N5G9	902-893-4141		670	Web: www.grinners.ca
Grip Ltd	179 John St 6th Fl	Toronto	ON	M5T1X4	416-340-7111		7	Web: www.griplimited.com
Grisham Industries Inc	13629 110th Ave	Davenport	IA	52804	563-381-3525	381-3075	189-1	Web: grishamind.com
Grismer Tire Co	1187 N Fairfield Rd	Beavercreek	OH	45432	937-426-0183		755	Web: www.grismertire.com
Griswold Cooperative Telephone Co (GCTC)	607 Main St	Griswold	IA	51535	712-778-2121	778-2500	224	Web: www.griswoldtelco.com
Griswold Industries	1701 Placentia Ave	Costa Mesa	CA	92627	949-722-4800		789	TF: 800-942-6326 ■ Web: www.cla-val.com
Griswold LLC	1 River St PO Box 638	Moosup	CT	06354	800-472-8788	564-9103*	676	*Fax Area Code: 860 ■ TF: 800-472-8788 ■ Web: griswoldllc.com
Griswold Machine & Engineering Inc	8530 M 60	Union City	MI	49094	517-741-4300		475	TF: 800-248-2054 ■ Web: gme-shields.com
Grit Commercial Printing Inc	80 Choate Cir	Montoursville	PA	17754	570-368-8021		627	TF: 800-872-0409 ■ Web: www.gritprinting.com
Grit Technologies LLC	39373 Garfield Rd	Clinton Township	MI	48038	586-286-8324		177	Web: grittechs.com
Grizzly & Wolf Discovery Ctr	201 S Canyon St	West Yellowstone	MT	59758	406-646-7001	646-7004	823	TF: 800-257-2570 ■ Web: www.grizzlydiscoveryctr.org
Grizzly Oil Sands ULC	605 - 5 Ave SW Ste 2600	Calgary	AB	T2P3H5	403-930-6400		536	Web: www.grizzlyoilsands.com
Grizzly Peak Brewing Co	120 W Washington St	Ann Arbor	MI	48104	734-741-7325		671	Web: www.grizzlypeak.net
GRM (Grand River Mutual)	1001 Kentucky St	Princeton	MO	64673	660-748-3231		224	TF: 800-451-2301 ■ Web: www.grm.net
GRMC (Gateway Regional Medical Ctr)	2100 Madison Ave	Granite City	IL	62040	618-798-3000		374-3	Web: www.gatewayregional.net
GRO (Grandparents Rights Organization)	1760 S Telegraph Rd Ste 300	Bloomfield Hills	MI	48302	248-646-7177		48-6	Web: www.grandparentsrights.org
Gro Group Distributors	68 Tadmuck Rd Unit 3	Westford	MA	01886	978-692-9102	692-9270	139	Web: grogroup.com
Grob Inc	1731 Tenth Ave	Grafton	WI	53024	262-377-1400	377-2106	455	TF: 800-225-6481 ■ Web: www.grobinc.com
Grob Systems Inc	1070 Navajo Dr	Bluffton	OH	45817	419-358-9015	369-3332	207	Web: grobgroup.com
Grobet File Company of America Inc	750 Washington Ave	Carlstadt	NJ	07072	201-939-6700	939-5067	758	TF: 800-847-4188 ■ Web: www.grobetusa.com
Grobmyer Associates Inc	632 Apalachee Cir NE	Saint Petersburg	FL	33702	727-570-8500	570-8300	196	Web: www.grobmyerassociates.com
Grocers Supply Company Inc, The	3131 E Holcombe Blvd PO Box 14200	Houston	TX	77021	713-747-5000		297-8	Web: www.grocerssupply.com
Grocery People Ltd, The (TGP)	14505 Yellowhead Trl	Edmonton	AB	T5L3C4	780-447-5700		297-8	TF: 800-461-9401 ■ Web: www.tgp.ca

Company	Phone	Fax	Class
Grocery Supply Co 130 Hillcrest Dr PO Box 638. . . . . Sulphur Springs TX 75482 *TF:* 800-231-1938 ■ *Web:* www.grocerysupply.com	903-885-7621	439-3249	297-8
Grocery, The 288 Smith St . . . . Brooklyn NY 11231 *Web:* www.thegroceryrestaurant.com	718-596-3335		671
Groendyke Transport Inc 2510 Rock Island Blvd . . . . .Enid OK 73701 *TF:* 800-843-2103 ■ *Web:* www.groendyke.com	580-234-4663		780
Groezinger Provisions Inc 1200 Seventh Ave. . . . . Neptune City NJ 07753 *Web:* alexianpate.com	732-775-3220		473
Groff NetWorks LLC 11 State St . . . . Troy NY 12180 *Web:* www.groffnetworks.com	518-320-8906		196
Grohe America Inc 200 N Gary Ave Ste G. . . . . Bloomingdale IL 60108 *TF:* 800-444-7643 ■ *Web:* www.grohe.com	630-582-7711	582-7722	609
Grolen Communications Inc 814 Elm St . . . . Manchester NH 03101 *Web:* www.grolen.com	603-645-0101		173-2
Groople Inc 990 Hwy 287 N Ste 106 No 214 . . . . .Mansfield TX 76063 *TF:* 844-476-6753 ■ *Web:* groople.com	844-476-6753		393
Groove 99.3 FM 3651 Pegasus Dr Ste 107. . . . . .Bakersfield CA 93308 *Web:* www.groove993.com	661-393-1900		645-14
Groovfold Inc 1050 W State St. . . . . Newcomerstown OH 43832 *TF:* 800-367-1133 ■ *Web:* www.groovfold.com	740-498-8363	498-8782	309
Gros Ventre River Ranch PO Box 151. . . . . .Moose WY 83012 *Web:* www.grosventreriverranch.com	307-733-4138	733-4272	239
Grosh Scenic Rentals 4114 Sunset Blvd . . . . .Los Angeles CA 90029 **Fax Area Code:* 323 ■ *TF:* 877-363-7998 ■ *Web:* www.grosh.com	877-363-7998	664-7526*	722
Gross Chandelier Co 9777 Reavis Park Dr . . . . Saint Louis MO 63123 *TF:* 800-331-2425 ■ *Web:* glighting.com	314-631-6000	631-7800	439
Gross Electric Inc 2807 N Reynolds Rd . . . . Toledo OH 43615 *Web:* www.grosselectric.com	419-537-1818		246
Gross Mendelsohn & Associates PA 36 S Charles St 18th Fl. . . . . .Baltimore MD 21201 *TF:* 800-899-4623 ■ *Web:* www.gma-cpa.com	410-685-5512		2
Gross Mortgage Finance Inc (GMF) 3325 S University Dr Ste 200. . . . . .Davie FL 33328 *Web:* www.grossmortgage.com	954-475-7784	688-2522	509
Grosse Ile Township Schools 23276 E River Rd . . . . Grosse Ile MI 48138 *Web:* www.gischools.org	734-362-2555		685
Grosse Pointe Historical Society Resource Ctr 381 Kercheval Ave Ste 2. . . . . .Grosse Pointe Farms MI 48236 *Web:* www.gphistorical.org	313-884-7010	884-7699	434-3
Grosse Pointe News 16980 Kercheval Ave McCourt Bldg. . . Grosse Pointe Farms MI 48230 *Web:* www.grossepointenews.com	313-882-6900	882-1585	532-4
Grossel Tool Co 34190 Doreka . . . . Fraser MI 48026 *Web:* www.grosseltool.com	586-294-3660	294-7134	811
Grossenburg Implement Inc 31341 US Hwy 18. . . . . .Winner SD 57580 *TF:* 800-658-3440 ■ *Web:* www.grossenburg.com	605-842-2040	842-3485	274
Grossman & Grossman LLP 4 Executive Park Dr. . . . . Albany NY 12203 *Web:* www.ggcpallp.com	518-438-3509		2
Grossman & Keith Engineering Co 10408 Greenbriar Pl .Oklahoma City OK 73159 *Web:* grossman-keith.com	405-691-3213		261
Grossman Iron & Steel 5 N Market St . . . . Saint Louis MO 63102 *TF:* 800-969-9423 ■ *Web:* www.grossmaniron.com	314-231-9423	231-6983	686
Grossman, Tucker, Perreault & Pfleger PLLC 55 S Commercial St . . . . Manchester NH 03101 *Web:* www.gtpp.com	603-668-6560		428
Grossmont College 8800 Grossmont College Dr. . . . . .El Cajon CA 92020 *Web:* grossmont.edu	619-644-7000	644-7933	162
Grossmont Ctr 5500 Grossmont Center Dr. . . . . .La Mesa CA 91942 *Web:* www.grossmontcenter.com	619-465-2900		460
Grote Industries Inc 2600 Lanier Dr . . . . Madison IN 47250 *TF:* 800-628-0809 ■ *Web:* www.grote.com	812-273-1296	265-8440	60
Groth Corp 13650 N Promenade Blvd. . . . . Stafford TX 77477 *TF:* 800-354-7684 ■ *Web:* www.grothcorp.com	281-295-6800	295-6999	789
Groth Gates Heating & Sheet Metal Inc 2614 SE Hwy 101 . . . . .Lincoln City OR 97367 *Web:* grothgates.com	541-994-2631	994-2960	610
Groth Vineyards & Winery LLC 750 Oakville Cross Rd . . . . Oakville CA 94562 *Web:* grothwines.com	707-944-0290		102
Grothman Glenn (Rep R - WI) 1427 Longworth House Office Bldg . . . . .Washington DC 20515 *Web:* www.grothman.house.gov	202-225-2476	225-2356	342-2
Groton Ag Partners Inc 1202 N First St Ste 2 . . . . Groton SD 57445 *Web:* grotonag.com	614-249-7111		390
Groton Partners LLC 640 Fifth Ave Ste 1700 . . . . .New York NY 10019 *Web:* www.grotonpartners.com	212-430-1800		194
Groton Public Library 52 Newtown Rd. . . . . Groton CT 06340 *TF:* 800-989-0900 ■ *Web:* www.groton-ct.gov	860-441-6750	448-0363	434-3
Groton School 282 Farmers Row PO Box 991 . . . . Groton MA 01450 *Web:* www.groton.org	978-448-3363		622
Grotto 37 Bowdoin St . . . . .Boston MA 02114 *Web:* www.grottorestaurant.com	617-227-3434		671
Grotto Pizza Inc 20376 Coastal Hwy. . . . . .Rehoboth Beach DE 19971 *Web:* www.grottopizza.com	302-227-3567	227-4566	670
Grotto Ristorante c/o Landry's Inc 4715 Westheimer . . . . .Houston TX 77027 *Web:* www.grottorestaurants.com	713-622-3663		670
Grotto, The 8840 NE Skidmore St . . . . .Portland OR 97220 *Web:* thegrotto.org	503-254-7371	254-7948	97
Ground Control Systems Inc 3100 El Camino Real . . . . .Atascadero CA 93422 *Web:* www.groundcontrol.com	805-783-4600		681
Ground Hog Inc 1470 S Victoria Ct . . . . San Bernardino CA 92408 *TF:* 800-922-4680 ■ *Web:* www.groundhoginc.com	909-478-5700	478-5710	190
Ground Penetrating Radar Systems Inc 7540 New West Rd . . . . Toledo OH 43617 *Web:* www.gp-radar.com	419-843-9804		727
Ground Swell Surf Shop Inc 811 Donald Ross Rd. . . . . Juno Beach FL 33408 *Web:* groundswellsurfshop.com	561-622-7878		711
Ground Water Protection Council (GWPC) 13308 N MacArthur Blvd . . . . .Oklahoma City OK 73142 *Web:* www.gwpc.org	405-516-4972	516-4973	48-13
Ground Zero Pharmaceuticals Inc (GZP) 5405 Alton Pky Ste A-464 . . . . Irvine CA 92604 *Web:* www.groundzerous.com	949-419-6136	861-9797	582
GroundMetrics Inc 4217 Ponderosa Ave Ste A . . . . San Diego CA 92123 *Web:* www.groundmetrics.com	619-786-8023		407
Grounds For Play Inc 1050 Columbia Dr . . . . Carrollton GA 30117 **Fax Area Code:* 817 ■ *TF:* 800-552-7529 ■ *Web:* groundsforplay.com	800-552-7529	477-1140*	346
Groundspeed Analytics Inc 2373 Oak Valley Dr Ste 150 . . . . Ann Arbor MI 48103 *Web:* groundspeed.com	734-369-9299		391-4
GroundSwell Inc 1776 Park Ave Ste 4-175 . . . . Park City UT 84060 *Web:* www.groundswellinc.com	435-214-2997		528
Groundwater & Environmental Services Inc (GES) 1599 Rte 34 Ste 1. . . . . .Wall Township NJ 07727 *TF:* 800-220-3068 ■ *Web:* www.gesonline.com	800-220-3068		192
Group 1 Automotive Inc 800 Gessner Ste 500 . . . . .Houston TX 77024 *NYSE:* GPI ■ *Web:* www.group1corp.com	713-647-5700		57
Group 22 Inc 1201 E Grand Ave. . . . . El Segundo CA 90245 *Web:* www.group22.com	310-322-2210		344
Group 55 Marketing Inc 3011 W Grand Blvd 329 Fisher Bldg . . . . Detroit MI 48202 *Web:* group55.com	313-875-1155		5
Group Builders Inc 511 Mokauea St. . . . . Honolulu HI 96819 *Web:* groupbuilders.net	808-832-0888		189-9
Group Delta Consultants 370 Amapola Ave Ste 212. . . . . .Torrance CA 90501 *Web:* groupdelta.com	310-320-5100		256
Group for Organizational Effectiveness Inc, The 727 Waldens Pond Rd . . . . .Albany NY 12203 *Web:* groupoe.com	518-456-7738		195
Group Health Cooperative of Eau Claire 2503 N Hillcrest Pky. . . . . Altoona WI 54720 *TF:* 888-203-7770 ■ *Web:* www.group-health.com	715-552-4300	836-7683	390
Group Health Solutions Inc 148 Madison Ave . . . . .New York NY 10016 *Web:* grouphealthsolutions.com	212-779-4158		226
Group Industries Inc 7580 Garfield Blvd . . . . .Cleveland OH 44125 *Web:* www.drumpartsinc.com	216-271-0702	271-5044	350
Group Insurance Solutions Inc 33 Boston Post Rd W Ste 120. . . . . Marlborough MA 01752 *Web:* sullivan-benefits.com	508-278-1730		390
Group Management Services Inc 3296 Columbia Rd Ste 101. . . . . Richfield OH 44286 *TF:* 888-823-2084 ■ *Web:* www.groupmgmt.com	330-659-0100		463
Group Manufacturing Services Inc 1928 Hartog Dr. . . . . San Jose CA 95131 *Web:* www.groupmanufacturing.com	408-436-1040		697
Group O Inc 4905 77th Ave . . . . Milan IL 61264 *TF:* 800-752-0730 ■ *Web:* www.groupo.com	309-736-8300		113
Group One Trading LP 440 S La Salle Ste 3232. . . . . .Chicago IL 60605 *Web:* www.group1.com	312-922-2620		690
Group Voyagers Inc 5301 S Federal Cir . . . . Littleton CO 80123 *Web:* www.globusandcosmos.com	303-703-7000		760
Group Wellesley 307 S Dithridge St . . . . Pittsburgh PA 15213 *Web:* www.groupwellesley.com	412-363-3481		194
Groupe BBA Inc 375 Sir-Wilfrid-Laurier Blvd . . . . .Mont-Saint-Hilaire QC J3H6C3 *Web:* www.bba.ca	450-464-2111		463
Groupe Canimex 285 Saint-Georges St . . . . Drummondville QC J2C4H3 *TF:* 855-777-1335 ■ *Web:* www.groupecanimex.com	819-477-1335		358
Groupe de Scieries GDS Inc 207 Rt 295. . . . . Degelis QC G5T1R1 *Web:* www.groupgds.com	418-853-2566		820
Groupe Deschenes 3901 Jarry St E Ste 250 . . . . Montreal QC H1Z2G1 *Web:* www.groupedeschenes.com	514-253-3110	253-3666	612
Groupe Desgagnes Inc 21 March-Champlain St . . . . .Quebec City QC G1K8Z8 *TF:* 800-463-0680 ■ *Web:* desgagnes.com	418-692-1000		313
Groupe Focus Lionel-Boulet 1567 Boul. . . . . Boucherville QC J4B5H3 *Web:* www.groupefocus.com	514-644-5551		321
Groupe HELIOS 2099 Fernand-Lafontaine Blvd . . . . Longueuil QC J4G2J4 *Web:* www.groupehelios.com	450-646-1903		393
Groupe Lacasse LLC 99 St-Pierre St . . . . Sainte-Pie QC J0H1W0 **Fax Area Code:* 888 ■ *TF:* 888-522-2773 ■ *Web:* www.groupelacasse.com	450-772-2495	248-1865*	319-1
Groupe Lelys Inc 3275 Ave Francis Hughes. . . . . Laval QC H7L5A5 *TF:* 800-361-3961 ■ *Web:* www.lelys.com	450-662-7161		627
Groupe Lou-Tec Inc 8500 Jules Leger . . . . .Anjou QC H1J1A7 *Web:* www.loutec.com	514-356-0047		23
Groupe Maskatel Lp 770 Casavant Ouest Bd. . . . . .Saint-Hyacinthe QC J2S7S3 *TF:* 877-627-5283 ■ *Web:* maskatel.ca	450-250-5050	250-5000	224

Name / Address	Phone	Fax	Class
Groupe Meloche Inc 491 Boul Des Rables, Salaberry-de-Valleyfield QC J6T6G3 *Web:* www.melocheinc.com	450-371-4646	371-4957	454
Groupe PARIMA Inc 4450 Cousens Rue, Montreal QC H4S1X6 *Web:* groupeparima.com	514-338-3780		743
Groupe Plombaction Inc 575 Boul Pierre-Roux est, Victoriaville QC G6T1S7 *Web:* www.groupeplombaction.com	819-752-6064		186
Groupe Sante Sedna Inc 1010 Sherbrooke W Ste 2405, Montreal QC H3A2R7 *Web:* www.groupesedna.ca	514-844-8760		194
Groupe Savoie Inc 251 Rt 180, Saint-Quentin NB E8A2K9 *Web:* groupesavoie.com	506-235-2228	235-3200	683
Groupe SYGIF Inc 112 Montee Industrielle-et-Commerciale Office 100, Rimouski QC G5M1B1 *Web:* www.groupesygif.ca	418-721-5353	721-5356	180
Groupon Inc 600 W Chicago Ave Ste 620, Chicago IL 60654 *Web:* www.groupon.com	312-676-5773		345
Groupspark Inc 111 S Bedford St Ste 200, Burlington MA 01803 *TF:* 877-546-7227 ■ *Web:* www.groupspark.com	781-273-6245		225
Grouse Mountain Resorts Ltd 6400 Nancy Greene Way, North Vancouver BC V7R4K9 *Web:* www.grousemountain.com	604-984-0661		707
Grove Bank & Trust 2701 S Bayshore Dr, Miami FL 33133 *Web:* www.coconutgrovebank.com	305-858-6666		70
Grove City College 100 Campus Dr, Grove City PA 16127 *Web:* www.gcc.edu	724-458-2135	458-3395	166
Grove Collaborative 1301 Sansome St, San Francisco CA 94111 *TF:* 844-476-8375 ■ *Web:* www.grove.co	844-476-8375		788
Grove Consultants Intl, The 1000 Oreilly Ave, San Francisco CA 94129 *Web:* www.thegrove.com	415-561-2500		463
Grove Gear 1524 15th Ave, Union Grove WI 53182 *Web:* www.grovegear.com	262-878-1221		709
Grove Grill 4550 Poplar Ave, Memphis TN 38117 *Web:* www.thegrovegrill.com	901-818-9951		671
Grove Hotel, The 245 S Capitol Blvd, Boise ID 83702 *Web:* www.grovehotelboise.com	208-333-8000	333-8800	379
Grove Printing Corp 4225 Howard Ave, Kensington MD 20895 *TF:* 877-290-5793 ■ *Web:* www.groveprinting.com	301-571-1024		627
Grove Street Advisors 2221 Washington St Bldg 1 Ste 201, Newton MA 02462 *Web:* www.grovestreet.com	781-263-6100	263-6101	792
Grove Tools Inc 3230 Dodge St, Dubuque IA 52003 *Web:* www.grovetools.com	563-588-0536	588-0302	454
Grove, The 189 The Grove Dr, Los Angeles CA 90036 *Web:* thegrovela.com	323-900-8080		460
Grove/Atlantic Inc 154 W 14th St 12th Fl, New York NY 10011 *Web:* groveatlantic.com	212-614-7850	614-7886	637-2
Grover Brothers Equipment Inc 1500 N Main St, Hattiesburg MS 39401 *Web:* www.groverbros.net	601-545-3505	544-4801	665
Grover Cleveland Birthplace State Historic Site 207 Bloomfield Ave, Caldwell NJ 07006 *Web:* www.njparksandforests.org	973-226-0001		565
Grover Corp 2759 S 28th St, Milwaukee WI 53234 *TF:* 800-776-3602 ■ *Web:* www.grovercorp.com	414-716-5900	384-0201	128
Grover Landscape Services Inc 6224 Stoddard Rd, Modesto CA 95356 *Web:* groverlandscapeservices.com	209-545-4401	545-3315	776
Grover Machine Co 207 Prospect Ave, Saint Louis MO 63122 *TF:* 888-554-7683 ■ *Web:* grovermachine.com	314-965-6808	968-7046	456
Groves Inc 818 Trakk Ln, Woodstock IL 60098 *TF:* 800-991-2120 ■ *Web:* www.groves.com	815-338-8640		393
Groves Industrial Supply Inc 7301 Pinemont Dr, Houston TX 77040 *TF:* 800-343-8923 ■ *Web:* www.grovesindustrial.com	713-675-4747		111
Grow Cedar Valley 360 Westfield Ave Ste 200, Waterloo IA 50701 *Web:* www.growcedarvalley.com	319-232-1156	233-4580	139
Grow In America PO Box 3667, Champaign IL 61826 *Web:* www.growinamerica.org	217-352-6989		48-21
Grow (Norfolk, VA) 427 Granby St, Norfolk VA 23510 *Web:* thisisgrow.com	757-431-7710		5
Grower Direct Fresh Cut Flowers 6303 Wagner Rd, Edmonton AB T6E4N4 *TF:* 877-277-4787 ■ *Web:* www.growerdirect.com	780-436-7774	436-3336	292
Grower, Ketcham Advocates, Counselors & Litigators 901 N Lake Destiny Rd Ste 450, Maitland FL 32751 *Web:* www.growerketcham.com	407-423-9545		428
Growers Co-operative Grape Juice Company Inc 112 N Portage St, Westfield NY 14787 *Web:* www.concordgrapejuice.com	716-326-3161	326-6566	296-20
Growers Express LLC 150 Main St Ste 210, Salinas CA 93901 *Web:* www.growersexpress.com	831-757-9951		315-4
Growers Ice Co 1060 Growers St, Salinas CA 93901 *TF:* 855-424-5781 ■ *Web:* www.growersice.com	831-424-5781	424-4280	380
GroWind Inc 800 Oneida St Ste A, Storm Lake IA 50588 *Web:* www.kenhach.com	712-213-3351		194
Growing Field Books 3815 Precision Dr Unit A, Fort Collins CO 80528 *TF:* 866-465-4211 ■ *Web:* www.growingfield.com	970-988-4208		637-2
Growing Leaders Inc 190 Technology Pkwy Ste 100, Peachtree Corners GA 30092 *Web:* growingleaders.com	770-495-3332		393
GROWMARK Inc 1701 Towanda Ave, Bloomington IL 61701 *Web:* www.growmark.com	309-557-6000		276
Growth Association of Southwestern Illinois Alden Hall 5800 Godfrey Rd, Godfrey IL 62035 *TF:* 855-852-9460 ■ *Web:* www.growthassociation.com	618-467-2280	466-8289	139
Growth Coach, The 10700 Montgomery Rd, Montgomery OH 45242 *TF:* 855-300-2622 ■ *Web:* thegrowthcoach.com	855-300-2622		310
Growth Energy 701 Eighth St NW Ste 450, Washington DC 20001 *Web:* growthenergy.org	202-545-4000		192
Growth Engine Co, The 1 Selleck St, Norwalk CT 06855 *Web:* www.growth-engine.com	203-857-4494		194
Growth Fund Guide 4020 Jackson Blvd, Rapid City SD 57702 *Web:* www.marketwatch.com	605-341-1971		531-9
Growth Industries Inc 12523 Third St PO Box 900, Grandview MO 64030 *Web:* www.growthind.com	816-763-7676	765-4925	22
Growth Products Ltd 80 Lafayette Ave, White Plains NY 10603 *TF:* 800-648-7626 ■ *Web:* www.growthproducts.com	914-428-1316		276
Growth Properties Investment Managers Inc 1329 Bristol Pk Ste 182, Bensalem PA 19020 *Web:* www.gpim.net	215-546-5980		656
GrowthForce LLC 800 Rockmead Ste 200, Kingwood TX 77339 *TF:* 877-735-7693 ■ *Web:* www.growthforce.com	281-358-2007	358-4120	194
Growthpoint Inc 5045 Timber Lake Trl, Clarkston MI 48346 *Web:* growthpoint-inc.com	248-467-6680		195
GRPS (Grand Rapids Public Schools) 1331 Franklin St SE PO Box 117, Grand Rapids MI 49506 *Web:* www.grps.org	616-819-2000	819-2104	685
GRR (Giant Resource Recovery - Harleyville Inc) 654 Judge St PO Box 352, Harleyville SC 29448 **Fax Area Code:* 803 ■ *TF:* 800-786-0477 ■ *Web:* www.grr-giant.com	800-786-0477	496-2200*	192
GRS (Gabriel Roeder Smith & Co) 1 Towne Sq Ste 800, Southfield MI 48076 *TF:* 800-521-0498 ■ *Web:* www.grsconsulting.com	248-799-9000	799-9020	193
GRTC Transit System 301 E Belt Blvd, Richmond VA 23224 *Web:* www.ridegrtc.com	804-358-3871	342-1933	468
Grubb Company Inc, The 1960 Mountain Blvd, Oakland CA 94611 *Web:* www.grubbco.com	510-339-0400		652
Grubbs Infiniti Ltd 1661 Airport Fwy, Euless TX 76040 *Web:* www.grubbsinfiniti.com	817-318-1200	359-4100	57
Grubbs, Hoskyn, Barton & Wyatt Inc 1 Trigon Pl, Little Rock AR 72209 *Web:* grubbsengineers.com	501-455-2536		261
Gruber Systems Inc 25636 Ave Stanford, Valencia CA 91355 *TF:* 800-257-4070 ■ *Web:* grubersystems.com	661-257-4060	257-4791	604
Gruber, Colabella, Liuzza & Thompson 41 Lakeside Blvd, Hopatcong NJ 07843 *Web:* gruberlaw-nj.com	973-398-7500		41
Grudi Associates Inc PO Box 626, Palmyra PA 17078 *Web:* grudiassociates.com	717-838-5022		463
Gruenberg & Kelly Pc 700 Koehler Ave, Ronkonkoma NY 11779 *TF:* 888-305-6372 ■ *Web:* newyorklawgroup.com	631-737-4110		41
Gruet Winery 8400 Pan American Fwy NE, Albuquerque NM 87113 *Web:* www.gruetwinery.com	505-821-0055		50-7
Gruett's Inc 101 Main St, Potter WI 54160 *Web:* www.gruettspowercenter.com	920-853-3516	853-7168	274
Gruhn Guitars 400 Broadway, Nashville TN 37204 *Web:* guitars.com	615-256-2033	255-2021	526
Gruma Corp 1159 Cottonwood Ln Ste 200, Irving TX 75038 *Web:* www.gruma.com	972-232-5000	232-5176	11-1
Grunau Company Inc 1100 W Anderson Ct, Oak Creek WI 53154 *TF:* 800-365-1920 ■ *Web:* www.grunau.com	414-216-6900		189-10
Grundfos Pumps Corp 17100 W 118th Terr, Olathe KS 66061 *Web:* www.grundfos.com	913-227-3400	227-3500	641
Grundmann's Athletic Co 3018 Galleria Dr, Metairie LA 70001 *Web:* www.grundmanns.com	504-833-6602	833-6899	710
Grundy County 68 Cumberland St PO Box 177, Altamont TN 37301 *Web:* www.grundycountytn.net	931-692-3721	692-3718	338
Grundy County 706 G Ave, Grundy Center IA 50638 *Web:* www.grundycountyiowa.gov	319-824-5229		338
Grundy County 1320 Union St, Morris IL 60450 *Web:* www.grundyco.org	815-941-3400		338
Grundy County 700 Main St, Trenton MO 64683 *Web:* www.grundycountymo.com	660-359-4040	359-6786	338
Grundy County Chamber of Commerce & Industry 909 Liberty St, Morris IL 60450 *Web:* grundychamber.com	815-942-0113	942-0117	139
Grundy County Rural Electric Co-op 303 N Park Ave PO Box 39, Grundy Center IA 50638 *TF:* 800-390-7605 ■ *Web:* www.grundycountyrecia.com	319-824-5251	824-3118	245
Grundy Electric Co-opeartive Inc 4100 Oklahoma Ave, Trenton MO 64683 *TF:* 800-279-2249 ■ *Web:* www.grundyec.com	660-359-3941	359-6030	245
Grunley Construction Company Inc 15020 Shady Grove Rd Ste 500, Rockville MD 20850 *Web:* www.grunley.com	240-399-2000	399-2001	186
Grunwald Printing Co 1418 Morgan Ave, Corpus Christi TX 78404 *Web:* www.gpprint.com	361-882-5654	882-7394	627
Grunyk & Associates PC 200E E 5th Ave Ste 125, Naperville IL 60563 *Web:* grunyklaw.com	630-428-3300		41
Grupe Co, The 3255 W March Ln Ste 400, Stockton CA 95219 *Web:* www.grupe.com	209-473-6000		187
Grupo Antolin Kentucky Inc 208 Commerce Ct, Hopkinsville KY 42240 *Web:* www.grupoantolin.com	270-885-2703		61
Grupo Uno 2199 Ponce De Leon Blvd Ste 649, Coral Gables FL 33134 *Web:* www.grupouno.com	305-448-6111	448-5553	7
GRUS Inc 3209 East 3rd Ave Unit 160, Tampa FL 33602 **Fax Area Code:* 888 ■ *Web:* www.gruspersonnel.com	727-791-6205	230-9909*	260

Name / Address	City	State	Zip	Phone	Fax	Class
Gruter Institute for Law and Behavioral Research 158 Goya Rd *Web:* gruterinstitute.org	Portola Valley	CA	94028	650-854-1191	854-1192	166
GRW Engineers Inc 801 Corporate Dr *Web:* www.grwinc.com	Lexington	KY	40503	859-223-3999		261
Gryphon Investment Counsel Inc 20 Bay St Ste 1905 *Web:* www.gryphon.ca	Toronto	ON	M5J2N8	416-364-2299		528
Gryphtech Inc 2595 Skymark Ave Ste 206 *Web:* www.gryphtech.com	Mississauga	ON	L4W4L5	416-362-0543		180
GS & F 209 10th Ave S Ste 222 *Web:* gsandf.com	Nashville	TN	37203	615-385-1100		4
GS Blodgett Corp 44 Lakeside Ave *Web:* www.blodgett.com	Burlington	VT	05401	802-658-6600	864-0183	298
GS Communications USA Inc 179 Greenpoint Ave *Web:* www.gscomm.net	Brooklyn	NY	11222	718-389-7371		173-2
G-S Company Inc, The 7920 Stansbury Rd *Web:* www.g-sco.com	Baltimore	MD	21222	410-284-9549		693
GS Engineering Consultants Inc 2080 N Talbot Rd RR 1 *Web:* www.gsengineering.ca	Windsor	ON	N9A6J3	519-737-9162		256
GS Engineering Inc 47500 US Hwy 41 *Web:* www.gsengineering.com	Houghton	MI	49931	906-482-1235	482-1236	261
GS Foods Inc 5925 S Alcoa Ave *Web:* www.gsfoods.com	Vernon	CA	90058	323-581-6161	589-2106	345
GS Precision Inc Exit One Industrial Pk 101 John Seitz Dr *Web:* www.gsprecision.com	Brattleboro	VT	05301	802-257-5200		112
G-S Supplies 1150 University Ave Ste 5 *TF:* 800-295-3050 ■ *Web:* gssupplies.com	Rochester	NY	14607	585-241-2370	241-2375	544
GSA (General Services Administration) 1275 F St NE *Web:* www.gsa.gov	Washington	DC	20417	202-501-0800		340-20
GSA (Geological Society of America, The) 3300 Penrose Pl PO Box 9140 *TF:* 800-472-1988 ■ *Web:* geosociety.org	Boulder	CO	80301	303-357-1000	357-1070	49-19
GSAT Inc 100 W Oak St Ste 200 *TF:* 866-977-4728 ■ *Web:* gsati.com	Denton	TX	76201	469-287-6771	464-1234	180
GSB (Guilford Savings Bank) PO Box 369 *TF:* 866-878-1480 ■ *Web:* www.gsb-yourbank.com	Guilford	CT	06437	203-453-3290		70
GSB (Great Southern Bank) 1451 E Battlefield St *TF:* 800-749-7113 ■ *Web:* www.greatsouthernbank.com	Springfield	MO	65804	417-887-4400		70
GSB Digital 28 E 28th St Concourse Level *Web:* gsbdigital.com	New York	NY	10016	212-684-3600		344
GSC W189 N11161 Kleinmann Dr *TF:* 800-454-2233 ■ *Web:* www.gsc-3d.com	Germantown	WI	53022	262-790-1080	790-1060	180
GSC (Golden Sufi Ctr) PO Box 456 *Web:* www.goldensufi.org	Point Reyes Station	CA	94956	415-663-0100	663-0103	48-20
GSC GROUP 10 905 Louis-H Lafontaine Ste 200 *Web:* groupe-gsc.qc.ca	Montreal	QC	H1J2E8	514-354-4222	354-3312	180
GSC Logistics Inc 530 Water St 5th Fl *TF:* 800-366-2769 ■ *Web:* gsclogistics.com	Oakland	CA	94607	510-844-3700		803-1
GSD (Gem State Distributors Inc) 350 Industrial Ln *TF:* 800-234-1525 ■ *Web:* www.gemstatedist.com	Pocatello	ID	83201	208-237-5151	237-0802	393
GSD & M Idea City 828 W 6th St *Web:* www.gsdm.com	Austin	TX	78703	512-242-4736		4
GSE Construction Company Inc 6950 Preston Ave *Web:* www.gseconstruction.com	Livermore	CA	94551	925-447-0292	447-0962	188-10
GSE Dynamics Inc 25 Corporate Dr *Web:* www.gsedynamics.com	Hauppauge	NY	11788	631-231-1044		22
GSE Lining Technology Inc 19103 Gundle Rd *TF:* 800-435-2008 ■ *Web:* www.gseworld.com	Houston	TX	77073	281-443-8564	875-6010	600
GSE Systems Inc 1332 Londontown Blvd Ste 200 *NASDAQ: GVP* ■ *TF:* 800-638-7912 ■ *Web:* www.gses.com	Sykesville	MD	21784	410-970-7800	970-7997	178-1
GSG Inc 4601 Spring Valley Rd **Fax Area Code:* 800 ■ *TF:* 800-366-1776 ■ *Web:* www.gogsg.com	Dallas	TX	75244	214-748-3271	676-0034*	328
GSI (Graphic Systems Inc) 7200 Goodlet Farms Pky Ste 102 *Web:* www.yesgsi.com	Cordova	TN	38016	901-937-5500	937-5555	534
GSI (Geo-Synthetics Inc) 2401 Pewaukee Rd *TF:* 800-444-5523 ■ *Web:* www.geo-synthetics.com	Waukesha	WI	53188	262-524-7979	524-7961	192
GSI (Globetrotter Services Inc) PO Box 154801 *Web:* www.mwradio.com	Waco	TX	76715	254-799-9556		192
GSI (Ghiorsi & Sorrenti Inc) 255 Madison Ave *Web:* www.gsiphilanthropy.com	Wyckoff	NJ	07481	201-307-1970	307-5632	194
GSI Engineering 2960 N Diers Ave *Web:* gsinetwork.com	Grand Island	NE	68803	308-381-1987		261
GSI Group Inc 1004 E Illinois St *TF:* 888-474-2467 ■ *Web:* www.grainsystems.com	Assumption	IL	62510	888-474-2467		273
GSI Interactive 935 1st Ave	King of Prussia	PA	19406	610-496-7000	265-1730	195
GSI Technology Inc 2360 Owen St *NASDAQ: GSIT* ■ *Web:* www.gsitechnology.com	Santa Clara	CA	95054	408-980-8388	980-8377	696
GSL Electric 8540 S Sandy Pkwy *Web:* www.gslelectric.com	Sandy	UT	84070	801-565-0088	565-0099	189-4
GSL Fine Lithographers 8386 Rovana Cir *Web:* www.gslitho.com	Sacramento	CA	95828	916-231-1410	231-1411	627
GSL Solutions Inc 1411 N Westshore Blvd Ste 204 *Web:* www.gslsolutions.com	Tampa	FL	33607	813-637-8535		177
Gsolutionz Inc 625 E Santa Clara St Ste 100 *Web:* www.gsolutionz.com	Ventura	CA	93001	805-662-1500		246
GSP (Greenville-Spartanburg Airport) 2000 GSP Dr Ste 1 *TF:* 800-331-1212 ■ *Web:* gspairport.com	Greer	SC	29651	864-877-7426	848-6225	27
GSP Group Inc 1343 Boswall Dr *Web:* gspgroup.com	Worthington	OH	43085	614-888-7502		195
Gsp International Inc 90 Woodbridge Center Dr Ste 110 *Web:* gspintl.com	Woodbridge	NJ	07095	732-602-0100		260
GSP Marketing Technologies Inc 14055 46th St N Ste 1112 *Web:* www.gspretail.com	Clearwater	FL	33760	727-532-0647		344
GSPANN Technologies Inc 362 Fairview Way *Web:* www.gspann.com	Milpitas	CA	95035	408-263-3435		196
GSS Infotech Inc 1699 Wall St Ste 201 *Web:* www.gssinfotech.com	Mount Prospect	IL	60056	847-640-1157		196
GST AutoLeather Inc 20 Oak Hollow Dr Ste 300 *Web:* www.gstautoleather.com	Southfield	MI	48033	248-436-2300	436-2390	432
GST Inc 12881 166th St *TF:* 800-833-0128 ■ *Web:* gstes.com	Cerritos	CA	90703	562-345-8700	345-8701	177
Gstek Inc 911 Cedar Rd *Web:* www.gstekinc.com	Chesapeake	VA	23322	757-548-1597		261
GSVlabs Inc 585 Broadway St *Web:* gsvlabs.com	Redwood City	CA	94063	650-421-2000		463
GSW Worldwide 500 Old Worthington Rd *Web:* gsw-w.com	Westerville	OH	43082	614-848-4848		4
GT Advanced Technologies Inc 243 Daniel Webster Hwy *Web:* gtat.com	Merrimack	NH	03054	603-883-5200		696
GT Church 1110 Snyder Rd *Web:* gtchurch.online	Reading	PA	19609	610-678-0266		48-20
GT Distributors Inc 2545 Brockton Dr Ste 100 *TF:* 800-443-6283 ■ *Web:* www.gtdist.com	Austin	TX	78758	512-451-8298	453-6149	237
GT Grandstands Inc 2810 Sydney Rd *Web:* www.gtgrandstands.com	Plant City	FL	33566	813-305-1415		320
GT Plastics Inc 4681 N Industrial Row *Web:* gtplastics.com	Oscoda	MI	48750	989-739-1112	739-7393	604
GT Technologies Inc 5859 Executive Dr. *Web:* www.gttechnologies.com	Westland	MI	48185	734-467-8371		256
GT Water Products Inc 5239 N Commerce Ave **Fax Area Code:* 805 ■ *TF:* 800-862-5647 ■ *Web:* www.gtwaterproducts.com	Moorpark	CA	93021	800-862-5647	529-4558*	607
GTC (Grand Telephone Company Inc) 226 S 4th St *TF:* 888-400-5587 ■ *Web:* www.grand.net	Jay	OK	74346	918-253-4231	253-3400	224
GTC Technology Inc 1001 S Dairy Ashford Ste 500 *Web:* www.gtctech.com	Houston	TX	77077	281-597-4800		146
GTCO CalComp Inc 14557 N 82nd St *TF:* 800-220-1137 ■ *Web:* www.gtcocalcomp.com	Scottsdale	AZ	85260	800-220-1137		173-1
GTCR LLC 300 N Lasalle Ste 5600 *Web:* www.gtcr.com	Chicago	IL	60654	312-382-2200		792
GTE Federal Credit Union PO Box 172599 *Web:* www.gtefinancial.org	Tampa	FL	33672	813-871-2690		219
Gtek Communications 4111 FM 2986 *Web:* gtek.biz	Portland	TX	78374	361-777-1400	777-1405	175
G-TEL Enterprises Inc 16840 Clay Rd Ste 118 *TF:* 800-884-4835 ■ *Web:* www.payphone.com	Houston	TX	77084	281-550-5592	550-1028	246
GTELCO (Gunnison Telecommunications Co) 29 S Main St *Web:* www.gtelco.net	Gunnison	UT	84634	435-528-7236		224
GTFM LLC 37 Spring Valley Ave *TF:* 800-676-4836 ■ *Web:* gtfmllc.com	Paramus	NJ	07652	201-343-7383		116
GTI (Gas Technology Institute) 1700 S Mt Prospect Rd *Web:* www.gti.energy	Des Plaines	IL	60018	847-768-0500	768-0501	668
GTI (Global Titanium Inc) 19300 Filer Ave **Fax Area Code:* 313 ■ *TF:* 800-762-7602 ■ *Web:* www.globaltitanium.com	Detroit	MI	48234	800-762-7602	366-5305*	723
GTI (Graham Trucking Inc) 722 S Chicago *Web:* www.grahamtrucking.com	Seattle	WA	98108	206-763-9734		780
GTI Corporate Travel 111 Township Line Rd *TF:* 800-223-3863 ■ *Web:* www.gtitravel.com	Jenkintown	PA	19046	215-379-6800		772
GTJ Consulting 22955 Industrial Dr W *Web:* gtjonline.com	Roseville	MI	48066	586-293-9600		196
GTM (Grand Traverse Machine) 1247 Boon St *Web:* www.gtmachine.com	Traverse City	MI	49686	231-946-8006		621
Gtm Wholesale Liquidators Inc 2025 Gillespie Wy Ste 108 *Web:* www.gtmstores.com	San Diego	CA	92154	619-596-7486		175
GTO 2000 Inc PO Box 2819 *TF:* 800-966-0801 ■ *Web:* gto2000.com	Gainesville	GA	30503	770-287-9233	287-7878	311
GTR Enterprises Inc 6352 Corte Del Abeto E *Web:* www.gtrnet.com	Carlsbad	CA	92011	760-931-1192	931-1297	454
GTR Manufacturing Inc 1 Jonathan Dr *Web:* gtrmfg.com	Brockton	MA	02301	508-588-3240		697
GTRI (Georgia Tech Research Institute) *Georgia Institute of Technology* 250 14th St NW *Web:* gtri.gatech.edu	Atlanta	GA	30318	404-407-7400		668
GTS (George T. Sanders Co) 10201 W 49th Ave *Web:* www.gtsanders.com	Wheat Ridge	CO	80033	303-940-5290		612
GTS Communications & Cabling Co 11953 Prospect Rd *Web:* www.gtscommunications.com	Strongsville	OH	44149	440-878-8866		179
GTS Consultants 2 Monmouth Ave *Web:* gtsconsultants.com	Freehold	NJ	07728	732-409-0900	409-0927	317

				Phone	Fax	Class
GTSI Corp 2553 Dulles View Dr Ste 100 *NASDAQ: GTSI* ■ *TF:* 800-999-4874 ■ *Web:* www.unicomgov.com	Herndon	VA	20171	800-999-4874		174
GTT Communications Inc 7900 Tysons One Pl Ste 1450 *NYSE: GTT* ■ *Web:* www.gtt.net	McLean	VA	22102	703-442-5500		736
GTT Global 600 Data Dr Ste 101 *TF:* 800-485-6828 ■ *Web:* www.gttglobal.com	Plano	TX	75075	972-490-3394		16
GTX Corp 117 W Ninth St Ste 1214 *Web:* gtxcorp.com	Los Angeles	CA	90015	213-489-3019		736
GTX Inc 175 Toyota Plz 7th Fl *NASDAQ: GTXI* ■ *Web:* www.gtxinc.com	Memphis	TN	38103	901-523-9700	844-8075	85
GU (Generations United) 1333 H St NW Ste 500-W *Web:* www.gu.org	Washington	DC	20005	202-289-3979	289-3952	48-6
Guadalajara Family Mexican 17 N 29th St *Web:* guadalajararestaurantmt.com	Billings	MT	59101	406-259-8930		671
Guadalajara Restaurant 314 W Sioux Ave *Web:* www.eatguads.com	Pierre	SD	57501	605-224-2771		671
Guadalupe Credit Union 3601 Mimbres Ln *TF:* 800-540-5382 ■ *Web:* guadalupecu.org	Santa Fe	NM	87507	505-982-8942		219
Guadalupe Cultural Arts Ctr 1301 Guadalupe St *Web:* www2.guadalupeculturalarts.org	San Antonio	TX	78207	210-271-3151		50-2
Guadalupe Mountains National Park 400 Pine Canyon Rd *Web:* www.nps.gov	Salt Flat	TX	79847	915-828-3251	828-3269	564
Guadalupe River Park & Gardens 438 Coleman Ave *Web:* www.grpg.org	San Jose	CA	95110	408-298-7657	288-9048	97
Guadalupe River State Park 3350 Park Rd 31 *Web:* tpwd.texas.gov	Spring Branch	TX	78070	830-438-2656		565
Guadalupe Valley Electric Co-opeartive Inc 825 E Sarah Dewitt Dr *TF:* 800-223-4832 ■ *Web:* www.gvec.org	Gonzales	TX	78629	830-857-1200		245
Guadalupe Valley Telephone Co-op (GVTC) 36101 FM 3159 *TF:* 800-367-4882 ■ *Web:* gvtc.com	New Braunfels	TX	78132	830-885-4411	885-2400	736
Guadalupe-Blanco River Authority (GBRA) 933 E Ct St *Web:* www.gbra.org	Seguin	TX	78155	830-379-5822	379-9718	245
Guajillo 1727 Wilson Blvd *Web:* guajillomexican.com	Arlington	VA	22201	703-807-0840		671
Guam *Secretary of State* Ricardo J Bordallo Complex 513 W Marine Corps Dr *Web:* www.governor.guam.gov	Hagatna	GU	96910	671-472-8931		337
Guarantee Electrical Co 3405 Bent Ave *Web:* www.geco.com	Saint Louis	MO	63116	314-772-5400		189-4
Guarantee Real Estate Corp 5380 N Fresno Ave Ste 103 *Web:* www.guarantee.com	Fresno	CA	93710	559-650-6088		652
Guarantee Specialties Inc 9401 Carr Ave *Web:* gps1usa.com	Cleveland	OH	44108	216-451-9744		488
Guarantee Trust Life Insurance Co 1275 Milwaukee Ave *TF:* 800-338-7452 ■ *Web:* www.gtlic.com	Glenview	IL	60025	847-699-0600	699-2355	391-2
Guaranteed Industries 5420 Pare *Web:* www.guaranteedindustries.com	Montreal	QC	H4P1R3	514-342-3400	342-2486	610
Guaranteed Rate Inc 3940 N Ravenswood *TF:* 866-934-7283 ■ *Web:* www.guaranteedrate.com	Chicago	IL	60613	773-290-0505		217
Guaranteed Supply Co 1211 Rotherwood Rd *TF:* 800-326-0810 ■ *Web:* guaranteedsupply.com	Greensboro	NC	27406	336-273-3491		191-1
Guarantors Agency, The 7 World Trade Ctr 46th Fl *Web:* theguarantors.com	New York	NY	10007	212-266-0020		653
Guaranty Bancshares Inc 100 W Arkansas St PO Box 1158 *TF:* 888-572-9881 ■ *Web:* www.gnty.com	Mount Pleasant	TX	75455	903-572-9881	572-9658	360-2
Guaranty State Bank & Trust Company Beloit Kansas, The 201 S Mill St PO Box 607 *TF:* 888-738-8000 ■ *Web:* www.guarantystate.com	Beloit	KS	67420	785-738-3501	738-3530	70
Guard Systems Inc 1190 Monterey Pass Rd *TF:* 800-606-6711 ■ *Web:* www.guardsystemsinc.com	Monterey Park	CA	91754	323-881-6711	261-7841	693
Guardair Corp 47 Veterans Dr *TF:* 800-482-7324 ■ *Web:* www.guardair.com	Chicopee	MA	01022	413-594-4400	594-4884	172
Guardian Alarm 20800 Southfield Rd *TF:* 800-782-9688 ■ *Web:* guardianalarm.com	Southfield	MI	48075	248-423-1000	423-3009	692
Guardian Angels HomeCare LLC 405 Maple Ave *TF:* 877-439-7731 ■ *Web:* www.myguardianangelshomecare.com	Cheshire	CT	06410	203-439-7731	250-7788	363
Guardian Credit Union 4501 W Greenfield Ave *Web:* www.guardiancu.org	West Milwaukee	WI	53214	414-546-7450		219
Guardian Energy LLC 4745 380th Ave *Web:* www.guardiannrg.com	Janesville	MN	56048	507-234-5000		580
Guardian Finance Co 2495 Hilliard-Rome Rd *TF:* 877-277-0345 ■ *Web:* www.guardianfinancecompany.com	Hilliard	OH	43026	877-277-0345		217
Guardian Industries Corp 2300 Harmon Rd *TF:* 800-822-5599 ■ *Web:* www.guardian.com	Auburn Hills	MI	48326	248-340-1800	340-9988	329
Guardian Interlock Systems 228 Church St *TF:* 800-499-0994 ■ *Web:* guardianinterlock.com	Marietta	GA	30060	800-499-0994		407
Guardian Jet LLC 102A Broad St *Web:* www.guardianjet.com	Guilford	CT	06437	203-453-0800		21
Guardian Life Insurance Company of America 7 Hanover Sq *TF:* 888-600-4667 ■ *Web:* www.guardianlife.com	New York	NY	10004	888-482-7342		391-2
Guardian Lima LLC 2485 Houx Pkwy *Web:* www.guardianlima.com	Lima	OH	45804	567-940-9500		580
Guardian Mobility Corp 43 Auriga Dr *TF:* 888-817-8159 ■ *Web:* www.guardianmobility.com	Ottawa	ON	K2E7Y8	613-225-8885		647
Guardian Packaging Industries, LP 3615 Security St *TF:* 800-259-1502 ■ *Web:* www.guardianpackaging.com	Garland	TX	75042	214-349-1500		601
Guardian Protection Services Inc 174 Thorn Hill Rd *TF:* 877-314-7092 ■ *Web:* www.guardianprotection.com	Warrendale	PA	15086	855-779-2001		693
Guardian Software Systems Inc 109 S Concord St *Web:* www.guardiansoft.com	Oconomowoc	WI	53066	262-567-0341	567-8552	178-1
Guardian Technologies LLC 7700 St Clair Ave *TF:* 866-603-5900 ■ *Web:* www.guardiantechnologies.com	Mentor	OH	44060	866-603-5900		35
Guardian, The 165 Prince St *Web:* www.theguardian.pe.ca	Charlottetown	PE	C1A4R7	902-629-6000	566-3808	532-1
Guard-Line Inc 215 S Louise St PO Box 1030 *TF:* 800-527-8822 ■ *Web:* www.guardline.com	Atlanta	TX	75551	903-796-4111	796-7262	155-8
Guatemalan Embassy 2220 R St NW Ste 102 *Web:* www.consulateofguatemalaindenver.org	Washington	DC	20008	202-745-4953	745-1908	257
Gud Marketing 1223 Turner St Ste 101 *Web:* www.gudmarketing.com	Lansing	MI	48906	517-267-9800	267-9815	7
Guelph Chamber of Commerce 111 Farquhar St *Web:* www.guelphchamber.com	Guelph	ON	N1H3N4	519-822-8081	822-8451	137
Guelph General Hospital 115 Delhi St *TF:* 855-329-5684 ■ *Web:* www.gghorg.ca	Guelph	ON	N1E4J4	519-822-5350	837-6773	374-2
Guenther House 205 E Guenther St *TF:* 800-235-8186 ■ *Web:* www.guentherhouse.com	San Antonio	TX	78204	210-227-1061		50-3
Guerbet LLC 120 W Seventh St Ste 108 *TF:* 877-729-6679 ■ *Web:* www.guerbet-us.com	Bloomington	IN	47404	812-333-0059		231
Guernsey County 801 Wheeling Ave *Web:* www.guernseycounty.org	Cambridge	OH	43725	740-432-9200	432-9359	338
Guernsey Inc 46070 Old Ox Rd *TF:* 800-818-5765 ■ *Web:* www.shop.buyguernsey.com	Dulles	VA	20100	703-968-8200	689-2809	535
Guernsey Industries Inc 60772 Southgate Rd **Fax Area Code:* 844 ■ *TF:* 855-692-7247 ■ *Web:* guernseyindustries.com	Byesville	OH	43723	740-439-5017	809-1160*	88
Guernsey State Park 2187 Lakeside Shore Dr	Guernsey	WY	82214	307-836-2900		565
Guernsey's 65 E 93rd St *Web:* www.guernseys.com	New York	NY	10128	212-794-2280	744-3638	393
Guernsey-Muskingum Electric Co-op 17 S Liberty St *TF:* 800-521-9879 ■ *Web:* www.gmenergy.com	New Concord	OH	43762	740-826-7661	826-7171	245
Guerra Publishing Inc PO Box 1128 *Web:* www.guerrapublishing.com	Spring Branch	TX	78070	830-228-5047	885-5098	637-2
Guest Communications Corp 15009 W 101st Terr *TF:* 800-637-8525 ■ *Web:* www.gcckc.com	Shawnee Mission	KS	66215	913-888-1217	888-4947	637-6
Guest Michael (Rep R - MS) 230 Cannon House Office Bldg *Web:* www.guest.house.gov	Washington	DC	20515	202-225-5031		342-2
Guest Services Inc 3055 Prosperity Ave *TF:* 800-345-7534 ■ *Web:* www.guestservices.com	Fairfax	VA	22031	703-849-9300		299
Guest Supply Inc 300 Davidson Ave **Fax Area Code:* 800 ■ *TF:* 800-772-7676 ■ *Web:* www.guestsupply.com	Somerset	NJ	08873	732-868-2200	480-7878*	214
GuestCounts Hospitality 1 Reed St Ste 200 *Web:* www.guestcounts.com	Philadelphia	PA	19147	215-922-3200	922-7429	671
Guestlogix Inc 111 Peter St Ste 407 *Web:* www.guestlogix.com	Toronto	ON	M5V2H1	647-317-1517		253
Guest-tek Ltd 777 8 Ave SW Ste 600 *Web:* www.guesttek.com	Calgary	AB	T2P3R5	403-509-1010		177
Guggenheim Hermitage Museum Venetian Resort Hotel & Casino 3355 Las Vegas Blvd S *Web:* www.guggenheim.org	Las Vegas	NV	89109	212-423-3575		520
Guggisberg Cheese Inc 5060 SR- 557 *TF:* 800-262-2505 ■ *Web:* www.babyswiss.com	Millersburg	OH	44654	330-893-2500		292
Guhring Inc 1445 Commerce Ave *TF:* 800-776-6170 ■ *Web:* www.guhring.com	Brookfield	WI	53045	262-784-6730	784-9096	493
Guida's Dairy 433 Park St *TF:* 800-832-8929 ■ *Web:* guidas.com	New Britain	CT	06051	800-832-8929		296-27
Guida, Slavich & Flores PC 750 N St Paul St Ste 200 *Web:* www.guidaslavichflores.com	Dallas	TX	75201	214-692-0009	692-6610	428
Guidance Charter School, The 38007 6th St E *Web:* www.thegcs.org	Palmdale	CA	93550	661-272-1701	272-1728	685
Guidance Solutions Inc 4134 Del Rey Ave *Web:* www.guidance.com	Marina	CA	90292	310-754-4000	754-4010	736
Guidant Law PLC 402 E S Ave *Web:* kuzmichlegal.com	Tempe	AZ	85282	480-422-4991		41
Guidant Partners 2 Maryland Farms Ste 195 *Web:* www.guidantpartners.com	Brentwood	TN	37027	615-327-9111		196
Guide Book Publishing 322 Sovereign Ct *TF:* 800-597-3037 ■ *Web:* www.guidebookpublishing.com	Saint Louis	MO	63101	636-391-2121	391-3172	637-10
Guide Dog Foundation for the Blind Inc 371 E Jericho Tkpe *TF:* 800-548-4337 ■ *Web:* www.guidedog.org	Smithtown	NY	11787	631-930-9000	930-9009	48-17
Guide Dogs for the Blind 350 Los Ranchitos Rd *TF:* 800-295-4050 ■ *Web:* www.guidedogs.com	San Rafael	CA	94903	415-499-4000	499-4035	48-17
Guide Dogs of America 13445 Glenoaks Blvd *TF:* 800-459-4843 ■ *Web:* www.guidedogsofamerica.org	Sylmar	CA	91342	818-362-5834	362-6870	48-17
Guide Technologies LLC 250 E 96th St Ste 525 *Web:* guidetechnologies.com	Indianapolis	IN	46240	317-844-3162		180

Name / Address	City	State	ZIP	Phone	Fax	Class
Guide, The 24904 Sussex Hwy PO Box 1210 *TF:* 800-984-8433 ■ *Web:* www.theguide.com	Seaford	DE	19973	302-629-5060	628-9207	627
Guidecraft USA 55508 Hwy 19 W *TF:* 800-524-3555 ■ *Web:* guidecraft.com	Winthrop	MN	55396	507-647-5030	647-3254	762
Guided Discoveries 27282 Calle Arroyo **Fax Area Code:* 909 ■ *TF:* 800-645-1423 ■ *Web:* guideddiscoveries.org	San Juan Capistrano	CA	92675	800-645-1423	625-7305*	239
Guided Therapeutics Inc 5835 Peachtree Corners E Ste D *OTC:* GTHP ■ *Web:* www.guidedinc.com	Norcross	GA	30092	770-242-8723	242-8639	477
Guided Wave Inc 3033 Gold Canal Dr *Web:* guided-wave.com	Rancho Cordova	CA	95670	916-638-4944	635-8458	201
Guideline Technologies 3050 S Delaware St Ste 202 *TF:* 888-228-3491 ■ *Web:* www.guideline.com	San Mateo	CA	94403	888-228-3491		113
Guidelines International Ministries 26161 Marguerite Pkwy Ste F *Web:* www.guidelines.org	Mission Viejo	CA	92692	949-582-5001		48-20
Guidemark Health Inc 6 Campus Dr *Web:* www.guidemarkhealth.com	Parsippany	NJ	07054	201-740-6160		5
GuideOne Mutual Insurance Co 1111 Ashworth Rd *TF:* 877-448-4331 ■ *Web:* www.guideone.com	West Des Moines	IA	50265	877-448-4331		391-4
Guidepoint Global LLC 730 Third Ave 11th Fl *Web:* www.guidepoint.com	New York	NY	10017	212-375-2980		466
Guidepoint Systems 25307 Dequindre Rd *Web:* www.guidepointsystems.com	Madison Heights	MI	48071	248-399-4543		690
Guideposts Books 110 William St Ste 901 *Web:* www.guideposts.org	New York	NY	10038	212-251-8100		637-2
Guidesoft Inc 5875 Castle Creek Pkwy Ste 400 *TF:* 877-256-6948 ■ *Web:* www.knowledgeservices.com	Indianapolis	IN	46250	317-578-1700		41
Guiding Light Video Co 3649 Mill Rd *Web:* www.guidinglightvideo.com	Collegeville	PA	19426	610-489-0746		459
Guidry's Catfish Inc 1093 Henderson Hwy *TF:* 800-867-4750 ■ *Web:* www.guidryscatfish.com	Breaux Bridge	LA	70517	337-228-7545	228-7544	297-5
Guild Associates Inc, The 389 Main St Ste 202 *Web:* www.guildassoc.com	Malden	MA	02148	781-397-8870	397-8887	47
Guild Education Republic Plaza 370 17th St *Web:* www.guildeducation.com	Denver	CO	80202	720-378-5452		49-5
Guild for Psychological Studies PO Box 29385 *Web:* www.guildsf.org	San Francisco	CA	94129	415-561-2385		49-19
Guild Hotel, San Diego, a Tribute Portfolio Hotel, The 500 W Broadway *Web:* theguildhotel.com	San Diego	CA	92101	619-234-5252	234-5272	379
Guild Investment Management Inc 12400 Wilshire Blvd Ste 1080 *TF:* 800-645-4100 ■ *Web:* guildinvestment.com	Los Angeles	CA	90025	310-826-8600		528
Guild Mortgage Co 5898 Copley Dr 4th Fl PO Box 85304 *TF:* 800-365-4441 ■ *Web:* www.guildmortgage.com	San Diego	CA	92111	800-365-4441		509
Guild of American Luthiers 8222 S Park Ave *Web:* www.luth.org	Tacoma	WA	98408	253-472-7853		48-4
Guild Shop of The Church of st John The Divine, The 2009 Dunlavy St *Web:* www.theguildshop.org	Houston	TX	77006	713-528-5095		48-20
Guilderland Chamber of Commerce 2050 Western Ave Ste 109 *Web:* www.guilderlandchamber.com	Guilderland	NY	12084	518-456-6611	456-6690	139
Guilford College 5800 W Friendly Ave *TF:* 800-992-7759 ■ *Web:* www.guilford.edu	Greensboro	NC	27410	336-316-2000	316-2954	166
Guilford County 301 W Market St PO Box 3427 *Web:* www.myguilford.com	Greensboro	NC	27401	336-641-3383		338
Guilford County Schools 712 N Eugene St *TF:* 866-286-7337 ■ *Web:* www.gcsnc.com	Greensboro	NC	27401	336-370-8100	370-8398	685
Guilford Press 370 7th Ave Ste 1200 **Fax Area Code:* 212 ■ *TF:* 800-365-7006 ■ *Web:* www.guilford.com	New York	NY	10001	800-365-7006	966-6708*	637-2
Guilford Savings Bank (GSB) PO Box 369 *TF:* 866-878-1480 ■ *Web:* www.gsb-yourbank.com	Guilford	CT	06437	203-453-3290		70
Guilford Technical Community College 601 E Main St PO Box 309 *Web:* www.gtcc.edu	Jamestown	NC	27282	336-334-4822		162
Guilford Veterinary Hospital LLP 81 Saw Mill Rd *Web:* guilfordvet.com	Guilford	CT	06437	203-453-2707		794
Guill Tool & Engineering Company Inc 10 Pike St *Web:* www.guill.com	West Warwick	RI	02893	401-828-7600	823-5310	757
Guillon Inc 2550 Lakewest Dr Ste 50 *Web:* gbrealestate.net	Chico	CA	95928	530-897-6452		653
Guinea Embassy 2112 Leroy Pl NW *Web:* guineaembassyusa.org	Washington	DC	20008	202-986-4300		257
Guinness World Records Museum 4943 Clifton Hill *TF:* 866-656-0310 ■ *Web:* falls.com	Niagara Falls	ON	L2G3N5	905-357-4330		520
Guiry's Paint 5475 Leetsdale Dr *Web:* www.guirys.com	Denver	CO	80246	303-757-5435	759-5036	802
Guitar Center Inc 5795 Lindero Canyon Rd *Web:* www.guitarcenter.com	Westlake Village	CA	91362	818-735-8800		526
Guitar Player Magazine 28 E 28th St 12th Fl *TF:* 800-289-9839 ■ *Web:* www.guitarplayer.com	New York	NY	10016	212-378-0400		457 9

Name / Address	City	State	ZIP	Phone	Fax	Class
Guittard Chocolate Co 10 Guittard Rd *TF:* 800-468-2462 ■ *Web:* www.guittard.com	Burlingame	CA	94010	650-697-4427	692-2761	296-8
Gulf & Ohio Railways Inc PO Box 2408 *Web:* www.gulfandohio.com	Knoxville	TN	37901	865-525-9400		360-3
Gulf & Pacific Equities Corp 1300 Bay St Ste 300 *Web:* www.gpequities.com	Toronto	ON	M5R3K8	416-968-3337		186
Gulf Asphalt Corp 4116 US Hwy 231 *Web:* www.gaccontractors.com	Panama City	FL	32404	850-785-4675	769-3456	188-4
Gulf Bay 8156 Fiddler's Creek Pkwy *Web:* www.gulfbay.com	Naples	FL	34114	239-732-9402		378
Gulf Beaches Historical Museum 115 Tenth Ave *Web:* gulfbeachesmuseum.com	Saint Pete Beach	FL	33706	727-552-1610		520
Gulf Branch Nature Center & Park Grounds 3608 N Military Rd *Web:* www.arlingtonva.us	Arlington	VA	22207	703-228-3403		50-5
Gulf Breeze News Inc 913 Gulf Breeze Pkwy Ste 35 *Web:* www.gulfbreezenews.com	Gulf Breeze	FL	32561	850-932-8986		177
Gulf Breeze Zoo 5701 Gulf Breeze Pkwy *Web:* gulfbreezezoo.org	Gulf Breeze	FL	32563	850-932-2229		823
Gulf Business Forms Inc 2460 IH 35 S *TF:* 800-433-4853 ■ *Web:* gulfforms.com	San Marcos	TX	78666	512-353-8313	353-8866	110
Gulf Coast Assisting Hands 2203 N Lois Ave Ste G450 *Web:* www.assistinghands.com	Tampa	FL	33607	813-868-6782		363
Gulf Coast Autoplex LLC 414 W Fred & Ruth Zingler Memorial Dr *TF:* 888-526-2391 ■ *Web:* www.sterlingchryslerdodgejeepramwest.com	Jennings	LA	70546	888-526-2391		57
Gulf Coast Bank 4310 Johnston St *TF:* 800-722-5363 ■ *Web:* www.gcbank.com	LaFayette	LA	70503	337-989-1133		70
Gulf Coast Bank & Trust Co 200 St Charles Ave *TF:* 800-223-2060 ■ *Web:* gulfbank.com	New Orleans	LA	70130	504-561-6100		685
Gulf Coast Chemical Inc 2 Magdalen Ctr *TF:* 800-264-4853 ■ *Web:* www.gulfcoastchemical.com	Abbeville	LA	70511	337-740-7414	893-9927	145
Gulf Coast Collection Bureau Inc 5630 Marquesas Cir *TF:* 888-839-6999 ■ *Web:* gulfcoastcollection.com	Sarasota	FL	34233	941-927-6999		160
Gulf Coast Community College 5230 W Hwy 98 *TF:* 800-311-3685 ■ *Web:* www.gulfcoast.edu	Panama City	FL	32401	850-769-1551	913-3308	162
Gulf Coast Electric Co-opeartive Inc 722 W Hwy 22 PO Box 220 *TF:* 800-333-9392 ■ *Web:* www.gcec.com	Wewahitchka	FL	32465	850-639-2216	639-5061	245
Gulf Coast Exploreum Science Ctr 65 Government St *Web:* www.exploreum.com	Mobile	AL	36602	251-208-6893	208-6889	521
Gulf Coast Machine Services LLC 436 N Eola Rd *Web:* gulfcoastmachineservices.com	Broussard	LA	70518	337-837-3175	837-6044	539
Gulf Coast Manufacturing LLC 3622 W Main St *Web:* gulfcoastmfg.com	Gray	LA	70359	985-872-0187		537
Gulf Coast Marine LLC 2626 N Arnoult Rd *Web:* g-c-m.com	Metairie	LA	70002	504-883-2600		390
Gulf Coast Medical Ctr (GCMC) 10141 US 59 Rd *Web:* www.gulfcoastmedical.com	Wharton	TX	77488	979-532-2500		374-3
Gulf Coast Mental Health Ctr 1600 Broad Ave *TF:* 800-681-0798 ■ *Web:* www.gcmhc.com	Gulfport	MS	39501	228-863-1132		726
Gulf Coast Office Products Inc 5801 River Oaks Rd S *Web:* www.gcopnet.com	New Orleans	LA	70123	504-733-3830	733-3840	112
Gulf Coast Paper Company Inc 3705 Houston Hwy *TF:* 800-876-5076 ■ *Web:* shop.gulfcoastpaper.com	Victoria	TX	77901	361-576-1237	575-8468	612
Gulf Coast Pharmaceuticals Inc 995A N Halstead Rd **Fax Area Code:* 228 ■ *TF:* 888-574-7366 ■ *Web:* www.gulfcoastpharmaceuticalsplus.com	Ocean Springs	MS	39564	888-574-7366	875-5596*	238
Gulf Coast Pre-stress Inc 494 Market St *Web:* www.gcprestress.com	Pass Christian	MS	39571	228-452-9486	452-9495	183
Gulf Coast Regional Blood Ctr 1400 La Concha Ln *TF:* 888-482-5663 ■ *Web:* www.giveblood.org	Houston	TX	77054	713-790-1200		89
Gulf Coast Research Laboratory 703 E Beach Dr *Web:* gcrl.usm.edu	Ocean Springs	MS	39564	228-872-4200		40
Gulf Coast Signs of Sarasota Inc 1713 Northgate Blvd *Web:* gulfcoastsigns.com	Sarasota	FL	34234	941-355-8841		701
Gulf Coast Tmc 7670 Hwy 10 *Web:* www.gulfcoasttmc.com	Ethel	LA	70730	225-683-6636		636
Gulf Coast Treatment Ctr 1015 Mar-Walt Dr *TF:* 800-537-5433 ■ *Web:* gulfcoasttc.com	Fort Walton Beach	FL	32547	850-863-4160	863-8576	374-1
Gulf Coast Village 1333 Santa Barbara Blvd *Web:* www.gulfcoastvillage.com	Cape Coral	FL	33991	239-772-1333		672
Gulf Compress 201 N 19th St PO Box 1378 *Web:* www.gulfcompress.com	Corpus Christi	TX	78408	361-882-5489	882-8081	803-1
Gulf Copper & Manufacturing Corp 5700 Procter St Ext *Web:* www.gulfcopper.com	Port Arthur	TX	77642	409-989-0300		698
Gulf Correctional Institution 500 Ike Steele Rd *Web:* dc.state.fl.us	Wewahitchka	FL	32465	850-639-1000	639-1182	213

Name / Address	Phone	Fax	Class
Gulf County 1000 Cecil Costin Sr Blvd Rm 148 . . . Port Saint Joe FL 32456 *Web:* www.gulfcounty-fl.gov	850-229-6112	229-6174	338
Gulf Craft LLC 320 Boro Ln . . . Franklin LA 70538 *Web:* www.gulfcraft.com	337-828-2580	828-2586	698
Gulf Crane Services Inc 73413 Bollfield Dr . . . Covington LA 70435 *TF:* 800-394-0093 ■ *Web:* gulfcraneservices.com	985-892-0056	892-4061	190
Gulf Crown Seafood Company Inc 306 Jon Floyd Rd . . . Delcambre LA 70528 *Web:* gulfcrown.us	337-685-4721		296-14
Gulf District Schools 150 Middle School Rd . . . Port Saint Joe FL 32456 *Web:* www.gulfcoschools.com	850-229-8256	229-6089	685
Gulf Electric Company Incorporated of Mobile PO Box 2385 . . . Mobile AL 36652 *Web:* www.gulfelec.com	251-666-0654	666-6323	189-4
Gulf Energy Information 2 Greenway Plz Ste 1020 . . . Houston TX 77046 *Web:* www.gulfenergyinfo.com	713-529-4301		637-9
Gulf Engineering LLC 611 Hill St . . . Jefferson LA 70121 *TF:* 800-347-4749 ■ *Web:* www.gulfengineering.com	504-733-4868		188
Gulf Hills Hotel 13701 Paso Rd . . . Ocean Springs MS 39564 *TF:* 866-875-4211 ■ *Web:* www.gulfhillshotel.com	228-875-4211	875-4213	669
Gulf Interstate Engineering 16010 Barkers Pt Ln Ste 600 . . . Houston TX 77079 *TF:* 800-521-8879 ■ *Web:* gie.com	713-850-3400	850-3579	261
Gulf Island Fabrication Inc 16225 Park Ten Pl . . . Houston TX 77084 *Web:* www.gulfisland.com	713-714-6100	714-6130	698
Gulf Islands National Seashore (Florida) 1801 Gulf Breeze Pkwy . . . Gulf Breeze FL 32563 *Web:* www.nps.gov	850-934-2600		564
Gulf Islands National Seashore (Mississippi) 3500 Park Rd . . . Ocean Springs MS 39564 *Web:* www.nps.gov	228-230-4100		564
Gulf Machine Shop Inc 5337 E Broad St . . . Lake Charles LA 70616 *Web:* gulfmachineshop.com	337-436-9411	436-9515	454
Gulf Manufacturing LLC 1221 Indiana St . . . Humble TX 77396 *TF:* 800-333-4493 ■ *Web:* www.gmigroup.com	281-446-0093	446-7971	567
Gulf Marine & Industrial Supplies Inc 5501 Jefferson Hwy . . . New Orleans LA 70123 *Web:* www.gulfmarine.net	504-525-6252	525-4761	770
Gulf Marine Repair Corp 1800 Grant St . . . Tampa FL 33605 *Web:* gulfmarinerepair.com	813-247-3153		698
Gulf of Maine Research Institute, The 350 Commercial St . . . Portland ME 04101 *Web:* www.gmri.org	207-772-2321		466
Gulf Offshore Logistics LLC 4535 Hwy 308 PO Box 309 . . . Raceland LA 70394 *TF:* 866-532-1060 ■ *Web:* www.gulf-log.com	866-532-1060		539
Gulf Oil LP 80 William St Ste 400 . . . Wellesley MA 02481 *TF:* 800-774-4853 ■ *Web:* gulfoil.com	339-933-7200		579
Gulf Regional Planning Commission 1635-G Popps Ferry Rd . . . Biloxi MS 39531 *Web:* www.grpc.com	228-864-1167		261
Gulf Seaboard General Contractors Inc 629 N Washington Hwy . . . Ashland VA 23005 *Web:* gulfseaboard.com	804-752-7600		186
Gulf South Machine Inc 39611 SW I 55 Service Rd . . . Ponchatoula LA 70454 *Web:* gulfsouthmachine.com	985-386-9401	386-9206	454
Gulf South Research Corp 8081 G S R I Rd . . . Baton Rouge LA 70820 *Web:* www.gsrcorp.com	225-757-8088		463
Gulf State Park 20115 Alabama 135 . . . Gulf Shores AL 36542 *Web:* www.alapark.com	251-948-7275	948-7726	565
Gulf States Distributors Inc 6000 E Shirley Ln . . . Montgomery AL 36117 *Web:* gulfstatesdist.com	334-271-2010		711
Gulf States Engineering Inc 4110 Moffett Rd . . . Mobile AL 36618 *TF:* 866-325-4646 ■ *Web:* www.gseeng.com	251-460-4646	460-4649	791
Gulf Stream Coach Inc 503 S Oakland Ave PO Box 1005 . . . Nappanee IN 46550 *TF:* 800-289-8787 ■ *Web:* www.gulfstreamcoach.com	800-289-8787		120
Gulf Winds International Inc 411 Brisbane St . . . Houston TX 77061 *TF:* 866-238-4909 ■ *Web:* www.gwii.com	713-747-4909	747-5330	803-1
Gulfland Office Supplies Inc 801 Brashear Ave . . . Morgan City LA 70380 *Web:* www.gulflandoffice.com	985-384-3250		535
GulfMark Energy Inc 17 S Briar Hollow Ln Ste 100 . . . Houston TX 77027 *TF:* 800-340-1495 ■ *Web:* gulfmarkenergy.com	800-340-1495		538
Gulfport Energy Corp 3001 Quail Springs Pkwy Ste 100 . . . Oklahoma City OK 73134 *Web:* www.gulfportenergy.com	405-252-4600		536
Gulfport/Biloxi International Airport 14035 - L Airport Rd . . . Gulfport MS 39503 *Web:* www.flygpt.com	228-863-5951	863-5953	27
Gulfside Hospice Inc 6224 Lafayette St . . . New Port Richey FL 34652 *TF:* 800-561-4883 ■ *Web:* www.gulfside.org	800-561-4883		371
GulfSlope Energy Inc 1331 Lamar St Ste 1665 . . . Houston TX 77010 *Web:* www.gulfslope.com	281-918-4100		536
Gulfstream Aerospace Corp 500 Gulfstream Rd . . . Savannah GA 31408 *Web:* www.gulfstream.com	912-965-3000	395-8222	20
Gulfstream Park 901 S Federal Hwy . . . Hallandale Beach FL 33009 *Web:* www.gulfstreampark.com	954-454-7000		133
Gull Assoc 14 Victoria Ln . . . Old Lyme CT 06371 *Web:* gullassociates.com	860-434-8214		366
Gull Industries 3404 4th Ave S . . . Seattle WA 98134	206-624-5900		579
Gullett & Associates Inc 7135 Office City Dr . . . Houston TX 77087 *Web:* gullettservices.com	713-644-3219		536
Gullett, Sanford, Robinson & Martin PLLC 150 Third Ave S Ste 1700 . . . Nashville TN 37201 *Web:* www.gsrm.com	615-244-4994		428
Gulley And Associates 2911 E 77th Pl . . . Tulsa OK 74136 *Web:* www.gulleyassociates.com	918-744-0100	488-8450	357
Gullickson Group, The 2310 Jersey Ridge Rd . . . Davenport IA 52803 *Web:* gullicksongroup.com	563-823-1500		390
Gulliver's Travel Service Inc 2800 S Hulen Ste 110 . . . Fort Worth TX 76109 *TF:* 800-796-7766 ■ *Web:* gullivers.com	817-924-7766	924-3100	772
Gully Transportation Inc 3820 Wismann Ln . . . Quincy IL 62305 *TF:* 800-566-8950 ■ *Web:* www.gullyicx.com	217-224-0770	224-9885	780
Gulo Solutions LLC 1467 N Elston Ave Ste 105 . . . Chicago IL 60642 *Web:* www.gulosolutions.com	773-276-8066		177
Gulph Creek Hotels Inc 150 Strafford Ave Ste 215 . . . Wayne PA 19087 *Web:* gulphcreekhotels.com	610-687-9283		132
Gumas Advertising LLC 99 Shotwell St . . . San Francisco CA 94103 *Web:* gumas.com	415-621-7575		393
Gumbiner Savett Inc 1723 Cloverfield Blvd . . . Santa Monica CA 90404 *Web:* gscpa.com	310-828-9798		2
Gumbo Limbo Nature Ctr 1801 N Ocean Blvd . . . Boca Raton FL 33432 *Web:* www.gumbolimbo.org	561-544-8605	544-8617	50-5
Gumbo Pot Inc, The 6333 W 3rd St Ste 312 . . . Los Angeles CA 90036	323-933-0358		671
Gump's 135 Post St . . . San Francisco CA 94108 *TF:* 800-766-7628 ■ *Web:* www.gumps.com	415-984-9250	984-9374	362
Gun Barrel Steak & Game House 862 West Broadway . . . Jackson WY 83001 *Web:* jackson.gunbarrel.com	307-733-3287	733-6090	671
Gun Parts Corp 226 Williams Ln . . . Kingston NY 12401 **Fax Area Code:* 877 ■ *TF:* 866-686-7424 ■ *Web:* www.gunpartscorp.com	845-679-4867	486-7278*	284
Gund Co 2121 Walton Rd . . . Saint Louis MO 63114 *TF:* 800-265-2957 ■ *Web:* www.thegundcompany.com	314-423-5200	423-9009	816
Gund Inc 1 Runyons Ln . . . Edison NJ 08817 *TF:* 800-448-4863 ■ *Web:* www.gundbusiness.com	732-248-1500		762
Gunda Corporation LLC 11750 Katy Fwy Ste 300 . . . Houston TX 77079 *Web:* gundacorp.com	713-541-3530	541-0032	186
Gundersen Credit Union 1910 S Ave . . . La Crosse WI 54601 *TF:* 800-362-9567 ■ *Web:* gundersencu.org	608-775-4715		219
Gunderson Dettmer Stough Villeneuve Franklin & Hachigian LLP 1200 Seaport Blvd . . . Redwood City CA 94063 *Web:* www.gunder.com	650-321-2400		41
Gunderson Palmer Nelson & Ashmore LLP 506 Sixth St . . . Rapid City SD 57701 *Web:* gpna.com	605-720-1080		445
Gundlach Champion Inc 180 Traders Mine Rd . . . Iron Mountain MI 49801 *Web:* www.gcfirst.com	906-779-2303		186
Gunlocke Co 1 Gunlocke Dr . . . Wayland NY 14572 *TF:* 800-828-6300 ■ *Web:* www.gunlocke.com	585-728-5111		319-1
Gunn Automotive Group 227 Broadway . . . San Antonio TX 78205 *TF:* 888-452-2856 ■ *Web:* www.gunnauto.com	210-988-9598		57
Gunn Memorial Public Library 161 Main St E . . . Yanceyville NC 27379 *Web:* www.caswellcountync.gov	336-694-6241	694-9846	434-3
Gunnchamberlain CPA Firm Pl 4350 Pablo Professional Ct Ste 200 . . . Jacksonville FL 32224 *Web:* gunnchamberlain.com	904-296-2024		2
Gunnebo-Johnson Corp 1240 N Harvard Ave . . . Tulsa OK 74115 *TF:* 800-331-5460 ■ *Web:* www.gunnebojohnson.com	918-832-8933	834-0984	470
Gunnery, The 99 Green Hill Rd . . . Washington Depot CT 06793 *Web:* www.gunnery.org	860-868-7334		622
Gunnison Country Times 218 N Wisconsin St . . . Gunnison CO 81230 *Web:* www.gunnisontimes.com	970-641-1414		532-2
Gunnison County 221 N Wisconsin St Ste C . . . Gunnison CO 81230 *Web:* www.gunnisoncounty.org	970-641-1516	641-7956	338
Gunnison County Electric Association Inc 37250 W Hwy 50 PO Box 180 . . . Gunnison CO 81230 *TF:* 800-726-3523 ■ *Web:* www.gcea.coop	970-641-3520		245
Gunnison Telecommunications Co (GTELCO) 29 S Main St . . . Gunnison UT 84634 *Web:* www.gtelco.net	435-528-7236		224
Gunn-Mowery LLC 650 N 12th St . . . Lemoyne PA 17043 *Web:* gunnmowery.com	717-761-4600		390
Gunnoe Sausage Company Inc 3989 Cifax Rd . . . Goode VA 24556 *Web:* www.gunnoesausage.com	540-586-1091		296-26
Gunpowder Falls State Park 2813 Jerusalem Rd . . . Kingsville MD 21087 *Web:* www.dnr.maryland.gov	410-592-2897		565
Gunsite Academy Inc 2900 W Gunsite Rd . . . Paulden AZ 86334 *Web:* www.gunsite.com	928-636-4565		711
Gunster Yoakley & Stewart Pa 777 S Flagler Dr Ste 500 E . . . West Palm Beach FL 33401 **Fax Area Code:* 561 ■ *TF:* 800-749-1980 ■ *Web:* gunster.com	305-367-2324	655-5677*	428
Gunstock Recreation Area 719 Cherry Valley Rd . . . Gilford NH 03249 *Web:* www.gunstock.com	603-293-4341		378
Guntersville City Schools Board of Education 4200 Alabama 79 S . . . Guntersville AL 35976 *Web:* www.guntersvilleboe.com	256-582-3159	582-6158	186
Guntersville Public Library 1240 O'Brig Ave . . . Guntersville AL 35976 *Web:* guntersvillelibrary.org	256-571-7595		434-3

	Phone	Fax	Class
Guntert & Zimmerman Construction Div Inc 222 E Fourth St . . . Ripon CA 95366 *TF:* 800-733-2912 ■ *Web:* www.guntert.com	209-599-0066		190
Gunther Douglas Inc 1430 Larimer St Ste 208 . . . Denver CO 80211 *Web:* www.guntherdouglas.com	303-534-4441		260
Gunther Mele Ltd 30 Craig St . . . Brantford ON N3R7J1 *TF:* 888-486-8437 ■ *Web:* www.gunthermele.com	519-756-4330		601
Gunze USA 2113 Wells Branch Pkwy Ste 5400 . . . Austin TX 78728 *Web:* www.gunzeusa.com	512-990-3400	252-1181	173-4
Gupton Marrs International Inc 245 Park Ave 39th Fl . . . New York NY 10167 *Web:* www.guptonmarrs.com	212-372-8880		463
Gupton-Jones College of Funeral Service 5141 Snapfinger Woods Dr . . . Decatur GA 30035 *TF:* 800-848-5352 ■ *Web:* www.gupton-jones.edu	770-593-2257	593-1891	800
Guralnick & Gilliland LLP 40004 Cook St Ste 3 . . . Palm Desert CA 92211 *Web:* gghoalaw.com	760-340-1515	568-3053	41
Gurecky Manufacturing Service Inc 2420 3rd St . . . Rosenberg TX 77471 *Web:* www.gurecky.com	281-342-5926		454
Gurley Leep Automotive Group 4004 N Grape Rd . . . Mishawaka IN 46545 *TF:* 888-702-8974 ■ *Web:* www.gurleyleep.com	574-272-0990	256-5427	57
Gurley Motor Co 701 W Coal . . . Gallup NM 87301 *Web:* www.gurleymotorford.com	505-722-6621		57
Gurley's Foods 1118 E Hwy 12 . . . Willmar MN 56201 *TF:* 800-426-7845 ■ *Web:* www.gurleysfoods.com	320-235-0600		296-9
Gurney Brothers Construction Inc 19 Gurney Rd . . . North Springfield VT 05150 *Web:* www.gurneybros.com	802-886-2210	886-2249	189-5
Gurney Productions Inc 8929 S Sepulveda Blvd Ste 510 . . . Los Angeles CA 90045 *Web:* gurneyproductions.com	310-645-1499		514
Gurney's Montauk Resort & Seawater Spa 290 Old Montauk Hwy . . . Montauk NY 11954 *TF:* 800-848-7639 ■ *Web:* www.gurneysresorts.com	631-668-2345		669
Gurney's Star Island Resort & Marina 32 Star Island Rd . . . Montauk NY 11954 *TF:* 888-692-8668 ■ *Web:* www.montaukyachtclub.com	631-668-3100		669
Gurnick Academy of Medical Arts 7335 N Palm Bluffs Ave . . . Fresno CA 93711 *Web:* www.gurnick.edu	559-222-1903	222-2672	230
Gurstel Chargo LLP 6681 Country Club Dr . . . Golden Valley MN 55427 *TF:* 877-750-6335 ■ *Web:* www.gurstel.com	877-344-4002		428
Guru Labs 1148 W Legacy Crossing Blvd Ste 200 . . . Centerville UT 84014 *TF:* 800-833-3582 ■ *Web:* www.gurulabs.com	801-298-5227	298-1149	94
Guru Studio 500-110 Spadina Ave . . . Toronto ON M5V2K4 *Web:* www.gurustudio.com	416-599-4878		514
Guru Technologies Inc North American Building 121 S Broad St 11th Fl . . . Philadelphia PA 19107 *Web:* getguru.com	267-469-0264		39
Gurucom 5001 Baum Blvd Ste 760 . . . Pittsburgh PA 15213 **Fax Area Code:* 412 ■ *TF:* 888-678-0136 ■ *Web:* www.guru.com	888-678-0136	687-4466*	260
Gurus Information Technology Services LLC 517 Georges Rd . . . North Brunswick NJ 08902 *Web:* www.gurusit.com	732-247-7747	247-7078	196
Gurwin Jewish Nursing & Rehabilitation Ctr 68 Hauppauge Rd . . . Commack NY 11725 *Web:* www.gurwin.org	631-715-2000		363
Gus Harrison Correctional Facility 2727 E Beecher St . . . Adrian MI 49221 *Web:* www.michigan.gov	517-265-3900		213
Gusher Pumps 115 Industrial Dr . . . Williamstown KY 41097 *Web:* www.gusher.com	859-824-3100	824-7248	641
Gusmer Enterprises Inc 1165 Globe Ave . . . Mountainside NJ 07092 *TF:* 866-213-1131 ■ *Web:* www.gusmerenterprises.com	908-301-1811	301-1812	14
Gust Rosenfeld PLC 1 E Washington St Ste 1600 . . . Phoenix AZ 85004 *TF:* 800-258-4878 ■ *Web:* www.gustlaw.com	602-257-7422	254-4878	41
Gustave A. Larson Co W233 N2869 Roundy Cir W . . . Pewaukee WI 53072 *TF:* 800-829-9609 ■ *Web:* www.galarson.com	262-542-0200	542-1400	665
Gustavson Associates LLC 5665 Flatiron Pkwy Ste 250 . . . Boulder CO 80301 *Web:* www.gustavson.com	303-443-2209	443-3156	668
Gustavus Adolphus College 800 W College Ave . . . Saint Peter MN 56082 *TF:* 800-487-8288 ■ *Web:* gustavus.edu	507-933-8000	933-7474	166
Gustman Chevrolet Sales Inc 1450 Delanglade St . . . Kaukauna WI 54130 *Web:* www.gustman.com	920-766-3581		57
Gusto 525 20th St . . . San Francisco CA 94107 *TF:* 800-936-0383 ■ *Web:* gusto.com	800-936-0383		178-8
Gutenberg College 1883 University St . . . Eugene OR 97403 *Web:* hello.gutenberg.edu	541-683-5141		166
Guth Laboratories Inc 590 N 67th St . . . Harrisburg PA 17111 *TF:* 800-233-2338 ■ *Web:* guthlabs.com	717-564-5470	564-2555	472
Guthrie & Associates Meeting & Event Management Inc 10889 La Alberca Ave . . . San Diego CA 92127 *Web:* www.guthrie-meetings-events.com	858-487-7759	487-8516	5
Guthrie County 200 N Fifth St . . . Guthrie Center IA 50115 *Web:* guthriecounty.org	641-747-3415		338
Guthrie Healthcare System 1011 N Elmer Ave . . . Sayre PA 18840 *TF:* 888-448-8474 ■ *Web:* www.guthrie.org	570-887-4401		353
Guthrie S. Brett (Rep R - KY) 2434 Rayburn House Office Bldg . . . Washington DC 20515 *Web:* guthrie.house.gov	202-225-3501	226-2019	342-2
Guthrie Theater 818 S Second St . . . Minneapolis MN 55415 *TF:* 877-447-8243 ■ *Web:* www.guthrietheater.org	612-377-2224		572
Guthrie, Nonemaker, Yingst & Hart LLP 40 York St . . . Hanover PA 17331 *Web:* gnyh.com	717-632-5315	632-5734	41
Guthy-Renker 100 N Sepulveda Blvd Ste 1600 . . . El Segundo CA 90245 *Web:* www.guthy-renker.com	310-581-6250	581-3232	514
Gutierrez Canales Engineering PC 1851 W 24th St Ste 201 . . . Yuma AZ 85364 *Web:* gce-pc.com	928-317-1401		261
Gutirrez Co, The 200 Summit Dr Ste 400 . . . Burlington MA 01803 *Web:* www.gutierrezco.com	781-272-7000	272-3130	186
Gutknecht Construction Co 2280 Citygate Dr . . . Columbus OH 43219 *Web:* www.gutknecht.com	614-532-5410		186
Gutman, Mintz, Baker & Sonnenfeldt 813 Jericho Tpke . . . New Hyde Park NY 11040 *Web:* www.gmbspc.com	516-775-7007	775-7052	428
Gutsy Women Travel LLC 801 E Katella Ave . . . Anaheim CA 92805 *TF:* 866-464-8879 ■ *Web:* www.gutsywomentravel.com	866-464-8879		760
Guttenberg Industries Inc 603 S Lincoln St . . . Garnavillo IA 52049 *Web:* www.guttenbergindustries.com	563-964-1000	964-1007	604
Guttenplans Frozen Dough 100 Hwy 36 . . . Middletown NJ 07748 *TF:* 888-422-4357 ■ *Web:* www.guttenplan.com	732-495-9480		296-2
Guttmacher Institute (AGI) 125 Maiden Ln 7th Fl . . . New York NY 10038 *TF:* 800-355-0244 ■ *Web:* www.guttmacher.org	212-248-1111	248-1951	48-5
Guttman Development Strategies Inc 400 Valley Rd Ste 103 . . . Mount Arlington NJ 07856 *Web:* www.guttmandev.com	973-770-7177		194
Guttman Group LLC, The 200 Speers St . . . Belle Vernon PA 15012 *Web:* www.guttmangroup.com	724-483-3533		539
Guttmann & Blaevoet 2351 Powell St . . . San Francisco CA 94133 *Web:* www.gb-eng.com	415-655-4000		539
Guy & O'Neill Inc 200 Industrial Dr . . . Fredonia WI 53021 *Web:* www.guyandoneill.com	262-692-2469		231
Guy Chemical Company Inc 150 Dominion Dr . . . Somerset PA 15501 *Web:* www.guychemical.com	814-443-9455	443-9470	88
Guy Engineering Services Inc 10759 E Admiral Pl . . . Tulsa OK 74116 *Web:* www.guyengr.com	918-437-0282		256
Guy Evans Inc 82585 Showcase Pkwy . . . Indio CA 92203	760-262-6300		499
Guy Hurley Blaser & Heuer LLC 1080 Kirts Blvd Ste 500 . . . Troy MI 48084 *Web:* ghbh.com	248-519-1400		390
Guy M. Turner Inc 4514 S Holden Rd PO Box 7776 . . . Greensboro NC 27406 *TF:* 800-432-4859 ■ *Web:* guymturner.com	336-294-4660	294-6668	780
Guy Shavender Trucking Inc PO Box 206 . . . Pantego NC 27860 *TF:* 800-682-2447 ■ *Web:* www.shavender.com	252-943-3379	943-6434	685
Guy's Academy Hair Skin & Nails 1141 Shreveport Barksdale Hwy . . . Shreveport LA 71105 *Web:* www.guysacademy.com	318-865-5591	869-1038	167-3
Guyana			
Consulate General 308 W 38th St . . . New York NY 10018 *Web:* www.guyana.org	212-947-5110	947-5163	257
Embassy 2490 Tracy Pl NW . . . Washington DC 20008 *Web:* www.guyana.org	202-265-6900		257
Guyer the Mover Inc 1050 Industrial Pky . . . Peru IN 46970 *TF:* 800-382-0605 ■ *Web:* www.guyerthemover.com	800-382-0605		803-1
Guzman & Co 101 Aragon Ave . . . Coral Gables FL 33134 *Web:* guzman.com	305-374-3600		690
Guzman's Machine Works Inc 3720 Nicole St . . . Paulina LA 70763 *Web:* www.guzmansmachine.com	225-869-3542	869-9840	454
Guzzler Manufacturing Inc 1621 S Illinois St . . . Streator IL 61364 *TF:* 800-627-3171 ■ *Web:* www.guzzler.com	815-672-3171	672-2779	386
GVC Capital LLC 5350 S Roslyn St Ste 400 . . . Greenwood Village CO 80111 *Web:* www.gvccap.com	303-694-0862	694-6287	690
GVD Commercial Properties Inc 1915 E Katella Ave Ste A . . . Orange CA 92867 *Web:* www.gvdcommercialproperties.com	714-639-2131	633-9602	652
Gvd Corp 45 Spinelli Pl . . . Cambridge MA 02138 *Web:* www.gvdcorp.com	617-661-0060		603
GVM (Grand Valley Manufacturing Co) 701 E Spring St Bldg 52 . . . Titusville PA 16354 *Web:* grandvalleymfg.com	814-827-2707	827-4349	454
GVNW Consulting 2270 La Montana Way Ste 200 . . . Colorado Springs CO 80918 *Web:* gvnw.com	719-594-5800		196
GVTC (Guadalupe Valley Telephone Co-op) 36101 FM 3159 . . . New Braunfels TX 78132 *TF:* 800-367-4882 ■ *Web:* gvtc.com	830-885-4411	885-2400	736
GVW (GVW Group LLC) 625 Roger Williams Ave . . . Highland Park IL 60035 *Web:* www.gvwgroup.com	847-681-8417	681-8515	360-3
GVW Group LLC (GVW) 625 Roger Williams Ave . . . Highland Park IL 60035 *Web:* www.gvwgroup.com	847-681-8417	681-8515	360-3
GW & Wade LLC 93 Worcester St . . . Wellesley MA 02481 *Web:* www.gwwade.com	781-239-1188		194
GW Berkheimer Company Inc 6000 Southport Rd . . . Portage IN 46368 *Web:* www.gwberkheimer.com	219-764-5200	764-5203	612
GW Fins 808 Bienville St . . . New Orleans LA 70112 *Web:* gwfins.com	504-581-3467		671
GW Hatchet, The 609 21st St NW . . . Washington DC 20052 *Web:* www.gwhatchet.com	202-854-0925		532-3
GW Hoffman Marketing 45 W 45th St . . . New York NY 10036 *Web:* www.gwhoffman.com	212-921-8005		7

Company / Address	City	State	ZIP	Phone	Fax	Class
GW Lisk Company Inc 2 South St. TF: 800-776-9528 ■ Web: gwlisk.com	Clifton Springs	NY	14432	315-462-2611	462-7661	253
GW Plastics Inc 239 Pleasant St. Web: www.gwplastics.com	Bethel	VT	05032	802-234-9941	234-9940	604
GW Services Inc PO Box 6476 Web: www.gwserviceshhi.com	Hilton Head Island	SC	29938	843-686-4052	686-4055	463
Gwa Electrical Engineers Inc 168 Laurelhurst Ave Web: www.gwainc.net	Columbia	SC	29210	803-252-6919	799-5494	261
Gwaii Haanas National Park Reserve & Haida Heritage Site 60 Second Beach Rd. Web: www.pc.gc.ca	Queen Charlotte	BC	V0T1S0	250-559-8818	559-8366	563
GWC Injury Lawyers LLC 1 E Upper Wacker Dr Ste 3800 TF: 800-464-4772 ■ Web: www.gwclaw.com	Chicago	IL	60601	312-464-1234		428
Gweenie's Old Alaska Restaurant 4333 Spenard Rd Web: gwenniesrestaurant.com	Anchorage	AK	99517	907-243-2090		671
GWI (Great Works Internet) 43 Landry St. TF: 866-494-2020 ■ Web: www.gwi.net	Biddeford	ME	04005	207-494-2000		608
GWI Engineering Inc 1411 Michigan St NE Web: gwiengineering.com	Grand Rapids	MI	49503	616-459-8274		386
Gwin Dobson & Foreman Inc 3121 Fairway Dr Web: gdfengineers.com	Altoona	PA	16602	814-943-5214	943-8494	261
Gwin's Commercial Printing & Engraving 957 Spring Hill Ave. Web: gwins.cc	Mobile	AL	36604	251-438-2226		687
Gwin's Travel Planners Inc 212 N Kirkwood Rd. TF: 888-254-7775 ■ Web: www.gwins.com	Saint Louis	MO	63122	314-822-1958		771
Gwinnett Chamber of Commerce 6500 Sugarloaf Pkwy Web: www.gwinnettchamber.org	Duluth	GA	30097	770-232-3000	232-8807	139
Gwinnett College of Business 4230 Lawrenceville Hwy NW Ste 11 Web: www.gwinnettcollege.edu	Lilburn	GA	30047	770-381-7200		166
Gwinnett County Gwinnett Justice & Administration Ctr 75 Langley Dr Web: www.gwinnettcounty.com	Lawrenceville	GA	30045	770-822-8000	822-7097	338
Gwinnett County Public Library 1001 Lawrenceville Hwy Web: www.gwinnettpl.org	Lawrenceville	GA	30046	770-822-4522		434-3
Gwinnett Daily Post 725 Old Norcross Rd Web: www.gwinnettdailypost.com	Lawrenceville	GA	30045	770-963-9205	339-8081	532-2
Gwinnett Medical Center Lawrenceville 1000 Medical Center Blvd Web: www.gwinnettmedicalcenter.org	Lawrenceville	GA	30046	678-312-1000		374-3
Gwinnett Technical College 5150 Sugarloaf Pky Web: www.gwinnetttech.edu	Lawrenceville	GA	30043	770-962-7580		167-3
GWK Enterprises 123 S Center St. Web: www.fourseasonsdirect.com	Geneseo	IL	61254	309-686-0124		157-6
GWN Securities Inc 11440 N Jog Rd Web: www.gwnsecurities.com	Palm Beach Gardens	FL	33418	561-472-2700		690
GWPC (Ground Water Protection Council) 13308 N MacArthur Blvd Web: www.gwpc.org	Oklahoma City	OK	73142	405-516-4972	516-4973	48-13
GWS (GWS Supply Inc) 2375 W Nordale Dr Web: www.gwssupply.com	Appleton	WI	54912	920-739-6066	739-6319	385
GWS Supply Inc (GWS) 2375 W Nordale Dr Web: www.gwssupply.com	Appleton	WI	54912	920-739-6066	739-6319	385
Gwynedd-Mercy College 1325 Sunneytown Pk PO Box 901 TF: 800-342-5462 ■ Web: www.gmercyu.edu	Gwynedd Valley	PA	19437	215-646-7300	641-5556	166
Gwynn Group 600 E Las Colinas Blvd Ste 520 TF: 877-941-7075 ■ Web: www.gwynngroup.com	Irving	TX	75039	214-941-7075		177
GX Technology Corp 2105 City West Blvd Ste 900 Web: www.iongeo.com	Houston	TX	77042	713-789-7250		727
GY & K Antler 175 Canal St. Web: gykantler.com	Manchester	NH	03101	617-303-1615		195
GYC (Greater Yellowstone Coalition) 215 S Wallace Ave TF: 800-775-1834 ■ Web: greateryellowstone.org	Bozeman	MT	59715	406-586-1593	556-2839	48-13
Gyford Productions 891 Trademark Dr. Web: www.standoffsystems.com	Reno	NV	89521	775-829-7272	201-7200	393
Gym Source 40 E 52nd St. TF: 800-496-7687 ■ Web: www.gymsource.com	New York	NY	10022	212-688-4222		711
GYMA Laboratories of America Inc 135 Cantiague Rock Rd Web: gyma.com	Westbury	NY	11590	516-933-0900	933-1075	479
Gymboree Corp 500 Howard St. NASDAQ: GYMB ■ *Fax Area Code: 415 ■ TF: 877-449-6932 ■ Web: www.gymboree.com	San Francisco	CA	94105	877-449-6932	278-7100*	157-1
GYMVMT 7222 Edgemont Blvd NW TF: 866-278-4131 ■ Web: gymvmt.com	Calgary	AB	T3A2X7	403-278-2499		354
Gynecologic Oncology Group (GOG) 1600 JFK Blvd Ste 1020 TF: 800-225-3053 ■ Web: www.gog.org	Philadelphia	PA	19103	215-854-0770	854-0716	49-8
Gyotaku 1824 King St. Web: www.gyotakuhawaii.com	Honolulu	HI	96826	808-949-4584		671
Gypsum Assn 6525 Belcrest Rd Ste 480 Web: www.gypsum.org	Hyattsville	MD	20782	301-277-8686	277-8747	49-13
Gypsum Express Ltd 8280 Sixty Rd PO Box 268 TF: 800-621-7901 ■ Web: www.gypsumexpress.com	Baldwinsville	NY	13027	315-638-2201		449
Gypsum Supply Company Inc 859 74th St. *Fax Area Code: 734 ■ Web: gypsum-supply.com	Byron Center	MI	49315	616-583-9300	545-7994*	191-1
Gypsy Den 125 N Broadway Web: www.thedencafeoc.com	Santa Ana	CA	92701	714-835-8840		671
Gyration Inc 160 Commerce Way TF: 888-340-0033 ■ Web: www.gyration.com	Walnut	CA	91789	909-839-2929	839-2930	173-1
Gyro Creative Group 400 Grand River Ave. Web: gyrocreative.com	Detroit	MI	48226	313-964-0100		5
Gyrodata Inc 23000 Northwest Lake Dr TF: 800-348-6063 ■ Web: www.gyrodata.com	Houston	TX	77095	281-213-6300		190
Gyrodyne Company of America Inc 1 Flowerfield Ste 24 NASDAQ: GYRO ■ Web: www.gyrodyne.com	Saint James	NY	11780	631-584-5400	584-7075	655
GyroHSR 7755 Montgomery Rd Ste 300 Web: www.gyro.com	Cincinnati	OH	45236	513-671-3811		4
Gyrus Medical Inc ENT Div 136 Turnpike Rd. TF: 800-757-2942 ■ Web: medical.olympusamerica.com	Southborough	MA	01772	508-804-2600		477
GZA GeoEnvironmental Inc 249 Vanderbilt Ave Web: www.gza.com	Norwood	MA	02062	781-278-3700	278-5701	261
GZP (Ground Zero Pharmaceuticals Inc) 5405 Alton Pky Ste A-464 Web: www.groundzerous.com	Irvine	CA	92604	949-419-6136	861-9797	582

H

Company / Address	City	State	ZIP	Phone	Fax	Class
H & B Mechanical Inc 111 Cal Ave	Barstow	CA	92311	760-256-8401		350
H & B Tool & Engineering Company Inc 481 Sullivan Ave. Web: h-btool.com	South Windsor	CT	06074	860-528-0341		261
H & C Tool Supply Corp 235 Mt Read Blvd TF: 800-323-4624 ■ Web: www.hctoolsupply.com	Rochester	NY	14611	585-235-5700		350
H & E Equipment Services Inc 7500 Pecue Ln NASDAQ: HEES ■ TF: 866-467-3682 ■ Web: www.he-equipment.com	Baton Rouge	LA	70809	225-298-5200		264-3
H & G Sales Inc 11635 Lackland Rd TF: 866-432-8188 ■ Web: www.h-gschultzdoor.com	Saint Louis	MO	63146	866-432-8188		499
H & H Chevrolet LLC 4645 S 84 St. TF: 855-866-1733 ■ Web: www.hhchevy.com	Omaha	NE	68127	888-350-0363		57
H & H Chief Sales Inc 1309 Hwy 35 N. Web: www.hhchiefsales.com	Carthage	MS	39051	601-267-9643	267-9645	61
H & H Color Lab Inc 8906 E 67th St TF: 800-821-1305 ■ Web: www.hhcolorlab.com	Raytown	MO	64133	816-358-6677	313-1480	588
H & H Diesel Repair Inc 1410 46th Ave E TF: 800-929-2335 ■ Web: www.hhdiesel.com	Fife	WA	98424	253-922-8786	922-7137	61
H & H General Excavating Inc 660 Old Hanover Rd PO Box 141 Web: h-hgenexc.com	Spring Grove	PA	17362	717-225-4669	225-4958	683
H & H Group, The 854 N Prince St TF: 866-338-7569 ■ Web: www.thehandhgroup.com	Lancaster	PA	17603	717-393-3941		344
H & H Industrial Corp 7612 Rt 130 TF: 800-982-0341 ■ Web: www.hhindustrial.com	Pennsauken Township	NJ	08110	856-663-4444	663-4446	697
H & H Publishing Company Inc 1231 Kapp Dr. TF: 800-366-4079 ■ Web: www.hhpublishing.com	Clearwater	FL	33765	727-442-7760	442-2195	244
H & H Sales Company Inc 16339 Lima Rd. TF: 800-551-9341 ■ Web: www.hhsalescompany.com	Huntertown	IN	46748	260-637-3177	637-6880	516
H & H Swiss Screw Machine Products Company Inc 1478 Chestnut Ave *Fax Area Code: 908 ■ TF: 800-826-9985 ■ Web: www.hhswiss.com	Hillside	NJ	07205	800-826-9985	688-3503*	621
H & H Total Care Services Inc 8382 156 St Web: thehamlets.ca	Surrey	BC	V3S3R7	604-597-7931		672
H & H Tube 579 Garfield Ave Web: www.h-htube.com	Vanderbilt	MI	49795	989-983-2800	983-4530	595
H & H Veterinary Care LLC 1259 Willamette St. Web: handhvetcare.com	Eugene	OR	97401	541-343-3419		794
H & H X-Ray Services Inc 104 Enterprise St TF: 800-551-5093 ■ Web: www.hhxray.com	West Monroe	LA	71292	800-551-5093		743
H & K International Inc 2200 Skyline Dr Web: www.hki.com	Mesquite	TX	75149	214-818-3596		298
H & L Advantage Inc 3500 Busch Dr SW. TF: 800-581-2343 ■ Web: hladvantage.com	Grandville	MI	49418	616-532-1012		350
H & L Partners Inc 655 Montgomery St 7th Fl Web: www.handlpartners.com	San Francisco	CA	94111	415-434-8500		4
H & L Tool Company Inc 32701 Dequindre Rd. Web: www.hltool.com	Madison Heights	MI	48071	248-585-7474	585-5774	621
H & L Tooth Company Inc 10055 E 56 St N. *Fax Area Code: 918 ■ TF: 800-458-6684 ■ Web: www.hltooth.com	Tulsa	OK	74117	800-458-6684	272-0163*	483
H & M Construction Company Inc 50 Security Dr. Web: hmcompany.com	Jackson	TN	38305	731-664-6300		188-7
H & M International Transportation Inc 485-C US 1 S Ste 330 TF: 800-446-4685 ■ Web: www.hmit.net	Iselin	NJ	08830	732-510-4640		780
H & M Shared Services Inc 985 Jolly Rd Web: www.henkelsgroup.com	Blue Bell	PA	19422	215-283-7600	283-7659	188-10
H & M Systems Software Inc 600 E Crescent Ave Ste 203 Web: www.hm-software.com	Upper Saddle River	NJ	07458	201-934-3414	934-9206	178-11

Company	Address	City	State	ZIP	Phone	Fax	Class
H & O Centerless Grinding Inc	45 Bathurst Dr *Web:* www.cylindricalprecision.com	Waterloo	ON	N2V1N2	519-884-0322		393
H & P LLC	1 N LaSalle St Ste 1015	Chicago	IL	60602	312-782-6008	782-2356	379
H & P Sales Inc	2022 Victory Dr *Web:* handpsales.com	Vista	CA	92084	760-727-2614	727-2616	292
H & P Trailer Leasing Inc	1849 Flowood Dr *TF:* 877-377-7052 ■ *Web:* www.hptrailerleasing.com	Flowood	MS	39232	601-939-2200	939-9037	393
H & R 1871	40 E Broadwy. *TF:* 866-776-9292 ■ *Web:* www.hr1871.com	Gardner	MA	01440	866-776-9292		284
H & R Agri-Power Inc	4900 Eagle Way *TF:* 800-844-3918 ■ *Web:* www.hragripower.com	Hopkinsville	KY	42240	270-886-3918	886-4389	190
H & R Block Tax Services Inc	4400 Main St *TF:* 800-472-5625 ■ *Web:* www.hrblock.com	Kansas City	MO	64111	800-472-5625		734
H & R Carpets Inc	608 E Main *Web:* hrcarpets.com	Waunakee	WI	53597	608-849-7482		290
H & R Construction Parts & Equipment Inc	20 Milburn St *TF:* 800-333-0650 ■ *Web:* www.hrparts.com	Buffalo	NY	14212	716-891-4311	891-4346	358
H & R Mechanical Contractors Inc	106 Demand Ct. *Web:* hrmech.com	Georgetown	KY	40324	502-863-4955		189-10
H & R Retail Inc	1 W Pennsylvania Ave Ste 320 *Web:* www.hrretail.com	Baltimore	MD	21204	410-308-0800	486-2733	655
H & S Bakery Inc	601 S Caroline St *TF:* 800-959-7655 ■ *Web:* www.hsbakery.com	Baltimore	MD	21231	410-276-7254		296-1
H & S Constructors Inc	1616 Valero Way *TF:* 800-727-8602 ■ *Web:* hsconstructors.com	Corpus Christi	TX	78469	361-289-5272		256
H & S Floors & Furnishings Inc	210 Russell St	Darlington	SC	29532	843-393-0456		131
H & S Heat Treating	133 S St N *Web:* hsheat.com	Port Robinson	ON	L0S1K0	905-384-9355		484
H & S Manufacturing Co	2913 Singleton St *Web:* www.hsmfg.com	Rowlett	TX	75088	972-475-4747		697
H & S Manufacturing Company Inc	2608 S Hume *Web:* www.hsmfgco.com	Marshfield	WI	54449	715-387-3414	384-5463	125
H & S Sports Plus	8015 Summerfield Rd *Web:* www.hssportsplus.com	Lambertville	MI	48144	734-847-3881		711
H & S Swansons' Tool Co	9000 68th St N *Web:* www.hsswansons.com	Pinellas Park	FL	33782	727-541-3575		454
H & W Computer Systems Inc	6154 N Meeker Pl Ste 100 *TF:* 800-338-6692 ■ *Web:* www.hwcs.com	Boise	ID	83713	208-377-0336	377-0069	177
H & W Management Co	300 W Vine St Ste 806 *Web:* hwhotels.com	Lexington	KY	40507	859-263-0106	263-0506	463
H & W Solutions	1724 Sands Pl *Web:* www.hwsolutions.com	Marietta	GA	30067	770-951-9800		627
H & W Trucking Company Inc	2519 N Andy Griffith Pkwy PO Box 1545 *Web:* www.hwtrucking.com	Mount Airy	NC	27030	336-789-2188	786-2483	780
H A M Media Group	1058 N Tamiami Tl Ste 108-302 *Web:* www.hammedia.com	Sarasota	FL	34236	917-407-6014		401
H B Fuller Construction Products Inc	1105 S Frontenac Rd *TF:* 800-832-9002 ■ *Web:* www.tecspecialty.com	Aurora	IL	60504	800-832-9002		3
H Barber & Sons Inc	15 Raytkwich Rd *TF:* 800-355-8318 ■ *Web:* www.hbarber.com	Naugatuck	CT	06770	203-729-9000		667
H C Olsen Construction Company Inc	710 Los Angeles Ave *Web:* hcolsen.com	Monrovia	CA	91016	626-359-8900		186
H Chambers Co	1800 Washington Blvd Ste 111 *Web:* www.chambersusa.com	Baltimore	MD	21230	410-727-4535	727-6982	393
H E Anderson Company Inc	2025 Anderson Dr *TF:* 800-331-9620 ■ *Web:* www.heanderson.com	Muskogee	OK	74403	918-687-4426		143
H E Whitlock Inc	PO Box 8030 *TF:* 866-933-0709 ■ *Web:* www.hewhitlock.com	Pueblo	CO	81008	719-544-9475	544-1832	449
H Gr Industrial Surplus	20001 Euclid Ave *TF:* 866-447-7117 ■ *Web:* hgrinc.com	Euclid	OH	44117	216-486-4567		358
H H Ellis Technical High School	613 Upper Maple St *Web:* ellis.cttech.org	Danielson	CT	06239	860-412-7500	779-2565	685
H Hotel, The	111 W Main St *Web:* www.thehhotel.com	Midland	MI	48640	989-839-0500	837-6000	377
H I M on Call Inc	1033 Hamilton St. *Web:* www.himoncall.com	Allentown	PA	18101	610-435-5724		196
H Ka Staffing Services	800 Waukegan Rd Ste 200 *Web:* hkastaffing.com	Glenview	IL	60025	847-998-9300		260
H Kramer & Co	1345 W 21st St *TF:* 800-621-2305 ■ *Web:* hkramer.com	Chicago	IL	60608	312-226-6600	226-4713	485
H Krevit & Company Inc	73 Welton St. *Web:* www.hkrevit.com	New Haven	CT	06511	203-772-3350	776-0730	145
H L Group Inc	16690 Swingley Ridge Rd Ste 100 *Web:* mobileplusgroup.com	Chesterfield	MO	63017	636-590-2900	536-9844	177
H Lee Moffitt Cancer Center & Research Institute Blood & Marrow Transplantation Program	12902 Magnolia Dr. *TF:* 888-663-3488 ■ *Web:* moffitt.org	Tampa	FL	33612	888-663-3488		769
H Muehlstein & Company Inc	10 Westport Rd *Web:* www.muehlstein.com	Wilton	CT	06897	203-855-6000	855-6221	603
H O Wolding Inc	9642 Western Way *TF:* 800-950-0054 ■ *Web:* www.howolding.com	Amherst	WI	54406	715-824-5513		780
H Pearce Real Estate Co	393 State St *TF:* 800-373-3411 ■ *Web:* www.joelgalvin.com	North Haven	CT	06473	203-281-3400	288-9645	652
H R Office Inc, The	2437 Commercial Blvd Ste 5 *Web:* www.thehrofficeinc.com	State College	PA	16801	814-238-3750		193
H S C Foundation Inc	2013 H St NW *Web:* www.hschealth.org	Washington	DC	20006	202-454-1220	454-1251	463
H Sattler Plastics Company Inc	5410 W Roosevelt Rd *Web:* www.sattlerplastics.com	Chicago	IL	60644	312-733-2900	733-5290	603
H Schultz & Sons Inc	777 Lehigh Ave *Web:* www.housewaresandthings.com	Union	NJ	07083	908-687-5400	687-1788	38
H Smith Packing Corp	99 Ft Fairfield Rd *TF:* 800-393-9898 ■ *Web:* www.smithsfarm.com	Presque Isle	ME	04769	207-764-4540	764-2816	297-7
H Stern Jewelers Inc	645 Fifth Ave *TF:* 800-747-8376 ■ *Web:* www.hstern.net	New York	NY	10022	212-688-0300		410
H Trucking Inc	96 Curtis St **Fax Area Code:* 618 ■ *TF:* 800-844-2984 ■ *Web:* hansentrucking.com	Jerseyville	IL	62052	800-844-2984	498-4879*	780
H. B. Smith Company Inc, The	61 Union St Ste 201 *Web:* hbsmith.com	Westfield	MA	01085	413-568-3148		91
H. B. Van Duzer Forest State Scenic Corridor	8300 Salmon River Hwy *Web:* stateparks.oregon.gov	Otis	OR	97368	541-994-7341		565
H. E. Long Co	3910 Anderson Rd. *Web:* www.helongco.com	Morrow	OH	45152	513-899-2610	899-4094	493
H. E. Murdock Company Inc	88 Main St **Fax Area Code:* 888 ■ *TF:* 800-439-3297 ■ *Web:* daysjewelers.com	Waterville	ME	04901	800-439-3297	974-1805*	410
H. Lamm Industries Inc	4425 NE 6th Ter *Web:* hlamm.com	Fort Lauderdale	FL	33334	954-491-8929	491-7346	189-10
H. M. Carter Broadcasting	44 Music Sq E *Web:* www.wnah.com	Nashville	TN	37203	615-254-7611		647
H. M. Dunn Co	3301 House Anderson Rd *Web:* www.hmdunn.com	Euless	TX	76040	817-283-3722		454
H. O. T. Printing & Graphics Inc	2595 Tracy Ct *TF:* 800-848-8259 ■ *Web:* hotgraphics.us	Northwood	OH	43619	419-242-7000	242-3299	627
H. P. Cummings Construction Co	14 Prospect St PO Box 29 *Web:* www.hpcummings.com	Ware	MA	01082	413-967-6251		186
H. P. White Laboratory Inc	3114 Scarboro Rd *Web:* www.hpwhite.com	Street	MD	21154	410-838-6550	838-2802	743
H. S. Crocker Company Inc	12100 Smith Dr *Web:* www.hscrocker.com	Huntley	IL	60142	847-669-3600		548
H. T. Berry Company Inc	PO Box B *TF:* 800-736-2206 ■ *Web:* www.htberry.com	Canton	MA	02021	781-828-6000	828-9788	559
H. T. Lyons Inc	7165 Ambassador Dr *Web:* www.engiemep.com	Allentown	PA	18106	610-530-2600		261
H. T. Specialty Inc	70 Bermar Pk *Web:* www.htspecialtyinc.com	Rochester	NY	14624	585-458-4060	458-7592	454
H. W. Culp Lumber Co	PO Box 235 *Web:* www.culplumber.com	New London	NC	28127	704-463-7311	463-4100	191-3
H. Wayne Judge, Attorney At Law	1 Broad St Plz PO Box 2850 *Web:* wjudgelaw.com	Glens Falls	NY	12801	518-745-5030		41
H.B. Davis Seed Co	50 Railroad Ave. *Web:* www.hbdavisseed.com	Albany	NY	12205	518-489-5411		323
H.B. Engineers Inc	2900 Hamilton Blvd Ste 200 *Web:* hbengineersinc.com	Allentown	PA	18103	610-395-0130	395-0101	261
H.F. Hauff Company Inc	2921 Sutherland Dr *TF:* 855-855-0318 ■ *Web:* www.hfhauff.com	Yakima	WA	98903	509-248-0318	248-0914	274
H.G. Reynolds Company Inc (HGR)	113 Contract Dr *Web:* www.hgreynolds.net	Aiken	SC	29801	803-641-1401	641-1037	186
H.J. High Construction Co	1015 W Amelia St *Web:* www.hjhigh.com	Orlando	FL	32805	407-422-8171		186
H.M. Payson and Co	1 Portland Sq 5th Fl Union St *TF:* 800-456-6710 ■ *Web:* www.hmpayson.com	Portland	ME	04101	207-772-3761	871-7508	401
H.M. Yonge & Associates Inc	51 E Gregory St	Pensacola	FL	32502	850-434-2661		261
H.N. Funkhouser & Company Inc	2150 S Loudoun St *TF:* 800-343-6556 ■ *Web:* www.hnfunkhouser.com	Winchester	VA	22601	540-662-9000		579
H.Q.C. Inc	230 Kendall Pt Dr *Web:* www.hqcinc.com	Oswego	IL	60543	630-820-5550	820-5549	608
H.R. Lewis Petroleum Co	Chevron 9148 San Jose Blvd *TF:* 800-638-6551 ■ *Web:* lewispetroleum.com	Jacksonville	FL	32257	904-356-0731		579
H.S. Industrial Equipment Inc	55 Mushroom Blvd. *Web:* www.hsindustrialequipment.com	Rochester	NY	14623	585-424-4800		385
H2 Plains LLC	10500 E Berkeley Sq Ste 100 *Web:* www.hartmanoil.com	Wichita	KS	67206	316-636-2090	636-1155	536
H2 Pre-Cast Inc	3835 N Clemons *Web:* h2precast.com	East Wenatchee	WA	98802	509-884-6644	884-4567	183
H2 Surveying LLC	7600 N Mineral Dr *Web:* www.h2survey.com	Coeur d'Alene	ID	83815	208-772-6600	772-6619	727
H2O Consulting Inc	5870 Hwy 6 N Ste 215 *Web:* www.h2oconsulting.net	Houston	TX	77084	281-861-6215		196
H2F Comedy Productions	102 E Magnolia Blvd *Web:* www.flapperscomedy.com	Burbank	CA	91502	818-845-9721		708
H2HP (House to House Publications)	11 Toll Gate Rd *TF:* 800-848-5892 ■ *Web:* www.h2hp.com	Lititz	PA	17543	717-627-1996	627-4004	637-2

Phone | Fax | Class

H2K Technologies Inc
7550 Commerce St. . . . . Corcoran MN 55340 763-746-9900 746-9903 261
Web: h2ktech.com

H2O Concepts International Inc
22405 N 19th Ave. . . . . Phoenix AZ 85027 623-582-5222 582-4465 364
TF: 888-275-4261 ■ *Web:* www.h2oconcepts.com

H2O.ai 2307 Leghorn St . . . . . Mountain View CA 94043 650-429-8337 39
Web: www.h2o.ai

H3 Ranch 105 E Exchange Ave . . . . . Fort Worth TX 76164 817-624-1246 624-2571 671
Web: www.h3ranch.com

H3 Solutions Inc
10432 Balls Ford Rd Ste 230 . . . . . Manassas VA 20109 855-464-5914 196
TF: 855-464-5914 ■ *Web:* www.h3s-inc.com

H3R Aviation 103 H St. . . . . Petaluma CA 94952 800-249-4289 366
TF: 800-249-4289 ■ *Web:* h3rcleanagents.com

H5 Colo 12712 Park Central Dr Ste 200 . . . . . Dallas TX 75251 469-533-0270 492
Web: www.h5colo.com

HA Guden Company Inc 99 Raynor Ave . . . . . Ronkonkoma NY 11779 631-737-2900 737-2933 350
TF: 800-344-6437 ■ *Web:* www.guden.com

Ha Ha Tonka State Park
1491 State Rd D . . . . . Camdenton MO 65020 573-346-2986 565
Web: mostateparks.com

HA Logistics Inc 5175 Johnson Dr. . . . . Pleasanton CA 94588 925-251-9300 251-9333 311
TF: 800-449-5778 ■ *Web:* www.halogistics.com

Haag Engineering Co 4949 W Royal Ln. . . . . Irving TX 75063 214-614-6500 261
TF: 800-527-0168 ■ *Web:* haagengineering.com

Haakon Industries 11851 Dyke Rd. . . . . Richmond BC V7A4X8 604-273-0161 273-8397 14
Web: www.haakon.com

Haaland Debra (Rep D - NM)
1237 Longworth House Office Bldg . . . . . Washington DC 20515 202-225-6316 342-2
Web: www.haaland.house.gov

Haapanen Brothers Inc 1400 St Paul Ave . . . . . Gurnee IL 60031 847-336-4200 687
Web: hb-graphics.net

Haartz Corp, The 87 Hayward Rd . . . . . Acton MA 01720 978-264-2600 264-2601 745-2
Web: www.haartz.com

Haas & Haynie Corp 250 Stockton Ave. . . . . San Jose CA 95126 650-588-5600 653
Web: www.hh1808.com

Haas & Wilkerson Inc
4300 Shawnee Mission Pkwy. . . . . Fairway KS 66205 913-432-4400 432-6159 390
TF: 800-821-7703 ■ *Web:* www.hwins.com

Haas Automation Inc 2800 Sturgis Rd. . . . . Oxnard CA 93030 805-278-1800 278-2255 454
TF: 800-331-6746 ■ *Web:* www.haascnc.com

Haas Cabinet Company Inc
625 W Utica St . . . . . Sellersburg IN 47172 812-246-4431 115
TF: 800-457-6458 ■ *Web:* www.haascabinet.com

Haas Printing Company Inc
1000 Hummel Ave . . . . . Lemoyne PA 17043 717-761-0277 761-7109 627
Web: www.haas-printing.com

Haas Trucking Inc 1940 E Michigan Ave . . . . . Albion MI 49224 517-629-2326 629-8632 311
Web: haastrucking.com

Habana 2728 S Congress Ave. . . . . Austin TX 78704 512-443-4253 671
Web: www.habanaaustin.com

Habana Inn 2200 NW 40th St. . . . . Oklahoma City OK 73112 405-528-2221 379
TF: 800-988-2221 ■ *Web:* www.habanainn.com

Habanero Consulting Group Inc
510-1111 Melville St . . . . . Vancouver BC V6E3V6 604-709-6201 225
TF: 866-841-6201 ■ *Web:* www.habaneroconsulting.com

Habasit ABT Inc
150 Industrial Park Rd . . . . . Middletown CT 06457 860-632-2211 632-1710 370
TF: 800-522-2358 ■ *Web:* www.habasit.com

Habbersett Scrapple Inc
103 S Railroad Ave. . . . . Bridgeville DE 19933 800-338-4727 296-26
TF: 800-338-4727 ■ *Web:* www.habbersettscrapple.com

Habco 501 Gordon Baker Rd. . . . . Toronto ON M2H2S6 416-491-6008 491-6982 803-1
TF: 800-448-0244 ■ *Web:* habcomfg.com

Habegger Corp, The 4995 Winton Rd . . . . . Cincinnati OH 45232 513-681-5600 681-9892 612
TF: 800-459-4822 ■ *Web:* www.habeggercorp.com

Habelman Bros Company Inc
10688 Estate Rd . . . . . Tomah WI 54660 608-372-2444 315-1
Web: www.habelmancranberries.com

Habenicht Novak & Birckbichler
287 Pittsburgh Rd. . . . . Butler PA 16002 724-283-8661 283-9647 2
Web: www.hnbcpa.net

Haber Vision LLC
15710 W Colfax Ave Ste 204 . . . . . Golden CO 80401 303-459-2220 45
TF: 800-621-4381 ■ *Web:* www.habervision.com

Haberfeld Associates Inc
206 S 13th St Ste 1500. . . . . Lincoln NE 68508 402-475-1191 196
Web: www.haberfeld.com

Haberman Machine Inc
6290 Hwy 36 Blvd N. . . . . Oakdale MN 55128 651-777-4511 454
Web: www.habermanmachine.com

Habersham County
555 Monroe St Unit 20. . . . . Clarkesville GA 30523 706-839-0160 839-1272 338
Web: www.habershamga.com

Habersham County Board of Education
132 W Stanford Mill Rd PO Box 70 . . . . . Clarkesville GA 30523 706-754-2118 754-1549 685
Web: www.habershamschools.com

Habersham County Chamber of Commerce
668 Clarkesville St . . . . . Cornelia GA 30531 706-778-4654 776-1416 139
TF: 800-835-2559 ■ *Web:* www.habershamchamber.com

Habersham Electric Membership Corp
6135 Georgia 115. . . . . Clarkesville GA 30523 706-754-2114 839-6325 245
TF: 800-640-6812 ■ *Web:* www.habershamemc.com

Habersham Funding LLC
3495 Piedmont Rd NE Ste 910. . . . . Atlanta GA 30305 404-233-8275 796
TF: 888-874-2402 ■ *Web:* www.habershamfunding.com

Habersham Metal Products Co
264 Stapleton Rd . . . . . Cornelia GA 30531 706-778-2212 778-2769 234
Web: www.habershammetal.com

Habib American Bank 99 Madison Ave. . . . . New York NY 10016 212-532-4444 532-8273 70
Web: www.habbank.com

Habitat Company LLC, The
350 W Hubbard St Ste 500. . . . . Chicago IL 60654 312-527-5400 652
Web: www.habitat.com

Habitat for Humanity Intl
121 Habitat St. . . . . Americus GA 31709 229-924-6935 410-7443 48-5
TF: 800-422-4828 ■ *Web:* www.habitat.org

Habitat Housewares
800 E Dimond Blvd Ste 3-207 . . . . . Anchorage AK 99515 907-561-1856 362
TF: 800-770-1856 ■ *Web:* www.habitathousewares.com

Habitat Suites
500 E Highland Mall Blvd. . . . . Austin TX 78752 512-467-6000 379
TF: 800-535-4663 ■ *Web:* www.habitatsuites.com

Habitec Security Inc
1545 Timberwolf Dr . . . . . Holland OH 43528 419-537-6768 693
TF: 888-422-4832 ■ *Web:* www.habitecsecurity.com

Habush Habush & Rottier S C
US Bank Ctr 777 E Wisconsin Ave Ste 2300. . . . . Milwaukee WI 53202 414-271-0900 445
Web: www.habush.com

HAC (Housing Assistance Council)
1025 Vermont Ave NW Ste 606. . . . . Washington DC 20005 202-842-8600 347-3441 48-5
TF: 866-234-2689 ■ *Web:* www.ruralhome.org

HACC (Howell Area Chamber of Commerce)
123 E Washington St . . . . . Howell MI 48843 517-546-3920 546-4115 139
Web: www.howell.org

HACC (Hellenic-American Chamber of Commerce)
370 Lexington Ave 27th Fl . . . . . New York NY 10017 212-629-6380 564-9281 138
Web: hellenicamerican.cc

HACDC (Haitian American Community Development)
181 NE 82 St . . . . . Miami FL 33138 305-759-2542 754-9200 194
Web: www.haitianamericancdc.org

Hach Co PO Box 389. . . . . Loveland CO 80539 970-669-3050 669-2932 419
TF: 800-227-4224 ■ *Web:* www.hach.com

Hachette Book Group 237 Park Ave. . . . . New York NY 10017 800-759-0190 331-1664 637-2
TF: 800-759-0190 ■ *Web:* www.hachettebookgroup.com

HACI Mechanical Contractors Inc
2108 W Shangri La Rd . . . . . Phoenix AZ 85029 602-944-1555 678-0266 189-10
Web: www.hacimechanical.com

Hacienda La Puente Adult Education - Willow Campus
14101 E Nelson St . . . . . La Puente CA 91746 626-934-2801 167-3
Web: www.hlpae.com

Hacienda Mexican Restaurant
711 N First Ave. . . . . Evansville IN 47710 812-423-6355 671
Web: haciendafiesta.com

Hacienda Restaurant 102 McLean Blvd . . . . . Paterson NJ 07514 973-345-1255 671
Web: haciendanj.com

Hacienda The at Hotel Santa Fe
1501 Paseo del Peralta . . . . . Santa Fe NM 87501 505-955-7805 379
TF: 855-825-9876 ■ *Web:* hotelsantafe.com

Hacienda, The 1725 College Ave . . . . . Santa Ana CA 92706 714-558-1304 671
Web: the-hacienda.com

Hack Piro
30 Columbia Tpke PO Box 168. . . . . Florham Park NJ 07932 973-301-6500 301-0094 445
Web: www.hpomlaw.com

Hackbarth Delivery Service Inc
3504 Brookdale Dr N . . . . . Mobile AL 36618 251-478-1401 479-9900 314
TF: 800-277-3322 ■ *Web:* www.hackbarthdelivery.com

Hackensack University Medical Ctr
30 Prospect Ave . . . . . Hackensack NJ 07601 201-996-2000 374-3
Web: www.hackensackumc.org

Hacker Group Inc
1215 Fourth Ave Ste 2100 . . . . . Seattle WA 98161 206-805-1500 7
Web: hal2l.com

Hacker Johnson & Smith PA
500 N Wshore Blvd Ste 1000 . . . . . Tampa FL 33609 813-286-2424 2
TF: 800-366-7126 ■ *Web:* www.hackerjohnson.com

Hackett Publishing Company Inc
3333 Massachusetts Ave . . . . . Indianapolis IN 46218 317-635-9250 635-9292 637-2
TF: 800-783-9213 ■ *Web:* www.hackettpublishing.com

Hacklebarney State Park
119 Hacklebarney Rd . . . . . Long Valley NJ 07853 908-638-8572 565
Web: www.njparksandforests.org

Hackley School 293 Benedict Ave. . . . . Tarrytown NY 10591 914-631-0128 622
TF: 877-723-3512 ■ *Web:* www.hackleyschool.org

Hackney 911 W Fifth St PO Box 880 . . . . . Washington NC 27889 252-946-6521 975-8340 516
TF: 800-763-0700 ■ *Web:* hackneyusa.com

Hackney Ladish Inc 400 E Willow . . . . . Enid OK 73701 580-237-4212 608
Web: www.hackneyladish.com

Hackworth Reprographics
1700 Liberty St. . . . . Chesapeake VA 23324 757-545-7675 113
TF: 800-676-2424 ■ *Web:* www.hackworth.co

HACU (Hispanic Association of Colleges & Universities)
8415 Datapoint Dr Ste 400. . . . . San Antonio TX 78229 210-692-3805 692-0823 49-5
TF: 800-780-4228 ■ *Web:* www.hacu.net

Hadady Corp 510 W 172nd St . . . . . South Holland IL 60473 708-596-5168 621
Web: www.hadadycorp.com

Haddad's Fine Arts Inc
3855 E Mira Loma Ave . . . . . Anaheim CA 92806 714-996-2100 996-4153 520
TF: 800-942-3323 ■ *Web:* www.haddadsfinearts.com

Haddox Reid Burkes & Calhoun PLLC
188 E Capitol St Ste 500 PO Box 22507. . . . . Jackson MS 39225 601-948-2924 2
Web: www.haddoxreid.com

Hader-Seitz Inc
15600 W Lincoln Ave . . . . . New Berlin WI 53151 262-641-6000 223
TF: 877-388-2101 ■ *Web:* www.hader-seitz.com

Hadley Capital
1200 Central Ave Ste 300 Chase Bank Bldg . . . . . Wilmette IL 60091 847-906-5300 906-5301 528
Web: www.hadleycapital.com

Hadley Exhibits Inc 1700 Elmwood Ave. . . . . Buffalo NY 14207 716-874-3666 874-9994 232
TF: 800-962-8088 ■ *Web:* hadleyexhibitsinc.com

Hadley Farms Inc 47 S Main St . . . . . Smithsburg MD 21783 301-824-2558 824-3917 296-2
TF: 800-346-3494 ■ *Web:* hadleyfarms.com

Hadley House Co PO Box 245. . . . . Madison Lake MN 56063 952-983-8208 243-3698* 637-10
**Fax Area Code:* 507 ■ *TF:* 800-423-5390 ■ *Web:* www.hadleyhouse.com

Hadron Technologies Inc
4941 Allison St Ste 15 . . . . . Arvada CO 80002 303-431-7798 431-6168 249
Web: www.hadrontechnologies.com

Hadronics Inc 4570 Steel Pl . . . . . Cincinnati OH 45209 513-321-9350 481
TF: 800-829-0826 ■ *Web:* www.hadronics.com

HAECO Americas MRO 623 Radar Rd. . . . . Greensboro NC 27410 336-668-4410 319-3
Web: www.haeco.aero

Haedrich & Company Inc
358 Hartnell Ave Ste A . . . . . Redding CA 96002 530-221-1127 652
Web: haedrich.com

Haefele Tv Inc 24 E Tioga St. . . . . Spencer NY 14883 607-589-6235 116
TF: 800-338-6330 ■ *Web:* www.htva.net

	Phone	Fax	Class

Haematologic Technologies Inc
57 River Rd Ste 1021 Essex Junction VT 05452 802-878-1777 878-1776 479
Web: www.haemtech.com
Haemonetics Corp 400 Wood Rd Braintree MA 02184 781-848-7100 860-1512* 476
NYSE: HAE ■ **Fax Area Code:* 800 ■ *TF:* 800-225-5242 ■ *Web:* www.haemonetics.com
Haemo-Sol Inc 7301 York Rd Baltimore MD 21204 410-821-5676 828-8461 146
TF: 800-821-5676 ■ *Web:* www.haemo-sol.com
HAF (Historic Alexandria Foundation)
218 N Lee St Ste 310 Alexandria VA 22314 703-549-5811 637-2
Web: www.historicalexandriafoundation.org
Hafele America Company Inc
3901 Cheyenne Dr Archdale NC 27263 336-434-2322 325-6197* 491
**Fax Area Code:* 800 ■ *TF:* 800-423-3531 ■ *Web:* www.hafele.com
Hafeli, Staran & Christ PC
2055 Orchard Lake Rd Sylvan Lake MI 48320 248-731-3080 731-3081 41
Web: hsc-law.com
Hafetz & Associates LLC 609 New Rd Linwood NJ 08221 609-872-0001 390
Web: hafetzandassociates.com
Hagadone Directories Inc
201 N 2nd St Coeur d'Alene ID 83816 208-667-8744 765-2616 637-10
Web: www.blackphonebook.com
Hagadone Printing Company Inc
274 Puuhale Rd Honolulu HI 96819 808-847-5310 626
Web: www.hagadoneprinting.com
Hagans Plastics Company Inc
121 W Rock Island Rd Grand Prairie TX 75050 972-790-9001 790-1164 604
TF: 800-259-9007 ■ *Web:* www.hagansus.com
Hagedorn Jim (Rep R - MN)
325 Cannon House Office Bldg Washington DC 20515 202-225-2472 342-2
Web: www.hagedorn.house.gov
Hagemeyer North America Inc
1460 Tobias Gadson Blvd Charleston SC 29407 843-745-2400 745-6942 385
TF: 877-462-7070
Hagen Wilka & Archer LLP
600 S Main Ave Ste 102 Sioux Falls SD 57104 605-334-0005 334-4814 428
Web: hwalaw.com
Hagens Berman Sobol Shapiro LLP
1918 Eighth Ave Ste 3300 Seattle WA 98101 206-623-7292 428
TF: 888-381-2889 ■ *Web:* www.hbsslaw.com
Hager Co 139 Victor St Saint Louis MO 63104 314-772-4400 782-0149* 350
**Fax Area Code:* 800 ■ *TF:* 800-325-9995 ■ *Web:* www.hagerco.com
Hager Sharp Inc
1030 15th St NW Ste 600 E Washington DC 20005 202-842-3600 636
Web: hagersharp.com
Hager, Dewick & Zuengler SC
200 S Washington St Ste 401 Green Bay WI 54301 920-430-1900 41
Web: hdz-law.com
Hagerman & Company Inc
505 Sunset Ct PO Box 139 Mount Zion IL 62549 217-864-2326 864-2281 809
Web: www.hagerman.com
Hagerman Fossil Beds National Monument
221 N State St PO Box 570 Hagerman ID 83332 208-933-4100 837-4857 564
Web: www.nps.gov
Hagerman Inc 510 W Washington Blvd Fort Wayne IN 46802 260-424-1470 177
Web: www.thehagermangroup.com
Hagerstown Community College
11400 Robinwood Dr Hagerstown MD 21742 301-790-2800 791-9165 162
Web: www.hagerstowncc.edu
Hagerstown/Washington County Convention & Visitors Bureau
16 Public Sq Hagerstown MD 21740 301-791-3246 206
TF: 888-257-2600 ■ *Web:* www.visithagerstown.com
Hagerty Insurance Agency LLC
141 River's Edge Dr Ste 200
PO Box 1303 Traverse City MI 49684 800-922-4050 941-8227* 391-4
**Fax Area Code:* 231 ■ *TF:* 877-922-9701 ■ *Web:* www.hagerty.com
Hagerty Peterson & Company LLC
18 E Dundee Rd Bldg 5 Ste 201 Barrington IL 60010 847-277-9900 401
Web: www.hagertypeterson.com
Hagerty Steel & Aluminum Co
601 N Main East Peoria IL 61611 309-699-7251 697
TF: 800-322-2600 ■ *Web:* www.hagertysteel.com
Hagey Coach & Tours Nrt
210 Schoolhouse Rd Souderton PA 18964 215-723-4381 760
TF: 800-544-2439 ■ *Web:* hagey.com
Haggar Clothing Co
1507 LBJ Fwy Ste 100 Farmers Branch TX 75234 972-481-1579 956-4561* 155-12
**Fax Area Code:* 214 ■ *TF:* 877-841-2219 ■ *Web:* www.haggar.com
Haggard & Stocking Assoc
5318 Victory Dr Indianapolis IN 46203 317-788-4661 788-1645 385
TF: 800-622-4824 ■ *Web:* www.haggard-stocking.com
Haggen Inc 2900 Woburn St Bellingham WA 98226 360-676-5300 345
TF: 800-995-1902 ■ *Web:* www.haggen.com
Haggin Museum, The
1201 N Pershing Ave Stockton CA 95203 209-940-6300 462-1404 520
Web: www.hagginmuseum.org
Hagie Manufacturing Co
721 Central Ave W Clarion IA 50525 515-532-2861 532-3553 273
TF: 800-247-4885 ■ *Web:* www.hagie.com
Hagiwara America Inc
38777 W Six Mile Rd Ste 307 Livonia MI 48152 734-462-0260 61
Web: www.hagiwara.co.jp
Hagle Lumber Company Inc
3100 Somis Rd PO Box 120 Somis CA 93066 805-987-3887 987-7564 191-3
Web: www.haglelumber.com
Hagley Museum & Library
298 Buck Rd E Wilmington DE 19807 302-658-2400 658-0568 520
Web: www.hagley.org
Hagopian & Sons Inc
14000 W 8 Mile Rd Oak Park MI 48237 800-424-6742 545-2521* 290
**Fax Area Code:* 248 ■ *TF:* 800-424-6742 ■ *Web:* www.originalhagopian.com
HAGR (Hamilton Grange National Memorial)
122 St Riverside Dr New York NY 10027 212-666-1640 564
Web: www.nps.gov
Hague Sahady & Company PC
126 President Ave Ste 201 Fall River MA 02720 508-675-7889 675-7859 2
Web: www.hague-sahady.com
Hague Water Conditioning Inc
4581 Homer Ohio Ln Groveport OH 43125 614-836-2195 366
TF: 800-282-3515 ■ *Web:* haguewaterconditioning.com

Hagyard-Davidson-McGee Associates PSC
4250 Iron Works Pk Lexington KY 40511 859-255-8741 253-0196 11-2
TF: 888-323-7798 ■ *Web:* www.hagyard.com
Hahl Inc 126 Glassmaster Rd Lexington SC 29072 803-359-0706 596
Web: www.perlon.com
Hahn & Bowersock Corp
151 Kalmus Dr Ste L1 Costa Mesa CA 92626 800-660-3187 445
TF: 800-660-3187 ■ *Web:* www.hahnbowersock.com
Hahn & Clay Ltd 5100 Clinton Dr Houston TX 77020 713-672-1671 672-9420 91
Web: www.hahnclay.com
Hahn Automotive Warehouse Inc
415 W Main St Rochester NY 14608 585-235-1595 61
Web: hahnauto.com
Hahn Capital Management LLC
601 Montgomery St Ste 840 San Francisco CA 94111 415-394-6512 401
Web: www.hahncap.com
Hahn Engineering Inc
3060 S Dale Mabry Hwy Tampa FL 33629 813-831-8599 261
Web: www.hahneng.com
Hahn Loeser & Parks LLP
200 Public Sq Ste 2800 Cleveland OH 44114 216-621-0150 241-2824 445
Web: www.hahnlaw.com
Hahn Manufacturing Co
5332 Hamilton Ave Cleveland OH 44114 216-391-9300 757
Web: hahnmfg.com
Hahn Supply Inc 2101 Main St Lewiston ID 83501 208-743-1577 612
Web: www.hahnsupply.com
Hahn Systems LLC
8416 Zionsville Rd Indianapolis IN 46268 317-243-3796 244-9079 385
TF: 800-201-4246 ■ *Web:* www.hahnsystems.com
Hahnel Bros Co
46 Strawberry Ave PO Box 1160 Lewiston ME 04243 207-784-6477 782-9859 189-12
Web: hahnelbrosco.com
Hahnemann College for Homeopathy & Heilkunst
9-4338 Innes Rd Ottawa ON K4A3W3 613-692-1700 692-0183 166
Web: www.homeopathy.com
Hahnemann University Hospital
230 N Broad St Philadelphia PA 19102 215-762-7000 374-3
Web: www.hahnemannhospital.com
HAI (Hightech American Industrial Laboratories Inc)
320 Massachusetts Ave Lexington MA 02420 781-862-9884 860-7722 477
Web: hailabs.com
HAI (Helicopter Association Intl)
1920 Ballenger Ave 4th Fl Alexandria VA 22314 703-683-4646 683-4745 49-21
TF: 800-435-4976 ■ *Web:* www.rotor.org
HAI (Hohman Associates LLC)
6951 W Little York Houston TX 77040 713-896-0978 896-9419 48-2
TF: 800-324-0978 ■ *Web:* www.hohmanassociates.com
Haida Corp PO Box 89 Hydaburg AK 99922 907-285-3721 752
TF: 800-478-3721 ■ *Web:* www.haidacorporation.com
Haidar Capital Management LLC
Carnegie Hall Tower 152 W 57th St New York NY 10019 212-752-5077 401
Web: www.haidarcapital.com
Haidar Inc 565 Dakota St Unit C Crystal Lake IL 60012 815-788-1337 477-2749 472
Web: www.haidar-inc.com
Haig's Quality Printing
6360 Sunset Corporate Dr Las Vegas NV 89120 702-966-1000 627
Web: www.haigsprinting.com
Haight Brown & Bonesteel LLP
555 S Flower St Los Angeles CA 90071 213-542-8000 542-8100 428
Web: www.hbblaw.com
Haight Law Group PLC
6080 Center Dr Ste 725 Los Angeles CA 90045 310-910-9880 41
Web: haightlaw.com
Haight-Ashbury Publications (HAP)
856 Stanyan St San Francisco CA 94117 415-752-7601 637-9
Web: www.journalofpsychoactivedrugs.com
Hail & Cotton Inc 2500 S Main St Springfield TN 37172 615-384-9576 384-6461 756
Web: hailcotton.com
Hailey, McNamara, Hall, Larmann & Papale LLP
1 Galleria Blvd Ste 1400 Metairie LA 70001 504-836-6500 428
Web: www.hmhlp.com
Hain Celestial Group Inc
4600 Sleepytime Dr Boulder CO 80301 877-612-4246 297-11
NASDAQ: HAIN ■ *TF:* 877-612-4246 ■ *Web:* www.hain.com
Hainen Ford Inc 800 Hwy 5 S Tipton MO 65081 660-433-5545 57
Web: www.hainenford.net
Haines & Company Inc
8050 Freedom Ave North Canton OH 44720 800-843-8452 637-6
TF: 800-843-8452 ■ *Web:* www.haines.com
Haines & Kibblehouse Inc
4747 S Broad St Philadelphia PA 19019 610-584-8500 584-5059 189-5
Web: www.hkgroup.com
Haines Borough
103 Third Ave S PO Box 1209 Haines AK 99827 907-766-2231 766-2716 338
TF: 800-572-8006 ■ *Web:* www.hainesalaska.gov
Haines City Citrus Growers Assn (HCCGA)
8 Railroad Ave PO Box 337 Haines City FL 33845 863-422-1174 11-1
TF: 800-327-6676
Haines Equipment Inc 20 Carrington St Avoca NY 14809 607-566-2234 566-2240 273
Web: www.hainesequipment.com
HAIR 1839 Monroe St Madison WI 53711 608-259-1111 77
Web: hairmonroe.com
Hair Academy 8435 Annapolis Rd New Carrollton MD 20784 301-459-2509 577-3479 167-3
Web: www.hairacademymd.com
Hair Club for Men Limited Inc
1515 S Federal Hwy Ste 401 Boca Raton FL 33432 561-361-7600 77
TF: 800-251-2658 ■ *Web:* www.hairclub.com
Hair Design Institute 375 86th St Brooklyn NY 11209 718-745-1000 167-3
Web: www.hairdesigninstitute.edu
Hair It Is 977 Perry Hwy Ste 4 Pittsburgh PA 15237 412-366-5511 77
Hair Professionals Career College
10321 S Roberts Rd Palos Hills IL 60465 708-430-1755 166
Web: www.hairpros.edu
Hair Salon Body & Soul Inc
29 South St New Providence NJ 07974 908-522-9080 77
Web: hairsalonbodyandsoul.com

Phone | Fax | Class

Hair Tech Beauty College
2509 W Kingshighway .... Paragould AR 72450 870-236-6086 167-3
Web: www.hairtechcosmo.com

Hairart International Inc
400 W 157th St .... Gardena CA 90248 310-217-8900 77
Web: hairartproducts.com

Haiti
Consulate General
545 Boylston St Ste 201 .... Boston MA 02116 617-266-3660 257
Web: www.haiticgboston.org
Consulate General
815 Second Ave 6th Fl .... New York NY 10017 212-697-9767 681-6991 257
Web: www.embassypages.com
Consulate General
11 E Adams St Ste 1400 .... Chicago IL 60603 312-922-4006 922-7122 257
Web: www.haitianconsulate.org
Embassy 2311 Massachusetts Ave NW .... Washington DC 20008 202-332-4090 745-7215 257
Web: haiti.org

Haitian American Community Development (HACDC)
181 NE 82 St .... Miami FL 33138 305-759-2542 754-9200 194
Web: www.haitianamericancdc.org

Hajoca Corp
Keenan Supply Div 127 Coulter Ave .... Ardmore PA 19003 610-649-1430 649-1798 612
Web: www.hajoca.com

Hakanson Anderson Associates Inc
3601 Thurston Ave .... Anoka MN 55303 763-427-5860 427-0520 261
Web: www.haa-inc.com

Hakim Optical Laboratory Ltd
128 Hazelton Ave .... Toronto ON M5R2E5 416-924-5600 543
Web: hakimoptical.ca

Hal & Mal's 200 Commerce St .... Jackson MS 39201 601-948-0888 355-1794 671
Web: www.halandmals.com

HAL Communications Corp
3111 Village Office Pl .... Champaign IL 61822 217-367-7373 367-1701 647
Web: www.halcomm.com

Hal Hays Construction Inc
4181 Latham St .... Riverside CA 92501 951-788-0703 275-0752 302
Web: www.halhays.com

HAL Inc 11109 Cutten Rd Ste 200 .... Houston TX 77066 281-260-8181 177
Web: www.hal-inc.com

Hal Leonard Corp 960 E Mark St .... Winona MN 55987 507-454-2920 637-7
TF: 800-321-3408 ■ *Web:* www.halleonard.com

Hal Smith Restaurant Group Inc
3101 W Tecumseh Rd .... Norman OK 73072 405-321-2600 670
Web: halsmith.com

Hal's "The Steakhouse" 30 Old Ivy Rd .... Atlanta GA 30342 404-261-0025 671
Web: hals.net

Halabi Inc 2100 Huntington Dr .... Fairfield CA 94533 800-660-4167 115
TF: 800-660-4167 ■ *Web:* www.duracite.com

Halbert Construction Company Inc
330 S Magnolia Ave Ste 203 .... El Cajon CA 92020 619-593-3527 186
Web: halbertco.com

Halbrecht Lieberman Associates Inc
32 Surf Rd .... Westport CT 06880 203-222-4890 222-4895 266
Web: www.hlassoc.com

HALCO Industries LLC
1015 Norcross Industrial Ct .... Norcross GA 30071 770-840-3480 579
TF: 800-766-5665 ■ *Web:* www.halcolubricants.com

Halco Products
100 Gordon St .... Elk Grove Village IL 60007 847-956-1600 186
Web: www.halco-products.com

Haldeman-Homme Inc
430 Industrial Blvd NE .... Minneapolis MN 55413 612-331-4880 320
Web: www.haldemanhomme.com

Halden Group, The
5940 Harbour Park Dr .... Midlothian VA 23112 804-595-2295 177
Web: www.haldengroup.com

Haldex Brake Products Corp
10930 N Pomona Ave .... Kansas City MO 64153 816-891-2470 891-9447 60
TF: 800-533-1941 ■ *Web:* www.haldex.com

Haldor Topsoe Inc 17629 El Cam Ste 300 .... Houston TX 77058 281-228-5000 228-5019 143
Web: www.topsoe.com

Hale Center Theater Orem 225 W 400 N .... Orem UT 84057 801-226-8600 852-3189 572
Web: www.haletheater.org

Hale Centre Theater 9900 S Monroe St .... Sandy UT 84070 801-984-9000 984-9009 572
Web: www.hct.org

Hale County 1001 Main St PO Box 160 .... Greensboro AL 36744 334-624-3081 338
Web: www.halecoso.com

Hale County 500 Broadway .... Plainview TX 79072 806-291-5261 291-5310 338
Web: www.halecounty.org

Hale County Board of Education
1115 Powers St .... Greensboro AL 36744 334-624-8836 624-3415 685
Web: www.halek12.org

Hale Engineering Inc 7910 Convoy Ct .... San Diego CA 92111 858-715-1420 261
Web: haleengineering.com

Hale Farm & Village
2686 Oakhill Rd PO Box 296 .... Bath OH 44210 330-666-3711 520
TF: 877-425-3327 ■ *Web:* www.wrhs.org

Hale Group Ltd, The 8 Cherry St .... Danvers MA 01923 978-777-9077 463
Web: www.halegroup.com

Hale Products Inc
700 Spring Mill Ave .... Conshohocken PA 19428 800-533-3569 825-6440* 641
*Fax Area Code: 610 ■ *TF:* 800-220-4253 ■ *Web:* www.haleproducts.com

Hale Trailer Brake & Wheel Inc
76 Cooper Rd PO Box 1400 .... Voorhees NJ 08043 856-768-1330 126
TF: 800-232-6535 ■ *Web:* haletrailer.com

Haleakala National Park PO Box 369 .... Makawao HI 96768 808-572-4400 572-1304 564
Web: www.nps.gov

Halekulani Hotel 2199 Kalia Rd .... Honolulu HI 96815 808-923-2311 926-8004 379
TF: 800-367-2343 ■ *Web:* www.halekulani.com

Hales Machine Tool Inc
2730 Niagara Ln N .... Plymouth MN 55447 763-553-1711 553-9467 358
Web: www.halesmachinetool.com

Halex Co 23901 Aurora Rd .... Bedford Heights OH 44146 800-749-3261 439-1792* 308
*Fax Area Code: 440 ■ *TF:* 800-749-3261 ■ *Web:* www.halexco.com

Haley & Aldrich Inc
465 Medford St Ste 2200 .... Boston MA 02129 617-886-7400 261
Web: www.haleyaldrich.com

Haley Bros Inc
6291 Orangethorpe Ave .... Buena Park CA 90620 714-670-2112 994-6971 236
TF: 800-854-5951 ■ *Web:* www.haleybros.com

Haley Construction Inc
9 Aviator Way .... Ormond Beach FL 32174 386-944-0470 186
Web: rescongroup.com

Haley Marketing Group
6028 Sheridan Dr PO Box 410 .... Williamsville NY 14221 888-696-2900 195
TF: 888-696-2900 ■ *Web:* www.haleymarketing.com

Haley-Greer Inc 2257-C Lombardy Ln .... Dallas TX 75220 972-556-1177 556-1384 186
Web: www.haleygreer.com

Haleyville Drapery Manufacturing Co
1050 Hill Ave .... Haleyville AL 35565 205-486-9257 486-4788 746
Web: www.haleyvilledrapery.com

Half Hitch Tackle Company Inc
2206 Thomas Dr .... Panama City FL 32408 850-234-2621 711
TF: 888-668-9810 ■ *Web:* www.halfhitch.com

Half Hollow Hills Community Library
55 Vanderbilt Pkwy .... Dix Hills NY 11746 631-421-4530 434-3
Web: hhhlibrary.org

Half Moon Bay Lodge & Conference Ctr
2400 S Cabrillo Hwy .... Half Moon Bay CA 94019 650-726-9000 726-7951 379
TF: 800-710-0778 ■ *Web:* www.pacificahotels.com

Half Moon Outfitters
15 E Broughton St .... Savannah GA 31401 912-201-9393 711
Web: www.halfmoonoutfitters.com

Half Moon Pond State Park
1621 Black Pond Rd .... Fair Haven VT 05743 802-273-2848 565
Web: www.vtstateparks.com

Half Price Books Records & Magazines Inc
5803 E Northwest Hwy .... Dallas TX 75231 214-360-0833 95
Web: www.hpb.com

Half Yard Productions LLC
4922 Fairmont Ave Ste 300 .... Bethesda MD 20814 240-223-3400 514
Web: www.halfyardproductions.com

Halfacre Construction Co
7015 Professional Pkwy E .... Sarasota FL 34240 941-907-9099 186
Web: www.halfacreconstruction.com

Halfaker & Associates LLC
2900 S Quincy St Ste 410 .... Arlington VA 22206 703-434-3900 225
Web: www.halfaker.com

Halff Associates Inc
1201 N Bowser Rd .... Richardson TX 75081 214-346-6200 739-0095 261
Web: www.halff.com

Halibut Point State Park Gott Ave .... Rockport MA 01966 978-546-2997 565
Web: www.mass.gov

Halifax Community College
100 College Dr PO Box 809 .... Weldon NC 27890 252-536-2551 536-4144 162
TF: 800-228-8443 ■ *Web:* www.halifaxcc.edu

Halifax County 33 S Granville St .... Halifax NC 27839 252-583-1131 583-9921 338
Web: www.halifaxnc.com

Halifax County PO Box 699 .... Halifax VA 24558 434-476-3300 476-3384 338
Web: www.halifaxcountyva.gov

Halifax County Chamber of Commerce
820 Bruce St PO Box 399 .... South Boston VA 24592 434-572-3085 139
Web: www.halifaxchamber.net

Halifax County Library System
PO Box 97 .... Halifax NC 27839 252-583-3631 583-8661 434-3
Web: www.halifaxnc.com

Halifax County Public Schools
1030 Mary Bethune St Ste 100 PO Box 1849 .... Halifax VA 24558 434-476-2171 476-1858 685
Web: www.halifax.k12.va.us

Halifax Electric Membership Corp
208 Whitfield St .... Enfield NC 27823 252-445-5111 245
TF: 800-600-0522 ■ *Web:* www.halifaxemc.com

Halifax Group
1133 Connecticut Ave NW Ste 300 .... Washington DC 20036 202-530-8300 296-7133 792
Web: www.thehalifaxgroup.com

Halifax Mutual Insurance Co
114 SW Railroad St .... Enfield NC 27823 252-445-4201 390
Web: halifaxmutualins.com

Halifax Port Authority
1215 Marginal Rd PO Box 336 .... Halifax NS B3J2P6 902-426-8222 426-7335 618
Web: www.portofhalifax.ca

Halifax Regional Medical Ctr
250 Smith Church Rd PO Box 1089 .... Roanoke Rapids NC 27870 252-535-8011 535-8466 374-3
Web: vidantnorthhospital.com

Halifax Stanfield International Airport (HIAA)
1 Bell Blvd .... Enfield NS B2T1K2 902-873-4422 873-4750 27
TF: 800-753-1051 ■ *Web:* halifaxstanfield.ca

Haliimaile General Store
900 Haliimaile Hwy .... Makawao HI 96768 808-572-2666 345
Web: hgsmaui.com

Hall & Evans 1001 17th St Ste 300 .... Denver CO 80202 303-628-3300 428
Web: www.hallevans.com

Hall Capital Partners LLC
1 Maritime Plz 6th Fl .... San Francisco CA 94111 415-288-0544 401
Web: www.hallcapital.com

Hall Communications Inc
404 W Lime St .... Lakeland FL 33815 863-682-8184 643
Web: www.hallradio.com

Hall Contracting Corp
6415 Lakeview Rd .... Charlotte NC 28269 704-598-0818 188-10
Web: www.hallcontracting.com

Hall County 225 Green St SE .... Gainesville GA 30501 770-531-7025 531-7070 338
Web: www.hallcounty.org

Hall County
County Courthouse 512 W Main St Ste 8 .... Memphis TX 79245 806-259-2627 259-5078 338
Web: www.texasfile.com

Hall County Schools
711 Green St NW Ste 100 .... Gainesville GA 30501 770-534-1080 535-7404 685
Web: www.hallco.org

Hall Dielectric Machinery Company Inc
698 Bryant Blvd .... Rock Hill SC 29732 803-324-0202 695
Web: www.halldielectric.com

Hall Environmental Consultants LLC
1376 Danville Loop 1 Rd .... Nicholasville KY 40356 859-885-3331 302
Web: consultantnicholasvilleky.com

Name / Address	City	State	ZIP	Phone	Fax	Class
Hall Family Foundation PO Box 419580 MD 323 *Web:* www.hallfamilyfoundation.org	Kansas City	MO	64141	816-274-8516	274-8547	305
HALL Group 2323 Ross Ave Ste 200 *Web:* hallgroup.com	Dallas	TX	75201	214-269-9500		655
Hall Hodges & Associates Inc 700 N Brand Blvd Ste 650 *TF:* 800-490-1447 ■ *Web:* hall-hodges.com	Glendale	CA	91203	800-490-1447		463
Hall Industries Inc 514 Mecklem Ln *Web:* hallindustries.com	Ellwood City	PA	16117	724-752-2000	758-1558	621
Hall Kistler & Company LLP 220 Market Ave S Ste 700 *Web:* www.hallkistler.com	Canton	OH	44702	330-453-7633	453-9366	2
Hall Laughlin China Co 672 Fiesta Dr **Fax Area Code:* 800 ■ *TF:* 800-452-4462 ■ *Web:* www.hlcdinnerware.com	Newell	WV	26050	330-385-2900	533-8918*	730
Hall Letter Shop Inc 5200 Rosedale Hwy *Web:* www.hallprintmail.com	Bakersfield	CA	93308	661-327-3228	327-5140	627
Hall Mark Global Technologies Inc 262 Chapman Rd Ste 101 *Web:* hgtechinc.net	Newark	DE	19702	302-366-8960		177
Hall MileOne Autogroup 441 Viking Dr *TF:* 877-206-9666 ■ *Web:* www.hallauto.com	Virginia Beach	VA	23452	877-206-9666		57
Hall of Flame Museum of Firefighting 6101 E Van Buren St *Web:* www.hallofflame.org	Phoenix	AZ	85008	602-275-3473	275-0896	520
Hall Render Killian Heath & Lyman Pc 500 N Meridian St Ste 400 *Web:* www.hallrender.com	Indianapolis	IN	46204	317-633-4884	633-4878	428
Hall Signs Inc 4495 W Vernal Pk **Fax Area Code:* 812 ■ *TF:* 800-284-7446 ■ *Web:* store.hallsigns.com	Bloomington	IN	47404	800-284-7446	332-9816*	701
Hall, Estill, Hardwick, Gable, Golden & Nelson PC 320 S Boston Ave Ste 200 *Web:* www.hallestill.com	Tulsa	OK	74103	918-594-0400		428
Hallamore Corp, The 795 Plymouth St *Web:* www.hallamore.com	Holbrook	MA	02343	781-767-2000		780
Hallandale Beach Chamber of Commerce 400 S Federal Hwy Ste 192 *Web:* hallandalebeachchamber.org	Hallandale Beach	FL	33009	954-454-0541	454-0930	139
Hallcon Corp 3280 Bloor St W Ste 250 *Web:* hallcon.com	Toronto	ON	M8X2X3	416-964-9191		393
Hallcrest Inc 1911 Pickwick Ln *Web:* www.hallcrest.com	Glenview	IL	60026	847-998-8580	998-6866	202
Haller Enterprises Inc 212 Bucky Dr *TF:* 888-565-0546 ■ *Web:* www.hallerent.com	Lititz	PA	17543	717-207-9813		610
Hallett & Perrin PC 1445 Ross Ave Ste 2400 *Web:* www.hallettperrin.com	Dallas	TX	75202	214-953-0053	922-4142	445
Halliburton 3000 N Sam Houston Pkwy E *Web:* www.halliburton.com	Houston	TX	77032	281-871-4000		316
Halliburton House Inn 5184 Morris St *TF:* 888-512-3344 ■ *Web:* www.thehalliburton.com	Halifax	NS	B3J1B3	902-420-0658	423-2324	379
Hallman/Lindsay Paints 1717 N Bristol St *Web:* www.hallmanlindsay.com	Sun Prairie	WI	53590	608-834-8844	837-1064	550
Hallmark Cards Inc 2501 McGee St *Web:* www.hallmark.com	Kansas City	MO	64108	800-425-5627		130
Hallmark Ch 12700 Ventura Blvd *TF:* 888-390-7474 ■ *Web:* www.hallmarkchannel.com	Studio City	CA	91604	818-755-2400		740
Hallmark College of Aeronautics 8901 Wetmore Rd *TF:* 800-880-6600 ■ *Web:* hallmarkuniversity.edu	San Antonio	TX	78216	210-690-9000		167-3
Hallmark Financial Services Inc 777 Main St Ste 1000 *NASDAQ: HALL* ■ *Web:* www.hallmarkgrp.com	Fort Worth	TX	76102	817-348-1600		360-4
Hallmark Inns & Resorts 1400 S Hemlock St *TF:* 888-448-4449 ■ *Web:* www.hallmarkinns.com	Cannon Beach	OR	97110	503-436-1566		379
Hallmark Nameplate Inc 1717 E Lincoln Ave *TF:* 800-874-9063 ■ *Web:* www.hallmarknameplate.com	Mount Dora	FL	32757	800-874-9063		701
Hallock Coin Jewelry 2060 W Lincoln Ave **Fax Area Code:* 714 ■ *TF:* 800-854-3232 ■ *Web:* www.hallockjewelry.com	Anaheim	CA	92801	800-854-3232	635-8247*	702
Halloran & Sage LLP 1 Goodwin Sq 225 Asylum St *Web:* www.halloransage.com	Hartford	CT	06103	860-522-6103	548-0006	445
Hall-Richardson Agency Inc 31080 Lankford Hwy PO Box 250	Keller	VA	23401	757-787-2791		390
Halls Atlanta Wholesale Florist Inc 630 Angier Ave *Web:* www.hallsatlanta.com	Atlanta	GA	30308	404-688-9397	522-0623	293
Hallwalls Contemporary Arts Ctr 341 Delaware Ave *Web:* www.hallwalls.org	Buffalo	NY	14202	716-854-1694	854-1696	50-2
Halma Holdings Inc 11500 Northlake Dr Ste 306 *Web:* www.halma.com	Cincinnati	OH	45249	513-772-5501		201
Halmar International LLC 421 E Rte 59 *Web:* www.halmarinternational.com	Nanuet	NY	10954	845-735-3511	735-3388	188
Halo Branded Solutions Inc 1500 Halo Way *Web:* www.halo.com	Sterling	IL	61081	815-625-0980	632-6900	86
Halo Group LLC 35055 W 12 Mile Rd Ste 215 *TF:* 877-456-4256 ■ *Web:* ettaingroup.com	Farmington Hills	MI	48331	877-456-4256		194
Halo Pharmaceutical Inc 30 N Jefferson Rd *Web:* www.halopharma.com	Whippany	NJ	07981	973-428-4000		231
Halocarbon Products Corp 6525 The Corners Pkwy Ste 200 *TF:* 800-338-5803 ■ *Web:* www.halocarbon.com	Peachtree Corners	GA	30092	470-419-6364		582
Halox Technologies Inc 304 Bishop Ave *Web:* www.haloxtech.com	Bridgeport	CT	06610	203-334-6278	334-6198	52
Halozyme Therapeutics Inc 11388 Sorrento Valley Rd *NASDAQ: HALO* ■ *Web:* www.halozyme.com	San Diego	CA	92121	858-794-8889	704-8311	582
Halron Lubricants Inc 1618 State St *TF:* 800-236-5845 ■ *Web:* www.halron.com	Green Bay	WI	54304	920-436-4000		579
Halsey Food Service 401 Lanier Rd *TF:* 800-621-0240 ■ *Web:* www.halseyfoodservice.com	Madison	AL	35758	256-772-9691	461-8386	297-8
Halstad Telephone Co (HTC) 345 2nd Ave W *TF:* 800-457-2125 ■ *Web:* www.halstadtel.com	Halstad	MN	56548	218-456-2125		224
Halstead Bank, The 314 Main St *Web:* halsteadbank.com	Halstead	KS	67056	316-835-2226		70
Halstead International Inc 15 Oakwood Ave *TF:* 866-843-8453 ■ *Web:* halsteadintl.com	Norwalk	CT	06850	866-843-8453		361
Halstead Property LLC 770 Lexington Ave *TF:* 800-765-2692 ■ *Web:* www.halstead.com	New York	NY	10065	212-317-7800		652
Halsted Corp 51 Commerce Dr Ste 3 *TF:* 800-843-5184 ■ *Web:* www.halstedbag.com	Cranbury	NJ	08512	800-843-5184		67
Halston LLC 1201 W Fifth St 11th Fl *TF:* 844-425-7866 ■ *Web:* www.halston.com	Los Angeles	CA	90017	844-425-7866		157-2
Haltom City Public Library 5024 Broadway Ave *Web:* www.haltomcitytx.com	Haltom City	TX	76117	817-222-7786		434-3
Haltoms Jewelers 317 Main St *Web:* www.haltoms.com	Fort Worth	TX	76102	817-336-4051		410
Halton Group Americas Inc 103 Industrial Dr *Web:* www.halton.com	Scottsville	KY	42164	270-393-7214		14
Halton Hills Chamber of Commerce 328 Guelph St *Web:* www.haltonhillschamber.on.ca	Georgetown	ON	L7G4B5	905-877-7119	877-5117	137
Halverson Co 235 Paxton Ave *Web:* www.halversoncompany.com	Salt Lake City	UT	84101	801-467-9423		362
Halverson Construction Company Inc 620 N 19th St *Web:* www.halversonconstruction.com	Springfield	IL	62702	217-753-0027	753-1904	188-4
Halverson, Mahlen & Wright PC 1001 S 24th St W Creekside Ste 301 *Web:* hglaw.net	Billings	MT	59108	406-652-1011		41
Halvor Lines Inc 217 Grand Ave *TF:* 800-233-2914 ■ *Web:* www.halvorlines.com	Superior	WI	54880	715-392-8161	392-1418	780
Halvorson's Upstreet Cafe 16 Church St *Web:* www.halvorsonsupstreetcafe.com	Burlington	VT	05401	802-658-0278		671
Halyard Health Inc 5405 Windward Pkwy *Web:* www.halyardhealth.com	Alpharetta	GA	30004	678-425-9273		475
Ham & McCreight Supply Inc 614 E Ave A *Web:* hmsupply.org	Temple	TX	76503	254-778-4747		612
Ham, Langston & Brezina LLP 11550 Fuqua St Ste 475 *Web:* www.hlb-cpa.com	Houston	TX	77034	281-481-1040	481-8485	2
Hamacher Resource Group Inc N 29 W 22769 Marjean Ln *TF:* 800-888-0889 ■ *Web:* hamacher.com	Waukesha	WI	53186	414-355-1330	355-1032	363
Hamamatsu Corp 360 Foothill Rd *Web:* www.hamamatsu.com	Bridgewater	NJ	08807	908-231-0960		246
Hamasaku 11043 Santa Monica Blvd *Web:* www.hamasakula.com	Los Angeles	CA	90025	310-479-7636		671
Hamblen County 2415 N Davy Crockett Pkwy *Web:* www.hamblencountytn.gov	Morristown	TN	37814	423-318-1536	318-2508	338
Hamblen County Board of Education 210 E Morris Blvd *Web:* www.hcboe.net	Morristown	TN	37813	423-586-7700	586-7747	685
Hambro Forest Products Inc 445 Elk Valley Rd *Web:* www.hambrowsg.com	Crescent City	CA	95531	707-464-6131		291
Hamburg Area School District (HASD) 701 Windsor St *Web:* www.hasdhawks.org	Hamburg	PA	19526	610-562-2241	562-2634	685
Hamburg Chamber of Commerce 6122 S Park Ave *TF:* 877-322-6890 ■ *Web:* www.hamburg-chamber.org	Hamburg	NY	14075	716-649-7917	649-6362	139
Hamburg State Park 6071 Hamburg State Park Rd *Web:* gastateparks.org	Mitchell	GA	30820	478-552-2393		565
Hamburg Sud North America Inc 465 S St **Fax Area Code:* 770 ■ *TF:* 888-228-8241 ■ *Web:* www.hamburgsud-line.com	Morristown	NJ	07960	973-775-5300	916-5901*	313
Hamburg, Karic, Edwards & Martin LLP 1900 Avenue of the Stars Ste 1800 *Web:* hkemlaw.com	Los Angeles	CA	90067	310-552-9292		41
Hamdard Center for Health & Human Services 228 E Lake St *Web:* www.hamdardcenter.org	Addison	IL	60101	630-835-1430	835-1433	317
Hamden Chamber of Commerce 2260 Whitney Ave *Web:* hamdenregionalchamber.com	Hamden	CT	06518	203-288-6431	288-4499	139
Hamden Library 2901 Dixwell Ave *Web:* www.hamdenlibrary.org	Hamden	CT	06518	203-287-2686		434-3
Hamel, Marcin, Dunn, Reardon & Shea PC 24 Federal St *Web:* hmdrslaw.com	Boston	MA	02110	617-482-0007		41
Hamer Enterprises 4200-A N Bicentennial Dr *Web:* hamerenterprises.com	McAllen	TX	78504	956-682-3466		174
Hamill Manufacturing Co 500 Pleasant Valley Rd *Web:* www.hamillmfg.com	Trafford	PA	15085	724-744-2131	744-3121	454
Hamilton Advisors Inc 373 Stanwich Rd *Web:* hamiltonadvisors.com	Greenwich	CT	06830	203-629-1112	629-1469	401
Hamilton Area YMCA Inc 1315 Whitehorse-Mercerville Rd *Web:* www.hamiltonymca.org	Hamilton Township	NJ	08619	609-581-9622	581-4737	354

Name / Address	City	State	Zip	Phone	Fax	Class
Hamilton Associates Inc 11403 Cronridge Dr *Web:* www.atitest.com	Owings Mills	MD	21117	410-363-9696		544
Hamilton Beach/Proctor-Silex Inc 4421 Waterfront Dr *TF:* 800-851-8900 ■ *Web:* www.hamiltonbeach.com	Glen Allen	VA	23060	804-273-9777		37
Hamilton Branch State Recreation Area 111 Campground Rd *Web:* southcarolinaparks.com	Plum Branch	SC	29845	864-333-2223		565
Hamilton Bulldogs Hockey Club 101 York Blvd *Web:* hamiltonbulldogs.com	Hamilton	ON	L8R3L4	905-529-8500		706
Hamilton Capital Management 5025 Arlington Centre Blvd *TF:* 888-833-5951 ■ *Web:* www.hamiltoncapital.com	Columbus	OH	43220	614-273-1000		401
Hamilton Caster & Manufacturing Co 1637 Dixie Hwy *Web:* www.hamiltoncaster.com	Hamilton	OH	45011	513-863-3300	863-5508	350
Hamilton Center Inc 620 Eighth Ave *TF:* 800-742-0787 ■ *Web:* www.hamiltoncenter.org	Terre Haute	IN	47804	800-742-0787		374-5
Hamilton Chamber of Commerce 120 King St W Plz level *Web:* www.hamiltonchamber.ca	Hamilton	ON	L8P4V2	905-522-1151	522-1154	137
Hamilton Chevrolet 5800 E 14 Mile Rd *TF:* 800-290-8018 ■ *Web:* www.hamiltonchevy.com	Warren	MI	48092	586-838-1537		57
Hamilton City School District (HCSD) 533 Dayton St PO Box 627 *Web:* hamiltoncityschools.com	Hamilton	OH	45012	513-887-5000	887-5014	685
Hamilton Co 4970 Energy Way *TF:* 800-648-5950 ■ *Web:* www.hamiltoncompany.com	Reno	NV	89502	775-858-3000		419
Hamilton Co, The 39 Brighton Ave *Web:* www.thehamiltoncompany.com	Allston	MA	02134	617-783-0039	783-0568	653
Hamilton College 198 College Hill Rd *TF:* 800-843-2655 ■ *Web:* www.hamilton.edu	Clinton	NY	13323	315-859-4421	859-4457	166
Hamilton Communications Group 20 N Wacker Dr	Chicago	IL	60606	312-321-5000		4
Hamilton Correctional Facility 10650 SW 46th St *Web:* www.dc.state.fl.us	Jasper	FL	32052	386-792-5151	792-5159	213
Hamilton County 1111 13th St Ste 1 *Web:* hamiltoncountyne.com	Aurora	NE	68818	402-694-3443	694-2297	338
Hamilton County 625 Georgia Ave *Web:* www.hamiltontn.gov	Chattanooga	TN	37402	423-209-6500	209-6501	338
Hamilton County 138 E Ct St Rm 603 *Web:* www.hamilton-co.org	Cincinnati	OH	45202	513-946-4550	946-4475	338
Hamilton County County Courthouse 102 N Rice Ste 107 *Web:* www.co.hamilton.tx.us	Hamilton	TX	76531	254-386-3518	386-8727	338
Hamilton County 207 NE 1st St Rm 106 *Web:* hamiltoncountyfl.com	Jasper	FL	32052	386-792-1060		338
Hamilton County 102 County View Dr *TF:* 800-533-8443 ■ *Web:* www.hamiltoncounty.com	Lake Pleasant	NY	12108	518-548-7111	548-9740	338
Hamilton County 1 Hamilton County Sq Ste 106 *Web:* www.hamiltoncounty.in.gov	Noblesville	IN	46060	317-776-9629		338
Hamilton County PO Box 1167 *Web:* www.syracuseks.gov	Syracuse	KS	67878	620-384-5629		338
Hamilton County 2300 Superior St *Web:* www.hamiltoncounty.org	Webster City	IA	50595	515-832-9535	832-9514	338
Hamilton County Convention & Visitors Bureau Inc 37 E Main St *TF:* 800-776-8687 ■ *Web:* www.visithamiltoncounty.com	Carmel	IN	46032	317-848-3181		206
Hamilton County Department of Education 3074 Hickory Valley Rd *Web:* www.hcde.org	Chattanooga	TN	37421	423-209-0400		685
Hamilton County Educational Service Ctr (HCESC) 11083 Hamilton Ave *Web:* www.hcesc.org	Cincinnati	OH	45231	513-674-4200	742-8339	685
Hamilton County Electric Cooperative Assn 420 N Rice St PO Box 753 *TF:* 800-595-3401 ■ *Web:* www.hamiltonelectric.coop	Hamilton	TX	76531	254-386-3123		245
Hamilton County Speedway 1200 Bluff St *TF:* 800-873-1507 ■ *Web:* www.hamiltoncospeedway.com	Webster City	IA	50595	515-832-6000		515
Hamilton County State Fish & Wildlife Area 10279 Sunrise Point Rd *Web:* www2.illinois.gov	McLeansboro	IL	62859	618-773-4340		565
Hamilton Designs LLC 11988 Fishers Crossing Dr Ste 154 *Web:* hamilton-designs.com	Fishers	IN	46038	317-570-8800		261
Hamilton Engineering & Surveyi 3409 W Lemon St *Web:* www.hamiltonengineering.us	Tampa	FL	33609	813-250-3535		261
Hamilton Equipment Inc 567 S Reading Rd PO Box 478 *Web:* www.haminc.com	Ephrata	PA	17522	717-733-7951		274
Hamilton Form Company Ltd 7009 Midway Rd *TF:* 800-332-7090 ■ *Web:* www.hamiltonform.com	Fort Worth	TX	76118	817-590-2111	595-1110	697
Hamilton Grange National Memorial (HAGR) 122 St Riverside Dr *Web:* www.nps.gov	New York	NY	10027	212-666-1640		564
Hamilton Group 100 Elwood Davis Rd *TF:* 800-351-3066 ■ *Web:* www.hamiltongroup.net	North Syracuse	NY	13212	315-413-0086	413-0087	272
Hamilton Health Sciences 1200 Main St W *TF:* 800-680-9868 ■ *Web:* www.hamiltonhealthsciences.ca	Hamilton	ON	L8N3Z5	905-522-3863		374-2
Hamilton Mall 4403 Black Horse Pk *Web:* www.shophamilton.com	Mays Landing	NJ	08330	609-646-8326		460
Hamilton Medical Ctr 1200 Memorial Dr PO Box 1168 *Web:* www.hamiltonhealth.com	Dalton	GA	30720	706-272-6000		374-3
Hamilton Oshawa Port Authority 605 James St N *TF:* 800-263-2131 ■ *Web:* www.hopaports.ca	Hamilton	ON	L8L1K1	905-525-4330		618
Hamilton Park Hotel & Conference Ctr 175 Park Ave *TF:* 877-999-3223 ■ *Web:* www.hamiltonparkhotel.com	Florham Park	NJ	07932	973-377-2424		377
Hamilton Partners Inc 300 Park Blvd Ste 500 *Web:* www.hamiltonpartners.com	Itasca	IL	60143	630-250-9700		653
Hamilton Place 2100 Hamilton Pl Blvd *Web:* www.hamiltonplace.com	Chattanooga	TN	37421	423-894-7177		460
Hamilton Plastics Inc 2641 Riverport Rd *Web:* www.hamiltonplasticsinc.com	Chattanooga	TN	37406	423-622-2200	264-6240	548
Hamilton Software Inc 6432 E Mineral Pl *Web:* www.hamiltonsoftware.com	Centennial	CO	80112	303-847-8092		178-1
Hamilton Sorter Company Inc 3158 Production Dr **Fax Area Code:* 800 ■ *TF:* 800-503-9966 ■ *Web:* www.hamiltoncs.com	Fairfield	OH	45014	513-870-4400	503-9963*	286
Hamilton System Distributors PO Box 58 *Web:* www.hamiltonsystem.com	Ridgefield Park	NJ	07660	551-237-5305		96
Hamilton Telecommunications 1001 12th St *TF:* 800-821-1831 ■ *Web:* www.hamiltontel.com	Aurora	NE	68818	402-694-5101		116
Hamilton Vopelak PC 450 Houston St *Web:* foundationtaxlaw.com	Coppell	TX	75019	972-393-8511		41
Hamilton Watch Company Inc 1200 Harbor Blvd Ste 7 *Web:* www.hamiltonwatch.com	Weehawken	NJ	07086	201-271-4680		153
Hamler State Bank 210 Randolph St PO Box 358 *TF:* 888-508-3955 ■ *Web:* hamlerstatebank.com	Hamler	OH	43524	419-274-3955		70
Hamlet Homes 308 East 4500 South Ste 200 *Web:* hamlethomes.com	Salt Lake City	UT	84107	801-281-2223	281-2224	653
Hamlet Title Agency Inc 601 Portion Rd Ste 207 *Web:* hamlettitle.com	Lake Ronkonkoma	NY	11779	631-654-5000	654-8555	653
Hamlet Village 200 Hamlet Hills Dr Ofc *Web:* hamletretirement.com	Chagrin Falls	OH	44022	440-247-4201		371
Hamlin Beach State Park 1 Hamlin Beach Blvd W *Web:* www.parks.ny.gov	Hamlin	NY	14464	585-964-2462		565
Hamlin County 300 Fourth St PO Box 237 *Web:* www.hamlincountysd.org	Hayti	SD	57241	605-783-3201		338
Hamlin County Herald Enterprise PO Box 207 *Web:* www.hamlincountypublishing.com	Hayti	SD	57241	605-783-3636	793-9140	532-2
Hamlin Newco LLC 2741 Wingate Ave *Web:* www.hnmetalstamping.com	Akron	OH	44314	330-753-7791	753-5577	489
Hamline University 1536 Hewitt Ave *TF:* 800-753-9753 ■ *Web:* www.hamline.edu	Saint Paul	MN	55104	651-523-2207	523-2458	166
Hamm Inc 609 Perry Pl PO Box 17 *Web:* www.nrhamm.com	Perry	KS	66073	785-597-5111		503-5
Hamm Memorial Psychiatric Clnc 408 St Peter St Ste 429 *Web:* www.hammclinic.org	Saint Paul	MN	55102	651-224-0614		726
Hammacher Schlemmer & Co 9307 N Milwaukee Ave *TF:* 800-321-1484 ■ *Web:* www.hammacher.com	Niles	IL	60714	847-581-8600		362
Hammel Green & Abrahamson Inc 420 N 5th St Ste 100 *TF:* 888-442-8255 ■ *Web:* www.hga.com	Minneapolis	MN	55401	612-758-4000	758-4199	261
Hammelmann Corp 436 Southpointe Dr *TF:* 800-783-4935 ■ *Web:* www.hammelmann.com	Miamisburg	OH	45449	800-783-4935		641
Hammer & Hand Inc 1020 SE Harrison St *Web:* hammerandhand.com	Portland	OR	97214	503-232-2447		186
Hammer Company Inc 7500 Greenway Center Dr Ste 1500 *Web:* www.hammers.com	Greenbelt	MD	20770	301-345-5300		81-3
Hammer Creative Inc 1020 Cole Ave Ste 4400 *Web:* www.hammercreative.com	Hollywood	CA	90038	323-606-4700		4
Hammer Data Systems LLC 8138 Main St *Web:* www.hammerdata.com	Garrettsville	OH	44231	330-527-4018		177
Hammer Museum 10899 Wilshire Blvd *Web:* hammer.ucla.edu	Los Angeles	CA	90024	310-443-7000	443-7099	520
Hammer Nutrition Ltd 4952 Whitefish Stage Rd **Fax Area Code:* 406 ■ *TF:* 800-336-1977 ■ *Web:* www.hammernutrition.com	Whitefish	MT	59937	800-336-1977	862-4543*	799
Hammer Packaging Corp 200 Lucius Gordon Dr *Web:* www.hammerpackaging.com	West Henrietta	NY	14586	585-424-3880	424-3886	627
Hammerman & Hultgren PC 3101 N Central Ave Ste 500 *Web:* hammerman-hultgren.com	Phoenix	AZ	85012	602-264-2566	266-3488	41
Hammerman Bros Inc 50 W 57th St 12th Fl *TF:* 800-223-6436 ■ *Web:* hammermanjewels.com	New York	NY	10019	212-956-2806	956-2769	409
Hammersmith Manufacturing & Sales Inc 401 Central Ave *TF:* 800-375-8245 ■ *Web:* www.vailproducts.com	Horton	KS	66439	800-375-8245		91
Hammock Beach Resort 200 Ocean Crest Dr *TF:* 866-841-0287 ■ *Web:* www.hammockbeach.com	Palm Coast	FL	32137	866-841-0287		669
Hammock Dunes Club Inc 30 Ave Royale *Web:* hammockdunesclub.com	Palm Coast	FL	32137	386-445-0747		653
Hammocks Beach State Park 1572 Hammock Beach Rd *Web:* www.ncparks.gov	Swansboro	NC	28584	910-326-4881		565
Hammonasset Beach State Park 1288 Boston Post Rd PO Box 271 *Web:* portal.ct.gov	Madison	CT	06443	203-245-2785	245-9201	565
Hammond & Irving Inc 254 N St *Web:* www.hammond-irving.com	Auburn	NY	13021	315-253-6265	253-3136	483

Name / Address	Phone	Fax	Class
Hammond & Tobler PC 1400 E Southern Ave Ste 935 .... Tempe AZ 85282 *Web:* hammondandtoblerpc.com	480-756-2224	752-2293	41
Hammond Communications Group Inc 173 Trade St .... Lexington KY 40511 *TF:* 888-424-1878 ■ *Web:* hammondcg.com	859-254-1878		513
Hammond Drives & Equipment Inc 8527 Midland Rd .... Freeland MI 48623 *TF:* 888-695-2239 ■ *Web:* www.hammondeqp.com	989-695-2239	695-2819	358
Hammond Electronics Inc 1230 W Central Blvd .... Orlando FL 32805 *TF:* 800-929-3672 ■ *Web:* www.hammondelec.com	407-849-6060	872-0826	246
Hammond Manufacturing Company Ltd 394 Edinburgh Rd N .... Guelph ON N1H1E5 *Web:* www.hammfg.com	519-822-2960		201
Hammond North Condominium Assn 5300 Hamilton Ave .... Cincinnati OH 45224 *Web:* www.hammondnorthcondos.com	513-541-5252		803-3
Hammond Public Library 564 State St .... Hammond IN 46320 *Web:* www.hammond.lib.in.us	219-931-5100	931-3474	434-3
Hammond Roto-Finish 1600 Douglas Ave .... Kalamazoo MI 49007 *Web:* hammondroto.com	269-345-7151	345-1710	455
Hammond Steakhouse 1402 N Fifth St .... Superior WI 54880 *Web:* hammondliquor.com	715-392-3269		671
Hammond Suzuki USA Inc 743 Annoreno Dr .... Addison IL 60101 *Web:* www.hammondorganco.com	630-543-0277		527
Hammond Travers & Tuttle Pc 6263 N Scottsdale Rd Ste 250 .... Scottsdale AZ 85250 *Web:* httcpa.com	480-998-2755	998-4235	2
Hammond-Harwood House 19 Maryland Ave .... Annapolis MD 21401 *Web:* www.hammondharwoodhouse.org	410-263-4683		520
Hammonds House 503 Peeples St SW .... Atlanta GA 30310 *Web:* www.hammondshouse.org	404-612-0500		50-3
Hampden County 50 State St PO Box 559 .... Springfield MA 01102 *Web:* hcbar.org	413-748-8600		338
Hampden Papers Inc 100 Water St .... Holyoke MA 01040 *Web:* www.hampdenpapers.com	413-536-1000	532-9161	554
Hampden-Sydney College PO Box 667 .... Hampden Sydney VA 23943 *TF:* 800-755-0733 ■ *Web:* www.hsc.edu	434-223-6120		166
Hampel Oil Distributors Inc 3727 S W St .... Wichita KS 67217 *TF:* 800-530-5848 ■ *Web:* www.hampeloil.com	800-530-5848		581
Hampshire College 893 W St .... Amherst MA 01002 *Web:* www.hampshire.edu	413-549-4600	559-5631	166
Hampshire Country School 28 Patey Cir .... Rindge NH 03461 *Web:* hampshirecountryschool.org	603-899-3325	899-6521	622
Hampshire County 19 E Main St PO Box 806 .... Romney WV 26757 *Web:* hampshirecountyclerk.weebly.com	304-822-5112	822-4039	338
Hampshire Fire Protection Company Inc 8 N Wentworth Ave .... Londonderry NH 03053 *Web:* www.hampshirefire.com	603-432-8221		189-10
Hampson Aerospace Inc 2700 112th St Ste 300 .... Grand Prairie TX 75050	214-988-0630		529
Hampson Archeological Museum State Park PO Box 156 .... Wilson AR 72395 *Web:* www.arkansasstateparks.com	870-655-8622		565
Hampstead Hospital 218 E Rd .... Hampstead NH 03841 *Web:* www.hampsteadhospital.com	603-329-5311	329-4746	374-5
Hampton Area Chamber of Commerce 1 Layfayette Rd .... Hampton NH 03842 *Web:* www.hamptonchamber.com	603-926-8718	926-9977	139
Hampton Beach State Park 160 Ocean Blvd .... Hampton NH 03842 *Web:* www.nhstateparks.org	603-926-8990		565
Hampton Behavioral Health Ctr 650 Rancocas Rd .... Westampton NJ 08060 *TF:* 800-603-6767 ■ *Web:* hamptonhospital.com	800-603-6767		726
Hampton Coliseum 1000 Coliseum Dr .... Hampton VA 23666 *Web:* www.hamptoncoliseum.org	757-838-4203	838-2595	720
Hampton Company Inc 12709 M 60 E .... Burlington MI 49029 *Web:* www.hamptongames.net	517-765-2222		762
Hampton Conventions & Visitors Bureau 1919 Commerce Dr Ste 290 .... Hampton VA 23666 *TF:* 800-487-8778 ■ *Web:* visithampton.com	757-722-1222	896-4600	206
Hampton County 200 Jackson Ave E .... Hampton SC 29924 *Web:* www.hamptoncountysc.org	803-914-2100	914-2107	338
Hampton Golf Inc 10401 Deerwood Park Blvd Ste 2130 .... Jacksonville FL 32256 *Web:* hampton.golf	904-564-9129		760
Hampton Homecare 50 Alexander Ct Ste 3 .... Ronkonkoma NY 11779 *Web:* www.hamptonhomecare.com	631-820-8220	820-8221	363
Hampton (Independent City) 22 Lincoln St .... Hampton VA 23669 *TF:* 800-555-3930 ■ *Web:* hampton.gov	757-727-8311		338
Hampton Inn 2300 Carlisle NE .... Albuquerque NM 87110 *Web:* hamptoninn3.hilton.com	505-837-9300	837-2211	378
Hampton Inn & Suites Atlanta Downtown Hotel 161 Spring St NW .... Atlanta GA 30303 *Web:* hamptoninn3.hilton.com	404-589-1111		379
Hampton Inn Brookhaven 2000 N Ocean Ave .... Farmingville NY 11738 *Web:* hamptoninn3.hilton.com	631-732-7300		378
Hampton Inn Phoenix-Biltmore 2310 E Highland Ave .... Phoenix AZ 85016 *Web:* hamptoninn3.hilton.com	602-956-5221	468-7220	379
Hampton Jitney Inc (HJ) 395 County Rd .... Southampton NY 11968 *Web:* www.hamptonjitney.com	631-283-4600		107
Hampton Lumber 9600 SW Barnes Rd Ste 200 .... Portland OR 97225 *Web:* www.hamptonlumber.com	503-297-7691		683
Hampton Machine Shop Inc 900 39th St .... Newport News VA 23607 *Web:* www.hampmach.com	757-380-8500	380-0101	757
Hampton Marina Hotel 700 Settlers Landing Rd .... Hampton VA 23669 *Web:* www.hamptonmarinahotel.com	757-727-9700		378
Hampton National Cemetery Cemetery Rd at Marshall Ave .... Hampton VA 23669 *Web:* www.cem.va.gov	757-723-7104		136
Hampton National Historic Site 535 Hampton Ln .... Towson MD 21286 *Web:* www.nps.gov	410-823-1309	823-8394	564
Hampton Office Products Inc 248 Donohoe Rd .... Greensburg PA 15601 *Web:* www.hamptonoffice.com	724-836-6430		321
Hampton Paper & Transfer Printing Inc 2230 Eddie Williams Rd .... Johnson City TN 37601 *Web:* www.hamptonprints.com	423-928-7247		627
Hampton Plantation State Historic Site 1950 Rutledge Rd .... McClellanville SC 29458 *Web:* southcarolinaparks.com	843-546-9361		565
Hampton Ponds State Park 1048 N Rd .... Westfield MA 01085 *Web:* www.mass.gov	413-532-3985		565
Hampton Press Inc 23 Broadway .... Cresskill NJ 07626 *TF:* 800-894-8955 ■ *Web:* www.hamptonpress.com	800-894-8955		637-2
Hampton Public Library 4207 Victoria Blvd .... Hampton VA 23669 *Web:* hampton.gov	757-727-1154	727-1152	434-3
Hampton Roads Chamber of Commerce 500 E Main St Ste 700 .... Norfolk VA 23510 *Web:* www.hrchamber.com	757-622-2312	622-5563	139
Hampton Roads Naval Museum 1 Waterside Dr Ste 248 .... Norfolk VA 23510 *Web:* www.history.navy.mil	757-322-2987	445-1867	520
Hampton Securities Ltd 141 Adelaide St W Ste 1800 .... Toronto ON M5H3L5 *TF:* 877-225-0229 ■ *Web:* www.hamptonsecurities.com	416-862-7800		690
Hampton Street Vineyard 1201 Hampton St .... Columbia SC 29202 *Web:* www.hamptonstreetvineyard.com	803-252-0850	931-0193	671
Hampton Technologies LLC 19 Scouting Blvd .... Medford NY 11763 *Web:* www.hamptontech.net	631-924-1335		467
Hampton University 100 E Queen St .... Hampton VA 23668 *TF:* 800-624-3341 ■ *Web:* www.hamptonu.edu	757-727-5000		166
Hampton, Lenzini & Renwick Inc 380 Shepard Dr .... Elgin IL 60123 *Web:* www.hlrengineering.com	847-697-6700		261
Hamptons Magazine 67 Hampton Rd Ste 5 .... Southampton NY 11968 *Web:* mlhamptons.com	631-283-7125	283-7854	457-22
Hamrick Inc 742 Peachoid Rd .... Gaffney SC 29341 *Web:* www.hamricks.com	864-487-7505		155-3
Hamrick Mills Inc 515 W Buford St PO Box 48 .... Gaffney SC 29341 *TF:* 800-600-4305 ■ *Web:* www.hamrickmills.com	864-489-4731		745-1
Hamrick School 1156 Medina Rd .... Medina OH 44256 *TF:* 800-470-4753 ■ *Web:* www.hamrickschool.edu	330-239-2229	239-2443	685
Hamrock Inc 12521 Los Nietos Rd .... Santa Fe Springs CA 90670 *Web:* www.hamrock.com	562-944-0255		488
Hana Microdisplay Technologies 2061 Case Pkwy S .... Twinsburg OH 44087 *Web:* hanaoh.com	330-405-4600		180
Hana Tropicals 4228 Hana Hwy .... Hana HI 96713 *TF:* 800-456-4262 ■ *Web:* www.hanatropicals.com	808-248-7533		293
Hana Yori 3601 Grape Rd .... Mishawaka IN 46545 *Web:* www.hanayori.com	574-258-5817		671
Hanalei Bay Resort & Suites 5380 Honoiki Rd .... Princeville HI 96722 *TF:* 877-344-0688 ■ *Web:* www.hanaleibayresort.com	808-826-6522		669
Hanapin Marketing LLC 501 N Morton St Ste 212 .... Bloomington IN 47404 *Web:* www.hanapinmarketing.com	812-330-3134		195
Hanauma Bay Nature Preserve 100 Hanauma Bay Rd .... Honolulu HI 96825 *TF:* 800-690-6200 ■ *Web:* www.honolulu.gov	808-396-4229	395-0468	50-5
Hanchett Manufacturing Inc 20000 19 Mile Rd .... Big Rapids MI 49307 *Fax Area Code: 231 ■ *TF:* 800-454-7463 ■ *Web:* www.hanchett.com	800-454-7463	796-4851*	455
Hancock & Moore PO Box 3444 .... Hickory NC 28603 *Web:* www.hancockandmoore.com	828-495-8235	495-3021	319-2
Hancock Concrete Products Inc 17 Atlantic Ave .... Hancock MN 56244 *Web:* www.hancockconcrete.com	320-392-5207	392-5155	183
Hancock County 854 Hwy 90 Ste A .... Bay Saint Louis MS 39520 *Web:* hancockcounty.ms.gov	228-467-2100	466-5994	338
Hancock County PO Box 189 .... Carthage IL 62321 *Web:* www.hancockcounty-il.gov	217-357-2616		338
Hancock County 50 State St Ste 10 .... Ellsworth ME 04605 *Web:* co.hancock.me.us	207-667-9542	667-1412	338
Hancock County 300 S Main St .... Findlay OH 45840 *TF:* 888-534-1432 ■ *Web:* www.co.hancock.oh.us	419-424-7037	424-7801	338
Hancock County PO Box 70 .... Garner IA 50438 *Web:* www.hancockcountyia.org	641-923-2532		338
Hancock County 225 Main Cross St .... Hawesville KY 42348 *Web:* www.hancockky.us	270-927-6117		338
Hancock County PO Box 367 .... New Cumberland WV 26047 *Web:* www.hancockcountywv.org	304-564-3311	564-5941	338
Hancock County 418 Harrison St PO Box 575 .... Sneedville TN 37869 *TF:* 800-332-0900 ■ *Web:* www.hancockcountytn.com	423-733-2519	733-4509	338
Hancock County 12630 Broad St .... Sparta GA 31087 *TF:* 800-255-0135 ■ *Web:* hancockcountyga.gov	706-444-5746	444-6221	338
Hancock County Cooperative Oil Assn 245 State St .... Garner IA 50438 *TF:* 800-924-2667 ■ *Web:* www.hancockcountycoop.com	641-923-2635		345

Phone | Fax | Class

Hancock County Library
312 Hwy 90 . . . . . Bay Saint Louis MS 39520 228-467-5282 467-5503 434-3
Web: www.hancocklibraries.info
Hancock County-Bar Harbor Airport
115 Caruso Dr . . . . . Trenton ME 04605 207-667-7329 27
Web: www.bhbairport.com
Hancock Herald PO Box 519. . . . . Hancock NY 13783 607-637-3591 637-4383 532-2
Web: www.hancockherald.com
Hancock Holding Co 2510 14th St. . . . . Gulfport MS 39501 228-868-4727 360-2
Web: www.hancockwhitney.com
Hancock House State Historic Site
3 Front St PO Box 139 . . . . . Hancocks Bridge NJ 08038 856-935-4373 565
Web: www.njparksandforests.org
Hancock International Corp
351 Main Pl . . . . . Carol Stream IL 60188 630-510-7697 311
Web: hancock-international.com
Hancock Park Associates
10350 Santa Monica Blvd Ste 295 . . . . . Los Angeles CA 90025 310-228-6900 228-6939 401
Web: www.hpcap.com
Hancock Regional Hospital School of Radiologic Technology
801 N State St. . . . . Greenfield IN 46140 317-468-4468 685
Web: www.hancockregionalhospital.org
Hancock State Prison 701 Prison Blvd . . . . . Sparta GA 31087 706-444-1000 444-1137 213
Web: dcor.state.ga.us
Hancock Telephone Co 34 Read St . . . . . Hancock NY 13783 607-637-9911 637-9999 224
TF: 800-360-4664 ■ *Web:* www.hancocktelephone.com
Hancor Inc PO Box 1047 . . . . . Findlay OH 45839 419-422-6521 596
TF: 888-892-2694 ■ *Web:* www.hancor.com
Hand County Clerk of Court
415 W 1st Ave Ste 11 . . . . . Miller SD 57362 605-853-3337 853-3779 338
Web: ujs.sd.gov
Hand Industries Inc 315 S Hand Ave . . . . . Warsaw IN 46580 574-267-3525 267-7349 146
Web: www.handindustries.com
Handa Travel Services Ltd
2269 Riverside Dr Billings Bridge Plz. . . . . Ottawa ON K1H8K2 613-731-1111 570-1885* 772
**Fax Area Code:* 866 ■ *Web:* www.handatravel.com
Handbill Printers Inc
820 E Parkridge Ave . . . . . Corona CA 92879 951-547-5910 627
Web: www.handbillprinters.com
Handel & Haydn Society 9 Harcourt St . . . . . Boston MA 02116 617-262-1815 266-4217 573-3
Web: handelandhaydn.org
Handel Group LLC 247 Limestone Rd . . . . . Ridgefield CT 06877 917-670-8782 463
TF: 800-617-7040 ■ *Web:* www.handelgroup.com
Handgards Inc 901 Hawkins Blvd . . . . . El Paso TX 79915 800-351-8161 576
TF: 800-351-8161 ■ *Web:* www.handgards.com
Handi Medical Supply Inc
2505 University Ave W . . . . . Saint Paul MN 55114 651-644-9770 237
Web: handimedical.com
Handi-Clean Products Inc
301 S Swing Rd . . . . . Greensboro NC 27409 336-292-3083 292-3086 151
Web: www.handi-clean.com
Handi-foil Corp 135 E Hintz Rd . . . . . Wheeling IL 60090 847-520-1000 295
Web: www.handi-foil.com
Handi-Ramp 510 N Ave . . . . . Libertyville IL 60048 847-680-7700 816-7689 358
TF: 800-876-7267 ■ *Web:* www.handiramp.com
Handke's Cuisine 520 S Front St . . . . . Columbus OH 43215 614-621-2500 671
Web: www.chefhandke.com
Handler, Henning & Rosenberg LLP
1300 Linglestown Rd . . . . . Harrisburg PA 17110 717-775-7514 41
TF: 888-498-3023 ■ *Web:* hhrlaw.com
Handlery Hotel & Resort
950 Hotel Cir N. . . . . . San Diego CA 92108 619-298-0511 669
TF: 800-676-6567 ■ *Web:* www.handlery.com
Handley Industries Inc
2101 Brooklyn Rd. . . . . Jackson MI 49203 517-787-8821 787-3946 199
TF: 800 070 5000 ■ *Web:* www.handleyind.com
Handling Systems Inc
2659 E Magnolia St . . . . . Phoenix AZ 85034 602-275-2228 770
TF: 800-229-9977 ■ *Web:* www.handlingsystems.com
Han-D-Pac Products Inc
9420 Carnegie Ave . . . . . El Paso TX 79925 915-595-2212 297-8
Web: www.han-d-pac.com
Handpicked 150C Harbison Blvd. . . . . Columbia SC 29212 803-749-6024 410
TF: 800-386-9117 ■ *Web:* behandpicked.com
Hands of Heartland 211 Galvin Rd N . . . . . Bellevue NE 68005 402-933-0680 371
Web: www.handsofheartland.com
Hands On Books 1117 Lenora Ct. . . . . Bellingham WA 98225 360-671-9079 637-2
Web: www.woodshop4kids.com
Hands on Central Ohio
195 N Grant Ave . . . . . Columbus OH 43215 614-221-6766 224-6866 637-10
Web: www.handsoncentralohio.org
Hands on Children's Museum
414 Jefferson St NE . . . . . Olympia WA 98501 360-956-0818 754-8626 521
Web: www.hocm.org
Hands on Mailing & Fulfillment
6840 Orangethorpe Ave Ste L. . . . . Buena Park CA 90620 714-522-3979 522-3238 5
Web: www.handsonmailing.com
Hands on Technology Transfer Inc
14 Fletcher St 1 Village Sq Ste 8 . . . . . Chelmsford MA 01824 978-250-4299 250-4372 764
TF: 800-413-0939 ■ *Web:* traininghott.com
Hands On! Regional Museum
315 E Main St. . . . . Johnson City TN 37601 423-434-4263 928-6915 521
Web: visithandson.org
Hands-On House Children's Museum of Lancaster
721 Landis Valley Rd . . . . . Lancaster PA 17601 717-569-5437 521
Web: www.handsonhouse.org
Handweavers Guild of America (HGA)
1255 Buford Hwy Ste 211. . . . . Suwanee GA 30024 678-730-0010 730-0836 48-18
Web: www.weavespindye.org
Handy & Handy PC
2150 South 1300 East Ste 300 . . . . . Salt Lake City UT 84106 801-264-6677 41
Web: handylawutah.com
Handy Industries
600 W Second Ave PO Box 223 . . . . . Sully IA 50251 855-752-5446 697
TF: 855-752-5446 ■ *Web:* www.handyindustries.com
Handy Kenlin Group, The (HKG)
29 E Hintz Rd . . . . . Wheeling IL 60090 847-459-0900 459-0902 261
Web: www.handykenlin.com

Handy Networks LLC
1801 Calif St Ste 240 . . . . . Denver CO 80202 303-414-6910 224
Web: www.handynetworks.com
Handy Store Fixtures Inc
337 Sherman Ave . . . . . Newark NJ 07114 800-631-4280 286
TF: 800-631-4280 ■ *Web:* www.handystorefixtures.com
Handy Tv Inc 224 Oxmoor Cir . . . . . Birmingham AL 35209 205-290-0300 429
Web: www.handytv.com
Handyman Connection Inc
11115 Kenwood Rd . . . . . Blue Ash OH 45242 513-771-3003 771-6439 189-11
TF: 800-466-5530 ■ *Web:* www.handymanconnection.com
HandyTrac Systems LLC
510 Staghorn Ct . . . . . Alpharetta GA 30004 678-990-2305 692
TF: 800-665-9994 ■ *Web:* www.handytrac.com
Hanes Companies Inc
500 N McLin Creek Rd . . . . . Conover NC 28613 828-464-4673 594
TF: 877-252-3052 ■ *Web:* www.hanescompanies.com
Hanes Erie Inc 7601 Klier Dr S . . . . . Fairview PA 16415 814-474-1999 627
Web: haneserie.com
Hanes Mall
3320 Silas Creek Pkwy Ste 264 . . . . . Winston-Salem NC 27103 336-765-8321 460
Web: www.shophanesmall.com
Haney Technical Ctr 3016 Hwy 77 N. . . . . Panama City FL 32405 850-767-5500 747-5555 167-3
Web: www.bayschools.com
Hanford Chamber of Commerce 113 Ct St . . . . . Hanford CA 93230 559-582-0483 139
Web: hanfordchamber.com
Hanford Nursing & Rehabilitation Hospital
1007 W Lacey Blvd. . . . . Hanford CA 93230 559-582-2871 450
Web: www.nursinghomes.com
Hanford Pharmaceuticals LLC
304 Oneida St. . . . . Syracuse NY 13202 315-476-7418 476-7434 231
TF: 800-234-4263 ■ *Web:* hanford.com
Hang Masters Peachtree St NW. . . . . Atlanta GA 30303 770-565-4264 393
Web: www.hangmasters.com
Hangar On The Wharf
2 Marine Way Ste 106 . . . . . Juneau AK 99801 907-586-5018 586 8173 671
Web: www.hangaronthewharf.com
Hangawi 12 E 32nd St . . . . . New York NY 10016 212-213-0077 689-0780 671
Web: www.hangawirestaurant.com
Hanger Inc 10910 Domain Dr Ste 300 . . . . . Austin TX 78758 512-777-3800 477
TF: 877-442-6437 ■ *Web:* www.hanger.com
Hangley Aronchick Segal & Pudlin PC
1 Logan Sq 18th & Cherry Sts . . . . . Philadelphia PA 19103 215-568-6200 428
Web: www.hangley.com
Hangman Products Inc
6400 Variel Ave. . . . . Woodland Hills CA 91367 818-610-0487 320
Web: hangmanproducts.com
Hangsterfer's Laboratories Inc
175 Ogden Rd. . . . . Mantua NJ 08051 856-468-0216 468-0200 541
TF: 800-433-5823 ■ *Web:* hangsterfers.com
Hani Shatila
9353 Clairemont Mesa Blvd Ste Q . . . . . San Diego CA 92123 858-268-0044 794
Web: tierramesavet.com
HANK AM 1550 & 97.7 FM
730 Ray O Vac Dr. . . . . Madison WI 53711 608-273-1000 274 0100 645-92
TF: 888-974-4265 ■ *Web:* www.hankonline.net
Hank's Seafood Restaurant
10 Hayne St . . . . . Charleston SC 29401 843-723-3474 671
Web: hanksseafoodrestaurant.com
Hanken-Wolfe Imports Company Inc
7140 N Dixie Dr . . . . . Dayton OH 45414 937-264-1800 264-8456 293
TF: 800-783-0852 ■ *Web:* hankenimports.com
Hankin & Mazel PLLC
60 Cutter Mill Rd Ste 505. . . . . Great Neck NY 11021 516-499-5800 41
Web: hankinmazel.com
Hankins Lumber Company Inc
PO Box 1397 . . . . . Grenada MS 38902 662-226-2961 191-3
Web: www.hankinslumber.com
Hankook Tire America Corp
1450 Valley Rd . . . . . Wayne NJ 07470 973-633-9000 754
TF: 800-426-5665 ■ *Web:* www.hankooktire.com
Hankscraft Inc 300 Wengel Dr . . . . . Reedsburg WI 53959 608-524-4341 524-4342 518
Web: www.hankscraft.com
Hanley House 7600 Westmoreland St . . . . . Clayton MO 63105 314-467-0712 50-3
Web: hanleyhouse.blogspot.com
Hanley Industries Inc
3640 Seminary Rd PO Box 1058 . . . . . Alton IL 62002 618-465-8892 465-3195 268
Web: www.hanleyindustries.com
Hanlin-Rainaldi Construction
6610 Singletree Dr . . . . . Columbus OH 43229 614-436-4204 186
Web: hanlinrainaldi.com
Hanlo Gages & Engineering Co
34403 Glendale . . . . . Livonia MI 48150 734-422-4224 422-2244 493
Web: www.hanlogages.com
Hanlon Engineering & Architecture Inc
2502 N Huachuca Dr . . . . . Tucson AZ 85745 520-326-0062 261
Web: hanlonengineering.com
Hanmi Bank
3660 Wilshire Blvd PH-A . . . . . Los Angeles CA 90010 213-382-2200 360-2
TF: 877-808-4266 ■ *Web:* www.hanmi.com
Hanna and Morton LLP
444 S Flower St Ste 2530. . . . . Los Angeles CA 90071 213-628-7131 623-3379 41
Web: www.hanmor.com
Hanna Andersson Corp 608 NE 19th Ave. . . . . Portland OR 97209 800-222-0544 459
TF: 800-222-0544 ■ *Web:* www.hannaandersson.com
Hanna Cylinders
804 E Park Ave Ste 101 . . . . . Libertyville IL 60048 847-990-7700 680-6991 223
TF: 866-950-6257 ■ *Web:* www.hannacylinders.com
Hanna Instruments Inc
584 Park East Dr. . . . . Woonsocket RI 02895 401-765-7500 696
Web: hannainst.com
Hanna Lind Ltd
10125 Crosstown Cir Ste 315. . . . . Eden Prairie MN 55344 952-931-1242 366
Web: hannalind.com
Hanna Plumbing & Supply Co
643 S Santa Fe Ave. . . . . Vista CA 92083 760-726-2002 189-10
TF: 800-246-1119 ■ *Web:* www.hannaplumbing.com

Name / Address	City	State	Zip	Phone	Fax	Class
Hanna Steel Corp						
3812 Commerce Ave PO Box 558	Fairfield	AL	35064	205-780-1111	783-8368	490
TF: 800-633-8252 ■ Web: www.hannasteel.com						
Hannacroix Creek Books Inc						
1127 High Ridge Rd Ste 110B	Stamford	CT	06905	203-968-8098	968-0193	637-2
Web: www.hannacroixcreekbooks.com						
Hannaford Bros Company LLC						
145 Pleasant Hill Rd	Scarborough	ME	04074	800-213-9040		297-8
TF: 800-213-9040 ■ Web: www.hannaford.com						
Hannah Lindahl Children's Museum						
1402 S Main St	Mishawaka	IN	46544	574-254-4540	254-4585	521
Web: www.hlcm.org						
Hannay Reels Inc 553 SR-143	Westerlo	NY	12193	518-797-3791	797-3259	117
TF: 877-467-3357 ■ Web: www.hannay.com						
Hannibal Carbide Tool Inc						
5000 Paris Gravel Rd	Hannibal	MO	63401	573-221-2775	221-1140	493
TF: 800-451-9436 ■ Web: www.hannibalcarbide.com						
Hannibal Convention & Visitors Bureau						
505 N Third St	Hannibal	MO	63401	573-221-2477		206
Web: www.visithannibal.com						
Hannibal Courier-Post 200 N 3rd St	Hannibal	MO	63401	573-221-2800		532-2
TF: 800-748-7025 ■ Web: www.hannibal.net						
Hannibal Industries Inc						
3851 S Santa Fe Ave	Los Angeles	CA	90058	323-588-4261		490
TF: 866-513-1200 ■ Web: hannibalindustries.com						
Hannibal Regional Hospital						
6500 Hospital Dr	Hannibal	MO	63401	573-248-1300		374-3
TF: 888-426-6425 ■ Web: hospital.hannibalregional.org						
Hannibal-LaGrange Univ						
2800 Palmyra Rd	Hannibal	MO	63401	573-221-3675	221-6594	166
TF: 800-454-1119 ■ Web: www.hlg.edu						
Hanning Construction Inc						
815 Swan St	Terre Haute	IN	47807	812-235-6218	235-1218	685
Web: www.hannigconstruction.com						
Hannon Co, The 1605 Waynesburg Dr SE	Canton	OH	44707	330-456-4728	456-3323	518
Web: www.hanco.com						
Hannon Hydraulics LLC 625 N Loop 12	Irving	TX	75061	800-333-4266		223
TF: 800-333-4266 ■ Web: www.hannonhydraulics.com						
Hannon-Murphy Insurance Associates Inc						
166 Center St	Pembroke	MA	02359	781-293-5500		390
Web: hannonmurphy.com						
Hannover House 1428 Chester St	Springdale	AR	72764	479-751-4500	751-4999	514
Web: www.hannoverhouse.com						
Hannover Life Reassurance Company of America						
200 S Orange Ave Ste 1900	Orlando	FL	32801	407-649-8411		391-2
Web: www.hannover-re.com						
Hanor Co 4005 E Owen K Garriott	Enid	OK	73701	580-599-6300		10-6
Web: hanorcompany.com						
Hanover Architectural Products						
5000 Hanover Rd	Hanover	PA	17331	717-637-0500		183
TF: 800-426-4242 ■ Web: www.hanoverpavers.com						
Hanover Area Chamber of Commerce						
146 Carlisle St	Hanover	PA	17331	717-637-6130	637-9127	139
Web: hanoverchamber.com						
Hanover College 484 Ball Dr	Hanover	IN	47243	812-866-7000	866-7098	166
TF: 800-213-2178 ■ Web: www.hanover.edu						
Hanover County 7497 County Complex Rd	Hanover	VA	23069	804-365-6000	365-6234	338
Web: www.hanovercounty.gov						
Hanover Design Services PA						
1123 Floral Pkwy	Wilmington	NC	28403	910-343-8002		727
Web: www.hanoverdesignserviceswilmingtonnc.com						
Hanover Engineering Associates Inc						
252 Brodhead Rd Ste 100	Bethlehem	PA	18017	610-691-5644		256
Web: www.hanovereng.com						
Hanover Foods Corp PO Box 334	Hanover	PA	17331	717-632-6000		296-36
OTC: HNFSA ■ Web: hanoverfoods.com						
Hanover Inn Dartmouth 2 E Wheelock St	Hanover	NH	03755	603-643-4300	643-4433	379
TF: 800-443-7024 ■ Web: www.hanoverinn.com						
Hanover Insurance Co 440 Lincoln St	Worcester	MA	01653	508-855-1000		391-4
TF: 800-853-0456 ■ Web: www.hanover.com						
Hanover Juvenile Correctional Ctr						
7093 Broadneck Rd	Hanover	VA	23069	804-537-5316	537-5907	412
Web: www.djj.virginia.gov						
Hanover Law PC						
2751 Prosperity Ave Ste 150	Fairfax	VA	22031	703-402-2723		41
Web: hanoverlawpc.com						
Hanover Mall 1775 Washington St	Hanover	MA	02339	781-826-7386		460
Web: thehanovercrossing.com						
Hanover Partners Inc						
425 California St Ste 2000	San Francisco	CA	94104	415-788-8680	788-8444	690
Web: hanoverpartners.com						
Hanover Public School District						
403 Moul Ave	Hanover	PA	17331	717-637-9000	630-4617	685
Web: www.hpsd.k12.pa.us						
Hanover Research						
1700 K St NW 8th Fl	Washington	DC	20006	202-559-0050		196
Web: www.hanoverresearch.com						
Hanovia 6 Evans St	Fairfield	NJ	07004	973-651-5510	651-5550	437
Web: www.hanovia-uv.com						
Hanrahan Carey & Company PLC						
306 S Troy St PO Box 1049	Royal Oak	MI	48068	248-544-1484	544-0529	2
Web: www.hccplc.com						
Hans Herr House & Museum						
1849 Hans Herr Dr	Willow Street	PA	17584	717-464-4438		50-3
Web: www.hansherr.org						
Hans Johnsen Co 8901 Chancellor Row	Dallas	TX	75247	214-879-1550	879-1520	351
TF: 800-879-1515 ■ Web: www.hjc.com						
Hans Kissle Company LLC						
9 Creek Brook Dr	Haverhill	MA	01832	978-556-4500	556-4612	123
Web: www.hanskissle.com						
Hans P. Kraus Jr Inc 962 Park Ave	New York	NY	10028	212-794-2064		42
Web: www.sunpictures.com						
Hans Rudolph Inc 8325 Cole Pkwy	Shawnee	KS	66227	913-422-7788		477
TF: 800-456-6695 ■ Web: www.rudolphkc.com						
Hansa GCR LLC 308 SW First Ave	Portland	OR	97204	503-241-8036		195
TF: 800-755-7683 ■ Web: www.hansagcr.com						
Hansa Language Centre of Toronto Inc						
51 Eglinton Ave E	Toronto	ON	M4P1G7	416-487-8643		148
Web: www.hansacanada.com						
Hanscom Air Force Base						
55 Grenier St	Hanscom AFB	MA	01731	781-225-1110		497-1
Web: www.hanscom.af.mil						
Hanscom Inc 331 Market St	Warren	RI	02885	401-247-1999	247-4575	608
TF: 877-725-6788 ■ Web: www.hanscominc.com						
Hanseatic Management Services Inc						
5600 Wyoming N E Ste 220	Albuquerque	NM	87109	505-828-2824		401
Web: www.hanseaticgroup.com						
Hansel 'n Gretel Brand Inc						
79-36 Cooper Ave	Glendale	NY	11385	718-326-0041	326-2069	473
Hansell Tierney						
2955 80th Ave SE Ste 103	Mercer Island	WA	98040	206-232-3080		260
Web: www.hanselltierney.com						
Hansen Architectural Systems						
5500 SE Alexander St	Hillsboro	OR	97123	800-599-2965		492
TF: 800-599-2965 ■ Web: www.aluminumrailing.com						
Hansen Balk Steel Treating Co						
1230 Monroe Ave NW	Grand Rapids	MI	49505	616-458-1414		484
Web: www.hansenbalk.com						
Hansen Beverage Co 1 Monster Way	Corona	CA	92879	951-739-6200		297-8
Web: www.hansens.com						
Hansen Company Inc, The						
5665 Greendale Rd Ste A	Johnston	IA	50131	515-270-1117	270-3829	186
Web: hansencompany.com						
Hansen Corp 901 S First St	Princeton	IN	47670	812-385-3415	385-3013	518
TF: 800-328-8996 ■ Web: www.hansen-motor.com						
Hansen Engineering Company Inc						
24050 Frampton Ave	Harbor City	CA	90710	310-534-3870	539-3066	22
Web: www.hansenengineering.com						
Hansen International Inc						
130 Zenker Rd	Lexington	SC	29072	803-695-1500	695-8847	697
TF: 800-850-8070 ■ Web: www.hansenint.com						
Hansen Mechanical Contractors						
4475 W Quail	Las Vegas	NV	89118	702-361-5111	361-6753	610
Web: www.hansenmechanical.com						
Hansen Plastic Corp 2758 Alft Ln	Elgin	IL	60124	847-741-4510		608
Web: www.hansenplastics.com						
Hansen Software Corp						
1855 Kirschner Rd Ste 380	Kelowna	BC	V1Y4N7	877-795-2274		525
TF: 877-795-2274 ■ Web: www.hansensoftware.com						
Hansen Surfboards						
1105 S Coast Hwy 101	Encinitas	CA	92024	800-480-4754		711
TF: 800-480-4754 ■ Web: www.hansensurf.com						
Hansen Technologies Corp						
6827 High Grove Blvd	Burr Ridge	IL	60527	630-325-1565	325-1572	202
TF: 800-426-7368 ■ Web: www.hantech.com						
Hansen Thorp Pellinen Olson Inc						
7510 Market Pl Dr	Eden Prairie	MN	55344	952-829-0700	829-7806	256
Web: htpo.com						
Hansen Wholesale						
11132 Winners Cir Ste 100	Los Alamitos	CA	90720	562-594-1249	626-8270	38
TF: 800-201-1193 ■ Web: www.hansenwholesale.com						
Hansen's Cakes Inc						
1072 S Fairfax Ave	Los Angeles	CA	90019	323-936-4332	934-3018	296-1
Web: www.hansencake.com						
Hansen, Dordell, Bradt, Odlaug & Bradt PLLP						
3900 Northwoods Dr Ste 250	Saint Paul	MN	55112	651-482-8900		41
Web: hansendordell.com						
Hansen, Jacobson, Teller, Hoberman, Newman, Warren, Richman, Rush & Kaller LLP						
450 N Roxbury Dr 8th Fl	Beverly Hills	CA	90210	310-271-8777	276-8310	428
Web: www.hjth.com						
Hansen-Mueller Co 12231 Emmet St Ste 1	Omaha	NE	68164	402-491-3385		690
TF: 800-964-7246 ■ Web: www.hansenmueller.com						
Hanser & Assoc						
1001 Office Park Rd Ste 210	West Des Moines	IA	50265	515-224-1086		636
Web: hanser.com						
Hanser Music Group						
9615 Inter-Ocean Dr	Cincinnati	OH	45246	859-817-7100	817-7150	527
TF: 800-999-5558 ■ Web: www.hansermusicgroup.com						
Hanset Stainless Inc						
1729 NE Argyle St	Portland	OR	97211	503-283-8822	283-8875	189-12
Web: www.hansetcorp.com						
Hansford County 15 Northwest Ct	Spearman	TX	79081	806-659-4110	659-4168	338
Web: www.co.hansford.tx.us						
Hansford County Feeders LP						
13800 County Rd 19	Spearman	TX	79081	806-477-1900	477-1910	10-1
Web: hcflp.com						
Hansgrohe Inc						
1490 Bluegrass Lakes Pkwy	Alpharetta	GA	30004	800-334-0455	360-9887*	609
*Fax Area Code: 770 ■ TF: 800-334-0455 ■ Web: www.hansgrohe-usa.com						
Hansome Energy Systems Inc						
365 Dalziel Rd	Linden	NJ	07036	908-862-9044		518
Web: www.hanenergy.com						
Hanson & Mouri, Personal Injury Lawyers						
3850 Vine St Ste 130	Riverside	CA	92507	951-688-0006		41
Web: attorneyhanson.com						
Hanson Bolkcom Law Group Ltd						
527 Marquette Ave Ste 2300	Minneapolis	MN	55402	612-342-2880		41
Web: hanson-law.net						
Hanson County Clerk of Court						
720 5th St PO Box 127	Alexandria	SD	57311	605-239-4446	239-9446	338
Web: ujs.sd.gov						
Hanson Directory Service Inc						
1501 N 15th Ave E	Newton	IA	50208	641-792-2855		4
Web: hansondirectory.com						
Hanson Distributing Co 975 W Eighth St	Azusa	CA	91702	626-224-9800	579-4053	61
Web: www.hansondistributing.com						
Hanson House						
380 E Paseo El Mirador	Palm Springs	CA	92262	760-416-5070	416-5071	372
Web: www.hansonhouse.org						
Hanson Information System						
2433 W White Oaks Dr	Springfield	IL	62704	217-726-2400		177
TF: 888-245-8468 ■ Web: hansoninfosys.com						
Hanson Logistics 2900 S State St	Saint Joseph	MI	49085	269-982-1390	982-1506	449
TF: 888-772-1197 ■ Web: www.hansonlogisticsgroup.com						
Hanson Professional Services Inc						
1525 S Sixth St	Springfield	IL	62703	217-788-2450		261
Web: www.hanson-inc.com						

Company	City	State	ZIP	Phone	Fax	Class
Hanson Sign Cos 82 Carter St *TF:* 800-522-2009 ■ *Web:* hansonsign.com	Falconer	NY	14733	716-661-3900		687
Hanson Silo Co 11587 County Rd 8 SE *Web:* www.hansonsilo.com	Lake Lillian	MN	56253	320-664-4171	664-4140	273
Hanson Watson Assoc 1411 15th St *Web:* www.hansonwatson.com	Moline	IL	61265	309-764-8315	764-8336	4
Hantronix Inc 10080 Bubb Rd *TF:* 800-525-0811 ■ *Web:* www.hantronix.com	Cupertino	CA	95014	408-252-1100	252-1123	173-4
Hantz Group Inc 26200 America Dr *Web:* hantzgroup.com	Southfield	MI	48034	248-304-2855		390
Hantzmon Wiebel LLP 818 E Jefferson St *Web:* www.hantzmonwiebel.com	Charlottesville	VA	22902	434-296-2156	977-4629	2
Hanwa American Corp 400 Kelby St Parker Plz 12th Fl *Web:* www.hanwa.co.jp	Fort Lee	NJ	07024	201-363-4500	346-9890	191-3
Hanwha Aerospace USA 5 McKee Pl *Web:* www.hanwhaaerospaceusa.com	Cheshire	CT	06410	203-806-2090		529
HAP (Haight-Ashbury Publications) 856 Stanyan St *Web:* www.journalofpsychoactivedrugs.com	San Francisco	CA	94117	415-752-7601		637-9
Hapa Sushi Grill & Sake Bar 2780 E Second Ave *Web:* hapasushi.com	Denver	CO	80206	303-322-9554		671
Hapag-Lloyd America Inc 401 E Jackson St Ste 3300 *TF:* 800-282-8977 ■ *Web:* www.hapag-lloyd.com	Tampa	FL	33602	813-276-4600		313
Hapco Inc 26252 Hillman Hwy *TF:* 800-368-7171 ■ *Web:* www.hapco.com	Abingdon	VA	24210	276-628-7171		491
Hapman 6002 E N Ave *TF:* 800-427-6260 ■ *Web:* www.hapman.com	Kalamazoo	MI	49048	269-382-8228	349-2477	207
Happenings Communications Group Inc PO Box 61 *Web:* www.happeningsmagazinepa.com	Clarks Summit	PA	18411	570-587-3532	586-7374	637-9
Happy & Healthy Products Inc 1600 S Dixie Hwy Ste 200 *Web:* www.fruitfull.com	Boca Raton	FL	33432	561-367-0730	300-5207	297-0
Happy Chef Systems Inc 51646 US Hwy 169	Mankato	MN	56001	507-345-4571	345-4585	670
Happy Faces Personnel Group Inc 4333 Lynburn Dr *Web:* www.happyfaces.net	Tucker	GA	30084	770-414-9071		260
Happy Hollow Park & Zoo 748 Story Rd *Web:* happyhollow.org	San Jose	CA	95112	408-794-6400		823
Happy Joe's Inc 2705 Happy Joe Dr *Web:* www.happyjoes.com	Bettendorf	IA	52722	563-332-8811	332-5822	670
Happy Mexican Restaurant & Cantina 6080 Primacy Pkwy *Web:* www.happymexican.com	Memphis	TN	38119	901-683-0000		671
Happy Software Inc 11 Federal St **Fax Area Code:* 518 ■ *TF:* 888-484-2779 ■ *Web:* www.happysoftware.com	Saratoga Springs	NY	12866	888-484-2779	584-5388*	177
Happy Sumo 4801 N University Ave *Web:* www.happysumosushi.com	Provo	UT	84604	801-225-9100	225-9102	671
Happy Time Tours & Travel 1475 Walsh St W *TF:* 800-473-5955 ■ *Web:* www.httours.com	Thunder Bay	ON	P7E4X6	807-473-5955		772
Happys Potato Chip Co 3900 Chandler Dr	Minneapolis	MN	55421	612-781-3121		123
Hara CPA Professional Services Inc 5935 Cornerstone Ct W Ste 120 *Web:* haracpaservices.com	San Diego	CA	92121	858-450-9155		2
Harada Industry of America Inc 22925 Venture Dr *Web:* www.harada.com	Novi	MI	48375	248-374-9000	374-9100	61
Haralson County 70 Murphy Campus Blvd *TF:* 800-955-7766 ■ *Web:* www.haralson.org	Waco	GA	30182	770-537-5594	537-5873	338
Haram-Christensen Corp 125 Asia Pl *Web:* www.haramchris.com	Carlstadt	NJ	07072	201-507-8544		360-3
Harbar LLC 320 Turnpike St *Web:* www.harbar.com	Canton	MA	02021	781-828-0848		68
Harbec Inc 358 Timothy Ln *TF:* 888-521-4416 ■ *Web:* www.harbec.com	Ontario	NY	14519	585-265-0010	265-1306	608
Harben Inc 2010 Ronald Regan Blvd *Web:* harben.com	Cumming	GA	30041	770-889-9535	887-9411	641
Harbert Management Corp 2100 Third Ave N Ste 600 *Web:* www.harbert.net	Birmingham	AL	35203	205-987-5500		580
Harbin Hot Springs 18424 Harbin Springs Rd PO Box 782 *Web:* harbin.org	Middletown	CA	95461	707-987-2477	987-0616	673
Harbinger Group Inc 450 Park Ave 29th Fl *NYSE:* SPB ■ *Web:* www.harbingergroupinc.com	New York	NY	10022	212-906-8555		296-12
HarbisonWalker Intl *ANH Refractories Co* 1305 Cherrington Pkwy Ste 100 *Web:* thinkhwi.com	Moon Township	PA	15108	412-375-6600	375-6962	662
Harbor Bay Club 200 Packet Landing Rd *Web:* harborbayclub.com	Alameda	CA	94502	510-521-5414		354
Harbor Capital Advisors Inc 111 S Wacker Dr 34th Fl *TF:* 800-422-1050 ■ *Web:* www.harborfunds.com	Chicago	IL	60606	312-443-4400		196
Harbor Capital Management Inc 831 E Morehead St Ste 350 *TF:* 800-431-3500 ■ *Web:* harborcapitalmgmt.com	Charlotte	NC	28202	704-377-6945	319-3189	528
Harbor Court Hotel 165 Steuart St *TF:* 877-989-5861 ■ *Web:* www.harborcourthotel.com	San Francisco	CA	94105	415-882-1300	882-1313	379
Harbor Cruises LLC 1 Long Wharf *Web:* www.bostonharborcruises.com	Boston	MA	02110	617-227-4321		760
Harbor Defense Museum 230 Sheridan Loop *Web:* harbordefensemuseum.com	Brooklyn	NY	11252	718-630-4349		520
Harbor Electronic Publishing (HEP) 80 E 11th St *TF:* 800-269-6422 ■ *Web:* www.hepdigital.com	New York	NY	10003	800-269-6422		637-10
Harbor Engineering Inc 41 S Main St *Web:* harborengineering.com	Manheim	PA	17545	717-665-9000	665-9001	261
Harbor Express Inc 501 Quay Ave *Web:* www.harbor-express.com	Wilmington	CA	90744	310-513-6478	835-3794	780
Harbor Freight Tools 3491 Mission Oaks Blvd *TF:* 800-444-3353 ■ *Web:* www.harborfreight.com	Camarillo	CA	93011	800-444-3353		351
Harbor Freight Transport Corp 301 Craneway St *Web:* www.harborusa.com	Newark	NJ	07114	973-589-6700	589-6677	311
Harbor Health Systems LLC PO Box 11779 *TF:* 888-626-1737 ■ *Web:* www.harborsys.com	Newport Beach	CA	92658	949-273-7020	242-2893	239
Harbor Hotel Provincetown 698 Commercial St Cape Cod *Web:* harborhotelptown.com	Provincetown	MA	02657	508-487-1711		378
Harbor House 28 Pier 21 *Web:* www.harborhousepier21.com	Galveston	TX	77550	409-763-3321	765-6421	379
Harbor House Law Press Inc PO Box 480 **Fax Area Code:* 202 ■ *TF:* 877-529-4332 ■ *Web:* www.harborhouselaw.com	Hartfield	VA	23071	804-758-8400	318-3239*	637-10
Harbor House Seafood 2510 N Roan St *Web:* www.harborhousejc.com	Johnson City	TN	37601	423-282-5122		671
Harbor Ind 14130 172nd Ave *Web:* www.harborretail.com	Grand Haven	MI	49417	616-842-5330	842-1385	233
Harbor Light Hospice 1 N 131 County Farm Rd *TF:* 800-419-0542 ■ *Web:* www.harborlighthospice.com	Winfield	IL	60190	630-682-3871	682-4492	371
Harbor Manufacturing Inc 8300 W 185th St *Web:* www.harbormfg.com	Tinley Park	IL	60487	708-614-6400	614-6444	295
Harbor Packaging Inc 13100 Danielson St *Web:* www.harborpackaging.com	Poway	CA	92064	858-513-1800	513-0800	100
Harbor Playhouse 1802 N Chaparral Bldg Ste 2 *Web:* www.harborplayhouse.com	Corpus Christi	TX	78401	361-882-5500		572
Harbor Rail Services Co 1550 W Colorado Blvd *Web:* www.harborservices.com	Pasadena	CA	91105	626-398-4065		188
Harbor Sales 1000 Harbor Ct *TF:* 800-345-1712 ■ *Web:* www.harborsales.net	Sudlersville	MD	21668	800-345-1712	868-9257	613
Harbor Shores Hotel Management Inc 300 Wrigley Dr *Web:* harborshoreslg.com	Lake Geneva	WI	53147	262-248-9181		378
Harbor Steel & Supply Corp 1115 E Broadway *Web:* www.harborsteel.com	Muskegon	MI	49444	231-739-7152		492
Harbor Technologies LLC 681 Riverside Dr *Web:* www.harbortech.us	Augusta	ME	04330	207-512-8739		106
Harbor View Hotel 131 N Water St PO Box 7 *TF:* 800-225-6005 ■ *Web:* www.harborviewhotel.com	Edgartown	MA	02539	844-248-1167		379
Harbor View Restaurant 301 Savannah Hwy *Web:* harborviewdining.com	Charleston	SC	29407	843-556-7100		671
Harbor Wholesale Grocery Inc 3901 Hogum Bay Rd NE *TF:* 800-624-3614 ■ *Web:* www.harborwholesale.com	Lacey	WA	98516	360-754-4484	705-2594	297-8
HarborLink Network Ltd 3131 S Dixie Dr Ste 500 *Web:* www.harborlink.net	Dayton	OH	45439	937-294-2954		387
HarborOne Credit Union 770 Oak St PO Box 720 *TF:* 800-244-7592 ■ *Web:* www.harborone.com	Brockton	MA	02301	508-895-1000		219
Harbors Home Health & Hospice 201 Seventh St *TF:* 800-772-1319 ■ *Web:* myhhhh.org	Hoquiam	WA	98550	360-532-5454		371
Harborside Event Ctr 1375 Monroe St *Web:* www.harborsideevents.com	Fort Myers	FL	33901	239-321-8110		205
Harborside Hotel & Marina 55 West St *Web:* www.theharborsidehotel.com	Bar Harbor	ME	04609	207-288-5033	288-3661	379
Harborside Inn 1 Christie's Landing *TF:* 800-427-9444 ■ *Web:* www.newportharborsideinn.com	Newport	RI	02840	401-846-6600		379
Harborside Inn of Boston 185 State St *Web:* harborsideinnboston.com	Boston	MA	02109	617-723-7500	670-6015	379
Harborside Suites At Little Harbor 536 Bahia Beach Blvd **Fax Area Code:* 813 ■ *TF:* 800-327-2773 ■ *Web:* www.staylittleharbor.com	Ruskin	FL	33570	800-327-2773	922-6171*	669
Harbortown Industries Inc 28477 N Ballard Dr *Web:* harbortown.net	Lake Forest	IL	60045	847-327-9900		820
Harbor-UCLA Medical Ctr 1000 W Carson St *Web:* www.humc.edu	Torrance	CA	90509	310-222-2345		374-3
Harbour Construction 23830 W Main St *Web:* www.harbour-cm.com	Plainfield	IL	60544	815-254-5500	254-5505	186
Harbour Homes LLC 400 N 34th St Ste 300 *Web:* harbourhomes.com	Seattle	WA	98103	206-315-8130		653
Harbour Industries Inc 4744 Shelburne Rd PO Box 188 *TF:* 800-659-4733 ■ *Web:* www.harbourind.com	Shelburne	VT	05482	802-985-3311	985-9534	814
Harbour Investments Inc 575 D'Onofrio Dr Ste 300 *TF:* 888-855-6960 ■ *Web:* harbourinv.com	Madison	WI	53719	608-662-6100	662-6116	401
Harbour Sixty Steakhouse 60 Harbour St *Web:* harbour60.com	Toronto	ON	M5J1B7	416-777-2111		671
Harbour Towers Hotel & Suites 345 Quebec St *Web:* www.harbourtowers.com	Victoria	BC	V8V1W4	250-385-2405		378
Harbour, Smith, Harris & Merritt PC 222 N Fredonia St *Web:* www.harbourlaw.com	Longview	TX	75601	903-757-4001		428

				Phone	Fax	Class
HarbourVest Partners LLC 1 Financial Ctr *Web:* www.harbourvest.com	Boston	MA	02111	617-348-3707	350-0305	792
HARC (Houston Advanced Research Ctr) 4800 Research Forest Dr *Web:* www.harcresearch.org	The Woodlands	TX	77381	281-364-6000	363-7914	668
HARC (Hawaii Agriculture Research Ctr) PO Box 100 *Web:* www.harc-hspa.com	Kunia	HI	96759	808-621-1350	621-1399	668
Harch Capital Management LLC 7400 N Federal Hwy Ste A5 *Web:* www.harchcapital.com	Boca Raton	FL	33487	561-226-6199		690
Harco Company Ltd 5610 McAdam Rd *TF:* 800-387-9503 ■ *Web:* www.harcoco.com	Mississauga	ON	L4Z1P1	905-890-1220	890-7039	35
Harco Laboratories Inc 186 Cedar St *TF:* 800-240-7041 ■ *Web:* harcosemco.com	Branford	CT	06405	203-483-3700		201
Harcourt Equipment 313 Hwy 169 & 175 E *TF:* 800-445-5646 ■ *Web:* www.kcnielsen.com	Harcourt	IA	50544	515-332-2545		274
Harcourt Outlines Inc 7765 S 175 W PO Box 128 *TF:* 800-428-6584 ■ *Web:* www.harcourtoutlinesstore.com	Milroy	IN	46156	800-428-6584	278-5165	55
Harcros 5200 Speaker Rd *Web:* harcros.com	Kansas City	KS	66106	913-321-3131	621-7718	146
Harcrow Surveying LLC 2314 W Main St *Web:* harcrowsurveying.com	Artesia	NM	88210	575-746-2158		727
Harcum College 750 Montgomery Ave *TF:* 800-537-3000 ■ *Web:* www.harcum.edu	Bryn Mawr	PA	19010	610-525-4100	526-6147	162
Hard Chrome Plating Consultant Inc 2196 W 59th St & Walworth Ave *Web:* hard-chromesystems.com	Cleveland	OH	44102	216-631-9090	631-9060	194
Hard Labor Creek State Park 5 Hard Labor Creek Rd *Web:* gastateparks.org	Rutledge	GA	30663	706-557-3001		565
Hard Manufacturing Company Inc 230 Grider St *TF:* 800-873-4273 ■ *Web:* www.hardmfg.com	Buffalo	NY	14215	800-873-4273		319-3
Hard Rock Cafe International Inc 5701 Stirling Rd *TF:* 888-519-6683 ■ *Web:* www.hardrock.com	Davie	FL	33314	954-585-5703		671
Hard Rock Hotel & Casino Biloxi 777 Beach Blvd *TF:* 877-877-6256 ■ *Web:* www.hrhcbiloxi.com	Biloxi	MS	39530	228-374-7625		133
Hard Rock Hotel Chicago 230 N Michigan Ave *Web:* www.hardrockhotels.com	Chicago	IL	60601	312-345-1000		379
Hard Rock Hotel San Diego 207 Fifth Ave *TF:* 866-751-7625 ■ *Web:* www.hardrockhotelsd.com	San Diego	CA	92101	619-702-3000	702-3007	379
Hard Rock Stadium 347 Don Shula Dr *Web:* hardrockstadium.com	Miami Gardens	FL	33056	305-943-7275		720
Hard Times Cafe 1404 King St *Web:* www.hardtimes.com	Alexandria	VA	22314	703-837-0050	837-0057	670
Hardaway Group 615 Main St *Web:* www.hardaway.net	Nashville	TN	37206	615-254-5461		187
Hard-E Foods Inc 3228 N Broadway *Web:* hardefoods.com	Saint Louis	MO	63147	314-533-2211	533-2656	297-4
Hardee County 412 W Orange St Rm 103 *Web:* www.hardeecounty.net	Wauchula	FL	33873	863-773-9430	773-0958	338
Hardee County School District 1009 N Sixth Ave PO Box 1678 *Web:* www.hardee.k12.fl.us	Wauchula	FL	33873	863-773-9058	773-0069	685
Hardeman County 100 N Main St *TF:* 800-336-2036 ■ *Web:* hardemancounty.org	Bolivar	TN	38008	731-658-3541		338
Hardeman County 1410 Shaw St *Web:* hardemantx.com	Quanah	TX	79252	940-663-2911	663-6302	338
Hardeman County Correctional Facility 2520 Union Springs Rd PO Box 549 *Web:* www.tn.gov	Whiteville	TN	38075	731-254-6000	254-6060	213
Harden Furniture Inc 8550 Mill Pond Way *Web:* www.hardenfurniture.com	McConnellsville	NY	13401	315-245-1000	245-2884	319-2
Harden House, The 626 Grand Central St *Web:* www.thehardenhouse.com	Clearwater	FL	33756	727-442-7546	445-9537	321
Hardenbergh Insurance Group Inc 8000 Sagemore Dr Ste 8101 *Web:* hig.net	Marlton	NJ	08053	856-489-9100		390
Harder AG Products Inc 608 W 9th St *Web:* www.grainbinsusa.com	Peabody	KS	66866	620-983-2158	983-2911	273
Harder Corp 7029 Raywood Rd *TF:* 800-261-3400 ■ *Web:* www.hardercorp.com	Monona	WI	53713	608-271-5127	271-4677	559
Harder Josh (Rep D - CA) 131 Cannon House Office Bldg *Web:* www.harder.house.gov	Washington	DC	20515	202-225-4540		342-2
Harder Mechanical Contractors Inc 2148 NE M L King Blvd *Web:* www.harder.com	Portland	OR	97212	503-281-1112		189-10
Hardesty & Havover LLP 1501 Broadway Ste 310 *Web:* www.hardestyhanover.com	New York	NY	10036	212-944-1150	391-0297	261
HARDI Hydronic Heating & Cooling Council 445 Hutchinson Ave Ste 550 *TF:* 888-253-2128 ■ *Web:* www.hardinet.org	Columbus	OH	43235	614-345-4328		49-18
Hardi Inc 1500 W 76th St *TF:* 866-770-7063 ■ *Web:* www.hardi-us.com	Davenport	IA	52806	563-386-1730	386-1280	273
Hardin & Company Ltd 113 S 19th Ave Ste C	Bozeman	MT	59718	406-587-1211		652
Hardin County 1215 Edgington Ave County Courthouse *Web:* www.hardincountyia.gov	Eldora	IA	50627	641-858-2328	858-2320	338
Hardin County PO Box 124 *Web:* www.hardincountyil.org	Elizabethtown	IL	62931	618-287-4333		338
Hardin County 150 N Provident Way *Web:* www.hccoky.org	Elizabethtown	KY	42701	270-765-2171	765-6193	338
Hardin County 1 Courthouse Sq Ste 370 *Web:* www.hardincourts.com	Kenton	OH	43326	419-674-2256	674-2264	338
Hardin County 495 Main St *TF:* 800-552-3866 ■ *Web:* www.tourhardincounty.org	Savannah	TN	38372	731-925-8181	925-6987	338
Hardin County Bank, The (HCB) 235 Wayne Rd *Web:* www.hardincountybank.bank	Savannah	TN	38372	731-925-9001	925-8106	70
Hardin County Chamber & Business Alliance (HCCBA) 225 S Detroit St *Web:* hardincountyoh.org	Kenton	OH	43326	419-673-4131	674-4876	139
Hardin County Public Library 100 Jim Owen Dr *Web:* www.hcpl.info	Elizabethtown	KY	42701	270-769-6337		434-3
Hardin Library for the Health Sciences 100 Main Library 125 W Washington St *Web:* www.lib.uiowa.edu	Iowa City	IA	52242	319-335-9871	353-3752	434-1
Hardin Memorial Hospital 913 W Dixie Ave *TF:* 800-955-9455 ■ *Web:* www.hmh.net	Elizabethtown	KY	42701	270-706-1212		374-3
Hardin's Wholesale Florist Supply 329 W Bowman Ave *Web:* www.hardins.com	Liberty	NC	27298	336-622-3035		292
Hardin, Kundla, McKeon & Poletto PA 673 Morris Ave *Web:* www.hkmpp.com	Springfield	NJ	07081	973-912-5222		428
Harding & Associates PC 730 17th St Ste 650 *Web:* www.hlaw.com	Denver	CO	80202	303-762-9500		41
Harding & Carbone Inc 3903 Bellaire Blvd *Web:* www.hctax.com	Houston	TX	77025	713-664-1215	664-2928	734
Harding Brooks Assoc 441 Commerce Rd *Web:* hardingbrooks.com	Vestal	NY	13850	607-729-9292		390
Harding County 410 Ramsland St PO Box 534 *Web:* ujs.sd.gov	Buffalo	SD	57720	605-375-3351	375-3432	338
Harding Instruments 7741 Wagner Rd NW *TF:* 888-792-1171 ■ *Web:* www.harding.ca	Edmonton	AB	T6E5B1	780-462-7100	450-8396	201
Harding Lake State Recreation Area c/o Northern Area Ofc 3700 Airport Way *Web:* www.dnr.alaska.gov	Fairbanks	AK	99709	907-451-2670	451-2690	565
Harding Poorman 4923 W 78th St *TF:* 888-809-7741 ■ *Web:* www.hardingpoorman.com	Indianapolis	IN	46268	317-876-3355		174
Harding Road Pharmacy Inc 400 W Harding Rd *Web:* hardingroadrx.com	Springfield	OH	45504	937-399-8531	399-4911	237
Harding School of Theology (HST) 1000 Cherry Rd *TF:* 800-680-0809 ■ *Web:* www.hst.edu	Memphis	TN	38117	901-761-1356	761-1358	637-2
Harding Shymanski & Company PSC 21 SE Third St Ste 500 *TF:* 800-880-7800 ■ *Web:* www.hsccpa.com	Evansville	IN	47708	812-464-9161	465-7811	2
Harding University 915 E Market Ave *TF:* 800-477-4407 ■ *Web:* harding.edu	Searcy	AR	72149	501-279-4000	279-4129	166
Hardinge Inc 1 Hardinge Dr *NASDAQ: HDNG* ■ *TF:* 800-843-8801 ■ *Web:* www.hardinge.com	Elmira	NY	14902	607-734-2281		455
Hardings Inc 109 W Commercial Ave *TF:* 866-776-7176 ■ *Web:* www.hardingsinc.com	Lowell	IN	46356	219-696-8911	696-8915	358
Hardings Market 533 Allegan St *Web:* www.hardings.com	Plainwell	MI	49080	269-685-5883		297-8
Hardin-Simmons University 2200 Hickory St *TF:* 877-464-7889 ■ *Web:* www.hsutx.edu	Abilene	TX	79698	325-670-1206	671-2115	166
Hardline Installation Inc 1759 Green Cove Rd St B *Web:* www.hardlineinstallation.com	Brasstown	NC	28902	828-835-8209		317
Hardrives Inc 14475 Quiram Dr *Web:* hardrivesinc.com	Rogers	MN	55374	763-428-8886	428-8868	188-4
Hardrives of Delray Inc 2101 S Congress Ave *Web:* www.hardrivespaving.com	Delray Beach	FL	33445	561-278-0456	278-2147	188-4
Hardscratch Press 2358 Banbury Pl *Web:* www.hardscratchpress.com	Walnut Creek	CA	94598	925-935-3422		637-2
Hardsuit Labs 4025 Delridge Way SW Ste 210 *Web:* www.hardsuitlabs.com	Seattle	WA	98106	206-785-6869		178-1
Hardware & Forging Co 3270 E 79th St *TF:* 800-321-1874 ■ *Web:* www.clevelandhardware.com	Cleveland	OH	44104	216-641-5200		483
Hardware Imagination 5012 W Knollwood St *TF:* 800-722-4409 ■ *Web:* www.hardwareimagination-tech.com	Tampa	FL	33634	813-882-0322	882-0264	115
Hardware Sales Inc 2034 James St *Web:* www.hardwaresales.net	Bellingham	WA	98225	360-734-6140		350
Hardwick Clothes Inc 3800 Old Tasso Rd *TF:* 800-251-6392 ■ *Web:* hardwick.com	Cleveland	TN	37312	800-251-6392		155-12
Hardwire LLC 1947 Clarke Ave *Web:* www.hardwirellc.com	Pocomoke City	MD	21851	410-957-3669		492
Hardwoods of Michigan Inc 430 Div St *TF:* 800-327-2812 ■ *Web:* www.hmilumber.com	Clinton	MI	49236	517-456-7431	456-4931	683
Hardy Bros Inc 6406 Siloam Rd *TF:* 800-525-5354 ■ *Web:* www.hardybros.com	Siloam	NC	27047	800-525-5354		186
Hardy Corp 350 Industrial Dr *TF:* 800-289-4822 ■ *Web:* www.hardycorp.com	Birmingham	AL	35211	205-252-7191	326-6268	189-10
Hardy County 204 Washington St Rm 111 *Web:* hardycounty.com	Moorefield	WV	26836	304-530-1786	530-0251	338
Hardy Diagnostics Inc 1430 W Mccoy Ln *Web:* hardydiagnostics.com	Santa Maria	CA	93455	805-346-2766		475
Hardy Insurance Agency Inc 10507-D Braddock Rd *Web:* hardyinsuranceagency.com	Fairfax	VA	22032	703-503-3100	503-9028	390
Hardy Lake 4171 E Harrod Rd *Web:* www.in.gov	Scottsburg	IN	47170	812-794-3800		565
Harford Bank 8 W Bel Air Ave *Web:* www.harfordbank.com	Aberdeen	MD	21001	410-272-5000	272-0533	70

	Phone	Fax	Class
Harford Community College 401 Thomas Run Rd .... Bel Air MD 21015 *Web:* www.harford.edu	410-879-8920		162
Harford County Chamber of Commerce 108 S Bond St .... Bel Air MD 21014 *Web:* www.harfordchamber.org	410-838-2020		139
Harford County Public Library 1221-A Brass Mill Rd .... Belcamp MD 21017 *TF:* 800-944-7403 ■ *Web:* www.hcplonline.org	410-575-6761	273-5606	434-3
Harford Refrigeration Company Inc 7915 Philadelphia Rd .... Rosedale MD 21237 *Web:* www.harfordrefrigeration.com	410-866-6200		189-10
Harford Systems Inc 2225 Pulaski Hwy PO Box 700 .... Aberdeen MD 21001 *Web:* harfordsystems.com	410-272-3400		482
Harger Inc 301 Ziegler Dr .... Grayslake IL 60030 *TF:* 800-842-7437 ■ *Web:* www.harger.com	847-548-8700		815
Hargis Engineers Inc 1201 Third Ave Ste 600 .... Seattle WA 98101 *Web:* hargis.biz	206-448-3376		256
Hargrave Military Academy (HMA) 200 Military Dr .... Chatham VA 24531 *TF:* 800-432-2480 ■ *Web:* www.hargrave.edu	434-432-2481	432-3129	622
Hargray Communications 870-C William Hilton Pkwy .... Hilton Head Island SC 29938 *TF:* 877-427-4729 ■ *Web:* www.hargray.com	843-341-1501		736
Hargreaves & Taylor LLP 750 B St Ste 2300 .... San Diego CA 92101 *Web:* www.htfamlaw.com	619-238-5501	235-4415	428
Hargrove & Associates Inc 100 N Sixth St Ste 306B .... Minneapolis MN 55403 *Web:* www.haiint.com	612-436-5500		396
Hargrove Electric Company Inc 1522 Market Center Blvd .... Dallas TX 75207 *Web:* www.hargroveelectric.com	214-742-8665	744-0846	189-4
Hargrove Inc 1 Hargrove Dr .... Lanham MD 20706 *Web:* hargroveinc.com	301-306-9000		232
Hari World Travel Inc 3400 Peachtree Rd NE Ste 815 .... Atlanta GA 30326 *Web:* www.hariworld.com	212-997-3300		772
Harig Manufacturing Corp 5423 Fargo Ave .... Skokie IL 60077 *Web:* www.harigmfg.com	847-647-9500	647-8351	757
Harkcon 1140 International Pkwy Ste B .... Fredericksburg VA 22406 *TF:* 800-499-6456 ■ *Web:* www.harkcon.com	800-499-6456		463
Harken Energy Corp 180 State St Ste 200 .... Southlake TX 76092 *OTC: HKNI* ■ *Web:* www.hkninc.com	817-424-2424		536
Harker's Distribution Inc 801 Sixth St SW .... Le Mars IA 51031 *Web:* www.lemarssentinel.com	712-546-8171		297-10
Harkess-Ord 263 W 38th St 8th Fl .... New York NY 10018 *Web:* www.harkess-ord.com	212-704-9989		463
Harkins Builders Inc 10490 Little Patuxent Pkwy Ste 400 .... Columbia MD 21044 *Web:* www.harkinsbuilders.com	410-750-2600	480-4299	186
Harkins Theatres 7511 E Mcdonald Dr .... Scottsdale AZ 85250 *Web:* www.harkins.com	480-627-7777		748
Harkness Pharmaceuticals Inc 4401 Eastgate Mall .... San Diego CA 92121 *Web:* www.harknesspharmaceuticals.com	858-550-6061	677-0800	668
Harlan Bakeries-Avon LLC 7597 E US Hwy 36 .... Avon IN 46123 *Web:* www.harlanbakeries.com	317-272-3600		297-11
Harlan Cabinets Inc 12707 Spencerville Rd .... Harlan IN 46743 *Web:* www.harlancabinets.com	260-657-5154	657-5151	115
Harlan Community Television Inc 124 S First St .... Harlan KY 40831 *Web:* www.harlanonline.net	606-573-8700		116
Harlan Consulting Services Inc 2515 Briarpark Dr .... Houston TX 77042 *Web:* www.harlanconsulting.com	713-464-2484		463
Harlan County 201 S Main St .... Harlan KY 40831 *TF:* 800-988-4660 ■ *Web:* www.harlancountytrails.com	606-573-4495	573-9485	338
Harlan County Chamber of Commerce PO Box 268 .... Harlan KY 40831 *Web:* www.harlancountychamber.com	606-573-4717		139
Harlan Global Manufacturing LLC 27 Stanley Rd .... Kansas City KS 66115 *TF:* 800-255-4262 ■ *Web:* www.harlan-corp.com	913-342-5650	321-5802	470
Harlan Graphic Arts Services Inc 4752 River Rd .... Cincinnati OH 45233 *Web:* www.harlangraphics.com	513-251-5700	251-5703	781
Harlan Harlan & Still 515 Cherry St Ste 300 .... Columbia MO 65201 *Web:* harlan-still.com	573-874-2402		41
Harland Technology Services 2020 S 156th Cir .... Omaha NE 68130 *TF:* 800-228-3628 ■ *Web:* www.harlandts.com	402-697-3000		180
Harlandale ISD 114 E Gerald .... San Antonio TX 78214 *Web:* www.harlandale.net	210-989-4300		685
Harlem Children's Zone Inc 35 E 125th St .... New York NY 10035 *Web:* hcz.org	212-360-3255	289-0661	685
Harlem Globetrotters International Inc 400 E Van Buren St Ste 300 .... Phoenix AZ 85004 **Fax Area Code:* 602 ■ *TF:* 800-641-4667 ■ *Web:* www.harlemglobetrotters.com	208-568-6644	258-5925*	181
Harlem Hospital Ctr 506 Lenox Ave .... New York NY 10037 *Web:* www1.nyc.gov	212-939-1000		374-3
Harlequin 233 Broadway Ste 1001 .... New York NY 10279 *TF:* 800-873-8635 ■ *Web:* www.harlequin.com	212-553-4200	227-8969	637-2
Harlequin Enterprises Ltd Bay Adelaide Centre East Tower 22 Adelaide St W 41st Fl .... Toronto ON M5H4E3 *TF:* 888-432-4879 ■ *Web:* www.corporate.harlequin.com	888-432-4879		637-2
Harley Gray Stone Co 5375 E Drake Rd .... Paulden AZ 86334 *Web:* www.harleygraystone.com	928-636-2436	636-0704	503-6
Harley Marine Services Inc 910 SW Spokane St .... Seattle WA 98134 *Web:* www.harleymarine.com	206-628-0051		803-1
Harley-Davidson Financial Services Inc PO Box 21489 .... Carson City NV 89721 *TF:* 888-691-4337 ■ *Web:* www.harley-davidson.com	888-691-4337		217
Harleysville Bank 271 Main St .... Harleysville PA 19438 *NASDAQ: HARL* ■ *TF:* 888-256-8828 ■ *Web:* www.harleysvillebank.com	215-256-8828	513-9393	360-2
Harleysville Mutual Insurance Co 355 Maple Ave .... Harleysville PA 19438 *Web:* www.harleysville.com	215-256-5000		391-2
Harleysville Veterinary Hospital 391 Main St .... Harleysville PA 19438 *Web:* harleysvillevet.com	215-256-4664		794
Harlick & Company Inc 893 American St .... San Carlos CA 94070 *Web:* www.harlick.com	650-593-2093	593-9704	710
Harlingen Area Chamber of Commerce 311 E Tyler St .... Harlingen TX 78550 *TF:* 800-225-5345 ■ *Web:* www.harlingen.com	956-423-5440	425-3870	139
Harlingen High School 1201 Marshall St .... Harlingen TX 78550 *Web:* hcisd.org	956-427-3600		685
Harlingen Public Library 410 76th Dr .... Harlingen TX 78550 *Web:* www.harlingenlibrary.org	956-216-5800		434-3
Harllee Packing Inc PO Box 08 .... Palmetto FL 34220 *Web:* www.harlleepacking.com	941-722-7747		11-1
Harlo Corp 4210 Ferry St SW .... Grandville MI 49468 *Web:* www.harlocorporation.com	616-538-0550		190
Harlow Aerostructures LLC 1501 McLean Blvd S .... Wichita KS 67213 *Web:* www.harlowair.com	316-265-5268		22
Harlow's Casino 4280 Harlow Blvd .... Greenville MS 38701 *TF:* 866-524-5825 ■ *Web:* www.harlowscasino.com	662-335-9797		42
Harlow, Adams & Friedman PC 1 New Haven Ave Ste 100 .... Milford CT 06460 *Web:* harlowadamsfriedman.com	203-878-0661		41
Harmac Medical Products Inc 2201 Bailey Ave .... Buffalo NY 14211 *Web:* www.harmac.com	716-897-4500	897-0016	476
Harman Construction Inc 1633 Rogers Rd .... Fort Worth TX 76107 *Web:* harmanconstructioninc.net	817-336-5780	336-5797	186
Harman International Industries Inc 400 Atlantic St 15th Fl .... Stamford CT 06901 *NYSE: HAR* ■ *TF:* 800-473-0602 ■ *Web:* www.harman.com	203-328-3500		52
Harman Management Corp 199 1st St Ste 212 .... Los Altos CA 94022	650-941-5681		670
Harman Music Group 8760 S Sandy Pkwy .... Sandy UT 84070 *Web:* www.dbxpro.com	801-566-8800	566-7005	52
Harman Press Inc, The 6840 Vineland Ave .... North Hollywood CA 91605 *Web:* harmanpress.com	818-432-0570	432-0578	627
Harman, Claytor, Corrigan & Wellman PC PO Box 70280 .... Richmond VA 23255 *TF:* 877-747-4229 ■ *Web:* www.hccw.com	804-747-5200		428
Harmelin Media 525 Righters Ferry Rd .... Bala Cynwyd PA 19004 *Web:* www.harmelin.com	610-668-7900		6
Harmer Assoc 150 S Wacker Dr Ste 2700 .... Chicago IL 60606 *Web:* www.harmer.com	312-407-7180		390
Harmon Brewing Co 1938 Pacific Ave .... Tacoma WA 98402 *Web:* www.harmonbrewingco.com	253-383-2739		671
Harmon Curran Spielberg & Eisenberg 1726 M St NW Ste 600 .... Washington DC 20036 *Web:* www.harmoncurran.com	202-328-3500	328-6918	428
Harmon Electric Association Inc (HEA) 114 N First St PO Box 393 .... Hollis OK 73550 *TF:* 800-643-7769 ■ *Web:* www.harmonelectric.com	580-688-3342		245
Harmon Medical & Rehabilitation Hospital 2170 E Harmon Ave .... Las Vegas NV 89119 *Web:* fundltc.com	702-794-0100	794-0041	374-6
Harmon Stores Inc 650 Liberty Ave .... Union NJ 07083 *TF:* 866-427-6661 ■ *Web:* www.harmondiscount.com	866-427-6661		237
Harmonia Inc 2020 Kraft Dr Ste 1000 .... Blacksburg VA 24060 *Web:* www.harmonia.com	540-951-5900		177
Harmonic Drive LLC 247 Lynnfield St .... Peabody MA 01960 *TF:* 800-921-3332 ■ *Web:* www.harmonicdrive.net	978-532-1800		61
Harmonic Inc 4300 N First St .... San Jose CA 95134 *NASDAQ: HLIT* ■ *Web:* www.harmonicinc.com	408-542-2500	542-2511	647
Harmonie State Park 3451 Harmonie State Park Rd .... New Harmony IN 47631 *TF:* 866-622-6746 ■ *Web:* www.in.gov	812-682-4821		565
Harmonix Music Systems Inc 625 Massachusetts Ave .... Cambridge MA 02139 *Web:* harmonixmusic.com	617-491-6144		177
Harmonix Technologies Inc 4915 Paseo De Norte NE Ste A .... Albuquerque NM 87113 *Web:* www.harmonixtechnologies.com	505-205-1585	217-1854	180
Harmons Grocery 3540 S 4000 W .... West Valley City UT 84120 *Web:* www.harmonsgrocery.com	801-969-8261	964-1299	345
Harmony Biosciences 630 W Germantown Pke .... Plymouth Meeting PA 19462 *Web:* www.harmonybiosciences.com	484-539-9800		634
Harmony Castings LLC 251 Perry Hwy .... Harmony PA 16037 *Web:* www.harmonycastings.com	724-452-5811	452-0118	308
Harmony Federal Cu 504 Court Rd .... Grand Junction CO 81501 *Web:* harmonyfcu.org	970-242-3100		219
Harmony Foundation Inc 1600 Fish Hatchery Rd .... Estes Park CO 80517 *TF:* 866-686-7867 ■ *Web:* harmonyfoundationinc.com	970-586-4491		726
Harmony Gold Music Inc 7655 W Sunset Blvd .... Los Angeles CA 90046 *Web:* harmonygold.com	323-851-4900		514

Phone | Fax | Class

Harmony Ink Press
5032 Capital Circle SW Ste 2 Tallahassee FL 32305 850-632-4648 308-3739* 637-2
*Fax Area Code: 888 ■ TF: 800-970-3759 ■ Web: www.harmonyinkpress.com

Harmony Nursing & Rehabilitation Center Inc
3919 W Foster Ave Chicago IL 60625 773-588-9500 371
Web: www.harmonychicago.com

Harmony Park Safari
431 Clouds Cove Rd Huntsville AL 35803 256-723-3880 823
Web: www.harmonyparksafari.com

Harmony Press 717 W Berwick St Easton PA 18042 610-559-9800 627
Web: www.harmonypress.net

Harms Oil Co 337 22nd Ave S Brookings SD 57006 605-696-5000 580
TF: 800-376-8476 ■ Web: www.harmsoil.com

Harmsco Inc PO Box 14066 North Palm Beach FL 33408 561-848-9628 845-2474 806
TF: 800-327-3248 ■ Web: www.harmsco.com

Harn Homestead & 1889er Museum
1721 N Lincoln Blvd Oklahoma City OK 73105 405-235-4058 235-4041 520
Web: harnhomestead.com

Harnack Co, The 6016 Nordic Dr Cedar Falls IA 50613 319-277-0660 772-2027* 429
*Fax Area Code: 800 ■ TF: 800-772-2022 ■ Web: www.harnack.net

Harness Racing Museum & Hall of Fame
240 Main St Goshen NY 10924 845-294-6330 294-3463 522
Web: www.harnessmuseum.com

Harnett Correctional Institution
1210 McNeil St Lillington NC 27546 910-893-2751 893-6432 213
Web: www.ncdps.gov

Harnett County PO Box 759 Lillington NC 27546 910-893-7555 814-2662 338
Web: www.harnett.org

Harnett County Board of Education
1008 S 11th St Lillington NC 27546 910-893-8151 893-8839 685
TF: 800-342-9647 ■ Web: www.harnett.k12.nc.us

Harnett County Public Library
601 S Main St Lillington NC 27546 910-893-2191 893-3001 434-3
Web: www.harnett.libguides.com

Harney County 450 N Buena Vista Ste 14 Burns OR 97720 541-573-6641 573-8370 338
Web: www.co.harney.or.us

Harney Electric Co-opeartive Inc
277 Lottery Ln PO Box 587 Hines OR 97738 541-573-2061 573-3930 245
Web: www.harneyelectric.org

Harney Rock & Paving Co 457 S Date Ave Burns OR 97720 541-573-7855 573-3532 503-5
TF: 888-298-2681 ■ Web: harneyrock.com

Harnois Energies 80 Rt 158 Saint Thomas QC J0K3L0 450-759-7979 579
Web: harnoisenergies.com

Haro Bicycles 1230 Avenida Chelsea Vista CA 92081 800-289-4276 599-1237* 82
*Fax Area Code: 760 ■ TF: 800-289-4276 ■ Web: harobikes.com

Harodite Industries Inc 66 South St Taunton MA 02780 508-824-6961 880-0696 745-7
Web: www.harodite.com

Harold & Belle's
2920 W Jefferson Blvd Los Angeles CA 90018 323-735-9023 671
Web: haroldandbelles.com

Harold Beck & Sons Inc 11 Terry Dr Newtown PA 18940 215-968-4600 203
Web: www.haroldbeck.com

Harold D. Carr PS 4239 Martin Way E Olympia WA 98516 360-455-0030 41
TF: 800-700-8082 ■ Web: haroldcarrattorney.com

Harold G. Butzer Inc
730 Wicker Ln Jefferson City MO 65109 573-636-4115 636-7053 189-10
TF: 800-769-1065 ■ Web: hgbutzer.com

Harold Import Company Inc
747 Vassar Ave Lakewood NJ 08701 800-526-2163 360-3
TF: 800-526-2163 ■ Web: www.haroldskitchen.com

Harold K. Scholz Co 7800 Serum Ave Ralston NE 68127 402-339-7600 339-1821 729
Web: www.hkscholz.com

Harold L. King & Company Inc
1420 Stafford St Redwood City CA 94063 650-368-2233 368-3547 297-8
Web: king-coffee.com

Harold L. Lee & Sons Inc 31 Pell St New York NY 10013 212-962-2232 233-1421 390
TF: 800-352-1707 ■ Web: leeins.com

Harold Levinson Assoc (HLA)
19 Banfi Plaza North Farmingdale NY 11735 631-962-2400 962-9000 297-3
TF: 800-325-2512 ■ Web: www.hlacigars.com

Harold Parker State Forest
305 Middleton Rd North Andover MA 01845 978-686-3391 565
Web: www.mass.gov

Harp Advertising + Interactive
555 Waters Edge Ste 130 Lombard IL 60148 630-691-9500 691-9525 180
Web: www.harpinteractive.com

Harp Enterprises Inc
2400 Merchant St Lexington KY 40511 859-253-2601 233-9457 76
Web: www.harpenterprisesinc.com

Harp of the Spirit PO Box 1320 Los Alamos NM 87544 866-661-8760 592
TF: 866-661-8760 ■ Web: www.harpofthespirit.com

Harp, The 4408 Detroit Ave Cleveland OH 44113 216-939-0200 671
Web: www.the-harp.com

Harper & Pearson Company PC
1 Riverway Ste 1900 Houston TX 77056 713-622-2310 622-5613 2
Web: www.harperpearson.com

Harper Bates Champion LLP
5910 N Central Expwy Ste 1050 Dallas TX 75206 214-238-8400 41
Web: harperbates.com

Harper Brush Works Inc
400 N Second St Fairfield IA 52556 641-472-5186 472-3187 103
TF: 800-223-7894 ■ Web: www.harperbrush.com

Harper Chevrolet-Buick-GMC 200 Hwy 531 Minden LA 71055 318-268-3320 667-4007* 57
*Fax Area Code: 313 ■ TF: 800-259-0395 ■ Web: www.harperminden.com

Harper Co 1648 Petersburg Rd Hebron KY 41048 859-586-8890 586-8891 188-4
Web: harperco.com

Harper College 1200 W Algonquin Rd Palatine IL 60067 847-925-6000 162
Web: www.harpercollege.edu

Harper Construction Company Inc
2241 Kettner Blvd Ste 300 San Diego CA 92101 619-233-7900 186
Web: www.harperconstruction.com

Harper Contracting Inc
8201 W 5400 S Salt Lake City UT 84118 801-326-1016 326-1019 188-4
Web: www.harpercontractinginc.com

Harper Corp - General Contractors, The
35 W Court St Ste 400 Greenville SC 29601 864-527-2500 527-2536 187
Web: www.harpergc.com

Harper Corporation of America
11625 Steele Creek Rd Charlotte NC 28273 704-588-3371 629
Web: www.harperimage.com

Harper County 201 N Jennings Ave Anthony KS 67003 620-842-5555 842-3455 338
TF: 877-537-2110 ■ Web: www.harpercountyks.gov

Harper Engraving & Printing Co
2626 Fisher Rd Columbus OH 43204 800-848-5196 627
TF: 800-848-5196 ■ Web: www.harperengraving.com

Harper Grey LLP
3200 Vancouver Centre 650 W Georgia St Vancouver BC V6B4P7 604-687-0411 428
Web: www.harpergrey.com

Harper Houf Peterson Righ
205 SE Spokane St Portland OR 97202 503-221-1131 256
Web: www.hhpr.com

Harper Industries Inc 616 Northview Paducah KY 42001 270-442-2753 443-9154 188-4
TF: 800-669-0077 ■ Web: harper1.com

Harper Love Adhesives Corp
11101 Westlake Dr Charlotte NC 28273 704-588-1350 3
Web: www.harperlove.com

Harper Trucks Inc PO Box 12330 Wichita KS 67277 316-942-1381 942-8508 470
TF: 800-835-4099 ■ Web: harpertrucks.com

Harper's Bazaar Magazine
300 W 57th St New York NY 10019 212-903-5000 457-11
Web: www.harpersbazaar.com

Harper's Magazine
666 Broadway 11th Fl New York NY 10012 212-420-5720 457-11
TF: 800-444-4653 ■ Web: harpers.org

Harper, Kynes, Geller & Greenleaf PA
1253 Park St Ste 200 Clearwater FL 33756 727-799-4840 41
Web: harperkynes.com

Harpers Ferry National Historic Park
PO Box 65 Harpers Ferry WV 25425 304-535-6029 564
Web: www.nps.gov

Harpeth Capital LLC
3100 W End Ave Ste 710 Nashville TN 37203 615-296-9850 690
Web: www.harpethcapital.com

Harpo Productions Inc 110 N Carpenter Chicago IL 60607 312-633-1000 514
Web: www.oprah.com

Harpoon Brewery 306 Northern Ave Boston MA 02210 617-574-9551 102
Web: www.harpoonbrewery.com

Harps Food Stores Inc
918 S Gutensohn Rd Springdale AR 72762 479-751-7601 345
Web: www.harpsfood.com

Harrah's Rincon Casino & Resort
777 Harrah's Rincon Way Funner CA 92082 760-751-3100 669

Harrang Long Gary Rudnick PC
360 E Tenth Ave Ste 300 Eugene OR 97401 541-485-0220 428
TF: 800-315-4172 ■ Web: harrang.com

Harraseeket Inn 162 Main St Freeport ME 04032 207-865-9377 379
TF: 800-342-6423 ■ Web: www.harraseeketinn.com

Harri Plumbing & Heating Inc
5245 Glacier Hwy Juneau AK 99801 907-586-3190 612

Harriet Brasserie, The
2724 W 43rd St Minneapolis MN 05510 612-354-2197 671
Web: www.lakeharrietbrasserie.com

Harrietts Energy Solutions Inc
101 S Main St Medford NJ 08055 609-654-2035 316
Web: harriettses.com

Harrigan Lumber Company Inc
1033 Hornady Dr Monroeville AL 36460 251-575-4821 683
Web: www.harriganlumber.com

Harriman State Park
3489 Green Canyon Rd Island Park ID 83429 208-558-7368 565
Web: www.stateparks.com

Harriman State Park
Palisades Pkwy Exit 17 Bear Mountain NY 10911 845-942-2560 565
Web: parks.ny.gov

Harrington & Rhodes Ltd
2750 S County Trail East Greenwich RI 02818 401-885-9393 885-9399 41
Web: h-rlaw.com

Harrington Beach State Park
531 County Rd D Belgium WI 53004 262-285-3015 565
Web: dnr.wi.gov

Harrington Co 4248 Pk Glen Rd Minneapolis MN 55416 952-928-7477 47
Web: www.harringtoncompany.com

Harrington College of Design
c/o Columbia College Chicago 600 S Michigan Ave
Chicago IL 60605 312-369-3700 167-3
Web: www.harrington.edu

Harrington Corp, The 3721 Cohen Pl Lynchburg VA 24501 434-845-7094 596
Web: www.harcofittings.com

Harrington Group, The
873 Inverness Cir Spartanburg SC 29306 864-585-5850 193
Web: harringtongroup.net

Harrington Hoists Inc 401 W End Ave Manheim PA 17545 717-665-2000 665-2861 386
TF: 800-233-3010 ■ Web: www.harringtonhoists.com

Harrington Hospital (HMH)
100 South St Southbridge MA 01550 508-765-9771 765-3147 374-3
TF: 800-416-6072 ■ Web: www.harringtonhospital.org

Harrington Industrial Plastics LLC
14480 Yorba Ave Chino CA 91710 909-597-8641 597-9826 385
TF: 800-213-4528 ■ Web: www.hipco.com

Harrington Investments Inc
1001 Second St Ste 325 Napa CA 94559 800-788-0154 401
TF: 800-788-0154 ■ Web: www.harringtoninvestments.com

Harrington Museum 106 Dorman St Harrington DE 19952 302-398-3530 520
Web: harrington.delaware.gov

Harrington Raceway 15 W Rider Rd Harrington DE 19952 888-887-5687 642
TF: 888-887-5687 ■ Web: casino.harringtonraceway.com

Harrington Signal Co 2519 Fourth Ave Moline IL 61265 309-762-0731 283
Web: www.harringtonsignal.com

Harrington Trucking Inc
510 S Delong St Salt Lake City UT 84104 801-972-4974 975-1266 780
Web: www.harringtontrucking.com

Harris & Associates Inc
1401 Willow Pass Rd Concord CA 94520 925-827-4900 261
TF: 866-356-0998 ■ Web: www.weareharris.com

Name / Address	City	State	ZIP	Phone	Fax	Class
Harris & Bowker LLP 10300 SW Greenburg Rd Ste 530 *Web:* harrisbowker.com	Portland	OR	97223	503-293-0073		41
Harris & Hart Inc 1759 W 1200 S *Web:* www.harris-hart.com	Ogden	UT	84404	801-731-0577		189-10
Harris & Sloan 2295 Gateway Oaks Dr Ste 200 *Web:* harrisandsloan.com	Sacramento	CA	95833	916-921-2441		256
Harris Andy (Rep R - MD) 2334 Rayburn House Office Bldg *Web:* harris.house.gov	Washington	DC	20515	202-225-5311	225-0254	342-2
Harris Associates LP 111 S Wacker Dr Ste 4600 *Web:* www.harrisassoc.com	Chicago	IL	60606	312-646-3600		401
Harris Barber College 803 S Blount St *Web:* www.hbccollege.com	Raleigh	NC	27616	919-834-3134		167-3
Harris Beach LLP 99 Garnsey Rd 130 E Main St *Web:* www.harrisbeach.com	Pittsford	NY	14534	585-419-8800		445
Harris Beach State Park 1655 Hwy 101 N *Web:* stateparks.oregon.gov	Brookings	OR	97415	541-469-0224		565
Harris Civil Engineers LLC 1200 Hillcrest St Ste 200 *Web:* www.harriscivilengineers.com	Orlando	FL	32803	407-629-4777		261
Harris Co 909 Montreal Cir *Web:* www.himec.com	Saint Paul	MN	55102	651-602-6500	602-6699	189-10
Harris Computer Systems Inc 1 Antares Dr Ste 400 *TF:* 866-450-6696 ■ *Web:* www.harriscomputer.com	Ottawa	ON	K2E8C4	613-226-5511		180
Harris Corp *RF Communications Div* 1680 University Ave *TF:* 866-264-8040 ■ *Web:* www.harris.com	Rochester	NY	14610	585-244-5830	242-4755	647
Harris County 159 S College St PO Box 426 *TF:* 888-478-0010 ■ *Web:* harriscountychamber.org	Hamilton	GA	31811	706-628-0010	628-4429	338
Harris County 1019 Congress St 1st Fl *Web:* www.harriscountytx.gov	Houston	TX	77002	713-755-5000		338
Harris County Federal Credit Union 1400 Franklin St *Web:* hcfcu.com	Houston	TX	77002	713-755-5160	755-8982	219
Harris County Public Library System 8080 El Rio St *Web:* www.hcpl.net	Houston	TX	77054	713-749-9000		434-3
Harris D. McKinney & Zoomedia HDMZ (HDMZ) 1620 Montgomery St *Web:* www.hdmz.com	San Francisco	CA	94111	415-474-1192	474-8146	177
Harris Discount Supply 1318 Fretz Dr *TF:* 800-227-8524 ■ *Web:* www.harrisdiscount.com	Edmond	OK	73003	847-726-3800	726-3803	475
Harris Environmental Systems Inc 11 Connector Rd *Web:* www.harrisenv.com	Andover	MA	01810	978-470-8600	475-7903	664
Harris Farms Inc 27366 W Oakland Ave *TF:* 800-311-6211 ■ *Web:* harrisfarms.com	Coalinga	CA	93210	559-884-2859	884-2855	10-11
Harris Financial Services Inc 940 Spokane Ave *TF:* 800-735-7895 ■ *Web:* www.harrisfsi.com	Whitefish	MT	59937	406-862-4400		690
Harris Frazier Government Relations 511 Union St Ste 710 *Web:* www.harrisfrazier.com	Nashville	TN	37219	615-255-2643	254-4866	41
Harris Freeman & Company LP 3110 E Miraloma Ave *Web:* www.harrisfreeman.com	Anaheim	CA	92806	714-765-1190		296-37
Harris Goldman Productions Inc 8885 Rio San Diego Dr Ste 335 *Web:* www.harrisgoldman.com	San Diego	CA	92108	619-299-7951		31
Harris Group Inc 300 Elliott Ave W *Web:* www.harrisgroup.com	Seattle	WA	98119	206-494-9400		261
Harris Harris Bauerle Ziegler Lopez 1201 E Robinson St *Web:* hhbzlflorida.com	Orlando	FL	32801	407-843-0404		787
Harris Industrial Gases 8475 Auburn Blvd *Web:* harrisgas.com	Citrus Heights	CA	95610	916-725-2168		789
Harris Industries Inc 5181 Argosy Ave *TF:* 800-222-6866 ■ *Web:* www.harrisind.com	Huntington Beach	CA	92649	714-898-8048	898-7108	732
Harris Instrument Corp 155 Johnson Dr *Web:* harris-instrument.com	Delaware	OH	43015	740-369-3580	369-2653	495
Harris Kamala D (Sen D - CA) 112 Hart Senate Office Bldg *Web:* www.harris.senate.gov	Washington	DC	20510	202-224-3553	224-2200	342-2
Harris Kocher Engineering Grou 1120 Lincoln St Ste 1000 *Web:* harriskochersmith.com	Denver	CO	80203	303-623-6300		261
Harris Law Firm PC 1125 17th St Ste 450 *Web:* www.harrisfamilylaw.com	Denver	CO	80202	303-622-5502		428
Harris Levy Inc 98 Forsyth St *TF:* 800-221-7750 ■ *Web:* www.harrislevy.com	New York	NY	10002	800-221-7750		157-4
Harris Machine Co 8623 Hwy 1 *Web:* www.harrismachineco.com	Oakes	ND	58474	701-742-2536		480
Harris Manufacturing Inc 4775 E Vine Ave *Web:* www.harrismfg.com	Fresno	CA	93725	559-268-7422		482
Harris Marketing Group Inc 700 Forest Ave *Web:* www.harris-hmg.com	Birmingham	MI	48009	248-723-6300		4
Harris Miller Miller & Hanson Inc 77 S Bedford St *Web:* hmmh.com	Burlington	MA	01803	781-229-0707	229-7939	196
Harris Miniature Golf 141 W Burk Ave *TF:* 888-294-6530 ■ *Web:* www.harrisminigolf.com	Wildwood	NJ	08260	609-522-4200	729-0100	188-3
Harris Originals of NY Inc 800 Prime Pl *Web:* www.harrisjewelry.com	Hauppauge	NY	11788	631-348-0303		410
Harris Packaging Corp 1600 Carson St *Web:* www.harrispackaging.com	Haltom City	TX	76117	817-429-6262		100
Harris Pharmaceutical Inc 9090 Park Royal Dr *TF:* 800-983-4708 ■ *Web:* harrispharmaceutical.com	Fort Myers	FL	33908	239-278-4749	936-9328	237
Harris Powers & Cunningham P L 361 E Coronado Rd Ste 101 *Web:* hpclawyers.com	Phoenix	AZ	85004	602-271-9344		41
Harris Products Group 4501 Quality Pl *TF:* 800-733-4043 ■ *Web:* www.harrisproductsgroup.com	Mason	OH	45040	513-754-2000	754-8778	811
Harris Ranch Beef Co 16277 S McCall Ave PO Box 220 *TF:* 800-742-1955 ■ *Web:* www.harrisranchbeef.com	Selma	CA	93662	800-742-1955		473
Harris Real Estate School c/o Arnold Century 21-Perras 481 Dalton Ave *Web:* www.harrisrealestateschool.com	Pittsfield	MA	01201	413-442-0109		685
Harris Real Estate School c/o Bob Simmons Premier Properties/GMAC 10 Commerce Way *Web:* www.harrisrealestateschool.com	Raynham	MA	02767	508-822-7444		685
Harris Real Estate School 150 Newburyport Tpke Rte 1 *Web:* www.harrisrealestateschool.com	Rowley	MA	01969	978-948-5578		685
Harris Smariga & Associates Inc 125 S Carroll St Ste 100 *Web:* www.harrissmariga.com	Frederick	MD	21701	301-662-4488		261
Harris Steel Co 1223 S 55th Ct *Web:* www.harrissteelco.com	Cicero	IL	60804	708-656-5500	656-0151	723
Harris Tea Co 344 New Albany Rd *Web:* www.harristea.com	Moorestown	NJ	08057	856-793-0290		123
Harris Technology Services Inc 1603 Golf Course Rd SE Ste B *Web:* www.htsusa.com	Rio Rancho	NM	87124	505-892-7364		180
Harris Teeter Inc PO Box 10100 *TF:* 800-432-6111 ■ *Web:* www.harristeeter.com	Matthews	NC	28106	800-432-6111		185
Harris Transport Co 1166 Curtis St *TF:* 800-444-4168 ■ *Web:* www.harristransport.com	Monroe	NC	28112	704-289-5447	296-9067	780
Harris Winick Harris LLP 333 W Wacker Dr Ste 2060 *Web:* hwhlegal.com	Chicago	IL	60606	312-662-4600		41
Harris Woolf California Almonds 26060 Colusa Rd *Web:* www.harriswoolfalmonds.com	Coalinga	CA	93210	559-884-2147		11-1
Harris Wyatt & Amala Attorneys at Law 5778 Commercial St SE *TF:* 800-853-2144 ■ *Web:* www.salemattorneys.com	Salem	OR	97306	503-378-7744		428
Harris' Restaurant 2100 Van Ness Ave *Web:* www.harrisrestaurant.com	San Francisco	CA	94109	415-673-1888	673-8817	671
Harris, Deville & Associates Inc 521 Laurel St *Web:* hdaissues.com	Baton Rouge	LA	70801	225-344-0381		636
Harrisburg Area Community College 1 HACC Dr *TF:* 800-222-4222 ■ *Web:* www.hacc.edu	Harrisburg	PA	17110	717-780-2300	231-7674	162
Harrisburg City Hall 10 N Second St *Web:* www.harrisburgpa.gov	Harrisburg	PA	17101	717-255-3060	255-3081	337
Harrisburg Dairies Inc 2001 Herr St **Fax Area Code:* 717 ■ *TF:* 800-692-7429 ■ *Web:* www.harrisburgdairies.com	Harrisburg	PA	17105	800-692-7429	231-4584*	296-27
Harrisburg District Offices of the Central Region *Probation & Parole Board* 1101 S Front St Ste 5950 *Web:* www.parole.pa.gov	Harrisburg	PA	17104	717-787-5699	230-8019	339-39
Harrisburg International Airport 1 Terminal Dr Ste 300 *Web:* www.flyhia.com	Middletown	PA	17057	717-948-3900	948-4636	27
Harrisburg Regional Chamber 3211 N Front St Ste 201 *TF:* 877-883-8339 ■ *Web:* www.harrisburgregionalchamber.org	Harrisburg	PA	17110	717-232-4099	232-5184	139
Harrisburg School District Inc 1601 State St *Web:* www.hbgsd.k12.pa.us	Harrisburg	PA	17103	717-703-4000		685
Harrisburg Symphony Orchestra 800 Corporate Cir Ste 101 *Web:* www.harrisburgsymphony.org	Harrisburg	PA	17110	717-545-5527	545-6501	573-3
Harrisburg University of Science & Technology 326 Market St *Web:* harrisburgu.edu	Harrisburg	PA	17101	717-901-5100		166
HarrisData 13555 Bishops Ct Ste 300 *TF:* 800-225-0585 ■ *Web:* www.harrisdata.com	Brookfield	WI	53005	262-784-9099	784-5994	178-1
Harrison & Held LLP 333 W Wacker Dr Ste 1700 **Fax Area Code:* 217 ■ *Web:* www.harrisonheld.com	Chicago	IL	60606	312-332-1111	546-6945*	428
Harrison & Lear Inc 2310 Tower Pl Ste 105 *Web:* www.harrison-lear.com	Hampton	VA	23666	757-825-9100	838-2574	655
Harrison & Star 75 Varick St *Web:* www.harrisonandstar.com	New York	NY	10013	212-727-1330		4
Harrison Accountancy 1503 S Coast Dr Ste 311 *Web:* harrison-accountancy.business.site	Costa Mesa	CA	92626	714-966-0644		734
Harrison Audio LLC 1024 Firestone Pkwy *TF:* 800-449-5919 ■ *Web:* harrisonconsoles.com	La Vergne	TN	37086	615-641-7200		52
Harrison Bay State Park 8411 Harrison Bay Rd *Web:* www.state.tn.us	Harrison	TN	37341	423-344-6214		565
Harrison County 1501 Central St PO Box 169 *Web:* www.harrisoncountysheriffmo.org	Bethany	MO	64424	660-425-3199		338
Harrison County 301 W Main St *TF:* 888-509-6568 ■ *Web:* www.harrisoncountywv.com	Clarksburg	WV	26301	304-624-8500	624-8673	338
Harrison County 300 N Capitol Ave *TF:* 866-972-9427 ■ *Web:* harrisoncounty.in.gov	Corydon	IN	47112	812-738-4289	738-3126	338

Phone | Fax | Class

Harrison County 313 Oddville Ave .... Cynthiana KY 41031 859-234-7130 234-8049 338
Web: www.harrisoncountyfiscalcourt.com

Harrison County 1801 23rd Ave .... Gulfport MS 39501 228-865-4036 868-1480 338
Web: co.harrison.ms.us

Harrison County PO Box 91 .... Logan IA 51546 712-644-3123 644-2643 338
Web: www.harrisoncountyia.org

Harrison County Chamber of Commerce
520 W Main St .... Clarksburg WV 26301 304-624-6331 624-5190 139
Web: www.harrisoncountychamber.com

Harrison County Clerk
200 W Houston Ste 143 PO Box 1365 .... Marshall TX 75671 903-935-8403 338
Web: harrisoncountytexas.org

Harrison County Public Library District
105 N Capital Ave .... Corydon IN 47112 812-738-4110 434-3
Web: www.hcpl.lib.in.us

Harrison County Rural Electric Co-op
105 Enterprise Dr PO Box 2 .... Woodbine IA 51579 712-647-2727 245
TF: 800-822-5591 ■ *Web:* www.hcrec.coop

Harrison Edwards Inc
80 Business Park Dr Ste 303 .... Armonk NY 10504 914-242-0010 466
Web: www.harrison-edwardspr.com

Harrison Hot Springs Resort & Spa
100 Esplanade Ave .... Harrison Hot Springs BC V0M1K0 604-796-2244 796-3682 669
TF: 800-663-2266 ■ *Web:* www.harrisonresort.com

Harrison Orr Air Conditioning LLC
4100 N Walnut .... Oklahoma City OK 73105 405-528-3333 610
Web: www.harrisonorr.com

Harrison Paint Co 1329 Harrison Ave SW .... Canton OH 44706 330-455-5125 454-1750 550
TF: 800-321-0680 ■ *Web:* harrisonpaint.com

Harrison Radio Station Inc
600 S Pine St .... Harrison AR 72601 870-741-1402 647
TF: 866-853-5293 ■ *Web:* www.kcwdradio.com

Harrison Regional Library
50 Lester St .... Columbiana AL 35051 205-669-3910 669-3940 434-3
Web: www.shelbycounty-al.org

Harrison Senior Living Inc
300 Strode Ave .... Coatesville PA 19320 610-384-6310 383-3945 271
Web: harrisonseniorliving.com

Harrison Steel Castings Company Inc
900 S Mound St .... Attica IN 47918 765-762-2481 762-2487 307
TF: 800-659-4722 ■ *Web:* www.hscast.com

Harrison's Harbor Watch Restaurant
806 S Boardwalk .... Ocean City MD 21842 410-289-5121 671
Web: www.harborwatchrestaurant.com

Harrison, Eichenberg & Murphy LLP
PO Box 640 .... Agoura Hills CA 91376 805-495-7379 428
Web: www.hem-law.com

Harrisonburg City Public Schools (HCPS)
317 S Main St .... Harrisonburg VA 22801 540-434-9916 434-5196 780
Web: www.harrisonburg.k12.va.us

Harrisonburg (Independent City)
345 S Main St .... Harrisonburg VA 22801 540-432-7701 432-7778 338
TF: 800-272-9829 ■ *Web:* www.harrisonburgva.gov

Harrisonburg-Rockingham Chamber of Commerce
800 Country Club Rd .... Harrisonburg VA 22802 540-434-3862 434-4508 139
Web: www.hrchamber.org

Harrison-Nichols Company Ltd
501 W Foothill Blvd .... Azusa CA 91702 626-337-5020 338-1610 780
TF: 800-451-6054 ■ *Web:* www.harrisonnichols.com

Harrisonville Telephone Co
213 S Main St PO Box 149 .... Waterloo IL 62298 618-939-6112 736
Web: www.htc.net

Harriss & Covington Hosiery Mills Inc
1250 Hickory Chapel Rd .... High Point NC 27260 336-882-6811 155-10
Web: www.harrissandcov.com

Harris-Stowe State University
3026 Laclede Ave .... Saint Louis MO 63103 314-340-3366 340-3555 166
Web: www.hssu.edu

Harris-Teller Inc 7400 S Mason Ave .... Chicago IL 60638 708-496-2130 526
Web: www.harristeller.com

Harristown Development Corp
320 Market St Ste 273 E .... Harrisburg PA 17101 717-255-1047 653
Web: www.harristown.net

Harrodsburg Herald, The
101 W Broadway .... Harrodsburg KY 40330 606-734-2726 532-2
TF: 800-803-1184 ■ *Web:* harrodsburgherald.com

Harrogate 400 Locust St .... Lakewood NJ 08701 732-905-7070 672
Web: www.harrogatelifecare.org

Harrow Sports Inc 600 W Bayaud .... Denver CO 80223 303-893-1401 893-1408 710
TF: 800-541-2905 ■ *Web:* www.harrowsports.com

Harry & David Holdings Inc
2500 S Pacific Hwy .... Medford OR 97501 541-864-2121 233-2300* 336
*Fax Area Code: 877 ■ *TF:* 877-322-1200 ■ *Web:* www.harryanddavid.com

Harry & Jeanette Weinberg Foundation Inc, The
7 Park Center Ct .... Owings Mills MD 21117 410-654-8500 305
Web: hjweinbergfoundation.org

Harry & Sons 820 N Highland Ave .... Atlanta GA 30306 404-873-2009 671
Web: surinofthailand.com

Harry Brainum Jr Inc
360 McGuinness Blvd .... Brooklyn NY 11222 718-389-4080 383-1646 697
TF: 800-540-7272 ■ *Web:* www.hbsteel.com

Harry Browne's 66 State Cir .... Annapolis MD 21401 410-263-4332 671
Web: www.harrybrownes.com

Harry Cooper Supply Company Inc
605 N Sherman Pkwy .... Springfield MO 65802 417-865-8392 612
TF: 800-426-6737 ■ *Web:* www.harrycooper.com

Harry Davis & Co
1725 Blvd of Allies .... Pittsburgh PA 15219 412-765-1170 765-0910 51
TF: 800-775-2289 ■ *Web:* harrydavis.com

Harry G. Barr Co 6500 S Zero St .... Fort Smith AR 72903 479-646-7891 646-8591 235
TF: 800-829-2277 ■ *Web:* www.weatherbarr.com

Harry Green Chevrolet Inc
1858 E Pike St .... Clarksburg WV 26302 304-624-6304 57
TF: 800-352-4389 ■ *Web:* www.harrygreenchevy.com

Harry Grodsky & Company Inc
33 Shaws Ln PO Box 880 .... Springfield MA 01101 413-785-1947 737-9870 189-10
TF: 800-843-4424 ■ *Web:* www.grodsky.com

Harry Hynes Memorial Hospice
313 S Market St .... Wichita KS 67202 316-265-9441 265-6066 371
TF: 800-767-4965 ■ *Web:* www.hynesmemorial.org

Harry Jernigan CPA Attorney PC
5101 Cleveland St Ste 200 .... Virginia Beach VA 23462 757-490-2200 490-0280 466
Web: www.hjlaw.com

Harry K. Dupree Stuttgart National Aquaculture Research Ctr
2955 Hwy 130 E PO Box 1050 .... Stuttgart AR 72160 870-673-4483 673-7710 668
Web: www.ars.usda.gov

Harry Kahn Associates Inc
13126 Pa Ave Ste 104 .... Hagerstown MD 21742 301-797-3390 797-3392 196
Web: harrykahn.com

Harry Klitzner Inc
530 Wellington Ave Ste 11 .... Cranston RI 02910 800-621-0161 622-9802 409
TF: 800-621-0161 ■ *Web:* www.klitzner.com

Harry L. Murphy Inc
42 Bonaventura Dr .... San Jose CA 95134 408-955-1100 955-1111 290
Web: www.harrylmurphyinc.com

Harry London Candies Inc
5353 Lauby Rd .... North Canton OH 44720 330-494-0833 296-8
TF: 800-333-3629 ■ *Web:* www.fanniemay.com

Harry Lundeberg Seamanship School Inc
45353 St George's Ave PO Box 75 .... Piney Point MD 20674 301-994-0010 685
Web: www.seafarers.org

Harry Miller Company Inc 19 Hampden St .... Boston MA 02119 617-427-2300 442-1152 733
Web: www.harrymiller.com

Harry N. Abrams Inc
115 W 18th St 6th Fl .... New York NY 10011 212-206-7715 519-1210 637-2
Web: www.abramsbooks.com

Harry P. Leu Gardens
1920 N Forest Ave .... Orlando FL 32803 407-246-2620 246-2849 97
Web: www.leugardens.org

Harry Ritchie's Jewelers Inc
956 Willamette St .... Eugene OR 97401 541-686-1787 485-8841 410
TF: 800-935-2850 ■ *Web:* harryritchies.com

Harry S. Truman Birthplace State Historic Site
1009 Truman St .... Lamar MO 64759 417-682-2279 565
Web: mostateparks.com

Harry S. Truman Memorial Veterans Hospital
800 Hospital Dr .... Columbia MO 65201 573-814-6000 814-6600 374-8
Web: www.columbiamo.va.gov

Harry S. Truman National Historic Site
223 N Main St .... Independence MO 64050 816-254-2720 254-4491 564
Web: www.nps.gov

Harry S. Truman Presidential Library & Museum
500 W Hwy 24 .... Independence MO 64050 816-268-8200 268-8295 434-2
TF: 800-833-1225 ■ *Web:* www.trumanlibrary.gov

Harry S. Truman Scholarship Foundation
712 Jackson Pl NW .... Washington DC 20006 202-395-4831 395-6995 725
Web: www.truman.gov

Harry S. Truman State Park
28761 State Park Rd .... Warsaw MO 65355 660-438-7711 565
Web: mostateparks.com

Harry S. Truman's Little White House Museum
111 Front St .... Key West FL 33040 305-294-9911 294-9988 520
Web: www.trumanlittlewhitehouse.com

Harry W. Gorst Company Inc
9310 Topanga Canyon Blvd .... Chatsworth CA 91311 818-507-0900 390
Web: gorstcompass.com

Harry Walker Agency Inc (HWA)
355 Lexington Ave .... New York NY 10017 646-227-4900 708
Web: www.harrywalker.com

Harry Winston Inc 718 Fifth Ave .... New York NY 10019 212-399-1000 409
TF: 800-988-4110 ■ *Web:* www.harrywinston.com

Harry's Continental Kitchens
525 St Judes Dr .... Longboat Key FL 34228 941-383-0777 383-2029 671
Web: harryskitchen.com

Harry's Nurses Registry
88-25 163rd St .... Jamaica NY 11432 718-739-0045 739-0102 363
Web: harryhomecare.com

Harry's Savoy Grill
2020 Naamans Rd .... Wilmington DE 19810 302-475-3000 475-9990 671
Web: www.harryshospitalitygroup.com

Harsco Corp 350 Poplar Church Rd .... Camp Hill PA 17011 717-763-7064 763-6424 185
NYSE: HSC ■ *TF:* 866-470-3900 ■ *Web:* www.harsco.com

Harsco Rail
2401 Edmund Rd PO Box 20 .... West Columbia SC 29171 803-822-9160 822-8107 650
Web: www.harscorail.com

Harsh International Inc 600 Oak Ave .... Eaton CO 80615 970-454-2291 273
Web: www.harshenviro.com

Hart & Price Corp PO Box 36368 .... Dallas TX 75235 214-521-9129 350-4143 665
TF: 800-777-9129 ■ *Web:* www.hartprice.com

Hart Associates Inc 811 Madison Ave .... Toledo OH 43604 419-893-9600 893-9070 4
Web: www.hartinc.com

Hart County 800 Chandler St .... Hartwell GA 30643 706-376-2024 376-9477 338
Web: www.hartcountyga.org

Hart County
10337 Cub Run Hwy PO Box 277 .... Munfordville KY 42765 270-524-2751 524-0458 338
Web: hartcounty.ky.gov

Hart County Charter System
284 Campbell Dr PO Box 696 .... Hartwell GA 30643 706-376-5141 376-7046 685
Web: www.hart.k12.ga.us

Hart Crowser Inc
3131 Elliott Ave Ste 600 .... Seattle WA 98109 206-324-9530 328-5581 261
Web: www.hartcrowser.com

Hart Davis Hart Wine Co
363 W Erie St Ste 500W .... Chicago IL 60654 312-482-9996 443
Web: www.hdhwine.com

Hart Electric Membership Corp
1071 Elberton Hwy .... Hartwell GA 30643 706-376-4714 245
TF: 800-241-4109 ■ *Web:* www.hartemc.com

Hart Engineering Corp
800 Scenic View Dr .... Cumberland RI 02864 401-658-4600 658-4609 256
Web: www.hartcompanies.com

Hart Hotels Inc 617 Dingens St .... Buffalo NY 14206 716-893-6551 194
Web: harthotels.com

Hart Industries Inc
11412 Cronridge Dr .... Owings Mills MD 21117 410-581-1900 627
TF: 800-638-2700 ■ *Web:* www.hartind.com

Name / Address	City	State	ZIP	Phone	Fax	Class
Hart InterCivic 15500 Wells Port Dr *TF:* 800-223-4278 ■ *Web:* www.hartintercivic.com	Austin	TX	78728	800-223-4278		801
Hart Interim Library 214 N Church St *Web:* www.rockfordpubliclibrary.org	Rockford	IL	61101	815-965-7606	963-7834	434-3
Hart King 4 Hutton Centre Dr Ste 900 *TF:* 866-718-7148 ■ *Web:* www.hartkinglaw.com	Santa Ana	CA	92707	714-432-8700	546-7457	445
Hart Medical Equipment 2001 Holland Ave *Web:* hartmedical.org	Port Huron	MI	48060	810-982-0700	982-0126	374-3
Hart Precision Products Inc 12700 Marion *Web:* hart-precision.com	Redford	MI	48239	313-537-0490		22
Hart Publications Inc 1616 S Voss Rd Ste 1000 *TF:* 800-874-2544 ■ *Web:* www.hartenergy.com	Houston	TX	77057	713-260-6400	840-8585	637-9
Hart Ranch Camping Resort Club 23756 Arena Dr *TF:* 800-605-4278 ■ *Web:* www.hrresort.org	Rapid City	SD	57702	605-399-2582		121
Hart Realty Advisers Inc 92 Hopmeadow St 3rd Fl *Web:* www.hartadvisers.com	Simsbury	CT	06089	860-651-4000	651-4016	652
Hart Schaffner & Marx (HSM) 101 N Wacker Dr *Web:* www.hartschaffnermarx.com	Chicago	IL	60606	847-257-4644		155-12
Hart Scientific Inc 799 E Utah Vly Dr *Web:* us.flukecal.com	American Fork	UT	84003	801-763-1600	763-1010	201
Hart Specialties Inc 5000 New Horizons Blvd *TF:* 800-221-6966 ■ *Web:* www.newyorkeye.net	Amityville	NY	11701	631-226-5600	226-5884	543
Hart Telephone Co (HTC) 196 N Forest Ave *TF:* 800-276-3925 ■ *Web:* www.htconline.net	Hartwell	GA	30643	706-376-4701		224
Harte Nissan 165 W Service Rd *TF:* 866-687-8971 ■ *Web:* www.hartenissan.com	Hartford	CT	06120	860-549-2800		57
Harte-Hanks Inc 9601 McAllister Fwy Ste 610 *NYSE: HHS* ■ *TF:* 800-456-9748 ■ *Web:* www.hartehanks.com	San Antonio	TX	78216	210-829-0000	829-0403	5
Harter Industries Inc 401 W Gemini Dr *Web:* www.harter.aero	Tempe	AZ	85283	480-345-9595	345-9211	22
Harter Secrest & Emery LLP (HSE) 1600 Bausch & Lomb Pl *Web:* www.hselaw.com	Rochester	NY	14604	585-232-6500	232-2152	428
Hartford Area Career & Technology Ctr 1 Gifford Rd *Web:* www.hactc.com	White River Junction	VT	05001	802-295-8630	295-8631	800
Hartford Beach State Park 13672 Hartford Beach Rd *Web:* gfp.sd.gov	Corona	SD	57227	605-432-6374		565
Hartford Casualty Insurance Co 690 Asylum Ave *TF:* 800-243-5860 ■ *Web:* www.thehartford.com	Hartford	CT	06155	866-553-5663		391-4
Hartford City Hall 550 Main St *Web:* www.hartfordct.gov	Hartford	CT	06103	860-757-9311		337
Hartford Computer Group Inc 10440 Little Patuxent Pkwy Ste 810 *Web:* hcgi.com	Columbia	MD	21044	410-202-8042	740-8732	180
Hartford Correctional Ctr 177 Weston St *Web:* portal.ct.gov	Hartford	CT	06120	959-200-3000	200-3008	213
Hartford Courant 285 Broad St *TF:* 800-524-4242 ■ *Web:* www.courant.com	Hartford	CT	06115	860-241-6200	520-6941	532-2
Hartford Despatch Moving & Storage Inc 225 Prospect St *Web:* www.hartforddespatch.com	East Hartford	CT	06108	860-528-9551		519
Hartford Electric Supply Co (HESCO) 30 Inwood Rd Ste 1 *TF:* 800-969-5444 ■ *Web:* www.hesconet.com	Rocky Hill	CT	06067	860-236-6363	236-0233	246
Hartford Foundation for Public Giving 10 Columbus Blvd 8th Fl *Web:* www.hfpg.org	Hartford	CT	06106	860-548-1888	524-8346	303
Hartford Funds 30 Dan Rd Ste 55022 *TF:* 888-843-7824 ■ *Web:* www.hartfordfunds.com	Canton	MA	02021	000-043-7024		528
Hartford Hospital 80 Seymour St *TF:* 800-545-7664 ■ *Web:* hartfordhospital.org	Hartford	CT	06102	860-545-5000	545-3622	374-3
Hartford Investment Management Co 1 Hartford Plz *TF:* 866-403-4733 ■ *Web:* www.himco.com	Hartford	CT	06155	860-297-6700		401
Hartford News 563 Franklin Ave *Web:* www.hartfordpublicationscom.wordpress.com	Hartford	CT	06114	860-296-6128		532-4
Hartford Public Library 500 Main St *Web:* www.hplct.org	Hartford	CT	06103	860-695-6300	722-6900	434-3
Hartford Public Schools 960 Main St *Web:* www.hartfordschools.org	Hartford	CT	06103	860-695-8000		685
Hartford Seminary 77 Sherman St *TF:* 877-860-2255 ■ *Web:* www.hartsem.edu	Hartford	CT	06105	860-509-9500	509-9509	166
Hartford Stage Co 50 Church St *Web:* www.hartfordstage.org	Hartford	CT	06103	860-527-5151	247-8243	749
Hartford Steam Boiler Inspection and Insurance Co, The 1 State St *Web:* www.munichre.com	Hartford	CT	06103	860-722-1866	722-5106	391-4
Hartford Technologies Inc 1022 Elm St *Web:* www.hartfordtechnologies.com	Rocky Hill	CT	06067	860-571-3602	571-3604	75
Hartgrove Hospital 5730 W Roosevelt Rd *TF:* 888-536-9589 ■ *Web:* www.hartgrovehospital.com	Chicago	IL	60644	773-413-1700		374-5
Hartig Drug Co 703 Main St *Web:* www.hartigdrug.com	Dubuque	IA	52001	563-588-8700	588-8750	237
Hartle & Rees LLC 448 E Winche Ste 225 *Web:* hrtaxcpa.com	Salt Lake City	UT	84107	801-904-2070	904-3809	2
Hartley County 900 Main St *Web:* www.co.hartley.tx.us	Channing	TX	79018	806-235-3582	235-2316	338
Hartley Data Service Inc (HDS) 1807 Glenview Rd Ste 201 *Web:* hartleydata.com	Glenview	IL	60025	847-724-9280	729-2199	225
Hartley Michon Robb LLP 155 Seaport Blvd 2nd Fl *Web:* hartleymichonrobb.com	Boston	MA	02210	617-723-8000		41
Hartley, Rowe & Fowler PC 6622 Broad St *Web:* www.hrflegal.com	Douglasville	GA	30134	770-920-2000		428
Hartley-Racon 1987 Placentia Ave *Web:* www.hartleyraconusa.com	Costa Mesa	CA	92627	949-646-9643	548-1220	571
Hartline Barger LLP 8750 N Central Expy Ste 1600 *Web:* hartlinebarger.com	Dallas	TX	75231	214-369-2100		428
Hartman Blitch & Gartside 4929 Atlantic Blvd *Web:* www.hbgcpa.com	Jacksonville	FL	32207	904-396-9802	396-1528	2
Hartman Creek State Park N2480 Hartman Creek Rd *Web:* dnr.wi.gov	Waupaca	WI	54981	715-258-2372		565
Hartman Enterprises Inc 455 Elizabeth St *Web:* www.hartmanenterprises.com	Oneida	NY	13421	315-363-7300	363-0314	454
Hartman Publishing Inc 8529 Indian School Rd NE **Fax Area Code:* 800 ■ *TF:* 800-999-9534 ■ *Web:* www.hartmanonline.com	Albuquerque	NM	87112	505-291-1274	474-6106*	637-2
Hartman, Simons, Spielman & Wood LLP 6400 Powers Ferry Rd NW Ste 400 *Web:* www.hartmansimons.com	Atlanta	GA	30339	770-955-3555		428
Hartman-Walsh Painting Co 7144 N Market St *Web:* www.hartmanwalsh.com	Saint Louis	MO	63133	314-863-1800	863-6964	189-8
Hartnell College 156 Homestead Ave *Web:* www.hartnell.edu	Salinas	CA	93901	831-755-6700	759-6014	162
Hartness House Inn 30 Orchard St *Web:* hartnesshouseinn.com	Springfield	VT	05156	802-885-2115		379
Hartness International Inc 500 Hartness Dr PO Box 26509 *TF:* 800-845-8791 ■ *Web:* www.hartness.com	Greenville	SC	29615	864-297-1200	297-4486	547
Hartnett Law Firm, The 2920 N Pearl St *TF:* 800-900-9702 ■ *Web:* www.hartnettlawfirm.com	Dallas	TX	75201	214-742-4655		428
Hartselle Big LLC 8200 113th St N Ste 201 *TF:* 800-749-6213 ■ *Web:* hartselleinsurance.com	Seminole	FL	33772	727-393-5000	391-1204	390
Hartselle Enquirer PO Box 929 *Web:* www.hartselleenquirer.com	Hartselle	AL	35640	256-773-6566	773-1953	532-4
Hartsfield-Jackson Atlanta International Airport 6000 N Terminal Pkwy Ste 4000 *Web:* www.atl.com	Atlanta	GA	30320	404-530-6600	530-6803	27
Hartson-kennedy Cabinet Top Company Inc 522 W 22nd St PO Box 3095 **Fax Area Code:* 765 ■ *TF:* 800-388-8144 ■ *Web:* www.hartson-kennedy.com	Marion	IN	46953	800-388-8144	662-3452*	599
Hartsville Oil Mill 311 Washington St	Darlington	SC	29532	843-393-2855		296-29
Hartt Transportation Systems Inc 262 Bomarc Rd *TF:* 800-341-1586 ■ *Web:* www.hartt-trans.com	Bangor	ME	04402	207-992-5900		780
Hartung Bros Inc 708 Heartland Trl Ste 2000 *TF:* 800-362-2522 ■ *Web:* www.hartungbrothers.com	Madison	WI	53717	608-829-6000	829-6001	10-11
Hartung Glass Industries 10450 SW Ridder Rd *TF:* 800-552-2227 ■ *Web:* hartung-glass.com	Wilsonville	OR	97070	503-682-3846		329
Hartwell Corp 900 Richfield Rd *Web:* www.hartwellcorp.com	Placentia	CA	92870	714-993-4200	579-4419	350
Hartwell Medical Corp 6354 Corte del Abeto Ste F *TF:* 800-633-5900 ■ *Web:* www.hartwellmedical.com	Carlsbad	CA	92011	760-438-5500		476
Hartwell Vineyards 5795 Silverado Trail *Web:* www.hartwellvineyards.com	Napa	CA	94558	707-255-4269		443
Hartwick College 1 Hartwick Dr *TF:* 888-427-8942 ■ *Web:* www.hartwick.edu	Oneonta	NY	13820	607-431-4150	431-4154	166
Hartwick Pines State Park 4216 Ranger Rd *Web:* www.michigan.org	Grayling	MI	49738	989-348-7068		565
Hartwig Inc 10617 Trenton Ave *TF:* 866-646-3660 ■ *Web:* www.hartwiginc.com	Saint Louis	MO	63132	314-426-5300	426-5311	358
Hartwood Mansion 200 Hartwood Acres *Web:* alleghenycounty.us	Pittsburgh	PA	15238	412-767-9200		50-3
Harty Integrated Solutions 25 James St *TF:* 800-654-0562 ■ *Web:* www.hartynet.com	New Haven	CT	06513	203-562-5112	782-9168	627
Hartz Construction Company Inc 9026 Heritage Pkwy *Web:* www.hartzhomes.com	Woodridge	IL	60517	630-228-3800		653
Hartz Mountain Corp, The 400 Plaza Dr *TF:* 800-275-1414 ■ *Web:* www.hartz.com	Secaucus	NJ	07094	800-275-1414		578
Hartz Mountain Industries Inc 400 Plaza Dr PO Box 1515 *Web:* www.hartzmountain.com	Secaucus	NJ	07096	201-348-1200	348-4358	360-3
Hartzell Engine Technologies LLC 2900 Selma Hwy *TF:* 877-359-5355 ■ *Web:* hartzell.aero	Montgomery	AL	36108	334-386-5400		21
Hartzell Fan Inc 910 S Downing St *TF:* 800-336-3267 ■ *Web:* hartzellairmovement.com	Piqua	OH	45356	937-773-7411	773-8994	18
Hartzell Hardwoods 1025 S Roosevelt Ave *Web:* www.hartzellhardwoods.com	Piqua	OH	45356	937-773-7054	773-6160	683
Hartzell Machine Works Inc 3354 Market St *Web:* www.hartzellmachineworks.com	Upper Chichester	PA	19014	610-485-3502	485-7471	454
Hartzell Propeller Inc 1 Propeller Pl *TF:* 800-942-7767 ■ *Web:* www.hartzellprop.com	Piqua	OH	45356	937-778-4200	778-4321	22
Hartzler Vicky (Rep R - MO) 2235 Rayburn House Office Bldg *Web:* www.hartzler.house.gov	Washington	DC	20515	202-225-2876		342-2
Haruki East 172 Wayland Ave *Web:* harukisushi.com	Providence	RI	02906	401-223-0332		671
Harvard Bioscience Inc 84 October Hill Rd Ste 10 *NASDAQ: HBIO* ■ *TF:* 800-272-2775 ■ *Web:* www.harvardbioscience.com	Holliston	MA	01746	508-893-8999	429-5732	419

	Phone	Fax	Class
Harvard Book Store Inc 1256 Massachusetts Ave, Cambridge MA 02138 — *TF:* 800-542-7323 ■ *Web:* www.harvard.com	617-661-1515		95
Harvard Business Review 60 Harvard Way, Boston MA 02163 — *TF:* 800-274-3214 ■ *Web:* hbr.org	617-783-7500		457-5
Harvard Business School Publishing 60 Harvard Way, Boston MA 02163 — *TF:* 800-795-5200 ■ *Web:* www.harvardbusiness.org	800-795-5200		637-4
Harvard Collection Services Inc 4839 N Elston Ave, Chicago IL 60630 — *Web:* www.harvardcollect.com	773-283-7500		160
Harvard Crimson Inc, The 14 Plympton St, Cambridge MA 02138 — *Web:* www.thecrimson.com	617-576-6600		557
Harvard Drug Group LLC 17177 N Laurel Pk Ste 233, Livonia MI 48152 — *TF:* 800-875-0123 ■ *Web:* www.theharvarddruggroup.com	800-875-0123		238
Harvard Educational Review 8 Story St 1st Fl, Cambridge MA 02138 — *TF:* 888-437-1437 ■ *Web:* hepg.org	617-495-3432	496-3584	457-8
Harvard Law Review 1511 Massachusetts Ave Gannett House, Cambridge MA 02138 — *Web:* harvardlawreview.org	617-495-4650		457-15
Harvard Law School Library (HLSL) 1563 Massachusetts Ave, Cambridge MA 02138 — *Web:* hls.harvard.edu	617-495-3100	495-1110	637-2
Harvard Management Company Inc 600 Atlantic Ave, Boston MA 02210 — *Web:* www.hmc.harvard.edu	617-523-4400		792
Harvard Medical School 25 Shattuck St, Boston MA 02115 — *TF:* 866-606-0573 ■ *Web:* hms.harvard.edu	617-432-1550		167-2
Harvard Museum of Natural History Harvard University 26 Oxford St, Cambridge MA 02138 — *Web:* www.mcz.harvard.edu	617-495-5891	496-8308	520
Harvard Pilgrim Health Care Inc 93 Worcester St, Wellesley MA 02481 — **Fax Area Code:* 617 ■ *TF:* 888-888-4742 ■ *Web:* www.harvardpilgrim.org	866-750-2074	509-2515*	391-3
Harvard Square Co-opeartive Society 1400 Massachusetts Ave, Cambridge MA 02238 — *Web:* www.harvardsquare.com	617-499-2000		95
Harvard Square Hotel Harvard Sq 110 Mt Auburn St, Cambridge MA 02138 — *TF:* 800-458-5886 ■ *Web:* www.harvardsquarehotel.com	617-864-5200	864-2409	379
Harvard Student Agencies Inc 67 Mt Auburn St, Cambridge MA 02138 — *Web:* www.hsa.net	617-495-3030	496-8015	260
Harvard Ukrainian Research Institute (HURI) 34 Kirkland St, Cambridge MA 02138 — *Web:* www.huri.harvard.edu	617-495-4053	495-8097	637-2
Harvard University 12 Holyoke St, Cambridge MA 02138 — *Web:* www.harvard.edu	617-495-1000	495-8821	166
Harvard University Press 79 Garden St, Cambridge MA 02138 — **Fax Area Code:* 800 ■ *Web:* www.hup.harvard.edu	617-495-2600	406-9145*	637-4
Harvard Women's Health Watch PO Box 9308, Big Sandy TX 75755 — *TF:* 877-649-9457 ■ *Web:* www.health.harvard.edu	877-649-9457		531-8
Harvard-Smithsonian Center for Astrophysics 60 Garden St, Cambridge MA 02138 — *Web:* www.cfa.harvard.edu	617-495-7301	495-7468	668
Harvest 44 Brattle St, Cambridge MA 02138 — *Web:* harvestcambridge.com	617-868-2255		671
Harvest Christian Fellowship 6115 Arlington Ave, Riverside CA 92504 — *Web:* harvest.church	951-687-6902		48-20
Harvest Health Foods 1944 Eastern Ave SE, Grand Rapids MI 49507 — *Web:* harvesthealthfoods.com	616-245-6268		297-8
Harvest Inn 1 Main St, Saint Helena CA 94574 — *TF:* 800-950-8466 ■ *Web:* www.harvestinn.com	707-963-9463		379
Harvest Moon Studio 3516 Dover St, Los Angeles CA 90039 — *Web:* www.harvestmoonstudio.com	323-660-3444		514
Harvest Operations Corp 700 Second St SW Ste 1500, Calgary AB T2P2W1 — *TF:* 866-666-1178 ■ *Web:* www.harvestoperations.com	403-265-1178	265-3490	675
Harvest Partners 280 Park Ave 25th Fl, New York NY 10017 — *TF:* 866-771-1000 ■ *Web:* harvestpartners.com	212-599-6300	812-0100	792
Harvest Vine 2701 E Madison St, Seattle WA 98112 — *Web:* www.harvestvine.com	206-320-9771		671
Harvest Word of Life Ministries International Inc 2260 Lake Ave PO Box 5734, Fort Wayne IN 46845	260-422-5750		48-20
Harvester Financial Credit Union 7020 Brookville Rd, Indianapolis IN 46239 — *TF:* 800-326-2279 ■ *Web:* harvesterfcu.org	317-352-0455	351-2351	219
Harvey 952 Ridgebrook Rd Ste 1000, Sparks MD 21152 — *Web:* www.harveyagency.com	410-771-5566		7
Harvey & Company LLC 5000 Birch St Ste 9200, Newport Beach CA 92660 — *Web:* www.harveyllc.com	949-757-0400	757-0404	405
Harvey & Lewis Company of Hartford Inc 45 Asylum St, Hartford CT 06103 — *Web:* harveyandlewis.com	860-522-2020		543
Harvey Alpert & Company Inc 2014 S Sepulveda Blvd Ste 200, Los Angeles CA 90025 — *Web:* www.haco.us.com	310-689-6000		297-8
Harvey Cadillac Co 2600 28th St SE, Grand Rapids MI 49512 — *TF:* 877-845-1557 ■ *Web:* www.harveycadillac.com	616-949-1140	954-1201	57
Harvey County 800 N Main PO Box 687, Newton KS 67114 — *Web:* www.harveycounty.com	316-284-6840	284-6856	338
Harvey Hohauser & Assoc 5600 New King Dr Ste 355, Troy MI 48098 — *Web:* www.hohauser.com	248-641-1400		196
Harvey Industries Inc 1400 Main St, Waltham MA 02451 — *TF:* 800-598-5400 ■ *Web:* www.harveybp.com	800-598-5400		191-4
Harvey Klinger Inc 300 W 55th St, New York NY 10019 — *Web:* www.harveyklinger.com	212-581-7068		444
Harvey Mudd College 301 Platt Blvd, Claremont CA 91711 — *TF:* 877-827-5462 ■ *Web:* www.hmc.edu	909-621-8000	607-7046	166

	Phone	Fax	Class
Harvey School 260 Jay St, Katonah NY 10536 — *Web:* www.harveyschool.org	914-232-3161		622
Harvey Software Inc 7050 Winkler Rd Ste 104, Fort Myers FL 33919 — *TF:* 800-231-0296 ■ *Web:* www.harveysoft.com	800-231-0296		177
Harvey Vogel Manufacturing Co 425 Weir Dr, Woodbury MN 55125 — *Web:* www.harveyvogel.com	651-739-7373	739-8666	488
Harvey Watt & Co 475 N Central Ave, Atlanta GA 30354 — *TF:* 800-241-6103 ■ *Web:* www.harveywatt.com	404-767-7501	761-8326	391-2
Harvey Wheeler Community Ctr 1276 Main St, Concord MA 01742 — *Web:* www.concordma.gov	978-318-3020		720
Harvey-Cleary Builders 6710A Rockledge Dr Ste 430, Bethesda MD 20817 — *Web:* harveycleary.com	301-519-2288		186
Harvill's Produce Co 8775 S Orange Ave, Orlando FL 32824 — *TF:* 800-356-0918 ■ *Web:* www.harvillsproduce.com	407-843-4331	648-4991	297-7
Harvin Clarendon County Library 215 N Brooks St, Manning SC 29102 — *Web:* www.clarendoncountylibrary.com	803-435-8633		434-3
Harwood Engineering Consultant 255 N 21st St, Milwaukee WI 53233 — *Web:* www.hecl.com	414-475-5554		256
Harwood International Corp 4713 Gann Store Rd 100 Northshore Office Pk, Hixson TN 37343 — *TF:* 800-390-2567 ■ *Web:* www.harwood-intl.com	423-870-5500	870-5199	174
Harwood Lloyd LLC 130 Main St, Hackensack NJ 07601 — *Web:* www.harwoodlloyd.com	201-487-1080		428
Hasbro Inc 1027 Newport Ave, Pawtucket RI 02861 — *NASDAQ: HAS* ■ *TF:* 800-242-7276 ■ *Web:* www.hasbro.com	401-431-8697	431-8082	762
Hasbrouck Geophysics Inc 12 Woodside Dr, Prescott AZ 86305 — *Web:* www.hasgeo.com	928-778-6320		192
Hasbrouck Heights School District 379 Blvd, Hasbrouck Heights NJ 07604 — *Web:* www.hhschools.org	201-288-6150		187
Hascall Steel Co 4165 Spartan Industrial Dr, Grandville MI 49418 — *Web:* www.hascallsteel.com	616-531-8600	531-7555	492
HASCO America Inc 270 Rutledge Rd Unit B, Fletcher NC 28732 — *Web:* www.hasco.com	828-650-2600		697
Hasco Oil Company Inc 2800 Temple Ave, Long Beach CA 90806 — *TF:* 800-456-8491 ■ *Web:* www.hascooil.com	562-595-8491		579
Hasco Relays & Electronics International Corp 906 Jericho Tpke, New Hyde Park NY 11040 — *Web:* www.hascorelays.com	516-328-9292		203
HASD (Hamburg Area School District) 701 Windsor St, Hamburg PA 19526 — *Web:* www.hasdhawks.org	610-562-2241	562-2634	685
Hasd & ic 5575 Ruffin Rd Ste 225, San Diego CA 92123 — *Web:* hasdic.org	858-614-0200	614-0201	466
Haselden Construction LLC 6950 S Potomac St, Centennial CO 80112 — *Web:* www.haselden.com	303-751-1478		186
Hashi Corp 101 2nd St Ste 700, San Francisco CA 94105 — *Web:* www.hashicorp.com	415-301-3250		657
Haskel International Inc 100 E Graham Pl, Burbank CA 91502 — *TF:* 800-743-2720 ■ *Web:* www.haskel.com	818-843-4000	841-4291	641
Haskel Thompson & Associates LLC 12734 Kenwood Ln Ste 74, Fort Myers FL 33907 — *TF:* 800-470-4226 ■ *Web:* haskelthompson.com	239-437-4600		260
Haskell & White LLP 300 Spectrum Center Dr Ste 300, Irvine CA 92618 — *Web:* www.hwcpa.com	949-450-6200		2
Haskell Co 111 Riverside Ave, Jacksonville FL 32202 — *TF:* 800-622-4326 ■ *Web:* www.haskell.com	904-791-4500	791-4699	188-7
Haskell Corp 1001 Meador Ave PO Box 917, Bellingham WA 98229 — *Web:* www.haskellcorp.com	360-734-1200	734-5538	186
Haskell County 1 Ave D, Haskell TX 79521 — *Web:* www.co.haskell.tx.us	940-864-3448		338
Haskell County PO Box 518, Sublette KS 67877 — *Web:* www.haskellcounty.org	620-675-2263	675-2681	338
Haskell Indian Nations University 155 Indian Ave PO Box 5031, Lawrence KS 66046 — *Web:* www.haskell.edu	785-749-8454	749-8429	165
Haskett Law Firm Pc 5820 Stoneridge Mall Rd Ste 207, Pleasanton CA 94588 — *Web:* haskettlaw.com	925-460-8850	460-9987	41
Haskins Laboratories Library 300 George St Ste 900, New Haven CT 06511 — *Web:* www.haskins.yale.edu	203-865-6163		434-3
Haskris Co 100 Kelly St, Elk Grove Village IL 60007 — *Web:* haskris.com	847-956-6420		14
Haslett Public School 5593 Franklin St, Haslett MI 48840 — *Web:* www.haslett.k12.mi.us	517-339-8242	339-1360	685
Hass Avocado Board 38 Discovery Ste 150, Irvine CA 92618 — *Web:* www.hassavocadoboard.com	949-341-3250		138
Hassan Margaret Wood (Sen D - NH) 324 Hart Senate Office Bldg, Washington DC 20510 — *Web:* www.hassan.senate.gov	202-224-3324		342-2
Hassayampa Inn 122 E Gurley St, Prescott AZ 86301 — *TF:* 800-322-1927 ■ *Web:* www.hassayampainn.com	928-778-9434	445-8590	379
Hassett Air Express 18W100 22nd St Ste 109, Oakbrook Terrace IL 60181 — *Web:* www.hassettexpress.com	630-530-6515		311
Hastings Alcee L (Rep D - FL) 2353 Rayburn House Office Bldg, Washington DC 20515 — *Web:* www.alceehastings.house.gov	202-225-1313	225-1171	342-2
Hastings Area Chamber of Commerce & Tourism Bureau 314 Vermillion St Ste 100, Hastings MN 55033 — *Web:* www.hastingsmn.org	651-437-6775	437-2697	139

				Phone	Fax	Class
Hastings Automotive Inc 3625 Vermillion St *TF:* 888-218-6155 ■ *Web:* www.hastingsautos.com	Hastings	MN	55033	651-437-4030		57
Hastings Bus Co 425 E 31st St *Web:* www.hastingsbuscompany.com	Hastings	MN	55033	651-437-1888		109
Hastings College 710 N Turner Ave *TF:* 800-532-7642 ■ *Web:* www.hastings.edu	Hastings	NE	68901	402-463-2402	461-7490	166
Hastings Co-operative Creamery Co 1701 Vermillion St PO Box 217 *Web:* www.hastingscreamery.com	Hastings	MN	55033	651-437-9414		345
Hastings Equity Mfg 1900 Summit Ave PO Box 1007 *TF:* 888-883-2189 ■ *Web:* www.hastingstank.com	Hastings	NE	68901	402-462-2189	462-2900	273
Hastings Fiber Glass Products Inc 770 Cook Rd PO Box 218 *Web:* www.hfgp.com	Hastings	MI	49058	269-945-9541	945-4623	758
Hastings Floor Covering Inc 919 Salem St *Web:* hastingsfloor.com	Groveland	MA	01834	978-521-8848		290
Hastings House Country House Hotel 160 Upper Ganges Rd *TF:* 800-661-9255 ■ *Web:* www.hastingshouse.com	Salt Spring Island	BC	V8K2S2	800-661-9255		379
Hastings HVAC Inc 3606 Yost Ave *TF:* 800-228-4243 ■ *Web:* www.hastingshvac.com	Hastings	NE	68901	402-463-9821	463-6273	14
Hastings Manufacturing Co 325 N Hanover St *TF:* 800-776-1088 ■ *Web:* www.hastingspistonrings.com	Hastings	MI	49058	269-945-2491	945-4667	128
Hastings Pavement Company LLC 200 Henry St *Web:* www.hastingsarchitectural.com	Lindenhurst	NY	11757	631-669-0600	669-8052	183
Hastings Pork 301 S Burlington Ave *Web:* www.hastingschamber.com	Hastings	NE	68901	402-461-8400		10-6
Hastings Public Library 314 N Denver Ave *Web:* hastingslibrary.us	Hastings	NE	68901	402-461-2346		434-3
Hastings Water Works Inc 10331 Brecksville Rd *Web:* www.hastingswaterworks.com	Brecksville	OH	44141	440-832-7700		104
Hastings, Jamieson & Lipschutz Family Law Group LLP 859 Turnpike St Ste 232 *Web:* nalegal.com	North Andover	MA	01845	978-681-5665		41
Hasty Plywood Co 100 N Austin St	Maxton	NC	28364	910-844-5267		613
Hat World Corp 7555 Woodland Dr **Fax Area Code: 317* ■ *TF:* 888-564-4287 ■ *Web:* www.lids.com	Indianapolis	IN	46278	888-564-4287	337-1428*	157-5
Hatboro Federal Savings 221 S York Rd *Web:* www.hatborofed.com	Hatboro	PA	19040	215-675-4000	672-6684	70
Hatboro-Horsham School District 229 Meetinghouse Rd *Web:* www.hatboro-horsham.org	Horsham	PA	19044	215-672-5660	420-5262	685
Hatch & Bailey Company Inc 1 Meadow St Ext *Web:* www.hatchandbailey.com	Norwalk	CT	06854	203-866-5515	854-1712	191-3
Hatch & Kirk Inc 5111 Leary Ave NW *TF:* 800-426-2818 ■ *Web:* www.hatchkirk.com	Seattle	WA	98107	206-783-2766	782-6482	262
Hatch Stamping Co 635 E Industrial Dr *Web:* www.hatchstamping.com	Chelsea	MI	48118	734-475-8628	475-6255	489
HatchBeauty Brands LLC 10951 W Pico Blvd Ste 300 *TF:* 855-895-6980 ■ *Web:* www.hatchbeautybrands.com	Los Angeles	CA	90064	855-895-6980		195
Hatcher Consultants Inc (HCI) 2955 SW Wanamaker Dr *Web:* www.hatcherci.com	Topeka	KS	66614	785-271-5557	271-8333	463
Hatchik Supply Co 5260 Port Royal Rd *Web:* hatchiksupplyonline.com	Springfield	VA	22151	703-321-7699	321-8478	189-11
Hatfield & Dawson 9500 Greenwood Ave N *Web:* hatdaw.com	Seattle	WA	98103	206-783-9151		261
Hatfield Enterprizes Inc 16715 E Euclid Ave *Web:* hatfieldent.com	Spokane Valley	WA	99216	509-927-8357		780
Hatfield Marine Science Ctr 2030 SE Marine Science Dr *Web:* www.hmsc.oregonstate.edu	Newport	OR	97365	541-867-0100	867-0138	668
Hatfield Quality Meats Inc 2700 Clemens Rd *TF:* 800-743-1191 ■ *Web:* www.hatfieldqualitymeats.com	Hatfield	PA	19440	215-368-2500		473
Hathaway Dinwiddie Construction Co 275 Battery St Ste 300 *Web:* www.hathawaydinwiddie.com	San Francisco	CA	94111	415-986-2718		186
Hathaway Inc 347 S Oak Ln *TF:* 800-323-2138 ■ *Web:* www.hathawaypaper.com	Waynesboro	VA	22980	540-949-8285	943-7619	559
Hathaway-Sycamores Child & Family Services 210 S DeLacey Ave Ste 110 *Web:* www.hathaway-sycamores.org	Pasadena	CA	91105	626-395-7100		726
Hattenbach Co, The 5309 Hamilton Ave *TF:* 800-966-5204 ■ *Web:* www.hattenbach.com	Cleveland	OH	44114	216-881-5200		115
Hatteras 56 Park Rd *Web:* www.hatteras.us	Tinton Falls	NJ	07724	732-223-9888		627
Hatteras Hammocks Inc 305 Industrial Blvd *TF:* 800-643-3522 ■ *Web:* www.hatterashammocks.com	Greenville	NC	27834	252-758-0641	758-0375	319-4
Hatteras Inc 12801 Prospect St *Web:* www.4hatteras.com	Dearborn	MI	48126	313-624-3300	624-3350	627
Hatteras Yachts Inc 110 N Glenburnie Rd *Web:* www.hatterasyachts.com	New Bern	NC	28560	252-633-3101		90
Hattiesburg American 825 N Main St *TF:* 800-844-2637 ■ *Web:* www.hattiesburgamerican.com	Hattiesburg	MS	39401	800-844-2637		532-2
Hattiesburg Zoo 107 S 17th Ave *Web:* www.hattiesburgms.com	Hattiesburg	MS	39401	601-545-4500		823
Hattiesburg-Laurel Regional Airport 1002 Terminal Dr *Web:* www.flypib.com	Moselle	MS	39459	601-649-2444	545-3155	27
Hatton Brown Publishers Inc PO Box 2268 *TF:* 800-669-5613 ■ *Web:* www.hattonbrown.net	Montgomery	AL	36102	334-834-1170		637-9
Hatzel & Buehler Inc PO Box 7499 *Web:* www.hatzelandbuehler.com	Wilmington	DE	19810	302-478-4200	478-2750	189-4
Hauck & Associates Inc 1000 Potomac St NW Ste 108 *Web:* www.hauck.com	Washington	DC	20007	202-521-6725	833-3636	47
Haug Communications Inc 622 Neptune Dr *Web:* www.bbwi.net	Seneca	KS	66538	785-336-3579		225
Haulsey Engineering Inc 10755 Scripps Poway Pkwy Ste 466 *Web:* www.haulseyengr.com	San Diego	CA	92131	858-271-1780	271-4360	256
Haumiller Engineering 445 Renner Dr *Web:* haumiller.com	Elgin	IL	60123	847-695-9111	695-2092	256
Haun-Magruder Inc 214 N Main St *Web:* haunmagruder.com	Woodstock	VA	22664	540-459-2145		390
Hauppauge Computer Works Inc 91 Cabot Ct *Web:* www.hauppauge.com	Hauppauge	NY	11788	631-434-1600	434-3198	625
Hauppauge School District (HSD) 495 Hoffman Ln *Web:* www.hauppauge.k12.ny.us	Hauppauge	NY	11788	631-761-8208		685
Hauptly Construction Co 2906 Violet Dr *Web:* www.hauptlyconstruction.com	Waterloo	IA	50701	319-240-7253	296-2282	189-11
Haury Plumbing & Heating Inc 1816 N Market St *Web:* www.hauryplumbing.com	Sparta	IL	62286	618-443-2416		189-10
Haus Murphy's 5739 W Glendale Ave *Web:* www.hausmurphys.com	Glendale	AZ	85301	623-939-2480		671
Hause Machines 809 S Pleasant St *TF:* 800-932-8665 ■ *Web:* www.hausemachines.com	Montpelier	OH	43543	419-485-3158	485-3146	455
Hauser & Wirth Inc 32 E 69th St *Web:* hauserwirth.com	New York	NY	10021	212-794-4970		42
Hauser Agency Inc 16 S Church St	Mount Pleasant	PA	15666	724-547-3536		390
Hausermann Abrading Process Co 300 Laura Dr *Web:* www.hausermann.net	Addison	IL	60101	630-543-6688	543-6689	455
Hausmann Industries Inc 130 Union St *TF:* 888-428-7626 ■ *Web:* www.hausmann.com	Northvale	NJ	07647	201-767-0255	767-1369	319-1
Hausted Patient Handling Systems LLC 2511 Midpark Rd *Web:* www.hausted.com	Montgomery	AL	36109	770-368-4700		567
Hautly Cheese Company Inc 251 Axminister Dr *Web:* www.hautly.com	Fenton	MO	63026	636-533-4400	533-4401	297-4
Havana 318 Main St *Web:* www.havanamaine.com	Bar Harbor	ME	04609	207-288-2822		671
Havana Central 151 W 46th St between 6th & 7th Aves *Web:* havanacentral.com	New York	NY	10036	212-398-7441	398-7449	407
Havana National Bank, The 112 S Orange St *Web:* www.havanabank.com	Havana	IL	62644	309-543-3361		70
Havas Worldwide 200 Hudson St *Web:* havas.com	New York	NY	10013	212-886-2000	886-5013	4
Havasu Newspapers Inc 2225 Acoma Blvd W *Web:* www.havasunews.com	Lake Havasu City	AZ	86403	928-453-4237		387
Havasu Pest Control Inc 2761 Maricopa Ave *Web:* www.havasupestcontrol.com	Lake Havasu City	AZ	86406	928-855-1054		577
Havasu Regional Medical Ctr 101 Civic Center Ln *Web:* www.havasuregional.com	Lake Havasu City	AZ	86403	928-855-8185		374-3
Havco Wood Products LLC 3200 E Outer Rd *TF:* 800-792-4040 ■ *Web:* www.havco.com	Scott City	MO	63780	573-334-6024		499
Haven 1441 Dresden Dr NE Ste 160 *Web:* www.havenrestaurant.com	Atlanta	GA	30319	404-969-0700	969-0701	671
Haven Homes Inc 195 Airport Rd *Web:* www.lockhaven.com	Beech Creek	PA	16822	570-962-2111		106
Haven Manor Health Care Center LLC 1441 Gateway Blvd *Web:* www.profiles.health.ny.gov	Far Rockaway	NY	11691	718-471-1500		450
Haven Restaurant 2208 W Morrison Ave *Web:* haventampa.com	Tampa	FL	33606	813-258-2233		671
Haven Steel Products Inc 13206 S Willison Rd *Web:* havensteel.com	Haven	KS	67543	620-465-2573		492
Havenwood-Heritage Heights Havenwood Campus 33 Christian Ave *TF:* 800-457-6833 ■ *Web:* www.hhhinfo.com	Concord	NH	03301	603-224-5363		672
Havenwoods State Forest 6141 N Hopkins St *Web:* dnr.wi.gov	Milwaukee	WI	53209	414-527-0232	527-0761	565
Havenwyck Hospital 1525 University Dr *TF:* 800-401-2727 ■ *Web:* havenwyckhospital.com	Auburn Hills	MI	48326	248-373-9200	377-8160	374-5
Haverford College 370 Lancaster Ave *Web:* www.haverford.edu	Haverford	PA	19041	610-896-1000	896-1338	166
Haverford Trust Co, The 3 Radnor Corp Ctr 100 Matsonford Rd Ste 450 *TF:* 888-995-1979 ■ *Web:* haverfordquality.com	Radnor	PA	19087	610-995-8700	995-8796	405
Havergal College 1451 Ave Rd *Web:* www.havergal.on.ca	Toronto	ON	M5N2H9	416-483-3519		622
Haverhill Public Library 99 Main St *Web:* www.haverhillpl.org	Haverhill	MA	01830	978-373-1586	373-8466	434-3
Haverly Systems Inc (HSI) 12 Hinchman Ave *Web:* www.haverly.com	Denville	NJ	07834	973-627-1424	625-2296	177
Havers Law Offices Incorporated PS 9226 Bayshore Dr NW Ste 220 *Web:* haverslaw.com	Silverdale	WA	98383	360-337-4040		41
Haverstock & Owens LLP 162 N Wolfe Rd *Web:* www.hollp.com	Sunnyvale	CA	94086	408-530-9700	530-9797	428

Name / Address	City	State	ZIP	Phone	Fax	Class
Haverty Furniture Companies Inc						
780 Johnson Ferry Rd NE Ste 800	Atlanta	GA	30342	888-428-3789	443-4169*	321
NYSE: HVT ■ **Fax Area Code:* 404 ■ *TF:* 888-428-3789 ■ *Web:* www.havertys.com						
Haviland Enterprises Inc						
421 Ann St NW	Grand Rapids	MI	49504	800-456-1134	361-9772*	146
**Fax Area Code:* 616 ■ *TF:* 800-456-1134 ■ *Web:* www.havilandusa.com						
Haviland Telephone Co 104 N Main St	Haviland	KS	67059	620-862-5211		224
TF: 800-339-8052 ■ *Web:* www.havilandtelco.com						
Havre Daily News 119 Second St	Havre	MT	59501	406-265-6795		532-3
TF: 800-993-2459 ■ *Web:* www.havredailynews.com						
Havre Laundry & Dry Cleaning Company Inc						
34 First St	Havre	MT	59501	406-265-2234		426
Web: northernmontanatextileservices.com						
Hawaii						
Aging Office (HCOA)						
250 S Hotel St Ste 406	Honolulu	HI	96813	808-643-2372		339-12
Web: www.hcoahawaii.org						
Agriculture Dept 1428 S King St	Honolulu	HI	96814	808-973-9560		339-12
Web: hdoa.hawaii.gov						
Attorney General 425 Queen St	Honolulu	HI	96813	808-586-1500	586-1239	339-12
Web: ag.hawaii.gov						
Bill Status 415 S Beretania St	Honolulu	HI	96813	808-587-0478		433
Web: www.capitol.hawaii.gov						
Budget & Finance Dept						
250 S Hotel St No 1 Capitol District Bldg	Honolulu	HI	96813	808-586-1518	586-1976	339-12
Web: portal.ehawaii.gov						
Business Economic Development & Tourism Dept						
PO Box 2359	Honolulu	HI	96804	808-586-2355		339-12
Web: www.hawaii.gov						
Child Support Enforcement Agency						
Kakuhihewa Bldg 601 Kamokila Blvd Ste 251	Kapolei	HI	96707	808-692-8265	692-7060	339-12
TF: 888-317-9081 ■ *Web:* ag.hawaii.gov						
Civil Defense Div						
3949 Diamond Head Rd	Honolulu	HI	96816	808-733-4260	733-4238	339-12
Web: www.dod.hawaii.gov						
Commerce & Consumer Affairs Dept						
335 Merchant St	Honolulu	HI	96813	808-586-2790		339-12
Web: cca.hawaii.gov						
Department of Accounting & General Services						
1151 Punchbowl St	Honolulu	HI	96813	808-586-0380	586-0775	339-12
Web: www.hawaii.gov						
Education Dept 1390 Miller St	Honolulu	HI	96813	808-586-3230	586-3234	339-12
Web: www.hawaiipublicschools.org						
Forestry & Wildlife Div						
1151 Punchbowl St Rm 325	Honolulu	HI	96813	808-587-0166		339-12
Web: hawaii.gov						
Historic Preservation Div						
601 Kamokila Blvd Ste 555	Kapolei	HI	96707	808-692-8015	692-8020	339-12
Web: dlnr.hawaii.gov						
Human Resources Development Dept						
235 S Beretania St 11th Fl	Honolulu	HI	96813	808-587-1100		339-12
TF: 877-447-5990 ■ *Web:* dhrd.hawaii.gov						
Human Services Dept						
1390 Miller St Rm 209	Honolulu	HI	96809	808-586-4993	586-4890	339-12
Web: humanservices.hawaii.gov						
Information Consortium						
201 Merchant St Ste 1805	Honolulu	HI	96813	808-695-4620	695-4618	339-12
Web: portal.ehawaii.gov						
Labor & Industrial Relations Dept						
830 Punchbowl St	Honolulu	HI	96813	808-586-8600		339-12
Web: labor.hawaii.gov						
Land & Natural Resources Dept						
1151 Punchbowl St Kalanimoku Bldg	Honolulu	HI	96813	808-587-0400	587-0390	339-12
Web: dlnr.hawaii.gov						
Lieutenant Governor						
415 S Beretania St 5th Fl	Honolulu	HI	96813	808-586-0255	586-0231	339-12
Web: ltgov.hawaii.gov						
Measurement Standards Branch						
1851 Auiki St	Honolulu	HI	96819	808-832-0690	832-0683	339-12
Web: www.hdoa.hawaii.gov						
Motor Vehicle Safety Office						
601 Kamokila Blvd Rm 511	Kapolei	HI	96707	808-692-7650	692-7665	339-12
Web: hidot.hawaii.gov						
Paroling Authority						
1177 Alakea St Ground Fl	Honolulu	HI	96813	808-587-1300		339-12
Web: www.hawaii.gov						
Professional & Vocational Licensing Div						
335 Merchant St Rm 301	Honolulu	HI	96813	808-586-3000		339-12
Web: cca.hawaii.gov						
Public Safety Dept						
919 Ala Moana Blvd 4th Fl	Honolulu	HI	96814	808-587-1288	587-1282	339-12
Web: dps.hawaii.gov						
Public Utilities Commission						
465 S King St Ste 103	Honolulu	HI	96813	808-586-2020	586-2066	339-12
Web: puc.hawaii.gov						
Secretary of State						
415 S Beretania St Ste 5	Honolulu	HI	96813	808-586-0034		340-16
Web: www.governor.hawaii.gov						
Securities Compliance Div						
335 Merchant St Rm 205	Honolulu	HI	96813	808-586-2744	586-3977	339-12
Web: cca.hawaii.gov						
Sheriffs Div 1177 Alakea St Rm 418	Honolulu	HI	96813	808-587-2652		339-12
Web: dps.hawaii.gov						
State Foundation for Culture & the Arts						
250 S Hotel St 2nd Fl	Honolulu	HI	96813	808-586-0300	586-0308	339-12
Web: sfca.hawaii.gov						
Supreme Court 417 S King St	Honolulu	HI	96813	808-539-4919	539-4928	339-12
Web: www.courts.state.hi.us						
Taxation Dept 830 Punchbowl St Rm 221	Honolulu	HI	96813	808-587-4242	587-1488	339-12
Web: tax.hawaii.gov						
Teacher Standards Board						
650 Iwilei Rd Ste 201	Honolulu	HI	96817	808-586-2600	586-2606	339-12
Web: hawaiiteacherstandardsboard.org						
Tourism Authority						
1801 Kalakaua Ave 1st Fl	Honolulu	HI	96815	808-973-2255	973-2253	339-12
Web: www.hawaiitourismauthority.org						
Transportation Dept 869 Punchbowl St	Honolulu	HI	96813	808-587-2220	587-2313	339-12
Web: www.hawaii.gov						
Veterans Services Office						
459 Patterson Rd E-Wing Rm 1-A103	Honolulu	HI	96819	808-433-0420	433-0385	339-12
Web: dod.hawaii.gov						
Vocational Rehabilitation Div						
1901 Bachelot St	Honolulu	HI	96817	808-586-9744		339-12
TF: 800-316-8005 ■ *Web:* www.humanservices.hawaii.gov						
Workforce Development Div						
1505 Dillingham Blvd Rm 110	Honolulu	HI	96817	808-586-8877		259
Web: www.hawaii.gov						
Hawaii Agriculture Research Ctr (HARC)						
PO Box 100	Kunia	HI	96759	808-621-1350	621-1399	668
Web: www.harc-hspa.com						
Hawaii Association of Realtors						
1259 A'Ala St Ste 300	Honolulu	HI	96817	808-733-7060	737-4977	656
Web: www.hawaiirealtors.com						
Hawaii Bar Journal						
1100 Alakea St Ste 1000	Honolulu	HI	96813	808-537-1868	521-7936	457-15
TF: 888-586-1056 ■ *Web:* hsba.org						
Hawaii Biotech Inc						
650 Iwilei Rd Ste 204	Honolulu	HI	96817	808-486-5333	792-1343	668
Web: www.hibiotech.com						
Hawaii Children's Discovery Ctr						
111 Ohe St	Honolulu	HI	96813	808-524-5437	524-5400	521
Web: www.discoverycenterhawaii.org						
Hawaii Coffee Co 1555 Kalani St	Honolulu	HI	96817	808-847-3600	487-3600	159
TF: 800-338-8353 ■ *Web:* www.hawaiicoffeecompany.com						
Hawaii Community College 1175 Manono St	Hilo	HI	96720	808-934-2500	934-2501	162
Web: www.hawcc.hawaii.edu						
Hawaii Community Foundation						
65-1279 Kawaihae Rd	Kamuela	HI	96743	808-537-6333	521-6286	303
TF: 888-731-3863 ■ *Web:* www.hawaiicommunityfoundation.org						
Hawaii Convention Ctr						
1801 Kalakaua Ave	Honolulu	HI	96815	808-943-3500	943-3599	205
TF: 800-295-6603 ■ *Web:* www.meethawaii.com						
Hawaii County 1055 Kinoole St Ste 101	Hilo	HI	96720	808-961-8255	961-8603	338
Web: www.hawaiicounty.gov						
Hawaii Democratic Party						
627 S St Ste 105	Honolulu	HI	96813	808-596-2980		616-1
TF: 844-596-2980 ■ *Web:* hawaiidemocrats.org						
Hawaii Dental Assn						
1345 S Beretania St Ste 301	Honolulu	HI	96814	808-593-7956	593-7636	227
TF: 800-359-6725 ■ *Web:* www.hawaiidentalassociation.net						
Hawaii Dental Service						
700 Bishop St Ste 700	Honolulu	HI	96813	808-521-1431	529-9368	391-3
TF: 800-232-2533 ■ *Web:* www.hawaiidentalservice.com						
Hawaii Department of Transportation Harbors Div						
79 S Nimitz Hwy	Honolulu	HI	96813	808-587-1928		618
Web: hidot.hawaii.gov						
Hawaii Engineering Group Inc						
1088 Bishop St Ste 2506	Honolulu	HI	96813	808-533-2092		261
Web: hawaiiengineering.net						
Hawaii Federal Credit Union						
1244 Kaumualii St	Honolulu	HI	96817	808-847-1371		219
Web: www.hawaiifcu.org						
Hawaii Gas 515 Kamake'e St	Honolulu	HI	96814	808-535-5933	535-5934	787
TF: 866-499-3941 ■ *Web:* www.hawaiigas.com						
Hawaii Healing Arts College						
407 Uluniu St						
Kailua Medical Arts Bldg Ste 204	Kailua-Kona	HI	96734	808-266-2462	266-2460	167-3
TF: 877-881-8884 ■ *Web:* www.hhacdirect.com						
Hawaii Health Systems Corp						
3675 Kilauea Ave	Honolulu	HI	96816	808-733-4020	733-4028	374-3
Web: www.hhsc.org						
Hawaii Insitute of Geophysics & Planetology						
1680 E W Rd Pacific Ocean Science & Technology (POST) Bldg Rm 602						
PO Box 602B	Honolulu	HI	96822	808-956-8760	956-3188	668
Web: www.higp.hawaii.edu						
Hawaii Institute of Hair Design						
1128 Nuuanu Ave Ste 102	Honolulu	HI	96817	808-533-6596		167-3
Web: www.hihdhawaii.net						
Hawaii Island Chamber of Commerce						
117 Keawe St	Hilo	HI	96720	808-935-7178	961-4435	139
TF: 877-482-4411 ■ *Web:* hicc.biz						
Hawaii Legislative Reference Bureau (LRB)						
Hawaii State Capitol	Honolulu	HI	96813	808-587-0690	587-0699	434-3
Web: www.lrbhawaii.org						
Hawaii Lions Eye Bank & Makana Foundation						
405 N Kuakini St Ste 801	Honolulu	HI	96817	808-536-7416		269
Web: www.hlebmf.org						
Hawaii Medical Assn						
1360 S Beretania St	Honolulu	HI	96816	808-536-7702		474
TF: 888-536-2792 ■ *Web:* www.hawaiimedicalassociation.org						
Hawaii Medical Service Assn						
818 Keeaumoku St	Honolulu	HI	96814	808-948-6111		391-3
TF: 800-776-4672 ■ *Web:* hmsa.com						
Hawaii Modular Space Inc						
91-282 Kalaeloa Blvd	Kapolei	HI	96707	808-682-5559	682-5199	187
Web: www.willscothawaii.com						
Hawaii National Bank 45 N King St	Honolulu	HI	96817	808-528-7711		69
TF: 800-528-2273 ■ *Web:* www.hawaiinational.bank						
Hawaii Nurses Assn (HNA)						
949 Kapiolani Blvd Ste 107	Honolulu	HI	96814	808-531-1628		533
TF: 800-617-2677 ■ *Web:* www.hawaiinurses.org						
Hawaii Nut & Bolt Inc 905 Ahua St	Honolulu	HI	96819	808-834-1919	836-8778	351
TF: 800-764-6887 ■ *Web:* www.hawaiinutandbolt.com						
Hawaii Opera Theatre						
848 S Beretania St Ste 301	Honolulu	HI	96813	808-596-7372	596-0379	573-2
TF: 800-836-7372 ■ *Web:* www.hawaiiopera.org						
Hawaii Pacific Federal Credit Union						
1441 Kapiolani Blvd Ste 1318	Honolulu	HI	96814	808-955-5933		219
Web: hawaiipacific.org						
Hawaii Pacific Teleport LP						
91-340 Farrington Hwy	Kapolei	HI	96707	808-674-9157		116
Web: www.hawaiiteleport.com						
Hawaii Pacific University						
1164 Bishop St Ste 200	Honolulu	HI	96813	808-544-0200	544-1136	166
TF: 866-225-5478 ■ *Web:* www.hpu.edu						
Hawaii Petroleum 16 Railroad Ave Ste 202	Hilo	HI	96720	808-935-6641	934-7197	579
Web: www.hawaiipetroleum.com						

Listing	City	State	ZIP	Phone	Fax	Class
Hawaii Planing Mill Ltd (HPM) 16-166 Melekahiwa St *TF:* 877-841-7633 ■ *Web:* www.hpmhawaii.com	Keaau	HI	96749	808-966-5693	966-7564	191-3
Hawaii Preparatory Academy 65-1692 Kohala Mountain Rd *TF:* 800-644-4481 ■ *Web:* www.hpa.edu	Kamuela	HI	96743	808-885-7321	881-4045	622
Hawaii Public Television 2350 Dole St *TF:* 800-238-4847 ■ *Web:* www.pbshawaii.org	Honolulu	HI	96822	808-973-1000	973-1090	632
Hawaii Republican Party 725 Kapiolani Blvd Ste C105 *Web:* www.gophawaii.com	Honolulu	HI	96813	808-593-8180		616-2
Hawaii Reserves Inc 55-510 Kamehameha Hwy *Web:* www.hawaiireserves.com	Laie	HI	96762	808-293-9201	293-6456	655
Hawaii State Ballet 1418 Kapiolani Blvd *Web:* www.hawaiistateballet.com	Honolulu	HI	96814	808-947-2755		573-1
Hawaii State Hospital 45-710 Keaahala Rd *Web:* www.health.hawaii.gov	Kaneohe	HI	96744	808-247-2191	247-7335	374-5
Hawaii State Parks Kalanimoku Bldg 1151 Punchbowl St Rm 310 *Web:* dlnr.hawaii.gov	Honolulu	HI	96813	808-587-0300	587-0311	565
Hawaii State Public Library System (HSPLS) 44 Merchant St *Web:* www.librarieshawaii.org	Honolulu	HI	96813	808-586-3700		434-5
Hawaii Stevedores Inc 1601 Sand Island Pkwy *Web:* www.hawaiistevedores.com	Honolulu	HI	96819	808-527-3400		465
Hawaii Technology Institute 1130 N Nimitz Hwy Ste A 226 *Web:* www.hti.edu	Honolulu	HI	96817	808-522-2700	522-2707	167-3
Hawaii Tribune-Herald 355 Kinoole St *Web:* www.hawaiitribune-herald.com	Hilo	HI	96720	808-935-6621		532-2
Hawaii Tropical Botanical Garden 27-717 Old Mamalahoa Hwy PO Box 80 *Web:* www.hawaiigarden.com	Papaikou	HI	96781	808-964-5233	964-1338	97
Hawaii Visitors & Convention Bureau 2270 Kalakaua Ave Ste 801 *TF:* 800-464-2924 ■ *Web:* www.gohawaii.com	Honolulu	HI	96815	800-464-2924		206
Hawaii Volcanoes National Park PO Box 52 *Web:* www.nps.gov	Hawaii National Park	HI	96718	808-985-6101	985-6004	564
Hawaii's Best Bed & Breakfasts 571 Pauku St *TF:* 800-262-9912 ■ *Web:* www.bestbnb.com	Kailua-Kona	HI	96734	808-263-3100	262-5030	376
Hawaii's Plantation Village (HPV) 94-695 Waipahu St *Web:* www.hawaiiplantationvillage.org	Waipahu	HI	96797	808-677-0110	676-6727	520
Hawaiian Airlines HawaiianMiles PO Box 30008 **Fax Area Code:* 808 ■ *TF:* 877-426-4537 ■ *Web:* www.hawaiianairlines.com	Honolulu	HI	96820	877-426-4537	838-6777*	26
Hawaiian Cement 99-1300 Halawa Vly St *Web:* www.hawaiiancement.com	Aiea	HI	96701	808-532-3400	532-3499	182
Hawaiian Dredging & Construction Co 605 Kapiolani Blvd *Web:* www.hdcc.com	Honolulu	HI	96813	808-735-3211		188-5
Hawaiian Electric Industries Inc 1001 Bishop St Ste 2900 *TF:* 877-871-8461 ■ *Web:* www.hei.com	Honolulu	HI	96813	808-543-5662		787
Hawaiian Express Service Inc 3623 Munster Ave *Web:* www.hawaiianexpress.com	Hayward	CA	94545	510-783-6100	782-5794	311
Hawaiian Falls Waterparks 4550 N Garland Ave *Web:* hfalls.com	Garland	TX	75040	972-675-0000		31
Hawaiian Gardens Casino 11871 Carson St *Web:* www.thegardenscasino.com	Hawaiian Gardens	CA	90716	562-860-5887		133
Hawaiian Greenhouse Inc PO Box 4400 *Web:* www.hawaiiangreenhouse.com	Hilo	HI	96720	808-959-7780		293
Hawaiian Housewares Ltd 96-1282 Waihona St *Web:* hansenhawaii.com	Pearl City	HI	96782	808-456-3334	455-5666	361
Hawaiian Inn 2301 S Atlantic Ave *TF:* 800-922-3023 ■ *Web:* www.hawaiianinn.com	Daytona Beach	FL	32118	386-255-5411	253-1209	379
Hawaiian Island Creations Inc 348 Hahani St *Web:* hicsurf.com	Kailua-Kona	HI	96734	808-266-6730		711
Hawaiian Islands Medical Corp 841 Pohukaina St Ste 8 *TF:* 866-264-4633 ■ *Web:* www.himed.cc	Honolulu	HI	96813	808-597-8087	597-8474	475
Hawaiian Isles Kona Coffee Co 2839 Mokumoa St *TF:* 800-657-7716 ■ *Web:* www.hawaiianisles.com	Honolulu	HI	96819	800-657-7716		296-7
Hawaiian Sun Products Inc 259 Sand Island Access Rd *Web:* www.hawaiiansunproducts.com	Honolulu	HI	96819	808-845-3211	842-0532	296-20
Hawaiian Telcom Holdco Inc 1177 Bishop St *Web:* www.hawaiiantel.com	Honolulu	HI	96813	808-643-3456		787
Hawk Inn & Mountain Resort 75 Billings Rd *TF:* 800-685-4295 ■ *Web:* www.hawkresort.com	Plymouth	VT	05056	802-672-3811	672-5585	669
Hawk Isolutions Group Inc 6439 Plymouth Ave Ste 112 *Web:* www.hawkisg.com	Saint Louis	MO	63133	314-727-1174		180
Hawk Mountain Lab Inc 201 W Clay Ave *Web:* hawkmtnlabs.com	Hazle Township	PA	18202	570-455-6011		743
Hawk Mountain Sanctuary (HMS) 1700 Hawk Mtn Rd *Web:* www.hawkmountain.org	Kempton	PA	19529	610-756-6961	756-4468	48-3
Hawk Quality Products Inc 125 Rockingham Rd *Web:* www.hawkquality.com	Derry	NH	03038	603-432-3319	437-6955	454
Hawk Steel Industries Inc 4010 S Eden Rd *Web:* www.hawksteel.com	Kennedale	TX	76060	817-572-4466	516-0200	492
Hawk Technology Ltd 8080 Centennial Expy *Web:* www.hawktechnology.com	Rock Island	IL	61201	309-787-6200		261
Hawk's Cay Resort & Marina 61 Hawk's Cay Blvd **Fax Area Code:* 305 ■ *TF:* 888-395-5539 ■ *Web:* www.hawkscay.com	Duck Key	FL	33050	866-347-2675	743-5215*	669
Hawken House, The 1155 S Rock Hill Rd *Web:* thehotelnexus.com	Saint Louis	MO	63119	314-968-1857		50-3
Hawker Pacific Aerospace 11240 Sherman Way *Web:* www.hawker.com	Sun Valley	CA	91352	818-765-6201	765-8073	24
Hawker Powersource Inc 9404 Ooltewah Industrial Dr PO Box 808 *TF:* 800-238-8658 ■ *Web:* www.hawkerpowersource.com	Ooltewah	TN	37363	423-238-5700		74
Hawkeye Community College 1501 E Orange Rd *TF:* 800-670-4769 ■ *Web:* www.hawkeyecollege.edu	Waterloo	IA	50704	319-296-2320	296-2874	162
Hawkeye Hotels Inc 320 2nd St *Web:* www.hawkeyehotels.com	Burlington	IA	52601	319-752-7400		378
Hawkeye Industries Inc 1126 N Eason Blvd *Web:* hawkeye.ws	Tupelo	MS	38804	662-842-3333		697
Hawkeye Information Systems Inc PO Box 2167 *Web:* www.hawkinfo.com	Fort Collins	CO	80521	970-498-9000	498-9096	178-1
Hawkeye International Ltd 5760 VT Rt 100 *Web:* www.hawkeyeintl.com	North Hyde Park	VT	05665	802-635-7500	635-7900	732
Hawkeye LLC 100 Marcus Blvd Ste 1 *Web:* www.elecnorhawkeye.com	Hauppauge	NY	11788	631-447-3100	447-3830	539
Hawkeye Stages Inc 703 Dudley St *TF:* 877-464-2954 ■ *Web:* www.hawkeyestages.com	Decorah	IA	52101	877-464-2954		107
Hawkeye Telephone Co 115 W Main St *TF:* 800-369-9131 ■ *Web:* www.hawkeyetelephone.com	Hawkeye	IA	52147	563-427-3222		224
Hawkhill Associates 125 E Gilman St *Web:* www.hawkhill.com	Madison	WI	53703	608-467-7003		525
Hawking Technologies Inc 35 Hammond Ste 150 *Web:* hawkingtech.com	Irvine	CA	92618	949-206-6900		246
Hawkins & Associates Engineering Inc 436 Mitchell Rd *Web:* hawkins-eng.com	Modesto	CA	95354	209-575-4295		261
Hawkins Construction Co 2516 Deer Pk Blvd *Web:* www.hawkins1.com	Omaha	NE	68105	402-342-1607		186
Hawkins County 110 E Main St Rm 202 *Web:* www.hawkinscountytn.gov	Rogersville	TN	37857	423-272-8304	921-3170	338
Hawkins County Library System 407 E Main St *Web:* hawkinslibraries.org	Rogersville	TN	37857	423-272-8710	272-9261	434-3
Hawkins Harrison Insurance 103 S 1st St *TF:* 800-505-5335 ■ *Web:* www.hawkinsharrison.com	Edina	MO	63537	660-397-2251		390
Hawkins Inc 3100 E Hennepin Ave *NASDAQ: HWKN* ■ *TF:* 800-328-5460 ■ *Web:* hawkinsinc.com	Minneapolis	MN	55413	612-331-6910	331-5304	143
Hawkins Parnell & Young LLP 303 Peachtree St NE Ste 4000 *Web:* www.hpylaw.com	Atlanta	GA	30308	404-614-7400		428
Hawkins Personnel Group 909 NE Loop 410 Ste 104 *Web:* www.hawkinspersonnel.com	San Antonio	TX	78209	210-349-9911	349-3393	721
Hawkins Point Partners N 7 Technology Dr Ste 103 *Web:* hawkinspointpartners.com	North Chelmsford	MA	01863	978-455-4110		193
Hawkins-Weir Engineers Inc 110 S 7th St PO Box 648 *Web:* hawkins-weir.com	Van Buren	AR	72956	479-474-1227		261
Hawks Giffels & Pullin (Hgp) Inc (HGP) 1308 Altamont Rd *Web:* hgp-inc.com	Greenville	SC	29608	864-370-0213		463
Hawks Nest State Park PO Box 857 *Web:* wvstateparks.com	Ansted	WV	25812	304-658-5212		565
Hawley Josh (Sen R - MO) 212 Russell Senate Office Bldg *Web:* www.hawley.senate.gov	Washington	DC	20510	202-224-6154		342-2
Hawley Mountain Guest Ranch 4188 Main Boulder Rd *TF:* 877-496-7848 ■ *Web:* www.hawleymountain.com	McLeod	MT	59052	406-932-5791		239
Hawley Products Inc 1567 N 8th St *Web:* hawleyproducts.com	Paducah	KY	42001	270-442-2344	442-9029	52
Hawley Troxell Ennis & Hawley LLP 877 Main St Ste 1000 *Web:* www.hawleytroxell.com	Boise	ID	83702	208-344-6000		428
Hawn State Park 12096 Pk Dr *TF:* 877-422-6766 ■ *Web:* mostateparks.com	Sainte Genevieve	MO	63670	573-883-3603		565
Haworth Inc 1 Haworth Ctr *TF:* 800-344-2600 ■ *Web:* www.haworth.com	Holland	MI	49423	616-393-3000	393-1570	319-1
Haworth Marketing & Media Co 45 S 7th St Ste 2400 *Web:* www.haworthmedia.com	Minneapolis	MN	55402	612-677-8900		6
Haworth, Bradshaw, Stallknecht & Barber Inc 4380 Auburn Blvd *Web:* www.haworthlaw.com	Sacramento	CA	95841	916-484-4354	487-4348	428
Haws Corp 1455 Kleppe Ln *TF:* 888-640-4297 ■ *Web:* www.hawsco.com	Sparks	NV	89431	775-359-4712	359-7424	664
Hawthorn Bancshares Inc 300 SW Longview Blvd *NASDAQ: HWBK* ■ *Web:* www.exchangebancshares.com	Lee's Summit	MO	64081	816-347-8100		360-2
Hawthorn Ctr 18471 Haggerty Rd *Web:* www.michigan.gov	Northville	MI	48167	248-349-3000	349-8259	374-1
Hawthorn Group LC 625 Slaters Ln Ste 100 *Web:* www.hawthorngroup.com	Alexandria	VA	22314	703-299-4499	299-4488	636

	Phone	Fax	Class
Hawthorne Advertising 2280 W Tyler Ave Ste 200 Fairfield IA 52556 *Web:* www.hawthorneadvertising.com	310-844-0606		720
Hawthorne Animal Hospital 1516 Alarth Dr Troy IL 62294 *Web:* hawthorneanimals.com	618-667-4900		794
Hawthorne Chamber of Commerce 471 Lafayette Ave PO Box 331 Hawthorne NJ 07506 *Web:* www.hawthornechamber.org	973-427-5078		139
Hawthorne Executive Search 1319 Military Cutoff Rd Wilmington NC 28403 *Web:* hawthornesearch.com	910-798-1800		260
Hawthorne Hotel 18 Washington Sq W Salem MA 01970 *Web:* www.hawthornehotel.com	978-744-4080		379
Hawthorne Machinery Co 16945 Camino San Bernardo San Diego CA 92127 *TF:* 800-437-4228 ■ *Web:* www.hawthornecat.com	858-674-7000		264-3
Hawthorne Race Course 3501 S Laramie Ave Cicero IL 60804 *Web:* www.hawthorneracecourse.com	708-780-3700		642
Hay Communications 72863 Blind Line PO Box 99 Zurich ON N0M2T0 *Web:* www.hay.net	519-236-4333		224
Hay House Inc PO Box 5100 Carlsbad CA 92018 *Fax Area Code: 800 ■ *TF:* 800-654-5126 ■ *Web:* www.hayhouse.com	760-431-7695	650-5115*	637-3
Hay-Adams Hotel 800 16th St NE Washington DC 20006 *TF:* 800-853-6807 ■ *Web:* www.hayadams.com	202-638-6600	638-2716	379
Haycock Petroleum Co 4825 N Sloan Ln Las Vegas NV 89115 *Web:* www.haycockpetroleum.com	702-382-1620		580
Hayden Automotive 1801 Waters Ridge Dr Lewisville TX 75057 *TF:* 888-505-4567 ■ *Web:* www.haydenauto.com	888-505-4567		60
Hayden Consulting Engineers Inc 12480 SW 68th Ave Tigard OR 97223 *Web:* hayden-engineers.com	503-968-9994		261
Hayden Planetarium 200 Central Pk W New York NY 10024 *Web:* www.amnh.org	212-769-5100	769-5427	598
Hayden Technologies Inc 333 Sandy Springs Cir Ste 127 Atlanta GA 30328 *Web:* www.haydentechnologies.com	404-303-9935		180
Hayden Twist Drill & Tool Company Inc 22822 Globe St Warren MI 48089 *Web:* www.haydendrills.com	586-754-7700		493
Haydon Building Corp 4640 E Cotton Gin Loop Phoenix AZ 85040 *Web:* haydonbc.com	602-296-1496		186
Hayes & Stolz Industrial Manufacturing Co 6500 Cirrus Dr Highpoint Business Pk Burleson TX 76028 *TF:* 800-725-7272 ■ *Web:* www.hayes-stolz.com	817-926-3391	926-4133	298
Hayes Barton Press 227 Fayetteville St Ste 400 Raleigh NC 27601 *TF:* 855-200-4146 ■ *Web:* www.vitalsource.com	855-200-4146		637-2
Hayes Beer 1819 Elmwood Rd Rockford IL 61103 *Web:* www.hayesbeer.com	815-877-0221	877-0225	81-1
Hayes Bolt & Supply Inc 2950 National Ave San Diego CA 92113 *Web:* www.hayesbolt.com	619-231-5966		351
Hayes Convalescent Hospital 1250 Hayes St San Francisco CA 94117 *Web:* hayesconvalescent.com	415-931-8806	931-2918	371
Hayes County 505 Troth St PO Box 370 Hayes Center NE 69032 *Web:* hayescounty.ne.gov	308-286-3413	286-3208	338
Hayes Group International Inc, The 4400 Silas Creek Pkwy Ste 301 Winston-Salem NC 27104 *Web:* www.thehayesgroupintl.com	336-765-6764		463
Hayes Handpiece Franchises Inc 5375 Avenida Encinas Ste C Carlsbad CA 92008 *TF:* 800-228-0521 ■ *Web:* www.hayeshandpiece.com	800-228-0521		310
Hayes Jahana (Rep D - CT) 1415 Longworth House Office Bldg Washington DC 20515 *Web:* www.hayes.house.gov	202-225-4476		342-2
Hayes James & Associates Inc 4145 Shackleford Rd Ste 300 Norcross GA 30093 *Web:* www.hayesjames.com	770-923-1600	923-4202	261
Hayes Lake State Park 48990 County Rd 4 Roseau MN 56751 *Web:* www.dnr.state.mn.us	218-425-7504		565
Hayes Pump Inc 66 Old Powder Mill Rd West Concord MA 01742 *TF:* 800-343-5020 ■ *Web:* hayespump.com	800-343-5020		358
Hayes Specialties Corp 1761 E Genesee Saginaw MI 48601 *TF:* 800-248-3603 ■ *Web:* www.ehayes.com	989-755-6541	755-2341	328
Hayes, Schloss & Alcocer PA 1401 Forum Way Ste 210 West Palm Beach FL 33401 *Web:* flworkcompdefense.com	561-775-1770		41
Hayfield Minnesota 18 W Main St Hayfield MN 55940 *Web:* www.hayfieldmn.com	507-374-9327		532-2
Haylex Manufacturing LLC 4401 S Delaware Dr Muncie IN 47302 *Web:* www.haylexmanufacturing.com	765-288-1818	288-2346	454
Haylor Freyer & Coon 231 Salina Meadows North Syracuse NY 13212 *TF:* 800-289-1501 ■ *Web:* www.haylor.com	315-451-1500		390
Hayman Capital Management LP 2101 Cedar Springs Rd Ste 1400 Dallas TX 75201 *Web:* www.haymancapital.com	214-347-8050		360-3
Haynes & Boone LLP 2323 Victory Ave Ste 700 Dallas TX 75219 *Web:* www.haynesboone.com	214-651-5000	651-5940	428
Haynes Furniture Company Inc 5324 Virginia Beach Blvd Virginia Beach VA 23462 *Web:* www.haynesfurniture.com	757-497-9681		321
Haynes International Inc 1020 W Park Ave PO Box 9013 Kokomo IN 46904 *NASDAQ: HAYN* ■ *TF:* 800-354-0806 ■ *Web:* www.haynesintl.com	765-456-6000	456-6905	485
Haynes Manufacturing Co 24142 Detroit Rd Westlake OH 44145 *TF:* 800-992-2166 ■ *Web:* www.haynesmfg.com	440-871-2188	871-0855	541
Haynesville Correctional Ctr 421 Barnfield Rd PO Box 129 Haynesville VA 22472 *Web:* www.vadoc.virginia.gov	804-333-3577		213
Hayneville Telephone Company Inc 210 E Tuskeena St Hayneville AL 36040 *Web:* htcnet.net	334-548-2101		736
Haynsworth Sinkler Boyd PA 134 Meeting St 3rd Fl Charleston SC 29401 *Web:* www.hsblawfirm.com	843-722-3366		428
Hays Academy of Hair Design 115 S 5th St Salina KS 67401 *Web:* www.haysacademy.edu	785-833-2280		166
Hays Consolidated I S D 21003 I- 35 Kyle TX 78640 *Web:* www.hayscisd.net	512-268-2141	268-2147	685
Hays Convention & Visitors Bureau 2700 Vine St PO Box 490 Hays KS 67601 *TF:* 800-569-4505 ■ *Web:* www.haysusa.com	785-628-8202	628-1471	206
Hays County 712 S Stagecoach Trl San Marcos TX 78666 *Web:* hayscountytx.com	512-393-7779	393-7735	338
Hays Financial Consulting LLC Atlanta Financial Ctr 3343 Peachtree Rd Ste 200 Atlanta GA 30326 *Web:* haysconsulting.net	404-926-0060		196
Hays Fluid Controls 114 Eason Rd Dallas NC 28034 *TF:* 800-354-4297 ■ *Web:* www.haysfluidcontrols.com	704-922-9565	922-9595	790
Hays Medical Ctr (HMC) 2220 Canterbury Dr Hays KS 67601 *TF:* 800-248-0073 ■ *Web:* haysmed.com	785-650-2759		374-3
Hays Oil Co 1890 S Pacific Hwy PO Box 1220 Medford OR 97501 *Web:* haysoil.com	541-772-2053	779-2602	579
Haysite Reinforced Plastics 5599 Perry Hwy Erie PA 16509 *Web:* www.haysite.com	814-868-3691	864-7803	606
Hayward Chamber of Commerce 22561 Main St Hayward CA 94545 *Web:* www.hayward.org	510-537-2424		139
Hayward Enterprises 6574 N State Rd 7 Ste 230 Coconut Creek FL 33073 *Web:* www.haywardenterprises.com	954-935-5555		214
Hayward Lumber Co 429 Front St Salinas CA 93901 *Web:* www.haywardlumber.com	831-755-8800	755-8821	364
Hayward Pool Products Inc 620 Div St Elizabeth NJ 07207 *Web:* www.hayward-pool.com	908-351-5400	351-5675	357
Hayward Public Library 835 C St Hayward CA 94541 *Web:* www.hayward-ca.gov	510-293-8685		434-3
Hayward Quartz Technology Inc 1700 Corporate Way Fremont CA 94539 *Web:* www.haywardquartz.com	510-657-9605	657-6404	454
Hayward Tyler Inc 480 Roosevelt Hwy Colchester VT 05446 *Web:* haywardtyler.com	802-655-4444	655-4682	641
Hayward Unified School District (HUSD) 24411 Amador St Hayward CA 94544 *Web:* www.husd.us	510-784-2600	784-2641	685
Haywood Builders Supply Inc 100 Charles St Waynesville NC 28786 *Web:* www.haywoodbuilders.com	828-456-6051		364
Haywood Community College 185 Freedlander Dr Clyde NC 28721 *Web:* www.haywood.edu	828-627-2821	627-3606	162
Haywood County 1 N Washington St Brownsville TN 38012 *TF:* 800-273-8712 ■ *Web:* www.haywoodcountybrownsville.com	731-772-1432	772-3864	338
Haywood County 1233 N Main St Annex II Waynesville NC 28786 *Web:* www.haywoodnc.net	828-452-6633	452-6750	338
Haywood County Chamber of Commerce 28 Walnut St Waynesville NC 28786 *Web:* haywoodchamber.com	828-456-3021		139
Haywood County Public Library 678 S Haywood St Waynesville NC 28786 *Web:* www.haywoodlibrary.org	828-452-5169		434-3
Haywood County School District 900 E Main St Brownsville TN 38012 *Web:* haywoodschools.com	731-772-9613		187
Haywood Electric Membership Corp 376 Grindstone Rd Waynesville NC 28785 *TF:* 800-951-6088 ■ *Web:* www.haywoodemc.com	828-452-2281		245
Haywood Hall House & Gardens 211 New Bern Pl Raleigh NC 27601 *Web:* www.haywoodhall.org	919-832-8357		50-3
Haywood Park Hotel 1 Battery Park Ave Asheville NC 28801 *Web:* www.haywoodpark.com	828-252-2522		379
Haywood Securities Inc Waterfront Centre 200 Burrard St Ste 700 Vancouver BC V6C3L6 *TF:* 800-663-9499 ■ *Web:* www.haywood.com	604-697-7100		401
Hayzlett Companies Inc, The 4912 S Technopolis Dr Sioux Falls SD 57106 *Web:* hayzlett.com	605-275-4075		636
Hazard Communication Systems LLC 190 Old Milford Rd Milford PA 18337 *TF:* 877-748-0244 ■ *Web:* www.clarionsafety.com	570-296-5686		627
Hazard Community & Technical College 1 Community College Dr Hazard KY 41701 *TF:* 800-246-7521 ■ *Web:* hazard.kctcs.edu	606-436-5721		162
Hazel Ridge Veterinary Clinic 4347 Hazel Ave Fair Oaks CA 95628 *Web:* hazelridgevet.com	916-965-8200		794
Hazelden Betty Ford Foundation 15251 Pleasant Valley Rd Center City MN 55012 *TF:* 877-281-4211 ■ *Web:* www.hazeldenbettyford.org	877-281-4211		354
Hazelett Strip-Casting Corp 135 W Lakeshore Dr PO Box 600 Colchester VT 05446 *Web:* www.hazelett.com	802-863-6376		787
Hazelnut Growers of Oregon 21260 Butteville Road NE Aurora OR 97002 *Web:* www.hazelnut.com	503-648-4176		11-1

Name / Address	City	State	Zip	Phone	Fax	Class
Hazelwood Enterprises Inc 402 N 32nd St *Web:* hazelwoods.com	Phoenix	AZ	85008	602-275-7709		327
Hazelwood Historic Home Museum 1008 S Monroe Ave *Web:* www.browncohistoricalsoc.org	Green Bay	WI	54301	920-437-1840	455-4518	520
Hazen & Sawyer PC 498 Seventh Ave 11th Fl *TF:* 888-514-2936 ■ *Web:* www.hazenandsawyer.com	New York	NY	10018	212-539-7000	614-9049	261
Hazen Paper Co 240 S Water St PO Box 189 *Web:* hazen.com	Holyoke	MA	01041	413-538-8204	533-1420	554
Hazen Research Inc 4601 Indiana St *Web:* www.hazenresearch.com	Golden	CO	80403	303-279-4501	278-1528	668
Hazle Park Packing Co 260 Washington Ave Hazle Pk *TF:* 800-238-4331 ■ *Web:* www.hazlepark.com	Hazleton	PA	18202	570-455-7571	455-6030	296-26
Hazleton Standard Speaker 21 N Wyoming St *TF:* 800-843-6680 ■ *Web:* www.standardspeaker.com	Hazleton	PA	18201	570-455-3636	455-4244	532-2
Hazlett Burt & Watson Inc 1300 Chapline St *TF:* 800-537-8985 ■ *Web:* www.hazlettburt.com	Wheeling	WV	26003	304-233-3312	233-3870	690
Hazmat Environmental Group Inc 60 Commerce Dr *Web:* www.hazmatinc.com	Buffalo	NY	14218	716-827-7200		194
HazMat Systems Inc 501 Slaters Ln Ste 1024 *Web:* www.hazmatsystems.com	Alexandria	VA	22314	703-652-4512	734-0961	809
Hazmateam Inc 12 Kimball Hill Rd *Web:* www.hazmateam.com	Hudson	NH	03051	603-882-1112		196
Hazmed Inc 1050 Connecticut Ave NW Ste 500 Fifth Fl *Web:* www.hazmed.com	Washington	DC	20036	202-742-6521	772-3101	463
H&B (Horse & Buggy Press) 1116 Broad St Middle Ste *Web:* www.horseandbuggypress.com	Durham	NC	27705	919-949-4847		626
HB & G Inc PO Box 589 *TF:* 800-264-4424 ■ *Web:* www.hbgcolumns.com	Troy	AL	36081	334-566-5000	566-4629	499
HB Communications Inc 60 Dodge Ave *Web:* hbcommunications.com	North Haven	CT	06473	203-234-9246		38
HB Frazer Co 514 Shoemaker Rd *Web:* www.hbfrazer.com	King of Prussia	PA	19406	610-768-0400	992-5070	189-4
HB Fuller Co 1200 Willow Lake Blvd PO Box 64683 *NYSE: FUL* ■ *TF:* 888-423-8553 ■ *Web:* www.hbfuller.com	Saint Paul	MN	55164	651-236-5900		3
HB Management Group Inc 7100 Broadway Ste 6L *TF:* 866-440-1100 ■ *Web:* www.hbmgmt.com	Denver	CO	80221	866-440-1100		104
HB McClure Co 600 S 17th St *Web:* hbmcclure.com	Harrisburg	PA	17104	717-232-4328		697
HB Mellot Estate Inc 100 Mellott Dr *TF:* 800-634-5634 ■ *Web:* www.mellottcompany.com	Warfordsburg	PA	17267	301-678-2050	678-2051	503-5
HB Rentals LC 5813 Hwy 90 E *TF:* 800-262-6790 ■ *Web:* www.hbrentals.com	Broussard	LA	70518	337-839-1641		264-3
Hba Architecture Engineering & Interior Design 1 Columbus Ctr Ste 1000 *Web:* www.hbaonline.com	Virginia Beach	VA	23462	757-490-9048		393
HBD Construction Inc 5517 Manchester Ave *Web:* hbdgc.com	Saint Louis	MO	63110	314-781-8000	781-5214	186
HBD Inc 3901 Riverdale Rd *TF:* 800-403-2247 ■ *Web:* www.hbdinc.com	Greensboro	NC	27406	336-275-4800		67
HBD Industries Inc 5200 Upper Metro Pl Ste 110 *Web:* www.hbdindustries.com	Dublin	OH	43017	614-526-7000	526-7020	610
HBD/Thermoid Inc 1301 W Sandusky Ave *TF:* 800-543-8070 ■ *Web:* www.thermoid.com	Bellefontaine	OH	43311	937-593-5010	593-4354	370
HBI (Hickory Brands Inc) 429 27th St NW **Fax Area Code:* 800 ■ *TF:* 800-438-5777 ■ *Web:* hickorybrands.com	Hickory	NC	28601	828-322-2600	422-3279*	745-5
HBM (Heavner, Beyers & Mihlar LLC) 111 E Main St *Web:* www.hsbattys.com	Decatur	IL	62523	217-422-1719	422-1754	428
HBP (Huttig Building Products Inc) 555 Maryville University Dr Ste 400 *NASDAQ: HBP* ■ *TF:* 800-325-4466 ■ *Web:* www.huttig.com	Saint Louis	MO	63141	314-216-2600	216-2601	499
HBP Inc 952 Frederick St *TF:* 800-638-3508 ■ *Web:* www.hbp.com	Hagerstown	MD	21740	301-733-2000		627
HBPL (Huntington Beach Public Library) 7111 Talbert Ave *TF:* 800-565-0148 ■ *Web:* www.huntingtonbeachca.gov	Huntington Beach	CA	92648	714-842-4481	375-5180	434-3
HBSC Strategic Services 100 N Hill Dr Bldg 26 *TF:* 800-970-7995 ■ *Web:* www.hbsconsult.com	Brisbane	CA	94005	415-715-8767		196
HC Davis Sons' Manufacturing Company Inc PO Box 395 *Web:* hcdavis.com	Bonner Springs	KS	66012	913-422-3000	422-7220	190
HC Miller Press 3030 Lowell Dr *Web:* hcmillerpress.com	Green Bay	WI	54311	920-465-3030		86
HC Nutting Co *Terracon* 611 Lunken Pk Dr *Web:* www.terracon.com	Cincinnati	OH	45226	513-321-5816	321-0294	261
HC Starck Inc 45 Industrial Pl *Web:* www.hcstarck.com	Newton	MA	02461	617-630-5800		485
HC Wainwright & Company Inc 430 Park Ave 4th Fl *Web:* hcwco.com	New York	NY	10022	212-356-0500		690
HC&A (Hettrick Cyr & Assoc) 59 Sycamore St *TF:* 888-805-0300 ■ *Web:* www.hettrickcyr.com	Glastonbury	CT	06033	860-652-9997	657-8193	400
HCA Gulf Coast 3737 Buffalo Speedway Ste 1400 *Web:* hcagulfcoast.com	Houston	TX	77098	713-852-1500		363
HCA Healthcare 1 Park Plz *NYSE: HCA* ■ *Web:* hcahealthcare.com	Nashville	TN	37203	615-344-9551		353
HCA Houston Healthcare 710 Cypress Creek Pkwy *Web:* hcahoustonhealthcare.com	Houston	TX	77090	281-440-1000		374-3
HCA Houston Healthcare Clear Lake 500 W Medical Center Blvd *Web:* clearlakermc.com	Webster	TX	77598	281-332-2511		374-3
HCA Houston Healthcare Southeast 4000 Spencer Hwy *Web:* hcahoustonhealthcare.com	Pasadena	TX	77504	713-359-2000	359-1004	374-3
HCA Midwest Health 2316 E Meyer Blvd Ste 500 *TF:* 800-386-9355 ■ *Web:* hcamidwest.com	Kansas City	MO	64132	816-508-4000		353
HCAA (National CPA Health Care Advisors Assn) 1801 W End Ave Ste 800 *TF:* 800-231-2524 ■ *Web:* hcaa.com	Nashville	TN	37203	615-373-9880	377-7092	49-1
HCB (Hardin County Bank, The) 235 Wayne Rd *Web:* www.hardincountybank.bank	Savannah	TN	38372	731-925-9001	925-8106	70
HCC (Highland Community College) 606 W Main *TF:* 800-985-9781 ■ *Web:* highlandcc.edu	Highland	KS	66035	785-442-6000	442-6106	162
HCC Inc 1501 First Ave *TF:* 800-548-6633 ■ *Web:* www.hccincorporated.com	Mendota	IL	61342	815-539-9371	539-3135	273
HCCBA (Hardin County Chamber & Business Alliance) 225 S Detroit St *Web:* hardincountyoh.org	Kenton	OH	43326	419-673-4131	674-4876	139
HCCC (Elizabethtown-Hardin County Chamber of Commerce) 111 W Dixie Ave *Web:* hardinchamber.com	Elizabethtown	KY	42701	270-765-4334	737-0690	139
HCCC (Radcliff) *Hardin County Chamber of Commerce* 306 N Wilson Rd *Web:* www.hardinchamber.com	Radcliff	KY	40160	270-351-4450	352-4449	139
HCCGA (Haines City Citrus Growers Assn) 8 Railroad Ave PO Box 337 *TF:* 800-327-6676	Haines City	FL	33845	863-422-1174		11-1
HCD Research Inc 260 US Hwy 202/31 Ste 1000 *Web:* www.hcdi.net	Flemington	NJ	08822	908-788-9393		466
HCDA Engineering Inc 9 S Weber St *Web:* hcdaengineering.com	Colorado Springs	CO	80903	719-633-7784		261
HCDPL (Holmes County District Public Library) 3102 Glen Dr *Web:* www.holmeslibrary.org	Millersburg	OH	44654	330-674-5972	674-1938	434-3
HCEA (Healthcare Convention & Exhibitors Assn) 7918 Jones Branch Dr Ste 300 *Web:* www.hcea.org	McLean	VA	22102	703-935-1961	506-3266	49-18
HCESC (Hamilton County Educational Service Ctr) 11083 Hamilton Ave *Web:* www.hcesc.org	Cincinnati	OH	45231	513-674-4200	742-8339	685
HCF Management Inc 1100 Shawnee Rd *Web:* hcfinc.com	Lima	OH	45805	419-999-2010	999-6284	451
HCH Institute 3746 Mt Diablo Blvd Ste 200 *Web:* www.hypnotherapytraining.com	Lafayette	CA	94549	925-283-3941		167-3
HCHS (Hunterdon County Historical Society) 114 Main St *Web:* hunterdonhistory.org	Flemington	NJ	08822	908-782-1091		48-13
HCI (Health Communications Inc) 3201 SW 15th St *TF:* 800-441-5569 ■ *Web:* www.hcibooks.com	Deerfield Beach	FL	33442	954-360-0909	360-0034	637-2
HCI (Hatcher Consultants Inc) 2955 SW Wanamaker Dr *Web:* www.hatcherci.com	Topeka	KS	66614	785-271-5557	271-8333	463
HCI Equity Partners 1730 Pennsylvania Ave NW Ste 525 *Web:* www.hciequity.com	Washington	DC	20006	202-371-0150	312-5300	792
HCI Group, The 6440 Southpoint Pkwy Ste 300 *TF:* 866-793-2484 ■ *Web:* www.thehcigroup.com	Jacksonville	FL	32216	904-337-6300		196
HCL (Hennepin County Library) 12601 Ridgedale Dr **Fax Area Code:* 952 ■ *Web:* hclib.org	Minnetonka	MN	55305	612-543-8800	847-8600*	434-3
HCL (Hennepin County Library) 300 Nicollet Mall *Web:* www.supporthclib.org	Minneapolis	MN	55401	612-543-8100		434-3
HCL America Inc 330 Potrero Ave *Web:* www.hcltech.com	Sunnyvale	CA	94085	408-733-0480	733-0482	180
Hcl Global Systems Inc 24543 Indoplex Cir Ste 220 *Web:* hclglobal.com	Farmington	MI	48335	248-473-0720		180
HCM (Henry Community Health) 1000 N 16th St *Web:* www.hchcares.org	New Castle	IN	47362	765-521-0890	521-1555	374-3
HCM Wealth Advisors 6116 Harrison Ave *TF:* 877-598-5120 ■ *Web:* hcmwealthadvisors.com	Cincinnati	OH	45247	513-598-5120		401
HCMC (Hennepin County Medical Ctr) 701 Park Ave *Web:* www.hennepinhealthcare.org	Minneapolis	MN	55415	612-873-3000		374-3
HCP (Honig Conte Porrino Insurance Agency Inc) 129 W 27th St *Web:* honigconte.com	New York	NY	10001	212-777-7113		390
HCP Packaging USA Inc 370 Monument Rd *Web:* www.hcpackaging.com	Hinsdale	NH	03451	603-256-3141	256-6979	548
Hcpro Inc 75 Sylvan St Ste A-10 *TF:* 800-650-6787 ■ *Web:* www.hcpro.com	Danvers	MA	01923	800-650-6787		195
HCPS (Harrisonburg City Public Schools) 317 S Main St *Web:* www.harrisonburg.k12.va.us	Harrisonburg	VA	22801	540-434-9916	434-5196	780
Hcr Inc 80207 US Hwy 87 *Web:* www.hcr-inc.com	Lewistown	MT	59457	406-538-7781	538-5506	202
HCR Manor Care 333 N Summit St PO Box 10086 *Web:* www.hcr-manorcare.com	Toledo	OH	43699	419-252-5500		451
HCR ManorCare 333 N Summit St *Web:* www.heartland-manorcare.com	Toledo	OH	43604	937-429-1106		450

	Phone	Fax	Class
HCS (Health Care Software) 1599 Rt 34 S Ste 2 .... Wall Township NJ 07727 *TF:* 800-524-1038 ■ *Web:* www.hcsinteractant.com	800-524-1038		177
HCS (Healthcare Cost Solutions Inc) 1200 Newport Center Dr Ste 190 .... Newport Beach CA 92660 *TF:* 866-427-7828 ■ *Web:* www.hcsstat.com	949-721-2795	759-1253	194
Hcs Group Inc 1030 E First St .... Humble TX 77338 *Web:* www.hcsgroup.com	281-540-4838	540-6105	261
HCSD (Hamilton City School District) 533 Dayton St PO Box 627 .... Hamilton OH 45012 *Web:* hamiltoncityschools.com	513-887-5000	887-5014	685
HCSG (Healthcare Services Group Inc) 3220 Tillman Dr Ste 300 .... Bensalem PA 19020 *Web:* www.hcsgcorp.com	215-639-4274	639-2152	442
HCTec LLC 5106 Maryland Way Ste 208 .... Franklin TN 37067 *Web:* hctec.com	615-577-4030		260
HCV Pacific Partners 530 Bush St Ste 801 .... San Francisco CA 94108 *Web:* www.hcv-vytc.com	415-249-0800	249-0801	653
HD Electric Co 1475 Lakeside Dr .... Waukegan IL 60085 *Web:* hdelectriccompany.com	847-473-4980	473-4981	248
H-D Electric Co-opeartive Inc 423 Third Ave S .... Clear Lake SD 57226 *TF:* 800-781-7474 ■ *Web:* h-delectric.coop	605-874-2171	874-8173	245
HD Hudson Manufacturing Co 500 N Michigan Ave .... Chicago IL 60611 *TF:* 800-977-7293 ■ *Web:* www.adaptasprayer.com	312-644-2830	644-7989	273
HDE (Hewitt Development Enterprises) 1717 N Bayshore Dr Ste 2154 .... Miami FL 33132 *Web:* www.hewittdevelopment.com	305-372-0941		194
HDF (Hereditary Disease Foundation) 3960 Broadway 6th Fl .... New York NY 10032 *Web:* www.hdfoundation.org	212-928-2121	928-2172	48-17
HDF Group 1800 S Oak St Ste 203 .... Champaign IL 61820 *Web:* www.hdfgroup.org	217-531-6100		177
HDI Solutions LLC 1550 Pumphrey Ave .... Auburn AL 36832 *TF:* 800-282-0999 ■ *Web:* www.hdisolutions.com	800-282-0999		225
HDL Cos 1340 Vly Vista Dr Ste 200 .... Diamond Bar CA 91765 *TF:* 888-861-0220 ■ *Web:* www.hdlcompanies.com	909-861-4335		463
HDM (Houston Drilling Management LLC) 900 Rockmead Dr Ste 220 .... Kingwood TX 77339 *Web:* www.hdm-us.com	281-312-1024	312-1064	196
HDM Hydraulics LLC 125 Fire Tower Dr .... Tonawanda NY 14150 *Web:* www.hdmhydraulics.com	716-694-8004	694-4164	262
HDMG 555 First Ave NE .... Minneapolis MN 55413 *Web:* www.hdmg.com	612-224-9500	224-9515	512
HDMZ (Harris D. McKinney & Zoomedia HDMZ) 1620 Montgomery St .... San Francisco CA 94111 *Web:* www.hdmz.com	415-474-1192	474-8146	177
HDR Engineering Inc 1917 S 67th St .... Omaha NE 68114 *TF:* 800-366-4411 ■ *Web:* www.hdrinc.com	402-399-1000	548-5015	261
HDS (Hartley Data Service Inc) 1807 Glenview Rd Ste 201 .... Glenview IL 60025 *Web:* hartleydata.com	847-724-9280	729-2199	225
HDS Truck Driving Institute 6251 S Wilmot Rd .... Tucson AZ 85756 *TF:* 877-205-2141 ■ *Web:* www.hdstruckdrivinginstitute.com	877-205-2141		167-3
HDSA (Huntington's Disease Society of America) 505 Eigth Ave Ste 902 .... New York NY 10018 *TF:* 800-345-4372 ■ *Web:* www.hdsa.org	212-242-1968	239-3430	48-17
HDSB (Holmes District School Board) 701 E Pennsylvania Ave .... Bonifay FL 32425 *Web:* www.hdsb.org	850-547-9341		685
HDSP (High Desert State Prison) 475-750 Rice Canyon Rd PO Box 750 .... Susanville CA 96127 *Web:* cdcr.ca.gov	530-251-5100		213
HDT Global 30500 Aurora Rd Ste 100 .... Solon OH 44139 **Fax Area Code: 440* ■ *TF:* 800-969-8527 ■ *Web:* www.hdtglobal.com	216-438-6111	248-1691*	15
HE Forum Newspaper Inc 155-19 Lahn St .... Howard Beach NY 11414 *Web:* www.theforumnewsgroup.com	718-845-3221	738-7645	532-4
HE Neumann Inc 100 Middle Creek Rd .... Triadelphia WV 26059 *TF:* 800-627-5312 ■ *Web:* www.heneumann.com	304-232-3040	232-7858	189-10
HE Press & Sun-Bulletin 33 Lewis Rd Ste 9 .... Binghamton NY 13905 *TF:* 800-253-5343 ■ *Web:* pressconnects.com	607-798-1234		532-3
HE Williams Inc 831 W Fairview Ave .... Carthage MO 64836 *TF:* 866-358-4065 ■ *Web:* www.hew.com	417-358-4065	358-6015	439
HEA (Harmon Electric Association Inc) 114 N First St PO Box 393 .... Hollis OK 73550 *TF:* 800-643-7769 ■ *Web:* www.harmonelectric.com	580-688-3342		245
HEAB (Wisconsin Higher Educational Aids Board) 131 W Wilson S PO Box 7885 .... Madison WI 53703 *Web:* www.heab.state.wi.us	608-267-2206	267-2808	725
Head in the Cloud Inc 220A Twin Dolphin Dr .... Redwood City CA 94065 *Web:* hitcloud.com	650-234-7100		196
Head Inc 4477 E 5th Ave .... Columbus OH 43219 *Web:* www.headinc.com	614-338-8501	338-8514	187
Head Injury Hotline 212 Pioneer Bldg .... Seattle WA 98104 *TF:* 888-644-2667 ■ *Web:* www.headinjury.com	206-621-8558		48-17
Head Insurance Agency LLC W579 Castle Dr .... Sherwood WI 54169 *Web:* headinsurance.biz	920-989-1473	989-2473	390
Head Johnson & Kachigian Pc 228 W 17th Pl .... Tulsa OK 74119 *Web:* www.hjkwlaw.com	918-587-2000		445
Head Start of Greater Dallas Inc 3954 Gannon Ln .... Dallas TX 75237 *Web:* www.hsgd.org	972-283-6400		148
Head USA Inc 3125 Sterling Cir Ste 101 .... Boulder CO 80301 *TF:* 800-874-3235 ■ *Web:* www.head.com	800-874-3235		710
Headcovers Unlimited 35 Tiffany Plz .... Ardmore OK 73401 *Web:* www.headcovers.com	580-226-5871		348
Header Die and Tool Inc 3022 Eastrock Ct .... Rockford Il 61109 *Web:* www.header.com	815-397-0123	397-7672	757
Headington Oil Co 2711 N Haskell Ave Ste 2800 .... Dallas TX 75204 *Web:* www.headington.com	214-696-0606		536
Headley Insurance Agency LLC 3544 S Florida Ave .... Lakeland FL 33803 *Web:* headleyinsurance.net	863-701-7411		390
Headley-Whitney Museum of Art 4435 Old Frankfort Pk .... Lexington KY 40510 *Web:* www.headley-whitney.org	859-255-6653		520
Headlight Audio Visual Inc 74 Evergreen Dr .... Portland ME 04103 *TF:* 800-247-0540 ■ *Web:* www.headlightav.com	207-774-5998	774-4917	23
Headliner Talent Marketing 45778 375th St .... Perham MN 56573 *Web:* headlinertalent.com	715-254-1977		50-6
Headlines Academy 333 Omaha St Ste 6-7 .... Rapid City SD 57701 *Web:* www.headlinesacademy.com	605-348-4247		167-3
Headmasters School of Hair Design 602 Main St .... Lewiston ID 83501 *Web:* www.headmasters.edu	208-743-1512		685
Headquarter Toyota 5895 NW 167th St .... Miami FL 33015 *TF:* 800-549-0947 ■ *Web:* headquartertoyota.com	305-600-4663		57
HeadquartersCom Inc 625 Walnut Ridge Dr Ste 108 .... Hartland WI 53029	262-369-0600		809
Headquist International Inc 230 Florence St .... Crystal Lake IL 60014 *Web:* www.hedquistintl.com	815-479-1700		260
Headrick Companies Inc, The 1 Freedom Sq .... Laurel MS 39440 *TF:* 800-933-1365 ■ *Web:* www.headricks.com	601-649-1977		5
Heads Up Technologies Inc 2033 Chenault Dr Ste 100 .... Carrollton TX 75006 *TF:* 800-367-4770 ■ *Web:* www.heads-up.com	972-980-4890	980-4843	438
Headset Zone 406 164th St SW Ste A .... Lynnwood WA 98037 *TF:* 800-533-4014 ■ *Web:* www.headsetzone.com	800-533-4014		459
Headsets Direct Inc 1454 W Gurley St Ste A .... Prescott AZ 86305 *TF:* 800-914-7996 ■ *Web:* www.headsetsdirect.com	928-777-9100		246
Headstart Hair For Men Inc 3395 Cypress Gardens Rd .... Winter Haven FL 33884 *TF:* 800-645-6525 ■ *Web:* www.headstarthairformen.com	863-324-5559	324-5673	348
Headwall Photonics Inc 601 River St .... Fitchburg MA 01420 *Web:* www.headwallphotonics.com	978-353-4100		639
Headwater Exploration Inc 5475 Spring Garden Rd .... Halifax NS B3J3T2 *TF:* 888-429-4511 ■ *Web:* headwaterexp.com	902-429-4511		536
Headwaters 1001 SW Broadway .... Portland OR 97205 *Web:* www.headwaterspdx.com	503-790-7752		671
Headwaters Builders Assn PO Box 1074 ...... Minocqua WI 54548 *Web:* www.headwatersbuilders.com	715-542-3557		48-13
Headwaters Health Care Ctr 100 Rolling Hills Dr .... Orangeville ON L9W4X9 *Web:* www.headwatershealth.ca	519-941-2410	942-0483	374-2
Headwaters Inc 10701 S River Front Pkwy Ste 300 .... South Jordan UT 84095 *NYSE: HW* ■ *Web:* www.headwaters.com	801-984-9400		804
Headway Technologies Inc 682 S Hillview Dr .... Milpitas CA 95035 *Web:* headway.com	408-934-5300	942-6916	173-8
Headway Workforce Solutions 421 Fayetteville St Ste 1020 .... Raleigh NC 27601 *TF:* 800-948-9379 ■ *Web:* www.headwaywfs.com	919-376-4929		721
Headwest Inc 15650 S Avalon Blvd .... Compton CA 90220 *Web:* headwestinc.com	310-532-5420	532-5920	332
Heale Manufacturing Company Inc 1231 The Strand .... Waukesha WI 53186 *Web:* www.healemfg.com	262-542-4496	542-6928	253
Healing Arts Ctr 10073 Manchester Rd No 100 .... Saint Louis MO 63122 *Web:* www.thehealingartscenter.com	314-647-8080		167-3
Healing Hands Institute 2141 SW 1 St Ste 201 .... Miami FL 33135 *Web:* www.hhi.edu	786-401-6270	401-6294	167-3
Healing Hands School of Holistic Health 125 W Mission Ave No 212 .... Escondido CA 92025 *TF:* 800-355-6463 ■ *Web:* hhs.edu	760-746-9364	839-0504	685
Healing Mountain Massage School 363 South 500 East Ste 210 .... Salt Lake City UT 84102 *TF:* 800-407-3251 ■ *Web:* www.healingmountain.org	801-355-6300		685
Healing Spirits Massage Training Program 550 Mohawk Dr 3825 Iris Ave Ste 300 No 65 ...... Boulder CO 80301 *Web:* www.healingspirits.net	303-525-5213	543-0093	167-3
Healing the Children (HTC) 2624 W Beacon Ave .... Spokane WA 99208 *Web:* www.healingthechildren.org	509-327-4281	327-4284	48-5
Healogics Inc 5220 Belfort Rd Ste 130 .... Jacksonville FL 32256 *TF:* 800-379-9774 ■ *Web:* www.healogics.com	800-379-9774		374-3
Health & Education Federal Credit Union, The 424 Park Pl .... Lexington KY 40511 *Web:* thefcu.com	859-231-8262		219
Region 1 200 Independence Ave .... Washington DC 20201 *Web:* www.hrsa.gov	301-443-3376		340-10
Health & Safety Institute Inc 1450 Westec Dr .... Eugene OR 97402 *TF:* 800-447-3177 ■ *Web:* www.hsi.com	800-447-3177		764
Health Advocacy Strategies LLC 601 Union St Ste 4840 .... Seattle WA 98101 *Web:* hastrategies.com	206-861-1000		636
Health Alliance of MidAmerica LLC, The 2345 Grand Bvd Ste 2400 .... Kansas City MO 64108 *Web:* www.allianceweb.org	816-941-3800		474
Health Alliance Plan 2850 W Grand Blvd .... Detroit MI 48202 *TF:* 800-422-4641 ■ *Web:* www.hap.org	313-872-8100	664-5866	391-3
Health and Care Professional Network 4850 W Flamingo Rd Ste 25 .... Las Vegas NV 89103 *Web:* www.healthandcareprofessionals.com	702-871-9917	582-0887	363

Name / Address	City	State	Zip	Phone	Fax	Class
Health Care Credit Union 769 E South Temple *TF:* 800-283-4550 ■ *Web:* gwcu.org	Salt Lake City	UT	84102	800-283-4550		219
Health Care Family Credit Union 2114 S Big Bend Blvd. *Web:* healthcarefamilycreditunion.org	Richmond Heights	MO	63117	314-645-5851		219
Health Care Software (HCS) 1599 Rt 34 S Ste 2 *TF:* 800-524-1038 ■ *Web:* www.hcsinteractant.com	Wall Township	NJ	07727	800-524-1038		177
Health Care Unlimited Inc 1100 E Laurel Ave. *TF:* 877-994-9923 ■ *Web:* www.hcuinc.com	Mcallen	TX	78501	956-994-9911	488-1343	237
Health Career Institute 1764 N Congress Ave. *Web:* www.hci.edu	West Palm Beach	FL	33409	561-586-0121	471-4010	167-3
Health Coalition Inc 8320 NW 30th Terr *TF:* 800-456-7283 ■ *Web:* www.healthcoalition.com	Doral	FL	33122	305-662-2988	667-5389	238
Health Communications Inc (HCI) 3201 SW 15th St *TF:* 800-441-5569 ■ *Web:* www.hcibooks.com	Deerfield Beach	FL	33442	954-360-0909	360-0034	637-2
Health Connect Partners Inc 65 Business Park Dr. *Web:* www.hlthcp.com	Lebanon	TN	37090	615-449-6234	449-5030	184
Health Decisions Inc 2510 Meridian Pkwy. *TF:* 888-779-3771 ■ *Web:* healthdec.com	Durham	NC	27713	919-967-2399	967-1145	463
Health Design Plus Inc 1755 Georgetown Rd *Web:* www.hdplus.com	Hudson	OH	44236	330-656-1072	656-9387	390
Health Dimensions Group 4400 Baker Rd Ste 100. *Web:* healthdimensionsgroup.com	Minnetonka	MN	55343	763-537-5700		194
Health First 6450 US Highway 1 *Web:* www.hf.org	Rockledge	FL	32955	321-434-4335		352
Health Hut 1512 First Ave NE. *Web:* www.healthhutcr.com	Cedar Rapids	IA	52402	319-362-7345		296-11
Health Industry Business Communications Council (HIBCC) 2525 E Arizona Biltmore Cir Ste 127 *TF:* 800-755-5505 ■ *Web:* www.hibcc.org	Phoenix	AZ	85016	602-381-1091	381-1093	49-8
Health Industry Distributors Assn (HIDA) 310 Montgomery St *TF:* 800-549-4432 ■ *Web:* www.hida.org	Alexandria	VA	22314	703-549-4432		49-18
Health Information Designs Inc 391 Industry Dr.	Auburn	AL	36832	334-502-3262		177
Health Insurance Specialists Inc 17620 A Redlands Rd. *Web:* his-inc.com	Rockville	MD	20855	301-590-0006		390
Health Integrated 10008 N Dale Mabry Hwy. **Fax Area Code:* 813 ■ *TF:* 877-267-7577 ■ *Web:* www.healthintegrated.com	Tampa	FL	33618	877-267-7577	388-4001*	194
Health iPASS Inc 1111 22nd St Ste 222. *TF:* 855-484-4727 ■ *Web:* healthipass.com	Oak Brook	IL	60523	855-484-4727		387
Health IQ 2513 Charleston Rd Ste 102. *TF:* 800-549-1664 ■ *Web:* www.healthiq.com	Mountain View	CA	94043	800-549-1664		391-1
Health Management Services Inc 9100 SW Fwy Ste 114 **Fax Area Code:* 832 ■ *Web:* www.hmssleep.com	Houston	TX	77074	713-541-2727	201-0196*	194
Health Management Systems Inc 401 Park Ave S *TF:* 877-357-3268 ■ *Web:* www.hms.com	New York	NY	10016	212-725-7965	857-5004	225
Health Mart of Gueydan Inc 200 Main. *Web:* gueydanhealthmart.com	Gueydan	LA	70542	337-536-9600		237
Health Medical Equipment Inc 2694 SW 87th Ave *Web:* www.healthmedical.com	Miami	FL	33165	305-223-7222	223-0122	475
Health Metrics Inc (HMI) 6929 N Hayden Rd Ste C4-600. *Web:* www.healthmetrics.com	Scottsdale	AZ	85250	801-566-1899	880-1160	352
Health Net of Arizona Inc 1230 W Washington St. *TF:* 800-291-6911 ■ *Web:* www.healthnet.com	Tempe	AZ	85281	602-794-1400		353
Health Net of West Michigan 620 Century SW Ste 210 *Web:* healthnetwm.org	Grand Rapids	MI	49503	616-726-8204	726-8205	363
Health Network America Inc 745 Hope Rd. *Web:* www.healthnetworkamerica.com	Tinton Falls	NJ	07724	732-676-2630	676-2657	390
Health Partners 8170 33rd Ave S *TF:* 800-247-7015 ■ *Web:* www.healthpartners.com	Minneapolis	MN	55425	952-883-6877		371
Health Physics Society 1313 Dolley Madison Blvd Ste 402 *TF:* 888-624-8373 ■ *Web:* www.hps.org	McLean	VA	22101	703-790-1745	790-2672	48-17
Health Plan of Nevada Inc PO Box 15645 *Web:* www.healthplanofnevada.com	Las Vegas	NV	89114	702-242-7300		391-3
Health Plan of San Joaquin 7751 S Manthey Rd **Fax Area Code:* 209 ■ *TF:* 888-936-7526 ■ *Web:* www.hpsj.com	French Camp	CA	95231	888-936-7526	942-6305*	391-3
Health Products Corp 1060 Nepperhan Ave. *Web:* healthproductscorporation.com	Yonkers	NY	10703	914-423-2900		799
Health Professions Press (HPP) PO Box 10624 *TF:* 888-337-8808 ■ *Web:* www.healthpropress.com	Baltimore	MD	21285	410-337-9585	337-8539	637-2
Health Resources & Services Administration (HRSA) 5600 Fishers Ln *TF:* 888-275-4772 ■ *Web:* www.hrsa.gov	Rockville	MD	20857	301-443-2216		340-10
Health Resources Inc PO Box 659 *TF:* 800-727-1444 ■ *Web:* www.insuringsmiles.com	Evansville	IN	47704	812-424-1444	424-2096	352
Health Revenue Assurance Assn 8551 W Sunrise Blvd Ste 304.	Plantation	FL	33322	954-472-2340		317
Health Sciences Ctr 820 Sherbrook St *Web:* www.hsc.mb.ca	Winnipeg	MB	R3A1R9	204-787-3661		374-2
Health Systems 2000 1901 Oak Park Blvd *Web:* www.hhc2000.com	Lake Charles	LA	70601	337-562-1140		363
Health Tradition Health Plan 1808 E Main St. *TF:* 800-545-8499 ■ *Web:* www.healthtradition.com	Onalaska	WI	54650	608-781-9692		391-3
Health Union 1218 Chestnut St 2nd Fl. *Web:* health-union.com	Philadelphia	PA	19107	484-985-9715		48-17
Health Unit Brant County 194 Ter Hill St. *TF:* 800-565-8603 ■ *Web:* www.bchu.org	Brantford	ON	N3R1G7	519-753-4937		138
HealthAlliance Leominster Hospital 60 Hospital Rd *Web:* www.umassmemorialhealthcare.org	Leominster	MA	01453	978-466-2000		374-3
HealthAxis Inc 7301 N State Hwy 161. *TF:* 888-974-2947 ■ *Web:* www.healthaxis.com	Irving	TX	75039	435-381-5443		463
HealthCap Partners LLC 4849 Greenville Ave Ste 1480. *Web:* healthcap.com	Dallas	TX	75206	214-953-1722		528
HealthCap Risk Management Services 130 S First St No 400. *TF:* 877-855-4227 ■ *Web:* www.healthcapusa.com	Ann Arbor	MI	48104	734-996-2700	996-1261	194
Healthcare Administrative Partners LLC 112 Chesley Dr. *TF:* 800-889-4447 ■ *Web:* www.hapusa.com	Media	PA	19063	610-892-8889		225
Healthcare Business Management LLC 1752 Howell Branch Rd *Web:* www.hbmorlando.com	Winter Park	FL	32789	407-645-1150	645-2178	194
Healthcare Commons Inc 500 S Pennsville-Auburn Rd *Web:* www.hcommons.com	Carneys Point	NJ	08069	856-299-3200		374-5
Healthcare Consultancy Group 488 Madison Ave 5th Fl *Web:* www.hcg-int.com	New York	NY	10022	212-849-7900		4
Healthcare Convention & Exhibitors Assn (HCEA) 7918 Jones Branch Dr Ste 300. *Web:* www.hcea.org	McLean	VA	22102	703-935-1961	506-3266	49-18
Healthcare Cost Solutions Inc (HCS) 1200 Newport Center Dr Ste 190 *TF:* 866-427-7828 ■ *Web:* www.hcsstat.com	Newport Beach	CA	92660	949-721-2795	759-1253	194
Healthcare Distribution Alliance 901 N Glebe Rd Ste 1000 *Web:* www.hda.org	Arlington	VA	22203	703-787-0000		49-18
Healthcare Environment 888 County Rd D W *Web:* www.hcenvironment.com	New Brighton	MN	55112	651-633-6519		194
Healthcare Financial Management Assn (HFMA) 2 Westbrook Corporate Ctr Ste 700 **Fax Area Code:* 708 ■ *TF:* 800-252-4362 ■ *Web:* www.hfma.org	Westchester	IL	60154	800-252-4362	531-0032*	49-8
Healthcare Information & Management Systems Society (HIMSS) 230 E Ohio St Ste 500 *Web:* www.himss.org	Chicago	IL	60611	312-664-4467	664-6143	49-8
Healthcare Leadership Council (HLC) 750 Ninth St NW Ste 500 *Web:* www.hlc.org	Washington	DC	20001	202-452-8700	296-9561	48-17
Healthcare Realty Trust Inc 3310 W End Ave Ste 700 *NYSE:* HR ■ *Web:* www.healthcarerealty.com	Nashville	TN	37203	615-269-8175		655
Healthcare Services Credit Union 946 E Third St. *Web:* hscu.net	Chattanooga	TN	37403	423-242-4728	242-1940	219
Healthcare Services Group Inc (HCSG) 3220 Tillman Dr Ste 300. *Web:* www.hcsgcorp.com	Bensalem	PA	19020	215-639-4274	639-2152	442
Healthcare Ventures LLC 47 Thorndike St Ste B1-1 *Web:* hcven.com	Cambridge	MA	02141	617-252-4343		360-3
HealthCareSource Inc 100 Sylvan Rd Ste 100 *TF:* 800-869-5200 ■ *Web:* www.healthcaresource.com	Woburn	MA	01801	800-869-5200	829-6600	260
Healthcom 1600 W Jackson St *TF:* 800-525-6237 ■ *Web:* www.healthcominc.com	Sullivan	IL	61951	800-525-6237		475
HealthDrive Corp 888 Worcester St *TF:* 888-964-6681 ■ *Web:* www.healthdrive.com	Wellesley	MA	02482	888-964-6681	662-0859	352
HealthEdge Investment Partners 5550 W Executive Dr Ste 230 *Web:* www.healthedgepartners.com	Tampa	FL	33609	813-490-7100		401
HEALTHeLINK 2475 George Urban Blvd Ste 202 *TF:* 877-895-4724 ■ *Web:* wnyhealthelink.com	Depew	NY	14043	716-206-0993		415
HEALTHEON Inc 201 St Charles Ave Ste 4310 *Web:* healtheoninc.com	New Orleans	LA	70170	504-599-5982		415
HealthFocus Intl 100 Second Ave N Ste 220. *Web:* www.healthfocus.com	Saint Petersburg	FL	33701	727-821-7499	821-7764	466
HealthForce Ontario Marketing & Recruitment Agency 163 Queen St E. *TF:* 800-596-4046 ■ *Web:* www.healthforceontario.ca	Toronto	ON	M5A1S1	416-862-2200		260
Healthforce Partners Inc 18323 Bothell Everett Hwy *TF:* 877-437-2497 ■ *Web:* www.healthforcepartners.com	Bothell	WA	98012	425-806-5700		194
Healthhelp LLC 16945 Northchase Dr Ste 1300. *TF:* 877-795-0373 ■ *Web:* www.healthhelp.com	Houston	TX	77060	281-447-7000		196
HealthInsight Inc 756 E Winchester St Ste 200 *Web:* healthinsight.org	Salt Lake City	UT	84107	801-892-0155		194
HealthLink Inc 1831 Chestnut St. *TF:* 877-284-0101 ■ *Web:* www.healthlink.com	Saint Louis	MO	63103	877-284-0101		390
Healthlinx Transitional Leadership Inc 1404 Goodale Blvd Ste 400 *TF:* 800-980-4820 ■ *Web:* healthlinx.com	Columbus	OH	43212	800-980-4820		463
HealthMarkets Inc 9151 Blvd 26 *TF:* 800-827-9990 ■ *Web:* www.healthmarketsinc.com	North Richland Hills	TX	76180	800-827-9990		360-4
Healthpac Computer Systems Inc 1010 E Victory Dr *Web:* www.healthpac.net	Savannah	GA	31405	912-341-7420		225

	Phone	Fax	Class
Healthpeak Properties Inc 1920 Main St Ste 1200......Irvine CA 92614 *Web:* www.healthpeak.com	949-407-0700		655
Healthplex Inc 333 Earl Ovington Blvd......Uniondale NY 11553 *TF:* 800-468-0608 ■ *Web:* www.healthplex.com	516-542-2200		391-3
HealthSCOPE Benefits Inc 27 Corporate Hill Dr......Little Rock AR 72205 *TF:* 800-884-0287 ■ *Web:* www.healthscopebenefits.com	501-225-1551		390
Healthshare Inc 1108 Lavaca......Austin TX 78701 *Web:* www.healthshare-tha.com	512-465-1028		138
HealthSmart Intl 1931 Norman Dr......Waukegan IL 60085 *TF:* 800-526-4753 ■ *Web:* www.livehealthsmart.com	800-526-4753	479-7968	475
HealthSource Saginaw 3340 Hospital Rd......Saginaw MI 48603 *TF:* 800-662-6848 ■ *Web:* www.healthsourcesaginaw.org	989-790-7700		726
Healthspace USA Inc 4860 Cox Rd Ste 200......Glen Allen VA 23060 *TF:* 866-860-4224 ■ *Web:* www.healthspace.ca	804-935-8532		201
HealthStaff Training Institute 1970 Old Tustin Ave Ste C......Santa Ana CA 92705 *Web:* healthstaff.training	714-543-9828	543-9835	167-3
HealthSTAR Communications Inc 1000 Wyckoff Ave......Mahwah NJ 07430 *Web:* www.healthstarcom.com	201-560-5370		4
HealthStream Inc 209 Tenth Ave S Ste 450......Nashville TN 37203 *NASDAQ: HSTM* ■ *TF:* 800-933-9293 ■ *Web:* www.healthstream.com	615-301-3100	301-3200	765
Healthtrax Fitness & Wellness 100 Simsbury Rd......Avon CT 06001 *TF:* 800-505-5000 ■ *Web:* www.healthtrax.com	860-284-1190	652-7066	354
HealthTronics Inc 9825 Spectrum Dr Bldg 3......Austin TX 78717 *TF:* 888-252-6575 ■ *Web:* www.healthtronics.com	512-328-2892	439-8303	250
Healthways WholeHealth Network Inc 21251 Ridgetop Cir Ste 150......Sterling VA 20166 *Web:* www.wholehealthpro.com	888-492-1027		391-3
Healthwise Home Care Solutions Inc 1100 N Ventura Rd Ste 102......Oxnard CA 93030 *Web:* www.healthwisehomesolutions.com	805-983-0086	983-0079	363
Healthwise Inc 2601 N Bogus Basin Rd......Boise ID 83702 *TF:* 800-706-9646 ■ *Web:* www.healthwise.org	800-706-9646		637-2
HealthWorks! Kids' Museum 111 W Jefferson Blvd......South Bend IN 46601 *Web:* www.healthworkskids.org	574-647-5437		521
Healthy 'N Fit International Inc 435 Yorktown Rd......Croton-on-Hudson NY 10520 *TF:* 800-338-5200 ■ *Web:* www.behealthynfit.com	914-271-6040	271-6042	231
Healthy Back Store LLC 10300 Southard Dr......Beltsville MD 20705 *TF:* 800-469-2225 ■ *Web:* www.healthyback.com	800-469-2225		321
Healthy Baking Co, The 1205 Stanford Ave......Emeryville CA 94608 *TF:* 800-830-0309 ■ *Web:* www.thehealthybakingcompany.com	510-658-3700	652-2361	296-9
Healthy Companies Intl 2107 Wilson Blvd Ste 530......Arlington VA 22201 *Web:* healthycompanies.com	703-351-9901		194
Healthy Directions LLC 7811 Montrose Rd......Potomac MD 20854 *TF:* 866-599-9491 ■ *Web:* www.healthydirections.com	866-599-9491		637-9
Healthy Heart Nurse Inc 6006 W 159th St Bldg D......Oak Forest IL 60452 *Web:* healthyheartnurse.com	708-367-1300	535-1575	363
Healthy Pet 6960 Salashan Pkwy......Ferndale WA 98248 *TF:* 800-242-2287 ■ *Web:* www.healthy-pet.com	360-734-7415	671-1588	578
Healthy Pets of Westgate Inc 3588 W Broad St......Columbus OH 43228 *Web:* healthypetsofohio.com	614-279-8415		794
Healthy Petz Veterinary Clinic 109 Enola Rd......Morganton NC 28655 *Web:* myhealthypetz.com	828-437-4524		794
Healthy Solutions Insurance Services 55 Independence Cir Ste 108......Chico CA 95973 *Web:* healthysolutionsinsuranceservices.com	530-895-3882		390
Healthy Teen Network 1501 St Paul St Ste 124......Baltimore MD 21202 *Web:* www.healthyteennetwork.org	410-685-0410		48-6
Healy Brothers Insurance Agency Inc 10 Common St PO Box 99......Barre MA 01005 *Web:* healybros.com	978-355-4536		390
Healy Group Inc, The 17535 Generations Dr......South Bend IN 46635 *TF:* 800-667-4613 ■ *Web:* healygroup.com	574-271-6000	243-3214	390
Healy Long & Jevin Inc 2000 Rodman Rd......Wilmington DE 19805 *Web:* www.healylongjevin.com	302-654-8039	654-8153	189-3
Healy Tibbitts Builders Inc 99-994 Iwaena St Ste A......Aiea HI 96701 *Web:* www.healytibbitts.com	808-487-3664	487-3660	188-3
Heapy Engineering Inc 1400 W Dorothy Ln......Dayton OH 45409 *Web:* heapy.com	937-224-0861		261
Heard & Medack PC 9494 SW Fwy Ste 700......Houston TX 77074 *Web:* heardmedackpc.com	713-772-6400		41
Heard & Smith LLP 3737 Broadway Ste 310......San Antonio TX 78209 *TF:* 800-584-3700 ■ *Web:* www.heardandsmith.com	210-820-3737		428
Heard County 215 E Court Sq......Franklin GA 30217 *Web:* www.heardcountyga.com	706-675-3821	675-2493	338
Heard Museum 2301 N Central Ave......Phoenix AZ 85004 *Web:* heard.org	602-252-8840	252-9757	520
Heard Natural Science Museum & Wildlife Sanctuary 1 Nature Pl......McKinney TX 75069 *Web:* www.heardmuseum.org	972-562-5566	548-9119	520
Heard, McElroy and Vestal LLP 333 Texas St Ste 1525......Shreveport LA 71101 *TF:* 800-241-0151 ■ *Web:* www.hmvcpa.com	318-429-1525	429-2070	2
Hearing Health Foundation 363 Seventh Ave......New York NY 10001 *TF:* 888-435-6104 ■ *Web:* hearinghealthfoundation.org	212-257-6140		48-17
Hearing Loss Association of America 7910 Woodmont Ave Ste 1200......Bethesda MD 20814 *TF:* 800-221-6827 ■ *Web:* www.hearingloss.org	301-657-2248	913-9413	48-17
Hearn Co, The 875 N Michigan Ave Ste 4100......Chicago IL 60611 *Web:* www.hearncompany.com	312-408-3000	408-3010	653
Hearn Kirkwood 7251 Standard Dr......Hanover MD 21076 *Web:* www.hearnkirkwood.com	410-712-6000		297-7
Hearn Paper Co 556 N Meridian Rd......Youngstown OH 44509 **Fax Area Code:* 330 ■ *TF:* 800-225-2989 ■ *Web:* www.hearnpaper.com	800-225-2989	792-4762*	553
Hearst Autos Inc 550 Kearny St Ste 500......San Francisco CA 94108 *Web:* www.hearstautos.com	415-844-6300		317
Hearst Corp *Hearst Magazines Div* 300 W 57th St......New York NY 10019 *Web:* www.hearst.com	212-649-2275		637-9
Hearst Foundation, The 300 W 57th St 26th Fl......New York NY 10019 *TF:* 800-841-7048 ■ *Web:* www.hearstfdn.org	212-649-3750	586-1917	305
Hearst San Simeon State Historical Monument 750 Hearst Castle Rd......San Simeon CA 93452 *TF:* 800-444-4445 ■ *Web:* www.parks.ca.gov	805-927-2020		565
Heart & Crown 67 Clarence St......Ottawa ON K1N5P5 *Web:* heartandcrown.pub	613-562-0674		671
Heart & Soul Magazine 15480 Annapolis Rd Ste 202-225......Bowie MD 20715 *TF:* 800-834-8813 ■ *Web:* www.heartandsoul.com	800-834-8813		457-13
Heart O' Texas Speedway 784 N McLennan Dr......Elm Mott TX 76640 *Web:* www.heartotexasspeedway.com	254-829-2294		515
Heart of Hope Asian American Hospice Care 1922 The Alameda Ste 215......San Jose CA 95126 *TF:* 888-663-8585 ■ *Web:* en.heartofhopehospice.org	408-986-8584	986-8581	363
Heart of Iowa Communications Coop 502 Main St......Union IA 50258 *Web:* www.home.heartofiowa.net	641-486-2211	486-2205	224
Heart of Texas Electric Co-op 1111 Johnson Dr PO Box 357......McGregor TX 76657 *TF:* 800-840-2957 ■ *Web:* www.hotec.coop	254-840-2871	840-4250	245
Heart of the House Hospitality 2346 S Lynhurst Dr Ste A-201......Indianapolis IN 46241 *TF:* 888-365-1440 ■ *Web:* www.heartofthehouse.com	888-365-1440		260
Heart of the Matter Expertise 2451 Brickell Ave 12-C......Miami FL 33129 *Web:* heartofyourcase.com	786-908-2438		194
Heart of the Valley Chamber of Commerce 101 E Wisconsin Ave......Kaukauna WI 54130 *Web:* heartofthevalleychamber.com	920-766-1616	766-5504	139
Heart of Virginia Council Incorporated Boy Scouts of America 4015 Fitzhugh Ave......Richmond VA 23230 *Web:* hovc.org	804-355-4306	353-6109	138
Heart of Wisconsin Business & Economic Alliance 1120 Lincoln St......Wisconsin Rapids WI 54494 *Web:* www.wisconsinrapidschamber.com	715-423-1830		139
Heart Rhythm Society 1400 K St NW Ste 500......Washington DC 20005 *Web:* www.hrsonline.org	202-464-3400	464-3401	49-8
Heart Six Ranch 16985 Buffalo Valley Rd......Moran WY 83013 *Web:* heartsix.com	307-543-2477		239
Heart to Heart Intl 13250 W 98th St......Lenexa KS 66215 *Web:* www.hearttoheart.org	913-764-5200		48-5
HEARTBEAT/Survivors After Suicide Inc 2015 Devon St......Colorado Springs CO 80909 *Web:* heartbeatsurvivorsaftersuicide.org	719-596-2575		48-21
Hearth & Home Technologies Inc 7571 215th St W......Lakeville MN 55044 *TF:* 888-427-3973 ■ *Web:* www.hearthnhome.com	952-985-6000		357
Hearth Patio & Barbecue Assn (HPBA) 1901 N Moore St Ste 600......Arlington VA 22209 *Web:* www.hpba.org	703-522-0086	522-0548	49-4
Hearthstone at Green Lake, The 6720 E Green Lake Way N......Seattle WA 98103 *Web:* www.hearthstone.org	206-525-9666		672
Hearthstone of Round Rock 401 Oakwood Blvd......Round Rock TX 78681 *Web:* abrihealthcare.com	512-388-7494	388-2166	450
Heartland Aviation 3800 Starr Ave......Eau Claire WI 54703 *TF:* 800-767-3181 ■ *Web:* www.heartlandaviation.com	715-835-3181	835-7150	167-3
Heartland Bank & Trust Co 606 S Main St......Princeton IL 61356 *OTC: PNBC* ■ *TF:* 888-897-2276 ■ *Web:* www.hbtbank.com	815-875-4444		360-2
Heartland Behavioral Healthcare 3000 S Erie St......Massillon OH 44646 *TF:* 800-783-9301 ■ *Web:* mha.ohio.gov	330-833-3135	833-6564	374-5
Heartland Blood Centers 1200 N Highland Ave......Aurora IL 60506 *TF:* 800-786-4483 ■ *Web:* www.versiti.org	630-892-7055	892-4590	89
Heartland Brewery 1430 Broadway Ste 1513......New York NY 10018 *Web:* www.heartlandbrewery.com	212-400-2300		670
Heartland Building Center Inc 2510 General Hays Rd......Hays KS 67601 *Web:* heartlandbuildingcenter.com	785-625-6554		351
Heartland Building Company Inc 119 William St......Middlesex NJ 08846 *Web:* www.njheartland.com	732-302-9277	356-9286	186
Heartland Community College 1500 W Raab Rd......Normal IL 61761 *Web:* www.heartland.edu	309-268-8000	268-7992	162
Heartland Co-op 2829 Westown Pkwy Ste 350......West Des Moines IA 50266 *TF:* 800-513-3938 ■ *Web:* www.heartlandcoop.com	515-225-1334	225-8511	275
Heartland Credit Union 5500 S Robert Trl......Inver Grove Heights MN 55077 *Web:* heartlandcu.com	651-451-5160		219
Heartland Equipment Inc 2100 N Falls Blvd......Wynne AR 72396 **Fax Area Code:* 870 ■ *TF:* 800-530-7617 ■ *Web:* www.tractorscraper.com	800-530-7617	238-8545*	273

Name / Address	City	State	ZIP	Phone	Fax	Class
Heartland Express Inc 901 N Kansas Ave. *NASDAQ: HTLD* ■ **Fax Area Code:* 319 ■ *TF:* 800-654-1175 ■ *Web:* www.heartlandexpress.com	North Liberty	IA	52317	800-654-1175	626-3311*	780
Heartland Film Festival 1043 Virginia Ave Ste 2 *Web:* heartlandfilm.org	Indianapolis	IN	46203	317-464-9405	464-9409	282
Heartland Financial USA Inc 1398 Central Ave *NASDAQ: HTLF* ■ *Web:* www.htlf.com	Dubuque	IA	52001	563-589-2100		360-2
Heartland Funds 789 N Water St Ste 500 *TF:* 800-432-7856 ■ *Web:* www.heartlandadvisors.com	Milwaukee	WI	53202	414-347-7777		528
Heartland Horseshoeing School 327 SW 1st Ln *Web:* www.heartlandhorseshoeing.com	Lamar	MO	64759	417-682-6896		685
Heartland Industrial Partners LP 177 Broad St 10th Fl. *Web:* www.heartlandpartners.com	Stamford	CT	06901	203-327-1202		360-3
Heartland Inns 87-2nd St *TF:* 800-334-3277 ■ *Web:* www.heartlandinns.com	Coralville	IA	52241	319-351-8132		379
Heartland Institute 3939 N Wilke Rd. *Web:* heartland.org	Arlington Heights	IL	60004	312-377-4000	277-4122	634
Heartland Investment Associates Inc 2202 Heritage Green Dr *Web:* www.heartlandinv.com	Hiawatha	IA	52233	319-393-8913		690
Heartland Label Printers LLC 1700 Stephen St *TF:* 800-236-3584 ■ *Web:* www.hrtlp.com	Little Chute	WI	54140	920-788-7720	788-7733	246
Heartland Lawns LLC 14320 Industrial Rd *Web:* heartlandlawns.com	Omaha	NE	68144	402-492-8800		422
Heartland Meat Company Inc 3461 Main St *TF:* 888-407-3668 ■ *Web:* heartlandmeat.com	Chula Vista	CA	91911	619-407-3668	407-3678	297-9
Heartland Multiple Listing Service Inc 11150 Overbrook Rd Ste 100 *Web:* www.heartlandmls.com	Leawood	KS	66211	913-661-1600	661-1618	652
Heartland National Life Insurance Co PO Box 2878 **Fax Area Code:* 801 ■ *TF:* 866-916-7971 ■ *Web:* www.heartlandnational.net	Salt Lake City	UT	84110	866-916-7971	931-6375*	796
Heartland Optical Inc 1012 N 27th St *Web:* heartlandoptical.com	Lincoln	NE	68503	402-476-3311		543
Heartland Paper Co 808 W Cherokee St. *TF:* 800-843-7922 ■ *Web:* www.heartland-paper.com	Sioux Falls	SD	57104	605-336-1190	332-8378	559
Heartland Park Topeka 7530 SW Topeka Blvd. *TF:* 844-200-6472 ■ *Web:* heartlandpark.com	Topeka	KS	66619	785-862-4781		515
Heartland Plays Inc 88 Howard Beer Rd *Web:* heartlandplays.com	Clancy	MT	59634	406-431-7680		637-10
Heartland Power Co-op 216 Jackson St PO Box 65 *TF:* 888-584-9732 ■ *Web:* www.heartlandpower.com	Thompson	IA	50478	641-584-2251	584-2253	245
Heartland Precision Fasteners Inc 301 Prairie Village Dr *Web:* www.heartlandfasteners.com	New Century	KS	66031	913-829-4447	829-7282	22
Heartland Publishing PO Box 402 *Web:* www.goheartland.com	Seymour	MO	65746	417-343-6354		637-2
Heartland Rural Electric Co-op 110 N Enterprise St. **Fax Area Code:* 620 ■ *TF:* 888-835-9585 ■ *Web:* www.heartland-rec.com	Girard	KS	66743	800-835-9586	724-8253*	245
Heartland Steel Products 355 Industrial Dr. *Web:* heartlandsteel.com	Harrison	OH	45030	513-367-0080		480
Heartland Steel Products LLC 2420 Wills St *TF:* 800-333-0080 ■ *Web:* www.heartlandsteel.com	Marysville	MI	48040	810-364-7421		723
Heartland Video Systems Inc 1311 Pilgrim Rd *TF:* 800-332-7088 ■ *Web:* www.hvs-inc.com	Plymouth	WI	53073	920-893-4204	893-3106	116
Heartlight Girls Publications LLC 6770 S Dawson Cir Ste 750 **Fax Area Code:* 303 ■ *TF:* 855-296-8624 ■ *Web:* www.byoumagazine.com	Centennial	CO	80112	855-296-8624	578-1234*	637-9
Heartline Fitness Products Inc 8041 Cessna Ave Ste 200 *TF:* 800-262-3348 ■ *Web:* heartlinefitness.com	Gaithersburg	MD	20879	301-921-0661		267
HeartSine Technologies Inc 121 Friends Ln Ste 400 *TF:* 866-478-7463 ■ *Web:* heartsine.com	Newtown	PA	18940	215-860-8100	860-8192	476
Heartstrings Card Co PO Box 4716 *Web:* www.heartstringscards.com	Boulder	CO	80306	303-447-2332		637-10
Heartwood College of Art PO Box 7027 *Web:* www.heartwoodcollegeofart.org	Cape Porpoise	ME	04014	207-205-7150		167-3
Heartwood Home Health & Hospice LLC 6671 S Redwood Ste 101 *Web:* heartwood.info	West Jordan	UT	84084	801-261-9490		363
Heartwood School Johnson Hill Rd *Web:* www.heartwoodschool.com	Washington	MA	01223	413-623-6677	623-0277	685
Heat & Control Inc 21121 Cabot Blvd *TF:* 800-227-5980 ■ *Web:* www.heatandcontrol.com	Hayward	CA	94545	510-259-0500	259-0600	298
Heat Pipe Technology Inc 4340 NE 49th Ave. *Web:* www.heatpipe.com	Gainesville	FL	32609	352-367-0999		14
Heat Seal LLC 4580 E 71st St Ste 100 *TF:* 800-342-6329 ■ *Web:* www.heatsealco.com	Cleveland	OH	44125	216-341-2022	341-2163	547
Heat Transfer Products Group LLC 201 Thomas French Dr *TF:* 800-288-9488 ■ *Web:* www.htpg.com	Scottsboro	AL	35769	256-259-7400		610
Heat Transfer Sales of the Carolinas Inc 4101 Beechwood Dr *TF:* 800-842-3328 ■ *Web:* heattransfersales.com	Greensboro	NC	27410	336-294-3838		612
Heat USA Inc PO Box 560240 *Web:* www.heatusa.com	College Point	NY	11356	212-254-4328		538
Heatcon Composite Systems Inc 480 Andover Pk E. *Web:* www.heatcon.com	Seattle	WA	98188	206-575-1333	575-0856	203
Heatcraft Refrigeration Products 2175 W Pk Pl Blvd *TF:* 800-321-1881 ■ *Web:* www.heatcraftrpd.com	Stone Mountain	GA	30087	770-465-5600	465-5990	664
Heateflex Corp 405 Santa Clara St *Web:* www.heateflex.com	Arcadia	CA	91006	626-599-8566	599-9567	14
Heater Designs Inc 2211 S Vista Ave. *Web:* www.heaterdesigns.com	Bloomington	CA	92316	909-421-0971	421-1547	318
Heater Specialists LLC 3171 N Toledo Ave *Web:* www.hsi-llc.com	Tulsa	OK	74115	918-835-3126		662
Heath Ceramics Ltd 400 Gate Five Rd *Web:* www.heathceramics.com	Sausalito	CA	94965	415-361-5552		361
Heath Consultants Inc 9030 Monroe Rd *TF:* 800-432-8487 ■ *Web:* www.heathus.com	Houston	TX	77061	713-844-1300	844-1309	192
Heath Outdoor Products 140 Mill St *TF:* 800-678-8183 ■ *Web:* www.heathmfg.com	Coopersville	MI	49404	616-997-8181	997-9491	578
Heath Village 430 Schooley's Mtn Rd *Web:* www.heathvillage.com	Hackettstown	NJ	07840	908-852-4801	852-3748	371
Heath, Overbey, Verser & Old PLC 11832 Rock Landing Dr Ste 201 *Web:* hovplc.com	Newport News	VA	23606	757-599-0734		41
Heathco's Pizza & Variety 375 Court St *Web:* heathcos.com	Auburn	ME	04210	207-689-9175		204
Heathcote Botanical Gardens 210 Savannah Rd *Web:* www.heathcotebotanicalgardens.org	Fort Pierce	FL	34982	772-464-4672		97
Heather Thies Insurance Agency Inc 525 West Hwy 50 *Web:* heatherthies.com	Clermont	FL	34711	352-394-6933		390
Heathman Lodge 7801 NE Greenwood Dr. *Web:* www.heathmanlodge.com	Vancouver	WA	98662	360-254-3100		379
Heathwood Hall Episcopal School 3000 S Beltline Blvd *Web:* www.heathwood.org	Columbia	SC	29201	803-765-2309		48-20
Heating & Plumbing Engineers Inc 407 Fillmore Pl. *Web:* www.hpeinc.com	Colorado Springs	CO	80907	719-633-5414	633-4031	189-10
Heaton Fontano Ltd 7285 Dean Martin Dr Ste 180 *Web:* heatonfontano.com	Las Vegas	NV	89118	702-329-9901		41
Heaton Pecan Farm 309 Sunrise Blvd *TF:* 800-446-3531 ■ *Web:* www.heaton.com	Clanton	AL	35045	205-755-8654		459
Heatrex Inc PO Box 515 *TF:* 800-394-6589 ■ *Web:* www.heatrex.com	Meadville	PA	16335	814-724-1800	333-6580	318
Heatron Inc 3000 Wilson *Web:* www.heatron.com	Leavenworth	KS	66048	913-651-4420		697
Heat-Timer Corp 20 New Dutch Ln *Web:* www.heat-timer.com	Fairfield	NJ	07004	973-575-4004	575-4052	407
Heaven Group Inc 245 8th Ave *Web:* www.relateloop.com	New York	NY	10011	508-878-7734		5
Heaven Sent By Home Town Health 23 Dunlop Village Cir *Web:* heavensentservices.com	Colonial Heights	VA	23834	804-526-3600		363
Heaven's Best Carpet & Upholstery Cleaning PO Box 607 *TF:* 800-359-2095 ■ *Web:* www.heavensbest.com	Rexburg	ID	83440	208-359-1106	359-1236	152
Heavener Runestone State Park 18365 Runestone Rd *Web:* www.travelok.com	Heavener	OK	74937	918-653-2241		565
Heavenhill Distilleries Inc 1064 Loretto Rd *Web:* www.heavenhill.com	Bardstown	KY	40004	502-348-3921		80-1
Heavenly Gold Card 1724 N State *Web:* www.novamediainc.com	Big Rapids	MI	49307	231-796-4637		303
Heavenly Home Health Care Inc 4430 Santa Monica Blvd Ste 201 *Web:* www.heavenlyhhc.com	Los Angeles	CA	90029	323-662-7071	662-0189	363
Heavner, Beyers & Mihlar LLC (HBM) 111 E Main St. *Web:* www.hsbattys.com	Decatur	IL	62523	217-422-1719	422-1754	428
Heavy Machines Inc 3926 E Raines Rd *TF:* 888-366-9028 ■ *Web:* heavymachinesinc.com	Memphis	TN	38118	901-260-2200		358
Heavy Parts Intl 1803 E 2nd Ave *Web:* www.heavyparts.com	Tampa	FL	33605	813-991-7001	626-7004	61
HEB Engineers 2605 White Mtn Hwy. *Web:* www.hebengineers.com	North Conway	NH	03860	603-356-6936	356-7715	261
Hebaragi & Lemi Bus Inc 606 W 140th St. *Web:* hebaragibus.com	Gardena	CA	90248	310-715-2400		107
Hebeler Corp 2000 Military Rd *TF:* 800-486-4709 ■ *Web:* www.hebeler.com	Tonawanda	NY	14150	716-873-9300	873-7538	620
Heberly & Assoc 615 First W *Web:* heberlyeng.com	Havre	MT	59501	406-265-6741	265-6787	261
Hebrew Academy of The Five Towns & Rockaway Inc 389 Central Ave *Web:* www.haftr.org	Lawrence	NY	11559	516-569-3370		685
Hebrew Hospital Home Continuum of Care 61 Grasslands Rd *TF:* 866-663-6877 ■ *Web:* www.hebrewhospitalhome.org	Valhalla	NY	10595	914-681-8400		374-7
Hebrew Immigrant Aid Society (HIAS) 1300 Spring St Ste 500 *Web:* www.hias.org	Silver Spring	MD	20910	301-844-7300		48-5
Hebrew Senior Care Inc 1 Abrahms Blvd *Web:* www.hebrewhealthcare.org	West Hartford	CT	06117	860-523-3800	523-3949	450
Hebrew Theological College 7135 Carpenter Rd *Web:* www.htc.edu	Skokie	IL	60077	847-982-2500	674-6381	165
Hebrew Union College 3101 Clifton Ave. *Web:* www.huc.edu	Cincinnati	OH	45220	513-221-1875	221-0321	800
Hebron Academy 339 Rd PO Box 309 *TF:* 888-432-7664 ■ *Web:* www.hebronacademy.org	Hebron	ME	04238	207-966-2100		622
Hebron Savings Bank (HSB) 101 N Main St PO Box 59. *TF:* 844-378-7081 ■ *Web:* www.hebronsavingsbank.com	Hebron	MD	21830	410-749-1185		70

Company	Phone	Fax	Class
Heceta Head Lighthouse State Scenic Viewpoint 91784 Oregon Coast Hwy....................Florence OR 97439 *Web:* stateparks.oregon.gov	541-547-3416		565
Hecht & Norman LLP 329 E Eighth Ave ....Eugene OR 97401 *Web:* immigrationoregon.com	541-465-2173		41
Hecht Solberg Robinson Goldberg & Bagley LLP 600 W Broadway Ste 800..................San Diego CA 92101 *Web:* www.hechtsolberg.com	619-239-3444	232-6828	445
Heck Denny (Rep D - WA) 2452 Rayburn House Office Bldg ....Washington DC 20515 *Web:* www.dennyheck.house.gov	202-225-9740		342-2
Heck's Direct Mail & Printing Service Inc 417 Main St ....Toledo OH 43605 *Web:* www.hecksprinting.com	419-661-6000	661-6036	5
Heckaman Homes Inc 2676 E Market St ....Nappanee IN 46550 *Web:* www.heckamanhomes.com	574-773-4167		106
Hecker Law Group, The 1925 Century Pk E Ste 2300................Los Angeles CA 90067 *Web:* heckerlaw.com	310-286-0377		41
Heckler & Koch Inc 5675 Transport Blvd ....Columbus GA 31907 *Web:* hk-usa.com	706-568-1906	568-9151	284
Heckscher Museum of Art 2 Prime Ave ....Huntington NY 11743 *Web:* www.heckscher.org	631-351-3250	423-2145	520
Heckscher State Park Heckscher Pkwy Field 1 ....East Islip NY 11730 *Web:* parks.ny.gov	631-581-2100		565
Hecla Mining Co 6500 N Mineral Dr Ste 200...............Coeur d'Alene ID 83815 *NYSE: HL* ■ *TF:* 800-432-5291 ■ *Web:* www.hecla-mining.com	208-769-4100		502
HECO Inc 2350 Del Monte St ....West Sacramento CA 95691 *Web:* www.hecogear.com	916-372-5411	373-0952	709
Hectic Digital LLC 599 Eighth Ave ....San Francisco CA 94118 *Web:* hecticdigital.com	415-592-8729		52
Hector International Airport 2801 32nd Ave NW...........................Fargo ND 58102 *TF:* 800-451-5333 ■ *Web:* www.fargoairport.com	701-241-8168	241-1538	27
HED Cycling Products 1735 Terrace Dr ....Roseville MN 55113 *TF:* 888-246-3639 ■ *Web:* www.hedcycling.com	888-246-3639		517
Hedback, Arendt & Carlson PLLC 2855 Anthony Ln S Ste 201 ....Saint Anthony MN 55418 *Web:* hac-mnlaw.com	612-789-1331	789-2109	41
Hedberg Aggregates Inc 1205 Nathan Ln N..........................Plymouth MN 55441 *Web:* www.hedbergaggregates.com	763-545-4400	545-7121	191-1
Hedberg Public Library (HPL) 316 S Main St............................Janesville WI 53545 *Web:* www.hedbergpubliclibrary.org	608-758-6600	758-6583	434-3
Hedberg, Batara & Vaughan-Sarandi LLC 1003 Bishop St Ste 1925...................Honolulu HI 96813 *Web:* hbvsllc.com	808-523-6955		2
Hedgehog Hosting 25050 Riding Plz Ste 130-644 ....Chantilly VA 20152 *Web:* www.hedgehoghosting.com	703-218-4170	218-4172	396
Hedges Engineering & Consulting Inc 913 Kincaid Ave ....Sumner WA 98390	253-891-9365		261
Hedgeye Risk Management LLC 1 High Ridge Pk ....Stamford CT 06905 *Web:* app.hedgeye.com	203-562-6500		401
HEDK Architects 4202 Beltway Dr..............Addison TX 75001 *Web:* hedk.com	214-520-8878		393
Hedrick Associates Inc 2360 Oak Industrial Dr NE ....Grand Rapids MI 49505 *Web:* www.hedrickassoc.com	616-454-1218		180
Hedrick Brothers Construction Company Inc 2200 Centrepark W Dr Ste 100.........West Palm Beach FL 33409 *Web:* hedrickbrothers.com	561-689-8880		186
Hedstrom Lumber Company Inc 1504 Gunflint Trl.......................Grand Marais MN 55604 *Web:* www.hedstromlumber.com	218-387-2995	387-2204	683
Hedy Holmes Staffing Services 4747 Feather River Dr Ste 2 ....Stockton CA 95219 *Web:* www.hedyholmesstaffing.com	209-957-9630		260
Hee Hing 449 Kapahulu Ave ....Honolulu HI 96815 *Web:* www.heehinghawaii.com	808-735-5544	732-6026	671
HeeBeen Restaurant 6231 Little River Tpke.....................Alexandria VA 22312 *Web:* heebeen.com	703-941-3737		671
Heeia State Park 46-465 Kamehameha Hwy ....Kaneohe HI 96744 *Web:* www.heeiastatepark.org	808-235-6509		565
Heely-Brown Company Inc 1280 Chattahoochee Ave ....Atlanta GA 30318 *TF:* 800-241-4628 ■ *Web:* heelybrown.com	404-352-0022		46
Heerema Co 200 Sixth Ave..................Hawthorne NJ 07506 *TF:* 800-346-4729 ■ *Web:* www.heeremacompany.com	973-423-0505		189-10
Heeren Bros Inc 1055 7 Mile Rd NW ....Comstock Park MI 49321 *Web:* www.heerenbros.com	616-452-2101	243-7070	297-7
HEF USA Corp 2015 Progress Rd.............Springfield OH 45505 *Web:* www.hefusa.net	937-323-2556	323-5787	261
Heffel Gallery Ltd 2247 Granville St ....Vancouver BC V6H3G1 *TF:* 800-528-9608 ■ *Web:* www.heffel.com	604-732-6505	732-4245	42
Heffernan Law Firm PLLC 1201 Market St.............................Kirkland WA 98033 *Web:* heffernanlawgroup.com	425-284-1150		41
Hefren - Tillotson Inc 308 Seventh Ave..........................Pittsburgh PA 15222 *Web:* www.hefren.com	412-434-0990		194
Hegemony Inc 920 Curtiss St PO Box 37...............Downers Grove IL 60515 *Web:* hegemony.com	630-690-5200		261
HEHR International Inc 3333 Casitas Ave PO Box 39160 ....Los Angeles CA 90039 *Web:* www.hehrintl.com	323-663-1261	666-2372	234

Company	Phone	Fax	Class
HEI Hospitality LLC 101 Merritt 7 Corporate Pk 1st Fl..............Norwalk CT 06851 *Web:* www.heihotels.com	203-849-8844		378
HEICO Corp 3000 Taft St.....................Hollywood FL 33021 *NYSE: HEI* ■ *Web:* www.heico.com	954-987-4000	987-8228	21
Heid Music Company Inc 308 E College Ave..........................Appleton WI 54911 *Web:* www.heidmusic.com	920-734-1969		526
Heide & Cook Ltd 1714 Kanakanui St...........Honolulu HI 96819 *Web:* heidecook.com	808-841-6161		189-10
Heidecke Lake State Fish & Wildlife Area 5010 N Jugtown Rd ....Morris IL 60450 *Web:* www2.illinois.gov	815-942-6352		565
Heidel House Resort 643 Illinois Ave..........................Green Lake WI 54941 *TF:* 800-444-2812 ■ *Web:* www.heidelhouse.com	920-294-3344	294-6128	669
Heidelberg Distributing Co 1518 Dalton St ....Cincinnati OH 45214 *Web:* www.heidelbergdistributing.com	513-421-5000	421-5194	81-1
Heidelberg University 310 E Market St............Tiffin OH 44883 *TF:* 800-434-3352 ■ *Web:* www.heidelberg.edu	419-448-2000	448-2334	166
Heidelberg USA Inc 1000 Gutenberg Dr........Kennesaw GA 30144 *TF:* 888-472-9655 ■ *Web:* www.heidelberg.com	770-419-6500	419-6550	629
Heidell, Pittoni, Murphy & Bach LLP 99 Park Ave..............................New York NY 10016 *Web:* www.hpmb.com	212-286-8585		428
Heidenhain Corp 333 E State Pky ....Schaumburg IL 60173 *Web:* www.heidenhain.us	847-490-1191	490-3931	385
Heidenreich & Heidenreich CPAS PLLC 10201 S 51st St Ste 170.....................Phoenix AZ 85044 *Web:* ahwatukeecpas.com	480-704-6301		2
Heidi's 3485 Lake Tahoe Blvd ....South Lake Tahoe CA 96150 *Web:* heidislaketahoe.com	530-544-8113		671
Heidler Roofing Services Inc 2120 Alpha Dr ....York PA 17408 *TF:* 866-792-3549 ■ *Web:* www.heidlerroofing.com	717-792-3549	792-4660	189-12
Heidman Law Firm LLP 1128 Fourth St ....Sioux City IA 51101 *Web:* heidmanlaw.com	712-255-8838		41
Heidner Law Firm PC 60 E 42d St Ste 3200 ....New York NY 10165 *Web:* heidnerlaw.com	212-302-9867		41
Heidrick & Struggles International Inc 233 S Wacker Dr Willis Twr Ste 4900...........Chicago IL 60606 *NASDAQ: HSII* ■ *Web:* www.heidrick.com	312-496-1000	496-1048	266
Heidtman Steel Products Inc 2401 Front St ....Toledo OH 43605 *TF:* 800-521-9531 ■ *Web:* www.heidtman.com	419-691-4646	698-1150	723
Heifer Intl 1 World Ave.....................Little Rock AR 72202 *TF:* 800-422-0474 ■ *Web:* www.heifer.org	501-907-2600	907-2902	48-5
Height Capital Markets 1775 Pennsylvania Ave NW 11th Fl ....Washington DC 20006 *Web:* www.heightllc.com	202-629-0000		401
Heights Insurance Group Inc 2148 S Hacienda Blvd ....Hacienda Heights CA 91745 *Web:* kcal.net	626-855-8288		390
Heights-Usa Inc 1445 Lower Ferry Rd ....Trenton NJ 08628 *Web:* heights-usa.com	609-530-1300		177
Heigl Adhesive Sales 7667 Cahill Rd Ste 100.........................Edina MN 55439 **Fax Area Code: 952* ■ *TF:* 800-401-1441 ■ *Web:* www.heigladhesive.com	800-401-1441	943-1255*	146
Heil Environmental Ltd 2030 Hamilton Pl Blvd Ste 200............Chattanooga TN 37421 *TF:* 866-367-4345 ■ *Web:* www.heil.com	423-899-9100		516
Heil Trailer International Co 1125 Congress Pkwy NE ....Athens TN 37303 *Web:* www.heiltrailer.com	423-745-5830		779
HEILBrice Inc 9840 Irvine Center Dr ....Irvine CA 92618 *Web:* www.heilbrice.com	949-336-8800		4
Heilig Misfeldt & Armstrong LLP 310 NW Seventh St Ste 101 ....Corvallis OR 97330 *Web:* hmalaw.net	541-754-7477		41
Heilind Electronics Inc 58 Jonspin Rd ....Wilmington MA 01887 *TF:* 800-400-7041 ■ *Web:* www.heilind.com	978-657-4870	658-0278	246
Heim LP 6360 W 73rd St.......................Chicago IL 60638 *TF:* 800-927-9393 ■ *Web:* www.theheimgroup.com	708-496-7450	496-7428	456
Heimerl & Lammers LLC 11100 Wayzata Blvd Ste 211 ....Minnetonka MN 55305 *Web:* hllawfirm.com	612-294-2200	294-2201	41
Heineken USA 360 Hamilton Ave Ste 1103 ....White Plains NY 10601 *Web:* www.heineken.com	914-681-4100		102
Heinemann 361 Hanover St.................Portsmouth NH 03801 *TF:* 800-541-2086 ■ *Web:* www.heinemann.com	603-431-7894	431-7840	637-2
Heinen Obstetrics & Gynecology LLC 3448 Hwy 190 ....Eunice LA 70535 *Web:* femmhealth.org	337-546-6237		41
Heinen's Inc 4540 Richmond Rd..............Cleveland OH 44128 **Fax Area Code: 216* ■ *TF:* 855-475-2300 ■ *Web:* www.heinens.com	855-475-2300	514-4788*	345
Heinfeld Meech & Company PC 10120 N Oracle Rd............................Tucson AZ 85704 *Web:* www.heinfeldmeech.com	520-742-2611		2
Heinrich Envelope Corp 925 Zane Ave N........................Minneapolis MN 55422 *TF:* 800-346-7957 ■ *Web:* www.heinrichenvelope.com	763-544-3571	544-6287	263
Heinrich Marketing Inc 2228 Blake St Ste 200 ....Denver CO 80205 *Web:* www.heinrich.com	303-233-8660		4
Heinrich Martin (Sen D - NM) 303 Hart Senate Office Bldg ....Washington DC 20510 *Web:* www.heinrich.senate.gov	202-224-5521	228-2841	342-2
Heintz & Weber Company Inc 150 Reading Ave............................Buffalo NY 14220 *TF:* 800-438-6878 ■ *Web:* www.webersmustard.com	716-852-7171	852-7173	296-41
Heinzeroth Marketing Group 415 Y Blvd ....Rockford IL 61107 *Web:* heinzeroth.com	815-967-0929	967-0983	195

				Phone	Fax	Class
Heirloom catering co 1306 Old County Rd *Web:* heirloomcatering.co	Belmont	CA	94002	650-622-4171		149
Heise Industries Inc 196 Commerce St *Web:* www.heiseindustries.com	East Berlin	CT	06023	860-828-6538	828-4997	757
Heisler Industries Inc 224 Passaic Ave *TF:* 800-496-7621 ■ *Web:* www.heislerind.com	Fairfield	NJ	07004	973-227-6300	227-7627	547
Heisler's Cloverleaf Dairy 743 Catawissa Rd *Web:* www.heislersdairy.com	Tamaqua	PA	18252	570-668-3399	668-3041	296-25
Hei-Tek Automation 2102 W Quail Ave Ste 4 *TF:* 800-926-2099 ■ *Web:* www.heitek.com	Phoenix	AZ	85027	800-926-2099		358
Heiter Truck Line Inc 1835 340th St *TF:* 800-245-1966 ■ *Web:* www.heitertruckline.com	Spencer	IA	51301	712-262-2845	262-3856	780
Heitman LLC 191 N Wacker Dr Ste 2500 *Web:* www.heitman.com	Chicago	IL	60606	312-855-5700		655
Heizer Aerospace Inc 8750 Pevely Industrial Dr *Web:* haiusa.org	Pevely	MO	63070	636-475-6300		22
Hekman Furniture 860 E Main Ave *Web:* www.hekman.com	Zeeland	MI	49464	616-748-2660	772-1670	319-2
Helbling & Associates Inc 8000 Brooktree Rd Ste 100 *Web:* www.helblingsearch.com	Wexford	PA	15090	724-935-7500		721
Helco Federal Credit Union 1437 Kilauea Ave Ste 105 *Web:* helcofcu.org	Hilo	HI	96720	808-238-3500	238-3220	219
Heldenfels Enterprises Inc 5700 IH-35 S *Web:* heldenfels.com	San Marcos	TX	78666	512-396-2376	396-2381	183
Helen B. Hoffman Plantation Library 501 N Fig Tree Ln *Web:* www.plantation.org	Plantation	FL	33317	954-797-2140	797-2767	434-3
Helen Brett Enterprises Inc 5111 Academy Dr *Web:* www.helenbrett.com	Lisle	IL	60532	630-241-9865	241-9870	188-3
Helen DeVos Children's Hospital 100 Michigan St NE *TF:* 866-989-7999 ■ *Web:* www.spectrumhealth.org	Grand Rapids	MI	49503	616-391-9000		769
Helen Hall Library (HHL) 600 W Walker St *Web:* www.leaguecity.com	League City	TX	77573	281-554-2994		434-3
Helen Keller Hospital 1300 S Montgomery Ave *Web:* www.helenkeller.com	Sheffield	AL	35660	256-386-4196		374-3
Helen Keller Intl 352 Park Ave S Ste 1200 *Web:* www.hki.org	New York	NY	10010	212-532-0544		48-5
Helen L. Wagner Insurance Agency Inc 5360 Arapahoe Ave Ste A-1 *Web:* helenwagner.com	Boulder	CO	80302	303-442-7844		390
Helen M. Plum Memorial Library 110 W Maple St *Web:* www.helenplum.org	Lombard	IL	60148	630-627-0316	627-0336	434-3
Helen of Troy 400 Donald Lynch Blvd *TF:* 800-477-0457 ■ *Web:* www.helenoftroy.com	Marlborough	MA	01752	800-477-0457		17
Helen's 2527 W Main St *Web:* www.helensrva.com	Richmond	VA	23220	804-358-4370		671
Helena Area Chamber of Commerce 225 Cruse Ave *TF:* 800-743-5362 ■ *Web:* www.helenachamber.com	Helena	MT	59601	406-442-4120	447-1532	139
Helena Chemical Co 225 Schilling Blvd Ste 300 *Web:* helenaagri.com	Collierville	TN	38017	901-761-0050	821-5455	280
Helena Civic Ctr 340 Neill Ave *Web:* www.helenaciviccenter.com	Helena	MT	59601	406-447-8481	447-8480	205
Helena Laboratories Inc 1530 Lindbergh Dr *TF:* 800-231-5663 ■ *Web:* www.helena.com	Beaumont	TX	77704	409-842-3714		231
Helena Regional Airport 2850 Skyway Dr *Web:* www.helenaairport.com	Helena	MT	59602	406-442-2821	449-2340	27
Helena Regional Medical Ctr 1801 ML King Dr *Web:* www.helenarmc.com	Helena	AR	72342	870-338-5800		374-3
Helene Fuld College of Nursing 24 E 120th St *Web:* www.helenefuld.edu	New York	NY	10035	212-616-7200	616-7299	800
Helfrich Bros Boiler Works Inc 39 Merrimack St *Web:* hbbwinc.com	Lawrence	MA	01843	978-683-7244		492
Helga's German Restaurant 14197 E Exposition Ave *Web:* www.helgasdeli.com	Aurora	CO	80012	303-344-5488		671
Helgesen 1055 W Sumner St *Web:* helgesen.com	Hartford	WI	53027	262-709-4444	709-4409	386
Heliae Development LLC 578 E Germann Rd *TF:* 800-373-4187 ■ *Web:* heliaeglobal.com	Gilbert	AZ	85297	480-424-2875		466
Helical Products Company Inc 901 W McCoy Ln *TF:* 877-353-9873 ■ *Web:* www.heli-cal.com	Santa Maria	CA	93455	805-928-3851	928-2369	620
Helicopter Association Intl (HAI) 1920 Ballenger Ave 4th Fl *TF:* 800-435-4976 ■ *Web:* www.rotor.org	Alexandria	VA	22314	703-683-4646	683-4745	49-21
Helicopter Support Inc (HSI) 124 Quarry Rd	Trumbull	CT	06611	203-416-4000	416-4291	770
Helicopter Tech Inc 452 Swedeland Rd *Web:* www.helicoptertechinc.com	King of Prussia	PA	19406	610-272-8090		25
Helicopter Transport Services Inc (HTS) 701 Wilson Pt Rd *Web:* www.htshelicopters.com	Baltimore	MD	21220	410-391-7722		359
Heliene Inc 520 Allen'S Side Rd *Web:* www.heliene.ca	Sault Sainte Marie	ON	P6A6K4	705-575-6556	575-4432	253
Heli-Mart Inc 3184 Airway Ave Unit E *TF:* 800-826-6899 ■ *Web:* helimart.com	Costa Mesa	CA	92626	714-755-2999	755-2995	770
Helinet Aviation Services LLC 16303 Waterman Dr *Web:* helinet.com	Van Nuys	CA	91406	818-902-0229		359
Heliodyne Corp 4910 Seaport Ave *TF:* 888-878-8750 ■ *Web:* www.heliodyne.com	Richmond	CA	94804	510-237-9614		321
Heli-One 120 NE Frontage Rd *Web:* www.heli-one.com	Fort Collins	CO	80524	970-492-1000		20
HelioPower Inc 25767 Jefferson Ave *Web:* heliopower.com	Murrieta	CA	92562	951-677-7755		35
Helios & Matheson North America Inc 350 5th Ave Ste 7520 *Web:* www.hmny.com	New York	NY	10018	212-979-8228		180
Helios Care Inc 297 River Street Service Rd Ste 1 *TF:* 800-306-3870 ■ *Web:* helioscare.org	Oneonta	NY	13820	607-432-5525		371
Helitune Inc 190 Gordon St *Web:* www.helitune.com	Elk Grove Village	IL	60007	847-228-0985	228-1164	407
HeliValue$ Inc 1001 N Old Rand Rd Unit 101 *Web:* www.helivalues.com	Wauconda	IL	60084	847-487-8258	487-0206	637-2
Helix Biopharma Corp 3-305 Industrial Pkwy S *TSE: HBP* ■ *Web:* www.helixbiopharma.com	Aurora	ON	L4G6X7	905-841-2300	841-2244	85
Helix Commerce International Inc c/o Dr Cindy Gordon 117 Melrose Ave *Web:* helixcommerce.com	Toronto	ON	M5M1Y8	647-477-6254	477-6256	196
Helix Computer Systems Inc 2401 Hydraulic Rd *Web:* www.helixsystems.com	Charlottesville	VA	22901	434-963-4900	963-9744	177
Helix Design Inc 175 Lincoln St Ste 201 **Fax Area Code:* 603 ■ *TF:* 800-511-5593 ■ *Web:* helixdesign.com	Manchester	NH	03103	800-511-5593	644-1409*	463
Helix Energy Solutions Inc 400 N Sam Houston Pkwy E Ste 400 *NYSE: HLX* ■ *TF:* 888-345-2347 ■ *Web:* www.helixesg.com	Houston	TX	77060	281-618-0400	618-0500	539
HELIX Environmental Planning Inc 7578 El Cajon Blvd Ste 200 *Web:* www.helixepi.com	La Mesa	CA	91942	619-462-1515	462-0552	194
Helix Technologies Inc 8550 W Main St *TF:* 877-849-2875 ■ *Web:* helixtec.net	French Lick	IN	47432	812-936-2525	936-2006	175
Helixstorm Inc 27238 Via Industria *TF:* 888-434-3549 ■ *Web:* www.helixstorm.com	Temecula	CA	92590	888-434-3549		387
Hella Corporate Center USA Inc 43811 Plymouth Oaks Blvd *Web:* www.hella.com	Plymouth	MI	48170	734-414-0900		48-20
Hellam Varon & Company Incorporated PS 1750 112th Ave NE *Web:* hellamvaron.com	Bellevue	WA	98004	425-453-9192		2
Hellas Construction Inc 12710 Research Blvd Ste 240 *TF:* 800-233-5714 ■ *Web:* www.hellasconstruction.com	Austin	TX	78759	512-250-2910	250-1960	186
Hellenic College-Holy Cross School of Theology 50 Goddard Ave *Web:* www.hchc.edu	Brookline	MA	02445	617-731-3500	850-1460	166
Hellenic Heritage Museum 1650 Senter Rd *Web:* www.hhisj.org	San Jose	CA	95112	408-247-4685		520
Hellenic Museum & Cultural Ctr 333 S Halsted Ave *Web:* www.nationalhellenicmuseum.org	Chicago	IL	60661	312-655-1234	655-1221	520
Hellenic-American Chamber of Commerce (HACC) 370 Lexington Ave 27th Fl *Web:* hellenicamerican.cc	New York	NY	10017	212-629-6380	564-9281	138
Heller Consulting Inc 1736 Franklin St Ste 600 *Web:* teamheller.com	Oakland	CA	94612	510-841-4222		177
Heller Jewelers Inc 2005 Crow Canyon Pl 168 *Web:* hellerjewelers.com	San Ramon	CA	94583	925-904-0200		410
Heller Law Firm LLC, The 1108 Olive St 5th Fl *Web:* sallyhellerlaw.com	Saint Louis	MO	63101	314-219-5959	219-5964	41
Heller Real Estate Group Inc, The 171 Saxony Rd Ste 205 *TF:* 800-800-2978 ■ *Web:* www.hellerthehomeseller.com	Encinitas	CA	92024	760-632-8408		652
Hellerwork Intl 300 Carlsbad Village Dr 108A Ste 256 *Web:* www.hellerwork.com	Carlsbad	CA	92008	714-873-6131		167-3
Hellman 1225 W Fourth St *Web:* www.hellman.com	Waterloo	IA	50702	319-234-7055		7
Hellman & Friedman LLC 1 Maritime Plz 12th Fl *Web:* hf.com	San Francisco	CA	94111	415-788-5111	788-0176	405
Hello Alfred 61 Broadway *Web:* www.helloalfred.com	New York	NY	10006	646-756-4877		374-3
Hello Direct Inc 77 NE Blvd *TF:* 800-435-5634 ■ *Web:* www.hellodirect.com	Nashua	NH	03062	800-435-5634	456-2566	459
Hello Inc 2315 W Broad St *TF:* 877-435-5646 ■ *Web:* www.helloinc.com	Richmond	VA	23220	804-353-5566	353-7335	393
Hello World Communications 118 W 22nd St 2nd Fl *Web:* hwc.tv	New York	NY	10011	212-243-8800		514
HelloWorld 3000 Town Ctr Ste 2100 *TF:* 877-837-7493 ■ *Web:* www.helloworld.com	Southfield	MI	48075	877-837-7493		7
Hells Canyon Preservation Council 105 First St Ste 327 PO Box 2768 *Web:* www.hellscanyon.org	La Grande	OR	97850	541-963-3950		48-13
Hells Gate State Park 5100 Hells Gate Rd *Web:* parksandrecreation.idaho.gov	Lewiston	ID	83501	208-799-5015		565
Helly Hansen US Inc 3703 I St NW *TF:* 800-435-5901 ■ *Web:* www.hellyhansen.com	Auburn	WA	98001	800-435-5901		155-5
Helm Inc 47911 Halyard Dr Ste 200 **Fax Area Code:* 734 ■ *TF:* 800-782-4356 ■ *Web:* www.helminc.com	Plymouth	MI	48170	800-782-4356	468-3704*	88

Name / Address	City	State	ZIP	Phone	Fax	Class
Helm Precision Ltd 2426 E Washington St *Web:* helmprecision.com	Phoenix	AZ	85034	602-275-2122	220-9669	454
Helm US Chemical Corp 1110 Centennial Ave *Web:* www.helmus.com	Piscataway	NJ	08854	732-981-1116	981-0528	146
Helmand Restaurant 143 First St *Web:* www.helmandrestaurant.com	Cambridge	MA	02142	617-492-4646		671
Helmand, The 806 N Charles St *Web:* www.helmand.com	Baltimore	MD	21201	410-752-0311		671
Helmel Engineering Products Inc 6520 Lockport Rd *TF:* 800-237-8266 ■ *Web:* www.helmel.com	Niagara Falls	NY	14305	716-297-8644		174
Helmerich & Payne Inc 1437 S Boulder Ave *NYSE:* HP ■ *TF:* 800-205-4913 ■ *Web:* www.hpinc.com	Tulsa	OK	74119	918-742-5531		540
Helmet House Inc 26855 Malibu Hill Rd *Web:* www.helmethouse.com	Calabasas	CA	91301	818-880-0000		576
Helmut Guenschel Inc 10 Emala Ave *TF:* 800-852-2525 ■ *Web:* www.guenschel.com	Baltimore	MD	21220	410-686-5900		115
Help At Home Inc 1 N State St Ste 800 **Fax Area Code:* 312 ■ *TF:* 800-404-3191 ■ *Web:* www.helpathome.com	Chicago	IL	60602	800-404-3191	704-0022*	363
Help Button, The 3109 W Market St *Web:* www.thehelpbutton.net	Akron	OH	44333	330-867-4357		809
Help Foundation Inc 26900 EuclidAve *Web:* www.helpfoundationinc.org	Cleveland	OH	44132	216-432-4810		305
HELP USA Inc 115 E 13th St *Web:* www.helpusa.org	New York	NY	10003	212-400-7000		48-5
Helping Hand Home Health Services Inc 261Old York Rd *Web:* www.helpinghandhomehealthservices.com	Jenkintown	PA	19046	215-572-6466	572-7939	363
Helping Hand Nursing Service Inc 8305 S Saginaw St Ste 1 *Web:* helpinghandhealthcare.com	Grand Blanc	MI	48439	810-606-8400		260
Helping Hands Home Care 456 SW Monroe Ave Ste 103 *Web:* www.helpinghandshomecare.com	Corvallis	OR	97333	541-757-0214		363
Helpjuice Inc 211 E Seventh St *TF:* 888-230-3420 ■ *Web:* helpjuice.com	Austin	TX	78701	888-230-3420		387
Help-U-Sell Real Estate 240 N Washington Blvd *Web:* www.helpusell.com	Sarasota	FL	34236	941-951-7707		652
Helser Industries Inc 10750 Sw Tualatin Rd *Web:* www.helser.com	Tualatin	OR	97062	503-692-6909		91
Helvoet Pharma Inc 9012 Pennsauken Hwy *Web:* www.datwyler.com	Pennsauken Township	NJ	08110	856-663-2202	663-2636	477
Helwig Carbon Products Inc 8900 W Tower Ave *TF:* 800-365-3113 ■ *Web:* www.helwigcarbon.com	Milwaukee	WI	53224	414-354-2411	354-2421	127
Helzberg Diamonds 1825 Swift Ave *TF:* 800-435-9237 ■ *Web:* www.helzberg.com	North Kansas City	MO	64116	816-531-4100		410
Hemacare Corp 15350 Sherman Way Ste 350 **Fax Area Code:* 818 ■ *TF:* 877-310-0717 ■ *Web:* www.hemacare.com	Van Nuys	CA	91406	877-397-3087	251-5300*	89
Hemagen Diagnostics Inc 9033 Red Branch Rd *OTC:* HMGN ■ **Fax Area Code:* 410 ■ *TF:* 800-436-2436 ■ *Web:* www.hemagen.com	Columbia	MD	21045	443-367-5500	997-7812*	231
HemaSource Inc 485 S 5700 W Ste 400 *TF:* 888-844-4362 ■ *Web:* www3.hemasource.com	Salt Lake City	UT	84104	888-844-4362		475
Hemco Industries Inc 2408 Karbach St *TF:* 877-394-3626 ■ *Web:* www.hemcoind.com	Houston	TX	77092	713-681-2426		480
Hemenway's Seafood Grille 121 S Main St *TF:* 888-759-5557 ■ *Web:* www.hemenwaysrestaurant.com	Providence	RI	02903	401-351-8570		671
Hemet Jacinto Valley Chamber of Commerce 615 N San Jacinto St *Web:* hemetsanjacintochamber.com	Hemet	CA	92543	951-658-3211	766-5013	139
Hemet Public Library 300 E Latham Ave *Web:* www.hemetca.gov	Hemet	CA	92543	951-765-2440		434-3
Hemingway Apparel Manufacturing Inc 60 Apparel Dr *Web:* www.hemingwayapparel.com	Hemingway	SC	29554	843-558-2525		157-6
Hemingway's Blue Water Cafe 1935 S Campbell *Web:* restaurants.basspro.com	Springfield	MO	65898	417-891-5100	887-5204	671
Hemisphere 9300 Jeff Fuqua Blvd *Web:* hemisphereorlando.com	Orlando	FL	32827	407-825-1344		671
Hemispheres Restaurant & Bistro 110 Chestnut St *Web:* www.hemispheres.com	Toronto	ON	M5G1R3	416-599-8000		671
Hemlock Bluffs Nature Preserve 2616 Kildaire Farm Rd *Web:* townofcary.org	Cary	NC	27518	919-387-5980		50-5
Hemlock Public Schools District 835 N Pine St *Web:* www.hemlock.k12.mi.us	Hemlock	MI	48626	989-642-5282	642-8008	685
Hemlock Semiconductor Corp 12334 Geddes Rd *Web:* www.hscpoly.com	Hemlock	MI	48626	989-301-5000		696
Hemmelgarn And Sons Inc 3763 Philothea Rd	Coldwater	OH	45828	419-678-2351		297-10
Hemmer Defrank Wessels PLLC 250 Grandview Dr Ste 500 *Web:* hemmerlaw.com	Fort Mitchell	KY	41017	859-344-1188	578-3869	41
Hemmings Motor News 222 Main St *TF:* 800-227-4373 ■ *Web:* www.hemmings.com	Bennington	VT	05201	802-442-3101	447-9631	457-3
HemoShear LLC 501 Locust Ave Ste 301 *Web:* www.hemoshear.com	Charlottesville	VA	22902	434-872-0196	872-0199	668
Hempel (USA) Inc 600 Conroe Park North Dr *Web:* www.hempel.com	Conroe	TX	77303	936-523-6000		550
Hemphill County 400 Main St *Web:* co.hemphill.tx.us	Canadian	TX	79014	806-323-6521	323-5260	338
Hempstead & Company Inc 807 Haddon Ave *Web:* www.hempsteadco.com	Haddonfield	NJ	08033	856-795-6026		463
Hempstead County 400 S Washington *Web:* www.hempsteadcountyar.com	Hope	AR	71801	870-777-6164		338
Hempstead Lake State Park Lakeside Dr *Web:* parks.ny.gov	West Hempstead	NY	11552	516-766-1029		565
Hempstead Public Library 115 Nichols Ct *Web:* www.hempsteadlibrary.info	Hempstead	NY	11550	516-481-6990	481-6719	434-3
Hempt Bros Inc 205 Creek Rd *Web:* hemptbros.com	Camp Hill	PA	17011	717-737-3411	761-5019	188-4
Hemstreet Development Corp 7440 E Pinnacle Peak Rd Ste 142 *Web:* www.hemstreet.com	Scottsdale	AZ	85255	480-719-1500	269-8745	655
Henak Law Office Sc 316 N Milwaukee St Ste 535 *Web:* henaklaw.net	Milwaukee	WI	53202	414-283-9300		41
Hencorp Inc 777 Brickell Ave Ste 1010 *Web:* www.hencorp.com	Miami	FL	33131	305-373-9000		463
Hendee Enterprises Inc 9350 S Point Dr *TF:* 800-231-7275 ■ *Web:* www.hendee.com	Houston	TX	77054	713-796-2322	796-0494	361
Henderson Area Chamber of Commerce 201 N Main St *Web:* www.hendersontx.com	Henderson	TX	75652	903-657-5528	657-9454	139
Henderson Auctions 13340 Florida Blvd PO Box 336 *TF:* 800-334-7443 ■ *Web:* www.hendersonauctions.com	Livingston	LA	70754	225-686-2252	686-0647	51
Henderson Beach State Park 17000 Emerald Coast Pkwy *Web:* www.floridastateparks.org	Destin	FL	32541	850-837-7550		565
Henderson Chamber of Commerce 777 W Lake Mead Pkwy Cancun Rm *Web:* www.hendersonchamber.com	Henderson	NV	89015	702-565-8951	565-3115	139
Henderson Community College 2660 S Green St *TF:* 800-696-9958 ■ *Web:* henderson.kctcs.edu	Henderson	KY	42420	270-827-1867	831-9612	162
Henderson County 125 N Prairieville St Rm 101 *Web:* www.henderson-county.com	Athens	TX	75751	903-675-6140	675-6105	338
Henderson County 383 Sam Ball Way *Web:* hendersoncountykyfair.com	Henderson	KY	42420	270-827-5753		338
Henderson County 1 Historic Courthouse Sq *Web:* www.hendersoncountync.gov	Hendersonville	NC	28792	828-697-4808	692-9855	338
Henderson County 17 Monroe Ave *Web:* hendersoncountytn.gov	Lexington	TN	38351	731-968-7777	968-6644	338
Henderson County 307 Warren St PO Box 308 *Web:* www.hendersoncountyedc.com	Oquawka	IL	61469	309-867-2911	867-2033	338
Henderson County Conservation Area PO Box 118 *Web:* www2.illinois.gov	Keithsburg	IL	61442	309-374-2496		565
Henderson County CW Murchison Memorial Library 121 S Prairieville St *Web:* www.henderson-county.com	Athens	TX	75751	903-677-7295		434-3
Henderson County Public Library 301 N Washington St *Web:* www.hendersoncountync.gov	Hendersonville	NC	28739	828-697-4725		434-3
Henderson County Tourist Commission 101 N Water St Ste B *TF:* 800-648-3128 ■ *Web:* www.hendersonky.org	Henderson	KY	42420	270-826-3128	826-0234	206
Henderson Glass Inc 715 S Blvd E *TF:* 800-694-0672 ■ *Web:* www.hendersonglass.com	Rochester Hills	MI	48307	800-694-0672		332
Henderson Hills Baptist Church 1200 E I 35 Frontage Rd *TF:* 877-901-4639 ■ *Web:* www.hhbc.com	Edmond	OK	73034	405-341-4639		48-20
Henderson House Museum 602 Deschutes Way *Web:* www.ci.tumwater.wa.us	Tumwater	WA	98501	360-754-4160		520
Henderson Implement Co 2929 N Bluff St *Web:* www.hendersonimp.com	Fulton	MO	65251	573-642-5777		45
Henderson Isd PO Box 728 *Web:* www.hendersonisd.org	Henderson	TX	75653	903-655-5000	657-9271	685
Henderson Properties Inc 919 Norland Rd *Web:* www.hendersonproperties.com	Charlotte	NC	28205	704-535-1122	569-9669	652
Henderson Sewing Machine Company Inc Waits Dr Industrial Pk *TF:* 800-824-5113 ■ *Web:* www.hendersonsewing.com	Andalusia	AL	36420	334-222-2451		358
Henderson State University 1100 Henderson St *TF:* 800-228-7333 ■ *Web:* www.hsu.edu	Arkadelphia	AR	71999	870-230-5000	230-5066	166
Henderson, Caverly, Pum & Charney LLP 12750 High Bluff Dr Ste 300 *Web:* www.hcesq.com	San Diego	CA	92130	858-755-3000		428
Henderson-Johnson Company Inc 918 Canal St *TF:* 800-492-3434 ■ *Web:* www.hjcoinc.com	Syracuse	NY	13210	315-479-5561	479-5585	189-9
Henderson-Vance County Chamber of Commerce 414 S Garnett St *Web:* hendersonvance.org	Henderson	NC	27536	252-438-8414		139
Hendersonville Area Chamber of Commerce 100 Country Dr Ste 104 *Web:* www.hendersonvillechamber.com	Hendersonville	TN	37075	615-824-2818	250-3637	139
Hendersonville County Chamber of Commerce 204 Kanuga Rd *Web:* www.hendersoncountychamber.org	Hendersonville	NC	28739	828-692-1413	693-8802	139
Hendersonville Public Library 140 Saundersville Rd *Web:* www.hendersonvillelibrary.org	Hendersonville	TN	37075	615-824-0656		434-3
Hendlin Visual Communications Inc 129 N 2nd St Ste 101 *Web:* www.hendlin.com	Minneapolis	MN	55401	612-338-1663		514
Hendren Plastics Inc 1607 Hwy 72 SE *TF:* 877-529-5300 ■ *Web:* www.hendrenplastics.com	Gravette	AR	72736	877-529-5300		601

Phone | Fax | Class

Hendrick Automotive Group
6000 Monroe Rd Ste 100 Charlotte NC 28212 704-568-5550 57
Web: www.hendrickauto.com

Hendrick Health System 1900 Pine St Abilene TX 79601 325-670-2000 374-3
Web: www.hendrickhealth.org

Hendrick Hospice Care 1682 Hickory St Abilene TX 79601 325-677-8516 371
TF: 800-622-8516 ■ *Web:* www.hendrickhospice.org

Hendrick Hudson Free Library
185 Kings Ferry Rd Montrose NY 10548 914-674-3600 434-3
Web: www.westchesterlibraries.org

Hendrick Inc
1201 NE Peachtree St 400 Colony Sq Ste 1900 Atlanta GA 30361 404-261-9383 240-9398 393
Web: www.hendrickinc.com

Hendrick Manufacturing Co
1 Seventh Ave Carbondale PA 18407 800-225-7373 282-1506* 488
**Fax Area Code:* 570 ■ *TF:* 800-225-7373 ■ *Web:* www.hendrickcorp.com

Hendrick Motorsports Museum
4400 Papa Joe Hendrick Blvd Charlotte NC 28262 877-467-4890 522
TF: 877-467-4890 ■ *Web:* www.hendrickmotorsports.com

Hendrick-Long Publishing Co
10635 Tower Oaks Blvd Ste D Houston TX 77070 800-544-3770 637-2
TF: 800-544-3770 ■ *Web:* www.hendricklongpublishing.com

Hendricks & Associates Inc
190 W Huffaker Ln Ste 403 Reno NV 89511 775-674-6000 390
Web: www.hendricks-inc.com

Hendricks County 355 S Washington St Danville IN 46122 317-745-9231 338
Web: www.co.hendricks.in.us

Hendricks Holding Company Inc
690 Third St Beloit WI 53511 608-362-8000 360-3
Web: www.hendricksholding.com

Hendricks Park & Gardens
Summit Ave & Skyline Blvd Eugene OR 97403 541-510-4636 97
Web: www.eugene-or.gov

Hendricks Power Co-op
86 N County Rd 500 E Avon IN 46123 317-745-5473 245
TF: 800-876-5473 ■ *Web:* www.hendrickspower.com

Hendricks Regional Health Danville
1000 E Main St Danville IN 46122 317-745-4451 374-3
Web: www.hendricks.org

Hendrickson Intl 800 S Frontage Rd Woodridge IL 60517 630-910-2800 910-2899 60
TF: 855-743-3733 ■ *Web:* www.hendrickson-intl.com

Hendrickson USA LLC 500 Pk Blvd Ste 450 Itasca IL 60143 630-773-9111 875-1204 360-3
TF: 800-668-5360 ■ *Web:* hendrickson-intl.com

Hendrix Batting Co 2310 Surrett Dr High Point NC 27263 336-431-1181 361
Web: hendrixbatting.com

Hendrix College 1600 Washington Ave Conway AR 72032 501-329-6811 450-3843 166
TF: 800-277-9017 ■ *Web:* www.hendrix.edu

Hendrix Consulting Engineers
115 E Main Round Rock TX 78664 512-218-0060 261
Web: hcengineer.com

Hendry County PO Box 1760 LaBelle FL 33975 863-675-5217 338
Web: www.hendryfla.net

Hendy Woods State Park
18599 Philo-Greenwood Rd Philo CA 95466 707-895-3141 565
Web: www.parks.ca.gov

Hene Health Brokerage LLC
2323 Cumberland Pkwy SE Ste 103 Atlanta GA 30339 678-384-3000 390
Web: healthquotesmadeez.com

Heneghan & Associates PC
1004 State Hwy 16 Jerseyville IL 62052 618-498-6418 261
Web: haengr.com

Henggeler Packing Company Inc
6730 Elmore Rd Fruitland ID 83619 208-452-4212 315-3
Web: www.henggelerpacking.com

Henglong USA Corp 2546 Elliott Dr Troy MI 48083 248-577-0353 577-0351 60
Web: www.caas-usa.com

Henig Inc 4135 Carmichael Rd Montgomery AL 36106 334-277-7610 157-6
TF: 800-521-2037 ■ *Web:* www.henigfurs.com

Henke Manufacturing Corp
3070 Wilson Ave Leavenworth KS 66048 913-682-9000 190
Web: henkemfg.com

Henkel & Cohen PA
7480 SW 40th St Ste 450 Miami FL 33155 305-971-9474 534-2607* 41
**Fax Area Code:* 786 ■ *Web:* miamibusinesslitigators.com

Henkel Corp 1 Henkel Way Rocky Hill CT 06067 860-218-2300 571-5465 3
TF: 800-243-4874 ■ *Web:* www.henkel.com

Henkel Harris Company Inc
2983 S Pleasant Valley Rd Winchester VA 22601 540-667-4900 319-2
Web: www.henkelharris.com

Henley & Company LLC 1290 RXR Plz Uniondale NY 11556 516-794-5520 794-6207 690
TF: 800-753-8688 ■ *Web:* www.henleyandcompany.com

Henley Group 2876 Hwy 9 Cheraw SC 29520 843-537-5924 537-5646 188-3
Web: www.henleygroup.com

Henley Park Hotel, The
926 Massachusetts Ave NW Washington DC 20001 202-638-5200 379
TF: 800-222-8474 ■ *Web:* www.henleypark.com

Henlopen Hotel 511 N Boardwalk Rehoboth Beach DE 19971 302-227-2551 227-8147 379
TF: 800-441-8450 ■ *Web:* www.henlopenhotel.com

Henna Chevrolet Inc 8805 N Ih 35 Austin TX 78753 512-832-1888 57
Web: www.hennachevyaustin.com

Henneman Engineering
1605 S State St Champaign IL 61820 217-359-1531 359-9354 261
Web: henneman.com

Hennen & Associates PLC
230 Hardman Ave S South Saint Paul MN 55075 651-255-3200 255-3205 2
Web: hennenassociates.com

Hennepin County 300 S Sixth St Minneapolis MN 55487 612-348-3081 348-8701 338
Web: www.hennepin.us

Hennepin County Library (HCL)
12601 Ridgedale Dr Minnetonka MN 55305 612-543-8800 847-8600* 434-3
**Fax Area Code:* 952 ■ *Web:* hclib.org

Hennepin County Library (HCL)
300 Nicollet Mall Minneapolis MN 55401 612-543-8100 434-3
Web: www.supporthclib.org

Hennepin County Medical Ctr (HCMC)
701 Park Ave Minneapolis MN 55415 612-873-3000 374-3
Web: www.hennepinhealthcare.org

Hennepin History Museum
2303 Third Ave S Minneapolis MN 55404 612-870-1329 520
Web: hennepinhistory.org

Hennepin Technical College
9000 Brooklyn Blvd Brooklyn Park MN 55445 952-995-1300 488-2944* 800
**Fax Area Code:* 763 ■ *TF:* 800-345-4655 ■ *Web:* www.hennepintech.edu

Hennepin Theatre Trust
900 Hennepin Ave Minneapolis MN 55403 612-455-9500 184
Web: www.hennepintheatretrust.org

Hennessee Group LLC
500 Fifth Ave 47th Fl New York NY 10110 212-857-4400 401
Web: www.hennesseegroup.com

Hennessey & Bienstock LLP
551 Madison Ave 11th Fl New York NY 10022 212-512-0808 41
Web: hblawny.com

Hennessy Construction Services Corp
2300 22nd St N Saint Petersburg FL 33713 727-821-3223 186
Web: hcsfl.com

Hennessy Industries Inc
1601 JP Hennesey Dr La Vergne TN 37086 855-876-3864 60
TF: 800-688-6359 ■ *Web:* www.hennessyind.com

Hennessy River View Ford
2200 US Hwy 30 Oswego IL 60543 630-897-8900 57
Web: www.riverviewford.com

Henning Construction Company Inc
PO Box 394 Johnston IA 50131 515-253-0943 253-0942 186
Web: www.henningcompanies.com

Henning Industrial Software Inc
102 1st St Ste 211 Hudson OH 44236 330-650-4212 177
Web: henningsoftware.com

Henninger Media Services Inc
1320 N Courthouse Rd Arlington VA 22201 703-243-3444 243-5697 512
TF: 888-243-3444 ■ *Web:* www.henninger.com

Hennings Super Market Inc
290 Main St Harleysville PA 19438 215-256-9533 345
Web: henningsmarket.com

Henningsen Foods Inc
14334 Industrial Rd Omaha NE 68144 402-330-2500 330-0875 619
Web: www.henningsenfoods.com

Hennis Care Ctr 1720 Cross St Dover OH 44622 330-364-8849 364-2128 450
Web: www.henniscarecentre.com

Henny Penny Corp 1219 US 35 W PO Box 60 Eaton OH 45320 937-456-8400 417-8402* 298
**Fax Area Code:* 800 ■ *TF:* 800-417-8417 ■ *Web:* www.hennypenny.com

Henri Bendel Inc 712 Fifth Ave New York NY 10019 212-247-1100 157-6
TF: 866-875-7975 ■ *Web:* www.lb.com

Henri Stern Watch Agency Inc
45 Rockefeller Plz Ste 401 New York NY 10111 212-218-1240 218-1283 153
Web: www.patek.com

Henricksen & Co
1101 W River Pkwy Ste 100 Minneapolis MN 55415 612-455-2200 877-3300 320
Web: www.henricksen.com

Henrico County 4301 E Parham Rd Henrico VA 23228 804-501-4000 501-5214 338
Web: henrico.us

Henrico County Public Library
1001 N Laburnum Ave Richmond VA 23223 804-501-1900 270-2982 434-3
Web: www.henricolibrary.org

Henrico Doctor's Hospital
1602 Skipwith Rd Richmond VA 23229 804-289-4500 374-3
Web: careers.hcahealthcare.com

Henricus Historical Park
251 Henricus Park Rd Chester VA 23836 804-748-1611 520
Web: henricus.org

Henrietta Public Library
455 Calkins Rd Rochester NY 14623 585-359-7092 334-6369 434-3
Web: www.hpl.org

Henriott Group Inc
250 Main St Ste 650 LaFayette IN 47901 765-429-5000 390
Web: henriott.com

Henry & Peters PC
3310 S Broadway Ste 100 Tyler TX 75701 903-597-6311 2
TF: 877-880-3348 ■ *Web:* henrypeters.com

Henry A. Fox Sales Co
4494 36th St SE Grand Rapids MI 49512 616-949-1210 81-1
Web: henryfoxsales.com

Henry A. Strobel
10878 Mill Creek Rd Aumsville OR 97325 503-749-1742 575-5367* 637-2
**Fax Area Code:* 708 ■ *Web:* www.henrystrobel.com

Henry Adams LLC
600 Baltimore Ave Ste 400 Baltimore MD 21204 410-296-6500 261
Web: henryadams.com

Henry Art Gallery
15th Ave NE & NE 41st St PO Box 351410 Seattle WA 98195 206-543-2280 520
Web: www.henryart.org

Henry B. Ball Co 5254 Dressler Rd NW Canton OH 44718 330-499-3000 410
Web: henrybball.com

Henry B. Gonzalez Convention Ctr
900 E Market St San Antonio TX 78205 210-207-8500 223-1495 205
Web: www.sahbgcc.com

Henry B. Plant Museum
401 W Kennedy Blvd Tampa FL 33606 813-254-1891 520
Web: www.plantmuseum.com

Henry Brewster LLC 205 N Conception St Mobile AL 36603 251-338-0630 41
Web: brewsterlaw.net

Henry Brick Company Inc 3409 Water Ave Selma AL 36703 334-875-2600 150
TF: 800-218-3906 ■ *Web:* www.henrybrick.com

Henry C. Smither Roofing Company Inc
6850 E 32nd St Indianapolis IN 46226 317-545-1304 546-4764 189-12
Web: www.smitherroofing.com

Henry Carlson Co
1205 W Russell St Sioux Falls SD 57104 605-336-2410 332-1314 685
Web: henrycarlson.com

Henry Co
909 N Sepulveda Blvd Ste 650 El Segundo CA 90245 310-955-9200 223-1285* 46
**Fax Area Code:* 866 ■ *TF:* 800-598-7663 ■ *Web:* www.henry.com

Henry Community Health (HCM)
1000 N 16th St New Castle IN 47362 765-521-0890 521-1555 374-3
Web: www.hchcares.org

Henry County 101 Ct Sq Ste B Abbeville AL 36310 334-585-2753 338
Web: henrycountyal.com

Name / Address	City	State	ZIP	Phone	Fax	Class
Henry County 307 W Center St *Web:* www.henrycty.com	Cambridge	IL	61238	309-937-3578		338
Henry County 100 W Franklin *Web:* www.henrycomo.com	Clinton	MO	64735	660-885-7204		338
Henry County PO Box 7 *Web:* www.henrycountyva.gov	Collinsville	VA	24078	276-634-4601	634-4781	338
Henry County 140 Henry Pkwy *Web:* www.co.henry.ga.us	McDonough	GA	30253	770-288-6535	288-7616	338
Henry County 100 E Washington St *Web:* www.henrycountyiowa.us	Mount Pleasant	IA	52641	319-385-2632	385-4144	338
Henry County 1853 Oakwood Ave *Web:* www.henrycountyohio.gov	Napoleon	OH	43545	419-592-4876	592-4016	338
Henry County 1215 Race St PO Box B *Web:* www.henryco.net	New Castle	IN	47362	765-529-6401	521-7046	338
Henry County 37 E Cross Main St *Web:* www.henrycountyky.com	New Castle	KY	40050	502-845-5750		338
Henry County 101 W Washington St *Web:* henrycountytn.org	Paris	TN	38242	731-642-5212	642-6531	338
Henry County Chamber of Commerce 1709 Hwy 20 W *Web:* www.henrycounty.com	McDonough	GA	30253	770-957-5786	957-8030	139
Henry County Medical Ctr 301 Tyson Ave *Web:* www.hcmc-tn.org	Paris	TN	38242	731-642-1220		374-3
Henry Cowell Redwoods State Park c/o Santa Cruz District Ofc 303 Big Trees Park Rd *Web:* www.parks.ca.gov	Felton	CA	95018	831-335-4598		565
Henry Doorly Zoo 3701 S Tenth St *Web:* www.omahazoo.com	Omaha	NE	68107	402-733-8401	733-7868	823
Henry Equestrian Insurance Brokers Ltd 53 Prospect St *TF:* 800-565-4321 ■ *Web:* www.hep.ca	Newmarket	ON	L3Y3T1	905-727-1144	898-0303	391-1
Henry F. Teichmann Inc 3009 Washington Rd *Web:* www.hft.com	McMurray	PA	15317	724-941-9550	941-3479	318
Henry Ford Bi-County Hospital 13355 E Ten-Mile Rd *Web:* www.hospital-data.com	Warren	MI	48089	586-759-7300		374-3
Henry Ford Centennial Library 16301 Michigan Ave *Web:* dearbornlibrary.org	Dearborn	MI	48126	313-943-2330		434-3
Henry Ford Community College 5101 Evergreen Rd *TF:* 800-585-4322 ■ *Web:* www.hfcc.edu	Dearborn	MI	48128	313-845-9600	845-9891	162
Henry Ford Health System 1 Ford Pl *TF:* 800-436-7936 ■ *Web:* www.henryford.com	Detroit	MI	48202	800-436-7936		353
Henry Frank & Co 160 Rock Hill Rd 2nd Fl *Web:* henryfrank.com	Bala Cynwyd	PA	19004	610-667-8480		2
Henry H. Armstrong Associates Inc 1 Gateway Ctr 420 Ft Duquesne Blvd Ste 1825 *Web:* henryarmstrong.com	Pittsburgh	PA	15222	412-471-1551		690
Henry Horton State Resort Park 4358 Nashville Hwy *Web:* tnstateparks.com	Chapel Hill	TN	37034	931-364-2222		565
Henry J. Kaiser Family Foundation 2400 Sand Hill Rd *Web:* www.kff.org	Menlo Park	CA	94025	650-854-9400	854-4800	305
Henry John Drewal Deptartment of Art History Chazen Museum of Art 800 University Ave UW-Madison *Web:* www.henrydrewal.com	Madison	WI	53706	608-263-2340		192
Henry Levy Group, The 5940 College Ave Ste F *Web:* hlgcpa.com	Oakland	CA	94618	510-652-1000		2
Henry Luce Foundation Inc 51 Madison Ave 30th Fl *Web:* www.hluce.org	New York	NY	10010	212-489-7700	581-9541	305
Henry M. Jackson Foundation For the Advancement of Military Medicine 6720-A Rockledge Dr Ste 100 *TF:* 866-687-2321 ■ *Web:* www.hjf.org	Bethesda	MD	20817	240-694-2000		305
Henry Margu Inc 540 Commerce St *TF:* 800-345-8284 ■ *Web:* www.henrymargu.com	Yeadon	PA	19050	610-622-0515		348
Henry Mayo Newhall Memorial Hospital 23845 McBean Pkwy *Web:* www.henrymayo.com	Valencia	CA	91355	661-253-8000		374-3
Henry Morrison Flagler Museum 1 Whitehall Way *Web:* www.flaglermuseum.us	Palm Beach Gardens	FL	33480	561-655-2833	655-2826	520
Henry O. Heiser III 104 Baltimore St *Web:* heiserlawoffice.com	Gettysburg	PA	17325	717-334-1990		41
Henry Pratt Co 401 S Highland Ave *TF:* 877-436-7977 ■ *Web:* www.henrypratt.com	Aurora	IL	60506	630-844-4000	844-4124	790
Henry Products Inc 302 S 23rd Ave *TF:* 800-525-5533 ■ *Web:* www.henryproducts.com	Phoenix	AZ	85009	602-253-3191	254-2325	191-1
Henry Quentzel Plumbing Supply Co 379 Throop Ave *TF:* 800-889-2294 ■ *Web:* www.quentzel.com	Brooklyn	NY	11221	718-455-6600		612
Henry Reeves Park 528 NW 10 St *Web:* miamigov.com	Miami	FL	33136	305-579-6970		564
Henry Schein Inc 135 Duryea Rd *NASDAQ: HSIC* ■ *TF:* 800-582-2702 ■ *Web:* www.henryschein.com	Melville	NY	11747	631-843-5500	843-5652	475
Henry Schmieder Arboretum *Delaware Valley College* 700 E Butler Ave *Web:* www.delval.edu	Doylestown	PA	18901	215-489-2283	489-2404	97
Henry Street Settlement 265 Henry St *TF:* 800-800-8000 ■ *Web:* www.henrystreet.org	New York	NY	10002	212-766-9200		363
Henry Technologies 701 S Main St *TF:* 800-964-3679 ■ *Web:* www.henry-group.net	Chatham	IL	62629	217-483-2406	483-2408	14
Henry Troemner LLC 201 Wolf Dr *TF:* 800-352-7705 ■ *Web:* www.troemner.com	Thorofare	NJ	08086	856-686-1600		476
Henry V. Events 6360 NE ML K Jr Blvd *Web:* www.henry-v.com	Portland	OR	97211	503-232-6666		184
Henry Vilas Zoo 702 S Randall Ave *Web:* www.henryvilaszoo.gov	Madison	WI	53715	608-266-4732		823
Henry W. Coe State Park 9000 E Dunne Ave *Web:* www.parks.ca.gov	Morgan Hill	CA	95037	408-779-2728		565
Henry Waldinger Memorial Library 60 Verona Pl *Web:* www.nassaulibrary.org	Valley Stream	NY	11582	516-825-6422		434-3
Henry Whitfield State Museum 248 Old Whitfield St *Web:* portal.ct.gov	Guilford	CT	06437	203-453-2457	453-7544	520
Henry's Foods Inc 234 McKay Ave N *TF:* 800-726-5299 ■ *Web:* www.henrysfoods.com	Alexandria	MN	56308	320-763-3194		297-8
Henry's Hi-life 301 W St John St *Web:* www.template.citycheers.com	San Jose	CA	95110	408-295-5414		671
Henry's Originals W Rosecrans Ave *Web:* henrysoriginal.com	Gardena	CA	90247	530-307-8377		479
Henry's Smokehouse 240 Wade Hampton Blvd *Web:* www.henryssmokehouse.com	Greenville	SC	29607	864-232-7774	232-7237	671
Henry-Madison Research Inc PO Box 84908 *Web:* www.chaostan.com	Phoenix	AZ	85071	602-252-4477	943-2363	637-2
Henrys Lake State Park 3917 E 5100 N *Web:* parksandrecreation.idaho.gov	Island Park	ID	83429	208-558-7532		565
Henschen & Associates Inc 432 W Gypsy Ln *Web:* henschen.com	Bowling Green	OH	43402	419-352-5454		177
Hensel Phelps 420 Sixth Ave *Web:* www.henselphelps.com	Greeley	CO	80631	970-352-6565	346-7252	186
Hensley Beverage Co 4201 N 45th Ave *Web:* hensley.com	Phoenix	AZ	85031	602-264-1635		81-1
Hensley Industries Inc 2108 Joe Field Rd *TF:* 888-406-6262 ■ *Web:* www.hensleyind.com	Dallas	TX	75229	972-241-2321	241-0915	190
Hensley, Elam & Associates LLC 163 E Main St Ste 401 *Web:* hea.biz	Lexington	KY	40507	859-389-8182		177
Henson & Efron PA 220 S Sixth St Ste 1800 *Web:* www.hensonefron.com	Minneapolis	MN	55402	612-339-2500		428
Henson Media Inc 1930 Bishop Ln Ste 1009 *Web:* Www.hensonmedia.com	Louisville	KY	40218	502-458-4222	458-4999	645-141
Henson Robinson Zoo 1100 E Lake Dr *Web:* www.springfieldparks.org	Springfield	IL	62712	217-585-1821	529-8748	823
Hentzen Coatings Inc 6937 W Mill Rd *TF:* 800-236-6589 ■ *Web:* www.hentzen.com	Milwaukee	WI	53218	414-353-4200	353-0286	550
HEP (Harbor Electronic Publishing) 80 E 11th St *TF:* 800-269-6422 ■ *Web:* www.hepdigital.com	New York	NY	10003	800-269-6422		637-10
HEPA Corp 3071 E Coronado St *Web:* www.hepa.com	Anaheim	CA	92806	714-630-5700		18
Hepaco Inc 2711 Burch Dr PO Box 26308 *TF:* 800-888-7689 ■ *Web:* www.hepaco.com	Charlotte	NC	28269	704-598-9782	598-7823	693
Hepatitis Foundation Intl (HFI) 504 Blick Dr *TF:* 800-891-0707 ■ *Web:* www.hepatitisfoundation.org	Silver Spring	MD	20904	301-622-4200		48-17
HeplerBroom LLC 211 N Broadway Ste 2700 *Web:* www.heplerbroom.com	Saint Louis	MO	63102	314-241-6160	241-6116	445
Heppner Molds Inc 1420 E 3rd Ave *Web:* www.heppnermolds.com	Post Falls	ID	83854	208-773-4055	773-6895	604
Her Interactive Inc 1150 114th Ave SE Ste 200 *TF:* 800-461-8787 ■ *Web:* www.herinteractive.com	Bellevue	WA	98004	425-460-8787	460-8788	178-6
Her Own Words LLC PO BOX 5264 *Web:* www.herownwords.com	Madison	WI	53705	608-271-7083	271-0209	514
Heraeus Medical Components LLC 5030 Centerville Rd *Web:* www.heraeus.com	Saint Paul	MN	55127	651-792-8500		718
Heral Enterprises Inc 9110 Lew Dr *Web:* www.heral.com	Little Rock	AR	72209	501-568-2090		300
Herald & Review 601 E Williams St *Web:* herald-review.com	Decatur	IL	62523	217-429-5151	421-6913	532-2
Herald Bulletin 1133 Jackson St *TF:* 800-750-5049 ■ *Web:* www.heraldbulletin.com	Anderson	IN	46016	765-622-1212	640-4815	532-2
Herald Democrat 331 W Woodard *Web:* www.heralddemocrat.com	Denison	TX	75020	903-465-7171		532-2
Herald Journal, The 1068 W 130 S *TF:* 800-275-0423 ■ *Web:* www.hjnews.com	Logan	UT	84321	435-752-2121	753-6642	532-2
Herald News 207 Pocasset St **Fax Area Code:* 973 ■ *Web:* www.northjersey.com	Fall River	MA	02722	508-676-8211	569-7268*	532-2
Herald Publishing Co PO Box 153 *TF:* 888-421-1866 ■ *Web:* www.jhvonline.com	Houston	TX	77001	713-630-0391	630-0404	637-8
Herald Times Reporter 902 Franklin St *TF:* 800-783-7323 ■ *Web:* local.htrnews.com	Manitowoc	WI	54220	920-684-4433		532-2
Herald, The 102 Manatee Ave W *Web:* www.bradenton.com	Bradenton	FL	34205	941-748-0411		532-2
Herald, The 52 S Dock St *TF:* 800-981-1692 ■ *Web:* www.sharonherald.com	Sharon	PA	16146	724-981-6100	981-5116	532-2
Herald, The 132 W Main St *Web:* www.heraldonline.com	Rock Hill	SC	29730	803-329-4000		532-2
Herald, The 1800 41st St S-300 *Web:* www.heraldnet.com	Everett	WA	98203	425-339-3000	339-3049	532-2
Herald-Dispatch 946 Fifth Ave *TF:* 800-444-2446 ■ *Web:* www.herald-dispatch.com	Huntington	WV	25701	304-781-6910	526-2857	532-2
Herald-Mail Co, The 100 Summit Ave PO Box 439 *TF:* 800-626-6397 ■ *Web:* www.heraldmailmedia.com	Hagerstown	MD	21741	301-733-5123	714-0245	637-8
Herald-Palladium 3450 Hollywood Rd *TF:* 800-356-4262 ■ *Web:* www.heraldpalladium.com	Saint Joseph	MI	49085	269-429-2400	429-4398	532-2
Herald-Progress 11159 Air Park Rd Ste 1 *Web:* www.herald-progress.com	Ashland	VA	23005	804-798-9031	798-9036	532-2

Name / Address	City	State	Zip	Phone	Fax	Class
Herald-Republican 45 S Public Sq *Web:* www.kpcnews.com	Angola	IN	46703	260-347-0400		532-2
Herald-Standard 8 E Church St *TF:* 800-342-8254 ■ *Web:* www.heraldstandard.com	Uniontown	PA	15401	724-439-7500	439-7559	532-2
Herald-Star 401 Herald Sq *TF:* 800-526-7987 ■ *Web:* www.heraldstaronline.com	Steubenville	OH	43952	740-283-4711	284-7355	637-8
Herald-Sun, The 1530 N Gregson St Ste 2a *Web:* www.heraldsun.com	Durham	NC	27701	919-419-6500		532-2
Herald-Times, The PO Box 909 *TF:* 800-422-0070 ■ *Web:* www.hoosiertimes.com	Bloomington	IN	47402	812-332-4401	331-4285	637-8
Herb Chambers 259 McGrath Hwy *TF:* 855-889-0839 ■ *Web:* www.herbchambers.com	Somerville	MA	02145	617-666-8333		57
Herb Chambers Chevrolet 90 Andover St Rt 114 *TF:* 877-907-1965 ■ *Web:* www.herbchamberschevrolet.com	Danvers	MA	01923	978-774-2000		57
Herb Easley 1125 Central Fwy *Web:* www.herbeasley.com	Wichita Falls	TX	76306	940-723-6631		57
Herb Gordon Nissan 3131 Automobile Blvd *TF:* 877-345-9869 ■ *Web:* www.herbgordonnissan.com	Silver Spring	MD	20904	877-345-9869		57
Herb Growing & Marketing Network (HGMN) PO Box 245 *TF:* 800-753-9199 ■ *Web:* www.herbworld.com	Silver Spring	PA	17575	717-393-3295	393-9261	48-2
Herb Pharm LLC 20260 Williams Hwy *TF:* 800-348-4372 ■ *Web:* www.herb-pharm.com	Williams	OR	97544	541-846-6262		345
Herb Redl Properties 80 Washington St Ste 100 *Web:* www.hredlproperties.com	Poughkeepsie	NY	12601	845-471-3388	471-3851	655
Herb Research Foundation (HRF) 4140 15th St *TF:* 800-748-2617 ■ *Web:* www.herbs.org	Boulder	CO	80304	303-449-2265	449-7849	48-17
Herbal Magic Inc 2180 Matheson Blvd E Ste 1 **Fax Area Code:* 416 ■ *TF:* 866-514-0786 ■ *Web:* herbalmagic.ca	Mississauga	ON	L4W5E1	866-514-0786	487-4569*	194
Herbalist, The 2106 NE 65th St *TF:* 800-694-3727 ■ *Web:* store.theherbalist.com	Seattle	WA	98115	206-523-2600	522-3253	799
Herbein & Company Inc 2763 Century Blvd *Web:* www.herbein.com	Reading	PA	19610	610-378-1175		2
Herber Aircraft Service Inc 1401 E Franklin Ave *TF:* 800-544-0050 ■ *Web:* www.herberaircraft.com	El Segundo	CA	90245	310-322-9575		480
Herberger Theater Ctr 222 E Monroe St *Web:* www.herbergertheater.org	Phoenix	AZ	85004	602-254-7399	258-9521	572
Herbert F. Johnson Museum of Art 114 Central Ave *Web:* www.museum.cornell.edu	Ithaca	NY	14853	607-255-6464		520
Herbert H. & Grace A. Dow Foundation 1018 W Main St *Web:* www.hhdowfoundation.org	Midland	MI	48640	989-631-3699	631-0675	305
Herbert H. Landy Insurance Agency Inc 75 Second Ave Ste 410 **Fax Area Code:* 781 ■ *TF:* 800-336-5422 ■ *Web:* www.landy.com	Needham	MA	02494	800-336-5422	449-7908*	390
Herbert Hoover National Historic Site 110 Parkside Dr PO Box 607 *Web:* www.nps.gov	West Branch	IA	52358	319-643-2541		564
Herbert Hoover Presidential Library & Museum 210 Parkside Dr *Web:* hoover.archives.gov	West Branch	IA	52358	319-643-5301	643-6045	434-2
Herbert K. Horita Realty Inc 98-150 Kaonohi St Ste B128 *Web:* www.hicentral.com	Aiea	HI	96701	808-487-1561		652
Herbert Mines Assoc (HMA) 600 Lexington Ave 2nd Fl *Web:* www.herbertmines.com	New York	NY	10022	212-355-0909		266
Herbert Rowland & Grubic Inc (HRG) 369 E Pk Dr *Web:* www.hrg-inc.com	Harrisburg	PA	17111	717-564-1121	564-1158	261
Herbert Smith Freehills New York LLP 450 Lexington Ave 14th Fl *Web:* herbertsmithfreehills.com	New York	NY	10017	917-542-7600	542-7601	41
Herbert Yentis & Company Inc 7300 City Line Ave *Web:* yentis.com	Philadelphia	PA	19151	215-878-7300	877-0955	652
Herbfarm, The 14590 NE 145th St *Web:* www.theherbfarm.com	Woodinville	WA	98072	425-485-5300	424-2925	671
Herbsaint Bar & Restaurant 701 St Charles Ave *Web:* herbsaint.com	New Orleans	LA	70130	504-524-4114		671
Herbst Oil Inc 230 S Orchard St *Web:* herbstoil.com	Thiensville	WI	53092	262-242-3660		316
Hercky-Pasqua-Herman Inc 324 Chestnut St *Web:* www.hph-comm.com	Roselle Park	NJ	07204	908-241-9474	241-8961	4
Hercon Laboratories Corp 101 Sinking Springs Ln *Web:* www.herconpharma.com	Emigsville	PA	17318	717-764-1191		583
Hercules Engine Components Co 2770 S Erie St *Web:* www.herculesmanufacturing.com	Massillon	OH	44646	330-830-2498		262
Hercules Industries Inc 1310 W Evans Ave *TF:* 800-356-5350 ■ *Web:* www.herculesindustries.com	Denver	CO	80223	303-937-1000	937-0903	612
Hercules Machine Tool & Die Co 13920 E Ten-Mile Rd *Web:* www.hmtd.com	Warren	MI	48089	586-778-4120	778-0070	757
Hercules Manufacturing Co 800 Bob Posey St *TF:* 800-633-3031 ■ *Web:* www.herculesvanbodies.com	Henderson	KY	42420	270-826-9501	826-0439	516
Hercules Technology Growth Capital Inc 400 Hamilton Ave Ste 310 *NYSE: HTGC* ■ *Web:* www.htgc.com	Palo Alto	CA	94301	650-289-3060	473-9194	792
Hercules Tire & Rubber Co 16380 E US Rt 224 - 200 *TF:* 800-677-9535 ■ *Web:* www.herculestire.com	Findlay	OH	45840	419-425-6400		754
Hercules Tire Sales Inc 10130 E 51st St *Web:* herculestiresales.com	Tulsa	OK	74146	918-627-7353		754
Herc-U-Lift Inc 5655 Hwy 12 W *TF:* 800-362-3500 ■ *Web:* www.herculift.com	Maple Plain	MN	55359	763-479-2501	479-2296	385
Herculite Products Inc 105 E Sinking Springs Ln *TF:* 800-772-0036 ■ *Web:* www.herculite.com	Emigsville	PA	17318	717-764-1192	764-5211	745-2
Herd Co Cattle Co 83973 489th Ave	Bartlett	NE	68622	402-482-5931		10-1
Herdrich Petroleum 210 E US Hwy 52 Ste E *Web:* herdrich.com	Rushville	IN	46173	765-932-3224		579
Here-4-You Consulting 109 E 6th St **Fax Area Code:* 413 ■ *TF:* 866-437-3481 ■ *Web:* www.npfunds.com	Front Royal	VA	22630	540-635-3518	702-9031*	192
Hereditary Disease Foundation (HDF) 3960 Broadway 6th Fl *Web:* www.hdfoundation.org	New York	NY	10032	212-928-2121	928-2172	48-17
Hereford Brand 313 N Lee *Web:* www.herefordbrand.com	Hereford	TX	79045	806-364-2030	364-8364	532-2
Hereford Independent School District 601 N 25 Mile Ave *Web:* www.herefordisd.net	Hereford	TX	79045	806-363-7600	363-7699	685
Heriaud & Genin Ltd 135 S Lasalle St Ste 2140 *Web:* hgtrustlaw.com	Chicago	IL	60603	312-616-1809		41
Heritage Animal Hospital Ltd 751 Main St *Web:* heritageanimal.com	Hortonville	WI	54944	920-779-4343		794
Heritage Auctions Inc 3500 Maple Ave 17th Fl *Web:* www.ha.com	Dallas	TX	75219	214-528-3500	409-1425	626
Heritage Bags 1648 Diplomat Dr *TF:* 800-527-2247 ■ *Web:* www.heritage-bag.com	Carrollton	TX	75006	800-527-2247		66
Heritage Bank 101 N Main St *TF:* 866-971-0106 ■ *Web:* www.heritagebank.com	Jonesboro	GA	30236	770-478-8881		360-2
Heritage Bank 201 Fifth Ave SW *TF:* 800-455-6126 ■ *Web:* www.heritagebanknw.com	Olympia	WA	98501	503-306-5400		360-2
Heritage Bank of Nevada 2330 S Virginia St *Web:* heritagebanknevada.com	Reno	NV	89502	775-348-1000		70
Heritage Bank of Schaumburg 1535 W Schaumburg Rd *Web:* hbschaumburg.com	Schaumburg	IL	60194	847-524-4000		70
Heritage Bible College 1747 Bud Hawkins Rd PO Box 1628 *TF:* 800-297-6351 ■ *Web:* www.heritagebiblecollege.edu	Dunn	NC	28334	910-892-3178		166
Heritage Christian University 3625 Helton Dr PO Box HCU *TF:* 800-367-3565 ■ *Web:* www.hcu.edu	Florence	AL	35630	256-766-6610		161
Heritage College & Seminary 175 Holiday Inn Dr *TF:* 800-465-1961 ■ *Web:* discoverheritage.ca	Cambridge	ON	N3C3T2	519-651-2869	651-2870	785
Heritage Commerce Corp 150 Almaden Blvd *NASDAQ: HTBK* ■ *Web:* www.heritagecommercecorp.com	San Jose	CA	95113	408-947-6900	947-6910	360-2
Heritage Corridor Convention & Visitors Bureau 339 W Jefferson St *TF:* 800-926-2262 ■ *Web:* www.heritagecorridorcvb.com	Joliet	IL	60435	815-727-2323	727-2324	206
Heritage Ctr 1201 W Buena Vista Rd *TF:* 800-704-0700 ■ *Web:* holidayhealthcare.com	Evansville	IN	47710	812-429-0700	429-1849	450
Heritage Dairy Stores Inc 376 Jessup Rd *Web:* www.heritages.com	Thorofare	NJ	08086	856-845-2855	845-8392	204
Heritage Distilling Co 3118 Harborview Dr *Web:* heritagedistilling.com	Gig Harbor	WA	98335	253-514-8120		49-13
Heritage Environmental Services Inc 7901 W Morris St *Web:* www.heritage-enviro.com	Indianapolis	IN	46231	317-243-0811		804
Heritage Equipment Co 9000 Heritage Dr *TF:* 800-282-7961 ■ *Web:* www.heritage-equipment.com	Plain City	OH	43064	614-873-3941		358
Heritage Farmstead Museum 1900 W 15th St *Web:* www.heritagefarmstead.org	Plano	TX	75075	972-881-0140	422-6481	520
Heritage Financial Consultants LLC 307 International Cir Ste 390 *TF:* 866-529-1324 ■ *Web:* heritageconsultants.com	Hunt Valley	MD	21030	410-785-0033	785-0044	194
Heritage Ford Inc 2100 Sisk Rd *TF:* 844-362-1446 ■ *Web:* www.heritagefordmodesto.com	Modesto	CA	95350	209-529-5110		57
Heritage Foundation 214 Massachusetts Ave NE *TF:* 800-546-2843 ■ *Web:* www.heritage.org	Washington	DC	20002	202-546-4400		634
Heritage FS Inc 1381 S Crescent St *Web:* www.heritagefs.com	Gilman	IL	60938	815-265-4751	265-4769	276
Heritage Gas Ltd 238 Brownlow Ave Ste 200 *TF:* 877-836-7427 ■ *Web:* www.heritagegas.com	Dartmouth	NS	B3B1Y2	902-466-2003		580
Heritage Global Solutions Inc 230 N Maryland Ave *TF:* 800-915-4474 ■ *Web:* www.heritageglobalsolutions.com	Glendale	CA	91206	818-547-4474		196
Heritage Group Inc 1101 12th St *TF:* 888-463-6611 ■ *Web:* www.bankonheritage.com	Aurora	NE	68818	402-694-3136		70
Heritage Hill Historic District 126 College Ave SE *Web:* www.heritagehillweb.org	Grand Rapids	MI	49503	616-459-8950	459-2409	50-3
Heritage Hill State Historical Park 2640 S Webster Ave *TF:* 800-721-5150 ■ *Web:* heritagehillgb.org	Green Bay	WI	54301	920-448-5150		565
Heritage Hills Golf Resort & Conference Ctr 2700 Mt Rose Ave *Web:* www.heritagehillsresort.com	York	PA	17402	717-755-0123		669
Heritage Home Services LLC 4060 Executive Dr *Web:* homeservicestitle.com	Dayton	OH	45430	937-435-2580		652
Heritage Hospice Inc 120 Enterprise Dr PO Box 1213 *TF:* 800-203-6633 ■ *Web:* www.heritagehospice.com	Danville	KY	40423	859-236-2425	236-6152	371
Heritage Hospital 111 Hospital Dr *Web:* www.vidanthealth.com	Tarboro	NC	27886	252-641-7700		374-3

Name / Address	City	State	ZIP	Phone	Fax	Class
Heritage Hotel 522 Heritage Rd *Web:* www.heritagesouthbury.com	Southbury	CT	06488	203-264-8200		377
Heritage Hotels & Resorts Inc 201 Third St NW Ste 1150 *TF:* 877-901-7666 ■ *Web:* www.hhandr.com	Albuquerque	NM	87102	505-836-6700	212-9255	379
Heritage India 3238 Wisconsin Ave NW	Washington	DC	20016	202-333-3120		671
Heritage Inn, The 34521 Postal Ln *TF:* 800-669-9399 ■ *Web:* www.rehobothheritage.com	Lewes	DE	19958	800-669-9399		379
Heritage Insurance Managers 919 Isom Rd Ste A	San Antonio	TX	78216	210-829-7467		391-5
Heritage Lace Inc 309 S St *Web:* www.heritagelace.com	Pella	IA	50219	641-628-4949		361
Heritage Makers Inc 370 W Center St *TF:* 866-694-3763 ■ *Web:* www.heritagemakers.com	Orem	UT	84057	801-437-8000		637-2
Heritage Manufacturing Inc 16175 NW 49th Ave *Web:* www.heritagemfg.com	Miami Lakes	FL	33014	305-685-5966	687-6721	284
Heritage Mechanical Services Inc 305 Suburban Ave **Fax Area Code:* 631 ■ *TF:* 800-734-0384 ■ *Web:* www.heritagemech.com	Deer Park	NY	11729	516-558-2000	667-8613*	189-10
Heritage Mint Ltd PO Box 13750 *TF:* 888-860-6245 ■ *Web:* www.heritagemint.com	Scottsdale	AZ	85267	480-860-1300		730
Heritage Mortgage Banking Corp 25 Lindsley Dr Ste 209 *Web:* hmbcdirect.com	Morristown	NJ	07960	973-539-9898		652
Heritage Museum of Orange County, The 3101 W Harvard St *Web:* heritagemuseumoc.org	Santa Ana	CA	92704	714-540-0404	540-1932	520
Heritage of the Americas Museum 12110 Cuyamaca College Dr W *Web:* www.heritageoftheamericasmuseum.com	El Cajon	CA	92019	619-670-5194		520
Heritage Office Furnishings 1588 Rand Ave *TF:* 888-775-4555 ■ *Web:* www.heritageoffice.com	Vancouver	BC	V6P3G2	604-688-2381		320
Heritage Optical Center Inc 19010 Livernois Ave *Web:* heritageoptical.com	Detroit	MI	48221	313-863-9581		543
Heritage Petroleum LLC 516 N Seventh Ave *TF:* 800-422-3645 ■ *Web:* www.heritageoil.com	Evansville	IN	47710	812-422-3251	422-3291	579
Heritage Place Inc 2829 S MacArthur *TF:* 888-343-9831 ■ *Web:* www.heritageplace.com	Oklahoma City	OK	73128	405-682-4551	686-1267	51
Heritage Plastics Inc 1002 Hunt St *TF:* 800-245-4623 ■ *Web:* www.heritage-plastics.com	Picayune	MS	39466	601-798-8663		605-2
Heritage Press Intl 204 Jefferson St *Web:* usmcpress.com	Plum Branch	SC	29845	864-443-5081	443-5572	637-2
Heritage Products Inc 2000 Smith Ave *Web:* www.heritageproductsinc.com	Crawfordsville	IN	47933	765-364-9002		489
Heritage Rehabilitation Ctr 21414 S Vermont Ave *Web:* hrcsnf.com	Torrance	CA	90502	310-320-8714	320-1809	450
Heritage Square Museum 3800 Homer St *Web:* www.heritagesquare.org	Los Angeles	CA	90031	323-225-2700	225-2725	520
Heritage State Bank 2201 James St *Web:* heritagesb.com	Lawrenceville	IL	62439	618-943-1038		70
Heritage Strategies LLC 135 Crossways Park Dr Ste 402 *Web:* heritagesllc.com	Woodbury	NY	11797	212-485-1536		390
Heritage Summit HealthCare of Florida Inc PO Box 2928 *TF:* 800-282-7644 ■ *Web:* www.summitholdings.com	Lakeland	FL	33806	863-665-6629	665-5177	391-3
Heritage Texas Properties LP 14340 Memorial Dr *TF:* 800-856-7797 ■ *Web:* heritagetexas.com	Houston	TX	77079	281-493-3880	493-0003	652
Heritage University 3240 Ft Rd *TF:* 888-272-6190 ■ *Web:* www.heritage.edu	Toppenish	WA	98948	509-865-8500	865-8659	166
Heritage Usa Community Federal Credit Union 5507 W Wadley *Web:* heritage-usa.net	Midland	TX	79707	432-681-1050		219
Heritage Valley Health System 1000 Dutch Ridge Rd *TF:* 877-771-4847 ■ *Web:* www.heritagevalley.org	Beaver	PA	15009	724-728-7000		374-3
Heritage Valley Kennedy 25 Heckel Rd Kennedy Twp *Web:* ohiovalleyhospital.org	McKees Rocks	PA	15136	412-777-6161		374-3
Heritage Village Museum 11450 Lebanon Pk *Web:* www.heritagevillagecincinnati.org	Cincinnati	OH	45241	513-563-9484	563-0914	520
Heritage Vision Plans Inc 1 Woodward Ave Ste 2020 *TF:* 800-252-2053 ■ *Web:* www.heritagevisionplans.com	Detroit	MI	48226	800-252-2053		391-3
Heritage-Crystal Clean Inc 2175 Pt Blvd Ste 375 *TF:* 877-938-7948 ■ *Web:* www.crystal-clean.com	Elgin	IL	60123	847-836-5670		151
Herker Industries Inc N57 W13760 Carmen Ave *Web:* www.herker.com	Menomonee Falls	WI	53051	262-781-8270		621
Herkimer County 109 Mary St Ste 1111 *Web:* www.herkimercounty.org	Herkimer	NY	13350	315-867-1129	867-1349	338
Herkimer County Chamber of Commerce 28 W Main St *TF:* 877-984-4636 ■ *Web:* www.herkimercountychamber.com	Mohawk	NY	13407	315-866-7820	866-7833	139
Herkimer County Community College 100 Reservoir Rd *TF:* 844-464-4375 ■ *Web:* www.herkimer.edu	Herkimer	NY	13350	315-866-0300	866-0062	162
Herkimer Home State Historic Site 200 SR- 169 *Web:* parks.ny.gov	Little Falls	NY	13365	315-823-0398		565
Herman & Kittle Properties Inc 500 E 96th St Ste 300 *Web:* www.hermankittle.com	Indianapolis	IN	46240	317-846-3111		652
Herman Goldner Company Inc 7777 Brewster Ave *TF:* 800-355-5997 ■ *Web:* goldner.com	Philadelphia	PA	19153	215-365-5400	492-6486	189-10
Herman Grant Company Inc 1100 Ashmore Ave **Fax Area Code:* 423 ■ *TF:* 800-472-6826 ■ *Web:* www.hermangrant.com	Chattanooga	TN	37415	800-472-6826	266-7227*	358
Herman H. Sticht Company Inc 45 Main St Ste 701 *TF:* 800-221-3203 ■ *Web:* www.stichtco.com	Brooklyn	NY	11201	718-852-7602	852-7915	472
Herman Herman Katz & Cotlar LLP 820 Okeefe Ave *TF:* 844-943-7626 ■ *Web:* hhklawfirm.com	New Orleans	LA	70113	504-581-4892		428
Herman Katz Cangemi Wilkes & Clyne LLP 538 Broadhollow Rd Ste 307 *Web:* www.hermankatz.com	Melville	NY	11747	631-501-5011		41
Herman Miller Inc 855 E Main Ave *NASDAQ:* MLHR ■ *TF:* 888-443-4357 ■ *Web:* www.hermanmiller.com	Zeeland	MI	49464	616-654-3000		319-1
Herman Seekamp Inc 1120 W Fullerton Ave *TF:* 888-874-6814 ■ *Web:* www.clydesdonuts.com	Addison	IL	60101	888-874-6814		296-1
Herman Strauss Inc 35th & McColloch St *Web:* www.strauss-ind.com	Wheeling	WV	26003	304-748-0699		791
Herman Weissker Inc 1645 Brown Ave *Web:* www.hermanweissker.com	Riverside	CA	92509	951-826-8800		194
Hermann Financial Services Inc 505 Lakeview Ave *Web:* hermannfinancial.com	Milford	DE	19963	302-424-1748		390
Hermann Oak Leather Co 4050 N First St *TF:* 800-325-7950 ■ *Web:* www.hermannoakleather.com	Saint Louis	MO	63147	314-421-1173	421-6152	432
Hermann Sons Life 515 S St Marys St PO Box 1941 *TF:* 800-234-4124 ■ *Web:* www.hermannsonslife.org	San Antonio	TX	78205	210-226-9261	892-0299	707
Hermanoff Public Relations 23537 Shagwood Dr *Web:* www.hermanoff.net	Bingham Farms	MI	48025	248-330-7829	485-6033	317
Hermanos Cocina Mexicana 11 Hills Ave *Web:* www.hermanosmexican.com	Concord	NH	03301	603-224-5669		671
Hermary Opto Electronics Inc 104-1500 Hartley Ave *Web:* www.hermary.com	Coquitlam	BC	V3K7A1	604-517-4625		256
Hermell Products Inc 9 Britton Dr *TF:* 800-233-2342 ■ *Web:* www.hermell.com	Bloomfield	CT	06002	860-242-6550		477
Hermes Abrasives Ltd 524 Viking Dr *TF:* 800-464-8314 ■ *Web:* www.hermes-schleifwerkzeuge.com	Virginia Beach	VA	23452	757-486-6623	431-2370	1
Hermes Music 401 S Broadway *TF:* 800-994-9150 ■ *Web:* en.hermesmusic.com	Pharr	TX	78501	800-693-8472		526
Hermetic Coil Company Inc 12005 E Davis Ln *Web:* www.hermeticcoil.com	Bicknell	IN	47512	812-735-2400		757
Hermetician Press 680 Fox St *Web:* www.jamesbraha.com	Longboat Key	FL	34228	941-387-9101	387-8029	637-2
Hermiston Chamber of Commerce 415 S Hwy 395 PO Box 185 *Web:* www.hermistonchamber.com	Hermiston	OR	97838	541-567-6151	564-9109	139
Hermitage 335 N Franklin Tpke *Web:* www.thehermitage.org	Ho-Ho-Kus	NJ	07423	201-445-8311		565
Hermitage Foundation Museum 7637 N Shore Rd *Web:* www.thehermitagemuseum.org	Norfolk	VA	23505	757-423-2052	423-2410	520
Hermitage Hotel 231 Sixth Ave N *TF:* 888-888-9414 ■ *Web:* www.thehermitagehotel.com	Nashville	TN	37219	615-244-3121	254-6909	379
Hermitage The (Home of Andrew Jackson) 4580 Rachel's Ln *Web:* thehermitage.com	Hermitage	TN	37076	615-889-2941	889-9289	520
Hermitage, The 1600 Westwood Ave *Web:* www.hermitagerichmond.org	Richmond	VA	23227	804-474-1800		672
Hermosa Inn 5532 N Palo Cristi Rd *TF:* 800-241-1210 ■ *Web:* www.hermosainn.com	Paradise Valley	AZ	85253	602-955-8614		379
Hern Kevin (Rep R - OK) 1019 Longworth House Office Bldg *Web:* www.hern.house.gov	Washington	DC	20515	202-225-2211		342-2
Hernandez & Associates PC 1490 Lafayette St Ste 307 *Web:* hdezlaw.com	Denver	CO	80218	303-623-1122	893-6116	41
Hernandez Companies Inc 3734 E Anne St *Web:* www.hernandezcompanies.com	Phoenix	AZ	85040	602-438-7825		187
Hernandez Consulting LLC 3221 Tulane Ave *Web:* www.hernandezconsulting.com	New Orleans	LA	70119	504-305-8571		196
Hernandez Office Solution 119 N 17th St *TF:* 866-724-0135 ■ *Web:* hernandezofficesolutions.com	Nederland	TX	77627	409-724-0135	724-0210	321
Hernando Correctional Institution 16415 Spring Hill Dr *Web:* www.dc.state.fl.us	Brooksville	FL	34604	352-754-6715	797-5794	213
Hernando County 16110 Aviation Loop Dr *TF:* 800-601-4580 ■ *Web:* www.hernandocounty.us	Brooksville	FL	34604	352-754-4000	754-4477	338
Hernando County Public Library System 238 Howell Ave *Web:* hernandocountylibrary.us	Brooksville	FL	34601	352-754-4043		434-3
Hernco Fabrication & Service 2131 Commerce Dr *Web:* herncoinc.com	Midland	TX	79703	432-522-1444		538
Herndon Career Ctr 11501 E 350 Hwy *Web:* www.raytownschools.org	Raytown	MO	64138	816-268-7140	268-7149	167-3
Herndon Plant Oakley Ltd 800 N Shoreline Blvd Ste 2200 S *TF:* 800-888-4894 ■ *Web:* hpo.com	Corpus Christi	TX	78401	361-888-7611	888-9342	401
Hero Systems Inc 700 N Hayden Island Dr Ste 290 **Fax Area Code:* 503 ■ *Web:* bigtownhero.com	Portland	OR	97217	360-823-9922	296-5808*	670
Heroix Corp 165 Bay State Dr *TF:* 800-229-6500 ■ *Web:* www.heroix.com	Braintree	MA	02184	781-848-1701		178-12

Company / Address	Phone	Fax	Class
Herold & Sager, Attorneys at Law 550 Second St Ste 200 ...... Encinitas CA 92024 *Web:* www.heroldsagerlaw.com	760-487-1047		428
Herold Precision Metals LLC 1370 Hammond Rd ...... White Bear Township MN 55110 *Web:* www.heroldprecision.com	651-490-5550		697
Herold's Salads Inc 17512 Miles Ave ...... Cleveland OH 44128 *Web:* www.heroldssalads.com	216-991-7500		296-33
Heron Systems Inc 22685 Three Notch Rd Unit B ...... California MD 20619 *Web:* heronsystems.com	301-866-0330		743
Heron Therapeutics Inc 123 Saginaw Dr ...... Redwood City CA 94063 *NASDAQ: HRTX* ■ *Web:* www.herontx.com	650-366-2626		582
HEROweb Marketing & Design Inc 1976 Garden Ave ...... Eugene OR 97403 *TF:* 888-257-2567 ■ *Web:* www.heroweb.com	541-746-6418		5
Herpes Resource Ctr (HRC) PO Box 13827 ...... Research Triangle Park NC 27709 *Web:* www.ashasexualhealth.org	919-361-8400	361-8425	48-17
Herr Foods Inc 20 Herr Dr PO Box 300 ...... Nottingham PA 19362 *TF:* 800-344-3777 ■ *Web:* www.herrs.com	610-932-9330		296-35
Herr Industrial Inc 610 E Oregon Rd ...... Lititz PA 17543 *Web:* www.herrindustrial.com	717-569-6619		697
Herr Tavern & Public House 900 Chambersburg Rd ...... Gettysburg PA 17325 *TF:* 800-362-9849 ■ *Web:* www.innatherrridge.com	717-334-4332		671
Herrera Beutler Jaime (Rep R - WA) 2352 Rayburn House Office Bldg ...... Washington DC 20515 *Web:* jhb.house.gov	202-225-3536	225-3478	342-2
Herrera Law Firm Inc, The 1800 W Commerce St ...... San Antonio TX 78207 *TF:* 800-455-1054 ■ *Web:* herreralaw.com	210-224-1054		41
Herrero Brothers Inc 2100 Oakdale Ave ...... San Francisco CA 94124 *Web:* www.herrero.com	415-824-7675		186
Herrick & White Ltd 3 Flat St ...... Cumberland RI 02864 *Web:* www.herrick-white.com	401-658-0440		499
Herrick Corp 3003 E Hammer Ln ...... Stockton CA 95212 *Web:* www.herricksteel.com	209-956-4751	956-1004	480
Herrick Feinstein LLP 2 Park Ave ...... New York NY 10016 *Web:* www.herrick.com	212-592-1400		428
Herrick Global 72 Main St ...... Burlington VT 05401 *Web:* herrickltd.com	802-864-4514	860-2210	2
Herrington Manor State Park 222 Herrington Ln ...... Oakland MD 21550 *Web:* www.dnr.maryland.gov	301-334-9180		565
Herrling Clark Hartzheim & Siddall Ltd 800 N Lynndale Dr ...... Appleton WI 54914 *Web:* www.herrlingclark.com	920-739-7366		445
Herrman & Goetz Inc 225 S Lafayette Blvd ...... South Bend IN 46601 *TF:* 800-528-1696 ■ *Web:* www.hgservices.com	574-282-2596	282-2645	610
Herrman Lumber Co 1917 S State Hwy N ...... Springfield MO 65802 *Web:* www.herrmanlumber.com	417-862-3737		364
Herrod Technology Inc 4500 Ridgecrest Dr ...... Arlington TX 76017 *Web:* www.herrodtech.com	214-202-0999		180
Herron Rail Video 2016 N Village Ave ...... Tampa FL 33612 **Fax Area Code:* 813 ■ *TF:* 800-783-3886 ■ *Web:* www.herronrail.com	800-783-3886	932-6173*	514
Herrschners Inc 2800 Hoover Rd ...... Stevens Point WI 54481 **Fax Area Code:* 715 ■ *TF:* 800-713-1239 ■ *Web:* www.herrschners.com	855-279-4701	341-2250*	258
Herr-Voss Corp 130 Main St ...... Callery PA 16024 *Web:* www.herr-voss.com	724-538-3180		295
HERS (Hysterectomy Educational Resources & Services Foundation) 422 Bryn Mawr Ave ...... Bala Cynwyd PA 19004 *TF:* 888-750-4377 ■ *Web:* www.hersfoundation.org	610-667-7757	667-8096	48-17
Hersam Acorn Newspapers 16 Bailey Ave ...... Ridgefield CT 06877 *TF:* 800-372-2790 ■ *Web:* www.hersamacorn.com	203-438-6544		637-8
Herschend Family Entertainment Corp (HFE) 5445 Triangle Pkwy Ste 200 ...... Peachtree Corners GA 30092 *Web:* www.hfecorp.com	770-441-3266		31
Hersha Hospitality Trust 510 Walnut St 9th Fl ...... Philadelphia PA 19106 *NYSE: HT* ■ *Web:* www.hersha.com	215-238-1046	238-0157	655
Hershey Co 100 Crystal A Dr ...... Hershey PA 17033 *NYSE: HSY* ■ *TF:* 800-468-1714 ■ *Web:* www.thehersheycompany.com	800-468-1714		296-8
Hershey Creamery Co 301 S Cameron St ...... Harrisburg PA 17101 *TF:* 888-240-1905 ■ *Web:* www.hersheyicecream.com	717-238-8134	233-7195	296-25
Hershey Entertainment & Resorts Co 27 W Chocolate Ave ...... Hershey PA 17033 *Web:* www.hersheypa.com	717-534-3887		669
Hershey Federal Credit Union 232 Hershey Rd ...... Hummelstown PA 17036 *Web:* hersheyfcu.org	717-533-9174	533-5241	219
Hershey Gardens 170 Hotel Rd ...... Hershey PA 17033 *Web:* www.hersheygardens.org	717-534-3492		97
Hershey Harrisburg Region Visitors Bureau 3211 N Front St Ste 301-A ...... Harrisburg PA 17110 *TF:* 877-727-8573 ■ *Web:* www.visithersheyharrisburg.org	717-231-7788		206
Hershey Lodge 325 University Dr ...... Hershey PA 17033 *TF:* 844-330-1802 ■ *Web:* www.hersheylodge.com	717-533-3311	533-9642	379
Hershey Trust Co 100 Mansion Rd E ...... Hershey PA 17033 *Web:* www.hersheytrust.com	717-520-1100		401
Hersheypark Arena & Stadium 550 W Hersheypark Dr ...... Hershey PA 17033 *Web:* www.hersheyentertainment.com	717-534-3911	534-8996	720
Hershner Hunter LLP 180 E 11th Ave ...... Eugene OR 97401 *Web:* www.hershnerhunter.com	541-686-8511		428
Herson's Inc 1396 Rockville Pke ...... Rockville MD 20855 *TF:* 888-203-8318 ■ *Web:* www.hersonsauto.com	301-279-8600		57
Hertford County School District 701 N Martin St ...... Winton NC 27986 *Web:* www.hertford.k12.nc.us	252-358-1761	358-4745	685
Hertrich Family of Automobile Dealerships 26905 Sussex Hwy ...... Seaford DE 19973 *TF:* 855-975-3690 ■ *Web:* www.hertrichs.com	855-975-3690		57
Hertz Global Holdings Inc 225 Brae Blvd ...... Park Ridge NJ 07656 *NYSE: HTZ* ■ *TF:* 800-654-3131 ■ *Web:* www.hertz.com	201-307-2000		126
Hertz Schram & Saretsky Pc 1760 S Telegraph Rd Ste 300 ...... Bloomfield Hills MI 48302 *TF:* 866-775-5987 ■ *Web:* www.hertzschram.com	248-335-5000		428
Herweck's 300 Broadway St ...... San Antonio TX 78205 *TF:* 800-725-1349 ■ *Web:* www.artdoggie.com	210-227-1349		45
Herzing College *Atlanta* 3393 Peachtree Rd Ste 1003 ...... Atlanta GA 30326 *TF:* 800-573-4533 ■ *Web:* www.herzing.edu	404-816-4533	816-5576	800
Herzing College Toronto 220 Yonge St Eaton Centre Galleria Offices Ste 202 ...... Toronto ON M5B2H1 *Web:* www.herzing.ca	416-599-6996		162
Herzog & Co 4640 Lankershim Blvd Ste 600 ...... North Hollywood CA 91602 *Web:* www.herzogcompany.com	818-762-4640	762-4648	41
Herzog Contracting Corp 600 S Riverside Rd ...... Saint Joseph MO 64507 *Web:* www.herzog.com	816-233-9001		188-4
Herzog Engineering LLC 530 N Third St Ste 230 ...... Minneapolis MN 55401 *Web:* herzogengineering.com	612-844-1234		261
Herzum North America Inc 175 N Franklin St Ste 301 ...... Chicago IL 60606 *Web:* www.herzum.com	312-602-1001		180
HESCO (Hartford Electric Supply Co) 30 Inwood Rd Ste 1 ...... Rocky Hill CT 06067 *TF:* 800-969-5444 ■ *Web:* www.hesconet.com	860-236-6363	236-0233	246
Heska Corp 3760 Rocky Mtn Ave ...... Loveland CO 80538 *NASDAQ: HSKA* ■ *Web:* www.heska.com	970-493-7272		584
Hesley Shoquist & Company Ltd 2607 White Bear Ave N ...... Maplewood MN 55109 *Web:* heshcpa.com	651-770-8505	770-0627	2
Heslin, Rothenberg, Farley, & Mesiti PC 5 Columbia Cir ...... Albany NY 12203 *Web:* www.hrfmlaw.com	518-452-5600		428
Hesperia Animal Hospital Inc 9540 I Ave ...... Hesperia CA 92345 *Web:* hesperiaanimalhospital.com	760-948-1553		794
Hesperia Chamber of Commerce 16816 Main St Ste D ...... Hesperia CA 92345 *Web:* www.hesperiacc.com	760-244-2135	244-1333	139
Hesperia Resorter PO Box 400937 ...... Hesperia CA 92345 *Web:* www.valleywidenewspaper.com	760-244-0021	244-6609	532-4
Hess Agency Inc, The 2990 Mt Joy Rd ...... Manheim PA 17545 *Web:* hessagency.com	717-665-2770		390
Hess Construction + Engineering Services Inc 804 W Diamond Ave Ste 200 ...... Gaithersburg MD 20878 *Web:* www.hessconstruction.com	301-670-9000		256
Hess Corp 1185 Avenue of the Americas ...... New York NY 10036 *TF:* 866-203-6215 ■ *Web:* www.hess.com	212-997-8500		304
Hess Sweitzer Inc 714 Rose Dr ...... Hartland WI 53029 *Web:* www.hesssweitzerpainting.com	262-641-9100		189-8
Hesse Inc 6700 St John Ave ...... Kansas City MO 64123 *TF:* 800-821-5562 ■ *Web:* www.grouphesse.com	816-483-7808	241-9010	779
Hesser Toyota Scion 1811 Humes Rd ...... Janesville WI 53545 *Web:* www.hessertoyota.com	608-754-7754		57
Hesston College 325 S College Dr PO Box 3000 ...... Hesston KS 67062 *TF:* 800-995-2757 ■ *Web:* www.hesston.edu	620-327-4221	327-8300	162
HET (Historic Elsinore Theatre) 170 High St SE ...... Salem OR 97301 *Web:* www.elsinoretheatre.com	503-375-3574	375-0284	572
Hethcoat & Davis Inc 278 Franklin Rd Ste 200 ...... Brentwood TN 37027 *Web:* www.hdengr.com	615-577-4300		261
Hetherington Engineering 5365 Avenida Encinas Ste A ...... Carlsbad CA 92008 *Web:* hetheringtonengineering.com	760-931-1917		261
Hetran Inc 70 Pinedale Industrial Rd ...... Orwigsburg PA 17961 *Web:* www.hetranb.com	570-366-1411	366-1829	455
Hetronic USA 3905 NW 36th St ...... Oklahoma City OK 73112 *Web:* www.hetronic.com	405-749-1270	749-1429	392
Hettinger County 336 Pacific Ave ...... Mott ND 58646 *Web:* www.hettingercountynd.com	701-824-4227	824-4387	338
Hettrick Cyr & Assoc (HC&A) 59 Sycamore St ...... Glastonbury CT 06033 *TF:* 888-805-0300 ■ *Web:* www.hettrickcyr.com	860-652-9997	657-8193	400
Heubel Shaw 6311 NE Equitable Rd ...... Kansas City MO 64120 **Fax Area Code:* 816 ■ *TF:* 800-283-4177 ■ *Web:* www.heubelshaw.com	800-283-4177	241-4217*	770
Heuer Insurance Agency Inc 5050 Vista Blvd Ste 101 ...... Sparks NV 89436 *Web:* www.heuerinsurance.com	775-358-5554	358-5596	390
Heuristic Park Inc 1900 Century Blvd Ste 17 ...... Atlanta GA 30345 *Web:* www.heuristicpark.com	404-373-7786		177
Heuristic Workshop Inc 203 W Jackson Ave ...... Knoxville TN 37902 *Web:* www.heuristicworkshop.com	865-523-9867		321
Heuss Printing Inc 903 N Second St ...... Ames IA 50010 *TF:* 800-232-6710 ■ *Web:* www.heuss.com	515-232-6710		627
Hewitt Development Enterprises (HDE) 1717 N Bayshore Dr Ste 2154 ...... Miami FL 33132 *Web:* www.hewittdevelopment.com	305-372-0941		194
Hewlett Packard 1501 Page Mill Rd ...... Palo Alto CA 94304 *NYSE: HPQ* ■ *Web:* www.hp.com	650-857-1501		173-2
Hewlett Packard Enterprise (Canada) Co (HP) 5150 Spectrum Way ...... Mississauga ON L4W5G2 *TF:* 888-447-4636 ■ *Web:* hpe.com	905-206-4725		173-2
Hewlett-Packard Co 3000 Hanover St ...... Palo Alto CA 94304 *NYSE: HPQ* ■ *TF:* 800-752-0900 ■ *Web:* www8.hp.com	650-857-1501	857-5518	173-2

Name / Address	City	State	Zip	Phone	Fax	Class
Hewson Landscape Inc 601 N Ave *Web:* www.hewsonland.com	Plainfield	NJ	07060	908-222-3616		422
Hexacon Electric Co 161 W Clay Ave *Web:* www.hexaconelectric.com	Roselle Park	NJ	07204	908-245-6200	245-6176	758
Hexagon Manufacturing Intelligence 250 Circuit Dr *TF:* 800-274-9433 ■ *Web:* www.hexagonmi.com	North Kingstown	RI	02852	401-886-2000	886-2727	472
Hexavest Inc 1250 Rene Levesque Blvd W Ste 4200 *Web:* www.hexavest.com	Montreal	QC	H3B4W8	514-390-8484	390-1184	463
Hexaware Technologies Inc 1095 Cranbury Rd *Web:* hexaware.com	Jamesburg	NJ	08831	609-409-6950	409-6910	180
Hexcel Corp 281 Tresser Blvd 16th Fl *NYSE: HXL* ■ *TF:* 800-444-3923 ■ *Web:* www.hexcel.com	Stamford	CT	06901	800-688-7734		605-1
Heyburn State Park 57 Chatcolet Rd *TF:* 866-634-3246 ■ *Web:* parksandrecreation.idaho.gov	Plummer	ID	83851	208-686-1308		565
Heyco Metals Inc 1069 Stinson Dr *Web:* heycometals.com	Reading	PA	19605	610-926-4131	926-4134	481
Heyco Products 1800 Industrial Way N *TF:* 800-526-4182 ■ *Web:* www.heyco.com	Toms River	NJ	08755	732-286-1800	244-8843	488
Heyer, Gruel & Associates PA 236 Broad St *Web:* hgapa.com	Red Bank	NJ	07701	732-741-2900		261
Heyl & Patterson Inc 2000 Cliff Mine Rd Ste 300 *Web:* www.heylpatterson.com	Pittsburgh	PA	15275	412-788-9810	788-9822	470
Heyl Royster Voelker & Allen Pc 124 SW Adams St Ste 600 *Web:* www.secure.heylroyster.com	Peoria	IL	61602	309-676-0400		428
Heyl Truck Lines Inc 220 Norka Dr *TF:* 800-324-4395 ■ *Web:* www.heyl.net	Akron	IA	51001	712-568-2451		780
Heymann Performing Arts Ctr 1373 S College Rd *Web:* www.heymanncenter.com	LaFayette	LA	70503	337-291-5540	291-5580	572
Heyrman Printing LLC 2083 Holmgren Way *Web:* heyrman.com	Green Bay	WI	54304	920-499-4815		627
HeyTutor Figueroa at Wilshire 601 S Figueroa St Ste 4050 *Web:* heytutor.com	Los Angeles	CA	90017	213-805-7854		242
Heywood Hospital 242 Green St *Web:* www.heywood.org	Gardner	MA	01440	978-632-3420		374-3
Hezel Associates LLC 731 James St Ste 410 *Web:* www.hezel.com	Syracuse	NY	13203	315-422-3512	422-3513	463
HF Group Inc 203 W Artesia Blvd *TF:* 800-421-5000 ■ *Web:* www.hf76.com	Compton	CA	90220	310-605-0755		496
HF Group, The 8844 Mayfield Rd *TF:* 800-444-7534 ■ *Web:* www.hfgroup.com	Chesterland	OH	44026	440-729-2445		92
HF Lenz Co 1407 Scalp Ave *Web:* www.hflenz.com	Johnstown	PA	15904	814-269-9300		261
HF Rubber Machinery Inc 1701 N Topeka Blvd *Web:* hf-group.com	Topeka	KS	66608	785-235-2336	235-1331	456
HF scientific Inc 16260 Airport Park Dr Ste 140 *TF:* 888-203-7248 ■ *Web:* www.watts.com	Fort Myers	FL	33913	888-203-7248		203
HFA (Humane Farming Assn) PO Box 3577 *Web:* www.hfa.org	San Rafael	CA	94912	415-485-1495	485-0106	48-3
HFA (Hospice Foundation of America) 1707 L St NW Ste 220 *TF:* 800-854-3402 ■ *Web:* www.hospicefoundation.org	Washington	DC	20036	202-457-5811	457-5815	49-8
HFE (Herschend Family Entertainment Corp) 5445 Triangle Pkwy Ste 200 *Web:* www.hfecorp.com	Peachtree Corners	GA	30092	770-441-3266		31
HFES (Human Factors & Ergonomics Society) 1124 Montana Ave Ste B PO Box 1369 *Web:* hfes.org	Santa Monica	CA	90406	310-394-1811	394-2410	48-17
HFI (Hepatitis Foundation Intl) 504 Blick Dr *TF:* 800-891-0707 ■ *Web:* www.hepatitisfoundation.org	Silver Spring	MD	20904	301-622-4200		48-17
HFI Enterprises Inc 2 S 181 County Line Rd	Maple Park	IL	60151	630-557-2406		280
HFI LLC 2421 McGaw Rd *TF:* 866-649-1400 ■ *Web:* www.hfi-inc.com	Obetz	OH	43207	614-491-0700		745-3
HFIA (Home Furnishings Independents Assn) 500 Giuseppe Ct Ste 6 *TF:* 800-422-3778 ■ *Web:* myhfa.org	Roseville	CA	95678	800-422-3778		49-4
HFKF (Historic Florida Keys Foundation) Old City Hall 510 Greene St *Web:* www.historicfloridakeys.org	Key West	FL	33040	305-292-6718		637-2
HFMA (Healthcare Financial Management Assn) 2 Westbrook Corporate Ctr Ste 700 **Fax Area Code: 708* ■ *TF:* 800-252-4362 ■ *Web:* www.hfma.org	Westchester	IL	60154	800-252-4362	531-0032*	49-8
HFN Inc 1315 W 22nd St Ste 300 *Web:* www.hfninc.com	Oak Brook	IL	60523	630-954-1232	954-1308	374-3
HFPA (Hollywood Foreign Press Assn) 646 N Robertson Blvd *Web:* www.goldenglobes.com	West Hollywood	CA	90069	310-657-1731		48-4
HFS Chicago Scholars 1074 W Taylor St Ste 201 *Web:* www.hfschicagoscholars.com	Chicago	IL	60607	312-421-4070	421-4071	196
HFTP (Hospitality Financial & Technology Professionals) 11709 Boulder Ln Ste 110 *TF:* 800-646-4387 ■ *Web:* www.hftp.org	Austin	TX	78726	512-249-5333	249-1533	49-1
HFW Industries Inc 196 Philadelphia St PO Box 8 *Web:* www.hfwindustries.com	Buffalo	NY	14207	716-875-3380	875-3385	386
HG Energy LLC 5260 Dupont Rd *Web:* hgenergyllc.com	Parkersburg	WV	26101	304-420-1100	863-3175	536
HG Engineers 142 Eglin Pkwy SE *Web:* www.hgengineers.com	Fort Walton Beach	FL	32548	850-243-6723		261
HG Marketing Group LLC 150 E State St	Doylestown	PA	18901	215-340-3606		636
HG Weber & Company Inc 725 Fremont St *Web:* www.holwegweber.com	Kiel	WI	53042	920-894-2221		556
HGA (Handweavers Guild of America) 1255 Buford Hwy Ste 211 *Web:* www.weavespindye.org	Suwanee	GA	30024	678-730-0010	730-0836	48-18
HGBD (Hussey Gay Bell) 329 Commercial Dr Ste 200 *Web:* www.husseygaybell.com	Savannah	GA	31406	912-354-4626		261
HGI Skydyne 100 River Rd *TF:* 800-428-2273 ■ *Web:* www.skydyne.com	Port Jervis	NY	12771	800-428-2273		199
HGI Technologies 1000 Park Centre Blvd Ste 128 *Web:* www.hgitechnologies.com	Miami Gardens	FL	33169	305-623-1921		535
HGK Asset Management Inc 525 Washington Blvd Newport Tower Ste 2000 *Web:* www.hgk.com	Jersey City	NJ	07310	201-659-3700		401
HGM Associates Inc 640 Fifth Ave *Web:* www.hgmonline.com	Council Bluffs	IA	51501	712-323-0530		261
HGMI (Hutar Growth Management Institute) 1701 E Lake Ave Ste 407 *Web:* www.hutar.com	Glenview	IL	60025	847-724-1910		194
HGMN (Herb Growing & Marketing Network) PO Box 245 *TF:* 800-753-9199 ■ *Web:* www.herbworld.com	Silver Spring	PA	17575	717-393-3295	393-9261	48-2
HGP (Hawks Giffels & Pullin (Hgp) Inc) 1308 Altamont Rd *Web:* hgp-inc.com	Greenville	SC	29608	864-370-0213		463
HGR (H.G. Reynolds Company Inc) 113 Contract Dr *Web:* www.hgreynolds.net	Aiken	SC	29801	803-641-1401	641-1037	186
HGS Engineering Inc 1121 Noble St *Web:* hgsengineeringinc.com	Anniston	AL	36201	256-236-1848		261
Hgs Financial Services 680 Craig Rd Ste 250 *Web:* www.hgsfinancialservices.com	Saint Louis	MO	63141	314-432-5341		226
HH Angus & Associates Ltd 1127 Leslie St *TF:* 866-955-8201 ■ *Web:* www.hhangus.com	Toronto	ON	M3C2J6	416-443-8200		256
HH Arnold Company Inc 529 Liberty St *TF:* 866-868-9603 ■ *Web:* www.hharnold.com	Rockland	MA	02370	781-878-0346	878-7944	744
HH Brown Shoe Company Inc 124 W Putnam Ave *Web:* www.hhbrown.com	Greenwich	CT	06830	203-661-2424	661-1818	301
HH Technologies Inc 1733 County Rd 68 *Web:* www.hhtech.net	Bremen	AL	35033	256-287-7000		596
Hhawaii Media 900 Fort Street Mall Ste 450 *Web:* www.hhawaiimedia.com	Honolulu	HI	96813	808-538-1180	538-9548	647
HHI (Hoag Hospital Irvine) 16200 Sand Canyon Ave *TF:* 800-309-9729 ■ *Web:* www.hoag.org	Irvine	CA	92618	949-764-4624		374-3
HHI Corp 736 W Harrisville Rd *Web:* www.hhicorp.com	Ogden	UT	84404	385-333-4400		186
HHL (Helen Hall Library) 600 W Walker St *Web:* www.leaguecity.com	League City	TX	77573	281-554-2994		434-3
HHMC Tax Inc 6955 San Luis Ave *Web:* haynertax.com	Atascadero	CA	93422	805-466-8800	466-4947	2
HHP (Horizon House Publications Inc) 685 Canton St *TF:* 800-966-8526 ■ *Web:* www.horizonhouse.com	Norwood	MA	02062	781-769-9750	762-9071	637-9
HHR (Home Health Resources Inc) 18338 Kingsland Blvd Ste 100 *TF:* 800-720-6592 ■ *Web:* www.homehealthresources.com	Houston	TX	77094	281-398-3444	398-6830	363
HHS (Department of Health & Human Services) 330 Independence Ave SW *TF:* 877-696-6775 ■ *Web:* www.hhs.gov	Washington	DC	20201	202-619-0150		340-10
HHS Indian Health Service (IHS) 801 Thompson Ave Ste 400 *TF:* 800-447-3368 ■ *Web:* www.ihs.gov	Rockville	MD	20852	303-443-3593		340-10
HI Development Corp 111 W Fortune St *Web:* www.hidevelopment.com	Tampa	FL	33602	813-229-6686		379
HI Nabor Supermarket Inc 7201 Winbourne Ave *Web:* www.hinabor.com	Baton Rouge	LA	70805	225-357-1448		345
HI Rel Connectors Inc 760 Wharton Dr *Web:* www.hirelco.net	Claremont	CA	91711	909-626-1820	399-0626	815
HI Roller 4511 N Northview Ave *TF:* 800-328-1785 ■ *Web:* www.aggrowth.com	Sioux Falls	SD	57107	605-332-3200		207
Hi Tech Data Floors Inc 164 Northfield Ave *Web:* hitechdatafloors.com	Edison	NJ	08837	732-905-1799	905-1442	290
Hi Tech International Group Inc 279 Goolsby Blvd *Web:* www.htig.com	Deerfield Beach	FL	33442	954-426-8512	426-8778	475
Hi Tech Profiles Inc 401 Main St *TF:* 800-342-5495 ■ *Web:* www.hitechprofiles.com	Ashaway	RI	02804	401-377-2040	377-2423	676
Hi Tech Seals Inc 9211-41 Ave *TF:* 800-661-6055 ■ *Web:* www.hitechseals.com	Edmonton	AB	T6E6R5	780-438-6055	434-5866	350
HI TecMetal Group Inc 1101 E 55th St *TF:* 877-484-2867 ■ *Web:* htgmetals.com	Cleveland	OH	44103	216-881-8100	426-6690	484
HIAA (Halifax Stanfield International Airport) 1 Bell Blvd *TF:* 800-753-1051 ■ *Web:* halifaxstanfield.ca	Enfield	NS	B2T1K2	902-873-4422	873-4750	27
Hialeah Chamber of Commerce & Industries 240 E 1st Ave Ste 217 *Web:* www.hialeahchamber.org	Hialeah	FL	33010	305-888-7780		139
Hialeah City Hall 501 Palm Ave *Web:* www.hialeahfl.gov	Hialeah	FL	33010	305-883-5800	883-5814	337
HIAS (Hebrew Immigrant Aid Society) 1300 Spring St Ste 500 *Web:* www.hias.org	Silver Spring	MD	20910	301-844-7300		48-5
Hiasun Inc 5218 Atlantic Ave PO Box 785 *Web:* hiasun.com	Mays Landing	NJ	08330	609-625-0565		177

	Phone	Fax	Class
Hiatus Spa & Retreat 1611 W Fifth St Ste 155 .... Austin TX 78703 *Web:* hiatusspa.com	512-362-5777		354
Hiawatha Homes Inc 1820 Valkyrie Dr NW .... Rochester MN 55901 *Web:* www.hiawathahomes.org	507-289-7222	289-8683	192
Hiawatha Rubber 1700 67th Ave N........ Minneapolis MN 55430 *TF:* 800-782-7776 ■ *Web:* hiawatharubber.com	763-566-0900	566-9537	677
Hiawatha World 411Oregon St .... Hiawatha KS 66434 *Web:* www.cityofhiawatha.org	785-742-2111	742-2276	532-2
HI-AYH (Hostelling International USA - American Youth Hostels) 8401 Colesville Rd Ste 600 .... Silver Spring MD 20910 *TF:* 888-449-8727 ■ *Web:* www.hiusa.org	240-650-2100	650-2094	48-23
Hibachi Japanese Steak House 3000 W 12th St........ Erie PA 16505 *Web:* www.hibachijapan.com	814-838-2495		671
Hibachi Master 8160 Beechmont Ave........ Cincinnati OH 45255 *Web:* hibachimaster.com	513-474-9888		671
Hibachi Steak House 108 S Fairmont Blvd........ Anaheim CA 92808	714-998-4110		671
Hi-Ball Trucking Inc 6925 Commercial Ave........ Billings MT 59101 *TF:* 800-423-6253 ■ *Web:* www.hiballtrucking.com	406-656-6700	656-9953	780
Hibar Systems Ltd 35 Pollard St........ Richmond Hill ON L4B1A8 *Web:* www.hibar.com	905-731-2400		547
Hibbert Company Inc, The 400 Pennington Ave........ Trenton NJ 08650 *Web:* www.hibbert.com	609-394-7500		5
Hibbett Sports 2700 Milan Ct........ Birmingham AL 35211 *Web:* www.hibbett.com	205-942-4292	912-7290	711
Hibbing Community College 1515 E 25th St .... Hibbing MN 55746 *TF:* 800-224-4422 ■ *Web:* hibbing.edu	218-262-7200	262-6717	162
Hibbs Hallmark & Co 501 Shelley Dr........ Tyler TX 75701 **Fax Area Code:* 903 ■ *TF:* 800-765-6767 ■ *Web:* www.hibbshallmark.com	800-765-6767	581-5988*	390
HIBCC (Health Industry Business Communications Council) 2525 E Arizona Biltmore Cir Ste 127 .... Phoenix AZ 85016 *TF:* 800-755-5505 ■ *Web:* www.hibcc.org	602-381-1091	381-1093	49-8
Hibco Plastics Inc 1820 Us 601 Hwy PO Box 157........ Yadkinville NC 27055 **Fax Area Code:* 336 ■ *TF:* 800-849-8683 ■ *Web:* hibco.com	800-849-8683	463-5591*	601
Hibernia Bancorp Inc 325 Carondelet St........ New Orleans LA 70130 *TF:* 888-297-3416 ■ *Web:* www.hibernia.bank	504-522-3203	301-9707	70
Hibernia Management & Development Company Ltd 100 New Gower St Ste 1000........ Saint John NL A1C6K3 *Web:* www.hibernia.ca	709-778-7000		536
Hibl Insurance Services Inc 1620 N Carpenter Rd Ste D46A .... Modesto CA 95351 *Web:* hiblinsurance.com	209-521-4440	521-0331	390
Hibon Inc 12055 Cote de Liesse........ Dorval QC H9P1B4 *Web:* www.hibon.com	514-631-3501		358
Hicaps Inc 600 N Regional Rd .... Greensboro NC 27409 *TF:* 800-498-9577 ■ *Web:* www.hicaps.com	336-665-1234		194
Hice Jody (Rep R - GA) 409 Cannon House Office Bldg........ Washington DC 20515 *Web:* hice.house.gov	202-225-4101	226-0776	342-2
Hickel Investment Co 939 W 5th Ave .... Anchorage AK 99501 *Web:* www.hickelinvestment.com	907-343-2400		655
Hicken, Scott, Howard & Anderson PA 2150 Third Ave N .... Anoka MN 55303 *Web:* hshalaw.com	763-421-4110	421-1040	428
Hickey Cianciolo Finn & Atkins PC 901 Wilshire Dr Ste 550........ Troy MI 48084 *Web:* www.michiganbusinesslawyers.com	248-247-3300		41
Hickey College 2700 N Lindbergh Blvd........ Saint Louis MO 63114 *TF:* 800-777-1544 ■ *Web:* www.hickeycollege.edu	314-434-2212	434-1974	167-3
Hickey Freeman 1155 N Clinton Ave .... Rochester NY 14621 *TF:* 844-755-7344 ■ *Web:* www.hickeyfreeman.com	585-467-7021		155-12
Hickman County 114 N Central Ave Ste 202 .... Centerville TN 37033 *Web:* hickmanco.com	931-729-2492	729-9951	338
Hicko CPA Group PC, The 310 E 90th Dr........ Merrillville IN 46410 *Web:* www.hickocpa.com	219-738-2863	738-2893	2
Hickok Waekon LLC 10514 Dupont Ave........ Cleveland OH 44108 *OTC:* HICKA ■ *TF:* 800-342-5080 ■ *Web:* www.hickok-inc.com	216-541-8060	761-9879	248
Hickory Brands Inc (HBI) 429 27th St NW........ Hickory NC 28601 **Fax Area Code:* 800 ■ *TF:* 800-438-5777 ■ *Web:* hickorybrands.com	828-322-2600	422-3279*	745-5
Hickory Bridge Farm 96 Hickory Bridge Rd .... Orrtanna PA 17353 *Web:* www.hickorybridgefarm.com	717-642-5261		671
Hickory County Library 18376 New Hermitage Dr .... Hermitage MO 65668 *Web:* hickorylibrary.org	417-745-6939	745-2132	338
Hickory Farms Inc 811 Madison Ave .... Toledo OH 43604 **Fax Area Code:* 419 ■ *TF:* 800-753-8558 ■ *Web:* www.hickoryfarms.com	800-753-8558	893-0164*	336
Hickory Grove Press 3151 Treeco Ln........ Bellevue IA 52031 *Web:* www.hickorygrovepress.com	563-583-4767		637-2
Hickory House Ribs *Aspen* 730 W Main St .... Aspen CO 81611 *Web:* www.hickoryhouseribs.com	970-925-2313		671
Hickory Knob State Resort Park 1591 Resort Dr........ McCormick SC 29835 *TF:* 800-491-1764 ■ *Web:* southcarolinaparks.com	864-391-2450		565
Hickory Metro Convention & Visitors Bureau 1960 13th Ave Dr SE........ Hickory NC 28602 *TF:* 800-509-2444 ■ *Web:* www.visithickorymetro.com	828-322-1335		206
Hickory Motor Speedway 3130 Hwy 70 SE........ Newton NC 28658 *TF:* 800-843-8725 ■ *Web:* www.hickorymotorspeedway.com	828-464-3655	465-5017	515
Hickory Park Furniture Galleries Inc 2220 Hwy 70 E Ste 370 .... Hickory NC 28602 *Web:* hickorypark.com	828-322-4440		321
Hickory Point Bank & Trust FSB 225 N Water Street........ Decatur IL 62525 *TF:* 800-872-0081 ■ *Web:* www.hickorypointbank.com	217-875-3131		70
Hickory Record 1100 11th Ave Blvd SE .... Hickory NC 28602 *Web:* www.hickoryrecord.com	828-322-4510		532-2
Hickory Ridge Mall 6075 Winchester Rd........ Memphis TN 38115 *Web:* www.hickoryridge.com	901-795-8844		460
Hickory Run State Park PO Box 81........ White Haven PA 18661 *Web:* www.dcnr.pa.gov	570-443-0400		565
Hickory Springs Manufacturing Co 235 Second Ave NW........ Hickory NC 28601 *TF:* 800-438-5341 ■ *Web:* www.hsmsolutions.com	800-438-5341		719
Hickory Telephone Co (HTC) 75 Main St .... Hickory PA 15340 *TF:* 888-721-3569 ■ *Web:* www.hky.com	724-356-2000		224
Hickory Veterinary Hospital 2303 Hickory Rd........ Plymouth Meeting PA 19462 *Web:* hickoryvet.com	610-828-3054	828-0811	794
Hickory Yarns Inc 1025 Tenth St NE PO Box 1975 .... Hickory NC 28601 *TF:* 800-713-1484 ■ *Web:* www.hickoryyarns.com	828-322-1550	322-1627	745-9
Hicks & Company Inc 1504 W 5th St Ste 109 .... Austin TX 78703 *Web:* hicksenv.com	512-478-0858		196
Hicks Guerry Group PA 119 S Acline St........ Lake City SC 29560 *Web:* hggcpa.com	843-374-3200		2
Hicks Oils & Hicksgas Inc 845 N Hickory St .... Du Quoin IL 62832 *Web:* www.hicksoils.com	618-542-5431		581
Hicks Partners LLC 21 E State St Ste 2200 .... Columbus OH 43215 *Web:* hickspartners.com	614-221-2800		636
Hicks Plastics Company Inc 51308 Industrial Dr........ Macomb MI 48042 *Web:* www.hicksplastics.com	586-786-5640	786-1199	608
Hicksville Chamber of Commerce 10 W Marie St........ Hicksville NY 11801 *Web:* www.hicksvillechamber.com	516-931-7170	931-8546	139
HICO America Sales & Technology Inc 3 Penn Ctr W Ste 300........ Pittsburgh PA 15276 *Web:* www.hicoamerica.com	412-787-1170		246
Hi-Craft Engineering Inc 33105 Kelly Rd........ Fraser MI 48026 *Web:* hicraftengineering.com	586-293-0551	293-2550	757
HID Global 3950 RCA Blvd Ste 5001 .... Palm Beach Gardens FL 33410 **Fax Area Code:* 650 ■ *TF:* 866-725-3926 ■ *Web:* www.hidglobal.com	561-622-1650	298-8313*	84
HID Inc 119 Starwood Cir Lot 16........ Jacksonville NC 28540	910-459-0800		401
HIDA (Health Industry Distributors Assn) 310 Montgomery St .... Alexandria VA 22314 *TF:* 800-549-4432 ■ *Web:* www.hida.org	703-549-4432		49-18
Hidalgo County 100 N Closner .... Edinburg TX 78539 *TF:* 888-318-2811 ■ *Web:* www.hidalgocounty.us	956-318-2100	318-2105	338
Hiday & Ricke PA 4100 E Southpoint Dr Ste 3 .... Jacksonville FL 32216 *Web:* hidayricke.com	904-363-2769		428
Hidden America PO Box 4262........ River Edge NJ 07661 *Web:* journeysinto.com	201-487-1190		773
Hidden Lake Gardens 6214 Monroe Rd........ Tipton MI 49287 *Web:* www.canr.msu.edu	517-431-2060	431-9148	97
Hidden Springs State Forest 2438 E 700N Rd........ Strasburg IL 62465 *Web:* www2.illinois.gov	217-644-3091		565
Hidden Valley Lake Realty 17568 Spruce Grove Rd .... Hidden Valley Lake CA 95467 *Web:* hiddenvalleylake.com	707-987-4485		652
Hidden Valley Resort & Conference Ctr 1 Craighead Dr PO Box 4420 .... Hidden Valley PA 15502 *TF:* 800-452-2223 ■ *Web:* www.hiddenvalleyresort.com	814-443-8000		377
Hidden Variable Studios LLC (HV3) 1800 S Brand Blvd .... Glendale CA 91204 *Web:* www.hiddenvariable.com	818-985-1080		225
Hideaway, The 197 Park Ave........ Rochester NY 14607 *Web:* www.thehideawayroc.com	585-434-0511		671
Hideout Lodge & Guest Ranch, The PO Box 206 .... Shell WY 82441 *TF:* 800-354-8637 ■ *Web:* thehideout.com	307-765-2080		239
Hi-Desert Publishing Co 56445 29 Palms Hwy .... Yucca Valley CA 92284 *Web:* www.hidesertstar.com	760-365-3315		637-8
HIDI Group, The 155 Gordon Baker Rd Ste 200 .... Toronto ON M2H3N5 *Web:* hidi.com	416-364-2100		463
Hiebing Group, The 315 Wisconsin Ave........ Madison WI 53703 *Web:* www.hiebing.com	608-256-6357		225
Higdon Florist 201 E 32nd St .... Joplin MO 64804 *TF:* 800-641-4726 ■ *Web:* www.higdonflorist.com	417-624-7171		292
Higgins Brian (Rep D - NY) 2459 Rayburn House Office Bldg .... Washington DC 20515 *Web:* www.higgins.house.gov	202-225-3306	226-0347	342-2
Higgins Clay (Rep R - LA) 424 Cannon House Office Bldg........ Washington DC 20515 *Web:* clayhiggins.house.gov	202-225-2031		342-2
Higgins Electric 1360 Columbia Hwy........ Dothan AL 36301 *Web:* higginselectric.com	334-793-4859		246
Higgins Restaurant & Bar 1239 SW Broadway .... Portland OR 97205 *Web:* higginsportland.com	503-222-9070		671
Higgins Supply Company Inc 18-25 South St........ Mcgraw NY 13101 *Web:* www.higginssupply.com	607-836-6474	836-6913	250
Higgins, Marcus & Lovett Inc 800 S Figueroa St Ste 710 .... Los Angeles CA 90017 *Web:* hmlinc.com	213-617-7775		41
Higginson Book Co 10 Colonial Rd Ste 5-6 .... Salem MA 01970 *Web:* www.higginsonbooks.com	978-745-7170	745-8025	637-2
Higgs Fletcher and Mack LLP 401 W A St Ste 2600 .... San Diego CA 92101 *Web:* www.higgslaw.com	619-236-1551	696-1410	41
High & Associates Inc 105 Old Hewitt Rd Ste 400 .... Waco TX 76712 *Web:* www.highandassociates.net	254-776-7283		390

Phone | Fax | Class

High Arctic Energy Services Inc
700-2nd St SW Ste 500 .... Calgary AB T2P2T8 403-508-7836 262-5176 540
TF: 800-668-7143 ■ *Web:* haes.ca

High Choice Feeders LLC
553 W Rd 40........ Scott City KS 67871 620-872-7271 10-1
Web: highchoicefeeders.com

High Cliff State Park
N7630 State Park Rd........ Sherwood WI 54169 920-989-1106 565
Web: dnr.wi.gov

High Concrete Structures Inc
125 Denver Rd........ Denver PA 17517 717-336-9300 336-9301 183
TF: 800-773-2278 ■ *Web:* www.highconcrete.com

High Country Bancorp Inc
7360 W Hwy 50 PO Box 309........ Salida CO 81201 719-539-2516 360-2
OTC: HCBC ■ *Web:* www.highcountrybank.net

High Country Beverage Corp
5706 Wright Dr........ Loveland CO 80538 970-622-8444 297-8
Web: www.highcountrybeverage.com

High Country Furniture & Design
3232 Dellwood Rd........ Waynesville NC 28786 828-926-1722 321
Web: highcountry.com

High Country News 119 Grand Ave........ Paonia CO 81428 970-527-4898 532-3
TF: 800-311-5852 ■ *Web:* www.hcn.org

High Country Performance 4x4 Inc
1695 W Hamilton Pl........ Englewood CO 80110 303-761-7379 57
Web: hcp4x4.com

High Country Transportation Inc
1425 N Dallas Ave Ste 200A........ Lancaster TX 75134 469-759-2300 780
Web: www.highcountrytrans.com

High Desert Museum 59800 US-97........ Bend OR 97702 541-382-4754 382-5256 520
Web: www.highdesertmuseum.org

High Desert State Prison (HDSP)
475-750 Rice Canyon Rd PO Box 750........ Susanville CA 96127 530-251-5100 213
Web: cdcr.ca.gov

High End Systems Inc
2105 Gracy Farms Ln........ Austin TX 78758 512-836-2242 837-5290 439
TF: 800-890-8989 ■ *Web:* www.highend.com

High Falls Film Festival Office
45 E Ave Ste 400........ Rochester NY 14604 585-279-8312 282
Web: highfallsfilmfestival.com

High Falls Museum 60 Browns Race........ Rochester NY 14614 585-287-5555 50-3
Web: www.cityofrochester.gov

High Falls State Park
76 High Falls Pk Dr........ Jackson GA 30233 478-993-3053 565
Web: gastateparks.org

High Grade Beverage Inc
891 Georges Rd........ Monmouth Junction NJ 08852 732-821-7600 821-2898 81-1
Web: www.highgradebeverage.com

High Hampton 1525 Hwy 107 S........ Cashiers NC 28717 800-334-2551 669
TF: 800-334-2551 ■ *Web:* highhamptonnc.com

High Impact Inc
8008 E Arapahoe Ct Ste 200........ Centennial CO 80112 800-749-2184 573-7418* 514
**Fax Area Code:* 303 ■ *TF:* 800-749-2184 ■ *Web:* www.highimpact.com

High Industries Inc
1853 William Penn Way........ Lancaster PA 17601 717-293-4444 189-14
Web: www.high.net

High Liner Foods Inc (HLF)
High Liner Foods Inc 100 Battery Pt
PO Box 910........ Lunenburg NS B0J2C0 902-634-8811 296-13
NYSE: HLF ■ *TF:* 877-991-3474 ■ *Web:* www.highlinerfoods.com

High Meadows Camp 1055 Willeo Rd........ Roswell GA 30075 770-993-7975 993-8331 239
TF: 800-344-8328 ■ *Web:* highmeadows.org

High Mesa Consulting Group
6010 Midway Park Blvd NE Ste B........ Albuquerque NM 87109 505-345-4250 345-4254 261
Web: hmcg.noaviv.studio

High Mowing School 222 Isaac Frye Hwy........ Wilton NH 03086 603-654-2391 654-6588 622
Web: www.highmowing.org

High Museum of Art
1280 Peachtree St NE........ Atlanta GA 30309 404-733-4400 520
Web: www.high.org

High Peaks Resort
2384 Saranac Ave........ Lake Placid NY 12946 518-523-4411 523-1120 669
TF: 800-755-5598 ■ *Web:* www.highpeaksresort.com

High Performance Computing Collaboratory
2 Research Blvd........ Starkville MS 39759 662-325-8278 325-7692 668
TF: 800-521-4041 ■ *Web:* www.hpc.msstate.edu

High Plains Power Inc
1775 E Monroe PO Box 713........ Riverton WY 82501 307-856-9426 856-4207 245
TF: 800-445-0613 ■ *Web:* www.highplainspower.org

High Plains Press PO Box 123........ Glendo WY 82213 800-552-7819 735-4590* 637-2
**Fax Area Code:* 307 ■ *TF:* 800-552-7819 ■ *Web:* www.highplainspress.com

High Plains Publishers Inc
1500 W Wyatt Earp Blvd........ Dodge City KS 67801 620-227-7171 227-7173 637-8
TF: 800-452-7171 ■ *Web:* www.hpj.com

High Point Enterprise
213 Woodbine St........ High Point NC 27262 336-888-3500 532-2
Web: www.hpenews.com

High Point Furniture Industries Inc
1104 Bedford St PO Box 2063........ High Point NC 27261 800-447-3462 434-1964* 319-1
**Fax Area Code:* 336 ■ *TF:* 800-447-3462 ■ *Web:* www.hpfi.com

High Point Precision Products Inc
1 First St........ Sussex NJ 07461 973-875-6229 875-1116 455
Web: www.highpointprecision.com

High Point Solutions Inc 5 Gail Ct........ Sparta NJ 07871 973-940-0040 940-0041 176
Web: www.highpoint.com

High Point Sprinkler Inc
2 Regency Industrial Blvd........ Thomasville NC 27360 336-475-6181 189-13

High Point State Park 1480 Rt 23........ Sussex NJ 07461 973-875-4800 565
Web: www.njparksandforests.org

High Point University
833 Montlieu Ave........ High Point NC 27262 336-841-9216 888-6382 166
TF: 800-345-6993 ■ *Web:* www.highpoint.edu

High Power Technical Services Inc (HPTS)
2230 Ampere Dr........ Louisville KY 40299 502-271-2469 116
TF: 866-398-3474 ■ *Web:* www.hpts.tv

High Purity Systems Inc
8432 Quarry Rd........ Manassas VA 20110 703-330-5094 189-10
Web: www.highpurity.com

High Q Lighting Inc
11439 E Lakewood Blvd........ Holland MI 49424 616-396-3591 439
Web: hql.net

High Ridge Partners LLC
140 S Dearborn St Ste 420........ Chicago IL 60603 312-456-5636 194
Web: www.high-ridge.com

High Road Craft Ice Cream Inc
1730 W Oak Commons Ct........ Marietta GA 30062 678-701-7623 296-25
Web: www.highroadcraft.com

High Speed Productions Inc
1303 Underwood Ave........ San Francisco CA 94124 415-822-3083 514
Web: www.juxtapoz.com

High Standards Technology
17000 El Camino Real........ Houston TX 77058 281-990-9422 225
Web: weredown.com

High Steel Service Center LLC
400 Steel Way........ Lancaster PA 17601 717-299-8989 299-5155 492
TF: 800-732-0346 ■ *Web:* highsteelservicecenter.com

High Steel Structures Inc
1915 Old Philadelphia Pk PO Box 10008........ Lancaster PA 17605 717-390-4270 399-4102 189-14
Web: www.highsteel.com

High Swartz LLP 40 E Airy St........ Norristown PA 19404 610-275-0700 275-5290 445
Web: www.highswartz.com

High Tech Design Safety LLC
15304 Rainbow One St Ste 101........ Austin TX 78734 512-266-0222 317
Web: hightechdesignsafety.com

High Tech Fire Protection Company Inc
84 Hackett Mills Rd........ Poland ME 04274 207-998-2551 610
Web: www.htfp.me

High Tech Tool Inc 7803 S Loop E........ Houston TX 77012 713-641-2303 641-6664 493
Web: www.hightechtool.com

High Technology Inc 109 Production Rd........ Walpole MA 02081 508-660-2221 535
Web: www.htmed.com

High Tide Creative 208 Bridge St........ Bridgeton NC 28519 252-671-7087 195
Web: www.hightidecreative.com

High Tide Seafoods 808 Marine Dr........ Port Angeles WA 98363 360-452-8488 296-14
Web: hightideseafoods.com

High Tor State Park
417 S Mountain Rd........ New City NY 10956 845-634-8074 565
Web: parks.ny.gov

High Touch Technologies
110 S Main St Ste 600........ Wichita KS 67202 316-462-4001 393
TF: 800-326-6059 ■ *Web:* hightouchtechnologies.com

High Vacuum Apparatus LLC (HVA)
12880 Moya Blvd........ Reno NV 89506 775-359-4442 359-1369 789
TF: 800-551-4422 ■ *Web:* www.highvac.com

High Velocity Communications LLC
1720 Dolphin Dr Ste D........ Waukesha WI 53186 262-544-6600 4
Web: www.highvelocitycommunications.com

High West Energy Inc (HWE)
6270 County Rd 212 PO Box 519........ Pine Bluffs WY 82082 307-245-3261 245-9292 245
TF: 888-834-1657 ■ *Web:* www.highwestenergy.coop

High Winds Casino 61475 E 100 Rd........ Miami OK 74354 918-541-9463 541-9405 452
Web: www.highwindscasino.com

HighBar Consulting
Carol Henriques 2952 Npaulina........ Chicago IL 60657 312-543-0300 194
Web: www.highbarconsulting.com

HighCom Armor Solutions Inc
2901 E 4th Ave........ Columbus OH 43219 614-500-6035 693
TF: 800-987-9098 ■ *Web:* www.highcomarmor.com

Higher Dimension Research Inc
570 Hale Ave........ Oakdale MN 55128 651-730-6203 463
Web: www.superfabric.com

Higher Education Assistance Group Inc, The
60 Walnut St 4th Fl........ Wellesley MA 02481 617-928-1975 244-6511 194
Web: www.heag.us

Higher Gear Group Inc, The
145 W Central Rd........ Schaumburg IL 60195 847-843-6800 179
Web: www.onecommand.com

Higher Technology Solutions
1547 Old Forge Rd........ Bartlett IL 60103 312-543-5296 809

Highfield Manufacturing Co
5144 S Intl Dr........ Cudahy WI 53110 414-489-7700 595
TF: 855-443-4353 ■ *Web:* www.highfield-mfg.com

Highgate
545 E John W Carpenter Fwy Ste 1400........ Irving TX 75062 972-444-9700 378
Web: highgate.com

Highgate Road Social Science Research Station (HRSSRS)
2601 Hilltop Dr Apt 217........ Richmond CA 94806 510-262-9189 466
Web: www.molokane.org

HighJump Software
5600 W 83rd St Ste 600........ Minneapolis MN 55437 952-947-4088 178-1
TF: 800-328-3271 ■ *Web:* www.highjump.com

Highland Area Chamber of Commerce
27255 Messina St........ Highland CA 92346 909-864-4073 864-4583 139
Web: www.highlandchamber.org

Highland Associates Ltd
102 Highland Ave........ Clarks Summit PA 18411 570-586-4334 256
Web: www.highlandassociates.com

Highland Capital Management LP
300 Crescent Ct Ste 700........ Dallas TX 75201 972-628-4100 405
Web: www.highlandcapital.com

Highland Capital Partners
92 Hayden Ave........ Lexington MA 02421 781-861-5500 792
Web: www.hcp.com

Highland Central School District
320 Pancake Hollow Rd........ Highland Falls NY 12528 845-691-1000 685
Web: www.highland-k12.org

Highland Community Bank
307 Thacker Ave PO Box 1059........ Covington VA 24426 540-962-2265 70
Web: www.highlandscommunitybank.com

Highland Community College
2998 W Pearl City Rd........ Freeport IL 61032 815-235-6121 235-6130 162
Web: highland.edu

Highland Community College (HCC)
606 W Main........ Highland KS 66035 785-442-6000 442-6106 162
TF: 800-985-9781 ■ *Web:* highlandcc.edu

	City	State	ZIP	Phone	Fax	Class
Highland Computer Forms Inc						
1025 W Main St	Hillsboro	OH	45133	937-393-4215	842-6485*	110
*Fax Area Code: 800 ■ TF: 800-669-5213 ■ Web: hcf.com						
Highland County						
119 Governor Foraker Pl	Hillsboro	OH	45133	937-393-1911	393-5850	338
TF: 800-774-1202 ■ Web: www.co.highland.oh.us						
County Offices 165 W Main St	Monterey	VA	24465	540-468-2551	468-3447	338
Web: www.highlandcova.org						
Highland County Chamber of Commerce						
PO Box 183	Hillsboro	OH	45133	937-393-1111	393-9604	139
Web: www.highlandcountychamber.com						
Highland County District Library						
10 Willettsville Pk	Hillsboro	OH	45133	937-393-3114	393-2985	434-3
Web: www.highlandco.org						
Highland Engineering & Surveying Inc						
1426 Memorial Dr	Oakland	MD	21550	301-334-6185		256
Web: highland-engineering.com						
Highland Engineering Inc						
1153 Grand Oaks Dr	Howell	MI	48843	517-548-4372	548-4423	207
Web: www.high-eng.com						
Highland Falls-Ft Montgomery School District						
PO Box 287	Highland Falls	NY	10928	845-446-9575		685
Web: www.hffmcsd.org						
Highland Fruit Growers Inc						
8304 Wide Hollow Rd	Yakima	WA	98908	509-966-3990		315-3
Web: www.highlandfruitgrowers.com						
Highland Hardwoods 407 Rte 125	Brentwood	NH	03833	603-679-1230	679-8248	191-3
TF: 800-442-1812 ■ Web: www.highlandhardwoods.com						
Highland Helicopters Ltd						
4240 Agar Dr	Richmond	BC	V7B1A3	604-273-6161	273-6088	359
Web: www.highland.ca						
Highland Homes 5601 Democracy Dr Ste 300	Plano	TX	75024	972-789-3500		653
TF: 888-379-1635 ■ Web: www.highlandhomes.com						
Highland Lakes Newspapers Inc						
304-A Highlander Cir PO Box 1000	Marble Falls	TX	78654	830-693-4367	693-3650	532-3
Web: www.highlandernews.com						
Highland Machine 700 Fifth St	Highland	IL	62249	618-654-2103	654-8016	621
Web: www.highlandmachine.com						
Highland Machine Tool Inc						
3461 E Luther Rd	Floyds Knobs	IN	47119	812-923-8884	923-8886	454
Web: www.highlandmachinetool.com						
Highland Mills Inc 340 E 16th St	Charlotte	NC	28206	704-375-3333	342-0391	155-10
Web: www.highlandmills.com						
Highland Nursing Home Inc						
182 Highland Rd	Massena	NY	13662	315-769-9956	769-9955	371
Web: www.highlandnursinghome.com						
Highland Park Chamber of Commerce						
508 Central Ave Ste 206	Highland Park	IL	60035	847-432-0284	432-2802	139
Web: www.chamberhp.com						
Highland Park Market of Farmington LLC						
317 Highland St	Manchester	CT	06040	860-646-4277		345
Web: www.highlandparkmarket.com						
Highland Park Public Library						
494 Laurel Ave	Highland Park	IL	60035	847-432-0216		434-3
Web: www.hplibrary.org						
Highland Recreation Area						
5200 Highland Rd	White Lake	MI	48383	248-889-3750		565
Web: www.michigan.org						
Highland Ridge Hospital 7309 S 180 W	Midvale	UT	84047	801-845-9544		726
Web: www.highlandridgehospital.com						
Highland Rim Regional Library Ctr						
2118 E Main St	Murfreesboro	TN	37130	615-893-3380	895-6727	434-3
Highland Tank & Manufacturing Co						
1 Highland Rd	Stoystown	PA	15563	814-893-5701	893-6126	91
Web: www.highlandtank.com						
Highland Threads Inc 11700 Gloger St	Houston	TX	77039	800-847-5713	986-5151*	350
*Fax Area Code: 281 ■ TF: 800-847-5713 ■ Web: www.highlandthreads.com						
Highland Title Agency						
6622 South 1300 East	Salt Lake City	UT	84121	801-858-0033		653
Web: highlandtitleutah.com						
Highlander Charter School						
42 Lexington Ave	Providence	RI	02907	401-277-2600		237
Web: www.highlandercharter.org						
Highlands Bar & Grill						
2011 11th Ave S	Birmingham	AL	35205	205-939-1400		671
Web: www.highlandsbarandgrill.com						
Highlands County 600 S Commerce Ave	Sebring	FL	33870	863-402-6500	402-6507	338
Web: www.highlandsfl.gov						
Highlands Diversified Services Inc						
250 Westinghouse Dr	London	KY	40741	606-878-1856		198
Web: www.hds-usa.com						
Highlands Fuel Delivery LLC						
190 Commerce Way	Portsmouth	NH	03801	603-559-8700		579
TF: 888-310-1924 ■ Web: www.irvingoil.com						
Highlands Hammock State Park						
5931 Hammock Rd	Sebring	FL	33872	863-386-6094	386-6095	565
Web: www.floridastateparks.org						
Highlands Medical Ctr						
380 Woods Cove Rd	Scottsboro	AL	35768	256-259-4444		374-3
Web: www.highlandsmedcenter.com						
Highlands News-Sun 315 US 27 N	Sebring	FL	33870	863-385-6155	385-1954	532-4
Web: www.midfloridanewspapers.com						
Highlands Pathology Consultants Pc						
2175 Hwy 75 Ste 4	Blountville	TN	37617	423-323-5290		415
Web: www.highlandspath.com						
Highlight Inc 1120 Hoeschler Dr	Sparta	WI	54656	608-269-3191	269-7830	261
Web: www.highlight-inc.com						
Highlights for Children Inc						
1800 Watermark Dr	Columbus	OH	43216	614-486-0631	324-1630	637-9
TF: 800-255-9517 ■ Web: www.highlights.com						
Highline College 2400 S 240th St	Des Moines	WA	98198	206-878-3710		800
Web: www.highline.edu						
Highline Electric Assn						
1300 S Interocean Ave	Holyoke	CO	80734	970-854-2236	854-3652	245
TF: 800-816-2236 ■ Web: www.hea.coop						
Highline Medical Ctr						
16251 Sylvester Rd SW	Burien	WA	98166	206-244-9970		374-3
TF: 888-825-3227 ■ Web: www.chifranciscan.org						
Highline Portafab Inc						
20105 Broadway Ave SE	Snohomish	WA	98296	425-486-8031		480
Web: www.hpf.com						
Highline SeaTac Botanical Gardens						
13735 24th Ave S PO Box 69384	SeaTac	WA	98168	206-391-4003		97
Web: highlinegarden.org						
Highline United Methodist Church						
13015 First Ave S	Burien	WA	98168	206-241-5520		48-20
Web: highlineunitedmethodistchurch.org						
Highlines Construction						
701 Bridge City Ave	Bridge City	LA	70094	504-436-3961		189-4
High-Lonesome Books PO Box 878	Silver City	NM	88062	575-388-7518	388-5705	637-2
TF: 800-380-7323 ■ Web: www.high-lonesomebooks.com						
Highmark Blue Cross Blue Shield						
PO Box 226	Pittsburgh	PA	15230	800-294-9568		391-3
TF: 800-294-9568 ■ Web: www.highmarkbcbs.com						
Highmark blue shield PO Box 890173	Camp Hill	PA	17089	800-345-3806		391-3
Web: www.highmarkblueshield.com						
Highmark Inc 120 Fifth Ave Pl	Pittsburgh	PA	15222	412-544-7000		391-3
TF: 800-992-0246 ■ Web: www.highmark.com						
Highpoint Community Bank						
150 W Court St	Hastings	MI	49058	888-422-2280		70
TF: 888-422-2280 ■ Web: www.highpointcommunitybank.com						
HighPoint Technology Solutions Inc						
2332 Galiano St 2nd Fl	Coral Gables	FL	33134	800-767-0893		260
TF: 800-767-0893 ■ Web: www.mhighpoint.com						
HighPointe Hotel Corp						
311 Gulf Breeze Pkwy	Gulf Breeze	FL	32561	850-932-9314		378
Web: www.highpointe.com						
HighQuest Group						
300 Rosewood Dr Ste 260	Danvers	MA	01923	978-887-8800		463
Web: www.highquestgroup.com						
HighRes Biosolutions Inc						
299 Washington St	Woburn	MA	01801	781-932-1912		256
Web: highresbio.com						
Highroad Press 220 Anderson Ave	Moonachie	NJ	07074	201-708-6900	727-0474*	627
*Fax Area Code: 212 ■ Web: www.highroadpress.com						
Highsmith Insurance Agency Inc						
3700 Glenwood Ave Ste 430	Raleigh	NC	27612	919-878-9412		390
Web: highsmithinsurance.com						
Highspot 2211 Elliott Ave Ste 400	Seattle	WA	98121	888-916-7768		178-1
TF: 888-916-7768 ■ Web: www.highspot.com						
Highstead Arboretum						
127 Lonetown Rd PO Box 1097	Redding	CT	06875	203-938-8809		97
Web: highstead.net						
Hightech American Industrial Laboratories Inc (HAI)						
320 Massachusetts Ave	Lexington	MA	02420	781-862-9884	860-7722	477
Web: hailabs.com						
HighTech Passport Ltd						
1590 Oakland Rd Ste B202	San Jose	CA	95131	408-453-6303	453-9434	194
Web: www.htpassport.com						
Hightech Signs						
1201 S Redwood Rd Ste 1	Salt Lake City	UT	84104	801-972-6464		9
Web: www.hightechsigns.com						
Hightower Advertising Agency						
970 Ebenezer Blvd PO Box 622	Madison	MS	39110	601-853-1822		7
Web: www.hightoweragency.com						
Hightower Reff Law LLC						
1625 Farnam St Ste 830	Omaha	NE	68102	402-932-9550		41
Web: hrlawomaha.com						
Hightowers Petroleum Co						
3577 Commerce Dr	Middletown	OH	45005	513-423-4272		579
Web: hpc1952.businesscatalyst.com						
Highview Custom Fabricating Inc						
3369 Bay Ridge Ct	Oneida	WI	54155	920-869-1900		480
TF: 800-336-1999 ■ Web: www.highviewfab.com						
HighVista Strategies LLC						
200 Clarendon St 50th Fl	Boston	MA	02116	617-406-6500		194
Web: www.highvistastrategies.com						
Highway Equipment Co						
1330 76th Ave SW	Cedar Rapids	IA	52404	319-363-8281	286-3350	190
Web: newleader.com						
Highway Handyman Products Inc						
4881 Biscayne Ave	Eagan	MN	55123	651-423-1968	493-8996	9
Web: www.highwayhandyman.com						
Highway Machine Company Inc (HMC)						
3010 S Old US Hwy 41	Princeton	IN	47670	812-385-3639	385-8186	454
TF: 866-990-9462 ■ Web: www.hmcgears.com						
Highway Radio Corp						
101 Convention Center Dr P119	Las Vegas	NV	89109	702-737-9899		647
Web: www.highwayradio.com						
Highway Safety Corp						
239 Commerce St	Glastonbury	CT	06033	860-633-9445		567
Web: www.highwaysafety.net						
Highway To Health Inc						
1 Radnor Corporate Ctr Ste 100	Radnor	PA	19087	888-243-2358	254-8797*	391-7
*Fax Area Code: 610 ■ TF: 888-243-2358 ■ Web: www.hthtravelinsurance.com						
Highway Transport Logistics Inc (HTL)						
6420 Baum Dr	Knoxville	TN	37919	865-584-8631		780
Web: hytt.com						
Highwire Public Relations Inc						
727 Sansome St	San Francisco	CA	94111	415-963-4174		636
Web: www.highwirepr.com						
Highwood Die & Engineering Inc						
1353 Highwood Blvd	Pontiac	MI	48340	248-338-1807		488
Web: www.highwooddie.com						
Highwood USA LLC 87 Tide Rd	Tamaqua	PA	18252	570-225-7501		820
Web: www.highwood-usa.com						
Highwoods Properties Inc						
3100 Smoketree Ct Ste 600	Raleigh	NC	27604	919-872-4924		655
NYSE: HIW ■ TF: 866-449-6637 ■ Web: www.highwoods.com						
Higley Flow State Park						
442 Cold Brook Dr	Colton	NY	13625	315-262-2880		565
Web: parks.ny.gov						
Hignell Book Printing 488 Burnell St	Winnipeg	MB	R3G2B4	204-784-1030		393
Web: www.hignell.mb.ca						
Hikaru 607 S Second St	Philadelphia	PA	19147	215-627-7110		671
Web: hikaruphilly.com						

Name / Address	City	State	Zip	Phone	Fax	Class
Hikma 246 Industrial Way W *TF:* 800-631-2174 ■ *Web:* www.hikma.com	Eatontown	NJ	07724	800-631-2174		583
Hikvision USA Inc 18639 Railroad St *Web:* hikvision.com	City of Industry	CA	91748	909-895-0400		692
Hiland Toyota 5500 45th Ave Dr *TF:* 866-286-2664 ■ *Web:* www.hilandtoyota.com	Moline	IL	61265	309-764-2481		57
Hilbert College 5200 S Park Ave *TF:* 800-649-8003 ■ *Web:* www.hilbert.edu	Hamburg	NY	14075	716-649-7900	649-1152	166
Hilborn Werner Carter & Associates Inc 1627 S Myrtle Ave *Web:* hwceng.com	Clearwater	FL	33756	727-584-8151		261
Hilburn & Lein CPAS 5520 S Ft Apache *Web:* www.hilburn-lein.com	Las Vegas	NV	89148	702-597-1945		2
Hilco Electric Co-opeartive Inc 115 E Main PO Box 127 *TF:* 800-338-6425 ■ *Web:* hilco.coop	Itasca	TX	76055	254-687-2331		245
Hilco Federal Credit Union PO Box 291717 *Web:* www.hilcocu.com	Kerrville	TX	78029	830-257-8238	792-6865	219
Hilco Industrial 171 Monroe Ave Ste 500 *Web:* www.hilcoind.com	Grand Rapids	MI	49503	616-732-1800	732-7100	690
Hilco Technologies Inc 4172 Danvers Ct SE *Web:* hilcotech.com	Grand Rapids	MI	49512	616-957-1081		608
Hilco Transport Inc 7700 Kenmont Rd *Web:* www.hilcotransport.com	Greensboro	NC	27409	336-273-9441	273-9701	186
Hildy Licht Inc 897 Independence Ave 3B *Web:* www.hildy.com	Mountain View	CA	94043	650-962-9300	254-1855	625
Hile Group 1100 Beech St Bldg 15 *Web:* www.hilegroup.com	Normal	IL	61761	309-888-4453		196
Hileman Enterprises LLC 2217 E Ninth St Ste 200 *Web:* www.hilemangroup.com	Cleveland	OH	44115	216-923-1445		393
Hi-Lex America Inc 5200 Wayne Rd *Web:* www.hi-lex.com	Battle Creek	MI	49037	269-968-0781		516
Hilford Moving & Storage 1595 Arundell Ave *TF:* 800-739-6683 ■ *Web:* www.hilfordmoving.com	Ventura	CA	93003	805-210-8252		519
Hilgard House Hotel & Suites 927 Hilgard Ave *TF:* 800-826-3934 ■ *Web:* www.hilgardhouse.com	Los Angeles	CA	90024	310-208-3945	208-1972	379
Hilgraeve Inc 1287 N Telegraph Rd *TF:* 800-826-2760 ■ *Web:* www.hilgraeve.com	Monroe	MI	48162	734-243-0576	243-0645	178-7
Hi-Line Inc 2121 Valley View Ln *TF:* 800-944-5463 ■ *Web:* www.hi-line.com	Dallas	TX	75234	800-944-5463		246
Hilite International Inc 250 Kay Industrial Dr *Web:* www.hilite.com	Orion	MI	48359	248-475-4580	475-4581	61
Hill & Company Real Estate Inc 1880 Lombard St *Web:* www.hill-co.com	San Francisco	CA	94123	415-921-6000	931-0984	652
Hill & Griffith Co 1085 Summer St *TF:* 800-543-0425 ■ *Web:* www.hillandgriffith.com	Cincinnati	OH	45204	513-921-1075	244-4199	500
Hill & Ponton PA 605 E Robinson St Ste 635 *TF:* 888-373-9436 ■ *Web:* www.hillandponton.com	Orlando	FL	32801	386-257-2100		445
Hill & Stone Insurance Agency Inc 900 N Shore Dr Ste 225 *Web:* www.hillandstone.com	Lake Bluff	IL	60044	847-295-3030		390
Hill & Valley Premium Bakery 320 44th St *TF:* 800-480-0055 ■ *Web:* www.hillandvalley.net	Rock Island	IL	61201	309-793-0161	793-0183	68
Hill Aerospace Museum 7961 Wardleigh Rd Bldg 1955 *Web:* www.hill.af.mil	Hill AFB	UT	84056	801-825-5817	775-3034	520
Hill Aerosystems Inc 911 Battersby Ave *Web:* www.hillaerosystems.com	Enumclaw	WA	98022	360-802-8300		22
Hill Barth & King LLC 6603 Summit Dr *TF:* 800-733-8613 ■ *Web:* www.hbkcpa.com	Canfield	OH	44406	330-758-8613	758-0357	2
Hill Bros Chemical Co 1675 N Main St *TF:* 800-994-8801 ■ *Web:* www.hillbrothers.com	Orange	CA	92867	714-998-8800	998-6310	146
Hill City Oil Company Inc 1409 Dunn St *TF:* 800-492-8377 ■ *Web:* www.hillcityoil.net	Houma	LA	70360	985-851-4000		579
Hill College 112 Lamar Dr *Web:* www.hillcollege.edu	Hillsboro	TX	76645	254-659-7500	582-7591	162
Hill Correctional Ctr 600 S Linwood Rd PO Box 1700 *Web:* www2.illinois.gov	Galesburg	IL	61402	309-343-4212	343-4287	213
Hill Country Christian School of Austin 12124 Ranch Rd 620 N *Web:* www.hillcountrychristianschool.org	Austin	TX	78750	512-331-7036		148
Hill Country Furniture Partners Ltd 1431 Fm 1101 *TF:* 877-314-8457 ■ *Web:* hillcountryholdings.com	New Braunfels	TX	78130	877-314-8457		321
Hill Country State Natural Area 10600 Bandera Creek Rd *Web:* tpwd.texas.gov	Bandera	TX	78003	830-796-4413		565
Hill County 315 4th St *Web:* www.hillcounty.us	Havre	MT	59501	406-265-5481		338
Hill County PO Box 398 *Web:* www.co.hill.tx.us	Hillsboro	TX	76645	254-582-4030	582-4003	338
Hill County Electric Co-opeartive Inc PO Box 2330 *TF:* 877-394-7804 ■ *Web:* www.hcelectric.com	Havre	MT	59501	877-394-7804		245
Hill Crest Behavioral Health Services 6869 5th Ave S *TF:* 800-292-8553 ■ *Web:* www.hillcrestbhs.com	Birmingham	AL	35212	205-833-9000		374-5
Hill French (Rep R - AR) 1533 Longworth House Office Bldg *Web:* hill.house.gov	Washington	DC	20515	202-225-2506	225-5903	342-2
Hill Group, The 11045 Gage Ave *Web:* www.hillgrp.com	Franklin Park	IL	60131	847-451-5000	451-5011	189-10
Hill Home Furnishings Inc 116 N 5th St *Web:* www.scheerqualityfurniture.com	Beatrice	NE	68310	402-228-4085		321
Hill International Inc 303 Lippincott Ctr *NYSE: HIL* ■ *Web:* www.hillintl.com	Marlton	NJ	08053	856-810-6200	810-1309	261
Hill Laboratories Co 3 N Bacton Hill Rd *TF:* 877-445-5020 ■ *Web:* www.hilllabs.com	Frazer	PA	19355	610-644-2867	647-6297	476
Hill Larson Walth & Benda PA 326 N Main St *Web:* hlwb-cpa.com	Austin	MN	55912	507-433-2264	437-8251	2
Hill Manufacturing Company Inc 1500 Jonesboro Rd SE *TF:* 800-445-5123 ■ *Web:* www.hillmfg.com	Atlanta	GA	30315	404-522-8364	522-9694	151
Hill Manufacturing Inc 318 W Chestnut St *Web:* www.hillmfginc.com	Wauseon	OH	43567	419-335-5006	335-7953	488
Hill Meat Co 1503 NW 50th St *TF:* 800-929-7621 ■ *Web:* www.hillmeat.com	Pendleton	OR	97801	541-276-7621	276-9253	473
Hill Museum & Manuscript Library PO Box 7300 *Web:* hmml.org	Collegeville	MN	56321	320-363-3514		434-3
Hill Phoenix Inc 1003 Sigman Rd *TF:* 800-518-6630 ■ *Web:* www.hillphoenix.com	Conyers	GA	30013	770-285-3264	285-3080	664
Hill Physicians Medical Group Inc 2409 Camino Ramon PO Box 5080 *TF:* 800-445-5747 ■ *Web:* www.hillphysicians.com	San Ramon	CA	94583	925-820-8300		463
Hill School 860 Beech St *TF:* 877-651-2800 ■ *Web:* www.thehill.org	Pottstown	PA	19464	610-326-1000	705-1753	622
Hill Street Veterinary Hospital 555 Hill St *Web:* hillstreetvet.com	York	PA	17403	717-843-6060		794
Hill Times 69 Sparks St *Web:* www.hilltimes.com	Ottawa	ON	K1P5A5	613-232-5952		532-3
Hill View Retirement Ctr 1610 Twenty-Eighth St *Web:* www.hillviewretirement.org	Portsmouth	OH	45662	740-354-3135	353-5511	371
Hill Ward Henderson 101 E Kennedy Blvd Ste 3700 *Web:* www.hwhlaw.com	Tampa	FL	33602	813-221-3900	221-2900	428
Hill Wood Products Inc 9483 Ashawa Rd **Fax Area Code:* 218 ■ *TF:* 800-788-9689 ■ *Web:* www.hillwoodproducts.com	Cook	MN	55723	800-788-9689	666-5726*	551
Hill's Lexington Barbecue 4005 Patterson Ave *Web:* ncbbqsociety.com	Winston-Salem	NC	27105	336-767-2184		671
Hill's Pet Nutrition Inc 400 SW Eigth St *Web:* www.hillspet.com	Topeka	KS	66603	785-354-8523		578
Hill, Farrer & Burrill LLP 300 S Grand Ave 37th Fl *Web:* www.hillfarrer.com	Los Angeles	CA	90071	213-620-0460		428
Hill, Rugh, Keller & Main PL 390 N Orange Ave Ste 1610 *Web:* hrkmlaw.com	Orlando	FL	32802	407-926-7460		41
Hillcraft Ltd 2202 Advance Rd *Web:* hillcraft.com	Madison	WI	53718	608-221-3220	221-1897	225
Hillcrest Aircraft Company Inc 540 O'Connor Rd *Web:* hillcrestaircraft.com	Lewiston	ID	83501	208-746-8271		302
Hillcrest Church of Christ 307 Oak St	Tunnel Hill	GA	30755	706-673-2234		48-20
Hillcrest Foods 2695 E 40th St *Web:* www.hillcrestfoods.com	Cleveland	OH	44115	216-361-4625		297-4
Hillcrest Garden 95 W Century Rd *TF:* 800-437-7000 ■ *Web:* www.kennicott.com	Paramus	NJ	07652	201-599-3030		292
Hillcrest Homes 2705 Mtn View Dr *Web:* livingathillcrest.org	La Verne	CA	91750	909-392-4375		672
Hillcrest Hospital South 8801 S 101st E Ave *Web:* hillcrestsouth.com	Tulsa	OK	74133	918-294-4000		374-3
Hillcrest Medical Ctr 1120 S Utica Ave *Web:* hillcrest.com	Tulsa	OK	74104	918-579-1000		374-3
Hillcrest Youth Correctional Facility 2450 Strong Rd SE *Web:* www.oregon.gov	Salem	OR	97302	503-986-0406		412
Hilldale Church of Christ Inc 501 Hwy 76 *Web:* hilldalecc.org	Clarksville	TN	37043	931-647-5264		48-20
Hillel: The Foundation for Jewish Campus Life 800 Eighth St NW *Web:* www.hillel.org	Washington	DC	20001	202-449-6500		48-20
Hillenbrand Industries Inc 1 Batesville Blvd *NYSE: HI* ■ *Web:* www.hillenbrand.com	Batesville	IN	47006	812-934-7000		250
Hill-Engineers, Architects, Planners Inc 50 Depot St *Web:* hillengineers.com	Dalton	MA	01226	413-684-0925	684-0267	261
Hiller Aviation Museum 601 Skyway Rd *TF:* 888-500-1555 ■ *Web:* www.hiller.org	San Carlos	CA	94070	650-654-0200		520
Hiller Inc 630 N Washington *Web:* www.hillerinc.com	Wichita	KS	67214	316-264-8022		22
Hillerich & Bradsby Company Inc 800 W Main St *Web:* www.slugger.com	Louisville	KY	40202	502-585-5226		710
Hillfield Strathallan College 299 Fennell Ave W *Web:* www.hsc.on.ca	Hamilton	ON	L9C1G3	905-389-1367		623
Hilliard Corp 100 W Fourth St *Web:* www.hilliardcorp.com	Elmira	NY	14902	607-733-7121		620
Hilliard Energy Inc 3001 W Loop 250 N Ste E103 *TF:* 800-287-0014 ■ *Web:* www.hilliardenergy.com	Midland	TX	79705	432-683-9100		539
Hilliard's House of Candy 316 Main St *TF:* 800-286-8533 ■ *Web:* www.hilliardscandy.com	North Easton	MA	02356	508-238-6231		296-8

	Phone	Fax	Class
Hilliker Corp 1401 S Brentwood Blvd Ste 650 . . . . . Saint Louis MO 63144 *Web:* hillikercorp.com	314-781-0001	781-1159	652
Hillis, Clark, Martin & Peterson PS 1221 Second Ave Ste 500 . . . . . Seattle WA 98101 *Web:* www.hcmp.com	206-623-1745		428
Hillman & Glorioso PLLC 1950 Old Gallows Rd Ste 700 . . . . . Vienna VA 22182 *Web:* hillmanandglorioso.com	703-902-9600		2
Hillman Group Inc 10590 Hamilton Ave . . . . . Cincinnati OH 45231 *TF:* 800-800-4900 ■ *Web:* www.hillmangroup.com	513-851-4900	851-4997	351
Hillman, Brown & Darrow PA 221 Duke of Gloucester St . . . . . Annapolis MD 21401 *Web:* www.hbdlaw.com	410-263-3131		428
Hillmann & Carr Inc 2233 Wisconsin Ave NW Ste 425 . . . . . Washington DC 20007 *Web:* www.hillmanncarr.com	202-342-0001		514
Hill-Rom Services Inc 1069 SR 46 E . . . . . Batesville IN 47006 *TF:* 800-267-2337 ■ *Web:* www.hillrom.com	812-934-7777	934-8189	319-3
Hills Bank & Trust Co 131 Main St PO Box 70 . . . . . Hills IA 52235 **Fax Area Code:* 319 ■ *TF:* 800-445-5725 ■ *Web:* www.hillsbank.com	800-445-5725	679-2180*	70
Hills Creek State Park 111 Spillway Rd . . . . . Wellsboro PA 16901 *Web:* www.dcnr.pa.gov	570-724-4246		565
Hills Inc 7785 Ellis Rd . . . . . West Melbourne FL 32904 *Web:* www.hillsinc.net	321-724-2370		111
Hills Properties 4901 Hunt Rd Ste 300 . . . . . Blue Ash OH 45242 *Web:* www.hillsproperties.com	513-984-0300		653
Hillsboro Argus 1500 SW First Ave . . . . . Portland OR 97201 *TF:* 800-544-0505 ■ *Web:* www.oregonlive.com	503-796-9806	648-9191	532-4
Hillsboro Bank 509 W Alexander St . . . . . Plant City FL 33563 *Web:* hillsborobank.com	813-707-6506		70
Hillsboro Chamber of Commerce 5193 NE Elam Young Pkwy Ste A . . . . . Hillsboro OR 97124 *Web:* hillsborochamberor.com	503-648-1102	681-0535	139
Hillsboro City Schools 39 Willetsville Pk . . . . . Hillsboro OH 45133 *Web:* www.hillsboro.k12.oh.us	937-393-3475		685
Hillsboro Community Unit School District 3 1311 Vandalia Rd . . . . . Hillsboro IL 62049 *Web:* www.hillsboroschools.net	217-532-2942	532-3137	685
Hillsboro Equipment Inc E18898 Hwy 33 . . . . . Hillsboro WI 54634 *TF:* 800-521-5133 ■ *Web:* www.hillsboroequipment.com	608-489-2275	489-2717	274
Hillsboro Industries Inc 220 Industrial Rd . . . . . Hillsboro KS 67063 *TF:* 800-835-0209 ■ *Web:* www.hillsboroindustries.com	620-947-3127	947-3366	516
Hillsboro Public Library 2850 NE Brookwood Pkwy . . . . . Hillsboro OR 97124 *Web:* www.wccls.org	503-615-6500		434-3
Hillsboro School District 3083 NE 49th Pl . . . . . Hillsboro OR 97124 *Web:* www.hsd.k12.or.us	503-844-1500	844-1540	685
Hillsborough Community College *Plant City* 1206 N Park Rd . . . . . Plant City FL 33566 *Web:* hccfl.edu	813-757-2102		162
Hillsborough County 329 Mast Rd Ste 120 . . . . . Goffstown NH 03045 *Web:* hcnh.org	603-627-5600	627-5603	338
Hillsborough County 601 E Kennedy Blvd . . . . . Tampa FL 33602 *Web:* www.hillsboroughcounty.org	813-272-5900		338
Hillsborough County Public Schools 901 E Kennedy Blvd . . . . . Tampa FL 33602 *Web:* www.sdhc.k12.fl.us	813-272-4000	272-4073	685
Hillsborough River State Park 15402 US 301 N . . . . . Thonotosassa FL 33592 *Web:* www.floridastateparks.org	813-987-6771		565
Hillsdale Beauty College Inc 64 Waldron St . . . . . Hillsdale MI 49242 *Web:* www.hillsdalebeautycollege.com	517-437-4670		167-3
Hillsdale College 33 E College St . . . . . Hillsdale MI 49242 *TF:* 888-886-1174 ■ *Web:* www.hillsdale.edu	517-437-7341	437-3923	166
Hillsdale County 29 N Howell St . . . . . Hillsdale MI 49242 *Web:* www.co.hillsdale.mi.us	517-437-3391	437-3392	338
Hillsdale Fabricators 2150 Kienlen Ave . . . . . Saint Louis MO 63121 *Web:* www.hillsdalefabricators.com	314-553-8205	553-8215	189-14
Hillsdale Investment Management Inc 100 Wellington St W Ste 2100 TD Centre . . . . . Toronto ON M5K1J3 *Web:* www.hillsdaleinv.com	416-913-3900	913-3901	401
Hillsdale Shopping Ctr 60 31st Ave . . . . . San Mateo CA 94403 *Web:* hillsdale.com	650-345-8222		460
Hillsdale State Park 26001 W 255th St . . . . . Paola KS 66071 *Web:* ksoutdoors.com	913-594-3600		565
Hillside Animal Clinic Inc 4745 Paoli Pk . . . . . Floyds Knobs IN 47119 *Web:* hillsideanimalclinic.com	812-923-8825		794
Hillside Apples E2237 Hwy 54 . . . . . Casco WI 54205 *Web:* www.hillsideapples.com	920-837-7440		296-20
Hillside Candy Co 35 Hillside Ave . . . . . Hillside NJ 07205 *TF:* 800-524-1304 ■ *Web:* www.hillsidecandy.com	973-926-2300	926-4440	296-8
Hillside Cemetery Assn 1401 Woodland Ave . . . . . Scotch Plains NJ 07076 *Web:* hillsidecemetery.com	908-756-1729		510
Hillside Plastics Corp 125 Long Ave . . . . . Hillside NJ 07205 *Web:* www.hillsideplasticscorp.com	973-923-2700		600
Hillside Plastics Inc 262 Millers Falls Rd . . . . . Turners Falls MA 01376 *Web:* www.plasticind.com	413-863-2222		98
Hillside Rehabilitation Hospital (HRH) 8747 Squires Lane NE . . . . . Warren OH 44484 *Web:* hillsiderehabhospital.org	330-841-3700		374-6
Hillside School 404 Robin Hill Rd . . . . . Marlborough MA 01752 *Web:* www.hillsideschool.net	508-485-2824	485-4420	622
Hill-Stead Museum 35 Mountain Rd . . . . . Farmington CT 06032 *Web:* www.hillstead.org	860-677-4787	677-0174	520

	Phone	Fax	Class
Hillstone Restaurant Group 147 S Beverly Dr . . . . . Beverly Hills CA 90212 *TF:* 800-230-9787 ■ *Web:* www.hillstone.com	800-230-9787		670
Hilltop Arboretum 11855 Highland Rd . . . . . Baton Rouge LA 70810 *Web:* www.sites01.lsu.edu	225-767-6916	768-7740	97
Hilltop Basic Resources Inc 1 W 4th St Ste 1100 . . . . . Cincinnati OH 45202 *Web:* hilltopcompanies.com	513-651-5000	684-8222	182
Hilltop Elementary School 2615 W Lincoln Rd . . . . . Mchenry IL 60051 *Web:* www.d15.org	815-385-4421		685
Hilltop Environmental Solutions 1585 McDaniel Dr Ste 102 . . . . . West Chester PA 19380 *Web:* www.hilltopes.com	610-430-6920		192
Hilltop Garden & Nature Ctr *Indiana University Campus* 2367 E 10th St . . . . . Bloomington IN 47408 *Web:* hilltop.indiana.edu	812-855-8808		97
Hilltop Inn of Vermont 3472 Airport Rd . . . . . Montpelier VT 05602 *TF:* 877-609-0003 ■ *Web:* www.hilltopinnvt.net	802-229-5766		379
Hilltop Lodge Retirement Community 815 N Independence . . . . . Beloit KS 67420 *Web:* hilltoplodgehc.com	785-738-3516		371
Hilltop Slate Inc 3 County Rt 21 . . . . . Middle Granville NY 12849 *Web:* www.hilltopslate.com	518-642-2270	642-1220	724
Hilltop Village 25900 Euclid Ave . . . . . Euclid OH 44132 *Web:* www.hilltopvillage.com	216-261-8383	261-6816	672
Hilltown Pork Inc 12948 SR-22 . . . . . Canaan NY 12029 *Web:* hilltownpork.com	518-781-4050		473
Hillview Books PO Box 3473 . . . . . Los Altos CA 94024 *Web:* www.hillviewbooks.com	650-967-4933		637-2
Hillview Capital Advisors LLC 777 3rd Ave 28th Fl . . . . . New York NY 10017 *Web:* www.hillviewcap.com	484-708-4720		401
Hillwig-Goodrow Inc 31407 Outer Hwy 10 . . . . . Redlands CA 92373 *TF:* 888-626-5137 ■ *Web:* hillwig-goodrow.com	909-794-2673		727
Hillwood Development Company LLC 3090 Olive St Ste 420 . . . . . Dallas TX 75219 *Web:* www.hillwood.com	214-303-5535	303-5525	536
Hillwood Estate Museum & Gardens 4155 Linnean Ave NW . . . . . Washington DC 20008 *Web:* www.hillwoodmuseum.org	202-686-5807	966-7846	520
Hillyard Chemical Company Inc 302 N Fourth St PO Box 909 . . . . . Saint Joseph MO 64501 **Fax Area Code:* 800 ■ *TF:* 800-365-1555 ■ *Web:* www.hillyard.com	816-233-1321	861-0256*	151
Hillyard Technical Ctr 3434 Faraon St . . . . . Saint Joseph MO 64506 *Web:* hillyardtech.sjsd.k12.mo.us	816-671-4170	671-4479	167-3
Hilman Inc 12 Timber Ln . . . . . Marlboro NJ 07746 *TF:* 888-276-5548 ■ *Web:* www.hilmanrollers.com	732-462-6277	462-6355	470
Hilmar Cheese Company Inc PO Box 910 . . . . . Hilmar CA 95324 *TF:* 800-577-5772 ■ *Web:* www.hilmarcheese.com	209-667-6076	634-1408	296-5
Hilo Medical Ctr 1190 Waianuenue Ave . . . . . Hilo HI 96720 *Web:* www.hilomedicalcenter.org	808-932-3000	974-4746	374-3
Hilscher Clarke Electric Co 519 Fourth St NW . . . . . Canton OH 44703 *Web:* www.hilscher-clarke.com	330-452-9806		189-4
Hilti Inc 5400 S 122nd E Ave . . . . . Tulsa OK 74146 *TF:* 800-879-8000 ■ *Web:* www.hilti.com	800-879-8000	879-7000	759
Hilton Akron Fairlawn 3180 W Market St . . . . . Akron OH 44333 *Web:* www3.hilton.com	330-867-5000		707
Hilton Garden Inn Baton Rouge Airport 3330 Harding Blvd . . . . . Baton Rouge LA 70807 *Web:* hiltongardeninn3.hilton.com	225-357-6177	357-6175	378
Hilton Garden Inn (Burlington Canada) 985 Syscon Rd . . . . . Burlington ON L7L5S3 *Web:* hiltongardeninn3.hilton.com	905-631-7000		379
Hilton Garden Inn Greenville 108 Carolina Point Pkwy . . . . . Greenville SC 29607 *Web:* hiltongardeninn3.hilton.com	864-284-0111	284-0112	379
Hilton Grand Vacations Company LLC 6355 Metro W Blvd Ste 180 . . . . . Orlando FL 32835 *TF:* 800-230-7068 ■ *Web:* www.hiltongrandvacations.com	407-613-3100		753
Hilton Head Health Institute 14 Valencia Rd . . . . . Hilton Head Island SC 29928 *TF:* 800-292-2440 ■ *Web:* www.hhhealth.com	843-785-3919		706
Hilton Head Island Beach & Tennis Resort 40 Folly Field Rd . . . . . Hilton Head Island SC 29928 *TF:* 800-475-2631 ■ *Web:* www.hhibeachandtennis.com	843-842-4402		669
Hilton Head Island Visitor & Convention Bureau, The 1 Chamber of Commerce Dr PO Box 5647 . . . . . Hilton Head Island SC 29938 *TF:* 800-523-3373 ■ *Web:* www.hiltonheadisland.org	843-785-3673	785-7110	139
Hilton Head Library 11 Beach City Rd . . . . . Hilton Head Island SC 29926 *Web:* www.beaufortcountylibrary.org	843-255-6500		434-3
Hilton Head Regional Medical Ctr 25 Hospital Center Blvd . . . . . Hilton Head Island SC 29926 *Web:* www.hiltonheadregional.com	843-681-6122		374-3
Hilton Orlando Buena Vista Palace 1900 E Buena Vista Dr . . . . . Lake Buena Vista FL 32830 *Web:* www.buenavistapalace.com	407-827-2727		669
Hilton Orrington/Evanston 1710 Orrington Ave . . . . . Evanston IL 60201 *TF:* 888-677-4648 ■ *Web:* www.hotelorrington.com	847-866-8700	866-8724	379
Hilton Sandestin Beach Golf Resort & Spa 4000 Sandestin Blvd S . . . . . Miramar FL 32550 *TF:* 800-559-1805 ■ *Web:* www.hiltonsandestinbeach.com	850-267-9500	267-3076	669
Hilton Santa Barbara Beachfront Resort 633 E Cabrillo Blvd . . . . . Santa Barbara CA 93103 *TF:* 800-879-2929 ■ *Web:* www.hiltonsantabarbarabeachfrontresort.com	805-564-4333		669
Hilton Savannah Desoto 15 E Liberty St . . . . . Savannah GA 31401 *TF:* 844-257-3520 ■ *Web:* thedesotosavannah.com	844-257-3520		378

Entry	City	State	ZIP	Phone	Fax	Class
Hilton Tool Company Inc 9980 SE Hwy 212 *Web:* www.hiltontool.com	Clackamas	OR	97015	503-657-9312	657-8939	757
Hilton Waikoloa Village 425 Waikoloa Beach Dr *TF:* 866-931-1679 ■ *Web:* www.hiltonwaikoloavillage.com	Waikoloa	HI	96738	808-886-1234	886-2900	669
Hilton Whistler Resort & Spa 4050 Whistler Way *TF:* 800-515-4050 ■ *Web:* www3.hilton.com	Whistler	BC	V8E1H9	604-932-1982	966-5093	669
Hilton Worldwide 7930 Jones Branch Dr *TF:* 800-445-8667 ■ *Web:* www.hilton.com	McLean	VA	22102	703-883-1000		379
Hiltons Tent City Inc 272 Friend St *TF:* 800-362-8368 ■ *Web:* www.hiltonstentcity.com	Boston	MA	02114	800-362-8368		711
HIM (HIM Mechanical Systems Inc) 90 First St *Web:* www.trustthisbiz.com	Bridgewater	MA	02324	508-697-5000	697-5812	665
HIM Mechanical Systems Inc (HIM) 90 First St *Web:* www.trustthisbiz.com	Bridgewater	MA	02324	508-697-5000	697-5812	665
Himalayan Institute Center for Health & Healing 952 Bethany Tpke *TF:* 800-822-4547 ■ *Web:* www.himalayaninstitute.org	Honesdale	PA	18431	570-253-5551		706
Himalayan Sherpa House 2227 N 56th St *Web:* www.himalayansherpahouse.com	Seattle	WA	98103	206-633-3538		671
Himebaugh Consulting Inc 4940 Munson St NW *Web:* www.hcd.net	Canton	OH	44718	330-493-9700		196
Himes Jim (Rep D - CT) 1227 Longworth House Office Bldg *TF:* 866-453-0028 ■ *Web:* himes.house.gov	Washington	DC	20515	202-225-5541	225-9629	342-2
Himes Vending Inc 4654 Groves Rd *Web:* himesvending.com	Columbus	OH	43232	614-868-6931	868-0028	113
Himoinsa Power Systems Inc 16002 W 110th St *TF:* 866-710-2988 ■ *Web:* www.hipowersystems.com	Lenexa	KS	66219	913-495-5557		518
Hims and Hers 340 Bryant St Ste 300 *TF:* 800-368-0038 ■ *Web:* www.forhims.com	San Francisco	CA	94107	800-368-0038		354
HIMSS (Healthcare Information & Management Systems Society) 230 E Ohio St Ste 500 *Web:* www.himss.org	Chicago	IL	60611	312-664-4467	664-6143	49-8
Hinchcliff Products Co 13550 Falling Water Rd *Web:* www.hinchcliffproducts.com	Strongsville	OH	44136	440-238-5200	238-5202	551
Hinckley Allen & Snyder LLP 28 State St *Web:* www.hinckleyallen.com	Boston	MA	02109	617-345-9000		428
Hinda Incentives Inc 2440 W 34th St *Web:* www.hinda.com	Chicago	IL	60608	773-890-5900	890-4606	765
Hinderliter Construction Inc 3601 N St Joseph Ave *Web:* www.hinderliterconstruction.com	Evansville	IN	47720	812-425-4137		186
Hindley Manufacturing Company Inc 9 Havens St *TF:* 800-323-9031 ■ *Web:* www.hindley.com	Cumberland	RI	02864	401-722-2550	722-3083	350
Hinds Community College 501 E Main St PO Box 1100 *TF:* 800-446-3722 ■ *Web:* hindscc.edu	Raymond	MS	39154	601-857-3212	857-3539	162
Hinds County 316 S President St *Web:* www.co.hinds.ms.us	Jackson	MS	39201	601-968-6587	353-1261	338
Hinds County School District 13192 Hwy 18 W *Web:* www.hinds.k12.ms.us	Raymond	MS	39154	601-857-5222	857-8548	685
Hinds Hospice 1616 W Shaw Ste C-1 *Web:* www.hindshospice.org	Fresno	CA	93711	559-248-8591	222-4782	371
Hindsdale Nurseries Inc 7200 S Madison Rd *Web:* www.hinsdalenurseries.com	Willowbrook	IL	60527	630-323-1411		422
Hinduja Global Solutions Inc 4355 Weaver Pkwy Ste 310 *Web:* www.teamhgs.com	Warrenville	IL	60555	630-791-9070		393
Hines 1050 Corporate Grove Dr *Web:* www.hinessupply.com	Buffalo Grove	IL	60089	847-353-7700	229-3781	191-3
Hines Corp 1218 Pontaluna Rd Ste B *Web:* hinescorp.com	Spring Lake	MI	49456	231-799-6240	799-6298	360-3
Hines Group Inc, The 5680 Old Hwy 54 E *Web:* www.thehinesgroup.com	Philpot	KY	42366	270-729-4242	729-4216	489
Hines Interest LP 2800 Post Oak Blvd *Web:* www.hines.com	Houston	TX	77056	713-621-8000		653
Hines Nut Company Inc 990 S St Paul St	Dallas	TX	75201	214-939-0253		296-28
Hines Park Lincoln Inc 40601 Ann Arbor Rd *Web:* www.hinesparklincoln.com	Plymouth	MI	48170	734-619-6272		57
Hinge Health Inc 465 California St 14th Fl *Web:* hingehealth.com	San Francisco	CA	94104	415-349-7757		48-17
Hingham Institution for Savings 55 Main St *NASDAQ: HIFS* ■ *Web:* www.hinghamsavings.com	Hingham	MA	02043	781-749-2200	740-4889	70
Hingham Jewelers Inc 35 Whiting St *Web:* hinghamjewelers.com	Hingham	MA	02043	781-749-2108		410
Hingham School District 220 Central St *Web:* www.hingham-ma.gov	Hingham	MA	02043	781-741-1500		685
Hiniker Co 58766 240th St *TF:* 800-433-5620 ■ *Web:* www.hiniker.com	Mankato	MN	56002	507-625-6621	625-5883	273
Hinkle Chair Company Inc 4669 Mount Sharon Rd *Web:* hinklechaircompany.com	Springfield	TN	37172	615-384-8477		319-2
Hinkle Contracting Company LLC 395 N Middletown Rd *Web:* www.hinklecontracting.com	Paris	KY	40361	859-987-3670	987-0727	188-4
Hinkle Insurance Agency Inc 705 Olde Hickory Rd *TF:* 877-408-1418 ■ *Web:* hinkleinsurance.com	Lancaster	PA	17601	717-560-9733		390
Hinkle Law Firm LLC 1617 N Waterfront Pkwy Ste 400 *Web:* www.hinklaw.com	Wichita	KS	67206	316-267-2000	630-8466	428
Hinkle Metals & Supply Company Inc 3300 11th Ave N *Web:* hinklemetals.com	Birmingham	AL	35234	205-326-3300		612
Hinkley Inc 33000 Pin Oak Pkwy **Fax Area Code:* 216 ■ *TF:* 800-446-5539 ■ *Web:* www.hinkley.com	Avon Lake	OH	44012	440-653-5500	671-4537*	439
Hinman, Howard & Kattell LLP 80 Exchange St PO Box 5250 *Web:* www.hhk.com	Binghamton	NY	13901	607-723-5341		428
Hinsdale County Sheriff 311 N Henson St *TF:* 877-944-7575 ■ *Web:* hinsdalecountysheriff.com	Lake City	CO	81235	970-944-2291	944-2744	338
Hinshaw & Culbertson LLP 222 N LaSalle St Ste 300 *Web:* www.hinshawlaw.com	Chicago	IL	60601	312-704-3000		428
Hinshaw Music Inc PO Box 470 *TF:* 800-568-7805 ■ *Web:* www.hinshawmusic.com	Chapel Hill	NC	27514	919-933-1691	967-3399	637-2
Hinshaws Acura/Honda 5955 20th St E *Web:* www.hinshawsacura.com	Fife	WA	98424	253-922-8830		57
Hinterland Brewery & Restaurant 313 Dousman St *Web:* hinterlandbeer.com	Green Bay	WI	54303	920-438-8050		671
Hinton Barber & Beauty College 1800 Springs Rd *Web:* www.hintonbarberbeauty.com	Vallejo	CA	94591	707-647-2800	647-2888	166
HIP-HOP 103.9 FM 2 Bala Plz Ste 700 *Web:* 1039hiphop.com	Bala Cynwyd	PA	19004	610-538-1100		645
Hippo Insurance 150 Forest Ave *Web:* www.hippo.com	Palo Alto	CA	94301	925-895-9184		391-2
Hippocrates Health Institute 1466 Hippocrates Way *TF:* 800-842-2125 ■ *Web:* hippocratesinst.org	West Palm Beach	FL	33411	561-471-8876		706
Hippodrome State Theatre 25 SE Second Pl *Web:* thehipp.org	Gainesville	FL	32601	352-375-4477		720
HipSwap Inc 1112 Montana Ave Ste 323 *Web:* www.hipswap.com	Santa Monica	CA	90403	310-396-5400		387
Hiram College PO Box 67 *TF:* 800-362-5280 ■ *Web:* www.hiram.edu	Hiram	OH	44234	330-569-5169	569-5944	166
Hire Demand LLC 20436 Rte 19 Ste 620 **Fax Area Code:* 866 ■ *Web:* hiredemand.com	Cranberry Township	PA	16066	724-538-3434	344-8014*	260
Hire Dynamics LLC 1845 Satellite Blvd Ste 800 *Web:* hiredynamics.com	Duluth	GA	30097	678-482-0200	482-8799	193
Hire Image LLC 6 Alcazar Ave *TF:* 888-433-0090 ■ *Web:* www.hireimage.com	Johnston	RI	02919	401-490-2202		721
Hire Priority 1800 St James Pl Ste 208 *TF:* 888-906-4473 ■ *Web:* www.hirepriority.com	Houston	TX	77056	713-960-9906		631
Hire Quest Inc 111 Springhall Dr *TF:* 800-835-6755 ■ *Web:* www.hirequestllc.com	North Charleston	SC	29418	843-723-7400	577-5742	260
Hire Source, The 24 Wooster Ave *Web:* www.thehiresource.com	Waterbury	CT	06708	203-757-4000	759-7145	260
HireAbilitycom LLC 25 Nashua Rd Ste C6 *Web:* www.hireability.com	Londonderry	NH	03053	603-432-6653		387
Hired 1200 Plymouth Ave N *Web:* www.hired.org	Minneapolis	MN	55411	612-529-3342		260
Hired Inc 303 Second St South Tower Ste 600 *Web:* hired.com	San Francisco	CA	94107	415-813-4987		260
Hireko Trading Company Inc 16185 Stephens St *TF:* 800-367-8912 ■ *Web:* www.hirekogolf.com	City of Industry	CA	91745	800-367-8912		710
Hireology 303 E Wacker Dr Ste 400 *TF:* 844-383-2633 ■ *Web:* hireology.com	Chicago	IL	60601	312-253-7870		387
HireRight Inc 5151 California Ave *TF:* 800-400-2761 ■ *Web:* www.hireright.com	Irvine	CA	92617	800-400-2761		635
Hirnis Wayside Gardens Inc 9950 SW 57th Ave *Web:* hirnisflorist.net	Miami	FL	33156	305-661-6266		70
HIRO 88 Restaurants 3655 N 129th St *Web:* hiro88.com	Omaha	NE	68164	402-933-0091		671
Hirono Mazie K (Sen D - HI) 713 Hart Senate Office Bldg *Web:* www.hirono.senate.gov	Washington	DC	20510	202-224-6361	224-2126	342-2
Hirose Electric (USA) Inc 2688 Westhills Ct *Web:* www.hirose.com	Simi Valley	CA	93065	805-522-7958		253
Hirotec America Inc 4567 Glenmeade Ln *Web:* www.hirotecamerica.com	Auburn Hills	MI	48326	248-836-5100	836-5101	386
Hirschbach Motor Lines Inc 18355 US Hwy 20 *TF:* 800-554-2969 ■ *Web:* www.hirschbach.com	East Dubuque	IL	61025	402-494-5000		780
Hirschfeld Industries LP 112 W 29th St PO Box 3768 *Web:* www.carolinasteel.com	San Angelo	TX	76903	325-486-4201		480
Hirschhaut & Schmidt LLC 47 E Chicago Ave Ste 380 *Web:* hirschhaut-schmidt.com	Naperville	IL	60540	630-873-2290		41
Hirschl & Adler Galleries Inc 730 Fifth Ave *Web:* www.hirschlandadler.com	New York	NY	10019	212-535-8810	772-7237	42
Hirschvogel Inc 2230 S Third St *Web:* www.hirschvogel.com	Columbus	OH	43207	614-445-6060		483
Hirsh Industries Inc 3636 Westown Pkwy Ste 100 *TF:* 800-383-7414 ■ *Web:* www.hirshindustries.com	West Des Moines	IA	50266	515-299-3200	299-3300	319-1
Hirshfield's Inc 725 Second Ave N *TF:* 800-432-3701 ■ *Web:* www.hirshfields.com	Minneapolis	MN	55405	612-377-3910		550
Hirzel Canning Company & Farms 411 Lemoyne Rd *TF:* 800-837-1631 ■ *Web:* www.deifratelli.com	Northwood	OH	43619	419-693-0531	693-4859	296-20
Hirzel Capital Management LLC 3963 Maple Ave Ste 170 *Web:* www.hirzelcapital.com	Dallas	TX	75219	214-999-0014	999-0020	690

Listing	City	State	ZIP	Phone	Fax	Class
H-I-S Paint Manufacturing Company Inc 1801 W Reno Ave *Web:* www.hispaint.com	Oklahoma City	OK	73106	405-232-2077	232-2083	550
HIS Radio 89.3 2420 Wade Hampton Blvd *TF:* 800-447-7234 ■ *Web:* www.hisradio.com	Greenville	SC	29615	864-292-6040	292-8428	645-65
HIS Tackle Box 40 Chestnut Ave *Web:* www.histacklebox.com	South San Francisco	CA	94080	650-588-1200		711
Hisada America Inc 1191 S Walnut St *Web:* www.hisada-g.co.jp	Edinburgh	IN	46124	812-526-0756	526-0766	247
Hisco Inc 6650 Concord Park Dr *TF:* 877-447-2650 ■ *Web:* www.hisco.com	Houston	TX	77040	713-934-1700		246
Hiskes, Dillner, O'Donnell, Marovich & Lapp Ltd 16231 Wausau Ave *Web:* hdoml.com	South Holland	IL	60473	708-333-1234	333-9246	41
Hispanic Association of Colleges & Universities (HACU) 8415 Datapoint Dr Ste 400 *TF:* 800-780-4228 ■ *Web:* www.hacu.net	San Antonio	TX	78229	210-692-3805	692-0823	49-5
Hispanic Communications Network 50 F St NW 8th Fl *Web:* www.hcnmedia.com	Washington	DC	20001	202-637-8800		644
Hispanic Information & Telecommunications Network Inc (HITN) 63 Flushing Ave Bld 292 Ste 211 *Web:* www.hitn.org	Brooklyn	NY	11205	646-731-3520		740
Hispanic Society of America 613 W 155th St *Web:* www.hispanicsociety.org	New York	NY	10032	212-926-2234		48-14
Hispanics in Philanthropy 414 13th St Ste 200 *Web:* hiponline.org	Oakland	CA	94612	415-837-0427		305
Hispec Wheel & Tire Inc 1655 E 12th St *Web:* www.hispecwheel.com	Mishawaka	IN	46544	574-807-8588	807-8596	779
Hissey Mulderig & Friend PLLC One Arboretum Plz 9442 Capital of Texas Hwy N Ste 400 *Web:* www.hmf-law.com	Austin	TX	78759	512-222-6352		41
Histopath Inc 3853 S Alameda St	Corpus Christi	TX	78411	361-992-4040		415
Historic Aircraft Restoration Museum 14301 Creve Coeur Airport Rd *Web:* www.historicaircraftrestorationmuseum.org	Saint Louis	MO	63146	314-434-3368	878-6453	520
Historic Alexandria Foundation (HAF) 218 N Lee St Ste 310 *Web:* www.historicalexandriafoundation.org	Alexandria	VA	22314	703-549-5811		637-2
Historic Annapolis Foundation Museum 77 Main St *Web:* www.annapolis.org	Annapolis	MD	21401	410-267-6656		520
Historic Arkansas Museum 200 E Third St *Web:* www.historicarkansas.org	Little Rock	AR	72201	501-324-9351		520
Historic Brownsville Museum 641 E Madison St *Web:* mitteculturaldistrict.org	Brownsville	TX	78520	956-548-1313		520
Historic Bullock Hotel 633 Main St *TF:* 800-336-1876 ■ *Web:* www.historicbullock.com	Deadwood	SD	57732	605-578-1745		379
Historic Camden *South Carolina* 222 Broad St PO Box 710 *Web:* historiccamden.org	Camden	SC	29020	803-432-9841		564
Historic Cherry Hill 523 1/2 S Pearl St *Web:* www.historiccherryhill.org	Albany	NY	12202	518-434-4791		520
Historic Columbia 1601 Richland St *Web:* www.historiccolumbia.org	Columbia	SC	29201	803-252-7742		520
Historic Crags Lodge 300 Riverside Dr *TF:* 800-438-2929 ■ *Web:* www.diamondresortsandhotels.com	Estes Park	CO	80517	800-438-2929		379
Historic Deerfield PO Box 321 *Web:* www.historic-deerfield.org	Deerfield	MA	01342	413-774-5581	775-7220	520
Historic Elsinore Theatre (HET) 170 High St SE *Web:* www.elsinoretheatre.com	Salem	OR	97301	503-375-3574	375-0284	572
Historic Florida Keys Foundation (HFKF) Old City Hall 510 Greene St *Web:* www.historicfloridakeys.org	Key West	FL	33040	305-292-6718		637-2
Historic Fort Worth Inc 1110 Penn St *Web:* historicfortworth.org	Fort Worth	TX	76102	817-332-5875		520
Historic French Market Inn 509 Decatur St *TF:* 800-366-2743 ■ *Web:* www.frenchmarketinn.com	New Orleans	LA	70130	504-561-5621	581-3802	379
Historic Governors' Mansion 300 E 21st St *Web:* www.capitolcomplex.wyo.gov	Cheyenne	WY	82001	307-777-7878		565
Historic Hack House Museum 775 County St *Web:* www.michigan.org	Milan	MI	48160	734-439-7522		520
Historic Heritage Square 115 N Sixth St *Web:* www.phoenix.gov	Phoenix	AZ	85004	602-261-8063		50-3
Historic Hudson Valley 639 Bedford Rd *Web:* www.hudsonvalley.org	Pocantico Hills	NY	10591	914-631-8200	631-0089	50-3
Historic Indian Agency House 1490 Agency House Rd *Web:* www.agencyhouse.org	Portage	WI	53901	608-742-6362		393
Historic Inns of Annapolis 58 State Cir *TF:* 800-847-8882 ■ *Web:* www.historicinnsofannapolis.com	Annapolis	MD	21401	410-263-2641	268-3613	379
Historic Jonesborough Visitors Center & Museum 117 Boone St *Web:* jonesborough.com	Jonesborough	TN	37659	423-753-1010		520
Historic Latta Plantation 5225 Sample Rd *Web:* www.lattaplantation.org	Huntersville	NC	28078	704-875-2312	875-1724	50-3
Historic Mill Creek Discovery Park 9001 W US Hwy 23 **Fax Area Code:* 906 ■ *Web:* www.mackinacparks.com	Mackinaw City	MI	49701	231-436-4100	847-3815*	565
Historic New England 141 Cambridge St *TF:* 800-722-2256 ■ *Web:* www.historicnewengland.org	Boston	MA	02114	617-227-3956	227-9204	48-13
Historic New Orleans Collection 533 Royal St *TF:* 800-535-9595 ■ *Web:* www.hnoc.org	New Orleans	LA	70130	504-523-4662	598-7108	520
Historic Northampton 46 Bridge St *Web:* www.historic-northampton.org	Northampton	MA	01060	413-584-6011	584-7956	49-19
Historic Old Town Fort Collins 19 Old Town Sq Ste 230 *Web:* downtownfortcollins.com	Fort Collins	CO	80524	970-484-6500		460
Historic Pantages Theatre 710 Hennepin Ave *Web:* hennepintheatretrust.org	Minneapolis	MN	55403	612-339-7007		572
Historic Pensacola Village 120 Church St PO Box 12866 *Web:* www.historicpensacola.org	Pensacola	FL	32502	850-595-5985	595-5989	50-3
Historic Rock Ford 881 Rockford Rd *Web:* historicrockford.org	Lancaster	PA	17602	717-392-7223		50-3
Historic Roswell District 617 Atlanta St *TF:* 800-776-7935 ■ *Web:* www.visitroswellga.com	Roswell	GA	30075	800-776-7935		50-3
Historic Tours of America Inc 201 Front St *TF:* 800-844-7601 ■ *Web:* www.historictours.com	Key West	FL	33040	855-629-8777		760
Historic Trinity Lutheran Church 1345 Gratiot Ave *Web:* www.historictrinity.org	Detroit	MI	48207	313-567-3100	567-3209	50-1
Historic Union Pacific Rail Trail State Park PO Box 754 *Web:* utah.com	Park City	UT	84060	435-649-6839		565
Historic Valley Junction 128 Fifth St *Web:* www.valleyjunction.com	West Des Moines	IA	50265	515-222-3642	274-8407	460
Historic Washington State Park 103 Franklin St *Web:* www.arkansasstateparks.com	Washington	AR	71862	870-983-2684	983-2736	565
Historical Folk Toys LLC 10100 Park Cedar Dr Ste 134 **Fax Area Code:* 800 ■ *TF:* 800-871-1984 ■ *Web:* www.historicalfolktoys.com	Charlotte	NC	28210	704-543-0204	871-1899*	761
Historical Glass Museum 1157 Orange St *Web:* historicalglassmuseum.com	Redlands	CA	92374	909-798-0868		520
Historical Research Center Inc 2107 Corporate Dr *TF:* 800-985-9956 ■ *Web:* www.names.com	Boynton Beach	FL	33426	800-985-9956		327
Historical Society of Carroll County, Maryland Inc 210 E Main St *Web:* www.hsccmd.org	Westminster	MD	21157	410-848-6494		637-2
Historical Society of Erie County, The Hagen History Center 356 W 6th St *Web:* www.eriehistory.org	Erie	PA	16507	814-454-1813	454-6890	520
Historical Society of Marshall County Research Library 202 E Church St *Web:* www.marshallhistory.org	Marshalltown	IA	50158	515-752-6664		434-3
Historical Society of Palm Beach County, The 300 N Dixie Hwy Ste 471 *Web:* www.hspbc.org	West Palm Beach	FL	33401	561-832-4164		520
Historical Society of Pennsylvania (HSP) 1300 Locust St *Web:* hsp.org	Philadelphia	PA	19107	215-732-6200	732-2680	48-13
Historical Society of Washington DC 555 Pennsylvania Ave NW *Web:* www.dchistory.org	Washington	DC	20001	202-249-3955		520
History Center of Olmsted County 1195 W Cir Dr SW *Web:* olmstedhistory.com	Rochester	MN	55902	507-282-9447	289-5481	50-3
History Ch *A & E Television Networks LLC* 235 E 45th St *TF:* 888-371-5848 ■ *Web:* www.aenetworks.com	New York	NY	10017	212-210-1400		740
History Ctr 302 E Berry St *Web:* www.fwhistorycenter.com	Fort Wayne	IN	46802	260-426-2882	424-4419	520
History Museum of Mobile 111 S Royal St *Web:* www.museumofmobile.com	Mobile	AL	36602	251-208-7569		637-2
History Museum On The Square 155 Park Central Sq PO Box 2963 *Web:* historymuseumonthesquare.org	Springfield	MO	65806	417-831-1976		520
History Publishing Company LLC PO Box 700 *Web:* www.historypublishingco.com	Palisades	NY	10964	845-398-8161		637-2
History San Jose Research Library 1650 Senter Rd *Web:* historysanjose.org	San Jose	CA	95112	408-287-2290	287-2291	434-3
History Theatre 30 E Tenth St *Web:* www.historytheatre.com	Saint Paul	MN	55101	651-292-4323	292-4322	572
HistoryMiami Museum 101 W Flagler St *Web:* www.historymiami.org	Miami	FL	33130	305-375-1492		520
Hit Promotional Products Inc 7150 Bryan Dairy Rd *TF:* 800-237-6305 ■ *Web:* www.hitpromo.net	Largo	FL	33777	727-541-5561	541-5130	9
Hitachi America Ltd 50 Prospect Ave *Web:* www.hitachi.com	Tarrytown	NY	10591	914-332-5800	332-5555	185
Hitachi America Ltd *Computer Div* 2000 Sierra Pt Pkwy **Fax Area Code:* 650 ■ *TF:* 800-448-2244 ■ *Web:* www.hitachi.us	Brisbane	CA	94005	619-591-5301	244-7776*	173-8
Hitachi Automotive Systems Americas Inc 955 Warwick Rd *Web:* www.hap.com	Harrodsburg	KY	40330	859-734-9451	734-5309	247
Hitachi Canada Ltd 501 - 5450 Explorer Dr Ste 501 *Web:* www.hitachi.ca	Mississauga	ON	L4W5N1	905-629-9300	290-0141	253
Hitachi Chemical Company America Ltd 2150 N First St Ste 350 *Web:* www.hitachi-chemical.com	San Jose	CA	95131	408-873-2200	873-2284	145
Hitachi Chemical Diagnostics 630 Clyde Ct *TF:* 800-233-6278 ■ *Web:* www.hcdiagnostics.com	Mountain View	CA	94043	650-961-5501	969-2745	231

Company / Address	City	State	Zip	Phone	Fax	Class
Hitachi Construction Machinery Loaders America Inc 60 Amlajack Blvd *Web:* www.kcmcorp.com	Newnan	GA	30265	770-499-7000	421-6842	190
Hitachi Consulting Corp 14643 Dallas Pkwy Ste 800 *Web:* www.hitachiconsulting.com	Dallas	TX	75254	214-665-7000	665-7010	178-1
Hitachi Credit America Ltd 800 Connecticut Ave *TF:* 866-718-4222 ■ *Web:* www.hitachicapitalamerica.com	Norwalk	CT	06854	203-956-3000	956-3103	264-1
Hitachi High Technologies America Inc 10 N Martingale Rd Ste 500 *Web:* www.hitachi-hightech.com	Schaumburg	IL	60173	847-273-4141		419
Hitachi ID Systems Inc 1401 - First St SE Ste 500 *TF:* 877-386-0372 ■ *Web:* hitachi-id.com	Calgary	AB	T2G2J3	403-233-0740		177
Hitachi Kokusai Electric America Ltd 150 Crossways Pk Dr *TF:* 855-490-5124 ■ *Web:* www.hitachikokusai.us	Woodbury	NY	11797	516-921-7200	496-3718	647
Hitachi Medical Systems America Inc 1959 Summit Commerce Pk *TF:* 800-800-3106 ■ *Web:* www.hitachimed.com	Twinsburg	OH	44087	330-425-1313	425-1410	382
Hitachi Metals America Ltd 2 Manhattanville Rd Ste 301 *TF:* 800-777-5757 ■ *Web:* www.hitachimetals.com	Purchase	NY	10577	914-694-9200	694-9279	307
Hitachi Systems Security Inc 955 Michele-Bohec Blvd Ste 244 *TF:* 866-430-8166 ■ *Web:* www.hitachi-systems-security.com	Blainville	QC	J7C5J6	450-430-8166		364
Hitchcock County 229 E D St *Web:* hitchcockcounty.ne.gov	Trenton	NE	69044	308-334-5646	334-5398	338
Hitchcock Fleming & Associates Inc 500 Wolf Ledges Pkwy *Web:* www.teamhfa.com	Akron	OH	44311	330-376-2111		7
Hitchiner Manufacturing Company Inc 594 Elm St *Web:* www.hitchiner.com	Milford	NH	03055	603-673-1100	673-7960	306
Hi-Tec Industries Inc 1000 Sixth Ave NE PO Box 1127 *Web:* hitecindustries.ca	Portage La Prairie	MB	R1N3C5	204-239-4270	239-4271	261
Hi-Tech Electric Inc 11116 W Little York Rd Bldg 8 *Web:* hitechelectric.com	Houston	TX	77041	832-243-0345	467-0132	189-4
Hi-Tech Inc 11 Sunnyside Ave *Web:* www.hi-techstampings.com	Johnston	RI	02919	401-331-0781	331-4740	488
Hi-tech Machining & Engineering LLC 1075 E Wieding Rd *Web:* www.hi-techmachining.net	Tucson	AZ	85706	520-889-8325		261
Hi-tech Optical Inc 3139 Christy Way S *Web:* www.hi-techoptical.com	Saginaw	MI	48603	989-799-9390		543
Hi-Tech Systems Engineering Co 2700 Old Centre Rd *Web:* www.htse.com	Portage	MI	49024	269-488-7788		261
Hitech Systems Inc C/O Pulsiam 16030 Ventura Blvd Ste 250 *Web:* www.pulsiam.com	Encino	CA	91436	310-282-9919	282-9929	178-1
Hi-Tech Wire Inc 631 E Washington St *Web:* hi-techwire.com	Saint Henry	OH	45883	419-678-8376	678-2287	723
Hi-Techniques Inc 2515 Frazier Ave *Web:* www.hi-techniques.com	Madison	WI	53713	608-221-7500		246
Hi-Tek Manufacturinginc 6050 Hi-Tek Ct *Web:* www.hitekmfg.com	Mason	OH	45040	513-459-1094		454
Hi-Temp Insulation Inc 4700 Calle Alto *Web:* www.hi-tempinsulation.com	Camarillo	CA	93012	805-484-2774	389-3443	389
Hitemp Products Co 14936 Grover St *Web:* www.hitempinc.com	Omaha	NE	68144	402-330-5919		151
Hi-Test Laboratories Inc 1104 Arvon Rd *Web:* hitestlabs.com	Arvonia	VA	23004	434-581-3204		261
Hither Hills State Park 164 Old Montauk Hwy *Web:* parks.ny.gov	Montauk	NY	11954	631-668-2554		565
HITN (Hispanic Information & Telecommunications Network Inc) 63 Flushing Ave Bld 292 Ste 211 *Web:* www.hitn.org	Brooklyn	NY	11205	646-731-3520		740
Hitran Corp 362 SR- 31 *Web:* www.hitrancorp.com	Flemington	NJ	08822	908-782-5525	782-9733	767
HITS Inc 319 Main St *Web:* www.hitsshows.com	Saugerties	NY	12477	845-246-8833	246-6371	31
Hitt Contracting Inc 2900 Fairview Park Dr *Web:* www.hitt-gc.com	Falls Church	VA	22042	703-846-9000	846-9110	186
Hitt Marking Devices Inc 3231 W MacArthur Blvd *TF:* 800-969-6699 ■ *Web:* www.hittmarking.com	Santa Ana	CA	92704	714-979-1405	979-1407	467
Hi-Vac Corp 117 Industry Rd *TF:* 800-752-2400 ■ *Web:* hi-vac.com	Marietta	OH	45750	740-374-2306	374-5447	427
Hive Modern Design 820 NW Glisan St *TF:* 866-663-4483 ■ *Web:* hivemodern.com	Portland	OR	97209	866-663-4483		138
Hivelocity Ventures Corp 8010 Woodland Center Blvd Ste 700 *TF:* 888-869-4678 ■ *Web:* www.hivelocity.net	Tampa	FL	33614	813-471-0355		225
Hively 6601 Owens Dr Ste 100 *Web:* behively.org	Pleasanton	CA	94588	925-417-8733	730-4942	148
Hivemine 1200 5th Ave Ste 1800A *Web:* www.hivemine.com	Seattle	WA	98101	206-512-1000		178-1
Hiwassee College 225 Hiwassee College Dr *TF:* 800-356-2187 ■ *Web:* www.hiwassee.edu	Madisonville	TN	37354	423-442-2001	442-8521	162
Hi-Way Paving Inc 4343 Weaver Ct N PO Box 550 *Web:* www.hiwaypaving.com	Hilliard	OH	43026	614-876-1700	876-1899	188-4
Hix Corp 1201 E 27th Terr *TF:* 800-835-0606 ■ *Web:* www.hixcorp.com	Pittsburg	KS	66762	620-231-8568	231-1598	744
Hixardt Technologies Inc 119 W Intendencia St *TF:* 866-985-3282 ■ *Web:* www.hixardt.com	Pensacola	FL	32502	850-439-3282		180
Hixson's School of Floral Design 14125 Detroit Ave *Web:* www.hixsonsinc.com	Cleveland	OH	44107	216-521-9277		685
Hiya Inc 2211 Elliott Ave Ste 300 *Web:* hiya.com	Seattle	WA	98121	501-425-4492		178-8
HJ (Hampton Jitney Inc) 395 County Rd *Web:* www.hamptonjitney.com	Southampton	NY	11968	631-283-4600		107
HJ Baker & Bros Inc 2 Corporate Dr Ste 545 *Web:* hjbaker.com	Shelton	CT	06484	203-682-9200	227-8351	280
H-J Enterprises Inc 3010 High Ridge Blvd *Web:* www.h-j.com	High Ridge	MO	63049	636-677-3421		308
HJ Russell & Co 171 17th St NW Ste 1600 *Web:* www.hjrussell.com	Atlanta	GA	30363	404-330-1000		186
HJM Precision Inc 9 New Tpke Rd *Web:* www.hjmprecision.com	Troy	NY	12182	518-235-7407		385
HKA Enterprises Inc 337 Spartangreen Blvd *TF:* 800-825-5452 ■ *Web:* www.hkaa.com	Duncan	SC	29334	864-661-5100		192
HKG (Handy Kenlin Group, The) 29 E Hintz Rd *Web:* www.handykenlin.com	Wheeling	IL	60090	847-459-0900	459-0902	261
Hkm Direct Market Communications Inc 5501 Cass Ave *TF:* 800-860-4456 ■ *Web:* www.hkmdirectmarket.com	Cleveland	OH	44102	216-651-9500	961-6330	5
Hkm Employment Attorneys LLP 600 Stewart St Ste 901 *Web:* hkm.com	Seattle	WA	98101	206-838-2504		41
HKS Inc 350 N St Paul St Ste 100 *Web:* www.hksinc.com	Dallas	TX	75201	214-969-5599	969-3397	261
HL Dalis Inc 35-35 24th St *TF:* 800-453-2547 ■ *Web:* www.hldalis.com	Long Island City	NY	11106	718-361-1100	392-7654	246
HL Turner Group Inc, The 27 Locke Rd *TF:* 800-305-2289 ■ *Web:* hlturner.com	Concord	NH	03301	603-228-1122		261
HLA (Harold Levinson Assoc) 19 Banfi Plaza North *TF:* 800-325-2512 ■ *Web:* www.hlacigars.com	Farmingdale	NY	11735	631-962-2400	962-9000	297-3
HL-A Company Inc 902 Ravenwood Dr *Web:* www.hondalock.co.jp	Selma	AL	36701	334-874-9010	874-9014	350
Hla Engineers Inc 8617 Ambassador Row Ste 100 *Web:* hlaengineers.com	Dallas	TX	75247	214-267-0930	267-0970	261
HLB Cinnamon Jang Willoughby Metro Tower II 900-4720 Kingsway *Web:* www.cjw.com	Burnaby	BC	V5H4N2	604-435-4317		401
Hlb Systems Solutions 291 Woodlawn Rd W Unit C1 *Web:* www.hlbsolutions.com	Guelph	ON	N1H7L6	519-822-3450	822-8861	180
HLC (Healthcare Leadership Council) 750 Ninth St NW Ste 500 *Web:* www.hlc.org	Washington	DC	20001	202-452-8700	296-9561	48-17
HLC Hotels Inc 123 Habersham St *Web:* www.hlchotels.com	Savannah	GA	31416	912-352-4493	352-0314	379
HLE (Holton Livestock Exchange Inc) 13788 K-16 Hwy *Web:* www.holtonlivestock.com	Holton	KS	66436	785-364-4114	364-3088	446
HLF (High Liner Foods Inc) High Liner Foods Inc 100 Battery Pt PO Box 910 *NYSE: HLF* ■ *TF:* 877-991-3474 ■ *Web:* www.highlinerfoods.com	Lunenburg	NS	B0J2C0	902-634-8811		296-13
HLG Health Communications 1700 Market St Ste 610 *Web:* www.hlgagency.com	Philadelphia	PA	19103	215-990-6848		4
HLI (Human Life Intl) 4 Family Life Ln *TF:* 800-549-5433 ■ *Web:* www.hli.org	Front Royal	VA	22630	540-635-7884	622-6247	48-6
Hli Properties Inc 1003 Central Ave *TF:* 800-247-2000 ■ *Web:* www.hlipublishing.com	Fort Dodge	IA	50501	515-955-1600		637-9
HLM Venture Partners 116 Huntington Ave 9th Fl *Web:* hlmvp.com	Boston	MA	02116	617-266-0030		792
HLN Consulting LLC 7072 Santa Fe Canyon Pl *Web:* www.hln.com	San Diego	CA	92129	858-538-2220		180
HLSL (Harvard Law School Library) 1563 Massachusetts Ave *Web:* hls.harvard.edu	Cambridge	MA	02138	617-495-3100	495-1110	637-2
HLT Ltd 1419 11th St N *Web:* hltlimitedtrailers.com	Humboldt	IA	50548	515-332-1802	332-1833	763
HLW Intl 5 Penn Plz *Web:* www.hlw.design	New York	NY	10001	212-353-4600	353-4666	261
HM Graphics Inc 7840 W Hicks St *Web:* hmgraphics.com	Milwaukee	WI	53219	414-321-6600	546-8692	627
HM Kelly Inc PO Box 186 *TF:* 800-399-0466 ■ *Web:* www.hmkellyinc.com	New Oxford	PA	17350	717-624-4421	624-9327	780
HM Richards Inc PO Box 373 *Web:* www.hmrichards.com	Baldwyn	MS	38824	662-365-9485		321
HM Royal Inc 689 Pennington Ave *TF:* 800-257-9452 ■ *Web:* www.hmroyal.com	Trenton	NJ	08601	609-396-9176	396-3185	146
HM Stauffer & Sons Inc 33 Glenola Dr PO Box 567 *TF:* 800-662-2226 ■ *Web:* hmstauffer.com	Leola	PA	17540	717-656-2811	656-4392	817
HM White Inc 12855 Burt Rd *Web:* hmwhite.com	Detroit	MI	48223	313-531-8477		697
HMA (Hargrave Military Academy) 200 Military Dr *TF:* 800-432-2480 ■ *Web:* www.hargrave.edu	Chatham	VA	24531	434-432-2481	432-3129	622
HMA (Herbert Mines Assoc) 600 Lexington Ave 2nd Fl *Web:* www.herbertmines.com	New York	NY	10022	212-355-0909		266
HMA Public Relations 3610 N 44th St Ste 110 *Web:* hmapr.com	Phoenix	AZ	85018	602-957-8881		636

	Phone	Fax	Class
HMC (Highway Machine Company Inc) 3010 S Old US Hwy 41 ... Princeton IN 47670 *TF:* 866-990-9462 ■ *Web:* www.hmcgears.com	812-385-3639	385-8186	454
HMC (Hays Medical Ctr) 2220 Canterbury Dr ... Hays KS 67601 *TF:* 800-248-0073 ■ *Web:* haysmed.com	785-650-2759		374-3
HMC Advertising LLC 65 Millet St 3rd Fl ... Richmond VT 05477 *Web:* www.wearehmc.com	802-434-7141	434-7140	4
HMC Archtiect 3546 Councours St ... Ontario CA 91764 *TF:* 800-350-9979 ■ *Web:* www.hmcarchitects.com	909-989-9979	483-1400	261
HMC Corp 284 Maple St ... Contoocook NH 03229 *Web:* www.hmccorp.com	603-746-4691	746-4819	821
Hmc Products Inc 7165 Greenlee Dr ... Caledonia IL 61011 *Web:* hmcproducts.org	815-885-1900		88
HMCS Haida National Historic Site 57 Discovery Dr ... Hamilton ON L8L8K4 *Web:* www.pc.gc.ca	905-526-6742	526-9734	563
HME Inc 1950 Byron Center Ave SW ... Wyoming MI 49519 *TF:* 800-269-7335 ■ *Web:* www.firetrucks.com	616-534-1463	534-1967	516
HMG/Courtland Properties Inc 1870 S Bayshore Dr ... Coconut Grove FL 33133 *AMEX:* HMG ■ *Web:* hmgcourtland.com	305-854-6803	856-7342	654
HMH (Harrington Hospital) 100 South St ... Southbridge MA 01550 *TF:* 800-416-6072 ■ *Web:* www.harringtonhospital.org	508-765-9771	765-3147	374-3
HMI (Health Metrics Inc) 6929 N Hayden Rd Ste C4-600 ... Scottsdale AZ 85250 *Web:* www.healthmetrics.com	801-566-1899	880-1160	352
HMN Financial Inc 1016 Civic Center Dr NW ... Rochester MN 55901 *NASDAQ:* HMNF ■ *TF:* 888-257-2000 ■ *Web:* www.justcallhome.com	507-535-1309		360-2
HMS (Hawk Mountain Sanctuary) 1700 Hawk Mtn Rd ... Kempton PA 19529 *Web:* www.hawkmountain.org	610-756-6961	756-4468	48-3
HMS Agency Inc 454 Sand Creek Rd ... Albany NY 12205 *TF:* 800-673-2465 ■ *Web:* hmsagency.com	518-690-0360	690-0355	390
HMS Products Co 1200 E Big Beaver Rd ... Troy MI 48083 *Web:* www.hmsproducts.com	248-689-8120		454
HMS Technologies Inc 1 Discovery Pl ... Martinsburg WV 25403 *Web:* www.hmstech.com	304-596-5583		180
HMSHost Corp 6905 Rockledge Dr Ste 1 ... Bethesda MD 20817 *TF:* 877-672-7467 ■ *Web:* www.hmshost.com	240-694-4100		299
HN Precision 601 N Skokie Hwy ... Lake Bluff IL 60044 *Web:* www.hnprecision.com	847-473-1300		128
HNA (Hawaii Nurses Assn) 949 Kapiolani Blvd Ste 107 ... Honolulu HI 96814 *TF:* 800-617-2677 ■ *Web:* www.hawaiinurses.org	808-531-1628		533
HNA (Hockey North America) 45570 Shepard Dr ... Sterling VA 20164 *TF:* 800-446-2539 ■ *Web:* www.hna.com	703-430-8100	421-9205	48-22
HNC (Hospice of Northern Colorado) 2726 W 11th St Rd ... Greeley CO 80634 *TF:* 800-564-5563 ■ *Web:* www.hospiceofnortherncolorado.org	970-352-8487	475-0037	371
HNH Machine Ltd 110 Towerline Pl ... London ON N6E2T1 *Web:* www.hnhmachine.com	519-680-3880	680-3884	454
HNTB Corp 715 Kirk Dr ... Kansas City MO 64105 *Web:* www.hntb.com	816-472-1201	472-4060	261
HNW (Houston Northwest Chamber of Commerce) 3920 Cypress Creek Pkwy ... Houston TX 77068 *Web:* www.houstonnwchamber.org	281-440-4160	440-5302	139
HO Bostrom Company Inc 818 Progress Ave ... Waukesha WI 53186 *TF:* 800-332-5415 ■ *Web:* www.hobostrom.com	262-542-0222	542-3784	689
Ho Chow Restaurant 47966 Warm Springs Blvd ... Fremont CA 94539 *Web:* www.hochow.com	510-657-0683		671
HO Penn Machinery Company Inc 122 Noxon Rd ... Poughkeepsie NY 12603 *TF:* 888-736-8228 ■ *Web:* www.hopenn.com	845-452-1200		358
HO Trerice Co 12950 W Eight-Mile Rd ... Oak Park MI 48237 *TF:* 888-873-7423 ■ *Web:* www.trerice.com	248-399-8000	399-7246	201
HO2 Partners 13455 Noel Rd 2 Galleria Tower Ste 1670 ... Dallas TX 75240 *Web:* www.ho2.com	972-702-1107	702-8234	792
Hoachlander Davis Photography LLC 5110 1/2 Macarthur Blvd NW ... Washington DC 20016 *Web:* hdphoto.com	202-364-9306		794
Hoag Hospital Irvine (HHI) 16200 Sand Canyon Ave ... Irvine CA 92618 *TF:* 800-309-9729 ■ *Web:* www.hoag.org	949-764-4624		374-3
Hoagland, Longo, Moran, Dunst & Doukas 40 Paterson St ... New Brunswick NJ 08903 *Web:* www.hoaglandlongo.com	732-545-4717	545-4579	428
Hoar Construction Inc 2 Metroplex Dr Ste 400 ... Birmingham AL 35209 *Web:* www.hoar.com	205-803-2121	423-2323	186
Hoard Historical Museum Research Library & Archive 401 Whitewater Ave ... Fort Atkinson WI 53538 *Web:* www.hoardmuseum.org	920-563-7769	568-3203	434-3
Hoard's Dairyman Magazine 28 Milwaukee Ave W PO Box 801 ... Fort Atkinson WI 53538 *TF:* 800-245-8222 ■ *Web:* hoards.com	920-563-5551	563-7298	457-1
HOB (House of Batteries) 10910 Talbert Ave ... Fountain Valley CA 92708 *TF:* 800-432-3385 ■ *Web:* www.houseofbatteries.com	714-962-7600	962-7644	246
Hobart & William Smith Colleges 300 Pulteney St ... Geneva NY 14456 *TF:* 800-852-2256 ■ *Web:* www.hws.edu	315-781-3000		166
Hobart Bros Co 101 Trade Sq E ... Troy OH 45373 *TF:* 800-424-1543 ■ *Web:* www.hobartbrothers.com	937-332-4000	332-5178	811
Hobart Institute of Welding Technology 400 Trade Sq E ... Troy OH 45373 **Fax Area Code:* 937 ■ *TF:* 800-332-9448 ■ *Web:* www.welding.org	800-332-9448	332-9550*	167-3
Hobas Pipe USA LP 1413 E Richey Rd ... Houston TX 77073 *TF:* 800-856-7473 ■ *Web:* www.hobaspipe.com	281-821-2200	821-7715	596
Hobblebush Books 17-A Old Milford Rd ... Brookline NH 03033 *Web:* www.hobblebush.com	603-672-4317		637-2
Hobbs & Towne Inc 1288 Vly Forge Rd PMB 269 PO Box 987 ... Valley Forge PA 19482 *Web:* hobbstowne.com	610-783-4600		193
Hobbs Bonded Fibers Inc 200 Commerce Dr ... Waco TX 76710 *TF:* 800-433-3357 ■ *Web:* www.hobbsbondedfibers.com	254-741-0040	772-7238	745-6
Hobbs Chamber of Commerce 400 N Marland Blvd ... Hobbs NM 88240 *Web:* www.hobbschamber.org	575-397-3202	397-1689	139
Hobbs Herder 2240 University Dr ... Newport Beach CA 92660 *Web:* www.hobbsherder.com	949-515-5000		7
Hobbs Medical Inc 8 Spring St ... Stafford Springs CT 06076 **Fax Area Code:* 203 ■ *Web:* www.hobbsmedical.com	860-684-5875	684-7574*	476
Hobbs Public Library 509 N Shipp St ... Hobbs NM 88240 *Web:* www.hobbspubliclibrary.org	575-397-9328		434-3
Hobbs State Park-Conservation Area 21392 E Hwy 12 ... Rogers AR 72756 *Web:* www.arkansasstateparks.com	479-789-2380		565
Hobby Center for the Performing Arts 800 Bagby St Ste 300 ... Houston TX 77002 *Web:* www.thehobbycenter.org	713-315-2400	315-2402	572
Hobby Lobby 7717 SW 44th St ... Oklahoma City OK 73179 *TF:* 800-888-0321 ■ *Web:* www.hobbylobby.com	405-745-1275		44
Hobbytown USA 4107 Pioneer Woods Dr Ste 108 ... Lincoln NE 68512 *Web:* www.hobbytown.com	402-434-5050	434-5055	761
Hobe & Lucas 4807 Rockside Rd Ste 510 ... Independence OH 44131 *Web:* www.hobe.com	216-524-8900		2
Hobe Sound Bible College PO Box 1065 ... Hobe Sound FL 33475 *TF:* 800-881-5534 ■ *Web:* hsbc.edu	772-546-5534	545-1422	161
Hobes Country Hams Inc 389 Elledge Mill Rd ... North Wilkesboro NC 28659 *Web:* www.hobescountryham.com	336-670-3401		296-26
HOBI International Inc 1202 Nagel Blvd ... Batavia IL 60510 *TF:* 877-814-2620 ■ *Web:* hobi.com	630-761-0500		174
Hobie Cat Co 4925 Oceanside Blvd ... Oceanside CA 92056 *Web:* www.hobie.com	760-758-9100	758-1841	90
Hobin & Hobin LLP 1011 A St ... Antioch CA 94509 *Web:* hobinlaw.com	925-757-7585		41
Hob-Nob Hill 2271 First Ave ... San Diego CA 92101 *Web:* hobnobhill.com	619-239-8176		671
Hoboken Public Library (HPL) 500 Park Ave ... Hoboken NJ 07030 *Web:* www.hobokenfol.org	201-420-2346		434-3
Hobson & Motzer Inc 30 Air Line Dr ... Durham CT 06422 *TF:* 800-476-5111 ■ *Web:* www.hobsonmotzer.com	860-349-1756	349-3602	488
Hobsons 50 E-Business Way Ste 300 ... Cincinnati OH 45241 *Web:* www.hobsons.com	513-891-5444		177
HOC Industries Inc 3511 N Ohio ... Wichita KS 67219 *TF:* 800-999-9645 ■ *Web:* hocindustries.com	316-838-4663	832-1211	581
Hochman, Salkin, Rettig, Toscher & Perez PC 9150 Wilshire Blvd Ste 300 ... Beverly Hills CA 90212 *Web:* www.taxlitigator.com	310-281-3200		428
Ho-Chunk Builders 1505 Stable Dr ... South Sioux City NE 68776 *Web:* hochunkconstructiongroup.com	402-494-0222	494-3110	189-5
Ho-Chunk Inc 1 Mission Dr ... Winnebago NE 68071 *TF:* 800-439-7008 ■ *Web:* www.hochunkinc.com	402-878-2809		317
Hockaday School 11600 Welch Rd ... Dallas TX 75229 *Web:* www.hockaday.org	214-363-6311		622
Hocker Tool and Die Inc 5161 Webster St ... Dayton OH 45414 *Web:* www.hockertoolanddie.com	937-274-3443	274-5860	454
Hockey Hall of Fame 30 Yonge St ... Toronto ON M5E1X8 *Web:* www.hhof.com	416-360-7765	360-1316	522
Hockey News Magazine 25 Sheppard Ave Ste 100 ... Toronto ON M2N6S7 *Web:* www.thehockeynews.com	514-848-7000		457-20
Hockey North America (HNA) 45570 Shepard Dr ... Sterling VA 20164 *TF:* 800-446-2539 ■ *Web:* www.hna.com	703-430-8100	421-9205	48-22
Hockeytown Cafe 2301 Woodward Ave ... Detroit MI 48201 *Web:* hockeytowncafe.com	313-471-3400		671
Hocking & Schulenberg LLC 5757 S 34th St Ste 100 ... Lincoln NE 68516	402-441-0140		2
Hocking College 3301 Hocking Pkwy ... Nelsonville OH 45764 *TF:* 877-462-5464 ■ *Web:* www.hocking.edu	740-753-3591	753-7065	800
Hocking County Treasurer 1 E Main St PO Box 28 ... Logan OH 43138 *Web:* www.co.hocking.oh.us	740-385-3517	385-8236	338
Hocking Hills Chamber of Commerce 96 W Hunter St ... Logan OH 43138 *Web:* hockinghillschamber.com	740-385-6836	385-7259	139
Hocking Hills State Park 19852 SR-664 S ... Logan OH 43138 *Web:* www.thehockinghills.org	740-385-6842		565
Hocking Valley Bank 7 W Stimson Ave ... Athens OH 45701 *TF:* 888-482-5854 ■ *Web:* www.hvbonline.com	740-592-4441		70
Hockley County 802 Houston St ... Levelland TX 79336 *Web:* www.co.hockley.tx.us	806-894-4404		338
Hocon Gas Inc 6 Armstrong Rd ... Shelton CT 06484 *Web:* www.hocongas.com	203-925-0600	944-0300	579
Hodel Wilks LLP 4 Park Plz Ste 640 ... Irvine CA 92614 *Web:* hodelwilks.com	949-450-4470		41
Hodell-natco Industries Inc 7825 Hub Pkwy ... Cleveland OH 44125 *TF:* 800-321-4862 ■ *Web:* www.hodell-natco.com	216-447-0165		351
Hodgdon Powder Company Inc 6430 Vista Dr ... Shawnee KS 66218 *Web:* www.hodgdon.com	913-362-9455	362-1307	268
Hodgdon Yachts Inc PO Box 505 ... East Boothbay ME 04544 *Web:* hodgdonyachts.com	207-633-4194		698
Hodge Engineering Inc 2615 Jahn Ave NW Ste E5 ... Gig Harbor WA 98335 *Web:* hodgeengineering.squarespace.com	253-857-7055		261

Name / Address	Phone	Fax	Class
Hodge Products Inc PO Box 1326 .... El Cajon CA 92022 *TF:* 800-778-2217 ■ *Web:* www.hpionline.com	800-778-2217		295
Hodgeman County PO Box 247 .... Jetmore KS 67854 *TF:* 877-357-6330 ■ *Web:* www.hodgemancountyks.com	620-357-6421	357-6313	338
Hodges & Associates PLLC 13642 Omega Rd .... Dallas TX 75244 *Web:* www.hodgesarchitecture.biz	972-387-1000		7
Hodges Harbin Newberry & Tribble 3920 Arkwright Rd .... Macon GA 31210 *Web:* www.hhnt.com	478-743-7175		261
Hodges University 2655 Northbrooke Dr .... Naples FL 34119 *TF:* 800-466-8017 ■ *Web:* www.hodges.edu	239-513-1122		166
Hodges-Mace Benefits Group Inc 5775-D Glenridge Dr Ste 350 .... Atlanta GA 30328 *Web:* www.hodgesmace.com	404-574-6110		260
Hodgson Mill Inc 1100 Stevens Ave .... Effingham IL 62401 *Web:* www.hodgsonmill.com	217-347-0105		296-23
Hodgson Russ LLP 140 Pearl St The Guaranty Bldg Ste 100 .... Buffalo NY 14202 *Web:* www.hodgsonruss.com	716-856-4000		428
Hodnett Cooper Real Estate Inc 520 Ocean Blvd .... Saint Simons Island GA 31522 *TF:* 844-402-8686 ■ *Web:* hodnettcooper.com	912-638-4750		652
Hoefferle-Butler Engineering Inc 8714 S Roberts Rd .... Hickory Hills IL 60457 *Web:* hbeconsulting.com	708-599-8980		261
Hoegemeyer Hybrids Inc 1755 Hoegemeyer Rd .... Hooper NE 68031 *TF:* 800-245-4631 ■ *Web:* www.therightseed.com	402-654-3399		10-5
HOERBIGER Engine Division 3350 Gateway Dr .... Pompano Beach FL 33069 *Web:* www.hoerbiger.com	954-623-2103	623-2299	789
Hoeven John (Sen R - ND) 338 Russell Senate Office Bldg .... Washington DC 20510 *Web:* www.hoeven.senate.gov	202-224-2551	228-5112	342-2
HOF Construction Inc 3137 Jamieson Ave .... Saint Louis MO 63139 *Web:* www.hofconstruction.com	314-645-2200		186
Hof's Hut Restaurants Inc 2601 E Willow St .... Signal Hill CA 90755 *Web:* www.hofshut.com	562-596-0200		670
Hoff Companies Inc 1840 N Lakes Ave .... Meridian ID 83646	208-884-2002		499
Hoff Enterprises Inc 151 Freidhoff Ln .... Johnstown PA 15902 *Web:* hoffent.com	814-535-8371		115
Hoffbrau Steaks 7203-G IH-40 W .... Amarillo TX 79106 *Web:* hoffbrausteakandgrill.com	806-358-6595		671
Hoffer Flow Controls Inc 107 Kitty Hawk Ln .... Elizabeth City NC 27909 *Web:* www.hofferflow.com	252-331-1997	331-2886	201
Hoffer Pest Solutions 12329 NW 35 St .... Coral Springs FL 33065 *Web:* www.hofferpest.com	954-753-1222		577
Hoffer Plastics Corp 500 N Collins St .... South Elgin IL 60177 *Web:* www.hofferplastics.com	847-741-5740		604
Hoffinger Industries Inc 315 Sebastian St .... West Helena AR 72390	870-572-3466		728
Hoffland Environmental Inc 10391 Silver Springs Rd .... Conroe TX 77303 *Web:* heienv.com	936-856-4515		201
Hoffman & Blasco LLC 9360 Glacier Hwy Ste 202 .... Juneau AK 99801 *Web:* hoffmanblasco.com	907-586-3340		41
Hoffman & Hoffman PA 3 Cliffdewller Ct .... Owings Mills MD 21117 *Web:* hoffmanandhoffmanmd.com	410-685-1156		41
Hoffman Alvary & Company LLC 7 Wells Ave .... Newton MA 02459 *Web:* hoffmanalvary.com	617-758-0500	758-0510	428
Hoffman Brown Company, An Insurance Agency 5000 Van Nuys Blvd 6th Fl .... Sherman Oaks CA 91403 *Web:* hoffmanbrown.com	818-986-8200		390
Hoffman California Fabrics Inc 25792 Obrero Dr .... Mission Viejo CA 92691 **Fax Area Code:* 949 ■ *TF:* 800-547-0100 ■ *Web:* hoffmancaliforniafabrics.net	800-547-0100	770-4022*	594
Hoffman Car Wash & Hoffman Jiffy Lube 1757 Central Ave .... Albany NY 12205 *TF:* 877-446-3362 ■ *Web:* www.hoffmancarwash.com	518-862-1658	869-3574	62-1
Hoffman Construction Corp 805 SW Broadway Ste 2100 .... Portland OR 97205 *Web:* www.hoffmancorp.com	503-221-8811		186
Hoffman Engineering Corp PO Box 4430 .... Stamford CT 06907 *Web:* www.hoffmanengineering.com	203-425-8900	425-8910	743
Hoffman Equipment Inc 300 S Randolphville Rd .... Piscataway NJ 08854 *Web:* hoffmanequip.com	732-752-3600		358
Hoffman Estates Chamber of Commerce 2200 W Higgins Rd Ste 201 .... Hoffman Estates IL 60169 *Web:* hechamber.com	847-781-9100		139
Hoffman Hills State Recreation Area 921 Brickyard Rd .... Menomonie WI 54751 *Web:* dnr.wi.gov	715-232-1242		565
Hoffman Homes for Youth 815 Orphanage Rd .... Littlestown PA 17340 *Web:* www.hoffmanhomes.com	717-359-7148	359-2600	653
Hoffman House 7550 E State St .... Rockford IL 61108 *Web:* www.hoffmanhouserockford.com	815-397-5800		671
Hoffman Planning, Design, & Construction Inc 122 E College Ave Ste 1G .... Appleton WI 54911 *TF:* 800-236-2370 ■ *Web:* www.hoffman.net	920-731-2322		186
Hoffman Products 9600 Vly View Rd .... Macedonia OH 44056 **Fax Area Code:* 866 ■ *TF:* 800-645-2014 ■ *Web:* www.tpcwire.com	216-525-4320	896-3017*	815
Hoffman, Comfort, Offutt, Scott & Halstad LLP 24 N Court St .... Westminster MD 21157 *Web:* carrollcountymarylandlawfirm.com	410-848-4444		41
Hoffman, Hamer & Associates PLLC 118 First Ave NE .... Faribault MN 55021 *Web:* jphoffmanlaw.com	507-332-4001		41
Hoffmann & Baron LLP 6900 Jericho Tpke .... Syosset NY 11791 *Web:* www.hbiplaw.com	516-822-3550		428
Hoffmann & Feige Inc 3 Fallsview Ln .... Brewster NY 10509 *Web:* hoffmann-feige.com	845-277-4401	277-4701	261
Hoffmann Die Cast Corp 229 Kerth St .... Saint Joseph MI 49085 *Web:* www.hoffmanndc.com	269-983-1102	983-2928	308
Hoffmann Hospice of the Valley 8501 Brimhall Rd Bldg 100 .... Bakersfield CA 93312 *Web:* www.hoffmannhospice.org	661-410-1010	410-1110	371
Hoffmann-LaRoche Inc 340 Kingsland St .... Nutley NJ 07110 *Web:* www.roche.com	973-235-5000		582
Hoffmaster 2920 N Main St .... Oshkosh WI 54901 **Fax Area Code:* 920 ■ *TF:* 800-327-9774 ■ *Web:* www.hoffmaster.com	800-558-9300	235-1642*	558
Hoffmeier Inc 3210 N Lewis Ave .... Tulsa OK 74110 *Web:* www.hoffmeier.com	918-388-6917	430-0820	685
Hofmann Industries Inc 3145 Shillington Rd .... Sinking Spring PA 19608 *Web:* www.hofmann.com	610-678-8051	670-2221	490
Hofstra University 206 Memorial Hall .... Hempstead NY 11549 *TF:* 800-463-7872 ■ *Web:* www.hofstra.edu	516-463-6600	463-5100	166
Hofwyl-Broadfield Plantation State Historic Site 5556 US Hwy 17 N .... Brunswick GA 31525 *Web:* gastateparks.org	912-264-7333		565
Hog Heaven 115 27th Ave N .... Nashville TN 37203 *Web:* www.hogheavenbbq.com	615-329-1234		671
Hog Heaven Bar-B-Q 2419 Guess Rd .... Durham NC 27705 *Web:* www.hogheavenbarbecue.com	919-286-7447		671
Hog Island Oyster Co 1 Ferry Bldg Ste 11A The Embarcadero ..... San Francisco CA 94111 *Web:* hogislandoysters.com	415-391-7117		671
Hog Slat Inc PO Box 300 .... Newton Grove NC 28366 *TF:* 800-949-4647 ■ *Web:* www.hogslat.com	910-594-0219	594-1392	10-6
Hog's Breath Saloon Key West 400 Front St .... Key West FL 33040 *TF:* 800-826-6969 ■ *Web:* www.hogsbreath.com	305-296-4222		671
Hogan Assessment Systems Inc 2622 E 21st St .... Tulsa OK 74114 *Web:* www.hoganassessments.com	918-749-0632		463
Hogan Flavors & Fragrances Inc c/o Founder, President & CEO - Ray Hogan 111 E 14th St Ste 340 .... New York NY 10003 *Web:* www.hoganff.com	212-598-4310	477-4711	214
Hogan Marren Babbo & Rose Ltd 321 N Clark St Ste 1301 .... Chicago IL 60654 *Web:* www.hmltd.com	312-946-1800	946-9818	428
Hogan-Knotts Financial Group, The 298 Broad St .... Red Bank NJ 07701 *TF:* 800-801-3190 ■ *Web:* hkfg.biz	732-842-7400		690
Hoge Lumber Co 701 S Main St .... New Knoxville OH 45871 *Web:* hoge.com	419-753-2263	753-2963	683
Hoggan Scientific LLC 3653 W 1987 S .... Salt Lake City UT 84104 **Fax Area Code:* 800 ■ *TF:* 800-678-7888 ■ *Web:* hogganscientific.com	801-572-6500	915-3439*	267
Hogue Cellars 2800 Lee Rd .... Prosser WA 99350 **Fax Area Code:* 509 ■ *TF:* 800-565-9779 ■ *Web:* www.hoguecellars.com	800-565-9779	786-4580*	80-3
H-O-H Water Technology Inc 500 S Vermont St .... Palatine IL 60067 *Web:* www.hohwatertechnology.com	847-358-7400		806
Hohl Industrial Services Inc 770 Riverview Blvd .... Tonawanda NY 14150 *Web:* www.hohlind.com	716-332-0466	332-0467	186
Hohl Machine & Conveyor Company Inc 1580 Niagara St .... Buffalo NY 14213 *Web:* www.hohlmachine.com	716-882-7210		207
Hohman Associates LLC (HAI) 6951 W Little York .... Houston TX 77040 *TF:* 800-324-0978 ■ *Web:* www.hohmanassociates.com	713-896-0978	896-9419	48-2
Hohmann & Barnard Inc 30 Rasons Ct .... Hauppauge NY 11788 *TF:* 800-645-0616 ■ *Web:* www.h-b.com	631-234-0600	234-0683	278
Hoigaards Inc 5425 Excelsior Blvd .... Minneapolis MN 55416 *TF:* 800-266-8157 ■ *Web:* hoigaards.com	952-929-1351		711
Hoist Fitness Systems Inc 11900 Community Rd .... Poway CA 92064 *TF:* 800-548-5438 ■ *Web:* www.hoistfitness.com	858-578-7676	578-9558	267
Hoke County Sand Company Inc 580 Doc Brown Rd .... Raeford NC 28376 *Web:* www.hoke-raeford.com	910-875-8751		338
Hoke Inc 405 Centura Ct PO Box 4866 .... Spartanburg SC 29305 *Web:* www.hoke.com	864-574-7966	587-5608	790
Hoku's 5000 Kahala Ave .... Honolulu HI 96816 *TF:* 866-318-4579 ■ *Web:* www.kahalaresort.com	808-739-8888		671
Holabird Sports LLC 9220 Pulaski Hwy .... Middle River MD 21220 *TF:* 866-860-1416 ■ *Web:* www.holabirdsports.com	410-687-6400		711
Holaday Circuits Inc 11126 Bren Rd W .... Minnetonka MN 55343 *TF:* 800-362-3303 ■ *Web:* www.holaday.com	952-933-3303		625
Holaday-Parks Inc 4600 S 134 Pl .... Tukwila WA 98168 *Web:* www.holadayparks.com	206-248-9700		189-10
HolaDoctor Inc 30 Mansell Ct Ste 215 .... Roswell GA 30076 *Web:* holadoctor.net	770-649-0298		353
Holben, Martin & White Consulting Structural Engineers Inc 3501 E Speedway Blvd Ste 225 .... Tucson AZ 85716 *Web:* www.hmwstructural.com	520-327-9491	795-6140	194
Holbrook Auto Parts 71 W Mcnichols Rd .... Highland Park MI 48203 *Web:* www.holbrookautoparts.com	313-868-6000		61
Holbrook Manufacturing Inc 291 Province St .... Franklin IN 46131 *TF:* 888-736-9387 ■ *Web:* www.holbrookmfg.com	317-736-9387	736-4395	697
Holbrook Tool & Molding Inc 10696 Perry Hwy .... Meadville PA 16335 *Web:* www.holbrooktool.com	814-336-4113	337-0910	604

Name / Address	City	State	ZIP	Phone	Fax	Class
Holcomb & Hoke Manufacturing Company Inc 1545 Van Buren St *Web:* www.foldoor.com	Indianapolis	IN	46203	317-784-2448	781-9164	286
Holcomb Bridge at Grimes Bridge 690 Holcomb Bridge Rd *Web:* www.myfriendsplacedeli.com	Roswell	GA	30076	770-594-9117		670
Holcomb Enterprises 25108 Marguerite Pkwy B-206 *Web:* www.holcombenterprises.com	Mission Viejo	CA	92692	949-458-0292		180
Hold Brothers Capital 10 W 46th St **Fax Area Code:* 646 ■ *Web:* www.holdbrothers.com	New York	NY	10036	212-792-0900	745-2150*	405
Holden Advisors Corp 2250 Main St Ste 2 *Web:* www.holdenadvisors.com	Concord	MA	01742	978-405-0020		195
Holden Arboretum 9500 Sperry Rd *Web:* www.holdenarb.org	Kirtland	OH	44094	440-946-4400	602-3857	97
Holden Industries Inc 5624 S State Hwy 43 *TF:* 800-488-4487 ■ *Web:* www.holdentrailers.com	South West City	MO	64863	417-762-3218		779
Holden Machine & Fabrication Inc 515 Batchhelder Rd *Web:* www.holdenmachine.com	Holden	WV	25625	304-239-6302	239-2133	358
Holden Oil Inc 91 Lynnfield St *Web:* holdenoil.com	Peabody	MA	01960	978-531-2984	531-4321	316
Holden, Carpenter & Roscow Pl 5608 NW 43rd St *Web:* gnv-law.com	Gainesville	FL	32653	352-373-7788		41
Holder & Jacobs PC 24725 W Twelve Mile Rd Ste 107 *Web:* holderandjacobscpas.com	Southfield	MI	48034	248-353-3050		2
Holder Construction Co 3333 Riverwood Pkwy Ste 400 *Web:* www.holderconstruction.com	Atlanta	GA	30339	770-988-3000		186
Holder Group Inc, The 150 Clove Rd 1st Fl *Web:* www.holdergroup.com	Little Falls	NJ	07424	973-227-2008		194
Holderness School 33 Chapel Ln *TF:* 877-262-1492 ■ *Web:* www.holderness.org	Holderness	NH	03245	603-536-1257	536-1267	622
Holding George (Rep R - NC) 1110 Longworth House Office Bldg *Web:* www.holding.house.gov	Washington	DC	20515	202-225-3032	225-0181	342-2
Holdrege & Kull Consulting Engineers & Geologists 792 Searls Ave	Nevada City	CA	95959	530-478-1305		261
Holdrege Daily Citizen 418 Garfield *Web:* www.holdregechamber.com	Holdrege	NE	68949	308-995-4441		532-2
Holdren Brothers Inc 301 Runkle *Web:* www.holdrenbrothers.com	West Liberty	OH	43357	937-465-7050		757
Holdsworth Financial Group 40 Eagle Vly Ct *Web:* www.holdsworthfinancial.com	Broadview Heights	OH	44147	440-746-8100		463
Hole in One Intl 6195 Ridgeview Ct Ste A *TF:* 800-827-2249 ■ *Web:* www.holeinoneinternational.com	Reno	NV	89519	775-828-4653		760
Holiday Acres Resort 4060 S Shore Dr PO Box 460 *TF:* 800-261-1500 ■ *Web:* www.holidayacres.com	Rhinelander	WI	54501	715-369-1500		669
Holiday Automotive 321 N Rolling Meadows Dr *TF:* 855-304-4768 ■ *Web:* www.holidayautomotive.com	Fond Du Lac	WI	54937	920-921-8898		516
Holiday Builders Inc 2293 W Eau Gallie Blvd *TF:* 866-431-2533 ■ *Web:* www.holidaybuilders.com	Melbourne	FL	32935	866-431-2533		653
Holiday Diver Inc 180 Gulf Stream Way *TF:* 800-348-3872 ■ *Web:* www.diversdirect.com	Dania Beach	FL	33004	954-925-7630		711
Holiday Express Corp 721 S 28th St *TF:* 800-831-5078 ■ *Web:* holidayexpresstrucking.com	Estherville	IA	51334	712-362-5012	362-3019	805
Holiday Hair 7201 Metro Blvd *TF:* 800-345-7811 ■ *Web:* www.signaturestyle.com	Minneapolis	MN	55439	800-345-7811		77
Holiday Ice Inc 204 Short Ave *Web:* www.holiday-ice.com	Longwood	FL	32750	407-831-2077	834-3359	14
Holiday Image Inc 760 First St *Web:* www.holidayimagellc.com	Harrison	NJ	07029	718-369-3212	369-3262	344
Holiday Inn By the Bay 88 Spring St *TF:* 800-345-5050 ■ *Web:* www.innbythebay.com	Portland	ME	04101	207-775-2311		378
Holiday Inn Resort Daytona Beach Oceanfront 1615 S Atlantic Ave *TF:* 877-834-3613 ■ *Web:* www.hiresortdaytona.com	Daytona Beach	FL	32118	386-255-0921		379
Holiday Inn Resort Lake Buena Vista 13351 SR 535 *Web:* www.hiresortlbv.com	Orlando	FL	32821	407-239-4500		669
Holiday Isle Beach Resort & Marina 84001 Overseas Hwy *TF:* 855-314-2829 ■ *Web:* www.holidayisle.com	Islamorada	FL	33036	305-664-2321	664-2523	669
Holiday Lanes 3316 Old Minden Rd *Web:* www.bowlholidaylanes.com	Bossier City	LA	71112	318-746-7331		99
Holiday Oil Co 3115 W 2100 S *Web:* www.holidayoil.com	West Valley City	UT	84119	801-973-7002	973-7398	579
Holiday Retirement 480 N Orlando Ave Ste 236 *TF:* 800-322-0999 ■ *Web:* www.holidaytouch.com	Winter Park	FL	32789	800-322-0999		655
Holiday River Expeditions 544 East 3900 South *TF:* 800-624-6323 ■ *Web:* www.bikeraft.com	Salt Lake City	UT	84107	801-266-2087		760
Holiday Stationstores LLC 4567 American Blvd W *TF:* 800-745-7411 ■ *Web:* www.holidaystationstores.com	Bloomington	MN	55437	952-830-8700		204
Holiday Tins and Containers 4025 Willowbend Blvd Ste 330 *TF:* 800-749-9911 ■ *Web:* www.e-holidaytins.com	Houston	TX	77025	832-518-2700	518-2799	459
Holiday Tours Inc 10367 Randleman Rd *Web:* holidaytoursinc.com	Randleman	NC	27317	336-498-9000	498-2204	760
Holiday Trails Resorts (Western) Inc 53730 Bridal Falls Rd *Web:* www.holidaytrailsresorts.com	Rosedale	BC	V0X1X1	604-794-7876	794-3756	121
Holiday Travel of America 6405 El Camino Real *Web:* www.htoa.com	Carlsbad	CA	92009	760-431-8600		772
Holiday Tree Farms Inc 800 NW Cornell Ave *TF:* 800-289-3684 ■ *Web:* www.holidaytreefarm.com	Corvallis	OR	97330	541-753-3236	757-8028	752
Holiday Valley Resort 6557 Holiday Valley Rd PO Box 370 *TF:* 800-323-0020 ■ *Web:* www.holidayvalley.com	Ellicottville	NY	14731	716-699-2345	699-5204	669
Holiday World & Splashin' Safari 452 E Christmas Blvd *TF:* 877-463-2645 ■ *Web:* www.holidayworld.com	Santa Claus	IN	47579	812-937-4401		32
Holihan Law 1101 N Lake Destiny Rd Ste 275 *Web:* www.holihanlaw.com	Maitland	FL	32751	407-660-8575		428
Holladay Corp 3400 Idaho Ave NW Ste 500 *Web:* holladaycorp.com	Washington	DC	20016	202-362-2400		655
Holland & Knight LLP 2115 Harden Blvd *Web:* www.hklaw.com	Lakeland	FL	33803	863-682-1161		41
Holland America Line 450 Third Ave W *TF:* 800-426-0327 ■ *Web:* www.hollandamerica.com	Seattle	WA	98119	206-281-3535	281-7110	220
Holland Area Chamber of Commerce 272 E Eigth St *Web:* www.westcoastchamber.org	Holland	MI	49423	616-392-2389	392-7379	139
Holland Area Convention & Visitors Bureau 76 E Eighth St *TF:* 800-506-1299 ■ *Web:* www.holland.org	Holland	MI	49423	616-394-0000	394-0122	206
Holland Bowl Mill 120 James St *Web:* hollandbowlmill.com	Holland	MI	49424	616-396-6513	396-0642	279
Holland College 140 Weymouth St *TF:* 800-446-5265 ■ *Web:* www.hollandcollege.com	Charlottetown	PE	C1A4Z1	902-629-4214	629-4239	162
Holland Communications Inc 7866 Deering Ave *Web:* www.holland-comm.com	Canoga Park	CA	91304	818-854-6136		4
Holland Community Hospital 602 Michigan Ave *Web:* www.hollandhospital.org	Holland	MI	49423	616-392-5141		374-3
Holland Enterprises Inc 500 Carl Olson St *TF:* 800-800-2635 ■ *Web:* www.hollandent.com	Mapleton	ND	58059	701-280-2634	280-1804	780
Holland Land Title & Abstract Company Inc 110 Pearl St *Web:* hollandtitle.com	Buffalo	NY	14202	716-853-6529	853-9870	390
Holland Law Firm LLC 300 N Tucker Blvd Ste 801 *Web:* www.hollandtriallawyers.com	Saint Louis	MO	63101	877-255-3352		41
Holland Litho Printing Service Inc 10972 Chicago Dr *TF:* 800-652-6567 ■ *Web:* www.hollandlitho.com	Zeeland	MI	49464	616-392-4644		592
Holland LP 1000 Holland Dr *TF:* 800-895-4389 ■ *Web:* www.hollandco.com	Crete	IL	60417	708-672-2300	672-0119	650
Holland Manufacturing Company Inc 15 Main St PO Box 404 *TF:* 800-345-0492 ■ *Web:* www.hollandmfg.com	Succasunna	NJ	07876	973-584-8141		732
Holland Manufacturing Company Inc 5115 W State Hwy 52 *TF:* 800-814-0937 ■ *Web:* www.hollandmfgcrane.com	Dothan	AL	36305	334-792-0937		454
Holland Patent Central School District 9601 Main St *Web:* www.hpschools.org	Holland Patent	NY	13354	315-865-7200	865-8978	685
Holland Public Schools 320 W 24th St *Web:* www.hollandpublicschools.org	Holland	MI	49423	616-494-2000	392-8225	685
Holland Sentinel 54 W Eigth St *Web:* www.hollandsentinel.com	Holland	MI	49423	616-546-4200	392-3526	532-2
Holland Society of New York (HSNY) 708 3rd Ave 6th Fl *Web:* www.hollandsociety.org	New York	NY	10017	212-758-1675	758-2232	48-13
Holland State Park 2215 Ottawa Beach Rd *Web:* www.michigan.org	Holland	MI	49424	616-399-9390		565
Holland Transportation Management Inc 305 N Center St *Web:* www.hollandtms.com	Statesville	NC	28677	704-872-4269		311
Holland's Rose 132 Griegos Rd NW *Web:* www.hollandsrose.com	Albuquerque	NM	87107	505-345-2020		372
Hollander Consultants Inc 18010 SW McEwan Rd *Web:* hollanderconsultants.wordpress.com	Lake Oswego	OR	97035	503-726-1810	726-1719	194
Hollander Glass Inc 10579 Dale Ave *Web:* www.hollanderglassinc.com	Stanton	CA	90680	714-761-5501	761-0183	191-2
Hollander Home Fashions Corp 6501 Congress Ave Ste 300 *TF:* 800-233-7666 ■ *Web:* www.hollander.com	Boca Raton	FL	33487	561-997-6900		746
Hollandia Dairy Inc 622 E Mission Rd *TF:* 888-883-2479 ■ *Web:* www.hollandiadairy.com	San Marcos	CA	92069	760-744-3222		10-3
Hollar & Greene Produce Company Inc 230 Cabbage Rd *TF:* 800-222-1077 ■ *Web:* www.hollarandgreene.com	Boone	NC	28607	828-264-2177	264-4413	297-7
Hollar Co 2012 Rainbow Dr *Web:* www.shell.com	Gadsden	AL	35901	256-547-1644		204
Holler Classic 1150 N Orlando Ave *TF:* 866-937-1398 ■ *Web:* www.hollerclassic.com	Winter Park	FL	32789	407-645-4969		57
Holley Credit Union 1107 Mineral Wells Ave *TF:* 800-426-5004 ■ *Web:* holleycreditunion.org	Paris	TN	38242	731-644-9031	642-4631	219
Holley Performance Products Inc 1801 Russellville Rd *TF:* 866-464-6553 ■ *Web:* www.holley.com	Bowling Green	KY	42101	270-782-2900	781-9940	128
Holley, Rosen, & Beard LLC 440 W South Grand Ave *TF:* 877-671-5884 ■ *Web:* holleyrosenbeard.com	Springfield	IL	62704	217-544-3368	544-5262	41
Holliday Lake State Park 2759 State Park Rd *Web:* www.dcr.virginia.gov	Appomattox	VA	24522	434-248-6308		565
Hollidaysburg Veterans Home 500 Municipal Dr *Web:* www.dmva.pa.gov	Hollidaysburg	PA	16648	814-696-5201		793

Name / Address	Phone	Fax	Class
Hollingsworth & Vose Co 112 Washington St ... East Walpole MA 02032 *Web:* www.hollingsworth-vose.com	508-850-2000		557
Hollingsworth Concrete Products Inc 920 Kingsbridge Rd ... Carrollton GA 30117 *Web:* www.hollingsworthconcreteproducts.com	770-832-2521		182
Hollingsworth Trey (Rep R - IN) 1641 Longworth House Office Bldg ... Washington DC 20515 *Web:* hollingsworth.house.gov	202-225-5315		342-2
Hollins Organic Products Inc 6247 Falls Rd ... Baltimore MD 21209 *Web:* hollinsorganic.com	410-828-0210	823-7645	274
Hollins University 7916 Williamson Rd ... Roanoke VA 24020 *TF:* 800-456-9595 ■ *Web:* www.hollins.edu	540-362-6401	362-6218	166
Hollis D. Segur Inc 156 Knotter Dr ... Cheshire CT 06410 *Web:* www.hdsegur.com	203-699-4500		390
Hollis Electronics Company LLC 5 N Blvd Ste 13 ... Amherst NH 03031 *Web:* www.holliselectronics.com	603-598-4640	598-3428	668
Hollis Industries Inc 1485 Washington St ... Holliston MA 01746	508-429-4328		454
Hollis Marketing 2130 Brenner St ... Saginaw MI 48602 *TF:* 866-797-3301 ■ *Web:* hollismarketing.com	989-797-3300		195
Hollis Social Library 2 Monument Sq ... Hollis NH 03049 *Web:* www.hollislibrary.org	603-465-7721	465-3507	434-3
Hollister Hills State Vehicular Recreation Area 7800 Cienega Rd ... Hollister CA 95023 *Web:* www.parks.ca.gov	831-637-8186		565
Hollister Inc 2000 Hollister Dr ... Libertyville IL 60048 *TF:* 800-323-4060 ■ *Web:* www.hollister.com	847-680-1000		477
Hollister Moving & Storage 2300 Technology Pkwy Ste 2 ... Hollister CA 95023 *Web:* www.hollistermovers.com	831-636-5000		519
Hollister-Whitney Elevator Corp 2603 N 24th St ... Quincy IL 62305 *Web:* www.hollisterwhitney.com	217-222-0466	222-0493	256
Holliway Insurance Agency Inc 5765 Olde Wadsworth Blvd ... Arvada CO 80002 *Web:* www.holliwayinsurance.com	303-421-3046		390
Holloman Corp 333 N Sam Houston Pkwy E Ste 600 ... Houston TX 77060 *TF:* 800-521-2461 ■ *Web:* www.hollomancorp.com	281-878-2600		186
Hollow Inn 278 S Main St ... Barre VT 05641 *Web:* www.hollowinn.com	802-479-9313	476-5242	379
Holloway Credit Solutions LLC 1286 Carmichael Way ... Montgomery AL 36106 *TF:* 800-264-2700 ■ *Web:* hollowaycredit.com	334-396-1200		218
Holloway Houston Inc 5833 Armour Dr ... Houston TX 77020 *Web:* www.hhilifting.com	713-674-5631		770
Holloway Odegard & Kelly PC 3020 E Camelback Rd Ste 201 ... Phoenix AZ 85016 *Web:* hoklaw.com	602-240-6670		41
Holloway Shunts Inc PO Box 727 ... Edna TX 77957 *Web:* www.hollowayshunts.com	361-782-3471	782-3517	248
Holloway's Real Estate Institute Inc 1161 E Clark Rd Ste 158 ... DeWitt MI 48820 *TF:* 800-292-5945 ■ *Web:* www.hollowaysinstitute.biz	517-668-6955	668-6958	167-3
Holly C. Roundtree 5001 Spring Valley Rd Ste 250E ... Dallas TX 75244 *Web:* hcroundtreecpa.com	972-404-4434		2
Holly Carlin CPA 1912 Sidewinder Ste 211A ... Park City UT 84060 *Web:* carlincpa.com	435-649-0909	608-6550	2
Holly Energy Partners LP 100 Crescent Ct Ste 1600 ... Dallas TX 75201 *TF:* 800-642-1687 ■ *Web:* www.hollyenergy.com	214-871-3555		360-5
Holly Hill Hospital 3019 Falstaff Rd ... Raleigh NC 27610 *TF:* 800-447-1800 ■ *Web:* hollyhillhospital.com	919-250-7000		374-5
Holly Hill Nursing Home 203 Lafayette St ... Anna IL 62906	618-833-3322		371
Holly Poultry Inc 2221 Berlin St ... Baltimore MD 21230 *TF:* 800-342-9464 ■ *Web:* www.hollypoultry.com	410-727-6210	727-1099	345
Holly Recreation Area 8100 Grange Hall Rd ... Holly MI 48442 *Web:* www.michigan.org	248-634-8811		565
Holly River State Park 680 State Park Rd ... Hacker Valley WV 26222 *Web:* wvstateparks.com	304-493-6353		565
Holly Shores Best Holiday 491 Rt 9 ... Cape May NJ 08204 *TF:* 877-494-6559 ■ *Web:* www.hollyshores.com	877-494-6559		707
HollyFrontier Corp *Tulsa Refinery* 1700 S Union Ave ... Tulsa OK 74107 *Web:* www.hollyfrontier.com	918-594-6000		324
Hollyhock PO Box 127 ... Mansons Landing BC V0P1K0 *TF:* 800-933-6339 ■ *Web:* hollyhock.ca	250-935-6576	935-6424	673
Hollyhock Hill 8110 N College Ave ... Indianapolis IN 46240 *Web:* www.hollyhockhill.com	317-251-2294		671
Hollymatic Corp 600 E Plainfield Rd ... Countryside IL 60525 *Web:* www.hollymatic.com	708-579-3700	579-1057	298
Hollywood & Highland 6801 Hollywood Blvd ... Hollywood CA 90028 *Web:* hollywoodandhighland.com	323-817-0200	460-6003	50-6
Hollywood Barber College 1336 W Prince Rd ... Tucson AZ 85705 *Web:* hollywoodbarbercollege.net	520-887-0532		167-3
Hollywood Bed & Spring Manufacturing Co 5959 Corvette St ... Commerce CA 90040 *Web:* www.hollywoodbed.com	323-887-9500		321
Hollywood Blvd a Cinema Bar & Eatery 1001 75th St ... Woodridge IL 60517 *Web:* www.hollywoodblvdcinema.com	630-427-1880		748
Hollywood Bowl 2301 N Highland Ave ... Hollywood CA 90068 **Fax Area Code:* 323 ■ *Web:* www.hollywoodbowl.com	213-972-3034	850-2155*	572
Hollywood Casino at Charles Town Races 750 Hollywood Dr ... Charles Town WV 25414 *TF:* 800-795-7001 ■ *Web:* www.hollywoodcasinocharlestown.com	304-725-7001		642
Hollywood Casino at Penn National Race Course 777 Hollywood Blvd ... Grantville PA 17028 *Web:* www.hollywoodpnrc.com	717-469-2211		642
Hollywood Casino Baton Rouge 1717 River Rd N ... Baton Rouge LA 70802 *TF:* 800-447-6843 ■ *Web:* hollywoodbr.com	225-709-7777		133
Hollywood Casino Bay Saint Louis 711 Hollywood Blvd ... Bay Saint Louis MS 39520 *TF:* 866-758-2591 ■ *Web:* www.hollywoodgulfcoast.com	866-758-2591		133
Hollywood Casino Joliet 777 Hollywood Blvd ... Joliet IL 60436 *TF:* 800-426-2537 ■ *Web:* www.hollywoodcasinojoliet.com	800-426-2537		133
Hollywood Chamber of Commerce 6255 Sunset Blvd Ste 150 ... Hollywood CA 90028 *Web:* www.walkoffame.com	323-469-8311		139
Hollywood Foreign Press Assn (HFPA) 646 N Robertson Blvd ... West Hollywood CA 90069 *Web:* www.goldenglobes.com	310-657-1731		48-4
Hollywood Institute of Beauty Careers 420 S State Rd 7 ... Hollywood FL 33020 *Web:* www.hi.edu	954-922-5505	922-5453	167-3
Hollywood Museum 1660 N Highland Ave ... Hollywood CA 90028 *Web:* thehollywoodmuseum.com	323-464-7776		520
Hollywood Park Land Company LLC 1050 S Prairie Ave ... Inglewood CA 90301 *Web:* www.hollywoodparklife.com	310-330-3515		642
Hollywood Records Inc 500 S Buena Vista St ... Burbank CA 91521 *Web:* www.hollywoodrecords.com	818-560-5670		657
Hollywood Reporter 5055 Wilshire Blvd Ste 500 ... Los Angeles CA 90036 *TF:* 866-525-2150 ■ *Web:* www.hollywoodreporter.com	323-525-2000	525-1453	457-9
Hollywood Roosevelt Hotel 7000 Hollywood Blvd ... Los Angeles CA 90028 *Web:* www.thehollywoodroosevelt.com	323-856-1970		379
Hollywood Scriptwriter Magazine PO Box 3761 ... Cerritos CA 90703 **Fax Area Code:* 562 ■ *Web:* www.hollywoodscriptwriter.com	310-283-1630	926-2060*	457-9
Hollywood Standard Hotel 8300 Sunset Blvd ... West Hollywood CA 90069 *Web:* www.standardhotels.com	323-650-9090		379
Hollywood Super Market Inc 2670 W Maple Rd ... Troy MI 48084 *Web:* hollywoodmarkets.com	248-643-6770	643-0309	345
Hollywood Wax Museum 3030 W Hwy 76 ... Branson MO 65616 *TF:* 800-214-3661 ■ *Web:* www.hollywoodwaxmuseum.com	417-337-8277	334-8202	520
Hollywood Woodwork Inc 2951 Pembroke Rd ... Hollywood FL 33020 *Web:* www.hollywoodwoodwork.com	954-920-5009		499
Hollywoodcom LLC 560 Broadway Ste 404 ... New York NY 10012 *Web:* www.hollywood.com	212-817-9105		387
Hol-Mac Corp PO Box 349 ... Bay Springs MS 39422 *TF:* 800-844-3019 ■ *Web:* www.hol-mac.com	601-764-4121	764-4282	223
Holman Aviation Co 1940 Airport Ct ... Great Falls MT 59404 *Web:* holmanaviation.com	406-453-7613		63
Holman Cadillac Co 1200 Rt 73 S ... Mount Laurel NJ 08054 *TF:* 866-865-6973 ■ *Web:* www.holmancadillac.com	877-209-6052		57
Holman Distribution Center of Oregon Inc 2300 SE Beta St ... Milwaukie OR 97222 *Web:* www.holmanusa.com	503-652-1912		803-1
Holman Group 9451 Corbin Ave ... Northridge CA 91324 *TF:* 800-321-2843 ■ *Web:* www.holmangroup.com	818-704-1444	704-9339	462
Holman Transportation Services Inc 1010 Holman Ct ... Caldwell ID 83605 *TF:* 800-375-2416 ■ *Web:* www.holmantransport.com	208-454-0779		780
Holman'S of Nevada Inc 3320 Sunrise Ave Ste 111 ... Las Vegas NV 89101 *Web:* www.holmansnv.com	702-222-1818		180
Holmatro Inc 505 Mccormick Dr ... Glen Burnie MD 21061 *Web:* www.holmatro.com	410-768-9662	768-4878	386
Holmberg Farms Inc 13430 Hobson Simmons Rd ... Lithia FL 33547	800-282-3562		293
Holmberg Galbraith LLP 118 N Tioga St Ste 304 ... Ithaca NY 14851 *Web:* cglawoffices.com	607-273-5475		41
Holmes Cheese Co 9444 SR 39 ... Millersburg OH 44654 *Web:* holmescheese.com	330-674-6451		296-5
Holmes Community College 1 Hill St PO Box 399 ... Goodman MS 39079 *TF:* 800-465-6374 ■ *Web:* holmescc.edu	662-472-2312		162
Holmes County Chamber of Commerce 106 E Byrd Ave ... Bonifay FL 32425 *Web:* www.chamberholmescountyflorida.com	850-547-6155		338
Holmes County Chamber of Commerce 104 W China St ... Lexington MS 39095 *Web:* holmescountymississippi.com	662-834-3372	834-4544	338
Holmes County District Public Library (HCDPL) 3102 Glen Dr ... Millersburg OH 44654 *Web:* www.holmeslibrary.org	330-674-5972	674-1938	434-3
Holmes County Law Library 1 E Jackson St Courthouse 2nd Fl Rm 204 ... Millersburg OH 44654 *Web:* cocll.ohio.gov	330-763-2956		434-3
Holmes County State Park 5369 State Park Rd ... Durant MS 39063 *Web:* www.mdwfp.com	662-653-3351		565
Holmes District School Board (HDSB) 701 E Pennsylvania Ave ... Bonifay FL 32425 *Web:* www.hdsb.org	850-547-9341		685
Holmes Firm Pc 14911 Quorum Dr ... Dallas TX 75254 *Web:* theholmesfirm.com	469-916-7700		41
Holmes Foods Inc 101 S Liberty Ave ... Nixon TX 78140 *Web:* holmesfoods.com	830-582-1551		619
Holmes Limestone Co 4255 SR 39 ... Millersburg OH 44654 *Web:* www.holmeslimestone.com	330-893-2721	893-2941	501
Holmes Murphy & Associates Inc 2727 Grand Prairie Pkwy ... Waukee IA 50263 *TF:* 800-247-7756 ■ *Web:* www.holmesmurphy.com	515-223-6800		390

				Phone	Fax	Class
Holmes Public Library 470 Plymouth St *Web:* holmespubliclibrary.org	Halifax	MA	02338	781-293-2271	294-8518	434-3
Holmes Tile & Marble Company Inc 1202 Falls St *Web:* www.holmestile.com	Jonesboro	AR	72401	870-932-8011	932-9730	290
Holmes Tool & Engineering Inc 1019 N Waukesha St *Web:* www.holmestool.com	Bonifay	FL	32425	850-547-4417	547-9329	454
Holmes-Wayne Electric Co-opeartive Inc 6060 Ohio 83 *TF:* 866-674-1055 ■ *Web:* www.hwecoop.com	Millersburg	OH	44654	330-674-1055	674-1869	245
Holming Fan & Fabrication LLC 6900 N Teutonia Ave *Web:* www.holming.com	Milwaukee	WI	53209	414-352-3250	352-1833	18
Holocaust Memorial Ctr 28123 Orchard Lake Rd *Web:* www.holocaustcenter.org	Farmington Hills	MI	48334	248-553-2400	553-2433	520
Holocaust Memorial of the Greater Miami Jewish Federation 1933-1945 Meridian Ave *Web:* www.holocaustmmb.org	Miami Beach	FL	33139	305-538-1663		50-4
Holocaust Museum Houston 5401 Caroline St *Web:* www.hmh.org	Houston	TX	77004	713-942-8000	942-7953	520
Holocaust Resource Ctr, The 601 Jefferson Ave *Web:* jewishnepa.org	Scranton	PA	18510	570-961-2300	346-0471	520
Holorad 2929 S Main St *Web:* www.holorad.com	Salt Lake City	UT	84115	801-983-6075	319-2387	382
Holsinger Law LLC 1800 Glenarm Pl Ste 500 *Web:* holsingerlaw.com	Denver	CO	80202	303-722-2828	496-1025	41
Holsted Jewelers Inc 112 W 34th St Ste 1405	New York	NY	10120	212-686-8537		195
Holstein Association USA Inc 1 Holstein Pl PO Box 808 *TF:* 800-952-5200 ■ *Web:* www.holsteinusa.com	Brattleboro	VT	05302	802-254-4551	254-8251	48-2
Holston Electric Co-opeartive Inc 1200 W Main St *Web:* www.holstonelectric.com	Rogersville	TN	37857	423-272-8821		245
Holston Gases Inc 545 W Baxter Ave *Web:* holstongases.com	Knoxville	TN	37920	865-573-1917	573-0063	385
Holsum of Fort Wayne Inc 136 Murray St *Web:* www.holsum.com	Fort Wayne	IN	46803	260-456-2130		297-8
Holt & Bugbee Co 1600 Shawsheen St **Fax Area Code:* 978 ■ *TF:* 800-325-6010 ■ *Web:* www.holtandbugbee.com	Tewksbury	MA	01876	800-325-6010	851-3941*	191-3
Holt County 204 N Fourth St PO Box 329 *Web:* www.co.holt.ne.us	O'Neill	NE	68763	402-336-1762		338
Holt County 102 W Nodaway St PO Box 437 *Web:* holtcounty.org	Oregon	MO	64473	660-446-3303	446-3353	338
Holt Integrated Circuits Inc 23351 Madero *Web:* www.holtic.com	Mission Viejo	CA	92691	949-859-8800	859-9643	696
Holt Marketing Services Inc 3075 Boardwalk Ste 2 *TF:* 800-698-2449 ■ *Web:* www.marketingholt.com	Saginaw	MI	48603	989-791-2475		463
Holt of California 7310 Pacific Ave *TF:* 800-452-5888 ■ *Web:* www.holtca.com	Pleasant Grove	CA	95668	916-921-8800	991-8290	264-3
Holt Texas Ltd 3302 S WW White Rd *TF:* 800-275-4658 ■ *Web:* www.holtcat.com	San Antonio	TX	78222	210-648-1111	648-0079	274
Holten Meat Inc 1682 Sauget Industrial Blvd *TF:* 800-851-4684 ■ *Web:* bih-us.com	Sauget	IL	62206	800-851-4684		296-26
Holter Museum of Art 12 E Lawrence St *Web:* www.holtermuseum.org	Helena	MT	59601	406-442-6400		520
Holthouse Carlin & Van Trigt LLP 355 S Grand Ave Ste 1710 *Web:* www.hcvt.com	Los Angeles	CA	90071	213-683-8790		2
Holton Livestock Exchange Inc (HLE) 13788 K-16 Hwy *Web:* www.holtonlivestock.com	Holton	KS	66436	785-364-4114	364-3088	446
Holts Cigar Co 1522 Walnut St *TF:* 800-523-1641 ■ *Web:* www.holts.com	Philadelphia	PA	19102	215-732-8500		756
Holtzman Enterprises Inc 5084 W 92nd Ave *Web:* greatclips.com	Westminster	CO	80031	303-657-6122		77
Holy Apostles College & Seminary 33 Prospect Hill Rd *Web:* www.holyapostles.edu	Cromwell	CT	06416	860-632-3077		166
Holy Apostles Convent 29001 County Road 187 *Web:* www.holyapostlesconvent.org	Buena Vista	CO	81211	719-395-8898	395-9422	637-2
Holy Cross College 54515 SR 933 N *Web:* www.hcc-nd.edu	Notre Dame	IN	46556	574-239-8400	239-8323	166
Holy Cross Energy PO Box 2150 *TF:* 877-833-2555 ■ *Web:* www.holycross.com	Glenwood Springs	CO	81602	970-945-5491	945-4081	245
Holy Cross Family Ministries 518 Washington St *TF:* 800-299-7729 ■ *Web:* www.hcfm.org	North Easton	MA	02356	508-238-4095		48-20
Holy Cross Hospital 2701 W 68th St *Web:* www.holycrosshospital.org	Chicago	IL	60629	773-884-9000		374-3
Holy Cross Hospital 4725 N Federal Hwy *Web:* www.holy-cross.com	Fort Lauderdale	FL	33308	954-771-8000	492-5741	374-3
Holy Cross Hospital 1500 Forest Glen Rd *Web:* www.holycrosshealth.org	Silver Spring	MD	20910	301-754-7000	754-7012	374-3
Holy Cross Monastery 1615 Rt 9W *Web:* holycrossmonastery.com	West Park	NY	12493	845-384-6660		673
Holy Cross Village At Notre Dame 54515 SR 933N *Web:* www.holycrossvillage.com	Notre Dame	IN	46556	574-287-1838		672
Holy Family Institute 8235 Ohio River Blvd *Web:* www.hfi-pgh.org	Pittsburgh	PA	15202	412-766-4030		242

				Phone	Fax	Class
Holy Family Memorial 2300 Western Ave PO Box 1450 *TF:* 800-994-3662 ■ *Web:* hfmhealth.org	Manitowoc	WI	54221	920-320-2011		48-5
Holy Family University 9801 Frankford Ave *TF:* 800-422-0010 ■ *Web:* www.holyfamily.edu	Philadelphia	PA	19114	215-637-7700		166
Holy Land Restaurant 677 Rand Ave *Web:* www.orderholylandrestaurant.com	Oakland	CA	94610	510-272-0535		671
Holy Name Hospital 718 Teaneck Rd *Web:* www.holyname.org	Teaneck	NJ	07666	201-833-3000		374-3
Holy Names University 3500 Mountain Blvd *TF:* 800-430-1321 ■ *Web:* www.hnu.edu	Oakland	CA	94619	510-436-1000	436-1325	166
Holy Redeemer Home Care & Hospice 12265 Townsend Rd Ste 400 *TF:* 888-678-8678 ■ *Web:* www.holyredeemer.com	Philadelphia	PA	19154	888-678-8678		371
Holy See 25 E 39th St *Web:* holyseemission.org	New York	NY	10016	212-370-7885	370-9622	784
Holy Spirit Catholic School 540 N 7th Ave *Web:* hscssa.org	Pocatello	ID	83201	208-232-5763		48-20
Holy Trinity Catholic Church 315 Marshall St *Web:* www.holytrinity-shreveport.com	Shreveport	LA	71101	318-221-5990		50-1
Holy Trinity Seminary Library PO Box 36 *Web:* www.hts.edu	Jordanville	NY	13361	315-858-0945		434-3
Holyoke Community College 303 Homestead Ave *TF:* 800-325-3252 ■ *Web:* www.hcc.edu	Holyoke	MA	01040	413-538-7000	552-2192	162
Holyoke Heritage State Park 221 Appleton St *Web:* www.mass.gov	Holyoke	MA	01040	413-534-1723		565
Holyoke Machine Co 514 Main St PO Box 988 *Web:* www.holyokemachine.com	Holyoke	MA	01040	413-534-5612	532-9244	556
Holyoke Mall at Ingleside 50 Holyoke St *Web:* www.holyokemall.com	Holyoke	MA	01040	413-536-1441		460
Holyoke Medical Ctr 575 Beech St *Web:* www.holyokehealth.com	Holyoke	MA	01040	413-534-2500		374-3
Holyoke Public Library 250 Chestnut St *Web:* www.holyokelibrary.org	Holyoke	MA	01040	413-420-8101		434-3
Holyoke Soldiers Home 110 Cherry St *Web:* www.mass.gov	Holyoke	MA	01040	413-532-9475	538-7968	793
Holz Motors Inc 5961 S 108th Pl *Web:* www.holzmotors.com	Hales Corners	WI	53130	414-425-2400		57
Holz Rubber Company Inc 1129 S Sacramento St *TF:* 800-285-1600 ■ *Web:* www.holzrubber.com	Lodi	CA	95240	209-368-7171	368-3246	677
Holzer Health Systems 100 Jackson Pk *Web:* www.holzer.org	Gallipolis	OH	45631	740-446-5000		374-3
Holzmueller Productions 1000 25th St *Web:* www.holzmueller.com	San Francisco	CA	94107	415-826-8383	826-2608	722
Homa & Sekey Books 140 E Ridgewood Ave Mack-Cali Center III 3rd Fl North Twr *TF:* 800-870-4662 ■ *Web:* www.homabooks.com	Paramus	NJ	07652	201-261-8810	384-6055	637-2
Homak Manufacturing LLC 1605 Old Rt 18 Ste 4-36 *TF:* 800-874-6625 ■ *Web:* www.homak.com	Wampum	PA	16157	800-874-6625		350
Homark Company Inc, The PO Box 309 *TF:* 800-382-1154 ■ *Web:* www.homark.com	Red Lake Falls	MN	56750	218-253-2777	253-2116	505
Homasote Co 932 Lower Ferry Rd PO Box 7240 *OTC:* HMTC ■ *TF:* 800-257-9491 ■ *Web:* www.homasote.com	West Trenton	NJ	08628	609-883-3300	883-3497	819
Homax Oil Sales Inc 605 S Poplar St *TF:* 800-269-9824 ■ *Web:* www.homaxoil.com	Casper	WY	82601	307-237-5800		579
Homax Products Inc 1835 Barkley Blvd Ste 101 *TF:* 888-890-9029 ■ *Web:* www.homaxproducts.com	Bellingham	WA	98226	800-729-9029		146
Homcare Inc 875 W Summit Ave *Web:* homcareinc.com	Muskegon	MI	49441	231-755-6951	755-4507	363
Home & Away Magazine 10703 J St Ste 100 *Web:* www.homeandawaymagazine.com	Omaha	NE	68127	402-592-5000		457-22
Home & Garden Showplace 8600 W Bryn Mawr *Web:* www.truevaluecompany.com	Chicago	IL	60631	773-695-5000		323
Home & Hearth 2090 E Main St *Web:* www.homeandhearth-mainst.com	Cortlandt Manor	NY	10567	914-734-9773		321
Home & Truck Accessory Centers 43 Airpark Ct *TF:* 888-232-8358 ■ *Web:* www.hhsales.com	Alabaster	AL	35007	888-232-8358	443-6878	61
Home Accents Mart 5521 McFarland Blvd *Web:* www.homeaccentsonline.com	Northport	AL	35476	205-339-6550		362
Home Aides of Central New York Inc 723 James St *TF:* 888-477-4663 ■ *Web:* www.nascentiahealth.org	Syracuse	NY	13203	315-476-4295		363
Home Automated Living Inc 14401 Sweitzer Ln Ste 600 *TF:* 800-935-5313 ■ *Web:* www.automatedliving.com	Laurel	MD	20707	301-498-7000	498-4619	174
Home Automation Inc 4330 Michoud Blvd *Web:* www.leviton.com	New Orleans	LA	70129	504-736-9810	253-2955	425
Home Bank 601 N Hwy 175 *Web:* www.homebanktx.com	Seagoville	TX	75159	972-287-2030		70
Home Banking Co 795 E Poplar *Web:* homebankingco.com	Selmer	TN	38375	731-645-6166		70
Home Bound Healthcare Inc 14216 McCarthy Rd *TF:* 800-444-7028 ■ *Web:* www.homeboundhealth.com	Lemont	IL	60439	708-798-0800		363
Home Care Equipment Inc 1135 Lester St *TF:* 800-457-4131 ■ *Web:* homecareinc.net	Poplar Bluff	MO	63901	573-686-3720	686-2929	475

	Phone	Fax	Class
Home Care Network Inc 190A E Spring Valley Rd.....Centerville OH 45458 *TF:* 800-417-0291 ■ *Web:* www.hcnmidwest.net	937-435-1142		363
Home Care Partners 1234 Massachusetts Ave NW Ste C-1002.....Washington DC 20005 *Web:* www.homecarepartners.org	202-638-2382		363
Home Care Specialists Inc 113 Neck Rd.....Haverhill MA 01835 **Fax Area Code:* 866 ■ *TF:* 800-698-8113 ■ *Web:* www.hcshme.com	978-373-7771	372-0380*	475
Home City Development Inc 261 Oak Grove Ave.....Springfield MA 01109 *Web:* homecitydevelopment.org	413-785-5312		653
Home Comfort Furniture & Mattress Center Inc 7016 Glenwood Ave.....Raleigh NC 27612 *Web:* www.homecomfortfurniture.com	919-781-3900		321
Home Crafts Inc 760 Railroad Ave.....West Babylon NY 11704 *Web:* www.chimneyco.com	631-669-0141	669-0351	612
Home Crest Cabinetry 1002 Eisenhower Dr N.....Goshen IN 46526 *Web:* www.homecrestcabinetry.com	574-535-9300		115
Home Depot Inc 2455 Paces Ferry Rd NW.....Atlanta GA 30339 *NYSE: HD* ■ *TF:* 800-553-3199 ■ *Web:* www.homedepot.com	770-433-8211		364
Home Depot Supply 2455 Paces Ferry Rd SE Ste B3.....Atlanta GA 30339 *Web:* www.hdsupply.com	770-852-9000		351
Home Design Outlet Ctr 400 County Ave.....Secaucus NJ 07094 *TF:* 800-701-0388 ■ *Web:* homedesignoutletcenter.com	800-701-0388		361
Home Dynamix 100 Porete Ave.....North Arlington NJ 07031 *TF:* 800-726-9290 ■ *Web:* www.homedynamix.com	800-726-9290		131
Home Entertainment 120 Shawmut Rd.....Canton MA 02021 *Web:* www.homeentertainment-canton-ma.brandsdirect.com	781-821-0087		38
Home Essentials & Beyond Inc 200 Theodore Conrad Dr.....Jersey City NJ 07305 *TF:* 800-417-6218 ■ *Web:* www.homeessentials.com	732-590-3600		361
Home Federal Bank 1602 Cumberland Ave.....Middlesboro KY 40965 *OTC: HFBA* ■ *TF:* 800-354-0182 ■ *Web:* www.homefederalbank.com	606-248-1095	242-1010	360-2
Home Federal Bank 221 S Locust St.....Grand Island NE 68801 *Web:* www.homefederalne.bank	308-382-4000		71
Home Federal Savings Bank 303 W Main St.....Marshalltown IA 50158 *Web:* www.justcallhome.com	641-754-6198	754-6161	70
Home Furnishings Independents Assn (HFIA) 500 Giuseppe Ct Ste 6.....Roseville CA 95678 *TF:* 800-422-3778 ■ *Web:* myhfa.org	800-422-3778		49-4
Home Furniture Mart 5301 Sheila St.....Commerce CA 90040 *TF:* 800-610-6605 ■ *Web:* www.homefurnituremart.com	800-610-6605		791
Home Hardware Inc 140 Center St.....Ashland OH 44805 *Web:* farmandhomehardware.com	419-281-4663		351
Home Health & Hospice Care 7 Executive Park Dr.....Merrimack NH 03054 *TF:* 800-887-5973 ■ *Web:* www.hhhc.org	603-882-2941		371
Home Health Management Services Inc 30 Broad St 12th Fl.....New York NY 10004 *Web:* profiles.health.ny.gov	212-952-9292		363
Home Health Mates 5421 Beaumont Center Blvd Ste 620.....Tampa FL 33634 *Web:* www.homehealthmates.com	813-884-5040	884-5168	363
Home Health Resources Inc (HHR) 18338 Kingsland Blvd Ste 100.....Houston TX 77094 *TF:* 800-720-6592 ■ *Web:* www.homehealthresources.com	281-398-3444	398-6830	363
Home Healthcare, Hospice & Community Services Inc 312 Marlboro St.....Keene NH 03431 *TF:* 800-541-4145 ■ *Web:* hcsservices.org	603-352-2253		363
Home Hospice of Grayson County 505 W Center St.....Sherman TX 75090 *TF:* 888-233-7455 ■ *Web:* www.homehospice.org	903-868-9315	893-2772	371
Home Instead Inc 13323 California St.....Omaha NE 68154 *TF:* 888-484-5759 ■ *Web:* www.homeinstead.com	402-498-4466		363
Home Light 100 1st St Ste 2600.....San Francisco CA 94105 *TF:* 855-999-7971 ■ *Web:* www.homelight.com	855-999-7971		509
Home Loan Advocates Inc 143 Triunfo Canyon Rd Ste 227.....Westlake Village CA 91361 *Web:* homeloanadvocates.com	805-413-8000		217
Home Loan Financial Corp 413 Main St.....Coshocton OH 43812 *OTC: HLFN* ■ *Web:* www.homeloansavingsbank.com	740-622-0444	623-6000	360-2
Home Lumber Company Inc 60 Ky Hwy 451.....Hazard KY 41702 *TF:* 800-467-0185 ■ *Web:* www.homelumberhazard.com	606-436-3185		364
Home Market Foods Inc 140 Morgan Dr.....Norwood MA 02062 *TF:* 800-367-8325 ■ *Web:* www.homemarketfoods.com	781-948-1500		296-36
Home Medix Inc 3811 Atlantic Ave.....Long Beach CA 90807 **Fax Area Code:* 888 ■ *TF:* 800-403-1010 ■ *Web:* www.homemedix.com	800-403-1010	553-0051*	45
Home Meridian Intl 2485 Penny Rd.....High Point NC 27265 *Web:* www.homemeridian.com	336-819-7200		787
Home News Enterprises 333 Second St.....Columbus IN 47201 *TF:* 800-876-7811 ■ *Web:* homenewsenterprises.com	800-876-7811		637-8
Home News Tribune 92 E Main St.....Somerville NJ 08876 *Web:* www.mycentraljersey.com	908-243-6600		532-2
Home Nursing Company Inc Russell Co Shopping Center 1770 E Main St.....Lebanon VA 24266 *TF:* 800-344-2668 ■ *Web:* www.homenursinginc.com	276-889-4318	889-0403	363
Home Nursing With Heart PC 7602 Park Dr.....Ralston NE 68127 *Web:* homenursingwithheart.com	402-614-4622	614-4726	363
Home of Franklin D Roosevelt National Historic Site 4097 Albany Post Rd.....Hyde Park NY 12538 *Web:* www.nps.gov	845-229-9115		564
Home Paramount Pest Control Companies Inc PO Box 850.....Forest Hill MD 21050 *TF:* 888-888-4663 ■ *Web:* www.homeparamount.com	410-510-0700		577
Home Patient Services 8240 McCormick Blvd.....Skokie IL 60076 *TF:* 877-946-6362 ■ *Web:* www.homepatientservices.com	847-673-5511	673-5566	363
Home Place Inc 9604 Hwy 31.....Warrior AL 35180 *Web:* www.thehomeplaceinc.com	205-543-6556		505
Home Pro Systems Inc 2841 Hartland Rd Ste 200.....Falls Church VA 22043 *TF:* 800-466-3776 ■ *Web:* www.homeproservices.com	703-560-4663	992-7927	393
Home Products International Inc 4501 W 47th St.....Chicago IL 60632 *TF:* 800-457-9881 ■ *Web:* www.homzproducts.com	773-890-8923		607
Home Properties Inc 850 Clinton Sq.....Rochester NY 14604 *NYSE: HME*	585-546-4900		655
Home Ranch PO Box 822.....Clark CO 80428 *Web:* www.homeranch.com	970-879-1780	879-1795	239
Home Reporter Inc 9733 4th Ave.....Brooklyn NY 11209 *Web:* brooklynreporter.com	718-238-6600		532-2
Home Run Auto Group 2627 Morse St.....Saint Janesville WI 53545 *Web:* www.homerunautogroup.com	715-341-2440		57
Home Run Inn Frozen Foods Corp 1300 International Pkwy.....Woodridge IL 60517 *Web:* www.homeruninnpizza.com	630-783-9696		296-36
Home Staff Health Services 40 Millbrook St.....Worcester MA 01606 *TF:* 800-779-3312 ■ *Web:* www.homestaffma.com	800-779-3312		363
Home Staff Inc 5509 N Cumberland Ave Ste 514.....Chicago IL 60656 *TF:* 888-806-6924 ■ *Web:* homestaffinc.com	773-467-6002	467-6003	363
Home State Bank 202 Third Ave PO Box 79.....Royal IA 51357 *Web:* hsbroyal.com	712-933-5511		70
Home Style Media LLC 2040 S Alma School Rd.....Chandler AZ 85286 *Web:* www.homestylemedia.com	615-916-1149		637-9
Home Team Marketing LLC 812 Huron Rd E Ste 205.....Cleveland OH 44115 *TF:* 866-810-2111	216-566-8326		195
Home Tester, The 10555 SW Tigard St Apt 57.....Tigard OR 97223 *Web:* www.thehometester.com	503-515-1833		104
Home Training Tools Ltd 665 Carbon St.....Billings MT 59102 *TF:* 800-860-6272 ■ *Web:* homesciencetools.com	800-860-6272		366
Home Trends Magazine 107 N Kirby St.....Garland TX 75042 **Fax Area Code:* 833 ■ *Web:* hometrendsmag.net	469-445-1544	712-3980*	637-9
HomeAdvisor Inc 14023 Denver W Pkwy Ste 200.....Golden CO 80401 *TF:* 800-474-1596 ■ *Web:* www.homeadvisor.com	303-963-7200	980-3003	397
Homeart 6419 Mc Pherson.....Laredo TX 78045 *Web:* www.homearte.com	956-791-8453	727-0986	115
HomeCare & Hospice 1225 W State St.....Olean NY 14760 *TF:* 800-339-7011 ■ *Web:* www.homecare-hospice.org	716-372-5735		371
Homecare Homebase LLC 6688 N Central Expy Ste 800.....Dallas TX 75206 *TF:* 866-535-4242 ■ *Web:* www.hchb.com	214-239-6700	239-6799	363
Homecare of Mid Missouri Inc 102 W Reed St.....Moberly MO 65270 *TF:* 800-246-6400 ■ *Web:* homecaremidmo.com	660-263-1517		363
Homecare Pharmacy LLC 1006 Woodward Ave.....Beloit WI 53511 *TF:* 800-579-6700 ■ *Web:* www.homecarepharmacy.net	608-362-1234	362-2744	237
Homecrest Outdoor Living 1250 Homecrest Ave.....Wadena MN 56482 *Web:* www.homecrest.com	218-631-1000		319-4
Homed Care Inc 419 W 49 St Ste 200.....Hialeah FL 33012 *Web:* www.homedcareinc.com	305-769-3334		363
Homee Inc 1413 S Howard Ave Ste 220.....Tampa FL 33606 *TF:* 855-964-6633 ■ *Web:* www.homee.com	855-964-6633		652
HomeGaincom Inc 1820 Bonanza St.....Walnut Creek CA 94596 *TF:* 888-542-0800 ■ *Web:* www2.homegain.com	510-655-0800	655-0848	652
Homegate Realty of Reno LLC 8755 Technology Way Ste I.....Reno NV 89521 *Web:* homegaterealty.com	775-826-9696		652
Homeland Vinyl Products Inc 3300 Pinson Valley Pkwy.....Birmingham AL 35217 *TF:* 800-999-6813 ■ *Web:* homelandvinyl.com	800-999-6813		596
Homelegance Inc 495 S Grand Central Pkwy Ste 625A.....Las Vegas NV 89106 *Web:* www.homelegance.com	702-384-2740		321
Homeplace Ranch RR 1 Site 2.....Priddis AB T0L1W0 *Web:* www.homeplaceranch.com	403-969-4444		239
HomEquity Bank 1881 Yonge St Ste 300.....Toronto ON M4S3C4 *TF:* 866-522-2447 ■ *Web:* www.homequitybank.ca	416-925-4757		69
Homer Central School District 80 S W St.....Homer NY 13077 *Web:* www.homercentral.org	607-749-7241		685
Homer Electric Association Inc 3977 Lake St.....Homer AK 99603 *TF:* 800-478-8551 ■ *Web:* www.homerelectric.com	907-235-8551	235-3313	245
Homer Group, The 2605 Egypt Rd.....Trooper PA 19403 *Web:* www.homergroup.com	610-539-8400		344
Homer Optical Company Inc 2401 Linden Ln.....Silver Spring MD 20910 *TF:* 800-627-2710 ■ *Web:* www.homeroptical.com	301-585-9060	585-5934	542
Homer Public Library 500 Hazel Ave.....Homer AK 99603 *TF:* 800-478-4441 ■ *Web:* www.cityofhomer-ak.gov	907-235-3180	235-3136	434-3
Homes & Land Magazine Affiliates LLC 1830 E Park Ave.....Tallahassee FL 32301 *TF:* 800-277-7800 ■ *Web:* www.homesandland.com	850-701-2300		637-9
Homes by Keystone Inc 13338 Midvale Rd PO Box 69.....Waynesboro PA 17268 *TF:* 800-890-7926 ■ *Web:* homesbykeystone.com	800-890-7926		106
Homescom 150 Granby St.....Norfolk VA 23510 *Web:* www.homes.com	757-351-7000		387
HomeServices of America Inc 333 S Seventh St 27th Fl.....Minneapolis MN 55402 *TF:* 888-485-0018 ■ *Web:* www.homeservices.com	888-485-0018		652
Homeside Hospice LLC 67 Walnut Ave Ste 205.....Clark NJ 07066 *Web:* www.homesidehospice.com	732-381-3444	381-3445	450
Homeslice Media Group 660 Flormann St Ste 100.....Rapid City SD 57701 *Web:* www.thehomeslicegroup.com	605-343-6161		647

Company	Address	City	State	ZIP	Phone	Fax	Class	Additional
HomeSmart International LLC	8388 E Hartford Dr Ste 100	Scottsdale	AZ	85255	602-230-7600		652	*TF:* 800-865-9025 ■ *Web:* homesmart.com
Homesnap	7200 Wisconsin Ave Ste 200	Bethesda	MD	20814	800-431-5509		652	*TF:* 800-431-5509 ■ *Web:* www.homesnap.com
Homestate Mortgage Company LLC	3801 Centerpoint Dr Ste 100	Anchorage	AK	99503	907-273-7390		653	*Web:* krishughes.net
Homestead	PO Box 29	Napoleon	ND	58561	701-754-2212		532-2	*Web:* www.napoleonnd.com
Homestead Baking Co	145 N Broadway	Rumford	RI	02916	401-434-0551	438-0542	296-1	*TF:* 800-556-7216 ■ *Web:* homesteadbaking.com
Homestead Custom Computing	PO Box 49 HC 70	Hay Springs	NE	69347	308-638-4690		180	*Web:* www.homesteadcustom.com
Homestead Inn	420 Field Pt Rd	Greenwich	CT	06830	203-869-7500	869-7502	379	*Web:* www.homesteadinn.com
Homestead Mills	221 N River St PO Box 1115	Cook	MN	55723	218-666-5233	666-5236	296-4	*TF:* 800-652-5233 ■ *Web:* www.homesteadmills.com
Homestead National Monument of America	8523 W State Hwy 4	Beatrice	NE	68310	402-223-3514	228-4231	564	*Web:* www.nps.gov
Homestead Pasta Co	315 S Maple Ave Ste 106	South San Francisco	CA	94080	650-615-0750	615-0764	296-36	*Web:* homesteadpasta.com
Homestead Resort	700 N Homestead Dr	Midway	UT	84049	435-654-1102		669	*TF:* 800-327-7220 ■ *Web:* homesteadresort.com
Homestead Resort, The	1 Wood Ridge Rd	Glen Arbor	MI	49636	231-334-5000	334-5246	669	*Web:* www.thehomesteadresort.com
Homestead Technologies Inc	180 Jefferson Dr	Menlo Park	CA	94025	888-888-8888		808	*TF:* 800-797-2958 ■ *Web:* www.homestead.com
Homesteaders Life Co	PO Box 1756	Des Moines	IA	50306	515-440-7777	440-7695	510	*TF:* 800-477-3633 ■ *Web:* www.homesteaderslife.com
Homestead-Miami Speedway	1 Ralph Sanchez Speedway Blvd	Homestead	FL	33035	305-230-5000	230-5140	515	*TF:* 866-409-7223 ■ *Web:* www.homesteadmiamispeedway.com
HomeSteps	500 Plano Pkwy	Carrollton	TX	75010	800-972-7555		509	*TF:* 800-972-7555 ■ *Web:* www.homesteps.com
HomeStreet Bank	601 Union St Ste 2000	Seattle	WA	98101	206-623-3050		70	*TF:* 800-654-1075 ■ *Web:* www.homestreet.com
Homestyles Media Inc	451 Hungerford Dr Ste 350	Rockville	MD	20850	240-328-6275	499-8362	637-9	*Web:* www.homeanddesign.com
HomeTeam Inspection Service Inc	575 Chamber Dr	Milford	OH	45150	800-598-5297		365	*TF:* 800-598-5297 ■ *Web:* www.hometeam.com
Hometown America LLC	150 N Wacker Dr Ste 2800	Chicago	IL	60606	312-604-7500	604-7501	505	*TF:* 877-941-2602 ■ *Web:* www.hometownamerica.com
Hometown Bank	245 N Peters Ave	Fond du Lac	WI	54935	920-907-2220		70	*Web:* www.htbwi.com
Hometown Bank of Pennsylvania	638 E Pitt St	Bedford	PA	15522	814-623-6093		70	*Web:* hometownbankpa.com
Hometown Foods USA Inc	11800 NW 102nd Rd Ste 6	Medley	FL	33178	305-887-5200		296-1	*Web:* hometownfoodsusa.com
Hometown News Corp	PO Box 789	Zebulon	GA	30295	770-567-3446	567-8814	532-2	*Web:* www.pikecountygeorgia.com
Hometown Quotes LLC	304 Inverness wy S Ste 395	Englewood	CO	80112	800-820-2981	601-1851*	390	**Fax Area Code:* 310 ■ *TF:* 800-820-2981 ■ *Web:* hometownquotes.com
Hometown Radio Inc	4712 State Rte 9	Plattsburgh	NY	12901	518-563-1340	563-1343	645-141	*Web:* www.wiry.com
Hometown Sportswear	3692 Us Rt 60 E	Barboursville	WV	25504	304-736-4021		711	*Web:* www.htswr.com
Hometown Toys LLC	6817 French Hill Rd NW	Dover	OH	44622	330-343-8699		327	
Hometrust Bank, The	10 Woodfin St PO Box 10	Asheville	NC	28802	828-259-3939		70	*TF:* 800-627-1632 ■ *Web:* www.htb.com
HomeVestors of America Inc	6500 Greenville Ave Ste 400	Dallas	TX	75206	972-761-0046	761-9022	310	*TF:* 866-200-6475 ■ *Web:* www.homevestors.com
Homewatch CareGivers	6251 Greenwood Plz Blvd Ste 250	Greenwood Village	CO	80111	844-220-0887		363	*TF:* 800-777-9770 ■ *Web:* www.homewatchcaregivers.com
Homewood at Williamsport	16505 Virginia Ave	Williamsport	MD	21795	301-582-1750		672	*TF:* 877-849-9244 ■ *Web:* www.homewood.com
Homewood Disposal Service Inc	1501 W 175th St	Homewood	IL	60430	708-798-1004		804	*Web:* www.mydisposal.com
Homewood FSB	3228-30 Eastern Ave	Baltimore	MD	21224	410-327-5220	558-1719	70	*Web:* www.homewoodfsb.com
Homewood Museum	Johns Hopkins University 3400 N Charles St	Baltimore	MD	21218	410-516-5589	516-7859	520	*Web:* www.museums.jhu.edu
HomeworkNOW.com	6 Elton Ave	Stratham	NH	03885	888-397-6297		178-1	*TF:* 888-397-6297 ■ *Web:* www.homeworknow.com
Hominy Grill	207 Rutledge Ave	Charleston	SC	29403	843-937-0930		671	*Web:* hominygrill.com
Homosassa Springs Wildlife State Park	4150 S Suncoast Blvd	Homosassa	FL	34446	352-628-5343	628-4243	565	*Web:* www.floridastateparks.org
Homrich & Berg Inc	3060 Peachtree Rd Ste 830	Atlanta	GA	30305	404-264-1400		194	*Web:* www.homrichberg.com
Homtex Inc	15295 Al Hwy 157	Vinemont	AL	35179	256-734-3937		745-1	*Web:* www.homtex.com
HON Co	200 Oak St	Muscatine	IA	52761	563-272-7100		319-1	*TF:* 800-553-8230 ■ *Web:* www.hon.com
HonBlue Inc	501 Sumner St Ste 3B1	Honolulu	HI	96817	808-531-4611	528-1248	112	*Web:* www.honblue.com
Honda Aircraft Company Inc	6430 Ballinger Rd	Greensboro	NC	27410	336-662-0246		20	*TF:* 888-453-5937 ■ *Web:* www.hondajet.com
Honda Carland	11085 Alpharetta Hwy	Roswell	GA	30076	770-993-2805		57	*Web:* www.hondacarland.com
Honda Ctr	2695 E Katella Ave	Anaheim	CA	92806	714-704-2400		720	*Web:* www.hondacenter.com
Honda Manufacturing of Alabama LLC	1800 Honda Dr	Lincoln	AL	35096	205-355-5000		59	*Web:* www.hondaalabama.com
Honda of Santa Monica	1301 Santa Monica Blvd	Santa Monica	CA	90404	800-269-2031		57	*TF:* 800-269-2031 ■ *Web:* www.hondaofsantamonica.com
Honda of Tiffany Springs	9200 NW Prairie View Rd	Kansas City	MO	64153	816-452-7000		516	*Web:* www.hondaoftiffanysprings.com
Honda Precision Parts of Georgia LLC	550 Honda Pkwy	Tallapoosa	GA	30176	770-574-3400		489	
Honda World	10645 Studebaker Rd	Downey	CA	90241	562-929-7000		57	*TF:* 888-458-9404 ■ *Web:* www.lahondaworld.com
Hondros College of Nursing	4140 Executive Pkwy	Westerville	OH	43081	855-906-8773		166	*TF:* 855-906-8773 ■ *Web:* www.hondros.edu
Honduras	*Embassy* 3007 Tilden St NW	Washington	DC	20008	202-966-7702	966-9751	257	*Web:* www.hondurasemb.org
Honduras Consulate General	3550 Wilshire Blvd Ste 918	Los Angeles	CA	90010	213-995-6406	995-6407	257	*Web:* www.consulate-los-angeles.com
Honegger Ringger & Company Inc	1905 N Main St	Bluffton	IN	46714	260-824-4107		2	*TF:* 888-853-5906 ■ *Web:* www.hrc-cpa.com
Honey	963 E 4th St	Los Angeles	CA	90013	213-375-4244		39	*Web:* www.joinhoney.com
Honey Acres	1557 Hwy 67 N	Ashippun	WI	53003	800-558-7746		296-24	*TF:* 800-558-7745 ■ *Web:* www.honeyacres.com
Honey Baked Ham Company LLC, The	1081 E Long Lake Rd	Troy	MI	48098	248-689-4890	689-1913	345	*TF:* 800-367-7720 ■ *Web:* www.honeybaked.com
Honey Bee Manufacturing Ltd	PO Box 120	Frontier	SK	S0N0W0	306-296-2297	296-2165	274	*TF:* 855-330-2019 ■ *Web:* www.honeybee.ca
Honey Creek State Park	12194 Honey Creek Pl	Moravia	IA	52571	641-724-3739	724-9846	565	*Web:* www.iowadnr.gov
Honey Creek State Park	901 State Park Rd	Grove	OK	74344	918-786-9447	787-5634	565	*Web:* www.travelok.com
Honey Dew Associates Inc	2 Taunton St	Plainville	MA	02762	508-699-3900	699-3949	68	*TF:* 800-946-6393 ■ *Web:* www.honeydewdonuts.com
Honey Farms Inc	505 Pleasant St	Worcester	MA	01609	508-753-7678		297-8	*Web:* www.myhoneyfarms.com
Honeycomb Company of America Inc	1950 Limbus Ave	Sarasota	FL	34243	941-756-8781		22	*Web:* www.hcoainc.com
Honeygo Animal Hospital Inc	11541 Philadelphia Rd	White Marsh	MD	21162	410-248-0442		794	*Web:* honeygoanimalhospital.com
Honeyman Aluminum Products Co	7715 NE 21st Ave	Portland	OR	97211	503-285-6446	285-6200	470	*Web:* www.honeymanaluminum.com
Honeys Place Inc	640 Glenoaks Blvd	San Fernando	CA	91340	800-910-3246		231	*TF:* 800-910-3246 ■ *Web:* www.honeysplace.com
Honeytree Inc	8570 W Monroe Rd	Onsted	MI	49265	517-467-2482		296-24	*TF:* 800-968-1889 ■ *Web:* www.honeytreehoney.com
Honeyville Grain Inc	1040 W 600 N	Ogden	UT	84404	385-374-9400	298-0133	296-4	*TF:* 888-810-3212 ■ *Web:* honeyville.com
Honeyville Metal Inc	4200 South 900 West	Topeka	IN	46571	800-593-8377	593-2486*	18	**Fax Area Code:* 260 ■ *TF:* 800-593-8377 ■ *Web:* www.honeyvillemetal.com
Honeyware Inc	244 Dukes St	Kearny	NJ	07032	201-997-5900	997-4420	604	*TF:* 800-525-5905 ■ *Web:* www.honeyware.com
Honeywell International Inc	115 Tabor Rd	Morris Plains	NJ	07950	480-353-3020		246	*TF:* 877-841-2840 ■ *Web:* www.honeywell.com
Honeywood Winery	1350 Hines St SE	Salem	OR	97302	503-362-4111		50-7	*TF:* 800-726-4101 ■ *Web:* www.honeywoodwinery.com
Hong Kong Buffet	927 E N St	Rapid City	SD	57701	605-716-4664		671	
Hong Kong Chinese Restaurant	1055 E Interstate Ave	Bismarck	ND	58503	701-223-2130		671	*Web:* www.hongkongnd.com
Hong Kong Tea House	565 W 200 S	Salt Lake City	UT	84101	801-531-7010	531-7033	671	*Web:* hongkongteahouse.yolasite.com
Hong Kong Tourism Board	115 E 54th St 2nd Fl	New York	NY	10022	212-421-3382		775	*Web:* www.discoverhongkong.com
Honig Conte Porrino Insurance Agency Inc (HCP)	129 W 27th St	New York	NY	10001	212-777-7113		390	*Web:* honigconte.com
Honigman Miller Schwartz & Cohn LLP	660 Woodward Ave Ste 2290	Detroit	MI	48226	313-465-7000		41	*Web:* www.honigman.com
Honiron Corp	400 Canal St	Jeanerette	LA	70544	337-276-6314		273	*Web:* www.honiron.com
Honkamp Krueger & Company PC	2345 JFK Rd PO Box 699	Dubuque	IA	52004	563-556-0123	556-8762	2	*TF:* 888-556-0123 ■ *Web:* www.honkamp.com
Honolulu Academy of Arts	900 S Beretania St	Honolulu	HI	96814	808-532-8700		520	*Web:* honolulumuseum.org
Honolulu Advertiser	500 Ala Moana Blvd Ste 7-210	Honolulu	HI	96813	808-529-4747		532-2	*TF:* 800-801-5999 ■ *Web:* staradvertiser.com

Phone | Fax | Class

Honolulu Botanical Gardens
50 N Vineyard Blvd — Honolulu HI 96817 — 808-768-3003 768-3053 97
Web: www.honolulu.gov

Honolulu City & County
832 S Hotel St — Honolulu HI 96813 — 808-768-3810 768-3835 338
Web: www.honolulu.gov

Honolulu City Hall 530 S King St — Honolulu HI 96813 — 808-768-4141 768-5552 337
Web: www.honolulu.gov

Honolulu Ford Lincoln & Mercury
1370 N King St — Honolulu HI 96817 — 808-824-3973 57
Web: www.honoluluford.com

Honolulu Information Service Inc
1136 Union Mall Ste 301 — Honolulu HI 96813 — 808-524-4488 524-4499 387
Web: www.honinfo.com

Honolulu Magazine
1000 Bishop St Ste 405 — Honolulu HI 96813 — 808-534-7546 457-22
TF: 800-788-4230 ■ *Web:* www.honolulumagazine.com

Honolulu Nail Academy
438 Hobron Ln Ste 207-208 — Honolulu HI 96815 — 808-944-1121 944-1131 167-3
Web: www.honolulunailacademy.com

Honolulu Publishing Company Ltd
707 Richards St Ste PH3 — Honolulu HI 96813 — 808-524-7400 531-2306 637-9
TF: 800-272-5245 ■ *Web:* honolulupublishing.com

Honolulu Wood Treating LLC
91-291 Hanua St — Kapolei HI 96707 — 808-682-5704 818
Web: hwthawaii.com

Honolulu Zoo 151 Kapahulu Ave — Honolulu HI 96815 — 808-971-7171 823
Web: honoluluzoo.org

Honolulu-Japanese Chamber of Commerce
2454 S Beretania St Ste 201 — Honolulu HI 96826 — 808-949-5531 949-3020 138
Web: hjcc.org

Honor Foods 1801 N Fifth St — Philadelphia PA 19122 — 215-236-1700 297-8
TF: 800-462-2890 ■ *Web:* www.honorfoods.com

HonorHealth John C Lincoln Medical Ctr
250 E Dunlap Ave — Phoenix AZ 85020 — 623-580-5800 374-3
TF: 800-223-3131 ■ *Web:* www.honorhealth.com

Honsa Rodd Landry PA
333 S Seventh St Ste 2360 — Minneapolis MN 55402 — 612-767-7300 41
Web: honsalaw.com

Honsa-Binder Printing Inc
320 Spruce St — Saint Paul MN 55101 — 651-222-0251 627
Web: www.h-bprint.com

Honshy Electric Company Inc
7345 SW 41st St — Miami FL 33155 — 305-264-5500 266-3159 189-4
Web: www.honshyelectric.com

Hontoon Island State Park
2309 River Ridge Rd — DeLand FL 32720 — 386-736-5309 565
Web: www.floridastateparks.org

Hoober Inc
3452 Old Philadelphia Pk PO Box 518 — Intercourse PA 17534 — 717-768-8231 768-3005 274
TF: 800-446-6237 ■ *Web:* www.hoober.com

Hood College 401 Rosemont Ave — Frederick MD 21701 — 301-696-3400 696-3819 166
TF: 800-922-1599 ■ *Web:* www.hood.edu

Hood Companies Inc
623 Main St PO Box 1828 — Hattiesburg MS 39401 — 601-582-4486 582-3989 613

Hood Construction Company Inc
1050 Shop Rd Ste A — Columbia SC 29201 — 803-765-2940 186
Web: www.hoodconstruction.com

Hood County 100 E Pearl St — Granbury TX 76048 — 817-579-3200 579-3213 338
Web: www.co.hood.tx.us

Hood County Genealogical Society
PO Box 1623 — Granbury TX 76048 — 817-279-0740 48-13
Web: www.granburydepot.org

Hood County News 1501 S Morgan St — Granbury TX 76048 — 817-573-7066 532-3
Web: www.hcnews.com

Hood Distribution
3890 Veterans Memorial Dr — Hattiesburg MS 39402 — 601-264-2559 296-4766 191-3
Web: www.hooddistribution.com

Hood Packaging Corp 25 Woodgreen Pl — Madison MS 39110 — 601-853-7260 853-7299 65
TF: 800-321-8115 ■ *Web:* www.hoodpkg.com

Hood River County 601 State St — Hood River OR 97031 — 541-386-3970 386-9392 338
Web: www.co.hood-river.or.us

Hood Theological Seminary
1810 Lutheran Synod Dr — Salisbury NC 28144 — 704-636-7611 167-3
Web: www.hoodseminary.edu

Hook Industrial Sales Inc
2731 Brooklyn Ave — Fort Wayne IN 46802 — 260-432-9441 436-4152 386
Web: www.hookindustrialsales.com

Hooker County PO Box 184 — Mullen NE 69152 — 308-546-2244 546-2490 338
Web: www.co.hooker.ne.us

Hooker Furniture Corp
440 E Commonwealth Blvd — Martinsville VA 24112 — 276-632-0459 388-2289* 319-2
NASDAQ: HOFT ■ **Fax Area Code:* 800 ■ *TF:* 800-422-1511 ■ *Web:* www.hookerfurniture.com

Hookflash Solutions Inc
6679 1A Ave Unit 1 — Delta BC V4M3B3 — 604-613-3726 224
Web: www.hookflash.ca

Hooley Inc
331 N Alexander St
Shop 4401 Bienville Ave — New Orleans LA 70119 — 504-482-3619 488-2680 723
Web: hooleyinc.com

Hoop Group, The
1930 Heck Ave Bldg 3 — Neptune City NJ 07753 — 732-502-2255 196
Web: www.hoopgroup.com

Hooper Corp 2030 Pennsylvania Ave — Madison WI 53704 — 608-249-0451 249-7360 189-10
TF: 877-630-7554 ■ *Web:* www.hoopercorp.com

Hooper Handling Inc 5590 Camp Rd — Hamburg NY 14075 — 716-649-5590 358
TF: 800-649-5590 ■ *Web:* www.hooperhandling.com

Hooray Agency 18261 McDurmott W — Irvine CA 92614 — 949-442-9850 195
Web: www.hooray.agency

Hoosac School 14 Pine Valley Rd — Hoosick Falls NY 12089 — 518-686-7331 622
Web: www.hoosac.org

Hoosick Street Discount Beverage Ctr
2200 19th St — Troy NY 12180 — 518-273-0877 81-1
Web: www.hoosickstreetbeverage.com

Hoosier Co
5421 W 86th St PO Box 681064 — Indianapolis IN 46268 — 317-872-8125 872-7183 286
TF: 800-521-4184 ■ *Web:* www.hoosierco.com

Hoosier Gasket Corp
2400 Enterprise Pk Pl — Indianapolis IN 46218 — 317-545-2000 545-5500 326
Web: www.hoosiergasket.com

Hoosier Hills Credit Union
630 Lincoln Ave — Bedford IN 47421 — 812-279-6644 219
Web: hoosierhills.com

Hoosier Tank & Manufacturing Inc
1710 N Sheridan St — South Bend IN 46628 — 574-232-8368 480
Web: www.hoosiertank.com

Hoosier Tire Mid-Atlantic (HTMA)
2931 Industrial Park Dr — Finksburg MD 21048 — 410-833-2061 833-5921 755
TF: 800-651-5164 ■ *Web:* www.hoosiermidatlantic.com

Hoosier Village
9875 Cherryleaf Dr — Indianapolis IN 46268 — 317-873-3349 672
Web: www.hoosiervillage.com

Hooven-Dayton Corp 511 Byers Rd — Miamisburg OH 45342 — 937-233-4473 627
Web: www.hoovendayton.com

Hoover & Strong Inc
10700 Trade Rd — North Chesterfield VA 23236 — 804-794-3700 616-9997* 485
**Fax Area Code:* 800 ■ *TF:* 800-759-9997 ■ *Web:* www.hooverandstrong.com

Hoover Chamber
1694 Montgomery Hwy Ste 108 — Hoover AL 35236 — 205-988-5672 139
TF: 888-349-4139 ■ *Web:* hooverchamber.org

Hoover Construction Co
302 S Hoover Rd PO Box 1007 — Virginia MN 55792 — 218-741-3280 741-6804 188-4
TF: 800-741-0970 ■ *Web:* hoov3r.com

Hoover Dam Lodge 18000 Hwy 93 — Boulder City NV 89005 — 702-293-5000 378
TF: 800-245-6380 ■ *Web:* hooverdamlodge.com

Hoover Ferguson Group Inc
2135 Hwy Six S — Houston TX 77077 — 281-870-8402 295
Web: www.hooverferguson.com

Hoover Inc 1205 Bridgestone Pkwy — La Vergne TN 37086 — 615-896-2531 182
TF: 800-944-9200 ■ *Web:* www.hoover.com

Hoover Institution on War Revolution & Peace
Stanford University 434 Galvez Mall — Stanford CA 94305 — 650-723-1754 723-1687 634
Web: www.hoover.org

Hoover Precision Products Inc
2200 Pendley Rd — Cumming GA 30041 — 770-889-9223 889-0828 485
Web: www.hooverprecision.com

Hoover Public Library (HPL)
200 Municipal Dr — Hoover AL 35216 — 205-444-7800 444-7878 434-3
Web: www.hooverlibrary.org

Hoover Toyota 2686 John Hawkins Pkwy — Hoover AL 35244 — 205-978-2600 57
Web: www.hoovertoyota.com

Hoover Treated Wood Products Inc
154 Wire Rd — Thomson GA 30824 — 706-595-1264 818
Web: www.frtw.com

HOP Energy LLC 1011 Hudson Ave — Ridgefield NJ 07657 — 877-448-3799 316
TF: 800-951-2941 ■ *Web:* www.metroenergynj.com

Hop-A-Jet
5525 NW 15th Ave Ste 150 — Fort Lauderdale FL 33309 — 954-771-5779 772-6981 13
TF: 800-556-6633 ■ *Web:* hopajetworldwide.com

Hopatcong State Park PO Box 8519 — Landing NJ 07850 — 973-398-7010 565
Web: www.njparksandforests.org

Hope College 69 E Tenth St PO Box 9000 — Holland MI 49422 — 616-395-7850 395-7130 166
TF: 800-968-7850 ■ *Web:* hope.edu

Hope Consulting Inc 117 S Market St — Benton AR 72015 — 501-315-2626 261
Web: hopeconsulting.com

Hope Global Engineered Textile Solutions
50 Martin St — Cumberland RI 02864 — 401-333-8990 334-6442 745-5
Web: www.hopeglobal.com

Hope Group 70 Bearfoot Rd — Northborough MA 01532 — 508-393-7660 393-8203 385
Web: www.thehopegroup.com

Hope Hospice 9470 Healthpark Cir — Fort Myers FL 33908 — 239-482-4673 371
TF: 800-835-1673 ■ *Web:* www.hopehospice.org

Hope Hospice 611 N Walnut Ave — New Braunfels TX 78130 — 830-625-7500 606-1388 371
TF: 800-499-7501 ■ *Web:* www.hopehospice.net

Hope International University
2500 E Nutwood Ave — Fullerton CA 92831 — 714-879-3901 526-0231 166
TF: 866-722-4673 ■ *Web:* www.hiu.edu

Hope Network
3075 Orchard Vista Dr SE — Grand Rapids MI 49546 — 616-301-8000 301-8010 450
TF: 800-695-7273 ■ *Web:* hopenetwork.org

Hope Pharmaceuticals Inc
16416 N 92nd St Ste 125 — Scottsdale AZ 85260 — 480-607-1970 607-1971 582
TF: 800-755-9595 ■ *Web:* hopepharm.com

Hope Worldwide
4231 Balboa Ave Ste 330 — San Diego CA 92117 — 610-254-8800 254-8989 48-5
TF: 866-551-7327 ■ *Web:* www.hopeww.org

Hope's Windows Inc
84 Hopkins Ave PO Box 580 — Jamestown NY 14702 — 716-665-5124 665-3365 234
Web: www.hopeswindows.com

HopeHealth 1085 N Main St — Providence RI 02904 — 401-415-4200 371
Web: www.hopehealthco.org

Hopesouth Federal Credit Union
807 W Greenwood St — Abbeville SC 29620 — 864-366-9602 366-8318 219
TF: 855-314-1049 ■ *Web:* hopesouth.org

Hopeville Pond State Park
193 Roode Rd — Jewett City CT 06351 — 860-376-2920 565
Web: portal.ct.gov

Hopewell Culture National Historical Park
16062 SR-104 — Chillicothe OH 45601 — 740-774-1126 774-1140 564
Web: www.nps.gov

Hopewell Furnace National Historic Site
2 Mark Bird Ln — Elverson PA 19520 — 610-582-8773 582-2768 564
Web: www.nps.gov

Hopewell Veterinary Group Inc
230 Hopewell Pennington Rd — Hopewell NJ 08525 — 609-466-0131 466-2314 794
Web: www.hvgpets.com

Hopewell/Prince George Chamber & Visitor Ctr
PO Box 1297 — Hopewell VA 23860 — 804-541-2461 139
Web: www.hpgchamber.org

Hopital Jean-Talon
1385 Jean-Talon St E — Montreal QC H2E1S6 — 514-495-6767 374-2
Web: www.ciusssnordmtl.ca

Hopkes Logging Company Inc
1115 Main Ave — Tillamook OR 97141 — 503-842-2491 448

Name / Address	City	State	ZIP	Phone	Fax	Class
Hopkins & Carley A Law Corp PO Box 1469 *Web:* www.hopkinscarley.com	San Jose	CA	95109	408-286-9800	998-4790	428
Hopkins County 118 Church St *TF:* 866-575-9014 ■ *Web:* www.hopkinscountytx.org	Sulphur Springs	TX	75482	903-438-4074	438-4099	338
Hopkins County Chamber of Commerce 300 Connally St *Web:* www.hopkinschamber.org	Sulphur Springs	TX	75482	903-885-6515	885-6516	139
Hopkins County Clerk 24 Union St *Web:* www.hopkinscountyclerk.com	Madisonville	KY	42431	270-821-7361	326-2091	338
Hopkins County Schools 320 S Seminary St *Web:* www.hopkins.kyschools.us	Madisonville	KY	42431	270-825-6000	825-6072	685
Hopkins Financial Corp 100 E Havens *Web:* www.cortrustbank.com	Mitchell	SD	57301	605-996-7775		70
Hopkins Floor Co 2323 Hwy 67 *Web:* www.hopkinsfloorco.com	Festus	MO	63028	636-937-2400	931-0910	290
Hopkins Furniture Inc 1509 NW 28th St *Web:* hopkinsfurniture.com	Fort Worth	TX	76164	817-624-8444	624-2812	321
Hopkins Manufacturing Corp 428 Peyton St *TF:* 800-524-1458 ■ *Web:* www.hopkinsmfg.com	Emporia	KS	66801	620-342-7320	340-8590	60
Hopkins Printing Inc 2246 CityGate Dr *TF:* 800-319-3352 ■ *Web:* www.hopkinsprinting.com	Columbus	OH	43219	614-509-1080	509-1081	627
Hopkins Sporting Goods Inc 5485 NW Beaver Dr *TF:* 800-362-2937 ■ *Web:* www.hopkinssportinggoods.com	Johnston	IA	50131	515-270-0132		711
Hopkins-Carter Company Inc 3300 NW 21st St *TF:* 800-595-9656 ■ *Web:* www.hopkins-carter.com	Miami	FL	33142	305-635-7377	633-1310	465
Hopkinsville Community College 720 N Dr *TF:* 866-534-2224 ■ *Web:* hopkinsville.kctcs.edu	Hopkinsville	KY	42240	270-886-3921	886-0237	162
Hopkinsville Milling Co PO Box 669 *Web:* www.sunflourflour.com	Hopkinsville	KY	42241	270-886-1231	886-6407	296-23
Hopkinsville-Christian County Chamber of Commerce 2800 Port Campbell Blvd *TF:* 800-842-9959 ■ *Web:* www.christiancountychamber.com	Hopkinsville	KY	42240	270-885-9096	886-2059	139
Hopkinton State Park 164 Cedar St *Web:* www.mass.gov	Hopkinton	MA	01748	508-435-4303		565
Hop-on Inc PO Box 940 Ste 222 *Web:* hop-on.com	Temecula	CA	92593	949-756-9008	335-0604	736
Hoppe North America Inc 205 E Blackhawk Dr *Web:* www.hoppe.com	Fort Atkinson	WI	53538	920-563-2626		350
Hoppe Technologies Inc 107 1st Ave *Web:* www.precinmac.com	Chicopee	MA	01020	413-592-9213	592-4688	493
Hopper Engineering Associates Inc 300 Vista Del Mar *Web:* www.hopperengineering.com	Redondo Beach	CA	90277	310-373-5573		256
Hopper, Hicks & Wrenn PLLC 111 Gilliam St PO Box 247 *Web:* www.hickswrennlaw.com	Oxford	NC	27565	919-693-8161		41
Hopsports Inc 24715 Ave Rockefeller *Web:* hopsports.com	Valencia	CA	91355	661-702-8946		514
Hoque & Associates Inc 4325 S 34th St *Web:* hoqueandassociates.com	Phoenix	AZ	85040	480-921-1368	921-0194	256
Hoquiam Plywood Products Inc 1000 Woodlawn St	Hoquiam	WA	98550	408-779-7354		613
Horace Mann Life Insurance Co 1 Horace Mann Plz *TF:* 800-999-1030 ■ *Web:* www.horacemann.com	Springfield	IL	62715	217-789-2500		391-2
Horan Associates Inc 4990 E Galbraith Rd *Web:* www.horanassoc.com	Cincinnati	OH	45236	513-745-0707		690
Horan Capital Management LLC 20 Wight Ave Ste 115 *TF:* 800-592-7534 ■ *Web:* horancm.com	Hunt Valley	MD	21030	410-494-4380		194
HORIBA ABX Inc 34 Bunsen Dr *Web:* www.horiba.com	Irvine	CA	92618	949-453-0500	453-0600	743
Horix Manufacturing Co 1384 Island Ave *Web:* horix.net	McKees Rocks	PA	15136	412-771-1111	331-8599	298
Horizen 3103 E Strong St *Web:* www.horizenpensacola.com	Pensacola	FL	32503	850-432-7899		671
Horizon Air Freight Inc 152-15 Rockaway Blvd *TF:* 800-221-6028 ■ *Web:* www.haf.com	Jamaica	NY	11434	718-528-3800	949-0655	449
Horizon Bank 515 Franklin Sq *Web:* www.horizonbank.com	Michigan City	IN	46360	219-874-9245		360-2
Horizon Books 243 E Front St *TF:* 800-587-2147 ■ *Web:* www.horizonbooks.com	Traverse City	MI	49684	231-946-7290		95
Horizon Business Solutions Inc 1589 Brice Rd *Web:* horizonbiz.com	Reynoldsburg	OH	43068	614-577-1700		2
Horizon Christian Fellowship PO Box 17480 *Web:* hcf.org	San Diego	CA	92177	858-277-4991		48-20
Horizon Consulting Inc 44135 Woodridge Pkwy Ste 100 *Web:* www.horizon-inc.com	Lansdowne	PA	19050	703-726-6430	783-0351	196
Horizon Convention Ctr 401 S High St PO Box 842 *TF:* 888-288-8860 ■ *Web:* www.horizonconvention.com	Muncie	IN	47305	888-288-8860		205
Horizon Credit Union 13224 E Mansfield Ste 300 *TF:* 800-808-6402 ■ *Web:* www.hzcu.org	Spokane Valley	WA	99216	800-852-5316		219
Horizon Dart Supply 2415 S 50th St *Web:* www.horizondarts.com	Kansas City	KS	66106	913-236-9111		761
Horizon Distribution Inc PO Box 1021 *Web:* www.horizondistribution.com	Yakima	WA	98907	509-453-3181	457-5769	351
Horizon Distributors Inc 5214 S 30th St **Fax Area Code:* 480 ■ *Web:* www.horizononline.com	Phoenix	AZ	85040	602-305-6046	337-6701*	422

Name / Address	City	State	ZIP	Phone	Fax	Class
Horizon Equipment 72 Bus Brown Dr *Web:* www.horizonequip.com	Woodbine	IA	51579	712-647-2702		274
Horizon Flight Center L L C 2801 Airport Dr *Web:* www.horizonflightcenter.com	Chesapeake	VA	23323	757-421-9000	421-7165	800
Horizon Freight Lines Inc 6579 S US Hwy 31 *Web:* www.horizonfreightlines.com	Edinburgh	IN	46124	812-526-3380		314
Horizon Freight System Inc 6600 Bessemer Ave *TF:* 800-480-6829 ■ *Web:* www.horizonfreightsystem.com	Cleveland	OH	44127	216-341-7410	429-3523	468
Horizon Group Properties Inc 5000 Hakes Dr *Web:* www.horizongroup.com	Norton Shores	MI	49441	231-798-9100	798-5100	655
Horizon Health Corp 1965 Lakepointe Dr Ste 100 *TF:* 800-727-2407 ■ *Web:* www.horizonhealth.com	Lewisville	TX	75057	972-420-8300		194
Horizon Healthcare Dental 3 Penn Plz E PP13Y **Fax Area Code:* 973 ■ *TF:* 800-433-6825 ■ *Web:* dental.horizonblue.com	Newark	NJ	07105	800-433-6825	274-2202*	391-3
Horizon Healthcare Services 3 Penn Plz E PP-16C *TF:* 800-355-2583 ■ *Web:* www.horizonblue.com	Newark	NJ	07105	800-355-2583		352
Horizon Helicopters Inc 2035 Sunset Lake Rd *Web:* horizonhelo.com	Newark	DE	19702	302-368-5135	368-4438	167-3
Horizon Hobby LLC 4710 E Guasti Rd *TF:* 888-899-5674 ■ *Web:* www.losi.com	Ontario	CA	91761	909-390-9595	390-5356	762
Horizon Holding Inc 6101 S 58th St Ste B *Web:* www.horizonholding.com	Lincoln	NE	68516	402-421-6400		360-3
Horizon Holdings LLC 1 Bush St Ste 650 *Web:* www.horizonholdings.com	San Francisco	CA	94104	415-788-2000	778-2030	401
Horizon Home Care & Hospice 11400 W Lake Park Dr *Web:* horizonhomecareandhospice.org	Milwaukee	WI	53224	414-365-8300	365-8330	371
Horizon Hotels Ltd 99 Corbett Way Ste 302 *Web:* www.horizonhotels.com	Eatontown	NJ	07724	732-935-9553		707
Horizon House Publications Inc (HHP) 685 Canton St *TF:* 800-966-8526 ■ *Web:* www.horizonhouse.com	Norwood	MA	02062	781-769-9750	762-9071	637-9
Horizon Juvenile Ctr 560 Brook Ave *Web:* www1.nyc.gov	Bronx	NY	10455	718-533-4620		412
Horizon Manufacturing Industries Inc 17925B 59th Ave NE **Fax Area Code:* 425 ■ *Web:* www.horizonman.com	Arlington	WA	98223	360-322-7368	493-0042*	621
Horizon NJ Health 210 Silvia St *TF:* 800-682-9094 ■ *Web:* www.horizonnjhealth.com	Trenton	NJ	08628	800-682-9094		391-3
Horizon Paper Company Inc 1010 Washington Blvd *TF:* 866-358-0855 ■ *Web:* www.horizonpaper.com	Stamford	CT	06901	203-358-0855		552-1
Horizon Publications Inc 1120 N Carbon St Ste 100	Marion	IL	62959	618-993-1711		532-3
Horizon Publishers' Bookstore 191 N 650 E *Web:* www.ldshorizonpublishers.com	Bountiful	UT	84010	801-292-7102		637-2
Horizon Services Co 250 Governor St *TF:* 800-949-5323 ■ *Web:* www.horizonsvcs.com	East Hartford	CT	06108	800-949-5323		104
Horizon Snack Foods Inc 16875 W Bernardo Dr Ste 100 *TF:* 800-229-2552	San Diego	CA	92127	800-229-2552		68
Horizon Software International LLC 2850 Premier Pkwy Ste 100 *TF:* 800-741-7100 ■ *Web:* horizonsoftware.com	Duluth	GA	30097	770-554-6353	554-6331	177
Horizon Solutions LLC 175 Josons Dr *TF:* 800-724-4750 ■ *Web:* www.horizonsolutions.com	Rochester	NY	14623	585-424-7376		180
Horizon Systems 615 Pennsylvania Ave Ste 4 *Web:* horizonsinsurancesystems.com	Sheboygan	WI	53081	920-803-8000		177
Horizon Telcom Inc 68 E Main St *TF:* 800-686-1570 ■ *Web:* www.horizontel.com	Chillicothe	OH	45601	740-772-8200		224
Horizon Termite & Pest Control Corp 45 Cross Ave *TF:* 888-612-2847 ■ *Web:* horizonpestcontrol.com	Midland Park	NJ	07432	201-447-2530		577
Horizon Utah Fcu 225 South 200 West *Web:* myhorizoncu.com	Farmington	UT	84025	801-451-5064		219
Horizon Wealth Management 8280 Ymca Plaza Dr Bldg 5 *Web:* www.horizonfg.com	Baton Rouge	LA	70810	225-612-3820		401
Horizon Wellness Group 20 Jerusalem Ave 3rd Fl *Web:* www.horizonhealthfairs.com	Hicksville	NY	11801	516-326-2020	358-7133	507
Horizons Conference Ctr 6200 State St *Web:* www.horizonscenter.com	Saginaw	MI	48603	989-799-4122	799-4188	205
Horizons Video & Film Inc 4000 Horizons Dr *Web:* horizonscompanies.com	Columbus	OH	43220	614-481-7200		514
Horizons Window Fashions Inc 1705 Waukegan Rd *TF:* 800-858-2352 ■ *Web:* horizonshades.com	Waukegan	IL	60085	800-858-2352		361
Horizontech Inc 417 Bridge St *Web:* horizontech.com	Danville	VA	24541	434-857-3200		177
Horn 1600 Steeles Ave W Ste 412 *TF:* 855-761-8015 ■ *Web:* www.horn.com	Concord	ON	L4K4M2	905-761-8000		445
Horn Drafting & CAD Ctr 3100 Wilcrest Dr Ste 120 *Web:* www.horncadcenter.com	Houston	TX	77042	832-831-0689		261
Horn Kendra (Rep D - OK) 415 Cannon House Office Bldg *Web:* www.horn.house.gov	Washington	DC	20515	202-225-2132		342-2
Horn Plastics Inc (HP) 712 38th St N Ste D *TF:* 800-373-7448 ■ *Web:* www.superslide.com	Fargo	ND	58102	701-282-7447	281-0439	603
Horn Williamson LLC 1500 Jfk Blvd 2 Penn Ctr Ste 1700 *Web:* hornwilliamson.com	Philadelphia	PA	19102	215-987-3800		41

	Phone	Fax	Class
Hornady Manufacturing Co 3625 W Old Potash Hwy .... Grand Island NE 68803 TF: 800-338-3220 ■ Web: www.hornady.com	308-382-1390	382-5761	284
Hornbacher's 2510 N Broadway .... Fargo ND 58102 Web: www.hornbachers.com	701-293-5444		345
Hornbeck Offshore Services Inc 103 Northpark Blvd Ste 300 .... Covington LA 70433 NYSE: HOS ■ TF: 800-642-9816 ■ Web: hornbeckoffshore.com	985-727-2000	727-2006	465
Hornby Zeller Associates Inc 48 Fourth St Ste 300 .... Troy NY 12180 Web: www.hornbyzeller.com	518-273-1614	273-0431	463
Horne LLP 26 Security Dr .... Jackson TN 38305 TF: 866-283-6150 ■ Web: hornellp.com	731-668-7070		2
Horne Properties Inc 412 Cedar Bluff Rd Ste 205 .... Knoxville TN 37923 Web: hpiknox.com	865-560-1100		652
Horner & Shifrin Inc 401 S 18th St Ste 400 .... Saint Louis MO 63103 Web: hornershifrin.com	314-531-4321		261
Horner Millwork Corp 1255 Grand Army Hwy .... Somerset MA 02726 Web: www.hornermillwork.com	508-679-6479		499
Hornerxpress Inc 5755 Powerline Rd .... Fort Lauderdale FL 33309 TF: 800-432-6966 ■ Web: www.hornerxpress.com	954-772-6966	772-6970	728
Horning Bros 3333 14th St NW Ste 300 .... Washington DC 20010 TF: 833-240-1206 ■ Web: www.horningbrothers.com	202-659-0700		655
Hornor Townsend & Kent Inc (HTK) 600 Dresher Rd Ste C1C .... Horsham PA 19044 *Fax Area Code: 215 ■ TF: 800-289-9999 ■ Web: www.htk.com	800-289-9999	956-7750*	402
Hornsby Tire Distributors Inc 5235 Kooiman Rd .... Theodore AL 36582 Web: www.hornsbytire.com	251-375-1292	375-1291	755
Hornthal, Riley, Ellis & Maland LLP 301 E Main St .... Elizabeth City NC 27909 Web: hrem.com	252-335-0871		41
Hornung's Golf Products Inc 815 Morris St .... Fond du Lac WI 54935 TF: 800-323-3569 ■ Web: www.hornungs.com	920-922-2640		328
Hornwood Inc 766 Hailey's Ferry Rd .... Lilesville NC 28091 TF: 800-225-6350 ■ Web: www.hornwoodinc.com	704-848-4121	848-4555	745-4
Horovitz, Rudoy and Roteman 875 Greentree Rd 7 Parkway Ctr Ste 1000 ...... Pittsburgh PA 15220 Web: www.hrrcpa.com	412-391-2920	391-4703	2
Horowitt, Darryl J - Coleman & Horowitt LLP 499 W Shaw Ave Ste 116 .... Fresno CA 93704 TF: 800-891-8362 ■ Web: www.ch-law.com	559-248-4820		428
Horrocks Engineers Inc 2162 Grove Pkwy Ste 400 .... Pleasant Grove UT 84062 Web: www.horrocksengineers.com	801-763-5100		256
Horry County 1301 Second Ave .... Conway SC 29526 Web: www.horrycounty.org	843-915-5080	915-6081	338
Horry County Solid Waste Authority Inc 1886 Hwy 90 .... Conway SC 29526 TF: 800-768-7348 ■ Web: www.solidwasteauthority.org	843-347-1651		660
Horry Electric Cooperative Inc 2774 Cultra Rd .... Conway SC 29526 Web: www.horryelectric.com	843-369-2211		245
Horry Telephone Co-opeartive Inc (HTC) 3480 Hwy 701 N PO Box 1820 .... Conway SC 29528 TF: 800-824-6779 ■ Web: www.htcinc.net	843-365-2151	365-0855	736
Horry-Georgetown Technical College 2050 E Hwy 501 .... Conway SC 29526 TF: 855-544-4482 ■ Web: www.hgtc.edu	843-347-3186	347-4207	800
Horsburgh & Scott Co 5114 Hamilton Ave .... Cleveland OH 44114 TF: 800-424-6514 ■ Web: www.horsburgh-scott.com	216-431-3900	432-2172	709
Horse & Buggy Press (H&B) 1116 Broad St Middle Ste .... Durham NC 27705 Web: www.horseandbuggypress.com	919-949-4847		626
Horse Hollow Press Inc PO Box 456 .... Goshen NY 10924 Web: horsehollowpress.com	845-294-0656		637-2
Horse Illustrated 4101 Tates Creek Centre Dr Ste 150-324 .... Lexington KY 40517 TF: 844-330-6373 ■ Web: www.horseillustrated.com	844-330-6373		457-14
Horse of Course Inc, The 514 W Will Rogers Blvd .... Claremore OK 74017 Web: thehorseofcourse.com	918-341-6293		711
Horseheads Printing 2077 Grand Central Ave .... Horseheads NY 14845 Web: www.horseheadsprinting.com	607-796-2681		627
Horseless Carriage Carriers 61 Iowa Ave .... Paterson NJ 07503 TF: 800-631-7796 ■ Web: www.horselesscarriage.com	973-742-2692	742-8369	780
HorseLoverZ com 254 N Cedar St .... Hazleton PA 18201 TF: 877-804-7810 ■ Web: www.horseloverz.com	570-399-3469		157-5
Horsemen's Park 6303 Q St .... Omaha NE 68117 Web: www.horsemenspark.com	402-731-2900	731-5122	133
Horseneck Beach State Reservation 5 John Reed Rd .... Westport Point MA 02791 Web: www.mass.gov	508-636-8816		565
Horseshoe Bend National Military Park 11288 Horseshoe Bend Rd .... Daviston AL 36256 Web: www.nps.gov	256-234-7111		564
Horseshoe Bend Regional Library 207 NW St .... Dadeville AL 36853 Web: www.horseshoebendlibrary.org	256-825-9232		434-3
Horseshoe Lake State Fish & Wildlife Area (Alexander County) 21204 Promised Land Rd .... Miller City IL 62962 Web: www2.illinois.gov	618-776-5689		565
Horseshoe Lake State Park (Madison County) 3321 Hwy 111 .... Granite City IL 62040 Web: www2.illinois.gov	618-931-0270		565
Horseshoe Valley Resort Ltd 1101 Horseshoe Valley Rd - Comp 10 RR 1 .... Barrie ON L4M4Y8 TF: 800-461-5627 ■ Web: horseshoeresort.com	800-461-5627		378

	Phone	Fax	Class
Horsford Steven (Rep D - NV) 1330 Longworth House Office Bldg .... Washington DC 20515 Web: www.horsford.house.gov	202-225-9894		342-2
Horsham Clinic 722 Butler Pk .... Ambler PA 19002 TF: 800-237-4447 ■ Web: www.horshamclinic.com	215-643-7800	654-1148	374-5
Horsley Co, The 1630 South 4800 West Ste D .... Salt Lake City UT 84104 Web: www.horsleyco.com	801-401-5500		207
Horsley Witten Group Inc 90 Rt 6A Unit 1 .... Sandwich MA 02563 Web: www.horsleywitten.com	508-833-6600		196
Horspool & Romine Manufacturing Inc 5850 Marshall St .... Oakland CA 94608 *Fax Area Code: 510 ■ TF: 800-446-2263 ■ Web: www.horspool.com	800-446-2263	652-3455*	621
Horst Engineering & Manufacturing Co 36 Cedar St .... East Hartford CT 06108 Web: horstengineering.com	860-289-8209		22
Horst Excavating Inc 320 Granite Run Dr .... Lancaster PA 17604 TF: 866-467-7848 ■ Web: www.horstexcavating.com	717-581-9910	581-9999	189-5
Horst Group Inc 320 Granite Run Dr PO Box 3330 .... Lancaster PA 17604 Web: www.horstgroup.com	717-581-9800	581-9816	186
Horst Insurance 320 Granite Run Dr .... Lancaster PA 17604 Web: www.horstinsurance.com	717-560-1919	581-9812	390
Hortau Inc 3485 Sacramento Dr Ste B .... San Luis Obispo CA 93401 Web: hortau.com	418-839-2852		407
Hortica Insurance 1 Horticultural Ln PO Box 428 .... Edwardsville IL 62025 TF: 800-851-7740 ■ Web: www.hortica.com	618-656-4240	656-7581	391-4
Horton & Horton Printing Co 12412 Sardis Rd .... Mabelvale AR 72103 Web: hortonandhorton.com	501-455-3168		627
Horton Emergency Vehicles 3800 McDowell Rd .... Grove City OH 43123 TF: 800-282-5113 ■ Web: www.hortonambulance.com	614-539-8181	539-8165	59
Horton Grand Hotel 311 Island Ave .... San Diego CA 92101 TF: 800-542-1886 ■ Web: www.hortongrand.com	619-544-1886		379
Horton Group 136 Rosa L Parks Blvd .... Nashville TN 37203 Web: www.hortongroup.com	615-292-8642		177
Horton Group, The 10320 Orland Pkwy .... Orland Park IL 60467 TF: 800-383-8283 ■ Web: www.thehortongroup.com	708-845-3000	845-3001	390
Horton Haven Christian Camp 3711 Reed Harris Rd .... Lewisburg TN 37091 Web: www.hortonhaven.org	931-364-7656		239
Horton Homes Inc PO Box 4410 .... Eatonton GA 31024	706-485-8506	485-4446	505
Horton Inc 2565 Walnut St .... Saint Paul MN 55113 TF: 800-621-1320 ■ Web: www.hortonww.com	651-361-6400		620
Horton International LLC 29 S Main St .... West Hartford CT 06107 Web: www.hortoninternational.com	860-521-0101		266
Horton, Oberrecht, Kirkpatrick & Martha, Attorneys At Law A Professional Corp NBC Bldg 225 Broadway Ste 2200 .... San Diego CA 92101 Web: www.hortonfirm.com	619-232-1183		428
Horvath Communications Inc 312 W Colfax Ave .... South Bend IN 46601 TF: 877-424-8693 ■ Web: www.horvathcommunications.com	574-237-0464	217-4357	116
Horvitz & Levy LLP 3601 W Olive Ave 8th Fl .... Burbank CA 91505 *Fax Area Code: 844 ■ Web: www.horvitzlevy.com	818-995-0800	497-6592*	428
Horwath Hotel Tourism & Leisure Consulting 1200 Ashwood Pkwy Ste 185 .... Atlanta GA 30338 Web: horwathhtl.com	404-410-7800		463
Horween Leather Co 2015 N Elston Ave .... Chicago IL 60614 Web: www.horween.com	773-772-2026	772-9235	432
Horwith Trucks Inc PO Box 7 .... Northampton PA 18067 TF: 800-220-8807 ■ Web: horwithfreightliner.com	610-261-2220	261-2916	57
Horwitz 7400 49th Ave N .... New Hope MN 55428 Web: www.horwitzinc.com	763-533-1900	235-9810	189-10
Horwitz & Zim Law Group 260 Madison Ave 16th Fl .... New York NY 10016 Web: hzlaw.com	212-644-1857	644-6553	41
Hosanna 2421 Aztec Rd NE .... Albuquerque NM 87107 TF: 800-545-6552 ■ Web: www.faithcomesbyhearing.com	505-881-3321		95
Hosanna Health Care PO Box 1257 .... Mission TX 78573	956-519-1000		363
Hose & Fittings Etc Inc 1811 Enterprise Blvd .... West Sacramento CA 95691 Web: www.hoseandfittingsetc.com	916-372-3888	371-5777	612
Hose Master LLC 1233 E 222nd St .... Cleveland OH 44117 TF: 800-221-2319 ■ Web: www.hosemaster.com	216-481-2020	481-7557	790
Hoselton Chevrolet Inc 909 Fairport Rd .... East Rochester NY 14445 Web: www.hoselton.com	585-586-7373		57
Hoshino USA Inc 1726 Winchester Rd .... Bensalem PA 19020 Web: www.hoshinogakki.co.jp	215-638-8670	245-8583	523
Hoshizaki America Inc 618 Hwy 74 S .... Peachtree City GA 30269 TF: 800-438-6087 ■ Web: hoshizakiamerica.com	770-487-2331		14
Hosie Rice LLP 600 Montgomery St 34th Fl .... San Francisco CA 94111 Web: hosielaw.com	415-247-6000		41
Hosley International Trdg Corp 20530 Stony Island Ave .... Chicago Heights IL 60411	708-758-1000	758-3243	361
Hosokawa Micron Powder Systems 10 Chatham Rd .... Summit NJ 07901 Web: www.hosokawamicron.co.jp	908-277-9300	273-9377	386
Hosokawa Polymer Systems 63 Fuller Way .... Berlin CT 06037 TF: 800-233-6112 ■ Web: www.polysys.com	860-828-0541	829-1313	386
Hosparus Inc 502 Hausfeldt Ln .... New Albany IN 47150 Web: www.hosparushealth.org	812-945-4596	945-4733	371
Hospicare of Tompkins County 172 E King Rd .... Ithaca NY 14850 Web: www.hospicare.org	607-272-0212	272-0237	371
Hospice & Palliative Care of Buffalo 225 Como Pk Blvd .... Cheektowaga NY 14227 Web: www.hospicebuffalo.com	716-686-1900	686-8181	371

Name / Address	City	State	ZIP	Phone	Fax	Class
Hospice & Palliative Care of Western Colorado 2754 Compass Dr Ste 377 *TF:* 866-310-8900 ■ *Web:* www.hopewestco.org	Grand Junction	CO	81506	970-241-2212	257-2400	371
Hospice Alliance 10220 Prairie Ridge Blvd *TF:* 800-830-8344 ■ *Web:* www.hospicealliance.org	Pleasant Prairie	WI	53158	262-652-4400	652-4516	371
Hospice at Charlotte 1420 E Seventh St *TF:* 800-835-5306 ■ *Web:* www.hpccr.org	Charlotte	NC	28204	704-375-0100	375-8623	371
Hospice at Home 4025 Health Pk Ln *TF:* 800-717-3811 ■ *Web:* www.spectrumhealthlakeland.org	Saint Joseph	MI	49085	269-429-7100	428-3499	371
Hospice at the Texas Medical Ctr 1905 Holcombe Blvd *Web:* www.houstonhospice.org	Houston	TX	77030	713-467-7423		371
Hospice Atlanta-Visiting Nurse Health System 1244 Pk Vista Dr *Web:* vnhs.org	Atlanta	GA	30319	404-869-3000	215-6005	371
Hospice Austin 4107 Spicewood Springs Rd Ste 100 *TF:* 800-445-3261 ■ *Web:* www.hospiceaustin.org	Austin	TX	78759	512-342-4700	795-9053	371
Hospice Brazos Valley 502 W 26th St *TF:* 800-824-2326 ■ *Web:* www.hospicebrazosvalley.org	Bryan	TX	77803	979-821-2266	821-0041	371
Hospice by the Bay 17 E Sir Francis Drake Blvd *Web:* hospicebythebay.org	Larkspur	CA	94939	415-927-2273		371
Hospice Care Inc 4277 Middle Settlement Rd *TF:* 800-317-5661 ■ *Web:* hospicecareinc.org	New Hartford	NY	13413	315-735-6484	793-8852	371
Hospice Care Network 99 Sunnyside Blvd *TF:* 800-405-6731 ■ *Web:* www.hospicecarenetwork.org	Woodbury	NY	11797	516-832-7100	832-7160	371
Hospice Care of Southwest Michigan 222 N Kalamazoo Mall Ste 100 *TF:* 800-304-0273 ■ *Web:* www.hospiceswmi.org	Kalamazoo	MI	49007	269-345-0273		371
Hospice Care Team 1708 N Amburn Rd Ste C *Web:* www.hospicecareteam.org	Texas City	TX	77591	409-938-0070	832-3312	371
Hospice Caring Project of Santa Cruz County 940 Disc Dr *Web:* www.hospicesantacruz.org	Scotts Valley	CA	95066	831-430-3000	430-9272	371
Hospice Chautauqua County 20 W Fairmount Ave *Web:* chpc.care	Lakewood	NY	14750	716-753-5383		371
Hospice Community Care PO Box 993 *TF:* 800-895-2273 ■ *Web:* hospicecommunitycare.org	Rock Hill	SC	29731	803-329-1500	329-5935	371
Hospice De La Luz 3812 Academy Pky NE *Web:* www.hospicedelaluz.com	Albuquerque	NM	87109	505-217-2490	873-1060	450
Hospice Family Care 1550 S Alma School Rd *Web:* www.hfc-az.com	Mesa	AZ	85210	480-461-3144		371
Hospice Foundation of America (HFA) 1707 L St NW Ste 220 *TF:* 800-854-3402 ■ *Web:* www.hospicefoundation.org	Washington	DC	20036	202-457-5811	457-5815	49-8
Hospice Hawaii 860 Iwilei Rd *Web:* www.hospicehawaii.org	Honolulu	HI	96817	808-924-9255	922-9161	371
Hospice Home Care 2200 S Bowman *Web:* www.hospicehomecare.com	Little Rock	AR	72211	501-296-9043	296-9978	371
Hospice House Foundation Inc 619 N Grant Ste 120 *Web:* www.homehospicewtx.com	Odessa	TX	79761	432-580-0067		371
Hospice In His Care LLC 3233 S Sherwood Forest Blvd Ste 102 *TF:* 888-362-6604 ■ *Web:* hospiceinhiscare.com	Baton Rouge	LA	70816	225-214-0010		363
Hospice Life Care 575 Beech St *Web:* www.holyokevna.org	Holyoke	MA	01040	413-533-3923		371
Hospice Longview Inc 4351 Mccann Rd *Web:* heartswayhospice.org	Longview	TX	75605	903-295-1680		363
Hospice Midland 911 W Texas Ave *Web:* hospiceofmidland.org	Midland	TX	79701	432-682-2855	682-2989	371
Hospice Ministries 450 Towne Center Blvd *TF:* 800-273-7724 ■ *Web:* www.hospiceministries.org	Ridgeland	MS	39157	601-898-1053		371
Hospice of Acadiana 2600 Johnston St *Web:* hospiceacadiana.com	LaFayette	LA	70503	337-232-1234	232-1297	371
Hospice of Anchorage 2612 E Northern Lights Blvd *Web:* www.hospiceofanchorage.org	Anchorage	AK	99508	907-561-5322		371
Hospice of Baton Rouge 3600 Florida Blvd *Web:* www.hospicebr.org	Baton Rouge	LA	70806	225-767-4673	769-8113	371
Hospice of Bend-La Pine 2075 NE Wyatt Ct *Web:* www.partnersbend.org	Bend	OR	97701	541-382-5882		371
Hospice of Boulder County 2594 Trlridge Dr E *TF:* 877-986-4766 ■ *Web:* www.trucare.org	LaFayette	CO	80026	303-449-7740		371
Hospice of Burke County 1721 Enon Rd *Web:* www.burkehospice.org	Valdese	NC	28690	828-879-1601	879-3500	371
Hospice of Central New York and Hospice of the Finger Lakes 1130 Corporate Dr *Web:* www.hospicecny.org	Auburn	NY	13021	315-255-2733		363
Hospice of Central Ohio 2269 Cherry Valley Rd *TF:* 800-804-2505 ■ *Web:* hospiceofcentralohio.org	Newark	OH	43055	740-788-1400		371
Hospice of Central Pennsylvania 1320 Linglestown Rd *TF:* 866-779-7374 ■ *Web:* hospiceofcentralpa.org	Harrisburg	PA	17110	717-732-1000		371
Hospice of Chattanooga 4411 Oakwood Dr *TF:* 800-267-6828 ■ *Web:* www.hospiceofchattanooga.org	Chattanooga	TN	37416	423-892-4289		371
Hospice of Cincinnati 4360 Cooper Rd *Web:* hospiceofcincinnati.org	Cincinnati	OH	45242	513-891-7700	792-6980	371
Hospice of Cleveland County 951 Wendover Heights Dr *Web:* www.hospicecares.cc	Shelby	NC	28150	704-487-4677	481-8050	371

Name / Address	City	State	ZIP	Phone	Fax	Class
Hospice of Dayton 324 Wilmington Ave *TF:* 800-653-4490 ■ *Web:* www.hospiceofdayton.org	Dayton	OH	45420	937-256-4490	256-9802	371
Hospice of East Texas 4111 University Blvd *TF:* 800-777-9860 ■ *Web:* www.hospiceofeasttexas.org	Tyler	TX	75701	903-266-3400		371
Hospice of El Paso 1440 Miracle Way *Web:* www.hospiceelpaso.org	El Paso	TX	79925	915-532-5699	532-7822	371
Hospice of Gaston County 258 E Garrison Blvd PO Box 3984 *Web:* www.caromonthealth.org	Gastonia	NC	28054	704-861-8405	865-0590	371
Hospice of Hilo 1011 Waianuenue Ave *Web:* www.hawaiicarechoices.org	Hilo	HI	96720	808-969-1733		371
Hospice of Holland Inc 270 Hoover Blvd *TF:* 800-255-3522 ■ *Web:* www.hollandhospice.org	Holland	MI	49423	616-396-2972	396-2808	371
Hospice of Huntington 1101 Sixth Ave *TF:* 800-788-5480 ■ *Web:* www.hospiceofhuntington.org	Huntington	WV	25701	304-529-4217	523-6051	371
Hospice of Jefferson County 1398 Gotham St *Web:* jeffersonhospice.org	Watertown	NY	13601	315-788-7323	788-9653	371
Hospice of Kankakee Valley Inc 482 Main St NW *TF:* 855-871-4695 ■ *Web:* www.hkvcares.org	Bourbonnais	IL	60914	815-939-4141		371
Hospice of Lake Cumberland 100 Pkwy Dr *TF:* 800-937-9596 ■ *Web:* hospicelc.org	Somerset	KY	42503	606-679-4389		371
Hospice of Lancaster 901 Meeting St Ste 201 *Web:* www.homecareoflancaster.com	Lancaster	SC	29720	803-286-1472	286-1378	363
Hospice of Lancaster County 685 Good Dr PO Box 4125 *TF:* 888-236-9563 ■ *Web:* www.hospiceandcommunitycare.org	Lancaster	PA	17604	717-295-3900	391-9582	371
Hospice of Lansing 3186 Pine Tree Rd *Web:* hospiceoflansing.org	Lansing	MI	48911	517-882-4500	882-3010	371
Hospice of Marion County 3231 SW 34th Ave *TF:* 888-482-5018 ■ *Web:* www.hospiceofmarion.com	Ocala	FL	34474	352-873-7400	873-7435	371
Hospice of Medina County 5075 Windfall Rd *TF:* 800-700-4771 ■ *Web:* www.hospiceofmedina.org	Medina	OH	44256	216-383-5291		371
Hospice of Miami County 550 Summit Ave Ste 101 *Web:* www.hospiceofmiamicounty.org	Troy	OH	45373	937-335-5191		371
Hospice of Michigan 400 Mack Ave *TF:* 888-247-5701 ■ *Web:* www.hom.org	Detroit	MI	48201	313-578-6259		371
Hospice of NE Georgia Medical Ctr 2150 Limestone Pkwy Ste 222 *TF:* 888-572-3900 ■ *Web:* www.nghs.com	Gainesville	GA	30501	770-533-8888	219-8887	371
Hospice of New Jersey 400 Broadacres Dr 1St Fl *Web:* www.nj.gov	Bloomfield	NJ	07003	973-893-0818	893-0828	371
Hospice of North Central Ohio 1050 Dauch Dr *TF:* 800-952-2207 ■ *Web:* www.hospiceofnorthcentralohio.org	Ashland	OH	44805	419-281-7107		371
Hospice of North Ottawa Community 1309 Sheldon Rd *Web:* www.noch.org	Grand Haven	MI	49417	616-842-3600		371
Hospice of Northern Colorado (HNC) 2726 W 11th St Rd *TF:* 800-564-5563 ■ *Web:* www.hospiceofnortherncolorado.org	Greeley	CO	80634	970-352-8487	475-0037	371
Hospice of Northwest Ohio 30000 E River Rd *TF:* 866-661-4001 ■ *Web:* www.hospicenwo.org	Perrysburg	OH	43551	419-661-4001	661-4015	371
Hospice of Orange & Sullivan Counties 800 Stony Brook Ct *TF:* 800-924-0157 ■ *Web:* hospiceoforange.com	Newburgh	NY	12550	845-561-6111	561-2170	371
Hospice of Randolph County 416 Vision Dr *Web:* www.hospiceofrandolph.org	Asheboro	NC	27203	336-672-9300	672-0868	371
Hospice of Redlands Community Hospital 350 Terracina Blvd *TF:* 888-397-4999 ■ *Web:* www.redlandshospital.org	Redlands	CA	92373	909-335-5643		371
Hospice of Reno County 1600 N Lorraine Ste 203 *Web:* hospice.io	Hutchinson	KS	67501	620-665-2473	669-5959	371
Hospice of Rockingham County Inc 2150 NC Hwy 65 PO Box 281 *Web:* hospiceofrockinghamcounty.com	Reidsville	NC	27320	336-427-9022	427-9030	371
Hospice of Saint Francis Inc 1250 Grumman Pl Ste B *TF:* 866-269-4240 ■ *Web:* www.hospiceofstfrancis.com	Titusville	FL	32780	321-269-4240		371
Hospice of Saint Lawrence Valley 6805 State Hwy 11 *Web:* hospiceslv.org	Potsdam	NY	13676	315-274-9336		371
Hospice of San Angelo 36 E Twohig Ave PO Box 471 *TF:* 800-499-6524 ■ *Web:* westtexasrehab.org	San Angelo	TX	76903	325-658-6524	658-8895	371
Hospice of San Joaquin 3888 Pacific Ave *Web:* www.hospicesj.org	Stockton	CA	95204	209-957-3888	922-0321	371
Hospice of Siouxland 4300 Hamilton Blvd *TF:* 800-383-4545 ■ *Web:* hospiceofsiouxland.com	Sioux City	IA	51104	712-233-4144	233-1123	371
Hospice of South Louisiana 6500 W Main St *TF:* 888-893-3829 ■ *Web:* www.hospiceofsouthlouisiana.com	Houma	LA	70360	985-868-3095	868-3910	371
Hospice of South Texas 605 E Locust Ave *TF:* 800-874-6908 ■ *Web:* hospice-vic.org	Victoria	TX	77901	361-572-4300		371
Hospice of Southeastern Connecticut Inc 227 Dunham St *TF:* 877-654-4035 ■ *Web:* www.hospicesect.org	Norwich	CT	06360	860-848-5699	848-6898	371
Hospice of Southern Illinois 305 S Illinois St *TF:* 800-233-1708 ■ *Web:* hospice.org	Belleville	IL	62220	618-235-1703		371
Hospice of Southern Kentucky 5872 Scottsville Rd *Web:* hospicesoky.org	Bowling Green	KY	42104	270-782-3402	782-3496	371

Name / Address	Phone	Fax	Class
Hospice of Southwest Georgia 114 A Mimosa Dr Thomasville GA 31792 *TF:* 800-290-6567 ■ *Web:* archbold.org	229-584-5500		371
Hospice of Spokane 121 S Arthur St Spokane WA 99202 *Web:* www.hospiceofspokane.org	509-456-0438		371
Hospice of Stanly County 960 N First St Albemarle NC 28001 *TF:* 800-230-4236 ■ *Web:* hospiceofstanly.org	704-983-4216	983-6662	371
Hospice of the Calumet Area 600 Superior Ave Munster IN 46321 *Web:* www.hospicecalumet.org	219-922-2732	922-1947	371
Hospice of the Carolina Foothills 374 Hudlow Rd PO Box 336 Forest City NC 28043 *TF:* 800-218-2273 ■ *Web:* hocf.org	828-245-0095	248-1035	371
Hospice of the Chesapeake John & Cathy Belcher Campus 90 Ritchie Hwy Pasadena MD 21122 *TF:* 877-462-1101 ■ *Web:* www.hospicechesapeake.org	410-987-2003		371
Hospice of the North Shore 75 Sylvan St Ste B-102 Danvers MA 01923 **Fax Area Code:* 978 ■ *TF:* 888-283-1722 ■ *Web:* www.caredimensions.org	888-283-1722	774-4389*	371
Hospice of the Panhandle 330 Hospice Ln Kearneysville WV 25430 *TF:* 800-345-6538 ■ *Web:* www.hospiceotp.org	304-264-0406	264-0409	371
Hospice of the Piedmont 675 Peter Jefferson Pkwy Ste 300 Charlottesville VA 22911 *TF:* 800-975-5501 ■ *Web:* www.hopva.org	434-817-6900	245-0187	371
Hospice of the Red River Valley 1701 38th St S Ste 101 Fargo ND 58103 *TF:* 800-237-4629 ■ *Web:* www.hrrv.org	800-237-4629		371
Hospice of the Upstate 1835 Rogers Rd Anderson SC 29621 *TF:* 800-261-8636 ■ *Web:* hospiceoftheupstate.com	864-224-3358		371
Hospice of the Valley 5190 Market St Youngstown OH 44512 *Web:* www.hospiceofthevalley.com	330-788-1992	788-1998	371
Hospice of the Valley 240 Johnston St SE PO Box 2745 Decatur AL 35602 *TF:* 877-260-3657 ■ *Web:* www.hospiceofthevalley.net	256-350-5585	350-5567	371
Hospice of The West 21410 N 19th Ave Ste 100 Phoenix AZ 85027 *TF:* 888-490-0377 ■ *Web:* hospicewestaz.com	602-343-6422		363
Hospice of the Western Reserve 300 E 185th St Cleveland OH 44119 *TF:* 800-707-8922 ■ *Web:* www.hospicewr.org	216-383-2222	383-3750	371
Hospice of Wake County Inc 250 Hospice Cir Raleigh NC 27607 *TF:* 888-900-3959 ■ *Web:* transitionslifecare.org	919-828-0890		371
Hospice of Warren County 1 Main Ave Warren PA 16365 *Web:* www.hospiceofwarrencounty.com	814-723-2455	723-6259	450
Hospice of Washington County Inc 747 N Ave Hagerstown MD 21742 *Web:* hospiceofwc.org	301-791-6360		374-7
Hospice of West Alabama 3851 Loop Rd Tuscaloosa AL 35404 *TF:* 877-362-7522 ■ *Web:* hospiceofwestal.com	205-523-0101	523-0102	371
Hospice of Westchester 1025 Westchester Ave Ste 200 White Plains NY 10604 *TF:* 800-860-9808 ■ *Web:* www.hospiceofwestchester.org	914-682-1484	682-9425	371
Hospice of Wichita Falls 4909 Johnson Rd Wichita Falls TX 76310 *TF:* 800-378-2822 ■ *Web:* www.howf.org	940-691-0982	691-1608	371
Hospice Savannah Inc PO Box 13190 Savannah GA 31416 *Web:* www.hospicesavannah.org	912-355-2289		371
Hospicomm 41 N Third St Ste 200 Philadelphia PA 19106 *Web:* www.hospicomm.com	215-925-5158	925-6055	463
Hospital & Healthcare Compensation Service PO Box 376 Oakland NJ 07436 *Web:* www.hhcsinc.com	201-405-0075	405-2110	637-9
Hospital Association of Southern California 515 S Figueroa St Ste 1300 Los Angeles CA 90071 *Web:* www.hasc.org	213-538-0700		78
Hospital Billing & Collection Service Ltd 118 Lukens Dr New Castle DE 19720	302-552-8000		160
Hospital Complex Sagamie, The 305 Ave St Vallier CP 5006 Chicoutimi QC G7H5H6 *Web:* www.usherbrooke.ca	418-541-1000		374-2
Hospital Cooperative Laundry Inc 6225 E 38th Ave Denver CO 80207 *Web:* hospitalcooperative.com	303-329-6662		363
Hospital De La Concepcion Carr 2 Km 1734 Bo Cain Alto San German PR 00683 *Web:* www.hospitaldelaconcepcion.com	787-659-5959		127
Hospital for Special Care 2150 Corbin Ave New Britain CT 06053 *Web:* www.hfsc.org	860-223-2761	612-6304	374-6
Hospital for Special Surgery 535 E 70th St New York NY 10021 *Web:* www.hss.edu	212-606-1328		374-7
Hospital Forms & Systems Corp 8900 Ambassador Row Dallas TX 75247 *TF:* 800-221-2825 ■ *Web:* www.hforms.com	800-221-2825		110
Hospital Hospitality House of Louisville 120 W Broadway Louisville KY 40202 *Web:* hhhlouisville.org	502-625-1360	625-1363	372
Hospital Hospitality House of SW Michigan Inc 527 W S St Kalamazoo MI 49007 *Web:* hhhkz.org	269-341-7811	341-7817	372
Hospital of Saint Raphael 1450 Chapel St New Haven CT 06511 *TF:* 888-700-6543 ■ *Web:* www.ynhh.org	203-789-3000		374-3
Hospital of the University of Pennsylvania 3400 Spruce St Philadelphia PA 19104 *Web:* www.pennmedicine.org	215-662-4000		374-3
Hospital Sisters Health System 4936 Laverna Rd Springfield IL 62707 *Web:* www.hshs.org	217-523-4747		353
Hospitality Builders Inc 150 Knollwood Dr Rapid City SD 57701 *Web:* www.hospitalitybuilders.com	605-791-3400		186
Hospitality Enterprises 4220 Howard Ave New Orleans LA 70125 *TF:* 888-546-1456 ■ *Web:* www.bigeasy.com	504-529-4567	592-0529	773
Hospitality Financial & Technology Professionals (HFTP) 11709 Boulder Ln Ste 110 Austin TX 78726 *TF:* 800-646-4387 ■ *Web:* www.hftp.org	512-249-5333	249-1533	49-1
Hospitality House of Charlotte 1400 Scott Ave Charlotte NC 28203 *Web:* www.hospitalityhouseofcharlotte.org	704-376-0060	376-0059	372
Hospitality House of Tulsa 1135 S Victor Ave Tulsa OK 74104 *Web:* hhtulsa.org	918-794-0088		372
Hospitality Inn 3709 NW 39th St Oklahoma City OK 73112 *Web:* www.hospitality-inn-oklahoma-city-us.book.direct	405-942-7730		379
Hospitality International Inc 1726 Montreal Cir Tucker GA 30084 *TF:* 800-251-1962 ■ *Web:* www.hifranchise.com	800-892-8405		379
Hospitality Investments LP 16114 E Indiana Ave Ste 200 Spokane Valley WA 99216 *Web:* www.hospitalityassociates.com	509-928-3736		610
Hospitality Real Estate Counselors 6400 S Fiddler'S Green Cir Ste 1730 Greenwood Village CO 80111 *Web:* www.hrec.com	303-267-0057	267-0105	652
Hospitality Sales & Marketing Association Intl (HSMAI) 7918 Jones Branch Dr Ste 300 McLean VA 22102 *Web:* global.hsmai.org	703-506-3280	610-9005	49-18
Hospitality Unlimited Investments Inc 17785 Center Court Dr Ste 720 Cerritos CA 90703 *Web:* huihotels.com	562-865-6411		652
Hospitality Ventures Management Group 990 Hammond Dr Ste 325 Atlanta GA 30328 *Web:* www.hvmg.com	404-467-9299	467-1962	463
Hospitals & Health Networks Magazine 155 N Wacker Ste 400 Chicago IL 60606 *Web:* www.hhnmag.com	312-893-6800	422-4500	457-5
Hoss's Steak & Sea House 110 Patchway Rd Duncansville PA 16635 *Web:* www.hosss.com	814-695-8543	695-3865	670
Host Analytics Inc 555 Twin Dolphin Dr Ste 400 Redwood City CA 94065 *Web:* www.hostanalytics.com	650-249-7100		178-1
Host Color LLC 746 S Arnold St South Bend IN 46619 *Web:* www.hostcolor.com	574-367-2393		225
Host Department LLC 45277 Fremont Blvd Ste 11 Fremont CA 94538 *TF:* 866-887-4678 ■ *Web:* www.hostdepartment.com	866-887-4678		387
Host Depot Inc 12524 W Atlantic Blvd Ste 227 Coral Springs FL 33067 *TF:* 888-340-3527 ■ *Web:* www.hostdepot.com	954-340-3527	340-3539	808
Host Engineering Inc 593 Aa Deakins Rd Jonesborough TN 37659 *Web:* hosteng.com	423-913-2587	913-3287	256
Host Healthcare 4225 Executive Sq Ste 1500 La Jolla CA 92037 *TF:* 800-585-1299 ■ *Web:* www.hosthealthcare.com	800-585-1299		89
Host Hotels & Resorts Inc 6903 Rockledge Dr Ste 1500 Bethesda MD 20817 *NYSE: HST* ■ *Web:* www.hosthotels.com	240-744-1000		654
Host T. Parker of Maryland Inc 2200 Broening Hwy Ste 102 Baltimore MD 21224 *Web:* www.tparkerhost.com	410-633-4666		23
Hostar International Inc 15000 Cross Creek Pky Newbury OH 44065 *Web:* hostar.com	440-564-7400		207
Hostcentric Inc 70 Blanchard Rd 3rd Fl Burlington MA 01803 *TF:* 866-897-5418 ■ *Web:* www.hostcentric.com	602-716-5396		808
Hostelling International USA - American Youth Hostels (HI-AYH) 8401 Colesville Rd Ste 600 Silver Spring MD 20910 *TF:* 888-449-8727 ■ *Web:* www.hiusa.org	240-650-2100	650-2094	48-23
Hosteria Romana 429 Espanola Way Miami Beach FL 33139 *Web:* www.hosteriaromana.com	305-532-4299		671
Hosting 4 Less 9586 Topanga Canyon Blvd Chatsworth CA 91311 *TF:* 888-818-0444 ■ *Web:* www.hosting4less.com	888-818-0444		681
Hostmark Hospitality Group 1300 E Woodfield Rd Ste 400 Schaumburg IL 60173 *Web:* careers.hostmark.com	847-517-9100	517-9797	379
HostMySite Inc 650 Pencader Dr Newark DE 19702 *TF:* 877-215-4678 ■ *Web:* www.hostmysite.com	302-731-4948		396
Hostos Community College 500 Grand Concourse Bronx NY 10451 *Web:* www.hostos.cuny.edu	718-518-4444	518-4256	162
Hostvedt Pavoni Inc 30 S Pine St Doylestown PA 18901 *Web:* www.hpisales.com	215-489-7300		518
Hostway Corp 100 N Riverside Plz 8th Fl Chicago IL 60606 *TF:* 866-467-8929 ■ *Web:* hostway.com	866-273-0585		808
Hostwinds 12101 Tukwila International Blvd Ste 320 Seattle WA 98168 *TF:* 888-404-1279 ■ *Web:* www.hostwinds.com	888-404-1279		225
Hot & Hot Fish Club 2180 11th Ct S Birmingham AL 35205 *Web:* www.hotandhotfishclub.com	205-933-5474		671
Hot 103.9 93.9 1900 Pineview Rd Columbia SC 29209 *Web:* www.hot1039fm.com	803-695-8600		645-38
Hot 104-9 3000 Olson Rd Tallahassee FL 32308 *Web:* hot1049.com	850-386-8004		645-159
Hot 106.3 1502 Wampanoag Trl East Providence RI 02915 *Web:* www.hot1063.com	401-433-4200		645
Hot 106.7 FM 2300 Vartan Way Ste 130 Harrisburg PA 17110 *Web:* www.hot1067fm.com	717-238-1041		645-68
Hot 107.9 1749 Bertrand Dr LaFayette LA 70506 *Web:* 1079ishot.com	337-234-1079		645-83
Hot 89.9 6 Antares Dr Phase 1 Ste 100 Ottawa ON K2E8A9 *Web:* www.hot899.com	613-723-8990		647
Hot 96 FM 1162 Mt Auburn Rd Evansville IN 47720 *TF:* 888-685-1961 ■ *Web:* hot96.com	812-491-9468	426-7928	645-54

Name / Address	City	State	Zip	Phone	Fax	Class
Hot Dog on a Stick 5942 Priestly Dr *TF:* 877-922-9215 ■ *Web:* hotdogonastick.com	Carlsbad	CA	92008	877-922-9215		670
Hot Graphics & Printing Inc 5241 Elmore Rd *Web:* www.hot-graphics.com	Memphis	TN	38134	901-387-1717		781
Hot Melt Technologies Inc 1723 W Hamlin Rd *Web:* hotmelt-tech.com	Rochester Hills	MI	48309	248-853-2011	853-6650	283
Hot Rooms 444 N Michigan Ave Ste 1200 **Fax Area Code:* 312 ■ *TF:* 800-468-3500 ■ *Web:* www.hotrooms.com	Chicago	IL	60611	773-468-7666	649-0559*	376
Hot Shot Final Mile 12333 Sowden Rd *TF:* 866-261-3184 ■ *Web:* hotshotfinalmile.com	Houston	TX	77080	713-869-5525	862-6354	546
Hot Shots Distributing Inc 4733 Dwight Evans Rd *Web:* www.hotshotshotsauce.com	Charlotte	NC	28217	704-527-2422		297-8
Hot Springs City Hall 133 Convention Blvd *Web:* www.cityhs.net	Hot Springs	AR	71901	501-321-6843	321-6809	337
Hot Springs Convention Ctr (HSCVB) 134 Convention Blvd PO Box 6000 *TF:* 800-625-7576 ■ *Web:* www.hotsprings.org	Hot Springs	AR	71902	501-321-2277		205
Hot Springs County 415 Arapahoe St *Web:* www.hscounty.com	Thermopolis	WY	82443	307-864-3515	864-3333	338
Hot Springs Documentary Film Festival (HSDFF) 659 Ouachita Ave *Web:* www.hsdfi.org	Hot Springs	AR	71901	501-538-0452		282
Hot Springs Lodge & Pool 415 E Sixth St *TF:* 800-537-7946 ■ *Web:* www.hotspringspool.com	Glenwood Springs	CO	81601	970-945-6571	947-2950	669
Hot Springs National Park 101 Reserve St *TF:* 800-582-2244 ■ *Web:* www.nps.gov	Hot Springs	AR	71901	501-620-6715		564
Hot Springs Telephone Co (HSTC) 216 Main St *Web:* hotsprgs.net	Hot Springs	MT	59845	406-741-2751	741-7766	224
Hot Stuff Pizza 2930 W Maple St *TF:* 800-336-1320 ■ *Web:* www.hotstuffpizza.com	Sioux Falls	SD	57107	605-336-6961		68
Hot Tuna Bar & Grill 2817 Shore Dr *Web:* www.hottunavb.com	Virginia Beach	VA	23451	757-481-2888		671
Hot Water Products 7500 N 81st St **Fax Area Code:* 877 ■ *TF:* 877-377-0011 ■ *Web:* www.hotwaterproducts.com	Milwaukee	WI	53223	414-434-1371	280-0022*	612
Hotaling Investment Management LLC 100 W Lancaster Ave Ste 105 *Web:* hotalingllc.com	Wayne	PA	19087	610-688-0616		528
Hotan Corp 789 NCanyons Pkwy *TF:* 800-656-1888 ■ *Web:* www.hotan.com	Livermore	CA	94551	925-290-1000		246
Hotcards Com Inc 2400 Superior Ave *TF:* 800-787-4831 ■ *Web:* hotcards.com	Cleveland	OH	44114	216-241-4040		344
Hotchkis & Wiley Capital Management LLC 725 S Figueroa St 3rd Fl *Web:* www.hwcm.com	Los Angeles	CA	90017	213-430-1000	430-1001	463
Hotchkiss School 11 Interlaken Rd PO Box 800 *Web:* www.hotchkiss.org	Lakeville	CT	06039	860-435-3102		622
Hotel & Restaurant Supply Inc 5020 Arundel Rd PO Box 6 *TF:* 800-782-6651 ■ *Web:* www.hnrsupply.com	Meridian	MS	39302	601-482-7127	482-7170	300
Hotel & Suites Normandin 4700 Pierre-Bertrand Blvd *TF:* 800-463-6721 ■ *Web:* www.hotelnormandin.com	Quebec City	QC	G2J1A4	418-622-1611	622-9277	379
Hotel & Travel Industry Federal Credit Union 1600 Kapiolani Blvd Ste 110 *TF:* 877-267-6941 ■ *Web:* htifcu.com	Honolulu	HI	96814	808-942-5115		219
Hotel 140 140 Clarendon St *Web:* www.hotel140.com	Boston	MA	02116	617-585-5600		379
Hotel 43 981 Grove St *TF:* 800-243-4622 ■ *Web:* www.hotel43.com	Boise	ID	83702	208-342-4622	344-5751	379
Hotel 71 71 St Pierre St *TF:* 888-692-1171 ■ *Web:* www.hotel71.ca	Quebec City	QC	G1K4A4	418-692-1171		379
Hotel Abri 127 Ellis St *Web:* www.hotelabrisf.com	San Francisco	CA	94102	415-392-8800		379
Hotel Alex Johnson 523 Sixth St *Web:* www.alexjohnson.com	Rapid City	SD	57701	605-342-1210		379
Hotel Allegro Chicago 171 W Randolph St *TF:* 800-643-1500 ■ *Web:* www.allegrochicago.com	Chicago	IL	60601	312-236-0123		379
Hotel Ambassadeur 3401 Blvd Ste-Anne **Fax Area Code:* 418 ■ *TF:* 800-363-4619 ■ *Web:* www.hotelambassadeur.ca	Quebec City	QC	G1E3L4	800-363-4619	666-2775*	379
Hotel Andra 2000 Fourth Ave *TF:* 877-448-8600 ■ *Web:* www.hotelandra.com	Seattle	WA	98121	206-448-8600	441-7140	379
Hotel Andrew Jackson 919 Royal St *Web:* www.andrewjacksonhotel.com	New Orleans	LA	70116	504-561-5881		379
Hotel Angeleno 170 N Church Ln *Web:* www.hotelangeleno.com	Los Angeles	CA	90049	310-476-6411		379
Hotel Arcata 708 Ninth St *Web:* hotelarcata.com	Arcata	CA	95521	707-826-0217		378
Hotel Arts Kensington 1126 Memorial Dr NW *TF:* 877-313-3733 ■ *Web:* www.hotelartskensington.com	Calgary	AB	T2N3E3	403-228-4442	228-9608	379
Hotel Astor 956 Washington Ave *Web:* www.hotelastor.com	Miami Beach	FL	33139	305-531-8081	531-3193	379
Hotel at Auburn University & Dixon Conference Ctr, The 241 S College St *TF:* 800-228-2876 ■ *Web:* www.auhcc.com	Auburn	AL	36830	334-821-8200	826-8746	377
Hotel at Old Town Wichita 830 E First St *TF:* 877-265-3869 ■ *Web:* www.hotelatoldtown.com	Wichita	KS	67202	316-267-4800	267-4840	379
Hotel Beacon 2130 Broadway *TF:* 800-572-4969 ■ *Web:* www.beaconhotel.com	New York	NY	10023	212-787-1100		379
Hotel Bethlehem 437 Main St *Web:* www.hotelbethlehem.com	Bethlehem	PA	18018	610-625-5000		379
Hotel Bijou 111 Mason St *TF:* 800-771-1022 ■ *Web:* www.hotelbijou.com	San Francisco	CA	94102	415-771-1200	346-3196	379
Hotel Blake 500 S Dearborn St *Web:* www.hotelblake.com	Chicago	IL	60605	312-986-1234		379
Hotel Blue 717 Central Ave NW *TF:* 877-878-4868 ■ *Web:* www.thehotelblue.com	Albuquerque	NM	87102	505-924-2400		378
Hotel Bonaparte 447 Rue Saint-Francois-Xavier *Web:* bonaparte.com	Montreal	QC	H2Y2T1	514-844-1448	844-0272	377
Hotel Boulderado 2115 13th St *TF:* 800-433-4344 ■ *Web:* www.boulderado.com	Boulder	CO	80302	303-442-4344	442-4378	379
Hotel Captain Cook 939 W Fifth Ave *TF:* 800-843-1950 ■ *Web:* www.captaincook.com	Anchorage	AK	99501	907-276-6000		379
Hotel Casa del Mar 1910 Ocean Way *Web:* www.hotelcasadelmar.com	Santa Monica	CA	90405	310-581-5533		379
Hotel Chateau Bellevue 16 Rue de la Porte *TF:* 877-849-1877 ■ *Web:* www.hotelvieux-quebec.com	Quebec City	QC	G1R4M9	418-692-2573	692-4876	379
Hotel Chateau Laurier 1220 Pl George-V Ouest *TF:* 877-522-8108 ■ *Web:* www.hotelchateaulaurier.com	Quebec City	QC	G1R5B8	418-522-8108	524-8768	379
Hotel Cheribourg 2603 Chemin du Parc *TF:* 877-845-5344 ■ *Web:* www.hotelsvillegia.com	Orford	QC	J1X8C8	819-843-3308	843-2639	669
Hotel Classique 2815 Laurier Blvd *TF:* 800-463-1885 ■ *Web:* www.hotelclassique.com	Quebec City	QC	G1V4H3	800-463-1885		379
Hotel Cleaning Services Inc 9609 N 22nd Ave *Web:* hotelcleaningservices.com	Phoenix	AZ	85021	602-588-0864	588-9960	192
Hotel Colorado 526 Pine St *TF:* 800-544-3998 ■ *Web:* hotelcolorado.com	Glenwood Springs	CO	81601	970-945-6511	945-7030	379
Hotel Commonwealth 500 Commonwealth Ave *TF:* 866-784-4000 ■ *Web:* www.hotelcommonwealth.com	Boston	MA	02215	617-933-5000	266-6888	379
Hotel Congress 311 E Congress St *TF:* 800-722-8848 ■ *Web:* hotelcongress.com	Tucson	AZ	85701	520-622-8848	792-6366	379
Hotel Contessa 306 W Market St *TF:* 866-435-0900 ■ *Web:* www.thehotelcontessa.com	San Antonio	TX	78205	210-229-9222		379
Hotel Crescent Court 400 Crescent Ct *Web:* www.rosewoodhotels.com	Dallas	TX	75201	214-871-3200	871-3272	379
Hotel De La Monnaie Owners Association Inc 405 Esplanade Ave *Web:* www.hoteldelamonnaie.com	New Orleans	LA	70116	504-947-0009		379
Hotel Deca 4507 Brooklyn Ave NE *TF:* 800-899-0251 ■ *Web:* www.graduatehotels.com	Seattle	WA	98105	206-634-2000		379
Hotel Del Coronado 1500 Orange Ave *TF:* 800-468-3533 ■ *Web:* hoteldel.com	Coronado	CA	92118	619-435-6611		669
Hotel Deluxe 729 SW 15th Ave *Web:* www.hoteldeluxeportland.com	Portland	OR	97205	503-219-2094		379
Hotel Dieu Hospital 166 Brock St *TF:* 855-544-3400 ■ *Web:* kingstonhsc.ca	Kingston	ON	K7L5G2	613-544-3400		374-2
Hotel Drisco 2901 Pacific Ave *TF:* 800-634-7277 ■ *Web:* hoteldrisco.com	San Francisco	CA	94115	415-346-2880		379
Hotel Edison 228 W 47th St *TF:* 800-637-7070 ■ *Web:* www.edisonhotelnyc.com	New York	NY	10036	212-840-5000		379
Hotel El Convento 100 Cristo St *Web:* www.elconvento.com	San Juan	PR	00901	787-723-9020		379
Hotel Elegante Event & Conference Ctr 2886 South Cir Dr *Web:* www.hotelelegante.com	Colorado Springs	CO	80906	719-576-5900		707
Hotel Elysee 60 E 54th St *Web:* www.elyseehotel.com	New York	NY	10022	212-753-1066		379
Hotel Encanto de Las Cruces 705 S Telshor Blvd *TF:* 866-383-0443 ■ *Web:* www.hotelencanto.com	Las Cruces	NM	88011	575-522-4300		379
Hotel Equities Inc 41 Perimeter Ctr E Ste 510 **Fax Area Code:* 770 ■ *Web:* www.hotelequities.com	Atlanta	GA	30346	678-578-4444	220-7779*	378
Hotel Fusion 140 Ellis St *TF:* 866-753-4244 ■ *Web:* hotelfusionsf.com	San Francisco	CA	94102	415-568-2525		132
Hotel Gault 449 Rue St-Helene St *TF:* 866-904-1616 ■ *Web:* www.hotelgault.com	Montreal	QC	H2Y2K9	514-904-1616		379
Hotel George 15 East St NW *TF:* 800-576-8331 ■ *Web:* www.hotelgeorge.com	Washington	DC	20001	202-347-4200	347-4213	379
Hotel Grand Pacific 463 Belleville St *TF:* 800-663-7550 ■ *Web:* www.hotelgrandpacific.com	Victoria	BC	V8V1X3	250-386-0450	380-4475	379
Hotel Grand Victorian 2325 W Hwy 76 *Web:* www.hotelgrandvictorian.com	Branson	MO	65616	417-336-2935		379
Hotel Granduca 1080 Uptown Pk Blvd *TF:* 888-472-6382 ■ *Web:* www.granducahouston.com	Houston	TX	77056	713-418-1000		379
Hotel Griffon 155 Steuart St *TF:* 800-321-2201 ■ *Web:* www.hotelgriffon.com	San Francisco	CA	94105	415-495-2100		379
Hotel Group, The (THG) 201 Fifth Ave S Ste 200 *Web:* www.thehotelgroup.com	Edmonds	WA	98020	425-771-1788	672-8280	379
Hotel Hershey, The 100 Hotel Rd *TF:* 844-330-1711 ■ *Web:* www.thehotelhershey.com	Hershey	PA	17033	717-533-2171	534-8887	669
Hotel Huntington Beach 7667 Center Ave *Web:* www.hotelhb.com	Huntington Beach	CA	92647	714-891-0123	895-4591	379
Hotel Icon 220 Main St *Web:* hotelicon.com	Houston	TX	77002	713-224-4266		379
Hotel Indigo San Diego 509 Ninth Ave *Web:* www.hotelinsd.com	San Diego	CA	92101	619-727-4000		379
Hotel La Rose 308 Wilson St *TF:* 800-527-6738 ■ *Web:* www.hotellarose.com	Santa Rosa	CA	95401	707-579-3200		379
Hotel Le Bleu 370 Fourth Ave *TF:* 866-427-6073 ■ *Web:* www.hotellebleu.com	Brooklyn	NY	11215	718-625-1500		379
Hotel Le Cantlie Suites 1110 Sherbrooke St W *TF:* 800-567-1110 ■ *Web:* www.hotelcantlie.com	Montreal	QC	H3A1G9	514-842-2000	844-7808	379
Hotel Le Capitole 972 Rue St-Jean *TF:* 800-261-9903 ■ *Web:* www.lecapitole.com	Quebec City	QC	G1R1R5	418-694-4444		379
Hotel Le Clos Saint-Louis 69 St Louis St *TF:* 800-461-1311 ■ *Web:* www.clossaintlouis.com	Quebec City	QC	G1R3Z2	418-694-1311	694-9411	379
Hotel Le Marais 717 Conti St *TF:* 800-935-8740 ■ *Web:* www.hotellemarais.com	New Orleans	LA	70130	504-525-2300		379

Name / Address	City	State	Zip	Phone	Fax	Class
Hotel le Priori						
15 Sault-au-Matelot St	Quebec City	QC	G1K3Y7	418-692-3992		379
TF: 800-351-3992 ■ *Web:* www.hotellepriori.com						
Hotel Le Soleil 567 Hornby St	Vancouver	BC	V6C2E8	604-632-3000	632-3001	379
TF: 877-632-3030 ■ *Web:* www.hotellesoleil.com						
Hotel Le St-James 355 St Jacques St	Montreal	QC	H2Y1N9	514-841-3111	841-1232	379
TF: 866-841-3111 ■ *Web:* www.hotellestjames.com						
Hotel Lombardy						
2019 Pennsylvania Ave NW	Washington	DC	20006	202-828-2600		379
TF: 800-424-5486 ■ *Web:* www.hotellombardy.com						
Hotel Lucia 400 SW Broadway	Portland	OR	97205	503-225-1717	225-1919	379
TF: 877-225-1717 ■ *Web:* hotellucia.com						
Hotel Madera						
1310 New Hampshire Ave NW	Washington	DC	20036	202-296-7600	293-2476	379
TF: 800-430-1202 ■ *Web:* www.hotelmadera.com						
Hotel Majestic 1500 Sutter St	San Francisco	CA	94109	415-441-1100	673-7331	379
Web: www.thehotelmajestic.com						
Hotel Manoir Victoria						
44 Cote du Palais	Quebec City	QC	G1R4H8	418-692-1030	692-3822	379
TF: 800-463-6283 ■ *Web:* www.manoir-victoria.com						
Hotel Marlowe Cambridge						
25 Edwind H Land Blvd	Cambridge	MA	02141	617-868-8000	868-8001	379
TF: 800-825-7140 ■ *Web:* www.hotelmarlowe.com						
Hotel Max 620 Stewart St	Seattle	WA	98101	206-728-6299		379
TF: 866-833-6299 ■ *Web:* www.hotelmaxseattle.com						
Hotel Mead 451 E Grand Ave	Wisconsin Rapids	WI	54494	800-843-6323		379
TF: 800-843-6323 ■ *Web:* www.hotelmead.com						
Hotel Mela 120 W 44th St	New York	NY	10036	212-710-7000		379
TF: 877-452-6352 ■ *Web:* www.hotelmela.com						
Hotel Metro 411 E Mason St	Milwaukee	WI	53202	414-272-1937		379
Web: www.hotelmetro.com						
Hotel ML, The 915 Rt 73	Mount Laurel	NJ	08054	856-234-7300		378
Web: thehotelml.com						
Hotel Monaco Chicago 225 N Wabash Ave	Chicago	IL	60601	312-960-8500	960-1883	379
TF: 866-610-0081 ■ *Web:* www.monaco-chicago.com						
Hotel Monaco Denver 1717 Champa St	Denver	CO	80202	303-296-1717	296-1818	379
TF: 800-990-1303 ■ *Web:* www.monaco-denver.com						
Hotel Monaco Portland						
506 SW Washington at Fifth Ave	Portland	OR	97204	503-222-0001	222-0004	379
TF: 866-861-9514 ■ *Web:* www.monaco-portland.com						
Hotel Monaco Salt Lake City						
15 West 200 South	Salt Lake City	UT	84101	801-595-0000	532-8500	379
TF: 800-805-1801 ■ *Web:* www.monaco-saltlakecity.com						
Hotel Monaco Seattle 1101 Fourth Ave	Seattle	WA	98101	206-621-1770	621-7779	379
TF: 800-715-6513 ■ *Web:* www.monaco-seattle.com						
Hotel Monte Vista						
100 N San Francisco St	Flagstaff	AZ	86001	928-779-6971	779-2904	379
TF: 800-545-3068 ■ *Web:* www.hotelmontevista.com						
Hotel Monteleone 214 Royal St	New Orleans	LA	70130	504-523-3341		379
TF: 866-338-4684 ■ *Web:* hotelmonteleone.com						
Hotel Mortagne 1228 Rue Nobel	Boucherville	QC	J4B5H1	450-655-9966		707
TF: 877-655-9966 ■ *Web:* www.hotelmortagne.com						
Hotel Murano 1320 Broadway Plz	Tacoma	WA	98402	253-238-8000		379
Web: hotelmuranotacoma.com						
Hotel Nelligan						
106 Rue Saint-Paul Ouest	Montreal	QC	H2Y1Z3	514-788-2040		707
Web: www.hotelnelligan.com						
Hotel Nikko San Francisco						
222 Mason St	San Francisco	CA	94102	415-394-1100	394-1102	671
Web: www.hotelnikkosf.com						
Hotel Northampton 36 King St	Northampton	MA	01060	413-584-3100		379
TF: 800-547-3529 ■ *Web:* www.hotelnorthampton.com						
Hotel Ocean 1230 Ocean Dr	Miami Beach	FL	33139	305-672-2579	352-8058*	379
**Fax Area Code:* 786 ■ *TF:* 844-319-3854 ■ *Web:* hotelocean.com						
Hotel Oceana						
Oceana Santa Monica						
849 Ocean Ave	Santa Monica	CA	90403	310-393-0486		379
Web: www.hoteloceanasantamonica.com						
Santa Barbara						
202 W Cabrillo Blvd	Santa Barbara	CA	93101	805-965-4577		379
TF: 800-965-9776 ■ *Web:* www.hotelmilosantabarbara.com						
Hotel of Rivington 107 Rivington St	New York	NY	10002	212-475-2600		378
Web: www.hotelonrivington.com						
Hotel One Sixty-six Magnificent Mile						
166 E Superior St	Chicago	IL	60611	312-787-6000		707
Web: hotel166magmile.com						
Hotel Pacific 300 Pacific St	Monterey	CA	93940	831-373-5700	373-6921	379
Web: www.hotelpacific.com						
Hotel Palomar Washington DC						
2121 P St NW	Washington	DC	20037	202-448-1800		378
Web: www.hotelpalomar-dc.com						
Hotel Park City (HPC) 2001 Park Ave	Park City	UT	84060	435-200-2000	940-5001	379
TF: 888-999-0098 ■ *Web:* www.hotelparkcity.com						
Hotel Plaza Athenee 37 E 64th St	New York	NY	10065	212-734-9100	772-0958	379
TF: 800-447-8800 ■ *Web:* www.plaza-athenee.com						
Hotel Plaza Quebec						
3031 Laurier Blvd	Quebec City	QC	G1V2M2	418-658-2727	658-6587	379
TF: 800-567-5276 ■ *Web:* www.hotelsjaro.com						
Hotel Plaza Real 125 Washington Ave	Santa Fe	NM	87501	505-988-4900	983-9322	379
TF: 855-752-9273 ■ *Web:* www.hotelchimayo.com						
Hotel Plaza Valleyfield						
40 Du Centenaire Ave	Salaberry-de-Valleyfield	QC	J6S3L6	450-373-1990		377
TF: 877-882-8818 ■ *Web:* hotelplazavalleyfield.com						
Hotel Portsmouth 40 Ct St	Portsmouth	NH	03801	603-433-1200		379
Web: www.thehotelportsmouth.com						
Hotel Preston 733 Briley Pkwy	Nashville	TN	37217	615-361-5900		379
Web: www.hotelpreston.com						
Hotel Pro Staffing LLC						
1950 N Park Pl Ste 330	Atlanta	GA	30339	770-937-9007		260
Web: www.gohotelpro.com						
Hotel Provincial						
1024 Rue Chartres	New Orleans	LA	70116	504-581-4995	581-1018	379
TF: 800-535-7922 ■ *Web:* www.hotelprovincial.com						
Hotel Roanoke & Conference Ctr						
110 Shenandoah Ave	Roanoke	VA	24016	540-985-5900	853-8264	377
TF: 866-594-4722 ■ *Web:* www.hotelroanoke.com						
Hotel Rodney 142 Second St	Lewes	DE	19958	302-645-6466		379
TF: 800-824-8754 ■ *Web:* www.hotelrodneydelaware.com						
Hotel Roger Williams 131 Madison Ave	New York	NY	10016	212-448-7000	448-7007	379
TF: 888-448-7788 ■ *Web:* www.therogernewyork.com						
Hotel Rose 50 SW Morrison St	Portland	OR	97204	503-221-0711		377
Web: www.hotelfifty.com						
Hotel Ruby Foo's 7655 Decarie Blvd	Montreal	QC	H4P2H2	514-731-7701		379
TF: 800-361-5419 ■ *Web:* www.hotelrubyfoos.com						
Hotel Saint Francis						
210 Don Gaspar Ave	Santa Fe	NM	87501	505-983-5700	989-7690	379
TF: 800-529-5700 ■ *Web:* www.hotelstfrancis.com						
Hotel Saint Marie 827 Toulouse St	New Orleans	LA	70112	504-561-8951		379
TF: 888-626-4812 ■ *Web:* www.hotelstmarie.com						
Hotel Saint Pierre						
911 Burgundy St	New Orleans	LA	70116	504-524-4401		379
Web: www.hotelstpierre.com						
Hotel Saint Regis Detroit						
3071 W Grand Blvd	Detroit	MI	48202	313-873-3000	481-8408	379
TF: 855-408-7738 ■ *Web:* www.hotelstregisdetroit.com						
Hotel San Carlos 202 N Central Ave	Phoenix	AZ	85004	602-253-4121	253-6668	379
TF: 866-253-4121 ■ *Web:* www.hotelsancarlos.com						
Hotel Santa Barbara						
533 State St	Santa Barbara	CA	93101	805-957-9300	962-2412	379
TF: 800-549-9869 ■ *Web:* www.hotelsantabarbara.com						
Hotel Sepia 3135 Ch St-Louis	Sainte-Foy	QC	G1W1R9	418-653-4941	653-0774	379
TF: 888-301-6837 ■ *Web:* www.hotelsepia.ca						
Hotel Shangri La 1301 Ocean Ave	Santa Monica	CA	90401	310-394-2791	496-0891	378
Web: www.shangrila-hotel.com						
Hotel Shelley 844 Collins Ave	Miami Beach	FL	33139	305-531-3341	674-0811	379
TF: 877-762-3477 ■ *Web:* www.hotelshelley.com						
Hotel Solamar 435 Sixth Ave	San Diego	CA	92101	619-819-9500	531-8742	379
TF: 877-230-0300 ■ *Web:* www.hotelsolamar.com						
Hotel Spero 405 Taylor St	San Francisco	CA	94102	415-885-2500	474-4879	379
TF: 866-575-9941 ■ *Web:* www.hotelspero.com						
Hotel St Germain 2516 Maple Ave	Dallas	TX	75201	214-871-2516	871-0740	379
Web: www.hotelstgermain.com						
Hotel st James Inc 109 W 45th St	New York	NY	10036	212-730-9444		379
Web: www.hotelstjames.net						
Hotel Strasburg, The						
213 S Holliday St	Strasburg	VA	22657	540-465-9191	465-4788	379
TF: 800-348-8327 ■ *Web:* www.hotelstrasburg.com						
Hotel Supplies Online 4040 N Blvd	Montgomery	AL	36110	215-554-3817	855-9533*	76
**Fax Area Code:* 775 ■ *Web:* www.hotelsupplies-online.com						
Hotel Teatro 1100 Fourteenth St	Denver	CO	80202	303-228-1100		379
TF: 888-727-1200 ■ *Web:* www.hotelteatro.com						
Hotel The Queen Mary						
1126 Queens Hwy	Long Beach	CA	90802	562-499-1739		379
TF: 877-342-0742 ■ *Web:* www.queenmary.com						
Hotel Triton 342 Grant Ave	San Francisco	CA	94108	415-394-0500	394-0555	379
TF: 800-800-1299 ■ *Web:* www.hoteltriton.com						
Hotel Tybee 1401 Strand Ave	Tybee Island	GA	31328	912-786-7777	786-4531	379
Web: www.hoteltybee.com						
Hotel Universel 2300 Ch St-Foy	Quebec City	QC	G1V1S5	800-463-4495	653-4486*	379
**Fax Area Code:* 418 ■ *TF:* 800-463-4495 ■ *Web:* www.hoteluniversel.qc.ca						
Hotel Valencia Riverwalk						
150 E Houston St	San Antonio	TX	78205	210-227-9700		707
TF: 855-596-3387 ■ *Web:* www.hotelvalencia-riverwalk.com						
Hotel Valencia Santana Row						
355 Santana Row	San Jose	CA	95128	408-551-0010		379
TF: 855-596-3396 ■ *Web:* www.hotelvalencia-santanarow.com						
Hotel Valley Ho 6850 E Main St	Scottsdale	AZ	85251	480-376-2600	421-7782	379
TF: 866-882-4484 ■ *Web:* www.hotelvalleyho.com						
Hotel Victoria 56 Yonge St	Toronto	ON	M5E1G5	416-363-1666		379
TF: 800-363-8228 ■ *Web:* www.hotelvictoria-toronto.com						
Hotel Viking 1 Bellevue Ave	Newport	RI	02840	401-847-3300		379
TF: 800-556-7126 ■ *Web:* www.hotelviking.com						
Hotel Villagio 6481 Washington St	Yountville	CA	94599	707-944-8877		707
Web: www.villagio.com						
Hotel Vintage Park 1100 Fifth Ave	Seattle	WA	98101	206-624-8000	623-0568	379
TF: 800-853-3914 ■ *Web:* www.hotelvintage-seattle.com						
Hotel Wales 1295 Madison Ave	New York	NY	10128	212-876-6000		379
TF: 866-925-3746 ■ *Web:* www.hotelwalesnyc.com						
Hotel Weatherford, The						
23 N Leroux St	Flagstaff	AZ	86001	928-779-1919		379
Web: www.weatherfordhotel.com						
Hotel Wolcott 4 W 31st St	New York	NY	10001	212-268-2900	563-0096	379
Web: www.wolcott.com						
Hotel Zags Portland, The						
515 SW Clay St	Portland	OR	97201	855-523-6914		378
Web: www.thehotelzags.com						
Hotel ZaZa Dallas 2332 Leonard St	Dallas	TX	75201	214-468-8399	468-8397	379
TF: 800-597-8399 ■ *Web:* www.hotelzaza.com						
Hotel, The 801 Collins Ave	Miami Beach	FL	33139	305-531-2222	531-3222	379
Web: www.thehotelofsouthbeach.com						
Hotel-Dieu d'Arthabaska						
5 Rue des Hospitalieres	Victoriaville	QC	G6P6N2	819-357-2030	758-7281	374-2
Web: www.csssae.qc.ca						
Hotel-Dieu de Sorel						
400 Ave Hotel-Dieu	Sorel-Tracy	QC	J3P1N5	450-746-6003		374-2
TF: 888-297-5970 ■ *Web:* fondationhoteldieusorel.org						
Hotel-Dieu Grace Hospital						
1030 Ouellette Ave	Windsor	ON	N9A1E1	519-973-4411		374-2
Web: www.hdgh.org						
Hotelroomscom Inc						
108-18 Queens Blvd	Forest Hills	NY	11375	718-730-6000	261-4598	397
TF: 800-486-7000 ■ *Web:* www.hotelrooms.com						
Hotels at Home Inc 208 Passaic Ave	Fairfield	NJ	07004	973-882-8437		707
Web: www.hotelsathome.com						
Hotels Etc Inc						
910 Athens Hwy Ste K-214	Loganville	GA	30052	877-967-7283	461-5637*	377
**Fax Area Code:* 866 ■ *TF:* 877-967-7283 ■ *Web:* www.hotelsetc.com						
Hotels Unlimited Inc						
399 Monmouth St	East Windsor	NJ	08520	609-632-0006		379
Web: www.hotelsunlimited.com						
HOT-FM 96.3 (CHR)						
21 E St Joseph St	Indianapolis	IN	46204	317-266-9600		645-74
Web: hot963.com						
HOT-FM 98.3 (Urban) 3202 N Oracle Rd	Tucson	AZ	85705	520-618-2100		645-165
Web: hot983.iheart.com						

	Phone	Fax	Class
Hot-Line Freight System Inc PO Box 205 . . . . . West Salem WI 54669 *TF:* 800-468-4686 ■ *Web:* www.hotlinefreight.com	608-486-1600	486-1601	780
Hotline to HR 110 Confederation Pkwy 2nd Fl . . . . . Concord ON L4K4T8	416-619-7867		260
HotLink Inc 3130 De La Cruz Blvd Ste 211 . . . . . Santa Clara CA 95054 *Web:* www.hotlink.com	408-463-6130		7
Hotronic USA Inc 25 Omega Dr. . . . . . Williston VT 05495 *Web:* www.hotronic.com	802-862-7403	863-6519	37
Hotspex Inc 40 Eglinton Ave E Ste 801 . . . . . Toronto ON M4P3A2 *Web:* www.hotspex.com	416-487-5439		466
HotSpot for Birds 1135 N Poinsettia Dr . . . . . Los Angeles CA 90046 **Fax Area Code:* 323 ■ *TF:* 888-246-8776	888-246-8776	927-1770*	297-8
Hotwatt Inc 128 Maple St . . . . . Danvers MA 01923 *Web:* www.hotwatt.com	978-777-0070	774-2409	318
Hotwire Communications LLC 2100 W Cypress Creek Rd . . . . . Fort Lauderdale FL 33309 *TF:* 800-355-5668 ■ *Web:* hotwirecommunications.com	800-355-5668		224
Hotwire Development LLC 15354 N 83rd Way Ste 102. . . . . Scottsdale AZ 85260 *Web:* productdevelopmentangel.com	480-250-4563		393
Hotwire Inc PO Box 26285. . . . . San Francisco CA 94126 **Fax Area Code:* 415 ■ *TF:* 866-468-9473 ■ *Web:* www.hotwire.com	866-381-3981	343-8401*	773
Houchen Bindery Ltd 340 First St . . . . . Utica NE 68456 *TF:* 800-869-0420 ■ *Web:* www.houchenbindery.com	402-534-2261		626
Houchens Industries Inc 700 Church St . . . . . Bowling Green KY 42101 *TF:* 800-846-3252 ■ *Web:* www.houchensindustries.com	270-843-3252		345
Houchin Community Blood Bank 5901 Truxtun Ave . . . . . Bakersfield CA 93309 *Web:* westcoastblood.org	661-323-4222		89
Houdini Museum 1433 N Main Ave. . . . . Scranton PA 18508 *Web:* www.houdini.org	570-342-5555		520
Houff Transfer Inc 46 Houff Rd . . . . . Weyers Cave VA 24486 *TF:* 800-476-4683 ■ *Web:* www.houff.com	540-234-9233	234-9011	780
Hougen Manufacturing Inc 3001 Hougen Dr. . . . . . Swartz Creek MI 48473 *TF:* 800-426-7818 ■ *Web:* hougen.com	810-635-7111	635-8277	493
Hough Petroleum Corp 340 Fourth St . . . . . Ewing NJ 08638 *TF:* 800-400-7154 ■ *Web:* houghpetroleum.com	609-771-1022		580
Houghton Academy 9790 Thayer St. . . . . Houghton NY 14744 *Web:* www.houghtonacademy.org	585-567-8115	567-8048	622
Houghton Chemical Corp 52 Cambridge St. . . . . Allston MA 02134 *TF:* 800-777-2466 ■ *Web:* www.houghton.com	617-254-1010		145
Houghton College 1 Willard Ave PO Box 128 . . . . . Houghton NY 14744 *TF:* 800-777-2556 ■ *Web:* www.houghton.edu	585-567-9200	567-9522	166
Houghton County 401 E Houghton Ave. . . . . Houghton MI 49931 *Web:* www.houghtoncounty.net	906-482-1150	483-0364	338
Houghton Financial Partners LLC 210 N Campbell . . . . . El Paso TX 79901 *Web:* houghtonfinancialpartners.com	915-541-7055		390
Houghton International Inc 945 Madison Ave PO Box 930 . . . . . Valley Forge PA 19482 *TF:* 888-459-9844 ■ *Web:* www.houghtonintl.com	610-666-4000	666-0174	3
Houghton Mifflin Harcourt 222 Berkeley St. . . . . Boston MA 02116 **Fax Area Code:* 617 ■ *TF:* 800-225-5425 ■ *Web:* www.eduplace.com	800-225-5425	351-3546*	637-2
Houlahan Chrissy (Rep D - PA) 1218 Longworth House Office Bldg . . . . . Washington DC 20515 *Web:* www.houlahan.house.gov	202-225-4315		342-2
Houlihan Capital LLC 500 W Madison St Ste 2600. . . . . Chicago IL 60661 *Web:* www.houlihancapital.com	312-450-8600		690
Houlihan Valuation Advisors Inc 28662 W Northwest Hwy Ste 3 . . . . . Lake Barrington IL 60010 *Web:* www.houlihan-hva.com	847-381-3616		70
Houlihan's Restaurants Inc 8700 State Line Rd Ste 100 . . . . . Leawood KS 66206 *Web:* www.houlihans.com	913-901-2500		670
Houma Area Convention & Visitors Bureau 114 Tourist Dr. . . . . . Gray LA 70359 *TF:* 800-688-2732 ■ *Web:* houmatravel.com	985-868-2732		206
Houmas House Plantation & Gardens 40136 Hwy 942 . . . . . Darrow LA 70725 *Web:* houmashouse.com	225-473-9380		50-3
Houma-Terrebonne Chamber of Commerce 6133 Louisiana 311 . . . . . Houma LA 70360 *TF:* 800-649-7346 ■ *Web:* houmachamber.com	985-876-5600	876-5611	139
Hound Ears Club 328 Shulls Mill Rd. . . . . Boone NC 28607 *TF:* 800-243-8652 ■ *Web:* houndears.com	828-963-4321		669
Hour of Harvest Inc 219 WLJC Dr PO Box Y . . . . . Beattyville KY 41311 *Web:* www.wljc.com	606-464-3600		647
Hour, The 301 Merritt 7 . . . . . Norwalk CT 06851 *Web:* www.thehour.com	203-846-3281		532-2
Housatonic Community College 900 Lafayette Blvd . . . . . Bridgeport CT 06604 *Web:* www.hctc.commnet.edu	203-332-5000	332-5123	162
Housatonic Meadows State Park 90 Rte 7 N. . . . . Sharon CT 06069 *Web:* portal.ct.gov	860-672-6772		565
Housatonic Museum of Art Housatonic Community College 900 Lafayette Blvd . . . . . Bridgeport CT 06604 *Web:* www.housatonic.edu	203-332-5052		520
Housatonic Partners 800 Boylston St Ste 2220. . . . . Boston MA 02199 *Web:* housatonicpartners.com	617-399-9200	267-5565	792
Hou-scape Inc 17725 Telge Rd . . . . . Cypress TX 77429 *Web:* www.hou-scape.com	281-579-6741		776
House 1230 Grant Ave. . . . . San Francisco CA 94133 *Web:* www.thehse.com	415-986-8612		671
House Chevrolet Co 410 Main St S . . . . . Stewartville MN 55976 *Web:* www.housechevrolet.net	507-533-4255		57

	Phone	Fax	Class
House Committee on veterans Affairs *Veterans Affairs Committee* 335 Cannon Bldg. . . . . Washington DC 20515 *Web:* veterans.house.gov	202-225-3527		342-1
House Foods America Corp 7351 Orangewood Ave . . . . . Garden Grove CA 92841 *TF:* 877-333-7077 ■ *Web:* www.house-foods.com	714-901-4350		296-20
House of Batteries (HOB) 10910 Talbert Ave. . . . . Fountain Valley CA 92708 *TF:* 800-432-3385 ■ *Web:* www.houseofbatteries.com	714-962-7600	962-7644	246
House of Blues Entertainment Inc 7060 Hollywood Blvd . . . . . Hollywood CA 90028 *Web:* www.houseofblues.com	323-769-4600		181
House of Brick Technologies LLC 9300 Underwood Ave Ste 300 . . . . . Omaha NE 68114 *TF:* 877-780-7038 ■ *Web:* houseofbrick.com	402-445-0764		180
House of Broel's Historic Mansion & Dollhouse Museum 2220 St Charles Ave . . . . . New Orleans LA 70130 *Web:* www.houseofbroel.com	504-522-2220		520
House of Clean Inc 332 Gallatin Park Dr . . . . . Bozeman MT 59715 *TF:* 800-223-5082 ■ *Web:* www.house-of-clean.com	406-587-5012	586-9210	76
House of Diamonds Inc 11805 College Blvd . . . . . Overland Park KS 66210 *Web:* mybigrock.com	913-469-0111		410
House of Dynasty 7550 Telegraph Rd . . . . . Alexandria VA 22315 *Web:* houseofdynasty.com	703-922-5210		671
House of Flavors Inc 110 N William St . . . . . Ludington MI 49431 *TF:* 800-930-7740 ■ *Web:* www.houseofflavors.com	231-845-7369	845-7371	380
House of Hunan 18 Public Sq . . . . . Medina OH 44256 *Web:* thehouseofhunan.com	330-722-1899	722-6566	671
House of India 8501 Delmar Blvd . . . . . Saint Louis MO 63124 *Web:* www.hoistl.com	314-567-6850		671
House of Ing 4113 S Cedar St . . . . . Lansing MI 48910 *Web:* www.houseofing.com	517-393-4848		671
House of Lights LLC 418 Payne Rd. . . . . Scarborough ME 04074 *Web:* houseoflights.com	207-883-0174		362
House of Prime Rib 1906 Van Ness Ave. . . . . San Francisco CA 94109 *Web:* houseofprimerib.net	415-885-4605		671
House of Raeford Farms Inc PO Box 699. . . . . Raeford NC 28376 *Web:* www.houseofraeford.com	910-875-5161		619
House of Schwan Inc 3636 Comotara St . . . . . Wichita KS 67226 *Web:* wichitabeer.com	316-636-9100		81-1
House of Shaw-Espresso Cafe 227 Dorris Pl . . . . . Stockton CA 95204 *Web:* www.houseofshawespresso.top-cafes.com	209-948-4300		671
House of Tang 114 River St. . . . . Montpelier VT 05602 *Web:* houseoftang.com	802-223-6020		671
House of the Good Shepherd, The 1550 Champlin Ave . . . . . Utica NY 13502 *Web:* www.hgs-utica.com	315-235-7600		48-15
House of the Seven Gables 115 Derby St. . . . . Salem MA 01970 *Web:* 7gables.org	978-744-0991	741-4350	50-3
House of Tricks 114 E Seventh St. . . . . Tempe AZ 85281 *Web:* www.houseoftricks.com	480-968-1114	968-0080	671
House of Webster Inc, The 1013 N Second St. . . . . Rogers AR 72756 *Web:* www.houseofwebster.com	479-636-4640		345
House Park & Dobratz Pc 605 W 47th St Ste 301 . . . . . Kansas City MO 64112 *Web:* www.hpdco.com	816-931-3393	931-9636	2
House to House Publications (H2HP) 11 Toll Gate Rd. . . . . Lititz PA 17543 *TF:* 800-848-5892 ■ *Web:* www.h2hp.com	717-627-1996	627-4004	637-2
House-Autry Mills Inc 7000 US Hwy 301 S . . . . . Four Oaks NC 27524 *TF:* 800-849-0802 ■ *Web:* www.house-autry.com	800-849-0802		296-23
Housecall Providers Inc 5100 SW Macadam Ave Ste 200. . . . . Portland OR 97239 *Web:* housecallproviders.org	971-202-5500		363
House-Hasson Hardware Inc 3125 Water Plant Rd. . . . . Knoxville TN 37914 *TF:* 800-333-0520 ■ *Web:* www.househasson.com	800-333-0520		351
Household & Commercial Products Assn 1667 K St NW Ste 300 . . . . . Washington DC 20006 *Web:* www.thehcpa.org	202-872-8110	223-2636	615
HouseLens Inc 150 Fourth Ave N 20th Fl . . . . . Nashville TN 37219 *TF:* 888-552-3851 ■ *Web:* www.houselens.com	888-552-3851		5
HouseMaster 92 E Main St Ste 301. . . . . Somerville NJ 08876 *TF:* 800-526-3939 ■ *Web:* housemaster.com	732-469-6565	469-7405	365
Houser & Allison APC 9970 Research Dr. . . . . Irvine CA 92618 *Web:* www.houser-law.com	949-679-1111		428
Houser Transport Inc 2809 Sam Houser Rd. . . . . Vale NC 28168 *TF:* 800-304-6122 ■ *Web:* www.housertransport.com	704-276-3500		780
Housh-the Home Energy Experts 18 S Main St. . . . . Monroe OH 45050 *TF:* 800-793-6374 ■ *Web:* www.houshhomeenergy.com	513-793-6374		610
Housing Assistance Council (HAC) 1025 Vermont Ave NW Ste 606. . . . . Washington DC 20005 *TF:* 866-234-2689 ■ *Web:* www.ruralhome.org	202-842-8600	347-3441	48-5
Housing Authority Risk Retention Group Inc 189 Commerce Ct PO Box 189. . . . . Cheshire CT 06410 *TF:* 800-873-0242 ■ *Web:* www.housingcenter.com	800-873-0242		390
Housing Data Systems PO Box 883. . . . . West Salem WI 54669 *Web:* www.housingdatasystems.com	608-786-2366		179
Housing Enterprises Inc 51 College St . . . . . Enfield CT 06082 *Web:* housingenterprises.com	860-741-9837		653
Housing First Minnesota 2960 Centre Pointe Dr . . . . . Roseville MN 55113 *Web:* housingfirstmn.org	651-697-1954		78
Housley Communications Inc 3550 S Bryant Blvd. . . . . San Angelo TX 76903 *Web:* housleygroup.com	325-944-9905		186
Houston Academy of Medicine - Texas Medical Ctr 1133 John Freeman Blvd . . . . . Houston TX 77030 *Web:* library.tmc.edu	713-795-4200	790-7052	434-1

Name	Address	City	State	ZIP	Phone	Fax	Class
Houston Advanced Research Ctr (HARC)	4800 Research Forest Dr *Web:* www.harcresearch.org	The Woodlands	TX	77381	281-364-6000	363-7914	668
Houston Apartment Association Inc	4810 Westway Park Blvd. *Web:* www.haaonline.org	Houston	TX	77041	713-595-0300		138
Houston Arboretum & Nature Ctr	4501 Woodway Dr *TF:* 866-510-7219 ■ *Web:* houstonarboretum.org	Houston	TX	77024	713-681-8433		50-5
Houston Area Safety Council	1301 W 13th St. *TF:* 888-955-7233 ■ *Web:* www.hasc.com	Deer Park	TX	77536	281-476-9900		138
Houston Arts Alliance	3201 Allen Pkwy Ste 250 *Web:* www.houstonartsalliance.com	Houston	TX	77019	713-527-9330	630-5210	720
Houston Asset Management Inc	1800 W Loop S. *Web:* allworthfinancial.com	Houston	TX	77027	713-629-1534		690
Houston Ballet	601 Preston St *TF:* 800-828-2787 ■ *Web:* www.houstonballet.org	Houston	TX	77002	713-523-6300	523-4038	573-1
Houston Baptist University	7502 Fondren Rd *TF:* 800-969-3210 ■ *Web:* www.hbu.edu	Houston	TX	77074	281-649-3000	649-3217	166
Houston Chronicle	801 Texas Ave *TF:* 800-735-3800 ■ *Web:* www.chron.com	Houston	TX	77002	713-362-7171	362-6806	532-2
Houston City Hall	901 Bagby St *Web:* www.houstontx.gov	Houston	TX	77002	713-837-0311		337
Houston City Legal Department Law Library	900 Bagby St 4th Fl PO Box 368 *Web:* www.houstontx.gov	Houston	TX	77002	832-393-6491		434-3
Houston Comets	1730 Jefferson St. *Web:* www.wnba.com	Houston	TX	77003	713-739-7442	739-7709	714-2
Houston Community College	*Northeast College* 4638 Airline Dr. *Web:* www.hccs.edu	Houston	TX	77022	713-718-8100	718-7500	162
Houston County	401 E Houston Ave PO Box 370 *TF:* 800-275-8777 ■ *Web:* www.co.houston.tx.us	Crockett	TX	75835	936-544-3255	544-8061	338
Houston County	4 Court Sq. *Web:* houstoncochamber.com	Erin	TN	37061	931-289-5100		338
Houston County	200 Carl Vinson Pkwy *Web:* www.houstoncountyga.org	Warner Robins	GA	31088	478-542-2115	923-5697	338
Houston Crating Inc	18941 Aldine Westfield. *Web:* www.houstoncrating.com	Houston	TX	77073	281-443-3222	443-3234	549
Houston Drilling Management LLC (HDM)	900 Rockmead Dr Ste 220 *Web:* www.hdm-us.com	Kingwood	TX	77339	281-312-1024	312-1064	196
Houston Dynamic Service Inc	8150 Lawndale *Web:* houstondynamic.com	Houston	TX	77012	713-928-6200		757
Houston Dynamo	1001 Avenida de las Americas Ste 200 *Web:* www.houstondynamo.com	Houston	TX	77010	713-276-7500		717
Houston Endowment Inc	600 Travis St Ste 6400 *Web:* www.houstonendowment.org	Houston	TX	77002	713-238-8100	238-8101	303
Houston Fire Museum	2403 Milam St. *Web:* www.houstonfiremuseum.org	Houston	TX	77006	713-524-2526	520-7566	520
Houston Foam Plastics Inc	2019 Brooks St. *Web:* www.houstonfoam.com	Houston	TX	77026	713-224-3484	224-5511	601
Houston Food Bank, The	535 Portwall St. *TF:* 866-384-4277 ■ *Web:* www.houstonfoodbank.org	Houston	TX	77029	713-223-3700		324
Houston Forward Times	4411 Almeda *Web:* forwardtimes.com	Houston	TX	77004	713-526-4727	526-3170	532-4
Houston Graduate School of Theology	4300-C W Bellfort Blvd. *Web:* www.hgst.edu	Houston	TX	77035	713-942-9505	942-9506	167-3
Houston Grand Opera	510 Preston St *TF:* 800-626-7372 ■ *Web:* www.houstongrandopera.org	Houston	TX	77002	713-546-0200		573-2
Houston Grinding & Manufacturing Co	3544 W 12th St.	Houston	TX	77008	713-869-3573		641
Houston Harris Div Patrol Inc	5600 NW Central Dr *TF:* 877-975-9922 ■ *Web:* www.hhdpi.com	Houston	TX	77092	832-649-4440		693
Houston Independent School District	228 McCarty St. *TF:* 800-446-2821 ■ *Web:* www.houstonisd.org	Houston	TX	77029	713-556-6000	556-6006	685
Houston Intercontinental Chamber of Commerce	550 Greens Pkwy Ste 230. *TF:* 855-839-4422 ■ *Web:* www.houstonicc.org	Houston	TX	77067	281-408-0866	248-4388	139
Houston LifeStyle Magazine	10707 Corporate Dr Ste 170. *TF:* 866-505-4456 ■ *Web:* www.houstonlifestyles.com	Stafford	TX	77477	281-240-2445	240-5079	457-22
Houston Livestock Show & Rodeo Inc	NRG Ctr Three NRG Pk. *Web:* www.rodeohouston.com	Houston	TX	77054	832-667-1000		446
Houston Manufacturing Specialty Company Inc	9909 Wallisville Rd. *TF:* 800-231-6030 ■ *Web:* www.houmfg.com	Houston	TX	77013	713-675-7400		326
Houston Maritime Museum	2204 Dorrington St. *Web:* houstonmaritime.org	Houston	TX	77030	713-666-1910		520
Houston Medical Ctr	1601 Watson Blvd. *Web:* www.hhc.org	Warner Robins	GA	31093	478-922-4281		374-3
Houston Medical Records Inc	2211 Norfolk St Ste 950 *Web:* www.houmedicalbilling.com	Houston	TX	77098	713-850-1190		180
Houston Montessori Ctr	7807 Long Point Rd Ste 100. *Web:* www.houstonmontessoricenter.org	Houston	TX	77055	713-465-7670	465-8577	167-3
Houston Motorsports Park	11620 N Lake Houston Pkwy *Web:* www.houstonmotorsportspark.com	Houston	TX	77044	281-458-1972	458-2836	515
Houston Museum of Decorative Arts	201 High St *Web:* www.thehoustonmuseum.org	Chattanooga	TN	37403	423-267-7176		520
Houston Museum of Natural Science	5555 Hermann Pk Dr *Web:* www.hmns.org	Houston	TX	77030	713-639-4629		520
Houston National Cemetery	10410 Veterans Memorial Dr *Web:* www.cem.va.gov	Houston	TX	77038	281-447-8686	447-0580	136
Houston Newspapers- Herald & The Messenger	113 N Grand Ave. *Web:* www.houstonherald.com	Houston	MO	65483	417-967-2000		532-3
Houston Northwest Chamber of Commerce (HNW)	3920 Cypress Creek Pkwy *Web:* www.houstonnwchamber.org	Houston	TX	77068	281-440-4160	440-5302	139
Houston Numismatic Exchange	2486 Times Blvd. *Web:* www.hnex.com	Houston	TX	77005	713-528-2135		459
Houston Pilots	203 Deerwood Glen Dr *Web:* www.houston-pilots.com	Deer Park	TX	77536	713-645-9620		465
Houston Pipe Benders	14500 E Hardy Rd *Web:* www.hpbenders.com	Houston	TX	77039	281-449-8241		595
Houston Press	1621 Milam St Ste 100 *Web:* www.houstonpress.com	Houston	TX	77002	713-280-2400	280-2444	532-5
Houston Production Guide Film	2054 W Main St *Web:* www.houstonproductionguide.com	Houston	TX	77098	713-523-5387		5
Houston Public Library	500 McKinney St *Web:* www.houstonlibrary.org	Houston	TX	77002	832-393-1313	393-1324	434-3
Houston Public Media	4343 Elgin. *Web:* www.houstonpublicmedia.org	Houston	TX	77204	713-743-8888		6
Houston Raceway Park	2525 FM 565 S *Web:* www.royalpurpleraceway.com	Baytown	TX	77523	281-383-7223		515
Houston Rockets	1510 Polk St. *TF:* 866-446-8849 ■ *Web:* www.toyotacenter.com	Houston	TX	77002	713-758-7200		714-1
Houston Symphony Orchestra	615 Louisiana St Ste 102 *Web:* www.houstonsymphony.org	Houston	TX	77002	713-224-7575		573-3
Houston Texans	2 NRG Pk *Web:* www.houstontexans.com	Houston	TX	77054	832-667-2002		715-3
Houston Ticket Brokers	118 Vintage Park Blvd Ste 221 *Web:* houstonticketbrokers.com	Houston	TX	77070	713-397-8193		232
Houston Trust Co	1001 Fannin St Ste 700 *Web:* houstontrust.com	Houston	TX	77002	713-651-9400		401
Houston West Chamber of Commerce	10370 Richmond Ave Ste 125 *TF:* 877-455-5468 ■ *Web:* www.hwcoc.org	Houston	TX	77042	713-785-4922	785-4944	139
Houston Wiper & Mill Supply Co	9800 Market St. *Web:* www.houstonwiper.com	Houston	TX	77029	713-672-0571	673-7637	508
Houston Wire & Cable Co (HWC)	10201 N Loop E *TF:* 800-468-9473 ■ *Web:* www.houwire.com	Houston	TX	77029	713-609-2100	609-2101	246
Houston Zoo Inc	1513 Cambridge. *Web:* www.houstonzoo.org	Houston	TX	77030	713-533-6500		823
Houstonian Hotel Club & Spa	111 N Post Oak Ln *TF:* 800-231-2759 ■ *Web:* www.houstonian.com	Houston	TX	77024	713-680-2626	680-2992	669
Houston-Pasadena Apache Oil Company LP	5136 Spencer Hwy *TF:* 800-248-6388 ■ *Web:* www.apacheoilcompany.com	Pasadena	TX	77505	800-248-6388		581
Hovair Systems Inc	6912 S 220th St *TF:* 800-237-4518 ■ *Web:* www.hovair.com	Kent	WA	98032	253-872-0405	872-0406	207
Hovenweep National Monument	McElmo Rt. *Web:* www.nps.gov	Cortez	CO	81321	970-562-4282		564
Hover Inc	634 2nd St *TF:* 844-754-6837 ■ *Web:* www.hover.to	San Francisco	CA	94107	844-754-6837		178-8
Hover Networks Inc	40 Gardenville Pkwy w *TF:* 855-552-8900 ■ *Web:* www.hovernetworks.com	Buffalo	NY	14224	855-552-8900		224
Hoveround Corp	2151 Whitfield Industrial Way. *TF:* 800-542-7236 ■ *Web:* www.hoveround.com	Sarasota	FL	34243	800-542-7236		477
Hovione LLC	40 Lake Dr. *Web:* www.hovione.com	East Windsor	NJ	08520	609-918-2600	918-2615	231
Hovland & Rasmus PLLC	6800 France Ave S Ste 190. *Web:* hovlandrasmus.com	Edina	MN	55435	612-874-8550		41
Hovnanian Enterprises Inc	1806 S Highland Ave *Web:* www.khov.com	Lombard	IL	60148	630-953-2222		187
How It Works	1014 4th St *TF:* 800-664-6623 ■ *Web:* www.howitworks.com	Anacortes	WA	98221	360-293-3515		344
Howard & Howard Attorneys Pc	450 W 4th St. *Web:* howardandhoward.com	Royal Oak	MI	48067	248-645-1483		428
Howard Bros Florists	8700 S Pennsylvania Ave *TF:* 800-648-0524 ■ *Web:* howardbrothersflorist.com	Oklahoma City	OK	73159	405-632-4747		292
Howard College	1001 Birdwell Ln. *TF:* 877-898-3833 ■ *Web:* howardcollege.edu	Big Spring	TX	79720	432-264-5000	264-5082	162
Howard Community College	10901 Little Patuxent Pkwy. *Web:* www.howardcc.edu	Columbia	MD	21044	410-772-4800	876-8855	162
Howard County	300 Main St *Web:* www.co.howard.tx.us	Big Spring	TX	79720	432-264-2213	264-2215	338
Howard County	3430 Courthouse Dr. *Web:* www.howardcountymd.gov	Ellicott City	MD	21043	410-313-2001		338
Howard County	1 Courthouse Sq *Web:* www.mocounties.com	Fayette	MO	65248	660-248-2284		338
Howard County	104 N Buckeye Rm 104B *Web:* www.howardcountyin.gov	Kokomo	IN	46901	765-456-2204	456-2267	338
Howard County	421 N Main St *Web:* howardcountytaxcollection.com	Nashville	AR	71852	870-845-7508	845-7505	338

Name / Address	Phone	Fax	Class
Howard County 830 Hardy Rd PO Box 25 Saint Paul NE 68873 *Web:* www.howardcounty.ne.gov	308-754-4343	754-4266	338
Howard County Central Library 10375 Little Patuxent Pkwy. Columbia MD 21044 *Web:* hclibrary.org	410-313-7800	313-7864	434-3
Howard County Chamber of Commerce 5560 Sterrett Pl Ste 105 Columbia MD 21044 *Web:* www.howardchamber.com	410-730-4111	730-4584	139
Howard County Library 500 Main St Big Spring TX 79720 *TF:* 844-829-2843 ■ *Web:* howard-county.ploud.net	432-264-2260	264-2263	434-3
Howard County Tourism Council 3430 Court House Dr Ellicott City MD 21043 *TF:* 866-313-6300 ■ *Web:* www.howardcountymd.gov	410-313-1900		206
Howard Cunningham Houchin & Turner LLP 6901 Quaker Ave Ste 100 Lubbock TX 79413 *Web:* hchtcpa.com	806-799-6699		2
Howard Design Group 707 State Rd Ste 103 Princeton NJ 08540 *Web:* www.howarddesign.com	609-924-1106		344
Howard E. Nyhart Company Inc, The 8415 Allison Pointe Blvd Ste 300 Indianapolis IN 46250 *TF:* 800-428-7106 ■ *Web:* www.nyhart.com	317-845-3500		260
Howard Electric Co-op 205 Hwy 5 & 240 N PO Box 391 Fayette MO 65248 *TF:* 877-352-0122 ■ *Web:* www.howardelectric.com	660-248-3311		245
Howard Engineering Company Inc 687 Wooster St PO Box 1315 Naugatuck CT 06770 *Web:* www.howardengineering.com	203-729-5213	729-3843	454
Howard Fischer Associates Intl 1800 Kennedy Blvd Ste 702 Philadelphia PA 19103 *Web:* www.hfischer.com	215-568-8363	568-4815	266
Howard Foster Ltd 150 N Wacker Dr Ste 2150 Chicago IL 60606 *Web:* fosterpc.com	312-726-1600		41
Howard Greeley Rural Public Power District 422 Howard Ave PO Box 105 Saint Paul NE 68873 *TF:* 800-280-4062 ■ *Web:* www.howardgreeleyrppd.com	308-754-4457	754-4230	245
Howard Hughes Medical Institute 4000 Jones Bridge Rd Chevy Chase MD 20815 *Web:* www.hhmi.org	301-215-8500		668
Howard I. Bleiwas & Associates CPA PLLC 39500 High Pointe Blvd Ste 145 Novi MI 48375 *Web:* hibassociates.com	248-380-1811		2
Howard Industries Inc 3225 Pendorff Rd. Laurel MS 39440 *TF:* 800-663-5598 ■ *Web:* www.howard-ind.com	601-425-3151	649-8090	767
Howard Kaye Insurance Agency LLC 1800 N Military Trail Ste 170 Boca Raton FL 33431 *Web:* howardkayeinsurance.com	561-417-5883		390
Howard Lumber Co 475 Columbia Industrial Blvd Evans GA 30809 *Web:* www.howardlumbercompany.com	706-868-8400		191-3
Howard McLeod Correctional Ctr 19603 E Whippoorwill Ln Atoka OK 74525 *Web:* doc.ok.gov	580-889-6651	889-2264	213
Howard Miller Clock Co 860 E Main Ave Zeeland MI 49464 *Web:* www.howardmiller.com	616-772-9131	772-1670	153
Howard Payne University 1000 Fisk St Brownwood TX 76801 *TF:* 800-950-8465 ■ *Web:* www.hputx.edu	325-646-2502		166
Howard Precision Metals Inc PO Box 240127 Milwaukee WI 53224 *TF:* 800-444-0311 ■ *Web:* www.howardprecision.com	414-355-9611	355-2637	492
Howard Price Turf Equipment Inc 18155 Edison Ave. Chesterfield MO 63005 *Web:* www.howardpriceturf.com	636-532-7000	532-0201	429
Howard Printing Company Inc 7419 S Sprinkle Rd. Portage MI 49002 *TF:* 800-968-4726 ■ *Web:* howardprinting.com	269-329-0022	329-1966	627
Howard R. Green Inc 8710 Earhart Ln SW Cedar Rapids IA 52404 *Web:* www.hrgreen.com	319-841-4390	841-4012	261
Howard Regional Health System Main Campus (HRHS) 3500 S Lafountain St Kokomo IN 46902 *Web:* www.ecommunity.com	765-453-0702		374-3
Howard Sheppard Inc PO Box 797 Sandersville GA 31082 *TF:* 800-846-1726 ■ *Web:* www.howardsheppard.com	478-552-5127		780
Howard Simon & Associates Inc 304 Saunders Rd Riverwoods IL 60015 *Web:* hsimon.com	847-945-0340		463
Howard Systems Intl 2777 Summer St Stamford CT 06905 *Fax Area Code: 203 ■ *TF:* 800-326-4860 ■ *Web:* www.howardsystems.com	800-326-4860	324-7722*	180
Howard Ternes Packaging Co 12285 Dixie Redford MI 48239 *Web:* www.ternespackaging.com	313-531-5867	531-5868	546
Howard Uniform Co 1915 Annapolis Rd Baltimore MD 21230 *TF:* 800-628-8299 ■ *Web:* howarduniform.com	410-727-3086		155-19
Howard University 2400 Sixth St NW Washington DC 20059 *TF:* 800-822-6363 ■ *Web:* www.howard.edu	202-806-6100	806-4465	166
Howard University College of Medicine 520 W St NW Washington DC 20059 *Web:* healthsciences.howard.edu	202-806-6270	806-7934	167-2
Howard University Hospital 2041 Georgia Ave Washington DC 20060 *Web:* www.huhealthcare.com	202-865-6100	865-1360	374-3
Howard University School of Law 2900 Van Ness St NW. Washington DC 20008 *Web:* law.howard.edu	202-806-8000	806-8162	167-1
Howard V. Katz 161 Madison Ave 33rd St New York NY 10016 *Web:* orthodoc.aaos.org	212-889-5914	889-1963	475
Howard, Kohn, Sprague & FitzGerald LLP 237 Buckingham St Hartford CT 06126 *Web:* hksflaw.com	860-525-3101		428
Howard, Tate, Sowell, Wilson, Leath Ers & Johnson PLLC 201 Fourth Ave N Ste 1900 Nashville TN 37219 *Web:* howardtatelaw.com	615-256-1125	244-5467	41
HowardSoft 7852 Ivanhoe Ave La Jolla CA 92037 *Web:* www.howardsoft.com	858-454-0121		178-9

Name / Address	Phone	Fax	Class
Howco Metals Management 9611 Telge Rd. Houston TX 77095 *TF:* 800-392-7720 ■ *Web:* www.howcogroup.com	281-649-8800		307
Howe Barnes Hoefer & Arnett Inc 222 S Riverside Plz 7th Fl. Chicago IL 60606	312-655-3000	655-2700	690
Howe Caverns Inc 255 Discovery Dr Howes Cave NY 12092 *Web:* howecaverns.com	518-296-8900		129
Howe Corp 1650 N Elston Ave Chicago IL 60642 *Web:* www.howecorp.com	773-235-0200	235-1530	664
Howe Electric Inc 4682 E Olive Ave Fresno CA 93702 *Web:* www.howe-electric.com	559-255-8992	255-9745	189-4
Howe Library 13 South St Hanover NH 03755 *Web:* www.thehowe.org	603-643-4120		434-3
Howe School Inc, The 5755 N State Rd PO Box 240 Howe IN 46746 *TF:* 888-462-4693	260-562-2131	562-3678	622
Howell Area Chamber of Commerce (HACC) 123 E Washington St Howell MI 48843 *Web:* www.howell.org	517-546-3920	546-4115	139
Howell Care Ctr 3003 W Grand River Ave Howell MI 48843 *Web:* www.medilodgeoflivingston.com	517-546-4210	546-7661	450
Howell Chamber of Commerce 103 W Second St Howell Township NJ 07731 *Web:* www.howellchamber.com	732-363-4114	363-8747	139
Howell County 911 35 Court Sq West Plains MO 65775 *Web:* howellcounty911.com	417-256-0209		338
Howell Engine Developments Inc 6201 Industrial Way Marine City MI 48039 *Web:* www.howellefi.com	810-765-5100	765-1503	60
Howell Furniture Galleries Inc 6095 Folsom Dr Beaumont TX 77706 *Web:* www.howellfurniture.com	409-832-2544		321
Howell Instruments Inc 8945 S Fwy Fort Worth TX 76140 *Web:* www.howellinst.com	817-336-7411	336-7874	472
Howell International Enterprises PO Box 1630 Castle Rock CO 80104 *TF:* 800-441-4748 ■ *Web:* www.miningrecord.com	303-663-7820	663-7823	627
Howell Tractor & Equipment LLC 480 Blaine St Gary IN 46406 *TF:* 800-852-8816 ■ *Web:* www.howelltractor.com	800-852-8816		791
Howell's Floral 6030 NE 112th Ave. Portland OR 97220 *Web:* howellsonline.com	503-255-2001		44
Howell's Motor Freight Inc 51 Simmons Dr Cloverdale VA 24077 *TF:* 800-444-0585 ■ *Web:* www.howellsmotor.com	540-966-3200		780
Howell-Oregon Electric Co-opeartive Inc 6327 N US Hwy 63 PO Box 649 West Plains MO 65775 *TF:* 855-385-9903 ■ *Web:* www.hoecoop.org	417-256-2131		245
Howen Enterprise 590-B Dillingham Blvd Honolulu HI 96817 *Web:* www.howenenterprise.com	808-841-1882	847-8818	156
Hower House Museum - University of Akron 60 Fir Hill Akron OH 44325 *Web:* howerhouse.org	330-972-6909	384-2635	520
Howerton Engineering & Surveying 404 Main St Greenup KY 41144 *Web:* www.howertoneng.com	606-473-5684		256
Howes & Jefferies Realtors 345 Fifth Ave S Clinton IA 52732 *Web:* www.howesandjefferies.com	563-242-3265		652
Howes and Howes Trucking Inc 5301 M 37 N Mesick MI 49668 *TF:* 800-800-4952 ■ *Web:* www.howesandhowes.com	231-885-1630	885-1840	780
Howe-Woods Technical Services Inc 241 Willow St Frankfort IL 60423 *Web:* www.hwts.com	815-474-8769		261
HowGood Inc 99 Commercial St PO Box 159 Brooklyn NY 11222 *TF:* 888-601-3015	888-601-3015		463
Howick Assoc 111 N Fairchild St Madison WI 53703 *Web:* www.howickassociates.com	608-233-3377		463
Howison & Arnott LLP 5420 Lbj Fwy Ste 660 Dallas TX 75240 *Web:* dalpat.com	972-479-0462		41
Howland Capital Management Inc 75 Federal St Ste 1100 Boston MA 02110 *Web:* www.howlandcapital.com	617-357-9110	357-5540	401
Howman Engineering 291 US Hwy 22 Ste 40 Lebanon NJ 08833 *Web:* www.howmaneng.com	908-534-2247	534-9357	203
Howred Corp 7887 San Felipe St Ste 122 Houston TX 77063 *Web:* www.howred.com	713-781-3980	784-3985	191-4
Howrey LLP 1299 Pennsylvania Ave NW Washington DC 20004	202-783-0800		428
Howson & Howson 350 Sentry Pkwy 5 Sentry E Ste 160 Blue Bell PA 19422 *Web:* www.howsoniplaw.com	215-540-9200		41
Howson & Simon LLP 101 Ygnacio Valley Rd Ste 310 Walnut Creek CA 94596	925-977-9060		2
Hoxie House 18 Water St Sandwich MA 02563 *Web:* www.sandwichhistory.org	508-888-1173		50-3
Hoxie Implement Company Inc 933 Oak Ave PO Box 587 Hoxie KS 67740 *Web:* www.hoxieimplement.com	785-675-3201	675-3438	274
Hoxworth Blood Ctr University of Cincinnati Medical Ctr 3130 Highland Ave ML0055 Cincinnati OH 45267 *TF:* 800-265-1515 ■ *Web:* www.hoxworth.org	513-451-0910	558-1209	89
Hoya Holdings Inc 680 N McCarthy Blvd Ste 120 Milpitas CA 95035 *Web:* www.hoya.co.jp	408-654-2300		542
HOYA Vision Care 651 E Corporate Dr. Lewisville TX 75057 *Web:* www.hoyavision.com	972-221-4141		543
Hoyer Steny H (Rep D - MD) 1705 Longworth House Office Bldg Washington DC 20515 *Web:* hoyer.house.gov	202-225-4131	225-4300	342-2
Hoyt Arboretum 4000 SW Fairview Blvd Portland OR 97221 *Web:* www.hoytarboretum.org	503-865-8733		97

Name / Address	City	State	ZIP	Phone	Fax	Class
Hoyt Archery 543 N Neil Armstrong Rd *TF:* 800-474-8733 ■ *Web:* hoyt.com	Salt Lake City	UT	84116	801-363-2990	537-1470	710
Hoyt Group, The 760 US Hwy One The Hoyt Ctr Ste 300 *Web:* hoytgroup.org	North Palm Beach	FL	33408	561-694-7621		463
Hoyt Livery Inc 21 Cross St *TF:* 800-342-0343 ■ *Web:* hoytlivery.com	New Canaan	CT	06840	203-966-5466		441
Hoyt Sherman Place 1501 Woodland Ave *Web:* www.hoytsherman.org	Des Moines	IA	50309	515-244-0507		520
Hoyt, Shepston & Sciaroni Inc 161a Starlite St Ste B *Web:* www.hoyt-shepston.com	South San Francisco	CA	94080	650-952-6930		449
HP (Hewlett Packard Enterprise (Canada) Co) 5150 Spectrum Way *TF:* 888-447-4636 ■ *Web:* hpe.com	Mississauga	ON	L4W5G2	905-206-4725		173-2
HP (Horn Plastics Inc) 712 38th St N Ste D *TF:* 800-373-7448 ■ *Web:* www.superslide.com	Fargo	ND	58102	701-282-7447	281-0439	603
HP Hotels Inc 1 Chase Corporate Dr Ste 210 *Web:* www.hp-hotels.com	Birmingham	AL	35244	205-879-7004		379
HP Industries Inc 415 W Hickory St *Web:* hpind.com	Kirksville	MO	63501	660-627-2000		506
HP Investments Inc 1149 Cherry St Ste 14 **Fax Area Code:* 707 ■ *Web:* www.hpifinancial.com	San Carlos	CA	94070	650-741-9797	237-2151*	652
H-P Products Inc 512 W Gorgas St *TF:* 800-822-8356 ■ *Web:* www.h-pproducts.com	Louisville	OH	44641	330-875-5556		595
HP2 Products & promotions 2880 E Northern Ave *Web:* hp2promo.com	Phoenix	AZ	85028	602-235-9099		366
HPA Development Group Inc 7800 Cooper Rd Ste 204 *Web:* www.hpadg.com	Cincinnati	OH	45242	513-793-2400		401
HPBA (Hearth Patio & Barbecue Assn) 1901 N Moore St Ste 600 *Web:* www.hpba.org	Arlington	VA	22209	703-522-0086	522-0548	49-4
HPC (Hotel Park City) 2001 Park Ave *TF:* 888-999-0098 ■ *Web:* www.hotelparkcity.com	Park City	UT	84060	435-200-2000	940-5001	379
HPC Foods Ltd 288 Libby St *TF:* 877-370-0919 ■ *Web:* www.hpcfoods.com	Honolulu	HI	96819	808-848-2431		296-21
Hpf Consultants Inc 3106 N Big Spring St *Web:* hpfconsultants.com	Midland	TX	79705	432-685-4143		261
HPG International Inc 2121 N California Blvd Ste 625 *Web:* www.higginspurchasing.com	Walnut Creek	CA	94596	925-949-5700		393
HPH Corp 1529 SE 47th Terr *TF:* 800-654-9884 ■ *Web:* www.discounthairpiece.com	Cape Coral	FL	33904	239-540-0085		348
HPI LLC 15503 W Hardy Rd *Web:* www.hpi-llc.com	Houston	TX	77060	713-457-7500		610
HPI Manufacturing Inc 375 Morse St *Web:* www.highprecisioninc.com	Hamden	CT	06517	203-777-5395	773-1976	621
HPL (Hoboken Public Library) 500 Park Ave *Web:* www.hobokenfol.org	Hoboken	NJ	07030	201-420-2346		434-3
HPL (Hoover Public Library) 200 Municipal Dr *Web:* www.hooverlibrary.org	Hoover	AL	35216	205-444-7800	444-7878	434-3
HPL (Hyannis Public Library) 401 Main St *Web:* www.hyannislibrary.org	Hyannis	MA	02601	508-775-2280	790-0087	434-3
HPL (Hedberg Public Library) 316 S Main St *Web:* www.hedbergpubliclibrary.org	Janesville	WI	53545	608-758-6600	758-6583	434-3
HPL Stampings Inc 425 Enterprise Pkwy *TF:* 800-927-0397 ■ *Web:* www.hplstampings.com	Lake Zurich	IL	60047	847-540-1400	540-1422	488
HPM (Hawaii Planing Mill Ltd) 16-166 Melekahiwa St *TF:* 877-841-7633 ■ *Web:* www.hpmhawaii.com	Keaau	HI	96749	808-966-5693	966-7564	191-3
HPM Corp 4304 W 24th Ave Ste 100 *Web:* www.hpmcorporation.com	Kennewick	WA	99338	509-737-8939		463
Hpn Worldwide Inc 119 W Vallette St *Web:* www.hpn.com	Elmhurst	IL	60126	630-941-9030		463
HPP (Health Professions Press) PO Box 10624 *TF:* 888-337-8808 ■ *Web:* www.healthpropress.com	Baltimore	MD	21285	410-337-9585	337-8539	637-2
HPPL (City of High Point Public Library) 901 N Main St *Web:* www.highpointnc.gov	High Point	NC	27262	336-883-3660	883-3636	434-3
HPTS (High Power Technical Services Inc) 2230 Ampere Dr *TF:* 866-398-3474 ■ *Web:* www.hpts.tv	Louisville	KY	40299	502-271-2469		116
HPV (Hawaii's Plantation Village) 94-695 Waipahu St *Web:* www.hawaiiplantationvillage.org	Waipahu	HI	96797	808-677-0110	676-6727	520
HR & A Advisors Inc 99 Hudson St 3rd Fl *Web:* www.hraadvisors.com	New York	NY	10013	212-977-5597		196
HR & P 9621 W Sam Houston Pkwy N Ste 100 *TF:* 877-880-4477 ■ *Web:* www.hrp.net	Houston	TX	77064	281-880-6525		2
HR Advisors Inc 25411 Cabot Rd Ste 212 **Fax Area Code:* 949 ■ *TF:* 877-344-8324 ■ *Web:* www.hradvisors.com	Laguna Hills	CA	92653	877-344-8324	598-9410*	260
HR Affiliates 1930 Bishop Ln Ste 111 *Web:* hraffiliates.com	Louisville	KY	40218	502-485-9675		631
HR Alliance LLC 580 W Main St *Web:* hralliancewithyou.com	Wytheville	VA	24382	276-223-1718		195
HR Answers Inc 7650 SW Beveland St Ste 130 *TF:* 877-287-4476 ■ *Web:* hranswers.com	Tigard	OR	97223	503-885-9815		195
HR Consultants Inc 160 Jari Dr Ste 180 *Web:* www.hrconsults.com	Johnstown	PA	15904	814-266-3818		195
HR Focal Point LLC 3948 Legacy Dr Ste 106 PO Box 369 *TF:* 855-464-4737 ■ *Web:* www.hrfocalpoint.com	Plano	TX	75023	855-464-4737		196
HR Insights Ltd 110 Brinker Rd *TF:* 866-506-4474 ■ *Web:* www.hrinsights.com	Barrington	IL	60010	866-506-4474		194
HR Investment Consultants Inc 305 W Chesapeake Ave Ste 205 *TF:* 888-401-3089 ■ *Web:* www.401kadvisor.com	Baltimore	MD	21204	410-296-1081	296-4042	401
HR Knowledge Inc 15 Berkshire Rd *Web:* hrknowledge.com	Mansfield	MA	02048	508-339-1300		570
HR Law 1560 Orange Ave Ste 500 *Web:* www.hrlawflorida.com	Winter Park	FL	32789	407-571-7400		428
HR ONE Inc 17199 N Laurel Park Dr Ste 306 *Web:* www.hroneinc.com	Livonia	MI	48152	734-464-6600	464-6644	194
HR People & Strategy (HRPS) 1800 Duke St *TF:* 888-602-3270 ■ *Web:* www.hrps.org	Alexandria	VA	22314	703-535-6056	535-6490	49-12
HR Resolutions 5441 Jonestown Rd *Web:* www.hrresolutions.com	Harrisburg	PA	17112	717-652-5187	652-2187	226
HR Strategies & Solutions 49663 Draper Cir Ste 200 *Web:* www.yourhrteam.net	Plymouth	MI	48170	734-455-1185		196
HR Wentzel Sons Inc 5521 Waggoners Gap Rd	Landisburg	PA	17040	717-789-3306		296-23
HR Works Inc 200 WillowBrook Ofc Pk *TF:* 877-219-9062 ■ *Web:* www.hrworks-inc.com	Fairport	NY	14450	585-381-8340		260
HR1 Services Inc 2030 Powers Ferry Rd Ste 120 *Web:* hr1.com	Atlanta	GA	30339	770-541-7823		260
HRA - Healthcare Research & Analytics 400 Lanidex Plz *TF:* 800-929-5400 ■ *Web:* id34111.securedata.net	Parsippany	NJ	07054	973-240-1200	240-1220	466
HRC (Herpes Resource Ctr) PO Box 13827 *Web:* www.ashasexualhealth.org	Research Triangle Park	NC	27709	919-361-8400	361-8425	48-17
HRC (Humboldt Redwood Co) 125 Main St PO Box 565 *TF:* 888-225-7339 ■ *Web:* www.getredwood.com	Scotia	CA	95565	707-764-4472	764-4444	820
HRCG Inc 1202 E Dover Dr *Web:* hrcgtest.newsite.hrconsultinggroup.com	Provo	UT	84604	801-765-4417		260
HRDQ 827 Lincoln Ave Ste B-10 *TF:* 800-633-4533 ■ *Web:* www.hrdqstore.com	West Chester	PA	19380	610-279-2002		196
Hrezo Engineering Inc 1025 Ridge Ave *Web:* www.hrezoengineering.com	Greendale	IN	47025	812-537-4700	537-5054	261
HRF (Herb Research Foundation) 4140 15th St *TF:* 800-748-2617 ■ *Web:* www.herbs.org	Boulder	CO	80304	303-449-2265	449-7849	48-17
HRG (Herbert Rowland & Grubic Inc) 369 E Pk Dr *Web:* www.hrg-inc.com	Harrisburg	PA	17111	717-564-1121	564-1158	261
HRG PLLC Surveying & Engineering 510 W Second St *Web:* www.hrgpllc.com	Owensboro	KY	42301	270-683-7558	683-9277	727
HRH (Hillside Rehabilitation Hospital) 8747 Squires Lane NE *Web:* hillsiderehabhospital.org	Warren	OH	44484	330-841-3700		374-6
HRHS (Howard Regional Health System Main Campus) 3500 S Lafountain St *Web:* www.ecommunity.com	Kokomo	IN	46902	765-453-0702		374-3
HRI Inc 1750 W College Ave *TF:* 877-474-9999 ■ *Web:* www.hrico.com	State College	PA	16801	814-238-5071		188-4
Hribar Logistics LLC 1521 Waukesha Rd *Web:* hribarlogistics.com	Caledonia	WI	53108	262-835-4401	835-1744	780
Hrizons 10749 108th Ave N *Web:* hrizons.com	Hanover	MN	55341	612-326-9677		393
HRL Laboratories LLC 3011 Malibu Canyon Rd *Web:* www.hrl.com	Malibu	CA	90265	310-317-5000	317-5483	261
HRM USA Inc 1044 Pulinski Rd *TF:* 800-403-8285 ■ *Web:* www.heartratemonitorsusa.com	Warminster	PA	18974	215-259-2700	259-2706	475
HRMC (Huron Regional Medical Ctr) 172 Fourth St SE *TF:* 800-529-0115 ■ *Web:* www.huronregional.org	Huron	SD	57350	605-353-6200	353-6300	374-3
HRO Partners LLC 855 Willow Tree Cir Ste 100 *TF:* 866-822-0123 ■ *Web:* hro-partners.com	Cordova	TN	38018	866-822-0123		260
HROplus com 65 Water St *Web:* hroplus.com	Laconia	NH	03246	603-524-8762		393
HRP Associates Inc 197 Scott Swamp Rd *TF:* 800-246-9021 ■ *Web:* hrpassociates.com	Farmington	CT	06032	800-246-9021		261
HRPS (HR People & Strategy) 1800 Duke St *TF:* 888-602-3270 ■ *Web:* www.hrps.org	Alexandria	VA	22314	703-535-6056	535-6490	49-12
hrQ Inc 2859 Umatilla St *Web:* www.hrqinc.com	Denver	CO	80211	303-455-1118		317
HRSA (Health Resources & Services Administration) 5600 Fishers Ln *TF:* 888-275-4772 ■ *Web:* www.hrsa.gov	Rockville	MD	20857	301-443-2216		340-10
HRSSRS (Highgate Road Social Science Research Station) 2601 Hilltop Dr Apt 217 *Web:* www.molokane.org	Richmond	CA	94806	510-262-9189		466
HRU Incorporated Technical Resources 3451 Dunckel Rd *TF:* 888-205-3446 ■ *Web:* hrutech.com	Lansing	MI	48911	517-272-5888		463
HRV Conformance Verification Associates Inc 420 Rouser Rd Ste 400 *Web:* www.hrvinc.com	Moon Township	PA	15108	412-299-2000		41
HRValue LLC 1010 E 20th St *Web:* www.4hrv.com	Tulsa	OK	74120	614-266-5926		463
HRVillage 651 W Washington Blvd Ste 302 *Web:* www.hrvillage.com	Chicago	IL	60661	312-902-1606	902-1612	194
HS Inc 215 Lake Michigan Dr NW *Web:* hsinc.us	Grand Rapids	MI	49534	616-453-5451		697

	Phone	Fax	Class
HS Intl 9871 Irvine Center Dr . . . . . Irvine CA 92618	949-753-9153		731
Web: www.hsi.net			
HS Strygler & Company Inc			
37 W 20th St Ste 1210 . . . . . New York NY 10011	212-727-7840		411
HSA Commercial Inc			
100 S Wacker Dr Ste 950 . . . . . Chicago IL 60606	312-332-3555		653
Web: hsacommercial.com			
HSA Engineering Consulting Services Inc			
5701 Euper Ln Ste A. . . . . Fort Smith AR 72903	479-452-8922		261
Web: hsaconsultants.com			
HSA Lps			
1520 S Beverly Glen Blvd Ste 305 . . . . . Los Angeles CA 90024	310-286-2722		193
Web: www.hsa-lps.com			
HSB (Hebron Savings Bank)			
101 N Main St PO Box 59. . . . . Hebron MD 21830	410-749-1185		70
TF: 844-378-7081 ■ *Web:* www.hebronsavingsbank.com			
HSBC Bank USA 2929 Walden Ave. . . . . Depew NY 14043	866-379-5621		509
TF: 800-975-4722 ■ *Web:* www.us.hsbc.com			
HSC Pediatric Ctr			
1731 Bunker Hill Rd NE . . . . . Washington DC 20017	202-832-4400		374-1
TF: 800-226-4444 ■ *Web:* hschealth.org			
HSCVB (Hot Springs Convention Ctr)			
134 Convention Blvd PO Box 6000 . . . . . Hot Springs AR 71902	501-321-2277		205
TF: 800-625-7576 ■ *Web:* www.hotsprings.org			
HSD (Hauppauge School District)			
495 Hoffman Ln . . . . . Hauppauge NY 11788	631-761-8208		685
Web: www.hauppauge.k12.ny.us			
HSDFF (Hot Springs Documentary Film Festival)			
659 Ouachita Ave . . . . . Hot Springs AR 71901	501-538-0452		282
Web: www.hsdfi.org			
HSE (Harter Secrest & Emery LLP)			
1600 Bausch & Lomb Pl. . . . . Rochester NY 14604	585-232-6500	232-2152	428
Web: www.hselaw.com			
HSE Integrated Ltd			
630-6th Ave SW Ste 1000 . . . . . Calgary AB T2P0S8	403-266-1833		539
Web: hseintegrated.com			
HSHS St Joseph's Hospital			
2661 County Hwy I . . . . . Chippewa Falls WI 54720	715-723-1811		374-3
TF: 877-723-1811 ■ *Web:* www.stjoeschipfalls.org			
HSHS St Vincent Hospital			
835 S Van Buren St. . . . . Green Bay WI 54301	800-211-2209		374-3
TF: 800-211-2209 ■ *Web:* www.stvincenthospital.org			
HSI (Helicopter Support Inc)			
124 Quarry Rd . . . . . Trumbull CT 06611	203-416-4000	416-4291	770
HSI (Haverly Systems Inc)			
12 Hinchman Ave . . . . . Denville NJ 07834	973-627-1424	625-2296	177
Web: www.haverly.com			
HSI Sensing Inc 3100 S Norge Rd. . . . . Chickasha OK 73018	405-224-4046	224-9423	253
Web: hsisensing.com			
HSM (Hart Schaffner & Marx)			
101 N Wacker Dr. . . . . Chicago IL 60606	847-257-4644		155-12
Web: www.hartschaffnermarx.com			
HSMAI (Hospitality Sales & Marketing Association Intl)			
7918 Jones Branch Dr Ste 300. . . . . McLean VA 22102	703-506-3280	610-9005	49-18
Web: global.hsmai.org			
HSMC Orizon LLC 16924 Frances St . . . . . Omaha NE 68130	402-330-7008	330-6851	177
Web: www.hsmcorizon.com			
HSNY (Holland Society of New York)			
708 3rd Ave 6th Fl . . . . . New York NY 10017	212-758-1675	758-2232	48-13
Web: www.hollandsociety.org			
HSP (Historical Society of Pennsylvania)			
1300 Locust St . . . . . Philadelphia PA 19107	215-732-6200	732-2680	48-13
Web: hsp.org			
HSPLS (Hawaii State Public Library System)			
44 Merchant St. . . . . Honolulu HI 96813	808-586-3700		434-5
Web: www.librarieshawaii.org			
HSQ Technology 26227 Research Rd. . . . . Hayward CA 94545	510-259-1334	259-1391	201
TF: 800-486-6684 ■ *Web:* www.hsq.com			
HSS LLC 5310 Hampton Pl Ste 1 . . . . . Saginaw MI 48604	989-777-2983		393
Web: valuepointsolutions.com			
HST (Harding School of Theology)			
1000 Cherry Rd . . . . . Memphis TN 38117	901-761-1356	761-1358	637-2
TF: 800-680-0809 ■ *Web:* www.hst.edu			
HSTC (Hot Springs Telephone Co)			
216 Main St . . . . . Hot Springs MT 59845	406-741-2751	741-7766	224
Web: hotsprgs.net			
HSU's Gourmet Chinese Restaurant			
303 Peachtree Center Ave. . . . . Atlanta GA 30303	404-659-2788		671
Web: www.hsus.com			
HSUS (Humane Society of the US)			
1255 23rd St NW Ste 450. . . . . Washington DC 20037	202-452-1100	778-6132	48-3
TF: 866-720-2676 ■ *Web:* www.humanesociety.org			
HT Hackney Co 502 S Gay St Ste 100. . . . . Knoxville TN 37902	305-685-6232	546-1501*	185
**Fax Area Code:* 865 ■ *TF:* 800-406-1291 ■ *Web:* www.hthackney.com			
HTC (Healing the Children)			
2624 W Beacon Ave . . . . . Spokane WA 99208	509-327-4281	327-4284	48-5
Web: www.healingthechildren.org			
HTC (Horry Telephone Co-opeartive Inc)			
3480 Hwy 701 N PO Box 1820. . . . . Conway SC 29528	843-365-2151	365-0855	736
TF: 800-824-6779 ■ *Web:* www.htcinc.net			
HTC (Hickory Telephone Co) 75 Main St . . . . . Hickory PA 15340	724-356-2000		224
TF: 888-721-3569 ■ *Web:* www.hky.com			
HTC (Hart Telephone Co)			
196 N Forest Ave . . . . . Hartwell GA 30643	706-376-4701		224
TF: 800-276-3925 ■ *Web:* www.htconline.net			
HTC (Halstad Telephone Co) 345 2nd Ave W . . . . . Halstad MN 56548	218-456-2125		224
TF: 800-457-2125 ■ *Web:* www.halstadtel.com			
HTC Extraction Systems			
002 2305 Victoria Ave. . . . . Regina SK S4P0S7	306-352-6132		539
Web: htcextraction.com			
HTC Global Services Inc			
3270 W Big Beaver Rd . . . . . Troy MI 48084	248-786-2500	786-2516	177
Web: www.htcinc.com			
HTI Cybernetics			
6701 Center Dr. . . . . Sterling Heights MI 48312	586-826-8346		454
Web: www.hticybernetics.com			
HTK (Hornor Townsend & Kent Inc)			
600 Dresher Rd Ste C1C. . . . . Horsham PA 19044	800-289-9999	956-7750*	402
**Fax Area Code:* 215 ■ *TF:* 800-289-9999 ■ *Web:* www.htk.com			
HTL (Highway Transport Logistics Inc)			
6420 Baum Dr . . . . . Knoxville TN 37919	865-584-8631		780
Web: hytt.com			
HTM Area Credit Union 847 W Main St. . . . . Troy OH 45373	937-335-8591	339-2467	219
Web: htmcu.com			
HTMA (Hoosier Tire Mid-Atlantic)			
2931 Industrial Park Dr. . . . . Finksburg MD 21048	410-833-2061	833-5921	755
TF: 800-651-5164 ■ *Web:* www.hoosiermidatlantic.com			
HTS (Helicopter Transport Services Inc)			
701 Wilson Pt Rd . . . . . Baltimore MD 21220	410-391-7722		359
Web: www.htshelicopters.com			
HTS 115 Norfinch Dr . . . . . Toronto ON M3N1W8	416-661-3400		111
Web: www.hts.com			
HTS Incorporated Consultants			
416 Pickering St. . . . . Houston TX 77091	713-692-8373		261
Web: htshouston.com			
HTT Inc 1828 Oakland Ave . . . . . Sheboygan WI 53081	920-453-5300	453-5301	488
Web: www.htt-inc.com			
Hu's Szechwan Restaurant			
10450 National Blvd . . . . . Los Angeles CA 90034	310-837-0252		671
Web: husszechwan.com			
Hualalai Resort Corp PO Box 5440 . . . . . Kailua-Kona HI 96745	808-325-8400	325-8210	707
Web: www.hualalairesort.com			
Hub City Press 186 W Main St . . . . . Spartanburg SC 29306	864-577-9349	577-0188	637-2
Web: www.hubcity.org			
Hub Folding Box Company Inc			
774 Norfolk St . . . . . Mansfield MA 02048	800-334-1113		101
TF: 800-334-1113 ■ *Web:* www.hubfoldingbox.com			
Hub Group Inc 2000 Clearwater Dr . . . . . Oak Brook IL 60523	630-271-3600	964-6475	449
NASDAQ: HUBG ■ *TF:* 800-377-5833 ■ *Web:* www.hubgroup.com			
HUB International Insurance Services			
333 W El Camino Real Ste 330. . . . . Sunnyvale CA 94087	650-964-8000	560-6390	390
TF: 877-530-8897 ■ *Web:* www.hubinternational.com			
Hub Plastics Inc			
725 Reynoldsburg-New Albany Rd . . . . . Blacklick OH 43004	614-861-1791	861-7176	604
Web: hubplastics.com			
Hub Strategy & Communication			
30 Mesa St Ste 212 . . . . . San Francisco CA 94129	415-561-4345		7
Web: hubsanfrancisco.com			
Hubbard & Drake General Mechanical Contractors Inc			
PO Box 1867 . . . . . Decatur AL 35602	256-353-9244	350-5043	189-10
TF: 800-353-9245 ■ *Web:* www.hubbarddrake.com			
Hubbard & Kurtz LLP 1718 Walnut. . . . . Kansas City MO 64108	816-472-5464		41
Web: mokanlaw.com			
Hubbard and Hoke Inc 401 W Main. . . . . Blytheville AR 72315	870-763-4409	763-4421	321
Web: www.hubbardandhokefurniture.com			
Hubbard Construction Co			
1936 Lee Rd . . . . . Winter Park FL 32789	407-645-5500		188-4
Web: hubbard.com			
Hubbard County 301 Court Ave. . . . . Park Rapids MN 56470	218-732-2300	732-3645	338
Web: www.co.hubbard.mn.us			
Hubbard Feeds Inc			
111 W Cherry St Ste 500 . . . . . Mankato MN 56001	507-388-9400		447
TF: 800-869-7219 ■ *Web:* www.hubbardfeeds.com			
Hubbard Funeral Home Inc			
4107 Wilkens Ave. . . . . Baltimore MD 21229	410-242-3300		510
Web: www.hubbardfuneralhome.com			
Hubbard ISA 195 Main St. . . . . Walpole NH 03608	603-756-3311	756-9034	10-8
Web: www.hubbardbreeders.com			
Hubbard Museum of the American West			
26301US-70. . . . . Ruidoso Downs NM 88346	575-378-4142		520
Web: www.hubbardmuseum.org			
Hubbard Pipe & Supply Inc			
463 Robeson St . . . . . Fayetteville NC 28301	910-484-9015		612
Web: www.hubbardkitchenandbath.com			
Hubbard Publishing Co			
127 E Chillicothe Ave PO Box 40 . . . . . Bellefontaine OH 43311	937-592-3060	592-4463	637-8
Web: www.examiner.org			
Hubbard Radio LLC			
3415 University Ave . . . . . Saint Paul MN 55114	651-642-4656	647-2932	645-141
Web: corporate.hubbardradio.com			
Hubbard Street Dance Chicago			
1147 W Jackson Blvd. . . . . Chicago IL 60607	312-850-9744	455-8240	573-1
Web: hubbardstreetdance.com			
Hubbard Systems Inc			
130 Inverness Plz . . . . . Birmingham AL 35242	205-871-5155		177
TF: 800-933-7995 ■ *Web:* www.jimhubbard.com			
Hubbard's Impala Parts Inc			
1676 Anthony Rd . . . . . Burlington NC 27215	336-227-1589		791
TF: 800-846-7252 ■ *Web:* www.impalaparts.com			
Hubbard/Young Pharmacy Inc			
402 College Ave . . . . . Clemson SC 29631	864-654-1771		237
Web: hubbardyoungpharmacy.com			
Hubbard-Hall Inc 563 S Leonard St . . . . . Waterbury CT 06708	866-441-5831	756-9017*	146
**Fax Area Code:* 203 ■ *TF:* 800-331-6871 ■ *Web:* www.hubbardhall.com			
Hubbell Entertainment Inc			
719 Pepperhill Cir . . . . . Myrtle Beach SC 29588	843-742-0664		572
Web: hubbellent.com			
Hubbell Group Inc, The			
859 Willard St One Adams Pl Ste 201 . . . . . Quincy MA 02169	781-878-8882		636
Web: www.hubbellgroup.com			
Hubbell Inc 40 Waterview Dr . . . . . Shelton CT 06484	203-882-4800	882-4852	815
NYSE: HUBB ■ *TF:* 800-288-6000 ■ *Web:* www.hubbell.com			
Hubbell Roth & Clark Inc			
555 Hulet Dr PO Box 824 . . . . . Bloomfield Hills MI 48303	248-454-6300	338-2592	261
Web: hrcengr.com			
Hubbell Trading Post National Historic Site			
1/2 Mile W Hwy 191 on Hwy 264 PO Box 150 . . . . . Ganado AZ 86505	928-755-3475	755-3405	564
Web: www.nps.gov			
Hubbinette-Cowell Associates Inc			
1003 Park Blvd . . . . . Massapequa Park NY 11762	516-795-1330		390
Web: hubbinettecowell.com			
Hubbuch & Co 324 W Main St. . . . . Louisville KY 40202	502-583-2713	582-7375	393
Web: www.hubbuch.com			
Hubco Inc 215 S Poplar . . . . . Hutchinson KS 67501	620-663-8301		67
Web: www.hubcoinc.com			
Huber & Associates Inc			
1400 Edgewood Dr. . . . . Jefferson City MO 65109	573-634-5000		180
TF: 888-634-5000 ■ *Web:* www.teamhuber.com			

Phone | Fax | Class

Huber Heights Chamber of Commerce
4707 Brandt Pk PO Box 24006 . . . Huber Heights OH 45424 937-233-5700 233-5769 139
Web: huberheightschamber.com

Huber's Orchard & Winery
19816 Huber Rd . . . Borden IN 47106 812-923-9463 50-7
TF: 800-345-9463 ■ *Web:* www.huberwinery.com

Hubert Distributors Inc
1200 Auburn Rd . . . Pontiac MI 48342 248-858-2340 81-1

Hubert H. Humphrey Metrodome
900 S Fifth St . . . Minneapolis MN 55415 612-332-0386 332-8334 720
Web: msfa.com

HubNetic
6 Westowne Dr Ste 602 PO Box 148 . . . Liberty MO 64068 816-452-4222 179
Web: www.hubnetic.com

Hubris Communications Inc
209 N Main . . . Garden City KS 67846 316-858-3000 387
TF: 888-267-4638 ■ *Web:* www.hubris.net

HubSpot 25 First St . . . Cambridge MA 02141 877-929-0687 178-2
NYSE: HUBS ■ *TF:* 877-929-0687 ■ *Web:* www.hubspot.com

HubTech 44 Norfolk Ave Ste 4 . . . South Easton MA 02375 877-482-8324 238-1146* 180
**Fax Area Code:* 508 ■ *TF:* 877-482-8324 ■ *Web:* www.hubtech.com

Hubtrucker Inc 315 Freeport St Ste B . . . Houston TX 77015 713-547-5482 311
TF: 866-913-6553 ■ *Web:* hubtrucker.com

Huck Group, The
4470 W Sunset Blvd Ste 107 . . . Los Angeles CA 90027 213-955-8080 344
Web: www.juliethuck.com

Huckabee, Weiler & Levengood PC
1136 Penn Ave . . . Wyomissing PA 19610 610-378-1933 378-9896 41
TF: 888-434-9531 ■ *Web:* hwllawpc.com

Huckleberry House PO Box 460928 . . . Escondido CA 92046 760-738-2040 637-2
Web: www.huckleberryhousebooks.com

Huckstep & Associates LLC
1661 W Swallow St Ste E . . . Springfield MO 65810 417-886-3820 2

HUD Office of Fair Housing & Equal Opportunity
451 Seventh St SW . . . Washington DC 20410 202-708-4252 340-12
Web: www.hud.gov

Hudapack Metal Treating Inc
979 Koopman Ln . . . Elkhorn WI 53121 262-723-3345 484
Web: hudapack.com

Huddle House Inc
5901 Peachtree Dunwoody Ste B450 . . . Atlanta GA 30328 770-325-1300 670
Web: www.huddlehouse.com

Huddles, Jones, Sorteberg & Dachille PC
10211 Wincopin Cir Ste 200 . . . Columbia MD 21044 410-720-0072 41
Web: constructionlaw.com

Hudson Advisors LLC
2711 N Haskell Ave Ste 1800 . . . Dallas TX 75204 214-754-8400 390
Web: www.hudson-advisors.com

Hudson Bros Trailer Manufacturing Inc
1508 Hwy 218 W . . . Indian Trail NC 28079 704-753-4723 779
Web: www.hudsontrailers.com

Hudson Color Concentrates Inc
50 Francis St . . . Leominster MA 01453 978-537-3538 550
TF: 888-858-9065 ■ *Web:* www.hudsoncolor.com

Hudson Community Enterprises
68-70 Tuers Ave . . . Jersey City NJ 07306 201-434-3303 434-3660 226
TF: 866-324-3337 ■ *Web:* hce.works

Hudson Company Inc, The
4660 Hwy 321 Hagerhill . . . Paintsville KY 41240 606-789-8884 789-1357 755
TF: 800-633-2244 ■ *Web:* www.thehudsontire.com

Hudson Cook LLP 7037 Ridge Rd Ste 300 . . . Hanover MD 21076 410-684-3200 684-2001 428
TF: 888-422-7529 ■ *Web:* www.hudsoncook.com

Hudson County
257 Cornelison Ave 4th Fl . . . Jersey City NJ 07302 201-369-3470 338
Web: www.hudsoncountyclerk.org

Hudson County Chamber of Commerce
857 Bergen Ave 3rd Fl . . . Jersey City NJ 07306 201-386-0699 386-8480 139
Web: www.hudsonchamber.org

Hudson County Community College
162 Sip Ave . . . Jersey City NJ 07306 201-714-7200 714-2136 162
Web: www.hccc.edu

Hudson Fusion 30 State St . . . Ossining NY 10562 914-762-0900 4
Web: www.hudsonfusion.com

Hudson Gardens & Event Ctr
6115 S Santa Fe Dr . . . Littleton CO 80120 303-797-8565 797-8647 97
Web: www.hudsongardens.org

Hudson Global Inc
53 Forest Ave 1st Fl . . . Old Greenwich CT 06870 203-409-5628 351-7401* 193
NASDAQ: HSON ■ **Fax Area Code:* 212 ■ *Web:* am.hudsonrpo.com

Hudson Group
1 Meadowlands Plz . . . East Rutherford NJ 07073 201-939-5050 530
TF: 800-326-7711 ■ *Web:* www.hudsongroup.com

Hudson Institute
1201 Pennsylvania Ave NW Ste 400 . . . Washington DC 20004 202-974-2400 974-2410 634
Web: www.hudson.org

Hudson International Group Inc
1339 Chestnut St . . . Philadelphia PA 19107 610-975-4600 975-4699 196
TF: 800-735-0030 ■ *Web:* www.hudsonies.com

Hudson Library & Historical Society
96 Library St . . . Hudson OH 44236 330-653-6658 434-3
Web: www.hudsonlibrary.org

Hudson Liquid Asphalts Inc
89 Ship St . . . Providence RI 02903 401-274-2200 191-1

Hudson Lock Inc 81 Apsley St . . . Hudson MA 01749 800-434-8960 562-9859* 350
**Fax Area Code:* 978 ■ *TF:* 800-434-8960 ■ *Web:* www.hudsonlock.com

Hudson Mann Inc
710 Johnnie Dodds Blvd . . . Mount Pleasant SC 29464 843-884-5557 463
Web: hudsonmann.com

Hudson Mohawk Press LLC
400 Broadway No1726 . . . Troy NY 12180 518-618-4651 637-2
Web: www.hudsonmohawkpress.com

Hudson Paper Co, The
1341 W Broad St . . . Stratford CT 06615 203-378-0123 378-7109 559
Web: www.hudsonpaper.com

Hudson Printing & Graphic Design
611 S Mobberly Ave . . . Longview TX 75602 903-758-1773 344
TF: 800-530-4888 ■ *Web:* www.hudsonprint.com

Hudson Richard (Rep R - NC)
2112 Rayburn House Office Bldg . . . Washington DC 20515 202-225-3715 225-4086 342-2
Web: www.hudson.house.gov

Hudson River Fruit Distributors
65 Old Indian Rd . . . Milton NY 12547 800-640-2774 315-3
TF: 800-640-2774 ■ *Web:* www.hudsonriverfruit.com

Hudson River Healthcare Inc
1037 Main St . . . Peekskill NY 10566 844-474-2273 352
TF: 844-474-2273 ■ *Web:* www.hrhcare.org

Hudson River Islands State Park
Schodack Island State Pk . . . Schodack Landing NY 12156 518-732-0187 565
Web: parks.ny.gov

Hudson River Museum 511 Warburton Ave . . . Yonkers NY 10701 914-963-4550 963-8558 520
Web: hrm.org

Hudson Tool & Die Co
Hudson Technologies 1327 N US 1 . . . Ormond Beach FL 32174 386-672-2000 676-6212 757
TF: 866-241-4448 ■ *Web:* www.hudson-technologies.com

Hudson Valley Community College
80 Vandenburgh Ave . . . Troy NY 12180 518-629-4822 629-4576 162
TF: 877-325-4822 ■ *Web:* www.hvcc.edu

Hudson Valley Credit Union
159 Barnegat Rd . . . Poughkeepsie NY 12601 845-463-3011 463-3613 219
TF: 800-468-3011 ■ *Web:* www.hvcu.org

Hudson Valley Gateway Chamber of Commerce
1 S Div St . . . Peekskill NY 10566 914-737-3600 737-0541 139
Web: www.hvgatewaychamber.com

Hudson Valley Homestead
102 Sheldon Ln . . . Craryville NY 12521 518-851-7336 851-7553 296-19
Web: www.hudsonvalleyhomestead.us

Hudson Valley Magazine
12 Vassar St . . . Poughkeepsie NY 12601 845-463-0542 463-1544 457-22
Web: www.hvmag.com

Hudson Valve Company Inc
5301 Office Pk Dr Ste 330 . . . Bakersfield CA 93309 661-869-1126 607-8731* 789
**Fax Area Code:* 800 ■ *TF:* 800-748-6218 ■ *Web:* www.hudsonvalve.com

Hudson's Bar & Grill
7805 NW Greenwood Dr . . . Vancouver WA 98662 360-816-6100 671
Web: hudsonsbarandgrill.com

Hudson's Furniture Showroom Inc
3290 W State Rd 46 . . . Sanford FL 32771 407-708-5970 321
Web: www.hudsonsfurniture.com

Hudson's Seafood House on the Docks
1 Hudsons Rd . . . Hilton Head Island SC 29926 843-681-2772 671
Web: www.hudsonsonthedocks.com

HudsonAnalytix
1800 Chapel Ave W Ste 360 . . . Cherry Hill NJ 08002 856-342-7500 342-8888 463
Web: hudsonanalytix.com

Hudson-Webber Foundation
333 W Ft St Ste 1310 . . . Detroit MI 48226 313-963-7777 305
Web: www.hudson-webber.org

Hudspeth County 109 Brown St . . . Sierra Blanca TX 79851 915-369-2331 369-3005 338
TF: 888-368-4689 ■ *Web:* www.txdmv.gov

Huebsch Laundry Co 3605 White Ave . . . Eau Claire WI 54703 715-835-3101 426
Web: huebsch-services.com

Hueco Tanks State Historic Site
6900 Hueco Tanks Rd Ste 1 . . . El Paso TX 79938 915-857-1135 845-1794* 565
**Fax Area Code:* 979 ■ *TF:* 800-792-1112 ■ *Web:* tpwd.texas.gov

Hueneme Elementary School Dist
205 N Ventura Rd . . . Port Hueneme CA 93041 805-488-3588 488-1779 685
TF: 866-431-2478 ■ *Web:* www.huensd.k12.ca.us

Huerfano County 401 Main St Ste 201 . . . Walsenburg CO 81089 719-738-2370 738-3996 338
Web: www.huerfano.us

Huerfano World 508 Main St . . . Walsenburg CO 81089 719-738-1415 532-2
Web: huerfanoworldjournal.com

Huestis ARI 106 Industrial Dr . . . Gilberts IL 60136 847-426-1055 385
TF: 800-747-2786 ■ *Web:* www.huestis.com

Hueston Mcnulty PC
256 Columbia Turnipke Ste 207 . . . Florham Park NJ 07932 973-377-0200 377-6328 41
TF: 800-276-9982 ■ *Web:* huestonmcnulty.com

Hueston Woods Lodge & Conference Ctr
5201 Lodge Rd . . . College Corner OH 45003 513-664-3500 523-1522 669
TF: 800-282-7275 ■ *Web:* www.huestonwoodslodge.com

Hueston Woods State Park
6301 Pk Office Rd . . . College Corner OH 45003 513-523-6347 565
Web: ohiodnr.gov

Huey's 115 E River St . . . Savannah GA 31401 912-234-7385 671
Web: hueysontheriver.net

Huey's 1927 Madison Ave . . . Memphis TN 38104 901-726-4372 671
Web: hueyburger.com

Hueytown Public Library
1372 Hueytown Rd . . . Hueytown AL 35023 205-491-1443 434-3
Web: www.hueytown.com

Hufcor Inc 2101 Kennedy Rd . . . Janesville WI 53545 608-756-1241 756-1246 286
TF: 800-356-6968 ■ *Web:* www.hufcor.com

Huffman Jared (Rep D - CA)
1527 Longworth House Office Bldg . . . Washington DC 20515 202-225-5161 225-5163 342-2
Web: huffman.house.gov

Huffman Laboratories Inc
4630 Indiana St . . . Golden CO 80403 303-278-4455 743
TF: 877-886-6225 ■ *Web:* www.huffmanlabs.com

Huffman Welding & Machine Inc
6224 Ave O . . . Fort Madison IA 52627 319-372-7232 372-3469 454
Web: huffmanwelding.com

Huffman, Kelley, Brock & Gottschalk LLC
540 W Market St . . . Lima OH 45801 419-227-3423 227-0582 41
TF: 800-687-3423 ■ *Web:* 540westmarket.com

Huffmaster 1055 W Maple Rd . . . Clawson MI 48017 800-446-1515 693
TF: 800-446-1515 ■ *Web:* huffmaster.com

Huffy Bicycle Co
6551 Centerville Business Pkwy . . . Centerville OH 45459 937-865-2800 82
TF: 800-872-2453 ■ *Web:* www.huffybikes.com

Hu-Friedy Manufacturing Company Inc
3232 N Rockwell St . . . Chicago IL 60618 773-975-6100 228
TF: 800-483-7433 ■ *Web:* www.hu-friedy.com

HUGE Inc 45 Main St 2nd Fl . . . Brooklyn NY 11201 718-625-4843 463
Web: www.hugeinc.com

Huggins & Company CPA PA
6148-D Brookshire Blvd Ste D . . . Charlotte NC 28216 704-394-2364 2
Web: www.hugginscpa.com

Name / Address	City	State	Zip	Phone	Fax	Class
Huggins Actuarial Services Inc 111 Veterans Sq 2nd Fl *Web:* hugginsactuarial.com	Media	PA	19063	610-892-1824	892-1827	390
Huggins Metal Finishing Inc 995 N Service Rd W *TF:* 877-754-8049 ■ *Web:* www.spmf.com	Sullivan	MO	63080	573-468-8049	468-2182	743
Huggy Bear's Cupboards Inc 2731 N Hayden Island Dr *Web:* huggybear.com	Portland	OR	97217	503-289-5541		321
Hugh Chatham Memorial Hospital 180 Parkwood Dr PO Box 560 *Web:* www.hughchatham.org	Elkin	NC	28621	336-527-7000		374-3
Hugh M. Cunningham Inc 13755 Benchmark Dr *Web:* hughcunningham.com	Dallas	TX	75234	972-888-3800		612
Hugh Taylor Birch State Park 3109 E Sunrise Blvd *Web:* www.floridastateparks.org	Fort Lauderdale	FL	33304	954-564-4521		565
Hughes Agency, The 700 E 13th St *Web:* www.hughesstaffingagency.com	North Little Rock	AR	72114	501-791-3303		260
Hughes Bros Inc 210 N 13th St *TF:* 800-869-0359 ■ *Web:* www.hughesbros.com	Seward	NE	68434	402-643-2991	643-2149	816
Hughes Capital Management Inc 916 Prince St 3rd Fl	Alexandria	VA	22314	703-684-7222	684-7799	401
Hughes Commercial Properties Inc 110 E Court St Ste 501 PO Box 10440 *Web:* hughescommercial.com	Greenville	SC	29603	864-233-0079		652
Hughes Corp *Weschler Instruments Div* 16900 Foltz Pkwy *TF:* 800-557-0064 ■ *Web:* www.weschler.com	Cleveland	OH	44149	440-238-2550	238-0660	248
Hughes County Courthouse 104 E Capitol Ave PO Box 1238 *Web:* ujs.sd.gov	Pierre	SD	57501	605-773-3713	773-3875	338
Hughes Design Assoc 7160 Beneva Rd *Web:* www.hughesdes.com	Sarasota	FL	34238	941-922-4767		41
Hughes Federal Credit Union Inc PO Box 11900 *TF:* 866-760-3156 ■ *Web:* www.hughesfcu.org	Tucson	AZ	85734	520-794-8341		219
Hughes Furniture Industries Inc 952 S Stout Rd *Web:* www.hughesfurniture.com	Randleman	NC	27317	336-498-8700		319-2
Hughes Group Inc 6200 E Hwy 62 *Web:* hughesdevelopmentllc.com	Jeffersonville	IN	47130	812-282-4393	283-0142	188-4
Hughes Group LLC 3701 S Lawrence St *TF:* 866-988-2626 ■ *Web:* www.hughesgroup.biz	Tacoma	WA	98409	253-588-2626	592-6127	463
Hughes Hardwood International Inc 500 Hwy 13 S *Web:* www.hugheshardwood.com	Collinwood	TN	38450	931-724-6258	724-6259	683
Hughes Hubbard & Reed LLP 1 Battery Park Plz *Web:* www.hugheshubbard.com	New York	NY	10004	212-837-6000	422-4726	428
Hughes Law LLC 2221 Rio Grande Blvd NW Ste 100 *Web:* www.hugheslawllc.com	Albuquerque	NM	87104	505-842-6700	764-0012	41
Hughes Machinery Co 14400 College Blvd *Web:* www.hughesmachinery.com	Lenexa	KS	66215	913-492-0355	492-1420	385
Hughes Marino Inc 1450 Front St *Web:* hughesmarino.com	San Diego	CA	92101	619-238-2111		652
Hughes Network Systems LLC 11717 Exploration Ln *TF:* 866-347-3292 ■ *Web:* www.hughes.com	Germantown	MD	20876	301-428-5500	428-1868	735
Hughes Parker Industries LLC 1604 Mahr Ave *Web:* hughesparker.com	Lawrenceburg	TN	38464	931-762-9403		483
Hughes Production PO Box 3556 *Web:* www.hughesproduction.com	Jackson	WY	83001	307-733-6505	733-0542	184
Hughes Supply Company of Thomasville Inc 175 Kanoy Rd PO Box 1003 *TF:* 800-747-8141 ■ *Web:* www.hughessupplyco.com	Thomasville	NC	27360	336-475-8146		454
Hughes Supply Inc 600 Ferguson Dr *Web:* hughessupply.com	Orlando	FL	32805	407-843-9100		612
Hughes Western Sales Inc PO Box 65457	Salt Lake City	UT	84165	801-262-2900		361
Hughes-Anderson Heat Exchangers Inc 1001 N Fulton Ave *Web:* www.hughesanderson.com	Tulsa	OK	74115	918-836-1681	836-5967	91
Hugo Boss Fashions Inc 601 W 26th St Ste M281 **Fax Area Code: 212* ■ *TF:* 800-484-6267 ■ *Web:* www.hugoboss.com	New York	NY	10001	800-484-6267	940-0619*	155-12
Hugo Neu Corp 120 Fifth Ave Ste 600 *Web:* www.hugoneu.com	New York	NY	10011	646-467-6700		492
Hugo's 1600 Westheimer Rd *Web:* www.hugosrestaurant.net	Houston	TX	77006	713-524-7744		671
Hugo's Restaurant 88 Middle St *Web:* www.hugosmaine.com	Portland	ME	04101	207-774-8538		671
Hugo's Restaurante 161 Stillwater Ave	Stamford	CT	06902	203-323-5577		671
Hugoton Royalty Trust 2911 Turtle Creek Blvd Ste 850 PO Box 962020 *NYSE: HGT* ■ *TF:* 855-588-7839 ■ *Web:* www.hgt-hugoton.com	Dallas	TX	75219	855-588-7839		675
Huguley Memorial Medical Ctr 11801 S Fwy *Web:* www.texashealthhuguley.org	Burleson	TX	76028	817-293-9110		374-3
Huhtamaki Incorporated North America 9201 Packaging Dr *TF:* 800-255-4243 ■ *Web:* www.huhtamaki.com	De Soto	KS	66018	913-583-3025	583-8725	548
Huitt-Zollars Inc 1717 McKinney Ave Ste 1400 *Web:* www.huitt-zollars.com	Dallas	TX	75202	214-871-3311	871-0757	261
Huizenga Bill (Rep R - MI) 2232 Rayburn House Office Bldg *Web:* huizenga.house.gov	Washington	DC	20515	202-225-4401	226-0779	342-2
Hula Hut 3825 Lake Austin Blvd *Web:* www.hulahut.com	Austin	TX	78703	512-476-4852	477-4852	671
Hulbert & Associates LLC 326 Main St *Web:* hulbertassociates.com	Sterling	CO	80751	970-425-1275		41
Hulen Mall 4800 S Hulen St *Web:* www.hulenmall.com	Fort Worth	TX	76132	817-294-1200		460
Hull & Associates Inc 6397 Emerald Pkwy Ste 200 *Web:* www.hullinc.com	Dublin	OH	43016	614-793-8777		261
Hull Lift Truck Inc 28747 Old US 33 W *TF:* 888-284-0364 ■ *Web:* hullllifttruck.com	Elkhart	IN	46516	574-293-8651	293-9769	385
Hull Street Blues 1222 Hull St *Web:* www.hullstreetblues.com	Baltimore	MD	21230	410-727-7476	576-2343	671
Hulman & Co 900 Wabash Ave *Web:* www.clabbergirl.com	Terre Haute	IN	47807	812-232-9446		360-2
Hulsey Harwood & Sheridan LLC 1900 Roselawn Ave *Web:* www.hhcpa.net	Monroe	LA	71201	318-325-6500		2
Hult Center for the Performing Arts 1 Eugene Ctr *Web:* www.hultcenter.org	Eugene	OR	97401	541-682-5087	682-5426	572
Human Capital 2055 Crooks Rd Level B *TF:* 888-736-9071 ■ *Web:* www.human-capital.com	Rochester Hills	MI	48309	888-736-9071		631
Human Development Foundation 2775 Algonquin Rd Ste 240 *Web:* www.hdf.com	Rolling Meadows	IL	60008	847-490-0100		305
Human Factors & Ergonomics Society (HFES) 1124 Montana Ave Ste B PO Box 1369 *Web:* hfes.org	Santa Monica	CA	90406	310-394-1811	394-2410	48-17
Human Factors International Inc 1680 hwy 1 Ste 3600 PO Box 2020 *TF:* 800-242-4480 ■ *Web:* www.humanfactors.com	Fairfield	IA	52556	641-472-4480	472-5412	177
Human Growth Foundation 997 Glen Cove Ave Ste 5 *TF:* 800-451-6434 ■ *Web:* www.hgfound.org	Glen Head	NY	11545	516-671-4041	671-4055	48-17
Human Interest 655 Montgomery St Ste 1800 *TF:* 855-622-7824 ■ *Web:* humaninterest.com	San Francisco	CA	94111	855-622-7824		390
Human International Academy 123 Camino de la Reina W-200 *Web:* hajl.athuman.com	San Diego	CA	92108	619-501-8091		423
Human Kinetics 1607 N Market St *TF:* 800-747-4457 ■ *Web:* www.humankinetics.com	Champaign	IL	61820	217-351-5076	351-2674	637-2
Human Life Intl (HLI) 4 Family Life Ln *TF:* 800-549-5433 ■ *Web:* www.hli.org	Front Royal	VA	22630	540-635-7884	622-6247	48-6
Human Network Systems Inc 1805 S Bellaire St Ste 325 *Web:* humannetworksystems.com	Denver	CO	80222	303-758-8182		363
Human Resource Development Press Inc 22 Amherst Rd *TF:* 800-822-2801 ■ *Web:* www.hrdpress.com	Amherst	MA	01002	800-822-2801		194
Human Resource Executive Magazine 747 Dresher Rd Ste 500 *TF:* 800-386-4176 ■ *Web:* hrexecutive.com	Horsham	PA	19044	215-784-0910	784-0275	457-5
Human Resources Inc 2127 Espey Ct Ste 306 *Web:* www.hri-online.com	Crofton	MD	21114	410-451-4202	451-4206	631
Human Resources Research Organization (HUMRRO) 66 Canal Center Plz Ste 400 *Web:* www.humrro.org	Alexandria	VA	22314	703-549-3611	549-9025	668
Human Rights Campaign 1640 Rhode Island Ave NW *TF:* 800-777-4723 ■ *Web:* www.hrc.org	Washington	DC	20036	202-628-4160	347-5323	48-8
Human Rights Watch 350 Fifth Ave 34th Fl *Web:* www.hrw.org	New York	NY	10118	212-290-4700	736-1300	48-8
Human Touch 3030 Walnut Ave *TF:* 800-742-5493 ■ *Web:* www.humantouch.com	Long Beach	CA	90807	562-426-8700	426-9690	319-2
Humana Inc 500 W Main St *NYSE: HUM* ■ *TF:* 800-486-2620 ■ *Web:* www.humana.com	Louisville	KY	40202	502-580-1000		391-3
Humane Farming Assn (HFA) PO Box 3577 *Web:* www.hfa.org	San Rafael	CA	94912	415-485-1495	485-0106	48-3
Humane Society of Macomb Animal Clinic Inc 11350 Twenty Two Mile Rd *Web:* humanesocietyofmacomb.org	Utica	MI	48317	586-731-9210		794
Humane Society of the US (HSUS) 1255 23rd St NW Ste 450 *TF:* 866-720-2676 ■ *Web:* www.humanesociety.org	Washington	DC	20037	202-452-1100	778-6132	48-3
Humanetics II Ltd 1700 Columbian Club Dr *Web:* www.humanetics.com	Carrollton	TX	75006	972-416-1304		697
HumanGood 6120 Stoneridge Mall Rd Ste 100 *Web:* www.humangood.org	Pleasanton	CA	94588	925-924-7100		363
HumanGood - Community Support Ctr 2000 Joshua Rd *TF:* 877-977-3729 ■ *Web:* www.humangoodpa.org	Lafayette Hill	PA	19444	610-834-1001		48-20
Humantech Inc 1161 Oak Vly Dr *Web:* www.humantech.com	Ann Arbor	MI	48108	734-663-6707	663-7747	261
HumanZyme Inc 2201 W Campbell Park Dr Ste 24 *Web:* humanzyme.com	Chicago	IL	60612	312-738-0127		231
Humber Arboretum 205 Humber College Blvd *Web:* www.humber.ca	Toronto	ON	M9W5L7	416-675-6622	675-2755	97
Humble Independent School District PO Box 2000 *Web:* www.humbleisd.net	Humble	TX	77347	281-641-1000	641-1050	685
Humboldt Bay Harbor District 601 Startare Dr *Web:* humboldtbay.org	Eureka	CA	95501	707-443-0801	443-0800	618
Humboldt Botanical Gardens 7707 Tompkins Hill Rd *Web:* www.hbgf.org	Eureka	CA	95503	707-442-5139		97
Humboldt Brews 856 Tenth St *Web:* www.humbrews.com	Arcata	CA	95521	707-826-2739		102
Humboldt County 203 Main St *Web:* www.humboldtcountyia.org	Dakota City	IA	50529	515-332-1571		338
Humboldt County 825 Fifth St *Web:* humboldtgov.org	Eureka	CA	95501	707-445-7256		338

Name / Address	City	State	ZIP	Phone	Fax	Class
Humboldt County 50 W Fifth St *Web:* www.hcnv.us	Winnemucca	NV	89445	775-623-6300	623-6302	338
Humboldt County Convention & Visitors Bureau 1034 Second St *TF:* 800-346-3482 ■ *Web:* www.visitredwoods.com	Eureka	CA	95501	707-443-5097	443-5115	206
Humboldt County Fair 1250 Fifth St *Web:* humboldtcountyfair.org	Ferndale	CA	95536	707-786-9511	786-9450	642
Humboldt County Library 1313 Third St *Web:* www.humboldtgov.org	Eureka	CA	95501	707-269-1910		434-3
Humboldt Manufacturing Co 875 Tollgate Rd *TF:* 800-544-7220 ■ *Web:* www.humboldtmfg.com	Elgin	IL	60123	800-544-7220		407
Humboldt Redwood Co (HRC) 125 Main St PO Box 565 *TF:* 888-225-7339 ■ *Web:* www.getredwood.com	Scotia	CA	95565	707-764-4472	764-4444	820
Humboldt Redwoods State Park 17119 Avenue of the Giants PO Box 100 *TF:* 800-444-7275 ■ *Web:* www.humboldtredwoods.org	Weott	CA	95571	707-946-2263		565
Humboldt State University 1 Harpst St *TF:* 866-850-9556 ■ *Web:* www.humboldt.edu	Arcata	CA	95521	707-826-3011	826-6190	166
Humbug Mountain State Park 39745 Hwy 101 S *Web:* stateparks.oregon.gov	Port Orford	OR	97465	541-332-6774		565
Humco Holding Group Inc 201 W Fifth St *TF:* 800-662-3435 ■ *Web:* www.humco.com	Austin	TX	78701	855-925-4736		582
Hume Lake Christian Camps Inc 5545 E Hedges Ave *Web:* hume.org	Fresno	CA	93727	559-305-7770		239
Hume Travel Corp 1130 W Pender St Ste 510 *TF:* 800-663-9787 ■ *Web:* www.hume-travel.com	Vancouver	BC	V6E4A4	604-682-7581	488-1138	772
Humidaire Company Inc 11500 Roosevelt Blvd Ste 4 *Web:* www.partshvac.com	Philadelphia	PA	19116	215-467-4646	467-1667	76
Hummel Brothers Inc 180 Sargent Dr *Web:* www.hummelbros.com	New Haven	CT	06511	203-787-4113	498-1755	296-26
Hummels Office Equipment Co 25 Canal St *Web:* www.hummelsop.com	Mohawk	NY	13407	315-866-3860		320
Hummer Winblad Venture Partners Pier 33 S The Embarcadero Ste 300 *Web:* hwvp.com	San Francisco	CA	94111	415-979-9600	979-9601	792
Hummer's Sports Cafe 2600 Paramount Blvd *Web:* www.hummerssportscafe.com	Amarillo	TX	79109	806-353-0723		671
Hummert International Inc 4500 Earth City Expy **Fax Area Code:* 314 ■ *TF:* 800-325-3055 ■ *Web:* www.hummert.com	Earth City	MO	63045	800-325-3055	506-4510*	276
Humphrey Company Ltd 6877 Wynnwood Ln *Web:* www.hclmechanicalservices.com	Houston	TX	77008	713-586-8140		189-10
Humphrey Products Co 5070 E N Ave PO Box 2008 **Fax Area Code:* 269 ■ *TF:* 800-477-8707 ■ *Web:* www.humphrey-products.com	Kalamazoo	MI	49048	800-477-8707	381-4113*	789
Humphrey's Building Supply Ctr 590 Main Rd *Web:* www.buildwiththeh.com	Tiverton	RI	02878	401-624-8800	625-6655	191-3
Humphrey's Half Moon Inn & Suites 2303 Shelter Island Dr *TF:* 800-542-7400 ■ *Web:* www.halfmooninn.com	San Diego	CA	92106	619-224-3411	224-3478	379
Humphreys College 6650 Inglewood Ave *Web:* www.humphreys.edu	Stockton	CA	95207	209-478-0800	478-8721	166
Humphreys County PO Box 547 *Web:* humphreys.msghn.org	Belzoni	MS	39038	662-247-1740		338
Humphreys County 102 Thompson St *Web:* www.humphreystn.com	Waverly	TN	37185	931-296-7795		338
Humphreys Restaurant 2241 Shelter Island Dr *Web:* humphreysrestaurant.com	San Diego	CA	92106	619-224-3577	224-9438	671
Humphrys Textile Products 5000 Paschall Ave *TF:* 800-645-2059 ■ *Web:* www.humphrys.biz	Philadelphia	PA	19143	215-724-8181		733
Humpty's Restaurants 2505 Macleod Terr S *Web:* www.humptys.com	Calgary	AB	T2G5J4	403-269-4675	266-1973	670
HUMRRO (Human Resources Research Organization) 66 Canal Center Plz Ste 400 *Web:* www.humrro.org	Alexandria	VA	22314	703-549-3611	549-9025	668
Hun School of Princeton 176 Edgerstoune Rd *Web:* www.hunschool.org	Princeton	NJ	08540	609-921-7600		622
Huna Totem Corp 9301 Glacier Hwy *Web:* myhunatotem.com	Juneau	AK	99801	907-789-8500		360-3
Hunan Gate 4233 N Fairfax Dr *Web:* hunangate.com	Arlington	VA	22203	703-243-5678		671
Hunan House 2350 E Dublin Granville Rd *Web:* www.hunancolumbus.com	Columbus	OH	43229	614-895-3330		671
Hunan Restaurant 1416 Missouri Blvd *Web:* www.hunan-restaurant.com	Jefferson City	MO	65101	573-634-5253		671
Hunan Springs 4939 Hamilton Blvd *Web:* hunansprings.com	Wescosville	PA	18106	610-366-8338		671
Hunan Village 3311 S Shepherd Dr *Web:* www.houstonhunanvillage.com	Houston	TX	77098	713-528-4651		671
Hunan Village Restaurant *Hunan Village Conroe* 1402 N Loop 336 W *Web:* www.hunanvillageconroe.com	Conroe	TX	77304	936-539-6811		671
Hundley Farms Inc 25849 CR 880 *Web:* www.hundleyfarms.com	Belle Glade	FL	33430	561-996-6855		10-11
Hundred Acre Consulting 1155 W 4th St Ste 225 *Web:* www.openresource.com	Reno	NV	89513	702-348-7299		180
Hunewill Guest Ranch PO Box 368 *Web:* www.hunewillranch.com	Bridgeport	CA	93517	760-932-7710		239
Hungary Consulate General 223 E 52nd St *Web:* www.newyork.mfa.gov.hu	New York	NY	10022	212-752-0669	755-5986	257
Hunger Project, The 5 Union Sq W *TF:* 800-228-6691 ■ *Web:* www.thp.org	New York	NY	10003	212-251-9100	532-9785	48-5

Name / Address	City	State	ZIP	Phone	Fax	Class
Hungerford & Terry Inc 226 N Atlantic Ave *Web:* www.hungerfordterry.com	Clayton	NJ	08312	856-881-3200	881-6859	806
Hungry Heart Franchise LLC 28202 Cabot Rd Ste 300 *TF:* 877-486-4797 ■ *Web:* thehungryheart.org	Laguna Niguel	CA	92677	949-887-2600		810
Hungry Howie's Pizza & Subs Inc 30300 Stephenson Hwy *Web:* www.hungryhowies.com	Madison Heights	MI	48071	248-414-3300	414-3301	670
Hungry Marketplace 4420 Fairfax Dr Ste 102 *TF:* 888-848-6479 ■ *Web:* tryhungry.com	Arlington	VA	22203	888-848-6479		670
Hungry Mother State Park 2854 Pk Blvd *Web:* www.dcr.virginia.gov	Marion	VA	24354	276-781-7400		565
Hungry Tiger Press 5995 Dandridge Ln Ste 121 *Web:* www.hungrytigerpress.com	San Diego	CA	92115	619-582-5106		637-9
Hungry Valley State Vehicular Recreation Area 46001 Orwin Way *Web:* www.parks.ca.gov	Gorman	CA	93243	661-248-7007		565
Hunsaker & Associates Irvine Inc 3 Hughes *Web:* www.hnagi.com	Irvine	CA	92618	949-583-1010	583-0759	261
Hunt & Behrens Inc 30 Lakeville St *Web:* hbfeeds.com	Petaluma	CA	94952	707-762-4594	762-9164	447
Hunt & Faherty 40 Delaware Ave *Web:* hunt-faherty.hub.biz	Lambertville	NJ	08530	609-397-0900		445
Hunt & Sons Inc 5750 S Watt Ave *TF:* 800-734-2999 ■ *Web:* www.huntnsons.com	Sacramento	CA	95829	916-383-4868	383-1005	324
Hunt Adkins 15 S 5th St 12th Fl Ste 300 *Web:* www.huntadkins.com	Minneapolis	MN	55402	612-339-8003		7
Hunt Brothers Inc 2404 Hunt Bros Rd	Lake Wales	FL	33898	863-676-9471		11-1
Hunt Conference Group Inc 611 S Main St Ste 410 *Web:* www.huntconferencegroup.com	Grapevine	TX	76051	817-527-8464		196
Hunt Construction Group Inc 2450 S Tibbs Ave *Web:* www.huntconstructiongroup.com	Indianapolis	IN	46241	317-227-7800		186
Hunt Consulting 9015 Maier Rd Ste B *Web:* www.huntconsulting.net	Laurel	MD	20723	301-490-3355	490-3833	196
Hunt Country Furniture Inc 16 Dog Tail Corners Rd *Web:* huntcountryfurniture.com	Wingdale	NY	12594	845-832-6601		319-2
Hunt County PO Box 1316 *Web:* www.huntcounty.net	Greenville	TX	75403	903-408-4130		338
Hunt Design & Manufacturing Inc 2581 Us Hwy 231 *Web:* www.hdmonline.com	Arab	AL	35016	256-586-2519	586-2520	427
Hunt Design Associates Inc 25 N Mentor Ave *Web:* www.huntdesign.com	Pasadena	CA	91106	626-793-7847		344
Hunt Electric Corp 7900 Chicago Ave S *Web:* www.huntelec.com	Bloomington	MN	55420	651-646-2911		189-4
Hunt Engine Inc (PEMCO) 14805 S Main St *Web:* www.huntengine.com	Houston	TX	77035	713-721-9400	721-7346	386
Hunt Forest Products 401 E Reynolds Dr PO Box 1263 *TF:* 800-390-8589 ■ *Web:* www.huntforpro.com	Ruston	LA	71273	318-255-2245	255-4048	683
Hunt Guillot & Associates LLC 603 Reynolds Dr *TF:* 866-255-6825 ■ *Web:* www.hga-llc.com	Ruston	LA	71270	318-255-6825		256
Hunt Insurance Agency Inc 12000 S Harlem Ave *TF:* 800-772-6484 ■ *Web:* thehuntgroup.com	Palos Heights	IL	60463	708-361-5300		390
Hunt Jrt Inc 1107 W Geneva Dr *Web:* www.jrthunt.com	Tempe	AZ	85282	480-968-5928	967-5929	454
Hunt Oil Co 1900 N Akard St *Web:* www.huntoil.com	Dallas	TX	75201	214-978-8000	978-8888	580
Hunt Pan Am Aviation Inc 505 Amelia Earhart Dr *TF:* 800-888-7524 ■ *Web:* huntpanam.com	Brownsville	TX	78521	956-542-9111	542-9133	63
Hunt Refining Co 2200 Jack Warner Pkwy Ste 400 *Web:* www.huntrefining.com	Tuscaloosa	AL	35401	205-391-3300	758-8371	580
Hunt Regional Healthcare 4215 Joe Ramsey Blvd *Web:* www.huntregional.org	Greenville	TX	75401	903-408-5000		374-3
Hunt Valve Company Inc 1913 E State St *TF:* 800-321-2757 ■ *Web:* www.huntvalve.com	Salem	OH	44460	330-337-9535	337-3754	790
Hunt, Spillman & Associates PC 125 S Howes St 7th Fl *Web:* huntspillman.com	Fort Collins	CO	80521	970-482-2272		2
Hunter Arts Publishing PO Box 66578 *Web:* www.headhuntersrevealed.com	Los Angeles	CA	90066	310-842-8864	842-8868	637-2
Hunter Banks Company Inc 29 Montford Ave *Web:* www.hunterbanks.com	Asheville	NC	28801	828-252-3005		711
Hunter Benefits Consulting Group Inc 119 E Palatine Rd Ste 104 *Web:* hunterbenefits.com	Palatine	IL	60067	847-776-2125		196
Hunter Business Group LLC 4650 N Port Washington Rd **Fax Area Code:* 414 ■ *TF:* 800-423-4010 ■ *Web:* www.hunterbusiness.com	Milwaukee	WI	53212	800-423-4010	203-8225*	195
Hunter Co, The 3300 W 71st Ave *TF:* 800-676-4868 ■ *Web:* www.huntercompany.com	Westminster	CO	80030	303-427-4626		710
Hunter College 695 Park Ave *Web:* www.hunter.cuny.edu	New York	NY	10065	212-772-4000	650-3472	166
Hunter Contracting Co 701 N Cooper Rd *Web:* www.huntercontracting.com	Gilbert	AZ	85233	480-892-0521	892-4932	188-4
Hunter Display 14 Hewlett Ave *Web:* hunterdisplays.com	East Patchogue	NY	11772	631-475-5900	475-5950	233
Hunter Duncan D (Rep R - CA) 2429 Rayburn House Office Bldg *Web:* clerk.house.gov	Washington	DC	20515	202-225-5672	225-0235	342-2

Name	Address	City	State	ZIP	Phone	Fax	Class
Hunter Engineering Co	11250 Hunter Dr *TF:* 800-448-6848 ■ *Web:* www.hunter.com	Bridgeton	MO	63044	314-731-3020	731-1776	62-5
Hunter Events	1686 Union St Ste 305 *Web:* hunterevents.net	San Francisco	CA	94123	415-563-8704		366
Hunter Fan Co	7130 Goodlett Farms Pkwy Ste 400 *TF:* 888-830-1326 ■ *Web:* www.hunterfan.com	Cordova	TN	38016	888-830-1326		37
Hunter Hamersmith	725 NE 125th St *Web:* www.hhadvertising.net	North Miami	FL	33161	305-895-8430		4
Hunter Heavy Equipment Inc	2829 Texas Ave *TF:* 800-562-7368 ■ *Web:* www.hunterheavyequipment.com	Texas City	TX	77590	409-945-2382	945-9145	190
Hunter House Victorian Museum	240 W Freemason St *Web:* www.hunterhousemuseum.org	Norfolk	VA	23510	757-623-9814		520
Hunter Medical Services Inc	1666 N Hampton Rd Ste 200 *TF:* 888-883-8678 ■ *Web:* www.huntermed.com	Desoto	TX	75115	972-780-9233	780-8690	363
Hunter Museum of American Art	10 Bluff View St *Web:* www.huntermuseum.org	Chattanooga	TN	37403	423-267-0968	267-9844	520
Hunter Presbyterian Church	109 Rosemont Garden *Web:* hunterlex.org	Lexington	KY	40503	859-277-5126		48-20
Hunter Public Relations	41 Madison Ave 5th Fl *Web:* www.hunterpr.com	New York	NY	10010	212-679-6600	679-6607	636
Hunter Research Inc	120 W State St *Web:* hunterresearch.com	Trenton	NJ	08608	609-695-0122		727
Hunter Woodworks Inc	21038 S Wilmington Ave PO Box 4937 *TF:* 800-966-4751 ■ *Web:* www.hunterpallets.com	Carson	CA	90749	323-775-2544	775-2540	551
Hunter World Travel	4683 Chabot Dr Ste 385 *TF:* 800-876-8785 ■ *Web:* www.hunterworldtravel.com	Pleasanton	CA	94588	925-463-0560		772
Hunter's Animal Hospital PA	7200 Sheridan Rd *Web:* huntersanimalhospital.vetstreet.com	White Hall	AR	71602	870-247-3283		794
Hunter's Friend LLC	340 Low Gap Frk *Web:* www.huntersfriend.com	Oil Springs	KY	41238	606-297-1011		711
Hunter's Specialties Inc	6000 Huntington Ct NE *Web:* hunterspec.com	Cedar Rapids	IA	52402	319-395-0321	395-0326	710
Hunter, Smith & Davis LLP	1212 N Eastman Rd *Web:* www.hsdlaw.com	Kingsport	TN	37664	423-378-8800	378-8801	428
Hunter-Dawson State Historic Site	PO Box 308 *Web:* mostateparks.com	New Madrid	MO	63869	573-748-5340		565
Hunterdon County	71 Main St *Web:* www.co.hunterdon.nj.us	Flemington	NJ	08822	908-788-1221	782-4068	338
Hunterdon County Chamber of Commerce	14 Mine St *Web:* www.hunterdon-chamber.org	Flemington	NJ	08822	908-782-7115	782-7283	139
Hunterdon County Historical Society (HCHS)	114 Main St *Web:* hunterdonhistory.org	Flemington	NJ	08822	908-782-1091		48-13
Hunterdon County Library	314 State Hwy 12 Bldg Ste 3 *Web:* www.hclibrary.us	Flemington	NJ	08822	908-788-1444	806-4862	434-3
Hunterdon Distributors	12 Coddingon Rd *Web:* www.hunterdonbrewing.com	Whitehouse Station	NJ	08889	908-454-7445	454-5921	81-1
Hunterdon Land Trust	111 Mine St *Web:* hunterdonlandtrust.org	Flemington	NJ	08822	908-237-4582		302
Hunterdon Medical Ctr	2100 Westcott Dr *Web:* www.hunterdonhealthcare.org	Flemington	NJ	08822	908-788-6100		374-3
Hunterdon Transformer Co	75 Industrial Dr *Web:* www.hunterdontransformer.com	Alpha	NJ	08865	908-454-2400	454-6266	767
Hunters Ambulance Service Inc	450 W Main St *Web:* www.huntersamb.com	Meriden	CT	06451	203-235-3369	514-5122	30
Hunting Energy Services Inc	16825 Northchase Dr Ste 600 *Web:* www.hunting-intl.com	Houston	TX	77060	281-442-7382	442-3993	253
Hunting Island State Park	2555 Sea Island Pkwy *Web:* southcarolinaparks.com	Saint Helena Island	SC	29920	843-838-2011		565
Huntingdon College	1500 E Fairview Ave *TF:* 800-763-0313 ■ *Web:* www.huntingdon.edu	Montgomery	AL	36106	334-833-4497		166
Huntingdon County	223 Penn St *TF:* 800-373-0209 ■ *Web:* www.huntingdoncounty.net	Huntingdon	PA	16652	814-643-3091	643-8152	338
Huntingdon County Business & Industry	9136 William Penn Hwy *Web:* www.hcbi.com	Huntingdon	PA	16652	814-506-8287		139
Huntingdon County Visitors Bureau	6993 Seven Pt Rd Ste 2 *TF:* 888-729-7869 ■ *Web:* www.raystown.org	Hesston	PA	16647	814-658-0060		206
Huntington Bancshares Inc	7 Easton Oval *NASDAQ: HBAN* ■ *TF:* 800-480-2265 ■ *Web:* www.huntington.com	Columbus	OH	43219	800-480-4862		360-2
Huntington Beach Arts Ctr	538 Main St *Web:* www.huntingtonbeachartcenter.org	Huntington Beach	CA	92648	714-374-1650		50-2
Huntington Beach Chamber of Commerce	2134 Main St Ste 100 *Web:* hbchamber.com	Huntington Beach	CA	92648	714-536-8888	960-7654	139
Huntington Beach City Hall	2000 Main St *Web:* www.huntingtonbeachca.gov	Huntington Beach	CA	92648	714-536-5511	374-1557	337
Huntington Beach Marketing & Visitors Bureau	301 Main St Ste 212 *TF:* 800-729-6232 ■ *Web:* www.surfcityusa.com	Huntington Beach	CA	92648	714-969-3492		206
Huntington Beach Pet Hospital	8851 Adams Ave *Web:* huntingtonpet.com	Huntington Beach	CA	92646	714-962-3639		794
Huntington Beach Public Library (HBPL)	7111 Talbert Ave *TF:* 800-565-0148 ■ *Web:* www.huntingtonbeachca.gov	Huntington Beach	CA	92648	714-842-4481	375-5180	434-3
Huntington Beach State Park	16148 Ocean Hwy *Web:* southcarolinaparks.com	Murrells Inlet	SC	29576	843-237-4440		565
Huntington College of Health Sciences	118 Legacy View Way *TF:* 800-290-4226 ■ *Web:* www.huhs.edu	Knoxville	TN	37918	865-524-8079	524-8339	167-3
Huntington County	201 N Jefferson St *Web:* www.huntington.in.us	Huntington	IN	46750	260-358-4804	358-4823	338
Huntington County Visitors & Convention Bureau	407 N Jefferson St *TF:* 800-848-4282 ■ *Web:* visithuntington.org	Huntington	IN	46750	260-359-8687		206
Huntington Hotel Group LLC	105 Decker Ct Ste 500 *Web:* www.huntingtonhotelgroup.com	Irving	TX	75062	972-510-1200		194
Huntington Ingalls Industries	4101 Washington Ave *NYSE: HII* ■ *TF:* 877-871-2058 ■ *Web:* www.huntingtoningalls.com	Newport News	VA	23607	757-380-2000		698
Huntington Ingalls Industries Inc	1000 Access Rd *Web:* ingalls.huntingtoningalls.com	Pascagoula	MS	39568	228-935-1122		698
Huntington Junior College	900 Fifth Ave *TF:* 800-344-4522 ■ *Web:* www.huntingtonjuniorcollege.com	Huntington	WV	25701	304-697-7550	697-7554	800
Huntington Learning Centers Inc	496 Kinderkamack Rd *TF:* 800-653-8400 ■ *Web:* huntingtonhelps.com	Oradell	NJ	07649	201-261-8400		148
Huntington Library Art Collections & Botanical Gardens, The	1151 Oxford Rd *Web:* www.huntington.org	San Marino	CA	91108	626-405-2100		97
Huntington Memorial Hospital	100 W California Blvd *TF:* 800-903-9233 ■ *Web:* www.huntingtonhospital.org	Pasadena	CA	91109	626-397-5000		374-3
Huntington Museum of Art Inc	2033 McCoy Rd *Web:* www.hmoa.org	Huntington	WV	25701	304-529-2701	529-7447	520
Huntington Park Rubber Stamp Co	2761 E Slauson Ave PO Box 519 *TF:* 800-882-0129 ■ *Web:* www.hprubberstamp.com	Huntington Park	CA	90255	323-582-6461	582-8046	467
Huntington Regional Chamber of Commerce	720 Fourth Ave *Web:* www.huntingtonchamber.org	Huntington	WV	25701	304-525-5131	525-5158	139
Huntington State Beach	21601 Pacific Coast Hwy *Web:* www.parks.ca.gov	Huntington Beach	CA	92646	714-536-1454		565
Huntington State Park	PO Box 1343 *TF:* 800-322-3770 ■ *Web:* utah.com	Huntington	UT	84528	435-384-2552		565
Huntington Steel	100 Third Ave *Web:* www.huntingtonsteel.com	Huntington	WV	25701	304-522-8218		492
Huntington Theatre Co	264 Huntington Ave *Web:* www.huntingtontheatre.org	Boston	MA	02115	617-266-7900	353-8300	749
Huntington Township Chamber of Commerce	164 Main St *Web:* www.huntingtonchamber.com	Huntington	NY	11743	631-423-6100	351-8276	139
Huntington Union Free School District 3	PO Box 1500 *Web:* www.hufsd.edu	Huntington	NY	11743	631-673-2185		685
Huntington University	2303 College Ave *TF:* 800-642-6493 ■ *Web:* www.huntington.edu	Huntington	IN	46750	260-356-6000	358-3699	166
Huntington University	935 Ramsey Lake Rd *Web:* huntington.laurentian.ca	Sudbury	ON	P3E2C6	705-673-4126		785
Huntington Valley Health Care Ctr	8382 Newman Ave *Web:* www.hvhcc.com	Huntington Beach	CA	92647	714-842-5551	848-5359	450
Huntington Veterans Affairs Medical Ctr	1540 Spring Valley Dr *TF:* 800-827-8244 ■ *Web:* www.huntington.va.gov	Huntington	WV	25704	304-429-6741		374-8
Huntington's Disease Society of America (HDSA)	505 Eigth Ave Ste 902 *TF:* 800-345-4372 ■ *Web:* www.hdsa.org	New York	NY	10018	212-242-1968	239-3430	48-17
Huntleigh Securities Corp	7800 Forsyth Blvd 5th Fl *TF:* 800-727-5405 ■ *Web:* www.hntlgh.com	Saint Louis	MO	63105	314-236-2400	236-2401	690
Huntley-Sheehy Inc	520 Olive St *Web:* hbzinsurance.com	Marysville	CA	95901	530-743-9264		390
Hunt-Morgan House	201 N Mill St *Web:* www.bluegrasstrust.org	Lexington	KY	40507	859-253-0362	259-9210	50-3
Hunton Andrews Kurth LLP	Riverfront Plz E Twr 951 E Byrd St *Web:* www.huntonak.com	Richmond	VA	23219	804-788-8200	788-8218	428
Hunton Group, The	10555 Westpark Dr *Web:* www.huntongroup.com	Houston	TX	77042	713-266-3900		14
Huntsinger & Jeffer Inc	809 Brook Hill Cir *Web:* www.huntsinger-jeffer.com	Richmond	VA	23227	804-266-2499	266-8563	5
Huntsman Corp	500 Huntsman Way *NYSE: HUN* ■ *TF:* 888-490-8484 ■ *Web:* www.huntsman.com	Salt Lake City	UT	84108	801-584-5700	584-5781	605-2
Huntsman, Lofgran & Fuller PLLC	623 E Fort Union Blvd Ste 201 *Web:* hla-law.net	Midvale	UT	84047	801-838-8900		41
Huntsville Ballet	800 Regal Dr SW *Web:* www.huntsvilleballet.org	Huntsville	AL	35801	256-539-0961		573-1
Huntsville Board of Education	200 White St *TF:* 877-517-0020 ■ *Web:* huntsvillecityschools.org	Huntsville	AL	35801	256-428-6800	428-6838	685
Huntsville Botanical Garden	4747 Bob Wallace Ave *TF:* 877-930-4447 ■ *Web:* www.hsvbg.org	Huntsville	AL	35805	256-830-4447	830-5314	97

Name / Address	City	State	Zip	Phone	Fax	Class
Huntsville City Hall						
308 Fountain Cir.	Huntsville	AL	35801	256-427-5240	427-5245	337
Web: www.huntsvilleal.gov						
Huntsville Hospital 101 Sivley Rd	Huntsville	AL	35801	256-265-1000		374-3
Web: www.huntsvillehospital.org						
Huntsville International Airport						
1000 Glenn Hearn Blvd Ste 20008	Huntsville	AL	35824	256-772-9395		27
Web: www.flyhuntsville.com						
Huntsville Item, The 1409 10th St.	Huntsville	TX	77320	936-295-5407	435-0135	532-2
Web: www.itemonline.com						
Huntsville Memorial Hospital						
110 Memorial Hospital Dr	Huntsville	TX	77340	936-291-3411		374-3
Web: www.huntsvillememorial.com						
Huntsville Museum of Art						
300 Church St SW	Huntsville	AL	35801	256-535-4350	532-1743	520
TF: 800-786-9095 ■ *Web:* www.hsvmuseum.org						
Huntsville State Park PO Box 508.	Huntsville	TX	77342	936-295-5644		565
Web: tpwd.texas.gov						
Huntsville Symphony Orchestra						
700 Monroe St PO Box 2400	Huntsville	AL	35801	256-539-4818	539-4819	573-3
Web: www.hso.org						
Huntsville/Madison County Convention & Visitor's Bureau						
500 Church St NW Ste 1.	Huntsville	AL	35801	256-551-2230	551-2324	206
TF: 800-843-0468 ■ *Web:* www.huntsville.org						
Huntsville-Madison County Public Library						
915 Monroe St	Huntsville	AL	35801	256-532-5940		434-3
Web: hmcpl.org						
Huntsville-Walker County Chamber of Commerce						
1327 11th St.	Huntsville	TX	77340	936-295-8113	295-0571	139
TF: 800-289-0389 ■ *Web:* www.chamber.huntsville.tx.us						
Hunt-Wilde Corp 2835 Overpass Rd	Tampa	FL	33619	813-623-2461	621-0664	655
Web: huntwilde.com						
Huntwood Industries						
23800 E Apple Way.	Liberty Lake	WA	99019	509-924-5858		115
TF: 800-873-7350 ■ *Web:* www.huntwood.com						
Huntzinger Management Group Inc, The						
72 Glenmaura National Blvd Ste 105	Moosic	PA	18507	570-824-4721		41
Web: www.huntzingergroup.com						
Hunzinger Construction Co						
21100 Enterprise Ave	Brookfield	WI	53045	262-797-0797		186
Web: hunzinger.com						
Huot Manufacturing Co						
550 Wheeler St N	Saint Paul	MN	55104	651-646-1869	646-0457	319-1
TF: 800-832-3838 ■ *Web:* www.huot.com						
Hupp & Associates Inc						
1690 Summit St	New Haven	IN	46774	260-748-8282		124
Web: www.huppaerospace.com						
Huppert Industries Inc						
16808 S Lathrop Ave	Harvey	IL	60426	708-339-2020	339-2225	318
Web: www.huppert.com						
Hurckman Mechanical Industries Inc						
1450 Velp Ave.	Green Bay	WI	54303	920-499-8771		189-10
TF: 844-499-8771 ■ *Web:* www.hurckman.com						
Hurco Companies Inc						
1 Technology Way.	Indianapolis	IN	46268	317-293-5309	298-2621	455
NASDAQ: HURC ■ *TF:* 800-634-2416 ■ *Web:* www.hurco.com						
Hurco Design & Manufacturing						
200 W 33rd St	Ogden	UT	84401	801-394-9471		286
Hurco Technologies Inc						
409 Enterprise St	Harrisburg	SD	57032	800-888-1436		480
TF: 800-888-1436 ■ *Web:* hurcotech.com						
Hurd It Communications						
2106 Gallows Rd A.	Vienna	VA	22182	703-442-3422	288-9246	180
Web: www.hurdit.com						
Hurd State Park						
c/o Eastern District HQ 209 Hebron Rd.	Marlborough	CT	06447	860-295-9523		565
Web: portal.ct.gov						
Hurd Will (Rep R - TX)						
317 Cannon House Office Bldg.	Washington	DC	20515	202-225-4511	225-2237	342-2
Web: hurd.house.gov						
Hurdman Communications						
1344 W 75 N	Centerville	UT	84014	801-292-7673		180
Web: hurdman.com						
HURI (Harvard Ukrainian Research Institute)						
34 Kirkland St.	Cambridge	MA	02138	617-495-4053	495-8097	637-2
Web: www.huri.harvard.edu						
Hurlen Corp						
9841 Bell Ranch Dr.	Santa Fe Springs	CA	90670	562-941-5330	941-4750	690
Web: www.hurlen-kenig.com						
Hurley Communications Inc						
1113 Washington St	Norwood	MA	02062	781-762-3313	762-8730	463
Web: hurleycommunications.com						
Hurley Medical Ctr 1 Hurley Plz.	Flint	MI	48503	810-262-9000		374-3
TF: 800-336-8999 ■ *Web:* www.hurleymc.com						
Hurley, Toevs, Styles, Hamblin & Panter PA						
4155 Montgomery Blvd NE.	Albuquerque	NM	87109	505-888-1188		428
Web: hurleyfirm.com						
Huron Automatic Screw Co						
PO Box 610068	Port Huron	MI	48061	810-364-6636	364-6639	621
Web: huronauto.com						
Huron Casting Inc						
7050 Hartley St PO Box 679.	Pigeon	MI	48755	989-453-3933	453-3319	307
Web: www.huroncasting.com						
Huron Chamber & Visitors Bureau						
1725 Dakota Ave S	Huron	SD	57350	605-352-0000	352-8321	206
TF: 800-487-6673 ■ *Web:* www.huronsd.com						
Huron Community Bank 301 Newman St.	East Tawas	MI	48730	989-362-6700	362-8982	70
TF: 888-226-5422 ■ *Web:* bankhcb.com						
Huron Consulting Services LLC						
550 W Van Buren St Ste 1700	Chicago	IL	60607	312-583-8700		463
Web: www.huronconsultinggroup.com						
Huron County 250 E Huron Ave Rm 303	Bad Axe	MI	48413	989-269-6431	269-6152	338
TF: 800-358-4862 ■ *Web:* huroncounty.com						
Huron County						
County Courthouse 2 E Main St	Norwalk	OH	44857	419-668-5113		338
TF: 800-808-5092 ■ *Web:* www.hccommissioners.com						
Huron Daily Tribune						
211 N Heisterman St.	Bad Axe	MI	48413	989-269-6461	269-9435	532-2
TF: 800-322-1184 ■ *Web:* www.michigansthumb.com						
Huron Inc 6554 Lakeshore Rd.	Lexington	MI	48450	810-359-5344	359-7521	621
Web: huroninc.com						
Huron Machine Products Inc						
228 SW 21st Terr	Fort Lauderdale	FL	33312	954-587-4541	583-2154	493
TF: 800-327-8186 ■ *Web:* huronmachine.com						
Huron Regional Medical Ctr (HRMC)						
172 Fourth St SE	Huron	SD	57350	605-353-6200	353-6300	374-3
TF: 800-529-0115 ■ *Web:* www.huronregional.org						
Huron Technologies International Inc						
550 Parkside Dr Unit B6.	Waterloo	ON	N2L5V4	519-886-9013		743
Web: www.hurondigitalpathology.com						
Huron University College 1349 W Rd	London	ON	N6G1H3	519-438-7224	438-3938	785
Web: huronatwestern.ca						
Huron Valley Chamber of Commerce						
317 Union St	Milford	MI	48381	248-685-7129	685-9047	139
Web: www.huronvcc.com						
Huron Valley Correctional Facility						
3201 Bemis Rd.	Ypsilanti	MI	48197	734-572-9900		213
Web: www.michigan.gov						
Huron Valley Financial Inc						
2395 Oak Vly Dr Ste 200	Ann Arbor	MI	48103	734-669-8000		528
TF: 800-650-7441 ■ *Web:* www.huronvalleyfinancial.com						
Huron Valley Steel Corp						
1650 W Jefferson Ste 100.	Trenton	MI	48183	734-479-3500	479-3413	723
Web: www.hvsc.net						
Hurricane Convention & Visitors Bureau						
3255 Teays Valley Rd PO Box 1086	Hurricane	WV	25526	304-562-5896	562-5858	206
Web: www.hurricanewv.com						
Hurricane Electric Internet Services						
760 Mission Ct.	Fremont	CA	94539	510-580-4100	580-4151	808
Web: www.he.com						
Hurricane Electronics Lab Inc						
331 N 2260 W	Hurricane	UT	84737	435-635-2003		253
Web: www.hurricaneelectronics.com						
Hurricane Express Inc 5624 Hwy 412.	Colcord	OK	74338	912-262-6025	262-6037*	780
**Fax Area Code:* 918 ■ *TF:* 877-379-7383 ■ *Web:* www.hurricaneexpressinc.com						
Hurst Boiler & Welding Company Inc						
100 Boilermaker Ln	Coolidge	GA	31738	229-346-3545	346-3874	91
TF: 877-994-8778 ■ *Web:* www.hurstboiler.com						
Hurst Chemical Co 2020 Cunningham Rd	Rockford	IL	61102	815-964-0451	723-2005*	628
**Fax Area Code:* 800 ■ *TF:* 800-723-2004 ■ *Web:* www.hurstchemical.com						
Hurst Farm Supply Inc 105 Ave D	Abernathy	TX	79311	806-298-2541	298-2936	274
TF: 800-535-8903 ■ *Web:* www.hurstfs.com						
Hurst Group 500 Buck Pl	Lexington	KY	40511	859-255-4422	255-4421	535
TF: 800-926-4423 ■ *Web:* shop.hurstgroup.net						
Hurst Public Library						
901 Precinct Line Rd	Hurst	TX	76053	817-788-7300	590-9515	434-3
TF: 800-344-8377 ■ *Web:* www.hursttx.gov						
Hurst Rosche Engineers Inc						
601 N Bruns Ln Ste B	Springfield	IL	62702	217-787-1199		256
Web: www.hurst-rosche.com						
Hurst-Euless-Bedford Chamber of Commerce						
2109 Martin Dr.	Bedford	TX	76021	817-283-1521	267-5111	139
Web: www.heb.org						
Hurth Yeager Sisk & Blakemore LLP						
4860 Riverbend Rd.	Boulder	CO	80301	303-443-7900	443-8733	445
Web: www.hurth.com						
Hurtigruten 405 Park Ave Ste 904	New York	NY	10022	212-319-1300		220
Hurwitz & Assoc 13A Highland Cir.	Needham	MA	02494	617-597-1724		463
Web: hurwitz.com						
Hurwitz-Mintz Furniture Co						
1751 Airline Dr.	Metairie	LA	70001	504-378-1000		321
TF: 888-957-9555 ■ *Web:* hurwitzmintz.com						
Husar's House of Fine Diamonds						
131 N Main St	West Bend	WI	53095	262-334-3453		410
Web: www.husars.com						
Husch & Husch Inc 8031 Branch Rd.	Harrah	WA	98933	509-848-2951		276
Web: www.huschandhusch.com						
Husch Blackwell LLP						
4801 Main St Ste 1000.	Kansas City	MO	64108	816-983-8000	983-8080	428
Web: www.huschblackwell.com						
HUSCO International Inc						
2239 Pewaukee Rd	Waukesha	WI	53188	262-513-4200	513-4514	790
Web: www.husco.com						
HUSD (Hayward Unified School District)						
24411 Amador St	Hayward	CA	94544	510-784-2600	784-2641	685
Web: www.husd.us						
Huseman Law Firm						
615 N Upper Broadway St Ste 2000	Corpus Christi	TX	78401	361-883-3563		41
Web: www.husemanlawfirm.com						
Huskin Machinery Company LLC						
377 S Long Hollow Rd	Maryville	TN	37801	269-598-0670	983-0736*	757
**Fax Area Code:* 865 ■ *Web:* www.huskinmc.com						
Husky Corp 2325 Husky Way	Pacific	MO	63069	636-825-7200	257-4962	482
TF: 800-325-3558 ■ *Web:* www.husky.com						
Husky Energy Inc						
5505 17 Ave SE PO Box 6525 Stn D.	Calgary	AB	T2P1H5	403-298-6111	298-7464	536
TSE: HSE ■ *TF:* 877-262-2111 ■ *Web:* www.huskyenergy.com						
Husky Envelope Products Inc						
1225 E W Maple Rd	Walled Lake	MI	48390	248-624-7070	624-5990	263
Web: huskyenvelope.com						
Husky Injection Molding Systems Ltd						
500 Queen St S.	Bolton	ON	L7E5S5	905-951-5000	951-5384	386
TF: 800-465-4875 ■ *Web:* www.husky.co						
Husky Rack & Wire						
6146 Denver Industrial Pk	Denver	NC	28037	704-483-1900		567
Web: huskyrackandwire.com						
Husky Spring						
5463 Mountain Iron Dr Ste 100	Virginia	MN	55792	800-826-3318		62-5
TF: 800-826-3318 ■ *Web:* www.huskyspring.com						
Husqvarna Construction Products						
17400 W 119th St.	Olathe	KS	66061	913-928-1000	825-0028*	493
**Fax Area Code:* 800 ■ *TF:* 800-288-5040 ■ *Web:* www.husqvarna.com						
Hussey Copper Ltd 100 Washington St	Leetsdale	PA	15056	724-251-4200	251-4243	485
TF: 800-733-8866 ■ *Web:* www.husseycopper.com						
Hussey Gay Bell (HGBD)						
329 Commercial Dr Ste 200	Savannah	GA	31406	912-354-4626		261
Web: www.husseygaybell.com						

				Phone	Fax	Class
Hussey Seating Co 38 Dyer St Ext *TF:* 800-341-0401 ■ *Web:* www.husseyseating.com	North Berwick	ME	03906	207-676-2271	676-2222	319-3
Hussmann Corp 12999 St Charles Rock Rd *TF:* 800-592-2060 ■ *Web:* www.hussmann.com	Bridgeton	MO	63044	314-291-2000	298-4756	664
Husson College 229 State St *TF:* 800-448-7766 ■ *Web:* www.husson.edu	Bangor	ME	04401	207-941-7000	941-7935	166
Hussong Manufacturing Company Inc 204 Industrial Park Rd *TF:* 800-253-4904 ■ *Web:* www.kozyheat.com	Lakefield	MN	56150	507-662-6641		362
Hussung Mechanical Contractors 6913 Enterprise Dr *TF:* 800-446-2738 ■ *Web:* hussung.com	Louisville	KY	40214	502-375-3500		610
Hustler Conveyor Co 4101 Crusher Dr *Web:* www.hustler-conveyor.com	O'Fallon	MO	63368	636-441-8600		207
Huston-Patterson Corp 123 W N St PO Box 260 *TF:* 800-866-5692 ■ *Web:* www.hustonpatterson.com	Decatur	IL	62522	800-866-5692		112
Huston-Tillotson University 900 Chicon St *TF:* 800-343-3822 ■ *Web:* www.htu.edu	Austin	TX	78702	512-505-3000	505-3190	166
Hutar Growth Management Institute (HGMI) 1701 E Lake Ave Ste 407 *Web:* www.hutar.com	Glenview	IL	60025	847-724-1910		194
Hutch & Son Inc 300 N Main St *TF:* 800-457-3520 ■ *Web:* www.hutch-and-son.com	Evansville	IN	47711	812-425-7201	421-4620	246
Hutch's 1375 Delaware Ave *Web:* www.hutchsrestaurant.com	Buffalo	NY	14209	716-885-0074		671
Hutch, The Nichols Hills 6437 Avondale Dr *Web:* www.hutchokc.com	Oklahoma City	OK	73116	405-842-1000		671
Hutchens Construction Co 1007 Main St *TF:* 888-728-3482 ■ *Web:* hutchensconstruction.com	Cassville	MO	65625	417-847-2489	847-5561	188-4
Hutchens Industries Inc 215 N Patterson Ave *TF:* 800-654-8824 ■ *Web:* www.hutchensindustries.com	Springfield	MO	65802	417-862-5012	862-2317	60
Hutchens Petroleum Corp 22 Performance Dr *TF:* 800-537-7433 ■ *Web:* www.hutchenspetro.com	Stuart	VA	24171	276-694-7000		580
Hutcheson Engineering Products Inc 6405 Pershing Dr *Web:* hutchesonengineering.com	Omaha	NE	68112	402-455-2000		261
Hutchings Museum 153 North 100 East *Web:* www.lehi-ut.gov	Lehi	UT	84043	385-201-1020		520
Hutchins State Jail 1500 E Langdon Rd *Web:* www.tdcj.texas.gov	Dallas	TX	75241	972-225-1304		213
Hutchinson & Bloodgood LLP 579 Auto Center Dr *Web:* www.hbllp.com	Watsonville	CA	95076	818-637-5000		2
Hutchinson Aerospace & Industry Inc 82 South St *TF:* 800-227-7962 ■ *Web:* www.hutchinsonai.com	Hopkinton	MA	01748	508-417-7000	417-7224	676
Hutchinson Community College & Area Vocational School 1300 N Plum St *TF:* 800-289-3501 ■ *Web:* www.hutchcc.edu	Hutchinson	KS	67501	620-665-3500	728-8199	162
Hutchinson Contracting Co 621 Chapel Ave E *TF:* 866-953-8728 ■ *Web:* www.hutchbiz.com	Cherry Hill	NJ	08034	866-953-8728		189-10
Hutchinson Co-Op 1060 5th Ave SE *TF:* 800-795-1299 ■ *Web:* www.hutchcoop.com	Hutchinson	MN	55350	320-587-4647		276
Hutchinson Correctional Facility PO Box 1568 *Web:* www.doc.ks.gov	Hutchinson	KS	67504	620-662-2321	728-3473	213
Hutchinson County PO Box 1186 *Web:* www.co.hutchinson.tx.us	Stinnett	TX	79083	806-273-0130		338
Hutchinson Leader Inc 36 Washington Ave W *Web:* www.crowrivermedia.com	Hutchinson	MN	55350	320-587-2146	587-6104	637-8
Hutchinson Manufacturing Inc 720 Hwy 7 W PO Box 487 *TF:* 800-795-1276 ■ *Web:* www.hutchmfg.com	Hutchinson	MN	55350	320-587-4653		697
Hutchinson News 300 W Second St *TF:* 800-766-3311 ■ *Web:* www.hutchnews.com	Hutchinson	KS	67504	620-669-7202	662-4186	532-2
Hutchinson Public Library 901 N Main St *Web:* www.hutchpl.org	Hutchinson	KS	67501	620-663-5441		434-3
Hutchinson Regional Healthcare System 1701 E 23rd Ave *TF:* 800-267-6891 ■ *Web:* hutchregional.com	Hutchinson	KS	67502	620-665-2000		374-3
Hutchinson Shockey Erley & Co 222 W Adams St Ste 1700 *Web:* www.hsemuni.com	Chicago	IL	60606	312-443-1550		690
Hutchinson Zoo 6 Emerson Loop E *Web:* hutchgov.com	Hutchinson	KS	67501	620-694-2672	694-1980	823
Hutchinson/Mayrath/TerraTrack Industries 514 W Crawford St *TF:* 800-523-6993 ■ *Web:* www.aggrowth.com	Clay Center	KS	67432	785-632-2161	632-5964	273
Hutchison Engineering Inc 1801 W Lafayette Ave *Web:* hutchisoneng.com	Jacksonville	IL	62650	217-245-7164		256
Hutchison Inc 7460 Hwy 85 PO Box 1158 *TF:* 800-525-0121 ■ *Web:* www.hutchison-inc.com	Adams City	CO	80022	303-287-2826		191-3
Hutson 306 Andrus Dr *TF:* 866-488-7662 ■ *Web:* www.hutsoninc.com	Murray	KY	42071	270-886-3994		429
Hutson Company Inc 2211 Corinth Ave Ste 300 *Web:* hutsoncompany.com	Los Angeles	CA	90064	310-566-0400	566-0405	2
Hutter Construction Corp 810 Turnpike Rd *Web:* hutterconstruction.com	New Ipswich	NH	03071	603-878-2300	878-3519	186
Huttig Building Products Inc (HBP) 555 Maryville University Dr Ste 400 *NASDAQ:* HBP ■ *TF:* 800-325-4466 ■ *Web:* www.huttig.com	Saint Louis	MO	63141	314-216-2600	216-2601	499
Hutton Communications Inc 2520 Marsh Ln **Fax Area Code:* 972 ■ *TF:* 800-725-5264 ■ *Web:* www.hol4g.com	Carrollton	TX	75006	888-248-8866	417-0180*	246

				Phone	Fax	Class
Hutton Construction Corp 2229 S W St *Web:* huttonbuilds.com	Wichita	KS	67213	316-942-8855		186
Hutton Hotel, The 1808 W End Ave *Web:* www.huttonhotel.com	Nashville	TN	37203	615-340-9333		707
Huvepharma Inc 525 Westpark Dr Ste 230 *Web:* www.huvepharma.com	Peachtree City	GA	30269	770-486-7212		231
Huxley Communications Co-op 102 N Main Ave *TF:* 800-231-4922 ■ *Web:* huxcomm.net	Huxley	IA	50124	515-597-2212		224
Huy Fong Foods Inc 4800 Azusa Canyon Rd *Web:* www.huyfong.com	Irwindale	CA	91706	626-286-8328	286-8522	297-8
Huynh Insurance & Financial Services 462 N Springboro Pk *Web:* daytonsfagent.com	Dayton	OH	45449	937-434-9999		390
HV Food Products Co 1221 Broadway **Fax Area Code:* 510 ■ *TF:* 877-853-7262 ■ *Web:* www.hiddenvalley.com	Oakland	CA	94612	877-853-7262	832-1463*	296-19
HVA (High Vacuum Apparatus LLC) 12880 Moya Blvd *TF:* 800-551-4422 ■ *Web:* www.highvac.com	Reno	NV	89506	775-359-4442	359-1369	789
HVAC Technical Institute 4532 S Kolin Ave 2nd Fl *Web:* www.hvac-tech.com	Chicago	IL	60632	773-927-9562		167-3
HVF West LLC 6581 E Drexel Rd *Web:* www.hvfwest.com	Tucson	AZ	85756	520-750-9454		660
HVH Transportation Inc 5630 Franklin *TF:* 866-723-0586 ■ *Web:* www.hvhtransportation.com	Denver	CO	80216	303-292-3644		780
HVS (Hidden Variable Studios LLC) 1800 S Brand Blvd *Web:* www.hiddenvariable.com	Glendale	CA	91204	818-985-1080		225
HVS Executive Search 372 Willis Ave *Web:* www.hvs.com	Mineola	NY	11501	516-248-8828		463
HW Fairway International Inc 716 N Mantua St **Fax Area Code:* 330 ■ *TF:* 888-813-4654 ■ *Web:* www.hwfairway.com	Kent	OH	44240	888-813-4654	673-0120*	425
HW Home Inc 4246 Carson St Ste 101 *Web:* hwhome.com	Denver	CO	80239	720-564-1286		321
HW Metal Products Inc 19480 SW 118th Ave *Web:* www.hwmetals.com	Tualatin	OR	97062	503-692-1690	692-5716	295
HWA (Harry Walker Agency Inc) 355 Lexington Ave *Web:* www.harrywalker.com	New York	NY	10017	646-227-4900		708
HWA Fong Rubber Co 14290 Lochridge Blvd *Web:* www.durotire.com	Covington	GA	30014	770-788-2060	788-2099	754
HWC (Houston Wire & Cable Co) 10201 N Loop E *TF:* 800-468-9473 ■ *Web:* www.houwire.com	Houston	TX	77029	713-609-2100	609-2101	246
HWE (High West Energy Inc) 6270 County Rd 212 PO Box 519 *TF:* 888-834-1657 ■ *Web:* www.highwestenergy.coop	Pine Bluffs	WY	82082	307-245-3261	245-9292	245
HWH Corp 2096 Moscow Rd *TF:* 800-321-3494 ■ *Web:* www.hwhcorp.com	Moscow	IA	52760	563-724-3396	724-3408	60
Hx5 LLC 212 Eglin Pkwy SE *Web:* www.hxfive.com	Fort Walton Beach	FL	32548	850-362-6551	362-6550	177
Hy Cite Enterprises LLC 333 Holtzman Rd *TF:* 877-494-2289 ■ *Web:* www.hycite.com	Madison	WI	53713	877-494-2289		362
HY Connect 200 N Water St *Web:* hoffmanyork.com	Milwaukee	WI	53202	414-289-9700		7
Hy Tech Forming Systems Inc 2425 W Desert Cove *Web:* www.hytechusa.com	Phoenix	AZ	85029	602-944-1526		604
Hy's Steak House 2440 Kuhio Ave *Web:* hyswaikiki.com	Honolulu	HI	96815	808-922-5555	926-5089	671
Hy's Steakhouse & Cocktail Bar 1 Lombard Pl Main Fl Richardson Bldg *Web:* www.hyssteakhouse.com	Winnipeg	MB	R3B0X3	204-942-1000		671
Hyannis Area Chamber of Commerce 397 Main St *Web:* hyannis.com	Hyannis	MA	02601	508-775-2201		139
Hyannis Holiday Motel 131 Ocean St *TF:* 800-423-1551 ■ *Web:* www.hyannisholiday.com	Hyannis	MA	02601	508-775-1639	775-1672	379
Hyannis Public Library (HPL) 401 Main St *Web:* www.hyannislibrary.org	Hyannis	MA	02601	508-775-2280	790-0087	434-3
Hyannis Travel Inn 18 North St *TF:* 800-352-7190 ■ *Web:* www.hyannistravelinn.com	Hyannis	MA	02601	508-775-8200	775-8201	379
Hyatt & Weber P A 200 Westgate Cir Ste 500 *TF:* 866-590-8719 ■ *Web:* www.hwlaw.com	Annapolis	MD	21401	410-266-0626	841-5065	445
Hyatt Die Cast & Engineering Corp 4656 Lincoln Ave *Web:* hyattdiecast.com	Cypress	CA	90630	714-826-7550	761-4057	256
Hyatt Hotels Corp 150 N Riverside Plz *NYSE:* H ■ *TF:* 888-591-1234 ■ *Web:* www.hyatt.com	Chicago	IL	60606	312-750-1234		379
Hyatts Market Inc Rte 1 BOX 209	Addison	AL	35540	256-747-6005		345
Hybrid Design Associates LLC 1140 W Warner Rd Ste 101 *Web:* www.hda-smc.com	Tempe	AZ	85284	480-967-8989	894-2578	729
Hybrid Design Services 2479 Elliott Dr *Web:* www.hybriddesignservices.com	Troy	MI	48083	248-298-3400		196
Hybrid Plastics 55 WL Runnels Industrial Dr *Web:* www.hybridplastics.com	Hattiesburg	MS	39401	601-544-3466	545-3103	145
Hybrid Transit Systems Inc 818 Dows Rd SE *TF:* 888-860-6448 ■ *Web:* www.hybridtrans.com	Cedar Rapids	IA	52403	319-261-0749		478
Hy-capacity Engineering & Manufacturing Inc 1404 13th St S *Web:* www.hy-capacity.com	Humboldt	IA	50548	515-332-2125		256
Hycomp Inc 17960 Englewood Dr *Web:* hycompinc.com	Cleveland	OH	44130	440-234-2002		608
Hycor Biomedical Inc 7272 Chapman Ave *TF:* 800-382-2527 ■ *Web:* www.hycorbiomedical.com	Garden Grove	CA	92841	714-933-3000	933-3222	231

Name / Address	City	State	Zip	Phone	Fax	Class
Hydac Technology Corp						
2660 City Line Rd	Bethlehem	PA	18017	610-266-0100		223
TF: 877-464-9322 ■ *Web:* www.hydac-na.com						
Hyde & Hyde Inc 300 El Sobrante Rd	Corona	CA	92879	951-817-2300		296-4
Web: hydeandhyde.com						
Hyde Collection 161 Warren St	Glens Falls	NY	12801	518-792-1761	792-9197	520
Web: www.hydecollection.org						
Hyde County 20791 US Highway 264	Swanquarter	NC	27885	252-926-4178	926-3701	338
Web: hydecountync.gov						
Hyde Hall State Historic Site						
PO Box 721	Cooperstown	NY	13326	518-486-1868		565
Web: parks.ny.gov						
Hyde Marine Inc						
2000 McClaren Woods Dr	Coraopolis	PA	15108	724-218-7001	695-3442	806
Web: www.hydemarine.com						
Hyde Park 4073 Medina Rd	Akron	OH	44333	330-670-6303	670-6174	671
Web: www.hydeparkrestaurants.com						
Hyde Park Art Ctr 5020 S Cornell Ave	Chicago	IL	60615	773-324-5520		522
Web: www.hydeparkart.org						
Hyde Park Bar & Grill 4206 Duval St	Austin	TX	78751	512-458-3168		671
Web: hpbng.com						
Hyde Park Chamber of Commerce						
5501 S Everett Ave	Chicago	IL	60637	773-288-0124	288-0464	139
Web: www.hydeparkchamberchicago.org						
Hyde Park Chamber of Commerce						
PO Box 17	Hyde Park	NY	12538	845-229-8612	229-8638	139
Web: www.hydeparkchamber.org						
Hyde Park Jewelers Inc						
3000 E First Ave Ste 237	Denver	CO	80206	303-333-4446		410
Web: www.hydeparkjewelers.com						
Hyde Park Landscaping Inc						
5055 Wooster Rd	Cincinnati	OH	45226	513-731-1334		422
Web: hydeparklandscaping.com						
Hyde Park Prime Steakhouse						
569 N High St	Columbus	OH	43215	831-536-1790		671
Web: hydeparkrestaurants.com						
Hyde Park Village 744 S Village Cir	Tampa	FL	33606	813-251-3500		50-6
Web: www.hydeparkvillage.com						
Hyde School 616 High St	Bath	ME	04530	207-443-7101		622
Web: www.hyde.edu						
Hyde Street Seafood House						
1509 Hyde St	San Francisco	CA	94109	415-931-3474		671
Web: www.hydestseafoodhouse.com						
Hyde Tools Co 54 Eastford Rd	Southbridge	MA	01550	508-764-4344	765-5250	758
TF: 800-872-4933 ■ *Web:* www.hydetools.com						
Hyden Citizens Bank						
22023 Main St PO Box 948	Hyden	KY	41749	606-672-2344	672-3627	70
Web: hydencitizensbank.com						
Hyde-Smith Cindy (Sen R - MS)						
702 Hart Senate Office Bldg	Washington	DC	20510	202-224-5054		342-2
Web: www.hydesmith.senate.gov						
Hydra Baths 1632 W 139th St	Gardena	CA	90249	714-556-9133	707-4633	375
Web: www.hydrabaths.com						
Hydra-Electric Co 3151 Kenwood St	Burbank	CA	91505	818-843-6211	843-1209	729
Web: hydraelectric.com						
Hydra-Fab Fluid Power Inc						
3585 Laird Rd Unit 5	Mississauga	ON	L5L5Z8	905-569-1819		358
TF: 866-466-9866 ■ *Web:* www.hydrafab.com						
Hydraflow Inc 1881 W Malvern Ave	Fullerton	CA	92833	714-773-2600	773-6351	350
Web: hydraflow.com						
Hydraforce Inc 500 Barclay Blvd	Lincolnshire	IL	60069	847-793-2300	793-0087	790
Web: www.hydraforce.com						
Hydratech Engineered Products LLC						
10448 Chester Rd	Cincinnati	OH	45215	513-827-9169		481
Web: hydratechllc.com						
Hydraulic Component Services Inc						
1760 S Springdale Rd	New Berlin	WI	53146	262-549-1760	549-3701	223
Web: www.hydraulicrepair.com						
Hydraulic Controls Inc						
4700 San Pablo Ave	Emeryville	CA	94608	510-658-8300		358
TF: 800-847-6900 ■ *Web:* www.hydraulic-controls.com						
Hydraulic Specialists Inc						
5655 Gundy Dr	Midvale	OH	44653	740-922-3343		91
Web: www.sun-source.com						
Hydraulic Technology Inc						
3833 Cincinnati Ave	Rocklin	CA	95765	916-645-3317	645-8343	697
Web: www.hydraulictechnology.com						
Hydraulics International Inc						
9201 Independence Ave	Chatsworth	CA	91311	818-998-1231	718-2459	385
Web: www.hiinet.com						
Hydreco Inc 200 Oakland Ave Ste D	Rock Hill	SC	29730	704-295-7575	210-9845*	128
**Fax Area Code:* 864 ■ *Web:* www.hydreco.com						
Hydrite Chemical Co						
300 N Patrick Blvd	Brookfield	WI	53045	262-792-1450	792-8721	146
Web: www.hydrite.com						
Hydro Carbide 4439 SR-982	Latrobe	PA	15650	724-539-9701		757
TF: 800-245-2476 ■ *Web:* www.hydrocarbide.com						
Hydro Geo Chem Inc						
6340 E Thomas Rd Ste 224	Scottsdale	AZ	85251	480-421-1501		196
Web: www.hgcinc.com						
Hydro One Networks Inc						
483 Bay St S Tower 8th Fl Reception	Toronto	ON	M5G2P5	888-664-9376		787
TF: 877-955-1155 ■ *Web:* www.hydroone.com						
Hydro Systems 29132 Ave Paine	Valencia	CA	91355	661-775-0686	775-0668	375
Web: hydrosystem.com						
Hydro Tube Enterprises Inc						
137 Artino St	Oberlin	OH	44074	440-774-1022	774-1482	595
TF: 800-226-3553 ■ *Web:* hydrotube.com						
HydroCAD Software Solutions LLC						
PO Box 477	Chocorua	NH	03817	603-323-8666	323-7467	178-8
TF: 800-927-7246 ■ *Web:* www.hydrocad.net						
Hydrocephalus Assn						
870 Market St Ste 705	San Francisco	CA	94102	415-732-7040		533
Web: www.hydroassoc.org						
HYDRO-FIT Inc 160 Madison St	Eugene	OR	97402	541-484-4361	484-1443	267
TF: 800-346-7295 ■ *Web:* www.hydrofit.com						
Hydro-flo Products Inc						
3655 N 124th St	Brookfield	WI	53005	262-781-2810	781-2228	612
TF: 800-843-3569 ■ *Web:* www.hydro-flo.com						
Hydroform USA Inc 2848 E 208th St	Long Beach	CA	90810	310-632-6353		483
Web: www.hydroforming.net						
Hydrol Chemical Company Inc						
520 Commerce Dr	Yeadon	PA	19050	610-622-3603	284-4448	144
TF: 800-345-8200 ■ *Web:* hydrolchemical.com						
Hydrolevel Co 83 Water St	New Haven	CT	06511	203-776-0473		203
TF: 800-654-0768 ■ *Web:* hydrolevel.com						
Hydromantis Environmental Software Solutions Inc						
407 King St W	Hamilton	ON	L8P1B5	905-522-0012		261
Web: www.hydromantis.com						
Hydromat Inc 11600 Adie Rd	Maryland Heights	MO	63043	314-432-4644	432-7552	455
Web: hydromat.com						
Hydromatic Pump Co 740 E 9th St	Ashland	OH	44805	888-957-8677		641
TF: 888-957-8677 ■ *Web:* www.pentair.com						
Hydromotion Inc 85 E Bridge St	Spring City	PA	19475	610-948-4150		641
Web: www.hydromotion.com						
Hydro-Pac Inc 7470 Market Rd	Fairview	PA	16415	814-474-1511	474-3421	172
Web: www.hydropac.com						
HydroPoint Data Systems Inc						
1720 Corporate Cir	Petaluma	CA	94954	800-362-8774		407
TF: 800-362-8774 ■ *Web:* www.hydropoint.com						
HydroPressure Cleaning Inc						
413 Dawson Dr	Camarillo	CA	93012	800-934-2399		641
TF: 800-934-2399 ■ *Web:* www.hydropressure.com						
Hydroscience Engineers Inc						
10569 Old Plrville Rd	Sacramento	CA	95827	916-364-1490		256
Web: www.hydroscience.com						
Hydro-stat Inc						
1111 SW First Way	Deerfield Beach	FL	33441	954-428-7677		743
Web: hydrostat.com						
Hydrotex Inc 12920 Senlac Dr	Farmers Branch	TX	75234	800-527-9439		541
TF: 800-527-9439 ■ *Web:* www.hydrotexlube.com						
Hydro-Thermal Corp 400 Pilot Ct	Waukesha	WI	53188	262-548-8900	548-8908	386
TF: 800-952-0121 ■ *Web:* www.hydro-thermal.com						
Hydrox Laboratories Inc 825 Tollgate Rd	Elgin	IL	60123	847-468-9400		743
Web: www.hydroxlabs.com						
Hydrozonix LLC						
333 N Rivershire Dr Ste 270	Conroe	TX	77304	936-441-0071		192
Web: www.hydrozonix.com						
Hygenic Corp 1245 Home Ave	Akron	OH	44310	330-633-8460	633-9359	228
TF: 800-321-2135 ■ *Web:* www.hygenic.com						
Hygieia Home Health Inc						
17100 S Pioneer Blvd Ste 270	Artesia	CA	90701	866-749-0948	749-0949	363
TF: 866-749-0948 ■ *Web:* www.hhhi.net						
Hygiena LLC 941 Avenida Acaso	Camarillo	CA	93012	805-388-8007		419
TF: 877-494-4364 ■ *Web:* www.hygiena.com						
Hygieneering Inc 7575 Plaza Ct	Willowbrook	IL	60527	630-654-2550		463
TF: 800-444-7154 ■ *Web:* www.hygieneering.com						
Hygolet Inc 349 SE Second Ave	Deerfield Beach	FL	33441	954-481-8601	481-8669	608
TF: 800-494-6538 ■ *Web:* www.hygolet.com						
Hygrade Metal Moulding Manufacturing Corp						
1990 Highland Ave	Bethlehem	PA	18020	610-866-2441	866-3761	234
TF: 800-645-9475 ■ *Web:* www.hygrademetal.com						
Hy-Grade Precast Concrete						
2411 First St	Saint Catharines	ON	L2R6P7	905-684-8568		183
TF: 800-229-8568 ■ *Web:* www.hygradeprecast.com						
Hygrade Precision Technologies Inc						
329 Cooke St	Plainville	CT	06062	860-747-5773	747-3179	757
TF: 800-457-1666 ■ *Web:* www.hygrade.com						
Hygun Group Inc						
4180 Providence Rd Ste 109	Marietta	GA	30062	770-973-0838		261
Web: www.hygun.com						
Hy-Ko Products Co 60 Meadow Ln	Northfield	OH	44067	330-467-7446	467-7442	701
TF: 800-292-0550 ■ *Web:* www.hy-ko.com						
Hykon Manufacturing Co						
163 E State St	Alliance	OH	44601	330-821-8889	821-2320	482
Web: www.hykon.com						
Hyland Levin LLP						
6000 Sagemore Dr Ste 6301	Marlton	NJ	08053	856-355-2900	355-2901	428
Web: www.hylandlevin.com						
Hyland Screw Machine Products						
1900 Kuntz Rd	Dayton	OH	45404	937-233-8600	233-7067	621
Web: www.hylandmach.com						
Hylant Group 811 Madison Ave	Toledo	OH	43604	419-255-1020	255-7557	390
TF: 800-249-5268 ■ *Web:* www.hylant.com						
Hy-Line Intl						
1755 W Lakes Pkwy	West Des Moines	IA	50266	515-225-6030	225-6425	10-8
Web: www.hyline.com						
Hyman Phelps & Mcnamara Pc						
700 13th St NW Ste 1200	Washington	DC	20005	202-737-5600	737-9329	428
TF: 800-628-2112 ■ *Web:* hpm.com						
Hyndman Industrial Products						
4031 Merchant Rd	Fort Wayne	IN	46818	260-483-6042	483-1722	425
TF: 888-496-3626 ■ *Web:* resistancewire.com						
Hyner View State Park						
c/o Hyner Run State Pk 86 Hyner Park Rd	Hyner	PA	17738	570-923-6000		565
Web: www.dcnr.pa.gov						
Hynes Industries 3760 Oakwood	Youngstown	OH	44515	800-321-9257	799-9098*	492
**Fax Area Code:* 330 ■ *TF:* 800-321-9257 ■ *Web:* www.hynesindustries.com						
Hynix Semiconductor America Inc						
3101 N First St	San Jose	CA	95134	408-232-8000	232-8103	696
Web: www.hynix.com						
Hype Agency LLC, The 2 Dyer Ave	Salem	NH	03079	603-328-9019		195
Web: thehypeagency.com						
Hyper/Word Services 101 Emily Rd	Tewksbury	MA	01876	978-657-5464		180
Web: www.hyperword.com						
HyperBranch Medical Technology Inc						
800-12 Capitola Dr	Durham	NC	27713	919-433-3325		475
Web: www.hyperbranch.com						
Hyperdynamics Corp						
12012 Wickchester Ln Ste 475	Houston	TX	77079	713-353-9400	353-9421	536
OTC: HDYN						
Hypergen Inc 7810 Carvin St	Roanoke	VA	24019	800-497-3744		177
TF: 800-497-3744 ■ *Web:* hypergeninc.com						
Hyperion Biotechnology Inc						
12002 Warfield Ste 101	San Antonio	TX	78216	210-493-7452		668
Web: hyperionbiotechnology.com						
Hyperion Inc 1660 Intl Dr	McLean	VA	22102	703-848-8850		225
Web: www.hyperioninc.com						

Company / Address	City	State	ZIP	Phone	Fax	Class
Hyperlogistics Group Inc 9301 Intermodal Ct N *Web:* www.hyperlog.com	Columbus	OH	43217	614-491-0800		803-1
Hyperquake LLC 205 W Fourth St Ste 1010 *Web:* www.hyperquake.com	Cincinnati	OH	45202	513-563-6555		7
Hyperride Technologies Inc 3746 NW 124th Ave *TF:* 888-994-9737 ■ *Web:* www.hyperride.com	Coral Springs	FL	33065	954-369-4184	344-4284	180
Hypertec BCDR 9300 Trans Canada Hwy *Web:* hypertec.com	Saint-Laurent	QC	H4S1K5	514-745-4540	745-0937	393
Hypertension Diagnostics Inc 730 Bldg Ste 295 *Web:* www.hypertensiondiagnostics.com	Minneapolis	MN	55402	612-361-5287		476
Hypertherm Inc 21 Great Hollow Rd PO Box 5010 *TF:* 800-643-0030 ■ *Web:* www.hypertherm.com	Hanover	NH	03755	603-643-3441	643-5352	455
Hyphen Digital 488 Madison Ave 5th Fl *Web:* hyphendigital.com	New York	NY	10022	212-849-7700		4
Hypneumat Inc 5900 W Franklin Dr *TF:* 800-228-9949 ■ *Web:* www.hypneumat.com	Franklin	WI	53132	414-423-7400	423-7414	455
Hypnosis & Wellness Training Ctr 20 S Main St Ste 29 *Web:* www.hypnosistrainingcenter.com	Janesville	WI	53546	608-757-0716	745-2517	230
Hypnosis Motivation Institute 18607 Ventura Blvd Ste 310 *TF:* 800-479-9464 ■ *Web:* www.hypnosis.edu	Tarzana	CA	91356	818-758-2747	344-2262	167-3
Hypotenuse Enterprises Inc 1545 East Ave *Web:* www.hypot.com	Rochester	NY	14610	585-473-7799	473-7465	463
HyPro Inc 600 S Jefferson St PO Box 370 *Web:* www.hypro.com	Waterford	WI	53185	262-534-5141	534-4151	295
Hy-Production Inc 6000 Grafton Rd *Web:* hy-production.com	Valley City	OH	44280	330-273-2400	273-6602	262
Hyrum State Park 405 W 300 S *Web:* utah.com	Hyrum	UT	84319	435-245-6866		565
Hy-Safe Technology Inc 960 Commerce Dr *TF:* 800-642-0775 ■ *Web:* www.hysafe.com	Union Grove	WI	53182	800-642-0775		693
Hyson Products 10367 Brecksville Rd *TF:* 800-876-4976 ■ *Web:* www.hysonsolutions.com	Brecksville	OH	44141	440-526-5900		790
Hyspan Precision Products Inc 1685 Brandywine Ave *Web:* www.hyspan.com	Chula Vista	CA	91911	619-421-1355	421-1702	480
Hysterectomy Educational Resources & Services Foundation (HERS) 422 Bryn Mawr Ave *TF:* 888-750-4377 ■ *Web:* www.hersfoundation.org	Bala Cynwyd	PA	19004	610-667-7757	667-8096	48-17
Hy-Tape Intl PO Box 540 **Fax Area Code:* 845 ■ *TF:* 800-248-0101 ■ *Web:* hytape.com	Patterson	NY	12563	800-248-0101	878-4104*	477
Hytech Spring & Machine Corp 950 Lincoln Pkwy *Web:* www.hytechspring.com	Plainwell	MI	49080	269-685-1768		492
Hytek Finishes Co 8127 S 216th St *Web:* www.hytekfinishes.com	Kent	WA	98032	253-872-7160		481
Hy-Tek Material Handling Inc 2222 Rickenbacker Pkwy W *TF:* 800-837-1217 ■ *Web:* hy-tek.com	Columbus	OH	43217	800-837-1217		770
Hy-Ten Plastics Inc 38 Powers St *Web:* www.hy-ten.com	Milford	NH	03055	603-673-1611	673-0970	604
Hy-Test Packaging Corp 515 E 41st St *Web:* www.hy-testpackaging.com	Paterson	NJ	07504	973-754-7000		88
Hythane Company LLC 12420 N Dumont Way *Web:* edeninnovations.com	Littleton	CO	80125	303-486-1705		580
Hytrol Conveyor Company Inc 2020 Hytrol St *TF:* 800-852-3233 ■ *Web:* www.hytrol.com	Jonesboro	AR	72401	870-935-3700	852-3233	207
Hytrust Inc 1975 W El Camino Real Ste 203 *TF:* 844-681-8100 ■ *Web:* hytrust.com	Mountain View	CA	94040	844-681-8100		180
Hyundai Motor America 10550 Talbert Ave *TF:* 800-633-5151 ■ *Web:* www.hyundaiusa.com	Fountain Valley	CA	92708	714-965-3000		59
Hyundai Repair by Rally Sport Engineering Inc 2136 Newport Blvd *Web:* hyundairepair.net	Costa Mesa	CA	92627	949-548-0978		256
HyVee Arena 1800 Genessee *Web:* www.visitkc.com	Kansas City	MO	64102	816-746-9100		720
Hy-Vee Inc 5820 Westown Pkwy *Web:* www.hy-vee.com	West Des Moines	IA	50266	515-267-2800		345

I

Company / Address	City	State	ZIP	Phone	Fax	Class
I & I Sling Inc PO Box 2423 *TF:* 800-874-3539 ■ *Web:* slingmax.com	Aston	PA	19014	610-485-8500		208
I & M Heating & Appliance Service Inc 1628 S Michigan St *Web:* www.imheatingandcooling.com	South Bend	IN	46613	574-288-3351		189-10
I & S Group Inc 115 E Hickory St Ste 300 *Web:* www.isginc.com	Mankato	MN	56001	507-387-6651	387-3583	261
I Am Athlete LLC 6701 Center Dr Ste 700 *TF:* 877-462-7979 ■ *Web:* www.imathlete.com	Los Angeles	CA	90045	877-462-7979		387
I C C Logistics Services Inc 960 S Broadway Ste 110 *Web:* icclogistics.com	Hicksville	NY	11801	516-822-1183		314
I C Group 3985 Pinedale Ct *Web:* ic-group.net	Highlands Ranch	CO	80126	303-972-2111	404-8896	627
I C S Solutions Inc 11964 Oak Creek Pkwy *Web:* www.icss.com	Huntley	IL	60142	847-515-8000		177
I Care Private Homecare Services 155 Westridge Pkwy Ste 208 *Web:* icarephcs.com	Mcdonough	GA	30253	678-782-5400		363
I D Booth Inc 620 William St PO Box 579 *TF:* 888-432-6684 ■ *Web:* www.idbooth.com	Elmira	NY	14902	607-733-9121	733-9111	612
I E T Inc 3539 Glendale Ave *TF:* 800-278-1031 ■ *Web:* www.ieteng.com	Toledo	OH	43614	419-385-1233		261
I Fratelli 7701 N MacArthur Blvd *Web:* www.ifratellipizza.com	Irving	TX	75063	972-501-9700		671
I Have a Dream Foundation (IHAD) 322 8th Ave Ste 202 *Web:* www.ihaveadreamfoundation.org	New York	NY	10001	212-293-5480		48-5
I J White Corp 20 Executive Blvd *Web:* www.ijwhite.com	Farmingdale	NY	11735	631-293-2211	293-3788	207
I Janvey & Sons Inc 218 Front St *Web:* www.janvey.com	Hempstead	NY	11550	516-489-9300		406
I Love Bracelets 8940 Ellis Ave *Web:* www.ilovebracelets.com	Los Angeles	CA	90034	310-839-5683		411
I Love Mr Sushi 9443 Olive Blvd *Web:* www.mrsushistl.com	Saint Louis	MO	63132	314-432-8898		671
I Macc 900 E Diehl Rd Ste 110 *Web:* imacc.net	Naperville	IL	60563	630-527-9052		196
I Reservoir Com Corp 1490 W Canal Ct Ste 2000 *Web:* ireservoir.com	Littleton	CO	80120	303-713-1112		539
I Ricchi 1220 19th St NW *Web:* iricchidc.com	Washington	DC	20036	202-835-0459		671
I Rice & Company Inc 11500 Roosevelt Blvd Bldg D *TF:* 800-232-6022 ■ *Web:* www.iriceco.com	Philadelphia	PA	19116	215-673-7423	673-2616	296-15
I Sc International Ltd 9700 W Bluemound Rd *Web:* iscfax.com	Milwaukee	WI	53226	877-472-4525		225
I See Me! Inc 4305 Chimo E St *TF:* 877-744-3210 ■ *Web:* www.iseeme.com	Deephaven	MN	55391	952-473-3939		637-2
I Spiewak & Sons Inc 225 W 37th St *Web:* www.spiewak.com	New York	NY	10018	212-695-1620		155-19
I. C. System Inc PO Box 64378 *TF:* 800-443-4123 ■ *Web:* www.icsystem.com	Saint Paul	MN	55164	800-443-4123		2
I. F. Engineering Corp 3 Foshay Rd **Fax Area Code:* 508 ■ *Web:* www.ifengineering.com	Dudley	MA	01571	860-935-0280	943-0400*	392
I. M. Systems Group Inc 3206 Tower Oaks Blvd Ste 300 *TF:* 866-368-9880 ■ *Web:* imsg.com	Rockville	MD	20852	240-833-1889		180
I.E.-Pacific Inc 150 W Crest St *Web:* www.iepacific.com	Escondido	CA	92025	760-294-7097	294-7098	261
I.T.M. Electronics Inc 20675 N Friends Rd **Fax Area Code:* 888 ■ *TF:* 888-884-2843 ■ *Web:* www.solargauge.com	Greenleaf	ID	83626	208-453-1714	884-4145*	189-4
I/O Magic Corp 20512 Crescent Bay Dr Ste 106 *OTC:* IOMG ■ *Web:* www.iomagic.com	Lake Forest	CA	92630	949-707-4888		173-8
i2c Inc 1300 Island Dr Ste 105 *Web:* www.i2cinc.com	Redwood City	CA	94065	650-593-5400		80-3
i2E Inc 840 Research Pkwy Research Pk Ste 250 *Web:* i2e.org	Oklahoma City	OK	73104	405-235-2305		466
i2M Inc 755 Oak Hill Rd Crestwood Industrial Pk *TF:* 800-242-3909 ■ *Web:* www.i2m.us.com	Mountain Top	PA	18707	800-242-3909		600
i3 Product Development 1869 Haynes Dr *Web:* i3pd.com	Sun Prairie	WI	53590	608-825-4700		261
I4DM 8227 Cloverleaf Dr Ste 312 *Web:* i4dm.com	Millersville	MD	21108	410-729-7920		225
i4i Inc 720 King St W Ste 805 *Web:* www.i4i.com	Toronto	ON	M5V2T3	416-504-0141	504-1785	180
I-95 95.7 FM 49 Acme Rd *Web:* i95rocks.com	Brewer	ME	04412	207-989-5631		645
IA (Irrigation Assn) 6540 Arlington Blvd *Web:* www.irrigation.org	Falls Church	VA	22042	703-536-7080	536-7019	48-2
IA (Idyll Arbor Inc) 39129 264th Ave SE *Web:* www.idyllarbor.com	Enumclaw	WA	98022	360-825-7797	825-5670	637-2
Ia Construction Corp 24 Gibb Rd **Fax Area Code:* 724 ■ *Web:* www.iaconstruction.com	Franklin	PA	16323	814-432-3184	452-0514*	188-4
IAABO (International Association of Approved Basketball Officials Inc) PO Box 355 *Web:* www.iaabo.org	Carlisle	PA	17013	717-713-8129	718-6164	48-22
IAAI (International Association of Arson Investigators) 2111 Baldwin Ave Ste 203 *TF:* 800-468-4224 ■ *Web:* www.firearson.com	Crofton	MD	21114	410-451-3473	451-9049	49-7
IAAO (International Association of Assessing Officers) 314 W Tenth St *TF:* 800-616-4226 ■ *Web:* iaao.org	Kansas City	MO	64105	816-701-8100	701-8149	49-7
IAAP (International Association of Administrative Professionals) 10502 NW Ambassador Dr Ste 100 *Web:* www.iaap-hq.org	Kansas City	MO	64153	816-891-6600	891-9118	49-12
IAAPA (International Association of Amusement Parks & Attractions) 1448 Duke St *Web:* www.iaapa.org	Alexandria	VA	22314	703-836-4800	836-6742	48-23
IAATI (International Association of Auto Theft Investigators) PO Box 223 *Web:* www.iaati.org	Clinton	NY	13323	315-853-1913		49-7
IABC (International Association of Business Communicators) 155 Montgomery St Ste 1210 *TF:* 800-776-4222 ■ *Web:* www.iabc.com	San Francisco	CA	94104	415-544-4700	544-4747	49-12
IAC Industries 895 Beacon St *TF:* 800-989-1422 ■ *Web:* www.iacindustries.com	Brea	CA	92821	714-990-8997	990-0557	319-1
IAC/InterActiveCorp 555 W 18th St *NASDAQ:* IAC ■ *Web:* www.iac.com	New York	NY	10011	212-314-7300	314-7309	185
IACC (International Association of Conference Centers) 35 E Wacker Dr Ste 850 *Web:* www.iacconline.org	Chicago	IL	60601	312-224-2580	644-8557	49-12

Name / Address	City	State	Zip	Phone	Fax	Class
IACC (Italian-American Chamber of Commerce Midwest) 1656 W CHICAGO Ave — *Web:* www.iacc-chicago.com	Chicago	IL	60622	312-553-9137	553-9142	138
IACC (International AntiCounterfeiting Coalition) 727 15th St NW 9th Fl — *Web:* www.iacc.org	Washington	DC	20005	202-223-6667		49-13
IACP (International Association of Culinary Professionals) 45 Rockefeller Plz Ste 2000 — *TF:* 855-738-4227 ■ *Web:* www.iacp.com	New York	NY	10111	855-738-4227		49-6
IACP (International Association of Chiefs of Police) 44 Canal Center Plz Ste 200 — *TF:* 800-843-4227 ■ *Web:* www.theiacp.org	Alexandria	VA	22314	703-836-6767	836-4543	49-7
IADA Services Inc 1111 Office Park Rd — *TF:* 800-869-1900 ■ *Web:* www.iada.com	West Des Moines	IA	50265	515-440-7621		138
IADC (International Association of Defense Counsel) 303 W Madison St Ste 925 — *Web:* www.iadclaw.org	Chicago	IL	60606	312-368-1494	368-1854	49-10
IADC (International Association of Drilling Contractors) 3657 Briarpark Dr Ste 760 — *Web:* www.iadc.org	Houston	TX	77042	713-292-1945	292-1946	49-3
IADR (International Association for Dental Research) 1619 Duke St — *Web:* www.iadr.org	Alexandria	VA	22314	703-548-0066	548-1883	49-8
iAdvantage Software Inc 219 E Chatham St Ste 200 — *Web:* www.iadvantagesoftware.com	Cary	NC	27511	919-469-3888		177
IAEA (International Atomic Energy Agency) 1 UN Plz Rm DC1-1155 — **Fax Area Code:* 917 ■ *Web:* www.iaea.org	New York	NY	10017	212-963-6010	367-4046*	783
IAEE (International Association of Exhibitions & Events) 12700 Park Central Dr Ste 308 — *Web:* www.iaee.com	Dallas	TX	75251	972-458-8002	458-8119	49-18
IAEI (International Association of Electrical Inspectors) 901 Waterfall Way Ste 602 — *TF:* 800-786-4234 ■ *Web:* www.iaei.org	Richardson	TX	75080	972-235-1455	235-6858	49-3
IAF (Institute for Alternative Futures) 2331 Mill Rd Ste 100 — *Web:* www.altfutures.org	Alexandria	VA	22314	703-684-5880		49-12
IAF (Inter-American Foundation) 901 N Stuart St 10th Fl — **Fax Area Code:* 703 ■ *Web:* www.iaf.gov	Arlington	VA	22203	202-360-4530	306-4365*	340-20
IAFC (International Association of Fire Chiefs) 4025 Fair Ridge Dr Ste 300 — *TF:* 866-385-9110 ■ *Web:* www.iafc.org	Fairfax	VA	22033	703-273-0911	273-9363	49-7
IAFE (International Association of Fairs & Expositions, The) 3043 E Cairo St — *TF:* 800-516-0313 ■ *Web:* www.fairsandexpos.com	Springfield	MO	65802	417-862-5771		48-23
IAFF (International Association of Fire Fighters) 1750 New York Ave NW Ste 300 — *Web:* www.iaff.org	Washington	DC	20006	202-737-8484	737-8418	414
IAFP (International Association for Food Protection) 6200 Aurora Ave Ste 200W — *TF:* 800-369-6337 ■ *Web:* www.foodprotection.org	Des Moines	IA	50322	515-276-3344	276-8655	49-6
IAFWA (International Association of Fish & Wildlife Agencies) 444 N Capitol St NW Ste 725 — *Web:* www.fishwildlife.org	Washington	DC	20001	202-624-7890	624-7891	49-7
IAI (Integrity Applications Inc) 15020 Conference Center Dr Ste 100 — *Web:* www.integrity-apps.com	Chantilly	VA	20151	703-378-8672	378-8978	261
IAI (Information Assets Inc) 9211 W Rd Ste 143-191 — *Web:* www.infoassets.com	Houston	TX	77064	713-443-9914		180
IAIA (International Association for Impact Assessment) 1330 23rd St S Ste C — *Web:* www.iaia.org	Fargo	ND	58103	701-297-7908	297-7917	49-12
IAIA (Institute of American Indian Arts) 83 Avan Nu Po Rd — *TF:* 800-804-6422 ■ *Web:* iaia.edu	Santa Fe	NM	87508	505-424-2300	424-0505	165
IAMAT (International Association for Medical Assistance to Travellers) 67 Mowat Ave Ste 036 — *Web:* www.iamat.org	Toronto	ON	M6K3E3	416-652-0137	652-1983	48-23
IAMGOLD Corp 401 Bay St Ste 3200 PO Box 153 — *TSE: IMG* ■ *TF:* 888-464-9999 ■ *Web:* www.iamgold.com	Toronto	ON	M5H2Y4	416-360-4710		502
IAMO Telephone Company Inc 104 Crook St — *TF:* 888-582-3232 ■ *Web:* www.iamotelephone.com	Coin	IA	51636	712-583-3232	583-3202	224
IAMS Co 3700 Ohio 65 — *TF:* 800-675-3849 ■ *Web:* www.iams.com	Leipsic	OH	45856	419-943-4267		578
Ian Ryan & Associates Inc 1400 E Touhy Ave Ste 220 — *Web:* ianryan.com	Des Plaines	IL	60018	847-803-2050		514
IANA (Intermodal Association of North America) 11785 Beltsville Dr Ste 1100 — *TF:* 877-438-8442 ■ *Web:* www.intermodal.org	Calverton	MD	20705	301-982-3400	982-4815	49-21
Ian-Conrad Bergan LLC 1001 E Belmont St — *Web:* bergan-blue.com	Pensacola	FL	32501	850-434-1286	434-1246	201
IAO Valley State Monument 54 S High St Rm 101 — *Web:* dlnr.hawaii.gov	Wailuku	HI	96793	808-984-8109	984-8111	565
Iap Inc W6905 Paradise Ln — *Web:* www.iapfan.com	Phillips	WI	54555	715-339-3024		18
IAP Worldwide Services Inc 7315 N Atlantic Ave — *Web:* www.iapws.com	Cape Canaveral	FL	32920	321-784-7100	784-7336	271
IAPA (Inter American Press Assn) 3511 NW 91st Ave — *Web:* www.sipiapa.org	Doral	FL	33172	305-634-2465	860-4264	49-14
IAPA (International Airline Passengers Assn) PO Box 700188 — *TF:* 800-821-4272 ■ *Web:* www.iapa.com	Dallas	TX	75370	972-404-9980	233-5348	48-23
IAPD (International Association of Plastics Distribution) 6734 W 121 St — *Web:* www.iapd.org	Overland Park	KS	66209	913-345-1005	345-1006	49-18
IAPES (International Association of Workforce Professionals) 1801 Louisville Rd — *Web:* iawponline.org	Frankfort	KY	40601	502-223-4459	223-4127	49-12
IAPMO (International Association of Plumbing & Mechanical Officials) 4755 E Philadelphia St — *TF:* 877-427-6601 ■ *Web:* www.iapmo.org	Ontario	CA	91761	909-472-4100	472-4150	49-7
IAPP (International Association of Privacy Professionals) 75 Rochester Ave Ste 4 — *TF:* 800-266-6501 ■ *Web:* iapp.org	Portsmouth	NH	03801	603-427-9200	427-9249	533
IAR Systems Software Inc 1065 E Hillsdale Blvd Century Plz — *Web:* www.iar.com	Foster City	CA	94404	650-287-4250	287-4253	174
IARC (International Arctic Research Ctr) 2160 Koyukuk Dr PO Box 757340 — *Web:* uaf-iarc.org	Fairbanks	AK	99775	907-474-6016	474-5662	668
Iaria's Italian Restaurant 317 S College Ave — *Web:* www.iariasrestaurant.com	Indianapolis	IN	46202	317-638-7706		671
IASP (International Association for the Study of Pain) 111 Queen Anne Ave N Ste 501 — *TF:* 866-574-2654 ■ *Web:* www.iasp-pain.org	Seattle	WA	98109	206-283-0311	283-9403	48-17
IATSE PAC 100 Centennial St Ste 2186 — *Web:* www.iatse.net	La Plata	MD	20646	212-730-1770		615
IAVM (International Association of Venue Managers Inc) 635 Fritz Dr Ste 100 — *TF:* 800-935-4226 ■ *Web:* www.iavm.org	Coppell	TX	75019	972-906-7441	906-7418	49-12
IAWF (International Association of Wildland Fire) 3416 Primm Ln — *Web:* www.iawfonline.org	Birmingham	AL	35216	205-824-7614		48-13
IB.I.S. Inc 420 Technology Pkwy Ste 100 — *TF:* 866-714-8422 ■ *Web:* ibisinc.com	Peachtree Corners	GA	30092	770-368-4000		695
Ibaset 27442 Portola Pkwy — *TF:* 877-422-7381 ■ *Web:* www.ibaset.com	Foothill Ranch	CA	92610	949-598-5200	598-2600	180
iBASIS Inc 10 Maguire Rd Bldg 3 — *Web:* www.ibasis.com	Lexington	MA	02421	781-505-7500		736
IBB Design Group 5798 Genesis Ct — *TF:* 800-355-9195 ■ *Web:* ibbdesign.com	Frisco	TX	75034	214-618-6600		138
IBBA (International Brangus Breeders Assn) 8870 US Hwy 87 E — *Web:* gobrangus.com	San Antonio	TX	78263	210-696-8231	696-8718	48-2
IBC 5700 Cromo Dr — *Web:* www.ibcelpaso.edu	El Paso	TX	79912	915-842-0422	585-2584	167-3
IBC Advanced Alloys Corp 401 Arvin Rd — *TF:* 800-423-5612 ■ *Web:* ibcadvancedalloys.com	Franklin	IN	46131	317-738-2558		502
IBC Advanced Technologies Inc 856 E Utah Valley Dr — *Web:* www.ibcmrt.com	American Fork	UT	84003	801-763-8400	763-8491	145
IBC Coating Technologies 902 Hendricks Dr — *Web:* www.ibccoatings.com	Lebanon	IN	46052	765-482-9802	482-9805	481
IBCC Industries Inc 4630 S Brust Ave — *Web:* www.ibccind.com	Saint Francis	WI	53235	414-486-5460	486-5464	194
IBE (Industrial Battery Engineering Inc) 9121 DeGarmo Ave — *Web:* www.ibe-inc.com	Sun Valley	CA	91352	818-767-7067	767-7173	74
Ibe Trade Corp 950 Third Ave Ste 2502 — *Web:* www.ibetrade.com	New York	NY	10022	212-593-3255	308-3642	280
I-Behavior Inc 2051 Dogwood St Ste 220 — *Web:* www.kbmg.com	Louisville	CO	80027	303-228-5000		194
IBERDROLA Group 1125 NW Couch Ste 700 — *Web:* www.avangridrenewables.com	Portland	OR	97209	503-796-7000	796-6901	620
Iberia Medical Ctr (IMC) 2315 E Main St — *Web:* www.iberiamedicalcenter.com	New Iberia	LA	70560	337-364-0441		374-3
Iberia Parish 300 Iberia St Ste 400 — *Web:* www.iberiaparishgovernment.com	New Iberia	LA	70560	337-365-8246	369-4470	338
Iberia Parish Library 445 E Main St — *Web:* iberialibrary.org	New Iberia	LA	70560	337-364-7024		434-3
Iberia Peninsula Restaurant 67 Ferry St — *Web:* www.iberiarestaurants.com	Newark	NJ	07105	973-344-5611	344-2067	671
Iberia Tiles Corp 2975 NW 77 Ave — *Web:* www.iberiatiles.com	Miami	FL	33122	305-591-3880		191-1
IBERIABANK Corp 200 W Congress St — *NASDAQ: IBKC* ■ *TF:* 800-968-0801 ■ *Web:* www.iberiabank.com	LaFayette	LA	70501	800-968-0801		360-2
Ibero-American Action League Inc 817 E Main St — *Web:* www.iaal.org	Rochester	NY	14605	585-256-8900		48-14
Iberville Parish 58050 Meriam St — *Web:* www.ibervilleparish.com	Plaquemine	LA	70764	225-687-5190		338
Iberville Parish Chamber of Commerce 23675 Church St — *TF:* 800-266-2692 ■ *Web:* www.ibervillechamber.com	Plaquemine	LA	70764	225-687-3560	687-3575	139
Iberville Parish Library 24605 J Gerald Berret Blvd — *Web:* myipl.org	Plaquemine	LA	70764	225-687-2520	687-9719	434-3
IBEW Local 125 17200 NE Sacramento St — *Web:* www.ibew125.com	Portland	OR	97230	503-262-9125		414
Ibex Insurance Agency 27750 Stansbury Blvd Ste 100 — *Web:* ibexagency.com	Farmington Hills	MI	48334	248-538-0470		390
IBEX Systems 150 Greenfield Dr — *Web:* www.ibexsystems.com	Bloomingdale	IL	60108	630-307-3634		194
IBFD Office for Americas 8300 Boone Blvd Ste 380 — *Web:* www.ibfd.org	Vienna	VA	22182	703-442-7757	442-7758	637-2
IBH (Institute for Better Health) PO Box 5710 — *TF:* 800-258-8411 ■ *Web:* www.ibh.com	Santa Rosa	CA	95402	707-595-9010	755-3133	49-8
IBHS (Institute for Business & Home Safety) 4775 E Fowler Ave — *TF:* 866-657-4247 ■ *Web:* disastersafety.org	Tampa	FL	33617	813-286-3400		49-9
IBI Armored Services Inc 37-06 61st St — *Web:* www.ibiarmored.com	Woodside	NY	11377	718-458-4000	458-5371	693

	Phone	Fax	Class
IBIS Communications 1024 17th Ave S . . . . Nashville TN 37212 *Web:* www.ibiscommunications.com	615-777-1900	777-1906	4
IBISWorld Inc 11755 Wilshire Blvd 11th Fl . . . . Los Angeles CA 90025 *TF:* 800-330-3772 ■ *Web:* www.ibisworld.com	800-330-3772		387
Ibiza Food & Wine Bar 2450 Louisiana St . . . . Houston TX 77006 *Web:* www.ibizafoodandwinebar.com	713-524-0004		671
IBJ (Indianapolis Business Journal) 41 E Washington St Ste 200 . . . . Indianapolis IN 46204 *TF:* 800-428-7081 ■ *Web:* www.ibj.com	317-634-6200	263-5060	457-5
IBM (International Business Machines Corp) 1 New Orchard Rd . . . . Armonk NY 10504 *NYSE: IBM* ■ *TF:* 800-426-4968 ■ *Web:* www.ibm.com	914-499-1900		173-2
IBMGS (Institute for Byzantine and Modern Greek Studies) 115 Gilbert Rd . . . . Belmont MA 02478 *Web:* ibmgs.org	617-484-8584	876-3600	637-2
IBML (Imaging Business Machines LLC) 2750 Crestwood Blvd . . . . Birmingham AL 35210 *TF:* 877-627-8325 ■ *Web:* www.ibml.com	205-956-4071	956-5309	111
IBPA (Independent Book Publishers Assn, The) 1020 Manhattan Beach Blvd Ste 204 . . . . . Manhattan Beach CA 90266 *TF:* 800-327-5113 ■ *Web:* www.ibpa-online.org	310-546-1818	546-3939	49-16
IBPO (International Brotherhood of Police Officers) 159 Burgin Pkwy . . . . Quincy MA 02169 *TF:* 866-412-7762 ■ *Web:* www.ibpo.org	617-376-0220	376-0285	414
IBS (International Biometric Society) 1444 'I' St NW Ste 700 . . . . Washington DC 20005 *Web:* www.biometricsociety.org	202-712-9049	216-9646	49-19
IBS (Institute of Buddhist Studies) 2140 Durant Ave . . . . Berkeley CA 94704 *Web:* www.shin-ibs.edu	510-809-1444	809-1443	637-2
IBS (International Bible Society) *Biblica* 1820 Jet Stream Dr . . . . Colorado Springs CO 80921 *TF:* 800-524-1588 ■ *Web:* www.biblica.com	719-488-9200		48-20
IBS Electronics Inc Lake Center Dr . . . . Santa Ana CA 92704 *TF:* 800-527-2888 ■ *Web:* www.ibselectronics.com	714-751-6633	751-8159	246
IBT Enterprises LLC 1770 Indian Trail Rd Ste 300 . . . . Norcross GA 30093 *TF:* 877-242-8428 ■ *Web:* www.ibtenterprises.com	770-381-2023		194
IBT Inc 9400 W 55th St . . . . Merriam KS 66203 *TF:* 800-332-2114 ■ *Web:* www.ibtinc.com	913-677-3151	677-3752	385
IBTTA (International Bridge Tunnel & Turnpike Assn) 1146 19th St NW Ste 600 . . . . Washington DC 20036 *Web:* www.ibtta.org	202-659-4620	659-0500	49-7
IBU (Inlandboatmen's Union of the Pacific) 1711 W Nickerson St Ste D . . . . Seattle WA 98119 *Web:* www.ibu.org	206-284-6001		414
I-Bus Corp 3350 Scott Blvd Bldg 54 . . . . Santa Clara CA 95054 *Web:* www.ibus.com	408-450-7880	450-7881	625
I-Business Network LLC 2617 Sandy Plains Rd Ste B . . . . Marietta GA 30066 *Web:* www.i-bn.com	678-627-0646	627-0688	39
IBWA (International Bottled Water Assn) 1700 Diagonal Rd Ste 650 . . . . Alexandria VA 22314 *TF:* 800-928-3711 ■ *Web:* www.bottledwater.org	703-683-5213	683-4074	49-6
IC Assemblies Inc 2250 NW 102nd Ave . . . . Doral FL 33172 *Web:* www.icassemblies.com	305-477-0387	594-7332	489
IC Distribution 11860 Fishing Point Dr . . . . Newport News VA 23606 *Web:* www.icdistribution.com	757-873-8288		174
IC Medical Inc 2340 W Shangri La Rd . . . . Phoenix AZ 85029 *TF:* 800-766-5336 ■ *Web:* icmedical.com	623-780-0700		475
IC Thomasson Associates Inc 2950 Kraft Dr Ste 500 . . . . Nashville TN 37204 *Web:* www.icthomasson.com	615-346-3400		201
ICA (International Communication Assn) 1500 21st St NW . . . . Washington DC 20036 *Web:* www.icahdq.org	202-955-1444	955-1448	49-14
ICA (International Chiropractors Assn) 6400 Arlington Blvd Ste 800 . . . . Falls Church VA 22042 *TF:* 800-423-4690 ■ *Web:* www.chiropractic.org	703-528-5000	528-5023	49-8
ICAC (Institute of Clean Air Cos) 1730 M St NW Ste 206 . . . . Washington DC 20036 *TF:* 800-631-9505 ■ *Web:* www.icac.com	202-478-6188	367-2114	48-12
iCAD Inc 98 Spit Brook Rd Ste 100 . . . . Nashua NH 03062 *NASDAQ: ICAD* ■ *TF:* 866-280-2239 ■ *Web:* www.icadmed.com	603-882-5200	880-3843	382
Icahn Enterprises LP 767 Fifth Ave 47th Fl . . . . New York NY 10153 *NASDAQ: IEP* ■ *TF:* 800-255-2737 ■ *Web:* www.ielp.com	212-702-4300	750-5841	360-3
ICAIR (International Center for Advanced Internet Research) 750 N Lake Shore Dr Ste 600 . . . . Chicago IL 60611 *Web:* www.icair.org	312-503-0735		668
ICAM Technologies Corp 21500 Nassr St . . . . Sainte-Anne-de-Bellevue QC H9X4C1 *TF:* 800-827-4226 ■ *Web:* icam.com	514-697-8033		179
ICANN (Internet Corporation for Assigned Names & Numbers) 4676 Admiralty Way Ste 330 . . . . Marina CA 90292 *Web:* www.icann.org	310-301-5800	823-8649	48-9
iCare Health Network 341 Bidwell St . . . . Manchester CT 06040 *Web:* www.icarehn.com	860-570-2140		371
Icare Industries Inc 4399 35th St N . . . . Saint Petersburg FL 33714 *TF:* 877-422-7352 ■ *Web:* www.icarelabs.com	727-526-0501		542
ICAT Logistics Inc 6805 Douglas Legum Dr . . . . Elkridge MD 21075 **Fax Area Code:* 410 ■ *TF:* 800-572-1324 ■ *Web:* www.icatlogistics.com	443-459-8070	799-0115*	311
ICBA (Independent Community Bankers of America) 1615 L St NW Ste 900 . . . . Washington DC 20036 *TF:* 800-422-8439 ■ *Web:* www.icba.org	202-659-8111		49-2
ICC (International Code Council) 500 New Jersey Ave NW 6th Fl . . . . Washington DC 20001 *TF:* 888-422-7233 ■ *Web:* www.iccsafe.org	202-370-1800	783-2348	49-3
ICC (Industrial Control Concepts Inc) 301 N Memorial Dr . . . . Saint Louis MO 63102 *Web:* www.icc-inc.net	314-621-0076	621-2111	203
ICC Chemicals 4660 Spring Grove Ave . . . . Cincinnati OH 45232 *Web:* icc-chemicals.com	513-541-7100	541-6880	145
ICC Industries Inc 460 Park Ave . . . . New York NY 10022 *TF:* 800-422-1720 ■ *Web:* www.iccchem.com	212-521-1700	521-1970	144
ICC Northwest Inc 390 S Redwood St . . . . Canby OR 97013 *Web:* jvnw.com	503-263-2858		480
ICCFA (International Cemetery Cremation & Funeral Assn) 107 Carpenter Dr Ste 100 . . . . Sterling VA 20164 *TF:* 800-645-7700 ■ *Web:* iccfa.com	703-391-8400	391-8416	49-4
ICCG Capital Inc 555 Republic Dr Ste 109 PO Box 861498 . . . . Plano TX 75074 *Web:* www.iccgcapital.com	972-424-5600		196
ICCLOS (Indiana Convention Center & Lucas Oil Stadium) 100 S Capitol Ave . . . . Indianapolis IN 46225 *Web:* icclos.com	317-262-3400	262-3685	205
ICCP (Institute for Certification of Computing Professionals) 2400 E Devon Ave Ste 281 . . . . Des Plaines IL 60018 *TF:* 800-843-8227 ■ *Web:* www.iccp.org	847-299-4227		48-9
ICD (International College of Dentists) 51 Monroe St Ste 1400 . . . . Rockville MD 20850 *Web:* www.icd.org	301-251-8861	738-9143	49-8
ICD (Industrial Controls Distributors Inc) 1776 Bloomsbury Ave . . . . Wanamassa NJ 07712 *TF:* 800-281-4788 ■ *Web:* www.industrialcontrolsonline.com	732-918-9000	922-4417	385
ICD Group International Inc 150 E 52nd St . . . . New York NY 10022 *Web:* www.icdgroup.com	212-644-1500	644-1480	360-3
ICE (U.S. Immigration & Customs Enforcement) 425 'I' St NW . . . . Washington DC 20536 *TF:* 866-347-2423 ■ *Web:* www.ice.gov	866-347-2423		340-11
ICE (International Crystal Exchange) 13325 Prospect Rd . . . . Strongsville OH 44149 **Fax Area Code:* 440 ■ *TF:* 800-443-8223 ■ *Web:* www.ice4crystal.com	800-443-8223	238-3553*	411
Ice Air LLC 80 Hartford Ave . . . . Mount Vernon NY 10553 *Web:* www.ice-air.com	914-668-4700	668-5643	664
Ice Cream Specialties (ICS) 8419 Hanley Industrial Ct . . . . Saint Louis MO 63144 *Web:* northstarfrozentreats.com	314-962-2550		296-25
Ice House Museum and Cultural Ctr 818 Earnest Ave . . . . Silsbee TX 77656 *Web:* www.icehousemuseum.org	409-385-2444		50-2
Ice Industries Inc 3810 Herr Rd . . . . Sylvania OH 43560 *Web:* www.iceindustries.com	419-842-3600		483
Ice Recycling LLC 431 Cedar St . . . . Lake City SC 29560 *TF:* 877-423-7373 ■ *Web:* www.icerecycling.com	843-374-0217		686
Ice Services Inc 2606 Center St . . . . Anchorage AK 99503 *Web:* www.iceservices.net	907-644-0835		393
Ice Specialty Entertainment Inc 409 Santa Monica Blvd Ste E . . . . Santa Monica CA 90401 *Web:* www.iceoplex.com	805-520-7465		354
Ice Sports Industry (ISI) 6000 Custer Rd Bldg 9 . . . . Plano TX 75023 *Web:* www.skateisi.org	972-735-8800	735-8815	48-22
Ice Systems & Supplies Inc (ISSI) 163 E Mount Gallant Rd . . . . Rock Hill SC 29730 *TF:* 800-662-1273 ■ *Web:* www.issionline.com	803-324-8791		14
Ice Technologies Inc 411 SE 9th St . . . . Pella IA 50219 *TF:* 877-754-8420 ■ *Web:* www.icetechnologies.com	877-754-8420		180
Icebox Cafe 1855 Purdy Ave . . . . Miami Beach FL 33139 *Web:* iceboxcafe.com	305-538-8448		671
ICECORP Logistics Inc 1600 Courtneypark Dr E . . . . Mississauga ON L5T2W8 *Web:* icecorp.ca	905-672-7400		314
Iceland *Consulate General* 800 Third Ave 36th Fl . . . . New York NY 10022 *Web:* www.iceland.is	646-282-9360	282-9369	257
Icelandair North America 1900 Crown Colony Dr . . . . Quincy MA 02169 *TF:* 800-223-5500 ■ *Web:* www.icelandair.com	800-223-5500		26
Icelandic State Park 13571 Hwy 5 . . . . Cavalier ND 58220 *Web:* www.parkrec.nd.gov	701-265-4561		565
Icemakers Inc 3711 5th Ct N . . . . Birmingham AL 35222 *Web:* www.icemakers.net	205-591-2791	591-2389	380
Ice-O-Matic 11100 E 45th Ave . . . . Denver CO 80239 *TF:* 800-423-3367 ■ *Web:* www.iceomatic.com	303-576-2940	371-6296	664
Icepts Technology Group Inc 1301 Fulling Mill Rd . . . . Middletown PA 17057 *Web:* www.icepts.com	717-704-1000		174
ICF (International Contract Furnishings Inc) 19 Ohio Ave . . . . Norwich CT 06360 **Fax Area Code:* 888 ■ *TF:* 800-237-1625 ■ *Web:* www.icfsource.com	860-886-1700	784-8209*	321
ICF International Inc 9300 Lee Hwy . . . . Fairfax VA 22031 *NASDAQ: ICFI* ■ *Web:* www.icf.com	703-934-3000	934-3740	261
ICF International Inc 420 N 5th St . . . . Minneapolis MN 55401 *Web:* www.icf.com	612-215-9800		4
ICFG (International Church of the Foursquare Gospel) 1910 W Sunset Blvd PO Box 26902 . . . . Los Angeles CA 90026 *TF:* 888-635-4234 ■ *Web:* www.foursquare.org	213-989-4234	989-4590	48-20
ICFL (Idaho Commission for Libraries) 325 W State St . . . . Boise ID 83702 *TF:* 800-458-3271 ■ *Web:* www.libraries.idaho.gov	208-334-2150	334-4016	434-5
ICG Consulting Inc 8570 E Shea Blvd Ste 110 . . . . Scottsdale AZ 85260 *Web:* www.icgconsulting.com	480-607-4040		463
ICG Link Inc 7003 Chadwick Dr Ste 111 . . . . Brentwood TN 37027 *TF:* 877-397-7605 ■ *Web:* www.icglink.net	615-370-1530		353
ICG/Holliston 905 Holliston Mills Rd . . . . Church Hill TN 37642 **Fax Area Code:* 800 ■ *TF:* 800-251-0451 ■ *Web:* www.holliston.com	423-357-6141	325-0351*	745-2
ICGS (Iroquois County Genealogical Society) Old Courthouse Museum 103 W Cherry St . . . . Watseka IL 60970 *Web:* www.iroquoiscountygenealogy.org	815-432-3730	432-3732	49-19
Ichetucknee Springs State Park 12087 SW US Hwy 27 . . . . Fort White FL 32038 *Web:* www.floridastateparks.org	386-497-4690		565

Company	City	State	Zip	Phone	Fax	Class
Ichiban 338 Central Ave *Web:* www.ichibanjapanesechinese.com	Albany	NY	12206	518-432-0358		671
Ichiban 226 Union St *Web:* www.bangorichiban.com	Bangor	ME	04401	207-262-9308		671
Ichiban 1449 University Ave *Web:* ichibansushisandiego.com	San Diego	CA	92103	619-299-7203	299-7514	671
Ichiban 1914 Catasauqua Rd *Web:* ichibanpa.com	Allentown	PA	18109	610-266-7781	266-7783	671
Ichiban 189 Carlton St *Web:* www.lakeviewhotels.com	Winnipeg	MB	R3C3H7	204-925-7400	957-1697	671
ICHM (Iron County Historical Museum) 100 Brady Ave *Web:* www.ironcountyhistoricalmuseum.org	Caspian	MI	49915	906-265-2617		637-2
ICHP Building Company LLC 4055 N Perryville Rd *TF:* 800-363-8012 ■ *Web:* ichpnet.org	Loves Park	IL	61111	815-227-9292		533
ICI (Investment Company Institute) 1401 H St NW Ste 1200 *Web:* www.ici.org	Washington	DC	20005	202-326-5800	326-5841	49-2
ICI (Investment Casting Institute) 136 Summit Ave *Web:* www.investmentcasting.org	Montvale	NJ	07645	201-573-9770	573-9771	49-13
ICI (Imaging Concepts Inc) 2818 Hungary Rd *TF:* 800-228-0060 ■ *Web:* www.imagingconcepts.com	Richmond	VA	23228	804-755-8701	755-8711	475
ICI (Intercultural Communication Institute) 8835 SW Canyon Ln Ste 238 *Web:* www.intercultural.org	Portland	OR	97225	503-297-4622	297-4695	167-3
ICI Mutual Insurance Co 1401 H St NW Ste 1000 *TF:* 800-643-4246 ■ *Web:* www.icimutual.com	Washington	DC	20005	800-643-4246		390
ICI Services Corp 500 Viking Dr Ste 400 *Web:* www.icisrvcs.com	Virginia Beach	VA	23452	757-340-6970	340-2293	196
Icicle Seafoods Inc 4019 21st Ave W *Web:* www.icicleseafoods.com	Seattle	WA	98199	206-282-0988	282-7222	296-13
iCIMS Inc 90 Matawan Rd Pkwy 120 5th Fl *Web:* www.icims.com	Matawan	NJ	07747	732-847-1941	876-0422	178-1
ICIO Inc 1373 Ridge Commons Blvd *Web:* www.icioinc.com	Hanover	MD	21076	410-850-0884		225
ICL Express 2307 Coney Island Ave *Web:* www.icl-express.com	Brooklyn	NY	11223	718-376-1023	376-1073	12
ICL Imaging Corp 51 Mellen St *TF:* 800-660-3280 ■ *Web:* www.icl-imaging.com	Framingham	MA	01702	508-872-3280		174
ICLE (Institute of Continuing Legal Education in Georgia) 104 Marietta St NW *TF:* 800-422-0893 ■ *Web:* www.iclega.org	Atlanta	GA	30303	706-369-5664	466-0886	49-19
ICM Controls Corp 7313 William Barry Blvd *TF:* 800-365-5525 ■ *Web:* www.icmcontrols.com	North Syracuse	NY	13212	315-233-5266	233-5276	203
ICM Inc 310 N First St *TF:* 877-456-8588 ■ *Web:* www.icminc.com	Colwich	KS	67030	316-796-0900	796-0570	463
ICMA (International Card Manufacturers Assn) 191 Clarksville Rd *Web:* icma.com	Princeton Junction	NJ	08550	609-799-4900	799-7032	49-4
ICMA (International Center of Medieval Art) The Cloisters Fort Tryon Pk *Web:* www.medievalart.org	New York	NY	10040	212-928-1146	928-9946	48-4
ICMA (International City/County Management Assn) 777 N Capitol St NE Ste 500 *TF:* 800-745-8780 ■ *Web:* icma.org	Washington	DC	20002	202-289-4262	962-3500	49-7
ICMARC 777 N Capitol St NE Ste 600 *TF:* 800-669-7471 ■ *Web:* www.icmarc.org	Washington	DC	20002	202-962-4600	962-4601	528
ICNC (Industrial Council of Nearwest Chicago) 320 N Damen Ave 1st Fl *Web:* www.industrialcouncil.com	Chicago	IL	60612	312-421-3941	421-1871	393
ICNY (Interfaith Center of New York) 475 Riverside Dr Ste 540 *Web:* interfaithcenter.org	New York	NY	10115	212-870-3510	870-3499	637-10
ICO (Inter City Oil Company Inc) 1921 S St *TF:* 800-642-5542 ■ *Web:* www.intercityoil.com	Duluth	MN	55812	218-728-3641		579
ICOI (International Congress of Oral Implantologists) 55 Ln Rd Ste 305 *TF:* 800-442-0525 ■ *Web:* www.icoi.org	Fairfield	NJ	07004	973-783-6300	783-1175	49-8
iCollector.com 103-2071 Kingsway Ave *TF:* 866-313-0123 ■ *Web:* www.icollector.com	Port Coquitlam	BC	V3C6N2	604-941-2221		51
ICOM America Inc 2380 116th Ave NE *TF:* 800-872-4266 ■ *Web:* www.icomamerica.com	Bellevue	WA	98004	425-454-8155	454-1509	647
Icomm 7321 W Madison Ste 200 *Web:* icomm.co	Forest Park	IL	60130	708-434-1000		681
Icon Advisers Inc 5299 DTC Blvd Ste 1200 *TF:* 800-828-4881 ■ *Web:* iconadvisers.com	Greenwood Village	CO	80111	303-790-1600		401
Icon Health & Fitness Inc 1500 S 1000 W *TF:* 800-999-3756 ■ *Web:* www.iconfitness.com	Logan	UT	84321	435-750-5000		267
Icon Interactive 220 Felch St *Web:* iconinteractive.com	Ann Arbor	MI	48103	734-707-9245		393
Icon International Inc 1 E Weaver St *Web:* www.icon-intl.com	Greenwich	CT	06831	203-328-2300	328-2333	463
Icon International Inc 345 N Beacon St *TF:* 800-734-1819 ■ *Web:* www.sdmarinehardware.com	San Pedro	CA	90731	310-831-9261	831-4442	770
Icon Laboratories Inc 123 Smith St *Web:* www.iconplc.com	Farmingdale	NY	11735	631-777-8833		225
Icon Media Direct Inc 5910 Lemona Ave *Web:* www.iconmediadirect.com	Sherman Oaks	CA	91411	818-995-6400		5
Icon Productions LLC 808 Wilshire Blvd	Santa Monica	CA	90401	310-434-7300		514
Icon Ventures 505 Hamilton Ave Ste 310 *Web:* iconventures.com	Palo Alto	CA	94301	650-463-8800	463-8801	792
Icon West Inc 520 S La Fayette Park Pl Ste 503 *Web:* icon-west.com	Los Angeles	CA	90057	213-385-0027		187
Icona Avalon 7849 Dune Dr *Web:* www.icona.com	Avalon	NJ	08202	609-368-5155		378
Iconixx Software 3420 Executive Center Dr Ste 250 *TF:* 877-426-6499 ■ *Web:* iconixx.com	Austin	TX	78731	877-426-6499		180
Iconma LLC 850 Stephenson Hwy Ste 612 *TF:* 888-451-2519 ■ *Web:* www.iconma.com	Troy	MI	48083	888-451-2519		631
iConnected Marketing 125 Tech Park Dr *Web:* www.iconnectedmarketing.com	Rochester	NY	14623	585-444-8500		5
Iconomics Inc 1 Dundas St W Ste 2108 *TF:* 855-703-6547 ■ *Web:* www.iconomics-inc.com	Toronto	ON	M5G1Z3	416-703-6547		180
Icor Technology Inc 935 Ages Dr *TF:* 877-483-7978 ■ *Web:* icortechnology.com	Ottawa	ON	K1G6L3	613-745-3600		690
ICO-RALLY Corp 2575 E Bayshore Rd *Fax Area Code: 800 ■ *Web:* www.icorally.com	Palo Alto	CA	94303	650-856-9900	856-2006*	816
Icotech Inc PO Box 210424 *Fax Area Code: 888 ■ *Web:* www.icotechinc.com	Montgomery	AL	36121	334-386-9996	696-5403*	203
ICP (International Comfort Products) 650 Heil Quaker Ave *Web:* www.icpusa.com	Lewisburg	TN	37091	931-359-3511	270-3312	15
ICP Construction 150 Dascomb Rd *TF:* 800-225-1141 ■ *Web:* www.californiapaints.com	Andover	MA	01810	800-225-1141	533-6788	550
ICP Inc 20 Clifton Ave *Web:* www.icpcorp.com	Staten Island	NY	10305	718-556-6700		174
ICP Inc 1815 W Country Rd 54 *TF:* 800-228-8278 ■ *Web:* www.icppharm.com	Tiffin	OH	44883	800-228-8278		237
ICPA (International Commission for the Prevention of Alcoholism and Drug Dependency) 12501 Old Columbia Pke *Web:* icpaworld.org	Silver Spring	MD	20904	301-680-6719	680-6707	49-19
ICPI (Interlocking Concrete Pavement Institute) 14801 Murdock St Ste 230 *TF:* 800-241-3652 ■ *Web:* www.icpi.org	Chantilly	VA	20151	703-657-6900	657-6901	49-3
ICPM (Institute of Certified Professional Managers) James Madison University MSC 5504 *Web:* www.icpm.biz	Harrisonburg	VA	22807	540-568-3247		49-12
ICRCO Inc 26 Coromar Dr *Fax Area Code: 805 ■ *TF:* 866-907-7740 ■ *Web:* www.icrco.com	Goleta	CA	93117	310-921-9559	685-1308*	201
Icreon Tech 433 5th Ave Fl 4 12th Fl *Web:* www.icreon.us	New York	NY	10017	212-706-6023		196
iCrossing Inc 300 W 57th St *Web:* www.icrossing.com	New York	NY	10019	212-649-3900		466
ICRW (International Center for Research on Women) 1120 20th St NW Ste 500-N *Web:* www.icrw.org	Washington	DC	20036	202-797-0007	797-0020	48-24
ICS (International College of Surgeons) 1516 N Lake Shore Dr *Web:* www.icsglobal.org	Chicago	IL	60610	312-642-3555		49-8
ICS (Integrated Computer Solutions Inc) 54 Middlesex Tpke Ste B *Web:* www.ics.com	Bedford	MA	01730	617-621-0060	621-9555	178-2
ICS (Ice Cream Specialties) 8419 Hanley Industrial Ct *Web:* northstarfrozentreats.com	Saint Louis	MO	63144	314-962-2550		296-25
ICS (Information & Computing Services Inc) 1650 Prudential Dr Ste 300 *TF:* 800-676-4427 ■ *Web:* www.icsfl.com	Jacksonville	FL	32207	904-399-8500		178-1
ICS (Implementation & Consulting Services Inc) 500 Office Center Dr Ste 400 *TF:* 844-432-8326 ■ *Web:* www.ics-corporate.com	Fort Washington	PA	19034	844-432-8326		177
ICS (International Counterintelligence Services Inc) 8283 N Hayden Rd Ste 128 *TF:* 800-828-9198 ■ *Web:* www.icsworld.com	Scottsdale	AZ	85258	480-990-8888	675-8800	693
ICS Blount Inc 4909 SE International Way *Fax Area Code: 503 ■ *TF:* 800-321-1240 ■ *Web:* www.icsdiamondtools.eu	Portland	OR	97222	800-321-1240	653-4393*	682
ICS Corp 100 Friars Blvd *Web:* ics-corporation.com	West Deptford	NJ	08086	215-427-3355		626
ICS Marketing Services Inc 4225 Legacy Pkwy *TF:* 888-394-1890 ■ *Web:* www.icshq.com	Lansing	MI	48911	517-394-1890		195
ICS Publications 2131 Lincoln Rd NE *TF:* 800-832-8489 ■ *Web:* www.icspublications.org	Washington	DC	20002	202-832-8489	832-8967	637-2
ICS Worldwide 1099 Morse Ave *Web:* www.icsworldwide.com	Elk Grove Village	IL	60007	847-718-9998		311
ICSA Labs 1000 Bent Creek Blvd Ste 200 *Web:* www.icsalabs.com	Mechanicsburg	PA	17050	717-790-8100		387
ICSC (International Council of Shopping Centers) 1251 Ave of the Americas 45th Fl *Fax Area Code: 212 ■ *Web:* www.icsc.org	New York	NY	10020	646-728-3800	589-5555*	49-12
ICSNetwork LLC 17450 Long Meadow Trl *Fax Area Code: 440 ■ *Web:* www.icsnetwork.com	Chagrin Falls	OH	44023	216-509-6000	543-8206*	41
ICT (International City Theatre) 67 Long Beach Blvd *Web:* www.ictlongbeach.org	Long Beach	CA	90802	562-495-4595		573-4
ICT (Industrial Ceramic Technology Inc) 37 Enterprise Dr *Web:* www.indceramictech.com	Ann Arbor	MI	48103	734-761-8137	996-0808	500
ICT Northumberland College 1888 Brunswick St 5th Fl *TF:* 888-862-2230 ■ *Web:* www.ictschools.com	Halifax	NS	B3J3J8	902-425-2869	425-2858	167-3
ICTA (International Center for Technology Assessment) 303 Sacramento St 2nd Fl *Web:* www.icta.org	San Francisco	CA	94111	415-826-2770		49-19
ICTA (Industry Council for Tangible Assets) 1510 Circle Dr *Web:* www.ictaonline.org	Annapolis	MD	21409	410-626-7005		49-2
ICTC (Inter-Community Telephone Co) PO Box 8 *TF:* 800-350-9137 ■ *Web:* www.ictc.com	Nome	ND	58062	701-924-8815	924-8808	736

				Phone	Fax	Class
ICTV Brands Inc						
489 Devon Park Dr Ste 315	Wayne	PA	19087	484-598-2300		225
TF: 800-839-4906 ■ *Web:* ictvbrands.com						
ICU Medical Inc						
951 Calle Amanecer	San Clemente	CA	92673	949-366-2183	366-8368	477
NASDAQ: ICUI ■ *TF:* 800-824-7890 ■ *Web:* www.icumed.com						
ICV Digital Media 3908 Valley Ave	Pleasanton	CA	94566	925-426-8230		514
Web: www.icvdm.com						
ICVM Group Inc						
320 Love Ln Ste B 2nd Fl	Mattituck	NY	11952	631-298-5505	298-5479	225
Web: www.icvmgroup.com						
IcwUSACom Inc 1487 Kingsley Dr	Medford	OR	97504	541-608-2824		321
TF: 800-558-4435 ■ *Web:* www.icwusa.com						
ICX Group Inc						
SunTrust Tower 76 S Laura St Ste 1300	Jacksonville	FL	32202	904-208-2200	208-2201	317
Web: www.icxgroup.com						
ID Group LLC, The 2641 Irving Blvd	Dallas	TX	75207	214-638-6800		393
Web: www.idgroupdallas.com						
ID Tech Inc						
910 E Hamilton Ave Ste 300	Campbell	CA	95008	408-871-3700		425
TF: 888-709-8324 ■ *Web:* www.idtech.com						
IDA (Institute for Defense Analyses)						
4850 Mark Center Dr	Alexandria	VA	22311	703-845-2000	845-2588	668
Web: www.ida.org						
IDA (In Defense of Animals)						
3010 Kerner Blvd	San Rafael	CA	94901	415-448-0048	454-1031	48-3
TF: 800-705-0425 ■ *Web:* www.idausa.org						
IDA (Industrial Diamond Association of America)						
PO Box 29460	Columbus	OH	43229	614-797-2265	797-2264	49-13
Web: www.superabrasives.org						
IDA (International Downtown Assn)						
910 17th St NW Ste 1050	Washington	DC	20006	202-393-6801	393-6869	49-17
Web: www.ida-downtown.org						
IDA (International Dyslexia Assn, The)						
40 York Rd 4th Fl	Towson	MD	21204	410-296-0232	321-5069	48-17
Web: dyslexiaida.org						
IDA County 401 Moorehead St	Ida Grove	IA	51445	712-364-3146		338
Web: idacounty.org						
IDA Rupp Public Library						
310 Madison St	Port Clinton	OH	43452	419-732-3212		434-3
Web: www.idarupp.org						
IDACORP Inc 1221 W Idaho St	Boise	ID	83702	208-388-2200		360-5
NYSE: IDA ■ *TF:* 800-242-0681 ■ *Web:* www.idacorpinc.com						
Idaho						
Accountancy Board 3101 W Main St Ste 210	Boise	ID	83702	208-334-2490	334-2615	339-13
Web: isba.idaho.gov						
Aging Commission (ICOA)						
341 W Washington 3rd Fl	Boise	ID	83702	208-334-3833		339-13
TF: 877-471-2777 ■ *Web:* www.idahoaging.com						
Agriculture Dept						
2270 Old Penitentiary Rd	Boise	ID	83712	208-332-8500	334-2170	339-13
Web: agri.idaho.gov						
Arts Commission						
2410 Old Penitentiary Rd	Boise	ID	83712	208-334-2119		339-13
TF: 800-278-3863 ■ *Web:* arts.idaho.gov						
Bill Status PO Box 83720	Boise	ID	83720	208-332-1000	334-2320	433
Web: legislature.idaho.gov						
Board of Medicine						
1755 N Westgate Dr Ste 140 PO Box 83720	Boise	ID	83704	208-327-7000	327-7005	339-13
Web: www.bom.idaho.gov						
Consumer Protection Unit PO Box 83720	Boise	ID	83720	208-332-0102		339-13
Web: www.state.id.us						
Correction Board						
1299 N Orchard St Ste 110	Boise	ID	83706	208-658-2000	327-7404	339-13
Web: www.idoc.idaho.gov						
Crime Victims Compensation Program						
PO Box 83720	Boise	ID	83720	208-334-6000	334-2321	339-13
TF: 800-950-2110 ■ *Web:* iic.idaho.gov						
Department of Commerce						
700 W State St PO Box 83720	Boise	ID	83720	208-334-2470	334-2631	339-13
TF: 800-842-5858 ■ *Web:* commerce.idaho.gov						
Education Dept 650 W State St	Boise	ID	83702	208-332-6800	334-2228	339-13
Web: www.sde.idaho.gov						
Finance Dept						
800 Pk Blvd Ste 200 PO Box 83720	Boise	ID	83712	208-332-8000		339-13
TF: 888-346-3378 ■ *Web:* www.finance.idaho.gov						
Fish & Game Dept 600 S Walnut St	Boise	ID	83712	208-334-3700	334-2114	339-13
Web: idfg.idaho.gov						
Health & Welfare Dept						
450 W State St 10th Fl PO Box 83720	Boise	ID	83720	877-456-1233	334-5926*	339-13
**Fax Area Code:* 208 ■ *TF:* 877-456-1233 ■ *Web:* www.healthandwelfare.idaho.gov						
Historical Society						
2205 Old Penitentiary Rd	Boise	ID	83712	208-334-2682	334-2774	339-13
Web: history.idaho.gov						
Housing & Finance Assn 565 W Myrtle Ave	Boise	ID	83702	208-331-4700		339-13
TF: 800-526-7145 ■ *Web:* www.idahohousing.com						
Insurance Dept 700 W State St 3rd Fl	Boise	ID	83720	208-334-4250	334-4398	339-13
TF: 800-247-4422 ■ *Web:* doi.idaho.gov						
Lands Dept						
300 N Sixth St Ste 103 PO Box 83720	Boise	ID	83702	208-334-0200	334-5342	339-13
Web: www.idl.idaho.gov						
Legislature PO Box 83720	Boise	ID	83720	208-334-2475	334-2125	339-13
Web: legislature.idaho.gov						
Lieutenant Governor State Capitol	Boise	ID	83720	208-334-2200	334-3259	339-13
Web: lgo.idaho.gov						
Lottery 1199 Shoreline Ln Ste 100	Boise	ID	83702	208-334-2600		452
TF: 800-432-5688 ■ *Web:* www.idaholottery.com						
Occupational Licenses Bureau						
700 W State St	Boise	ID	83702	208-334-3233		339-13
Web: www.ibol.idaho.gov						
Office of Emergency Management						
4040 W Guard St Bldg 600	Boise	ID	83705	208-258-6500	422-3044	339-13
Web: ioem.idaho.gov						
Pardon & Parole Commission						
7155 W Denton St	Boise	ID	83705	208-334-2520		339-13
Web: www.parole.idaho.gov						
Parks & Recreation Dept						
5657 Warm Springs Ave	Boise	ID	83716	208-334-4199		339-13
Web: parksandrecreation.idaho.gov						

				Phone	Fax	Class
Public Utilities Commission						
472 W Washington PO Box 83720	Boise	ID	83720	208-334-0300	334-3762	339-13
TF: 800-432-0369 ■ *Web:* www.puc.idaho.gov						
Racing Commission 700 S Stratford Dr	Meridian	ID	83642	208-884-7080	884-7098	712
Web: isp.idaho.gov						
Real Estate Commission						
575 E Parkcenter Blvd Ste 180	Boise	ID	83706	208-334-3285	334-2050	339-13
Web: irec.idaho.gov						
Secretary of State						
700 W Jefferson Rm E205	Boise	ID	83702	208-334-2300		339-13
Web: sos.idaho.gov						
State Treasurer's						
700 W Jefferson St Ste E-110	Boise	ID	83702	208-334-3200	332-2959	339-13
Web: sto.idaho.gov						
Supreme Court PO Box 83720	Boise	ID	83720	208-334-2210		339-13
Web: isc.idaho.gov						
Veterans Services Div 351 Collins Rd	Boise	ID	83702	208-577-2310	780-1300	339-13
Web: www.veterans.idaho.gov						
Vocational Rehabilitation Div						
650 W State St Rm 150	Boise	ID	83720	208-334-3390	334-5305	339-13
Web: vr.idaho.gov						
Weights & Measures Bureau						
2270 Old Penitentiary Rd PO Box 790	Boise	ID	83712	208-332-8690	334-2170	339-13
Web: agri.idaho.gov						
Idaho Association of Realtors						
10116 W Overland Rd	Boise	ID	83709	208-342-3585	336-7958	656
TF: 800-621-7553 ■ *Web:* idahorealtors.com						
Idaho Black History Museum						
508 Julia Davis Dr	Boise	ID	83702	208-789-2164		520
Web: www.ibhm.org						
Idaho Botanical Garden						
2355 N Penitentiary Rd	Boise	ID	83712	208-343-8649	343-3601	97
TF: 877-527-8233 ■ *Web:* www.idahobotanicalgarden.org						
Idaho Cedar Sales LLC 221 Main St	Troy	ID	83871	208-835-2161	835-2772	820
Web: www.cedar.idahotimber.com						
Idaho Commission for Libraries (ICFL)						
325 W State St	Boise	ID	83702	208-334-2150	334-4016	434-5
TF: 800-458-3271 ■ *Web:* www.libraries.idaho.gov						
Idaho Community Foundation Inc						
210 W State St	Boise	ID	83702	208-342-3535		305
TF: 800-657-5357 ■ *Web:* www.idahocf.org						
Idaho Correctional Industries						
1301 N Orchad Ste 110	Boise	ID	83706	208-577-5555	577-5545	630
Web: www.ci.idaho.gov						
Idaho County 320 W Main St Rm 5	Grangeville	ID	83530	208 983-2751		338
Web: www.idahocounty.org						
Idaho County Free Press						
900 W Main St	Grangeville	ID	83530	208-983-1200	983-1336	532-2
Web: idahocountyfreepress.com						
Idaho County Light & Power Co-op						
1065 Hwy 13	Grangeville	ID	83530	208-983-1610		245
TF: 877-212-0424 ■ *Web:* www.iclp.coop						
Idaho Democratic Party						
812 W Franklin St	Boise	ID	83701	208-336-1815		616-1
TF: 800-626-0471 ■ *Web:* idahodems.org						
Idaho Department of Labor 317 W Main St	Boise	ID	83735	208-332-3576	334-6300	259
TF: 800-448-2977 ■ *Web:* www2.labor.idaho.gov						
Idaho Falls Public Library						
457 West Broadway	Idaho Falls	ID	83402	208-612-8460		434-3
Web: www.ifpl.org						
Idaho Falls School District 91 Education Foundation Inc						
690 John Adams Pkwy	Idaho Falls	ID	83401	208-525-7500	525-7596	685
TF: 888-993-7120 ■ *Web:* www.d91.k12.id.us						
Idaho gov 999 Main St Ste 910	Boise	ID	83702	580-255-0977		339-13
Web: www.idaho.gov						
Idaho Historical Museum						
610 N Julia Davis Dr	Boise	ID	83702	208-334-2120	334-4059	520
Web: history.idaho.gov						
Idaho Innovation Center Inc						
2300 N Yellowstone	Idaho Falls	ID	83401	208-523-1026	528-7127	194
Web: innovateidaho.org						
Idaho Maximum Security Institution (IMSI)						
PO Box 51	Boise	ID	83707	208-338-1635		213
Web: www.idoc.idaho.gov						
Idaho Medical Assn 305 W Jefferson St	Boise	ID	83702	208-344-7888	344-7903	474
Web: www.idmed.org						
Idaho Military History Museum						
4692 W Harvard St	Boise	ID	83705	208-272-4841		520
Web: museum.mil.idaho.gov						
Idaho Milk Transport Inc PO Box 1185	Burley	ID	83318	208-878-5000	878-5001	468
Web: www.idahomilktransport.com						
Idaho National Laboratory (INL)						
2525 Fremont Ave	Idaho Falls	ID	83402	866-495-7440		668
TF: 866-495-7440 ■ *Web:* www.inl.gov						
Idaho Northern & Pacific Railroad						
119 N Commercial Ave	Emmett	ID	83617	208-365-6353	365-6336	649
Web: rgpc.com						
Idaho Pacific Lumber Company Inc (IDAPAC)						
1770 Spanish Sun Way	Meridian	ID	83642	800-231-2310	375-3054*	191-3
**Fax Area Code:* 208 ■ *TF:* 800-231-2310 ■ *Web:* www.idapac.com						
Idaho Press-Tribune 1618 N Midland Blvd	Nampa	ID	83651	208-467-9251	467-9562	532-2
Web: www.idahopress.com						
Idaho Primary Care Association Inc						
1087 W River St Ste 160	Boise	ID	83702	208-345-2335		533
Web: www.idahopca.org						
Idaho Public Television (IPTV)						
1455 N Orchard St	Boise	ID	83706	208-373-7220	373-7245	632
TF: 800-543-6868 ■ *Web:* idahoptv.org						
Idaho Republican Party						
101 S Capitol Blvd Ste 302	Boise	ID	83702	208-343-6405		616-2
Web: www.idgop.org						
Idaho River Publications LLC						
76 E Fork Rd	Hailey	ID	83333	208-788-1346		637-2
Web: www.idahoriverpublications.com						
Idaho Scholarship Office						
650 W State St PO Box 83720	Boise	ID	83720	208-334-2270	334-2632	725
Web: boardofed.idaho.gov						

Name / Address	City	State	Zip	Phone	Fax	Class
Idaho School of Massage Therapy 3551 E Overland Rd Web: www.idschoolmassage.com	Meridian	ID	83642	208-343-1847		685
Idaho State Bar 525 W Jefferson St TF: 800-221-3295 ■ Web: isb.idaho.gov	Boise	ID	83702	208-334-4500	334-4515	72
Idaho State Civic Symphony 921 S Eigth Ave S- 8099 Web: www.thesymphony.us	Pocatello	ID	83209	208-282-3595		573-3
Idaho State Correctional Institution 13500 S Pleasant Valley Rd Web: www.idoc.idaho.gov	Kuna	ID	83634	208-336-0740	334-2748	213
Idaho State Dental Assn 1220 W Hays St Web: www.theisda.org	Boise	ID	83702	208-343-7543		227
Idaho State Journal 305 S Arthur Ave TF: 800-669-9777 ■ Web: www.idahostatejournal.com	Pocatello	ID	83204	208-232-4161	233-8007	532-2
Idaho State Parks & Recreation PO Box 83720 TF: 855-514-2429 ■ Web: parksandrecreation.idaho.gov	Boise	ID	83720	855-514-2429		565
Idaho State Pharmacy Assn (ISPA) 816 W Bannock St Ste 60 Web: www.ourispa.com	Boise	ID	83702	208-870-8312		585
Idaho State University 353 N 4th Ave Ste 210 Web: www.isu.edu	Pocatello	ID	83209	208-282-2475	282-4511	166
Idaho State Veterans Home-Boise 320 Collins Rd Web: veterans.idaho.gov	Boise	ID	83702	208-780-1600	780-1601	793
Idaho State Veterans Home-Lewiston 821 21st Ave Web: veterans.idaho.gov	Lewiston	ID	83501	208-750-3600	799-3414	793
Idaho State Veterans Home-Pocatello 1957 Alvin Ricken Dr TF: 855-488-8440 ■ Web: veterans.idaho.gov	Pocatello	ID	83201	208-235-7800	235-7801	793
Idaho Statesman PO Box 40 TF: 800-635-8934 ■ Web: www.idahostatesman.com	Boise	ID	83707	208-389-4769		532-2
Idaho Steel Products 255 E Anderson St Web: www.idahosteel.com	Idaho Falls	ID	83401	208-522-1275	522-6041	298
Idaho Supreme Potatoes Inc 614 E 800 N PO Box 246 Web: idahosupreme.com	Firth	ID	83236	208-346-6841	346-4104	296-18
Idaho Technology Council Inc 101 S Capitol Blvd Ste 206 Web: www.idahotechcouncil.org	Boise	ID	83702	208-917-5700		463
Idaho-Pacific Corp 4723 E 100 N PO Box 478 TF: 800-238-5503 ■ Web: www.idahopacific.com	Ririe	ID	83443	208-538-6971	538-5082	296-18
Idamerica 941 Corporate Ln Web: idamerica.com	Chesapeake	VA	23320	757-549-2300		344
IDAPAC (Idaho Pacific Lumber Company Inc) 1770 Spanish Sun Way *Fax Area Code: 208 ■ TF: 800-231-2310 ■ Web: www.idapac.com	Meridian	ID	83642	800-231-2310	375-3054*	191-3
iData Research 4211 Kingsway Ste 308 Web: idataresearch.com	Burnaby	BC	V5H1Z6	604-266-6933	266-6934	466
IDBB (Israel Discount Bank of New York) 511 Fifth Ave Web: www.idbny.com	New York	NY	10017	212-551-8500	551-8540	70
IDC 5 Speen St TF: 800-343-4952 ■ Web: www.idc.com	Framingham	MA	01701	508-872-8200	424-4829	466
IDC Communications 1385 Niakwa Rd E TF: 800-474-7771 ■ Web: idccommunications.com	Winnipeg	MB	R2J3T3	204-254-8282		736
IDD Process & Packaging 5450 Tech Cir TF: 800-621-4144 ■ Web: www.iddeas.com	Moorpark	CA	93021	805-529-9890		547
IDDBA (International Dairy-Deli-Bakery Assn) 636 Science Dr TF: 877-399-4925 ■ Web: www.iddba.org	Madison	WI	53711	608-310-5000	238-6330	49-6
IDEA (International District Energy Assn) 24 Lyman St Ste 230 Web: www.districtenergy.org	Westborough	MA	01581	508-366-9339	366-0019	49-3
Idea & Design Works LLC 2765 Truxtun Rd Web: idwpublishing.com	San Diego	CA	92106	858-270-1315		637
Idea Channel 2002 Filmore Ave Web: www.freetochoosenetwork.org	Erie	PA	16506	814-833-7140		740
Idea Engineering Inc 21 E Carrillo St Web: www.ideaengineering.com	Santa Barbara	CA	93101	805-963-5399		256
Idea Foundry Inc 4551 Forbes Ave Ste 200 Web: ideafoundry.org	Pittsburgh	PA	15213	412-208-3832		260
Idea Inc 10455 Pacific Center Ct TF: 800-999-4332 ■ Web: www.ideafit.com	San Diego	CA	92121	858-535-8979	535-8234	48-22
Idea Lab Marketing 37 E Main St Web: www.idealabdigital.com	Moorestown	NJ	08057	856-642-0007		7
Idea Works Inc, The 3809 Trefoil Dr TF: 888-444-5772 ■ Web: www.ideaworks.com	Columbia	MO	65203	573-514-5932		177
Ideacom Mid-America Inc 30 W Water St TF: 800-433-6208 ■ Web: www.idea-ma.com	Saint Paul	MN	55107	651-292-0102	252-0144	189-4
Ideacom Midwest Inc 1283 Research Blvd Web: www.ideacommidwest.com	Saint Louis	MO	63132	314-961-5002		224
Ideal Adv & Printing 116 N Winnebago St TF: 800-208-0294 ■ Web: www.idealad.com	Rockford	IL	61101	815-965-1713		4
Ideal Appliance Parts Inc 3417 Division St TF: 800-452-7665 ■ Web: www.idealappliance.com	Metairie	LA	70002	504-888-4232	888-4258	246
Ideal Builders Inc 1406 Emil St Web: idealbuilders.com	Madison	WI	53713	608-271-8111		186
Ideal Chemical & Supply Co 4025 Air Park St TF: 800-232-6776 ■ Web: www.idealchemical.com	Memphis	TN	38118	901-363-7720	366-0864	146
Ideal Clamp Products Inc 8100 Tridon Dr TF: 800-251-3220 ■ Web: idealtridon.com	Smyrna	TN	37167	615-459-5000	223-1550	350
Ideal Computer Services Inc 88 Wright Brothes Ave TF: 800-862-8787 ■ Web: www.icsgroup.com	Livermore	CA	94551	925-447-4747	447-4780	180
Ideal Consulting Services Inco 521 American Legion Hwy TF: 866-254-6136 ■ Web: idealconsultingservices.com	Westport	MA	02790	508-636-6615		196
Ideal Data Inc 420 River Rd Web: www.idealdata.com	North Arlington	NJ	07031	201-998-9440		396
Ideal Fastener Corp 603 W Industry Dr Web: www.idealfastener.com	Oxford	NC	27565	919-693-3115	693-3118	594
Ideal Image 1 N Dale Mabry Hwy Ste 1200 *Fax Area Code: 866 ■ Web: www.idealimage.com	Tampa	FL	33609	813-286-8100	866-4390*	77
Ideal Industries Inc 1375 Park Ave TF: 800-435-0705 ■ Web: www.idealindustries.com	Sycamore	IL	60178	815-895-5181		816
Ideal Innovations Inc 950 N Glebe Rd Ste 800 Web: www.idealinnovations.com	Arlington	VA	22203	703-528-9101	528-1913	194
Ideal Integrations Inc 800 Regis Ave Web: www.idealintegrations.net	Pittsburgh	PA	15236	412-349-6680		180
Ideal Interiors Inc 450 Seventh Ave Web: www.ideal-interiors.com	New York	NY	10123	212-262-7005		186
Ideal Jacobs Corp 515 Valley St TF: 877-873-4332 ■ Web: www.idealjacobs.com	Maplewood	NJ	07040	973-275-5100		627
Ideal Manufacturing Inc 2011 Harnish Blvd TF: 800-523-3888 ■ Web: www.idealmfginc.com	Billings	MT	59101	406-656-4360		492
Ideal Pet Products Inc 24735 Ave Rockefeller TF: 800-378-4385 ■ Web: www.idealpetproducts.com	Valencia	CA	91355	661-294-2266		608
Ideal Pipe Ltd 1100 Ideal Dr PO Box 100 Web: www.idealpipe.ca	Thorndale	ON	N0M2P0	519-473-2669		350
Ideal Power Inc 4120 Freidrich Ln Ste 100 Web: www.idealpower.com	Austin	TX	78744	512-264-1542		767
Ideal Printers Inc 645 Olive St Web: www.idealprint.com	Saint Paul	MN	55130	651-855-1100	855-1055	174
Ideal Ready Mix Company Inc 3902 W Mt Pleasant St Web: www.idealrm.com	West Burlington	IA	52655	319-754-4747		182
Ideal Shield 2525 Clark St TF: 866-825-8659 ■ Web: www.idealshield.com	Detroit	MI	48209	313-842-7290		295
Ideal Snacks Corp 89 Mill St Web: www.idealsnacks.com	Liberty	NY	12754	845-292-7000		296-35
Ideal Software Systems Inc 3839 Hwy 45 N TF: 800-964-3325 ■ Web: idealss.com	Meridian	MS	39305	601-693-1673		177
Ideal Supply Company Inc 2935 S Highland Dr Web: idealsupplylv.net	Las Vegas	NV	89109	702-731-3445	796-7467	612
Ideal Welders Ltd 660 Caldew St Web: www.idealwelders.com	Delta	BC	V3M5S2	604-525-5558	525-5313	595
Ideal Window Manufacturing Inc 100 W Seventh St TF: 800-631-3400 ■ Web: www.idealwindow.com	Bayonne	NJ	07002	800-631-3400		596
Idealab 130 W Union St Web: www.idealab.com	Pasadena	CA	91103	626-585-6900	535-2701	792
Idealease Inc 430 N Rand Rd TF: 800-435-3273 ■ Web: www.idealease.com	North Barrington	IL	60010	847-304-6000	304-0076	778
Idealliance 1800 Diagonal Rd Ste 320 Web: www.idealliance.org	Alexandria	VA	22314	703-837-1070	837-1072	49-16
Idealogical Systems Inc 2900 John St Web: www.idealogical.com	Markham	ON	L3R5G3	905-474-0772		180
Ideal-Pmt Machine Inc 1 Tannery St Web: www.idealpmt.com	Great Bend	PA	18821	570-879-2165		454
Idealstor LLC 12400 St Hwy 71 W Ste 350-364 TF: 888-864-3257 ■ Web: www.idealstor.com	Austin	TX	78738	512-279-4321	279-4322	173-8
Ideaology Advertising Inc 4223 Glencoe Ave Ste A127 Web: ideaologyinc.com	Marina	CA	90292	310-306-6501		7
Ideas To Go Inc 1 Main St SE 5th Fl Web: www.ideastogo.com	Minneapolis	MN	55414	612-331-1570		463
Ideastream 1375 Euclid Ave Web: wviz.ideastream.org	Cleveland	OH	44115	216-916-6100		741-31
IdeaTek 111 Old Mill St TF: 855-433-2835 ■ Web: www.ideatek.com	Buhler	KS	67522	855-433-2835		387
Ideation International Inc 32000 NW Hwy Ste 145 Web: www.whereinnovationbegins.net	Farmington Hills	MI	48334	248-613-3251	737-8929	177
IdeaVillage Products Corp 155 Rt 46 W 4th Fl Web: www.ideavillage.com	Wayne	NJ	07470	973-826-8418		76
Ideaworks 1110 N Palafox St Web: ideaworks.co	Pensacola	FL	32501	850-434-9095		7
IDEC Corp 1175 Elko Dr TF: 800-262-4332 ■ Web: www.idec.com	Sunnyvale	CA	94089	408-747-0550	744-9055	203
Idegy Inc 226 N Fifth St Ste 220 TF: 888-421-2288 ■ Web: www.idegy.com	Columbus	OH	43215	614-545-5000	545-4000	184
Idem Translations Inc 550 California Ave Ste 310 Web: www.idemtranslations.com	Palo Alto	CA	94306	650-858-4336		393
Iden Cosmetics Inc 15500 Texaco St Web: www.idencosmetics.com	Paramount	CA	90723	562-630-2580		238
Ident-A-Kid Services of America 1780 102nd Ave N Ste 100 TF: 800-890-1000 ■ Web: identakid.com	Saint Petersburg	FL	33716	727-577-4646	576-8258	310
Identatronics Inc 165 N Lively Blvd TF: 800-323-5403 ■ Web: www.identatronics.com	Elk Grove Village	IL	60007	847-437-2654		591
IDenticard Systems Inc 25 Race Ave 1st Fl *Fax Area Code: 717 ■ TF: 800-233-0298 ■ Web: www.identicard.com	Lancaster	PA	17603	800-233-0298	569-2390*	692
Identification Plates Inc 1555 High Point Dr *Fax Area Code: 800 ■ TF: 800-395-2570 ■ Web: www.idplates.com	Mesquite	TX	75149	972-216-1616	934-8304*	411

Phone Fax Class

Identifix Inc 2714 Patton Rd . . . . Saint Paul MN 55113 651-633-8007 624
TF: 800-745-9649 ■ *Web:* www.identifix.com

Identigene LLC
2495 S West Temple. .Salt Lake City UT 84115 888-404-4363 418
TF: 888-404-4363 ■ *Web:* dnatesting.com

Identigraphix Inc 19866 Quiroz Ct. . . . . Walnut CA 91789 909-468-4741 468-4755 344
Web: www.identigraphix.com

Identity Automation LP
8833 N Sam Houston Pkwy W . . . . Houston TX 77064 877-221-8401 358
TF: 877-221-8401 ■ *Web:* www.identityautomation.com

Identity Genetics Inc 1720 6th St . . . . Brookings SD 57006 605-697-5300 697-5307 417
TF: 800-861-1054 ■ *Web:* www.identitygenetics.com

Identity Links Inc 6211 W Howard St. . . . . Niles IL 60714 888-282-9507 366
TF: 888-282-9507 ■ *Web:* identity-links.com

Identity Theft Resource Ctr
3625 Ruffin Rd Ste 204. San Diego CA 92123 888-400-5530 631
TF: 888-400-5530 ■ *Web:* www.idtheftcenter.org

IDEO 100 Forest Ave. . . . . Palo Alto CA 94301 650-289-3400 261
Web: www.ideo.com

Idera Inc
Brookhollow Central III 2950 N Loop Fwy W
Ste 700. . . . . .Houston TX 77092 713-862-5210 177
Web: www.idera.com

Idera Pharmaceuticals Inc
167 Sidney St. . . . . .Cambridge MA 02139 617-679-5500 679-5592 85
NASDAQ: IDRA ■ *Web:* www.iderapharma.com

Idesco Corp 37 W 26th St . . . . New York NY 10010 212-889-2530 358
TF: 800-336-1383 ■ *Web:* www.idesco.com

Idesign Solutions Inc
14 Steinway Blvd Ste 5. . . . . Toronto ON M9W6M6 416-213-8445 180
TF: 877-730-4770 ■ *Web:* www.idesignsol.com

IDEX Corp 1925 W Field Ct Ste 200 . . . . Lake Forest IL 60045 847-498-7070 641
NYSE: IEX ■ *TF:* 866-292-2089 ■ *Web:* www.idexcorp.com

IDEXX Laboratories Inc 1 IDEXX Dr . . . . Westbrook ME 04092 207-556-0300 556-4346 231
NASDAQ: IDXX ■ *TF:* 800-548-6733 ■ *Web:* www.idexx.com

IDF (Immune Deficiency Foundation)
40 W Chesapeake Ave Ste 308 . . . . Towson MD 21204 800-296-4433 321-9165* 48-17
*Fax Area Code: 410 ■ *TF:* 800-296-4433 ■ *Web:* www.primaryimmune.org

IDFW (Institute for a Drug-Free Workplace)
10701 Parkridge Blvd Ste 300 . . . . Reston VA 20191 703-391-7222 391-7223 49-12
Web: www.drugfreeworkplace.org

IDG World Expo 3 Speen St Ste 320 . . . . Framingham MA 01701 508-879-0700 184
Web: www.idgworldexpo.com

IDI Distributors Inc
8303 Audubon Rd. . . . . .Chanhassen MN 55317 952-279-6400 690
TF: 888-843-1318 ■ *Web:* www.idi-insulation.com

IDI Group Cos
1700 N Moore St Ste 2020. . . . . Arlington VA 22209 703-558-7300 558-7377 653
Web: www.idigroup.com

Ididit Inc 610 S Maumee St . . . . .Tecumseh MI 49286 517-424-0577 59
Web: www.ididitinc.com

iDirect Marketing Inc
6789 Quail Hill Pkwy Ste 550. Irvine CA 92603 949-753-7300 269-0198 5
Web: www.idirectmarketing.com

iDirect Technologies Inc
13865 Sunrise Valley Dr Ste 100 . . . . .Herndon VA 20171 703-648-8118 735
TF: 888-362-5475 ■ *Web:* www.idirect.net

Idlewild & Soak Zone Rt 30 E PO Box C . . . . .Ligonier PA 15658 724-238-3666 238-6544 32
Web: www.idlewild.com

Idm Computer Solutions Inc
5559 Eureka Dr. . . . . Hamilton OH 45011 513-892-8600 225
Web: www.ultraedit.com

Ido Bar & Grill 1537 S Main St . . . . Akron OH 44301 330-773-1724 671
Web: www.idobar.com

IDOM Consulting LLC
55 Madison Ave Ste 400. . . . . Morristown NJ 07960 973-285-3328 538-0503 463
Web: www.idomusa.com

IDP (Insurance Data Processing Inc)
8101 Washington Ln. . . . . Wyncote PA 19095 215-885-2150 887-4621 178-11
TF: 800-523-6745 ■ *Web:* www.idpnet.com

Idp Housing Lp
1709 A Gornto Rd PMB 343. . . . . .Valdosta GA 31601 229-219-6760 653
Web: www.idpproperties.com

IDPR (Winchester Lake State Park)
1786 Forest Rd. . . . . .Winchester ID 83555 208-924-7563 565
Web: parksandrecreation.idaho.gov

IDQ Holdings Inc 2901 W Kingsley Rd . . . . Garland TX 75041 214-778-4600 3
Web: rechargeac.com

IDRA (Intercultural Development Research Assn)
5815 Callaghan Rd Ste 101 . . . . San Antonio TX 78228 210-444-1710 444-1714 48-11
Web: www.idra.org

IDS Group Inc 1 Peters Canyon Rd. . . . . Irvine CA 92606 949-387-8500 261
Web: www.idsgi.com

IDSA 1300 Wilson Blvd Ste 300. . . . . Arlington VA 22209 703-299-0200 299-0204 49-8
Web: www.idsociety.org

IDSA (Industrial Designers Society of America)
45195 Business Ct Ste 250 . . . . Dulles VA 20166 703-707-6000 787-8501 49-13
Web: www.idsa.org

IDT (Integrated Document Technologies Inc)
1009 W Hawthorn Dr . . . . .Itasca IL 60143 630-875-1100 875-1101 196
TF: 877-722-6438 ■ *Web:* www.idt-inc.com

IDT Corp 520 Broad St . . . . .Newark NJ 07102 973-438-1000 736
NYSE: IDT ■ *Web:* www.idt.net

IDX Corp
1 Rider Trail Plaza Dr Ste 400. . . . . .Earth City MO 63045 314-739-4120 739-4129 286
Web: www.idxcorporation.com

Idyll Arbor Inc (IA) 39129 264th Ave SE. . . . . Enumclaw WA 98022 360-825-7797 825-5670 637-2
Web: www.idyllarbor.com

Idyllwild Arts Academy
52500 Temecula Rd PO Box 38 . . . . .Idyllwild CA 92549 951-659-2171 622
Web: www.idyllwildarts.org

Idyllwild OnLine 25225 Hwy 243 . . . . .Idyllwild CA 92549 951-468-5674 224
TF: 800-297-1410 ■ *Web:* www.idyllwild.com

IEA 6325 Digital Way Ste 460 . . . . .Indianapolis IN 46278 800-688-3775 256
TF: 800-688-3775 ■ *Web:* iea.net

IEA Inc 9625 55th St. . . . . .Kenosha WI 53144 262-942-1414 61
Web: www.iearad.com

Phone Fax Class

IEAP (Interface EAP Inc)
2424 Wilcrest Dr Ste 230 PO Box 421879 . . . . .Houston TX 77042 713-781-3364 784-0425 462
TF: 800-324-4327 ■ *Web:* www.ieap.com

IEC (International Environmental Corp)
PO Box 2598 . . . . Oklahoma City OK 73101 405-605-5000 605-5001 14
TF: 800-264-5329 ■ *Web:* iec-okc.com

IEC Electronics Corp 105 Norton St. . . . . .Newark NY 14513 315-331-7742 331-3547 625
NYSE: IEC ■ *TF:* 888-688-3570 ■ *Web:* www.iec-electronics.com

IEC Group 3449 E Copper Point Dr. . . . . Meridian ID 83642 208-344-7900 463
TF: 888-716-4482 ■ *Web:* www.iecgroup.com

IECA (Independent Educational Consultants Assn)
3251 Old Lee Hwy Ste 510. . . . . Fairfax VA 22030 703-591-4850 591-4860 49-5
Web: www.iecaonline.com

IEDC (International Economic Development Council)
734 15th St NW Ste 900. . . . . Washington DC 20005 202-223-7800 223-4745 49-12
Web: www.iedconline.org

IEEE 3 Park Ave 17th Fl . . . . New York NY 10016 212-419-7900 752-4929 49-19
Web: www.ieee.org

IEEE Computational Intelligence Society
445 Hoes Ln. . . . . .Piscataway NJ 08855 732-465-5892 455-1560* 49-19
*Fax Area Code: 858 ■ *Web:* cis.ieee.org

IEEE Computer Society
2001 L St NW Ste 700 . . . . Washington DC 20036 202-371-0101 728-9614 49-19
TF: 800-272-6657 ■ *Web:* www.computer.org

IEEE Industry Applications Society
445 Hoes Ln. . . . . .Piscataway NJ 08854 732-465-5804 49-19
Web: ias.ieee.org

IEEE Instrumentation & Measurement Society (IM)
445 Hoes Ln. . . . . .Piscataway NJ 08854 732-562-3844 981-9019 49-19
Web: www.ieee-ims.org

IEEE Microwave Theory & Techniques Society (MTT-S)
5829 Bellanca Dr . . . . .Elkridge MD 21075 410-796-5866 49-19
TF: 800-678-4333 ■ *Web:* www.mtt.org

IEEE Nuclear & Plasma Sciences Society (NPSS)
445 Hoes Ln. . . . . .Piscataway NJ 08854 732-981-0060 49-19
Web: ieee-npss.org

IEEE Signal Processing Society
445 Hoes Ln. . . . . .Piscataway NJ 08854 732-562-3888 867-9953 49-19
Web: signalprocessingsociety.org

IEEE Solid State Circuits Society (SSCS)
445 Hoes Ln. . . . . .Piscataway NJ 08854 732-981-3400 49-19
Web: sscs.ieee.org

IEEI (International Electronic Enterprises Inc)
110 Agate Ave. . . . . .Newport Beach CA 92662 949-673-2943 673-0249 174
Web: www.ieei.com

IEF (International Eye Foundation)
10801 Connecticut Ave. . . . . Kensington MD 20895 240-290-0263 290-0269 48-5
Web: iefusa.org

IEG (Image Engineering Group Ltd)
1301 Solana Blvd Bldg 1 Ste 1420. . . . . Westlake TX 76262 817-410-2858 261
Web: www.iegltd.com

Ieh Laboratories & Consulting Group
15300 Bothell Way NE . . . . Lake Forest Park WA 98155 800-491-7745 794
TF: 800-491-7745 ■ *Web:* www.iehinc.com

IEHA (International Executive Housekeepers Assn)
1001 Eastwind Dr Ste 301 . . . . .Westerville OH 43081 614-895-7166 895-1248 49-4
TF: 800-200-6342 ■ *Web:* www.ieha.org

IEI (Interstate Electronics Inc)
1394 State Rte 36. . . . . .Hazlet NJ 07730 732-264-3900 38
Web: www.interstateelectronics.com

IEI (Institutional Equipment Inc)
704 Veterans Pky Ste B. . . . . .Bolingbrook IL 60440 630-771-0990 771-0994 300
Web: www.ieiusa.net

ieLinks Inc 2701 E Thomas Rd Ste B. . . . . Phoenix AZ 85016 602-852-0101 463
Web: ecampuslynx.com

IEM (International Electronic Machines Corp)
850 River St . . . . Troy NY 12180 518-268-1636 268-1639 261
Web: www.iem.net

I-engineeringcom Inc 4 Armstrong Rd . . . . Shelton CT 06484 203-402-0800 402-0801 387
Web: www.i-engineering.com

IEntertainment Network Inc PO Box 3897. . . . . .Cary NC 27519 919-238-4090 178-6
OTC: IENT ■ *Web:* corporate-ient.com

IEP Technologies LLC 400 Main St . . . . Ashland MA 01721 855-793-8407 667
TF: 855-793-8407 ■ *Web:* www.ieptechnologies.com

IER Fujikura Inc 8271 Bavaria Rd . . . . .Macedonia OH 44056 330-425-7121 425-7596 677
Web: ierfujikura.com

IES (Institute of Ecosystem Studies)
2801 Sharon Tpke PO Box AB . . . . .Millbrook NY 12545 845-677-5343 677-5976 668
Web: www.caryinstitute.org

IES (Institute of Education Sciences)
550 12th St SW . . . . .Washington DC 20024 202-245-6940 219-1466 668
Web: ies.ed.gov

IES (Industrial Electronic Supply Inc)
2321 Texas Ave. . . . . .Shreveport LA 71103 318-222-1911 246
Web: www.goies.com

IES (International Education Systems)
1814 Hillcrest Ave Ste 300 . . . . Saint Paul MN 55116 651-227-2052 637-2
Web: www.marybosrock.com

IESCO (International Electrical Sales Corp)
7540 NW 66th St . . . . Miami FL 33166 305-591-8390 246
Web: iescomia.com

IeSmart Systems LLC 15200 E Hardy Rd . . . . .Houston TX 77032 281-447-6278 196
TF: 866-437-6278 ■ *Web:* www.iesmartsystems.com

IESNA (Illuminating Engineering Society of North America)
120 Wall St 17th Fl. . . . . New York NY 10005 212-248-5000 248-5017 49-13
Web: www.ies.org

IEST (Institute of Environmental Sciences & Technology)
1827 Walden Office Sq Ste 400 . . . . Schaumburg IL 60173 847-981-0100 981-4130 49-19
Web: www.iest.org

IET Labs Inc
1 Expressway Plz Ste 120. . . . . Roslyn Heights NY 11577 516-334-5959 334-5988 248
Web: www.ietlabs.com

IEWC (Industrial Electric Wire & Cable Inc)
5001 S Towne Dr . . . . .New Berlin WI 53151 877-613-4392 246
TF: 800-344-2323 ■ *Web:* www.iewc.com

IEX Group Inc
4 World Trade Ctr 44th Fl . . . . New York NY 10007 646-568-2320 690
Web: iextrading.com

Company	Address	City	State	Zip	Phone	Fax	Class
IFAC (International Federation of Accountants)	545 Fifth Ave 14th Fl *TF:* 888-272-2001 ■ *Web:* www.ifac.org	New York	NY	10017	212-286-9344	286-9570	49-1
IFAD (International Fund for Agricultural Development)	1775 K St NW Ste 410 *Web:* www.ifad.org	Washington	DC	20006	202-331-9099	331-9366	783
IFAI (Industrial Fabrics Association Intl)	1801 County Rd 'B' W *TF:* 800-225-4324 ■ *Web:* www.ifai.com	Roseville	MN	55113	651-222-2508	631-9334	49-13
IFAW (International Fund for Animal Welfare)	290 Summer St *TF:* 800-932-4329 ■ *Web:* www.ifaw.org	Yarmouth Port	MA	02675	508-744-2000		48-3
IFC Stone Crab	81532 Overseas Hwy PO Box 283 **Fax Area Code:* 305 ■ *TF:* 800-258-2559 ■ *Web:* www.ifcstonecrab.com	Islamorada	FL	33036	800-258-2559	664-5071*	671
IFCA Intl	3520 Fairlane Ave SW *TF:* 800-347-1840 ■ *Web:* www.ifca.org	Grandville	MI	49418	616-531-1840	531-1814	48-20
IFCO (Interreligious Foundation for Community Organization)	418 W 145th St *Web:* ifconews.org	New York	NY	10031	212-926-5757	926-5842	48-7
Ifco Systems	3030 N Rocky Point Dr Ste 300 *Web:* www.ifco.com	Tampa	FL	33607	813-463-4100	286-2070	551
IFDA (International Foodservice Distributors Assn)	1410 Spring Hill Rd Ste 210 *Web:* www.ifdaonline.org	McLean	VA	22102	703-532-9400	538-4673	49-18
IFEA (International Festivals & Events Assn)	2603 W Eastover Terr *Web:* www.ifea.com	Boise	ID	83706	208-433-0950	433-9812	48-23
IFF (International Flavors & Fragrances Inc)	521 W 57th St *NYSE:* IFF ■ *Web:* www.iff.com	New York	NY	10019	212-765-5500	708-7132	144
IFG Corp	100 W 33rd St Ste 1105	New York	NY	10001	212-594-5511	564-0174	155-4
IFIC (International Fidelity Insurance Co)	1 Newark Ctr 1111 Raymond Blvd 20th Fl **Fax Area Code:* 973 ■ *TF:* 800-333-4167 ■ *Web:* www.ific.com	Newark	NJ	07102	800-333-4167	624-1408*	391-5
IFIC (International Food Information Council Foundation)	1100 Connecticut Ave NW Ste 430 *Web:* foodinsight.org	Washington	DC	20036	202-296-6540	296-6547	49-6
Ifland Engineers Inc	5300 Soquel Ave Live Oak Business Pk Ste 101 *Web:* iflandengineers.com	Santa Cruz	CA	95062	831-426-5313	426-1763	261
iFly Holdings LLC	31310 Alvarado-Niles Rd *TF:* 800-759-3861 ■ *Web:* www.iflyworld.com	Union City	CA	94587	510-489-4359		31
IFMA (International Facility Management Assn)	800 Gessner Rd Ste 900 *Web:* www.ifma.org	Houston	TX	77024	713-623-4362	623-6124	49-12
IFMA (International Foodservice Manufacturers Assn)	180 N Stetson Ave 2 Prudential Plz Ste 850 *Web:* www.ifmaworld.com	Chicago	IL	60601	312-540-4400	540-4401	49-6
Ifocus Consulting Inc	100 39th St Ste 201 *TF:* 888-308-6192 ■ *Web:* www.ifocus.us	Astoria	OR	97103	503-338-7443		196
Ifonoclast Inc	4620 Fortran Dr Ste 207 *Web:* www.phonevite.com	San Jose	CA	95134	408-946-9700		387
IFOS Inc	4425 Fortran Dr *Web:* www.ifos.com	San Jose	CA	95134	408-565-9002	565-9005	668
IFPRI (International Food Policy Research Institute)	2033 K St NW *Web:* www.ifpri.org	Washington	DC	20006	202-862-5600	467-4439	634
IFPW (International Federation of Pharmaceutical Wholesalers)	10569 Crestwood Dr *Web:* www.ifpw.com	Manassas	VA	20109	703-331-3714	331-3715	49-18
IFRA (International Furniture Rental Assn)	950 F St NW 10th Fl *Web:* www.ifra.org	Washington	DC	20004	202-239-3818	654-4818	49-4
Ifrah Financial Services Inc	17300 Chenal Pkwy Ste 150 *TF:* 800-954-3724 ■ *Web:* ifrahfinancial.com	Little Rock	AR	72223	501-821-7733		251
IFS Benefits LLC	220 Continental Dr *Web:* ifs-benefits.com	Newark	DE	19713	302-652-2355	652-5722	390
IFS Financial Services Inc	250 Brownlow Ave Ste 1 *TF:* 800-565-1153 ■ *Web:* www.ifs-finance.com	Dartmouth	NS	B3B1W9	902-481-6106		317
IFS North America Inc	300 Pk Blvd Ste 555 *TF:* 888-437-4968 ■ *Web:* www.ifs.com	Itasca	IL	60143	888-437-4968		178-1
IFSCO (Independent Foundry Supply Co)	6463 E Canning St *Web:* www.foundry-supplies.com	Commerce	CA	90040	323-725-1051	725-0664	492
IFSI (Illinois Foundation Seeds Inc)	1083 County Rd 900 N *Web:* www.ifsi.com	Tolono	IL	61880	217-485-6260		10-5
IFT (Institute of Food Technologists)	525 W Van Buren St Ste 1000 *TF:* 800-438-3663 ■ *Web:* www.ift.org	Chicago	IL	60607	312-782-8424	782-8348	49-6
IFTA (Independent Film & Television Alliance)	10850 Wilshire Blvd 9th Fl *Web:* www.ifta-online.org	Los Angeles	CA	90024	310-446-1000	446-1600	48-4
IG Inc	720 S Sara Rd *TF:* 800-654-8433 ■ *Web:* www.igok.com	Mustang	OK	73064	405-376-9393	376-3933	326
IG Publishing	PO Box 2547 *Web:* www.igpub.com	New York	NY	10163	718-797-0676		637-2
IGA Inc	8745 W Higgins Rd Ste 350 *TF:* 800-321-5442 ■ *Web:* www.iga.com	Chicago	IL	60631	773-693-4520	693-4533	345
iGan Partners	60 Bloor St W 9th Fl *Web:* iganpartners.com	Toronto	ON	M4W3B8	416-928-4349		528
Igarashi Motor Sales USA LLC	710 Colomba Ct *Web:* www.jp-igarashi.com	Saint Charles	IL	60174	630-587-1177		57
IGAS (International Graphoanalysis Society)	842 Fifth Ave **Fax Area Code:* 509 ■ *Web:* www.igas.com	New Kensington	PA	15068	724-472-9701	271-1149*	49-12
IGD Industries Inc	4150 C St SW *Web:* www.igdindustries.com	Cedar Rapids	IA	52404	319-396-2222	396-0422	61
IGEL Technology Inc	5353 NW 35th Ave *Web:* www.igel.com	Fort Lauderdale	FL	33309	954-739-9990		177
Igenex	795 San Antonio Rd *TF:* 800-832-3200 ■ *Web:* igenex.com	Palo Alto	CA	94303	650-424-1191		418
IGFA Fishing Hall of Fame	300 Gulf Stream Way *Web:* www.igfa.org	Dania Beach	FL	33004	954-927-2628	924-4299	522
IGI (Information Gatekeepers Inc)	1340 Soldiers Field Rd Ste 2 *TF:* 800-323-1088 ■ *Web:* www.igigroup.com	Brighton	MA	02135	617-782-5033	782-5735	637-11
IGI (Insight Global Inc)	4170 Ashford Dunwoody Rd Ste 250 *TF:* 888-336-7463 ■ *Web:* www.insightglobal.com	Atlanta	GA	30319	404-257-7900	257-1004	193
Iglesia Adventista Del Septimo Dia	4606 Mangum Rd *Web:* www.little-york-iglesia-adventista-del-septimo-dia.business.site	Houston	TX	77092	713-937-1200		48-20
Iglesia Ni Cristo Church of Christ	770 Airport Blvd **Fax Area Code:* 650 ■ *Web:* iglesianicristo.net	Burlingame	CA	94010	310-872-3487	548-1128*	48-20
Igloo Products Corp	777 Igloo Rd *TF:* 866-509-3503 ■ *Web:* www.igloocoolers.com	Katy	TX	77494	281-394-6800		607
Iglou Internet Services Inc	3315 Gilmore Industrial Blvd *TF:* 800-436-4456 ■ *Web:* www.iglou.com	Louisville	KY	40213	502-966-3848	968-9306	224
IGLTA (International Gay & Lesbian Travel Assn)	1201 NE 26th St Ste 103 *Web:* www.iglta.org	Fort Lauderdale	FL	33305	954-630-1637	630-1652	48-23
Igneous	2401 4th Ave Ste 200 *Web:* www.igneous.ioo	Seattle	WA	98121	206-504-3685		178-1
Ignite Restaurant Group Inc	9900 Westpark Dr Ste 300 *Web:* igniterestaurants.com	Houston	TX	77063	713-366-7500		670
Ignite Technical Resources Ltd	1295 - 355 Burrard St *Web:* ignitetechnical.com	Vancouver	BC	V6C2G8	604-687-6795		260
Ignite! Entertainment	PO Box 641131 *Web:* www.ignite-ent.com	Los Angeles	CA	90064	310-806-0325	822-5652	637-2
Ignite! Learning Inc	4030 W Braker Ln Ste 175 *Web:* www.ignitelearning.com	Austin	TX	78759	512-697-7000		177
Ignited LLC	2150 Park Pl Ste 100 *Web:* www.ignitedusa.com	El Segundo	CA	90245	310-773-3100		7
Ignition Commerce	3820 Mansell Rd Ste 250 *Web:* www.ignitioncommerce.com	Alpharetta	GA	30022	770-640-6382		631
Ignition Systems & Controls LP	6300 W Hwy 80 *TF:* 800-777-5559 ■ *Web:* www.ignition-systems.com	Midland	TX	79706	432-697-6472	697-0563	247
Ignitus Worldwide	132 Roucourt Lp *Web:* www.ignitusworldwide.org	College Station	TX	77845	979-574-6176		48-6
iGo Inc	590 Madison Ave 32 nd Fl *NASDAQ:* IGOI ■ **Fax Area Code:* 480 ■ *TF:* 888-205-0093 ■ *Web:* igo.com	New York	NY	10022	212-520-2300	596-0349*	176
IGO Insurance Agency Inc	8117 Ebenezer Church Rd *TF:* 800-243-1560 ■ *Web:* igoinsurance.com	Raleigh	NC	27612	919-782-1560	782-5706	390
I-Go Van & Storage	9820 S 142nd St *TF:* 800-228-9276 ■ *Web:* www.igovanandstorage.com	Omaha	NE	68138	402-891-1222		519
iGov	9211 Palm River Rd Ste 110 *TF:* 800-777-9375 ■ *Web:* www.igov.com	Tampa	FL	33619	813-612-9470	622-3861	226
IGS (Institute of General Semantics)	72-11 Austin St *TF:* 800-346-1359 ■ *Web:* www.generalsemantics.org	Forest Hills	NY	11375	212-729-7973		48-11
IGS (Industrial Gasket & Shim Company Inc)	200 Country Club Rd *TF:* 800-229-1447 ■ *Web:* www.igsind.com	Meadow Lands	PA	15347	724-222-5800		326
IGSHPA (International Ground Source Heat Pump Assn)	Oklahoma State University 374 Cordell S *TF:* 800-626-4747 ■ *Web:* igshpa.org	Stillwater	OK	74078	405-744-5175	744-5283	49-13
IGT (International Game Technology)	9295 Prototype Dr *NYSE:* IGT ■ *Web:* www.igt.com	Reno	NV	89521	775-448-7777		322
IGT Media Holdings Inc	8395 Ne 2nd Ave *Web:* www.igtmh.com	Miami	FL	33131	305-573-2800		5
IGTI (ASME International Gas Turbine Institute)	6525 the Corners Pkwy *Web:* www.asme.org	Norcross	GA	30092	404-847-0072	847-0151	49-19
Iguana Inc	PO Box 101 *Web:* www.iguanaware.com	Crystal Bay	NV	89402	530-546-3113	546-3119	681
IH Services Inc	PO Box 5033 *Web:* www.ihservices.com	Greenville	SC	29606	864-297-3748	297-9219	152
IHA (International Housewares Assn)	6400 Shafer Ct Ste 650 *TF:* 800-752-1052 ■ *Web:* www.housewares.org	Rosemont	IL	60018	847-292-4200	292-4211	49-4
IHA (Iowa Hospital Assn)	100 E Grand Ave Ste 100 *Web:* www.ihaonline.org	Des Moines	IA	50309	515-288-1955	283-9366	49-19
IHAD (I Have a Dream Foundation)	322 8th Ave Ste 202 *Web:* www.ihaveadreamfoundation.org	New York	NY	10001	212-293-5480		48-5
IHC (International Homes of Cedar Inc)	PO Box 886 *TF:* 800-767-7674 ■ *Web:* www.ihoc.com	Woodinville	WA	98072	360-668-8511	668-5562	106
iHealth Labs Inc	719 N Shoreline Blvd *TF:* 855-816-7705 ■ *Web:* ihealthlabs.com	Mountain View	CA	94043	855-816-7705		743
iHeartMedia Inc	20880 Stone Oak Pkwy *TF:* 800-829-6551 ■ *Web:* www.iheartmedia.com	San Antonio	TX	78258	210-822-2828		185
iHeartMedia San Diego	9660 Granite Ridge Dr Ste 100 **Fax Area Code:* 210 ■ *Web:* star941fm.iheart.com	San Diego	CA	92123	858-292-2000	832-3149*	645-141
IHFRA (International Home Furnishings Representatives Assn)	209 S Main St PO Box 670 *Web:* www.ihfra.org	High Point	NC	27261	336-889-3920		49-18

Name / Address	City	State	Zip	Phone	Fax	Class
IHI (Institute for Healthcare Improvement)						
20 University Rd 7th Fl	Cambridge	MA	02138	617-301-4800	301-4848	49-8
TF: 866-787-0831 ■ *Web:* www.ihi.org						
IHI Inc 150 E 52nd St 24th Fl	New York	NY	10022	212-599-8100	599-8111	770
Web: www.ihiincus.com						
I-Hire Inc 307 Sonora Dr	San Mateo	CA	94402	650-678-2808		260
Web: www.i-hire.com						
IHL Group						
1650 Murfreesboro Rd Ste 206	Franklin	TN	37067	615-591-2955		463
TF: 888-445-6777 ■ *Web:* ihlservices.com						
IHLIC (Investors Heritage Life Insurance Co)						
200 Capital Ave	Frankfort	KY	40601	502-223-2361	875-7084	391-2
TF: 800-422-2011 ■ *Web:* www.ihlic.com						
IHM Academy of EMS 2500 Abbott Pl	Saint Louis	MO	63143	314-768-1234	768-1595	167-3
TF: 888-281-1212 ■ *Web:* ihmacademyofems.com						
IHMM (Institute of Hazardous Materials Management)						
11900 Parklawn Dr Ste 450	Rockville	MD	20852	301-984-8969	984-1516	48-12
Web: www.ihmm.org						
IHO (Institute of Human Origins)						
951 S Cady Mall PO Box 874101	Tempe	AZ	85287	480-727-6580	727-6570	668
Web: iho.asu.edu						
IHOP Corp 450 N Brand Blvd	Glendale	CA	91203	818-240-6055	637-4730	670
TF: 866-444-5144 ■ *Web:* www.ihop.com						
IHP Industrial Inc						
1701 S Eigth St PO Box 578	Saint Joseph	MO	64502	816-364-1581	232-4473	189-10
Web: www.ihpindustrial.com						
IHRIM (International Association for Human Resource Information Management Inc)						
PO Box 1086	Burlington	MA	01803	800-804-3983	998-8011*	49-12
**Fax Area Code:* 781 ■ *TF:* 800-804-3983 ■ *Web:* ihrim.org						
IHRSA (International Health Racquet & Sportsclub Assn)						
70 Fargo St	Boston	MA	02210	617-951-0055	951-0056	48-22
TF: 800-228-4772 ■ *Web:* www.ihrsa.org						
iHRSource						
7734 Silver Sage Ct Ste 100	Springfield	VA	22153	800-766-0745	330-0720*	194
**Fax Area Code:* 208 ■ *TF:* 800-766-0745 ■ *Web:* www.ihrsource.com						
IHRY Insurance Agency Inc						
1291 - 13th Ave E	West Fargo	ND	58078	701-402-2228	532-0570	390
TF: 800-726-7929 ■ *Web:* ihryins.com						
IHS (International Hearing Society)						
16880 Middlebelt Rd Ste 4	Livonia	MI	48154	734-522-7200	522-0200	48-17
Web: www.ihsinfo.org						
IHS (HHS Indian Health Service)						
801 Thompson Ave Ste 400	Rockville	MD	20852	303-443-3593		340-10
TF: 800-447-3368 ■ *Web:* www.ihs.gov						
IHS Professional Services Inc						
1632 Byron Nelson Pkwy	Southlake	TX	76092	847-447-7700		474
Web: www.ihsrs.com						
IHT Health Products Inc						
225 Long Ave Bldg 15	Hillside	NJ	07205	888-232-5267	926-1735*	237
**Fax Area Code:* 973 ■ *TF:* 888-232-5267 ■ *Web:* www.ibiopharma.com						
II Stanley Company Inc						
1500 Hill Brady Rd	Battle Creek	MI	49037	269-660-7777		247
Web: www.iistanley.com						
IIA (Institute of Internal Auditors, The)						
247 Maitland Ave	Altamonte Springs	FL	32701	407-937-1100	937-1101	49-1
Web: na.theiia.org						
IIABA (Independent Insurance Agents & Brokers of America Inc)						
127 S Peyton St	Alexandria	VA	22314	703-683-4422	683-7556	49-9
TF: 800-221-7917 ■ *Web:* www.independentagent.com						
IIB (Institute of International Bankers)						
299 Park Ave 17th Fl	New York	NY	10171	212-421-1611	421-1119	49-2
Web: www.iib.org						
IIC (Indotronix International Corp)						
331 Main St	Poughkeepsie	NY	12601	845-473-1137	473-1197	180
Web: www.iic.com						
IICL (Institute of International Container Lessors)						
1990 M St NW Ste 650	Washington	DC	20036	202-223-9800	223-9810	49-21
Web: www.iicl.org						
IICRC (Institute of Inspection Cleaning & Restoration Certification)						
4043 S E Ave	Las Vegas	NV	89119	844-464-4272		49-4
TF: 844-464-4272 ■ *Web:* www.iicrc.org						
IID (Imperial Irrigation District)						
PO Box 937	Imperial	CA	92251	760-482-9600	482-9611	203
TF: 800-303-7756 ■ *Web:* www.iid.com						
IIDA (International Interior Design Assn)						
222 Merchandise Mart Plz Ste 567	Chicago	IL	60654	312-467-1950	467-0779	48-4
TF: 888-799-4432 ■ *Web:* www.iida.org						
IIE (Institute of Industrial & Systems Engineers)						
3577 Parkway Ln Ste 200	Norcross	GA	30092	770-449-0461	441-3295	49-13
TF: 800-494-0460 ■ *Web:* www.iise.org						
IIE (Institute of International Education)						
809 United Nations Plz Ste 1	New York	NY	10017	212-883-8200		48-11
Web: www.iie.org						
IIF (Institute of International Finance)						
1333 H St NW Ste 800-E	Washington	DC	20005	202-857-3600	775-1430	49-2
Web: www.iif.com						
IIF Data Solutions Inc						
7000 Gateway Ct Unit 130	Manassas	VA	20109	703-531-1180	531-1189	809
Web: www.iifdata.com						
III (Insurance Information Institute Inc)						
110 William St	New York	NY	10038	212-346-5500	732-1916	49-9
TF: 877-263-7995 ■ *Web:* www.iii.org						
III Forks 111 Lavaca St	Austin	TX	78701	512-474-1776		671
Web: www.3forks.com						
IIJ America Inc (IIJA)						
55 E 59th St Ste 18C	New York	NY	10022	212-440-8080	869-9829	180
Web: iijamerica.com						
IIJA (IIJ America Inc)						
55 E 59th St Ste 18C	New York	NY	10022	212-440-8080	869-9829	180
Web: iijamerica.com						
IIMC (International Institute of Municipal Clerks)						
8331 Utica Ave Ste 200	Rancho Cucamonga	CA	91730	909-944-4162	944-8545	49-7
TF: 800-251-1639 ■ *Web:* www.iimc.com						
IIP Insurance Agency 823 Clinton St	Ottawa	IL	61350	815-433-2680	433-2681	390
TF: 888-252-4626 ■ *Web:* mylocalagent.com						
IIRR (International Institute of Rural Reconstruction)						
601 W 26th St Ste 325-1	New York	NY	10001	917-410-7891		48-5
Web: www.iirr.org						
IISRP (International Institute of Synthetic Rubber Producers Inc)						
3535 Briarpark Dr Ste 250	Houston	TX	77042	713-783-5046	783-7253	49-13
Web: iisrp.com						
IIT Research Institute (IITRI)						
10 W 35th St	Chicago	IL	60616	312-567-4487		668
Web: iitri.org						
IITF (International Institute of Tropical Forestry)						
Jardin Botanico Sur 1201 Calle Ceiba	San Juan	PR	00926	787-766-5335	766-6302	668
Web: www.fs.usda.gov						
IITRI (IIT Research Institute)						
10 W 35th St	Chicago	IL	60616	312-567-4487		668
Web: iitri.org						
II-VI Inc 375 Saxonburg Blvd	Saxonburg	PA	16056	724-352-4455		544
NASDAQ: IIVI ■ *TF:* 888-558-1504 ■ *Web:* www.ii-vi.com						
IJ Research Inc 2919 Tech Center Dr	Santa Ana	CA	92705	714-546-8522		256
Web: www.ijresearch.com						
Ijams Nature Ctr						
2915 Island Home Ave	Knoxville	TN	37920	865-577-4717	577-1683	50-5
Web: www.ijams.org						
IJO (Independent Jewelers Organization)						
136 Old Post Rd	Southport	CT	06890	800-624-9252	254-7429*	49-4
**Fax Area Code:* 203 ■ *TF:* 800-624-9252 ■ *Web:* www.ijo.com						
Ikaros 4901 Eastern Ave	Baltimore	MD	21224	410-633-3750	633-7881	671
Web: www.ikarosrestaurant.com						
Ika-Works Inc						
2635 Northchase Pkwy SE	Wilmington	NC	28405	910-452-7059	452-7693	420
TF: 800-733-3037 ■ *Web:* www.ika.com						
Ike International Corp 500 E Maple St	Stanley	WI	54768	715-644-5777	644-5786	191-3
Web: www.ikeinternational.com						
Ike Kinswa State Park 873 SR 122	Silver Creek	WA	98585	360-983-3402		565
Web: parks.state.wa.us						
IKEA 420 Alan Wood Rd	Conshohocken	PA	19428	809-567-4532		321
TF: 800-434-4532 ■ *Web:* www.ikea.com						
Ikegami Electronics USA Inc						
300E SR-17S	Mahwah	NJ	07430	201-368-9171	569-1626	647
Web: www.ikegami.com						
IKG Industries 1514 S Sheldon Rd	Channelview	TX	77530	281-452-6637	378-3987*	491
**Fax Area Code:* 713 ■ *Web:* ikg.com						
I-K-I Manufacturing Company Inc						
116 Swift St	Edgerton	WI	53534	608-884-3411	884-4712	145
Web: www.ikimfg.com						
Iknow LLC 100 Overlook Ctr 2nd Fl	Princeton	NJ	08540	609-419-0500		317
Web: www.iknow.us						
IKO International Inc						
91 Walsh Dr Fox Hill Industrial Pk	Parsippany	NJ	07054	973-402-0254		385
TF: 800-922-0337 ■ *Web:* www.ikont.com						
Ikonisys Inc 5 Science Pk	New Haven	CT	06511	203-776-0791		743
Web: www.ikonisys.com						
IL Bistro 93-A Pike St	Seattle	WA	98101	206-682-3049		671
Web: ilbistro.net						
IL Capriccio 888 Main St	Waltham	MA	02453	781-894-2234		671
Web: www.bostonchefs.com						
IL Fornaio 400 Capitol Mall	Sacramento	CA	95814	916-446-4100		671
Web: www.ilfornaio.com						
IL Fornello Management Ltd						
576 Danforth Ave	Toronto	ON	M4K1R1	416-920-9410		707
Web: www.ilfornello.com						
IL Gatto Nero 720 College St	Toronto	ON	M6G1C3	416-536-3132		671
IL Giardino 910 Atlantic Ave	Virginia Beach	VA	23451	757-422-6464		671
Web: www.ilgiardino.com						
IL MITO Trattoria e Enoteca						
6913 W N Ave	Wauwatosa	WI	53213	414-443-1414		671
Web: www.ilmitotrattoriaeenoteca.com						
IL Mulino 86 W Third St	New York	NY	10012	212-673-3783		671
Web: www.ilmulino.com						
IL Mulino 1800 E Sunrise Blvd	Fort Lauderdale	FL	33304	954-524-1800		671
Web: www.ilmulinofl.com						
IL Porto Ristorante 121 King St	Alexandria	VA	22314	703-836-8833		671
Web: www.ilportoristorante.com						
IL Terrazzo Carmine 411 First Ave S	Seattle	WA	98104	206-467-7797		671
Web: www.ilterrazzocarmine.com						
IL Vicino 321 W San Francisco St	Santa Fe	NM	87501	505-986-8700		671
Web: www.ilvicino.com						
IL Vicino 11 S Tejon St	Colorado Springs	CO	80903	719-475-9224		671
Web: ilvicino.com						
ILA (Illinois Library Assn)						
33 W Grand Ave Ste 401	Chicago	IL	60654	312-644-1896	644-1899	435
TF: 877-565-1896 ■ *Web:* www.ila.org						
ILAA (International Lawyers in Alcoholics Anonymous)						
537 Sherbrooke St	Vancouver	BC	V5W3M6	604-324-7424		48-21
Web: www.ilaa.org						
Ilan Systems Inc						
1107 Fair Oaks Ave Ste 304	South Pasadena	CA	91030	626-304-9021		180
Web: www.ilan.com						
Ilani Shoes Ltd 311 E 43rd St	New York	NY	10017	212-947-5830		301
ILAO (Illinois Legal Aid Online)						
17 N State St Ste 1380	Chicago	IL	60602	312-977-9047		428
Web: www.illinoislegalaid.org						
ILC Dover Inc 1 Moonwalker Rd	Frederica	DE	19946	302-335-3911	335-0762	576
TF: 800-631-9567 ■ *Web:* www.ilcdover.com						
ILC Resources 3301 106th Cir	Urbandale	IA	50322	515-243-8106	244-3200	503-3
TF: 800-247-2133 ■ *Web:* www.ilcresources.com						
iLeads.com						
567 San Nicolas Dr Ste 180	Newport Beach	CA	92660	877-245-3237		224
TF: 877-245-3237 ■ *Web:* ileads.com						
iLearning Gateway Inc						
2650 Vly View Ln Bldg 1 Ste 200	Dallas	TX	75234	888-464-2672	464-0260	387
TF: 888-464-2672 ■ *Web:* www.ilearninggateway.com						
Ilene Industries Inc						
301 Stanley Blvd	Shelbyville	TN	37160	931-684-8731	684-8735	326
TF: 800-251-1602 ■ *Web:* www.ileneindustries.com						
Ilex Construction & Woodworking						
3801 Northampton St NW Ste 3	Washington	DC	20015	410-820-4393	820-4394	685
TF: 866-551-4539 ■ *Web:* www.ilexconstruction.com						
ILF (Indiana Library Federation)						
941 E 86th St Ste 260	Indianapolis	IN	46240	317-257-2040	257-1389	435
TF: 800-326-0013 ■ *Web:* www.ilfonline.org						

Phone | Fax | Class

ILHS (Illinois Labor History Society)
430 S Michigan Ave Rm WB 1806 ....Chicago IL 60605 312-341-2247 637-2
Web: www.illinoislaborhistory.org

ILI (International Law Institute)
1055 Thomas Jefferson St NW Ste M-100 .....Washington DC 20007 202-247-6006 247-6010 49-10
Web: www.ili.org

Iliff School of Theology
2201 S University Blvd.......................Denver CO 80210 303-744-1287 777-0164 167-3
TF: 800-678-3360 ■ *Web:* www.iliff.edu

Ilikai Hotel & Suites
1777 Ala Moana Blvd......................Honolulu HI 96815 808-949-3811 947-0892 379
TF: 866-536-7973 ■ *Web:* www.ilikaihotel.com

Iliniwek Village State Historic Site
c/o Battle of Athens State Historic Site Rt 1
PO Box 26 ....Revere MO 63465 660-877-3871 565
Web: mostateparks.com

Ilink Technology Inc
9840 Willows Rd Ste 202...................Redmond WA 98052 425-869-8104 175
Web: www.ilink-systems.com

Ilio DiPaolo's Restaurant & Banquet
3785 S Park Ave............................Buffalo NY 14219 716-825-3675 825-1054 671
Web: iliodipaolos.com

Ilios Noche 11508 Providence Rd .... Charlotte NC 28277 704-814-9882 671
Web: www.xeniahospitality.com

Ilisagvik College
100 Stevenson St PO Box 749 ....Barrow AK 99723 907-852-3333 852-2729 167-3
TF: 800-478-7337 ■ *Web:* www.ilisagvik.edu

Illahee State Park
3540 NE Sylvan Way...................... Bremerton WA 98310 360-478-6460 565
Web: www.parks.state.wa.us

ILLCO Inc 535 S River St....................... Aurora IL 60506 630-892-7904 892-0318 612
Web: www.illco.com

Illegal Pete's 1447 Pearl St.................... Boulder CO 80302 303-440-3955 671
Web: illegalpetes.com

Illig Construction Co
444 S Flower St Ste 2360..................Los Angeles CA 90071 323-227-1411 227-8257 186
Web: www.illigconstruct.com

Illingworth Engineering Co
6855 Phillips Pkwy Dr S..................Jacksonville FL 32256 904-262-4700 610
Web: boiler.publishpath.com

Illini State Park 2660 E 2350th Rd............ Marseilles IL 61341 815-795-2448 565
Web: www.dnr.illinois.gov

Illinois

Administrative Office of the Illinois Courts
3101 Old Jacksonville Rd ....Springfield IL 62704 217-558-4490 785-3905 339-14
Web: www.illinoiscourts.gov

Aging Dept
1 Natural Resources Way Ste 100 ....Springfield IL 62701 800-252-8966 785-4477* 339-14
**Fax Area Code: 217* ■ *TF:* 800-252-8966 ■ *Web:* www2.illinois.gov

Attorney General 500 S Second St...........Springfield IL 62701 217-782-1090 339-14
TF: 800-964-3013 ■ *Web:* www.illinoisattorneygeneral.gov

Children & Family Services Dept
406 E Monroe St ....Springfield IL 62701 217-785-2509 339-14
Web: www2.illinois.gov

Commerce Commission
527 E Capitol Ave ....Springfield IL 62701 217-557-5213 339-14
TF: 800-524-0795 ■ *Web:* www.icc.illinois.gov

Community College Board
401 E Capitol Ave ....Springfield IL 62701 217-785-0123 524-4981 339-14
Web: www.iccb.org

Crime Victims Services Div
100 W Randolf Rd 13th Fl ....Chicago IL 60601 312-814-2581 814-7105 339-14
TF: 800-228-3368 ■ *Web:* illinoisattorneygeneral.gov

Department of Public Health
535 W Jefferson St 5th Fl Conference Rm ....Springfield IL 62761 217-782-4977 339-14
Web: www.dph.illinois.gov

Driver Services Office
2701 S Dirksen Pkwy....................Springfield IL 62723 217-782-6212 339-14
Web: www.cyberdriveillinois.com

Emergency Management Agency
2420 S State St ....Springfield IL 62703 217-782-2700 339-14
Web: www2.illinois.gov

Environmental Protection Agency
1021 N Grand Ave E.....................Springfield IL 62794 217-782-3397 339-14
TF: 800-782-7860 ■ *Web:* www2.illinois.gov

Financial & Professional Regulation
320 W Washington St 3rd Fl ....Springfield IL 62786 888-473-4858 339-14
TF: 888-473-4858 ■ *Web:* www.idfpr.com

General Assembly
705 Stratton Bldg.......................Springfield IL 62706 217-782-3944 339-14
Web: www.ilga.gov

Governor 207 State House.................Springfield IL 62706 217-782-6830 339-14
Web: www2.illinois.gov

Healthcare & Family Services Dept
201 S Grand Ave E......................Springfield IL 62763 217-782-1200 339-14
Web: www.illinois.gov

Housing Development Authority
401 N Michigan Ave Ste 700 ....Chicago IL 60611 312-836-5200 339-14
Web: www.ihda.org

Insurance Div 320 W Washington St..........Springfield IL 62767 217-782-4515 782-5020 339-14
TF: 877-527-9431 ■ *Web:* insurance.illinois.gov

Labor Dept 160 N LaSalle St C-1300 ....Chicago IL 60601 312-793-2800 793-5257 339-14
Web: www2.illinois.gov

Lottery 101 W Jefferson St ....Springfield IL 62702 217-524-6435 452
TF: 800-252-1775 ■ *Web:* www.illinoislottery.com

Mental Health Div
100 W Randolph 16-100 Ste 3-400...........Chicago IL 60601 312-814-2121 339-14
TF: 800-252-2923 ■ *Web:* www2.illinois.gov

Military Affairs Dept
1301 N MacArthur Blvd...................Springfield IL 62702 217-761-3515 339-14
Web: www2.illinois.gov

Natural Resources Dept
1 Natural Resources Way.................Springfield IL 62702 217-782-6302 339-14
Web: www2.illinois.gov

Racing Board
100 W Randolph St Ste 5-700...............Chicago IL 60601 312-814-2600 814-5062 712
Web: www2.illinois.gov

Revenue Dept 101 W Jefferson St ....Springfield IL 62702 217-782-3336 339-14
TF: 800-732-8866 ■ *Web:* www2.illinois.gov

State Police 801 S Seventh St...............Springfield IL 62794 217-782-7263 339-14
Web: www.isp.state.il.us

Student Assistance Commission
1755 Lake Cook Rd .... Deerfield IL 60015 800-899-4722 519-4652 725
TF: 877-877-3724 ■ *Web:* www.collegeillinois.org

Supreme Court 200 E Capitol Ave............Springfield IL 62701 217-782-2035 339-14
Web: illinoiscourts.gov

Tourism Bureau
100 W Randolph St Ste 3-400...............Chicago IL 60601 312-814-4732 814-6175 339-14
TF: 800-226-6632 ■ *Web:* www.enjoyillinois.com

Treasurer
219 Statehouse Capitol Bldg ....Springfield IL 62706 866-458-7327 785-2777* 339-14
**Fax Area Code: 217* ■ *TF:* 866-458-7327 ■ *Web:* illinoistreasurer.gov

Veterans Affairs Dept
69 W Washington Ste 1620.................Chicago IL 60602 312-814-2460 814-2764 339-14
TF: 800-437-9824 ■ *Web:* www2.illinois.gov

Vital Records Div
605 W Jefferson St......................Springfield IL 62702 217-782-6553 339-14
Web: www.idph.state.il.us

Workers' Compensation Commission
807 W Van Buren St Ste 8-200 ....Chicago IL 60601 312-814-6611 814-6523 339-14
TF: 866-352-3033 ■ *Web:* www2.illinois.gov

Illinois Alcoholism & Drug Dependence Assn
937 S Second St..........................Springfield IL 62704 217-528-7335 533
Web: www.ilabh.org

Illinois Association of Chamber of Commerce Executives
PO Box 9436 ....Springfield IL 62791 217-585-2995 139
Web: www.iacce.org

Illinois Association of Realtors
522 S Fifth St ....Springfield IL 62701 217-529-2600 529-3904 656
Web: www.illinoisrealtors.org

Illinois Auto Electric Co
2115 W Diehl Rd .... Naperville IL 60563 630-862-3300 385
Web: illinoisautoelectric.com

Illinois Beach State Park Lake Frnt ....Zion IL 60099 847-662-4811 662-6433 565
Web: www2.illinois.gov

Illinois Blueprint Corp
800 SW Jefferson Ave......................... Peoria IL 61605 309-676-1300 676-1310 240
TF: 800-747-7070 ■ *Web:* www.illinoisblue.com

Illinois Board of Higher Education
1 N Old State Capitol Plz Ste 333............Springfield IL 62701 217-782-2551 782-8548 339-14
TF: 888-261-2881 ■ *Web:* www.ibhe.org

Illinois Broaching Co
4200 Grace St.......................... Schiller Park IL 60176 847-678-3080 678-5445 455
TF: 888-427-6224 ■ *Web:* www.ilbroach.com

Illinois Capacitor Inc
3757 W Touhy Ave .... Lincolnwood IL 60712 847-675-1760 673-2850 253
Web: www.illinoiscapacitor.com

Illinois Carbide Tool Co
1322 Belvidere Rd .... Waukegan IL 60085 847-244-1118 249-0693 385
TF: 800-323-2414 ■ *Web:* corbaltusa.net

Illinois Caverns State Natural Area
4369 G Rd .... Waterloo IL 62298 618-458-6699 565
Web: www2.illinois.gov

Illinois Cement Company LLC
1601 Rockwell Rd...........................LaSalle IL 61301 815-224-2112 224-4358 135
Web: www.illinoiscement.com

Illinois Center for Broadcasting - Lombard Campus
455 Eisenhower Ln S Ste 200................ Lombard IL 60148 630-916-1700 167-3
Web: www.beonair.com

Illinois College
1101 W College Ave.....................Jacksonville IL 62650 217-245-3030 245-3034 166
TF: 866-464-5265 ■ *Web:* www.ic.edu

Illinois Crane Inc 1621 W Chanute Rd............ Peoria IL 61615 309-692-0856 207
Web: www.illinoiscrane.com

Illinois Eastern Community Colleges
233 East Chestnut............................Olney IL 62450 618-393-2982 162
Web: www.iecc.edu

Illinois Fair Plan Assn
180 N Stetson Ste 2800 ....Chicago IL 60601 312-861-0385 861-0485 690
TF: 800-972-4480 ■ *Web:* www.illinoisfairplan.com

Illinois Foundation Seeds Inc (IFSI)
1083 County Rd 900 N.......................Tolono IL 61880 217-485-6260 10-5
Web: www.ifsi.com

Illinois Glove Co 650 Anthony Trl .... Northbrook IL 60062 847-291-1700 291-7722 155-8
TF: 800-342-5458 ■ *Web:* www.illinoisglove.com

Illinois Hammer Injury Law Firm, The
134 N Lasalle St Ste 650 ....Chicago IL 60602 888-442-6637 41
Web: www.illinoishammer.com

Illinois Health Care Assn
1029 S Fourth St ....Springfield IL 62703 217-528-6455 533
TF: 800-252-8988 ■ *Web:* www.ihca.com

Illinois Historic Preservation Agency
One Natural Resources Way ....Springfield IL 62702 217-782-4836 339-14
Web: www2.illinois.gov

Illinois Institute of Technology
10 W 33rd St ....Chicago IL 60616 312-567-3000 567-6939 166
TF: 800-448-2329 ■ *Web:* www.iit.edu

Illinois Institute of Technology

IIT Paul V. Galvin Library
35 W 33rd St............................Chicago IL 60616 312-567-3616 567-5318 434-6
Web: library.iit.edu

Rice 201 E Loop Rd....................... Wheaton IL 60189 630-682-6000 682-6010 166
Web: appliedtech.iit.edu

Illinois International Port District
3600 E 95th St ....Chicago IL 60617 773-646-4400 221-7678 618
Web: iipd.com

Illinois Labor History Society (ILHS)
430 S Michigan Ave Rm WB 1806 ....Chicago IL 60605 312-341-2247 637-2
Web: www.illinoislaborhistory.org

Illinois Legal Aid Online (ILAO)
17 N State St Ste 1380.....................Chicago IL 60602 312-977-9047 428
Web: www.illinoislegalaid.org

Illinois Library Assn (ILA)
33 W Grand Ave Ste 401......................Chicago IL 60654 312-644-1896 644-1899 435
TF: 877-565-1896 ■ *Web:* www.ila.org

Illinois Mutual Life Insurance Co
300 SW Adams St.......................... Peoria IL 61634 309-674-8255 391-2
TF: 800-380-6688 ■ *Web:* www.illinoismutual.com

Phone | Fax | Class

Illinois National Bank
322 E Capitol ... Springfield IL 62701 217-747-5500 70
TF: 877-771-2316 ■ *Web:* www.inb.com

Illinois Nurses Assn (INA)
105 W Adams St Ste 2101 ... Chicago IL 60603 312-419-2900 419-2920 533
TF: 800-262-2500 ■ *Web:* www.illinoisnurses.com

Illinois Pharmacists Assn (IPHA)
204 W Cook St ... Springfield IL 62704 217-522-7300 522-7349 585
Web: www.ipha.org

Illinois Principals Assn
2940 Baker Dr ... Springfield IL 62703 217-525-1383 533
Web: ilprincipals.org

Illinois Rack Enterprises Inc
480 Scotland Rd ... Lakemoor IL 60051 815-385-5750 385-5760 286
Web: illinoisrack.com

Illinois Radio Network
200 W Madison St Ste 2100 ... Chicago IL 60603 312-943-6363 647
Web: www.illinoisradionetwork.com

Illinois Rural Electric Co-op
2 S Main St ... Winchester IL 62694 217-742-3128 245
TF: 800-468-4732 ■ *Web:* e-co-op.com

Illinois Safe Schools Alliance
180 N Michigan Ave Ste 1220 ... Chicago IL 60601 312-368-9070 423
Web: www.ilsafeschools.org

Illinois South Tourism
4387 N Illinois St Ste 200 ... Swansea IL 62226 618-257-1488 257-3403 206
TF: 800-442-1488 ■ *Web:* www.illinoisouth.org

Illinois Soybean Assoc
1605 Commerce Pkwy ... Bloomington IL 61704 309-663-7692 138
Web: www.ilsoy.org

Illinois State Bar Assn
424 S Second St ... Springfield IL 62701 217-525-1760 525-0712 72
TF: 800-252-8908 ■ *Web:* www.isba.org

Illinois State Board of Education
100 N 1st St ... Springfield IL 62777 217-782-4321 339-14
TF: 866-262-6663 ■ *Web:* www.isbe.net

Illinois State Chamber of Commerce
300 S Wacker Dr Ste 1600 ... Chicago IL 60606 312-983-7100 983-7101 140
Web: www.ilchamber.org

Illinois State Dental Society
1010 S Second St ... Springfield IL 62704 217-525-1406 525-8872 227
TF: 888-286-2447 ■ *Web:* www.isds.org

Illinois State Fairgrounds
801 E Sangamon Ave ... Springfield IL 62702 217-782-6661 524-6194 642
TF: 866-287-2999 ■ *Web:* www2.illinois.gov

Illinois State Genealogical Society (ISGS)
PO Box 10195 ... Springfield IL 62791 217-789-1968 637-2
Web: www.ilgensoc.org

Illinois State Historical Society (ISHS)
5255 Shepherd Rd ... Springfield IL 62703 217-525-2781 49-19
TF: 866-244-0626 ■ *Web:* www.historyillinois.org

Illinois State Medical Society
20 N Michigan Ave Ste 700 ... Chicago IL 60602 312-782-1654 782-2023 474
TF: 800-782-4767 ■ *Web:* www.isms.org

Illinois State Museum
502 S Spring St ... Springfield IL 62706 217-782-7386 782-1254 520
Web: www.illinoisstatemuseum.org

Illinois State Police Federal Credit Union
730 Engineering Ave ... Springfield IL 62703 800-255-0886 219
TF: 800-255-0886 ■ *Web:* ispfcu.org

Illinois State University
100 N University St ... Normal IL 61761 309-438-2111 438-3032 166
TF: 800-366-2478 ■ *Web:* illinoisstate.edu

Illinois State Veterinary Medical Assn
1121 Chatham Rd ... Springfield IL 62704 217-546-0301 540-5033 795
Web: www.isvma.org

Illinois State Water Survey (ISWS)
2204 Griffith Dr ... Champaign IL 61820 217-333-2210 637-2
Web: www.isws.illinois.edu

Illinois Symphony Orchestera
524 E Capitol Ave ... Springfield IL 62701 217-522-2838 573-3
TF: 800-401-7222 ■ *Web:* www.ilsymphony.org

Illinois Tool Works 155 Harlem Ave ... Glenview IL 60025 224-661-8870 385
Web: www.itw.com

Illinois Truck Center Inc
700 E Devon Ave ... Elk Grove Village IL 60007 847-437-8900 311
TF: 866-981-5252 ■ *Web:* illinoistruck.com

Illinois Valley Area Chamber of Commerce & Economic Development
1320 Peoria St ... Peru IL 61354 815-223-0227 223-4827 139
Web: www.ivaced.org

Illinois Valley Community College
815 N Orlando Smith Ave ... Oglesby IL 61348 815-224-2720 224-3033 162
Web: www.ivcc.edu

Illinois Valley Community Hospital
925 W St ... Peru IL 61354 815-223-3300 374-3
TF: 877-874-8813 ■ *Web:* www.ivch.org

Illinois Veterans Home-Anna
792 N Main St ... Anna IL 62906 618-833-6302 793
Web: www2.illinois.gov

Illinois Veterans Home-La Salle
1015 O'Connor Ave ... LaSalle IL 61301 815-223-0303 793
Web: www2.illinois.gov

Illinois Veterans Home-Manteno
1 Veterans Dr ... Manteno IL 60950 815-468-6581 793
Web: www.vfwil.org

Illinois Veterans Home-Quincy
1707 N 12th St ... Quincy IL 62301 217-222-8641 793
Web: quincyivh.org

Illinois Welding School
1315 Enterprise Dr ... Romeoville IL 60446 630-679-0566 679-9757 685
TF: 888-632-9353 ■ *Web:* ilws.edu

Illinois Wesleyan University
1312 Park St ... Bloomington IL 61701 309-556-3031 556-3820 166
TF: 800-332-2498 ■ *Web:* www.iwu.edu

Illinois Wholesale Cash Register Inc
2790 Pinnacle Dr ... Elgin IL 60124 847-310-4200 310-8490 112
TF: 800-544-5493 ■ *Web:* www.illinoiswholesale.com

Illinois Youth Center Harrisburg
1201 W Poplar St ... Harrisburg IL 62946 618-252-8681 795-6869* 412
**Fax Area Code:* 815 ■ *Web:* www2.illinois.gov

Illinois Youth Center Saint Charles
3825 Campton Hills Rd ... Saint Charles IL 60175 630-584-0506 584-1014 412
Web: www2.illinois.gov

Illumina Inc 9885 Towne Centre Dr ... San Diego CA 92121 858-202-4500 202-4545 419
NASDAQ: ILMN ■ *TF:* 800-809-4566 ■ *Web:* www.illumina.com

Illumina Partners Inc
67 Yonge St Ste 600 ... Toronto ON M5E1J8 416-861-1717 528
Web: www.illuminapartners.com

Illuminate Education Inc
47 Discovery Ste 100 ... Irvine CA 92618 949-242-0343 387
Web: www.illuminateed.com

Illuminating Engineering Society of North America (IESNA)
120 Wall St 17th Fl ... New York NY 10005 212-248-5000 248-5017 49-13
Web: www.ies.org

Illuminous Enterprises Inc
3129 S Hacienda Blvd Ste 691 ... Hacienda Heights CA 91745 626-600-2087 196
Web: www.illuminousinc.com

ILMA (Independent Lubricant Manufacturers Assn)
400 N Columbus St Ste 201 ... Alexandria VA 22314 703-684-5574 836-8503 49-13
Web: www.ilma.org

ILMO Products Company Inc
7 Eastgate Dr ... Jacksonville IL 62650 217-245-2183 358
TF: 888-243-9353 ■ *Web:* ilmoproducts.com

Ilmor Engineering Inc
43939 Plymouth Oaks Blvd ... Plymouth MI 48170 734-456-3600 60
Web: www.ilmor.com

ILO (International Labour Organization)
220 E 42nd St Ste 3101 ... New York NY 10017 212-697-0150 697-5218 783
Web: www.ilo.org

iLOOKABOUT Inc 383 Richmond St Ste 408 ... London ON N6A3C4 519-963-2015 177
TF: 866-963-2015 ■ *Web:* www.ilookabout.com

ILPEA Industries Inc
745 S Gardner St ... Scottsburg IN 47170 812-752-2526 600
Web: www.ilpeaindustries.com

ILS (International Launch Services)
12110 Sunset Hills Rd Ste 450 ... Reston VA 20190 703-435-5689 435-2671 504
TF: 800-852-4980 ■ *Web:* beta.ilslaunch.com

ILS Associates Inc 79 Galli Dr ... Novato CA 94947 415-883-9200 261
Web: ilscels.com

ILSC Education Group Inc, The
555 Richards St ... Vancouver BC V6B2Z5 604-689-9095 423
TF: 866-266-4572 ■ *Web:* www.ilsc.com

ILSCO 4730 Madison Rd ... Cincinnati OH 45227 513-533-6200 815
TF: 800-776-9775 ■ *Web:* www.ilsco.com

ILTA (Independent Liquid Terminals Assn)
1005 N Glebe Rd Ste 600 ... Arlington VA 22201 703-875-2011 875-2018 49-21
Web: www.ilta.org

ILX Lightwave Corp
31950 E Frontage Rd ... Bozeman MT 59715 800-459-9459 586-9405* 248
**Fax Area Code:* 406 ■ *TF:* 800-459-9459 ■ *Web:* www.newport.com

IM (IEEE Instrumentation & Measurement Society)
445 Hoes Ln ... Piscataway NJ 08854 732-562-3844 981-9019 49-19
Web: www.ieee-ims.org

IM Group, The 1903 Post Rd Ste 201 ... Fairfield CT 06824 203-307-2151 463
Web: www.the-imgroup.com

IMA (International Marketing Assn)
3509 Virginia Beach Blvd ... Virginia Beach VA 23452 757-490-9860 490-0716 301
Web: imacorporate.com

IMA (Institute of Management Accountants Inc)
10 Paragon Dr Ste 1 ... Montvale NJ 07645 201-573-9000 474-1600 49-1
TF: 800-638-4427 ■ *Web:* www.imanet.org

IMA (International Magnesium Assn)
1000 N Rand Rd Ste 214 ... Wauconda IL 60084 651-379-7305 526-3993* 49-13
**Fax Area Code:* 847 ■ *Web:* www.intlmag.org

IMA (Interchurch Medical Assistance Inc)
1730 M St NW Ste 1100 ... Washington DC 20036 202-888-6200 470-3370 48-5
TF: 877-241-7952 ■ *Web:* www.imaworldhealth.org

IMA Financial Group Inc
8200 E 32nd St N PO Box 2992 ... Wichita KS 67226 316-267-9221 390
TF: 800-813-0203 ■ *Web:* www.imacorp.com

IMA LIFE North America Inc
2175 Military Rd ... Tonawanda NY 14150 716-695-6354 610
Web: ima.it

IMA Technologies Inc
990 Reserve Dr Ste 200 ... Roseville CA 95678 916-757-1444 781-0168 178-1
Web: www.casetrakker.com

ImaCor Inc 50 Jericho Tpke Ste 105 ... Jericho NY 11753 516-393-0970 476
Web: imacorinc.com

Image Access Inc 543 NW 77th St ... Boca Raton FL 33487 561-886-2900 431-2766 173-1
TF: 800-378-5432 ■ *Web:* www.imageaccess.com

Image Air 2933 E Empire St ... Bloomington IL 61704 309-663-2303 167-3
TF: 800-232-4360 ■ *Web:* www.imageair.com

Image API LLC
2002 Old St Augustine Rd Bldg D ... Tallahassee FL 32301 850-222-1400 224-3367 177
Web: www.imageapi.com

Image Architects Inc
784 Morris Tpke ... Short Hills NJ 07078 973-912-9334 177
Web: imagearch.com

Image Builders Inc PO Box 243 ... Mantoloking NJ 08738 732-899-9121 714-9167 7
Web: www.image-builders.com

Image Craft LLC
3401 E Broadway Rd Ste 15 ... Phoenix AZ 85040 602-276-2082 592
Web: www.imcraft.com

Image Custom Engineering Solutions LLC
5011 E Fifth St ... Katy TX 77493 281-829-4000 261
Web: www.image-ces.com

Image Data Inc 18 Petra Ln ... Albany NY 12205 518-862-2740 225
Web: www.imgdata.com

Image Diagnostics Inc
310 Authority Dr ... Fitchburg MA 01420 978-829-0009 723
Web: imagediagnostics.com

Image Engineering Group Ltd (IEG)
1301 Solana Blvd Bldg 1 Ste 1420 ... Westlake TX 76262 817-410-2858 261
Web: www.iegltd.com

Image Group, The 973 Bluebell Dr ... Holland MI 49423 616-393-9588 4
Web: www.imagegroup.com

	Phone	Fax	Class
Image Intl 4959 Hamilton Blvd. .... Allentown PA 18106 *Web:* www.imageintl.com	610-391-9133		167-3
Image Iv Systems Inc 512 S Varney St .... Burbank CA 91502 *TF:* 800-473-5424 ■ *Web:* www.imageiv.com	818-841-0756		366
Image Labs Intl PO Box 1545 .... Belgrade MT 59714 *TF:* 800-785-5995 ■ *Web:* www.imagelabs.com	406-585-7225		178-8
Image Marketing & Communications Inc (IMC) 2140 W Fulton St Ste B .... Chicago IL 60612 *Web:* image-communications.com	312-421-5680	421-5708	194
Image Matters Inc 3017 Sutherland Ave. .... Knoxville TN 37919 *Web:* imagemattersinc.com	865-212-3600		535
Image Matters LLC 201 Loudoun St SW .... Leesburg VA 20175 *Web:* www.imagemattersllc.com	703-669-5510		195
Image National Inc 16265 Star Rd .... Nampa ID 83687 *Web:* www.imagenational.com	208-345-4020	336-9886	701
Image One Corp 13201 Capital St. .... Oak Park MI 48237 *TF:* 800-799-5377 ■ *Web:* www.imageoneway.com	248-414-9955	414-9951	628
Image Process Design LLC 3155 W Big Beaver Rd Ste 200 .... Troy MI 48084 *Web:* ipdsolution.com	248-723-9733		177
Image Resource Group 130 Pinnacle Point Ct Ste 101 .... Columbia SC 29223 *Web:* www.imageresourcegroup.com	803-790-2121		463
Image Sensing Systems Inc 500 Spruce Tree Centre 1600 University Ave .... Saint Paul MN 55104 *Web:* www.imagesensing.com	651-603-7700		407
Image Studios Inc 1100 S Lynndale Dr .... Appleton WI 54914 *TF:* 877-738-4080 ■ *Web:* www.imagestudios.com	877-738-4080		592
Image Works PO Box 443 .... Woodstock NY 12498 *TF:* 800-475-8801 ■ *Web:* www.theimageworks.com	845-679-8500	679-0606	593
Imagecat Inc 400 Oceangate Ste 1050 .... Long Beach CA 90802 *Web:* www.imagecatinc.com	562-628-1675		225
Imagecom Inc 4120 Peachwood Dr. .... Arlington TX 76016 *Web:* www.aspire3d.com	817-572-2824		178-1
Imagemakers Inc 514 Lincoln Ave PO Box 368 .... Wamego KS 66547 **Fax Area Code:* 785 ■ *TF:* 888-865-8511 ■ *Web:* imagemakers-inc.com	888-865-8511	380-2556*	4
ImageMark Business Services Inc 3145 Northwest Blvd .... Gastonia NC 28052 *TF:* 800-632-9513 ■ *Web:* www.imagemarkonline.com	800-632-9513		627
imageMEDIA 425 E Spruce St .... Tarpon Springs FL 34689 **Fax Area Code:* 727 ■ *TF:* 866-885-4468 ■ *Web:* www.imagemedia.com	866-885-4468	234-1068*	627
Imagenation Systems 549 Pylon Dr .... Raleigh NC 27604 *Web:* imagenationsystems.com	919-834-3440	834-3441	196
Imagenet Consulting 6411 S 216th St. .... Kent WA 98032 *Web:* www.imagenetconsulting.com	253-395-0110		225
Imager Software Inc 2932 Wellington Cir .... Tallahassee FL 32309 *Web:* goisc.com	850-893-6741		180
Images Press 27920 Roble Alto Dr .... Los Altos Hills CA 94022 *Web:* www.imagespress.com	650-948-8251	941-6114	637-2
Imageset 6611 Portwest Dr Ste 190 .... Houston TX 77024 *Web:* imageset.com	713-869-7700	869-7707	627
ImageShack Corp 236 N Santa Cruz Ave Ste 100 .... Los Gatos CA 95030 *Web:* imageshack.com	408-612-3954		387
ImageSource Inc 612 Fifth Ave SW .... Olympia WA 98501 *Web:* imagesourceinc.com	360-943-9273		225
ImageTech Marketing 10388 S Randall St .... Orange CA 92869 *Web:* www.imagetechmarketing.com	714-639-5411		179
ImageWare Systems Inc 10815 Rancho Bernardo Rd Ste 310 .... San Diego CA 92127 *Web:* www.iwsinc.com	858-673-8600	673-1770	178-10
Imagewerks Marketing 1600 Gervais Ave Ste 5 .... Arden Hills MN 55112 *Web:* www.iwmarketing.com	651-770-1319		624
ImageWorks 250 Clearbrook Rd .... Elmsford NY 10523 *TF:* 800-592-6666 ■ *Web:* www.imageworkscorporation.com	914-592-6100	592-6148	382
Imageworks Manufacturing Inc 49 South St. .... Park Forest IL 60466 *Web:* www.imageworksmfg.com	708-503-1122	503-1133	9
Imaginarium of South Texas 5300 San Dario Ste 505 .... Laredo TX 78041 *Web:* www.imaginariumstx.org	956-728-0404	725-7776	521
Imaginary Forces LLC 2254 S Sepulveda Blvd. .... Los Angeles CA 90064 *Web:* www.imaginaryforces.com	323-957-6868		514
Imaginasium Inc 320 N Broadway Ste 330 .... Green Bay WI 54303 *TF:* 800-820-4624 ■ *Web:* www.imaginasium.com	920-431-7872		4
Imagination Publishing 600 W Fulton St Ste 600 .... Chicago IL 60661 *Web:* www.imaginepub.com	312-887-1000		637-10
Imagination Realty Inc 617 Celebration Ave .... Celebration FL 34747 *Web:* imaginationrealty.net	321-939-0493		652
Imagine Advertising & Publishing Inc 3100 Medlock Bridge Rd Ste 370 .... Norcross GA 30071 *TF:* 866-832-3214 ■ *Web:* www.imagineadv.com	770-734-0966		393
Imagine Air Jet Services LLC 460 Briscoe Blvd Ste 210 .... Lawrenceville GA 30046 *TF:* 877-359-4242 ■ *Web:* www.imagineair.com	877-359-4242		21
Imagine Business Development 485 Ritchie Hwy Ste 201 .... Severna Park MD 21146 *Web:* www.imaginellc.com	410-544-7878		463
Imagine Entertainment Inc 150 S El Camino Dr 7th Fl .... Beverly Hills CA 90212 *Web:* www.imagine-entertainment.com	310-858-2000		514
Imagine Express 2633 Minnehaha Ave .... Minneapolis MN 55406 *Web:* imagine-express.com	612-728-1500		658
Imagine GPS Inc 6847 S Ea Ste 104 .... Las Vegas NV 89119 *TF:* 800-800-1020 ■ *Web:* www.gpscity.com	702-990-5600	990-5603	647
Imagine IT! 21730 Nordhoff St. .... Chatsworth CA 91311 *TF:* 800-569-2260 ■ *Web:* www.imagineit.com	818-368-2604	322-1322	180

	Phone	Fax	Class
Imagine Nation Books Ltd 282 Century Pl Ste 2000 .... Louisville CO 80027 *TF:* 888-516-3431 ■ *Web:* shopedu.collectivegoods.com	888-516-3431		96
Imagine One Technology & Management Ltd 416 Colonial Ave .... Colonial Beach VA 22443 *Web:* imagine-one.com	301-866-4098		261
Imagine Schools 1005 N Glebe Rd Ste 610 .... Arlington VA 22201 *Web:* www.imagineschools.org	703-527-2600		242
Imagine That Inc 6830 Via Del Oro Ste 230 .... San Jose CA 95119 *Web:* www.extendsim.com	408-365-0305	629-1251	178-1
Imagine! Print Solutions Inc 1000 Vly Park Dr .... Shakopee MN 55379 *Web:* www.imagineps.com	952-903-4400	641-2111	627
Imagineering Machine Inc 6851 Oxford St .... Saint Louis Park MN 55426 *Web:* www.imagineeringmachine.com	952-922-9311	922-2157	454
Imaginet Resources Corp 233 Portage Ave .... Winnipeg MB R3B2A7 *TF:* 800-989-6022 ■ *Web:* www.imaginet.com	204-989-6022		177
ImagineThis 1147 Oberlin Ave SW .... Massillon OH 44647 *Web:* imaginetr.ordersentry.net	330-481-1102		459
Imaging & Microfilm Access Inc 150 Knickerbocker Ave .... Bohemia NY 11716 *Web:* www.scanyourdocs.com	631-589-8100	589-8119	396
Imaging Associates Inc 11110 Westlake Dr .... Charlotte NC 28273 *TF:* 877-720-9210 ■ *Web:* imaginga.com	704-522-8094	522-8098	590
Imaging Business Machines LLC (IBML) 2750 Crestwood Blvd .... Birmingham AL 35210 *TF:* 877-627-8325 ■ *Web:* www.ibml.com	205-956-4071	956-5309	111
Imaging Concepts Inc (ICI) 2818 Hungary Rd .... Richmond VA 23228 *TF:* 800-228-0060 ■ *Web:* www.imagingconcepts.com	804-755-8701	755-8711	475
Imaging Diagnostic Systems Inc 1291-B NW 65th Pl .... Fort Lauderdale FL 33309 *OTC: IMDS* ■ *Web:* www.imds.com	954-581-9800	979-2420	382
Imaging Dynamics Company Ltd 3510 - 29 St NE .... Calgary AB T1Y7E5 *Web:* www.imagingdynamics.com	403-251-9939		476
Imaging Healthcare Specialists Medical Group Inc 6256 Greenwich Dr Ste 150 .... San Diego CA 92122 *TF:* 866-558-4320 ■ *Web:* www.imaginghealthcare.com	866-558-4320		415
Imaging Office Systems Inc 4505 E Park 30 Dr .... Columbia City IN 46725 *TF:* 800-878-7731 ■ *Web:* www.imagingoffice.com	260-248-9696		45
Imaging Supplies Company Inc 804 Woodland Ave .... Sanford NC 27330 *TF:* 800-518-1152 ■ *Web:* www.imagingsuppliesco.com	919-776-1152		589
Imaging Systems Technology Inc 4750 W Bancroft St. .... Toledo OH 43615 *Web:* www.isttouch.com	419-536-5741		180
Imagize LLC 2855 Telegraph Ave Ste 510 .... Berkeley CA 94705 *Web:* www.imagizellc.com	510-540-0260		256
IMAj Institute 8370 E Via de Ventura Ste K200 .... Scottsdale AZ 85258 *Web:* www.imajschool.org	480-361-8585	699-5607	167-3
iMakeNews Inc 7400 Wilshire Place Dr .... Houston TX 77040 **Fax Area Code:* 781 ■ *TF:* 866-964-6397 ■ *Web:* www.imninc.com	937-485-8030	890-4701*	180
Imalux Corp 11000 Cedar Ave Ste 250 .... Cleveland OH 44106	216-502-0755		476
Iman Academy 10929 Almeda Genoa Rd. .... Houston TX 77034 *Web:* www.imanacademy.org	713-910-3626		685
IMANA (Islamic Medical Association of North America) 101 W 22nd St Ste 104 .... Lombard IL 60148 *Web:* imana.org	630-932-0000	932-0005	49-8
Imanami Corp 2301 Armstrong St Ste 211 .... Livermore CA 94551 *TF:* 800-684-8515 ■ *Web:* www.imanami.com	925-371-3000		196
Imani Lee Translations Services 11297 Senda Luna Llena Bldg B .... San Diego CA 92130 *Web:* imanilee.com	858-523-9733		768
IMAPS (International Microelectronics & Packaging Society) PO Box 110127 .... Research Triangle Park NC 27709 *Web:* www.imaps.org	202-548-4001	548-6115	49-19
Imark Molding Inc 104 Park Ave .... Woodville WI 54028 *Web:* www.imarkmolding.com	715-698-3144		608
Imata & Associates Inc 1750 Kalakaua Ave Ste 115 .... Hilo HI 96720 *Web:* www.imata.biz	808-935-6827		261
iMatch 1417 Fourth Ave Ste 810 .... Seattle WA 98101 *Web:* www.imatch.com	206-262-1661		260
IMAX Corp 2525 Speakman Dr. .... Mississauga ON L5K1B1 *NYSE: IMAX* ■ *Web:* imax.com	905-403-6500	403-6450	748
IMBA (International Mountain Bicycling Assn) PO Box 20280 .... Boulder CO 80308 *Web:* www.imba.com	303-545-9011		48-23
Imbellus 1085 Gayley Ave .... Culver City CA 90024 *Web:* www.imbellus.com	617-775-1747		178-1
IMC (Institute of Management Consultants USA Inc) 2025 M St NW Ste 800 .... Washington DC 20036 **Fax Area Code:* 202 ■ *TF:* 800-221-2557 ■ *Web:* www.imcusa.org	800-793-4992	367-2134*	49-12
IMC (InterAmerican Motor Corp) 8901 Canoga Ave .... Canoga Park CA 91304 *TF:* 800-874-8925 ■ *Web:* www.imcparts.net	818-678-1200		61
IMC 233 S Wacker Dr Ste 4300 .... Chicago IL 60606 *Web:* www.imc.com	312-244-3300	244-3301	225
IMC (Iberia Medical Ctr) 2315 E Main St. .... New Iberia LA 70560 *Web:* www.iberiamedicalcenter.com	337-364-0441		374-3
IMC (Image Marketing & Communications Inc) 2140 W Fulton St Ste B .... Chicago IL 60612 *Web:* image-communications.com	312-421-5680	421-5708	194
IMC (International Medical Corp) 1919 Santa Monica Blvd Ste 400 .... Santa Monica CA 90404 *TF:* 800-481-4462 ■ *Web:* internationalmedicalcorps.org	310-826-7800	442-6622	48-5

Name / Address	City	State	ZIP	Phone	Fax	Class
IMC Resort Services INC 2 Corpus Christie Pl Ste 302 *TF:* 800-955-4474 ■ *Web:* www.imchhi.com	Hilton Head Island	SC	29928	843-785-4775	785-3901	707
IMCA (Insurance Marketing Communications Assn) 4248 Park Glen Rd *Web:* www.imcanet.com	Minneapolis	MN	55416	952-928-4644	929-1318	49-9
Imc-Metalsamerica LLC 135 Old Boiling Springs Rd *Web:* www.imc-ma.com	Shelby	NC	28152	704-482-8200		567
IMCO Carbide Tool Inc 28170 Cedar Park Blvd *TF:* 800-765-4626 ■ *Web:* www.imcousa.com	Perrysburg	OH	43551	419-661-6313	661-6314	186
IMCO General Construction Inc 2116 Buchanan Loop *Web:* imcoconstruction.com	Ferndale	WA	98248	360-671-3936	671-8808	186
IMCOR-Interstate Mechanical Corp 1841 E Washington St *TF:* 800-628-0211 ■ *Web:* www.imcor-az.com	Phoenix	AZ	85034	602-257-1319	271-0674	189-10
IMCU (Indiana Members Credit Union) 7110 W Tenth St *TF:* 800-556-9268 ■ *Web:* www.imcu.com	Indianapolis	IN	46214	317-248-8556		219
IMD Inc 560 Hwy 39 *Web:* www.imd-inc.com	Huntsville	UT	84317	801-745-4700		270
IMDbcom Inc 410 Terry Ave N *Web:* www.imdb.com	Seattle	WA	98109	206-266-4784	266-7010	387
IME (Institute of Makers of Explosives) 1212 New York Ave NW Ste 650 *Web:* www.ime.org	Washington	DC	20036	202-429-9280	293-2420	49-13
IME (Intermountain Electric Inc) 5050 Osage St Ste 500 *Web:* imelect.com	Denver	CO	80221	303-733-7248	722-2410	189-4
IME (Inberg-Miller Engineers) 124 E Main St *Web:* www.inberg-miller.com	Riverton	WY	82501	307-856-8136	856-3851	192
IMEC (Industrial Machine and Engineering Co) 1716 N 9th St *Web:* www.imecmonett.com	Monett	MO	65708	417-235-3053	235-3054	454
IMEC Technologies Inc 702 Bloomington Rd *Web:* www.imectechnologies.com	Champaign	IL	61820	217-643-7488	903-2517	177
I-MED Pharma Inc 1601 St Regis Blvd *TF:* 800-463-1008 ■ *Web:* imedpharma.com	Dollard-Des-Ormeaux	QC	H9B3H7	514-685-8118	685-8998	543
Imedex Inc 4325 Alexander Dr *Web:* www.imedex.com	Alpharetta	GA	30022	770-751-7332	751-7334	800
iMemories Inc 9181 E Bell Rd **Fax Area Code:* 480 ■ *TF:* 800-845-7986 ■ *Web:* www.imemories.com	Scottsdale	AZ	85260	800-845-7986	767-2511*	588
Imerys Clays Inc 100 Mansell Ct E Ste 300	Roswell	GA	30076	770-594-0660	645-3384	503-2
IMETCO (Innovative Metals Company Inc) 4648 S Old Peachtree Rd *TF:* 800-646-3826 ■ *Web:* www.imetco.com	Norcross	GA	30071	770-908-1030	908-2264	46
iMethods 8787 Perimeter Park Blvd **Fax Area Code:* 904 ■ *TF:* 888-306-2261 ■ *Web:* www.imethods.com	Jacksonville	FL	32216	888-306-2261	398-4148*	196
IMEX Research 1474 Camino Robles *Web:* www.imexresearch.com	San Jose	CA	95120	408-268-0800		463
IMEX Veterinary Inc 1001 Mckesson Dr *TF:* 800-828-4639 ■ *Web:* www.imexvet.com	Longview	TX	75604	903-295-2196		794
IMF (International Monetary Fund) 700 19th St NW *TF:* 800-548-5384 ■ *Web:* www.imf.org	Washington	DC	20431	202-623-7000	623-4661	783
IMFAB Inc 1249 Ave R *Web:* www.imfabinc.com	Grand Prairie	TX	75050	903-717-3115		492
IMG (International Motor Coach Group Inc) 12351 W 96th Ter **Fax Area Code:* 913 ■ *TF:* 888-447-3466 ■ *Web:* imgcoach.com	Lenexa	KS	66215	888-447-3466	906-0115*	49-21
IMG Artists 7 W 54th St *Web:* imgartists.com	New York	NY	10019	212-994-3500	994-3550	731
IMG Inc 9601 Wilshire Blvd *Web:* img.com	Beverly Hills	CA	90210	310-285-9000		731
IMG Models 304 Park Ave S PH N *Web:* www.imgmodels.com	New York	NY	10010	212-253-8884	253-8883	506
IMH Financial Corp 7001 N Scottsdale Rd Ste 2050 *TF:* 800-510-6445 ■ *Web:* www.imhfc.com	Scottsdale	AZ	85253	480-840-8400		216
IMHA-RVIC (Indiana Manufactured Housing Association-Recreation Vehicle Indiana Council) 3210 Rand Rd *Web:* www.imharvic.org	Indianapolis	IN	46241	317-247-6258	243-9174	139
IMI (Irving Materials Inc) 8032 N SR-9 *Web:* irvmat.com	Greenfield	IN	46140	317-536-6650	326-3105	182
IMI (International Masonry Institute) 17101 Science Dr *TF:* 800-803-0295 ■ *Web:* imiweb.org	Bowie	MD	20715	301-291-2124	261-2855	49-3
IMI (Integrated Medical Inc) 7012 S Revere Pky Ste 140 *TF:* 800-333-7617 ■ *Web:* www.integratedmedicalonline.com	Centennial	CO	80112	303-792-0069	799-3516	475
IMI Association Executives 110 Horizon Dr Ste 210 *Web:* www.imiae.com	Raleigh	NC	27615	919-459-2070	459-2075	47
IMI Cornelius Inc 101 Broadway St W *TF:* 800-238-3600 ■ *Web:* www.cornelius.com	Osseo	MN	55369	800-238-3600		664
IMI Data Search Inc 4333 Park Terrace Dr Ste 220 *TF:* 866-984-1736 ■ *Web:* imidatasearch.com	Westlake Village	CA	91361	805-920-8617	495-0310	635
IMI Precision Engineering 5400 S Delaware St *Web:* www.norgren.com	Littleton	CO	80120	303-794-2611		386
IMIC Hotels 1 Surrey Ct *Web:* www.imichotels.com	Columbia	SC	29212	803-772-2629		377
I-Minerals Inc 880 - 580 Hornby St *TF:* 877-303-6573 ■ *Web:* www.imineralsinc.com	Vancouver	BC	V6C3B6	604-303-6573		503-2
iMirus 7715 E 111th St Ste 100 *Web:* www.imirus.com	Tulsa	OK	74133	918-492-0660		393
IMKO 900 N Belt Hwy *Web:* www.imko.com	Saint Joseph	MO	64506	816-233-4040		260
IMLA (International Municipal Lawyers Assn) 51 Monroe St Ste 404 *TF:* 800-942-7732 ■ *Web:* www.imla.org	Rockville	MD	20850	202-466-5424	785-0152	49-10
Imlay City Ford Inc 1788 S Cedar St *TF:* 888-577-0437 ■ *Web:* www.imlaycityfordsales.com	Imlay City	MI	48444	810-724-5900		57
IMM Inc 758 Isenhauer Rd *TF:* 855-202-6384 ■ *Web:* www.immmi.com	Grayling	MI	49738	989-344-7662	344-7619	697
Immaculata University 1145 King Rd *Web:* www.immaculata.edu	Immaculata	PA	19345	610-647-4400	640-0836	166
Immanuel Home Care Services 712 E 47th St **Fax Area Code:* 773 ■ *Web:* www.immanuelhcs.com	Chicago	IL	60653	815-545-7350	285-3033*	363
Immanuel Lutheran Church 2120 Lakewood Ave *Web:* www.wcoil.com	Lima	OH	45805	419-222-2541		48-20
Immanuel Lutheran Communities 185 Crestline Ave *Web:* www.ilcorp.org	Kalispell	MT	59901	406-752-9622		48-20
Immanuel Lutheran High School, College, & Seminary 501 Grover Rd *Web:* ilc.edu	Eau Claire	WI	54701	715-836-6621		166
IMMC (International Museum of Muslim Cultures) 201 E Pascagoula St *Web:* www.muslimmuseum.org	Jackson	MS	39201	601-960-0440		520
Immecor 1650 Northpoint Pkwy *Web:* www.immecor.com	Santa Rosa	CA	95407	707-636-2550	636-2565	173-2
Immediate HomeCare Inc 2920 Olga Ave *Web:* www.immediatehomecareinc.com	Bensalem	PA	19020	215-638-2223		363
Immediatek 3301 Airport Fwy Ste 200 *TF:* 888-661-6565 ■ *Web:* www.immediatek.com	Bedford	TX	76021	888-661-6565		224
Immersion Corp 30 Rio Robles *NASDAQ: IMMR* ■ *Web:* www.immersion.com	San Jose	CA	95134	408-467-1900	467-1901	173-1
Immigrant & Employee Rights Section-US Department of Justice Civil Rights Division 950 Pennsylvania Ave NW Ste 4706 *TF:* 800-255-7688 ■ *Web:* www.justice.gov	Washington	DC	20530	202-616-5594	616-5509	340-14
Immigrant Law Group LLP 333 SW Fifth Ave Ste 525 *Web:* ilgrp.com	Portland	OR	97204	503-241-0035	241-7733	41
Immix Law Group PC 600 NW Naito Pkwy Ste G *Web:* immixlaw.com	Portland	OR	97209	503-802-5533		41
IMMS (Insurance Marketing and Management Services) PO Box 542 **Fax Area Code:* 909 ■ *TF:* 800-753-4467 ■ *Web:* www.imms.com	Big Bear City	CA	92314	800-753-4467	547-6212*	194
Immtech Pharmaceuticals 1 N End Ave *TF:* 877-898-8038 ■ *Web:* www.immtechpharma.com	New York	NY	10282	212-791-2911	791-2917	582
ImmucorGamma Inc 3130 Gateway Dr PO Box 5625 *NASDAQ: BLUD* ■ *TF:* 800-829-2553 ■ *Web:* www.immucor.com	Norcross	GA	30091	770-441-2051	441-3807	231
Immunalysis Corp 829 Towne Center Dr *TF:* 888-664-8378 ■ *Web:* immunalysis.com	Pomona	CA	91767	909-482-0840	482-0850	476
Immune Deficiency Foundation (IDF) 40 W Chesapeake Ave Ste 308 **Fax Area Code:* 410 ■ *TF:* 800-296-4433 ■ *Web:* www.primaryimmune.org	Towson	MD	21204	800-296-4433	321-9165*	48-17
Immune Design Corp 1616 Eastlake Ave E Ste 310	Seattle	WA	98102	206-682-0645		668
Immuno Concepts NA Ltd 9825 Goethe Rd Ste 350 *TF:* 800-251-5115 ■ *Web:* immunoconcepts.com	Sacramento	CA	95827	916-363-2649		743
ImmunoDiagnostics Inc 1 Presidential Way Ste 104 *TF:* 800-573-1700 ■ *Web:* www.immunodx.com	Woburn	MA	01801	781-938-6300	938-7300	231
ImmunoGen Inc 830 Winter St *NASDAQ: IMGN* ■ *Web:* www.immunogen.com	Waltham	MA	02451	781-895-0600		85
Immunomedics Inc 300 The American Rd *NASDAQ: IMMU* ■ *Web:* immunomedics.com	Morris Plains	NJ	07950	973-605-8200	605-8282	85
ImmunoScience Inc 6670 Owens Dr *Web:* immunoscience.com	Pleasanton	CA	94588	925-828-1000	397-2114	476
Immunotope Inc The Pennsylvania Biotechnology Ctr 3805 Old Easton *Web:* www.immunotope.com	Doylestown	PA	18902	215-253-4180		668
Immunovision Inc 1820 Ford Ave *TF:* 800-541-0960 ■ *Web:* www.immunovision.com	Springdale	AR	72764	479-751-7005	751-7002	231
Immuta Inc 8400 Baltimore Ave Ste 100 *TF:* 800-655-0982 ■ *Web:* immuta.com	College Park	MD	20740	800-655-0982		177
IMMY 2701 Corporate Centre Dr *TF:* 800-654-3639 ■ *Web:* www.immy.com	Norman	OK	73069	405-360-4669		231
IMO Pump 1710 Airport Rd *TF:* 877-853-7867 ■ *Web:* www.imo-pump.com	Monroe	NC	28110	704-289-6511	289-9273	641
iModules Software Inc 5101 College Blvd *Web:* www.imodules.com	Leawood	KS	66211	913-888-0772		180
ImOn Communications LLC 625 First St SE *Web:* www.imon.net	Cedar Rapids	IA	52401	319-298-6484		116
IMP Holdings LLC 409 Growth Pkwy *Web:* www.indianamarine.com	Angola	IN	46703	260-665-6112		253
Impac Intl 11445 Pacific Ave *TF:* 800-227-9591 ■ *Web:* www.impac-international.com	Fontana	CA	92337	951-685-9660		8
Impac Mortgage Holdings Inc 19500 Jamboree Rd *NYSE: IMH* ■ *TF:* 800-597-4101 ■ *Web:* www.impaccompanies.com	Irvine	CA	92612	949-475-3600		654
Impact - Proven Solutions 4600 Lyndale Ave N *Web:* www.impactconnects.com	Minneapolis	MN	55412	612-521-6245		4
Impact Christian Books Inc 332 Leffingwell Ave Ste 101 *Web:* www.impactchristianbooks.com	Kirkwood	MO	63122	314-822-3309	822-3325	637-2
Impact Consulting Solutions Inc 300 Cedar Ridge Dr Ste 306 *Web:* www.impactcsi.com	Pittsburgh	PA	15205	412-937-1000	763-8187	180
Impact Credit Union Inc 1455 W McPherson Hwy *Web:* impactcu.org	Clyde	OH	43410	419-547-7781		219

Name / Address	City	State	ZIP	Phone	Fax	Class
Impact Directories 1251 N Cole Rd *Web:* www.impactyp.com	Boise	ID	83704	208-375-2220		5
Impact Drug & Alcohol Treatment Ctr 1680 N Fair Oaks Ave *TF:* 866-734-4200 ■ *Web:* www.impacthouse.com	Pasadena	CA	91103	626-798-0884	798-6970	726
Impact Group 12977 N Outer 40 Dr Ste 300 *TF:* 800-420-2420 ■ *Web:* www.impactgrouphr.com	Saint Louis	MO	63141	314-453-9002		260
Impact Guns 2710 S 1900 W *TF:* 800-917-7137 ■ *Web:* www.impactguns.com	Ogden	UT	84401	800-917-7137		683
Impact Hub DC 419 7th St NW Ste 300 *Web:* washington.impacthub.net	Washington	DC	20004	202-545-6745		180
Impact Hub Salt Lake 150 State St Ste 1 *Web:* hubsaltlake.com	Salt Lake City	UT	84111	385-202-6008		192
Impact Incentives 552 Valley Rd *Web:* www.impactincentives.com	West Orange	NJ	07052	973-952-9052	325-1119	384
Impact Industries Inc 5120 Mills Industrial Pkwy *Web:* impactindustries.com	North Ridgeville	OH	44039	440-327-2360		488
Impact Interactive 5400 Laurel Springs Pkwy Ste 1003 *TF:* 800-768-6856 ■ *Web:* impact.amwins.com	Suwanee	GA	30024	800-768-6856		177
Impact International Inc 2600 Lockheed Way *Web:* www.impactmenusystems.com	Carson City	NV	89706	775-882-7834		596
Impact Label Corp 8875 Krum Ave *TF:* 800-820-0362 ■ *Web:* www.impactlabel.com	Galesburg	MI	49053	800-820-0362		413
Impact Mailing Services Inc 100 Forsyth Hall Dr Ste A1 *Web:* impactmailingservices.com	Charlotte	NC	28273	704-583-9490	583-9495	5
Impact Makers Inc 1707 Summit Ave Ste 201 *Web:* www.impactmakers.com	Richmond	VA	23230	804-774-2600		180
Impact Management Services 29792 Telegraph Rd Ste 150 *Web:* www.theimpactanswer.com	Southfield	MI	48034	248-262-5200	344-2901	193
Impact Marketing Inc 10340 Viking Dr Ste 100 *Web:* impactmn.com	Eden Prairie	MN	55344	952-562-6000	562-6001	525
Impact Planning Group 11 Grumman Hill Rd *Web:* www.impactplan.com	Wilton	CT	06897	203-854-1011		195
Impact Plastics Inc 1070 S Industrial Dr A *Web:* www.impact-plastics.com	Erwin	TN	37650	423-743-3561		604
Impact Products LLC 2840 Centennial Rd *TF:* 800-333-1541 ■ *Web:* www.impact-products.com	Toledo	OH	43617	419-841-2891	841-7861	151
Impact Publications Inc PO Box 322 *TF:* 800-350-4422 ■ *Web:* www.impact-publications.com	Waupaca	WI	54981	715-258-2448	258-9048	637-9
IMPACT Recruiting Group 18325 N Allied Way Ste 210 *Web:* go-impact.com	Phoenix	AZ	85054	480-307-9000		260
Impact Resources Inc 5910 Lone Oak Dr *Web:* www.ir-tech.com	Bethesda	MD	20814	301-581-9676		463
Impact Science & Technology Inc 85 NW Blvd	Nashua	NH	03063	603-459-2200		193
Impact Seven Inc 147 Lake Almena Dr *TF:* 800-685-9353 ■ *Web:* www.impactseven.org	Almena	WI	54805	715-357-3334	357-6233	402
Impact Solutions Inc 3810 McKnight E Dr *TF:* 800-858-8330 ■ *Web:* www.membermax.com	Pittsburgh	PA	15237	412-367-8833	367-2344	178-1
Impact Venture Capital 345 Lorton Ave *TF:* 888-292-4748 ■ *Web:* impactvc.com	Burlingame	CA	94010	888-292-4748		393
Impaq 7785 W Sunset Blvd *Web:* impaqcorp.com	Los Angeles	CA	90046	323-969-0088	969-0089	195
Impastato's 3400 16th St *Web:* www.impastatos.com	Metairie	LA	70002	504-455-1545		671
Impatica Inc 2430 Don Reid Dr Ste 200 *TF:* 800-548-3475 ■ *Web:* www.impatica.com	Ottawa	ON	K1H1E1	613-736-9982		225
Impatto Custom Marketing Inc 23235 Telegraph Rd *Web:* impatto.com	Southfield	MI	48033	248-415-5000		195
Impax Asset Management 30 Penhallow St Ste 400 *TF:* 800-767-1729 ■ *Web:* impaxam.com	Portsmouth	NH	03801	603-431-8022		528
Impax Laboratories Inc 30831 Hun2od Ave *TF:* 877-994-6729 ■ *Web:* www.impaxlabs.com	Hayward	CA	94544	510-240-6000		583
IMPCO Machine Tools 3417 W St Joseph St *Web:* www.impco.com	Lansing	MI	48917	517-484-9411	484-0502	455
IMPCO Technologies 5757 Farinon Dr *TF:* 800-325-4534 ■ *Web:* www.impcotechnologies.com	San Antonio	TX	78240	210-495-9772	495-9791	128
Impelsys Inc 116 W 23rd St Ste 500 **Fax Area Code:* 917 ■ *Web:* www.impelsys.com	New York	NY	10011	212-239-4138	591-9536*	261
Imperfect Foods 1616 Donner Ave *Web:* www.imperfectfoods.com	San Francisco	CA	94124	510-595-6683		296-11
Imperial Agency Inc, The 193 W City Ave *Web:* imperialagency.com	Bala Cynwyd	PA	19004	610-617-8850	617-8635	390
Imperial Beach Chamber of Commerce & Visitors Bureau 702 Seacoast Dr *Web:* www.ib-chamber.com	Imperial Beach	CA	91932	619-424-3151	424-3008	139
Imperial Bedding Co 720 11th St PO Box 5347 *TF:* 800-529-3321 ■ *Web:* imperialbedding.com	Huntington	WV	25703	304-529-3321		471
Imperial Beverage Co 3825 Emerald Dr *Web:* www.imperialbeverage.com	Kalamazoo	MI	49001	269-382-4200		81-1
Imperial Brown Inc 2271 NE 194th *TF:* 800-238-4093 ■ *Web:* imperialbrown.com	Portland	OR	97230	503-665-5539	665-2929	106
Imperial Building Materials Inc 1000 S Cypress St *Web:* www.imperialbm.com	La Habra	CA	90631	714-526-4373	526-4473	191 1
Imperial Calcasieu Museum 204 W Sallier St *Web:* www.imperialcalcasieumuseum.org	Lake Charles	LA	70601	337-439-3797		520
Imperial Capital LLC 10100 Santa Monica Blvd Ste 2400 *TF:* 800-929-2299 ■ *Web:* www.imperialcapital.com	Los Angeles	CA	90067	310-246-3700	777-3000	401
Imperial Carbide Inc 10826 Mercer Pk *Web:* www.imperialcarbide.com	Meadville	PA	16335	814-724-3732		350
Imperial Counters LLLP 725 Spiral Blvd	Hastings	MN	55033	651-437-3903	438-3855	286
Imperial County 940 W Main St Ste 202 **Fax Area Code:* 760 ■ *Web:* imperialcounty.org	El Centro	CA	92243	442-265-1148	482-4271*	338
Imperial Dax Company Inc 120 New Dutch Ln *TF:* 866-329-9297 ■ *Web:* www.daxhaircare.com	Fairfield	NJ	07004	973-227-6105	808-8533	88
Imperial Distributors Inc 33 Sword St *Web:* www.imperialdist.com	Auburn	MA	01501	508-756-5156	756-0085	214
Imperial Electric Co 1503 Exeter Rd *Web:* www.imperialelectric.com	Akron	OH	44306	330-734-3600	734-3601	518
Imperial Electronic Assembly Inc 1000 Federal Rd *Web:* www.impea.com	Brookfield	CT	06804	203-740-8425	740-8450	261
Imperial Fabricators Co 9119 Medill Ave *Web:* www.imperialfabricatorsco.com	Franklin Park	IL	60131	847-455-5544	455-1744	816
Imperial foods Inc 115 N Brandon Dr *Web:* www.imperial-foods.com	Glendale Heights	IL	60139	877-467-3003		297-3
Imperial Graphics Inc 3100 Walkent Dr NW *TF:* 800-777-2591 ■ *Web:* www.imperialcrs.com	Grand Rapids	MI	49544	800-777-2591		110
Imperial Hardware Company Inc 1041 N Imperial *Web:* www.imperialhardwarecompany.com	El Centro	CA	92243	760-353-5280		321
Imperial High School 517 W Barioni Blvd *Web:* imperialhighschool.org	Imperial	CA	92251	760-355-3220		685
Imperial Industries Inc 505 Industrial Park Ave *TF:* 800-558-2945 ■ *Web:* www.imperialind.com	Rothschild	WI	54474	715-359-0200	355-5349	105
Imperial Irrigation District (IID) PO Box 937 *TF:* 800-303-7756 ■ *Web:* www.iid.com	Imperial	CA	92251	760-482-9600	482-9611	203
Imperial Machine & Tool Co 8 W Crisman Rd *Web:* www.imperialmachine.com	Columbia	NJ	07832	908-496-8100		248
Imperial Manufacturing Group Inc 40 Industrial Park St *TF:* 800-561-3100 ■ *Web:* www.imperialgroup.ca	Richibucto	NB	E4W4A4	506-523-9117		610
Imperial Mechanical Inc 30685 Solon Industrial Pkwy *Web:* imperialhvac.com	Solon	OH	44139	440-498-1788		610
Imperial Metal Products Co 835 Hall St Sw *Web:* www.imperialmetalproducts.com	Grand Rapids	MI	49503	616-452-1700		621
Imperial Metals Corp 580 Hornby St Ste 200 *TSX:* III ■ *Web:* www.imperialmetals.com	Vancouver	BC	V6C3B6	604-669-8959		502
Imperial of Waikiki 205 Lewers St *TF:* 800-347-2582 ■ *Web:* imperialofwaikiki.com	Honolulu	HI	96815	808-923-1827	921-7586	379
Imperial Oil Resources Ltd 237 Fourth Ave SW PO Box 2480 Stn M *TF:* 800-567-3776 ■ *Web:* www.imperialoil.ca	Calgary	AB	T2P3M9	800-567-3776		580
Imperial Palace 701 N 27th St *Web:* www.imperialpalacene.net	Lincoln	NE	68503	402-474-2688		671
Imperial Palace 4878 Princess Anne Rd *Web:* www.imperialpalacevb.com	Virginia Beach	VA	23462	757-493-8838		671
Imperial Parking Corp 601 W Cordova St Ste 300 *Web:* www.impark.com	Vancouver	BC	V6B1G1	604-681-7311	681-4098	562
Imperial PFS 1055 Broadway Blvd Fl 11	Kansas City	MO	64105	816-627-0500		216
Imperial Plastics Inc 21320 Hamburg Ave W *Web:* www.imperialplastics.com	Lakeville	MN	55044	952-469-4951		596
Imperial Pools Inc 33 Wade Rd *TF:* 800-444-9977 ■ *Web:* www.imperialpoolsb2b.com	Latham	NY	12110	518-786-1200	786-0954	728
Imperial Realty Company Inc 4747 W Peterson Ave *Web:* imperialrealtyco.com	Chicago	IL	60646	773-736-4100		655
Imperial Salon & Spa Inc 3 Suntree Pl *Web:* www.imperialsalonandspa.com	Melbourne	FL	32940	321-254-4432		77
Imperial Sprinkler Supply Inc 1485 N Manassero St **Fax Area Code:* 925 ■ *Web:* www.imperialsprinklersupply.com	Anaheim	CA	92807	714-792-2925	667-2197*	429
Imperial Swan Hotel 4141 S Florida Ave	Lakeland	FL	33813	863-647-3000		379
Imperial Teacher's Store 2347 Main St *TF:* 800-947-9701 ■ *Web:* www.imperialteachersstore.com	Wheeling	WV	26003	304-233-0711	233-9424	535
Imperial Theatre 749 Broad St *Web:* www.imperialtheatre.com	Augusta	GA	30901	706-722-8293	312-1202	572
Imperial Trading Company Inc 701 Edwards Ave *TF:* 800-775-4504 ■ *Web:* www.imperialtrading.com	Elmwood	LA	70123	504-733-1400		297-8
Imperial Valley College 380 E Atten Rd PO Box 158 *TF:* 800-336-1642 ■ *Web:* www.imperial.edu	Imperial	CA	92251	760-352-8320	355-2663	162
Imperial Valley Press 205 N Eigth St *Web:* www.ivpressonline.com	El Centro	CA	92243	760-337-3400		532-2
Imperial Valley Rop 687 W State St *Web:* www.ivrop.org	El Centro	CA	92243	760-482-2600		685

Name / Address	Phone	Fax	Class
Imperial Woodworking Co 310 N Woodwork Ln . . . Palatine IL 60067 *Web:* www.imperialwoodworking.com	847-358-6920	358-0905	499
Imperial Woodworks Inc PO Box 7835 . . . Waco TX 76714 **Fax Area Code: 254* ■ *TF:* 800-234-6624 ■ *Web:* www.pews.com	800-234-6624	741-0736*	319-3
Imperium Inc 5901-F Ammendale Rd . . . Beltsville MD 20705 *Web:* www.imperiuminc.com	301-431-2900		250
Impetus Capital LLC 145 W 57th St 16th Fl . . . New York NY 10019 *Web:* www.impetuscapital.com	212-258-2782		691
Impinj Inc 400 Fairview Ave N Ste 1200 . . . Seattle WA 98109 *Web:* www.impinj.com	206-517-5300	517-5262	696
Implantech Dental Laboratory 72415 Parkview Dr . . . Palm Desert CA 92260 *Web:* www.implantechlab.com	760-341-7388	674-5746	415
Implement Sales Company LLC 1574 Stone Ridge Dr . . . Stone Mountain GA 30083 *TF:* 800-955-9592 ■ *Web:* implementsales.com	770-908-9439	908-8123	274
Implementation & Consulting Services Inc (ICS) 500 Office Center Dr Ste 400 . . . Fort Washington PA 19034 *TF:* 844-432-8326 ■ *Web:* www.ics-corporate.com	844-432-8326		177
Implementix Inc 4850 Ward Rd . . . Wheat Ridge CO 80033 *TF:* 800-433-2257 ■ *Web:* www.implement-ix.com	888-831-2536		627
IMPO PO Box 639 . . . Santa Maria CA 93456 *TF:* 800-367-4676 ■ *Web:* impo.com	800-367-4676		301
Import Auto World 21571 Mission Blvd . . . Hayward CA 94541 *Web:* importautoworldinc.com	510-581-1200	581-1228	57
Impreglon Tennessee Inc 162 Corporate Dr . . . Cleveland TN 37311 *Web:* www.impreglon.us	423-559-9900	559-1239	481
IMPRES Technology Solutions Inc 10330 Pioneer Blvd Ste 280 . . . Santa Fe Springs CA 90670 *Web:* www.imprestechnology.com	562-298-4030		196
Impression 5 Science Ctr 200 Museum Dr . . . Lansing MI 48933 *Web:* impression5.org	517-485-8116		520
Impressive Image Works Inc 2901 Teague Dr . . . Tyler TX 75701 *Web:* www.impressiveimageworks.com	903-597-4599	593-6647	110
Imprex Inc 3260 S 108th St . . . Milwaukee WI 53227 *Web:* imprexusa.com	414-321-9300	321-9086	480
Imprimis Group Inc 4835 Lyndon B Johnson Fwy . . . Dallas TX 75244 *Web:* www.imprimis.com	972-419-1700	419-1799	344
Imprimis International Inc Ben F Hord III or Margaret A Martin 111 S Alfred St 2nd Fl . . . Alexandria VA 22314 *Web:* www.imprimisinternational.com	703-549-3131	931-5143	194
Impro Products Inc 3 Allamakee St . . . Waukon IA 52172 *TF:* 800-626-5536 ■ *Web:* www.improproducts.com	563-568-3401		582
Improper Bostonian 142 Berkeley St 3rd Fl . . . Boston MA 02116 *Web:* www.improper.com	617-859-1400	859-1446	532-3
Improv Asylum 216 Hanover St . . . Boston MA 02113 *TF:* 888-396-6887 ■ *Web:* www.improvasylum.com	617-263-6887		522
Improve Group Inc, The 661 LaSalle St Ste 300 . . . Saint Paul MN 55114 *TF:* 877-467-7847 ■ *Web:* theimprovegroup.com	651-315-8919	927-8085	196
Improved Construction Methods 1040 N Redmond Rd . . . Jacksonville AR 72076 *TF:* 877-494-5793 ■ *Web:* www.improvedconstructionmethods.com	877-494-5793		358
Impulse Point LLC 5650 Breckenridge Park Dr Ste 201 . . . Tampa FL 33610 *Web:* impulse.com	813-607-2770		180
Impulse Technologies Ltd 920 Gana Crt . . . Mississauga ON L5S1Z4 *TF:* 800-667-5475 ■ *Web:* impulsetechnologies.com	905-564-9266		196
IMR Environmental Equipment Inc 3632 Central Ave . . . Saint Petersburg FL 33711 *TF:* 800-746-4467 ■ *Web:* www.imrusa.com	727-328-2818	328-2826	385
IMS (Innovative Media Systems) 7121 Washington Ave S . . . Edina MN 55439 *Web:* www.innovativemediasystems.com	952-960-2915		189-4
IMS Buhrke-Olson 511 W Algonquin Rd . . . Arlington Heights IL 60005 *Web:* www.metalstamper.com	847-981-7550		492
IMS inc 245 Commerce Blvd . . . Liverpool NY 13088 *TF:* 800-466-4189 ■ *Web:* imsdirect.com	800-466-4189		5
IMS Productions 4555 W 16th St . . . Indianapolis IN 46222 *Web:* www.imsproductionstv.com	317-492-8770		513
IMS Worldwide Inc 309 Henrietta . . . Webster TX 77598 *Web:* www.imsw.com	281-554-9099		463
IMSA (International Municipal Signal Assn) 165 E Union St PO Box 539 . . . Newark NY 14513 *TF:* 800-723-4672 ■ *Web:* www.imsasafety.org	315-331-2182	331-8205	49-7
IMshopping Inc 6220 STONERIDGE MALL Rd . . . Pleasanton CA 94588	408-641-1654		387
IMSI (Idaho Maximum Security Institution) PO Box 51 . . . Boise ID 83707 *Web:* www.idoc.idaho.gov	208-338-1635		213
IMSolutions LLC 3600 Pointe Center Ct Ste 200 . . . Dumfries VA 22026 *Web:* www.imsolutionsllc.com	703-221-2685		463
IMT (Iowa Mold Tooling Company Inc) 500 W US Hwy 18 . . . Garner IA 50438 *TF:* 800-247-5958 ■ *Web:* www.imt.com	641-923-3711	923-6063	470
IMT (Lomont In-Mold Technologies) 1516 E Mapleleaf Dr . . . Mount Pleasant IA 52641 *TF:* 800-776-0380 ■ *Web:* www.lomontimt.com	319-385-1528	385-1533	601
IMT (Infomagnetics Technologies Corp) 900-330 St Mary Ave . . . Winnipeg MB R3C3Z5 *Web:* imt.ca	204-989-4630		261
IMT Precision Inc 31902 Hayman St . . . Hayward CA 94544 *Web:* www.imtp.com	510-324-8926	324-8943	454
Imtec Acculine Inc 49036 Milmont Dr . . . Fremont CA 94538 *Web:* www.imtecacculine.com	510-770-1800	770-1400	695
Imtech Graphics Inc 545 Dell Rd . . . Carlstadt NJ 07072 *TF:* 800-468-3240 ■ *Web:* imtechgraphics.com	800-468-3240		781
Imtek Inc 175 Amherst St . . . Nashua NH 03064 *TF:* 877-889-7610 ■ *Web:* imtek.com	603-889-7610		7
Imtronics Industries Inc 11930 31st Ct N . . . Saint Petersburg FL 33716 *Web:* www.imtronics.com	727-572-9010	572-9012	246
IMV (Institute for Molecular Virology) 1525 Linden Dr 413 RM Bock Laboratories . . . Madison WI 53706 *Web:* virology.wisc.edu	608-262-4540	262-4570	668
In a Nutshell 753 Montague St . . . San Leandro CA 94577 *Web:* www.inanutshell.com	510-895-2010		297-3
In Business Magazine 200 River Pl Ste 250 . . . Madison WI 53716 *Web:* www.ibmadison.com	608-204-9655	204-9656	457-5
In Defense of Animals (IDA) 3010 Kerner Blvd . . . San Rafael CA 94901 *TF:* 800-705-0425 ■ *Web:* www.idausa.org	415-448-0048	454-1031	48-3
In Demand 345 Hudson St 17th Fl . . . New York NY 10014 *Web:* www.indemand.com	646-638-8200		740
In Plain English 14501 Antigone Dr . . . Gaithersburg MD 20878 *TF:* 800-274-9645 ■ *Web:* www.inplainenglish.com	301-340-2821	279-0115	194
In Record Time Inc 1901 SE 4th Ave . . . Fort Lauderdale FL 33316 *TF:* 800-788-4960 ■ *Web:* www.inrecordtime.net	800-788-4960	834-1038	194
In The Game Freedom Station 2992 N Park Ave Ste A . . . Prescott Valley AZ 86314 *Web:* prescottvalley.inthegame.net	928-775-4040		31
In The Line of Duty 10786 Indian Head Industrial Blvd . . . Saint Louis MO 63132 *TF:* 800-462-5232 ■ *Web:* lineofduty.com	314-890-8733		95
In the Raw Sushi 3321 S Peoria . . . Tulsa OK 74105 *Web:* www.intherawsushi.com	918-744-1300		671
In The Swim Inc 320 Industrial Dr . . . West Chicago IL 60185 *TF:* 800-288-7946 ■ *Web:* www.intheswim.com	630-876-1080		711
In Touch Marketing Inc 2793 Deerhaven Dr . . . Cincinnati OH 45244 *Web:* intouchmarketinginc.net	513-235-3847	474-6316	195
In Touch Weekly Magazine 270 Sylvan Ave . . . Englewood Cliffs NJ 07632 *Web:* www.intouchweekly.com	201-569-6699		457-11
In Zone Brands 2859 Paces Ferry Rd SE Ste 2100 . . . Atlanta GA 30339 *Web:* www.good2grow.com	678-718-2000		98
INA (Illinois Nurses Assn) 105 W Adams St Ste 2101 . . . Chicago IL 60603 *TF:* 800-262-2500 ■ *Web:* www.illinoisnurses.com	312-419-2900	419-2920	533
INA (Iowa Nurses Assn) 2400 86th St Ste 32 . . . Urbandale IA 50322 *Web:* www.iowanurses.org	515-225-0495		533
Inabata America Corp 1270 Ave of the Americas Ste 602 . . . New York NY 10020 *Web:* us.inabata.com	212-586-7764		696
Inaho 157 Rt 6A . . . Yarmouth Port MA 02675 *Web:* www.inaho-sushi.com	508-362-5522		671
Inair Aviation Services Co 8225 Country Club Pl . . . Indianapolis IN 46214 *Web:* inairaviation.com	317-271-0195		22
Inanovate Inc 1304 Adams Mountain Rd . . . Raleigh NC 27614 *Web:* inanovate.com	919-410-8973		419
InApp Inc 999 Commercial St Ste 210 . . . Palo Alto CA 94303 *Web:* inapp.com	650-283-8282		225
Inberg-Miller Engineers (IME) 124 E Main St . . . Riverton WY 82501 *Web:* www.inberg-miller.com	307-856-8136	856-3851	192
InBios International Inc 562 First Ave S Ste 600 . . . Seattle WA 98104 *Web:* www.inbios.com	206-344-5821		466
Inbound Call Experts LLC 700 Banyan Trl Ste 200 . . . Boca Raton FL 33431 *Web:* www.inboundcallexperts.com	561-705-0700		196
Inbox Group LLC 2100 W NW Hwy Ste 114-1135 . . . Grapevine TX 76051 *Web:* www.inboxgroup.com	214-530-5972	530-5973	366
Inc Magazine 7 World Trade Ctr . . . New York NY 10007 *TF:* 800-234-0999 ■ *Web:* www.inc.com	212-389-5377		457-5
Inc ommand Technologies Inc 21 W William St . . . Corning NY 14830 *Web:* www.incommandtech.com	607-936-5066		180
Inc Solayre Inc 4568 N Hiatus Rd . . . Sunrise FL 33351 *TF:* 877-825-5028 ■ *Web:* www.solayre.com	954-389-4779		463
INCA Engineers Inc 400 112th Ave NE Ste 400 . . . Bellevue WA 98004	425-635-1000	635-1150	194
Incapital LLC 200 S Wacker Dr Ste 3700 . . . Chicago IL 60606 *Web:* www.incapital.com	312-379-3700		690
Incarnate Word High School 727 E Hildebrand Ave . . . San Antonio TX 78212 *Web:* www.incarnatewordhs.org	210-829-3100	829-3101	622
Incarnation Lutheran Church 4880 Hodgson Rd . . . Shoreview MN 55126 *Web:* www.incarnationmn.org	651-484-7213	484-0260	48-20
Incas 3312 S Holly Ave . . . Sioux Falls SD 57105 *Web:* www.incamexicanrestaurantsf.com	605-367-1992	367-1993	671
Incenta Federal Credit Union 175 W Wenger Rd . . . Englewood OH 45322 *TF:* 800-678-4943 ■ *Web:* incentafcu.org	937-223-4943	429-5375	219
Incentia Design Systems Inc 3080 Olcott St Ste C250 . . . Santa Clara CA 95054 *Web:* incentia.com	408-727-8988		225
Incentive Group Inc, The 399 Knollwood Rd . . . White Plains NY 10603 *Web:* www.incentivegroup.com	914-948-0904		463
Incentive Publications Inc 2400 Crestmoor Dr . . . Nashville TN 37215 *TF:* 800-967-5325 ■ *Web:* incentivepublications.com	615-385-2934		243
Incentive Research Foundation 100 Chesterfield Business Pkwy Ste 200 . . . Chesterfield MO 63005 *Web:* theirf.org	314-473-5601		305

	Phone	Fax	Class
Incentive Travel & Meetings (ITM) 970 Clementstone Dr Ste 100 .... Atlanta GA 30342 *Web:* usaitm.com	404-847-9021	855-4863	384
INCERTEC LLC 160 83rd Ave NE .... Fridley MN 55432 *TF:* 800-638-2573 ■ *Web:* incertec.com	763-717-7016		256
InCharge Debt Solutions 5750 Major Blvd Ste 300 .... Orlando FL 32819 *TF:* 888-734-6229 ■ *Web:* www.incharge.org	888-734-6229		218
Inchcape Shipping Services Inc 11 N Water St Ste 9290 .... Mobile AL 36602 *Web:* www.iss-shipping.com	251-461-2747		313
Inclinator Company of America 601 Gibson Blvd .... Harrisburg PA 17104 *TF:* 800-343-9007 ■ *Web:* www.inclinator.com	717-939-8420		256
Inclind Incorporated Web Development Services 119 W 3rd St Ste 6 .... Lewes DE 19958 *Web:* www.inclind.com	800-604-8139		177
Incline Village/Crystal Bay Visitors Bureau 969 Tahoe Blvd .... Incline Village NV 89451 *TF:* 800-468-2463 ■ *Web:* www.gotahoenorth.com	775-832-1606	832-1605	206
Inclusiv 39 Broadway Ste 2140 .... New York NY 10006 *TF:* 800-437-8711 ■ *Web:* www.inclusiv.org	212-809-1850	809-3274	49-2
Incoe Corp 1740 E Maple Rd .... Troy MI 48083 *Web:* www.incoe.com	248-616-0220	616-0225	757
Incom Integrated Computer Systems Inc 7353 Austin Powder Dr .... Glenwillow OH 44139 *TF:* 800-414-6266 ■ *Web:* netincom.com	440-439-7000	439-7001	180
Incom USA Inc 294 Southbridge Rd .... Charlton MA 01507 *Web:* www.incomusa.com	508-765-9151	765-0041	330
Income Research & Management 100 Federal St 30th Fl .... Boston MA 02110 *Web:* www.incomeresearch.com	617-330-9333		401
InComm Conferencing Inc 208 Harristown Rd Ste 202 .... Glen Rock NJ 07452 *TF:* 877-804-2062 ■ *Web:* www.incommconferencing.com	201-612-9696	612-9692	387
INCON Process Systems LLC PO Box 268 .... Saint Charles IL 60174 *Web:* www.ips-gigk.com	630-305-8556	477-0333	479
Incontact Inc 7730 S Union Park Ave Ste 500 .... Midvale UT 84047 *NASDAQ: SAAS* ■ *TF:* 877-401-7227 ■ *Web:* www.niceincontact.com	877-401-7227		178-11
Incontrol Technology Inc 1651 E Main St .... El Cajon CA 92021 *Web:* incontroltechnology.com	619-270-1260		225
Increte Systems Inc 1611 Gunn Hwy .... Odessa FL 33556 *TF:* 800-752-4626 ■ *Web:* www.increte.com	813-886-8811	920-1516	183
InCycle Software Inc 1120 Avenue of The Americas 4th Fl .... New York NY 10036 *TF:* 800-565-0510 ■ *Web:* www.incyclesoftware.com	212-626-2608	626-6558	180
Incyte Corp 1801 Augustine Cut-Off .... Wilmington DE 19803 *NASDAQ: INCY* ■ *TF:* 800-783-3711 ■ *Web:* www.incyte.com	302-498-6700		85
Incyte Diagnostics 13103 E Mansfield Ave .... Spokane Valley WA 99216 *TF:* 800-403-6749 ■ *Web:* www.incytediagnostics.com	509-892-2700	892-2740	415
INDA: Association of the Nonwoven Fabrics Industry 1100 Crescent Green Ste 125 .... Cary NC 27518 *Web:* inda.org	919-459-3700	459-3701	49-13
Indaba Capital Management LP 1 Letterman Dr Bldg D The Presidio of San Francisco Ste DM700 .... San Francisco CA 94129 *Web:* www.indabacapital.com	415-680-1180		401
Indaco Metal 3 American Way .... Shawnee OK 74804 *TF:* 877-750-5614 ■ *Web:* www.indacometals.com	405-273-9200		106
Indak Manufacturing Corp 1915 Techny Rd .... Northbrook IL 60062 *Web:* www.indak.com	847-272-0343		729
Indal Technologies Inc 3570 Hawkestone Rd .... Mississauga ON L5C2V8 *Web:* www.indaltech.cwfc.com	905-275-5300		21
Indalco Alloys Inc 939 Gana Ct .... Mississauga ON L5S1N9 *Web:* www.indalco.com	905-564-1151		811
Indco Cable TV Inc PO Box 3799 .... Batesville AR 72503 *TF:* 800-364-0831 ■ *Web:* www.indco.net	870-793-4174		116
Indco Inc 4040 Earnings Way .... New Albany IN 47150 *TF:* 800-942-4383 ■ *Web:* www.indco.com	800-942-4383		190
Indeck Energy Services Inc 600 N Buffalo Grove Rd Ste 300 .... Buffalo Grove IL 60089 *Web:* indeckenergy.com	847-520-3212		91
Indeck Keystone Energy LLC 5340 Fryling Rd Ste 200 .... Erie PA 16510 *Web:* www.indeck-keystone.com	814-452-6421		612
Indeck Power Equipment Co 1111 Willis Ave .... Wheeling IL 60090 *TF:* 800-446-3325 ■ *Web:* www.indeck.com	847-541-8300	541-9984	385
Indeco North America Inc 135 Research Dr .... Milford CT 06460 *Web:* indeco-breakers.com	203-713-1030	713-1040	532-3
Indelco Plastics Corp 6530 Cambridge St .... Minneapolis MN 55426 *TF:* 800-486-6456 ■ *Web:* www.indelco.com	952-925-5075		605-2
Indepak Inc 2136 NE 194th Ave .... Portland OR 97230 *TF:* 800-338-1857 ■ *Web:* www.indepak.com	800-338-1857		596
Independant Insurance Services In 3956 N Pine St .... Davenport IA 52806 *TF:* 800-373-1562 ■ *Web:* qcfreequote.com	563-383-5555		390
Independence 4 Seniors Inc 5 W Second St Ste 4 .... Hinsdale IL 60521 *Web:* independence4seniors.com	630-323-4665	323-4669	363
Independence Blue Cross 1901 Market St .... Philadelphia PA 19103 **Fax Area Code: 215* ■ *TF:* 800-275-2583 ■ *Web:* www.ibx.com	800-275-2583	241-0403*	391-3
Independence Bowl Foundation 401 Market St .... Shreveport LA 71101 *TF:* 888-414-2695 ■ *Web:* www.radiancetechnologiesindependencebowl.com	318-221-0712	221-7366	720
Independence Chamber of Commerce 210 W Truman Rd .... Independence MO 64050 *TF:* 800-222-6400 ■ *Web:* ichamber.biz	816-252-4745	252-4917	139
Independence City Hall 111 E Maple Ave .... Independence MO 64050 *Web:* www.ci.independence.mo.us	816-325-7000	325-7012	337
Independence College of Cosmetology 815 W 23rd S St .... Independence MO 64055	816-252-4247		167-3
Independence Community College 1057 W College Ave PO Box 708 .... Independence KS 67301 *TF:* 800-842-6063 ■ *Web:* www.indycc.edu	620-332-5460	331-0946	162
Independence County 192 E Main St .... Batesville AR 72501 *Web:* www.independencecounty.com	870-793-8800	793-8803	338
Independence Excavating 5720 Schaaf Rd .... Independence OH 44131 *TF:* 800-524-3478 ■ *Web:* www.indexc.com	216-524-1700	524-1701	189-5
Independence Lumber Inc 407 Lumber Ln .... Independence VA 24348 *Web:* www.independencelumberinc.com	276-773-3744	773-3723	683
Independence Mall 3500 Oleander Dr .... Wilmington NC 28403 *Web:* www.shopindependencemall.com	910-392-1776		460
Independence Media Group PO Box 364 .... Broomall PA 19008 *Web:* www.independencemg.com	610-325-2310	325-2312	637-10
Independence National Historical Park 143 S Third St .... Philadelphia PA 19106 *TF:* 800-537-7676 ■ *Web:* www.nps.gov	215-597-8787		564
Independence Seaport Museum 211 S Columbus Blvd .... Philadelphia PA 19106 *Web:* www.phillyseaport.org	215-413-8655	925-6713	520
Independence Tube Corp 6226 W 74th St .... Chicago IL 60638 *TF:* 800-376-6000 ■ *Web:* www.independencetube.com	800-376-6000		492
Independence University 4021 South 700 East Ste 400 .... Salt Lake City UT 84107 *TF:* 800-972-5149 ■ *Web:* www.independence.edu	801-290-3240	263-0345	786
Independent Bank Corp 230 W Main St .... Ionia MI 48846 *NASDAQ: IBCP* ■ *TF:* 888-300-3193 ■ *Web:* www.independentbank.com	616-527-2400	527-4004	360-2
Independent Book Publishers Assn, The (IBPA) 1020 Manhattan Beach Blvd Ste 204 .... Manhattan Beach CA 90266 *TF:* 800-327-5113 ■ *Web:* www.ibpa-online.org	310-546-1818	546-3939	49-16
Independent Can Co 1300 Brass Mill Rd .... Belcamp MD 21017 *Web:* www.independentcan.com	410-272-0090	273-7500	124
Independent Capital Management 4141 Inland Empire Blvd Ste 301 .... Ontario CA 91764 *Web:* www.icmfinancial.com	909-948-1608		401
Independent Chemical Corp 79-51 Cooper Ave .... Glendale NY 11385 *TF:* 800-892-2578 ■ *Web:* www.independentchemical.com	718-894-0700	894-9224	146
Independent Coach Corp 25 Wanser Ave .... Inwood NY 11096 *Web:* independentcoach.com	516-239-1100		109
Independent Coast Observer Inc PO Box 1200 .... Gualala CA 95445 *Web:* www.mendonoma.com	707-884-3501	884-1710	532-2
Independent Community Bankers of America (ICBA) 1615 L St NW Ste 900 .... Washington DC 20036 *TF:* 800-422-8439 ■ *Web:* www.icba.org	202-659-8111		49-2
Independent Educational Consultants Assn (IECA) 3251 Old Lee Hwy Ste 510 .... Fairfax VA 22030 *Web:* www.iecaonline.com	703-591-4850	591-4860	49-5
Independent Electric Supply Inc 1370 Bayport Ave .... San Carlos CA 94070 *Web:* www.iesupply.com	650-594-9440		246
Independent Film & Television Alliance (IFTA) 10850 Wilshire Blvd 9th Fl .... Los Angeles CA 90024 *Web:* www.ifta-online.org	310-446-1000	446-1600	48-4
Independent Food Corp 2072 Orchard Dr E .... Twin Falls ID 83301 *Web:* www.independentmeat.com	208-733-0980		473
Independent Forge Co 692 N Batavia St .... Orange CA 92868 *Web:* www.independentforge.com	714-997-7337	997-7546	483
Independent Foundry Supply Co (IFSCO) 6463 E Canning St .... Commerce CA 90040 *Web:* www.foundry-supplies.com	323-725-1051	725-0664	492
Independent Graphics Inc 242 W 8th St .... West Wyoming PA 18644 *Web:* independentgraphics.com	570-609-5267	654-9799	627
Independent Health 511 Farber Lakes Dr .... Buffalo NY 14221 *TF:* 800-247-1466 ■ *Web:* www.independenthealth.com	716-631-3001		391-3
Independent Ink Inc 13700 Gramercy Pl .... Gardena CA 90249 *TF:* 800-446-5538 ■ *Web:* www.independentink.com	310-523-4657	329-0943	388
Independent Institute 100 Swan Way .... Oakland CA 94621 *TF:* 800-927-8733 ■ *Web:* www.independent.org	510-632-1366	568-6040	634
Independent Insurance Agents & Brokers of America Inc (IIABA) 127 S Peyton St .... Alexandria VA 22314 *TF:* 800-221-7917 ■ *Web:* www.independentagent.com	703-683-4422	683-7556	49-9
Independent Jewelers Organization (IJO) 136 Old Post Rd .... Southport CT 06890 **Fax Area Code: 203* ■ *TF:* 800-624-9252 ■ *Web:* www.ijo.com	800-624-9252	254-7429*	49-4
Independent Liquid Terminals Assn (ILTA) 1005 N Glebe Rd Ste 600 .... Arlington VA 22201 *Web:* www.ilta.org	703-875-2011	875-2018	49-21
Independent Living Resource Center Inc, The 423 W Victoria St .... Santa Barbara CA 93101 *Web:* www.ilrc-trico.org	805-963-0595		768
Independent Lubricant Manufacturers Assn (ILMA) 400 N Columbus St Ste 201 .... Alexandria VA 22314 *Web:* www.ilma.org	703-684-5574	836-8503	49-13
Independent Mechanical Industries Inc 4155 N Knox Ave .... Chicago IL 60641 *Web:* www.independentmech.com	773-282-4500	282-2046	189-10
Independent Office Products & Furniture Dealers Assn (IOPFDA) 3601 E Joppa Rd .... Baltimore MD 21234 *Web:* www.nopanet.org	410-931-8100	931-8111	49-4
Independent Order of Foresters (IOF) 789 Don Mills Rd .... Toronto ON M3C1T9 *TF:* 800-828-1540 ■ *Web:* www.foresters.com	416-429-3000		48-5
Independent Order of Odd Fellows 422 N Trade St .... Winston-Salem NC 27101 *TF:* 800-235-8358 ■ *Web:* www.ioof.org	336-725-5955	722-7317	48-15
Independent Packing Services Inc 7600 32nd Ave N .... Crystal MN 55427 *Web:* www.ipsipack.com	763-425-7155	425-0451	549

Phone | Fax | Class

Independent Petroleum Association of America (IPAA)
1201 15th St NW Ste 300 .... Washington DC 20005 202-857-4722 857-4799 48-12
TF: 800-433-2851 ■ *Web:* www.ipaa.org

Independent Pipe & Supply Corp
Whitman Rd .... Canton MA 02021 781-828-8500 612
Web: www.indpipe.com

Independent Protection Company Inc
1607 S Main St .... Goshen IN 46526 574-533-4116 534-3719 815
TF: 800-860-8388 ■ *Web:* www.ipclp.com

Independent Record PO Box 4249 .... Helena MT 59604 406-447-4000 447-4052 532-2
TF: 800-523-2272 ■ *Web:* helenair.com

Independent Rental
2020 S Cushman St .... Fairbanks AK 99701 907-456-6595 264-2
Web: www.independentrental.com

Independent Roofing Consultants
2901 Tullman St .... Santa Ana CA 92705 949-476-8626 476-9810 193
Web: www.irctech.com

Independent Sector
1602 L St NW Ste 900 .... Washington DC 20036 202-467-6100 467-6101 48-5
Web: independentsector.org

Independent Stave Company Inc
1078 S Jefferson Ave .... Lebanon MO 65536 417-588-4151 200
TF: 800-797-2688 ■ *Web:* www.independentstavecompany.com

Independent Technology Service Inc
9182 Independence Ave .... Chatsworth CA 91311 818-727-1500 727-1750 175
TF: 800-342-3475 ■ *Web:* itscnc.com

Independent Television Service (ITVS)
651 Brannan St Ste 410 .... San Francisco CA 94107 415-356-8383 356-8391 742
TF: 888-572-8918 ■ *Web:* itvs.org

Independent Title Agency
200 Canal View Blvd Ste 206 .... Rochester NY 14623 585-424-3750 424-3775 653
TF: 877-363-4958 ■ *Web:* fasttitles.com

Independent Tribune, The
363 Church St N Ste 140 .... Concord NC 28025 704-789-9162 532-2
Web: www.independenttribune.com

Independent Weekly PO Box 2690 .... Durham NC 27715 919-286-1972 286-4274 532-5
Web: www.indyweek.com

Independent, The 2250 First St .... Livermore CA 94550 925-447-8700 447-0212 532-4
TF: 877-952-3588 ■ *Web:* www.independentnews.com

Independents Service Co
2710 Market St .... Hannibal MO 63401 573-221-4615 194
TF: 800-325-3694 ■ *Web:* www.isco.net

Indera Mills Co
350 W Maple St PO Box 309 .... Yadkinville NC 27055 800-334-8605 679-4475* 155-18
*Fax Area Code: 336 ■ *TF:* 800-334-8605 ■ *Web:* www.inderamills.com

Inderbitzin Distributors Inc
901 Valley Ave NW .... Puyallup WA 98371 253-922-2592 922-8807 297-8
TF: 800-998-9218 ■ *Web:* www.inderbitzin.com

Indesign LLC 8225 E 56th St Ste A .... Indianapolis IN 46216 317-377-5450 261
TF: 877-561-0274 ■ *Web:* www.indesign-llc.com

Index Analytics
3700 Koppers St Ste 535 .... Baltimore MD 21227 667-309-3192 39
Web: www.index-analytics.com

Index Engines Inc 960 Holmdel Rd .... Holmdel NJ 07733 732-817-1060 54
Web: www.indexengines.com

Index Fresh Inc 18184 Slover Ave .... Bloomington CA 92316 909-877-0999 877-0495 11-1
TF: 800-352-6931 ■ *Web:* indexfresh.com

Index Funds Advisors Inc
19200 Von Karman Ave Ste 150 .... Irvine CA 92612 949-502-0050 690
TF: 888-643-3133 ■ *Web:* www.ifa.com

Index Journal 610 Phoenix St .... Greenwood SC 29648 864-223-1411 223-7331 532-2
Web: www.indexjournal.com

Index Packaging Inc 1055 White Mtn Hwy .... Milton NH 03851 800-662-3626 601
TF: 800-662-3626 ■ *Web:* www.indexpackaging.com

Indexing Partners LLC
19266 Coastal Hwy Ste 4-52 .... Rehoboth Beach DE 19971 302-644-7466 102
Web: www.indexingpartners.com

Indexing Technologies Inc
37 Orchard St .... Ramsey NJ 07446 201-934-6333 358
Web: www.ititooling.com

Indexx Inc 303 Haywood Rd .... Greenville SC 29607 864-234-1024 627
TF: 800-252-8227 ■ *Web:* www.indexx.com

India
Consulate General
540 Arguello Blvd .... San Francisco CA 94118 415-668-0662 668-9764 257
Web: www.cgisf.org
Embassy 2107 Massachusetts Ave NW .... Washington DC 20008 202-939-7000 265-4351 257
Web: www.indianembassy.org

India Bistro 2301 NW Market St .... Seattle WA 98107 206-783-5080 297-9069 671
Web: www.seattleindiabistro.com

India Community Center Inc
525 Los Coches St .... Milpitas CA 95035 408-934-1130 354
Web: www.indiacc.org

India Garden
830 Broad Ripple Ave .... Indianapolis IN 46220 317-253-6060 253-2832 671
Web: www.indiagardenindy.com

India Garden Restaurant
1107 N Broadway .... Rochester MN 55906 507-288-6280 671
Web: www.india-garden-restaurant-halal-restaurant.business.site

India Globalization Capital Inc
4336 Montgomery Ave .... Bethesda MD 20814 301-983-0998 465-0273* 188-4
NYSE: IGC ■ *Fax Area Code: 240 ■ *Web:* www.igcinc.us

India K'Raja 9051 W Broad St .... Richmond VA 23294 804-965-6345 671
Web: www.indiakraja.com

India Mahal 5970 Brainerd Rd .... Chattanooga TN 37421 423-634-8899 671
Web: www.dinnerdeliveredonline.org

India Oven 1031 Patricia Dr .... San Antonio TX 78213 210-366-1030 671
Web: www.indiaovensa.com

India Palace 227 Don Gaspar Ave .... Santa Fe NM 87501 505-986-5859 671

India Palace 4213 Lafayette Rd .... Indianapolis IN 46254 317-298-0773 671
Web: www.indiapalaceindy.com

India Palace 1720 Poplar Ave .... Memphis TN 38104 901-278-1199 671
Web: www.indiapalacememphis.com

India Palace 377 Ct St .... Salem OR 97301 503-371-4808 671
Web: www.indiapalacesalem.com

India Palace 2941 W Bell Rd .... Phoenix AZ 85053 602-942-4224 671
Web: indiapalacephoenix.com

India Palace 319 W Superior St .... Duluth MN 55802 218-727-8767 671
Web: www.indiapalaceduluth.com

India Palace Restaurant
12817 Preston Rd Ste 105 .... Dallas TX 75230 972-392-0190 671
Web: www.indiapalacedallas.com

India Palace Restaurant
6963 S Lewis Ave .... Tulsa OK 74136 918-492-8040 671
Web: theindiapalacetulsa.com

India Palace Restaurant
8474 Fredericksburg Rd .... San Antonio TX 78229 210-692-5262 671
Web: www.indiapalacesatx.com

India Quality 484 Commonwealth Ave .... Boston MA 02215 617-267-4499 267-4477 671
Web: www.indiaquality.com

India Tourist Office
1270 Ave of the Americas Ste 303 .... New York NY 10020 212-586-4901 775
Web: tourism.gov.in

India's Oven 11645 Wilshire Blvd .... Los Angeles CA 90025 310-207-5522 671
Web: www.laindiasoven.com

India's Restaurant 5230 Essen Ln .... Baton Rouge LA 70809 225-769-0600 671
Web: www.indiasbr.com

India's Restaurant 8921 E Hampden Ave .... Denver CO 80231 303-755-4284 752-9814 671
Web: www.indiasrestaurant.com

India's Tandoori
5468 Wilshire Blvd .... Los Angeles CA 90036 323-936-2050 936-0187 671
Web: www.indiastandoori.net

Indian Arts & Crafts Board
1849 C St NW MS 2528-MIB .... Washington DC 20240 202-208-3773 208-5196 340-20
TF: 888-278-3253 ■ *Web:* www.doi.gov

Indian Bible College
2237 E Cedar Ave .... Flagstaff AZ 86004 928-774-3890 774-2655 166
TF: 866-503-7789 ■ *Web:* www.indianbible.org

Indian Capital Technology Ctr
2403 N 41st St E .... Muskogee OK 74403 918-687-6383 800
TF: 800-757-0877 ■ *Web:* www.ictctech.com

Indian Creek Fabricators
1350 Commerce Pk Dr .... Tipp City OH 45371 937-667-5818 667-4093 757
TF: 877-769-5880 ■ *Web:* www.indiancreekfab.com

Indian Creek Foundation
420 Cowpath Rd .... Souderton PA 18964 267-203-1500 726
Web: www.indcreek.org

Indian Creek Nature Ctr
6665 Otis Rd SE .... Cedar Rapids IA 52403 319-362-0664 50-5
Web: www.indiancreeknaturecenter.org

Indian Creek Recreation Area
12905 288th Ave .... Glenham SD 57631 605-845-7112 565
Web: gfp.sd.gov

Indian Electric Co-opeartive Inc
2506 E Hwy 64 .... Cleveland OK 74020 918-295-9500 245
TF: 800-482-2750 ■ *Web:* www.iecok.com

Indian Garden 247 E Ontario St 2nd Fl .... Chicago IL 60611 312-280-4910 280-4934 671
Web: www.indiangardenchicago.com

Indian Grinding Rock State Historic Park
14881 Pine Grove-Volcano Rd .... Pine Grove CA 95665 209-296-7488 565
Web: www.parks.ca.gov

Indian Harvest Specialtifoods Inc
1012 Paul Bunyan Dr SE .... Bemidji MN 56601 800-346-7032 751-8519* 296-23
*Fax Area Code: 218 ■ *TF:* 800-346-7032 ■ *Web:* www.inharvest.com

Indian Head Industries Inc
8530 Cliff Cameron Dr .... Charlotte NC 28269 704-547-7411 547-9367 60
TF: 800-527-1534 ■ *Web:* mgmbrakes.com

Indian Hills Community College
525 Grandview Ave .... Ottumwa IA 52501 641-683-5111 683-5741 162
TF: 800-726-2585 ■ *Web:* www.indianhills.edu

Indian Hills Resort 7276 14th NW .... Garrison ND 58540 701-743-4122 565
Web: www.fishindianhills.com

Indian Hot Springs
302 Soda Creek Rd PO Box 1990 .... Idaho Springs CO 80452 303-989-6666 669
TF: 800-884-3201 ■ *Web:* www.indianhotsprings.com

Indian Hotels Company Ltd, The
1270 Avenue of the Americas 7th Fl .... New York NY 10020 646-330-4557 379
Web: www.tajhotels.com

Indian King Tavern State Historic Site
233 Kings Hwy .... Haddonfield NJ 08033 856-429-6792 565
Web: www.njparksandforests.org

Indian Lake State Park
8970W County Rd 442 .... Manistique MI 49854 906-341-2355 565
Web: www.michigan.org

Indian Mountain School
211 Indian Mtn Rd .... Lakeville CT 06039 860-435-0871 435-0641 622
Web: www.indianmountain.org

Indian Mountain State Park
143 State Pk Cir .... Jellico TN 37762 423-566-5870 565
Web: tnstateparks.com

Indian Oven 1010 Howard St .... Omaha NE 68102 402-342-4856 671
Web: www.findmeglutenfree.com

Indian Oven 233 Fillmore St .... San Francisco CA 94117 415-626-1628 255-6116 671
Web: www.indianovensf.com

Indian Oven 427 E Main St .... Columbus OH 43215 614-220-9390 671
Web: www.indianoven.com

Indian Pueblo Cultural Ctr
2401 12th St NW .... Albuquerque NM 87104 505-843-7270 520
TF: 866-855-7902 ■ *Web:* www.indianpueblo.org

Indian River County 1801 27th St .... Vero Beach FL 32960 772-567-8000 978-1822 338
Web: www.ircgov.com

Indian River County Chamber of Commerce
1216 21st St .... Vero Beach FL 32960 772-567-3491 778-3181 139
Web: www.indianriverchamber.com

Indian River County Library (IRCL)
1600 21st St .... Vero Beach FL 32960 772-770-5060 770-5066 434-3
Web: www.irclibrary.org

Indian River Exchange Packers Inc
7355 9th St SW .... Vero Beach FL 32968 772-562-2252 11-1
Web: irexp.com

Indian River Home Care Inc
65 Royal Palm Pt Ste A .... Vero Beach FL 32960 772-569-3885 363
Web: indianriverhomecare.com

Indian River Juvenile Correctional Facility
2775 Indian River Rd SW .... Massillon OH 44646 330-837-4211 837-4740 412
Web: www.dys.ohio.gov

Name / Address	City	State	ZIP	Phone	Fax	Class
Indian River Lifesaving Station Museum 25039 Costal Hwy *Web:* www.destateparks.com	Rehoboth Beach	DE	19971	302-227-6991	227-6438	520
Indian River Medical Ctr 1000 36th St *Web:* www.indianrivermedicalcenter.com	Vero Beach	FL	32960	772-567-4311	562-5628	374-3
Indian River State College (IRSC) 3209 Virginia Ave *TF:* 866-792-4772 ■ *Web:* www.irsc.edu	Fort Pierce	FL	34981	772-462-4772	462-4699	162
Indian River Transport Co 2580 Executive Rd *TF:* 800-877-2430 ■ *Web:* www.indianrivertransport.com	Winter Haven	FL	33884	863-324-2430	326-9702	780
Indian Rocks Road Acute Rehabilitation 2025 Indian Rocks Rd *Web:* largomedical.com	Largo	FL	33774	727-588-5200		374-3
Indian Springs Manufacturing Company Inc 2095 W Genesse Rd *Web:* www.indiansprings.com	Baldwinsville	NY	13027	315-635-6101		326
Indian Springs Resort & Spa 1712 Lincoln Ave *TF:* 800-877-3623 ■ *Web:* www.indianspringscalistoga.com	Calistoga	CA	94515	707-709-8139	942-4919	669
Indian Springs School 190 Woodward Dr *TF:* 888-843-9477 ■ *Web:* www.indiansprings.org	Pelham	AL	35124	205-988-3350	988-3797	622
Indian Springs State Park 678 Lake Clark Rd *Web:* gastateparks.org	Flovilla	GA	30216	770-504-2277		565
Indian Summer Carpet Mills Inc 601 Callahan Rd PO Box 3577 *TF:* 800-824-4010 ■ *Web:* www.southwindcarpet.com	Dalton	GA	30719	706-277-6277	279-1884	131
Indian Temple Mound Museum 107 Miracle Strip Pkwy SW *TF:* 866-847-1301 ■ *Web:* www.fwb.org	Fort Walton Beach	FL	32548	850-833-9500	833-9640	520
Indian Trails Inc 109 E Comstock St *TF:* 800-292-3831 ■ *Web:* www.indiantrails.com	Owosso	MI	48867	989-725-5105		107
Indian Valley Bulk Carriers Inc 74 Ridge Rd *Web:* www.ivbulk.com	Tylersport	PA	18971	215-257-5151		519
Indian Valley Chamber of Commerce 100 Penn Ave *Web:* www.indianvalleychamber.com	Telford	PA	18969	215-723-9472	723-2490	139
Indian Valley Industries Inc PO Box 810 *TF:* 800-659-5111 ■ *Web:* www.iviindustries.com	Johnson City	NY	13790	607-729-5111	729-5158	67
Indian Well State Park c/o Osbornedale State Pk 555 Roosevelt Dr *Web:* portal.ct.gov	Derby	CT	06418	203-735-4311		565
Indian Wells Resort Hotel 76-661 Hwy 111 *TF:* 800-248-3220 ■ *Web:* www.indianwellsresort.com	Indian Wells	CA	92210	760-345-6466	772-5083	669
Indiana						
Consumer Protection Div 402 W Washington St Rm W-478 *Web:* www.in.gov	Indianapolis	IN	46204	317-232-3001	233-4613	339-15
Disability Aging & Rehabilitative Services Div 402 W Washington St Ste W453 PO Box 7083 *TF:* 800-545-7763 ■ *Web:* www.in.gov	Indianapolis	IN	46207	317-542-3449	232-1240	339-15
Economic Development Corp 1 N Capitol Ave Ste 700 *TF:* 800-463-8081 ■ *Web:* www.iedc.in.gov	Indianapolis	IN	46204	317-232-8800	232-4146	339-15
Education Dept 115 W Washington St South Tower Ste 600 *Web:* www.doe.in.gov	Indianapolis	IN	46204	317-232-6610	232-8004	339-15
Finance Authority 302 W Washington St Rm E120 *Web:* www.in.gov	Indianapolis	IN	46204	317-233-4332	232-6786	339-15
Health Dept 2 N Meridian St *TF:* 800-382-9480 ■ *Web:* www.in.gov	Indianapolis	IN	46204	317-233-7451		339-15
Higher Education Commission 402 W Washington St Rm W160 *Web:* www.in.gov	Indianapolis	IN	46204	317-464-4400	464-4410	339-15
Horse Racing Commission 1302 N Meridian Ste 175 *Web:* www.in.gov	Indianapolis	IN	46204	317-233-3119		712
Housing Finance Authority 30 S Meridian St Ste 1000 *TF:* 800-872-0371 ■ *Web:* www.in.gov	Indianapolis	IN	46204	317-232-7777		339-15
Insurance Dept 311 W Washington St Ste 300 *TF:* 800-622-4461 ■ *Web:* www.in.gov	Indianapolis	IN	46204	317-232-2385	232-5251	339-15
Labor Dept 402 W Washington St Rm W195 *Web:* www.in.gov	Indianapolis	IN	46204	317-233-4613		339-15
Lieutenant Governor 302 W Washington St Rm E018 *Web:* in.gov	Indianapolis	IN	46204	317-232-4711		339-15
Port Commission 150 W Market St Ste 100 *TF:* 800-232-7678 ■ *Web:* www.portsofindiana.com	Indianapolis	IN	46204	317-232-9200	232-0137	618
Revenue Dept 100 N Senate Ave Rm N105 *TF:* 800-677-9800 ■ *Web:* www.in.gov	Indianapolis	IN	46204	800-453-4756		339-15
Secretary of State 200 W Washington St Rm 201 *Web:* www.in.gov	Indianapolis	IN	46204	317-232-2688	233-3283	339-15
Securities Div 302 W Washington St 5th Fl *TF:* 800-382-5516 ■ *Web:* www.in.gov	Indianapolis	IN	46204	317-232-6201	232-7979	339-15
State Court Administration Div 30 S Meridian St Ste 500 *Web:* www.in.gov	Indianapolis	IN	46204	317-232-2542	233-6586	339-15
Students Assistance Commission 150 W Market St Rm 414 *TF:* 888-528-4719 ■ *Web:* www.in.gov	Indianapolis	IN	46204	317-233-2100	232-3260	725
Supreme Court 200 W Washington St *Web:* www.in.gov	Indianapolis	IN	46204	317-232-2540		339-15
Technology Office 100 N Senate Ave Rm N551 *TF:* 800-382-1095 ■ *Web:* www.in.gov	Indianapolis	IN	46204	317-233-2072		339-15
Tourism Development Office 1 N Capitol Ave Ste 600 *TF:* 800-457-8283 ■ *Web:* www.in.gov	Indianapolis	IN	46204	317-232-8860	233-6887	339-15
Transportation Dept 100 N Senate Ave Rm N755 *Web:* www.in.gov	Indianapolis	IN	46204	317-232-5533	232-0238	339-15
Treasurer 200 W Washington St Ste 242 *Web:* www.in.gov	Indianapolis	IN	46204	317-232-0002		339-15
Veterans' Affairs Dept 302 W Washington St Rm E418 *TF:* 800-400-4520 ■ *Web:* www.in.gov	Indianapolis	IN	46204	317-232-3910	232-7721	339-15
Victims Services Div 101 W Washington St East Tower Ste 1170 *TF:* 800-353-1484 ■ *Web:* www.in.gov	Indianapolis	IN	46204	317-232-1289	233-3912	339-15
Vital Records Office PO Box 7125 *Web:* www.cdc.gov	Indianapolis	IN	46206	317-233-2700		339-15
Workforce Development Dept 402 W Washington St Rm W160 *TF:* 800-891-6499 ■ *Web:* www.in.gov	Indianapolis	IN	46204	317-232-4200		259
Indiana Association of Realtors 320 N Meridian St Ste 428 *TF:* 800-284-0084 ■ *Web:* www.indianarealtors.com	Indianapolis	IN	46204	800-284-0084		656
Indiana Association of School Principals Inc 11025 E 25th St *Web:* www.iasp.org	Indianapolis	IN	46229	317-891-9900		533
Indiana Automotive Fasteners Inc 1300 Anderson Blvd *Web:* www.iafi.com	Greenfield	IN	46140	317-467-0100		278
Indiana Bankers Assn 8425 Woodfield Crossing Blvd Ste 155E *Web:* indianabankers.org	Indianapolis	IN	46240	317-387-9380		70
Indiana Basketball Hall of Fame 408 Trojan Ln *Web:* www.hoopshall.com	New Castle	IN	47362	765-529-1891	529-0273	522
Indiana Beach 5224 E Indiana Beach Rd *Web:* www.indianabeach.com	Monticello	IN	47960	574-583-4141		32
Indiana Black Expo Inc 3145 N Meridian St *Web:* www.indianablackexpo.com	Indianapolis	IN	46208	317-925-2702	925-6624	138
Indiana Bottle Company Inc 300 W Lovers Ln *Web:* indianabottle.com	Scottsburg	IN	47170	812-752-8700		604
Indiana Carbon Company Inc 3164 N Shadeland Ave *TF:* 800-547-2233 ■ *Web:* www.iccbusinessproducts.com	Indianapolis	IN	46226	317-547-9621	543-5738	174
Indiana Convention Center & Lucas Oil Stadium (ICCLOS) 100 S Capitol Ave *Web:* icclos.com	Indianapolis	IN	46225	317-262-3400	262-3685	205
Indiana County 825 Philadelphia St 3rd Fl *TF:* 888-559-6355 ■ *Web:* www.countyofindiana.org	Indiana	PA	15701	724-465-3805	465-3953	338
Indiana County Chamber of Commerce 1019 Philadelphia St *Web:* www.indianacountychamber.us	Indiana	PA	15701	724-465-2511		139
Indiana County Tourist Bureau 2334 Oakland Ave Ste 68 *TF:* 877-746-3426 ■ *Web:* visitindianacountypa.org	Indiana	PA	15701	724-463-7505	465-3819	206
Indiana Credit Union League 5975 Castle Creek Pkwy N Ste 300 *TF:* 800-285-5300 ■ *Web:* www.icul.org	Indianapolis	IN	46250	317-594-5300		219
Indiana Democratic Party 115 W Washington St Ste 1165 *TF:* 800-223-3387 ■ *Web:* www.indems.org	Indianapolis	IN	46204	317-231-7100	231-7129	616-1
Indiana Dental Assn 1319 East S-10 Rd *TF:* 800-562-5646 ■ *Web:* indental.org	Indianapolis	IN	46227	317-634-2610	634-2612	227
Indiana Dimension Inc 1621 W Market St *TF:* 888-875-4434 ■ *Web:* indianadimension.com	Logansport	IN	46947	888-875-4434		683
Indiana Donor Network 3760 Guion Rd *TF:* 888-275-4676 ■ *Web:* indianadonornetwork.org	Indianapolis	IN	46222	888-275-4676		545
Indiana Dunes National Lakeshore 1100 N Mineral Springs Rd *Web:* www.nps.gov	Porter	IN	46304	219-395-1767	926-7561	564
Indiana Dunes State Park 1600 N 25 E *Web:* www.in.gov	Chesterton	IN	46304	219-926-1952		565
Indiana Dunes the Casual Coast 1215 N State Rd 49 *TF:* 800-283-8687 ■ *Web:* www.indianadunes.com	Porter	IN	46304	219-926-2255	929-5395	206
Indiana Farm Bureau Insurance Co 225 SE St PO Box 1250 *TF:* 800-723-3276 ■ *Web:* www.infarmbureau.com	Indianapolis	IN	46206	317-692-7200		391-2
Indiana Farmers Mutual Insurance Co 10 W 106th St *TF:* 800-477-1660 ■ *Web:* insurance.indianafarmers.com	Indianapolis	IN	46290	800-477-1660		391-4
Indiana Football Hall of Fame 815 N A St PO Box 40 *Web:* www.indiana-football.org	Richmond	IN	47375	765-966-2235	966-5700	522
Indiana Furniture 1224 Mill St *TF:* 800-422-5727 ■ *Web:* www.indianafurniture.com	Jasper	IN	47546	812-482-5727	482-9035	319-1
Indiana Gazette, The 899 Water St *Web:* www.indianagazette.com	Indiana	PA	15701	724-465-5555	465-8267	637-8
Indiana Harbor Belt Railroad Co 2721 161st St *Web:* www.ihbrr.com	Hammond	IN	46323	219-989-4703	989-4707	651
Indiana Hardwood Specialists Inc 4341 N US Hwy 231 *Web:* indianahardwoodspec.com	Spencer	IN	47460	812-829-4866	829-4860	683
Indiana Health Information Exchange Inc 846 N Senate Ave Ste 300 *Web:* www.ihie.org	Indianapolis	IN	46202	317-644-1750		194

				Phone	Fax	Class
Indiana Heat Transfer Corp						
500 W Harrison St	Plymouth	IN	46563	574-936-3171	935-8200	61
Web: www.ihtc.net						
Indiana Knitwear Corp						
230 E Osage St	Greenfield	IN	46140	317-462-4413		155-12
Indiana Landmarks						
1201 Central Ave	Indianapolis	IN	46202	317-639-4534	639-6734	50-3
TF: 800-450-4534 ■ *Web:* indianalandmarks.org						
Indiana Library Federation (ILF)						
941 E 86th St Ste 260	Indianapolis	IN	46240	317-257-2040	257-1389	435
TF: 800-326-0013 ■ *Web:* www.ilfonline.org						
Indiana Manufactured Housing Association-Recreation Vehicle Indiana Council (IMHA-RVIC)						
3210 Rand Rd	Indianapolis	IN	46241	317-247-6258	243-9174	139
Web: www.imharvic.org						
Indiana Medical History Museum						
3045 W Vermont St	Indianapolis	IN	46222	317-635-7329		520
Web: imhm.org						
Indiana Members Credit Union (IMCU)						
7110 W Tenth St	Indianapolis	IN	46214	317-248-8556		219
TF: 800-556-9268 ■ *Web:* www.imcu.com						
Indiana Memorial Union Board						
900 E Seventh St Rm 270	Bloomington	IN	47405	812-855-4682		379
Web: imu.indiana.edu						
Indiana Mills & Manufacturing Inc						
18881 US 31 N	Westfield	IN	46074	317-896-9531	896-2142	576
Web: www.imminet.com						
Indiana Oxygen Company Inc						
6099 W Corporate Way	Indianapolis	IN	46278	317-290-0003	328-5009	146
TF: 800-325-7314 ■ *Web:* www.indianaoxygen.com						
Indiana Pharmacists						
9449 Priority Way W Dr Ste 230	Indianapolis	IN	46240	317-634-4968	632-1219	585
Web: www.indianapharmacists.org						
Indiana Philanthropy Alliance (IPA)						
32 E Washington St Ste 1100	Indianapolis	IN	46204	317-630-5200	630-5210	48-13
Web: www.inphilanthropy.org						
Indiana Rail Road Co, The						
1500 S Senate Ave Ste 1600	Indianapolis	IN	46225	317-262-5140		649
TF: 888-596-2121 ■ *Web:* www.inrd.com						
Indiana Regional Medical Ctr						
835 Hospital Rd	Indiana	PA	15701	724-357-7000	357-7449	374-3
Web: www.indianarmc.org						
Indiana Repertory Theatre Inc						
140 W Washington St	Indianapolis	IN	46204	317-635-5277	236-0767	573-4
Web: www.irtlive.com						
Indiana Republican Party						
101 W Ohio St Ste 2200	Indianapolis	IN	46204	317-635-7561	632-8510	616-2
Web: indiana.gop						
Indiana Ribbon Inc 106 N Second St	Wolcott	IN	47995	219-279-2112		548
TF: 800-531-3100 ■ *Web:* www.giftwrapgifts.com						
Indiana Rural Health Assn						
2901 Ohio Blvd Ste 240	Terre Haute	IN	47803	812-478-3919		78
Web: www.indianaruralhealth.org						
Indiana Soybean Alliance (ISA)						
8425 Keystone Crossing Ste 200	Indianapolis	IN	46240	317-347-3620	347-3626	139
TF: 800-735-0195 ■ *Web:* www.indianasoybean.com						
Indiana State Afl-Cio						
2917 Roosevelt Ave	Indianapolis	IN	46218	317-529-9839		414
Web: inaflcio.org						
Indiana State Bar Assn						
1 Indiana Sq Ste 530	Indianapolis	IN	46204	317-639-5465	266-2588	72
TF: 800-266-2581 ■ *Web:* www.inbar.org						
Indiana State Chamber of Commerce						
115 W Washington St Ste 850-S	Indianapolis	IN	46204	317-264-3110	264-6855	140
TF: 800-824-6885 ■ *Web:* www.indianachamber.com						
Indiana State Fairgrounds						
1202 E 38th St	Indianapolis	IN	46205	317-927-7500	927-7695	642
Web: www.in.gov						
Indiana State Medical Assn						
322 Canal Walk	Indianapolis	IN	46202	317-261-2060	261-2076	474
TF: 800-257-4762 ■ *Web:* www.ismanet.org						
Indiana State Museum						
650 W Washington St	Indianapolis	IN	46204	317-232-1637		520
TF: 800-382-9842 ■ *Web:* www.in.gov						
Indiana State Nurses Assn (ISNA)						
2915 N High School Rd	Indianapolis	IN	46224	317-299-4575	297-3525	533
Web: www.indiananurses.org						
Indiana State Prison 1 Pk Row	Michigan City	IN	46360	219-874-7258		213
Web: www.in.gov						
Indiana State University						
200 N Seventh St	Terre Haute	IN	47809	800-468-6478	237-8023*	166
**Fax Area Code:* 812 ■ *TF:* 800-468-6478 ■ *Web:* indstate.edu						
Indiana Steel Fabricating Inc						
4545 W Bradbury Ave	Indianapolis	IN	46241	317-247-4545		480
Web: indianasteelfabricating.com						
Indiana Sugars Inc 911 Virginia St	Gary	IN	46402	219-886-9151	886-5124	297-11
Web: www.sugars.com						
Indiana Tech						
1600 E Washington Blvd	Fort Wayne	IN	46803	260-422-5561	422-7696	166
TF: 800-937-2448 ■ *Web:* www.indianatech.edu						
Indiana Trust & Investment Management Co						
4045 Edison Lakes Pkwy Ste 100	Mishawaka	IN	46545	574-271-3400		796
TF: 800-362-7905 ■ *Web:* www.indtrust.com						
Indiana Tube Corp						
2100 Lexington Ave	Evansville	IN	47720	812-424-9028	424-8195	595
Web: www.indianatube.com						
Indiana University						
107 S Indiana Ave	Bloomington	IN	47405	812-855-4848		167-3
Web: www.indiana.edu						
Indiana University						
East 2325 Chester Blvd	Richmond	IN	47374	765-973-8208	973-8288	166
TF: 800-959-3278 ■ *Web:* www.iue.edu						
Kokomo 2300 S Washington St PO Box 9003	Kokomo	IN	46904	765-455-9217	455-9537	166
TF: 888-875-4485 ■ *Web:* www.iuk.edu						
Northwest 3400 Broadway	Gary	IN	46408	219-980-6500	981-4219	166
TF: 888-968-7486 ■ *Web:* www.iun.edu						
South Bend						
1700 Mishawaka Ave PO Box 7111	South Bend	IN	46634	574-520-4870		166
TF: 877-462-4872 ■ *Web:* www.iusb.edu						

				Phone	Fax	Class
Southeast 4201 Grant Line Rd	New Albany	IN	47150	812-941-2212	941-2595	166
TF: 800-852-8835 ■ *Web:* www.ius.edu						
Indiana University Archives of African American Music and Culture						
2805 E 10th St Ste 180-181	Bloomington	IN	47408	812-855-8547	856-0333	434-3
Web: aaamc.indiana.edu						
Indiana University Auditorium						
1211 E Seventh St	Bloomington	IN	47405	812-855-1103	855-4244	572
Web: www.iuauditorium.com						
Indiana University Bloomington						
Libraries 1320 E Tenth St	Bloomington	IN	47405	812-855-8028	855-2576	434-6
Web: libraries.indiana.edu						
Indiana University Hospital						
550 N University Blvd	Indianapolis	IN	46202	317-274-5000		374-3
TF: 800-248-1199 ■ *Web:* iuhealth.org						
Indiana University Melvin & Bren Simon Cancer Ctr						
535 Barnhill Dr	Indianapolis	IN	46202	317-278-0070		769
TF: 888-600-4822 ■ *Web:* cancer.iu.edu						
Indiana University of Pennsylvania						
1011 South Dr	Indiana	PA	15705	724-357-2100	357-6281	166
TF: 800-442-6830 ■ *Web:* www.iup.edu						
Indiana University Press						
1320 E 10th St E4	Bloomington	IN	47405	812-855-8817	855-8507	637-4
TF: 800-842-6796 ■ *Web:* iupress.org						
Indiana University School of Law Bloomington						
211 S Indiana Ave	Bloomington	IN	47405	812-855-7995	855-0555	167-1
Web: www.law.indiana.edu						
Indiana University School of Law Indianapolis						
Lawrence W Inlow Hall 530 W New York St	Indianapolis	IN	46202	317-274-8523	274-3955	167-1
Web: mckinneylaw.iu.edu						
Indiana University School of Medicine						
340 W Tenth St Ste 6200	Indianapolis	IN	46202	317-274-8157		167-2
TF: 888-484-3258 ■ *Web:* medicine.iu.edu						
Indiana University-Purdue University						
Columbus 4601 Central Ave	Columbus	IN	47203	812-348-7271	348-7257	166
Web: www.iupuc.edu						
Fort Wayne 2101 E Coliseum Blvd	Fort Wayne	IN	46805	260-481-6100	481-6880	166
TF: 800-324-4739 ■ *Web:* www.pfw.edu						
Indianapolis 425 University Blvd	Indianapolis	IN	46202	317-274-5555		166
Web: www.iupui.edu						
Indiana University-Purdue University Indianapolis						
Library 755 W Michigan St	Indianapolis	IN	46202	317-274-0462	278-2300	434-6
TF: 888-422-0499 ■ *Web:* www.ulib.iupui.edu						
Indiana Veterans Home						
3851 N River Rd	West Lafayette	IN	47906	765-463-1502		793
Web: www.in.gov						
Indiana Veterinary Medical Assn						
1202 E 38th St Discovery Hall Ste 200	Indianapolis	IN	46205	317-974-0888	974-0985	795
TF: 800-270-0747 ■ *Web:* invma.org						
Indiana Wesleyan University						
4201 S Washington St	Marion	IN	46953	765-677-2138	677-2333	166
TF: 800-332-6901 ■ *Web:* www.indwes.edu						
Indiana Women's Prison						
2596 N Girls School Rd	Indianapolis	IN	46214	317-244-3387	244-4670	213
Web: www.in.gov						
Indianapolis Art Ctr						
820 E 67th St	Indianapolis	IN	46220	317-255-2464		50-2
Web: www.indplsartcenter.org						
Indianapolis Artsgarden						
924 N Pennsylvania St	Indianapolis	IN	46204	317-624-2563		572
Web: indyarts.org						
Indianapolis Business Journal (IBJ)						
41 E Washington St Ste 200	Indianapolis	IN	46204	317-634-6200	263-5060	457-5
TF: 800-428-7081 ■ *Web:* www.ibj.com						
Indianapolis Colts						
7001 W 56th St	Indianapolis	IN	46254	317-297-2658	297-8971	715-3
TF: 800-805-2658 ■ *Web:* www.colts.com						
Indianapolis Convention & Visitors Assn						
200 S Capitol Ave Ste 300	Indianapolis	IN	46225	317-262-3000		206
TF: 800-862-6912 ■ *Web:* www.visitindy.com						
Indianapolis Fruit Company Inc						
4501 Massachusetts Ave	Indianapolis	IN	46218	317-546-2425		297-7
TF: 800-377-2425 ■ *Web:* indyfruit.com						
Indianapolis International Airport						
7800 Col H Weir Cook Memorial Dr	Indianapolis	IN	46241	317-487-5025	487-5325	194
Web: www.indianapolisairport.com						
Indianapolis Monthly Magazine						
40 Monument Cir Ste 100	Indianapolis	IN	46204	317-237-9288	684-2080	457-22
TF: 888-403-9005 ■ *Web:* www.indianapolismonthly.com						
Indianapolis Motor Speedway & Hall of Fame Museum						
4790 W 16th St	Indianapolis	IN	46222	317-492-6747		520
Web: www.indianapolismotorspeedway.com						
Indianapolis Opera						
4011 N Pennsylvania St	Indianapolis	IN	46205	317-283-3531		573-2
Web: www.indyopera.org						
Indianapolis Power & Light Co						
1 Monument Cir	Indianapolis	IN	46204	317-261-8261		787
TF: 888-261-8222 ■ *Web:* www.iplpower.com						
Indianapolis Public Schools						
120 E Walnut St	Indianapolis	IN	46204	317-226-4000		685
Web: www.myips.org						
Indianapolis Public Transportation Corp						
1501 W Washington St	Indianapolis	IN	46222	317-635-2100	634-6585	108
Web: www.indygo.net						
Indianapolis Star						
307 N Pennsylvania St	Indianapolis	IN	46204	317-444-8045		532-2
TF: 800-669-7827 ■ *Web:* www.indystar.com						
Indianapolis Symphony Orchestra						
45 Monument Cir	Indianapolis	IN	46204	317-262-1100		573-3
TF: 800-366-8457 ■ *Web:* www.indianapolissymphony.org						
Indianapolis Zoo						
1200 W Washington St	Indianapolis	IN	46222	317-630-2001	630-5153	823
Web: www.indianapoliszoo.com						
Indianhead Federated Library System						
1538 Truax Blvd	Eau Claire	WI	54703	715-839-5082	839-5151	434-3
TF: 800-321-5427 ■ *Web:* iflsweb.org						
Indiantown Gap National Cemetery						
Indiantown Gap Rd RR 2 PO Box 484	Annville	PA	17003	717-865-5254	865-5256	136
Web: www.cem.va.gov						

Name / Address	City	State	Zip	Phone	Fax	Class
Indice Mode						
5401 Boul Des Galeries Ste 243	Quebec City	QC	G2K1N4	418-624-9330		157-6
Web: www.indicemode.com						
Indicom Buildings Inc						
721 N Burleson Blvd	Burleson	TX	76028	817-447-1213	447-2751	106
Web: www.indicombuildings.com						
Indicon Corp 6125 Center Dr	Sterling Heights	MI	48312	586-274-0505		729
Web: www.indicon.com						
Indiemark LLC 801 Broad St Ste 603	Augusta	GA	30901	917-558-5264		5
Web: www.indiemark.com						
Indiggo Associates Inc						
4600 E W Hwy Ste 875	Bethesda	MD	20814	240-314-0533		193
Web: indiggolead.com						
Indigo 3013 Lindbergh Blvd	Springfield	IL	62704	217-726-3487		671
Web: www.indigocuisine.com						
Indigo BioSystems Inc						
385 City Center Dr Ste 200	Carmel	IN	46032	317-493-2400		177
Web: www.indigobio.com						
Indigo Books & Music Inc						
468 King St W Ste 500	Toronto	ON	M5V1L8	416-364-4499	364-0355	95
TSX: IDG ■ *TF:* 800-832-7569 ■ *Web:* www.chapters.indigo.ca						
Indigo Dynamic Networks LLC						
2413 W Algonquin Rd	Algonquin	IL	60102	888-464-6344		180
TF: 888-464-6344 ■ *Web:* ezbookit.com						
Indigo Inn 1 Maiden Ln	Charleston	SC	29401	843-577-5900		379
Web: www.indigoinn.com						
Indigo ORB Inc 2454 Alton Pkwy	Irvine	CA	92606	949-784-0303		475
Web: www.indigo-orb.com						
Indigo Rose Corp						
123 Bannatyne Ave Ste 200	Winnipeg	MB	R3B0R3	204-946-0263		179
TF: 800-665-9668 ■ *Web:* www.indigorose.com						
Indika 516 Westheimer Rd	Houston	TX	77006	713-524-2170	984-1755	671
Web: indikausa.com						
Indio Chamber of Commerce						
82921 Indio Blvd	Indio	CA	92201	760-347-0676		139
Web: www.gcvcc.org						
Indique 3512 Connecticut Ave NW	Washington	DC	20008	202-244-6600		671
Web: www.indique.com						
Indira Publishing House						
PO Box 250456	West Bloomfield	MI	48325	248-661-2529		637-9
Web: www.indirapublishinghouse.com						
IndiSoft LLC 5550 Sterrett Pl Ste 311	Columbia	MD	21044	410-730-0667		174
Web: www.indisoft.us						
Indital USA Ltd 7947 Mesa Dr	Houston	TX	77028	800-772-4706		191-1
TF: 800-772-4706 ■ *Web:* www.indital.com						
Individual Commercial Brokerage Inc						
500 International Dr Ste 305	Budd Lake	NJ	07828	800-422-0696		390
TF: 800-422-0696 ■ *Web:* icbinsures.com						
Individual Software Inc						
4255 Hopyard Rd Ste 2	Pleasanton	CA	94588	925-734-6767	734-8337	178-3
TF: 800-822-3522 ■ *Web:* www.individualsoftware.com						
Individualized Shirts						
581 Cortland St	Perth Amboy	NJ	08861	732-826-8400		155-12
Web: individualizedshirts.com						
Indmar Products Company Inc						
5400 Old Millington Rd	Millington	TN	38053	901-353-9930		698
Web: www.indmar.com						
Indochine Asian Dining Lounge						
1924 Pacific Ave	Tacoma	WA	98402	253-272-8200		671
Web: www.indochinedowntown.com						
Indoff Inc 11816 Lackland Rd	Saint Louis	MO	63146	314-997-1122	812-3932	385
TF: 800-486-7867 ■ *Web:* www.indoff.com						
Indonesia						
Consulate General						
211 W Wacker Dr 8th Fl	Chicago	IL	60606	312-920-1880	920-1881	257
Web: www.indonesiachicago.org						
Consulate General 5 E 68th St	New York	NY	10065	212-879-0600	570-6206	257
Web: www.kemlu.go.id						
Embassy 2020 Massachusetts Ave NW	Washington	DC	20036	202-775-5200	775-5365	257
Web: www.embassyofindonesia.org						
Indoor Purification Systems Inc						
Surround Air Div						
334 N Marshall Way Ste C	Layton	UT	84041	801-547-1162	991-4838	17
TF: 888-812-1516 ■ *Web:* www.surroundair.com						
Indotronix International Corp (IIC)						
331 Main St	Poughkeepsie	NY	12601	845-473-1137	473-1197	180
Web: www.iic.com						
Indros Group 210 Richardson St	Brooklyn	NY	11222	866-463-7671	202-6119*	396
**Fax Area Code:* 212 ■ *TF:* 866-463-7671 ■ *Web:* www.indrosgroup.com						
IndSoft Inc						
3755 E Main St Ste 180	Saint Charles	IL	60174	630-324-0006	524-0009	180
Web: www.indsoft.com						
Indtai Inc 2095 Chain Bridge Rd Ste 300	Vienna	VA	22182	877-912-6672	823-1407	180
TF: 877-912-6672 ■ *Web:* www.indtai.com						
Inductoheat Inc						
32251 N Avis Dr	Madison Heights	MI	48071	800-624-6297	589-1062*	318
**Fax Area Code:* 248 ■ *TF:* 800-624-6297 ■ *Web:* www.inductoheat.com						
Inductotherm Group						
10 Indel Ave PO Box 157	Rancocas	NJ	08073	609-267-9000		318
TF: 800-257-9527 ■ *Web:* www.inductotherm.com						
Indufast Industrial Fasteners Ltd						
111b-81 Golden Dr	Coquitlam	BC	V3K6R2	604-464-6164		351
Web: indufast.com						
Induron Coatings Inc						
3333 Richard Arrington Jr Blvd N	Birmingham	AL	35234	205-521-9602	320-5220	146
TF: 800-324-9584 ■ *Web:* www.induron.com						
Indus Corp 1951 Kidwell Dr	Vienna	VA	22182	703-506-6700	506-6776	177
Web: www.induscorp.com						
Indus Instruments 721 Tristar Dr Ste C	Webster	TX	77598	281-286-1130	461-8168	196
Web: www.indusinstruments.com						
Indus International Inc						
340 S Oak St PO Box 890	West Salem	WI	54669	608-786-0300	786-0786	496
TF: 800-843-9377 ■ *Web:* www.indususa.com						
Indus Technology Inc						
2243 San Diego Ave	San Diego	CA	92110	619-299-2555	299-2444	261
Web: www.industechnology.com						
Indusco Group 1200 W Hamburg St	Baltimore	MD	21230	800-727-0665	666-0757	470
TF: 800-727-0665 ■ *Web:* www.induscowirerope.com						
Indusol Inc 11 Depot St	Sutton	MA	01590	508-865-9516	865-9518	605-2
Web: www.indusolinc.com						
Industrial Acoustics Company Inc						
1160 Commerce Ave	Bronx	NY	10462	630-270-1790	863-1138*	389
**Fax Area Code:* 718 ■ *Web:* www.iacacoustics.com						
Industrial Air Centers Inc						
731 E Market St	Jeffersonville	IN	47130	812-280-7070	280-7072	172
Web: www.iacserv.com						
Industrial Air Inc						
428 Edwardia Dr PO Box 8769	Greensboro	NC	27409	336-292-1030	855-7763	697
Web: industrialairinc.com						
Industrial Alliance Insurance & Financial Services Inc						
1080 Grande Allee W						
PO Box 1907 Sta Terminus	Quebec City	QC	G1K7M3	418-684-5405	688-0705	391-2
TF: 888-266-2224 ■ *Web:* www.ia.ca						
Industrial Bank NA						
4812 Georgia Ave NW	Washington	DC	20011	202-722-2000	461-5056*	70
**Fax Area Code:* 800 ■ *Web:* www.industrial-bank.com						
Industrial Battery & Charger Inc						
5831 Orr Rd	Charlotte	NC	28213	704-597-7330		74
TF: 800-833-8412 ■ *Web:* www.ibcipower.com						
Industrial Battery Engineering Inc (IBE)						
9121 DeGarmo Ave	Sun Valley	CA	91352	818-767-7067	767-7173	74
Web: www.ibe-inc.com						
Industrial Brush Company Inc						
105 Clinton Rd	Fairfield	NJ	07004	973-575-0455	575-6169	103
TF: 800-241-9860 ■ *Web:* indbrush.com						
Industrial Ceramic Technology Inc (ICT)						
37 Enterprise Dr	Ann Arbor	MI	48103	734-761-8137	996-0808	500
Web: www.indceramictech.com						
Industrial Chemicals Inc						
2042 Montreat Dr	Vestavia Hills	AL	35216	205-823-7330	978-0485	146
TF: 800-476-2042 ■ *Web:* www.industrialchem.com						
Industrial Chrome Inc 834 NE Madison	Topeka	KS	66608	785-235-3463		247
Web: www.industrialchrome.com						
Industrial Clutch 2800 Fisher Rd	Waukesha	WI	53186	262-547-3357		620
TF: 800-964-3262 ■ *Web:* www.indclutch.com						
Industrial Coatings Contractors Inc						
36545 Perkins Rd	Prairieville	LA	70769	225-673-4490	673-3572	189-11
Web: industrialcoating.com						
Industrial Combustion Inc 351 21st St	Monroe	WI	53566	608-325-3141	325-4379	318
Web: www.ind-comb.com						
Industrial Commodities Inc						
4134 Innslake Dr	Glen Allen	VA	23060	800-523-7902		297-11
TF: 800-523-7902 ■ *Web:* www.industrialcommodities.com						
Industrial Communications & Electronics Inc						
40 Lone St	Marshfield	MA	02050	781-319-1100	837-4000	647
TF: 800-822-9999 ■ *Web:* www.induscom.com						
Industrial Container & Supply Company Inc						
1845 South 5200 West	Salt Lake City	UT	84104	801-972-1561		333
TF: 800-748-4250 ■ *Web:* www.industrialcontainer.com						
Industrial Container Services						
7152 First Ave S	Seattle	WA	98108	206-763-2345		198
TF: 800-273-3786 ■ *Web:* www.iconserv.com						
Industrial Contractors Inc						
7401 Yukon Dr	Bismarck	ND	58501	701-258-9908	258-9988	189-10
TF: 800-467-3089 ■ *Web:* www.icinorthdakota.com						
Industrial Control Concepts Inc (ICC)						
301 N Memorial Dr	Saint Louis	MO	63102	314-621-0076	621-2111	203
Web: www.icc-inc.net						
Industrial Controls Distributors Inc (ICD)						
1776 Bloomsbury Ave	Wanamassa	NJ	07712	732-918-9000	922-4417	385
TF: 800-281-4788 ■ *Web:* www.industrialcontrolsonline.com						
Industrial Controls Inc						
837 W Trindle Rd	Mechanicsburg	PA	17055	717-697-7555	691-9693	196
Web: industrialcontrolsinc.com						
Industrial Council of Nearwest Chicago (ICNC)						
320 N Damen Ave 1st Fl	Chicago	IL	60612	312-421-3941	421-1871	393
Web: www.industrialcouncil.com						
Industrial Custom Products Inc						
2801 37th Ave NE	Minneapolis	MN	55421	612-781-2255	781-1144	326
TF: 800-654-0886 ■ *Web:* www.industrialcustom.com						
Industrial Data Systems Inc						
3822 E La Palma Ave	Anaheim	CA	92807	714-921-9212	399-0286	684
TF: 800-854-3311 ■ *Web:* www.industrialdata.com						
Industrial Design & Fabrication Inc						
350 Fortner Rd	McEwen	TN	37101	931-582-8844		695
Web: www.idf-tn.com						
Industrial Designers Society of America (IDSA)						
45195 Business Ct Ste 250	Dulles	VA	20166	703-707-6000	787-8501	49-13
Web: www.idsa.org						
Industrial Diamond Association of America (IDA)						
PO Box 29460	Columbus	OH	43229	614-797-2265	797-2264	49-13
Web: www.superabrasives.org						
Industrial Dielectrics Inc						
407 S Seventh St PO Box 357	Noblesville	IN	46061	317-773-1766	773-3877	605-2
Web: www.idicomposites.com						
Industrial Diesel Inc						
8705 Harmon Rd	Fort Worth	TX	76177	817-232-1071	232-0354	385
TF: 800-323-3659 ■ *Web:* www.industrialdiesel.net						
Industrial Door Company Inc						
360 Coon Rapids Blvd	Minneapolis	MN	55433	763-786-4730		236
TF: 888-798-0199 ■ *Web:* www.idc-automatic.com						
Industrial Door Contractors Inc						
820 Mayberry Springs Rd	Columbia	TN	38401	931-380-0463		492
Web: hangardoor.com						
Industrial Dynamics Company Ltd						
3100 Fujita St	Torrance	CA	90505	310-325-5633	530-1000	472
Web: www.filtec.com						
Industrial Electric Wire & Cable Inc (IEWC)						
5001 S Towne Dr	New Berlin	WI	53151	877-613-4392		246
TF: 800-344-2323 ■ *Web:* www.iewc.com						
Industrial Electronic Supply Inc (IES)						
2321 Texas Ave	Shreveport	LA	71103	318-222-1911		246
Web: www.goies.com						
Industrial Employees Credit Union						
1513 S 18th St	Centerville	IA	52544	641-437-7109		219
Web: industrialemployeescu.com						

	Phone	Fax	Class
Industrial Engineers Inc 267 Raymond Hill Rd . . . Uncasville CT 06382 *Web:* www.industrialengineersinc.com	860-848-8558	848-7140	261
Industrial Fabricators Inc 403 N Cemetery St . . . Thorp WI 54771 *Web:* www.industrialfabinc.com	715-669-5512	669-5514	386
Industrial Fabrics Association Intl (IFAI) 1801 County Rd 'B' W. . . . Roseville MN 55113 *TF:* 800-225-4324 ■ *Web:* www.ifai.com	651-222-2508	631-9334	49-13
Industrial Finishing Products Inc 465 Logan St . . . Brooklyn NY 11208 *Web:* www.industrialfinishings.com	718-277-3333	827-6321	550
Industrial Furnace Interiors Inc 35160 Stanley Dr . . . Sterling Heights MI 48312 *Web:* ifi-inc.com	586-977-9600	977-9601	318
Industrial Gasket & Shim Company Inc (IGS) 200 Country Club Rd . . . Meadow Lands PA 15347 *TF:* 800-229-1447 ■ *Web:* www.igsind.com	724-222-5800		326
Industrial Growth Partners 100 Spear St Ste 1500 . . . San Francisco CA 94105 *Web:* www.igpequity.com	415-882-4550	882-4551	792
Industrial Hardware & Specialties Inc 17-B Kentucky Ave . . . Paterson NJ 07503 *TF:* 800-684-4010 ■ *Web:* www.industrialhardware.com	973-684-4010		351
Industrial Health Council 3513 Seventh Ave S . . . Birmingham AL 35222 *Web:* i-h-c.org	205-326-4109		415
Industrial Heater Corp 30 Knotter Dr. . . . Cheshire CT 06410 *Web:* www.industrialheater.com	203-250-0500	250-0599	318
Industrial Inspection & Analysis Inc 6766 Culebra Rd. . . . San Antonio TX 78238 *Web:* industrial-ia.com	210-256-4100		261
Industrial Instruments & Supplies Inc 125 James Way. . . . Southampton PA 18966 *Web:* www.iisusa.com	215-396-0822	396-0833	459
Industrial Insurance Associates Inc 1632 Colonial Pkwy . . . Inverness IL 60067 *Web:* webiia.com	847-705-6600		390
Industrial Kinetics Inc 2535 Curtiss St. . . . Downers Grove IL 60515 *TF:* 800-655-0306 ■ *Web:* www.iki.com	630-655-0300	655-1720	207
Industrial Laboratories Company Inc, The 4046 Youngfield St. . . . Wheat Ridge CO 80033 *Web:* www.industriallabs.net	303-287-9691	287-0964	416
Industrial Laminates/Norplex Inc 665 Lybrand St. . . . Postville IA 52162 *Web:* www.norplex-micarta.com	563-864-7321	864-4231	604
Industrial Logic Inc 829 Bancroft Way . . . Berkeley CA 94710 *Web:* www.industriallogic.com	510-540-8336		177
Industrial Louvers Inc 511 Seventh St S . . . Delano MN 55328 *TF:* 800-328-3421 ■ *Web:* www.industriallouvers.com	763-972-2981	972-2911	697
Industrial Machine and Engineering Co (IMEC) 1716 N 9th St. . . . Monett MO 65708 *Web:* www.imecmonett.com	417-235-3053	235-3054	454
Industrial Machine Work Inc 27530 Hwy 31 . . . Flomaton AL 36441 *Web:* www.industrialmachineworksinc.com	251-296-5342	296-9199	454
Industrial Maintenance Welding & Machining Company Inc 2nd & Hupp Rd. . . . Kingsbury IN 46345 *Web:* imwnet.com	219-393-5531	393-3178	386
Industrial Manufacturing & Machining 5495 E 69th Ave . . . Commerce City CO 80022	303-287-2125		595
Industrial Manufacturing Specialties Inc 1268 Hwy 67 S. . . . Decatur AL 35603 *Web:* www.imsprecisionmachining.com	256-350-9334	350-9391	723
Industrial Marking Products 1415 Grovenburg Rd . . . Holt MI 48842 *Web:* www.industrialmarking.com	517-699-2160	699-1505	467
Industrial Material Corp 7701 Harborside Dr . . . Galveston TX 77554 *TF:* 800-701-4462 ■ *Web:* www.industrialmaterial.com	409-744-4538	744-1844	492
Industrial Molds Inc 5175 27th Ave. . . . Rockford IL 61109 *Web:* www.industrialmolds.com	815-397-2971	397-0380	757
Industrial Motion Control LLC 1444 S Wolf Rd. . . . Wheeling IL 60090 *Web:* www.destaco.com	847-459-5200		709
Industrial Networking Solutions (INS) 16415 Addison Rd Ste 550. . . . Addison TX 75001 *TF:* 800-889-1461 ■ *Web:* www.industrialnetworking.com	972-248-7466	248-9533	174
Industrial Nut Corp 1425 Tiffin Ave . . . Sandusky OH 44870 *Web:* www.industrialnut.com	419-625-8543		350
Industrial Paper Tube Inc 1335 E Bay Ave. . . . Bronx NY 10474 **Fax Area Code:* 718 ■ *TF:* 800-345-0960 ■ *Web:* www.mailingtubes-ipt.com	800-345-0960	378-0055*	125
Industrial Paramedic Services Ltd 630 4th Ave SW Ste 100. . . . Calgary AB T2P0J9 *TF:* 877-947-7367 ■ *Web:* ipsems.com	403-264-6435		30
Industrial Partnership for Research in Interfacial & Materials Engineering (IPRIME) 151 Amundson Hall 421 Washington Ave SE . . . Minneapolis MN 55455 *TF:* 800-822-6757 ■ *Web:* www.iprime.umn.edu	612-625-1269	626-1686	668
Industrial Parts Depot LLC 23231 Normandie Ave . . . Torrance CA 90501 *Web:* www.ipdparts.com	310-530-1900		262
Industrial Parts Specialties (IPS) 630 Lot Rd . . . Port Allen LA 70767 *TF:* 800-272-3019 ■ *Web:* www.indparts.com	225-408-7500	408-3081	454
Industrial Pipe & Supply Company Inc 1779 Martin Luther King Junior Blvd . . . Gainesville GA 30501 *TF:* 800-426-1458 ■ *Web:* www.industrialpipega.com	770-536-0517		612
Industrial Plastic Products Inc 14025 Nw 58th Ct. . . . Miami Lakes FL 33014 *Web:* www.industrialplasticproducts.com	305-822-3223		604
Industrial Plastic Systems Inc 4225 Drane Field Rd. . . . Lakeland FL 33811 *Web:* www.ips-frp.com	863-646-8551	644-1534	595

	Phone	Fax	Class
Industrial Power & Lighting Corp 60 Depost St. . . . Buffalo NY 14206 *TF:* 800-639-3702 ■ *Web:* www.iplcorp.com	716-854-1811	854-1828	189-4
Industrial Property Trust 518 17th St 17th Fl. . . . Denver CO 80202 *TF:* 866-324-7348 ■ *Web:* www.industrialpropertytrust.com	303-339-3650	339-3651	690
Industrial Realty Group LLC 11100 Santa Monica Blvd Ste 850 . . . Los Angeles CA 90025 *Web:* www.industrialrealtygroup.com	562-803-4761		652
Industrial Research Institute Inc (IRI) 2200 Clarendon Blvd Ste 1102. . . . Arlington VA 22201 *Web:* www.iriweb.org	703-647-2580	647-2581	49-19
Industrial Resources Inc PO Box 2648. . . . Fairmont WV 26554 *Web:* www.indres.com	304-363-4100		186
Industrial Revolution Inc 5835 Segale Park Dr C . . . Tukwila WA 98188 **Fax Area Code:* 206 ■ *TF:* 888-297-6062 ■ *Web:* www.industrialrev.com	888-297-6062	812-2250*	697
Industrial Roller Co 218 N Main St . . . Smithton IL 62285 *Web:* industrialrollerco.com	618-234-0740	234-0237	676
Industrial Rubber Inc 11801 S Meridian Ave . . . Oklahoma City OK 73173 *TF:* 800-457-4851 ■ *Web:* www.iri-oiltool.com	405-703-7048		537
Industrial Scientific Corp 7848 Steubenville Pk . . . Oakdale PA 15071 *TF:* 800-338-3287 ■ *Web:* www.indsci.com	412-788-4353	788-8353	201
Industrial Shredders 448 Geiger St . . . Berea OH 44017 *Web:* www.industrialshredders.com	330-549-9960	549-9961	111
Industrial Soap Co 722 S Vandeventer Ave. . . . Saint Louis MO 63110 *TF:* 800-405-7627 ■ *Web:* www.industrialsoap.com	314-241-6363	533-5556	406
Industrial Source Inc 1574 W Sixth Ave . . . Eugene OR 97402 *Web:* www.industrialsource.com	541-344-1438		811
Industrial Specialty Contractors LLC 20480 Highland Rd. . . . Baton Rouge LA 70817 *Web:* www.iscgrp.com	225-756-8001		189-4
Industrial Steel Construction Inc 86 N Bridge St . . . Gary IN 46404 *Web:* www.iscbridge.com	219-885-7600		480
Industrial Steel Inc 3561 Industrial Rd . . . Titusville FL 32796 *Web:* www.industrial-steel.com	321-267-2341		480
Industrial Steel Treating Inc 613 Carroll St. . . . Jackson MI 49202 **Fax Area Code:* 866 ■ *TF:* 800-253-9534 ■ *Web:* www.indstl.com	800-253-9534	550-7045*	484
Industrial Supply Solutions Inc 520 Elizabeth St . . . Charleston WV 25311 *TF:* 800-346-5341 ■ *Web:* weareissi.com	304-346-5341	346-5347	385
Industrial Systems Laboratory 58 Logan Ave S. . . . Renton WA 98055 *Web:* www.islab.com	425-226-7585	226-2210	178-1
Industrial Tech Services Inc 321 Triport Rd. . . . Georgetown KY 40324 *Web:* www.itslex.com	502-863-4941		261
Industrial Tectonics Inc 7222 Huron River Dr. . . . Dexter MI 48130 *TF:* 866-816-8904 ■ *Web:* www.itiball.com	734-426-4681		485
Industrial Thermoform Inc 1211 Industrial Way . . . Cedar Hill TX 75104 *Web:* www.industrialthermoform.com	972-299-5391		596
Industrial Tool Inc 9210 52nd Ave N . . . New Hope MN 55428 *TF:* 800-776-4455 ■ *Web:* www.industrial-tool.com	763-533-7244		454
Industrial Tool Services Inc 109 Williams St . . . Bristol VA 24201 *Web:* www.indtools.net	276-669-6571	669-8429	385
Industrial Tools Inc (ITI) 1111 S Rose Ave. . . . Oxnard CA 93033 *TF:* 800-266-5561 ■ *Web:* www.iti-abrasives.com	805-483-1111	483-6302	493
Industrial Tube & Steel Corp 4658 Crystal Pkwy . . . Kent OH 44240 *TF:* 800-662-9567 ■ *Web:* www.industrialtube.com	330-474-5530		490
Industrial Vehicles International Inc (IVI) 6737 E 12th St . . . Tulsa OK 74112 *Web:* www.indvehicles.com	918-836-6516	838-9529	470
Industrial Ventilation Inc W6395 Speciality Dr. . . . Greenville WI 54942 *Web:* www.ivinc.com	920-757-6001	757-6004	610
Industrial Welding Academy 11001 Wallisville Rd. . . . Houston TX 77013 *Web:* www.iwatraining.com	713-672-9353		167-3
Industries Bonneville Ltee 601 Rue de l'Industrie. . . . Beloeil QC J3G4S5 *TF:* 877-964-1001 ■ *Web:* www.maisonsbonneville.com	450-464-1001		106
Industries for the Blind 445 S Curtis Rd . . . West Allis WI 53214 *TF:* 800-642-8778 ■ *Web:* www.ibmilwaukee.com	414-778-3040	778-3041	103
Industries of the Blind Inc 920 W Lee St . . . Greensboro NC 27403 *TF:* 800-909-7086 ■ *Web:* www.industriesoftheblind.com	336-274-1591		103
Industrios Software Inc 2150 Winston Park Dr Ste 214. . . . Oakville ON L6H5V1 *Web:* www.industrios.com	905-829-2525		174
Industrious 215 Park Ave S 11th Fl . . . New York NY 10003 *Web:* www.industriousoffice.com	646-776-2823		652
Industronics Service Co 489 Sullivan Ave. . . . South Windsor CT 06074 *TF:* 800-878-1551 ■ *Web:* www.industronics.com	860-289-1551	289-3526	318
Industry Council for Tangible Assets (ICTA) 1510 Circle Dr . . . Annapolis MD 21409 *Web:* www.ictaonline.org	410-626-7005		49-2
Industry Products Co 500 E Statler Rd. . . . Piqua OH 45356 *Web:* www.industryproductsco.com	937-778-0585		247
Industry Specific Solutions LLC 24901 Northwestern Hwy Ste 400. . . . Southfield MI 48075 *TF:* 877-356-3450 ■ *Web:* industryspecificstaffing.com	877-356-3450		260
Industry Telephone Co (ITC) 17105 Fordtran Blvd. . . . Industry TX 78944 *TF:* 888-212-8872 ■ *Web:* www.industrytelco.com	979-357-4411	278-3600	224

Company / Address	City	State	ZIP	Phone	Fax	Class
Industry-Railway Suppliers Inc 577 W Lamont Rd *TF:* 800-728-0029 ■ *Web:* industryrailway.com	Elmhurst	IL	60126	630-766-5708	766-0017	770
Indy Gov 200 E Washington S Ste 1942 *Web:* www.indy.gov	Indianapolis	IN	46204	317-327-4740	327-3893	339-15
Indy Honda 8455 US 31 S *Web:* www.indyhonda.com	Indianapolis	IN	46227	317-887-0800		57
Indyne Inc 11800 Sunrise Vly Dr Ste 250 *Web:* www.indyneinc.com	Reston	VA	20191	703-903-6900	903-4997	743
Indyvet Emergency & Specialty 5425 Victory Dr *TF:* 800-551-4879 ■ *Web:* indyvet.com	Indianapolis	IN	46203	317-782-4484		794
InEdge 9800 Cavendish Blvd Ste 250 *Web:* www.inedge.com	Montreal	QC	H4M2V9	514-333-6600		463
Inertech Supply Inc 641 Monterey Pass Rd *Web:* inertech.com	Monterey Park	CA	91754	626-282-2000		326
Inertia Dynamics Inc 31 Industrial Park Rd *TF:* 800-800-6445 ■ *Web:* www.idicb.com	New Hartford	CT	06057	860-379-1252	379-1137	203
Inertia Engineering 6665 Hardaway Rd *TF:* 800-791-9997 ■ *Web:* www.inertiaworks.com	Stockton	CA	95215	209-931-1670		729
INETCO Systems Ltd 4664 Lougheed Hwy Ste 258 *Web:* www.inetco.com	Burnaby	BC	V5C5T5	604-451-1567		174
InetSolution Inc 2075 W Big Beaver Rd Ste 222 *TF:* 855-728-5839 ■ *Web:* www.inetsolution.com	Troy	MI	48084	855-728-5839		180
Infaith Community Foundation 625 Fourth Ave S Ste 1500 *TF:* 800-365-4172 ■ *Web:* www.infaithfound.org	Minneapolis	MN	55415	612-844-4110	844-4109	304
Infantino LLC 4920 Carroll Canyon Rd Ste 200 *TF:* 800-840-4916 ■ *Web:* www.infantino.com	San Diego	CA	92121	800-840-4916		64
Infax Inc 4250 River Green Pkwy Ste D *Web:* infax.com	Duluth	GA	30096	770-209-9925		177
inferno LLC 505 Tennessee St Ste 108 *Web:* creativeinferno.com	Memphis	TN	38103	901-278-3773		7
Infi Net Solutions Inc 6430 S 84th St *Web:* www.omahait.com	Omaha	NE	68127	402-895-5777		225
INFICON Inc 2 Technology Pl *Web:* www.inficon.com	East Syracuse	NY	13057	315-434-1100	437-3803	201
Infinedi LLC 1437 S Boulder Ave Ste 1030 *TF:* 800-688-8087 ■ *Web:* www.infinedi.net	Tulsa	OK	74119	918-249-4450	249-4460	708
Infinera Corp 140 Caspian Ct *NASDAQ: INFN* ■ *TF:* 877-742-3427 ■ *Web:* www.infinera.com	Sunnyvale	CA	94089	408-572-5200		735
Infinia Group LLC 135 Madison Ave 8th Fl *Web:* www.infiniagroup.com	New York	NY	10016	212-463-5100		195
Infinigy Engineering 1033 Watervliet-Shaker Rd *Web:* www.infinigy.com	Albany	NY	12205	518-690-0790		261
Infinite Campus Inc 4321 109th Ave NE *TF:* 800-850-2335 ■ *Web:* www.infinitecampus.com	Blaine	MN	55449	651-631-0000		177
Infinite Convergence Solutions Inc 3231 N Wilke Rd *Web:* www.infinite-convergence.com	Arlington Heights	IL	60004	224-764-3535		224
Infinite Dimensions Inc 1760 Reston Pkwy Ste 500 *Web:* www.infdim.com	Reston	VA	20191	703-435-9500		396
Infinite Graphics Inc 4611 E Lake St *OTC: INFG* ■ *TF:* 800-679-0676 ■ *Web:* www.igi.com	Minneapolis	MN	55406	612-721-6283	721-3802	178-5
Infinite Scale Design Group LLC 16 E Exchange Pl *Web:* www.infinitescale.com	Salt Lake City	UT	84111	801-363-1881		393
Infinite Wellness Solutions 3119 Fincham Rd *Web:* infinitewellnesssolutions.com	Seekonk	MA	02771	336-725-8624		466
Infiniti HR LLC 3905 National Dr Ste 400 **Fax Area Code:* 240 ■ *TF:* 866-552-6360 ■ *Web:* infinitihr.com	Burtonsville	MD	20866	301-841-6380	722-0090*	734
INFINITT North America Inc 755 Memorial Pkwy Hillcrest Professional Plz Ste 304 *TF:* 877-387-6960 ■ *Web:* www.infinittna.com	Phillipsburg	NJ	08865	908-387-6960	387-6965	624
Infinitude Creative Group LP 1820 Preston Park Blvd Ste 2100 *Web:* nfnitude.com	Plano	TX	75093	972-867-6800		514
Infinity Capital Partners LLC 1075 Peachtree St NE Ste 2125 *Web:* infinityfunds.com	Atlanta	GA	30309	404-458-4448		401
Infinity Compounding Solutions LLC 1204 SE 28th St Ste 2 PO Box 699 *TF:* 888-414-5805 ■ *Web:* icsrx.com	Bentonville	AR	72712	888-414-5805		237
Infinity Contractors International Ltd 2563 E Loop 820 N *Web:* www.infinitycontractors.com	Fort Worth	TX	76118	817-838-8700		610
Infinity Direct Inc 13220 County Rd 6 Ste 200 *Web:* infinitydirect.com	Plymouth	MN	55441	763-559-1111		41
Infinity Engineering Consultants L L C 4001 DIVISION St *Web:* www.infinityec.com	Metairie	LA	70002	504-304-0548		256
Infinity Fasteners Inc 11028 Strang Line Rd *TF:* 800-762-5948 ■ *Web:* www.infinityfasteners.com	Lenexa	KS	66215	913-438-2252	438-2292	351
Infinity Federal Credit Union 202 Larabee Rd *Web:* infinityfcu.com	Westbrook	ME	04092	207-854-6000		219
Infinity Hospice Care LLC 5110 N 40th St Ste 107 *Web:* www.infinityhospicecare.com	Phoenix	AZ	85018	602-381-0375	381-0385	371
Infinity International Properties Inc 1209 E Las Olas Blvd *Web:* infinityprops.com	Fort Lauderdale	FL	33301	954-653-5000		652

Company / Address	City	State	ZIP	Phone	Fax	Class
Infinity Marketing Team Inc 8575 Higuera St *Web:* www.infinitymarketing.com	Culver City	CA	90232	323-962-4784		195
Infinity Pharmaceuticals Inc 784 Memorial Dr *NASDAQ: INFI* ■ *Web:* www.infi.com	Cambridge	MA	02139	617-453-1000	453-1001	582
Infinity Publishing 1094 New Dehaven St Ste 100 *TF:* 877-289-2665 ■ *Web:* www.infinitypublishing.com	West Conshohocken	PA	19428	610-941-9999	941-9959	637-10
Infinity Software Development Inc 1901 Commonwealth Ln *Web:* www.infinity-software.com	Tallahassee	FL	32303	850-383-1011		180
Infinova Corp 51 Stouts Ln *Web:* www.infinova.com	Monmouth Junction	NJ	08852	732-355-9100	355-9101	692
Infitec Inc 6500 Badgley Rd *TF:* 800-334-0837 ■ *Web:* www.infitec.com	East Syracuse	NY	13057	315-433-1150		203
Inflection Point Ventures (IPV) 1 Innovation Way Ste 302 *Web:* www.inflectpoint.com	Newark	DE	19711	302-452-1120	452-1122	792
Influence Technologies Inc 3457 Ringsby Ct Ste 111 *Web:* www.influence.tv	Denver	CO	80216	303-495-6980		393
InfluxData 799 Market St Ste 400 *Web:* www.influxdata.com	San Francisco	CA	94103	415-295-1901		178-8
Influxis 28110 Ave Stanford Unit D *Web:* influxis.com	Valencia	CA	91355	661-775-3936		225
Info Cubic LLC 116 Inverness Dr E Ste 206 *TF:* 877-360-4636 ■ *Web:* www.infocubic.net	Englewood	CO	80112	303-220-0171		317
Info Net Publishing 21142 Canada Rd Unit 7-J *Web:* www.infonetpublishing.com	Lake Forest	CA	92630	949-462-0224	462-9595	637-2
Info Quality Healthcare 385b Highland Colony Pkwy Ste 504 *Web:* www.iqh.org	Ridgeland	MS	39157	601-957-1575		138
Info Quest 6300 Powers Ferry Rd Ste 600-294 *Web:* www.thecasefile.com	Atlanta	GA	30339	770-235-1664		637-2
Info Tech Inc 2970 SW 50th Ter *Web:* www.infotechfl.com	Gainesville	FL	32608	352-381-4400		178-10
Info X Distribution LLC 3 Aspen Dr Ste 1 *TF:* 800-463-9998 ■ *Web:* www.info-x.com	Randolph	NJ	07869	973-386-1411		196
InfoAdvantage LLC 10900 NE 8th St Ste 215 *Web:* www.infoadvantage.com	Bellevue	WA	98004	425-869-2157		194
Infocast Inc 20931 Burbank Blvd Ste B *Web:* www.infocastinc.com	Woodland Hills	CA	91367	818-888-4444	888-4440	196
InfoCision Management Corp 325 Springside Dr *TF:* 800-210-6269 ■ *Web:* www.infocision.com	Akron	OH	44333	330-668-1400		737
InfoCommerce Group Inc 2 Bala Plz Ste 300 *Web:* infocommercegroup.com	Bala Cynwyd	PA	19004	610-649-1200	471-0515	637-10
InFocus Corp 13190 SW 68th Pkwy Ste 200 *TF:* 877-388-8385 ■ *Web:* www.infocus.com	Portland	OR	97223	503-207-4700	207-1937	591
INFOCUS Marketing Inc 4245 Sigler Rd *TF:* 800-708-5478 ■ *Web:* www.infocusmarketing.com	Warrenton	VA	20187	800-708-5478		463
InfoData Corp 181 Waukegan Rd Ste 300 *Web:* www.infodatacorp.com	Northfield	IL	60093	847-486-0000	386-7166	194
InfoExpress Inc 170 S Whisman Rd Ste B *Web:* www.infoexpress.com	Mountain View	CA	94041	650-623-0260		177
Infoflex Inc PO Box 1596 *Web:* www.infoflex.com	Burlingame	CA	94011	650-270-1019	433-8897	178-1
Infogain Corp 485 Alberto Way *Web:* www.infogain.com	Los Gatos	CA	95032	408-355-6000		39
Infoglide Software 6500 River Pl Blvd Bldg 2 *Web:* www.infoglide.com	Austin	TX	78730	512-532-3500	532-3505	178-1
InfoGroup Inc 1020 E First St *TF:* 866-414-7848 ■ *Web:* www.hilldonn.com	Papillion	NE	68046	402-836-5290		5
Infogrow 2140 Front St *Web:* www.infogrowcorp.com	Cuyahoga Falls	OH	44221	330-929-1353		196
Infolab Inc 17400 Hwy 61 N	Clarksdale	MS	38614	662-627-2283		419
Infolink Exp 2880 Zanker Rd Ste 203 *TF:* 800-280-7703 ■ *Web:* infolink-exp.com	San Jose	CA	95134	915-577-9466		180
Info-Link Technologies Inc 601 Pittsburgh Ave *Web:* www.infolinktechnologies.net	Mount Vernon	OH	43050	740-393-3100		180
Infomagnetics Technologies Corp (IMT) 900-330 St Mary Ave *Web:* imt.ca	Winnipeg	MB	R3C3Z5	204-989-4630		261
InfoMart Inc 1582 Terrell Mill Rd *TF:* 800-800-3774 ■ *Web:* www.infomart-usa.com	Marietta	GA	30067	770-984-2727		193
Infomax Office Systems Inc 1010 Illinois St *TF:* 800-727-4629 ■ *Web:* www.infomaxoffice.com	Des Moines	IA	50314	515-244-5203		535
Infomax Shelf Management Inc 1000 Nevada Hwy Ste 204 *Web:* www.infomaxshelfmgmt.com	Boulder City	NV	89005	702-513-8503		195
Infomedia 2081 Columbiana Rd *Web:* www.infomedia.com	Birmingham	AL	35216	205-823-4440		225
InfoMine Inc 580 Hornby St Ste 900 *TF:* 888-683-2037 ■ *Web:* www.infomine.com	Vancouver	BC	V6C3B6	604-683-2037		531-13
Info-Power International Inc 3345 Silverstone Dr *Web:* www.abw.com	Plano	TX	75023	972-424-4447		177
InfoPro Inc 8200 Greensboro Dr Ste 1450	McLean	VA	22102	703-226-2520		360-3
Infopro Systems Inc 2752 Forgue Dr Ste 100A *Web:* infoprosystemsinc.com	Naperville	IL	60564	630-355-3750	355-9895	177
Infopros 12325 Oracle Blvd Ste 100 *TF:* 888-235-3231 ■ *Web:* infopros.com	Colorado Springs	CO	80921	888-235-3231		809

Company / Address	City	State	ZIP	Phone	Fax	Class
Infoquest Consulting Group Inc 68 Culver Rd Ste 106 — *Web:* www.infoquestgroup.com	Monmouth Junction	NJ	08852	609-409-5151	409-5155	196
Infor 641 Ave of the Americas — *TF:* 866-244-5479 ■ *Web:* www.infor.com	Newyork	NY	10011	646-336-1700		261
Inforeem Inc 1 Quality Pl — *Web:* www.inforeem.com	Edison	NJ	08820	732-494-4100		180
Informa 75 West St — *Web:* informatp.com	Walpole	MA	02081	508-668-0288		507
Informa 605 3rd Ave — *Web:* www.informa.com	New York	NY	10158	212-520-2700		184
Informant Technologies Inc 1571 Sumneytown Pke — *TF:* 877-503-4636 ■ *Web:* informant.tech	Lansdale	PA	19446	877-529-6883		177
Information & Computing Services Inc (ICS) 1650 Prudential Dr Ste 300 — *TF:* 800-676-4427 ■ *Web:* www.icsfl.com	Jacksonville	FL	32207	904-399-8500		178-1
Information Analysis Inc 11240 Waples Mill Rd Ste 201 — *Web:* www.infoa.com	Fairfax	VA	22030	703-383-3000	293-7979	180
Information Assets Inc (IAI) 9211 W Rd Ste 143-191 — *Web:* www.infoassets.com	Houston	TX	77064	713-443-9914		180
Information Builders Inc 2 Penn Plz — *TF:* 800-969-4636 ■ *Web:* www.ibi.com	New York	NY	10121	212-736-4433	967-6406	178-7
Information Consultants Inc 1320 Tower Rd — *Web:* www.financialportrait.com	Schaumburg	IL	60173	847-397-0088		178-1
Information Gatekeepers Inc (IGI) 1340 Soldiers Field Rd Ste 2 — *TF:* 800-323-1088 ■ *Web:* www.igigroup.com	Brighton	MA	02135	617-782-5033	782-5735	637-11
Information Management Systems Inc 114 W Main St Ste 211 PO Box 2924 — *TF:* 888-403-8347 ■ *Web:* www.imswebb.com	New Britain	CT	06050	860-229-1119	225-5524	635
Information Network Associates Inc 5235 N Front St — *TF:* 800-443-0824 ■ *Web:* www.ina-inc.com	Harrisburg	PA	17110	717-599-5505		693
Information Resources Inc 150 N Clinton St — *TF:* 866-262-5973 ■ *Web:* www.iriworldwide.com	Chicago	IL	60661	312-726-1221		466
Information Station Specialists Inc 3368 88th Ave — *Web:* www.theradiosource.com	Zeeland	MI	49464	616-772-2300	772-2966	647
Information Systems & Networks Corp (ISN) 10411 Motor City Dr Ste 700 — *Web:* www.isncorp.com	Bethesda	MD	20817	301-469-0400	469-0767	180
Information Systems Audit & Control Assn (ISACA) 3701 Algonquin Rd Ste 1010 — *Web:* www.isaca.org	Rolling Meadows	IL	60008	847-253-1545	253-1443	48-9
Information Systems Laboratories Inc 10070 Barnes Canyon Rd — *Web:* www.islinc.com	San Diego	CA	92121	858-535-9680	535-9848	28
Information Technology Industry Council (ITI) 1101 K St NW Ste 610 — *Web:* www.itic.org	Washington	DC	20005	202-737-8888	638-4922	48-9
Information Technology Solutions Corp 336 Main St Ste 204 — *Web:* its-gj.com	Grand Junction	CO	81501	970-255-0480		180
Information Television Network 6650 Pk of Commerce Blvd — *TF:* 877-697-2926 ■ *Web:* www.itvisus.com	Boca Raton	FL	33487	561-997-7771	997-5208	742
Information Today Inc 143 Old Marlton Pk — *Web:* www.infotoday.com	Medford	NJ	08055	609-654-6266	654-4309	637-9
Information Tycoon 1455 Old Alabama Rd Ste 140 — *Web:* infotycoon.com	Roswell	GA	30076	404-267-1506		387
Informatix Inc 2485 Natomas Park Dr Ste 430 — *Web:* www.informatixinc.com	Sacramento	CA	95833	916-830-1400	830-1403	178-1
INFORMS (Institute for Operations Research & the Management Sciences) 7240 Pkwy Dr Ste 300 — *TF:* 800-446-3676 ■ *Web:* www.informs.org	Hanover	MD	21076	443-757-3500	757-3515	49-19
Infortrend Corp 435 Lakeside Dr — *TF:* 800-829-8678 ■ *Web:* www.infortrend.com	Sunnyvale	CA	94085	408-988-5088	988-6288	173-8
Infosat Communications Inc 3130-114 Ave SE — *TF:* 888-524-3038 ■ *Web:* infosat.com	Calgary	AB	T2Z3V6	403-543-8188		246
InfoSearch Media 6041 Bristol Pkwy 1st Fl	Culver City	CA	90230	310-437-7380		224
Infosec Inc 14001c St Germain Dr — *Web:* infosecinc.com	Centreville	VA	20121	703-825-1202		225
Infosemantics Inc 2605 Sagebrush Dr Ste 207 — *Web:* infosemantics.com	Flower Mound	TX	75028	469-941-0266	941-0267	177
InfoSend Inc 4240 E La Palma Ave — *TF:* 800-955-9330 ■ *Web:* www.infosend.com	Anaheim	CA	92807	714-993-2690		393
Infoshred LLC 3 Craftsman Rd — *Web:* infoshred.com	East Windsor	CT	06088	860-627-5800		317
Infosight Corp PO Box 5000 — *TF:* 800-401-0716 ■ *Web:* www.infosight.com	Chillicothe	OH	45601	740-642-3600	642-5001	467
Infosilem 99 Emilien-Marcoux Ste 201 — *TF:* 866-420-5585 ■ *Web:* www.infosilem.com	Blainville	QC	J7C0B4	450-420-5585	420-5565	177
Infosmart Systems Inc 5850 Town & Country Blvd Ste 1102 — *Web:* www.infosmartsys.com	Frisco	TX	75034	972-267-5900		196
Infosoft Group Inc 1123 N Water St Ste 400 — *TF:* 800-984-3775 ■ *Web:* www.milwaukeejobs.com	Milwaukee	WI	53202	414-278-0700		180
InfoSonics Corp 4435 Eastgate Mall Ste 320 — *NASDAQ: IFON* ■ *Web:* www.infosonics.com	San Diego	CA	92122	858-373-1600	373-1503	246
Infosource Inc 1300 City View Ctr — *TF:* 800-393-4636 ■ *Web:* www.simplek12.com	Oviedo	FL	32765	407-796-5200	796-5190	177
InfoSpace Inc 601 108th Ave NE Ste 1200 — *Web:* www.infospaceinc.com	Bellevue	WA	98004	425-201-6100	201-6150	397
Infostretch Corp 3200 Patrick Henry Dr Ste 250 — *Web:* www.infostretch.com	Santa Clara	CA	95054	408-727-1100		177
InfoSystems Inc 1317 Hickory Valley Rd — *Web:* www.infosystems.biz	Chattanooga	TN	37421	423-624-6551		180
InfoTech Enterprises America Inc 330 Roberts St Ste 102 — *Web:* www.cyient.com	East Hartford	CT	06108	860-528-5430		256
Infotech Global Inc 371 Hoes Ln — *Web:* www.igiusa.com	Piscataway	NJ	08854	732-271-0600		225
Infotex Inc 299 Dayton Rd PO Box 469 — **Fax Area Code:* 866 ■ *TF:* 800-466-9939 ■ *Web:* www.infotex.com	Dayton	IN	47941	800-466-9939	271-2831*	196
Infotier 350 Clark Dr Ste 302 — *TF:* 866-713-0555 ■ *Web:* infotier.com	Budd Lake	NJ	07828	973-520-1800		196
InfoTree Inc 30 Nagog Pk — *Web:* www.infotreeinc.com	Acton	MA	01720	978-263-8558		178-1
InfoUSA Inc 1020 E 1st St — **Fax Area Code:* 402 ■ *TF:* 800-321-0869 ■ *Web:* www.infousa.com	Omaha	NE	68127	800-835-5856	331-1505*	387
Infovine Inc 1100 W 23rd St Ste 100 — *Web:* www.infovine.com	Houston	TX	77008	713-223-9994		627
InfoVista Corp 12950 Worldgate Dr Ste 250 — *TF:* 866-921-9219 ■ *Web:* www.infovista.com	Herndon	VA	20170	703-435-2435		178-1
Infoweb Systems Inc 3435 Asbury Rd Ste 175 — *Web:* infowebsystems.com	Dubuque	IA	52002	563-582-5042	556-7990	177
Infoworks Inc 102 Woodmont Blvd Ste 500 — *Web:* infoworks-tn.com	Nashville	TN	37205	615-356-2686		180
InfoWorld 501 Second St 6th Fl — *Web:* www.infoworld.com	San Francisco	CA	94107	415-243-0500		457-7
InfoZen Inc 6700A Rockledge Dr Ste 300 — *Web:* www.infozen.com	Bethesda	MD	20817	301-605-8000		196
Infra Metals Co 4501 Curtis Ave — **Fax Area Code:* 410 ■ *TF:* 800-235-3979 ■ *Web:* www.infra-metals.com	Baltimore	MD	21225	800-235-3979	355-9395*	492
Infradant LLC 1514 Flora Lee Dr — *Web:* www.infradant.com	Leesburg	FL	34748	352-693-3581		463
Infralogix 1315 Jamestown Rd Ste 201 — *Web:* www.infralogix.com	Williamsburg	VA	23185	757-229-2965		365
InfraReDx Inc 34 Third Ave — *TF:* 888-680-7339 ■ *Web:* www.infraredx.com	Burlington	MA	01803	781-221-0053		476
Infrastructure Alternatives 7888 Childsdale NE — *Web:* iaiwater.com	Rockford	MI	49341	616-866-1600		261
Infratech Corp 2036 Baker Ct — *TF:* 800-574-6372 ■ *Web:* infratechcorp.com	Kennesaw	GA	30144	800-574-6372		256
Infuse Medical Digital Agency 3369 W Mayflower Ave — *Web:* www.infusemed.com	Lehi	UT	84043	801-331-8610		415
Infusion Nurses Society (INS) 315 Norwood Pk S — *TF:* 800-694-0298 ■ *Web:* www.ins1.org	Norwood	MA	02062	781-440-9408	440-9409	49-8
Infusion Options Inc 5924 13th Ave — *Web:* www.infusionoptions.net	Brooklyn	NY	11219	718-283-7233	283-6990	237
Infusive Solutions Inc 50 Harrison St Ste 204B — *Web:* www.infusivesolutions.com	Hoboken	NJ	07030	646-213-2000		193
Infutor Data Solutions 1 Lincoln Ctr 18W140 Butterfield Rd Ste 1020 — *Web:* infutor.com	Oakbrook Terrace	IL	60181	312-348-7900		225
InfySource Ltd 8345 NW 66th St — *TF:* 800-275-7503 ■ *Web:* www.infy-source.com	Miami	FL	33166	800-275-7503		024
ING Financial Markets LLC 1133 Avenue of the Americas — *Web:* www.ingwb.com	New York	NY	10036	646-424-6000		690
ING Funds 7337 E Doubletree Ranch Rd — *Web:* investments.voya.com	Scottsdale	AZ	85258	800-999-2018		528
INGAA (Interstate Natural Gas Association of America) 10 G St NE Ste 700 — *Web:* www.ingaa.org	Washington	DC	20002	202-216-5900	216-0870	49-21
Ingalls Feed Yard 10505 US Hwy 50 — *Web:* www.irsikanddoll.com	Ingalls	KS	67853	620-335-5174		10-1
Ingalls Memorial Hospital 1 Ingalls Dr — *TF:* 888-824-0200 ■ *Web:* www.ingalls.org	Harvey	IL	60426	708-333-2300		374-3
Ingenicomm Inc 14120 Parke Long Ct Ste 210 — *Web:* www.ingenicomm.net	Chantilly	VA	20151	703-665-4333		736
Ingenium PO Box 9724 Station T — **Fax Area Code:* 613 ■ *TF:* 866-442-4416 ■ *Web:* www.ingeniumcanada.org	Ottawa	ON	K1G5A3	866-442-4416	993-7923*	520
Ingenium Aerospace LLC 5389 International Dr — *Web:* www.ingeniumaerospace.com	Rockford	IL	61109	815-525-2000		350
Ingenium Technologies Corp 4216 Maray Dr — *Web:* www.ingeniumtech.com	Rockford	IL	61107	815-399-8803		256
InGenius Prep 50 Mitchell Dr — *TF:* 800-722-3105 ■ *Web:* www.ingeniusprep.com	New Haven	CT	06511	800-722-3105		113
Ingenuite Inc 7701 S Western Ave Ste 204 — *Web:* ingenuite.com	Oklahoma City	OK	73139	405-636-1802		177
Ingenuity Inc 8137 Helena Rd Ste 200 — *Web:* teamingenuity.com	Pelham	AL	35124	205-263-1560	263-1570	180
Ingerman & Horwitz LLP 20 Park Ave — *Web:* ihlaw.com	Baltimore	MD	21201	410-539-1200		41
Ingersoll Watson & Mcmachen Inc 1133 E Milham Rd — *Web:* iwmeng.com	Portage	MI	49002	269-344-6165	344-0555	727
Ingham County 315 S Jefferson St PO Box 179 — *Web:* www.ingham.org	Mason	MI	48854	517-676-7201	676-7254	338
Ingk Labs LLC 101 5th Ave Fl 8 — *Web:* www.digital.nyc	New York	NY	10003	646-350-3004		196
Ingle Intl 460 Richmond St W Ste 100 — *Web:* www.ingleinternational.com	Toronto	ON	M5V1Y1	416-730-8488		391-7

	Phone	Fax	Class
Ingles Markets Inc 2913 US Hwy 70 W .... Black Mountain NC 28711 *NASDAQ: IMKTA* ■ *TF:* 800-635-5066 ■ *Web:* www.ingles-markets.com	828-669-2941		345
Ingleside By The Lake 10630 W Front Rd .... Atascadero CA 93422 *Web:* inglesideal.com	805-460-6541		363
Ingleside High School 2807 Mustang Dr .... Ingleside TX 78362 *Web:* www.inglesideisd.org	361-776-2712		685
Ingleside Inn 200 W Ramon Rd............ Palm Springs CA 92264 *TF:* 800-772-6655 ■ *Web:* inglesideinn.com	760-325-0046		379
Ingleside Plantation Nurseries 5870 Leedstown Rd .... Oak Grove VA 22443 *Web:* inglesidenurseries.com	804-224-7111		369
Ingleside Rock Creek 3050 Military Rd NW .... Washington DC 20015 *Web:* www.ircdc.org	202-363-8310		672
IngletBlair LLC 8716 N Mopac Expwy Ste 310 .... Austin TX 78759 *Web:* www.ingletblair.com	512-732-0498	732-0488	225
Inglett & Stubbs LLC 5200 Riverview Rd .... Mableton GA 30126 *Web:* www.inglett-stubbs.com	404-881-1199	872-3101	189-4
Inglewood Associates LLC 9242 Headlands Rd .... Mentor OH 44060 *Web:* www.ingw.com	216-672-5560		193
Inglewood Park Cemetery Inc 720 E Florence Ave......................... Inglewood CA 90301 *Web:* www.inglewoodparkcemetery.org	310-412-6500		510
Inglewood Public Library 101 W Manchester Blvd .... Inglewood CA 90301 *Web:* www.cityofinglewood.org	310-412-5380		434-3
Ingomar Packing Co 9950 S Ingomar Grade PO Box 1448 .... Los Banos CA 93635 *TF:* 800-328-0026 ■ *Web:* www.ingomarpacking.com	209-826-9494	854-6292	296-20
Ingot Metal Company Ltd 111 Fenmar Dr........ Weston ON M9L1M3 *TF:* 800-567-7774 ■ *Web:* www.ingot.ca	416-749-1372		481
Ingram Barge Co 4400 Harding Rd............. Nashville TN 37205 *Web:* www.ingrambarge.com	615-298-8200		314
Ingram Entertainment Inc 2 Ingram Blvd .... La Vergne TN 37089 *TF:* 800-621-1333 ■ *Web:* www.ingramentertainment.com	615-287-4000		511
Ingram Financial Group Inc 799 Overlook Dr .... Winter Haven FL 33884 *Web:* ingramfinancialgroup.com	863-326-9833		390
Ingram Readymix Inc 3580 Fm 482........ New Braunfels TX 78132 *Web:* www.ingramreadymixinc.com	830-625-9156		182
Ingredient Exchange Co 401 N Lindbergh Blvd Ste 315 .... Saint Louis MO 63141 *Web:* www.ingexchange.com	314-872-8850	872-7500	297-2
Inhance Corp 609 8th St.................. Fort Madison IA 52627 *Web:* www.inhancecorp.com	319-372-4920		379
Inhance Digital 8057 Beverly Blvd .... Los Angeles CA 90048 *Web:* inhance.com	323-297-7700		514
Inhand Electronics 30 W Gude Dr Ste 550 .... Rockville MD 20850 *Web:* www.inhand.com	240-558-2014		261
Inhofe James M (Sen R - OK) 205 Russell Senate Office Bldg............. Washington DC 20510 *Web:* www.inhofe.senate.gov	202-224-4721	228-0380	342-2
inhouseIT 3193 Red Hill Ave .... Costa Mesa CA 92626 *TF:* 866-999-2638 ■ *Web:* inhouseit.com	949-660-5655	660-5688	177
Initial Group Inc 6556 Jocelyn Hollow Rd..................... Nashville TN 37205 *TF:* 866-295-6586 ■ *Web:* www.initialgroup.com	615-352-8721	352-8782	391-3
Initial Outfitters Inc 3325 Skyway Dr .... Auburn AL 36832 *Web:* www.initialoutfitters.com	334-887-1856		195
Initiative Corp 5700 Wilshire Blvd Ste 400 .... Los Angeles CA 90036 *Web:* initiative.com	323-370-8000		742
Initiative for a Competitive Inner City 200 High St 3rd Fl .... Boston MA 02110 *Web:* icic.org	617-292-2363		194
Initio Inc 350 Passaic St Ste 2............. Rochelle Park NJ 07662 *Web:* initioinc.com	201-621-0400		463
Injen Technology Company Ltd 244 Pioneer Pl .... Pomona CA 91768 *Web:* www.injen.com	909-839-0706		57
Injured Workers Insurance Fund 8722 Loch Raven Blvd .... Towson MD 21286 *TF:* 800-264-4943 ■ *Web:* www.ceiwc.com	410-494-2000		391-4
InjuryFree Inc 20250 144th Ave NE Ste 305 .... Woodinville WA 98072 **Fax Area Code:* 425 ■ *Web:* www.ergostat.com	206-363-7676	481-2998*	260
Ink Custom Tees 400 Casey Dr................ Maumelle AR 72113 *Web:* www.inkcustomtees.com	501-851-6916		687
Ink Inc 10561 Barkley St Ste 600 .... Overland Park KS 66212 *Web:* inkincpr.com	913-602-8531		636
Ink Spot Inc, The 40 Oval Rd Ste 1............... Quincy MA 02170 *Web:* www.theinkspot.com	617-773-7605		627
Ink Technologies Printer Supplies LLC 7600 Mcewen Rd .... Dayton OH 45459 *Web:* inktechnologies.com	937-630-3083		180
Inka Dinka Ink Children's Press PO Box 747 .... Miamitown OH 45041 *Web:* www.halotoys.com	513-477-0007		762
Inks Lake State Park 3630 Park Rd 4 .... Burnet TX 78611 *Web:* tpwd.texas.gov	512-793-2223		565
Inkstone Printing Inc 129 Liberty St .... Brockton MA 02301 *Web:* www.inkstone.com	508-587-5200		627
Inktel Contact Center Solutions 13975 NW 58th Ct .... Miami Lakes FL 33014 *Web:* www.inktel.com	305-523-1100		737
InkWell Management 521 Fifth Ave Ste 2600...................... New York NY 10175 *Web:* www.inkwellmanagement.com	212-922-3500	922-0535	444
INL (Idaho National Laboratory) 2525 Fremont Ave......................... Idaho Falls ID 83402 *TF:* 866-495-7440 ■ *Web:* www.inl.gov	866-495-7440		668
Inland 2009 W Ave S........................ La Crosse WI 54601 *Web:* www.inlandpackaging.com	608-788-5800		627
Inland Aerial Surveys Inc 7117 Arlington Ave Ste A.................... Riverside CA 92503 *Web:* inlandaerial.com	951-687-4252		727
Inland Arts & Graphics Inc 14440 Edison Dr.......................... New Lenox IL 60451 *TF:* 800-437-6003 ■ *Web:* www.inlandautoforms.com	800-437-6003		627
Inland Empire Magazine 3400 Central Ave Ste 160.................... Riverside CA 92506 *Web:* www.inlandempiremagazine.com	951-682-3026	682-0246	457-22
Inland Empire Paper Co 3320 N Argonne Rd .... Millwood WA 99212 *TF:* 866-437-7711 ■ *Web:* www.iepco.com	509-924-1911	927-8461	557
Inland Inc 209 Peterson Dr................. Elizabethtown KY 42701 *TF:* 800-626-4403 ■ *Web:* inland-inc.com	270-737-6757	737-6241	3
Inland Lakes Machine Inc 314 Haynes St .... Cadillac MI 49601 *Web:* www.inlandlakes.com	231-775-6543		454
Inland Marine Industries Inc 3245 Depot Rd .... Hayward CA 94545 *Web:* www.inlandmetal.com	510-785-8555		567
Inland Massage Institute Holland Professional Bldg Ste 110............. Spokane WA 99218 **Fax Area Code:* 888 ■ *Web:* www.inlandmassage.edu	509-465-3033	872-9791*	167-3
Inland Pacific Ballet 5050 Arrow Hwy........................... Montclair CA 91763 *Web:* www.ipballet.org	909-482-1590	482-1589	573-1
Inland Plastics Inc 201 Center St .... Rosedale AB T0J0Y0 *TF:* 800-997-6299 ■ *Web:* www.inlandplastics.com	403-823-6252		601
Inland Plywood Co 375 N Cass Ave............. Pontiac MI 48342 *TF:* 800-521-4355 ■ *Web:* www.inlandplywood.com	248-334-4706	338-7407	613
Inland Power & Light Company Inc 10110 W Hallett Rd.......................... Spokane WA 99224 *TF:* 800-747-7151 ■ *Web:* www.inlandpower.com	509-747-7151	747-7987	245
Inland Press Assn 701 Lee St Ste 925........................ Des Plaines IL 60016 *Web:* inlandpress.org	847-795-0380		138
Inland Productivity Solutions Inc 1153 W Ninth St............................. Upland CA 91786 *Web:* www.inland-prod.com	909-981-4500		177
Inland Sea Inc, The 9601 Carnegie Ave.......... El Paso TX 79925 *TF:* 800-434-7146 ■ *Web:* www.tis-worldwide.com	915-592-1517		780
Inland Seafood Corp 1651 Montreal Cir .... Tucker GA 30084 *TF:* 800-883-3474 ■ *Web:* www.inlandseafood.com	404-350-5850		297-5
Inland Technologies Inc 14 Queen St PO Box 253 .... Truro NS B2N5C1 *TF:* 877-633-5263 ■ *Web:* www.inlandgroup.ca	902-895-6346		192
Inland Truck Parts Co (ITP) 4400 College Blvd Ste 145............... Overland Park KS 66211 *TF:* 800-448-8436 ■ *Web:* www.inlandtruck.com	913-345-9664	345-8745	61
Inland Valley Arbitration & Mediation Service (IVAMS) 8287 White Oak Ave .... Rancho Cucamonga CA 91730 *Web:* www.ivams.com	909-466-1665	466-1796	41
Inland Valley Daily Bulletin 2041 E Fourth St............................ Ontario CA 91764 *Web:* www.dailybulletin.com	909-987-6397		532-2
Inlandboatmen's Union of the Pacific (IBU) 1711 W Nickerson St Ste D .... Seattle WA 98119 *Web:* www.ibu.org	206-284-6001		414
Inlet Tower Hotel & Suites 1020 W 12th Ave .... Anchorage AK 99501 *TF:* 800-544-0786 ■ *Web:* www.inlettower.com	907-276-0110		379
InLine 10802 Executive Center Dr Benton Bldg Ste 300................................ Little Rock AR 72211 *TF:* 877-652-2321 ■ *Web:* uniti.com	501-850-0820		174
Inline Fibreglass Ltd 30 Constellation Ct.......................... Toronto ON M9W1K1 *TF:* 866-566-5656 ■ *Web:* www.inlinefiberglass.com	416-679-1171	679-1150	499
Inline Filling Systems Inc 216 Seaboard Ave............................ Venice FL 34285 *Web:* www.fillers.com	941-486-8800		547
Inline Packaging LLC 1205 18th Ave S........................... Princeton MN 55371 *Web:* www.inlinepkg.com	763-631-1555	631-1557	317
Inline Plastics Corp 42 Canal St .... Shelton CT 06484 *TF:* 800-826-5567 ■ *Web:* www.inlineplastics.com	203-924-5933	924-0370	602
Inline Services Inc 27731 Commercial Park Rd .... Tomball TX 77375 *Web:* www.inlineservices.com	281-401-8142		358
inlingua Intl 551 Fifth Ave.................... New York NY 10176 *Web:* www.inlinguametrony.com	212-682-8585		423
Inman 75 N Woodward Ave Ste 80368 .... Tallahassee FL 32313 *TF:* 800-775-4662 ■ *Web:* www.inman.com	510-658-9252		530
Inman Mills 300 Park Rd PO Box 207 .... Inman SC 29349 *Web:* www.inmanmills.com	864-472-2121		745-1
Inman-EMJ Construction 88 Union Ave Ste 400....................... Memphis TN 38103 *Web:* www.inmanemj.com	901-682-4100		186
INMED Partnerships for Children 21240 Ridgetop Cir Ste 115.................. Ashburn VA 20147 **Fax Area Code:* 703 ■ *Web:* inmed.org	571-293-9380	858-7253*	48-5
Inmediata Health Group Corp 636 San Patricio Ave 2nd Fl.................. San Juan PR 00920 *Web:* portal.inmediata.com	787-774-0606		225
Inn & Club at Harbour Town, The 7 Lighthouse Ln .... Hilton Head Island SC 29928 *Web:* www.seapines.com	843-363-8100		379
Inn & Spa at Loretto 211 Old Santa Fe Trl........................ Santa Fe NM 87501 *TF:* 800-727-5531 ■ *Web:* www.hotelloretto.com	505-988-5531	984-7968	379
Inn Above Tide, The 30 El Portal .... Sausalito CA 94965 *TF:* 800-893-8433 ■ *Web:* innabovetide.com	415-332-9535		379
Inn At 500 Capitol LLC 500 S Capitol Blvd .... Boise ID 83702 *Web:* innat500.com	208-227-0500		378
Inn at Bay Harbor, The 3600 Village Harbor Dr..................... Bay Harbor MI 49770 *TF:* 866-585-8123 ■ *Web:* www.innatbayharbor.com	866-585-8123		669

	Phone	Fax	Class
Inn at Camachee Harbor 201 Yacht Club Dr, Saint Augustine FL 32084 *TF:* 800-688-5379 ■ *Web:* www.camacheeinn.com	904-825-0003	825-0048	379
Inn at Cherry Hill 500 17th Ave., Seattle WA 98122 *Web:* www.swedish.org	206-320-2164		372
Inn at Gig Harbor 3211 56th St NW, Gig Harbor WA 98335 *TF:* 800-795-9980 ■ *Web:* www.innatgigharbor.com	253-858-1111	851-5402	379
Inn at Henderson's Wharf 1000 Fell St, Baltimore MD 21231 *Web:* www.hendersonswharf.com	410-522-7777		379
Inn at Lambertville Station 11 Bridge St, Lambertville NJ 08530 *Web:* www.lambertvillestation.com	609-397-4400		379
Inn at Langley 400 First St PO Box 835, Langley WA 98260 *Web:* innatlangley.com	360-221-3033		379
Inn at Little Washington Middle & Main St PO Box 300, Washington VA 22747 *Web:* theinnatlittlewashington.com	540-675-3800		379
Inn at Longshore 260 Compo Rd S., Westport CT 06880 *Web:* www.innatlongshore.com	203-226-3316		379
Inn at Mamas Fish House 799 Poho Pl., Paia HI 96779 *TF:* 800-860-4852 ■ *Web:* www.mamasfishhouse.com	808-579-8488		378
Inn at Montchanin Village 528 Montchanin Rd, Montchanin DE 19710 *Web:* www.montchanin.com	302-888-2133	691-0198	379
Inn at Montpelier, The 147 Main St, Montpelier VT 05602 *Web:* www.innatmontpelier.com	802-223-2727	223-0722	379
Inn at Morro Bay 60 State Park Rd, Morro Bay CA 93442 *TF:* 800-321-9566 ■ *Web:* www.innatmorrobay.com	805-772-5651	772-4779	379
Inn at Mystic 3 Williams Ave PO Box 526, Mystic CT 06355 *TF:* 800-237-2415 ■ *Web:* innatmystic.com	860-536-9604	572-1635	379
Inn at Nichols Village 1101 Northern Blvd, Clarks Summit PA 18411 *Web:* www.nicholsvillage.com	570-587-1135		379
Inn at Ohio Northern University Management Co, The 401 W College Ave, Ada OH 45810 *Web:* innatonu.com	419-772-2500		378
Inn at Otter Crest 301 Otter Crest Loop, Otter Rock OR 97369 *TF:* 800-452-2101 ■ *Web:* www.innatottercrest.com	541-765-2111		379
Inn at Pelican Bay 800 Vanderbilt Beach Rd., Naples FL 34108 *TF:* 800-597-8770 ■ *Web:* www.innatpelicanbay.com	239-597-8777	597-8012	379
Inn at Perry Cabin 308 Watkins Ln., Saint Michaels MD 21663 *TF:* 800-722-2949 ■ *Web:* www.innatperrycabin.com	410-745-2200	745-3348	379
Inn at Queen Anne 505 First Ave N., Seattle WA 98109 *Web:* www.innatqueenanne.com	206-282-7357		379
Inn at Rancho Santa Fe 5951 Linea Del Cielo PO Box 869, Rancho Santa Fe CA 92067 *TF:* 800-843-4661 ■ *Web:* www.theinnatrsf.com	858-756-1131		669
Inn at Reading, The 1040 N Park Rd, Wyomissing PA 19610 *Web:* www.innatreading.com	610-372-7811		379
Inn at Saint John 939 Congress St., Portland ME 04102 *TF:* 800-636-9127 ■ *Web:* www.innatstjohn.com	207-773-6481		379
Inn at Saint Mary's 53993 US Hwy 31-33 N, South Bend IN 46637 *Web:* www.innatsaintmarys.com	574-232-4000		379
Inn at Spanish Head 4009 SW Hwy 101, Lincoln City OR 97367 *TF:* 800-452-8127 ■ *Web:* www.spanishhead.com	541-996-2161	996-4089	379
Inn at Tallgrass, The 2280 N Tara Cir, Wichita KS 67226 *Web:* www.theinnattallgrass.com	316-684-3466		379
Inn at the Market 86 Pine St, Seattle WA 98101 *TF:* 800-446-4484 ■ *Web:* www.innatthemarket.com	206-443-3600		379
Inn at The Quay 900 Quayside Dr., New Westminster BC V3M6G1 *TF:* 800-663-2001 ■ *Web:* www.innatwestminsterquay.com	604-520-1776	520-5645	379
Inn at the Tides, The 800 Coast Hwy 1, Bodega Bay CA 94923 *TF:* 800-541-7788 ■ *Web:* www.innatthetides.com	707-875-2751	875-2669	379
Inn at Virginia Mason 1006 Spring St, Seattle WA 98104 *TF:* 800-283-6453 ■ *Web:* www.innatvirginiamason.com	800-283-6453		372
Inn at Virginia Tech & Skelton Conference Ctr 901 Prices Fork Rd, Blacksburg VA 24061 *TF:* 877-200-3360 ■ *Web:* www.innatvirginiatech.com	540-231-8000		377
Inn by the Sea 40 Bowery Beach Rd., Cape Elizabeth ME 04107 *Web:* www.innbythesea.com	207-799-3134		669
Inn of Chicago Magnificent Mile 162 E Ohio St, Chicago IL 60611 *Web:* www.theinnofchicago.com	312-787-3100		379
Inn of Long Beach 185 Atlantic Ave, Long Beach CA 90802 *TF:* 800-230-7500 ■ *Web:* www.innoflongbeach.com	562-435-3791	436-7510	379
Inn of the Governors 101 W Alameda St, Santa Fe NM 87501 *TF:* 800-234-4534 ■ *Web:* innofthegovernors.com	505-982-4333		379
Inn of the Hills River Resort 1001 Junction Hwy, Kerrville TX 78028 *TF:* 800-292-5690 ■ *Web:* www.innofthehills.com	830-895-5000		669
Inn of the Mountain Gods 287 Carrizo Canyon Rd., Mescalero NM 88340 *TF:* 800-545-9011 ■ *Web:* innofthemountaingods.com	800-545-9011		669
Inn on Biltmore Estate 1 Antler Hill Rd., Asheville NC 28803 *TF:* 800-411-3812 ■ *Web:* www.biltmore.com	828-225-1600		379
Inn on Fifth 699 Fifth Ave S, Naples FL 34102 *TF:* 888-403-8778 ■ *Web:* www.innonfifth.com	239-403-8777	403-8778	379
Inn on Gitche Gumee 8517 Congdon Blvd., Duluth MN 55804 *TF:* 800-317-4979 ■ *Web:* www.innongitchegumee.com	218-525-4979		379
Inn on Lake Superior 350 Canal Pk Dr., Duluth MN 55802 *TF:* 888-668-4352 ■ *Web:* www.theinnonlakesuperior.com	218-726-1111	727-3976	379
Inn on Long Wharf 5 Washington St, Newport RI 02840 *Web:* www.extraholidays.com	401-847-7800		669
Inn on the Alameda 303 E Alameda St, Santa Fe NM 87501 *TF:* 888-984-2121 ■ *Web:* www.innonthealameda.com	888-984-2121		379
Inn on the Paseo 630 Paseo de Peralta, Santa Fe NM 87501 *TF:* 855-984-8200 ■ *Web:* www.innonthepaseo.com	505-984-8200		379
Inner City Law Ctr 1309 E Seventh St, Los Angeles CA 90021 *Web:* www.innercitylaw.org	213-891-2880	891-2888	428
Inner Path 200 Commercial St., Nevada City CA 95959 *TF:* 866-665-7765 ■ *Web:* innerpath.org	530-470-6057		239
Inner State Beauty School 5150 Mayfield Rd, Lyndhurst OH 44124 *Web:* www.innerstatebeautyschool.com	440-442-4500	442-4630	685
Inner Traditions Intl 1 Park St, Rochester VT 05767 **Fax Area Code:* 802 ■ *TF:* 800-246-8648 ■ *Web:* www.innertraditions.com	800-246-8648	767-3726*	637-2
Innerchoice Publishing 15079 Oak Chase Ct, Wellington FL 33414 *Web:* www.innerchoicepublishing.com	561-790-0132		637-2
InnerCite PO Box 22310, Salt Lake City UT 84122 **Fax Area Code:* 801 ■ *TF:* 866-700-3245 ■ *Web:* www.isp.com	866-700-3245	924-1092*	224
InnerLight Publishing c/o K. Alexander PO Box 370002, Decatur GA 30037 *Web:* innerlightpublishing.com	404-298-1018	298-1845	637-2
Innerspec Technologies Inc 2940 Perrowville Rd, Forest VA 24551 *Web:* www.innerspec.com	434-948-1301		463
Innerstave LLC 21660 Eighth St E, Sonoma CA 95476 *Web:* www.innerstave.com	707-996-8781		385
Innerworkings Inc 600 W Chicago Ave Ste 850, Chicago IL 60654 *NASDAQ: INWK* ■ *Web:* www.inwk.com	312-642-3700		687
Innis Maggiore Group Inc 4715 Whipple Ave NW, Canton OH 44718 *TF:* 800-460-4111 ■ *Web:* innismaggiore.com	330-492-5500	492-5568	4
Innisbrook Resort & Golf Club 36750 US Hwy 19 N, Palm Harbor FL 34684 *TF:* 800-492-6899 ■ *Web:* www.innisbrookgolfresort.com	727-942-2000	942-5576	669
Inniswood Metro Gardens 940 S Hempstead Rd, Westerville OH 43081 *Web:* www.inniswood.org	614-895-6216	895-6352	97
Innkeepers USA Trust 340 Royal Poinciana Way Ste 306, Palm Beach Gardens FL 33480	561-835-1800	835-0457	654
Innocean USA 180 5th St Ste 200, Huntington Beach CA 92648 *Web:* www.innoceanusa.com	714-861-5200		5
Innocence Project of Florida Inc 1100 E Park Ave, Tallahassee FL 32301 *Web:* www.floridainnocence.org	850-561-6767		428
Innolect Inc 2764 Pleasant Rd Ste 11503, Fort Mill SC 29708 *Web:* innolectinc.com	803-396-8500		193
InnoMark Inc 982 E Factory Dr, Saint George UT 84790 *TF:* 866-486-6642 ■ *Web:* www.innomarkinc.com	435-627-8464	627-8463	393
InnoMedia Inc 1901 McCarthy Blvd, Milpitas CA 95035 *Web:* www.innomedia.com	408-432-5400	941-8152	735
Innonet LLC 2 Huntley Rd., Old Lyme CT 06371 *Web:* www.innonetllc.com	860-395-0700		180
Innophos Holdings Inc 259 Prospect Plains Rd, Cranbury NJ 08512 *NASDAQ: IPHS* ■ *Web:* www.innophos.com	609-495-2495		146
Innosight LLC 92 Hayden Ave, Lexington MA 02421 *TF:* 877-934-7787 ■ *Web:* www.innosight.com	781-652-7200	652-7202	463
InnoSource Inc 5600 Blazer Pkwy Ste 200, Dublin OH 43017 *Web:* www.innosource.com	614-775-1400		260
Innospec Inc 8375 S Willow St, Littleton CO 80124 *NASDAQ: IOSP* ■ *Web:* www.innospecinc.com	303-792-5554		144
Innosphere Systems Development Group Ltd 147 Wyndham St N Ste 306, Guelph ON N1H4E9 *Web:* innosphere.ca	519-766-9726		180
Innotech-Execaire Aviation Group 10225 Ryan Ave, Dorval QC H9P1A2 *Web:* www.innotechaviation.com	514-636-8484		21
Innotek Corp 9140 Zachary Ln N., Maple Grove MN 55369 *Web:* www.innotek-ep.com	763-488-9904		454
In-N-Out Burger Inc 4199 Campus Dr 9th Fl, Irvine CA 92612 *TF:* 800-786-1000 ■ *Web:* www.in-n-out.com	949-509-6200		670
Innova Engineering Inc 2 Park Plz Ste 680, Irvine CA 92614 *Web:* innovaengineering.com	949-975-9965	975-9969	256
Innova Medical Ophthalmics Inc 48 Carnforth Rd, Toronto ON M4A2K7 *Web:* www.innovamed.com	416-615-0185		543
Innova Technologies Inc 1432 S Jones Blvd, Las Vegas NV 89146 *Web:* www.innovanv.com	702-220-6640		261
InnoVactiv Inc 265 2E Rue E, Rimouski QC G5L9H3 *Web:* innovactiv.com	418-721-2308		146
Innovadex LLC 7930 Santa Fe 3rd Fl, Overland Park KS 66204 *Web:* www.ulprospector.com	913-307-9010		393
Innovage LLC 19511 Pauling, Foothill Ranch CA 92610	949-587-9207		4
Innovairre Communications LLC 825 Hylton Rd., Pennsauken Township NJ 08110 *Web:* www.innovairre.com	856-663-2500		466
Innovara Inc 105 Middle St, Hadley MA 01035 *Web:* innovara.com	413-387-6188	387-6772	41
Innovasium Inc 55 Albert St Ste 200, Markham ON L3P2T4 *Web:* www.innovasium.com	905-479-5555		225
Innovasys 36735 Metro Ct, Sterling Heights MI 48312 *Web:* innovasys1.com	586-795-3000		358
Innovasystems International LLC 2385 Northside Dr Ste 300, San Diego CA 92108 *Web:* www.innovasi.com	619-955-5800	955-5801	177
Innovate E-Commerce Inc 1000 Brooktree Rd Ste 110, Wexford PA 15090 *Web:* innovateec.com	412-681-7090		631
InnovaTech Inc 1800 Diagonal Rd, Alexandria VA 22314	703-418-3919		177
Innovated Packaging Company Inc 38505 Cherry St Ste C, Newark CA 94560 *TF:* 866-745-8180 ■ *Web:* www.innovpak.com	510-745-8180	745-8294	88
Innovatia Inc 1 Germain St, Saint John NB E2L4V1 *TF:* 800-363-3358 ■ *Web:* www.innovatia.net	506-640-4000		463

	Phone	Fax	Class
Innovation Capital LLC 222 N Sepulveda Blvd Ste 1300 . . . . El Segundo CA 90245 *Web:* www.innovation-capital.com	310-335-9333		194
Innovation Connector 1208 W White River Blvd . . . . Muncie IN 47303 *Web:* innovationconnector.com	765-285-4900		196
Innovation Genesis LLC 75 Arlington St Ste 500 . . . . Boston MA 02116 *Web:* www.productgenesis.com	617-234-0070		261
Innovation Tap LLC 200 N Warner Rd Ste 210. . . . . King of Prussia PA 19406 *TF:* 855-438-4666 ■ *Web:* www.innotap.com	855-438-4666		225
Innovation Works Inc Nova Tower 2 2 Allegheny Ctr Ste 100 . . . . Pittsburgh PA 15212 *Web:* www.innovationworks.org	412-681-1520	681-2625	792
Innovations International Inc 1416 E Farm Meadow Ln . . . . Salt Lake City UT 84117 **Fax Area Code:* 800 ■ *TF:* 800-693-3594 ■ *Web:* www.innovint.com	801-671-8392	693-9430*	196
Innovative Air Inc 747 S 13th St . . . . Boise ID 83702 *Web:* innovativeairinc.com	208-331-3303		362
Innovative Artists 1505 Tenth St . . . . Santa Monica CA 90401 *Web:* www.innovativeartists.com	310-656-0400		731
Innovative Benefit Solutions Inc 11057 N Towne Sq Rd . . . . Mequon WI 53092 *Web:* ibsinc.ws	262-241-2500		390
Innovative Brick Systems LLC 11625 Reed Ct . . . . Broomfield CO 80020 *TF:* 800-413-4588 ■ *Web:* www.mbrick.com	720-890-6032	890-6038	191-1
Innovative Circuits Arizona Inc 130 N Pasadena St . . . . Gilbert AZ 85233 *Web:* www.icaz.com	480-497-6681	497-8366	625
Innovative Circuits Inc 311a S Pky St. . . . . Corinth MS 38834 *TF:* 866-887-7381 ■ *Web:* www.icimfg.com	662-287-2007	665-9275	425
Innovative Coatings Inc 24 Jayar Rd . . . . Medway MA 02053 *Web:* www.innovativecoatings.com	508-533-6101	533-5722	481
Innovative Communications Inc 528-F Bypass 123 . . . . Seneca SC 29678 *TF:* 888-846-6682 ■ *Web:* www.innova.net	864-888-4911	882-9638	224
Innovative Components Inc 1050 National Pkwy . . . . Schaumburg IL 60173 *Web:* www.innovative-components.com	847-885-9050		596
Innovative Composite Engineering Inc 1265 N Main Ave . . . . White Salmon WA 98672 *Web:* www.innovativecomposite.com	509-493-4484		180
Innovative Concepts 3440 Roberto Ct . . . . San Luis Obispo CA 93401 *TF:* 877-545-9562 ■ *Web:* www.in-con.com	805-545-9562	545-5730	180
Innovative Consulting Inc 5320 Eagleswatch Ct . . . . Cincinnati OH 45230 *TF:* 800-837-7224 ■ *Web:* www.billradin.com	800-837-7224		196
Innovative Control Systems Inc 10125 S 52nd St. . . . . Franklin WI 53132 **Fax Area Code:* 414 ■ *TF:* 800-356-2671 ■ *Web:* www.accutechsecurity.com	800-356-2671	423-4448*	253
Innovative Data Management Systems LLC 4006 W Azeele St . . . . Tampa FL 33609 *TF:* 866-706-4588 ■ *Web:* idmsystems.com	813-207-2025		177
Innovative Employee Solutions Inc 9665 Granite Ridge Dr Ste 420. . . . . San Diego CA 92123 *Web:* www.innovativeemployeesolutions.com	858-715-5100		734
Innovative Engineering Solutions Inc 26200 Adams Ave. . . . . Murrieta CA 92562 *Web:* iesnet.com	951-304-7600		261
Innovative Enterprises Inc 25 Town & Country Dr . . . . Washington MO 63090 *TF:* 800-280-0300 ■ *Web:* www.innovative-1.com	636-390-0300	390-4004	548
Innovative Fluid Handling Systems 3300 E Rock Falls Rd . . . . Rock Falls IL 61071 **Fax Area Code:* 815 ■ *TF:* 800-435-7003 ■ *Web:* www.ifhgroup.com	800-435-7003	626-1438*	198
Innovative Industrial Solutions Inc 208 S Phoenix Ave . . . . Russellville AR 72801 *TF:* 888-684-8249	479-968-4266		693
Innovative Information Solutions Inc 61 Interstate Ln. . . . . Waterbury CT 06705 *Web:* www.innovativeis.com	203-756-4243		179
Innovative Injection Technologies Inc 2360 Grand Ave . . . . West Des Moines IA 50265 *Web:* www.i2-tech.com	515-225-6707	225-9673	604
Innovative Insurance Group LLC 3062 Main St . . . . Green Lane PA 18054 *TF:* 877-691-7188 ■ *Web:* innovativeig.com	877-691-7188		390
Innovative Lighting Inc 109 Progressive Ave. . . . . Roland IA 50236 **Fax Area Code:* 515 ■ *TF:* 800-949-4888 ■ *Web:* www.innovativelight.com	800-949-4888	388-5549*	60
Innovative Media Systems (IMS) 7121 Washington Ave S . . . . Edina MN 55439 *Web:* www.innovativemediasystems.com	952-960-2915		189-4
Innovative Metals Company Inc (IMETCO) 4648 S Old Peachtree Rd . . . . Norcross GA 30071 *TF:* 800-646-3826 ■ *Web:* www.imetco.com	770-908-1030	908-2264	46
Innovative Mold Inc 12500 31 Mile Rd. . . . . Washington MI 48095 *Web:* www.innovativemoldinc.com	586-752-2996		757
Innovative Office Solutions 711 W Russell St . . . . Sioux Falls SD 57104 *Web:* www.innovativeos.com	605-336-1960		320
Innovative Optics Inc 6812 Hemlock Ln . . . . Maple Grove MN 55369 *Web:* innovativeoptics.com	763-425-7789		475
Innovative Plastech Inc 1260 Kingsland Dr . . . . Batavia IL 60510 *Web:* www.thinkipi.com	630-232-1808		596
Innovative Plastics Corp 400 Rt 303 . . . . Orangeburg NY 10962 *Web:* www.innovative-plastics.com	845-359-7500	359-0237	601
Innovative Routines International Inc 2194 Hwy A1A 3rd Fl . . . . Melbourne FL 32937 *TF:* 800-333-7678 ■ *Web:* www.iri.com	321-777-8889	777-8886	178-1
Innovative Sciences Inc 401 Cascade Point Ln. . . . . Cary NC 27513 **Fax Area Code:* 919 ■ *TF:* 800-243-9169 ■ *Web:* www.thinkingmaps.com	800-243-9169	678-8782*	637-2
Innovative Software Services Inc 157 S Main St. . . . . Eaton Rapids MI 48827 *Web:* issi-central.com	517-663-5710		177
Innovative Solutions & Support Inc 720 Pennsylvania Dr. . . . . Exton PA 19341 *NASDAQ: ISSC* ■ *Web:* innovative-ss.com	610-646-9800	646-0149	529
Innovative Stamping Corp 2068 E Gladwick St. . . . . Compton CA 90220 *TF:* 800-400-0047 ■ *Web:* www.innovative-sys.com	310-537-6996	537-0312	488
Innovative Surfaces Inc 2620 Industrial Ct. . . . . Hastings MN 55033 *Web:* www.innovativesurfaces.com	651-437-1004		115
Innovative Systems Group Inc 799 Roosevelt Rd . . . . Glen Ellyn IL 60137 *TF:* 800-739-2400 ■ *Web:* www.innovativesys.com	630-858-8500		177
Innovative Systems Inc 790 Holiday Dr . . . . Pittsburgh PA 15220 *TF:* 800-622-6390 ■ *Web:* www.innovativesystems.com	412-937-9300		178-1
Innovative Technologies Corp (ITC) 1020 Woodman Dr Ste 100 . . . . Dayton OH 45432 *TF:* 800-745-8050 ■ *Web:* www.itc-1.com	937-252-2145	254-6853	178-10
Innovative Technology Ltd 105 Carter Rd . . . . Elk City OK 73644 *Web:* www.itlnet.net	580-243-1559	243-2810	393
Innovative Telecom Solutions Inc 9 Vela Way . . . . Edgewater NJ 07020 *TF:* 800-510-3000 ■ *Web:* www.innovativetel.com	800-510-3000		387
Innovent Air Handling Equipment 60 28th Ave N. . . . . Minneapolis MN 55411 *TF:* 877-218-4129 ■ *Web:* www.innoventair.com	612-877-4800		358
Innovest Portfolio Solutions LLC 4643 S Ulster St Ste 1040 . . . . Denver CO 80237 *Web:* www.innovestinc.com	303-694-1900		401
Innovid 30 Irving P 1st Fl . . . . New York NY 10003 **Fax Area Code:* 646 ■ *Web:* www.innovid.com	212-966-7555	349-3639*	5
Innovital Systems Inc 3901 Calverton Blvd Ste 155 . . . . Calverton MD 20705 *Web:* innovitalsystems.com	240-790-0598		261
Innovize Inc 500 Oak Grove Pkwy . . . . Saint Paul MN 55127 *TF:* 877-605-6580 ■ *Web:* www.innovize.com	877-605-6580		602
Innovus Pharmaceuticals Inc 1981 Murray Holladay Rd Ste 100 . . . . Salt Lake City UT 84117 *Web:* innovuspharma.com	801-272-9294		85
InnoZen Inc 6429 Independence Ave . . . . Woodland Hills CA 91367	818-593-4880		231
InnQuest Software Corp 5300 W Cypress Ste 160 . . . . Tampa FL 33607 *Web:* www.innquest.com	813-288-4900		174
Inns By The Sea PO Box 101. . . . . Carmel By The Sea CA 93921 *Web:* www.innsbythesea.com	831-624-0101		379
InnSuites Hospitality Trust InnSuites Hotels & Suites 475 N Granada Ave. . . . . Tucson AZ 85701 *TF:* 800-842-4242 ■ *Web:* www.innsuites.com	520-622-0923		379
InoCom Inc 228 Park Ave S Ste 320. . . . . New York NY 10003 *TF:* 800-538-7424 ■ *Web:* www.ino.com	410-867-2100		463
Inogen Inc 326 Bollay Dr . . . . Goleta CA 93117 *Web:* www.inogen.com	855-631-2438		476
Inolex Chemical Co 2101 S Swanson St . . . . Philadelphia PA 19148 *TF:* 800-521-9891 ■ *Web:* www.inolex.com	215-271-0800	271-6282	144
Inova Diagnostics Inc 9900 Old Grove Rd . . . . San Diego CA 92131 *TF:* 800-545-9495 ■ *Web:* www.inovadx.com	858-586-9900	586-9911	231
Inova Federal Credit Union 358 S Elkhart Ave . . . . Elkhart IN 46516 *Web:* www.inovafederal.org	574-294-6553		70
Inova Geophysical Equipment Ltd 12200 Parc Crest Dr . . . . Stafford TX 77477 *Web:* www.inovageo.com	281-568-2000		539
Inova Health System 8110 Gatehouse Rd . . . . Falls Church VA 22042 **Fax Area Code:* 703 ■ *TF:* 855-694-6682 ■ *Web:* www.inova.org	855-694-6682	504-6607*	353
Inova Payroll Inc 636 Grassmere Pk Ste 110 . . . . Nashville TN 37211 *TF:* 888-244-6106	615-921-0600		734
Inova Solutions Inc 110 Avon St . . . . Charlottesville VA 22902 *TF:* 800-637-1077 ■ *Web:* www.inovasolutions.com	434-817-8000	817-8002	178-1
Inovalon Inc 4321 Collington Rd. . . . . Bowie MD 20716 *TF:* 877-831-8171 ■ *Web:* www.inovalon.com	301-809-4000		363
Inovar Inc 1073 W 1700 N. . . . . Logan UT 84321 *TF:* 866-898-4949 ■ *Web:* www.inovar-inc.com	435-792-4949		393
Inovar Packaging Group LLC 10470 Miller Rd . . . . Dallas TX 75238 *TF:* 800-285-2235 ■ *Web:* inovarpkg.com	817-277-6666	275-2770	627
In-O-Vate Technologies Inc 810 Saturn St Ste 21. . . . . Jupiter FL 33477 *TF:* 888-443-7937 ■ *Web:* dryerbox.com	561-743-8696		191-1
Inovatia Laboratories LLC 120 E Davis St . . . . Fayette MO 65248 *TF:* 800-280-1912 ■ *Web:* www.inovatia.com	660-248-1911		743
Invent Engineering Inc 8877 Fwy Dr. . . . . Macedonia OH 44056 *Web:* inoventengineering.com	330-468-0011		261
Inovex Industries Inc 45681 Oakbrook Ct Ste 102 . . . . Sterling VA 20166 *TF:* 888-374-3366 ■ *Web:* www.ride-on.com	703-421-9778		3
Inovex Information Systems Inc 390 Interlocken Cres Ste 350 . . . . Broomfield CO 80021 *TF:* 800-469-9705 ■ *Web:* inovexcorp.com	443-782-1452		180
Inovio Pharmaceuticals Inc 660 W Germantown Pk Ste 110 . . . . Plymouth Meeting PA 19462 *NASDAQ: INO* ■ *TF:* 877-446-6846 ■ *Web:* www.inovio.com	267-440-4200		250
Inovise Medical Inc 8770 SW Nimbus Ave Ste D. . . . . Beaverton OR 97008 *TF:* 877-466-8473 ■ *Web:* inovise.com	503-431-3800		476

Company	Phone	Fax	Class
Inovity Inc 5775 Peachtree Dunwoody Rd Ste D-550 Atlanta GA 30342 *Fax Area Code: 674 ■ TF: 800-452-7418 ■ Web: inovity.com	678-904-9040	904-9041*	180
Inovo Inc 401 Leonard Blvd N Lehigh Acres FL 33971 TF: 888-446-6862 ■ Web: www.inovoinc.com	239-643-6577	643-6530	476
Inovo LLC 213 S Ashley St Ste 300 Ann Arbor MI 48104 TF: 888-464-6686 ■ Web: www.theinovogroup.com	888-464-6686		463
Inovonics Corp 397 S Taylor Ave Louisville CO 80027 Web: www.inovonics.com	303-939-9336		693
In-place Machining Company Inc 3811 N Holton St Milwaukee WI 53212 Web: www.inplace.com	414-562-2000		697
Inpower LLC 3555 Africa Rd Galena OH 43021 TF: 866-548-0965 ■ Web: www.inpowerdirect.com	740-548-0965		350
Inprov Ltd 2150 E Continental Blvd Southlake TX 76092 Web: www.inprov.biz	817-748-0300		463
Input 1 LLC 6200 Canoga Ave Ste 400 Woodland Hills CA 91367 TF: 888-882-2554 ■ Web: www.input1.com	818-713-2203		178-10
Input Solutions Inc 9250 Gaither Rd Gaithersburg MD 20877 Web: www.inputsolutions.com	301-948-6620		225
In-Q-Tel 2107 Wilson Blvd Ste 1100 Arlington VA 22201 Web: www.iqt.org	703-248-3000		792
InQuest Marketing Inc 9100 Ward Pkwy Kansas City MO 64114 Web: inquestmarketing.com	816-994-0994		636
Inquipco 2730 N Nellis Blvd Las Vegas NV 89115 Web: inquipco.com	702-644-1700		190
Inquir 1702 E McNair Dr Tempe AZ 85283 TF: 866-433-8532 ■ Web: inquir.com	833-346-7847		449
Inquiries Inc 129 N West St Frnt Easton MD 21601 TF: 866-987-3767 ■ Web: www.inquiriesinc.com	866-987-3767		400
Inquiry Press 7550 Eastman Ave Midland MI 48642 TF: 800-748-0188 ■ Web: www.inquirypress.com	989-631-0009	631-9280	637-2
Inquiry Systems Inc 1195 Goodale Blvd Columbus OH 43212 TF: 800-508-1116 ■ Web: www.inquirysys.com	614-464-3800		195
Inrad Inc 4375 Donker Ct SE Kentwood MI 49512 TF: 800-558-4647 ■ Web: www.inradinc.com	616-301-7800		476
Inrad Optics Inc 181 Legrand Ave Northvale NJ 07647 Web: www.inradoptics.com	201-767-1910	767-9644	253
In-Rel Properties Inc 2328 Tenth Ave N Ste 401 Lake Worth FL 33461 Web: in-rel.com	561-533-0344		652
inRESONANCE Inc 32 Industrial Dr E Ste 100 Northampton MA 01060 Web: www.inresonance.com	413-587-0236	587-0238	177
INRIX Inc 10210 NE Points Dr Ste 300 Kirkland WA 98033 Web: www.inrix.com	425-284-3800		393
INS (Infusion Nurses Society) 315 Norwood Pk S Norwood MA 02062 TF: 800-694-0298 ■ Web: www.ins1.org	781-440-9408	440-9409	49-8
INS (International Neuropsychological Society) 700 Ackerman Rd Ste 625 Columbus OH 43202 *Fax Area Code: 614 ■ Web: www.the-ins.org	801-487-0475	263-4366*	49-15
INS (Industrial Networking Solutions) 16415 Addison Rd Ste 550 Addison TX 75001 TF: 800-889-1461 ■ Web: www.industrialnetworking.com	972-248-7466	248-9533	174
Insaco Inc 1365 Canary Rd Quakertown PA 18951 Web: www.insaco.com	215-536-3500	536-7750	621
Insbank 2106 Crestmoor Rd Nashville TN 37215 Web: insbanktn.com	615-515-2265		70
Inscape Publishing Inc 6465 Wayzata Blvd Ste 800 Minneapolis MN 55426 Web: everythingdisc.com	763-765-2222	765-2277	178-3
Insco Distributing Inc 12501 Network Blvd San Antonio TX 78249 TF: 855-282-4295 ■ Web: www.insco.com	210-690-8400	690-1524	665
Insegment Inc 313 Washington St Ste 401 Newton MA 02458 Web: www.insegment.com	617-965-0800		5
Insequence Inc 750 Jim Parker Dr Smyrna TN 37167 Web: www.insequence.com	615-459-8943		177
Inserts East Inc 7045 Central Hwy Pennsauken Township NJ 08109 Web: insertseast.com	856-663-8181	663-3288	174
In-Shape Health Clubs 6 S El Dorado St Ste 600 Stockton CA 95210 TF: 877-446-7427 ■ Web: www.inshape.com	209-472-2450	472-2235	354
Inside Edition Inc PO Box 1323 New York NY 10101 Web: www.insideedition.com	212-817-5555		116
Inside Ideas Inc 49 Broadway St Ste 202 Asheville NC 28801 Web: www.thegossagency.com	828-225-6888		7
Inside Publications 6221 N Clark St Chicago IL 60660 Web: www.insideonline.com	773-465-9700	465-9800	532-4
Inside Self Storage Magazine 3300 N Central Ave Ste 300 Phoenix AZ 85012 Web: www.insideselfstorage.com	480-990-1101	990-0819	457-21
Inside Source Inc 985 Industrial Rd Ste 101 San Carlos CA 94070 Web: www.insidesource.com	650-508-9101		321
Inside Washington Publishers 1919 S Eads St Ste 201 Arlington VA 22202 Web: www.iwpnews.com	703-416-8500	416-8543	637-9
InsideFlyer Magazine 1930 Frequent Flyer Pt Colorado Springs CO 80915 Web: insideflyer.com	719-597-8889		457-22
Insider Marketing 10801 E Northwest Hwy Dallas TX 75238 Web: www.insidermarketing.com	214-348-4350		195
InsideUp Inc 8880 Rio San Diego Ste 800 San Diego CA 92108 TF: 800-889-6178 ■ Web: www.insideup.com	858-397-5733		393
Insight 6820 S Harl Ave Tempe AZ 85283 TF: 800-467-4448 ■ Web: www.ips.insight.com	800-467-4448		366
In-Sight Books Inc 4141 NW Expy Ste 110 Oklahoma City OK 73116 TF: 800-658-9262 ■ Web: www.insightbooks.com	405-810-9501	810-9504	637-2

Company	Phone	Fax	Class
Insight Capital Investment Company Ltd 4101 Gateway Dr Colleyville TX 76034	817-545-1959		690
Insight Computing LLC 448 Ignacio Blvd Ste 490 Novato CA 94949 *Fax Area Code: 415 ■ TF: 800-380-8985 ■ Web: www.insight-computing.com	800-380-8985	532-2439*	175
Insight Designs Web Solutions 2006 Broadway St 300 Boulder CO 80302 Web: www.insightdesigns.com	303-449-8567		180
Insight Editions PO Box 3088 San Rafael CA 94912 Web: www.insighteditions.com	415-526-1370		637-2
Insight Global Inc (IGI) 4170 Ashford Dunwoody Rd Ste 250 Atlanta GA 30319 TF: 888-336-7463 ■ Web: www.insightglobal.com	404-257-7900	257-1004	193
Insight Information 214 King St W Ste 300 Toronto ON M5H3S6 *Fax Area Code: 866 ■ TF: 888-777-1707 ■ Web: www.insightinfo.com	888-777-1707	777-1292*	765
Insight Investments Corp 611 Anton Blvd Ste 700 Costa Mesa CA 92626 Web: www.insightinvestments.com	714-939-2300		624
Insight Marketing Design Inc 401 E 8th St Ste 304 Sioux Falls SD 57103 Web: insightmarketingdesign.com	605-275-0011		195
Insight Medical Holdings Ltd 200 Meadowlark Health Ctr 156 St & 89 Ave Edmonton AB T5R5W9 TF: 866-771-9446 ■ Web: x-ray.ca	780-669-2222		415
Insight Outcomes LLC 1325 13th St NW Ste 47 Washington DC 20005 Web: www.insightoutcomes.org	202-258-5025	797-7912	194
Insight Performance Inc 990 Washington St Ste S109 Dedham MA 02026 Web: insightperformance.com	781-326-8201		463
Insight Product Development 4660 N Ravenswood Ave Chicago IL 60640 Web: insightpd.com	773-907-9500		256
Insight Resource Group 3468 Mt Diablo Blvd Ste B120 LaFayette CA 94549 Web: www.insightresourcegroup.com	925-254-4114		317
Insight Service 20338 Progress Dr Strongsville OH 44149 TF: 800-465-4329 ■ Web: testoil.com	216-251-2510		743
Insight Sourcing Group Inc (ISG) 5555 Triangle Pky Ste 300 Norcross GA 30092 TF: 888-973-0208 ■ Web: www.insightsourcing.com	888-973-0208		393
Insight Technology Inc 9 Akira Way Londonderry NH 03053 TF: 866-509-2040 ■ Web: www.insighttechnology.com	866-509-2040		21
Insight Technology Solutions Inc 17251 Melford Blvd Ste 100 Bowie MD 20715 TF: 800-908-1121 ■ Web: www.insighttsi.com	301-860-1121		177
Insights in Marketing LLC 444 Skokie Blvd Ste 200 Wilmette IL 60091 Web: www.insightsinmarketing.com	847-853-0500		195
Insignia Systems Inc 8799 Brooklyn Blvd Minneapolis MN 55445 NASDAQ: ISIG ■ TF: 800-874-4648 ■ Web: www.insigniasystems.com	763-392-6200	392-6222	701
Insigniam Performance 345 Third St Laguna Beach CA 92651 Web: insigniam.com	949-494-4553		195
Insinger Machine Co 6245 State Rd Philadelphia PA 19135 TF: 800-344-4802 ■ Web: insingermachine.com	215-624-4800	624-6966	298
In-Sink-Erator 4700 21st St Racine WI 53406 TF: 800-845-8345 ■ Web: www.insinkerator.com	262-554-5432		36
Insite Managed Solutions LLC 1616 W Cape Coral Pkwy Ste 102 PMB 165 Cape Coral FL 33914 Web: www.callinsite.com	239-338-8719		463
Insite Real Estate Inc 714 Grand Central St Clearwater FL 33756 Web: insiterei.com	727-445-9331	445-9225	652
InSite Vision Inc 965 Atlantic Ave Alameda CA 94501 NASDAQ: ISV ■ Web: www.insitevision.com	510-865-8800	865-5700	231
InSitu Technologies Inc 539 Phalen Blvd Saint Paul MN 55139 Web: insitu-tech.com	651-389-1017		476
Insmed Inc 10 Finderne Ave Bldg 10 Bridgewater NJ 08807 NASDAQ: INSM ■ Web: www.insmed.com	908-977-9900		85
Insparisk LLC 18-10 Whitestone Expy 3rd Fl Whitestone NY 11357 TF: 888-464-6772 ■ Web: insparisk.com	888-464-6772		365
Inspec Group LLC 140 SW Arthur St Portland OR 97201	503-595-6540		186
Inspectech Ltd 450 Midwest Rd Toronto ON M1P3A9 Web: inspectech.ca	416-757-1179		112
Inspection Depot Inc 3131 St Johns Bluff Rd Jacksonville FL 32246 TF: 888-589-2112 ■ Web: www.inspectiondepot.com	888-589-2112		365
Inspection Oilfield Services 7814 Miller Rd 3 Houston TX 77049 Web: www.iosinspection.com	281-452-9015		580
Insperity Inc 19001 Crescent Springs Dr Kingwood TX 77339 TF: 800-237-3170 ■ Web: www.insperity.com	866-715-3552		463
Inspira Care Connect LLC 165 Bridgeton Pike Mullica Hill NJ 08062 Web: www.inspirahealthnetwork.org	856-641-6275		353
Inspirage Inc 600 108th Ave NE Ste 540 Bellevue WA 98004 TF: 855-517-4250 ■ Web: www.inspirage.com	855-517-4250		631
Inspiration Software Inc 6663 SW Beaverton Hillsdale Hwy Ste 370 Portland OR 97221 TF: 800-877-4292	503-297-3004	297-4676	178-1
Inspirato LLC 1625 Wazee St Denver CO 80202 TF: 855-481-5405 ■ Web: www.inspirato.com	303-586-7771		652
Inspire Excellence 657 N West Ave Elmhurst IL 60126 Web: www.inspireexcellence.com	630-279-7500		463
Inspired eLearning Inc 4630 N Loop 1604 W Ste 401 San Antonio TX 78249 TF: 800-631-2078 ■ Web: inspiredelearning.com	210-579-0224		225
InspireHealth 200-1330 West 8th Ave Vancouver BC V6H4A6 Web: www.inspirehealth.ca	604-734-7125		353

	Phone	Fax	Class
Inspirica Ltd 850 Seventh Ave Ste 403, New York NY 10019 *Web:* www.inspirica.com	212-245-3888		765
Inspiring Wellness LLC 8830 S Tamiami Trl Ste 100, Sarasota FL 34238 *Web:* www.babybootcamp.com	941-953-5000		310
Inspironix Inc 3400 Cottage Way, Sacramento CA 95825 *TF:* 866-684-3669 ■ *Web:* www.inspironix.com	916-488-3222	488-3210	179
INSTAAR (Institute of Arctic & Alpine Research) 4001 Discovery Dr, Boulder CO 80303 *Web:* instaar.colorado.edu	303-492-6387	492-6388	668
InstaGift LLC 1500 First Ave N Ste 65, Birmingham AL 35203 *TF:* 877-870-3463 ■ *Web:* instagift.com	877-870-3463		393
InstaMed Communications LLC 1880 John F Kennedy Blvd 12th Fl, Philadelphia PA 19103 *TF:* 800-507-3800 ■ *Web:* www.instamed.com	215-789-3680		360-3
Instanet Solutions 100 Wellington St Ste 201, London ON N6B2K6 *TF:* 800-668-8768 ■ *Web:* www.instanetsolutions.com	800-668-8768		179
Instant Imprints 6615 Flanders Dr Ste B, San Diego CA 92121 *TF:* 800-542-3437 ■ *Web:* instantimprints.com	858-642-4848	453-6513	310
Instant Recall Inc 8180 Greensboro Dr Ste 700, McLean VA 22102 *Web:* www.irecall.com	703-714-1332		178-1
Instant Sign Ctr 1400 Providence Hwy Ste 2500, Norwood MA 02062 **Fax Area Code:* 978 ■ *Web:* www.instantsigncenter.com	781-278-0150	521-2192*	627
Instantel Inc 309 Legget Dr, Ottawa ON K2K3A3 *TF:* 800-267-9111 ■ *Web:* www.instantel.com	613-592-4642		253
Instantiations Inc Officers Row Ste 1325B, Vancouver WA 98661 *TF:* 855-476-2558 ■ *Web:* www.instantiations.com	503-649-3836		178-2
Instantwhip Foods Inc 2200 Cardigan Ave, Columbus OH 43215 **Fax Area Code:* 614 ■ *TF:* 800-544-9447 ■ *Web:* instantwhip.com	877-576-7320	488-0307*	296-10
INSTEC 1811 Centre Pt Cir Ste 115, Naperville IL 60563 *Web:* www.instec-corp.com	630-955-9200		178-10
Insteel Industries Inc 1373 Boggs Dr, Mount Airy NC 27030 *NASDAQ:* IIIN ■ *TF:* 800-334-9504 ■ *Web:* www.insteel.com	336-786-2141	786-2144	813
InStep Health 111 Water St, East Dundee IL 60118 *Web:* www.leveragepointmedia.com	847-879-6036		195
InStil Health Insurance Co PO Box 100294, Columbia SC 29202 *TF:* 877-446-7845 ■ *Web:* www.myinstil.com	877-446-7845		390
Instinct Marketing 7460 Warren Pky Ste 255, Frisco TX 75034 *Web:* www.instinctmarketing.com	214-269-1700		4
Institech Inc 12521 W Hampton Ave, Butler WI 53007 *TF:* 800-430-4808 ■ *Web:* www.institech.com	262-252-8484	252-8494	631
Institut Canadien-Francais d'Ottawa Bibliotheque 316 rue Dalhousie, Ottawa ON K1N1B4 *Web:* www.institutcfottawa.ca	613-241-3522		434-3
Institute for a Drug-Free Workplace (IDFW) 10701 Parkridge Blvd Ste 300, Reston VA 20191 *Web:* www.drugfreeworkplace.org	703-391-7222	391-7223	49-12
Institute for Alternative Futures (IAF) 2331 Mill Rd Ste 100, Alexandria VA 22314 *Web:* www.altfutures.org	703-684-5880		49-12
Institute for American Indian Studies, The 38 Curtis Rd PO Box 1260, Washington Depot CT 06793 *Web:* www.iaismuseum.org	860-868-0518	868-1649	520
Institute for Astronomy Institute for Astronomy 2680 Woodlawn Dr, Honolulu HI 96822 *Web:* www.ifa.hawaii.edu	808-956-8312	988-2790	668
Institute for Basic Research in Developmental Disabilities 1050 Forest Hill Rd, Staten Island NY 10314 *Web:* opwdd.ny.gov	718-494-0600		668
Institute for Better Health (IBH) PO Box 5710, Santa Rosa CA 95402 *TF:* 800-258-8411 ■ *Web:* www.ibh.com	707-595-9010	755-3133	49-8
Institute for Business & Home Safety (IBHS) 4775 E Fowler Ave, Tampa FL 33617 *TF:* 866-657-4247 ■ *Web:* disastersafety.org	813-286-3400		49-9
Institute for Byzantine and Modern Greek Studies (IBMGS) 115 Gilbert Rd, Belmont MA 02478 *Web:* ibmgs.org	617-484-8584	876-3600	637-2
Institute for Certification of Computing Professionals (ICCP) 2400 E Devon Ave Ste 281, Des Plaines IL 60018 *TF:* 800-843-8227 ■ *Web:* www.iccp.org	847-299-4227		48-9
Institute for Corporate Productivity Inc 411 First Ave S Ste 403, Seattle WA 98104 *Web:* www.i4cp.com	206-624-6565		466
Institute for Defense Analyses (IDA) 4850 Mark Center Dr, Alexandria VA 22311 *Web:* www.ida.org	703-845-2000	845-2588	668
Institute for Foreign Policy Analysis Inc 675 Massachusetts Ave 10th Fl, Cambridge MA 02139 *Web:* www.ifpa.org	617-492-2116	492-8242	634
Institute for Health Freedom 1825 K St NW Ste 1200, Washington DC 20006 *Web:* www.forhealthfreedom.org	202-534-3700	534-3731	48-8
Institute for Healthcare Improvement (IHI) 20 University Rd 7th Fl, Cambridge MA 02138 *TF:* 866-787-0831 ■ *Web:* www.ihi.org	617-301-4800	301-4848	49-8
Institute for Humane Studies 3434 Washington Blvd MS 1C5, Arlington VA 22201 *TF:* 800-697-8799 ■ *Web:* theihs.org	703-993-4880	993-4890	634
Institute for Justice 901 N Glebe Rd Ste 900, Arlington VA 22203 *Web:* www.ij.org	703-682-9320	682-9321	634
Institute for Molecular Virology (IMV) 1525 Linden Dr 413 RM Bock Laboratories, Madison WI 53706 *Web:* virology.wisc.edu	608-262-4540	262-4570	668
Institute For Natural Resources PO Box 5757, Concord CA 94524 *TF:* 877-246-6336 ■ *Web:* www.inrseminars.com	925-609-2820		21
Institute for Operations Research & the Management Sciences (INFORMS) 7240 Pkwy Dr Ste 300, Hanover MD 21076 *TF:* 800-446-3676 ■ *Web:* www.informs.org	443-757-3500	757-3515	49-19
Institute for Participatory Management & Planning (IPMP) PO Box 1937, Monterey CA 93942 *Web:* www.consentbuilding.com	831-373-4292	373-0760	393
Institute for Policy Studies (IPS) 1112 16th St NW Ste 600, Washington DC 20036 *Web:* ips-dc.org	202-234-9382		634
Institute for Professionals in Taxation (IPT) 600 Northpark Town Ctr 1200 Abernathy Rd Ste L-2, Atlanta GA 30328 *Web:* www.ipt.org	404-240-2300	240-2315	49-10
Institute for Research on Poverty University of Wisconsin Madison 1180 Observatory Dr 3412 William H Sewell Social Sciences Bldg, Madison WI 53706 *Web:* www.irp.wisc.edu	608-262-6358	265-3119	668
Institute for Research on the Economics of Taxation (IRET) 529 14th St NW Ste 420, Washington DC 20045 *Web:* www.iret.org	202-464-5113		634
Institute for Scientific Analysis 390 Fourth St Ste D, San Francisco CA 94107 *Web:* www.scientificanalysis.org	415-777-2352		668
Institute for Simulation & Training (IST) 3100 Technology Pkwy, Orlando FL 32826 *Web:* www.ist.ucf.edu	407-882-1300	658-5059	668
Institute for Social Behavioral & Economic Research University of California 2201 N Hall, Santa Barbara CA 93106 *Web:* isber.ucsb.edu	805-893-2548	893-7995	668
Institute for Social Research ISR-Thompson 426 Thompson St PO Box 1248, Ann Arbor MI 48106 *Web:* home.isr.umich.edu	734-764-8354	647-4575	668
Institute for Southern Studies PO Box 531, Durham NC 27702 *Web:* www.facingsouth.org	919-419-8311		49-19
Institute for Supply Management (ISM) 309 W Elliot Rd Ste 113, Tempe AZ 85284 *TF:* 800-888-6276 ■ *Web:* www.instituteforsupplymanagement.org	480-752-6276	752-7890	49-12
Institute for Systems Research University of Maryland 2173 Av Williams Bldg, College Park MD 20742 *Web:* www.isr.umd.edu	301-405-1000	314-9920	668
Institute for Telecommunications Sciences 325 Broadway, Boulder CO 80305 *Web:* www.its.bldrdoc.gov	303-497-5216		668
Institute for the North 1675 C St Ste 106, Anchorage AK 99501 *Web:* institutenorth.org	907-786-6324		634
Institute for Tomorrow 2601 Floyd Ave, Richmond VA 23220 *Web:* www.institutefortomorrow.com	804-690-4837		194
Institute of American Indian Arts (IAIA) 83 Avan Nu Po Rd, Santa Fe NM 87508 *TF:* 800-804-6422 ■ *Web:* iaia.edu	505-424-2300	424-0505	165
Institute of Arctic & Alpine Research (INSTAAR) 4001 Discovery Dr, Boulder CO 80303 *Web:* instaar.colorado.edu	303-492-6387	492-6388	668
Institute of Beauty & Wellness, The 327 E St Paul Ave, Milwaukee WI 53202 *Web:* www.ibw.edu	414-227-2889		76
Institute of Buddhist Studies (IBS) 2140 Durant Ave, Berkeley CA 94704 *Web:* www.shin-ibs.edu	510-809-1444	809-1443	637-2
Institute of Certified Professional Managers (ICPM) James Madison University MSC 5504, Harrisonburg VA 22807 *Web:* www.icpm.biz	540-568-3247		49-12
Institute of Clean Air Cos (ICAC) 1730 M St NW Ste 206, Washington DC 20036 *TF:* 800-631-9505 ■ *Web:* www.icac.com	202-478-6188	367-2114	48-12
Institute of Consumer Financial Education PO Box 34070, San Diego CA 92163 *Web:* www.financial-education-icfe.org	619-239-1401	923-3284	48-11
Institute of Contemporary Art University of Pennsylvania 118 S 36th St Philadelphia PA 19104 *Web:* www.icaphila.org	215-898-7108	898-5050	520
Institute of Continuing Legal Education in Georgia (ICLE) 104 Marietta St NW, Atlanta GA 30303 *TF:* 800-422-0893 ■ *Web:* www.iclega.org	706-369-5664	466-0886	49-19
Institute of Corporate Directors 2701 - 250 Yonge St, Toronto ON M5B2L7 *TF:* 877-593-7741 ■ *Web:* www.icd.ca	416-593-7741		162
Institute of Culinary Education 50 W 23rd St, New York NY 10010 *TF:* 800-522-4610 ■ *Web:* www.ice.edu	212-847-0700	847-0723	163
Institute of Ecosystem Studies (IES) 2801 Sharon Tpke PO Box AB, Millbrook NY 12545 *Web:* www.caryinstitute.org	845-677-5343	677-5976	668
Institute of Education Sciences (IES) 550 12th St SW, Washington DC 20024 *Web:* ies.ed.gov	202-245-6940	219-1466	668
Institute of Environmental Sciences & Technology (IEST) 1827 Walden Office Sq Ste 400, Schaumburg IL 60173 *Web:* www.iest.org	847-981-0100	981-4130	49-19
Institute of Food Technologists (IFT) 525 W Van Buren St Ste 1000, Chicago IL 60607 *TF:* 800-438-3663 ■ *Web:* www.ift.org	312-782-8424	782-8348	49-6
Institute of General Semantics (IGS) 72-11 Austin St, Forest Hills NY 11375 *TF:* 800-346-1359 ■ *Web:* www.generalsemantics.org	212-729-7973		48-11
Institute of Government & Public Affairs Univ of Illinois 1007 W Nevada St, Urbana IL 61801 *Web:* igpa.uillinois.edu	217-333-3340	244-4817	634
Institute of Hazardous Materials Management (IHMM) 11900 Parklawn Dr Ste 450, Rockville MD 20852 *Web:* www.ihmm.org	301-984-8969	984-1516	48-12
Institute of Human Origins (IHO) 951 S Cady Mall PO Box 874101, Tempe AZ 85287 *Web:* iho.asu.edu	480-727-6580	727-6570	668

	Phone	Fax	Class
Institute of Industrial & Systems Engineers (IIE) 3577 Parkway Ln Ste 200 .... Norcross GA 30092 *TF:* 800-494-0460 ■ *Web:* www.iise.org	770-449-0461	441-3295	49-13
Institute of Inspection Cleaning & Restoration Certification (IICRC) 4043 S E Ave .... Las Vegas NV 89119 *TF:* 844-464-4272 ■ *Web:* www.iicrc.org	844-464-4272		49-4
Institute of Internal Auditors, The (IIA) 247 Maitland Ave .... Altamonte Springs FL 32701 *Web:* na.theiia.org	407-937-1100	937-1101	49-1
Institute of International Bankers (IIB) 299 Park Ave 17th Fl .... New York NY 10171 *Web:* www.iib.org	212-421-1611	421-1119	49-2
Institute of International Container Lessors (IICL) 1990 M St NW Ste 650 .... Washington DC 20036 *Web:* www.iicl.org	202-223-9800	223-9810	49-21
Institute of International Education (IIE) 809 United Nations Plz Ste 1 .... New York NY 10017 *Web:* www.iie.org	212-883-8200		48-11
Institute of International Finance (IIF) 1333 H St NW Ste 800-E .... Washington DC 20005 *Web:* www.iif.com	202-857-3600	775-1430	49-2
Institute of Makers of Explosives (IME) 1212 New York Ave NW Ste 650 .... Washington DC 20036 *Web:* www.ime.org	202-429-9280	293-2420	49-13
Institute of Management Accountants Inc (IMA) 10 Paragon Dr Ste 1 .... Montvale NJ 07645 *TF:* 800-638-4427 ■ *Web:* www.imanet.org	201-573-9000	474-1600	49-1
Institute of Management Consultants USA Inc (IMC) 2025 M St NW Ste 800 .... Washington DC 20036 **Fax Area Code:* 202 ■ *TF:* 800-221-2557 ■ *Web:* www.imcusa.org	800-793-4992	367-2134*	49-12
Institute of Materials Science University of Connecticut 97 N Eagleville Rd .... Storrs CT 06269 *Web:* www.ims.uconn.edu	860-486-4623	486-4745	668
Institute of Medicine 500 Fifth St NW .... Washington DC 20001 *Web:* www.nationalacademies.org	202-334-2352	334-1412	49-8
Institute of Navigation Inc (ION) 8551 Rixlew Ln Ste 360 .... Manassas VA 20109 *Web:* www.ion.org	703-366-2723	366-2724	49-21
Institute of Nuclear Power Operations 700 Galleria Pkwy SE Ste 100 .... Atlanta GA 30339 *Web:* www.inpo.info	770-644-8000		48-12
Institute of Packaging Professionals (IOPP) 1833 Centre Point Cir Ste 123 .... Naperville IL 60563 *TF:* 800-432-4085 ■ *Web:* www.iopp.org	630-544-5050	544-5055	49-13
Institute of Real Estate Management (IREM) 430 N Michigan Ave .... Chicago IL 60611 **Fax Area Code:* 800 ■ *TF:* 800-837-0706 ■ *Web:* irem.org	312-329-6000	338-4736*	49-17
Institute of Scrap Recycling Industries Inc (ISRI) 1250 H St NW Ste 400 .... Washington DC 20005 *Web:* www.isri.org	202-662-8500	626-0900	48-12
Institute of Texan Cultures 801 E Durango Blvd .... San Antonio TX 78205 *Web:* www.texancultures.com	210-458-2300		520
Institute of Transportation Engineers (ITE) 1627 Eye St NW Ste 600 .... Washington DC 20006 *Web:* www.ite.org	202-785-0060	785-0609	49-21
Institute of World Politics 1521 16th St NW .... Washington DC 20036 *Web:* www.iwp.edu	202-462-2101	464-0335	634
Institute on Education & the Economy 525 W 120th St .... New York NY 10027 *Web:* www.tc.columbia.edu	212-678-3000	678-3699	634
Institutional Equipment Inc (IEI) 704 Veterans Pky Ste B .... Bolingbrook IL 60440 *Web:* www.ieiusa.net	630-771-0990	771-0994	300
Institutional Real Estate Inc 2274 Camino Ramon .... San Ramon CA 94583 *Web:* irei.com	925-244-0500		652
Institutional Shareholder Services Inc 702 King Farm Blvd Ste 400 .... Rockville MD 20850 *Web:* www.issgovernance.com	301-556-0500		401
Institutional Venture Partners 3000 Sand Hill Rd Bldg 2 Ste 250 .... Menlo Park CA 94025 *Web:* www.ivp.com	650-854-0132	854-2009	792
Institutional Wholesale Co 535 Dry Valley Rd .... Cookeville TN 38506 *TF:* 800-239-9588 ■ *Web:* goiwc.com	931-537-4000	537-4017	299
InStor Solutions 44053 S Grimmer Blvd .... Fremont CA 94538 *TF:* 877-441-2234 ■ *Web:* www.instor.com	510-490-7475	490-9359	658
Instron Corp 825 University Ave .... Norwood MA 02062 *Web:* www.instron.us	781-828-2500	575-5750	472
Instructional Resources Co PO Box 111704 .... Anchorage AK 99511 *Web:* www.susancanthony.com	907-345-6689		637-2
Instrumar Ltd 39 Pippy Pl 3rd Fl .... Saint John NL A1B3X2 *Web:* www.instrumar.com	709-726-8460		261
Instrument 3529 N Williams Ave .... Portland OR 97227 *Web:* www.instrument.com	503-928-3188		201
Instrument Development Corporation Inc 820 Swan Dr .... Mukwonago WI 53149 *Web:* www.idcwi.com	262-363-7307		653
Instrument Sales & Service Inc 16427 NE Airport Way .... Portland OR 97230 *TF:* 800-333-7976 ■ *Web:* www.instrumentsales.com	503-239-0754		61
Instrument Technology Inc 33 Airport Rd .... Westfield MA 01085 *Web:* www.scopes.com	413-562-3606		542
Instrumentation Laboratory Inc 180 Hartwell Rd .... Bedford MA 01730 *TF:* 800-955-9525 ■ *Web:* www.instrumentationlaboratory.com	781-861-0710	861-1908	419
Instruments Inc 7263 Engineer Rd Ste G .... San Diego CA 92111 *Web:* www.instrumentsinc.com	858-571-1111	571-0188	729
Instyle Hair Designs Inc 175 Littleton Rd .... Westford MA 01886 *Web:* www.instylehd.com	978-692-7851		77

	Phone	Fax	Class
Insulation Specialties of America Inc 1095 Kabert Dr .... Wanatah IN 46390 *Web:* www.insulationspecialties.com	219-733-2502	733-2300	500
Insulectro 20362 Windrow Dr .... Lake Forest CA 92630 *TF:* 800-279-7686 ■ *Web:* www.insulectro.com	949-587-3200	454-0066	246
Insulet Corp 9 Oak Park Dr .... Bedford MA 01730 *TF:* 800-591-3455 ■ *Web:* investor.insulet.com	781-457-5000		476
Insulfab Plastics Inc 834 Hayne St .... Spartanburg SC 29301 *TF:* 800-845-7599 ■ *Web:* www.insulfab.com	864-582-7506	582-5215	599
Insultab Inc 45 Industrial Pkwy .... Woburn MA 01801 *TF:* 800-468-4822 ■ *Web:* www.insultab.com	781-935-0800	935-0879	599
Insur IQ LLC 2 Corporate Dr Ste 636 .... Shelton CT 06484 *TF:* 800-882-2824 ■ *Web:* www.insuriq.com	203-446-8050		387
Insurance & Financial Ser. Limited of De 1523 Concord Pk Ste 400 .... Wilmington DE 19803 *TF:* 800-598-0420 ■ *Web:* trustifs.com	800-598-0420		390
Insurance Alliance Network, The 3425 Simpson Ferry Rd Ste 101 .... Camp Hill PA 17011 *Web:* tiacp.com	717-230-1910		390
Insurance Auto Auctions Inc 2 Westbrook Corporate Ctr 10th Fl .... Westchester IL 60154 *TF:* 800-872-1501 ■ *Web:* www.iaai.com	708-492-7000		51
Insurance Center of North Jersey Inc, The 25 E Spring Valley Ave Ste 275 .... Maywood NJ 07607 *Web:* icnj.com	201-525-1100		390
Insurance Center of The Se Inc 1296 Westgate Pkwy .... Dothan AL 36302 *Web:* insctr.net	334-793-0014		390
Insurance Company of the West 11455 El Camino Real .... San Diego CA 92130 *TF:* 800-877-1111 ■ *Web:* www.icwgroup.com	858-350-2400	350-2616	391-4
Insurance Consultants Intl 1840 Deer Creek Rd Ste 200 .... Monument CO 80132 **Fax Area Code:* 603 ■ *TF:* 800-576-2674 ■ *Web:* www.globalhealthinsurance.com	719-573-9080	843-6662*	391-7
Insurance Corporation of British Columbia Library 151 W Esplanade .... North Vancouver BC V7M3H9 *Web:* www.icbc.com	604-982-6210		434-3
Insurance Data Processing Inc (IDP) 8101 Washington Ln .... Wyncote PA 19095 *TF:* 800-523-6745 ■ *Web:* www.idpnet.com	215-885-2150	887-4621	178-11
Insurance Educational Assn 3611 S Harbor Blvd Ste 180 .... Santa Ana CA 92704 *TF:* 800-655-4432 ■ *Web:* www.ieatraining.com	714-689-0090	689-0167	167-3
Insurance Exchange Inc, The 9713 W West Ave Ste 401 .... Rockville MD 20850 *Web:* tie-inc.com	301-279-5500		390
Insurance Information Institute Inc (III) 110 William St .... New York NY 10038 *TF:* 877-263-7995 ■ *Web:* www.iii.org	212-346-5500	732-1916	49-9
Insurance Institute for Highway Safety 1005 N Glebe Rd Ste 800 .... Arlington VA 22201 *Web:* www.iihs.org	703-247-1500	247-1588	49-9
Insurance Management Group Inc 109 77th St .... Ocean City MD 21842 *Web:* imgoc.com	410-524-5700		390
Insurance Marketing Agencies Inc 306 Main St .... Worcester MA 01608 *TF:* 800-891-1226 ■ *Web:* www.imaagency.com	508-753-7233		391-2
Insurance Marketing and Management Services (IMMS) PO Box 542 .... Big Bear City CA 92314 **Fax Area Code:* 909 ■ *TF:* 800-753-4467 ■ *Web:* www.imms.com	800-753-4467	547-6212*	194
Insurance Marketing Center Inc 6101 Executive Blvd Ste 120 .... Rockville MD 20852 *Web:* www.imctr.com	301-468-8888		390
Insurance Marketing Communications Assn (IMCA) 4248 Park Glen Rd .... Minneapolis MN 55416 *Web:* www.imcanet.com	952-928-4644	929-1318	49-9
Insurance Partners LLC 32 W St Ste 200 .... Towson MD 21204 *Web:* www.insurancepartnersllc.com	812-352-8385		390
Insurance Services Office Inc (ISO) 545 Washington Blvd .... Jersey City NJ 07310 *Web:* www.verisk.com	201-748-1472		390
Insurance Specialties Services Inc 946 Town Ctr .... New Britain PA 18901 *TF:* 800-533-4579 ■ *Web:* issisvs.com	800-533-4579		390
Insurance Technology Consultants Inc (ITC) 2090 N Tustin Ave Ste 260 .... Santa Ana CA 92705 *Web:* www.itc-systems.com	714-442-8702		177
Insurance Unlimited of LA Inc 3111 Ryan St .... Lake Charles LA 70601 *Web:* www.insunlimited.com	337-477-6922		390
InsurBanc 10 Executive Dr .... Farmington CT 06032 *TF:* 866-467-2262 ■ *Web:* www.insurbanc.com	860-677-9701	677-9793	70
Insured Aircraft Title Services Inc 4848 SW 36th St .... Oklahoma City OK 73179 *TF:* 800-654-4882 ■ *Web:* www.insuredaircraft.com	405-681-6663		569
Insurity Inc 170 Huyshope Ave .... Hartford CT 06106 *Web:* insurity.com	860-616-7721		177
InsurMark Inc 820 Gessner Ste 970 .... Houston TX 77024 *TF:* 800-752-0207 ■ *Web:* www.insurmark.net	713-973-7575	973-5252	393
Insync 90 Eglinton Ave E Ste 403 .... Toronto ON M4P2Y3 *TF:* 877-847-7341 ■ *Web:* www.insyncstrategy.com	416-932-0921		668
InSync Plus 3530 Wilshire Blvd Ste 1500 .... Los Angeles CA 90010 *Web:* insync.plus	323-965-4800		4
In-Sys Solutions Inc 14047 Petronella Dr Unit 101 .... Libertyville IL 60048 *Web:* in-sys.com	847-996-0400		180
Insyst Inc 271 Rte 46 W Ste A201 .... Fairfield NJ 07004 *Web:* www.insystus.com	973-227-6582		180
Insyst Inc 140 Littleton Rd Ste 303 .... Parsippany NJ 07054 *Web:* insystus.com	973-917-4848		177
Insystech Inc 3949 Pender Dr Ste 125 .... Fairfax VA 22030 *Web:* www.insystechinc.com	703-657-0472		396
INTA (International Trademark Assn) 655 Third Ave 10th Fl .... New York NY 10017 *TF:* 800-995-3579 ■ *Web:* www.inta.org	212-768-9887	768-7796	49-12

Company / Address	City	State	Zip	Phone	Fax	Class
Intact Info 3 Pointe Dr Ste 218 *TF:* 888-986-7736 ■ *Web:* www.intactinfo.com	Brea	CA	92821	888-986-7736		196
Intact Insurance 700 University Ave *Web:* www.intact.ca	Toronto	ON	M5G0A1	416-341-1464	344-8030	391-4
Intag Inc 11469 Olive Bld Ste 400 *Web:* www.appliedws.com	Saint Louis	MO	63141	314-822-1102		175
Intaglio LLC 3106 Three Mile Rd NW *TF:* 800-632-9153 ■ *Web:* www.intaglioav.com	Grand Rapids	MI	49534	616-243-3300		513
Intalere Inc 2060 Craigshire Rd *TF:* 800-388-2638 ■ *Web:* www.intalere.com	Saint Louis	MO	63146	800-388-2638		194
Intarcia Therapeutics Inc 24650 Industrial Blvd *Web:* www.intarcia.com	Hayward	CA	94545	510-782-7800	782-7801	85
Intat Precision Inc 2148 N State Rd 3 PO Box 488 *Web:* www.intat.com	Rushville	IN	46173	765-932-5323	932-3032	621
Intcomex Inc 3505 NW 107th Ave *Web:* www.intcomex.com	Miami	FL	33178	305-477-6230		174
Intec Group Inc 666 S Vermont St *Web:* www.intecgrp.com	Palatine	IL	60067	847-358-0088	358-4391	604
Intec Video Systems Inc 23301 Vista Grande Dr *TF:* 800-468-3254 ■ *Web:* www.intecvideo.com	Laguna Hills	CA	92653	949-859-3800		693
Intech Direct 105 E Marquardt Dr *Web:* intechdirect.com	Wheeling	IL	60090	847-850-5999		255
Intech Enterprises Inc 3825 Grant St *Web:* www.intechenterprises.com	Washougal	WA	98671	360-835-8785	835-5144	463
Intech Inc 2802 Belle Arbor Ave *Web:* www.intech-intl.com	Chattanooga	TN	37406	423-622-3700		261
Intech Inc 375 East Dr *Web:* go-intech.com	Melbourne	FL	32904	321-951-2326	951-2511	177
Intecon LLC 5080 Mark Dabling Blvd *Web:* www.inteconusa.com	Colorado Springs	CO	80918	719-597-2275	597-7120	180
Intedge Manufacturing 1875 Chumley Rd Po Box 969 *TF:* 866-969-9605 ■ *Web:* intedge.com	Woodruff	SC	29388	864-969-9605	969-9604	300
INTEG Process Group Inc 2919 E Hardies Rd 1st Fl *Web:* www.integpg.com	Gibsonia	PA	15044	724-933-9350		225
Intega IT 210-1900 Merivale Rd *Web:* www.intega.ca	Ottawa	ON	K2G4N4	613-260-1114		196
Integer Group 7245 W Alaska Dr *Web:* www.integer.com	Lakewood	CO	80226	303-393-3000		4
Integra Capital Ltd 2020 Winston Park Dr Ste 200 *TF:* 800-363-2480 ■ *Web:* www.integra.com	Oakville	ON	L6H6X7	905-829-1131		401
Integra Cincinnati/Columbus Inc 8241 Cornell Rd Ste 210 *Web:* irr.com	Cincinnati	OH	45249	513-561-2305		652
Integra Graphix 160 Koser Rd *Web:* www.yourvisitorguide.com	Lititz	PA	17543	717-626-7895		627
Integra Group 16 Triangle Park Dr Ste 1600 *TF:* 800-424-8384 ■ *Web:* www.integragrp.com	Cincinnati	OH	45246	513-326-5600	326-5614	463
Integra Information Technologies Inc PO Box 8304	Boise	ID	83707	208-336-2720		196
Integra Insurance Services LLC 5702 Mancuso Ln *Web:* integragroup.us	Baton Rouge	LA	70809	225-400-6400		390
Integra Land Co 1525 International Pkwy Ste 20 *Web:* integralandcompany.com	Lake Mary	FL	32746	407-833-3927		652
Integra LifeSciences Corp 311 Enterprise Dr *TF:* 800-654-2873 ■ *Web:* www.integralife.com	Plainsboro	NJ	08536	609-275-0500		475
Integra Marketing Group 206 Jackson St *Web:* integramarketinggroup.com	New Galilee	PA	16141	724-200-0005		7
Integra Realty Resources Inc 7800 East Union Ave Ste 400 **Fax Area Code:* 646 ■ *Web:* www.irr.com	Denver	CO	80237	212-575-2935	424-1869*	653
Integra Services Technologies Inc 5000 E 2nd Unit E *TF:* 800-779-2658 ■ *Web:* www.integratechnologies.com	Benicia	CA	94510	707-751-0685	751-0678	385
Integra Technologies LLC 3450 N Rock Rd Bldg 100 Ste 111 *Web:* integra-tech.com	Wichita	KS	67226	316-630-6800		70
Integra Telecom Inc 1201 NE Lloyd Blvd Ste 750 *TF:* 866-468-3472 ■ *Web:* www.integratelecom.com	Portland	OR	97232	866-468-3472		736
Integral Automation Inc 16w171 Shore Ct *Web:* www.premiertool.com	Burr Ridge	IL	60527	630-654-4300	654-8519	189-1
Integral Building Systems Inc 717 Post Rd 1st Fl *Web:* ibsystemsinc.com	Madison	WI	53713	608-467-9193		180
Integral Group Inc 427 13th St *Web:* www.integralgroup.com	Oakland	CA	94612	510-663-2070		261
Integral Group LLC, The 191 Peachtree St NE Ste 4100 *Web:* www.integral-online.com	Atlanta	GA	30303	404-224-1860		401
Integral Hospitality Solutions 3516 Vann Rd Ste 106 *Web:* www.integralhospitality.com	Birmingham	AL	35235	205-655-2097	206-9473	463
Integral Marketing Inc 2139 Espey Ct Ste 7 *Web:* www.integralmkting.com	Crofton	MD	21114	410-721-0645	721-0768	177
Integral Networks Inc 4960 Rocklin Rd Ste 100 *Web:* www.integralnetworks.com	Rocklin	CA	95677	916-626-4000		174
Integral Products Inc 24030 Frampton Ave *Web:* www.integralproducts.com	Harbor City	CA	90710	310-326-8889		3
Integral Transportation Networks Corp 6975 D Pacific Cir *TF:* 888-594-4244 ■ *Web:* www.itn-logistics.com	Mississauga	ON	L5T2H3	905-362-1111		314
Integranetics 325 Park Plaza Dr 2b *TF:* 800-291-9307 ■ *Web:* integranetics.net	Owensboro	KY	42301	270-685-6016		175
integraSoft Inc 2547 Tech Dr *Web:* integrasoft.com	Bettendorf	IA	52722	563-332-5030		196
Integrasys Inc 786 Mountain Blvd Ste 101 *Web:* integrasys.com	Watchung	NJ	07069	908-686-5200		180
Integrated Alliances LLC 1701 Wynkoop St Ste 239 *Web:* integratedalliances.com	Denver	CO	80202	720-897-8254		177
Integrated Biometrics Inc 121 Broadcast Dr *TF:* 888-840-8034 ■ *Web:* integratedbiometrics.com	Spartanburg	SC	29303	864-990-3711		692
Integrated BioPharma Inc 225 Long Ave *OTC:* INBP ■ *TF:* 888-319-6962 ■ *Web:* www.chemintl.com	Hillside	NJ	07205	973-926-0816		799
Integrated BioTherapeutics Inc 4 Research Ct Ste 300 **Fax Area Code:* 301 ■ *TF:* 877-411-2041 ■ *Web:* www.integratedbiotherapeutics.com	Rockville	MD	20850	877-411-2041	515-0324*	743
Integrated Business Systems & Services Inc 1601 Shop Rd Ste E *TF:* 800-553-1038 ■ *Web:* www.ibss.net	Columbia	SC	29201	803-736-5595		178-1
Integrated Computer Solutions Inc (ICS) 54 Middlesex Tpke Ste B *Web:* www.ics.com	Bedford	MA	01730	617-621-0060	621-9555	178-2
Integrated Decisions & Systems Inc 8500 Normandale Lake Blvd Ste 1200 *Web:* ideas.com	Minneapolis	MN	55437	952-698-4200	698-4299	178-1
Integrated Design Tools Inc 1202 E Park Ave *Web:* idtvision.com	Tallahassee	FL	32301	850-222-5939	222-4591	591
Integrated Device Technology Inc 6024 Silver Creek Valley Rd *NASDAQ:* IDTI ■ *TF:* 800-345-7015 ■ *Web:* www.idt.com	San Jose	CA	95138	408-284-8200	284-2775	696
Integrated Digital Technologies Corp 1501 S Brand Blvd *Web:* www.idt.edu	Glendale	CA	91204	818-396-3511		177
Integrated Document Technologies Inc (IDT) 1009 W Hawthorn Dr *TF:* 877-722-6438 ■ *Web:* www.idt-inc.com	Itasca	IL	60143	630-875-1100	875-1101	196
Integrated Engineers & Contractors Corp 8795 Folsom Blvd Ste 205 *Web:* iec-corporation.com	Sacramento	CA	95826	916-383-6000		261
Integrated Flow Solutions LLC 6461 Reynolds Rd *TF:* 800-859-7867 ■ *Web:* ifsolutions.com	Tyler	TX	75708	903-595-6511		641
Integrated Health Management Services LLC 4647 N 32nd St Ste B150 *Web:* www.ihmsllc.com	Phoenix	AZ	85018	602-279-1109		194
Integrated Industrial Technologies 221 Seventh St Ste 200 *Web:* www.isquaredt.com	Pittsburgh	PA	15238	412-828-1200		256
Integrated Logistical Support, I 5130 Tchoupitoulas St *Web:* ilsiengineering.com	New Orleans	LA	70115	504-523-1619		261
Integrated Logistics Solutions Inc 3317 Triana Blvd SW *Web:* ilogsol.com	Huntsville	AL	35805	256-650-4105	650-4106	803-1
Integrated Magnetics Inc 11248 Playa Ct *TF:* 800-421-6692 ■ *Web:* www.intemag.com	Culver City	CA	90230	310-391-7213		253
Integrated Management Services PA 126 E Amite St *Web:* imsengineers.com	Jackson	MS	39201	601-968-9194		256
Integrated Management Systems Inc PO Box 1058 *Web:* www.imsicorp.com	Seabrook	TX	77586	281-474-3565		178-1
Integrated Marketing Services Inc 279 Wall St Research Pk *Web:* www.imsworld.com	Princeton	NJ	08540	609-683-9055		194
Integrated Medical Inc (IMI) 7012 S Revere Pky Ste 140 *TF:* 800-333-7617 ■ *Web:* www.integratedmedicalonline.com	Centennial	CO	80112	303-792-0069	799-3516	475
Integrated Microwave Corp 11353 Sorrento Valley Rd *Web:* www.imcsd.com	San Diego	CA	92121	858-259-2600		253
Integrated Office Solutions (IOS) PO Box 90212 *Web:* www.e-ios.com	Santa Barbara	CA	93190	805-252-4564		175
Integrated Orbital Implants Inc (IOI) 11230 Sorrento Valley Rd Ste 135 *TF:* 800-424-6537 ■ *Web:* www.ioi.com	San Diego	CA	92121	858-677-9990	677-9993	475
Integrated Paper Services Inc 3211 E Capitol Dr *Web:* ipstesting.com	Appleton	WI	54911	920-749-3040	749-3046	743
Integrated Power Designs Inc 300 Stewart Rd *Web:* www.ipdpower.com	Wilkes-Barre	PA	18701	570-824-4666	824-4843	253
Integrated Print & Graphics (IPG) 645 Stevenson Rd *Web:* www.ipandginc.com	South Elgin	IL	60177	847-695-6777		110
Integrated Procurement Technologies Inc 7230 Hollister Ave *Web:* www.iptsb.com	Goleta	CA	93117	805-682-0842		770
Integrated Regional Laboratories 5361 NW 33rd Ave **Fax Area Code:* 954 ■ *TF:* 800-522-0232 ■ *Web:* irlfl.com	Fort Lauderdale	FL	33309	800-522-0232	777-0211*	415
Integrated Sensing Systems Inc 391 Airport Industrial Dr *Web:* mems-iss.com	Ypsilanti	MI	48198	734-547-9896	547-9964	472
Integrated Service Company LLC 1900 N 161st E Ave Ste B *Web:* inservusa.com	Tulsa	OK	74116	918-234-4150		539
Integrated Services Inc 15115 SW Sequoia Pkwy Ste 110 *TF:* 800-922-3099 ■ *Web:* www.ints.com	Portland	OR	97224	800-922-3099		174
Integrated Solution Group Inc, The 10 Cedar St *Web:* www.intsolgrp.com	Woburn	MA	01801	781-938-0712		225

	Phone	Fax	Class
Integrated Solutions Inc 16602 N 23rd Ave Ste 109 .... Phoenix AZ 85023 *Web:* www.isiaz.com	602-437-5209		256
Integrated Surface Technologies 3475-F Edison Way .... Menlo Park CA 94025 *Web:* insurftech.com	650-324-1824		481
Integrated Technologies Inc 186 College St 4th Fl .... Burlington VT 05401 *Web:* www.processengineer.com	802-497-3990	497-1325	261
Integrated Textile Solutions Inc 865 Cleveland Ave .... Salem VA 24153 *Web:* www.intextile.com	540-389-8113	387-5855	155-19
Integrated Thermoforming Systems Inc 305 Hankes Ave .... Aurora IL 60505 *Web:* www.itspackaging.com	630-906-6895		596
Integrated Title Insurance Services LLC 1092 E South Union Ave...................... Midvale UT 84047 *Web:* www.itstitle.com	801-307-0160		194
Integrated Tower Systems 2703 Dawson Rd .... Tulsa OK 74110 *Web:* www.itstowers.com	918-749-8535		387
Integrated Wealth Counsel LLC 5375 Kietzke Ln PO Box 21389 .... Reno NV 89511 *TF:* 866-898-1860 ■ *Web:* www.integratedwealth.com	866-898-1860		401
Integration Partners Inc 12 Hayden Ave ....Lexington MA 02421 *Web:* www.integrationpartners.com	781-357-8100		180
Integration Technologies Group Inc 2745 Hartland Rd Ste 200................. Falls Church VA 22043 *TF:* 800-835-7823 ■ *Web:* www.itgonline.com	703-698-8282	698-0305	175
Integrative Logic Inc 2397 Huntcrest Way Ste 200 ....Lawrenceville GA 30043 *Web:* www.integrativelogic.com	678-638-2600	638-2601	4
Integri Net Solutions Inc 925 S Allante Pl .... Boise ID 83709 *Web:* www.insllc.net	208-376-0500		180
IntegriChain Inc 1628 JFK Blvd ....Philadelphia PA 19103 *Web:* www.integrichain.com	609-806-5005		177
Integridata Inc 122 E 42nd St Ste 2900 ....New York NY 10168 *Web:* integri-data.com	212-302-6200		180
Integris Federal Credit Union 2525 NW Expy Ste 108..................Oklahoma City OK 73112 *Web:* integrisfcu.org	405-947-3730		219
INTEGRIS Health Inc 3300 NW Expy ....Oklahoma City OK 73112 *TF:* 888-951-2277 ■ *Web:* integrisok.com	405-951-2277		353
Integrity Applications Inc (IAI) 15020 Conference Center Dr Ste 100........... Chantilly VA 20151 *Web:* www.integrity-apps.com	703-378-8672	378-8978	261
Integrity Building Systems Inc 2435 Housels Run Rd......................... Milton PA 17847	570-522-3600		106
Integrity Business Solutions Inc 9470 Annapolis Rd.......................... Lanham MD 20706 *Web:* www.integritybsi.com	301-306-3100		180
Integrity Construction Maintenance Inc 3531 Gravenstein Hwy S...................Sebastopol CA 95472 *Web:* icmconstruction.com	707-829-5300		104
Integrity Marketing Solutions 1311 Interquest Pkwy Ste 215 .... Colorado Springs CO 80921 *TF:* 877-352-2021 ■ *Web:* www.integritymarketingsolutions.com	877-352-2021		195
Integrity Music 1646 Westgate Cir Ste 106.................. Brentwood TN 37027 *TF:* 888-888-4726 ■ *Web:* www.integritymusic.com	888-888-4726		657
Integrity Parking Systems LLC 9828 E Washington St ....Chagrin Falls OH 44023 *Web:* integrityparking.com	440-543-4123		562
Integrity Rotational Molding LLC 701 Carr Rd .... Plainfield IN 46168 *Web:* www.integrityrotational.com	317-837-1101		608
Integrity Saw & Tool Inc 217 E Larsen Dr ....Fond du Lac WI 54937 *TF:* 800-779-8782 ■ *Web:* www.integritysaw.com	920-922-4474		454
Integrity Staffing Solutions Inc 700 Prides Crossing Ste 300 ....Newark DE 19713 *TF:* 888-458-8367 ■ *Web:* www.integritystaffing.com	302-661-8776	661-8779	721
Integrity Systems & Solutions LLC 1247 Highland Ave Ste 202 .... Cheshire CT 06410 *TF:* 866-446-8797 ■ *Web:* www.integrityss.com	866-446-8797		177
Integrity Tech Solutions 816 S Eldorado Rd Ste 4.................. Bloomington IL 61704 *Web:* www.integrityts.com	309-662-7723		180
Integro Technologies Corp 301 S Main St Ste 200 ....Salisbury NC 28144 *Web:* integro-tech.com	704-636-9666		261
Integron Corp 35 Bermar Pk ....Rochester NY 14624 *Web:* www.integron.com	585-426-6200		175
Intek Plastic Inc 1000 Spiral Blvd............. Hastings MN 55033 **Fax Area Code:* 651 ■ *TF:* 888-468-3531 ■ *Web:* www.intekplastics.com	888-468-3531	437-3805*	326
Intel Corp 2200 Mission College Blvd .... Santa Clara CA 95054 *NASDAQ: INTC* ■ *TF:* 800-628-8686 ■ *Web:* www.intel.in	408-765-8080		696
Intelametrix 6246 Preston Ave .... Livermore CA 94551 *Web:* www.intelametrix.com	925-606-7044		639
IntelCenter PO Box 22572................... Alexandria VA 22304 *TF:* 800-217-0610 ■ *Web:* www.intelcenter.com	703-370-2962	370-1571	637-9
InteleCom Solutions Inc 155 Knickerbocker Ave...................... Bohemia NY 11716 *Web:* www.intelecomsolutions.com	631-240-9100		224
Intelect Corp 4000 Dillon St..................Baltimore MD 21224 *Web:* www.intelectcorp.com	410-327-0020		180
Intelegain Technologies North Dallas Business Centre 3010 LBJ Freeway Ste 1200.................... Dallas TX 75234 *TF:* 888-235-8964 ■ *Web:* www.intelegain.com	214-233-0880		180
Intelemark LLC 4545 E Shea Blvd Ste 280 .... Phoenix AZ 85028 *Web:* www.intelemark.com	602-943-7111		737
InteleSystems 17400 Dallas Pkwy .... Dallas TX 75287 *Web:* www.intelesystems.com	972-852-8200		387
Inteletravel.com 777 E Atlantic Ave Ste 300 ....Delray Beach FL 33483 *TF:* 800-873-5353 ■ *Web:* www.inteletravel.com	561-272-9666	272-0813	771
Intelex Technologies Inc 905 King St W Ste 600....................... Toronto ON M6K3G9 *Web:* www.intelex.com	416-599-6009		179
Inteliport 103 N Church St.................... Hertford NC 27944 *Web:* inteliport.net	252-426-4600		396
Intelisearch Inc 60 Long Ride Rd............. Stamford CT 06902 *Web:* www.isimpact.com	203-325-1389		193
Intelitech Group, The 4800 NW Camas Meadows Dr Ste 220........... Camas WA 98607 *Web:* www.intelitechgroup.com	360-260-9780		261
Intellect Resources Inc 3824 N Elm St Ste 102..................... Greensboro NC 27455 *TF:* 877-554-8911 ■ *Web:* www.intellectresources.com	877-554-8911		260
Intelletrace Inc 936 B Seventh St................Novato CA 94945 *TF:* 800-618-5877 ■ *Web:* intelletrace.com	415-493-2200	598-2108	387
Intellex Consulting Services Inc 4 Apple Row .... Kennett Square PA 19348 *Web:* www.intellexinc.com	610-388-3939		194
Intellicents Inc 100 N Broadway Ave....................... Albert Lea MN 56007 *Web:* www.intellicents.com	507-377-9344		734
IntelliChoice Energy LLC 2355 W Utopia Rd ....Phoenix AZ 85027 *Web:* iceghp.com	623-879-4664		664
Intellicom Computer Consulting 1702 Second Ave .... Kearney NE 68847 *TF:* 877-501-3375 ■ *Web:* intellicominc.com	308-237-0684		180
Intellicomm Inc 575 E Swedesford Rd .... Wayne PA 19087 **Fax Area Code:* 267 ■ *Web:* www.intellicomm.com	610-687-8020	295-8000*	174
Intellicor Communications 330 Eden Rd.............................Lancaster PA 17601 *Web:* www.intellicor.com	800-233-0107		627
Intelligence Press Inc 22648 Glenn Dr Ste 305...................... Sterling VA 20164 *TF:* 800-427-5747 ■ *Web:* www.naturalgasintel.com	703-318-8848	318-0597	6
Intelligencer, The 1500 Main St ....Wheeling WV 26003 *Web:* www.theintelligencer.net	304-233-0100	232-1399	532-2
Intelligent Automation Inc 15400 Calhoun Dr Ste 400.................. Rockville MD 20855 *Web:* www.i-a-i.com	301-294-5200	294-5201	261
Intelligent Capital Inc Market at Third St The Hearst Bldg Ste 810.............................. San Francisco CA 94103 *Web:* www.intelligentcapital.com	415-974-1000		401
Intelligent Computer Solutions Inc 9350 Eton Ave.......................... Chatsworth CA 91311 *TF:* 888-994-4678 ■ *Web:* ics-iq.com	818-998-5805		174
Intelligent Decisions Inc 21445 Beaumeade Cir ....Ashburn VA 20147 *TF:* 800-929-8331 ■ *Web:* www.intelligent.net	703-554-1600		180
Intelligent Interiors Inc 16837 Addison Rd Ste 500....................Addison TX 75001 *Web:* iispaces.com	972-716-9979		321
Intelligent Lighting Controls Inc 5229 Edina Industrial Blvd ....Minneapolis MN 55439 *Web:* www.ilc-usa.com	952-829-1900		203
Intelligent Marketing Inc 200 Merrimack St.......................... Haverhill MA 01830 *Web:* inmarketing.com	978-702-0100		180
Intelligent Mechatronic Systems Inc 445 Wes Graham Way Ste 101 .... Waterloo ON N2L6R2 *TF:* 877-579-9699 ■ *Web:* www.intellimcc.com	519-745-8887		668
Intelligent Optical Systems 2520 W 237th St...........................Torrance CA 90505 **Fax Area Code:* 310 ■ *Web:* www.intopsys.com	424-263-6300	530-7417*	385
Intelligent Product Solutions Inc 700 Veterans Hwy Ste 100 .... Hauppauge NY 11788 *Web:* intelligentproduct.solutions	631-676-7744		261
Intelligent Systems Corp 4355 Shackleford Rd .... Norcross GA 30093 *NYSE: INS* ■ *TF:* 800-937-5449 ■ *Web:* www.intelsys.com	770-381-2900	381-2808	792
Intelligent Transportation Society of America (ITS) 1100 New Jersey Ave SE Ste 850...........Washington DC 20003 *TF:* 800-374-8472 ■ *Web:* www.itsa.org	202-484-4847	484-3483	49-21
Intelligentsia Coffee Inc 1850 W Fulton St...........................Chicago IL 60612 *TF:* 888-945-9786 ■ *Web:* www.intelligentsiacoffee.com	312-563-0023		296-7
Intelligrated Products 475 E High St PO Box 899 .... London OH 43140 *TF:* 866-936-7300 ■ *Web:* www.intelligrated.com	740-490-0300		207
IntelliGuard 6451 El Camino Real Ste C................... Carlsbad CA 92009 *Web:* www.ig.solutions	760-448-9500	448-9599	475
Intellimar Inc 7560 Main St .... Sykesville MD 21784 *Web:* www.intellimar.com	410-552-9940	552-9939	195
Intellimed International Corp 1825 E Northern Ave Ste 175 ....Phoenix AZ 85020 *Web:* www.intellimed.com	602-230-0333		194
Intellimeter Canada Inc 1125 Squires Beach Rd ....Pickering ON L1W3T9 *Web:* intellimeter.on.ca	905-839-9199	839-9198	317
Intelli-Mine Inc 1200 Quail St Ste 270..................Newport Beach CA 92660 *Web:* www.intelli-mine.com	949-528-3830		180
IntelliNet Technologies Inc 1990 W New Haven Ave Ste 303.............Melbourne FL 32904 *Web:* www.diametriq.com	321-726-0686	726-0683	178-7
Intellinetics 2190 Dividend Dr .... Columbus OH 43228 *Web:* www.intellinetics.com	614-921-8170		177
IntelliPower Inc 1746 N St Thomas Cir ....Orange CA 92865 *Web:* www.intellipower.com	714-921-1580	921-4023	767
IntelliShop LLC 2025 Michael Owens Way...................Perrysburg OH 43551 *Web:* www.intelli-shop.com	419-872-5103		195
IntelliSoft Group LLC 61 Spit Brook Rd .... Nashua NH 03060 *TF:* 888-634-4464 ■ *Web:* www.intellisoftgroup.com	888-634-4464		180

Phone Fax Class

Intellisoft Solutions Inc
PO Box 260883 ... Pembroke Pines FL 33026 305-471-5111 178-1
TF: 800-246-3232 ■ *Web:* www.managemore.com

IntelliSpring Technologies Inc
4038 Flowers Rd Ste 300 ... Atlanta GA 30360 678-291-0711 291-0669 177
Web: www.intellispring.com

Intelliswift Software Inc
2201 Walnut Ave ... Fremont CA 94538 510-490-9240 180
Web: www.intelliswift.com

Intellisys Technology LLC
1000 Jorie Blvd Ste 200 ... Oak Brook IL 60523 630-928-1111 990-1333 180
Web: intellisystechnology.com

IntelliTec College
772 Horizon Dr ... Grand Junction CO 81506 970-639-0093 243-8074 166
Web: www.intellitec.edu

Intellithink LLC
1225 N 78 St Ste A ... Kansas City KS 66112 913-766-0303 463
Web: www.intelli-think.com

Intellyk Inc 15 Corporate Pl S ... Piscataway NJ 08854 732-399-9510 178-1
Web: intellyk.com

Intellys Corp 621 W College St ... Grapevine TX 76051 972-929-9000 180
Web: www.intellys.com

Intelsat General Corp
6550 Rock Spring Dr Ste 450 ... Bethesda MD 20817 301-571-1210 387
Web: www.intelsatgeneral.com

Intelsat Ltd
3400 International Dr NW ... Washington DC 20008 703-559-6800 681
Web: www.intelsat.com

Intematix Corp 46410 Fremont Blvd ... Fremont CA 94538 510-933-3300 668-0793 668
Web: www.intematix.com

Intensity Corp
12730 High Bluff Dr Ste 300 ... San Diego CA 92130 858-876-9101 138
Web: intensity.com

Intent IQ LLC
37-18 N Blvd Ste 404 ... Long Island City NY 11101 646-583-1376 349-2778 4
Web: www.intentiq.com

Intepros Consulting Inc
750 Marrett Rd ... Lexington MA 02421 781-761-1140 177
Web: intepros.com

Inter American Press Assn (IAPA)
3511 NW 91st Ave ... Doral FL 33172 305-634-2465 860-4264 49-14
Web: www.sipiapa.org

Inter City Oil Company Inc (ICO)
1921 S St ... Duluth MN 55812 218-728-3641 579
TF: 800-642-5542 ■ *Web:* www.intercityoil.com

Inter Mountain Cable Inc
20 Laynesville Rd PO Box 159 ... Harold KY 41635 606-478-9406 116
TF: 800-635-7052

Inter Parfums Inc
551 Fifth Ave Ste 1500 ... New York NY 10176 212-983-2640 983-4197 574
NASDAQ: IPAR ■ *Web:* www.interparfumsinc.com

Inter Trans Insurance Services Inc
9311 Irvine Blvd ... Irvine CA 92618 949-387-9220 387-9241 390
TF: 800-251-0678 ■ *Web:* intertransins.com

Inter Valley Escrow Inc
447 Burchett St ... Glendale CA 91203 818-547-9999 653
Web: intervalleyescrow.com

InterAct Ministries 31000 SE Kelso Rd ... Boring OR 97009 800-258-3464 48-20
TF: 800-258-3464 ■ *Web:* interactministries.org

Interact One Inc
4665 Cornell Rd Ste 255 ... Cincinnati OH 45241 513-469-7042 196
Web: www.interactone.com

Interact Performance Systems Inc
180 N Rverview Dr Ste 165 ... Anaheim CA 92808 714-283-8288 463
TF: 800-944-7553 ■ *Web:* www.inter-ps.com

InterAct PMTI 260 Maple Ct Ste 210 ... Ventura CA 93003 805-658-5600 658-5605 539
Web: www.pacificmti.com

InterAction 1400 16th St NW ... Washington DC 20036 202-667-8227 667-8236 48-5
Web: www.interaction.org

Interaction Assoc 70 Fargo St Ste 908 ... Boston MA 02210 800-625-8049 535-7099* 194
**Fax Area Code:* 617 ■ *TF:* 800-625-8049 ■ *Web:* www.interactionassociates.com

Interaction Research Institute Inc
4428 Rockcrest Dr ... Fairfax VA 22032 703-978-0313 978-1776 180
TF: 800-782-8626 ■ *Web:* irism.com

Interactive Business Systems Inc
2625 Butterfield Rd ... Oak Brook IL 60523 630-571-9100 571-2490 180
Web: www.ibs.com

Interactive College of Technology
1580 Southlake Pky Ste C ... Morrow GA 30260 770-960-1298 166
Web: www.ict.edu

Interactive Digital Solutions Inc
14701 Cumberland Rd Ste 400 ... Noblesville IN 46060 317-770-3500 770-3528 52
TF: 877-880-0022 ■ *Web:* www.e-idsolutions.com

Interactive Management Inc
12011 Tejon St Ste 700 ... Westminster CO 80234 303-433-4446 47
Web: www.imigroup.org

Interactive Media Communications Inc
PO Box 401002 ... Cambridge MA 02140 617-868-8288 868-7227 637-10
Web: www.safetysite.com

Interactive One LLC 4 NY Plz Ste 501 ... New York NY 10004 212-431-4477 6
Web: www.ionedigital.com

Interactive Tracking Systems Inc
820 51st St E Ste 150 ... Saskatoon SK S7K0X8 306-665-5026 225
TF: 888-525-5026 ■ *Web:* www.itracks.com

Interagency Council on Homelessness
409 Third St SW Ste 310 ... Washington DC 20024 202-708-4663 340-20
Web: www.usich.gov

Inter-American Commission of Women (CIM)
1889 F St NW ... Washington DC 20006 202-458-6084 458-6094 48-24
Web: www.oas.org

Inter-American Development Bank
1300 New York Ave NW ... Washington DC 20577 202-523-7344 623-3096 783
TF: 877-782-7432 ■ *Web:* www.iadb.org

Inter-American Dialogue
1211 Connecticut Ave NW Ste 510 ... Washington DC 20036 202-822-9002 822-9553 634
Web: www.thedialogue.org

Inter-American Foundation (IAF)
901 N Stuart St 10th Fl ... Arlington VA 22203 202-360-4530 306-4365* 340-20
**Fax Area Code:* 703 ■ *Web:* www.iaf.gov

InterAmerican Motor Corp (IMC)
8901 Canoga Ave ... Canoga Park CA 91304 818-678-1200 61
TF: 800-874-8925 ■ *Web:* www.imcparts.net

Interamerican Trading And Products Company LLC
1800 Sunset Harbour Dr Ste P ... Miami Beach FL 33139 305-885-9666 297-5

Inter-American Trading Inc
PO Box 370183 ... Denver CO 80237 303-696-2613 750-3403 594
TF: 800-279-4534 ■ *Web:* www.i-at.com

InterBank 4921 N May Ave ... Oklahoma City OK 73112 405-782-4200 225-5570* 70
**Fax Area Code:* 580 ■ *TF:* 855-599-5745 ■ *Web:* www.interbank.com

InterBase Corp
22485 La Palma Ave Ste 200D ... Yorba Linda CA 92887 714-701-3600 701-6330 196
Web: www.interbasecorp.com

Interbel Telephone Cooperative Inc
300 Dewey Ave ... Eureka MT 59917 406-889-3311 224
Web: www.interbel.com

Interboro Systems Corp
206 San Jorge St ... San Juan PR 00912 787-641-7777 641-7790 196
Web: www.interboropr.com

Interbrand Design Forum LLC
7575 Paragon Rd ... Dayton OH 45459 937-439-4400 7
Web: www.interbranddesignforum.com

InterCall 8420 W Bryn Mawr Ste 1100 ... Chicago IL 60631 773-399-1600 736
TF: 800-374-2441 ■ *Web:* shop.west.com

Interceramic USA 1950 E Parker Rd ... Carrollton TX 75010 214-503-5500 751
Web: interceramicusa.com

Interchange Institute
292 Newbury St Ste 301 ... Boston MA 02115 617-566-2227 277-0889 637-2
Web: www.interchangeinstitute.org

Interchem Corp 120 Rt 17 N ... Paramus NJ 07652 201-261-7333 479
TF: 800-261-7332 ■ *Web:* www.interchem.com

InterChez Logistics Systems Inc
600 Alpha Pkwy ... Stow OH 44224 330-923-5080 449
TF: 800-780-4707 ■ *Web:* interchez.com

Interchurch Medical Assistance Inc (IMA)
1730 M St NW Ste 1100 ... Washington DC 20036 202-888-6200 470-3370 48-5
TF: 877-241-7952 ■ *Web:* www.imaworldhealth.org

Inter-City Printing Company Inc
614 Madison St ... Oakland CA 94607 510-451-4775 451-5039 627
Web: www.madisonstreetpress.com

Intercoast Colleges
2235 E Garvey Ave N ... West Covina CA 91791 626-337-6800 167-3
TF: 888-718-8282 ■ *Web:* www.intercoast.edu

Intercollegiate Studies Institute (ISI)
3901 Centerville Rd ... Wilmington DE 19807 302-652-4600 48-11
TF: 800-526-7022 ■ *Web:* home.isi.org

Inter-Commercial Business Systems Inc
601 Century Pky ... Allen TX 75013 800-886-6642 649-4959* 246
**Fax Area Code:* 972 ■ *TF:* 800-886-6642 ■ *Web:* www.icbsrepair.com

Inter-Community Telephone Co (ICTC)
PO Box 8 ... Nome ND 58062 701-924-8815 924-8808 736
TF: 800-350-9137 ■ *Web:* www.ictc.com

Intercomp Co 3839 County Rd 116 ... Medina MN 55340 763-476-2531 476-2613 684
TF: 800-328-3336 ■ *Web:* www.intercompcompany.com

Intercon Inc 1222 Corporate Park Dr ... Forest VA 24551 434-525-3390 525-8418 253
Web: www.interconinc.com

Interconnect Services Inc
661 Everhart Rd ... Corpus Christi TX 78411 361-884-3447 882-2280 178-1
TF: 800-460-0546 ■ *Web:* www.interconnect.net

Interconnect Wiring Harnesses Inc
5024 W Vickery Blvd ... Fort Worth TX 76107 817-377-9473 732-8667 247
Web: www.interconnect-wiring.com

Intercontinental Asset Management Group Ltd
112 E Pecan St Ste 525 ... San Antonio TX 78205 210-271-7947 271-0309 690
TF: 800-292-0898 ■ *Web:* www.intercontl.com

Intercontinental Exchange Inc
5660 New Northside Dr NW 3rd Fl ... Atlanta GA 30328 770-857-4700 937-0020 387
Web: www.intercontinentalexchange.com

InterContinental Hotels Group
3315 Peachtree Rd NE ... Atlanta GA 30326 404-946-9000 379
Web: www.ihg.com
Staybridge Suites 3 Ravinia Dr Ste 100 ... Atlanta GA 30346 770-604-2000 379
Web: www.ihgplc.com

InterContinental Insurance Brokers LLC
175 Federal St Ste 725 ... Boston MA 02110 617-648-5100 390
Web: intercobrokers.com

Intercontinental Marble Corp
8228 NW 56th St ... Doral FL 33166 305-591-2207 724
Web: www.intercontinentalmarble.com

InterContinental Mark Hopkins San Francisco
999 California St ... San Francisco CA 94108 415-392-3434 378
Web: www.intercontinentalmarkhopkins.com

InterContinental Montreal
360 St-Antoine St W ... Montreal QC H2Y3X4 514-987-9900 378
TF: 877-660-8550 ■ *Web:* montreal.intercontinental.com

Intercontinental San Francisco
888 Howard St ... San Francisco CA 94103 888-811-4273 378
TF: 888-811-4273 ■ *Web:* www.intercontinentalsanfrancisco.com

InterContinental Stephen F Austin Hotel
701 Congress Ave ... Austin TX 78701 512-457-8800 457-8896 378
TF: 800-424-6835 ■ *Web:* www.austin.intercontinental.com

InterCorr International Inc
14503 Bammel N Houston Rd Ste 300 ... Houston TX 77014 281-444-2282 444-0246 743
Web: www.intercorr.com

Intercosmos Media Group Inc
3500 N Causeway Blvd Ste 160 ... Metairie LA 70002 504-355-0081 564-7373* 180
**Fax Area Code:* 888 ■ *TF:* 877-856-9598 ■ *Web:* www.directnic.com

Inter-County Bakers Inc
1095 Long Island Ave ... Deer Park NY 11729 631-957-1350 957-1013 70
TF: 800-696-1350 ■ *Web:* www.icbakers.com

Intercounty Electric Co-op
102 Maple Ave ... Licking MO 65542 573-674-2211 674-2888 245
TF: 866-621-3679 ■ *Web:* www.ieca.coop

Inter-County Energy Co-op
1009 Hustonville Rd ... Danville KY 40422 859-236-4561 236-3627 245
TF: 888-266-7322 ■ *Web:* www.intercountyenergy.net

Intercrowd LLC 3100 Technology Pkwy ... Orlando FL 32826 561-212-3548 178-1
Web: www.intecrowd.com

Phone | Fax | Class

Intercultural Communication Institute (ICI)
8835 SW Canyon Ln Ste 238 Portland OR 97225 503-297-4622 297-4695 167-3
Web: www.intercultural.org

Intercultural Communications College
810 Richards St Ste 200 Honolulu HI 96813 808-946-2445 946-2231 423
Web: www.icchawaii.edu

Intercultural Development Research Assn (IDRA)
5815 Callaghan Rd Ste 101 San Antonio TX 78228 210-444-1710 444-1714 48-11
Web: www.idra.org

Intercultural Institute of California
1362 Post St San Francisco CA 94109 415-359-9099 359-9033 167-3
Web: www.iicesl.org

Interdenominational Theological Ctr
700 Martin Luther King Jr Dr Atlanta GA 30314 404-527-7700 527-0901 168
Web: www.itc.edu

InterDent Inc
9800 S La Cienega Blvd Ste 800 Inglewood CA 90301 310-765-2400 463
Web: www.interdent.com

InterDev LLC
2650 Holcomb Bridge Rd Ste 310 Alpharetta GA 30022 770-643-4400 180
TF: 877-841-8069 ■ *Web:* www.interdev.com

InterDigital Communications Corp
781 Third Ave King of Prussia PA 19406 610-878-7800 696
Web: www.interdigital.com

Interdyn 875 Sixth Avenue 20th Fl New York NY 10001 800-289-7830 180
TF: 800-289-7830 ■ *Web:* interdyncorp.wordpress.com

Interdynamix 620-10180 101 St NW Edmonton AB T5J3S4 780-423-7005 423-7811 177
Web: www.interdynamix.com

Interdyne Inc 530 Industrial Pky Jonesville MI 49250 517-849-2281 849-7557 676
Web: www.interdyneinc.com

Intereal Corp 500 3rd St Ste 505 San Francisco CA 94107 415-778-3900 652

Intereum 9800 8th Ave N Plymouth MN 55441 763-417-3300 417-3309 320
Web: intereum.com

InterEx Exhibits 34 S Hunt Rd Amesbury MA 01913 978-388-8755 393
Web: www.interex.com

Interface Construction Corp
8401 Wabash Ave Saint Louis MO 63134 314-522-1011 522-1022 186
Web: www.interfaceconstruction.com

Interface EAP Inc (IEAP)
2424 Wilcrest Dr Ste 230 PO Box 421879 Houston TX 77042 713-781-3364 784-0425 462
TF: 800-324-4327 ■ *Web:* www.ieap.com

Interface Inc 7401 E Butherus Dr Scottsdale AZ 85260 480-948-5555 948-1924 472
TF: 800-947-5598 ■ *Web:* www.interfaceforce.com

Interface Inc
2859 Paces Ferry Rd Ste 2000 Atlanta GA 30339 770-437-6800 131
NASDAQ: TILE ■ *Web:* www.interface.com

Interface Logic Systems Inc
3311 E Livingston Ave Columbus OH 43227 614-236-8388 362
Web: www.interfacelogic.com

Interface Media Group Inc
1233 20th St NW Washington DC 20036 202-861-0500 514
Web: www.interfacemedia.com

Interface Multimedia Inc
4330 EW Hwy Ste 220 Silver Spring MD 20814 301-585-0068 225
Web: www.ifmm.com

Interface Precision Benchworks Inc
150 Quabbin Blvd Orange MA 01364 978-544-8866 523-5363 253
Web: www.ipbconnect.com

Interface Security Systems LLC
6340 International Pkwy Ste 101 Plano TX 75093 972-996-2800 996-2801 692
Web: www.interfacesystems.com

Interface Solutions Inc
216 Wohlsen Way Lancaster PA 17603 800-942-7538 207-6080* 326
**Fax Area Code: 717* ■ *TF:* 800-942-7538 ■ *Web:* www.interfacematerials.com

Interfaith Action of Greater Saint Paul
1671 Summit Ave Saint Paul MN 55105 651-646-8805 646-6866 48-20
Web: interfaithaction.org

Interfaith Alliance
2101 L St NW Ste 400 Washington DC 20037 202-466-0567 238-3301 48-7
Web: interfaithalliance.org

Interfaith Center of New York (ICNY)
475 Riverside Dr Ste 540 New York NY 10115 212-870-3510 870-3499 637-10
Web: interfaithcenter.org

Interfaith Medical Ctr
1545 Atlantic Ave Brooklyn NY 11213 718-613-4000 374-3
Web: www.interfaithmedical.com

Interfaith Ministries for Greater Houston
3303 Main St Houston TX 77002 713-533-4900 48-20
Web: www.imgh.org

Interfoods of America Inc
9500 S Dadeland Blvd Ste 800 Miami FL 33156 305-670-0746 670

Interfor Pacific Inc
2211 Rimland Dr Ste 220 Bellingham WA 98226 360-788-2299 683
Web: www.interfor.com

Intergen 30 Corporate Dr Burlington MA 01803 781-993-3000 245
Web: www.intergen.com

Intergraph Corp 19 Interpro Rd Madison AL 35758 256-730-2000 730-2048 178-5
TF: 800-345-4856 ■ *Web:* www.intergraph.com

InterGreet.com PO Box 9830 Anaheim CA 92812 714-956-8706 130
TF: 888-600-9354 ■ *Web:* www.intergreet.com

Interim HealthCare Inc
1601 Sawgrass Corporate Pkwy Sunrise FL 33323 800-338-7786 721
TF: 800-338-7786 ■ *Web:* www.interimhealthcare.com

Interim Healthcare of Spokane
1625 W Fourth Ave Spokane WA 99201 509-456-5665 363
Web: interimhealthcare.com

Interinvest Corporation Inc
192 S St Ste 600 Boston MA 02111 617-723-7870 401
Web: www.interinvest.com

Interior Architects Inc
1750 15th St 3rd Fl Denver CO 80202 303-292-4963 292-4971 466
Web: www.interiorarchitects.com

Interior Construction Services Ltd
2930 Market St Saint Louis MO 63103 314-534-6664 534-6663 189-9
Web: www.ics-stl.com

Interior Crafts Inc
2513 W Cullerton Ave Chicago IL 60608 773-376-8160 376-9578 319-2
Web: interiorcraftsinc.com

Interior Creations Inc
700 E Erie Ave Philadelphia PA 19134 215-425-9390 820
Web: interiorcreationsinc.com

Interior Design
1271 Avenue of the Americas New York NY 10020 917-934-2882 637-9
TF: 800-900-0804 ■ *Web:* www.interiordesign.net

Interior Designers Institute
1061 Camelback Rd Newport Beach CA 92660 949-675-4451 759-0667 167-3
Web: www.idi.edu

Interior Finishes Abbey Carpet of North Royalton
9591 York-Alpha Dr North Royalton OH 44133 440-237-8120 290
Web: www.northroyalton.abbeycarpet.com

Interior Health Authority
505 Doyle Ave Kelowna BC V1Y0C5 250-469-7070 469-7068 352
Web: www.interiorhealth.ca

Interior Move Consultants Inc
5 W 19th St Rm 2C New York NY 10011 212-343-8624 343-8767 463
Web: www.moveconsultants.com

Interior Region EMS Council
2503 18th Ave Fairbanks AK 99709 907-456-3978 456-3970 167-3
Web: www.iremsc.org

Interior Systems Contract Group Inc
612 N Main St Royal Oak MI 48067 248-399-1600 399-1601 393
Web: www.iscginc.com

Interiors by Steven G Inc
2818 Centre Port Cir Pompano Beach FL 33064 954-735-8223 393
Web: www.interiorsbysteveng.com

Interiors Inc 1325 N Dutton Ave Santa Rosa CA 95401 707-544-4770 544-0722 320
Web: www.interiorsincorporated.com

Interkal Inc 5981 E Cork St Kalamazoo MI 49048 269-349-1521 349-6530 319-3
Web: www.interkal.com

Interlake Steamship Co, The
7300 Engle Rd Middleburg Heights OH 44130 440-260-6900 260-6945 313
Web: www.interlake-steamship.com

Interlaken Capital Inc
475 Steamboat Rd 2nd Fl Greenwich CT 06830 203-629-8750 629-8554 401
Web: www.interlakencapital.com

Interlaken Inn
74 Interlaken Rd Rt 12 Lakeville CT 06039 860-435-9878 435-2980 669
TF: 800-222-2909 ■ *Web:* www.interlakeninn.com

Interlectric Corp 1401 Lexington Ave Warren PA 16365 814-723-6061 723-1074 437
TF: 800-722-2184 ■ *Web:* www.interlectric.com

Interlex Communications
4005 Broadway St San Antonio TX 78209 210-930-3339 7
Web: interlexusa.com

Interllnc Direct Corp
6411 Edwards Blvd Mississauga ON L5T2P7 905-677-2620 224

Interline Creative Group
553 N North Ct Ste 160 Palatine IL 60067 847-358-4848 358-8089 7
TF: 800-222-1208 ■ *Web:* www.interlinegroup.com

Interlink Electronics Inc
546 Flynn Rd Camarillo CA 93012 805-484-8855 173-1
NASDAQ: LINK ■ *Web:* www.interlinkelectronics.com

Interlink Network Systems Inc
495 Cranbury Rd East Brunswick NJ 08816 732-846-2226 256
TF: 877-872-6947 ■ *Web:* www.ilinknet.com

Interlink Networks Inc
2531 Jackson Rd Ste 306 Ann Arbor MI 48103 734-821-1200 821-1235 179
Web: www.interlinknetworks.com

interlinkONE Inc
260-A Fordham Rd Ste 100 Wilmington MA 01887 978-694-9992 178-1
Web: interlinkone.com

Interlochen Center for the Arts
4000 Michigan 137 Interlochen MI 49643 231-276-7200 276-7444 572
Web: www.interlochen.org

Interlochen State Park
4167 Hwy M-137 Interlochen MI 49643 231-276-9511 565
Web: www.michigan.org

InterLock Industries Inc
545 S Third St Ste 310 Louisville KY 40202 502-569-2007 480
Web: www.interlockindustries.com

Interlocking Concrete Pavement Institute (ICPI)
14801 Murdock St Ste 230 Chantilly VA 20151 703-657-6900 657-6901 49-3
TF: 800-241-3652 ■ *Web:* www.icpi.org

Interlog USA Inc
9380 Central Ave NE Ste 350 Minneapolis MN 55434 800-603-6030 313
TF: 800-603-6030 ■ *Web:* www.interlogusa.com

Interlude Home Inc 25 Trefoil Dr Trumbull CT 06611 203-445-7617 361
Web: www.interludehome.com

Intermap Technologies Inc
8310 S Vly Hwy Ste 400 Englewood CO 80112 303-708-0955 727
Web: www.intermap.com

Intermarine LLC
365 Canal St One Canal Pl Ste 2400 New Orleans LA 70130 504-529-2100 312
Web: www.intermarine.com

Intermark Group 101 25th St N Birmingham AL 35203 800-624-9239 4
TF: 800-624-9239 ■ *Web:* www.intermarkgroup.com

Intermarket Insurance Agency Inc
205 E Main St Ste 3-4 Huntington NY 11743 631-421-2424 421-2004 390
Web: intermarketins.com

Intermatic Inc 7777 Winn Rd Spring Grove IL 60081 815-675-7000 675-7001 203
Web: www.intermatic.com

Intermax Pharmaceuticals Inc
228 Sherwood Ave Farmingdale NY 11735 631-777-3318 231

InterMetro Communications Inc
2685 Park Center Dr Bldg A Simi Valley CA 93065 805-433-8000 582-1006 681
Web: www.intermetro.net

InterMetro Industries Corp
651 N Washington St Wilkes-Barre PA 18705 570-825-2741 73
TF: 800-992-1776 ■ *Web:* www.metro.com

Intermodal Association of North America (IANA)
11785 Beltsville Dr Ste 1100 Calverton MD 20705 301-982-3400 982-4815 49-21
TF: 877-438-8442 ■ *Web:* www.intermodal.org

Intermodal Cartage Company Inc
5707 E Holmes Rd Memphis TN 38141 901-363-0050 432-6174 468
Web: www.imcg.com

Intermolecular Inc 3011 N First St San Jose CA 95134 408 582-5700 696
TF: 877-251-1860 ■ *Web:* intermolecular.com

	Phone	Fax	Class
Intermotive Inc 12840 Earhart Ave . . . . Auburn CA 95602 *Web:* www.intermotive.net	530-823-1048		350
Intermountain Business Forms Inc 22 S 1400 W . . . . Centerville UT 84014 *TF:* 800-488-7961 ■ *Web:* www.interform.net	801-292-7971	292-7990	534
Intermountain Electric Inc (IME) 5050 Osage St Ste 500 . . . . Denver CO 80221 *Web:* imelect.com	303-733-7248	722-2410	189-4
Intermountain Farmers Assn 1147 West 2100 South . . . . Salt Lake City UT 84119 *TF:* 800-748-4432 ■ *Web:* ifacountrystores.com	801-972-2122	972-2186	276
Intermountain Gas Company Inc 555 S Cole Rd . . . . Boise ID 83709 *TF:* 800-548-3679 ■ *Web:* www.intgas.com	208-377-6840	377-6081	787
Intermountain Healthcare Logan Regional Hospital 500 E 1400 N . . . . Logan UT 84341 *TF:* 800-442-4845 ■ *Web:* intermountainhealthcare.org	435-716-1000	716-5409	374-3
Intermountain Livestock Inc 60654 Livestock Rd . . . . La Grande OR 97850 *Web:* imlivestock.com	541-963-2158		446
InterMountain Management LLC 2390 Tower Dr . . . . Monroe LA 71201 *Web:* www.intermountainhotels.com	318-325-5561	812-0090	379
Intermountain Rural Electric Assn 5496 Hwy 85 . . . . Sedalia CO 80135 **Fax Area Code:* 720 ■ *TF:* 800-332-9540 ■ *Web:* irea.coop	303-688-3100	733-5872*	245
Intermountain Wood Products Inc 2316 E Iona Rd . . . . Salt Lake City UT 84115 *Web:* www.intermountainwood.com	801-486-5414	466-0428	820
Internal Audit Services Inc 6231 PGA Blvd Ste 136 . . . . Palm Beach Gardens FL 33418 *Web:* internalauditservices.com	561-626-7746		2
Internal Environment Institute 910 Broadway St Ste 112 . . . . Santa Monica CA 90401 *Web:* www.gentlewellnesscenter.com	310-576-6360		167-3
Internal Intelligence Security Service 1767 Morris Ave Ste 220 . . . . Union NJ 07083	973-242-5400		693
Internal Medicine News 5635 Fishers Ln Ste 6000 . . . . Rockville MD 20852 *TF:* 877-524-9336 ■ *Web:* www.mdedge.com	240-221-2400	221-4400	457-16
Internal Revenue Service (IRS) 1111 Constitution Ave NW . . . . Washington DC 20224 *Web:* www.irs.gov	202-622-5000		340-18
Taxpayer Advocate Service 77 K St NE Ste 1500 . . . . Washington DC 20002 **Fax Area Code:* 855 ■ *TF:* 877-777-4778 ■ *Web:* www.irs.gov	202-803-9800	810-2125*	340-18
Internal Sound and Communications Inc (ISC) 10500 Chicago Dr Ste 80 . . . . Zeeland MI 49464 **Fax Area Code:* 800 ■ *TF:* 800-777-1905 ■ *Web:* www.isc-inc.com	616-772-4875	772-4995*	246
Internap Network Services Corp 250 Williams St Ste E-100 . . . . Atlanta GA 30303 *NASDAQ: INAP* ■ *TF:* 877-843-7627 ■ *Web:* www.inap.com	404-302-9700	475-0520	39
International Academy 2550 S Ridgewood Ave . . . . South Daytona FL 32119 *TF:* 888-893-3636 ■ *Web:* www.iahd.net	386-767-4600	271-0009	167-3
International Aid Inc 17011 W Hickory St . . . . Spring Lake MI 49456 *TF:* 800-968-7490 ■ *Web:* www.internationalaid.org	616-846-7490	846-3842	48-5
International Air Cargo Assn (TIACA) 5600 NW 36th St Ste 620 . . . . Miami FL 33122 *Web:* tiaca.org	786-265-7011	265-7012	49-21
International Air Response Inc 6250 S Taxiway Cir . . . . Mesa AZ 85212 *Web:* www.internationalairresponse.com	480-840-9860	840-9866	302
International Air Transport Assn 800 Pl Victoria PO Box 113 . . . . Montreal QC H4Z1M1 *TF:* 800-716-6326 ■ *Web:* www.iata.org	514-874-0202	874-9632	49-21
International Airline Passengers Assn (IAPA) PO Box 700188 . . . . Dallas TX 75370 *TF:* 800-821-4272 ■ *Web:* www.iapa.com	972-404-9980	233-5348	48-23
International Alliance for Women (TIAW) 1101 Pennsylvania Ave NW 3rd Fl . . . . Washington DC 20004 *TF:* 888-712-5200 ■ *Web:* www.tiaw.org	888-712-5200		48-24
International AntiCounterfeiting Coalition (IACC) 727 15th St NW 9th Fl . . . . Washington DC 20005 *Web:* www.iacc.org	202-223-6667		49-13
International Arctic Research Ctr (IARC) 2160 Koyukuk Dr PO Box 757340 . . . . Fairbanks AK 99775 *Web:* uaf-iarc.org	907-474-6016	474-5662	668
International Armoring Corp 80 N 1400 W . . . . Centerville UT 84014 *Web:* www.armormax.com	801-393-1075		59
International Association for Dental Research (IADR) 1619 Duke St . . . . Alexandria VA 22314 *Web:* www.iadr.org	703-548-0066	548-1883	49-8
International Association for Food Protection (IAFP) 6200 Aurora Ave Ste 200W . . . . Des Moines IA 50322 *TF:* 800-369-6337 ■ *Web:* www.foodprotection.org	515-276-3344	276-8655	49-6
International Association for Human Resource Information Management Inc (IHRIM) PO Box 1086 . . . . Burlington MA 01803 **Fax Area Code:* 781 ■ *TF:* 800-804-3983 ■ *Web:* ihrim.org	800-804-3983	998-8011*	49-12
International Association for Impact Assessment (IAIA) 1330 23rd St S Ste C . . . . Fargo ND 58103 *Web:* www.iaia.org	701-297-7908	297-7917	49-12
International Association for Medical Assistance to Travellers (IAMAT) 67 Mowat Ave Ste 036 . . . . Toronto ON M6K3E3 *Web:* www.iamat.org	416-652-0137	652-1983	48-23
International Association for the Study of Pain (IASP) 111 Queen Anne Ave N Ste 501 . . . . Seattle WA 98109 *TF:* 866-574-2654 ■ *Web:* www.iasp-pain.org	206-283-0311	283-9403	48-17
International Association of Administrative Professionals (IAAP) 10502 NW Ambassador Dr Ste 100 . . . . Kansas City MO 64153 *Web:* www.iaap-hq.org	816-891-6600	891-9118	49-12
International Association of Amusement Parks & Attractions (IAAPA) 1448 Duke St . . . . Alexandria VA 22314 *Web:* www.iaapa.org	703-836-4800	836-6742	48-23
International Association of Approved Basketball Officials Inc (IAABO) PO Box 355 . . . . Carlisle PA 17013 *Web:* www.iaabo.org	717-713-8129	718-6164	48-22
International Association of Arson Investigators (IAAI) 2111 Baldwin Ave Ste 203 . . . . Crofton MD 21114 *TF:* 800-468-4224 ■ *Web:* www.firearson.com	410-451-3473	451-9049	49-7
International Association of Assessing Officers (IAAO) 314 W Tenth St . . . . Kansas City MO 64105 *TF:* 800-616-4226 ■ *Web:* iaao.org	816-701-8100	701-8149	49-7
International Association of Auto Theft Investigators (IAATI) PO Box 223 . . . . Clinton NY 13323 *Web:* www.iaati.org	315-853-1913		49-7
International Association of Bridge Structural Ornamental & Reinforcing Iron Workers 1750 New York Ave NW Ste 400 . . . . Washington DC 20006 *TF:* 800-368-0105 ■ *Web:* www.ironworkers.org	202-383-4800	638-4856	414
International Association of Business Communicators (IABC) 155 Montgomery St Ste 1210 . . . . San Francisco CA 94104 *TF:* 800-776-4222 ■ *Web:* www.iabc.com	415-544-4700	544-4747	49-12
International Association of Chiefs of Police (IACP) 44 Canal Center Plz Ste 200 . . . . Alexandria VA 22314 *TF:* 800-843-4227 ■ *Web:* www.theiacp.org	703-836-6767	836-4543	49-7
International Association of Conference Centers (IACC) 35 E Wacker Dr Ste 850 . . . . Chicago IL 60601 *Web:* www.iacconline.org	312-224-2580	644-8557	49-12
International Association of Culinary Professionals (IACP) 45 Rockefeller Plz Ste 2000 . . . . New York NY 10111 *TF:* 855-738-4227 ■ *Web:* www.iacp.com	855-738-4227		49-6
International Association of Defense Counsel (IADC) 303 W Madison St Ste 925 . . . . Chicago IL 60606 *Web:* www.iadclaw.org	312-368-1494	368-1854	49-10
International Association of Drilling Contractors (IADC) 3657 Briarpark Dr Ste 760 . . . . Houston TX 77042 *Web:* www.iadc.org	713-292-1945	292-1946	49-3
International Association of Electrical Inspectors (IAEI) 901 Waterfall Way Ste 602 . . . . Richardson TX 75080 *TF:* 800-786-4234 ■ *Web:* www.iaei.org	972-235-1455	235-6858	49-3
International Association of Exhibitions & Events (IAEE) 12700 Park Central Dr Ste 308 . . . . Dallas TX 75251 *Web:* www.iaee.com	972-458-8002	458-8119	49-18
International Association of Fairs & Expositions, The (IAFE) 3043 E Cairo St . . . . Springfield MO 65802 *TF:* 800-516-0313 ■ *Web:* www.fairsandexpos.com	417-862-5771		48-23
International Association of Fire Chiefs (IAFC) 4025 Fair Ridge Dr Ste 300 . . . . Fairfax VA 22033 *TF:* 866-385-9110 ■ *Web:* www.iafc.org	703-273-0911	273-9363	49-7
International Association of Fire Fighters (IAFF) 1750 New York Ave NW Ste 300 . . . . Washington DC 20006 *Web:* www.iaff.org	202-737-8484	737-8418	414
International Association of Fish & Wildlife Agencies (IAFWA) 444 N Capitol St NW Ste 725 . . . . Washington DC 20001 *Web:* www.fishwildlife.org	202-624-7890	624-7891	49-7
International Association of Heat & Frost Insulators & Allied Workers 9602 ML King Jr Hwy . . . . Lanham MD 20706 *Web:* www.insulators.org	301-731-9101	731-5058	414
International Association of Machinists & Aerospace Workers 9000 Machinists Pl . . . . Upper Marlboro MD 20772 *Web:* www.goiam.org	301-967-4520		414
International Association of Plastics Distribution (IAPD) 6734 W 121 St . . . . Overland Park KS 66209 *Web:* www.iapd.org	913-345-1005	345-1006	49-18
International Association of Plumbing & Mechanical Officials (IAPMO) 4755 E Philadelphia St . . . . Ontario CA 91761 *TF:* 877-427-6601 ■ *Web:* www.iapmo.org	909-472-4100	472-4150	49-7
International Association of Privacy Professionals (IAPP) 75 Rochester Ave Ste 4 . . . . Portsmouth NH 03801 *TF:* 800-266-6501 ■ *Web:* iapp.org	603-427-9200	427-9249	533
International Association of Venue Managers Inc (IAVM) 635 Fritz Dr Ste 100 . . . . Coppell TX 75019 *TF:* 800-935-4226 ■ *Web:* www.iavm.org	972-906-7441	906-7418	49-12
International Association of Wildland Fire (IAWF) 3416 Primm Ln . . . . Birmingham AL 35216 *Web:* www.iawfonline.org	205-824-7614		48-13
International Association of Workforce Professionals (IAPES) 1801 Louisville Rd . . . . Frankfort KY 40601 *Web:* iawponline.org	502-223-4459	223-4127	49-12
International Assurance of Tennessee Inc 123 Seventh Ave S . . . . Franklin TN 37064 *Web:* iatmgu.com	615-790-6908		390
International Atomic Energy Agency (IAEA) 1 UN Plz Rm DC1-1155 . . . . New York NY 10017 **Fax Area Code:* 917 ■ *Web:* www.iaea.org	212-963-6010	367-4046*	783
International Auction School 241 Greenfield Rd Rt 5 . . . . South Deerfield MA 01373 *Web:* www.douglasauctioneers.com	413-665-2877	665-3297	685
International Automotive Technicians' Network Inc PO Box 1599 . . . . Brea CA 92822 *Web:* www.iatn.net	714-257-1335		387
International Bakers Service Inc 1902 N Sheridan St . . . . South Bend IN 46628 *Web:* www.internationalbakers.com	574-287-7111		345
International Bancshares Corp 1200 San Bernardo Ave . . . . Laredo TX 78040 *NASDAQ: IBOC* ■ *TF:* 888-999-1091 ■ *Web:* www.ibc.com	956-722-7611	726-6637	360-2
International Bank of Chicago 5069 N Broadway . . . . Chicago IL 60640 *Web:* www.inbk.com	773-769-2899	769-2686	70
International Baptist College 2211 W Germann Rd . . . . Chandler AZ 85286 *Web:* tricityministries.org	480-245-7900		166
International Bar Code Systems Inc 160 Oak St . . . . Glastonbury CT 06033 *Web:* www.internationalbarcode.com	860-659-9660	657-3860	173-1
International Bible Society (IBS) *Biblica* 1820 Jet Stream Dr . . . . Colorado Springs CO 80921 *TF:* 800-524-1588 ■ *Web:* www.biblica.com	719-488-9200		48-20
International Billiards Inc 2311 Washington Ave . . . . Houston TX 77007 *Web:* www.intlbilliards.com	713-869-3237		710
International Biometric Society (IBS) 1444 'I' St NW Ste 700 . . . . Washington DC 20005 *Web:* www.biometricsociety.org	202-712-9049	216-9646	49-19

	Phone	Fax	Class
International Board of Jewish Missions Inc 5106 Genesis Ln. . . . . Hixson TN 37343 *Web:* www.ibjm.org	423-876-8150	876-8156	520
International Bottled Water Assn (IBWA) 1700 Diagonal Rd Ste 650 . . . . . Alexandria VA 22314 *TF:* 800-928-3711 ■ *Web:* www.bottledwater.org	703-683-5213	683-4074	49-6
International Boundary & Water Commission - US & Mexico 2616 W Paisano Dr Ste C-100 . . . . . El Paso TX 79922 *TF:* 800-262-8857 ■ *Web:* www.ibwc.gov	915-351-1030	832-4190	340-16
International Boundary Commission - US & Canada 1717 H St NW Ste 845 . . . . . Washington DC 20006 *Web:* www.internationalboundarycommission.org	202-736-9100	632-2008	340-16
International Bowling Museum & Hall of Fame 621 Six Flags Dr. . . . . Arlington TX 76011 *TF:* 800-514-2695 ■ *Web:* www.bowlingmuseum.com	817-385-8215		522
International Boxing Hall of Fame Museum 1 Hall of Fame Dr . . . . . Canastota NY 13032 *Web:* www.ibhof.com	315-697-7095	697-5356	522
International Brangus Breeders Assn (IBBA) 8870 US Hwy 87 E . . . . . San Antonio TX 78263 *Web:* gobrangus.com	210-696-8231	696-8718	48-2
International Bridge Tunnel & Turnpike Assn (IBTTA) 1146 19th St NW Ste 600 . . . . . Washington DC 20036 *Web:* www.ibtta.org	202-659-4620	659-0500	49-7
International Brotherhood of Boilermakers Iron Shipbuilders Blacksmiths Forgers & Helpers 753 State Ave Ste 570 . . . . . Kansas City KS 66101 *Web:* boilermakers.org	913-371-2640	281-8101	414
International Brotherhood of Electrical Workers 900 7th St NW . . . . . Washington DC 20001 *Web:* www.ibew.org	202-833-7000		414
International Brotherhood of Police Officers (IBPO) 159 Burgin Pkwy . . . . . Quincy MA 02169 *TF:* 866-412-7762 ■ *Web:* www.ibpo.org	617-376-0220	376-0285	414
International Business College 7205 Shadeland Sta . . . . . Indianapolis IN 46256 *TF:* 800-589-6363 ■ *Web:* www.ibcfortwayne.edu	260-459-4500		800
International Business Machines Corp (IBM) 1 New Orchard Rd. . . . . Armonk NY 10504 *NYSE: IBM* ■ *TF:* 800-426-4968 ■ *Web:* www.ibm.com	914-499-1900		173-2
International Carbonic Inc 16630 Koala Rd . . . . . Adelanto CA 92301 **Fax Area Code:* 760 ■ *TF:* 800-854-1177 ■ *Web:* www.ici.us	800-854-1177	246-4044*	55
International Card Manufacturers Assn (ICMA) 191 Clarksville Rd . . . . . Princeton Junction NJ 08550 *Web:* icma.com	609-799-4900	799-7032	49-4
International Carwash Assn 230 E Ohio St . . . . . Chicago IL 60611 *TF:* 888-422-8422 ■ *Web:* www.carwash.org	888-422-8422		49-21
International Cemetery Cremation & Funeral Assn (ICCFA) 107 Carpenter Dr Ste 100 . . . . . Sterling VA 20164 *TF:* 800-645-7700 ■ *Web:* iccfa.com	703-391-8400	391-8416	49-4
International Center for Advanced Internet Research (ICAIR) 750 N Lake Shore Dr Ste 600 . . . . . Chicago IL 60611 *Web:* www.icair.org	312-503-0735		668
International Center for Language Studies Inc 1133 15th St NW Ste 600 . . . . . Washington DC 20005 *Web:* www.icls.edu	202-639-8800		423
International Center for Research on Women (ICRW) 1120 20th St NW Ste 500-N . . . . . Washington DC 20036 *Web:* www.icrw.org	202-797-0007	797-0020	48-24
International Center for Technology Assessment (ICTA) 303 Sacramento St 2nd Fl . . . . . San Francisco CA 94111 *Web:* www.icta.org	415-826-2770		49-19
International Center of Medieval Art (ICMA) The Cloisters Fort Tryon Pk . . . . . New York NY 10040 *Web:* www.medievalart.org	212-928-1146	928-9946	48-4
International Center of Photography 1133 Avenue of the Americas . . . . . New York NY 10036 *Web:* www.icp.org	212-857-0000		520
International Ceramic Engineering 235 Brooks St. . . . . Worcester MA 01606 *TF:* 800-779-3321 ■ *Web:* www.intlceramics.com	508-853-4700	852-4101	249
International Chauffeured Service Worldwide 53 E 34th St . . . . . New York NY 10016 *TF:* 800-266-5254 ■ *Web:* www.bookalimo.com	212-213-0302	213-1373	441
International Checker Hall of Fame 220 Lynn Ray Rd. . . . . Petal MS 39465 *Web:* nccheckers.org	601-582-7090		520
International Chemical Co 2628-48 N Mascher St . . . . . Philadelphia PA 19133 *Web:* www.e-icc.com	215-739-2313	423-7171	145
International Chemical Workers Union Council 1655 W Market St 6th Fl. . . . . Akron OH 44313 *Web:* www.icwuc.org	330-926-1444	926-0816	414
International Chimney Corp 55 S Long St. . . . . Williamsville NY 14221 *TF:* 800-828-1446 ■ *Web:* www.internationalchimney.com	716-634-3967	634-3983	189-7
International Chiropractors Assn (ICA) 6400 Arlington Blvd Ste 800. . . . . Falls Church VA 22042 *TF:* 800-423-4690 ■ *Web:* www.chiropractic.org	703-528-5000	528-5023	49-8
International Church of the Foursquare Gospel (ICFG) 1910 W Sunset Blvd PO Box 26902 . . . . . Los Angeles CA 90026 *TF:* 888-635-4234 ■ *Web:* www.foursquare.org	213-989-4234	989-4590	48-20
International City Theatre (ICT) 67 Long Beach Blvd . . . . . Long Beach CA 90802 *Web:* www.ictlongbeach.org	562-495-4595		573-4
International City/County Management Assn (ICMA) 777 N Capitol St NE Ste 500. . . . . Washington DC 20002 *TF:* 800-745-8780 ■ *Web:* icma.org	202-289-4262	962-3500	49-7
International Civil Rights Center & Museum 134 S Elm St. . . . . Greensboro NC 27401 *TF:* 800-748-7116 ■ *Web:* www.sitinmovement.org	336-274-9199	274-6244	520
International Coatings Co 13929 166th St. . . . . Cerritos CA 90703 *TF:* 800-423-4103 ■ *Web:* iccink.com	562-926-1010	926-9486	388
International Code Council (ICC) 500 New Jersey Ave NW 6th Fl. . . . . Washington DC 20001 *TF:* 888-422-7233 ■ *Web:* www.iccsafe.org	202-370-1800	783-2348	49-3
International Coil Inc 15 Jonathan Dr. . . . . Brockton MA 02301 *Web:* www.internationalcoil.com	508-580-8515	580-8511	767
International Cold Storage Company Inc 215 E 13th St . . . . . Andover KS 67002 *TF:* 800-835-0001 ■ *Web:* www.everidge.com	316-733-1385	733-2434	664
International College of Dentists (ICD) 51 Monroe St Ste 1400. . . . . Rockville MD 20850 *Web:* www.icd.org	301-251-8861	738-9143	49-8
International College of Surgeons (ICS) 1516 N Lake Shore Dr . . . . . Chicago IL 60610 *Web:* www.icsglobal.org	312-642-3555		49-8
International Comfort Products (ICP) 650 Heil Quaker Ave . . . . . Lewisburg TN 37091 *Web:* www.icpusa.com	931-359-3511	270-3312	15
International Commission for the Prevention of Alcoholism and Drug Dependency (ICPA) 12501 Old Columbia Pke . . . . . Silver Spring MD 20904 *Web:* icpaworld.org	301-680-6719	680-6707	49-19
International Communication Assn (ICA) 1500 21st St NW . . . . . Washington DC 20036 *Web:* www.icahdq.org	202-955-1444	955-1448	49-14
International Conference of Funeral Service Examining Boards Inc 1885 Shelby Ln . . . . . Fayetteville AR 72704 *Web:* theconferenceonline.org	479-442-7076	442-7090	49-7
International Congress of Oral Implantologists (ICOI) 55 Ln Rd Ste 305 . . . . . Fairfield NJ 07004 *TF:* 800-442-0525 ■ *Web:* www.icoi.org	973-783-6300	783-1175	49-8
International Contact Technologies Inc 1432 Old Waterbury Rd . . . . . Southbury CT 06488 *Web:* www.ict-probe.com	203-264-5757	264-5707	248
International Contract Furnishings Inc (ICF) 19 Ohio Ave . . . . . Norwich CT 06360 **Fax Area Code:* 888 ■ *TF:* 800-237-1625 ■ *Web:* www.icfsource.com	860-886-1700	784-8209*	321
International Contractors Inc 977 S Rt 83. . . . . Elmhurst IL 60126 *Web:* iciinc.com	630-834-8043		186
International Control Services Inc 606 W Imboden Dr . . . . . Decatur IL 62521 *Web:* www.internationalcontrolservices.com	217-422-6700	422-3205	253
International Converter Inc 17153 Industrial Hwy . . . . . Caldwell OH 43724 *Web:* www.i-convert.com	740-732-5665		554
International Copper Assn 260 Madison Ave 16th Fl . . . . . New York NY 10016 *Web:* copperalliance.org	212-251-7240	251-7245	49-13
International Council of Shopping Centers (ICSC) 1251 Ave of the Americas 45th Fl. . . . . New York NY 10020 **Fax Area Code:* 212 ■ *Web:* www.icsc.org	646-728-3800	589-5555*	49-12
International Council on Hotel Restaurant & Institutional Education (CHRIE) 2810 N Parham Rd Ste 230 . . . . . Richmond VA 23294 *Web:* www.chrie.org	804-346-4800	346-5009	49-5
International Counterintelligence Services Inc (ICS) 8283 N Hayden Rd Ste 128. . . . . Scottsdale AZ 85258 *TF:* 800-828-9198 ■ *Web:* www.icsworld.com	480-990-8888	675-8800	693
International Crystal Exchange (ICE) 13325 Prospect Rd . . . . . Strongsville OH 44149 **Fax Area Code:* 440 ■ *TF:* 800-443-8223 ■ *Web:* www.ice4crystal.com	800-443-8223	238-3553*	411
International Culinary Consultants 747 Vassar Ave. . . . . Lakewood NJ 08701 *Web:* www.chefharvey.com	732-886-1444	886-5885	637-2
International Daily News 870 Monterey Pass Rd . . . . . Monterey Park CA 91754 *Web:* chinesetoday.com	323-265-1317	262-1425	532-2
International Dairy-Deli-Bakery Assn (IDDBA) 636 Science Dr. . . . . Madison WI 53711 *TF:* 877-399-4925 ■ *Web:* www.iddba.org	608-310-5000	238-6330	49-6
International Delivery Solutions 7340 S Howell Ave . . . . . Oak Creek WI 53154 *TF:* 877-437-8722 ■ *Web:* www.idstrac.com	877-437-8722		5
International District Energy Assn (IDEA) 24 Lyman St Ste 230. . . . . Westborough MA 01581 *Web:* www.districtenergy.org	508-366-9339	366-0019	49-3
International Diving Career Institute at Hall's 5050 Overseas Hwy . . . . . Marathon FL 33050 *TF:* 800-331-4255 ■ *Web:* www.hallsdiving.com	305-743-5929		167-3
International Diving Institute 2340 Ave F . . . . . North Charleston SC 29405 *Web:* www.idicharleston.edu	843-740-1124	740-5598	167-3
International Division Inc (REMC) PO Box 1275 . . . . . Springfield MO 65801 *Web:* www.indiv.com	417-862-2673	862-5434	297-10
International Down & Feather Testing Laboratory 1455 S 1100 E . . . . . Salt Lake City UT 84105 *Web:* www.idfl.com	801-467-7611		743
International Downtown Assn (IDA) 910 17th St NW Ste 1050. . . . . Washington DC 20006 *Web:* www.ida-downtown.org	202-393-6801	393-6869	49-17
International Dyslexia Assn, The (IDA) 40 York Rd 4th Fl . . . . . Towson MD 21204 *Web:* dyslexiaida.org	410-296-0232	321-5069	48-17
International Economic Development Council (IEDC) 734 15th St NW Ste 900. . . . . Washington DC 20005 *Web:* www.iedconline.org	202-223-7800	223-4745	49-12
International Education Systems (IES) 1814 Hillcrest Ave Ste 300 . . . . . Saint Paul MN 55116 *Web:* www.marybosrock.com	651-227-2052		637-2
International Electrical Sales Corp (IESCO) 7540 NW 66th St . . . . . Miami FL 33166 *Web:* iescomia.com	305-591-8390		246
International Electronic Enterprises Inc (IEEI) 110 Agate Ave. . . . . Newport Beach CA 92662 *Web:* www.ieei.com	949-673-2943	673-0249	174
International Electronic Machines Corp (IEM) 850 River St . . . . . Troy NY 12180 *Web:* www.iem.net	518-268-1636	268-1639	261
International Engraved Graphics Assn 305 Plus Pk Blvd . . . . . Nashville TN 37217 *TF:* 800-821-3138 ■ *Web:* www.iega.org	800-821-3138		49-4

Name / Address	City	State	Zip	Phone	Fax	Class
International Enterprises Inc 108 Allen St *TF:* 866-362-8562 ■ *Web:* www.ieionline.com	Talladega	AL	35160	256-362-8562		21
International Environmental Corp (IEC) PO Box 2598 *TF:* 800-264-5329 ■ *Web:* iec-okc.com	Oklahoma City	OK	73101	405-605-5000	605-5001	14
International Executive Housekeepers Assn (IEHA) 1001 Eastwind Dr Ste 301 *TF:* 800-200-6342 ■ *Web:* www.ieha.org	Westerville	OH	43081	614-895-7166	895-1248	49-4
International Exotic Feline Sanctuary 3901E Hwy 114 **Fax Area Code:* 940 ■ *Web:* www.bigcat.org	Boyd	TX	76023	254-826-6500	433-5092*	823
International Extrusions Inc 5800 Venoy Rd *TF:* 800-242-8876 ■ *Web:* www.extrusion.net	Garden City	MI	48135	734-427-8700	427-9319	482
International Eye Foundation (IEF) 10801 Connecticut Ave *Web:* iefusa.org	Kensington	MD	20895	240-290-0263	290-0269	48-5
International Eyecare Center Inc 2445 Broadway *TF:* 877-457-6485 ■ *Web:* iec2020.com	Quincy	IL	62301	217-222-8800		237
International Facility Management Assn (IFMA) 800 Gessner Rd Ste 900 *Web:* www.ifma.org	Houston	TX	77024	713-623-4362	623-6124	49-12
International Federation of Accountants (IFAC) 545 Fifth Ave 14th Fl *TF:* 888-272-2001 ■ *Web:* www.ifac.org	New York	NY	10017	212-286-9344	286-9570	49-1
International Federation of Pharmaceutical Wholesalers (IFPW) 10569 Crestwood Dr *Web:* www.ifpw.com	Manassas	VA	20109	703-331-3714	331-3715	49-18
International Federation of Professional & Technical Engineers 8630 Fenton St Ste 400 *Web:* www.ifpte.org	Silver Spring	MD	20910	301-565-9016	565-0018	414
International Festivals & Events Assn (IFEA) 2603 W Eastover Terr *Web:* www.ifea.com	Boise	ID	83706	208-433-0950	433-9812	48-23
International Fiber Corp 50 Bridge St *TF:* 888-698-1936 ■ *Web:* www.ifcfiber.com	North Tonawanda	NY	14120	716-693-4040	693-3528	605-1
International Fidelity Insurance Co (IFIC) 1 Newark Ctr 1111 Raymond Blvd 20th Fl **Fax Area Code:* 973 ■ *TF:* 800-333-4167 ■ *Web:* www.ific.com	Newark	NJ	07102	800-333-4167	624-1408*	391-5
International Financial Group 2530 Meridian Pkwy 2nd Fl *Web:* www.ifg-global.com	Raleigh	NC	27713	919-806-4458	806-4829	260
International Fire Equipment Corp 500 Telser Rd *Web:* intlfire.com	Lake Zurich	IL	60047	847-438-2343	438-1869	679
International Flavors & Fragrances Inc (IFF) 521 W 57th St *NYSE: IFF* ■ *Web:* www.iff.com	New York	NY	10019	212-765-5500	708-7132	144
International Foam Products Inc 10530 Westlake Dr *Web:* www.internationalfoam.com	Charlotte	NC	28273	704-588-0080		34
International Food Information Council Foundation (IFIC) 1100 Connecticut Ave NW Ste 430 *Web:* foodinsight.org	Washington	DC	20036	202-296-6540	296-6547	49-6
International Food Policy Research Institute (IFPRI) 2033 K St NW *Web:* www.ifpri.org	Washington	DC	20006	202-862-5600	467-4439	634
International Foodservice Distributors Assn (IFDA) 1410 Spring Hill Rd Ste 210 *Web:* www.ifdaonline.org	McLean	VA	22102	703-532-9400	538-4673	49-18
International Foodservice Manufacturers Assn (IFMA) 180 N Stetson Ave 2 Prudential Plz Ste 850 *Web:* www.ifmaworld.com	Chicago	IL	60601	312-540-4400	540-4401	49-6
International Fraternity of Phi Gamma Delta 1201 Red Mile Rd PO Box 4599 *Web:* www.phigam.org	Lexington	KY	40544	859-255-1848	253-0779	48-16
International Fund for Agricultural Development (IFAD) 1775 K St NW Ste 410 *Web:* www.ifad.org	Washington	DC	20006	202-331-9099	331-9366	783
International Fund for Animal Welfare (IFAW) 290 Summer St *TF:* 800-932-4329 ■ *Web:* www.ifaw.org	Yarmouth Port	MA	02675	508-744-2000		48-3
International Furniture Rental Assn (IFRA) 950 F St NW 10th Fl *Web:* www.ifra.org	Washington	DC	20004	202-239-3818	654-4818	49-4
International Game Technology (IGT) 9295 Prototype Dr *NYSE: IGT* ■ *Web:* www.igt.com	Reno	NV	89521	775-448-7777		322
International Gay & Lesbian Travel Assn (IGLTA) 1201 NE 26th St Ste 103 *Web:* www.iglta.org	Fort Lauderdale	FL	33305	954-630-1637	630-1652	48-23
International Gourmet Foods Inc 7520 Fullerton Rd *TF:* 800-522-0377 ■ *Web:* www.igf-inc.com	Springfield	VA	22153	703-569-4520		345
International Graphoanalysis Society (IGAS) 842 Fifth Ave **Fax Area Code:* 509 ■ *Web:* www.igas.com	New Kensington	PA	15068	724-472-9701	271-1149*	49-12
International Ground Source Heat Pump Assn (IGSHPA) Oklahoma State University 374 Cordell S *TF:* 800-626-4747 ■ *Web:* igshpa.org	Stillwater	OK	74078	405-744-5175	744-5283	49-13
International Group Inc 85 Old Eagle School Rd *TF:* 800-852-6537 ■ *Web:* www.igiwax.com	Wayne	PA	19087	610-687-9030		580
International Guide Academy 8700 E Jefferson Ave 370190 *Web:* www.bepaidtotravel.com	Denver	CO	80237	303-780-0131		167-3
International Health Racquet & Sportsclub Assn (IHRSA) 70 Fargo St *TF:* 800-228-4772 ■ *Web:* www.ihrsa.org	Boston	MA	02210	617-951-0055	951-0056	48-22
International Hearing Society (IHS) 16880 Middlebelt Rd Ste 4 *Web:* www.ihsinfo.org	Livonia	MI	48154	734-522-7200	522-0200	48-17
International Herald Tribune 229 W 43rd St *Web:* www.nytimes.com	New York	NY	10036	212-556-7707		532-2
International Historic Films Inc PO Box 5796 *Web:* ihffilm.com	Chicago	IL	60680	773-927-2900	927-9211	511
International Home Furnishings Representatives Assn (IHFRA) 209 S Main St PO Box 670 *Web:* www.ihfra.org	High Point	NC	27261	336-889-3920		49-18
International Homes of Cedar Inc (IHC) PO Box 886 *TF:* 800-767-7674 ■ *Web:* www.ihoc.com	Woodinville	WA	98072	360-668-8511	668-5562	106
International House Hotel 221 Camp St *Web:* www.ihhotel.com	New Orleans	LA	70130	504-553-9550	553-9560	379
International House of Music Inc 339 S Broadway *Web:* ihomi.com	Los Angeles	CA	90013	213-628-9161		526
International Housewares Assn (IHA) 6400 Shafer Ct Ste 650 *TF:* 800-752-1052 ■ *Web:* www.housewares.org	Rosemont	IL	60018	847-292-4200	292-4211	49-4
International Imaging Materials Inc 310 Commerce Dr *TF:* 888-464-4625 ■ *Web:* www.iimak.com	Amherst	NY	14228	716-691-6333		534
International Immunology Corp 25549 Adams Ave *TF:* 800-843-2853 ■ *Web:* www.nittobous.com	Murrieta	CA	92562	951-677-5629	677-6752	231
International Industrial Contracting Corp 35900 Mound Rd *Web:* www.iiccusa.com	Sterling Heights	MI	48310	586-264-7070	264-7088	189-1
International Ingredient Corp 150 Larkin Williams Industrial Ct PO Box 26377 *Web:* www.iicag.com	Fenton	MO	63026	636-343-4111	349-4845	447
International Institute of Ammonia Refrigeration 1001 N Fairfax St Ste 503 *Web:* www.iiar.org	Alexandria	VA	22314	703-312-4200	312-0065	49-3
International Institute of Metropolitan Detroit 111 E Kirby St *Web:* www.iimd.org	Detroit	MI	48202	313-871-8600	871-1651	520
International Institute of Municipal Clerks (IIMC) 8331 Utica Ave Ste 200 *TF:* 800-251-1639 ■ *Web:* www.iimc.com	Rancho Cucamonga	CA	91730	909-944-4162	944-8545	49-7
International Institute of Rural Reconstruction (IIRR) 601 W 26th St Ste 325-1 *Web:* www.iirr.org	New York	NY	10001	917-410-7891		48-5
International Institute of Synthetic Rubber Producers Inc (IISRP) 3535 Briarpark Dr Ste 250 *Web:* iisrp.com	Houston	TX	77042	713-783-5046	783-7253	49-13
International Institute of Tropical Forestry (IITF) Jardin Botanico Sur 1201 Calle Ceiba *Web:* www.fs.usda.gov	San Juan	PR	00926	787-766-5335	766-6302	668
International Interior Design Assn (IIDA) 222 Merchandise Mart Plz Ste 567 *TF:* 888-799-4432 ■ *Web:* www.iida.org	Chicago	IL	60654	312-467-1950	467-0779	48-4
International Investigators Inc 3216 N Pennsylvania St *TF:* 800-403-8111 ■ *Web:* www.iiiweb.net	Indianapolis	IN	46205	317-925-1496		400
International Isotopes Inc 4137 Commerce Cir *OTC: INIS* ■ *TF:* 800-699-3108 ■ *Web:* www.intisoid.com	Idaho Falls	ID	83401	208-524-5300	524-1411	231
International Jet Aviation Services 8511 Aviator Ln *TF:* 800-858-5891 ■ *Web:* www.internationaljet.com	Centennial	CO	80112	303-790-0414	790-4144	13
International Label & Printing Company Inc 2550 United Ln **Fax Area Code:* 630 ■ *TF:* 800-244-1442 ■ *Web:* www.internationallabel.com	Elk Grove Village	IL	60007	800-244-1442	595-1747*	413
International Labour Organization (ILO) 220 E 42nd St Ste 3101 *Web:* www.ilo.org	New York	NY	10017	212-697-0150	697-5218	783
International Labs Inc 2701 75th St N *Web:* www.internationallabs.com	Saint Petersburg	FL	33710	727-343-1548		583
International Language Institute 1717 Rhode Island Ave NW Ste 100 *Web:* ilidc.com	Washington	DC	20036	202-362-2505		423
International Launch Services (ILS) 12110 Sunset Hills Rd Ste 450 *TF:* 800-852-4980 ■ *Web:* beta.ilslaunch.com	Reston	VA	20190	703-435-5689	435-2671	504
International Law Institute (ILI) 1055 Thomas Jefferson St NW Ste M-100 *Web:* www.ili.org	Washington	DC	20007	202-247-6006	247-6010	49-10
International Lawyers Co PO Box 40335 *TF:* 800-529-5478 ■ *Web:* www.lawlistil.com	Cleveland	OH	44140	800-529-5478	254-9187	637-10
International Lawyers in Alcoholics Anonymous (ILAA) 537 Sherbrooke St *Web:* www.ilaa.org	Vancouver	BC	V5W3M6	604-324-7424		48-21
International Longshore & Warehouse Union 1188 Franklin St 4th Fl *TF:* 866-266-0013 ■ *Web:* www.ilwu.org	San Francisco	CA	94109	415-775-0533	775-1302	414
International Magnesium Assn (IMA) 1000 N Rand Rd Ste 214 **Fax Area Code:* 847 ■ *Web:* www.intlmag.org	Wauconda	IL	60084	651-379-7305	526-3993*	49-13
International Manufacturing Group Inc 879 F St STE 120A *TF:* 800-775-6412	West Sacramento	CA	95605	800-775-6412		475
International Marine Industries Inc 221 3rd St *TF:* 800-235-2248 ■ *Web:* imifish.com	Newport	RI	02840	401-849-4982		297-5
International Market Centers 209 S Main St *Web:* www.imchighpointmarket.com	High Point	NC	27260	336-888-3700		321
International Marketing Assn (IMA) 3509 Virginia Beach Blvd *Web:* imacorporate.com	Virginia Beach	VA	23452	757-490-9860	490-0716	301
International Masonry Institute (IMI) 17101 Science Dr *TF:* 800-803-0295 ■ *Web:* imiweb.org	Bowie	MD	20715	301-291-2124	261-2855	49-3
International Meat Inspection Consultants Inc PO Box 264 **Fax Area Code:* 240 ■ *Web:* www.thefoodtrainer.com	Germantown	MD	20875	301-570-1058	821-5939*	196

Name / Address	City	State	ZIP	Phone	Fax	Class
International Medical Corp (IMC) 1919 Santa Monica Blvd Ste 400 *TF:* 800-481-4462 ■ *Web:* internationalmedicalcorps.org	Santa Monica	CA	90404	310-826-7800	442-6622	48-5
International Medical Device Regulatory Monitor 300 N Washington St Ste 200 *TF:* 888-838-5578 ■ *Web:* www.fdanews.com	Falls Church	VA	22046	703-538-7600	538-7676	531-8
International Medical Group Inc 2960 N Meridian St *TF:* 800-628-4664 ■ *Web:* www.imglobal.com	Indianapolis	IN	46208	317-655-4500	655-4505	390
International Medical Industries Inc 2981 Gateway Dr *TF:* 800-344-2554 ■ *Web:* www.imiweb.com	Pompano Beach	FL	33069	954-917-9570	917-9244	476
International Medical Laboratory Inc 6419 Parkland Dr *Web:* www.internationalmedicallab.com	Sarasota	FL	34243	941-756-0000		415
International Meeting Managers Inc 4550 Post Oak Pl Ste 342 *TF:* 800-423-7175 ■ *Web:* www.meetingmanagers.com	Houston	TX	77056	713-965-0566	960-0488	184
International Metal Hose Co 520 Goodrich Rd *TF:* 800-458-6855 ■ *Web:* www.metalhose.com	Bellevue	OH	44811	419-483-7690	483-8225	490
International Microelectronics & Packaging Society (IMAPS) PO Box 110127 *Web:* www.imaps.org	Research Triangle Park	NC	27709	202-548-4001	548-6115	49-19
International Mold Steel Inc 6796 Powerline Dr *TF:* 800-625-6653 ■ *Web:* www.imsteel.com	Florence	KY	41042	859-342-6000		492
International Monetary Fund (IMF) 700 19th St NW *TF:* 800-548-5384 ■ *Web:* www.imf.org	Washington	DC	20431	202-623-7000	623-4661	783
International Montessori Council & The Montessori Foundation 19600 E State Rd 64 *TF:* 800-655-5843 ■ *Web:* www.montessori.org	Bradenton	FL	34212	941-729-9565		48-11
International Motor Coach Group Inc (IMG) 12351 W 96th Ter **Fax Area Code:* 913 ■ *TF:* 888-447-3466 ■ *Web:* imgcoach.com	Lenexa	KS	66215	888-447-3466	906-0115*	49-21
International Motorsports Hall of Fame & Museum 3198 Speedway Blvd *Web:* www.motorsportshalloffame.com	Talladega	AL	35160	256-362-5002		522
International Mountain Bicycling Assn (IMBA) PO Box 20280 *Web:* www.imba.com	Boulder	CO	80308	303-545-9011		48-23
International Municipal Lawyers Assn (IMLA) 51 Monroe St Ste 404 *TF:* 800-942-7732 ■ *Web:* www.imla.org	Rockville	MD	20850	202-466-5424	785-0152	49-10
International Municipal Signal Assn (IMSA) 165 E Union St PO Box 539 *TF:* 800-723-4672 ■ *Web:* www.imsasafety.org	Newark	NY	14513	315-331-2182	331-8205	49-7
International Museum of Cultures 411 US Hwy 67 Southbound Frontage Rd *Web:* www.internationalmuseumofcultures.org	Duncanville	TX	75137	972-572-0462		520
International Museum of Muslim Cultures (IMMC) 201 E Pascagoula St *Web:* www.muslimmuseum.org	Jackson	MS	39201	601-960-0440		520
International Museum of Surgical Science 1524 N Lake Shore Dr *Web:* imss.org	Chicago	IL	60610	312-642-6502		520
International Museum of the Horse 4089 Iron Works Pkwy *Web:* www.imh.org	Lexington	KY	40511	859-259-4232		520
International Musician 120 Walton St Ste 300 *Web:* internationalmusician.org	Syracuse	NY	13202	315-422-4488	422-3837	457-9
International Network of Golf 556 Teton St *Web:* www.inggolf.com	Lake Mary	FL	32795	407-328-0500	878-4928	317
International Neuropsychological Society (INS) 700 Ackerman Rd Ste 625 **Fax Area Code:* 614 ■ *Web:* www.the-ins.org	Columbus	OH	43202	801-487-0475	263-4366*	49-15
International OCD Foundation (OCF) PO Box 961029 *TF:* 800-331-3131 ■ *Web:* iocdf.org	Boston	MA	02196	617-973-5801	973-5803	48-17
International Order of the Golden Rule (OGR) 3520 Executive Center Dr Ste 300 *TF:* 800-637-8030 ■ *Web:* www.ogr.org	Austin	TX	78731	512-334-5504	334-5514	49-4
International Order-Hoo-Hoo 207 E Main St *Web:* www.hoohoo.org	Gurdon	AR	71743	870-353-4997		48-2
International Organization for Migration 1752 North St NW Ste 700 *Web:* www.iom.int	Washington	DC	20036	202-862-1826	862-1879	48-8
International Organization of Masters Mates & Pilots 700 Maritime Blvd *TF:* 877-667-5522 ■ *Web:* www.bridgedeck.org	Linthicum Heights	MD	21090	410-850-8700	850-0973	414
International Orthodox Christian Charities (IOCC) 110 W Rd Ste 360 *TF:* 877-803-4622 ■ *Web:* www.iocc.org	Towson	MD	21204	410-243-9820	243-9824	48-5
International Paper Co 6400 Poplar Ave *NYSE:* IP ■ *TF:* 800-223-1268 ■ *Web:* www.internationalpaper.com	Memphis	TN	38197	901-419-9000		557
International Parking Institute (IPI) 1330 Braddock Pl Ste 350 *Web:* www.parking.org	Alexandria	VA	22314	571-699-3011		49-21
International Pentecostal Holiness Church (IPHC) PO Box 12609 *TF:* 888-474-2966 ■ *Web:* iphc.org	Oklahoma City	OK	73157	405-787-7110	789-3957	48-20
International Photography Hall of Fame & Museum 3415 Olive St *Web:* www.iphf.org	Saint Louis	MO	63103	314-535-1999		520
International Planned Parenthood Federation - Western Hemisphere Region (IPPF/WHR) 125 Maiden Ln 9th Fl *Web:* www.ippfwhr.org	New York	NY	10038	212-248-6400	248-4221	48-5
International Plant Nutrition Institute (IPNI) 3500 Parkway Ln Ste 550 *Web:* www.ipni.net	Norcross	GA	30092	770-447-0335	448-0439	48-2
International Plastics Inc 185 Commerce Ctr *TF:* 800-820-4722 ■ *Web:* www.interplas.com	Greenville	SC	29615	864-297-8000		345
International Playthings Inc 75D Lackawanna Ave *TF:* 800-631-1272 ■ *Web:* www.intplay.com	Parsippany	NJ	07054	973-316-2500	316-5883	762
International Plaza & Bay Street 2223 NW Shore Blvd *Web:* www.shopinternationalplaza.com	Tampa	FL	33607	813-342-3790		50-6
International Poly Bag Inc 900 Park Center Dr Ste F & G *TF:* 800-976-5922 ■ *Web:* intlpolybag.com	Vista	CA	92081	760-598-2468	598-2469	66
International Port of Dutch Harbor 43 Raven Way *Web:* www.ci.unalaska.ak.us	Unalaska	AK	99685	907-581-1251		618
International Precious Metals Institute (IPMI) 5101 N 12th Ave Ste C *Web:* www.ipmi.org	Pensacola	FL	32504	850-476-1156	476-1548	49-4
International Precision Inc 9526 Vassar Ave PO Box 4839 *Web:* www.intlprecision.com	Chatsworth	CA	91313	818-882-3933	882-0319	22
International Precision Machining 511 Sundial Dr *Web:* www.ipminc.com	Waite Park	MN	56387	320-656-1241	656-1242	454
International Primate Protection League (IPPL) 120 Primate Ln *Web:* www.ippl.org	Summerville	SC	29483	843-871-2280	871-7988	48-3
International Process Plants (IPP) 410 Princeton Hightstown Rd *Web:* www.ippe.com	West Windsor	NJ	08550	609-586-8004	586-0002	385
International Procurement Agency Inc 4322 Avondale Ln NW *Web:* www.usaipa.com	Canton	OH	44708	330-477-5020	477-1210	449
International Production Specialists Inc 35006 Washington Ave *Web:* www.ipstanks.com	Honey Creek	WI	53138	262-534-3130	534-4748	480
International Professional Rodeo Assn (IPRA) 1412 S Agnew *TF:* 800-639-9002 ■ *Web:* www.ipra-rodeo.com	Oklahoma City	OK	73108	405-235-6540		48-22
International Programs Group PO Box 45058 *Web:* www.ipgclaims.com	Little Rock	AR	72214	501-228-0900	228-0967	466
International Propeller Club of the United States 3927 Old Lee Hwy *Web:* www.propellerclub.us	Fairfax	VA	22030	703-691-2777		49-21
International Public Management Association for Hum Res (IPMA-HR) 1617 Duke St *TF:* 800-381-8378 ■ *Web:* www.ipma-hr.org	Alexandria	VA	22314	703-549-7100	684-0948	49-12
International Radio & Television Society Foundation Inc (IRTS) 1697 Broadway 10th Fl *Web:* www.irtsfoundation.org	New York	NY	10019	212-867-6650		49-14
International Reprographic Assn (IRGA) 401 N Michigan Ave Ste 2200 **Fax Area Code:* 312 ■ *TF:* 800-833-4742 ■ *Web:* www.apdsp.org	Chicago	IL	60611	877-226-6839	673-6724*	49-16
International Rescue Committee (IRC) 122 E 42nd St *Web:* www.rescue.org	New York	NY	10168	212-551-3000	551-3179	48-5
International Restaurant Management Group Inc (IRMG) 4531 Ponce de Leon Blvd Ste 300 *Web:* www.irmgusa.com	Coral Gables	FL	33146	305-476-1611	476-9622	670
International Revolving Door Co 2138 N Sixth Ave *TF:* 800-745-4726 ■ *Web:* www.intlentrance.com	Evansville	IN	47710	812-425-3311	426-2682	234
International Risk Management Institute Inc (IRMI) 12222 Merit Dr Ste 1600 *TF:* 800-827-4242 ■ *Web:* www.irmi.com	Dallas	TX	75251	972-960-7693	371-5120	401
International Road Federation (IRF) 500 Mongomery St 5th Fl *Web:* www.irfnet.ch	Alexandria	VA	22314	703-535-1001	535-1007	49-3
International Safe Transit Assn (ISTA) 1400 Abbott Rd Ste 160 *TF:* 888-299-2208 ■ *Web:* www.ista.org	East Lansing	MI	48823	517-333-3437	333-3813	49-21
International Salon & Spa Academy 5707 N Academy Blvd *Web:* www.csbeautyschools.com	Colorado Springs	CO	80918	719-419-5829		166
International Sanitary Supply Assn (ISSA) 3300 Dundee Rd *TF:* 800-225-4772 ■ *Web:* issa.com	Northbrook	IL	60062	847-982-0800	982-1012	49-18
International Satellite Services Inc 1004 Collier Ctr Way Ste 204 *Web:* www.internationalsatelliteservices.com	Naples	FL	34110	239-598-2241		681
International School of Colon Hydrotherapy Inc 13901 US Highway 1 Ste 2 *Web:* www.cathysheaschool.com	Juno Beach	FL	33408	561-775-9912	625-3775	685
International School of Midwifery 140 NE 119 St *Web:* www.flexidomains.net	Miami	FL	33161	305-754-2354		685
International School of Professional Bartending 2001 Baltimore *TF:* 800-227-8363 ■ *Web:* www.kansascitybartendingschool.com	Kansas City	MO	64108	816-753-3900		685
International School of Skin Nail Care & Massage Therapy 5600 Roswell Rd NE 014 *TF:* 877-843-1005 ■ *Web:* www.beautyschoolatlanta.com	Atlanta	GA	30342	404-594-8957		685
International Sensor Systems Inc 103 Grant St *TF:* 800-260-6287 ■ *Web:* www.internationalsensor.com	Aurora	NE	68818	402-694-6111	694-6180	253
International Sensor Technology Inc 3 Whatney *TF:* 800-478-4271 ■ *Web:* www.intlsensor.com	Irvine	CA	92618	949-452-9000	452-9009	472
International Sew-Right Co 6190 Don Murie St *Web:* www.safetyclothing.com	Niagara Falls	ON	L2G0B4	905-374-3600	374-6121	576
International Ship Repair & Marine Services Inc 1616 Penny St *Web:* internationalship.com	Tampa	FL	33605	813-247-1118		698
International Sign Assn (ISA) 1001 N Fairfax St Ste 301 *Web:* www.signs.org	Alexandria	VA	22314	703-836-4012	836-8353	49-4
International Sleep Products Assn (ISPA) 501 Wythe St *Web:* www.sleepproducts.org	Alexandria	VA	22314	703-683-8371	683-4503	49-4

Name	Address	City	State	ZIP	Phone	Fax	Class
International Snowmobile Hall of Fame	1521 N Railroad St *Web:* www.ishof.com	Eagle River	WI	54521	715-479-2186		522
International Society for Animal Rights (ISAR)	PO Box F *TF:* 888-589-6397 ■ *Web:* www.isaronline.org	Clarks Summit	PA	18411	570-586-2200	586-9580	48-3
International Society for Heart & Lung Transplantation (ISHLT)	14673 Midway Rd Ste 200 *Web:* www.ishlt.org	Addison	TX	75001	972-490-9495	490-9499	49-8
International Society for Magnetic Resonance in Medicine (ISMRM)	2030 Addison St Ste 700 *Web:* www.ismrm.org	Berkeley	CA	94704	510-841-1899	841-2340	49-8
International Society for Performance Improvement (ISPI)	PO Box 13035 *TF:* 800-825-7550 ■ *Web:* ispi.org	Silver Spring	MD	20910	301-587-8570	587-8573	49-12
International Society for Peritoneal Dialysis (ISPD)	66 Martin St *TF:* 888-834-1001 ■ *Web:* ispd.org	Milton	ON	L9T2R2	905-875-2456	875-2864	49-8
International Society for Pharmaceutical Engineering (ISPE)	3109 W Dr ML King Jr Blvd Ste 250 *Web:* www.ispe.org	Tampa	FL	33607	813-960-2105	264-2816	49-19
International Society for Pharmacoepidemiology (ISPE)	5272 River Rd Ste 500 *Web:* www.pharmacoepi.org	Bethesda	MD	20816	301-718-6500	656-0989	49-8
International Society for Technology in Education (ISTE)	1530 Wilson Blvd Ste 730 *TF:* 800-336-5191 ■ *Web:* www.iste.org	Arlington	VA	22209	800-336-5191		49-5
International Society for Traumatic Stress Studies (ISTSS)	111 Deer Lake Rd Ste 100 *TF:* 877-469-7873 ■ *Web:* www.istss.org	Deerfield	IL	60015	847-480-9028	480-9282	49-15
International Society of Arboriculture (ISA)	PO Box 3129 *TF:* 888-472-8733 ■ *Web:* www.isa-arbor.com	Champaign	IL	61826	217-355-9411	355-9516	48-2
International Society of Automation, The	67 Alexander Dr PO Box 12277 *Web:* www.isa.org	Research Triangle Park	NC	27709	919-549-8411	549-8288	49-19
International Society of Bassists (ISB)	14070 Proton Rd Ste 100 *Web:* www.isbworldoffice.com	Dallas	TX	75244	972-233-9107	490-4219	48-4
International Society of Certified Electronics Technicians (ISCET)	3608 Pershing Ave *TF:* 800-946-0201 ■ *Web:* www.iscet.org	Fort Worth	TX	76107	817-921-9101	921-3741	49-19
International Society of Certified Employee Benefits (ISCEBS)	18700 W Bluemond Rd PO Box 209 *TF:* 888-334-3327 ■ *Web:* www.iscebs.org	Brookfield	WI	53008	262-786-8771	786-8650	49-12
International Society of Fire Service Instructors (ISFSI)	14001C St Germain Dr *TF:* 800-435-0005 ■ *Web:* www.isfsi.org	Centreville	VA	20121	800-435-0005	235-9153	49-7
International Society of Political Psychology (ISPP)	126 Ward St Ste 1213 PO Box 1213 *Web:* www.ispp.org	Columbus	NC	28722	828-894-5422		48-7
International Society of Refractive Surgery (ISRS)	655 Beach St PO Box 7424 *Web:* www.isrs.org	San Francisco	CA	94109	415-561-8581	561-8575	49-8
International Society of Travel Medicine (ISTM)	315 W Ponce de Leon Ave Ste 245 *Web:* www.istm.org	Decatur	GA	30030	404-373-8282	373-8283	49-8
International Society of Tropical Foresters (ISTF)	5400 Grosvenor Ln **Fax Area Code:* 877 ■ *Web:* www.istf-bethesda.org	Bethesda	MD	20814	301-530-4514	665-6473*	48-13
International Software Products	7128 Parkside Ln Unit 111 *TF:* 800-295-7608 ■ *Web:* www.ispinfo.com	Racine	WI	53406	800-295-7608	295-7609	177
International SOS	3600 Horizon Blvd Ste 300 *TF:* 800-523-6586 ■ *Web:* www.internationalsos.com	Trevose	PA	19053	215-942-8000		391-7
International Specialized Book Services Inc (ISBS)	920 NE 58th Ave Ste 300 *Web:* www.isbs.com	Portland	OR	97213	503-287-3093	280-8832	96
International Spy Museum	800 F St NW *Web:* www.spymuseum.org	Washington	DC	20004	202-393-7798	393-7797	520
International Studies Assn (ISA)	University of Arizona 324 Social Sciences *Web:* www.isanet.org	Tucson	AZ	85721	520-621-2327		48-11
International Submarine Engineering Ltd	1734 Broadway St *Web:* ise.bc.ca	Port Coquitlam	BC	V3C2M8	604-942-5223	942-7577	698
International Sulphur Inc	PO Box 611 *Web:* www.internationalsulphur.com	Mount Pleasant	TX	75456	903-577-5500		280
International Surfing Museum	411 Olive Ave *Web:* www.huntingtonbeachsurfingmuseum.org	Huntington Beach	CA	92648	714-465-4350		520
International Swaps & Derivatives Assn (ISDA)	360 Madison Ave 16th Fl *Web:* www.isda.org	New York	NY	10017	212-901-6000		49-2
International Swimming Hall of Fame	1 Hall of Fame Dr *Web:* ishof.org	Fort Lauderdale	FL	33316	954-462-6536	525-4031	522
International TechneGroup Inc (ITI)	5303 DuPont Cir **Fax Area Code:* 513 ■ *TF:* 800-783-9199 ■ *Web:* www.iti-oh.com	Milford	OH	45150	800-783-9199	576-3994*	178-1
International Technology Education Assn (ITEA)	1914 Assn Dr Ste 201 *Web:* www.iteea.org	Reston	VA	20191	703-860-2100	860-0353	49-5
International Technology Law Assn	7918 Jones Branch Dr Ste 300 *Web:* www.itechlaw.org	McLean	VA	22102	781-876-8877		48-9
International Tennis Hall of Fame & Museum	194 Bellevue Ave *Web:* www.tennisfame.com	Newport	RI	02840	401-849-3990		522
International Textile Group	804 Green Valley Rd Ste 300 *Web:* www.itg-global.com	Greensboro	NC	27408	336-379-6220		360-3
International Thermal Systems LLC (ITS)	4697 W Greenfield Ave *Web:* www.internationalthermalsystems.com	Milwaukee	WI	53214	414-672-7700	672-8800	318
International Ticketing Assn (INTIX)	5868 E 71st St Ste E 365 *Web:* www.intix.org	Indianapolis	IN	46220	212-629-4036		48-4
International Titanium Assn	11674 Huron St *Web:* titanium.org	Northglenn	CO	80234	303-404-2221	404-9111	49-19
International Tour Management Institute	14 W Pier *TF:* 800-442-4864 ■ *Web:* www.itmitourtraining.com	Sausalito	CA	94965	415-957-9489		167-3
International Towing & Recovery Hall of Fame & Museum	3315 Broad St *Web:* www.internationaltowingmuseum.org	Chattanooga	TN	37408	423-267-3132	267-0867	520
International Trade Administration	1401 Constitution Ave NW *Web:* www.ita.doc.gov	Washington	DC	20230	202-482-0140	482-5819	340-2
International Trade Information Inc (ITI)	900 Las Vegas Blvd S Unit 908 *Web:* internationaltradeinformation.com	Las Vegas	NV	89101	818-591-2255		184
International Trademark Assn (INTA)	655 Third Ave 10th Fl *TF:* 800-995-3579 ■ *Web:* www.inta.org	New York	NY	10017	212-768-9887	768-7796	49-12
International Training Inc	1321 SE Decker Ave **Fax Area Code:* 877 ■ *TF:* 888-778-9073 ■ *Web:* www.tdisdi.com	Stuart	FL	34994	207-729-4201	436-7096*	31
International Transplant Nurses Society (ITNS)	8735 W Higgins Rd Ste 300 *TF:* 800-776-8636 ■ *Web:* www.itns.org	Chicago	IL	60631	847-375-6340	375-6341	49-8
International Transportation Service Inc	1281 Pier J Way *Web:* www.itslb.com	Long Beach	CA	90802	562-435-7781	590-6761	465
International Travel Systems Inc	64 Madison Ave *TF:* 800-258-0135 ■ *Web:* international-travel-systems.com	Wood-Ridge	NJ	07075	201-727-0470		16
International Tsunami Information Ctr	1845 Wasp Blvd Bldg 176 *Web:* www.itic.ioc-unesco.org	Honolulu	HI	96818	808-725-6050	532-5576	783
International Union of Bricklayers & Allied Craftworkers (BAC)	620 F St NW *TF:* 888-880-8222 ■ *Web:* www.bacweb.org	Washington	DC	20004	202-783-3788		414
International Union of Elevator Constructors (IUEC)	7154 Columbia Gateway Dr *Web:* www.iuec.org	Columbia	MD	21046	410-953-6150		49-3
International Union of Operating Engineers	1125 17th St NW *Web:* www.iuoe.org	Washington	DC	20036	202-429-9100		414
International Union of Painters & Allied Trades (IUPAT)	7234 Pkwy Dr *TF:* 800-554-2479 ■ *Web:* iupat.org	Hanover	MD	21076	410-564-5900		414
International Union of Police Assn	1549 Ringling Blvd Ste 600 *TF:* 800-247-4872 ■ *Web:* iupa.org	Sarasota	FL	34236	941-487-2560	487-2570	414
International Union Security Police & Fire Professionals of America (SPFPA)	25510 Kelly Rd *TF:* 800-228-7492 ■ *Web:* www.spfpa.org	Roseville	MI	48066	586-772-7250	772-9644	414
International Union United Automobile Aerospace & Agricultural Implement Workers of America	8000 E Jefferson Ave *Web:* uaw.org	Detroit	MI	48214	313-926-5000	823-6016	414
International University Line (IUL)	PO Box 2525 *Web:* www.iul-world.com	La Jolla	CA	92038	858-457-0595	581-9073	637-2
International Veterinary Acupuncture Society (IVAS)	1730 S College Ave Ste 301 *Web:* www.ivas.org	Fort Collins	CO	80525	970-266-0666	266-0777	48-3
International Violin Company Ltd	1421 Clarkview Rd *TF:* 800-542-3538 ■ *Web:* www.internationalviolin.com	Baltimore	MD	21209	410-832-2525	832-2528	526
International Visual Corp (IVC)	11500 Blvd Armand Bombardier *TF:* 866-643-0570 ■ *Web:* www.ivcweb.com	Montreal	QC	H1E2W9	514-643-0570	643-4867	286
International Warehouse Logistics Assn (IWLA)	2800 S River Rd Ste 260 *Web:* www.iwla.com	Des Plaines	IL	60018	847-813-4699	813-0115	49-21
International Webmasters Assn (IWA)	119 E Union St Ste A *TF:* 866-607-1773 ■ *Web:* www.iwanet.org	Pasadena	CA	91103	626-449-3709		48-9
International Wholesale Inc	21170 W 8 Mile Rd *TF:* 855-549-7253 ■ *Web:* www.internationalwholesale.com	Southfield	MI	48075	248-262-7414	353-8801	238
International Wildlife Museum	4800 W Gates Pass Rd *Web:* www.thewildlifemuseum.org	Tucson	AZ	85745	520-629-0100		520
International Window Corp	5625 E Firestone Blvd *TF:* 800-477-4032 ■ *Web:* www.intlwindow.com	South Gate	CA	90280	562-928-6411	928-3492	234
International Wine Ctr	350 7th Ave Ste 1201 *Web:* www.internationalwinecenter.com	New York	NY	10001	212-239-3055	239-3051	167-3
International Wireless Industry Consortium, The (IWPC)	610 Louis Dr *Web:* www.iwpc.org	Warminster	PA	18974	215-293-9000		463
International Women's Air & Space Museum	Burke Lakefront Airport 1501 N Marginal Rd *TF:* 877-287-4752 ■ *Web:* www.iwasm.org	Cleveland	OH	44114	216-623-1111	623-1113	520
International Wood Products Assn (IWPA)	4214 King St *TF:* 855-435-0005 ■ *Web:* www.iwpawood.org	Alexandria	VA	22302	703-820-6696	820-8550	49-3
International Wrestling Institute & Museum	303 Jefferson St *Web:* nwhof.org	Waterloo	IA	50701	319-233-0745	233-3477	522
International, The	220 4th Ave SW *TF:* 800-661-8627 ■ *Web:* www.minto.com	Calgary	AB	T2P0H5	825-258-5010		379
Internet Archive	300 Funston Ave *Web:* archive.org	San Francisco	CA	94118	415-561-6767	840-0391	397
Internet Brands Inc	909 N Sepulveda Blvd 11th Fl *Web:* www.internetbrands.com	El Segundo	CA	90245	310-280-4000		393

Company / Address	City	State	ZIP	Phone	Fax	Class
Internet Business Network 303 Ross Dr *Web:* www.interbiznet.com	Mill Valley	CA	94941	415-377-2255	380-8245	637-9
Internet Business Systems Inc 25 N 14th St Ste 710 *Web:* www.ibsystems.com	San Jose	CA	95112	408-882-6554		4
Internet Corporation for Assigned Names & Numbers (ICANN) 4676 Admiralty Way Ste 330 *Web:* www.icann.org	Marina	CA	90292	310-301-5800	823-8649	48-9
Internet Creations Inc 2000 Waterview Dr Ste 100 *Web:* www.internetcreations.com	Hamilton Township	NJ	08691	609-570-7200		225
Internet Employment Linkage Inc 934 Bellaforte Ave Ste 106 *Web:* www.ielinc.net	Oak Park	IL	60302	708-848-4351		225
Internet Exposure Inc 1101 Washington Ave S *Web:* www.iexposure.com	Minneapolis	MN	55415	612-676-1946		344
Internet Expressway PO Box 3976 *TF:* 888-311-7769 ■ *Web:* www.ieway.com	Spokane	WA	99202	509-456-4691		224
Internet Matrix Inc 10179 Huennekens St *TF:* 800-462-8749 ■ *Web:* imatrix.com	San Diego	CA	92121	800-462-8749		7
Internet Nebraska Inc 330 S 21st St PO Box 5301 *Web:* inebraska.com	Lincoln	NE	68505	402-434-8680		225
Internet Society (ISOC) 11710 Plz America Dr Ste 400 *Web:* www.internetsociety.org	Reston	VA	20190	703-439-2120	326-9881	48-9
Internet2 1000 Phoenix Dr Ste 111 *Web:* www.internet2.edu	Ann Arbor	MI	48108	734-913-4250	913-4255	48-9
InternetSpeech 6980 Santa Teresa Blvd Ste 201 *Web:* www.internetspeech.com	San Jose	CA	95119	408-360-7730		617
Internexus 220 South 200 East Ste 200 *TF:* 800-209-5010 ■ *Web:* internexus.edu	Salt Lake City	UT	84111	801-487-2499	487-2198	423
InterNiche Technologies Inc 1999 S Bascom Ave Ste 700 *Web:* www.iniche.com	Campbell	CA	95008	408-540-1160		180
Internovo Inc PO Box 26258 *Web:* www.internovo.com	Collegeville	PA	19426	610-409-9120		463
Interocean Systems 3738 Ruffin Rd *Web:* www.interoceansystems.com	San Diego	CA	92123	858-565-8400		407
Interop Technologies LLC 13500 Powers Ct *Web:* www.interoptechnologies.com	Fort Myers	FL	33912	239-425-3000	425-6845	736
Inter-Pacific Corp 2257 Colby Ave *Web:* inter-pacific.com	Los Angeles	CA	90064	310-473-7591		301
Interpak Inc 7278 Justin Way *TF:* 800-768-6665 ■ *Web:* www.rotomold.com	Mentor	OH	44060	440-974-8999	974-3383	604
InterPark 200 N LaSalle St Ste 1400 *Web:* www.interparkholdings.com	Chicago	IL	60601	312-935-2800		562
Interpex Ltd PO Box 839 *Web:* www.interpex.com	Golden	CO	80402	303-278-9124	278-4007	177
Interplastic Corp 1225 Wolters Blvd *TF:* 800-736-5497 ■ *Web:* www.interplastic.com	Saint Paul	MN	55110	651-481-6860	481-9836	605-2
Interplex Engineered Products 231 Ferris Ave *Fax Area Code: 508 ■ *Web:* interplex.com	Rumford	RI	02916	401-434-6543	399-7655*	481
Interplex Medical LLC 25 Whitney Dr *Web:* interplexmedical.com	Milford	OH	45150	513-248-5120		475
Interpoint 10301 Willows Rd NE PO Box 97005 *Web:* www.interpoint.com	Redmond	WA	98052	425-882-3100	882-1990	253
INTERPOL (U.S. National Central Bureau of INTERPOL) 950 Pennsylvania Ave NW *Web:* www.justice.gov	Washington	DC	20530	202-616-9000	616-8400	340-14
Interpress Technologies Inc 1120 Del Paso Rd *Web:* interpresstechnologies.com	Sacramento	CA	95834	916-929-9771		561
Interpreters Unlimited Inc 10650 Treena St Ste 308 *TF:* 800-726-9891 ■ *Web:* interpretersunlimited.com	San Diego	CA	92131	800-726-9891		768
Interpretive Laboratory Data Inc PO Box 341 *Web:* www.bakermanbooks.com	Scottsdale	AZ	85252	480-947-2604	947-2381	637-2
Interprint LLC 7111 Hayvenhurst Ave *TF:* 800-926-9873 ■ *Web:* www.interprintusa.com	Van Nuys	CA	91406	818-989-3600		627
Interprint web Printing 12350 US Hwy 19 N *TF:* 800-749-5152 ■ *Web:* www.printerusa.com	Clearwater	FL	33764	727-531-8957		627
InterPro Translation Solutions Inc 4200 Commerce Ct Ste 204 *TF:* 877-232-3277 ■ *Web:* www.interproinc.com	Lisle	IL	60532	630-245-7150		393
Interprose Inc 2635 Steeplechase Dr *Web:* interprosepr.com	Reston	VA	20191	703-860-0577		636
Interpublic Group 909 Third Ave *NYSE: IPG* ■ *TF:* 800-908-5395 ■ *Web:* www.interpublic.com	New York	NY	10036	212-704-1200		4
Inter-quest Corp 304 S Spring St *Web:* wemaketechsimple.com	Beaver Dam	WI	53916	920-885-0141		175
Interra Credit Union 300 W Lincoln Ave *Web:* www.interracu.com	Goshen	IN	46526	574-534-2506		219
Interrad Medical Inc 181 Cheshire Ln Ste 100 *Web:* securacath.com	Plymouth	MN	55441	763-225-6699		476
InterraTech Corp PO Box 4 *TF:* 888-589-4889 ■ *Web:* www.interratech.com	Mount Ephraim	NJ	08059	856-854-5100	854-5102	178-1
InterRel Consulting Inc The Rangers Ballpark in Arlington 1000 Ballpark Wa Ste 304 *Web:* www.interrel.com	Arlington	TX	76011	972-735-8716		180
Interreligious Foundation for Community Organization (IFCO) 418 W 145th St *Web:* ifconews.org	New York	NY	10031	212-926-5757	926-5842	48-7
Inter-Rock Minerals Inc 2 Toronto St 5th Fl *TF:* 888-848-8178 ■ *Web:* www.interrockminerals.com	Toronto	ON	M5C2B6	416-367-3003	367-3638	503-6

Company / Address	City	State	ZIP	Phone	Fax	Class
Interroll Corp 3000 Corporate Dr *Web:* www.interroll.us	Wilmington	NC	28405	910-799-1100		207
Interrupt Marketing 6622 Maplewood Ave *Web:* www.interruptdelivers.com	Sylvania	OH	43560	419-724-9900		5
Interschola School And Government Surplus Sales Via Online Auctions 1004 Oreilly Ave Fl 3rd *TF:* 888-653-7360	San Francisco	CA	94129	888-653-7360		387
Interscience Laboratories Inc 199 Weymouth St *Web:* www.interscience.com	Rockland	MA	02370	781-792-2134		420
Interscope Pathology Medical Group Inc 21114 Vanowen St *Web:* www.interscopepath.com	Canoga Park	CA	91303	818-992-7848	992-7943	415
Interscope Records 2220 Colorado Ave *Web:* www.interscope.com	Santa Monica	CA	90404	310-865-1000		657
Intersect ENT Inc 1555 Adams Dr *TF:* 866-531-6004 ■ *Web:* www.intersectent.com	Menlo Park	CA	94025	650-641-2100		476
Intersect Media Solutions 610 Crescent Executive Ct Ste 112 *TF:* 866-404-5913 ■ *Web:* www.intersectmediasolutions.com	Lake Mary	FL	32746	866-404-5913		195
Interserve USA PO Box 418 *TF:* 800-809-4440 ■ *Web:* interserveusa.org	Upper Darby	PA	19082	610-352-0581		48-20
Intersoft Corp 20367 Leutar Ct	Saratoga	CA	95070	408-733-5300	733-5303	809
InterSoft International Inc PO Box 218794 *Fax Area Code: 866 ■ *TF:* 888-823-1541 ■ *Web:* www.securenetterm.com	Houston	TX	77218	888-823-1541	701-1260*	180
Intersog Inc 220 N Green St Ste 2011 *Web:* intersog.com	Chicago	IL	60607	773-305-0885		177
Intersol Industries Inc 241 James St *Web:* www.intersolind.com	Bensenville	IL	60106	630-238-0385	238-9131	203
InterStar Communications 3900 N US 421 Hwy *TF:* 800-706-6538 ■ *Web:* www.starcom.net	Clinton	NC	28329	910-564-4194		224
Inter-State Aviation 4800 Airport Complex N *TF:* 800-653-8420 ■ *Web:* inter-stateaviation.com	Pullman	WA	99163	509-332-6596	334-1751	63
Interstate Aviation Inc 62 Johnson Ave *TF:* 800-573-5519 ■ *Web:* www.interstateaviation.com	Plainville	CT	06062	860-747-5519	747-5939	63
Interstate Bank SSB 301 S Main *TF:* 800-757-4071 ■ *Web:* interstatebankssb.com	Perryton	TX	79070	806-435-4071		70
Interstate Batteries 12770 Merit Dr *Web:* www.interstatebatteries.com	Dallas	TX	75251	972-991-1444		61
Interstate Billing Service Inc 2114 Veterans Dr SE *TF:* 800-332-9140 ■ *Web:* www.interstatebilling.com	Decatur	AL	35609	800-332-9140		160
Interstate Castings Co 3823 Massachusetts Ave *Web:* www.iscastings.com	Indianapolis	IN	46218	317-546-2427	546-4004	307
Interstate Chemical Company Inc 2797 Freedland Rd *TF:* 800-422-2436 ■ *Web:* www.interstatechemical.com	Hermitage	PA	16148	724-981-3771	981-8383	143
Interstate Connecting Components Inc 120 Mt Holly By Pass *Fax Area Code: 856 ■ *TF:* 800-422-3911 ■ *Web:* www.connecticc.com	Lumberton	NJ	08048	800-422-3911	722-9425*	246
Interstate Contract Cleaning Services Inc 509 Blairhill Rd	Charlotte	NC	28217	704-522-7773	522-7731	104
Interstate Diesel Service Inc 5300 Lakeside Ave *TF:* 800-321-4234 ■ *Web:* www.interstate-mcbee.com	Cleveland	OH	44114	216-881-0015	881-0805	60
Interstate Electrical Supply Inc 2300 Second Ave *TF:* 800-903-4409 ■ *Web:* www.interstate-electrical.com	Columbus	GA	31901	706-324-1000	576-5821	246
Interstate Electronics Inc (IEI) 1394 State Rte 36 *Web:* www.interstateelectronics.com	Hazlet	NJ	07730	732-264-3900		38
Interstate Foam & Supply Inc 302 Comfort Dr NE *Web:* www.interstatefoamandsupply.com	Conover	NC	28613	828-459-9700	459-0300	676
Interstate Glass Inc 1621 S Brightleaf Blvd *TF:* 855-969-4527	Smithfield	NC	27577	919-934-4121		329
Interstate Insurance Management Inc 2307 Menoher Blvd *Fax Area Code: 814 ■ *TF:* 800-452-0297 ■ *Web:* interstate-insurance.com	Johnstown	PA	15905	800-452-0297	255-6010*	390
Interstate Meat Distributors Inc 15501 SE Piazza Ave	Clackamas	OR	97015	971-377-4171		296-26
Interstate Mechanical Contractors Inc 3200 Henson Rd *Web:* www.interstatemechanical.com	Knoxville	TN	37921	865-588-0180	602-4124	189-10
Interstate NationaLease 2700 Palmyra Rd *Web:* inlleasing.com	Albany	GA	31707	229-883-7250		778
Interstate Natural Gas Association of America (INGAA) 10 G St NE Ste 700 *Web:* www.ingaa.org	Washington	DC	20002	202-216-5900	216-0870	49-21
Interstate Oil & Gas Compact Commission (IOGCC) 900 NE 23rd St PO Box 53127 *Web:* iogcc.ok.gov	Oklahoma City	OK	73105	405-522-8380	525-3592	48-12
Interstate Optical Co 680 Lindaire Ln *TF:* 800-472-5790 ■ *Web:* www.interstateoptical.com	Ontario	OH	44906	800-472-5790		237
Interstate Paper Supply Company Inc (IPSCO) 103 Good St PO Box 670 *Web:* www.ipscoinc.com	Roscoe	PA	15477	724-938-2218	938-3415	554
Interstate Plastic Inc 3375 E Seltice Way *Fax Area Code: 888 ■ *TF:* 800-776-7537 ■ *Web:* interstateplastic.com	Post Falls	ID	83854	208-773-4538	206-3012*	596
Interstate Printing Co 2002 N 16th St *Web:* www.interstateprinting.com	Omaha	NE	68110	402-341-8028	341-6168	627
Interstate Registration Service Inc (IRS) PO Box 200005 *TF:* 800-383-5829 ■ *Web:* www.fueltax.net	Arlington	TX	76006	469-733-1620	733-1621	192
Interstate SignWays 7415 Lindsey Rd *Web:* www.interstatesigns.com	Little Rock	AR	72206	501-490-4242		701

	Phone	Fax	Class
Interstate State Park 307 Milltown Rd PO Box 254.............. Taylors Falls MN 55084 *Web:* www.dnr.state.mn.us	651-465-5711		565
Interstate State Park PO Box 703 .... Saint Croix Falls WI 54024 *Web:* dnr.wi.gov	715-483-3747		565
Interstate Telecommunications Cooperative Inc (ITC) 312 4th St W.............................. Clear Lake SD 57226 *TF:* 800-417-8667 ■ *Web:* www.itc-web.com	605-874-2181	874-2014	224
Interstate Transport Inc 324 1st Ave N........................ Saint Petersburg FL 33701 *TF:* 866-281-1281 ■ *Web:* www.interstate-transport.com	727-822-9999		650
Interstate Warehouse Services 1901 Krug St .... Albany GA 31705 *Web:* interstatewarehouse.com	229-888-3922	434-1276	803-1
Interstates Construction Services Inc 1520 N Main Ave .... Sioux Center IA 51250 *Web:* www.interstates.com	712-722-1662	722-1667	189-4
Interstock Premium Cabinets LLC 6300 Bristol Pk............................. Levittown PA 19057 *TF:* 800-896-9842 ■ *Web:* www.interstockcabinets.com	267-442-0026	288-1206	745-9
Interstyle Ceramics & Glass Ltd 3625 Brighton Ave .... Burnaby BC V5A3H5 *TF:* 800-667-1566 ■ *Web:* interstyleglass.com	604-421-7229	421-7544	751
Intersyn Technologies LP 2736 Albans ....Houston TX 77005 **Fax Area Code:* 832 ■ *Web:* www.orbitaltraction.com	713-866-4808	456-0004*	226
InterSystems Corp 1 Memorial Dr ....Cambridge MA 02142 *TF:* 800-753-2571 ■ *Web:* www.intersystems.com	617-621-0600	494-1631	178-1
Intertape Polymer Group 3647 Cortez Rd W.......................... Bradenton FL 34210 *Web:* www.itape.com	941-727-5788		124
InterTech Computer Products Inc 5225 S 39th St .... Phoenix AZ 85040 *Web:* www.allcovered.com	602-437-0035		174
Intertech Corp 3240 N O'Henry Blvd.......... Greensboro NC 27405 *TF:* 800-364-2255 ■ *Web:* www.intertechcorp.com	336-621-1891	621-1893	596
Intertech Development Co 7401 N Linder Ave .... Skokie IL 60077 *Web:* intertechdevelopment.com	847-679-3377	679-3391	386
InterTech Group Inc 4838 Jenkins Ave .... North Charleston SC 29405 *Web:* www.theintertechgroup.com	843-744-5174		605-1
Intertech Inc 1575 Thomas Center Dr.............. Eagan MN 55122 *Web:* intertech.com	651-994-8558		177
Intertech Plastics Inc 12850 E 40th Ave .... Denver CO 80239 *Web:* www.intertechplastics.com	303-371-4270	371-4901	596
Intertech Training & Consulting Inc 25 Barcelona Ste 202 .... Irvine CA 92614 *Web:* www.intertechconsulting.net	949-852-1165		180
Intertek Group PLC 801 Travis St............... Houston TX 77002 *Web:* www.intertek.com	713-407-3500		261
Interthinx 30005 Ladyface Ct................ Agoura Hills CA 91301 *TF:* 800-333-4510 ■ *Web:* www.interthinx.com	800-333-4510		391-6
Intertractor America Corp 960 Proctor Dr .... Elkhorn WI 53121 *Web:* www.intertractoramerica.com	262-723-6000	741-6655	190
Intertrade Industries Inc 14600 Hoover St......................... Westminster CA 92683 *Web:* intertradeindustries.com	714-894-5566		601
InterTrust Technologies Corp 920 Stewart Dr Ste 100..................... Sunnyvale CA 94085 *TF:* 800-393-2272 ■ *Web:* www.intertrust.com	408-616-1600	616-1626	178-12
Interuniversity Services Inc 1550 Bedford Hwy .... Bedford NS B4A1E6 *Web:* interuniversity.ns.ca	902-453-2470		317
Interurban Railway Museum 901 E 15th St ....Plano TX 75074 *Web:* www.plano.gov	972-941-2117		520
Inter-Urban Transit Partnership 300 Ellsworth St SW.....................Grand Rapids MI 49503 *Web:* www.ridetherapid.org	616-776-1100	456-1941	468
Interval International Inc 6262 Sunset Dr.............................. Miami FL 33143 **Fax Area Code:* 305 ■ *TF:* 800-828-8200 ■ *Web:* www.intervalworld.com	888-784-3447	667-2072*	753
Interval Management Inc 515 Nichols Blvd .... Sparks NV 89431 *Web:* www.qmcorp.com	775-355-4040		463
Interval Servicing International Co 3363 W Commercial Blvd Ste 202 .... Fort Lauderdale FL 33309 *Web:* www.intervalservicing.com	954-485-5400		772
InterVarsity Christian Fellowship/USA 6400 Schroeder Rd.......................... Madison WI 53711 *TF:* 866-734-4823 ■ *Web:* intervarsity.org	608-274-9001	274-7882	48-20
Interventional Spine Inc 13700 Alton Pkwy Ste 160 .... Irvine CA 92618	949-472-0006		476
Intervest Construction Inc 2379 Beville Rd ....Daytona Beach FL 32119 *TF:* 855-215-2974 ■ *Web:* icihomes.com	844-349-6401		653
Intervideo Duplication Services 3533 S Archer Ave .... Chicago IL 60609 *Web:* www.intervideoduplication.com	773-927-9091	927-9211	512
Interview Magazine 575 Broadway Ste 5........ New York NY 10012 *TF:* 800-925-9574 ■ *Web:* www.interviewmagazine.com	212-941-2900		457-11
Intervision PO Box 268 .... Eugene OR 97440 *Web:* www.intervisionmedia.com	541-343-7993		178-1
InterVision Systems Technologies Inc 2270 Martin Ave......................... Santa Clara CA 95050 *TF:* 800-787-6707 ■ *Web:* www.intervision.com	408-980-8550		180
Interwest Capital Corp 4275 Executive Sq Ste 1020.................... La Jolla CA 92037 *TF:* 800-792-9639 ■ *Web:* www.interwestcapital.com	858-622-4900		690
InterWest Insurance Services Inc 8950 Cal Center Dr Bldg 3 Ste 200............ Sacramento CA 95826 *TF:* 800-444-4134 ■ *Web:* www.iwins.com	916-488-3100	979-7992	390
InterWest Partners 2710 Sand Hill Rd Ste 200.................. Menlo Park CA 94025 *TF:* 866-803-9204 ■ *Web:* interwest.com	650-854-0585	854 4706	792

	Phone	Fax	Class
Interwest Safety Supply Inc (IW) 724 E 1860 S .... Provo UT 84606 *TF:* 800-955-1996 ■ *Web:* www.iwsafety.com	801-375-6321	377-2739	523
Inter-Wire Products (IWP) 355 Main St .... Armonk NY 10504 *TF:* 800-699-6633 ■ *Web:* www.interwiregroup.com	914-273-6633	273-6848	813
InterWorks Inc 1425 S Sangre Rd............. Stillwater OK 74074 *TF:* 866-490-9643 ■ *Web:* www.interworks.com	405-624-3214		180
inTEST Corp 804 E Gate Dr Ste 200.......... Mount Laurel NJ 08054 *NYSE:* INTT ■ *Web:* www.intest.com	856-505-8800	505-8801	253
Intevac Inc 3560 Bassett St................. Santa Clara CA 95054 *NASDAQ:* IVAC ■ *Web:* www.intevac.com	408-986-9888		544
Intex Recreation Corp 1665 Hughes Way....................... Long Beach CA 90810 *TF:* 800-234-6839 ■ *Web:* www.intexcorp.com	800-234-6839		710
Intex Solutions Inc 110 A St .... Needham MA 02494 *Web:* www.intex.com	781-449-6222	444-2318	177
INTIX (International Ticketing Assn) 5868 E 71st St Ste E 365 .... Indianapolis IN 46220 *Web:* www.intix.org	212-629-4036		48-4
Intone Networks 10 Austin Ave................... Iselin NJ 08830 *Web:* intonenetworks.com	732-721-3002	721-3024	196
In-Touch Insight Systems Inc 400 March Rd............................... Ottawa ON K2K3H4 *TF:* 800-263-2980 ■ *Web:* www.intouchinsight.com	800-263-2980		177
Intoximeters Inc 2081 Craig Rd .... Saint Louis MO 63146 *TF:* 800-451-8639 ■ *Web:* www.intox.com	314-429-4000		407
Intra Corp 885 Manufacturers Dr .... Westland MI 48186 *Web:* www.intra-corp.net	734-326-7030	326-1410	472
Intracare North Hospital 1120 Cypress Stn........................... Houston TX 77090 *Web:* www.intracarehospital.com	713-790-0949		374-5
Intraco Corp 530 Stephenson Hwy .... Troy MI 48083 *Web:* www.intracousa.com	248-585-6900		61
Intracon Na Inc 250 S 5 St Ste 840................ Boise ID 83702 *Web:* www.intracon.com	208-672-0888		78
Intracorp 550 Burrard St Ste 600.............. Vancouver BC V6C2B5 *Web:* intracorphomes.com	604-801-7000		656
Intrada Technologies 31 Ashler Manor Dr......... Muncy PA 17756 *TF:* 800-858-5745 ■ *Web:* www.intradatech.com	800-858-5745		396
Intradiem 3650 Mansell Rd Ste 500............ Alpharetta GA 30022 *TF:* 888-566-9457 ■ *Web:* www.intradiem.com	678-356-3500		178-10
IntraEdge Inc 80 N McClintock Dr Ste 2.................... Chandler AZ 85226 *Web:* intraedge.com	480-240-5240		196
IntraLinks Inc 150 E 42nd St.................. New York NY 10017 *TF:* 888-546-5383 ■ *Web:* www.intralinks.com	212-543-7700	543-7978	39
Intralox LLC 7157 Ridge Rd .... Hanover MD 21076 *TF:* 800-100-1029 ■ *Web:* www.intralox.com	301-575-2200		207
Intraoptics Inc 1611c Owen Dr.............. Fayetteville NC 28304 *Web:* www.intraoptics.com	910-484-6178		542
Intraprisetechknowlogies LLC 1110 Nuuanu Ave Ste 18 .... Honolulu HI 96817 *TF:* 866-737-9991 ■ *Web:* www.intraprise.us	866-737-9991		180
Intraspek Inc 8707 Timber Oak Ln .... Laurel MD 20723 *Web:* www.intraspek.com	301-617-0521		175
IntraSystems Inc 35 Braintree Hill Office Pk Ste 302 .... Braintree MA 02184 *Web:* www.intrasystems.com	781-986-1700	986-1001	180
Intratek Computer Inc 5431 Industrial Dr................... Huntington Beach CA 92649 *TF:* 800-892-8282 ■ *Web:* www.intrapc.com	714-892-0892		175
Intrawest ULC 1621 18th St Ste 300.............. Denver CO 80202 *Web:* www.alterramtnco.com	303-749-8370		669
InTren Inc 18202 W Union Rd .... Union IL 60180 *Web:* www.intren.com	815-923-2300		256
Intrepid Advisors LLC 290 Donald Lynch Blvd Ste 302 .... Marlborough MA 01752 *Web:* intrepid-advisors.com	508-219-4550		261
Intrepid Aviation Group Holdings LLC 263 Tresser Blvd One Stamford Plz............. Stamford CT 06901 *Web:* www.intrepidaviation.com	203-905-4220		791
Intrepid Control Systems Inc 31601 Research Park Dr............... Madison Heights MI 48071 *TF:* 800-859-6265 ■ *Web:* www.intrepidcs.com	586-731-7950		180
Intrepid Enterprises Inc 1848 Industrial Blvd .... Harvey LA 70058 *Web:* intrepidstone.com	504-348-2861	340-7018	191-1
Intrepid Potash Inc 700 17th St Ste 1700 .... Denver CO 80202 *NYSE:* IPI ■ *Web:* www.intrepidpotash.com	303-296-3006	298-7502	280
Intrepid Powerboats 11700 S Belcher Rd .... Largo FL 33773 *Web:* www.intrepidpowerboats.com	727-548-1260	544-1796	90
Intrepid Sea-Air-Space Museum W 46th St & 12th Ave Pier 86................. New York NY 10036 *TF:* 877-957-7447 ■ *Web:* intrepidmuseum.org	212-245-0072		520
IntriCon Corp 1260 Red Fox Rd.............. Arden Hills MN 55112 *NASDAQ:* IIN ■ *Web:* www.intricon.com	651-636-9770	636-9503	318
Intrigue Media Solutions Inc 55 Delhi St .... Guelph ON N1E4J3 *Web:* intrigueme.ca	519-265-4933		5
Intrinsic Therapeutics Inc 30 Commerce Way .... Woburn MA 01801 *Web:* www.barricaid.com	781-932-0222		475
Intrinsix Corp 100 Campus Dr.............. Marlborough MA 01752 *TF:* 800-783-0330 ■ *Web:* www.intrinsix.com	508-658-7600		261
Intrinzic 1 Levee Way Ste 3121 .... Newport KY 41071 *Web:* intrinzicbrands.com	859-261-2200	261-2100	195
introNetworks Inc 1482 E Valley Rd Ste 446................ Santa Barbara CA 93108 *Web:* intronetworks.com	805-722-1040		225
Intronix Technologies Inc 26 McEwan Dr W Unit 15...................... Bolton ON L7E1E6 *TF:* 800-819-9996 ■ *Web:* www.intronixtech.com	905-951-3361		317
Introtek International LP 150 Executive Dr.......................... Edgewood NY 11717 *Web:* introtek.com	631-242-5425		743

Company	Phone	Fax	Class
Introworks Inc 13911 Ridgedale Dr Ste 280 Minnetonka MN 55305 *Web:* intro.works	952-593-1800		7
Intrusion Inc 1101 E Arapaho Rd Richardson TX 75081 *TF:* 888-637-7770 ■ *Web:* www.intrusion.com	972-234-6400		178-12
Intsel Steel Distributors LP 11310 W Little York Houston TX 77041 *TF:* 800-762-3316 ■ *Web:* www.intselsteel.com	713-937-9500	937-1091	723
Intuit Inc 2632 Marine Way Mountain View CA 94043 *NASDAQ: INTU* ■ *TF:* 800-446-8848 ■ *Web:* www.intuit.com	650-944-6000	944-5656	178-9
Intuit Inc 2675 Coast Ave Ste 11 Mountain View CA 94043 *NASDAQ: INTU* ■ *Web:* about.intuit.com	650-944-6000		178-1
Intuit The Center for Intuitive & Outsider 756 N Milwaukee Ave Chicago IL 60642 *Web:* www.art.org	312-243-9088		520
Intuition Design Inc 508 2nd St Chesapeake City MD 21915 *Web:* www.intuitiondesign.com	410-885-2513		194
Intuition LLC 6735 Southpoint Dr S Ste 300 Jacksonville FL 32216 *Web:* www.intuitionllc.com	904-421-7220		569
Intuitive Research & Technology Corp 5030 Bradford Dr NW Ste 205 Huntsville AL 35805 *Web:* www.irtc-hq.com	256-922-9300	922-1122	178-1
Intuitive Surgical Inc 1020 Kifer Rd Sunnyvale CA 94086 *NASDAQ: ISRG* ■ *TF:* 888-868-4647 ■ *Web:* www.intuitivesurgical.com	408-523-2100	523-1390	476
Inuit Broadcasting Corp 309 Cooper St Ste 310 Ottawa ON K2P0G5 *Web:* inuitbroadcasting.ca	613-235-1892	230-8824	647
Inuit Gallery of Vancouver Ltd 206 Cambie St Gastown Vancouver BC V6B2M9 *TF:* 888-615-8399 ■ *Web:* inuit.com	604-688-7323		42
Inuvialuit Regional Corp Bag Service Ste 21 Inuvik NT X0E0T0 *Web:* www.irc.inuvialuit.com	867-777-2737		787
Invacare Canada LP 570 Matheson Blvd E Unit 8 Mississauga ON L4Z4G4 *Web:* www.invacare.ca	905-890-8300		363
Invacare Corp 1 Invacare Way Elyria OH 44036 *NYSE: IVC* ■ **Fax Area Code:* 877 ■ *TF:* 800-333-6900 ■ *Web:* www.invacare.com	440-329-6000	619-7996*	477
Invaluable LLC 38 Everett St Ste 101 Allston MA 02134 *Web:* www.invaluable.com	617-746-9800		809
Invena Corp 416 E Fifth St Eureka KS 67045 *Web:* www.invena.com	620-583-8630		454
Invenio Marketing Solutions Inc 2201 Donley Dr Ste 200 Austin TX 78758 *TF:* 800-926-1754 ■ *Web:* www.inveniomarketing.com	800-926-1754		195
Invenshure LLC 807 Broadway St NE Ste 350 Minneapolis MN 55413 *TF:* 844-663-6635 ■ *Web:* invenshure.com	844-663-6635		528
Inventis Group Ltd 8400 Sugar Maple Dr Ste 305 Mason OH 45040 *Web:* www.inventisgroup.com	513-518-6691		466
Inventive Systems Inc 21797C N Coral Dr Lexington Park MD 20653 **Fax Area Code:* 301 ■ *TF:* 800-873-5153 ■ *Web:* www.oilinwater.org	800-873-5153	863-7583*	201
Inventory Operations Consulting LLC 723 58th St Ste 100 Kenosha WI 53140 *TF:* 800-849-1081 ■ *Web:* www.inventoryops.com	800-849-1081		194
Inventory Sales Co 9777 Reavis Rd Saint Louis MO 63123 *TF:* 866-417-3801 ■ *Web:* www.inventorysales.com	866-417-3801		350
Inver Hills Community College 2500 80th St E Inver Grove Heights MN 55076 *TF:* 866-576-0689 ■ *Web:* inverhills.edu	651-450-3000		162
Inverness Management LLC 21 Locust Ave Ste 1D New Canaan CT 06840 *Web:* www.invernessmanagement.com	203-966-4177		402
Invesco 11 Greenway Plz Ste 100 Houston TX 77046 *TF:* 800-959-4246 ■ *Web:* www.invesco.com	713-626-1919		528
Invesco Canada Ltd 5140 Yonge St Ste 800 Toronto ON M2N6X7 *TF:* 800-874-6275 ■ *Web:* www.invesco.ca	416-590-9855		528
Invesco Ltd 225 Liberty St New York NY 10281 *TF:* 800-525-7048 ■ *Web:* www.invesco.com	800-525-7048		528
Invesco Ltd 1555 Peachtree St NE Ste 1800 Atlanta GA 30309 *Web:* www.invesco.com	404-479-1095		192
Invesco Private Capital Inc 1166 Avenue of the Americas 26th Fl New York NY 10036 *Web:* www.invesco.com	212-278-9000	278-9822	792
Invest/O - Registered Investment Advisors PO Box 5996 Bend OR 97708 *Web:* www.riskfactor.com	541-389-3676		401
Investco Financial Corp 1302 Puyallup St Sumner WA 98390 **Fax Area Code:* 206 ■ *Web:* www.investco.com	253-863-6200	264-0121*	463
Investcorp 6 Montgomery Village Ave Ste 320 Gaithersburg MD 20879 *Web:* investcorponline.com	301-740-2550		390
Investcorp International Inc 280 Park Ave New York NY 10017 *Web:* www.investcorp.com	212-599-4700	983-7073	401
Investec 200 E Carrillo St Ste 200 Santa Barbara CA 93101 *Web:* www.investecre.com	805-962-8989		652
Investec Ernst & Co 10 E 53rd St 22nd Fl New York NY 10022 *Web:* www.investec.com	212-259-5610		690
Investedge Inc 1151 Freeport Rd Ste 396 Pittsburgh PA 15238 *TF:* 800-830-1839 ■ *Web:* investedge.com	610-747-0123		180
Investigative Services Inc 4381 S 153rd Cir Omaha NE 68137	402-894-5625		400
Investing Daily 7600A Leesburg Pk W Bldg Ste 300 Falls Church VA 22043 *TF:* 800-832-2330 ■ *Web:* www.investingdaily.com	703-394-4931	905-8100	531-9

Company	Phone	Fax	Class
Investment Casting Institute (ICI) 136 Summit Ave Montvale NJ 07645 *Web:* www.investmentcasting.org	201-573-9770	573-9771	49-13
Investment Company Institute (ICI) 1401 H St NW Ste 1200 Washington DC 20005 *Web:* www.ici.org	202-326-5800	326-5841	49-2
Investment Counselors of Maryland LLC 803 Cathedral St Baltimore MD 21201 *Web:* www.icomd.com	410-539-3838	625-9016	401
Investment Metrics LLC 3 Parklands Dr Darien CT 06820 *Web:* www.invmetrics.com	203-662-8400		466
Investment Partners Ltd 419 W High Ave New Philadelphia OH 44663 *Web:* invp.com	330-308-9707		690
Investment Performance Services LLC 570 E York St Savannah GA 31401 *Web:* ips-net.com	912-352-2862		401
Investment Planners Inc 226 W Eldorado St Decatur IL 62522 *Web:* www.investment-planners.com	217-425-6340		401
Investment Planning Counsel 5015 Spectrum Way Ste 200 Mississauga ON L4W0E4 **Fax Area Code:* 844 ■ *TF:* 877-212-9799 ■ *Web:* www.ipcc.ca	905-212-9799	378-6244*	2
Investment Quality Trends (IQT) 2888 Loker Ave E Ste 116 Carlsbad CA 92010 *TF:* 866-927-5250 ■ *Web:* iqtrends.com	866-927-5250	927-5251	531-9
Investments & Wealth Institute 5619 DTC Pkwy Ste 500 Greenwood Village CO 80111 *TF:* 800-250-9083 ■ *Web:* www.investmentsandwealth.org	303-770-3377	770-1812	49-2
Investor Group Services LLC 855 Boylston St 6th Fl Boston MA 02116 *Web:* www.igsboston.com	617-371-4000		194
Investor Protection Trust 750 1st St NE Ste 1140 Washington DC 20002 *Web:* www.investorprotection.org	202-775-2111		49-2
Investor Responsibility Research Center Institute (IRRC) 40 Wall St 28th Fl New York NY 10005 *Web:* www.irrcinstitute.org	646-612-5807		637-2
Investor's Business Daily 12655 Beatrice St Los Angeles CA 90066 *TF:* 800-831-2525 ■ *Web:* www.investors.com	310-448-6000		532-2
Investorideas.com 1385 Gulf Rd Ste 102 Point Roberts WA 98281 *TF:* 800-665-0411 ■ *Web:* www.investorideas.com	800-665-0411		466
InvestorPlace Media LLC 9201 Corporate Blvd Ste 200 Rockville MD 20850 *TF:* 800-219-8592 ■ *Web:* www.jimwoodsinvesting.stockinvestor.com	800-219-8592		531-9
Investors Bank 101 Wood Ave S Iselin NJ 08830 *NASDAQ: ISBC* ■ *TF:* 855-422-6548 ■ *Web:* www.myinvestorsbank.com	973-924-5100	765-0921	70
Investors Group Inc 447 Portage Ave Winnipeg MB R3B3H5 *TSE: IGM* ■ **Fax Area Code:* 866 ■ *TF:* 888-746-6344 ■ *Web:* www.investorsgroup.com	888-746-6344	202-1923*	401
Investors Heritage Life Insurance Co (IHLIC) 200 Capital Ave Frankfort KY 40601 *TF:* 800-422-2011 ■ *Web:* www.ihlic.com	502-223-2361	875-7084	391-2
Investors Management Corp 801 N West St Raleigh NC 27603 *Web:* www.investorsmanagement.com	919-653-7499	653-7498	360-3
Investors Title Co 121 N Columbia St Chapel Hill NC 27514 *NASDAQ: ITIC* ■ *TF:* 800-326-4842 ■ *Web:* www.invtitle.com	919-968-2200		360-4
Investrade Discount Securities 950 N Milwaukee Ave Ste 102 Glenview IL 60025 **Fax Area Code:* 877 ■ *TF:* 800-498-7120 ■ *Web:* www.investrade.com	847-375-6080	367-8466*	690
Invetech 9980 Huennekens St Ste 140 San Diego CA 92121 *TF:* 866-969-3232 ■ *Web:* www.invetech.us	858-768-3232	768-3299	194
Invincible Office Furniture Co 842 S 26th St PO Box 1117 Manitowoc WI 54220 *TF:* 877-682-4601 ■ *Web:* www.invinciblefurniture.com	920-682-4601	683-2970	319-1
Invisible Hand Networks Inc 670 Broadway Ste 302 New York NY 10012 *TF:* 866-637-5286 ■ *Web:* www.invisiblehand.net	212-400-7416		393
Invisible Theatre 1400 N First Ave Tucson AZ 85719 *Web:* www.invisibletheatre.com	520-882-9721	884-5410	573-4
InVision Communications Inc 1280 Civic Dr 3rd Fl Walnut Creek CA 94596 *Web:* www.iv.com	925-944-1211		195
InVision Software Inc 110 Lake Ave S Ste 35 Nesconset NY 11767 *Web:* www.invisionsoft.com	631-360-3400		177
INVISTA 4123 E 37th St N Wichita KS 67220 *TF:* 877-446-8478 ■ *Web:* www.invista.com	316-828-1000		605-1
InVite Health Inc 1 Garden State Plz Paramus NJ 07652 *TF:* 800-349-0929 ■ *Web:* www.invitehealth.com	201-587-2222		345
Invitechange LLC 110 Third Ave N Ste 102 Edmonds WA 98020 *Web:* www.invitechange.com	425-778-3505		765
Inviting Homecom 4700 SW 51st St Unit 219 Davie FL 33314 **Fax Area Code:* 954 ■ *TF:* 866-751-6606 ■ *Web:* www.invitinghome.com	781-444-8001	616-8037*	321
InVitro Intl 330 E Orangethorpe Ave Ste D Placentia CA 92870 *TF:* 800-246-8487 ■ *Web:* invitrointl.com	949-851-8356	851-4985	231
Invivo Therapeutics Holdings Corp 1 Kendall Sq Ste B14402 Cambridge MA 02139 *Web:* www.invivotherapeutics.com	617-863-5500		250
Invivoscribe Technologies Inc 6330 Nancy Ridge Dr Ste 106 San Diego CA 92121 *TF:* 866-623-8105 ■ *Web:* www.invivoscribe.com	858-224-6600		231
Invoke Solutions Inc 395 Totten Pond Rd Ste 403 Waltham MA 02451 *Web:* invoke.com	781-810-2700		466
Involve LLC 130 E Chestnut St Ste 401 Columbus OH 43215 *Web:* getinvolve.com	614-545-3464		5
Invotec Engineering Inc 10909 Industry Ln Miamisburg OH 45342 *Web:* www.invotec.com	937-886-3232	886-2131	256
InVue Security Products Inc 10715 Sikes Pl Ste 200 Charlotte NC 28277 *TF:* 888-257-4272 ■ *Web:* alphaworld.com	704-206-7849		253

Name / Address	City	State	ZIP	Phone	Fax	Class
Invuity Inc 444 De Haro St *TF:* 866-711-7768 ■ *Web:* invuity.com	San Francisco	CA	94107	415-655-2100		475
INW Solutions 4500 Holland Office Pk Ste 301 *Web:* www.inwsolutions.com	Virginia Beach	VA	23452	757-563-3572		196
Inwood Animal Clinic PC 4846 Broadway *Web:* inwoodanimalclinic.com	New York	NY	10034	212-304-8387		794
Inwood National Bank 7621 Inwood Rd *Web:* www.inwoodbank.com	Dallas	TX	75209	214-358-5281		70
InXile Entertainment Inc 2727 Newport Blvd *Web:* inxile-entertainment.com	Newport Beach	CA	92663	949-675-3690		225
Inyo County PO Box N *TF:* 800-447-4696 ■ *Web:* www.inyocounty.us	Independence	CA	93526	760-878-0292	878-2241	338
Inyo-Mono Title Co 873 N Main St *Web:* inyomonotitle.com	Bishop	CA	93514	760-872-4741		653
Inyxa LLC 3501 W Algonguin Rd Ste 608 *Web:* www.inyxa.com	Rolling Meadows	IL	60008	224-325-4699		180
I-O Corp 14852 S Heritage Crest Way 1-A *TF:* 800-871-9998 ■ *Web:* www.iocorp.com	Bluffdale	UT	84065	801-973-6767		696
IO Environmental & Infrastructure Inc 2840 Adams Ave Ste 301 *Web:* www.iosdv.com	San Diego	CA	92116	619-280-3278		610
IO Industries Inc 1510 Woodcock St *Web:* www.ioindustries.com	London	ON	N6H5S1	519-663-9570		201
IO Integration Inc 20480 Pacifica Dr Ste 1C *Web:* www.iointegration.com	Cupertino	CA	95014	408-996-3420	996-3425	180
IO Semiconductor 4350 Executive Dr Ste 200	San Diego	CA	92121	858-373-0440		201
IOA Re Inc 190 W Germantown Pk Ste 200 *TF:* 800-462-2300 ■ *Web:* www.ioare.com	East Norriton	PA	19401	610-940-9000		391-3
IOActive Inc 701 Fifth Ave Ste 6850 *TF:* 866-760-0222 ■ *Web:* ioactive.com	Seattle	WA	98104	206-784-4313		180
IOCC (International Orthodox Christian Charities) 110 W Rd Ste 360 *TF:* 877-803-4622 ■ *Web:* www.iocc.org	Towson	MD	21204	410-243-9820	243-9824	48-5
IOF (Independent Order of Foresters) 789 Don Mills Rd *TF:* 800-828-1540 ■ *Web:* www.foresters.com	Toronto	ON	M3C1T9	416-429-3000		48-5
IOGCC (Interstate Oil & Gas Compact Commission) 900 NE 23rd St PO Box 53127 *Web:* iogcc.ok.gov	Oklahoma City	OK	73105	405-522-8380	525-3592	48-12
ioGenetics LLC 3591 Anderson St Ste 218 *Web:* www.iogenetics.com	Madison	WI	53704	608-310-9540		85
IOI (Integrated Orbital Implants Inc) 11230 Sorrento Valley Rd Ste 135 *TF:* 800-424-6537 ■ *Web:* www.ioi.com	San Diego	CA	92121	858-677-9990	677-9993	475
Iolani Palace State Monument 364 S King St *Web:* www.iolanipalace.org	Honolulu	HI	96813	808-522-0822		565
Iolani School 563 Kamoku St *Web:* www.iolani.org	Honolulu	HI	96826	808-949-5355		623
Ioline Corp 14140 NE 200th St *TF:* 800-598-0029 ■ *Web:* ioline.com	Woodinville	WA	98072	425-398-8282	398-8383	744
I-Ology Inc 16767 N Perimeter Dr Ste 230 *Web:* www.i-ology.com	Scottsdale	AZ	85260	480-850-2800		180
IOMEDIA Inc 640 W 28th St 9th Fl *Web:* www.io-media.com	New York	NY	10001	212-352-1115	352-1117	7
Iomer Internet Solutions 10110 107 St NW Ste 202 *Web:* www.iomer.com	Edmonton	AB	T5J1J4	780-424-3122		180
Iomosaic Corp 93 Stiles Rd *TF:* 844-466-6724 ■ *Web:* www.iomosaic.com	Salem	NH	03079	603-893-7009		196
ION (Institute of Navigation Inc) 8551 Rixlew Ln Ste 360 *Web:* www.ion.org	Manassas	VA	20109	703-366-2723	366-2724	49-21
ION Art 407 Radam Ln Ste 100 *Web:* www.ionart.com	Austin	TX	78745	512-326-9333		8
ION Brand Design 948 W Seventh Ave W *TF:* 888-336-2466 ■ *Web:* iondesign.ca	Vancouver	BC	V5Z1C3	604-682-6787		7
ION Corp 7500 Equitable Dr *Web:* www.ioncorp.com	Eden Prairie	MN	55344	952-936-9490		21
ION Media Networks Inc 601 Clearwater Park Rd *TF:* 888-467-2988 ■ *Web:* ionmedia.com	West Palm Beach	FL	33401	561-659-4122	659-4754	741-140
ION Networks Inc 120 Corporate Blvd Ste A *TF:* 800-722-8986 ■ *Web:* apitech.com	South Plainfield	NJ	07080	908-546-3900	546-3901	178-7
ION Physics Corp 373 Main St *TF:* 800-223-0466 ■ *Web:* www.ionphysics.com	Fremont	NH	03044	800-223-0466		518
ION Trading Inc 1345 Avenue of the Americas *Web:* iongroup.com	New York	NY	10105	212-906-0050		177
Iona College 715 N Ave *TF:* 800-264-6350 ■ *Web:* www.iona.edu	New Rochelle	NY	10801	914-633-2502	633-2486	166
IonBond LLC 200 Roundhill Dr *Web:* www.ionbond.com	Rockaway	NJ	07866	973-586-4700	586-4729	481
IonField Systems LLC 1 Executive Dr Ste 8 *Web:* ionfieldsystems.com	Moorestown	NJ	08057	856-437-0330	823-1426	419
Ionia County 100 W Main St *TF:* 800-649-3777 ■ *Web:* ioniacounty.org	Ionia	MI	48846	616-527-5322	527-8201	338
Ionia Maximum Correctional Facility 1576 W Bluewater Hwy *Web:* www.michigan.gov	Ionia	MI	48846	616-527-6331	527-6863	213
Ionia Recreation Area 2880 W David Hwy *Web:* www.michigan.org	Ionia	MI	48846	616-527-3750		565
Ionic Services Inc 7012 Harrison Ave Ste 6 *TF:* 866-496-3470 ■ *Web:* ionicservices.com	Cincinnati	OH	45247	513-744-6800		225
IonIdea Inc 3913 Old Lee Hwy Ste 33B *Web:* www.ionidea.com	Fairfax	VA	22030	703-691-0400		180
IonSense Inc 999 Broadway Ste 404 *Web:* www.ionsense.com	Saugus	MA	01906	781-484-1043		419
IOPFDA (Independent Office Products & Furniture Dealers Assn) 3601 E Joppa Rd *Web:* www.nopanet.org	Baltimore	MD	21234	410-931-8100	931-8111	49-4
IOPP (Institute of Packaging Professionals) 1833 Centre Point Cir Ste 123 *TF:* 800-432-4085 ■ *Web:* www.iopp.org	Naperville	IL	60563	630-544-5050	544-5055	49-13
IOS (Integrated Office Solutions) PO Box 90212 *Web:* www.e-ios.com	Santa Barbara	CA	93190	805-252-4564		175
IOS Partners 311 Mendoza Ave *Web:* iospartners.com	Coral Gables	FL	33134	305-648-2877	446-7122	401
Iosco County 422 W Lake St *Web:* www.iosco.net	Tawas City	MI	48763	989-362-3497		338
Iostudio 565 Marriott Dr Ste 820 *Web:* www.iostudio.com	Nashville	TN	37214	615-256-6282		225
Iovation Inc 555 SW Oak St Ste 300 *Web:* www.iovation.com	Portland	OR	97204	503-224-6010		395
Iowa						
Adult Children & Family Services Div 1305 E Walnut St *Web:* dhs.iowa.gov	Des Moines	IA	50319	515-281-8977		339-16
Agriculture & Land Stewardship Dept 502 E Ninth St *Web:* www.iowaagriculture.gov	Des Moines	IA	50319	515-281-5321		339-16
Arts Council 600 E Locust St *Web:* iowaculture.gov	Des Moines	IA	50319	515-281-5111	242-6498	339-16
Attorney General 1305 E Walnut St 2nd Fl *TF:* 866-448-4605 ■ *Web:* www.state.ia.us	Des Moines	IA	50319	515-281-5164	281-4209	339-16
Banking Div 200 E Grand Ave Ste 300 *Web:* www.idob.state.ia.us	Des Moines	IA	50309	515-281-4014	281-4862	339-16
Child Support Recovery Unit PO Box 9125 *TF:* 888-229-9223 ■ *Web:* www.secureapp.dhs.state.ia.us	Des Moines	IA	50306	888-229-9223		339-16
Consumer Protection Div 1305 E Walnut St 2nd Fl *TF:* 888-777-4590 ■ *Web:* www.iowaattorneygeneral.gov	Des Moines	IA	50319	515-281-5926	281-6771	339-16
Department on Aging 510 E 12th St Ste 2 *TF:* 800-532-3213 ■ *Web:* www.iowaaging.gov	Des Moines	IA	50319	515-725-3333		339-16
Economic Development Dept 200 E Grand Ave *Web:* www.iowaeconomicdevelopment.com	Des Moines	IA	50309	515-725-3000		339-16
Education Dept 400 E 14th St *Web:* www.iowa.gov	Des Moines	IA	50319	515-281-3436	242-5988	339-16
Emergency Management Div 7900 Hickman Rd Ste 500 *Web:* www.homelandsecurity.iowa.gov	Windsor Heights	IA	50324	515-725-3231	725-3260	339-16
Environmental Services Div 11101 Aurora Ave *Web:* www.iesiowa.com	Urbandale	IA	50322	515-279-8042	279-1853	339-16
Ethics & Campaign Disclosure Board 510 E 12th St Ste 1-A *Web:* www.iowa.gov	Des Moines	IA	50319	515-281-4028	281-4073	265
General Assembly State Capitol 1007 E Grand Ave *Web:* www.legis.iowa.gov	Des Moines	IA	50319	515-802-3004		339-16
Governor 1007 E Grand Ave State Capitol *Web:* governor.iowa.gov	Des Moines	IA	50319	515-281-5211		339-16
Human Services Dept 1305 E Walnut St 5th Fl SE *TF:* 800-362-2178 ■ *Web:* dhs.iowa.gov	Des Moines	IA	50319	515-242-5880	242-6036	339-16
Insurance Div 601 Locust St 4th Fl *TF:* 877-955-1212 ■ *Web:* iid.iowa.gov	Des Moines	IA	50309	515-281-5705	281-3059	339-16
Lottery 13001 University Ave *Web:* ialottery.com	Clive	IA	50325	515-725-7900		452
Medical Examiners Board 400 SW Eigth St Ste C *TF:* 844-474-4321 ■ *Web:* medicalboard.iowa.gov	Des Moines	IA	50309	515-281-5171	242-5908	339-16
Motor Vehicle Div 100 Euclid Ave PO Box 9204 *Web:* www.dmv.com	Des Moines	IA	50306	515-244-1052		339-16
Natural Resource Dept 502 E Ninth St 4th Fl *Web:* www.iowadnr.gov	Des Moines	IA	50319	515-725-8200	725-8202	339-16
Office of the Chief Information Officer 1305 E Walnut St *Web:* ocio.iowa.gov	Des Moines	IA	50319	515-281-5503		339-16
Parole Board 510 E 12th St Ste 3 *Web:* bop.iowa.gov	Des Moines	IA	50319	515-725-5757		339-16
Professional Licensing & Regulation Div 200 E Grand Ave Ste 350 *Web:* plb.iowa.gov	Des Moines	IA	50309	515-725-9022	725-9032	339-16
Public Health Dept 321 E 12th St *Web:* www.idph.state.ia.us	Des Moines	IA	50319	515-281-6225		339-16
Regents Board 11260 Aurora Ave *Web:* www.iowaregents.edu	Urbandale	IA	50322	515-281-3934	281-6420	339-16
Secretary of State 321 E 12th St Lucas Bldg First Fl *Web:* sos.iowa.gov	Des Moines	IA	50319	515-281-5204		339-16
State Court Administration 1111 E Ct Ave *Web:* www.iowacourts.gov	Des Moines	IA	50319	515-281-5241		339-16
State Patrol Div 215 E 7th St *Web:* www.dps.state.ia.us	Des Moines	IA	50319	515-725-6090		339-16
Supreme Court 4645 NE 7th St Iowa Judicial Branch Bldg. *Web:* iowautility.org	Des Moines	IA	50319	515-348-4700		339-16
Treasurer State Treasurer's Ofc Capitol Bldg *TF:* 888-672-9116 ■ *Web:* www.iowatreasurer.gov	Des Moines	IA	50319	515-281-5368	281-7562	339-16
Utilities Board 1375 E Ct Ave Rm 69 *TF:* 877-565-4450 ■ *Web:* www.state.la.us	Des Moines	IA	50319	515-963-0606	725-7399	339-16

Name / Address	City	State	ZIP	Phone	Fax	Class
Veterans Affairs Dept 7105 NW 70th Ave Camp Dodge Bldg 3465 *Web:* va.iowa.gov	Johnston	IA	50131	515-252-4698	727-3713	339-16
Vocational Rehabilitation Services Div 510 E 12th St *TF:* 800-532-1486 ■ *Web:* www.ivrs.iowa.gov	Des Moines	IA	50319	515-281-4311	281-7645	339-16
Workforce Development 1000 E Grand Ave *TF:* 866-239-0843 ■ *Web:* www.iowaworkforcedevelopment.gov	Des Moines	IA	50319	866-239-0843		259
Iowa 80 Group Inc 515 Sterling Dr PO Box 639 *Web:* iowa80group.com	Walcott	IA	52773	563-284-6965		324
Iowa Arboretum 1875 Peach Ave *Web:* iowaarboretum.org	Madrid	IA	50156	515-795-3216		97
Iowa Association of Business & Industry 400 E Ct Ave Ste 100 *TF:* 800-383-4224 ■ *Web:* www.iowaabi.org	Des Moines	IA	50309	515-280-8000		140
Iowa Association of Realtors 1370 NW 114th St Ste 100 *TF:* 800-532-1515 ■ *Web:* www.iowarealtors.com	Clive	IA	50325	515-453-1064	453-1070	656
Iowa Beef Steakhouse 1201 E Euclid Ave *Web:* www.iowabeefsteakhouse.com	Des Moines	IA	50316	515-262-1138		671
Iowa Braille & Sight Saving School 1002 G Ave *TF:* 800-645-4579 ■ *Web:* www.iowa-braille.k12.ia.us	Vinton	IA	52349	319-472-5221		166
Iowa Central Community College 2031 Quail Ave *TF:* 800-362-2793 ■ *Web:* www.iowacentral.edu	Fort Dodge	IA	50501	800-362-2793		162
Iowa City Area Chamber of Commerce 325 E Washington St *Web:* www.iowacityarea.com	Iowa City	IA	52240	319-337-9637	338-9958	139
Iowa City Hospice Inc 1025 Wade St *Web:* iowacityhospice.org	Iowa City	IA	52240	319-351-5665		363
Iowa City Public Library 123 S Linn St *Web:* www.icpl.org	Iowa City	IA	52240	319-356-5200	356-5494	434-3
Iowa City/Coralville Area Convention & Visitors Bureau 900 1st Ave/Hayden Fry Way *TF:* 800-283-6592 ■ *Web:* www.thinkiowacity.com	Coralville	IA	52241	319-337-6592	337-9953	206
Iowa College Student Aid Commission 430 E Grand Ave 3rd Fl *TF:* 800-383-4222 ■ *Web:* www.iowacollegeaid.gov	Des Moines	IA	50309	515-725-3400	725-3401	725
Iowa Communications Network Inc Grimes State Office Bldg 400 E 14th St *Web:* icn.iowa.gov	Des Moines	IA	50319	515-725-4692		387
Iowa Correctional Institution for Women 420 Mill St SW *Web:* mitchellvilleprison.org	Mitchellville	IA	50169	515-725-5042	725-5015	213
Iowa County 222 N Iowa St *Web:* www.iowacounty.org	Dodgeville	WI	53533	608-935-0318	935-3024	338
Iowa County PO Box 266 *Web:* www.co.iowa.ia.us	Marengo	IA	52301	319-642-3914		338
Iowa Democratic Party 5661 Fleur Dr *Web:* www.iowademocrats.org	Des Moines	IA	50321	515-244-7292	244-5051	616-1
Iowa Dental Assn 8797 NW 54th Ave Ste 100 *TF:* 800-828-2181 ■ *Web:* www.iowadental.org	Johnston	IA	50131	515-331-2298	334-8007	227
Iowa Dot Administration 800 Lincoln Way *Web:* iowadot.gov	Ames	IA	50010	515-239-1101	239-1639	339-16
Iowa Employment Solutions 430 E Grand Ave *Web:* www.iowaemploymentsolutions.com	Des Moines	IA	50309	515-281-9700		193
Iowa Farm Bureau Spokesman Magazine 5400 University Ave *TF:* 866-598-3693 ■ *Web:* www.iowafarmbureau.com	West Des Moines	IA	50266	515-225-5413	225-5419	457-1
Iowa Farmer Today 1065 Sierra Ct NE Ste B *TF:* 800-475-6655 ■ *Web:* www.iowafarmertoday.com	Cedar Rapids	IA	52402	800-475-6655		532-2
Iowa Gold Star Military Museum 7105 NW 70th Ave *TF:* 800-294-6607 ■ *Web:* www.iowanationalguard.com	Johnston	IA	50131	515-252-4531		520
Iowa Heartland Credit Union 1602 S Monroe Ave *Web:* iowaheartland.org	Mason City	IA	50401	641-424-5391		219
Iowa Hospital Assn (IHA) 100 E Grand Ave Ste 100 *Web:* www.ihaonline.org	Des Moines	IA	50309	515-288-1955	283-9366	49-19
Iowa Interstate Railroad 5900 Sixth St SW *TF:* 800-321-3891 ■ *Web:* iaisrr.com	Cedar Rapids	IA	52404	319-298-5400		648
Iowa Lakes Community College 300 S 18th St *TF:* 800-242-5106 ■ *Web:* www.iowalakes.edu	Estherville	IA	51334	712-362-2604	362-8363	162
Iowa Lakes Electric Co-op 702 S First St *TF:* 800-225-4532 ■ *Web:* www.ilec.coop	Estherville	IA	51334	800-225-4532		245
Iowa Legal Aid 1111 Ninth St Ste 230 *TF:* 800-992-8161 ■ *Web:* www.iowalegalaid.org	Des Moines	IA	50314	515-243-1193		428
Iowa Masonic Library & Museum 813 1st Ave SE *Web:* www.gl-iowa.org	Cedar Rapids	IA	52402	319-365-1438		520
Iowa Medical Society 515 E Locust St Ste 400 *TF:* 800-747-3070 ■ *Web:* www.iowamedical.org	Des Moines	IA	50309	515-223-1401	223-0590	474
Iowa Mold Tooling Company Inc (IMT) 500 W US Hwy 18 *TF:* 800-247-5958 ■ *Web:* www.imt.com	Garner	IA	50438	641-923-3711	923-6063	470
Iowa Mortgage Assn 8800 NW 62nd Ave *TF:* 800-800-2353 ■ *Web:* iowama.org	Johnston	IA	50131	800-987-7365		533
Iowa Northern Railway Co 201 Tower Park Dr Ste 300 *TF:* 800-392-3342 ■ *Web:* www.iowanorthern.com	Waterloo	IA	50701	319-297-6000		649
Iowa Nurses Assn (INA) 2400 86th St Ste 32 *Web:* www.iowanurses.org	Urbandale	IA	50322	515-225-0495		533
Iowa Pharmacy Assn 8515 Douglas Ave Ste 16 *Web:* www.iarx.org	Des Moines	IA	50322	515-270-0713	270-2979	585
Iowa Precision Industries Inc 5480 Sixth St SW *Web:* www.mestekmachinery.com	Cedar Rapids	IA	52404	319-364-9181		493
Iowa Prison Industries (IPI) 1445 E Grand Ave *TF:* 800-670-4537 ■ *Web:* www.iaprisonind.com	Des Moines	IA	50316	515-242-5770	242-5779	630
Iowa Public Interest Research Group 2643 Beaver Ave Ste 120 *Web:* iowapirg.webaction.org	Des Moines	IA	50310	515-236-3257		633
Iowa Public Television 6450 Corporate Dr PO Box 6450 *TF:* 800-532-1290 ■ *Web:* www.iptv.org	Johnston	IA	50131	515-725-9700	725-9836	741
Iowa Realty Company Inc 3501 Westown Pkwy *TF:* 800-247-2430 ■ *Web:* www.iowarealty.com	West Des Moines	IA	50266	515-453-6222		652
Iowa Republican Party 621 E Ninth St *Web:* www.iowagop.org	Des Moines	IA	50309	515-282-8105		616-2
Iowa Rotocast Plastics Inc 1712 Moellers Dr *Web:* www.irpinc.com	Decorah	IA	52101	563-382-9636	382-3016	604
Iowa School of Beauty 3320 Line Dr *Web:* www.iowaschoolofbeauty.com	Sioux City	IA	51106	712-274-9733		685
Iowa Select Farms 811 S Oak St PO Box 400 *Web:* www.iowaselect.com	Iowa Falls	IA	50126	641-648-4479	648-4251	10-6
Iowa Soybean Assn 4554 114th St *TF:* 800-383-1423 ■ *Web:* www.iasoybeans.com	Urbandale	IA	50322	515-251-8640		138
Iowa Speedway LLC 3333 Rusty Wallace Dr *Web:* www.iowaspeedway.com	Newton	IA	50208	641-791-8000		642
Iowa Spring Manufacturing & Sales Co 2112 Greene St *TF:* 800-022-2203 ■ *Web:* www.iowaspring.com	Adel	IA	50003	515-993-4791		492
Iowa State Association of Counties 5500 Westown Pkwy *Web:* www.iowacounties.org	West Des Moines	IA	50266	515-244-7181		615
Iowa State Bar Assn 625 E Ct Ave *TF:* 800-457-3729 ■ *Web:* www.iowabar.org	Des Moines	IA	50309	515-243-3179	243-2511	72
Iowa State Fair (state House) PO Box 57130 *Web:* www.iowastatefair.org	Des Moines	IA	50317	515-262-3111		720
Iowa State Library 1007 E Grand Ave *TF:* 800-248-4483 ■ *Web:* www.statelibraryofiowa.org	Des Moines	IA	50319	515-281-4105	281-6191	434-5
Iowa State Penitentiary 2111 330th Ave PO Box 316 *TF:* 800-382-0019 ■ *Web:* www.iowastatepen.com	Fort Madison	IA	52627	319-372-5432	372-2856	213
Iowa State Savings Bank 401 W Adams St *TF:* 888-508-0142 ■ *Web:* www.issbbank.com	Creston	IA	50801	641-782-1000		70
Iowa State University 100 Alumni Hall *TF:* 800-262-3810 ■ *Web:* www.iastate.edu	Ames	IA	50011	515-294-4111	294-2592	166
Iowa State University Parks Library Osborn Dr & Morrill Rd *Web:* www.lib.iastate.edu	Ames	IA	50011	515-294-3642	294-5525	434-6
Iowa State University Research Park Corp 1805 Collaboration Pl Ste 1250 *Web:* www.isupark.org	Ames	IA	50010	515-296-7275	296-9924	166
Iowa Steel & Wire Co 1500 W Van Buren St **Fax Area Code:* 641 ■ *TF:* 800-325-5118 ■ *Web:* iowasteel.com	Centerville	IA	52544	800-325-5118	437-1667*	813
Iowa Trust & Savings Bank 2101 Tenth St *Web:* iowatrustbank.com	Emmetsburg	IA	50536	712-852-3451		70
Iowa Veterinary Medical Assn 1605 N Ankeny Blvd Ste 110 *TF:* 800-369-9564 ■ *Web:* www.iowavma.org	Ankeny	IA	50023	515-965-9237	965-9239	795
Iowa Wesleyan College 601 N Main St **Fax Area Code:* 319 ■ *TF:* 800-582-2383 ■ *Web:* www.iw.edu	Mount Pleasant	IA	52641	800-582-2383	385-6240*	166
Iowa Western Community College *Clarinda* 923 E Washington St *TF:* 800-521-2073 ■ *Web:* www.iwcc.cc.ia.us	Clarinda	IA	51632	712-542-5117	542-4608	162
IP Casino Resort & Spa 850 Bayview Ave *TF:* 888-946 2847 ■ *Web:* www.ipbiloxi.com	Biloxi	MS	39530	228-436-3000		133
IP Convergence Inc PO Box 107 Ste 5 *TF:* 800-813-5106 ■ *Web:* ipcnv.com	Argyle	TX	76226	800-813-5106		180
IP Fabrics Inc 3720 SW 141st Ave Ste 201 *Web:* www.ipfabrics.com	Beaverton	OR	97005	503-444-2400		225
IP Network Solutions Inc 13921 Park Center Rd Ste 400 *Web:* www.ipnsinc.com	Herndon	VA	20171	703-787-0095		180
IPA (Indiana Philanthropy Alliance) 32 E Washington St Ste 1100 *Web:* www.inphilanthropy.org	Indianapolis	IN	46204	317-630-5200	630-5210	48-13
IPAA (Independent Petroleum Association of America) 1201 15th St NW Ste 300 *TF:* 800-433-2851 ■ *Web:* www.ipaa.org	Washington	DC	20005	202-857-4722	857-4799	48-12
IPAC Services Corp 8701 102 St *Web:* www.ipacservices.com	Clairmont	AB	T0H0W0	780-532-7350		186
ipaint.us 1999 Elizabeth St *Web:* www.ipaint.us	North Brunswick	NJ	08902	732-821-8180		550
iPass Inc 3800 Bridge Pkwy *NASDAQ: IPAS* ■ *TF:* 877-236-3807 ■ *Web:* www.ipass.com	Redwood City	CA	94065	650-232-4100	232-4111	394
IPayStation LLC 213 School St Ste 101 *Web:* www.paystation.com	Gardner	MA	01440	978-632-6798		387
IPC Systems Inc Harborside Financial Plz 10 15th Fl *Web:* www.ipc.com	Jersey City	NJ	07311	201-253-2000	253-2361	178-10
IPC Technologies Inc 7200 Glen Forest Dr Ste 100 *TF:* 877-947-2835 ■ *Web:* www.ipctech.com	Richmond	VA	23226	877-947-2835		721

Name / Address	City	State	Zip	Phone	Fax	Class
ipCapital Group Inc						
426 Industrial Ave Ste 150	Williston	VT	05495	802-859-7800	859-0183	463
TF: 888-853-2212 ■ *Web:* www.ipcg.com						
IPD Analytics LLC						
1170 Kane Concourse Ste 300	Bay Harbor Islands	FL	33154	305-662-8515		463
Web: www.ipdanalytics.com						
IPD Company Inc						
11744 NE Ainsworth Cir	Portland	OR	97220	800-444-6473		61
TF: 800-444-6473 ■ *Web:* www.ipdusa.com						
IPG (Integrated Print & Graphics)						
645 Stevenson Rd	South Elgin	IL	60177	847-695-6777		110
Web: www.ipandginc.com						
IPG Photonics Corp 50 Old Webster Rd	Oxford	MA	01540	508-373-1100	373-1103	425
NASDAQ: IPGP ■ *TF:* 877-980-1550 ■ *Web:* www.ipgphotonics.com						
IPHA (Illinois Pharmacists Assn)						
204 W Cook St	Springfield	IL	62704	217-522-7300	522-7349	585
Web: www.ipha.org						
IPHC (International Pentecostal Holiness Church)						
PO Box 12609	Oklahoma City	OK	73157	405-787-7110	789-3957	48-20
TF: 888-474-2966 ■ *Web:* iphc.org						
Iphorgan Ltd						
195 Arlington Heights Rd Ste 125	Buffalo Grove	IL	60089	847-808-5500		428
Web: iphorgan.com						
IPI (Iowa Prison Industries)						
1445 E Grand Ave	Des Moines	IA	50316	515-242-5770	242-5779	630
TF: 800-670-4537 ■ *Web:* www.iaprisonind.com						
IPI (International Parking Institute)						
1330 Braddock Pl Ste 350	Alexandria	VA	22314	571-699-3011		49-21
Web: www.parking.org						
iPipeline Canada						
5500 N Service Rd Ste 1107	Burlington	ON	L7L6W6	905-333-3353		179
TF: 877-565-1828 ■ *Web:* www.ipipeline.ca						
Iplastics LLC 300 N Cummings Ln	Washington	IL	61571	309-444-8884		604
TF: 888-618-9627 ■ *Web:* www.ivpplastics.com						
IPMA-HR (International Public Management Association for Hum Res)						
1617 Duke St	Alexandria	VA	22314	703-549-7100	684-0948	49-12
TF: 800-381-8378 ■ *Web:* www.ipma-hr.org						
IPMI (International Precious Metals Institute)						
5101 N 12th Ave Ste C	Pensacola	FL	32504	850-476-1156	476-1548	49-4
Web: www.ipmi.org						
IPMP (Institute for Participatory Management & Planning)						
PO Box 1937	Monterey	CA	93942	831-373-4292	373-0760	393
Web: www.consentbuilding.com						
IPNI (International Plant Nutrition Institute)						
3500 Parkway Ln Ste 550	Norcross	GA	30092	770-447-0335	448-0439	48-2
Web: www.ipni.net						
IPOfferings LLC 75 Montebello Rd	Suffern	NY	10901	845-337-6911		225
Web: www.ipofferings.com						
IPP (International Process Plants)						
410 Princeton Hightstown Rd	West Windsor	NJ	08550	609-586-8004	586-0002	385
Web: www.ippe.com						
IPPF/WHR (International Planned Parenthood Federation - Western Hemisphere Region)						
125 Maiden Ln 9th Fl	New York	NY	10038	212-248-6400	248-4221	48-5
Web: www.ippfwhr.org						
IPPL (International Primate Protection League)						
120 Primate Ln	Summerville	SC	29483	843-871-2280	871-7988	48-3
Web: www.ippl.org						
IPRA (International Professional Rodeo Assn)						
1412 S Agnew	Oklahoma City	OK	73108	405-235-6540		48-22
TF: 800-639-9002 ■ *Web:* www.ipra-rodeo.com						
IPRIME (Industrial Partnership for Research in Interfacial & Materials Engineering)						
151 Amundson Hall 421 Washington Ave SE	Minneapolis	MN	55455	612-625-1269	626-1686	668
TF: 800-822-6757 ■ *Web:* www.iprime.umn.edu						
IPRO (Island Peer Review Organization Inc)						
1979 Marcus Ave	Lake Success	NY	11042	516-326-7767	328-2310	353
TF: 888-880-9976 ■ *Web:* ipro.org						
IPRO Tech LLC 1700 N Desert Dr Ste 101	Tempe	AZ	85281	877-324-4776	324-4784*	179
**Fax Area Code:* 602 ■ *TF:* 877-324-4776 ■ *Web:* iprotech.com						
Iprocess Online Inc						
1050 Hull St Ste 100	Baltimore	MD	21230	410-547-3270		2
Web: www.iprocessonline.com						
IPS (Institute for Policy Studies)						
1112 16th St NW Ste 600	Washington	DC	20036	202-234-9382		634
Web: ips-dc.org						
IPS (Industrial Parts Specialties)						
630 Lot Rd	Port Allen	LA	70767	225-408-7500	408-3081	454
TF: 800-272-3019 ■ *Web:* www.indparts.com						
IPS Corp 455 W Victoria St	Compton	CA	90220	310-898-3300	853-5008*	3
**Fax Area Code:* 901 ■ *TF:* 800-888-8312 ■ *Web:* www.ipscorp.com						
IPS Group Inc 4343 Easton Rd	Saint Joseph	MO	64503	816-233-1800		207
Web: www.continentalscrew.com						
IPS Worldwide LLC						
265 Clyde Morris Blvd Ste 100	Ormond Beach	FL	32174	386-672-7727		225
Web: www.ipsww.com						
IPSCO (Interstate Paper Supply Company Inc)						
103 Good St PO Box 670	Roscoe	PA	15477	724-938-2218	938-3415	554
Web: www.ipscoinc.com						
Ipsen Biopharmaceuticals Inc						
106 Allen Rd 3rd Fl	Basking Ridge	NJ	07920	908-275-6300	275-6301	85
TF: 866-837-2422 ■ *Web:* www.ipsenus.com						
Ipsen Inc PO Box 6266	Rockford	IL	61125	815-332-4941	332-4995	318
TF: 800-727-7625 ■ *Web:* www.ipsenusa.com						
Ipsenault Co, The 3791 River Rd N Ste F	Keizer	OR	97303	503-390-8968	390-5934	195
TF: 866-240-7032 ■ *Web:* ipsenault.com						
Ipsos 160 Bloor St E Ste 300	Toronto	ON	M4W1B9	416-324-2900		466
Web: www.ipsos.com						
Ipsos 3550 Columbia Pkwy	Cincinnati	OH	45226	513-872-4300		193
Web: www.ipsos.com						
Ipsos-ASI Inc						
Corporate Pk 301 Merritt 7	Norwalk	CT	06851	203-840-3400		466
Web: www.ipsos.com						
Ipss Inc 150 Isabella St	Ottawa	ON	K1S1V7	613-232-2228	231-4888	693
TF: 866-532-2207 ■ *Web:* www.ipss.ca						
Ipswich Shellfish Group 8 Hayward St	Ipswich	MA	01938	978-356-4371	356-9235	297-5
TF: 800-477-9424 ■ *Web:* www.ipswichshellfish.com						
Ipswich State Bank						
301 First Ave PO Box 8	Ipswich	SD	57451	605-426-6031	426-6035	70
Web: isbipswich.com						
Ipswitch Inc 83 Hartwell Ave	Lexington	MA	02421	781-676-5700	676-5710	178-12
TF: 800-793-4825 ■ *Web:* www.ipswitch.com						
IPT (Institute for Professionals in Taxation)						
600 Northpark Town Ctr						
1200 Abernathy Rd Ste L-2	Atlanta	GA	30328	404-240-2300	240-2315	49-10
Web: www.ipt.org						
IPTV (Idaho Public Television)						
1455 N Orchard St	Boise	ID	83706	208-373-7220	373-7245	632
TF: 800-543-6868 ■ *Web:* idahoptv.org						
IPV (Inflection Point Ventures)						
1 Innovation Way Ste 302	Newark	DE	19711	302-452-1120	452-1122	792
Web: www.inflectpoint.com						
IQ BackOffice LLC						
2121 Rosecrans Ave Ste 3350	El Segundo	CA	90245	310-322-2311		194
Web: www.iqbackoffice.com						
IQ Technology Solutions						
5595 Equity Ave Ste 300	Reno	NV	89502	775-352-2301	352-2344	463
TF: 866-842-4748 ■ *Web:* www.iqisit.com						
IQE Inc 119 Technology Dr	Bethlehem	PA	18015	610-861-6930	861-5273	696
Web: www.iqep.com						
IQMax Inc						
15720 Brixham Hill Ave Ste 300	Charlotte	NC	28277	704-377-2202		177
IQMS Inc 2231 Wisteria Ln	Paso Robles	CA	93446	805-227-1122		177
Web: www.iqms.com						
Iqr Consulting Inc						
1915 Gardenview Cir	Santa Rosa	CA	95403	707-328-3475		225
Web: iqrconsulting.com						
Iqs Inc						
24950 Country Club Blvd Ste 120	North Olmsted	OH	44070	440-333-1344	508-2315	177
TF: 800-635-5901 ■ *Web:* iqs.com						
IQT (Investment Quality Trends)						
2888 Loker Ave E Ste 116	Carlsbad	CA	92010	866-927-5250	927-5251	531-9
TF: 866-927-5250 ■ *Web:* iqtrends.com						
IQVIA 16720 Trans-Canada Hwy	Kirkland	QC	H9H5M3	514-428-6000		582
TF: 866-267-4479 ■ *Web:* www.iqvia.com						
IQware Inc						
5850 Coral Ridge Dr Ste 309	Coral Springs	FL	33076	954-698-5151		180
TF: 877-698-5151 ■ *Web:* www.iqwareinc.com						
IR Engraving LLC 5901 Lewis Rd	Sandston	VA	23150	804-222-2821	226-3462	481
Web: irengraving.com						
Ira G. Steffy & Son Inc 460 Wenger Dr	Ephrata	PA	17522	717-733-2001	733-0971	363
Web: www.iragsteffyandson.com						
Ira Green Inc 177 Georgia Ave	Providence	RI	02905	800-663-7487		409
TF: 800-663-7487 ■ *Web:* www.iragreen.com						
Ira H. Weinstock PC						
800 N Second St	Harrisburg	PA	17102	717-238-1657		41
Web: paworkerscompensation.law						
Ira Higdon 150 Iga Way	Cairo	GA	39828	229-377-1272		345
Web: www.irahigdongc.com						
IRA Services Trust Co						
1160 Industrial Rd Ste 1	San Carlos	CA	94070	650-593-2221		225
TF: 800-248-8447 ■ *Web:* www.iraservices.com						
Iracore International LLC						
3516 E 13th Ave	Hibbing	MN	55746	218-262-5211	263-9731	676
Web: www.irproducts.com						
Irashiai Sushi Pub & Japanese Restaurant						
115 Pelham Rd	Greenville	SC	29615	864-271-0900		671
Web: www.irashiai.com						
Racing Board						
100 W Randolph St Ste 5-700	Chicago	IL	60601	312-814-2600	814-5062	712
Web: www2.illinois.gov						
Irby Construction Co						
318 Old Hwy 49 S	Richland	MS	39218	601-709-4729		188-10
TF: 800-872-0615 ■ *Web:* www.irbyconst.com						
IRC (International Rescue Committee)						
122 E 42nd St	New York	NY	10168	212-551-3000	551-3179	48-5
Web: www.rescue.org						
IRC Building Sciences Group						
2121 Argentia Rd Ste 401	Mississauga	ON	L5N2X4	905-607-7244		463
TF: 888-607-5245 ■ *Web:* www.ircgroup.com						
IRCL (Indian River County Library)						
1600 21st St	Vero Beach	FL	32960	772-770-5060	770-5066	434-3
Web: www.irclibrary.org						
IRD LLC 4740 Allmond Ave	Louisville	KY	40209	502-366-0916	238-1001	407
TF: 888-473-2251 ■ *Web:* www.irdbalancing.com						
Iredale Mineral Cosmetics Ltd						
50 Church St	Great Barrington	MA	01230	413-644-9900		238
TF: 877-869-9420 ■ *Web:* janeiredale.com						
Iredell County						
200 S Center St PO Box 788	Statesville	NC	28687	704-878-3000	878-5355	338
Web: www.co.iredell.nc.us						
Iredell County Library						
201 N Tradd St	Statesville	NC	28677	704-878-3090		434-3
Web: www.iredell.lib.nc.us						
Iredell Health System						
557 Brookdale Dr	Statesville	NC	28677	704-873-5661		374-3
Web: www.iredellhealth.org						
Ireland						
Consulate General						
100 Pine St Ste 3350	San Francisco	CA	94111	415-392-4214	392-0885	257
TF: 800-777-0133 ■ *Web:* www.dfa.ie						
Ireland Army Community Hospital						
289 Ireland Ave	Fort Knox	KY	40121	502-624-9333		374-4
Web: www.iach.knox.amedd.army.mil						
Ireland Bank 33 Bannock St	Malad City	ID	83252	208-766-2254		70
Web: ireland-bank.com						
Irell & Manella LLP						
1800 Avenue of the Stars Ste 900	Los Angeles	CA	90067	310-277-1010	203-7199	428
Web: irell.com						
iRely LLC 4242 Flagstaff Cove	Fort Wayne	IN	46815	800-433-5724	486-5187*	178-1
**Fax Area Code:* 260 ■ *TF:* 800-433-5724 ■ *Web:* www.irely.com						
IREM (Institute of Real Estate Management)						
430 N Michigan Ave	Chicago	IL	60611	312-329-6000	338-4736*	49-17
**Fax Area Code:* 800 ■ *TF:* 800-837-0706 ■ *Web:* irem.org						
Irene's 529 Bienville St	New Orleans	LA	70130	504-529-8811		671
Web: www.irenesnola.com						
Irene's Myomassology Institute Inc						
26061 Franklin Rd	Southfield	MI	48033	248-350-1400	350-8068	167-3
Web: www.imieducation.com						

	Phone	Fax	Class
IRET 1400 31st Ave SW Ste 60 .... Minot ND 58702 *NYSE: IRET* ■ *TF:* 888-478-4738 ■ *Web:* www.iretapartments.com	701-837-4738	838-7785	654
IRET (Institute for Research on the Economics of Taxation) 529 14th St NW Ste 420 .... Washington DC 20045 *Web:* www.iret.org	202-464-5113		634
Irex Contracting Group 120 N Lime St .... Lancaster PA 17608 *TF:* 800-487-7255 ■ *Web:* www.irexcontracting.com	800-487-7255		189-9
IRF (International Road Federation) 500 Mongomery St 5th Fl .... Alexandria VA 22314 *Web:* www.irfnet.ch	703-535-1001	535-1007	49-3
IRGA (International Reprographic Assn) 401 N Michigan Ave Ste 2200 .... Chicago IL 60611 **Fax Area Code:* 312 ■ *TF:* 800-833-4742 ■ *Web:* www.apdsp.org	877-226-6839	673-6724*	49-16
IRI (Industrial Research Institute Inc) 2200 Clarendon Blvd Ste 1102 .... Arlington VA 22201 *Web:* www.iriweb.org	703-647-2580	647-2581	49-19
Iridescence 2901 Grand River Ave .... Detroit MI 48201 *Web:* www.motorcitycasino.com	313-237-6732		671
Iridex Corp 1212 Terra Bella Ave .... Mountain View CA 94043 *NASDAQ: IRIX* ■ *TF:* 800-388-4747 ■ *Web:* www.iridex.com	650-940-4700	940-4710	424
Iridian Asset Management LLC 276 Post Rd W .... Westport CT 06880 *Web:* www.iridian.com	203-341-7800		194
Iridium Satellite LLC 6701 Democracy Blvd .... Bethesda MD 20817 *Web:* www.iridium.com	301-571-6200	571-6250	736
Irina S. Shea, Attorney At Law LLC 88 W Main St .... Ramsey NJ 07446 *Web:* irinashea.com	201-327-7000		41
Irina Sprishen CPA PC 101 E Pennsylvania Blvd .... Feasterville-Trevose PA 19053 *Web:* sprishen.com	215-942-2980		2
Irion County 209 N Parkview PO Box 736 .... Mertzon TX 76941 *Web:* www.co.irion.tx.us	325-835-2421	835-7941	338
Iris Films 2600 Tenth St Ste 413 .... Berkeley CA 94710 *Web:* www.irisfilms.org	510-845-5415	841-3336	513
Iris Group Inc, The 1675 Faraday Ave .... Carlsbad CA 92008 *TF:* 800-347-1103 ■ *Web:* www.irisgroup.com	760-431-1103		4
Iris Molecular Diagnostics Inc 9172 Eton Ave .... Chatsworth CA 91311 **Fax Area Code:* 818	760-438-9923	700-9661*	743
Iris Software Inc 200 Metroplex Dr Ste 300 .... Edison NJ 08817 *Web:* www.irissoftware.com	732-393-0034		180
Iris Telehealth 114 W 7th St .... Austin TX 78701 *TF:* 888-285-2269 ■ *Web:* www.iristelehealth.com	888-285-2269		89
Iris USA Inc 11111 80th Ave .... Pleasant Prairie WI 53158 **Fax Area Code:* 262 ■ *TF:* 800-320-4747 ■ *Web:* www.irisusainc.com	800-320-4747	612-1010*	607
iRise 2301 Rosecrans Ave Ste 4100 .... El Segundo CA 90245 *TF:* 800-556-0399 ■ *Web:* www.irise.com	800-556-0399		177
Irish American Heritage Ctr 4626 N Knox Ave .... Chicago IL 60630 *Web:* irish-american.org	773-282-7035		50-2
Irish Classical Theatre 625 Main St .... Buffalo NY 14203 *Web:* www.irishclassicaltheatre.com	716-853-1380	853-0592	573-4
Irish Construction Inc 2641 River Ave .... Rosemead CA 91770 *Web:* www.irishteam.com	626-288-8530		188-10
Irish Cultural & Heritage Center of Wisconsin 2133 W Wisconsin Ave .... Milwaukee WI 53233 *Web:* www.ichc.net	414-345-8800		50-2
Irish Democrat Pub 3207 First Ave SE .... Cedar Rapids IA 52402 *Web:* www.irishdemocrat.net	319-364-9896		671
Irish Lion 212 W Kirkwood Ave 1/2 Block West of the Sq .... Bloomington IN 47404 *Web:* www.irishlion.com	812-336-9076		671
IrishCentral LLC 875 Sixth Ave .... New York NY 10001 *Web:* www.irishcentral.com	212-871-0111		387
IRMG (International Restaurant Management Group Inc) 4531 Ponce de Leon Blvd Ste 300 .... Coral Gables FL 33146 *Web:* www.irmgusa.com	305-476-1611	476-9622	670
IRMI (International Risk Management Institute Inc) 12222 Merit Dr Ste 1600 .... Dallas TX 75251 *TF:* 800-827-4242 ■ *Web:* www.irmi.com	972-960-7693	371-5120	401
Iron & Metals Inc 5555 Franklin St .... Denver CO 80216 *TF:* 800-776-7910 ■ *Web:* www.ironandmetals.com	303-292-5555	292-0513	686
Iron Bridge Resources Inc 1500 308 Fourth Ave SW .... Calgary AB T2P0H7 *TF:* 877-414-7782 ■ *Web:* www.ironbridgeres.com	403-930-6300		536
Iron City Workplace Services 6640 Frankstown Ave .... Pittsburgh PA 15206 *TF:* 800-532-2010 ■ *Web:* www.ironcityuniform.com	412-661-2001	661-9356	442
Iron County 2 S Sixth St Ste 7 .... Crystal Falls MI 49920 *Web:* www.ironmi.org	906-875-3301	875-0655	338
Iron County 300 Taconite St Ste 101 .... Hurley WI 54534 *Web:* www.co.iron.wi.gov	715-561-3636	561-2128	338
Iron County 220 S Shepherd St .... Ironton MO 63650 *Web:* www.icsomo.org	573-546-7051		338
Iron County 68 S 100 E .... Parowan UT 84761 *Web:* www.ironcounty.net	435-477-8360	477-8847	338
Iron County Community Credit Union 5702 W Us Hwy 2 .... Hurley WI 54534 *Web:* ironcccu.com	715-561-2842		219
Iron County Historical Museum (ICHM) 100 Brady Ave .... Caspian MI 49915 *Web:* www.ironcountyhistoricalmuseum.org	906-265-2617		637-2
Iron County Miner 216 Copper St .... Hurley WI 54534 *Web:* www.ironcountyminer.com	715-561-3405		532-2
Iron Design Inc 120 N Aurora St Ste 5A .... Ithaca NY 14850 *Web:* www.irondesign.com	607-275-9544	275-0370	344
Iron Hill Brewery 2502 W Sixth St .... Wilmington DE 19805 *Web:* www.ironhillbrewery.com	302-472-2739		670
Iron Horse 6034 SE Milwaukie Ave .... Portland OR 97202 *Web:* www.portlandironhorse.com	503-232-1826		671
Iron Horse Energy Services Inc 1901 Dirkson Dr NE .... Redcliff AB T0J2P0 *TF:* 877-526-4666 ■ *Web:* www.ihes.ca	403-526-4600		540
Iron Island Museum 998 E Lovejoy St .... Buffalo NY 14206 *Web:* www.ironislandmuseum.com	716-892-3084		520
Iron Monkey 99 Greene St .... Jersey City NJ 07302 *Web:* www.ironmonkey.com	201-435-5756	433-0762	671
Iron Mountain 745 Atlantic Ave .... Boston MA 02111 *NYSE: IRM* ■ *TF:* 800-899-4766 ■ *Web:* www.ironmountain.com	800-899-4766		803-1
Iron Range Historical Society 5454 Grand Ave .... McKinley MN 55741 *Web:* www.ironrangehistoricalsociety.org	218-749-3150		48-13
Iron Range Tourism Bureau 111 Stn 44 Rd .... Eveleth MN 55734 *TF:* 800-777-8497 ■ *Web:* ironrange.org	218-749-8161		206
Iron Road Healthcare 1040 N 2200 W PO Box 161020 .... Salt Lake City UT 84116 *TF:* 800-547-0421 ■ *Web:* www.uphealth.com	801-595-4300	595-4399	391-3
Iron Skillet Restaurant, The 2489 W 30th St .... Indianapolis IN 46222 *Web:* www.ironskillet.net	317-923-6353		671
Iron Systems Inc 980 Mission Ct .... Fremont CA 94539 **Fax Area Code:* 408 ■ *Web:* www.ironsystems.com	714-408-4700	943-8222*	631
Iron Tribe Franchise LLC 300 27th St S .... Birmingham AL 35233 *Web:* www.irontribefitness.com	205-226-8669		354
Iron Workers Local 377 570 Barneveld Ave .... San Francisco CA 94124 *Web:* ironworkers377.com	415-285-3880		414
Iron-a-way Inc 220 W Jackson St .... Morton IL 61550 *TF:* 800-536-9495 ■ *Web:* ironaway.com	309-266-7232		362
Ironclad Inc 71 Stevenson St Ste 600 .... San Francisco CA 94105 *TF:* 855-999-4766 ■ *Web:* www.ironcladapp.com	855-999-4766		113
Irondequoit Public Library 1290 Titus Ave .... Rochester NY 14617 *Web:* www.irondoquoitlibrary.org	585-336-6062		434-3
Ironmark Inc 9040 Jct Dr .... Annapolis Junction MD 20701 *TF:* 888-775-3737 ■ *Web:* ironmarkusa.com	888-775-3737		627
IronMaster LLC 14562 167th Ave SE .... Monroe WA 98272 *TF:* 800-533-3339 ■ *Web:* www.ironmaster.com	360-217-7780	217-8415	267
Ironmind Enterprises Inc 11992 Charles Dr .... Grass Valley CA 95945 *Web:* www.ironmind.com	530-272-3579		711
Ironplanet Inc 5667 Gibraltar Dr Ste 200 .... Pleasanton CA 94588 *TF:* 888-433-5426 ■ *Web:* www.ironplanet.com	925-225-8800	225-8610	51
Ironrock Capital Inc 1201 Millerton St SE .... Canton OH 44707 *Web:* www.ironrock.com	330-484-4887	484-3584	751
Ironspeed 2870 Zanker Rd Ste 210 .... San Jose CA 95134 *Web:* www.ironspeed.com	408-228-3400		177
Irontite Products Inc 2525 18th St SW Ste D .... Cedar Rapids IA 52404 *Web:* www.irontite.com	319-377-9421		3
Ironwood Capital Ltd 45 Nod Rd .... Avon CT 06001 *Web:* ironwoodcap.com	860-409-2100		690
Ironwood Grille 400 Avenue of the Champions .... Palm Beach Gardens FL 33418 *Web:* www.pgaresort.com	561-627-4852		671
Ironwood Industries Inc 115 S Bradley Rd .... Libertyville IL 60048 *Web:* www.ironind.com	847-362-8681	362-9190	604
Ironwood Lithographers Inc 455 S 52nd St .... Tempe AZ 85281 *Web:* www.ironwoodlitho.com	480-829-7700		627
Ironwood Plastics Inc 1235 Wall St .... Ironwood MI 49938 *Web:* www.ironwood.com	906-932-5025		608
Ironwood State Prison 19005 Wiley's Well Rd .... Blythe CA 92225 *Web:* www.cdcr.ca.gov	760-921-3000		213
Iroquois County 1001 E Grant St Rm 104 .... Watseka IL 60970 *Web:* www.co.iroquois.il.us	815-432-6978	432-6999	338
Iroquois County Genealogical Society (ICGS) Old Courthouse Museum 103 W Cherry St .... Watseka IL 60970 *Web:* www.iroquoiscountygenealogy.org	815-432-3730	432-3732	49-19
Iroquois County State Wildlife Area RR 1 2803 E 3300 N Rd .... Beaverville IL 60912 *Web:* www.dnr.illinois.gov	815-435-2218		565
Iroquois Gas Transmission System LP 1 Corporate Dr Ste 600 .... Shelton CT 06484 *TF:* 800-888-3982 ■ *Web:* www.iroquois.com	203-925-7200	929-9501	325
Iroquois Indian Museum 324 Caverns Rd .... Howes Cave NY 12092 *Web:* www.iroquoismuseum.org	518-296-8949		520
Iroquois Industries Inc 25101 Groesbeck Hwy .... Warren MI 48089 *Web:* www.iroquoisind.com	586-771-5734		489
Iroquois New York 49 W 44th St .... New York NY 10036 *TF:* 800-332-7220 ■ *Web:* www.iroquoisny.com	212-840-3080		379
Iroquois Products of Chicago 2220 W 56th St .... Chicago IL 60636 *TF:* 800-453-3355 ■ *Web:* www.iroquoisproducts.com	800-453-3355		199
Irosoft 3100 Boul De La Cote-vertu Ste 510 .... Montreal QC H4R2J8 *Web:* www.irosoft.com	514-920-0020		180
Irpinia Kitchens 278 Newkirk Rd .... Richmond Hill ON L4C3G7 *Web:* irpinia.com	905-780-7722		321
Irr Supply Centers Inc 908 Niagara Falls Blvd .... North Tonawanda NY 14120 *Web:* irrsupply.com	716-692-1600	692-1611	612
IRRC (Investor Responsibility Research Center Institute) 40 Wall St 28th Fl .... New York NY 10005 *Web:* www.irrcinstitute.org	646-512-5807		637-2
Irregardless Cafe 901 W Morgan St .... Raleigh NC 27603 *Web:* www.irregardless.com	919-833-8898		671
Irresistibles 7 Hawkes St .... Marblehead MA 01945 *TF:* 800-555-9865 ■ *Web:* www.irresistibles.com	781-631-8903		157-6

Name / Address	Phone	Fax	Class
Irrigation Assn (IA) 6540 Arlington Blvd .... Falls Church VA 22042 *Web:* www.irrigation.org	703-536-7080	536-7019	48-2
Irrigation By Design Inc 175 James Ave N .... Minneapolis MN 55405 *Web:* irrigationbydesign.com	763-559-7771		422
Irrometer Company Inc 1425 Palmyrita Ave......................... Riverside CA 92507 *Web:* www.irrometer.com	951-682-9505	682-9501	472
IRS (Internal Revenue Service) 1111 Constitution Ave NW................. Washington DC 20224 *Web:* www.irs.gov	202-622-5000		340-18
IRS (Interstate Registration Service Inc) PO Box 200005 .... Arlington TX 76006 *TF:* 800-383-5829 ■ *Web:* www.fueltax.net	469-733-1620	733-1621	192
IRSC (Indian River State College) 3209 Virginia Ave......................... Fort Pierce FL 34981 *TF:* 866-792-4772 ■ *Web:* www.irsc.edu	772-462-4772	462-4699	162
Irsfeld Pharmacy PC 33 Ninth St W........... Dickinson ND 58601 *TF:* 800-279-6053 ■ *Web:* www.irsfeldpharmacy.com	701-483-4858	483-4926	237
IRTS (International Radio & Television Society Foundation Inc) 1697 Broadway 10th Fl...................... New York NY 10019 *Web:* www.irtsfoundation.org	212-867-6650		49-14
Irvin Automotive Products Inc 2600 Centerpoint Pkwy....................... Pontiac MI 48341 *Web:* www.irvinautomotive.com	248-451-4100	451-4101	60
Irvin Dick Inc 475 Wilson Ave................... Shelby MT 59474 *Web:* dickirvininc.com	406-434-5862		780
Irvin Simon Photographers Inc 146 Meacham Ave .... Elmont NY 11003 *TF:* 800-540-4701 ■ *Web:* www.irvinsimon.com	800-540-4701		592
Irvine Access Floors Inc 9425 Washington Blvd .... Laurel MD 20723 *TF:* 800-969-8870 ■ *Web:* www.irvineaccessfloors.com	301-617-9333	617-9907	491
Irvine Barclay Theatre 4242 Campus Dr........... Irvine CA 92612 *Web:* www.thebarclay.org	949-854-4646		572
Irvine Co 550 Newport Center Dr .... Newport Beach CA 92660 *TF:* 844-238-2579 ■ *Web:* www.irvinecompany.com	949-720-2000		653
Irvine Company Apartment Communities 2500 Baypointe Dr .... Newport Beach CA 92660 *TF:* 844-718-2918 ■ *Web:* www.irvinecompanyapartments.com	844-354-7395		655
Irvine Electronics Inc 1601 Alton Pky Ste A .... Irvine CA 92606 *Web:* www.irvine-electronics.com	949-250-0315	250-0318	625
Irvine Sensors Corp 3001 Red Hill Ave Bldg 3-108 .... Costa Mesa CA 92626 *Web:* www.irvine-sensors.com	714-444-8700	444-8773	696
Irvine Technology Corp 17900 Von Karman Ste 100 .... Irvine CA 92614 **Fax Area Code:* 714 ■ *TF:* 866-322-4482 ■ *Web:* www.irvinetechcorp.com	866-322-4482	434-8869*	194
Irvine Valley College 5500 Irvine Center Dr.......................... Irvine CA 92618 *Web:* www.ivc.edu	949-451-5100		162
Irving A. Miller Inc 2550 W Chester Pk.......................... Broomall PA 19008 *Web:* www.irvingamiller.com	610-356-1130		652
Irving Arts Ctr 3333 N MacArthur Blvd............. Irving TX 75062 *Web:* www.irvingartscenter.com	972-252-7558	570-4962	572
Irving Burton Associates Inc 3150 Fairview Park Dr Ste 301 .... Falls Church VA 22042 *Web:* www.ibacorp.us	703-575-8359		466
Irving City Hall 825 W Irving Blvd................. Irving TX 75060 *Web:* www.ci.irving.tx.us	972-721-2600	721-2420	337
Irving Convention & Visitors Bureau 500 W Las Colinas Blvd........................ Irving TX 75039 *TF:* 800-247-8464 ■ *Web:* www.irvingtexas.com	972-252-7476		206
Irving Mall 3880 Irving Mall .... Irving TX 75062 *Web:* shopirvingmall.com	972-255-0572		460
Irving Materials Inc (IMI) 8032 N SR-9............................. Greenfield IN 46140 *Web:* irvmat.com	317-536-6650	326-3105	182
Irving Materials Inc 8032 N State Road 9....................... Greenfield IN 46140 *Web:* www.irvmat.com	317-326-3101		182
Irving Michael Gustilo CPA 140 E Walnut Ave Ste A .... Monrovia CA 91016 *Web:* imgcpas.com	626-305-3110	305-3115	2
Irving Shipbuilding Inc 3099 Barrington St........................... Halifax NS B3K5M7 *Web:* www.irvingshipbuilding.com	902-423-9271		698
Irving Tool & Manufacturing Company Inc 2249 Wall St............................... Garland TX 75041 *Web:* www.irvingtool.com	972-926-4000	926-4099	697
Irvington Public Library 5 Civic Sq............ Irvington NJ 07111 *Web:* www.irvingtonpubliclibrary.org	973-372-6400	372-6860	434-3
Irwin Army Community Hospital 600 Caisson Hill Rd .... Fort Riley KS 66442	785-239-7000		374-4
Irwin Car & Equipment 9953 Broadway St .... Irwin PA 15642 *Web:* www.irwincar.com	724-864-8900		480
Irwin County 620 S Irwin Ave .... Ocilla GA 31774 *Web:* www.ocillachamber.net	229-468-0050		338
Irwin Electric Membership Corp 915 W Fourth St.............................. Ocilla GA 31774 *TF:* 800-237-3745 ■ *Web:* www.irwinemc.com	229-468-7415		245
Irwin Engineers Inc 33 W Central St .... Natick MA 01760 *Web:* irwinengineers.com	508-653-8007		261
Irwin Industries Inc 3201 International Airport Dr Ste 600........... Charlotte NC 28208 *Web:* www.irwinindustries.com	704-898-1338		186
Irwin Manufacturing Corp 398 Fitzgerald Hwy............................ Ocilla GA 31774	229-468-9481		155-4
Irwin Naturals 5310 Beethoven St............ Los Angeles CA 90066 *TF:* 800-297-3273 ■ *Web:* www.appliednutrition.com	310-306-3636		799
Irwin Seating Company Inc 3251 Fruit Ridge NW .... Grand Rapids MI 49544 *TF:* 866-464-7946 ■ *Web:* www.irwinseating.com	616-574-7400		319-3
ISA (International Sign Assn) 1001 N Fairfax St Ste 301.................... Alexandria VA 22314 *Web:* www.signs.org	703-836-4012	836-8353	49-4
ISA (International Society of Arboriculture) PO Box 3129 .... Champaign IL 61826 *TF:* 888-472-8733 ■ *Web:* www.isa-arbor.com	217-355-9411	355-9516	48-2
ISA (International Studies Assn) University of Arizona 324 Social Sciences .... Tucson AZ 85721 *Web:* www.isanet.org	520-621-2327		48-11
ISA (Indiana Soybean Alliance) 8425 Keystone Crossing Ste 200 .... Indianapolis IN 46240 *TF:* 800-735-0195 ■ *Web:* www.indianasoybean.com	317-347-3620	347-3626	139
Isa Restaurant 3324 Steiner St............ San Francisco CA 94123 *Web:* www.isarestaurant.com	415-567-9588		671
Isaac Farrar Mansion 17 Second St .... Bangor ME 04401 *Web:* www.bangory.org	207-941-2808	941-2812	50-3
Isaac's Deli Inc 354 N Prince St Ste 220..................... Lancaster PA 17603 *Web:* www.isaacsrestaurants.com	717-394-0623	393-0955	670
Isaacs Friedberg LLP 555 S Flower St Ste 4250.................. Los Angeles CA 90071 *Web:* ifcounsel.com	213-929-5550		41
Isaacson & Arfman PA 128 Monroe St NE .... Albuquerque NM 87108 *Web:* iacivil.com	505-268-8828		256
Isaak Bond Investments Inc 3900 S Wadsworth Blvd Ste 590 .... Lakewood CO 80235	303-623-7500		690
Isabel Bloom LLC 736 Federal St Ste 2100.................... Davenport IA 52803 *TF:* 800-273-5436 ■ *Web:* www.ibloom.com	800-273-5436		183
Isabella County 200 N Main St........... Mount Pleasant MI 48858 *Web:* www.isabellacounty.org	989-772-0911	773-7431	338
Isabella Freedman Jewish Retreat Ctr 116 Johnson Rd......................... Falls Village CT 06031 *TF:* 800-398-2630 ■ *Web:* www.hazon.org	860-824-5991		673
Isabella Medical Care Facility 1222 North Dr........................ Mount Pleasant MI 48858 *Web:* mcf.isabellacounty.org	989-772-2957	772-3669	450
Isabella Stewart Gardner Museum 25 Evans Way............................... Boston MA 02115 *Web:* www.gardnermuseum.org	617-566-1401		520
ISACA (Information Systems Audit & Control Assn) 3701 Algonquin Rd Ste 1010 .... Rolling Meadows IL 60008 *Web:* www.isaca.org	847-253-1545	253-1443	48-9
I-Safe America 6189 El Camino Real Ste 201................. Carlsbad CA 92009 *Web:* www.isafe.org	760-603-7911	603-8382	41
Isagenix International LLC 2225 S Price Rd........................... Chandler AZ 85286 *TF:* 877-877-8111 ■ *Web:* www.isagenix.com	480-889-5747	636-5386	296-11
Isaksen Promotional Specialties 4620 Churchill St .... Shoreview MN 55126 *Web:* www.isaksenpromotions.com	651-481-9092	481-1509	7
Isani Consultants 3143 Yellowstone Blvd........................ Houston TX 77054 *Web:* www.isaniconsultants.com	713-747-2399		261
Isanti County 555 18th Ave SW.............. Cambridge MN 55008 *Web:* www.co.isanti.mn.us	763-689-3859	689-8226	338
ISAR (International Society for Animal Rights) PO Box F .... Clarks Summit PA 18411 *TF:* 888-589-6397 ■ *Web:* www.isaronline.org	570-586-2200	586-9580	48-3
ISB (International Society of Bassists) 14070 Proton Rd Ste 100...................... Dallas TX 75244 *Web:* www.isbworldoffice.com	972-233-9107	490-4219	48-4
ISBS (International Specialized Book Services Inc) 920 NE 58th Ave Ste 300 .... Portland OR 97213 *Web:* www.isbs.com	503-287-3093	280-8832	96
ISBX Corp 3415 S Sepulveda Blvd Ste 1250 .... Los Angeles CA 90034 *Web:* www.isbx.com	310-437-8010		177
ISC (Internal Sound and Communications Inc) 10500 Chicago Dr Ste 80 .... Zeeland MI 49464 **Fax Area Code:* 800 ■ *TF:* 800-777-1905 ■ *Web:* www.isc-inc.com	616-772-4875	772-4995*	246
ISC Consultants Inc 345 Hoyt St Ste 1000 .... Brooklyn NY 11231 *Web:* www.isc.com	212-477-8800	477-9895	449
ISC Engineering 4351 Schaefer Ave .... Chino CA 91710 *Web:* www.iscengineering.com	909-203-1121		256
ISC Group Inc 3500 Oak Lawn Ave Ste 400......... Dallas TX 75219 *Web:* iscgroup.com	214-520-1115		401
ISC Kentucky 12305 Westport Rd Ste 1 .... Louisville KY 40245 *Web:* www.iscky.com	502-292-5097		174
ISC Sales Inc 4421 Tradition Trl.................. Plano TX 75093 *TF:* 800-836-7472 ■ *Web:* iscsales.com	972-964-2700		177
ISCAR Metals 300 Wway Pl................... Arlington TX 76018 *Web:* www.iscarmetals.com	817-258-3200		360-2
ISCEBS (International Society of Certified Employee Benefits) 18700 W Bluemond Rd PO Box 209........... Brookfield WI 53008 *TF:* 888-334-3327 ■ *Web:* www.iscebs.org	262-786-8771	786-8650	49-12
ISCET (International Society of Certified Electronics Technicians) 3608 Pershing Ave .... Fort Worth TX 76107 *TF:* 800-946-0201 ■ *Web:* www.iscet.org	817-921-9101	921-3741	49-19
Isco Industries 100 Witherspoon St 2 W.................... Louisville KY 40202 *TF:* 800-345-4726 ■ *Web:* www.isco-pipe.com	502-583-6591		596
ISCO International LLC 444 E State Pkwy Ste 123................ Schaumburg IL 60173 **Fax Area Code:* 224 ■ *TF:* 888-948-4726 ■ *Web:* www.iscointl.com	630-283-3100	222-1691*	735
iScreen Vision Inc 110 Timber Creek Dr Ste 2.................... Cordova TN 38018 *Web:* www.iscreenvision.com	901-201-6132		743
ISD Inc 2500 W Higgins Rd Ste 250............. Hoffman Estates IL 60169 *Web:* www.isdinc.com	847-519-1150	519-1159	225
ISDA (International Swaps & Derivatives Assn) 360 Madison Ave 16th Fl .... New York NY 10017 *Web:* www.isda.org	212-901-6000		49-2
ISE America Inc PO Box 267.................... Galena MD 21635 *Web:* www.iseamerica.com	410-755-6300	755-6367	619

	Phone	Fax	Class
ISEC Inc 6000 Greenwood Plaza Blvd Ste 200 Greenwood Village CO 80111 *Web:* www.isecinc.com	303-790-1444		248
isee systems Inc Wheelock Office Pk 31 Old Etna Rd Ste 7N Lebanon NH 03766 *Web:* www.iseesystems.com	603-448-4990		177
iSelect Internet Inc 1420 W Kettleman Ln Ste E Lodi CA 95242 **Fax Area Code:* 877 ■ *Web:* www.iselect.net	209-334-0496	837-1427*	398
Iseli Co 402 N Main St Walworth WI 53184 *TF:* 800-403-8665 ■ *Web:* iseli.com	262-275-2108	275-6094	621
ISFSI (International Society of Fire Service Instructors) 14001C St Germain Dr Centreville VA 20121 *TF:* 800-435-0005 ■ *Web:* www.isfsi.org	800-435-0005	235-9153	49-7
ISG (Insight Sourcing Group Inc) 5555 Triangle Pky Ste 300 Norcross GA 30092 *TF:* 888-973-0208 ■ *Web:* www.insightsourcing.com	888-973-0208		393
ISG Prime LLC 12723 Mill Heights Ct Herndon VA 20171 *Web:* www.isgprime.com	703-624-9409	935-4777	180
ISG Technologies 3333 St Rd Ste 330 Bensalem PA 19020 *TF:* 800-566-3310 ■ *Web:* isgtechnologies.com	800-566-3310		175
ISG Technology & Data Ctr 127 N Seventh St Salina KS 67401 *Web:* www.isgtech.com	785-823-1555		178-10
Isgett Distributors Inc 51 Highland Center Blvd Asheville NC 28806 *TF:* 800-358-0080 ■ *Web:* www.isgettdistributors.com	828-667-9846		579
ISGN (ISGN Corp) 1333 Gateway Dr Ste 1000 Melbourne FL 32901 *TF:* 800-462-5545 ■ *Web:* www.isgn.com	860-656-7550		178-1
ISGN Corp (ISGN) 1333 Gateway Dr Ste 1000 Melbourne FL 32901 *TF:* 800-462-5545 ■ *Web:* www.isgn.com	860-656-7550		178-1
ISGS (Illinois State Genealogical Society) PO Box 10195 Springfield IL 62791 *Web:* www.ilgensoc.org	217-789-1968		637-2
ISH Entertainment LLC 34 W 27th St 7th Fl New York NY 10001 *Web:* ish.tv	212-377-3845		260
Isham-Terry House 211 High St Hartford CT 06103 *Web:* www.ctlandmarks.org	860-247-8996		50-3
Ishihara Corporation USA 601 California St Ste 1700 San Francisco CA 94108 *Web:* www20.inetba.com	415-421-8207	397-5403	280
ISHLT (International Society for Heart & Lung Transplantation) 14673 Midway Rd Ste 200 Addison TX 75001 *Web:* www.ishlt.org	972-490-9495	490-9499	49-8
ISHS (Illinois State Historical Society) 5255 Shepherd Rd Springfield IL 62703 *TF:* 866-244-0626 ■ *Web:* www.historyillinois.org	217-525-2781		49-19
ISI (Intercollegiate Studies Institute) 3901 Centerville Rd Wilmington DE 19807 *TF:* 800-526-7022 ■ *Web:* home.isi.org	302-652-4600		48-11
ISI (Ice Sports Industry) 6000 Custer Rd Bldg 9 Plano TX 75023 *Web:* www.skateisi.org	972-735-8800	735-8815	48-22
ISI Commercial Refrigeration LP 640 W Sixth St Houston TX 77007 *TF:* 800-777-5070 ■ *Web:* www.isi-texas.com	214-631-7980	631-6813	665
ISI-Biz Inc PO Box 3968 Evergreen CO 80437 *Web:* www.isi-biz.com	303-526-1662		178-1
Isine Inc 47 Winter St Ste 4 Boston MA 02108 *Web:* www.isine.com	617-695-2700		261
Isis Papyrus America Inc 301 Bank St Southlake TX 76092 *Web:* www.isis-papyrus.com	817-416-2345	416-1223	177
ISK Biosciences Corp 7474 Auburn Rd Ste A Painesville OH 44077 *TF:* 877-706-4640 ■ *Web:* www.iskbc.com	440-357-4640		317
Iskalo Development Corp Harbinger Sq 5166 Main St Williamsville NY 14221 *Web:* www.iskalo.com	716-633-2096	633-5776	653
ISKME 323 Harvard Ave Half Moon Bay CA 94019 *Web:* iskme.org	650-728-3322		507
ISky Inc 1700 Pennsylvania Ave NW Ste 560 Washington DC 20006 *Web:* www.isky.com	240-456-4300		737
Islamic Center of Hawthorne 12227 Hawthorne Way Hawthorne CA 90250 *Web:* ichla.org	310-973-8000	978-4036	685
Islamic Medical Association of North America (IMANA) 101 W 22nd St Ste 104 Lombard IL 60148 *Web:* imana.org	630-932-0000	932-0005	49-8
Islamorada Chamber of Commerce PO Box 915 Islamorada FL 33036 *TF:* 800-322-5397 ■ *Web:* www.islamoradachamber.com	305-664-4503	664-4289	139
Island Beach State Park PO Box 37 Seaside Park NJ 08752 *Web:* www.njparksandforests.org	732-793-0506		565
Island County 1 NE Seventh St Coupeville WA 98239 *Web:* www.islandcountywa.gov	360-679-7354	679-7381	338
Island Delight Caribbean 323 Airbase Blvd Montgomery AL 36108	334-264-0041		671
Island Drafting & Technical Institute 128 Broadway Amityville NY 11701 *Web:* www.idti.edu	631-691-8733		668
Island Express Helicopter Service 1175 Queens Hwy S Long Beach CA 90802 *TF:* 800-228-2566 ■ *Web:* iexhelicopters.com	310-510-2525		359
Island Federal Credit Union 120 Motor Pkwy Hauppauge NY 11788 *TF:* 800-475-5263 ■ *Web:* www.islandfcu.org	631-851-1100		219
Island Global Yachting 717 5th Ave 18th Fl New York NY 10022 *Web:* www.igymarinas.com	212-705-5000	705-5001	31
Island Hammock Pet Hospital 98175 Overseas Hwy Key Largo FL 33037 *Web:* ihph.net	305-852-5252		794
Island Health 1952 Bay St Victoria BC V8R1J8 *Web:* www.islandhealth.ca	250-370-8699		352
Island Hotel, The 690 Newport Center Dr Newport Beach CA 92660 *TF:* 866-554-4620 ■ *Web:* www.fashionislandhotel.com	949-759-0808	759-0568	379
Island Key Computer Ltd 938 Howe St Vancouver BC V6Z1N9 *Web:* www.islandkey.com	604-669-8178		177
Island Lincoln-Mercury Inc 1850 E Merritt Island Cswy Merritt Island FL 32952 *Web:* www.islandlincoln.net	321-452-9220		57
Island Micro Solutions Inc 3375 Koapaka St Ste B282 Honolulu HI 96819 *Web:* solutionshawaii.com	808-833-6048		177
Island Nature Trust PO Box 265 Charlottetown PE C1A7K4 *Web:* www.islandnaturetrust.ca	902-892-7513	628-6331	48-13
Island Pacific Distributors Inc 500 Alakawa St Ste 114 Honolulu HI 96817 *Web:* ipdhawaii.com	808-955-1126		364
Island Pacific Inc 17310 Red Hill Ave Ste 320 Irvine CA 92614 *TF:* 800-994-3847 ■ *Web:* www.islandpacific.com	250-250-1000		178-10
Island Packet, The 10 Buck Island Rd Bluffton SC 29910 *TF:* 877-706-8100 ■ *Web:* www.islandpacket.com	877-706-8100		532-2
Island Peer Review Organization Inc (IPRO) 1979 Marcus Ave Lake Success NY 11042 *TF:* 888-880-9976 ■ *Web:* ipro.org	516-326-7767	328-2310	353
Island Press 2000 M St NW Ste 650 Washington DC 20036 *Web:* islandpress.org	202-232-7933	234-1328	637-2
Island Pro Digital 35 Davids Dr Hauppauge NY 11788 *Web:* www.islandprodigital.com	631-293-4217		627
Island Ready-Mix Concrete Inc 91-047 Hanua St Kapolei HI 96707 *Web:* www.islandreadymix.com	808-682-1305		182
Island Real Estate of Anna Maria Island Inc 6101 Marina Dr Holmes Beach FL 34217 *Web:* islandreal.com	941-778-6066		653
Island Staffing 1895 Avenida Del Oro Ste 5947 Oceanside CA 92052 *Web:* www.islandstaffing.us	760-547-5018		260
Island Surf 1450 Miracle Strip Pkwy SE Fort Walton Beach FL 32548 *TF:* 800-272-2065 ■ *Web:* www.islandersoutfitter.com	800-272-2065		711
Island Technologies 17408 Chatsworth St Ste 200 Granada Hills CA 91344 *Web:* www.islandtechnologies.net	818-832-2310		177
Island Timberlands LP 65 Front St 4th Fl Nanaimo BC V9R5H9 *TF:* 800-663-5555 ■ *Web:* www.islandtimberlands.com	250-755-3500		454
Island View Casino Resort PO Box 1600 Gulfport MS 39502 *TF:* 877-774-8439 ■ *Web:* www.islandviewcasino.com	228-314-2100		133
Island Windjammers Inc 165 Shaw Dr Acworth GA 30102 *TF:* 877-772-4549 ■ *Web:* www.islandwindjammers.com	877-772-4549		31
Islander 3537 US Rte 2 North Hero VT 05474 *Web:* www.lakechamplainislander.com	802-372-5600	372-3025	532-2
Islander Resort 82100 Overseas Hwy PO Box 766 Islamorada FL 33036 *TF:* 800-753-6002 ■ *Web:* www.islanderfloridakeys.com	305-664-2031		377
Islandport Press Inc PO Box 10 Yarmouth ME 04096 *Web:* www.islandportpress.com	207-846-3344	846-3955	637-2
Islands in the Sun Cruises & Tours Inc 348 Thompson Creek Mall Ste 107 Stevensville MD 21666 **Fax Area Code:* 443 ■ *TF:* 800-278-7786 ■ *Web:* www.crus-sun.com	410-827-3812	782-2371*	771
Islands Restaurants 5750 Fleet St Ste 120 Carlsbad CA 92008 *Web:* www.islandsrestaurants.com	760-268-1800		670
IslandWeb Inc 4 Devon Rd Bar Harbor ME 04609 *Web:* www.islandwebinc.com	207-288-4725		225
ISLC Inc 14 Savannah Hwy Beaufort SC 29906 *TF:* 888-828-4752 ■ *Web:* www.islc.net	843-770-1000		387
Isle of Capri Casino Hotel Lake Charles 100 W Lake Ave Westlake LA 70669 *TF:* 800-843-4753	800-843-4753		133
Isle of Capri Casinos Inc 600 Emerson Rd Ste 300 Saint Louis MO 63141 *Web:* www.eldoradoresorts.com	314-813-9200		379
Isle of Wight County 17090 Monument Cir Ste 123 Isle of Wight VA 23397 *Web:* www.co.isle-of-wight.va.us	757-365-6204		338
Isle Royale National Park 800 E Lakeshore Dr Houghton MI 49931 *Web:* www.nps.gov	906-482-0984	482-8753	564
Islip Public Library 71 Monell Ave Islip NY 11751 *Web:* isliplibrary.org	631-581-5933		434-3
ISM (Institute for Supply Management) 309 W Elliot Rd Ste 113 Tempe AZ 85284 *TF:* 800-888-6276 ■ *Web:* www.instituteforsupplymanagement.org	480-752-6276	752-7890	49-12
ISMRM (International Society for Magnetic Resonance in Medicine) 2030 Addison St Ste 700 Berkeley CA 94704 *Web:* www.ismrm.org	510-841-1899	841-2340	49-8
ISN (Information Systems & Networks Corp) 10411 Motor City Dr Ste 700 Bethesda MD 20817 *Web:* www.isncorp.com	301-469-0400	469-0767	180
ISN Global Enterprises Inc PO Box 1391 Claremont CA 91711 *TF:* 877-376-4476 ■ *Web:* www.isnglobal.com	909-670-0601		192
ISNA (Indiana State Nurses Assn) 2915 N High School Rd Indianapolis IN 46224 *Web:* www.indiananurses.org	317-299-4575	297-3525	533
iSnap 808 R St Sacramento CA 95811 *Web:* www.isnap.com	916-333-0330		387
ISO (Insurance Services Office Inc) 545 Washington Blvd Jersey City NJ 07310 *Web:* www.verisk.com	201-748-1472		390
iSOA Group Inc 8 Keller St Petaluma CA 94952 *Web:* www.isoagroup.com	707-773-1198		525
Isobunkers LLC 5353 E Princess Anne Rd Ste F Norfolk VA 23502 *Web:* www.isoindustries.com	757-855-0900	855-6200	579

Name / Address	City	State	ZIP	Phone	Fax	Class
ISOC (Internet Society) 11710 Plz America Dr Ste 400 — *Web:* www.internetsociety.org	Reston	VA	20190	703-439-2120	326-9881	48-9
ISOFlex Packaging 101 ISO Pkwy — *TF:* 866-295-8290 ■ *Web:* www.isoflexpackaging.com	Gray Court	SC	29645	864-876-4300		601
Isoflux Inc PO Box 190 — *Web:* www.isofluxinc.com	Pittsford	NY	14534	585-349-0640		350
Isolatek Intl 41 Furnace St — *TF:* 800-631-9600 ■ *Web:* www.isolatek.com	Stanhope	NJ	07874	973-347-1200	347-9170	389
iSold It 1196 E Walnut St — *Web:* www.isolditpasadena.com	Pasadena	CA	91106	626-584-0844		310
ISOMEDIA Inc 12842 Interurban Ave S — *TF:* 877-638-9277 ■ *Web:* www.isomedia.com	Seattle	WA	98168	425-869-5411	869-9437	224
Isomet Corp 5263 Port Royal Rd — *OTC:* IOMT ■ *Web:* www.isomet.com	Springfield	VA	22151	703-321-8301	321-8546	425
Isometric Tool & Design Inc 240 Wisconsin Dr — *Web:* www.isotool.com	New Richmond	WI	54017	715-246-7005	246-3462	711
IsoRay Medical Inc 350 Hills St Ste 106 — *Web:* isoray.com	Richland	WA	99354	509-375-5329	267-3670	360-3
Isotec International Inc 201 Longview Dr — *TF:* 800-234-6300 ■ *Web:* isotecintl.com	Canton	GA	30114	770-479-4775	479-1566	605-2
Isotech Laboratories Inc 1308 Parkland Ct — *TF:* 877-362-4190 ■ *Web:* www.isotechlabs.com	Champaign	IL	61821	217-398-3490	398-3493	743
Isotech Pest Management Inc 12881 Ramona Blvd — *TF:* 888-392-8443 ■ *Web:* isotechpest.com	Baldwin Park	CA	91706	888-392-8443		577
Iso-Tex Diagnostics Inc 1511 County Rd 129 — *TF:* 800-477-4839 ■ *Web:* www.isotexdiagnostics.com	Pearland	TX	77581	281-481-1232	482-1070	231
Isothermal Community College 286 ICC Loop Rd PO Box 804 — *Web:* www.isothermal.edu	Spindale	NC	28160	828-286-3636	286-4014	162
Isotropic Networks Inc 2492 Crest Dr — *Web:* isosat.net	Lake Geneva	WI	53147	262-248-9600		116
ISP Optics Corp 50 S Buckhout St — *TF:* 800-472-3486 ■ *Web:* www.ispoptics.com	Irvington	NY	10533	914-591-3070		544
ISPA (Idaho State Pharmacy Assn) 816 W Bannock St Ste 60 — *Web:* www.ourispa.com	Boise	ID	83702	208-870-8312		585
ISPA (International Sleep Products Assn) 501 Wythe St — *Web:* www.sleepproducts.org	Alexandria	VA	22314	703-683-8371	683-4503	49-4
ISPA Inc 2000 Powers Ferry Rd SE Ste 300 — *Web:* www.ispainc.com	Atlanta	GA	30339	770-690-2900		463
iSparks Inc 2657 Windmill Pky Ste 175 — *TF:* 888-355-4376 ■ *Web:* www.spamhero.com	Henderson	NV	89074	702-800-4911		681
ISPD (International Society for Peritoneal Dialysis) 66 Martin St — *TF:* 888-834-1001 ■ *Web:* ispd.org	Milton	ON	L9T2R2	905-875-2456	875-2864	49-8
ISPE (International Society for Pharmacoepidemiology) 5272 River Rd Ste 500 — *Web:* www.pharmacoepi.org	Bethesda	MD	20816	301-718-6500	656-0989	49-8
ISPE (International Society for Pharmaceutical Engineering) 3109 W Dr ML King Jr Blvd Ste 250 — *Web:* www.ispe.org	Tampa	FL	33607	813-960-2105	264-2816	49-19
ISPI (International Society for Performance Improvement) PO Box 13035 — *TF:* 800-825-7550 ■ *Web:* ispi.org	Silver Spring	MD	20910	301-587-8570	587-8573	49-12
ISPN Network Services 14303 W 95th St — *TF:* 866-584-4776 ■ *Web:* www.ispn.net	Lenexa	KS	66215	866-584-4776		393
ISPnet Inc 82-04 218th St — *TF:* 800-806-6387 ■ *Web:* www.ispnetinc.net	Hollis Hills	NY	11427	718-464-4747	217-9407	225
ISPOR 505 Lawrence Sq Blvd S — *TF:* 800-992-0643 ■ *Web:* www.ispor.org	Lawrenceville	NJ	08648	609-586-4981	219-0774	49-8
ISPP (International Society of Political Psychology) 126 Ward St Ste 1213 PO Box 1213 — *Web:* www.ispp.org	Columbus	NC	28722	828-894-5422		48-7
iSqFt Inc 3825 Edwards Rd Ste 800 — *TF:* 800-364-2059 ■ *Web:* www.isqft.com	Cincinnati	OH	45209	513-645-8004	645-8005	178-10
Isr Inc 264 Main St	Sugar Grove	IL	60554	630-466-7800		693
ISR Info Way Inc 559 Donofrio Dr Ste 101 & 102 — *Web:* www.isrinfo.com	Madison	WI	53719	608-827-7884	833-0527	177
Isra Surface Vision Inc 4470 Peachtree Lakes Dr — *Web:* www.lasorsystronics.com	Berkeley Lake	GA	30096	770-449-7776		472
Israel 800 Second Ave — *Web:* embassies.gov.il	New York	NY	10017	212-499-5000	499-5515	784
Israel Discount Bank of New York (IDBB) 511 Fifth Ave — *Web:* www.idbny.com	New York	NY	10017	212-551-8500	551-8540	70
ISRI (Institute of Scrap Recycling Industries Inc) 1250 H St NW Ste 400 — *Web:* www.isri.org	Washington	DC	20005	202-662-8500	626-0900	48-12
ISRS (International Society of Refractive Surgery) 655 Beach St PO Box 7424 — *Web:* www.isrs.org	San Francisco	CA	94109	415-561-8581	561-8575	49-8
ISS Facilities Services Inc 1019 Central Pkwy N Ste 100 — *Web:* www.us.issworld.com	San Antonio	TX	78232	210-495-6021		104
ISS Inc Aspen Corporate Pk 1480 US Hwy 9 N Ste 202 — *Web:* issivs.com	Woodbridge	NJ	07095	732-855-1111		692
ISS LLC 820 E 20th St — *Web:* www.sproutnet.com	Cookeville	TN	38501	931-526-1106		273
ISS Software Solutions Inc 5 Great Vly Pkwy Ste 110 — *Web:* www.intsoftinc.com	Malvern	PA	19355	610-560-4300		225
ISS Technologies 22 Business Park Cir — *Web:* www.isstechnologies.com	Arden	NC	28704	828-684-4248	684-4249	463
ISSA (International Sanitary Supply Assn) 3300 Dundee Rd — *TF:* 800-225-4772 ■ *Web:* issa.com	Northbrook	IL	60062	847-982-0800	982-1012	49-18
Issaquah Dental Lab Inc 640 NW Gilman Blvd — *Web:* www.issaquah-dl.com	Issaquah	WA	98027	425-392-5125		228
Issaquah Law Group PLLC 410 Newport Way NW Ste C — *Web:* issaquahlaw.com	Issaquah	WA	98027	425-313-1184		41
Issaquah Press, The 1085 12th Ave NW Ste D1 PO Box 1328 — *Web:* www.issaquah-press.com	Issaquah	WA	98027	425-392-6434	392-1695	532-4
ISSI (Ice Systems & Supplies Inc) 163 E Mount Gallant Rd — *TF:* 800-662-1273 ■ *Web:* www.issionline.com	Rock Hill	SC	29730	803-324-8791		14
Isspro Inc 2515 NE Riverside Way — *Web:* www.issproinc.com	Portland	OR	97211	503-288-4488		495
Issue Insurance Agency Inc 407 Corporate Center Dr Ste A — *Web:* issueins.com	Vandalia	OH	45377	937-890-4991		390
Issuer Direct Corp 500 Perimeter Park Dr Ste D — *TF:* 877-481-4014 ■ *Web:* www.issuerdirect.com	Morrisville	NC	27560	919-481-4000		317
Issues & Answers Network Inc 5151 Bonney Rd Ste 100 — *Web:* www.issans.net	Virginia Beach	VA	23462	757-456-1100		668
IST (Institute for Simulation & Training) 3100 Technology Pkwy — *Web:* www.ist.ucf.edu	Orlando	FL	32826	407-882-1300	658-5059	668
IS&T (Society for Imaging Science & Technology) 7003 Kilworth Ln — *TF:* 800-654-2240 ■ *Web:* www.imaging.org	Springfield	VA	22151	703-642-9090	642-9094	49-16
ISTA (International Safe Transit Assn) 1400 Abbott Rd Ste 160 — *TF:* 888-299-2208 ■ *Web:* www.ista.org	East Lansing	MI	48823	517-333-3437	333-3813	49-21
ISTA Advocate Magazine 150 W Market St Ste 900 — *TF:* 800-382-4037 ■ *Web:* www.ista-in.org	Indianapolis	IN	46204	317-263-3400	655-3700	457-8
Istaff Inc 1325 Satellite Blvd Ste 1305 — *Web:* www.istaff.com	Suwanee	GA	30024	770-962-9604		260
iStar Inc 1114 Avenue of the Americas 39th Fl — *NYSE:* STAR ■ *Web:* www.istar.com	New York	NY	10036	212-930-9400	930-9494	216
ISTE (International Society for Technology in Education) 1530 Wilson Blvd Ste 730 — *TF:* 800-336-5191 ■ *Web:* www.iste.org	Arlington	VA	22209	800-336-5191		49-5
Istech Inc 4691 Raycom Rd — *TF:* 800-555-4880 ■ *Web:* www.istech-inc.com	Dover	PA	17315	717-764-5565		261
ISTF (International Society of Tropical Foresters) 5400 Grosvenor Ln — **Fax Area Code:* 877 ■ *Web:* www.istf-bethesda.org	Bethesda	MD	20814	301-530-4514	665-6473*	48-13
ISTM (International Society of Travel Medicine) 315 W Ponce de Leon Ave Ste 245 — *Web:* www.istm.org	Decatur	GA	30030	404-373-8282	373-8283	49-8
iStreet Solutions LLC 1911 Douglas Blvd 85-200 — *TF:* 866-976-3976 ■ *Web:* www.istreetsolutions.com	Roseville	CA	95661	866-976-3976		196
ISTSS (International Society for Traumatic Stress Studies) 111 Deer Lake Rd Ste 100 — *TF:* 877-469-7873 ■ *Web:* www.istss.org	Deerfield	IL	60015	847-480-9028	480-9282	49-15
ISTT Inc 846 Broadway Ave — *Web:* isttechnology.com	Bowling Green	KY	42101	270-781-5096		177
ISU Petasys Corp 12930 Bradley Ave — *Web:* www.petasys.com	Sylmar	CA	91342	818-833-5800		625
ISWS (Illinois State Water Survey) 2204 Griffith Dr — *Web:* www.isws.illinois.edu	Champaign	IL	61820	217-333-2210		637-2
ISYS Technologies Inc 801 W Mineral Ave Ste 105 — *Web:* isystechnologies.com	Littleton	CO	80120	303-290-8922		681
IT America Inc 100 Metroplex Dr Ste 207 — *Web:* www.itamerica.com	Edison	NJ	08817	732-985-5100	985-5101	196
IT Blueprint Solutions Consulting Inc 170-422 Richards St — *TF:* 866-261-8981 ■ *Web:* itblueprint.ca	Vancouver	BC	V6B2Z4	866-261-8981		196
IT Cadre LLC 43777 Central Station Dr Ste 450 — *Web:* itcadre.com	Ashburn	VA	20147	703-724-5400		177
IT Co, The 16 Emory Pl Ste 100 — *Web:* www.theitco.net	Knoxville	TN	37917	865-392-9200		196
IT Direct LLC 67 Prospect Ave Ste 202 — *Web:* www.gettingyouconnected.com	West Hartford	CT	06106	860-249-1200	371-2097	624
IT Healthtrack Inc 6500 Main St Ste 3 — *Web:* ithealthtrack.com	Williamsville	NY	14221	716-630-0063		354
It is Written Inc 11291 Pierce St — *TF:* 888-664-5573 ■ *Web:* www.itiswritten.com	Riverside	CA	92505	805-433-0210		557
It Pitstop Inc 10120 S E Ave	Henderson	NV	89052	702-777-4445		396
It Pro Source 2600 Kitty Hawk Rd Ste 115 — *Web:* www.itprosource.com	Livermore	CA	94551	925-455-7701		396
iT Services 2 2340 E Trinity Mills Rd Ste 300 — *TF:* 877-400-0293 ■ *Web:* itservices2.com	Carrollton	TX	75006	877-400-0293		196
IT Staffing Inc 5 Bliss Ct Ste 200 — *Web:* www.itstaffinc.com	Woodcliff Lake	NJ	07677	201-505-0493		631
IT Weapons 7965 Goreway Dr Unit 1 — *TF:* 866-202-5298 ■ *Web:* www.itweapons.com	Brampton	ON	L6T5T5	905-494-1040		180
It's Just Lunch! Inc 121 W Wacker Dr Ste 663 — *Web:* www.itsjustlunch.com	Chicago	IL	60601	312-644-9999		226
It4la Inc 8033 Sunset Blvd 228 — *Web:* it4la.com	Los Angeles	CA	90046	323-936-4900		396
Ita Inc 2162 Dana Ave — **Fax Area Code:* 513 ■ *TF:* 800-899-8877 ■ *Web:* ita.com	Cincinnati	OH	45207	800-899-8877	631-8877*	525

Name / Address	City	State	Zip	Phone	Fax	Class
Ita Software Inc 5 Cambridge Ctr	Cambridge	MA	02142	617-714-2100	621-3913	178-10
Web: www.itasoftware.com						
ITAC Solutions LLC						
700 Montgomery Hwy Ste 148	Birmingham	AL	35216	205-326-0004		193
TF: 877-651-4822 ■ *Web:* www.itacsolutions.com						
ITAGroup 4600 Westown Pkwy	West Des Moines	IA	50266	800-257-1985		384
TF: 800-257-1985 ■ *Web:* www.itagroup.com						
Italgrani USA Inc						
7900 Van Buren St	Saint Louis	MO	63111	314-638-1447	752-7621	275
TF: 800-274-1274 ■ *Web:* www.italgraniusa.com						
Italian Cafe						
387 Las Colinas Blvd E Ste 120	Irving	TX	75039	972-401-0000	401-9193	671
Web: www.italianitaliancafe.com						
Italian Government Tourist Board						
10850 Wilshire Blvd Ste 575	Los Angeles	CA	90024	310-820-1898	470-7788	775
Web: www.italiantourism.com						
Italian Moon 810 S Washington St	Grand Forks	ND	58201	701-772-7277		671
Web: italianmoon.com						
Italian Village Pizza						
711 Vandiver Dr Ste B	Columbia	MO	65202	573-442-8821		671
Web: www.theitalianvillagepizza.com						
Italian-American Chamber of Commerce Midwest (IACC)						
1656 W CHICAGO Ave	Chicago	IL	60622	312-553-9137	553-9142	138
Web: www.iacc-chicago.com						
iTalkBB CA						
245 W Beaver Creek Rd Unit 9	Richmond Hill	ON	L4B1L1	877-482-5522		224
TF: 877-482-5522 ■ *Web:* www.italkbb.com						
Italy						
885 Second Ave One Dag Hammarskjold Plz						
49th Fl	New York	NY	10017	212-486-9191	486-1036	784
Web: italyun.esteri.it						
Italy						
Consulate General						
1300 Post Oak Blvd Ste 660	Houston	TX	77056	713-850-7520	850-9113	257
Web: www.conshouston.esteri.it						
Consulate General						
2590 Webster St	San Francisco	CA	94115	415-292-9200	931-7205	257
Web: www.conssanfrancisco.esteri.it						
Consulate General						
4000 Ponce de Leon Ste 590	Coral Gables	FL	33146	305-374-6322	374-7945	257
Web: www.consmiami.esteri.it						
Consulate General 690 Park Ave	New York	NY	10065	212-737-9100		257
Web: www.consnewyork.esteri.it						
Embassy 3000 Whitehaven St NW	Washington	DC	20008	202-612-4427	462-9406	257
Web: ambwashingtondc.esteri.it						
Italy-America Chamber of Commerce Inc						
730 Fifth Ave Ste 502	New York	NY	10019	212-459-0044	459-0090	138
Web: www.italchamber.org						
Italy-America Chamber of Commerce of Texas Inc						
1800 W Loop S Ste 1120	Houston	TX	77027	713-626-9303		138
Web: www.iacctexas.com						
Italy-America Chamber of Commerce Southeast Inc						
999 Brickell Ave Ste 1002	Miami	FL	33131	305-577-9868	577-3956	138
Web: iacc-miami.com						
Italy-America Chamber of Commerce West Inc						
10537 Santa Monica Blvd Ste 210	Los Angeles	CA	90025	310-557-3017	557-1217	138
Web: www.iaccw.net						
ITAMCO 6100 Michigan Rd	Plymouth	IN	46563	574-936-2112		454
Web: www.itamco.com						
Itasca Community College						
1851 E US Hwy 169	Grand Rapids	MN	55744	800-966-6422	327-4350*	162
**Fax Area Code:* 218 ■ *TF:* 800-996-6422 ■ *Web:* www.itascacc.edu						
Itasca County 123 NE Fourth St	Grand Rapids	MN	55744	218-327-7363	327-2848	338
TF: 800-422-0312 ■ *Web:* www.co.itasca.mn.us						
Itasca State Park						
36750 Main Park Dr	Park Rapids	MN	56470	218-699-7251		565
Web: www.dnr.state.mn.us						
Itasca-Mantrap Cooperative Electrical Assn						
16930 County Rd 6	Park Rapids	MN	56470	218-732-3377	732-5890	245
TF: 888-713-3377 ■ *Web:* www.itasca-mantrap.com						
Itawamba Community College						
Fulton 602 W Hill St	Fulton	MS	38843	662-862-8000	862-8234	162
Web: www.iccms.edu						
Itawamba County 107 W Wiygul St	Fulton	MS	38843	662-862-4571		338
Web: itawambams.com						
ITB Group Ltd						
39555 Orchard Hill Pl Ste 157	Novi	MI	48375	248-380-6310		256
Web: www.itbgroup.com						
ITC (Innovative Technologies Corp)						
1020 Woodman Dr Ste 100	Dayton	OH	45432	937-252-2145	254-6853	178-10
TF: 800-745-8050 ■ *Web:* www.itc-1.com						
ITC (Insurance Technology Consultants Inc)						
2090 N Tustin Ave Ste 260	Santa Ana	CA	92705	714-442-8702		177
Web: www.itc-systems.com						
ITC (Industry Telephone Co)						
17105 Fordtran Blvd	Industry	TX	78944	979-357-4411	278-3600	224
TF: 888-212-8872 ■ *Web:* www.industrytelco.com						
ITC (Interstate Telecommunications Cooperative Inc)						
312 4th St W	Clear Lake	SD	57226	605-874-2181	874-2014	224
TF: 800-417-8667 ■ *Web:* www.itc-web.com						
ITC Engineering Services Inc						
9959 Calaveras Rd	Sunol	CA	94586	925-862-2944	862-9013	256
Web: itcemc.com						
ITC Holding Company LLC						
1791 O G Skinner Dr Ste A	West Point	GA	31833	706-645-8714		360-3
Web: www.itchold.com						
ITC Learning Corp						
444 NW 1st Ave Ste 503	Fort Lauderdale	FL	33301	703-286-0756		765
TF: 800-638-3757 ■ *Web:* www.itclearning.com						
ITC Systems Inc						
800 Fee Fee Rd	Maryland Heights	MO	63043	314-872-7772	872-3353	569
Web: www.itcsystems.com						
ITCO Solutions Inc						
1003 Whitehall Ln	Redwood City	CA	94061	650-366-2761		317
Web: itcosolutions.com						
Itcon Services LLC						
501 School St SW Ste 300	Washington	DC	20024	844-559-0534	852-3955*	180
**Fax Area Code:* 703 ■ *TF:* 844-559-0534 ■ *Web:* www.itcon-inc.com						
ITE (Institute of Transportation Engineers)						
1627 Eye St NW Ste 600	Washington	DC	20006	202-785-0060	785-0609	49-21
Web: www.ite.org						
ITE LLC 424 Wards Corner Rd	Loveland	OH	45140	513-576-6200	576-6324	261
Web: ite.com						
ITEA (International Technology Education Assn)						
1914 Assn Dr Ste 201	Reston	VA	20191	703-860-2100	860-0353	49-5
Web: www.iteea.org						
Itech Consulting Partners						
8 Wedgewood Ct	Newtown	CT	06470	203-270-0051		196
Web: www.itechcp.com						
Itech Digital LLC 4287 W 96th St	Indianapolis	IN	46268	317-704-0440		693
TF: 866-733-6673 ■ *Web:* www.itechdigital.com						
Iteck Solutions LLC						
4909 Morning Glory Ct Ste 250	Rockville	MD	20853	301-929-1852		180
TF: 866-483-2544 ■ *Web:* www.itecksolutions.com						
ITEL Laboratories Inc						
6676 Corporate Center Pkwy Ste 107	Jacksonville	FL	32216	800-890-4835	363-2379*	743
**Fax Area Code:* 904 ■ *TF:* 800-890-4835 ■ *Web:* www.itelinc.com						
itelligence Inc						
10856 Reed Hartman Hwy	Cincinnati	OH	45242	513-956-2000		196
TF: 888-381-7878 ■ *Web:* www.itelligencegroup.com						
Item House Inc 2920 S Steele St	Tacoma	WA	98409	253-627-7168	627-1070	155-5
Web: itemhouseinc.com						
Item, The 20 N Magnolia St PO Box 1677	Sumter	SC	29151	803-774-1200	774-1210	532-2
Web: www.theitem.com						
Iten Industries 4602 Benefit Ave	Ashtabula	OH	44004	440-997-6134	992-4966	599
TF: 800-227-4836 ■ *Web:* www.itenindustries.com						
Iterable 71 Stevenson St Ste 300	San Francisco	CA	94105	415-723-5230		49-18
Web: iterable.com						
Itergy 2075 University Ste 700	Montreal	QC	H3A2L1	514-845-5881	789-0445	180
TF: 866-522-5881 ■ *Web:* itergy.com						
Iteris Inc 1700 Carnegie Ave Ste 100	Santa Ana	CA	92705	949-270-9400		647
NASDAQ: ITI ■ *TF:* 888-254-5487 ■ *Web:* www.iteris.com						
Iterna 2600 Beverly Dr	Aurora	IL	60502	630-585-7400	805-0748*	253
**Fax Area Code:* 866 ■ *Web:* www.iternacorp.com						
ITG Electronics Inc						
175 Clearbrook Rd	Elmsford	NY	10523	914-347-2474		246
Web: www.itg-electronics.com						
Itgroove Professional Services Ltd						
101-7161 W Saanich Rd	Brentwood Bay	BC	V8M1P7	250-220-4575		317
Web: itgroove.net						
Ithaca College 953 Danby Rd	Ithaca	NY	14850	607-274-3124	274-1900	166
TF: 800-429-4274 ■ *Web:* www.ithaca.edu						
Ithaca College Library 953 Danby Rd	Ithaca	NY	14850	607-274-3206		434-6
Web: library.ithaca.edu						
Ithaca Journal 123 W State St	Ithaca	NY	14850	607-272-2321		532-2
TF: 866-254-3068 ■ *Web:* www.ithacajournal.com						
Ithaca Times 109 N Cayuga St	Ithaca	NY	14850	607-277-7000		532-5
Web: www.ithaca.com						
Ithaca/Tompkins County Convention & Visitors Bureau						
904 E Shore Dr	Ithaca	NY	14850	607-272-1313		206
TF: 800-284-8422 ■ *Web:* www.visitithaca.com						
iTHINK Financial Credit Union						
1000 NW 17th Ave	Delray Beach	FL	33445	561-982-4700		219
Web: www.ithinkfi.org						
ITI (Information Technology Industry Council)						
1101 K St NW Ste 610	Washington	DC	20005	202-737-8888	638-4922	48-9
Web: www.itic.org						
ITI (Industrial Tools Inc)						
1111 S Rose Ave	Oxnard	CA	93033	805-483-1111	483-6302	493
TF: 800-266-5561 ■ *Web:* www.iti-abrasives.com						
ITI (International Trade Information Inc)						
900 Las Vegas Blvd S Unit 908	Las Vegas	NV	89101	818-591-2255		184
Web: internationaltradeinformation.com						
ITI (International TechneGroup Inc)						
5303 DuPont Cir	Milford	OH	45150	800-783-9199	576-3994*	178-1
**Fax Area Code:* 513 ■ *TF:* 800-783-9199 ■ *Web:* www.iti-oh.com						
ITI Technical College						
13944 Airline Hwy	Baton Rouge	LA	70817	225-752-4233		167-3
TF: 888-211-7165 ■ *Web:* www.iticollege.edu						
ITI TranscenData 5303 DuPont Cir	Milford	OH	45150	513-576-3900		387
Web: www.iti-global.com						
ITM (Incentive Travel & Meetings)						
970 Clementstone Dr Ste 100	Atlanta	GA	30342	404-847-9021	855-4863	384
Web: usaitm.com						
ITM Marketing Inc						
470 Downtowner Plz	Coshocton	OH	43812	740-295-3575	295-3581	624
Web: www.itmmarketing.com						
ITN Energy Systems Inc						
8130 Shaffer Pkwy	Littleton	CO	80127	303-420-1141		668
Web: www.itnes.com						
ITneer Inc						
1880 S Lee Ct South Lee Business Pk	Buford	GA	30519	678-541-0712	840-7680	178-1
TF: 844-648-6337 ■ *Web:* www.itneer.com						
ITNS (International Transplant Nurses Society)						
8735 W Higgins Rd Ste 300	Chicago	IL	60631	847-375-6340	375-6341	49-8
TF: 800-776-8636 ■ *Web:* www.itns.org						
ITO EN (North America) Inc						
20 Jay St Ste 530	Brooklyn	NY	11201	888-832-7832	246-1325*	671
**Fax Area Code:* 718 ■ *TF:* 888-832-7832 ■ *Web:* www.itoen.com						
ITOCHU Techno-Solutions America Inc						
3945 Freedom Cir Ste 640	Santa Clara	CA	95054	408-727-8810	727-9391	174
Web: www.ctc-america.com						
ITP (Inland Truck Parts Co)						
4400 College Blvd Ste 145	Overland Park	KS	66211	913-345-9664	345-8745	61
TF: 800-448-8436 ■ *Web:* www.inlandtruck.com						
ITP of Usa Inc						
520 E Bainbridge St	Elizabethtown	PA	17022	717-367-3670		627
Web: www.itpofusa.com						
ITR Economics						
77 Sundial Ave Ste 510w	Manchester	NH	03103	603-796-2500		466
Web: www.itreconomics.com						
ITR Group Inc						
2520 Lexington Ave S Ste 500	Saint Paul	MN	55120	866-290-3423		193
TF: 866-290-3423 ■ *Web:* itrgroup.com						
ITR of Georgia Inc 3346 Montreal	Tucker	GA	30084	770-496-0366		317
Web: itrps.com						

Company / Address	City	State	Zip	Phone	Fax	Class
ITRenew Inc 8356 Central Ave.	Newark	CA	94560	408-744-9600		225
TF: 866-744-9860 ■ *Web:* itrenew.com						
ITRI International Inc						
2870 Zanker Rd Ste 140	San Jose	CA	95134	408-428-9988	428-9388	48-13
Web: www.itri.com						
Itron Inc 2111 N Molter Rd	Liberty Lake	WA	99019	509-924-9900	891-3355	248
NASDAQ: ITRI ■ *TF:* 800-635-5461 ■ *Web:* www.itron.com						
ITS (Intelligent Transportation Society of America)						
1100 New Jersey Ave SE Ste 850	Washington	DC	20003	202-484-4847	484-3483	49-21
TF: 800-374-8472 ■ *Web:* www.itsa.org						
ITS (International Thermal Systems LLC)						
4697 W Greenfield Ave	Milwaukee	WI	53214	414-672-7700	672-8800	318
Web: www.internationalthermalsystems.com						
ITS Logistics LLC 555 Vista Blvd	Sparks	NV	89434	775-358-5300		314
TF: 844-668-3487 ■ *Web:* www.its4logistics.com						
ITS Technologies Inc						
7060 Spring Meadows Dr W Ste D	Holland	OH	43528	800-432-6607	842-2100*	260
**Fax Area Code:* 419 ■ *TF:* 800-432-6607 ■ *Web:* www.wehirepeople.com						
ITSource Technology Inc						
899 Northgate Dr Ste 304	San Rafael	CA	94903	866-548-4911		180
TF: 866-548-4911 ■ *Web:* www.itsourcetek.com						
ITT Aerospace Controls						
28150 Industry Dr.	Valencia	CA	91355	661-295-4000	294-1750	790
Web: www.ittaerospace.com						
ITT Educational Services Inc						
13000 N Meridian St	Carmel	IN	46032	317-706-9200		242
NYSE: ESINQ ■ *Web:* www.ittesi.com						
ITT Industries Inc						
4 W Red Oak Ln	White Plains	NY	10604	914-641-2000	696-2950	253
NYSE: ITT ■ *TF:* 800-254-2823 ■ *Web:* www.itt.com						
ITT Industries Inc						
Engineered Valves Div						
33 Centerville Rd	Lancaster	PA	17603	717-509-2200	509-2336	789
TF: 800-366-1111 ■ *Web:* www.engvalves.com						
ITT Standard 175 Standard Pkwy	Cheektowaga	NY	14227	800-281-4111	897-1777*	91
**Fax Area Code:* 716 ■ *TF:* 800-447-7700 ■ *Web:* www.ittstandard.com						
Ittig & Ittig PC 1420 Ninth St NW	Washington	DC	20001	202-387-5508	232-1334	41
Web: ittig-ittig.com						
ITU AbsorbTech Inc 2700 S 160th St	New Berlin	WI	53151	888-729-4884		442
TF: 888-729-4884 ■ *Web:* www.ituabsorbtech.com						
Ituran USA Inc						
1700 NW 64th St Ste 100	Fort Lauderdale	FL	33309	954-484-3806		224
TF: 866-543-5433 ■ *Web:* www.ituranusa.com						
ITV America Inc						
15303 Ventura Blvd Bldg C Ste 800	Sherman Oaks	CA	91403	818-455-4600		116
Web: itv-america.com						
ITVS (Independent Television Service)						
651 Brannan St Ste 410	San Francisco	CA	94107	415-356-8383	356-8391	742
TF: 888-572-8918 ■ *Web:* itvs.org						
ITW Brands						
955 National Pkwy Ste 95500	Schaumburg	IL	60173	847-944-2260	619-8344	278
Web: www.itwbrands.com						
ITW Buildex 1349 W Bryn Mawr	Itasca	IL	60143	800-848-5611	595-3549*	278
**Fax Area Code:* 630 ■ *TF:* 800-848-5611 ■ *Web:* www.itwbuildex.com						
ITW Coding Products 111 W Pk Dr	Kalkaska	MI	49646	231-258-5521	258-6120	628
TF: 800-793-3649 ■ *Web:* www.codingproducts.com						
ITW Drawform 500 Fairview	Zeeland	MI	49464	616-772-1910	772-9572	489
Web: www.drawform.com						
ITW Fluids North America						
475 N Gary Ave.	Carol Stream	IL	60188	800-452-5823	397-8704*	541
**Fax Area Code:* 913 ■ *TF:* 800-452-5823 ■ *Web:* www.itwprobrands.com						
ITW Food Equipment Group 701 S Ridge Ave.	Troy	OH	45374	937-332-3000	332-2852	298
Web: www.hobartcorp.com						
ITW Hi-Cone 1140 W Bryn Mawr Ave.	Itasca	IL	60143	630-438-5300	438-5315	548
Web: www.hicone.com						
ITW Highland 1240 Wolcott St.	Waterbury	CT	06722	203-574-3200	754-4019	489
Web: www.itwhighland.com						
ITW Industrial Finishing						
195 International Blvd.	Glendale Heights	IL	60139	630-237-5000		172
ITW Linx 425 N Gary Ave	Carol Stream	IL	60188	630-315-2151		392
Web: www.itwlinx.com						
ITW Minigrip Inc 8125 Cobb Center Dr	Kennesaw	GA	30152	770-422-4187		601
Web: www.minigrip.com						
ITW Polymers Sealants North America						
111 S Nursery R	Irving	TX	75060	972-438-9111	554-3939	3
TF: 800-878-7876 ■ *Web:* itwsealants.com						
ITW Sexton Can Company Inc						
3101 Sexton Rd	Decatur	AL	35603	256-355-5850		393
Web: www.sextoncan.com						
ITW Switches 195 E Algonquin Rd	Des Plaines	IL	60016	847-876-9400	876-9440	729
TF: 800-544-3354 ■ *Web:* www.itwswitches.com						
ITW United Silicone 4471 Walden Ave.	Lancaster	NY	14086	716-681-8222	681-8789	386
Web: www.unitedsilicone.com						
ITW Vortec 10125 Carver Rd	Cincinnati	OH	45242	513-891-7485	891-4092	14
TF: 800-441-7475 ■ *Web:* www.itw-air.com						
ITX Corp						
1169 Pittsford Victor Rd Ste 100	Pittsford	NY	14534	585-899-4888		224
TF: 800-600-7785 ■ *Web:* www.itx.com						
IUEC (International Union of Elevator Constructors)						
7154 Columbia Gateway Dr	Columbia	MD	21046	410-953-6150		49-3
Web: www.iuec.org						
IUL (International University Line)						
PO Box 2525	La Jolla	CA	92038	858-457-0595	581-9073	637-2
Web: www.iul-world.com						
iUniverse Inc 1663 Liberty Dr	Bloomington	IN	47403	812-330-2909	355-4085	637-2
TF: 800-288-4677 ■ *Web:* www.iuniverse.com						
Iuoe Local 420 1140 W Anderson Ct.	Oak Creek	WI	53154	414-570-0420		414
Web: local420oe.com						
IUPAT (International Union of Painters & Allied Trades)						
7234 Pkwy Dr	Hanover	MD	21076	410-564-5900		414
TF: 800-554-2479 ■ *Web:* iupat.org						
IV Most Consulting Inc 33 Park Dr	Mount Kisco	NY	10549	914-864-2781		177
TF: 800-448-6678 ■ *Web:* www.ivmost.com						
iv3 Solutions Corp						
50 Minthorn Blvd Ste 301	Markham	ON	L3T7X8	877-995-2651		365
TF: 877-995-2651 ■ *Web:* www.iv3solutions.com						
Ivalley Technology Partners Inc						
1170 Aberdeen Ave.	Livermore	CA	94550	510-305-1390		180
Web: ivalleytech.com						

Company / Address	City	State	Zip	Phone	Fax	Class
IVAMS (Inland Valley Arbitration & Mediation Service)						
8287 White Oak Ave	Rancho Cucamonga	CA	91730	909-466-1665	466-1796	41
Web: www.ivams.com						
Ivan C. Dutterer Inc 115 Ann St.	Hanover	PA	17331	717-637-8977		499
Web: ivancdutterer.com						
Ivan Franko Museum 200 McGregor St	Winnipeg	MB	R2W2K4	204-589-4397	942-3749	520
TF: 866-747-9323 ■ *Web:* www.museumsmanitoba.com						
Ivanhoe Broadcast News						
2211 Lee Rd Ste 107	Winter Park	FL	32789	407-740-0789	740-5320	742
Web: www.ivanhoe.com						
Ivanhoe Cambridge Inc						
1001 Sq Victoria Bureau C-500	Montreal	QC	H2Z2B5	514-841-7600		205
Web: www.ivanhoecambridge.com						
Ivanhoe Mines Ltd 654-999 Canada Pl	Vancouver	BC	V6C3E1	604-688-6630		502
Web: www.ivanhoemines.com						
Ivanhoe Tool & Die Company Inc						
590 Thompson Rd	Thompson	CT	06277	860-923-9541	923-2497	757
Web: www.ivanhoetool.com						
i-Vantage Inc 400 Talcott Ave	Watertown	MA	02472	617-393-2338	679-2959*	260
**Fax Area Code:* 253 ■ *Web:* www.i-vantage.com						
Ivanti 8660 E Hartford Dr Ste 300	Scottsdale	AZ	85255	480-970-1025	970-6323	225
TF: 888-725-7828 ■ *Web:* www.ivanti.com						
Ivar Jacobson Consulting LLC						
211 N Union St Ste 100	Alexandria	VA	22314	703-434-3344		196
Web: www.ivarjacobson.com						
Ivar's Acres of Clams						
1001 Alaskan Way Pier 54	Seattle	WA	98104	206-624-6852	624-4895	671
Web: www.ivars.com						
Ivarson Inc 3100 W Green Tree Rd	Milwaukee	WI	53209	414-351-0700	351-4551	757
Web: ivarsoninc.com						
IVAS (International Veterinary Acupuncture Society)						
1730 S College Ave Ste 301	Fort Collins	CO	80525	970-266-0666	266-0777	48-3
Web: www.ivas.org						
IVC (International Visual Corp)						
11500 Blvd Armand Bombardier	Montreal	QC	H1E2W9	514-643-0570	643-4867	286
TF: 866-643-0570 ■ *Web:* www.ivcweb.com						
IVCi LLC 601 Old Willets Path	Hauppauge	NY	11788	631-273-5800	273-7277	736
TF: 800-224-7083 ■ *Web:* ivci.com						
IVDiagnostics Inc						
9800 Connecticut Dr	Crown Point	IN	46307	219-840-0007		743
Web: ivdiagnostics.com						
Iventure Solutions Inc						
7775 Belfort Pkwy	Jacksonville	FL	32256	904-332-8645	332-8647	180
TF: 888-380-1235 ■ *Web:* iventuresolutions.com						
Ivenuecom 9925 Painter Ave Ste A	Whittier	CA	90605	800-683-8314		177
TF: 800-683-8314 ■ *Web:* www.ivenue.com						
Iverify Inc 150 Iverify Dr.	Charlotte	NC	28217	704-525-2701	523-7578	246
TF: 800-763-0314 ■ *Web:* www.iverify.us						
Iverson Language Associates Inc						
111 W Pleasant St Ste 102	Milwaukee	WI	53212	414-271-1144		768
Web: iversonlang.com						
Ives Group Inc 9 Main St Ste 2F	Sutton	MA	01590	508-476-7007		225
Web: www.ivesinc.com						
Ivey, Barnum & O'mara LLC						
170 Mason St	Greenwich	CT	06830	203-661-6000		428
Web: www.ibolaw.com						
IVG Energy Ltd						
20 E Greenway Pl Ste 400	Houston	TX	77046	713-554-3700		194
Web: www.ivgenergy.com						
IVI (Industrial Vehicles International Inc)						
6737 E 12th St	Tulsa	OK	74112	918-836-6516	838-9529	470
Web: www.indvehicles.com						
IVID Communications						
9265 Dowdy Dr Ste 201	San Diego	CA	92126	858-217-5465	309-4748	4
Web: www.ivid.com						
Ivie & Associates Inc						
601 Silveron Blvd	Flower Mound	TX	75028	972-899-5000	899-5050	195
Web: www.ivieinc.com						
Ivision Inc 1430 W Peachtree St NW	Atlanta	GA	30309	678-999-3002	495-1454	225
Web: ivision.com						
Ivory Consulting Corp						
325 Lennon Ln	Walnut Creek	CA	94598	925-926-1100		177
Web: www.ivorycc.com						
Ivory Homes 970 E Woodoak Ln	Salt Lake City	UT	84117	888-455-5561	747-7090*	653
**Fax Area Code:* 801 ■ *TF:* 888-455-5561 ■ *Web:* ivoryhomes.com						
Ivory Jack's 2581 Goldstream Rd	Fairbanks	AK	99709	907-455-6665		671
Web: www.ivoryjacksrestaurant.com						
Ivy at the Shore						
113 N Robertson Blvd.	Los Angeles	CA	90048	310-393-3113		671
Web: theivyrestaurants.com						
IVY Biomedical Systems Inc						
11 Business Pk Dr	Branford	CT	06405	203-481-4183	481-8734	250
TF: 800-247-4614 ■ *Web:* www.ivybiomedical.com						
Ivy Planning Group						
15204 Omega Dr Ste 110	Rockville	MD	20850	301-963-1669		463
Web: www.ivyplanninggroup.com						
Ivy Software Inc						
1146 Richmond-Tappahannock Hwy.	Manquin	VA	23106	800-342-5489		178-1
TF: 800-342-5489 ■ *Web:* www.ivysoftware.com						
Ivy Tech Columbus College						
4475 Central Ave	Columbus	IN	47203	812-372-9925	372-0311	800
TF: 800-922-4838 ■ *Web:* www.ivytech.edu						
IW (Interwest Safety Supply Inc)						
724 E 1860 S	Provo	UT	84606	801-375-6321	377-2739	523
TF: 800-955-1996 ■ *Web:* www.iwsafety.com						
IWA (International Webmasters Assn)						
119 E Union St Ste A	Pasadena	CA	91103	626-449-3709		48-9
TF: 866-607-1773 ■ *Web:* www.iwanet.org						
Iwaki America Inc 5 Boynton Rd	Holliston	MA	01746	508-429-1110	429-7433	641
Web: www.walchem.com						
IWCO Direct 7951 Powers Blvd	Chanhassen	MN	55317	952-474-0961	474-6467	195
Web: www.iwco.com						
iWeb Technologies Inc						
20 Place du Commerce	Montreal	QC	H3E1Z6	800-100-3276	286-1292*	225
**Fax Area Code:* 514 ■ *TF:* 800-100-3276 ■ *Web:* iweb.com						
IWITTS (National Institute for Women in Trades Technology & Science)						
1150 Ballena Blvd Ste 102	Alameda	CA	94501	510-749-0200	749-0500	49-19
Web: www.iwitts.org						

Listing	City	State	ZIP	Phone	Fax	Class
IWK Health Centre Health Sciences Library 5980 University Ave Rm 2048 PO Box 9700 *Web:* www.iwk.nshealth.ca	Halifax	NS	B3K6R8	902-470-8888		434-3
IWLA (International Warehouse Logistics Assn) 2800 S River Rd Ste 260 *Web:* www.iwla.com	Des Plaines	IL	60018	847-813-4699	813-0115	49-21
IWLA (Izaak Walton League of America) 707 Conservation Ln *TF:* 800-453-5463 ■ *Web:* www.iwla.org	Gaithersburg	MD	20878	301-548-0150	548-0146	48-13
IWM International LLC 500 E Middle St *TF:* 800-323-5585 ■ *Web:* www.iwmesh.com	Hanover	PA	17331	800-323-5585		688
iWORKS 2501 S Malt Ave *Web:* www.iworksus.com	Los Angeles	CA	90040	323-278-8363		480
IWorld of Travel 25 Broadway 9th Fl *Fax Area Code: 212 ■ *TF:* 800-223-7460 ■ *Web:* www.iworldoftravel.com	New York	NY	10004	800-223-7460	370-1477*	760
IWP (Inter-Wire Products) 355 Main St *TF:* 800-699-6633 ■ *Web:* www.interwiregroup.com	Armonk	NY	10504	914-273-6633	273-6848	813
IWPA (International Wood Products Assn) 4214 King St *TF:* 855-435-0005 ■ *Web:* www.iwpawood.org	Alexandria	VA	22302	703-820-6696	820-8550	49-3
IWPC (International Wireless Industry Consortium, The) 610 Louis Dr *Web:* www.iwpc.org	Warminster	PA	18974	215-293-9000		463
IWS (Robert E. Webber Institute for Worship Studies, The) 4001 Hendricks Ave *TF:* 800-282-2977 ■ *Web:* iws.edu	Jacksonville	FL	32207	904-264-2172	379-5534	685
IWT (Anita Borg Institute for Women & Technology) 1501 Page Mill Rd MS 1105 *Web:* anitab.org	Palo Alto	CA	94304	650-352-7500	852-8172	48-9
IWV Insurance Agency 1310 N Norma St	Ridgecrest	CA	93555	760-446-3544		390
IX Ctr 1-X Center Dr *Web:* www.ixcenter.com	Cleveland	OH	44135	216-676-6000		205
IXI Technology 23231 La Palma Ave *Web:* ixitech.com	Yorba Linda	CA	92887	714-692-3800	692-3838	625
I-XL Building Products Ltd 4900 102 Ave SE *Web:* ixlbuild.com	Calgary	AB	T2X2X8	403-526-5901		150
IXP Corp Princeton Forrestal Vlg 103 Main St *Web:* www.ixpcorp.com	Princeton	NJ	08540	609-759-5100		194
IXYS Corp 3540 Bassett St *NASDAQ: IXYS* ■ *Web:* www.ixys.com	Santa Clara	CA	95054	408-982-0700	748-9788	696
Iyka Enterprises Inc 3890 E Main St *Web:* iyka.com	Saint Charles	IL	60174	630-372-3900		177
Izaak Walton League of America (IWLA) 707 Conservation Ln *TF:* 800-453-5463 ■ *Web:* www.iwla.org	Gaithersburg	MD	20878	301-548-0150	548-0146	48-13
Izard County 80 E Main St PO Box 327 *Web:* www.izardcountyar.org	Melbourne	AR	72556	870-368-4316	368-3183	338
Izatys Golf Resort 40005 85th Ave *Web:* www.izatys.com	Onamia	MN	56359	320-532-4574		669
IZEA Inc 480 N Orlando Ave Ste 200 *Web:* izea.com	Winter Park	FL	32789	407-674-6911		7
Izumo Sushi 4412 Ming Ave	Bakersfield	CA	93309	661-398-0608		671
Izzard Ink LLC PO Box 522251 *Web:* izzardink.com	Salt Lake City	UT	84152	415-889-6100		637-2
Izzo Insurance Services 150 S Bloomingdale Rd *TF:* 800-800-1704 ■ *Web:* izzoinsurance.com	Bloomingdale	IL	60108	630-582-2800	582-2803	390

J

Listing	City	State	ZIP	Phone	Fax	Class
J & A Freight Systems Inc 4704 Irving Park Rd Ste 8 *TF:* 877-668-3378 ■ *Web:* jandafreight.com	Chicago	IL	60641	773-205-7720	205-7725	311
J & A Industries Inc 11918 Grandview Rd *TF:* 800-748-7722 ■ *Web:* www.railmart.com	Grandview	MO	64030	913-281-5722	281-1401	650
J & A Manufacturing Inc 2805 E Centerville Rd *Web:* www.jamfg.com	Garland	TX	75040	972-494-5552	494-0244	697
J & A Printing Inc PO Box 457 *TF:* 800-793-1781 ■ *Web:* www.japrinting.com	Hiawatha	IA	52233	319-393-1781		627
J & B Importers Inc 11925 SW 128th St *Web:* www.jbi.bike	Miami	FL	33186	305-238-1866		710
J & B International Trucks Inc 964 Hercules Dr PO Box 678 *Web:* jbinternational.org	Colchester	VT	05446	802-655-1290		311
J & B Medical Supply Company Inc 50496 W Pontiac Trl *TF:* 800-980-0047 ■ *Web:* www.jandbmedical.com	Wixom	MI	48393	800-737-0045		238
J & B Supply Inc 4915 S Zero PO Box 10450 *TF:* 800-262-2028 ■ *Web:* jandbsupply.com	Fort Smith	AR	72917	479-649-4915	649-4911	612
J & C Co 5000 N 72nd St *Web:* www.jccompany.net	Lincoln	NE	68507	402-467-4837	467-5137	625
J & D Enterprises 12000 Basswood Ave NW *Web:* www.jdenterprises.com	Uniontown	OH	44685	330-699-0203		7
J & D Interiors Inc 2015 N Main *Web:* ilovejd.com	Fort Worth	TX	76164	817-626-2365	626-9725	362
J & D Trucking Inc 3526 NW Blvd *Web:* janddtruckinginc.com	Vineland	NJ	08360	856-691-5145	691-5134	780
J & E Earl Manufacturing Co 7925 215th St W *Web:* www.jecompanies.com	Lakeville	MN	55044	952-469-3933		483
J & E Metal Fabricators 1 Coan Pl *Web:* www.metalfab.com	Metuchen	NJ	08840	732-548-9650		697
J & E Supply & Fastner Company Inc 1903 SE 59th St *TF:* 800-677-7922 ■ *Web:* www.jandesupply.com	Oklahoma City	OK	73129	405-670-1234		351
J & E Wholesale Floral Co 515 Crockett St *Web:* www.jandewholesaleamarillo.com	Amarillo	TX	79106	806-372-2301		293
J & G Sales Inc 440 Miller Valley Rd *Web:* www.jgsales.com	Prescott	AZ	86301	928-445-9650	445-9658	711
J & G Steel Corp 2429 Industrial Rd *Web:* www.jgsteel.com	Sapulpa	OK	74066	918-227-3131		480
J & G's Steakhouse 6000 E Camelback Rd *Web:* www.jgsteakhousescottsdale.com	Scottsdale	AZ	85251	480-214-8000	214-8001	671
J & H Dry Clean Express Inc 1008 Vestavia Pkwy *Web:* inthehamper.com	Vestavia Hills	AL	35216	205-823-1265		426
J & H Oil Company Inc 1619 Chicago Dr SW *Web:* jhoil.com	Wyoming	MI	49519	616-245-1114		324
J & J Foods Inc 1075 Jesse Jewell Pkwy SW *Web:* www.jandjfoods.com	Gainesville	GA	30501	770-287-7217		297-8
J & J Industries Inc 818 J & J Dr PO Box 1287 *TF:* 800-241-4586 ■ *Web:* www.jjflooringgroup.com	Dalton	GA	30721	706-529-2100	275-4433	131
J & J Machine Inc 12655 Industrial Blvd *TF:* 866-435-6716 ■ *Web:* jandjmachine.com	Elk River	MN	55330	763-421-0114	421-1605	757
J & J Material Handling Systems Inc 1820 Franklin St *TF:* 800-821-1054 ■ *Web:* jnjmaterial.com	Columbia	PA	17512	717-449-5153		261
J & J Security Services Corp 2922 Howland Blvd Ste 2 *Web:* www.jandjsecurity.com	Deltona	FL	32725	386-789-5555		693
J & J Sheetmetal Works LLC 414 Commerce Rd *Web:* www.jjsheetmetalworks.com	Vestal	NY	13850	607-729-3566		567
J & J Snack Foods Corp 6000 Central Hwy *NASDAQ: JJSF* ■ *TF:* 800-486-9533 ■ *Web:* www.jjsnack.com	Pennsauken Township	NJ	08109	856-665-9533	665-6718	296-25
J & K Distributors PO Box 1431 *Fax Area Code: 770 ■ *TF:* 800-780-4767 ■ *Web:* www.jandkdistributors.com	Kennesaw	GA	30144	800-780-4767	419-2453*	534
J & K Ingredients Inc 160 E 5th St *Web:* www.jkingredients.com	Paterson	NJ	07524	973-340-8700	340-4994	296-15
J & L Marketing 2100 Nelson Miller Pkwy *TF:* 800-651-5508 ■ *Web:* www.jandlmarketing.com	Louisville	KY	40223	800-651-5508		4
J & L Plastic Molding 368 N Cherry St Ext *Web:* www.jlmolding.com	Wallingford	CT	06492	203-265-6237		757
J & L Self Defense Products Inc 70 Defense Dr *Web:* www.selfdefenseproducts.com	Berkeley Springs	WV	25411	304-258-2900		148
J & M Brown Company Inc 267 Amory St *Web:* www.jmbco.com	Jamaica Plain	MA	02130	617-522-6800	522-6422	189-4
J & M Industries Inc 300 Ponchatoula Pkwy *TF:* 800-989-1002 ■ *Web:* www.jm-ind.com	Ponchatoula	LA	70454	985-386-6000		67
J & M Industries Inc 8045 Bond St *Web:* www.jmiinc.com	Lenexa	KS	66214	913-362-8994	362-0609	178-1
J & M Machine Products Inc 1821 Manor Dr *Web:* www.jmmachine.com	Muskegon	MI	49441	231-755-1622		757
J & M Plating Inc 4500 Kishwaukee St *TF:* 877-344-3044 ■ *Web:* www.jmplating.com	Rockford	IL	61109	815-964-4975		481
J & S Cafeteria Inc 110 Westover Dr *Web:* jandscafeteria.com	High Point	NC	27265	336-884-0404		670
J & S Electronic Business System Inc 878 Jefferson St *Web:* www.jselectronics.com	Burlington	IA	52601	319-752-5603		175
J & S Grinding Company Inc 224 River Rd *Web:* www.jsgrinding.com	Ridgway	PA	15853	814-776-1113		454
J A Piper Roofing Co 209 Commerce Rd *Web:* www.piperroofing.com	Greenville	SC	29611	864-269-6645	269-6648	697
J A Sauer Co 4559 Peoples Rd *Web:* jasauerco.com	Pittsburgh	PA	15237	412-931-7200		189-10
J A T of Fort Wayne Inc 5031 Industrial Rd *Web:* www.jatoffortwayne.com	Fort Wayne	IN	46825	260-482-8447	482-9990	780
J Alexander's Corp 3401 W End Ave Ste 260 *NASDAQ: JAX* ■ *TF:* 888-528-1991 ■ *Web:* www.jalexandersholdings.com	Nashville	TN	37203	615-269-1900		670
J B M Inc 2651 Scottish Pk *Web:* www.jbmincorporated.com	Knoxville	TN	37920	865-573-9800		480
J B Poindexter & Company Inc 600 Travis St Ste 200 *Web:* www.jbpoindexter.com	Houston	TX	77002	713-655-9800	951-9038	60
J Bailey & Co 10010 Sanctuary Blvd *Web:* www.jbaileyinc.com	Ocean Springs	MS	39564	228-348-1719		196
J Bar B Foods 1078 US-90 *Web:* www.jbfoods.com	Weimar	TX	78962	830-788-7511	788-7279	296-36
J Brand Holdings LLC 1318 E Seventh St Ste 260 *Web:* www.jbrandjeans.com	Los Angeles	CA	90021	212-228-8181		157-6
J Bulow Campbell Foundation 4401 Northside Pkwy NW Ste 950 *Web:* www.jbcf.org	Atlanta	GA	30327	404-658-9066		305
J Byrne Agency Inc 5200 New Jersey Ave *Web:* jbyrneagency.com	Wildwood	NJ	08260	609-522-3406		390
J C Bamford Excavators Ltd 2000 Bamford Blvd *Web:* www.jcb.com	Pooler	GA	31322	912-447-2000	447-2299	358

Company / Address	City	State	Zip	Phone	Fax	Class
J C Foodservice Inc 415 S Atlantic Blvd *TF:* 800-328-6688 ■ *Web:* www.actionsales.com	Monterey Park	CA	91754	626-308-1988	308-9780	111
J C Hanlon Consulting Inc 52611 Jessie Dr *Web:* www.jchci.com	Chesterfield	MI	48051	586-435-6231		196
J C Holliday Library 217 Graham St *Web:* www.sampsonnc.com	Clinton	NC	28328	910-592-4153		434-3
J C Machine Works & Fabricating Inc 1070 Neosho Ave *Web:* www.jcmachineworks.com	Baton Rouge	LA	70802	225-359-6117	381-0025	454
J C Marketing Associates Inc 467 Main St PO Box 289 *Web:* jcmarketingassociates.com	Wakefield	MA	01880	781-245-7070		195
J C Millwork Inc 501 Lakeside Pkwy Ste 150 *Web:* www.jcmillwork.com	Flower Mound	TX	75028	469-702-2570		499
J C Snavely & Sons Inc 150 Main St *Web:* www.jcsnavely.com	Landisville	PA	17538	717-394-7277	898-5208	817
J C Steele & Sons Inc 710 S Mulberry St *TF:* 800-278-3353 ■ *Web:* www.jcsteele.com	Statesville	NC	28677	704-872-3681		454
J C Taylor Antique Automobile Agency Inc 320 S 69th St *TF:* 800-345-8290 ■ *Web:* www.jctaylor.com	Upper Darby	PA	19082	800-345-8290		390
J C Wilkins Plumbing Company Inc 840 Massengill Pond Rd *Web:* www.jcwilkinsplumbing.com	Angier	NC	27501	919-639-6201		610
J Calnan & Associates Inc 3 Batterymarch Pk 5th Fl *Web:* jcalnan.com	Quincy	MA	02169	617-801-0200	801-0201	463
J Carter Marketing Inc 205 Smithtown Blvd *Web:* www.jcartermarketing.com	Nesconset	NY	11767	631-979-5620		195
J Chester & Associates Inc 5418 St Charles Ave *Web:* jchestercpa.com	Dallas	TX	75223	214-330-4682		734
J Crew Group Inc 770 Broadway *TF:* 800-562-0258 ■ *Web:* www.jcrew.com	New York	NY	10003	212-209-2500		459
J D H Contracting 8109 Network Dr *TF:* 877-839-0520 ■ *Web:* www.jdhcontracting.com	Plainfield	IN	46168	317-839-0520	838-0925	186
J D Products Inc 405 Commerce Ct *Web:* www.jdproductsinc.com	Vadnais Heights	MN	55127	651-483-9166		596
J D Rush C Inc 5900 E Lerdo Hwy *Web:* jdrush.com	Shafter	CA	93263	661-392-1900	399-2728	490
J D'Addario & Company Inc 595 Smith St *TF:* 800-323-2746 ■ *Web:* www.daddario.com	Farmingdale	NY	11735	631-439-3300	439-3333	527
J E B Advertising Inc 616-618 E Market St **Fax Area Code: 800* ■ *Web:* www.jebadvertising.com	Louisville	KY	40202	502-625-1800	251-9483*	7
J Edgar Eubanks & Assoc 1 Windsor Cove Ste 305 *TF:* 800-445-8629 ■ *Web:* www.jee.com	Columbia	SC	29223	803-252-5646	765-0860	47
J Edward Roush Lake 517 N Warren Rd *Web:* www.in.gov	Huntington	IN	46750	260-468-2165		565
J Ennis Fabrics Ltd 12122 - 68 St *TF:* 800-663-6647 ■ *Web:* www.ennisfabrics.com	Edmonton	AB	T5B1R1	800-663-6647		406
J Erik Jonsson Central Library 1515 Young St *Web:* www.dallaslibrary2.org	Dallas	TX	75201	214-670-1400		434-3
J F C Construction Inc 4901 Pacheco Blvd *Web:* www.jfcconstruction.com	Martinez	CA	94553	925-228-0924		186
J F Jacobs Inc 31523 W 8 Mile Rd *Web:* jfjacobsinc.net	Livonia	MI	48152	248-476-7888		189-10
J F Sato & Associates Inc 5878 S Rapp St *Web:* www.jfsato.com	Littleton	CO	80120	303-797-1200		256
J Fletcher Creamer & Son Inc 101 E Broadway *TF:* 800-835-9801 ■ *Web:* www.jfcson.com	Hackensack	NJ	07601	201-488-9800	488-2901	189-5
J Frank Schmidt & Son Company Inc 9500 SE 327th Ave *Web:* www.jfschmidt.com	Boring	OR	97009	503-663-4128		192
J Freirich Foods Inc 815 W Kerr St PO Box 1529 *TF:* 800-554-4788 ■ *Web:* www.freirich.com	Salisbury	NC	28144	800-221-1315		473
J Gilbert's Wood Fired Steaks 1 E Campus View Blvd *Web:* www.jgilberts.com	Columbus	OH	43235	614-840-9090		670
J H I Engineering 3420 SW Macadam Ave *Web:* www.jhiengineering.com	Portland	OR	97239	503-223-7799		256
J Hall & Associates CPAs Inc 327 S Market St	Troy	OH	45373	937-339-8417		2
J Horst Manufacturing Co, The 279 E Main St *Web:* www.jhorst.com	Dalton	OH	44618	330-828-2216	828-8107	454
J J Curran Crane Co 865 S Ft St *Web:* www.jjcurran.com	Detroit	MI	48217	313-842-1700		190
J J Plumbing LLC 4210 B St NW *Web:* www.jjplumbingllc.com	Auburn	WA	98001	253-939-1390		189-10
J Joseph Consulting 21732 Hardy Oak Blvd *Web:* jjc.com	San Antonio	TX	78258	210-587-2750		463
J Josephson Inc 35 Horizon Blvd *Web:* www.jjosephson.com	South Hackensack	NJ	07606	201-440-7000	440-7109	802
J K Consulting 988 E 9th St *Web:* jkconsulting.net	Lockport	IL	60441	815-588-4530		196
J K Datta Consultants Inc 711 W 40th St Ste 355	Baltimore	MD	21211	410-243-2882		180
J K Financial Services Inc 149 Cross Rail Ln Ste 102 *Web:* lilyho.com	Norco	CA	92860	714-704-1010		690
J Knipper & Company Inc 1 Healthcare Way *TF:* 888-564-7737 ■ *Web:* www.knipper.com	Lakewood	NJ	08701	732-905-7878	905-0469	195
J Kokolakis Contracting Inc 1500 Ocean Ave *Web:* www.jkokolakis.com	Bohemia	NY	11716	631-744-6147	744-6156	186
J Krug & Associates Inc 1350 W Northwest Hwy Ste 100 *Web:* www.jkrug.com	Mount Prospect	IL	60056	847-392-8585		393
J L A Consulting 1013 N Causeway Blvd *Web:* jlaconsulting.net	Metairie	LA	70001	504-835-9639	835-7850	196
J L Business Interiors Inc 515 Schoenhaar Dr PO Box 303 *TF:* 866-338-5524 ■ *Web:* www.jlbusinessinteriors.com	West Bend	WI	53090	262-338-2221	338-2269	320
J L Clark 923 23rd Ave *TF:* 888-452-3342 ■ *Web:* www.jlclark.com	Rockford	IL	61104	815-962-8861		547
J L Manufacturing Inc 2300 Merrill Creek Pkwy	Everett	WA	98203	425-355-3330	355-9856	295
J L Wallace Inc 9111 W College Pointe Dr *Web:* www.jlwallaceinc.com	Fort Myers	FL	33919	239-437-1111		186
J Lawrence Hall Company Inc 17 Progress Ave *Web:* jlawrencehall.com	Nashua	NH	03062	603-882-2021		189-10
J Lewis & Assoc 3985 University Ave Ste 2 *TF:* 855-804-6049 ■ *Web:* jlewislaw.com	Riverside	CA	92501	951-682-0488		41
J Lohr Vineyards & Wines 1000 Lenzen Ave *Web:* www.jlohr.com	San Jose	CA	95126	408-288-5057	993-2276	50-7
J Lorber Company Inc 2659 Bristol Pk *Web:* www.jlorber.com	Bensalem	PA	19020	215-638-2300		610
J M Brennan Inc 2101 W St Paul Ave *Web:* jmbrennan.com	Milwaukee	WI	53201	414-342-3829	342-3209	610
J M Field Marketing Inc 3570 NW 53rd Ct *TF:* 844-523-1957 ■ *Web:* www.jmfieldmarketing.com	Fort Lauderdale	FL	33309	954-523-1957		317
J M Fox Associates Inc 616 Dekalb St *Web:* jmfox.com	Norristown	PA	19401	610-275-5957		7
J McLaughlin 236250 Greenpoint Ave 2nd Fl Bldg 6 *TF:* 844-532-5625 ■ *Web:* www.jmclaughlin.com	Brooklyn	NY	11222	718-532-9000		157-4
J Michael Brill & Associates Inc 5053 Ritter Rd Ste 200 PO Box 298 *Web:* www.jmichaelbrill.com	Mechanicsburg	PA	17055	717-691-0200	691-7654	727
J N Machinery Corp (JN) 1081 Rock Rd Ln *Web:* jnmachinery.com	East Dundee	IL	60118	224-699-9161	699-9286	318
J Nick Leitch & Co 1109 Rhode Island St NE *Web:* jnickleitch.com	Albuquerque	NM	87110	505-884-8744		2
J P Diamond Co 25 E James St *Web:* www.jpdiamond.com	Falconer	NY	14733	716-665-4100		116
J P Kane's Town & Country Furniture 641 Missouri Ave N *Web:* jpkfurniture.com	Largo	FL	33770	727-584-2121		321
J P Noonan Transportation Inc 415 W St *TF:* 800-922-8026 ■ *Web:* www.jpnoonan.com	West Bridgewater	MA	02379	800-922-8026		780
J P R Communications 19029 Dorlon Dr *Web:* www.jprcom.com	Tarzana	CA	91356	818-884-8282		636
J Paul Getty Museum 1200 Getty Center Dr *Web:* www.getty.edu	Los Angeles	CA	90049	310-440-7300	440-7720	520
J Paul Leonard Library 1630 Holloway Ave *Web:* library.sfsu.edu	San Francisco	CA	94132	415-469-6100	338-1504	434-6
J Polep Distribution Services Inc 705 Meadow St *TF:* 800-447-6537 ■ *Web:* www.jpolep.com	Chicopee	MA	01013	413-592-4141	592-5870	756
J R C Transportation Inc 47 Maple Ave *Web:* www.jrctransportation.com	Thomaston	CT	06787	860-283-0207		780
J R D Systems Inc 42450 Hayes Rd Ste 3 *Web:* www.jrdsi.com	Clinton Township	MI	48038	586-416-1500	416-1600	463
J R Miller & Assoc 2700 Saturn St *Web:* www.jrma.com	Brea	CA	92821	714-524-1870		256
J R O'Dwyer Company Inc 271 Madison Ave Ste 600 *Web:* www.odwyerpr.com	New York	NY	10016	212-679-2471		531-11
J Reese Construction Inc 10805 Thornmint Rd *Web:* www.debconstruct.com	San Diego	CA	92127	858-592-6500		188-4
J Reynolds 365 Sansom Blvd *Web:* www.jreynolds.com	Saginaw	TX	76179	817-306-9596		708
J Robert Scott Inc 500 N Oak St *TF:* 877-207-5130 ■ *Web:* www.jrobertscott.com	Inglewood	CA	90302	310-680-4300		319-4
J Rockcliff Realtors 15 Railroad Ave *Web:* www.rockcliff.com	Danville	CA	94526	925-855-4000		652
J S Redpath Ltd 710 McKeown Ave *Web:* www.redpathmining.com	North Bay	ON	P1A7M2	705-474-2461		787
J Sargeant Reynolds Community College PO Box 85622 *TF:* 800-922-3420 ■ *Web:* www.reynolds.edu	Richmond	VA	23285	804-371-3000	371-3650	162
J Smith Lanier & Co 300 W Tenth St *TF:* 800-226-4522 ■ *Web:* www.jsmithlanier.com	West Point	GA	31833	706-645-2211	643-0606	390
J Stokes & Associates Inc 1444 N Main St *Web:* jstokes.com	Walnut Creek	CA	94596	925-933-1624		195
J T M Technologies Inc 160 County Road 979 *Web:* jtmtechnologies.com	Royse City	TX	75189	972-429-6575	635-6905	621
J T Turner Construction Company Inc 319 Tattnall St PO Box 3403 *Web:* www.jttconst.com	Savannah	GA	31799	912-356-5611	356-5615	186

Company / Address	City	State	ZIP	Phone	Fax	Class
J Walter Miller Co 411 E Chestnut St *Web:* www.jwaltermiller.com	Lancaster	PA	17602	717-392-7428		492
J Wda 2359 Fourth Ave Ste 300 *Web:* jwdainc.com	San Diego	CA	92101	619-233-6777	237-0541	196
J. & J. Carbide & Tool Inc 5656 W 120th St *Web:* www.jandjcarbide.com	Alsip	IL	60803	708-489-0300	489-0396	493
J. & M. Golf Inc 319 Industrial Dr *Web:* jandmgolf.com	Griffith	IN	46319	219-922-1787		711
J. & W. Instruments Inc 4800 Mustang Cir *Web:* www.jwinst.com	New Brighton	MN	55112	763-784-5708	784-5751	385
J. A. Riggs Tractor Company Inc 9125 Interstate 30 *TF:* 800-759-3140 ■ *Web:* www.riggscat.com	Little Rock	AR	72209	501-570-3100		23
J. Aaron Cooper CPA LLC 106 W Nezpique PO Box 918	Jennings	LA	70546	337-824-5007		2
J. C. Macelroy Company Inc PO Box 850 *TF:* 800-622-3576 ■ *Web:* www.macelroy.com	Piscataway	NJ	08855	732-572-7100	572-7112	480
J. C. Watts Cos 600 13th St NW Ste 790 *Web:* www.wattsconsultinggroup.com	Washington	DC	20005	202-207-2854		636
J. Christopher Haircutters Inc 65 Park St *Web:* jchristopherhaircutters.com	Andover	MA	01810	978-475-4884		77
J. Cruz & Associates LLC 216 W Village Blvd Ste 202 *TF:* 877-513-1373 ■ *Web:* jca-law.com	Laredo	TX	78041	956-717-1300		41
J. D. Seibert & Company Inc 20 W Ninth St *Web:* jdseibertandco.com	Cincinnati	OH	45202	513-241-8888		690
J. F. Brennan Company Inc 818 Bainbridge St *TF:* 800-658-9027 ■ *Web:* www.jfbrennan.com	La Crosse	WI	54603	608-784-7173	785-2090	465
J. F. Smith Group 735 E Glenn Ave *Web:* jfsg.com	Auburn	AL	36831	334-502-5374	502-5370	463
J. Good-In Inc 576 Explorer St *TF:* 800-397-6821 ■ *Web:* www.jgoodin.com	Brea	CA	92821	714-257-9391		411
J. H. Bennett & Company Inc PO Box 8028 *TF:* 800-837-5426 ■ *Web:* www.jhbennett.com	Novi	MI	48376	248-596-5100	596-0640	385
J. J. Sullivan Inc 229 River St *Web:* jjsullivaninc.com	Guilford	CT	06437	203-453-2781		316
J. Kings Food Service Professionals Inc 700 Furrows Rd *Web:* www.jkings.com	Holtsville	NY	11742	631-289-8401	758-0187	297-8
J. Levine Books & Judaica 5 W 30th St *TF:* 800-553-9474 ■ *Web:* www.levinejudaica.com	New York	NY	10001	212-695-6888	643-1044	95
J. M. Bozeman Enterprises Inc 166 Seltzer Ln *TF:* 800-472-1836 ■ *Web:* jmbozeman.com	Malvern	AR	72104	800-472-1836		685
J. M. Huber Corp 499 Thornall St 8th Fl *TF:* 800-535-2687 ■ *Web:* www.huber.com	Edison	NJ	08837	732-549-8600		536
J. M. Smucker Co, The 1 Strawberry Ln *Web:* www.smuckers.com	Orrville	OH	44667	330-682-3000		296-20
J. N. White Associates Inc 129 N Center St PO Box 219 *TF:* 800-227-5718 ■ *Web:* jnwhiteusa.com	Perry	NY	14530	800-227-5718		687
J. P. Farley Corp 29055 Clemens Rd *TF:* 800-634-0173 ■ *Web:* www.jpfarley.com	Westlake	OH	44145	440-250-4300		463
J. P. King Auction Company Inc 414 Broad St *TF:* 800-558-5464 ■ *Web:* www.jpking.com	Gadsden	AL	35901	800-558-5464		41
J. P. Pattern Inc 5038 N 125th St *Web:* www.jppattern.com	Butler	WI	53007	262-781-2040	781-7698	567
J. Philip Tyler CPA LLC 2910 Russ St *Web:* tylercpafirm.com	Marianna	FL	32446	850-482-7333	482-3085	2
J. R. Henry Consulting Inc PO Box 9724 *Web:* psmarketing.com	Pittsburgh	PA	15229	412-931-2833	291-3434	463
J. R. Schneider Company Inc 849 Jackson St *Web:* www.jrschneider.com	Benicia	CA	94510	707-745-0404	745-1246	386
J. R. Setina Manufacturing Company Inc 2926 Yelm Hwy SE *TF:* 800-426-2627 ■ *Web:* setina.com	Olympia	WA	98501	360-491-6197		393
J. Reed Jordan PC 1500 Citywest Blvd Ste 450 *Web:* reedjordanpc.com	Houston	TX	77042	713-278-5982	278-5989	2
J. Robin Haynes & Company PA 5446 Sunset Blvd Ste 202 *Web:* jrhaynescpa.com	Lexington	SC	29072	803-951-8586		2
J. S. McCarthy Printers Inc 15 Darin Dr *TF:* 888-465-6241 ■ *Web:* jsmccarthy.com	Augusta	ME	04330	207-622-6241		627
J. W. Allen Company Inc 111 John St Ste 1801 *Web:* jwallenco.com	New York	NY	10038	212-227-6875		390
J. W. Hirschfeld Agency Inc 326 New York Ave *Web:* jwhinsurance.com	Huntington	NY	11743	631-421-2525		390
J.A. Optronics LLC 7337 Old Alexandria Ferry Rd *Web:* www.jaoptronics.biz	Clinton	MD	20735	301-868-5316	868-9402	543
J.A. Swanson Agency 140 Hwy 219 PO Box 147 *Web:* jaswansonagency.com	Pendroy	MT	59467	406-469-2276	469-2283	390
J.B. Merritt & Associates LLC 220 Swartz Rd *Web:* jbmerritt.com	Lexington	SC	29072	803-359-1041		2
J.B.L. International Inc 417 E 29th St *Web:* www.pagetequipment.com	Marshfield	WI	54449	715-384-3158	387-0720	91
J.C. Choate Publications PO Box 72 *Web:* www.worldevangelism.org	Winona	MS	38967	662-283-1192		637-2
J.C. Licht 901 S Rohlwing Rd Ste M *Web:* www.jclicht.com	Addison	IL	60101	630-351-0400		802
J.C. Sales Inc 2500 Hollywood Blvd Ste 412 *Web:* www.jcsales.com	Hollywood	FL	33020	954-341-8636	345-1909	44
J.E. Abercrombie Inc 9111 Galveston Ave *Web:* www.jeabercrombie.net	Jacksonville	FL	32211	904-727-9521		189-9
J.E. Shekell Inc 424 W Tennessee St *TF:* 800-473-4215 ■ *Web:* www.shekell.com	Evansville	IN	47710	812-425-9131		189-10
J.G. Edelen Company Inc 8901 Kelso Dr *Web:* www.jgedelen.com	Baltimore	MD	21221	410-918-1200	918-0964	351
J.H. Dowling Inc 3019 Jackson Bluff Rd *Web:* www.jhdowling.com	Tallahassee	FL	32304	850-222-2616	222-2617	191-3
J.H. Lynch & Sons Inc 50 Lynch Pl *TF:* 800-545-9624 ■ *Web:* jhlynch.com	Cumberland	RI	02864	401-333-4300	334-2830	188-4
J.H. Strain and Sons Inc PO Box 277 *Web:* www.jhstrain.net	Tye	TX	79563	325-692-0067		188-4
J.I. Garcia Construction Co 4717 E Hedges Ave *Web:* www.jigarcia.com	Fresno	CA	93703	559-276-7726		186
J.J. Collins Printers 2300 Warrenville Rd Ste 190 *Web:* www.jjcollins.com	Downers Grove	IL	60515	630-960-2525	960-7487	627
J.L. Cohen & Associates Ltd 2925 William Penn Hwy Ste 103 *Web:* jlcohencpa.com	Easton	PA	18045	610-258-0819		2
J.L. Rothrock Inc 3111 Southbrook Dr *Web:* www.rothrocktrucking.com	Greensboro	NC	27406	336-854-6050		780
J.L. Souser & Associates Inc 3495 Industrial Dr *TF:* 800-757-0181 ■ *Web:* www.jlsautomation.com	York	PA	17402	717-505-3800		358
J.M. Ahle Company Inc 2 Hermann St *Web:* www.jmahle.com	South River	NJ	08882	732-238-1700	238-9663	480
J.M. Rodgers Company Inc 1975 Linden Blvd *Web:* www.jmrodgers.com	Elmont	NY	11003	516-872-5570	872-5587	314
J.R. Roberts/Deacon Inc 7745 Greenback Ln Ste 250 *Web:* www.jrrobertsdeacon.com	Citrus Heights	CA	95610	916-729-5600	729-5666	186
J.R. Tallman & Company Inc 12 Court St *Web:* jrtallman.com	Taunton	MA	02780	508-824-4051	822-7654	390
J.S. Fleming Associates Inc (RDA) 28 Lord Rd *TF:* 800-498-0904 ■ *Web:* jsfleming.com	Marlborough	MA	01752	508-460-0904	460-0909	179
J.T. Cullen Company Inc 901 31st Ave *Web:* www.jtcullenco.com	Fulton	IL	61252	815-589-2412		91
J.T. Engineering Inc 1077 Centennial Centre Blvd *Web:* jt-engineering.com	Hobart	WI	54155	920-468-4771		261
J.T. Neal Insurance Agency Inc 611 C Ave	Lawton	OK	73501	580-355-6595		390
J.T. Smith Cos 5285 Meadows Rd Ste 171 *Web:* jtsmithco.com	Lake Oswego	OR	97035	503-657-3402		653
J.V. Manufacturing Inc 701 Butterfield Coach Rd *Web:* www.cram-a-lot.com	Springdale	AR	72764	479-751-7320	751-7774	806
J.V. Plastics Inc 2723 S Great SW Pky *Web:* www.jvplastics.com	Grand Prairie	TX	75052	972-606-0500		604
J.V. Precision Machine Co 71 Cogwheel Ln *Web:* www.jvprecision.net	Seymour	CT	06483	203-888-0748	888-7433	454
J.V. Rigging Inc 740 Greensburg Rd *Web:* www.jvrigging.com	New Kensington	PA	15068	724-339-8900	339-3903	189-11
J.W. Childs Associates LP (JWC) 500 Totten Pond Rd 6th Fl *Web:* www.jwchilds.com	Waltham	MA	02451	617-753-1100	753-1101	792
J.W. Design & Construction Inc 3563 Sueldo St Ste I *Web:* www.jwdci.com	San Luis Obispo	CA	93401	805-544-3130		186
J.W. Performance Transmission Inc 1826 Baldwin St *Web:* www.racewithjw.com	Rockledge	FL	32955	321-632-6205	632-0247	60
J.W.Reedy Realty Ltd 1136 S Main St *Web:* jwreedy.com	Lombard	IL	60148	630-629-0016	629-0024	652
J2 Global Communications Inc 6922 Hollywood Blvd *TF:* 888-718-2000 ■ *Web:* www.j2global.com	Hollywood	CA	90028	323-860-9200		736
J2 Interactive LLC 2 13th St *Web:* www.j2interactive.com	Boston	MA	02129	617-241-7266		398
J2 Retail Systems Inc 15042 Parkway Loop Bldg D *Web:* www.aures-pos.fr	Tustin	CA	92780	714-669-3111		173-1
J2E Technology LLC 925 St Germain Rd *Web:* j2etech.com	Chula Vista	CA	91913	619-861-8039		180
J2t Recruiting Consultants Inc 4101 S Quebec St Ste 2128 **Fax Area Code:* 866 ■ *Web:* j2t-recruiting.com	Denver	CO	80237	303-741-6122	839-6629*	721
J4 Systems Inc 2521 Warren Dr Ste A *TF:* 866-547-9783 ■ *Web:* www.j4systems.com	Rocklin	CA	95677	916-303-7200		180
JA (Jenkins Arboretum) 631 Berwyn Baptist Rd *Web:* www.jenkinsarboretum.org	Devon	PA	19333	610-647-8870	647-6664	97
JA (Jewelers of America) 120 Broadway Ste 2820 *TF:* 800-223-0673 ■ *Web:* www.jewelers.org	New York	NY	10271	646-658-0246	658-0256	49-4
JA & Kathryn Albertson Foundation 501 Baybrook Ct *Web:* www.jkaf.org	Boise	ID	83706	208-424-2600		305

Name / Address	City	ST	ZIP	Phone	Fax	Class
JA Apparel Corp 424 Madison Ave	New York	NY	10017	212-872-1340		157-3
Web: www.josephabboud.com						
JA Billipp Co 6925 Portwest Dr Ste 130	Houston	TX	77024	713-426-5000		653
TF: 800-216-9013 ■ *Web:* www.jabillipp.com						
JA Reinhardt & Company Inc						
Spruce Cabin Rd	Mountainhome	PA	18342	570-595-7491		487
Web: jareinhardt.bethermalandpower.com						
JA Solar USA Inc						
2570 N 1st St Ste 360	San Jose	CA	95131	408-586-0000	956-9505	696
Web: www.jasolar.com						
JA Street & Associates Inc						
245 Birch St	Blountville	TN	37617	423-323-8017		186
Web: jastreet.com						
JA Tiberti Construction Co						
1806 Industrial Rd	Las Vegas	NV	89102	702-382-7071		186
Web: www.tiberti.com						
JA Woollam Company Inc						
645 M St Ste 102	Lincoln	NE	68508	402-477-7501	477-8214	256
Web: www.jawoollam.com						
Jaapharm Canada Inc						
510 Rowntree Dairy Rd Bldg B	Woodbridge	ON	L4L8H2	905-851-7885	856-5838	582
TF: 800-465-9587 ■ *Web:* www.jaapharm.com						
JAARS Inc 7405 Jaars Rd	Waxhaw	NC	28173	800-890-0628	843-6000*	393
**Fax Area Code:* 704 ■ *TF:* 800-890-0628 ■ *Web:* www.jaars.org						
JAAS Systems Ltd						
5011 Pine Creek Dr	Westerville	OH	43081	614-759-4167		177
Web: jaas.net						
Jabil Circuit Inc						
10560 ML King St N	Saint Petersburg	FL	33716	727-577-9749		625
NYSE: JBL ■ *TF:* 877-217-6328 ■ *Web:* www.jabil.com						
Jabo Supply Corp						
5164 County Rd 64/66	Huntington	WV	25705	304-736-8333	736-8551	385
TF: 800-334-5226 ■ *Web:* www.jabosupply.com						
J-A-C Electric Co-opeartive Inc						
1784 FM 172	Bluegrove	TX	76352	940-895-3311	895-3321	245
Web: www.jacelectric.com						
JAC Manufacturing Inc						
701 Industrial Blvd	Palmyra	WI	53156	262-495-2141	495-4631	729
Web: www.jacmfg.com						
JACAN (Junior Achievement of Canada)						
161 Bay St 27th Fl	Toronto	ON	M5J2S1	416-622-4602	622-6861	48-11
TF: 800-265-0699 ■ *Web:* jacanada.org						
JaCiva's Chocolate						
4733 SE Hawthorne Ave	Portland	OR	97215	503-234-8115		123
Web: www.jacivas.com						
Jack & Giulio's 2391 San Diego Ave	San Diego	CA	92110	619-294-2074	294-4188	671
Web: www.jackandgiulios.com						
Jack & Mary's Restaurant 655 N 114th St	Omaha	NE	68154	402-496-2090		671
Web: www.jackandmarysrestaurant.com						
Jack A. Farrior Inc						
9585 US Hwy 264A	Farmville	NC	27828	252-753-2020	753-7851	697
Web: www.farriorsteelworks.com						
Jack B. Keenan Inc 1820 Georgetta Dr	San Jose	CA	95125	408-448-4686		507
Web: jackbkeenan.com						
Jack Becker Distributors Inc						
6800 Suemac Pl	Jacksonville	FL	32254	800-488-8411		581
TF: 800-488-8411 ■ *Web:* www.jackbecker.com						
Jack Bros Inc 551 W Main St Ste 5	Brawley	CA	92227	760-344-3781		10-11
Jack Brown Produce Inc						
8035 Fruit Ridge Ave NW	Sparta	MI	49345	616-887-9568	887-9765	297-7
Web: www.jackbrownproduce.com						
Jack Conway 137 Washington St	Norwell	MA	02061	781-871-0080	878-2632	652
TF: 800-283-1030 ■ *Web:* www.jackconway.com						
Jack Cooper Transport Company Inc						
1100 Walnut St Ste 2400	Kansas City	MO	64106	816-983-4000		780
Web: www.jackcooper.com						
Jack County 100 Main St Ste 208	Jacksboro	TX	76458	940-567-2111	567-6441	338
Web: www.jackcounty.org						
Jack Cust Baseball Academy						
5B Bartles Corner Rd	Flemington	NJ	08822	908-284-1778		48-22
Web: www.diamondnation.com						
Jack Engle and Co						
8440 S Alameda St	Los Angeles	CA	90001	323-589-8111	589-9189	686
Web: www.jackengleco.com						
Jack FM 180 N Stetson Ste 900	Chicago	IL	60601	312-870-6400		647
Web: www.khitschicago.cbslocal.com						
Jack Giambalvo Motor Co 1390 Eden Rd	York	PA	17402	717-781-2154		57
Web: www.jackgiambalvo.com						
Jack Gray Transport Inc 4600 E 15th Ave	Gary	IN	46403	219-938-7020		780
TF: 800-426-1827 ■ *Web:* jackgray.com						
Jack Green Assoc 242 W 36th St	New York	NY	10018	212-629-0850		261
Web: jackgreenassoc.com						
Jack Henry & Associates Inc						
663 W Hwy 60 PO Box 807	Monett	MO	65708	417-235-6652	235-8406	178-11
NASDAQ: JKHY ■ *TF:* 800-299-4222 ■ *Web:* www.jackhenry.com						
Jack in the Box Inc 9330 Balboa Ave	San Diego	CA	92123	858-571-2121		670
NASDAQ: JACK ■ *TF:* 800-955-5225 ■ *Web:* www.jackinthebox.com						
Jack Jones Jefferson County Juvenile Detention Ctr						
101 E Barraque St	Pine Bluff	AR	71611	870-541-5351		412
Web: www.jeffcoso.org						
Jack Kent Cooke Foundation						
44325 Woodridge Pkwy	Lansdowne	VA	20176	703-723-8000	723-8030	303
Web: jkcf.org						
Jack Kilgore & Company Inc						
154 E 71st St 3rd Fl	New York	NY	10021	212-650-1149		42
Web: www.kilgoregallery.com						
Jack Laurence Corp						
12831 W Golden Ln	San Antonio	TX	78249	210-696-0273		189-10
Jack Lawton Webb Convention Ctr						
4000 S Range Line	Joplin	MO	64804	417-623-4600		205
Web: www.jlwcenter.weebly.com						
Jack London Inn 444 Embarcadero W	Oakland	CA	94607	510-444-2032		379
Web: www.jacklondoninn.com						
Jack London State Historic Park						
2400 London Ranch Rd	Glen Ellen	CA	95442	707-938-5216		565
Web: www.parks.ca.gov						
Jack M. Shuck Agency Inc						
427 Washington St	Huntingdon	PA	16652	814-643-3020		390
Web: shuckagency.com						
Jack Morton Inc 909 3rd Ave 11th Fl	New York	NY	10022	212-401-7000		393
Web: www.jackmorton.com						
Jack Nadel International Inc						
8701 Bellanca Ave	Los Angeles	CA	90045	310-815-2600		5
Web: www.nadel.com						
Jack Nicklaus Museum						
2355 Olentangy River Rd	Columbus	OH	43210	614-247-5959	247-5906	522
Web: nicklausmuseum.org						
Jack O'Reilly Tuxedos LLC						
2701 Fifth St Hwy	Reading	PA	19605	610-929-9409		157-3
Web: www.jackoreillytuxedos.com						
Jack of All Trades Personnel Services						
2701 Franklin Ave	Waco	TX	76710	254-754-7997		260
Web: joatwaco.com						
Jack Powell Ford-Mercury Inc						
1418 SE 1 St	Mineral Wells	TX	76067	940-325-1331		57
Web: www.jackpowellford.net						
Jack Richeson & Company Inc						
557 Marcella Dr	Kimberly	WI	54136	920-738-0744	738-9156	43
TF: 800-233-2404 ■ *Web:* www.richesonart.com						
Jack Schwartz Shoes Inc						
155 Avenue of the Americas	New York	NY	10013	212-691-4700		301
Web: www.lugz.com						
Jack Tilton Gallery 8 E 76th St	New York	NY	10021	212-737-2221	396-1725	42
Web: www.jacktiltongallery.com						
Jack Tire & Oil 1795 N Main	Logan	UT	80216	435-752-7897		755
TF: 866-804-8473 ■ *Web:* www.jackstireandoil.com						
Jack Williams Tire Company Inc						
PO Box 3655	Scranton	PA	18505	800-833-5051		62-5
TF: 800-833-5051 ■ *Web:* www.jackwilliams.com						
Jack's Bar-B-Que 334 W Trinity Ln	Nashville	TN	37207	615-228-4600	228-4700	671
Web: jacksbarbque.com						
Jack's Diving Locker Inc						
75-5813 Alii Dr	Kailua-Kona	HI	96740	808-329-7585	329-7588	423
TF: 800-345-4807 ■ *Web:* www.jacksdivinglocker.com						
Jack's Family Restaurants Inc						
2831 19th St S	Homewood	AL	35209	205-879-9321	945-8167	670
Web: www.eatatjacks.com						
Jack's Oyster House 42 State St	Albany	NY	12207	518-465-8854	434-2134	671
Web: www.jacksoysterhouse.com						
Jackalope 2820 Cerrillos Rd	Santa Fe	NM	87507	505-471-8539		362
Web: jackalope.com						
Jackburn Manufacturing Inc						
438 Church St	Girard	PA	16417	814-774-3573	774-2854	491
Web: www.jackburn.com						
Jackdaw Publications 29 E 21st St	New York	NY	10010	800-237-9932	436-4643*	637-2
**Fax Area Code:* 888 ■ *TF:* 800-237-9932 ■ *Web:* www.jackdaw.com						
Jackie B Lovett Trucking Co						
4236 Hwy 24 S	Waynesboro	GA	30830	706-554-6732	554-3045	780
Web: www.lovetttrucking.com						
Jackie Gleason Theater of the Performing Arts						
1700 Washington Ave	Miami Beach	FL	33139	305-673-7300		572
Web: www.fillmoremb.com						
Jackie Matchett Personnel Inc						
519 Heritage Rd Ste 2B	Southbury	CT	06488	203-405-6111	583-4930	260
Web: www.jackiematchett.com						
Jacklin Steel Supply Co						
2410 Aero Park Dr	Traverse City	MI	49686	231-946-8434		480
Web: www.jacklinsteel.com						
Jacknob Corp 290 Oser Ave	Hauppauge	NY	11788	631-231-9400	231-0330	350
TF: 888-231-9333 ■ *Web:* www.jacknob.com						
Jacko Law Group PC						
5920 Friars Rd Ste 208	San Diego	CA	92108	619-298-2880		428
TF: 866-497-2298 ■ *Web:* www.jackolg.com						
Jackpot Junction Casino Hotel						
39375 County Hwy 24 PO Box 420	Morton	MN	56270	800-946-2274		133
TF: 800-946-2274 ■ *Web:* www.jackpotjunction.com						
Jacksboro National Bank						
910 N Main St	Jacksboro	TX	76458	940-567-5551		70
Web: mybanktexas.com						
Jacksboro Public Library						
585 Main St	Jacksboro	TN	37757	423-562-3675	562-9587	434-3
Web: www.jacksboropubliclibrary.org						
Jackson & Associates Inc						
15460 Herriman Blvd	Noblesville	IN	46060	317-773-6660		366
TF: 800-262-4108 ■ *Web:* jackson-assoc.us						
Jackson & Bergman LLP						
32 W State St	Binghamton	NY	13901	607-296-4190		41
Web: jacksonbergman.com						
Jackson & Blanc Inc 7929 Arjons Dr	San Diego	CA	92126	858-831-7900	527-1502	189-10
Web: www.jacksonandblanc.com						
Jackson & Campbell 1120 20th St NW	Washington	DC	20036	202-457-1600		445
Web: jackscamp.com						
Jackson & Hertogs LLP						
201 Mission St Ste 700	San Francisco	CA	94105	415-986-4559	986-1871	428
TF: 800-780-2008 ■ *Web:* www.jackson-hertogs.com						
Jackson & Jackson Insurance						
302 E Foothill Blvd	San Dimas	CA	91773	626-914-9944		390
Web: jjinsurance.com						
Jackson & Perkins 2 Floral Ave	Hodges	SC	29653	800-292-4769		459
TF: 800-292-4769 ■ *Web:* www.jacksonandperkins.com						
Jackson & Tull Chartered Engineers						
12201 Distribution Way	Beltsville	MD	20705	301-937-8255		256
Web: www.jnt.com						
Jackson Area Chamber of Commerce						
197 Auditorium St	Jackson	TN	38301	731-423-2200	424-4860	139
Web: jacksontn.com						
Jackson Area Chamber of Commerce						
234 Broadway St	Jackson	OH	45640	740-286-2722	286-8443	139
Web: www.jacksonohio.org						
Jackson Community College						
1376 N Main St	Jackson	MI	49201	517-787-0800	796-8631	162
TF: 888-522-7344 ■ *Web:* www.jccmi.edu						
Jackson Correctional Institution						
5563 Tenth St	Malone	FL	32445	850-569-5260	569-5996	213
Web: dc.state.fl.us						
Jackson County 307 Main St	Black River Falls	WI	54615	715-284-0208	284-0270	338
Web: www.co.jackson.wi.us						

Name / Address	City	State	Zip	Phone	Fax	Class
Jackson County PO Box 318 *Web:* www.jacksoncounty.in.gov	Brownstown	IN	47220	812-358-6116	358-6187	338
Jackson County 115 W Main Rm 101 *Web:* www.co.jackson.tx.us	Edna	TX	77957	361-782-3563		338
Jackson County 101 E Hull Ave *Web:* www.jacksoncotn.com	Gainesboro	TN	38562	931-268-9212	268-4149	338
Jackson County 405 Fourth St *Web:* www.co.jackson.mn.us	Jackson	MN	56143	507-847-2763	847-4718	338
Jackson County 275 Portsmouth St *Web:* www.jacksoncountyohio.us	Jackson	OH	45640	740-286-3301	286-4754	338
Jackson County 67 Athens St *Web:* www.jacksoncountygov.com	Jefferson	GA	30549	706-367-6312		338
Jackson County 700 Main St PO Box 128 *Web:* www.ujs.sd.gov	Kadoka	SD	57543	605-837-2122	837-2120	338
Jackson County 415 E 12th St *Web:* www.16thcircuit.org	Kansas City	MO	64106	816-881-3000		338
Jackson County 201 W Platt St *Web:* www.co.jackson.ia.us	Maquoketa	IA	52060	563-652-3144	652-4738	338
Jackson County PO Box 175 *Web:* www.jacksoncounty.ky.gov	McKee	KY	40447	606-287-8562	287-7190	338
Jackson County 10 S Oakdale Ave *Web:* jacksoncountyor.org	Medford	OR	97501	541-774-6152	774-6714	338
Jackson County 215 N 14th St *Web:* www.jacksoncounty-il.gov	Murphysboro	IL	62966	618-687-7370	687-4046	338
Jackson County 3300 Theater Dr PO Box 647 *Web:* www.jacksonsheriff.org	Newport	AR	72112	870-523-5842	523-7418	338
Jackson County 3104 Magnolia St PO Box 998 *Web:* www.co.jackson.ms.us	Pascagoula	MS	39567	228-769-3040	769-3180	338
Jackson County PO Box 800 *Web:* www.jacksoncounty.wv.gov	Ripley	WV	25271	304-373-2220	373-0245	338
Jackson County 102 E Laurel St *Web:* www.jacksoncountyal.gov	Scottsboro	AL	35768	256-574-9320		338
Jackson County 401 Grindstaff Cove Rd *Web:* www.jacksonnc.org	Sylva	NC	28779	828-586-4055		338
Jackson County 404 4th St PO Box 1019 *Web:* www.jacksoncountycogov.com	Walden	CO	80480	970-723-4660		338
Jackson County Area Chamber of Commerce 270 Athens St PO Box 629 *Web:* www.jacksoncountyga.com	Jefferson	GA	30549	706-387-0300	387-0304	139
Jackson County Chamber of Commerce 720 Krebs Ave *Web:* jcchamber.com	Pascagoula	MS	39567	228-762-3391	769-1726	139
Jackson County Chamber of Commerce 773 W Main St *TF:* 800-962-1911 ■ *Web:* www.mountainlovers.com	Sylva	NC	28779	828-586-2155		139
Jackson County Chamber of Commerce 4318 Lafayette St *Web:* www.jacksoncounty.com	Marianna	FL	32446	850-482-8060		338
Jackson County Courthouse, The 101 N Main St *Web:* jackson.okcounties.org	Altus	OK	73521	580-482-2370		338
Jackson County Intermediate School District (JCISD) 6700 Browns Lake Rd *Web:* www.jcisd.org	Jackson	MI	49201	517-768-5200	787-2844	685
Jackson County Law Library (JCLL) Kessler Bldg 1301 Oak St Ste 310 *Web:* jcll.org	Kansas City	MO	64106	816-221-2221		434-3
Jackson County Library System 205 S Central Ave *Web:* www.jcls.org	Medford	OR	97501	541-774-8689		434-3
Jackson County Memorial Hospital 1200 E Pecan St *TF:* 800-595-0455 ■ *Web:* www.jcmh.com	Altus	OK	73521	580-379-5000		374-3
Jackson County Public Library 208 Church St N *Web:* jackson.park.lib.wv.us	Ripley	WV	25271	304-372-5343	372-7935	434-3
Jackson County Public Library (JCPL) 303 W Second St *Web:* www.myjclibrary.org	Seymour	IN	47274	812-522-3412	522-5456	434-3
Jackson County Rural Electric Membership Corp 274 E Base Rd *TF:* 800-288-4458 ■ *Web:* www.jacksonremc.com	Brownstown	IN	47220	812-358-4458	358-5719	245
Jackson County School District 6 300 Ash St *Web:* www.district6.org	Central Point	OR	97502	541-494-6200	664-1637	685
Jackson County School District 9 11 N Royal PO Box 548 *Web:* www.eaglepnt.k12.or.us	Eagle Point	OR	97524	541-830-1200	830-6550	685
Jackson County School System 1660 Winder Hwy *TF:* 800-760-3727 ■ *Web:* www.jacksonschoolsga.org	Jefferson	GA	30549	706-367-5151	367-9457	685
Jackson District Library 244 W Michigan Ave *Web:* www.myjdl.com	Jackson	MI	49201	517-788-4087		434-3
Jackson Electric Co-op N6868 County Rd F PO Box 546 *TF:* 800-370-4607 ■ *Web:* www.jackelec.com	Black River Falls	WI	54615	715-284-5385	284-7143	245
Jackson Electric Co-opeartive Inc 8925 State Hwy 111 S *Web:* www.jecec.com	Ganado	TX	77962	361-771-4400		245
Jackson Electric Membership Corp 850 Commerce Rd *TF:* 800-462-3691 ■ *Web:* www.jacksonemc.com	Jefferson	GA	30549	706-367-5281		245
Jackson Energy Authority 119 E College St *TF:* 800-351-1111 ■ *Web:* www.jaxenergy.com	Jackson	TN	38301	731-422-7500		787
Jackson Energy Co-op 115 Jackson Energy Ln *TF:* 800-262-7480 ■ *Web:* www.jacksonenergy.com	McKee	KY	40447	606-364-1000		245
Jackson Federal Savings & Loan Assn 414 Second St PO Box 46 *Web:* jacksonfederalsl.com	Jackson	MN	56143	507-847-4714	847-4766	70
Jackson George N Ltd 1139 Mcdermot Ave *TF:* 800-665-8978 ■ *Web:* www.jackson.ca	Winnipeg	MB	R3E0V2	204-786-3821		361
Jackson Griffin Insurance Co 103 W Jackson St *Web:* www.jacksonsfh.com	Harrisburg	AR	72432	870-578-2452	578-3360	510
Jackson Grill 3736 W Mitchell St *Web:* www.thejacksongrill.com	Milwaukee	WI	53215	414-384-7384		671
Jackson Group Media LLC 206 N Washington St Ste 10 *Web:* www.jacksongroupmedia.com	Alexandria	VA	22314	703-548-3100		194
Jackson Healthcare LLC 2655 Northwinds Pkwy *Web:* jacksonhealthcare.com	Alpharetta	GA	30009	770-643-5500		631
Jackson Hewitt Inc 3 Sylvan Way Ste 301 *OTC:* JHTXQ ■ *TF:* 800-234-1040 ■ *Web:* www.jacksonhewitt.com	Parsippany	NJ	07054	973-630-1040	630-0710	734
Jackson Hole Airport 1250 E Airport Rd PO Box 159 *Web:* www.jacksonholeairport.com	Jackson	WY	83001	307-733-7682	733-9270	27
Jackson Hole Central Reservations (JHCR) 140 E Broadway Ste 24 PO Box 2618 *TF:* 888-838-6606 ■ *Web:* www.jacksonholewy.com	Jackson	WY	83001	307-733-4005	733-1286	376
Jackson Hole Chamber of Commerce 130 N Cache St *Web:* www.jacksonholechamber.com	Jackson	WY	83001	307-733-3316	733-5585	139
Jackson Hole Historical Society & Museum 105 N Glenwood St *Web:* jacksonholehistory.org	Jackson	WY	83001	307-733-2414		520
Jackson Hole Lodge 420 W Broadway PO Box 1805 *TF:* 800-604-9404 ■ *Web:* www.jacksonholelodge.com	Jackson	WY	83001	307-733-2992	739-2144	379
Jackson Hole Mountain Resort 3395 Cody Ln PO Box 290 *TF:* 800-450-0477 ■ *Web:* www.jacksonhole.com	Teton Village	WY	83025	307-733-2292	739-2737	669
Jackson Hole News & Guide 1225 Maple Way *Web:* www.jhnewsandguide.com	Jackson	WY	83001	307-733-2047	733-2138	532-4
Jackson Hole Playhouse 145 W Deloney Ave *Web:* jacksonholeplayhouse.com	Jackson	WY	83001	307-733-6994		572
Jackson HoleResort Lodging 3200 W McCollister Dr PO Box 510 *TF:* 800-443-8613 ■ *Web:* www.jhrl.com	Teton Village	WY	83025	307-733-3990		669
Jackson Hospital 1725 Pine St *Web:* www.jackson.org	Montgomery	AL	36106	334-293-8000		374-3
Jackson Hospital 4250 Hospital Dr *Web:* www.jacksonhosp.com	Marianna	FL	32446	850-526-2200	482-6374	374-3
Jackson ImmunoResearch Laboratories Inc 872 W Baltimore Pk PO Box 9 *Fax Area Code: 610 ■ *TF:* 800-367-5296 ■ *Web:* www.jacksonimmuno.com	West Grove	PA	19390	800-367-5296	869-0171*	231
Jackson International Airport 100 International Dr Ste 300 *TF:* 800-227-7368 ■ *Web:* jmaa.com	Jackson	MS	39208	601-939-5631	939-3713	27
Jackson Kelly PLLC PO Box 553 *Web:* www.jacksonkelly.com	Charleston	WV	25322	304-340-1172		428
Jackson Laboratory, The 600 Main St *TF:* 800-422-6423 ■ *Web:* www.jax.org	Bar Harbor	ME	04609	207-288-6000		668
Jackson Lake State Park 26363 County Rd 3 *Web:* cpw.state.co.us	Orchard	CO	80649	970-645-2551		565
Jackson Lee Sheila (Rep D - TX) 2079 Rayburn House Office Bldg *Web:* jacksonlee.house.gov	Washington	DC	20515	202-225-3816	225-3317	342-2
Jackson Livestock Auction LLC 205 S Koke St *Web:* jacksonlivestock.net	De Graff	OH	43318	937-585-5701		446
Jackson Local Schools District (JLSD) 7602 Fulton Dr *Web:* www.jackson.stark.k12.oh.us	Massillon	OH	44646	330-830-8000	830-8008	186
Jackson Lumber & Millwork Company Inc PO Box 449 *Web:* www.jacksonlumber.com	Lawrence	MA	01842	978-686-4141		364
Jackson Marketing Group Inc 1068 Holland Rd *Web:* www.jacksonmg.com	Simpsonville	SC	29681	864-272-3000		7
Jackson Marking Products Co 9105 N Rainbow Ln *TF:* 800-782-6722 ■ *Web:* www.rubber-stamp.com	Mount Vernon	IL	62864	618-242-1334	242-7732	467
Jackson Mattress Company Inc 3154 Camden Rd *TF:* 800-763-7378 ■ *Web:* restonic.com	Fayetteville	NC	28306	910-425-0131	425-1602	471
Jackson Memorial Hospital 1611 NW 12th Ave *Web:* www.jacksonhealth.org	Miami	FL	33136	305-585-1111	326-9470	374-3
Jackson National Life Insurance Co 1 Corporate Way *TF:* 800-644-4565 ■ *Web:* www.jackson.com	Lansing	MI	48951	517-381-5500		391-2
Jackson O'Keefe 433 Silas Deane Hwy *Web:* jacksonokeefe.com	Wethersfield	CT	06109	860-278-4040		41
Jackson Oil & Solvents Inc 1970 Kentucky Ave *TF:* 800-221-4603 ■ *Web:* jacksonoilsolvents.com	Indianapolis	IN	46221	317-636-4421	685-2403	541
Jackson Parish 500 E Ct St Rm 301 *Web:* www.jacksonparishpolicejury.org	Jonesboro	LA	71251	318-259-2361	259-5660	338
Jackson Public Schools 662 S President St *Web:* www.jackson.k12.ms.us	Jackson	MS	39201	601-960-8700	960-8713	685
Jackson Purchase Ag Credit Assn PO Box 309 *TF:* 877-422-4203 ■ *Web:* www.rivervalleyagcredit.com	Mayfield	KY	42066	270-247-5613		216
Jackson Purchase Energy Corp 2900 Irvin Cobb Dr *TF:* 800-633-4044 ■ *Web:* www.jpenergy.com	Paducah	KY	42002	270-442-7321	442-5337	245
Jackson Purchase Medical Ctr 1099 Medical Center Cir *Web:* www.jacksonpurchase.com	Mayfield	KY	42066	270-251-4100	251-4507	374-3
Jackson Ready Mix Concrete Inc 100 W Woodrow Wilson Dr *Web:* www.delta-ind.com	Jackson	MS	39213	601-354-3801		182

Name / Address	City	State	ZIP	Phone	Fax	Class
Jackson River Community Credit Union 347 N Court Ave	Covington	VA	24426	540-962-6154		219
TF: 833-809-9815 ■ *Web:* yourvirtualcu.com						
Jackson State Community College *Lexington-Henderson Ctr* 932 E Church St	Lexington	TN	38351	731-968-5722	968-1539	162
Web: www.jscc.edu						
Jackson State University 1400 John R Lynch St	Jackson	MS	39217	601-979-2121	979-3445	166
TF: 800-848-6817 ■ *Web:* www.jsums.edu						
Jackson State University Information Services Library 1325 J R Lynch St	Jackson	MS	39217	601-432-6313		434-3
Web: www.sampson.jsums.edu						
Jackson Sun 245 W LaFayette St	Jackson	TN	38301	731-427-3333	425-9639	532-2
TF: 800-372-3922 ■ *Web:* www.jacksonsun.com						
Jackson Technical LLC 427 S Boston Ave Ste 1010	Tulsa	OK	74103	918-585-8324		180
Web: www.jacksontechnical.com						
Jackson Tidus A Law Corp 2030 Main St 12th Fl	Irvine	CA	92614	949-752-8585	752-0597	428
Web: www.jacksontidus.law						
Jackson Tube Service Inc 8210 Industry Pk Dr	Piqua	OH	45356	937-773-8550	773-8806	490
TF: 800-543-8910 ■ *Web:* www.jackson-tube.com						
Jackson Typesetting Company Inc 1820 W Ganson St	Jackson	MI	49202	517-784-0576		781
Jackson Wholesale Co 129 Armory Dr	Jackson	KY	41339	606-666-2495	666-2280	297-8
TF: 800-874-7964 ■ *Web:* www.jacksonwholesale.com						
Jackson WWS Inc 6209 N US Higway 25E	Gray	KY	40734	888-800-5672	523-1799*	806
**Fax Area Code:* 606 ■ *TF:* 888-800-5672 ■ *Web:* www.jacksonwws.com						
Jackson (WY) Town Hall 150 E Pearl Ave	Jackson	WY	83001	307-733-3932	739-0919	337
Web: www.jacksonwy.gov						
Jackson Zoological Park 2918 W Capitol St	Jackson	MS	39209	601-352-2580	352-2594	823
Web: www.jacksonzoo.org						
Jackson's Bistro 601 S Harbour Island Blvd Ste 100	Tampa	FL	33602	813-277-0112		671
Web: jacksonsbistro.com						
Jackson's Steakhouse 400 S Palafox St	Pensacola	FL	32502	850-469-9898		671
Web: greatsouthernrestaurants.com						
Jackson-George Regional Library System 3214 S Pascagoula St	Pascagoula	MS	39567	228-769-3060	769-3146	434-3
Web: www.jgrls.org						
Jackson-Lloyd Insurance Agency Ltd 1615 Judson Rd	Longview	TX	75601	903-758-6206		390
Web: jackson-lloyd.com						
Jackson-Madison County General Hospital 620 Skyline Dr	Jackson	TN	38301	731-541-5000		374-3
Web: www.wth.org						
Jackson-Madison County Library 433 E Lafayette St	Jackson	TN	38301	731-425-8600	425-8609	434-3
Web: www.jmclibrary.org						
Jacksonport State Park 205 Ave St	Newport	AR	72112	870-523-2143		565
Web: www.arkansasstateparks.com						
Jacksonville Area Chamber of Commerce 310 E State St	Jacksonville	IL	62650	217-243-5678		139
TF: 800-593-5678 ■ *Web:* jacksonvilleil.org						
Jacksonville Area Chamber of Commerce 155 W Morton	Jacksonville	IL	62650	217-245-2174	245-0661	140
Web: www.jacksonvilleareachamber.org						
Jacksonville Area Legal Aid (JALA) 126 W Adams St	Jacksonville	FL	32202	904-356-8371	356-8285	428
TF: 866-356-8371 ■ *Web:* www.jaxlegalaid.org						
Jacksonville Chamber of Commerce 200 Dupree Dr	Jacksonville	AR	72076	501-982-1511	982-1464	139
TF: 877-815-3111 ■ *Web:* www.jacksonville-arkansas.com						
Jacksonville College 105 BJ Albritton Dr	Jacksonville	TX	75766	903-586-2518	586-0743	162
Web: www.jacksonville-college.edu						
Jacksonville Correctional Ctr 2268 E Morton Ave	Jacksonville	IL	62650	217-245-1481		213
TF: 800-526-0844 ■ *Web:* www.illinois.gov						
Jacksonville Independent School District 800 College Ave	Jacksonville	TX	75766	903-586-6511	586-3133	685
TF: 800-583-6908 ■ *Web:* www.jisd.org						
Jacksonville International Airport 2400 Yankee Clipper Dr	Jacksonville	FL	32218	904-741-4902	741-2224	27
Web: www.flyjacksonville.com						
Jacksonville Magazine 1261 King St	Jacksonville	FL	32204	904-389-3622	389-3628	457-22
TF: 800-962-0214 ■ *Web:* www.jacksonvillemag.com						
Jacksonville Municipal Stadium 1 EverBank Field Dr	Jacksonville	FL	32202	904-633-6000		720
Web: www.jaguars.com						
Jacksonville Museum of Modern Art 333 N Laura St	Jacksonville	FL	32202	904-366-6911	366-6901	520
Web: www.mocajacksonville.org						
Jacksonville School District 117 516 Jordan St	Jacksonville	IL	62650	217-243-9411	243-6844	685
Web: jsd117.org						
Jacksonville State University 700 Pelham Rd N	Jacksonville	AL	36265	256-782-5781	782-5953	166
TF: 800-231-5291 ■ *Web:* www.jsu.edu						
Jacksonville Steel Inc 310 W Dewitt Henry Dr	Beebe	AR	72012	501-882-3563		480
Web: www.jacksonvillesteel.com						
Jacksonville Symphony Orchestra (JSO) 300 Water St Ste 200	Jacksonville	FL	32202	904-354-5547		573-3
Web: www.jaxsymphony.org						
Jacksonville University 2800 University Blvd N	Jacksonville	FL	32211	904-256-8000	256-7012	166
TF: 800-225-2027 ■ *Web:* www.ju.edu						
Jacksonville Veterans Memorial Arena 300 A Philip Randolph Blvd	Jacksonville	FL	32202	904-630-3900		720
Web: www.jaxevents.com						
Jacksonville Zoo & Gardens 370 Zoo Pkwy	Jacksonville	FL	32218	904-757-4463	757-4315	823
TF: 800-241-4113 ■ *Web:* www.jacksonvillezoo.org						
Jacksonville/Onslow Chamber of Commerce 1099 Gum Branch Rd	Jacksonville	NC	28540	910-347-3141		139
Web: www.jacksonvilleonline.org						
JACL (Japanese American Citizens League) 1765 Sutter St	San Francisco	CA	94115	415-921-5225	931-4671	48-14
Web: jacl.org						
Jacmar Food Service Distribution 300 N Baldwin Park Blvd	City of Industry	CA	91746	800-834-8806	430-2342*	297-8
**Fax Area Code:* 626 ■ *TF:* 800-834-8806 ■ *Web:* jacmar.com						
Jacmel Jewelry Inc 1385 Broadway 8th Fl	New York	NY	10018	800-945-4300		409
TF: 800-945-4300 ■ *Web:* www.jacmel.com						
Jaco Electronics Inc 415 Oser Ave	Hauppauge	NY	11788	877-373-5226	231-1051*	246
OTC: JACO ■ **Fax Area Code:* 631 ■ *TF:* 877-373-5226 ■ *Web:* www.jacoelect.com						
Jaco Engineering 879 S E St	Anaheim	CA	92805	714-991-1680		757
Web: www.jacoengineering.com						
Jaco Manufacturing Co 468 Geiger St	Berea	OH	44017	440-234-4000	234-7007	604
Web: www.jacomfg.com						
Jacob Group, The 6190 Virginia Pkwy One Jacob Pl Ste 100	Mckinney	TX	75071	214-544-9030		260
Web: www.jacobgroup.com						
Jacob Holtz Co Airport Business Complex B 10 Industrial Hwy MS-6	Lester	PA	19029	215-423-2800	634-7454	350
TF: 800-445-4337 ■ *Web:* www.jacobholtz.com						
Jacob K. Javits Convention Ctr 655 W 34th St	New York	NY	10001	212-216-2000		205
TF: 800-272-7469 ■ *Web:* javitscenter.com						
Jacob Leinenkugel Brewing Co 124 E Elm St	Chippewa Falls	WI	54729	888-534-6437		102
TF: 888-534-6437 ■ *Web:* www.leinie.com						
Jacob Securities Inc 199 Bay St Ste 2901	Toronto	ON	M5L1G1	416-866-8300		401
Jacob Stern & Sons Inc PO Box 50740	Santa Barbara	CA	93150	805-565-1411	565-1415	296-12
Web: www.jacobstern.com						
Jacob White Construction 2000 W Parkwood	Friendswood	TX	77546	281-286-6666		186
Web: www.jacobwhitecc.com						
Jacobi Building Materials Inc 21341 Vanowen St	Canoga Park	CA	91303	818-346-4150	346-0817	191-1
Web: www.jacobibuilding.com						
Jacobi Sales Inc 425 Main St NE PO Box 67	Palmyra	IN	47164	812-364-6141	364-6157	274
Web: www.jacobisales.com						
Jacobi-Lewis Co 622 S Front St	Wilmington	NC	28401	910-763-6201	763-5610	300
TF: 800-763-2433 ■ *Web:* www.jacobi-lewis.com						
Jacobs 155 N Lake Ave	Pasadena	CA	91101	626-578-3500	578-6988	261
NYSE: JEC ■ *Web:* www.jacobs.com						
Jacobs 8096 Excelsior Blvd	Hopkins	MN	55343	877-582-3325		360-3
TF: 877-582-3325 ■ *Web:* invest.jacobs.com						
Jacobs & Associates Inc 12782 Prospect Rd 1st Fl	Strongsville	OH	44149	440-625-2690		390
Web: jacobsnow.org						
Jacobs & Bell 19 Engle St	Tenafly	NJ	07670	201-568-2200		41
Web: jacobsandbell.com						
Jacobs & Clevenger Inc 303 E Wacker Dr Ste 2030	Chicago	IL	60601	312-894-3000	894-3005	5
Web: www.jacobsclevenger.com						
Jacobs & Schlesinger LLP 1620 5th Ave Ste 750	San Diego	CA	92101	619-900-6778		41
Web: jsslegal.com						
Jacobs Agency Inc 325 W Huron St Ste 310	Chicago	IL	60654	312-664-5000		7
Web: jacobsagency.com						
Jacobs Entertainment Inc 17301 W Colfax Ave Ste 250	Golden	CO	80401	303-215-5200		322
Web: jacobsentertainmentinc.com						
Jacobs Financial Group, The 20 Wind Trace Ct	The Woodlands	TX	77381	281-298-6545		391-4
Web: www.thejacobsfinancialgroup.com						
Jacobs Insurance Agency Inc 2021 E Main St	Owosso	MI	48867	989-725-7117		390
Web: jacobsinsurance.com						
Jacobs Management Group Inc 1420 Walnut St	Philadelphia	PA	19102	215-732-6400	732-4042	260
Web: www.jacobsmgt.com						
Jacobs Mechanical Inc 4500 W Mitchell Ave	Cincinnati	OH	45232	513-681-6800	681-6855	189-10
Web: jacobsmech.com						
Jacobs Music Company Inc 1718 Chestnut St	Philadelphia	PA	19103	215-568-7800		526
Web: jacobsmusic.com						
Jacobs Publishers 9600 Great Hills Trl Ste 150 W	Austin	TX	78759	512-400-0398		637-9
Web: www.jacobspublishers.com						
Jacobs Trading Co 8090 Exceksior Blvd	Hopkins	MN	55343	763-843-2000	843-2101	361
Web: www.jacobstrading.com						
Jacobs Vehicle Systems Inc 22 E Dudley Town Rd	Bloomfield	CT	06002	860-243-1441		60
Web: www.jacobsvehiclesystems.com						
Jacobs, Nones & Company CPAS 6401 SW 87th Ave Ste 115	Miami	FL	33173	305-274-1200	274-0191	2
Web: jnccpas.com						
Jacobsburg Environmental Education Ctr 835 Jacobsburg Rd	Wind Gap	PA	18091	610-746-2801		565
Web: www.dcnr.pa.gov						
Jacobsen 11108 Quality Dr	Charlotte	NC	28273	704-504-6600	504-6661	429
TF: 800-848-1636 ■ *Web:* www.jacobsen.com						
Jacobsen & Horan Engineering PC 990 S Second St Ste 2	Ronkonkoma	NY	11779	631-580-6100		261
Web: jhepc.com						
Jacobsen Homes 600 Packard Ct	Safety Harbor	FL	34695	727-726-1138		505
TF: 800-843-1559 ■ *Web:* www.jachomes.com						

Name / Address	City	State	Zip	Phone	Fax	Class
Jacobson & Company Inc 1079 E Grand St PO Box 511 *Web:* jacobsoncompany.com	Elizabeth	NJ	07207	908-355-5200	355-8680	189-9
Jacobson Brotman Pc 984 First Colonial Rd Ste 305 *Web:* jwbcpas.com	Virginia Beach	VA	23454	757-422-4445	491-8431	2
Jacobson Companies Inc, The 1334 S 5th Ave *Web:* jacobsoncompanies.com	Yuma	AZ	85364	928-782-1801		656
Jacobson Floral Supply Inc 500 Albany St *Web:* jacobsonfloral.com	Boston	MA	02118	617-426-4287		292
Jacobson Hat Company Inc 1301 Ridge Row *TF:* 800-233-4690 ■ *Web:* www.jhats.com	Scranton	PA	18510	800-233-4690	882-5428	155-9
Jacobson Holman PLLC 400 Seventh St NW *Web:* www.jhip.com	Washington	DC	20004	202-638-6666	393-5350	428
Jacobson Plastics 1401 Freeman Ave *Web:* www.jacobsonplastics.com	Long Beach	CA	90804	562-433-4911		608
Jacobson Press & Fields PC 168 N Meramec Ave Ste 150 *Web:* archcitylawyers.com	Saint Louis	MO	63105	314-899-9789		41
Jacobson Rost Inc 233 N Water St Ste 6 *Web:* www.jacobsonrost.com	Milwaukee	WI	53202	414-220-4888		7
Jacobson Transport Inc 924 4th Ave S *TF:* 800-726-8615 ■ *Web:* www.jtitransport.com	Wahpeton	ND	58074	701-642-4770		780
Jacoby/Storm Productions Inc 47 Ridgeline Rd *Web:* www.jacobystorm.com	Easton	CT	06612	203-261-1988	261-1970	681
Jacom Inc 5310 N State Rd *Web:* www.wqbx.biz	Alma	MI	48801	989-463-3175	463-6674	645-141
Jacquelyn Wigs 15 W 37th St 4th Fl *TF:* 800-272-2424 ■ *Web:* www.jacquelynwigs.com	New York	NY	10018	212-302-2266		348
Jacques Marchais Museum of Tibetan Art 338 Lighthouse Ave *Web:* www.tibetanmuseum.org	Staten Island	NY	10306	718-987-3500		520
Jacques-Imo's Cafe 8324 Oak St *Web:* jacques-imos.com	New Orleans	LA	70118	504-861-0886		671
Jacquette Consulting 413 Walnut Hill Rd *Web:* www.jacquette.com	West Chester	PA	19382	610-357-5611	280-3922	225
Jacquinot Consulting Inc (JCI) 2615 George Busbee Pky Ste 11-312 **Fax Area Code:* 206 ■ *Web:* www.jacquinot.com	Kennesaw	GA	30144	770-514-8039	309-0058*	177
Jacuzzi Brands LLC 13925 City Center Dr Ste 200 *TF:* 866-234-7727 ■ *Web:* www.jacuzzi.com	Chino Hills	CA	91709	866-234-7727		401
Jadcore Inc 300 N Fruitridge *Web:* www.jadcore.com	Terre Haute	IN	47803	812-234-2724		596
Jade Corp 3063 Philmont Ave *Web:* www.jadecorp.com	Huntingdon Valley	PA	19006	215-947-3333		757
Jade Engineered Plastic Inc 121 Broadcommon Rd *TF:* 800-557-9155 ■ *Web:* www.jadeplastics.com	Bristol	RI	02809	401-253-4440		326
Jade Garden Chinese Restaurant 1200 Battlefield Blvd N Ste 119 *Web:* www.jadegardenchesapeake.com	Chesapeake	VA	23320	757-436-1010		671
Jade Garden Helena 3128 N Montana Ave *Web:* jadegardenhelena.com	Helena	MT	59602	406-443-8899	443-8390	671
Jade Palace 2320 W 21st Ave *Web:* www.jadepalaceeugene.com	Eugene	OR	97402	541-344-9523		671
Jade Palace 820 W Spring Creek Pkwy Ste 214 *Web:* www.jadepalacechinese.com	Plano	TX	75023	972-424-5578		671
Jade Palace 1659 Rte 9 *Web:* www.jadepalacewappingersfalls.com	Wappingers Falls	NY	12590	845-297-1188		671
Jade Tours 1650 Elgin Mills Rd E Unit 403 *TF:* 800-387-0387 ■ *Web:* en.jadetours.com	Richmond Hill	ON	L4S0B2	905-787-9288	787-9299	760
Jadoo Power Systems Inc 181 Blue Ravine Rd	Folsom	CA	95630	209-326-1814		194
Jadtec Computer Group 1520 W Yale Ave *Web:* www.jadtec.com	Orange	CA	92867	714-282-0828		175
JAE Electronics Inc 142 Technology Dr Ste 100 *Web:* www.jaeusa.com	Irvine	CA	92618	949-753-2600		246
JAE Oregon Inc 11555 SW Leveton Dr *Web:* jaeoregon.com	Tualatin	OR	97062	503-692-1333		596
Jaeckle Wholesale Inc 4101 Owl Creek Dr *TF:* 800-236-7225 ■ *Web:* www.jaeckledistributors.com	Madison	WI	53718	608-838-5400		191-1
Jaekle Group Inc, The 1410 Highland Rd E *Web:* www.jaeklegroup.com	Macedonia	OH	44056	330-405-9353		180
JAF Consulting Inc PO Box 925 *Web:* www.jafconsulting.com	Mullica Hill	NJ	08062	856-241-1900		587
Jaffe Communications Inc 312 North Ave E Ste 5 *Web:* www.jaffecom.com	Cranford	NJ	07016	908-789-0700	292-1177	636
Jaffe PR 1300 Pennsylvania Ave NW Ste 700 **Fax Area Code:* 208 ■ *TF:* 877-808-9600 ■ *Web:* www.jaffeassociates.com	Washington	DC	20004	877-808-9600	439-6173*	41
Jaffe Raitt Heuer & Weiss PC 27777 Franklin Rd Ste 2500 *Web:* www.jaffelaw.com	Southfield	MI	48034	248-351-3000		428
Jaffrey-Rindge School District 81 Fitzgerald Dr Unit 2 *Web:* www.sau47.org	Jaffrey	NH	03452	603-532-8100		685
Jafra Cosmetics Intl 2451 Townsgate Rd *Web:* www.jafra.com	Westlake Village	CA	91361	805-449-3000		214
Jaftex Corp 49 W 37th St	New York	NY	10018	212-686-5194		594
JAG Advisors 9841 Clayton Rd *TF:* 800-966-4596 ■ *Web:* jaglynn.com	Saint Louis	MO	63124	314-997-1277		528
JaGee Holdings LLP 2918 Wingate St *Web:* www.jagee.com	Fort Worth	TX	76107	817-335-5881	335-1905	463
Jagemann Stamping Co 5757 W Custer St *TF:* 888-337-7853 ■ *Web:* www.jagemann.com	Manitowoc	WI	54220	920-682-4633		488
Jaguar Computer Systems Inc 4135 Indus Way *Web:* www.jaguar.net	Riverside	CA	92503	951-273-7950	734-5615	175
Jaguar Design Studio Inc 9039 Soquel Dr *Web:* www.jaguardesignstudio.com	Aptos	CA	95003	831-662-9991		344
Jaguar Industries Inc 89 Broadway *Web:* www.jaguarind.com	Haverstraw	NY	10927	845-947-1800		253
Jailhouse Inn 13 Marlborough St *Web:* www.jailhouse.com	Newport	RI	02840	401-847-4638		379
Jaipur Living Inc 1800 Cherokee Pkwy **Fax Area Code:* 678 ■ *TF:* 888-676-7330 ■ *Web:* www.jaipurrugsco.com	Acworth	GA	30102	404-351-2360	551-6677*	131
Jaipur, The 10922 Elm St *Web:* jaipurindianfood.com	Omaha	NE	68144	402-392-7331		671
JAIR LYNCH Development Partners 1508 U St NW *Web:* www.jairlynch.com	Washington	DC	20009	202-462-1092		653
Jajo Inc 131 N Rock Is *Web:* jajo.agency	Wichita	KS	67202	316-267-6700		7
JAK Enterprises Inc 8309 N Knoxville Ave *TF:* 800-752-3295 ■ *Web:* www.bardoptical.com	Peoria	IL	61615	309-692-8222		543
JaK's Grill 3701 NE 45th St *Web:* jaksgrill.com	Seattle	WA	98105	206-985-8545		671
Jake & Telly's Greek Taverna 2616 W Colorado Ave *Web:* www.jakeandtellys.com	Colorado Springs	CO	80904	719-633-0406		671
Jake A. Parrott Insurance Agency Inc 2508 N Herritage St *TF:* 800-727-7688 ■ *Web:* www.parrottins.com	Kinston	NC	28501	252-523-1041		390
Jake's 221 Canyon St *Web:* www.jakesbillings.com	Billings	MT	59101	406-259-9375		671
Jake's Good Time Place 620 S Cleveland *Web:* www.dexknows.com	Pierre	SD	57501	605-945-0485		671
Jake's Seafood House 19178 Coastal Hwy *Web:* www.jakesseafoodhouse.com	Rehoboth Beach	DE	19971	302-644-7711		671
Jake's Tex-Mex Cafe 1710 Oak St *Web:* jakestexmex.com	Bakersfield	CA	93301	661-322-6380	322-3731	671
Jaken Company Inc 14420 Myford Rd Ste 150 *TF:* 800-401-7225 ■ *Web:* www.jaken.com	Irvine	CA	92606	714-522-1700		286
Jakes Archery 765 S Orem Blvd *Web:* www.jakesarchery.com	Orem	UT	84058	801-225-9202	225-9509	711
JAKKS Pacific Inc 21749 Baker Pkwy *TF:* 877-875-2557 ■ *Web:* www.jakks.com	Walnut	CA	91789	909-594-7771		762
Jakprints Inc 3133 Chester Ave *TF:* 877-246-3132 ■ *Web:* www.jakprints.com	Cleveland	OH	44114	216-622-6360		627
JALA (Jacksonville Area Legal Aid) 126 W Adams St *TF:* 866-356-8371 ■ *Web:* www.jaxlegalaid.org	Jacksonville	FL	32202	904-356-8371	356-8285	428
Jalapeno Inferno 23587 N Scottsdale Rd *Web:* jalapenoinferno.com	Scottsdale	AZ	85255	480-585-6442		671
Jalapenos 85 Forest Dr *Web:* jalapenosonline.com	Annapolis	MD	21401	410-266-7580		671
Jaleo 480 Seventh St NW *Web:* www.jaleo.com	Washington	DC	20004	202-628-7949		671
Jalpak International Hawaii Inc 2270 Kalakaua Ave Ste 1600	Honolulu	HI	96815	808-926-4500		760
Jam Productions Ltd 205 W Goethe *Web:* jamusa.com	Chicago	IL	60610	312-440-9191		181
JAM'N 107.5 13333 SW 68th Pkwy Ste 310 *Web:* jamn1075.iheart.com	Tigard	OR	97223	503-248-1075		646-126
JAM'N 94.5 1 Cabot Rd Ste 302 *Web:* jamn945.iheart.com	Medford	MA	02155	781-663-2500		647
JAMA (Japan Automobile Manufacturers Association Inc) 888 17th St NW Ste 609 *Web:* www.jama.org	Washington	DC	20006	202-296-8537	872-1212	49-21
JAMA (Journal of the American Medical Assn) PO Box 10946 *TF:* 800-262-2350 ■ *Web:* www.jamanetwork.com	Chicago	IL	60654	312-670-7827		457-16
Jamac 422 Buchanan St *Web:* www.jamac.com	Sandusky	OH	44870	419-625-9790		552-1
Jamac Frozen Foods 570 Grand St *TF:* 800-631-0440 ■ *Web:* www.jamacfoods.com	Jersey City	NJ	07302	201-333-6200		345
Jamaica Bay Riding Academy Inc 7000 Shore Pkwy *Web:* www.horsebackride.com	Brooklyn	NY	11234	718-531-8949		148
Jamaica Chamber of Commerce 15711 Rockaway Blvd *Web:* www.jamaicachambernyc.com	Jamaica	NY	11434	718-877-7704		139
Jamaica Embassy 1520 New Hampshire Ave NW *Web:* www.embassyofjamaica.org	Washington	DC	20036	202-452-0660	452-0036	257
Jamaica Hospital Medical Ctr 8900 Van Wyck Expy *Web:* jamaicahospital.org	Jamaica	NY	11418	718-206-6000		374-3
Jamaica Jamaica 4857 Nc Hwy 55 *Web:* www.jamaicajamaicartp.com	Durham	NC	27713	919-544-1532		671
Jamaica State Park 48 Salmon Hole Ln *Web:* www.vtstateparks.com	Jamaica	VT	05343	802-874-4600		565
Jamaica Tourist Board 5201 Blue Lagoon Dr Ste 670 *TF:* 800-526-2422 ■ *Web:* www.visitjamaica.com	Miami	FL	33126	305-665-0557		775
Jamak Fabrication Inc 1401 N Bowie Dr *TF:* 800-543-4747 ■ *Web:* jamak.com	Weatherford	TX	76086	817-594-8771	594-8324	677
Jamar Co, The 4701 Mike Colalillo Dr *TF:* 800-644-3624 ■ *Web:* www.jamarcompany.com	Duluth	MN	55807	218-628-1027	628-1174	189-10
Jamba Juice Co 6475 Christie Ave Ste 150 *Web:* www.jambajuice.com	Emeryville	CA	94608	510-596-0100		345
Jamco Aerospace Inc 121 E Industry Ct *Web:* www.jamco-aerospace.com	Deer Park	NY	11729	631-586-7900		454

Listing	City	State	ZIP	Phone	Fax	Class
Jamco America Inc 1018 80th St SW *Web:* www.jamco-america.com	Everett	WA	98203	425-347-4735	355-0237	22
Jamcracker Inc 5201 Great America Pkwy Ste 320 *Web:* www.jamcracker.com	Santa Clara	CA	95054	408-496-5500		39
James & Springgate PLC 490 W South St *Web:* jscpas.com	Kalamazoo	MI	49007	269-384-0219		2
James A- Sewell and Associates LLC 600 4th St W *Web:* jasewell.com	Newport	WA	99156	509-447-3626	447-2112	261
James A. Connors Associates Inc 225 Madison Ave PO Box 336 *Web:* jamesaconnors.com	Morristown	NJ	07963	973-539-9300		390
James A. Garfield National Historic Site 8095 Mentor Ave *Web:* www.nps.gov	Mentor	OH	44060	440-255-8722		564
James A. Murphy & Son Inc 50 Colorado Ave *Web:* www.jambeads.com	Warwick	RI	02886	508-761-5060		407
James Agee Film Project PO Box 73 *Web:* www.ageefilms.org	Riverdale	MD	20738	301-277-3880		514
James Alexander Corp 845 Rt 94 *Web:* www.james-alexander.com	Blairstown	NJ	07825	908-362-9266		88
James Allyn Inc 6575 Trinity Ct Ste B *TF:* 877-828-5530 ■ *Web:* www.jamesallyn.com	Dublin	CA	94568	925-828-5530		627
James Arthur Vineyards & Winery 2001 W Raymond Rd *Web:* www.jamesarthurvineyards.com	Raymond	NE	68428	402-783-5255		50-7
James Austin Co 115 Downieville Rd PO Box 827 *TF:* 800-245-1942 ■ *Web:* austinsbleach.com	Mars	PA	16046	724-625-1535	625-3288	151
James Avery Craftsman Inc 145 Avery Rd N *TF:* 800-283-1770 ■ *Web:* www.jamesavery.com	Kerrville	TX	78029	830-895-6800		409
James B. Mcevoy CPA 280 N Bedford Rd *Web:* jmcevoycpa.com	Mount Kisco	NY	10549	914-241-0460		2
James Baird State Park 14 Maintenance Ln *Web:* parks.ny.gov	Pleasant Valley	NY	12569	845-452-1489		565
James Bradshaw State Jail 3900 W Loop 571 N PO Box 9000 *Web:* www.tdcj.texas.gov	Henderson	TX	75653	903-655-0880	655-0500	213
James C. Hailey & Co 7518 Hwy 70 S Ste 100 *Web:* jchengr.com	Nashville	TN	37221	615-883-4933	883-4937	261
James Candy Co 1519 Boardwalk *TF:* 800-441-1404 ■ *Web:* www.jamescandy.com	Atlantic City	NJ	08401	609-344-1519	344-0246	296-8
James Chicago, The 55 E Ontario *TF:* 888-526-3778 ■ *Web:* www.jameshotels.com	Chicago	IL	60611	312-337-1000	337-7217	379
James City County 4600 Opportunity Way PO Box 8784 *Web:* www.jamescitycountyva.gov	Williamsburg	VA	23188	757-253-6728	253-6833	338
James City County Government Ctr 101 Mounts Bay Rd *Web:* www.jamescitycountyva.gov	Williamsburg	VA	23185	757-253-6630		338
James Coney Island Inc 1750 Stebbins Dr *Web:* www.jamesconeyisland.com	Houston	TX	77043	713-932-1500	932-0061	670
James Crabtree Correctional Ctr 216 N Murray St *Web:* doc.ok.gov	Helena	OK	73741	580-852-3221		213
James Craft & Son Inc 2780 York Haven Rd PO Box 8 *Web:* www.jamescraftson.com	York Haven	PA	17370	717-266-6629	266-6623	189-10
James D. Morrissey Inc 300 Keiser Rd *TF:* 877-536-6857 ■ *Web:* www.jdm-inc.com	Philadelphia	PA	19114	215-708-8420	338-3225	188-4
James Davis 400 S Grove Park Rd *Web:* www.jamesdavisstore.com	Memphis	TN	38117	901-767-4640		157-4
James Dee Johnson & Company CPA PC 3608 NW 58th St Ste 100 *Web:* jdjcpa.com	Oklahoma City	OK	73112	405-943-1272		2
James E. Conner Jr Plumbing 505 Rte 168 Ste B & C *Web:* jameseconnerjrplumbing.com	Turnersville	NJ	08012	856-784-0004		189-10
James E. Moore Insurance Agency Inc 1508 Military Cutoff Rd Ste 104 *Web:* jamesemoore.com	Wilmington	NC	28403	910-256-5333		390
James E. Roberts-obayashi Corp 20 Oak Ct *Web:* www.jerocorp.com	Danville	CA	94526	925-820-0600		190
James Eagen Sons Co PO Box 4097 *Web:* jameseagen.com	Wyoming	PA	18644	570-693-2100	693-3829	207
James Excavating Inc 476 Hildebrand St *Web:* jamesexcavating.com	Johnstown	PA	15909	814-539-1903		422
James F. Molleur LLC 419 Alfred St *Web:* molleurlaw.com	Biddeford	ME	04005	207-283-3777		41
James F. Turner Engineers LP 8340 Meadow Rd Ste 160 *Web:* jfte.com	Dallas	TX	75231	214-750-2900		261
James Farris Associates Ltd 7100 N Classen Blvd Ste 301 *Web:* www.jamesfarris.com	Oklahoma City	OK	73116	405-525-5061	525-5069	260
James Fisher Technologies LLC 5821 Langley Ave *Web:* jftechgroup.com	Loveland	CO	80538	720-408-0100		261
James Flanagan, Attorney At Law, A Prof Corp 14912 S Eastern Ave Ste 106 *Web:* flanaganlawfirm.com	Plainfield	IL	60544	815-254-1100		41
James G. Davis Construction Corp 12530 Parklawn Dr *Web:* www.davisconstruction.com	Rockville	MD	20852	301-881-2990	468-3918	186
James G. Hardy & Co 24919 148th Rd	Jamaica	NY	11422	212-689-6680		361
James G. Whitley PC 679 E 2nd Ave Ste E-1 2 *Web:* 4cornerslaw.com	Durango	CO	81301	970-385-9130		41
James Gettys Hotel 27 Chambersburg St *TF:* 888-900-5275 ■ *Web:* jamesgettyshotel.com	Gettysburg	PA	17325	717-337-1334	334-2103	379
James Goodman Gallery 41 E 57th St Ste 802 *Web:* www.jamesgoodmangallery.com	New York	NY	10022	212-593-3737	980-0195	42
James Graham Brown Cancer Ctr 529 S Jackson St *TF:* 866-530-5516 ■ *Web:* uoflbrowncancercenter.org	Louisville	KY	40202	502-562-4158		769
James Greene & Associates Inc 275 W Kiehl Ave *TF:* 800-422-3384 ■ *Web:* jamesgreeneins.com	Sherwood	AR	72120	501-834-4001		390
James Group Intl 4335 W Ft St *Web:* www.jamesgroupintl.com	Detroit	MI	48209	313-841-0070		449
James Gutheim & Associates Inc 16400 Ventura Blvd *Web:* www.gutheim.com	Encino	CA	91436	818-784-7189	784-4916	195
James H Clark and Son Inc 4100 S 500 W *TF:* 800-453-7222 ■ *Web:* www.jameshclark.com	Salt Lake City	UT	84123	801-266-9322	269-1553	780
James H. Drew Corp 8701 Zionsville Rd *Web:* jameshdrew.com	Indianapolis	IN	46268	317-876-3739	876-3829	188-4
James H. Magee 1108 N Sixth St *Web:* washingtonbankruptcy.com	Tacoma	WA	98403	253-383-1001		41
James H. Quillen Veterans Affairs Medical Ctr Corner of Lamont & Veterans Way *TF:* 877-573-3529 ■ *Web:* www.mountainhome.va.gov	Mountain Home	TN	37684	423-926-1171	979-3519	374-8
James H. Sloppy Floyd State Park 2800 Sloppy Floyd Lake Rd *Web:* gastateparks.org	Summerville	GA	30747	706-857-0826		565
James Hardie Building Products 26300 La Alameda Ave Ste 400 *TF:* 888-542-7343 ■ *Web:* www.jameshardie.com	Mission Viejo	CA	92691	888-542-7343		191-4
James Hook & Co 15-17 N Ave *Web:* www.jameshooklobster.com	Boston	MA	02210	617-423-5501	423-5505	297-5
James Investment Research Inc PO Box 8 *TF:* 800-995-2637 ■ *Web:* www.jamesinvestment.com	Alpha	OH	45301	888-426-7640		401
James Irvine Foundation 1 Bush St Ste 800 *Web:* www.irvine.org	San Francisco	CA	94104	415-777-2244	777-0869	305
James J. Eagan Civic Ctr 1 James J Eagan Dr *Web:* www.florissantmo.com	Florissant	MO	63033	314-921-5700		720
James J. Peters Veterans Affairs Medical Ctr 130 W Kingsbridge Rd *Web:* www.bronx.va.gov	Bronx	NY	10468	718-584-9000		374-8
James Jordan Middle School 7911 Winnetka Ave *Web:* www.jamesjordanms.com	Winnetka	CA	91306	818-882-2496	882-1798	685
James Joyce Authentic Irish Pub 114 Eigth Ave SW *Web:* www.stthomasac.com	Calgary	AB	T2P1B3	403-262-0708		671
James K. Polk Memorial State Historic Site 12031 Lancaster Hwy *Web:* www.jameskpolk.net	Pineville	NC	28134	704-889-7145	889-3057	50-3
James L. Druffner CPA PC 1912 Sidewinder Dr Ste 200A *Web:* druffner.com	Park City	UT	84060	435-649-4592		2
James L. Goodwin State Forest 23 Potter Rd *Web:* portal.ct.gov	Hampton	CT	06247	860-455-9534		565
James L. Howard & Co 10 Britton Dr *Web:* www.jameslhoward.com	Bloomfield	CT	06002	860-242-3581		350
James L. Knight International Ctr 400 SE Second Ave *Web:* www.jlkc.com	Miami	FL	33131	305-416-5970	350-7910	572
James L. Maher Ctr 120 Hillside Ave *Web:* www.mahercenter.org	Newport	RI	02840	401-846-0340		104
James L. Miniter Insurance Agency Inc 400 Hingham St *Web:* miniter.com	Rockland	MA	02370	781-982-3100		390
James L. Taylor Manufacturing Co 108 Parker Ave *TF:* 800-952-1320 ■ *Web:* www.jamesltaylor.com	Poughkeepsie	NY	12601	845-452-3780	452-0764	821
James L. West Alzheimer Ctr 1111 Summit Ave *Web:* www.jameslwest.org	Fort Worth	TX	76102	817-877-1199		371
James Lane Air Conditioning Company Inc 5024 Old Jacksboro Hwy *TF:* 800-460-2204 ■ *Web:* jameslane.com	Wichita Falls	TX	76302	940-766-0244		610
James M. Fishman PA 9655 S Dixie Hwy Ste 102 *Web:* fishmanlawfl.com	Miami	FL	33156	305-661-1680		41
James M. Polyak Attorney At Law 645 Penn St *Web:* polyaklawoffice.com	Reading	PA	19601	610-376-5250		41
James M. Robb - Colorado River State Park PO Box 700 *Web:* cpw.state.co.us	Clifton	CO	81520	970-434-3388		565
James M. Wesolowski CPA PA 2503 Del Prado Blvd S Ste 500 *TF:* 800-275-4975 ■ *Web:* jwesocpa.com	Cape Coral	FL	33904	239-574-4449	574-5716	2
James M. Wood CPA 603 B Omni Dr *Web:* jmwoodcpa.com	Hillsborough	NJ	08844	908-431-1700		2
James Machine Works LLC 1521 Adams St *TF:* 800-259-6104 ■ *Web:* jamesmachineworks.com	Monroe	LA	71201	318-322-6104	388-4245	189-1
James Madison University 800 S Main St *Web:* www.jmu.edu	Harrisonburg	VA	22807	540-568-6211	568-3332	166
James Madison's Montpelier 13384 Laundry Rd *Web:* www.montpelier.org	Montpelier Station	VA	22957	540-672-2728		50-3
James Magno CPA 51 Monroe St Ste 402	Rockville	MD	20850	240-778-6041		2
James Marine Inc (JMI) 4500 Clarks River Rd PO Box 2305 *Web:* www.jamesmarine.com	Paducah	KY	42002	270-898-7392		465

Name / Address	City	State	Zip	Phone	Fax	Class
James Marta & Co 701 Howe Ave Ste E3 *Web:* jpmcpa.com	Sacramento	CA	95825	916-993-9494	993-9489	2
James Martin Signature Vanities LLC 1229 Slocum St *Web:* jamesmartinfurniture.com	Dallas	TX	75207	512-795-4171		362
James McHugh Construction Co 1737 S Michigan Ave *Web:* www.mchughconstruction.com	Chicago	IL	60616	312-986-8000	431-8518	188-4
James New York - NoMad, The 88 Madison Ave *TF:* 800-601-8500 ■ *Web:* www.jameshotels.com	New York	NY	10016	212-532-4100	696-9758	379
James Pappas Investment Counsel PO Box 475 *TF:* 800-546-7277 ■ *Web:* www.jpic.net	Redding Ridge	CT	06876	203-938-8916		401
James Pate Philip State Park 2050 W Stearns Rd *Web:* www.bartlettparks.org	Bartlett	IL	60103	847-608-3100		565
James Paton Memorial Hospital 125 Trans Canada Hwy *Web:* centralhealth.nl.ca	Gander	NL	A1V1P7	709-256-2500	256-7800	374-2
James Posey Associates Inc 3112 Lord Baltimore Dr *Web:* www.jamesposey.com	Baltimore	MD	21244	410-265-6100		256
James Printing Inc 1340 Taney *Web:* www.jamesprinting.com	North Kansas City	MO	64116	816-561-6211	561-9827	627
James R. Hill Inc 2500 County Rd 42 W Ste 120 *Web:* jrhinc.com	Burnsville	MN	55337	952-890-6044		261
James R. Mclauchlen Real Estate Inc 789 Hill St *Web:* www.mclauchlen.com	Southampton	NY	11968	631-283-0448		652
James Reynolds Transport Inc 360 S Eaton St *Web:* www.jamesreynoldstransport.com	Berwick	PA	18603	570-752-3500	752-8420	780
James Richardson Intl (JRI) 2415 2A Ave N *Web:* www.richardson.ca	Winnipeg	MB	R3B0X8	204-934-5961		275
James River Coal Co 901 E Byrd St Ste 1600 *NASDAQ: JRVR* ■ *TF:* 877-283-6545 ■ *Web:* www.jamesrivercoal.com	Richmond	VA	23219	804-780-3000		501
James River Convalescent Ctr 540 Aberthaw Ave *Web:* www.vahs.com	Newport News	VA	23601	757-595-2273		450
James River Equipment 11047 Leadbetter Rd *Web:* www.jamesriverequipment.com	Ashland	VA	23005	804-798-6001	752-7111	274
James Rumsey Technical Institute 3274 Hedgesville Rd *Web:* www.jamesrumsey.com	Martinsburg	WV	25401	304-754-7925	754-7933	167-3
James S. Rogers 1500 Fourth Ave Ste 500 *Web:* jsrogerslaw.com	Seattle	WA	98101	206-621-8525		41
James Screw Machine Products 36 Nettleton Ave *Web:* colescrew.com	North Haven	CT	06473	203-772-6675	773-9526	621
James Sewell Ballet 528 Hennepin Ave Ste 215 *Web:* jsballet.org	Minneapolis	MN	55403	612-672-0480		573-1
James Sprunt Community College 133 James Sprunt Dr *Web:* www.jamessprunt.edu	Kenansville	NC	28349	910-296-2400		162
James Steele Construction Co 1410 Sylvan St *Web:* www.jamessteeleconstruction.com	Saint Paul	MN	55117	651-488-6755	488-4787	188-5
James Thompson & Company Inc 381 Park Ave S Ste 718 *Web:* www.jamesthompson.com	New York	NY	10016	212-686-4242	686-9528	208
James Tool Machine & Engineering Inc 130 Reep Dr *Web:* www.jamestool.com	Morganton	NC	28655	828-584-8722		256
James V. Brown Library of Williamsport & Lycoming County 19 E Fourth St *Web:* jvbrown.edu	Williamsport	PA	17701	570-326-0536	326-1671	434-3
James W. Bell Company Inc 1755 I Ave NE *Web:* jwbell.biz	Cedar Rapids	IA	52402	319-362-1151	365-3649	358
James W. Glover Ltd PO Box 579 *Web:* www.gloverltd.com	Honolulu	HI	96809	808-591-8977	591-8978	188-4
James Walker Co 7109 Milford Industrial Rd *Web:* jameswalker.com	Baltimore	MD	21215	410-486-3950		470
James Walker Manufacturing Co 511 W 195th St *Web:* www.jameswalker.biz	Glenwood	IL	60425	708-754-4020		326
James Whitcomb Riley Museum Home 528 Lockerbie St *Web:* www.rileykids.org	Indianapolis	IN	46202	317-631-5885		520
James White Construction Company Inc 4156 Freedom Way *Web:* jameswhiteconstruction.com	Weirton	WV	26062	304-748-8181	748-8183	188-10
James White's Fort 205 E Hill Ave *Web:* www.jameswhitesfort.org	Knoxville	TN	37915	865-525-6514		520
James Wood Motors 2111 US Hwy 287 S *TF:* 866-232-6058 ■ *Web:* jameswood.com	Decatur	TX	76234	940-627-2177		57
James, House,Downing & Lueken PA 801 W Third St PO Box 3585 *Web:* jameshousedowning.com	Little Rock	AR	72203	501-372-6555		41
James, McElroy & Diehl PA 525 N Tryon St Ste 700 *Web:* www.jmdlaw.com	Charlotte	NC	28202	704-372-9870		428
James, Stevens & Daniels Inc 1283 College Park Dr *TF:* 800-305-0773 ■ *Web:* www.jsdinc.net	Dover	DE	19904	302-735-4628		160
James, The 460 W Tenth Ave **Fax Area Code:* 614 ■ *TF:* 800-293-5066 ■ *Web:* cancer.osu.edu	Columbus	OH	43210	800-293-5066	293-9449*	374-7

Name / Address	City	State	Zip	Phone	Fax	Class
Jameson & Dunagan PC 5429 LBJ Fwy Ste 700 *Web:* www.jdlawtx.com	Dallas	TX	75240	214-369-6422		428
Jameson Annex 1600 N Dr PO Box 5911 *Web:* www.doc.sd.gov	Sioux Falls	SD	57117	605-367-5051	367-5585	213
Jameson Commercial Real Estate 425 W N Ave *Web:* www.jamesoncommercial.com	Chicago	IL	60610	312-216-8000	751-2808	652
Jameson Group 287 S Robertson Blvd Ste 474 *Web:* www.thejamesongroup.com	Beverly Hills	CA	90211	310-289-5085	289-5086	393
Jameson LLC 1451 Old N Main St *TF:* 877-278-2601 ■ *Web:* www.spartacogroup.com	Clover	SC	29710	803-222-6400		253
Jamestown Area Chamber of Commerce 120 Second St SE PO Box 1530 *Web:* www.jamestownchamber.com	Jamestown	ND	58402	701-252-4830	952-4837	139
Jamestown Business College 7 Fairmount Ave PO Box 429 *Web:* www.jbc.edu	Jamestown	NY	14702	716-664-5100	664-3144	800
Jamestown College 6000 College Ln *TF:* 800-336-2554 ■ *Web:* www.uj.edu	Jamestown	ND	58405	701-252-3467	253-4318	166
Jamestown Community College 525 Falconer St *TF:* 800-388-8557 ■ *Web:* www.sunyjcc.edu	Jamestown	NY	14702	716-338-1000		162
Jamestown Livestock Auction 3443 82nd Ave SE *Web:* www.jamestownlivestock.com	Jamestown	ND	58401	701-252-2111	252-1520	446
Jamestown Plastics Inc 8806 Highland Ave *Web:* www.jamestownplastics.com	Brocton	NY	14716	716-792-4144	792-4154	602
Jamesville Office Furniture Inc 11309 Folsom Blvd Ste B *Web:* jamesvillefurniture.com	Rancho Cordova	CA	95742	916-638-4050		321
Jamesway Incubator Company Inc 30 High Ridge Ct *TF:* 800-438-8077 ■ *Web:* www.jamesway.com	Cambridge	ON	N1R7L3	519-624-4646		273
Jamie Gibbs & Assoc 120 W 73rd St *Web:* www.jamiegibbsassociates.com	Indianapolis	IN	46260	917-862-5313		393
Jamie Oil Company Inc 171 Main St *Web:* jamieoil.com	Ashland	MA	01721	508-231-1400		316
Jamie Whitten Delta States Research Ctr 141Experiment Stn Rd *Web:* www.ars.usda.gov	Stoneville	MS	38776	662-686-5265	686-5459	668
Jamieson Management Company Inc 627 Main St Ste One *Web:* jamiesonproperties.com	Woburn	MA	01801	781-933-5783		653
Jamison Bedding Inc PO Box 681948 *TF:* 800-255-1883 ■ *Web:* www.jamisonbedding.com	Franklin	TN	37068	615-794-1883		471
Jamison Door Co 55 JV Jamison Dr **Fax Area Code:* 240 ■ *TF:* 800-532-3667 ■ *Web:* www.jamisondoor.com	Hagerstown	MD	21740	301-733-3100	329-5155*	234
Jamko Technical Solutions Inc 932 Sohn Alloway Rd *Web:* jamkocorp.com	Lyons	NY	14489	315-871-4420		261
Jammin-FM 99.5 (Alt) 75153 Merle Dr Ste G *Web:* www.jammin995fm.com	Palm Desert	CA	92211	760-568-4550		645-117
Jampro Antennas Inc 6340 Sky Creek Dr *TF:* 800-732-7665 ■ *Web:* www.jampro.com	Sacramento	CA	95828	916-383-1177	383-1182	647
JAMS/Endispute 500 N State College Blvd 14th Fl *Web:* www.jamsadr.com	Orange	CA	92868	714-939-1300	939-8710	41
Jamsan Hotel Management Inc 83 Hartwell Ave *TF:* 800-523-5549 ■ *Web:* www.jhmus.com	Lexington	MA	02421	781-863-8500		463
Jan Companies, The 35 Sockanosset Cross Rd *Web:* www.jancompanies.com	Cranston	RI	02920	401-946-4000	946-4392	670
Jan Dils Attorneys at Law Lc 107 Lb & T Way *TF:* 877-526-3457 ■ *Web:* www.jandils.com	Logan	WV	25601	304-831-0000		428
Jan Marini Skin Research Inc 5883 Rue Ferrari *TF:* 800-347-2223 ■ *Web:* www.janmarini.com	San Jose	CA	95138	408-362-0130	362-0140	214
Jan Packaging Inc 100 Harrison St *Web:* www.janpackaging.net	Dover	NJ	07801	973-361-7200		311
Jan's Mountain Outfitters 1600 Park Ave PO Box 280 *TF:* 800-745-1020 ■ *Web:* www.jans.com	Park City	UT	84060	435-649-4949	649-7511	711
Jana Foods LLC 100 Wood Ave S Ste 206 *Web:* www.janafoods.com	Iselin	NJ	08830	201-866-5001		297-8
Jan-Air Inc 10815 Commercial St *Web:* www.jan-air.com	Richmond	IL	60071	815-678-4516		18
Janas Consulting 141 S Lake Ave Ste 102 *Web:* www.janascorp.com	Pasadena	CA	91101	626-432-7000	432-7050	708
Janazzo Services Corp 140 Norton St Rt 10 PO Box 469 *TF:* 800-297-3931 ■ *Web:* www.janazzo.com	Milldale	CT	06467	860-621-7381	621-7529	189-10
Janco Supply Inc 723 N Highland Ave	Aurora	IL	60506	630-896-4651		366
Jancyn Inc 1100 Lincoln Ave Ste 367 **Fax Area Code:* 866 ■ *TF:* 800-339-2861 ■ *Web:* www.jancyn.com	San Jose	CA	95125	800-339-2861	266-3140*	506
Jane Goodall Institute for Wildlife Research Education (JGI) 1595 Spring Hill Rd Ste 550 *TF:* 800-592-5263 ■ *Web:* www.janegoodall.org	Vienna	VA	22182	703-682-9220		48-3
Jane Maughan PC 726 Ann St *Web:* roachmaughanlaw.com	Stroudsburg	PA	18360	570-421-7009	421-7039	41
Jane Rose Reporting 80 Fifth Ave **Fax Area Code:* 800 ■ *TF:* 800-825-3341 ■ *Web:* janerosereporting.com	New York	NY	10011	212-727-7773	825-9055*	445
Jane Rotrosen Agency 318 E 51st St *Web:* janerotrosen.com	New York	NY	10022	212-593-4330	935-6985	444
Janell Inc 6130 Cornell Rd *TF:* 888-489-9111 ■ *Web:* janell.com	Cincinnati	OH	45242	513-489-9111		358
Janes Island State Park 26280 Alfred Lawson Dr *Web:* www.dnr.maryland.gov	Crisfield	MD	21817	410-968-1565		565

Name / Address	City	State	Zip	Phone	Fax	Class
Janesville Sand & Gravel Co (JSG) 1110 Harding St PO Box 427 *TF:* 800-955-7702 ■ *Web:* www.jsandg.com	Janesville	WI	53547	608-754-7701	754-8555	503-4
Janesville Tool & Manufacturing Inc 3930 Enterprise Dr *Web:* www.janesvilletool.com	Janesville	WI	53546	608-314-1620		757
Janet Mcafee Real Estate 9889 Clayton Rd *TF:* 888-991-4800 ■ *Web:* www.janetmcafee.com	Saint Louis	MO	63124	314-997-4800	997-0647	652
Janet's Antiques 2545 Central Ave	Saint Petersburg	FL	33713	727-823-5700		460
Jang & Associates LLP 1766 Lacassie Ave Ste 200 *Web:* janglit.com	Walnut Creek	CA	94596	925-937-1400		41
Janicki Industries Inc 719 Metcalf St *TF:* 888-856-5143 ■ *Web:* www.janicki.com	Sedro-Woolley	WA	98284	360-856-5143		454
Jani-King International Inc 16885 Dallas Pkwy *Web:* www.janiking.com	Addison	TX	75001	972-991-0900		152
Janis Plastics Inc 330 N Ave *Web:* janisplastics.com	Antioch	IL	60002	847-838-5500	838-0200	9
Janitor's Closet Ltd 3301 N Markey Ave *TF:* 800-658-2244 ■ *Web:* www.janclo.com	Sioux Falls	SD	57107	605-334-4387	334-4911	76
Janitronics Building Services 29 Sawyer Rd *Web:* www.janitronics.com	Waltham	MA	02453	781-647-5570	893-5878	104
Janitronics Inc 1988 Central Ave *Web:* www.janitronicsinc.com	Albany	NY	12205	518-456-8484		256
Janko Hospitality LLC 3050 Finley Rd Ste 300D-1 *Web:* www.jankohotels.com	Downers Grove	IL	60515	630-434-9400		463
Jankovich Co, The Berth 74 *Web:* www.jankovichcompany.com	San Pedro	CA	90731	310-547-3305		538
Janlynn Corp 2070 Westover Rd *TF:* 800-445-5565 ■ *Web:* www.janlynn.com	Chicopee	MA	01022	413-206-0002		594
Janney Montgomery Scott LLC 1801 Market St *TF:* 800-526-6397 ■ *Web:* www.janney.com	Philadelphia	PA	19103	215-665-6000		690
Jannus Inc 1607 W Jefferson St *Web:* www.jannus.org	Boise	ID	83702	208-336-5533	336-0880	48-17
Janos Technology LLC 55 Black Brook Rd *Web:* www.janostech.com	Keene	NH	03431	603-757-0070	757-0069	544
Janou Pakter Inc 108 W 39th St *Fax Area Code: 310 ■ *Web:* pakter.com	New York	NY	10018	212-989-1288	359-0232*	721
Jan-Pro Cleaning Systems Minneapolis 33 Tenth Ave S Ste 200 *Web:* jan-pro.com	Hopkins	MN	55343	952-238-1005		256
Jan-Pro International Inc (JPI) 4221 S Santa Rita Ave Ste 101 *TF:* 866-355-1064 ■ *Web:* jan-pro.com	Alpharetta	GA	30009	678-336-1780		152
Janson Industries 1200 Garfield Ave SW *TF:* 800-548-8982 ■ *Web:* www.jansonindustries.com	Canton	OH	44706	330-455-7029	455-5919	722
Janson Media Inc 118 Main St *Web:* www.janson.com	Tappan	NY	10983	845-359-8488		194
Janssen Clinic for Animals 1624 N High Point Rd *Web:* www.janssenclinic.com	Middleton	WI	53562	608-836-0600		794
Janssen Consulting Inc 1704 Mission Ave Ste 1 *Web:* www.janssenconsulting.com	Carmichael	CA	95608	916-716-2326		179
Janssen Malloy LLP 730 Fifth St *Web:* janssenlaw.com	Eureka	CA	95502	707-445-2071		41
Janssen Pharmaceutica Inc 1125 Trenton-Harbourton Rd *Fax Area Code: 609 ■ *TF:* 800-526-7736 ■ *Web:* www.janssen.com	Titusville	NJ	08560	908-218-6095	730-2378*	582
Jantek Industries 230 Rt 70 *TF:* 888-782-7937 ■ *Web:* jantekwindows.com	Medford	NJ	08055	609-654-1030	654-1083	234
Jantzen Beach SuperCtr N Hayden Island Dr *Web:* www.jantzenbeachpdx.shopkimco.com	Portland	OR	97217	503-286-9103		460
January Co 5851 S 194th St *Web:* www.kyjusa.com	Kent	WA	98032	253-872-9919	872-9927	296-26
Janus Consulting Inc 115 Ellis Rd *Web:* www.janusconsulting.com	Havertown	PA	19083	610-996-1809		196
Janus Corp 1081 Shary Cir *Web:* www.januscorp.com	Concord	CA	94518	925-969-9200	969-9290	186
Janus Group Inc, The 2744 US Hwy 1 S *Web:* www.janusgroup.com	Saint Augustine	FL	32086	904-797-1181		194
Janus Henderson Investors 720 S S Colorado Blvd Ste 900 *Web:* www.janushenderson.com	Denver	CO	80246	800-525-3713		401
Janus Hotels & Resorts Inc 2300 Corporate Blvd NW Ste 232 *Web:* www.janushotels.com	Boca Raton	FL	33431	561-997-2325	997-5331	379
Janus Research Group Inc 600 Ponder Pl Dr *Web:* janusresearch.com	Evans	GA	30809	706-364-9100	364-9004	194
Japan 866 UN Plz 2nd Fl *Web:* www.un.emb-japan.go.jp	New York	NY	10017	212-223-4300	521-0676	784
Japan						
Consulate General 1225 17th St Ste 3000 *Web:* www.denver.us.emb-japan.go.jp	Denver	CO	80202	303-534-1151	534-3393	257
Consulate General 3601 C St Ste 1300 *Web:* www.anchorage.us.emb-japan.go.jp	Anchorage	AK	99503	907-562-8424	562-8434	257
Consulate General 1742 Nuuanu Ave *Web:* www.honolulu.us.emb-japan.go.jp	Honolulu	HI	96817	808-543-3111	543-3170	257
Consulate General 1801 W End Ave Ste 900 *Web:* www.nashville.us.emb-japan.go.jp	Nashville	TN	37203	615-340-4300	340-4311	257
Consulate General 400 Renaissance Ctr Ste 1600 *Web:* www.detroit.us.emb-japan.go.jp	Detroit	MI	48243	313-567-0120	567-0274	257
Consulate General Wells Fargo Ctr 1300 SW Fifth Ave Ste 2700 *Web:* www.portland.us.emb-japan.go.jp	Portland	OR	97201	503-221-1811	224-8936	257

Name / Address	City	State	Zip	Phone	Fax	Class
Consulate General 350 S Grand Ave Ste 1700 *Web:* www.la.us.emb-japan.go.jp	Los Angeles	CA	90071	213-617-6700	617-6727	257
Consulate General 299 Park Ave 18th Fl *Web:* www.ny.us.emb-japan.go.jp	New York	NY	10171	212-371-8222	371-1294	257
Consulate General 601 Union St Ste 500 *Web:* www.seattle.us.emb-japan.go.jp	Seattle	WA	98101	206-682-9107	624-9097	257
Consulate General 80 SW Eigth St Ste 3200 *Web:* www.miami.us.emb-japan.go.jp	Miami	FL	33130	305-530-9090	530-0950	257
Consulate General 600 Atlantic Ave 22nd Fl *Web:* www.boston.us.emb-japan.go.jp	Boston	MA	02210	617-973-9772	542-1329	257
Japan Automobile Manufacturers Association Inc (JAMA) 888 17th St NW Ste 609 *Web:* www.jama.org	Washington	DC	20006	202-296-8537	872-1212	49-21
Japan Canada Oil Sands Ltd 639-5th Ave SW Ste 2300 *Web:* www.jacos.ca	Calgary	AB	T2P0M9	403-264-9046		536
Japan National Tourist Organization 1 Grand Central Pl 60 E 42nd St Ste 448 *Web:* us.jnto.go.jp	New York	NY	10165	212-757-5640	307-6754	775
Japan Samurai 12233 Jefferson Ave *Web:* www.japansamurainn.com	Newport News	VA	23602	757-249-4400		671
Japan Society 333 E 47th St *Web:* www.japansociety.org	New York	NY	10017	212-832-1155	755-6752	48-14
Japan Travel Bureau USA Inc (JTB) 2 W 45th St Ste 305 *TF:* 800-223-6104 ■ *Web:* www.jtbusa.com	New York	NY	10036	212-698-4900	586-9686	771
Japan-America Institute of Management Science 6660 Hawaii Kai Dr *Web:* www.jaims.org	Honolulu	HI	96825	808-395-2314	396-7111	242
Japanese American Citizens League (JACL) 1765 Sutter St *Web:* jacl.org	San Francisco	CA	94115	415-921-5225	931-4671	48-14
Japanese American National Library 1619 Sutter St *Web:* www.janlibrary.org	San Francisco	CA	94159	415-567-5006		434-3
Japanese American National Museum 369 E First St *TF:* 800-461-5266 ■ *Web:* www.janm.org	Los Angeles	CA	90012	213-625-0414		520
Japanese Chamber of Commerce & Industry of Chicago 541 N Fairbanks Ct Ste 2050 *Web:* www.jccc-chi.org	Chicago	IL	60611	312-245-8344	245-8355	138
Japanese Chamber of Commerce & Industry of Hawaii 714 Kanoelehua Ave *Web:* jccih.org	Hilo	HI	96720	808-934-0177	934-0178	138
Japanese Chamber of Commerce & Industry of New York Inc 145 W 57th St *Web:* www.jcciny.org	New York	NY	10019	212-246-8001	246-8002	138
Japanese Chamber of Commerce of Northern California 1875 S Grant St Ste 760 *Web:* www.jccnc.org	San Mateo	CA	94402	650-522-8500	522-8300	138
Japanese Cultural Center of Hawaii 2454 S Beretania St *Web:* www.jcch.com	Honolulu	HI	96826	808-945-7633	944-1123	520
Japanese Garden 611 SW Kingston Ave *TF:* 800-955-8352 ■ *Web:* japanesegarden.org	Portland	OR	97205	503-223-1321	223-8303	97
Japanese-American Museum 535 N Fifth St *Web:* www.jamsj.org	San Jose	CA	95112	408-294-3138	294-1657	520
Japango 1136 Pearl St *Web:* boulderjapango.com	Boulder	CO	80302	303-938-0330		671
Japan-US Friendship Commission 1201 15th St NW Ste 330 *Web:* www.jusfc.gov	Washington	DC	20005	202-653-9800	653-9802	340-20
Jaquith Industries Inc 600 E Brighton Ave *Web:* www.jaquith.com	Syracuse	NY	13210	315-478-5700	478-5707	697
JAR 8225 Beverly Blvd *Web:* www.thejar.com	Los Angeles	CA	90048	323-655-6566		671
Jarboe Sales Co 315 S 85th E Ave *Web:* www.jarboesales.com	Tulsa	OK	74112	918-836-2511		80-3
Jarco Supply LLC 100 Ag Dr *Web:* www.jarcosupply.com	Youngsville	NC	27596	919-562-0123		191-1
Jardine, Logan & O'Brien PLLP 8519 Eagle Point Blvd Ste 100 *Web:* www.jlolaw.com	Lake Elmo	MN	55042	651-290-6500	223-5070	428
Jarecki Valves 6910 W Ridge Rd *Web:* jareckivalves.net	Fairview	PA	16415	814-474-2666	474-3645	789
Jared Coffin House 29 Broad St *Web:* www.jaredcoffinhouse.com	Nantucket	MA	02554	508-228-2400	228-8549	379
Jargon Software 708 N First St Ste 432 *Fax Area Code: 866 ■ *TF:* 866-568-4291 ■ *Web:* www.jargonsoft.com	Minneapolis	MN	55401	952-426-0858	426-0858*	179
Jarlette Health Services 711 Yonge St *Web:* www.jarlette.com	Midland	ON	L4R2E1	705-549-4889	549-2494	463
Jaro Transportation Services Inc 975 Post Rd *TF:* 800-451-3447 ■ *Web:* www.jarotrans.com	Warren	OH	44483	330-393-5659	393-5906	780
JARP Industries Inc 1051 Pine St PO Box 923 *Web:* www.jarpind.com	Schofield	WI	54476	715-359-4241	355-4960	223
Jarrard Phillips Cate & Hancock Inc 219 Ward Cir *TF:* 888-844-6274 ■ *Web:* jarrardinc.com	Brentwood	TN	37027	312-419-0575		353
Jarrell Plantation State Historic Site 711 Jarrell Plantation Rd *Web:* gastateparks.org	Juliette	GA	31046	478-986-5172		565
Jarret Inc 1037 Country Club Dr Ste A *Web:* www.jarrett-inc.com	Auburn	AL	36830	334-270-0046	270-8815	186
Jarrett Industries of The Carolinas Inc 11511 Cronridge Dr *Web:* www.jarrettindustries.com	Owings Mills	MD	21117	410-581-0303		344
Jarrett Logistics Systems 1347 N Main St *TF:* 877-392-9811 ■ *Web:* www.gojarrett.com	Orrville	OH	44667	877-392-9811		449

	Phone	Fax	Class
Jarrow Formulas Inc 1824 S Robertson Blvd, Los Angeles CA 90035 *TF:* 800-726-0886 ■ *Web:* www.jarrow.com	310-204-6936	204-2520	799
J-Art Iron Co 9435 Jefferson Blvd, Culver City CA 90232 *Web:* www.jartiron.com	310-202-1126	202-1642	319-2
Jarvis Airfoil Inc 528 Glastonbury Tpke, Portland CT 06480 *Web:* www.jarvisairfoil.com	860-342-5000		22
Jarvis Caster Co 203 Kerth St, Saint Joseph MI 49085 *TF:* 800-253-0868 ■ *Web:* jarviscaster.com	800-253-0868		350
Jarvis Christian College PO Box 1470, Hawkins TX 75765 *Web:* www.jarvis.edu	903-769-5700	769-1282	166
Jarvis Press Inc, The 9112 Viscount Row, Dallas TX 75247 *Web:* www.jarvispress.com	214-637-2340		627
Jarvis Products Corp 33 Anderson Rd, Middletown CT 06457 *Web:* www.jarvisproducts.com	860-347-7271	347-6978	298
JAS (Jo-Ann Stores Inc) 5555 Darrow Rd, Hudson OH 44236 **Fax Area Code:* 330 ■ *TF:* 888-739-4120 ■ *Web:* www.joann.com	888-739-4120	463-6760*	270
Jas Forwarding USA Inc 6165 Barfield Rd, Atlanta GA 30328 *Web:* www.jas.com	770-688-1206	688-1229	311
JASA (Jewish Association for Services for the Aged) 247 W 37th St, New York NY 10018 *Web:* www.jasa.org	212-273-5272		48-6
JASCO Inc 28600 Mary's Ct, Easton MD 21601 *TF:* 800-333-5272 ■ *Web:* jascoinc.com	410-822-1220		407
Jasco Products Co 10 E Memorial Rd Bldg B, Oklahoma City OK 73114 *TF:* 800-654-8483 ■ *Web:* byjasco.com	405-752-0710	752-1537	246
Jasculca/Terman & Assoc (JTPR) 730 N Franklin St Ste 510, Chicago IL 60654 *Web:* jtpr.com	312-337-7400		636
JASINT Consulting & Technologies LLC 9730 Patuxent Woods Dr Ste 500, Columbia MD 21046 **Fax Area Code:* 443 ■ *Web:* jasint.com	410-969-5573	557-1694*	180
Jasmine 1330 Niagara Falls Blvd, Tonawanda NY 14150 *Web:* www.jasthai.com	716-838-3011	332-0280	671
Jasmine 4609 Convoy St, San Diego CA 92111 *Web:* jasmineseafood.com	858-268-0888		671
Jasmine 7231 Radio Rd, Naples FL 34104 *Web:* www.jasminechinesefood.com	239-352-5528		671
Jasmine Asian Cuisine 9938 Bellaire Blvd Ste D, Houston TX 77036 *Web:* jasmineasianrestaurant.com	713-272-8188		671
Jasmine Creek Florist 753 Jamacha Rd, El Cajon CA 92019 *TF:* 800-354-8614 ■ *Web:* www.jasminecreekflorist.com	619-588-2377		293
Jasmine Engineering Inc 115 E Travis St Ste 1020, San Antonio TX 78205 *Web:* jasmineengineering.com	210-227-3000		186
Jasmine Hill Gardens & Outdoor Museum 3001 Jasmine Hill Rd, Wetumpka AL 36093 *Web:* www.jasminehill.org	334-567-6463		520
Jason Hertel State Farm 197 SE Fifth St, Madras OR 97741 *Web:* jasonhertel.com	541-475-2264		390
Jason Inc 833 E Michigan St Ste 900, Milwaukee WI 53202 *Web:* www.jasoninc.com	414-277-9300		60
Jason Industrial Inc 340 Kaplan Dr, Fairfield NJ 07004 *Web:* www.jasonindustrial.com	973-227-4904	227-1651	370
Jason International Inc 8328 MacArthur Dr, North Little Rock AR 72118 *TF:* 800-255-5766 ■ *Web:* www.jasoninternational.com	501-771-4477	771-2333	375
Jason McCoy Inc 41 E 57th St 11th Fl, New York NY 10022 *Web:* www.jasonmccoyinc.com	212-319-1996	319-4799	42
Jaspan Schlesinger Hoffman LLP 300 Garden City Plz, Garden City NY 11530 *Web:* www.jaspanllp.com	516-746-8000		428
Jasper County PO Box 1047, Bay Springs MS 39422 *Web:* www.co.jasper.ms.us	601-764-3368	764-3999	338
Jasper County 302 S Main St Rm 102, Carthage MO 64836 *Web:* www.jaspercounty.org	417-358-0416	358-0415	338
Jasper County 121 N Austin, Jasper TX 75951 *Web:* www.co.jasper.tx.us	409-384-6226	384-7198	338
Jasper County 126 W Greene St Ste 18, Monticello GA 31064 *Web:* jaspercountyga.org	706-468-4900	468-4942	338
Jasper County 101 First St N, Newton IA 50208 *Web:* www.co.jasper.ia.us	641-792-7016	792-1053	338
Jasper County 223 W Kellner Blvd, Rensselaer IN 47978 *Web:* www.jaspercountyin.com	219-866-3080		338
Jasper County PO Box 248, Ridgeland SC 29936 *Web:* jaspersc.org	843-726-7710		338
Jasper County Public Library (JCPL) 208 W Susan St, Rensselaer IN 47978 *Web:* www.jasperco.lib.in.us	219-866-5881		434-3
Jasper County Rural Electric Membership Corp 280 E 400 S, Rensselaer IN 47978 *TF:* 888-866-7362 ■ *Web:* www.jasperremc.com	219-866-4601	866-2199	245
Jasper Desk Co 415 E Sixth St, Jasper IN 47546 *TF:* 800-365-7994 ■ *Web:* www.jasperdesk.com	812-482-4132	482-9552	319-1
Jasper Engineering & Equipment Co 3800 5th Ave W Ste 1, Hibbing MN 55746 *TF:* 800-776-6184 ■ *Web:* www.jaspereng.com	218-262-3421	262-4936	358
Jasper Engines & Transmissions 815 Wernsing Rd PO Box 650, Jasper IN 47547 *TF:* 800-827-7455 ■ *Web:* www.jasperengines.com	812-482-1041	634-1820	60
Jasper Lumber Company Inc 2700 Hwy 78 W, Jasper AL 35501 *Web:* www.jasperlumber.com	205-384-9088	384-0000	683
Jasper Rubber Products Inc 1010 First Ave, Jasper IN 47546 *TF:* 800-457-7457 ■ *Web:* www.jasperrubber.com	812-482-3242	482-0816	677
Jasper Seating Company Inc *Jasper Group* 225 Clay St, Jasper IN 47546 *TF:* 800-622-5661 ■ *Web:* www.jaspergroup.us.com	812-482-3204	482-1548	319-1
Jasper Wyman & Son PO Box 100, Milbridge ME 04658 *TF:* 800-341-1758 ■ *Web:* www.wymans.com	833-487-1367		315-1
Jasper's 1201 W 103rd St, Kansas City MO 64114 *TF:* 800-810-3708 ■ *Web:* jasperskc.com	816-941-6600		671
Jasper-Dubois County Public Library 1116 Main St, Jasper IN 47546 *Web:* jdcpl.us	812-482-2712	482-7123	434-3
Jasper-Newton Electric Co-opeartive Inc (JNEC) 812 S Margaret Ave, Kirbyville TX 75956 *Web:* www.jnec.com	409-423-2241		245
Jaspers, Moriarty & Wetherille PA 206 Scott St S, Shakopee MN 55379 *Web:* jmwlaw.com	952-445-2817		41
Jat Oil Inc 600 W Main St, Chattanooga TN 37402 *Web:* jatoil.com	423-629-6611	629-9459	579
Jatco Inc 725 Zwissig Way, Union City CA 94587 *Web:* www.jatco.com	510-487-0888		608
Jatheon Technologies Inc 90 Richmond St E Ste 200, Toronto ON M5C1P1 *Web:* jatheon.com	416-840-0418	849-9971	401
Jatom Systems Inc 99 Michael Cowpland Dr, Kanata ON K2M1X3 *Web:* www.jsitelecom.com	613-591-5910	591-5969	224
Jaurigue Law Group APC 300 W Glenoaks Blvd Ste 300, Glendale CA 91202 *Web:* jlglawyers.com	818-630-7280		41
Java Dave's Executive Coffee Service 6239 E 15th St, Tulsa OK 74112 *TF:* 800-725-7315 ■ *Web:* javadavescoffee.com	918-836-5570		113
Java Estate Roastery Inc 261 Sloop Point Loop Rd, Hampstead NC 28443 *TF:* 800-573-5282 ■ *Web:* www.javaestate.com	910-270-0266	270-3370	297-2
Javan Engineering Inc 465 Maryland Dr Ste 100, Fort Washington PA 19034 *Web:* javanengineering.com	215-654-7890	654-7893	261
Javelina Partners 616 Texas St, Fort Worth TX 76102	817-336-7109		652
Javier's Gourmet Mexicano 4912 Cole Ave, Dallas TX 75205 *Web:* www.javiers.net	214-521-4211		671
Javiers 703 Washington Blvd, Ogden UT 84404 *Web:* javiersmexicanfood.com	801-393-4747		671
Javitch Block LLP 700 Walnut St Ste 302, Cincinnati OH 45202 *TF:* 800-837-0109 ■ *Web:* www.jbllc.com	513-744-9600	744-9602	428
JAX Chamber 3 Independent Dr, Jacksonville FL 32202 *Web:* www.myjaxchamber.com	904-366-6600		139
Jax Fish House 928 Pearl St, Boulder CO 80302 *Web:* www.jaxfishhouse.com	303-444-1811		671
Jax Fish House 1539 17th St, Denver CO 80202 *Web:* www.jaxfishhouse.com	303-292-5767		671
Jax Kneppers Associates Inc 2125 Ygnacio Valley Rd, Walnut Creek CA 94598 *Web:* jaxkneppers.com	925-933-3914		463
Jay & Rose Phillips Family Foundation, The 615 First Ave NE Ste 330, Minneapolis MN 55413 *Web:* phillipsfamilymn.org	612-623-1654		303
Jay Advertising Inc 170 Linden Oaks, Rochester NY 14625 *Web:* jayww.com	585-264-3600		7
Jay C Food Stores 1181 W Tipton St, Seymour IN 47274 *Web:* www.jaycfoods.com	812-522-2883		345
Jay Cashman Inc 549 S St, Quincy MA 02269 *Web:* www.jaycashman.com	617-890-0600		194
Jay Cee Sales & Rivet Inc 32861 Chesley Dr, Farmington MI 48336 *TF:* 800-521-6777 ■ *Web:* rivetsinstock.com	248-478-2150		351
Jay Cooke State Park 780 Hwy 210, Carlton MN 55718 *Web:* www.dnr.state.mn.us	218-384-4610		565
Jay County 500 W Votaw St Ste 2, Portland IN 47371 *Web:* www.co.jay.in.us	260-726-8080	726-2220	338
Jay County Rural Electric Membership Corp 484 S 200 W PO Box 904, Portland IN 47371 *TF:* 800-835-7362 ■ *Web:* www.jayremc.com	260-726-7121	726-6240	245
Jay Dee Contractors Inc 38777 Schoolcraft Rd, Livonia MI 48150 *Web:* www.jaydee.us	734-591-3400	464-6868	188-4
Jay Franco & Sons Inc 295 Fifth Ave 3rd Fl, New York NY 10016 *Web:* www.jfranco.com	212-679-3022		361
Jay Industrial Repair 5300 E Lake Blvd, Birmingham AL 35217 *Web:* jayindustrial.com	205-595-9910	595-9970	463
Jay Packaging Group (JPG) 100 Warwick Industrial Dr, Warwick RI 02886 *Web:* www.jaypack.com	401-739-7200		88
Jay Peak Resort 830 Jay Peak Rd, Jay VT 05859 *TF:* 800-451-4449 ■ *Web:* jaypeakresort.com	802-988-2611		669
Jay Roberts Jewelers 515 Rt 73 S, Marlton NJ 08053 *TF:* 888-828-8463 ■ *Web:* www.jayrobertsjewelers.com	856-596-8600		410
Jay Sons Screw Machine Products Inc 197 Burritt St, Milldale CT 06467 *Web:* www.jaysons.com	860-621-0141	621-0142	621
Jay Wolfe Automotive Group 1011 W 103rd St, Kansas City MO 64114 *Web:* www.jaywolfe.com	816-943-6060		57
Jay's Bistro 135 W Oak St, Fort Collins CO 80524 *Web:* www.jaysbistro.com	970-482-1876		671
Jay's Sporting Goods Inc 8800 S Clare Ave, Clare MI 48617 *Web:* jayssportinggoods.com	989-386-3475	386-3496	711
Jayapal Pramila (Rep D - WA) 1510 Longworth House Office Bldg, Washington DC 20515 *Web:* www.jayapal.house.gov	202-225-3106	225-6197	342-2
Jayco Inc 903 S Main St, Middlebury IN 46540 *TF:* 800-283-8267 ■ *Web:* www.jayco.com	574-825-5861	825-7354	120
Jaydecom 2549 Richmond Rd 2nd Fl, Lexington KY 40509 *Web:* www.jayde.com	859-514-2720	219-9065	397
Jayhawk Bowling Supply & Equipment Inc 355 N Iowa St PO Box 685, Lawrence KS 66044 *TF:* 800-255-6436 ■ *Web:* www.jayhawkbowling.com	785-842-3237	842-9667	710
Jay-K Cabinet 8448 Seneca Tpke, New Hartford NY 13413 *Web:* www.jay-k.com	315-735-4475	735-0049	321

Company	Phone	Fax	Class
Jayman MasterBUILT Inc 200 3132 - 118 Ave SE ... Calgary AB T2Z3X1 *Web:* www.jayman.com	403-258-3772		186
Jaymie Scotto & Assoc PO Box 20 ... Middlebrook VA 24459 **Fax Area Code:* 201 ■ *TF:* 866-695-3629 ■ *Web:* www.jsa.net	866-695-3629	624-7316*	636
Jayna Inc 15 Marybill Dr S ... Troy OH 45373 *Web:* www.jaynainc.com	937-335-8922	339-7581	454
Jaynes Corp 2906 Broadway NE ... Albuquerque NM 87107 *Web:* www.jaynescorp.com	505-345-8591	345-8598	186
Jaypee International Inc 30 S Wacker Dr Ste 1700 ... Chicago IL 60606 *Web:* www.jaypeeusa.com	312-655-7606		690
Jaypro Sports Inc 976 Hartford Tpke ... Waterford CT 06385 **Fax Area Code:* 860 ■ *TF:* 800-243-0533 ■ *Web:* www.jaypro.com	800-243-0533	444-1779*	346
JayRay 535 Dock St Ste 205 ... Tacoma WA 98402 *Web:* www.jayray.com	253-627-9128	627-6548	7
Jayson Home & Garden 1885 N Clybourn Ave ... Chicago IL 60614 *TF:* 800-472-1885 ■ *Web:* www.jaysonhome.com	773-248-8180		321
Jazz A Louisiana Kitchen 1421 Farnam St ... Omaha NE 68102 *Web:* www.jazzkitchen.com	402-342-3662		671
Jazz Pharmaceuticals Inc 3180 Porter Dr ... Palo Alto CA 94304 *TF:* 866-997-3688 ■ *Web:* www.jazzpharma.com	650-496-3777		582
Jazzeppi's 195 B Porter Ave ... Biloxi MS 39530 *Web:* jazzeppisbiloxi.com	228-374-9660		671
Jazzercise Inc 2460 Impala Dr ... Carlsbad CA 92010 *TF:* 800-348-4748 ■ *Web:* www.jazzercise.com	760-476-1750	602-7180	810
JB Coxwell Contracting Inc 6741 Lloyd Rd W ... Jacksonville FL 32254 *Web:* www.jbcoxwell.com	904-786-1120	783-2970	188-4
JB Goodwin Real Estate Company Inc 3933 Steck Ave Ste B-110 ... Austin TX 78759 *Web:* www.jbgoodwin.com	512-502-7800	346-3711	652
JB Hunt Transport Services Inc 615 JB Hunt Corporate Dr ... Lowell AR 72745 *NASDAQ: JBHT* ■ *TF:* 800-643-3622 ■ *Web:* www.jbhunt.com	479-820-0000		449
JB Kreider Printing R J Casey Industrial Pk 1800 Columbus Ave ... Pittsburgh PA 15233 *Web:* kreiderprinting.com	412-246-0343	246-0307	627
JB Martin Co 645 Fifth Ave Ste 400 ... New York NY 10022 *TF:* 800-223-0525 ■ *Web:* www.jbmartin.com	212-421-2020	421-1460	745-1
JB Moving Services Inc 222A Selleck St ... Stamford CT 06902 *TF:* 800-776-6833 ■ *Web:* www.movejb.com	203-602-7979	602-7984	780
JB Nottingham & Company Inc *Duraline Div* 1731 Patterson Ave ... DeLand FL 32724 *Web:* jbn-duraline.com	631-234-2002		815
JB Wholesale Roofing & Building Supplies Inc 21524 Nordhoff St ... Chatsworth CA 91311 *TF:* 800-464-2461 ■ *Web:* jbwholesale.com	818-998-0440		191-3
Jba Intl 1192 N Lake Ave ... Pasadena CA 91104 *Web:* jba.com	626-844-1400		180
Jbar A/C 15501 Chatfield Ave ... Cleveland OH 44111 *Web:* www.jbar-ac.com	216-941-7766		247
JBC Inc 1502 Tenth St PO Box 556 ... Gering NE 69341 *Web:* www.jbc1.com	308-635-0455		581
JBCConnect 8437 Warner Dr ... Culver City CA 90232 *Web:* jbcconnect.com	310-601-7231		260
JBCStyle Inc 108 W 39th St 7th Fl ... New York NY 10018 *Web:* jbcstyle.com	212-355-3197		194
J-Berd Mechanical Contractors 3308 Southway Dr ... Saint Cloud MN 56301 *Web:* j-berd.com	320-656-0847	656-0312	189-10
JBL Energy Partners LLC 23902 FM 2978 Ste B ... Tomball TX 77375	281-516-3137	516-3139	536
JBL Enterprises International Inc 3219 Roymar Rd ... Oceanside CA 92058 *Web:* www.jblspearguns.com	760-754-2727		454
JBL Professional 8500 Balboa Blvd ... Northridge CA 91329 **Fax Area Code:* 818 ■ *TF:* 800-852-5776 ■ *Web:* www.jblpro.com	800-397-1881	830-1220*	52
JBL Studios 21434 Wyandotte St ... Canoga Park CA 91303 *Web:* www.jbistudios.com	818-592-0056		657
Jbl Systems Inc 51935 Filomena Dr ... Shelby Township MI 48315 *Web:* jblsys.com	586-802-6700	802-6705	177
JBM (JBM Sales & Marketing) 125 Washington St ... Foxboro MA 02035 *Web:* www.jbmsales.com	508-543-3611		297-2
JBM Patrol & Protection Corp 3110 Kingsley Way ... Madison WI 53713 *TF:* 800-765-3755 ■ *Web:* jbmpatrol.com	608-222-5156		693
JBM Sales & Marketing (JBM) 125 Washington St ... Foxboro MA 02035 *Web:* www.jbmsales.com	508-543-3611		297-2
JBMH (Joseph Brant Memorial Hospital) 1230 N Shore Blvd ... Burlington ON L7S1W7 *TF:* 800-810-0000 ■ *Web:* www.josephbranthospital.ca	905-632-3737	336-6480	374-2
JBoss Inc 3340 Peachtree Rd Ste 1200 ... Atlanta GA 30326 *Web:* www.redhat.com	404-467-8555		177
JBR Clinical Research 650 E 4500 S Ste 100 ... Salt Lake City UT 84107 *Web:* www.jbrclinicalresearch.com	801-261-2000	261-4539	231
JBRND 10525 Mopac Dr ... San Antonio TX 78217 *Web:* jbrnd.com	210-590-3133		22
JBS Five Rivers Cattle Feeding LLC 1770 Promontory Cir ... Greeley CO 80634 *Web:* www.fiveriverscattle.com	970-506-8363		473
JBS GROUP US Inc 444 E Huntington Dr Ste 212 ... Arcadia CA 91006 *Web:* www.jbshotels.com	626-397-2886	397-2881	393
JBT (Jewelers Board of Trade) 95 Jefferson Blvd ... Warwick RI 02888 *Web:* www.jewelersboard.com	401-467-0055	467-6070	49-4
JBT 70 W Madison Ste 4400 ... Chicago IL 60602 *TF:* 800-835-3230 ■ *Web:* www.jbtc.com	312-861-5900	861-5897	296
JC Audiology 1519 Dale Mabry Hwy Ste 105 ... Lutz FL 33548 *Web:* www.jc-audiology.com	813-949-1331	949-6132	352
JC Blair Memorial Hospital 1225 Warm Springs Ave ... Huntingdon PA 16652	814-643-2290		374-3
JC Higgins Corp 70 Hawes Way ... Stoughton MA 02072 *Web:* jchigginscorp.com	781-341-1500	344-6075	189-10
JC Horizon Ltd 825 E State St ... Ontario CA 91761 *Web:* www.jchorizonltd.com	626-446-1819	446-5129	360-3
JC Jones & Associates LLC 145 Sully's Trl Ste 6 ... Pittsford NY 14534 **Fax Area Code:* 866 ■ *Web:* www.jcjones.com	585-899-4072	498-9625*	193
JC Newman Cigar Co 2701 16th St ... Tampa FL 33605 *Web:* www.cigarfamily.com	813-248-2124	247-2135	756
JC Penney Company Inc 6501 Legacy Dr ... Plano TX 75024 *NYSE: JCP* ■ *Web:* www.jcpenney.com	972-431-1000		229
JC Penney Optical Co 821 N Central Expy ... Plano TX 75075 *TF:* 866-435-7111 ■ *Web:* www.jcpenneyoptical.com	866-435-7111		543
JC Raulston Arboretum 4415 Beryl Rd CB 7522 ... Raleigh NC 27695 *TF:* 888-842-2442 ■ *Web:* jcra.ncsu.edu	919-515-3132	515-5361	97
JC Resorts LLC 533 Coast Blvd S ... La Jolla CA 92037 *Web:* www.jcresorts.com	858-605-2700		379
JC Smith Inc 345 Peat St ... Syracuse NY 13210 *Web:* www.jcsmithinc.com	315-428-9903	428-9841	358
JCAHO (Joint Commission on Accreditation of Healthcare Organizations) 1 Renaissance Blvd ... Oakbrook Terrace IL 60181 *Web:* www.jointcommission.org	630-792-5000	792-5005	48-1
JCCA (Jewish Child Care Association of New York) 858 E 29th St ... Brooklyn NY 11210 *Web:* www.jccany.org	917-808-4800		147
JCConnect LLC 7825 Langwood Dr ... Indianapolis IN 46268 *Web:* www.jcconnect.net	317-339-6532	872-6492	177
JCD Sports Group Inc 1300 Park of Commerce Ste 272 ... Delray Beach FL 33445 *Web:* www.jcdsportsgroup.com	561-265-0255		720
JCG Technologies Inc 50 S Belcher Rd ... Clearwater FL 33765 *Web:* jcgtech.com	727-461-3776	461-3235	196
JCHS 1033 Massachusetts Ave ... Cambridge MA 02138 *Web:* www.jchs.harvard.edu	617-495-7908	496-9957	634
JCHS (Jefferson County Historical Society) 540 Water St ... Port Townsend WA 98368 *Web:* jchsmuseum.org	360-385-1003		48-13
JCI (Journal of Clinical Investigation) 15 Research Dr ... Ann Arbor MI 48103 *Web:* jci.org	734-222-6050	222-6058	49-8
JCI (Jacquinot Consulting Inc) 2615 George Busbee Pky Ste 11-312 ... Kennesaw GA 30144 **Fax Area Code:* 206 ■ *Web:* www.jacquinot.com	770-514-8039	309-0058*	177
JCISD (Jackson County Intermediate School District) 6700 Browns Lake Rd ... Jackson MI 49201 *Web:* www.jcisd.org	517-768-5200	787-2844	685
JCJ (JCJ Architecture) 120 Huyshope Ave Ste 400 ... Hartford CT 06106 *Web:* www.jcj.com	860-247-9226		261
JCJ Architecture (JCJ) 120 Huyshope Ave Ste 400 ... Hartford CT 06106 *Web:* www.jcj.com	860-247-9226		261
JCL Insurance Agency 3351 San Gabriel Blvd ... Rosemead CA 91770 *TF:* 888-378-0998 ■ *Web:* jclinsagency.com	626-307-4588		390
JCLL (Jackson County Law Library) Kessler Bldg 1301 Oak St Ste 310 ... Kansas City MO 64106 *Web:* jcll.org	816-221-2221		434-3
JCM Associates Inc 301C Prince Georges Blvd ... Upper Marlboro MD 20774 *Web:* www.gojcm.com	301-390-5500	390-5510	35
JCM Engineering Corp 2690 E Cedar St ... Ontario CA 91761 *Web:* jcmcorp.com	909-923-3730	923-0355	256
JCM Mutual Insurance Assn 50 South PO Box 430 ... Fairfield IA 52556 *TF:* 888-554-3352 ■ *Web:* jcmmutual.com	641-472-2136	469-6711	390
JCMS Inc 1741 Whitehorse Mercerville Rd ... Mercerville NJ 08619 *Web:* www.jcms.com	609-631-0700		196
JCN Construction Company Inc 155 Dow St ... Manchester NH 03101 *Web:* www.jcnconstruction.com	603-624-7080		186
JCO Inc 1828 Pearl St ... Boulder CO 80302 *Web:* www.jco-online.com	303-443-1720	443-9356	637-9
JCPL (Jackson County Public Library) 303 W Second St ... Seymour IN 47274 *Web:* www.myjclibrary.org	812-522-3412	522-5456	434-3
JCPL (Jasper County Public Library) 208 W Susan St ... Rensselaer IN 47978 *Web:* www.jasperco.lib.in.us	219-866-5881		434-3
JCPLL (Jefferson County Public Law Library) Old Jail Bldg 514 W Liberty Ste 240 ... Louisville KY 40202 *Web:* www.jcpll.net	502-574-5943		434-3
J-C-R Tech Inc 936 E Cherry St ... Blanchester OH 45107 *Web:* jcrtech.com	937-783-2296	783-4109	455
JCS Enterprises Inc 3501 Moreland Ave ... Conley GA 30288 *TF:* 800-664-3325 ■ *Web:* www.jcsenterprises.net	800-664-3325		779
JCS Family 1704 Cape Horn ... Julian CA 92036 *TF:* 866-853-0003 ■ *Web:* www.jcs-inc.org	760-765-5500		685
JCSI Corporate Staffing 2 South St ... Grafton MA 01519 **Fax Area Code:* 508 ■ *Web:* jcsi.net	774-760-1800	749-6032*	260
JCVB (Johnston County Visitors Bureau) 234 Venture Dr ... Smithfield NC 27577 *TF:* 800-441-7829 ■ *Web:* www.johnstoncountync.org	919-989-8687	989-6295	206
JD & Billy Hines Trucking Inc 407 Hines Blvd ... Prescott AR 71857 *TF:* 800-264-6693 ■ *Web:* www.hinestrucking.com	870-887-9400	887-5126	311
JD Abrams LP 111 Congress Ave Ste 2400 ... Austin TX 78701 *Web:* www.jdabrams.com	512-322-4000	322-4018	188-4
JD Biggs & Associates Inc 12602 Bear Creek Terr ... Beltsville MD 20705	202-596-8245		180
JD Calato Manufacturing Company Inc 4501 Hyde Pk Blvd ... Niagara Falls NY 14305 *TF:* 800-358-4590 ■ *Web:* www.regaltip.com	716-285-3546	285-2710	527

Name / Address	City	State	ZIP	Phone	Fax	Class
JD Donovan Inc 7805 County Rd 75 *Web:* www.jddonovan.com	Saint Cloud	MN	56301	320-251-1213	251-3220	780
JD Equipment Inc 1660 State Rte US 42 NE *TF:* 800-659-5646	London	OH	43140	614-879-6620		274
JD Events LLC 5520 Park Ave Ste 305 *Web:* www.jdevents.com	Trumbull	CT	06611	203-371-6322		195
JD Fields & Company Inc 55 Waugh Dr Ste 1250 *Web:* jdfields.com	Houston	TX	77007	281-558-7199	870-9918	791
JD Gould Company Inc 4707 Massachusetts Ave **Fax Area Code:* 317 ■ *TF:* 800-634-6853 ■ *Web:* www.gouldvalve.com	Indianapolis	IN	46218	800-634-6853	547-5234*	790
JD Heiskell & Co 1939 Hillman St *Web:* www.heiskell.com	Tulare	CA	93274	559-685-6100		447
JD Long Masonry Inc 7044 Colchester Park Dr *Web:* www.jdlongmasonry.com	Manassas	VA	20112	703-550-8880	730-5210	189-7
JD McCarty Center for Children with Developmental Disabilities 2002 E Robinson St *TF:* 800-777-1272 ■ *Web:* jdmc.org	Norman	OK	73071	405-307-2800	307-2801	374-1
JD Merit & Co 650 S Cherry St Ste 1100 *Web:* jdmerit.com	Denver	CO	80246	303-333-3673		690
JD Norman Industries Inc 787 W Belden Ave *Web:* www.jdnorman.com	Addison	IL	60101	630-458-3700		483
JD Power & Assoc 2625 Townsgate Rd Ste 100 *TF:* 800-274-5372 ■ *Web:* www.jdpower.com	Westlake Village	CA	91361	805-418-8000	418-8900	466
JD Squared Inc 2244 Eddie Williams Rd *Web:* www.jd2.com	Johnson City	TN	37601	423-979-0309		595
JD Streett & Company Inc 144 Weldon Pkwy *Web:* www.jdstreett.com	Maryland Heights	MO	63043	314-432-6600	432-4248	541
JD Young 116 W Third St *Web:* www.jdyoung.com	Tulsa	OK	74103	918-582-9955		45
JDA Professional Services Inc 6464 Savoy Dr Ste 777 *Web:* www.jdapsi.com	Houston	TX	77036	713-548-5400		260
JDA Software Group Inc 15059 N Scottsdale Rd Ste 400 *NASDAQ: JDAS* ■ *Web:* blueyonder.com	Scottsdale	AZ	85254	480-308-3000	308-3001	178-10
JDB (John Dallas Bowers LLC) 219 Radnor-Chester Rd *Web:* www.johndallasbowers.com	Villanova	PA	19085	610-989-9234	989-9236	4
JDB Capital Partners LLC 20645 N Pima Rd Ste 110 *Web:* www.jdbcapital.com	Scottsdale	AZ	85255	480-502-9200		691
JDC (American Jewish Joint Distribution Committee) 711 Third Ave *Web:* www.jdc.org	New York	NY	10017	212-687-6200	370-5467	48-5
JDC Group 980 Hammond Dr Ste 1250 *Web:* www.jdc-group.com	Atlanta	GA	30328	404-601-3310	601-3316	41
JDG (Justice Design Group) 500 S Grand Ave Ste 110 *Web:* jdg.com	Los Angeles	CA	90071	213-437-0102	437-0860	439
JDH Pacific Inc 14821 Artesia Blvd *Web:* www.jdhpacific.com	La Mirada	CA	90638	562-926-8088	926-8066	492
JDI (Journal of Drug Issues) College of Criminology & Criminal Justice Florida State University *Web:* criminology.fsu.edu	Tallahassee	FL	32306	850-644-4050		637-9
JDi Data Corp 100 W Cypress Creek Rd Ste 1052 *Web:* www.jdidata.com	Fort Lauderdale	FL	33309	954-938-9100		177
J-Dig Cards Inc 2701 Fondren Ste 110 *Web:* shop.j-digcards.com	Dallas	TX	75206	214-821-2769		130
JDK Consulting 4924 Balboa Blvd Ste 487 *TF:* 855-535-7877 ■ *Web:* jdkconsulting.com	Encino	CA	91316	818-705-8050		196
JDK Management Company Inc 1388 SR- 487 *Web:* www.jdkmgt.com	Bloomsburg	PA	17815	570-784-0111	784-4785	463
JDL Technologies Inc 5450 NW 33rd Ave Ft Lauderdale Commerce Ste 106 *TF:* 888-493-7833 ■ *Web:* www.jdltech.com	Fort Lauderdale	FL	33309	954-334-0650		393
JDM Systems Consultants Inc 33117 Hamilton Ct *Web:* www.jdmconsulting.com	Farmington Hills	MI	48334	248-324-1937		225
JDR Microdevices Inc 229 Polaris Ave Ste 17 **Fax Area Code:* 800 ■ *TF:* 800-538-5000 ■ *Web:* www.jdr.com	Mountain View	CA	94043	650-625-1400	538-5005*	459
JDRF 26 Broadway *TF:* 800-533-2873 ■ *Web:* www.jdrf.org	New York	NY	10004	212-785-9500	785-9595	48-17
JDW Distributors 612 N Ecknoff St *Web:* www.jdwdist.com	Orange	CA	92868	714-634-3478	634-4424	297-8
JE & LE Mabee Foundation Inc 401 S Boston Ave Ste 3001 *Web:* www.mabeefoundation.com	Tulsa	OK	74103	918-584-4286		305
JE Adams Industries Ltd 1025 63rd Ave SW *TF:* 800-553-8861 ■ *Web:* www.jeadams.com	Cedar Rapids	IA	52404	319-363-0237		54
JE Dunn Construction Co 1001 Locust St *Web:* www.jedunn.com	Kansas City	MO	64106	816-474-8600		186
JE Herndon Company Inc 1020 J E Herndon Access Rd *TF:* 800-277-0500 ■ *Web:* jeherndon.com	Kings Mountain	NC	28086	704-739-4711	734-0621	745-8
JE Sawyer & Company Inc 64 Glen St *TF:* 800-724-3983 ■ *Web:* vpsupply.com	Glens Falls	NY	12801	800-724-3983		612
Jean Georges 1 Central Pk W *Web:* www.jean-georges.com	New York	NY	10023	212-299-3900		671
Jean Lafitte National Historical Park & Preserve 419 Decatur St *Web:* www.nps.gov	New Orleans	LA	70130	504-589-3882		564
Jean Madeline Aveda Institute Queen Village 315A Bainbridge St *TF:* 877-729-5326 ■ *Web:* www.jeanmadeline.edu	Philadelphia	PA	19147	215-574-9670		167-3
Jean Mayer USDA Human Nutrition Research Center on Aging 711 Washington St *TF:* 800-738-7555 ■ *Web:* hnrca.tufts.edu	Boston	MA	02111	617-556-3000	556-3344	668
Jean Paree Weegs Inc 4041 South 700 East Ste 2 *TF:* 800-422-9447 ■ *Web:* jeanparee.net	Salt Lake City	UT	84107	800-422-9447		348
Jean Simpson Personnel Services Inc 1318 Shreveport Barksdale *Web:* jeansimpson.com	Shreveport	LA	71105	318-869-3494	862-3392	721
Jean V. Naggar Literary Agency Inc 216 E 75th St Ste 1E *Web:* www.jvnla.com	New York	NY	10021	212-794-1082		444
Jean's Jewelers Inc 407 E Main St *Web:* jeansjewelers.com	Front Royal	VA	22630	540-622-6166		410
Jeans Warehouse Inc 2612 Waiwai Loop *Web:* www.jeanswarehousehawaii.com	Honolulu	HI	96819	808-839-2421		157-6
Jeansonne & Remondet LLC 200 W Congress St Ste 1100 PO Box 91530 *TF:* 800-446-2745 ■ *Web:* www.jeanrem.com	LaFayette	LA	70509	337-237-4370	235-2011	428
JEBCO Industries Inc 111 Ellis Dr *Web:* www.jebcointl.com	Barrie	ON	L4N8Z3	705-797-8888		480
JEBCO Seismic LP 2450 Fondren Rd Ste 112 *Web:* www.jebcoseis.com	Houston	TX	77063	713-975-0202	975-9293	539
Jeck, Harris, Raynor & Jones PA 790 Juno Ocean Walk Ste 600 *Web:* jhrjpa.com	Juno Beach	FL	33408	561-331-2597	775-0270	41
Jeckel Pork Farm Inc 600 N Sherman St	Delavan	IL	61734	309-244-7281		10-6
Jeco Plastic Products LLC 885 Andico Rd *Web:* www.jecoplastics.com	Plainfield	IN	46168	317-839-4943		604
Jeda Technologies Inc 2900 Gordon Ave Ste 100 *Web:* www.jedatechnologies.net	Santa Clara	CA	95051	408-912-1856	912-1855	177
Jedco Inc 1615 Broadway NW	Grand Rapids	MI	49504	616-459-5161		57
Jedson Engineering 705 Central Ave *TF:* 866-729-3945 ■ *Web:* jedson.com	Cincinnati	OH	45202	513-965-5999		256
Jeeps Unlimited USA 4245 County Rd 6 *Web:* jeepsunlimited.net	Erie	CO	80516	303-666-9020		62
Jeff Anderson Regional Medical Ctr 2124 14th St *Web:* www.andersonregional.org	Meridian	MS	39301	601-553-6000		374-3
Jeff Avery State Farm Insurance Cos 1822 Buenaventura Blvd Ste 107 *Web:* jeffavery.net	Redding	CA	96001	530-243-4600		390
Jeff Davis Bancshares Inc 507 N Main St PO Box 730 *OTC: JDVB* ■ *TF:* 800-789-5159 ■ *Web:* jdbank.com	Jennings	LA	70546	337-824-3424	824-7283	70
Jeff Davis County 100 Court Ave *Web:* www.co.jeff-davis.tx.us	Fort Davis	TX	79734	432-426-3251		338
Jeff Evans Insurance 3973 Massillon Rd *Web:* jeffevansins.com	Uniontown	OH	44685	330-896-1173	896-1172	390
Jeff Ruby's Steakhouse 700 Walnut St *Web:* www.jeffruby.com	Cincinnati	OH	45202	513-321-8080		671
Jeff Schmitt Auto Group 1001 N Broad St *TF:* 877-800-5333 ■ *Web:* www.jeffdeals.com	Fairborn	OH	45324	877-800-5333		57
Jeff Schrantz 313 Sw 2nd St Ste A *Web:* jeffschrantz.com	Newport	OR	97365	541-265-2011		390
Jeff's Movers and Storage 8900 Louisiana St *TF:* 800-533-4947 ■ *Web:* www.jeffsmoversandstorage.com	Merrillville	IN	46410	800-533-4947		780
Jeffco Fibres Inc 12 Park St *Web:* www.jeffcofibres.com	Webster	MA	01570	508-943-0440		601
Jefferds Corp 2070 Winfield Rd *TF:* 888-848-6216 ■ *Web:* jefferds.com	Saint Albans	WV	25177	304-755-8111		385
Jefferies Group Inc 520 Madison Ave *NYSE: JEF* ■ *Web:* www.jefferies.com	New York	NY	10022	212-284-2300		690
Jefferies Socks 2203 Tucker St **Fax Area Code:* 800 ■ *TF:* 800-334-6831 ■ *Web:* www.jefferiessocks.com	Burlington	NC	27215	336-226-7315	727-5502*	155-10
Jeffers Inc 310 W Saunders Rd PO Box 100 *TF:* 800-533-3377 ■ *Web:* www.jefferspet.com	Dothan	AL	36301	334-793-6257	793-5179	578
Jeffers, Danielson, Sonn & Aylward PS 2600 Chester Kimm Rd *Web:* www.jdsalaw.com	Wenatchee	WA	98801	509-662-3685	662-2452	428
Jefferson Area Local School District 906 W Main St *Web:* www.west-jefferson.k12.oh.us	West Jefferson	OH	43162	614-879-7654		685
Jefferson Chamber of Commerce 3421 N Cswy Blvd Ste 203 *Web:* jeffersonchamber.org	Metairie	LA	70002	504-835-3880	835-3828	139
Jefferson Cherry Hill Hospital 2201 Chapel Ave W *TF:* 866-224-0264 ■ *Web:* newjersey.jeffersonhealth.org	Cherry Hill	NJ	08002	856-488-6500	488-6526	374-3
Jefferson City - City Hall 320 E McCarty St *Web:* www.jeffersoncitymo.gov	Jefferson City	MO	65101	573-634-6304	634-6329	337
Jefferson City Area Chamber of Commerce 213 Adams St *TF:* 866-223-6535 ■ *Web:* www.jcchamber.org	Jefferson City	MO	65101	573-634-3616	634-3805	139
Jefferson City Convention & Visitors Bureau 700 E Capitol Ave *TF:* 800-769-4183 ■ *Web:* www.visitjeffersoncity.com	Jefferson City	MO	65101	573-632-2820	638-4892	206
Jefferson City Correctional Ctr 8200 No More Victims Rd *Web:* www.mo.gov	Jefferson City	MO	65101	573-751-3224		213
Jefferson City News Tribune 210 Monroe St *Web:* www.newstribune.com	Jefferson City	MO	65101	573-636-3131		532-2
Jefferson College 1000 Viking Dr *Web:* www.jeffco.edu	Hillsboro	MO	63050	636-481-3281	789-5103	162

Name / Address	City	State	Zip	Phone	Fax	Class
Jefferson Community & Technical College 109 E Broadway *TF:* 855-246-5282 ■ *Web:* jefferson.kctcs.edu	Louisville	KY	40202	502-213-5333	213-2540	162
Jefferson Community College 1220 Coffeen St *TF:* 888-435-6522 ■ *Web:* www.sunyjefferson.edu	Watertown	NY	13601	315-786-2200	786-2459	162
Jefferson County PO Box 1151 *Web:* www.co.jefferson.tx.us	Beaumont	TX	77704	409-835-8475	839-2394	338
Jefferson County 716 Richard Arrington Jr Blvd N *Web:* www.jccal.org	Birmingham	AL	35203	205-325-5555		338
Jefferson County 102 S Monroe St PO Box H *Web:* www.jeffersoncounty-mt.gov	Boulder	MT	59632	406-225-4020	225-4149	338
Jefferson County 155 Main St 2nd Fl *TF:* 800-852-8036 ■ *Web:* www.jeffersoncountypa.com	Brookville	PA	15825	814-849-3696	849-4084	338
Jefferson County PO Box 208 *Web:* www.jeffersoncountywv.org	Charles Town	WV	25414	304-728-3215		338
Jefferson County 411 Fourth St *Web:* www.co.jefferson.ne.us	Fairbury	NE	68352	402-793-5585	729-2904	338
Jefferson County 51 W Briggs Ave *Web:* www.jeffersoncountyiowa.com	Fairfield	IA	52556	641-472-3454	472-9472	338
Jefferson County 1483 Main St PO Box 145 *Web:* www.jeffersoncountyms.com	Fayette	MS	39069	601-786-3021	786-6009	338
Jefferson County 100 Jefferson County Pkwy *Web:* www.jeffco.us	Golden	CO	80419	303-279-6511	271-8197	338
Jefferson County 302 E Broad St PO Box 630 *TF:* 866-527-2642 ■ *Web:* jeffersoncounty.org	Louisville	GA	30434	478-625-8134		338
Jefferson County 300 E Main St *Web:* jeffersoncounty.in.gov	Madison	IN	47250	812-265-8900	265-8955	338
Jefferson County 66 SE 'D' St Ste D *Web:* www.jeffco.net	Madras	OR	97741	541-475-4451	325-5018	338
Jefferson County 300 Jefferson St PO Box 458 *TF:* 800-332-6633 ■ *Web:* www.jfcountyks.com	Oskaloosa	KS	66066	785-403-0000	403-0748	338
Jefferson County 1820 Jefferson St *Web:* www.co.jefferson.wa.us	Port Townsend	WA	98368	360-385-9100	385-9382	338
Jefferson County 210 Courthouse Way Ste 120 *TF:* 888-588-2328 ■ *Web:* www.co.jefferson.id.us	Rigby	ID	83442	208-745-7736	745-6636	338
Jefferson County Courthouse 301 Market St *Web:* www.jeffersoncountyoh.com	Steubenville	OH	43952	740-283-8500		338
Jefferson County 175 Arsenal St *Web:* www.co.jefferson.ny.us	Watertown	NY	13601	315-785-3081	785-5145	338
Jefferson County Chamber of Commerce 630 Market St *Web:* www.jeffersoncountychamber.com	Steubenville	OH	43952	740-282-6226		139
Jefferson County Chamber of Commerce 200 Potomac Blvd *Web:* www.southernillinois.com	Mount Vernon	IL	62864	618-242-5725	242-5130	139
Jefferson County Chamber of Commerce 201 E Washington St *TF:* 800-624-0577 ■ *Web:* www.jeffersoncountywvchamber.org	Charles Town	WV	25414	304-725-2055		139
Jefferson County Chamber of Commerce 532 Patriot Dr *Web:* jeffersoncountytennessee.com	Jefferson City	TN	37760	865-397-9642		139
Jefferson County Convention & Visitors Bureau 4328 William L Wilson Fwy *TF:* 866-435-5698 ■ *Web:* discoveritallwv.com	Harpers Ferry	WV	25425	304-535-2627		206
Jefferson County Historical Society 228 Washington St *Web:* jeffersoncountyhistory.org	Watertown	NY	13601	315-782-3491	782-2913	520
Jefferson County Historical Society (JCHS) 540 Water St *Web:* jchsmuseum.org	Port Townsend	WA	98368	360-385-1003		48-13
Jefferson County Journal 1405 N Truman Blvd *TF:* 800-365-0820 ■ *Web:* www.stltoday.com	Festus	MO	63028	636-933-2243	931-2638	532-4
Jefferson County Public Law Library (JCPLL) Old Jail Bldg 514 W Liberty Ste 240 *Web:* www.jcpll.net	Louisville	KY	40202	502-574-5943		434-3
Jefferson County Public Library 420 W Main St *Web:* www.mjcpl.org	Madison	IN	47250	812-265-2744		434-3
Jefferson County Teachers Credit Union 1500 W Washington St *Web:* jctcuonline.org	Monticello	FL	32344	850-342-0250		219
Jefferson County Visitor's Bureau PO Box 274 *Web:* www.visitoregontrail.org	Fairbury	NE	68352	402-729-3000		206
Jefferson Ctr 541 Luck Ave Ste 221 *TF:* 866-345-2550 ■ *Web:* www.jeffcenter.org	Roanoke	VA	24016	540-343-2624	343-3744	572
Jefferson Custom Home Design Studio 405 S Main St *Web:* www.wausauhomes.com	Jefferson	WI	53549	920-723-8946		751
Jefferson Davis Community College *Brewton* 220 Alco Dr *Web:* www.jdcc.edu	Brewton	AL	36426	251-867-4832	809-1596	162
Jefferson Davis County 1025 Third St PO Box 342 *Web:* www.jeffdavisms.com	Prentiss	MS	39474	601-792-5903	792-0291	338
Jefferson Davis Electric Co-op 906 N Lake Arthur Ave PO Box 1229 *TF:* 800-256-5332 ■ *Web:* www.jdec.org	Jennings	LA	70546	337-824-4330	824-8936	245
Jefferson Davis Memorial State Historic Site 338 Jeff Davis Park Rd *Web:* gastateparks.org	Fitzgerald	GA	31750	229-831-2335		565
Jefferson Davis Parish Public Library 118 W Plaquemine St *Web:* jdplibrary.org	Jennings	LA	70546	337-824-1210	824-5444	434-3
Jefferson Davis Parish Schools 203 E Plaquemine St PO Box 640 *Web:* www.jeffersondavis.org	Jennings	LA	70546	337 824 1834		685
Jefferson Electric Inc 9650 S Franklin Dr *TF:* 800-892-3755 ■ *Web:* jeffersonelectric.com	Franklin	WI	53132	414-209-1620	209-1621	767
Jefferson Energy Cooperative 3077 Hwy 17 N PO Box 457 *TF:* 877-533-3377 ■ *Web:* www.jec.coop	Wrens	GA	30833	706-547-2167		245
Jefferson Forwarding 2222 Jefferson St *Web:* casaduana.com	Laredo	TX	78040	956-723-0111		311
Jefferson Hotel 101 W Franklin St *TF:* 800-424-8014 ■ *Web:* www.jeffersonhotel.com	Richmond	VA	23220	804-649-4750	225-0334	379
Jefferson Hotel Washington Dc, The 1200 16th St NW *TF:* 877-313-9749 ■ *Web:* www.jeffersondc.com	Washington	DC	20036	202-448-2300		707
Jefferson Industries Corp 6670 Ohio 29 *Web:* www.jic-ohio.com	West Jefferson	OH	43162	614-879-5300		59
Jefferson Ip Law LLP 1130 Conn Ave NW Ste 420 *Web:* jeffersonip.com	Washington	DC	20036	202-293-0804	293-1644	41
Jefferson Mall 4801 Outerloop Rd *Web:* www.shopjefferson-mall.com	Louisville	KY	40219	502-968-4101		460
Jefferson Medical College of Thomas Jefferson University 1015 Walnut St *TF:* 800-533-3669 ■ *Web:* www.jefferson.edu	Philadelphia	PA	19107	215-955-6983	955-5151	167-2
Jefferson Millwork & Design 44098 Mercure Ci *Web:* jeffersonmillwork.com	Sterling	VA	20166	703-260-3370		499
Jefferson National Expansion Memorial 11 N Fourth St *TF:* 855-733-4522 ■ *Web:* www.nps.gov	Saint Louis	MO	63102	314-655-1750		564
Jefferson Parish 200 Derbigny St Ste 3100 *Web:* www.jeffparish.net	Gretna	LA	70053	504-364-2777		338
Jefferson Parish Library 4747 W Napoleon Ave *Web:* www.jefferson.lib.la.us	Metairie	LA	70001	504-838-1100	838-1110	434-3
Jefferson Partners LP 2100 E 26th St *TF:* 800-767-5333 ■ *Web:* www.jeffersonlines.com	Minneapolis	MN	55404	612-359-3400	359-3437	108
Jefferson Regional Medical Ctr (JRMC) 1600 W 40th Ave *Web:* www.jrmc.org	Pine Bluff	AR	71603	870-541-7100		374-3
Jefferson Restaurant 1453 Richmond Rd *Web:* www.jeffersonrestaurantva.com	Williamsburg	VA	23185	757-229-2296		671
Jefferson Schools 5707 Williams Rd *Web:* www.jeffersonschools.org	Newport	MI	48166	734-289-5550		685
Jefferson State Community College 2601 Carson Rd *TF:* 800-239-5900 ■ *Web:* www.jeffersonstate.edu	Birmingham	AL	35215	205-853-1200	856-6070	162
Jefferson Telecom 105 W Harrison St *Web:* www.jeffersontelephone.com	Jefferson	IA	50129	515-386-4141	386-2600	224
Jefferson Urian Doane & Sterner Inc 651 N Bedford St Extn PO Box 830 *Web:* www.juds.com	Georgetown	DE	19947	302-856-3900	856-3018	2
Jefferson Valley Mall 650 Lee Blvd *Web:* www.jeffersonvalleymall.com	Yorktown Heights	NY	10598	914-245-4688		460
Jefferson Vineyards LP 1353 Thmas Jefferson Pkwy *Web:* www.jeffersonvineyards.com	Charlottesville	VA	22902	434-977-3042		80-3
Jefferson-Madison Regional Library 201 E Market St *TF:* 866-979-1555 ■ *Web:* jmrl.org	Charlottesville	VA	22902	434-979-7151	971-7035	434-3
Jeffersontown Chamber of Commerce 10434 Watterson Tr *Web:* www.jtownchamber.com	Jeffersontown	KY	40299	502-267-1674		139
Jeffersonville Bancorp 4866 SR-52 PO Box 398 *OTC: JFBC* ■ *Web:* www.jeffbank.com	Jeffersonville	NY	12748	845-482-4000	482-3544	360-2
Jeffrey A. Aronsky PC 800 Second Ave Ste 301 *Web:* aronskylaw.com	New York	NY	10017	212-577-6600	577-6776	41
Jeffrey Court Inc 620 Parkridge Ave *Web:* www.jeffreycourt.com	Norco	CA	92860	951-340-3383		191-1
Jeffrey Hale Saint Brigid's 1250 ch Sainte-Foy *TF:* 888-984-5333 ■ *Web:* www.jhsb.ca	Quebec City	QC	G1S2M6	418-684-5333		374-2
Jeffrey M. Brown Associates LLC 2337 Philmont Ave *Web:* jmbassociates.com	Huntingdon Valley	PA	19006	215-938-5000		186
Jeffrey Matthews Financial Group LLC, The 30B Vreeland Rd Ste 210 *TF:* 888-467-3636 ■ *Web:* www.jeffreymatthews.com	Florham Park	NJ	07932	973-805-6222		401
Jeffrey N. Fink 462 Washington St *Web:* jfinklawadr.com	Wellesley	MA	02482	781-237-0338		41
Jeffrey N. Powers PC 3557 Vineville Ave *Web:* powerslawgroup.com	Macon	GA	31204	478-738-8884		41
Jeffrey Scott Nightly, The 1544 Fulton St *Web:* wearejsa.com	Fresno	CA	93721	559-268-9741		7
Jeffrey's Restaurant 1204 W Lynn St *Web:* www.jeffreysofaustin.com	Austin	TX	78703	512-477-5584		671
Jeffries Hakeem (Rep D - NY) 2433 Rayburn House Office Bldg *Web:* www.jeffries.house.gov	Washington	DC	20515	202-225-5936		342-2
Jeffries, Kube, Forrest & Monteleone Company LPA 26021 Center Ridge Rd Ste 200 *TF:* 888-341-5854 ■ *Web:* jkfmlaw.com	Westlake	OH	44145	216-771-4050	771-0732	41
JEGI Capital LLC 150 E 52nd St 18th Fl *Web:* www.jegi.com	New York	NY	10022	212-754-0710		792
JEGS Performance Auto Parts 101 Jeg'S Pl *TF:* 800-345-4545 ■ *Web:* www.jegs.com	Delaware	OH	43015	614-294-5050		61
Jekyll Island Club Hotel 371 Riverview Dr *TF:* 800-535-9547 ■ *Web:* www.jekyllclub.com	Jekyll Island	GA	31527	912-635-2600	635-2818	669

Name / Address	Phone	Fax	Class
Jekyll Island Convention Ctr 1 N Beachview Dr . . . . Jekyll Island GA 31527 *Web:* www.jekyllisland.com	912-635-3636		205
Jel Sert Co 501 Conde St . . . . West Chicago IL 60185 *TF:* 800-323-2592 ■ *Web:* jelsert.com	630-876-4838		296-15
Jeld-Wen Inc PO Box 1329 . . . . Klamath Falls OR 97601 *TF:* 800-535-3936 ■ *Web:* www.jeld-wen.com	800-535-3936		499
Jelec Usa Inc 16901 Park Row . . . . Houston TX 77084 *Web:* jelec.com	713-977-6500		570
Jellico Chemical Company Inc PO Box 11459 . . . . Louisville KY 40251 *Web:* jellicocoatings.com	502-772-2547	772-2552	550
Jelliff Corp 354 Pequot Ave . . . . Southport CT 06890 *TF:* 800-243-0052 ■ *Web:* www.jelliff.com	203-259-1615	255-7908	688
Jelly Belly Candy Co 1 Jelly Belly Ln . . . . Fairfield CA 94533 *TF:* 800-323-9380 ■ *Web:* www.jellybelly.com	707-428-2838		296-8
Jellyvision Lab Inc, The 848 W Eastman St . . . . Chicago IL 60642 *Web:* www.jellyvision.com	312-340-6402		809
Jem Engineering LLC 8683 Cherry Ln . . . . Laurel MD 20707 *TF:* 877-317-1070 ■ *Web:* www.jemengineering.com	301-317-1070		647
Jem Group LLC 509 N Second St . . . . Harrisburg PA 17101 *Web:* www.jemgroup.net	717-238-7709		610
Jem Strapping Systems 116 Shaver St . . . . Brantford ON N3T5M1 *TF:* 877-536-6584 ■ *Web:* www.jemline.com	519-754-5432		656
Jemez Mountains Electric Co-op PO Box 128 . . . . Espanola NM 87532 *TF:* 888-755-2105 ■ *Web:* www.jemezcoop.org	505-753-2105	753-6958	245
Jen's Restaurant 701 W 36th Ave . . . . Anchorage AK 99503 *Web:* www.jensrestaurant.com	907-561-5367		671
Jenco Productions Inc 401 S J St . . . . San Bernardino CA 92410 *Web:* www.jencoproductions.com	909-381-9453		88
Jendoco Construction Corp 2000 Lincoln Rd . . . . Pittsburgh PA 15235 *Web:* www.jendoco.com	412-361-4500		186
Jenike & Johanson Inc 400 Business Park Dr . . . . Tyngsboro MA 01879 *Web:* jenike.com	978-649-3300		261
Jenison Public Schools (JPS) 8375 20th Ave . . . . Jenison MI 49428 *Web:* www.jpsonline.org	616-457-1402	457-8090	685
Jenkins & Wynne 2655 Trenton Rd . . . . Clarksville TN 37040 *Web:* jenkinsandwynne.com	931-542-4886		57
Jenkins Arboretum (JA) 631 Berwyn Baptist Rd . . . . Devon PA 19333 *Web:* www.jenkinsarboretum.org	610-647-8870	647-6664	97
Jenkins County 548 Cotton Ave . . . . Millen GA 30442 *TF:* 800-262-0128 ■ *Web:* www.jenkinscountyga.com	478-982-5595		338
Jenkins Electric Co 5933 Brookshire Blvd . . . . Charlotte NC 28216 *TF:* 800-438-3003 ■ *Web:* www.jenkinselectric.com	800-438-3003		253
Jenkins Fenstermaker PLLC 325 Eighth St . . . . Huntington WV 25701 *TF:* 866-617-4736 ■ *Web:* www.jenkinsfenstermaker.com	304-523-2100		428
Jenkins Landscape Co 12260 SE Dixie Hwy . . . . Hobe Sound FL 33455 *Web:* jenkinslandscape.com	772-546-2861		422
Jenkins Oil 1100 W Industrial Rd . . . . Cedar City UT 84721 *Web:* rallystopcstores.com	435-586-6931		579
Jenkins Systems LLC 4336 Gateway Dr . . . . Sheboygan WI 53081 *Web:* www.jenkins-systems.com	920-452-2110		821
Jenkins, Wilson, Taylor & Hunt PA 3015 Carrington Mill Blvd Ste 550 . . . . Morrisville NC 27560 *Web:* www.jwth.com	919-493-0000	419-0383	428
Jenks Beauty College 535 W Main St . . . . Jenks OK 74037 *Web:* www.sandspringsbeautycollege.com	918-299-0901	299-7053	167-3
Jenn's House Inc 3250 S Cedar Crest Blvd . . . . Emmaus PA 18049 *Web:* jennshouse.org	610-965-1777		372
Jenner & Block LLP 353 N Clark St . . . . Chicago IL 60654 *Web:* jenner.com	312-222-9350	527-0484	428
Jennerjahn Machine Inc 901 Massachusetts Ave . . . . Matthews IN 46957 *Web:* jennerjahn.com	765-998-2733	998-2468	556
Jenness State Beach 2280 Ocean Blvd . . . . Rye NH 03870 *Web:* www.nhstateparks.org	603-436-1552		565
Jennie Edmundson Hospital 933 E Pierce St . . . . Council Bluffs IA 51503 *TF:* 800-958-6498 ■ *Web:* www.bestcare.org	712-396-6000		374-3
Jennie Rubenstein, Dvm PC 3 Joskey Hollow Rd PO Box 208 . . . . New Milford NY 10959 *Web:* jhvet.com	845-986-9900		794
Jennie Stuart Health 320 W 18th St . . . . Hopkinsville KY 42240 *TF:* 800-887-5762 ■ *Web:* www.jenniestuarthealth.org	270-887-0100		374-3
Jennie-O Turkey Store 2505 Willmar Ave SW PO Box 778 . . . . Willmar MN 56201 *TF:* 800-621-3505 ■ *Web:* www.jennieo.com	320-235-2622	214-2885	619
Jennifer A. Jones CPA Ltd 10615 Judicial Dr Ste 701 . . . . Fairfax VA 22030 *Web:* jajonescpa.com	703-352-1587		2
Jennifer Fairfax LLC 827 Woodside Pkwy . . . . Silver Spring MD 20910 *Web:* jenniferfairfax.com	301-221-9651		41
Jennifer L. Wilkerson A Professional Corp 140 Litton Dr Ste 204 . . . . Grass Valley CA 95945 *Web:* jwilkerson.net	530-272-4292		41
Jennifer Paris Insurance Agency Inc 1325 Dry Creek Dr Ste 102 . . . . Longmont CO 80503 *Web:* jenniferparis.com	303-772-2969		390
Jennings & Assoc 2121 Palomar Airport Rd Ste 220 . . . . Carlsbad CA 92011 *Web:* jandacommunications.com	760-431-7466		4
Jennings County PO Box 383 . . . . Vernon IN 47282 *Web:* jenningscounty-in.gov	812-352-3070		338
Jennings County *Indiana Government* 200 East Brown St . . . . Vernon IN 47282 *Web:* www.jenningscounty-in.gov	812-352-3024	352-3030	339-15
Jennings County Chamber of Commerce 524 N State St Ste B PO Box 340 . . . . North Vernon IN 47265 *TF:* 866-382-4968 ■ *Web:* www.jenningscountychamber.org	812-346-2339		139
Jennings County Schools 34 W Main St . . . . North Vernon IN 47265 *Web:* www.jcsc.org	812-346-4483		685
Jennings Environmental Education Ctr 2951 Prospect Rd . . . . Slippery Rock PA 16057 *Web:* www.dcnr.pa.gov	724-794-6011		565
Jennings International Corp 3 Blue Heron Dr . . . . Collegeville PA 19426 *Web:* www.jenningsinternational.com	610-831-1600		757
Jennings Sigmond PC 1835 Market St Ste 2800 . . . . Philadelphia PA 19103 *Web:* jslex.com	215-922-6700		41
Jennings Teague PC 204 N Robinson Ste 1000 . . . . Oklahoma City OK 73102 *Web:* jenningsteague.com	405-609-6000		41
Jennings Technology 970 McLaughlin Ave . . . . San Jose CA 95122 *TF:* 800-292-4025 ■ *Web:* new.abb.com	408-292-4025	286-1789	203
Jennmar Corp 258 Kappa Dr . . . . Pittsburgh PA 15238 *Web:* www.jennmar.com	412-963-9071	963-9767	190
Jenny Jump State Forest 330 State Park Rd . . . . Hope NJ 07844 *Web:* www.njparksandforests.org	908-459-4366		565
Jenny Lea Academy 74 Parkway Plaza Loop . . . . Whitesburg KY 41858 *Web:* www.jennyleaacademy.edu	606-633-8784		167-3
Jensen Baird Gardner & Henry 10 Free St . . . . Portland ME 04112 *TF:* 800-756-1166 ■ *Web:* www.jensenbaird.com	207-775-7271	775-7935	428
Jensen Bridge & Supply Co 400 Stoney Creek Dr PO Box 151 . . . . Sandusky MI 48471 *TF:* 800-270-2852 ■ *Web:* jensenbridge.com	810-648-3000	648-3549	697
Jensen Builders Ltd 1175 S 32nd St . . . . Fort Dodge IA 50501 *Web:* www.jensenbuilders.com	515-573-3292		186
Jensen Distribution Services PO Box 3708 . . . . Spokane WA 99220 **Fax Area Code:* 509 ■ *TF:* 800-234-1321 ■ *Web:* www.jensenonline.com	800-234-1321	838-2432*	351
Jensen Meat Co 2550 Britannia Blvd Ste 101 . . . . San Diego CA 92154 *Web:* www.jensenmeat.com	619-754-6400	754-6450	297-9
Jensen Mixers International Inc 5354 S Garnett Rd . . . . Tulsa OK 74146 *Web:* jensenmixers.com	918-627-5770		190
Jensen Precast 521 Dunn Cir . . . . Sparks NV 89431 **Fax Area Code:* 775 ■ *TF:* 800-648-1134 ■ *Web:* www.jensenprecast.com	855-468-5600	359-1038*	183
Jensen Tire & Auto 2820 S 84th St . . . . Omaha NE 68124 *Web:* jensentireandauto.com	402-391-7280		62-5
Jensen USA Inc 99 Aberdeen Loop . . . . Panama City FL 32405 *Web:* www.jensen-group.com	850-271-5959		14
Jensen's Inc 715 W Jackson St . . . . Shelbyville TN 37160	931-684-5021	685-9229	571
Jensen-Alvarado Historic Ranch & Museum 4307 Briggs St . . . . Riverside CA 92509 *TF:* 800-234-7275 ■ *Web:* www.rivcoparks.org	951-369-6055		520
Jenson USA Inc 1615 Eastridge Ave . . . . Riverside CA 92507 *TF:* 888-880-3811 ■ *Web:* www.jensonusa.com	909-947-9036		517
Jentec Engineering Company Inc 2820 E Coronado St . . . . Anaheim CA 92806	714-632-6762		608
Jenzabar Inc 101 Huntington Ave Ste 2200 . . . . Boston MA 02199 *TF:* 800-593-0028 ■ *Web:* www.jenzabar.com	617-492-9099	492-9081	178-10
Jeo Consulting Group Inc 142 W 11th St . . . . Wahoo NE 68066 *Web:* www.pdiowa.com	402-443-4661		256
JEOL USA Inc 11 Dearborn Rd . . . . Peabody MA 01960 *Web:* www.jeolusa.com	978-535-5900	536-2205	419
Jeopardy Productions Inc 10202 Washington Blvd . . . . Culver City CA 90232 *Web:* www.jeopardy.com	310-244-8855		52
JEPC (Jim Edgar Panther Creek State Fish and Wildlife Area) 10149 County Hwy 11 . . . . Chandlerville IL 62627 *Web:* www2.illinois.gov	217-452-7741		565
Jeppesen 55 Inverness Dr E . . . . Englewood CO 80112 *TF:* 800-353-2107 ■ *Web:* ww2.jeppesen.com	303-799-9090	328-4153	637-2
Jepson Technologies Inc 14900 Ventura Blvd Ste 210 . . . . Sherman Oaks CA 91403 *Web:* www.jepsontech.com	818-990-0601		226
Jerauld County Clerk of Court 205 S Wallace PO Box 435 . . . . Wessington Springs SD 57382 *Web:* www.ujs.sd.gov	605-539-1202	539-1203	338
Jerdon Style 1820 N Glenville Dr Ste 124 . . . . Richardson TX 75081 **Fax Area Code:* 972 ■ *TF:* 800-223-3571 ■ *Web:* www.jerdonstyle.com	800-223-3571	644-2957*	76
Jeremiah's 1307 W 1200 S . . . . Ogden UT 84404 *Web:* jeremiahsutah.com	801-394-3273	627-6579	671
Jergens Inc 15700 S Waterloo Rd . . . . Cleveland OH 44110 **Fax Area Code:* 216 ■ *TF:* 800-537-4367 ■ *Web:* www.jergensinc.com	877-486-1454	481-6193*	493
Jericho Road Ministries Inc 1090 Mondon Hill Rd . . . . Brooksville FL 34601 *Web:* www.jericho-road.net	352-799-2912		48-20
Jerith Manufacturing Company Inc 14400 McNulty Rd . . . . Philadelphia PA 19154 *TF:* 800-344-2242 ■ *Web:* www.jerith.com	215-676-4068	676-9756	491
Jernigan Oil Company Inc 415 E Main St PO Box 688 . . . . Ahoskie NC 27910 *Web:* www.jerniganoil.com	252-332-2131		581
Jero Manufacturing Inc 5117 S 100th E Ave . . . . Tulsa OK 74146 *TF:* 800-525-6415 ■ *Web:* www.jeromfg.com	918-628-0230	628-1603	806
Jerome Cheese 547 W Nez Perce . . . . Jerome ID 83338 *Web:* www.agropurcheese.com	208-324-8806	324-8892	296-5
Jerome County 300 N Lincoln Ave . . . . Jerome ID 83338 *Web:* jeromecountyid.us	208-644-2715		338
Jerome County Fairgrounds 205 N Fir St . . . . Jerome ID 83338 *Web:* jeromecountyfair.com	208-324-7209		642

Name / Address	City	State	ZIP	Phone	Fax	Class
Jerome County Historical Society Museum Research Library 212 1st Ave E PO Box 50 *Web:* www.historicaljeromecounty.com	Jerome	ID	83338	208-324-5641		434-3
Jerome Distributing Inc 455 23rd Ave E *Web:* www.jeromedistributing.com	Dickinson	ND	58601	701-225-3187		81-1
Jerome State Historic Park 100 Douglas Rd *Web:* azstateparks.com	Jerome	AZ	86331	928-634-5381		565
Jerome's Furniture Warehouse 16960 Mesamint St *TF:* 866-633-4094 ■ *Web:* www.jeromes.com	San Diego	CA	92127	866-633-4094		321
Jerpbak-Bayless Co 34150 Solon Rd *Web:* www.jerpbakbayless.com	Solon	OH	44139	440-248-5387	248-1070	454
Jerry Bruckheimer Films 1631 10th St *Web:* www.jbfilms.com	Santa Monica	CA	90404	310-664-6260	664-6261	514
Jerry G. Williams & Sons Inc 524 Brogden Rd *Web:* www.jerrygwilliamslumber.com	Smithfield	NC	27577	919-934-4115		683
Jerry Haag Motors Inc 1475 N High St *Web:* www.jerryhaagmotors.com	Hillsboro	OH	45133	937-402-2090		57
Jerry Jackson Associates Ltd 37 N Orange Ave Ste 500 *Web:* www.maisy.com	Orlando	FL	32801	979-204-7821		178-1
Jerry Jungels 10920 Fry Rd Ste 700 *Web:* www.jerryjungels.com	Cypress	TX	77433	281-256-3330		390
Jerry L. Pettis Memorial Veterans' Hospital 11201 Benton St *Web:* www.lomalinda.va.gov	Loma Linda	CA	92357	909-825-7084		374-8
Jerry Lipps Inc 3888 Nash Rd *TF:* 800-325-3331 ■ *Web:* www.jerrylippsinc.com	Cape Girardeau	MO	63702	573-335-0196	335-4483	780
Jerry MacNeish 5750 Kinsmen Courage Ct *Web:* www.z28camaro.com	Eldersburg	MD	21784	410-781-0418		393
Jerry Pate Turf & Irrigation Inc 301 Schubert Dr *TF:* 800-700-7004 ■ *Web:* jerrypate.com	Pensacola	FL	32504	850-479-4653	484-8596	274
Jerry Pittman & Associates Inc 12504 Hwy 57 *Web:* www.jerrypittman.com	Vancleave	MS	39565	228-826-9255		261
Jerry Sorbara Furs Inc 21 Mulberry Ln Ste 1400 *Web:* sorbarafur.com	Cos Cob	CT	06807	212-594-3897		155-7
Jerry Trimble Helicopters 4050 SE Nimbus Loop *Web:* www.jerrytrimblehelicopters.com	McMinnville	OR	97128	503-557-6371		167-3
Jerry's Artarama Inc 6104 Maddry Oaks Ct *TF:* 800-827-8478 ■ *Web:* www.jerrysartarama.com	Raleigh	NC	27616	800-827-8478		45
Jerry's Famous Deli Inc 12711 Ventura Blvd Ste 400 *Web:* www.jerrysdeli.com	Studio City	CA	91604	818-766-8311	766-8315	670
Jerry's Foods 5125 Vernon Ave S *Web:* www.jerrysfoods.com	Edina	MN	55436	952-929-2685		345
Jerry's Iron Works Inc 16015 Main St Ne *Web:* www.sanitech.net	Duvall	WA	98019	425-788-1467	844-8625	806
Jerry's Marine Service 100 SW 16th St *TF:* 800-432-2231 ■ *Web:* jerrysmarineservice.com	Fort Lauderdale	FL	33315	800-432-2231		770
Jerry's Sport Center Inc 100 Capital Rd *TF:* 800-234-2612 ■ *Web:* www.jerryssportscenter.com	Jenkins Township	PA	18640	800-234-2612		710
Jerry's Supermarkets Inc 532 W Jefferson Blvd *Web:* www.jerryssupermarkets.com	Dallas	TX	75208	214-941-8110		345
Jersey Cape Realty Inc 739 Washington St *TF:* 800-643-0043 ■ *Web:* www.jerseycaperealty.com	Cape May	NJ	08204	609-884-5800		652
Jersey Cape Yachts Inc 2143 River Rd *Web:* jerseycapeyachts.com	Lower Bank	NJ	08215	609-965-8650	965-7480	90
Jersey City - City Hall 280 Grove St *Web:* jerseycitynj.gov	Jersey City	NJ	07302	201-547-5000	547-5461	337
Jersey City Free Public Library 472 Jersey Ave *TF:* 800-443-0315 ■ *Web:* jclibrary.org	Jersey City	NJ	07302	201-547-4501	547-4584	434-3
Jersey City Museum 350 Montgomery St *Web:* jerseycityonline.com	Jersey City	NJ	07302	201-413-0303	413-9922	520
Jersey County 209 N Lafayette St *Web:* www.jerseycountyillinois.us	Jerseyville	IL	62052	217-248-8811		338
Jersey Journal 1 Harmon Plz Ste 1010 *Web:* www.jjournal.com	Secaucus	NJ	07094	201-653-1000		532-2
Jersey Precast Corp 853 Nottingham Way *Web:* www.mydigitalarchitect.com	Trenton	NJ	08638	609-689-3700		183
Jersey Printing Associates Inc 153 First Ave *Web:* www.jerseyprinting.com	Atlantic Highlands	NJ	07716	732-872-9654	872-9309	627
Jersey Shore Chamber of Commerce 2510 Belmar Blvd Ste I-20 *Web:* www.jerseyshorechambernj.com	Wall	NJ	07719	732-280-8800	280-8505	139
Jersey Shore State Bank 300 Market St *TF:* 888-412-5772 ■ *Web:* www.jssb.com	Williamsport	PA	17701	570-322-1111		70
Jersey Shore Steel Co 70 Maryland Ave PO Box 5055 *TF:* 800-833-0277 ■ *Web:* www.jssteel.com	Jersey Shore	PA	17740	570-753-3000	753-3782	723
Jersey Shore University Medical Ctr 1945 Rt 33 *Web:* www.jerseyshoreuniversitymedicalcenter.com	Neptune City	NJ	07753	732-775-5500	751-5120	374-3
Jersey State Bank 1000 S State St *Web:* www.jerseystatebank.com	Jerseyville	IL	62052	618-498-6466		70
Jersey Strong 762 SR-18 *TF:* 888-564-6969 ■ *Web:* www.jerseystrong.com	East Brunswick	NJ	08816	732-390-7390		354
Jerusalem Restaurant & Cafe 106 E Evergreen Blvd *Web:* www.thejerusalemcafe.com	Vancouver	WA	98660	360-906-0306		671
JES Publishing c/o Boca Raton Magazine 1000 Clint Moore Rd Ste 103 *TF:* 877-553-5363 ■ *Web:* www.bocamag.com	Boca Raton	FL	33487	561-997-8683	997-8909	637-9
JES Search Firm Inc 1021 Stovall Blvd Ste 600 *Web:* www.jessearch.com	Atlanta	GA	30319	404-812-0622		260
JESCO Inc 2020 McCullough Blvd *Web:* www.jescoinc.net	Tupelo	MS	38801	662-842-3240		186
Jesco Inc 1001 Industrial Dr **Fax Area Code:* 410 ■ *Web:* www.jesco.us	Middletown	DE	19709	302-376-0784	918-5112*	358
Jesco-Wipco Industries Inc 950 Anderson Rd PO Box 388 *TF:* 800-455-0019 ■ *Web:* www.jescoonline.com	Litchfield	MI	49252	517-542-2903	542-2501	286
Jeskell Systems LLC 6201 Chevy Chase Dr *Web:* www.jeskell.com	Laurel	MD	20707	301-230-1533	230-7195	463
Jeson Enterprises Inc 687 NW 12th St Ste 1E *Web:* craftwarehouse.com	Camas	WA	98607	360-834-7728		761
Jess & Jim's Steakhouse 517 E 135th St *Web:* www.jessandjims.com	Kansas City	MO	64145	816-941-9499		671
Jess Dunn Correctional Ctr 601 S 124th St W PO Box 316 *Web:* doc.ok.gov	Taft	OK	74463	918-682-7841	682-4372	213
Jesse Duplantis Ministries 1973 Ormond Blvd *Web:* www.jdm.org	Destrehan	LA	70047	985-764-2000		48-20
Jesse Engineering Co 1840 Marine View Dr *TF:* 800-468-3595 ■ *Web:* www.jesse-co.com	Tacoma	WA	98422	253-922-7433	922-1998	480
Jesse H. Jones Hall for the Performing Arts 901 Bagby St 1st Fl City Hall *Web:* www.houstontx.gov	Houston	TX	77002	832-487-7050	487-7051	572
Jessee Brothers Machine Shop Inc 1640 Dell Ave *Web:* www.jesseebrothersinc.com	Campbell	CA	95008	408-866-1755	866-2697	454
Jessen Mfg 1409 W Beardsley Ave PO Box 1729 *Web:* www.jessenmfg.com	Elkhart	IN	46515	574-295-3836	522-2962	621
Jessen Press Inc 3982 Alabama Ave S *Web:* www.jessenpress.com	Minneapolis	MN	55416	952-929-0346		627
Jessie Lord Bakery LLC 21100 S Western Ave *Web:* www.jessielordbakery.com	Torrance	CA	90501	310-533-6010		68
Jessup Engineering Inc 2745 Bond St *Web:* www.jessupengineering.com	Rochester Hills	MI	48309	248-853-5600	853-7530	695
Jestine's Kitchen 251 Meeting St *Web:* jestineskitchen.com	Charleston	SC	29401	843-722-7224		671
JestMaster Productions Inc 434 Tenafly Rd *TF:* 877-255-3665 ■ *Web:* www.Jestmaster.com	Englewood	NJ	07631	201-568-7782	567-1610	459
Jesto Transmissions 3642 W Cypress *Web:* www.jestotransmissions.com	Tampa	FL	33607	813-873-2433	875-3286	62-5
Jesuit Center for Spiritual Growth 501 N Church Rd *Web:* jesuitcenter.org	Wernersville	PA	19565	610-670-3642		673
Jesuit Refugee Service/USA (JRS) 1016 16th St NW Ste 500 *Web:* jrsusa.org	Washington	DC	20036	202-629-5906		48-5
Jesuit Retreat House 300 Manresa Way *Web:* www.jrclosaltos.org	Los Altos	CA	94022	650-917-4000		673
Jesuit Spiritual Ctr 5361 S Milford Rd *Web:* jesuitspiritualcenter.com	Milford	OH	45150	513-248-3500		673
Jet Aviation 112 Charles A Lindbergh Dr *TF:* 800-538-0832 ■ *Web:* www.jetaviation.com	Teterboro	NJ	07608	201-288-8400	462-4005	24
Jet Engineering Inc 1241 Park Pl NE Ste E *Web:* www.jetinc.net	Cedar Rapids	IA	52402	319-294-6106	382-0160	256
Jet Food Stores of Georgia 1106 S Harris St *Web:* www.jetfoodstores.com	Sandersville	GA	31082	478-552-2588		204
Jet Grinding & Manufacturing Inc 2309 E Oakton St *Web:* www.jetgrinding.com	Arlington Heights	IL	60005	847-956-8646	956-0142	454
Jet Harbor Inc 2860 NW 59th St *Web:* www.jetharbor.com	Fort Lauderdale	FL	33309	954-772-2863		63
Jet Industries Inc 1935 Silverton Rd NE PO Box 7362 *TF:* 800-659-0620 ■ *Web:* jet.industries	Salem	OR	97303	503-363-2334		610
Jet International Company LLC 1811 Elmdale Ave *Web:* jetinternational.com	Glenview	IL	60026	847-657-8666	657-9197	770
Jet Logistics Inc 5400 Airport Dr *TF:* 866-824-9394 ■ *Web:* www.jetlogistics.us	Charlotte	NC	28208	866-824-9394		196
Jet Parts Engineering Inc 4772 Ohio Ave S *Web:* www.jetpartsengineering.com	Seattle	WA	98134	206-281-0963		256
Jet PCB 2055 Junction Ave Ste 135 *Web:* www.jetpcb.com	San Jose	CA	95131	408-922-3991	922-7285	625
Jet Plastics 941 NE Ave *TF:* 800-375-2784 ■ *Web:* www.jetplastics.com	Los Angeles	CA	90063	323-268-6706	268-8262	604
Jet Propulsion Laboratory (JPL) 4800 Oak Grove Dr *Web:* www.jpl.nasa.gov	Pasadena	CA	91109	818-354-9314		668
Jet Rubber Company Inc 4457 Tallmadge Rd *Web:* www.jetrubber.com	Rootstown	OH	44272	330-325-1821	325-2876	676

Company / Address	City	State	Zip	Phone	Fax	Class
Jet Set Sports PO Box 366 *Web:* www.jetsetsports.com	Far Hills	NJ	07931	908-766-1001	766-4646	707
Jet Specialty Inc 211 Market Ave *Web:* jetspecialty.com	Boerne	TX	78006	830-331-9457		538
Jet Star Inc 10825 Andrade Dr *TF:* 800-969-4222 ■ *Web:* www.jetstarinc.com	Zionsville	IN	46077	317-873-4222		780
Jet Support Services Inc (JSSI) 180 N Stetson Ave *Web:* www.jetsupport.com	Chicago	IL	60601	312-644-4444		194
Jet Technologies Inc 2120 S Calhoun Rd *TF:* 800-869-0684 ■ *Web:* www.gojet.com	New Berlin	WI	53151	262-796-5050	796-5054	625
Jet X Aerospace 400 N York Rd *Web:* www.jetxaerospace.com	Bensenville	IL	60106	847-750-8888		57
Jet's America Inc 37501 Mound Rd *Web:* jetspizza.com	Sterling Heights	MI	48310	586-268-5870	268-6762	670
JetBlue Airways Corp 118-29 Queens Blvd *NASDAQ: JBLU* ■ *TF:* 800-538-2583 ■ *Web:* www.jetblue.com	Forest Hills	NY	11375	718-286-7900		360-1
Jetlease Inc 5718 Westheimer 17th Fl *Web:* jetleaseinc.com	Houston	TX	77057	713-952-5100	974-2813	21
Jetline Engineering 15 Goodyear St *Web:* www.millerwelds.com	Irvine	CA	92618	949-951-1515	951-9237	811
Jet-Lube Inc 4849 Homestead Rd Ste 232 *TF:* 800-538-5823 ■ *Web:* www.jetlube.com	Houston	TX	77226	713-670-5700	678-4604	541
Jetmore Fireplace Ctr 3343 Merrick Rd *Web:* www.jetmore.com	Wantagh	NY	11793	516-826-1166		362
Jetnet LLC 101 1st St 2nd Fl *TF:* 800-553-8638 ■ *Web:* www.jetnet.com	Utica	NY	13501	315-797-4420	797-4798	387
Jetstream Capital LLC 12 Cadillac Dr Ste 280 *Web:* www.jetstreamcapital.com	Brentwood	TN	37027	615-425-3400	425-3401	401
Jetstream of Houston LLP 4930 Cranswick *TF:* 800-231-8192 ■ *Web:* www.waterblast.com	Houston	TX	77041	713-462-7000	462-5387	790
JetSuite 18952 MacArthur Blvd *TF:* 866-779-7770 ■ *Web:* www.jetsuite.com	Irvine	CA	92612	866-779-7770		13
Jetta Corp 425 Centennial Blvd **Fax Area Code:* 918 ■ *TF:* 800-288-7771 ■ *Web:* www.jettacorp.com	Edmond	OK	73013	405-340-6661	574-2141*	362
Jetta Operating Company Inc 777 Taylor St Ft Worth Club Tower Ste P1 *Web:* www.jettaoperating.com	Fort Worth	TX	76102	817-335-1179		539
Jeunesse Global LLC 650 Douglas Ave *Web:* www.jeunesseglobal.com	Altamonte Springs	FL	32714	407-215-7414		76
Jewel Box Theatre 3700 N Walker Ave *Web:* fccokc.org	Oklahoma City	OK	73118	405-521-1786		572
Jewel Case Corp 110 Dupont Dr *TF:* 800-441-4447 ■ *Web:* www.jewelcase.com	Providence	RI	02907	401-943-1400	943-1426	199
Jewel Cave National Monument 11149 US Hwy 16 Bldg B-12 *Web:* www.nps.gov	Custer	SD	57730	605-673-8300		564
Jewel-Craft Inc 4122 Olympic Blvd *TF:* 800-525-5482 ■ *Web:* www.jewel-craft.com	Erlanger	KY	41018	859-282-2400		411
Jewelers Board of Trade (JBT) 95 Jefferson Blvd *Web:* www.jewelersboard.com	Warwick	RI	02888	401-467-0055	467-6070	49-4
Jewelers Inc, The 2400 Western Ave *Web:* www.thejewelers.com	Las Vegas	NV	89102	702-382-1234	382-3307	410
Jewelers of America (JA) 120 Broadway Ste 2820 *TF:* 800-223-0673 ■ *Web:* www.jewelers.org	New York	NY	10271	646-658-0246	658-0256	49-4
Jewelers Shipping Assn (JSA) 125 Carlsbad St *TF:* 800-688-4572 ■ *Web:* www.jewelersshipping.com	Cranston	RI	02920	401-943-6020		49-21
Jewelex New York Ltd 529 Fifth Ave *Web:* jewelexgroup.com	New York	NY	10017	212-840-3500		411
JewelFM 1415 Fulton St *Web:* www.kjwl.com	Fresno	CA	93721	559-497-5118		645-61
Jewell Associates Engineers Inc 560 Sunrise Dr *Web:* www.jewellassoc.com	Spring Green	WI	53588	608-588-7484		261
Jewell Group 130 Research Pkwy *TF:* 800-831-8665 ■ *Web:* www.jewellgroup.com	Davenport	IA	52806	563-355-5010	355-4817	454
Jewell Instruments LLC 850 Perimeter Rd *TF:* 800-227-5955 ■ *Web:* jewellinstruments.com	Manchester	NH	03103	603-669-6400	669-5962	529
Jewel-Osco 150 Pierce Rd *Web:* www.jewelosco.com	Itasca	IL	60143	630-948-6000		410
Jewelry Concepts 41 W Industrial Dr *Web:* www.jewelryconcepts.com	Cranston	RI	02921	401-228-8586		410
JewelryWebcom Inc 98 Cuttermill Rd Ste 464 **Fax Area Code:* 800 ■ *TF:* 800-955-9245 ■ *Web:* www.jewelryweb.com	Great Neck	NY	11021	516-482-3982	955-2520*	410
Jewett-Cameron Trading Company Ltd 32275 NW Hillcrest PO Box 1010 *NASDAQ: JCTCF* ■ *TF:* 800-547-5877 ■ *Web:* www.jewettcameron.com	North Plains	OR	97133	503-647-0110	647-2272	191-3
Jewish Alcoholics Chemically Dependent Persons & Significant Others 135 W 50th St 6th Fl *TF:* 888-523-2769 ■ *Web:* jewishboard.org	New York	NY	10020	212-632-4600	399-3525	48-21
Jewish Association for Services for the Aged (JASA) 247 W 37th St *Web:* www.jasa.org	New York	NY	10018	212-273-5272		48-6
Jewish Child Care Association of New York (JCCA) 858 E 29th St *Web:* www.jccany.org	Brooklyn	NY	11210	917-808-4800		147
Jewish Community Centers Association of North America 520 Eigth Ave *Web:* www.jcca.org	New York	NY	10018	212-532-4949	481-4174	48-20
Jewish Genealogical Society of Illinois (JGSI) PO Box 515 *Web:* www.jgsi.org	Northbrook	IL	60065	312-666-0100		48-13
Jewish General Hospital 3755 Cote Sainte-Catherine *Web:* www.jgh.ca	Montreal	QC	H3T1E2	514-340-8222		374-2
Jewish Heritage Center of Western Canada C116-123 Doncaster St *Web:* www.jhcwc.org	Winnipeg	MB	R3N2B2	204-477-7460	477-7465	50-2
Jewish Home Lifecare 120 W 106th St *TF:* 800-544-0304 ■ *Web:* jewishhome.org	New York	NY	10025	212-870-5000	870-4715	450
Jewish Museum 1109 Fifth Ave *Web:* thejewishmuseum.org	New York	NY	10128	212-423-3200	423-3232	520
Jewish Museum of Florida 301 Washington Ave *Web:* jmof.fiu.edu	Miami Beach	FL	33139	305-672-5044	672-5933	520
Jewish Museum of Maryland 15 Lloyd St *TF:* 800-235-4045 ■ *Web:* jewishmuseummd.org	Baltimore	MD	21202	410-732-6400	732-6451	520
Jewish National Fund (JNF) 42 E 69th St *TF:* 800-542-8733 ■ *Web:* www.jnf.org	New York	NY	10021	212-879-9300		48-20
Jewish Press Inc 4915 16th Ave *TF:* 800-992-1600 ■ *Web:* www.jewishpress.com	Brooklyn	NY	11204	718-330-1100		532-3
Jewish Publication Society 2100 Arch St *TF:* 800-234-3151 ■ *Web:* jps.org	Philadelphia	PA	19103	215-832-0600	568-2017	637-3
Jewish Reconstructionist Federation (JRF) 101 Greenwood Ave *TF:* 877-226-7573 ■ *Web:* archive.jewishrecon.org	Jenkintown	PA	19046	215-885-5601	885-5603	48-20
Jewish Senior Services of Fairfield County Inc 175 Jefferson St *Web:* jseniors.org	Fairfield	CT	06825	203-365-6400	374-8082	450
Jewish Telegraphic Agency 24 W 30th St 4th Fl *Web:* www.jta.org	New York	NY	10001	212-643-1890	643-8499	530
Jewish United Fund/Jewish Federation of Metropolitan Chicago (JUF) 30 S Wells St *TF:* 855-275-5237 ■ *Web:* www.juf.org	Chicago	IL	60606	312-346-6700	444-2086	48-20
JewishCard 7360 Viewpoint Rd *Web:* www.jewishcard.com	Aptos	CA	95003	831-469-8883	662-2746	130
Jews for Jesus 60 Haight St *TF:* 800-366-5521 ■ *Web:* jewsforjesus.org	San Francisco	CA	94102	415-864-2600	552-8325	48-20
Jezic & Moyco LLC 2730 University Blvd W Ste 604 *Web:* jezicfirm.com	Wheaton	MD	20902	240-292-7200		41
JF Ahern Co 855 Morris St *TF:* 800-532-0155 ■ *Web:* www.jfahern.com	Fond du Lac	WI	54935	920-921-9020	921-8632	189-10
JF Drake State Technical College 3421 Meridian St N *TF:* 888-413-7253 ■ *Web:* www.drakestate.edu	Huntsville	AL	35811	256-539-8161	551-3142	800
JF Electric Inc 100 Lakefront Pkwy PO Box 570 *Web:* www.jfelectric.com	Edwardsville	IL	62025	618-797-5353		189-4
JF Fredericks Aero LLC 25 Spring Ln *Web:* www.jffaero.com	Farmington	CT	06032	860-677-2646		454
JF O'neill Packing Co 3120 G St	Omaha	NE	68107	402-733-1200		473
JF Petroleum Group 100 Perimeter Park Dr Ste H *TF:* 800-286-4133 ■ *Web:* jfpetrogroup.com	Morrisville	NC	27560	919-231-1998		539
JF Shea Company Inc 655 Brea Canyon Rd *TF:* 800-685-6494 ■ *Web:* www.jfshea.com	Walnut	CA	91789	909-594-9500		503-5
JF Taylor Inc 21610 S Essex Dr *Web:* jfti.com	Lexington Park	MD	20653	301-862-3939		261
JF White Contracting Co 10 Burr St **Fax Area Code:* 617 ■ *TF:* 866-539-4400 ■ *Web:* www.jfwhite.com	Framingham	MA	01701	508-879-4700	558-0460*	188-4
JFC International Inc 7101 E Slauson Ave *TF:* 800-633-1004 ■ *Web:* jfc.com	Los Angeles	CA	90040	323-721-6100	721-6133	297-11
JFE Steel USA Inc 350 Park Ave *Web:* www.jfe-steel.co.jp	New York	NY	10022	212-935-8710	308-9292	723
JFK (John F. Kennedy International Airport) 150 Greenwich St **Fax Area Code:* 201 ■ *Web:* www.jfkairport.com	New York	NY	10007	212-435-7000	871-2343*	27
JFK Medical Ctr 65 James St *Web:* www.jfkmc.org	Edison	NJ	08818	732-321-7000		374-3
JFK Window & Door Co 2110 Schappelle Ln *Web:* jfkwindowanddoor.com	Cincinnati	OH	45240	513-851-1000		366
JFKL (John F. Kennedy Library) 190 W 49th St *Web:* www.hialeahfl.gov	Hialeah	FL	33012	305-821-2700		434-3
JFM Enterprises Inc 1770 Corporate Dr Ste 530 *TF:* 800-462-3449 ■ *Web:* www.jfm.net	Norcross	GA	30093	770-447-9740	409-1013	787
JFM Inc 4276 Lakeland Dr *Web:* www.jfminc.net	Flowood	MS	39232	601-664-7177		204
JFP (Joyner Fine Properties) 2727 Enterprise Pkwy *Web:* www.joynerfineproperties.com	Richmond	VA	23294	804-270-9440	967-2770	652
JG Boswell Co 101 W Walnut St *OTC: BWEL*	Pasadena	CA	91103	626-583-3000		10-2
JG Tax Group 1430 S Federal Hwy *TF:* 866-477-5291 ■ *Web:* www.jgtaxgroup.com	Deerfield Beach	FL	33441	866-477-5291		734
JG Van Holten & Son Inc 703 W Madison St PO Box 66 *Web:* www.vanholtenpickles.com	Waterloo	WI	53594	920-478-2144	478-2316	296-19
JGB Enterprises Inc 115 Metropolitan Dr *Web:* www.jgbhose.com	Liverpool	NY	13088	315-451-2770	451-8503	370
JGI (Jane Goodall Institute for Wildlife Research Education) 1595 Spring Hill Rd Ste 550 *TF:* 800-592-5263 ■ *Web:* www.janegoodall.org	Vienna	VA	22182	703-682-9220		48-3
JGPG (Joe Goode Performance Group) 499 Alabama St Ste 150 *Web:* joegoode.org	San Francisco	CA	94110	415-561-6565	561-6562	573-1
JGSI (Jewish Genealogical Society of Illinois) PO Box 515 *Web:* www.jgsi.org	Northbrook	IL	60065	312-666-0100		48-13
JH Baxter & Co PO Box 5902 *TF:* 800-556-1098 ■ *Web:* www.jhbaxter.com	San Mateo	CA	94402	650-349-0201	570-6878	818
JH Berra Construction Company Inc 5091 Baumgartner Rd *Web:* www.jhberra.com	Saint Louis	MO	63129	314-487-5617	487-5817	188-10

Name / Address	Phone	Fax	Class
JH Fletcher & Company Inc 402 High St ... Huntington WV 25705 TF: 800-327-6203 ■ Web: www.jhfletcher.com	304-525-7811	525-3770	190
JH Industries Inc 1981 E Aurora Rd ... Twinsburg OH 44087 TF: 800-321-4968 ■ Web: copperloy.com	330-963-4105	963-4111	480
JH Kelly 821 Third Ave ... Longview WA 98632 Web: www.jhkelly.com	360-423-5510	423-9170	189-10
JH Larson Co 10200 51st Ave N ... Plymouth MN 55442 Web: www.jhlarson.com	763-545-1717	545-1144	246
JH Routh Packing Company Inc 4413 W Bogart Rd ... Sandusky OH 44870 TF: 800-446-6759 ■ Web: routhpacking.com	419-626-2251	625-4782	473
JH Technology Inc 5107 Lena Rd Unit 111 ... Bradenton FL 34211 Web: www.jhtechnology.com	941-758-7710		194
JH Walker Trucking Company Inc 152 N Hollywood Rd ... Houma LA 70364 TF: 800-581-2600 ■ Web: www.jhwalkertrucking.com	985-868-8330		780
JH Whitney & Co 130 Main St ... New Canaan CT 06840 Web: www.whitney.com	203-716-6100		792
JH Williams Oil Company Inc 1237 E Twiggs St ... Tampa FL 33602 Web: www.jhwoil.com	813-228-7776	224-9413	579
JHCR (Jackson Hole Central Reservations) 140 E Broadway Ste 24 PO Box 2618 ... Jackson WY 83001 TF: 888-838-6606 ■ Web: www.jacksonholewy.com	307-733-4005	733-1286	376
JHL Digital Direct 3100 Borham Ave ... Stevens Point WI 54481 TF: 800-236-0581 ■ Web: www.jhl.com	715-341-0581		195
JHL Industries 10012 Nevada Ave ... Chatsworth CA 91311 TF: 800-255-6636 ■ Web: www.jhlindustries.com	818-882-2233	882-4350	732
JHOC Inc 323 Cash Memorial Blvd ... Forest Park GA 30297 TF: 800-927-6460 ■ Web: www.premiertransportation.com	404-675-1950	675-1963	311
JHPIEGO Corp 1615 Thames St ... Baltimore MD 21231 Web: www.jhpiego.org	410-537-1800		463
Jibe Media LLC 774 South 300 West Unit B ... Salt Lake City UT 84101 Web: jibemedia.com	801-433-5423		7
JIC (Johnston Investment Counsel Ltd) 2714 N Knoxville ... Peoria IL 61614 *Fax Area Code: 888 ■ TF: 877-848-3330 ■ Web: www.jicinvest.com	309-674-3330	301-0514*	194
Jiffy Lube PO Box 4427 ... Houston TX 77210 TF: 800-344-6933 ■ Web: www.jiffylube.com	800-344-6933		62-5
Jif-Pak Manufacturing 1451 Engineer St ... Vista CA 92081 TF: 800-777-6613 ■ Web: jifpak.kallegroup.com	760-597-2665		601
Jifram Extrusions Inc 320 Forest Ave ... Sheboygan Falls WI 53085 Web: www.jifram.com	920-467-2477	467-2530	604
JILA (JILA Science) University of Colorado 440 UCB ... Boulder CO 80309 Web: jila.colorado.edu	303-492-7789	492-5235	668
JILA Science (JILA) University of Colorado 440 UCB ... Boulder CO 80309 Web: jila.colorado.edu	303-492-7789	492-5235	668
Jill Newhouse Gallery 4 E 81st St ... New York NY 10028 Web: www.jillnewhouse.com	212-249-9216	734-4098	42
Jill R. Featherstonhaugh PC 1158 High St Ste 101 ... Eugene OR 97401 Web: businesslawcentre.com	541-345-2778		41
Jim & Dude's Plumbing Heating Inc 724 W Clark St ... Albert Lea MN 56007 Web: www.jimanddudes.com	507-373-6161		189-10
Jim & Jennie's Greek Village 3026 N 90th St ... Omaha NE 68134 Web: www.jimandjennies.com	402-571-2857		671
Jim 'N Nick's 7004 Charlotte Pk ... Nashville TN 37209 Web: jimnnicks.com	615-352-5777		671
Jim 'N Nick's Bar-B-Q 7791 Gateway Ln NW ... Concord NC 28027 Web: www.jimnnicks.com	704-453-2791		671
Jim Appley's Tru-Arc Inc 5140 110th Ave N ... Clearwater FL 33760 Web: www.jimappleystruarc.com	727-571-3007	571-3219	454
Jim Bishop Cabinets Inc 5640 Bell Rd ... Montgomery AL 36116 TF: 800-410-2444 ■ Web: www.bishopcabinets.com	800-410-2444		115
Jim Click Ford Inc 6244 E 22nd St ... Tucson AZ 85711 TF: 888-563-3932 ■ Web: www.jimclickford.com	888-563-3932		57
Jim Edgar Panther Creek State Fish and Wildlife Area (JEPC) 10149 County Hwy 11 ... Chandlerville IL 62627 Web: www2.illinois.gov	217-452-7741		565
Jim Ellis Auto Dealerships 5901 Peachtree Industrial Blvd S ... Atlanta GA 30341 Web: www.jimellis.com	770-458-6811		57
Jim Hawk Truck-Trailers Inc 3515 Adventureland Dr ... Altoona IA 50009 TF: 800-992-3355 ■ Web: www.jhtt.com	800-992-3355		470
Jim Henson's Creature Shop 1416 N LaBrea Ave ... Hollywood CA 90028 Web: creatureshop.com	323-802-1557		33
Jim Hogg County Abstract Company In PO Box 125 ... Hebbronville TX 78361	361-527-3015		338
Jim House & Associates Inc 1401 Georgia Rd ... Irondale AL 35210 TF: 800-292-6335 ■ Web: jimhouse.com	205-592-6302	951-0291	261
Jim Jordan & Associates Lp 12941 N Fwy Ste 226 ... Houston TX 77060	281-877-7009		466
Jim Marshall Insurance Inc 2084 Ninth St Ste D ... Los Osos CA 93402 Web: www.jimmarshallinsurance.com	805-528-4739		390
Jim McKay Chevrolet Inc 3509 University Dr ... Fairfax VA 22030 TF: 833-822-4212 ■ Web: www.jimmckaychevrolet.com	833-822-4212		57
Jim Neely's Interstate Barbeque 2265 S Third St ... Memphis TN 38109 Web: www.interstatebarbecue.com	901-775-2304	775-3149	671
Jim Palmer Trucking 9730 Derby Dr ... Missoula MT 59808 TF: 888-698-3422 ■ Web: www.jimpalmertrucking.com	888-698-3422		780
Jim Pattison Group 1067 W Cordova St Ste 1800 ... Vancouver BC V6C1C7 Web: jimpattison.com	604-688-6764		185
Jim Spachman State Farm Agency 2501 E College ... Bloomington IL 61704 Web: jimspachman.com	309-661-1700		390
Jim Turner Chevrolet 1015 E Mcgregor Dr ... Mcgregor TX 76657 Web: www.jimturnerchevrolet.com	254-236-6232		57
Jim Wells County PO Box 1459 ... Alice TX 78333 Web: www.co.jim-wells.tx.us	361-668-5702	668-8681	338
Jim Whitten Roof Consultants LLC PO Box 200925 ... Austin TX 78720 Web: www.jimwhitten.com	512-250-0999		463
Jim Wilson & Associates LLC 2660 Eastchase Ln Ste 100 ... Montgomery AL 36117 Web: jwacompanies.com	334-260-2500	260-2533	655
Jim's Farm Meat Inc PO Box 1098 ... Winton CA 95388 Web: jimsfarmmeat.com	209-358-3535	667-4597	473
Jim's Seafood 950 Wilkinson Blvd ... Frankfort KY 40601 Web: www.jimseafood1.wixsite.com	502-223-7448	227-7419	671
Jim's Steakhouse 110 SW Jefferson Ave ... Peoria IL 61602 Web: www.jimssteakhouse.net	309-673-5300		671
Jim's Travel Link Inc 500 Middlefork ... Irving TX 75063 TF: 800-395-8855 ■ Web: www.jimstravel.com	214-720-1000	720-1022	771
Jimbo's Pit BBQ 4103 W Kennedy Blvd ... Tampa FL 33609 Web: www.jimbosbarbq.com	813-289-9724	289-1006	671
Jimcor Agency 60 Craig Rd ... Montvale NJ 07645 Web: jimcor.com	856-866-8858		390
Jiminy Peak Mountain Resort LLC 37 Corey Rd ... Hancock MA 01237 TF: 800-835-2364 ■ Web: www.jiminypeak.com	413-738-5500		707
Jimmie Davis State Park 1209 State Park Rd ... Chatham LA 71226 TF: 888-677-2263 ■ Web: crt.state.la.us	318-249-2595		565
Jimmy Carter Library & Museum 441 Freedom Pkwy ... Atlanta GA 30307 Web: www.jimmycarterlibrary.gov	404-865-7100	865-7102	434-2
Jimmy Carter National Historic Site 300 N Bond St ... Plains GA 31780 Web: www.nps.gov	229-824-4104		564
Jimmy John's Franchise Inc 2212 Fox Dr ... Champaign IL 61820 TF: 800-546-6904 ■ Web: www.jimmyjohns.com	217-356-9900	359-2956	670
Jimmy Swaggart Ministries (JSM) 8919 World Ministry Blvd PO Box 262550 ... Baton Rouge LA 70810 TF: 800-288-8350 ■ Web: www.jsm.org	225-768-8300		48-20
Jimmy Whittington Lumber Co 3637 Jackson Ave ... Memphis TN 38108 Web: www.whittingtonlumber.com	901-386-2800		364
Jimmy's Family Steak House 3101 S Providence Rd ... Columbia MO 65203 Web: www.jimmysfamilysteakhouse.com	573-443-1796		671
Jims Formal Wear LLC 804 E Broadway ... Trenton IL 62293 Web: www.jimsformalwear.com	618-224-9211	224-7924	156
Jims Place Grille 3660 S Houston Levee ... Collierville TN 38017 Web: jimsplacegrille.com	901-861-5000		671
Jin Ju 5203 N Clark St ... Chicago IL 60640 Web: jinjurestaurant.com	773-334-6377		671
Jinbeh 301 E Las Colinas Blvd ... Irving TX 75039 Web: www.jinbeh.com	972-869-4011	869-4311	671
JinkoSolar (US) Inc 595 Market St Ste 2200 ... San Francisco CA 94105 Web: www.jinkosolar.com	415-402-0502	402-0703	696
Jireh Metal Inc 3635 Nardin St ... Grandville MI 49418 Web: jirehmetal.com	616-531-7581		295
Jiten Hotel Management Inc 495 Westgate Dr ... Brockton MA 02301 Web: jitenhotels.com	508-427-1667		463
Jitlada 5233 1/2 W Sunset Blvd ... Los Angeles CA 90027 Web: jitladala.com	323-667-9809		671
Jivamukti Yoga Center Inc 841 Broadway ... New York NY 10003 Web: jivamuktiyoga.com	212-353-0214		148
JJ Bender LLC 457 Castle Ave ... Fairfield CT 06825 *Fax Area Code: 203 ■ TF: 800-367-9673 ■ Web: www.jjbender.com	800-367-9673	336-4034*	112
JJ Cassone Bakery Inc 202 S Regent St ... Port Chester NY 10573 TF: 800-331-7504 ■ Web: www.jjcassone.com	914-939-1568		345
JJ Gumberg Company Inc 1051 Brinton Rd ... Pittsburgh PA 15221 Web: www.jjgumberg.com	412-244-4000	244-4018	655
JJ Haines & Company Inc 6950 Aviation Blvd ... Glen Burnie MD 21061 *Fax Area Code: 410 ■ TF: 800-922-9248 ■ Web: www.jjhaines.com	800-922-9248	760-4045*	361
JJ Kane 1000 Lenola Rd Bldg 1 Ste 203 ... Maple Shade NJ 08052 TF: 855-462-5263 ■ Web: www.jjkane.com	855-462-5263		138
JJ Keller & Associates Inc 3003 Breezewood Ln PO Box 368 ... Neenah WI 54957 *Fax Area Code: 800 ■ TF: 800-558-5011 ■ Web: www.jjkeller.com	877-564-2333	727-7516*	637-11
JJ MacKay Canada Ltd 1342 Abercrombie Rd PO Box 338 ... New Glasgow NS B2H5C6 TF: 888-462-2529 ■ Web: www.mackaymeters.com	902-752-5124	752-5955	770
JJ Neilson Arboretum University of Guelph 120 Main St E Ridgetown College ... Ridgetown ON N0P2C0 Web: www.ridgetownc.com	519-674-1500	674-1515	97
JJ Nichting Company Inc 1342 Pilot Grove Rd ... Pilot Grove IA 52648 Web: jjnichting.com	319-469-4461	469-4703	274
JJ Powell Inc 109 W Presqueisle St ... Philipsburg PA 16866 TF: 800-432-0866 ■ Web: www.jjpowell.com	814-342-3190		579
JJ Taylor Companies Inc 655 N AIA ... Jupiter FL 33477 Web: www.jjtaylor.com	561-354-2900		81-1

	City	State	Zip	Phone	Fax	Class
JJ's Bistro de Paris 330 A1A N Ste 209 *Web:* www.jjbistro.com	Ponte Vedra Beach	FL	32082	904-996-7557		671
JJDS Environmental Inc 40 Woodview Dr *Web:* www.jjdsenvironmental.com	Doylestown	PA	18901	267-880-2325		194
JJJ Floor Covering Inc 4831 Passons Blvd Ste A *Web:* www.jjjfloorcovering.com	Pico Rivera	CA	90660	562-692-9008	692-5979	290
JK & B Capital 180 N Stetson Ave Ste 4500 *Web:* www.jkbcapital.com	Chicago	IL	60601	312-946-1200	946-1103	792
JK Design Inc 465 Amwell Rd *Web:* www.jkdesign.com	Hillsborough	NJ	08844	908-428-4700		344
J-K Prosthetics & Orthotics Inc 699 N Macquesten Pky *Web:* www.jkpando.com	Mount Vernon	NY	10552	914-699-2077	699-0676	477
JK Pulley Company Inc 3805 Bates St *Web:* www.jkpulley.com	Saint Louis	MO	63116	314-843-4388	481-9004	350
JK Tool & Die Inc 148 Prominence Dr *Web:* www.jktoolinc.com	New Kensington	PA	15068	724-339-1858	339-1453	757
JKL Technologies Inc 3245 Grande Vista Dr *Web:* www.cos-jkl.com	Newbury Park	CA	91320	805-375-5820	375-5830	180
JKmicrosystems Inc 12228 E Bennett Rd *Web:* www.jkmicro.com	Grass Valley	CA	95945	530-297-6073	297-6074	174
JL (Junior League of Pueblo) 421 N Main St Ste 415 *Web:* www.jlofpueblo.org	Pueblo	CO	81003	719-542-0491		637-2
JL Darling LLC 2614 Pacific Hwy E *Web:* www.riteintherain.com	Tacoma	WA	98424	253-922-5000		535
JL Industries Inc 4450 W 78th St Cir *TF:* 800-554-6077 ■ *Web:* www.activarcpg.com	Bloomington	MN	55435	952-835-6850	835-2218	286
JL Media Inc 1600 Rt 22 E 2nd Fl *Web:* jlmedia.com	Union	NJ	07083	908-302-1285		6
JL Properties Inc 813 D St Ste 200 *Web:* www.jlproperties.com	Anchorage	AK	99501	907-279-8068	279-8066	652
JL Richards & Associates Ltd 864 Lady Ellen Pl *Web:* www.jlrichards.ca	Ottawa	ON	K1Z5M2	613-728-3571		256
JL Shandy Transportation Inc 10115 Ravenwood *TF:* 888-274-2639 ■ *Web:* www.jlshandy.com	Saint John	IN	46373	219-365-2000		780
JL Smith Group Inc, The 36610 Detroit Rd *Web:* jlsmithgroup.com	Avon	OH	44011	440-934-9181		390
JLA (Junior League of Augusta) Surrey Ctr 375 Highland Ave *Web:* www.jlaugusta.org	Augusta	GA	30909	706-736-0033	736-6526	48-6
JLC (Junior League of Charleston) 51 Folly Rd *Web:* www.jlcharleston.org	Charleston	SC	29407	843-763-5284	763-1626	48-6
JLC (Junior League of Charlotte Inc) 1332 Maryland Ave *Web:* www.jlcharlotte.org	Charlotte	NC	28209	704-375-5993	375-9730	48-6
JLC Associates Inc 3198-A Airport Loop Dr *Web:* www.jlcassoc.com	Costa Mesa	CA	92626	714-241-4430		186
JLCM (Junior League of Cobb-Marietta) 505 Kennesaw Ave *Web:* www.jlcm.org	Marietta	GA	30060	770-422-5266	427-2253	48-6
JLCooper Electronics 142 Arena St *Web:* www.jlcooper.com	El Segundo	CA	90245	310-322-9990	335-0110	253
J-Lenco Inc 664 N High St **Fax Area Code:* 614 ■ *Web:* jlenco.com	La Rue	OH	43332	740-499-2260	499-2631*	567
JLG (Junior League of Greenville Inc) 120 Greenacre Rd *Web:* www.jlgreenville.org	Greenville	SC	29607	864-233-2663	233-9092	48-6
Jlg Harvesting Inc 1450 S Atlantic Ave	Yuma	AZ	85365	928-329-7548		11-1
JLG Industries Inc 1 JLG Dr *Web:* www.jlg.com	McConnellsburg	PA	17233	717-485-5161	485-6417	190
JLL (Junior League of Lafayette) 504 Richland Ave *TF:* 800-757-3651 ■ *Web:* www.juniorleagueoflafayette.com	Lafayette	LA	70508	337-988-2739	988-1079	48-6
Jll Partners Inc 450 Lexington Ave 31st Fl *Web:* www.jllpartners.com	New York	NY	10017	212-286-8600		405
JLM (Junior League of Monroe Inc) 2811 Cameron St *Web:* www.jlmonroe.org	Monroe	LA	71201	318-322-3236	322-3299	48-6
JLM (Junior League of McAllen) 514 E Dove Ave *Web:* www.juniorleaguemcallen.org	McAllen	TX	78502	956-682-0071		48-6
JLM (Junior League of Mobile) 57 N Sage Ave *Web:* www.juniorleaguemobile.org	Mobile	AL	36607	251-471-3348	471-3340	48-6
JLM Couture Inc 525 Seventh Ave Ste 1703 *Web:* www.jlmcouture.com	New York	NY	10018	212-221-8203		155-21
JLM Educational Training PO Box 4845 *Web:* www.reflexologyusa.com	Seminole	FL	33775	727-319-6818	319-6911	637-10
JLM Wholesale 3095 Mullins Ct *TF:* 800-522-2940 ■ *Web:* www.jlmwholesale.com	Oxford	MI	48371	248-628-6440	628-6733	351
JLN MD Associates LLC 4939 Chestnut St *Web:* www.jln-md.com	New Orleans	LA	70115	504-899-7893	899-7557	192
JLO (Junior League of Odessa Inc) 2707 Kermit Hwy *Web:* www.jlodessa.org	Odessa	TX	79764	432-332-0095	333-6515	48-6
JLP (Junior League of Peoria) 114 State St Ste 2A *Web:* www.juniorleagueofpeoria.org	Peoria	IL	61602	309-685-9312		48-6
JLPB (Junior League of the Palm Beaches) 470 Columbia Dr Bldg F *Web:* www.jlpb.org	West Palm Beach	FL	33409	561-689-7590		48-6
JLR (Junior League of Rochester) 110 Linden Oaks Dr Ste A *Web:* www.jlroch.org	Rochester	NY	14625	585-385-8590	385-1873	48-6
JLS (Junior League of Springfield) 2574 E Bennett St *Web:* www.jlspringfield.org	Springfield	MO	65804	417-887-9422		637-2
JLS (Junior League of Springfield) 2800 Montvale *Web:* www.jlsil.org	Springfield	IL	62704	217-544-5557		48-6
JLS Language Corp 135 Willow Rd *Web:* www.jls.com	Menlo Park	CA	94025	650-321-9832		768
JLS Mailing Services 672 Crescent St *TF:* 866-557-6245 ■ *Web:* www.jlsms.com	Brockton	MA	02302	866-557-6245		5
JLSD (Jackson Local Schools District) 7602 Fulton Dr *Web:* www.jackson.stark.k12.oh.us	Massillon	OH	44646	330-830-8000	830-8008	186
JLT (Junior League of Tampa Inc) 87 Columbia Dr *Web:* www.jltampa.org	Tampa	FL	33606	813-254-1734		48-22
JLT (Junior League of Tulsa Inc) 3633 S Yale Ave *Web:* www.jltulsa.org	Tulsa	OK	74135	918-663-6100	627-9588	48-6
JLT Mobile Computers Inc 7402 W Detroit St Ste 150 *TF:* 844-705-4200 ■ *Web:* www.jltmobile.com	Chandler	AZ	85226	480-705-4200	397-1214	173-2
JM Davis Arms & Historical Museum 330 N J M Davis Blvd *Web:* www.thegunmuseum.com	Claremore	OK	74017	918-341-5707	341-5771	520
JM Digitalworks 2460 Impala Dr	Carlsbad	CA	92008	760-476-1783		530
JM Family Enterprises Inc 100 Jim Moran Blvd *TF:* 800-565-3987 ■ *Web:* www.jmfamily.com	Deerfield Beach	FL	33442	954-429-2000		57
JM Furniture 3333 N Carson St *Web:* www.jmfurniture.net	Carson City	NV	89706	775-883-3333		320
JM Indexing 118 E 92nd St By-Pass S *Web:* www.jmindexing.com	New York	NY	10128	212-427-7375		192
JM Manufacturing Company Inc 5200 W Century Blvd *TF:* 800-621-4404 ■ *Web:* www.jmeagle.com	Los Angeles	CA	90045	800-621-4404		596
JM Search & Company Inc 1045 First Ave Ste 110 *Web:* jmsearch.com	King of Prussia	PA	19406	610-964-0200		194
JM Smith Corp 101 W St John St Ste 305 *Web:* www.jmsmithcorp.com	Spartanburg	SC	29306	864-542-9419		238
JM Sorge Inc 57 Fourth St *Web:* jmsorge.com	Somerville	NJ	08876	908-218-0066		192
JM Swank LLC 395 Herky St *TF:* 800-593-6375 ■ *Web:* www.jmswank.com	North Liberty	IA	52317	319-626-3683		297-8
JM Test Systems Inc 7323 Tom Dr *TF:* 800-353-3411 ■ *Web:* jmtest.com	Baton Rouge	LA	70806	225-925-2029		743
JM Turner Engineering Inc 1325 College Ave *TF:* 800-514-4220 ■ *Web:* www.jmteng.com	Santa Rosa	CA	95404	707-528-4503		256
JMA Energy Company LLC 1021 NW Grand Blvd *TF:* 844-265-0062 ■ *Web:* jmaenergy.com	Oklahoma City	OK	73118	405-947-4322	418-2550	536
Jma Engineering Corp Garden 531 E Bethany Home Rd *Web:* jmaengineering.com	Phoenix	AZ	85012	602-248-0286		261
JMA Railroad Supply Co 835 E Tenth St *Web:* www.jmarail.com	Seymour	IN	47274	812-522-7200	522-1150	770
J-MacLumber Inc 4154 Faust St *Web:* www.maclumber.com	Bamberg	SC	29003	803-245-1700	245-1701	661
J-Mar Enterprises Inc PO Box 4143 *TF:* 800-446-8283 ■ *Web:* www.j-mar-enterprises.com	Bismarck	ND	58502	701-222-4518	255-7587	780
JMC Communities 2201 Fourth St N Ste 200 *Web:* www.jmccommunities.com	Saint Petersburg	FL	33704	727-823-0022		653
JMD Communications Inc 760 Calle Bolivar *Web:* www.jmdcom.com	San Juan	PR	00909	787-728-3030		387
JME of Monticello Inc 1401 Fallon Ave *TF:* 800-450-3122 ■ *Web:* jmecompanies.com	Monticello	MN	55362	763-295-3122	295-8765	519
JMF Co 2735 62nd St Ct *TF:* 800-397-3739 ■ *Web:* www.jmfcompany.com	Bettendorf	IA	52722	563-332-9200	332-9880	612
JMFA (John M. Floyd & Associates Inc) 125 N Burnett Dr *TF:* 800-809-2307 ■ *Web:* www.jmfa.com	Baytown	TX	77520	281-424-3800	424-8864	194
JMG Financial Group 2001 Butterfield Rd Ste 1400 *Web:* www.jmgfinancial.com	Downers Grove	IL	60515	630-571-5252		401
JMG Realty Inc 5605 Glenridge Dr Ste 1010 *Web:* www.jmgrealty.com	Atlanta	GA	30342	404-995-1111	995-1112	655
JMG Security Systems Inc 17150 Newhope St Ste 109 *Web:* www.jmgsecurity.com	Fountain Valley	CA	92708	714-545-8882		693
JMH (Johnson Memorial Hospital) 1125 W Jefferson St *Web:* www.johnsonmemorial.org	Franklin	IN	46131	317-736-3300	736-2692	374-3
JMI (James Marine Inc) 4500 Clarks River Rd PO Box 2305 *Web:* www.jamesmarine.com	Paducah	KY	42002	270-898-7392		465
JMI Corporation - Venture Services 2516 Via Tejon 3rd Fl *Web:* www.jmicorp.com	Palos Verdes Peninsula	CA	90274	310-373-6540	919-2903	631
JMK Intl 1401 N Bowie Dr	Weatherford	TX	76086	817-737-3703		360-3
JMK Nippon 2551 N Perryville Rd *Web:* jmkrockford.com	Rockford	IL	61107	815-877-0505		671
JMK Systems Solutions Inc 20 Broadway Ave *Web:* jmkssi.com	Ipswich	MA	01938	978-356-8888		180
JML Optical Industries LLC 820 Linden Ave *Web:* www.jmloptical.com	Rochester	NY	14625	585-248-8900	248-8924	544

Listing	City	State	ZIP	Phone	Fax	Class
JMMC (John Muir Medical Ctr) 1601 Ygnacio Valley Rd *TF:* 844-398-5376 ■ *Web:* www.johnmuirhealth.com	Walnut Creek	CA	94598	925-939-3000	308-8944	374-3
JMP IT Services 535 W 152 St *Web:* www.jmpits.com	New York	NY	10031	646-397-8117		196
JMP Solutions 4026 Meadowbrook Dr Unit 143 *Web:* www.jmpsolutions.com	London	ON	N6L1C9	519-652-2741		261
JMR Electronics Inc 8968 Fullbridht Ave *Web:* jmr.com	Chatsworth	CA	91311	818-993-4801		254
JMS Elite 5900 Som Center Rd Ste 12 *Web:* jmselite.com	Willoughby	OH	44094	440-943-9200		195
JMS North America Corp 22320 Foothill Blvd Ste 350 *Web:* www.jmsna.net	Hayward	CA	94541	510-888-9090	888-9099	729
JMS Southeast Inc 105 Temperature Ln *TF:* 800-873-1835 ■ *Web:* www.jms-se.com	Statesville	NC	28677	800-873-1835		201
JMT (Johnson Mirmiran & Thompson) 72 Loveton Cir *TF:* 800-472-2310 ■ *Web:* www.jmt.com	Sparks	MD	21152	410-329-3100	472-2200	261
JMT Consulting Group Inc 2200-2202 Rt 22 *TF:* 888-368-2463 ■ *Web:* jmtconsulting.com	Patterson	NY	12563	845-278-9262	278-9266	528
JN (J N Machinery Corp) 1081 Rock Rd Ln *Web:* jnmachinery.com	East Dundee	IL	60118	224-699-9161	699-9286	318
JNA Institute of Culinary Arts 1212 S Broad St *Web:* www.culinaryarts.com	Philadelphia	PA	19146	215-468-8800		163
JNEC (Jasper-Newton Electric Co-opeartive Inc) 812 S Margaret Ave *Web:* www.jnec.com	Kirbyville	TX	75956	409-423-2241		245
JNF (Jewish National Fund) 42 E 69th St *TF:* 800-542-8733 ■ *Web:* www.jnf.org	New York	NY	10021	212-879-9300		48-20
JNJ Express Inc 3935 Old Getwell Rd *TF:* 888-383-7157 ■ *Web:* www.jnjexpress.com	Memphis	TN	38118	901-362-3444	362-2331	780
JNJ Mobile Inc 745 Atlantic Ave Fl 8 *Web:* www.jnjmobile.com	Boston	MA	02111	617-542-1614		387
JNK Securities Corp 902 Broadway 20th Fl *Web:* www.jnksecurities.com	New York	NY	10010	212-885-6300		401
JNL Glass Inc 618 E Gutierrez St *Web:* jnlglass.com	Santa Barbara	CA	93103	805-957-1685	957-1689	329
Jo Ann Hoffman & Associates PA 4403 W Tradewinds Ave *TF:* 800-273-5297 ■ *Web:* joannhoffman.com	Lauderdale-by-the-Sea	FL	33308	954-772-2845		41
JO Daviess County 330 N Bench St *Web:* www.jodaviess.org	Galena	IL	61036	815-777-0037	776-9146	338
Jo-Ad Industries Inc 31465 Stephenson Hwy *TF:* 800-331-8923 ■ *Web:* www.jo-ad.com	Madison Heights	MI	48071	248-588-4810	588-3448	757
Joan C. Edwards School of Medicine at Marshall University 1600 Medical Center Dr *TF:* 877-691-1600 ■ *Web:* jcesom.marshall.edu	Huntington	WV	25701	304-691-1700	691-1726	167-2
Joan of Arc Academy 2221 Elmira Dr *Web:* joanofarcacademy.com	Ottawa	ON	K2C1H3	613-728-6364		685
Joan Shorenstein Center on the Press Politics & Public Policy 79 John F Kennedy St *Web:* shorensteincenter.org	Cambridge	MA	02138	617-495-8269	495-8696	634
Jo-Ann Stores Inc (JAS) 5555 Darrow Rd **Fax Area Code:* 330 ■ *TF:* 888-739-4120 ■ *Web:* www.joann.com	Hudson	OH	44236	888-739-4120	463-6760*	270
Joat Company Inc 60 Huntley Way *Web:* thejoatcompany.com	Bridgewater	NJ	08807	908-253-9233	253-9575	637-2
Job Cost Inc 208 N Washington St *Web:* www.jobcost.com	Naperville	IL	60540	630-355-8188	355-8675	178-1
Job Finders Employment Service Co 1729 W Broadway Ste 4 *TF:* 844-228-5627 ■ *Web:* www.jobfindersusa.com	Columbia	MO	65203	573-446-4250		260
Job Performance Systems Inc 1240 N Pitt St Ste 200 *Web:* www.jps-usa.com	Alexandria	VA	22314	703-683-5805	683-6181	463
Job Shop Managers 28966 Hancock Pkwy *Web:* www.skmindustries.com	Valencia	CA	91355	661-294-8373		350
Job Squad Inc 102 Second St *Web:* jobsquadinc.org	Bridgeport	WV	26330	304-848-0850		104
Jobaline 620 Kirkland Way Ste 208 *Web:* www.jobalign.com	Kirkland	WA	98033	425-947-2707		387
Jobast Holdings Inc 377 Oak St Ste 402	Garden City	NY	11530	516-997-4490		690
Jobbers Meat Packing Company Inc 3336 Fruitland Ave	Vernon	CA	90058	323-585-6328		473
JobDiva 116 John St Ste 1406 *TF:* 866-562-3482 ■ *Web:* www.jobdiva.com	New York	NY	10038	866-562-3482		393
Jobe & Company Inc 9004 Yellow Brick Rd Ste F *TF:* 855-805-2599 ■ *Web:* jobeandcompany.com	Rosedale	MD	21237	410-288-0560	285-8651	358
Jobe Hastings & Associates CPA's 745 S Church St Ste 105 *TF:* 866-207-2384 ■ *Web:* www.jobehastings.com	Murfreesboro	TN	37133	615-893-7777		2
Jobelephantcom Inc 5443 Fremontia Ln *TF:* 800-311-0563 ■ *Web:* www.jobelephant.com	San Diego	CA	92115	619-795-0837	243-1484	7
JobGiraffe 8430 W Bryn Mawr Ste 777 *Web:* www.jobgiraffe.com	Chicago	IL	60631	773-693-9070	693-9071	631
JobMonkey Inc 1409 Post Alley *TF:* 800-230-1095 ■ *Web:* www.jobmonkey.com	Seattle	WA	98101	800-230-1095		260
Jobscope Corp 355 Woodruff Rd *TF:* 800-443-5794 ■ *Web:* www.jobscope.com	Greenville	SC	29607	800-443-5794		178-11
JobsOhio 41 S High St Ste 1500 *TF:* 855-874-2530 ■ *Web:* www.jobsohio.com	Columbus	OH	43215	614-215-9323		463
JobTarget LLC 15 Thames St *Web:* www.jobtarget.com	Groton	CT	06340	860-440-0635	447-4562	260
Jo-Carroll Energy 793 US Hwy 20 W **Fax Area Code:* 815 ■ *TF:* 800-858-5522 ■ *Web:* www.jocarroll.com	Elizabeth	IL	61028	800-858-5522	858-3731*	245
Jockey Club, The 40 E 52nd St *Web:* www.jockeyclub.com	New York	NY	10022	212-371-5970	371-6123	48-22
Jockey International Inc 2300 60th St PO Box 1417 *TF:* 800-562-5391 ■ *Web:* www.jockey.com	Kenosha	WI	53140	800-562-5391		155-18
Jockeys' Guild Inc 448 Lewis Hargett Cir Ste 220 *TF:* 866-465-6257 ■ *Web:* www.jockeysguild.com	Lexington	KY	40503	859-523-5625	219-9892	48-22
Jocks & Jills Sports Grill 4109 S Stream Blvd *Web:* jocksandjills.com	Charlotte	NC	28217	704-423-0001		670
Jodon Engineering 62 Enterprise Dr *Web:* www.jodon.com	Ann Arbor	MI	48103	734-761-4044		425
Joe Allen 326 W 46th St *Web:* joeallenrestaurant.com	New York	NY	10036	212-581-6464		671
Joe Allen's Pit Bar-B-Que 301 S 11th St *Web:* www.joeallensbbq.com	Abilene	TX	79602	325-672-6082	672-5131	671
Joe Blasco Make-Up Ctr 195 Raymond Hill Rd Ste C *Web:* www.joeblasco.com	Newnan	GA	30265	407-363-1234	354-2435	167-3
Joe Christensen Inc 1540 Adams St *TF:* 800-228-5030 ■ *Web:* www.christensenprinting.com	Lincoln	NE	68521	402-476-7535	476-3094	626
Joe Fazio Bakery Inc 1717 Sublette Ave *Web:* www.faziosbakery.com	Saint Louis	MO	63110	314-645-6239	645-2410	296-1
Joe Gibbs Racing 13415 Reese Blvd W *Web:* www.joegibbsracing.com	Huntersville	NC	28078	704-944-5000		642
Joe Goode Performance Group (JGPG) 499 Alabama St Ste 150 *Web:* joegoode.org	San Francisco	CA	94110	415-561-6565	561-6562	573-1
Joe Holland Chevrolet Inc 210 Maccorkle Ave SW *TF:* 800-627-8249 ■ *Web:* www.joeholland.com	South Charleston	WV	25303	304-744-1561		57
Joe Jackson Realty Corp 100 E Wilson Bridge Rd *Web:* thejacksonteam.net	Worthington	OH	43085	614-431-1220		652
Joe Kegans State Jail 707 Top St *Web:* www.tdcj.texas.gov	Houston	TX	77002	713-224-6584		213
Joe Krentzman & Son Inc 3175 Back Maitland Rd *Web:* www.krentzman.net	Lewistown	PA	17044	717-543-4000		686
Joe L. Wheeler PO Box 1246 *Web:* www.joewheelerbooks.com	Conifer	CO	80433	303-838-2333		637-2
Joe Roots Grill 2826 W Eigth St *Web:* www.joerootsgrill.com	Erie	PA	16505	814-836-7668		671
Joe Smith Company Inc 902 E Jefferson St *Web:* joesmithcompany.com	Pittsburg	KS	66762	620-231-3610		756
Joe T. Garcia's 2201 N Commerce St *Web:* joetgarcias.com	Fort Worth	TX	76164	817-626-4356		671
Joe Tahan's Furniture Liquidation Centers Inc 5125 Commercial Dr *Web:* www.tahans.com	Rome	NY	13440	315-339-2330		321
Joe W. Taylor CPAS 1733 Campus Plaza Ct Ste 4 *Web:* joewtaylorcpas.com	Bowling Green	KY	42102	270-781-0324	781-0325	2
Joe Wheeler Electric Membership Corp 25700 AL-24 *Web:* www.jwemc.org	Trinity	AL	35673	256-552-2300	355-0631	245
Joe Wheeler Resort Lodge & Convention Ctr 4401 McLean Dr *TF:* 800-544-5639 ■ *Web:* www.alapark.com	Rogersville	AL	35652	256-247-5461	247-5471	669
Joe's Crab Shack 5802 W Loop S 289 *Web:* www.joescrabshack.com	Lubbock	TX	79424	806-797-8600		671
Joe's Hardware 640 S Main Ave *Web:* joeshardwareonline.com	Fallbrook	CA	92028	760-728-4265	728-6286	351
Joe's Jeans Inc 2340 S E Ave *NASDAQ: JOEZ* ■ *Web:* www.joesjeans.com	Commerce	CA	90040	323-837-3700		157-4
Joe's Seafood Prime Steak & Stone Crab 60 E Grand Ave *Web:* leye.com	Chicago	IL	60611	312-379-5637		671
Joe's Stone Crab 11 Washington Ave *TF:* 800-780-2722 ■ *Web:* www.joesstonecrab.com	Miami Beach	FL	33139	305-673-0365		671
Joe's Tv & Appliance 223 Central Ave NE *Web:* joestvandappliance.com	Orange City	IA	51041	712-737-4254		35
Joel Asher Studio 13448 Albers St *Web:* www.joelasherstudio.com	Sherman Oaks	CA	91401	818-785-1551		423
Joel B. Castro Inc, A Professional Law Corp 11766 Wilshire Blvd Ste 250 *Web:* defectlaw.com	Los Angeles	CA	90025	310-966-6060		41
Joel Lane House Museum & Gardens 728 W Hargett St *Web:* www.joellane.org	Raleigh	NC	27603	919-833-3431		520
Joeris Inc 823 Arion Pky *Web:* www.joeris.com	San Antonio	TX	78216	210-494-1639		187
Joes Auto Parks 808 S Olive St **Fax Area Code:* 213 ■ *TF:* 855-895-0872 ■ *Web:* joesautoparks.com	Los Angeles	CA	90014	855-388-3496	742-7550*	714-1
Joes Sporting Goods - Ski Shop Inc 33 County Rd B E *Web:* www.joessportinggoods.com	Saint Paul	MN	55117	651-209-7800		711
Joester Loria Group Inc, The 30 Irving Pl 10th Fl *Web:* joesterloriagroup.com	New York	NY	10003	212-683-5150		226
JOEY Restaurants Rideau Centre Rideau St *Web:* joeyrestaurants.com	Ottawa	ON	K1N9J7	613-680-5639		671
Joey's Restaurant 6594 Thompson Rd *Web:* www.joeysitalianrestaurant.com	Syracuse	NY	13206	315-432-0315		671
Joey's Seafood Restaurants 3048 - 9 St SE *TF:* 800-661-2123 ■ *Web:* joeys.ca	Calgary	AB	T2G3B9	403-243-4584	243-8989	670
Joffrey Ballet of Chicago 10 E Randolph St *Web:* joffrey.org	Chicago	IL	60601	312-739-0120	739-0119	573-1

Name	Address	City	State	ZIP	Phone	Fax	Class
Joffrey's Coffee & Tea Co	3803 Corporex Pk Dr *TF:* 800-458-5282 ■ *Web:* www.joffreys.com	Tampa	FL	33619	813-250-0404		297-11
JOH	1 Progress Rd *Web:* www.johare.com	Billerica	MA	01821	978-663-9000	262-2200	297-8
Johanna Foods Inc	Johanna Farm Rd PO Box 272 *TF:* 800-727-6700 ■ *Web:* www.johannafoods.com	Flemington	NJ	08822	908-788-2200		296-20
Johannes Flowers Inc	4990 Foothill Rd *Web:* www.johannesflowers.com	Carpinteria	CA	93013	805-684-5686	566-2199	369
Johannes Leonardo	628 Broadway 6th Fl *Web:* johannesleonardo.com	New York	NY	10012	212-462-8120		7
Johannesen-Farrar Inc	512 E Walworth Ave *Web:* jfinsurance.com	Delavan	WI	53115	262-728-2631		390
JohannesRestaurants.com	196 S Indian Canyon Dr *Web:* johannespalmsprings.com	Palm Springs	CA	92262	760-778-0017		671
Johanson & Yau Accountancy Corp	160 W Santa Clara St Ste 900 *Web:* www.jyac.com	San Jose	CA	95113	408-288-5111		41
Johanson Dielectrics	4001 Calle Tecate *Web:* www.johansondielectrics.com	Camarillo	CA	93012	805-389-1166		696
Johanson Transportation Service Inc	5583 E Olive Ave. *TF:* 800-742-2053 ■ *Web:* www.johansontrans.com	Fresno	CA	93727	559-458-2200		311
John & Mable Ringling Museum of Art	5401 Bay Shore Rd *Web:* www.ringling.org	Sarasota	FL	34243	941-359-5700	360-7326	520
John A. Culhane CPA	755 Main St Bldg 1 *Web:* www.culhanecpa.com	Monroe	CT	06468	203-268-4431	268-6146	2
John A. Gupton College	1616 Church St *Web:* guptoncollege.edu	Nashville	TN	37203	615-327-3927	321-4518	800
John A. Jurgiel & Associates Inc	123 N Main St *Web:* www.jurgiel.com	Saint Charles	MO	63301	636-757-3060	757-3064	196
John A. Knapp & Associates Inc	3920 California Ave SW *Web:* jknappinc.com	Seattle	WA	98116	206-937-1551		734
John A. Logan College	700 Logan College Rd *Web:* www.jalc.edu	Carterville	IL	62918	618-985-2828		162
John A. Marshall Co	10930 Lackman Rd *Web:* www.jamarshall.com	Lenexa	KS	66219	913-599-4700	599-4838	320
John A. Martin & Association Inc	950 S Grand Ave 4th Fl. *TF:* 800-776-2368 ■ *Web:* www.johnmartin.com	Los Angeles	CA	90015	213-483-6490	483-3084	261
John A. Penney Company Inc	270 Sidney St *Web:* johnpenney.com	Cambridge	MA	02139	617-547-7744		189-4
John A. Van Den Bosch Co	4511 Holland Ave *TF:* 800-968-6477 ■ *Web:* vboschhome.com	Holland	MI	49424	616-848-2000		447
John A. Volpe National Transportation Systems Ctr	55 Broadway *Web:* www.volpe.dot.gov	Cambridge	MA	02142	617-494-2000		668
John Abbott College	21 275 Lakeshore Rd *Web:* www.johnabbott.qc.ca	Sainte-Anne-de-Bellevue	QC	H9X3L9	514-457-6610	457-4730	166
John Amico School of Hair Design	15301 S Cicero Ave *Web:* www.johnamicoschoolofhairdesign.com	Oak Forest	IL	60452	708-687-7800		685
John B. Malouf Inc	8201 Quaker Ave Ste 106 *TF:* 800-658-9500 ■ *Web:* www.maloufs.com	Lubbock	TX	79424	806-794-9500		157-4
John B. Sanfilippo & Son Inc	1703 N Randall Rd *NASDAQ: JBSS* ■ *Web:* jbssinc.com	Elgin	IL	60123	847-289-1800	289-1843	296-28
John B. Wright Agency Inc	64 Union Ave *Web:* johnbwright.com	Manasquan	NJ	08736	732-223-6611		390
John Ball Zoological Garden	1300 W Fulton St *Web:* www.jbzoo.org	Grand Rapids	MI	49504	616-336-4301	336-3907	823
John Bean Co	309 Exchange Ave. *TF:* 800-225-5786 ■ *Web:* www.johnbean.com	Conway	AR	72032	501-450-1500		60
John Berggruen Gallery	228 Grant Ave *Web:* www.berggruen.com	San Francisco	CA	94108	415-781-4629	781-0126	42
John Boos & Co	3601 S Banker St PO Box 609 *TF:* 888-431-2667 ■ *Web:* johnboos.com	Effingham	IL	62401	217-347-7701	347-7705	286
John Bouchard & Sons Co	1024 Harrison St *Web:* jbouchard.com	Nashville	TN	37203	615-256-0112		189-10
John Boyd Thacher State Park	1 Hailes Cave Rd *Web:* parks.ny.gov	Voorheesville	NY	12186	518-872-1237		565
John Brown Farm State Historic Site	115 John Brown Rd *Web:* parks.ny.gov	Lake Placid	NY	12946	518-523-3900		565
John Brown House Museum	52 Power St *Web:* www.rihs.org	Providence	RI	02906	401-273-7507		50-3
John Brown Limited Inc	PO Box 296 *Web:* www.johnbrownlimited.com	Peterborough	NH	03458	603-924-3834	924-7998	317
John Brown University	2000 W University St *TF:* 877-528-4636 ■ *Web:* www.jbu.edu	Siloam Springs	AR	72761	479-524-9500	524-4196	166
John Bryan State Park	3790 SR- 370 *Web:* ohiodnr.gov	Yellow Springs	OH	45387	937-767-1274		565
John Buchan Homes LLC	2821 Northup Way Ste 110 *Web:* www.buchan.com	Bellevue	WA	98004	425-827-2266		653
John Buck Co	151 N Franklin St Ste 300 *Web:* www.tjbc.com	Chicago	IL	60606	312-993-9800		653
John Bunning Transfer Company Inc	1600 Elk St *TF:* 800-443-2753 ■ *Web:* www.bunningtransfer.com	Rock Springs	WY	82901	307-362-3791		780
John Burns Construction Company Inc	17601 SW Hwy *Web:* www.jbconstructionco.com	Orland Park	IL	60467	708-326-3500		186
John C. Dolph Co	320 New Rd *TF:* 800-654-7652 ■ *Web:* www.dolphs.com	Monmouth Junction	NJ	08852	732-329-2333		481
John C. Flanagan House	942 NE Glen Oak Ave *Web:* www.peoriahistoricalsociety.com	Peoria	IL	61603	309-674-1921		50-3
John C. Hall	1200 Truxtun Ave Ste 114 *Web:* johnhalllaw.com	Bakersfield	CA	93301	661-328-1200		41
John C. Hart Memorial Library	1130 E Main St *Web:* www.yorktownlibrary.org	Shrub Oak	NY	10588	914-245-5262		434-3
John C. Heath, Attorney at Law PLLC	2875 S Decker Lake Dr *TF:* 833-333-8277 ■ *Web:* www.lexingtonlaw.com	West Valley City	UT	84119	833-333-8277		428
John C. Mallett Insurance Agency Inc	15 Mallett Way *Web:* johnmallett.com	Bluffton	SC	29910	843-815-4888		390
John C. Nordt Company Inc	1420 Coulter Dr NW *Web:* www.jcnordt.com	Roanoke	VA	24012	540-362-9717		409
John C. Proctor Endowment	2724 W Reservoir Blvd *Web:* proctorplace.org	Peoria	IL	61615	309-685-6580	566-4292	450
John C. R. Kelly Realty	3535 Blvd of the Allies *Web:* www.jcrkelly.com	Pittsburgh	PA	15213	412-683-7300		652
John C. Willis, IV PA	801 N Orange Ave Ste 830 *Web:* jcwillislaw.com	Orlando	FL	32801	407-712-2599		41
John Cannon Homes Inc	6710 Professional Pkwy W *Web:* www.johncannonhomes.com	Sarasota	FL	34240	941-924-5935	924-4129	187
John Carlo Inc	45000 River Ridge Dr	Clinton Township	MI	48038	586-465-4661	226-5645	188-4
John Carroll School, The	703 Churchville Rd *Web:* johncarroll.org	Bel Air	MD	21014	410-879-2480	836-8514	685
John Carroll University	20700 N Pk Blvd *TF:* 888-335-6800 ■ *Web:* www.jcu.edu	Cleveland	OH	44118	216-397-1886	397-4981	166
John Chadds House	1736 N Creek Rd PO Box 27 *Web:* www.chaddsfordhistory.org	Chadds Ford	PA	19317	610-388-7376	388-7480	50-3
John Colegrove Inc	3613 Braselton Hwy Ste 102 *Web:* caldercolegrove.com	Suwanee	GA	30024	678-482-0686		217
John Cooper School	1 John Cooper Dr *TF:* 800-295-1162 ■ *Web:* www.johncooper.org	The Woodlands	TX	77381	281-367-0900		685
John Crane Canada Inc	423 Green Rd N *Web:* www.johncrane.com	Stoney Creek	ON	L8E3A1	905-662-6191		326
John D. & Catherine T. MacArthur Foundation	140 S Dearborn St *Web:* www.macfound.org	Chicago	IL	60603	312-726-0000	920-6258	305
John D. Bradshaw PC	107 W Michigan Ave 6th Fl *Web:* johndbradshawpc.com	Kalamazoo	MI	49007	269-373-4400	373-4550	41
John D. MacArthur Beach State Park	10900 SR 703 (A1A) *Web:* www.floridastateparks.org	North Palm Beach	FL	33408	561-624-6950		565
John D. Rockefeller Jr Memorial Parkway	PO Box 170 *Web:* www.nps.gov	Moose	WY	83012	307-739-3300	739-3438	564
John D. Sileo LLC	320 N Carrollton Ave Ste 101 *Web:* johnsileolaw.com	New Orleans	LA	70119	504-486-4343		41
John D. Smith Company LPA	140 N Main St *Web:* johndsmith.com	Springboro	OH	45066	937-748-2522	748-2712	41
John Dallas Bowers LLC (JDB)	219 Radnor-Chester Rd *Web:* www.johndallasbowers.com	Villanova	PA	19085	610-989-9234	989-9236	4
John Day Co	6263 Abbott Dr *TF:* 800-767-2273 ■ *Web:* www.johnday.com	Omaha	NE	68110	402-455-8000		274
John Day Fossil Beds National Monument	32651 Hwy 19 *Web:* www.nps.gov	Kimberly	OR	97848	541-987-2333		564
John Degrand & Son Inc	430 Island Ln *Web:* degrandandson.com	West Haven	CT	06516	203-933-7726		311
John Deklewa & Sons Inc	1273 Washington Pke PO Box 158	Bridgeville	PA	15017	412-257-9000		186
John Dickinson Plantation	340 Kitts Hummock Rd *Web:* history.delaware.gov	Dover	DE	19901	302-739-3277		50-3
John E. Biggiani, Esq. LLC	40 Parker Rd Ste 101 *Web:* biggilaw.com	Elizabeth	NJ	07208	908-469-3710	469-3712	41
John E. Campbell & Associates Ltd	1801 Mill St Ste H *Web:* cfgrp.net	Naperville	IL	60563	630-420-1231		734
John E. Green	220 Victor Ave *TF:* 888-918-7002 ■ *Web:* www.johnegreen.com	Highland Park	MI	48203	313-868-2400	868-0011	189-10
John E. Jones Oil Company Inc	1016 S Cedar PO Box 546 *TF:* 800-323-9821 ■ *Web:* www.jonesoil.net	Stockton	KS	67669	785-425-6746	425-6323	186
John E. Koerner & Company Inc	4820 Jefferson Hwy *TF:* 800-333-1913 ■ *Web:* www.koerner-co.com	New Orleans	LA	70121	800-333-1913		297-11

	Phone	Fax	Class
John E. Sharts 5 Fairway Dr PO Box 350 Springboro OH 45066 *Web:* shartslaw.com	937-748-2761		41
John E. Virga Inc 721 Eleventh St. Sacramento CA 95814 *Web:* virgalawfirm.com	916-444-6595		41
John Elway Chevrolet 5200 S Broadway Englewood CO 80113 *TF:* 866-273-4757 ■ *Web:* www.johnelwaychevrolet.com	720-259-0395		57
John Ernst Agency 126 N 30th St Ste 103 Quincy IL 62301	217-223-4127		390
John Evans' Sons Inc 1 Spring Ave PO Box 885 Lansdale PA 19446 *Web:* www.springcompany.com	215-368-7700	368-9019	719
John F. Kennedy Space Ctr. Merritt Island FL 32899 *TF:* 866-737-5235 ■ *Web:* www.nasa.gov	321-867-5000		668
John F. Kennedy Hyannis Museum 397 Main St Hyannis MA 02601 *Web:* jfkhyannismuseum.org	508-790-3077		520
John F. Kennedy International Airport (JFK) 150 Greenwich St New York NY 10007 **Fax Area Code:* 201 ■ *Web:* www.jfkairport.com	212-435-7000	871-2343*	27
John F. Kennedy Library 500 Hoes Ln Piscataway NJ 08854 *Web:* piscatawaylibrary.org	732-463-1633		434-3
John F. Kennedy Library (JFKL) 190 W 49th St. Hialeah FL 33012 *Web:* www.hialeahfl.gov	305-821-2700		434-3
John F. Kennedy National Historic Site 83 Beals St Brookline MA 02446 *Web:* www.nps.gov	617-566-7937	730-9884	564
John F. Kennedy Presidential Library & Museum Columbia Pt Boston MA 02125 *TF:* 866-535-1960 ■ *Web:* www.jfklibrary.org	617-514-1600	514-1652	434-2
John F. Kennedy University 100 Ellinwood Way Pleasant Hill CA 94523 *TF:* 800-696-5358 ■ *Web:* www.jfku.edu	925-969-3300	969-3101	166
John F. Little 49 E Center St Ste 101 Nazareth PA 18064 *Web:* johnflittle.com	610-759-6400		390
John F. Long Properties LLLP 1118 E Missouri Ave Ste A Phoenix AZ 85014 **Fax Area Code:* 623 ■ *Web:* www.jflongproperties.com	602-272-0421	846-7208*	655
John F. Otto Inc 1717 Second St. Sacramento CA 95811 *Web:* ottoconstruction.com	916-441-6870	441-6138	188-10
John F. Sutherland & Associates Insurance Services Inc 6275 Lusk Blvd San Diego CA 92121	858-535-1139		390
John F. Trompeter Co 314 E Burnett Ave Louisville KY 40208 *Web:* trompeters.com	502-585-5852		756
John Fabick Tractor Co 1 Fabick Dr Fenton MO 63026 *TF:* 800-845-9188 ■ *Web:* www.fabickcat.com	636-343-5900	343-4910	358
John G. Cleminshaw Inc 3928 Clock Pointe Trl Ste 103 Stow OH 44224 *TF:* 888-650-4300 ■ *Web:* johngcleminshawinc.com	888-650-4300	650-4301	192
John G. Riley Center/Museum of African American History & Culture 419 E Jefferson St. Tallahassee FL 32301 *Web:* www.rileymuseum.org	850-681-7881	681-7000	520
John G. Shedd Aquarium 1200 S Lake Shore Dr. Chicago IL 60605 *Web:* www.sheddaquarium.org	312-939-2438		40
John G. Ullman & Associates Inc 51 E Market St Corning NY 14830 *TF:* 800-936-3785 ■ *Web:* jgua.com	607-936-3785		401
John Gallin & Son Inc 102 Madison Ave 9th Fl New York NY 10016 *Web:* www.gallin.com	212-252-8900		186
John Gerlach & Company LLP 37 W Broad St Ste 530 Columbus OH 43215 *Web:* www.johngerlach.com	614-224-2164	224-1391	2
John Gorrie Museum State Park 46 Sixth St PO Box 267 Apalachicola FL 32320 *Web:* www.floridastateparks.org	850-653-9347		565
John H. Fisher PC 278 Wall St Kingston NY 12401 *Web:* protectingpatientrights.com	845-802-0047		41
John H. Hampshire Inc 320 W 24th St. Baltimore MD 21211 *Web:* www.jhhampshire.com	410-366-8900	467-7391	189-2
John Hancock Financial Services Inc 601 Congress St. Boston MA 02210 *Web:* www.johnhancock.com	617-572-6000	663-2470	360-4
John Hancock Funds 601 Congress St Boston MA 02210 *TF:* 800-338-8080 ■ *Web:* www.jhinvestments.com	617-572-9167		528
John Harris-Simon Cameron Mansion, The 219 S Front St Harrisburg PA 17104 *TF:* 800-732-0099 ■ *Web:* www.dauphincountyhistory.org	717-233-3462	233-6059	50-3
John Heath & Company Inc 950 S Tamiami Trl Ste 102 Sarasota FL 34236 *Web:* www.jheathco.com	941-955-5005	955-5252	796
John Henry Co 5800 W Grand River Ave Lansing MI 48906 *TF:* 800-748-0517 ■ *Web:* www.jhc.com	517-323-9000		626
John Henry Foster Minnesota Inc 3103 Mike Collins Dr Eagan MN 55121 *TF:* 800-582-5162 ■ *Web:* jhfoster.com	651-452-8452		172
John Henry's Cafe 1785 E Tahquitz Canyon Way Palm Springs CA 92262 *Web:* www.johnhenryscafe.com	760-327-7667		671
John Hersey High School 1900 E Thomas St Arlington Heights IL 60004 *Web:* jhhs.d214.org	847-718-4800		685
John Hine Mazda Inc 1545 Camino Del Rio S San Diego CA 92108 *Web:* www.johnhine.com	619-297-4251		57
John Hoadley & Sons Inc 672 Union St Rockland MA 02370 *Web:* hoadleyandsons.com	781-878-8098		189-10
John Hofmeister & Son Inc 2386 S Blue Island Ave. Chicago IL 60608 *TF:* 800-923-4267 ■ *Web:* www.hofhaus.com	773-847-0700		296-26
John Holmlund Nursery LLC 29285 SE Hwy 212 Boring OR 97009 *TF:* 800-643-6650 ■ *Web:* www.jhnsy.com	503-663-6650	663-2350	192

	Phone	Fax	Class
John Hsu Capital Group Inc 747 3rd Ave 26th Fl New York NY 10017 *Web:* www.johnhsucapital.com	212-223-7515		401
John J. Campbell Company Inc 6012 Resources Dr Memphis TN 38134 *Web:* www.campbellroofing.com	901-372-8400		189-12
John J. Hoober Inc 3216 Mill Ln Gordonville PA 17529 *Web:* www.hooberfeeds.com	717-768-3216		276
John J. Palmeri Attorney At Law LLC 515 Highland Ave PO Box 297 Cheshire CT 06410 *Web:* palmerilaw.com	203-699-9132	699-9235	41
John J. Pershing Veterans Affairs Medical Ctr 1500 N Westwood Blvd. Poplar Bluff MO 63901 *TF:* 888-557-8262 ■ *Web:* www.poplarbluff.va.gov	573-686-4151		374-8
John J. Smith Masonry Co 9200 Green Park Rd Saint Louis MO 63123 *Web:* www.smithmasonry.com	314-894-9500	894-1172	189-7
John James Audubon State Park 3100 US Hwy 41 N Henderson KY 42419 *Web:* parks.ky.gov	270-826-2247		565
John Jasperse Projects 140 Second Ave Ste 501 New York NY 10003 *Web:* johnjasperse.org	646-642-9572		573-1
John Jay Homestead State Historic Site PO Box 832 Katonah NY 10536 *Web:* parks.ny.gov	914-232-5651		565
John K. Zaid & Associates PLLC 16951 Feather Craft Ln Houston TX 77058 *Web:* zaidlaw.com	281-333-8959		41
John Keal Music Company Inc 819 Livingston Ave Albany NY 12206 *TF:* 800-544-6631 ■ *Web:* www.johnkealmusic.com	518-482-4405	482-4426	526
John Knox Village 651 SW 6th St. Pompano Beach FL 33060 *TF:* 800-998-5669 ■ *Web:* johnknoxvillage.com	954-783-4040		672
John Knox Village of the Rio Grande Valley 1300 S Border Ave Weslaco TX 78596 *Web:* johnknoxvillagergv.com	956-968-4575		672
John Levy Consulting 505 Mesa Rd PO Box 1419 Point Reyes Station CA 94956 *Web:* johnlevyconsulting.com	415-663-1818		463
John Lyman Center for the Performing Arts 501 Crescent St New Haven CT 06515 *Web:* tickets.southernct.edu	203-392-6154		572
John M. Browning Firearms Museum 2501 Wall Ave. Ogden UT 84401 *Web:* theunionstation.org	801-393-9890		520
John M. Campbell & Co 1215 Crossroads Blvd Norman OK 73072 *TF:* 800-821-5933 ■ *Web:* www.jmcampbell.com	405-321-1383		261
John M. Cichelero PC 8008 Carondelet Ave Ste 304 Clayton MO 63105 *TF:* 877-449-7325	314-205-2886		41
John M. Floyd & Associates Inc (JMFA) 125 N Burnett Dr. Baytown TX 77520 *TF:* 800-809-2307 ■ *Web:* www.jmfa.com	281-424-3800	424-8864	194
John M. Hartel & Company Inc 144 N Kinderkamack Rd Montvale NJ 07645 *Web:* jmhartel.com	845-735-3666		38
John M. Leask II CPA LLC 765 Post Rd Fairfield CT 06824 *Web:* www.leaskbv.com	203-255-3805	380-1289	2
John Manlove Marketing & Communications 5125 Preston Rd. Pasadena TX 77505 *Web:* www.johnmanlove.com	281-487-6767		627
John Masters Organic Hair Care Inc 77 Sullivan St. New York NY 10012 *Web:* johnmasters.com	212-343-9590		77
John Matouk Company Inc 118 W 22nd S 9th Fl. New York NY 10011 *Web:* www.matouk.com	212-683-9242		361
John Michael Kohler Arts Ctr 608 New York Ave. Sheboygan WI 53081 *Web:* www.jmkac.org	920-458-6144		520
John Morrell & Co 805 E Kemper Rd Cincinnati OH 45246 *TF:* 800-722-1127 ■ *Web:* www.johnmorrell.com	513-346-3540		473
John Motta 312 N Ave E Ste 1 Cranford NJ 07016 *Web:* johnmottalaw.com	908-272-4300		41
John Muir Medical Ctr (JMMC) 1601 Ygnacio Valley Rd Walnut Creek CA 94598 *TF:* 844-398-5376 ■ *Web:* www.johnmuirhealth.com	925-939-3000	308-8944	374-3
John Muir National Historic Site 4202 Alhambra Ave. Martinez CA 94553 *Web:* www.nps.gov	925-228-8860	228-8192	564
John Mullen and Company Inc 677 Ala Moana Blvd Ste 910 Honolulu HI 96813 *Web:* www.johnmullen.com	808-531-9733	531-0053	390
John N John Truck Line 1213 W 2nd St Crowley LA 70527 *TF:* 800-467-8222 ■ *Web:* www.johnnjohn.net	800-467-8222		780
John N. Calvino, Esq. Ltd 373 Elmwood Ave. Providence RI 02907 *Web:* calvinolaw.com	401-785-9400		41
John Nagle & Co 306 N Ave Boston MA 02210 *Web:* www.johnnagle.com	617-542-9418	423-7830	297-5
John Newcombe Tennis Ranch Inc 325 Mission Valley Rd New Braunfels TX 78132 *TF:* 800-444-6204 ■ *Web:* www.newktennis.com	830-625-9105	625-2004	379
John Nuzzo 7428 W Belmont Chicago IL 60634 *Web:* johnnuzzo.com	773-889-3900		390
John Patrick Publishing Company Inc 1707 4th St. Trenton NJ 08638 *TF:* 800-333-3166 ■ *Web:* www.jppc.net	609-883-2700	883-8821	637-10
John Paul Mitchell Systems 1888 Century Pk E Ste 1600 Los Angeles CA 90067 *TF:* 800-793-8790 ■ *Web:* www.paulmitchell.com	800-027-4066		214
John Peter Smith Hospital 1500 S Main St. Fort Worth TX 76104 *Web:* www.jpshealthnet.org	817-702-1100		374-3

Name / Address	City	State	ZIP	Phone	Fax	Class
John Q. Hammons Hotels and Resorts 300 John Q Hammons Pky *Web:* www.jqhhotels.com	Springfield	MO	65806	417-864-4300		379
John R. Hess & Company Inc 400 Stn St PO Box 3615 *TF:* 800-828-4377 ■ *Web:* www.jrhessco.com	Cranston	RI	02910	401-785-9300	785-2510	146
John R. Ianelli PC 804 Rt 9 Ste 2 *Web:* ianellilaw.com	Fishkill	NY	12524	845-896-7900		41
John R. Jurgensen Co 11641 Mosteller Rd *Web:* www.jrjnet.com	Cincinnati	OH	45241	513-771-0820		188-4
John R. Nalbach Engineering Co 621 E Plainfield Rd *Web:* www.nalbach.com	Countryside	IL	60525	708-579-9100	579-0122	547
John R. Wald Company Inc 10576 Fairgrounds Rd *Web:* www.jrwald.com	Huntingdon	PA	16652	814-643-3908	643-5300	295
John R. White Company Inc 200 Citation Ct Ste 100 *TF:* 800-245-1183 ■ *Web:* johnrwhite.com	Birmingham	AL	35202	205-595-8381	595-8386	146
John R. Williams & Associates LLC 51 Elm St *Web:* johnrwilliams.com	New Haven	CT	06510	203-562-9931		41
John Roberts Co 9687 E River Rd NW *TF:* 800-551-1534 ■ *Web:* www.johnroberts.com	Minneapolis	MN	55433	763-755-5500	755-0394	627
John Rohrer Contracting Company Inc 2820 Roe Ln *Web:* johnrohrercontracting.com	Kansas City	KS	66103	913-236-5005	236-7291	189-3
John S. & James L. Knight Foundation 200 S Biscayne Blvd Ste 3300 *Web:* knightfoundation.org	Miami	FL	33131	305-908-2600		305
John S. Grimm Inc 4559 Abbeyville Rd. *Web:* saltdistributormedinaoh.com	Medina	OH	44256	330-725-5334		311
John S. Knight Ctr 77 E Mill St. *TF:* 800-245-4254 ■ *Web:* www.johnsknightcenter.org	Akron	OH	44308	330-374-8900		205
John Sakash Company Inc 700 Walnut St. *TF:* 800-929-3940 ■ *Web:* www.johnsakash.com	Elmhurst	IL	60126	630-833-3940	833-9830	492
John Searcy & Associates Inc 6320 St Augustine Rd *Web:* searcyengineering.com	Jacksonville	FL	32217	904-739-1231		261
John Seybold & Company Ltd 800 Busse Hwy *Web:* www.johnseybold.com	Park Ridge	IL	60068	847-696-1060	696-2249	2
John Simon Guggenheim Memorial Foundation 90 Park Ave. *TF:* 800-232-0960 ■ *Web:* www.gf.org	New York	NY	10016	212-687-4470	697-3248	305
John Snow Inc 44 Farnsworth St. *Web:* www.jsi.com	Boston	MA	02210	617-482-9485	482-0617	194
John St 172 John St *Web:* www.johnst.com	Toronto	ON	M5T1X5	416-348-0048		7
John Staurulakis Inc (JSI) 7852 Walker Dr Ste 200 *Web:* www.jsitel.com	Greenbelt	MD	20770	301-459-7590		194
John Steinbeck Library 350 Lincoln Ave *Web:* www.salinaspubliclibrary.org	Salinas	CA	93901	831-758-7311		434-3
John Stewart Company Inc 1388 Sutter St 1st Fl. *Web:* jsco.net	San Francisco	CA	94109	415-345-4400	614-9175	652
John T. Costa Agency Inc 2025 Hamburg Tpke Ste J *Web:* burglaralarminsurance.com	Wayne	NJ	07470	973-835-8444		390
John T. Cyr & Sons Inc 153 Gilman Falls Ave *TF:* 800-244-2335 ■ *Web:* johntcyrandsons.com	Old Town	ME	04468	207-827-2335	827-6763	109
John T. Ferreira & Son Inc 500 Centre St *TF:* 800-940-8951 ■ *Web:* century21ferreira.com	Fernandina Beach	FL	32034	904-261-5571		652
John T. Lally CPA PC 69 Alden Rd *Web:* jtlcpa.net	Fairhaven	MA	02719	508-992-6500		2
John T. Mather Memorial Hospital 75 N Country Rd. *Web:* www.matherhospital.org	Port Jefferson	NY	11777	631-473-1320	476-2792	374-3
John Tanner State Park 354 Tanner's Beach Rd *Web:* gastateparks.org	Carrollton	GA	30117	770-830-2222		565
John Templeton Foundation 300 Conshohocken State Rd Ste 500 *Web:* www.templeton.org	West Conshohocken	PA	19428	610-941-2828	825-1730	305
John Tyler Community College 13101 Jefferson Davis Hwy *TF:* 800-552-3490 ■ *Web:* jtcc.edu	Chester	VA	23831	804-796-4000	796-4362	162
John U. Lloyd Beach State Park 6503 N Ocean Dr *Web:* www.floridastateparks.org	Dania Beach	FL	33004	954-923-2833		565
John Varvatos Enterprises Inc 26 W 17th St 12th Fl. *TF:* 800-780-5838 ■ *Web:* www.johnvarvatos.com	New York	NY	10011	800-780-5838		155-3
John Vena Inc 6700 Essington Ave Units F1 - F6 *Web:* www.johnvenaproduce.com	Philadelphia	PA	19153	215-336-0766	336-2812	297-2
John W. Bristol & Company Inc 48 Wall St 18th Fl. *Web:* www.jwbristol.com	New York	NY	10005	212-389-5880		401
John W. Danforth Co 300 Colvin Woods Pkwy *TF:* 800-888-6119 ■ *Web:* www.jwdanforth.com	Tonawanda	NY	14150	716-832-1940	832-2388	189-10
John W. Kyle State Park 4235 State Park Rd *Web:* www.mdwfp.com	Sardis	MS	38666	662-487-1345		565
John W. McDougall Company Inc (JWMCD) 3731 Amy Lynn Dr *Web:* www.jwmcd.com	Nashville	TN	37218	615-321-3900	329-9069	697
John W. Ramsey 8181 S Harvard *Web:* johnwramsey.com	Tulsa	OK	74137	918-481-1411		390
John W. Stone Oil Distributor LLC 87 First St **Fax Area Code:* 225 ■ *Web:* www.stoneoil.com	Gretna	LA	70053	504-366-3401	819-1943*	579
John Waddell & Company CPAS 3416 American River Dr Ste A *Web:* jwaddell.com	Sacramento	CA	95864	916-488-2460		2
John Watson Chevrolet 3535 Wall Ave *TF:* 866-647-9930 ■ *Web:* www.johnwatsonchevrolet.com	Ogden	UT	84401	801-394-2611		57
John Watts Associates Inc 45 Pratt St Ste 200 *Web:* jwatts.com	Hartford	CT	06103	860-528-1110		366
John Wayne Airport 18601 Airport Way *Web:* www.ocair.com	Santa Ana	CA	92707	949-252-5200		27
John Wayne Birthplace & Museum 205 S John Wayne Dr. *TF:* 877-462-1044 ■ *Web:* www.johnwaynebirthplace.museum	Winterset	IA	50273	515-462-1044		520
John Wesley International Barber & Beauty College 717 Pine Ave. *Web:* www.johnwesleybarberbeauty.com	Long Beach	CA	90813	562-435-7060	435-0480	166
John Wieland Homes & Neighborhoods 4125 Atlanta Rd SE *TF:* 800-376-4663 ■ *Web:* www.jwhomes.com	Smyrna	GA	30080	770-996-2400	907-3481	653
John Wiley & Sons Inc 111 River St *NYSE:* JW.A ■ **Fax Area Code:* 201 ■ *TF:* 800-225-5945 ■ *Web:* www.wiley.com	Hoboken	NJ	07030	877-762-2974	748-6088*	637-2
John Wingate Weeks Historic Site 200 Weeks State Park Rd *Web:* www.nhstateparks.org	Lancaster	NH	03584	603-788-4004		565
John Wolf Florist 6228 Waters Ave. *TF:* 800-944-6435 ■ *Web:* www.johnwolfflorist.com	Savannah	GA	31406	912-352-9843		292
John Wood Community College 1301 S 48th St *Web:* www.jwcc.edu	Quincy	IL	62305	217-224-6500	641-4192	162
John Zink Hamworthy Combustion 11920 E Apache St *TF:* 800-421-9242 ■ *Web:* www.johnzinkhamworthy.com	Tulsa	OK	74116	918-234-1800	234-2700	357
John's Pass Village & Boardwalk 150 John's Pass Boardwalk Pl *TF:* 800-853-1536 ■ *Web:* www.johnspass.com	Madeira Beach	FL	33708	727-398-6577		50-6
Johncarroll.com PO Box 2430 *Web:* www.johncarroll.com	Mount Pleasant	SC	29465	843-881-8815		194
JohnDow Industries Inc 151 Snyder Ave. *TF:* 800-433-0708 ■ *Web:* www.johndow.com	Barberton	OH	44203	330-753-6895		54
John-Kenyon Eye Ctr 1305 Wall St. *TF:* 800-342-5393 ■ *Web:* www.johnkenyon.com	Jeffersonville	IN	47130	800-342-5393		798
Johnny Appleseed Visitors' Ctr 1000 Rte 2 Westbound *Web:* www.visitnorthcentral.com	Lancaster	MA	01523	978-534-2302		138
Johnny Cupcakes 36 Finnell Dr Ste 1 *TF:* 866-606-2253 ■ *Web:* www.johnnycupcakes.com	Weymouth	MA	02188	866-606-2253		810
Johnny Janosik Inc 11151 Trussum Pond Rd *TF:* 888-875-8955 ■ *Web:* www.johnnyjanosik.com	Laurel	DE	19956	302-875-5955		321
Johnny Londoff Chevrolet Inc 1375 Dunn Rd *Web:* www.londoff.com	Florissant	MO	63031	314-837-1800		57
Johnny Rebs' Southern Roadhouse 4663 Long Beach Blvd *Web:* johnnyrebs.com	Long Beach	CA	90805	562-423-7327		671
Johnny Rockets 2 S Pointe Dr Ste 200	Lake Forest	CA	92630	949-643-6100		671
Johnny's 4245 W Fourth St. *Web:* www.johnnysristorante.com	Reno	NV	89523	775-747-4511		671
Johnny's Bar on Fulton 3164 Fulton Rd. *Web:* www.johnnyscleveland.com	Cleveland	OH	44109	216-281-0055		671
Johnny's Cafe 4702 S 27th St *Web:* www.johnnyscafe.com	Omaha	NE	68107	402-731-4774		671
Johnny's Dock 1900 E D St *Web:* www.johnnysdock.com	Tacoma	WA	98421	253-627-3186		671
Johnny's Fine Foods Inc 319 E 25th St. *TF:* 800-962-1462 ■ *Web:* johnnysfinefoods.com	Tacoma	WA	98421	253-383-4597		296-37
Johnny's Half Shell 1819 Columbia Rd NW *Web:* www.johnnyshalfshell.net	Washington	DC	20009	202-506-5257		671
Johnny's Pizza House Inc 230 N Glynn St *Web:* www.johnnyspizza.com	Fayetteville	GA	30214	770-461-4225		670
Johnny's Selected Seeds 955 Benton Ave. *TF:* 877-564-6697 ■ *Web:* www.johnnyseeds.com	Winslow	ME	04901	877-564-6697		694
Johns Dental Laboratory Inc 423 S 13th St *TF:* 800-457-0504 ■ *Web:* www.johnsdental.com	Terre Haute	IN	47807	812-232-6026		383
Johns Eastern Company Inc PO Box 110259 **Fax Area Code:* 813 ■ *TF:* 877-326-5326 ■ *Web:* www.johnseastern.com	Lakewood Ranch	FL	34211	941-907-3100	402-7913*	390
Johns Greenhouse & Florist Shop 517 Copeland St. *Web:* www.johnsgreenhouses-florist.com	Brockton	MA	02301	508-588-0955		292
Johns Hopkins Hospital 600 N Wolfe St *Web:* www.hopkinsmedicine.org	Baltimore	MD	21287	410-955-5000		374-3
Johns Hopkins University 3400 N Charles St *Web:* www.jhu.edu	Baltimore	MD	21218	410-516-8000	516-6025	166
Johns Hopkins University Applied Physics Laboratory 11100 Johns Hopkins Rd *Web:* www.jhuapl.edu	Laurel	MD	20723	240-228-5000	228-1093	668
Johns Hopkins University Press 2715 N Charles St *Web:* www.press.jhu.edu	Baltimore	MD	21218	410-516-6900	516-6998	637-4
Johns Manville Corp 717 17th St PO Box 5108 *TF:* 800-654-3103 ■ *Web:* www.jm.com	Denver	CO	80217	800-922-5922		389

Listing	City	State	ZIP	Phone	Fax	Class
Johns Monroe Mitsunaga Kolouskova PLLC 11201 SE Eighth St *Web:* jmmklanduselaw.com	Bellevue	WA	98004	425-451-2812		41
Johns Pharmacy Lllp 2001 Independence St *TF:* 800-540-9222 ■ *Web:* johnsrx.com	Cape Girardeau	MO	63703	573-334-1300		237
JohnsByrne Co 6701 W Oakton St *Web:* www.johnsbyrne.com	Niles	IL	60714	847-583-3100		627
Johnson & Bell Ltd 33 W Monroe St Ste 2700 *Web:* johnsonandbell.com	Chicago	IL	60603	312-372-0770	372-9818	428
Johnson & Johnson Consumer Products Co 199 Grandview Rd *TF:* 866-565-2229 ■ *Web:* www.johnsonsbaby.com	Skillman	NJ	08558	908-874-1000		214
Johnson & Johnson Development Corp 1 Johnson & Johnson Plz *NYSE: JNJ* ■ *Web:* www.jnj.com	New Brunswick	NJ	08933	732-524-0400		792
Johnson & Johnson Inc 890 Woodlawn Rd W *TF:* 877-223-9807 ■ *Web:* www.jnjcanada.com	Guelph	ON	N1K1A5	877-223-9807		214
Johnson & Johnson Vision Care Inc 7500 Centurion Pkwy *TF:* 800-843-2020 ■ *Web:* www.jnjvisionpro.com	Jacksonville	FL	32256	800-874-5278		542
Johnson & Jordan Inc 18 Mussey Rd *Web:* www.johnsonandjordan.com	Scarborough	ME	04074	207-883-8345	883-8619	610
Johnson & Mackowiak 70 E Main St *Web:* jma-cpas.com	Fredonia	NY	14063	716-672-4770	679-1512	2
Johnson & Martin PA 500 W Cypress Creek Rd Ste 430 *Web:* johnsonmartinlaw.com	Fort Lauderdale	FL	33309	954-790-6700		41
Johnson & Mock Attorneys at Law 307 N Oakland Ave *Web:* www.johnsonandmock.com	Oakland	NE	68045	402-685-5647		445
Johnson & Montas PA 1290 Federal Hwy 1 *Web:* jbclaw.com	Rockledge	FL	32955	321-636-9600		41
Johnson & Pace Inc 1201 W Loop 281 Ste 100 *Web:* www.johnsonpace.com	Longview	TX	75604	903-753-0663		261
Johnson - Prewitt & Associates Inc 850 W Ventura Ave *Web:* johnsonprewitt.com	Clewiston	FL	33440	863-983-9188		261
Johnson & Quin Inc 7460 N Lehigh Ave *Web:* j-quin.com	Niles	IL	60714	847-588-4800		5
Johnson & Rountree Premium Inc 6160 Lusk Blvd Ste C-203 *TF:* 800-578-3300 ■ *Web:* jrpremium.com	San Diego	CA	92121	858-259-5846	500-7206	160
Johnson & Sheldon PC 500 S Taylor Plz II Ste 200 *Web:* www.amacpas.com	Amarillo	TX	79105	806-371-7661		734
Johnson & Shute PS 11130 NE 33rd Pl Ste 102 *Web:* www.johnsonandshute.com	Bellevue	WA	98004	425-827-5755	827-3322	2
Johnson & Wales University *Providence* 8 Abbott Pk Pl *TF:* 800-342-5598 ■ *Web:* www.jwu.edu	Providence	RI	02903	401-598-1000		166
Johnson and Towers Inc 2021 Briggs Rd *Web:* www.johnsontowers.com	Mount Laurel	NJ	08054	856-234-6990	222-2414	385
Johnson Bank 4001 N Main St *TF:* 888-769-3796 ■ *Web:* www.johnsonfinancialgroup.com	Racine	WI	53402	262-639-6010		70
Johnson Bill (Rep R - OH) 2336 Rayburn House Office Bldg *Web:* www.billjohnson.house.gov	Washington	DC	20515	202-225-5705	225-5907	342-2
Johnson Brass & Machine Foundry Inc 270 N Mill St PO Box 80219 *Web:* johnsoncentrifugal.com	Saukville	WI	53080	262-377-9440	284-7066	308
Johnson Bros Bakery Supply Inc 10731 I H 35 N **Fax Area Code: 210* ■ *TF:* 800-590-2575 ■ *Web:* jbrosbakerysupply.com	San Antonio	TX	78233	800-590-2575	599-3102*	297-8
Johnson Bros Metal Forming Co 5744 McDermott Dr *Web:* www.johnsonrollforming.com	Berkeley	IL	60163	708-449-7050	449-0042	480
Johnson Bros Rubber Co 42 W Buckeye St PO Box 812 *Web:* www.johnsonbrosrubbercompany.com	West Salem	OH	44287	419-853-4122		677
Johnson Bros Wholesale Liquor Co 1999 Shepard Rd *Web:* www.johnsonbrothers.com	Saint Paul	MN	55116	651-649-5800		81-3
Johnson Brothers Lumber 2550 E Ballina Rd *Web:* www.johnsonbrotherslumber.com	Cazenovia	NY	13035	315-655-8824	655-4449	683
Johnson C. Smith University 100 Beatties Ford Rd *TF:* 800-782-7303 ■ *Web:* www.jcsu.edu	Charlotte	NC	28216	704-378-1000	378-1242	166
Johnson Carlier Inc 738 S 52nd St *Web:* www.johnsoncarlier.com	Tempe	AZ	85281	602-275-2222		780
Johnson City Press 204 W Main St *TF:* 800-949-3111 ■ *Web:* www.johnsoncitypress.com	Johnson City	TN	37604	423-929-3111	929-7484	532-2
Johnson City Public Library 100 W Millard St *Web:* www.jcpl.org	Johnson City	TN	37604	423-434-4450	434-4469	434-3
Johnson City Symphony Orchestra 172 W Springbrook Dr *Web:* www.jcsymphony.com	Johnson City	TN	37604	423-926-8742		573-3
Johnson City/Jonesborough/Washington County Chamber of Commerce 603 E Market St *Web:* www.johnsoncitytnchamber.com	Johnson City	TN	37601	423-461-8000		139
Johnson College 3427 N Main Ave *TF:* 800-293-9675 ■ *Web:* www.johnson.edu	Scranton	PA	18508	570-342-6404	348-2181	800
Johnson Concrete Products 217 Klumac Rd *Web:* www.johnsonproductsusa.com	Salisbury	NC	28144	704-636-5231		183
Johnson Contracting Company Inc 2750 Morton Dr *Web:* jccinc.com	East Moline	IL	61244	309-755-0601		189-10
Johnson Controls Fire & Security Solutions 5757 N Green Bay Ave PO Box 591 *Web:* www.johnsoncontrols.com	Milwaukee	WI	53201	414-524-1200		692
Johnson County 76 N Main St *Web:* www.johnsoncountywyoming.org	Buffalo	WY	82834	307-684-7272	684-2708	338
Johnson County 215 W Main St *Web:* johnsoncounty.arkansas.gov	Clarksville	AR	72830	479-754-2175		338
Johnson County 204 S Buffalo Ave *Web:* www.johnsoncountytx.org	Cleburne	TX	76033	817-556-6323	556-6849	338
Johnson County 5 E Jefferson St 1st Fl *Web:* co.johnson.in.us	Franklin	IN	46131	317-346-4700	736-3749	338
Johnson County 325 E Washington St Johnson County Administration Bldg Ste 100 *Web:* www.johnson-county.com	Iowa City	IA	52240	319-356-6093		338
Johnson County 222 W Main St *Web:* www.tn.gov	Mountain City	TN	37683	423-727-9633	727-7047	338
Johnson County 111 S Cherry St *Web:* jocogov.org	Olathe	KS	66061	913-715-5000	715-0800	338
Johnson County 351 Broadway *Web:* johnsoncounty.ne.gov	Tecumseh	NE	68450	402-335-6300	335-6311	338
Johnson County 117 N 5th St PO Box 96 *Web:* votejohnsoncounty.com	Vienna	IL	62995	618-658-3611	658-9665	338
Johnson County 300 N Holden *Web:* www.jococourthouse.com	Warrensburg	MO	64093	660-747-6161		338
Johnson County 2557 E Elm St *Web:* www.johnsonco.org	Wrightsville	GA	31096	478-864-3484	864-1343	338
Johnson County Clerk 230 Ct St Ste 124 *Web:* johnson.countyclerk.us	Paintsville	KY	41240	606-789-2557	789-2559	338
Johnson County Community College 12345 College Blvd *TF:* 866-896-5893 ■ *Web:* www.jccc.edu	Overland Park	KS	66210	913-469-8500	469-2524	162
Johnson County Library PO Box 2933 *TF:* 800-362-0699 ■ *Web:* www.jocolibrary.org	Shawnee Mission	KS	66201	913-826-4600	826-4471	434-3
Johnson County Public Library 401 S State St *Web:* www.pageafterpage.org	Franklin	IN	46131	317-738-2833	738-9635	434-3
Johnson County Rural Electric Membership Corp 750 International Dr *TF:* 800-382-5544 ■ *Web:* jcremc.com	Franklin	IN	46131	317-736-6174		245
Johnson design Group Inc 1000 N Halsted Ste 204 *Web:* www.jdg1.com	Chicago	IL	60642	312-649-1650		466
Johnson Dusty (Rep R - SD) 1508 Longworth House Office Bldg *Web:* www.dustyjohnson.house.gov	Washington	DC	20515	202-225-2801		342-2
Johnson Eddie Bernice (Rep D - TX) 2306 Rayburn House Office Bldg *Web:* ebjohnson.house.gov	Washington	DC	20515	202-225-8885	226-1477	342-2
Johnson Eiesland Law Offices PC 4020 Jackson Blvd *Web:* johnsoneiesland.com	Rapid City	SD	57702	605-348-7300	348-4757	41
Johnson Electric Coil Co 821 Watson St *TF:* 800-826-9741 ■ *Web:* www.johnsoncoil.com	Antigo	WI	54409	715-627-4367	623-2812	767
Johnson Engineering & Design Inc 5 Elm St Ste 14 *Web:* johnsonengineering.biz	Danvers	MA	01923	978-646-9001		261
Johnson Engineering Inc 2122 Johnson St *TF:* 866-367-4400 ■ *Web:* www.johnsonengineering.com	Fort Myers	FL	33901	239-334-0046	334-3661	256
Johnson Equipment Co 4674 Olin Rd *TF:* 877-376-7706 ■ *Web:* www.jequip.com	Dallas	TX	75244	972-661-9822		385
Johnson Fain 1201 N Broadway *Web:* johnsonfain.com	Los Angeles	CA	90012	323-224-6000	224-6030	261
Johnson Farm Machinery Company Inc 38574 W Kentucky Ave *Web:* www.jfmco.com	Woodland	CA	95695	530-662-1788	666-5585	273
Johnson Fitness & Wellness 1600 Landmark Dr *TF:* 800-964-0124 ■ *Web:* www.johnsonfitness.com	Cottage Grove	WI	53527	800-964-0124		267
Johnson Gas Appliance Co 520 E Ave NW *TF:* 800-553-5422 ■ *Web:* www.johnsongas.com	Cedar Rapids	IA	52405	319-365-5267	365-6282	318
Johnson Golf Course Builders LLC 497 Golf Rd	South Sioux City	NE	68776	402-494-4687		188-3
Johnson Graffe Keay Moniz & Wick LLP 2115 N 30th St Ste 101 *Web:* jgkmw.com	Tacoma	WA	98403	253-572-5323		41
Johnson Group, The 436 Market St *Web:* www.johngroup.com	Chattanooga	TN	37402	423-756-2608		4
Johnson Hall State Historic Site 139 Hall Ave *Web:* parks.ny.gov	Johnstown	NY	12095	518-762-8712		565
Johnson Henry C Jr (Rep D - GA) 2240 Rayburn House Office Bldg *Web:* hankjohnson.house.gov	Washington	DC	20515	202-225-1605	226-0691	342-2
Johnson Industrial Sheet Metal Inc 2131 Barstow St *Web:* www.johnson-ind.com	Sacramento	CA	95815	916-927-8244	927-3319	697
Johnson Investment Counsel Inc 3777 W Fork Rd *TF:* 800-541-0170 ■ *Web:* www.johnsoninv.com	Cincinnati	OH	45247	513-661-3100		401
Johnson Jackson LLC 100 N Tampa St Ste 2310 *Web:* johnsonjackson.com	Tampa	FL	33602	813-580-8400		41
Johnson Lambert & Company LLP 2650 Park Tower Dr Ste 801 *TF:* 877-576-4419 ■ *Web:* www.johnsonlambert.com	Vienna	VA	22180	703-842-1115		2
Johnson Level & Tool Manufacturing Company Inc 6333 W Donges Bay Rd *TF:* 888-953-8357 ■ *Web:* www.johnsonlevel.com	Mequon	WI	53092	262-242-1161	242-0189	758
Johnson Lexus of Raleigh 5839 Capital Blvd *TF:* 855-679-4891 ■ *Web:* www.johnsonlexusraleigh.com	Raleigh	NC	27616	855-679-4891		57
Johnson Litho Graphics of Eau Claire Ltd 2219 Galloway St *Web:* www.johnsonlitho.com	Eau Claire	WI	54703	715-832-3211		627

Name / Address	City	State	Zip	Phone	Fax	Class
Johnson March Systems Inc 220 Railroad Dr *Web:* www.johnsonmarch.com	Ivyland	PA	18974	215-364-2500		610
Johnson Matthey 1401 King Rd *Web:* matthey.com	West Chester	PA	19380	610-648-8000	648-8105	482
Johnson Media Inc 2475 Northwinds Pky Ste 200 *Web:* www.johnsonmedia.com	Alpharetta	GA	30009	404-487-6010		647
Johnson Memorial Hospital (JMH) 1125 W Jefferson St *Web:* www.johnsonmemorial.org	Franklin	IN	46131	317-736-3300	736-2692	374-3
Johnson Mike (Rep R - LA) 418 Cannon House Office Bldg. *Web:* mikejohnson.house.gov	Washington	DC	20515	202-225-2777		342-2
Johnson Mirmiran & Thompson (JMT) 72 Loveton Cir *TF:* 800-472-2310 ■ *Web:* www.jmt.com	Sparks	MD	21152	410-329-3100	472-2200	261
Johnson Motors Inc 1891 Blinker Pkwy *TF:* 800-537-1768 ■ *Web:* www.johnsonauto.com	DuBois	PA	15801	814-371-4444		57
Johnson Nursery Corp 985 Johnson Nursery Rd *TF:* 800-624-8174 ■ *Web:* www.johnson-nursery.com	Willard	NC	28478	910-285-7861		293
Johnson Oil Co 507 S Otsego Ave PO Box 629 *TF:* 800-292-3941 ■ *Web:* www.johnsonspropane.com	Gaylord	MI	49735	989-732-2451		581
Johnson Outdoors Inc 555 Main St *NASDAQ: JOUT* ■ *Web:* www.johnsonoutdoors.com	Racine	WI	53403	262-631-6600	631-6601	710
Johnson Pioneer, The 103 S Main *Web:* jon.stparchive.com	Johnson	KS	67855	620-492-6244		532-2
Johnson Plastics 9240 Grand Ave S. *TF:* 800-869-7800 ■ *Web:* www.johnsonplastics.com	Minneapolis	MN	55420	952-888-9507		481
Johnson Poss Government Relations Inc 511 Union St Ste 1530 *Web:* gomoto.net	Nashville	TN	37219	615-242-7406		41
Johnson Power Ltd 2530 Braga Dr. *TF:* 800-345-1411 ■ *Web:* www.johnsonpower.com	Broadview	IL	60155	708-345-4300	345-4315	54
Johnson Press of America Inc 800 N Court St *Web:* jpapontiac.com	Pontiac	IL	61764	815-844-5161		627
Johnson Publishing Company Inc 200 S Michigan Ave Fl 21 *Web:* www.johnsonpublishing.com	Chicago	IL	60604	312-322-9200	322-1099	637-9
Johnson Rice & Company LLC 639 Loyola Ave Ste 2775 *TF:* 800-443-5924 ■ *Web:* www.jrco.com	New Orleans	LA	70113	504-525-3767		194
Johnson Ron (Sen R - WI) 328 Hart Senate Office Bldg *Web:* www.ronjohnson.senate.gov	Washington	DC	20510	202-224-5323	228-6965	342-2
Johnson Scale Company Inc 36 Stiles Ln **Fax Area Code:* 973 ■ *TF:* 800-572-2531 ■ *Web:* www.johnsonscale.com	Pine Brook	NJ	07058	866-635-4741	882-8068*	684
Johnson School Bus Services Inc 2151 W Washington St PO Box 285 *Web:* www.johnsonschoolbus.com	West Bend	WI	53095	262-334-3146	334-8019	109
Johnson Screens Inc 1950 Old Hwy 8 NW *TF:* 800-833-9473 ■ *Web:* www.aqseptence.com	New Brighton	MN	55112	651-636-3900		295
Johnson Space Ctr 2101 Nasa Pkwy *Web:* www.nasa.gov	Houston	TX	77058	281-483-0123		668
Johnson Spellman & Associates Inc (JSA) 350 Research Ct *Web:* jsace.com	Norcross	GA	30092	770-447-4555		261
Johnson State College 337 College Hill *TF:* 800-635-2356 ■ *Web:* www.jsc.edu	Johnson	VT	05656	802-635-2356	635-1230	166
Johnson Storage & Moving Co 221 Broadway *TF:* 800-289-6683 ■ *Web:* www.johnsonstorage.com	Denver	CO	80202	800-289-6683		519
Johnson Supply Co (JSC) 50 SE St *TF:* 800-476-7103 ■ *Web:* www.johnsonsupplyco.com	Pensacola	FL	32502	850-434-7103	434-5647	770
Johnson Supply Inc 10151 Stella Link Rd *TF:* 800-833-5455 ■ *Web:* www.webstore.johnsonsupply.com	Houston	TX	77025	713-830-2499	662-5519	612
Johnson University 7900 Johnson Dr *TF:* 800-827-2122 ■ *Web:* www.johnsonu.edu	Knoxville	TN	37998	865-573-4517	251-2337	161
Johnson Victrola Museum 375 S New St *Web:* history.delaware.gov	Dover	DE	19901	302-739-3262		520
Johnson Window Films Inc 20655 Annalee Ave *TF:* 800-448-8468 ■ *Web:* www.johnsonwindowfilms.com	Carson	CA	90746	310-631-6672		361
Johnson Youth Ctr 3252 Hospital Dr *TF:* 800-780-9972 ■ *Web:* www.dhss.alaska.gov	Juneau	AK	99801	907-586-9433	463-4933	412
Johnson's Boiler & Control Inc 2440 S Gearhart Ave *Web:* www.johnsonsboiler.com	Fresno	CA	93725	559-237-7772	237-1745	612
Johnson's Garden Centers 2707 W 13th St. *TF:* 888-542-8463 ■ *Web:* www.johnsonsgarden.com	Wichita	KS	67203	316-942-1443		323
Johnson's Nursery Inc W180 N 6275 Marcy Rd *Web:* www.jniplants.com	Menomonee Falls	WI	53051	262-252-4988	252-4495	323
Johnson's Village Pharmacy Inc 99 E Chautauqua St *Web:* johnsonsvillagepharmacy.com	Mayville	NY	14757	716-753-3200		237
Johnson, Grossnickle & Associates LLC 29 S Park Blvd *Web:* www.jgacounsel.com	Greenwood	IN	46143	317-215-2400		193
Johnson, Vorhees & Martucci LLC 510 W Sixth St *Web:* 4stateslaw.com	Joplin	MO	64801	417-313-1130		41
Johnson-Doppler Lumber Co 3320 Llewellyn Ave. *TF:* 877-600-0857 ■ *Web:* www.johnsondoppler.com	Cincinnati	OH	45223	513-541-0050	853-3112	191-3
JohnsonKreis Construction 160 Village St. *Web:* www.johnsonkreis.com	Birmingham	AL	35242	205-981-9030		186
Johnson-Laird Inc 850 NW Summit Ave. *Web:* www.jli.com	Portland	OR	97210	503-274-0784	274-0512	180
Johnson-Nash Metal Products Inc 9265 Seward Rd *Web:* www.johnsonnash.com	Fairfield	OH	45014	513-874-7022	874-2700	697
JohnsonRauhoff 2525 Lake Pine Dr *Web:* johnsonrauhoff.com	Saint Joseph	MI	49085	269-428-3377		344
Johnson-Sauk Trail State Park 28616 Sauk Trl Rd *Web:* www.dnr.illinois.gov	Kewanee	IL	61443	309-853-2425		565
Johnsonville LLC PO Box 906 *TF:* 888-556-2728 ■ *Web:* www.johnsonville.com	Sheboygan Falls	WI	53085	888-556-2728		296-26
Johnsonville State Historic Park 90 Nell Beard Rd. *Web:* tnstateparks.com	New Johnsonville	TN	37134	931-535-2789		565
Johnstech International Corp 1210 New Brighton Blvd. *Web:* www.johnstech.com	Minneapolis	MN	55413	612-378-2020	378-2030	696
Johnston & Murphy Inc 1415 Murfreesboro Rd *TF:* 800-424-2854 ■ *Web:* www.johnstonmurphy.com	Nashville	TN	37217	615-367-7168		301
Johnston | Food Service & Cleaning Solutions 2 Eagle Dr. *TF:* 800-800-7123 ■ *Web:* www.johnston.biz	Auburn	NY	13021	315-253-8435	253-8744	559
Johnston Asset Management Corp 300 Atlantic St Ste 601 *Web:* hardmanjohnston.com	Stamford	CT	06901	203-324-4722		401
Johnston Boiler Co 300 Pine St *Web:* www.johnstonboiler.com	Ferrysburg	MI	49409	616-842-5050	842-1854	357
Johnston Community College 245 College Rd PO Box 2350 *TF:* 800-510-9132 ■ *Web:* johnstoncc.edu	Smithfield	NC	27577	919-934-3051	989-7862	162
Johnston Community School District PO Box 10 *Web:* www.johnstoncsd.org	Johnston	IA	50131	515-278-0470	278-5884	685
Johnston County 207 E Johnston St PO Box 451 *Web:* www.johnstonnc.com	Smithfield	NC	27577	919-989-5100	989-5179	338
Johnston County 403 W Main St *Web:* www.ltap.okstate.edu	Tishomingo	OK	73460	580-371-3058	371-2174	338
Johnston County Visitors Bureau (JCVB) 234 Venture Dr *TF:* 800-441-7829 ■ *Web:* www.johnstoncountync.org	Smithfield	NC	27577	919-989-8687	989-6295	206
Johnston Dandy Co 148 Main St *Web:* www.johnstondandy.com	Lincoln	ME	04457	207-794-6571		556
Johnston Investment Counsel Ltd (JIC) 2714 N Knoxville **Fax Area Code:* 888 ■ *TF:* 877-848-3330 ■ *Web:* www.jicinvest.com	Peoria	IL	61614	309-674-3330	301-0514*	194
Johnston Law Office PC 420 S Buchanan *TF:* 866-655-6789 ■ *Web:* pgjlaw.com	Edwardsville	IL	62025	618-655-1234	655-0624	41
Johnston Lemon & Company Inc 1101 Vermont Ave NW Ste 800	Washington	DC	20005	202-842-5500		690
Johnston Manufacturing Co 19406 E Parlier Ave *Web:* www.johnstonmfg.com	Reedley	CA	93654	559-638-2737		453
Johnston Memorial Hospital 509 N Bright Leaf Blvd *Web:* johnstonhealth.org	Smithfield	NC	27577	919-934-8171		374-3
Johnston's Bakery Inc 1227 Superior Ave *Web:* www.johnstonsbakery.com	Sheboygan	WI	53081	920-458-3342		296-1
Johnston's Trading Inc 11 N Pioneer Ave *Web:* johnstontrading.com	Woodland	CA	95776	530-661-6152		200
Johnston, Allison & Hord PA 1065 E Morehead St *Web:* www.jahlaw.com	Charlotte	NC	28204	704-332-1181	376-1628	428
Johnstone Adams Bailey Gordon & Harris L L C 1 St Louis St Ste 4000 *TF:* 844-682-7682 ■ *Web:* www.johnstoneadams.com	Mobile	AL	36602	251-432-7682	432-2800	445
Johnstown Flood National Memorial 733 Lake Rd *Web:* www.nps.gov	South Fork	PA	15956	814-886-6170	495-7463	564
Joie de Vivre Hospitality Inc 650 California St 7th Fl. *TF:* 800-738-7477 ■ *Web:* www.jdvhotels.com	San Francisco	CA	94108	407-734-7128		379
Joining Technologies Inc 17 Connecticut S Dr *Web:* www.joiningtech.com	East Granby	CT	06026	860-653-0111		539
Joint Base Myer 204 Lee Ave Bldg 59 *Web:* home.army.mil	Fort Myer	VA	22211	703-696-3353		497-2
Joint Chiefs of Staff *Chairman* 9999 Joint Chiefs of Staff Pentagon Rm 2D932 *Web:* www.jcs.mil	Washington	DC	20318	703-767-8267		340-3
Joint Clutch and Gear Service Inc 30200 Cypress Rd *TF:* 800-572-8249 ■ *Web:* www.jointclutchandgear.com	Romulus	MI	48174	734-641-7575	641-7599	61
Joint Commission on Accreditation of Healthcare Organizations (JCAHO) 1 Renaissance Blvd. *Web:* www.jointcommission.org	Oakbrook Terrace	IL	60181	630-792-5000	792-5005	48-1
Joint Institute for Marine & Atmospheric Research University of Hawaii at Manoa 1000 Pope Rd Marine Sciences Bldg 312 *Web:* www.soest.hawaii.edu	Honolulu	HI	96822	808-956-8083	956-4104	668
Joint Production Technology (JPT) 15381 Hallmark Ct *Web:* www.jptonline.com	Macomb	MI	48042	586-786-0080	786-0088	493
Joint Review Committee on Education in Radiologic Technology (JRCERT) 20 N Wacker Dr Ste 2850 *Web:* www.jrcert.org	Chicago	IL	60606	312-704-5300	704-5304	48-1
Joint Review Committee on Educational Programs in Nuclear Medicine Technology, The (JRCNMT) 820 W Danforth Rd Ste B1 *Web:* www.jrcnmt.org	Edmond	OK	73003	405-285-0546	285-0579	48-1
Joint Technology Solution Inc 9255 Center St Ste 300 *Web:* jointtechnologysolution.net	Manassas	VA	20110	703-218-0372		180

Name / Address	City	State	ZIP	Phone	Fax	Class
Joissu Products Inc 4627 L B Mcleod Rd *Fax Area Code: 407 ■ TF: 800-233-1681 ■ Web: www.joissu.com	Orlando	FL	32811	800-233-1681	649-8630*	44
JoJo Restaurant 160 E 64th St Web: www.jojorestaurantnyc.com	New York	NY	10065	212-223-5656		671
Jokake Construction Co 5013 E Washington St Ste 100 Web: www.jokake.com	Phoenix	AZ	85034	602-224-4500		187
Jolera Inc 365 Bloor St E 2nd Fl TF: 800-292-4078 ■ Web: www.jolera.com	Toronto	ON	M4W3L4	416-410-1011		177
Jolico/J-B Tool Inc 4325 22 Mile Rd Web: jolico.com	Utica	MI	48317	586-739-5555	739-4840	757
Joliet Area Community Hospice 250 Water Stone Cir TF: 800-360-1817 ■ Web: www.joliethospice.org	Joliet	IL	60431	815-740-4104	740-4107	371
Joliet Avionics Inc 43w730 US Hwy 30 TF: 800-323-5966 ■ Web: www.jaair.com	Sugar Grove	IL	60554	630-584-3200		246
Joliet Electric Motors LLC 1 Doris Ave TF: 800-435-9350 ■ Web: jolietelectricmotors.com	Joliet	IL	60433	815-727-6606	727-6626	518
Joliet Junior College 1215 Houbolt Rd Web: www.jjc.edu	Joliet	IL	60431	815-729-9020	280-2493	162
Joliet Metallurgical Laboratories Inc 305 N Republic Ave Web: www.jolietmetlab.com	Joliet	IL	60435	815-725-9500	725-9577	743
Joliet Public Library 150 N Ottawa St Web: www.jolietlibrary.org	Joliet	IL	60432	815-740-2660	740-6161	434-3
Joliet Public School District 86 420 N Raynor Ave Web: www.joliet86.org	Joliet	IL	60435	815-740-3196		685
Joliet Region Chamber of Commerce & Industry 63 N Chicago St Web: jolietchamber.com	Joliet	IL	60432	815-727-5371	727-5374	139
Jolley, Urga & Wirth Ltd 330 S Rampart Blvd Ste 380 Web: juwlaw.com	Las Vegas	NV	89145	702-699-7500		41
Jolt Consulting Group 112 Spring St Ste 301 TF: 877-249-6262 ■ Web: joltconsultinggroup.com	Saratoga Springs	NY	12866	877-249-6262		463
Jomax Drilling (1988) Ltd 140 - 4 Ave SW Ste 1750 Web: www.jomax.ca	Calgary	AB	T2P3N3	403-265-5312		540
Jomax Recovery Services 9242 W Union Hills Dr Ste 102 *Fax Area Code: 602 ■ TF: 888-866-0721 ■ Web: jomaxrecovery.com	Peoria	AZ	85382	888-866-0721	866-0722*	393
Jon D. Rigney A Professional Co 2333 Camino Del Rio S Ste 300 Web: rigneylaw.com	San Diego	CA	92108	619-236-0533		41
Jon Lancaster Inc 3501 Lancaster Dr Web: www.eastmadisontoyota.com	Madison	WI	53718	608-240-7900		57
Jon Peddie Research Inc 4 St Gabrielle Ct Web: www.jonpeddie.com	Tiburon	CA	94920	415-435-9368		449
Jon Renau Collection 2510 Island View Way TF: 800-462-9447 ■ Web: www.jonrenau.com	Vista	CA	92081	760-598-0067		348
Jon Wollen 152 N Main St TF: 800-824-6681 ■ Web: jonwollen.com	Kingman	KS	67068	620-532-3179	532-5658	390
Jon's Nursery Inc 24546 Nursery Way TF: 800-322-4289 ■ Web: jonsnursery.com	Eustis	FL	32736	352-357-4289		292
Jonah Energy LLC 707 17th St Ste 2700 Web: www.jonahenergy.com	Denver	CO	80202	720-577-1000		536
Jonah Group Ltd, The 461 King St W 3rd Fl TF: 888-594-6260 ■ Web: www.jonahgroup.com	Toronto	ON	M5V1K4	416-304-0860		179
Jonal Laboratories Inc PO Box 743 Web: www.jonal.com	Meriden	CT	06450	203-634-4444	634-4448	677
Jonar 55 Rue de Louvain W Ste 303 Web: www.jonar.com	Montreal	QC	H2N1A4	514-335-5525		180
Jonard Industries Corp 134 Marbledale Rd Web: www.jonard.com	Tuckahoe	NY	10707	914-793-0700	793-4527	758
Jonas Equities 725 Church Ave Web: www.jonasequities.com	Brooklyn	NY	11218	718-871-6020		655
Jonas Fitness Inc 16969 N Texas Ave TF: 800-324-9800 ■ Web: jonasfitness.com	Webster	TX	77598	800-324-9800		354
Jonathan Club Charitable Fund 545 S Figueroa St Web: www.jc.org	Los Angeles	CA	90071	213-624-0881		292
Jonathan Engineered Solutions 410 Exchange St Ste 200 Web: www.jonathanengr.com	Irvine	CA	92602	714-665-4400	368-7002	350
Jonathan Lord Cheesecakes & Desserts 87 Carlough Rd TF: 800-814-7517 ■ Web: www.jonathanlordny.com	Bohemia	NY	11716	631-517-1271	563-8505	297-8
Jonathan Louis International Ltd 544 W 130th St Web: www.jonathanlouis.net	Gardena	CA	90248	323-770-3330		321
Jonathan Publishing 660 Laurel St Ste B-103 Web: www.jonpub.com	Baton Rouge	LA	70802	225-205-5873		637-2
Jonathan's Tucson Cork 6320 E Tanque Verde Rd Web: jonathanscork.com	Tucson	AZ	85715	520-296-1631		671
Jonco Die Co 5201 Program Ave Web: www.joncodie.com	Mounds View	MN	55112	763-783-9300	783-9599	757
Jondo Ltd 22700 Savi Ranch Pkwy Web: jondo.com	Yorba Linda	CA	92887	714-279-2300		627
Jones & Assoc 6300 Wilshire Blvd Ste 860 Web: www.charityaccounting.com	Los Angeles	CA	90048	323-782-9391	782-9392	734
Jones & Beach Engineers Inc 85 Portsmouth Ave PO Box 219 Web: jonesandbeach.com	Stratham	NH	03885	603-772-4746		261
Jones & Henry Engineers Ltd 3103 Executive Pkwy Web: jheng.com	Toledo	OH	43606	419-473-9611		261
Jones & Jones Inc 4300 N 10th St Ste D	McAllen	TX	78504	956-687-1171	631-3345	229
Jones & Jones PC 1600 S Church St Web: jandjpc.com	Smithfield	VA	23430	757-357-2187		41
Jones & Kolb 3475 Piedmont Rd Ste 1500 Web: www.joneskolb.com	Atlanta	GA	30305	404-262-7920	237-4034	2
Jones & Peacock Inc 1812 Eastchester Dr Web: jonesandpeacock.com	High Point	NC	27265	336-889-8282		390
Jones & Roth PC 432 W 11th Ave Web: jrcpa.com	Eugene	OR	97401	541-687-2320	485-0960	401
Jones & Sons Inc PO Box 2357 Web: www.jonesandsons.com	Washington	IN	47501	812-254-4731	254-3293	182
Jones & Vining Inc 1115 W Chestnut St Web: www.jonesandvining.com	Brockton	MA	02301	508-232-7470	232-7477	604
Jones & Warren PA 243 US Route 1 Web: jwlawfirm.com	Scarborough	ME	04074	207-883-4167		41
Jones Agency, The 303 N Indian Canyon Dr Web: jonesagency.com	Palm Springs	CA	92262	760-325-1437		636
Jones Bank 203 S 6th St Web: jonesbank.com	Seward	NE	68434	402-643-3602		70
Jones Beach State Park 1 Ocean Pkwy Web: parks.ny.gov	Wantagh	NY	11793	516-785-1600		565
Jones Cassity Inc 302 Pine Tree Rd Web: cassityjones.com	Longview	TX	75604	903-759-0736	759-1406	364
Jones County 500 W Main St TF: 800-622-3849 ■ Web: www.jonescountyiowa.org	Anamosa	IA	52205	319-462-2282		338
Jones County PO Box 552 Web: www.co.jones.tx.us	Anson	TX	79501	325-823-3762	823-4223	338
Jones County 166Industrial Blvd PO Box 1359 Web: www.jonescountyga.org	Gray	GA	31032	478-986-6405	986-6462	338
Jones County PO Box 527 Web: jonescounty.com	Laurel	MS	39441	601-649-3031	428-2047	338
Jones County 418 Hwy 58 N Web: www.jonescountync.gov	Trenton	NC	28585	252-448-7571		338
Jones County Clerk of Court 310 Main St PO Box 448 Web: www.ujs.sd.gov	Murdo	SD	57559	605-669-2361	669-2641	338
Jones County Junior College 900 S Ct St Web: jcjc.edu	Ellisville	MS	39437	601-477-4000	477-4258	162
Jones CPA Group 120 Atlantic St Ste 300 Web: jonescpagroup.com	Norfolk	VA	23510	757-627-7672		2
Jones Dairy Farm 800 Jones Ave TF: 800-635-6637 ■ Web: www.jonesdairyfarm.com	Fort Atkinson	WI	53538	800-635-6637		296-26
Jones Day 51 Louisiana Ave NW Web: www.jonesday.com	Washington	DC	20001	202-879-3939	626-1700	428
Jones Doug (Sen D - AL) 330 Hart Senate Office Bldg Web: www.jones.senate.gov	Washington	DC	20510	202-224-4124		342-2
Jones Edmunds & Associates Inc 730 NE Waldo Rd Web: jonesedmunds.com	Gainesville	FL	32641	352-377-5821	377-3166	261
Jones Environmental Inc 708 Milam St Ste 100 Web: www.jonesenvironmentalinc.com	Shreveport	LA	71101	318-226-8444	226-0381	196
Jones Eye Clinic 4405 Hamilton Blvd TF: 800-334-2015 ■ Web: joneseye.com	Sioux City	IA	51104	712-239-3937	239-1305	798
Jones Family Foundation 31021 Lakeview Ave Web: jonesfamilyfoundation.org	Red Wing	MN	55066	651-388-7941		305
Jones Gap State Park 303 Jones Gap Rd Web: southcarolinaparks.com	Marietta	SC	29661	864-836-3647		565
Jones Ham & Cluff P C 14475 SW Allen Blvd Ste A Web: www.jonesandham.com	Beaverton	OR	97005	503-643-6333	643-6396	2
Jones Hamilton Co 30354 Tracy Rd TF: 888-858-4425 ■ Web: www.jones-hamilton.com	Walbridge	OH	43465	419-666-9838	666-1817	143
Jones Heavy Equipment Products Inc 4115 NE 148th Ave Web: www.joneshep.com	Portland	OR	97230	503-254-7346	257-0206	190
Jones Henle & Schunck 135 Town & Country Dr Web: www.jhs.com	Danville	CA	94526	925-820-1821		2
Jones Huyett Partners Inc 3200 SW Huntoon St Web: www.jhpadv.com	Topeka	KS	66604	785-228-0900		636
Jones Lake State Park 4117 NC 242 Hwy Web: www.ncparks.gov	Elizabethtown	NC	28337	910-588-4550		565
Jones Lang LaSalle IP Inc 200 E Randolph Dr Fl 43-48 NYSE: JLL ■ Web: www.us.jll.com	Chicago	IL	60601	312-782-5800	782-4339	655
Jones Library Inc 43 Amity St Web: www.joneslibrary.org	Amherst	MA	01002	413-259-3090	256-4096	434-3
Jones Lumber Company Inc 2438 Hwy 98 E TF: 844-500-2438 ■ Web: jonescompanies.com	Columbia	MS	39429	601-876-2427	876-2977	191-3
Jones Metal Products Co 200 N Center St TF: 888-868-6535 ■ Web: www.jmpforming.com	West Lafayette	OH	43845	740-545-6381		757
Jones Metal Products Inc 3201 Third Ave TF: 800-967-1750 ■ Web: jonesmetalinc.com	Mankato	MN	56001	507-625-4436	625-2994	697
Jones Mobile Television 5200 Northshore Dr Ste C Web: jmtv.com	North Little Rock	AR	72118	501-376-1993		514
Jones Motor Group 654 Enterprise Dr TF: 800-825-6637 ■ Web: www.jonesmotor.com	Limerick	PA	19468	610-948-7900	948-5660	780
Jones Nale & Mattingly PLC 642 S 4th St Ste 300 Web: www.jnmcpa.com	Louisville	KY	40202	502-583-0248	589-1680	463
Jones Petroleum Company Inc 407 E Second St Web: www.jonespetroleum.com	Jackson	GA	30233	770-775-2386	755-3893	581

Phone | Fax | Class

Jones Popcorn Inc 125 Quality Ave New Albany IN 47150 812-941-8810 941-8830 296-37
Web: www.clarksnacks.com

Jones Potato Chip Co 823 Bowman St Mansfield OH 44903 419-529-9424 529-6789 296-35
Web: www.joneschips.com

Jones Printing Service Inc
931 Ventures Way Chesapeake VA 23320 757-436-3331 627
Web: www.jones-printing.com

Jones Raczkowski Pc
2141 E Camelback Rd Ste 100 Phoenix AZ 85016 602-842-6297 41
Web: bojolaw.com

Jones Soda Co 66 S Hanford St Ste 150 Seattle WA 98134 206-624-3357 624-6857 80-2
OTC: JSDA ■ *Web:* www.jonessoda.com

Jones Stephens 3249 Moody Pkwy Moody AL 35004 800-355-6637 462-6991 610
TF: 800-355-6637 ■ *Web:* www.jonesstephens.com

Jones Travel 511 S Lincoln St Elkhorn WI 53121 262-723-4309 723-6268 772
TF: 800-236-3160 ■ *Web:* www.jonestravel.com

Jones, Allen & Fuquay LLP
8828 Greenville Ave Dallas TX 75243 214-343-7400 343-7455 428
Web: www.jonesallen.com

Jones, Childers, Donaldson & Webb PLLC
149 Welton Way Mooresville NC 28117 704-664-1127 41
Web: jcdwlaw.com

Jones, Foster, Johnston & Stubbs PA
Flagler Center Twr 505 S Flagler Dr West Palm Beach FL 33401 561-659-3000 650-5300 41
Web: www.jonesfoster.com

Jones, Haugh & Smith Inc
515 S Washington Albert Lea MN 56007 507-373-4876 261
Web: jhseng.com

Jones, Mcknight & Edmonson PC
1429 Business Center Dr Conyers GA 30094 770-922-5790 2
Web: jmecpa.net

Jonesboro Regional Chamber of Commerce
1709 E Nettleton Ave PO Box 789 Jonesboro AR 72403 870-932-6691 933-5758 139
Web: www.jonesborochamber.com

Jonesboro Sun 518 Carson St Jonesboro AR 72401 870-935-5525 935-5823 532-2
TF: 800-237-5341 ■ *Web:* www.jonesborosun.com

Jonesburg State Bank
110 First St PO Box E Jonesburg MO 63351 636-488-5441 488-5701 70
TF: 800-811-0991 ■ *Web:* jonesburgstatebank.com

Jones-Heroy & Associates Inc
13915 N Mopac Expy Ste 408 Austin TX 78728 512-989-2200 261
Web: jones-heroy.com

Jones-Onslow Electric Membership Corp
259 Western Blvd Jacksonville NC 28546 910-353-1940 245
TF: 800-682-1515 ■ *Web:* www.joemc.com

JonesTrading Institutional Services LLC
32133 Lindero Canyon Rd Ste 208 Westlake Village CA 91361 818-991-5500 707-2095 690
TF: 800-423-5933 ■ *Web:* www.jonestrading.com

Jonna S. Wooten 8148 Electric Ave Vienna VA 22182 703-560-7804 390
Web: autoinsurancedmv.com

Jons Flags & Poles Inc
3215 Chicago Ave Riverside CA 92507 951-682-0134 327
Web: jonsflags.com

Jons International Market Place
5315 Santa Monica Blvd Los Angeles CA 90029 323-460-4646 345
Web: www.jonsmarketplace.com

JoongAng Daily News
690 Wilshire Pl Los Angeles CA 90005 213-368-2500 532-3
Web: www.koreadaily.com

Jopari Solutions Inc
1855 Gateway Blvd Ste 500 Concord CA 94520 925-459-5200 459-5222 317
TF: 800-630-3060 ■ *Web:* www.jopari.com

Joplin Area Chamber of Commerce
320 E Fourth St Joplin MO 64801 417-624-4150 624-4303 139
Web: www.joplincc.com

Joplin Convention & Visitors Bureau
602 S Main St Joplin MO 64801 417-625-4789 624-7948 206
TF: 800-657-2534 ■ *Web:* www.visitjoplinmo.com

Joplin Globe 117 E Fourth St Joplin MO 64801 417-623-3480 532-2
TF: 800-444-8514 ■ *Web:* www.joplinglobe.com

Joplin Metro Credit Union
3301 Texas Ave Joplin MO 64804 417-623-9816 219
Web: joplinmcu.com

Joplin Public Library 300 S Main St Joplin MO 64801 417-623-7953 624-5217 434-3
Web: www.joplinpubliclibrary.org

Jordache Enterprises 1400 Broadway New York NY 10018 215-925-1800 155-11
Web: www.jordache.com

Jordan
Embassy 3504 International Dr NW Washington DC 20008 202-966-2664 966-3110 257
Web: www.jordanembassyus.org

Jordan Advertising
3111 Quail Springs Pkwy Ste 200 Oklahoma City OK 73134 405-840-3201 7
Web: jordanadvertising.com

Jordan Essentials 1520 N Commercial Rd Nixa MO 65714 877-662-8669 449-0027* 354
**Fax Area Code:* 417 ■ *TF:* 877-662-8669 ■ *Web:* www.jordanessentials.com

Jordan Hospital 275 Sandwich St Plymouth MA 02360 508-746-2000 374-3
TF: 800-256-7326 ■ *Web:* www.bidplymouth.org

Jordan Jim (Rep R - OH)
2056 Rayburn House Office Bldg Washington DC 20515 202-225-2676 226-0577 342-2
Web: www.jordan.house.gov

Jordan Lake State Recreation Area
280 State Park Rd Apex NC 27523 919-362-0586 565
Web: www.ncparks.gov

Jordan Lumber & Supply Inc
1939 NC Hwy 109 S Mount Gilead NC 27306 912-439-8142 191-3
Web: www.jordanlumber.com

Jordan Price Wall Gray Jones & Carlton PLLC
1951 Clark Ave Raleigh NC 27605 919-828-2501 428
Web: jordanprice.com

Jordan Ramis
2 Ctrpointe Dr Ste 600 Lake Oswego OR 97035 503-598-7070 598-7373 445
Web: jordanramis.com

Jordan Schnitzer Museum of Art
1430 Johnson Ln Eugene OR 97403 541-346-3027 346-0976 520
Web: jsma.uoregon.edu

Jordan Specialty Plastics LLC
1751 Lake Cook Rd Ste 550 Deerfield IL 60015 847-945-5591 604

Jordan Tourism Board (JTB)
1307 Dolley Madison Blvd Ste 2A McLean VA 22101 703-243-7404 243-7406 775
TF: 877-733-5673 ■ *Web:* www.visitjordan.com

Jordan Valley Medical Ctr
3460 S Pioneer Pkwy West Valley City UT 84120 801-964-3100 374-3
Web: www.jordanvalleymc.org

Jordan's Furniture Company Inc
450 Revolutionary Dr East Taunton MA 02718 508-828-4000 321
Web: www.jordans.com

Jordanelle State Park
SR 319 Ste 515 Heber City UT 84032 435-649-9540 565
Web: utah.com

Jordano Electric Company Inc
200 Hudson St Hackensack NJ 07601 201-489-4800 489-5071 189-4
Web: www.jordanoelectric.com

Jordano's Inc
550 S Patterson Ave Santa Barbara CA 93111 805-964-0611 964-3821 297-8
TF: 800-325-2278 ■ *Web:* www.jordanos.com

Jorg's Cafe Vienna 1037 E 15th St Plano TX 75074 972-509-5966 671
Web: jorgscafevienna.com

Jorgensen Conveyors Inc
10303 N Baehr Rd Mequon WI 53092 262-242-3089 242-4382 207
TF: 800-325-7705 ■ *Web:* www.jorgensenconveyors.com

Jorgensen Gibbons PA
4455 Central Ave Saint Petersburg FL 33713 727-327-6125 41
TF: 800-341-8338 ■ *Web:* jorgensengibbons.com

Jorgensen Laboratories Inc
1450 Van Buren Ave Loveland CO 80538 970-669-2500 663-5042 475
TF: 800-525-5614 ■ *Web:* www.jorvet.com

Jorgensen Tool & Stamping Inc
23 Fruite St Belmont NH 03220 603-524-5813 524-5223 454
Web: www.jorgensentool.com

Jorgenson's Inn & Suites 1714 11th Ave Helena MT 59601 406-442-1770 379
Web: www.jorgensonsinn.com

Jor-Mac Company Inc 155 E Main St Lomira WI 53048 920-269-8500 269-2217 697
Web: www.jor-mac.com

Jorstad Incorporated CPA
1000 Fourth St Ste 375 San Rafael CA 94901 415-459-6622 459-6104 2
Web: jorstad.com

Jos A. Bank Clothiers Inc
6380 Rogerdale Rd PO Box 1000 Houston TX 77072 800-285-2265 155-12
TF: 800-285-2265 ■ *Web:* www.josbank.com

Josam Co 525 W US Hwy 20 Michigan City IN 46360 800-365-6726 627-0008 609
TF: 800-365-6726 ■ *Web:* www.josam.com

JOSE 97.5 5426 N Mesa El Paso TX 79912 915-581-1126 645-52
Web: www.joseradio.com

Jose Matteo's Ballet Theatre
400 Harvard St Cambridge MA 02138 617-354-7467 573-1
Web: www.ballettheatre.org

Josef's School of Hair Design
2011 S Washington Grand Forks ND 58201 701-772-2728 685
Web: www.josefsschoolofhairdesign.com

Joseph A. Natoli Construction Corp
293 Changebridge Rd Pine Brook NJ 07058 973-575-1500 575-8216 186
Web: jnatoli.com

Joseph A. Paine Inc
4301 S Pine St Ste 26 Tacoma WA 98409 253-472-3055 390
Web: www.paineinsurance.com

Joseph A. Schudt & Associates Inc
9455 Enterprise Dr Mokena IL 60448 708-720-1000 727
Web: jaseng.com

Joseph B. Marzouk MD
4096 Piedmont Ave Ste 911 Oakland CA 94611 510-835-6225 192
Web: www.infectiousdiseasemd.com

Joseph Berning Printing Co
1850 Dalton Ave Cincinnati OH 45214 513-721-0781 721-0783 627
TF: 877-828-9864 ■ *Web:* www.josberningprinting.com

Joseph Blank Inc 62 W 47th St Ste 808 New York NY 10036 212-575-9050 302-8521 411
TF: 800-223-7666 ■ *Web:* www.josephblank.com

Joseph Brant Memorial Hospital (JBMH)
1230 N Shore Blvd Burlington ON L7S1W7 905-632-3737 336-6480 374-2
TF: 800-810-0000 ■ *Web:* www.josephbranthospital.ca

Joseph C. Sansone Co
18040 Edison Ave Chesterfield MO 63005 636-537-2700 317
TF: 800-394-0140 ■ *Web:* www.jcsco.com

Joseph Campione Garlic Bread
2201 W S Branch Blvd Oak Creek WI 53154 414-761-8944 761-2005 68
Web: www.josephcampione.com

Joseph Construction Company Inc
203 Letterman Rd Knoxville TN 37919 865-584-3945 186
Web: jcc1972.com

Joseph Crnkovich Jr CPA
1053 Mclaughlin Run Rd Bridgeville PA 15017 412-257-0844 2

Joseph D. Fail Engineering Company Inc
27 S 2nd St Bay Springs MS 39422 601-764-2195 261
Web: www.jdfec.com

Joseph Davis State Park
4143 Lower River Rd Lewiston NY 14092 716-754-4596 565
Web: parks.ny.gov

Joseph Finn Company Inc 188 Needham St Newton MA 02464 617-964-1886 366
Web: josephfinn.com

Joseph Flihan Co 418-426 Broad St Utica NY 13504 315-735-8519 724-4790 300
Web: www.josephflihanco.com

Joseph Freedman Company Inc
115 Stevens St Springfield MA 01104 413-781-4444 192
TF: 888-677-7818 ■ *Web:* jfrecycle.com

Joseph H. Stewart State Recreation Area
35251 OR-62 Trail OR 97541 800-452-5687 565
TF: 800-452-5687 ■ *Web:* stateparks.oregon.gov

Joseph Harp Correctional Ctr
16161 Moffat Rd PO Box 548 Lexington OK 73051 405-527-5593 527-4841 213
Web: doc.ok.gov

Joseph J. Henderson & Son Inc
4288 Old Grand Ave Gurnee IL 60031 847-244-3222 244-9572 187
Web: www.jjhenderson.com

Joseph J. Szela & Associates PC
426 Worcester Rd Charlton MA 01507 508-248-1040 2
Web: www.szelacpa.com

Listing	City	State	ZIP	Phone	Fax	Class
Joseph J. Tock 963 Rt 6 *Web:* tocklaw.com	Mahopac	NY	10541	845-628-8080	628-5450	41
Joseph L. Ertl Inc 502 5th St NW *Web:* www.scalemodeltoys.com	Dyersville	IA	52040	563-875-2436	875-8004	604
Joseph L. Stefanski CPA PA 305 W Chesapeake Ave Ste 100 *Web:* jlscpa-pa.com	Towson	MD	21204	410-252-0500		2
Joseph Machine Company Inc 595 Range End Rd *Web:* www.josephmachineco.com	Dillsburg	PA	17019	717-432-3442	432-0680	494
Joseph Mccormick Construction Company Inc 3340 Pearl Ave *Web:* www.jmccormickconstruction.com	Erie	PA	16510	814-899-3111	899-4278	188-4
Joseph Oat Corp 2500 Broadway Drawer 10 *Web:* www.josephoat.com	Camden	NJ	08104	856-541-2900	541-0864	91
Joseph P. Carrara & Sons Inc 167 N Shrewsbury Rd *Web:* www.jpcarrara.com	North Clarendon	VT	05759	802-775-2301		183
Joseph P. Day Realty Corp 9 E 40th St *Web:* jpday.com	New York	NY	10016	212-889-7460		652
Joseph P. Dipino LLC 30 N Lasalle St Ste 1530 *Web:* beverlypauselaw.com	Chicago	IL	60602	312-782-4803		41
Joseph P. O'brien Agency 454 New York Ave *Web:* www.jpoinsurance.com	Huntington	NY	11743	631-421-0505		390
Joseph P. Rigogliloso 375 Coram Ave *Web:* rigogliosolaw.com	Shelton	CT	06484	203-922-8100		41
Joseph Productions Inc 34525 Glendale St *Web:* www.jpitel.com	Livonia	MI	48150	734-266-0500		514
Joseph R. Paolino Jr 100 Westminster St Ste 1700 *Web:* paolinoproperties.com	Providence	RI	02903	401-274-6611		652
Joseph Skilken Organization 383 S 3rd St *Web:* www.jskilken.com	Columbus	OH	43215	614-221-4547	221-3091	655
Joseph's Beverage Ctr 4129 Talmadge Rd *Web:* www.josephsbeveragecenter.com	Toledo	OH	43623	419-841-3000	472-1913	81-1
Joseph's College : Cosmetology 1620 E 4th St *Web:* www.josephscollege.edu	North Platte	NE	69101	308-532-4664		166
Joseph's Steakhouse 360 Fairfield Ave *Web:* josephssteakhouse.com	Bridgeport	CT	06604	203-337-9944		671
Joseph, Greenwald & Laake PA 6404 Ivy Ln Ste 400 *TF:* 877-412-7429 ■ *Web:* www.jgllaw.com	Greenbelt	MD	20770	301-220-2200		428
Josephine County 500 NW Sixth St *Web:* www.co.josephine.or.us	Grants Pass	OR	97526	541-474-5240	474-5246	338
Josephine County Library System 200 NW 'C' St PO Box 1684 *Web:* josephinelibrary.org	Grants Pass	OR	97526	541-476-0571		434-3
Josephine's 503 N Humphreys St *Web:* www.josephinesrestaurant.com	Flagstaff	AZ	86001	928-779-3400	272-0744	671
Josephine's Personnel Services Inc 2158 Ringwood Ave *Web:* www.jps-inc.com	San Jose	CA	95131	408-943-0111	943-9649	260
Joshen Paper & Packaging Company Inc 5808 Grant Ave *Web:* www.joshen.com	Cleveland	OH	44105	216-441-5600	441-7647	548
Joshua Tree National Park 74485 National Pk Dr *Web:* www.nps.gov	Twentynine Palms	CA	92277	760-367-5500		564
Joslin Diabetes Ctr 1 Joslin Pl *Web:* www.joslin.org	Boston	MA	02215	617-732-2400		668
Joslyn Art Museum 2200 Dodge St *TF:* 800-965-2030 ■ *Web:* joslyn.org	Omaha	NE	68102	402-342-3300	342-2376	520
Joslyn Castle 3902 Davenport St *Web:* joslyncastle.com	Omaha	NE	68131	402-595-2199		50-3
Joso's 202 Davenport Rd *Web:* www.josos.com	Toronto	ON	M5R1J2	416-925-1903	925-6567	671
Joss Cafe & Sushi Bar 195 Main St *Web:* www.josssushi.com	Annapolis	MD	21401	410-263-4688		671
Jostens Inc 3601 Minnesota Ave Ste 400 *TF:* 800-235-4774 ■ *Web:* www.jostens.com	Minneapolis	MN	55435	952-830-3300		409
Jo-Thor's Dog Trainers Academy 12580 Crabapple Rd *Web:* www.agooddog.com	Alpharetta	GA	30004	770-667-0334		167-3
Jottan Inc PO Box 166 *TF:* 800-364-4234 ■ *Web:* www.jottan.com	Florence	NJ	08518	609-447-6200		189-12
Joule Inc 1235 Rt 1 S **Fax Area Code:* 732 ■ *TF:* 800-341-0341 ■ *Web:* www.jouleinc.com	Edison	NJ	08837	800-341-0341	494-6346*	721
Joule Technologies Inc 4167 W Orleans St *Web:* www.jouletechnologies.com	Mchenry	IL	60050	815-759-0600	759-6902	625
Journal & Courier 217 N Sixth St *TF:* 800-456-3223 ■ *Web:* www.jconline.com	LaFayette	IN	47901	765-423-5511		532-2
Journal & Topics Online Media Group 622 N Graceland Ave *Web:* www.journal-topics.com	Des Plaines	IL	60016	847-299-5511	298-8549	457-11
Journal Gazette 600 W Main St *TF:* 888-966-4532 ■ *Web:* www.journalgazette.net	Fort Wayne	IN	46802	260-461-8773	461-8648	532-2
Journal Graphics Inc 2840 NW 35th Ave *Web:* www.journalgraphics.com	Portland	OR	97210	503-790-9100		637-8
Journal Inquirer 306 Progress Dr PO Box 510 *TF:* 800-237-3606 ■ *Web:* www.journalinquirer.com	Manchester	CT	06045	860-646-0500	646-9867	532-2
Journal Mississippi State Medical Assn 408 W Parkway Pl *Web:* msmaonline.com	Ridgeland	MS	39157	601-853-6733		474
Journal News 1611 S Main St *Web:* www.journal-news.com	Hamilton	OH	45011	203-748-4704		532 2
Journal of Accountancy 220 Leigh Farm Rd **Fax Area Code:* 919 ■ *TF:* 888-777-7077 ■ *Web:* www.journalofaccountancy.com	Durham	NC	27707	888-777-7077	419-5241*	457-5
Journal of Business 429 E Third Ave *Web:* www.spokanejournal.com	Spokane	WA	99202	509-456-5257	456-0624	457-5
Journal of Clinical Investigation (JCI) 15 Research Dr *Web:* jci.org	Ann Arbor	MI	48103	734-222-6050	222-6058	49-8
Journal of Drug Issues (JDI) College of Criminology & Criminal Justice Florida State University *Web:* criminology.fsu.edu	Tallahassee	FL	32306	850-644-4050		637-9
Journal of Men's Studies PO Box 32 *Web:* www.mensstudies.info	Harriman	TN	37748	423-369-2375	369-1125	637-9
Journal of Philosophy Inc 2852 Broadway Rm 209 2nd Fl **Fax Area Code:* 434 ■ *TF:* 800-444-2419 ■ *Web:* www.journalofphilosophy.org	New York	NY	10025	212-854-3065	220-3300*	637-9
Journal of Practical Nursing (JPN) 2071 N Bechtle Ave PMB 307 *TF:* 800-995-5222 ■ *Web:* www.napnes.org	Springfield	OH	45504	703-933-1003	940-4089	457-16
Journal of Protective Coatings & Linings 2100 Wharton St Ste 310 *TF:* 800-837-8303 ■ *Web:* www.paintsquare.com	Pittsburgh	PA	15203	412-431-8300	431-5428	457-21
Journal of the American Dietetic Assn 1600 John F Kennedy Blvd **Fax Area Code:* 212 ■ *TF:* 800-654-2452 ■ *Web:* jandonline.org	Philadelphia	PA	19103	800-654-2452	633-3820*	457-16
Journal of the American Medical Assn (JAMA) PO Box 10946 *TF:* 800-262-2350 ■ *Web:* www.jamanetwork.com	Chicago	IL	60654	312-670-7827		457-16
Journal of the Louisiana State Medical Society 6767 Perkins Rd Ste 100 *TF:* 800-375-9508 ■ *Web:* www.lsms.site-ym.com	Baton Rouge	LA	70808	225-763-8500	768-5601	457-16
Journal of the San Juan Islands PO Box 519 *Web:* www.sanjuanjournal.com	Friday Harbor	WA	98250	360-378-5696		532-4
Journal Record Oklahoma City 101 N Robinson St Ste 101 *Web:* www.journalrecord.com	Oklahoma City	OK	73102	405-235-3100		532-2
Journal Times 212 Fourth St *TF:* 888-460-8725 ■ *Web:* www.journaltimes.com	Racine	WI	53403	888-460-8725		532-2
Journal, The 207 W King St *TF:* 800-448-1895 ■ *Web:* www.journal-news.net	Martinsburg	WV	25402	304-263-8931	267-2903	532-2
Journal-Patriot PO Box 70 *Web:* www.journalpatriot.com	North Wilkesboro	NC	28659	336-838-4117	838-9864	532-4
Journal-Standard 27 S State Ave *TF:* 800-325-6397 ■ *Web:* www.journalstandard.com	Freeport	IL	61032	815-232-1171	232-0105	532-2
Journey Aviation LLC 3700 Airport Rd Ste 202 *Web:* journeyflight.com	Boca Raton	FL	33441	561-826-9400		107
Journey Group Inc 418 Fourth St NE *Web:* www.journeygroup.com	Charlottesville	VA	22902	434-961-2500		637-9
Journey Museum & Learning Ctr 222 New York St *Web:* www.journeymuseum.org	Rapid City	SD	57701	605-394-6923	394-6940	520
JourneyEdcom Inc 80 E McDermott Dr *TF:* 800-876-3507 ■ *Web:* www.journeyed.com	Allen	TX	75002	972-481-2000	481-2069	174
Journyx Inc 7600 Burnet Rd Ste 300 *TF:* 800-755-9878 ■ *Web:* journyx.com	Austin	TX	78757	512-834-8888		39
Jova Solutions 1402 18th St *Web:* www.jovasolutions.com	San Francisco	CA	94107	415-816-4482		463
Joveo 1047 Whipple Ave Ste B *Web:* www.joveo.com	Redwood City	CA	94062	650-376-8100		4
JOWA USA Inc 59 Porter Rd *TF:* 800-861-1560 ■ *Web:* www.jowa-usa.com	Littleton	MA	01460	978-486-9800		246
Joy Cone Co 3435 Lamor Rd *TF:* 800-242-2663 ■ *Web:* joycone.com	Hermitage	PA	16148	724-962-5747		296-9
Joy Dog Food PO Box 305 **Fax Area Code:* 618 ■ *TF:* 800-245-4125 ■ *Web:* joydogfood.com	Pinckneyville	IL	62274	800-245-4125	357-3651*	578
Joy Equipment Protection Inc 5690 Casitas Pass Rd *Web:* joyequipment.com	Carpinteria	CA	93014	805-684-0805	684-2358	189-10
Joy FM 93.3, The 1175 Senoia Rd *TF:* 877-800-7729 ■ *Web:* georgia.thejoyfm.com	Tyrone	GA	30290	770-487-4500	486-6400	645
Joy FM Network PO Box 25775 *Web:* www.joyfm.org	Winston-Salem	NC	27114	336-788-1155	788-7199	647
Joy Health Services LLC 2825 E 96th St *Web:* joyhealthservices.com	Indianapolis	IN	46240	317-816-7300	816-7304	363
Joy Lucky 3467 Broadway *Web:* www.joyluckyoh.com	Grove City	OH	43123	614-277-0827		457-11
Joy of Life Adult Day Care Inc 15190 SW 136th St *Web:* joylifecenter.com	Miami	FL	33196	786-293-3310		363
Joy of Tokyo 15 Pelham Rd Ste A *Web:* joyoftokyo.tv	Greenville	SC	29615	864-232-2888		671
Joy Signal Technology LLC 1020 Marauder St *TF:* 888-891-3551 ■ *Web:* www.joysignal.com	Chico	CA	95973	530-891-3551	891-3599	815
Joyce & Associates Pc 205 Portland St 3rd Fl *Web:* joyceassociates.com	Boston	MA	02114	617-523-1500	523-2400	41
Joyce David (Rep R - OH) 1124 Longworth House Office Bldg *TF:* 800-447-0529 ■ *Web:* www.joyce.house.gov	Washington	DC	20515	202-225-5731	225-3307	342-2
Joyce Engineering Inc 1604 Ownby Ln *Web:* joyceengineering.com	Richmond	VA	23220	804-355-4520	355-4282	261
Joyce Florist 2729 S Hampton Rd *Web:* www.joyceflorist.com	Dallas	TX	75224	214-942-1776		292
Joyce Foundation 321 N CLARK St Ste 1500 *Web:* www.joycefdn.org	Chicago	IL	60654	312-782-2464	782-4160	305
Joyce Goldstein & Associates Company LPA 1111 Superior Ave E Ste 620 *Web:* goldsteingragel.com	Cleveland	OH	44114	216-771-6633		41
Joyce Honda 3166 SR-10 *TF:* 844-332-5955 ■ *Web:* www.joycehonda.com	Denville	NJ	07834	844-332-5955		57

Phone | Fax | Class

Joyce John (Rep R - PA)
1337 Longworth House Office Bldg ... Washington DC 20515 202-225-2431 342-2
Web: www.johnjoyce.house.gov

Joyce Koons Buick Gmc
10660 Automotive Dr ... Manassas VA 20109 866-755-0072 516
TF: 866-755-0072 ■ *Web:* www.joycekoonsbuickgmc.com

Joyce Theatre Foundation
175 Eighth Ave ... New York NY 10011 212-691-9740 305
Web: www.joyce.org

Joyce Windows
1125 Berea Industrial Pkwy ... Berea OH 44017 800-824-7988 234
TF: 800-824-7988 ■ *Web:* www.joycewindows.com

Joyent Inc
655 Montgomery St Ste 1600 ... San Francisco CA 94111 415-400-0600 225
TF: 855-456-9368 ■ *Web:* www.joyent.com

Joy-Mark Inc 5935 S Pennsylvania Ave ... Cudahy WI 53110 414-769-8155 769-1595 663
Web: www.joy-mark.com

Joyner Fine Properties (JFP)
2727 Enterprise Pkwy ... Richmond VA 23294 804-270-9440 967-2770 652
Web: www.joynerfineproperties.com

Joyner Keeny & Assoc
1051 N Winstead Ave ... Rocky Mount NC 27804 252-977-3124 256
Web: joynerkeeny.com

Joytv 5668 192 St Ste 204 ... Surrey BC V3S2V7 604-576-6880 647
Web: www.joytv.ca

Joyva Corp 53 Varick Ave ... Brooklyn NY 11237 718-497-0170 366-8504 296-8
Web: www.joyva.com

JP Carroll Company Inc
310 N Madison Ave ... Los Angeles CA 90004 323-660-9230 189-8
Web: www.myhomepro.org

JP Digital Imaging Inc
230 Polaris Ave ... Mountain View CA 94043 650-965-0803 393
Web: www.jpdigital.com

JP Flooring Systems Inc
9097 Union Centre Blvd ... West Chester OH 45069 513-346-4300 364
Web: jpflooring.com

JP Graphics Inc 3001 E Venture Dr ... Appleton WI 54911 920-733-4483 627
Web: www.jpinc.com

JP Harvey Engineering Solutions
29 Kings Way ... Hampton VA 23669 757-722-7074 261
Web: jphes.com

JP Maguire Associates Inc
266 Brookside Rd ... Waterbury CT 06708 203-755-2297 573-8547 83
TF: 877-576-2484 ■ *Web:* www.jpmaguire.com

JP Marketing 7589 N Wilson St Ste 103 ... Fresno CA 93711 559-438-2180 195
Web: jpmktg.com

JP Mchale Pest Management Inc
241 Bleakley Ave ... Buchanan NY 10511 800-479-2284 577
TF: 800-479-2284 ■ *Web:* www.nopests.com

JP Morgan Chase & Co 270 Park Ave ... New York NY 10017 212-270-6000 70
Web: www.jpmorganchase.com

JP Morgan Chase and Co 277 Park Ave ... New York NY 10172 212-272-2000 528
NYSE: JPM ■ *Web:* www.jpmorgan.com

JP Oil Holdings LLC
1604 W Pinhook Rd Ste 300 PO Box 52584 ... LaFayette LA 70508 337-234-1170 234-9891 536
Web: www.jpoll.com

JPB Engineering Inc
47-388 Hui Iwa St Ste 16 ... Kaneohe HI 96744 808-436-8108 261
Web: jpbengineering.com

JPG (Jay Packaging Group)
100 Warwick Industrial Dr ... Warwick RI 02886 401-739-7200 88
Web: www.jaypack.com

JPI (Jan-Pro International Inc)
4221 S Santa Rita Ave Ste 101 ... Alpharetta GA 30009 678-336-1780 152
TF: 866-355-1064 ■ *Web:* jan-pro.com

JPI Healthcare Solutions Inc
52 Newton Plz ... Plainview NY 11803 516-513-1330 476
Web: www.jpihealthcare.com

JPL (Jet Propulsion Laboratory)
4800 Oak Grove Dr ... Pasadena CA 91109 818-354-9314 668
Web: www.jpl.nasa.gov

JPL Integrated Communictions Inc
471 Jplwick Dr ... Harrisburg PA 17111 717-558-8048 514
Web: www.jplcreative.com

JPM Productions Inc 582 Etowah Dr NE ... Marietta GA 30060 770-941-0543 941-0554 514
Web: www.jpmproductions.com

JPMorgan Fleming Asset Management
PO Box 8528 ... Boston MA 02266 800-480-4111 471-3053* 401
**Fax Area Code:* 816 ■ *TF:* 800-480-4111 ■ *Web:* www.am.jpmorgan.com

JPMS Cox PLLC
11300 Cantrell Rd Ste 301 ... Little Rock AR 72212 501-227-5800 227-5851 2
Web: www.jpmscox.com

JPN (Journal of Practical Nursing)
2071 N Bechtle Ave PMB 307 ... Springfield OH 45504 703-933-1003 940-4089 457-16
TF: 800-995-5222 ■ *Web:* www.napnes.org

JPS (Jenison Public Schools)
8375 20th Ave ... Jenison MI 49428 616-457-1402 457-8090 685
Web: www.jpsonline.org

JPS Aviation L L C 5410 Operations Rd ... Monroe LA 71203 318-512-4218 605-4893 348
Web: www.jpsaviation.com

JPS Industries Inc
55 Beattie Pl Ste 1510 ... Greenville SC 29601 864-239-3900 191-4

JPS Technologies Inc
11110 Deerfield Rd ... Cincinnati OH 45242 513-984-6400 984-8204 385
Web: jpstechnologies.com

JPT (Joint Production Technology)
15381 Hallmark Ct ... Macomb MI 48042 586-786-0080 786-0088 493
Web: www.jptonline.com

JPW Riggers Inc 6376 Thompson Rd ... Syracuse NY 13206 315-432-1111 536
Web: www.jpwcompanies.com

JR Automation 13365 Tyler St ... Holland MI 49424 833-800-7630 494
Web: www.jrautomation.com

JR Barto Heating/Air- Conditioning/Sheet Metal Inc
PO Box 2720 ... Orcutt CA 93457 805-736-5160 189-10
Web: jrbarto.com

JR Cigar Inc 2589 Eric Ln ... Burlington NC 27215 800-574-3576 457-3299 756
TF: 800 574-3576 ■ *Web:* www.jrcigars.com

JR Filanc Construction Inc
740 N Andreasen Dr ... Escondido CA 92029 760-941-7130 941-3969 188-10
TF: 877-225-5428 ■ *Web:* www.filanc.com

JR Finishers Inc 616 Albion Ave ... Schaumburg IL 60193 847-301-2556 301-2559 92
Web: www.jrfinishers.com

Jr Gales & Associates Inc
2704 Brownsville Rd ... Pittsburgh PA 15227 412-885-8885 261
Web: jrgales.com

JR Merritt Controls Inc
55 Sperry Ave ... Stratford CT 06615 203-381-0100 381-0400 203
TF: 800-333-5762 ■ *Web:* jrmerritt.com

JR Pierce Plumbing Co
14481 Wicks Blvd ... San Leandro CA 94577 510-483-5473 483-1808 189-10
TF: 800-345-7887 ■ *Web:* www.jrpierceplumbing.com

JR Simplot Co PO Box 27 ... Boise ID 83707 208-336-2110 296-21
TF: 800-832-8893 ■ *Web:* www.simplot.com

JR's Texas Bar-B-Que 180 Otto Cir ... Sacramento CA 95822 916-424-3520 424-9915 671
Web: www.jrtexasbbq.com

Jr3 Inc 22 Harter Ave ... Woodland CA 95776 530-661-3677 661-3701 201
Web: www.jr3.com

JRCERT (Joint Review Committee on Education in Radiologic Technology)
20 N Wacker Dr Ste 2850 ... Chicago IL 60606 312-704-5300 704-5304 48-1
Web: www.jrcert.org

JRCNMT (Joint Review Committee on Educational Programs in Nuclear Medicine Technology, The)
820 W Danforth Rd Ste B1 ... Edmond OK 73003 405-285-0546 285-0579 48-1
Web: www.jrcnmt.org

JRF (Jewish Reconstructionist Federation)
101 Greenwood Ave ... Jenkintown PA 19046 215-885-5601 885-5603 48-20
TF: 877-226-7573 ■ *Web:* archive.jewishrecon.org

JRH GoldenState Software Inc
29011 Golden Meadow Dr ... Rancho Palos Verdes CA 90275 310-544-1497 178-1
Web: www.jrh-inc.com

JRI (James Richardson Intl)
2415 2A Ave N ... Winnipeg MB R3B0X8 204-934-5961 275
Web: www.richardson.ca

JRI America Inc 277 Park Ave ... New York NY 10172 212-224-4200 177
Web: www.jri-america.com

Jrlon Inc 4344 Fox Rd ... Palmyra NY 14522 315-597-4067 597-9781 605-2
Web: www.jrlon.com

Jrm Consultants Inc
PO Box 90310 ... Santa Barbara CA 93190 805-564-3119 180
Web: www.jrmconsultants.com

JRM Industries Inc 1 Mattimore St ... Passaic NJ 07055 973-779-9340 779-8017 745-5
TF: 800-533-2697 ■ *Web:* www.jrm.com

JRMC (Jefferson Regional Medical Ctr)
1600 W 40th Ave ... Pine Bluff AR 71603 870-541-7100 374-3
Web: www.jrmc.org

JRN Inc 209 W Seventh St ... Columbia TN 38401 931-381-3000 670
Web: www.kfc.com

JRS (Jesuit Refugee Service/USA)
1016 16th St NW Ste 500 ... Washington DC 20036 202-629-5906 48-5
Web: jrsusa.org

JRS Consulting Inc 2906 Central St ... Evanston IL 60201 847-920-1701 920-1702 317
Web: www.jrsconsulting.net

JS Chinese - Casper 116 W Second St ... Casper WY 82601 307-577-0618 671
Web: www.jschinesewy.com

JS Dyer & Associates Inc
8891 Research Dr ... Irvine CA 92618 949-296-8858 256
Web: www.jsdyer.com

JS Paluch Company Inc
3708 River Rd Ste 400 ... Franklin Park IL 60131 847-678-9300 41
TF: 800-621-5197 ■ *Web:* www.jspaluch.com

JS West Milling Company Inc
501 9th St ... Modesto CA 95354 209-577-3221 527-5406 447
TF: 800-675-9378 ■ *Web:* www.jswest.com

JS Woodhouse Company Inc
1314 Union St ... West Springfield MA 01090 413-736-5462 732-3786 274
Web: www.jswoodhouse.com

JSA (Junior State of America)
111 Anza Blvd Ste 109 ... Burlingame CA 94010 650-347-1600 347-7200 48-11
TF: 800-334-5353 ■ *Web:* www.jsa.org

JSA (Jewelers Shipping Assn)
125 Carlsbad St ... Cranston RI 02920 401-943-6020 49-21
TF: 800-688-4572 ■ *Web:* www.jewelersshipping.com

JSA (Johnson Spellman & Associates Inc)
350 Research Ct ... Norcross GA 30092 770-447-4555 261
Web: jsace.com

Jsa Technologies
201 Main St Ste 1320 ... Fort Worth TX 76102 877-572-8324 396
TF: 877-572-8324 ■ *Web:* www.jsatech.com

JSB Industries Inc 130 Crescent Ave ... Chelsea MA 02150 617-846-1565 345
Web: muffintown.com

JSC (Johnson Supply Co) 50 SE St ... Pensacola FL 32502 850-434-7103 434-5647 770
TF: 800-476-7103 ■ *Web:* www.johnsonsupplyco.com

JSD Professional Services Inc
161 Horizon Dr Ste 101 ... Verona WI 53593 608-848-5060 727
Web: www.jsdinc.com

JSFirm LLC
Aviation Search Group
11350 Cleveland Gibbs Rd ... Roanoke TX 76262 817-560-0300 260
Web: www.jsfirm.com

JSG (Janesville Sand & Gravel Co)
1110 Harding St PO Box 427 ... Janesville WI 53547 608-754-7701 754-8555 503-4
TF: 800-955-7702 ■ *Web:* www.jsandg.com

JSG School of Massage Therapy
207 Livingston St ... Northvale NJ 07647 201-394-9200 685
Web: www.jsgmassage.org

JSI (John Staurulakis Inc)
7852 Walker Dr Ste 200 ... Greenbelt MD 20770 301-459-7590 194
Web: www.jsitel.com

JSJ Corp 700 Robbins Rd ... Grand Haven MI 49417 616-842-6350 847-3112 319-1
Web: www.jsjcorp.com

JSL Foods Inc
6623 E Washington Blvd ... Los Angeles CA 90031 323-223-2484 123
Web: www.jslfoods.com

JSM (Jimmy Swaggart Ministries)
8919 World Ministry Blvd PO Box 262550 ... Baton Rouge LA 70810 225-768-8300 48-20
TF: 800-288-8350 ■ *Web:* www.jsm.org

Name / Address	City	State	ZIP	Phone	Fax	Class
JSM Communications Inc						
N5764 County Rd Ste Tt	Sheboygan Falls	WI	53085	920-467-7550	467-8686	681
TF: 800-876-1987 ■ *Web:* www.jsmcom.com						
JSMN International Inc						
591 Summit Ave Ste 522	Jersey City	NJ	07306	201-792-6800		260
Web: www.jsmninc.com						
JSO (Jacksonville Symphony Orchestra)						
300 Water St Ste 200	Jacksonville	FL	32202	904-354-5547		573-3
Web: www.jaxsymphony.org						
JSR Micro Inc 1280 N Mathilda Ave	Sunnyvale	CA	94089	408-543-8800		696
Web: www.jsrmicro.com						
JSR Power Systems International LLC						
5563 De Zavala Rd Ste 200	San Antonio	TX	78249	210-558-1943		226
Web: jsrpsi.com						
JSSI (Jet Support Services Inc)						
180 N Stetson Ave	Chicago	IL	60601	312-644-4444		194
Web: www.jetsupport.com						
J-Systems Franchising Corp						
2147 Market St	Nesquehoning	PA	18240	570-645-2015	645-2159	647
Web: www.wmgh.com						
JT Fennell Company Inc						
1104 N Front St	Chillicothe	IL	61523	309-274-2145		492
Web: www.jtfennell.com						
JT Mega 4020 Minnetonka Blvd	Minneapolis	MN	55416	952-929-1370		7
Web: jtmega.com						
JT Schmid's Restaurant & Brewery						
2610 E Katella Ave	Anaheim	CA	92806	714-634-9200		671
Web: www.jtschmidsrestaurants.com						
JT Thorpe & Son Inc 1060 Hensley St	Richmond	CA	94801	510-233-2500	233-2901	318
Web: www.jtthorpe.com						
JT Wein Inc 15548 Hwy 190	Opelousas	LA	70570	337-948-3939	948-8883	780
TF: 800-467-9346 ■ *Web:* www.jtwein.com						
JTB (Japan Travel Bureau USA Inc)						
2 W 45th St Ste 305	New York	NY	10036	212-698-4900	586-9686	771
TF: 800-223-6104 ■ *Web:* www.jtbusa.com						
JTB (Jordan Tourism Board)						
1307 Dolley Madison Blvd Ste 2A	McLean	VA	22101	703-243-7404	243-7406	775
TF: 877-733-5673 ■ *Web:* www.visitjordan.com						
JTD Stamping Company Inc						
403 Wyandanch Ave	West Babylon	NY	11704	631-643-4144	643-4016	488
TF: 800-927-7907 ■ *Web:* www.jtdstamping.com						
J-TEC Associates Inc						
5005 Blairs Forest Ln NE Ste L	Cedar Rapids	IA	52402	319-393-5200	393-5211	385
TF: 800-959-0872 ■ *Web:* www.j-tecassociates.com						
JTech Communications Inc						
1400 Northbrook Pkwy Ste 320	Suwanee	GA	30024	800-321-6221		735
TF: 800-321-6221 ■ *Web:* www.jtech.com						
Jtek Data Solutions LLC						
10411 Motor City Dr	Bethesda	MD	20817	301-469-1900		177
Web: jtekds.com						
JTEKT Corp 29570 Clemens Rd	Westlake	OH	44145	440-835-1000	835-9347	75
TF: 800-263-5163 ■ *Web:* jtekt-na.com						
JTJ Commercial Interiors						
200 Shady Grove Rd	Nashville	TN	37214	615-872-9363		291
Web: www.jtjci.com						
Jtl Technical Services LLC						
113 Crosby Rd U8 Ste 8	Dover	NH	03820	603-427-2500		177
Web: www.jtltechnicalservices.com						
JTM Foods Inc 2126 E 33rd St	Erie	PA	16510	814-899-0886		296-1
Web: www.jjsbakery.net						
JTM Provisions Company Inc						
200 Sales Dr	Harrison	OH	45030	800-626-2308	367-1132*	297-8
**Fax Area Code:* 513 ■ *TF:* 800-626-2308 ■ *Web:* www.jtmfoodgroup.com						
JTPR (Jasculca/Terman & Assoc)						
730 N Franklin St Ste 510	Chicago	IL	60654	312-337-7400		636
Web: jtpr.com						
JTS Direct LLC 1180 Walnut Ridge Dr	Hartland	WI	53029	877-387-9500		627
TF: 877-387-9500 ■ *Web:* www.jtsdirect.com						
JTS Farm Store 447 E 1st Ave	Glenns Ferry	ID	83623	208-366-2538	366-7527	755
Web: www.jtsfarmstore.com						
Juab County 160 N Main St	Nephi	UT	84648	435-623-3410		338
Web: www.co.juab.ut.us						
Juanita K. Hammons Hall for the Performing Arts						
901 S National Ave	Springfield	MO	65897	417-836-7678	836-6891	572
TF: 888-476-7849 ■ *Web:* www.hammonshall.com						
Juanita's Foods Inc PO Box 847	Wilmington	CA	90748	800-303-2965		296-36
TF: 800-303-2965 ■ *Web:* www.juanitas.com						
J-U-B Engineers Inc						
250 S Beechwood Ave Ste 201	Boise	ID	83709	208-376-7330		261
Web: web.jub.com						
Juban's 3739 Perkins Rd	Baton Rouge	LA	70808	225-346-8422	387-2601	671
Web: www.jubans.com						
Jubilant Life Sciences (USA) Inc						
790 Township Line Rd Ste 175	Yardley	PA	19067	908-658-9988	658-9927	146
Web: www.jubl.com						
Jubilee College State Park						
13921 W Rt 150	Brimfield	IL	61517	309-446-3758	446-3183	565
Web: www.dnr.illinois.gov						
Jubilee Foods Inc						
13050 N Wintzell Ave	Bayou La Batre	AL	36509	251-824-2110		296-14
Web: www.jubileeseafood.com						
Jubilee Theatre 506 Main St	Fort Worth	TX	76102	817-338-4204		573-4
Web: www.jubileetheatre.org						
Jubitz Corp 33 NE Middlefield Rd	Portland	OR	97211	503-283-1111		324
TF: 800-523-0600 ■ *Web:* www.jubitz.com						
Judaica Press Inc 123 Ditmas Ave	Brooklyn	NY	11218	718-972-6200		637-2
TF: 800-972-6201 ■ *Web:* www.judaicapress.com						
Judd & Black 3001 Hewitt Ave	Everett	WA	98201	425-258-2591		35
Web: juddblack.com						
Judd & Judd PLLC						
9700 Park Plaza Ave Ste 208	Louisville	KY	40241	502-292-5300		2
Web: juddcpa.com						
Judd Wire Inc 124 Tpke Rd	Turners Falls	MA	01376	413-863-4357	863-2305	814
TF: 800-545-5833 ■ *Web:* www.juddwire.com						
Judge CR Magney State Park						
4051 E Hwy 61	Grand Marais	MN	55604	218-387-6300		565
Web: www.dnr.state.mn.us						
Judge Group Inc						
300 Conshohocken State Rd Ste 300	West Conshohocken	PA	19428	610-667-7700	667-1058	721
TF: 888-228-7162 ■ *Web:* www.judge.com						
Judge Organization Companies, The						
201A Export St	Newark	NJ	07114	973-491-0600		41
Web: www.judgeorg.com						
Judicare Wisconsin Incorporated Attys						
401 Fifth St Ste 200	Wausau	WI	54403	715-842-1681		428
TF: 800-472-1638 ■ *Web:* www.judicare.org						
Judicate West						
1851 E First St Ste 1600	Santa Ana	CA	92705	714-834-1340	834-1344	41
TF: 800-488-8805 ■ *Web:* www.judicatewest.com						
Judicial Dispute Resolution LLC						
1425 Fourth Ave Ste 300	Seattle	WA	98101	206-223-1669	223-0450	41
Web: jdrllc.com						
Judicial Panel on Multidistrict Litigation						
Thurgood Marshall Federal Judiciary Bldg 1 Columbus Cir NE Rm G 255 N Lobby	Washington	DC	20544	202-502-2800	502-2888	341
Web: www.jpml.uscourts.gov						
Judicial Watch Inc						
425 Third St SW Ste 800	Washington	DC	20024	888-593-8442	646-5199*	48-7
**Fax Area Code:* 202 ■ *TF:* 888-593-8442 ■ *Web:* www.judicialwatch.org						
Judith Basin County						
91 Third St N PO Box 339	Stanford	MT	59479	406-566-2277		338
Web: www.co.judith-basin.mt.us						
Judson Center Inc 4410 W 13 Mile Rd	Royal Oak	MI	48073	248-549-4339		726
Web: www.judsoncenter.org						
Judson College 302 Bibb St	Marion	AL	36756	334-683-5110		166
TF: 800-447-9472 ■ *Web:* www.judson.edu						
Judson University 1151 N State St	Elgin	IL	60123	847-628-2500	628-2526	166
TF: 800-879-5376 ■ *Web:* www.judsonu.edu						
Judy Harris Cooking School						
2402 Nordok Pl	Alexandria	VA	22306	703-768-3767		685
Web: www.judyharris.com						
Judys Staffing Services Inc						
997 Governors Ln Ste 150	Lexington	KY	40503	859-223-5005		260
Web: www.thejssgroup.com						
JUF (Jewish United Fund/Jewish Federation of Metropolitan Chicago)						
30 S Wells St	Chicago	IL	60606	312-346-6700	444-2086	48-20
TF: 855-275-5237 ■ *Web:* www.juf.org						
JUGGLE Magazine						
3315 E Russell Rd Ste A4 203	Las Vegas	NV	89120	702-798-0099		530
Web: www.juggle.org						
Jugs Sports 11885 SW Herman Rd	Tualatin	OR	97062	800-547-6843	691-1100*	710
**Fax Area Code:* 503 ■ *TF:* 800-547-6843 ■ *Web:* www.jugssports.com						
Juice It Up! Franchise Corp						
17915 Sky Pk Cir Ste J	Irvine	CA	92614	949-475-0146	475-0137	310
Web: www.juiceitup.com						
Juice Mafia 2436 S 11th St	Niles	MI	49120	574-485-8073		756
Web: juicemafia.com						
Juice Studios Inc 1648 10th St	Santa Monica	CA	90404	310-460-7830		7
Web: www.juicestudios.tv						
Juilliard School, The						
Wallace Library						
60 Lincoln Center Plz	New York	NY	10023	212-799-5000		434-4
Web: www.juilliard.edu						
Juju Inc 151 First Ave Ste 19	New York	NY	10003	212-537-3898		260
Web: www.juju.com						
Jules Borel & Co 1110 Grand Blvd	Kansas City	MO	64106	816-421-6110		411
TF: 800-776-6858 ■ *Web:* julesborel.com						
Jules Saint-Michel Luthier - Economuseum of Violin-Making						
57 Ontario St W	Montreal	QC	H2X1Y8	514-288-4343	288-9296	520
Web: www.luthiersaintmichel.com						
Jules Seltzer Assoc						
9020 W Olympic Blvd	Beverly Hills	CA	90211	310-274-7243		320
Web: www.julesseltzer.com						
Julia Pfeiffer Burns State Park						
52801 California SR 1	Big Sur	CA	93920	831-667-2315		565
Web: www.parks.ca.gov						
Julian F. Keith Alcohol & Drug Abuse Treatment Ctr						
201 Tabernacle Rd	Black Mountain	NC	28711	828-257-6200	257-6300	726
Web: www.ncdhhs.gov						
Julian J. Rodriguez PA						
2600 S Douglas Rd Ste 900	Coral Gables	FL	33134	305-445-0777		2
Web: www.jjrpa.com						
Julian Tours 1721 Crestwood Dr	Alexandria	VA	22302	703-379-2300	379-5030	760
TF: 800-541-7936 ■ *Web:* juliantours.com						
Julian's 318 Broadway	Providence	RI	02909	401-861-1770		671
Web: www.juliansprovidence.com						
Juliano & Marks LLC						
1224 Farmington Ave	West Hartford	CT	06107	860-521-0569	521-0558	41
Web: jmattys.com						
Julie Inc 3275 Executive Dr	Joliet	IL	60431	815-741-5000		737
TF: 800-892-0123 ■ *Web:* www.illinois1call.com						
Julie Morgenstern Enterprises LLC						
850 7th Ave	New York	NY	10019	212-586-8084		194
Web: www.juliemorgenstern.com						
Juliette Gordon Low Girl Scout National Ctr						
10 E Oglethorpe Ave	Savannah	GA	31401	912-233-4501		50-3
Web: www.juliettegordonlowbirthplace.org						
Julin Printing Company Inc						
801 N Birch St	Monticello	IA	52310	319-465-3558		627
TF: 800-752-6782 ■ *Web:* www.julin.com						
Julio's Barrio 10450 82nd Ave	Edmonton	AB	T6E2A2	780-431-0774		671
Web: juliosbarrio.com						
Julio's Cantina LLC 54 State St	Montpelier	VT	05602	802-229-9348		671
Web: www.juliosmontpelier.com						
Julio's Mexican Food						
8050 Gateway Blvd E	El Paso	TX	79907	915-591-7676	592-1294	671
Web: www.juliosmexicanfood.com						
Julius Boehm Pool						
50 SE Clark St PO Box 1307	Issaquah	WA	98027	425-837-3350	897-3309	354
Web: www.issaquahwa.gov						
Julius Koch 1750 Satellite Blvd Ste 100	Buford	GA	30519	700-995-2222		745-5
TF: 800-252-2512 ■ *Web:* jkusa.com						
July Business Services						
400 Austin Ave Ste 1200 PO Box 2208	Waco	TX	76701	254-296-4015		41
TF: 888-333-5859 ■ *Web:* www.julyservices.com						

Name / Address	Phone	Fax	Class
Jumboshrimp Advertising Inc 544 Bryant St . . . San Francisco CA 94107 *Web:* jumboshrimp.com	415-369-0500		7
Jump Film Editing 625 Broadway Ste 7 . . . New York NY 10012 *Web:* www.jumpeditorial.tv	917-797-0151		434-3
Jump River Electric Co-op PO Box 99 . . . Ladysmith WI 54848 *TF:* 866-273-5111 ■ *Web:* www.jrec.net	715-532-5524	532-3065	245
Jump Start Press Inc 802 Cedar Ave . . . Point Pleasant Beach NJ 08742 *Web:* www.jumpstartpress.com	732-892-4994		637-2
JumpCloud 361 Centennial Pkwy Ste 300 . . . Louisville CO 80027 *TF:* 855-212-3122 ■ *Web:* jumpcloud.com	855-212-3122		178-1
Jumping Brook Country Club 210 Jumping Brook Rd . . . Neptune City NJ 07753 *Web:* www.jumpingbrookcc.com	732-922-8200		711
JumpSport Inc 2055 S Seventh St Ste A . . . San Jose CA 95112 *TF:* 888-567-5867 ■ *Web:* www.jumpsport.com	408-213-2551		41
JumpStart Partners Inc 3616 Far West Blvd Ste 117-294 . . . Austin TX 78731 *Web:* www.jumpstartpartners.com	512-576-9000		70
JumpstartMD Inc 595 Price Ave Ste 200 . . . Redwood City CA 94063 *Web:* www.jumpstartmd.com	650-701-1460		810
Jun Japanese Restaurant 1760 Dublin Blvd . . . Colorado Springs CO 80918 *Web:* www.jun-japanese.com	719-531-9368		671
Junction City Area Chamber of Commerce 222 W Sixth St PO Box 26 . . . Junction City KS 66441 *Web:* www.junctioncitychamber.org	785-762-2632		139
Junction Networks Inc 55 Broad St 20th Fl . . . New York NY 10004 *TF:* 800-801-3381 ■ *Web:* www.onsip.com	800-801-3381		387
June Kelly Gallery 166 Mercer St Ste 3C . . . New York NY 10012 *Web:* www.junekellygallery.com	212-226-1660		42
June L. Mazer Lesbian Archives 020 N Robertson Blvd . . . West Hollywood CA 90069 *Web:* www.mazerlesbianarchives.org	310-659-2478		48-13
Juneau Associates Incorporated PC 2100 State St . . . Granite City IL 62040 *Web:* www.jaipc.com	618-877-1400		261
Juneau Chamber of Commerce 9301 Glacier Hwy Ste 110 . . . Juneau AK 99801 *TF:* 888-581-2201 ■ *Web:* www.juneauchamber.com	907-463-3488	463-3489	139
Juneau Convention & Visitors Bureau 800 Glacier Ave Ste 201 . . . Juneau AK 99801 *Web:* www.traveljuneau.com	907-586-1737		206
Juneau County 220 E State St . . . Mauston WI 53948 *Web:* www.juneaucounty.com	608-847-9300		338
Juneau Empire 3100 Ch Dr . . . Juneau AK 99801 *Web:* juneauempire.com	907-586-3740	586-9097	532-2
Juneau Harbor 155 S Seward St . . . Juneau AK 99801 *Web:* www.beta.juneau.org	907-586-5255	586-2507	618
Juneau International Airport 1873 Shell Simmons Dr Ste 200 . . . Juneau AK 99801 *Web:* www.beta.juneau.org	907-789-7821	789-1227	27
Juneau Symphony Orchestra 522 W Tenth St PO Box 21236 . . . Juneau AK 99802 *Web:* www.juneausymphony.org	907-586-4676	463-2555	573-3
Juneau-Douglas City Museum 292 Marine Way . . . Juneau AK 99801 *Web:* beta.juneau.org	907-586-5249		520
Junex Inc 2795 Laurier Blvd Ste 200 . . . Quebec City QC G1V4M7 *Web:* www.junex.ca	418-654-9661		536
Junge Control Inc 640 29th Ave Sw . . . Cedar Rapids IA 52408 *TF:* 800-541-7834 ■ *Web:* www.jungecontrol.com	319-365-0686		201
Jungle Adventures 26205 E Colonial Dr . . . Christmas FL 32709 *TF:* 877-424-2867 ■ *Web:* www.jungleadventures.com	407-568-2885		823
Jungle Cat World Inc 3667 Concession Rd 6 . . . Orono ON L0B1M0 *Web:* www.junglecatworld.com	905-983-5016	983-9858	823
Jungle Gardens LA Hwy 329 . . . Avery Island LA 70513 *Web:* www.junglegardens.org	337-369-6243		97
Jungle Island 1111 Parrot Jungle Trl . . . Miami FL 33132 *Web:* www.jungleisland.com	305-400-7000	400-7291	823
Jungle Scout 2021 E 5th St Ste 150 . . . Austin TX 78702 *Web:* www.junglescout.com	512-644-2014		178-8
Jungle Theater 2951 Lindale Ave S . . . Minneapolis MN 55408 *Web:* www.jungletheater.org	612-822-7063		572
Juniata College 1700 Moore St . . . Huntingdon PA 16652 *TF:* 877-586-4282 ■ *Web:* www.juniata.edu	814-641-3000	641-3100	166
Juniata County Courthouse Bridge & Main St PO Box 68 . . . Mifflintown PA 17059 *Web:* www.juniataco.org	717-436-7704	436-7734	338
Juniata Valley Area Chamber of Commerce 1 W Market St . . . Lewistown PA 17044 *Web:* juniatarivervalley.org	717-248-6713	248-6714	139
Junior Achievement of Canada (JACAN) 161 Bay St 27th Fl . . . Toronto ON M5J2S1 *TF:* 800-265-0699 ■ *Web:* jacanada.org	416-622-4602	622-6861	48-11
Junior Chamber International Inc 15645 Olive Blvd . . . Chesterfield MO 63017 *Web:* www.jci.cc	636-449-3100	449-3107	48-7
Junior League of Augusta (JLA) Surrey Ctr 375 Highland Ave . . . Augusta GA 30909 *Web:* www.jlaugusta.org	706-736-0033	736-6526	48-6
Junior League of Charleston (JLC) 51 Folly Rd . . . Charleston SC 29407 *Web:* www.jlcharleston.org	843-763-5284	763-1626	48-6
Junior League of Charlotte Inc (JLC) 1332 Maryland Ave . . . Charlotte NC 28209 *Web:* www.jlcharlotte.org	704-375-5993	375-9730	48-6
Junior League of Cobb-Marietta (JLCM) 505 Kennesaw Ave . . . Marietta GA 30060 *Web:* www.jlcm.org	770-422-5266	427-2253	48-6
Junior League of Greenville Inc (JLG) 120 Greenacre Rd . . . Greenville SC 29607 *Web:* www.jlgreenville.org	864-233-2663	233-9092	48-6
Junior League of Lafayette (JLL) 504 Richland Ave . . . Lafayette LA 70508 *TF:* 800-757-3651 ■ *Web:* www.juniorleagueoflafayette.com	337-988-2739	988-1079	48-6
Junior League of McAllen (JLM) 514 E Dove Ave . . . McAllen TX 78502 *Web:* www.juniorleaguemcallen.org	956-682-0071		48-6
Junior League of Mobile (JLM) 57 N Sage Ave . . . Mobile AL 36607 *Web:* www.juniorleaguemobile.org	251-471-3348	471-3340	48-6
Junior League of Monroe Inc (JLM) 2811 Cameron St . . . Monroe LA 71201 *Web:* www.jlmonroe.org	318-322-3236	322-3299	48-6
Junior League of Odessa Inc (JLO) 2707 Kermit Hwy . . . Odessa TX 79764 *Web:* www.jlodessa.org	432-332-0095	333-6515	48-6
Junior League of Peoria (JLP) 114 State St Ste 2A . . . Peoria IL 61602 *Web:* www.juniorleagueofpeoria.org	309-685-9312		48-6
Junior League of Pueblo (JL) 421 N Main St Ste 415 . . . Pueblo CO 81003 *Web:* www.jlofpueblo.org	719-542-0491		637-2
Junior League of Rochester (JLR) 110 Linden Oaks Dr Ste A . . . Rochester NY 14625 *Web:* www.jlroch.org	585-385-8590	385-1873	48-6
Junior League of Springfield (JLS) 2574 E Bennett St . . . Springfield MO 65804 *Web:* www.jlspringfield.org	417-887-9422		637-2
Junior League of Springfield (JLS) 2800 Montvale . . . Springfield IL 62704 *Web:* www.jlsil.org	217-544-5557		48-6
Junior League of Tampa Inc (JLT) 87 Columbia Dr . . . Tampa FL 33606 *Web:* www.jltampa.org	813-254-1734		48-22
Junior League of the Palm Beaches (JLPB) 470 Columbia Dr Bldg F . . . West Palm Beach FL 33409 *Web:* www.jlpb.org	561-689-7590		48-6
Junior League of Tulsa Inc (JLT) 3633 S Yale Ave . . . Tulsa OK 74135 *Web:* www.jltulsa.org	918-663-6100	627-9588	48-6
Junior State of America (JSA) 111 Anza Blvd Ste 109 . . . Burlingame CA 94010 *TF:* 800-334-5353 ■ *Web:* www.jsa.org	650-347-1600	347-7200	48-11
Junior's Building Materials Inc 7574 Battlefield Pkwy . . . Ringgold GA 30736 *Web:* www.juniorsbuildingmaterials.com	706-937-3400		364
Juniper Advisory LLC 191 N Wacker Dr Ste 900 . . . Chicago IL 60606 *Web:* www.juniperadvisory.com	312-506-3000		690
Juniper Industries Inc 72-15 Metropolitan Ave PO Box 148 . . . Middle Village NY 11379 *Web:* juniperind.com	718-326-2546	326-3786	697
Juniper Networks Inc 1194 N Mathilda Ave . . . Sunnyvale CA 94089 *NYSE:* JNPR ■ *TF:* 888-586-4737 ■ *Web:* www.juniper.net	408-745-2000	745-2100	176
Juniper Payments 9440 E Boston . . . Wichita KS 67207 *TF:* 800-453-9400 ■ *Web:* www.juniperpayments.com	316-267-3200		174
Juniper Square 343 Sansome St Ste 600 . . . San Francisco CA 94104 *Web:* www.junipersquare.com	415-841-2722		652
Junipero Serra Museum 2727 Presidio Dr . . . San Diego CA 92103 *Web:* www.sandiegohistory.org	619-232-6203		520
Junkermier Clark Campanella Stevens PC 501 Park Dr S . . . Great Falls MT 59405 *Web:* jccscpa.com	406-761-2820	761-2825	2
Juno Pacific 1100 McKinley St . . . Anoka MN 55303 *Web:* junopacific.com	763-703-5000		604
Jupe Feeds Inc 405 S 2nd St . . . Temple TX 76504 *TF:* 800-792-3038 ■ *Web:* www.wendlands.com	254-773-5211		447
Jupe Mills Inc 107 S Roberts St . . . West TX 76691 *Web:* www.westfeeds.com	254-826-5301	826-3233	447
Jupiter Aluminum Corp 2800 S River Rd . . . Des Plaines IL 60018 **Fax Area Code:* 847 ■ *TF:* 800-392-7265 ■ *Web:* www.jupiteraluminum.com	219-932-3322	928-0795*	660
Jupiter Beach Resort 5 N Hwy A1A . . . Jupiter FL 33477 *TF:* 877-389-0571 ■ *Web:* www.jupiterbeachresort.com	561-746-2511		669
Jupiter Group, The 6565 W Loop S Ste 770 . . . Bellaire TX 77401 *Web:* www.jupgroup.com	832-778-1960	778-1933	693
Jupiter Marine International Holdings 1103 12th Ave E . . . Palmetto FL 34221 *Web:* jupitermarine.com	941-729-5000		698
Jupiter Medical Ctr 1210 S Old Dixie Hwy . . . Jupiter FL 33458 *Web:* www.jupitermed.com	561-263-2234		374-3
Jupiter Realty Company LLC 401 Michigan Ave 13th Fl . . . Chicago IL 60611 *Web:* www.jupiterrealty.com	312-642-6000	642-2316	653
Jupitor Corporation USA 55 Fairbanks . . . Irvine CA 92618 *Web:* www.jpus.com	949-588-0505		21
Juran Institute Inc 160 Main St . . . Southington CT 06489 *TF:* 800-338-7726 ■ *Web:* www.juran.com	800-338-7726		113
Jurupa Mountains Discovery Ctr 7621 Granite Hill Dr . . . Riverside CA 92509 *Web:* jmdc.org	951-685-5818	685-1240	50-2
Jury Research Institute 2617 Danville Blvd PO Box 100 . . . Alamo CA 94507 *TF:* 800-233-5879 ■ *Web:* www.juryresearchinstitute.com	925-932-5663	932-8409	445
Just Bagels Manufacturing Inc 527 Casanova St . . . Bronx NY 10474 *Web:* justbagels.com	718-328-9700	328-9997	297-8
Just Bead It 9514 Third Ave . . . Stone Harbor NJ 08247 *Web:* www.justbeadit.net	609-368-0400		411
Just Born Inc 1300 Stefko Blvd . . . Bethlehem PA 18017 *TF:* 800-445-5787 ■ *Web:* www.justborn.com	610-867-7568	867-3983	296-8

Name / Address	City	State	ZIP	Phone	Fax	Class
Just Click Media Group LLC 16782-B Red Hill Ave *TF:* 866-623-8777 ■ *Web:* www.justclickmedia.com	Irvine	CA	92606	866-623-8777		5
Just Desserts Inc 5000 Fulton Dr *Web:* www.justdesserts.com	Fairfield	CA	94534	415-780-6860	780-6861	68
Just Floors LLC 550 Poyner Dr *Web:* justfloorsinc.net	Longwood	FL	32750	407-332-7729		290
Just for Laughs Inc 2101 St-Laurent Blvd *Web:* www.hahaha.com	Montreal	QC	H2X2T5	514-845-3155	845-4140	514
Just For Wraps Inc 4871 S Santa Fe Ave *Web:* www.wrapper.com	Vernon	CA	90058	213-239-0503	239-0515	157-6
Just Four Paws Academy of Pet Styling 1530 W 26th St *Web:* www.justfourpawsacademy.com	Erie	PA	16508	814-456-7297	456-7299	167-3
Just Looking Gallery 746 Higuera St Ste 1 *Web:* justlookinggallery.com	San Luis Obispo	CA	93401	805-541-6663		42
Just Manufacturing Company Inc 9233 King St *Web:* www.justmfg.com	Franklin Park	IL	60131	847-678-5150		612
Just Packaging Inc 450 Oak Tree Ave Ste 1 *Web:* www.justpackaging.com	South Plainfield	NJ	07080	908-753-6700	753-6709	557
Just Service Inc 2940 N Clark St *Web:* www.justservice.com	Chicago	IL	60657	773-871-7171		175
Just Solutions Inc 7300 Pittsford Palmyra Rd (RT 31) PO Box 118 *Web:* www.justinc.com	Fairport	NY	14450	585-425-3420	425-3421	175
Justia Inc 1380 Pear Ave Unit 2b *TF:* 800-300-0001 ■ *Web:* www.justia.com	Mountain View	CA	94043	888-587-8421		428
Justice Design Group (JDG) 500 S Grand Ave Ste 110 *Web:* jdg.com	Los Angeles	CA	90071	213-437-0102	437-0860	439
Justice in Aging 1444 'I' St Ste 1100 *Web:* www.justiceinaging.org	Washington	DC	20005	202-289-6976		49-10
Justice Institute of British Columbia 715 McBride Blvd *TF:* 888-865-7764 ■ *Web:* www.jibc.ca	New Westminster	BC	V3L5T4	604-525-5422	528-5518	162
Justice Resource Institute Inc 160 Gould St Ste 300 **Fax Area Code:* 508 ■ *Web:* jri.org	Needham	MA	02494	781-559-4900	947-1569*	412
Justice Solutions of America Inc 2750 Taylor Ave Ste A-56 *TF:* 888-577-4766 ■ *Web:* www.federalprisonconsultants.com	Orlando	FL	32806	888-577-4766		463
Justice Systems Inc 4600 McLeod NE *Web:* www.justicesystems.com	Albuquerque	NM	87109	505-883-3987	883-2845	177
Justice Systems Press PO Box 2852 *TF:* 800-553-1903 ■ *Web:* www.justicesystemspress.com	Port Angeles	WA	98362	360-417-8845		637-2
Justifacts Credential Verification Inc 5250 Logan Ferry Rd *TF:* 800-356-6885 ■ *Web:* www.justifacts.com	Murrysville	PA	15668	800-356-6885		708
Justin Boot Inc 610 W Daggett Ave *TF:* 800-548-1021 ■ *Web:* www.justinbrands.com	Fort Worth	TX	76104	817-332-4385	348-2037	301
Justin Bradley 1725 I St NW Ste 300 *Web:* www.justinbradley.com	Washington	DC	20006	202-457-8400		721
Justin Electronics Corp 400 Oser Ave Ste 800 *Web:* www.justinelectronics.com	Hauppauge	NY	11788	631-951-4900	951-4747	246
Justin Seed Company Inc 524 S Hwy 156 *Web:* www.justinseed.com	Justin	TX	76247	940-648-2751		276
Justin Winter & Associates LLC 106 Cliffs South Pkwy *Web:* justinwinter.com	Salem	SC	29676	864-481-4444		652
Justiss Oil Company Inc 1120 E Oak St *TF:* 800-256-2501 ■ *Web:* www.justissoil.com	Jena	LA	71342	318-992-4111	992-7201	540
Justrite Manufacturing Co 2454 E Dempster St Ste 300 *TF:* 800-798-9250 ■ *Web:* www.justrite.com	Des Plaines	IL	60016	847-298-9250	298-9261	198
Just-Us Printers Inc 555 N Old Missouri Rd *Web:* www.justusprinters.com	Springdale	AR	72764	479-751-0385		627
Justworks Inc PO Box 7119 Church Street Sta *Web:* www.justworks.com	New York	NY	10008	646-663-1347		260
JUV Consulting LLC 1460 Broadway *Web:* www.juvconsulting.com	New York	NY	10036	609-575-1255		195
Juvenile Corrections Center-Nampa 1650 11th Ave N *Web:* www.idjc.idaho.gov	Nampa	ID	83687	208-465-8443		412
Juvenile Corrections Centre-Saint Anthony 2220 E 600 N PO Box 40 *Web:* www.governmentjobs.com	Saint Anthony	ID	83445	208-624-3462		412
JV Driver Installations Ltd 212- 3601 82 Ave *Web:* www.jvdriver.com	Leduc	AB	T9E0H7	780-980-5837	980-5890	261
JV Manufacturing Inc 1603 Burtner Rd *Web:* www.jvmfgco.com	Natrona Heights	PA	15065	724-224-1704	224-7728	386
JVA Consulting LLC 2465 Sheridan Blvd *TF:* 800-292-9551 ■ *Web:* www.jvaconsulting.com	Denver	CO	80214	303-477-4896		194
JVA Inc 1319 Spruce St *Web:* www.jvajva.com	Boulder	CO	80302	303-444-1951		261
JVC Professional Products Co 1700 Valley Rd *TF:* 800-252-5722 ■ *Web:* www.pro.jvc.com	Wayne	NJ	07470	973-317-5135	317-5030	52
Jviation Inc 35 S 400 W Ste 200 *Web:* jviation.com	Saint George	UT	84770	435-673-4677		261
JVKellyGroup Inc 14 Wall St *Web:* www.jvkg.com	Huntington	NY	11743	631-427-2888		196
JVLNET Internet Services Inc The Electrolarm Building 1220 W Court St *TF:* 800-570-6094 ■ *Web:* www.jvlnet.com	Janesville	WI	53545	608-758-8750	754-0015	224
JVT Advisors 35 New England Business Ctr *Web:* www.jvtadvisors.com	Andover	MA	01810	978-683-4555	681-4569	631
JW Aluminum 435 Old Mt Holly Rd *TF:* 877-586-5314 ■ *Web:* www.jwaluminum.com	Goose Creek	SC	29445	877-586-5314		485
JW Chalkley III PA 1130 SE 17th St *TF:* 866-629-7511 ■ *Web:* chalkleylaw.com	Ocala	FL	34471	352-629-7511		41
JW Hampton Jr & Company Inc 161-15 Rockaway Blvd *Web:* www.jwhampton.com	Jamaica	NY	11434	718-276-0301		311
JW Jones Lumber Co 1443 Northside Rd *Web:* www.jwjoneslumber.com	Elizabeth City	NC	27909	252-771-2497	771-8252	683
JW Jung Seed Co 335 S High St **Fax Area Code:* 800 ■ *TF:* 800-297-3123 ■ *Web:* www.jungseed.com	Randolph	WI	53956	920-326-5672	692-5864*	694
JW Marriott Orlando Grande Lakes Resort 4040 Central Florida Pkwy *TF:* 800-576-5750 ■ *Web:* www.grandelakes.com	Orlando	FL	32837	407-206-2300	206-2301	669
JW Mays Inc 9 Bond St *NASDAQ: MAYS* ■ *Web:* www.jwmays.com	Brooklyn	NY	11201	718-624-7400		655
JW Pepper & Son Inc 2480 Industrial Blvd *TF:* 800-345-6296 ■ *Web:* www.jwpepper.com	Paoli	PA	19301	610-648-0500	993-0563	526
JW Peters Inc 500 W Market St *TF:* 866-265-7888 ■ *Web:* journaltimes.com	Burlington	WI	53105	262-763-2401	763-2779	183
J-W Power Company Inc 16479 N Dallas Pkwy Ste 850 LB-8 *Web:* www.jwpower.net	Addison	TX	75001	972-233-8191		536
JW Speaker Corp N 120 W 19434 Freistadt Rd PO Box 1011 *TF:* 800-558-7288 ■ *Web:* www.jwspeaker.com	Germantown	WI	53022	262-251-6660	251-2918	438
JW Winco Inc 2815 S Calhoun Rd *TF:* 800-877-8351 ■ *Web:* www.jwwinco.com	New Berlin	WI	53151	262-786-8227		295
JWC (J.W. Childs Associates LP) 500 Totten Pond Rd 6th Fl *Web:* www.jwchilds.com	Waltham	MA	02451	617-753-1100	753-1101	792
JWF Industries 84 Iron St PO Box 1286 *Web:* www.jwfi.com	Johnstown	PA	15907	814-539-6922		811
JWMCD (John W. McDougall Company Inc) 3731 Amy Lynn Dr *Web:* www.jwmcd.com	Nashville	TN	37218	615-321-3900	329-9069	697
JWV-NMI (National Museum of American Jewish Military History) 1811 R St NW *Web:* nmajmh.org	Washington	DC	20009	202-265-6280		520
JXTA Juxtaposition Arts 2007 Emerson Ave N *Web:* juxtapositionarts.org	Minneapolis	MN	55411	612-588-1148		520
Jyoti 2433 18th St NW *Web:* www.jyotidc.com	Washington	DC	20009	202-518-5892		671
Jyoti Americas LLC 3575 Pollok Dr *Web:* www.jyotiamericas.com	Conroe	TX	77303	936-523-4700	494-4100	620
JZ Trend Academy Paul Mitchell Partner School 1320 Tacoma Ave *TF:* 800-767-5079 ■ *Web:* www.jztrendacademy.edu	Bismarck	ND	58504	701-223-8154		685
Jzanus Healthcare Financial Service 170 Jericho Tpke *Web:* jzanushomecare.com	Floral Park	NY	11001	516-437-4747	437-4902	196

K

Name / Address	City	State	ZIP	Phone	Fax	Class
K & A Tech Services 1215 Paramount Pkwy *Web:* www.katechservices.com	Batavia	IL	60510	630-879-1360	879-1361	180
K & B Industries 208 Rebecca's Pond Rd *Web:* www.kb-industries.com	Schriever	LA	70395	985-868-6730		386
K & D Pratt 126 Glencoe Dr *TF:* 800-563-9595 ■ *Web:* www.kdpratt.com	Mount Pearl	NL	A1N4S9	709-722-5690	722-6975	791
K & H Printers-Lithographers Inc 7720 Hardeson Rd *TF:* 800-451-5740 ■ *Web:* www.khprint.com	Everett	WA	98203	425-446-3300	446-3333	627
K & J Trucking Inc 1800 E 50th St N *TF:* 800-843-5624 ■ *Web:* www.kandjtrucking.com	Sioux Falls	SD	57104	605-332-5531	332-6016	780
K & K Die Inc 40700 Enterprise Dr *Web:* www.kandkdie.com	Sterling Heights	MI	48314	586-268-8812	268-2891	489
K & K Machine Shop Inc 161 Fleet Dr *TF:* 800-559-5632 ■ *Web:* kkmachineatlanta.com	Villa Rica	GA	30180	770-459-1377	459-3930	454
K & K Mine Products Inc 200 Airport Rd *Web:* www.kkmineproducts.com	Indiana	PA	15701	724-463-5000	463-5008	207
K & K Veterinary Supply Inc 675 Laura Ln *Web:* www.kkvet.com	Tontitown	AR	72770	479-361-1516		584
K & L Freight Management Inc 3813 Illinois Ave *TF:* 800-770-9007 ■ *Web:* www.kandlfreight.com	Saint Charles	IL	60174	630-607-1500		311
K & L Gates LLP 210 Sixth Ave *TF:* 800-452-8260 ■ *Web:* www.klgates.com	Pittsburgh	PA	15222	412-355-6500	355-6501	428
K & L Microwave Inc 2250 Northwood Dr *Web:* www.klmicrowave.com	Salisbury	MD	21801	410-749-2424		253
K & L Wine Merchants 855 Harrison St *Web:* www.klwines.com	San Francisco	CA	94107	415-896-1734		443
K & M Machine-Fabricating Inc 20745 Michigan 60 *Web:* www.k-mm.com	Cassopolis	MI	49031	269-445-2495		454

Company	City	State	ZIP	Phone	Fax	Class
K & M Printing Company Inc 1410 N Meacham Rd *Web:* www.kmprinting.com	Schaumburg	IL	60173	847-884-1100		627
K & M Technology Group LLC 480 Wildwood Forest Dr Ste 440 *Web:* www.kmtechnology.com	The Woodlands	TX	77380	281-298-6900	298-6875	261
K & M Tire Inc 965 Spencerville Rd PO Box 279 *TF:* 877-879-5407 ■ *Web:* www.kmtire.com	Delphos	OH	45833	419-695-1061		754
K & R Negotiation Associates LLC 908 Ethan Allen Hwy *Web:* www.negotiators.com	Ridgefield	CT	06877	203-431-7693		196
K & s Air Conditioning Inc 143 E Meats Ave *Web:* kandsair.com	Orange	CA	92865	714-685-0077		610
K & T Switching Services Inc 3901 Colorado Ave *Web:* www.ktswitching.com	Sheffield Village	OH	44054	440-949-1910	949-1912	393
K & W Tire Company Inc 735 N Prince St **Fax Area Code:* 717 ■ *TF:* 877-598-4731 ■ *Web:* www.kwtire.com	Lancaster	PA	17603	800-732-3563	397-4164*	755
K A Hamilton & Assoc 159 Perry Hwy Ste 100 *Web:* www.kahamilton.com	Pittsburgh	PA	15229	412-459-0122	459-0120	260
K B L Design Ctr 6710 N Big Hollow Rd *Web:* kbldesign.com	Peoria	IL	61615	309-692-8700	692-1170	321
K Bell Plumbing & Heating Inc 1676 W 2100 S *Web:* kbellplumbing.com	Ogden	UT	84401	801-731-6886		610
K D M Enterprise LLC 820 Commerce Pkwy *TF:* 877-591-9768 ■ *Web:* www.gokdm.com	Carpentersville	IL	60110	847-783-0333		557
K Financial Inc 940 Main St *Web:* kfinancial.com	Louisville	CO	80027	303-665-8060		2
K G B Communictions L L C 5935 E Pima St *Web:* www.kgbcommunications.com	Tucson	AZ	85712	520-743-3300		246
K L House Construction Company Inc 6409 Acoma Rd SE *Web:* www.klhouse.com	Albuquerque	NM	87108	505-268-4361	268-9266	186
K Light Radio 98 - 1016 Komo Mai Dr *Web:* www.klight.org	Aiea	HI	96701	808-524-1040		645
K Line America Inc 4860 Cox Rd Ste 300 *TF:* 800-609-3221 ■ *Web:* www.kline.com	Glen Allen	VA	23060	804-560-3600		313
K P Pharmaceutical Technology Inc 1212 W Rappel Ave *Web:* kppt.com	Bloomington	IN	47404	812-330-8121	330-8363	582
K R Consulting Group Ltd 298 Washington Pl *Web:* krgroupny.com	Lawrence	NY	11559	516-837-7558		196
K Restaurant 1710 Edgewater Dr *Web:* www.krestaurantorlando.com	Orlando	FL	32804	407-872-2332		671
K Wm Beach Manufacturing Company Inc 4655 Urbana Rd *Web:* www.kwmbeach.com	Springfield	OH	45502	937-399-3838		326
K Y Diamond Ltd 2645 Rue Diab *Web:* www.kydiamond.ca	Saint-Laurent	QC	H4S1E7	514-333-5606	339-5493	697
K. D. Analytical Consulting Inc 4460 Linglestown Rd *Web:* www.kdanalytical.com	Harrisburg	PA	17112	717-343-2984		196
K. L. Steven Company Inc 300 Frontage Rd NE Ste B *Web:* www.klsteven.com	Rio Rancho	NM	87124	505-892-1353		22
K.A.M. Tool & Die Inc 530 Industrial Dr *Web:* www.kamtool.com	Zebulon	NC	27597	919-269-5099	269-5709	757
K.B. Canham Cameras Inc 14406 N Lost Tank Trl *Web:* www.canhamcameras.com	Fort McDowell	AZ	85264	480-250-3990		628
K.E.Y. Animal Hospital 855 Warden Run Rd *Web:* keyanimal.com	Wheeling	WV	26003	304-242-7475		794
K.M. Biggs Inc 3550 E Elizabethtown Rd *Web:* www.kmbiggs.com	Lumberton	NC	28358	910-739-2871		274
K/E Electric Supply Co 146 N Groesbeck Hwy *Web:* www.keelectric.com	Mount Clemens	MI	48043	586-469-3005	469-3006	203
K/HC (Kore/Hi Com Inc) 3909 Leland Ave NE *Web:* www.korehicom.com	Comstock Park	MI	49321	616-647-6666	647-9971	180
K12 Inc 2300 Corporate Pk Dr *NYSE: LRN* ■ *TF:* 866-512-2273 ■ *Web:* www.k12.com	Herndon	VA	20171	703-483-7000		685
K2 Engineering Services Inc 85 Rangeway Rd *Web:* www.k2-eng.com	North Billerica	MA	01862	978-600-1333	600-1331	261
K2 Industrial Services 3838 N Sam Houston Pkwy E Ste 285 **Fax Area Code:* 850 ■ *TF:* 800-347-4813 ■ *Web:* www.k2industrial.com	Houston	TX	77032	800-347-4813	477-8670*	189-8
K2 Partnering Solutions 100 Montgomery St Ste 2200 *Web:* k2partnering.com	San Francisco	CA	94104	415-391-3804		193
K2 Project Control Systems 4330 E W Hwy Ste 320 *Web:* k2consulting.com	Bethesda	MD	20814	301-656-2228	656-0229	463
K2 Sports 413 Pine St Ste 300 *TF:* 800-426-1617 ■ *Web:* www.k2sports.com	Seattle	WA	98108	206-805-4800		710
K2 Studios 880 Apollo St Ste 239 *Web:* www.k2studios.us	El Segundo	CA	90245	310-524-9100	524-1540	225
K2Share LLC 1005 University Dr E *TF:* 866-527-4273 ■ *Web:* k2share.com	College Station	TX	77840	979-260-0030		225
K3 Enterprises Inc 504 Cumberland St Ste 300 *Web:* www.k3-enterprises.com	Fayetteville	NC	28301	910-307-3017	401-1121	317
K5 420 Waiakamilo Rd Ste 205 *Web:* www.hawaiinewsnow.com	Honolulu	HI	96817	808-847-3246	847-9315	647
K-97 2394 W Edmonton Mall (Entrance 55) 8882 - 170 St *Web:* www.k97.ca	Edmonton	AB	T5T4M2	780-437-4996		645-51
KA (Kraus-Anderson Co) 501 S Eigth St *Web:* www.krausanderson.com	Minneapolis	MN	55404	612-332-7281	332-8739	185
Kaady Car Washes 2545 SW Spring Garden St *Web:* www.kaady.com	Portland	OR	97219	503-246-7735	245-0851	62-1
KAAL-TV Ch 6 (ABC) 1701 Tenth Pl NE *Web:* www.kaaltv.com	Austin	MN	55912	507-437-6666	433-9560	741
KAAM-AM 770 (Nost) 3201 Royalty Row *Web:* www.770kaam.com	Irving	TX	75062	972-445-1700		645
Kaava Consulting Inc 15190 SW 136th St Ste 24 *Web:* www.kaavainc.com	Miami	FL	33196	305-255-5151		196
Kaba Mas 749 W Short St *Web:* www.mas-hamilton.com	Lexington	KY	40508	859-253-4744		350
Kaback Enterprises Inc 318 W 39th St 2nd Fl *Web:* www.kaback.com	New York	NY	10018	212-645-5100	645-8962	256
Kabam Inc 795 Folsom St Ste 600 *Web:* kabam.com	San Francisco	CA	94107	415-391-0817		366
Kabana Inc 616 Indian School Rd NW *TF:* 800-521-5986 ■ *Web:* kabana.com	Albuquerque	NM	87102	800-521-5986		411
KA-BAR Knives Inc 200 Homer St *TF:* 800-282-0130 ■ *Web:* www.kabar.com	Olean	NY	14760	716-372-5952	790-7188	222
KABB-TV 4335 NW Loop 410 *Web:* www.foxsanantonio.com	San Antonio	TX	78229	210-366-1129	377-4758	647
KABC-AM 790 (N/T) 8965 Lindblade St *TF:* 800-222-5222 ■ *Web:* www.kabc.com	Culver City	CA	90232	310-840-4900		645-42
KABC-TV Ch 7 (ABC) 500 Cir Seven Dr *Web:* www.abc7.com	Glendale	CA	91201	818-863-7777	863-7080	741
KABD-FM 426 N Hwy 281 Ste 4 *Web:* www.dakotabroadcasting.com	Aberdeen	SD	57401	605-725-5551	725-5553	647
Kabel Business Services 1454 30th St Ste 105 *TF:* 800-300-9691 ■ *Web:* www.kabelbiz.com	West Des Moines	IA	50266	515-224-9400	224-9256	113
KABF-FM 88.3 (Var) 2101 Main St Ste 200 **Fax Area Code:* 504 ■ *Web:* www.kabf.org	Little Rock	AR	72206	501-372-6119	376-3952*	645-88
Kabinart Corp 3650 Trousdale Dr *Web:* www.kabinart.com	Nashville	TN	37204	615-833-1961		115
Kable Link Communications 15273 Flight Path Dr *Web:* www.kablelink.com	Brooksville	FL	34604	352-796-7639		116
Kable Product Services Inc 4275 Thunderbird Ln *Web:* www.kablefulfillment.com	Fairfield	OH	45014	513-671-2800		96
Kablooe Design 8560 Cottonwood St NW Ste 100 *Web:* kablooe.com	Minneapolis	MN	55443	763-785-9595		187
Kabookaboo Marketing LLC 2222 Ponce de Leon Blvd Ste 07-112 *Web:* kabookaboo.com	Coral Gables	FL	33134	305-569-9154		195
Kabuki Japanese Restaurant 3539 E Foothill Blvd *Web:* kabukirestaurants.com	Pasadena	CA	91107	626-351-8963		671
Kabuki Japanese Steak House 3503 Franklin Rd SW *Web:* kabukiva.com	Roanoke	VA	24018	540-981-0222		671
Kabuki Japanese Steakhouse 8130 I 40 W *Web:* kabukiromanza.com	Amarillo	TX	79106	806-358-7799		671
Kabul Afghan Cuisine 2301 N 45th St *Web:* www.kabulrestaurant.com	Seattle	WA	98103	206-545-9000	545-4635	671
Kabuto Inc 13158 Midlothian Tpke *Web:* www.kabutorichmond.com	Midlothian	VA	23113	804-379-7979		671
Kabuto Restaurant 5121 Geary Blvd *Web:* www.kabutosf.com	San Francisco	CA	94118	415-752-5652		671
KABX-FM 97.5 (Oldies) 1020 W Main St *TF:* 800-350-3777 ■ *Web:* www.975kabx.com	Merced	CA	95340	209-723-2191	205-1013	645
KABZ-FM 103.7 (N/T) 2400 Cottondale Ln *TF:* 800-477-1037 ■ *Web:* www.1037thebuzz.com	Little Rock	AR	72202	501-661-1037	664-5871	645-88
KAC (Kansas Association of Counties) 300 SW Eigth St 3rd Fl *Web:* www.kansascounties.org	Topeka	KS	66603	785-272-2585	272-3585	49-7
KAC (Korean American Coalition) 3727 W Sixth St Ste 305 *Web:* www.kacla.org	Los Angeles	CA	90020	213-365-5999	380-7990	48-14
Kachina Aviation 4130 Heliport Rd *Web:* www.kachinaaviation.com	Nampa	ID	83687	208-318-0100		23
KACL-FM 98.7 (Oldies) 4303 Memorial Hwy *Web:* www.cool987fm.com	Mandan	ND	58554	701-663-9898		645
Kacoa Landscaping Inc 300 Jefferson Dr *Web:* kacoalandscaping.com	Kingston	IL	60145	815-784-3800		422
KACU-FM 89.7 (NPR) 1925 Campus Ct *Web:* kacu.org	Abilene	TX	79699	325-674-2441		645-1
KACV-FM 90 (Alt) PO Box 447 *TF:* 800-766-0176 ■ *Web:* www.kacvfm.org	Amarillo	TX	79178	800-766-0176		645-5
Kadant 1425 Kingsview Dr *Web:* www.kadant.com	Lebanon	OH	45036	513-229-8100		261
Kadant Inc 1 Technology Pk Dr *NYSE: KAI* ■ *Web:* www.kadant.com	Westford	MA	01886	978-776-2000	635-1593	556
Kadant Inc 15050 - 54A Ave Unit 8 *Web:* www.kadant.com	Surrey	BC	V3S5X7	604-299-3431		454
Kaddis Manufacturing Corp 293 Patriot Wy PO Box 92985 *Web:* www.kaddis.com	Rochester	NY	14692	585-464-9000	464-0008	621
KADI-FM 99.5 (Rel) 5431 W Sunshine St *Web:* kadi.com	Brookline	MO	65619	417-831-0995	831-4026	645

	Phone	Fax	Class
Kadlec Regional Medical Ctr 888 Swift Blvd ... Richland WA 99352 TF: 800-780-6067 ■ Web: www.kadlec.org	509-946-4611	942-2679	374-3
KADN-TV 1500 Eraste Landry Rd ... Lafayette LA 70506 TF: 800-448-6405 ■ Web: www.kadn.com	337-237-1500	237-2237	647
Kaeden Books PO Box 16190 ... Rocky River OH 44116 *Fax Area Code: 440 ■ TF: 800-890-7323 ■ Web: www.kaeden.com	800-890-7323	617-1403*	637-2
Kaepa USA Inc 9050 Autobahn Dr Ste 500 ... Dallas TX 75237 TF: 800-880-9200 ■ Web: www.kaepa.com	800-880-9200		301
Kaercher Insurance Agency Inc 9555 Hillwood Dr Ste 140 ... Las Vegas NV 89134 Web: kaercherinsurance.com	702-304-7800		390
Kaeser & Blair Inc 4236 Grissom Dr ... Batavia OH 45103 TF: 800-642-0790 ■ Web: kaeser-blair.com	800-642-0790		366
Kaeser Compressors Inc PO Box 946 ... Fredericksburg VA 22404 TF: 800-777-7873 ■ Web: www.kaeser.com	540-898-5500	898-5520	172
Kafafian Group Inc, The 2001 Rt 46 Ste 310 ... Parsippany NJ 07054 Web: kafafiangroup.com	973-299-0300	299-1002	734
KAFL Inc 85 Allen St Ste 300 ... Rochester NY 14608 TF: 800-272-6488 ■ Web: www.kafl.com	585-271-6400		390
KAFX-FM 1216 S 1st St ... Lufkin TX 75901 Web: www.kfox95.com	936-639-4455		647
Kagan 981 Calle Amanecer ... San Clemente CA 92673 TF: 800-933-2667 ■ Web: www.kaganonline.com	949-369-6310		530
Kagan Binder PLLC 221 Main St N Ste 200 ... Stillwater MN 55082 Web: www.kaganbinder.com	651-351-2900		428
KAGH-FM 117 E Wellfield Rd ... Crossett AR 71635 Web: www.crossettradio.com	870-364-2181	364-2183	647
Kagmo Electric Motor Co 2351 Rust Ave ... Cape Girardeau MO 63703 Web: www.kagmo.com	573-335-2562	335-3726	518
Kagome Creative Foods LLC 710 N Pearl St ... Osceola AR 72370 Web: www.kagomeusa.com	870-563-2601	563-3824	296-30
Kagome Inc 333 Johnson Rd ... Los Banos CA 93635 Web: www.kagome.co.jp	209-826-8850		296-20
Kahala Corp 9311 E Via de Ventura ... Scottsdale AZ 85258 Web: www.blimpie.com	480-362-4800	362-4812	670
Kahala Travel 3838 Camino Del Rio N Ste 300 ... San Diego CA 92108 TF: 800-852-8338 ■ Web: www.kahalatravel.com	619-282-8300		772
Kahan Jewelry Corp 20 W 47th St ... New York NY 10036	212-719-1055		407
KAHE-FM 2609 Central Ave ... Dodge City KS 67801 Web: www.rockingmradio.com	620-225-8080	225-6655	647
Kahiki Foods Inc 1100 Morrison Rd ... Gahanna OH 43230 TF: 855-524-4540 ■ Web: www.kahiki.com	855-524-4540		296-36
Kahlenberg Industries Inc 1700 12th St ... Two Rivers WI 54241 Web: www.kahlenberg.com	920-793-4507	793-1346	454
Kahler Grand Hotel, The 1517 16th St SW ... Rochester MN 55902 *Fax Area Code: 507 ■ TF: 800-533-1655 ■ Web: www.kahler.com	800-533-1655	285-2701*	671
Kahler Slater Inc 111 W Wisconsin Ave ... Milwaukee WI 53203 Web: www.kahlerslater.com	414-272-2000		195
Kahn & Kahn PC 1000 SW Broadway Ste 905 ... Portland OR 97205 Web: kahnattorneys.com	503-227-4488		41
Kahn Consulting Inc PO Box 1045 ... Highland Park IL 60035 Web: www.kahnconsultinginc.com	847-266-0722		463
Kahn Kruse Company LPA 1301 E Ninth St Ste 2200 ... Cleveland OH 44114 Web: kahnkruse.com	216-579-4114		41
Kahn Litwin Renza & Company Ltd 951 N Main St ... Providence RI 02904 TF: 888-557-8557 ■ Web: www.kahnlitwin.com	401-274-2001		2
Kahn Lucas Lancaster Inc 1412 Broadway 10th Fl ... New York NY 10018 Web: www.kahnlucas.com	212-244-4500		155-4
Kahn Media 11988 Challenger Ct Ste 102 ... Moorpark CA 93021 Web: www.kahnmedia.com	818-881-5246		636
Kahn Soares & Conway LLP 1415 L St Ste 400 ... Sacramento CA 95814 Web: www.ksclawyers.com	916-448-3826		428
Kahns Fine Wine & Spirits 5341 N Keystone Ave ... Indianapolis IN 46220 Web: kahnsfinewines.com	317-251-9463		443
Kahului Airport 1 Kahului Airport Rd ... Kahului HI 96732 TF: 800-321-3712 ■ Web: www.hawaii.gov	808-872-3830	872-3829	27
Kahului Federal Credit Union 25 W Kamehameha Ave ... Kahului HI 96732 Web: kahuluifcu.com	808-871-7705	877-4093	219
Kahului Trucking & Storage Inc 140 Hobron Ave ... Kahului HI 96732 Web: www.kahuluitrucking.com	808-877-5001	877-0572	780
Kahuna Inc 811 Hamilton St ... Redwood City CA 94063 TF: 844-465-2486 ■ Web: www.kahuna.com	844-465-2486		387
KAI USA ltd 18600 SW Teton Ave ... Tualatin OR 97062 TF: 800-325-2891 ■ Web: www.kaiusa.com	503-682-1966	682-7168	222
KAIL-TV Ch 7 1066 E Shaw Ave ... Fresno CA 93710 Web: www.kail.tv	559-230-1980	230-1981	741
Kailua Chamber of Commerce 600 Kailua Rd Ste 107 ... Kailua-Kona HI 96734 TF: 888-261-7997 ■ Web: kailuachamber.com	808-261-7997		139
Kaine Tim (Sen D - VA) 231 Russell Senate Office Bldg ... Washington DC 20510 Web: www.kaine.senate.gov	202-224-4024	228-6363	342-2
Kaiperm Northwest Federal Credit Union 500 NE Multnomah St Ste 320 ... Portland OR 97232 Web: kaipermnw.org	503-813-3242		219
Kairos Autonomi Inc 508 W 8360 S ... Sandy UT 84070 Web: www.kairosautonomi.com	801-255-2950		647
Kairos Power LLC 707 W Tower Ave ... Alameda CA 94501 Web: kairospower.com	510-808-5265		787
Kaiser Air Cond & Sheet Metal Inc 600 Pacific Ave ... Oxnard CA 93030 Web: kaiserac.com	805-988-1800		189-10
Kaiser Aluminum Canada Ltd 3021 Gore Rd ... London ON N5V5A9 Web: www.kaiseraluminum.com	519-457-3610		492
Kaiser Assoc 1615 L St NW 13th Fl ... Washington DC 20036 Web: kaiserassociates.com	202-454-2000		194
Kaiser Financial Services 3087 Winch Rd ... Springfield IL 62707 Web: www.kaiserfinancial.com	217-787-4845		251
Kaiser Foundation Health Plan Inc 1 Kaiser Plz ... Oakland CA 94612 *Fax Area Code: 510 ■ TF: 800-464-4000 ■ Web: healthy.kaiserpermanente.org	408-972-3000	271-6493*	391-3
Kaiser Grille 205 S Palm Canyon Dr ... Palm Springs CA 92262 Web: www.restaurantsofpalmsprings.com	760-323-1003		671
Kaiser Permanente 3495 Piedmont Rd NE 9 Piedmont Ctr ... Atlanta GA 30305 TF: 800-611-1811 ■ Web: medicare.kaiserpermanente.org	404-233-3700		391-3
Kaiser Permanente Hawaii 1292 Waianuenue Ave ... Hilo HI 96720 TF: 800-966-5955 ■ Web: www.kpinhawaii.org	808-334-4400		391-3
Kaiser Permanente Medical Center-South Sacramento 6600 Bruceville Rd ... Sacramento CA 95823 Web: mydoctor.kaiserpermanente.org	916-688-2000		374-3
Kaiser Permanente Medical Ctr 710 Lawrence Expy ... Santa Clara CA 95051 Web: thrive.kaiserpermanente.org	408-851-1000		374-3
KaiserAir Inc 8735 Earhart Rd ... Oakland CA 94621 TF: 800-538-2625 ■ Web: www.kaiserair.com	510-569-9622	255-5017	13
Kaiser-Francis Oil Co 6733 S Yale Ave ... Tulsa OK 74136 Web: www.kfoc.net	918-494-0000		539
Kaiyo Grill 81701 Old Hwy (MM 817) ... Islamorada FL 33036 Web: www.kaiyokeys.com	305-664-5556		670
KAJA-FM 20880 Stone Oak Pkwy 1st Flr ... San Antonio TX 78258 Web: kj97.iheart.com	210-736-9700	735-8811	647
KAJN-FM 102.9 (Rel) 110 W Third St PO Box 1469 ... Crowley LA 70527 Web: kajn.com	337-783-1560	783-1674	645
Kajun Kettle Foods 405 Alpha Dr ... Destrehan LA 70047 TF: 800-331-9612 ■ Web: www.kajunkettle.com	504-733-8800		345
Kakivik Asset Management LLC 5015 Business Park Blvd Ste 4000 ... Anchorage AK 99503 Web: www.kakivik.com	907-770-9400	770-9450	567
Kal Plastics 2050 E 48th St ... Vernon CA 90058 TF: 800-321-3925 ■ Web: www.kal-plastics.com	323-581-6194	581-1805	602
Kal Tire 1460 Kalamalka Lake Rd ... Vernon BC V1T6V2 Web: www.kaltire.com	250-545-2729	545-4740	754
Kalahari Resorts 1305 Kalahari Dr ... Wisconsin Dells WI 53965 TF: 877-525-2427 ■ Web: www.kalahariresorts.com	608-254-5466		378
Kalamarides & Lambert 750 W Second Ave Ste 200 ... Anchorage AK 99501 Web: kalamarides.com	907-276-2135		41
Kalamata's 3764 Hillsboro Pk ... Nashville TN 37215 Web: kalamatasnashville.com	615-383-8700		671
Kalamazoo College 1200 Academy St ... Kalamazoo MI 49006 TF: 800-253-3602 ■ Web: www.kzoo.edu	269-337-7166	337-7390	166
Kalamazoo Community Foundation 402 E Michigan Ave ... Kalamazoo MI 49007 Web: www.kalfound.org	269-381-4416	381-3146	48-20
Kalamazoo County 201 W Kalamazoo Ave ... Kalamazoo MI 49007 Web: www.kalcounty.com	269-383-8840	384-8143	338
Kalamazoo County Convention & Visitors Bureau 141 E Michigan Ave Ste 100 ... Kalamazoo MI 49007 TF: 800-888-0509 ■ Web: www.discoverkalamazoo.com	269-488-9000	488-0050	206
Kalamazoo Gospel Mission 448 N Burdick St ... Kalamazoo MI 49007 Web: www.kzoogospel.org	269-345-2974		48-20
Kalamazoo Institute of Arts (KIA) 314 S Park St ... Kalamazoo MI 49007 Web: www.kiarts.org	269-349-7775	349-9313	520
Kalamazoo Oil Co 2601 N Burdick St ... Kalamazoo MI 49007 Web: kalamazooil.com	269-381-3142		316
Kalamazoo Psychiatric Hospital 1312 Oakland Dr ... Kalamazoo MI 49008 TF: 888-509-7007 ■ Web: www.michigan.gov	269-337-3000		374-5
Kalamazoo Public Library 315 S Rose St ... Kalamazoo MI 49007 Web: www.kpl.gov	269-342-9837		434-3
Kalamazoo Speedway 7656 Ravine Rd ... Kalamazoo MI 49009 Web: www.kalamazoospeedway.com	269-349-3978		515
Kalamazoo Steel Processing 306 Peekstok Rd ... Kalamazoo MI 49001 Web: www.kalsteel.com	269-344-9778		492
Kalamazoo Symphony Orchestra 359 S Kalamazoo Mall Ste 100 ... Kalamazoo MI 49007 Web: www.kalamazoosymphony.com	269-349-7759	349-9229	573-3
Kalamazoo Valley Community College *Arcadia Commons* 202 N Rose St ... Kalamazoo MI 49007 Web: www.kvcc.edu	269-373-7800		162
Kalamazoo Valley Plant Growers Cooperative Inc 8937 Krum Ave ... Galesburg MI 49053 *Fax Area Code: 269 ■ TF: 800-253-4898 ■ Web: www.kvpg.com	800-253-4898	342-1644*	186
Kalan LP 97 S Union Ave ... Lansdowne PA 19050 *Fax Area Code: 610 ■ TF: 800-345-8138 ■ Web: www.kalanlp.com	800-345-8138	623-0366*	534
Kalani Oceanside Retreat 12-6860 Kapoho Kalapana Rd ... Pahoa HI 96778 TF: 800-800-6886 ■ Web: kalani.com	808-965-7828	965-0527	673
Kalas Manufacturing Inc 167 Greenfield Rd ... Lancaster PA 17601 Web: www.kalaswire.com	717-336-5575	945-1002	813
Kalaupapa National Historical Park PO Box 2222 ... Kalaupapa HI 96742 Web: www.nps.gov	808-567-6802	567-6729	564

Name / Address	City	State	ZIP	Phone	Fax	Class
Kalba International Inc						
116 McKinley Ave	New Haven	CT	06515	203-397-2199		196
Web: www.kalbainternational.com						
Kalbaugh, Pfund & Messersmith PC						
901 Moorefield Park Dr Ste 200	Richmond	VA	23236	804-320-6300		41
TF: 800-606-3350 ■ *Web:* kpmlaw.com						
Kal-blue Reprographics Inc						
914 E Vine St	Kalamazoo	MI	49001	800-522-0541	349-0940*	113
**Fax Area Code:* 269 ■ *TF:* 800-522-0541 ■ *Web:* www.kalblue.com						
Kalcor Coatings Company Inc						
37721 Stevens Blvd	Willoughby	OH	44094	440-946-4700		550
TF: 800-422-8484 ■ *Web:* www.kalcor.com						
Kaleel Jamison Consulting Group Inc, The						
5 3rd St Ste 230	Troy	NY	12180	518-271-7000		463
Web: kjcg.com						
Kaleida Health 100 High St	Buffalo	NY	14203	716-859-5600		374-3
Web: www.kaleidahealth.org						
Kaleidescape Inc 440 Potrero Ave	Sunnyvale	CA	94085	650-625-6100		52
Web: www.kaleidescape.com						
Kaleidoscope						
2500 Grand Blvd PO Box 419580	Kansas City	MO	64108	816-274-8301		521
Web: hallmarkkaleidoscope.com						
Kalenborn Abresist Corp						
5541 N State Road 13 PO Box 38	Urbana	IN	46990	260-774-3327		183
TF: 800-348-0717 ■ *Web:* kalenborn.us						
Kaleo Software Inc						
2041 Rosecrans Ave Ste 245	El Segundo	CA	90245	424-277-5597		387
Web: www.kaleosoftware.com						
Kaleva Telephone Co 9462 Osmo St	Kaleva	MI	49645	231-362-3111	362-2002	224
Web: www.kaltelnet.net						
Kali's Mezze 1606 Thames St	Baltimore	MD	21231	410-563-7600		671
Web: kalismezze.com						
Kalian Cos						
2 Hennessey Blvd	Atlantic Highlands	NJ	07716	732-741-0054	741-3404	187
Web: www.kalian.com						
Kalibrate Technologies PLC						
25B Hanover Rd	Florham Park	NJ	07932	973-549-1850		178-11
TF: 800-727-6774 ■ *Web:* www.kalibrate.com						
Kalida Telephone Co						
121 E Main St PO Box 267	Kalida	OH	45853	419-532-3218	532-3300	387
Web: www.kalidatel.com						
Kalimat Press						
1600 Sawtelle Blvd Ste 310	Los Angeles	CA	90025	310-479-5668		637-2
TF: 800-683-8081 ■ *Web:* www.kalimat.com						
Kalinich Fence Company Inc						
12223 Prospect Rd	Strongsville	OH	44149	440-238-6127	238-2178	279
Web: www.kalinichfenceco.com						
Kalinosky Landscaping Inc						
90 Northridge Ln	Wyoming	PA	18644	570-696-4606		422
Web: kalinoskylandscapinginc.com						
Kalispell Area Chamber of Commerce						
15 Depot Pk	Kalispell	MT	59901	406-758-2800	758-2805	139
Web: kalispellchamber.com						
Kalispell Regional Medical Ctr						
310 Sunnyview Ln	Kalispell	MT	59901	406-752-5111		374-3
TF: 800-228-1574 ■ *Web:* www.krh.org						
Kalitta Charters LLC						
843 Willow Run Airport	Ypsilanti	MI	48198	734-544-3400		21
TF: 800-525-4882 ■ *Web:* www.kalittacharters.com						
Kalitta Flying Service						
818 Willow Run Airport	Ypsilanti	MI	48198	734-484-0088	484-3640	12
TF: 800-521-1590 ■ *Web:* www.kalittaair.com						
Kalkaska County 605 N Birch St	Kalkaska	MI	49646	231-258-3336	258-3337	338
Web: www.kalkaskacounty.net						
Kalkomey Enterprises Inc						
14086 Proton Rd	Dallas	TX	75244	214-351-0461		05
TF: 800-830-2268 ■ *Web:* www.kalkomey.com						
Kallman & Co 125 S Barrington Pl	Los Angeles	CA	90049	310-909-1900		2
Kallman Worldwide Inc 4 N St Ste 800	Waldwick	NJ	07463	201-251-2600		206
TF: 877-492-7028 ■ *Web:* www.kallman.com						
Kallo Inc						
255 Duncan Mill Rd Ste 504	North York	ON	M3B3H9	416-246-9997		177
Web: www.kalloinc.ca						
Kalman Floor Company Inc						
1680 E 69th Ave	Denver	CO	80229	303-674-2290	674-1238	189-2
TF: 800-525-7840 ■ *Web:* kalmanfloor.com						
Kalmanowitz And Lee CPAs PLLC						
575 E Ave Ste 1706	New York	NY	10018	212-687-2628		2
Kalmar Nyckel Foundation						
1124 E Seventh St	Wilmington	DE	19801	302-429-7447	429-0350	520
Web: www.kalmarnyckel.org						
Kalmar RT Center LLC 103 Guadalupe Dr	Cibolo	TX	78108	210-599-6541		770
Web: www.kalmarrt.com						
Kalmbach Media						
21027 Crossroads Cir PO Box 1612	Waukesha	WI	53187	262-796-8776		658
Web: www.kalmbach.com						
Kalogridis International Ltd						
4819 Maple Ave	Dallas	TX	75219	214-637-0519		21
Web: kalogridis.com						
Kaloko-Honokohau National Historical Park						
73-4786 Kanalani St Ste 14	Kailua-Kona	HI	96740	808-329-6881		564
Web: www.nps.gov						
Kalona Cooperative Telephone Co (KCTC)						
510 B Ave	Kalona	IA	52247	319-656-3668	656-4484	681
TF: 800-656-8510 ■ *Web:* www.kctc.net						
Kalopa State Recreation Area						
44 3480 Kalaniai Rd	Honokaa	HI	96727	808-775-8852	961-9599	565
Web: hawaiistateparks.org						
Kalow Technologies Inc						
238 Innovation Dr	North Clarendon	VT	05759	802-775-4633		757
Web: www.kalowtech.com						
Kalsec Inc 3713 W Main St	Kalamazoo	MI	49006	269-349-9711	382-3060	296-15
TF: 800-323-9320 ■ *Web:* www.kalsec.com						
Kalsi Engineering Inc						
745 Park Two Dr	Sugar Land	TX	77478	281-240-6500	240-0255	256
Web: www.kalsi.com						
Kalt Manufacturing Co, The						
36700 Sugar Ridge Rd	North Ridgeville	OH	44039	440-327-2102		757
Web: www.kaltmfg.com						
Kalustyan Corp 855 Rahway Ave	Union	NJ	07083	908-688-6111		123
Web: www.kalustyan.com						
Kaluzny Bros Inc 2324 Mound Rd	Rockdale	IL	60436	815-744-1453		296-12
KALV-Live 101.5 phoenix						
840 N Central Ave	Phoenix	AZ	85004	602-452-1000	440-6530	645-121
Web: live1015phoenix.radio.com						
Kalwall Corp						
1111 Candia Rd PO Box 237	Manchester	NH	03105	603-627-3861	627-7905	608
TF: 800-258-9777 ■ *Web:* www.kalwall.com						
KALW-FM 91.7 (NPR)						
500 Mansell St	San Francisco	CA	94134	415-841-4121	841-4125	645-142
Web: www.kalw.org						
Kam Companies						
9035 Stellhorn Crossing Pkwy	Fort Wayne	IN	46835	260-432-4432		175
Kam's 4500 Montrose Blvd	Houston	TX	77006	713-529-5057	529-5486	671
Web: kamscuisine.com						
Kaman Aerospace Corp						
30 Old Windsor Rd PO Box 2	Bloomfield	CT	06002	860-242-4461	243-7514	20
Web: www.kaman.com						
Kamco Supply Corporation of Boston						
181 New Boston St	Woburn	MA	01801	781-938-0909	897-7206	191-1
Web: www.kamcoboston.com						
KAMC-TV Ch 28 (ABC)						
7403 S University Ave	Lubbock	TX	79423	806-745-2345	748-2250	741-78
Web: www.everythinglubbock.com						
KAMedDatacom Inc						
4400 Bayou Blvd Ste 12	Pensacola	FL	32503	850-477-2475		194
Web: www.kameddata.com						
Kamehameha Schools Press						
567 S King St Ste 118	Honolulu	HI	96813	808-541-5305		637-2
Web: www.kamehamehapublishing.org						
Kamerlink, Stark, Powers & Mcnicholas LLC						
221 N Lasalle St Ste 1800	Chicago	IL	60601	312-855-0324		41
Web: fam-atty.com						
Kamet Manufacturing Solutions						
1778 McCarthy Blvd	Milpitas	CA	95035	800 888 2080		454
TF: 800-888-2089 ■ *Web:* www.kamet.com						
Kamimoto String Instruments						
609 N Fourth St	San Jose	CA	95112	408-298-8168		526
Web: kamimotostrings.com						
Kaminsky & Associates Inc						
2340 Detroit Ave 3rd Fl	Maumee	OH	43537	419-535-5502		390
Web: teamkaminsky.com						
Kamiya Biomedical Co 12779 Gateway Dr	Seattle	WA	98168	206-575-8068	575-8094	231
TF: 800-526-4925 ■ *Web:* www.kamiyabiomedical.com						
Kamloops Chamber of Commerce						
615 Victoria St	Kamloops	BC	V2C2B3	250-372-7722	828-9500	137
Web: www.kamloopschamber.ca						
Kamloops Daily News 393 Seymour St	Kamloops	BC	V2C6P6	250-372-2331		532-1
Web: www.kamloopsnews.ca						
KAMM Consulting Inc						
1407 W Newport Center Dr	Deerfield Beach	FL	33442	954-949-2200		196
Web: kammconsulting.com						
KAMMCO 623 SW Tenth Ave	Topeka	KS	66612	785-232-2224	232-4704	391-5
TF: 800-232-2259 ■ *Web:* www.kammco.com						
Kammer Browning PLLC						
7700 Broadway Ste 202	San Antonio	TX	78209	210-832-0900		41
Web: kammerbrowning.com						
Kamminga & Roodvoets Inc						
3435 Broadmoor Ave SE	Grand Rapids	MI	49512	616-949-0800		189-5
Web: www.kammingaroodvoets.com						
KAMO Electric Cooperative Inc						
500 S Kamo Dr	Vinita	OK	74301	918-256-5551	256-8023	245
Web: www.kamopower.com						
Kampbell & Johnson PLLC						
4041 Ruston Way Ste 200	Tacoma	WA	98402	253-564-2088	722-1305	41
Web: www.kampbell-law.com						
Kamper Fabrication Inc 20107 N Ripon Rd	Ripon	CA	95366	209-599-7137		273
Web: www.kamperfab.com						
Kampgrounds of America Inc (KOA)						
PO Box 30558	Billings	MT	59114	888-562-0000		121
TF: 888-562-0000 ■ *Web:* koa.com						
Kamphaus, Henning & Hood CPA						
1046 Techne Center Dr	Milford	OH	45150	513-752-8350		2
TF: 866-760-0940 ■ *Web:* brixeyandmeyer.com						
Kampi Components Company Inc						
88 Canal Rd	Fairless Hills	PA	19030	215-736-2000	736-9000	770
Web: kampi.com						
KAMQ-AM 1609 Radio Blvd	Carlsbad	NM	88220	575-887-7563	887-7000	647
Web: www.carlsbadradio.com						
KAMR-TV Ch 4 (NBC)						
1015 S Fillmore St	Amarillo	TX	79101	806-383-3321	220-0941	741-4
Web: www.myhighplains.com						
Kamsky Associates Inc 563 Park Ave	New York	NY	10065	212-317-1116		194
Web: www.kamsky.com						
Kanabec County 18 N Vine St	Mora	MN	55051	320-679-6466	679-6431	338
Web: www.kanabeccounty.org						
Kanata Energy Group Ltd						
1900 112-4th Ave SW	Calgary	AB	T2P0H3	587-774-7000	774-6970	261
TF: 844-526-2822 ■ *Web:* www.kanataenergy.com						
Kanawha County 409 Virginia St E	Charleston	WV	25301	304-357-0130	357-0585	338
Web: www.kanawha.us						
Kanawha Hospice Care						
1606 Kanawha Blvd W	Charleston	WV	25387	304-768-8523		371
TF: 800-560-8523 ■ *Web:* www.hospicecarewv.org						
Kanawha Manufacturing Co						
1520 Dixie St	Charleston	WV	25311	304-342-6127		234
Web: www.kanawhamfg.com						
Kanawha Scales & Systems Inc						
Rock Branch Industrial Pk 303 Jacobson Dr	Poca	WV	25159	304-755-8321		361
TF: 800-955-8321 ■ *Web:* www.kanawhascales.com						
Kanawha State Forest						
7500 Kanawha State Forest Dr	Charleston	WV	25314	304-558-3500		565
Web: wvstateparks.com						
Kanawha Stone Company Inc						
409 Jacobson Dr	Poca	WV	25159	304-755-8271	755-8274	261
Web: www.kanawhastone.com						

	Phone	Fax	Class
Kandiyohi County, Minnesota 400 Benson Ave SW . . . Willmar MN 56201 *Web:* www.kcmn.us	320-231-6202	231-6263	338
Kane County 719 Batavia Ave Bldg A . . . Geneva IL 60134 *Web:* www.countyofkane.org	630-232-5930	232-9188	338
Kane County 78 S 100 E . . . Kanab UT 84741 *TF:* 800-733-5263 ■ *Web:* www.visitsouthernutah.com	435-644-5033		338
Kane Engineering Group Inc 3464 Springbrook Dr Nw . . . Grand Rapids MI 49544 *Web:* www.kaneinc.com	616-481-0559		196
Kane Furniture Corp 5700 70th Ave N . . . Pinellas Park FL 33781 *Web:* www.kanesfurniture.com	727-545-9555		321
Kane Graphical Corp 2255 W Logan Blvd . . . Chicago IL 60647 **Fax Area Code:* 773 ■ *TF:* 800-992-2921 ■ *Web:* www.kanegraphical.com	800-992-2921	384-1207*	344
Kane Manufacturing Corp 515 N Fraley St . . . Kane PA 16735 *TF:* 800-952-6399 ■ *Web:* www.kaneinnovations.com	814-837-6464		234
Kane Partners LLC 1816 W Point Pk Ste 221 . . . Lansdale PA 19446 *Web:* kanepartners.net	215-699-5500		260
Kane Transport Inc 40925 403rd Ave . . . Sauk Centre MN 56378 **Fax Area Code:* 320 ■ *TF:* 800-892-8557 ■ *Web:* www.kanetransport.com	877-532-2788	352-6141*	768
Kane, McKenna and Associates Inc 150 N Wacker Dr Ste 1600 . . . Chicago IL 60606 *Web:* www.kanemckenna.com	312-444-1702	444-9052	192
Kanebridge Corp 153 Bauer Dr . . . Oakland NJ 07436 *TF:* 888-222-9221 ■ *Web:* www.kanebridge.com	201-337-2300		350
Kanematsu USA Inc 500 Fifth Ave 29th Fl . . . New York NY 10110 **Fax Area Code:* 212 ■ *Web:* kanematsuusa.com	847-981-5600	704-9483*	386
Kanequip Inc 1451 S 2nd St . . . Dodge City KS 67801 *Web:* www.kanequip.com	620-225-0016	225-3635	429
Kaneva Inc 270 Carpenter Dr Ste 100 . . . Sandy Springs GA 30328 **Fax Area Code:* 770 ■ *Web:* www.kaneva.com	678-367-0555	352-0077*	387
Kanguru Solutions 1360 Main St . . . Millis MA 02054 *TF:* 888-526-4878 ■ *Web:* www.kanguru.com	508-376-4245	376-4462	173-8
Kankakee Community College 100 College Dr . . . Kankakee IL 60901 *Web:* www.kcc.edu	815-802-8100	802-8101	162
Kankakee County 3000 S Justice Way . . . Kankakee IL 60901 *Web:* www.co.kankakee.il.us	815-937-2990	939-8831	338
Kankakee Public Library 201 E Ct St . . . Kankakee IL 60901 *Web:* www.lions-online.org	815-939-4564		434-3
Kankakee River State Park 5314 W Rt 102 PO Box 37 . . . Bourbonnais IL 60914 *Web:* www.dnr.illinois.gov	815-933-1383		565
Kankakee Valley Construction Company Inc 4356 West Rt 17 . . . Kankakee IL 60901 *Web:* www.kvcci.com	815-937-8700	937-0402	188-4
Kanki Japanese House of Steak & Sushi 4325 Glenwood Ave . . . Raleigh NC 27612 *Web:* www.kanki.com	919-782-9708	787-4524	670
Kann Enterprises Inc 209 Amendodge Dr . . . Shorewood IL 60404 *Web:* www.kannenterprises.com	815-609-7170		358
Kann Manufacturing Corp PO Box 400 . . . Guttenberg IA 52052 *TF:* 800-806-5266 ■ *Web:* www.kannmfg.com	563-252-2035	252-3069	516
Kanomax Usa Inc 219 US Hwy 206 . . . Andover NJ 07821 *TF:* 800-247-8887 ■ *Web:* www.kanomax-usa.com	973-786-6386		743
Kanopolis State Park 200 Horsethief Rd . . . Marquette KS 67464 *Web:* www.ksoutdoors.com	785-546-2565		565
Kanpai of Tokyo 300 Winchester Pl . . . Spartanburg SC 29301 *Web:* www.kanpaioftokyo.com	864-574-3805		671
Kansas			
Accountancy Board 900 SW Jackson St Ste 556 . . . Topeka KS 66612 *Web:* www.ksboa.org	785-296-2162	291-3501	339-17
Attorney General Derek Schmidt 120 SW 10th Ave 2nd Fl . . . Topeka KS 66612 *TF:* 888-428-8436 ■ *Web:* ag.ks.gov	785-296-2215	296-6296	339-17
Banking Commissioner 700 SW Jackson St Ste 300 . . . Topeka KS 66603 *Web:* www.osbckansas.org	785-296-2266	296-0168	339-17
Bill Status 300 SW Tenth Ave Ste 551-S . . . Topeka KS 66612 *Web:* www.kslegislature.org	785-296-2391	296-1153	433
Board of Cosmetology 714 SW Jackson St Ste 100 . . . Topeka KS 66603 *Web:* www.kansas.gov	785-296-3155	296-3002	339-17
Chief Legal Governor's Office Capitol Bldg 2nd Fl . . . Topeka KS 66612 *Web:* portal.kansas.gov	785-368-8767		339-17
Commerce Dept 1000 SW Jackson St Ste 100 . . . Topeka KS 66612 *Web:* www.kansascommerce.gov	785-296-3481	296-5055	339-17
Department for Children & Families 915 SW Harrison St 6th Fl . . . Topeka KS 66612 *Web:* www.dcf.ks.gov	785-296-3959	296-2173	339-17
Department of Agriculture 900 SW Jackson Rm 456 . . . Topeka KS 66612 *Web:* agriculture.ks.gov	785-296-3556	564-6777	339-17
Department of Agriculture 1320 Research Park Dr . . . Manhattan KS 66502 *Web:* agriculture.ks.gov	785-564-6700		339-17
Healing Arts Board Lower Level 800 SW Jackson Ste A . . . Topeka KS 66612 *TF:* 888-886-7205 ■ *Web:* www.ksbha.org	785-296-7413	368-7102	339-17
Health & Environment Dept 1000 SW Jackson St . . . Topeka KS 66612 *Web:* www.kdheks.gov	785-296-0461	559-4269	339-17
Highway Patrol 122 SW Seventh St . . . Topeka KS 66603 *Web:* www.kansashighwaypatrol.org	785-296-6800		339-17
Historical Society 6425 SW Sixth Ave . . . Topeka KS 66615 *Web:* www.kshs.org	785-272-8681	272-8682	339-17
Housing Resources Corp 611 S Kansas Ave Ste 300 . . . Topeka KS 66603 *TF:* 800-766-3777 ■ *Web:* www.kshousingcorp.org	785-217-2001	232-8084	339-17
Judicial Administrator Kansas Judicial Ctr 301 S W Tenth St . . . Topeka KS 66612 *Web:* www.kscourts.org	785-296-2256	296-7076	339-17
Lottery 128 N Kansas Ave . . . Topeka KS 66603 *TF:* 800-544-9467 ■ *Web:* kslottery.com	785-296-5700		452
Rehabilitation Services Div 915 SW Harrison Docking State Office Bldg Ninth Fl N . . . Topeka KS 66612 *TF:* 866-213-9079 ■ *Web:* www.dcf.ks.gov	785-368-7471	368-7467	339-17
Revenue Dept 915 SW Harrison St . . . Topeka KS 66626 *Web:* www.ksrevenue.org	785-296-3909		339-17
Secretary of State 120 SW Tenth Ave 1st Fl . . . Topeka KS 66612 *Web:* www.kssos.org	785-296-4564	296-4570	339-17
Securities Commission 618 S Kansas Ave 2nd Fl . . . Topeka KS 66603 *Web:* www.ksc.ks.gov	785-296-3307	296-6872	339-17
Travel & Tourism Development Div 1020 S Kansas Ave Ste 200 . . . Topeka KS 66612 *Web:* www.travelks.com	785-296-1847	296-6988	339-17
Vital Statistics Div 1000 SW Jackson . . . Topeka KS 66612 *Web:* www.kdheks.gov	785-296-1400		339-17
Weights & Measures Div Forbes Field Bldg 282 PO Box 19282 . . . Topeka KS 66619 *Web:* www.kansas.gov	785-862-2415	862-2460	339-17
Kansas Action for Children Inc 720 SW Jackson St Ste 201 . . . Topeka KS 66603 *Web:* kac.org	785-232-0550		533
Kansas African American Museum 601 N Water St . . . Wichita KS 67203 *Web:* www.tkaamuseum.org	316-262-7651		520
Kansas Association of Counties (KAC) 300 SW Eigth St 3rd Fl . . . Topeka KS 66603 *Web:* www.kansascounties.org	785-272-2585	272-3585	49-7
Kansas Association of Realtors 3644 SW Burlingame Rd . . . Topeka KS 66611 *TF:* 800-366-0069 ■ *Web:* kansasrealtor.com	785-267-3610	267-1867	656
Kansas Aviation Museum 3350 S George Washington Blvd . . . Wichita KS 67210 *Web:* www.kansasaviationmuseum.org	316-683-9242		520
Kansas Bankers Assn 610 SW Corporate View . . . Topeka KS 66615 *TF:* 800-285-7878 ■ *Web:* www.ksbankers.com	785-272-7836		78
Kansas Beer Wholesalers Assn (KBWA) 100 SE 9th St Ste 100 . . . Topeka KS 66612 *Web:* www.ksbeer.com	785-408-8087		637-10
Kansas Board of Regents, The 1000 SW Jackson St Ste 520 . . . Topeka KS 66612 *Web:* kansasregents.org	785-296-3421	296-0983	725
Kansas Board of Technical Professions 900 SW Jackson St Ste 507 . . . Topeka KS 66612 *Web:* www.ksbtp.ks.gov	785-296-3053		339-17
Kansas Brick & Tile Inc 767 N US Hwy 281 . . . Hoisington KS 67544 *Web:* www.kansasbrick.com	620-653-2157	653-7609	150
Kansas Chamber of Commerce 835 SW Topeka Blvd . . . Topeka KS 66612 *Web:* www.kansaschamber.org	785-357-6321		140
Kansas Children's Service League (KCSL) 3545 SW Fifth St . . . Topeka KS 66606 *TF:* 877-530-5275 ■ *Web:* www.kcsl.org	785-274-3100		48-6
Kansas Christian Home 1035 SE Third St . . . Newton KS 67114 *Web:* www.kschristianhome.org	316-283-6600	283-6375	672
Kansas City Art Institute 4415 Warwick Blvd . . . Kansas City MO 64111 *TF:* 800-522-5224 ■ *Web:* www.kcai.edu	816-474-5224	802-3309	164
Kansas City Aviation Center Inc 15325 S Pflumm Rd . . . Olathe KS 66062 *Web:* www.kcac.com	913-782-0530		63
Kansas City Chiefs 1 Arrowhead Dr . . . Kansas City MO 64129 *Web:* www.chiefs.com	816-920-9300	923-4719	720
Kansas City Credit Union 5110 Ararat Dr . . . Kansas City MO 64129 *TF:* 844-318-2394 ■ *Web:* kccu.net	816-861-5700		219
Kansas City Electrical Supply Co (KCES) 14851 W 99th St . . . Lenexa KS 66215 *Web:* kcelectricalsupply.com	913-563-7000	563-7055	246
Kansas City Hospice & Palliative Care 1500 Meadow Lake Pkwy Ste 100 . . . Kansas City MO 64114 *Web:* www.kchospice.org	816-363-2600		371
Kansas City International Airport 601 Brasilia Ave PO Box 20047 . . . Kansas City MO 64153 *Web:* www.flykci.com	816-243-5237	243-3171	27
Kansas City Jazz Ambassadors (KCJA) PO Box 36181 . . . Kansas City MO 64171 *Web:* www.kcjazzambassadors.org	816-888-4503		48-4
Kansas City Kansas Community College 7250 State Ave . . . Kansas City KS 66112 *TF:* 800-640-0352 ■ *Web:* www.kckcc.edu	913-334-1100	288-7648	162
Kansas City Kansas Convention & Visitors Bureau Inc PO Box 171517 . . . Kansas City KS 66117 *TF:* 800-264-1563 ■ *Web:* www.visitkansascityks.com	913-321-5800	371-0204	206
Kansas City Life Insurance Co 3520 Broadway . . . Kansas City MO 64111 *OTC:* KCLI ■ *TF:* 800-821-6164 ■ *Web:* www.kclife.com	816-753-7000	753-4902	360-4
Kansas City Missouri School District 1211 McGee St . . . Kansas City MO 64106 *Web:* www.kcpublicschools.org	816-418-7000	418-7766	685
Kansas City (MO) City Hall 414 E 12th St . . . Kansas City MO 64106 *Web:* www.kcmo.gov	816-513-3360	513-3353	337
Kansas City Peterbilt Inc 8915 Woodend Rd . . . Kansas City KS 66111 *TF:* 800-489-1122 ■ *Web:* www.kcpete.com	913-441-2888	422-5029	62-5
Kansas City Public Library, The (KCPL) 14 W Tenth St . . . Kansas City MO 64105 *Web:* www.kclibrary.org	816-701-3400	701-3401	434-3

Name / Address	City	State	ZIP	Phone	Fax	Class
Kansas City Regional Association of Realtors Inc, The 11150 Overbrook Rd Ste 100 *Web:* kcrar.com	Leawood	KS	66211	913-498-1100		652
Kansas City Repertory Theatre 4949 Cherry St *Web:* www.kcrep.org	Kansas City	MO	64110	816-235-2700	235-5508	749
Kansas City Southern Railway Co 427 W 12th St *TF:* 800-468-6527 ■ *Web:* www.kcsouthern.com	Kansas City	MO	64105	816-983-1303		648
Kansas City Star 1601 McGee St *Web:* www.kansascity.com	Kansas City	MO	64108	816-234-4345		532-2
Kansas City Structural Steel Inc 3801 Raytown Rd *Web:* www.kcstructural.com	Kansas City	MO	64129	816-924-0977	924-3740	492
Kansas City Symphony 1703 Wyandotte Ste 200 *Web:* www.kcsymphony.org	Kansas City	MO	64108	816-471-1100	471-0976	573-3
Kansas City Zoo 6800 Zoo Dr *Web:* www.kansascityzoo.org	Kansas City	MO	64132	816-595-1234		823
Kansas Coliseum 1279 E 85th St N *Web:* www.kansascoliseum.com	Park City	KS	67147	316-440-0888		720
Kansas Commission on Veterans' Affairs Office 700 SW Jackson St Ste 1004 *Web:* kcva.ks.gov	Topeka	KS	66603	785-296-3976		339-17
Kansas Corporation Commission 1500 SW Arrowhead Rd *TF:* 800-662-0027 ■ *Web:* kcc.ks.gov	Topeka	KS	66604	785-271-3100	271-3354	339-17
Kansas Correctional Industries PO Box 2 *Web:* www.kancorind.com	Lansing	KS	66043	913-727-3249	727-2331	630
Kansas Cosmosphere 1100 N Plum St *TF:* 800-397-0330 ■ *Web:* www.cosmo.org	Hutchinson	KS	67501	620-662-2305		520
Kansas County Treasurers Assn 201 S New York Ave *Web:* www.kansastreasurers.org	Coldwater	KS	67029	620-582-2964	582-2426	48-5
Kansas Democratic Party 501 Jefferson St Ste 30 *Web:* www.kansasdems.org	Topeka	KS	66607	785-234-0425	234-8420	616-1
Kansas Department for Aging & Disability Services 503 S Kansas Ave *Web:* www.kdads.ks.gov	Topeka	KS	66603	785-296-4986		340
Kansas Department of Administration 900 SW Jackson Rm 401-N *Web:* www.da.ks.gov	Topeka	KS	66612	785-296-2376		339-17
Kansas Department of Corrections 714 SW Jackson Ste 300 *Web:* www.doc.ks.gov	Topeka	KS	66603	785-296-3317		339-17
Kansas Department of Health & Environment 300 W Douglas Ste 700 *TF:* 800-842-0078 ■ *Web:* www.kdheks.gov	Wichita	KS	67202	316-337-6020		804
Kansas Department of Wildlife, Parks and Tourism 1020 S Kansas Ave Rm 200 *Web:* ksoutdoors.com	Topeka	KS	66612	785-296-2281	296-6953	339-17
Kansas Division of Workers Compensation 401 SW Topeka Blvd Ste 2 *TF:* 800-332-0353 ■ *Web:* www.dol.ks.gov	Topeka	KS	66603	785-296-4000	296-0025	339-17
Kansas Gas Service 7421 W 129th St *TF:* 888-482-4950 ■ *Web:* www.kansasgasservice.com	Overland Park	KS	66213	888-482-4950		787
Kansas Genealogical Society (KGS) 2601 Central Ave *Web:* www.kgs-genlibrary.com	Dodge City	KS	67801	620-225-1951		49-19
Kansas Governmental Ethics Commission 901 S Kansas Ave *Web:* www.kansas.gov	Topeka	KS	66612	785-296-4219	296-2548	265
Kansas Health Foundation 309 E Douglas *TF:* 800-373-7681 ■ *Web:* kansashealth.org	Wichita	KS	67202	316-262-7676		305
Kansas Living Magazine 2627 KFB Plz *TF:* 800-406-3053 ■ *Web:* www.kfb.org	Manhattan	KS	66503	785-587-6000	587-6914	457-1
Kansas Medical Society 623 SW Tenth Ave *TF:* 800-332-0156 ■ *Web:* www.kmsonline.org	Topeka	KS	66612	785-235-2383	235-5114	474
Kansas Mutual Insurance Co 1435 SW Topeka Blvd *Web:* www.kansasmutual.net	Topeka	KS	66601	785-354-8452	354-0706	390
Kansas Pharmacists Assn 1020 SW Fairlawn Rd *Web:* kansaspharmacistsassociation.wildapricot.org	Topeka	KS	66604	785-228-2327		585
Kansas Press Association Inc 5423 Sw 7th St *TF:* 855-572-1863 ■ *Web:* www.kspress.com	Topeka	KS	66606	785-271-5304	271-7341	530
Kansas Real Estate Commission 700 SW Jackson St Ste 404 *Web:* www.krec.ks.gov	Topeka	KS	66603	785-296-3411	296-1771	339-17
Kansas Sports Hall of Fame 515 S Wichita St *Web:* www.kshof.org	Wichita	KS	67202	316-262-2038		522
Kansas State Library (KSL) Capitol Bldg 300 SW 10th Ave Rm 312-N *TF:* 800-432-3919 ■ *Web:* www.kslib.info	Topeka	KS	66612	785-296-3296		637-10
Kansas State Nurses Assn (KSNA) 1109 SW Topeka Blvd *Web:* www.ksnurses.com	Topeka	KS	66612	785-233-8638	233-5222	533
Kansas State University 119 Anderson Hall *TF:* 800-432-8270 ■ *Web:* www.k-state.edu	Manhattan	KS	66506	785-532-6250	532-6393	166
Kansas State University-Salina *Kansas State Polytechnic* 2310 Centennial Rd *Web:* polytechnic.k-state.edu	Salina	KS	67401	785-826-2640		166
Kansas Turnpike Authority (KTA) 9401 E Kellogg *Web:* www.ksturnpike.com	Wichita	KS	67207	316-682-4537		271
Kansas Venture Capital Inc (KVCI) 40 Corporate Woods 9401 Indian Creek Pkwy Ste 200 *Web:* kvci.com	Leawood	KS	66224	913-262-7117	262-3509	402
Kansas Veterinary Medical Assn PO Box 77 *Web:* www.ksvma.org	Lyndon	KS	66451	785-221-0312		795
Kansas Wesleyan University 100 E Claflin Ave *TF:* 800-874-1154 ■ *Web:* www.kwu.edu	Salina	KS	67401	785-827-5541	827-0927	166
Kansas.gov *Kansas Insurance Department* 1300 SW Arrowhead Rd *TF:* 800-432-2484 ■ *Web:* insurance.kansas.gov	Topeka	KS	66604	785-296-3071	296-7805	339-17
Kansaw Carvings PO Box 1214 *Web:* www.kansaw.com	Louisburg	KS	66053	913-548-9427		45
Kanson Electronics Inc 245 Forrest Ave *TF:* 800-233-9354 ■ *Web:* www.issc-kanson.com	Hohenwald	TN	38462	931-796-3050		45
Kanstul Musical Instruments Inc 1332 S Claudina St *Web:* www.kanstul.com	Anaheim	CA	92805	714-563-1000		526
Kantar Group and Affiliates 3 World Trade Center 175 Greenwich St 35th Fl *Web:* www.kantar.com	New York	NY	10007	866-471-1399		466
Kantar Media & SRDS (Standard Rate & Data Service) 5600 N River Rd Ste 900 *TF:* 800-851-7737 ■ *Web:* www.login.srds.com	Rosemont	IL	60018	800-851-7737		637-2
Kanto Corp 13424 N Woodrush Way *TF:* 866-609-5571 ■ *Web:* www.kantocorp.com	Portland	OR	97203	503-283-0405	240-0409	143
Kantola Productions LLC 55 Sunnyside Ave *TF:* 800-280-1180 ■ *Web:* www.kantola.com	Mill Valley	CA	94941	415-381-9363		514
Kantor, Davidoff, Mandelker, Twomey, Gallanty & Kesten PC 51 E 42nd St 16th Fl *Web:* kantordavidoff.com	New York	NY	10017	212-682-8383		41
KANU-FM 91.5 (NPR) Kansas Public Radio 1120 W 11th St *TF:* 888-577-5268 ■ *Web:* kansaspublicradio.org	Lawrence	KS	66044	785-864-4530		645
Kanza Bank 151 N Main St *TF:* 888-532-5821 ■ *Web:* kanzabank.com	Kingman	KS	67068	620-694-6767		70
Kanzaki Specialty Papers 20 Cummings St *TF:* 888-526-9254 ■ *Web:* kanzakiusa.com	Ware	MA	01082	413-967-6204		554
Kao Specialties Americas LLC 243 Woodbine St PO Box 2316 *TF:* 800-727-2214 ■ *Web:* chemical.kao.com	High Point	NC	27261	336-884-2214	884-8786	145
Kap Medical 1395 Pico St *Web:* www.kapmedical.com	Corona	CA	92881	951-340-4360		250
KAP Project Services Ltd 1200 Hwy 146 Ste 260 *TF:* 877-527-7762 ■ *Web:* www.kap.us.com	La Porte	TX	77571	281-842-8333	842-8335	180
Kapalua Realty Company Ltd 700 Office Rd *TF:* 800-545-8439 ■ *Web:* www.kapalua.com	Lahaina	HI	96761	808-665-5454		652
KAPCO Inc 1000 Badger Cir *Web:* kapcoinc.com	Grafton	WI	53024	262-377-6500	377-9345	483
KAPE-AM 901 S Kingshighway St *TF:* 800-467-1007 ■ *Web:* www.kaperadio1550.com	Cape Girardeau	MO	63703	573-339-7000	339-1550	647
Kapitan Engineering Inc 802 Franklin St *Web:* kapitan-eng.com	Sauk City	WI	53583	608-643-6477		256
Kaplan Computers LLC 61 Tolland Tpke *Web:* kaplancomputers.com	Manchester	CT	06042	860-643-6474		175
Kaplan Devries Inc 1903 Ashwood Ct *Web:* kaplandevries.com	Greensboro	NC	27455	336-288-8200	282-6878	463
Kaplan Early Learning Co 1310 Lewisville-Clemmons Rd **Fax Area Code:* 800 ■ *TF:* 800-334-2014 ■ *Web:* www.kaplanco.com	Lewisville	NC	27023	336-766-7374	452-7526*	243
Kaplan Home Inspection Training School 332 Front St S Ste 501 *TF:* 888-323-9235 ■ *Web:* www.kapre.com	La Crosse	WI	54601	888-323-9235		685
Kaplan Inc 6301 Kaplan University Ave **Fax Area Code:* 212 ■ *Web:* kaplan.com	Fort Lauderdale	FL	33309	954-515-3993	437-1159*	244
Kaplan Industries Inc 6255 Kilby Rd **Fax Area Code:* 513 ■ *TF:* 800-257-8299 ■ *Web:* www.kaplanindustries.com	Harrison	OH	45030	856-779-8181	367-0803*	385
Kaplan McLaughlin Diaz 222 Vallejo St *Web:* www.kmdarchitects.com	San Francisco	CA	94111	415-398-5191		261
Kaplan Mrd Inc 31 Chesley Rd *Web:* kaplanmrd.com	White Plains	NY	10605	914-686-1450		466
Kaplan Trucking Co 6600 Bessemer Ave *TF:* 800-352-2848 ■ *Web:* www.kaplantrucking.com	Cleveland	OH	44127	216-341-3322		780
Kaplansky Insurance Agency 10 Kearney Rd *TF:* 800-640-2020 ■ *Web:* kaplansky.com	Needham	MA	02494	800-640-2020		390
Kaplel 220 N Cushing Ave *TF:* 866-643-7171 ■ *Web:* kaptel.net	Kaplan	LA	70548	337-643-7171	643-6000	736
Kapok Press LLC PO Box 1861 *TF:* 866-445-2765 ■ *Web:* www.kapokpress.com	Fredericksburg	VA	22402	540-372-2033		637-2
Kapp Construction Company Inc 329 Mt Vernon Ave *Web:* www.kappconstruction.com	Springfield	OH	45501	937-324-0134	324-3406	186
Kapp Surgical Instrument Inc 4919 Warrensville Center Rd *TF:* 800-282-5277 ■ *Web:* www.kappsurgical.com	Cleveland	OH	44128	216-587-4400	587-0411	476
Kappa Alpha Order 115 Liberty Hall Rd PO Box 1865 *Web:* www.kappaalphaorder.org	Lexington	VA	24450	540-463-1865	463-2140	48-16
Kappa Alpha Psi Fraternity Inc 2322-24 N Broad St *Web:* kappaalphapsi1911.com	Philadelphia	PA	19132	215-228-7184	228-7181	48-16
Kappa Alpha Theta Fraternity 8740 Founders Rd **Fax Area Code:* 317 ■ *TF:* 800-526-1870 ■ *Web:* www.kappaalphatheta.org	Indianapolis	IN	46268	888-526-1870	876-1925*	48-16
Kappa Delta Pi 3707 Woodview Trace *TF:* 800-284-3167 ■ *Web:* www.kdp.org	Indianapolis	IN	46268	317-871-4900	704-2323	48-16
Kappa Delta Sorority 3205 Players Ln *TF:* 800-536-1897 ■ *Web:* www.kappadelta.org	Memphis	TN	38125	901-748-1897	748-0949	48-16

Phone | Fax | Class

Kappa Kappa Gamma PO Box 38 Columbus OH 43216 614-228-6515 228-7809 48-16
TF: 866-554-1870 ■ Web: www.kappakappagamma.org

Kappa Sigma Fraternity
1610 Scottsville Rd Charlottesville VA 22902 434-295-3193 296-9557 48-16
Web: kappasigma.org

Kappe Associates Inc
100 Wormans Mill Ct Frederick MD 21701 301-846-0200 641
Web: www.kappe-inc.com

Kappes, Cassiday & Associates Inc
7950 Security Cir Reno NV 89506 775-972-7575 261
Web: www.kcareno.com

Kappler Inc
55 Grimes Dr PO Box 490 Guntersville AL 35976 256-505-4005 505-4151 576
TF: 800-600-4019 ■ Web: www.kappler.com

Kappus Plastic Company Inc
61-65 NJ Rte 31 S Hampton NJ 08827 908-537-2288 537-7192 600
TF: 800-537-1175 ■ Web: kappusplastic.com

Kappy S. Liquors 325 Bennett Hwy Malden MA 02148 781-321-1000 443
Web: www.kappys.com

KAPS-ALL Packaging Systems Inc
200 Mill Rd Riverhead NY 11901 631-727-0300 369-5939 557
TF: 800-736-4512 ■ Web: kapsall.com

Kapstone Medical LLC 520 Elliot St Charlotte NC 28202 704-843-7852 475
Web: www.kapstonemedical.com

Kapta Inc 2220 1re Av Notre-Dame-des-Pins QC G0M1K0 418-774-5688 687
Web: www.kapta.ca

Kaptur Marcy (Rep D - OH)
2186 Rayburn House Office Bldg Washington DC 20515 202-225-4146 225-7711 342-2
Web: www.kaptur.house.gov

KAQC-TV 705b W Main St Atlanta TX 75551 903-796-4060 647
Web: www.casscountytoday.com

Kar's Nuts 1200 E 14 Mile Rd Madison Heights MI 48071 800-527-6887 296-28
TF: 800-527-6887 ■ Web: www.karsnuts.com

Karas & Karas Glass Company Inc
455 Dorchester Ave Boston MA 02127 617-268-8800 269-0536 189-6
TF: 800-888-1235 ■ Web: www.karasglass.com

Karas Insurance Agencies Inc
321 S Riverside Ave Croton-on-Hudson NY 10520 914-271-5188 390
Web: karasinsurance.com

Karavan Trailers Inc
100 Karavan Dr PO Box 27 Fox Lake WI 53933 920-928-6200 928-6201 763
Web: www.karavantrailers.com

Karbal, Cohen, Economou, Silk & Dunne LLC
150 S Wacker Dr 17th Fl Chicago IL 60606 312-431-3700 431-3670 428
Web: www.karballaw.com

Karbone 675 Third Ave Ste 3004 New York NY 10017 646-291-2900 219-7168 192
Web: karbone.com

Karcher Group Inc
14221a Willard Rd Ste 1500 Chantilly VA 20151 703-631-6626 180
Web: www.karchergroup.com

Kardium Inc 12851 Rowan Pl Ste 100 Richmond BC V6V2K5 604-248-8891 723
Web: kardium.com

Karen Ann Quinlan Hospice
99 Sparta Ave Newton NJ 07860 973-383-0115 383-6889 371
TF: 800-882-1117 ■ Web: www.karenannquinlanhospice.org

Karen Poling Law LLC
5354 Cemetery Rd Hilliard OH 43026 614-771-6000 41
Web: karenpolinglaw.com

Karen Temple, Attorney At Law Lllc
24 N Church St Ste 200 Wailuku HI 96793 808-244-8222 242-7621 41
Web: ktemplelaw.com

KARE-TV Ch 11 (NBC)
8811 Olson Memorial Hwy Minneapolis MN 55427 763-546-1111 546-8590 741
Web: www.kare11.com

Karges Furniture Company Inc
4047 Eastern Ave SE Grand Rapids MI 49508 616-243-3676 286
Web: www.karges.com

Karges-Faulconbridge Inc
670 County Rd B W Saint Paul MN 55113 651-771-0880 261
TF: 866-604-2390 ■ Web: www.kfi-eng.com

Karina Library Press PO Box 35 Ojai CA 93024 805-500-4535 637-2
Web: www.karinalibrary.com

KARK-TV
KARK 4 1401 W Capitol Ave Ste 104 Little Rock AR 72201 501-340-4444 647
Web: www.kark.com

Karl Chevrolet Accessories
1101 SE Oralabor Rd Ankeny IA 50021 515-299-4300 791
Web: www.karlchevrolet.com

Karl Ehmer Inc 48 S Ocean Ave Patchogue NY 11772 631-289-3448 296-26
Web: karlehmer.com

Karl Schmidt Manufacturing Inc
3900 E 68th Ave Commerce City CO 80022 303-287-7400 695
Web: www.karlschmidt.com

Karl Storz Endoscopy-america Inc
600 Corporate Pt Culver City CA 90230 310-338-8100 475
TF: 800-321-1304 ■ Web: www.karlstorz.com

Karl Storz Imaging Inc 175 Cremona Dr Goleta CA 93117 805-968-3568 963-0933 544
TF: 800-796-8909 ■ Web: www.optronics.com

Karl Truman Law Office LLC
420 Wall St Jeffersonville IN 47130 812-282-8500 428
TF: 877-492-1706 ■ Web: www.trumanlaw.com

Karl Tyler Chevrolet Inc
3663 N Reserve Missoula MT 59808 406-721-2438 57
TF: 866-503-1949 ■ Web: www.gmofmontana.com

Karl W. Richter Ltd
350 Middlefield Rd Scarborough ON M1S5B1 416-757-8951 757-7110 351
TF: 877-597-8665 ■ Web: www.kwrtools.com

Karl's Transport 975 Amron Ave Antigo WI 54409 715-623-2791 468
Web: www.karlstransport.com

Karla Colletto Swimwear Inc
319d Mill St NE Vienna VA 22180 703-281-3262 711
Web: karlacolletto.com

Karlitz and Co 200 W 41st St Ste 1004 New York NY 10036 646-289-8900 289-8911 393
Web: www.karlitz.com

Karls Mechanical Contractors Inc
954 Forward Ave Chilton WI 53014 920-849-2050 849-9446 189-10
Web: www.karlsmechanical.com

Karma 246 Market St Philadelphia PA 19106 215-925-1444 671
Web: karmaphiladelphia.com

Karman Rubber Co 2331 Copley Rd Akron OH 44320 330-864-2161 864-2124 677
Web: www.karman.com

Karnak Corp, The 330 Central Ave Clark NJ 07066 732-388-0300 388-9422 46
TF: 800-526-4236 ■ Web: www.karnakcorp.com

Karner Blue Marketing LLC
2 Nott Terr Schenectady NY 12308 518-935-4101 5
Web: www.karnerbluemarketing.com

Karnes County 210 W Calvert Ave Karnes City TX 78118 830-780-3938 780-4576 338
Web: www.co.karnes.tx.us

Karnes Electric Co-opeartive Inc
1007 N Hwy 123 Karnes City TX 78118 830-780-3952 780-2347 245
TF: 888-807-3952 ■ Web: karnesec.org

Karns Quality Foods Ltd
6001 Allentown Blvd Harrisburg PA 17112 717-545-4731 345
Web: www.karnsfoods.com

Karol Fulfillment
Hanover Industrial Estates 375 Stewart Rd
Wilkes-Barre PA 18706 570-822-8899 822-8226 627
TF: 800-526-4773 ■ Web: karolfulfillmentservices.com

Karpel Computer Systems Inc
9717 Landmark Pkwy Dr Ste 200 Saint Louis MO 63127 314-892-6300 892-8035 177
TF: 866-813-8305 ■ Web: www.karpel.com

Karpeles Manuscript Library
453 Porter Ave Buffalo NY 14201 716-885-4139 520
Web: www.rain.org

Karpeles Manuscript Library Museum
902 E First St Duluth MN 55805 218-728-0630 520
Web: www.rain.org

Karpen Steel Custom Doors & Frames
181 Reems Creek Rd Weaverville NC 28787 828-645-4821 645-3230 234
TF: 800-851-2131 ■ Web: www.karpensteel.com

Karpinski, Berry, Adler & Company PLC
5110 N 40th St Ste 201 Phoenix AZ 85018 602-244-8411 2
Web: phxcpa.net

Karr Barth Associates Inc
40 Monument Rd Bala Cynwyd PA 19004 610-660-4000 401
Web: www.karr-barthassociates.com

Karrass
8370 Wilshire Blvd Ste 300 Beverly Hills CA 90211 323-866-3800 782-1812 95
Web: www.karrass.com

Kartchner Caverns State Park
2980 Arizona 90 Benson AZ 85602 520-586-2283 565
Web: azstateparks.com

Kartemquin Films Ltd
1901 W Wellington Ave Chicago IL 60657 773-472-4366 472-3348 514
Web: www.kartemquin.com

Karthauser & Sons Inc
W 147 N 11100 Fond du Lac Ave Germantown WI 53022 262-255-7815 255-6920 293
TF: 800-338-8620 ■ Web: www.karthauser.net

Karuna Advisors
1550 El Camino Real Ste 250 Menlo Park CA 94025 650-328-2758 734
Web: www.karunaadvisors.com

Karuna Therapeutics 33 Arch St Ste 3110 Boston MA 02110 857-449-2244 994-3001* 582
NASDAQ: JNP ■ *Fax Area Code: 973 ■ TF: 866-566-5636 ■ Web: karunatx.com

KARVY Global Services (US)
115 Broadway Ste 1506 New York NY 10006 212-267-4334 267-4335 401
Web: www.karvyglobal.com

Karwoski and Courage
Fifth Street Towers 150 S 5th St Ste 900 Minneapolis MN 55402 612-342-9898 342-9700 317
Web: www.creativepr.com

KAS Inc 62 Veronica Ave Somerset NJ 08873 800-967-4254 131
TF: 800-967-4254 ■ Web: www.kasrugs.com

Kasa Companies Inc 418 E Ave B Salina KS 67401 785-404-3600 825-0590 729
TF: 800-755-5272 ■ Web: www.kasacompanies.com

Kasa Industrial Controls Inc
418 E Ave B Salina KS 67401 785-825-7181 729
Web: www.kasacontrols.com

Kasco Fab Inc 4529 S Chestnut Ave Fresno CA 93725 559-442-1018 492
Web: kascofab.com

Kasco-Sharptech Corp
1569 Tower Grove Ave Saint Louis MO 63110 314-771-1550 683
TF: 800-325-3251 ■ Web: www.kasco.com

Kase Equipment Corp 7400 Hub Pkwy Valley View OH 44125 216-642-9040 986-0678 628
Web: www.kaseequip.com

Kaseya Corp 400 Totten Pond Rd Ste 200 Waltham MA 02451 877-926-0001 196
TF: 877-926-0001 ■ Web: www.kaseya.com

Kasgro Rail Corp 121 Rundle Rd New Castle PA 16102 724-658-9061 650
TF: 888-203-5580 ■ Web: www.kasgro.com

KASH-FM 107.5 (Ctry)
800 E Dimond Blvd Ste 3-370 Anchorage AK 99515 907-522-1515 645-7
Web: kashcountry1075.iheart.com

Kashmir Fabrics + Furnishings
3191 Commonwealth Dr Dallas TX 75247 214-631-8040 631-8651* 361
*Fax Area Code: 800 ■ TF: 800-527-4630 ■ Web: www.kasmirfabrics.com

Kashrus Magazine PO Box 204 Brooklyn NY 11204 718-336-8544 336-8550 457-18
Web: www.kashrusmagazine.com

Kaskaskia College 27210 College Rd Centralia IL 62801 618-545-3090 162
TF: 800-642-0859 ■ Web: www.kaskaskia.edu

KASL Consulting Engineers Inc
7777 Greenback Ln Ste 104 Citrus Heights CA 95610 916-722-1800 256
Web: www.kasl.com

Kaslen Textiles 2140 E 51st St Vernon CA 90058 323-588-7700 838-0346 746
TF: 800-777-5789 ■ Web: kaslentextiles.com

KASM-AM 35223 238th Ave Albany MN 56307 320-845-2184 647
TF: 800-950-2148 ■ Web: www.mykasm.com

Kason Industries Inc 57 Amlajack Blvd Newnan GA 30265 770-304-3000 251-4854 350
TF: 800-935-3550 ■ Web: www.kasonind.com

Kaspar Broadcasting Co PO Box 220 Warrenton MO 63383 636-377-2300 645-141
TF: 877-259-7373 ■ Web: www.kwre.com

Kaspick & Co
203 Redwood Shores Pkwy Ste 300 Redwood City CA 94065 650-585-4100 401
Web: www.kaspick.com

Kass Brothers Inc 700 River Rd Westwego LA 70094 504-348-9018 189-5
Web: www.kassbros.com

Kass Uehling Inc 333 Seventh Ave New York NY 10001 212-465-9206 344
Web: www.kassuehling.com

Kassbohrer All Terrain Vehicles Inc
8850 Double Diamond Pkwy Reno NV 89521 775-857-5000 857-5010 516
Web: www.pistenbully.com

Name / Address	City	State	ZIP	Phone	Fax	Class
Kassirco 2027 Leo Ave *TF:* 888-995-9935 ■ *Web:* www.kassirco.com	Commerce	CA	90040	323-888-8880	889-1880	238
Kastner Kim LLP 1451 Grant Rd Ste 104 *Web:* kastnerkim.com	Mountain View	CA	94040	650-967-7854	386-1885	41
KAT 103.7FM 5010 Underwood Ave *Web:* thekat.iheart.com	Omaha	NE	68132	402-561-2000		645-113
Katahdin Federal Credit Union 1000 Central St *Web:* katahdinfcu.org	Millinocket	ME	04462	207-723-9718		219
Katahdin Iron Works State Historic Site *Peaks-Kenny State Park* 401 State Park Rd *Web:* www.maine.gov	Dover-Foxcroft	ME	04426	207-326-4012		565
Katahdin Restaurant 27 Forest Ave *Web:* www.katahdinrestaurant.com	Portland	ME	04101	207-774-1740		671
Katalyst Data Management LLC 10311 Westpark Dr *TF:* 855-529-6444 ■ *Web:* www.katalystdm.com	Houston	TX	77042	281-529-3200		539
Katalyst Surgical LLC 754 Goddard Ave *TF:* 888-452-8259 ■ *Web:* www.katalystsurgical.com	Chesterfield	MO	63005	888-452-8259		476
Kataman Metals 7733 Forsyth Blvd Ste 300 *Web:* www.kataman.com	Saint Louis	MO	63105	314-863-6699		791
Katana Software Inc 333 W Broadway Ste 105 *Web:* www.katanasoft.com	Long Beach	CA	90802	805-494-1651		178-1
Katapult Engineering Inc 54 Old York Rd *Web:* katapultengineering.com	Dillsburg	PA	17019	717-432-0716		261
KATB Life Changing Radio 2709 Boniface Pkwy *Web:* www.katb.org	Anchorage	AK	99504	907-333-5282		645-7
KATC-TV Ch 3 (ABC) 1103 Eraste Landry Rd *Web:* www.katc.com	LaFayette	LA	70506	337-235-3333	769-1050	741-70
Kate Aspen Inc 2700 Breckinridge Blvd *TF:* 866-316-2453 ■ *Web:* www.kateaspen.com	Duluth	GA	30097	770-613-0887		241
Kate B. Reynolds Charitable Trust 128 Reynolda Vlg *TF:* 800-485-9080 ■ *Web:* www.kbr.org	Winston-Salem	NC	27106	336-397-5500	723-7765	305
Kate Spade 135 5th Ave *TF:* 866-999-5283 ■ *Web:* www.katespade.com	New York	NY	10010	212-358-0420		349
Katech Inc 24324 Sorrentino Ct *Web:* katechengines.com	Clinton Township	MI	48035	586-791-4120		247
Katecho Inc 4020 Gannett Ave *Web:* www.katecho.com	Des Moines	IA	50321	515-244-1212		476
Kater-Crafts Bookbinders Inc 4860 Gregg Rd *Web:* www.katercrafts.com	Pico Rivera	CA	90660	562-692-0665	692-7920	92
Katherine Delmar Burke School 7070 California St *Web:* www.kdbs.org	San Francisco	CA	94121	415-751-0177	666-0535	685
Katherine Frazier Insurance Agency 1600 Lebanon Ave Ste 103 *Web:* katherinefrazier.com	Belleville	IL	62221	618-234-3680		390
Katherine L. Mcarthur LLC 6055 Lakeside Commons Dr Ste 400 *Web:* mcarthurlawfirm.com	Macon	GA	31210	478-796-9380	238-6607	41
Katherine Shaw Bethea Hospital 403 E First St *Web:* www.ksbhospital.com	Dixon	IL	61021	815-288-5531	285-5859	374-3
Katherman, Briggs & Greenberg LLP 110 N George St 3rd Fl *TF:* 800-509-1011 ■ *Web:* resultsyoudeserve.com	York	PA	17401	717-848-3838		41
Kathoderay Media Inc 20 Country Estates Rd *Web:* www.kathoderay.com	Greenville	NY	12083	518-966-5600	966-5629	344
KATH-TV Ch 5 (NBC) 1107 W Eigth St *Web:* www.kath.tv	Juneau	AK	99801	907-586-8384	586-8394	741-67
Kathy Leslie Wall 5600 W Lovers Ln Ste 200 *Web:* kathylwall.com	Dallas	TX	75209	214-350-2692		390
Kathy Sisk Enterprises Inc PO Box 1754 *TF:* 800-477-1278 ■ *Web:* www.kathysiskenterprises.com	Clovis	CA	93613	559-323-1472	323-9151	737
Kathy's Gazebo Cafe 4199 N Federal Hwy *Web:* www.kathysgazebo.com	Boca Raton	FL	33431	561-395-6033		671
Kathy's House Inc 600 N 103 St *Web:* www.kathys-house.org	Milwaukee	WI	53226	414-453-8290	453-8292	372
Katko John (Rep R - NY) 2457 Rayburn House Office Bldg *Web:* www.katko.house.gov	Washington	DC	20515	202-225-3701	225-4042	342-2
Katmai Coastal Bear Tours PO Box 1503 *Web:* www.katmaibears.com	Homer	AK	99603	907-235-8337		760
Katmai National Park & Preserve King Salmon Mall PO Box 7 *Web:* www.nps.gov	King Salmon	AK	99613	907-246-3305	246-2116	564
Kato Engineering Inc 2075 Howard Dr *Web:* www.emersonindustrial.com	Mankato	MN	56003	507-625-4011	345-2798	518
Katonah Museum of Art Inc 134 Jay St *Web:* www.katonahmuseum.org	Katonah	NY	10536	914-232-9555		520
KATP-FM 101.9 (Ctry) 6214 W 34th St *Web:* thebullamarillo.com	Amarillo	TX	79109	806-355-9777		645-5
Katsky Korins LLP 605 Third Ave *Web:* katskykorins.com	New York	NY	10158	212-953-6000		445
Katterman's Sand Point Pharmacy 5400 Sand Point Way NE *Web:* www.kattermans.com	Seattle	WA	98105	206-524-2211	524-8669	237
KATU-TV Ch 2 (ABC) 2153 NE Sandy Blvd *Web:* katu.com	Portland	OR	97232	503-231-4222		741-103
KATV ABC 7 PO Box 77 *Web:* katv.com	Little Rock	AR	72203	501-324-7777	372-1509	741-75
Katz & Doorakian Law Firm PL 625 N Flagler Dr Ste 605 *Web:* katzlawpl.com	West Palm Beach	FL	33401	561-721-6770		41
Katz & Korin PC 334 N Senate Ave The Emelie Bldg *TF:* 800-464-2427 ■ *Web:* www.kkclegal.com	Indianapolis	IN	46204	317-464-1100		428
Katz Abosch Windesheim Gershman & Freedman PA 9690 Deereco Rd Ste 500 *Web:* www.katzabosch.com	Lutherville Timonium	MD	21093	410-828-2727		2
Katz Cassidy 11400 W Olympic Blvd Ste 1050 *Web:* www.katzcassidy.com	Los Angeles	CA	90064	310-477-6300	626-9270	734
Katz Consulting Group LLC 179 Summers St Ste 213 *Web:* katzconsultinggroup.com	Charleston	WV	25301	304-346-1900		41
Katz Goldstein & Warren PC 2345 Waukegan Rd Ste 150 *Web:* kgwlaw.com	Bannockburn	IL	60015	847-317-9500	317-0286	428
Katz Group 10104-103 Ave 1702 Bell Twr *Web:* www.katzgroup.ca	Edmonton	AB	T5J0H8	780-990-0505		237
Katz Sapper & Miller 800 E 96th St Ste 500 *Web:* www.ksmcpa.com	Indianapolis	IN	46240	317-580-2000	580-2117	2
Katz Teller 255 E Fifth St Ste 2400 *Web:* katzteller.com	Cincinnati	OH	45202	513-721-4532	762-0000	41
Katzkin Leather Interiors Inc 6868 Acco St *Web:* katzkin.com	Montebello	CA	90640	323-725-1243		453
Kaua'i Chamber of Commerce 2970 Kele St Ste 112 *Web:* www.kauaichamber.org	Lihue	HI	96766	808-245-7363	245-8815	139
Kauai Community College 2444 Dole St *Web:* www.kauai.hawaii.edu	Honolulu	HI	96822	808-245-8311	245-8220	162
KAUAI KIAHUNA 2253 Poipu Rd *Web:* kauai-kiahuna.com	Koloa	HI	96756	808-742-2121	742-1570	377
Kauai Museum 4428 Rice St *Web:* www.kauaimuseum.org	Lihue	HI	96766	808-245-6931		637-2
Kauffman Engineering Inc 701 Ransdell Rd *Web:* www.kewire.com	Lebanon	IN	46052	765-402-5040		253
Kauffmann + Associates CPAS 4350 Brownsboro Rd Ste 170 *Web:* kaacpas.com	Louisville	KY	40207	502-893-8067	893-8068	2
Kaufman & Kabani CPA 811 Wilshire Blvd Ste 1850 *Web:* kkcpa.com	Los Angeles	CA	90017	213-488-6180	488-6188	2
Kaufman Borgeest & Ryan LLP (KBR) 120 Broadway 14th Fl *Web:* www.kbrlaw.com	New York	NY	10271	212-980-9600	980-9291	428
Kaufman Campaign Consultants (KCC) 1510 J St Ste 210 *Web:* www.kaufmancampaigns.com	Sacramento	CA	95814	916-443-7817		192
Kaufman Company Inc 19 Walkhill Rd *TF:* 800-338-8023 ■ *Web:* www.kaufmanco.com	Norwood	MA	02062	781-255-1000	619-1753	41
Kaufman County Courthouse 100 W Mulberry *Web:* www.kaufmancounty.net	Kaufman	TX	75142	469-376-4100		338
Kaufman Engineered Systems Inc 1260 Wtrville Monclova Rd *Web:* kaufmanengsys.com	Waterville	OH	43566	419-878-9727	878-9726	318
Kaufman Herald 300 N Washington *Web:* www.kaufmanherald.com	Kaufman	TX	75142	972-932-2171		532-2
Kaufman Lynn Construction (KL) 3185 S Congress Ave *Web:* www.kaufmanlynn.com	Delray Beach	FL	33445	561-361-6700	361-6979	186
Kaufman Manufacturing Co 547 S 29th St PO Box 1056 *TF:* 800-420-6641 ■ *Web:* www.kaufmanmfg.com	Manitowoc	WI	54221	920-684-6641	686-4103	455
Kaufman Rossin & Company PA 2699 S Bayshore Dr Ste 300 *TF:* 888-680-5726 ■ *Web:* kaufmanrossin.com	Miami	FL	33133	305-858-5600	856-3284	2
Kaufman Steinberg LLP 2020 Main St Ste 345 *Web:* kaufmansteinberg.com	Irvine	CA	92614	949-757-9000		41
Kaulkin Ginsberg Co 20251 Century Blvd Ste 160 **Fax Area Code:* 240 ■ *Web:* www.kaulkin.com	Germantown	MD	20874	301-907-0840	499-3801*	177
KAUS-AM 18431 State Hwy 105 *Web:* www.myaustinminnesota.com	Austin	MN	55912	507-437-7666		647
Kautex Inc 750 Stephenson Hwy *Web:* www.kautex.de	Troy	MI	48083	248-616-5100	616-5395	60
Kavaliro Staffing Services 12001 Research Pkwy Ste 344 *TF:* 800-562-1470 ■ *Web:* kavaliro.com	Orlando	FL	32826	407-243-6006		260
Kavanagh Assoc 10585 Rookwood Dr *Web:* kavassoc.com	San Diego	CA	92131	858-549-6744		261
Kavarna 143 N Broadway *Web:* kavarna.com	Green Bay	WI	54303	920-430-3200		671
Kaveri Madras Cuisine 1148 Fulton Ave *Web:* kaverimadrascuisine.com	Sacramento	CA	95825	916-481-9970		671
Kavinoky Theatre 320 Porter Ave *Web:* www.kavinokytheatre.com	Buffalo	NY	14201	716-829-7668		572
KAVU-TV 3808 N Navarro *Web:* www.crossroadstoday.com	Victoria	TX	77901	361-575-2500	572-0050	647
Kaw Valley Bank 1110 N Kansas Ave *Web:* kawvalleybank.com	Topeka	KS	66608	785-232-6062		70
Kawada Hotel 200 S Hill St *TF:* 800-752-9232 ■ *Web:* www.kawadahotel.com	Los Angeles	CA	90012	213-621-4455	687-4455	379
Kawai America Corp PO Box 9045 *Web:* www.kawaius.com	Rancho Dominguez	CA	90224	310-631-1771	604-6913	527
Kawailoa Development LLP PO Box 369 *Web:* www.kawailoa.com	Koloa	HI	96756	808-742-6300	742-7197	379
Kawasaki Heavy Industries USA Inc 60 E 42nd St Ste 2501 *Web:* www.khi.co.jp	New York	NY	10165	212-759-4950	759-6421	360-3
Kawasaki Motors Corporation USA PO Box 25252 *Web:* www.kawasaki.com	Santa Ana	CA	92799	949-460-5629		710

	Phone	Fax	Class
Kawasaki Rail Car Inc 29 Wells Ave Bldg 4 .... Yonkers NY 10701 Web: www.kawasakirailcar.com	914-376-4700	376-4779	650
Kawasaki Robotics Inc 28140 Lakeview Dr .... Wixom MI 48393 Web: robotics.kawasaki.com	248-446-4100	446-4200	386
Kaweah Delta 400 W Mineral King Ave........ Visalia CA 93291 Web: www.kaweahdelta.org	559-624-2000		374-3
Kawneer Company Inc 555 Guthridge Ct........ Norcross GA 30092 Web: www.kawneer.com	770-449-5555	734-1560	286
Kay & Associates Inc 165 N Arlington Heights Rd Ste 150........ Buffalo Grove IL 60089 Web: www.kayinc.com	847-255-8444		20
Kay Automotive Graphics 57 Kay Industrial Dr .... Lake Orion MI 48359 Web: www.kayautomotive.com	248-377-4999	377-2097	687
Kay Casto & Chaney PLLC 1500 Chase Tower 707 Virginia St E........ Charleston WV 25301 Web: www.kaycasto.com	304-345-8900	345-8909	428
Kay Chemical Co 8300 Capital Dr........ Greensboro NC 27409 *Fax Area Code: 651 ■ TF: 877-315-1115 ■ Web: www.ecolab.com	844-880-8355	225-3098*	151
Kay County 201 S Main St........ Newkirk OK 74647 TF: 800-255-9456 ■ Web: www.courthouse.kay.ok.us	580-362-2565	362-3668	338
Kay Dee Designs Inc 177 Skunk Hill Rd........ Hope Valley RI 02832 TF: 800-537-3433 ■ Web: www.kaydeedesigns.com	800-537-3433	272-0724	746
Kay Dee Feed Company Inc 1919 Grand Ave .... Sioux City IA 51106 TF: 800-831-4815 ■ Web: kaydeefeed.com	712-277-2011		447
Kay El Bar Guest Ranch 2655 S Kay El Bar Rd .... Wickenburg AZ 85390 TF: 800-684-7583 ■ Web: www.kayelbar.com	928-684-7593	684-4497	239
Kay Electric Co-op (KEC) 300 W Doolin Ave........ Blackwell OK 74631 TF: 800-535-1079 ■ Web: www.kayelectric.coop	580-363-1260	363-2308	245
Kay Green Design Inc 668 Cherry St Ste A .... Winter Park FL 32789 Web: kaygreendesign.com	407-246-7155	426-7873	393
Kay Jewelers 375 Ghent Rd........ Akron OH 44333 TF: 800-527-8029 ■ Web: www.kay.com	800-527-8029		410
Kay Manufacturing Co 602 State St .... Calumet City IL 60409 Web: kaymfg.com	708-862-6800		454
Kay Park Recreation Corp 1301 Pine St........ Janesville IA 50647 TF: 866-442-8161 ■ Web: www.kaypark.com	319-987-2313	987-2900	319-4
Kay Toledo Tag 6050 Benore Rd PO Box 5038 .... Toledo OH 43612 *Fax Area Code: 800 ■ TF: 800-822-8247 ■ Web: www.kaytag.com	419-729-5479	265-1948*	627
Kaya Associates Inc 806 Governors Dr Ste 201 .... Huntsville AL 35801 Web: www.kayacorp.com	256-382-8084		194
Kayaku Advanced Materials Inc 90 Oak St .... Newton MA 02464 Web: www.microchem.com	617-965-5511	965-5818	145
Kaydon Ring & Seal Inc 1600 Wicomico St .... Baltimore MD 21230 Web: www.skf.com	410-547-7700		326
Kaye Personnel Inc 1868 Marlton Pike E........ Cherry Hill NJ 08003 Web: kayepersonnel.com	856-489-1200		260
Kaye Rose & Partners LLP 9100 Wilshire Blvd Ste 420 W .... Beverly Hills CA 90212 Web: kayerose.com	310-551-6555	277-1220	445
Kayem Foods Inc 75 Arlington St........ Chelsea MA 02150 TF: 800-426-6100 ■ Web: www.kayem.com	617-889-1600		296-26
Kayes Inc 4601 16th Ave N .... Fargo ND 58102 *Fax Area Code: 800 ■ Web: www.forumprinting.com	701-476-2000	765-2937*	627
Kaye-Smith 4101 Oakesdale Ave SW........ Renton WA 98057 TF: 800-822-9987 ■ Web: www.kayesmith.com	425-228-8600		110
Kayline Processing Inc 31 Coates St .... Trenton NJ 08611 Web: www.kayline.com	609-695-1449	989-1094	600
Kaylor Dental Laboratory Inc 619 N Florence St........ Wichita KS 67212 TF: 800-657-2549 ■ Web: www.kaylordental.com	316-943-3226		415
Kayne Anderson Capital Advisors LP 1800 Avenue of the Stars 3rd Fl .... Los Angeles CA 90067 TF: 800-638-1496 ■ Web: www.kaynecapital.com	310-282-7900		401
Kays CPA Group PC 3021 E 98th St Ste 100........ Indianapolis IN 46280 Web: kayscpa.com	317-472-0525		2
Kaytee Products Inc 521 Clay St........ Chilton WI 53014 TF: 800-529-8331 ■ Web: www.kaytee.com	920-849-2321	849-7044	578
KAYU-TV Ch 28 (Fox) 4600 S Regal St........ Spokane WA 99223 Web: fox28spokane.com	509-448-2828		741-127
Kaz Sushi Bistro 1915 I St NW........ Washington DC 20006 Web: www.kazsushi.com	202-530-5500		671
Kazakhstan			
Consulate 26 W 17th St 19th Fl........ New York NY 10017 Web: kazconsulny.org	646-370-6331	370-6334	257
Embassy 1401 16th St NW .... Washington DC 20036 Web: www.kazakhembus.com	202-232-5488	232-5845	257
Kazal Fire Protection Inc 3499 E 34th St .... Tucson AZ 85713 TF: 833-242-1455 ■ Web: kazalfire.com	520-323-1518		610
Kazan, McClain, Satterley & Greenwood Jack London Market 55 Harrison St Ste 400........ Oakland CA 94607 TF: 877-995-6372 ■ Web: www.kazanlaw.com	877-995-6372		466
KAZI 88.7 FM 8906 Wall St Ste 203........ Austin TX 78754 Web: www.kazifm.org	512-836-9544	836-9563	645-13
Kazimierz World Wine Bar 7137 E Stetson Dr........ Scottsdale AZ 85251 Web: kazbar.net	480-946-3004		671
KAZN-AM 747 E Green St .... Pasadena CA 91101 Web: www.am1300.com	626-568-1300	568-3666	647
KAZR-FM 103.3 (Rock) 1416 Locust St........ Des Moines IA 50309 Web: www.lazer1033.com	515-280-1350	280-3011	645-47
KAZT-TV Ch 7 (Ind) 3211 Tower Rd........ Prescott AZ 86305 Web: aztv.com	928-778-6770	445-5210	741

	Phone	Fax	Class
KB (Kobalt Books) PO Box 1062........ Bala Cynwyd PA 19004 Web: www.kobaltbooks.com	314-503-5462		637-2
KB Environmental Sciences Inc 9500 Koger Blvd N Ste 211 .... Saint Petersburg FL 33702 Web: www.kbenv.com	727-578-5152		192
KB Home 10990 Wilshire Blvd 7th Fl .... Los Angeles CA 90024 NYSE: KBH ■ TF: 800-304-0657 ■ Web: www.kbhome.com	310-231-4000	231-4222	653
KB International LLC 735 Broad St Ste 209 .... Chattanooga TN 37402 Web: www.kbtech.com	423-266-6964		146
KB Partners LLC 600 Central Ave Ste 390........ Highland Park IL 60035 Web: www.kbpartners.com	847-681-1270	681-1370	792
KBA Engineering LLC 2157 Mohawk St........ Bakersfield CA 93308 Web: www.kbaeng.com	661-323-0487	328-0372	483
KBA Inc 11201 SE 8th St Ste 160........ Bellevue WA 98004 Web: www.kbacm.com	425-455-9720		261
KBA2 Inc 400 Treat Ave Ste E........ San Francisco CA 94110 Web: www.crowdoptic.com	415-528-5500		387
KBAC-FM 98.1 (AAA) 2502 Camino Entrada Ste C .... Santa Fe NM 87507 Web: santafe.com	505-988-5222		645-144
KBAI-AM 2219 Yew Street Rd .... Bellingham WA 98226 Web: www.sagacom.com	360-734-9790	733-4551	647
KBAK-TV 1901 Westwind Dr........ Bakersfield CA 93301 Web: www.bakersfieldnow.com	661-327-7955		647
KBAQ-FM 89.5 (Clas) 2323 W 14th St........ Tempe AZ 85281 Web: kbaq.org	480-833-1122	774-8475	645
KBBO-FM 92.1 (AC) 833 Gambell St........ Anchorage AK 99501 Web: www.921bob.com	907-344-4045	522-6053	645-7
KBBR-AM 320 Central Ave Ste 519........ Coos Bay OR 97420 Web: www.1340kbbr.com	541-267-2121		647
KBBY-FM 95.1 (AC) 1376 Walter St .... Ventura CA 93003 Web: www.951kbby.com	805-642-8595		645
KBC (KBC International Inc) 140 Venture Ct Ste 1........ Lexington KY 40511 *Fax Area Code: 859 ■ TF: 800-928-7777 ■ Web: www.kbchorsesupplies.com	800-928-7777	253-9669*	274
KBC International Inc (KBC) 140 Venture Ct Ste 1........ Lexington KY 40511 *Fax Area Code: 859 ■ TF: 800-928-7777 ■ Web: www.kbchorsesupplies.com	800-928-7777	253-9669*	274
KBC Tools & Machinery Inc 6300 18 Mile Rd........ Sterling Heights MI 48314 TF: 800-521-1740 ■ Web: www.kbctools.com	586-979-0500	979-4292	358
KBCB-TV 4164 Meridian St Ste 102 .... Bellingham WA 98226 TF: 877-335-3310 ■ Web: www.kbcbtv.com	360-647-8842		647
KBCO-FM 97.3 (AAA) 4695 S Monaco St........ Denver CO 80237 Web: kbco.iheart.com	303-444-5600		645
KBCS-FM 3000 Landerholm Cir SE........ Bellevue WA 98007 Web: www.kbcs.fm	425-564-2427		647
KBCW-TV 855 Battery St........ San Francisco CA 94111 Web: www.cwsanfrancisco.cbslocal.com	415-765-8144		647
KBCY-FM 99.7 (Ctry) 2525 S Danville Dr........ Abilene TX 79605 Web: www.kbcy.com	325-793-9700	692-1576	645-1
KBEAR 104.1 301 Arctic Slope Ave Ste 200........ Anchorage AK 99518 Web: www.listentothebear.com	907-275-2221		645-7
KBFB-FM 97.9 (Urban) 13760 Noel Rd Ste 1100........ Dallas TX 75240 TF: 844-787-1979 ■ Web: thebeatdfw.com	972-331-5400	331-5560	645-43
KBFD-TV 1188 Bishop St PH 1........ Honolulu HI 96813 Web: www.kbfd.com	808-521-8066	521-5233	647
KBH Corp, The 395 Anderson Blvd .... Clarksdale MS 38614 TF: 800-843-5241 ■ Web: www.kbhequipment.com	662-624-5471		273
KBIA-FM 91.3 (NPR) 78 McReynolds Hall........ Columbia MO 65211 TF: 800-292-9136 ■ Web: kbia.org	573-882-3431	882-2636	645
KBIM-FM PO Box 1953........ Roswell NM 88202 Web: www.kbimradio.com	575-623-9100		647
KBIQ-FM 102.7 (Rel) 7150 Campus Dr Ste 150........ Colorado Springs CO 80920 Web: kbiqradio.com	719-531-5438	531-5588	645-37
KBIZ-AM 416 E Main St .... Ottumwa IA 52501 Web: www.ottumwaradio.com	641-684-5563		647
KBJR-TV 246 S Lake Ave .... Duluth MN 55802 Web: kbjr6.com	218-720-9600		647
KBKB-FM 610 N Fourth St Ste 310........ Burlington IA 52601 TF: 855-372-5252 ■ Web: www.1017thebull.com	319-752-2701		647
KBL Merger Corporation IV 150 W 56th St Ste 5901 .... New York NY 10019 Web: kblmerger.com	212-319-5555		792
KBLI-AM 400 W Sunnyside Rd .... Idaho Falls ID 83402 Web: www.eastidahonews.com	208-523-3722		647
KBLJ-AM 116 Dalton PO Box 485........ La Junta CO 81050 Web: www.myhometeamsports.com	719-384-5450		647
KBLN-TV PO Box 766 .... Grants Pass OR 97528 TF: 877-741-2588 ■ Web: www.betterlifetv.tv	541-474-3089	474-9409	647
KBLP-FM 204 S Main St........ Lindsay OK 73052 Web: www.kblpsports.com	405-756-4438	756-2040	647
KBM Workspace 160 W Santa Clara St Ste 102........ San Jose CA 95113 Web: www.kbm-hogue.com	408-351-7100	938-0699	320
KBMQ-FM PO Box 3265........ Monroe LA 71210 Web: www.887thecross.com	318-387-1230		647
KBMW-AM 605 Dakota Ave PO Box 1115........ Wahpeton ND 58074 Web: www.kbmwam.com	701-642-8747	642-9501	647
KBMY-TV Ch 17 (ABC) 301 Eighth St S .... Fargo ND 58103 Web: www.wday.com	701-237-6500	241-5358	741-16
KBND-AM 63088 NE 18th St........ Bend OR 97701 Web: www.kbnd.com	541-382-5263	388-0456	647
KBNP-AM 1410 (N/T) 278 SW Arthur St........ Portland OR 97201 TF: 888-214-9237 ■ Web: www.kbnp.com	503-223-6769	223-4305	645-126
KBNW-FM 854 NE 4th St .... Bend OR 97701 Web: www.newsradiocentraloregon.com	541-323-1340		647
K-Bob's 135 W Palace Ave Ste 300........ Santa Fe NM 87501 Web: www.k-bobs.com	505-216-2838		670

Name / Address	City	State	Zip	Phone	Fax	Class
KBOE-AM PO Box 380 *Web:* www.kboeradio.com	Oskaloosa	IA	52577	641-673-3493	673-3495	647
KBOI-TV 140 N 16th St *Web:* idahonews.com	Boise	ID	83702	208-472-2222		647
KBOO-FM 90.7 (Var) 20 SE Eighth Ave *Web:* kboo.fm	Portland	OR	97214	503-231-8032	231-7145	645-126
KBR (Kaufman Borgeest & Ryan LLP) 120 Broadway 14th Fl *Web:* www.kbrlaw.com	New York	NY	10271	212-980-9600	980-9291	428
KBR Inc 601 Jefferson St *Web:* kbr.com	Houston	TX	77002	713-753-2000		261
KBR Rural Public Power District 374 N Pine St PO Box 187 *TF:* 800-672-0009 ■ *Web:* kbrpower.com	Ainsworth	NE	69210	402-387-1120	387-1033	245
KBRF-AM 728 Western Ave N PO Box 495 *Web:* www.kbrfradio.com	Fergus Falls	MN	56537	218-736-7596		647
KBRH-AM 2825 Government St *Web:* www.baton-rouge.com	Baton Rouge	LA	70806	225-383-0520		647
KBRK-AM 227 22nd Ave S *Web:* www.brookingsradio.com	Brookings	SD	57006	605-692-1430	692-6434	647
KBS (KBS Constructors Inc) 1701 SW 41st St *Web:* kbsci.com	Topeka	KS	66609	785-266-4222	266-3313	189
KBS Constructors Inc (KBS) 1701 SW 41st St *Web:* kbsci.com	Topeka	KS	66609	785-266-4222	266-3313	189
KBSI-TV 806 Enterprise St *Web:* www.kbsi23.com	Cape Girardeau	MO	63703	573-334-1223	334-1208	647
KBSX-FM 91.5 (NPR) 1910 University Dr *Web:* boisestatepublicradio.org	Boise	ID	83725	208-426-3663	344-6631	645-21
KBT Inc 3885 W Michigan St *Web:* www.quicktransportsolutions.com	Sidney	OH	45365	937-498-1151	498-5877	685
KBTC-TV Ch 28 (PBS) 2320 S 19th St *TF:* 888-596-5282 ■ *Web:* www.kbtc.org	Tacoma	WA	98405	253-680-7700	680-7725	741-123
KBTS Technologies Inc 41461 W 11 Mile Rd *Web:* kbtctooh.com	Novi	MI	48375	248-374-1230		196
KBUE-FM 105.5 (Span) 1845 Empire Ave *Web:* radiostationusa.fm	Burbank	CA	91504	323-520-1055		645
KBUF-AM PO Box 907 *Web:* radiostationnet.com	Valley City	ND	58072	620-276-2366	276-3568	647
KBUL-FM 595 E Plumb Ln *Web:* www.kbul.com	Reno	NV	89502	775-789-6700	789-6767	645-131
KBWA (Kansas Beer Wholesalers Assn) 100 SE 9th St Ste 100 *Web:* www.ksbeer.com	Topeka	KS	66612	785-408-8087		637-10
KBXL-FM 94.1 (Rel) 1440 S Weideman Ave *TF:* 877-207-2276 ■ *Web:* www.941thevoice.com	Boise	ID	83709	208-377-3790	377-3792	645-21
KBXX-FM 97.9 (Urban) 24 Greenway Plz Ste 900 *Web:* theboxhouston.com	Houston	TX	77046	713-623-2108	300-5763	645-72
KBXZ-AM 1016 W University Ave Ste 205 *Web:* www.reachoutthewindow.com	Flagstaff	AZ	86001	928-774-5250	774-5247	647
KBYZ-FM 4303 Memorial Hwy *TF:* 888-663-9650 ■ *Web:* www.965thefox.com	Mandan	ND	58554	701-663-9600	663-8790	647
KBZQ-FM 2331 Southwest Lee Blvd *Web:* www.breeze995.com	Lawton	OK	73505	580-357-9950		647
KBZY-AM 1490 (AC) 2659 Commercial St SE Ste 204 *Web:* kbzy.com	Salem	OR	97302	503-362-1490	362-6545	645-126
KC Electric Assn 422 Third Ave *TF:* 800-700-3123 ■ *Web:* www.kcelectric.coop	Hugo	CO	80821	719-743-2431	743-2396	245
KC Engineering & Land Surveying PC 7 Penn Plz Ste 1604 *Web:* kcepc.com	New York	NY	10001	212-947-4945		261
KC Hilites Inc 2843 W Avenida De Luces *Web:* www.kchilites.com	Williams	AZ	86046	928-635-2607	635-2486	438
KC Jones Plating Co 2845 E Ten Mile Rd *Web:* www.kcjplating.com	Warren	MI	48091	586-755-4900		481
KC Pharmaceuticals Inc 3201 Producer Way *Web:* kc-ph.com	Pomona	CA	91768	909-598-9499	595-9332	231
KC Robotics Inc 9000 Le St Dr *Web:* www.kcrobotics.com	West Chester	OH	45014	513-860-4442		358
KC Sign Express Inc 5033 Mackey St *Web:* kcsignexpress.com	Shawnee	KS	66203	913-432-2500	432-2882	8
KCA (Kelley Chunn & Associates) PO Box 190871 *Web:* www.kelleychunn.com	Boston	MA	02119	617-427-0046		317
KCAA-AM 254 Carousel Mall *TF:* 888-909-1050 ■ *Web:* www.kcaaradio.com	San Bernardino	CA	92401	909-885-8497		647
KCAL-FM 96.7 (Rock) 1940 Orange Tree Ln Ste 200 *Web:* www.kcalfm.com	Redlands	CA	92374	909-793-3554		645-130
KCB Real Estate Manamegment LLC 117 E Colorado Blvd Ste 400 *Web:* kcbrem.com	Pasadena	CA	91105	626-356-0944	356-0996	194
KCBD-TV Ch 11 (NBC) 5600 Ave A *Web:* www.kcbd.com	Lubbock	TX	79404	806-744-1414	749-1111	741-78
KCBI-FM 90.9 (Rel) 750 NSt Paul St Ste 1050 *Web:* www.kcbi.org	Dallas	TX	75201	469-801-7000		645
KCBS-AM 740 (N/T) 865 Battery St *Web:* sanfrancisco.cbslocal.com	San Francisco	CA	94111	415-765-8758	765-8935	645-142
KCC (Kaufman Campaign Consultants) 1510 J St Ste 210 *Web:* www.kaufmancampaigns.com	Sacramento	CA	95814	916-443-7817		192
KCC (Killion Communications Consultants Inc) 302 Palm St *TF:* 800-301-6672 ■ *Web:* www.kilco.com	Roodhouse	IL	62082	217-589-4713	589-4920	194
KCC Manufacturing 2716 Grassland Dr *Web:* www.kcccurbs.com	Louisville	KY	40299	502-491-9881	491-1739	697
KCC Transport Systems Inc 311 W Artesia Blvd *Web:* www.kccusa.com	Compton	CA	90220	310-764-5933		311
KCCI-TV Ch 8 (CBS) 888 Ninth St *Web:* www.kcci.com	Des Moines	IA	50309	515-247-8888		741-40
KCCR-AM 1240 106 W Capitol Ave *Web:* www.todayskccr.com	Pierre	SD	57501	605-224-1240	945-4270	645-122
KCD Financial Inc 3061 Allied St Ste B *Web:* www.kcdfinancial.com	Green Bay	WI	54304	920-347-3400	347-3402	401
KCEP-FM 88.1 330 W Washington Ave Ste 125 *Web:* power88lv.com	Las Vegas	NV	89106	702-648-0104		645-85
KCES (Kansas City Electrical Supply Co) 14851 W 99th St *Web:* kcelectricalsupply.com	Lenexa	KS	66215	913-563-7000	563-7055	246
KCET-TV Ch 28 (PBS) 2900 W Alameda Ave *TF:* 866-523-8200 ■ *Web:* www.kcet.org	Burbank	CA	91505	747-201-5238		741-76
KCF Technologies Inc 336 S Fraser St *Web:* www.kcftech.com	State College	PA	16801	814-867-4097		497
KCFJ-AM 1773 W San Bernardino Rd Bldg C31 *Web:* www.edimediainc.com	West Covina	CA	91790	626-856-3889	856-3895	647
KCFR-FM 90.1 (NPR) 7409 S Alton Ct *TF:* 800-722-4449 ■ *Web:* www.cpr.org	Centennial	CO	80112	303-871-9191	733-3319	645
KCG (Kowalenko Consulting Group Inc) 474 Central Ave Ste 205 **Fax Area Code:* 844 ■ *Web:* www.kowalenkogroup.com	Highland Park	IL	60035	847-433-8747	270-5522*	194
KCG Inc 15720 W 108th St Ste 100 *TF:* 855-858-3344 ■ *Web:* www.rewmaterials.com	Lenexa	KS	66219	855-858-3344		347
KCHA-FM 207 N Main St *Web:* www.kchanews.com	Charles City	IA	50616	641-228-1000	228-1200	647
KCHE-AM PO Box 141 *Web:* www.kcheradio.com	Cherokee	IA	51012	712-225-2511		647
KCHS-AM 217 E Third St **Fax Area Code:* 575 ■ *Web:* www.gpkmedia.com	Truth or Consequences	NM	87901	505-894-3088	894-3008*	647
KCI Aviation 2100 Aviation Way *Web:* www.kciaviation.com	Bridgeport	WV	26330	304-842-3591	842-4308	317
KCI Construction Co 10315 Lake Bluff Dr *Web:* www.kciconstruction.com	Saint Louis	MO	63123	314-894-8888		186
KCI Industries Inc 1111 Hill St *Web:* www.automagzonevalve.net	Jessup	PA	18434	570-383-2428		202
KCI Medical Canada Inc 75 Courtneypark Dr W Unit 403 *TF:* 800-668-5403 ■ *Web:* kci.acelity.ca	Mississauga	ON	L5W0E3	800-668-5403		475
KCI Sports Publishing LLC 3340 Whiting Ave Ste 5 **Fax Area Code:* 715 ■ *Web:* www.kcisports.com	Stevens Point	WI	54481	217-766-3390	344-2668*	637-2
KCI Technologies Inc 936 Ridgebrook Rd *TF:* 800-572-7496 ■ *Web:* www.kci.com	Sparks	MD	21152	410-316-7800		261
KCII-FM PO Box 524 *Web:* www.kciiradio.com	Washington	IA	52353	319-653-2113	653-3500	647
KCJA (Kansas City Jazz Ambassadors) PO Box 36181 *Web:* www.kcjazzambassadors.org	Kansas City	MO	64171	816-888-4503		48-4
KCJB-AM 1000 20th Ave SW *TF:* 800-472-2908 ■ *Web:* www.kcjb910.iheart.com	Minot	ND	58701	701-852-4646	852-1390	647
KCK Chamber 727 Minnesota Ave *Web:* www.kckchamber.com	Kansas City	KS	66101	913-371-3070	371-3732	139
KCKC-FM 102.1 (AC) 508 Westport Rd Ste 202 *Web:* www.kc1021.com	Kansas City	MO	64111	816-753-4000		645-80
KCL (Krause Consultants Ltd) 5225 N Ironwood Rd Ste 109 *Web:* www.ckrause.com	Glendale	WI	53217	414-963-8688	963-8699	194
KCLB-FM 93.7 (Rock) 1321 N Gene Autry Trl *TF:* 800-827-2946 ■ *Web:* www.937kclb.com	Palm Springs	CA	92262	760-322-7890		645-117
KCLR 3215 Lemone Industrial Blvd *TF:* 800-455-5257 ■ *Web:* clear99.com	Columbia	MO	65201	573-449-5257		645
KCLU 60 W Olsen Rd Ste 4400 *Web:* www.kclu.org	Thousand Oaks	CA	91360	805-493-3900		645
KCLY-FM 1815 Meadowlark Rd *Web:* www.kclyradio.com	Clay Center	KS	67432	785-632-5662	632-5661	647
KCM Investment Advisors LLC 750 Lindaro St Ste 350 *TF:* 888-287-5555 ■ *Web:* www.kcmadvisors.com	San Rafael	CA	94901	415-461-7788		401
KCMQ 3215 Lemone Industrial Blvd Ste 200 *TF:* 800-455-1967 ■ *Web:* www.kcmq.com	Columbia	MO	65201	573-875-1967		645
KCMS-FM 105.3 (Rel) 19319 Fremont Ave N *TF:* 877-275-1053 ■ *Web:* www.spirit1053.com	Shoreline	WA	98133	206-546-7350	546-7372	645-147
KCMT-FM 3301 BARHAM Blvd Ste 200 PO Box 2098 *Web:* www.kcmt.com	Los Angeles	CA	90068	323-461-8225		647
KCNI-AM PO Box 409 *Web:* www.kbbn.com	Broken Bow	NE	68822	308-872-2801		647
KCOS 13 9050 Viscount Blvd Ste A440 *TF:* 800-683-1899 ■ *Web:* kcostv.org	El Paso	TX	79925	915-590-1313	303-9800	741-43
KCP Wholesale Distributors 1070 Rte 34 S Ste 200 **Fax Area Code:* 732 ■ *Web:* www.kcpwholesale.com	Matawan	NJ	07747	908-601-2014	583-1422*	238
KCPL (Kansas City Public Library, The) 14 W Tenth St *Web:* www.kclibrary.org	Kansas City	MO	64105	816-701-3400	701-3401	434-3
KCPQ-TV Ch 13 (Fox) 1813 Westlake Ave N *Web:* q13fox.com	Seattle	WA	98109	206-674-1305		741-123
KCPS-AM 205 S Gear Ave PO Box 100 *Web:* www.kcpsradio.com	West Burlington	IA	52655	319-753-5277		647
KCPT-TV Ch 19 (PBS) 125 E 31st St *TF:* 800-343-4727 ■ *Web:* www.kcpt.org	Kansas City	MO	64108	816-756-3580		741-68
KCQL-AM 200 E Broadway *TF:* 866-345-8255 ■ *Web:* www.sports1340.iheart.com	Farmington	NM	87401	505-325-1716		647

Name / Address	City	State	ZIP	Phone	Fax	Class
KCRA-TV Ch 3 (NBC) 3 Television Cir *Web:* www.kcra.com	Sacramento	CA	95814	916-446-3333		741-113
KCRG-TV Ch 9 (ABC) 501 Second Ave SE *TF:* 800-332-5443 ■ *Web:* www.kcrg.com	Cedar Rapids	IA	52401	319-399-5999		741-23
KCRW-FM 89.9 (NPR) 1900 Pico Blvd *TF:* 888-600-5279 ■ *Web:* www.kcrw.com	Santa Monica	CA	90405	310-450-5183	450-7172	645
KCRX-AM 200 W 1st St *Web:* www.kcrx.tripod.com	Roswell	NM	88203	505-622-1432		647
KCSA Strategic Communications 420 5th Ave 3rd Fl *Web:* www.kcsa.com	New York	NY	10018	212-682-6300		636
KCSARC (King County Sexual Assault Resource Ctr) 200 Mill Ave S Ste 10 *TF:* 888-998-6423 ■ *Web:* www.kcsarc.org	Renton	WA	98057	425-226-5062	235-7422	637-2
KCSL (Kansas Children's Service League) 3545 SW Fifth St *TF:* 877-530-5275 ■ *Web:* www.kcsl.org	Topeka	KS	66606	785-274-3100		48-6
KCSM-FM 91.1 (Jazz) 1700 W Hillsdale Blvd *Web:* www.kcsm.org	San Mateo	CA	94402	650-574-6586		645
KCSP-AM 610 (Sports) 7000 Squibb Rd *TF:* 800-234-6860 ■ *Web:* 610sports.radio.com	Mission	KS	66202	913-744-3650		645
KCSR-AM 226 Bordeaux St *TF:* 800-266-4682 ■ *Web:* www.chadrad.com	Chadron	NE	69337	308-432-5545	432-5601	647
KCTC (Kalona Cooperative Telephone Co) 510 B Ave *TF:* 800-656-8510 ■ *Web:* www.kctc.net	Kalona	IA	52247	319-656-3668	656-4484	681
KCTN-FM PO Box 990 *TF:* 888-245-5286 ■ *Web:* www.kctn.com	Elkader	IA	52043	563-245-1400	245-1402	647
KCTR-FM 102.9 (Ctry) 27 N 27th St Crowne Plz 23rd Fl *Web:* catcountry1029.com	Billings	MT	59101	406-248-7827		645-18
KCTS-TV Ch 9 (PBS) 401 Mercer St *Web:* kcts9.org	Seattle	WA	98109	206-728-6463		741-123
KCUR-FM 89.3 (NPR) 4825 Troost Ave Ste 202 *TF:* 855-778-5437 ■ *Web:* www.kcur.org	Kansas City	MO	64110	816-235-1551		645-80
KCUV-AM 3091 S Jamaica Ct Ste 230 *Web:* www.onda1150am.com	Aurora	CO	80011	303-337-1150	696-5962	647
KCVB (Kingsport Convention & Visitors Bureau) 400 Clinchfield St Ste 100 *TF:* 800-743-5282 ■ *Web:* visitkingsport.com	Kingsport	TN	37660	423-392-8820	392-8833	206
KCVL-AM PO Box 111 *Web:* www.kcvl.com	Colville	WA	99114	509-684-5032	684-5034	647
KCWE-TV Ch 29 (CW) 6455 Winchester Ave *Web:* www.kmbc.com	Kansas City	MO	64133	816-221-9999		741-68
KCWY-TV 141 Progress Cir PO Box 1540 *Web:* www.wyomingnewsnow.tv	Mills	WY	82644	307-577-0013	577-5251	741
KCYT-FM 2704 American Streen *Web:* www.967thecoyote.com	Springdale	AR	72764	479-303-2034	303-2037	647
KD Scientific Inc 84 October Hill Rd *Web:* www.kdscientific.com	Holliston	MA	01746	508-429-6809		475
KDAE-AM PO Box 260715 *Web:* www.radiolibertad.net	Corpus Christi	TX	78426	361-299-1960		647
KDAQ-FM 89.9 (NPR) 8675 Youree Dr *TF:* 800-552-8502 ■ *Web:* www.redriverradio.org	Shreveport	LA	71115	318-798-0102	798-0107	645-148
KDAR-FM 98.3 (Rel) 500 E Esplanade Dr *Web:* 983fmtheword.com	Oxnard	CA	93036	805-485-8881	656-5330	645-116
KDB-TV 4501 Montgomery Blvd NE *Web:* www.kazq32.org	Albuquerque	NM	87109	505-884-8355	266-3836	647
KDC One Northern Labs 5800 W Dr PO Box 850 *Web:* www.kdc-one.com	Manitowoc	WI	54220	920-684-7137	684-4957	151
KDC Technologies 27201 Tourney Rd Ste 201 **Fax Area Code:* 661 ■ *TF:* 877-532-1112 ■ *Web:* www.kdctechnologies.com	Valencia	CA	91355	877-532-1112	977-4178*	196
KDDB-FM 102.7 (CHR) 1000 Bishop St Ste 200 *Web:* 1027dabomb.net	Honolulu	HI	96813	808-947-1500		645-70
KDDG-FM 35223 238th Ave *Web:* www.mybobcountry.com	Albany	MN	56307	763-450-7777		647
KDDI America Inc 825 Third Ave 3rd Fl *TF:* 866-348-3370 ■ *Web:* us.kddi.com	New York	NY	10022	212-295-1200	295-1080	736
KDEC-FM 110 Highland Dr *Web:* www.kdecradio.com	Decorah	IA	52101	563-382-4251		647
KDEP-FM 170 Third St W *Web:* www.tillamookradio.com	Tillamook	OR	97141	503-842-4422		647
KDF Electronic & Vacuum Services Inc 10 Volvo Dr *Web:* www.kdf.com	Rockleigh	NJ	07647	201-784-5005		695
KDF U.S. Inc 2301 W 205th St Ste 107 *Web:* www.kdfus.com	Torrance	CA	90501	310-320-6633	320-6116	228
KDFW FOX 4 400 N Griffin St *TF:* 800-677-5339 ■ *Web:* www.fox4news.com	Dallas	TX	75202	214-720-4444	720-3263	741-37
KDGI (Kuhlmann Design Group) 2043 Woodland Pkwy *Web:* kdginc.com	Saint Louis	MO	63146	314-434-8898		261
KDHL-AM 601 Central Ave *Web:* www.kdhlradio.com	Faribault	MN	55021	507-334-0061		647
KDI Capital Partners LLC 4101 Lake Boone Trl Ste 218 *Web:* kdicapitalpartners.com	Raleigh	NC	27607	919-573-4124		401
KDJL-FM PO Box 390 *Web:* www.ksdzfm.com	Gordon	NE	69343	308-282-2500	282-0061	647
KDJS-AM 730 NE Hwy 71 Service Dr *Web:* www.k-musicradio.com	Willmar	MN	56201	320-231-1600	235-7010	647
KDK Publications 1892 Fell St *Web:* www.kdk.org	San Francisco	CA	94117	415-752-5454		95
KDKA-AM Foster Plz 5 651 Holiday Dr *Web:* www.pittsburgh.cbslocal.com	Pittsburgh	PA	15220	412-920-9400		647
KDKB-FM 1167 W Javelina Ave *Web:* www.altaz933.com	Mesa	AZ	85210	480-897-9300		647
KDLH-TV 246 S Lake Ave *Web:* www.northlandsnewscenter.com	Duluth	MN	55802	218-529-7780		647
KDLT Television 325 S 1st Ave Ste 100 *TF:* 800-727-5358 ■ *Web:* www.dakotanewsnow.com	Sioux Falls	SD	57104	605-336-1300	361-3982	741-125
KDM Engineering LLC 35 E Wacker Dr Ste 800 *Web:* www.kdmengineering.com	Chicago	IL	60601	312-763-2198		261
KDM Signs Inc 10450 N Medallion Dr *TF:* 855-232-7799 ■ *Web:* www.kdmpop.com	Cincinnati	OH	45241	855-232-7799		627
KDMD-TV 1310 E 66th Ave *Web:* www.kdmd.tv	Anchorage	AK	99518	907-562-5363		647
KDNL-TV Ch 30 (ABC) 1215 Cole St *Web:* abcstlouis.com	Saint Louis	MO	63106	314-436-3030	361-7043	741-114
KDOC-TV 625 N Grand Ave *Web:* www.kdoc.tv	Santa Ana	CA	92701	949-442-9800	261-5956	647
KDOT-FM 104.5 (Rock) 690 E Plumb Ln *Web:* www.kdot.com	Reno	NV	89502	775-329-9261	323-1450	645-131
KDR (National Fraternity of Kappa Delta Rho) 331 S Main St *TF:* 800-536-5371 ■ *Web:* www.kdr.com	Greensburg	PA	15601	724-838-7100	838-7101	48-16
KDR Supply Inc PO Box 10130 *Web:* www.kdrsupply.com	Liberty	TX	77575	936-336-6267	336-1034	358
KDRO-AM 301 E Ohio St *Web:* www.kdro.com	Sedalia	MO	65301	660-826-5005		647
KDRV-TV 1090 Knutson Ave *Web:* www.kdrv.com	Medford	OR	97504	541-773-1212	779-9261	647
KDRY-AM 16414 San Pedro Ave Ste 575 *Web:* www.kdry.com	San Antonio	TX	78232	210-545-1100		647
KDSJ-AM 745 Main St *Web:* www.kdsj980.com	Deadwood	SD	57732	605-578-1826	578-1827	647
KDSM-TV Ch 17 (Fox) 4023 Fleur Dr *Web:* www.kdsm17.com	Des Moines	IA	50321	515-287-1717		741-40
KDSN-FM 1530 Ridge Rd PO Box 670 *Web:* www.kdsnradio.com	Denison	IA	51442	712-263-3141	263-2088	647
KDT Solutions Inc 1256 5th St N *Web:* www.kdtsolutions.com	West Palm Beach	FL	33409	561-688-9399	688-9609	175
KDTH-AM PO Box 659 *TF:* 800-422-5384 ■ *Web:* www.kdth.radiodubuque.com	Dubuque	IA	52004	563-690-0800		647
KDUK-FM 104.7 (CHR) 1500 Valley River Dr Ste 350 *TF:* 888-634-5385 ■ *Web:* www.kduk.com	Eugene	OR	97401	541-284-3600		645-94
KDUX-FM 1308 Coolidge Rd *Web:* www.kdux.com	Aberdeen	WA	98520	360-532-1047	532-0935	647
KDWN-AM 720 (N/T) 2920 S Durango Dr *Web:* kdwn.com	Las Vegas	NV	89117	702-730-0300	736-8447	645-85
KDXN-FM 26 W Villard St *Web:* www.themix1057.com	Dickinson	ND	58601	701-225-1057		647
KDYN-AM 9331 Puddin Ridge Rd PO Box 1086 **Fax Area Code:* 479 ■ *TF:* 888-325-5396 ■ *Web:* www.kdyn.com	Ozark	AR	72949	501-667-4567	667-5214*	647
KDZR-AM 6400 SE Lake Rd Ste 350 *Web:* thepatriotportland.com	Portland	OR	97222	503-652-8174		647
KDZY-FM 707 N Mission St PO Box 2114 *Web:* www.kdzy.tripod.com	McCall	ID	83638	208-634-3781	634-3799	647
KEA News 401 Capital Ave *TF:* 800-231-4532 ■ *Web:* www.kea.org	Frankfort	KY	40601	502-875-2889	227-8062	457-8
Keadle Lumber Enterprises Inc 889 Railroad St *Web:* www.keadlelumber.com	Thomaston	GA	30286	706-647-8982		683
KEAG-FM 97.3 301 Arctic Slope Ave Ste 200 *Web:* www.kool973.com	Anchorage	AK	99518	907-344-9622		645-7
Kealy Trucking Co 3184 E 79th St *TF:* 800-521-4750 ■ *Web:* www.kealytrucking.com	Cleveland	OH	44104	800-521-4750		780
Kean University 1000 Morris Ave Kean Hall *TF:* 800-882-1037 ■ *Web:* www.kean.edu	Union	NJ	07083	908-737-7100	737-7105	166
Keane Circuits Inc 341 Avondale Ave *Web:* www.keanecircuits.com	Haddonfield	NJ	08033	856-795-1181	795-9691	256
Keane Thummel Trucking Inc 419 Main St *Web:* www.keanethummel.com	New Market	IA	51646	712-585-3266	585-3766	780
KEAN-FM 105.1 (Ctry) 3911 S First St *TF:* 800-588-5326 ■ *Web:* keanradio.com	Abilene	TX	79605	325-676-5326		645-1
Kearfott Guidance & Navigation Corp 1150 McBride Ave *Web:* www.kearfott.com	Woodland Park	NJ	07424	973-785-6000	785-6025	529
Kearney Area Chamber of Commerce 1007 Second Ave PO Box 607 *TF:* 800-227-8340 ■ *Web:* www.kearneycoc.org	Kearney	NE	68848	308-237-3101	237-3103	139
Kearney County 424 N Colorado Ave *Web:* kearneycounty.ne.gov	Minden	NE	68959	308-832-2723		338
Kearney Electric Inc 3609 E Superior Ave *Web:* www.kearneyaz.com	Phoenix	AZ	85040	602-437-0235	437-2914	189-4
Kearney Hub 13 E 22nd PO Box 1988 *TF:* 800-950-6113 ■ *Web:* www.kearneyhub.com	Kearney	NE	68847	308-237-2152		530
Kearney Mansion Museum 7160 W Kearney Blvd *Web:* www.valleyhistory.org	Fresno	CA	93706	559-441-0862	441-1372	520
Kearney Public Library & Information Ctr 2020 First Ave *Web:* www.cityofkearney.org	Kearney	NE	68847	308-233-3282	233-3291	434-3
Kearns Duffy & Vaccaro PC 3648 Valley Rd *Web:* kdvlawyers.com	Liberty Corner	NJ	07938	908-647-7773		41
Kearny County PO Box 86 *Web:* www.kearnycountykansas.com	Lakin	KS	67860	620-355-6422	355-7382	338
Kearny FSB 120 Passaic Ave *TF:* 800-273-3406 ■ *Web:* www.kearnybank.com	Fairfield	NJ	07004	800-273-3406		70
Kearny Public Library 318 Kearny Ave *Web:* kearnylibrary.org	Kearny	NJ	07032	201-998-2666		434-3
Kearny Steel Container Corp 401 S St *Web:* www.kearnysteel.com	Newark	NJ	07105	973-589-2070		100

Name / Address	City	State	ZIP	Phone	Fax	Class
Keating 285 W Broadway Rm 460 — *Web:* www.keatingco.com	New York	NY	10013	212-925-6900		636
Keating Building Corp 1600 Arch St Ste 300 — *Web:* www.tutorperinibuilding.com	Philadelphia	PA	19103	610-668-4100		186
Keating Daniel J Co 134 N Narberth Ave — *Web:* www.djkeating.com	Narberth	PA	19072	610-664-4550		186
Keating Hotel, The 432 F St — *Web:* www.thekeating.com	San Diego	CA	92101	619-814-5700		378
Keating Muething & Klekamp Pll 1 E Fourth St Ste 1400 — *Web:* www.kmklaw.com	Cincinnati	OH	45202	513-579-6400	579-6457	428
Keating Technologies Inc 25 Royal Crest Ct Ste 120 — *TF:* 877-532-8464 ■ *Web:* www.keating.com	Markham	ON	L3R9X4	905-479-0230		463
Keating William (Rep D - MA) 2351 Rayburn House Office Bldg — *Web:* keating.house.gov	Washington	DC	20515	202-225-3111	225-5658	342-2
Keating, Bucklin & Mccormack Incorporated PS 801 Second Ave Ste 1210 — *Web:* kbmlawyers.com	Seattle	WA	98104	206-623-8861		41
Keats Manufacturing Co 350 Holbrook Dr — *Web:* www.keatsmfg.com	Wheeling	IL	60090	847-520-1133	520-0114	73
Keats, Connelly & Associates LLC 3336 N 32nd St Ste 100 — *TF:* 800-678-5007 ■ *Web:* www.keatsconnelly.com	Phoenix	AZ	85018	602-955-5007		401
Kebs Inc 2116 Haslett Rd — *Web:* www.kebs.com	Haslett	MI	48840	517-339-1014	339-8047	261
KEC (Kay Electric Co-op) 300 W Doolin Ave — *TF:* 800-535-1079 ■ *Web:* www.kayelectric.coop	Blackwell	OK	74631	580-363-1260	363-2308	245
KEC (Kiamichi Electric Co-opeartive Inc) 944 SW Hwy 2 PO Box 340 — *TF:* 800-888-2731 ■ *Web:* kiamichielectric.org	Wilburton	OK	74578	918-465-2338		245
KEC (Kilpatrick Equipment Co) 2612 Manor Way — *TF:* 800-929-2822 ■ *Web:* www.kec-dfw.com	Dallas	TX	75235	214-358-4346	358-3723	112
KEC Engineering 200 N Sherman Ave — *Web:* kecengineering.com	Corona	CA	92882	951-734-3010		261
KECH-FM 141 Citation Way Ste 8 — *Web:* kech95fm.com	Hailey	ID	83333	208-726-7118	726-7119	647
Kecia Parrish Dvm Llc T/A Hickory Ridge 10328 Owen Brown Rd — *Web:* hickoryridgeanimal.com	Columbia	MD	21044	410-730-7434		794
Keck-Craig Inc PO Box 93966 — *Web:* www.keckcraig.com	Pasadena	CA	91109	626-584-1688		695
KECO-FM 220 S Pioneer Rd — *Web:* www.kecofm.com	Elk City	OK	73644	580-225-9696		647
k-eCommerce 666 St-Martin W Blvd Ste 330 — *TF:* 855-532-6663 ■ *Web:* www.k-ecommerce.com	Laval	QC	H7M5G4	514-973-2510		387
KEDB-FM 402 N 12th St — *TF:* 800-373-4930 ■ *Web:* www.kedbradio.com	Centerville	IA	52544	800-373-4930		647
Keds Corp 1400 Industries Rd — *TF:* 800-680-0966 ■ *Web:* www.keds.com	Richmond	IN	47374	800-680-0966	446-1339	301
KEDT-TV Ch 16 (PBS) 3205 S Staples — *Web:* www.kedt.org	Corpus Christi	TX	78411	361-855-2213	855-3877	741-36
Kee Grill 17940 N Military Trl Ste 700 — *Web:* www.keegrillbocaraton.com	Boca Raton	FL	33496	561-995-5044		671
Keeco LLC 30736 Wiegman Rd — *Web:* keecohome.com	Hayward	CA	94544	510-324-8800		361
Keefe Bruyette & Woods Inc 787 Seventh Ave The Equitable Bldg 4th Fl — *TF:* 866-647-3745 ■ *Web:* www.kbw.com	New York	NY	10019	212-887-7777		690
Keefe McCullough & Company LLP CPA 6550 N Federal Hwy 4th Fl — *Web:* kmccpa.com	Fort Lauderdale	FL	33308	954-771-0896	938-9353	2
Keefe Real Estate 1155 E Geneva St — *TF:* 800-690-2292 ■ *Web:* www.keeferealestate.com	Delavan	WI	53115	262-728-8757		652
Keegan & Coppin Company Inc 1355 N Dutton Ave — *Web:* keegancoppin.com	Santa Rosa	CA	95401	707-528-1400		652
Keel Point Advisors LLC 8065 Leesburg Pk Ste 300 — *Web:* www.keelpoint.com	Vienna	VA	22182	703-807-2020		194
Keel Publications PO Box 160155 — *Web:* winningisntnormal.weebly.com	Austin	TX	78716	512-327-1280		637-2
Keeler Motor Car Co 1111 Troy Schenectady Rd — *TF:* 800-474-4197 ■ *Web:* www.keeler.com	Latham	NY	12110	518-785-4197		57
Keeley Investment Corp 401 S La Salle St Ste 1201 — *TF:* 800-533-5344 ■ *Web:* keeleyfunds.com	Chicago	IL	60605	312-786-5050	786-5002	169
Keeling Co PO Box 15310 — *TF:* 800-343-9464 ■ *Web:* keelingcompany.net	North Little Rock	AR	72231	501-945-4511		612
Keen Battle Mead & Co 7850 NW 146th St Ste 200 — *Web:* www.kbmco.com	Miami Lakes	FL	33016	305-558-1101	822-4722	391-4
Keen Compressed Gas Company Inc 4063 New Castle Ave — *Web:* www.keengas.com	New Castle	DE	19720	302-594-4545	594-4569	385
Keen Technical Solutions LLC 800 Cottage View Dr Ste 1042 PO Box 2109 — *TF:* 888-675-7772 ■ *Web:* www.keen-minds.com	Traverse City	MI	49685	888-675-7772		192
Keen Transport Inc 1951 Harrisbrug Pke — *TF:* 888-872-5336 ■ *Web:* www.keentransport.com	Carlisle	PA	17015	717-243-6622	243-8195	780
Keenan & Assoc PO Box 4328 — *TF:* 800-654-8102 ■ *Web:* www.keenan.com	Torrance	CA	90510	310-212-3344	212-0300	390
Keenan Agency Inc, The 6805 Avery Muirfield Dr Ste 200 — *Web:* www.keenanins.com	Dublin	OH	43016	614-764-7000	764-7227	390
Keene Beauty Academy 800 Park Ave — *Web:* www.keenebeautyacademy.edu	Keene	NH	03431	603-357-3736		167-3
Keene Promotions Inc 450 Lexington St Ste 102 — *Web:* www.keenepromostore.com	Newton	MA	02466	617-243-0101	243-0202	636
Keene Publishing Corp PO Box 546 — *TF:* 800-765-9994 ■ *Web:* www.sentinelsource.com	Keene	NH	03431	603-352-1234	352-0437	637-8
Keene State College 229 Main St — *TF:* 800-572-1909 ■ *Web:* www.keene.edu	Keene	NH	03435	603-358-2711	358-2767	166
Keene Valley Video Inc 1948 Nys Rt 73 — *Web:* www.kvvi.net	Keene Valley	NY	12943	518-576-4510		116
Keeneland Association Inc 4201 Versailles Rd — *TF:* 800-456-3412 ■ *Web:* www.keeneland.com	Lexington	KY	40510	859-254-3412		446
Keener Oil and Gas Co 1648 S Boston Ave Ste 200 — *Web:* www.keeneroil.com	Tulsa	OK	74119	918-587-4154	587-4981	538
Keener Printing Inc 401 E 200th St — *Web:* keenerprinting.com	Euclid	OH	44119	216-531-7595	531-5140	627
Keener Rubber Co 14700 Commerce St NE — *Web:* www.keenerrubber.com	Alliance	OH	44601	330-821-1880	821-4246	676
Keeney Manufacturing Co 1170 Main St — *TF:* 800-243-0526 ■ *Web:* www.keeneymfg.com	Newington	CT	06111	860-666-3342	665-0374	609
Keeney, Waite & Stevens 402 W Broadway Ste 1820 — *Web:* www.keenlaw.com	San Diego	CA	92101	619-238-1661		428
Keenline Conveyor Systems Inc 1936 Chase Dr — *Web:* www.keenline.com	Omro	WI	54963	920-685-0365	685-0506	207
Keep America Beautiful Inc 1010 Washington Blvd — *Web:* www.kab.org	Stamford	CT	06901	203-659-3000		48-7
Keep It Simple Computer Training Calvert Village Shopping Center 230 West Dares Beach Rd Ste 105 — *TF:* 866-727-5455 ■ *Web:* www.keepitsimple.net	Prince Frederick	MD	20678	410-535-1545	535-7543	180
Keep Me in Stitches 14833 N Dale Mabry Hwy — *Web:* kmisinc.com	Tampa	FL	33618	813-908-3889		594
Keep Truckin 55 Hawthorne St 4th Fl — *TF:* 855-434-3564 ■ *Web:* keeptruckin.com	San Francisco	CA	94105	855-434-3564		39
Keep Writing 4456 Manchester St — *TF:* 800-264-4900 ■ *Web:* www.keepwriting.com	Cedar Hills	UT	84062	801-492-7898		637-2
Keepers International Inc 9420 Eton Ave	Chatsworth	CA	91311	818-882-5000		155-10
Keer & Heyer 1001 Richmond Ave — *Web:* keerandheyer.com	Point Pleasant	NJ	08742	732-892-7700		390
Kees Inc 400 Industrial Dr — *Web:* www.kees.com	Elkhart Lake	WI	53020	920-876-3391		697
Keesal Young & Logan 400 Oceangate — *TF:* 800-877-7049 ■ *Web:* www.kyl.com	Long Beach	CA	90802	562-436-2000	436-7416	428
Keesler Federal Credit Union PO Box 7001 — *TF:* 888-533-7537 ■ *Web:* www.kfcu.org	Biloxi	MS	39534	228-385-5500	385-5535	219
Keeton's Office & Art Supply Co 817 Manatee Ave W — *TF:* 800-833-4735 ■ *Web:* www.keetonsonline.com	Bradenton	FL	34205	941-747-2995	746-5579	535
Keewaydin State Park 46165 NYS Rt 12 PO Box 247 — *Web:* parks.ny.gov	Alexandria Bay	NY	13607	315-482-3331		565
Keffeler Pharmaceutical Inc 260 Hospital Dr Ste 111 — *Web:* myersmedicalpharmacy.com	Ukiah	CA	95482	707-468-8991		237
Keg Steakhouse 10100 Shellbridge Way — *Web:* www.kegsteakhouse.com	Richmond	BC	V6X2W7	604-276-0242	276-2681	670
Kegel's Produce Inc 2851 Old Tree Dr — *TF:* 800-535-3435 ■ *Web:* www.kegels.com	Lancaster	PA	17603	717-392-6612		297-7
Kegel, Kelin, Almy & Lord LLP 24 N Lime St — *Web:* kkallaw.com	Lancaster	PA	17602	717-392-1100		41
Kegels German Inn 5901 W National Ave — *Web:* www.kegelsinn.com	Milwaukee	WI	53214	414-257-9999		671
Kegerreis Outdoor Advertising LLC 1310 Lincoln Way East — *TF:* 800-745-4166 ■ *Web:* kegerreis.com	Chambersburg	PA	17202	717-263-6700		8
Kegler, Brown, Hill & Ritter Company LPA 65 E State St Capitol Sq Ste 1800 — *Web:* www.keglerbrown.com	Columbus	OH	43215	614-462-5400		428
Kegworks 1460 Military Rd — *Web:* www.kegworks.com	Buffalo	NY	14217	716-301-5551		321
KEH Insurance Agency Inc 1415 Marlton Pike E Ste 501 — *Web:* keh4ins.com	Cherry Hill	NJ	08034	856-429-6000	429-8999	390
Kehoe Custom Wood Designs Inc 1320 N Miller St Ste D — *Web:* kehoecustomwood.com	Anaheim	CA	92806	714-993-0444		321
Kehrer Bielan Research & Consulting 510 Meadowmont Village Cir Ste 229 — *Web:* kehrerbielan.com	Chapel Hill	NC	27517	919-903-9043		463
Keicher Insurance Agency Inc 315 W Elm St — *TF:* 877-895-5178 ■ *Web:* jeffkeicher.com	Sycamore	IL	60178	815-895-1945		390
Keidel Supply Co 1150 Tennessee Ave — *Web:* keidel.com	Cincinnati	OH	45229	513-351-1600	351-9649	612
Keifer's 710 Poplar Blvd — *Web:* www.keifers.net	Jackson	MS	39202	601-355-6825		671
Keilson-Dayton Co 107 Commerce Park Dr — *TF:* 800-759-3174 ■ *Web:* keilsondayton.com	Dayton	OH	45404	937-236-1070	236-2124	756
KEIM (KEIM Mineral Systems) 102 Savannah Rd — *Web:* www.cohalancompany.com	Lewes	DE	19958	302-684-3299	684-5974	802
Keim Lumber Company Inc 4465 SR-557 PO Box 40 — *TF:* 800-362-6682 ■ *Web:* www.keimlumber.com	Charm	OH	44617	330-893-2251		752

	Phone	Fax	Class
KEIM Mineral Systems (KEIM) 102 Savannah Rd . . . . . Lewes DE 19958 *Web:* www.cohalancompany.com	302-684-3299	684-5974	802
Keim T. S. Inc 1249 N Ninth St PO Box 226 . . . . . Sabetha KS 66534 *TF:* 800-255-2450 ■ *Web:* keimts.com	800-255-2450		780
Keir Surgical Ltd 126-408 E Kent Ave S. . . . . Vancouver BC V5X2X7 *TF:* 800-663-4525 ■ *Web:* keirsurgical.com	604-261-9596	261-9549	475
Keiro Services 325 S Boyle Ave . . . . . Los Angeles CA 90033 *Web:* www.keiro.org	323-980-7555		463
Keiser University *Fort Lauderdale* 1500 W Commercial Blvd . . . . . Fort Lauderdale FL 33309 *TF:* 800-749-4456 ■ *Web:* www.keiseruniversity.edu	954-776-4456	771-4894	800
Keith A. Shibou CPA Accountancy 1900 E Tahquitz Canyon Way Ste B1 . . . . . Palm Springs CA 92262	760-325-1214		2
Keith County 511 N Spruce St Rm 205 . . . . . Ogallala NE 69153 *Web:* www.keithcountyne.gov	308-284-7776	284-3922	338
Keith D. Weiner & Associates Company LPA (KWA) 75 Public Sq Ste 400 . . . . . Cleveland OH 44113 *TF:* 866-368-6500 ■ *Web:* weinerlaw.com	216-771-6500	664-9830	445
Keith Smith Company Inc PO Box 3800 . . . . . Hot Springs AR 71914 *Web:* www.keith-smith.com	501-760-0100	760-9199	447
Keith Titus Corp PO Box 920 . . . . . Weedsport NY 13166 *TF:* 800-233-2126 ■ *Web:* www.pagetrucking.com	315-834-6681		780
Keith Watson Events 350 NW 39th Ave . . . . . Gainesville FL 32609 *TF:* 800-584-1709 ■ *Web:* www.keithwatsonevents.com	352-264-8814		33
Keithly-Williams Seeds Inc 420 Palm Ave . . . . . Holtville CA 92250 *TF:* 800-533-3465 ■ *Web:* www.keithlywilliams.com	760-356-5533		694
Keizer Heritage Museum 980 Chemawa Rd NE . . . . . Keizer OR 97303 *Web:* keizerculturalcenter.org	503-393-9660	393-0209	520
KEJO-AM 2840 Marion St SE . . . . . Albany OR 97322 *Web:* www.kejoam.com	541-926-8628	928-1261	647
Kejr Inc 1835 Wall St . . . . . Salina KS 67401 *TF:* 800-436-7762 ■ *Web:* geoprobe.com	785-825-1842		407
KEK Associates Inc 100 Josons Dr . . . . . Rochester NY 14623 *Web:* www.kekdesign.com	585-424-3380		463
Keker & Van Nest LLP 633 Battery St . . . . . San Francisco CA 94111 *Web:* www.keker.com	415-391-5400		428
Kelchner Inc 50 Advanced Dr . . . . . Springboro OH 45066 *Web:* www.kelchner.com	937-704-9890	704-9895	193
KELCO Industries 1425 Lake Ave . . . . . Woodstock IL 60098 *TF:* 800-762-0369 ■ *Web:* www.guardian-electric.com	815-334-3600	337-0377	203
Kelco Management & Development Inc 1020 Oriental Gardens Rd. . . . . Jacksonville FL 32207 *Web:* www.kelcohotels.com	904-858-9919		707
Kelderman Manufacturing Inc 2686 Hwy 92 E . . . . . Oskaloosa IA 52577 *Web:* kelderman.com	641-673-0468	673-4168	273
Kele Inc PO Box 34817 . . . . . Memphis TN 38184 *Web:* www.kele.com	901-382-4300		62
Kell Partners 303 Camp Craft Rd . . . . . Austin TX 78746 *Web:* www.kellpartners.com	512-732-2276		225
Kell's 112 SW Second Ave . . . . . Portland OR 97204 *Web:* www.kellsirish.com	503-227-4057		671
Kell, Alterman & Runstein LLP 520 SW Yamhill St Ste 600 . . . . . Portland OR 97204 *Web:* www.kelrun.com	503-222-3531		428
Kellam Berg Engineering & Surveys Ltd 5800 1A St SW . . . . . Calgary AB T2H0G1 *Web:* www.kellamberg.com	403-640-0900		261
Kelleher Associates LLC 265 Drummers Ln Ste 106 . . . . . Wayne PA 19087 *Web:* kelleherllc.com	610-293-1115		194
Kellen 3200 Windy Hill Rd SE Ste 600W . . . . . Atlanta GA 30339 *Web:* kellencompany.com	404-252-3663		47
Keller 8275 N W 80 St . . . . . Miami FL 33166 *TF:* 866-751-4545 ■ *Web:* www.keller-na.com	305-592-8181		188-2
Keller & Heckman LLP 1001 G St NW Ste 500w . . . . . Washington DC 20001 *Web:* www.khlaw.com	202-434-4100	434-4646	428
Keller & Kirkpatrick Inc 301 Gibraltar Dr Ste 2A . . . . . Morris Plains NJ 07950 *Web:* kellkirk.com	973-377-8500	887-0925	261
Keller America Inc 813 Diligence Dr Ste 120 . . . . . Newport News VA 23606 *Web:* www.kelleramerica.com	757-596-6680		201
Keller Army Community Hospital 900 Washington Rd . . . . . West Point NY 10996 *TF:* 800-552-2907 ■ *Web:* www.kach.amedd.army.mil	845-938-7992		374-4
Keller Associates Engineering Inc 131 SW Fifth Ave . . . . . Meridian ID 83642 *Web:* www.kellerassociates.com	208-288-1992		256
Keller Augusta Partners LLC 45 Newbury St Ste 204 . . . . . Boston MA 02116 *Web:* www.kelleraugusta.com	617-247-0505		260
Keller Equipment Supply Ltd 1228 26 Ave SE . . . . . Calgary AB T2G5S2 *TF:* 888-535-5373 ■ *Web:* keller.ca	403-243-8666		579
Keller Fred (Rep R - PA) 1717 Longworth House Office Bldg . . . . . Washington DC 20515 *Web:* www.keller.house.gov	202-225-3731		342-2
Keller Grain & Feed Inc 7977 Main St . . . . . Greenville OH 45331 *Web:* www.kellergrain.com	937-448-2284		276
Keller Inc N216 State Rd 55 . . . . . Kaukauna WI 54130 *TF:* 800-236-2534 ■ *Web:* www.kellerbuilds.com	920-766-5795		186
Keller Law Firm PC 50 S Last Chance Gulch Ste 4 . . . . . Helena MT 59601 *Web:* kellerlawmt.com	406-442-0230		41
Keller Law Office PA 126 E Olympia Ave Ste 200 . . . . . Punta Gorda FL 33950 *Web:* kellerlaw.biz	941-505-2555	505-4355	41
Keller Schroeder & Associates Inc 4920 Carriage Dr . . . . . Evansville IN 47715 *Web:* www.kellerschroeder.com	812-474-6825		177
Keller Supply Company Inc 3209 17th Ave W . . . . . Seattle WA 98119 *TF:* 800-285-3302 ■ *Web:* www.kellersupply.com	206-285-3300	283-8668	612
Keller Technology Corp 2320 Military Rd. . . . . Tonawanda NY 14150 *Web:* www.kellertechnology.com	716-693-3840		454
Keller Williams Realty Inc 807 Las Cimas Pkwy Ste 200 . . . . . Austin TX 78746 *Web:* www.kw.com	512-327-3070	328-1433	310
Keller, Turner, Andrews & Ghanem PLLC 20 Music Sq W Ste 200 . . . . . Nashville TN 37203 *Web:* www.ktaglaw.com	615-244-7600		41
Kellermeyer Bergensons Services LLC 1575 Henthorne Dr . . . . . Maumee OH 43537 *Web:* www.kbs-services.com	419-867-4300		192
Kellerstrass Oil Co 1500 W 2550 S . . . . . Ogden UT 84401 *Web:* www.kellerstrassoil.com	801-392-9516	392-9589	581
Kelley & Ferraro LLP Ernst & Young Tower 950 Main Ave Ste 1300 . . . . Cleveland OH 44113 *TF:* 800-398-1795 ■ *Web:* www.kelley-ferraro.com	216-202-3450	575-0799	428
Kelley Bean Company Inc 2407 Cir Dr. . . . . Scottsbluff NE 69361 *Web:* www.kelleybean.com	308-635-6438	635-7345	275
Kelley Beekeeping Co 807 W Main St. . . . . Clarkson KY 42726 *Web:* www.kelleybees.com	270-242-2012	242-4801	820
Kelley Blue Book Company Inc 195 Technology Dr . . . . . Irvine CA 92618 *TF:* 800-258-3266 ■ *Web:* www.kbb.com	949-770-7704		58
Kelley Chunn & Associates (KCA) PO Box 190871 . . . . . Boston MA 02119 *Web:* www.kelleychunn.com	617-427-0046		317
Kelley Dewatering & Construction 5175 Clay Ave SW . . . . . Wyoming MI 49548 *Web:* www.kelleydewatering.com	616-538-8010	538-0708	189-15
Kelley Drye & Warren LLP 101 Park Ave. . . . . New York NY 10178 *Web:* www.kelleydrye.com	212-808-7800	808-7897	428
Kelley Fuels Inc 250 Sarazin St . . . . . Shakopee MN 55379 *Web:* www.kelleyfuels.com	952-884-4100		579
Kelley Library 234 Main St . . . . . Salem NH 03079 *Web:* www.kelleylibrary.org	603-898-7064		434-3
Kelley Manufacturing Co 80 Vernon Dr PO Box 1467 . . . . . Tifton GA 31793 *TF:* 800-444-5449 ■ *Web:* www.kelleymfg.com	229-382-9393	382-5259	273
Kelley Technical Coatings Inc 1445 S 15th St PO Box 3726 . . . . . Louisville KY 40201 *TF:* 800-458-2842 ■ *Web:* www.kelleytech.com	502-636-2561	635-5170	550
Kelley-Ross Compounding Pharmacy 805 Madison St Ste 702 . . . . . Seattle WA 98104 *TF:* 866-622-3565 ■ *Web:* www.kelley-ross.com	206-622-3565	382-9727	237
Kelliher Samets Volk 212 Battery St . . . . . Burlington VT 05401 *Web:* www.ksvc.com	802-862-8261	863-4724	395
Kellmark Corp 2501 Ada Dr. . . . . Elkhart IN 46514 *Web:* kellmark.net	574-264-9695		627
Kellogg Co 1 Kellogg Sq PO Box 3599 . . . . . Battle Creek MI 49016 *NYSE: K* ■ *TF:* 800-962-1413 ■ *Web:* investor.kelloggs.com	269-961-2000		296-4
Kellogg Community College 450 N Ave . . . . . Battle Creek MI 49017 *Web:* www.kellogg.edu	269-965-3931	966-4089	162
Kellogg Garden Products 350 W Sepulveda Blvd . . . . . Carson CA 90745 *TF:* 800-232-2322 ■ *Web:* www.kellogggarden.com	800-232-2322		280
Kellogg Hotel & Conference Ctr Michigan State University 219 S Harrison Rd . . . . . East Lansing MI 48824 *TF:* 800-875-5090 ■ *Web:* kelloggcenter.com	517-432-4000	353-1872	379
Kellogg Marine Supply Inc 5 Enterprise Dr . . . . . Old Lyme CT 06371 **Fax Area Code: 800* ■ *TF:* 800-243-9303 ■ *Web:* www.kelloggmarine.com	860-434-6002	628-1304*	770
Kellogg School of Management *Northwestern University* 2211 Campus Dr . . . . . Evanston IL 60208 *Web:* www.kellogg.northwestern.edu	847-491-3300		685
Kellogg Smith 9499 NE 2nd Ave Ste 204 . . . . . Miami Shores FL 33138 *Web:* www.kelloggsmith.com	305-757-9801	757-9802	390
Kellogg, Huber, Hansen, Todd, Evans & Figel PLLC Sumner Sq 1615 M St NW Ste 400 . . . . . Washington DC 20036 *Web:* www.kellogghansen.com	202-326-7900	326-7999	428
Kelloggauto Supply 502 S Edgemoor St . . . . . Wichita KS 67218 *Web:* www.poormanautosupply.com	316-682-4525		791
Kellogg-Hubbard Library 135 Main St . . . . . Montpelier VT 05602 *Web:* www.kellogghubbard.org	802-223-3338		434-3
KellPro Inc 101 S 15th St. . . . . Duncan OK 73533 *TF:* 888-535-5776 ■ *Web:* www.okcountyrecords.com	888-535-5776		635
Kell-Strom Tool Co 214 Church St . . . . . Wethersfield CT 06109 *TF:* 800-851-6851 ■ *Web:* www.kell-strom.com	860-529-6851	257-9694	757
Kellwood Co 600 Kellwood Pkwy. . . . . Chesterfield MO 63017 *Web:* www.kellwood.com	314-576-3100		155-21
Kelly & Lemmons PA 223 Little Canada Rd E Ste 200 . . . . . Saint Paul MN 55117 *Web:* kellyandlemmons.com	651-224-3781		41
Kelly Advertising Inc 818 Fulton St . . . . . Fort Wayne IN 46802 *Web:* kellyadvertising.com	260-426-1843		7
Kelly Aerospace 1404 E S Blvd . . . . . Montgomery AL 36116 *TF:* 888-461-6077 ■ *Web:* www.kellyaerospace.com	334-286-8551	227-8596	247
Kelly Box & Packaging Corp 2801 Covington Rd. . . . . Fort Wayne IN 46802 *Web:* www.kellybox.com	260-432-4570		100
Kelly Collins & Gentry Inc 1700 N Orange Ave Ste 400 . . . . . Orlando FL 32804 *Web:* kcgcorp.com	407-898-7858	898-1488	256

Name / Address	City	State	Zip	Phone	Fax	Class
Kelly Inns Ltd 3205 W Sencore Dr *Web:* www.kellyinns.com	Sioux Falls	SD	57107	605-965-1440	965-1450	379
Kelly Loeffler (Sen R - GA) 131 Russell Senate Office Bldg *Web:* www.loeffler.senate.gov	Washington	DC	20510	202-224-3643	228-0724	342-2
Kelly Manufacturing Co 555 S Topeka St *Web:* www.kellymfg.com	Wichita	KS	67202	316-265-6868	265-6687	529
Kelly Mike (Rep R - PA) 1707 Longworth House Office Bldg *Web:* kelly.house.gov	Washington	DC	20515	202-225-5406	225-3103	342-2
Kelly Mitchell Group Inc 8229 Maryland Ave **Fax Area Code:* 314 ■ *TF:* 877-827-1700 ■ *Web:* www.kellymitchell.com	Saint Louis	MO	63105	877-827-1700	727-0107*	194
Kelly Paper Co 288 Brea Canyon Rd **Fax Area Code:* 909 ■ *TF:* 800-675-3559 ■ *Web:* www.kellypaper.com	Walnut	CA	91789	800-675-3559	859-8903*	553
Kelly Pipe Company LLC 11680 Bloomfield Ave *TF:* 800-305-3559 ■ *Web:* www.kellypipe.com	Santa Fe Springs	CA	90670	562-868-0456	863-4695	595
Kelly Press Inc 1701 Cabin Branch Dr *TF:* 888-535-5940 ■ *Web:* www.thekellycompanies.com	Cheverly	MD	20785	301-386-2800		627
Kelly Robin (Rep D - IL) 2416 Rayburn House Office Bldg *Web:* robinkelly.house.gov	Washington	DC	20515	202-225-0773	225-4583	342-2
Kelly Ryan Equipment Co 900 Kelly Ryan Dr *TF:* 800-640-6967 ■ *Web:* www.kryan.com	Blair	NE	68008	402-426-2151	426-2186	273
Kelly Sauder Rupiper Equipment LLC 805 E Howard St *Web:* www.ksrequipment.com	Pontiac	IL	61764	815-842-1149		274
Kelly Services Inc 999 W Big Beaver Rd *NASDAQ: KELYA* ■ *Web:* www.kellyservices.com	Troy	MI	48084	248-362-4444		721
Kelly Smertz Tires Inc 912 Wyoming Ave *Web:* kellysmertztires.com	Scranton	PA	18509	570-343-3925		755
Kelly Systems Inc 422 N Western Ave *TF:* 800-258-8237 ■ *Web:* www.kellytubesystems.com	Chicago	IL	60612	312-733-3224	733-6971	470
Kelly Trent (Rep R - MS) 1005 Longworth House Office Bldg *Web:* www.trentkelly.house.gov	Washington	DC	20515	202-225-4306	225-3549	342-2
Kelly Waters Inc 5 Clementine Pk *Web:* www.kellywaters.com	Dorchester Center	MA	02124	617-282-3620		652
Kelly Williams Insurance Agency Inc 4400 E Pacific Coast Hwy *Web:* kellywilliamsins.com	Long Beach	CA	90804	562-498-8661		390
Kelly's Janitorial Service Inc 228 Hazel Ave *TF:* 800-227-0366 ■ *Web:* www.kellysjanitorial.com	Trenton	NJ	08638	609-771-0365		256
Kelly's Pipe & Supply Company Inc 2124 Industrial Rd *Web:* kellyspipe.com	Las Vegas	NV	89102	702-382-4957	382-4879	612
Kelly's Pub & Eatery 1802 Cedar Ave *Web:* www.kpehotwings.com	Scranton	PA	18505	570-346-9758		671
Kelly, Remmel & Zimmerman PA 53 Exchange St PO Box 597 *Web:* krz.com	Portland	ME	04101	207-775-1020		41
Kelly, Sutter & Kendrick PC 3050 Post Oak Blvd Ste 200 *Web:* ksklawyers.com	Houston	TX	77056	713-595-6000		41
Kellyco Marketing 333 Hudson St *Web:* www.kellycomarketing.com	New York	NY	10013	212-243-9131		194
Kelly-Moore Paint Company Inc 987 Commercial St *TF:* 800-874-4436 ■ *Web:* kellymoore.com	San Carlos	CA	94070	650-592-8337		550
Kellys Roast Beef Inc 605 Broadway Ste 300 *Web:* www.kellysroastbeef.com	Saugus	MA	01906	781-233-5000		670
Kelly-Strayhorn Theater 5941 Penn Ave *Web:* kelly-strayhorn.org	Pittsburgh	PA	15206	412-363-3000	363-4320	573-1
Kelman-Lazarov Inc 5100 Poplar Ave Ste 2805 *Web:* www.kelman-lazarov.com	Memphis	TN	38137	901-685-8284	685-8013	401
KELO-AM 1320 (N/T) 500 S Phillips Ave *Web:* kelo.com	Sioux Falls	SD	57104	605-271-5838	336-0415	645-149
Kelowna Chamber of Commerce 544 Harvey Ave *Web:* www.kelownachamber.org	Kelowna	BC	V1Y6C9	250-861-3627	861-3624	137
KELP Christian Radio 6900 Commerce Ave *TF:* 800-658-6299 ■ *Web:* www.kelpradio.com	El Paso	TX	79915	915-779-0016	779-6641	645-52
Kelser Corp 43 Western Blvd *TF:* 800-647-5316 ■ *Web:* www.kelsercorp.com	Glastonbury	CT	06033	860-610-2200		225
Kelsey Construction Inc 306 E Princeton St *Web:* kelseyconstruction.com	Orlando	FL	32804	407-898-4101		186
Kelsey Furniture Company Inc 215 N Main St *Web:* www.kelseyfurniture.com	Tuscola	IL	61953	217-253-2142	253-4135	321
Kelsey Museum of Archaeology University of Michigan 434 S State St *TF:* 800-562-3559 ■ *Web:* lsa.umich.edu	Ann Arbor	MI	48109	734-763-3559	763-8976	520
Kelsey National Corp 3030 S Bundy Dr *Web:* www.kelsey.com	Los Angeles	CA	90066	310-390-1000		390
Kelso & Bradshaw 132 Hamilton St *Web:* kelsoburgess.com	New Brunswick	NJ	08901	732-246-4501		41
Kelso & Company Inc 320 Park Ave 24th Fl *Web:* www.kelso.com	New York	NY	10022	212-350-7700		690
Kelso Longview Chamber of Commerce 1563 Olympia Way *Web:* www.kelsolongviewchamber.org	Longview	WA	98632	360-423-8400	423-0432	139
Kelso-Burnett Co 5200 Newport Dr *Web:* www.kelso-burnett.com	Rolling Meadows	IL	60008	847-259-0720	259-0839	189-4
Keltic Transportation Inc 90 MacNaughton Ave Caledonia Industrial Pk *TF:* 888-854-1233 ■ *Web:* keltictransportation.com	Moncton	NB	E1H3L9	506-854-1233		314
Kelton House Museum & Garden 586 E Town St *Web:* www.keltonhouse.com	Columbus	OH	43215	614-464-2022		520
Kelty 6235 Lookout Rd *TF:* 800-423-2320 ■ *Web:* www.kelty.com	Boulder	CO	80301	800-535-3589	504-2745	64
Kelvyn Press Inc 2910 S 18th Ave *Web:* kelvynpress.com	Broadview	IL	60155	708-343-0448	343-0452	627
KELYN Group 1620 Sudbury Rd Ste 6 *Web:* www.thekelyngroup.com	Concord	MA	01742	978-369-7000		195
Kelyniam Global Inc 97 River Rd *TF:* 800-280-8192 ■ *Web:* www.kelyniam.com	Canton	CT	06019	800-280-8192		250
KEM Electric Co-opeartive Inc 107 S Broadway *TF:* 800-472-2673 ■ *Web:* www.kemelectric.com	Linton	ND	58552	701-254-4666	254-4975	245
Kem Equipment Inc 10800 SW Herman Rd *Web:* www.kemequipment.com	Tualatin	OR	97062	503-692-5012	692-1098	261
Kem Krest Corp 3221 Magnum Dr *TF:* 800-285-5916 ■ *Web:* www.kemkrest.com	Elkhart	IN	46516	574-389-2650	389-2694	311
Kemark Financial Services Inc 1 Blue Hill Plz 11th Fl *Web:* www.kemarkfinancial.com	Pearl River	NY	10965	845-620-9300	620-9340	180
Kemba Delta Federal Credit Union 3108 N Germantown Pkwy Ste 106 *TF:* 888-725-3622 ■ *Web:* kembadelta.org	Bartlett	TN	38133	901-795-9055	795-9063	219
Kemba Louisville Credit Union 4017 Poplar Level Rd *Web:* kembaky.org	Louisville	KY	40213	502-459-1411		219
Kemba Peoria Credit Union 2318 W Willow Knolls Dr *TF:* 800-927-6003 ■ *Web:* kembapeoria.com	Peoria	IL	61614	309-693-6000	693-7312	219
Kemble Interiors Inc 294 Hibiscus Ave *Web:* www.kembleinteriors.com	Palm Beach Gardens	FL	33480	561-659-5556	833-4843	393
KEMCO Industries LLC 70 Keyes Ct *Web:* www.kemco.com	Sanford	FL	32773	407-322-1230		203
Kemco Systems Inc 11500 47th St N *TF:* 800-633-7055 ■ *Web:* www.kemcosystems.com	Clearwater	FL	33762	727-573-2323	573-2346	427
Kemeny Overseas Products Corp 5237 Summerlin Commons Blvd *Web:* www.kemenyoverseas.com	Fort Myers	FL	33907	239-275-2550	275-2501	492
Kemerer Museum of Decorative Arts 427 N New St *Web:* historicbethlehem.org	Bethlehem	PA	18018	610-868-6868		520
KEMET Corp PO Box 5928 *NYSE: KEM* ■ *Web:* www.kemet.com	Greenville	SC	29606	864-963-6300		253
Kemin Industries Inc 2100 Maury St *TF:* 800-777-8307 ■ *Web:* www.kemin.com	Des Moines	IA	50317	515-559-5100	559-5232	447
Kemlon Products & Development Co 1424 N Main St *Web:* www.kemlon.com	Pearland	TX	77581	281-997-3300	997-1300	641
Kemoll's 211 N Broadway *Web:* www.kemolls.com	Saint Louis	MO	63102	314-421-0555		671
Kemp & Smith LLP 221 N Kansas Ste 1700 *Web:* www.kempsmith.com	El Paso	TX	79901	915-533-4424	546-5360	428
Kemp Bros Construction Inc 10135 Geary Ave *Web:* www.kempbros.com	Santa Fe Springs	CA	90670	562-236-5000		186
Kemp Hardware & Supply Co 7305 Madison St *Web:* www.kemphardware.com	Paramount	CA	90723	562-634-2553	634-2052	351
Kemp Manufacturing Co 4310 N Voss St Peoria Hts *Web:* www.kempmfg.com	Peoria	IL	61616	309-682-7292		454
Kemp Stone Inc PO Box 968 *Web:* www.kempquarries.com	Pryor	OK	74362	918-825-3370	825-3388	503-5
Kemp West Inc 3800 Sinclair Ave *Web:* kempwest.com	Snohomish	WA	98290	425-334-5572		422
Kempe Ctr 13123 E 16th Ave *Web:* www.kempe.org	Aurora	CO	80045	303-864-5300		48-6
Kemper County Mississippi Courthouse PO Box 188 *Web:* kemper.countycriminal.com	De Kalb	MS	39328	601-743-2754		338
Kemper Equipment Inc 5051 Horseshoe Pk *Web:* www.kemperequipment.com	Honey Brook	PA	19344	610-273-2066	273-3537	385
Kemper Lesnik Communications 500 Skokie Blvd 4th Fl *Web:* www.kemperlesnik.com	Northbrook	IL	60062	847-850-1818	559-0406	636
Kemper Museum of Contemporary Art 4420 Warwick Blvd *Web:* www.kemperart.org	Kansas City	MO	64111	816-753-5784	753-5806	520
Kempf House Museum 312 S Div St *Web:* www.kempfhousemuseum.org	Ann Arbor	MI	48104	734-994-4898		520
KemPharm Inc 2656Crosspark Rd Ste 100 *Web:* kempharm.com	Coralville	IA	52241	319-665-2575	665-2577	668
Kemp-Meek Manufacturing Inc 101 Park Central Rd *Web:* www.kempmeek.com	Mineola	TX	75773	903-569-9700	569-9696	495
Kempner Properties 257 Mamaroneck Ave *Web:* kempnerproperties.com	White Plains	NY	10605	914-946-3030		652
Kemps LLC 1270 Energy Ln *TF:* 800-322-9566 ■ *Web:* www.kemps.com	Saint Paul	MN	55108	800-322-9566		296-27
Kempsmith Machine Co 1819 S 71st St *Web:* www.kempsmith-dl.com	Milwaukee	WI	53214	414-256-8160	476-0564	556
Kempton Group 2 Garfield Pl Ste 1602 *Web:* www.kemptongroup.com	Cincinnati	OH	45202	513-651-5556		195
Kemron Environmental Services Inc 8521 Leesburg Pk Ste 175 *TF:* 888-429-3516 ■ *Web:* www.kemron.com	Vienna	VA	22182	703-893-4106	893-1741	192
Kemtah Group Inc 7601 Jefferson St NE Ste 120	Albuquerque	NM	87109	505-346-4900		180
Kemwel 39 Commercial St *TF:* 800-678-0678 ■ *Web:* www.kemwel.com	Portland	ME	04101	207-842-2285	842-2286	126

Name	Address	City	State	Zip	Phone	Fax	Class	Notes
Ken & Sue's	636 Main Ave	Durango	CO	81301	970-385-1810		671	*Web:* www.kenandsues.com
Ken Blanchard Companies Inc, The	125 State Pl	Escondido	CA	92029	760-839-8070		194	*TF:* 800-102-1345 ■ *Web:* www.kenblanchard.com
Ken Brady Construction Company Inc	4001 Turnagain Blvd	Anchorage	AK	99517	907-243-4604		186	*Web:* www.kenbrady.com
Ken Clark International Inc	630 Freedom Business Center Dr Ste 300	King of Prussia	PA	19406	610-768-7770		193	*Web:* www.kenclark.com
Ken Cook Co	2855 S Calhoun Rd	New Berlin	WI	53151	414-466-6060		637-11	*Web:* www.kencook.com
Ken Creative Inc	1500 Park Ave Ste 200	Emeryville	CA	94608	510-879-7977		195	*Web:* kencreative.com
Ken Die Cutting Supplies Inc	2280 Conestoga Dr	Carson City	NV	89706	775-882-4453	882-4782	757	*Web:* www.ameriken.com
Ken Forging Inc	1049 Griggs Rd	Jefferson	OH	44047	440-993-8091	992-0360	483	*TF:* 888-536-3674 ■ *Web:* www.kenforging.com
Ken Fowler Motors	1265 Airport Pk Blvd	Ukiah	CA	95482	707-468-0101	462-2475	57	*TF:* 800-287-0107 ■ *Web:* www.fowlergmcbuick.com
Ken Garff Automotive Group	405 S Main St	Salt Lake City	UT	84111	801-257-3200	257-3363	57	*Web:* www.kengarff.com
Ken Garner Manufacturing - Rho Inc	1201 E 28th St Ste B	Chattanooga	TN	37404	423-698-6200		470	*TF:* 888-454-7207 ■ *Web:* www.kgarnermfg.com
Ken Grody Ford	6211 Beach Blvd	Buena Park	CA	90621	714-521-3110		57	*Web:* www.kengrody.com
Ken Jones Tire Inc	73 Chandler St	Worcester	MA	01609	508-755-5255	755-4397	755	*TF:* 800-225-9513 ■ *Web:* www.kenjones.com
Ken Leiner Associates Inc	10401 Connecticut Ave Ste 140	Kensington	MD	20895	301-933-8800		193	*Web:* itsearch.com
Ken Nunn Law Office	104 S Franklin Rd	Bloomington	IN	47404	812-332-9451		428	*TF:* 800-225-5536 ■ *Web:* kennunn.com
Ken Perry State Farm Insurance	2724 24th St Ste 200	Sacramento	CA	95818	916-452-6668		390	*Web:* kensperry.com
Ken Stewart's Grille	1970 W Market St	Akron	OH	44313	330-867-2555		671	*Web:* www.kenstewartsgrille.com
Ken Ton Fabricators Inc	2505 Main St	Buffalo	NY	14214	716-832-1200		321	*Web:* www.kentonfab.com
Ken Wilson Ford Inc	769 Champion Dr	Canton	NC	28716	800-532-4631		57	*TF:* 800-532-4631 ■ *Web:* www.kenwilsonford.com
Ken's Flower Shop	140 W S Boundary St	Perrysburg	OH	43551	419-874-1333		292	*TF:* 800-253-0100 ■ *Web:* www.kensflowers.com
Ken's Foods Inc	1 D'Angelo Dr	Marlborough	MA	01752	508-485-7540		296-19	*Web:* www.kensfoods.com
Kenai Drilling Ltd	6430 Cat Canyon Rd	Santa Maria	CA	93454	805-937-7871		540	*Web:* www.kenaidrilling.com
Kenai Peninsula Borough	144 N Binkley St	Soldotna	AK	99669	907-262-4441		338	*Web:* www.kpb.us
Kenall Mfg	1020 Lakeside Dr	Gurnee	IL	60031	262-891-9700	360-1781*	439	**Fax Area Code:* 847 ■ *TF:* 800-453-6255 ■ *Web:* www.kenall.com
Ken-Bar Tool & Engineering Inc	3121 S Walnut St	Muncie	IN	47302	765-284-4408	284-4441	757	*Web:* ken-bartoolandengr.com
KenCast Inc	535 Connecticut Ave Ste 304	Norwalk	CT	06854	203-359-6984		116	*Web:* kencast.com
Kenco Group Inc	2001 Riverside Dr	Chattanooga	TN	37406	800-758-3289		449	*TF:* 800-758-3289 ■ *Web:* www.kencogroup.com
Kencoil Inc	2805 Engineers Rd	Belle Chasse	LA	70037	504-394-4010		518	*TF:* 800-221-8577 ■ *Web:* www.kencoil.com
KenCraft Manufacturing Inc	4155 Dixie Inn Rd	Wilson	NC	27893	252-291-0271		90	*Web:* www.kencraftboats.com
KenCrest Services Inc	960A Harvest Dr Ste 100	Blue Bell	PA	19422	610-825-9360	825-4127	48-15	*Web:* www.kencrest.org
Kenda USA	7095 Americana Pkwy	Reynoldsburg	OH	43068	614-866-9803	866-9805	755	*TF:* 866-536-3287 ■ *Web:* www.kendatire.com
Kendal at Hanover	80 Lyme Rd	Hanover	NH	03755	603-643-8900	643-7099	672	*Web:* kah.kendal.org
Kendal at Ithaca	2230 N Triphammer Rd	Ithaca	NY	14850	607-266-5300		672	*TF:* 800-253-6325 ■ *Web:* kai.kendal.org
Kendal at Oberlin	600 Kendal Dr	Oberlin	OH	44074	800-548-9469		672	*TF:* 800-548-9469 ■ *Web:* kao.kendal.org
Kendal Crosslands Communities	1109 E Baltimore Pk	Kennett Square	PA	19348	610-388-1441	388-5503	672	*TF:* 800-216-1920 ■ *Web:* kcc.kendal.org
Kendall College	900 N North Branch St	Chicago	IL	60642	312-752-2024		163	*TF:* 888-905-3632 ■ *Web:* www.kendall.edu
Kendall College of Art & Design of Ferris State University	17 Fountain St NW	Grand Rapids	MI	49503	800-676-2787	831-9689*	166	**Fax Area Code:* 616 ■ *TF:* 800-676-2787 ■ *Web:* kcad.ferris.edu
Kendall County	201 E San Antonio St	Boerne	TX	78006	830-249-9343	249-1763	338	*Web:* www.co.kendall.tx.us
Kendall County	111 W Fox St	Yorkville	IL	60560	630-553-4104	553-4119	338	*Web:* www.co.kendall.il.us
Kendall Electric Inc	131 Grand Trunk Ave	Battle Creek	MI	49037	269-965-6897		246	*TF:* 800-632-5422 ■ *Web:* www.kendallelectric.com
Kendall Fontenot	1110 W Laurel	Eunice	LA	70535	337-546-6501	546-0916	390	*Web:* kendallfontenot.com
Kendall News Gazette	6796 SW 62nd Ave	South Miami	FL	33143	305-669-7355		532-4	*Web:* communitynewspapers.com
Kendall Packaging Corp	10335 N Port Washington Rd	Mequon	WI	53092	262-404-1200	404-1221	600	*TF:* 800-237-0951 ■ *Web:* www.kendallpkg.com
Kendall Regional Medical Ctr	11750 SW 40th St	Miami	FL	33175	305-223-3000		374-3	*Web:* kendallmed.com
Kendall Toyota	10943 S Dixie Hwy	Miami	FL	33156	305-665-6581		57	*Web:* www.kendalltoyota.com
Kendall's Brasserie & Bar	135 N Grand Ave	Los Angeles	CA	90012	213-972-7322		671	*Web:* www.patinagroup.com
Kendall/Hunt Publishing Co	4050 Westmark Dr PO Box 1840	Dubuque	IA	52002	563-589-1000	772-9165*	637-2	**Fax Area Code:* 800 ■ *TF:* 800-228-0810 ■ *Web:* www.kendallhunt.com
Kendall-Jackson Wine Estates & Gardens	5007 Fulton Rd	Fulton	CA	95439	866-287-9818		80-3	*TF:* 800-769-3649 ■ *Web:* www.kj.com
Kendor Music Inc	21 Grove St	Delevan	NY	14042	716-492-1254	492-5124	637-10	*Web:* www.kendormusic.com
Kendra Scott LLC	1400 S Congress Ave Ste A-170	Austin	TX	78704	866-677-7023		411	*TF:* 866-677-7023 ■ *Web:* www.kendrascott.com
Kenedy County	139 N Main	Sarita	TX	78385	361-294-5785	294-5788	338	*Web:* www.co.kenedy.tx.us
Kenergy Corp	6402 Old Corydon Rd	Henderson	KY	42419	270-826-3991	826-3999	245	*TF:* 800-844-4832 ■ *Web:* www.kenergycorp.com
Kenilworth Aquatic Gardens	1550 Anacostia Ave NE	Washington	DC	20019	202-692-6080	426-5991	97	*Web:* www.nps.gov
Kenilworth Historical Society (KHS)	415 Kenilworth Ave	Kenilworth	IL	60043	847-251-2565		49-19	*Web:* kenilworthhistory.org
Kenilworth Steel	8700 E Market St Ste 11	Warren	OH	44484	330-373-1885	399-2144	492	*TF:* 800-537-5283 ■ *Web:* www.kenilworthsteel.com
Kenlake State Resort Park	542 Kenlake Rd	Hardin	KY	42048	270-474-2211		565	*TF:* 800-325-0143 ■ *Web:* parks.ky.gov
Kenlee Precision Corp	1701 Inverness Ave	Baltimore	MD	21230	410-525-3800	646-3278	621	*TF:* 800-969-5278 ■ *Web:* www.kenlee.com
Ken-Mac Metals Inc	17901 Englewood Dr	Cleveland	OH	44130	440-234-7500	234-4459	492	*TF:* 800-831-9503 ■ *Web:* www.thyssenkrupp-materials-na.com
Kenmar Corp	17515 W 9 Mile Rd Ste 1200	Southfield	MI	48075	248-424-8200		61	*Web:* www.ekenmar.com
Kenmark Co, The	83 River Rd	Canton	CT	06019	860-693-6818		422	*Web:* kenmarkcompany.com
Kenmode Tool & Engineering Co	820 W Algonquin Rd	Algonquin	IL	60102	847-658-5041	658-9150	757	*Web:* www.kenmode.com
Kenmore Air Harbor Inc	6321 NE 175th St	Kenmore	WA	98028	425-486-1257		25	*TF:* 866-435-9524 ■ *Web:* kenmoreair.com
Kenmore Camera Inc	6708 NE 181st St PO Box 82467	Kenmore	WA	98028	425-485-7447	489-2843	119	*TF:* 888-485-7447 ■ *Web:* www.kenmorecamera.com
Kenmore Construction Company Inc	700 Home Ave	Akron	OH	44310	330-762-9373	762-2135	186	*Web:* kenmorecompanies.com
Kenmore-Town of Tonawanda Chamber of Commerce	3411 Delaware Ave	Kenmore	NY	14217	716-874-1202	874-3151	139	*Web:* ken-ton.org
Kennametal Inc	600 Grant St Ste 5100	Pittsburgh	PA	15219	800-446-7738		1	*NYSE:* KMT ■ *TF:* 800-446-7738 ■ *Web:* www.kennametal.com
Kennebec County	125 State St	Augusta	ME	04330	207-622-0971	623-4083	338	*Web:* kennebeccounty.org
Kennebec Lumber Co	105 S Main PO Box 288	Solon	ME	04979	207-643-2110		311	*Web:* kennebeclumber.com
Kennebec Savings Bank	150 State St PO Box 50	Augusta	ME	04332	207-622-5801	626-2858	70	*TF:* 888-303-7788 ■ *Web:* www.kennebecsavings.bank
Kennebec Telephone Company Inc	220 S Main St PO Box 158	Kennebec	SD	57544	605-869-2220	869-2221	736	*TF:* 888-868-3390 ■ *Web:* www.kennebectelephone.com
Kennebec Valley Chamber of Commerce	21 University Dr	Augusta	ME	04330	207-623-4559	626-9342	139	*Web:* augustamaine.com
Kennebec Valley Community College	92 Western Ave	Fairfield	ME	04937	207-453-5000	453-5010	162	*TF:* 800-528-5882 ■ *Web:* www.kvcc.me.edu
Kennedy & Coe LLC	3030 Cortland Cir	Salina	KS	67401	785-825-1561	825-5371	2	*Web:* www.kcoe.com
Kennedy Consulting Inc	205 E University Ave Ste 450	Georgetown	TX	78626	512-864-2833		261	*Web:* www.kcitx.com
Kennedy III Joseph P (Rep D - MA)	304 Cannon House Office Bldg	Washington	DC	20515	202-225-5931	225-0182	342-2	*Web:* kennedy.house.gov
Kennedy John (Sen R - LA)	416 Russell Senate Office Bldg	Washington	DC	20510	202-224-4623		342-2	*Web:* www.kennedy.senate.gov
Kennedy Johnson Schwab & Roberge LLC	555 Long Wharf Dr	New Haven	CT	06511	866-689-1248		41	*TF:* 866-689-1248 ■ *Web:* kennedyjohnson.com
Kennedy Krieger Institute	707 N Broadway	Baltimore	MD	21205	443-923-9200		374-1	*TF:* 800-873-3377 ■ *Web:* www.kennedykrieger.org
Kennedy Manufacturing Co	1260 Industrial Dr	Van Wert	OH	45891	800-413-8665		488	*TF:* 800-413-8665 ■ *Web:* buykennedy.com
Kennedy Office Supply	4211-A Atlantic Ave	Raleigh	NC	27604	919-878-5400	790-9649	535	*TF:* 800-733-9401 ■ *Web:* kennedyoffice.com
Kennedy Political Items Collectors	PO Box 922	Clark	NJ	07066	732-382-4652		637-2	*Web:* www.apic.us
Kennedy Tank & Manufacturing Company Inc	833 E Sumner Ave	Indianapolis	IN	46227	317-787-1311		480	*TF:* 800-445-1344 ■ *Web:* www.kennedytank.com

Name / Address	City	State	ZIP	Phone	Fax	Class
Kennedy Tool & Die Inc 325 W Main St *Web:* www.ktdmold.com	Birdsboro	PA	19508	610-582-8735		757
Kennedy Valve 1021 E Water St *TF:* 800-782-5831 ■ *Web:* www.kennedyvalve.com	Elmira	NY	14902	607-734-2211	734-3288	789
Kennedy/Jenks Consultants 303 Second St Ste 300 S *Web:* www.kennedyjenks.com	San Francisco	CA	94107	415-243-2150	896-0999	261
Kennedy-Wilson Inc 151 S El Camino Dr *Web:* www.kennedywilson.com	Beverly Hills	CA	90212	310-887-6400	887-3410	51
Kenner Planetarium & MegaDome Cinema 1801 Williams Blvd *TF:* 800-555-5160 ■ *Web:* www.kenner.la.us	Kenner	LA	70062	504-468-7231	468-7213	598
Kennerley-Spratling Inc 2116 Farallon Dr *TF:* 800-523-5474 ■ *Web:* www.ksplastic.com	San Leandro	CA	94577	510-351-8230	352-9240	604
Kennesaw Mountain National Battlefield Park 900 Kennesaw Mtn Dr *Web:* www.nps.gov	Kennesaw	GA	30152	770-427-4686	528-8398	564
Kennesaw State University 1000 Chastain Rd **Fax Area Code:* 770 ■ *Web:* www.kennesaw.edu	Kennesaw	GA	30144	470-578-6000	420-4435*	166
Kenneth B. Murov, Attorney At Law 716 J Clyde Morris Blvd Ste B *Web:* kbmurovlaw.com	Newport News	VA	23601	757-595-2100		41
Kenneth Clark Company Inc 10264 Baltimore National Pk *TF:* 866-999-5116 ■ *Web:* www.kennethclark.com	Ellicott City	MD	21042	410-465-5116		195
Kenneth Cole Productions Inc 603 W 50th St *NYSE: KCP* ■ *TF:* 800-536-2653 ■ *Web:* www.kennethcole.com	New York	NY	10019	800-536-2653		301
Kenneth Hahn State Recreation Area 4100 S La Cienega Blvd *Web:* www.parks.ca.gov	Los Angeles	CA	90056	323-298-3660		565
Kenneth Honey Rubenstein Juvenile Ctr 141 Forestry Camp Rd *Web:* dcr.wv.gov	Davis	WV	26260	304-259-5241	259-4851	412
Kenneth J. Gerbino and Co 9595 Wilshire Blvd Ste 303 *Web:* www.kengerbino.com	Beverly Hills	CA	90212	310-550-6304		401
Kenneth R. Warner, Attorney At Law 910 Hampshire Rd Ste D *Web:* kwarnerlaw.com	Westlake Village	CA	91361	805-371-0567		41
Kenneth Rainin Foundation 155 Grand Ave *Web:* krfoundation.org	Oakland	CA	94612	510-625-5200		303
Kenneth Shuler School of Cosmetology & Hair Design Inc 449 St Andrews Rd *Web:* kennethshuler.com	Columbia	SC	29210	803-772-6042		77
Kennetic Productions 25 N Market St 300 D *Web:* www.kenneticproductions.com	Jacksonville	FL	32202	904-372-8570		514
Kennett School District No 39 - Kennett Career & Technology Ctr 1400 W Washington St *Web:* www.kennett.k12.mo.us	Kennett	MO	63857	573-717-1123	717-1147	685
Kennewick General Hospital (KGH) 900 S Auburn *Web:* www.trioshealth.org	Kennewick	WA	99336	509-586-5707		374-3
Kenney & Assn 1754 N Washington St Ste 112	Naperville	IL	60563	630-505-4333		390
Kenney Machinery Corp 8420 Zionsville Rd *Web:* kenneymachinery.com	Indianapolis	IN	46260	317-872-4793		429
Kenney Manufacturing Co 1000 Jefferson Blvd *TF:* 800-753-6639 ■ *Web:* www.kenney.com	Warwick	RI	02886	401-739-2200		87
Kennickell Printing Co 1700 E President St *TF:* 800-673-6455 ■ *Web:* www.kennickell.com	Savannah	GA	31404	912-233-4532		627
Kennicott Brothers Co 452 N Ashland Ave *TF:* 866-346-2826 ■ *Web:* kennicott.com	Chicago	IL	60622	312-492-8200	492-8201	293
Kennies Market Inc 217 W Middle St *Web:* www.kenniesmarket.com	Gettysburg	PA	17325	717-334-2179		345
Kenny Pipe & Supply Inc 811 Cowan St *Web:* www.kennypipe.com	Nashville	TN	37207	615-255-4810	255-5925	612
Kenny The Printer 17931 Sky Park Cir *Web:* www.kennytheprinter.com	Irvine	CA	92614	949-250-3212		627
Kenny's Kustom Kards Inc 5400 Airport Fwy Ste G *TF:* 800-229-8639 ■ *Web:* www.kennyskustomkards.com	Haltom City	TX	76117	817-332-8639	332-2708	627
Kenny, O'Keefe & Usseglio PC 21 Oak St *Web:* kou-law.com	Hartford	CT	06106	860-246-2700		41
Kennywood Park 4800 Kennywood Blvd *Web:* www.kennywood.com	West Mifflin	PA	15122	412-461-0500		32
KENO-AM 1460 (Sports) 3301 Barham Blvd	Los Angeles	CA	90028	702-247-1460	876-6685	645-85
Kenona Industries Inc 3044 Wilson Dr NW *Web:* www.kenona.net	Grand Rapids	MI	49534	616-735-6228		454
Kenora Daily Miner 33 Main St S *Web:* www.kenoraminerandnews.com	Kenora	ON	P9N3X7	807-468-5555	468-4318	532-1
Kenora District Services Board 211 Princess St *TF:* 800-461-5766 ■ *Web:* kdsb.on.ca	Dryden	ON	P8N3L5	807-223-2100		30
Kenosha Achievement Center Inc 1218 - 79th Street Kenosha *Web:* www.thekac.com	Kenosha	WI	53143	262-658-9500		393
Kenosha Area Chamber of Commerce 600 52nd St Ste 130 *Web:* kenoshaareachamber.com	Kenosha	WI	53140	262-654-1234	654-4655	139
Kenosha Area Convention & Visitors Bureau 812 56th St *TF:* 800-654-7309 ■ *Web:* www.visitkenosha.com	Kenosha	WI	53140	262-654-7307	654-0882	206
Kenosha County 1010 56th St *Web:* www.kenoshacounty.org	Kenosha	WI	53140	262-653-2552	653-2564	338
Kenosha Medical Ctr 6308 Eigth Ave *Web:* www.froedtertsouth.com	Kenosha	WI	53143	262-656-2011		374-3
Kenosha Metal Products Inc 8121 - 104th St *Web:* www.kenosha-metal.com	Pleasant Prairie	WI	53158	262-947-8840	947-8845	488
Kenosha News 5800 Seventh Ave *TF:* 800-292-2700 ■ *Web:* www.kenoshanews.com	Kenosha	WI	53140	262-657-1000	657-8455	532-2
Kenosha Public Library 7979 38th Ave *Web:* www.mykpl.info	Kenosha	WI	53142	262-564-6100		434-3
Kenosha Public Museum 5500 First Ave *TF:* 888-258-9966 ■ *Web:* www.kenosha.org	Kenosha	WI	53140	262-653-4140	653-4437	520
Kenosha Tire Inc 6005 75th St *Web:* www.kenoshatireinc.com	Kenosha	WI	53142	262-694-3332	694-0412	755
Kenrick-Glennon Seminary 5200 Glennon Dr *Web:* kenrick.edu	Saint Louis	MO	63119	314-792-6100	792-6500	167-3
Kenron Industrial A/C Inc 299 Gregory St *Web:* www.kenron.com	Rochester	NY	14620	585-442-5600		189-10
Kens Reproductions Lllp 2220 Curtis St *Web:* www.kensrepro.com	Denver	CO	80205	303-297-9191		113
Kensai International Ltd 75 Nottingham Rd *Web:* www.kensai.net	Malverne	NY	11565	516-593-0480		174
Kensico Capital Management Corp 55 Railroad Ave 2nd Fl *Web:* www.kensicocapital.com	Greenwich	CT	06830	203-862-5800	862-5801	401
Kensico Cemetery Inc, The 273 Lakeview Ave *Web:* www.kensico.org	Valhalla	NY	10595	914-949-0347		510
Kensington Community Church 1825 E Sq Lake Rd *Web:* kensingtonchurch.org	Troy	MI	48085	248-786-0600		48-20
Kensington Computer Products Group 1500 Fashion Island Blvd 3rd Fl *TF:* 800-535-4242 ■ *Web:* www.kensington.com	Redwood City	CA	94065	866 602 0054		173-1
Kensington Furniture & Mattress 200 Tilton Rd *Web:* www.kensingtonfurniture.com	Northfield	NJ	08225	609-241-0807		321
Kensington Hotel, The 3500 S State St *TF:* 800-344-7829 ■ *Web:* www.kcourtaa.com	Ann Arbor	MI	48108	734-761-7800		379
Kensington International Inc 1515 W 22nd St Ste 500 *Web:* www.kionline.com	Oak Brook	IL	60523	630-571-0123		194
Kensington Park Hotel 450 Post St *TF:* 800-553-1900 ■ *Web:* www.kensingtonparkhotel.com	San Francisco	CA	94102	800-553-1900		379
Kensington Realty Advisors Inc 401 N Michigan Ave Ste 1200 *Web:* www.kra-net.com	Chicago	IL	60606	312-993-7800	993-7801	652
Kensington Valley Chamber of Commerce 58000 Grand River Ave *Web:* www.kensingtonvalleychamber.com	New Hudson	MI	48165	248-617-3075		139
KENS-TV Ch 5 (CBS) 5400 Fredericksburg Rd *Web:* www.kens5.com	San Antonio	TX	78229	210-366-5000		741-116
Kent & Mcbride PC 1617 Jfk Blvd Ste 1140 *Web:* kentmcbride.com	Philadelphia	PA	19103	215-568-1800		41
Kent Area Chamber of Commerce 176 E Main St Ste 303 *Web:* www.kentbiz.com	Kent	OH	44240	330-673-9855		139
Kent Chamber of Commerce 524 W Meeker St Ste 1 *TF:* 800-321-2808 ■ *Web:* kentchamber.com	Kent	WA	98032	253-854-1770	854-8567	139
Kent Corp 4446 Pinson Valley Pkwy *Web:* www.kentcorp.com	Birmingham	AL	35215	205-853-3420	449-5810	286
Kent County 400 High St *Web:* www.kentcounty.com	Chestertown	MD	21620	410-778-7435	778-7482	338
Kent County 555 S Bay Rd *Web:* www.co.kent.de.us	Dover	DE	19901	302-744-2305	736-2279	338
Kent County 300 Monroe Ave NW *Web:* www.accesskent.com	Grand Rapids	MI	49503	616-632-7640	632-7645	338
Kent County PO Box 9 *Web:* www.kentcountytexas.us	Jayton	TX	79528	806-237-3881	237-2300	338
Kent District Library 814 W River Center Dr NE *TF:* 877-243-2466 ■ *Web:* www.kdl.org	Comstock Park	MI	49321	616-784-2007	647-3908	434-3
Kent Elastomer Products Inc 1500 St Claire Ave *TF:* 800-331-4762 ■ *Web:* www.kentelastomer.com	Kent	OH	44240	330-673-1011	673-1351	676
Kent Falls State Park c/o Macedonia Brook State Pk 159 Macedonia Brook Rd *Web:* portal.ct.gov	Kent	CT	06757	860-927-3238		565
Kent Hospital 455 Toll Gate Rd *TF:* 800-892-9291 ■ *Web:* www.kentri.org	Warwick	RI	02886	401-737-7000		374-3
Kent Hotel 1131 Collins Ave *Web:* www.thekenthotel.com	Miami Beach	FL	33139	305-604-5068		379
Kent Quality Foods Inc 703 Leonard St NW *TF:* 800-748-0141 ■ *Web:* www.kqf.com	Grand Rapids	MI	49504	800-748-0141		296-26
Kent School PO Box 2006 *TF:* 800-538-5368 ■ *Web:* www.kent-school.edu	Kent	CT	06757	860-927-6111	927-6109	622
Kent Scientific Corp 1116 Litchfield St *Web:* www.kentscientific.com	Torrington	CT	06790	860-626-1172		407
Kent Security Services Inc 14600 Biscayne Blvd *TF:* 800-273-5368 ■ *Web:* www.kentsecurity.com	North Miami Beach	FL	33181	305-919-9400	919-9590	693
Kent Sporting Goods Company Inc 433 Park Ave S *Web:* www.kentwatersports.com	New London	OH	44851	419-929-1142	929-1769	710
Kent State University 800 E Summit St PO Box 5190 *TF:* 800-988-5368 ■ *Web:* www.kent.edu	Kent	OH	44242	330-672-3000	672-2499	166

Name / Address	City	State	Zip	Phone	Fax	Class
Kent State University						
Libraries 1125 Risman Dr	Kent	OH	44242	330-672-3456	672-4811	434-6
Web: www.library.kent.edu						
Kent State University Press, The						
1118 Library	Kent	OH	44242	330-672-7913	672-3104	637-9
Web: www.kentstateuniversitypress.com						
Kent Supply Co 50 Jon Barrett Rd	Patterson	NY	12563	845-878-6940		612
Web: www.kentsupply.com						
Kent Sussex Industries Inc						
301 N Rehoboth Blvd	Milford	DE	19963	302-422-4014	422-5848	88
Web: www.ksiinc.org						
Kentec Communications Inc						
710 W Main St	Sterling	CO	80751	970-522-8107		736
Web: www.kci.net						
Kentec Medical Inc 17871 Fitch	Irvine	CA	92614	949-863-0810	833-9730	475
TF: 800-825-5996 ■ *Web:* www.kentecmedical.com						
Kentfield Hospital						
1125 Sir Francis Drake Blvd	Kentfield	CA	94904	415-853-9499		374-6
Web: www.vibrahealthcare.com						
Kenton County 303 Ct St	Covington	KY	41011	859-392-1600		338
Web: www.kentoncounty.org						
Kenton County Public Library						
502 Scott Blvd	Covington	KY	41011	859-962-4060		434-3
Web: www.kentonlibrary.org						
Ken-Tool Co 768 E N St	Akron	OH	44305	330-535-7177	872-4929*	758
**Fax Area Code:* 800 ■ *Web:* www.kentool.com						
Ken-Tron Manufacturing Inc						
PO Box 21250	Owensboro	KY	42304	270-684-0431		488
TF: 800-872-9336 ■ *Web:* www.ken-tron.com						
Kents Hill School 1614 Main St	Kents Hill	ME	04349	207-685-4914	685-9529	622
Web: www.kentshill.org						
Kentuck Museum 503 Main Ave	Northport	AL	35476	205-758-1257		520
Web: www.kentuck.org						
Kentuckiana Trucking Inc						
380 Emery Ln	Clarksville	IN	47129	812-282-0908		780
TF: 888-288-8785 ■ *Web:* www.kentuckianatrucking.com						
Kentucky						
Accountancy Board						
332 W Broadway Ste 310	Louisville	KY	40202	502-595-3037	595-4500	339-18
Web: www.cpa.ky.gov						
Aging Services Office						
275 E Main St Ste 3E-E	Frankfort	KY	40621	502-564-6930	564-4595	339-18
Web: chfs.ky.gov						
Attorney General						
700 Capitol Ave Ste 118	Frankfort	KY	40601	502-696-5300	564-2894	339-18
Web: ag.ky.gov						
Bill Status 702 Capitol Ave Rm 405F	Frankfort	KY	40601	502-564-8100		433
Web: kentuckyhouserepublicans.org						
Child Support Div 730 Schenkel Ln	Frankfort	KY	40601	800-248-1163		339-18
TF: 800-248-1163 ■ *Web:* www.chfs.ky.gov						
Consumer Protection Div						
1024 Capital Center Dr Ste 200	Frankfort	KY	40601	502-696-5389	573-8317	339-18
TF: 888-432-9257 ■ *Web:* ag.ky.gov						
Correctional Institution for Women						
3000 Ash Ave	Pewee Valley	KY	40056	502-241-8454	243-0079	213
TF: 877-687-6818 ■ *Web:* www.corrections.ky.gov						
Corrections Dept						
275 E Main St PO Box 2400	Frankfort	KY	40602	502-564-4726	564-5037	339-18
Web: www.corrections.ky.gov						
Department of Revenue						
501 High St Sta 32	Frankfort	KY	40601	502-564-4581	564-3875	339-18
Web: www.revenue.ky.gov						
Education Dept 300 Sower Blvd 5th Fl	Frankfort	KY	40601	502-564-4770		339-18
Web: www.education.ky.gov						
Education Professional Standards Board						
100 Airport Dr 3rd Fl	Frankfort	KY	40601	502-564-4606	564-7080	339-18
TF: 888-598-7667 ■ *Web:* www.epsb.ky.gov						
Emergency Management Div						
100 Minuteman Pkwy	Frankfort	KY	40601	800-255-2587	607-1614*	339-18
**Fax Area Code:* 502 ■ *TF:* 800-255-2587 ■ *Web:* www.kyem.ky.gov						
Finance & Administration Cabinet						
Capitol Annex Rm 383	Frankfort	KY	40601	502-564-4240	564-6785	339-18
Web: www.finance.ky.gov						
Fish & Wildlife Resources Dept						
1 Sportsman's Ln	Frankfort	KY	40601	502-564-3400	564-9845	339-18
TF: 800-858-1549 ■ *Web:* www.fw.ky.gov						
Governor 700 Capital Ave Ste 100	Frankfort	KY	40601	502-564-2611	564-2517	339-18
Web: governor.ky.gov						
Governor's Office for Technology						
101 Cold Harbor Dr	Frankfort	KY	40601	502-564-1201		339-18
Web: www.technology.ky.gov						
Hairdressers & Cosmetologists Board						
111 St James Ct Ste A	Frankfort	KY	40601	502-564-4262	564-0481	339-18
Web: kbc.ky.gov						
Health & Family Services Cabinet						
275 E Main St	Frankfort	KY	40601	502-564-7042	564-7091	339-18
TF: 800-372-2973 ■ *Web:* chfs.ky.gov						
Higher Education Assistance Authority						
PO Box 798	Frankfort	KY	40602	800-928-8926		725
TF: 800-928-8926 ■ *Web:* www.kheaa.com						
Historical Society 100 W Broadway	Frankfort	KY	40601	502-564-1792		339-18
TF: 877-444-7867 ■ *Web:* history.ky.gov						
Horse Racing Authority						
4063 Iron Works Pkwy Bldg B	Lexington	KY	40511	859-246-2040	246-2039	712
Web: www.khrc.ky.gov						
Housing Corp 1231 Louisville Rd	Frankfort	KY	40601	502-564-7630		339-18
TF: 800-633-8896 ■ *Web:* www.kyhousing.org						
Labor Cabinet						
1047 Old US Hwy 127 S Ste 4	Frankfort	KY	40601	502-564-3070		339-18
Web: www.labor.ky.gov						
Legislative Ethics Commission						
22 Mill Creek Pk	Frankfort	KY	40601	502-573-2863	573-2929	265
Web: www.klec.ky.gov						
Medical Licensure Board						
310 Whittington Pkwy Ste 1B	Louisville	KY	40222	502-429-7150	429-7158	339-18
Web: www.kbml.ky.gov						
Parole Board PO Box 2400	Frankfort	KY	40602	502-564-3620	564-8995	339-18
TF: 800-221-5991 ■ *Web:* www.justice.ky.gov						
Postsecondary Education Council						
1024 Capital Center Dr Ste 320	Frankfort	KY	40601	502-573-1555	573-1535	339-18
Web: www.cpe.ky.gov						
Real Estate Commission						
Mayo-Underwood Bldg 500 Mero St 2NE09	Frankfort	KY	40601	502-564-7760	564-1538	339-18
TF: 888-373-3300 ■ *Web:* krec.ky.gov						
Secretary of State						
The Capitol Bldg 700 Capital Ave Ste 152	Frankfort	KY	40601	502-564-3490	564-5687	339-18
Web: www.sos.ky.gov						
State Capital 700 Capitol Ave	Frankfort	KY	40601	502-564-3449		339-18
Web: capitol.ky.gov						
State Government Information						
229 W Main St Ste 400	Frankfort	KY	40601	502-875-3733	875-3722	339-18
Web: www.kentucky.gov						
Supreme Court 700 Capitol Ave Rm 235	Frankfort	KY	40601	502-564-5444		339-18
Web: www.kentucky.gov						
Travel & Tourism Dept						
100 Airport Rd 2nd Fl	Frankfort	KY	40601	502-564-4930	564-5695	339-18
TF: 800-225-8747 ■ *Web:* www.kentuckytourism.com						
Treasury 1050 US Hwy 127 S Ste 100	Frankfort	KY	40601	502-564-4722	564-6545	339-18
Web: www.treasury.ky.gov						
Vehicle Regulation Div 200 Mero St	Frankfort	KY	40601	502-564-1257	696-3900	339-18
Web: drive.ky.gov						
Veterans Affairs Dept (KDVA)						
1111B Louisville Rd	Frankfort	KY	40601	502-564-9203	564-9240	339-18
TF: 800-572-6245 ■ *Web:* www.veterans.ky.gov						
Vital Statistics Div						
275 E Main St 3E-E	Frankfort	KY	40621	502-564-4212		339-18
Web: www.chfs.ky.gov						
Vocational Rehabilitation Dept						
275 E Main St	Frankfort	KY	40601	502-564-4440	564-6745	339-18
TF: 800-372-7172 ■ *Web:* www.kcc.ky.gov						
Kentucky Arts Council						
500 Mero St 5th Fl	Frankfort	KY	40601	502-564-3757	212-5393	339-18
TF: 888-833-2787 ■ *Web:* artscouncil.ky.gov						
Kentucky Association of Realtors						
2801 Palumbo Dr Ste 202	Lexington	KY	40509	859-263-7377	263-7565	656
TF: 800-264-2185 ■ *Web:* www.kyrealtors.com						
Kentucky Association of School Administrators						
87 C Michael Davenport Blvd	Frankfort	KY	40601	502-875-3411		78
TF: 800-928-5272 ■ *Web:* server.kasa.org						
Kentucky Bank PO Box 157	Paris	KY	40362	859-987-1795		70
TF: 800-467-1939 ■ *Web:* www.kybank.com						
Kentucky Bankers Assn						
600 W Main St Ste 400	Louisville	KY	40202	502-582-2453		533
TF: 800-392-4045 ■ *Web:* www.kybanks.com						
Kentucky Bar Assn 514 W Main St	Frankfort	KY	40601	502-564-3795	564-3225	72
Web: www.kybar.org						
Kentucky Blood Ctr						
3121 Beaumont Centre Cir	Lexington	KY	40513	859-276-2534	233-4166	89
TF: 800-775-2522 ■ *Web:* kybloodcenter.org						
Kentucky Bourbon Distillers Ltd						
1869 Loretto Rd	Bardstown	KY	40004	502-348-0899		80-1
Web: www.kentuckybourbonwhiskey.com						
Kentucky Center for African American Heritage						
1701 W Muhammad Ali Blvd	Louisville	KY	40203	502-583-4100		50-2
Web: www.kcaah.org						
Kentucky Center for Performing Arts, The						
501 W Main St	Louisville	KY	40202	502-562-0100		572
TF: 800-775-7777 ■ *Web:* www.kentuckyperformingarts.org						
Kentucky Chamber of Commerce						
464 Chenault Rd	Frankfort	KY	40601	502-695-4700		140
Web: www.kychamber.com						
Kentucky Christian University						
100 Academic Pkwy	Grayson	KY	41143	800-522-3181	474-3155*	166
**Fax Area Code:* 606 ■ *TF:* 800-522-3181 ■ *Web:* www.kcu.edu						
Kentucky Claims Commission						
130 Brighton Pk Blvd	Frankfort	KY	40601	502-573-2290	573-4817	339-18
TF: 800-469-2120 ■ *Web:* kycc.ky.gov						
Kentucky Correctional Industries						
1041 Leestown Rd	Frankfort	KY	40601	502-573-1040	573-1050	630
TF: 800-828-9524 ■ *Web:* www.kci.ky.gov						
Kentucky Democratic Party						
PO Box 694	Frankfort	KY	40602	502-695-4828	695-7629	616-1
TF: 800-995-3386 ■ *Web:* kydemocrats.org						
Kentucky Department for Libraries & Archives						
300 Coffee Tree Rd	Frankfort	KY	40602	502-564-8300	564-5773	434-5
TF: 800-372-2968 ■ *Web:* www.kdla.ky.gov						
Kentucky Derby Museum						
704 Central Ave	Louisville	KY	40208	502-637-1111	636-5855	520
TF: 800-593-3729 ■ *Web:* www.derbymuseum.org						
Kentucky Downs LLC						
5629 Nashville Rd PO Box 405	Franklin	KY	42134	270-586-7778		642
Web: www.kentuckydowns.com						
Kentucky Educational Television (KET)						
600 Cooper Dr	Lexington	KY	40502	859-258-7000		741
TF: 800-432-0951 ■ *Web:* www.ket.org						
Kentucky Electronics Inc						
222 Riggs Ave	Portland	TN	37148	615-325-4127	325-3108	757
Web: www.precind.com						
Kentucky Enquirer 226 Grandview Dr	Covington	KY	41017	859-578-5500		532-2
Web: www.kentucky.gov						
Kentucky Exposition Ctr						
937 Phillips Ln	Louisville	KY	40209	502-367-5000	367-5139	720
Web: www.kyexpo.org						
Kentucky Farm Bureau						
9201 Bunsen Pkwy	Louisville	KY	40220	502-495-5000		276
Web: www.kyfb.com						
Kentucky Farmers Bank 6313 US Rte 60	Ashland	KY	41102	606-929-5000		70
Web: www.kfb.bank						
Kentucky Highlands Investment Corp						
362 Old Whitley Rd PO Box 1738	London	KY	40743	606-864-5175	864-5194	402
Web: www.khic.org						
Kentucky Horse Park						
4089 Iron Works Pkwy	Lexington	KY	40511	859-233-4303	254-0253	823
TF: 800-678-8813 ■ *Web:* www.kyhorsepark.com						
Kentucky Hospital Assn						
2501 Nelson Miller Pkwy	Louisville	KY	40223	502-426-6220		533
TF: 888-393-7353 ■ *Web:* www.kyha.com						

Name / Address	City	State	ZIP	Phone	Fax	Class
Kentucky International Convention Ctr						
221 S 4th St	Louisville	KY	40202	502-595-4381		205
TF: 800-701-5831 ■ *Web:* kyconvention.com						
Kentucky Lottery Corp						
1011 W Main St	Louisville	KY	40202	877-789-4532		452
Web: www.kylottery.com						
Kentucky Machine & Engineering Inc						
590 Glenwood Mill Rd	Cadiz	KY	42211	270-522-6061	522-8097	454
Web: www.kymachine.com						
Kentucky Medical Assn						
9300 Shelbyville Rd Ste 850	Louisville	KY	40222	502-426-6200	426-6877	474
Web: kyma.org						
Kentucky Mountain Bible College						
855 Hwy 541	Jackson	KY	41339	606-693-5000		161
TF: 800-879-5622 ■ *Web:* www.kmbc.edu						
Kentucky Museum of Art & Craft						
715 W Main St	Louisville	KY	40202	502-589-0102		50-2
Web: www.kmacmuseum.org						
Kentucky National Insurance Co						
2416 Sir Barton Way	Lexington	KY	40509	800-432-9310	367-5293*	390
**Fax Area Code:* 859 ■ *Web:* www.kynatins.com						
Kentucky New Era Inc						
1618 E Ninth St PO Box 729	Hopkinsville	KY	42240	270-887-3255		532-3
Web: kentuckynewera.com						
Kentucky Oil & Refining Co						
156 Kentucky Oil Vlg	Betsy Layne	KY	41605	606-478-9501		581
Web: teamkore.com						
Kentucky Opera Assn						
323 W Broadway Ste 601	Louisville	KY	40202	502-584-4500	561-7941	573-2
Web: kyopera.org						
Kentucky Organ Donor Affiliates (KODA)						
10160 Linn Station Rd	Louisville	KY	40223	502-581-9511	589-5157	545
TF: 800-525-3456 ■ *Web:* donatelifeky.org						
Kentucky Pharmacists Assn						
96 C Michael Davenport Blvd	Frankfort	KY	40601	502-227-2303	227-2258	585
Web: www.kphanet.org						
Kentucky Press Assn 101 Consumer Ln	Frankfort	KY	40601	502-223-8821	226-3867	624
TF: 800-264-5721 ■ *Web:* www.kypress.com						
Kentucky Republican Party						
PO Box 1068	Frankfort	KY	40602	502-875-5130	223-5625	616-2
Web: www.rpk.org						
Kentucky Science & Technology Corp						
200 W Vine St Ste 420	Lexington	KY	40507	859-233-3502		244
Web: www.kstc.com						
Kentucky Simpson County Clerk						
103 W Cedar St	Franklin	KY	42134	270-586-8161	586-6464	338
Web: www.simpsoncountyclerk.ky.gov						
Kentucky Speedway 1 Speedway Blvd	Sparta	KY	41086	859-578-2300	647-4307	515
TF: 888-652-7223 ■ *Web:* www.kentuckyspeedway.com						
Kentucky State Parks						
Jenny Wiley State Resort Park						
75 Theatre Ct	Prestonsburg	KY	41653	606-889-1790		565
TF: 800-325-0142 ■ *Web:* www.parks.ky.gov						
Kentucky State Reformatory						
3001 W Hwy 146	LaGrange	KY	40032	502-222-9441		213
Web: www.corrections.ky.gov						
Kentucky State University						
400 E Main St	Frankfort	KY	40601	502-597-6000	597-5814	166
TF: 800-325-1716 ■ *Web:* kysu.edu						
Kentucky Symphony Orchestra						
540 Linden Ave PO Box 72810	Newport	KY	41072	859-431-6216	431-3097	573-3
Web: kyso.org						
Kentucky Theater 214 E Main St	Lexington	KY	40507	859-231-7924		572
Web: www.kentuckytheater.com						
Kentucky Trailer 7201 Logistics Dr	Louisville	KY	40258	502-637-2551		779
TF: 800-463-6126 ■ *Web:* www.kytrailer.com						
Kentucky Veterinary Medical Assn						
108 Consumer Ln	Frankfort	KY	40601	502-226-5862	226-6177	795
TF: 800-552-5862 ■ *Web:* www.kvma.org						
Kentucky Wesleyan College						
3000 Frederica St	Owensboro	KY	42301	270-852-3120	852-3133	166
TF: 800-999-0592 ■ *Web:* kwc.edu						
Kentwood Office Furniture Inc						
3063 Breton Rd SE	Grand Rapids	MI	49512	616-957-2320		320
TF: 877-698-6250 ■ *Web:* www.kentwoodoffice.com						
Kentwood Public Schools						
5820 Eastern Ave	Kentwood	MI	49508	616-455-4400	455-4920	685
Web: www.kentwoodps.org						
KentWool 135 S Main St Ste 800	Greenville	SC	29601	877-577-6769	878-2723*	745-9
**Fax Area Code:* 864 ■ *Web:* www.kentwool.com						
Kenvirons Inc 452 Versailles Rd	Frankfort	KY	40601	502-695-4357	695-4363	261
Web: www.kenvirons.com						
Kenwal Steel Corp 8223 W Warren Ave	Dearborn	MI	48126	313-739-1000	739-1001	492
Web: www.kenwal.com						
Kenway Corp 681 Riverside Dr	Augusta	ME	04330	207-622-6229	622-6611	596
Web: www.kenway.com						
Kenway Distributors Inc						
6320 Strawberry Ln	Louisville	KY	40214	502-367-2201	368-5519	406
TF: 800-292-9478 ■ *Web:* www.kenway.net						
Kenwel Printers Inc						
4272 Indianola Ave	Columbus	OH	43214	614-261-1011	268-3299	627
Web: kenwelprinters.com						
Kenwood & Associates PC						
1 Sugar Creek Blvd Ste 300	Sugar Land	TX	77478	281-243-2300		2
Web: kenwoodpc.com						
Kenwood Publishing Group						
11060 Kenwood Rd	Cincinnati	OH	45242	513-793-6256		637-2
Web: m25m.org						
Kenwood Towne Ctr						
7875 Montgomery Rd	Cincinnati	OH	45236	513-745-9100		460
Web: www.kenwoodtownecentre.com						
Kenwood USA PO Box 22745	Long Beach	CA	90810	310-639-9000		647
TF: 800-536-9663 ■ *Web:* www.kenwood.com						
Kenworth Northwest Inc						
20220 International Blvd S	SeaTac	WA	98198	206-433-5911	878-7676	57
TF: 800-562-0060 ■ *Web:* www.papekwnw.com						
Kenworth of Indianapolis Inc						
2929 S Holt Rd	Indianapolis	IN	46241	317-247-8421	241-5742	57
TF: 800-827-8421 ■ *Web:* www.palmertrucks.com						

Name / Address	City	State	ZIP	Phone	Fax	Class
Kenworth Sales Co						
2125 Constitution Blvd	West Valley City	UT	84119	801-487-4161		780
TF: 800-222-7831 ■ *Web:* www.kenworthsalesco.com						
Kenworth Truck Co 10630 NE 38th Pl	Kirkland	WA	98033	425-828-5000		516
Web: kenworth.com						
Kenya Embassy 2249 R St NW	Washington	DC	20008	202-387-6101	462-3829	257
Web: kenyaembassydc.org						
Kenya Tourism Board						
6033 W Century Blvd Ste 900	Los Angeles	CA	90045	310-649-7718	914-6946*	775
**Fax Area Code:* 952 ■ *TF:* 800-223-6486 ■ *Web:* www.magicalkenya.com						
Kenyon College 103 College Dr	Gambier	OH	43022	740-427-5000	427-5770	166
TF: 800-848-2468 ■ *Web:* www.kenyon.edu						
Kenyon Disend PLLC 11 Front St S	Issaquah	WA	98027	425-392-7090		41
Web: kenyondisend.com						
Kenyon Plastering Inc						
4001 W Indian School Rd	Phoenix	AZ	85019	602-233-1191	278-6801	550
Web: www.kenyonweb.com						
Kenyon Press Inc						
1 Kenyon Press Dr PO Box 710	Sherburne	NY	13460	607-674-9066	674-4952	627
Web: www.kenyonpress.net						
Kenzer Group LLC 1 Penn Plz Ste 6300	New York	NY	10119	212-308-4300	534-6280*	266
**Fax Area Code:* 917 ■ *Web:* www.kenzer.com						
KEOGH Consulting Inc						
10217 Brecksville Rd	Brecksville	OH	44141	440-526-2002	526-9466	196
Web: keogh1.com						
Keogh, Cox & Wilson Ltd						
701 Main St	Baton Rouge	LA	70821	225-383-3796		41
Web: keoghcox.com						
Keokuk Area Chamber of Commerce						
511 Blondeau St Ste 3	Keokuk	IA	52632	319-524-5055	524-5016	139
Web: keokukchamber.com						
Keokuk County 101 S Main	Sigourney	IA	52591	641-622-2721	622-2171	338
Web: keokukcountyia.com						
Keokuk National Cemetery 1701 J St	Keokuk	IA	52632	319-524-1304	524-8118	136
Web: www.cem.va.gov						
Keough & Moody PC 114 E Van Buren	Naperville	IL	60540	630-369-2700		41
Web: kmlegal.com						
Keowee-Toxaway State Natural Area						
108 Residence Dr	Sunset	SC	29685	864-868-2605		565
Web: southcarolinaparks.com						
Kepco Inc 131-38 Sanford Ave	Flushing	NY	11355	718-461-7000	767-1102	253
TF: 800-526-2324 ■ *Web:* www.kepcopower.com						
Kepler Group LLC 6 E 32nd St 9th Fl	New York	NY	10016	646-524-6896		5
Web: www.keplergrp.com						
Kepler Press PO Box 400326	Cambridge	MA	02140	617-576-1577		637-2
Web: www.keplerpress.com						
Kepner Plastics Fabricators Inc						
3131 Lomita Blvd	Torrance	CA	90505	310-325-3162	326-8560	600
Web: www.kepnerplastics.com						
Kepner Products Co						
995 N Ellsworth Ave	Villa Park	IL	60181	630-279-1550	279-9669	790
Web: www.kepner.com						
Kepner-Tregoe Inc PO Box 704	Princeton	NJ	08542	609-921-2806	497-0130	194
TF: 800-537-6378 ■ *Web:* www.kepner-tregoe.com						
Keppel Union School District						
34004 128th St E PO Box 186	Pearblossom	CA	93553	661-944-2155	944-2933	685
Web: kusd-ca.schoolloop.com						
Keppler Speakers						
3030 Clarendon Blvd	Arlington	VA	22201	703-516-4000	516-4819	708
Web: www.kepplerspeakers.com						
KEPR-TV 2807 W Lewis St	Pasco	WA	99301	509-547-0547	547-2845	647
Web: www.keprtv.com						
Kepware Inc 400 Congress St 4th Fl	Portland	ME	04101	207-775-1660		177
Web: www.kepware.com						
Ker & Downey Inc 6703 Hwy Blvd	Katy	TX	77494	281-371-2500	371-2514	760
TF: 800-423-4236 ■ *Web:* kerdowney.com						
KERA-FM 90.1 (NPR)						
3000 Harry Hines Blvd	Dallas	TX	75201	214-871-1390	754-0635	645-43
TF: 800-456-5372 ■ *Web:* www.kera.org						
KERAMIDA Inc 401 N College Ave	Indianapolis	IN	46202	317-685-6600		192
TF: 800-508-8034 ■ *Web:* www.keramida.com						
Kerasotes ShowPlace Theatres LLC						
1011 S Delano Ct	Chicago	IL	60605	312-447-6304		748
Web: www.showplaceicon.com						
Keres Consulting Inc						
2700 San Pedro Dr NE	Albuquerque	NM	87110	505-837-2104	837-0575	196
Web: www.keresnm.com						
Kerkau Manufacturing Co						
1321 S Valley Center Dr	Bay City	MI	48706	989-686-0350	686-0399	483
TF: 800-248-5060 ■ *Web:* www.kerkau.com						
Kerkstra Precast Inc 3373 Busch Dr	Grandville	MI	49418	616-224-6176		106
Web: www.kerkstra.com						
Kerley & Sears Inc						
4331 Cement Valley Rd	Midlothian	TX	76065	972-775-3902		791
TF: 800-346-4381 ■ *Web:* www.kerleyandsears.com						
Kerley Ink Engineers Inc						
2700 S 12th Ave	Broadview	IL	60155	708-344-1295	865-5759	388
Web: www.kerleyink.com						
Kerlin Capital Group LLC						
624 S Grand Ave Ste 2450	Los Angeles	CA	90071	213-627-3300	094-7107	401
Web: www.kerlincapital.com						
Kern & Associates Ltd						
5421 Kietzke Ln Ste 200	Reno	NV	89511	775-324-5930		41
Web: kernltd.com						
Kern Community College District						
2100 Chester Ave	Bakersfield	CA	93301	661-336-5100		167
Web: www.kccd.edu						
Kern County						
1115 Truxtun Ave 5th Fl	Bakersfield	CA	93301	661-868-3198	868-3190	338
Web: www.kerncounty.com						
Kern County Board of Trade						
2101 Oak St	Bakersfield	CA	93301	661-868-5376	861-2017	139
Web: www.ridgecrestchamber.com						
Kern County High School District						
5801 Sundale Ave	Bakersfield	CA	93309	661-827-3100		685
Web: www.kernhigh.org						
Kern County Museum						
3801 Chester Ave	Bakersfield	CA	93301	661-437-3330		520
Web: kerncountymuseum.org						

Name	Address	Phone	Fax	Class
Kern Health Systems	9700 Stockdale Hwy Bakersfield CA 93311 *TF:* 888-466-2219 ■ *Web:* www.kernfamilyhealthcare.com	661-664-5000		231
Kern Meat Company Inc	2225 Cherokee St Saint Louis MO 63118 *Web:* www.kernmeatco.com	314-664-4467		297-9
Kern Medical Ctr	1700 Mt Vernon Ave Bakersfield CA 93306 *Web:* www.kernmedical.com	661-326-2000	326-2969	374-3
Kern Oil & Refining Co	7724 E Panama Ln Bakersfield CA 93307 *Web:* kernoil.com	661-845-0761		579
Kern Organization Inc	20955 Warner Center Ln Woodland Hills CA 91367 *Web:* kernagency.com	818-703-8775		4
Kern River Gas Transmission Co	2755 E Cottonwood Pkwy Ste 300 Salt Lake City UT 84121 *TF:* 800-420-7500 ■ *Web:* www.kernrivergas.com	801-937-6000		325
Kern Steel Fabrication Inc	627 Williams St Bakersfield CA 93305 *Web:* www.kernsteel.com	661-327-9588		480
Kern Valley Museum	49 Big Blue Rd PO Box 651 Kernville CA 93238 *Web:* kernvalleymuseum.org	760-376-6683		520
Kernel Press Inc	026 Grehan Journalism Bldg Lexington KY 40506 *Web:* www.kykernel.com	859-257-1915		532-2
Kerneos Inc	1316 Priority Ln Chesapeake VA 23324 *Web:* www.kerneosinc.com	757-284-3200		135
Kern-Liebers USA Inc	1510 Albon Rd Holland OH 43528 *Web:* www.kern-liebers.com	419-865-2437	865-2738	719
Kernodle Clinic Inc	1234 Huffman Mill Rd Burlington NC 27215 *Web:* www.kernodle.com	336-538-1234		374-3
Kerns Manufacturing Corp	37-14 29th St Long Island City NY 11101 *Web:* www.kernsmfg.com	718-784-4044	786-0534	488
Kernutt Stokes LLP	1600 Executive Pkwy Eugene OR 97401 *Web:* kernuttstokes.com	541-687-1170		2
KERO-TV Ch 23 (ABC)	321 21st St Bakersfield CA 93301 *Web:* www.turnto23.com	661-637-2323	323-5538	741-10
Kerr County	700 Main St Rm 122 Kerrville TX 78028 *Web:* www.co.kerr.tx.us	830-792-2255	792-2274	338
Kerr Lake State Recreation Area	6254 Satterwhite Pt Rd Henderson NC 27537 *Web:* www.ncparks.gov	252-438-7791		565
Kerr Lakeside Inc	26841 Tungsten Rd Euclid OH 44132 *TF:* 800-487-5377 ■ *Web:* www.kerrlakeside.com	216-261-2100	261-9798	621
Kerr Paper & Supply	6701 Interstate 30 Little Rock AR 72209 *Web:* www.kerrpaper.com	501-562-0005		559
Kerr Pump & Supply	12880 Cloverdale St Oak Park MI 48237 *TF:* 800-482-8259 ■ *Web:* www.kerrpump.com	248-543-3880	543-3236	641
Kerrington Group Inc	24 S Fifth St Fernandina Beach FL 32034 *Web:* www.kerringtongroup.com	904-491-1411	491-1414	180
Kerrville Chamber of Commerce	1700 Sidney Baker St Ste 100 Kerrville TX 78028 *Web:* www.kerrvilletx.com	830-896-1155	896-1175	139
Kerrville Convention & Visitors Bureau	2108 Sidney Baker St Kerrville TX 78028 *TF:* 800-221-7958 ■ *Web:* www.kerrvilletexascvb.com	830-792-3535	792-3230	206
Kerrville State Hospital	721 Thompson Dr Kerrville TX 78028 *Web:* www.dshs.texas.gov	830-896-2211	792-4926	374-5
Kerry Company Inc, The	3003 Wildwood Sample Rd Allison Park PA 15101 *Web:* kerrydocks.com	412-486-3388	486-7449	223
Kerry Group LLC, The	44 Soccer Park Rd Fenton MO 63026 *Web:* www.kerrygroup.net	636-203-5550		184
Kerrytown Concert House	415 N Fourth Ave Ann Arbor MI 48104 *Web:* www.kerrytownconcerthouse.com	734-769-2999		572
Kershaw Correctional Institution	4848 Gold Mine Hwy Kershaw SC 29067 *Web:* www.doc.sc.gov	803-475-5770		213
Kershaw County	1121 Broad St Rm 202 Camden SC 29020 *Web:* www.kershaw.sc.gov	803-425-7226	425-6044	338
Kershaw County Chamber of Commerce	607 S Broad St Camden SC 29020 *TF:* 800-968-4037 ■ *Web:* www.kershawcountychamber.org	803-432-2525	432-4181	139
Kershaw County School District	2029 W DeKalb St Camden SC 29020 *Web:* www.kcsdschools.net	803-432-8416	425-8918	685
KershawHealth Medical Ctr	1315 Roberts St Camden SC 29020 *Web:* www.kershawhealth.org	803-432-4311		374-3
Kershaw-Ryan State Park	PO Box 985 Caliente NV 89008 *Web:* parks.nv.gov	775-726-3564		565
Kerton Group	7901 Stoneridge Dr Ste 507 Pleasanton CA 94588 *Web:* www.kertongroup.com	408-935-8702		193
Kerusso Inc	402 Hwy 62 Spur Berryville AR 72616 *TF:* 800-424-0943 ■ *Web:* www.kerusso.com	870-423-6242		687
Kerzner International Ltd	31 Hudson Yards 11th Fl New York NY 10001 *Web:* www.kerzner.com	929-279-4096		132
Kesler-Schaefer Auto Auction Inc	5333 W 46th St PO Box 53203 Indianapolis IN 46254 *TF:* 800-959-5722 ■ *Web:* www.ksaa1.com	317-297-2300	297-6234	516
Kesling Home Health Care	1115 W Market St Logansport IN 46947 *Web:* www.keslinghomehealthcare.com	574-735-0082	753-3910	475
Kesluk, Silverstein & Jacob	9255 Sunset Blvd Ste 411 Los Angeles CA 90069 *Web:* californialaborlawattorney.com	310-273-3180		41
Kesner, Godes & Morrissey LLC	15 Pacella Park Dr Ste 200 Randolph MA 02368 *Web:* www.kgmcpa.com	781-961-2900	961-2927	2
KESQ-TV Ch 3 (ABC)	31276 Dunham Way Thousand Palms CA 92276 *Web:* www.kesq.com	760-773-0342	343-3512	741
Kesselman Jones	3411 Candelaria Rd NE Ste G Albuquerque NM 87107 *TF:* 866-219-4582 ■ *Web:* www.kessjones.com	505-266-3461		195
Kesselrun	8215 Roswell Rd Ste 925 Atlanta GA 30350 *TF:* 800-420-6687 ■ *Web:* www.kesselrunconsulting.com	800-420-6687		463
Kessington Aerospace	1020 County Rd 6 W Elkhart IN 46514 *Web:* www.kessington.com	574-266-4500	266-8899	454
Kessler & Associates Inc	31800 NW Hwy Farmington Hills MI 48334 *Web:* kesslercpa.com	248-855-4224	855-4405	194
Kessler Chemical Inc	77 W Broad St Bethlehem PA 18018 *TF:* 844-758-9602 ■ *Web:* www.kesslerchemical.com	610-758-9602	758-9615	146
Kessler Collection, The	4901 Vineland Rd Ste 650 Orlando FL 32811 *Web:* www.kesslercollection.com	407-996-9999	996-9998	379
Kessler Crane Inc	1901 Western Ave Plymouth IN 46563 *Web:* www.kesslercrane.com	574-936-3341		344
Kessler Industries	8600 Gateway Blvd E El Paso TX 79907 *Web:* www.kesslerind.com	915-591-8161	598-7353	319-2
Kessler Sign Co	5804 Poe Ave Dayton OH 45414 *TF:* 800-686-1870 ■ *Web:* www.kesslersignco.com	937-898-0633		701
Kessler's Food & Liquor	615 Sixth Ave SE Aberdeen SD 57401 *Web:* kesslersgrocery.com	605-225-1692		345
Kessler's Inc	1201 Hummel Ave Lemoyne PA 17043 *Web:* www.kesslerfoods.com	717-763-7162	763-4982	296-26
Kestenbaum & Mark	40 Cutter Mill Rd Great Neck NY 11021 *Web:* kmtaxlaw.com	516-466-0410	829-3729	41
Kester Inc	800 W Thorndale Ave Itasca IL 60143 *TF:* 800-253-7837 ■ *Web:* www.kester.com	630-616-4048	616-4044	145
Kestrel Consulting Ltd	1415 7th St W Saint Paul MN 55102 *TF:* 877-954-7818 ■ *Web:* www.kcl-group.com	952-903-0676	903-0678	631
Kestrel Institute	3260 Hillview Ave Palo Alto CA 94304 *Web:* kestrel.edu	650-493-6871	424-1807	177
Kestrel Labs Inc	3133 Indian Rd Ste K Boulder CO 80301 *Web:* www.kestrellabs.com	303-544-0660		177
Keswick Hall	701 Club Dr Keswick VA 22947 *Web:* www.keswick.com	434-979-3440		379
Keswick Multi-Care Ctr	700 W 40th St Baltimore MD 21211 *Web:* choosekeswick.org	410-235-8860	662-4324	450
KET (Kentucky Educational Television)	600 Cooper Dr Lexington KY 40502 *TF:* 800-432-0951 ■ *Web:* www.ket.org	859-258-7000		741
Ketcher & Company Inc	1717 E 5th North Little Rock AR 72114 *Web:* www.ketcherco.com	501-372-5216		189-12
Ketchikan Correctional Ctr	1201 Schoenbar Rd Ketchikan AK 99901 *Web:* www.correct.state.ak.us	907-228-7350	225-7031	213
Ketchikan Gateway Borough	1900 1st Ave Ste 118 Ketchikan AK 99901 *Web:* www.borough.ketchikan.ak.us	907-228-6620		338
Ketchikan Integrated Support Command	1300 Stedman St Ketchikan AK 99901 *Web:* www.uscg.mil	907-228-0340		158
Ketchikan Visitors Bureau	131 Front St Ketchikan AK 99901 *TF:* 800-770-3300 ■ *Web:* visit-ketchikan.com	907-225-6166	225-4250	206
Ketchmark & Associates Inc	145 Tower Dr Burr Ridge IL 60527	630-850-7774		261
Ketchum	1285 Avenue of the Americas New York NY 10019 *Web:* www.ketchum.com	646-935-3900		636
KETC-TV Ch 9 (PBS)	3655 Olive St Saint Louis MO 63108 *TF:* 855-482-5382 ■ *Web:* www.ninenet.org	314-512-9000	512-9005	741-114
Ketek Industries Ltd	20204 - 110 Ave NW Edmonton AB T5S1X8 *Web:* ketek.ca	780-447-5050		539
Ketron Optimization	45573 Shepard Dr Ste 201 Sterling VA 20164 *Web:* www.ketronms.com	703-636-4805		194
Kett Engineering Corp	15500 Erwin St Ste 1029 Van Nuys CA 91411 *Web:* www.ketteng.com	818-908-5388		743
Kettering College	3737 Southern Blvd Kettering OH 45429 *TF:* 800-433-5262 ■ *Web:* www.kc.edu	937-395-8601		167-3
Kettering Foundation (KF)	200 Commons Rd Dayton OH 45459 *TF:* 800-221-3657 ■ *Web:* kettering.org	937-434-7300		637-2
Kettering Health Network Credit Union	7740 Paragon Rd Dayton OH 45459 *Web:* khnetworkcu.com	937-558-9070		219
Kettering University	1700 University Ave Flint MI 48504 *TF:* 800-955-4464 ■ *Web:* www.kettering.edu	810-762-9500	762-9837	166
Kettering-Moraine-Oakwood Area Chamber of Commerce	2977 Far Hills Ave Kettering OH 45419 *TF:* 800-621-8931 ■ *Web:* www.kmo-coc.org	937-299-3852	299-3851	139
Kettle Creek State Park	97 Kettle Creek Pk Ln Renovo PA 17764 *Web:* www.dcnr.pa.gov	570-923-6004		565
Kettle Moraine Correctional Institution	PO Box 31 Plymouth WI 53073 *Web:* www.doc.wi.gov	920-526-3244	526-9320	213
Kettle Moraine State Forest - Northern Unit	N1765 Hwy G Campbellsport WI 53010 *Web:* dnr.wi.gov	262-626-2116		565

Name / Address	City	State	Zip	Phone	Fax	Class
Kettle Moraine State Forest - Pike Lake Unit 3544 Kettle Moraine Rd *Web:* dnr.wi.gov	Hartford	WI	53027	262-665-9780	670-3411	565
Kettle Moraine State Forest - Southern Unit S91 W39091 Hwy 59 *Web:* dnr.wi.gov	Eagle	WI	53119	262-594-6200		565
Kettle Moraine State Forest-Lapham Peak Unit W329 N846 County Hwy C *Web:* dnr.wi.gov	Delafield	WI	53018	262-646-3025		565
Kettler 8255 Greensboro Dr Ste 200 *TF:* 833-407-6280 ■ *Web:* www.kettler.com	McLean	VA	22102	703-641-9000	641-9630	653
Kettletown State Park 1400 Georges Hill Rd *Web:* portal.ct.gov	Southbury	CT	06488	203-264-5678		565
KETV-TV Ch 7 (ABC) 2665 Douglas St *TF:* 800-279-5388 ■ *Web:* www.ketv.com	Omaha	NE	68131	402-345-7777		741-94
Keuka College 141 Central Ave *Web:* www.keuka.edu	Keuka Park	NY	14478	315-279-5254	536-5386	166
Keuka Lake State Park 3560 Pepper Rd *Web:* parks.ny.gov	Keuka Park	NY	14478	315-536-3666		565
Keurig Dr Pepper Inc 53 S Ave *TF:* 866-901-2739 ■ *Web:* www.keurig.com	Burlington	MA	01803	866-901-2739		102
Keusch Glass Inc 403 E 23rd St *TF:* 800-677-2637 ■ *Web:* www.keuschglass.com	Jasper	IN	47546	812-482-2566	482-9635	191-2
Kevco Building Services Inc 7610 T Rickenbacker Dr **Fax Area Code:* 301 ■ *TF:* 800-315-3444 ■ *Web:* www.kevco1.com	Gaithersburg	MD	20879	800-315-3444	840-0790*	612
Kevin Ahrenholz Law Firm 620 Lafayette St Ste 300 *Web:* www.beecherlaw.com	Waterloo	IA	50703	319-433-0754		445
Kevin Guest House 782 Ellicott St *Web:* kevinguesthouse.com	Buffalo	NY	14203	716-882-1818	882-1291	372
Kevin J. Goering CPA PA 2201 W 25th St *Web:* goeringcpa.com	Lawrence	KS	66047	785-832-8300	832-0901	2
Kevin Panter Insurance Inc PO Box 1198 *Web:* kevinpanterinsurance.com	Blue Ridge	GA	30513	706-632-3400		390
KEVN Black Hills Fox 2001 Skyline Dr *Web:* www.blackhillsfox.com	Rapid City	SD	57701	605-394-7777		741-106
KEVU-TV 2940 Chad Dr *Web:* www.oregonsfox.com	Eugene	OR	97408	541-683-3434		647
Kewanna Metal Specialties Inc (KMS) 419 W Main St PO Box 367 *Web:* www.kmswire.com	Kewanna	IN	46939	574-653-2554	653-2556	73
Kewaskum Frozen Foods Inc 118 Forest Ave *Web:* www.kewaskumfrozenfoods.com	Kewaskum	WI	53040	262-626-2181	626-2183	297-9
Kewaunee County 613 Dodge St *Web:* www.kewauneeco.org	Kewaunee	WI	54216	920-388-7144		338
Kewaunee Fabrications 520 N Main St *Web:* www.kewauneefabrications.com	Kewaunee	WI	54216	920-388-2000	388-0263	454
Kewaunee Scientific Corp 2700 W Front St PO Box 1842 *NASDAQ:* KEQU ■ *TF:* 800-824-6626 ■ *Web:* www.kewaunee.com	Statesville	NC	28687	704-873-7202	873-5160	420
Keweenaw Bay Indian Community 16429 Bear Town Rd *Web:* www.kbic-nsn.gov	Baraga	MI	49908	906-353-6623		452
Keweenaw Bay Ojibwa Community College 111 Beartown Rd *Web:* www.kbocc.org	Baraga	MI	49908	906-353-4600	353-8107	165
Keweenaw County 902 College Ave *Web:* www.keweenaw.org	Houghton	MI	49931	906-482-5240		338
Keweenaw Financial Corp 235 Quincy St *TF:* 866-482-0404 ■ *Web:* www.snb-t.com	Hancock	MI	49930	906-482-0404	482-4403	360-2
Keweenaw National Historical Park 25970 Red Jacket Rd PO Box 471 *Web:* www.nps.gov	Calumet	MI	49913	906-337-3168	337-3169	564
Keweenaw Research Ctr 1400 Townsend Dr *Web:* www.mtukrc.org	Houghton	MI	49931	906-487-2750	487-2202	668
KEWF-FM Radio Billings LLC 222 N 32nd St 10th Fl *Web:* 985thewolf.com	Billings	MT	59101	406-238-1000		645-18
Kewin Consulting 62 Twenty Seventh St *Web:* www.kewin.ca	Toronto	ON	M8W2X4	416-802-2526		463
KEXA-FM 548 E Alisal St PO Box 1939 *Web:* www.wolfhouseradio.net	Salinas	CA	93905	831-757-1910		647
KEXL-FM 309 Braasch Ave PO Box 789 *Web:* norfolkdailynews.com	Norfolk	NE	68701	402-371-0780		647
Key Arena 305 Harrison St *Web:* www.seattlecenter.com	Seattle	WA	98109	206-684-7202		720
Key Bank 65 Dutch Hill Rd *TF:* 800-539-2968 ■ *Web:* www.key.com	Orangeburg	NY	10962	845-398-2280		70
Key Bellevilles Inc 100 Key Ln *TF:* 800-245-3600 ■ *Web:* www.keybellevilles.com	Leechburg	PA	15656	724-295-5111		492
Key Blue Prints Inc 195 E Livingston Ave *Web:* www.key-evidence.com	Columbus	OH	43215	614-228-3285		113
Key Cadillac Inc 6825 York Ave S *TF:* 800-235-3182 ■ *Web:* www.keycadillac.com	Edina	MN	55435	952-920-4300		57
Key Club Intl 3636 Woodview Trace *TF:* 800-549-2647 ■ *Web:* www.keyclub.org	Indianapolis	IN	46268	317-875-8755	879-0204	48-15
Key College 225 E Dania Beach Blvd *TF:* 877-421-6149 ■ *Web:* www.keycollege.edu	Dania Beach	FL	33004	954-246-4529	923-9226	167-3
Key Computing 85 Sea Ln *Web:* keycomputing.com	Farmingdale	NY	11735	631-264-0660	760-8316	225
Key Construction Inc 741 W Second *TF:* 800-280-9515 ■ *Web:* www.keyconstruction.com	Wichita	KS	67203	316-263-9515		186
Key Container Corp 21 Campbell St *TF:* 800-343-8811 ■ *Web:* keycontainercorp.com	Pawtucket	RI	02861	401-723-2000	725-5980	100
Key Corporate Services LLC 9746 Olympia Dr *Web:* www.kcsllc.net	Fishers	IN	46037	317-598-1950	849-5342	260
Key Curriculum Press 1150 65th St **Fax Area Code:* 800 ■ *Web:* www.keycurriculum.com	Emeryville	CA	94608	510-595-7000	541-2442*	637-2
Key Energy 2210 W Broadway *Web:* www.keyenergy.com	Sweetwater	TX	79556	325-236-6611		780
Key Engineering Inc 287 Woodall Rd *Web:* key-eng.com	Decatur	AL	35601	256-351-1350		261
Key Enterprise Solutions 58 Chandler St *Web:* www.keysolutions.com	Boston	MA	02116	617-338-6933	423-2399	180
Key Equipment Finance 1000 S McCaslin Blvd *TF:* 888-301-6238 ■ *Web:* www.keyequipmentfinance.com	Superior	CO	80027	888-301-6238		216
Key Events Inc 657 Mission St Ste 202 *Web:* keyevents.com	San Francisco	CA	94105	415-695-8000		179
Key Fasteners Corp 525 Key Way Dr *Web:* adamswells.com	Berne	IN	46711	260-589-2626		351
Key Fire Hose Corp (KFH) 2926 Columbia Hwy *TF:* 800-447-5666 ■ *Web:* keyhose.com	Dothan	AL	36302	800-447-5666	447-5664	370
Key Food Stores Co-opeartive Inc 1200 S Ave *Web:* www.keyfood.com	Staten Island	NY	10314	718-370-4200		297-8
Key High Vacuum Products Inc 36 S Blvd *Web:* keyhigh.com	Nesconset	NY	11767	631-360-3970	360-3973	806
Key Industries Inc 400 Marble Rd *TF:* 800-835-0365 ■ *Web:* www.keyapparel.com	Fort Scott	KS	66701	800-835-0365		155-19
Key Information Systems Inc 30077 Agoura Ct 1st Fl *TF:* 877-442-3249 ■ *Web:* www.keyinfo.com	Agoura Hills	CA	91301	818-992-8950	992-8970	178-11
Key Largo Chamber of Commerce 106000 Overseas Hwy *TF:* 800-822-1088 ■ *Web:* www.keylargochamber.org	Key Largo	FL	33037	305-451-1414	451-4726	139
Key Lime Air Corp 13252 E Control Tower Rd *Web:* www.keylimeair.com	Englewood	CO	80112	303-768-9626		13
Key Machine Tool Inc 53928 County Rd 5 *Web:* keymachinetool.com	Elkhart	IN	46514	574-262-1537	262-0787	385
Key Magazine of Memphis PO Box 111266 *Web:* www.keymemphis.com	Memphis	TN	38111	901-458-3912		457-22
Key Performance Petroleum 1558 N LaSalle St *TF:* 800-548-6671 ■ *Web:* www.kppetro.com	Navasota	TX	77868	936-825-6868	870-3355	316
Key Polymer Corp 17 Shepard St *Web:* www.keypolymer.com	Lawrence	MA	01843	978-683-9411	686-7729	3
Key Radio 307 S 1600 W *TF:* 855-539-4583 ■ *Web:* www.keyradio.org	Provo	UT	84601	801-374-5210		645
Key Realty School 3650 E Flamingo Rd *TF:* 800-472-3893 ■ *Web:* www.keyrealtyschool.com	Las Vegas	NV	89121	702-313-7000		685
Key Software Systems LLC 5100 Belmar Blvd *Web:* www.keysoftwaresystems.com	Farmingdale	NJ	07727	732-409-6068		180
Key Speakers Bureau Inc 250 Newport Center Dr Ste 202 *TF:* 800-675-1175 ■ *Web:* www.keyspeakers.com	Newport Beach	CA	92660	949-675-7856	675-1478	708
Key This Week in Chicago 222 W Ontario St Ste 420 *Web:* www.keymagazinechicago.com	Chicago	IL	60654	312-943-0838	664-6113	457-22
Key Tronic Corp 4424 N Sullivan Rd *NASDAQ:* KTCC ■ *Web:* www.keytronic.com	Spokane Valley	WA	99214	509-928-8000	927-5555	253
Key Trucking Inc 19657 78th Ave S *Web:* www.keytrucking.com	Kent	WA	98032	253-395-3677	872-0129	780
Key West Aloe 13095 N Telecom Pkwy *TF:* 800-445-2563 ■ *Web:* keywestaloe.com	Tampa	FL	33637	800-445-2563		214
Key West Aquarium 1 Whitehead St *TF:* 888-544-5927 ■ *Web:* www.keywestaquarium.com	Key West	FL	33040	888-544-5927		40
Key West Boats Inc 593 Ridgeville Rd PO Box 399 *Web:* www.keywestboatsinc.com	Ridgeville	SC	29472	843-873-0112	821-6334	90
Key West Botanical Garden 5210 College Rd *Web:* www.keywest.garden	Key West	FL	33040	305-296-1504		97
Key West Citizen 3420 Northside Dr *Web:* keysnews.com	Key West	FL	33040	305-292-7777		532-2
Key West City Hall 3132 Flagler Ave *TF:* 800-955-8770 ■ *Web:* www.cityofkeywest-fl.gov	Key West	FL	33040	305-809-3700	809-3833	337
Key West International Airport 3491 S Roosevelt Blvd *Web:* keywestinternationalairport.com	Key West	FL	33040	305-809-5200		27
Key West Key 726 Passover Ln **Fax Area Code:* 305 ■ *TF:* 800-881-7321 ■ *Web:* www.keywestkey.com	Key West	FL	33040	800-881-7321	294-2974*	376
Key West Visitors Ctr 510 Greene St 1st Fl *Web:* www.keywestchamber.org	Key West	FL	33040	305-294-2587	294-7806	206
Key2 Consulting 11555 Medlock Bridge Rd *Web:* key2consulting.com	Johns Creek	GA	30097	678-835-8539		631
Keya Paha County 310 Courthouse Dr PO Box 349 *Web:* www.co.keya-paha.ne.us	Springview	NE	68778	402-497-3791	497-3799	338
Keyano College 8115 Franklin Ave *TF:* 800-251-1408 ■ *Web:* www.keyano.ca	Fort McMurray	AB	T9H2H7	780-791-4800		95
Keyboard Workshop PO Box 700 *Web:* www.playpiano.com	Medford	OR	97501	541-664-7052		423
Keybridge Medical Revenue Management 2348 Baton Rouge Ave *TF:* 877-222-4114 ■ *Web:* www.keybridgemed.com	Lima	OH	45805	419-993-2900		160
Keybridge Research LLC 3050 K St NW Ste 220 *Web:* keybridgedc.com	Washington	DC	20007	202-965-9480		466
Keycentrix LLC 2420 N Woodlawn Bldg 500 *TF:* 800-444-8486 ■ *Web:* keycentrix.com	Wichita	KS	67220	800-444-8486		177

Name / Address	City	State	ZIP	Phone	Fax	Class
Keycom Technologies 1144 Solana Ave. *Web:* www.keycom.net	Winter Park	FL	32789	407-949-0600		225
Keyes Coverage Inc 5900 Hiatus Rd *Web:* www.keyescoverage.com	Tamarac	FL	33321	954-724-7000	724-7024	390
Keyes Insurance Services Inc 5075 South 1500 West *TF:* 800-331-0167 ■ *Web:* keyesinsuranceservices.com	Riverdale	UT	84405	801-394-2600		390
Keyes North Atlantic 459 Watertown St. *Web:* www.keyesweb.com	Newton	MA	02460	617-964-6180	965-8329	35
Keyes Packaging Group Inc 3715 State Hwy. *Web:* www.keyespackaging.com	Wenatchee	WA	98807	509-663-8537		601
Keyes Toyota 5855 Van Nuys Blvd *TF:* 844-781-4304 ■ *Web:* www.keyestoyota.com	Van Nuys	CA	91401	844-781-4304		57
KEYE-TV Ch 42 (CBS) 10700 Metric Blvd. *Web:* cbsaustin.com	Austin	TX	78758	512-835-0042	490-2111	741-9
KEYG-FM 58053 Spokane Blvd NE *Web:* www.kcsyfm.com	Grand Coulee	WA	99133	509-633-2020	633-1014	647
Keyhole State Park 22 Marina Rd *Web:* wyoparks.wyo.gov	Moorcroft	WY	82721	307-756-3596		565
KeyImpact Sales & Systems Inc 1701 Crossroads Dr *TF:* 800-955-0600 ■ *Web:* www.kisales.com	Odenton	MD	21113	800-955-0600		691
Keylogic Systems Inc 3168 Collins Ferry Rd. *TF:* 888-204-9649 ■ *Web:* keylogic.com	Morgantown	WV	26505	304-296-9100		225
KEYN-FM 103.7 (Oldies) 9111 E Douglas Ste 130 *Web:* keyn.radio.com	Wichita	KS	67207	316-869-1037		645-173
KeyPoint Credit Union 2805 Bowers Ave *TF:* 888-255-3637 ■ *Web:* kpcu.com	Santa Clara	CA	95051	408-731-4100	731-4485	219
KEYS (Keys Energy Services) 1001 James St *Web:* www.keysenergy.com	Key West	FL	33040	305-295-1000	295-1085	188-10
Keys Energy Services (KEYS) 1001 James St *Web:* www.keysenergy.com	Key West	FL	33040	305-295-1000	295-1085	188-10
Keys Federal Credit 3022 N Roosevelt Blvd *TF:* 866-820-7227 ■ *Web:* keysfcu.org	Key West	FL	33040	305-294-6622	293-6051	219
Keys Innovative Solutions 1004 Keys Dr *Web:* www.keysinnovativesolutions.com	Greenville	SC	29615	864-288-6560		627
Keys Realty Group Inc 3304 E Linwood Blvd *Web:* keysrealtygroupinc.com	Kansas City	MO	64128	816-337-8626		652
Keyser & Miller Ford Inc 8 E Main St. *Web:* www.keysermillerford.com	Collegeville	PA	19426	610-489-9366		57
Keysight Technologies 1400 Fountaingrove Pkwy *NYSE:* KEYS ■ *TF:* 800-829-4444 ■ *Web:* www.keysight.com	Santa Rosa	CA	95403	800-829-4444		201
Keysource Group Inc, The 1920 Georgetown Rd Ste C. *Web:* www.thekeysource.com	Hudson	OH	44236	330-342-4630		196
Keysource Medical Inc 7820 Palace Dr *Web:* www.keysourcemedical.com	Cincinnati	OH	45249	513-469-7881		231
Keyston Bros 2801 Academy Way *TF:* 800-453-1112 ■ *Web:* keystonbros.com	Sacramento	CA	95815	916-927-5851	921-9123	594
Keystone 1207 Roseneath Rd. *Web:* www.keystone.build	Richmond	VA	23230	804-358-5768		653
Keystone Adjustable Cap Co 1591 Hylton Rd. *Web:* www.beringer.net	Pennsauken Township	NJ	08110	856-663-5740		557
Keystone Aerial Surveys Inc 9800 Ashton Rd *Web:* kasurveys.com	Philadelphia	PA	19114	215-677-3119		727
Keystone Automotive Operations Inc 44 Tunkhannock Ave. *TF:* 800-521-9999 ■ *Web:* www.keystoneautomotive.com	Exeter	PA	18643	570-655-4514	603-2003	61
Keystone Cable Corp 8200 Lynch Rd. *Web:* www.keystonecable.net	Detroit	MI	48234	313-924-9720	924-0050	815
Keystone Capital Corp 1953 San Elijo Ave *Web:* kccbd.com	Cardiff-By-The-Sea	CA	92007	858-348-4405		401
Keystone Capital Inc 155 N Wacker Dr Ste 4150 *Web:* keystonecapital.com	Chicago	IL	60606	312-219-7900		401
Keystone Chevrolet Inc 8700 Charles Page Blvd *Web:* www.keystonechevrolet.com	Sand Springs	OK	74063	918-932-1706		516
Keystone Clearwater Solutions LLC 34 Northeast Dr *Web:* www.keystoneclear.com	Hershey	PA	17033	717-508-0550		539
Keystone College 1 College Green *TF:* 800-824-2764 ■ *Web:* www.keystone.edu	La Plume	PA	18440	570-945-5141	945-7916	166
Keystone Communications 86 Main St *TF:* 800-568-9584 ■ *Web:* www.keystonecommunications.com	Keystone	IA	52249	319-442-3241		224
Keystone Consolidated Industries Inc 7000 SW Adams St. **Fax Area Code:* 309 ■ *TF:* 800-447-6444 ■ *Web:* www.redbrand.com	Peoria	IL	61641	800-447-6444	697-7120*	813
KeyStone Ctr 2001 Providence Ave *TF:* 800-558-9600 ■ *Web:* keystonecenter.net	Chester	PA	19013	610-876-9000	876-5441	726
Keystone Ctr 1628 St John Rd. *Web:* www.keystone.org	Keystone	CO	80435	970-513-5800	262-0152	634
Keystone Dental Inc 144 Middlesex Tpke *TF:* 866-902-9272 ■ *Web:* www.keystonedental.com	Burlington	MA	01803	781-328-3490		228
Keystone Electrical Manufacturing Co 2511 Bell Ave *Web:* www.keystoneemc.com	Des Moines	IA	50321	515-283-2567	283-0418	729
Keystone Electronics Corp 31-07 20th Rd *TF:* 800-221-5510 ■ *Web:* www.keyelco.com	Astoria	NY	11105	718-956-8900	956-9040	350
Keystone Engineering 6310 Sidney St *Web:* www.keystoneeng.com	Houston	TX	77021	713-747-1478	747-8227	621

Name / Address	City	State	ZIP	Phone	Fax	Class
Keystone First 200 Stevens Dr *Web:* www.keystonefirstpa.com	Philadelphia	PA	19113	215-937-8000		391-3
Keystone Folding Box Company Inc 367 Verona Ave. *Web:* www.keyboxco.com	Newark	NJ	07104	973-483-1054		561
Keystone Food Products Inc PO Box 326 *Web:* www.keystonesnacks.com	Easton	PA	18044	610-258-0888	250-0721	296-35
Keystone Foods 905 Airport Rd Ste 400 *Web:* www.keystonefoods.com	West Chester	PA	19380	610-668-6700		296-26
Keystone Forging Co 215 Duke St *Web:* www.keystoneforging.com	Northumberland	PA	17857	570-473-3524	473-7273	483
Keystone Friction Hinge Co 520 Matthews Blvd. *Web:* www.kfhinge.com	South Williamsport	PA	17702	570-323-9479	326-0217	488
Keystone Fruit Marketing 11 N Carlisle St Ste 102 *Web:* www.keystonefruit.com	Greencastle	PA	17225	717-597-2112		194
Keystone Honing Co 1000 Industrial Dr.	Titusville	PA	16354	814-827-9641		454
Keystone Industries 480 S Democrat Rd. *TF:* 800-333-3131 ■ *Web:* keystoneindustries.com	Gibbstown	NJ	08027	856-663-4700		475
Keystone Information Systems 1000 S Lenola Rd *TF:* 800-735-4862 ■ *Web:* www.keyinfosys.com	Maple Shade	NJ	08052	856-722-0700		225
Keystone Insurance Services Inc 21301 Powerline Rd Ste 312 *Web:* keystone-ins.com	Boca Raton	FL	33433	561-852-1445		390
Keystone Law Group PC 11300 W Olympic Blvd Ste 910 *Web:* keystone-law.com	Los Angeles	CA	90064	310-444-9060	444-9092	41
Keystone Lime Co 1156 Christner Hollow Rd *Web:* www.keystonelime.com	Fort Hill	PA	15540	814-662-2711		188-4
Keystone Lodge & Spa PO Box 38. *TF:* 877-625-1556 ■ *Web:* www.keystoneresort.com	Keystone	CO	80435	970-496-4000		379
Keystone Marketing 709 N Main St *Web:* www.keystonemarketing.net	Winston-Salem	NC	27101	336-777-3473		195
Keystone Outdoors 186 Path Valley Rd *Web:* www.keystoneoutdoors.net	Fort Loudon	PA	17224	717-369-2970		791
Keystone Payroll 355-C Colonnade Blvd. *TF:* 877-717-2272 ■ *Web:* keystonepayroll.com	State College	PA	16803	814-234-2272	234-3304	2
Keystone Powdered Metal Co 251 State St *Web:* www.keystonepm.com	Saint Marys	PA	15857	814-781-1591		485
Keystone Pretzels 124 W Airport Rd *Web:* www.potatopro.com	Lititz	PA	17543	888-572-4500		296-9
Keystone Profiles Ltd 220 Seventh Ave. *TF:* 800-777-1533 ■ *Web:* www.keystoneprofiles.com	Beaver Falls	PA	15010	724-506-1500		492
Keystone Property Group 125 E Elm St Ste 400 *TF:* 866-980-1818 ■ *Web:* keystonepropertygroup.com	Conshohocken	PA	19428	610-980-7000	980-7009	652
Keystone Quality Transport Co 1260 E Woodland Ave. *Web:* www.keystonequalitytransport.com	Springfield	PA	19064	610-604-1421		30
Keystone Real Estate Group, Lp 444 E College Ave Ste 560 *Web:* kregcommercial.com	State College	PA	16801	814-234-6860		652
Keystone Retaining Wall Systems Inc 4444 W 78th St. *TF:* 800-747-8971 ■ *Web:* www.keystonewalls.com	Minneapolis	MN	55435	952-897-1040	897-3858	724
Keystone RV Co 2642 Hackberry Dr PO Box 2000 *Web:* www.keystonerv.com	Goshen	IN	46527	574-535-2100		120
Keystone School District 451 Huston Ave *Web:* www.keyknox.com	Knox	PA	16232	814-797-5921		685
Keystone Shipping Co 1 Bala Plz E Ste 600 *Web:* www.keyship.com	Bala Cynwyd	PA	19004	610-617-6800	617-6899	312
Keystone Sporting Arms LLC 155 Sodom Rd *TF:* 800-742-0455 ■ *Web:* www.keystonesportingarmsllc.com	Milton	PA	17847	570-742-2777		807
Keystone State Park 1926 S Hwy 151 *Web:* www.travelok.com	Sand Springs	OK	74063	918-865-4991	865-2083	565
Keystone State Park 1150 Keystone Park Rd. *Web:* www.dcnr.pa.gov	Derry	PA	15627	724-668-2939		565
KEYTEC Inc 520 Shepherd Dr. *TF:* 800-624-4289 ■ *Web:* www.magictouch.com	Garland	TX	75042	972-272-7555	272-7501	173-1
KEYU-TV 7900 Broadway PO Box 10 *Web:* www.telemundoamarillo.com	Amarillo	TX	79108	806-383-1010	383-7178	647
KEYW Corp 7740 Milestone Pkwy Ste 400 *TF:* 800-340-1001 ■ *Web:* www.keywcorp.com	Hanover	MD	21076	443-733-1600		177
Keyway Internet Services Inc 1030 N Mountain Ave Ste 335 *Web:* www.cpl.net	Ontario	CA	91762	909-933-3650	933-3660	224
Keywell LLC 1035 Commercial Dr *Web:* www.keywell.com	Matthews	NC	28104	708-608-8020		686
Keyword Connects LLC 77 Rumford Ave *Web:* www.keywordconnects.com	Waltham	MA	02453	781-899-3675	723-0403	195
Key-Z Productions 85343 Nestle Way. *Web:* www.key-z.com	Pleasant Hill	OR	97455	541-484-4315		514
KEYZ-AM 410 6th St E PO Box 2048. *Web:* www.keyzradio.com	Williston	ND	58802	701-572-5371		647
Kezber I. Solution 2685 Rue Hertel *Web:* www.kezber.com	Sherbrooke	QC	J1J2J4	819-566-6900		180
KEZI-TV Ch 9 (ABC) PO Box 7009. *Web:* www.kezi.com	Eugene	OR	97408	541-485-5611	686-8004	741-45
KEZK-FM 102.5 (AC) 1220 Olive St 3rd Fl *Web:* kezk.radio.com	Saint Louis	MO	63103	314-531-1025		645-138

				Phone	Fax	Class
KEZS-FM 324 Broadway TF: 800-455-5103 ■ Web: www.k103fm.com	Cape Girardeau	MO	63701	573-651-3003	335-4806	647
KEZW-AM 4700 S Syracuse St Ste 1050 Web: ez1430.radio.com	Denver	CO	80237	303-631-1430		647
KEZX-AM 511 Rossanley Dr Web: www.opusradio.com	Medford	OR	97501	541-772-0322		647
KF (Kettering Foundation) 200 Commons Rd TF: 800-221-3657 ■ Web: kettering.org	Dayton	OH	45459	937-434-7300		637-2
K-Fab Inc 1408 Vine St Web: kfabinc.com	Berwick	PA	18603	570-759-8411	759-0150	757
KFAN AM1270 1530 Greenview Dr SW Ste 200 Web: mykfan.iheart.com	Rochester	MN	55902	507-288-3888	288-7815	645-134
KFAX-AM 1100 (Rel) 39650 Liberty St Ste 340 Web: kfax.com	Fremont	CA	94538	510-713-1100	897-1453	645
KFAZ-TV 706 W Herndon Ave Web: www.kmsgtv.com	Fresno	CA	93650	559-255-0039	435-3201	647
KFBB-TV 3200 Old Havre Hwy Web: www.montanarightnow.com	Black Eagle	MT	59414	406-453-4377		741
KFBC-AM 1240 (N/T) 1806 Capital Ave Web: www.kfbcradio.com	Cheyenne	WY	82001	307-634-4462		645-33
KFBI-TV 820 Crater Lake Ave Web: kfbimy48.com	Medford	OR	97504	541-772-2600	732-0511	647
KFBW-FM The Brew 13333 SW 68th Pky Ste 310 TF: 866-445-1059 ■ Web: 1059thebrew.iheart.com	Portland	OR	97223	503-323-6400		647
KFBX-AM 970 (N/T) 546 Ninth Ave Web: 970kfbx.iheart.com	Fairbanks	AK	99701	907-450-1000		645-55
KFDI-FM 101.3 (Ctry) 4200 N Old Lawrence Rd Web: www.kfdi.com	Wichita	KS	67219	316-838-9141		645-173
KFDM Channel 6 2955 I-10 E Web: kfdm.com	Beaumont	TX	77702	409-892-6622	899-4639	116
KFFX-TV 6725 W Clearwater Ave Web: fox41yakima.com	Kennewick	WA	99336	509-735-1700		647
KFG Resources Ltd 150-A Providence Rd Web: kfgresources.com	Natchez	MS	39120	601-446-5219		538
KFH (Key Fire Hose Corp) 2926 Columbia Hwy TF: 800-447-5666 ■ Web: keyhose.com	Dothan	AL	36302	800-447-5666	447-5664	370
KFH-AM 1240 (N/T) 9111 E Douglas Ste 130 Web: kfh.radio.com	Wichita	KS	67207	316-685-2121		645-173
KFIS-FM & Salem Interactive Media 6400 SE Lake Rd Ste 350 Web: www.thefishportland.com	Portland	OR	97222	503-652-8172		643
K-Five Construction Corp 999 Oakmont Plz Dr Ste 200 Web: www.k-five.com	Westmont	IL	60559	630-257-5600	257-6788	188-4
KFJB-AM 123 W Main St Web: www.1230kfjb.com	Marshalltown	IA	50158	641-752-5352	752-7201	647
KFKA-AM 1002 31st Ave Web: www.1310kfka.com	Greeley	CO	80634	970-356-1310		647
KFLA-TV 701 Perdew Ave Web: www.kfla.tv	Ridgecrest	CA	93555	760-446-6794		647
Kfm International Industries 20277 Valley Blvd Ste L Web: www.kfmii.com	Walnut	CA	91789	626-369-9556	369-9856	358
KFMA-FM Radio 3871 N Commerce Dr Web: www.kfma.com	Tucson	AZ	85705	520-407-4500		645-165
KFMB-TV Ch 8 (CBS) 7677 Engineer Rd Web: www.cbs8.com	San Diego	CA	92111	858-571-8888	560-0627	741-119
KFMF-FM 1459 Humboldt Rd Ste A Web: www.939thehippo.com	Chico	CA	95928	530-899-3600		647
KFMO-AM 804 St Joe Dr Web: www.b104fm.com	Park Hills	MO	63601	573-431-1000		647
KFMR Katz Ferraro McMurtry PC 210 6th Ave Ste 200 Web: www.kfmr.com	Pittsburgh	PA	15222	412-471-0200		2
KFNW-FM 97.9 (Rel) 5702 52nd Ave S Web: life979.com	Fargo	ND	58104	701-356-0979	282-5781	645-56
Kforce Inc 1001 E Palm Ave NASDAQ: KFRC ■ TF: 877-453-6723 ■ Web: www.kforce.com	Tampa	FL	33605	813-552-5000	552-1482	721
KFOR-TV Ch 4 (NBC) 444 E Britton Rd Web: www.kfor.com	Oklahoma City	OK	73114	405-424-4444		741-93
K-Four Systems 1660 Washington St Web: www.kfoursystems.com	Holliston	MA	01746	774-233-0697		196
KFOX-TV Ch 14 (Fox) 200 S Alto Mesa St Web: www.kfoxtv.com	El Paso	TX	79912	915-833-8585	833-8973	741-43
KFRG-FM 95.1 900 E Washington St Ste 315 *Fax Area Code: 909 ■ TF: 888-431-3764 ■ Web: kfrog.radio.com	Colton	CA	92324	888-431-3764	825-0441*	645
KFS Inc 1840 W Airfield Dr TF: 800-364-4115 ■ Web: www.kfsinc.com	Dallas	TX	75261	817-488-4115	488-4350	24
KFSI-FM 92.9 (Rel) 4016 28th St SE Web: www.kfsi.org	Rochester	MN	55904	507-289-8585	529-4017	645-134
KFSM-TV Ch 5 (CBS) 318 N 13th St Web: 5newsonline.com	Fort Smith	AR	72901	479-783-3131	783-3295	741-50
KFSN-TV Ch 30 (ABC) 1777 G St TF: 800-423-3030 ■ Web: abc30.com	Fresno	CA	93706	559-442-1170		741-52
KFT Fire Trainer LLC 17 Philips Pky Web: kft.firetrainer.com	Montvale	NJ	07645	201-300-8100	300-8101	22
KFTM-AM 16041 US Hwy 34 PO Box 430 Web: www.kftm.net	Fort Morgan	CO	80701	970-867-5674	542-1023	647
KFTX-FM 97.5 (Ctry) 1520 S Port Ave Web: www.kftx.com	Corpus Christi	TX	78405	361-883-5987	883-3648	645-41
KFVS-TV 310 Broadway PO Box 100 TF: 800-455-5387 ■ Web: www.kfvs12.com	Cape Girardeau	MO	63701	573-335-1212	335-6303	647
KFWB 980AM La Mera Mera 5777 W Century Blvd Ste 980 Web: www.980lameramera.com	Los Angeles	CA	90045	323-851-5959		645-42
KFXE-FM 3505 Fredericksburg Rd Web: www.thefox965.com	Kerrville	TX	78028	830-896-4990	896-4991	647
KFXL-TV 1078 25 Rd Web: www.foxnebraska.com	Axtell	NE	68924	308-743-2494	743-2644	647
KFYR-TV Ch 5 (NBC) 200 N Fourth St Web: www.kfyrtv.com	Bismarck	ND	58501	701-255-5757	255-8220	741-16
KGAB-AM 650 (N/T) 1912 Capitol Ave Ste 300 Web: www.kgab.com	Cheyenne	WY	82001	307-632-4400		645-33
KGAF-AM PO Box 368 Web: www.1580kgaf.com	Gainesville	TX	76241	940-665-5546	665-1580	647
KGBT-TV Ch 4 (CBS) 9201 W Expy 83 Web: www.valleycentral.com	Harlingen	TX	78552	956-366-4444	366-4494	741
KGEB TV-53 7777 S Lewis Ave TF: 800-255-4407 ■ Web: kgeb.net	Tulsa	OK	74171	918-488-5300	495-7388	647
KGEC-TV 215 Lake Blvd Ste 26 Web: www.kgectv.com	Redding	CA	96003	530-941-7879		647
KGEM-AM 5601 Cassia Web: www.saltandlightradio.com	Boise	ID	83701	208-344-4774		647
KGET-TV 17 2120 L St Web: www.kget.com	Bakersfield	CA	93301	661-283-1700	283-1843	741-10
KGFW-AM 2223 Central Ave Web: www.kgfw.com	Kearney	NE	68847	308-698-2100	237-0312	647
KGGI-FM 99.1 (CHR) 2030 Iowa Ave Ste 100 TF: 866-991-5444 ■ Web: 991kggi.iheart.com	Riverside	CA	92507	951-684-1991	486-7335	645-130
KGGO-FM 4143 109th St Web: www.kggo.com	Urbandale	IA	50322	515-331-9200		647
KGH (Kennewick General Hospital) 900 S Auburn Web: www.trioshealth.org	Kennewick	WA	99336	509-586-5707		374-3
KGHS - 1230 AM 519 3rd St TF: 888-283-1041 ■ Web: network1sports.com	International Falls	MN	56649	218-283-3481	283-3087	647
KGJX-FM 2314 Hwy 6 & 50 TF: 888-429-7722 ■ Web: www.redrock101.com	Grand Junction	CO	81505	970-986-4900		647
KGLO-AM 341 South Yorktown Pke Web: www.kgloam.com	Mason City	IA	50401	641-423-1300		647
KGLX-FM 1632 S Second St Web: www.991kglx.iheart.com	Gallup	NM	87301	505-863-9391		647
KGMS-AM 3222 S Richey Ave Web: www.wilkinsradio.com	Tucson	AZ	85713	520-790-2440		647
KGNC-FM 97.9 (Ctry) 3505 Olsen Blvd Ste 117 Web: www.kgncfm.com	Amarillo	TX	79109	806-355-9801		645-5
KGNS-TV 120 W Delmar Blvd Web: www.kgns.tv	Laredo	TX	78045	956-727-8888		647
KGNU-FM 88.5 (Var) 4700 Walnut St TF: 800-737-3030 ■ Web: www.kgnu.org	Boulder	CO	80301	303-449-4885		645
KGNZ-FM 88.1 (Rel) 542 Butternut St Web: kgnz.com	Abilene	TX	79602	325-673-8801		645-1
KGO-TV Ch 7 (ABC) 900 Front St Web: abc7news.com	San Francisco	CA	94111	415-954-7770		741-120
KGOU-FM 106.3 (NPR) 860 Van Vleet Oval Rm 300 TF: 866-533-2470 ■ Web: www.kgou.org	Norman	OK	73019	405-325-3388	325-7129	645
KGPE CBS47 5035 E McKinley Ave Web: www.yourcentralvalley.com	Fresno	CA	93727	559-222-2411		741-52
KGPR-FM 89.9 (NPR) PO Box 3343 Web: kgpr.org	Great Falls	MT	59403	406-268-3739		645
KGPS-FM 500 Stowell Ave Web: www.calvarychapelkingman.com	Kingman	AZ	86401	928-753-3730		647
KGPT-TV 401 S Greenwood Web: kgpttv26.com	Wichita	KS	67211	316-201-4800	440-3997	647
KGRN-AM 909 1/2 Main St Web: www.myiowainfo.com	Grinnell	IA	50112	641-236-1410	236-8896	647
KGRT-FM 103.9 1355 California Ave Web: kgrt.com	Las Cruces	NM	88001	575-525-9298	525-9419	645
KGS (Kansas Genealogical Society) 2601 Central Ave Web: www.kgs-genlibrary.com	Dodge City	KS	67801	620-225-1951		49-19
KGS Steel Inc 3725 Pine Ln TF: 800-533-3846 ■ Web: kgssteel.com	Bessemer	AL	35022	205-425-0800		492
KGTO-AM 7030 S Yale Ave Web: tulsaheartandsoul.com	Tulsa	OK	74136	918-494-9886		647
KGTV-TV Ch 10 (ABC) 4600 Airway TF: 800-799-8881 ■ Web: www.10news.com	San Diego	CA	92102	619-237-1010	527-0369	741-119
KGUN-TV Ch 9 (ABC) 7280 E Rosewood St Web: www.kgun9.com	Tucson	AZ	85710	520-290-7700	733-7050	741-137
KGWC-TV Ch 14 (CBS) 1856 Skyview Dr Web: nocable.org	Casper	WY	82601	307-577-5923	577-5928	741-22
KGW-TV Ch 8 (NBC) 1501 SW Jefferson St Web: www.kgw.com	Portland	OR	97201	503-226-5000		741-103
KGY 95.3 1700 Marine Dr NE Web: www.kgyfm.com	Olympia	WA	98501	360-943-1240		645
Kha Accountants PLLC 4880 Long Prairie Rd Ste 100 Web: khaaccountants.com	Flower Mound	TX	75028	972-221-2500	436-8887	2
KHAFRA Engineering Consultants Inc 225 Peachtree St NE Ste 1600 Web: www.khafra.com	Atlanta	GA	30303	404-525-2120	522-7941	256
Khanna Ro (Rep D - CA) 221 Cannon House Office Bldg Web: khanna.house.gov	Washington	DC	20515	202-225-2631		342-2
Khazana 10177 107th St Web: khazanarestaurant.ca	Edmonton	AB	T5J1J5	780-702-0330		671
KHBS-TV Ch 40 (ABC) 2415 N Albert Pk Web: www.4029tv.com	Fort Smith	AR	72904	479-783-4040	785-5375	741-50
Higher Education Assistance Authority PO Box 798 TF: 800-928-8926 ■ Web: www.kheaa.com	Frankfort	KY	40602	800-928-8926		725
Khemia Software Co 33080 Industrial Rd Web: khemia.com	Livonia	MI	48150	734-513-9940	744-5022	179
Kheops International Inc 232 Rt 3 TF: 800-215-8705 ■ Web: kheopsinternational.com	Colebrook	NH	03576	603-237-8188	237-5855	327
KHFI-FM 3601 S Congress Ave Bldg F Web: www.967kissfm.iheart.com	Austin	TX	78704	512-684-7300		647

Name / Address	City	State	Zip	Phone	Fax	Class
KHHO-AM 645 Elliott Ave W Ste 400 *Web:* www.sportsradiokjr.iheart.com	Seattle	WA	98119	206-286-9595		647
KHMX-FM 96.5 (CHR) 24 Greenway Plz Ste 1900 *Web:* mix965houston.radio.com	Houston	TX	77046	713-881-5965		645-72
KHND-AM 718 Lincoln Ave PO Box 6 *Web:* www.khnd1470.com	Harvey	ND	58341	701-324-4848	324-2043	647
KHNR-AM 1160 N King St 2nd Fl *Web:* theanswerhawaii.com	Honolulu	HI	96817	808-954-4367		647
Khong Guan Corp 30068 Eigenbrodt Way *TF:* 877-889-8968 ■ *Web:* kgcusa.squarespace.com	Union City	CA	94587	510-487-7800	487-0301	195
KHON-TV Ch 2 (Fox) 88 Piikoi St *Web:* www.khon2.com	Honolulu	HI	96814	808-591-4278	593-2418	741-59
KHOP @ 95-1 3127 Transworld Dr Ste 270 *TF:* 800-548-0951 ■ *Web:* www.khop.com	Stockton	CA	95206	209-766-5000	522-2061	647
Khorporate Holdings Inc 6492 State Rd 205 *Web:* www.khorporateholdings.com	Laotto	IN	46763	260-357-3365	356-7891	73
Khoury Inc 1129 Webster Ave PO Box 1746 *TF:* 800-725-6765 ■ *Web:* www.khouryinc.com	Waco	TX	76703	254-754-5481	754-1606	319-1
KHOU-TV Ch 11 (CBS) 1945 Allen Pkwy *Web:* www.khou.com	Houston	TX	77019	713-526-1111		741-60
KHQA-TV 301 S 36th St *TF:* 800-929-3518 ■ *Web:* khqa.com	Quincy	IL	62301	217-222-6200	224-4909	647
KHQ-TV Ch 6 (NBC) 1201 W Sprague Ave *Web:* www.khq.com	Spokane	WA	99201	509-448-6000	448-4644	741-127
KHRI (Kresge Hearing Research Institute) 4605 Medical Science *Web:* medicine.umich.edu	Ann Arbor	MI	48109	734-764-8110	764-0014	668
KHRW-FM 324 Coffeen Ave *Web:* www.bighornmountainradio.com	Sheridan	WY	82801	307-672-2690	672-1722	647
KHS (Kenilworth Historical Society) 415 Kenilworth Ave *Web:* kenilworthhistory.org	Kenilworth	IL	60043	847-251-2565		49-19
KHS & S Contractors Inc 5422 Bay Center Dr Ste 200 *Web:* www.khss.com	Tampa	FL	33609	813-628-9330	628-4339	189-9
Khs USA Inc 880 Bahcall Ct *Web:* www.khs.com	Waukesha	WI	53186	262-797-7200		298
KHSL-TV 3460 Silverbell Rd *Web:* www.actionnewsnow.com	Chico	CA	95973	530-342-0141		647
KHTH-FM 101.7 (AC) 1410 Neotomas Ave Ste 200 *Web:* www.hot1017.com	Santa Rosa	CA	95405	707-543-0100	571-1097	645-71
KHTK-AM 1140 (Sports) 5244 Madison Ave *TF:* 800-920-1140 ■ *Web:* sacramento.cbslocal.com	Sacramento	CA	95841	916-339-1140		645-137
KHVN-AM 5787 S Hampton Ste 285 *TF:* 888-996-3970 ■ *Web:* www.khvnam.com	Dallas	TX	75232	214-331-5486	331-1908	647
KHYT-FM 575 W Roger Rd *Web:* www.khit1075.com	Tucson	AZ	85705	520-887-1000		645-165
KI 1330 Bellevue St *TF:* 800-424-2432 ■ *Web:* www.ki.com	Green Bay	WI	54302	920-468-8100	468-0280	319-1
Ki Ho Military Acquisition Consulting Inc 5501 Backlick Rd *Web:* kihomac.com	Springfield	VA	22151	703-960-5450		256
KI Industries Inc 5540 McDermott Dr *Web:* kiindustries.com	Berkeley	IL	60163	708-449-1990	449-1997	604
KIA (Kalamazoo Institute of Arts) 314 S Park St *Web:* www.kiarts.org	Kalamazoo	MI	49007	269-349-7775	349-9313	520
KIAH-TV 7700 Westpark Dr *Web:* www.cw39.com	Houston	TX	77063	713-781-3939		647
Kiamichi Electric Co-opeartive Inc (KEC) 944 SW Hwy 2 PO Box 340 *TF:* 800-888-2731 ■ *Web:* kiamichielectric.org	Wilburton	OK	74578	918-465-2338		245
Kiamichi Technology Ctr 107 S 15th St *TF:* 888-567-6641 ■ *Web:* www.ktc.edu	Hugo	OK	74743	580-326-6491	326-5696	230
Kianka & Zollo CPAs PC 521 Erie Blvd *Web:* kzcpas.com	West Syracuse	NY	13204	315-299-5247		2
Kiawah Island Golf Resort 1 Sancturay Beach Dr *TF:* 800-654-2924 ■ *Web:* kiawahresort.com	Kiawah Island	SC	29455	843-768-2121		669
Kibbey Wagner PLLC 416 SW Camden Ave *Web:* kibbeylaw.com	Stuart	FL	34994	772-286-0023		41
Kibble Equipment 1150 S Victory Dr *TF:* 800-624-8983 ■ *Web:* www.kibbleeq.com	Mankato	MN	56001	507-387-8201	388-3565	358
Kibel Green Inc 2001 Wilshire Blvd Ste 420 *Web:* kginc.com	Santa Monica	CA	90403	310-829-0255	453-6324	463
Kibow Biotech Inc 4781 W Chester Pike Newtown Business Ctr *TF:* 888-271-2560 ■ *Web:* www.kibowbiotech.com	Newtown Square	PA	19073	610-353-5130		231
Kibre & Horwitz LLP 9430 W Olympic Blvd Ste 400 *Web:* kandhlaw.net	Beverly Hills	CA	90212	310-557-1213		41
KIBZ-FM 104.1 3800 Cornhusker Hwy *Web:* www.kibz.com	Lincoln	NE	68504	402-466-1234		645-87
KICB-FM 1 Triton Cir *Web:* www.881thepoint.com	Fort Dodge	IA	50501	515-574-1213		647
Kice Industries Inc 5500 N Mill Heights Dr *TF:* 877-289-5423 ■ *Web:* www.kice.com	Wichita	KS	67219	316-744-7151	744-7355	207
Kichler Lighting 7711 E Pleasant Valley Rd PO Box 318010 *TF:* 866-558-5706 ■ *Web:* www.kichler.com	Cleveland	OH	44131	866-558-5706		439
Kickapoo Cavern State Park PO Box 705 *Web:* tpwd.texas.gov	Brackettville	TX	78832	830-563-2342		565
Kickapoo State Recreation Area 10906 Kickapoo Park Rd *Web:* www2.illinois.gov	Oakwood	IL	61858	217-442-4915		565
Kickapoo Traditional Tribe of Texas 2212 Rosita Valley Rd *Web:* kickapootexas.org	Eagle Pass	TX	78852	830-773-2105		132
Kickerillo Cos 1306 S Fry Rd *Web:* www.kickerillo.com	Katy	TX	77450	713-951-0666		186
Kickhaefer Manufacturing Co (KMC) 1221 S Park St PO Box 348 *TF:* 800-822-6080 ■ *Web:* www.kmcstampings.com	Port Washington	WI	53074	262-377-5030	284-9774	488
Kid to Kid 1244 Township Line Rd *Web:* kidtokid.com	Drexel Hill	PA	19026	610-446-2544		310
Kidambi & Associates PC 140 Monroe Tpke Ste A *Web:* kidambi.com	Trumbull	CT	06611	203-416-5300	590-3249	41
Kidango Inc 44000 Old Warm Springs Blvd *TF:* 800-262-4252 ■ *Web:* www.kidango.org	Fremont	CA	94538	408-258-3710		305
KidCo Inc 1013 Technology Way *TF:* 800-553-5529 ■ *Web:* www.kidco.com	Libertyville	IL	60048	847-549-8600	549-8660	64
Kidd & Company LLC 1455 E Putnam Ave *Web:* www.kiddcompany.com	Old Greenwich	CT	06870	203-661-0070		690
Kidd Carr LLP 1080 Marina Village Pkwy Ste 520 *Web:* kiddcarr.com	Alameda	CA	94501	510-268-8600		41
Kidd Kraddick Morning, The 220 Las Colinas Blvd E Ste C- 210 *TF:* 800-543-3548 ■ *Web:* www.kiddnation.com	Irving	TX	75039	972-432-9094		645-11
Kidde Aerospace 4200 Airport Dr NW *Web:* www.utcaerospacesystems.com	Wilson	NC	27896	252-237-7004	246-7181	283
Kidde-Fenwal Inc 400 Main St *TF:* 800-872-6527 ■ *Web:* www.kidde-fenwal.com	Ashland	MA	01721	508-881-2000		202
Kidder County Kidder County Courthouse *Web:* www.ndcourts.gov	Steele	ND	58482	701-475-2632	475-2202	338
Kiddesigns LLC 1299 Main St *TF:* 800-777-5206 ■ *Web:* www.kiddesigns.com	Rahway	NJ	07065	732-382-1760		246
KIDJ-FM 4745 N 7th St Ste 410 *Web:* www.hot975phoenix.com	Phoenix	AZ	85014	602-898-8881		647
KIDK-TV 1915 N Yellowstone Hwy *Web:* www.localnews8.com	Idaho Falls	ID	83401	208-528-2145	529-2443	647
Kidkusion Inc 623 River Rd *TF:* 800-845-9236 ■ *Web:* www.kidkusion.com	Washington	NC	27889	800-845-9236		601
Kidron Auction Inc 4885 Kidron Rd *Web:* www.kidronauction.com	Kidron	OH	44636	330-857-2641		446
Kidron Metal Products 13442 Emerson Rd **Fax Area Code:* 330 ■ *Web:* kidron.com	Dalton	OH	44618	800-763-0700	857-0505*	516
Kids Cancer Care Foundation of Alberta 609 14 St NW *Web:* www.kidscancercare.ab.ca	Calgary	AB	T2N2A1	403-216-9210		305
Kids Help Phone 300-439 University Ave *TF:* 800-268-3062 ■ *Web:* kidshelpphone.ca	Toronto	ON	M5G1Y8	416-586-5437		138
Kids Play Today LLC 837 Rt 6 Unit 5 *Web:* www.kidsplaytoday.com	Shohola	PA	18458	570-296-2313		31
Kids2 Inc 3333 Piedmont Rd Ste 1800 *TF:* 800-230-8190 ■ *Web:* www.kids2.com	Atlanta	GA	30305	800-230-8190		64
KidSafety of America 6288 Susana St *Web:* www.kidsafetystore.com	Chino	CA	91710	909-627-8700		523
KidsPeace Orchard Hills Campus 5300 Kids Peace Dr *TF:* 800-257-3223 ■ *Web:* www.kidspeace.org	Orefield	PA	18069	800-257-3223		374-1
Kidwick Books LLC 110 E 9th St Ste A698 *TF:* 866-543-9425 ■ *Web:* www.kidwick.com	Los Angeles	CA	90079	310-471-2472	861-8111	637-2
KIDX-FM 1086 Mechem Dr *Web:* www.985thewolf.com	Ruidoso	NM	88345	575-258-9922		647
Kieckhafer Dietzler & Hauser LLP 627 Elm St *Web:* kdhcpa.com	West Bend	WI	53095	262-334-2341	334-5773	2
Kiefer Specialty Flooring Inc 2910 Falling Waters Blvd *TF:* 800-322-5448 ■ *Web:* www.kieferusa.com	Lindenhurst	IL	60046	847-245-8450		361
Kieffer | Starlite Co 3322 Washington Ave *TF:* 877-543-3337 ■ *Web:* kiefferstarlite.com	Sheboygan	WI	53081	800-659-2493		701
Kiefner & Associates Inc 585 Scherers Ct *Web:* kiefner.com	Worthington	OH	43085	614-888-8220		256
Kieft Bros Inc 837 S Riverside Dr *Web:* www.kieftbros.com	Elmhurst	IL	60126	630-832-8090	834-5765	183
Kiely & Assoc 209 S LaSalle St Ste 1200 *Web:* www.jjkpc.com	Chicago	IL	60604	312-786-5961		41
Kiemle Hagood 601 W Main Ave Ste 400 *Web:* kiemlehagood.com	Spokane	WA	99201	509-838-6541		652
Kier & Wright Civil Engineers 2850 Collier Canyon Rd *Web:* www.kierwright.com	Livermore	CA	94551	925-245-8788		261
Kierland Commons 15205 N Kierland Blvd Ste 150 *Web:* www.kierlandcommons.com	Scottsdale	AZ	85254	480-348-1577		460
Kiernan, Plunkett & Redihan 146 Westminster St *Web:* kprlaw.com	Providence	RI	02903	401-831-2900		41
Kieve Wavus Education Inc 42 Kieve Rd *Web:* www.kwe.org	Nobleboro	ME	04555	207-563-5172		239
KIFT-FM 130 Ski Hill Rd Ste 240 *Web:* www.alwaysmountaintime.com	Breckenridge	CO	80424	970-453-2234		647
Kight Home Ctr 5521 Oak Grove Rd *Web:* www.kighthomecenter.com	Evansville	IN	47715	812-479-8281		191-3
Kightlinger Motors Inc 358 Rt 6 W *Web:* www.kightlingermotor.com	Coudersport	PA	16915	814-274-9660		57
KIII-TV Ch 3 (ABC) 5002 S Padre Island Dr *Web:* www.kiiitv.com	Corpus Christi	TX	78411	361-986-8300		741-36
KIIM-FM 99.5 (Ctry) 575 W Roger Rd *Web:* www.kiimfm.com	Tucson	AZ	85705	520-880-5446	887-6397	645-165
Kiip Inc 970 Folsom St *Web:* home.kiip.me	San Francisco	CA	94107	415-400-9479		4

Name / Address	City	State	ZIP	Phone	Fax	Class
KIK Custom Products 2730 Middlebury St TF: 800-479-6603 ■ Web: www.kikcorp.com	Elkhart	IN	46516	574-295-0000		145
KIK Pool Additives Inc 5160 E Airport Dr TF: 800-745-4536 ■ Web: www.kem-tek.com	Ontario	CA	91761	909-390-9912	390-9911	145
Kiki's Bistro 900 N Franklin St Web: www.kikisbistro.com	Chicago	IL	60610	312-335-5454		671
Kikiriki 215 Market St Web: kikirikirestaurant.com	Paterson	NJ	07505	973-225-0336		671
Kikkoman Foods Inc N 1365 Six Corners Rd Web: www.kikkoman.com	Walworth	WI	53184	262-275-6181	275-9452	296-19
KIKO 2722 Fulton Dr NW TF: 800-533-5456 ■ Web: www.kikoauctions.com	Canton	OH	44718	330-453-9187	453-1765	466
KIKO Wireless 33 W 27th St Web: www.kikowireless.com	New York	NY	10001	212-686-2198		246
Kiko's 5514 Everhart Rd Web: kikosmexicanfood.com	Corpus Christi	TX	78411	361-991-1211		671
Kiku Japanese Restaurant 225 W Station Square Dr Web: kikupittsburgh.net	Pittsburgh	PA	15219	412-765-3200		671
Kiku Obata & Co 6161 Delmar Blvd Ste 200 Web: kikuobata.com	Saint Louis	MO	63112	314-361-3110		344
Kikusui America Inc 3625 Del Amo Blvd Ste 160 TF: 877-876-2807 ■ Web: www.kikusuiamerica.com	Torrance	CA	90503	650-259-5900		246
KIKU-TV 737 Bishop St Ste1430 Web: www.kikutv.com	Honolulu	HI	96813	808-847-2021	841-3326	741-59
Kilby Correctional Facility 12201 Wares Ferry Rd Web: doc.alabama.gov	Montgomery	AL	36117	334-215-6600		213
Kildair Service ULC 1000 Montee des Pionniers Bureau 110 Web: www.kildair.com	Terrebonne	QC	J6V1S8	450-756-8091	756-4783	579
Kildee Daniel (Rep D - MI) 203 Cannon House Office Bldg Web: dankildee.house.gov	Washington	DC	20515	202-225-3611		342-2
Kildeer Countryside Community Consolidated School District 96 1050 Ivy Hall Ln Web: www.kcsd96.org	Buffalo Grove	IL	60089	847-459-4260	459-2344	780
Kildonan School 425 Morse Hill Rd Web: www.kildonan.org	Amenia	NY	12501	845-373-8111	373-2004	622
Kile & Kupiszewski Law Firm 8727 E Via De Commercio TF: 866-404-5085 ■ Web: kilekuplaw.com	Scottsdale	AZ	85258	480-348-1590		41
Kilen Woods State Park 50200 860th St Web: www.dnr.state.mn.us	Lakefield	MN	56150	507-832-6034		565
Kilgore College 1100 Broadway Web: www.kilgore.edu	Kilgore	TX	75662	903-984-8531		162
Kilgore Flares Co 155 Kilgore Dr Web: www.chemring.co.uk	Toone	TN	38381	731-658-5231	658-4173	268
Kilgore Manufacturing Company Inc 445 S Line St Web: kilgoremfg.com	Columbia City	IN	46725	260-248-2002	248-2882	476
Kilgore-Lewis House, The 560 N Academy St Web: www.kilgore-lewis.org	Greenville	SC	29601	864-232-3020		50-3
KILJ-AM 2411 Radio Dr Web: www.kilj.com	Mount Pleasant	IA	52641	319-385-8728	385-4517	647
Kil-Kare Speedway 1166 Dayton-Xenia Rd Web: www.kilkare.com	Xenia	OH	45385	937-429-2961		515
Kilkenny's Irish Pub & Eatery 1413 E 15th St Web: tulsairishpub.com	Tulsa	OK	74120	918-582-8282	582-3931	671
Kill Kare State Park 2714 Hathaway Point Rd Web: www.vtstateparks.com	Saint Albans	VT	05481	802-524-6021		565
Killam Oil Co 4320 University Blvd Web: www.killamco.com	Laredo	TX	78041	956-724-7141		538
Killdeer Mountain Manufacturing Inc (KMM) 233 Rodeo Dr Web: www.kmmnet.com	Killdeer	ND	58640	701-764-5651	764-5427	625
Killeen Civic & Conference Center & Visitors Bureau 3601 S WS Young Dr Web: www.visitkilleen.com	Killeen	TX	76542	254-501-3888		206
Killeen Daily Herald 1809 Florence Rd PO Box 1300 Web: www.kdhnews.com	Killeen	TX	76540	254-501-7525	200-7640	532-2
Killens Pond State Park 5025 Killens Pond Rd Web: www.destateparks.com	Felton	DE	19943	302-284-4526	284-4694	565
Killer Dana Surf Shop 24621 Del Prado Web: www.kdsurfshop.com	Dana Point	CA	92629	949-489-8380		711
Killian Branding 73 W Monroe St Web: www.killianbranding.com	Chicago	IL	60603	312-836-0050		4
Killian Construction Co 2664 E Kearney St Web: www.killco.com	Springfield	MO	65803	417-883-1204	887-7338	186
Killian, Davis, Richter & Mayle PC 202 N Seventh St Web: www.killianlaw.com	Grand Junction	CO	81501	970-241-0707	242-8375	428
Killington 4763 Killington Rd TF: 800-734-9435 ■ Web: www.killington.com	Killington	VT	05751	802-422-3333	422-6113	669
Killion Communications Consultants Inc (KCC) 302 Palm St TF: 800-301-6672 ■ Web: www.kilco.com	Roodhouse	IL	62082	217-589-4713	589-4920	194
Killion Industries Inc 1380 Poinsettia Ave TF: 800-421-5352 ■ Web: www.killionindustries.com	Vista	CA	92081	760-727-5102	727-5108	286
Killmer, Lane & Newman LLP 1543 Champa St Ste 400 Web: kln-law.com	Denver	CO	80202	303-571-1000		41
Kilmer Derek (Rep D - WA) 1410 Longworth House Office Bldg Web: www.kilmer.house.gov	Washington	DC	20515	202-225-5916		342-2
Kilmer, Voorhees & Laurick PC 732 NW 19th Ave Web: www.kilmerlaw.com	Portland	OR	97209	503-224-0055		428
Kiln Drying Systems & Components Inc 234 Industrial Dr TF: 800-274-5456 ■ Web: kdskilns.com	Etowah	NC	28729	828-891-8115	891-5451	695
KILO Radio 1805 E Cheyenne Rd TF: 800-727-5456 ■ Web: kilo943.com	Colorado Springs	CO	80905	719-633-5456	634-5837	645-37
Kilpatrick Equipment Co (KEC) 2612 Manor Way TF: 800-929-2822 ■ Web: www.kec-dfw.com	Dallas	TX	75235	214-358-4346	358-3723	112
Kilpatrick Life Insurance Co 1818 Marshall St TF: 800-235-0555 ■ Web: klic.com	Shreveport	LA	71101	800-235-0555		391-2
Kilpatrick Townsend & Stockton LLP 1100 Peachtree St Web: www.kilpatricktownsend.com	Atlanta	GA	30309	404-815-6500	815-6555	428
Kilroy Realty Corp 12200 W Olympic Blvd Ste 200 NYSE: KRC ■ Web: www.kilroyrealty.com	Los Angeles	CA	90064	310-481-8400	481-6501	655
Kilwins Quality Confections Inc (KQC) 1050 Bay View Rd TF: 888-454-5946 ■ Web: www.kilwins.com	Petoskey	MI	49770	888-454-5946		123
KIM (Kim International Manufacturing LP) 14840 Landmark Blvd *Fax Area Code: 800 ■ TF: 800-275-5555 ■ Web: www.kimint.com	Dallas	TX	75254	972-385-7555	608-3322*	409
Kim Andy (Rep D - NJ) 1516 Longworth House Office Bldg Web: www.kim.house.gov	Washington	DC	20515	202-225-4765		342-2
Kim Davidson Aviation Inc 2701 Airport Ave Web: www.kdasmo.com	Santa Monica	CA	90405	310-391-6293		359
Kim Engineering Inc 11900 Baltimore Ave Ste F Web: www.kimengineering.com	Beltsville	MD	20705	240-542-4238		256
Kim Hotstart Manufacturing Co 5723 E Alki Ave TF: 800-224-5550 ■ Web: www.hotstart.com	Spokane	WA	99212	509-536-8660		15
Kim International Manufacturing LP (KIM) 14840 Landmark Blvd *Fax Area Code: 800 ■ TF: 800-275-5555 ■ Web: www.kimint.com	Dallas	TX	75254	972-385-7555	608-3322*	409
Kim Phung 7601 N Lamar Blvd Web: www.kimphungaustin.com	Austin	TX	78752	512-451-2464		671
Kimal Lumber Co 400 Riverview Dr Web: kimallumber.com	Nokomis	FL	34275	941-484-9721	484-9593	191-3
Kimball County 114 E Third St TF: 800-369-2850 ■ Web: www.co.kimball.ne.us	Kimball	NE	69145	308-235-2241	235-3654	338
Kimball Electronics 13700 Reptron Blvd Web: www.kimballelectronics.com	Tampa	FL	33626	813-814-5000		625
Kimball Genetics Inc 8490 Upland Dr Ste 100 TF: 800-444-9111 ■ Web: www.kimballgenetics.com	Englewood	CO	80112	800-444-9111		415
Kimball Hospitality 1180 E 16th St TF: 800-634-9510 ■ Web: www.kimballhospitality.com	Jasper	IN	47549	276-666-8933		319-3
Kimball International Inc 1600 Royal St NASDAQ: KBAL ■ TF: 800-482-1616 ■ Web: www.kimball.com	Jasper	IN	47549	800-482-1616		185
Kimball Midwest 4800 Robert Rd *Fax Area Code: 614 ■ TF: 800-233-1294 ■ Web: www.kimballmidwest.com	Columbus	OH	43228	800-214-9440	219-6101*	385
Kimball Property Maintenance 12717 S 125 E Web: kimballpm.com	Draper	UT	84020	801-571-3351		776
Kimball Terrace Inn 10 Huntington Rd TF: 800-454-6225 ■ Web: www.kimballterraceinn.com	Northeast Harbor	ME	04662	207-276-3383		379
Kimball Union Academy 7 Campus Center Dr Web: www.kua.org	Meriden	NH	03770	603-469-2000	469-2040	622
Kimball, Tirey & St John LLP 7676 Hazard Center Dr TF: 800-564-6611 ■ Web: www.kts-law.com	San Diego	CA	92108	800-564-6611		428
Kimball-Jenkins Estate 266 N Main St Web: www.kimballjenkins.com	Concord	NH	03301	603-225-3932	225-9288	50-3
Kimbanet 613 D Liberty St TF: 877-666-9209 ■ Web: www.kimbanet.com	Martinsville	VA	24112	276-666-9209	666-0155	224
Kimbell Art Museum 3333 Camp Bowie Blvd Web: www.kimbellart.org	Fort Worth	TX	76107	817-332-8451	877-1264	520
Kimber Manufacturing Inc 555 Taxter Rd Ste 235 TF: 888-243-4522 ■ Web: www.kimberamerica.com	Elmsford	NY	10523	406-758-2222		326
Kimberly Crest House & Gardens 1325 Prospect Dr Web: www.kimberlycrest.org	Redlands	CA	92373	909-792-2111	798-1716	50-3
Kimberly Hotel 145 E 50th St TF: 800-683-0400 ■ Web: www.kimberlyhotel.com	New York	NY	10022	212-755-0400	355-4318	379
Kimberly Ries Ashley PS 415 W 3rd Ave Web: krashleylaw.com	Moses Lake	WA	98837	509-766-4234		41
Kimberly-Clark Corp 351 Phelps Dr NYSE: KMB ■ TF: 888-525-8388 ■ Web: www.kimberly-clark.com	Irving	TX	75038	972-281-1200		558
Kimble Chase Life Science & Research Products LLC 1022 Spruce St Web: www.kimble-chase.com	Vineland	NJ	08362	856-692-8500		419
Kimble Companies Inc 3596 SR-39 NW TF: 800-201-0005 ■ Web: www.kimblecompanies.com	Dover	OH	44622	800-201-0005		787
Kimble County 501 Main St Web: www.co.kimble.tx.us	Junction	TX	76849	325-446-3353	446-2986	338
Kimbro Oil Company Inc 2200 Clifton Ave Web: www.kimbrooil.com	Nashville	TN	37203	615-320-7484		579
Kimbrough Animal Hospital Inc 1613 Judson Rd Web: kimbroughanimalhospital.com	Longview	TX	75601	903-757-5543		794
Kimco Realty Corp 3333 New Hyde Park Rd NYSE: KIM ■ TF: 800-645-6292 ■ Web: www.kimcorealty.com	New Hyde Park	NY	11042	516-869-9000		655

Phone | Fax | Class

Kimco Staffing Services Inc
17872 Cowan Ave. . . . Irvine CA 92614 949-752-6996 721
TF: 800-649-5627 ■ Web: www.kimco.com

Kimley-Horn & Associates Inc
421 Fayetteville St Ste 600 . . . . Raleigh NC 27601 919-677-2000 194
Web: www.kimley-horn.com

Kimlor Mills Inc
2630 Saint Matthews Rd . . . . Orangeburg SC 29118 800-762-0007 232-9060 745-1
TF: 800-762-0007 ■ Web: www.kimlor.com

Kimmel & Associates Inc 25 Page Ave . . . . Asheville NC 28801 828-251-9900 251-9955 193
Web: kimmel.com

Kimmel Center for the Performing Arts
1500 Walnut St 1st Fl . . . . Philadelphia PA 19102 215-790-5800 790-5801 572
Web: www.kimmelcenter.org

Kimmins Contracting Corp
1501 E Second Ave . . . . Tampa FL 33605 813-248-3878 579-1081 188-10
Web: www.kimmins.com

Kimmons Investigative Services Inc
5177 Richmond Ave Ste 1190 . . . . Houston TX 77056 713-532-5881 266-4002 693
TF: 800-681-5046 ■ Web: www.kimmonsinv.com

KiMo Theater 423 Central Ave NW . . . . Albuquerque NM 87102 505-768-3589 572
Web: www.abqtickets.com

Kimoto Tech Inc 601 Canal St . . . . Cedartown GA 30125 770-748-2643 748-2648 600
Web: www.kimototech.com

Kimpton Hotel & Restaurant Group
422 SW Broadway . . . . Portland OR 97205 503-228-1212 228-3598 379
TF: 800-263-2305 ■ Web: www.hotelvintage-portland.com

Kimpton Hotel & Restaurant Group LLC
1733 N St NW . . . . Washington DC 20036 202-393-3000 331-8599 379
TF: 800-775-1202 ■ Web: www.topazhotel.com

Kimpton Key West
Kimpton Hotel & Restaurant Group LLC
725 Truman Ave . . . . Key West FL 33040 305-294-5229 379
TF: 800-549-4430 ■ Web: www.kimptonkeywest.com

Kimray Inc 52 NW 42nd St . . . . Oklahoma City OK 73118 405-525-6601 525-7520 790
Web: kimray.com

KIMT-TV Ch 3 (CBS)
112 N Pennsylvania Ave . . . . Mason City IA 50401 641-423-2540 423-9309 741
TF: 800-323-4883 ■ Web: www.kimt.com

Kimwood Corp 77684 Oregon 99 . . . . Cottage Grove OR 97424 541-942-4401 942-0719 821
TF: 800-942-4401 ■ Web: www.kimwood.com

KIMX-FM 302 S 2nd St Ste 204 . . . . Laramie WY 82070 307-745-5208 647
Web: imixwyoming.com

Kin Communications Inc
736 Granville St Ste 100 . . . . Vancouver BC V6Z1G3 604-684-6730 224
TF: 866-684-6730 ■ Web: kincommunications.com

Kin Insurance 55 W Monroe St . . . . Chicago IL 60603 855-717-0022 391-5
TF: 855-717-0022 ■ Web: www.kin.com

Kin On Health Care Ctr
4416 S Brandon St . . . . Seattle WA 98118 206-721-3630 371
Web: kinon.org

Kin's Wok
4001 Virginia Beach Blvd . . . . Virginia Beach VA 23452 757-340-6898 671
Web: kinswokvb.com

Kinamed Inc 820 Flynn Rd . . . . Camarillo CA 93012 805-384-2748 476
TF: 800-827-5775 ■ Web: www.kinamed.com

Kinamor Inc
63 N Plains Industrial Rd . . . . Wallingford CT 06492 203-269-0380 604
Web: www.kinamorinc.com

Kinaneco Inc 2925 Milton Ave . . . . Syracuse NY 13209 315-468-6201 468-6202 627
TF: 800-536-6201 ■ Web: www.kinaneco.com

Kinark Child 500 Hood Rd Ste 200 . . . . Markham ON L3R9Z3 905-474-9595 393
TF: 800-230-8533 ■ Web: www.kinark.on.ca

Kinaxis 700 Silver Seven Rd . . . . Ottawa ON K2V1C3 613-592-5780 592-0584 178-10
TF: 877-546-2947 ■ Web: www.kinaxis.com

Kincaid Coach Lines Inc
9207 Woodend Rd . . . . Kansas City KS 66111 913-441-6200 441-0068 760
TF: 800-998-1901 ■ Web: www.kincaidcoach.com

Kincaid Grill 6700 Jewel Lake Rd . . . . Anchorage AK 99502 907-243-0507 243-5110 671
Web: www.kincaidgrill.com

Kincaid Lake State Park
565 Kincaid Park Rd . . . . Falmouth KY 41040 859-654-3531 565
Web: parks.ky.gov

Kincaid Taylor & Geyer 50 N 4th St . . . . Zanesville OH 43701 740-454-2591 41
Web: kincaidlaw.com

Kincaid's American Dining
380 St Peter St Ste 125 . . . . Saint Paul MN 55102 651-602-9000 671
Web: kincaids.com

Kincannon & Reed LLC
40 Stoneridge Dr Ste 101 . . . . Waynesboro VA 22980 540-941-3460 301-6320 193
Web: www.krsearch.com

Kincardine Cable TV Ltd
223 Bruce Ave . . . . Kincardine ON N2Z2P2 519-396-8880 116
TF: 800-265-3064 ■ Web: www.tnt21.com

Kincel & Company Ltd 1100 Dunham Dr . . . . Dunmore PA 18512 570-961-8731 390
Web: kincel.com

Kinco Constructors LLC
12600 Lawson Rd . . . . Little Rock AR 72210 501-225-7606 186
Web: kincoconstructors.com

Kinco Intl 18792 NE Portal Way . . . . Portland OR 97230 800-547-8410 536-4905 155-8
TF: 800-547-8410 ■ Web: www.kinco.com

Kind Ron (Rep D - WI)
1502 Longworth House Office Bldg . . . . Washington DC 20515 202-225-5506 225-5739 342-2
Web: www.kind.house.gov

Kinder Morgan
1001 Louisiana St Ste 1000 . . . . Houston TX 77002 713-369-9000 230-5675 325
NYSE: KMI ■ TF: 800-247-4122 ■ Web: www.kindermorgan.com

KinderCare Learning Centers LLC
650 NE Holladay St Ste 1400 . . . . Portland OR 97232 800-633-1488 872-1427* 148
*Fax Area Code: 503 ■ TF: 800-633-1488 ■ Web: www.kindercare.com

Kinderdance International Inc
5238 Valleypointe Pkwy . . . . Roanoke VA 24019 540-904-2595 310
TF: 800-554-2334 ■ Web: kinderdance.com

Kindred Communications Inc
555 5th Ave Ste K . . . . Huntington WV 25701 304-523-8401 647
Web: www.kindredcom.net

Kindred Healthcare Inc
680 S Fourth Ave . . . . Louisville KY 40202 502-596-7300 353
NYSE: KND ■ TF: 800-545-0749 ■ Web: www.kindredhealthcare.com

Kindred Partners LLC
535 Mission St 22nd Fl Ste 2250 . . . . San Francisco CA 94105 650-573-5500 652
Web: www.kindredpartners.com

Kinecta Federal Credit Union
1440 Rosecrans Ave PO Box 10003 . . . . Manhattan Beach CA 90266 310-643-5400 219
TF: 800-854-9846 ■ Web: www.kinecta.org

Kinectrics Inc 800 Kipling Ave . . . . Toronto ON M8Z5G5 416-207-6000 261
Web: www.kinectrics.com

Kinefac Corp
156 Goddard Memorial Dr . . . . Worcester MA 01603 508-754-6891 756-5342 456
Web: www.kinefac.com

KINE-FM 105.1 (AC) 900 Ft St Ste 700 . . . . Honolulu HI 96813 808-275-1000 645-70
Web: www.hawaiian105.com

Kinematic Automation Inc
21085 Longeway Rd . . . . Sonora CA 95370 209-532-3200 532-0248 476
Web: www.kinematic.com

Kinemetrics Inc 222 Vista Ave . . . . Pasadena CA 91107 626-795-2220 795-0868 472
Web: kinemetrics.com

Kinemotive Corp 222 Central Ave . . . . Farmingdale NY 11735 631-249-6440 407
Web: www.kinemotive.com

Kinesis Corp 22030 20th Ave SE Ste 102 . . . . Bothell WA 98021 425-402-8100 402-8181 173-1
TF: 800-454-6374 ■ Web: www.kinesis-ergo.com

Kinetic Cafe Inc 934 - 1 Yonge St . . . . Toronto ON M5E1E5 416-899-0761 463
Web: www.kineticcommerce.com

Kinetic Instrument Inc
17 Berkshire Blvd . . . . Bethel CT 06801 203-743-0080 228
TF: 800-233-2346 ■ Web: www.kineticinc.com

Kinetic Systems Inc 20 Arboretum Rd . . . . Boston MA 02131 617-522-8700 256
Web: www.kineticsystems.com

Kinetic Technologies Inc
6399 San Ignacio Ave Ste 250 . . . . San Jose CA 95119 408-746-9000 261
Web: kinet-ic.com

Kinetico Inc 10845 Kinsman Rd . . . . Newbury OH 44065 440-564-9111 564-9541 806
TF: 800-944-9283 ■ Web: www.kinetico.com

Kineticorp
6070 Greenwood Plaza Blvd Ste 200 . . . . Greenwood Village CO 80111 303-733-1888 733-1902 743
TF: 877-805-4205 ■ Web: kineticorp.com

Kinetics Industries Inc
140 Stokes Ave . . . . Trenton NJ 08638 609-883-9700 883-0025 253
Web: www.kinetics-industries.com

Kinetics Mechanical Service Inc
6336 Patterson Pass Rd . . . . Livermore CA 94550 925-245-6200 245-6222 610
Web: www.kms-inc.com

Kinetix Technology Ctr
400 Murray St . . . . Alexandria LA 71301 318-487-8200 396
Web: www.400ktc.com

King & I 545 Broadbridge Rd . . . . Bridgeport CT 06610 203-374-2081 671
Web: www.kingandict.com

King & I 3157 S Grand Ave . . . . Saint Louis MO 63118 314-771-1777 671
Web: kingandistl.squarespace.com

King & I, The
830 N Old World Third St . . . . Milwaukee WI 53203 414-276-4181 671
Web: www.kingandirestaurant.com

King & Jurgens LLC
201 St Charles Ave 45th Fl . . . . New Orleans LA 70170 504-582-3800 582-1233 428
TF: 877-809-6912 ■ Web: www.kingjurgens.com

King & Partners PLC
170 College Ave Ste 230 . . . . Holland MI 49423 616-355-0400 355-9862 428
Web: www.king-partners.com

King & Prince Beach & Golf Resort
201 Arnold Rd . . . . Saint Simons Island GA 31522 912-638-3631 638-7699 669
TF: 800-342-0212 ■ Web: www.kingandprince.com

King & Prince Seafood Corp
1 King & Prince Blvd . . . . Brunswick GA 31520 888-391-5223 296-14
TF: 888-391-5223 ■ Web: www.kpseafood.com

King & Queen County
242 Allens Cir Ste L
PO Box 177 . . . . King and Queen Court House VA 23085 804-785-5975 785-5999 338
Web: www.kingandqueenco.net

King & Schickli PLLC
800 Corporate Dr Ste 200 . . . . Lexington KY 40503 859-274-4287 252-0779 428
TF: 888-364-5712 ■ Web: www.iplaw1.net

King & Spalding 1180 Peachtree St NE . . . . Atlanta GA 30309 404-572-4600 572-5100 428
Web: www.kslaw.com

KING 5 Television
1501 First Ave S Ste 300 . . . . Seattle WA 98134 206-448-5555 741-123
Web: www.king5.com

King Aerospace Inc 4500 Westgrove Dr . . . . Addison TX 75001 972-248-4886 21
Web: kingaerospace.com

King Agency Inc, The 3 N Lombardy St . . . . Richmond VA 23220 804-249-7500 4
Web: thekingagency.com

King Angus S Jr (Sen I - ME)
133 Hart Senate Office Bldg . . . . Washington DC 20510 202-224-5344 342-2
Web: www.king.senate.gov

King Architectural Metals Inc
PO Box 271169 . . . . Dallas TX 75227 800-542-2379 491
TF: 800-542-2379 ■ Web: kingmetals.com

King Arthur Flour Company Inc, The
135 Rt 5 S . . . . Norwich VT 05055 802-649-3361 649-3365 68
TF: 800-827-6836 ■ Web: www.kingarthurflour.com

King Arts Complex, The
867 Mt Vernon Ave . . . . Columbus OH 43203 614-645-5464 645-0672 50-2
Web: kingartscomplex.com

King Bio 3 Westside Dr . . . . Asheville NC 28806 855-739-7127 255-0940* 582
*Fax Area Code: 828 ■ TF: 800-237-4100 ■ Web: www.drkings.com

King Business Interiors Inc
1400 Goodale Blvd Ste 102 . . . . Columbus OH 43229 614-430-0020 317
Web: www.kbiinc.com

King City Union School District
104 S Vanderhurst Ave . . . . King City CA 93930 831-385-2940 685
Web: www.kcusd.org

King College 1350 King College Rd . . . . Bristol TN 37620 423-652-4861 166
TF: 800-362-0014 ■ Web: www.king.edu

King County 401 Fifth Ave 3rd Fl . . . . Seattle WA 98104 206-296-1586 296-0194 338
TF: 800-325-6165 ■ Web: www.kingcounty.gov

King County 516 3rd Ave . . . . Seattle WA 98104 206-205-9200 296-0910 270
Web: www.kingcounty.gov

Name / Address	City	State	ZIP	Phone	Fax	Class
King County Department of Transportation 201 S Jackson St *Web:* kingcounty.gov	Seattle	WA	98104	206-296-6590	684-1224	468
King County Library System 960 Newport Way NW *Web:* kcls.org	Issaquah	WA	98027	425-369-3224		434-3
King County Sexual Assault Resource Ctr (KCSARC) 200 Mill Ave S Ste 10 *TF:* 888-998-6423 ■ *Web:* www.kcsarc.org	Renton	WA	98057	425-226-5062	235-7422	637-2
King Ctr, The 449 Auburn Ave NE *Web:* www.thekingcenter.org	Atlanta	GA	30312	404-526-8900		48-8
King David's 129 Marshall St *Web:* www.kingdavids.com	Syracuse	NY	13210	315-471-5000		671
King Electrical Manufacturing Co 9131 Tenth Ave S *TF:* 800-603-5464 ■ *Web:* www.king-electric.com	Seattle	WA	98108	206-762-0400	763-7738	37
King Engineering Associates Inc 324 Nicholas Parkway W Unit A *Web:* www.kingengineering.com	Cape Coral	FL	33991	813-880-8881		261
King Engineering Corp 3201 S State St *TF:* 800-242-8871 ■ *Web:* www.king-gage.com	Ann Arbor	MI	48106	734-662-5691	662-6652	18
King Estate Winery 80854 Territorial Rd *TF:* 800-884-4441 ■ *Web:* www.kingestate.com	Eugene	OR	97405	541-942-9874	942-9867	50-7
King Features Syndicate Inc 300 W 57th St **Fax Area Code:* 646 ■ *Web:* www.kingfeatures.com	New York	NY	10019	212-969-7550	280-1550*	530
King Fuels Inc 14825 Willis St *Web:* www.kingfuels.com	Houston	TX	77039	281-449-9975		579
King George County 9483 Kings Hwy Ste 3 *Web:* www.kinggeorgecountyva.gov	King George	VA	22485	540-775-3322	775-5466	338
King George Hotel 334 Mason St *Web:* www.kinggeorge.com	San Francisco	CA	94102	415-781-5050	391-6976	378
King Hickory Furniture Co 1820 Main Ave SE *Web:* www.kinghickory.com	Hickory	NC	28602	828-322-6025		319-2
King Industries Inc 1 Science Rd *TF:* 800-431-7900 ■ *Web:* www.kingindustries.com	Norwalk	CT	06852	203-866-5551	866-1268	145
King Information Systems Inc 3 Edgewater Dr *Web:* kinginformationsystems.com	Norwood	MA	02062	781-762-6477		535
King Instrument Company Inc 12700 Pala Dr *Web:* kinginstrumentco.com	Garden Grove	CA	92841	714-891-0008		201
King Kamehameha V - Judiciary History Ctr 417 S King St *Web:* www.jhchawaii.net	Honolulu	HI	96813	808-539-4999		520
King Koil Licensing Company Inc 7501 S Quincy St *TF:* 800-525-8331 ■ *Web:* www.kingkoil.com	Willowbrook	IL	60527	800-525-8331		471
King Kold Inc 331-333 N Main St *TF:* 800-836-2797 ■ *Web:* kingkoldinc.com	Englewood	OH	45322	937-836-2731	836-5919	296-36
King Kullen Grocery Company Inc 185 Central Ave *Web:* www.kingkullen.com	Bethpage	NY	11714	516-733-7100		345
King Kutter inc 305 Commerce Dr PO Box 1200 *Web:* taylorpittsburgh.com	Winfield	AL	35594	205-487-3202		273
King Machine & Tool Co 1237 Sanders Ave SW *Web:* www.kmtco.com	Massillon	OH	44647	330-833-7217	833-2761	295
King Medical Supply (KMS) 20816 Higgins Ct **Fax Area Code:* 866 ■ *TF:* 800-488-6535 ■ *Web:* www.kingmedicalsupply.com	Torrance	CA	90501	800-488-6535	533-8810*	475
King Milling Co 115 S Broadway St *Web:* kingflour.com	Lowell	MI	49331	616-897-9264		296-23
King Mountain State Recreation Site King Mountain 33915 N Glenn Hwy *Web:* www.dnr.alaska.gov	Chickaloon	AK	99674	907-240-9797		565
King Nummy Trail Campground 205 Rt 47 S *Web:* rvonthego.com	Cape May	NJ	08210	609-465-4242		239
King Nut Co 31900 Solon Rd *TF:* 800-860-5464 ■ *Web:* www.kingnut.com	Solon	OH	44139	440-248-8484	248-0153	296-28
King Pacific Lodge 4850 Cowley Crescen *TF:* 855-825-9378 ■ *Web:* kingpacificlodge.com	Richmond	BC	V7E0B5	604-503-5474		379
King Pete (Rep R - NY) 302 Cannon House Office Bldg *Web:* www.peteking.house.gov	Washington	DC	20515	202-225-7896	226-2279	342-2
King Plastic Corp 1100 N Toledo Blade Blvd *TF:* 800-780-5502 ■ *Web:* www.kingplastic.com	North Port	FL	34288	941-493-5502	497-3274	608
King Plastics Inc 840 N Elm St *TF:* 800-363-9822 ■ *Web:* www.kingplastics.com	Orange	CA	92867	714-997-7540	997-0491	607
King Precision Glass Inc 177 S Indian Hill Blvd *Web:* www.kingprecisionglass.com	Claremont	CA	91711	909-626-3526	625-0173	332
King Printing Company Inc 181 Industrial Ave E *Web:* www.kingprinting.com	Lowell	MA	01852	978-458-2345	458-1441	626
King Ranch Inc 3 Riverway Ste 1600 **Fax Area Code:* 713 ■ *TF:* 800-762-0076 ■ *Web:* king-ranch.com	Houston	TX	77056	832-681-5700	287-2755*	10-1
King Relocation Services 13535 Larwin Cir *TF:* 800-854-3679 ■ *Web:* www.kingcompaniesusa.com	Santa Fe Springs	CA	90670	800-854-3679		519
King Steve (Rep R - IA) 2210 Rayburn House Office Bldg *Web:* steveking.house.gov	Washington	DC	20515	202-225-4426	225-3193	342-2
King Taco Restaurants Inc 1118 Cypress Ave *Web:* www.kingtaco.com	Los Angeles	CA	90065	323-223-2595		670
King Tiger Martial Arts Inc 13401 New Hampshire Ave *Web:* www.kingtigermartialarts.com	Silver Spring	MD	20904	301-989-2400		148
King Tut's Grill 4132 Martin Mill Pk	Knoxville	TN	37920	865-573-6021		671
King William County 351 Courthouse Ln Ste 201 *Web:* www.kingwilliamcounty.us	King William	VA	23086	804-769-4947	769-4971	338
King William Historic District 122 Madison St *Web:* www.kwfair.org	San Antonio	TX	78204	210-271-3247		50-3
King Wire Partitions Inc 6044 N Figueroa St PO Box 42220 *TF:* 800-789-9608 ■ *Web:* www.kingwireusa.com	Los Angeles	CA	90042	323-256-4848	256-1950	688
King's Academy Inc, The 8401 Belvedere Rd *Web:* www.tka.net	West Palm Beach	FL	33411	561-686-4244	686-8017	685
King's Cages International LLC 375 Old Bridge Tpke *TF:* 866-777-7303 ■ *Web:* www.kingscages.com	East Brunswick	NJ	08816	732-698-9800	698-9806	328
King's Chapel 58 Tremont St *Web:* www.kings-chapel.org	Boston	MA	02108	617-227-2155		50-1
King's College 133 N River St *TF:* 800-955-5777 ■ *Web:* www.kings.edu	Wilkes-Barre	PA	18711	570-208-5858	208-5971	166
King's College & Seminary 14344 Sherman Way *Web:* www.tku.edu	Van Nuys	CA	91405	818-779-8505		161
King's County Market 13735 Roundlake Blvd *Web:* kingscountymarket.com	Andover	MN	55304	763-422-1768		297-8
King's Daughters Medical Ctr 2201 Lexington Ave *TF:* 888-377-5362 ■ *Web:* www.kingsdaughtershealth.com	Ashland	KY	41101	606-408-8999		374-3
King's Daughters Medical Ctr 427 Hwy 51 N *Web:* kdmc.org	Brookhaven	MS	39601	601-833-6011		374-3
King's Daughters' Hospital 1373 E State Rd 62 *Web:* www.kdhmadison.org	Madison	IN	47250	812-801-0800	801-0680	374-3
King's Fish House 100 W Broadway *Web:* www.kingsfishhouse.com	Long Beach	CA	90802	562-432-7463		671
King's Head Pub 120 King St *Web:* www.kingshead.ca	Winnipeg	MB	R3B1H0	204-957-7710		671
King's Heating & Sheet Metal Inc 137 S Work St *Web:* www.kings-heating.com	Falconer	NY	14733	716-665-3102	665-5524	697
King's Jewelry & Loan 800 S Vermont Ave *TF:* 800-378-1111 ■ *Web:* www.kingspawn.com	Los Angeles	CA	90005	213-383-5555		410
King's Material Inc 650 12th Ave SW *TF:* 800-332-5298 ■ *Web:* www.kingsmaterial.com	Cedar Rapids	IA	52404	319-363-0233	366-0249	183
King's Medical Co 1894 Georgetown Rd *Web:* www.kingsmedical.com	Hudson	OH	44236	330-653-3968	656-0600	264-4
King's Palace Cafe 162 Beale St *Web:* www.kingspalacecafe.com	Memphis	TN	38103	901-521-1851		671
King's Seafood Co 3185 Airway Ave *Web:* www.kingsseafood.com	Costa Mesa	CA	92626	714-432-0400		670
King's University College 9125 50th St *TF:* 800-661-8582 ■ *Web:* www.kingsu.ca	Edmonton	AB	T6B2H3	780-465-3500	465-3534	166
Kingbridge Centre, The 12750 Jane St *TF:* 800-827-7221 ■ *Web:* kingbridgecentre.com	King City	ON	L7B1A3	905-833-3086	833-3075	377
KingChapman 3355 W Albama St Ste 1255 *Web:* kingchapman.com	Houston	TX	77098	713-223-7233		194
Kingdom Builders' Center, The 6011 W Orem Dr *Web:* www.thekbc.com	Houston	TX	77085	713-726-2500	726-2508	655
Kingdom Come State Park 502 Park Rd *Web:* parks.ky.gov	Cumberland	KY	40823	606-589-2478		565
Kingdom FM PO Box 61721 *Web:* www.kingdom.fm	Fort Myers	FL	33906	239-274-9150		645-141
Kingdom Inc 719 Lambs Creek Rd *TF:* 800-480-1011 ■ *Web:* www.kingdom.com	Mansfield	PA	16933	570-662-7515		174
Kingdom of Morocco, The *Consulate General* 10 E 40th St **Fax Area Code:* 646 ■ *TF:* 800-787-8806 ■ *Web:* www.moroccanconsulate.com	New York	NY	10016	212-758-2625	395-8077*	257
Kingdom Telephone Co 211 S Main St *TF:* 800-829-2452 ■ *Web:* www.kingdomtelco.com	Auxvasse	MO	65231	573-386-5847	386-5520	224
Kingery Construction Co 201 N 46th St *Web:* www.kccobuilders.com	Lincoln	NE	68503	402-465-4400		196
Kingery Printing Co 3012 S Banker PO Box 727 *Web:* www.kingeryprinting.com	Effingham	IL	62401	217-347-5151		627
Kingfish Grill 252 Yacht Club Dr *Web:* www.kingfishgrill.com	Saint Augustine	FL	32084	904-824-2111		671
Kingfisher Bar & Grill 2564 E Grant Rd *Web:* kingfishertucson.com	Tucson	AZ	85716	520-323-7739		671
Kingfisher County 101 S Main County Courthouse Rm 9 *Web:* ltap.okstate.edu	Kingfisher	OK	73750	405-375-3808	375-2366	338
KING-FM 98.1 (Clas) 10 Harrison St Ste 100 *TF:* 888-598-9810 ■ *Web:* www.king.org	Seattle	WA	98109	206-691-2981	691-2982	645-147
Kingman Area Chamber of Commerce 120 W Andy Devine Ave *Web:* www.kingmanchamber.com	Kingman	AZ	86401	928-753-6253	753-1049	139
Kingman Chevrolet Buick 3730 Stockton Hill Rd *Web:* www.kingmanchevrolet-buick.com	Kingman	AZ	86409	928-377-4150		57
Kingman County 130 N Spruce St *Web:* www.kingmancoks.org	Kingman	KS	67068	620-532-2521		338
Kingman Museum 175 Limit St *Web:* www.kingmanmuseum.org	Battle Creek	MI	49037	269-965-5117		520
Kingman Regional Medical Ctr (KRMC) 3269 Stockton Hill Rd *TF:* 877-757-2101 ■ *Web:* www.azkrmc.com	Kingman	AZ	86409	928-757-2101		374-3
King-o'rourke Cadillac Inc 756 Smithtown Byp *Web:* www.kingorourkeautogroup.com	Smithtown	NY	11787	631-724-4700	724-4784	57

Name / Address	City	State	ZIP	Phone	Fax	Class
Kings Aire Inc 1035 Kessler Dr *Web:* kingsaire.com	El Paso	TX	79907	915-592-2997		189-10
Kings Beach State Recreation Area c/o Sierra District Ofc PO Box 266 *Web:* www.parks.ca.gov	Tahoma	CA	96142	530-525-7232		565
Kings College 322 Lamar Ave *TF:* 800-768-2255 ■ *Web:* www.parchment.com	Charlotte	NC	28204	704-372-0266		166
Kings County 360 Adams St Rm 189 *Web:* www.nycourts.gov	Brooklyn	NY	11201	347-404-9772	401-9609	338
Kings County 680 Campus Dr *Web:* www.countyofkings.com	Hanford	CA	93230	559-582-3211	582-6639	338
Kings County Hospital Ctr 451 Clarkson Ave *Web:* www1.nyc.gov	Brooklyn	NY	11203	718-245-3131		374-3
Kings County Library 401 N Douty St *Web:* www.kingscountylibrary.org	Hanford	CA	93230	559-582-0261	583-6163	434-3
Kings Credit Services *KCS* 510 N Douty St *TF:* 800-366-0950 ■ *Web:* www.kcs-arm.com	Hanford	CA	93230	800-366-0950		160
Kings Dominion 16000 Theme Pkwy *Web:* www.kingsdominion.com	Doswell	VA	23047	804-876-5000	876-5864	32
Kings Gap Environmental Education Ctr 500 Kings Gap Rd *Web:* www.dcnr.pa.gov	Carlisle	PA	17015	717-486-5031		565
Kings Head 1246 N Van Buren St *Web:* kingshead.com	Milwaukee	WI	53202	414-273-7980		77
Kings Head British Pub 6460 US 1 *Web:* kingsheadbritishpub.com	Saint Augustine	FL	32095	904-823-9787		671
Kings Liquor Inc 2810 W Berry St *Web:* www.kingsliquor.com	Fort Worth	TX	76109	817-923-3737		443
Kings Mountain National Military Park 2625 Park Rd *Web:* www.nps.gov	Blacksburg	SC	29702	864-936-7921		564
Kings Mountain State Park 1277 Park Rd *Web:* southcarolinaparks.com	Blacksburg	SC	29702	803-222-3209		565
Kings Oil Tools Inc 2235 Spring St *Web:* kingsoiltools.com	Paso Robles	CA	93446	805-238-9311	238-9411	536
Kings Super Markets Inc 700 Lanidex Plz *TF:* 800-325-4647 ■ *Web:* kingsfoodmarkets.com	Parsippany	NJ	07054	973-463-6300		297-8
Kingsboro Psychiatric Ctr 681 Clarkson Ave *Web:* omh.ny.gov	Brooklyn	NY	11203	718-221-7700		374-5
Kingsborough Community College 2001 Oriental Blvd *Web:* www.kbcc.cuny.edu	Brooklyn	NY	11235	718-368-5000		162
Kingsbrook Jewish Medical Ctr 585 Schenectady Ave *Web:* www.kingsbrook.org	Brooklyn	NY	11203	718-604-5000		374-3
Kingsburg Apple Packers Inc 10363 E Davis Ave PO Box 38 *Web:* www.kingsburgorchards.com	Kingsburg	CA	93631	559-897-5132	897-4532	11-1
Kingsbury County Courthouse 202 2nd St SE *Web:* www.kingsburycountysd.org	De Smet	SD	57231	605-854-3811	854-9080	338
Kingsbury Electric Co-opeartive Inc 511 US Hwy 14 *TF:* 888-200-5243 ■ *Web:* www.kec-sd.coop	De Smet	SD	57231	605-854-3522		245
Kingsbury Inc 10385 Drummond Rd *TF:* 866-581-5464 ■ *Web:* www.kingsbury.com	Philadelphia	PA	19154	215-824-4000	824-4999	620
Kingsbury Printing Co Mt Royal Plz State Rte 9 *Web:* www.kingsburyprinting.com	Queensbury	NY	12804	518-747-6606	747-8852	627
Kingsdown Inc 126 W Holt St *TF:* 800-354-5464 ■ *Web:* kingsdown.com	Mebane	NC	27302	800-800-1353		471
Kingsford Broach & Tool Inc 2200 Maule Dr *Web:* kingsfordbroach.com	Kingsford	MI	49802	906-774-4917	774-6981	493
Kingsland Bay State Park 787 Kingsland Bay State Park Rd *Web:* www.vtstateparks.com	Ferrisburgh	VT	05456	802-877-3445		565
Kingsley Consulting Group Ltd 701 Papworth Ave Ste 207 *Web:* kingsleygroup.com	Metairie	LA	70005	504-834-6484		196
Kingsley Plantation 11676 Palmetto Ave *Web:* www.nps.gov	Jacksonville	FL	32226	904-251-3537	251-3577	520
Kingsley-Bate Ltd 7200 Gateway Ct *Web:* www.kingsleybate.com	Manassas	VA	20109	703-361-7000		319-4
Kingsmill Resort & Spa 1010 Kingsmill Rd *TF:* 800-832-5665 ■ *Web:* www.kingsmill.com	Williamsburg	VA	23185	757-253-1703	253-8246	669
Kingsport Chamber 400 Clinchfield St Ste 100 *Web:* www.kingsportchamber.org	Kingsport	TN	37660	423-392-8800	392-8834	139
Kingsport Convention & Visitors Bureau (KCVB) 400 Clinchfield St Ste 100 *TF:* 800-743-5282 ■ *Web:* visitkingsport.com	Kingsport	TN	37660	423-392-8820	392-8833	206
Kingsport Press Credit Union 528 W Center St *TF:* 800-748-9978 ■ *Web:* kpcu.org	Kingsport	TN	37660	423-378-9292	378-5424	219
Kingsport Public Library 400 Broad St *Web:* www.kingsportlibrary.org	Kingsport	TN	37660	423-224-2559		434-3
Kingsport Times-News 701 Lynn Garden Dr *TF:* 800-251-0328 ■ *Web:* www.timesnews.net	Kingsport	TN	37660	423-246-8121	392-1385	532-2
Kingstar Supplies Inc 19809 Hamilton Ave *TF:* 800-573-9352 ■ *Web:* www.smokengift.com	Torrance	CA	90502	310-515-9900	515-9901	756
Kingston Collegiate & Vocational Institute 235 Frontenac St *Web:* www.kcvi.limestone.on.ca	Kingston	ON	K7L3S7	613-544-4811	544-8795	800
Kingston Cos 477 Shoup Ave *Web:* kingstoncorp.com	Idaho Falls	ID	83402	208-522-2365	522-7488	11-1
Kingston Machine Tool Inc 5421 Business Dr *Web:* www.kingstonmachine.com	Huntington Beach	CA	92649	714-894-1648		523
Kingston National Bank 2 N Main St PO Box 613 *TF:* 800-337-4562 ■ *Web:* www.kingstonnationalbank.com	Kingston	OH	45644	740-642-2191		70
Kingston State Park 124 Main St *Web:* www.nhstateparks.org	Kingston	NH	03848	603-642-5471		565
Kingston Technology Co 17600 Newhope St *TF:* 800-835-6575 ■ *Web:* www.kingston.com	Fountain Valley	CA	92708	714-435-2600	435-2699	288
Kingston Whig-Standard, The 6 Cataraqui St *Web:* www.thewhig.com	Kingston	ON	K7L4Z7	613-544-5000	530-4122	532-1
Kingstone Companies Inc 15 Joys Ln *NASDAQ: KINS* ■ *Web:* www.kingstonecompanies.com	Kingston	NY	12401	516-374-7600		391-4
Kingsville Chamber of Commerce 635 E King Ave Ste 124 *Web:* www.kingsville.org	Kingsville	TX	78363	361-592-6438	592-0866	139
Kingsway Charities 1119 Commonwealth Ave *TF:* 800-321-9234 ■ *Web:* www.kingswaycharities.org	Bristol	VA	24201	276-466-3014	466-0955	48-20
Kingsway Christian School 7979 E County Rd 100 N *Web:* www.kingswaychurch.org	Avon	IN	46123	317-272-2227		623
Kingsway College School 4600 Dundas St W *Web:* www.kcs.on.ca	Etobicoke	ON	M9A1A5	416-234-5073		685
Kingsway Financial Services Inc 45 St Clair Ave W Ste 400 *TSE: KFS* ■ *Web:* kingsway-financial.com	Toronto	ON	M4V1K9	416-848-1171		391-4
Kingswood Senior Living Community 10000 Wornall Rd *Web:* www.kingswoodretirementliving.com	Kansas City	MO	64114	816-673-2835		672
Kingwood Center Gardens 50 N Trimble Rd *Web:* kingwoodcenter.org	Mansfield	OH	44906	419-522-0211		97
Kingwood Medical Ctr 22999 US Hwy 59 *Web:* hcahoustonhealthcare.com	Kingwood	TX	77339	281-348-8000		374-3
Kinkaid Lake Fish & Wildlife Area 52 Cinder Hill Dr *Web:* www2.illinois.gov	Murphysboro	IL	62966	618-684-2867		565
Kinkaid School, The 201 Kinkaid School Dr *Web:* www.kinkaid.org	Houston	TX	77024	713-782-1640		623
Kinloch Consulting Group Inc 25 Melville Park Rd Ste 260 *Web:* www.kinlochcg.com	Melville	NY	11747	631-773-6600		535
Kinnetic Laboratories Inc 307 Washington St *Web:* www.kinneticlabs.com	Santa Cruz	CA	95060	831-457-3950		668
Kinney & Lange PA 312 S Third St *Web:* www.kinney.com	Minneapolis	MN	55415	612-339-1863		428
Kinney Agency Inc, The 3027 SR-4 *Web:* kinneyinsurance.com	Hudson Falls	NY	12839	518-747-4136		390
Kinney Brick Co 100 Prosperity Rd PO Box 1804 *TF:* 800-464-4605 ■ *Web:* kinneybrickco.com	Albuquerque	NM	87103	505-877-4550		150
Kinney Construction Services Inc 121 E Birch Ave Ste 500 *Web:* www.kinneyconstruction.net	Flagstaff	AZ	86001	928-779-2820	773-4696	186
Kinney County 501 S Ann St *Web:* www.co.kinney.tx.us	Brackettville	TX	78832	830-563-2521		338
Kinney Drugs Inc 520 E Main St *Web:* www.kinneydrugs.com	Gouverneur	NY	13642	315-287-3600		237
Kinney Electrical Manufacturing Co 678 Buckeye St *Web:* www.kinneyelectric.com	Elgin	IL	60123	847-742-9600	742-3326	580
Kinney Lisovicz Reilly & Wolff Pc 299 Cherry Hill Rd Ste 300 *Web:* klrw.law	Parsippany	NJ	07054	973-957-2550		41
Kinnickinnic State Park W11983 820th Ave *Web:* dnr.wi.gov	River Falls	WI	54022	715-425-1129		565
Kinnucan Enterprises Inc 3365 Skyway Dr *Web:* www.kinnucans.com	Auburn	AL	36830	334-887-6100		711
Kino Flo Inc 2840 N Hollywood Way *Web:* www.kinoflo.com	Burbank	CA	91505	818-767-6528		362
Kinokuniya Book Stores of America Company Ltd 1581 Webster St *Web:* www.kinokuniya.com	San Francisco	CA	94115	415-673-7431		95
Kinokuniya Bookstores 1073 Avenue of the Americas *Web:* usa.kinokuniya.com	New York	NY	10018	212-869-1700		95
Kinray Inc 152-35 Tenth Ave *TF:* 800-854-6729 ■ *Web:* www.kinray.com	Whitestone	NY	11357	718-767-1234	767-4706	238
Kinross Correctional Facility 16770 S Watertower Dr *Web:* www.michigan.gov	Kincheloe	MI	49788	906-495-2282		213
Kinross Gold Corp 25 York St 17th Fl *TF:* 866-561-3636 ■ *Web:* kinross.com	Toronto	ON	M5J2V5	416-365-5123	363-6622	502
Kinsbursky Bros 125 E Commercial *TF:* 800-548-8797 ■ *Web:* www.kbirecycling.com	Anaheim	CA	92801	800-548-8797		196
Kinsel Forensic Accounting LLP 1222 Lincoln Ave *TF:* 855-202-2021 ■ *Web:* kinselcpa.com	Pasadena	CA	91103	855-202-2021		2
Kinsella Weitzman Iser Kump & Aldisert LLP 808 Wilshire Blvd Ste 300 *Web:* kwikalaw.com	Santa Monica	CA	90401	310-566-9800		41
Kinseth Hotel Corp 2 Quail Creek Cir *Web:* www.kinseth.com	North Liberty	IA	52317	319-626-5600		379
Kinseth Plumbing & Heating Inc 148 E Main St *Web:* www.kinsethplumbing.com	Belmond	IA	50421	641-444-4428		189-10
Kinsey & Kinsey Inc 26 N Park Blvd *Web:* www.kinsey.com	Glen Ellyn	IL	60137	630-858-4866		180

	Phone	Fax	Class
Kinsey Institute for Research in Sex, Gender, and Reproduction Inc Morrison Hall 302 1165 E 3rd St . . . . Bloomington IN 47405 *Web:* www.kinseyinstitute.org	812-855-7686		637-2
Kinsey's Floor Covering Inc 16222 Allisonville Rd . . . . .Noblesville IN 46060 *Web:* kinseysfloorcovering.com	317-773-2929		290
Kinship Books 305 Cedar Heights Rd . . . . Rhinebeck NY 12572 *Web:* www.kinshipny.com	845-876-4592		637-2
Kinsley & Sons Inc PO Box 549. . . . . .Union MO 63084 *Web:* www.gothic-jewelry.com	314-843-0400		409
Kinsley Construction Inc 1110 E Princess St . . . . .York PA 17403 *Web:* www.kinsleyconstruction.com	717-741-3841		186
Kinsman Robinson Galleries 108 Cumberland St. . . . . Toronto ON M5R1A6 *Web:* www.kinsmanrobinson.com	416-964-2374	964-9042	42
Kinston-Lenoir County Chamber of Commerce 301 N Queen St . . . . Kinston NC 28501 *Web:* www.kinstonchamber.com	252-527-1131	527-1914	139
Kintetsu Intl 1325 6th Ave 20th Fl. . . . . New York NY 10104 *Web:* www.kintetsu.com	212-259-9600	259-9625	771
Kintetsu World Express USA Inc 1 Jericho Plz Ste 100 . . . . .Jericho NY 11753 *TF:* 800-275-4045 ■ *Web:* www.kweusa.com	516-933-7100	933-7731	449
Kintronic Laboratories Inc 144 Pleasant Grove Rd . . . . Bluff City TN 37618 *Web:* www.kintronic.com	423-878-3141		647
Kinyo Company Inc 14235 Lomitas Ave . . . . .La Puente CA 91746 *TF:* 800-735-4696 ■ *Web:* www.kinyo.com	626-333-3711	961-9114	173-5
Kinze Manufacturing 2172 M Ave. . . . . Williamsburg IA 52361 *Web:* kinze.com	319-668-1300		273
Kinzelman Art Consulting LLC 3909 Main St . . . . .Houston TX 77002 *Web:* www.kinzelmanart.com	713-533-9923		196
Kinzie Hotel 20 W Kinzie St. . . . . .Chicago IL 60654 *Web:* www.kinziehotel.com	312-395-9000	395-9001	379
Kinzinger Adam (Rep R - IL) 2245 Rayburn House Office Bldg . . . . Washington DC 20515 *Web:* kinzinger.house.gov	202-225-3635	226-3521	342-2
Kinzler Construction Services 2335 230th St. . . . . .Ames IA 50014 *TF:* 888-292-2382 ■ *Web:* www.insulation.net	515-292-5714		189-9
Kinzua Environmental Inc 1176 E 38th St . . . . .Cleveland OH 44114 *TF:* 855-200-7011 ■ *Web:* kinzuachemical.com	216-881-4040	881-8968	151
Kiolbassa Provision Co 1325 S Brazos St . . . . .San Antonio TX 78207 *TF:* 800-456-5465 ■ *Web:* kiolbassa.com	800-456-5465		296-26
KIONIX Inc 36 Thornwood Dr . . . . .Ithaca NY 14850 *Web:* www.kionix.com	607-257-1080	257-1146	253
KION-TV 1550 Moffett St. . . . . .Salinas CA 93905 *Web:* kion546.com	831-757-6397		647
KIOS-FM 91.5 (NPR) 3230 Burt St . . . . Omaha NE 68131 *Web:* www.kios.org	402-557-2777	557-2559	645-113
Kiosk Information Systems Inc (KIS) 346 S Arthur Ave. . . . . .Louisville CO 80027 **Fax Area Code:* 303 ■ *TF:* 800-509-5471 ■ *Web:* kiosk.com	888-661-1697	466-6730*	614
KIOU-AM 292 S Pine St PO Box 444. . . . . .Spartanburg SC 29302 **Fax Area Code:* 864 ■ *TF:* 888-989-2299 ■ *Web:* www.wilkinsradio.com	888-989-2299	597-0687*	647
Kiowa County 1208 Maine St . . . . .Eads CO 81036 *Web:* www.onlinedmv.com	719-438-5421		338
Kiowa County 211 E Florida Ave . . . . Greensburg KS 67054 *Web:* kiowacountyks.org	620-723-3366	723-3234	338
Kip Inc 25740 Washington Ave. . . . . .Murrieta CA 92562 *Web:* www.kipincorporated.com	951-698-7890		188-10
Kipany Productions Ltd 32 E 39th St . . . . New York NY 10016 *Web:* www.kipany.com	212-883 8300		737
Kipin Industries Inc 4194 Green Garden Rd. . . . . .Aliquippa PA 15001 *Web:* kipin.com	724-495-6200	495-2219	189-16
Kiplinger Agriculture Letter 1729 H St NW. . . . . Washington DC 20006 *TF:* 800-544-0155 ■ *Web:* www.kiplinger.com	202-887-6400	778-8976	531-13
Kipp Foundation 135 Main St Ste 1700. . . . . San Francisco CA 94105 *Web:* www.kipp.org	415-399-1556		194
KippsDeSanto & Co 8000 Towers Crescent Dr Ste 1200. . . . . .Tysons VA 22182 *Web:* kippsdesanto.com	703-442-1400	442-1498	690
Kiptopeke State Park 3540 Kiptopeke Dr . . . . .Cape Charles VA 23310 *Web:* www.dcr.virginia.gov	757-331-2267		565
KIRA Inc 2595 Canyon Blvd Ste 240. . . . . Boulder CO 80306 *Web:* www.kira.com	303-402-1526	402-1528	186
Kiran's Houston 2925 Richmond Ave . . . . .Houston TX 77098 *Web:* kiranshouston.com	713-960-8472		671
Kirby Agri Inc 500 Running Pump Rd PO Box 6277 . . . . Lancaster PA 17607 *TF:* 800-745-7524 ■ *Web:* www.kirbyagri.com	717-299-2541	293-9306	280
Kirby Bates Assn 3452 Lake Lynda Dr Ste 200. . . . . Orlando FL 32817 *Web:* www.kirbybates.com	610-667-1800		463
Kirby Building Systems Inc 124 Kirby Dr. . . . . .Portland TN 37148 *TF:* 800-348-7799 ■ *Web:* www.kirbybuildingsystems.com	615-325-4165		105
Kirby Co 1920 W 114th St. .Cleveland OH 44102 *TF:* 800-437-7170 ■ *Web:* www.kirby.com	216-228-2400	529-6146	788
Kirby Electric Inc 415 Northgate D. . . . . .Warrendale PA 15086 *TF:* 800-767-3263 ■ *Web:* www.kirbyelectricinc.com	724-772-1800	772-2227	189-4
Kirby Foods Inc 4102-B Fieldstone Rd. . . . . Champaign IL 61826 *Web:* www.kirbyfoods.com	217-352-2600	352-9394	345
Kirby Manufacturing Inc 484 S Hwy 59 . . . . Merced CA 95340 *Web:* www.kirbymanufacturing.com	209-723-0778	723-3941	273
Kirby Risk Corp 1815 Sagamore Pkwy N PO Box 5089 . . . . LaFayette IN 47904 *TF:* 877-641-0929 ■ *Web:* www.kirbyrisk.com	765-448-4567	448-1342	246
Kirby's Steakhouse 123 N Loop 1604 E. . . . . .San Antonio TX 78232 *Web:* kirbyssteakhouse.com	210-404-2221	404-2225	671
Kirila Contractors Inc 505 Bedford Rd PO Box 179. . . . . Brookfield OH 44403 *Web:* www.kirila.com	330-448-4055		186
Kiriu USA Corp 359 Mitch Mcconnell Way . . . . .Bowling Green KY 42101 *Web:* www.kiriuusacorp.com	270-843-4160		518
Kirk Rankin Law Office 2601 University Blvd Ste 202 . . . . Wheaton MD 20902 *Web:* www.kirkrankin.com	301-933-4648		428
Kirk Rudy Inc 125 Lorraine Pkwy. . . . . .Woodstock GA 30188 *Web:* www.kirkrudy.com	770-427-4203	427-4036	547
Kirk Williams Company Inc 2734 Home Rd . . . . Grove City OH 43123 *Web:* www.kirkwilliamsco.com	614-875-9023	875-9214	697
Kirk's Folly 236 Chapman St . . . . .Providence RI 02905 *Web:* www.kirksfolly.com	401-941-4300		408
Kirkendall Public Library 1210 NW Prairie Ridge Dr . . . . .Ankeny IA 50023 *Web:* www.ankenyiowa.gov	515-965-6460	289-9122	434-3
Kirkham Michael Inc 12700 W Dodge Rd . . . . Omaha NE 68154 *Web:* www.kirkham.com	402-393-5630	255-3850	261
Kirkhill Manufacturing Co 12023 Woodruff Ave . . . . Downey CA 90241 *Web:* www.rubbersales.com	562-803-1117	803-3117	677
Kirkland Correctional Institution 4344 Broad River Rd. . . . . .Columbia SC 29210 *Web:* doc.sc.gov	803-896-1521	896-1766	213
Kirkland's Inc 5310 Maryland Way . . . . Brentwood TN 37027 *NASDAQ: KIRK* ■ *TF:* 877-541-4855 ■ *Web:* www.kirklands.com	877-541-4855		362
Kirkpatrick & Goldsborough PLLC 1233 Shelburne Rd Ste E-1 . . . . South Burlington VT 05403 *Web:* vtlawfirm.com	802-651-0960		41
Kirkpatrick Ann (Rep D - AZ) 309 Cannon House Office Bldg. . . . . Washington DC 20515 *Web:* www.kirkpatrick.house.gov	202-225-2542		342-2
Kirkpatrick Concrete Co 2000-A Southbridge Pkwy Ste 610. . . . . .Birmingham AL 35209 *Web:* www.nationalcement.com	205-423-2600	621-0952	182
Kirkpatrick Phillips & Miller 1445 E Republic Rd . . . . .Springfield MO 65804 *Web:* www.kpmcpa.com	417-882-4300	882-4343	2
Kirkridge Retreat & Study Ctr 2495 Fox Gap Rd . . . . .Bangor PA 18013 *Web:* www.kirkridge.org	610-588-1793		673
Kirksey 6909 Portwest Dr. . . . . .Houston TX 77024 *Web:* www.kirksey.com	713-850-9600		261
Kirksville Area Technical Ctr 1103 S Cottage Grove. . . . . Kirksville MO 63501 *Web:* www.kirksville.k12.mo.us	660-665-2865	626-1477	167-3
Kirksville Daily Express 110 E McPherson St. . . . . Kirksville MO 63501 *Web:* www.kirksvilledailyexpress.com	660-665-2808		532-2
Kirkwood 904 Main St . . . . Wilmington MA 01887 *Web:* www.kirkwoodus.com	978-658-4200	658-5547	627
Kirkwood Bank & Trust Co 2911 N 14th St . . . . Bismarck ND 58503 *TF:* 800-492-4955 ■ *Web:* www.kirkwoodbank.com	701-258-6550		70
Kirkwood Community College 6301 Kirkwood Blvd SW. . . . . .Cedar Rapids IA 52404 *TF:* 800-332-2055 ■ *Web:* www.kirkwood.edu	319-398-5411		162
Kirkwood Industries Inc 1239 Rockside Rd. . . . . Parma OH 44134 *Web:* www.kirkwoodholding.com	216-267-6200	351-3141	518
Kirkwood Mountain Resort LLC 1501 Kirkwood Meadows Dr. . . . . Kirkwood CA 95646 *TF:* 800-427-7623 ■ *Web:* www.kirkwood.com	209-258-6000		378
Kirkwood Public Library 140 E Jefferson Ave . . . . Kirkwood MO 63122 *Web:* kirkwoodpubliclibrary.org	314-821-5770	822-3755	434-3
Kirkwood School District 11289 Manchester Rd. . . . . Kirkwood MO 63122 *Web:* www.kirkwoodschools.org	314-213-6100	984-0002	685
Kirkwood-Des Peres Area Chamber of Commerce 108 W Adams Ave. . . . . Saint Louis MO 63122 *Web:* www.kirkwooddesperes.com	314-821-4161	821-5229	139
Kirlin Co 3401 E Jefferson Ave . . . . Detroit MI 48207 *Web:* www.kirlinlighting.com	313-259-6400	259-3121	439
KIRO-FM 97.3 1820 Eastlake Ave E . . . . Seattle WA 98102 *TF:* 800-756-5476 ■ *Web:* www.mynorthwest.com	206-726-7000		645-147
KIRO-TV Ch 7 (CBS) 2807 Third Ave . . . . Seattle WA 98121 *Web:* www.kiro7.com	206-728-7777		741-123
KIRQ-FM 21361 Hwy 30 . . . . .Twin Falls ID 83301 *Web:* www.q1067.com	208-735-8300		647
Kirr Marbach & Company Investment Management 621 Washington St. . . . . Columbus IN 47201 *TF:* 800-808-9444 ■ *Web:* www.kirrmar.com	812-376-9444		401
Kirsan Engineering Inc 8201 100th St. . . . . Pleasant Prairie WI 53158 *Web:* www.kirsan.com	262-658-1860	658-1870	455
Kirschman Realty LLC 3631 Canal St. . . . . New Orleans LA 70119 *Web:* kirschmanrealty.com	504-486-8951		653
KIRS-FM 1225 S St Ste B . . . . Stockton MO 65785 *Web:* www.vcyamerica.org	417-276-5253		647
Kirsh Foundry Inc 125 Rowell St . . . . Beaver Dam WI 53916 *Web:* www.kirshfoundry.com	920-887-0395		492
Kirsh Title Services Inc 112 E Cecil Ave. . . . . North East MD 21901 *Web:* kirshtitle.com	410-287-1510		41
Kirshon & Company PC 311 Mill St. . . . . Poughkeepsie NY 12601 *Web:* kirshoncpa.com	845-473-1811	473-2479	2
Kirtland Air Force Base 2000 Wyoming Blvd SE Ste A-1. . . . . Kirtland AFB NM 87117 *TF:* 877-246-1453 ■ *Web:* www.kirtland.af.mil	505-846-5991		497-1

Name / Address	Phone	Fax	Class
Kirtland Capital Partners 3201 Enterprise Pkwy Ste 200 Beachwood OH 44122 *Web:* www.kirtlandcapital.com	216-593-0100	593-0240	792
Kirtland Community College 10775 N St Helen Rd Roscommon MI 48653 *Web:* www.kirtland.edu	989-275-5000	275-6789	162
Kirtley-Cole Associates LLC 2820 Oakes Ave Ste B. Everett WA 98201 *Web:* www.kirtley-cole.com	425-609-0400	609-0410	186
Kirwan Surgical Products Inc 180 Enterprise Dr Marshfield MA 02050 *TF:* 888-547-9267 ■ *Web:* www.ksp.com	781-834-9500		476
KIS (Kiosk Information Systems Inc) 346 S Arthur Ave. Louisville CO 80027 **Fax Area Code:* 303 ■ *TF:* 800-509-5471 ■ *Web:* kiosk.com	888-661-1697	466-6730*	614
KIS (Knowledge Information Solutions Inc) 2877 Guardian Ln Ste 201 Virginia Beach VA 23452 *TF:* 877-547-7248 ■ *Web:* www.kisinc.net	757-463-3232	463-2318	179
Kisco Senior Living LLC 5790 Fleet St Ste 300 Carlsbad CA 92008 *Web:* www.kiscoseniorliving.com	760-804-5900		450
Kish Bancorp Inc 4255 E Main St PO Box 917 Belleville PA 17004 *OTC: KISB* ■ *TF:* 888-554-4748 ■ *Web:* www.kishbank.com	717-935-2191		70
Kishimoto.Gordon.Dalaya PC 1101 15th St NW Ste 200 Washington DC 20005 *Web:* www.kgdarchitecture.com	202-338-3800		393
Kishwaukee College 21193 Malta Rd Malta IL 60150 *TF:* 888-656-7329 ■ *Web:* www.kish.edu	815-825-2086	825-2306	162
Kisinger Campo & Associates Corp 201 N Franklin St Ste 400 Tampa FL 33602 *Web:* kisingercampo.com	813-871-5331	871-5135	261
Kiska Construction Corporation USA 43-10 11TH St Long Island City NY 11101 *Web:* www.kiskagroup.com	718-943-0400	943-0401	188-4
Kiski School 1888 Brett Ln Saltsburg PA 15681 *TF:* 877-547-5448 ■ *Web:* www.kiski.org	724-639-3586	639-8596	622
Kislak Company Inc, The 1000 Rt 9 N Woodbridge NJ 07095 *Web:* kislakrealty.com	732-750-3000		652
Kislak Organization, The 7900 Miami Lakes Dr W Miami Lakes FL 33016 *Web:* www.kislak.com	305-364-4100		509
Kisma Preserve PO Box 84 Mount Desert ME 04660 *Web:* www.kismapreserve.org	207-667-3244		823
KISS 96.1 4101-A Wall St Montgomery AL 36106 *Web:* kiss961.com	334-396-5477	279-9563	645-102
KISS 98.1 808 E Sprague Ave Spokane WA 99202 *TF:* 888-433-7950 ■ *Web:* kiss981.iheart.com	509-242-2400		645-151
KISS 98.5 500 Corporate Pkwy Ste 200 Amherst NY 14226 *Web:* kiss985.radio.com	716-843-0600		645
KISS 99.9 194 NW 187th St Miami FL 33169 *TF:* 866-954-0999 ■ *Web:* wkis.radio.com	305-654-1700	654-1715	645-96
KISS Country 93.7 6341 Westport Ave Shreveport LA 71129 *Web:* mykisscountry937.com	318-320-5477	687-8574	645-148
KISS FM 96.1 5010 Underwood Ave Omaha NE 68132 *Web:* 961kissonline.iheart.com	402-558-9696		645-113
Kiss the Cook Restaurant 72 Church St Burlington VT 05401 *Web:* kissthecook.net	802-863-4226		671
KISS-FM 99.5 (Rock) 8122 Datapoint Dr Ste 600 San Antonio TX 78229 *Web:* www.kissrocks.com	210-615-5400	615-5300	645-140
Kissimmee Prairie Preserve State Park 33104 NW 192 Ave. Okeechobee FL 34972 *Web:* www.floridastateparks.org	863-462-5360		565
Kissimmee Utility Authority Inc (KUA) 1701 W Carroll St Kissimmee FL 34741 *TF:* 877-582-7700 ■ *Web:* www.kua.com	407-933-7777		787
Kissimmee/Osceola County Chamber of Commerce 1425 E Vine St Kissimmee FL 34744 *TF:* 800-447-8206 ■ *Web:* kissimmeechamber.com	407-847-3174	870-8607	139
Kissinger & Fellman PC 3773 Cherry Creek N Dr Denver CO 80209 *Web:* www.kandf.com	303-320-6100	327-8601	428
Kist Livestock Auction Co 1715 40th Ave SE Mandan ND 58554 **Fax Area Code:* 701 ■ *TF:* 800-732-1163 ■ *Web:* www.kistlivestockauction.com	800-732-1163	663-9860*	446
Kistler Instrument Corp 75 John Glenn Dr Amherst NY 14228 *Web:* www.kistler.com	716-691-5100	691-5226	472
Kistler-Morse Corp 150 Venture Blvd Spartanburg SC 29306 *TF:* 800-426-9010 ■ *Web:* www.specialtyproducttechnologies.com	864-574-2763	574-8063	201
Kistner Concrete Products Inc 8713 Read Rd East Pembroke NY 14056 *TF:* 800-809-2801 ■ *Web:* www.kistner.com	585-762-8216	762-8315	183
KISU-TV Ch 10 (PBS) 921 S Eighth Ave S-8111 Pocatello ID 83209 *Web:* www.idahoptv.org	208-282-2857		741-101
Kiswire Pine Bluff Inc 5100 Industrial Dr Pine Bluff AR 71602 *Web:* www.kiswire.com	870-247-2444	247-1622	813
Kit Carson County 251 16th St Ste 103 Burlington CO 80807 *Web:* www.colorado.gov	719-346-8638	346-7242	338
KIT HomeBuilders West LLC 1124 Garber St Caldwell ID 83605 *TF:* 800-859-0347 ■ *Web:* www.kitwest.com	208-454-5000		106
Kitagawa & Ebert PC 300 Spectrum Center Dr Ste 960 Irvine CA 92618 *Web:* japanuslaw.com	949-788-9980		41
Kitamura Machinery of USA Inc 78 Century Dr Wheeling IL 60090 *Web:* www.kitamura-machinery.com	847-520-7755	520-7763	455
Kitano New York 66 Park Ave E 38th St New York NY 10016 *TF:* 800-548-2666 ■ *Web:* www.kitano.com	212-885-7000	885-7100	379
Kitch Drutchas Wagner Valitutti & Sherbrook 1 Woodward Ave Ste 2400 Detroit MI 48226 *Web:* www.kitch.com	313-965-7900	965-7403	428
Kitchell Corp 1707 E Highland Ave Phoenix AZ 85016 *Web:* www.kitchell.com	602-264-4411		186
Kitchen & Bath Studios Inc 7001 Wisconsin Ave Chevy Chase MD 20815 *Web:* www.kitchenbathstudios.com	301-657-1636	656-2086	362
Kitchen 24 1608 N Cahuenga Blvd Los Angeles CA 90028 *Web:* www.kitchen24.info	323-465-2424		362
Kitchen Advantage 7377 Transit Rd East Amherst NY 14051 *Web:* kitchenadvantageofwny.com	716-689-0805		321
Kitchen Art The Store for Cook 1550 Win Hentschel Blvd West Lafayette IN 47906 *Web:* k-art.com	765-497-3878		361
Kitchen Craft Cabinetry 1180 Springfield Rd Winnipeg MB R2C2Z2 *TF:* 866-856-4845 ■ *Web:* www.kitchencraft.com	866-856-4845		115
Kitchen Craft Cookware 4129 United Ave Mount Dora FL 32757 *TF:* 800-800-2850 ■ *Web:* www.cookforlife.com	800-800-2850		362
Kitchen Distributors Inc 1309 W Littleton Blvd Littleton CO 80120 *Web:* kitchendistributors.com	303-795-0665		362
Kitchen Expressions of Short Hills Inc 396 Springfield Ave Summit NJ 07901 *Web:* kitchenexpressions.com	908-273-4442		362
Kitchen Fantasy 27576 Ynez Rd Ste H9 Temecula CA 92591 *Web:* www.kitchenfantasy.com	951-693-4264	693-4265	362
Kitchen Kompact Inc 911 E 11th St Jeffersonville IN 47130 *Web:* www.kitchenkompact.com	812-282-6681	282-7880	115
Kitchen Musician, The 449 Hidden Valley Ln Cincinnati OH 45215 *Web:* www.kitchenmusician.net	513-761-7585		657
Kitchen Restaurant, The 2225 Hurley Way Sacramento CA 95825 *Web:* thekitchenrestaurant.com	916-568-7171		671
Kitchen Tune-Up 813 Cir Dr Aberdeen SD 57401 *TF:* 800-333-6385 ■ *Web:* kitchentuneup.com	605-225-4049		189-11
Kitchen Window Calhoun Sq 3001 Hennepin Ave Minneapolis MN 55408 *TF:* 888-824-4417 ■ *Web:* www.kitchenwindow.com	612-824-4417	824-8225	167-3
Kitchen World Inc 83 Ethan Allen Dr South Burlington VT 05403 *Web:* kitchenworldvermont.com	802-658-6971		362
Kitchen, The 4348 Fountain Ave Los Angeles CA 90029 *Web:* thekitchen.la	323-664-3663		671
KitchenAid Div 553 Benson Rd Benton Harbor MI 49022 *TF:* 800-422-1230 ■ *Web:* www.kitchenaid.com	800-422-1230		37
Kitchens By Kleweno Inc 4034 Broadway Blvd Kansas City MO 64111 *Web:* kleweno.com	816-531-3968		362
KitchenSync 7409 Beverly Blvd Los Angeles CA 90036 *Web:* kitchensync.us	424-248-9289		193
Kitchenworks Inc, The 1808 E Sunrise Blvd Fort Lauderdale FL 33304 *Web:* thekitchenworks.com	954-764-1482		35
Kitchin Neal Webb Webb & Futrell pa Attys 111 E Washington St Rockingham NC 28379	910-997-2206		445
KITCO Fiber Optics 5269 Cleveland St Ste 108 & 110 Virginia Beach VA 23462 *TF:* 866-643-5220 ■ *Web:* kitcofiberoptics.com	757-518-8100		610
Kitco Inc 1625 N Mountain Springs Pkwy Springville UT 84663 *Web:* www.kitcodefense.com	801-489-2000		22
Kite Realty Group Trust 30 S Meridian St Ste 1100 Indianapolis IN 46204 *NYSE: KRG* ■ *TF:* 888-577-5600 ■ *Web:* kiterealty.com	317-577-5600	577-5605	654
KITI-AM 1133 Kresky Centralia WA 98531 *Web:* www.live95.com	360-736-1355	736-4761	647
Kitsap County 614 Div St MS 4 Port Orchard WA 98366 *Web:* www.kitsapgov.com	360-377-9499	337-4632	338
Kitsap Mental Health Services 5455 Almira Dr NE Bremerton WA 98311 *TF:* 800-843-4793 ■ *Web:* www.kitsapmentalhealth.org	360-405-4010		450
Kitsap Publishing 1450 NW Finn Hill Rd Poulsbo WA 98370 *Web:* kitsap-publishing.myshopify.com	360-626-0256		637-2
Kitsap Regional Library 1301 Sylvan Way Bremerton WA 98310 *TF:* 877-883-9900 ■ *Web:* www.krl.org	360-405-9100	405-9156	434-3
Kitsap Sun 545 Fifth St Bremerton WA 98337 *Web:* www.kitsapsun.com	360-377-3711		532-2
KITS-FM 105.3 (Alt) 865 Battery St San Francisco CA 94111 *Web:* alt1053.radio.com	415-402-6700		645-142
Kitson LA 115 S Robertson Blvd Los Angeles CA 90048 *Web:* www.kitsonlosangeles.com	424-245-4003		292
Kittatinny Manufacturing Services Inc 160 Reading Rd Shippensburg PA 17257 *Web:* www.kittatinnymfg.com	717-530-1242		454
Kittatinny Valley State Park PO Box 621 Andover NJ 07821 *Web:* www.njparksandforests.org	973-786-6445		565
Kittelson & Associates Inc 610 SW Alder Ste 700 Portland OR 97205 *Web:* www.kittelson.com	503-228-5230		261
Kitten Krazy Inc 930 Lafeyette Rd Medina OH 44256 *Web:* kittenkrazy.org	330-558-1540		794
Kittery Trading Post 301 US 1 Kittery ME 03904 **Fax Area Code:* 207 ■ *TF:* 888-587-6246 ■ *Web:* www.kitterytradingpost.com	603-334-1157	439-8001*	157-2
Kittinger Business Machines 1024 N Mills Ave Orlando FL 32803 *Web:* www.kbmachines.com	407-894-1896	898-3117	112
Kittitas County 205 W Fifth Ave Ste 108 Ellensburg WA 98926 *Web:* www.co.kittitas.wa.us	509-962-7508	962-7679	338

Name / Address	City	State	Zip	Phone	Fax	Class
Kittle's Home Furnishings Center Inc 8600 Allisonville Rd. Web: www.kittles.com	Indianapolis	IN	46250	317-849-5300		321
Kittredge Equipment Company Inc 100 Bowles Rd. TF: 800-423-7082 ■ Web: www.kittredgeequipment.com	Agawam	MA	01001	413-304-4100	786-7086	300
Kittson County 1010 S Birch Ave. Web: visitnwminnesota.com	Hallock	MN	56728	218-843-2655		338
Kitty Askins Hospice Ctr 107 Handley Pk Ct. TF: 800-692-4442 ■ Web: www.3hc.org	Goldsboro	NC	27534	919-735-2145	735-5948	371
Kitty Hawk Kites Inc 306 W Lake Dr Unit K. TF: 877-359-8447 ■ Web: www.kittyhawk.com	Kill Devil Hills	NC	27948	252-441-4127	441-2498	711
KITV-TV Ch 4 (ABC) 801 S King St. Web: www.kitv.com	Honolulu	HI	96813	808-535-0400	536-8993	741-59
KITZ-AM 1700 Mile Hill Dr Ste 243. Web: www.kitz1400.com	Port Orchard	WA	98366	360-876-1400		647
Kivel & Howard LLP 111 SW Fifth Ave Ste 1900. Web: kivelhoward.com	Portland	OR	97204	503-796-0909		41
Kivell, Rayment & Francis PC 7666 E 61st St Ste 550. Web: www.kivell.com	Tulsa	OK	74133	918-254-0626	254-7915	428
KIVM-FM 1406 E Garden Ln. TF: 888-784-3476 ■ Web: www.grnonline.com	Midland	TX	79701	888-784-3476		647
Kivort Steel 380 Hudson River Rd. TF: 800-462-2616 ■ Web: kivortsteel.com	Waterford	NY	12188	518-590-7233	235-2042	492
Kiwi Coders Corp 265 E Messner Dr. Web: www.kiwicoders.com	Wheeling	IL	60090	847-541-4511	541-6332	627
Kiwi Ii Construction Inc 28177 Keller Rd. TF: 877-465-4942 ■ Web: www.kiwiconstruction.com	Murrieta	CA	92563	951-301-8975		186
Kiwi Partners Inc 30 Soundview Ln. Web: www.kiwipartners.com	Port Washington	NY	11050	516-767-6678		2
Kiwibox 330 W 38TH St Ste 1602. Web: www.kiwibox.com	New York	NY	10018	212-239-8210		387
Kiwiplan Inc 7870 E Kemper Rd Ste 200. Web: www.kiwiplan.com	Cincinnati	OH	45249	513-554-1500		177
KIWR-FM 2700 College Rd. Web: www.897theriver.com	Council Bluffs	IA	51503	712-328-8970		647
Kix 96.5 WJCL FM 214 Television Cir. Web: www.kix96.com	Savannah	GA	31406	912-947-9650	961-7070	645-145
Kixby Hotel 45 W 35th St. TF: 800-356-3870 ■ Web: www.kixby.com	New York	NY	10001	212-947-2500	279-1310	379
Kizan International Inc 100 W Hill Dr. Web: louisraphael.com	Brisbane	CA	94005	415-468-7360		157-3
KiZan Technologies LLC 1831 Williamson Ct. Web: www.kizan.com	Louisville	KY	40223	502-327-0333		180
Kizer Pharmacy LLC 1117 S Miles Ave Ste 1. Web: www.kizerpharmacy.com	Union City	TN	38261	731-885-2226		237
KIZN-FM 92.3 (Ctry) 1419 W Bannock. TF: 800-529-5264 ■ Web: www.kizn.com	Boise	ID	83702	208-336-3670	336-3734	645-21
KIZZ-FM 1000 20th Ave SW. Web: z94radio.iheart.com	Minot	ND	58701	701-852-2496	852-1390	647
KJ Energy LLC 5106 Knickerbocker Rd. Web: kjenergy.com	San Angelo	TX	76904	325-942-8792		360-3
KJ-108 505 University Ave. Web: kjkj.iheart.com	Grand Forks	ND	58203	701-746-1417		645-62
KJAA-AM 5734 S McKinney Ave. Web: www.jukebox1240.com	Globe	AZ	85501	928-425-8255	425-6397	647
KJAN-AM PO Box 389. TF: 800-283-5526 ■ Web: www.kjan.com	Atlantic	IA	50022	712-243-3920		647
KJB Security Products Inc 841-B Fessiers Pkwy. TF: 800-590-4272 ■ Web: www.kjbsecurity.com	Nashville	TN	37210	615-620-1370		246
KJCB-AM 770 (Urban) 413 Jefferson St. Web: www.radio.net	LaFayette	LA	70501	337-233-4262		645-83
KJCE-AM 1370 (N/T) 4301 Westbank Dr. TF: 866-408-7669 ■ Web: talk1370.radio.com	Austin	TX	78746	512-327-9595	329-6252	645-13
KJCS-FM 1026 S John Redditt Dr. Web: www.103thebull.com	Lufkin	TX	75904	936-564-2855		647
KJCT-TV 2531 Blichmann Ave. Web: www.kjct8.com	Grand Junction	CO	81505	970-245-8880		647
KJDL-FM 1500 Broadway St Ste 1208. Web: www.thereddirtrebel.com	Lubbock	TX	79401	806-438-4998		647
Kjeldsen Sinnock & Neudeck Inc 711 N Pershing Ave. Web: www.ksninc.com	Stockton	CA	95203	209-946-0268		256
Kjellstrom & Lee Inc 1607 Ownby Ln. Web: www.kjellstromandlee.com	Richmond	VA	23220	804-288-0082	285-4288	186
KJEM-FM 2049 E Joyce Blvd Ste 101. Web: www.933theeagle.iheart.com	Fayetteville	AR	72703	479-973-9339		647
KJIL 909 W Carthage PO Box 991. TF: 866-480-5545 ■ Web: www.kjil.com	Meade	KS	67864	620-873-2991	873-2755	647
KJJR-AM 2432 Hwy 2 E. Web: www.kjjr.com	Kalispell	MT	59901	406-755-8700		647
KJLA-TV Ch 57 (Ind) 2323 Corinth Ave. TF: 800-588-5788 ■ Web: www.kjla.com	Los Angeles	CA	90064	310-943-5288	943-5299	741-76
KJLH-FM 102.3 (Urban) 161 N La Brea Ave. Web: www.kjlhradio.com	Inglewood	CA	90301	310-330-2200		645
KJMO-FM 1002 Diamond Ridge Ste 400. Web: www.kjmo.com	Jefferson City	MO	65109	866-764-7460		647
KJNP-TV PO Box 56359. Web: www.mosquitonet.com	North Pole	AK	99705	907-488-2216		647
KJR-AM 950 (Sports) 645 Elliott Ave W Ste 400. TF: 800-829-0950 ■ Web: sportsradiokjr.iheart.com	Seattle	WA	98119	206-494-2000		645-147
KJRH-TV Ch 2 (NBC) 3701 S Peoria Ave. TF: 800-727-5574 ■ Web: www.kjrh.com	Tulsa	OK	74105	918-743-2222	748-1436	741-138
KJWM-FM 828 N Diers Ave. TF: 855-571-0200 ■ Web: www.spiritcatholicradio.com	Grand Island	NE	68803	855-571-0200		647
KJZZ-FM 91.5 (NPR) 2323 W 14th St. Web: kjzz.org	Tempe	AZ	85281	480-834-5627	774-8475	645
KJZZ-TV 299 S Main St Ste 150. Web: kjzz.com	Salt Lake City	UT	84111	801-839-1234	839-1101	741-115
KKAI-TV PO Box 15. Web: www.kkai.tv	Honolulu	HI	96810	808-593-5524		647
KKAL-FM 3620 Sacramento Dr Ste 204. Web: www.krush925.com	San Luis Obispo	CA	93401	805-781-2750		647
KKCO-TV 2531 Blichmann Ave. Web: www.nbc11news.com	Grand Junction	CO	81505	970-243-1111	243-1770	647
KKCT-FM 97.5 (CHR) 4303 Memorial Hwy. Web: www.hot975fm.com	Mandan	ND	58554	701-250-6602		645-20
KKDA-FM 104 621 NW Sixth St. Web: www.myk104.com	Grand Prairie	TX	75050	972-263-9911		645-43
KKFI-FM 90.1 (Var) 3901 Main St Ste 203. TF: 888-931-0901 ■ Web: www.kkfi.org	Kansas City	MO	64111	816-931-3122	931-7078	645-80
KKFS-FM 103.9 (Rel) 1425 River Pk Dr Ste 520. Web: thefishsacramento.com	Sacramento	CA	95815	916-924-0710		645-137
KKHQ-FM *Q92.3* 501 Sycamore St Ste 300. Web: q923fm.com	Waterloo	IA	50703	319-833-4800		647
KKHT-FM 100.0 (Rel) 6161 Savoy Dr Ste 1200. Web: www.kkht.com	Houston	TX	77036	713-260-3600		645-72
KKIQ-FM 7901 Stoneridge Dr Ste 525. TF: 800-398-1017 ■ Web: www.kkiq.com	Pleasanton	CA	94588	925-455-4500		647
KKIS-FM 40960 Kalifornsky Beach Rd. TF: 855-631-3995 ■ Web: www.radiokenai.net	Kenai	AK	99611	907-283-8700	283-9177	647
KKKJ-FM 1338 Oregon Ave. Web: www.klamathradio.com	Klamath Falls	OR	97601	541-882-4656	884-2845	647
KKMA-FM 2000 Indian Hills Dr. Web: classicrock995.com	Sioux City	IA	51104	712-239-2100	239-3346	647
KKMG-FM 98.9 (CHR) 6805 Corporate Dr Ste 130. Web: www.989magicfm.com	Colorado Springs	CO	80919	719-593-2700	593-2727	645-37
KKMI-FM 610 N Fourth St Ste 300. Web: www.935kkmi.com	Burlington	IA	52601	319-752-5402	752-4715	647
KKMS-AM 2110 Cliff Rd. Web: www.am980themission.com	Eagan	MN	55122	651-405-8800	405-8222	647
KKNU-FM 93.3 (Ctry) 925 Country Club Rd Ste 200. Web: www.kknu.fm	Eugene	OR	97401	541-484-9400	344-9424	645-94
KKNX-AM 1142 Willagillespie Rd Ste 28. Web: www.radio84.com	Eugene	OR	97401	541-342-1012	342-6201	647
KKO & Associates LLC 5 Vine St. Web: kko.com	Andover	MA	01810	978-475-4079		463
KKOL-FM 107.9 1160 N King St 2nd Fl. Web: 1079koolgold.com	Honolulu	HI	96817	808-533-0065		645-70
KKOW-AM 1162 E Hwy 126. Web: www.kkowam.com	Pittsburg	KS	66762	620-231-7200		647
KKPT-FM 94.1 2400 Cottondale Ln. TF: 800-844-0094 ■ Web: kkpt.com	Little Rock	AR	72202	501-664-9410		645-88
KKPZ-AM 9700 SE Eastview Dr. Web: www.kkpz.com	Happy Valley	OR	97086	503-242-1950		647
KKR Credit Advisors (US) LLC 555 California St 50th Fl. Web: www.kkr.com	San Francisco	CA	94104	415-315-3620		654
KKRT-AM 1124 N Miller St. Web: www.kkrt.com	Wenatchee	WA	98801	509-663-5186		647
KKSP-FM 415 N McKinley St Ste 700. Web: www.933fmthefish.com	Little Rock	AR	72205	501-332-6981	332-6984	647
KKTV 11 News 520 E Colorado. Web: www.kktv.com	Colorado Springs	CO	80903	719-634-2844	632-0808	741-32
KKTX-AM 501 Tupper Ln. Web: www.1360kktx.iheart.com	Corpus Christi	TX	78417	361-560-5589		647
KKTY-AM 247 Russell Ave. TF: 800-880-3208 ■ Web: www.kktyonline.com	Douglas	WY	82633	307-358-3636		647
KKVI-FM PO Box 1433. Web: www.kkvidfw.com	Wylie	TX	75098	972-487-6090		647
KKVV-AM 1060 (Rel) 3185 S Highland Dr Ste 13. Web: kkvv.com	Las Vegas	NV	89109	702-731-5588	731-5851	645-85
KKW Trucking Inc 3100 Pomona Blvd. TF: 800-955-4559 ■ Web: www.kkwtrucks.com	Pomona	CA	91768	909-869-1200	869-1215	780
KL (Kaufman Lynn Construction) 3185 S Congress Ave. Web: www.kaufmanlynn.com	Delray Beach	FL	33445	561-361-6700	361-6979	186
KL Communications Inc 50 English Plz Ste 6B. Web: www.klcommunications.com	Red Bank	NJ	07701	732-224-9991		466
KL Industries Inc 1790 Sun Dolphin Dr. TF: 800-733-2727 ■ Web: www.klindustries.com	Muskegon	MI	49444	231-733-2725	739-4502	710
KLA Laboratories Inc 6800 Chase Rd. Web: www.klalabs.com	Dearborn	MI	48126	313-846-3800		179
KlaasKids Foundation PO Box 925. Web: www.klaaskids.org	Sausalito	CA	94966	415-331-6867		48-6
KLAB-FM 110 N Broadway. Web: www.klrc.com	Siloam Springs	AR	72761	479-238-8600	238-8601	647
KLAD-FM 404 Main St Ste 4. Web: www.mybasin.com	Klamath Falls	OR	97601	541-882-8833		647
Klafter's Inc 216 N Beaver St. TF: 800-922-1233 ■ Web: www.klafters.com	New Castle	PA	16101	800-922-1233		756
Klamath Boat Co 5199 Fulton Dr Ste I. Web: klamathboats.com	Fairfield	CA	94534	707-643-0447		90
Klamath Community College 7390 S Sixth St. Web: www.klamathcc.edu	Klamath Falls	OR	97603	541-882-3521	885-7758	162
Klamath County 305 Main St. TF: 800-377-6094 ■ Web: www.klamathcounty.org	Klamath Falls	OR	97601	541-883-5134	883-5165	338

Name / Address	City	State	ZIP	Phone	Fax	Class
Klamath County Chamber of Commerce 205 Riverside Dr *Web:* klamath.org	Klamath Falls	OR	97601	541-884-5193	884-5195	139
Klamath County Library 126 S 3rd St *Web:* klamathlibrary.org	Klamath Falls	OR	97601	541-882-8894	882-6166	434-3
Klamath County Museum 1451 Main St *Web:* www.museum.klamathcounty.org	Klamath Falls	OR	97601	541-882-1000		520
Klamath Public Employees Federal Credit Union 3737 Shasta Way *TF:* 800-454-5525 ■ *Web:* kpefcu.com	Klamath Falls	OR	97603	541-882-5525	884-0653	219
KLAQ-FM 95.5 (Rock) 4180 N Mesa St *TF:* 844-305-6210 ■ *Web:* www.klaq.com	El Paso	TX	79902	915-880-4955	532-3334	645-52
Klarity Multimedia Inc 36 Maple St *TF:* 888-387-8273 ■ *Web:* www.klarity.com	North Vassalboro	ME	04962	207-873-3911	873-3924	393
Klass Ingredients Inc 3885 N Buffalo St *TF:* 800-662-6577 ■ *Web:* www.klassingredients.com	Orchard Park	NY	14127	716-662-6665	662-0285	345
Klassen Corp 2021 Westwind Dr *Web:* www.klassencorp.com	Bakersfield	CA	93301	661-324-3000		186
KLA-Tencor Corp 1 Technology Dr *NASDAQ: KLAC* ■ *TF:* 800-600-2829 ■ *Web:* www.kla-tencor.com	Milpitas	CA	95035	408-875-3000	875-4144	248
Klatzkin & Company Jr CPAS 1670 Whitehorse Hamilton Sq Rd *Web:* www.klatzkin.com	Hamilton Township	NJ	08690	609-890-9189		2
Klauber Bros Inc 253 W 35th St 11th Fl *Web:* www.klauberlace.com	New York	NY	10001	212-686-2531	481-7194	745-4
Klauer Manufacturing Co 1185 Roosevelt Ext PO Box 59 *Web:* www.klauer.com	Dubuque	IA	52004	563-582-7201		697
Klaus & Associates 2125 Parker St *Web:* peggyklaus.com	Berkeley	CA	94704	510-548-8828		194
Klaussner Home Furnishings 405 Lewallen Rd *Web:* www.klaussner.com	Asheboro	NC	27204	336-625-6174	625-5584	319-2
Klaviyo 225 Franklin St 10th Fl *TF:* 800-338-1744 ■ *Web:* www.klaviyo.com	Boston	MA	02110	800-338-1744		7
KLAX-AM 10281 W Pico Bl *Web:* www.979laraza.lamusica.com	Los Angeles	CA	90064	310-203-0900		647
KLAX-TV 1811 England Dr *Web:* www.klax-tv.com	Alexandria	LA	71303	318-473-0031		647
KLAY-AM 10025 Lakewood Dr SW Ste B *Web:* www.klay1180.com	Tacoma	WA	98499	253-581-0324		647
KLBC-TV 3100 S Needles Hwy *Web:* www.tv2klbc.com	Laughlin	NV	89029	702-298-2222	298-0011	647
KLBJ-FM 93.7 (Rock) 8309 N IH-35 *Web:* www.klbjfm.com	Austin	TX	78753	512-834-0937	832-4081	645-13
KLCC-FM 89.7 (NPR) 136 W Eighth Ave *TF:* 800-922-3682 ■ *Web:* klcc.org	Eugene	OR	97401	541-463-6000	463-6046	645-94
KLCK-AM 620 E 3rd St PO Box 1023 *TF:* 888-297-9102 ■ *Web:* gorgenewscenter.com	The Dalles	OR	97058	541-296-9102	298-7775	647
KLCS-TV Ch 58 (PBS) 1061 W Temple St *Web:* www.klcs.org	Los Angeles	CA	90012	213-241-4000	481-1019	741-76
KLCW-TV 9800 University Ave *Web:* www.lubbockcw.com	Lubbock	TX	79423	806-745-3434		647
Klean Image 13498 Pond Springs Rd *Web:* www.kisscleaning.com	Austin	TX	78729	512-258-7003		256
Klean Industries Inc 700 W Georgia St Ste 2500 *TF:* 866-302-5928 ■ *Web:* www.kleanindustries.com	Vancouver	BC	V7Y1K8	604-637-9609		192
Kleber & Assoc 1215 Hightower Trial Bldg C *Web:* kleberandassociates.com	Atlanta	GA	30350	770-518-1000		4
Kleberg County PO Box 1327 *Web:* www.co.kleberg.tx.us	Kingsville	TX	78364	361-595-8548	593-1355	338
Kleen Air Service Corp 5354 N Northwest Hwy *Web:* www.kleenair.com	Chicago	IL	60630	773-631-0007		612
Kleen Test Products Corp 1611 Sunset Rd *TF:* 800-634-7328 ■ *Web:* kleentest.com	Port Washington	WI	53074	262-284-6600	284-6623	558
Kleenair Products Co 14230 SE 98th Ct *Web:* www.kleenairusa.com	Clackamas	OR	97015	503-653-6925	659-0941	318
Kleen-Rite Inc 4444 Gustine Ave *Web:* kleen-rite.com	Saint Louis	MO	63116	314-353-1712	353-5340	427
KLEEN-TEX Industries Inc 50 Hurt Plz SE Ste 1040 *Web:* www.kleen-tex.com	Atlanta	GA	30303	404-991-5500	953-6444	508
Kleer Corp 19925 Stevens Creek Blvd Ste 111	Cupertino	CA	95014	408-973-7255	973-7256	696
Kleet Lumber Company Inc 777 Park Ave *Web:* www.kleet.com	Huntington	NY	11743	631-427-7060	427-4384	191-3
Klehm Arboretum & Botanic Garden 2715 S Main St *Web:* www.klehm.org	Rockford	IL	61102	815-965-8146	965-5914	97
Klein & Hoffman Inc 150 S Wacker Dr *Web:* www.kleinandhoffman.com	Chicago	IL	60606	312-251-1900		261
Klein Electronics 349 N Vinewood St *TF:* 800-959-2899 ■ *Web:* www.kleinelectronics.com	Escondido	CA	92029	760-781-3220		647
Klein Independent School District 7200 Spring Cypress Rd *TF:* 888-703-0083 ■ *Web:* kleinisd.net	Klein	TX	77379	832-249-4000		685
Klein Steel Service 105 Vanguarden Pkwy *TF:* 800-477-6789 ■ *Web:* www.kleinsteel.com	Rochester	NY	14606	585-328-4000	328-0470	492
Klein Tools Inc 450 Bond St *TF:* 800-553-4676 ■ *Web:* www.kleintools.com	Lincolnshire	IL	60069	800-553-4676		758
Klein, Hockel, Iezza & Patel PC 455 Market St Ste 1480 *Web:* khiplaw.com	San Francisco	CA	94105	415-951-0535	391-7808	41
Kleinfeld, Kaplan & Becker LLP 1850 M St NW Ste 800 *Web:* www.kkblaw.com	Washington	DC	20036	202-223-5120	223-5619	428
Kleingers Group Inc, The 6305 Centre Park Dr **Fax Area Code:* 614 ■ *Web:* www.kleingers.com	West Chester	OH	45069	513-779-7851	882-4479*	261
Kleinhans Music Hall 3 Symphony Cir *Web:* kleinhansbuffalo.org	Buffalo	NY	14201	716-883-3560		572
Kleinknecht Electrc 19 W 44th St Ste 500 *Web:* www.kecny.com	New York	NY	10036	212-728-1800		189-4
Kleinpeter & Schwartzberg LLC 6651 Jefferson Hwy *Web:* ksbrlaw.com	Baton Rouge	LA	70806	225-926-4130		41
Kleinpeter Farms Dairy LLC 14444 Airline Hwy *Web:* www.kleinpeterdairy.com	Baton Rouge	LA	70817	225-753-2121		296-27
Kleinschmidt Inc 450 Lake Cook Rd *TF:* 800-824-2330 ■ *Web:* www.kleinschmidt.com	Deerfield	IL	60015	847-945-1000	945-4619	39
Klemchuk LLP 8150 N Central Expy 10th Fl *Web:* klemchuk.com	Dallas	TX	75206	214-367-6000		41
Klement Sausage Company Inc 207 E Lincoln Ave *Web:* www.klements.com	Milwaukee	WI	53207	414-744-2330	744-2438	296-26
Klemmer 1340 Commerce St *TF:* 800-577-5447 ■ *Web:* www.klemmer.com	Petaluma	CA	94954	707-559-7722		463
Klenda Austerman LLC 1600 Epic Ctr 301 N Main St *Web:* klendalaw.com	Wichita	KS	67202	316-267-0331	267-0333	428
Klepadlo Winnell Nuorala PC 2301 Mitchell Park Dr *Web:* www.kwncpa.com	Petoskey	MI	49770	231-347-3963		2
Klerer Financial Services Inc 3272 Merrick Rd *Web:* klerer.com	Wantagh	NY	11793	516-409-5500	409-6100	390
Klett Consulting Group Inc 2488 N Landing Rd Ste 111 *Web:* kcg-inc.net	Virginia Beach	VA	23456	757-721-5040		261
KLFC-FM 88.1 205 W Atlantic St *TF:* 877-410-8592 ■ *Web:* www.klfcradio.com	Branson	MO	65616	417-334-5532	335-2437	645-24
KLFD-AM 234 N Sibley Ave *Web:* klfdradio.com	Litchfield	MN	55355	320-693-3281	693-3283	647
KLFY-TV Ch 10 (CBS) 1808 Eraste Landry Rd *Web:* www.klfy.com	LaFayette	LA	70506	337-981-4823		741-70
KLG Advisors 399 Park Ave 11th Fl *Web:* www.klgadvisors.com	New York	NY	10022	212-514-4600		463
KLH Audio Speakers 984 Logan St *TF:* 833-554-8326 ■ *Web:* www.klhaudio.com	Noblesville	IN	46060	833-554-8326		52
KLH Engineers Inc 5173 Campbells Run Rd *Web:* klhengineers.com	Pittsburgh	PA	15205	412-494-0510		261
KLH Industries Inc N117 W18607 Fulton Dr *TF:* 877-222-0850 ■ *Web:* www.klhindustries.com	Germantown	WI	53022	262-253-4990	253-4992	455
Klickitat County 205 S Columbus Ave Rm 204 *Web:* www.klickitatcounty.org	Goldendale	WA	98620	509-773-5744	773-4559	338
Klick-lewis Inc 720 E Main St *Web:* www.klicklewiscars.com	Palmyra	PA	17078	717-838-1353		57
Kliegel Machine Company LLC 104 Hibbard Rd *Web:* www.kliegelmachine.com	Big Flats	NY	14814	607-562-3275		454
Kliemann Bros Heating & Air Conditioning Inc 4703 116th St E *Web:* www.kliemannbros.com	Tacoma	WA	98446	253-537-0655		610
KLIK-AM 1240 (N/T) 1002 Diamond Rdg Ste 400 *Web:* www.klik1240.com	Jefferson City	MO	65109	573-893-5100		645-77
Kliklok LLC *Syntegon Co* 5224 Snapfinger Woods Dr *Web:* cartoning-casepacking.syntegon.com	Decatur	GA	30035	770-981-5200		547
Kline & Company Inc 35 Waterview Blvd Ste 305 *TF:* 800-290-5214 ■ *Web:* www.klinegroup.com	Parsippany	NJ	07054	973-435-6262	435-6291	194
Kline & Specter PC 1525 Locust St *TF:* 800-243-1100 ■ *Web:* klinespecter.com	Philadelphia	PA	19102	215-772-1000	772-1359	428
Kline Process Systems Inc 625 Spring St Ste 200 *Web:* www.kpsnet.com	Reading	PA	19610	610-371-0200		180
Kline Scott Visco Commercial Real Estate Inc 117 W Patrick St *Web:* klinescottvisco.com	Frederick	MD	21701	301-694-8444	694-6592	652
Klinedinst PC 801 K St *Web:* klinedinstlaw.com	Sacramento	CA	95814	916-444-7573		428
Klingberg Family Centers Inc 370 Linwood St *Web:* klingberg.org	New Britain	CT	06052	860-224-9113	827-8440	48-15
Klinge Corp 4075 E Market St *Web:* klingecorp.com	York	PA	17402	717-840-4500	840-4501	539
Klingelhofer Corp 165 Mill Ln *TF:* 800-879-5546 ■ *Web:* www.klingelhofer.com	Mountainside	NJ	07092	908-232-7200	232-1841	455
Klingensmith HealthCare 313 Ford St *Web:* www.klingensmiths.com	Ford City	PA	16226	724-763-1201	763-7571	352
Klingher Nadler LLP 580 Sylvan Ave Ste Ma *Web:* klinghernadler.com	Englewood Cliffs	NJ	07632	201-731-3025		2
Klink Citrus Assn 32921 Rd 159 *Web:* growers.sunkist.com	Ivanhoe	CA	93235	559-798-1881		11-1
Klink Trucking Inc 3320 W 800 S *Web:* www.klinktrucking.com	Ashley	IN	46705	260-587-9113		780
Klipsch LLC 137 Hempstead 278 **Fax Area Code:* 870 ■ *TF:* 888-250-8561 ■ *Web:* www.klipsch.com	Hope	AR	71801	888-250-8561	777-6753*	52
Klitzberg Associates Inc 600 Alexander Rd *Web:* klitzbergfundsolutions.com	Princeton	NJ	08540	609-452-2888		528
KLJ Computer Solutions Inc 10-3250 Ridgeway Dr *TF:* 888-455-5669 ■ *Web:* kljsolutions.com	Mississauga	ON	L5L5Y6	888-455-5669		179

Name / Address	City	State	ZIP	Phone	Fax	Class
KLJC-FM 88.5 8717 W 110th St Ste 480 *TF:* 855-474-8850 ■ *Web:* life885.com	Overland Park	KS	66210	913-451-8850		645-80
KLKK-FM *103.7 The Fox* 201 N Federal Ave *Web:* 1037thefoxrocks.com	Mason City	IA	50401	641-421-7744	421-7755	647
KLKN-TV Ch 8 (ABC) 3240 S Tenth St *Web:* www.klkntv.com	Lincoln	NE	68502	402-434-8000	436-2236	741-74
KLLM Inc 135 Riverview Dr *TF:* 800-925-5556 ■ *Web:* www.kllm.com	Richland	MS	39218	800-925-1000		780
KLM Creative Inc 1900 Powell St 6th Fl *Web:* klmcreative.com	Emeryville	CA	94608	415-503-4150		195
KLM Heating & Cooling 11216 Decimal Dr *Web:* www.klmheatingandcooling.com	Louisville	KY	40299	502-215-5981	955-2064	189-10
KLMP-FM 88.3 1853 Fountain Plaza Dr *Web:* www.klmp.com	Rapid City	SD	57702	605-342-6822	342-0854	645-129
KLMX-AM PO Box 547 *Web:* www.klmx.us	Clayton	NM	88415	575-374-2555	374-2557	647
KLN Klein Product Development Inc 19787 56 Ave *Web:* klnklein.com	Langley	BC	V3A3X8	604-530-1491		196
KLNC-FM 4343 O St *Web:* www.1053thebone.com	Lincoln	NE	68510	402-475-4567	479-1411	647
Klobuchar Amy (Sen D - MN) 425 Dirksen Senate Office Bldg *Web:* www.klobuchar.senate.gov	Washington	DC	20510	202-224-3244	228-2186	342-2
Klochko Equipment Rental Company Inc 2782 Corbin Ave *TF:* 800-783-7368 ■ *Web:* www.klochko.com	Melvindale	MI	48122	313-386-7220	386-2530	264-3
Klockner Pentaplast of America Inc 3585 Klockner Rd PO Box 500 *Web:* www.kpfilms.com	Gordonsville	VA	22942	540-832-3600	832-5656	599
Klocwork Inc 15 New England Executive Pk **Fax Area Code:* 613 ■ *TF:* 866-556-2967 ■ *Web:* www.klocwork.com	Burlington	MA	01803	215 556 2067	036 0000*	170-1
Klodowski Law LLC 6400 Brooktree Ct Ste 250 *Web:* www.bhklawpgh.com	Wexford	PA	15090	724-940-4000	940-4048	41
Kloepfer Concrete & Paving Co 505 E Ellis PO Box 840 *Web:* www.kloepfer.com	Paul	ID	83347	208-438-4525	438-5030	182
Klondike Cheese Co W7839 Hwy 81 *Web:* www.klondikecheese.com	Monroe	WI	53566	608-325-3021		296-5
Klondike Gold Rush National Historical Park - Seattle Unit 319 Second Ave S *Web:* www.nps.gov	Seattle	WA	98104	206-220-4240		564
Klondike PROMOTIONS 1900 W Benson Blvd *Web:* www.klondikepromotions.com	Anchorage	AK	99517	907-274-3535		7
Kloppenberg & Co 2627 W Oxford Ave *TF:* 800-346-3246 ■ *Web:* www.kloppenberg.com	Englewood	CO	80110	303-761-1615	789-1741	664
KLOS-FM 95.5 (CR) 2600 W Olive Ave 8th Fl *TF:* 800-955-5567 ■ *Web:* www.955klos.com	Burbank	CA	91505	818-953-4200	525-5001	645-42
Klosterman Baking Company Inc 4760 Paddock Rd *TF:* 877-301-1004 ■ *Web:* www.klostermanbakery.com	Cincinnati	OH	45229	513-242-1004		296-1
Klosterman Distributing Co 2930 Millcork St *Web:* www.klostermandistributing.com	Kalamazoo	MI	49001	269-381-0870		756
KLPW-AM 6501 Hwy BB *TF:* 866-570-1220 ■ *Web:* www.klpw.com	Washington	MO	63090	636-583-5155		647
KLPZ-AM 816 W 6th St *Web:* www.klpz1380.com	Parker	AZ	85344	928-669-9274	669-9300	647
KLRU-TV Ch 18 (PBS) 2504-B Whitis Ave PO Box 7158 *Web:* austinpbs.org	Austin	TX	78712	512-471-4811	471-5561	741-9
KLS Professional Advisors Group LLC 1325 Avenue of the Americas 14th Fl *Web:* www.klsadvisors.com	New York	NY	10019	212-355-0346	355-0413	41
KLSU-FM Louisiana State University B-39 Hodges Hall *Web:* www.lsureveille.com	Baton Rouge	LA	70803	225-578-5578		647
KLTG-FM 1733 S Brownlee Blvd *Web:* corpuschristirocks.com	Corpus Christi	TX	78404	361-883-1600	883-9303	647
KLTT-AM 2821 S Parker Rd Ste 1205 *Web:* www.670kltt.com	Aurora	CO	80014	303-433-5500	433-1555	647
KLTV-TV 105 W Ferguson *Web:* www.kltv.com	Tyler	TX	75702	903-597-5588	510-7847	647
KLTY-FM 94.9 (Rel) 6400 N Beltline Rd Ste 120 **Fax Area Code:* 214 ■ *Web:* www.klty.com	Irving	TX	75063	972-870-9949	561-2155*	645
Kluane National Park & Reserve of Canada PO Box 5495 *TF:* 877-852-3100 ■ *Web:* www.pc.gc.ca	Haines Junction	YT	Y0B1L0	867-634-7250	634-7208	563
Kluber Lubrication NA LP 32 Industrial Dr *TF:* 800-447-2238 ■ *Web:* www.klueber.com	Londonderry	NH	03053	603-647-4104	647-4106	541
KLUZ-TV 2725 Broadbent Pky NE Ste F *Web:* www.noticiasya.com	Albuquerque	NM	87107	505-341-6132	344-0891	647
KLVO-FM 8009 Marble Ave NE *Web:* www.radiolobo.net	Albuquerque	NM	87110	505-254-7100	254-7106	647
KLWB-FM 3501 NW Evangeline Thwy *Web:* www.1037thegame.com	Carencro	LA	70520	337-896-1600		647
KLWN-AM 3125 W Sixth St *Web:* www.klwn.com	Lawrence	KS	66049	785-843-1320		647
KLYD-FM 2301 Avenue R *Web:* www.bigstarradiogroup.com	Snyder	TX	79549	325-573-9322		647
KLYV-FM 5490 Saratoga Rd *Web:* www.y105music.com	Dubuque	IA	52002	563-556-5105		647
KLYY-FM 5700 Wilshire Blvd Ste 250 **Fax Area Code:* 818 ■ *Web:* www.superestrella.com	Los Angeles	CA	90036	323-900-6100	351-6218*	647
KM (Kramer Metals Inc) 1760 E Slauson Ave *Web:* www.kramermetals.com	Los Angeles	CA	90058	323-587-2277	588-8007	686
KM Fabrics Inc 2 Waco St *TF:* 800-845-1896 ■ *Web:* www.kmfabrics.com	Greenville	SC	29611	864-295-2550	295-3356	745-1
KM2 Solutions LLC 100 Park Ave Ste 1600 *Web:* www.km2solutions.com	New York	NY	10017	404-848-8886		463
KMA (Kubota Manufacturing of America Corp) 2715 Ramsey Rd Industrial Pk N *Web:* www.kubota-kma.com	Gainesville	GA	30501	770-532-0038	532-9057	274
KMA One 6815 Meadowridge Ct *TF:* 888-500-2536 ■ *Web:* www.kmaone.com	Alpharetta	GA	30005	770-886-4000		366
KMA Sunbelt Trading Corp 3696 Ulmerton Rd *Web:* shopidc.com	Clearwater	FL	33762	727-572-6323		411
K-Mac Enterprises Inc 1820 South Zero St *TF:* 800-947-9277 ■ *Web:* www.kmaccorp.com	Fort Smith	AR	72906	479-646-2053	646-8748	670
KMAG-FM 311 Lexington Ave *TF:* 866-503-1398 ■ *Web:* www.kmag991.iheart.com	Fort Smith	AR	72901	479-782-8888	782-0366	647
KMAH-TV 2232 Dell Range Blvd	Cheyenne	WY	82009	307-637-7777		647
KMAJ-AM 1440 825 S Kansas Ave Ste 100 *TF:* 877-297-1077 ■ *Web:* www.kmaj1440.com	Topeka	KS	66612	785-272-2122	272-6219	645-162
KMAN-AM 2414 Casement Rd *Web:* www.1350kman.com	Manhattan	KS	66502	785-776-1350	539-1000	647
KMAQ-FM 129 N Main St PO Box 940 *TF:* 800-747-0057 ■ *Web:* www.kmaq.com	Maquoketa	IA	52060	563-652-2426	652-6210	647
KMBR-FM 95.5 (Rock) 750 Dewey Blvd *Web:* 955kmbr.com	Butte	MT	59701	406-494-4442		645
KMC (Kickhaefer Manufacturing Co) 1221 S Park St PO Box 348 *TF:* 800-822-6080 ■ *Web:* www.kmcstampings.com	Port Washington	WI	53074	262-377-5030	284-9774	488
KMC (Knapp Medical Ctr) 1401 E Eigth St PO Box 1110 *Web:* www.knappmed.org	Weslaco	TX	78596	956-968-8567		374-3
KMC Controls Inc 19476 Industrial Dr *TF:* 877-444-5622 ■ *Web:* www.kmccontrols.com	New Paris	IN	46553	574-831-5250	831-5252	202
KMC Exim Corp 1 Harbor Park Dr	Port Washington	NY	11050	516-621-6565		237
KMCI-TV Ch 38 4720 Oak St *Web:* www.kshb.com	Kansas City	MO	64112	816-753-4141		741-68
KMCO LLC 16503 Ramsey Rd *Web:* kmcollc.com	Crosbyton	TX	77532	281-328-3501	328-9528	145
KMCS-FM 3218 Mulberry Ave *Web:* 931thebuzz.com	Muscatine	IA	52761	563-263-9393		647
KMCX-FM *Hot Country 106.5 FM* 113 W 4th St *Web:* kmcx.iheart.com	Ogallala	NE	69153	308-284-3633		647
KME Fire Apparatus 68 Sicker Rd *Web:* www.kmefire.com	Latham	NY	12110	518-785-0900		516
KMEA 964 5th Ave *Web:* www.kmea.net	San Diego	CA	92101	619-342-7377		194
KMEG-TV 100 Gold Cir *Web:* www.siouxlandnews.com	Dakota Dunes	SD	57049	712-277-3554	255-5250	647
KMEZ-FM 106.7 (Oldies) 201 St Charles Ave Ste 201 *Web:* www.kmez1029.com	New Orleans	LA	70170	504-581-7002		645-107
KMG-Bernuth Inc 9555 W Sam Houston Pkwy S Ste 600 *Web:* kmgchemicals.com	Houston	TX	77099	713-600-3800		146
KMGi Corp 228 Park Ave S Ste 16065 *Web:* kmgi.cc	New York	NY	10003	212-202-0793	202-4982	463
KMGV-FM 97.9 1071 W Shaw Ave *TF:* 800-265-6342 ■ *Web:* www.mega979.com	Fresno	CA	93711	559-490-5800		645-61
KMH Cardiology & Diagnostic Centres 2075 Hadwen Rd *Web:* kmhlabs.com	Mississauga	ON	L5K2L3	905-855-1860		415
KMHK FM 27 N 27th St Crowne Plz 23rd Fl *Web:* kmhk.com	Billings	MT	59101	406-294-1037		645-18
KMI Diagnostics Inc 8201 Central Ave NE Ste P *TF:* 888-564-3424 ■ *Web:* www.kmidiagnostics.com	Minneapolis	MN	55432	763-231-3313	780-2988	231
KMIR-TV Ch 6 (NBC) 72920 Parkview Dr *TF:* 888-422-9925 ■ *Web:* nbcpalmsprings.com	Palm Desert	CA	92260	760-340-1623		741
KMIZ-TV Ch 17 (ABC) 501 Business Loop 70 E *TF:* 800-345-4109 ■ *Web:* www.abc17news.com	Columbia	MO	65201	573-449-0917	875-7078	741
KMJ Consulting Inc 120 E Lancaster Ave Ste 105 *Web:* kmjinc.com	Ardmore	PA	19003	610-896-1996		194
KMJ Corbin & Co 555 Anton Blvd Ste 1000 *Web:* www.kmjpartnerscpa.com	Costa Mesa	CA	92626	714-380-6565	380-6566	734
KMJM-FM 1001 Highlands Plaza Dr W Ste 100 *Web:* www.thebeatstl.iheart.com	Saint Louis	MO	63110	314-333-8000		647
KMKS-FM 2309 5th St *Web:* www.kmks.com	Bay City	TX	77414	979-244-4242		647
KMM (Killdeer Mountain Manufacturing Inc) 233 Rodeo Dr *Web:* www.kmmnet.com	Killdeer	ND	58640	701-764-5651	764-5427	625
KMM Technologies Inc 2525 Emerson Dr Ste 101 *Web:* www.kmmtechnologies.com	Frederick	MD	21702	240-286-2321		194
KMMJ-AM 128 S 4th St *TF:* 888-920-5665 ■ *Web:* www.praisenetwork.info	O'Neill	NE	68763	888-920-5665		647
KMMM-AM 30129 E Hwy 54 PO Box 486 *Web:* www.themighty1290am.com	Pratt	KS	67124	620-672-5581		647
KMMO-FM 1190 N Lexington Ave (Hwy 65 N) PO Box 128 *TF:* 800-727-5666 ■ *Web:* www.kmmo.com	Marshall	MO	65340	660-886-7422	886-6291	647
KMMS-AM 125 W Mendenhall *Web:* www.kmmsam.com	Bozeman	MT	59715	406-586-2343	587-2202	647

Name	Address	City	State	ZIP	Phone	Fax	Class	Notes
KMND-AM	11300 Hwy 191 Bldg 2	Midland	TX	79707	432-563-9300		647	Web: foxsports1510.com
KMNG & Associates Inc	6243 W Ih 10 Ste 200	San Antonio	TX	78201	210-736-6623		261	
KMNV-AM	3003 27th Ave S Ste 400	Minneapolis	MN	55406	612-354-3282		647	Web: www.laraza1400.com
KMOD-FM 97.5 (Rock)	7136 S Yale Ave Ste 500	Tulsa	OK	74136	918-388-5100		645-166	Web: kmod.iheart.com
KMOG-AM	500 E Tyler Pkwy	Payson	AZ	85541	928-474-5214	474-0236	647	Web: www.kmogcountry.com
KMOS-TV Ch 6 (PBS)	University of Central Missouri	Warrensburg	MO	64093	800-753-3436	543-8863*	741	*Fax Area Code: 660 ■ TF: 800-753-3436 ■ Web: www.kmos.org
KMOU-TV	PO Box 670	Roswell	NM	88202	316-269-4160	884-8888*	647	*Fax Area Code: 573 ■ Web: www.komu.com
KMOV-TV Ch 4 (CBS)	1 Memorial Dr	Saint Louis	MO	63102	314-621-4444	621-4775	741-114	Web: www.kmov.com
KMP Designs Inc	7145 W Credit Ave Bldg 2 Ste 101	Mississauga	ON	L5N6J7	905-812-5635		180	Web: kmpdesigns.com
KMPH-TV Ch 26 (Fox)	5111 E McKinley Ave	Fresno	CA	93727	559-453-8850	255-9626	741-52	TF: 800-101-2045 ■ Web: kmph.com
KMR Scripts	PO Box 220	Valley Center	KS	67147	316-765-1957		637-10	Web: www.kmrscripts.com
KMRY-AM 1450 (Nost)	1957 Blairs Ferry Rd NE	Cedar Rapids	IA	52402	319-393-1450		645-28	Web: kmryradio.com
KMS (Kewanna Metal Specialties Inc)	419 W Main St PO Box 367	Kewanna	IN	46939	574-653-2554	653-2556	73	Web: www.kmswire.com
KMS (King Medical Supply)	20816 Higgins Ct	Torrance	CA	90501	800-488-6535	533-8810*	475	*Fax Area Code: 866 ■ TF: 800-488-6535 ■ Web: www.kingmedicalsupply.com
KMS Business Products Corp	3010 E Cervantes St	Pensacola	FL	32503	850-433-1131		180	Web: www.kmsbusiness.com
KMS Consulting Services Inc	92 Broadway Ste 206	Greenlawn	NY	11740	631-912-0200		196	Web: kmssolutions.com
KMS Inc	3761 Alabama Hwy 14	Millbrook	AL	36054	334-285-1637		297-8	Web: www.kms-inc.net
KMS Solutions LLC	205 S Whiting St Ste 400	Alexandria	VA	22304	703-823-8405		261	Web: www.kmssol.com
KMSP-TV Ch 9 (Fox)	11358 Viking Dr	Eden Prairie	MN	55344	952-946-5767		741	Web: www.fox9.com
KMSS-TV	3150 N Market St	Shreveport	LA	71107	318-629-7175	629-7158	647	Web: www.arklatexhomepage.com
KMSYS Worldwide Inc	PO Box 669695	Marietta	GA	30066	770-635-6363	635-6351	177	Web: www.kmsys.com
KMT Waterjet Systems Inc	635 W 12th St	Baxter Springs	KS	66713	620-856-2151	856-5050	493	TF: 800-826-9274 ■ Web: www.kmtwaterjet.com
Kmtelecom	18 Second Ave NW	Kasson	MN	55944	507-634-2511		116	Web: www.kmtel.com
KMTG (Kronick Moskovitz Tiedemann & Girard)	400 Capitol Mall 2nd Fl	Sacramento	CA	95814	916-321-4500	321-4555	428	Web: kmtg.com
KMTP-TV	719 Woodside Way	San Mateo	CA	94401	415-777-3232		647	Web: www.kmtp.tv
KMTR-TV	3825 International Ct	Springfield	OR	97477	541-746-1600		647	Web: nbc16.com
KMUW-FM 89.1 (NPR)	3317 E 17th St N	Wichita	KS	67208	316-978-6789		645-173	Web: kmuw.org
KMVT-TV	1100 Blue Lake Blvd N	Twin Falls	ID	83301	208-733-1100		647	Web: www.kmvt.com
KMW Ltd	PO Box 327	Sterling	KS	67579	620-278-3641	278-2388	273	TF: 800-445-7388 ■ Web: www.kmwloaders.com
KMWB-FM	1145 Kilauea Ave	Hilo	HI	96720	808-935-5461	935-7761	647	Web: www.b97hawaii.com
KMXB-FM 94.1 (AC)	7255 S Tenaya Way Ste 100	Las Vegas	NV	89113	702-257-9400		645-85	Web: mix941fm.radio.com
KMXI-AM	2654 Cramer Ln	Chico	CA	95928	530-345-0021	893-2121	647	Web: www.kpay.com
KMXJ-FM 94.1 (AC)	6214 W 34th St	Amarillo	TX	79109	806-320-0994		645-5	Web: mix941kmxj.com
KMXM-FM	100 W Lyndale Ave Ste B	Helena	MT	59601	406-442-6645		647	Web: mixhelena.com
KMXZ-FM 94.9	3871 N Commerce Dr	Tucson	AZ	85710	520-775-0949		645-165	Web: www.mixfm.com
KMYQ-TV	1813 Westlake Ave N	Seattle	WA	98109	206-674-1321		647	Web: www.q13fox.com
KMZL-FM	c/o SOS Radio 2201 S 6th St	Las Vegas	NV	89104	702-731-5452	731-1992	647	TF: 800-804-5452 ■ Web: www.sosradio.net
KN (Kubin-Nicholson)	8440 N 87th St	Milwaukee	WI	53224	414-586-4300	586-6802	8	TF: 800-858-9557 ■ Web: www.kubin.com
KN Rubber LLC	35 Cawthra Ave	Toronto	ON	M6N5B3	416-657-1111		605-3	Web: www.knrubber.com
KNA Structural Engineers	9931 Muirlands Blvd	Irvine	CA	92618	949-462-3200		261	Web: knastructural.com
Knaack Manufacturing Co	420 E Terra Cotta Ave	Crystal Lake	IL	60014	800-456-7865	459-9097*	488	*Fax Area Code: 815 ■ TF: 800-456-7865 ■ Web: www.knaack.com
Knack Systems	10 Woodbridge Ctr Dr Ste 425	Woodbridge	NJ	07095	732-596-0110		196	TF: 855-849-3109 ■ Web: knacksystems.com
Knaggs Brake PC	7521 Westshire Dr Ste 100	Lansing	MI	48917	517-622-0590		41	Web: khbslaw.com
Knape & Vogt Manufacturing Co	2700 Oak Industrial Dr NE	Grand Rapids	MI	49505	800-253-1561	459-3290*	350	*Fax Area Code: 616 ■ TF: 800-253-1561 ■ Web: www.knapeandvogt.com
Knapheide Manufacturing Co	1848 Westphalia Strasse PO Box 7140	Quincy	IL	62305	217-223-1848		516	Web: www.knapheide.com
Knapp & Associates Intl	712 Executive Dr	Princeton	NJ	08540	609-921-3478		463	Web: www.knappinternational.com
Knapp Medical Ctr (KMC)	1401 E Eigth St PO Box 1110	Weslaco	TX	78596	956-968-8567		374-3	Web: www.knappmed.org
Knapp Supply & Equipment Co	811 Winborne St	Casper	WY	82601	307-234-7323	235-7902	385	TF: 800-442-9214 ■ Web: www.knapprestaurantsupply.com
Knapp, Petersen & Clarke	550 N Brand Blvd Ste 1500	Glendale	CA	91203	818-547-5000		41	Web: kpclegal.com
Knappen Milling Co	110 S Water St	Augusta	MI	49012	269-731-4141		296-23	TF: 800-562-7736 ■ Web: knappenmilling.com
Knaster Technology Group, The	9233 Park Meadows Dr	Lone Tree	CO	80124	303-796-7626		525	Web: www.theknastergroup.com
Knauf Insulation	1 Knauf Dr	Shelbyville	IN	46176	317-398-4434	398-3675	389	TF: 800-825-4434 ■ Web: www.knaufinsulation.com
Knauff & Grove Inc	3523 S Eagle Valley Rd	Julian	PA	16844	814-355-2483		637-2	Web: www.eglider.org
KNAU-FM 88.7 (NPR)	PO Box 5764	Flagstaff	AZ	86011	928-523-5628	523-7647	645-57	TF: 800-523-5628 ■ Web: www.knau.org
KNBA-FM 90.3 (NPR)	3600 San Geronimo Dr Ste 480	Anchorage	AK	99508	907-793-3500	793-3536	645-7	TF: 800-996-2848 ■ Web: knba.org
KNBN-TV Ch 27 (NBC)	2424 S Plaza Dr	Rapid City	SD	57702	605-355-0024	355-9274	741-106	Web: www.newscenter1.tv
KNBR-AM	750 Battery St 3rd Fl	San Francisco	CA	94111	415-995-6800	995-6867	647	Web: www.knbr.com
KNCO-FM	1255 E Main St Ste A	Grass Valley	CA	95945	530-272-3424		647	Web: www.mystarradio.com
KNDO-TV	216 W Yakima Ave	Yakima	WA	98902	509-225-2300	225-2363	647	Web: www.nbcrightnow.com
KNDR-FM 104.7 (Rel)	PO Box 516	Mandan	ND	58554	701-663-2345		645	Web: kndr.fm
KNDY-FM	937 Jayhawk Rd	Marysville	KS	66508	785-562-2361		647	TF: 800-905-8020 ■ Web: www.kndyradio.com
Knecht's Auto Parts	3400 Main St	Springfield	OR	97478	541-746-4446		54	Web: www.knechts.com
KNEM-AM	414 E Walnut PO Box 447	Nevada	MO	64772	417-667-3113	667-9797	647	TF: 800-934-4584 ■ Web: www.knemknmo.com
Knepper Press	2251 Sweeney Dr	Clinton	PA	15026	724-899-4200	899-1331	627	Web: www.knepperpress.com
KNES-FM	627 W Commerce	Fairfield	TX	75840	903-389-5637	389-7172	647	Web: www.texas99.com
Knew Deal Inc	1528 Woodward Ave 4th Fl	Detroit	MI	48226	313-373-7844		387	Web: www.stik.com
KNF Flexpak Corp	734 W Penn Pk	Tamaqua	PA	18252	570-386-3550		601	Web: www.knfcorporation.com
Knf Neuberger Inc	2 Black Forest Rd	Trenton	NJ	08691	609-890-8600	890-2838	420	Web: www.knf.com
KNIA-AM	PO Box 31	Knoxville	IA	50138	641-842-3161	842-5606	647	Web: www.kniakrls.com
Knichel Logistics LP	5347 William Flynn Hwy 2nd Fl	Gibsonia	PA	15044	724-449-3300		311	TF: 888-386-7450 ■ Web: www.knichellogistics.com
Knickerbocker Baking Inc	26040 Pinehurst Dr	Madison Heights	MI	48071	248-541-2110	336-8963	296-1	Web: knickerbockerbaking.com
Knickerbocker on The Lake, The	1028 E Juneau Ave	Milwaukee	WI	53202	414-276-8500	276-3668	379	Web: www.knickerbockeronthelake.com
Knickerbocker Partition Corp	193 Hanse Ave	Freeport	NY	11520	516-546-0550	546-0549	286	Web: www.knickerbockerpartition.com
Knickerbocker Russell Company Inc	4759 Campbells Run	Pittsburgh	PA	15205	412-494-9233	787-7991	385	Web: bignick.biz
KNID-FM	*107.1 KNID-FM* 316 E Willow Rd	Enid	OK	73701	580-237-1390	242-1390	647	Web: www.1071knid.com
Knife & Fork Inn, The	3600 Atlantic Ave	Atlantic City	NJ	08401	609-344-1133	344-3533	671	Web: www.knifeandforkinn.com
Knife River - Central Minnesota Division	4787 Shadow Wood Dr NE	Sauk Rapids	MN	56379	320-251-9472	258-9328	182	Web: www.kniferiver.com
Knife River Indian Villages National Historic Site	564 County Rd 37 PO Box 9	Stanton	ND	58571	701-745-3300		564	Web: www.nps.gov
Knight Adjustment Bureau Inc	5525 South 900 East Ste 215	Salt Lake City	UT	84117	801-531-7251	359-1195	390	TF: 800-748-4113 ■ Web: knightadj.com
KNIGHT AGENCY Inc	130 S Orange Ave Ste 150	Orlando	FL	32801	407-206-1011		7	Web: www.knightagency.com
Knight Barry Title	204 N Main St	Crestview	FL	32536	850-689-8537		653	Web: www.knightbarry.com
Knight Broadband	301 S Missouri Ave	Clearwater	FL	33756	727-524-6235		116	Web: knight-broadband.com
Knight Dental Group	3659 Tampa Rd	Oldsmar	FL	34677	813-854-3333		415	TF: 800-359-2043 ■ Web: www.knightdentalgroup.com
Knight Electronics Inc	10557 Metric Dr	Dallas	TX	75243	214-340-0265		194	TF: 800-323-2439 ■ Web: www.orionfans.com
Knight Facilities Management Inc	5360 Hampton Pl	Saginaw	MI	48604	989-793-8820	399-9096	194	Web: www.knightfm.com
Knight Furniture Showrooms Inc	214 Second Loop Rd	Florence	SC	29505	843-662-2681		321	Web: knightfurn.com
Knight Global	2705 Commerce Pkwy	Auburn Hills	MI	48326	248-377-4950	377-2135	207	Web: knightglobal.com

Name / Address	City	State	ZIP	Phone	Fax	Class
Knight Hawk Coal LLC 500 Cutler-Trico Rd *Web:* www.knighthawkcoal.com	Percy	IL	62272	618-426-3662		501
Knight Inlet Grizzly Bear Adventure Tours 8841 Driftwood Rd *Web:* www.grizzlytours.com	Black Creek	BC	V9J1A8	250-337-1953	337-1914	760
Knight Printing LLC 16 S 16th St *TF:* 888-526-1121 ■ *Web:* www.knightprinting.com	Fargo	ND	58103	701-235-1121	235-9658	627
Knight Rifles 213 Dennis St *TF:* 866-518-4181 ■ *Web:* www.muzzleloaders.com	Athens	TN	37303	866-518-4181		284
Knight School of Welding 2017 S 39th St *Web:* www.knightschoolofwelding.com	Louisville	KY	40211	502-778-9767		685
Knight Security Systems LLC 10105 Technology Blvd W Ste 100 *TF:* 800-642-1632 ■ *Web:* knightsecurity.com	Dallas	TX	75220	214-350-1632		693
Knight Sky LLC 7470-F New Technology Way *Web:* www.knight-sky.com	Frederick	MD	21703	240-252-1950		647
Knight Transportation Inc 5601 W Buckeye Rd *NYSE:* KNX ■ *TF:* 800-489-2000 ■ *Web:* www.knighttrans.com	Phoenix	AZ	85043	602-269-2000		780
Knight's Action Park & Caribbean Water Adventure 1700 Recreation Dr *Web:* www.knightsactionpark.com	Springfield	IL	62711	217-546-8881		32
Knight's Armament Co 701 Columbia Blvd *Web:* www.knightarmco.com	Titusville	FL	32780	321-607-9900		807
Knight's Steak House 2324 Dexter Ave *Web:* www.knightsrestaurants.com	Ann Arbor	MI	48103	734-665-8644		671
Knight-Abbey Commercial Prntrs 315 Caillavet St *Web:* www.knightabbey.com	Biloxi	MS	39530	228-374-3298		627
Knighthawk Engineering Inc 17625 El Camino Real Ste 412 *Web:* www.knighthawk.com	Houston	TX	77058	281-282-9200		256
Knights Airport Limousine Service Inc 390 Hartford Tpke *Web:* knightslimo.com	Shrewsbury	MA	01545	508-839-6252		441
Knightsbridge Asset Management LLC 660 Newport Center Dr Ste 460 *Web:* www.knightsb.com	Newport Beach	CA	92660	949-644-4444		401
Knippelmier Chevrolet Inc 1811 E Hwy 62 E *TF:* 877-644-7255 ■ *Web:* www.knippelmier.com	Blanchard	OK	73010	405-485-3333		57
Knit Rite Inc 120 Osage Ave *TF:* 800-821-3094 ■ *Web:* www.knitrite.com	Kansas City	KS	66105	913-281-4600	281-5455	476
Knitney Lines Inc 411 Gilligan St *Web:* knitneylines.com	Scranton	PA	18508	570-457-5060	457-6725	311
KNLC-TV PO Box 924 *Web:* www.knlc.tv	Saint Louis	MO	63188	314-436-2424	436-2434	647
KNLX-FM PO Box 7408 *Web:* www.knlr.com	Bend	OR	97708	541-389-8873		647
KNME-TV Ch 5 (PBS) University of New Mexico 1130 University Blvd NE *TF:* 800-328-5663 ■ *Web:* www.newmexicopbs.org	Albuquerque	NM	87102	505-277-2121		741-3
Knob Hill Inn 960 N Main St PO Box 1327 *TF:* 800-526-8010 ■ *Web:* www.knobhillinn.com	Ketchum	ID	83340	208-726-8010		379
Knob Noster State Park 873 SE 10th *Web:* mostateparks.com	Knob Noster	MO	65336	660-563-2463		565
Knobbe, Martens, Olson & Bear LLP 2040 Main St 14th Fl *Web:* knobbe.com	Irvine	CA	92614	949-760-0404		41
Knock Inc 1315 Glenwood Ave *Web:* knockinc.com	Minneapolis	MN	55405	612-333-6511		514
Knock Lending LLC 335 Madison Ave 16th Fl *Web:* www.knock.com	New York	NY	10017	470-485-6625		652
Knockout Pest Control Inc 1009 Front St *TF:* 800-244-7378 ■ *Web:* knockoutpest.com	Uniondale	NY	11553	800-244-7378		577
Knoebels Amusement Resort 391 Knoebels Blvd *TF:* 800-487-4386 ■ *Web:* www.knoebels.com	Elysburg	PA	17824	570-672-2572		32
Knoll Inc 1235 Water St *NYSE:* KNL ■ *TF:* 800-343-5665 ■ *Web:* knoll.com	East Greenville	PA	18041	800-343-5665		319-1
Knollwood 6200 Oregon Ave NW *TF:* 800-541-4255 ■ *Web:* knollwoodcommunity.org	Washington	DC	20015	202-541-0400		672
Knopf Automotive 93 Shrewsbury Ave *Web:* www.mmknopf.com	Red Bank	NJ	07701	732-212-0444	212-0443	61
Knopp Inc 1307 66th St *Web:* www.knoppinc.com	Emeryville	CA	94608	510-653-1661		248
Knorr Associates Inc 10 Pk Pl PO Box 400 *Web:* www.knorrassociates.com	Butler	NJ	07405	973-492-8500	492-0453	178-10
Knorr Beeswax Products Inc 14906 Via De La Valle *TF:* 800-807-2337 ■ *Web:* www.knorrbeeswax.com	Del Mar	CA	92014	760-431-2007	431-8977	122
Knorr-Bremse 901 Cleveland St *Web:* www.knorr-bremse.com	Elyria	OH	44035	440-329-9609		650
Knot, The *XO Group Inc* 195 Broadway 25th Fl *Web:* www.theknot.com	New York	NY	10007	212-219-8555	219-1929	171
Knott House Museum 301 E Park Ave *Web:* museumoffloridahistory.com	Tallahassee	FL	32301	850-922-2459		520
Knott Laboratory LLC 7185 S Tucson Way *Web:* knottlab.com	Englewood	CO	80112	303-925-1900	925-1901	261
Knott's Berry Farm 8039 Beach Blvd *TF:* 800-742-6427 ■ *Web:* www.knotts.com	Buena Park	CA	90620	714-220-5200	220-5124	32
Knouse Foods Co-opeartive Inc 800 Peach Glen Rd - Idaville Rd *Web:* www.knouse.com	Peach Glen	PA	17375	717-677-8181	677-7069	296-20
Knovalent 3135 S State St Ste 300 *Web:* www.knovalent.com	Ann Arbor	MI	48108	734-996-8300		178-10
Knovation 3600 Park 42 Dr Ste 125A *Web:* www.knovationlearning.com	Cincinnati	OH	45241	513-731-4090		180
Know Before You Go Reservations 8000 International Dr *TF:* 800-749-1993 ■ *Web:* www.knowbeforeugo.com	Orlando	FL	32819	800-749-1993		376
Know It All Intelligence Group 1950 St Rd Ste 402 *Web:* knowitallgroup.com	Bensalem	PA	19020	215-245-1975		196
Know Labs Inc 500 Union St Ste 810 *Web:* www.knowlabs.co	Seattle	WA	98101	206-903-1351	903-1352	418
Knowcean Consulting Inc 10605 Stapleford Hall Dr *Web:* www.knowceanconsulting.com	Potomac	MD	20854	240-672-1699		177
Knowledge Anywhere Inc 3015 112th Ave NE Ste 210 *TF:* 800-850-2025 ■ *Web:* www.knowledgeanywhere.com	Bellevue	WA	98004	800-850-2025		194
Knowledge Information Solutions Inc (KIS) 2877 Guardian Ln Ste 201 *TF:* 877-547-7248 ■ *Web:* www.kisinc.net	Virginia Beach	VA	23452	757-463-3232	463-2318	179
Knowledge Relay LLC 5836 Corporate Ave Ste 130 *Web:* knowledgerelay.com	Cypress	CA	90630	714-761-6760		177
Knowledge Systems & Research Inc 120 Madison St 15th Fl *Web:* www.ksrinc.com	Syracuse	NY	13202	315-470-1350		668
KnowledgeBank Inc 20365 Exchange St *Web:* www.knowledgebank.us.com	Ashburn	VA	20147	703-448-8070		194
KnowledgeBroker Inc PO Box 17097 *Web:* www.kbi.com	Reno	NV	89511	626-441-0702		173-2
Knowles Corp 1151 Maplewood Dr	Itasca	IL	60143	630-250-5100	250-0575	253
Knox & Co 33 Riverside Ave 5th Fl *Web:* www.knoxandco.com	Westport	CT	06880	203-226-6288	226-8022	401
Knox Addley Art Design 1468 Smithland Cir *Web:* knoxaddley.com	Atlanta	GA	30318	404-603-8000		42
Knox College 59 St George St *Web:* www.utoronto.ca	Toronto	ON	M5S2E6	416-978-4500	971-2133	167-3
Knox College 2 E S St *Web:* www.knox.edu	Galesburg	IL	61401	309-341-7000	341-7806	166
Knox Community Hospital 1330 Coshocton Rd *TF:* 888-977-3319 ■ *Web:* www.kch.org	Mount Vernon	OH	43050	740-393-9000		374-3
Knox County PO Box 196 *Web:* www.knoxcountytexas.org	Benjamin	TX	79505	940-459-2441	459-2005	338
Knox County 400 Main St city county Bldg Ste 603 *Web:* www.knoxcounty.org	Knoxville	TN	37902	865-215-2534	215-2038	338
Knox County 117 E High St Ste 131 *Web:* www.co.knox.oh.us	Mount Vernon	OH	43050	740-393-6752	397-2723	338
Knox County 62 Union St *Web:* www.knoxcountymaine.gov	Rockland	ME	04841	207-594-0420	594-0443	338
Knox County 316 Main St *Web:* www.knoxcountychamber.com	Vincennes	IN	47591	812-882-6440		338
Knox County Chamber of Commerce 400 S Gay St *Web:* www.knoxchamber.com	Mount Vernon	OH	43050	740-393-1111	393-1590	139
Knox County Convention & Visitors Bureau 107 S Main St *TF:* 800-837-5282 ■ *Web:* www.visitknoxohio.org	Mount Vernon	OH	43050	740-392-6102	392-7840	206
Knox County Health Dept 11660 Upper Gilchrist Rd *Web:* www.knoxhealth.com	Mount Vernon	OH	43050	740-392-2200		804
Knox County Illinois 200 S Cherry St *TF:* 800-916-3330 ■ *Web:* co.knox.il.us	Galesburg	IL	61401	309-343-3121		338
Knox County Public Library 502 N Seventh St *Web:* kcpl.lib.in.us	Vincennes	IN	47591	812-886-4380		434-3
Knox Courthouse 206 Main St *Web:* co.knox.ne.us	Center	NE	68724	402-288-5604	288-5605	338
Knox Horticulture 940 Avalon Rd *TF:* 800-441-5669 ■ *Web:* www.knoxhort.com	Winter Garden	FL	34787	407-654-1972		369
Knox Kershaw Inc 11211 Trackwork St *Web:* knoxkershaw.com	Montgomery	AL	36117	334-387-5669		650
Knox Machine Company Inc 936 Eastern Rd *Web:* www.knoxmachine.com	Warren	ME	04864	207-273-2296		454
Knox McLaughlin Gornall & Sennett PC 120 W 10th St *TF:* 800-939-9886 ■ *Web:* www.kmgslaw.com	Erie	PA	16501	814-459-2800		428
Knox News Radio Old Belmont Rd S *Web:* knoxradio.com	Grand Forks	ND	58208	701-775-4611		645
Knox School 541 E Long Beach Rd *Web:* www.knoxschool.org	Saint James	NY	11780	631-686-1600	686-1650	622
Knox Services 2250 Fourth Ave *TF:* 800-995-6694 ■ *Web:* www.knoxservices.com	San Diego	CA	92101	800-995-6694		627
Knox's Headquarters State Historic Site 289 Old Forge Hill Rd *Web:* parks.ny.gov	Vails Gate	NY	12584	845-561-5498		565
Knoxville Area Chamber Partnership 17 Market Sq Ste 201 *Web:* www.knoxvillechamber.com	Knoxville	TN	37902	865-637-4550	523-2071	139
Knoxville Beverage Co 1335 E Weisgarber Rd *Web:* www.knoxvillebeverage.com	Knoxville	TN	37909	865-637-9411		81-3
Knoxville City Hall 305 S 3rd St *Web:* www.knoxvilleia.gov	Knoxville	IA	50138	865-215-2000	215-2085	337
Knoxville Civic Auditorium/Coliseum 500 Howard Baker Jr Ave *TF:* 877-995-9961 ■ *Web:* www.knoxvillecoliseum.com	Knoxville	TN	37915	865-215-8900	215-8989	572
Knoxville Convention Ctr 701 Henley St PO Box 2543 *Web:* kccasm.com	Knoxville	TN	37902	865-522-5669	329-0422	205
Knoxville Firefighters Federal Credit Union 5207 Schubert Rd *Web:* knoxfirefcu.com	Knoxville	TN	37912	865-688-0498		219

Name / Address	City	State	Zip	Phone	Fax	Class
Knoxville Hospital & Clinics 1002 S Lincoln St *Web:* knoxvillehospital.org	Knoxville	IA	50138	641-842-2151		363
Knoxville Locomotive Works 300 W Quincy Ave *TF:* 888-207-4576 ■ *Web:* www.goklw.com	Knoxville	TN	37917	865-522-7078	200-4939	41
Knoxville Museum of Art 1050 World Fair Pk Dr *Web:* www.knoxart.org	Knoxville	TN	37916	865-525-6101	546-3635	520
Knoxville News Sentinel, The 2332 News Sentinel Dr *TF:* 800-237-5821 ■ *Web:* www.knoxnews.com	Knoxville	TN	37921	844-900-7097		532-2
Knoxville Opera Co 612 E Depot Ave *Web:* www.knoxvilleopera.com	Knoxville	TN	37917	865-524-0795	524-7384	573-2
Knoxville Symphony Orchestra 100 S Gay St Ste 302 *TF:* 800-845-5665 ■ *Web:* www.knoxvillesymphony.com	Knoxville	TN	37902	865-291-3310	546-3766	573-3
Knoxville Teachers Federal Credit Union 711 N Hall of Fame Dr *Web:* ktfcu.org	Knoxville	TN	37917	865-582-2700	463-7482	219
Knoxville Tourism & Sports Corp 301 S Gay St *TF:* 800-727-8045 ■ *Web:* www.visitknoxville.com	Knoxville	TN	37902	865-523-7263		206
Knoxville Wholesale Furniture Company Inc 410 N Peters Rd *Web:* knoxvillewholesalefurniture.com	Knoxville	TN	37922	865-671-5300		321
Knoxville Zoological Gardens Inc 3500 Knoxville Zoo Dr *Web:* www.zooknoxville.org	Knoxville	TN	37914	865-637-5331		823
KNOZ-FM 203 Grand Ave *Web:* www.krydfm.com	Grand Junction	CO	81501	970-609-1200	609-5670	647
KNPB-TV Ch 5 (PBS) 1670 N Virginia St *Web:* www.pbsreno.org	Reno	NV	89503	775-784-4555	784-1438	741-107
KNRK-FM 94.7 0700 SW Bancroft St *TF:* 800-777-0947 ■ *Web:* 947.radio.com	Portland	OR	97239	503-733-5470		645-126
KNS Companies Inc 475 Randy Rd *Web:* www.knscompanies.com	Carol Stream	IL	60188	630-665-9010		481
KNSS-AM 1330/FM 98.7 9111 E Douglas Ste 130 *Web:* knss.radio.com	Wichita	KS	67207	316-869-1330		645-173
KNTU-FM 1155 Union Cir No 310881 *Web:* www.kntu.com	Denton	TX	76203	940-565-3688		647
KNTV-TV Ch 11 (NBC) 2450 N First St *Web:* www.nbcbayarea.com	San Jose	CA	95131	408-432-6221		741
Knupp & Watson & Wallman Inc 2010 Eastwood Dr *Web:* www.knupp-watson.com	Madison	WI	53704	608-232-2300	232-2301	7
KNUS-AM 710 (N/T) 3131 S Vaughn Way Ste 601 *Web:* 710knus.com	Aurora	CO	80014	303-750-5687		645
Knutson Construction Services Inc 7515 Wayzata Blvd *Web:* www.knutsonconstruction.com	Minneapolis	MN	55426	763-546-1400		186
KNWA-TV Ch 51 (NBC) 609 W Dickson St 3rd Fl *Web:* www.nwahomepage.com	Fayetteville	AR	72701	479-571-5100		741
KNWM-FM 3737 Woodland Ave Ste 300 *Web:* www.life1071.com	West Des Moines	IA	50266	515-327-1071		647
KNWS-FM 4880 Texas St *TF:* 866-515-1019 ■ *Web:* www.life1019.com	Waterloo	IA	50702	866-515-1019		647
KNXT-TV Ch 49 (Ind) 1550 N Fresno St *Web:* www.knxt.tv	Fresno	CA	93703	559-488-7440	488-7444	741-52
KNXV-TV Ch 15 (ABC) 515 N 44th St *Web:* www.abc15.com	Phoenix	AZ	85008	602-273-1500	683-5995	741-99
KNZA-FM 1828 South Hwy 73 PO Box 104 *Web:* www.knzafm.com	Hiawatha	KS	66434	785-547-3461	547-9900	647
K-O Products Co 1225 Milton St *Web:* www.koproducts.com	Benton Harbor	MI	49022	269-925-0657	925-9020	488
KOA (Kampgrounds of America Inc) PO Box 30558 *TF:* 888-562-0000 ■ *Web:* koa.com	Billings	MT	59114	888-562-0000		121
Koa Books PO Box 822 *Web:* www.koabooks.com	Kihei	HI	96753	808-875-7995		637-2
KOA Speer Electronics Inc 199 Bolivar Dr *Web:* www.koaspeer.com	Bradford	PA	16701	814-362-5536	362-8883	253
KOA-AM 850 (N/T) 4695 S Monaco St *Web:* koanewsradio.iheart.com	Denver	CO	80237	303-713-8000		645-46
KOAA-TV Ch 5/30 (NBC) 2200 Seventh Ave *Web:* www.koaa.com	Pueblo	CO	81003	719-544-5781	295-6677	741
KOAM 2950 NE Hwy 69 PO Box 659 *Web:* www.koamnewsnow.com	Pittsburg	KS	66762	417-782-1414	624-3115	647
KOAN-AM 814 WN Lights *Web:* www.1080koan.com	Anchorage	AK	99503	907-947-7344	522-1027	647
KOAT-TV Ch 7 (ABC) 3801 Carlisle Blvd NE *TF:* 877-871-0165 ■ *Web:* www.koat.com	Albuquerque	NM	87107	505-884-7777		741-3
Kobalt Books (KB) PO Box 1062 *Web:* www.kobaltbooks.com	Bala Cynwyd	PA	19004	314-503-5462		637-2
Kobayashi Travel Service 650 Iwilei Rd Ste 410 *Web:* www.kobay.com	Honolulu	HI	96817	808-593-9387		345
Kobayashi, Sugita & Goda LLP, Attorneys at Law 999 Bishop St Ste 2600 *Web:* ksglaw.com	Honolulu	HI	96813	808-535-5700		428
Kobe Japanese Steakhouse Inc 468 W Hwy 436 *Web:* kobesteakhouse.com	Altamonte Springs	FL	32714	407-862-2888		670
Kobe Sportswear Inc 791 Tapscott Rd *TF:* 888-898-5623 ■ *Web:* kobesportswear.com	Scarborough	ON	M1X1A2	416-754-7024		442
Kobe Steaks Nashville 210 25th Ave N Ste 100 *Web:* www.kobesteaks.net	Nashville	TN	37203	615-327-9081		671
Kobe Steel Ltd 535 Madison Ave *Web:* www.kobelco.co.jp	New York	NY	10022	212 751-9400	355-5564	723
Kobelco Compressors (America) Inc 3000 Hammond Ave *Web:* www.kobelcocompressors.com	Elkhart	IN	46516	574-295-3145	293-1641	14
Kobelco Stewart Bolling Inc (KSBI) 1600 Terex Rd *TF:* 800-464-0064 ■ *Web:* www.ksbiusa.com	Hudson	OH	44236	330-655-3111		386
Kobelt Manufacturing Company Ltd 8238 129th St *Web:* www.kobelt.com	Surrey	BC	V3W0A6	604-572-3935	590-8313	203
KOBF-TV 4 Broadcast Plz SW *Web:* www.kob.com	Albuquerque	NM	87104	505-764-2442	764-2522	647
Kobussen Buses Ltd W914 County Rd CE *TF:* 800-447-0116 ■ *Web:* www.kobussen.com	Kaukauna	WI	54130	920-766-0606	766-0797	109
KOCB CW34 1228 E Wilshire Blvd *Web:* cwokc.com	Oklahoma City	OK	73111	405-843-2525	478-4343	741-93
Koch & Company Inc 1809 North St *Web:* www.kochandco.com	Seneca	KS	66538	785-336-6022		115
Koch Air LLC 1900 W Lloyd Expy *Web:* kochair.com	Evansville	IN	47712	812-962-5200	962-5306	612
Koch Development 222 S Central Ave Ste 506 *Web:* www.kochdevelopment.com	Saint Louis	MO	63105	314-333-5624		205
Koch Enterprises Inc 14 S 11th Ave *Web:* kochenterprises.com	Evansville	IN	47712	812-465-9800	465-9613	185
KOCH EYE Assoc 566 Toll Gate Rd *Web:* www.kocheye.com	Warwick	RI	02886	401-738-4800	738-8153	374-3
Koch Family Children's Museum of Evansville 22 SE Fifth St *Web:* www.cmoekids.org	Evansville	IN	47708	812-464-2663	477-4339	521
Koch Filter Corp 625 W Hill St *TF:* 800-757-5624 ■ *Web:* www.kochfilter.com	Louisville	KY	40208	502-634-4796	637-2280	18
Koch Foods Inc 1300 Higgins Rd Ste 100 *TF:* 800-837-2778 ■ *Web:* www.kochfoods.com	Park Ridge	IL	60068	847-384-5940		619
Koch Foods of Mississippi LLC 4688 Hwy 80 E	Morton	MS	39117	601-732-8911		619
Koch Foundation Inc 4421 NW 39th Ave Bldg 1 Ste 1 *Web:* www.thekochfoundation.org	Gainesville	FL	32606	352-373-7491		304
Koch Group & Company LLP 333 7th Ave	New York	NY	10001	212-631-0700		2
Koch Heat Transfer Company LP 12602 FM 529 *Web:* www.kochheattransfer.com	Houston	TX	77041	713-466-3535	466-3701	91
Koch Industries Inc PO Box 2256 *Web:* www.kochind.com	Wichita	KS	67201	316-828-3756		185
Koch Knight LLC 5385 Orchard View Dr SE *Web:* www.kochknight.com	Canton	OH	44730	330-488-1651	488-1656	751
Koch Membrane Systems Inc 850 Main St *TF:* 888-677-5624 ■ *Web:* www.kochmembrane.com	Wilmington	MA	01887	978-657-4250	657-5208	386
Koch Modular Process Systems LLC 45 Eisenhower Dr *Web:* kochmodular.com	Paramus	NJ	07652	201-267-8670	368-8989	420
Koch Office Group 325 Grand Ave *TF:* 800-944-5624 ■ *Web:* kochofficegroup.com	Des Moines	IA	50309	515-283-2451	243-3147	535
Koch Specialty Plant Services 12221 E Sam Houston Pkwy N *TF:* 800-765-9177 ■ *Web:* www.kochservices.com	Houston	TX	77044	713-427-7700	427-7747	539
Koch Supply & Trading LP 20 Greenway Plz 8th Fl *Web:* www.ksandt.com	Houston	TX	77046	713-544-4123		391-4
KOCHAM (Korean Chamber of Commerce & Industry in the USA Inc) 460 Park Ave Ste 410 *Web:* www.kocham.org	New York	NY	10022	212-644-0140	644-9106	138
Koch-Glitsch LP 4111 E 37th St N *Web:* www.koch-glitsch.com	Wichita	KS	67220	316-828-5110	828-7985	169
KOCO-TV Ch 5 (ABC) 1300 E Britton Rd *TF:* 800-464-7928 ■ *Web:* www.koco.com	Oklahoma City	OK	73131	405-478-3000		741-93
Kocour Co 4800 S St Louis Ave *Web:* www.kocour.net	Chicago	IL	60632	773-847-1111	847-3399	500
KOCP-FM 95.9 (CR) 2284 S Victoria Ave *TF:* 877-440-1047 ■ *Web:* oldschool1047.com	Ventura	CA	93003	909-693-4929		645
KODA (Kentucky Organ Donor Affiliates) 10160 Linn Station Rd *TF:* 800-525-3456 ■ *Web:* donatelifeky.org	Louisville	KY	40223	502-581-9511	589-5157	545
Koddi 2821 W 7th St Ste 270 *Web:* www.koddi.com	Fort Worth	TX	76107	817-725-8248		4
Kodiak Electric Association Inc 515 E Marine Way *Web:* www.kodiakelectric.com	Kodiak	AK	99615	907-486-7700		245
Kodiak Island Borough 710 Mill Bay Rd *Web:* www.kodiakak.us	Kodiak	AK	99615	907-486-9300	486-9395	338
Kodiak Machining Company Inc 20 Hayward St *Web:* www.kodiakmachine.net	Ipswich	MA	01938	978-356-9876	356-9885	454
Kodiak Venture Partners PO Box 550225 **Fax Area Code:* 978 ■ *Web:* www.kodiakvp.com	Wellesley	MA	02481	781-214-6855	293-1003*	792
KODL-AM 620 E 3rd St *Web:* www.kodl.com	The Dalles	OR	97058	541-296-2101	296-3766	647
KODY-AM PO Box 1085 *Web:* www.huskeradio.com	North Platte	NE	69101	308-532-3344		647
Koegel Meats Inc 3400 W Bristol Rd *TF:* 800-678-1962 ■ *Web:* www.koegelmeats.com	Flint	MI	48507	810-238-3685	238-2467	296-26
Koehler & Dramm Institute of Floristry 2407 E Hennepin Ave *TF:* 800-298-0495 ■ *Web:* www.koehlerdramm.com	Minneapolis	MN	55413	612-331-4141		668
Koehler & Passarelli LLC 900 S Frontage Rd Ste 300 *Web:* k-pllc.com	Woodridge	IL	60517	630-505-9939		41
Koehler Instrument Company Inc 1595 Sycamore Ave *TF:* 800-878-9070 ■ *Web:* koehlerinstrument.com	Bohemia	NY	11716	631-589-3800	589-3815	743
Koehler Lighting Products 380 Stewart Rd *TF:* 800-788-1696 ■ *Web:* www.flashlight.com	Hanover Township	PA	18706	570-825-1900	825-7108	439

Name / Address	City	State	Zip	Phone	Fax	Class
Koellmann Gear Corp 8 Industrial Pk	Waldwick	NJ	07463	201-447-0200		709
Web: www.koellmann.com						
Koenig Jacobsen LLP 16300 Bake Pkwy	Irvine	CA	92618	949-756-0700		428
Web: kjattorneys.com						
Koeppel Direct Inc						
16200 Dallas Pkwy Ste 270	Dallas	TX	75248	972-732-6110		7
Web: www.koeppeldirect.com						
Koerner Distributors Inc						
1601 Pike Ave	Effingham	IL	62401	800-475-5162	347-8736*	81-1
**Fax Area Code:* 217 ■ *TF:* 800-475-5162 ■ *Web:* www.koernerdistributor.com						
Koerner Ford of Syracuse Inc						
805 W Genesee St	Syracuse	NY	13204	315-474-4275		57
Web: www.koernerford.net						
Koers-turgeon Consulting Service Inc						
2006 Ridgeview Rd	Salina	KS	67401	785-825-8192		196
Web: beef4u.com						
Koeze Co PO Box 9470	Grand Rapids	MI	49509	800-555-9688	817-0147*	296-8
**Fax Area Code:* 866 ■ *TF:* 800-555-9688 ■ *Web:* www.koeze.com						
Kofax PLC 15211 Laguna Canyon Rd	Irvine	CA	92618	949-783-1000	727-3144	178-8
Web: www.kofax.com						
Koffler Boats 90017 GreenHill Rd	Eugene	OR	97402	541-688-6093		90
Web: www.kofflerboats.com						
KOFY-TV 2500 Marin St	San Francisco	CA	94124	415-821-2020		647
Web: www.kofytv.com						
Koger Center for the Arts						
1051 Greene St	Columbia	SC	29201	803-777-7500	777-9774	572
Web: www.kogercenterforthearts.com						
Koger/Air Corp PO Box 2098	Martinsville	VA	24113	276-638-8821		151
TF: 800-368-2096 ■ *Web:* kogerair.com						
KOGT-AM PO Box 14	Orange	TX	77631	409-883-4381		647
Web: www.kogt.com						
Kohala Spa 69-425 Waikoloa Beach Dr	Waikoloa	HI	96738	808-886-2828	886-2953	706
KOHD-TV 63090 Sherman Rd	Bend	OR	97703	541-388-7704	996-3232*	647
**Fax Area Code:* 866 ■ *Web:* centraloregondaily.com						
Kohl & Frisch Ltd 7622 Keele St	Concord	ON	L4K2R5	800-265-2520		231
TF: 800-265-2520 ■ *Web:* www.kohlandfrisch.com						
Kohl Building Products						
1047 Old Bernville Rd	Reading	PA	19605	610-916-0582		364
Web: www.kohlbp.com						
Kohl's Corp						
N 56 W 17000 Ridgewood Dr	Menomonee Falls	WI	53051	262-703-7000		229
NYSE: KSS ■ *TF:* 855-564-5705 ■ *Web:* www.kohls.com						
Kohlberg Capital Corp						
295 Madison Ave 6th Fl	New York	NY	10017	212-455-8300	983-7654	690
Kohler & Eyre CPAS LLC						
1883 W Royal Hunte Dr	Cedar City	UT	84720	435-865-5866		2
Web: kohlereyrecpas.com						
Kohler Canada Co						
Hytec Plumbing Products Div						
4150 Spallumcheen Dr	Armstrong	BC	V0E1B6	250-546-3067	546-3170	610
TF: 800-871-8311 ■ *Web:* www.hytec.ca						
Kohler Co 444 Highland Dr	Kohler	WI	53044	920-457-4441		185
TF: 800-456-4537 ■ *Web:* www.kohlercompany.com						
Kohler Ronan LLC 93 Lake Ave 3rd Fl	Danbury	CT	06810	203-778-1017	778-1018	261
Web: kohlerronan.com						
Kohler-Andrae State Park						
1020 Beach Pk Ln	Sheboygan	WI	53081	920-451-4080	451-4086	565
Web: dnr.wi.gov						
KOHL-FM 89.3 (CHR) 43600 Mission Blvd	Fremont	CA	94539	510-659-6221	659-6001	645
Web: www.kohlradio.com						
Kohli & Kaliher Associates Inc						
2244 Baton Rouge Ave	Lima	OH	45805	419-227-1135		261
Web: kohlikaliher.com						
Kohlls Rx 12741 Q St	Omaha	NE	68132	402-553-8901		238
Web: kohllsrx.com						
Kohltech International Ltd						
583 MacElmon Rd	Debert	NS	B0M1G0	902-662-3100		752
TF: 800-565-4396 ■ *Web:* www.kohltech.com						
Kohn Pedersen Fox Associates PC						
11 W 42nd St	New York	NY	10036	212-977-6500	956-2526	261
Web: www.kpf.com						
Kohnami Japanese 313 S Guadalupe	Santa Fe	NM	87501	505-984-2002		671
Web: kohnamirestaurant.com						
Kohnen & Patton LLP						
201 E Fifth St PNC Ctr Ste 800	Cincinnati	OH	45202	513-381-0656		41
Web: kplaw.com						
Kohner Mann & Kailas SC						
4650 N Port Washington Rd Washington Bldg	Milwaukee	WI	53212	414-962-5110	962-8725	428
Web: kmksc.com						
Koho Pono LLC						
15024 SE Pinegrove Loop	Clackamas	OR	97015	503-723-7392		637-2
Web: kohopono.com						
Kohrs Lonnemann Heil Engineers Psc						
1538 Alexandria Pk	Fort Thomas	KY	41075	859-442-8050		261
KOI Auto Parts						
2701 Spring Grove Ave	Cincinnati	OH	45225	513-357-2400		54
TF: 800-354-0408 ■ *Web:* www.koiautoparts.com						
Koibito 1707 Harrison Ave NW	Olympia	WA	98502	360-352-4751		671
Web: www.koibitosushi.com						
Koike Aronson Inc						
635 W Main St PO Box 307	Arcade	NY	14009	585-492-2400	457-3517	455
TF: 800-252-5232 ■ *Web:* www.koike.com						
Koinonia House Inc 4055 E 3rd Ave	Post Falls	ID	83854	208-773-6310	773-6312	48-20
TF: 800-546-8731 ■ *Web:* www.khouse.org						
KOIN-TV Ch 6 (CBS)						
222 SW Columbia St	Portland	OR	97201	503-464-0600	464-0806	741-103
Web: www.koin.com						
Kois Bros Equipment Company Inc						
5200 Colorado Blvd	Commerce City	CO	80022	303-298-7370		386
TF: 800-672-6010 ■ *Web:* www.koisbrothers.com						
KOIT-FM 96.5 (AC)						
201 Third St Ste 1200	San Francisco	CA	94103	415-777-0965		645-142
Web: www.koit.com						
Kojak's House of Ribs 2808 W Gandy Blvd	Tampa	FL	33611	813-837-3774		671
Web: www.kojaksbbq.net						
Koji Osakaya 606 SW Broadway	Portland	OR	97205	503-294-1169		671
Web: www.koji.com						
Kokkari Estiatorio						
200 Jackson St	San Francisco	CA	94111	415-981-0983	982-0983	671
Web: kokkari.com						
Koko Inn LLC 4801 Ave Q	Lubbock	TX	79412	806-747-2591		379
KoKo LLC 1200 S Fordham St Ste B	Longmont	CO	80503	303-666-5555	666-5588	476
TF: 800-574-7374 ■ *Web:* www.nspirehealth.com						
Kokomo Opalescent Glass Co						
1310 S Market St	Kokomo	IN	46902	765-457-8136	459-5177	329
TF: 877-475-6329 ■ *Web:* www.kog.com						
Kokomo Tribune (KT)						
300 N Union St PO Box 9014	Kokomo	IN	46901	765-459-3121	854-6733	532-2
TF: 800-382-0696 ■ *Web:* www.kokomotribune.com						
Kokomo/Howard County Chamber of Commerce						
700 E Firmin St	Kokomo	IN	46901	765-457-5301	452-4564	139
Web: www.greaterkokomo.com						
Kokomo-Howard County Public Library						
220 N Union St	Kokomo	IN	46901	765-457-3242	457-3683	434-3
TF: 800-837-0971 ■ *Web:* www.khcpl.org						
Kokosing Construction Company Inc						
17531 Waterford Rd PO Box 226	Fredericktown	OH	43019	740-694-6315	694-1481	188-4
TF: 800-800-6315 ■ *Web:* www.kokosing.biz						
KOKR River Country 96.7 FM						
2025 McLarty Dr PO Box 768	Newport	AR	72112	870-523-5891	523-2967	643
Web: www.rivercountry967.com						
Kokua Services						
1226 Carpenter Rd SE Ste B1	Lacey	WA	98503	360-705-4665		363
Web: kokuaservices.org						
Kokusai Semiconductor Equipment Corp						
2460 N First St Ste 290	San Jose	CA	95131	408-456-2750	456-2760	695
TF: 800-800-5321 ■ *Web:* www.ksec.com						
Kolar Corp 412 S Washington Ste 200	Royal Oak	MI	48067	248-543-0500		261
Web: kolarcorp.com						
Kolberg Ocular Products Inc						
9663 Tierra Grande St Ste 201	San Diego	CA	92126	858-695-2021		543
Web: artificialeye.net						
Kolberg-Pioneer Inc 700 W 21st St	Yankton	SD	57078	605-665-9311		207
Web: www.kpijci.com						
Kolbrenner & Alexander LLC CPAS						
15 Valley Dr	Greenwich	CT	06831	203-869-3199		2
Web: kolbrenneralexander.com						
Kolcraft Enterprises Inc						
10832 NC Hwy 211 E	Aberdeen	NC	28315	910-944-9345		471
TF: 800-453-7673 ■ *Web:* www.kolcraft.com						
Kold-Draft 1525 E Lake Rd	Erie	PA	16511	814-453-6761	455-6336	664
TF: 800-840-9577 ■ *Web:* kold-draft.com						
KOLD-TV 7831 N Business Park Dr	Tucson	AZ	85743	520-744-1313	629-7185	647
Web: www.kold.com						
KOLEASECO Inc						
4265 Corporate Exchange Dr	Hudsonville	MI	49426	616-896-5170	896-5175	780
TF: 800-300-7935 ■ *Web:* www.koleaseco.com						
Kolene Corp 12890 Westwood Ave	Detroit	MI	48223	313-273-9220	273-5207	145
TF: 800-521-4182 ■ *Web:* www.kolene.com						
Kolenz Transport Inc 4319 State Rd	Peninsula	OH	44264	330-620-6242		311
Web: ktimulch.com						
Koler Financial Group						
6400 Pearl Rd	Parma Heights	OH	44130	440-884-7042	845-0065	401
Web: www.kolerfinancialgroup.com						
Kollabra 12760 Earhart Ave	Auburn	CA	95602	800-565-5227	565-5227*	195
**Fax Area Code:* 866 ■ *Web:* www.kollabra.com						
Koller & Company LLP						
206 S Iowa Ave	Washington	IA	52353	319-653-6561	653-6745	2
Web: kollerandcompany.com						
Koller Craft Plastic Products						
1400 S Old Hwy PO Box 718	Fenton	MO	63026	636-343-9220	343-1034	661
Web: www.koller-craft.com						
Kollmorgen Corp 203A W Rock Rd	Radford	VA	24141	540-633-3545		518
Web: www.kollmorgen.com						
Kolmar Americas Inc						
10 Middle St PH	Bridgeport	CT	06604	203-873-2051		169
Web: www.kolmargroup.com						
KOLN-TV Ch 10 (CBS) 840 N 40th	Lincoln	NE	68503	402-467-4321	467-9210	741-74
TF: 800-475-1011 ■ *Web:* www.1011now.com						
Kolomoki Mounds State Historic Park						
205 Indian Mounds Rd	Blakely	GA	39823	229-724-2150		565
Web: gastateparks.org						
Kolosso Toyota 3000 W Wisconsin Ave	Appleton	WI	54914	920-738-3666		57
TF: 877-756-2297 ■ *Web:* www.kolossotoyota.com						
Kolossos Printing Inc						
2055 W Stadium Blvd	Ann Arbor	MI	48103	734-994-5400		627
Web: www.kolossosprinting.com						
KOLO-TV Ch 8 (ABC) 4850 Ampere Dr	Reno	NV	89502	775-858-8888	858-8855	741-107
Web: www.kolotv.com						
Kolpak 2915 Tennessee Ave N	Parsons	TN	38363	731-847-5328	847-5387	664
TF: 800-826-7036 ■ *Web:* www.kolpak.com						
Kolpin Powersports 9955 59th Ave N	Plymouth	MN	55442	920-928-3118	928-3687	710
TF: 877-956-5746 ■ *Web:* www.kolpin.com						
KOLR-TV Ch 10 (CBS) 2650 E Div St	Springfield	MO	65803	417-862-1010	831-4209	741-130
Web: www.ozarksfirst.com						
Kolstad Co 8501 Naples St NE	Blaine	MN	55449	763-792-1033	792-3799	62-5
Web: www.kolstadco.com						
Kom Intl 5555 Westminster Ave Ste 414	Montreal	QC	H4W2J2	514-849-4000	849-8888	449
Web: www.komintl.com						
Koman Group, The						
8025 Bonhomme Ave Ste 200	Saint Louis	MO	63105	314-993-5800		653
Web: www.komangroup.com						
Komar Industries Inc						
4425 Marketing Pl	Groveport	OH	43125	614-836-2366		454
Web: www.komarindustries.com						
Komatsu America Industries LLC						
1701 Golf Rd Ste 1-100	Rolling Meadows	IL	60008	847-437-3888	437-1811	386
Web: www.komatsupress.com						
Komax Corp						
1100 Corporate Grove Dr	Buffalo Grove	IL	60089	847-537-6640		454
Web: www.komaxgroup.com						
Kombi 5711 Ferrier St	Montreal	QC	H4P1N3	514-341-4321		195
TF: 800-203-0695 ■ *Web:* www.kombicanada.com						
Komegashi 99 Town Square Pl	Jersey City	NJ	07302	201-433-4567		671
Web: www.komegashi.com						

				Phone	Fax	Class
KOMENAR Publishing 1756 Lacassie Ave Ste 202 *Web:* www.komenarpublishing.com	Walnut Creek	CA	94596	510-444-2261	834-2141	637-2
Komet of America Inc 2050 Mitchell Blvd *TF:* 800-656-6381 ■ *Web:* www.komet.com	Schaumburg	IL	60193	800-656-6381	865-6638	621
Komfort and Kare 424 N White Horse Pke *TF:* 888-852-0181 ■ *Web:* www.komfortkare.com	Magnolia	NJ	08049	856-854-3100		475
Komi Restaurant 1509 17th St NW *Web:* www.komirestaurant.com	Washington	DC	20036	202-332-9200	330-5909	671
Kominiarek Bressler Harvick & Gudmundson LLC 33 N Dearborn St Ste 1310 *Web:* www.kbhglaw.com	Chicago	IL	60602	312-322-1111	782-1432	428
Komline-Sanderson Engineering Corp 12 Holland Ave *TF:* 800-225-5457 ■ *Web:* www.komline.com	Peapack	NJ	07977	908-234-1000	234-9487	386
Komo Machine Inc 1 Komo Dr *TF:* 800-255-5670 ■ *Web:* komo.com	Lakewood	NJ	08701	732-719-6222	579-5443	683
KOMO News 140 4th Ave N Ste 370 *Web:* www.komonews.com	Seattle	WA	98109	206-404-4000	706-2603	531-5
KOMO-TV Ch 4 (ABC) 140 Fourth Ave N **Fax Area Code:* 206 ■ *Web:* sbgi.net	Seattle	WA	98109	443-517-3332	404-4422*	741-123
Kompass Integrated Solutions Inc 2083 Old Middlefield Way Ste 202 *Web:* kompassconsulting.com	Mountain View	CA	94043	650-938-5667		177
KOMP-FM 92.3 (Rock) 8755 W Flamingo Rd *Web:* www.komp.com	Las Vegas	NV	89147	702-876-3692		645-85
KomTeK Technologies 40 Rockdale St *Web:* www.komtektech.com	Worcester	MA	01606	508-853-4500	853-2753	483
Kona Grill & Sushi Bar 7014 E Camelback Rd *Web:* www.konagrill.com	Scottsdale	AZ	85251	480-429-1100		671
Kona International Airport 73-200 Kupipi St *Web:* www.hawaii.gov	Kailua-Kona	HI	96740	808-327-9520	838-8067	27
Kona Kai Resort 1551 Shelter Island Dr *TF:* 800-566-2524 ■ *Web:* www.resortkonakai.com	San Diego	CA	92106	619-221-8000		379
Kona Sports Ctr 103 E Rio Grande Ave *Web:* www.konasurfco.com	Wildwood	NJ	08260	609-522-7899		711
Kona Veterinary Service 73-4730 Old Mamalahoa Hwy *Web:* konavetservice.com	Kailua-Kona	HI	96740	808-325-6637		794
Kona, Daddy & Apres Jacks Inc 9419 N Meridian St *Web:* jacksarebetter.net	Indianapolis	IN	46260	317-843-1609	571-6987	671
Kona-Kohala Chamber of Commerce 75-5737 Kuakini Hwy Ste 208 *Web:* www.kona-kohala.com	Kailua-Kona	HI	96740	808-329-1758	329-8564	139
Konami Gaming Inc 585 Trade Center Dr *Web:* www.gaming.konami.com	Las Vegas	NV	89119	702-616-1400		322
Konark Software Solutions LLC 5741 Cleveland St Ste 200 *Web:* konarksoftware.com	Virginia Beach	VA	23462	757-497-3303		177
Konecranes 7300 Chippewa Blvd *TF:* 800-231-0241 ■ *Web:* www.konecranes.com	Houston	TX	77086	281-445-2225	445-9355	470
KONE-FM 101.1 *101.1 The Beard Rocks* 33 Briercroft Office Pk *Web:* www.101thebeard.com	Lubbock	TX	79412	806-762-3000		645-90
Koneta Inc 1400 Lunar Dr *TF:* 800-331-0775 ■ *Web:* knrubber.com	Wapakoneta	OH	45895	419-739-4200	739-4247	676
Kongregate Inc 660 Mission St Ste 400 *Web:* www.kongregate.com	San Francisco	CA	94105	415-618-0087		637-10
Kongsberg Maritime 10777 Westheimer Rd Ste 1200 *Web:* www.kongsberg.com	Houston	TX	77042	713-329-5580		647
Koni Ameri Tech Services Inc 15 Serina Dr *Web:* www.katsi.com	Plainsboro	NJ	08536	732-226-0727	875-0363	177
KONI North America 1961-A International Way *TF:* 800-965-5664 ■ *Web:* www.koni-na.com	Hebron	KY	41048	859-586-4100	334-3340	60
Koniag Services Inc 4100 Lafayette Dr Ste 303 *Web:* ksikoniag.com	Chantilly	VA	20151	703-488-9300		225
Konica Minolta Business Solutions 411 Newark Pompton Tpke *Web:* www.konicaminolta.com	Wayne	NJ	07470	973-633-1500	523-7408	382
Konica Minolta Business Solutions USA Inc 100 Williams Dr *TF:* 800-456-5664 ■ *Web:* kmbs.konicaminolta.us	Ramsey	NJ	07446	201-825-4000		589
Konicom Inc 1819 J St *Web:* www.konicom.com	Sacramento	CA	95811	916-441-7373		175
Konner, Harbus and Schwartz PC 80 E Rte 4 Ste 408 *Web:* www.khs-cpa.com	Paramus	NJ	07652	201-556-1311	556-1310	2
Konocti Harbor Resort 8727 Soda Bay Rd *Web:* konoctiharborresort.com	Kelseyville	CA	95451	707-279-4281		378
Konop Cos 1725 Industrial Dr *TF:* 800-770-0477 ■ *Web:* www.konopcompanies.com	Green Bay	WI	54302	920-468-8517		296-34
Konrad 469 King St W 2nd Fl *Web:* www.konrad.com	Toronto	ON	M5V1K4	416-551-3684		631
Konsultek 2230 Point Blvd Ste 800 *Web:* www.konsultek.com	Elgin	IL	60123	847-426-9355	426-9366	251
Konsyl Pharmaceuticals Inc 8050 Industrial Park Rd *TF:* 800-356-6795 ■ *Web:* www.konsyl.com	Easton	MD	21601	410-822-5192		582
Kontek Industries Inc 1200 Dawson Rd PO Box 98 *Web:* kontekindustries.com	New Madrid	MO	63869	573-748-5561		106
Kontiki Beach Resort 2290 N Fulton Beach Rd *TF:* 800-388-0649 ■ *Web:* www.kontikibeachresorts.com	Rockport	TX	78382	361-729-2318	729-3212	378
Kontos Inc 505 Nashua Rd	Dracut	MA	01826	978-957-0330		237
Kontron S & T AG 7631 Anagram Dr *TF:* 888-343-5396 ■ *Web:* kontron.com	Eden Prairie	MN	55344	952-974-7000	974-7199	173-2
Koochiching County 715 Fourth St *Web:* www.co.koochiching.mn.us	International Falls	MN	56649	218-283-1152	283-1151	338
KOOI-FM 210 S Broadway Ste 100 *Web:* www.1065jackfm.com	Tyler	TX	75702	903-581-9966		647
KOOL 101.7 14 E Central Entrance *Web:* kool1017.com	Duluth	MN	55811	218-727-5665		645-50
Kool Ice and Seafood Company Inc 110 Washington St *TF:* 800-437-2417 ■ *Web:* www.freshmarylandseafood.com	Cambridge	MD	21613	410-228-2300		296-13
KOOL-FM 100.7 (Oldies) 3911 S First St *Web:* koolfmabilene.com	Abilene	TX	79605	325-676-5100		645-1
KOOL-FM 94.5 (Oldies) 840 N Central Ave *Web:* kool.radio.com	Phoenix	AZ	85004	602-260-9494	440-6530	645-121
Kooltronic Inc 30 Pennington-Hopewell Rd *Web:* www.kooltronic.com	Pennington	NJ	08534	609-466-3400	466-1114	14
Koons Ford of Annapolis Inc 2540 Riva Rd *Web:* www.koonsford.com	Annapolis	MD	21401	410-224-2100		57
Koontz-Wagner Electric Company Inc 3801 Voorde Dr *TF:* 800-345-2051 ■ *Web:* www.koontz-wagner.com	South Bend	IN	46628	574-232-2051		189-4
Koopman Lumber Company Inc 665 Church St *TF:* 800-836-4545 ■ *Web:* www.koopmanlumber.com	Whitinsville	MA	01588	508-234-4545		752
Koopman Ostbo Inc 412 NW Eighth Ave *Web:* koopmanostbo.com	Portland	OR	97209	503-223-2168		4
Koops Inc 987 Productions Ct *Web:* koops.com	Holland	MI	49423	616-395-0230		190
Kooser State Park 943 Glades Pk *Web:* www.dcnr.pa.gov	Somerset	PA	15501	814-445-8673		565
Kootenai County 451 N Government Way PO Box 9000 *TF:* 800-325-7940 ■ *Web:* www.kcgov.us	Coeur d'Alene	ID	83814	208-446-1500	446-1501	338
Kootenai Electric Co-opeartive Inc 2451 W Dakota Ave *TF:* 800-240-0459 ■ *Web:* www.kec.com	Hayden	ID	83835	208-765-1200	772-5858	245
Kootenay Savings Credit Union 1199 Cedar Ave **Fax Area Code:* 250 ■ *TF:* 800-665-5728 ■ *Web:* kscu.com	Trail	BC	V1R4B8	800-665-5728	368-3754*	401
Koozoo Inc 1998 Broadway Ste 1106	San Francisco	CA	94107	415-778-6374		387
Kopachuck State Park 10712 56th St NW *Web:* parks.state.wa.us	Gig Harbor	WA	98335	253-265-3606		565
Kop-Coat Inc 3040 William Pitt Way *TF:* 800-221-4466 ■ *Web:* www.kop-coat.com	Pittsburgh	PA	15238	412-227-2426	227-2618	550
Kope & Associates LLC 3900 Market St *Web:* kopelaw.com	Camp Hill	PA	17011	717-761-7573		428
Kopec & White 801 S Macarthur Blvd *Web:* springfield-law.com	Springfield	IL	62704	217-726-7540		41
Kopelowitz Ostrow PA 1 W Las Olas Blvd Ste 500 *Web:* kolawyers.com	Fort Lauderdale	FL	33301	954-525-4100	525-4300	41
Kopf Builders Inc 420 Avon Belden Rd *TF:* 888-933-5673 ■ *Web:* www.kopf.net	Avon Lake	OH	44012	440-933-6908	933-6956	187
Kopin Corp 125 N Dr *NASDAQ: KOPN* ■ *Web:* www.kopin.com	Westborough	MA	01581	508-870-5959		696
Koplar Communications 50 Maryland Plz *Web:* www.koplar.com	Saint Louis	MO	63108	314-345-1000		224
KOPN-FM 89.5 (Var) 915 E Broadway *TF:* 800-895-5676 ■ *Web:* www.kopn.org	Columbia	MO	65201	573-874-1139	499-1662	645
Koppel & Associates PA 817 S University Dr *Web:* koppellaw.net	Plantation	FL	33324	954-370-7878		41
Koppers Inc 436 Seventh Ave *NYSE: KOP* ■ *TF:* 800-385-4406 ■ *Web:* www.koppers.com	Pittsburgh	PA	15219	412-227-2001	227-2333	818
Koppinger & Associates Inc 3060 Commerce Dr Ste 4 *Web:* koppingerins.com	Fort Gratiot	MI	48059	810-721-7223		390
Kopy-Rite 2175 Crooks Rd Ste 101 *Web:* www.kopyrite.com	Rochester Hills	MI	48309	248-298-7000		253
KOR Water Inc 95 Enterprise Ste 310 *TF:* 877-708-7567 ■ *Web:* www.korwater.com	Aliso Viejo	CA	92656	877-708-7567		124
Koral Industries Inc 1504 S Kaufman St *TF:* 800-627-2441 ■ *Web:* www.koralco.com	Ennis	TX	75119	972-875-6555	875-9558	375
Korber Hats Inc PO Box 336	Fall River	MA	02724	508-672-7033	673-0762	155-9
Kor-Chem Inc 5800 Bucknell Dr SW *Web:* www.kor-chem.com	Atlanta	GA	30336	404-344-9580	349-2240	151
Kord Technologies Inc 635 Discovery Dr NW *Web:* kordtechnologies.com	Huntsville	AL	35806	256-489-2346	489-2347	177
Kordes Retreat Ctr 802 E Tenth St *TF:* 800-880-2777 ■ *Web:* www.thedome.org	Ferdinand	IN	47532	812-367-2777		673
Kore Inc 355 Madison Ave *Web:* www.korecorp.com	Morristown	NJ	07960	973-883-0308		535
Kore Press 240 N Court Ave *Web:* www.korepress.org	Tucson	AZ	85701	520-327-2127		637-2
Kore Telematics Inc 3700 Mansell Rd Ste 250 *TF:* 877-710-5673 ■ *Web:* www.korewireless.com	Alpharetta	GA	30022	877-710-5673		387
Kore/Hi Com Inc (K/HC) 3909 Leland Ave NE *Web:* www.korehicom.com	Comstock Park	MI	49321	616-647-6666	647-9971	180
Korea House 2590 Royal Ln *Web:* www.koreahousedallas.com	Dallas	TX	75229	972-243-0434		671

Name / Address	City	State	Zip	Phone	Fax	Class
Korea Republic of						
Consulate General 3243 Wilshire Blvd. Web: south-korea.embassy-online.net	Los Angeles	CA	90010	213-385-9300	385-1849	257
Consulate General 2756 Pali Hwy. Web: www.overseas.mofa.go.kr	Honolulu	HI	96817	808-595-6109		257
Korea Republic of Consulate General 455 N City Front Plaza Dr NBC Tower Ste 2700. Web: www.overseas.mofa.go.kr	Chicago	IL	60611	312-822-9485	822-9849	257
Korea Times Los Angeles Inc, The 4525 Wilshire Blvd. Web: www.koreatimes.com	Los Angeles	CA	90010	323-692-2000	692-2020	532-3
Korea Tourism Organization (KTO) 2 Executive Dr Ste 750. Web: english.visitkorea.or.kr	Fort Lee	NJ	07024	201-585-0909	585-9041	775
Korean Air 6101 W Imperial Hwy. TF: 800-438-5000 ■ Web: www.koreanair.com	Los Angeles	CA	90045	310-417-5200		25
Korean American Chamber of Commerce of Los Angeles 3435 Wilshire Blvd Ste 2450. *Fax Area Code: 866 ■ Web: www.lakacc.com	Los Angeles	CA	90010	213-480-1115	936-4497*	138
Korean American Coalition (KAC) 3727 W Sixth St Ste 305. Web: www.kacla.org	Los Angeles	CA	90020	213-365-5999	380-7990	48-14
Korean Chamber of Commerce & Industry in the USA Inc (KOCHAM) 460 Park Ave Ste 410. Web: www.kocham.org	New York	NY	10022	212-644-0140	644-9106	138
Korean War Veterans Memorial 900 Ohio Dr SW. Web: www.nps.gov	Washington	DC	20024	202-426-6841		50-4
Korein Tillery LLC 505 N Seveth St Ste 3600. Web: koreintillery.com	Saint Louis	MO	63101	314-241-4844		445
Koren Rogers Four West Red Oak Ln Ste 312. Web: www.korenrogers.com	White Plains	NY	10604	914-686-5800		260
Koreshan State Historic Site 3800 Corkscrew Rd. Web: www.floridastateparks.org	Estero	FL	33928	239-992-0311	992-1607	565
Korey Kay & Partners 130 Fifth Ave. TF: 800-264-8590 ■ Web: www.koreykay.com	New York	NY	10011	212-620-4300		4
Korg USA Inc 316 S Service Rd. Web: www.korg.com	Melville	NY	11747	631-390-6500	390-6501	527
Kor-it Inc 1964 Auburn Blvd. TF: 888-727-4560 ■ Web: www.kor-it.com	Sacramento	CA	95815	888-727-4560		190
Korman Healthcare LLC 5783 W Erie St. TF: 800-306-8641 ■ Web: www.kormanhealthcare.com	Chandler	AZ	85226	800-306-8641		363
Korn Consulting Group Inc 151 E 83rd St Ste 4AB. Web: www.kornconsulting.com	New York	NY	10028	212-734-6200		196
Korn/Ferry Intl 1900 Avenue of the Stars Ste 2600. NYSE: KFY ■ TF: 877-345-3610 ■ Web: www.kornferry.com	Los Angeles	CA	90067	310-552-1834	553-6452	266
Korney Board Aids Sporting 312 Harrison Ave. TF: 800-842-7772 ■ Web: www.kbacoach.com	Roxton	TX	75477	903-346-3269		711
Kornit Digital North America Inc 10541-10601 N Commerce St. TF: 888-456-7648 ■ Web: www.kornit.com	Mequon	WI	53092	262-518-0200	518-0340	627
Kornitzer Capital Management Inc 5420 W 61st Pl. Web: kornitzercapitalmanagement.com	Mission	KS	66205	913-677-7778		401
Korns Galvanizing Co 75 Bridge St. Web: www.kornsgalvanizing.com	Johnstown	PA	15902	814-535-3293		481
Kornylak Corp 400 Heaton St. TF: 800-837-5676 ■ Web: www.kornylak.com	Hamilton	OH	45011	513-863-1277	863-7644	470
Koro Industries Inc 9530 85th Ave N. Web: www.koroind.com	Maple Grove	MN	55369	763-425-5247	425-5261	709
KORR-FM 544 N Arthur. Web: www.korr104.com	Pocatello	ID	83204	208-234-1290	234-9451	647
Korsch 18 Bristol Dr. Web: www.korsch.com	South Easton	MA	02375	508-238-9080		111
Korshak Kracoff Kong & Sugano LLP 1640 S Sepulveda Blvd Ste 520. Web: www.kkks.com	Los Angeles	CA	90025	310-996-2340	996-2334	428
Korte Co, The 9225 W Flamingo Rd Ste 100. Web: www.korteco.com	Las Vegas	NV	89147	702-228-9551	228-5852	186
Korte Consulting PLLC 15 Ionia Ave SW Ste 505. Web: korteandkowatch.com	Grand Rapids	MI	49503	616-774-2727		2
Korth Companies Inc, The 9101 Gaither Rd. Web: www.korthcos.com	Gaithersburg	MD	20877	301-921-9500		186
Kortick Manufacturing Co 2230 Davis Ct. Web: www.kortick.com	Hayward	CA	94545	510-856-3600		816
Korum Automotive Group 100 River Rd. TF: 888-443-0094 ■ Web: www.korum.com	Puyallup	WA	98371	253-845-6600		57
Koryu Books PO Box 86. *Fax Area Code: 877 ■ TF: 888-665-6798 ■ Web: www.koryu.com	Berkeley Heights	NJ	07922	908-363-7371	308-3478*	637-2
KOSA-TV 4101 E 42nd St Ste J7. Web: www.cbs7.com	Odessa	TX	79762	432-580-5672	580-8010	647
Kosciusko County 100 W Center St. TF: 800-840-8757 ■ Web: www.kcgov.com	Warsaw	IN	46580	574-372-2331		338
Kosciusko County Rural Electric Membership Corp 370 S 250 E. Web: kremc.com	Warsaw	IN	46582	574-267-6331		245
Kosciusko Home Care & Hospice Inc 1515 Provident Dr Ste 250. Web: koshomecare.org	Warsaw	IN	46580	574-372-3401		363
Koshii Maxelum America Inc 12 Van Kleeck Dr. Web: www.kmamax.com	Poughkeepsie	NY	12602	845-471-0500	471-7842	499
Koshin America Corp 1218 Remington Rd. TF: 800-634-4092 ■ Web: www.koshinamerica.com	Schaumburg	IL	60173	847-884-1570		641

Name / Address	City	State	Zip	Phone	Fax	Class
Koshland Pharmacy Inc 301 Folsom St Ste B. Web: koshlandpharm.com	San Francisco	CA	94105	415-344-0600	344-0607	237
KOSI-FM 101(AC) 7800 E Orchard Rd Ste 400. Web: kosi101.com	Greenwood Village	CO	80111	303-321-0950		645-46
Kositzka Wicks & Co 5500 Cherokee Ave Ste 400. Web: www.kwccpa.com	Alexandria	VA	22312	703-642-2700		2
Koskoff, Koskoff & Bieder PC 350 Fairfield Ave. TF: 877-645-2313 ■ Web: www.koskoff.com	Bridgeport	CT	06604	203-583-8634		428
Kosmos Energy LLC 8176 Park Ln Ste 500. Web: www.kosmosenergy.com	Dallas	TX	75231	214-445-9600	363-9024	536
Kosmos Tool Inc 2727 Rt 12. Web: www.kosmostool.com	Spring Grove	IL	60081	815-675-2200	675-2994	729
Koso Hammel Dahl 253 Pleasant St. Web: kosoamerica.com	West Bridgewater	MA	02379	774-517-5300	517-5230	223
Koss Construction Co 5830 SW Drury Ln. Web: www.kossconstruction.com	Topeka	KS	66604	785-228-2928	228-2927	188-4
Koss Corp 4129 N Port Washington Ave. NASDAQ: KOSS ■ TF: 800-872-5677 ■ Web: www.koss.com	Milwaukee	WI	53212	800-872-5677		52
Koss Industrial Inc 1943 Commercial Way. TF: 800-844-6261 ■ Web: www.kossindustrial.com	Green Bay	WI	54311	920-469-5300		296
Kossuth County 114 W State St. Web: www.co.kossuth.ia.us	Algona	IA	50511	515-295-2718	295-3071	338
Kosta's Cafe 4621 W Pk Blvd Ste 100. Web: kostascafe.com	Plano	TX	75093	972-596-8424		671
Koster Industries Inc 40 Daniel St Ste 2. Web: www.kosterindustries.com	Farmingdale	NY	11735	631-454-1766	454-1779	41
Kostopoulos Rodriguez PLLC 550 W Merrill St Ste 100. Web: korolaw.com	Birmingham	MI	48009	248-268-7800		41
KOSW-FM 189 Ocean Lake Way SE PO Box 2473. Web: www.koswradio.com	Ocean Shores	WA	98569	360-289-5679	289-3744	647
KOSY-AM 2324 Arkansas Blvd. Web: www.kosy790am.com	Texarkana	AR	71854	870-772-2753		647
KOTA 518 St Joseph St. Web: www.kotaradio.com	Rapid City	SD	57701	605-342-2000	721-5732	738
KotaPress PO Box 514. Web: www.kotapress.com	Vashon	WA	98070	206-251-6706		637-2
Kotecki Rock of Ages Memorials 3636 Pearl Rd. Web: www.koteckifamilymemorials.com	Cleveland	OH	44109	216-749-2880		724
Kotin, Crabtree & Strong LLP 1 Bowdoin Sq. Web: www.kcslegal.com	Boston	MA	02114	617-227-7031		428
Kotler Marketing Group 3509 Connecticut Ave Ste 1175. TF: 800-331-9110 ■ Web: www.kotlermarketing.com	Washington	DC	20008	202-331-0555	331-0544	195
Kotobuki 457 Summer St. Web: www.kotobukijapaneserestaurant.com	Stamford	CT	06901	203-359-4747	357-7522	671
Kotobuki 721 W 21st St. Web: kotobukisushibar.com	Norfolk	VA	23517	757-628-1025		671
KOTR-TV 2511 Garden Rd Ste C150. Web: www.mytvmonterey.com	Monterey	CA	93940	831-655-5687	649-5687	647
Kotter Intl 5 Bennett St. TF: 855-400-4712 ■ Web: www.kotterinc.com	Cambridge	MA	02130	617-600-6787		463
Kotzebue Electric Association Inc PO Box 44. Web: www.kea.coop	Kotzebue	AK	99752	907-442-3491	442-2482	245
Kountry Folks 3653 La Sierra Ave. Web: kountry.com	Riverside	CA	92505	951-354-0437	354-7728	671
Kourosh Jewelry Inc 606 S Hill St Ste 509. TF: 800-750-9555 ■ Web: www.kouroshjewelryinc.com	Los Angeles	CA	90014	213-623-2990	623-7161	410
Koury Engineering & Testing Inc 14280 Euclid Ave. *Fax Area Code: 909 ■ Web: www.kouryengineering.com	Chino	CA	91710	310-851-8685	606-6555*	365
Kova Fertilizer Inc 1330 N Anderson St. TF: 800-346-1569 ■ Web: www.ekova.com	Greensburg	IN	47240	812-663-5081	663-5370	276
Kovack Securities Inc 6451 N Federal Hwy Ste 1201. TF: 800-711-4078 ■ Web: www.kovacksecurities.com	Fort Lauderdale	FL	33308	954-782-4771	943-7331	690
Kovak Likly Communications Inc 23 Hubbard Rd. Web: www.klcpr.com	Wilton	CT	06897	203-762-8833		636
Koval Williamson 11208 47th Ave W. Web: www.kwawest.com	Mukilteo	WA	98275	425-347-4249		361
Kovalsky-Carr Electric Supply Company Inc 208 St Paul St. Web: www.kovalskycarr.com	Rochester	NY	14604	585-325-1950	546-6904	246
Kovash & Dasovick PC 148 W First St. Web: www.dickinsonndcpas.com	Dickinson	ND	58601	701-483-1156	483-1160	2
Kovasys Inc 165 Cross Ave Ste 300. *Fax Area Code: 888 ■ TF: 888-568-2747 ■ Web: www.kovasys.com	Oakville	ON	L6J0A9	416-800-4286	363-3992*	260
Kovatch Castings Inc 3743 Tabs Dr. TF: 888-568-2824 ■ Web: www.kovatchcastings.com	Uniontown	OH	44685	330-896-9944		492
Kovel/Fuller LLC 9925 Jefferson Blvd. Web: www.kovelfuller.com	Culver City	CA	90232	310-841-4444		4
Kovensky Daniels 1250 Connecticut Ave NW Ste 200. *Fax Area Code: 413 ■ Web: www.kovdan.com	Washington	DC	20036	202-261-3555	832-1838*	266
Kovitz Shifrin Nesbit, A Professional Corp 175 N Archer Ave. TF: 855-537-0500 ■ Web: ksnlaw.com	Mundelein	IL	60060	847-537-0500		41
KOVR-TV 2713 KOVR Dr. TF: 800-374-8813 ■ Web: www.sacramento.cbslocal.com	West Sacramento	CA	95605	916-374-1313	374-1304	647
Kowa Pharmaceuticals America Inc 530 Industrial Park Blvd. Web: www.kowapharma.com	Montgomery	AL	36117	334-288-1288	288-2788	231

	Phone	Fax	Class
Kowal & Associates Inc 620 Massachusetts Ave .Cambridge MA 02139	617-577-0700	577-0500	737
Kowalenko Consulting Group Inc (KCG) 474 Central Ave Ste 205. . . . . Highland Park IL 60035 **Fax Area Code:* 844 ■ *Web:* www.kowalenkogroup.com	847-433-8747	270-5522*	194
Kowalski Companies Inc 1261 Grand Ave . . . . Saint Paul MN 55105 *Web:* www.kowalskis.com	651-698-3366		345
Kowalski Heat Treating Co 3611 Detroit Ave. . . . . .Cleveland OH 44113 *Web:* www.khtheat.com	216-631-4411		484
Kowalski Sausage Company Inc 2270 Holbrook St. . . . . Hamtramck MI 48212 *Web:* www.kowality.com	313-873-8200		296-26
Koyal Wholesale 2325 Raymer Ave . . . . Fullerton CA 92833 *TF:* 888-985-6925 ■ *Web:* www.koyalwholesale.com	714-459-0600		44
Koyo Restaurant 2275 East 33rd South. . . . . .Salt Lake City UT 84109 *Web:* www.koyoslc.com	801-466-7111		671
Koza Inc 2910 S Main St . . . . Pearland TX 77581 *TF:* 800-594-5555 ■ *Web:* kozas.com	281-485-1462		627
Kozak, Davis & Renninger PC 355 Crawford St Ste 700. . . . . Portsmouth VA 23704 *Web:* kozakfirm.com	757-364-0923		41
Kozak, Pollekoff & Goldman PC 1950 Old Gallows Rd Ste 440. . . . . .Vienna VA 22182 *Web:* kpgcpas.com	703-506-9700		2
Kozeny-Wagner Inc 951 W Outer Rd . . . . Arnold MO 63010 *Web:* www.kozenywagner.com	636-296-2012	296-2409	194
KOZK-TV Ch 21 (PBS) 901 S National Ave. . . . . .Springfield MO 65897 *TF:* 866-684-5695 ■ *Web:* www.optv.org	417-836-3500	836-3569	741-130
KP Tissue Inc 1900 Minnesota Ct Ste 200 . . . . Mississauga ON L5N5R5 *TF:* 866-600-5869 ■ *Web:* kptissueinc.com	905-812-6900	812-6910	787
KPAM-AM 6605 SE Lake Rd. .Portland OR 97222 *TF:* 877-774-5726 ■ *Web:* www.kpam.com	503-223-4321	294-0074	647
K-Paul's Louisiana Kitchen 416 Chartres St. . . . . New Orleans LA 70130 *Web:* www.kpauls.com	504-596-2530		671
KPAX-TV 1049 W Central Ave. . . . . Missoula MT 59801 *Web:* www.kpax.com	406-542-4400	543-7111	647
KPBN-TV 5500 Florida Blvd Ste 105. . . . . Baton Rouge LA 70806 *Web:* www.pelicansportstv.com	225-248-0049		647
KPBS Public Media 5200 Campanile Dr. . . . . San Diego CA 92182 *TF:* 888-399-5727 ■ *Web:* www.kpbs.org	619-594-1515		645-141
KPC Healthcare Inc 1301 N Tustin Ave. . . . . Santa Ana CA 92705 *OTC:* IHCH ■ *Web:* www.ihhioc.com	714-953-3652	953-3384	353
Kpd Insurance Inc 1111 Gateway Loop . . . . .Springfield OR 97477 *TF:* 800-929-0191 ■ *Web:* kpdinsurance.com	541-741-0550		390
KPEF-FM 3939 Gentilly Blvd. . . . . New Orleans LA 70126 **Fax Area Code:* 504 ■ *TF:* 888-480-3600 ■ *Web:* www.lifesongs.com	888-480-3600	816-8580*	647
KPFF Consulting Engineers Inc 1601 Fifth Ave Ste 1600 . . . . Seattle WA 98101 *Web:* www.kpff.com	206-622-5822		261
KPG 3131 Elliott Ave Ste 400. . . . . Seattle WA 98121 *Web:* www.kpg.com	206-286-1640		256
KPHE-TV 2412 E University Dr . . . . .Phoenix AZ 85034 *Web:* www.kphetv.com	602-220-9944		647
KPHT 95.5 106 W 24th St. . . . . .Pueblo CO 81003 *Web:* kpht955.iheart.com	719-545-9555		643
KPI Partners 39899 Balentine Dr Ste 212 . . . . .Newark CA 94560 *Web:* www.kpipartners.com	510-818-9480		180
KPIC-TV 655 W Umpqua PO Box 1345. . . . . .Roseburg OR 97470 *Web:* www.kpic.com	541-672-4481		647
KPIG-FM 107.5 (AAA) 1110 Main St Ste 16. . . . . Watsonville CA 95076 *TF:* 877-744-5273 ■ *Web:* www.kpig.com	831-722-9000		645
KPIR-AM 1620 Weatherford Hwy . . . . Granbury TX 76048 *Web:* www.kpir.com	817-736-0360	736-0340	647
KPIT Infosystems Inc 379 Thornall St. . . . . Edison NJ 08837 *Web:* www.kpit.com	732-321-0921		177
KPIX-TV 855 Battery St. . . . . San Francisco CA 94111 *Web:* www.sanfrancisco.cbslocal.com	415-362-5550		647
KPLC-TV Ch 7 (NBC) 320 Div St . . . . Lake Charles LA 70601 *Web:* www.kplctv.com	337-439-9071	437-7600	741
KPM VIPER Consulting LLC South Shore Executive Pk 10 Forbes Rd. . . . . Braintree MA 02184 *Web:* www.kpm-us.com	781-380-3520		260
KPMG International Cooperative 333 Base St Ste 4600 . . . . Toronto ON M5H2R2 *Web:* home.kpmg	416-777-8500	777-8818	194
KPNT-FM 105.7 (Alt) 11647 Olive Blvd . . . . Saint Louis MO 63146 *Web:* 1057thepoint.com	314-231-1057		645-138
KPNW-AM 1500 Valley River Dr Ste 350. . . . . .Eugene OR 97401 *Web:* www.kpnw.com	541-485-5769	284-3693	647
KPRC AM 950 2000 W Loop S Ste 300 . . . . .Houston TX 77027 *Web:* kprcradio.iheart.com	713-212-5950		645-72
KPRC-TV Ch 2 (NBC) 8181 SW Fwy . . . . .Houston TX 77074 *Web:* www.click2houston.com	713-222-2222	771-4930	741-60
KPRS Construction Services Inc 2850 Saturn St . . . . .Brea CA 92821 *Web:* www.kprsinc.com	714-672-0800	672-0871	186
KPRZ-AM 9255 Towne Centre Dr Ste 535 . . . . San Diego CA 92121 *Web:* www.kprz.com	858-535-1210		647
KPS Special Situations Fund LP 485 Lexington Ave 31st Fl . . . . .New York NY 10166 **Fax Area Code:* 646 ■ *Web:* www.kpsfund.com	212-338-5100	307-7100*	792
KPS3 500 Ryland Ste 300 . . . . Reno NV 89502 *Web:* kps3.com	775-686-7439		7
KPST-FM 72920 Parkview Dr . . . . .Palm Desert CA 92260 *Web:* www.radiolatricolor.com	888-874-2656		647
KPTS-TV Ch 8 (PBS) 320 W 21 St. . . . . Wichita KS 67203 *TF:* 800-794-8498 ■ *Web:* www.kpts.org	316-838-3090	838-8586	741-142

	Phone	Fax	Class
KPTX-FM 316 S Cedar . . . . .Pecos TX 79772 *Web:* www.98xfm.com	432-445-2497		647
KPVI-TV Ch 6 (NBC) 902 E Sherman St. . . . . Pocatello ID 83201 *Web:* www.kpvi.com	208-232-6666	233-6678	741-101
KPVU-FM 91.3 Prairie View A & M University MS 1415 PO Box 519 . . . . .Prairie View TX 77446 *Web:* kpvu.org	936-261-3750	261-3769	645
Kpw Structural Engineers Inc 55 Harrison Ste 550 . . . . Oakland CA 94607 *Web:* kpwse.com	510-208-3300		261
KPYK-AM PO Box 157 . . . . .Terrell TX 75160 *Web:* www.kpyk.com	972-524-5795		647
KPYN-AM PO Box 900 . . . . Atlanta TX 75551 *Web:* www.kpyn.net	903-796-2817		647
KQ2 4000 Faraon . . . . Saint Joseph MO 64506 *Web:* www.kq2.com	816-364-2222	364-3787	647
KQBB-FM 307 San Augustine St. . . . . Center TX 75935 *Web:* www.cbc-radio.com	936-598-3304	598-9537	647
KQBT *93.7 The Beat* 2000 W Loop S Ste 300 . . . . .Houston TX 77027 *Web:* 937thebeathouston.iheart.com	713-212-8000		647
KQC (Kilwins Quality Confections Inc) 1050 Bay View Rd. . . . . Petoskey MI 49770 *TF:* 888-454-5946 ■ *Web:* www.kilwins.com	888-454-5946		123
KQCH-FM 94.1 (CHR) 10714 Mockingbird Dr. . . . . . . Omaha NE 68127 *Web:* www.channel941.com	402-938-9400		645-113
KQCW-TV *News On 6* 303 N Boston Ave . . . . Tulsa OK 74103 *TF:* 800-447-5688 ■ *Web:* www.newson6.com	918-732-6000	732-6185	647
KQED Inc 2601 Mariposa St . . . . San Francisco CA 94110 *Web:* www.kqed.org	415-864-2000		741
KQKQ-FM 5011 Capitol Ave . . . . Omaha NE 68132 *Web:* www.sweet985.com	402-342-2000		647
KQLB LA JOYA 106.9 FM 401-A Pacheco Blvd. . . . . Los Banos CA 93635 *Web:* www.kqlb.com	209-827-0123	826-1906	643
KQMG-AM 1812 3rd Ave SE . . . . Independence IA 50644 *Web:* kqmgfm.wixsite.com	319-332-1812	332-1300	647
KQNA-AM PO Box 26523 . . . . .Prescott Valley AZ 86312 *Web:* www.kqna.com	928-445-8289		647
KQNK-FM 17038 KQNK Rd . . . . Norton KS 67654 *Web:* www.kqnk.com	785-877-3378		647
KQOB-FM 4045 NW 64th Ste 600 . . . . .Oklahoma City OK 73116 *Web:* www.fun969fm.com	405-460-2623		647
KQRK-FM 36581 N Reservoir Rd. . . . . Polson MT 59860 *TF:* 800-750-5377 ■ *Web:* www.qcountry997.com	406-257-9430	883-4441	647
KQSK-FM 2703 Hall Ste 15. . . . . Hays KS 67601	785-625-4000		647
KQV-AM 1410 (N/T) PO Box 990. . . . . Greensburg PA 15601 *Web:* www.kqv.com	724-853-7000		645-123
KQWC-FM 1020 E Second St PO Box 550. . . . . Webster City IA 50595 *Web:* www.kqradio.com	515-832-1570	832-2079	647
KQXR-FM 100.3 (Rock) 5257 Fairview Ave . . . . Boise ID 83706 *Web:* www.xrock.com	208-344-3511	947-6765	645-21
KQXY-FM 755 S 11th St Ste 102. . . . . Beaumont TX 77701 *Web:* www.kqxy.com	409-833-9421	833-9296	647
KQYX-AM 2510 W 20th St . . . . Joplin MO 64804 *Web:* www.1450thedove.com	417-781-1313		647
KRA Insurance Agency Inc 871 Mountain Ave PO Box 266. . . . . .Springfield NJ 07081 *Web:* krainsurance.com	973-467-8850	467-5641	390
KRA International LLC 1810 Clover Rd. . . . . .Mishawaka IN 46545 *Web:* www.krainternational.com	574-259-3550		247
Krabloonik 4250 Divide Rd PO Box 5517. . . . . Snowmass Village CO 81615 *Web:* krabloonik.com	970-923-3953		671
Krack Corp 1300 N Arlington Heights Rd Ste 130. . . . . .Itasca IL 60143 *TF:* 855-487-7778 ■ *Web:* www.krack.com	630-629-7500	250-3537	14
Kraemer Bros LLC 925 Park Ave. . . . . Plain WI 53577 *Web:* www.kraemerbrothers.com	608-546-2411	546-2509	186
Kraemer Design Services Inc 4655 N Flowing Wells Rd . . . . .Tucson AZ 85705 *Web:* www.kdsaz.com	520-690-1669		261
Kraft Chemical Co 1975 N Hawthorne Ave. . . . . .Melrose Park IL 60160 *TF:* 800-345-5200 ■ *Web:* www.kraftchemical.com	708-345-5200	345-4005	146
Kraft Fluid Systems Inc 14300 Foltz Pkwy . . . . .Strongsville OH 44149 *TF:* 800-257-1155 ■ *Web:* www.kraftfluid.com	440-238-5545		641
Kraft Hat Manufacturers Inc 725 Whittier St . . . . .Bronx NY 10474 *Web:* www.krafthat.com	845-735-6200	735-2299	155-9
Kraft Heinz Co 200 E Randolph St Ste 7600. . . . . .Chicago IL 60601 *NASDAQ:* KHC ■ *TF:* 800-543-5335 ■ *Web:* www.kraftheinzcompany.com	800-543-5335		296-5
Kraft Miles & Tatum LLC 1650 W Harper St. . . . . Poplar Bluff MO 63901 *Web:* kmtcpas.com	573-785-6438		2
Kraft Power Corp 199 Wildwood Ave . . . . Woburn MA 01801 *TF:* 800-969-6121 ■ *Web:* www.kraftpower.com	781-938-9100	933-7812	518
KraftCPAs PLLC 555 Great Cir Rd . . . . Nashville TN 37228 **Fax Area Code:* 931 ■ *Web:* www.kraftcpas.com	615-242-7351	388-9998*	2
Kraft-Engel Management 15233 Ventura Blvd Ste 200. . . . . Sherman Oaks CA 91403 *Web:* kraft-engel.com	818-380-1918		731
Kraftmaid Cabinetry Inc 15535 S State Ave PO Box 1055. . . . . Middlefield OH 44062 *TF:* 888-562-7744 ■ *Web:* www.kraftmaid.com	888-562-7744		115
Kraftube Inc 925 E Church Ave. . . . . Reed City MI 49677 *Web:* www.kraftube.com	231-832-5562	832-2937	595
Kraftware Corp 270 Cox St. . . . . .Roselle NJ 07203 *TF:* 800-221-1728 ■ *Web:* www.kraftwarecorp.com	800-221-1728		607
Kraken Oil & Gas LLC 9821 Katy Fwy Ste 460. . . . . .Houston TX 77024 *Web:* krakenoil.com	713-360-7705		536

	Phone	Fax	Class
Kramer & Frank P C 9300 Dielman Industrial Dr Ste 100 .... Saint Louis MO 63132 *Web:* kramerandfrank.com	314-991-1177	991-0485	41
Kramer & Jensen LLC 7430 E Caley Ave Ste 300E.................. Centennial CO 80111 *TF:* 855-330-4215 ■ *Web:* kramerjensen.com	303-741-2253		2
Kramer Accountancy Corp 120 N Topanga Canyon Blvd Ste 111 ....Topanga CA 90290 *Web:* kramercpa.com	310-455-9300	455-2122	2
KRAMER aerotek Inc 580 Utica Ave............. Boulder CO 80304 *Web:* www.krameraerotek.com	303-247-1762		196
Kramer Fiduciary Services 1500 Ardmore Blvd Ste 205 .... Pittsburgh PA 15221 *Web:* www.kramerfiduciary.com	412-351-2150	351-2164	2
Kramer Gehlen & Associates Inc 400 Columbia St Ste 240 .... Vancouver WA 98660 *Web:* kramer-gehlen.com	360-693-1621		261
Kramer Graphics Inc 2408 W Dorothy Ln ....Dayton OH 45439 *Web:* www.kramergraphics.com	937-296-9600	296-7496	781
Kramer Huy PA 950 N Collier Blvd Ste 101................ Marco Island FL 34145 *Web:* marcoislandlaw.com	239-394-3900		41
Kramer Laboratories Inc 400 University Dr Ste 400................. Coral Gables FL 33134 *Web:* kramerlabs.com	305-223-1287		582
Kramer Metals Inc (KM) 1760 E Slauson Ave ....Los Angeles CA 90058 *Web:* www.kramermetals.com	323-587-2277	588-8007	686
Kramer, Dillof, Livingston & Moore 217 Broadway 10th Fl........................New York NY 10007 *Web:* www.kdlm.com	212-267-4177	233-8525	428
KRAM-FM PO Box 332 .... Montevideo MN 56265 *Web:* www.967kram.com	320-321-9671		647
Krannert Art Museum & Kinkead Pavilion 500 E Peabody Dr......................... Champaign IL 61820 *Web:* kam.illinois.edu	217-333-1861		520
Krannert Center for the Performing Arts 500 S Goodwin Ave ....Urbana IL 61801 *TF:* 800-527-2849 ■ *Web:* krannertcenter.com	217-333-6700	244-0810	572
Kranz Inc 2200 DeKoven Ave .... Racine WI 53403 *TF:* 888-638-2201 ■ *Web:* www.kranzinc.com	262-638-2200	638-2202	76
Krasl Art Ctr 707 Lake Blvd .... Saint Joseph MI 49085 *Web:* krasl.org	269-983-0271		522
Krasnoo Klehm & Falkner LLP 28 Andover St Ste 240 ....Andover MA 01810 *Web:* kkf-attorneys.com	978-296-5173		41
Krasnow, Keller & Boris PC 665 Franklin St.......................... Framingham MA 01702 *Web:* krasnowkellerboris.com	508-872-2710		41
Kraton Performance Polymers 2419 State Rte 618........................... Belpre OH 45714 *NYSE: KRA* ■ *Web:* kraton.com	740-423-7571		605-2
Kratos Analytical Inc 100 Red Schoolhouse Rd Bldg A .... Chestnut Ridge NY 10977 *Web:* www.kratos.com	845-426-6700		407
Kratos Defense & Security Solutions Inc 10680 Treena St 6th Fl .... San Diego CA 92131 *Web:* www.kratosdefense.com	717-397-2777	397-7079	504
Kraus 65 Northfield Dr W .... Waterloo ON N2L0A8 *Web:* www.krausflooring.com	519-884-2310		290
Kraus & Naimer Inc 760 New Brunswick Rd...................... Somerset NJ 08873 *Web:* www.krausnaimer.us	732-560-1240		350
Kraus Global Inc 25 Paquin Rd................Winnipeg MB R2J3V9 *Web:* krausglobal.com	204-663-3601		358
Kraus Manning Inc 7233 Lake Ellenor Dr .... Orlando FL 32809 *Web:* www.kraus-manning.com	407-251-0085		194
Kraus USA Inc 160 Amsler Ave ....Shippenville PA 16254 *Web:* krausflooring.com	814-226-9300		361
Kraus-Anderson Co (KA) 501 S Eigth St...........................Minneapolis MN 55404 *Web:* www.krausanderson.com	612-332-7281	332-8739	185
Kraus-Anderson Insurance 420 Gateway Blvd.......................... Burnsville MN 55337 *Web:* www.kainsurance.com	952-707-8200		390
Krause Consultants Ltd (KCL) 5225 N Ironwood Rd Ste 109................. Glendale WI 53217 *Web:* www.ckrause.com	414-963-8688	963-8699	194
Krause Gentle Corp 6400 Westown Pkwy..................West Des Moines IA 50266 *Web:* www.kumandgo.com	515-226-0128		204
Kraushaar Galleries Inc 15 E 71 St Ste 2B ....New York NY 10021 *Web:* www.kraushaargalleries.com	212-288-2558		42
Kravco Co 234 Mall Blvd .... King of Prussia PA 19406 *Web:* www.kravco.com	610-854-2800		655
Kravet Inc 225 Central Ave S Ste 6 .... Bethpage NY 11714 **Fax Area Code:* 800 ■ *Web:* www.kravet.com	516-293-2000	221-6981*	321
Krazan & Associates Inc 215 W Dakota Ave............................. Clovis CA 93612 *Web:* www.krazan.com	559-348-2200	348-2201	261
KRBC-TV Ch 9 (NBC) 4510 S 14th St .... Abilene TX 79605 *Web:* www.bigcountryhomepage.com	325-692-4242		741-1
KRBI-FM 1807 Lee Blvd ....North Mankato MN 56003 *Web:* www.river105.com	507-345-4646		647
KRCB FM 5850 Labath Ave................. Rohnert Park CA 94928	707-584-2020		645-11
KRCC-FM 91.5 (NPR) 912 N Weber St..................... Colorado Springs CO 80903 *TF:* 800-748-2727 ■ *Web:* krcc.org	719-473-4801	473-7863	645-37
KRCG-TV Ch 13 (CBS) 10188 Old Hwy 54 N ....New Bloomfield MO 65063 *TF:* 800-773-6180 ■ *Web:* krcgtv.com	573-896-5144	896-5193	741
KRCQ-FM 1340 Richwood Rd .... Detroit Lakes MN 56501 *TF:* 800-962-5590 ■ *Web:* www.realcountry102.com	218-847-5624		647
KRCR News Channel 755 Auditorium Dr ....Redding CA 96001 *TF:* 800-222-5727 ■ *Web:* krcrtv.com	530-243-7777	243-9382	742
KRCW-TV 10255 SW Arctic Dr ....Beaverton OR 97005 *Web:* www.portlandscw.com	503-644-3232	626-3576	647

	Phone	Fax	Class
KRCX-AM *KRCX Regis University Radio* 3333 Regis Blvd........................... Denver CO 80221 *Web:* www.krcx.org	303-964-5392		647
KRDO-TV 399 S Eighth St .... Colorado Springs CO 80905 *Web:* www.krdo.com	719-632-1515		647
Kream and Kream 536 Broad St Ste 5 .... East Weymouth MA 02189 *Web:* www.kreamandkream.com	781-331-9333	331-9549	428
Kreamer Feed Inc 215 Kreamer Ave.............Kreamer PA 17833 *TF:* 800-767-4537 ■ *Web:* www.kreamerfeed.com	570-374-8148	374-2007	276
Kreate & Print Inc 14 Central St............... Norwood MA 02062 *Web:* kreateandprint.com	781-255-0505		627
Krech Ojard & Assoc 227 W First St Ste 500 .... Duluth MN 55802 *Web:* www.krechojard.com	218-727-3282	727-1216	256
Kreeger Museum, The 2401 Foxhall Rd NW...................... Washington DC 20007 *Web:* www.kreegermuseum.org	202-338-3552	337-3051	520
KREG-TV 345 Hillcrest Ave .... Grand Junction CO 81501 *Web:* www.westernslopenow.com	970-242-5000		647
Kreher Steel Company LLC 1550 N 25th Ave........................ Melrose Park IL 60160 **Fax Area Code:* 708 ■ *TF:* 800-323-0745 ■ *Web:* www.kreher.com	800-323-0745	345-8293*	492
Krehling Industries Inc 1399 Hagy Way........................... Harrisburg PA 17110 *Web:* www.krehlingcountertops.com	717-232-7936	236-8810	182
Kreider Ayers & Associates Inc 1130 Patterson Ave SW ....Roanoke VA 24016	540-343-7612		189-10
Kreider Corp 2000 S Yellow Springs St...................Springfield OH 45506 *Web:* www.kreidercorp.com	937-325-8787		483
Kreider Farms 1461 Lancaster Rd .... Manheim PA 17545 **Fax Area Code:* 717 ■ *TF:* 888-665-4415 ■ *Web:* www.kreiderfarms.com	888-665-4415	665-9614*	10-3
Kreilkamp Trucking Inc 6487 Hwy 175..........Allenton WI 53002 *TF:* 800-558-1724 ■ *Web:* www.kreilkamp.com	800-558-1724		780
Kreinik Manufacturing Company Inc 1708 Gihon Rd ....Parkersburg WV 26101 *TF:* 800-537-2166 ■ *Web:* www.kreinik.com	304-422-8900		745-9
Kreis Enderle 8225 Moorsbridge Rd............. Portage MI 49024 *TF:* 800-535-4939 ■ *Web:* www.kreisenderle.com	269-324-3000	966-3022	428
Kreis' Restaurant 535 S Lindbergh Blvd...................... Saint Louis MO 63131 *Web:* www.kreissteakhouse.com	314-993-0735		671
Krell Industries LLC 45 Connair Rd ....Orange CT 06477 *Web:* www.krellhifi.com	203-799-9954	799-9796	52
Krell Institute 1609 Golden Aspen Dr Ste 101 .... Ames IA 50010 *Web:* www.krellinst.org	515-956-3696	956-3699	196
Kremblas Foster Phillips & Pollick 7632 Slate Ridge Blvd .... Reynoldsburg OH 43068 *Web:* ohiopatent.com	614-575-2100		428
Kremer & Associates Inc 6400 Brooktree Ct Ste 240 ....Wexford PA 15090 *Web:* www.kremerassociates.com	724-934-0808	934-0820	463
Kremer Wholesale 520 Lagonda Ave ....Lexington KY 40505 *Web:* www.kremerwholesale.com	859-255-3432		594
Krengel Enterprises 121 Tulton St............. New York NY 10038 *Web:* reviews.birdeye.com	212-227-1877		467
Krenz & Company Inc W132 N 10940 Eisenhower Dr .... Germantown WI 53022 *Web:* www.krcnzvcnt.com	262-255-2310	255-2904	18
Kresge Foundation 3215 W Big Beaver Rd........... Troy MI 48084 *Web:* kresge.org	248-643-9630		305
Kresge Hearing Research Institute (KHRI) 4605 Medical Science .... Ann Arbor MI 48109 *Web:* medicine.umich.edu	734-764-8110	764-0014	668
Kress Corp 227 W Illinois St .... Brimfield IL 61517 *Web:* www.kresscarrier.com	309-446-3395	446-9625	190
Kress Employment Screening 320 Westcott St Ste 108 ....Houston TX 77007 *TF:* 888-636-3693 ■ *Web:* kressinc.com	713-880-3693		635
Krestmark Industries Lp 3950 Bastille Rd .... Dallas TX 75212 *Web:* boralwindows.com	214-237-5055		234
Kretschmar & Smith Inc 6293 Pedley Rd .... Riverside CA 92509 *Web:* kandsmasonry.com	951-361-1405		189-7
Kretz Lumber Company Inc W11143 County Hwy G .... Antigo WI 54409 *Web:* www.kretzlumber.com	715-623-5410		683
Kreuzberger & Assoc 1000 Fourth St .... San Rafael CA 94901 *Web:* kreuzberger.com	415-459-2300		260
KRFO-AM 245 18th St SE ....Owatonna MN 55060 *Web:* www.krforadio.com	507-451-2250		647
KRGE-AM 2720 W Business 83..................Weslaco TX 78596 *Web:* www.radiovida.com	956-968-7777		647
KRGV-TV Ch 5 (ABC) 900 E Expy PO Box 5 ....Weslaco TX 78596 *Web:* www.krgv.com	956-968-5555	973-5016	741
Krieg DeVault Alexander & Capehart 1 Indiana Sq Ste 2800 ....Indianapolis IN 46204 *Web:* www.kriegdevault.com	317-636-4341	636-1507	428
Krieger Specialty Products Co 4880 Gregg Rd .... Pico Rivera CA 90660 *TF:* 866-203-5060 ■ *Web:* www.kriegerproducts.com	562-695-0645	692-0146	234
KRIG-FM 1200 SE Frank Phillips Blvd.................Bartlesville OK 74003 *TF:* 800-749-5936 ■ *Web:* www.bartlesvilleradio.com	918-336-1001	336-6939	647
Kring & Chung LLP 38 Corporate Pk............... Irvine CA 92606 *Web:* www.kringandchung.com	949-345-1621		428
Krinzman, Huss & Lubetsky LLP 800 Brickell Ave Ste 1501...................... Miami FL 33131 *Web:* khllaw.com	305-854-9700		41
KRIO-AM 4300 S Business Hwy 281............. Edinburg TX 78539 *TF:* 800-099-0333 ■ *Web:* radioesperanza.org	956-380-3435		647
Kripalu Center for Yoga & Health 57 Interlaken Rd ....Stockbridge MA 01262 *TF:* 800-741-7353 ■ *Web:* kripalu.org	413-448-3400	448-3384	706

Name	Address	City	State	ZIP	Phone	Fax	Class
Kris Way Truck Leasing Inc	43 Hemco Rd Ste 1 *Web:* www.kris-way.com	South Portland	ME	04106	207-799-8593	799-8657	778
KrisDee & Associates Inc	755 Schneider Dr *Web:* www.krisdee.com	South Elgin	IL	60177	847-608-8300	608-8400	295
Krise Transportation Inc	1325 Scotland Ave Ext *Web:* www.krisetran.info	Punxsutawney	PA	15767	814-938-6200	938-7545	109
Krishnamoorthi Raja (Rep D - IL)	115 Cannon House Office Bldg. *Web:* krishnamoorthi.house.gov	Washington	DC	20515	202-225-3711		342-2
Krishnamurti Foundation of America	PO Box 1560 *Web:* kfa.org	Ojai	CA	93024	805-646-2726		305
Krispy Kreme Doughnuts Corp	PO Box 83 *NYSE:* KKD ■ *TF:* 800-457-4779 ■ *Web:* www.krispykreme.com	Winston-Salem	NC	27102	336-725-2981		68
Krist Oil Co	303 Selden Rd *TF:* 800-722-6691 ■ *Web:* www.kristoil.com	Iron River	MI	49935	906-265-6144		345
Kristal Graphics	22001 Sherman Way *Web:* www.kristalgraphics.net	Canoga Park	CA	91303	818-342-7822	999-4982	627
Kristin Manwaring Insurance	2300 S Park Ave *Web:* kristinmanwaring.com	Port Townsend	WA	98368	360-385-4400		390
KRIS-TV Ch 6 (NBC)	301 Artesian St *Web:* www.kristv.com	Corpus Christi	TX	78401	361-886-6100		741-36
KRIV-TV Ch 26 (Fox)	4261 SW Fwy *Web:* www.fox26houston.com	Houston	TX	77027	713-479-2600	479-2859	741-60
KRLQ-FM	PO Box 2941 *Web:* www.krlqfm.com	Ruston	LA	71273	318-255-7941	255-8211	647
KRMC (Kingman Regional Medical Ctr)	3269 Stockton Hill Rd *TF:* 877-757-2101 ■ *Web:* www.azkrmc.com	Kingman	AZ	86409	928-757-2101		374-3
KRMD-FM 101.1	270 Plaza Loop	Bossier City	LA	71111	318-549-8500		645
KRMG-AM 740 (N/T)	7136 S Yale Ave Ste 500 *TF:* 855-297-9696 ■ *Web:* www.krmg.com	Tulsa	OK	74136	918-493-7400		645-166
KRMS-AM	5715 Osage Beach Pky PO Box 225 *Web:* www.krmsradio.com	Osage Beach	MO	65065	573-348-2772	348-2779	647
KRNV-TV	1790 Vassar St *Web:* www.mynews4.com	Reno	NV	89502	775-322-4444		647
KROC-AM 1340	122 SW 4th St *Web:* krocnews.com	Rochester	MN	55902	507-286-1010		645-134
Krochet Kids Intl	1630 Superior Ave Unit C *Web:* www.krochetkids.org	Costa Mesa	CA	92627	949-791-2560		305
Kroeschell Inc	3222 N Kennicott Ave *Web:* www.kroeschell.com	Arlington Heights	IL	60004	312-649-7980		261
Kroger Co	1014 Vine St *NYSE:* KR ■ *Web:* www.kroger.com	Cincinnati	OH	45202	513-762-4000		345
Krohn & Moss Ltd	10 N Dearborn St 3rd Fl *TF:* 800-875-3666 ■ *Web:* westopdebtcollectors.com	Chicago	IL	60602	800-875-3666		41
Krohn Conservatory	511 Fairfield Ave *Web:* www.cincinnatiparks.com	Cincinnati	OH	45202	513-421-4086		520
Krohn Industries Inc	PO Box 98 *TF:* 800-526-6299 ■ *Web:* www.krohnindustries.com	Carlstadt	NJ	07072	201-933-9696	933-9684	407
Krohne Inc	7 Dearborn Rd *Web:* www.krohne.com	Peabody	MA	01960	978-535-6060		639
KROK-FM	168 KVVP Dr *Web:* www.westcentralsbest.com	Leesville	LA	71446	337-537-5887	537-4152	647
Kroll Background America Inc	100 Centerview Dr Ste 300 *TF:* 800-697-7189 ■ *Web:* www.kroll.com	Nashville	TN	37214	800-679-7189		635
Kroll Direct Marketing Inc	3914 Netherlee Way *Web:* www.krolldirect.com	Wellington	FL	33449	609-275-2900		5
Kroll Ontrack Inc	9023 Columbine Rd *TF:* 800-872-2599 ■ *Web:* www.ontrack.com	Eden Prairie	MN	55347	952-937-5161	937-5750	178-12
Krolls West	1990 S Ridge Rd *Web:* www.krollswest.com	Green Bay	WI	54304	920-497-1111		671
Krome Communications Inc	925 Penn Ave *Web:* www.krome.com	Pittsburgh	PA	15222	412-471-0840		636
Kromet International Inc	200 Sheldon Dr *Web:* www.kromet.com	Cambridge	ON	N1R7K1	519-623-2511		488
Kromite LLC	243 N Union St Ste 117 *Web:* www.kromite.com	Lambertville	NJ	08530	267-983-6305		463
Krone North America	3363 Miac Cove *Web:* www.krone-northamerica.com	Memphis	TN	38118	901-842-6011		273
Kroner Publications Inc	1123 W Park Ave *Web:* thereviewnewspapers.com	Niles	OH	44446	330-544-5500	544-5511	532-2
Krones Inc	9600 S 58th St PO Box 321801 *TF:* 800-752-3787 ■ *Web:* www.krones.com	Franklin	WI	53132	414-409-4000	409-4100	547
Kronick Moskovitz Tiedemann & Girard (KMTG)	400 Capitol Mall 2nd Fl *Web:* kmtg.com	Sacramento	CA	95814	916-321-4500	321-4555	428
Kronos Inc	297 Billerica Rd *TF:* 888-293-5549 ■ *Web:* www.kronos.com	Chelmsford	MA	01824	978-250-9800	367-5900	178-11
Kronos Press	226 Richmond C *Web:* www.kronos-press.com	Deerfield Beach	FL	33442	954-421-8934		637-2
Kronos Products Inc	1 Kronos Dr *TF:* 800-621-0099 ■ *Web:* kronosfoodscorp.com	Glendale Heights	IL	60139	224-353-5353	353-5402	296-26
Kropp Equipment Inc	1020 Kennedy Ave *TF:* 866-402-2222 ■ *Web:* www.kroppequipment.com	Schererville	IN	46375	866-402-2222		358
Kropp Forge	5301 W Roosevelt Rd *Web:* www.kroppforge.com	Cicero	IL	60804	708-652-6691	652-9144	483
KROQ-FM 106.7 (Alt)	5901 Venice Blvd *TF:* 800-520-1067 ■ *Web:* www.kroq.radio.com	Los Angeles	CA	90034	323-930-1067		645-42
KROS-AM	870 13th Ave N **Fax Area Code:* 536 ■ *Web:* www.krosradio.com	Clinton	IA	52733	563-242-1252	242-4825*	647
Krove Corp	1373 SW 12th Ave *Web:* www.krove.com	Pompano Beach	FL	33069	954-741-2972		180
KROX-AM 1260 (Var)	208 S Main St *Web:* www.kroxam.com	Crookston	MN	56716	218-281-1140	281-5036	645
Kroy LLC	3830 Kelley Ave *TF:* 888-888-5769 ■ *Web:* www.kroy.com	Cleveland	OH	44114	216-426-5600		173-6
Krozak Information Technologies Inc	201 Linton Knoll Ct *Web:* www.krozak.com	Silver Spring	MD	20904	301-384-4340		396
KRPI-AM	5538 Imhof Rd *Web:* www.krpiradio.com	Ferndale	WA	98248	360-384-5117	380-4202	647
KRSC-TV	1701 W Will Rogers Blvd *TF:* 800-823-7210 ■ *Web:* www.rsu.tv	Claremore	OK	74017	918-343-7649		647
KRT Marketing Inc	3685 Mt Diablo Blvd Ste 255 *Web:* www.krtmarketing.com	LaFayette	CA	94549	925-284-0444		195
KRTH-FM 101.1 (Oldies)	5670 Wilshire Blvd Ste 200 *TF:* 800-232-5784 ■ *Web:* kearth101.radio.com	Los Angeles	CA	90036	323-936-5784	933-6072	645-42
KRTV-TV Ch 3 (CBS)	PO Box 2989 *Web:* www.krtv.com	Great Falls	MT	59403	406-329-3625		741-54
Kruckeberg Botanic Garden	20312 15th Ave NW *Web:* www.kruckeberg.org	Shoreline	WA	98177	206-546-1281		97
Krueger Bearings Inc	8811 W Dean Rd **Fax Area Code:* 414 ■ *TF:* 800-552-9077 ■ *Web:* www.kruegerbearings.com	Milwaukee	WI	53224	800-552-9077	357-7415*	454
Krueger Engineering & Manufacturing Co	12001 Hirsch Rd PO Box 11308 *Web:* www.kemcotx.com	Houston	TX	77293	281-442-2537	442-6668	91
Krueger Sheet Metal Co	6515 W Marginal Way SW *Web:* kruegersheetmetal.com	Spokane	WA	99202	509-489-0221	489-6539	697
Krueger Wholesale Florist Inc	10706 Tesch Ln *Web:* kruegerwholesale.com	Rothschild	WI	54474	715-359-7202		292
Krueger-Gilbert Health Physics Inc	809 Gleneagles Ct Ste 100 *Web:* kruegergilbert.com	Towson	MD	21286	410-339-5447		194
Kruepke Trucking Inc	2881 County Road P *TF:* 800-798-5000 ■ *Web:* kruepketrucking.com	Jackson	WI	53037	262-677-3155	677-3206	780
KRUF-FM 94.5 (CHR)	6341 W Port Ave *Web:* k945.com	Shreveport	LA	71129	318-688-1130		645-148
Kruger Digiovanni Aluisi LLC	127 Lubrano Dr Ste 300 *Web:* kdalawfirm.com	Annapolis	MD	21401	410-224-1332		41
Kruger Inc	3285 Ch Bedford *TF:* 877-526-2833 ■ *Web:* www.kruger.com	Montreal	QC	H3S1G5	514-737-1131	343-3124	557
Kruger Street Toy & Train Museum	144 Kruger St *TF:* 877-242-8133 ■ *Web:* www.toyandtrain.com	Wheeling	WV	26003	304-242-8133	242-1925	520
Kruggel Lawton & Company LLC	210 S Michigan St Ste 200 *Web:* www.klcpas.com	South Bend	IN	46601	574-289-4011		2
Krugliak, Wilkins, Griffiths & Dougherty Co	4775 Munson St NW *TF:* 877-876-9958 ■ *Web:* www.kwgd.com	Canton	OH	44735	330-497-0700		428
KRUI-AM	1086 Mechem Dr *Web:* www.mtdradio.com	Ruidoso	NM	88345	505-258-5784	258-2363	647
KRUI-FM	University of Iowa 379 Iowa Memorial Union *Web:* www.krui.fm	Iowa City	IA	52242	319-335-9525		647
Kru-Kel Company Inc	2125 Macon Ave *Web:* www.kru-kel.com	North Charleston	SC	29405	843-744-2558	744-8729	665
Krummrich Engineering Corp	590 Poli St *Web:* kecorp.us	Ventura	CA	93001	805-288-6360		261
Krung Thai	642 S Winchester Blvd *Web:* www.originalkrungthai.com	San Jose	CA	95128	408-260-8224		671
Kruse Adhesive Tape Inc	1610 E McFadden Ave *TF:* 800-992-7702 ■ *Web:* www.krusetape.com	Santa Ana	CA	92705	714-640-2130	640-2134	732
Kruse Asset Management	1 Kruse Plz 11202 Disco Dr Ste 100 *TF:* 800-952-1973 ■ *Web:* www.kruseasset.com	San Antonio	TX	78216	210-499-0777	499-4217	189-11
Krusinski Construction Co	2107 Swift Dr *Web:* www.krusinski.com	Oak Brook	IL	60523	630-573-7700		186
Krvn Transmitter	1007 Plum Crk Pkwy PO Box 880 *Web:* www.krvn.com	Lexington	NE	68850	308-324-2371		645-11
KRVV-FM	1109 Hudson Ln	Monroe	LA	71211	318-388-2323	388-0569	647
KRW Consulting Group LLC	1881 Commerce Dr Ste 111 *Web:* www.krweng.com	Elk Grove Village	IL	60007	847-734-0128		196
KRWA-FM	321 N Greenwood Ave *Web:* www.thefort945fm.com	Fort Smith	AR	72901	225-936-8016		647
KRWG-FM 90.7 (NPR)	2915 McFie Cir PO Box 30001 *Web:* krwg.org	Las Cruces	NM	88003	575-646-2222	646-1974	645
KRWM-FM	3650 131st Ave SE Ste 550 *TF:* 800-622-1069 ■ *Web:* www.warm1069.com	Bellevue	WA	98006	425-373-5545	373-5507	647
KRXA-AM	495 Elder Ave Ste 8 *Web:* www.radiomonterey.com	Sand City	CA	93955	831-394-5792		647
Kryptonite Kollectibles	1441 Plainfield Ave *TF:* 877-646-1728 ■ *Web:* kryptonitekollectibles.com	Janesville	WI	53545	608-758-2100		791
Krystal Klear Water Systems	10502 W 150th St *Web:* krystalklearh2o.com	Overland Park	KS	66221	913-558-1129		610

Name / Address	City	State	Zip	Phone	Fax	Class
Krystofiak & Associates Insur & Financial Services 50 Francisco St Ste 257 *Web:* prudential.com	San Francisco	CA	94133	415-291-0202		390
KRZR-FM 83 E Shaw Ave Ste 150 *Web:* powertalk967.iheart.com	Fresno	CA	93710	559-243-4300	243-4301	647
KS 107.5 4700 S Syracuse St Ste 1050 *Web:* ks1075.radio.com	Denver	CO	80237	303-967-2700		645
KS Energy Services LLC 19705 W Lincoln Ave *Web:* ksenergy.us	New Berlin	WI	53146	262-574-5100		261
KS Industries LP 6205 District Blvd *Web:* www.ksilp.com	Bakersfield	CA	93313	661-617-1700	617-1800	256
KS Kolbenschmidt U.S. Inc 1731 Industrial Pky *Web:* www.kspg.com	Marinette	WI	54143	715-732-0181	732-4163	128
KS Property Maintenance Inc 1166 Mckinley St *Web:* ksmanagementservices.com	Wyandotte	MI	48192	734-285-4442		422
KSA Engineers Inc 140 E Tyler St Ste 600 *TF:* 877-572-3647 ■ *Web:* www.ksaeng.com	Longview	TX	75601	903-236-7700	236-7779	261
KSAB-FM 501 Tupper Ln *Web:* ksabfm.iheart.com	Corpus Christi	TX	78417	360-289-0111		645-41
KSAS-TV Ch 24 (Fox) 316 NW St *Web:* foxkansas.com	Wichita	KS	67203	316-942-2424	942-8927	741-142
KSAX-TV 3415 University Ave *Web:* www.kstp.com	Saint Paul	MN	55114	651-646-5555		647
KSAZ-TV Ch 10 (Fox) 511 W Adams St *TF:* 888-369-4762 ■ *Web:* www.fox10phoenix.com	Phoenix	AZ	85003	602-257-1234		741-99
KSB SE & Co 4415 Sarellen Rd *Web:* www.ksb.com	Richmond	VA	23231	804-222-1818	226-6961	789
KSBI (Kobelco Stewart Bolling Inc) 1600 Terex Rd *TF:* 800-464-0064 ■ *Web:* www.ksbiusa.com	Hudson	OH	44236	330-655-3111		386
KSBJ Educational Foundation Inc 1722 Treblo Dr *Web:* www.ksbj.org	Humble	TX	77338	281-446-5725		116
KSBW-TV Ch 8 (NBC) 238 John St *Web:* www.ksbw.com	Salinas	CA	93901	831-758-8888	424-3750	741
Ksby-Tv 1772 Calle Joaquin *Web:* www.ksby.com	San Luis Obispo	CA	93405	805-541-6666		116
KSC Inc 40 Sarasota Center Blvd Ste 107 *Web:* kscadvpr.com	Sarasota	FL	34241	941-906-1555	906-1556	4
KSCE-TV 2201 E Wyoming Ave *Web:* lifechristian.tv	El Paso	TX	79903	915-585-8838		647
KSCJ-AM 2000 Indian Hills Dr *Web:* www.kscj.com	Sioux City	IA	51104	712-239-2101	239-3346	647
KSD Inc 161 W Lincoln St *Web:* www.ksdinc.net	Banning	CA	92220	951-849-7669	849-5913	454
KSDK-TV Ch 5 (NBC) 1000 Market St *Web:* www.ksdk.com	Saint Louis	MO	63101	314-444-5219	425-5348	741-114
KSDM-FM 519 3rd St *Web:* n.rjbroadcasting.com	International Falls	MN	56649	218-283-2622	283-3087	647
KSEM-FM 105 NW 11th St *Web:* www.kikzksem.com	Seminole	TX	79360	432-758-5879	758-5474	647
KSEV-AM 700 (N/T) 11451 Katy Fwy Ste 215 *Web:* www.ksevradio.com	Houston	TX	77079	281-588-4800		645-72
KSFO-AM 750 Battery St Ste 300 *TF:* 877-381-3811 ■ *Web:* www.ksfo.com	San Francisco	CA	94105	415-808-5600		647
KSGF 104.1 2330 W Grand St *Web:* springfieldadvertisingworks.com	Springfield	MO	65802	417-447-1821	865-9643	647
KSGN-FM 89.7 (Rel) 2048 Orange Tree Ln Ste 200 *TF:* 888-897-5746 ■ *Web:* www.ksgn.com	Redlands	CA	92374	909-583-2150	583-2170	645-130
KSHE 95 11647 Olive Blvd *TF:* 800-842-5743 ■ *Web:* www.kshe95.com	Saint Louis	MO	63141	314-621-0095		647
KSHK-FM 4271 Halenani St *Web:* www.shaka103.com	Lihue	HI	96766	808-245-9527		647
KSIB-AM 1409 Hwy 34 W PO Box 426 *Web:* www.ksibradio.com	Creston	IA	50801	641-782-2155	782-6963	647
KSIM-AM 324 Broadway *Web:* www.kzimksim.com	Cape Girardeau	MO	63701	573-335-8291		647
KSIR-AM 220 State St Ste 106 PO Box 917 *TF:* 888-556-5747 ■ *Web:* www.ksir.com	Fort Morgan	CO	80701	970-867-7271		647
KSIS-AM 2209 S Limit *TF:* 800-748-8354 ■ *Web:* www.ksisradio.com	Sedalia	MO	65301	660-826-1050	827-5072	647
KSJK-AM 1250 Siskiyou Blvd *TF:* 800-782-6191 ■ *Web:* www.ijpr.org	Ashland	OR	97520	541-552-6301		647
KSJX-AM 545 Parrott St *Web:* www.vienthao.com	San Jose	CA	95112	408-947-7517	947-0463	647
KSK Studios 307 W 38th St Ste 1201 *Web:* www.kskstudios.com	New York	NY	10018	212-481-3111	481-5404	637-10
KSKK-FM 11 SE Bryant Ave *Web:* www.kkradionetwork.com	Wadena	MN	56482	218-631-3441	631-3414	647
KSL (Kansas State Library) Capitol Bldg 300 SW 10th Ave Rm 312-N *TF:* 800-432-3919 ■ *Web:* www.kslib.info	Topeka	KS	66612	785-296-3296		637-10
KSL Media Inc 387 Park Ave S	New York	NY	10016	212-352-5800		195
KSL RADIO & TV 55 N 300 W *Web:* www.ksl.com	Salt Lake City	UT	84101	801-575-5555		645-139
KSL Resorts 50-905 Avenida Bermudas *Web:* www.kslresorts.com	La Quinta	CA	92253	760-564-8000		378
KSLA-TV Ch 12 (CBS) 1812 Fairfield Ave *TF:* 800-444-5752 ■ *Web:* www.ksla.com	Shreveport	LA	71101	318-222-1212	677-6703	741-124
KSLV-AM 109 Adams St PO Box 631 *Web:* www.kslvradio.com	Monte Vista	CO	81144	719-852-3581		647
KSLX-FM 100.7 (CR) 4343 E Camelback Rd Ste 200 *Web:* kslx.com	Phoenix	AZ	85018	602-260-1007		645-121
KSM Industries Inc N 115 W 19025 Edison Dr *Web:* www.ksmindustries.com	Germantown	WI	53022	262-251-9510	251-4865	697
KSM Technology Partners LLC 1010 Adams Ave Ste 200 *Web:* www.ksmpartners.com	Audubon	PA	19403	610-628-0550		177
KSMQ-TV Ch 15 (PBS) 2000 Eigth Ave NW *TF:* 800-658-2539 ■ *Web:* www.ksmq.org	Austin	MN	55912	507-481-2095		741
KSNA (Kansas State Nurses Assn) 1109 SW Topeka Blvd *Web:* www.ksnurses.com	Topeka	KS	66612	785-233-8638	233-5222	533
KSNH-FM 510 N Acoma Blvd *Web:* www.ksnh885.com	Lake Havasu City	AZ	86404	928-537-1111	453-8825	647
KSNQ-FM 415 Park Ave *Web:* www.983thesnake.com	Twin Falls	ID	83301	208-733-7512	737-6070	647
KSNT-TV Ch 27 (NBC) 6835 NW Hwy 24 *Web:* www.ksnt.com	Topeka	KS	66618	785-582-4000		741-135
KSOP Inc 1285 West 2320 South *Web:* www.cc1370.com	Salt Lake City	UT	84119	801-972-1370	974-0868	645-139
KSOP-FM 1285 W 2320 S *Web:* www.z104country.com	West Valley City	UT	84119	801-972-1043	974-0868	645-139
k-Space Associates Inc 2182 Bishop Cir E *Web:* www.k-space.com	Dexter	MI	48130	734-426-7977	426-7955	419
KSPS Public TV 3911 S Regal St *TF:* 800-735-2377 ■ *Web:* www.ksps.org	Spokane	WA	99223	509-443-7800		741-127
KSRZ-FM 10714 Mockingbird Dr *Web:* www.104star.com	Omaha	NE	68127	402-951-1045		647
KSSM-FM 108 East Ave E *Web:* www.mykiss1031.com	Copperas Cove	TX	76522	254-547-8889		647
KSSU-AM 6000 J St *Web:* www.kssu.com	Sacramento	CA	95819	916-278-3343		647
K-State Libraries 1117 Mid-Campus Dr N *Web:* www.lib.k-state.edu	Manhattan	KS	66506	785-532-6011		434-6
KSTC-TV 3415 University Ave *Web:* www.45tv.com	Saint Paul	MN	55114	651-645-4500		647
KSTF-TV 3385 N 10th St *Web:* www.msn.com	Gering	NE	69341	308-632-7535		647
KSTP-FM 3415 University Ave *Web:* www.ks95.com	Minneapolis	MN	55414	651-642-4267	647-2904	645-99
KSTU-TV Ch 13 (Fox) 5020 Amelia Earhart Dr *Web:* fox13now.com	Salt Lake City	UT	84116	801-536-1313		741-115
KSVP 317 W Quay Ave *Web:* www.ksvpradio.com	Artesia	NM	88210	575-746-2751	748-3748	647
KSWB-TV Ch 5 (Fox) 7191 Engineer Rd *Web:* www.fox5sandiego.com	San Diego	CA	92111	858-492-9269	268-0401	741-119
KSWO-TV 1401 SE 60th St *Web:* www.kswo.com	Lawton	OK	73501	580-355-6397	355-0059	647
K-Systems Inc 2104 Aspen Dr *TF:* 800-221-0204 ■ *Web:* www.ksystemsinc.com	Mechanicsburg	PA	17055	717-795-7711		178-1
KT (Kokomo Tribune) 300 N Union St PO Box 9014 *TF:* 800-382-0696 ■ *Web:* www.kokomotribune.com	Kokomo	IN	46901	765-459-3121	854-6733	532-2
KT Consulting Inc 4435 E Chandler Blvd *Web:* ktc-inc.com	Phoenix	AZ	85048	480-538-2668	538-2686	809
KT's Kitchens Inc 1065 E Walnut St Ste C *Web:* www.ktskitchens.com	Carson	CA	90746	310-764-0850	764-0855	296-19
KTA (Kansas Turnpike Authority) 9401 E Kellogg *Web:* www.ksturnpike.com	Wichita	KS	67207	316-682-4537		271
KTA Super Stores 321 Keawe St *Web:* www.ktasuperstores.com	Hilo	HI	96720	808-935-3751		345
KTAR-FM 98.7 7740 N 16th St Ste 200 *Web:* ktar.com	Phoenix	AZ	85020	602-274-6200		645-121
Kta-Tator Inc 115 Technology Dr *Web:* kta.com	Pittsburgh	PA	15275	800-245-6379		261
KTC Media Group 9891 Hamilton Ave *Web:* ktcmediagroup.com	Huntington Beach	CA	92646	714-378-1660		5
KTCK Sportsradio 1310 3090 Olive St W Victory Plz Ste 400 *TF:* 888-787-1310 ■ *Web:* www.theticket.com	Dallas	TX	75219	214-526-2400	525-2525	647
KTCS-FM 99.9 (Ctry) 5304 Hwy 45 E *Web:* www.ktcs.com	Fort Smith	AR	72916	479-646-6151		645-59
K-Tech Aviation Inc 6001 S Wilmot Rd *Web:* www.k-techav.com	Tucson	AZ	85756	520-747-4417	745-6139	20
KTED-FM 145 S Durbin St Ste 303 *Web:* www.kted1005.com	Casper	WY	82601	307-232-1005		647
KTEK-AM 6161 Savoy No 1200 *Web:* www.business1110ktek.com	Houston	TX	77036	713-979-2700		647
KTEL-AM 13 1/2 E Main St Ste 202 *Web:* www.mycolumbiabasin.com	Walla Walla	WA	99362	509-522-1383		647
KTEN-TV Ten Highpoint Cir *TF:* 800-375-5836 ■ *Web:* www.kten.com	Denison	TX	75020	903-337-4000	465-1368	647
KTEP-FM 88.5 (NPR) 500 W University Ave Cotton Memorial Bldg Ste 203 *Web:* ktep.org	El Paso	TX	79968	915-747-5152		645-52
KTFX-FM 501 N Main St Ste 4 *Web:* www.okiecountry1017.com	Muskogee	OK	74401	918-684-1022	686-6159	643
KTGA-FM PO Box 990 *Web:* www.bigfoot99.com	Saratoga	WY	82331	307-326-8642	326-8340	647
Kth Parts Industries Inc 1111 State Rte 235 N *Web:* kth.net	Saint Paris	OH	43072	937-663-5941	663-4996	60
KTHS-AM 1 Radio Dr *Web:* www.kthsradio.com	Berryville	AR	72616	870-423-2147		647
KTHT-FM 1990 Post Oak Blvd Ste 2300 *TF:* 844-892-5971 ■ *Web:* www.countrylegends971.com	Houston	TX	77056	713-963-1200	622-5457	645-72
KTHV-TV Ch 11 (CBS) 720 S Izard St *Web:* www.thv11.com	Little Rock	AR	72201	501-376-1111		741-75
Kti Kanatek Technologies Inc 359 Terry Fox Dr Ste 230 *TF:* 800-526-2821 ■ *Web:* www.kanatek.com	Kanata	ON	K2K2E7	613-591-1482		180
KTIS-FM 3003 Snelling Ave N *Web:* www.myktis.com	Saint Paul	MN	55113	651-631-5000		647

Name / Address	City	State	ZIP	Phone	Fax	Class
KTIV-TV 3135 Floyd Blvd *Web:* www.ktiv.com	Sioux City	IA	51108	712-239-4100	239-2621	647
KTKZ - AM 1380 The Answer 1425 River Pk Dr Ste 520 *TF:* 888-923-1380 ■ *Web:* www.am1380theanswer.com	Sacramento	CA	95815	916-924-9435	924-1587	645-137
KTLA-TV Ch 5 (CW) 5800 W Sunset Blvd *Web:* ktla.com	Los Angeles	CA	90028	323-460-5500	460-5333	741-76
KTLN-TV 100 Pelican Way Ste E *Web:* www.ktln.tv	San Rafael	CA	94901	415-485-5856	256-9262	647
KTLT-FM 3280 Peachtree Rd Nw Ste 2300 *Web:* www.98theticket.com	Atlanta	GA	30305	940-855-6924	855-4041	647
KTLV-AM 3336 SE 67th St *Web:* www.ktlv1220.com	Oklahoma City	OK	73135	405-672-3886		647
KTM Supermarkets Inc 1115 W Chester Pk *Web:* shoprite.com	West Chester	PA	19382	610-696-4066		345
KTMD-TV Ch 47 (Tele) 1235 N Loop W Ste 125 *Web:* www.telemundohouston.com	Houston	TX	77008	713-974-4848		741-60
KTMF-TV 2200 Stephens Ave *Web:* www.abcfoxmontana.com	Missoula	MT	59801	406-542-8900		647
KTMW-TV PO Box 2630 *Web:* www.tv20.tv	Rancho Santa Fe	CA	92067	858-442-0900		647
KTMY-FM 107.1 (N/T) 3415 University Ave *Web:* www.mytalk1071.com	Saint Paul	MN	55114	651-642-4107	647-3901	645
KTNK-AM PO Box 606 *Web:* www.radioktnk.com	Lompoc	CA	93438	805-736-5656	735-6000	647
KTNV-TV Ch 13 (ABC) 3355 S Valley View Blvd *Web:* www.ktnv.com	Las Vegas	NV	89102	702-876-1313	876-2237	741-72
KTNW-TV PO Box 642530 *TF:* 800-922-4220 ■ *Web:* www.nwptv.org	Pullman	WA	99164	509-335-6588	335-3772	647
KTO (Korea Tourism Organization) 2 Executive Dr Ste 750 *Web:* english.visitkorea.or.kr	Fort Lee	NJ	07024	201-585-0909	585-9041	775
KTOE-AM 59346 Madison Ave *Web:* www.ktoe.com	Mankato	MN	56001	507-345-4537	345-5364	647
KTOO KTOO Public Media 360 Egan Dr *Web:* www.ktoo.org	Juneau	AK	99801	907-586-1670		647
KTOR-FM 1787 Esplanade Way *Web:* www.radiomexicana997.com	Yuba City	CA	95993	530-755-9997	466-2656	647
KTOX-AM 100 Balboa Pl *Web:* www.ktox1340.com	Needles	CA	92363	760-326-4500		647
KTOY-FM 615-618 Olive St *Web:* www.ktoy1047.com	Texarkana	TX	75501	903-793-4671		647
KTPI-FM 570 E Ave Q-9 *TF:* 866-790-1031 ■ *Web:* www.ktpifm.com	Palmdale	CA	93550	805-942-1121	723-5512	647
KTRE-TV 358 TV Rd *Web:* www.ktre.com	Pollok	TX	75969	936-853-5873	853-3084	647
KTRK-TV Ch 13 (ABC) 3310 Bissonnet St *Web:* abc13.com	Houston	TX	77005	713-666-0713		741-60
KTRS-AM 550 (N/T) 638 Westport Plz *TF:* 888-550-5877 ■ *Web:* www.ktrs.com	Saint Louis	MO	63146	314-453-5500	453-9704	645-138
KTSA-AM 550 (N/T) 4050 Eisenhauer Rd *Web:* www.ktsa.com	San Antonio	TX	78218	210-654-5100		645-140
KTSF-TV Ch 26 (Ind) 100 Valley Dr *Web:* www.ktsf.com	Brisbane	CA	94005	415-468-2626	467-7559	741
KTSM-AM 690 (N/T) 4045 N Mesa *Web:* ktsmradio.iheart.com	El Paso	TX	79902	915-351-5400		645-52
KTSR-FM 900 N Lakeshore Dr *Web:* www.kissfm921.com	Lake Charles	LA	70601	337-433-1641		647
KTSS-TV 219 W 23rd St	Hope	AR	71801	870-777-1673		647
KTTC-TV Ch 10 (NBC) 6301 Bandel Rd NW *TF:* 800-288-1656 ■ *Web:* www.kttc.com	Rochester	MN	55901	507-288-4444	288-6324	741-110
KTTS-FM 94.7 (Ctry) 2330 W Grand St *Web:* www.ktts.com	Springfield	MO	65802	417-865-6614	865-9643	645-153
KTTW-TV Ch 7 (Fox) 2817 W 11th St *Web:* www.kttw.com	Sioux Falls	SD	57104	605-338-0017	338-7173	741-125
KTTZ-TV *Texas Tech University* 17th & Indiana *Web:* www.kttz.org	Lubbock	TX	79409	806-742-2209	742-1274	741-78
K-Tube Technologies 13400 Kirkham Way *TF:* 800-394-0058 ■ *Web:* www.k-tube.com	Poway	CA	92064	858-513-9229	513-9459	477
KTUL-TV Ch 8 (ABC) PO Box 8 *Web:* www.ktul.com	Tulsa	OK	74101	918-445-8888	445-9354	741-138
KTUU-TV 501 E 40th Ave *Web:* www.ktuu.com	Anchorage	AK	99503	907-762-9202	561-0874	741-5
KTVA-TV Ch 11 (CBS) 1001 Northway Dr St 202 *TF:* 800-408-3178 ■ *Web:* www.ktva.com	Anchorage	AK	99508	907-274-1111	334-9427	741-5
KTVB-TV Ch 7 (NBC) 5407 Fairview *TF:* 800-537-8939 ■ *Web:* www.ktvb.com	Boise	ID	83706	208-375-7277		741-17
KTVE-TV 200 Pavilion Rd *Web:* www.myarklamiss.com	West Monroe	LA	71292	318-323-1972	322-0926	647
KTVF-TV Ch 11 (NBC) 3650 Braddock St *Web:* www.webcenter11.com	Fairbanks	AK	99701	907-458-1800	458-1820	741-47
KTVH 100 W Lyndale Ave Ste A *Web:* www.ktvh.com	Helena	MT	59601	406-457-1212		741-58
KTVK-TV Ch 3 (Ind) 5555 N Seventh Ave *Web:* www.azfamily.com	Phoenix	AZ	85013	602-207-3333	207-3477	741-99
KTVL-TV 1440 Rossanley Dr PO Box 10 *Web:* www.ktvl.com	Medford	OR	97501	541-773-7373	779-0451	647
KTVN-TV Ch 2 (CBS) 4925 Energy Way *Web:* www.ktvn.com	Reno	NV	89502	775-858-2222	861-4298	741-107
KTVO-TV 15518 US Highway 63 N PO Box 949 *Web:* www.ktvo.com	Kirksville	MO	63501	660-627-3333	627-1885	647
KTVQ-TV Ch 2 (CBS) 3203 Third Ave N *Web:* www.ktvq.com	Billings	MT	59101	406-252-5611	252-9938	741-14
KTVU-TV Ch 2 (Fox) 2 Jack London Sq *Web:* www.ktvu.com	Oakland	CA	94607	510-834-1212		741
KTVZ-TV 62990 O B Riley Rd *Web:* www.ktvz.com	Bend	OR	97701	541-383-2121	382-1616	647
KTWB-FM 101.9 (Ctry) 500 S Phillips Ave *Web:* ktwb.com	Sioux Falls	SD	57104	605-331-5350	336-0415	645-149
KTWO-TV 1856 Skyview Dr *Web:* www.k2tv.com	Casper	WY	82601	307-237-3711	234-9866	741-22
KTWU-TV Ch 11 (PBS) 1700 College *TF:* 800-866-5898 ■ *Web:* ktwu.org	Topeka	KS	66621	785-670-1111	670-1112	741-135
KTWV-FM 5670 Wilshire Blvd Ste 200 *TF:* 800-520-9283	Los Angeles	CA	90036	323-937-9283	634-0947	647
KTXD-TV 15455 Dallas Pky Ste 100 *Web:* www.texas47.com	Addison	TX	75001	214-628-9900		647
KTXL-TV Ch 40 (Fox) 4655 Fruitridge Rd *Web:* www.fox40.com	Sacramento	CA	95820	916-454-4422		741-113
KTXR 101.3 The Outlaw 3000 E Chestnut Expy *TF:* 855-586-8852 ■ *Web:* 1013theoutlaw.com	Springfield	MO	65802	417-862-3751		645-153
KTXS-TV Ch 12 (ABC) 4420 N Clack St *Web:* ktxs.com	Abilene	TX	79601	325-677-2281		741-1
KTXX 912 S Capital of Texas Hwy Ste 400 *Web:* hornfm.com	Austin	TX	78746	512-804-1049		647
KUA (Kissimmee Utility Authority Inc) 1701 W Carroll St *TF:* 877-582-7700 ■ *Web:* www.kua.com	Kissimmee	FL	34741	407-933-7777		787
KUAC FM/TV PO Box 755620 *Web:* kuac.org	Fairbanks	AK	99775	907-474-7491	474-5064	632
KUAF 91.3 Public Radio 9 S School Ave *TF:* 800-522-5823 ■ *Web:* kuaf.com	Fayetteville	AR	72701	479-575-2556	575-8440	645
Kuakini Health System 347 N Kuakini St *Web:* www.kuakini.org	Honolulu	HI	96817	808-536-2236	547-9547	374-3
Kuali 3400 Ashton Blvd Ste 450 *Web:* kuali.co	Lehi	UT	84043	760-582-5401		177
KUAT-FM 90.5 (Clas) PO Box 210067 *Web:* about.azpm.org	Tucson	AZ	85721	520-621-1500	621-8136	645-165
KUBD-TV 2550 Denali St Ste 1000 *Web:* www.cbssoutheastak.com	Anchorage	AK	99503	907-868-5579		647
Kubera Partners LLC 1475 Franklin Ave *Web:* www.kuberapartners.com	Garden City	NY	11530	212-202-7657		401
Kuberre Systems Inc 805 Turnpark St *Web:* www.kudosedge.com	North Andover	MA	01845	978-203-0453		809
Kubert School, The 37 Myrtle Ave *Web:* www.kubertschool.edu	Dover	NJ	07801	973-361-1327	361-1844	685
Kubin-Nicholson (KN) 8440 N 87th St *TF:* 800-858-9557 ■ *Web:* www.kubin.com	Milwaukee	WI	53224	414-586-4300	586-6802	8
Kubisys 200 Wanaque Ave *Web:* www.kubisys.com	Pompton Lakes	NJ	07442	973-513-9350		41
KUBL-FM 93.3 (Ctry) 434 Bearcat Dr *Web:* www.kbull93.com	Salt Lake City	UT	84115	801-485-6700		645-139
Kubota Manufacturing of America Corp (KMA) 2715 Ramsey Rd Industrial Pk N *Web:* www.kubota-kma.com	Gainesville	GA	30501	770-532-0038	532-9057	274
Kubota Tractor Corp 3401 Del Amo Blvd *TF:* 888-458-2682 ■ *Web:* www.kubota.com	Torrance	CA	90503	310-370-3370		273
Kubotek USA 2 Mt Royal Ave Ste 500 *TF:* 800-372-3872 ■ *Web:* www.kubotek3d.com	Marlborough	MA	01752	508-229-2020	229-2121	178-5
KUBRA Data Transfer Ltd 5050 Tomken Rd *TF:* 800-766-6616 ■ *Web:* kubra.com	Mississauga	ON	L4W5B1	905-624-2220		177
Kucera International Inc 38133 Western Pkwy *Web:* www.kucerainternational.com	Willoughby	OH	44094	440-975-4230		13
Kuck Immigration Partners LLC 365 Northridge Rd Ste 300 *Web:* immigration.net	Atlanta	GA	30350	404-816-8611	816-8615	41
Kuck Mechanical Contractors Inc 395 W 67th St PO Box 388 *Web:* www.kuckmechanical.com	Loveland	CO	80538	970-461-3553		610
Kucker & Bruh LLP 747 Third Ave *Web:* kbllp.com	New York	NY	10017	212-869-5030		445
KUCR-FM 88.3 (Var) University of California *Web:* kucr.org	Riverside	CA	92521	951-827-3737	827-3240	645-130
KUCW-TV 2175 W 1700 S *Web:* www.abc4.com	Salt Lake City	UT	84104	801-975-4444	975-4440	647
Kuczmarski & Assoc 2001 N Halsted Ste 201 *Web:* www.kuczmarski.com	Chicago	IL	60614	312-988-1539		195
KUED-TV Ch 7 (PBS) 101 Wasatch Dr Rm 215 *TF:* 800-477-5833 ■ *Web:* www.kued.org	Salt Lake City	UT	84112	801-581-7777	585-5096	741-115
Kuehn Motor Inc 5020 Hwy 52 *TF:* 800-657-3208 ■ *Web:* www.kuehnmotors.com	Rochester	MN	55901	800-657-3208		57
KUEHNE + NAGEL 10 Exchange Pl *Web:* www.kn-portal.com	Jersey City	NJ	07302	201-413-5500	413-5777	449
KUER-FM 90.1 (NPR) 101 S Wasatch Dr *Web:* kuer.org	Salt Lake City	UT	84112	801-581-6625		645-139
Kuert Concrete Inc 3402 Lincoln Way W *Web:* www.kuert.com	South Bend	IN	46628	574-232-9911	232-9977	182
Kuest Corp PO Box 33007 *Web:* www.kuestcorp.com	San Antonio	TX	78265	210-655-1220		697
Kugler Co 209 W Third St PO Box 1748 *TF:* 800-445-9116 ■ *Web:* www.kuglercompany.com	McCook	NE	69001	308-345-2280	345-7756	276
KUGN-AM 590 (N/T) 1200 Executive Pkwy Ste 440 *TF:* 800-590-5846 ■ *Web:* www.kugn.com	Eugene	OR	97401	541-284-8500	485-0969	645-94
KUGR-AM 40 Shoshone *TF:* 800-254-5847 ■ *Web:* www.theradionetwork.net	Green River	WY	82935	307-875-6666		647

				Phone	Fax	Class
Kuhl Corp 39 Kuhl Rd PO Box 26 Web: www.kuhlcorp.com	Flemington	NJ	08822	908-782-5696	782-2751	298
Kuhl Insurance Agency Inc 632 W Jefferson St Web: kuhlinsurance.com	Morton	IL	61550	309-266-7300		390
Kuhl, Phillips, & Jans Inc 2401 Coral Ct Ste 2 Web: taxforu.com	Coralville	IA	52241	319-545-2215		2
Kuhlman Corp 1845 Indian Woods Cir TF: 800-669-3309 ■ Web: www.kuhlman-corp.com	Maumee	OH	43537	419-897-6000	897-6061	182
Kuhlman Inc N 56 W 16865 Ridgewood Dr Web: www.kuhlmaninc.com	Menomonee Falls	WI	53051	262-252-9400		189-10
Kuhlmann Design Group (KDGI) 2043 Woodland Pkwy Web: kdginc.com	Saint Louis	MO	63146	314-434-8898		261
Kuhn & Company CPAS 1730 Park St Ste 206 Web: kuhnandcompany.com	Naperville	IL	60563	630-416-7700	416-7717	2
Kuhn Flowers Inc 3802 Beach Blvd TF: 800-458-5846 ■ Web: www.kuhnflowers.com	Jacksonville	FL	32207	904-398-8601		292
Kuhn Knight Inc 1501 W 7th Ave PO Box 167 Web: www.kuhnnorthamerica.com	Brodhead	WI	53520	608-897-2131	897-2561	273
Kuhn Ltd 1733 W Third Ave Web: kuhnlimited.com	Columbus	OH	43212	614-481-3737		41
Kuhn Rikon Corp 16 Digital Dr Ste 220 Web: ch.kuhnrikon.com	Novato	CA	94949	415-883-1101	883-5985	362
Kuhns Brothers Securities Corp he Farm House 558 Lime Rock Rd Web: www.kuhnsbrothers.com	Lakeville	CT	06039	860-435-7000		401
Kuka Assembly & Test 5675 Dixie Hwy Web: www.kuka-at.com	Saginaw	MI	48601	989-777-2111		248
Kuka Systems Corporation North America LLC 6600 Center Dr Web: www.kuka.com	Sterling Heights	MI	48312	586-795-2000		494
KUKC-TV 5400 Antioch Dr Web: www.dlatinos.com	Mission	KS	66202	816-556-3900	556-3920	647
Kula Farm Flowers 1181 Pulehuiki Rd Web: www.kulafarm.com	Kula	HI	96790	502-383-9915		293
Kula Hospital 100 Keokea Pl TF: 800-845-6733 ■ Web: www.mauihealth.org	Kula	HI	96790	808-878-1221		450
Kulicke & Soffa Industries Inc 1005 Virginia Dr NASDAQ: KLIC ■ Web: www.kns.com	Fort Washington	PA	19034	215-784-6000	784-6001	695
Kulite Semiconductor Products Inc 1 Willow Tree Rd Web: www.kulite.com	Leonia	NJ	07605	201-461-0900	461-0990	472
Kuljian Corp 1880 JF Kennedy Blvd Web: www.kuljian.com	Philadelphia	PA	19103	215-243-1900	243-1942	261
Kulla, Ronnau, Schaub & Chambers Pc 2210 NE 22nd St Web: lincolncityattorneys.com	Lincoln City	OR	97367	541-996-2195		41
KULL-FM 92.5 (Oldies) 3911 S 1st Web: mix925abilene.com	Abilene	TX	79605	325-676-7711		645-1
KULR-TV Ch 8 (NBC) 2045 Overland Ave Web: www.kulr8.com	Billings	MT	59102	406-656-8000	652-8207	741-14
Kultur International Films Ltd PO Box 755 TF: 888-329-2580 ■ Web: www.kulturvideo.com	Forked River	NJ	08731	888-329-2580		513
Kulzer LLC 4315 S Lafayette Blvd TF: 800-431-1785 ■ Web: www.kulzerus.com	South Bend	IN	46614	800-431-1785		228
Kumagoro Restaurant 533 W Fourth Ave Web: www.kumagoroak.com	Anchorage	AK	99501	907-272-9905		671
Kumar & Associates Inc 2390 S Lipan St Web: www.kumarusa.com	Denver	CO	80223	303-742-9700		261
Kumarian Press Inc 1800 30th St Ste 314 Web: www.rienner.com	Boulder	CO	80301	303-444-6684	444-0824	637-2
Kumbrabow State Forest PO Box 65 Web: wvstateparks.com	Huttonsville	WV	26273	304-335-2219		565
KUMD 1201 Ordean Ct 130 Humanities TF: 800-566-5863 ■ Web: www.kumd.org	Duluth	MN	55812	218-726-7181	726-6571	645-50
Kumon North America Inc 300 Frank W Burr Blvd Ste 6 TF: 800-222-6284 ■ Web: www.kumon.com	Teaneck	NJ	07666	201-928-0444	928-0044	148
Kunath Karren Rinne & Atkin LLC 1000 Second Ave Ste 4000 Web: kkra.com	Seattle	WA	98104	206-621-7400		405
Kunau Implement Co 420 W White St Web: www.kunauimplement.com	Preston	IA	52069	563-689-3311	689-4621	274
Kunkleman & Lucente PLLC 4500 Cameron Valley Pkwy Web: kululaw.com	Charlotte	NC	28211	704-626-6799		41
KUNM-FM 89.9 (NPR) 1University of New Mexico MSC 06 3520 TF: 877-277-4806 ■ Web: kunm.org	Albuquerque	NM	87131	505-277-4806	277-6393	645-4
Kuno Creative Group LLC 36901 American Wy Ste 2A TF: 800-303-0806 ■ Web: www.kunocreative.com	Avon	OH	44011	800-303-0806		4
KUNS-TV 140 4th Ave N Ste 340 Web: www.univisionseattle.com	Seattle	WA	98109	206-404-6684		647
Kuntz Electroplating Inc 851 Wilson Ave Web: www.kuntz.com	Kitchener	ON	N2C1J1	519-893-7680	893-5431	481
KUOO-FM Hwy 9 West PO Box 528 Web: www.kuooradio.com	Spirit Lake	IA	51360	712-336-5800	336-1634	647
KUOW-FM 94.9 (NPR) 4518 University Way NE Ste 310 TF: 800-289-5869 ■ Web: kuow.org	Seattle	WA	98105	206-543-2710	543-2720	645-147
KUPD-FM 97.9 (Rock) 1900 W Carmen St Web: 98kupd.com	Tempe	AZ	85283	480-838-0400		645
Kuperus Trucking Inc 2225 Center Industrial Ct TF: 800-669-2710 ■ Web: kuperustrucking.com	Jenison	MI	49428	800-669-2710		311

				Phone	Fax	Class
Kupferle Foundry Co, The 2511 N Ninth St Web: hydrants.com	Saint Louis	MO	63102	314-231-8738		789
KUPS-FM 1500 N Warner St	Tacoma	WA	98416	253-879-2415		647
Kurama Seafood & Steakhouse 3644 Chapel Hill Blvd Web: www.kuramadurham.com	Durham	NC	27707	919-489-2669	489-4400	671
Kuraray America Inc 2625 Bay Area Blvd Ste 600 TF: 800-423-9762 ■ Web: www.kuraray.us.com	Houston	TX	77058	800-423-9762		745-1
KURB-FM 98.5 700 Wellington Hills Rd Web: www.b98.com	Little Rock	AR	72211	501-401-0200		645-88
Kureha America Inc 420 Lexington Ave Ste 2510 Web: www.kureha.com	New York	NY	10170	212-867-7040		360-3
Kuriyama of America Inc 360 E State Pkwy TF: 800-800-0320 ■ Web: www.kuriyama.com	Schaumburg	IL	60173	847-755-0360	885-0996	191-2
Kurkin Forehand Brandes LLP 18851 NE 29th Ave Ste 303 Web: kfb-law.com	Aventura	FL	33180	305-929-8500	675-0564	41
KURL-AM 730 (Rel) 636 Haugen St Web: www.kurlradio.com	Billings	MT	59101	406-245-3121	245-0822	645-18
Kurlan & Associates Inc 114 Turnpike Rd Web: www.kurlanassociates.com	Westborough	MA	01581	508-389-9350		194
Kurman Communications Inc 345 N Canal St Ste 1404 Web: kurman.com	Chicago	IL	60606	312-651-9000	651-9006	636
KURS-AM PO Box 471 Web: www.elsembradorministries.com	San Fernando	CA	91341	818-700-4938		647
Kurt A. Holmes PA 445 N Waco Ave Web: kaholmeslaw.com	Wichita	KS	67202	316-267-6711		41
Kurt E. Vragel Jr P C 1701 E Lake Ave Ste 170 Web: kevtrucks.com	Glenview	IL	60025	847-657-8551		41
Kurt J. Lesker Co 1925 Rt 51 TF: 800-245-1656 ■ Web: www.lesker.com	Jefferson Hills	PA	15025	800-245-1656		419
Kurt Manufacturing Co 5280 Main St NE TF: 800-458-7855 ■ Web: www.kurt.com	Minneapolis	MN	55421	763-572-1500		454
Kurt Orban Partners LLC 111 Anza Blvd Ste 350 Web: www.kurtorbanpartners.com	Burlingame	CA	94010	650-579-3959		360-3
Kurt S. Adler Inc 122 E 42nd St Web: www.kurtadlor.com	New York	NY	10168	212-924-0900		328
Kurt Versen Co 1 Paragon Dr Ste 157 Web: kurtversen.com	Montvale	NJ	07645	201-664-5283	664-4801	439
Kurt Weiss Greenhouses Inc 95 Main St Web: www.kurtweiss.com	Center Moriches	NY	11934	631-878-2500		369
Kurtz Bros Company Inc 400 Reed St PO Box 392 TF: 800-252-3811 ■ Web: www.kurtzbros.com	Clearfield	PA	16830	814-765-6561	765-8690	86
Kurtzon Lighting Inc 1420 S Talman Ave TF: 800-837-8937 ■ Web: www.kurtzon.com	Chicago	IL	60608	773-277-2121		439
Kuruma Zushi 7 E 47th St 2nd Fl Web: www.kurumazushi.com	New York	NY	10017	212-317-2802	317-2803	671
KURY-FM 605 Railroad St Web: www.kuryradio.com	Brookings	OR	97415	541-469-2111		647
Kurz Industrial Solutions 1325 McMahon Dr TF: 800-776-3629 ■ Web: www.kurz.com	Neenah	WI	54956	920-886-8200	886-8201	709
Kurz Instruments Inc 2411 Garden Rd TF: 800-424-7356 ■ Web: www.kurzinstruments.com	Monterey	CA	93940	831-646-5911	646-8901	201
Kurz Transfer Products Lp 3200 Woodpark Blvd Web: www.kurzusa.com	Charlotte	NC	28206	704-927-3700		658
Kurz-Kasch Inc 199 E State St Web: www.kurz-kasch.com	Newcomerstown	OH	43832	740-498-8343	498-6747	596
KUSA-TV Ch 9 (NBC) 500 Speer Blvd Web: www.9news.com	Denver	CO	80203	303-871-9999		741-39
KUSC 1149 S Hill St Ste H100 PO Box 7913 TF: 800-421-5872 ■ Web: www.kusc.org	Los Angeles	CA	90015	213-225-7400	225-7410	645-42
Kusel Equipment Co 820 W St Web: www.kuselequipment.com	Watertown	WI	53094	920-261-4112		429
Kushner Electroplating School 1170 Hawk Cir Web: www.platingschool.com	Anaheim	CA	92807	714-630-0965	632-1056	685
Kushner La Graize LLC 3330 W Esplanade Ave S Ste 100 Web: www.kl-cpa.com	Metairie	LA	70002	504-838-9991	833-7971	2
Kushnick Pallaci PLLC 630 Johnson Ave Ste 201 TF: 888-587-4529 ■ Web: nyconstructionlaw.com	Bohemia	NY	11716	631-752-7100	752-3654	41
KUSI-TV Ch 51 (Ind) 4575 Viewridge Ave Web: www.kusi.com	San Diego	CA	92123	858-571-5151	571-5711	741-119
KUSM-TV Ch 9 (PBS) Visual Communications Bldg Rm 183 TF: 800-426-8243 ■ Web: www.montanapbs.org	Bozeman	MT	59717	406-994-3437	994-6545	741
Kussmaul Electronics Company Inc 170 Cherry Ave TF: 800-346-0857 ■ Web: www.kussmaul.com	West Sayville	NY	11796	631-567-0314		256
Kuster Ann (Rep D - NH) 320 Cannon House Office Bldg Web: www.kuster.house.gov	Washington	DC	20515	202-225-5206	225-2946	342-2
Kustera Projects Red Hook 57 Wolcott St Web: annakustera.com	New York	NY	11231	212-989-0082		42
Kustoff David (Rep R - TN) 523 Cannon House Office Bldg Web: kustoff.house.gov	Washington	DC	20515	202-225-4714		342-2
Kustom Fit/Hi-Tech Seating 8990 Atlantic Ave TF: 800-624-6254 ■ Web: www.kustomfit.com	South Gate	CA	90280	323-564-4481		689

Name / Address	City	State	ZIP	Phone	Fax	Class
Kustom US 265 Hunt Park Ct *TF:* 866-679-0699 ■ *Web:* kustom.us	Longwood	FL	32750	866-679-0699		186
Kutak Rock LLP 1650 Farnam St *Web:* www.kutakrock.com	Omaha	NE	68102	402-346-6000	346-1148	428
Kutchins, Robbins, & Diamond Ltd 1101 Perimter Dr Ste 760 *Web:* www.krdcpas.com	Schaumburg	IL	60173	847-240-1040		2
KUT-FM 90.5 (NPR) 300 W Dean Keeton *Web:* kut.org	Austin	TX	78712	512-471-1631	471-3700	645-13
Kutir 37600 Central Ct Ste 280 *Web:* www.kutirtech.com	Newark	CA	94560	510-402-4526		180
Kutta Technologies Inc 2075 W Pinnacle Peak Rd Ste 102 *TF:* 866-574-9990 ■ *Web:* kuttatech.com	Phoenix	AZ	85027	602-896-1976		261
KUTU-TV 5101 S Shields *Web:* www.unidosok.com	Oklahoma City	OK	73129	405-429-5006		647
Kutztown University 15200 Kutztown Rd *TF:* 877-628-1915 ■ *Web:* kutztown.edu	Kutztown	PA	19530	610-683-4000	683-1375	166
Kuukpik Corp PO Box 89187 *TF:* 866-480-6220 ■ *Web:* www.kuukpik.com	Nuiqsut	AK	99789	907-480-6220		345
KUVI-TV Ch 45 5801 Truxtun Ave *Web:* www.45kuvi.com	Bakersfield	CA	93309	661-334-2600		741-10
KUVO-FM 89.3 (Jazz) 2900 Welton St Ste 200 *TF:* 800-574-5886 ■ *Web:* kuvo.org	Denver	CO	80205	303-480-9272		645-46
KUVR-AM 1007 Plum Creek Pkwy PO Box 880 *Web:* www.kuvr.com	Lexington	NE	68850	308-995-2202		647
Kuwait Parker Plaza 400 Kelby St 18th Fl *Web:* www.kuwaitmission.com	Fort Lee	NJ	07024	212-973-4300		784
Kuwait Airways Oasis Club 400 Kelby St Ste 41 *TF:* 800-458-9248 ■ *Web:* www.kuwaitairways.com	Fort Lee	NJ	07024	201-582-9222		26
Kuwait Embassy 2940 Tilden St NW *Web:* www.kuwaitembassy.us	Washington	DC	20008	202-966-0702	966-0517	257
Kuyper College 3333 E Beltline Ave NE *TF:* 800-511-3749 ■ *Web:* www.kuyper.edu	Grand Rapids	MI	49525	616-222-3000	222-3045	161
Kuzmich Law Firm Pc 335 W Main St *Web:* kuzmichlaw.com	Lewisville	TX	75057	972-434-1555		428
KUZZ AM 55 FM 107.9 3223 Sillect Ave *Web:* www.kuzz.com	Bakersfield	CA	93308	661-326-1011	328-7503	645-14
KVAL Inc 825 Petaluma Blvd So *TF:* 800-553-5825 ■ *Web:* www.kvalinc.com	Petaluma	CA	94952	707-762-4363	762-0621	821
KVAL-TV 4575 Blanton Rd *Web:* www.kval.com	Eugene	OR	97405	541-342-4961	342-2635	741-45
K-VA-T Food Stores Inc PO Box 1158 *TF:* 800-826-8451 ■ *Web:* www.foodcity.com	Abingdon	VA	24212	276-623-5100		345
KVCI (Kansas Venture Capital Inc) 40 Corporate Woods 9401 Indian Creek Pkwy Ste 200 *Web:* kvci.com	Leawood	KS	66224	913-262-7117	262-3509	402
KVCR-FM 91.9 (NPR) 701 S Mt Vernon Ave *Web:* www.empirenetwork.org	San Bernardino	CA	92410	909-384-4444	885-2116	645-130
KVCW-TV 1500 Foremaster Ln *Web:* www.cwlasvegas.com	Las Vegas	NV	89101	702-382-2121	952-4676	647
KVEG-FM 97.5 3999 Las Vegas Blvd S Ste K *Web:* www.kvegas.com	Las Vegas	NV	89119	702-736-6161	736-2986	645-85
KVGB-AM 1200 Baker St PO Box 609 *Web:* www.greatbendpost.com	Great Bend	KS	67530	620-792-3647	792-3649	647
KVH Industries Inc 50 Enterprise Ctr *NASDAQ: KVHI* ■ *Web:* www.kvh.com	Middletown	RI	02842	401-847-3327	849-0045	529
KVIA-TV Ch 7 (ABC) 4140 Rio Bravo St *Web:* www.kvia.com	El Paso	TX	79902	915-496-7777	532-0505	741-43
K-Video & Web Productions 212 Potomac Rd *Web:* kvideo.com	Wilmington	DE	19803	302-377-9936		514
KVIE-TV Ch 6 (PBS) 2030 W El Camino Ave *TF:* 800-347-5843 ■ *Web:* www.kvie.org	Sacramento	CA	95833	916-929-5843		741-113
KVII-TV 1 Broadcast Ctr *Web:* www.connectamarillo.com	Amarillo	TX	79101	806-373-1787		647
KVJM-FM 1716 Briarcrest Dr Ste 150 *Web:* www.kissfm1031.iheart.com	Bryan	TX	77802	979-846-5597		647
KVK-TECH Inc 110 Terry Dr Ste 200 *Web:* www.kvktech.com	Newtown	PA	18940	215-579-1842		231
KVLC-FM 101.1 (Oldies) 101 Perkins Dr *TF:* 877-527-1011 ■ *Web:* www.101gold.com	Las Cruces	NM	88005	575-527-1111		645
KVLY-TV Ch 11 (NBC) 1350 21st Ave S *TF:* 800-450-5844 ■ *Web:* www.valleynewslive.com	Fargo	ND	58103	701-237-5211	232-0493	741-48
KVM Switches Online LLC 2655 Crescent Dr Unit B *TF:* 877-586-6654 ■ *Web:* www.kvm-switches-online.com	Lafayette	CO	80026	877-586-6654		459
KVMY-TV 1500 Foremaster Ln *Web:* mylvtv.com	Las Vegas	NV	89101	702-642-3333	657-3152	647
KVNA-AM 1800 S Milton Rd Ste 105 *Web:* www.myradioplace.com	Flagstaff	AZ	86001	928-526-2700		647
KVNS-AM 901 E Pike Blvd *Web:* www.foxsports1700.com	Weslaco	TX	78596	956-973-9202		647
KVNU-AM 810 W 200 N *TF:* 800-369-5868 ■ *Web:* www.610kvnu.com	Logan	UT	84321	435-752-5141		647
KVOA-TV Ch 4 (NBC) 209 W Elm PO Box 5188 *Web:* www.kvoa.com	Tucson	AZ	85705	520-792-2270	620-1309	741-137
KVOC-AM 1230 (Nost) 218 N Wolcott St PO Box 2515 *Web:* www.kvoc1230am.com	Casper	WY	82601	307-265-1984		645-27
KVOE-FM PO Box 968 *Web:* www.kvoe.com	Emporia	KS	66801	620-342-1400	342-0804	647
KVOK-AM 1315 Mill Bay Rd *Web:* www.kvok.com	Kodiak	AK	99615	907-486-5159	406-3044	647
KVOM-AM PO Box 541 *Web:* www.kvom.com	Morrilton	AR	72110	501-354-2484	354-5629	647
KVOR-AM 740 (N/T) 6805 Corporate Dr Ste 130 *Web:* www.kvor.com	Colorado Springs	CO	80919	719-540-0740		645-37
KVOX-FM 99.9 (Ctry) 1020 S 25th St *Web:* www.froggyweb.com	Fargo	ND	58103	701-241-9936		645-56
KVPI-AM PO Box J *Web:* www.kvpionline.com	Ville Platte	LA	70586	337-363-2124	363-3574	647
KVRV-FM 1410 Neotomas Ave Ste 200 *Web:* www.977theriver.com	Santa Rosa	CA	95405	707-636-0977	571-1097	647
KVS Information Systems Inc 821 Maple Rd *TF:* 866-777-0069 ■ *Web:* www.kvsinfo.com	Williamsville	NY	14221	716-626-1976		177
KVSV-AM 3185 US 24 Hwy PO Box 7 *Web:* www.kvsvradio.com	Beloit	KS	67420	785-738-2206	738-2208	647
KVTO-AM 256 Laguna Honda Blvd Ste B *Web:* www.kvto.net	San Francisco	CA	94116	415-566-8808	566-8901	647
KVUE-TV Ch 24 (ABC) 3201 Steck Ave *Web:* www.kvue.com	Austin	TX	78757	512-459-6521	533-2233	741-9
KVVU-TV Ch 5 (Fox) 25 TV 5 Dr *Web:* www.fox5vegas.com	Henderson	NV	89014	702-435-5555	451-4220	741
KVWC Inc 302 E Wilbarger St PO Box 1419 *Web:* www.kvwc.com	Vernon	TX	76384	940-552-6221		647
KW Automotive North America Inc 300 W Pontiac Way **Fax Area Code: 559* ■ *TF:* 800-445-3767 ■ *Web:* www.kwsuspensions.com	Clovis	CA	93612	800-445-3767	876-2259*	350
KW Brock Directories Inc 1225 E Centennial Dr *TF:* 800-592-7625 ■ *Web:* www.namesandnumbers.com	Pittsburg	KS	66762	620-231-4000		637-10
KW Engineering 287 17th St Ste 300 *Web:* www.kw-engineering.com	Oakland	CA	94612	510-834-6420		463
KW International Inc 18655 S Bishop Ave *Web:* www.kwinternational.com	Carson	CA	90746	310-354-6944		311
KW Property Management LLC 8200 NW 33rd St Ste 300 *Web:* kwpmc.com	Miami	FL	33122	305-476-9188		652
KWA (Keith D. Weiner & Associates Company LPA) 75 Public Sq Ste 400 *TF:* 866-368-6500 ■ *Web:* weinerlaw.com	Cleveland	OH	44113	216-771-6500	664-9830	445
KWAM-AM 990 (N/T) 5495 Murray Rd *Web:* www.kwam990.com	Memphis	TN	38119	901-261-4200		645-95
Kwame Building Group Inc, The 1204 Washington Ave 200 *Web:* kwamebuildinggroup.com	Saint Louis	MO	63103	314-862-5344		196
KWAY-AM 110 29th Ave SW *Web:* www.kwayradio.com	Waverly	IA	50677	319-352-3550	352-3601	647
KWBG-AM 724 Story St Ste 201 *Web:* www.kwbg.com	Boone	IA	50036	515-432-2046		647
KWBW-AM 825 N Main *Web:* www.bwradio.biz	Hutchinson	KS	67501	620-662-4486	662-5357	647
KWCC-TV 205 1st St PO Box 582 *Web:* www.ncwlife.com	Wenatchee	WA	98801	509-293-4403	423-7491	647
KWCO-FM 627 W Chickasha Ave	Chickasha	OK	73018	405-224-1560	702-9495	647
KWD Manufacturing Co 2230 W Southcross Blvd *Web:* www.kwdmfg.com	San Antonio	TX	78211	210-924-5999		470
KWEM-TV PO Box 1604 *Web:* www.tv31.wordpress.com	Stillwater	OK	74075	405-377-8831		647
KWES-TV PO Box 60150 *Web:* www.newswest9.com	Midland	TX	79711	432-567-9999	567-9994	647
KWET-TV 7403 N Kelley Ave *TF:* 800-879-6382 ■ *Web:* www.oeta.tv	Oklahoma City	OK	73111	405-848-8501	841-9252	647
KWEY-AM 10040 N Hwy 54 *Web:* www.kwey.com	Weatherford	OK	73096	580-772-5939	772-1590	647
KWFS-FM 2525 Kell Blvd Ste 200 *Web:* www.1023blakefm.com	Wichita Falls	TX	76308	940-763-1111		647
KWHB TV-47 2208 N Yellowood *TF:* 866-223-4584 ■ *Web:* kwhbtv47.com	Broken Arrow	OK	74012	918-254-4701	254-5614	741-138
KWHE-TV 14 1188 Bishop St Ste 502 *TF:* 800-218-1414 ■ *Web:* kwhetv14.com	Honolulu	HI	96813	808-538-1414	526-0326	741-59
KWHS-TV Chapel Hills Mall 1710 Briargate Blvd Ste 423 *Web:* www.chapelhillsmall.com	Colorado Springs	CO	80920	719-228-0651		647
KWIC-FM 99.3 (Oldies) 825 S Kansas Ave Ste 100 **Fax Area Code: 785* ■ *TF:* 844-366-8993 ■ *Web:* www.eagle993.com	Topeka	KS	66612	913-795-2665	272-6219*	645-162
Kwik Goal Ltd 140 Pacific Dr **Fax Area Code: 800* ■ *TF:* 800-531-4252 ■ *Web:* www.kwikgoal.com	Quakertown	PA	18951	215-536-2200	778-8869*	710
Kwik Industries Inc 4725 Nall Rd *TF:* 800-442-5368 ■ *Web:* kwikind.com	Dallas	TX	75244	972-458-9761	458-0948	152
Kwik Kafe Company Inc 204 Furnace St *TF:* 800-533-4066 ■ *Web:* www.kwikkafeco.com	Bluefield	VA	24605	276-322-4691		366
Kwik Kopy Corp 12715 Telge Rd *Web:* www.kwikkopy.com	Cypress	TX	77429	281-256-4100		627
Kwik Kopy Printing Canada Corp 1550-16th Ave Bldg D *Web:* kkpcanada.ca	Richmond Hill	ON	L4B3K9	416-798-7007		627
Kwik Lok Corp PO Box 9548 *TF:* 800-688-5945 ■ *Web:* www.kwiklok.com	Yakima	WA	98909	509-248-4770	457-6531	298
Kwik Trip Inc 1626 Oak St PO Box 2107 *TF:* 800-305-6666 ■ *Web:* www.kwiktrip.com	La Crosse	WI	54602	608-781-8988	781-7517	204
Kwik-Covers 811 Ridge Rd Ste 100 *TF:* 866-586-9620 ■ *Web:* kwikcovers.com	Webster	NY	14580	585-787-9620		362
Kwik-Wall Co 1010 E Edwards St *TF:* 800-280-5945 ■ *Web:* www.kwik-wall.com	Springfield	IL	62703	217-522-5553	522-1170	286
KWIN-FM 97.7 (CHR) 3127 Transworld Dr Ste 270 *Web:* www.kwin.com	Stockton	CA	95206	209-507-8500		645-156
KWJ Engineering Inc 8430 Central Ave Ste C *TF:* 800-472-6626 ■ *Web:* www.kwjengineering.com	Newark	CA	94560	510-794-4296	574-8341	692

Name / Address	City	State	ZIP	Phone	Fax	Class
KWJJ-FM 99.5 (Ctry) 0700 SW Bancroft St *Web:* thewolfonline.radio.com	Portland	OR	97239	503-733-9653		645-126
KWLM-AM 1340 N 7th St NW PO Box 838 *Web:* www.willmarradio.com	Willmar	MN	56201	320-235-1340		647
Kwm Gutterman 795 S Larkin Ave *TF:* 888-729-4290 ■ *Web:* kwmgutterman.com	Rockdale	IL	60436	815-725-9205		358
KWMU-FM 90.7 (NPR) 3651 Olive St *TF:* 866-240-5968 ■ *Web:* news.stlpublicradio.org	Saint Louis	MO	63108	314-516-5968		645-138
KWNO-AM 752 Bluffview Cir PO Box 767 *TF:* 800-584-6782 ■ *Web:* www.winonaradio.com	Winona	MN	55987	507-452-4000	452-9494	647
KWPC-AM 3218 Mulberry Ave *Web:* voiceofmuscatine.com	Muscatine	IA	52761	563-263-2442	263-9206	647
KWPZ-FM 1843 Front St *TF:* 888-298-1065 ■ *Web:* www.praise1065.com	Lynden	WA	98264	360-354-5596	354-7517	647
KWQC-TV 805 Brady St *Web:* www.kwqc.com	Davenport	IA	52803	563-383-7000	383-7131	647
KWRU-AM 1415 Fulton St *Web:* www.940espnfresno.com	Fresno	CA	93721	559-452-0940	452-0948	647
KWS Manufacturing Company Ltd 3041 Conveyor Dr *TF:* 800-543-6558 ■ *Web:* www.kwsmfg.com	Burleson	TX	76028	817-295-2247	447-8528	207
KWSP-FM 795 Buckley Rd Ste 2 *TF:* 877-945-3106 ■ *Web:* www.wild1061.com	San Luis Obispo	CA	93401	805-786-2570		647
KWTX-AM 314 W State Hwy 6 *Web:* www.newstalk1230.com	Waco	TX	76712	254-776-3900		647
KWTX-FM 2625 S Memorial Dr Ste A *Web:* www.975online.com	Tulsa	OK	74129	918-664-4581		647
KWTX-TV 6700 American Plz PO Box 2636 *TF:* 800-749-5957 ■ *Web:* www.kwtx.com	Waco	TX	76712	254-776-1330	751-1088	647
KWUR 90.3 FM One Brookings Dr CB 1205 *Web:* www.kwur.com	Saint Louis	MO	63130	314-935-5952	935-8833	643
KWVR-AM 220 W Main St *Web:* www.kwvrradio.net	Enterprise	OR	97828	541-426-4577		647
KWVT-TV 17980 Brown Rd *Web:* www.kwvtsalem.com	Dallas	OR	97338	503-930-7228		647
KWWL-TV Ch 7 (NBC) 500 E Fourth St *TF:* 800-947-7746 ■ *Web:* www.kwwl.com	Waterloo	IA	50703	319-291-1200		741
KWYR PO Box 491 *TF:* 800-388-5997 ■ *Web:* www.kwyr.com	Winner	SD	57580	605-842-3333	842-3875	645
KWYS-AM 15 Madison Ave PO Box 9 *Web:* www.kwys920.com	West Yellowstone	MT	59758	406-646-7361		647
KX Systems 555 Bryant St Ste 375 *Web:* kx.com	Palo Alto	CA	94301	650-798-5155		387
KX Technologies LLC 55 Railroad Ave *Web:* www.kxtech.com	West Haven	CT	06516	203-799-9000	799-7000	806
KXAN News 908 W Martin Luther King Jr Bl *Web:* www.kxan.com	Austin	TX	78701	512-476-3636		741-9
KXAS-TV Ch 5 (NBC) 4805 Amon Carter Blvd *TF:* 800-232-5927 ■ *Web:* www.nbcdfw.com	Fort Worth	TX	76155	214-303-5119		741-37
KXDD-FM 17 N 3rd St Ste 103 *Web:* www.1041kxdd.com	Yakima	WA	98901	509-248-2900	452-9661	647
KXDI-FM 127 1st St W *Web:* www.kxdiradio.com	Dickinson	ND	58601	701-483-5547	483-5548	647
KXFM-FM c/o Point Broadcasting Co 6922 Wildlife Rd	Malibu	CA	90265	805-925-2582		647
KXGN-TV Broadcasting Bldg 210 S Douglas *Web:* www.kxgn.com	Glendive	MT	59330	406-377-3377		647
KXIA-FM 123 W Main St *Web:* www.kixweb.com	Marshalltown	IA	50158	641-753-6101	752-7201	647
KXII-TV 4201 Texoma Pky *Web:* www.kxii.com	Sherman	TX	75090	903-892-8123	893-7858	647
KXIT-AM 323 Denver Ave *Web:* www.kxit.com	Dalhart	TX	79022	806-249-4747	249-0123	647
KXIX-FM 345 SW Cyber Dr No 101 *Web:* www.power94.fm	Bend	OR	97702	541-388-3300		647
KXJK-AM 501 E Broadway St PO Box 707 *TF:* 800-246-5955 ■ *Web:* www.kxjkkbfc.com	Forrest City	AR	72335	870-633-1252	633-1259	647
KXKC-FM 202 Galbert Rd *Web:* www.nashfm991.com	Lafayette	LA	70506	337-232-1311	233-3779	647
KXLA-TV 2323 Corinth Ave *Web:* www.kxlatv.com	Los Angeles	CA	90064	310-478-0055	478-8070	647
KXLF-TV Ch 4 (CBS) 1003 S Montana St *Web:* www.kxlf.com	Butte	MT	59701	406-496-8400	782-8906	741
KXLH-TV 100 W Lyndale PO Box 7479 *Web:* www.kxlh.com	Helena	MT	59601	406-422-1018		647
KXLM-FM 102.9 (Span) 200 S A St Ste 400 *Web:* www.radiolazer.com	Oxnard	CA	93031	805-240-2070	240-5960	645-116
KXLT-TV Ch 47 (Fox) 6301 Bandel Rd NW *Web:* www.myfox47.com	Rochester	MN	55901	507-252-4747	252-5050	741-110
KXMB-TV 1811 N 15th St *Web:* www.kxnet.com	Bismarck	ND	58501	701-223-9197	223-3320	647
KXMX-FM 333 S Kerr Blvd *Web:* www.kxmx.com	Sallisaw	OK	74955	918-790-4444	790-1052	647
KXNT 840 AM 7255 S Tenaya Way Ste 100 *Web:* lasvegas.cbslocal.com	Las Vegas	NV	89113	702-889-5100	889-7555	645-85
KXNW-TV 4201 N Shiloh Dr Ste 169 *Web:* www.5newsonline.com	Fayetteville	AR	72703	479-521-1330		647
KXOJ-FM 100.9 (Rel) 2448 E 81st St Ste 5500 *Web:* kxoj.com	Tulsa	OK	74137	918-492-2660		645-166
KXOQ-FM 932 Country Rd 448	Poplar Bluff	MO	63901	573-686-3700		647
KXPS-AM 75-153 Merle Dr *Web:* www.team1010.com	Palm Desert	CA	92211	760-440-8255		647
KXRA-AM 1312 Broadway St PO Box 69 *Web:* www.voiceofalexandria.com	Alexandria	MN	56308	320-763-3131	763-5641	647
KXRC-FM 1135 Main Ave *Web:* www.xrock105.com	Durango	CO	81301	970-259-1364		647
KXRO-AM 1308 Coolidge Rd *Web:* www.kxro.com	Aberdeen	WA	98520	360-533-1320		647
KXSC-FM 104.9 (Alt) 3607 Trousdale Pkwy *TF:* 888-966-5332 ■ *Web:* kxsc.org	Los Angeles	CA	90089	213-740-1483		645-143
KXTE-FM 107.5 (Alt) 7255 S Tenaya Way Ste 100 *Web:* x1075lasvegas.radio.com	Las Vegas	NV	89113	702-257-1075	889-7555	645-85
KXTV-TV 400 Broadway *Web:* www.news10.net	Sacramento	CA	95818	916-321-3300		647
KXTX-TV 1601 Elm St Ste 3838 *Web:* www.telemundodallas.com	Dallas	TX	75201	214-220-2000		647
KXUL-FM 120 Stubbs Hall	Monroe	LA	71209	318-342-5986		647
KXVO-TV Ch 15 (CW) 4625 Farnam St *Web:* cw15kxvo.com	Omaha	NE	68132	402-558-4200	554-4290	741-94
KXXO Mixx 96.1 PO Box 7937 *Web:* www.mixx96.com	Olympia	WA	98507	360-943-9937	352-3643	645
KY3 999 W Sunshine St *TF:* 888-476-6988 ■ *Web:* www.ky3.com	Springfield	MO	65807	417-268-3000		741-130
Ky-Ani Sun Inc 1070 Riverwalk Dr Ste 350 *Web:* www.kyani.com	Idaho Falls	ID	83402	208-529-9872		195
Kyanite Mining Corp 30 Willis Mtn Ln *Web:* www.kyanite.com	Dillwyn	VA	23936	434-983-2085		503-2
KYB America LLC 180 N Meadow Rd *Web:* www.kybfluidpower.com	Addison	IL	60101	630-620-5555	620-8133	61
KYCC-FM 90.1 9019 W Ln *TF:* 800-654-5254 ■ *Web:* www.kycc.com	Stockton	CA	95210	209-477-3690	477-2762	645-156
Kycon Inc 305 Digital Dr *Web:* kycon.com	Morgan Hill	CA	95037	408-494-0330		52
Kycul Services Inc 3615 Newburg Rd *TF:* 833-338-8205 ■ *Web:* kycul.org	Louisville	KY	40218	502-459-8023		219
KYD Inc 2949 Koapaka St *Web:* www.kydinc.com	Honolulu	HI	96819	808-836-3221	833-8995	65
KYE Systems Corp 1301 NW 84th Ave Ste 127 *Web:* us.geniusnet.com	Doral	FL	33126	305-460-0250	460-9251	173-1
Kyfi Inc 4300 Fern Valley Rd *Web:* www.kyfi.com	Louisville	KY	40219	502-810-9800		311
KYIS-FM 98.9 (AC) 4045 NW 64th St Ste 600 *Web:* www.kyis.com	Oklahoma City	OK	73116	405-848-0100		645-112
KYJK-FM 2620 Radio Way Ste B *Web:* jackfmmissoula.com	Missoula	MT	59808	406-721-6800		647
KYKN-AM 1430 (N/T) PO Box 1430 *Web:* www.kykn.com	Salem	OR	97308	503-390-3014	390-3728	645-126
KYKZ-FM 425 Broad St *TF:* 800-737-3696 ■ *Web:* www.kykz.com	Lake Charles	LA	70601	337-439-3300		647
Kyle Busch Motorsports Inc 351 Mazeppa Rd *Web:* kylebuschmotorsports.com	Mooresville	NC	28115	704-662-0000		642
Kyma Technologies Inc 8829 Midway W Rd *Web:* www.kymatech.com	Raleigh	NC	27617	919-789-8880		696
Kymera Intl 901 Lehigh Ave *TF:* 800-232-3198 ■ *Web:* kymerainternational.com	Union	NJ	07083	908-851-4500		492
KYMG-FM 800 E Diamond Blvd Ste 3-370 *Web:* www.magic989fm.com	Anchorage	AK	99515	907-743-0989	743-5183	647
KYMX-FM 280 Commerce Cir	Sacramento	CA	95815	916-766-5969		647
Kynikos Associates LP 20 W 55th St *Web:* www.kynikos.com	New York	NY	10019	212-649-0200	649-0269	41
Kyocera Communications Inc 9520 Towne Centre Dr *TF:* 800-349-4188 ■ *Web:* www.kyoceramobile.com	San Diego	CA	92121	858-882-1400		647
Kyocera Industrial Ceramics Corp 5713 E Fourth Plain Rd *TF:* 888-955-0800 ■ *Web:* americas.kyocera.com	Vancouver	WA	98661	360-696-8950	696-9804	249
Kyocera International Inc 8611 Balboa Ave *TF:* 877-248-4237 ■ *Web:* global.kyocera.com	San Diego	CA	92123	858-576-2600	569-9412	360-3
Kyocera Mita Corp 225 Sand Rd PO Box 40008 *Web:* www.kyoceradocumentsolutions.com	Fairfield	NJ	07004	973-808-8444		589
KYOCERA Precision Tools 3565 Cadillac Ave *TF:* 888-848-9266 ■ *Web:* www.kyoceraprecisiontools.com	Costa Mesa	CA	92626	714-428-3600	428-3605	455
Kyocera Solar Inc 7812 E Acoma Dr *TF:* 800-544-6466 ■ *Web:* www.kyocerasolar.com	Scottsdale	AZ	85260	480-948-8003	483-6431	696
Kyoei Electronics America Inc 39555 Orchard Hill Pl Ste 137 *Web:* www.kyoei.co.jp	Novi	MI	48375	248-773-3690	773-3563	246
Kyosan USA Inc 1141 Ringwood Ct Ste 170 *Web:* www.kyosan.co.jp	San Jose	CA	95131	408-432-6267		392
Kyoto Japanese Steak House & Sushi Bar 1412 Greenbrier Pkwy *Web:* kyotochesapeakeva.com	Chesapeake	VA	23320	757-420-0950		671
KYOU-TV 820 W 2nd St *Web:* www.kyoutv.com	Ottumwa	IA	52501	641-684-5415	684-4433	647
Kyo-Ya Company Ltd 2255 Kalakaua Ave 2nd Fl *Web:* www.kyoyahotelsandresorts.com	Honolulu	HI	96815	808-931-8600		378
Kyra InfoTech Inc 4454 Florida National Dr *TF:* 877-561-5972 ■ *Web:* www.kyrasolutions.com	Lakeland	FL	33813	863-686-2271		196
KYS 700 E Market St *Web:* kys.com	Jeffersonville	IN	47130	812-282-2660		90
Kysela Pere Et Fils Ltd 331 Victory Rd *Web:* www.kysela.com	Winchester	VA	22602	540-722-9228		80-3
Kysor Panel Systems 4201 N Beach St *TF:* 800-633-3426 ■ *Web:* kpsglobal.com	Fort Worth	TX	76137	817-281-5121		664
Kysor Warren Corp 5201 Transport Blvd *TF:* 800-866-5596 ■ *Web:* www.kysorwarren.com	Columbus	GA	31907	706-568-1514		610
KYTS-FM 1949 Mountain View Dr *Web:* www.mybighornbasin.com	Cody	WY	82414	307-578-5000		647

	Phone	Fax	Class
KYTX-TV CBS 19 2211 Ese Loop 323 Tyler TX 75701 *Web:* www.cbs19.tv	903-581-2211		116
KYW-NEWSRADIO 1060 (N/T) 1555 Hamilton St Philadelphia PA 19130 *TF:* 800-223-8477 ■ *Web:* philadelphia.cbslocal.com	215-977-5333	977-5658	645-120
KYXY-FM 96.5 (AC) 8033 Linda Vista Rd San Diego CA 92111 *Web:* kyxy.radio.com	858-571-7600		645-141
Kyyba Inc 28230 Orchard Lake Rd Ste 130 Farmington Hills MI 48334 *Web:* www.kyyba.com	248-813-9665	813-9668	177
KZBT-FM 11300 State Hwy 191 Bldg 2 Midland TX 79707 *Web:* www.b93.net	432-563-5636		647
KZF Design Inc 700 Broadway St Cincinnati OH 45202 *Web:* kzf.com	513-621-6211		256
KZIA-FM 102.9 (CHR) 1110 26th Ave SW Cedar Rapids IA 52404 *Web:* www.kzia.com	319-363-2061		645-28
KZKS-FM 751 Horizon Ct Ste 225 Grand Junction CO 81506 *Web:* www.wscradio.net	970-241-6460		647
KZMN-FM 317 First Ave E Kalispell MT 59901 *Web:* www.monster1039.com	406-755-6690		647
KZNS-AM 1280 (Sports) 301 W South Temple Salt Lake City UT 84101 *TF:* 855-340-9663 ■ *Web:* www.1280thezone.com	801-325-2043		645-139
KZNT-AM 1750 Campus Dr Ste 150 Colorado Springs CO 80920 *Web:* www.newstalk1460.com	719-388-0394		647
KZOR-FM 619 North Turner St Hobbs NM 88240 *Web:* www.1radiosquare.com	575-397-4941		647
KZPickles.com 134 Kaighn Ave Camden NJ 08101 *Web:* kzpickles.patriotpickle.com	856-964-1083		296-19
KZPR-FM 1000 20th Ave SW Minot ND 58701 *Web:* www.1053thefox.com	701-838-1369		647
KZSN-FM 9323 E 37th St N Wichita KS 67226 *Web:* www.1021thebull.com	316-436-1021	494-6730	647
KZTH-FM PO Box 14 Ponca City OK 74602 *TF:* 800-324-8488 ■ *Web:* www.thehousefm.com	580-767-1400	765-1700	647
KZTW-FM PO Box 13703 Grand Forks ND 58208 *TF:* 877-795-0122 ■ *Web:* www.yourcatholicradiostation.com	877-795-0122		647
KZXY-FM 12370 Hesperia Rd No 16 Victorville CA 92395 *Web:* www.y102fm.com	760-241-1313	241-0205	647
KZZU-FM 500 W Boone Ave Spokane WA 99201 *TF:* 866-845-0929 ■ *Web:* www.929zzu.com	509-324-4000		647

L

	Phone	Fax	Class
L & B Realty Advisors LLP 5910 N Central Expy Ste 1200 Dallas TX 75206 *Web:* lbrealty.com	214-989-0800		655
L & B Transport LLC 708 US190 PO Box 74870 Port Allen LA 70767 *TF:* 800-545-9401 ■ *Web:* www.landbtransport.com	225-387-0894		449
L & C Meat Inc 1136 S Vista Ave Independence MO 64056 *Web:* www.lcmeats.com	816-796-6100	796-6107	297-9
L & D Mail Masters Inc 110 Security Pkwy New Albany IN 47150 *Web:* www.ldmailmasters.com	812-981-7161	981-7169	5
L & E Meridian 8000 Corporate Ct Springfield VA 22153 *Web:* www2.l-e.com	703-913-0300		225
L & H Boats Inc 3350 SE Slater St Stuart FL 34997 *Web:* www.lhboats.com	772-288-2291		90
L & H Industrial 913 L J Ct Gillette WY 82718 *TF:* 844-431-2363 ■ *Web:* www.lnh.net	307-682-7238	686-1646	709
L & J Cafe 3622 E Missouri St El Paso TX 79903 *Web:* www.landjcafe.com	915-566-8418		671
L & L Hawaiian Barbecue 931 University Ave Stev202 Honolulu HI 96826 *Web:* www.hawaiianbarbecue.com	808-951-9888		670
L & L Industries Inc 500 Industrial Dr NE White GA 30184 *Web:* llind.com	770-382-2861	386-1545	697
L & L Insulation 5525 NE 22nd St Des Moines IA 50313 *TF:* 800-747-5385 ■ *Web:* www.llinsulation.com	515-246-2070	266-0054	191-4
L & L Nursery Supply Company Inc 2552 Shenandoah Way San Bernardino CA 92407 *TF:* 800-624-2517 ■ *Web:* www.llsupply.net	909-591-0461		293
L & L Products Inc 160 McLean Dr Romeo MI 48065 *Web:* www.llproducts.com	586-336-1700	336-1699	3
L & L Redi Mix 1939 Rt 206 Southampton NJ 08088 *Web:* www.llredimix.com	609-859-2271		182
L & L Wings Inc 301 S Kings Hwy 2nd Fl Myrtle Beach SC 29575 *Web:* wingsbeachwear.com	212-481-8299	481-8218	157-6
L & M Botruc Rental Inc 18692 W Main St Galliano LA 70354 *Web:* www.botruc.com	985-475-5733	475-5669	314
L & M Fabrication and Machine Inc 6814 Chrisphalt Dr Bath PA 18014 *Web:* lmfab.com	610-837-1848	837-9180	91
L & M Mail Service Inc 2452 Truax Blvd PO Box 805 Eau Claire WI 54703 *TF:* 800-507-7070 ■ *Web:* www.lmmailservice.com	715-836-0138	836-7636	5
L & M Office Furniture Inc 4444 S 91st E Ave Tulsa OK 74145 *Web:* www.l-mofficefurn.com	918-664-1010		321
L & M Radiator Inc 1414 E 37th St Hibbing MN 55746 *TF:* 800-346-3500 ■ *Web:* mesabi.com	218-263-8993		61
L & M Technologies Inc 4209 Balloon Park Rd NE Albuquerque NM 87109 *Web:* www.lmtechnologies.com	505-343-0200	343-0300	271
L & N Federal Credit Union 9265 Smyrna Pkwy Louisville KY 40229 *TF:* 800-443-2479 ■ *Web:* www.lnfcu.com	502-368-5858		219
L & R Construction Services 16749 Dixie Hwy Ste 9 Davisburg MI 48350 **Fax Area Code:* 248 ■ *TF:* 888-824-7165 ■ *Web:* www.lrconstruction.com	888-824-7165	634-9401*	186
L & R Manufacturing Co 577 Elm St Kearny NJ 07032 *Web:* www.lrultrasonics.com	201-991-5330	991-5870	782
L & R Security Services Inc 3930 Old Gentilly Rd New Orleans LA 70126 *Web:* www.lrsecurity.com	504-943-3191	944-1142	400
L & S Packing Company Inc 101 Central Ave PO Box 709 East Farmingdale NY 11735 *Web:* www.paesana.com	631-845-1717	845-1788	123
L & S Truck Center of Appleton Inc 330 N Bluemound Dr Appleton WI 54914 *Web:* www.lstruck.com	920-749-1700	749-0818	57
L & S Video 45 Stornowaye Chappaqua NY 10514 *Web:* www.landsvideo.com	914-238-9366	238-6324	797
L & W Engineering Inc 107 Industrial Pkwy Middlebury IN 46540 *Web:* www.lw-eng.com	574-825-5351		256
L & Z Tool and Engineering Inc 1691 Us Hwy 22 Watchung NJ 07069 *Web:* www.lztool.com	908-322-2220	322-3758	757
L A Party Rents Inc 13520 Saticoy St Van Nuys CA 91402 *Web:* lapartyrents.com	818-989-4300	989-3593	129
L A Tews Realty Inc 13011 Lazdins Cir Cypress TX 77429 *Web:* www.latews.com	281-807-3444		652
L B L Group 3631 S Harbor Blvd Ste 200 Santa Ana CA 92704 *TF:* 800-451-8037 ■ *Web:* www.lblgroup.com	800-451-8037		690
L B L Strategies 6321 N Avondale Ave Ste 214 Chicago IL 60631 *Web:* www.lblstrategies.com	773-774-0240		195
L B Plastics Inc 482 E Plaza Dr Mooresville NC 28115 *TF:* 800-752-7739 ■ *Web:* www.lbplastics.com	704-663-1543	664-2989	610
L B Property Management 4730 Woodman Ave Ste 200 Sherman Oaks CA 91423 *Web:* lbpm.com	818-981-1802		652
L Bornstein & Company Inc 321 Washington St Somerville MA 02143 *TF:* 800-842-1111 ■ *Web:* www.lbornstein.com	617-776-3555		361
L C Industries 1 Signature Dr Hazlehurst MS 39083 *Web:* www.lcindustries.com	601-894-1771		508
L Catterton 599 W Putnam Ave Greenwich CT 06830 *Web:* www.lcatterton.com	203-629-4901	629-4903	792
L D Reeves & Associates Inc 1889 Manzana Ave Punta Gorda FL 33950 *Web:* ldreeves.com	941-575-3555		196
L E Coppersmith Inc 525 S Douglas St El Segundo CA 90245 *Web:* www.coppersmith.com	310-607-8000	607-8001	311
L E Peabody & Associates Inc 1501 Duke St Ste 200 Alexandria VA 22314 *Web:* lepeabody.com	703-836-0100	836-0285	194
L F L Veritas LLC 1086 Teaneck Rd Ste 2C Teaneck NJ 07666 *Web:* www.lflveritas.com	201-833-2266	833-0770	2
L H Industries Corp 4420 Clubview Dr Fort Wayne IN 46804 *Web:* www.lhindustries.com	260-432-5563	432-2503	43
L H Stamping Corp 4708 Clubview Dr Fort Wayne IN 46804 *Web:* www.lhindustries.com	260-432-9372		488
L H Thomson Company Inc, The 7800 NE Industrial Blvd Macon GA 31216 *Web:* www.lhthomson.com	478-788-5052	788-1956	483
L Keeley Construction 500 S Ewing Ave Ste G Saint Louis MO 63103 *TF:* 866-553-3539 ■ *Web:* www.lkeeley.com	866-553-3539		186
L L Pelling Co 1425 W Penn St PO Box 230 North Liberty IA 52317 *Web:* www.llpelling.com	319-626-4600	626-4605	186
L M Engineering Inc 2720 Intertech Dr Youngstown OH 44509 *Web:* lmcases.com	330-270-2400	270-2424	261
L M Scofield Co 6533 Bandini Blvd Los Angeles CA 90040 *TF:* 800-800-9900 ■ *Web:* www.scofield.com	323-720-3000		183
L Patrick Mulligan & Associates LPA 28 N Wilkinson St Dayton OH 45402 *Web:* www.patrickmulligan.com	937-685-7006		428
L Peres & Associates Inc 525 River Rd Edgewater NJ 07020 *Web:* lperes.com	201-943-7717		652
L Roy Papp & Associates LLP 2201 E Camelback Rd Ste 227B Phoenix AZ 85016 *Web:* www.roypapp.com	602-956-0980	956-1985	401
L Salon & Color Group 223 S San Mateo Dr San Mateo CA 94401 *Web:* www.lsalon.com	650-342-6668		77
L Suzio Concrete Company Inc 975 Westfield Rd Meriden CT 06450 *TF:* 888-789-4626 ■ *Web:* www.suzioyorkhill.com	203-237-8421	238-9177	182
L Tech Network Services Inc 9926 Pioneer Blvd Ste 101 Santa Fe Springs CA 90670 *Web:* www.ltechnet.com	562-222-1121	222-1533	225
L Thorn Co 6000 Grant Line Rd New Albany IN 47150 *Web:* lthorn.com	812-246-4461	246-2678	191-1
L' Appartement Hotel 455 Sherbrooke W Montreal QC H3A1B7 *TF:* 800-363-3010 ■ *Web:* www.appartementhotel.com	514-284-3634	287-1431	379
L'Academie de Cuisine 16006 Industrial Dr Gaithersburg MD 20877 *TF:* 800-664-2433 ■ *Web:* www.lacademie.com	301-670-8670		167-3
L'Acadie-Nouvelle 476 St-Pierre W PO Box 5536 Caraquet NB E1W1B7 *TF:* 800-561-2255 ■ *Web:* www.acadienouvelle.com	506-727-4444		532-1
L'Alouette 787 Massachusetts 28 Harwich MA 02646 *Web:* frenchbistrocapecod.com	508-430-0405		671

Name / Address	City	State	ZIP	Phone	Fax	Class
L'Angolo Ristorante 1415 Porter St *Web:* www.langolo-restaurant.com	Philadelphia	PA	19145	215-389-4252		671
L'Atelier 1739 Pearl St *Web:* www.latelierboulder.com	Boulder	CO	80302	303-442-7233		671
L'Auberge de Sedona 301 L'Auberge Ln. **Fax Area Code:* 928 ■ *TF:* 855-905-5745 ■ *Web:* www.lauberge.com	Sedona	AZ	86336	800-905-5745	282-2885*	671
L'Auberge Del Mar 1540 Camino del Mar PO Box 2889 *TF:* 800-245-9757 ■ *Web:* www.laubergedelmar.com	Del Mar	CA	92014	858-259-1515		669
L'Echaude 73 Rue Sault-au-Matelot St *Web:* www.echaude.com	Quebec City	QC	G1K3Y9	418-692-1299		671
L'Enfant Plaza 429 L'Enfant Plz SW *Web:* www.lenfantplaza.com	Washington	DC	20024	202-485-3300		379
L'Entrecote Saint Jean 1080 St Jean St *Web:* www.entrecotesaintjean.com	Quebec City	QC	G1R1S4	418-694-0234		671
L'Entrecote St-Jean 2022 Peel St *Web:* www.lentrecotestjean.com	Montreal	QC	H3A2W5	514-281-6492		671
L'Escale 500 Steamboat Rd. *Web:* www.lescalerestaurant.com	Greenwich	CT	06830	203-661-4600		671
L'Estaminet 1340 Fleury E *Web:* www.lestaminet.ca	Montreal	QC	H2C1R3	514-389-0596		671
L'etoile PO Box 2040 *Web:* www.letoile.net	Edgartown	MA	02539	508-627-5187		671
L'Etoile 1 S Pinckney St *Web:* www.letoile-restaurant.com	Madison	WI	53703	608-251-0500	251-7577	671
L'Express 3927 St Denis St *Web:* restaurantlexpress.com	Montreal	QC	H2W2M4	514-845-5333		671
L'Garde Inc 15181 Woodlawn Ave *Web:* www.lgarde.com	Tustin	CA	92780	714-259-0771	259-7822	504
L'Horizon Resort & Spa 1050 E Palm Canyon Dr *Web:* lhorizonpalmsprings.com	Palm Springs	CA	92264	760-323-1858		378
L'Hotel du Vieux-Quebec 1190 St Jean St *TF:* 800-361-7787 ■ *Web:* hvq.com	Quebec City	QC	G1R1S6	418-692-1850		379
L'Hotel Quebec 3115 des Hotels Ave *Web:* www.hotelsjaro.com	Quebec City	QC	G1W3Z6	418-658-5120	658-4504	379
L'Opera 101 Pine Ave *Web:* www.lopera.com	Long Beach	CA	90802	562-491-0066		671
L'Oreal USA 575 Fifth Ave *TF:* 800-322-2036 ■ *Web:* www.lorealusa.com	New York	NY	10017	212-818-1500		214
L'Usine Tactic Inc 127th St Ste 2050 *TF:* 800-933-5232 ■ *Web:* www.samplingproduct.com	Saint George	QC	G5Y2W8	800-933-5232		627
L. A. Hotel Downtown, The 333 S Figueroa St *Web:* thelahotel.com	Los Angeles	CA	90071	213-617-1133		707
L. Bissell & Son Inc PO Box 490 *Web:* lbissell.com	Southington	CT	06489	860-875-2555		390
L. De Geus & Associates Inc 227 N Hammes Ave *Web:* degeusinsurance.com	Joliet	IL	60435	815-744-2880		390
L. E. Goodgame & Associates Inc 8058 Corporate Center Dr Ste *Web:* legoodgame.com	Charlotte	NC	28226	704-831-6001		390
L. E. Sauer Machine Co 3535 Tree Crt Indus Blvd *TF:* 800-444-1349 ■ *Web:* www.sauermachine.com	Saint Louis	MO	63122	636-225-5358	225-3438	556
L. F. Manufacturing Inc 5528 E Hwy 290 **Fax Area Code:* 979 ■ *Web:* www.lfm-frp.com	Giddings	TX	78942	800-237-5791	542-0911*	604
L. G. & W. Federal Credit Union 1616 Whitten Rd *Web:* lgwfcu.com	Memphis	TN	38134	901-680-7995		219
L. G. Jordan Oil Company Inc 314 N Hughes St *Web:* www.lgjordanoil.com	Apex	NC	27502	919-362-8388		579
L. H. Frishkoff & Co 546 5th Ave 9th Fl *Web:* lhfcpa.com	New York	NY	10036	212-808-0070	808-0073	2
L. J. Engineering Inc 18192 Gothard St *Web:* www.ljengineering.com	Huntington Beach	CA	92648	714-848-8001	848-0973	420
L. J. Rogers Inc 421 Currant Rd *Web:* www.ljrogers.com	Fall River	MA	02720	508-672-8888		311
L. J. Thalmann Co 3132 Lake Ave *Web:* chaletnursery.com	Wilmette	IL	60091	847-256-0561		323
L. Milton Cancienne, Jr. (Aplc) 515 Barrow St *Web:* houmaestates.com	Houma	LA	70360	985-876-5656		41
L. W. Schneider Inc 1180 N 6th St *Web:* www.lwschneider.com	Princeton	IL	61356	815-875-3835		454
L.A. Silver Inc 330 Golden Shore Ste 230 *TF:* 800-624-8669 ■ *Web:* www.99centbodyjewelry.com	Long Beach	CA	90802	562-432-6776	432-7992	411
L.A.B. Equipment Inc 1549 Ardmore Ave *Web:* www.labequipment.com	Itasca	IL	60143	630-595-4288	595-5196	248
L.B. Carpenter PA 420 S Dixie Hwy Ste 2B *Web:* www.lbbeatsirs.com	Miami	FL	33146	305-232-8477		2
L.C. Smith Co 196 Morgan Ave *Web:* lcsmithco.com	Elyria	OH	44035	440-327-1251	353-0947	493
L.D. Oliver Seed Company Inc 26 Sunset Ave *Web:* www.ldoliverseed.com	Milton	VT	05468	802-893-1241	893-2194	276
L.D. Plastics Inc 1130 Pearl St *Web:* www.ldplastics.net	Brockton	MA	02301	508-584-7651		604
L.E. Myers Co 1655 Hubbard Ave *Web:* www.lemyers.com	Decatur	IL	62526	217-877-0430	875-2312	189-4
L.E. Warren Inc 1600 S Jackson St *Web:* www.lewarren.com	Jackson	MI	49203	517-784-8701		454
L.H.P. Transportation Services Inc 2740 N Mayfair *TF:* 800-642-1035 ■ *Web:* www.lhp-transport.com	Springfield	MO	65803	417-865-7577	865-7543	311
L.I.F. Industries Inc 5 Harbor Park Dr *Web:* lifd.com	Port Washington	NY	11050	516-390-6800	390-6848	499
L.J. Zucca Inc 760 S Delsea Dr *TF:* 800-552-2639 ■ *Web:* www.ljzucca.com	Vineland	NJ	08362	856-692-7425	696-7112	756
L.K. Wood Realty Inc 8460 Watson Rd Ste 112 *Web:* www.lkwood.com	Saint Louis	MO	63119	314-849-6300	403-7715	652
L.L. Lee Scouting Museum 395 Blondin Rd *Web:* scoutingmuseum.nhscouting.org	Manchester	NH	03109	603-867-2501		520
L.P. Publications 7119 E Shea Blvd Ste 109 *Web:* www.consciousnesswork.com	Scottsdale	AZ	85254	480-948-1800		637-2
L.P.I. Information Systems 10020 Fontana *TF:* 888-729-2020 ■ *Web:* www.datasmithpayroll.com	Overland Park	KS	66207	913-381-9118		2
L.S. Associates Risk Management Consultants 1973 Oak Tree Cove *TF:* 888-393-9115 ■ *Web:* lsassoc.net	Hernando	MS	38632	662-393-9115	393-9242	390
L.V.O. Manufacturing Inc 808 N 2nd Ave E *Web:* www.lvomfg.com	Rock Rapids	IA	51246	712-472-2203		806
L2 Consulting Services Inc 2100 E Hwy 290 *Web:* www.l2aviation.com	Dripping Springs	TX	78620	512-894-3414		256
L3 Advertising Inc 115 Bowery St 3rd Fl *Web:* www.L3advertising.com	New York	NY	10002	212-966-7050	431-1282	4
L3 Avionics Systems 5353 52nd St SE *TF:* 800-253-9525 ■ *Web:* l-3avionics.com	Grand Rapids	MI	49512	616-949-6600		529
L3 Communications Corp *Aviation Recorders Div* 100 Cattlemen Rd *Web:* www.l3aviationproducts.com	Sarasota	FL	34232	941-371-0811		529
L3 Kigre Inc 100 Marshland Rd *Web:* www.kigre.com	Hilton Head Island	SC	29926	843-681-5800	681-4559	425
L3 Payments LLC 30700 Russell Ranch Rd Ste 250 *Web:* www.l3payments.com	Westlake Village	CA	91362	805-449-1191	449-1103	463
L3 Technologies Inc 1 Federal St *TF:* 800-339-6197 ■ *Web:* www.l3t.com	Camden	NJ	08103	856-338-3000	338-6014	529
L3Harris Commercial Aviation *Florida Flight Academy* 2685 Flight line Ave *TF:* 800-822-6359 ■ *Web:* www.l3commercialaviation.com	Sanford	FL	32773	407-330-7020		167-3
L3Harris Technologies Inc 1025 W Nasa Blvd *Web:* www.l3harris.com	Melbourne	FL	32919	321-727-9100		504
L3Harris Unidyne 240 W 30th St *Web:* l-3mps.com	National City	CA	91950	619-336-2200		698
L5 Solutions LLC 7950 Castleway Dr Ste 160 *Web:* www.L5Solutions.com	Indianapolis	IN	46250	317-436-1044	577-3005	196
La Baguette Inc 1130 Rambling Oaks *Web:* www.labaguette.com	Norman	OK	73072	405-329-1101		670
La Barca 2414 S Vermont *Web:* www.labarcarestaurant.net	Los Angeles	CA	90007	323-735-6567		671
La Beau Bros Inc 295 N Harrison Ave *TF:* 800-747-9519 ■ *Web:* www.labeautrucks.com	Kankakee	IL	60901	815-933-5519	933-4366	57
La Bella 256 Broadway *Web:* www.labella.com	NEWBURGH	NY	12550	845-562-4400		253
La Bella Italia 402 York St	Gettysburg	PA	17325	717-334-1978		671
La Belle Dodge Chrysler Jeep Inc 501 S Main St *TF:* 800-226-1193 ■ *Web:* www.labelledodgechryslerjeep.com	Labelle	FL	33935	863-675-2701		57
La Bodega 703 SW Blvd *Web:* labodegakc.com	Kansas City	MO	64108	816-472-8272		671
La Bonne Bouchee 12344 Olive Blvd Westgate Ctr *Web:* www.labonnebouchee.com	Saint Louis	MO	63141	314-576-6606	576-3656	670
La Cabana 312 E 4th Ave *Web:* alaskalacabana.com	Anchorage	AK	99501	907-272-0135		671
La Cabanita Restaurant 3445 N Verdugo Rd *Web:* www.lacabanitarestaurant.com	Glendale	CA	91208	818-957-2711		671
La Caille at Quail Run 9565 Wasatch Blvd *Web:* www.lacaille.com	Sandy	UT	84092	801-942-1751	944-8990	671
La Camarilla Racquet Fitness & Swim Club 5320 E Shea Blvd *Web:* www.lacamarilla.com	Scottsdale	AZ	85254	480-998-3388		77
La Canasta Mexican Food Products Inc 3101 W Jackson *Web:* la-canasta.com	Phoenix	AZ	85009	602-269-7721		123
La Cantera Resort & Spa 16641 La Cantera Pkwy *Web:* www.lacanteraresort.com	San Antonio	TX	78256	210-558-6500	558-2405	378
La Capitol Federal Credit Union PO Box 3398 *TF:* 800-522-2748 ■ *Web:* www.lacapfcu.org	Baton Rouge	LA	70821	225-342-5055	342-9135	219
LA Care Health Plan 555 W Fifth St 29th Fl *TF:* 888-839-9909 ■ *Web:* www.lacare.org	Los Angeles	CA	90013	213-694-1250		391-3
La Carreta Mexican Restaurant 35 Manchester Rd Ste 5A *Web:* lacarretamex.com	Derry	NH	03038	603-421-0091		671
La Causa Inc PO Box 4188 *Web:* www.lacausa.org	Milwaukee	WI	53204	414-647-8750		48-8
La Cazuela Mexican Restaurants 4965 Lanier Islands Pkwy Ste 108 *Web:* lacazuela.com	Buford	GA	30519	770-614-6871		671
La Chambre de Commerce de Drummond 1502 Rue Jean-Berchmans-Michaud CP 188 *Web:* www.ccid.qc.ca	Drummondville	QC	J2C2Z5	819-477-7822		137

Name / Address	City	State	Zip	Phone	Fax	Class
La Chaumiere Restaurant 139 17th Ave SW *Web:* www.lachaumiere.ca	Calgary	AB	T2S0A1	403-228-5689	228-4448	671
La Chinita 1451 N Broadway St *Web:* www.lachinitamexicanrestaurant.com	Wichita	KS	67214	316-267-1552		671
La Chronique 104 Ave Laurier Ouest *Web:* www.lachronique.qc.ca	Montreal	QC	H2T2N7	514-271-3095		671
La Cie Canada Tire Inc 21500 Transcanadienne *TF:* 888-267-5097 ■ *Web:* canada-tire.ca	Baie-D'Urfe	QC	H9X4B7	514-457-0155		754
La Cita Country Club 777 Country Club Dr *Web:* www.lacitacc.com	Titusville	FL	32780	321-383-2582		669
La Citadelle International Academy of Arts & Science 36 Scarsdale Rd *Web:* www.lacitadelleacademy.com	North York	ON	M3B2R7	416-385-9685		685
La Cite 801 Aviation Dr *TF:* 800-267-2483 ■ *Web:* www.collegelacite.ca	Ottawa	ON	K1K4R3	613-742-2483	742-2481	165
La Clef De Sol Inc 445 av St-Jean Baptiste Ste 220 *Web:* www.laclefdesol.com	Quebec City	QC	G2E5N7	418-627-0840		246
La Colombe 554 Duluth E *Web:* lacolombe.ca	Montreal	QC	H2L1A9	514-849-8844		671
La Colombe D'Or Inn 3410 Montrose Blvd *Web:* www.lacolombedor.com	Houston	TX	77006	713-524-7999	524-8923	379
La Colonial Tortilla Products Inc 543 Monterey Pass Rd *Web:* lacolonial-la.com	Monterey Park	CA	91754	626-289-3647		123
La Costa 1600 E Second St *Web:* www.webs.com	Casper	WY	82601	307-235-6599		671
La Cote d'Or Cafe 6876 Lee Hwy *Web:* www.lacotedorarlington.com	Arlington	VA	22213	703-538-3033		671
La Crepe Nanou 1410 Robert St *Web:* lacrepenanou.com	New Orleans	LA	70115	504-899-2670		671
La Crete Sawmills Ltd Hwy 697 S PO Box 1090 *TF:* 888-928-2298 ■ *Web:* lacretesawmills.com	La Crete	AB	T0H2H0	780-928-2292	928-2288	683
La Cro Products Inc 1648 Liberty St *TF:* 877-811-2276 ■ *Web:* www.lacroproducts.com	La Crosse	WI	54603	608-781-1600		253
La Crosse Area Convention & Visitors Bureau 410 Veterans Memorial Dr *TF:* 800-658-9424 ■ *Web:* www.explorelacrosse.com	La Crosse	WI	54601	608-782-2366	782-4082	206
La Crosse County 212 6th St N Rm 1500 *Web:* www.lacrossecounty.org	La Crosse	WI	54601	608-785-9581	785-9741	338
La Crosse County Library 121 W Legion St PO Box 220 *Web:* www.lacrossecountylibrary.org	Holmen	WI	54636	608-526-9600		434-3
La Crosse Ctr 300 Harborview Plz *Web:* www.lacrossecenter.com	La Crosse	WI	54601	608-789-7400	789-7444	205
La Crosse Graphics Inc 3025 E Ave S *TF:* 800-832-2503 ■ *Web:* www.lacrossegraphics.com	La Crosse	WI	54601	608-788-2500		627
La Crosse Public Library 800 Main St *Web:* www.lacrosselibrary.org	La Crosse	WI	54601	608-789-7100	789-7106	434-3
La Crosse Tribune 401 N Third St *TF:* 800-262-0420 ■ *Web:* lacrossetribune.com	La Crosse	WI	54601	608-782-9710	782-9723	532-2
La Cucina Sul Mare 237 Main St *Web:* www.lacucinasulmare.com	Falmouth	MA	02540	508-548-5600		671
La Cueva 9742 E Colfax Ave *Web:* www.lacuevacolfax.com	Aurora	CO	80010	303-367-1422		671
La Cumbre Animal Hospital Inc 110 S La Cumbre Rd *Web:* lcah.com	Santa Barbara	CA	93105	805-967-0121		794
LA Darling Co 1401 Hwy 49B *TF:* 800-682-5730 ■ *Web:* www.ladarling.com	Paragould	AR	72450	870-239-9564		286
La Difference Salon & Day Spa 830 Paoli Pk *Web:* ladifferencesalon.com	West Chester	PA	19380	610-429-1808		77
La Dolce Vita 17546 Woodward *Web:* ldvrestaurant.net	Detroit	MI	48203	313-865-0331		671
La Duni Concepts LLC 4620 McKinney Ave *Web:* www.ladunihub.com	Dallas	TX	75219	214-520-7300	520-7390	671
La Fama Foods Inc 7566 Us Hwy 259 N *TF:* 800-256-4898 ■ *Web:* www.lafamafoods.com	Ore City	TX	75683	903-968-4500	759-8408	296-37
La Famiglia 8 S Front St *Web:* www.lafamiglia.com	Philadelphia	PA	19106	215-922-2803		671
La Familia Restaurant 841 Foch St *Web:* www.la-familia-mexican-restaurant.business.site	Fort Worth	TX	76107	817-870-2002		671
La Fenice 319 King St W *Web:* www.lafenice.ca	Toronto	ON	M5V1J5	416-585-2377		671
La Fiesta Brava 6168 Hwy 49 *Web:* www.lafiestabravarestaurants.com	Hattiesburg	MS	39401	601-584-9484		671
La Fiesta Grande 314 Versailles Rd *Web:* www.lafiestagrandeky.com	Frankfort	KY	40601	502-695-8378		671
La Fiesta Mexican Restaurant 9513 NW 39th Ave *Web:* www.lafiestagainesville.com	Gainesville	FL	32606	352-335-8484		671
La Fogata 2427 Vance Jackson Rd *Web:* www.lafogata.com	San Antonio	TX	78213	210-340-1337		671
La Folie 2316 Polk St *Web:* www.lafolie.com	San Francisco	CA	94109	415-776-5577	776-3431	671
La Follette Utilities Board 302 N Tennessee Ave PO Box 1411 *TF:* 800-352-1340 ■ *Web:* www.lub.org	La Follette	TN	37766	423-562-3316	566-0580	245
La Fonda 1900 N Second St *Web:* lafondaflg.com	Flagstaff	AZ	86004	928-779-0296		671
La Fonda 100 E San Francisco St *TF:* 800-523-5002 ■ *Web:* www.lafondasantafe.com	Santa Fe	NM	87501	505-982-5511	988-2952	379
La Fontaine Bleue Inc 7514 S Ritchie Hwy *Web:* www.lafontainebleue.com	Glen Burnie	MD	21061	410-760-4115		671
La Foret 21747 Bertram Rd *Web:* www.laforetrestaurant.com	San Jose	CA	95120	408-997-3458		671
La Fortaleza Inc 501 N Ford Blvd *Web:* lafortalezaproducts.net	Los Angeles	CA	90022	323-261-1211		345
LA Fuess Partners Inc 3333 Lee Pkwy Ste 300 *Web:* www.lafp.com	Dallas	TX	75219	214-871-7010		256
La Galerie French Quarter Hotel 131 Rue Decatur *Web:* www.lagaleriehotel.com	New Orleans	LA	70130	504-592-7700		379
La Gran Plaza 4200 S Fwy Ste 2500 *Web:* www.lagranplazamall.com	Fort Worth	TX	76115	817-922-8888		460
La Grand Industrial Supply Co 2620 SW 1st Ave *TF:* 800-574-5806 ■ *Web:* lagrandindustrial.net	Portland	OR	97201	503-224-5800	224-0639	679
La Grande FM 107.5 *CBS Radio Dallas* 4131 N Central Expy Ste 1000 *Web:* lagrande1075.radio.com	Dallas	TX	75204	214-525-7000		645-43
La Grande-Union County Chamber of Commerce 102 Elm St *TF:* 800-848-9969 ■ *Web:* www.cityoflagrande.org	La Grande	OR	97850	541-963-8588	963-3936	139
La Grenouille 3 E 52nd St *Web:* www.la-grenouille.com	New York	NY	10022	212-752-1495		671
La Griglia 2002 W Gray St *Web:* www.lagrigliarestaurant.com	Houston	TX	77019	713-526-4700		671
La Grolla 815 Cote d'Abraham *Web:* www.restaurantlagrolla.com	Quebec City	QC	G1R1A4	418-529-8107		671
La Grolla 452 Selby Ave *Web:* lagrollastpaul.com	Saint Paul	MN	55102	651-221-1061		671
La Grotta 2637 Peachtree Rd *Web:* www.la-grotta.com	Atlanta	GA	30305	404-231-1368		671
La Habra Area Chamber of Commerce 321 E La Habra Blvd *Web:* www.lahabrachamber.com	La Habra	CA	90631	562-697-1704	697-8359	139
La Habra City School District (LHCSD) 500 N Walnut St *Web:* www.lahabraschools.org	La Habra	CA	90631	562-690-2305	690-4154	186
La Habra Products Inc 4125 E La Palma Ave Ste 250 *TF:* 866-516-0061 ■ *Web:* www.lahabrastucco.com	Anaheim	CA	92807	714-778-2266	774-2079	500
La Hacienda Inc 515 S Park St	Madison	WI	53715	608-255-8227		671
La Hacienda Treatment Ctr 145 La Hacienda Way *TF:* 800-749-6160 ■ *Web:* www.lahacienda.com	Hunt	TX	78024	830-238-4222	238-3120	726
LA Hearne Company Inc 512 Metz Rd *Web:* www.hearneco.com	King City	CA	93930	831-385-5441		11-1
La James International College 8805 Chambery Blvd *TF:* 888-880-2106 ■ *Web:* www.ljic.edu	Johnston	IA	50131	888-880-2108		167-3
La Jicarita Rural Telephone Cooperative Inc 455 State Hwy 518 *TF:* 800-742-7232 ■ *Web:* www.lajicarita.com	Mora	NM	87732	575-387-2216	387-9010	224
La Jolla Beach & Tennis Club 2000 Spindrift Dr *TF:* 888-828-0948 ■ *Web:* www.ljbtc.com	La Jolla	CA	92037	858-454-7126	456-3805	669
La Jolla Bioengineering Institute 505 Coast Blvd S Ste 406 *Web:* www.ljbi.org	La Jolla	CA	92037	858-456-7505	456-7540	261
La Jolla Light Newspaper 565 Pearl St Ste 300 *TF:* 800-691-0952 ■ *Web:* www.lajollalight.com	La Jolla	CA	92037	858-459-4201		532-3
La Jolla Pharmaceutical Co 10182 Telesis Ct 6th Fl *Web:* lajollapharmaceutical.com	San Diego	CA	92121	858-207-4264		85
La Jolla Playhouse PO Box 12039 *Web:* www.lajollaplayhouse.org	La Jolla	CA	92039	858-550-1070	550-1075	573-4
La Jolla Sports Club Inc 7825 Fay Ave *Web:* lajollasportsclub.com	La Jolla	CA	92037	858-456-2595		194
La Jolla Town Council 7660 Fay Ave Ste H-274 *Web:* www.lajollatowncouncil.org	La Jolla	CA	92037	858-454-1444		139
La Lanterna 23 Grey Oaks Ave *Web:* www.lalanterna.com	Yonkers	NY	10710	914-476-3060	375-3008	671
LA Law Library 301 301 W First St *Web:* www.lalawlibrary.org	Los Angeles	CA	90012	213-785-2529		445
La Leche League International Inc (LLLI) 957 N Plum Grove Rd *TF:* 800-525-3243 ■ *Web:* www.llli.org	Schaumburg	IL	60173	847-519-7730	969-0460	48-17
La Ley 107.9 150 N Michigan Ave Ste 1040 *Web:* laley1079.lamusica.com	Chicago	IL	60601	312-920-9500	920-9515	645-34
La Loggia Restaurant 68 W Flagler St *Web:* www.laloggiarestaurantmenu.com	Miami	FL	33130	305-373-4800		671
La Lou Salon 15444 N Greenway Hayden Loop Ste 102 *Web:* lalousalon.com	Scottsdale	AZ	85260	480-776-5726		77
LA Louver Inc 45 N Venice Blvd *Web:* www.lalouver.com	Venice	CA	90291	310-822-4955		42
La Lumiere School 6801 N Wilhelm Rd *Web:* www.lalumiere.org	La Porte	IN	46350	219-326-7450	325-3185	622
La Madeleine de Corps Inc 12201 Merit Dr Ste 900 *Web:* lamadeleine.com	Dallas	TX	75251	214-696-6962		671
La Mar Lighting Company Inc 485 Smith St **Fax Area Code:* 516 ■ *Web:* www.lamarlighting.com	Farmingdale	NY	11735	631-777-7700	777-7705*	439
La Marche Manufacturing Co 106 Bradrock Dr *TF:* 888-232-9562 ■ *Web:* www.lamarchemfg.com	Des Plaines	IL	60018	847-299-1188	299-3061	253
La Margarita Co 545 Ferry St SE *Web:* www.lamargaritasalem.com	Salem	OR	97301	503-362-8861		671
La Medusa 4857 Rainier Ave S *Web:* www.lamedusarestaurant.com	Seattle	WA	98118	206-723-2192		671
La Mer 1840 ReneLevesque Est *Web:* www.lamer.ca	Montreal	QC	H2K4P1	514-522-3003	522-0467	671
La Mesa Arts Academy 4200 Parks Ave *Web:* lmsvsd.k12.ca.us	La Mesa	CA	91941	619-668-5730	668-8303	685
La Mesa Rv Center Inc 7430 Copley Pk Pl *TF:* 800-496-8778 ■ *Web:* www.lamesarv.com	San Diego	CA	92111	858-874-8000	874-8029	57

Name / Address	City	State	ZIP	Phone	Fax	Class
La Michoacana Meat Market Inc 4717 Telephone Rd *Web:* www.lamichoacanameatmarket.com	Houston	TX	77087	713-547-4600	645-6493	345
La Minestra 106 E Dakota Ave *Web:* www.laminestra.com	Pierre	SD	57501	605-224-8090		671
LA Models 7700 Sunset Blvd *Web:* www.latalent.com	Los Angeles	CA	90046	323-436-7700		506
La Opinion 700 S Flower St Ste 3000 *Web:* laopinion.com	Los Angeles	CA	90017	213-622-8332		532-2
La Palma Intercommunity Hospital 7901 Walker St *Web:* www.lapalmaintercommunityhospital.com	La Palma	CA	90623	714-670-7400		374-3
La Pantera 940 AM *KWBY* 1665 James St *Web:* lapantera940.com	Woodburn	OR	97071	503-981-9400		645-126
La Paz *La PazMexican Restaurant* 321 N Cotner Blvd *Web:* www.getintolapaz.com	Lincoln	NE	68505	402-466-9111		671
La Paz County 1108 S Joshua Ave *Web:* www.co.la-paz.az.us	Parker	AZ	85344	928-669-6115	669-9709	338
La Paz Regional Hospital & Clinics 1200 W Mohave Rd *Web:* www.lapazhospital.org	Parker	AZ	85344	928-669-9201	669-7417	374-3
La Penna Group Inc, The 2110 Enterprise SE **Fax Area Code:* 616 ■ *TF:* 800-527-3662 ■ *Web:* www.lapenna.com	Grand Rapids	MI	49508	800-527-3662	281-0573*	196
La Pensione Hotel 606 W Date St *TF:* 800-232-4683 ■ *Web:* www.lapensionehotel.com	San Diego	CA	92101	619-236-8000	236-8088	379
La Perla Cafe 5912 W Glendale Ave *Web:* www.laperlasportscantina.com	Glendale	AZ	85301	602-753-3896		671
La Petite Bretonne Inc 1210 Boul Mich Le-Bohec *TF:* 800-361-3381 ■ *Web:* www.petitebretonne.com	Blainville	QC	J7C5S4	450-435-3381	435-0944	297-8
La Petite Folie 1504 E 55th St *Web:* www.lapetitefolie.com	Chicago	IL	60615	773-493-1394		671
La Piñata Mexican Food Restaurant 5521 N 7th Ave *Web:* lapinatarestaurantaz.com	Phoenix	AZ	85013	602-279-1763		671
LA Pipeline Rental & Industrial Supply LLC 3210 E Napoleon St *Web:* www.lapipelinerentals.com	Sulphur	LA	70663	337-533-8184		190
La Plata County Courthouse 1060 E 2nd Ave Ste B10 *Web:* www.co.laplata.co.us	Durango	CO	81302	970-382-6280		338
La Plata Electric Association Inc 45 Stewart St *TF:* 888-839-5732 ■ *Web:* www.lpea.com	Durango	CO	81303	970-247-5786	247-2674	245
La Playa Beach & Golf Resort 9891 Gulf Shore Dr *TF:* 800-237-6883 ■ *Web:* www.laplayaresort.com	Naples	FL	34108	239-597-3123	597-6278	669
La Poderosa 860 Am 5030 Camino de la Siesta Ste 403 *Web:* www.lapoderosa860.com	San Diego	CA	92108	664-683-5288		645-141
La Porte County 809 State St *TF:* 800-654-3441 ■ *Web:* www.laportecounty.org	La Porte	IN	46350	219-326-6808		338
La Porte County Public Library 904 Indiana Ave *Web:* www.laportelibrary.org	La Porte	IN	46350	219-362-6156		434-3
La Porte Hospital (LPH) 1007 Lincolnway PO Box 250 *Web:* www.laportehealth.com	La Porte	IN	46350	219-326-1234		374-3
La Porte-Bayshore Chamber of Commerce 712 W Fairmont Pkwy *Web:* www.laportechamber.org	La Porte	TX	77571	281-471-1123	471-1710	130
La Posada at Park Ctr 350 E Morningside Rd *Web:* posadalife.org	Green Valley	AZ	85614	520-648-8131		672
La Posada de Santa Fe Resort & Spa 330 E Palace Ave **Fax Area Code:* 970 ■ *TF:* 866-280-3810 ■ *Web:* rockresorts.com	Santa Fe	NM	87501	505-986-0000	476-7425*	669
La Posada Hotel & Suites 1000 Zaragoza St *TF:* 800-444-2099 ■ *Web:* www.laposada.com	Laredo	TX	78040	956-722-1701		379
La Preferida Inc 3400 W 35th St *Web:* www.lapreferida.com	Chicago	IL	60632	773-254-7200		297-8
La Quinta Inn & Suites by Wyndham Boise Towne Square 7965 W Emerald St *TF:* 800-600-6001 ■ *Web:* www.laquintaboisetownesquare.com	Boise	ID	83704	208-378-7000		379
La Quinta Inn & Suites by Wyndham Pocatello 1440 Bench Rd *Web:* www.laquintapocatello.com	Pocatello	ID	83201	208-234-7500		379
La Quinta Inn & Suites by Wyndham Secaucus Meadowlands 350 Lighting Way *TF:* 800-753-3757 ■ *Web:* www.lq.com	Secaucus	NJ	07094	201-863-8700	863-6209	379
La Quinta Resort Leasing c/o California Lifestyle Realty 50200 Avenida Vista Bonita *Web:* www.californialifestylerealty.com	La Quinta	CA	92253	760-564-1200	564-0200	654
La Reina Inc 316 N Ford Blvd *TF:* 800-367-7522 ■ *Web:* www.lareinainc.com	Los Angeles	CA	90022	323-268-2791		296-36
La Roche College 9000 Babcock Blvd *TF:* 800-838-4572 ■ *Web:* laroche.edu	Pittsburgh	PA	15237	412-367-9300		166
LA Rockler Fur Co 16 N 4th St *Web:* www.rocklerfurco.com	Minneapolis	MN	55401	612-332-8643		155-7
LA Rockola 96.7FM 3101 W Fifth St *Web:* scba.com	Santa Ana	CA	92703	714-554-5000		645
La Rosa Del Monte Express Inc 1133-35 Tiffany St *TF:* 800-643-6684 ■ *Web:* www.larosadelmonte.com	Bronx	NY	10459	718-991-3300	893-1948	780
La Salle County 101 Courthouse Sq Ste 107 *Web:* www.co.la-salle.tx.us	Cotulla	TX	78014	830-483-5120	483-5101	338
La Salle University 1900 W Olney Ave *TF:* 800-328-1910 ■ *Web:* www.lasalle.edu	Philadelphia	PA	19141	215-951-1500	951-1656	166
La Scala of Little Italy 1012 Eastern Ave *Web:* lascaladining.com	Baltimore	MD	21202	410-783-9209		671
La Scogliera Restaurant 474 River Rd *Web:* www.lascoglierarestaurant.com	Shelton	CT	06484	203-922-1179		671
La Senorita Mexican Restaurants 2455 N US 31 S *Web:* lasfiesta.com	Traverse City	MI	49684	231-946-4545		671
La Sierra University 4500 Riverwalk Pkwy *TF:* 800-874-5587 ■ *Web:* lasierra.edu	Riverside	CA	92515	951-785-2000	785-2901	166
La Sirena 6316 S Dixie Hwy *Web:* lasirenaonline.com	West Palm Beach	FL	33405	561-585-3128		671
La Sportiva North America Inc 3850 Frontier Ave Ste 100 *Web:* www.sportiva.com	Boulder	CO	80301	303-443-8710		301
LA STAGE Alliance 4200 Chevy Chase Dr *Web:* lastagealliance.com	Los Angeles	CA	90039	213-614-0556		720
La Tapatia Tortilleria Inc 104 E Belmont Ave *Web:* www.tortillas4u.com	Fresno	CA	93701	559-441-1030	441-1712	296-36
La Tavola 248 Albemarle St *Web:* www.la-tavola.com	Baltimore	MD	21202	410-685-1859		671
La Tavola Trattoria 992 Virginia Ave *Web:* latavolatrattoria.com	Atlanta	GA	30306	404-873-5430		671
La Tercera Elementary School 1600 Albin Way *Web:* www.oldadobe.org	Petaluma	CA	94954	707-765-4303	765-4333	685
La Terre Federal Credit Union 701 Barrow St *Web:* laterrefcu.org	Houma	LA	70360	985-872-2836		219
La Tolteca Mexican Restaurant 3048 Richmond Rd *Web:* www.latoltecava.com	Williamsburg	VA	23185	757-253-2939		671
La Touraine Inc 625 Broadway Ste 700 *TF:* 800-893-8871 ■ *Web:* latouraineinc.com	San Diego	CA	92101	619-237-5014		225
La Trattoria 524 Duval St *Web:* www.latrattoria.us	Key West	FL	33040	305-296-1075		671
La Trattoria 522 Moosic St *Web:* thelatrattoria.com	Scranton	PA	18505	570-961-1504		671
La Traviata 314 Congress Ave *Web:* latraviatatx.com	Austin	TX	78701	512-479-8131		671
La Traviata Restaurant 301 N Cedar Ave *Web:* www.latraviata301.com	Long Beach	CA	90802	562-432-8022		671
La Tribune 1950 Roy St *Web:* www.latribune.ca	Sherbrooke	QC	J1K2X8	819-564-5450		532-1
La Valencia Hotel 1132 Prospect St *Web:* www.lavalencia.com	La Jolla	CA	92037	858-454-0771		379
La Valle Food Co 235 Murray Hill Pkwy *Web:* www.lavalleus.com	East Rutherford	NJ	07073	201-939-0005		345
La Verne Chamber of Commerce 2078 Bonita Ave *Web:* www.lavernechamber.org	La Verne	CA	91750	909-593-5265		139
La Veta/Cuchara Chamber of Commerce 132 W Ryus Ave *Web:* lavetacucharachamber.com	La Veta	CO	81055	719-742-3676		139
La Vida Llena 10501 Lagrima de Oro NE *TF:* 800-922-1344 ■ *Web:* www.lavidallena.com	Albuquerque	NM	87111	505-293-4001		672
La Vie Parisienne Corp 1837 Lincoln Blvd *Web:* lavieparisienne.com	Santa Monica	CA	90404	310-392-8428		411
La Viña Winery 4201 S Hwy 28 *Web:* lavina.wolfep.com	La Union	NM	88021	575-882-7632		50-7
La Vision 1394 Indian-Lilburn Rd Ste 202 *Web:* lavisionweb.com	Norcross	GA	30093	770-963-7521		532-2
La Vita E Bella 2411 Second Ave *Web:* www.lavitaebella.us	Seattle	WA	98121	206-441-5322		671
LA Vocational Institute 3540 Wilshire Blvd Ste 890 *Web:* www.lavocational.com	Los Angeles	CA	90010	213-480-4882		800
La Ward Telephone Exchange Inc 12991 ST Hwy 172 *TF:* 877-872-2213 ■ *Web:* www.laward.net	La Ward	TX	77970	361-872-2211		224
LA Weekly 6715 Sunset Blvd **Fax Area Code:* 323 ■ *TF:* 866-789-6188 ■ *Web:* www.laweekly.com	Los Angeles	CA	90028	866-789-6188	465-3220*	532-5
Lab Fabricators Co 1802 E 47th St *Web:* www.labfabricators.com	Cleveland	OH	44103	216-431-5444		420
Lab Lite LLC 8 S Main St *Web:* www.lablite.com	New Milford	CT	06776	860-355-8817		809
Lab LLC, The 637 W 27th St 8th Fl *Web:* thelabnyc.com	New York	NY	10001	212-209-1333		5
Lab Medical Manufacturing Inc 28 Cook St *Web:* www.labmedical.com	Billerica	MA	01821	978-663-2475		476
Lab Products Inc 742 Sussex Ave *TF:* 800-526-0469 ■ *Web:* labproductsinc.com	Seaford	DE	19973	302-628-4300	628-4309	73
Lab School of Washington, The 4759 Reservoir Rd NW *Web:* www.labschool.org	Washington	DC	20007	202-965-6600		685
Labatt Breweries of Canada 207 Queen's Quay W Ste 299 *TF:* 800-268-2337 ■ *Web:* www.labatt.com	Toronto	ON	M5J1A7	416-361-5050		102
Labatt Food Service 4500 Industry Pk Dr *Web:* www.labattfood.com	San Antonio	TX	78218	210-661-4216	661-0973	297-8
Labcon North America Inc 3700 Lkeville Hwy *TF:* 800-227-1466 ■ *Web:* www.labcon.com	Petaluma	CA	94954	707-766-2100	766-2199	419
Labconco Corp 8811 Prospect Ave *TF:* 800-821-5525 ■ *Web:* www.labconco.com	Kansas City	MO	64132	816-333-8811	363-0130	420
Label Graphics 1225 Carnegie St Ste 104B *Web:* www.labelgraphicscompany.com	Rolling Meadows	IL	60008	847-454-1005	454-1008	413

	Phone	Fax	Class
Label Impression Inc 1831 W Sequoia Ave. . . . . Orange CA 92868 *Web:* www.labelimpressions.com	714-634-3466	634-3468	627
Label Printers Lp, The 1710 N Landmark Rd . . . . . Aurora IL 60506 *TF:* 800-229-9549 ■ *Web:* thelabelprinters.com	630-897-6970		627
Label Systems Inc 4111 Lindbergh Dr . . . . . Addison TX 75001 *TF:* 800-220-9552 ■ *Web:* www.labelsystemsinc.com	972-387-4512	387-4935	627
Label Technology Inc 2050 Wardrobe Ave. . . . . Merced CA 95341 *TF:* 800-388-1990 ■ *Web:* www.labeltech.com	209-384-1000		627
Label Works 2025 Lookout Dr . . . . . North Mankato MN 56003 *TF:* 800-522-3558 ■ *Web:* www.navitor.com	800-522-3558	553-8698	627
Label-Aire Inc 550 Burning Tree Rd . . . . . Fullerton CA 92833 *Web:* www.label-aire.com	714-449-5155	526-0300	547
Labelcraft USA Inc 1410 Bunton Rd. . . . . Louisville KY 40213 **Fax Area Code:* 502 ■ *TF:* 866-248-9402 ■ *Web:* www.labelcraftusa.com	866-248-9402	454-4338*	554
LaBella Associates PC 300 State St Ste 201 . . . . . Rochester NY 14614 *Web:* www.labellapc.com	585-454-6110		261
LaBelle Management Inc 405 S Mission Rd. . . . . Mount Pleasant MI 48858 *Web:* www.labellemgt.com	989-772-2902	773-7521	670
Labelmaster Co 5724 N Pulaski Rd. . . . . Chicago IL 60646 *TF:* 800-621-5808 ■ *Web:* www.labelmaster.com	773-478-0900		413
Labeltape Inc 5100 Beltway Dr SE . . . . . Caledonia MI 49316 *TF:* 800-928-4537 ■ *Web:* www.labeltape-inc.com	616-698-1830	698-7831	413
Labeltronix 2419 E Winston Rd . . . . . Anaheim CA 92806 *TF:* 800-429-4321 ■ *Web:* labeltronix.com	800-429-4321		366
Labenz & Associates LLC 8555 Pioneers Blvd . . . . . Lincoln NE 68520 *Web:* www.labenz.com	402-437-8383	437-8399	2
Labette Bank 4th & Huston PO Box 497 . . . . . Altamont KS 67330 *TF:* 800-711-5311 ■ *Web:* labettebank.com	620-784-5311		70
Labette Community College 200 S 14th St . . . . . Parsons KS 67357 *TF:* 888-522-3883 ■ *Web:* www.labette.cc.ks.us	620-421-6700	421-0180	162
Labette County 501 Merchant St. . . . . Oswego KS 67356 *Web:* www.labettecounty.com	620-795-2138	795-2928	338
LABI College 14209 E Lomitas Ave . . . . . La Puente CA 91746 *Web:* www.labi.edu	626-968-1328	961-7253	167-3
Labomed Inc 2921 S La Cienega Blvd Ste A . . . . . Culver City CA 90232 *Web:* www.labomed.com	310-202-0814	202-7286	419
LabOne Inc 10101 Renner Blvd . . . . . Lenexa KS 66219 *TF:* 800-646-7788 ■ *Web:* www.labone.com	913-888-1770		418
Labor Finders 11426 N Jog Rd . . . . . Palm Beach Gardens FL 33418 *TF:* 800-864-7749 ■ *Web:* www.laborfinders.com	561-627-6507		721
Labor Law Center Inc 12534 Vly View St . . . . . Garden Grove CA 92845 *TF:* 800-745-9970 ■ *Web:* www.laborlawcenter.com	800-745-9970		138
Labor Party, The 216 N Mosley . . . . . Wichita KS 67202 *Web:* labor-party.com	316-712-4623		393
Labor Racketeering & Fraud Investigations Office 200 Constitution Ave NW Rm S-5506 . . . . . Washington DC 20210 *TF:* 800-347-3756 ■ *Web:* www.oig.dol.gov	202-693-6999	693-7020	340-15
Laboratoire Du-var Inc 1460 Rue Graham-Bell . . . . . Boucherville QC J4B6H5 *Web:* www.du-var.com	450-641-4740		231
Laboratory Corporation of America Holdings 1737 Tennessee Ave . . . . . Cincinnati OH 45229 *Web:* www.labcorpdna.com	513-985-9777		417
Laboratory for Laser Energetics 250 E River Rd . . . . . Rochester NY 14623 *Web:* www.lle.rochester.edu	585-275-5101	275-5960	668
Laboratory Institute of Merchandising 12 E 53rd St . . . . . New York NY 10022 *TF:* 800-677-1323 ■ *Web:* www.limcollege.edu	212-752-1530		166
Laborers National Pension Fund 14140 Midway Rd Ste 105 . . . . . Dallas TX 75244 *Web:* www.lnpf.org	972-233-4458		528
Laborers' International Union of North America 905 16th St NW . . . . . Washington DC 20006 *TF:* 800-548-6242 ■ *Web:* www.liuna.org	202-737-8320	737-2754	414
Laborie Medical Technologies Inc 6415 Northwest Dr Unit 11 . . . . . Mississauga ON L4V1X1 *Web:* www.laborie.com	905-612-1170		476
Laboure College 303 Adams St. . . . . Milton MA 02186 *Web:* www.laboure.edu	617-322-3575	690-3730	800
Labov & Beyond Inc 609 E Cook Rd. . . . . Fort Wayne IN 46825 *Web:* labov.com	260-497-0111		7
Labovitz Enterprises *Lion Hotel Group* 227 W 1st St 950 Missabe Bldg . . . . . Duluth MN 55802 *Web:* lionhotelgroup.com	218-727-7765	727-7362	707
Labrada Nutrition 403 Century Plaza Dr Ste 440 . . . . . Houston TX 77073 **Fax Area Code:* 281 ■ *TF:* 800-832-9948 ■ *Web:* www.labrada.com	800-832-9948	209-2135*	799
Labree's Inc 169 Gilman Falls Ave. . . . . Old Town ME 04468 *Web:* www.labrees.com	207-827-6121	827-2525	296-2
Labrie Enviroquip Group 175-B Rte Marie-Victorin . . . . . Levis QC G7A2T3 *TF:* 800-463-6638 ■ *Web:* www.labriegroup.com	418-831-8250	831-5255	516
LabRoots Inc 18340 Yorba Linda Blvd Ste 107 . . . . . Yorba Linda CA 92886 *Web:* www.labroots.com	714-463-4673		395
LABS Inc 6933 S Revere Pkwy . . . . . Centennial CO 80112 *TF:* 866-393-2244 ■ *Web:* labs-inc.org	720-528-4750	528-4786	417
Labsphere Inc 231 Shaker St. . . . . North Sutton NH 03260 *Web:* www.labsphere.com	603-927-4266	927-4694	407
Labstat International ULC 262 Manitou Dr . . . . . Kitchener ON N2C1L3 *Web:* www.labstat.com	519-748-5409		743
LabVantage Solutions Inc 265 Davidson Ave Ste 220 . . . . . Somerset NJ 08873 *Web:* www.labvantage.com	908-707-4100		177
Labware Inc 3 Mill Rd Ste 102 . . . . . Wilmington DE 19006 *Web:* www.labware.com	302-658-8444	658-7894	178-10
Lac Courte Oreilles Ojibwa Community College 13466 W Trepania Rd . . . . . Hayward WI 54843 *TF:* 888-526-6221 ■ *Web:* www.lco.edu	715-634-4790	634-5049	165
Lac du Flambeau Band of Lake Superior Chippewa Indians PO Box 67 . . . . . Lac du Flambeau WI 54538 *Web:* www.ldftribe.com	715-588-4265		379
Lac qui Parle County (LQP) 600 Sixth St . . . . . Madison MN 56256 *Web:* www.lqpco.com	320-598-7444	598-3125	338
Lac Qui Parle State Park 14047 20th St NW . . . . . Watson MN 56295 *Web:* dnr.state.mn.us	320-734-4450	734-4452	565
Lacamas Laboratories Inc 3625 N Suttle Rd . . . . . Portland OR 97217 *Web:* www.lacamaslabs.com	503-285-0360	289-1355	144
Lacasse & Weston Inc 203 Anderson St Ste 1 . . . . . Portland ME 04101 *Web:* www.lacwes.com	207-773-7711		261
Lacay Fabrication & Manufacturing Inc 52941 Glenview Dr . . . . . Elkhart IN 46514 *Web:* www.lacayfab.com	574-288-4678	288-2921	480
LaCaze Moss & Company CPAS LLC 2901 Ridgelake Dr Ste 110 S . . . . . Metairie LA 70002 *Web:* lmcocpa.com	504-835-8247		2
LACBA (Los Angeles County Bar Assn) PO Box 55020 . . . . . Los Angeles CA 90055 *Web:* www.lacba.org	213-243-1525	833-6717	49-19
Lace For Less Inc 1500 Main Ave. . . . . Clifton NJ 07011 *TF:* 800-533-5223 ■ *Web:* www.parislace.com	973-478-2955	478-8746	745-4
Lacework 700 E El Camino Real Ste 130 . . . . . Mountain View CA 94041 *TF:* 888-497-4531 ■ *Web:* www.lacework.com	888-497-4531		178-8
Lacey Drug Company Inc 4797 S Main St. . . . . Acworth GA 30101 *Web:* www.laceydrug.com	770-974-3131		237
Lacey Milling Co 231 W 5th St . . . . . Hanford CA 93230	559-584-6634		296-23
Lacey Museum 829 1/2 Lacey St SE . . . . . Lacey WA 98503 *Web:* www.ci.lacey.wa.us	360-438-0209		520
Lacey South Sound Chamber 420 Golf Club Rd SE . . . . . Lacey WA 98503 *Web:* www.laceysschamber.com	360-491-4141		139
Lachman Consultant Services Inc 1600 Stewart Ave Ste 604 . . . . . Westbury NY 11590 *Web:* www.lachmanconsultants.com	516-222-6222		194
Lachman Imports Inc 230 Fifth Ave Ste 900 . . . . . New York NY 10001 *Web:* www.guinotusa.com	212-532-1030	725-9692	237
Laciny Bros Inc 6622 Vernon Ave . . . . . Saint Louis MO 63130 *Web:* www.lacinybros.com	314-862-8330	862-8332	697
Lackawanna College 501 Vine St . . . . . Scranton PA 18509	570-961-7815		162
Lackawanna County 436 Spruce St . . . . . Scranton PA 18503 *Web:* www.lackawannacounty.org	570-963-6723	963-6387	338
Lackawanna County Convention & Visitors Bureau 99 Glenmaura National Blvd . . . . . Moosic PA 18507 *Web:* www.visitnepa.org	570-496-1701		206
Lackawanna State Park 1839 Abington Rd. . . . . North Abington Township PA 18414 *Web:* www.dcnr.pa.gov	570-945-3239		565
Lackenbach Siegel LLP 1 Chase Rd . . . . . Scarsdale NY 10583 *Web:* lackenbachsiegel.com	914-723-4300		41
Lackmann Culinary Services Inc 303 Crossways Pk Dr . . . . . Woodbury NY 11797	516-364-2300		299
Lacks Enterprises 5460 Cascade Rd SE . . . . . Grand Rapids MI 49546 *Web:* www.lacksenterprises.com	616-949-6570		604
Lacks Valley Stores Ltd 1300 San Patricia St . . . . . Pharr TX 78577 *TF:* 800-870-6999 ■ *Web:* www.lacks.com	956-702-3361	782-5740	321
Laclede Chain Manufacturing Company LLC 1549 Fenpark Dr. . . . . Fenton MO 63026 *TF:* 800-325-2699 ■ *Web:* lacledechain.com	800-325-2699		492
Laclede County 200 N Adams Ave . . . . . Lebanon MO 65536 *Web:* lacledecountymissouri.org	417-532-5471	588-9288	338
Laclede Electric Cooperative 1400 E Rt 66 . . . . . Lebanon MO 65536 *TF:* 800-299-3164 ■ *Web:* www.lacledeelectric.com	417-532-3164		245
Laclede Inc 2103 E University Dr. . . . . Rancho Dominguez CA 90220 *Web:* www.laclede.com	310-605-4280		743
Laclede's Landing 710 N Second St. . . . . Saint Louis MO 63102 *Web:* lacledeslanding.com	314-241-5875		50-6
La-Co/Markal Co 1201 Pratt Blvd. . . . . Elk Grove Village IL 60007 **Fax Area Code:* 800 ■ *TF:* 800-621-4025 ■ *Web:* markal.com	847-956-7600	448-5436*	467
Lacorte, Bundy, Varady & Kinsella 989 Bonnel Ct. . . . . Union NJ 07083 *Web:* lbvklaw.com	908-810-0500		41
Lacrimedics Inc 2620 Williamson Pl Ste 113 . . . . . Dupont WA 98327 *TF:* 800-367-8327 ■ *Web:* www.lacrimedics.com	253-964-0360	964-2699	542
Lacroix at the Rittenhouse 210 W Rittenhouse Sq . . . . . Philadelphia PA 19103 *Web:* www.rittenhousehotel.com	215-790-2533		671
LaCroix Precision Optics 50 LaCroix Dr . . . . . Batesville AR 72501 *Web:* lacroixoptics.com	870-698-1881		544
Lacrosse Fairgrounds Speedway N 4985 Cty Rd M . . . . . West Salem WI 54669 *Web:* lacrossespeedway.com	608-786-1525	786-1524	515
Lacrosse Hall of Fame & Museum 113 W University Pkwy. . . . . Baltimore MD 21210 *Web:* www.uslacrosse.org	410-235-6882	366-6735	520
Lacrosse Unlimited Inc 59 Gilpin Ave . . . . . Hauppauge NY 11788 *TF:* 877-800-5850 ■ *Web:* lacrosseunlimited.com	877-800-5850		711
Lacy Construction Co 3356 W Old Hwy 30 PO Box 188 . . . . . Grand Island NE 68801 *Web:* www.lacygc.com	308-384-2866	384-2883	186
Lacy Katzen LLP Attorneys at Law 130 E Main St. . . . . Rochester NY 14604 *Web:* www.lacykatzen.com	585-454-5650	269-3077	428

Phone | Fax | Class

Lad Drago Insurance & Financial Services I
7623 Spanish Fort Blvd .... Spanish Fort AL 36527 251-626-1237 390
Web: laddragoinsurance.com

Lad Global Enterprises Inc
1309 S Fountain Dr .... Olathe KS 66061 913-768-0888 787
Web: www.lad-global.com

Lad Lake Inc
W350s1401 Waterville Rd PO Box 158 .... Dousman WI 53118 262-965-2131 965-4107 148
TF: 877-965-2131 ■ *Web:* www.ladlake.org

Lad Truck Lines Inc
109 Barnett Shoals Rd .... Watkinsville GA 30677 706-769-4048 780
Web: www.ladtrucklines.com

Ladas & Parry LLP
1040 Avenue of the Americas .... New York NY 10018 212-708-1800 246-8959 428
Web: ladas.com

Ladco Company Ltd
200-40 Lakewood Blvd .... Winnipeg MB R2J2M6 204-982-5900 186
Web: www.ladco.mb.ca

Ladd Engineering Inc (LEI)
1127 Brookside Dr .... Lebanon IN 46052 765-482-9219 482-9224 261
TF: 877-437-6145 ■ *Web:* www.laddengr.com

Ladd Research Industries
83 Holly Ct .... Williston VT 05495 802-658-4961 253
TF: 800-451-3406 ■ *Web:* www.laddresearch.com

Ladder Capital Finance LLC
345 Park Ave 8th Fl .... New York NY 10154 212-715-3170 652
Web: www.laddercapital.com

Ladd-Peebles Stadium 1621 Virginia St .... Mobile AL 36604 251-208-2500 208-2514 720
Web: laddpeeblesstadium.com

Ladenburg Thalmann Financial Services Inc
4400 Biscayne Blvd 12th Fl .... Miami FL 33137 305-572-4100 572-4199 690
NYSE: LTS ■ *Web:* www.ladenburg.com

Ladew Topiary Gardens
3535 Jarettsville Pk .... Monkton MD 21111 410-557-9466 557-7763 97
Web: www.ladewgardens.com

Ladies Auxiliary VFW Magazine
406 W 34th St .... Kansas City MO 64111 816-561-8655 931-4753 457-10
Web: vfwauxiliary.org

Ladies Professional Golf Assn (LPGA)
100 International Golf Dr .... Daytona Beach FL 32124 386-274-6200 274-1099 48-22
Web: www.lpga.com

Lado International College
401 Ninth St NW Ste C100 .... Washington DC 20004 202-223-0023 337-1118 423
TF: 800-281-7710 ■ *Web:* lado.edu

Lady And Sons, The 102 W Congress St .... Savannah GA 31401 912-233-2600 233-8283 671
Web: www.ladyandsons.com

Lady Bird Johnson Wildflower Ctr
4801 La Crosse Ave .... Austin TX 78739 512-232-0100 232-0156 97
TF: 877-945-3357 ■ *Web:* www.wildflower.org

Lady Grace Stores Inc
238 W Cummings Pk .... Woburn MA 01801 877-381-4629 157-6
TF: 877-381-4629 ■ *Web:* www.ladygrace.com

Lady of The Sea General Hospital (LOSGH)
200 W 134th Pl .... Cut Off LA 70345 985-632-6401 374-3
Web: www.losgh.org

Laerdal Medical Corp
167 Myers Corners Rd PO Box 1840 .... Wappingers Falls NY 12590 845-297-7770 475
TF: 800-227-1143 ■ *Web:* www.laerdal.com

Laetitia Vineyards & Winery Inc
453 Laetitia Vineyard Dr .... Arroyo Grande CA 93420 805-481-1772 481-6920 80-3
Web: www.laetitiawine.com

Lafarge Fox River Decorative Stone
1300 S Rte Business 31 .... South Elgin IL 60177 847-888-6133 503-6
Web: www.foxriverstone.com

LafargeHolcim 8700 W Bryn Mawr Ave .... Chicago IL 60631 773-372-1000 191-2
Web: www.lafargeholcim.us

Lafave, White & Mcgivern LS PC
133 Commercial St .... Theresa NY 13691 315-628-4414 727
Web: lwmlspc.com

Lafayette College 730 High St .... Easton PA 18042 610-330-5000 330-5355 166
Web: www.lafayette.edu

Lafayette College Skillman Library
710 Sullivan Rd .... Easton PA 18042 610-330-5151 252-0370 434-6
Web: library.lafayette.edu

Lafayette Consolidated Government
705 W University Ave .... Lafayette LA 70506 337-291-8200 338
Web: www.lafayettela.gov

Lafayette Convention & Visitors Commission
1400 NW Evangeline Thwy .... LaFayette LA 70501 337-232-3737 232-0161 206
Web: www.lafayettetravel.com

Lafayette Copier Service & Sales
310 Farabee Dr .... LaFayette IN 47905 765-446-2230 535
Web: lafayettecopier.com

Lafayette County
626 Main St PO Box 40 .... Darlington WI 53530 608-776-4850 776-8893 338
Web: www.lafayettecountywi.org

Lafayette County 1001 Main St .... Lexington MO 64067 660-259-4315 259-6109 338
Web: www.lafayettecountymo.com

Lafayette County
300 N Lamar Blvd PO Box 1240 .... Oxford MS 38655 662-236-2717 234-5402 338
Web: lafayettems.com

Lafayette Data Systems LLC
605 S Buchanan PO Box 4301 .... LaFayette LA 70501 337-261-8999 180
Web: www.lafayettedata.com

Lafayette Federal Credit Union (Inc)
3535 University Blvd W .... Kensington MD 20895 301-929-7990 219
TF: 800-888-6560 ■ *Web:* www.lfcu.org

Lafayette General Medical Ctr
1214 Coolidge Blvd .... LaFayette LA 70505 337-289-7991 374-3
Web: www.lafayettegeneral.com

Lafayette Grinding LLC 115 Banker St .... Brooklyn NY 11222 718-388-5973 486-8636 393
Web: lafayettegrinding.com

Lafayette Hotel
600 St Charles Ave .... New Orleans LA 70130 504-524-4441 379
TF: 888-626-5457 ■ *Web:* www.lafayettehotelneworleans.com

Lafayette Hotel 101 Front St .... Marietta OH 45750 740-373-5522 379
TF: 800-331-9336 ■ *Web:* www.lafayettehotel.com

Lafayette Hotel & Suites San Diego
2223 El Cajon Blvd .... San Diego CA 92104 619-296-2101 296-0512 379
Web: www.lafayettehotelsd.com

Lafayette Instrument Company Inc (LIC)
3700 Sagamore Pky N .... Lafayette IN 47903 765-423-1505 423-4111 472
TF: 800-428-7545 ■ *Web:* www.lafayetteinstrument.com

Lafayette Natural History Museum & Planetarium
433 Jefferson St .... LaFayette LA 70501 337-291-5544 598
Web: lafayettesciencemuseum.org

Lafayette Parish Public Library
301 W Congress St .... LaFayette LA 70501 337-261-5787 261-5782 434-3
Web: lafayettepubliclibrary.org

Lafayette Parish School System
113 Chaplin Dr .... LaFayette LA 70508 337-521-7000 685
Web: www.lpssonline.com

Lafayette Park Hotel
3287 Mt Diablo Blvd .... LaFayette CA 94549 800-394-3112 379
TF: 855-382-8632 ■ *Web:* www.lafayetteparkhotel.com

Lafayette Printing Co 511 Ferry St .... Lafayette IN 47902 765-423-2578 742-1242 627
TF: 800-564-5294 ■ *Web:* www.lafayetteprinting.com

Lafayette Quality Products
111 Farabee Dr .... LaFayette IN 47905 765-447-3106 482
Web: www.lqp-mfg.com

Lafayette Regional Airport
222 Tower Dr .... LaFayette LA 70508 337-266-4400 272-0260 27
Web: www.lftairport.com

Lafayette School Corp 2300 Cason St .... Lafayette IN 47904 765-771-6000 685
Web: lsc.k12.in.us

Lafayette Sun, The PO Box 378 .... Lafayette AL 36862 334-864-8885 864-8310 532-2
Web: thelafayettesun.com

Lafayette Venetian Blind Inc
3000 Klondike Rd PO Box 2838 .... West Lafayette IN 47996 800-342-5523 87
TF: 800-342-5523 ■ *Web:* www.lafvb.com

Lafayette Wood-Works Inc
3004 Cameron St .... LaFayette LA 70506 337-233-5250 233-1147 499
TF: 800-960-3311 ■ *Web:* www.lafayettewood.com

LaFayette-Walker County Library
305 S Duke St .... LaFayette GA 30728 706-638-2992 434-3
Web: www.chrl.org

Lafayette-West Lafayette Convention & Visitors Bureau
301 Frontage Rd .... LaFayette IN 47905 765-447-9999 447-5062 206
TF: 800-872-6648 ■ *Web:* www.homeofpurdue.com

Lafferty, Gallagher & Scott LLC
116 W William .... Maumee OH 43537 419-241-5500 41
Web: lgslaw.net

Lafitte Cork & Capsule Inc
45 Executive Ct .... Napa CA 94558 800-343-2675 279
TF: 800-343-2675 ■ *Web:* www.lafitte-usa.com

Laflamme Doors & Windows
39 Industrielle St .... Saint Apollinaire QC G0S2E0 800-463-1922 463-3437 499
TF: 800-463-1922 ■ *Web:* www.laflamme.com

Lafontaine Honda 2245 S Telegraph Rd .... Dearborn MI 48124 866-567-5088 57
TF: 866-567-5088 ■ *Web:* www.lafontainehonda.com

LaForce inc 41 E 11th St 6th Fl .... New York NY 10003 212-367-8008 636
Web: laforce.nyc

LaForce Inc 1060 W Mason St .... Green Bay WI 54303 920-497-7100 497-4955 234
TF: 800-236-8858 ■ *Web:* laforceinc.com

Lafourche Chamber of Commerce, The
107 W 26th St .... Larose LA 70373 985-693-6700 693-6702 139
Web: www.lafourchechamber.com

Lafourche Parish
402 Green St PO Box 5548 .... Thibodaux LA 70302 985-446-8427 446-8459 338
TF: 800-834-8832 ■ *Web:* www.lafourchegov.org

LaFrance Corp
1 LaFrance Way PO Box 5002 .... Concordville PA 19331 610-361-4300 361-4301 701
Web: www.lafrancecorp.com

LaFrance Equipment Corp 516 Erie St .... Elmira NY 14904 607-733-5511 733-0482 679
TF: 800-873-8808 ■ *Web:* www.lafrance-equipment.com

Lafromboise Communications Inc
321 N Pearl St .... Centralia WA 98531 360-736-3311 532-3
TF: 800-356-4404 ■ *Web:* www.chronline.com

Lagerlof LLP
790 E Colorado Blvd Ste 300 .... Pasadena CA 91101 626-683-7234 683-7251 41
Web: www.lagerlof.com

Lago Mar Resort & Club
1700 S Ocean Ln .... Fort Lauderdale FL 33316 954-523-6511 669
TF: 855-209-5677 ■ *Web:* www.lagomar.com

Lagoon & Pioneer Village
375 N Lagoon Dr .... Farmington UT 84025 801-451-8000 32
TF: 800-748-5246 ■ *Web:* www.lagoonpark.com

Lagoon Information Systems Inc
PO Box 1763 .... Los Altos CA 94023 650-492-5474 393
Web: www.lagooninfo.com

LaGrange College 601 Broad St .... LaGrange GA 30240 706-880-8000 880-8005 166
TF: 800-593-2885 ■ *Web:* www.lagrange.edu

LaGrange County 114 W Michigan St .... LaGrange IN 46761 260-499-6300 338
Web: lagrangecounty.org

LaGrange County Chamber of Commerce
901 S Detroit St Ste A .... LaGrange IN 46761 260-463-2443 463-2683 139
Web: www.lagrangechamber.org

LaGrange County Public Library
203 W Spring St .... LaGrange IN 46761 260-463-2841 463-2843 434-3
Web: www.lagrange.lib.in.us

LaGrange County Rural Electric Membership Corp
1995 E US Hwy 20 .... LaGrange IN 46761 877-463-7165 463-4329* 245
*Fax Area Code: 260 ■ *TF:* 877-463-7165 ■ *Web:* www.lagrangeremc.com

Lagrange Products Inc 607 S Wayne St .... Fremont IN 46737 260-495-3025 770
TF: 800-369-6978 ■ *Web:* www.lagrangeproducts.com

LaGrange-Troup County Chamber of Commerce
111 Bull St .... LaGrange GA 30240 706-884-8671 882-8012 139
Web: www.lagrangechamber.com

LaGuardia Community College
31-10 Thomson Ave .... Long Island City NY 11101 718-482-5000 609-2033 162
Web: www.laguardia.edu

Laguna Beach Chamber of Commerce
357 Glenneyre .... Laguna Beach CA 92651 949-494-1018 139
Web: www.lagunabeachchamber.org

	Phone	Fax	Class
Laguna Beach Visitors & Conference Bureau 381 Forest Ave .... Laguna Beach CA 92651 *TF:* 800-877-1115 ■ *Web:* www.visitlagunabeach.com	949-497-9229		206
Laguna Brisas 1600 S Coast Hwy .... Laguna Beach CA 92651 *TF:* 855-502-2877 ■ *Web:* www.lagunabrisashotel.com	949-497-7272		379
Laguna College of Art & Design 2222 Laguna Canyon Rd .... Laguna Beach CA 92651 *TF:* 800-255-0762 ■ *Web:* www.lcad.edu	949-376-6000	376-6009	166
Laguna Honda Hospital and Rehabilitation Ctr 375 Laguna Honda Blvd .... San Francisco CA 94116 *Web:* www.lagunahonda.org	415-759-2363		374-6
Laguna Niguel Chamber of Commerce 28062 Forbes Rd Ste C .... Laguna Niguel CA 92677 *Web:* www.lnchamber.com	949-363-0136	363-9026	139
Laguna Playhouse, The 606 Laguna Canyon Rd PO Box 1747 .... Laguna Beach CA 92651 *Web:* www.lagunaplayhouse.com	949-497-2787	497-6948	749
Laguna Productions 20640 Plummer St .... Chatsworth CA 91311 *TF:* 800-852-9840 ■ *Web:* www.lagunaproductions.com	800-852-9840		572
Laguna Wilderness Press PO Box 149 .... Laguna Beach CA 92652 *Web:* www.lagunawildernesspress.com	951-827-1571		637-2
Lahey Clinic Foundation Inc 41 Mall Rd .... Burlington MA 01805 *TF:* 800-524-3955 ■ *Web:* www.lahey.org	781-744-8000		374-3
Lahontan State Recreation Area 16799 Lahontan Dam .... Fallon NV 89406 *Web:* www.parks.nv.gov	775-577-2226		565
LaHood Darin (Rep R - IL) 1424 Longworth House Office Bldg .... Washington DC 20515 *Web:* lahood.house.gov	202-225-6201	225-9249	342-2
LAI (Language Automation Inc) 1660 S Amphlett Blvd Ste 106 .... San Mateo CA 94402 *Web:* www.lai.com	650-571-7877		178-7
LAI International Inc 1110 Business Pky S .... Westminster MD 21157 *TF:* 800-840-1126 ■ *Web:* www.laico.com	800-840-1126		454
Lai Wah Heen 108 Chestnut St .... Toronto ON M5G1R3 *Web:* laiwahheen.com	416-977-9899		671
Laibe Corp 1414 Bates St .... Indianapolis IN 46201 *TF:* 800-942-3388 ■ *Web:* www.versa-drill.com	317-231-2250		492
Laico's 67 Terhune Ave .... Jersey City NJ 07305 *Web:* www.laicosjc.com	732-609-3432		671
Laika 22990 NW Bennett St .... Hillsboro OR 97124 *Web:* www.laika.com	503-906-5497		33
Laingsburg Community Schools Central 205 S Woodhull Rd .... Laingsburg MI 48848 *Web:* www.laingsburg.k12.mi.us	517-651-2705	651-9075	685
Laipac Technology Inc 20 Mural St Unit 5 .... Richmond Hill ON L4B1K3 *Web:* www.laipac.com	905-762-1228		246
Laird & Co 1 Laird Rd .... Eatontown NJ 07724 *Web:* www.lairdandcompany.com	732-542-0312	542-2244	80-1
Laird Noller Ford Inc 2245 SW Topeka Blvd .... Topeka KS 66611 *TF:* 877-803-1859 ■ *Web:* www.nollerford-topeka.com	785-235-9211		516
Laird Norton Tyee 801 Second Ave Ste 1600 .... Seattle WA 98104 *TF:* 800-426-5105 ■ *Web:* lairdnortonwm.com	800-426-5105		401
Laird Partners LLC 475 Tenth Ave 7th Fl .... New York NY 10018 *Web:* lairdandpartners.com	212-478-8181		4
Laird Plastics Inc 450 E 22nd St Ste 172 .... Lombard IL 60148 **Fax Area Code:* 561 ■ *TF:* 800-243-9696 ■ *Web:* www.lairdplastics.com	630-451-4688	443-9108*	603
LAITEK Inc 18101 Martin Ave .... Homewood IL 60430 *Web:* www.laitek.com	708-799-5000		177
Laitram LLC 200 Laitram Ln .... Harahan LA 70123 *TF:* 800-535-7631 ■ *Web:* www.laitram.com	504-733-6000	733-2143	529
LaJames College 24 2nd St NE .... Mason City IA 50401 *Web:* lajames.edu	641-424-2161		167-3
Lake & Cobb Plc 1095 W Rio Salado Pkwy Ste 206 .... Tempe AZ 85281 *Web:* www.lakeandcobb.com	602-523-3000		445
Lake Afton Public Observatory 25000 W 39th S .... Goddard KS 67052 *Web:* www.lakeafton.com	316-559-2899		598
Lake Agassiz Regional Library (LARL) 118 Fifth St S PO Box 900 .... Moorhead MN 56560 *TF:* 800-247-0449 ■ *Web:* www.larl.org	218-233-3757	233-7556	434-3
Lake Ahquabi State Park 1650 118th Ave .... Indianola IA 50125 *Web:* www.iowadnr.gov	515-961-7101		565
Lake Air 7709 Winpark Dr .... Minneapolis MN 55427 *TF:* 888-785-2422 ■ *Web:* www.lakeairmetals.com	763-546-0994	546-4469	489
Lake Anita State Park 55111 750th St .... Anita IA 50020 *Web:* www.iowadnr.gov	712-762-3564		565
Lake Anna State Park 6800 Lawyers Rd .... Spotsylvania VA 22551 *Web:* www.dcr.virginia.gov	540-854-5503		565
Lake Area Technical Institute 1201 Arrow Ave PO Box 730 .... Watertown SD 57201 *TF:* 800-657-4344 ■ *Web:* www.lakeareatech.edu	605-882-5284	882-6299	162
Lake Arrowhead Resort & Spa 27984 Hwy 189 .... Lake Arrowhead CA 92352 *TF:* 877-688-7182 ■ *Web:* www.lakearrowheadresort.com	909-336-1511	744-3088	669
Lake Arrowhead State Park 229 Park Rd 63 .... Wichita Falls TX 76310 *Web:* tpwd.texas.gov	940-528-2211		565
Lake Austin Spa Resort 1705 S Quinlan Park Rd .... Austin TX 78732 *TF:* 800-847-5637 ■ *Web:* www.lakeaustin.com	512-372-7380	266-1572	707
Lake Avenue Cafe 394 S Lake Ave .... Duluth MN 55802 *Web:* lakeaveduluth.com	218-722-2355		671
Lake Bank Shares Inc 437 Bridge Ave .... Albert Lea MN 56007 *Web:* www.securitybankmn.com	507 373 1481		70
Lake Barkley State Resort Park 3500 State Park Rd .... Cadiz KY 42211 *TF:* 800-325-1708 ■ *Web:* parks.ky.gov	800-325-1708		565
Lake Barkley Tourist Commission 82 Days Inn Dr .... Kuttawa KY 42055 *Web:* www.lakebarkley.org	270-388-5300		206
Lake Bemidji State Park 3401 State Pk Rd NE .... Bemidji MN 56601 **Fax Area Code:* 651 ■ *Web:* www.dnr.state.mn.us	218-308-2300	296-6047*	565
Lake Beverage Corp 900 John St .... West Henrietta NY 14586 *Web:* lakebeverage.com	585-427-0090		81-1
Lake Bistineau State Park 103 State Park Rd .... Doyline LA 71023 *TF:* 888-677-2478 ■ *Web:* crt.state.la.us	318-745-3503		565
Lake Bluff Public Library 123 E Scranton Ave .... Lake Bluff IL 60044 *Web:* lakebluffibrary.org	847-234-2540		435
Lake Bob Sandlin State Park 341 State Park Rd 2117 .... Pittsburg TX 75686 *Web:* tpwd.texas.gov	903-572-5531		565
Lake Book Manufacturing Inc 2085 N Cornell Ave .... Melrose Park IL 60160 *Web:* www.lakebook.com	708-345-7000	345-1544	92
Lake Breeze Motel Resort 9000 Congdon Blvd .... Duluth MN 55804 *TF:* 800-738-5884 ■ *Web:* www.lakebreeze.com	218-525-6808	525-2986	669
Lake Bronson State Park 3793 230th St PO Box 9 .... Lake Bronson MN 56734 *Web:* www.dnr.state.mn.us	218-754-2200	754-6141	565
Lake Brownwood State Park 200 Hwy Park Rd 15 .... Lake Brownwood TX 76801 *Web:* tpwd.texas.gov	325-784-5223		565
Lake Bruin State Park 201 State Park Rd .... Saint Joseph LA 71366 *TF:* 888-677-2784 ■ *Web:* crt.state.la.us	318-766-3530		565
Lake Buena Vista Factory Stores 15657 S Apopka Vineland Rd Sr 535 .... Orlando FL 32821 *Web:* www.lbvfs.com	407-238-9301		460
Lake Business Products Inc 37200 Research Dr .... Eastlake OH 44095 *TF:* 800-443-4583 ■ *Web:* www.lakebusinessproducts.com	440-953-1199	953-0645	112
Lake Capital 875 N Michigan Ave Ste 3520 .... Chicago IL 60611 *Web:* www.lakecapital.com	312-640-7050	640-7051	792
Lake Carlos State Park 2601 County Rd 38 NE .... Carlos MN 56319 *Web:* www.dnr.state.mn.us	320-852-7200		565
Lake Carmi State Park 460 Marsh Farm Rd .... Enosburg Falls VT 05450 *Web:* www.vtstateparks.com	802-933-8383		565
Lake Cascade State Park 970 Dam Rd .... Cascade ID 83611 *Web:* parksandrecreation.idaho.gov	208-382-6544		565
Lake Catherine Footwear 3770 Malvern Rd .... Hot Springs AR 71901 *TF:* 800-819-1901 ■ *Web:* www.munroshoes.com	800-819-1901		301
Lake Catherine State Park 1200 Catherine Park Rd .... Hot Springs AR 71913 *Web:* www.arkansasstateparks.com	501-844-4176		565
Lake Champlain Maritime Museum 4472 Basin Harbor Rd .... Vergennes VT 05491 *Web:* www.lcmm.org	802-475-2022	475-2953	520
Lake Champlain Regional Chamber of Commerce 60 Main St Ste 100 .... Burlington VT 05401 *TF:* 877-686-5253 ■ *Web:* www.vermont.org	802-863-3489	863-1538	139
Lake Charles Civic Ctr 900 Lakeshore Dr .... Lake Charles LA 70602 *TF:* 888-620-1749 ■ *Web:* www.lakecharlescivicenter.com	337-491-1256	491-1534	572
Lake Charles Memorial Health System (LCMH) 1701 Oak Pk Blvd .... Lake Charles LA 70601 *TF:* 800-494-5264 ■ *Web:* www.lcmh.com	337-494-3000		374-3
Lake Charles State Park 3705 Hwy 25 .... Powhatan AR 72458 *Web:* www.arkansasstateparks.com	870-878-6595		565
Lake Chatuge Animal Hospital 1619 State Hwy 17N .... Young Harris GA 30582 *Web:* lakechatugeanimalhospital.com	706-896-1244		794
Lake Chelan State Park 7544 S Lakeshore Rd .... Chelan WA 98816 *Web:* www.parks.state.wa.us	509-687-3710		565
Lake Chicot State Park 2542 Hwy 257 .... Lake Village AR 71653 *TF:* 800-264-2430 ■ *Web:* www.arkansasstateparks.com	870-265-5480		565
Lake City Correctional Facility 7906 E US Hwy 90 .... Lake City FL 32055 *Web:* www.corecivic.com	386-755-3379	752-7202	213
Lake City Printing Inc 1723 W Sale Rd .... Lake Charles LA 70605 *Web:* lcpmail.com	337-477-2595	474-4217	9
Lake City Supply Inc 502 7th St .... Lake Charles LA 70601 *Web:* www.lakecitysupply.com	337-439-8308	439-4365	146
Lake City Trucking 5700 BJ Cement Rd .... Lake Charles LA 70615 *TF:* 800-256-2785 ■ *Web:* www.lakecitytrucking.com	337-494-6900	436-4606	780
Lake City/Columbia County Chamber of Commerce 162 S Marion Ave .... Lake City FL 32025 *Web:* www.lakecitychamber.com	386-752-3690	755-7744	139
Lake Claiborne State Park 225 State Park Rd .... Homer LA 71040 *TF:* 888-677-2524 ■ *Web:* crt.state.la.us	318-927-2976		565
Lake Claremont Press (LCP) PO Box 711 .... Chicago IL 60690 *Web:* www.lakeclaremont.com	312-226-8400	226-8420	637-2
Lake Clark National Park & Preserve 240 W Fifth Ave Ste 236 .... Anchorage AK 99501 *TF:* 800-365-2267 ■ *Web:* www.nps.gov	907-644-3626	644-3810	564
Lake Colorado City State Park 4582 FM 2836 .... Colorado City TX 79512 *Web:* tpwd.texas.gov	325-728-3931		565
Lake Companies Inc, The 2980 Walker Dr .... Green Bay WI 54311 *Web:* www.lakeco.com	920-406-3030	406-3040	174

Phone | Fax | Class

Lake Compounce Family Theme Park
822 Lake Ave . . . Bristol CT 06010 860-583-3300 589-7974 32
Web: www.lakecompounce.com

Lake Corpus Christi State Park
23194 Park Rd 25 . . . Mathis TX 78368 361-547-2635 565
Web: tpwd.texas.gov

Lake Correctional Institution
19225 US Hwy 27 . . . Clermont FL 34711 352-394-6146 213
Web: dc.state.fl.us

Lake Country Engineering Inc
970 S Silver Lake St Ste 105 . . . Oconomowoc WI 53066 262-569-9331 569-9316 261
Web: lce.biz

Lake Country Power 2810 Elida Dr . . . Grand Rapids MN 55744 800-421-9959 326-8136* 245
*Fax Area Code: 218 ■ *TF:* 800-421-9959 ■ *Web:* lakecountrypower.coop

Lake County 2293 N Main St . . . Crown Point IN 46307 219-755-3000 755-3520 338
Web: www.lakecountyin.org

Lake County 513 Center St . . . Lakeview OR 97630 541-947-6006 947-6015 338
Web: www.lakecountyor.org

Lake County
505 Harrison Ave PO Box 28 . . . Leadville CO 80461 719-486-2426 486-3972 338
Web: www.lakecountyco.com

Lake County 200 E Center St . . . Madison SD 57042 605-256-7618 256-7624 338
Web: www.lake.sd.gov

Lake County 105 Main St . . . Painesville OH 44077 800-899-5253 338
TF: 800-899-5253 ■ *Web:* www.lakecountyohio.org

Lake County 601 3rd Ave . . . Two Harbors MN 55616 218-834-8300 834-8360 338
Web: www.co.lake.mn.us

Lake County 18 N County St . . . Waukegan IL 60085 847-377-2000 338
Web: www.lakecountyil.gov

Lake County Chamber
895 Michigan Ave PO Box 130 . . . Baldwin MI 49304 231-745-4331 338
Web: lakecountymichigan.com

Lake County Chamber of Commerce
1313 N Delany Rd 2nd Fl of Associated Bank . . . Gurnee IL 60031 847-249-3800 139
Web: www.lakecountychamber.com

Lake County Convention & Visitors Bureau
5465 W Grand Ave Ste 100 . . . Gurnee IL 60031 847-662-2700 662-2702 206
TF: 800-525-3669 ■ *Web:* www.visitlakecounty.org

Lake County Courthouse
106 Fourth Ave E . . . Polson MT 59860 406-883-7215 338
Web: www.lakemt.gov

Lake County Courthouse 550 W Main St . . . Tavares FL 32778 352-742-4100 338
Web: www.lakecountyclerk.org

Lake County Educational Federal Credit Union
1595 Mentor Ave . . . Painesville OH 44077 440-352-4732 219
Web: lakecountyedufcu.org

Lake County Educational Service Ctr
8221 Auburn Rd . . . Concord Township OH 44077 440-350-2563 242
Web: www.lcesc.k12.oh.us

Lake County Forest Preserve
1899 W Winchester Rd . . . Libertyville IL 60048 847-367-6640 367-6649 302
Web: www.lcfpd.org

Lake County Press Inc 98 Noll St . . . Waukegan IL 60085 847-336-4333 627
Web: www.lakecountypress.com

Lake County Public Library
1919 W 81st Ave . . . Merrillville IN 46410 219-769-3541 434-3
TF: 888-303-0180 ■ *Web:* www.lcplin.org

Lake Court Medical Supplies Inc
27733 Groesbeck Hwy . . . Roseville MI 48066 800-860-3130 41
TF: 800-860-3130 ■ *Web:* www.lakecourt.com

Lake Cumberland Regional Hospital
305 Langdon St . . . Somerset KY 42503 606-679-7441 678-9919 374-3
Web: lakecumberlandhospital.com

Lake Cumberland State Resort Park
5465 State Park Rd . . . Jamestown KY 42629 270-343-3111 669
Web: parks.ky.gov

Lake D'Arbonne State Park
3628 Evergreen Rd . . . Farmerville LA 71241 318-368-2086 565
Web: crt.state.la.us

Lake Dardanelle State Park
100 State Park Dr . . . Russellville AR 72802 479-967-5516 565
Web: www.arkansasstateparks.com

Lake Darling State Park
10 Lake Darling Rd . . . Brighton IA 52540 319-694-2323 565
Web: www.iowadnr.gov

Lake Data Center Inc 800 Lloyd Rd . . . Wickliffe OH 44092 440-944-2020 225
Web: www.lakedata.com

Lake Easton State Park
150 Lake Easton State Park Rd . . . Easton WA 98925 509-656-2230 565
Web: parks.state.wa.us

Lake Elmo State Park
2300 Lake Elmo Dr . . . Billings MT 59105 406-247-2955 565
Web: stateparks.mt.gov

Lake Elsinore Valley Chamber of Commerce
132 W Graham Ave . . . Lake Elsinore CA 92530 951-245-8848 245-9127 139
Web: www.lakeelsinorechamber.com

Lake EMS 2761 W Old US Hwy 441 . . . Mount Dora FL 32757 352-383-4554 30
Web: www.lakeems.org

Lake Engineering Inc
2085 Daniels St . . . Long Lake MN 55356 952-473-5485 454
TF: 800-215-5514 ■ *Web:* www.lakeengineering.com

Lake Erie Beach Hotels 8696 E Lake Rd . . . Erie PA 16511 814-899-6948 379
Web: www.lakeviewerie.com

Lake Erie College
391 W Washington St . . . Painesville OH 44077 440-375-7050 375-7005 166
TF: 800-533-4996 ■ *Web:* www.lec.edu

Lake Erie Construction Co
25 S Norwalk Rd E . . . Norwalk OH 44857 419-668-3302 663-3314 188-4
Web: www.lec-co.com

Lake Erie Electric 25730 First St . . . Westlake OH 44145 440-835-5565 835-5688 189-4
TF: 855-877-9393 ■ *Web:* www.lakeerieelectric.com

Lake Erie Frozen Foods Co
1830 Orange Rd . . . Ashland OH 44805 419-289-9204 345
TF: 800-766-8501 ■ *Web:* www.leffco.net

Lake Erie Graphics Inc
5372 W 130th St . . . Brook Park OH 44142 216-265-7575 627
TF: 888-293-7397 ■ *Web:* lakeeriegraphics.com

Lake Erie Shores & Islands Welcome Center - west
770 SE Catawba Rd . . . Port Clinton OH 43452 419-734-4386 734-9798 206
TF: 800-441-1271 ■ *Web:* www.shoresandislands.com

Lake Erie Speedway 10700 Delmas Dr . . . North East PA 16428 814-725-3303 725-3353 642
Web: www.lakeeriespeedway.com

Lake Erie State Park 5838 Rt 5 . . . Brocton NY 14716 716-792-9214 565
Web: parks.ny.gov

Lake Eufaula State Park
111563 Hwy 150 . . . Checotah OK 74426 918-689-5311 565
Web: www.travelok.com

Lake Forest Academy
1500 W Kennedy Rd . . . Lake Forest IL 60045 847-234-3210 622
Web: www.lfanet.org

Lake Forest College
555 N Sheridan Rd . . . Lake Forest IL 60045 847-234-3100 735-6271 166
TF: 800-828-4751 ■ *Web:* www.lakeforest.edu

Lake Fort Smith State Park
PO Box 4 . . . Mountainburg AR 72946 479-369-2469 565
Web: www.arkansasstateparks.com

Lake Frierson State Park 7904 Hwy . . . Jonesboro AR 72401 870-932-2615 565
Web: www.arkansasstateparks.com

Lake George Historical Assn (LGHA)
290 Canada St . . . Lake George NY 12845 518-668-5044 49-19
Web: www.lakegeorgehistorical.org

Lake Gogebic State Park
N9995 State Hwy M-64 . . . Marenisco MI 49947 906-842-3341 565
Web: www.michigan.org

Lake Granbury Area Chamber of Commerce
3408 E Hwy 377 . . . Granbury TX 76049 817-573-1114 573-0805 139
Web: www.granburychamber.com

Lake Greenwood State Recreation Area
302 State Park Rd . . . Ninety Six SC 29666 864-543-3535 565
Web: southcarolinaparks.com

Lake Griffin State Park
3089 US 441-27 . . . Fruitland Park FL 34731 352-360-6760 565
Web: www.floridastateparks.org

Lake Group Media Inc 1 Byram Brook Pl . . . Armonk NY 10504 914-925-2400 925-2499 5
Web: www.lakegroupmedia.com

Lake Harriet Veterinary PA
4249 Bryant Ave S . . . Minneapolis MN 55409 612-822-1545 794
Web: lakeharrietvet.com

Lake Hartwell State Recreation Area
19138 S Hwy 11 Ste A . . . Fair Play SC 29643 864-972-3352 565
Web: southcarolinaparks.com

Lake Havasu Area Chamber of Commerce
314 London Bridge Rd . . . Lake Havasu City AZ 86403 928-855-4115 680-0010 139
TF: 800-307-3610 ■ *Web:* www.havasuchamber.com

Lake Havasu State Park
699 London Bridge Rd . . . Lake Havasu City AZ 86403 928-855-2784 565
Web: golakehavasu.com

Lake Haven Utility District
31627-1st Ave S PO Box 4249 . . . Federal Way WA 98063 253-941-1516 787
Web: www.lakehaven.org

Lake Herman State Park
23409 State Pk Dr . . . Madison SD 57042 605-256-5003 565
Web: gfp.sd.gov

Lake House on Canandaigua, The
770 S Main St . . . Canandaigua NY 14424 585-394-7800 394-5003 379
TF: 800-228-2801 ■ *Web:* www.lakehousecanandaigua.com

Lake Houston Area Chamber of Commerce, The
110 W Main St . . . Humble TX 77338 281-446-2128 446-7483 139
Web: www.lakehouston.org

Lake Hudson Recreation Area
5505 Morey Hwy . . . Clayton MI 49235 517-445-2265 565
Web: www.michigan.org

Lake Immunogenics Inc 348 Berg Rd . . . Ontario NY 14519 800-648-9990 265-2306* 584
*Fax Area Code: 585 ■ *TF:* 800-648-9990 ■ *Web:* www.lakeimmunogenics.com

Lake James State Park 7321 NC Hwy 126 . . . Nebo NC 28761 828-584-7728 565
Web: www.ncparks.gov

Lake Junaluska Assembly
Lake Junaluska Conference Retreat Ctr 689 N Lakeshore Dr
. . . Lake Junaluska NC 28745 828-452-2881 48-20
TF: 800-482-1442 ■ *Web:* www.lakejunaluska.com

Lake Kegonsa State Park
2405 Door Creek Rd . . . Stoughton WI 53589 608-873-9695 873-0674 565
TF: 888-947-2757 ■ *Web:* dnr.wi.gov

Lake Keomah State Park
2720 Keomah Ln . . . Oskaloosa IA 52577 641-673-6975 673-0647 565
Web: www.iowadnr.gov

Lake Kissimmee State Park
14248 Camp Mack Rd . . . Lake Wales FL 33898 863-696-1112 565
Web: www.floridastateparks.org

Lake Land College 5001 Lake Land Blvd . . . Mattoon IL 61938 217-234-5253 234-5390 162
Web: www.lakelandcollege.edu

Lake Lawn Resort 2400 E Geneva St . . . Delavan WI 53115 262-728-7950 669
TF: 800-338-5253 ■ *Web:* www.lakelawnresort.com

Lake Le-Aqua-Na State Recreation Area
8542 N Lake Rd . . . Lena IL 61048 815-369-4282 565
Web: www2.illinois.gov

Lake Loramie State Park
4401 Ft Loramie Swanders Rd . . . Minster OH 45865 937-295-2011 565
Web: ohiodnr.gov

Lake Louisa State Park
7305 US Hwy 27 . . . Clermont FL 34714 352-394-3969 565
Web: www.floridastateparks.org

Lake Louise Inn
210 Village Rd PO Box 209 . . . Lake Louise AB T0L1E0 403-522-3791 522-2018 379
TF: 800-661-9237 ■ *Web:* www.lakelouiseinn.com

Lake Lowndes State Park
3319 Lake Lowndes Rd . . . Columbus MS 39702 662-328-2110 565
Web: www.mdwfp.com

Lake Lure Inn & Spa, The
2771 Memorial Hwy . . . Lake Lure NC 28746 828-625-2525 379
TF: 888-434-4970 ■ *Web:* www.lakelure.com

Lake Lurleen State Park
13226 Lake Lurleen Rd . . . Coker AL 35452 205-339-1558 339-8885 565
Web: www.alapark.com

Name	Address	City	State	ZIP	Phone	Fax	Class
Lake Macbride State Park	3525 Hwy 382 NE *Web:* www.iowadnr.gov	Solon	IA	52333	319-624-2200	624-2188	565
Lake Manatee State Park	20007 Hwy 64 E *Web:* www.floridastateparks.org	Bradenton	FL	34212	941-741-3028		565
Lake Manawa State Park	1100 S Shore Dr *Web:* www.iowadnr.gov	Council Bluffs	IA	51501	712-366-0220	366-0474	565
Lake Maria State Park	11411 Clementa Ave NW *Web:* www.dnr.state.mn.us	Monticello	MN	55362	763-878-2325		565
Lake Mary Ronan State Park	490 N Meridian Rd *Web:* www.fwp.mt.gov	Kalispell	MT	59901	406-752-5501		565
Lake McConaughy State Recreation Area	1450 NE Hwy 61N *TF:* 800-658-4390 ■ *Web:* ilovelakemac.com	Ogallala	NE	69153	308-284-8800		565
Lake Mead National Recreation Area	601 Nevada Hwy *Web:* www.nps.gov	Boulder City	NV	89005	702-293-8990	293-8936	564
Lake Merced Golf & Country Club	2300 Junipero Serra Blvd *Web:* www.lmgc.org	Daly City	CA	94015	650-755-2233		354
Lake Meritt, The	1800 Madison St *Web:* www.thelakemerritt.com	Oakland	CA	94612	510-903-3600		379
Lake Metigoshe State Park	2 Lake Metigoshe State Pk *Web:* www.parkrec.nd.gov	Bottineau	ND	58318	701-263-4651		565
Lake Michigan College	2755 E Napier Ave *TF:* 800-252-1562 ■ *Web:* www.lakemichigancollege.edu	Benton Harbor	MI	49022	269-927-1000	927-6875	162
Lake Michigan Mailers	3777 Sky King Blvd *Web:* www.lakemichiganmailers.com	Kalamazoo	MI	49009	269-383-9333		5
Lake Milton State Park	16801 Mahoning Ave *Web:* ohiodnr.gov	Lake Milton	OH	44429	330-654-4989		565
Lake Minatare State Recreation Area	PO Box 188 *Web:* outdoornebraska.gov	Minatare	NE	69356	308-783-2911		565
Lake Mineral Wells State Park & Trailway	100 Park Rd 71 *Web:* tpwd.texas.gov	Mineral Wells	TX	76067	940-328-1171		565
Lake Mission Viejo Assn	22555 Olympiad Rd *Web:* lakemissionviejo.org	Mission Viejo	CA	92692	949-770-1313		533
Lake Morey Resort	1 Clubhouse Rd *TF:* 800-423-1211 ■ *Web:* www.lakemoreyresort.com	Fairlee	VT	05045	802-333-4311		669
Lake Murray Resort Park	3323 Lodge Rd *Web:* www.travelok.com	Ardmore	OK	73401	580-223-6600		669
Lake Natoma Inn	702 Gold Lake Dr *Web:* lakenatomainn.com	Folsom	CA	95630	916-351-1500		378
Lake Natoma Ltd	702 Gold Lake Dr *Web:* www.lakenatomainn.com	Folsom	CA	95630	916-932-2769		707
Lake Norman Chamber of Commerce	19900 W Catawba Ave Ste 101 *Web:* www.lakenormanchamber.org	Cornelius	NC	28031	704-892-1922	892-5313	139
Lake Norman Regional Medical Ctr	171 Fairview Rd *Web:* www.lnrmc.com	Mooresville	NC	28117	704-660-4000	696-2929	374-3
Lake Norman State Park	759 State Park Rd *Web:* www.ncparks.gov	Troutman	NC	28166	704-528-6350		565
Lake of the Ozarks Convention & Visitors Bureau	985 KK Dr *TF:* 800-386-5253 ■ *Web:* www.funlake.com	Osage Beach	MO	65065	573-348-1599	348-2293	206
Lake of the Ozarks State Park	PO Box 170 *Web:* mostateparks.com	Kaiser	MO	65047	573-348-2694		565
Lake of the Torches Resort Casino	510 Old Abe Rd *Web:* www.lakeofthetorches.com	Lac du Flambeau	WI	54538	715-588-7070		133
Lake of the Woods County	206 Eigth Ave SE *Web:* www.co.lake-of-the-woods.mn.us	Baudette	MN	56623	218-634-4570		338
Lake of the Woods District Hospital (LWDH)	21 Sylvan St *Web:* www.lwdh.on.ca	Kenora	ON	P9N3W7	807-468-9861	468-3939	374-2
Lake of Three Fires State Park	2303 Lake Rd *Web:* www.iowadnr.gov	Bedford	IA	50833	712-523-2700	523-3104	565
Lake Orion Review	30 N Broadway *Web:* www.lakeorionreview.com	Lake Orion	MI	48362	248-693-8331		532-2
Lake Oroville State Recreation Area	917 Kelly Ridge Rd *Web:* www.parks.ca.gov	Oroville	CA	95966	530-538-2219		565
Lake Oswego Chamber of Commerce	459 3rd St *TF:* 800-518-0760 ■ *Web:* lakeoswegochamber.com	Lake Oswego	OR	97034	503-636-3634		139
Lake Oswego Public Library	706 Fourth St *Web:* www.ci.oswego.or.us	Lake Oswego	OR	97034	503-636-7628	635-4171	434-3
Lake Ouachita State Park	5451 Mtn Pine Rd *Web:* www.arkansasstateparks.com	Mountain Pine	AR	71956	501-767-9366		565
Lake Park Retirement Residences	1850 Alice St *TF:* 866-384-3130 ■ *Web:* www.lakeparkretirement.org	Oakland	CA	94612	510-835-5511		672
Lake Perris State Recreation Area	17801 Lake Perris Dr *Web:* www.parks.ca.gov	Perris	CA	92571	951-657-0676		565
Lake Placid Convention & Visitors Bureau	2608 Main St *Web:* www.lakeplacid.com	Lake Placid	NY	12946	518-523-2445	523-2605	206
Lake Placid Lodge	144 Lodge Way *TF:* 877-523-2700 ■ *Web:* www.lakeplacidlodge.com	Lake Placid	NY	12946	518 523 2700	523-1124	379
Lake Poinsett Recreation Area	45617 S Poinsett Recreation Area *Web:* gfp.sd.gov	Arlington	SD	57212	605-983-5085		565
Lake Poinsett State Park	5752 State Pk Ln *Web:* www.arkansasstateparks.com	Harrisburg	AR	72432	870-578-2064		565
Lake Powell Resorts & Marinas	100 Lake shore Dr *TF:* 888-896-3829 ■ *Web:* www.lakepowell.com	Page	AZ	86040	928-645-2433	645-1031	669
Lake Printing Company Inc	6815 Hwy 54 *Web:* www.lakeprinting.com	Osage Beach	MO	65065	573-346-0600		627
Lake Pueblo State Park	640 Pueblo Reservoir Rd *Web:* cpw.state.co.us	Pueblo	CO	81005	719-561-9320		565
Lake Quassapaug Park	2132 Middlebury Rd *Web:* www.quassy.com	Middlebury	CT	06762	203-758-2913		31
Lake Quinault Lodge	345 S Shore Rd *TF:* 800-562-6672 ■ *Web:* www.olympicnationalparks.com	Quinault	WA	98575	360-288-2900	288-2901	669
Lake Region Cooperative Electrical Assn	1401 S Broadway PO Box 643 *TF:* 800-552-7658 ■ *Web:* www.lrec.coop	Pelican Rapids	MN	56572	218-863-1171	863-1172	245
Lake Region Electric Association Inc	1212 Main St *TF:* 800-657-5869 ■ *Web:* www.lakeregion.coop	Webster	SD	57274	605-345-3379	345-4442	245
Lake Region Electric Co-opeartive Inc	516 S Lake Region Rd *TF:* 800-364-5732 ■ *Web:* www.lrecok.coop	Hulbert	OK	74441	918-772-2526		245
Lake Region Hospital	712 S Cascade St *TF:* 800-439-6424 ■ *Web:* www.lrhc.org	Fergus Falls	MN	56537	218-736-8000		374-3
Lake Region Packing Association Inc	1293 S Duncan Dr	Tavares	FL	32778	352-343-3111		11-1
Lake Region State College	1801 College Dr N *TF:* 800-443-1313 ■ *Web:* www.lrsc.edu	Devils Lake	ND	58301	701-662-1600	662-1581	162
Lake Regional Health System	54 Hospital Dr *Web:* www.lakeregional.com	Osage Beach	MO	65065	573-348-8000		374-3
Lake Roosevelt National Recreation Area	1008 Crest Dr *Web:* www.nps.gov	Coulee Dam	WA	99116	509-633-9441		564
Lake Saint Catherine State Park	3034 VT Rt 30 S *Web:* www.vtstateparks.com	Poultney	VT	05764	802-287-9158		565
Lake Saint George State Park	278 Belfast Augusta Rd *Web:* www.maine.gov	Liberty	ME	04949	207-589-4255		565
Lake Sammamish State Park	2000 NW Sammamish Rd *Web:* parks.state.wa.us	Issaquah	WA	98027	425-649-4275		565
Lake Scott State Park	520 W Scott Lake Dr *Web:* www.kansastravel.org	Scott City	KS	67871	620-872-2061		565
Lake Shaftsbury State Park	262 Shaftsbury State Park Rd *Web:* www.vtstateparks.com	Shaftsbury	VT	05262	802-375-9978		565
Lake Shetek State Park	163 State Park Rd *Web:* www.dnr.state.mn.us	Currie	MN	56123	507-763-3256		565
Lake Shore Athletic Club	2401 NW 94th St *Web:* lakeshoreac.com	Vancouver	WA	98665	360-574-1991		354
Lake Shore Bancorp Inc	128 E Fourth St *NASDAQ: LSBK* ■ *Web:* www.lakeshoresavings.com	Dunkirk	NY	14048	716-366-4070	366-2965	71
Lake Shore Cryotronics	575 McCorkle Blvd *Web:* www.lakeshore.com	Westerville	OH	43082	614-891-2243	818-1600	201
Lake Shore Industries Inc (LSI)	1817 Poplar St PO Box 3427 **Fax Area Code:* 814 ■ *TF:* 800-458-0463 ■ *Web:* www.lsisigns.com	Erie	PA	16508	800-458-0463	453-4293*	701
Lake Shore Railway Museum	31 Wall St *Web:* lakeshorerailway.com	North East	PA	16428	814-725-1911		520
Lake Shore Securities Lp	401 S La Salle St Ste 1000 *Web:* www.lakeshoresecurities.com	Chicago	IL	60605	312-663-1307		690
Lake Somerville State Park	1560 Thornberry Dr *Web:* tpwd.texas.gov	Somerville	TX	77879	979-535-7763		565
Lake State Railway Co	750 N Washington Ave *Web:* www.lsrc.com	Saginaw	MI	48607	989-393-9800	757-2134	648
Lake Superior College	2101 Trinity Rd *TF:* 800-432-2884 ■ *Web:* www.lsc.edu	Duluth	MN	55811	218-733-7600	733-5945	162
Lake Superior Ind Sch Dist 381	1640 2 Hwy *Web:* www.isd381.k12.mn.us	Two Harbors	MN	55616	218-834-8201	834-8239	685
Lake Superior Maritime Visitor Ctr (LSMVC)	600 Canal Park Dr *Web:* www.lsmma.com	Duluth	MN	55802	218-788-6430		520
Lake Superior Medical Equipment Inc	522 E 4th St *Web:* www.lakesuperiormedicalequipment.com	Duluth	MN	55805	218-727-0600		45
Lake Superior Railroad Museum	506 W Michigan St *Web:* www.lsrm.org	Duluth	MN	55802	218-727-8025		520
Lake Superior State University (LSSU)	650 W Easterday Ave *Web:* www.lssu.edu	Sault Sainte Marie	MI	49783	906-632-6841	635-2111	166
Lake Superior Zoo	7210 Fremont St *Web:* www.lszooduluth.org	Duluth	MN	55807	218-730-4500	723-3750	823
Lake Sylvia State Park	1812 N Lake Sylvia Rd *Web:* parks.state.wa.us	Montesano	WA	98563	360-249-3621		565
Lake Taghkanic State Park	1528 Rt 82 *Web:* parks.ny.gov	Ancram	NY	12502	518-851-3631	851-3633	565

				Phone	Fax	Class
Lake Tahoe Chamber of Commerce 169 Hwy 50 *Web:* tahoechamber.org	Stateline	NV	89449	775-588-1728	588-1941	139
Lake Tahoe Community College 1 College Dr *TF:* 800-877-1466 ■ *Web:* www.ltcc.edu	South Lake Tahoe	CA	96150	530-541-4660	542-1781	162
Lake Tahoe Nevada State Park PO Box 8867 *Web:* www.parks.nv.gov	Incline Village	NV	89452	775-831-0494	831-2514	565
Lake Tahoe Visitors Authority 3066 Lake Tahoe Blvd *TF:* 800-288-2463 ■ *Web:* tahoesouth.com	South Lake Tahoe	CA	96150	530-544-5050		206
Lake Tarleton State Park 949 Rt 25C *Web:* www.nhstateparks.org	Piermont	NH	03779	603-823-7722		565
Lake Tawakoni Regional Chamber of Commerce 100 W Hwy 276 *Web:* laketawakoniregionalchamberofcommerce.wildapricot.org	West Tawakoni	TX	75474	903-447-3020		139
Lake Tawakoni State Park 10822 Fm 2475 *Web:* tpwd.texas.gov	Wills Point	TX	75169	903-560-7123		565
Lake Taylor Transitional Hospital 1309 Kempsville Rd *Web:* www.laketaylor.org	Norfolk	VA	23502	757-461-5001	461-4282	374-7
Lake Technical College 2001 Kurt St *Web:* www.laketech.org	Eustis	FL	32726	352-589-2250		167-3
Lake Texana State Park 46 Park Rd 1 *Web:* tpwd.texas.gov	Edna	TX	77957	361-782-5718		565
Lake Thompson Recreation Area 21176 Flood Club Rd *Web:* gfp.sd.gov	Lake Preston	SD	57249	605-847-4893		565
Lake Thunderbird State Park 13101 Alameda Dr *Web:* www.travelok.com	Norman	OK	73026	405-360-3572	366-8150	565
Lake Travis Independent School District 3322 Ranch Rd 620 S *Web:* www.ltisdschools.org	Austin	TX	78738	512-533-6000	533-6001	685
Lake Union Drydock Co 1515 Fairview Ave E *Web:* ludd.com	Seattle	WA	98102	206-323-6400	324-0124	698
Lake Vermillion Recreation Area 26140 451st Ave *Web:* gfp.sd.gov	Canistota	SD	57012	605-296-3643		565
Lake View Cemetery 12316 Euclid Ave *Web:* lakeviewcemetery.com	Cleveland	OH	44106	216-421-2665	421-2415	520
Lake Villa Illinois Public Library District 1001 E Grand Ave *Web:* www.lvdl.org	Lake Villa	IL	60046	847-356-7711		434-3
Lake Waccamaw State Park 1866 State Pk Dr *Web:* www.ncparks.gov	Lake Waccamaw	NC	28450	910-646-4748		565
Lake Walcott State Park 959 E Minidoka Dam *Web:* parksandrecreation.idaho.gov	Rupert	ID	83350	208-436-1258		565
Lake Wales Area Chamber of Commerce 340 W Central Ave *TF:* 800-365-6380 ■ *Web:* www.lakewaleschamber.com	Lake Wales	FL	33859	863-676-3445	676-3446	139
Lake Wapello State Park 15248 Campground Rd *Web:* www.iowadnr.gov	Drakesville	IA	52552	641-722-3371		565
Lake Wappapello State Park MO Hwy 172 *Web:* mostateparks.com	Williamsville	MO	63967	573-297-3232		565
Lake Waramaug State Park 30 Lake Waramaug Rd *Web:* portal.ct.gov	New Preston	CT	06777	860-868-2592		565
Lake Warren State Park 1079 Lake Warren Rd *Web:* southcarolinaparks.com	Hampton	SC	29924	803-943-5051		565
Lake Washington School District 414 16250 NE 74th St PO Box 97039 *Web:* www.lwsd.org	Redmond	WA	98073	425-936-1200	936-1213	685
Lake Wateree State Recreation Area 881 State Park Rd *Web:* southcarolinaparks.com	Winnsboro	SC	29180	803-482-6401		565
Lake Wenatchee State Park 21588 A Hwy 207 *Web:* parks.state.wa.us	Leavenworth	WA	98826	509-763-3101		565
Lake White State Park 2767 State Ste 551 *Web:* ohiodnr.gov	Waverly	OH	45690	740-493-2212		565
Lake Whitney State Park PO Box 1175 *Web:* tpwd.texas.gov	Whitney	TX	76692	254-694-3793		565
Lake Wilderness Arboretum 22520 SE 248th St PO Box 72 *Web:* www.lakewildernessarboretum.org	Maple Valley	WA	98038	253-293-5103		97
Lake Winnepesaukah Amusement Park 1730 Lakeview Dr *Web:* lakewinnie.com	Rossville	GA	30741	706-866-5681		32
Lake Winnipesaukee Golf Club LLC 1 Lake Winnipesaukee Dr *Web:* www.lwgcnh.com	New Durham	NH	03855	603-569-3055		671
Lake Wissota State Park 18127 County Hwy O *Web:* dnr.wi.gov	Chippewa Falls	WI	54729	715-382-4574	382-5187	565
Lake Wister State Park 25567 US Hwy 270 *Web:* www.travelok.com	Wister	OK	74966	918-655-7212	655-7274	565
Lake Worth Beach Public Library 15 N M St *Web:* lakeworthbeachfl.gov	Lake Worth Beach	FL	33460	561-533-7354		434-3
Lake Worth Herald/Coastal & Greenacres Observer 1313 Central Terr *Web:* www.lwherald.com	Lake Worth	FL	33460	561-585-9387		532-4
Lake Worth Independent School District (LWISD) 6805 Telephone Rd *Web:* www.lwisd.org	Lake Worth	TX	76135	817-306-4200	237-2583	685
Lake Wyola State Park 94 Lake View Rd *Web:* www.mass.gov	Shutesbury	MA	01072	413-367-0317		565
Lake Zurich Area Chamber of Commerce 444 S Rand Rd Ste 308 *Web:* lzacc.com	Lake Zurich	IL	60047	847-438-5572	438-5574	139
Lake-Cook Distributors Inc 951 N Old Rand Rd Ste 114 *TF:* 800-677-6047 ■ *Web:* www.lake-cook.com	Wauconda	IL	60084	847-526-5877	526-5810	95
Lakefield College School 4391 County Rd 29 *Web:* www.lcs.on.ca	Lakefield	ON	K0L2H0	705-652-3324		622
Lakehead University 955 Oliver Rd *Web:* www.lakeheadu.ca	Thunder Bay	ON	P7B5E1	807-343-8110	343-8023	785
Lakeland Area Chamber of Commerce 35 Lake Morton Dr *Web:* www.lakelandchamber.com	Lakeland	FL	33801	863-688-8551	683-7454	139
Lakeland Bancorp Inc 250 Oak Ridge Rd *NASDAQ: LBAI* ■ *TF:* 866-224-1379 ■ *Web:* www.lakelandbank.com	Oak Ridge	NJ	07438	973-697-2000	697-8385	360-2
Lakeland College PO Box 359 *TF:* 800-569-2166 ■ *Web:* lakeland.edu	Sheboygan	WI	53082	920-565-2111	565-1215	166
Lakeland Community College 7700 Clocktower Dr *TF:* 800-589-8520 ■ *Web:* lakelandcc.edu	Kirtland	OH	44094	440-525-7000	525-7651	162
Lakeland Correctional Facility 141 First St *Web:* www.michigan.gov	Coldwater	MI	49036	517-278-6942		213
Lakeland Financial Corp 202 E Center St *NASDAQ: LKFN* ■ *TF:* 800-827-4522 ■ *Web:* www.lakecitybank.com	Warsaw	IN	46580	574-267-6144		360-2
Lakeland Industries Inc 3555 Veterans Memorial Hwy Ste C *NASDAQ: LAKE* ■ *TF:* 800-645-9291 ■ *Web:* www.lakeland.com	Ronkonkoma	NY	11779	631-981-9700	981-9751	576
Lakeland Plastics Inc (LP) 1550 McCormick Blvd *TF:* 800-454-4006 ■ *Web:* lakelandplastics.com	Mundelein	IL	60060	847-680-1550	680-1595	599
Lakeland Public Library 100 Lake Morton Dr *Web:* www.lakelandgov.net	Lakeland	FL	33801	863-834-4270		434-3
Lakeland Regional Health 1324 Lakeland Hills Blvd *Web:* mylrh.org	Lakeland	FL	33805	863-687-1100		374-3
Lakeland Regional Library 318 Williams Ave *Web:* www.lakelandregionallibrary.ca	Killarney	MB	R0K1G0	204-523-4949	523-7460	436
Lakeland Surgical & Diagnostic Center LLP 1315 N Florida Ave *Web:* lsdc.net	Lakeland	FL	33805	863-683-2268		418
Lakeland Tool & Engineering Inc 2939 Sixth Ave *Web:* www.lte.biz	Anoka	MN	55303	763-422-8866		604
Lakeland Village 3535 Lake Tahoe Blvd *TF:* 888-484-7094 ■ *Web:* www.skiheavenly.com	South Lake Tahoe	CA	96150	530-544-1685		669
Lakelands Concrete Products Inc 7520 E Main St *Web:* www.lakelandsconcrete.com	Lima	NY	14485	585-624-1990		183
Lakepoint Resort State Park 104 Lakepoint Dr *TF:* 800-544-5253 ■ *Web:* www.alapark.com	Eufaula	AL	36027	334-687-8011	687-3273	565
Lakeport Library 1425 N High St *Web:* library.lakecountyca.gov	Lakeport	CA	95453	707-263-8817		434-3
Lakeport Regional Chamber of Commerce 875 Lakeport Blvd *TF:* 866-525-3767 ■ *Web:* www.lakecochamber.com	Lakeport	CA	95453	707-263-5092	263-5104	139
Lakeport State Park 7605 Lakeshore Rd *Web:* www.michigan.gov	Lakeport	MI	48059	810-327-6224		565
Lakeridge Health Bowmanville 47 Liberty St S *Web:* www.lakeridgehealth.on.ca	Bowmanville	ON	L1C2N4	905-623-3331	743-5943	374-2
Lakes Area Chamber of Commerce 305 N Pontiac Trl Ste B *Web:* lakesareachamber.com	Walled Lake	MI	48390	248-624-2826	624-2892	139
Lakes Area Co-op 459 Third Ave SE PO Box 247 *TF:* 866-346-5601 ■ *Web:* lakesareacoop.com	Perham	MN	56573	218-346-6240	346-6241	276
Lakes Golf Course, The 19 Golf Dr *Web:* www.golfatthelakes.com	Wentworth	SD	57075	605-483-3535		121
Lakes Mall LLC, The 5600 Harvey St *Web:* www.thelakesmall.com	Muskegon	MI	49444	231-798-7104		710
Lakes Region Chamber 383 S Main St *Web:* www.lakesregionchamber.org	Laconia	NH	03246	603-524-5531		139
Lakes Region Community College (LRCC) 379 Belmont Rd *TF:* 800-357-2992 ■ *Web:* www.lrcc.edu	Laconia	NH	03246	603-524-3207	524-8084	162
Lakes Region General Hospital 80 Highland St *Web:* www.lrgh.org	Laconia	NH	03246	603-524-3211		374-3
Lakeshirts Inc 750 Randolph Rd *Web:* blue84.com	Detroit Lakes	MN	56501	800-627-2780		61
Lakeshore Chamber of Commerce 5246 Hohman Ave Ste 100 *Web:* www.lakeshorechamber.com	Hammond	IN	46320	219-931-1000	937-8778	139
Lakeshore Display Manufacturing Company Inc 2031 Washington Ave PO Box 983 *Web:* lakeshoredisplay.com	Sheboygan	WI	53081	920-457-3695	457-5673	233
Lakeshore General Hospital (LGH) 160 Stillview Ste 1249 *Web:* fondationlakeshore.ca	Pointe-Claire	QC	H9R2Y2	514-630-2081	630-2873	374-2
Lakeshore Group Ltd 5723 Superior Ste A1 *Web:* www.lakeshoregroup.com	Baton Rouge	LA	70816	225-292-7422		177
Lakeshore Learning Materials 2695 E Dominguez St **Fax Area Code: 800* ■ *TF:* 800-778-4456 ■ *Web:* www.lakeshorelearning.com	Carson	CA	90895	310-537-8600	537-5403*	534
Lakeshore State Park 2300 N Martin Luther King Jr Dr *Web:* dnr.wi.gov	Milwaukee	WI	53212	414-263-8500		565

Name / Address	Phone	Fax	Class
Lakeshore Talent 8400 E Prentice Ave Ste 1401 Greenwood Village CO 80111 *Web:* www.lakeshoretalent.com	303-483-1100		721
Lakeshore Technical College 1290 N Ave Cleveland WI 53015 *TF:* 888-468-6582 ■ *Web:* gotoltc.edu	920-693-1000	693-3561	800
Lakeshores Library System (LLS) 725 Cornerstone Crossing Ste C Waterford WI 53185 *Web:* www.lakeshores.lib.wi.us	262-514-4500		434-3
Lakeside Bank 55 W Wacker Dr Chicago IL 60601 *Web:* www.lakesidebank.com	312-435-5100		70
Lakeside Beach State Park Route 18 Waterport NY 14571 *Web:* parks.ny.gov	585-682-4888		565
Lakeside Behavioral Health System 2911 Brunswick Rd Memphis TN 38133 *TF:* 800-232-5253 ■ *Web:* lakesidebhs.com	901-377-4700		374-5
Lakeside Capital Management LLC 50 S 6th St Ste 1460 Minneapolis MN 55402 *Web:* gmbmezz.com	612-243-4400		401
Lakeside Chamber of Commerce 9924 Vine St Lakeside CA 92040 *Web:* lakesidechamber.org	619-561-1031	561-7951	139
Lakeside Credit Union 1008 Broadway Hwy New Johnsonville TN 37134 *TF:* 800-819-0792 ■ *Web:* lcu.coop	931-535-7269	535-7286	219
Lakeside Foods Inc 808 Hamilton St Manitowoc WI 54220 *TF:* 800-466-3834 ■ *Web:* www.lakesidefoods.com	920-684-3356	686-4033	296-20
Lakeside Industries Inc 6505 226th Pl SE Ste 200 Issaquah WA 98027 *Web:* lakesideindustries.com	425-313-2600	313-2620	188-4
Lakeside Inn 100 N Alexander St Mount Dora FL 32757 *TF:* 800-556-5016 ■ *Web:* www.lakeside-inn.com	352-383-4101	385-1615	379
Lakeside International LLC 11000 W Silver Spring Rd Milwaukee WI 53225 *Web:* www.lakesidetrucks.com	414-353-4800		57
Lakeside Lutheran High School 231 Woodland Beach Rd Lake Mills WI 53551 *Web:* www.llhs.org	920-648-2321		685
Lakeside Mall 14000 Lakeside Cir Sterling Heights MI 48313 *Web:* www.shop-lakesidemall.com	586-247-1590		460
Lakeside Manufacturing Inc 4900 W Electric Ave West Milwaukee WI 53219 *TF:* 800-558-8565 ■ *Web:* www.elakeside.com	414-902-6400	902-6446	319-1
Lakeside Medical Center Inc 129 Sixth Ave SE Pine City MN 55063 *Web:* lmc-pcac.com	320-629-2542		371
Lakeside Mills Inc 398 W Main St Spindale NC 28160 *Web:* www.lakesidemills.com	828-286-4866		296-23
Lakeside Place 7210 N Lakeside Dr Charlotte NC 28215 *Web:* lakesideplaceinc.com	704-563-1341		363
Lakeside Plastics Inc 450 W 33rd Ave Oshkosh WI 54902 *Web:* www.lakesideplastics.net	920-235-3620	235-6545	608
Lakeside Process Controls 2475 Hogan Dr Mississauga ON L5N0E9 *Web:* www.lakesidecontrols.com	800-265-1005		111
Lakeside Shopping Ctr 3301 Veterans Memorial Blvd Metairie LA 70002 *Web:* www.lakesideshopping.com	504-835-8000		460
Lakeside Toyota 3701 N Cswy Blvd Metairie LA 70002 *Web:* www.lakesidetoyota.com	504-833-3311		57
Lake-Sumter State College 1405 CR 526A Sumterville FL 33585 *Web:* www.lssc.edu	352-568-0001	568-7515	162
Lakeview College of Nursing 903 N Logan Ave Danville IL 61832 *Web:* www.lakeviewcol.edu	217-443-5238		166
Lakeview Construction Inc 10505 Corp Dr Ste 200 Pleasant Prairie WI 53158 *Web:* www.lvconstruction.com	262-857-3336	857-3424	186
Lakeview Forge Co 1725 Pittsburgh Ave Erie PA 16505 *Web:* lakeviewforge.com	814-454-4518	455-5875	483
Lakeview Golf Resort & Spa 1 Lakeview Dr Morgantown WV 26508 *TF:* 800-624-8300 ■ *Web:* www.lakeviewresort.com	304-594-1111		669
Lakeview Hospital 630 E Medical Dr Bountiful UT 84010 *Web:* lakeviewhospital.com	801-299-2200		374-3
Lakeview Industries Inc 1225 Lakeview Dr Chaska MN 55318 *Web:* www.lakeviewindustries.com	952-368-3500		326
Lakeview Lawn & Landscape Inc 4477 County Rd 1 Canandaigua NY 14424 *Web:* lakeviewlandscape.com	585-394-6701	394-0962	422
Lakeview Medical Ctr 1700 W Stout St Rice Lake WI 54868 *Web:* www.lakeviewmedical.com	715-236-6309		374-3
Lakeview Professional Services Inc 104 S Maple St Corona CA 92880 *TF:* 800-287-1371 ■ *Web:* lakeviewpro.com	951-371-3390		196
Lakeview Regional Medical Ctr 95 Judge Tanner Blvd Covington LA 70433 *Web:* lakeviewregional.com	985-867-3800		374-3
Lakeview Shock Incarceration Correctional Facility 9300 Lake Ave PO Box T Brocton NY 14716 *Web:* doccs.ny.gov	716-792-7100		213
Lakeview Veterinary Clinic 2020 W Havens Mitchell SD 57301 *Web:* lakeviewveterinary.com	605-996-5806		794
Lakeville Area Chamber of Commerce & Convention & Visitors Bureau 19950 Dodd Blvd Ste 101 Lakeville MN 55044 *Web:* www.lakevillechamber.org	952-469-2020	469-2028	139
Lakeway Broadcasting LLC 1181 N Hwy 92 PO Box 430 Jefferson City TN 37760 *Web:* www.wjfcradio.com	865-475-3825		647
Lakeway Container Inc 5715 Superior Dr Morristown TN 37814 *Web:* www.lakewaycontainer.com	423-581-2164	586-7044	100
Lakeway Resort & Spa 101 Lakeway Dr Austin TX 78734 *TF:* 844-822-2621 ■ *Web:* www.lakewayresortandspa.com	512-261-6600		377

Name / Address	Phone	Fax	Class
Lakewold Gardens 12317 Gravelly Lake Dr SW Lakewood WA 98499 *TF:* 888-858-4106 ■ *Web:* lakewoldgardens.org	253-584-4106	584-3021	97
Lakewood Brick and Tile Co 1325 Jay St Lakewood CO 80214 *Web:* www.summitbrick.com	303-238-5313		191-1
Lakewood Center Mall 500 Lakewood Ctr Lakewood CA 90712 *Web:* www.shoplakewoodcenter.com	562-531-6707		460
Lakewood Chamber of Commerce 4650 Steilacoom Blvd SW Ste 109 Lakewood WA 98499 *Web:* www.lakewood-chamber.com	253-582-9400	581-5241	139
Lakewood Chamber of Commerce 24 Lakewood Ctr Mall Lakewood CA 90712 *Web:* lakewoodchamber.com	562-531-9733	531-9737	139
Lakewood Chamber of Commerce 16017 Detroit Ave Lakewood OH 44107 *Web:* lakewoodchamber.org	216-226-2900	226-1340	139
Lakewood Health System 49725 County 83 Staples MN 56479 *TF:* 800-525-1033 ■ *Web:* www.lakewoodhealthsystem.com	218-894-1515		363
Lakewood Manor 1900 Lauderdale Dr Richmond VA 23238 *Web:* lakewoodwestend.org	804-729-5563		672
Lakewood Public Library 15425 Detroit Ave Lakewood OH 44107 *Web:* www.lakewoodpubliclibrary.org	216-226-8275		434-3
Lakewood Regional Medical Ctr 3700 S St Lakewood CA 90712 *Web:* www.lakewoodregional.com	562-531-2550		374-3
Lakewood School of Therapeutic Massage 1102 6th St Port Huron MI 48060 *Web:* lakewoodschool.edu	810-987-3959		685
Lakewood Shores Resort 7751 Cedar Lake Rd Oscoda MI 48750 *TF:* 800-882-2493 ■ *Web:* www.lakewoodshores.com	800-882-2493		669
Lakewood United Methodist Church of North Little Rock 1922 Topf Rd North Little Rock AR 72116 *Web:* www.expandingthelight.org	501-753-6186		48-20
Lakewood Veterinary Service 8840 Rt 243 Rushford NY 14777 *Web:* rushfordlakeveterinarian.com	585-437-5120		794
Lakewood Veterinary Services 6333 E Mockingbird Ln Ste 125 Dallas TX 75214 *Web:* lakewoodvetcenter.com	214-826-4800		794
Lakewoods Resort & Lodge 21540 County Hwy M Cable WI 54821 *Web:* www.lakewoodsresort.com	715-794-2561		379
Lakin General Corp 2044 N Dominick St Chicago IL 60614 *Web:* www.lakincorp.com	773-871-6675		755
Lakin Spears LLP 2400 Geng Rd Ste 110 Palo Alto CA 94303 *Web:* www.lakinspears.com	650-328-7000		428
Lakin Tire West Inc 15305 Spring Ave Santa Fe Springs CA 90670 *TF:* 800-488-2752 ■ *Web:* lakintire.com	562-802-2752	802-7584	755
Lakota American PO Box 507 Lakota ND 58344 *Web:* www.lakota-nd.com	701-247-2482		532-2
Lakota Books PO Box 140 Kendall Park NJ 08824 *Web:* www.lakotabooks.com	732-297-2253	940-9429	637-2
Lally Acoustical Consulting LLC 611 Broadway Ste 806 New York NY 10012 *Web:* lallyacoustics.com	212-614-3280		261
LallyPak Inc 1209 Central Ave Hillside NJ 07205 *TF:* 800-523-8484 ■ *Web:* www.lallypakusa.com	908-351-4141	351-4411	548
Lam 103.7 355 So 'A' St Ste 103 Oxnard CA 93030 *Web:* www.lam1037.com	805-385-5656	385-5690	645-116
LAM Design Associates Inc 409 Manville Rd Pleasantville NY 10570 *Web:* lamdesign.com	914-773-7600		344
Lam Research Corp 4650 Cushing Pkwy Fremont CA 94538 *NASDAQ:* LRCX ■ *TF:* 800-526-7678 ■ *Web:* www.lamresearch.com	510-572-0200		695
LaMalfa Doug (Rep R - CA) 322 Cannon House Office Bldg Washington DC 20515 *Web:* lamalfa.house.gov	202-225-3076		342-2
Lamamco Drilling Co PO Box 550 Skiatook OK 74070 *Web:* www.lamamco.net	918-396-3020		538
Lamar & Wallace Inc 7000 Old Landover Rd Landover Hills MD 20785 *Web:* www.lamarandwallace.com	301-772-2400		499
Lamar Advertising Co 5321 Corporate Blvd Baton Rouge LA 70808 *NASDAQ:* LAMR ■ *TF:* 800-235-2627 ■ *Web:* www.lamar.com	225-926-1000		8
Lamar Area Vocational-Technical School 501 Maple St Lamar MO 64759 *Web:* www.lamar.k12.mo.us	417-682-3384		800
Lamar Bank & Trust Co 1000 Broadway Lamar MO 64759 *Web:* lbt.com	417-682-3348		70
Lamar Community College 2401 S Main St Lamar CO 81052 *TF:* 800-968-6920 ■ *Web:* lamarcc.edu	719-336-2248	336-2400	162
Lamar County 408 Thomaston St Ste E Barnesville GA 30204 *Web:* www.lamarcountyga.com	770-358-5146	358-5149	338
Lamar County 119 N Main St Paris TX 75460 *Web:* www.co.lamar.tx.us	903-737-2420	782-1100	338
Lamar County 403 Main St Purvis MS 39475 *Web:* www.lamarcountyms.gov	601-794-8504	794-1049	338
Lamar County Chamber of Commerce 1125 Bonham St Paris TX 75460 *TF:* 800-727-4789 ■ *Web:* www.paristexas.com	903-784-2501	784-2503	139
Lamar Democrat 100 E 11th Lamar MO 64759 *Web:* www.lamardemocrat.com	417-682-5529		532-2
Lamar electric Coop 1485 N Main St PO Box 580 Paris TX 75461 *Web:* www.lamarelectric.coop	903-784-4303	784-7084	245
Lamar Graphics 1986 Beaumont Dr Baton Rouge LA 70806 *TF:* 800-952-3113 ■ *Web:* www.lamargraphics.com	225-923-3113	923-3147	9
Lamar Institute of Technology 855 E Lavaca PO Box 10043 Beaumont TX 77705 *TF:* 800-950-6989 ■ *Web:* www.lit.edu	409-880-8321	880-1711	167-3

	Phone	Fax	Class

Lamar National Bank
200 S Collegiate PO Box 1097 Paris TX 75460 903-785-0701 70
Web: lamarnationalbank.com
Lamar Soutter Library 55 Lake Ave N Worcester MA 01655 508-856-6099 856-5899 434-1
Web: library.umassmed.edu
Lamar State College
Orange 410 Front St Orange TX 77630 409-883-7750 882-3055 162
TF: 877-673-6839 ■ *Web:* www.lsco.edu
Port Arthur PO Box 310 Port Arthur TX 77641 409-983-4921 984-6025 162
TF: 800-477-5872 ■ *Web:* www.lamarpa.edu
Lamar University
4400 ML King Jr Pkwy Beaumont TX 77710 409-880-7011 880-8463 166
Web: www.lamar.edu
Lamarca Law Group PC
1820 NW 118th St Ste 200 Des Moines IA 50325 515-225-2600 41
Web: lamarcalandry.com
Lamart Corp 16 Richmond St Clifton NJ 07015 973-772-6262 772-3673 599
Web: www.lamartcorp.com
Lamartek Inc 175 NW Washington St Lake City FL 32055 386-752-1087 755-0613 710
TF: 800-495-1046 ■ *Web:* www.diverite.com
Lamaze Intl 2025 M St NW Ste 800 Washington DC 20036 202-367-1128 367-2128 49-8
TF: 800-368-4404 ■ *Web:* www.lamaze.org
Lamb & Barnosky LLP
534 Broadhollow Rd Ste 210 PO Box 9034 Melville NY 11747 631-694-2300 694-2309 428
Web: www.lambbarnosky.com
Lamb Conor (Rep D - PA)
1224 Longworth House Office Bldg Washington DC 20515 202-225-2301 225-1844 342-2
Web: lamb.house.gov
Lamb County
1101 E Waylon Jennings Blvd Littlefield TX 79339 806-385-4222 338
Web: www.co.lamb.tx.us
Lamb County Electric Co-op
2415 S Phelps Ave Littlefield TX 79339 806-385-5191 385-5197 245
Web: www.lcec.coop
Lamb McErlane PC
24 E Market St PO Box 565 West Chester PA 19381 610-430-8000 428
Web: www.lambmcerlane.com
Lamb Weston Inc 8701 W Gage Blvd Kennewick WA 99336 509-736-0437 296-21
Web: www.lambweston.com
Lamb's Lawn Service & Landscaping LLC
5343 Buck Creek Rd Floyds Knobs IN 47119 812-923-6894 422
Web: lambslawn.com
Lamb's Machine Works Inc
296 E Mallory Ave Memphis TN 38109 901-775-0663 454
Web: www.lambsmachineworks.com
Lamb's Tire & Automotive
501 W Slaughter Ln Austin TX 78748 512-291-8662 583-1441 62-5
Web: www.lambstire.com
Lambda Legal Defense & Education Fund
120 Wall St 19th Fl New York NY 10005 212-809-8585 809-0055 48-8
TF: 866-542-8336 ■ *Web:* www.lambdalegal.org
Lambda Publications Inc
5315 N Clark St Ste 192 Chicago IL 60640 773-871-7610 871-7609 637-9
Web: www.windycitymediagroup.com
Lambda Research Corp 25 Porter Rd Littleton MA 01460 978-486-0766 177
Web: www.lambdares.com
Lambda Research Optics Inc
1695 Macarthur Blvd Costa Mesa CA 92626 714-327-0600 327-0610 419
Web: www.lambda.cc
Lambda Solutions Inc
1700 Seventh Ave Ste 1200 Seattle WA 98104 604-398-0162 242
Web: www.lambdasolutions.net
Lambda Technologies
3929 Virginia Ave Cincinnati OH 45227 513-561-0883 743
Web: www.lambdatechs.com
Lambert Buick Pontiac-Gmc Truck Inc
2409 Front St Cuyahoga Falls OH 44221 330-923-9771 57
Web: www.lambertgm.com
Lambert Saint Louis International Airport
10701 Lambert International Blvd
PO Box 10212 Saint Louis MO 63145 314-426-8000 426-1221 27
Web: www.flystl.com
Lambert's Cafe Inc 2305 E Malone Sikeston MO 63801 573-471-4261 471-7563 670
Web: throwedrolls.com
Lambert, Riddle, Schimmel And Company Limited Partnership
3931 University Dr Fairfax VA 22030 703-691-1300 390
Lamborn Doug (Rep R - CO)
2371 Rayburn House Office Bldg Washington DC 20515 202-225-4422 226-2638 342-2
Web: lamborn.house.gov
Lambos Firm Llp, The
303 S Broadway Ste 410 Tarrytown NY 10591 212-381-9700 797-9213 41
Web: thelambosfirm.com
Lambro Industries Inc
115 Albany Ave Amityville NY 11701 631-842-8088 842-8083* 697
**Fax Area Code:* 516 ■ *Web:* www.lambro.net
Lambs & Ivy Inc
2040-2042 E Maple Ave El Segundo CA 90245 310-322-3800 361
Web: lambsivy.com
Lamb-Star Engineering LP
5700 W Plano Pkwy Ste 1000 Plano TX 75093 214-440-3600 440-3601 256
Web: lamb-star.com
Lambton College of Applied Arts & Technology, The
1457 London Rd Sarnia ON N7S6K4 519-542-7751 162
Web: www.lambtoncollege.ca
Lamchick Law Group PA
9350 So Dixie Hwy Ph3 Miami FL 33156 305-670-4455 670-4422 41
Web: lamchick.com
Lamco Inc, The
1202 Territorial Rd Benton Harbor MI 49022 269-926-6101 926-8066 548
Web: www.thelamco.com
Lamco Machine Tool Inc
135 Industrial Dr Morehead City NC 28557 252-247-4360 247-4633 695
Web: www.lamcomachine.com
Lamcom Technologies inc
2330 Rue Masson Montreal QC H2G2A6 514-271-2891 627
Web: www.lamcom.ca
Lamcraft Partition Company Inc
1231 County Rd 4781 Boyd TX 76023 817-840-3223 608
TF: 888-685-9404 ■ *Web:* www.lamcraftpartition.com

Lamers Bus Lines Inc
2407 S Point Rd Green Bay WI 54313 920-496-3600 107
TF: 800-236-1240 ■ *Web:* www.golamers.com
Lamesa Independent School District
212 N Houston Lamesa TX 79331 806-872-5461 872-6220 685
Web: www.lamesaisd.net
Lamesa National Bank, The
602 S First St Lamesa TX 79331 806-872-5457 70
Web: www.lamesanb.com
Lamey-Wellehan Inc 940 Turner St Auburn ME 04210 207-784-6595 784-9650 301
TF: 800-370-6900 ■ *Web:* www.lwshoes.com
Lamiglas Inc 1400 Atlantic Ave Woodland WA 98674 360-225-9436 710
Web: www.lamiglas.com
Laminar Consulting Services
424 S Olive St Orange CA 92866 888-531-9995 196
TF: 888-531-9995 ■ *Web:* laminarconsulting.com
Lamin-Art Inc 1670 Basswood Rd Schaumburg IL 60173 847-860-4300 596
TF: 800-323-7624 ■ *Web:* www.laminart.com
Laminate Technologies Inc 161 Maule Rd Tiffin OH 44883 800-231-2523 817
TF: 800-231-2523 ■ *Web:* lamtech.net
Laminated Wood Systems Inc (LWS)
1327 285th Rd PO Box 386 Seward NE 68434 800-949-3526 643-4374* 817
**Fax Area Code:* 402 ■ *TF:* 800-949-3526 ■ *Web:* www.lwsinc.com
Laminating Company of America
20322 Windrow Dr Lake Forest CA 92630 949-587-3300 599
Web: www.lcoa.com
Lamination Depot Inc
1601 Alton Pkwy Ste E Irvine CA 92606 714-954-0632 954-6053 535
TF: 800-925-0054 ■ *Web:* www.laminationdepot.com
Lamination Specialties Corp
235 N Artesian Ave Chicago IL 60612 312-243-2181 243-2873 767
Web: www.laminationspecialties.com
Laminations 3010 E Venture Dr Appleton WI 54911 800-925-2626 548
TF: 800-925-2626 ■ *Web:* www.laminationsonline.com
Laminators Inc 3255 Penn St Hatfield PA 19440 215-723-8107 721-4669 817
TF: 877-663-4277 ■ *Web:* www.laminatorsinc.com
Laminex Inc 4209 Pleasant Rd Fort Mill SC 29708 704-679-4170 679-8453 627
TF: 800-438-8850 ■ *Web:* www.laminex.com
Lamitech Inc 322 Half Acre Rd Cranbury NJ 08512 609-860-8037 561
Web: www.lamitech.com
Lamm Technical Resources LLC
917 S Limit Sedalia MO 65301 660-827-9944 180
TF: 888-566-9944 ■ *Web:* lammtech.com
Lammes Candies Since 1885 Inc
PO Box 1885 Austin TX 78767 512-310-2223 238-2019 296-8
TF: 800-252-1885 ■ *Web:* lammes.com
LAMMICO 1 Galleria Blvd Ste 700 Metairie LA 70001 504-831-3756 841-5300 391-5
Web: www.lammico.com
Lamms Machine Inc 3216 Berger St Allentown PA 18103 610-797-2023 454
Web: www.lammsmachine.com
Lamoille County PO Box 455 Morrisville VT 05661 802-888-5640 851-1136 338
Web: lamoilleeconomy.org
Lamoille Home Health & Hospice
54 Farr Ave Morrisville VT 05661 802-888-4651 363
Web: www.lhha.org
Lamoine State Park 23 State Park Rd Lamoine ME 04605 207-667-4778 565
Web: www.maine.gov
Lamons Gasket Co 7300 Airport Blvd Houston TX 77061 713-222-0284 547-9502 326
TF: 800-231-6906 ■ *Web:* www.lamons.com
Lamont Engineers 548 Main St Cobleskill NY 12043 518-234-4028 234-4613 194
TF: 800-882-9721 ■ *Web:* lamontengineers.com
Lamont Ltd 1530 Bluff Rd Burlington IA 52601 319-753-5131 753-0946 319-2
TF: 800-553-5621 ■ *Web:* www.lamonthome.com
Lamont, Hanley & Associates Inc
1138 Elm St Manchester NH 03105 603-625-5547 160
TF: 800-639-2204 ■ *Web:* www.lhainc.com
Lamont-Doherty Earth Observatory
61 Rt 9w Palisades NY 10964 845-359-2900 668
Web: www.ldeo.columbia.edu
Lamorinda Arts Council PO Box 121 Orinda CA 94563 925-359-9940 637-2
Web: lamorindaarts.org
Lamothe House Hotel
621 Esplanade Ave New Orleans LA 70116 800-535-7815 302-2019* 379
**Fax Area Code:* 504 ■ *TF:* 800-535-7815 ■ *Web:* www.frenchquarterguesthouses.com
LaMotte Co 802 Washington Ave Chestertown MD 21620 410-778-3100 778-6394 419
TF: 800-344-3100 ■ *Web:* www.lamotte.com
LaMoure County
202 Fourth Ave NE PO Box 128 La Moure ND 58458 701-883-5301 338
Web: www.lamourecountynd.com
Lamp Post Publishing Inc
1741 Tallman Hollow Rd Montoursville PA 17754 570-435-2804 637-2
TF: 800-326-9273 ■ *Web:* www.lamppostpublishing.com
Lamp Rynearson 14710 W Dodge Rd Ste 100 Omaha NE 68154 402-496-2498 727
Web: lamprynearson.com
Lampasas County 409 S Pecan St Lampasas TX 76550 512-556-8271 556-8270 338
Web: www.co.lampasas.tx.us
Lampasas Isd 207 W Eighth St Lampasas TX 76550 512-556-6224 556-8711 186
Web: www.lisdtx.org
Lampco Federal Credit Union
5411 Dr MLK Jr Blvd Anderson IN 46013 765-649-9226 622-0010 219
Web: lampco.com
Lampert Yards Inc 1850 Como Ave Saint Paul MN 55108 651-695-3600 364
Web: www.lampertlumber.com
Lamphere Schools
31201 Dorchester Ave Madison Heights MI 48071 248-589-1990 589-2618 685
Web: lamphereschools.org
Lampin Corp 38 River Rd Uxbridge MA 01569 508-278-2422 278-7863 483
TF: 800-657-6450 ■ *Web:* www.lampin.com
Lampire Biological Labs Inc
PO Box 270 Pipersville PA 18947 215-795-2838 795-0237 476
Web: lampire.com
Lamplighter Inn & Suites South
1772 S Glenstone Ave Springfield MO 65804 417-882-1113 379
Web: www.lamplighterhotels.com
Lamplighter Publishing PO Box 777 Waverly PA 18471 888-246-7735 637-2
TF: 888-246-7735 ■ *Web:* www.lamplighter.net

	Phone	Fax	Class
Lampo Group Inc, The 1749 Mallory Ln. . . . . Brentwood TN 37027 *Web:* www.daveramsey.com	615-371-8881		401
Lamppost Pizza Franchise Corp 3002 Dow Ave. . . . . Tustin CA 92780 *Web:* www.lamppost-backstreet.com	714-731-6171		670
Lamps Plus Inc 20250 Plummer St. . . . . Chatsworth CA 91311 *TF:* 800-782-1967 ■ *Web:* www.lampsplus.com	800-782-1967		362
Lampton-Love Inc PO Box 1607. . . . . Jackson MS 39215 *Web:* www.lamptonlove.com	601-939-8304	939-8309	787
Lampus Press 19611 Antioch Rd. . . . . White City OR 97503 *Web:* www.seven-rays.org	541-826-7418		637-2
Lamson & Goodnow Manufacturing Co 45 Conway St. . . . . Shelburne Falls MA 01370 *TF:* 800-872-6564 ■ *Web:* lamsonproducts.com	413-625-0201		222
Lamson Institute 5819 NW Loop 410 Ste 160. . . . . San Antonio TX 78238 *TF:* 888-547-5013 ■ *Web:* www.lamsoninstitute.com	210-465-1794		167-3
LAMSON OIL Co 5060 27th Ave . . . . . Rockford IL 61109 *Web:* www.lamsonoil.com	815-226-8090	226-9250	580
Lamson, Dugan & Murray LLP 10306 Regency Pkwy Dr. . . . . Omaha NE 68114 *Web:* www.ldmlaw.com	402-397-7300	397-7824	428
Lamvin Inc 4675 North Ave . . . . . Oceanside CA 92056 *TF:* 800-446-6329 ■ *Web:* www.lamvin.com	760-806-6400	806-3200	608
Lan Associates Engineering Planning Architecture Surveying Inc 445 Godwin Ave Ste 9 . . . . . Midland Park NJ 07432 *Web:* www.lanassociates.com	201-447-6400		256
Lan Do & Associates LLC 2171 Harbor Bay Pkwy . . . . . Alameda CA 94502 *Web:* landoassociates.com	510-748-9200		768
Lan Pan Asian Cafe 8332 S Dixie Hwy. . . . . Miami FL 33143 *Web:* www.lanpanasian.com	305-661-8141		671
Lanahan Publishers Inc 324 Hawthorn Rd . . . . . Baltimore MD 21210 *TF:* 866-354-1949 ■ *Web:* www.lanahanpublishers.com	410-366-2434	366-8798	637-2
Lanair Group LLC 620 N Brand Blvd 6th Fl. . . . . Glendale CA 91203 *TF:* 877-526-2471 ■ *Web:* www.lanairgroup.com	323-512-7363	512-7763	180
Lancair International LLC 250 SE Timber Ave. . . . . Redmond OR 97756 *Web:* lancair.com	541-923-2244		21
Lancaster Archery Supply Inc 2195-A Old Philadelphia Pk. . . . . Lancaster PA 17602 *TF:* 800-829-7408 ■ *Web:* www.lancasterarchery.com	800-829-7408		711
Lancaster Barnstormers & Keystone Baseball 650 N Prince St . . . . . Lancaster PA 17603 *Web:* www.lancasterbarnstormers.com	717-509-4487		713
Lancaster Beauty School 44646 10th St W. . . . . Lancaster CA 93534 *Web:* www.lancasterbeautyschool.com	661-948-1672		685
Lancaster Bible College 901 Eden Rd . . . . . Lancaster PA 17601 *TF:* 800-544-7335 ■ *Web:* www.lbc.edu	717-569-7071	560-8213	161
Lancaster Brewing Co 302 N Plum St. . . . . Lancaster PA 17602 *Web:* www.lancasterbrewing.com	717-391-6258	391-6015	671
Lancaster Chamber of Commerce & Industry PO Box 1558 . . . . . Lancaster PA 17608 *Web:* www.lancasterchamber.com	717-397-3531	293-3159	139
Lancaster City School District 345 E Mulberry St. . . . . Lancaster OH 43130 *Web:* www.lancaster.k12.oh.us	740-687-7300	687-7303	685
Lancaster Colony Corp 37 W Broad St . . . . . Columbus OH 43215 *NASDAQ: LANC* ■ *Web:* www.lancastercolony.com	614-224-7141		185
Lancaster Commercial Products Inc 2353 Westbrooke Dr. . . . . Columbus OH 43228 *TF:* 844-324-1444 ■ *Web:* www.lcpinc.com	614-263-2850		300
Lancaster County 150 N Queen St. . . . . Lancaster PA 17603 *Web:* co.lancaster.pa.us	717-299-8000	293-7208	338
Lancaster County 8265 Mary Ball Rd. . . . . Lancaster VA 22503 *Web:* www.courts.state.va.us	804-462-5611	462-9978	338
Lancaster County 575 S Tenth St 3rd Fl. . . . . Lincoln NE 68508 *Web:* www.lancaster.ne.gov	402-441-7481	441-8728	338
Lancaster County Association of Realtors 1930 Harrington Dr. . . . . Lancaster PA 17601 *Web:* lcar.com	717-569-4625	569-5994	653
Lancaster County Chamber of Commerce PO Box 430 . . . . . Lancaster SC 29721 *TF:* 800-532-0335 ■ *Web:* www.lancasterchambersc.org	803-283-4105	286-4360	139
Lancaster County Library 313 S White St . . . . . Lancaster SC 29720 *Web:* www.lanclib.org	803-285-1502	285-6004	434-3
Lancaster DHIA 1592 Old Line Rd. . . . . Manheim PA 17545 *Web:* www.lancasterdhia.com	717-665-5960		368
Lancaster Eagle Gazette 138 W Chestnut St . . . . . Lancaster OH 43130 *TF:* 877-513-7355 ■ *Web:* www.lancastereaglegazette.com	740-654-1321		532-2
Lancaster Farming PO Box 609. . . . . Ephrata PA 17522 *Web:* www.lancasterfarming.com	717-626-1164	733-6058	532-4
Lancaster General Hospital 555 N Duke St . . . . . Lancaster PA 17604 *Web:* www.lancastergeneralhealth.org	717-544-5511	544-5966	374-3
Lancaster Hotel 701 Texas St. . . . . Houston TX 77002 *TF:* 800-231-0336 ■ *Web:* www.thelancaster.com	713-228-9500	223-4528	379
Lancaster Knives Inc 165 Ct St. . . . . Lancaster NY 14086 *TF:* 800-869-9666 ■ *Web:* www.lancasterknives.com	716-683-5050	683-5068	493
Lancaster Mcaden Willis Smith Co 1320 Commerce Dr . . . . . New Bern NC 28562 *Web:* ticnc.com	252-637-4173		390
Lancaster Newspapers Inc 8 W King St PO Box 1328. . . . . Lancaster PA 17603 *Web:* lancasteronline.com	717-291-8811		637-8
Lancaster Pollard 65 E State St Ste 1600 . . . . . Columbus OH 43215	614-224-8800		401
Lancaster Public Library 125 N Duke St . . . . . Lancaster PA 17602 *Web:* lancasterpubliclibrary.org	717-394-2651	394-3083	434-3
Lancaster Pump Co 1340 Manheim Pk . . . . . Lancaster PA 17601 *TF:* 800-442-0786 ■ *Web:* lancasterwatergroup.com	717-397-3521	392-0266	806
Lancaster School of Cosmetology & Therapeutic Bodywork 50 Ranck Ave . . . . . Lancaster PA 17602 *Web:* www.lancasterschoolofcosmetology.com	717-299-0200		685
Lancaster School of Massage 313 W Liberty St Ste 326 . . . . . Lancaster PA 17603 *Web:* www.lancasterschoolofmassage.com	717-293-9698		685
Lancaster Systems Inc 411 Theodore Fremd Ave . . . . . Rye NY 10580 *Web:* www.lancastersys.com	914-967-5700		180
Lancaster Theological Seminary 555 W James St . . . . . Lancaster PA 17603 *TF:* 800-393-0654 ■ *Web:* www.lancasterseminary.edu	717-393-0654	393-4254	167-3
Lancaster Toyota Inc 5270 Manheim Pk . . . . . East Petersburg PA 17520 *TF:* 888-424-1295 ■ *Web:* www.lancastertoyota.com	888-424-1295		57
Lancaster-Fairfield County Chamber of Commerce 109 N Broad St Ste 100 . . . . . Lancaster OH 43130 *Web:* www.lancoc.org	740-653-8251	653-7074	139
LancasterHistory.org 230 N President Ave. . . . . Lancaster PA 17603 *Web:* www.lancasterhistory.org	717-392-4633		50-3
Lance Camper Manufacturing Corp 43120 Venture St . . . . . Lancaster CA 93535 *Web:* www.lancecamper.com	661-949-3322	949-1262	120
Lance Soll & Lunghard LLP 203 N Brea Blvd Ste 203. . . . . Brea CA 92821 *Web:* lslcpas.com	714-672-0022		2
Lance Trucking Company Inc 4246 E First St . . . . . Blue Ridge GA 30513 *Web:* www.lancetruckingcompany.com	706-632-2248	632-6235	780
Lancer Orthodontics Inc 1493 Poinsettia Ave Ste 143. . . . . Vista CA 92081 *NYSE: LANZ* ■ *TF:* 800-854-2896 ■ *Web:* www.lancerortho.com	760-744-5585	598-0418	228
Lancer Worldwide 6655 Lancer Blvd . . . . . San Antonio TX 78219 **Fax Area Code:* 210 ■ *TF:* 800-729-1500 ■ *Web:* www.lancercorp.com	888-676-5196	310-7250*	664
Lancet Capital 100 Technology Dr Ste 200 . . . . . Pittsburgh PA 15219 *Web:* lancetcapital.com	412-402-9914	452-9480	792
Lancia Homes 9430 Lima Rd. . . . . Fort Wayne IN 46818 *Web:* www.lanciahomes.com	260-489-4433		653
Lancione Law Firm, The 619 Linda St Ste 201 . . . . . Rocky River OH 44116 *Web:* www.lancionelaw.com	440-571-6862		41
Lanconnect Inc 623 W Washington St . . . . . Norristown PA 19401 *Web:* lanconnectinc.com	610-272-2044		116
Lancore Technologies 11211 Richmond Ave. . . . . Houston TX 77082 *TF:* 866-492-5800 ■ *Web:* www.lancoretech.com	281-493-5850	493-5815	177
Lancs Industries 12704 NE 124th St Bldg 36 . . . . . Kirkland WA 98034 *Web:* www.lancsindustries.com	425-823-6634	820-6784	596
Land & Legal Solutions Inc 300 S Hamilton Ave . . . . . Greensburg PA 15601	724-853-8992	853-3221	178-10
Land Coast Insulation Inc 4017 2nd St PO Box 14110 . . . . . New Iberia LA 70560	337-367-7741	367-7744	189-9
Land Design Consultants Inc 800 Royal Oaks Dr Ste 104. . . . . Monrovia CA 91016 *Web:* www.ldcla.com	626-578-7000		261
Land Development Consultants Inc 20210 142nd Ave NE . . . . . Woodinville WA 98072 *Web:* ldccorp.com	425-806-1869	482-2893	261
Land Home Financial Services Inc 1355 Willow Way Ste 250. . . . . Concord CA 94520 *TF:* 800-672-9470 ■ *Web:* lhfs.com	925-338-8200		652
Land Information Access Assn 324 Munson Ave. . . . . Traverse City MI 49686 *Web:* www.liaa.org	231-929-3696		41
Land Legal Group, Aplc 1900 Avenue of the Stars Ste 1800. . . . . Los Angeles CA 90067 *Web:* landlegalgroup.com	310-552-3500		41
Land Line Magazine & Land Line Now 1 Ooida dr PO Box 1000. . . . . Grain Valley MO 64029 *TF:* 800-444-5791 ■ *Web:* landline.media	816-229-5791	443-2227	457-21
Land O'Frost Inc 16850 Chicago Ave . . . . . Lansing IL 60438 *Web:* www.landofrost.com	708-474-7100		473
Land O'Lakes Finance Co PO Box 64408 . . . . . Saint Paul MN 55164 **Fax Area Code:* 651 ■ *TF:* 800-328-9680 ■ *Web:* www.landolakesfinance.com	800-328-9680	234-8215*	196
Land of Sleep 1285 US Hwy 41 By-Pass S . . . . . Venice FL 34285 *Web:* www.landofsleep.com	941-484-2688		361
Land of the Yankee Fork State Park PO Box 1086 . . . . . Challis ID 83226 *Web:* parksandrecreation.idaho.gov	208-879-5244		565
Land Precision Corp 2683 Sunset Point Rd. . . . . Clearwater FL 33759 *Web:* landprecision.com	727-796-2737		261
Land Rover North America Inc 555 MacArthur Blvd . . . . . Mahwah NJ 07430 *TF:* 800-637-6837 ■ *Web:* www.landrover.com	800-637-6837		59
Land Rover North Haven 525 Washington Ave. . . . . North Haven CT 06473 *TF:* 877-819-6922 ■ *Web:* www.landrovernorthhaven.com	203-453-7060		57
Land Rover of Calgary 175 Glendeer Cir SE. . . . . Calgary AB T2H2V4 *TF:* 866-274-4080 ■ *Web:* landrovercalgary.com	866-274-4080		57
Land Title Guarantee Company Inc 3033 E First Ave Ste 600 . . . . . Denver CO 80206 *TF:* 888-778-4853 ■ *Web:* www.ltgc.com	303-321-1880		390
Land Trust Alliance (LTA) 1660 L St NW Ste 1100 . . . . . Washington DC 20036 *Web:* www.landtrustalliance.org	202-638-4725	638-4730	48-13
Landa & Associates Inc 5128 E Thomas Rd Ste 100 . . . . . Phoenix AZ 85018 *Web:* landaandassociates.com	602-443-5515		256
Landaal Packaging Systems Inc 3256 B Iron St . . . . . Burton MI 48529 *TF:* 800-616-6619 ■ *Web:* www.landaal.com	800-616-6619		100

	City	State	ZIP	Phone	Fax	Class
Landaas & Co 411 E Wisconsin Ave 20th Fl *TF:* 800-236-1096 ■ *Web:* www.landaas.com	Milwaukee	WI	53202	414-223-1099		401
Landair Corp 1110 Myers St *TF:* 888-526-3247 ■ *Web:* www.landair.com	Greeneville	TN	37743	888-526-3247		780
LandaJob 222 W Gregory Blvd Ste 304 *TF:* 800-931-8806 ■ *Web:* www.landajobnow.com	Kansas City	MO	64114	816-523-1881		195
Landau Building Co 9855 Rinaman Rd *Web:* www.landau-bldg.com	Wexford	PA	15090	724-935-8800	935-6510	186
Landau Uniforms 8410 W Sandidge Rd *TF:* 800-238-7513 ■ *Web:* www.landau.com	Olive Branch	MS	38654	662-895-7200		155-19
Landavazo Bros Inc 29280 Pacific St	Hayward	CA	94544	510-581-7104		189-3
Landec Corp 3603 Haven Ave *NASDAQ: LNDC* ■ *Web:* www.landec.com	Menlo Park	CA	94025	650-306-1650		605-2
Landel Telecom 142 Martinvale Ln *TF:* 855-624-5284 ■ *Web:* landel.com	San Jose	CA	95119	855-624-5284		387
Lander & Lander PC 405 Cochituate Rd Ste 302 *Web:* landerandlander.com	Framingham	MA	01701	508-879-0046		41
Lander County 315 S Humboldt St *Web:* landercountynv.org	Battle Mountain	NV	89820	775-635-2610	635-5520	338
Lander University 320 Stanley Ave *TF:* 800-922-1117 ■ *Web:* www.lander.edu	Greenwood	SC	29649	864-388-8307	388-8125	166
Landers Premier Flooring Inc 2601 Mchale Ct Ste 140 *Web:* launderspremierflooring.com	Austin	TX	78758	512-873-9470		290
Landesa 1424 Fourth Ave Ste 300 *Web:* www.landesa.org	Seattle	WA	98101	206-528-5880	528-5881	305
Landfear & Brophy Inc 20 Assembly Dr Ste 107 *Web:* lbworldwide.com	Mendon	NY	14506	585-624-1470		261
Landice Inc 111 Canfield Ave *TF:* 800-526-3423 ■ *Web:* www.landice.com	Randolph	NJ	07869	973-927-9010		476
Landing School, The 286 River Rd *Web:* www.landingschool.edu	Arundel	ME	04046	207-985-7976	985-7942	685
Landings Club Inc 71 Green Island Rd *TF:* 800-841-7011 ■ *Web:* www.landingsclub.com	Savannah	GA	31411	912-598-8050		354
Landings Yacht Golf & Tennis Club Inc, The 4420 Flagship Dr *Web:* www.landingsygtc.com	Fort Myers	FL	33919	239-482-3211	482-1796	706
Landini Bros 115 King St *Web:* landinibrothers.com	Alexandria	VA	22314	703-836-8404	549-3596	671
Landis + Gyr 2800 Duncan Rd *TF:* 888-390-5733 ■ *Web:* www.landisgyr.de	LaFayette	IN	47904	765-742-1001	742-0936	248
Landis Arboretum 174 Lape Rd PO Box 186 *Web:* www.landisarboretum.org	Esperance	NY	12066	518-875-6935		97
Landis Block Co 711 N County Line Rd PO Box 64418 *Web:* www.landisbc.com	Souderton	PA	18964	215-723-5506	723-5500	183
Landis Construction LLC 8300 Earhart Blvd Ste 300 PO Box 4278 *TF:* 800-880-3290 ■ *Web:* www.landisllc.com	New Orleans	LA	70118	504-833-6070	833-6662	186
Landis Corp 6446 Fairway Ave SE *Web:* www.landisconsulting.com	Salem	OR	97306	503-584-1576		261
Landis Supermarket Inc 2685 County Line Rd *Web:* www.landismarket.com	Telford	PA	18969	215-723-1157		345
Landis Technologies LLC 1120 Division Hwy *Web:* landistechnologies.com	Ephrata	PA	17522	717-733-0793	798-3884	624
Landiscor 3401 E Broadway Rd *TF:* 866-221-0570 ■ *Web:* landiscor.com	Phoenix	AZ	85040	602-248-8989		727
Landmann Wire Rope Products Inc 1818 Gilbreth Rd Ste 148 *TF:* 800-331-0794 ■ *Web:* www.landmannwire.com	Burlingame	CA	94010	650-777-4210		492
Landmark College 19 River Rd S *Web:* www.landmark.edu	Putney	VT	05346	802-387-4767		162
Landmark Community Newspapers Inc 601 Taylorsville Rd *TF:* 800-939-9322 ■ *Web:* www.lcni.com	Shelbyville	KY	40065	502-633-4334		637-8
Landmark Construction Group LLC 13301 N Santa Fe Ave *Web:* landmarkokc.com	Oklahoma City	OK	73114	405-843-8041	843-1882	780
Landmark Consultants Inc 141 Ninth St *Web:* www.landmark-co.com	Steamboat Springs	CO	80477	970-871-9494		261
Landmark Credit Union 5445 S Westridge Dr PO Box 510910 *TF:* 800-801-1449 ■ *Web:* www.landmarkcu.com	New Berlin	WI	53151	262-796-4500	782-3422	219
Landmark Data Systems Inc 2 Old River Pl Ste L *TF:* 800-424-8178 ■ *Web:* www.landmarkdata.com	Jackson	MS	39202	601-362-0303	362-0347	178-1
Landmark Equipment Company Inc 1309 Haltom Rd **Fax Area Code:* 972 ■ *Web:* www.landmarkeq.com	Fort Worth	TX	76117	817-834-8131	579-7871*	429
Landmark Financial Group LLC 181 Old Post Rd *TF:* 800-437-4214 ■ *Web:* landmark-mortgage.com	Southport	CT	06890	203-254-8422		251
Landmark Ford Inc 12000 SW 66th Ave *TF:* 888-776-0542 ■ *Web:* www.landmarkford.com	Tigard	OR	97223	503-639-1131		516
Landmark Healthcare Inc 1750 Howe Ave Ste 300 *TF:* 800-638-4557 ■ *Web:* www.lmhealthcare.com	Sacramento	CA	95825	800-638-4557		194
Landmark Hotel Group LLC 249 Central Park Ave Ste 320 *Web:* www.landmarkhotelgroup.com	Virginia Beach	VA	23462	757-249-0200	440-3955	378
Landmark Imaging Medical Group Inc 11620 Wilshire Blvd Ste 100 *Web:* www.landmarkimaging.com	Los Angeles	CA	90025	310-914-7336	914-7326	415
Landmark Industries Ltd 11111 Wilcrest Green Dr Ste 100 *Web:* www.landmarkindustries.com	Houston	TX	77042	713-789-0310	789-2907	316
Landmark Inn 230 N Front St *TF:* 888-752-6362 ■ *Web:* www.thelandmarkinn.com	Marquette	MI	49855	906-228-2580	228-5676	379
Landmark Inn State Historic Site 402 E Florence St *Web:* www.thc.texas.gov	Castroville	TX	78009	830-931-2133		565
Landmark International Trucks Inc 4550 Rutledge Pk *TF:* 800-968-9999 ■ *Web:* landmarktrucks.com	Knoxville	TN	37914	865-637-4881		780
Landmark Lincoln-Mercury Inc 5000 S Broadway *TF:* 888-318-9692 ■ *Web:* www.landmarklincoln.com	Englewood	CO	80113	303-761-1560		57
Landmark Manufacturing Corp 28100 Quick Ave *Web:* landmarkfab.com	Gallatin	MO	64640	660-663-2185	663-2417	697
Landmark Medical Ctr 115 Cass Ave *Web:* www.landmarkmedical.org	Woonsocket	RI	02895	401-769-4100		374-3
Landmark on the Park 160 Central Pk W *Web:* www.landmarkonthepark.com	New York	NY	10023	212-971-5353		50-1
Landmark Parking Inc 33 S Gay St *Web:* landmarkparking.com	Baltimore	MD	21202	410-837-5600		562
Landmark Plastic Corp 1331 Kelly Ave *TF:* 800-242-1183 ■ *Web:* www.landmarkplastic.com	Akron	OH	44306	330-785-2200	785-9200	608
Landmark Publishing Inc N27 W5230 Hamilton Rd *Web:* www.landmarkpublishing.net	Cedarburg	WI	53012	262-377-7398		637-9
Landmark Realty LLC 2205 Beckett St *Web:* www.landmarkrealty.org	Bossier City	LA	71111	318-747-0052		652
Landmark Resort 7643 Hillside Rd *TF:* 800-273-7877 ■ *Web:* www.thelandmarkresort.com	Egg Harbor	WI	54209	920-868-3205	868-2569	669
Landmark Resort 1501 S Ocean Blvd *TF:* 800-845-0658 ■ *Web:* www.landmarkresort.com	Myrtle Beach	SC	29577	843-448-9441		669
Landmark School 429 Hale St PO Box 227 *TF:* 866-333-0859 ■ *Web:* www.landmarkschool.org	Prides Crossing	MA	01965	978-236-3010	927-7268	622
Landmark Society of Western New York (LSWNY) 133 S Fitzhugh St *Web:* www.landmarksociety.org	Rochester	NY	14608	585-546-7029	546-4788	48-6
Landmark Structures LP 1665 Harmon Rd *TF:* 800-888-6816 ■ *Web:* www.teamlandmark.com	Fort Worth	TX	76177	817-439-8888	439-9001	188-10
Landmark Testing & Engineering 795 E Factory Dr *Web:* landmarktesting.com	Saint George	UT	84790	435-986-0566	986-0568	261
Landmark Theaters 700 N San Vicente Blvd Ste G470 *TF:* 888-724-6362 ■ *Web:* landmarktheatres.com	West Hollywood	CA	90064	310-473-6701		748
Landmark Theatre 362 S Salina St *Web:* landmarktheatre.org	Syracuse	NY	13202	315-475-7979		572
Landmark Tours Inc 4001 Stinson Blvd Ste 430 *TF:* 888-231-8735 ■ *Web:* gowithlandmark.com	Minneapolis	MN	55421	651-490-5408		760
Landoll Corp 1900 North St **Fax Area Code:* 888 ■ *TF:* 800-446-5175 ■ *Web:* www.landoll.com	Marysville	KS	66508	785-562-5381	321-3865*	470
Landon Hotel Miami, The *Daddy O Miami* 9660 E Bay Harbor Dr *Web:* www.thelandon.com	Bay Harbor Islands	FL	33154	305-868-4141	723-7676	379
Landor 1001 Front St *Web:* landor.com	San Francisco	CA	94111	415-365-1700		195
Landpoint LLC 5486 Airline Dr *TF:* 800-348-5254 ■ *Web:* www.landpoint.net	Bossier City	LA	71111	318-226-0100		727
Landrum & Shouse LLP 106 W Vine St Ste 800 *TF:* 888-322-2505 ■ *Web:* www.landrumshouse.com	Lexington	KY	40507	859-554-4038	233-0308	428
Landrum's Homestead & Village 1356 Hwy 15 S *Web:* landrums.com	Laurel	MS	39443	601-649-2546		520
Landry & Associates CPAS PA 6 Chenell Dr *Web:* taxpronh.com	Concord	NH	03301	603-228-3004	715-1105	2
Landry's Inc 1510 W Loop South *TF:* 800-552-6379 ■ *Web:* www.landrysinc.com	Houston	TX	77027	713-850-1010		372
Landry's Seafood House 2900 W Missouri Hwy 76 *Web:* www.landrysseafood.com	Branson	MO	65616	417-339-1010		671
Lands' End Inc 1 Lands' End Ln *TF:* 800-963-4816 ■ *Web:* www.landsend.com	Dodgeville	WI	53595	608-935-9341		459
Landsberg Orora 1640 S Greenwood Ave *TF:* 888-526-3723 ■ *Web:* www.landsberg.com	Montebello	CA	90640	323-832-2000		559
Landsby, The 1576 Mission Dr Ofc *Web:* thelandsby.com	Solvang	CA	93463	805-688-3121		378
Landscape Communications Inc 14771 Plaza Dr Ste M *Web:* www.landscapeonline.com	Tustin	CA	92780	714-979-5276		637-9
Landscape Concepts Management 31745 Alleghany Rd *TF:* 866-655-3800 ■ *Web:* www.landscapeconcepts.com	Grayslake	IL	60030	847-223-3800	223-0169	422
Landscape Development Inc 28447 Witherspoon Pkwy *Web:* landscapedevelopment.com	Valencia	CA	91355	661-295-1970	295-1969	422
Landscape Structures Inc 601 Seventh St S *TF:* 800-328-0035 ■ *Web:* www.playlsi.com	Delano	MN	55328	763-972-3391	972-3185	346
Landscapes Unlimited LLC 1201 Aries Dr *Web:* www.landscapesunlimited.com	Lincoln	NE	68512	402-423-6653	423-4487	188-3
Landsford Canal State Park 2051 Pk Dr *Web:* southcarolinaparks.com	Catawba	SC	29704	803-789-5800		565
Landsman Law Firm LLC 33 N LaSalle St Ste 1400 *Web:* www.landsmanfirm.com	Chicago	IL	60602	312-801-5684	251-1147	445
Landstar Inway Inc 13410 Sutton Pk Dr S *TF:* 800-872-9400 ■ *Web:* www.landstar.com	Jacksonville	FL	32224	800-872-9400		780
Land-Tech Consultants Inc 518 Riverside Ave *Web:* landtechconsult.com	Westport	CT	06880	203-454-2110		261

	Phone	Fax	Class
LandTek Group Inc, The 235 County Line Rd . . . Amityville NY 11701 *Web:* www.landtekgroup.com	631-691-2381		188
LandUse USA LLC 6971 Westgate Dr . . . Laingsburg MI 48848 *Web:* www.landuseusa.com	517-290-5531		652
Lane & Waterman LLP 220 N Main St Ste 600 . . . Davenport IA 52801 *Web:* www.l-wlaw.com	563-324-3246	324-1616	428
Lane Aviation Corp 4389 International Gateway . . . Columbus OH 43219 *TF:* 800-848-6263 ■ *Web:* www.laneaviation.com	614-237-3747	231-4741	63
Lane Bryant Inc 3344 Morse Crossing Rd . . . Columbus OH 43219 *TF:* 866-886-4731 ■ *Web:* www.lanebryant.com	954-970-2205		157-6
Lane College 545 Ln Ave . . . Jackson TN 38301 *TF:* 800-960-7533 ■ *Web:* www.lanecollege.edu	731-426-7500	426-7559	166
Lane Community College 4000 E 30th Ave . . . Eugene OR 97405 *Web:* www.lanecc.edu	541-463-3000	463-3995	162
Lane Construction Company Inc 1 Indian Rd . . . Denville NJ 07834 *Web:* www.thelanegroup.us	973-586-2700	586-2965	188-4
Lane Construction Corp, The 90 Fieldstone Ct . . . Cheshire CT 06410 *Web:* www.laneconstruct.com	203-235-3351	237-4260	188-4
Lane County 125 E Eigth Ave . . . Eugene OR 97401 *TF:* 800-281-2800 ■ *Web:* www.lanecounty.org	541-682-4203	682-4616	338
Lane Electric 787 Bailey Hill Rd PO Box 21410 . . . Eugene OR 97402 *TF:* 877-562-5503 ■ *Web:* laneelectric.com	541-484-1151	484-7316	245
Lane Engineering LLC 117 Bay St . . . Easton MD 21601 *Web:* leinc.com	410-822-8003	822-2024	261
Lane Events Ctr 796 W 13th Ave . . . Eugene OR 97402 *Web:* www.atthefair.com	541-682-4292	682-3614	205
Lane Gorman Trubitt LLP 2626 Howell St Ste 700 . . . Dallas TX 75204 *Web:* www.lgt-cpa.com	214-871-7500	871-0011	2
Lane Group LLC, The 14-25 Plaza Rd . . . Fair Lawn NJ 07410 *Web:* www.tlgmeetings.com	201-398-9230		196
Lane Medical Library Stanford University Medical Ctr 300 Pasteur Dr Rm L-109 . . . Stanford CA 94305 *Web:* www.lane.stanford.edu	650-723-6831	725-7471	434-1
Lane Press Inc 1000 Hinesburg Rd . . . Burlington VT 05403 *TF:* 877-300-5933 ■ *Web:* www.lanepress.com	877-300-5933		627
Lane Public Library 300 N Third St . . . Hamilton OH 45011 *Web:* www.lanepl.org	513-894-7156		434-3
Lane Punch Corp 281 Ln Pkwy . . . Salisbury NC 28146 **Fax Area Code:* 800 ■ *Web:* www.lanepunch.com	704-633-3900	227-6725*	757
Lane Regional Medical Ctr 6300 Main St . . . Zachary LA 70791 *Web:* www.lanermc.org	225-658-4000	658-4287	374-3
Lane Steel Company Inc 4 River Rd . . . McKees Rocks PA 15136 *Web:* lanesteel.com	412-777-1700		492
Lane Supply Inc 120 Fairview . . . Arlington TX 76010 *Web:* www.lanesupplyinc.com	817-261-9116	275-1660	579
Lane's End 1500 Midway Rd PO Box 626 . . . Versailles KY 40383 *Web:* www.lanesend.com	859-873-7300	873-3746	368
Lane4 Property Group Inc 4705 Central St . . . Kansas City MO 64112 *Web:* www.lane4group.com	816-960-1444	960-1441	652
Lane-Scott Electric Co-opeartive Inc 410 S High . . . Dighton KS 67839 *TF:* 800-407-2217 ■ *Web:* www.lanescott.coop	620-397-5327		245
LaneTerralever 645 E Missouri Ave Ste 400 . . . Phoenix AZ 85012 *Web:* www.laneterralever.com	602-258-5263		466
Laney College 900 Fallon St . . . Oakland CA 94607 *Web:* laney.edu	510-834-5740		162
Laney's Inc 55 27 St S . . . Fargo ND 58103 *Web:* www.laneysinc.com	701-237-0543		787
Lang Asset Management Inc 171 Village Pkwy NE Bldg 8A . . . Marietta GA 30067 *Web:* www.langasset.com	404-256-4100	256-1473	194
Lang Dental Manufacturing Co 175 Messner Dr . . . Wheeling IL 60090 *TF:* 800-222-5264 ■ *Web:* www.langdental.com	800-222-5264		228
Lang Diesel Inc 1366 Toulon Ave . . . Hays KS 67601 *Web:* langdieselinc.com	785-735-2651	735-2656	429
Lang Pharma Nutrition Inc 20 Silva Ln . . . Middletown RI 02842 *Web:* www.langpni.com	401-848-7700	848-7701	297-8
Lang Realty 2901 Clint Moore Rd Ste 9 . . . Boca Raton FL 33496 *TF:* 877-357-0618 ■ *Web:* www.langrealty.com	561-998-0100	998-8875	652
Lang Richert & Patch Fig Garden Financial Ctr 5200 N Palm Ave 4th Fl . . . Fresno CA 93704 *Web:* www.lrplaw.net	559-228-6700	228-6727	41
Lang Stone Company Inc 707 Short St . . . Columbus OH 43215 *Web:* www.langstone.com	614-235-4099		191-1
Lang, Lang & Company CPAS 191 E Main St Ste 2A . . . Tustin CA 92780 *Web:* langlangco.com	714-380-6200	380-6442	2
Langan Engineering & Environmental Services Inc 300 Kimball Dr 4th Fl . . . Parsippany NJ 07054 *Web:* www.langan.com	973-560-4900	560-4901	261
Langan Products Inc 2660 California St . . . San Francisco CA 94115 *Web:* www.langan.biz	415-567-8087	398-7664	173-1
Langara College 100 W 49th Ave . . . Vancouver BC V5Y2Z6 *Web:* langara.ca	604-323-5511		162
Langboard Inc 320 Langboard Ln . . . Quitman GA 31643 *Web:* www.langboard.com	229-244-4154	263-5535	819
Langdale Forest Products Co PO Box 1088 . . . Valdosta GA 31603 *TF:* 800-864-6909 ■ *Web:* www.langdaleforest.com	229-333-2500	333-2533	683
Langdon & Company LLP 223 Us 70 Hwy E Ste 100 . . . Garner NC 27529 *Web:* www.langdoncpa.com	919-662-1001		2
Langdon Hall Country House Hotel & Spa 1 Langdon Dr . . . Cambridge ON N3H4R8 *TF:* 800-268-1898 ■ *Web:* www.langdonhall.ca	519-740-2100	740-8161	379
Langdon Wilson Architecture Planning Interiors 1055 Wilshire Blvd Ste 1500 . . . Los Angeles CA 90017 *Web:* www.langdonwilson.com	213-250-1186	482-4654	261
Langer Inc 2905 Veterans' Memorial Hwy . . . Ronkonkoma NY 11779 *TF:* 800-645-5520 ■ *Web:* www.langerbiomechanics.com	800-645-5520		477
Langers Juice Company Inc 16195 Stephens St . . . City of Industry CA 91745 *Web:* www.langers.com	626-336-3100	961-2021	296-20
Langevin Jim (Rep D - RI) 2077 Rayburn House Office Bldg . . . Washington DC 20515 *Web:* langevin.house.gov	202-225-2735	225-5976	342-2
Langham Boston, The 250 Franklin St . . . Boston MA 02110 *TF:* 800-791-7781 ■ *Web:* www.langhamhotels.com	617-451-1900	423-2844	379
Langhorne Carpet Company Inc 201 W Lincoln Hwy PO Box 7175 . . . Penndel PA 19047 *TF:* 800-372-6274 ■ *Web:* langhornecarpets.com	215-757-5155	757-2212	131
Langlade County 800 Clermont St . . . Antigo WI 54409 *Web:* www.co.langlade.wi.us	715-627-6200	627-6303	338
Langley & Mcdonald Inc 309 Lynnhaven Pkwy . . . Virginia Beach VA 23452 *Web:* langleymcdonald.com	757-463-4306		261
Langley Air Force Base 49 Spruce St . . . Langley AFB VA 23665 *Web:* www.jble.af.mil	757-764-1110		497-1
Langley Chamber of Commerce 8047 199 St Ste 207 . . . Langley BC V2Y0E2 *Web:* www.langleychamber.com	604-371-3770		137
Langley Federal Credit Union 1055 W Mercury Blvd . . . Hampton VA 23666 *TF:* 800-826-7490 ■ *Web:* langleyfcu.org	757-827-7200	825-7557	219
Langley Recycling 503 SE Branner St . . . Topeka KS 66607 *Web:* kcscrapyard.com	785-234-2691		686
Langley Research Ctr 2 Langley Blvd . . . Hampton VA 23681 *Web:* www.nasa.gov	757-864-2790		668
Langley Speedway 11 Dale Lemonds Dr . . . Hampton VA 23666 *Web:* langley-speedway.com	757-865-7223		515
Langlois Co, The 10810 San Sevaine Way . . . Mira Loma CA 91752 *Web:* www.langloiscompany.com	951-360-3900		296-16
Langlois Stores Inc 3000 Henry St . . . Muskegon MI 49441 *TF:* 800-606-7600 ■ *Web:* www.Langloisstore.com	231-733-2528		321
Langlois, Wilkins, Furtado & Metcald PC 200 Midway Rd Ste 169 . . . Cranston RI 02920 *Web:* lwfmlaw.com	401-351-9970		41
Lang-Mekra North America LLC 101 Tillessen Blvd . . . Ridgeway SC 29130 *Web:* www.lang-mekra.com	803-337-5264	337-5265	332
Langston Companies Inc 1760 S Third St . . . Memphis TN 38109 **Fax Area Code:* 901 ■ *TF:* 800-238-5798 ■ *Web:* langstonbag.com	800-238-5798	942-5402*	67
Langston Construction Company Inc 125 Langston Rd . . . Piedmont SC 29673 *Web:* www.langstonconstr.com	864-295-9156		186
Langston University 2017 Langston University PO Box 1500 . . . Langston OK 73050 *TF:* 877-466-2231 ■ *Web:* www.langston.edu	877-466-2231		166
Langstons Co 2034 NW Seventh St . . . Oklahoma City OK 73106 *TF:* 800-658-2831 ■ *Web:* www.langstons.com	405-235-9536		229
Langtech Systems Consulting Inc 733 Frnt St Ste 110 . . . San Francisco CA 94111 *TF:* 800-480-8488 ■ *Web:* www.langtech.com	415-364-9600		809
Language Academy 200 S Andrews Ave Ste 401 . . . Fort Lauderdale FL 33301 *Web:* www.languageacademy.com	954-462-8373	462-3738	423
Language Automation Inc (LAI) 1660 S Amphlett Blvd Ste 106 . . . San Mateo CA 94402 *Web:* www.lai.com	650-571-7877		178-7
Language Co 189 W 15th St . . . Edmond OK 73013 *Web:* www.thelanguagecompany.com	405-715-9996	715-1116	423
Language Door LLC 18103 Sky Park Cir Ste D2 . . . Irvine CA 92614 *Web:* www.languagedoor.com	949-833-0900		423
Language Engineering Company LLC 135 Beaver St . . . Waltham MA 02452 *TF:* 888-366-4532 ■ *Web:* www.lec.com	781-642-8900		178-3
Language Exchange Intl 500 NE Spanish River Blvd Ste 19 . . . Boca Raton FL 33431 *Web:* languageexchange.com	561-368-3913	368-9380	423
Language Line Solutions 1 Lower Ragsdale Dr Bldg 2 . . . Monterey CA 93940 *TF:* 800-752-6096 ■ *Web:* www.languageline.com	800-752-6096	648-0170	768
Language Plus Inc 1301 N Oregon St Ste 100 . . . El Paso TX 79902 *Web:* languageplus.edu	915-544-8600		423
Language Scientific 101 Station Landing Ste 500 . . . Medford MA 02155 *TF:* 800-240-0246 ■ *Web:* www.languagescientific.com	617-621-0940		393
Language Services Associates Inc 455 Business Center Dr - Ste 100 . . . Horsham PA 19044 *TF:* 800-305-9673 ■ *Web:* lsaweb.com	215-259-7000		768
Language World Services Inc 7220 Fair Oaks Blvd Ste D . . . Carmichael CA 95608 *Web:* languageworldservices.com	916-333-5247		768
Languages Canada 27282 - 12B Ave . . . Aldergrove BC V4W2P6 **Fax Area Code:* 888 ■ *Web:* www.languagescanada.ca	604-574-1532	277-0522*	49-5
Lanham Brothers General Contractors 2119 W Third St . . . Owensboro KY 42301 *Web:* www.lanhambros.com	270-683-4591		186
Lanier & Associates Consulting Engi Neers Inc 4101 Magazine St . . . New Orleans LA 70115 *Web:* www.lanier-engineers.com	504-895-0368		261

Phone | Fax | Class

Lanier County 56 W Main St Ste 9 . . . . Lakeland GA 31635 229-482-2088 482-8187 338
Web: www.laniercountyboc.com

Lanier County School 247 S Hway 221 . . . . Lakeland GA 31635 229-482-3966 482-3020 685
Web: www.lanier.k12.ga.us

Lanier Ford Shaver & Payne PC
2101 W Clinton Ave Ste 102. . . . . Huntsville AL 35805 256-535-1100 533-9322 428
Web: lanierford.com

Lanier Islands 6950 Holiday Rd . . . . Buford GA 30519 770-945-8787 669
Web: www.lanierislands.com

Lanier Law Group PA 600 S Duke St . . . . Durham NC 27701 919-682-2111 428
TF: 855-234-7619 ■ *Web:* www.lanierlawgroup.com

Lanier Parking Solutions
233 Peachtree St NE. . . . . Atlanta GA 30303 404-881-6076 881-6077 562
Web: www.lanierparking.com

Lanier Technical College
2990 Landrum Education Dr. . . . . Oakwood GA 30566 770-531-6300 531-6328 167-3
Web: www.laniertech.edu

Lanigan, Ryan, Malcolm & Doyle PC
555 Quince Orchard Rd Ste 600 . . . . Gaithersburg MD 20878 301-258-8900 258-1020 2
Web: www.lrmd-cpa.com

Lank Oil Co 2203 W McNab Rd . . . . .Pompano Beach FL 33069 954-978-6600 974-0854 579
Web: lankoil.com

Lankford James (Sen R - OK)
316 Hart Senate Office Bldg . . . . Washington DC 20510 202-224-5754 342-2
Web: www.lankford.senate.gov

Lankota Inc 270 Westpark Ave. . . . . Huron SD 57350 605-352-4550 273
TF: 866-526-5682 ■ *Web:* www.lankota.com

LANL (Los Alamos National Laboratory)
PO Box 1663 . . . . Los Alamos NM 87545 505-667-7000 668
TF: 877-723-4101 ■ *Web:* www.lanl.gov

Lanlogic Inc 248 Rickenbacker Cir . . . . Livermore CA 94551 925-273-2300 196
Web: lanlogic.com

Lanly Co, The 26201 Tungsten Rd. . . . . .Cleveland OH 44132 216-731-1115 731-7900 318
Web: www.lanly.com

Lanman Oil Company Inc PO Box 108. . . . . .Charleston IL 61920 800-677-2819 579
TF: 800-677-2819 ■ *Web:* www.lanmanoil.com

Lanmark Staffing Co 1002 Green Ave . . . . .Orange TX 77630 409-886-7676 193
Web: www.lanmarkstaffing.com

Lanner Group Inc
10777 Westheimer Rd Ste 1100 . . . . .Houston TX 77042 713-532-8008 532-3732 178-1
Web: www.lanner.com

Lannett Company Inc (LCI)
13200 Townsend Rd . . . . .Philadelphia PA 19154 215-333-9000 333-9004 479
NYSE: LCI ■ *TF:* 800-325-9994 ■ *Web:* www.lannett.com

Lanning's 826 N Cleveland-Massillon Rd. . . . . .Akron OH 44333 330-666-1159 671
Web: www.lannings-restaurant.com

Lano Equipment Inc 3021 W 133rd St . . . . .Shakopee MN 55379 952-445-6310 496-0263 274
TF: 877-753-6100 ■ *Web:* www.lanoequip.com

LANSA Inc
2001 Butterfield Rd Ste 102 . . . . Downers Grove IL 60515 630-874-7000 874-7001 178-2
TF: 800-457-4083 ■ *Web:* www.lansa.com

Lansberg, Gersick & Associates LLC
100 Whitney Ave Apt 1 . . . . .New Haven CT 06510 203-497-8855 195
Web: www.lgassoc.com

Lansco Colors
1 Blue Hill Plz 11th Fl PO Box 1685 . . . . .Pearl River NY 10965 845-735-2787 550
TF: 800-526-2783 ■ *Web:* www.pigments.com

Lansdale School of Business
290 Wissahickon Ave . . . . .North Wales PA 19454 215-699-5700 699-8770 800
TF: 800-219-0486 ■ *Web:* www.lsb.edu

Lansdale Semiconductor Inc
5245 S 39th St . . . . .Phoenix AZ 85040 602-438-0123 438-0138 695
Web: www.lansdale.com

Lansdowne-Moody Co 8445 E Fwy . . . . .Houston TX 77029 713-322-7965 274
TF: 888-489-7454 ■ *Web:* www.lmtractor.com

Lanshack.Com
Atcom Services Inc
155 Meadow Rd Ste 206 Unit A. . . . . .Toms River NJ 08753 732-396-3600 116
TF: 888-568-1230 ■ *Web:* www.lanshack.com

Lansing Art Gallery
119 N Washington Sq. . . . . Lansing MI 48933 517-374-6400 50-2
Web: www.lansingartgallery.org

Lansing Building Products
8501 Sanford Dr. . . . . Richmond VA 23228 804-266-8893 264-2124 191-4
Web: lansingbp.com

Lansing Chamber of Commerce
18155 Roy St Unit 3. . . . . Lansing IL 60438 708-474-4170 139
Web: www.chamberoflansing.com

Lansing City Hall
124 W Michigan Ave 9th Fl . . . . Lansing MI 48933 517-483-4131 377-0068 337
Web: www.lansingmi.gov

Lansing Community College
411 N Grand Ave. . . . . Lansing MI 48933 517-483-1957 483-9668 162
TF: 800-644-4522 ■ *Web:* lcc.edu

Lansing Ctr 333 E Michigan Ave . . . . Lansing MI 48933 517-483-7400 483-7439 205
Web: www.lansingcenter.com

Lansing Ice & Fuel 911 Center St. . . . . Lansing MI 48906 517-940-6584 316
TF: 800-678-7230 ■ *Web:* www.lansingiceandfuel.com

Lansing Regional Chamber of Commerce
500 E Michigan Ave Ste 200. . . . . Lansing MI 48912 517-487-6340 484-6910 139
Web: www.lansingchamber.org

Lansing State Journal
120 E Lenawee St . . . . Lansing MI 48919 517-267-1304 532-2
TF: 800-234-1719 ■ *Web:* www.lansingstatejournal.com

Lansing Symphony Orchestra (LSO)
104 S Washington Sq Ste 300 . . . . Lansing MI 48933 517-487-5001 487-0210 573-3
Web: www.lansingsymphony.org

Lansmont Corp 17 Mandeville Ct . . . . Monterey CA 93940 831-655-6622 344
Web: www.lansmont.com

LANSolutions LLC
6359 Nancy Ridge Dr . . . . San Diego CA 92121 858-587-8000 587-0712 196
Web: www.lansolutions.net

Lantal Textiles Inc
1300 Langenthal Dr PO Box 965 . . . . .Rural Hall NC 27045 336-969-9551 745-1
TF: 800-334-3309 ■ *Web:* www.lantal.com

Lantana Communications Corp
1700 Tech Centre Pkwy Ste 100. . . . . Arlington TX 76014 800-345-4211 45
TF: 800-345-4211 ■ *Web:* www.lantanacom.com

Lantec Products Inc
5302 Derry Ave Ste G . . . . .Agoura Hills CA 91301 818-707-2285 707-9367 601
Web: www.lantecp.com

Lantech Inc 11000 Bluegrass Pkwy. . . . . .Louisville KY 40299 502-815-9109 547
Web: www.lantech.com

Lantech LLC 1783 Tribute Rd Ste C . . . . Sacramento CA 95815 916-564-5455 180
Web: www.lantechllc.com

Lanter Delivery Systems Inc
1 Caine Dr . . . . Madison IL 62060 618-452-5300 452-5931 780
TF: 800-830-6126 ■ *Web:* www.lanterdeliverysystems.com

Lantern Lodge Motor Inn
411 N College St . . . . .Myerstown PA 17067 717-866-6536 866-8857 379
TF: 800-262-5564 ■ *Web:* www.thelanternlodge.com

Lantheus Medical Imaging Inc
331 Treble Cove Rd Bldg 200-2 . . . . North Billerica MA 01862 978-667-9531 231
Web: www.lantheus.com

Lantronix Inc 167 Technology Dr. . . . . Irvine CA 92618 949-453-3990 450-7249 735
NASDAQ: LTRX ■ *TF:* 800-526-8766 ■ *Web:* www.lantronix.com

Lantz Security Systems Inc
43440 Sahuayo St . . . . .Lancaster CA 93535 661-949-3565 693
Web: www.lantzsecurity.com

Lanxess Corp 111 Ridc Pk W Dr . . . . Pittsburgh PA 15275 412-809-1000 605-3
TF: 800-526-9377 ■ *Web:* lanxess.com

LanXpert Corp
605 Market St Ste 410 . . . . San Francisco CA 94105 415-543-1033 177
TF: 888-499-1703 ■ *Web:* www.intivix.com

Lanyx Corp 4824 Bridle Ct . . . . Antioch CA 94531 415-370-6406 2

Lanz & Mcardle Agency Inc
1022 17th Ave. . . . . Monroe WI 53566 608-325-9126 390
Web: lanzmcardle.com

Lanz Cabinet Shop Inc 3025 W 7th Pl . . . . .Eugene OR 97402 541-485-4050 361
TF: 800-788-6332 ■ *Web:* lanzcabinets.com

Lanz Heating & Cooling Inc
2718 Hundman Dr . . . . Champaign IL 61822 217-355-5512 411
Web: lanzinc.com

Lanza & Lanza LLP 5 Main St. . . . . Flemington NJ 08822 908-905-0183 41
Web: lanzaandlanza.com

Lanza & Smith 3 Park Plz Ste 1650. . . . . .Irvine CA 92614 949-221-0490 41
TF: 888-244-3934 ■ *Web:* lanzasmith.com

Lao Laan-Xang 1146 Williamson St . . . . Madison WI 53703 608-280-0104 671
Web: www.laolaan-xang.com

Lao People's Democratic Republic Embassy
2222 South St NW . . . . .Washington DC 20008 202-332-6416 332-4923 257
Web: www.laoembassy.com

Lao Tse Press 2049 NW Hoyt St . . . . .Portland OR 97209 503-223-8188 227-7003 637-2
Web: www.processwork.org

Lapakahi State Historical Park
75 Aupuni St Rm 204 . . . . Hilo HI 96720 808-327-4958 565
Web: dlnr.hawaii.gov

Lapco Inc 12995 Rue Du Parc . . . . Mirabel QC J7J0W5 450-971-0432 234
TF: 800-433-1988 ■ *Web:* www.lapcoinc.com

Lapco Manufacturing Inc
98 Glenwood St . . . . .Morgan City LA 70380 985-385-5380 155-19
Web: www.lapco.com

Lapeer Area Chamber of Commerce
108 W Park St. . . . . Lapeer MI 48446 810-969-4546 664-4349 139
Web: lapeerareachamber.org

Lapeer County 129 W Nepessing St . . . . Lapeer MI 48446 810-667-0356 338
Web: lapeercountyweb.org

Lapeer Industries Inc 400 Mccormick Dr . . . . Lapeer MI 48446 810-664-1816 538-0633 480
TF: 800-664-1816 ■ *Web:* lapeerind.com

Lapels Dry Cleaning 962 Washington St . . . . .Hanover MA 02339 781-829-9935 829-9546 426
TF: 866-695-2735 ■ *Web:* mylapels.com

Lapham-Hickey Steel Corp
5500 W 73rd St . . . . .Chicago IL 60638 708-496-6111 496-8504 492
TF: 800-323-8443 ■ *Web:* www.lapham-hickey.com

Lapham-Patterson House State Historic Site
626 N Dawson St . . . . .Thomasville GA 31792 229-226-7664 565
Web: www.gastateparks.org

Lapin Sheet Metal Co
3825 Gardenia Ave . . . . Orlando FL 32839 407-423-9897 697
Web: www.lapinsm.com

LaPine State Park
15800 State Recreation Rd . . . . La Pine OR 97739 541-536-2428 565
Web: stateparks.oregon.gov

Laplaca Cohen 520 Broadway 11th Fl. . . . . New York NY 10012 212-675-4106 4
Web: www.laplacacohen.com

Laplante & Sowa Ltd
272 W Exchange St. . . . . .Providence RI 02903 401-273-0200 41
Web: lsglaw.com

LapLink Software Inc
600 108th Ave NE Ste 610 .Bellevue WA 98004 425-952-6000 952-6002 178-12
TF: 800-527-5465 ■ *Web:* web.laplink.com

Lapmaster International LLC
501 W Algonquin Rd . . . . .Mount Prospect IL 60056 877-352-8637 491
TF: 877-352-8637 ■ *Web:* www.lapmaster-wolters.com

Lapolla Industries Inc
15402 Vantage Pkwy E Ste 322 . . . . .Houston TX 77032 281-219-4700 219-4106 3
OTC: LPAD ■ *TF:* 888-452-7655 ■ *Web:* lapolla.com

Laporte & Associates Inc
5515 SE Milwaukie Ave . . . . .Portland OR 97202 503-239-4116 231-9021 390
TF: 800-542-2125 ■ *Web:* www.laporte-insurance.com

LaPorte County Convention & Visitors Bureau
4073 S Franklin St . . . . Michigan City IN 46360 219-872-5055 206
TF: 800-634-2650 ■ *Web:* www.michigancitylaporte.com

LAPP Insulator Co 130 Gilbert St . . . . Le Roy NY 14482 585-768-6221 768-6219 249
Web: www.lappinsulators.com

Lapp, Fatch, Myers & Gallagher Accountants PC
2401 Professional Pkwy .Santa Maria CA 93455 805-934-0015 2
Web: lfmgcpas.com

LaPrairie Crane
235 Front St Ste 209. . . . . Tumbler Ridge BC V0C2W0 250-242-5561 242-4529 261
TF: 877-787-5438 ■ *Web:* laprairiegroup.com

Lar Lubovitch Dance Co
229 W 42nd St 8th Fl . . . . .New York NY 10036 212-221-7909 221-7938 573-1
Web: www.lubovitch.org

Larabida Children's Hospital
6501 S Promontory Dr . . . . .Chicago IL 60649 773-363-6700 374-1
Web: www.larabida.org

				Phone	Fax	Class
Laramie Area Chamber of Commerce 800 S Third St *TF:* 866-876-1012 ■ *Web:* laramie.org	Laramie	WY	82070	307-745-7339	745-4624	139
Laramie County 309 W 20th St *Web:* laramiecountyclerk.com	Cheyenne	WY	82001	307-633-4264	633-4240	338
Laramie County Community College 1400 E College Dr *Web:* www.lccc.cc.wy.us	Cheyenne	WY	82007	307-778-5222	778-1350	162
Laramie County Community College *Albany County* 1125 Boulder Dr *TF:* 800-522-2993 ■ *Web:* www.lccc.wy.edu	Laramie	WY	82070	307-721-5138		162
Laramie County Public Library 2200 Pioneer Ave *Web:* www.lclsonline.org	Cheyenne	WY	82001	307-634-3561	634-2082	434-3
Laramie Plains Museum 603 E Ivinson St *Web:* www.laramiemuseum.org	Laramie	WY	82070	307-742-4448		520
Laramie River Dude Ranch 25777 County Rd 103 *TF:* 800-551-5731 ■ *Web:* lrranch.com	Jelm	WY	82063	970-435-5716		239
Larch Corrections Ctr 15314 NE Dole Valley Rd *Web:* doc.wa.gov	Yacolt	WA	98675	360-260-6300		213
Larchmont Engineering & Irrigation Co 11 Larchmont Ln PO Box 66 *TF:* 877-862-2550 ■ *Web:* www.larchmont-eng.com	Lexington	MA	02420	781-862-2550	862-0173	274
Larco 210 NE Tenth Ave *Web:* larco.com	Brainerd	MN	56401	218-829-9797	829-0139	253
Lard Oil Company Inc 914 Florida Blvd SW *Web:* www.lardoil.com	Denham Springs	LA	70726	225-664-3311		579
Laredo & Smith LLP 101 Federal St Ste 650 *Web:* laredosmith.com	Boston	MA	02114	617-443-1100		41
Laredo Chamber of Commerce, The 2310 San Bernardo *TF:* 800-292-2122 ■ *Web:* www.laredochamber.com	Laredo	TX	78040	956-722-9895	791-4503	139
Laredo Community College (LCC) W End Washington St *Web:* www.laredo.edu	Laredo	TX	78040	956-722-0521	721-5493	162
Laredo Energy Arena 6700 Arena Blvd *Web:* www.learena.com	Laredo	TX	78041	956-791-9192	523-7777	720
Laredo Energy LP 840 W Sam Houston Pkwy N Ste 400 *Web:* www.laredoenergy.com	Houston	TX	77024	713-600-6000		580
Laredo Medical Ctr (LMC) 1700 E Saunders Ave *Web:* www.laredomedical.com	Laredo	TX	78041	956-796-5000		374-3
Laredo Morning Times 111 Esperanza Dr *TF:* 800-232-7907 ■ *Web:* www.lmtonline.com	Laredo	TX	78041	956-728-2500		532-2
Laredo Public Library 1120 E Calton Rd *Web:* www.laredolibrary.org	Laredo	TX	78041	956-795-2400	795-2403	434-3
Laredo's 694 S Whitney Way *Web:* laredosrestaurante.com	Madison	WI	53711	608-278-0585		671
Larimer County 200 W Oak St *Web:* www.larimer.org	Fort Collins	CO	80521	970-498-7860	498-7906	338
Larimer Square 1512 Larimer St Unit 10R No 200 *Web:* www.larimersquare.com	Denver	CO	80202	303-534-2367		50-6
Larimore Associates Inc 16091 Swingley Ridge Rd Ste 180 *Web:* www.larimore.net	Chesterfield	MO	63017	636-537-3112		177
Lario Oil & Gas Co 301 S Market St *Web:* www.lariooil.com	Wichita	KS	67202	316-265-5611	265-5610	536
Lark Builders Inc 409 Dixon St *Web:* www.larkbuilders.com	Vidalia	GA	30474	912-538-1888		105
Lark Sparrow Press 1726 Ashland Ave *Web:* www.larksparrowpress.com	Evanston	IL	60201	847-869-0085		637-2
Larkin Enterprises Inc 317 W Broadway PO Box 405 *TF:* 800-990-5418 ■ *Web:* larkinent.com	Lincoln	ME	04457	207-794-8700		188
Larkin Ervin & Shirley LLP 7 Grogan'S Park Dr *Web:* larkin-ervin.com	The Woodlands	TX	77380	281-931-8539	931-5128	2
Larkin Hoffman Daly & Lindgren Ltd 8300 Norman Center Dr Ste 1000 *Web:* larkinhoffman.com	Minneapolis	MN	55437	952-835-3800	896-3333	445
Larkin's on the River 318 S Main St *Web:* www.larkinsontheriver.com	Greenville	SC	29601	864-467-9777		671
Larksfield Place 7373 E 29th St N *Web:* www.larksfieldplace.org	Wichita	KS	67226	316-858-3910	636-5790	672
Larkspur Landing 550 W Hamilton Ave *Web:* www.larkspurhotels.com	Campbell	CA	95008	408-364-1514		379
Larkspur Restaurant & Grill 904 E Douglas Ave *Web:* www.larkspuronline.com	Wichita	KS	67202	316-262-5275	262-1292	671
LARL (Lake Agassiz Regional Library) 118 Fifth St S PO Box 900 *TF:* 800-247-0449 ■ *Web:* www.larl.org	Moorhead	MN	56560	218-233-3757	233-7556	434-3
Larmar Industries 3700 S County Rd 1295 *Web:* www.larmarindustries.com	Odessa	TX	79765	432-561-8700		358
Larned Correctional Mental Health Facility 1301 KS Hwy 264 *Web:* www.doc.ks.gov	Larned	KS	67550	620-285-6249	285-8070	412
LARON Inc 4255 Santa Fe Dr *TF:* 800-248-3430 ■ *Web:* www.laron.com	Kingman	AZ	86401	928-757-8424		256
LaRosa's Inc 2334 Boudinot Ave *Web:* www.larosas.com	Cincinnati	OH	45238	513-347-5660		670
Larowe Gerlach Taggart LLP 110 E Main St *Web:* lgtlawfirm.com	Reedsburg	WI	53959	608-524-8231		41
Larrabee Albi Coker LLP 9920 Pacific Heights Blvd Ste 300 *Web:* larrabee.com	San Diego	CA	92121	858-642-0420		41
Larrabee State Park 245 Chuckanut Dr *Web:* parks.state.wa.us	Bellingham	WA	98229	360-676-2093		565

				Phone	Fax	Class
Larrabee Ventures Inc PO Box 55007 *TF:* 800-232-3584 ■ *Web:* www.larrabeeventures.com	Sherman Oaks	CA	91413	800-232-3584		194
Larry Associates Inc 6136 170th St Ste M1 *Web:* www.accountingbylarry.com	Fresh Meadows	NY	11365	718-321-0384	321-0385	2
Larry Blumberg & Associates Inc 2733 Ross Clark Cir *Web:* lbaproperties.com	Dothan	AL	36301	334-793-6855		707
Larry Green Chevrolet Oldsmobile & Geo Inc 2050 E Rodeo Dr *Web:* www.larrygreenchevrolet.com	Cottonwood	AZ	86326	928-208-4675		57
Larry H. Miller Ford Commercial Vehicle Ctr 461 E Auto Center Dr *Web:* www.lhmfordmesafleet.com	Mesa	AZ	85204	480-497-1111		57
Larry H. Miller Group of Companies 9350 S 150 E Ste 1000 *Web:* www.lhm.com	Sandy	UT	84070	801-563-4100		185
Larry M. Jacobs & Associates Inc 328 E Gadsden *Web:* lmj-a.com	Pensacola	FL	32501	850-434-0846	433-7027	261
Larry Murphy Insurance Agency Inc 113 E Grand *TF:* 800-443-1520 ■ *Web:* larrymurphyinsurance.com	Ponca City	OK	74601	580-767-1520	767-1070	390
Larry Roesch Chrysler-jeep-dodge LLC 200 W Grand Ave *Web:* www.larryroeschchryslerjeepdodge.com	Elmhurst	IL	60126	630-333-9121		57
Larry Snyder & Company Inc 4820 N Towne Centre Dr *Web:* lscinc.com	Ozark	MO	65721	417-887-6897	447-3040	261
Larry V. Howell State Farm Ins Agncy 4156 Lincoln Ave *Web:* larryhowell.com	Cypress	CA	90630	714-821-5030		390
Larry's Main Entrance 1964 W Market St	Akron	OH	44313	330-864-8162		671
Larry's Sausage Co 1624 Middle River Loop *Web:* www.larryssausage.com	Fayetteville	NC	28312	910-483-5148		296-26
Larsen Farms 960 Pier View Dr Ste B *TF:* 800-767-6104 ■ *Web:* www.larsenfarms.com	Idaho Falls	ID	83402	208-662-5501		296-18
Larsen Manufacturing LLC 1201 Allanson Rd *Web:* larsenmfg.com	Mundelein	IL	60060	847-970-9600		483
Larsen Rick (Rep D - WA) 2113 Rayburn House Office Bldg *Web:* www.larsen.house.gov	Washington	DC	20515	202-225-2605	225-4420	342-2
Larsen Supply Company Inc 12055 E Slauson Ave PO Box 4388 *Web:* www.lasco.net	Santa Fe Springs	CA	90670	562-698-0731		612
Larson Berg & Perkins PLLC 105 N Third St *Web:* www.lbplaw.com	Yakima	WA	98901	509-457-1515		428
Larson Contracting Inc 508 W Main St *TF:* 800-765-1426 ■ *Web:* www.larsoncontracting.com	Lake Mills	IA	50450	641-592-5800	592-8610	189-3
Larson Data Communications Inc 220 S Kimball St PO Box 96 *TF:* 866-996-5521 ■ *Web:* www.larsondata.com	Mitchell	SD	57301	605-996-5521	996-5642	224
Larson Davis Inc 3425 Walden Ave *TF:* 888-258-3222 ■ *Web:* www.larsondavis.com	Depew	NY	14043	716-926-8243	926-8215	201
Larson Design Group Inc 1000 Commerce Park Dr 2nd Fl Ste 201 **Fax Area Code:* 570 ■ *TF:* 877-323-6603 ■ *Web:* www.larsondesigngroup.com	Williamsport	PA	17701	877-323-6603	323-9902*	261
Larson Engineering Inc 3524 Labore Rd *Web:* larsonengr.com	White Bear Lake	MN	55110	651-481-9120	481-9201	261
Larson Hardware Manufacturing Co PO Box E *Web:* www.larsonhardware.com	Sterling	IL	61081	815-625-0503	625-8786	350
Larson John B (Rep D - CT) 1501 Longworth House Office Bldg *Web:* www.larson.house.gov	Washington	DC	20515	202-225-2265	225-1031	342-2
Larson King LLP 30 E Seventh St Ste 2800 *TF:* 877-373-5501 ■ *Web:* www.larsonking.com	Saint Paul	MN	55101	651-312-6500	312-6618	428
Larson Kuper & Wenninghoff PC LLO 17021 Lakeside Hills Plz Ste 202 *Web:* lkwfirm.com	Omaha	NE	68130	402-932-0290	932-0301	41
Larson Manufacturing Co 2333 Eastbrook Dr *TF:* 888-483-3768 ■ *Web:* www.larsondoors.com	Brookings	SD	57006	605-692-6115		235
Larson Systems Inc 13847 Aberdeen St NE *Web:* www.larsonsystems.com	Ham Lake	MN	55304	763-780-2131		454
Larson Tool & Stamping Co 90 Olive St *Web:* www.larsontool.com	Attleboro	MA	02703	508-222-0897	226-7407	488
Larson-Danielson Construction Company Inc 302 Tyler St *Web:* www.ldconstruction.com	La Porte	IN	46350	219-362-2127	362-2848	186
Larson-Juhl 3900 Steve Reynolds Blvd **Fax Area Code:* 770 ■ *TF:* 800-221-4123 ■ *Web:* www.larsonjuhl.com	Norcross	GA	30093	800-221-4123	279-5297*	309
Larta Institute 606 S Olive St Ste 650 *Web:* www.larta.org	Los Angeles	CA	90014	213-694-2826		196
Larue Coffee 2631 S 156th Cir *TF:* 800-658-4498 ■ *Web:* www.laruecoffee.com	Omaha	NE	68130	402-333-9099		297-8
LaRue County 209 W High St *Web:* www.laruecounty.org	Hodgenville	KY	42748	270-358-3544	358-4528	338
LaRusso & McNeill LLC 550 Mamaroneck Ave Ste 402 *Web:* www.larussomcneill.com	Harrison	NY	10528	914-698-8303		2
Lary Archer & Associates Inc 1348 Palo Pinto Hwy *Web:* www.archerassoc.com	Palo Pinto	TX	76484	940-659-4069	659-4071	538
Larzelere Picou Wells Simpson Lonero LLC (LPWSL) 2 Lakeway Ctr 3850 N Causeway Blvd Ste 500 *Web:* lpwsl.com	Metairie	LA	70002	504-834-6500	834-6565	445

				Phone	Fax	Class
Las Animas County 200 E First St — *Web:* www.lasanimascounty.net	Trinidad	CO	81082	719-846-2981	845-2591	338
Las Casuelas Terraza 222 S Palm Canyon Dr — *Web:* www.lascasuelas.com	Palm Springs	CA	92262	760-325-2794		671
Las Cruces Bulletin 1740-A Calle de Mercado — *Web:* www.lascrucesbulletin.com	Las Cruces	NM	88005	575-524-8061	526-4621	532-4
Las Cruces Community Theatre 313 N Downtown Mall — *Web:* www.lcctnm.org	Las Cruces	NM	88001	575-523-1200		572
Las Cruces Convention & Visitors Bureau 211 N Water St — *Web:* www.lascrucescvb.org	Las Cruces	NM	88001	575-541-2444	541-2164	206
Las Cruces Public Schools Foundation 505 S Main St Ste 249 — *Web:* lcpsf.org	Las Cruces	NM	88001	575-527-5888		685
Las Cruces Sun News 256 W Las Cruces Ave — *TF:* 877-827-7200 ■ *Web:* www.lcsun-news.com	Las Cruces	NM	88004	575-541-5400	541-5498	532-2
Las Cruces Symphony Orchestra 1075 N Horseshoe St Ste 210 — *Web:* www.lascrucessymphony.com	Las Cruces	NM	88003	575-646-3709	646-1086	573-3
LAS Enterprises Inc 2413 L & A Rd — *TF:* 800-264-1527 ■ *Web:* lashome.com	Metairie	LA	70001	504-887-1515		187
Las Margaritas Restaurante 1999 W Fourth Ave — *Web:* www.lasmargaritas.com	Vancouver	BC	V6J1M7	604-734-7117		671
Las Palmas Medical Ctr 1801 N Oregon St — *Web:* laspalmasdelsolhealthcare.com	El Paso	TX	79902	915-521-1200		374-3
Las Positas College 3000 Campus Hill Dr — *Web:* www.laspositascollege.edu	Livermore	CA	94551	925-424-1000	443-0742	162
Las Vegas Asian Chamber of Commerce 6431 W Sahara Ave Ste 280 — *TF:* 800-468-7272 ■ *Web:* lvacc.org	Las Vegas	NV	89146	702-737-4300	735-0406	139
Las Vegas Athletic Club 2655 S Maryland Pkwy Ste 201 — *Web:* www.lvac.com	Las Vegas	NV	89109	702-734-8944		354
Las Vegas City Hall 495 S Main St — *Web:* www.lasvegasnevada.gov	Las Vegas	NV	89101	702-229-6011	386-9108	337
Las Vegas College 170 N Stephanie St — *TF:* 888-741-4270 ■ *Web:* lvcollege.edu	Henderson	NV	89074	702-567-1920	566-9725	166
Las Vegas Color Graphics Inc 4265 W Sunset Rd — *Web:* www.lasvegascolor.com	Las Vegas	NV	89118	702-617-9000		174
Las Vegas Convention & Visitors Authority 3150 Paradise Rd — *TF:* 877-847-4858 ■ *Web:* www.lvcva.com	Las Vegas	NV	89109	702-892-0711	837-0315	206
Las Vegas Cuban Cuisine 2807 E Oakland Pk Blvd — *Web:* www.lasvegascubancuisine.com	Fort Lauderdale	FL	33306	954-457-8383		671
Las Vegas Events 770 E Warm Springs Rd Ste 140 — *Web:* www.lasvegasevents.com	Las Vegas	NV	89119	702-260-8605		317
Las Vegas Floral & Plant Wholesale 2404 Western Ave Ste B — *Web:* floracouture.com	Las Vegas	NV	89102	702-221-1220		292
Las Vegas Motor Speedway 7000 Las Vegas Blvd N — *TF:* 800-644-4444 ■ *Web:* www.lvms.com	Las Vegas	NV	89115	702-644-4444		515
Las Vegas Natural History Museum 900 Las Vegas Blvd N — *Web:* www.lvnhm.org	Las Vegas	NV	89101	702-384-3466	384-5343	520
Las Vegas Paving Corp 4420 S Decatur Blvd — *Web:* www.lasvegaspaving.com	Las Vegas	NV	89103	702-251-5800	251-4891	188-4
Las Vegas Presort LLC 3655 E Patrick Ln Ste 300 — *Web:* lasvegaspresort.com	Las Vegas	NV	89120	702-320-0450	320-1226	317
Las Vegas Review-Journal 1111 W Bonanza Rd PO Box 70 — *Web:* www.reviewjournal.com	Las Vegas	NV	89106	702-383-0211	383-4676	532-2
Las Vegas Sands Corp 3355 Las Vegas Blvd S — *NYSE: LVS* ■ *Web:* www.sands.com	Las Vegas	NV	89109	702-414-1000		379
Las Vegas Sun 2275 Corporate Cir Ste 300 — *Web:* lasvegassun.com	Henderson	NV	89074	702-385-3111	383-7264	532-2
Lasalle College High School 8605 Cheltenham Ave — *Web:* www.lschs.org	Wyndmoor	PA	19038	215-233-2911	233-1418	305
LaSalle County 707 E Etna Rd — *TF:* 800-247-5243 ■ *Web:* www.lasallecounty.org	Ottawa	IL	61350	815-433-3366	433-9522	338
LaSalle Grill 115 W Colfax Ave — *Web:* www.lasallegrill.com	South Bend	IN	46601	574-288-1155		671
LaSalle Hotel 120 S Main St — *Web:* www.lasalle-hotel.com	Bryan	TX	77803	979-822-2000		379
LaSalle Lake State Fish & Wildlife Area 2660 E 2350th Rd — *Web:* www.stateparks.com	Marseilles	IL	61341	815-357-1608		565
LaSalle Parish PO Box 1288 — *Web:* www.lpgov.org	Jena	LA	71342	318-992-2101		338
Lasalle St Securities LLC 940 N Industrial Dr — *Web:* www.lasallest.com	Elmhurst	IL	60126	630-600-0500		690
LaSalle Systems Leasing Inc 6111 N River Rd — *Web:* lasallesolutions.com	Rosemont	IL	60018	847-823-9600	823-1646	264-1
Lasco Fittings Inc 414 Morgan St PO Box 116 — *TF:* 800-776-2756 ■ *Web:* www.lascofittings.com	Brownsville	TN	38012	731-772-3180	772-0835	596
Lasco Foods Inc 4553 Gustine Ave — *Web:* www.lascofoods.com	Saint Louis	MO	63116	314-832-1906		297-8
Lascom Solutions Inc 5473 Kearny Villa Rd Ste 255 — *Web:* lascom.com	San Diego	CA	92123	858-452-1300		177
Lasell College 1844 Commonwealth Ave — *TF:* 888-222-5229 ■ *Web:* www.lasell.edu	Newton	MA	02466	617-243-2225	243-2380	166
Laser & Computer Options Inc 3758 E Grove St — *Web:* www.laseroptionsinc.com	Phoenix	AZ	85040	480-968-8440		175
Laser App Software Inc 3190 Shelby St Ste D 100 — *Web:* www.laserapp.com	Ontario	CA	91764	909-985-2174		177
Laser Connection LLC 100 E Midland Rd — **Fax Area Code:* 989 ■ *TF:* 800-868-1154 ■ *Web:* www.laser-connection.com	Auburn	MI	48611	800-868-1154	662-2612*	628
Laser Diode Inc 4 Olsen Ave — *Web:* laserdiode.com	Edison	NJ	08820	732-549-9001	906-1559	696
Laser Electrolysis Ctr 943 S George Mason Dr — *Web:* www.laserelectrol.com	Arlington	VA	22204	703-979-2853		167-3
Laser Excel N6323 Berlin Rd — *TF:* 800-285-6544 ■ *Web:* laserexcel.com	Green Lake	WI	54941	800-285-6544		454
Laser Institute of America (LIA) 13501 Ingenuity Dr Ste 128 — *TF:* 800-345-2737 ■ *Web:* www.lia.org	Orlando	FL	32826	407-380-1553	380-5588	49-19
Laser Locators LLC 13933 Lynmar Blvd — *TF:* 877-924-2020 ■ *Web:* laserlocators.com	Tampa	FL	33626	813-855-0343		366
Laser Logic Inc 450 N Iowa Ste A3 — *TF:* 800-335-0505 ■ *Web:* www.laserlogic.com	Lawrence	KS	66044	785-865-0505		112
Laser Mechanisms Inc 25325 Regency Dr — *Web:* www.lasermech.com	Novi	MI	48375	248-474-9480	474-9277	425
Laser Plus Imaging 6739 Variel Ave — *TF:* 866-804-4418 ■ *Web:* laserplusimaging.com	Canoga Park	CA	91303	866-804-4418		535
Laser Print Plus 1261 First S Ext Ste A — *Web:* www.laserprintplus.com	Columbia	SC	29209	803-695-7090		627
Laser Pros Intl 1 International Ln — *TF:* 888-558-5277 ■ *Web:* www.laserpros.com	Rhinelander	WI	54501	715-369-5995	369-5910	174
Laser Quest 3415 American Dr — *Web:* www.laserquest.com	Mississauga	ON	L4V1T4	416-613-4555		31
Laser Technologies Inc 1120 N Frontenac Rd — *Web:* www.lasertechnologiesinc.com	Naperville	IL	60563	630-761-1200		454
Laser Technology Inc 7070 S Tucson Way — *TF:* 800-280-6113 ■ *Web:* www.lasertech.com	Englewood	CO	80112	303-649-1000	649-9710	495
Laser Tek Services Inc 742 19th St N — *Web:* lasertekservices.com	Fargo	ND	58102	701-239-4033		179
Laser Tool Inc 17763 State Hwy 198 — *Web:* www.laser-tool.com	Saegertown	PA	16433	814-763-2032	763-2521	757
Lasercycle USA Inc 528 S Taylor Ave — *TF:* 866-666-7776 ■ *Web:* lasercycleusa.com	Louisville	CO	80027	303-666-7776		589
Laserdome 2050 Auction Rd — *Web:* laserdome.com	Manheim	PA	17545	717-492-0002		31
Laserflex Corp, The 3649 Pkwy Ln — *Web:* www.laserflex-inc.com	Hilliard	OH	43026	614-850-9600		454
Lasergraphics Inc 4 Squire Rd — *Web:* www.laserg.com	Revere	MA	02151	781-289-2022	289-2027	781
Laserlinc Inc 777 Zapata Dr — *Web:* laserlinc.com	Fairborn	OH	45324	937-318-2440		180
LaserMax Corp 3495 Winton Pl — *TF:* 800-527-3703 ■ *Web:* www.lasermax.com	Rochester	NY	14623	585-272-5420		544
Lasership Inc 1912 Woodford Rd — *Web:* www.lasership.com	Vienna	VA	22182	804-414-2590		41
LaserVue Eye Ctr 3540 Mendocino Ave Ste 200 — *TF:* 888-527-3745 ■ *Web:* www.laservue.com	Santa Rosa	CA	95403	707-522-6200		798
Lashbrook Designs 131 E 13065 S — *TF:* 888-252-7388 ■ *Web:* www.lashbrookdesigns.com	Draper	UT	84020	888-252-7388		411
Lashley & Associates Inc 3215 Claymoore Park Dr — *TF:* 888-527-4539 ■ *Web:* www.lashleyinc.com	Houston	TX	77043	713-462-8888	462-8881	189-10
Lashley, Cohen, & Associates Inc 1800 Cedars Rd Ste 102 — *Web:* lashleycohen.com	Lawrenceville	GA	30045	770-962-0878		261
Lashly & Baer PC 714 Locust St — *Web:* www.lashlybaer.com	Saint Louis	MO	63101	314-621-2939	621-6844	428
Lasko Products LLC 820 Lincoln Ave — *TF:* 800-233-0268 ■ *Web:* www.lasko.com	West Chester	PA	19380	610-436-1455	696-4648	37
LasscoWizer Inc 485 Hague St — *TF:* 800-854-6595 ■ *Web:* www.lasscowizer.com	Rochester	NY	14606	585-436-1934	464-8665	629
Lassen Canyon Nursery Inc 1300 Salmon Creek Rd — *Web:* www.lassencanyonnursery.com	Redding	CA	96003	530-223-1075	223-6754	275
Lassen Community College 478-200 Hwy 139 PO Box 3000 — *TF:* 800-461-9389 ■ *Web:* www.lassencollege.edu	Susanville	CA	96130	530-257-6181	257-8964	162
Lassen County 221 S Roop St Ste 4 — *Web:* www.lassencounty.org	Susanville	CA	96130	530-251-8217	257-3480	338
Lassen County Chamber of Commerce 1516 Main St — *Web:* lassencountychamber.org	Susanville	CA	96130	530-257-4323		139
Lassen Volcanic National Park 38050 Hwy 36 E PO Box 100 — *Web:* www.nps.gov	Mineral	CA	96063	530-595-4480		564
Lassen's Health Food 2150 Thousand Oaks Blvd — *Web:* www.lassens.com	Thousand Oaks	CA	91362	805-620-4850		297
Lassiter Law Firm, PA, The 6100 Greenland Rd Ste 403 — *Web:* www.lassiterlawyers.com	Jacksonville	FL	32258	904-779-5585		428
Lassiter Transportation Group 1450 W Granada Blvd Ste 2 — *Web:* lassitertransportation.com	Ormond Beach	FL	32174	386-257-2571		261
Lassonde Pappas 1 Colons Dr Ste 200 — *TF:* 800-257-7019 ■ *Web:* lassondepappas.com	Carneys Point	NJ	08069	800-257-7019		296-20
Lassus Bros Oil Inc 1800 Magnavox Way — *Web:* www.lassus.com	Fort Wayne	IN	46804	260-436-1415		324

Name / Address	Phone	Fax	Class
Lassus Wherley & Associates Pc 1 Academy St ... New Providence NJ 07974 *TF:* 800-298-5420 ■ *Web:* www.lassuswherley.com	908-464-0102	464-9852	463
Lastick Furniture 269 E High St ... Pottstown PA 19464 *Web:* www.lastick.com	610-323-4000		321
Lasting Impressions Inc 7406 43rd Ave NE ... Marysville WA 98270 *TF:* 866-859-7625 ■ *Web:* www.lastingimp.com	360-659-1255		627
Lasting Legacy Ltd 812 Busse Hwy ... Park Ridge IL 60068	847-685-8402		690
Lastrapes Spangler & Pacheco PA 333 Rio Rancho Dr Ste 401 ... Rio Rancho NM 87124 *Web:* www.lsplegal.com	505-892-3607		428
LasVegasTickets.com 5030 Paradise Rd Ste B108 ... Las Vegas NV 89119 *TF:* 800-597-7469 ■ *Web:* lasvegastickets.com	702-597-1588		376
Latah County 522 S Adams St PO Box 8068 ... Moscow ID 83843 *Web:* www.latah.id.us	208-882-8580	883-7203	338
Latah Creek Winery 13030 E Indiana Ave ... Spokane WA 99216 *Web:* www.latahcreek.com	509-926-0164		50-7
Latch 450 W 33rd St ... New York NY 10001 *Web:* www.latch.com	646-833-0604		177
Latex Construction Co PO Box 917 ... Conyers GA 30012 *Web:* www.latexconstruction.com	770-760-0820	760-0852	188-10
Latham & Watkins LLP 885 Third Ave ... New York NY 10022 *Web:* www.lw.com	212-906-4532	751-4864	428
Latham Hotel, The 110 S 19th St Ste 300 ... Philadelphia PA 19103 **Fax Area Code:* 215 ■ *Web:* pearl-apartments.com	610-529-4444	568-0505*	379
Latham Pool Products Inc 787 Watervliet Shaker Rd ... Latham NY 12110 *TF:* 800-833-3800 ■ *Web:* www.lathampool.com	800-833-3800		187
Latham Seed Co 131 180th St ... Alexander IA 50420 *TF:* 877-465-2842 ■ *Web:* www.lathamseeds.com	641-692-3258	692-3250	694
Lathem Time Corp 200 Selig Dr SW ... Atlanta GA 30336 **Fax Area Code:* 800 ■ *TF:* 800-241-4990 ■ *Web:* www.lathem.com	404-691-0400	252-2208*	111
Lathrop Co 460 W Dussel Dr ... Maumee OH 43537 *Web:* www.turnerconstruction.com	419-893-7000		186
Lathrop Gage LLP 2345 Grand Blvd Ste 2200 ... Kansas City MO 64108 *Web:* www.lathropgage.com	816-292-2000	292-2001	41
Lathrop State Park 70 County Rd 502 ... Walsenburg CO 81089 *Web:* cpw.state.co.us	719-738-2376		565
Laticrete International Inc 91 Amity Rd ... Bethany CT 06524 *TF:* 800-243-4788 ■ *Web:* laticrete.com	203-393-0010	393-1684	3
Latigo Petroleum Inc 15 W Sixth St Ste 900 ... Tulsa OK 74119 *Web:* www.laredopetro.com	918-513-4570		538
Latigo Ranch 201 County Rd 1911 PO Box 237 ... Kremmling CO 80459 *TF:* 800-729-5521 ■ *Web:* www.latigotrails.com	970-724-9008		239
Latimer County 109 N Centra Rm 109 ... Wilburton OK 74578 *Web:* okcountytreasurers.com	918-465-3450	465-4005	338
Latin Business Assn (LBA) 120 S San Pedro St Ste 530 ... Los Angeles CA 90012 *Web:* www.lbausa.com	213-628-8510	628-8519	49-12
Latin Chamber of Commerce Nevada Inc 300 N 13th St ... Las Vegas NV 89101 *Web:* lvlcc.com	702-385-7367	385-2614	139
Latin Chamber of Commerce of the US (CAMACOL) 1401 W Flagler St ... Miami FL 33135 *Web:* www.camacol.org	305-642-3870	642-3961	138
Latin King 2200 Hubbell Ave ... Des Moines IA 50317 *Web:* www.tursislatinking.com	515-266-4466		671
Latin Press Inc 600 SW 22 Ave ... Miami FL 33135 *Web:* www.latinpressinc.com	305-285-3133		637-9
Latin School of Chicago 59 W N Blvd ... Chicago IL 60610 *Web:* www.latinschool.org	312-582-6000		623
Latina Media Ventures LLC 120 Broadway 34th Fl ... New York NY 10271 *TF:* 800-274-1521 ■ *Web:* www.latina.com	212-642-0200	575-3088	457-11
Latina Restaurant & Pizzeria 1370 W Bristol Rd ... Flint MI 48507 *Web:* latinarestaurant.com	810-767-8491		671
Latino Book & Family Festival (LBFF) 3445 Catalina Dr ... Carlsbad CA 92010 *Web:* lbff.us	760-434-1223	434-7476	281
Latino Communications LLC 3067 Waughtown St ... Winston-Salem NC 27107 *Web:* www.quepasamedia.com	336-784-9004	714-0435	681
Latitude Consulting Group Inc 100 E Michigan Ave Ste 200 ... Saline MI 48176 *TF:* 888-577-2797 ■ *Web:* www.latitudecg.com	888-577-2797		463
Latitude Management Real Estate Investors Inc 350 S Beverly Dr Ste 300 ... Beverly Hills CA 90212 *Web:* latitudeinvestors.com	310-234-2100	234-2150	509
Lat-Lon LLC 2300 S Jason St ... Denver CO 80223 *TF:* 877-300-6566 ■ *Web:* www.lat-lon.com	303-937-7406		770
LaTolteca 2209 Concord Pk ... Wilmington DE 19803 *Web:* www.authenticmex.com	302-778-4646		671
Latorra Paul & Mccann Inc 120 E Washington St University Bldg 10th Fl ... Syracuse NY 13202 *Web:* www.lpm-adv.com	315-476-1646		4
Latour Management Inc 2949 N Rock Rd ... Wichita KS 67226 *Web:* www.latourmanagement.com	316-524-2290		670
LatPro Inc 3980 N Broadway Ste 103-147 ... Boulder CO 80304 *Web:* www.latpro.com	954-727-3844		393
Latrobe Area Chamber of Commerce PO Box 463 ... Latrobe PA 15650 *Web:* www.latrobelaurelvalley.org	724-537-2671		139
Latrobe Federal Credit Union 1812 Ligonier St ... Latrobe PA 15650 *Web:* latrobefcu.com	724-537-2734		219
Latt Maxcy Corp 21299 US Hwy 27 ... Lake Wales FL 33859 *Web:* www.lattmaxcy.com	863-679-6700		652
Latta Harris Hanon & Penningroth LLP 2730 Naples Ave SW Ste 101 ... Iowa City IA 52240 *Web:* www.lattaharris.com	319-358-0520	358-0503	2
Latta Robert E (Rep R - OH) 2467 Rayburn House Office Bldg ... Washington DC 20515 *TF:* 800-541-6446 ■ *Web:* www.latta.house.gov	202-225-6405	225-1985	342-2
Latta's School Supplies 1502 4th Ave ... Huntington WV 25701 *Web:* www.lattas.com	304-523-8400	525-5038	535
Latter & Blum Inc 430 Notre Dame St ... New Orleans LA 70130 *Web:* www.latterblum.com	504-525-1311	569-9336	652
Latter Day Saints Business College 95 North 300 West ... Salt Lake City UT 84101 *TF:* 800-999-5767 ■ *Web:* ldsbc.edu	801-524-8159	524-1900	800
Lattice Inc 22 Battery St 11th Fl ... San Francisco CA 94111 *Web:* www.lattice.com	856-910-1166		178-12
Lattice Press PO Box 340 ... Sunset Beach CA 90742 *Web:* www.latticepress.com	714-840-5010		637-2
Lattice Semiconductor Corp 5555 NE Moore Ct ... Hillsboro OR 97124 *NASDAQ: LSCC* ■ *TF:* 800-528-8423 ■ *Web:* www.latticesemi.com	503-268-8000	268-8347	696
Lattice3d 582 Market St Ste 1215 ... San Francisco CA 94104 *Web:* www.lattice3d.com	415-274-1670		177
Lattimore Black Morgan & Cain PC 5250 Virginia Way ... Brentwood TN 37027 *Web:* www.lbmc.com	615-377-4600		2
Latva Machine Inc 744 John Stark Hwy ... Newport NH 03773 *Web:* www.latva.com	603-863-5155		454
Latvia 333 E 50th St ... New York NY 10022 *Web:* www.mfa.gov.lv	212-838-8877		784
Latvia Embassy 2306 Massachusetts Ave NW ... Washington DC 20008 *Web:* www.mfa.gov.lv	202-328-2840	328-2860	257
LAUDA-Noah LP 2501 SE Columbia Way Ste 140 ... Vancouver WA 98661 *Web:* www.lauda-noah.com	360-993-1395	993-1399	695
Lauderdale County 102 S Court St PO Box 1059 ... Florence AL 35631 *Web:* lauderdalecountyonline.com	256-760-5833	760-5839	338
Lauderdale County 410 Constitution Ave 11th Fl ... Meridian MS 39301 *Web:* www.lauderdalecounty.org	601-482-9746		338
Lauderdale County 123 S Jefferson St ... Ripley TN 38063 *Web:* www.lauderdalecountytn.org	731-635-9541		338
Laughing Elephant 3645 Interlake Ave N ... Seattle WA 98103 *TF:* 800-354-0400 ■ *Web:* laughingelephant.com	800-509-4166	838-1149	130
Laughing Loon 344 Gardiner Rd ... Jefferson ME 04348 *Web:* www.laughingloon.com	207-549-3531		710
Laughing Planet Cafe 322 E Kirkwood Ave ... Bloomington IN 47408 *Web:* thelaughingplanetcafe.com	812-323-2233		671
Laughing Seed Cafe 40 Wall St ... Asheville NC 28801 *Web:* laughingseed.com	828-252-3445		671
Laughlin Air Force Base 561 Liberty Dr Ste 3 ... Laughlin AFB TX 78843 *TF:* 866-966-1020 ■ *Web:* www.laughlin.af.mil	830-298-3511	298-4179	497-1
Laughlin Millea Hillman Architecture LLC 819 W Main St Ste 400 ... Louisville KY 40202 *Web:* lmharchitecture.com	502-581-0570		261
Laughlin River Lodge 2700 S Casino Dr ... Laughlin NV 89029 *TF:* 800-835-7903 ■ *Web:* www.laughlinriverlodge.com	702-298-2242		133
Laughlin Trucking Inc (LTC) 12850 NE Hendricks Rd ... Carlton OR 97111 *TF:* 800-452-9436 ■ *Web:* www.laughlintrucking.com	503-852-7186	852-7056	780
Laughlin/Constable Inc 207 E Michigan St ... Milwaukee WI 53202 *Web:* www.laughlin.com	414-272-2400		4
LaughlinCartrell Inc PO Box 399 ... Carlton OR 97111 *TF:* 800-547-3009 ■ *Web:* www.laughlincartrell.com	503-852-7151	852-7056	297-2
Laughter Works Seminars PO Box 1220 ... Folsom CA 95763 *Web:* www.laughterworks.com	916-985-6570		196
Laumeier Sculpture Park & Museum 12580 Rott Rd ... Saint Louis MO 63127 *Web:* www.laumeiersculpturepark.org	314-615-5278		520
Launch Academy 77 Summer St 7th Fl ... Boston MA 02111 *TF:* 844-745-2862 ■ *Web:* launchacademy.com	844-745-2862		764
Launch Agency LP 4100 Midway Rd Ste 2110 ... Carrollton TX 75007 *TF:* 866-427-5013 ■ *Web:* www.launchagency.com	972-818-4100		4
Launch Dynamic Media 1103 Rocky Dr Ste 202 ... Reading PA 19609 *Web:* launchdm.com	610-898-1330		180
Launch Incentives Inc 224 Greenfield Ave Ste B ... San Anselmo CA 94960 *Web:* www.launchinc.com	415-457-1701		232
Launch Pad 18130 Jorene Rd ... Odessa FL 33556 *TF:* 888-920-3450 ■ *Web:* www.launchpadonline.com	888-920-3450		179
Launch Technical Workforce Solutions LLC 700 Commerce Dr Ste 140 ... Oak Brook IL 60523 *TF:* 888-888-7195 ■ *Web:* www.launchtws.com	888-888-7195		193
LaunchCode Mentor Ctr 4811 Delmar Blvd ... St. Louis MO 63108 *Web:* www.launchcode.org	314-254-0107		113
Launchpad 119 W 24th St 4th Fl ... New York NY 10011 *Web:* www.lpnyc.com	212-303-7650	253-5709	4
Laura Davidson Public Relations Inc 72 Madison Ave 8th Fl ... New York NY 10016 *Web:* ldpr.com	212-696-0660		636
Laura Ingalls Wilder Museum & Home 3060 Hwy A ... Mansfield MO 65704 *TF:* 877-924-7126 ■ *Web:* www.lauraingallswilderhome.com	877-924-7126		520
Laura Kelly 300 S W 10th St ... Topeka KS 66612 *Web:* www.governor.kansas.gov	785-368-8500		339-17

Name	Address	City	State	ZIP	Phone	Fax	Class	Notes
Laura Margulies & Associates LLC	6205 Executive Blvd	Rockville	MD	20852	301-816-1600		41	*Web:* law-margulies.com
Laura S. Walker State Park	5653 Laura Walker Rd	Waycross	GA	31503	912-287-4900		565	*Web:* gastateparks.org
Laurdan Associates Inc	2305 Glenmore Ter	Rockville	MD	20850	301-762-5794		195	*Web:* www.laurdan.com
Laureate Education Inc	650 S Exeter St	Baltimore	MD	21202	410-843-6100		242	*TF:* 866-452-8732 ■ *Web:* www.laureate.net
Laurel Business Institute	11 E Penn St PO Box 877	Uniontown	PA	15401	724-439-4900	439-3607	167-3	*Web:* www.laurel.edu
Laurel County Clerk	101 S Main St Rm 203	London	KY	40741	606-864-5158	864-7369	338	*Web:* laurel.countyclerk.us
Laurel Grocery Company Inc	129 Barbourville Rd	London	KY	40744	606-878-6601	878-9361	297-8	*TF:* 800-467-6601 ■ *Web:* www.laurelgrocery.com
Laurel Highland Total Communications Inc (LHTC)	4157 Main St	Stahlstown	PA	15687	724-593-2411		224	*Web:* lhtcbroadband.com
Laurel Highlands Chamber of Commerce	537 W Main St	Mount Pleasant	PA	15666	724-547-7521		139	
Laurel Highlands Jet Ctr	148 Aviation Ln Ste 109	Latrobe	PA	15650	724-539-4533	539-5501	63	*TF:* 800-278-2710 ■ *Web:* www.laurelhighlandsjet.com
Laurel Highlands School District (LHSD)	304 Bailey Ave	Uniontown	PA	15401	724-437-4741	437-5653	685	*Web:* laurelhighlandssd.wixsite.com
Laurel Highlands Visitors Bureau	120 E Main St	Ligonier	PA	15658	724-238-5661	238-3673	206	*TF:* 800-333-5661 ■ *Web:* www.laurelhighlands.org
Laurel Hill State Park	1454 Laurel Hill Park Rd	Somerset	PA	15501	814-445-7725		565	*Web:* www.dcnr.pa.gov
Laurel Holdings Inc	111 Roosevelt Blvd	Johnstown	PA	15906	814-533-5782		360-3	*TF:* 888-838-4072 ■ *Web:* www.laurelmanagement.net
Laurel Lake Retirement Community	200 Laurel Lake Dr	Hudson	OH	44236	866-650-2100	655-1738*	672	**Fax Area Code:* 330 ■ *TF:* 866-650-2100 ■ *Web:* www.laurellake.org
Laurel Machine and Foundry Co	810 Front St	Laurel	MS	39440	601-428-0541	425-5617	454	*Web:* www.lmfco.com
Laurel Outlook, The	415 E Main PO Box 278	Laurel	MT	59044	406-628-4412		532-3	*Web:* www.laureloutlook.com
Laurel Park	Rt 198 & Racetrack Rd PO Box 130	Laurel	MD	20724	301-725-0400	792-7775*	642	**Fax Area Code:* 410 ■ *Web:* www.laurelpark.com
Laurel Rehabilitation Services	216 Haddon Ave Ste 702	Westmont	NJ	08108	856-869-7360		363	*Web:* laurelrehab.com
Laurel Ridge State Park	1117 Jim Mtn Rd	Rockwood	PA	15557	724-455-3744		565	*Web:* www.dcnr.pa.gov
Laurel Theatre	1538 Laurel Ave	Knoxville	TN	37916	865-522-5851		572	*Web:* www.jubileearts.org
Laurel-Jones County Library	530 Commerce St	Laurel	MS	39440	601-428-4313		434-3	*Web:* www.laurel.lib.ms.us
Laurels of University Park, The	2420 Pemberton Rd	Richmond	VA	23233	804-747-9200	747-1574	450	*Web:* www.laurelsofuniversitypark.com
Laurelville Mennonite Church Ctr	941 Laurelville Ln	Mount Pleasant	PA	15666	724-423-2056	423-2096	673	*Web:* www.laurelville.org
Lauren Davis & Company CPAS PC	54391 30th St	South Bend	IN	46635	574-272-1680	272-1780	2	
Lauren Engineers & Constructors	901 S 1st St	Abilene	TX	79602	325-670-9660	670-9663	261	*TF:* 800-948-0142 ■ *Web:* laurenec.com
Lauren Rogers Museum of Art	565 N Fifth Ave	Laurel	MS	39440	601-649-6374	649-6379	520	*Web:* www.lrma.org
Lauren Spencer Inc	40 Clairedan Dr	Powell	OH	43065	614-888-7773		410	*Web:* www.lauren-spencer.com
Laurence C. Zale Associates Inc	340 E 80th St Ste 18H	New York	NY	10075	212-772-2673		192	*Web:* www.visualartsadvisory.com
Laurence Miller Gallery	521 W 26th St 5th Fl	New York	NY	10001	212-397-3930		42	*Web:* www.laurencemillergallery.com
Laurendale Associates	15035 Wyandotte St	Van Nuys	CA	91405	818-994-6920	994-6958	526	*Web:* www.laurendale.com
Laurens County	117 E Jackson St	Dublin	GA	31040	478-272-4755	272-3895	338	*Web:* www.laurenscoga.org
Laurens County	100 Hillcrest Sq Ste B	Laurens	SC	29360	864-984-3538	984-3726	338	*TF:* 800-768-5858 ■ *Web:* laurenscounty.us
Laurens County Board of Education	467 Firetower Rd	Dublin	GA	31021	478-272-4767	277-2619	685	*Web:* www.lcboe.net
Laurens County Chamber of Commerce	291 Professional Park Rd	Clinton	SC	29325	864-833-2716	939-0016	139	*Web:* www.laurenscounty.org
Laurens County Library	1017 W Main St	Laurens	SC	29360	864-681-7323	681-0598	434-3	*Web:* www.lcpl.org
Laurens Electric Co-opeartive Inc	2254 S Carolina 14	Laurens	SC	29360	800-942-3141		245	*TF:* 800-942-3141 ■ *Web:* www.laurenselectric.com
Laurentian Bank of Canada	1981 McGill College Ave	Montreal	QC	H3A3K3	514-284-4500	284-3988	70	*TSE:* LB ■ *TF:* 800-252-1846 ■ *Web:* www.laurentianbank.ca
Laurentian University	935 Ramsey Lake Rd	Sudbury	ON	P3E2C6	705-675-1151		785	*TF:* 800-461-4030 ■ *Web:* laurentian.ca
Lauretano Sign Group	1 Tremco Dr	Terryville	CT	06786	860-582-0233		701	*Web:* www.lauretano.com
Laurie Raphael	117 Dalhousie St	Quebec City	QC	G1K9C8	418-692-4555	692-4175	671	*TF:* 877-876-4555 ■ *Web:* www.laurieraphael.com
Laurier House National Historic Site	335 Laurier Ave E	Ottawa	ON	K1N6R4	613-992-8142	947-4851	563	*Web:* www.pc.gc.ca
Laurin Publishing Company Inc	100 West St	Pittsfield	MA	01202	413-499-0514	442-3180	637-9	*Web:* www.photonics.com
Laurinburg/Scotland County Area Chamber of Commerce	606 Atkinson St	Laurinburg	NC	28352	910-276-7420	277-8785	139	*Web:* www.laurinburgchamber.com
Lauritzen Gardens Omaha's Botanical Ctr	100 Bancroft St	Omaha	NE	68108	402-346-4002	346-8948	97	*Web:* www.lauritzengardens.org
Laurus College	8693 El Camino Real	Atascadero	CA	93422	805-267-1690		166	*Web:* www.lauruscollege.edu
Laurus Systems	3460 Ellicott Ctr Dr Ste 101	Ellicott City	MD	21043	410-465-5558	465-5257	196	*TF:* 800-274-4212 ■ *Web:* www.laurussystems.com
Laury's	350 MacCorkle Ave SE	Charleston	WV	25314	304-343-0055		671	*Web:* www.laurysrestaurant.com
LAUSD (Los Angeles Unified School District)	333 S Beaudry Ave	Los Angeles	CA	90017	213-241-1000		685	*Web:* achieve.lausd.net
Lauterbach & Eilber	1721 Bethel Rd	Columbus	OH	43220	614-459-6500	459-6568	390	*Web:* www.lauterbachandeilber.com
Lauterbach Group Inc	W222 N5710 Miller Way	Sussex	WI	53089	262-820-8130		554	*TF:* 800-841-7301 ■ *Web:* www.lauterbachgroup.com
Lauth Investigations International Inc	201 N Illinois St Fl 16	Indianapolis	IN	46204	866-951-5288		41	*Web:* www.lauthinvestigations.com
Laux & Co	672 W Liberty St	Medina	OH	44256	330-721-0100		690	*Web:* www.lauxco.com
Laux Sporting Goods Inc	25 Pineview Dr	Amherst	NY	14228	716-691-3367	691-4393	711	*Web:* www.lauxsportinggoods.com
Lava Beds National Monument	1 Indian Well Headquarters	Tulelake	CA	96134	530-260-0537		564	*Web:* www.nps.gov
Lava Hot Springs State Foundation	430 E Main St PO Box 669	Lava Hot Springs	ID	83246	208-776-5221		50-5	*TF:* 800-423-8597 ■ *Web:* lavahotsprings.com
Lavaca County	412 N Texana	Hallettsville	TX	77964	361-798-3612	798-1610	338	*Web:* www.co.lavaca.tx.us
Laval Chamber of Commerce & Industry	1455 Michelin St	Laval	QC	H7L4S2	450-682-5255	682-5735	137	*Web:* www.ccilaval.qc.ca
Laval University	2325 Rue University	Quebec City	QC	G1V0A6	418-656-2131		785	*TF:* 877-785-2825 ■ *Web:* www.ulaval.ca
Lavalley Building Supply Inc	351 Sunapee St	Newport	NH	03773	603-863-1050	863-3964	290	*TF:* 800-528-2553 ■ *Web:* www.lavalleys.com
Lavanture Products Co	22825 Gallatin Way	Elkhart	IN	46515	574-264-0658	264-6601	600	*TF:* 800-348-7625 ■ *Web:* www.lavanture.com
Lavdas Jewelry Ltd	3671 E 12 Mile Rd	Warren	MI	48092	586-751-8275		410	*Web:* www.lavdas.com
Lavelle Industries Inc	665 McHenry St	Burlington	WI	53105	262-763-2434	763-5607	677	*TF:* 800-528-3553 ■ *Web:* www.lavelle.com
LaVelle Vineyards	89697 Sheffler Rd	Elmira	OR	97437	541-935-9406		50-7	*Web:* www.lavellevineyards.com
Lavelle's Bistro	575 First Ave	Fairbanks	AK	99701	907-450-0555	456-2064	671	*Web:* www.lavellesbistro.com
Lavendou	19009 Preston Rd Ste 200	Dallas	TX	75252	972-248-1911	248-1660	671	*Web:* www.lavendou.com
Lavery Automotive Sales & Service	1096 W State St	Alliance	OH	44601	330-823-1100		57	*Web:* laveryauto.com
LaVezzi Precision Inc	250 Madsen Dr	Bloomingdale	IL	60108	800-323-1772	582-1238*	454	**Fax Area Code:* 630 ■ *TF:* 800-323-1772 ■ *Web:* www.lavezziprecision.com
Lavidge Co, The	2777 E Camelback Rd Ste 300	Phoenix	AZ	85016	480-998-2600		7	*Web:* www.lavidge.com
Lavigne Oil Company LLC	11203 Proverbs Ave	Baton Rouge	LA	70816	800-349-0170		538	*TF:* 800-349-0170 ■ *Web:* www.lavigneoil.com
Lavin & Waldon P C	1849 Green Bay Rd Ste 440	Highland Park	IL	60035	312-670-4260		41	*Web:* lavinwaldon.com
Lavin O'Neil Ricci Cedrone & Disipio	190 N Independence Mall W	Philadelphia	PA	19106	215-627-0303	627-2551	428	*Web:* www.lavin-law.com
Lavine Lofgren Morris & Engelberg CPAs	4180 La Jolla Village Dr Ste 300	La Jolla	CA	92037	858-455-1200		2	*Web:* llme.com
Lavista Associates Inc	3475 Piedmont Rd NE Ste 1150	Atlanta	GA	30305	770-448-6400	729-2856	194	*Web:* lavista.com
Law & Stein LLP	2601 Main St Ste 1200	Irvine	CA	92614	949-501-4800		41	*Web:* lawandsteinllp.com
Law Bulletin Media	415 N State St	Chicago	IL	60654	312-644-7800	644-4255	637-8	*TF:* 877-556-0719 ■ *Web:* lawbulletinmedia.com
Law Care	1646 Westgate Cir Ste 101	Brentwood	TN	37027	615-661-0122	661-0197	41	*Web:* tennfamilylaw.com
Law Collaborative Los Angeles, The	5955 De Soto Ave Ste 125	Woodland Hills	CA	91367	818-348-6700	348-0961	41	*Web:* thelawcollaborative.com
Law Company Inc, The	345 Riverview St	Wichita	KS	67203	316-268-0200	268-0210	186	*Web:* www.law-co.com

Name	Address	City	State	Zip	Phone	Fax	Class
Law Elder Law	2275 Church Rd *TF:* 800-310-3100 ■ *Web:* lawelderlaw.com	Aurora	IL	60502	630-585-5200		687
Law Enforcement Associates Corp (LEA-AID)	120 Penmarc Dr Ste 113 *OTC:* LAWEQ ■ **Fax Area Code:* 844 ■ *TF:* 800-354-9669 ■ *Web:* www.leacorp.com	Raleigh	NC	27603	919-872-6210	201-2109*	52
Law Enforcement Supply Inc	10920 64th Ave *TF:* 800-346-3174 ■ *Web:* www.porta-clip.com	Allendale	MI	49401	800-346-3174		482
Law Enforcement Technology Magazine	1233 Janesville Ave *TF:* 800-547-7377 ■ *Web:* www.officer.com	Fort Atkinson	WI	53538	800-547-7377		457-5
Law Engine	7660-H Fay Ave Ste 342 *TF:* 800-894-2889 ■ *Web:* thelawengine.com	La Jolla	CA	92037	858-456-1234	454-3375	397
Law Firm of Jeremy Rosenthal, The	4100 E Mississippi Ave Ste 1900 *Web:* lawfirmofjeremyrosenthal.com	Denver	CO	80246	303-825-2223		41
Law Firm of John F Schaefer, The	380 N Old Woodward Ave Ste 320 *Web:* lfjfs.com	Birmingham	MI	48009	248-642-6655		428
Law Journal Press (LJP)	120 Broadway 5th Fl *TF:* 877-807-8076 ■ *Web:* www.lawjournalpress.com	New York	NY	10271	877-807-8076		637-2
Law Office of Anthony W. Greco, The	6810 Caine Rd *Web:* grecoatlaw.com	Columbus	OH	43235	614-792-7800		41
Law Office of Ball & Yorke	1001 Partridge Dr Ste 330 *Web:* ballandyorke.com	Ventura	CA	93003	805-642-5177		41
Law Office of Borah & Shaffer	20111 Stevens Creek Blvd Ste 230 *Web:* borahandshaffer.com	Cupertino	CA	95014	408-996-8650		41
Law Office of Bryan P. Lynch PC	734 N Wells St *TF:* 800-710-9478 ■ *Web:* blynchlaw.com	Chicago	IL	60610	312-573-2727	573-2728	41
Law Office of C. Nicholas Burke	3 Campbell St *Web:* cnburkelaw.com	Lebanon	NH	03766	603-448-9650		41
Law Office of Carol M. Thomas	5191 Hampton Pl *Web:* attorneycarolthomas.com	Saginaw	MI	48604	989-793-2300		41
Law Office of Channing Migner	446 Main St Ste 2104 *TF:* 800-332-0116 ■ *Web:* worcesterlaw.com	Worcester	MA	01608	508-792-6060		41
Law Office of Charles D. Hines	90 Enfield St Ste 205 *Web:* chineslaw.com	Enfield	CT	06082	860-741-8322		41
Law Office of Christopher A. Ferro LLC	160 E Market St *Web:* ferrolawfirm.com	York	PA	17401	717-668-8159		41
Law Office of Claudia Flower PLLC	3137 Mt Vernon Ave *Web:* claudiaflowerlaw.com	Alexandria	VA	22305	703-518-4458	518-3003	41
Law Office of Clifford Bush III LLC	28 Old Jericho Rd *TF:* 866-379-3432 ■ *Web:* lawofficeofcbushiii.com	Beaufort	SC	29906	843-379-9500	379-9550	41
Law Office of David J. Karbasian PC	900 N Kings Hwy Ste 308 *Web:* karbasianlaw.com	Cherry Hill	NJ	08034	856-667-4666		41
Law Office of Henry Gates Steen, Jr	3001 N Lamar Blvd Ste 306 *Web:* steenlaw.com	Austin	TX	78705	512-476-4688		41
Law Office of Hunter C. Piel LLC	502 Washington Ave Ste 730 *Web:* hunterpiel.com	Towson	MD	21204	410-849-4888		41
Law Office of Jacob J. Rivas	7473 N Ingram Ave Ste 105 *Web:* rivasinjurylaw.com	Fresno	CA	93711	559-263-9667		41
Law Office of Jennifer A. Wing PLLC	4041 Ruston Way Ste 200 *Web:* jwinglaw.com	Tacoma	WA	98402	253-627-1762		41
Law Office of Joann Wood LLC, The	23087 Three Notch Rd PO Box 70 *Web:* joannwoodlaw.com	California	MD	20619	301-737-8882		41
Law Office of Joel R. Spivack	1820 Chapel Ave W Ste 195 *Web:* spivacklaw.com	Cherry Hill	NJ	08002	856-488-1200		41
Law Office of John Karl Schwartz Jr	318 N John Young Pkwy Ste 6 *Web:* www.orlandoevictionservices.com	Kissimmee	FL	34744	407-932-2883		41
Law Office of John R. Solis	2620 San Bernardo Ave *TF:* 866-465-9093 ■ *Web:* lawofficeofjohnsolis.com	Laredo	TX	78040	956-718-2300		41
Law Office of John T. Benjamin, The	1115 Hillsborough St *Web:* lawjtb.com	Raleigh	NC	27603	919-755-0060		41
Law Office of Julie R. Glade, Rn, Jd	8035 Cleveland Pl *Web:* julieglade.com	Merrillville	IN	46410	219-736-0456		41
Law Office of Kathleen M. Toombs	157 Barrett St *Web:* toombslawny.com	Schenectady	NY	12305	518-688-2846	688-2849	41
Law Office of Kevin F. Gillespie A Professional Corp	411 Brookside Ave *Web:* www.kevinfgillespielaw.com	Redlands	CA	92373	909-792-2039		41
Law Office of Kevin P Flyn, The	100 N Main St Ste 301 *Web:* kevinpflynn.com	Elmira	NY	14901	607-732-8990	732-8999	41
Law Office of Kyle D. Brown PC	408 Lindberg Ave *Web:* kylebrownlaw.com	Mcallen	TX	78501	956-668-1690	668-1693	41
Law Office of Laura E. Shapiro PC	8751 E Hampden Ave Ste B-5 *Web:* shapirofamilylaw.com	Denver	CO	80231	303-695-0200		41
Law Office of Lawrence Hill LLC	3430 E Flamingo Rd Ste 232 *Web:* lvlegalhelp.com	Las Vegas	NV	89121	702-530-5688		41
Law Office of Lawrence L Washb	245 W Crogan St *Web:* llwlaw.com	Lawrenceville	GA	30046	770-963-4300		41
Law Office of Lisa A. Lee PA	14286 Beach Blvd Ste 19-194 *Web:* veteranslegalhelp.com	Jacksonville	FL	32250	904-223-1974		41
Law Office of Mark A. Vickness	1939 Harrison St Ste 715 *Web:* vicknesslawfirm.com	Oakland	CA	94612	510-452-0400		41
Law Office of Massey Mcclusky	3074 East Rd *TF:* 888-341-4226 ■ *Web:* masseymcclusky.com	Memphis	TN	38128	901-384-4004	937-8004	41
Law Office of Neil Otoole PC	226 W 12th Ave *Web:* otoole-sbarbaro.com	Denver	CO	80204	303-595-4777		41
Law Office of Sarah Heck LLC	21 N Green St *Web:* sarahhecklaw.com	Brownsburg	IN	46112	317-858-1118		41
Law Office of Steven Markan LLC	2124 Oak Tree Rd Ste 309 *Web:* markanlaw.com	Edison	NJ	08820	732-696-8700		41
Law Office of Timothy M. Osborn	2200 Truxtun Ave *Web:* osborn-law.com	Bakersfield	CA	93301	661-322-7400		41
Law Office of Usman B. Ahmad	47-40 21st St Ph A *Web:* usmanbahmad.com	Long Island City	NY	11101	718-482-7777		41
Law Office of Victor E. Perry	350 N Monroe St *Web:* www.lawofficesofvictorperry.com	Eagle Pass	TX	78852	830-758-1200	758-1204	41
Law Office of Victor N. Yamouti PLLC	216 E Concord St *TF:* 877-787-8766 ■ *Web:* yamoutilaw.com	Morganton	NC	28655	828-438-1166		41
Law Office of William F. Jaworski, The	1274 S Governors Ave *Web:* wfjlaw.com	Dover	DE	19904	302-730-8511		41
Law Office of William J. Fitzpatrick	525 Townline Rd Ste 1 *Web:* wjfitzlaw.com	Hauppauge	NY	11788	631-686-5970		41
Law Offices Michael Spector	2677 N Main St Ste 910 *Web:* michaelgspector.com	Santa Ana	CA	92705	714-835-3130		41
Law Offices of Aaron I. Katsman PC	70 E Sunrise Hwy Ste 608 *Web:* katsmanlaw.com	Valley Stream	NY	11581	516-295-9680	295-9685	41
Law Offices of Alan M. Cohen LLC	550 Worcester Rd *Web:* collections-law.com	Framingham	MA	01702	508-620-6900	620-9696	41
Law Offices of Allan W Lugg & Robert H. Lugg	350 E Water St *Web:* lugglaw.com	Lock Haven	PA	17745	570-748-2481		445
Law Offices of Allweiss & Mcmurt	18321 Ventura Blvd Ste 500 *Web:* allweissmcmurtry.com	Tarzana	CA	91356	818-343-7509		41
Law Offices of Andrew L. Crabtree Pc	225 Broadhollow Rd Ste 303 *Web:* crabtreesq.com	Melville	NY	11747	631-753-0200	753-0950	41
Law Offices of Andrew S Blumer	4255 Us Hwy 9 Ste D *Web:* blumerlaw.com	Freehold	NJ	07728	732-303-6430		41
Law Offices of Anne Frassetto Olsen	307 Main St Ste 310 *Web:* afolaw.com	Salinas	CA	93901	831-800-7298		41
Law Offices of Anthony J. Dipaula PA	34 S Main St *Web:* dipaulalaw.com	Bel Air	MD	21014	410-893-4255		41
Law Offices of Bennie D. Rush PC	1300 11th St Ste 300 *Web:* bdrushlaw.com	Huntsville	TX	77340	936-295-0700	295-3330	41
Law Offices of Brian Nelson	9401 Wilshire Blvd Ste 608 *Web:* briannelsonlaw.com	Beverly Hills	CA	90212	310-277-5300		41
Law Offices of Camilla T Morch	289 Main Ave *Web:* camillamorch.com	Stirling	NJ	07980	908-604-5981		41
Law Offices of Charles A. Matison, The	1640 Tilton Rd *Web:* cmatison.com	Northfield	NJ	08225	609-407-1100		41
Law Offices of Charles W. Arline PA	203 N Armenia Ave Ste 101 *Web:* charlesarline.com	Tampa	FL	33609	813-258-3500	601-6370	41
Law Offices of Cheryl K. David	528 College Rd *Web:* cheryldavid.com	Greensboro	NC	27410	336-547-9999		41
Law Offices of Cleveland Metz	9330 Baseline Rd Ste 100 *TF:* 800-397-7708 ■ *Web:* clevelandmetzlaw.com	Rancho Cucamonga	CA	91701	909-980-9703		41
Law Offices of Cohn & Smith PA	5599 S University Dr Ste 305 *Web:* cohnlaw.com	Davie	FL	33328	954-431-8100		41
Law Offices of Dana L. Reynolds LLC	30C Trolley Sq *Web:* danareynoldslaw.com	Wilmington	DE	19806	302-428-8900	397-0606	41
Law Offices of David J. Follin	950 County Square Dr Ste 202 *Web:* davidfollin.com	Ventura	CA	93003	805-658-8691		41
Law Offices of David J. Hoey PC	352 Park St Ste 105 *Web:* hoeylaw.com	North Reading	MA	01864	978-664-3633		41
Law Offices of Denis Alexandroff, The	16542 Ventura Blvd Ste 203 *Web:* lainjured.com	Encino	CA	91436	213-277-7777		41
Law Offices of Dennis J. Luca, The	1252 Park Ave *Web:* dennislucalaw.com	San Jose	CA	95126	408-287-7878		41
Law Offices of Frank L. Branson, The	Highland Park Pl 4514 Cole Ave Ste 1800 *TF:* 800-522-0216 ■ *Web:* www.flbranson.com	Dallas	TX	75205	972-263-7452		41
Law Offices of G.M. Rego PC	1166 N Main St *Web:* gmrego.com	Fall River	MA	02720	508-678-3400		41

Name / Address	Phone	Fax	Class
Law Offices of Gail M. Walton 690 Mace Ave ... Bronx NY 10467 *Web:* gmwaltonlaw.com	718-655-6000		41
Law Offices of Gary Green 1001 La Harpe Blvd ... Little Rock AR 72201 *TF:* 888-442-7947 ■ *Web:* ggreen.com	501-224-7400	224-2294	41
Law Offices of Gehrke, Baker, Doull & Kelly PLLC 22030 Seventh Ave S Ste 202 ... Des Moines WA 98198 *Web:* gehrkelawoffices.com	206-878-4100		41
Law Offices of Herbert Hafif 269 W Bonita Ave ... Claremont CA 91711 *Web:* www.hafif.com	909-624-1671	625-7772	41
Law Offices of Howard N Sobel PA, The 507 Kresson Rd PO Box 1525 ... Voorhees NJ 08043 *Web:* www.sobellaw.com	856-424-6400		428
Law Offices of James B. James 3835 Avocado Blvd Ste 270 ... La Mesa CA 91941 *Web:* james-law.net	619-521-2660		41
Law Offices of Jane Heath 1052 Main St Ste A ... Morro Bay CA 93442 *Web:* sloconflictmanagement.com	805-225-1773		41
Law Offices of Jay G. Putnam 523 B St ... Petaluma CA 94952 *Web:* jaygputnam.com	707-778-5000		41
Law Offices of Jay S. Marks LLC 836 Bonifant St ... Silver Spring MD 20910 *Web:* marksjustice.com	301-578-4444		41
Law Offices of Jeffrey R. Singer PC 77 Sugar Creek Center Blvd Ste 565 ... Sugar Land TX 77478 *Web:* jrsingerlaw.com	281-565-4242	565-4448	41
Law Offices of Jeremy Flachs 6601 Little River Tpke Ste 315 ... Alexandria VA 22312 *Web:* flachslaw.com	703-879-1998	462-9090	41
Law Offices of John Cooney & Associates PS 330 W Indiana Ave ... Spokane WA 99205 *Web:* jcooney.com	509-326-2613		41
Law Offices of John M. Boehnert Ltd 50 S Main St ... Providence RI 02903 *Web:* jmblawoffices.com	401-595-5995		41
Law Offices of Joseph W Campbell, The 1301 Marina Village Pkwy Ste 330 ... Alameda CA 94501 *Web:* jwc-law.com	510-865-5409	865-5410	41
Law Offices of Jotham S. Stein PC 214 S Third St ... Saint Charles IL 60174 *Web:* jotham.com	630-443-4390		41
Law Offices of Justin Tierney, The 2000 U St ... Sacramento CA 95818 *Web:* jtierneylaw.com	916-451-3426		41
Law Offices of Kamela James PLLC, The 209 Quince St NE ... Olympia WA 98506 *Web:* www.olyinjurylawyers.com	360-943-0555	943-0475	41
Law Offices of Kathryn M. Parakilas PC 10 School St ... Westfield MA 01085 *Web:* parakilaslaw.com	413-568-3553		41
Law Offices of Keith A. Minoff PC 1350 Main St Ste 1003 ... Springfield MA 01103 *Web:* minofflaw.com	413-301-0866		41
Law Offices of Lawrence M Rief 9 Old Sugar Hollow Rd ... Danbury CT 06810 *Web:* riefberglaw.com	203-744-8601		41
Law Offices of Leonard S. Roth PC, The 4265 San Felipe Ste 500 ... Houston TX 77027 *Web:* leonardsroth.com	713-622-4222		41
Law Offices of Lisa A. Ruggieri PC 27 Mica Ln Ste 101 ... Wellesley MA 02481 *Web:* lisaruggieri.com	781-239-8984		41
Law Offices of Lisa C. Bryant Inc 1625 The Alameda Ste 820 ... San Jose CA 95126 *TF:* 800-970-3414 ■ *Web:* sanjoseelderlaw.com	408-286-2122	286-2121	41
Law Offices of Lobeck & Hanson PA, The 2033 Main St Ste 403 ... Sarasota FL 34237 *Web:* lobeckhanson.com	941-955-5622	951-1469	41
Law Offices of Lutz, Shafranski, Gorman & Mahoney PA, The 77 Livingston Ave ... New Brunswick NJ 08901 *Web:* lsgmpa.com	732-249-0834		41
Law Offices of Marc S Ward LLC 1030 W Patrick St ... Frederick MD 21703 *Web:* wardlawoffices.com	301-662-2911		41
Law Offices of Marie Calla Quartell PA 4500 Pga Blvd Ste 206 ... Palm Beach Gardens FL 33418 *Web:* callalegal.com	561-622-1090		41
Law Offices of Marion M. Moses LLC 2909 Devine St ... Columbia SC 29205 *Web:* moseslawsc.com	803-771-7011	771-7022	41
Law Offices of Michael A Pines Apc 4660 La Jolla Village Dr Ste 575 ... San Diego CA 92122 *Web:* seriousaccidents.com	858-551-2090		41
Law Offices of Michael J. Gurfinkel Inc 219 N Brand ... Glendale CA 91203 *Web:* gurfinkel.com	818-543-5800		41
Law Offices of Michael Kuldiner PC 922 Bustleton Pk ... Feasterville-Trevose PA 19053 *Web:* phillyesquire.com	215-942-2100		41
Law Offices of Michael P. Sousa Apc 3232 Governor Dr Ste A ... San Diego CA 92122 *Web:* msousalaw.com	858-453-6122		41
Law Offices of Michael R. Kaiser 801 E Tahquitz Canyon Way Ste 101 ... Palm Springs CA 92262 *Web:* mkaiserlaw.com	760-322-0806	322-8979	41
Law Offices of Mitchell J. Devack PLLC 90 Merrick Ave Ste 500 ... East Meadow NY 11554 *Web:* devacklaw.com	516-794-2800		41
Law Offices of Mueller & Haller LLC 5312 W Main St ... Belleville IL 62226 *Web:* thebankruptcycenter.net	618-236-7000		41
Law Offices of Neil Crane LLC, The 2679 Whitney Ave ... Hamden CT 06518 *TF:* 888-249-3027 ■ *Web:* ctbankruptcyattorneys.com	203-230-2233	230-8484	41
Law Offices of Omar Baloch, The 8801 Fast Park Dr ... Raleigh NC 27617 *Web:* balochlaw.com	919-834-3535		41
Law Offices of Peter Miller PA 1601 S Broadway ... Little Rock AR 72206 *Web:* petermillerlaw.com	501-374-6300		41
Law Offices of Peter T. Nicholl 36 S Charles St Ste 1700 ... Baltimore MD 21201 *Web:* nichollaw.com	410-244-7005		41
Law Offices of R Ross Jacinto 690 EGreen St Ste 103 ... Pasadena CA 91101 *Web:* rossjacinto.com	626-304-1001		41
Law Offices of Richard Troutman Pa, The 1101 N Kentucky Ave ... Winter Park FL 32789 *Web:* richardtroutman.com	407-647-5002		41
Law Offices of Robert A. Levine 630 N Broadway ... Milwaukee WI 53202 *Web:* rlevinelaw.com	414-368-9100	271-8506	41
Law Offices of Salnick & Fuchs PA 1645 Palm Beach Lakes Blvd Ste 1000 Tenth Fl ... West Palm Beach FL 33401 *Web:* palmbeachcriminallawfirms.com	561-471-1000	659-0793	41
Law Offices of Samer Habbas & Associates Incorporated PC 200 Spectrum Center Dr Ste 1230 ... Irvine CA 92618 *Web:* habbaspilaw.com	949-727-9300		41
Law Offices of Sherwood Guernsey, The 69 E Housatonic St ... Pittsfield MA 01201 *Web:* sglawoffice.com	413-499-3520		41
Law Offices of Sonia Figueroa 2000 Riverside Dr ... Los Angeles CA 90039 *Web:* soniafiglaw.com	323-665-5770		41
Law Offices of Steven M. Goldfarb 233 Broadway ... New York NY 10279 *Web:* lawofficesofstevengoldfarb.com	212-227-4242		41
Law Offices of Travis R. Walker Pa, The 1235 SE Indian St Ste 101 ... Stuart FL 34997 *TF:* 844-487-9529 ■ *Web:* traviswalkerlaw.com	772-708-0952	673-3738	41
Law Offices of Victor Wu 10161 Bolsa Ave Ste 204C ... Westminster CA 92683 *Web:* vicwulaw.com	714-531-4411		41
Law Offices of Vladimir P. Devens LLC 707 Richards St ... Honolulu HI 96813 *Web:* pacificlaw.com	808-528-5003		41
Law Offices of W. Michael Young 4629 Cass St PO Box 78 ... San Diego CA 92109 *Web:* myecounsel.com	619-800-4718		41
Law Offices of William A. Bramley, Apc 110 Juniper St ... San Diego CA 92101 *Web:* bramleylaw.com	619-232-1400		41
Law Place Pllc, The 2445 Fruitville Rd ... Sarasota FL 34237 *Web:* thelawplace.com	941-444-4444		41
Law Society of Manitoba 219 Kennedy St ... Winnipeg MB R3C1S8 *Web:* www.lawsociety.mb.ca	204-942-5571		428
Law Writing PO Box 40312 ... Providence RI 02940 *TF:* 800-345-6470 ■ *Web:* www.lawwriting.com	401-383-7471		192
Lawes Coal Company Inc 499 Sycamore Ave ... Shrewsbury NJ 07702 *Web:* lawescompany.com	732-741-6300		316
Lawgical Inc 11693 San Vicente Blvd Ste 910 ... Los Angeles CA 90049 *TF:* 800-811-4458 ■ *Web:* www.lawgical.com	800-811-4458		195
Lawinger Consulting Inc (LCI) 106 Central Ave ... Osseo MN 55369 *Web:* www.lci-online.com	763-425-7567	425-5483	196
Lawler Dessert's PO Box 2558 ... Humble TX 77347 *Web:* www.dessertholdings.com	281-446-0059		296-1
Lawler Direct Inc 10300 Drummond Rd ... Philadelphia PA 19154 *Web:* www.lawlerdirect.com	215-824-3290	824-3299	5
Lawler Foundry Corp 4908 Powell Ave S ... Birmingham AL 35222 *TF:* 800-624-9512 ■ *Web:* www.lawlerfoundry.com	800-624-9512		492
Lawler-Wood LLC 900 S Gay St ... Knoxville TN 37902 *Web:* www.lawlerwood.com	865-637-7777	549-7400	652
Lawley Service Insurance 361 Delaware Ave ... Buffalo NY 14202 *TF:* 800-860-5741 ■ *Web:* www.lawleyinsurance.com	716-849-8618	849-8291	390
Lawman Heating & Cooling Inc PO Box 599 ... Sackets Harbor NY 13685 *Web:* www.lawmaninc.com	315-646-2919	646-2920	189-10
Lawn & Golf Supply Company Inc 647 Nutt Rd PO Box 447 ... Phoenixville PA 19460 *Web:* www.lawn-golf.com	610-933-5801		429
Lawn Care Specialists Inc 3016 Airport Rd ... La Crosse WI 54603 *Web:* lawncarespecialists.com	608-781-3217	781-3273	422
Lawn Doctor Inc 142 SR 34 ... Holmdel NJ 07733 *TF:* 800-845-0580 ■ *Web:* www.lawndoctor.com	732-946-4300		577
Lawn Equipment Parts Co 1475 River Rd PO Box 466 ... Marietta PA 17547 *TF:* 800-365-3726 ■ *Web:* lepco.com	717-426-5200	426-5201	429
Lawndale Art & Performance Ctr 4912 Main St ... Houston TX 77002 *Web:* lawndaleartcenter.org	713-528-5858	528-4140	520
Lawndale Logistics 1239 12th Ave ... Grafton WI 53024 *TF:* 888-375-3684 ■ *Web:* www.lawndalelogistics.com	262-375-3684		314
Lawns Unlimited Ltd 15089 Coastal Hwy ... Milton DE 19968 *Web:* lawnsunlimited.com	302-645-5296		422
Lawnwood Regional Medical Center & Heart Institute 1700 S 23rd St ... Fort Pierce FL 34950 *Web:* lawnwoodmed.com	772-461-4000		374-3
Lawrence & Company College of Cosmetology 810 N 10th Ave ... Hanford CA 93230 *Web:* www.lawrenceandco.net	559-584-1192	584-1876	167-3
Lawrence & Memorial Hospital 365 Montauk Ave ... New London CT 06320 *TF:* 800-579-3341 ■ *Web:* www.lmhospital.org	860-442-0711		374-3

Name / Address	City	State	ZIP	Phone	Fax	Class
Lawrence & Schiller Inc 3932 S Willow Ave *Web:* l-s.com	Sioux Falls	SD	57105	605-338-8000		4
Lawrence & Wheeler Inc 46 Main St *Web:* lawrenceandwheeler.com	Springfield	VT	05156	802-885-2178		390
Lawrence A. Mantell & Assocs Inc 16055 Ventura Blvd Ste 1100 *Web:* mantellinc.com	Encino	CA	91436	818-788-3995		390
Lawrence Academy Powderhouse Rd PO Box 992 *Web:* www.lacademy.edu	Groton	MA	01450	978-448-6535	448-9208	622
Lawrence Berkeley National Laboratory (LBNL) 1 Cyclotron Rd *Web:* www.lbl.gov	Berkeley	CA	94720	510-486-4000		668
Lawrence Berkeley National Laboratory *Advanced Light Source* Lawrence Berkeley National Laboratory 1 Cyclotron Rd *Web:* als.lbl.gov	Berkeley	CA	94720	510-486-7745	486-4773	668
Lawrence Brenda (Rep D - MI) 2463 Rayburn House Office Bldg *Web:* lawrence.house.gov	Washington	DC	20515	202-225-5802	226-2356	342-2
Lawrence Companies (LTS) 872 Lee Hwy Ste 100 **Fax Area Code:* 540 ■ *TF:* 800-336-9626 ■ *Web:* www.lawrencecompanies.com	Roanoke	VA	24019	800-336-9626	966-4555*	780
Lawrence Construction Company Inc 9002 N Moore Rd *Web:* www.lawrence-construction.com	Littleton	CO	80125	303-791-5642	791-5647	188-4
Lawrence County 916 15th St Rm 20 *Web:* www.bedfordonline.com	Bedford	IN	47421	812-275-7543	278-8845	338
Lawrence County 90 Sherman St *Web:* www.lawrence.sd.us	Deadwood	SD	57732	605-578-1941	578-1065	338
Lawrence County 12521 Hwy 157 Ste L *Web:* www.lawrencealabama.com	Moulton	AL	35650	256-974-1658	974-2400	338
Lawrence County 1 Courthouse Sq PO Box 188 *Web:* lawrencecountymoassessor.com	Mount Vernon	MO	65712	417-466-2831	466-3931	338
Lawrence County County Courthouse 430 Court St *TF:* 855-564-6116 ■ *Web:* co.lawrence.pa.us	New Castle	PA	16101	724-658-2541	652-9646	338
Lawrence County 315 W Main *Web:* www.lawrencecountysheriffsoffice.com	Walnut Ridge	AR	72476	870-886-2525		338
Lawrence County Chamber of Commerce 216 Collins Ave *TF:* 800-408-1334 ■ *Web:* lawrencecc.org	South Point	OH	45680	740-377-4550	377-2091	338
Lawrence County Public Library 519 E Gaines St *Web:* lawrencecountytn.gov	Lawrenceburg	TN	38464	931-762-4627	766-1597	434-3
Lawrence County Public Library 401 College St *Web:* sites.google.com	Moulton	AL	35650	256-974-0883	974-0890	434-3
Lawrence County Regional Chamber of Commerce 325 E Washington St *Web:* www.lawrencecounty.com	New Castle	PA	16101	724-658-1488		139
Lawrence County Tennessee Chamber of Commerce 25B Public Sqr *Web:* lawcotn.com	Lawrenceburg	TN	38464	931-762-4911	762-3153	139
Lawrence County Tourist Promotion Agency 229 S Jefferson St *TF:* 888-284-7599 ■ *Web:* visitlawrencecounty.com	New Castle	PA	16101	724-654-8408	654-2044	206
Lawrence Equipment Inc 2034 Peck Rd *TF:* 800-423-4500 ■ *Web:* www.lawrenceequipment.com	El Monte	CA	91733	626-442-2894	350-5181	298
Lawrence Foods Inc 2200 Lunt Ave *Web:* www.lawrencefoods.com	Elk Grove Village	IL	60007	847-437-2400	437-2567	296-20
Lawrence General Hospital 1 General St *Web:* www.lawrencegeneral.org	Lawrence	MA	01842	978-683-4000		374-3
Lawrence Green Fire Protection 18323 Weaver St	Detroit	MI	48228	313-835-5800		610
Lawrence Hall Chevrolet Inc 1385 S Danville Dr *Web:* www.lawrencehall.com	Abilene	TX	79605	325-695-8800		57
Lawrence Heritage State Park 1 Jackson St *Web:* www.mass.gov	Lawrence	MA	01840	978-794-1655		565
Lawrence Journal-World 1035 N 3rd St *Web:* www2.ljworld.com	Lawrence	KS	66044	800-578-8748		637-8
Lawrence Kamin LLC 300 S Wacker Dr Ste 500 *Web:* www.lawrencekaminlaw.com	Chicago	IL	60606	312-372-1947	372-2389	41
Lawrence Livermore National Laboratory (LLNL) 7000 E Ave PO Box 808 *Web:* www.llnl.gov	Livermore	CA	94550	925-422-1100	422-1370	668
Lawrence Memorial Hospital (LMH) 325 Maine St *TF:* 800-749-4144 ■ *Web:* www.lmh.org	Lawrence	KS	66044	785-505-5000		374-3
Lawrence Memorial Hospital of Medford 170 Governors Ave *TF:* 800-540-9191 ■ *Web:* www.melrosewakefield.org	Medford	MA	02155	781-306-6000		374-3
Lawrence Merchandising 1405 Xenium Ln N Ste 250 *TF:* 800-328-3967 ■ *Web:* www.lmsvc.com	Plymouth	MN	55441	763-383-5700	551-9990	463
Lawrence P. Lemieux & Associates LLC 1000 Bridgeport Ave *Web:* lemieuxcpa.com	Monroe	CT	06484	203-925-9600		2
Lawrence Paper Co 2801 Lakeview Rd *TF:* 800-535-4553 ■ *Web:* www.lpco.co	Lawrence	KS	66049	800-535-4553		100
Lawrence Printing Co 400 Stribling Ave PO Box 886 *TF:* 800-844-0338 ■ *Web:* laprico.com	Greenwood	MS	38935	662-453-6301	455-4746	627
Lawrence Public Library 707 Vermont St *Web:* lplks.org	Lawrence	KS	66044	785-843-3833	843-3368	434-3
Lawrence Public Schools 110 McDonald Dr *Web:* www.usd497.org	Lawrence	KS	66044	785-832-5000	832-5016	685
Lawrence Screw Products Inc 7230 W Wilson Ave *Web:* www.lawrencescrew.com	Harwood Heights	IL	60706	708-867-5150	867-7052	278
Lawrence Segal Attorney At Law 9100 Wilshire Blvd Ste 616-E *Web:* legalsegal.com	Beverly Hills	CA	90212	310-550-4840		41
Lawrence Solomon 1628 Jfk Blvd Ste 2200 *Web:* solomonsherman.com	Philadelphia	PA	19103	215-665-1100		41
Lawrence Technological University 21000 W 10-Mile Rd *TF:* 800-225-5588 ■ *Web:* www.ltu.edu	Southfield	MI	48075	248-204-3160	204-3188	166
Lawrence Tractor Company Inc 2530 E Main St *Web:* www.lawrencetractor.com	Visalia	CA	93292	559-734-7406	734-8325	274
Lawrence University 711 E Boldt Way *TF:* 800-432-5427 ■ *Web:* www.lawrence.edu	Appleton	WI	54911	920-832-7000	832-6782	166
Lawrenceburg Medical Supply 753 W Broadway St	Lawrenceburg	KY	40342	502-839-4557		238
Lawrenceville Correctional Ctr 1607 Planters Rd *Web:* vadoc.virginia.gov	Lawrenceville	VA	23868	434-848-9349		213
Lawrenceville School 2500 Main St PO Box 6008 *TF:* 800-735-2030 ■ *Web:* www.lawrenceville.org	Lawrenceville	NJ	08648	609-896-0400	895-2217	622
Lawrimore Communications Inc 1320 Fillmore Ave Unit 312 *Web:* lciweb.com	Charlotte	NC	28203	704-332-4344		195
Lawry's Restaurants Inc 225 S Lake Ave Ste 1500 *TF:* 888-552-9797 ■ *Web:* www.lawrysonline.com	Pasadena	CA	91101	888-552-9797		670
Lawson & Weitzen LLP 88 Black Falcon Ave *Web:* www.lawson-weitzen.com	Boston	MA	02210	617-439-4990		428
Lawson Al (Rep D - FL) 1406 Longworth House Office Bldg *Web:* lawson.house.gov	Washington	DC	20515	202-225-0123	225-2256	342-2
Lawson Health Research Institute Inc 268 Grosvenor St *Web:* www.lawsonresearch.ca	London	ON	N6A4V2	519-646-6005		415
Lawson Kroeker Investment Management Inc 450 Regency Pkwy Ste 410 *TF:* 800-810-5994 ■ *Web:* www.lawsonkroeker.com	Omaha	NE	68114	402-392-2606		401
Lawson Lundell LLP 925 W Georgia St Cathedral Pl Ste 1600 *Web:* www.lawsonlundell.com	Vancouver	BC	V6C3L2	604-685-3456		428
Lawson Mechanical Contractors 6090 S Watt Ave *Web:* www.lawsonmechanical.com	Sacramento	CA	95829	916-381-5000	381-5073	189-10
Lawson Products Inc 1666 E Touhy Ave *TF:* 800-323-5922 ■ *Web:* www.lawsonproducts.com	Des Plaines	IL	60018	847-827-9666	827-1525	385
Lawson State Community College *Bessemer* 1100 Ninth Ave SW *TF:* 800-373-4879 ■ *Web:* www.lawsonstate.edu	Bessemer	AL	35022	205-925-2515	929-3598	800
Lawson-Fisher Associates PC (LFA) 525 W Washington Ave *Web:* lawson-fisher.com	South Bend	IN	46601	574-234-3167		261
Lawson-Hemphill Inc 1658 G A R Hwy Ste 6 *Web:* www.lawsonhemphill.com	Swansea	MA	02777	508-679-5364	679-5396	744
Lawter & Lawter Attorneys At Law 5615 Kirby Ste 930 *Web:* lawterandlawter.com	Houston	TX	77005	713-522-9400		41
Lawter part of Harima Chemicals Inc 200 N LaSalle St Ste 2600 *Web:* www.lawter.com	Chicago	IL	60601	312-662-5700		388
Lawton & Cates SC 10 E Doty St Ste 400 *TF:* 800-900-4539 ■ *Web:* www.lawtoncates.com	Madison	WI	53703	608-282-6200		428
Lawton Brothers Inc 2515 Dinneen Ave *Web:* www.lawtonbros.com	Orlando	FL	32804	407-291-2501	290-0471	76
Lawton Constitution, The 102 SW Third St *Web:* www.swoknews.com	Lawton	OK	73501	580-357-9545		532-2
Lawton Group, The 4747 Viewridge Ave Ste 106 *Web:* www.lawtongrp.com	San Diego	CA	92123	858-569-6260		260
Lawton Industries Inc 4353 Pacific St *TF:* 800-692-2600 ■ *Web:* www.lawtonindustries.com	Rocklin	CA	95677	916-624-7894	624-7898	386
Lawton Public Library 110 SW 4th St *TF:* 855-895-8064 ■ *Web:* www.lawtonok.gov	Lawton	OK	73501	580-581-3450	248-0243	434-3
Lawton's Drug Stores Ltd 236 Brownlow Ave Ste 270 *TF:* 866-990-1599 ■ *Web:* lawtons.ca	Dartmouth	NS	B3B1V5	902-468-1000		231
Lawyer Referral Service 123 Remsen St *Web:* brooklynbar.org	Brooklyn	NY	11201	718-624-0843	797-1713	428
Lawyers Aid Service Inc 408 W 17th St Ofc 101 *Web:* lawyersaidservice.com	Austin	TX	78701	512-474-2002		445
Lawyers Diary & Manual 890 Mtn Ave Ste 300 *TF:* 800-444-4041 ■ *Web:* www.lawdiary.com	New Providence	NJ	07974	973-642-1440	642-4280	637-2
Lawyers for Civil Justice (LCJ) 1140 Connecticut Ave NW Ste 503 *Web:* www.lfcj.com	Washington	DC	20036	202-429-0045	429-6982	49-10
Lawyers Group Advertising Inc 28 Thorndal Cir *TF:* 800-948-1080 ■ *Web:* www.lawyersgroup.com	Darien	CT	06820	800-948-1080		445
Lawyers Weekly Inc 10 Milk St Ste 1000 *TF:* 800-444-5297 ■ *Web:* masslawyersweekly.com	Boston	MA	02108	617-451-7300		532-3
Lawyers' Committee for Civil Rights Under Law 1401 New York Ave NW Ste 400 *TF:* 888-299-5227 ■ *Web:* lawyerscommittee.org	Washington	DC	20005	202-662-8600	783-0857	49-10
Lawyerscom 121 Chanlon Rd Ste 110 **Fax Area Code:* 908 ■ *TF:* 800-526-4902 ■ *Web:* www.lawyers.com	New Providence	NJ	07974	800-526-4902	771-8704*	171
Lax & Company Inc 3616 Post Rd *Web:* laxandco.com	Warwick	RI	02886	401-738-7776		390

Company / Address	City	State	ZIP	Phone	Fax	Class
LAX Coastal Area Chamber of Commerce 9100 S Sepulveda Blvd Ste 210 *Web:* laxcoastal.com	Los Angeles	CA	90045	310-645-5151	645-0130	139
Layer 3 Communications LLC 109 Park of Commerce Dr Ste 1 **Fax Area Code:* 866 ■ *TF:* 844-352-9373 ■ *Web:* www.layer3com.com	Savannah	GA	31405	770-225-5279	535-3925*	252
Layer 3 Technologies Inc 1645 Lyell Ave Ste 200 *Web:* layer3.tech	Rochester	NY	14606	585-254-1966	254-2266	196
LayerZero Power Systems Inc 1500 Danner Dr *Web:* www.layerzero.com	Aurora	OH	44202	440-399-9000		729
Layher Inc 8225 Hansen Rd *Web:* layherna.com	Houston	TX	77075	713-947-1444		52
Laylalina Restaurant 5216 Wilson Blvd *Web:* layalinarestaurant.com	Arlington	VA	22205	703-525-1170	525-6561	671
Laynas & Georges Pc 1500 Jfk Blvd Ste 1300 *Web:* laynaslaw.com	Philadelphia	PA	19102	215-851-8700		41
Laynes Family Pharmacy 509 S Van Buren Rd *Web:* laynespharmacy.com	Eden	NC	27288	336-627-4600		237
Layser's Flowers Inc 501 W Washington Ave *Web:* www.laysersflowers.com	Myerstown	PA	17067	717-866-5746	866-6099	369
Layton Manufacturing Corp 825 Remsen Ave *TF:* 800-545-8002 ■ *Web:* www.laytonmfg.com	Brooklyn	NY	11236	718-498-6000		14
LAZ Parking Ltd 15 Lewis St *Web:* www.lazparking.com	Hartford	CT	06103	860-522-7641		562
Lazar Equipment Ltd 520 Ninth St W *Web:* lazarequipment.com	Meadow Lake	SK	S9X1Y4	306-236-5222		274
Lazard 30 Rockefeller Plz *NYSE: LAZ* ■ *TF:* 866-867-4070 ■ *Web:* www.lazard.com	New York	NY	10112	212-632-6000		690
Lazare Kaplan International Inc 19 W 44th St 16th Fl *OTC: LKII* ■ *Web:* www.lazarediamonds.com	New York	NY	10036	212-972-9700		407
La-Z-Boy Inc 1284 N Telegraph Rd *NYSE: LZB* ■ *TF:* 800-375-6890 ■ *Web:* www.la-z-boy.com	Monroe	MI	48162	734-242-1444		319-2
Lazear Capital Partners Ltd 401 N Front St Ste 350 *Web:* www.lazearcapital.com	Columbus	OH	43215	614-221-1616		691
Lazenby & Associates Inc 10300 W Charelston Blvd Ste 13-467 *Web:* www.lazenbyassociates.com	Las Vegas	NV	89135	702-498-8506		401
Lazer Grant Inc 309 Mcdermot Ave *TF:* 800-220-0005 ■ *Web:* www.lazergrant.ca	Winnipeg	MB	R3A1T3	204-942-0300	957-5611	2
Lazer Inc 971 Pinebrook Knolls Dr *Web:* www.lazerinc.com	Winston-Salem	NC	27105	336-744-8047		92
Lazlo's Brewery & Grill 210 N 7th St *Web:* lazlosbreweryandgrill.com	Lincoln	NE	68508	402-434-5636	434-3291	671
Lazo Technologies Inc 4818 Mill Run Rd	Dallas	TX	75244	214-652-9898	652-9889	246
Lazorpoint 737 Bolivar Rd Ste 100 *Web:* lazorpoint.com	Cleveland	OH	44115	216-325-5200		196
Lazy Acres Market 302 Meigs Rd *Web:* www.lazyacres.com	Santa Barbara	CA	93109	805-564-4410		345
Lazy K Bar Ranch PO Box 1550 *Web:* lkbranch.com	Big Timber	MT	59011	406-537-9450		239
Lazy L & B Ranch 1072 E Fork Rd *TF:* 800-453-9488 ■ *Web:* www.lazylb.com	Dubois	WY	82513	307-455-2839	455-2849	239
Lazy Shoppes of Winston-Salem Inc 700 Hanes Mall Blvd *Web:* la-z-boy.com	Winston-Salem	NC	27103	336-766-3336		321
Lazzari Fuel Company LLC 11 Industrial Way *TF:* 800-242-7265 ■ *Web:* www.lazzari.com	Brisbane	CA	94005	415-467-2970		316
LB Foster Co 415 Holiday Dr *NASDAQ: FSTR* ■ *TF:* 800-255-4500 ■ *Web:* www.lbfoster.com	Pittsburgh	PA	15220	800-255-4500		650
LB Furniture Industries LLC 99 S 3rd St *TF:* 800-221-8752 ■ *Web:* www.lbempire.com	Hudson	NY	12534	518-828-1501	828-3219	319-3
LB Sales LLC 50 Plant St	New London	CT	06320	860-437-3953		362
LB Steel LLC 15700 Lathrop Ave *Web:* www.lbsteel.com	Harvey	IL	60426	708-331-2600	331-8500	454
LB White Company Inc W 6636 LB White Rd *TF:* 800-345-7200 ■ *Web:* www.lbwhite.com	Onalaska	WI	54650	608-783-5691	783-6115	357
LBA (Latin Business Assn) 120 S San Pedro St Ste 530 *Web:* www.lbausa.com	Los Angeles	CA	90012	213-628-8510	628-8519	49-12
LBA Group Inc 3400 Tupper Dr *TF:* 800-522-4464 ■ *Web:* www.lbagroup.com	Greenville	NC	27834	252-757-0279	752-9155	261
LBA Networking Inc 2251 N Rampart Blvd Ste 375 *Web:* www.lvmedit.com	Las Vegas	NV	89128	702-553-3200		180
LBC (Lexington Ballet Co) 161 N Mill St *Web:* www.lexingtonballet.org	Lexington	KY	40507	859-233-3925		573-1
LBC Houston 11666 Port Rd *Web:* www.lbctt.com	Seabrook	TX	77586	281-474-4433		581
LBCH (Louisiana Baptist Children's Home Inc) 7200 DeSiard St *Web:* www.lbch.org	Monroe	LA	71203	318-343-2244		48-15
LBFF (Latino Book & Family Festival) 3445 Catalina Dr *Web:* lbff.us	Carlsbad	CA	92010	760-434-1223	434-7476	281
LBI Eyewear 9747 Independence Ave **Fax Area Code:* 818 ■ *Web:* shop.ltdeyewear.com	Chatsworth	CA	91311	800-423-5175	407-1895*	542
LBi Software Inc 7600 Jericho Tpke *Web:* www.lbisoftware.com	Woodbury	NY	11797	516-921-1500		177
LBIW Inc 2020 W 14th St *Web:* www.lbiw.com	Long Beach	CA	90813	562-432-5451		723
LBJ Library & Museum 2313 Red River St *TF:* 800-874-6451 ■ *Web:* www.lbjlibrary.org	Austin	TX	78705	512-721-0216	721-0170	434-2
LBL Architects Inc 1106 W Randol Mill Rd Ste 300 *Web:* www.lblarchitects.com	Arlington	TX	76012	817-265-1510		393
LBM (Lloyd Bilyeu McLellan Construction Company Inc) 11421 Blankenbaker Access Dr *Web:* www.lbmconstructionco.com	Louisville	KY	40299	502-452-1151	454-0291	186
LBNL (Lawrence Berkeley National Laboratory) 1 Cyclotron Rd *Web:* www.lbl.gov	Berkeley	CA	94720	510-486-4000		668
LBRG Law Firm 1509 FD Roosevelt Ave Ste 306 *Web:* www.lbrglaw.com	Guaynabo	PR	00968	787-724-0230		428
LBS (Library Binding Service) 1801 Thompson Ave **Fax Area Code:* 800 ■ *TF:* 800-247-5323 ■ *Web:* www.lbsbind.com	Des Moines	IA	50316	515-262-3191	262-4091*	92
LBSO (Long Beach Symphony Orchestra) 249 E Ocean Blvd Ste 200 *Web:* longbeachsymphony.org	Long Beach	CA	90802	562-436-3203	491-3599	573-3
LBT (London Bridge Trading Company Ltd) 585 London Bridge Rd *TF:* 800-229-0207 ■ *Web:* www.lbtinc.com	Virginia Beach	VA	23454	757-498-0207	498-0059	67
LBT Inc 11502 "I" St *TF:* 888-528-7278 ■ *Web:* www.lbt-inc.com	Omaha	NE	68137	402-333-4900	333-0685	779
LBU Inc 217 Brook Ave Ste 6 *Web:* lbuinc.com	Passaic	NJ	07055	973-773-4800		67
LC (LeChase Construction Services LLC) 205 Indigo Creek Dr *TF:* 888-953-2427 ■ *Web:* www.lechase.com	Rochester	NY	14626	585-254-3510	254-3871	186
LC Doane Co 110 Pond Meadow Rd PO Box 700 *Web:* www.lcdoane.com	Ivoryton	CT	06442	860-767-8295	767-1397	439
LC Engineering Group Inc 889 Pierce Ct Ste 101 **Fax Area Code:* 818 ■ *Web:* lcegroupinc.com	Thousand Oaks	CA	91360	805-497-1244	991-5942*	261
LC Engineers Inc 1471 Pinewood St *Web:* www.lcengineers.com	Rahway	NJ	07065	732-340-9190	340-9194	261
LC Industries 2781 Katherine Wy *Web:* lewisnclark.com	Elk Grove Village	IL	60007	312-455-0500		453
LC King Manufacturing Company Inc 24 Seventh St *TF:* 800-826-2510 ■ *Web:* lcking.com	Bristol	TN	37620	423-764-5188	764-6809	155-19
LC Sciences LLC 2575 W Bellfort St Ste 270 *TF:* 888-528-8818 ■ *Web:* www.lcsciences.com	Houston	TX	77054	713-664-7087	664-8181	668
LC Whitford Company Inc 164 N Main St *TF:* 800-321-3602 ■ *Web:* www.lcwhitford.com	Wellsville	NY	14895	585-593-3601	593-1876	188-4
LCA (Literacy Council of Alaska) 517 Gaffney Rd *Web:* www.literacycouncilofalaska.org	Fairbanks	AK	99701	907-456-6212	456-4302	48-6
LCA-Vision Inc 7840 Montgomery Rd *Web:* www.lasikplus.com	Cincinnati	OH	45236	513-792-9292		798
LCB Associates Inc 388 17th St Ste 200 *Web:* lcbassociates.com	Oakland	CA	94612	510-763-7016		652
LCC (Laredo Community College) W End Washington St *Web:* www.laredo.edu	Laredo	TX	78040	956-722-0521	721-5493	162
LCC (Legal Cost Control Inc) 8 Kings Hwy W Ste C *TF:* 800-493-7345 ■ *Web:* legalcost.com	Haddonfield	NJ	08033	856-216-0800	216-1736	445
LCCC (Loudon County Chamber of Commerce) 318 Angel Row *Web:* www.loudoncountychamberofcommerce.com	Loudon	TN	37774	865-458-2067	458-1206	139
LCCR (Leadership Conference on Civil Rights) 1620 L St NW Ste 1100 *Web:* www.civilrights.org	Washington	DC	20036	202-466-3311	466-3435	48-8
LCD Lighting Inc 37 Robinson Blvd *TF:* 800-826-9465 ■ *Web:* www.light-sources.com	Orange	CT	06477	203-795-1520	795-2874	437
LCEC 4980 Bayline Dr *TF:* 800-282-1643 ■ *Web:* www.lcec.net	North Fort Myers	FL	33917	239-995-2121	995-7904	245
LCF Systems Inc 7755 E Gelding Dr Ste 105 *Web:* www.lcfsystems.com	Scottsdale	AZ	85260	480-247-6303		770
LCG Associates Inc 400 Galleria Pkwy SE *Web:* www.lcgassociates.com	Atlanta	GA	30339	770-644-0100	644-0105	401
LCG Inc 6000 Executive Blvd Ste 410 *Web:* www.lcginc.com	Rockville	MD	20852	301-984-4004		177
LCH Paper Tube & Core Co 11930 Larc Industrial Blvd *TF:* 800-472-3477 ■ *Web:* www.lchpapertube.com	Burnsville	MN	55337	952-358-3587	224-0087	125
LCI (Lannett Company Inc) 13200 Townsend Rd *NYSE: LCI* ■ *TF:* 800-325-9994 ■ *Web:* www.lannett.com	Philadelphia	PA	19154	215-333-9000	333-9004	479
LCI (Lawinger Consulting Inc) 106 Central Ave *Web:* www.lci-online.com	Osseo	MN	55369	763-425-7567	425-5483	196
LCI Graphics Inc 2400 Main St Ext Ste 8 *Web:* www.lcigraphics.com	Sayreville	NJ	08872	973-893-2913		627
LCJ (Lawyers for Civil Justice) 1140 Connecticut Ave NW Ste 503 *Web:* www.lfcj.com	Washington	DC	20036	202-429-0045	429-6982	49-10
LCL Bulk Transport Inc 2100 Riverside Dr *TF:* 855-525-2855 ■ *Web:* www.lclbulk.com	Green Bay	WI	54307	920-431-3500	431-3501	780
LCME (Liaison Committee on Medical Education) 330 N Wabash Ave Ste 39300 *Web:* lcme.org	Chicago	IL	60611	312-464-4933		48-1
LCMH (Lake Charles Memorial Health System) 1701 Oak Pk Blvd *TF:* 800-494-5264 ■ *Web:* www.lcmh.com	Lake Charles	LA	70601	337-494-3000		374-3
LCMS (Lutheran Church Missouri Synod) 1333 S Kirkwood Rd *TF:* 888-843-5267 ■ *Web:* www.lcms.org	Saint Louis	MO	63122	314-965-9000		48-20
LCNB National Bank 3209 W Galbraith Rd *TF:* 800-344-2265 ■ *Web:* www.lcnb.com	Cincinnati	OH	45239	513-932-1414		70

Phone | Fax | Class

Lco Casino Lodge & Convention Ctr
13767 W County Rd B Hayward WI 54843 715-634-5643 452
Web: www.sevenwindscasino.com

L-Com Inc 50 High St North Andover MA 01845 978-682-6936 253
TF: 800-341-5266 ■ *Web:* www.l-com.com

LCOR Inc 850 Cassatt Rd Ste 300 Berwyn PA 19312 610-251-9110 653
Web: lcor.com

LCP (Lake Claremont Press) PO Box 711 Chicago IL 60690 312-226-8400 226-8420 637-2
Web: www.lakeclaremont.com

LCPS (Lenoir County Public School)
2017 W Vernon Ave PO Box 729 Kinston NC 28504 252-527-1109 527-6884 685
Web: www.lcpsnc.org

Lcptracker Inc 117 E Chapman Ave Orange CA 92866 714-669-0052 684-0145* 179
**Fax Area Code:* 562 ■ *Web:* www.lcptracker.com

LCS (Leon County Schools)
2757 W Pensacola St Tallahassee FL 32304 850-487-7100 685
Web: www.leonschools.net

LCS Precision Molding Inc
119 S 2nd St Waterville MN 56096 507-362-8685 608
Web: www.lcsplastics.com

LCS Technologies Inc
11230 Gold Express Dr Ste 310-140 Gold River CA 95670 855-277-5527 624
TF: 855-277-5527 ■ *Web:* www.lcs-technologies-inc.com

LD Amory & Company Inc 101 S King St Hampton VA 23669 757-722-1915 297-5
Web: virginiaseafood.org

LD Systems LP 407 Garden Oaks Houston TX 77018 713-695-9400 695-8015 179
TF: 800-416-9327 ■ *Web:* www.ldsystems.com

LDA (Learning Disabilities Association of America)
4156 Library Rd Pittsburgh PA 15234 412-341-1515 344-0224 48-17
TF: 888-300-6710 ■ *Web:* ldaamerica.org

LDA (Lisa Davis Associates)
33 Bradford St Concord MA 01742 978-254-6287 194
Web: www.davisplanning.com

Lddi LLC
Pauahi Twr 1003 Bishop St Ste 2115 Honolulu HI 96813 808-522-1040 2
Web: detorcpa.com

LDG Electronics Inc
1445 Parran Rd Saint Leonard MD 20685 410-586-2177 586-8475 173-2
Web: www.ldgelectronics.com

LDI Industries 1864 Nage Ave Manitowoc WI 54220 920-682-6877 684-7210 790
Web: www.ldi-industries.com

LDI Ltd 54 Monument Cir Ste 800 Indianapolis IN 46204 317-237-5400 237-2280 185
Web: lacydiversified.com

LDI Mechanical Inc 1587 Bentley Dr Corona CA 92879 951-340-9685 610

LDP Inc 75 Kiwanis Blvd PO Box O Hazleton PA 18201 800-522-8413 178-3
TF: 800-522-8413 ■ *Web:* www.leaderservices.com

LDR Industries Inc 600 N Kilbourn Ave Chicago IL 60624 773-265-3000 609
Web: www.ldrind.com

LDS Consulting Group LLC
233 Needham St Newton MA 02464 617-454-1144 653
Web: ldsconsultinggroup.com

LDS Group, The
9016 Bluebonnet Blvd Baton Rouge LA 70810 225-769-9923 391-2
Web: theldsgroup.com

LDS Vacuum Products Inc
773 Big Tree Dr Longwood FL 32750 407-862-4643 862-8723 806
Web: ldsvacuumshopper.com

LDX Solutions
60 Chastain Center Blvd Ste 60 Kennesaw GA 30144 770-429-5575 429-5556 18
TF: 800-647-6167 ■ *Web:* www.ldxsolutions.com

LE (Leff Electronics Inc)
455 N Center Ave New Stanton PA 15672 724-925-3001 925-3022 246
TF: 800-245-4200 ■ *Web:* www.leff.com

Le Baluchon Eco-resort
3550 Chemin des Trembles Saint-Paulin QC J0K3G0 819-268-2555 268-5234 707
TF: 800-789-5968 ■ *Web:* www.baluchon.com

Le Bas Intl 16152 Beach Blvd Huntington Beach CA 92647 805-593-0510 593-0509 21
Web: www.lebas.com

Le Bistro 4626 N Federal Hwy Lighthouse Point FL 33064 954-946-9240 671
Web: www.lebistrorestaurant.com

Le Bleu Corp 3134 Cornatzer Rd Advance NC 27006 336-998-2894 805
TF: 800-854-4471 ■ *Web:* www.lebleu.com

Le Boulanger Inc 305 N Mathilda Sunnyvale CA 94085 408-774-9000 68
Web: www.leboulanger.com

Le Chamois 4557 Blackcomb Way Whistler BC V0N1B4 604-932-8700 379
TF: 888-621-1177 ■ *Web:* www.lechamoiswhistler.com

Le Cheval Restaurant 1007 Clay St Oakland CA 94607 510-763-8495 671
Web: www.lecheval.co

Le Colonial 937 N Rush St Chicago IL 60611 312-255-0088 671
Web: www.lecolonialchicago.com

Le Continental 26 Rue St-Louis Quebec City QC G1R3Y9 418-694-9995 671
Web: www.restaurantlecontinental.com

LE Cooke Co 26333 Rd 140 Visalia CA 93292 559-732-9146 732-3702 461
Web: www.lecooke.com

Le Coq Au Vin 4800 S Orange Ave Orlando FL 32806 407-851-6980 671
Web: www.lecoqauvinrestaurant.com

Le Creuset of America Inc
114 Bob Gifford Blvd Early Branch SC 29916 877-273-8738 943-4510* 486
**Fax Area Code:* 803 ■ *TF:* 877-273-8738

Le Devoir 1265 Berri 8th Fl Montreal QC H2L4X4 514-985-3333 985-3360 532-1
TF: 800-463-7559 ■ *Web:* www.ledevoir.com

Le Fou Frog 400 E Fifth St Kansas City MO 64106 816-474-6060 671
Web: www.lefoufrog.com

Le Gourmand 4100 Fourth Ave S Seattle WA 98134 206-588-9728 671
Web: www.legourmandseattle.com

Le Groupe Genitique Inc
2655 boul of the Kingdom Ste 480 Jonquiere QC G7S4S9 418-548-4626 196
Web: www.genitique.com

LE Johnson Products Inc
2100 Sterling Ave Elkhart IN 46516 574-293-5664 294-4697 350
TF: 800-837-5664 ■ *Web:* www.johnsonhardware.com

LE Jones Co 1200 34th Ave Menominee MI 49858 906-863-4411 128
Web: www.lejones.com

Le Languedoc Bistro 24 Broad St Nantucket MA 02554 508-228-2552 671
Web: languedocbistro.com

Le Lapin Saute
52 ru du Petit-Champlain Quebec City QC G1K4H4 418-692-5325 671
Web: www.lapinsaute.com

Le Mars Insurance Co PO Box 1608 Le Mars IA 51031 800-545-6480 390
TF: 800-545-6480 ■ *Web:* www.lemm.com

Le Moyne College
1419 Salt Springs Rd Syracuse NY 13214 315-445-4100 445-4711 166
TF: 800-333-4733 ■ *Web:* www.lemoyne.edu

Le Nil Bleu 3706 St-Denis Montreal QC H2X3L7 514-285-4628 671
Web: www.nilbleurestaurant.com

Le Nouvel Montreal Hotel & Spa
1740 Rene-Levesque Blvd W Montreal QC H3H1R3 514-931-8841 931-5581 379
TF: 800-363-6063 ■ *Web:* www.lenouvelhotel.com

Le Papillon 410 Saratoga Ave San Jose CA 95129 408-296-3730 671
Web: www.lepapillon.com

Le Papillon on Front 69 Front St E Toronto ON M5E1B5 416-367-0303 671
Web: www.papillononfront.com

Le Parc Suite Hotel
733 N West Knoll Dr West Hollywood CA 90069 310-855-8888 659-7812 379
TF: 877-591-9556 ■ *Web:* www.leparcsuites.com

Le Pavillon Hotel 833 Poydras St New Orleans LA 70112 504-581-3111 620-4130 379
TF: 844-656-8636 ■ *Web:* www.lepavillon.com

Le Petit Cafe 308 W 6th St Bloomington IN 47404 812-334-9747 671

LE Phillips Memorial Public Library
400 Eau Claire St Eau Claire WI 54701 715-839-5004 434-3
Web: www.ecpubliclibrary.info

Le Pichet 1933 First Ave Seattle WA 98101 206-256-1499 671
Web: lepichetseattle.com

Le Port-Royal Hotel & Suites
144 St Pierre St Quebec City QC G1K8N8 418-692-2777 379
TF: 866-417-2777 ■ *Web:* www.leportroyal.com

Le Quotidien & Progres Dimanche
1051 Boul Talbot Chicoutimi QC G7H5C1 418-545-4664 532-1
TF: 800-866-3658 ■ *Web:* www.lequotidien.com

Le Refuge Restaurant
127 N Washington St Alexandria VA 22314 703-548-4661 671
Web: www.lerefugealexandria.com

Le Rendez-vous 3844 E Ft Lowell Rd Tucson AZ 85716 520-323-7373 671
Web: www.rendezvoustucson.com

Le Richelieu Hotel
1234 Chartres St New Orleans LA 70116 800-535-9653 524-8179* 379
**Fax Area Code:* 504 ■ *Web:* www.jcollectionhotels.com

Le Saint Sulpice 414 Rue St Sulpice Montreal QC H2Y2V5 514-288-1000 288-0077 379
TF: 877-785-7423 ■ *Web:* www.lesaintsulpice.com

Le Saint-Amour
48 Sainte-Ursule St Quebec City QC G1R4E2 418-694-0667 694-0967 671
Web: www.saint-amour.com

LE Schwartz & Son Inc 279 Reid St Macon GA 31206 478-745-6563 745-2711 189-12
Web: www.leschwartz.com

Le Smith Co, The 1030 E Wilson St Bryan OH 43506 419-636-4555 633-6616 350
Web: www.lesmith.com

Le Soleil
410 Blvd Charest E Branch Terminus Quebec City QC G1K7J6 418-686-3233 532-1
Web: www.lesoleil.com

Le Sueur County 88 S Park Ave Le Center MN 56057 507-357-2251 357-6375 338
Web: www.co.le-sueur.mn.us

Le Sueur Manufacturing Co
3220 Lorna Rd Birmingham AL 35216 205-822-0720 822-0721 203
Web: lesueurmoisturecontrols.com

Le Tourneau Plastics Inc
160 Charles St Oconto WI 54153 920-834-2777 596
Web: www.letourneauplastics.net

Le Vallauris
385 W Tahquitz Canyon Way Palm Springs CA 92262 760-325-5059 671
Web: palmsprings.com

Le Yaca 1430 High St Williamsburg VA 23185 757-220-3616 671
Web: www.leyacawilliamsburg.com

LEA Book Distributors 170-23 83rd Ave Jamaica NY 11432 718-291-9891 96
Web: www.leabooks.com

LEA Consulting 625 Cochrane Dr 9th Fl Markham ON L3R9R9 905-470-0015 194
Web: lea.ca

Lea County 100 N Main St Ste 11 Lovington NM 88260 575-396-8619 396-3293 338
TF: 800-658-9955 ■ *Web:* www.leacounty.net

Lea County Electric Cooperative Inc
1300 W Ave D Lovington NM 88260 575-396-3631 396-3634 245
TF: 800-510-5232 ■ *Web:* www.leacountyelectric.coop

Lea Regional Medical Ctr
5419 N Lovington Hwy Hobbs NM 88240 575-492-5000 492-5505 374-3
TF: 877-492-8001 ■ *Web:* www.learegionalmedical.com

LEA-AID (Law Enforcement Associates Corp)
120 Penmarc Dr Ste 113 Raleigh NC 27603 919-872-6210 201-2109* 52
OTC: LAWEQ ■ **Fax Area Code:* 844 ■ *TF:* 800-354-9669 ■ *Web:* www.leacorp.com

Leach Botanical Garden
6704 SE 122 Ave PO Box 90667 Portland OR 97236 503-823-9503 97
Web: www.leachgarden.org

Leach Enterprises 4304 Il Rt 176 Crystal Lake IL 60014 815-459-6917 57
Web: www.leach-ent.com

Leach Farms Inc
W1102 Buttercup Ct PO Box 192 Berlin WI 54923 920-361-1880 361-4474 10-11
Web: www.leachfarms.com

Leach International Corp
6900 Orangethorpe Ave Buena Park CA 90620 714-736-7598 739-1713 203
TF: 800-232-7700 ■ *Web:* leachcorp.com

Leaco 220 W Broadway Hobbs NM 88240 575-370-5010 224
Web: www.leaco.net

Lead Concepts Inc 1060 Texan Trl Grapevine TX 76051 800-238-0140 463
TF: 800-238-0140 ■ *Web:* leadconcepts.com

Lead IT Corp
1999 Wabash Ave Ste 210 Springfield IL 62704 217-726-7250 180
Web: www.leaditgroup.com

Lead Pulse Media
324 S Beverly Dr Ste 272 Beverly Hills CA 90212 424-245-4591 7
Web: www.leadpulsemedia.com

Lead Technologies Inc
1927 S Tryon St Ste 200 Charlotte NC 28203 704-332-5532 177
TF: 800-637-4699 ■ *Web:* www.leadtools.com

LeadCreations com LLC
12717 W Sunrise Blvd Ste 312 Fort Lauderdale FL 33323 305-831-0999 195
Web: www.leadcreations.com

Leader & Berkon LLP 630 Third Ave New York NY 10017 212-486-2400 486-3099 445
Web: www.leaderberkon.com

				Phone	Fax	Class
Leader Business Systems 35436 Mound Rd *Web:* www.leaderbusiness.com	Sterling Heights	MI	48310	586-264-4908		525
Leader Capital Corp 7412 SW Beaverton Hillsdale Hwy Ste 210 *TF:* 800-269-8810 ■ *Web:* www.leadercapital.com	Portland	OR	97232	503-294-1010		690
Leader Engineering Fabrication Inc 695 Independence Dr *Web:* www.lefusa.com	Napoleon	OH	43545	419-592-0008		757
Leader Global Technologies Inc 905 W 13th St *Web:* www.leadergt.com	Deer Park	TX	77536	281-542-0600		326
Leader Graphic Design Inc 5050 Newport Dr Ste 5 *Web:* www.leadergraphics.com	Rolling Meadows	IL	60008	847-564-5409		195
Leader Industries 10941 Weaver Ave *Web:* leaderambulance.com	South El Monte	CA	91733	626-575-0880		59
Leader Newspapers 3500 T C Jester Blvd PO Box 924487 *Web:* theleadernews.com	Houston	TX	77292	713-686-8494	686-0970	532-4
Leader Promotions Inc 790 E Johnstown Rd *TF:* 877-677-9988 ■ *Web:* www.leaderpromos.com	Columbus	OH	43230	614-416-6565		4
Leader Publications 217 N Fourth St *Web:* www.leaderpub.com	Niles	MI	49120	269-683-2100		532-3
Leader Union, The 229 S Fifth St *Web:* www.leaderunion.com	Vandalia	IL	62471	618-283-3374		637-8
Leader Vindicator, The 435 Broad St *Web:* www.thecourierexpress.com	New Bethlehem	PA	16242	814-275-3131	275-3531	532-2
Leader's Edge 2 Bala Plz Ste 300 *Web:* the-leaders-edge.com	Bala Cynwyd	PA	19004	610-660-6684		41
Leader, The 34 W Pulteney St *Web:* www.the-leader.com	Corning	NY	14830	607-936-4651		532-2
Leaders Bank, The 2001 York Rd Ste 150 *Web:* www.leadersbank.com	Oak Brook	IL	60523	630-572-5323		70
Leaders Casual Furniture 6303 126th Ave *Web:* leadersfurniture.com	Largo	FL	33773	727-538-5577		321
Leaders LLC 14 Maine St Ste 216G PO Box 18 *TF:* 888-583-7770 ■ *Web:* www.leaders-llc.com	Brunswick	ME	04011	207-318-1893		690
Leaders Magazine Inc 59 E 54th St *Web:* www.leadersmag.com	New York	NY	10022	212-758-0740		41
Leadership Conference on Civil Rights (LCCR) 1620 L St NW Ste 1100 *Web:* www.civilrights.org	Washington	DC	20036	202-466-3311	466-3435	48-8
Leadership Connect Inc 1407 Broadway Ste 318 *TF:* 800-627-0311 ■ *Web:* www.leadershipconnect.io	New York	NY	10018	212-627-4140	645-0931	637-2
Leadership Management International Inc 4567 Lake Shore Dr *TF:* 800-876-2389 ■ *Web:* lmi-world.com	Waco	TX	76710	254-776-2060	772-9588	765
Leadership Performance Solutions Inc 235 Court St *TF:* 800-511-6150 ■ *Web:* www.leadershipperformance.com	Newtown	PA	18940	800-511-6150		196
Leadership Public Schools 344 Thomas L Berkley Way *Web:* www.leadps.org	Oakland	CA	94612	510-830-3780	225-2575	685
Leading Age 2519 Connecticut Ave NW *TF:* 866-898-2624 ■ *Web:* www.leadingage.org	Washington	DC	20008	202-783-2242	783-2255	48-6
Leading Authorities Inc 1725 Eye St NW Ste 200 **Fax Area Code:* 202 ■ *TF:* 855-827-0943 ■ *Web:* www.leadingauthorities.com	Washington	DC	20006	855-827-0943	783-0301*	708
Leading Hotels of the World 485 Lexington Ave Ste 401 *TF:* 800-745-8883 ■ *Web:* www.lhw.com	New York	NY	10017	212-515-5600		376
Leading Jewelers Guild Inc 5601 W Slauson Ave Ste 244 *Web:* leadingjewelersguild.org	Culver City	CA	90230	310-216-9106		411
Leading Lady 24050 Commerce Pk *TF:* 800-321-4804 ■ *Web:* www.leadinglady.com	Beachwood	OH	44122	800-321-4804		155-18
Leading Market Technologies Inc 58 Winter St 5th Fl *Web:* www.lmtech.com	Boston	MA	02108	617-494-4747		204
Leading Systems Technologies Inc (LST) 2721 Prosperity Ave Ste 100	Fairfax	VA	22031	703-204-0404		463
Leading Technology Composites Inc 2626 W May *Web:* ltc-ltc.com	Wichita	KS	67213	316-944-0011		504
LeadingResponse LLC 4805 Independence Pkwy *TF:* 800-660-2550 ■ *Web:* www.leadingresponse.com	Tampa	FL	33634	800-660-2550		5
Leadman Electronic USA Inc 382 Laurelwood Dr *TF:* 877-532-3626 ■ *Web:* www.leadman.com	Santa Clara	CA	95054	408-738-1751	738-2620	174
LeadMD Inc 15001 N 74th St Ste A *Web:* www.leadmd.com	Scottsdale	AZ	85260	480-278-7205		195
LeadMinders LLC 1600 Hover St *Web:* www.leadminders.com	Longmont	CO	80501	720-552-5650		5
LeadRival 1207 S White Chapel Blvd Ste 250 *TF:* 800-332-8017 ■ *Web:* www.leadrival.com	Southlake	TX	76092	800-332-8017		5
LeadScope Inc 1393 Dublin Rd *Web:* www.leadscope.com	Columbus	OH	43215	614-675-3730	675-3732	177
LeadSwell PO Box 170432 *Web:* leadswell.com	San Francisco	CA	94117	415-518-6701		317
Leadtek Research Inc 910 Auburn Ct *Web:* www.leadtek.com	Fremont	CA	94538	510-490-8076		625
Leaf Chronicle 200 Commerce St **Fax Area Code:* 615 ■ *TF:* 877-424-0154 ■ *Web:* www.theleafchronicle.com	Clarksville	TN	37040	931-552-1808	259-8820*	637-8
LEAF Commercial Capital Inc 1 Commerce Sq 2005 Market St 14th Fl **Fax Area Code:* 267 ■ *TF:* 800-819-5556 ■ *Web:* www.leafnow.com	Philadelphia	PA	19103	800-819-5556	675-5750*	23
Leaf, Miele, Manganelli, Fortunato & Engel 310 Passaic Ave *Web:* www.leafsaltzman.com	Fairfield	NJ	07004	973-808-9500		2
League for Innovation in the Community College 4505 E Chandler Blvd Ste 250 *Web:* www.league.org	Phoenix	AZ	85048	480-705-8200	705-8201	48-11
League of American Bicyclists 1612 K St NW Ste 800 *Web:* www.bikeleague.org	Washington	DC	20006	202-822-1333	822-1334	48-22
League of American Orchestras 33 W 60th St 5th Fl *Web:* www.americanorchestras.org	New York	NY	10023	212-262-5161	262-5198	48-4
League of Arizona Cities and Towns 1820 W Washington St *Web:* www.azleague.org	Phoenix	AZ	85007	602-258-5786	253-3874	48-13
League of Conservation Voters 1920 L St NW Ste 800 *Web:* www.lcv.org	Washington	DC	20036	202-785-8683	835-0491	48-7
League of Kansas Municipalities, The 300 SW Eighth Ave Ste 100 *TF:* 800-445-5588 ■ *Web:* www.lkm.org	Topeka	KS	66603	785-354-9565	354-4186	533
League of Minnesota Cities (LMC) 145 University Ave W *TF:* 800-925-1122 ■ *Web:* www.lmc.org	Saint Paul	MN	55103	651-281-1200	281-1299	49-19
League of Resident Theatres (LORT) 1501 Broadway Ste 1801 *Web:* lort.org	New York	NY	10036	212-944-1501		48-4
League of Women Voters (LWV) 1730 M St NW Ste 1000 *Web:* www.lwv.org	Washington	DC	20036	202-429-1965	429-0854	48-7
League of Women Voters Minnesota (LWVMN) 550 Rice St *Web:* www.lwvmn.org	Saint Paul	MN	55103	651-224-5445		637-2
League of Women Voters of Atlanta-Fulton County PO Box 420705 *Web:* www.lwvaf.org	Atlanta	GA	30342	404-577-8683		615
League of Women Voters of Metropolitan Tulsa (LWV) 3336 E 32nd St Ste 4 *Web:* www.lwvtulsa.org	Tulsa	OK	74135	918-747-7933		48-13
League of Women Voters of New York State (LWVNYS) 62 Grand St *Web:* www.lwvny.org	Albany	NY	12207	518-465-4162	465-0812	615
League of Women Voters of Ohio Education Fund (LWVOEF) 17 S High St Ste 650 *TF:* 800-598-6446 ■ *Web:* www.lwvohio.org	Columbus	OH	43215	614-469-1505	469-7918	637-2
League to Save Lake Tahoe 2608 Lake Tahoe Blvd *Web:* www.keeptahoeblue.org	South Lake Tahoe	CA	96150	530-541-5388	541-5454	48-13
Leahy Patrick J (Sen D - VT) 437 Russell Senate Office Bldg *Web:* www.leahy.senate.gov	Washington	DC	20510	202-224-4242	224-3479	342-2
Leahy's Fuels Inc 130 White St *TF:* 800-932-8084 ■ *Web:* leahys.com	Danbury	CT	06810	203-748-3535	616-2100	316
Leake & Andersson 1100 Poydras St Ste 1700 *Web:* leakeandersson.com	New Orleans	LA	70163	504-585-7500	585-7775	41
Leaktite Corp 40 Francis St *TF:* 800-392-0039 ■ *Web:* www.leaktite.com	Leominster	MA	01453	978-537-8000	534-3539	608
Leal Trejo, A Professional Corp 3767 Worsham Ave *Web:* leal-law.com	Long Beach	CA	90808	213-628-0808	628-0818	41
Leam Drilling Systems Inc 2027A Airport Rd *TF:* 800-426-5349 ■ *Web:* leam.net	Conroe	TX	77301	800-426-5349		539
Leamington District Chamber of Commerce 318 Erie St S *Web:* leamingtonchamber.com	Leamington	ON	N8H3C5	519-326-2721	326-3204	137
Lean Horizons Consulting PO Box 1402 *Web:* leanhorizons.com	Glastonbury	CT	06033	860-430-1174		538
Leanin' Tree Inc 6055 Longbow Dr *TF:* 800-525-0656 ■ *Web:* www.leanintree.com	Boulder	CO	80301	800-525-0656		130
Leaning Pine Publishing Co 13236 W Chicago Bloomington Trl *Web:* www.mtnviewranch-cowles.com	Homer Glen	IL	60491	815-485-8161		637-2
Leanplum 1550 Bryant St Unit 545 *TF:* 844-532-6758 ■ *Web:* www.leanplum.com	San Francisco	CA	94103	844-532-6758		788
LeanTaaS 471 El Camino Real Ste 230 *Web:* www.leantaas.com	Santa Clara	CA	95050	650-409-3247		353
Leantrak Inc 1645 Indian Wood Cir Ste 101 *Web:* leantrak.com	Maumee	OH	43537	419-482-0797	482-6801	261
LEAP 2500 Technology Dr *Web:* www.leapagency.com	Louisville	KY	40299	502-212-1390		5
Leap/Carpenter/Kemps Insurance Agency 3187 Collins Dr *TF:* 800-221-0864 ■ *Web:* www.lckinsurance.com	Merced	CA	95348	209-384-0727		390
LeapFrog Enterprises Inc 6401 Hollis St Ste 100 *NYSE: LF* ■ *TF:* 800-701-5327 ■ *Web:* www.leapfrog.com	Emeryville	CA	94608	510-420-5000		762
Leapfrog Services Inc 1190 W Druid Hills Dr Ste 200 *TF:* 866-260-9478 ■ *Web:* leapfrogservices.com	Atlanta	GA	30329	404-870-2122	870-2123	180
LeapFrog Systems Inc 1 International Pl *Web:* www.leapfrogsystems.com	Boston	MA	02110	617-224-9700		177
Lear Capital Inc 1990 S Bundy Dr Ste 600 *TF:* 800-576-9355 ■ *Web:* www.learcapital.com	Los Angeles	CA	90025	800-576-9355		251
Lear Corp 21557 Telegraph Rd *Web:* www.lear.com	Southfield	MI	48033	248-447-1500		247
Learfield Communications Inc 505 Hobbs Rd *Web:* www.learfield.com	Jefferson City	MO	65109	573-893-7200		644
Learning A-Z 1840 E River Rd No 320 **Fax Area Code:* 520 ■ *TF:* 866-889-3729 ■ *Web:* www.learninga-z.com	Tucson	AZ	85718	866-889-3729	327-9934*	178-1
Learning Care Group Inc 21333 Haggerty Rd Ste 300 *TF:* 877-817-3883 ■ *Web:* www.learningcaregroup.com	Novi	MI	48375	248-697-9000	697-9002	148

	Phone	Fax	Class
Learning Co 1620 SW Taylor St No 100..........Portland OR 97205 *TF:* 800-580-4640 ■ *Web:* www.learning.com	800-580-4640		637-10
Learning Communications LLC 5520 Trabuco Rd..............................Irvine CA 92620 **Fax Area Code:* 949 ■ *TF:* 800-622-3610	800-622-3610	727-4323*	513
Learning Designs Inc 614 Main St Ste 305 PO Box 656..............Park City UT 84060 *Web:* www.learningdesigns.biz	435-645-9515		463
Learning Disabilities Association of America (LDA) 4156 Library Rd ....Pittsburgh PA 15234 *TF:* 888-300-6710 ■ *Web:* ldaamerica.org	412-341-1515	344-0224	48-17
Learning Edge, The PO Box 97041 ....Tacoma WA 98497 *Web:* www.lepublishing.com	253-588-5174	588-1594	637-2
Learning Express Inc 29 Buena Vista St ....Devens MA 01434 *TF:* 888-725-8697 ■ *Web:* learningexpress.com	978-889-1000		761
Learning Guild, The 120 Stony Point Rd Ste 200.................Santa Rosa CA 95401 *Web:* www.learningguild.com	707-566-8990		196
Learning Multi-Systems Inc 1402 Greenway Cross.......................Madison WI 53713 *TF:* 800-362-7323 ■ *Web:* www.lmssite.com	608-273-8060	273-8065	177
Learning Network, The 401 Glenneyre St Ste C..................Laguna Beach CA 92651 *TF:* 866-798-5897 ■ *Web:* learning.net	949-221-8600	497-5569	463
Learning Objects LLC 1528 Connecticut Ave NW ....Washington DC 20036 *Web:* www.learningobjects.com	202-265-3276		177
Learning Research & Development Ctr (LRDC) University of Pittsburgh 3939 O'Hara St........Pittsburgh PA 15260 *Web:* www.lrdc.pitt.edu	412-624-7020	624-9149	668
Learning Resources 380 N Fairway Dr ....Vernon Hills IL 60061 *TF:* 800-222-3909 ■ *Web:* www.learningresources.com	847-573-8400	573-8425	243
Learning Services 2095 Laura St Ste H ....Springfield OR 97477 *TF:* 800-877-9378 ■ *Web:* www.learningservicesus.com	800-877-9378	815-5154	174
Learning Source Ltd 644 Tenth St ....Brooklyn NY 11215 *Web:* www.learningsourceltd.com	718-768-0231	369-3467	94
Learning Systems Institute 4600 University Ctr.......................Tallahassee FL 32306 *Web:* www.lsi.fsu.edu	850-644-2570		668
Learning Tree International Inc 1831 Michael Faraday Dr ....Reston VA 20190 *OTC:* LTRE ■ *TF:* 800-843-8733 ■ *Web:* www.learningtree.com	703-709-9119		764
Learning Tree School 9100 Diceman Dr ....Dallas TX 75218 *Web:* www.thelearningtreeschool.net	214-320-9690		637-2
Learning Unlimited 4137 S Harvard Ave Ste A........................Tulsa OK 74135 *TF:* 888-622-4203 ■ *Web:* learningunlimited.com	918-622-3292		463
Learning Works 181 Brackett St ....Portland ME 04102 *Web:* www.learningworks.me	207-775-0105		243
Learning Worlds Inc 2647 Broadway Ste 5W......................New York NY 10025 *Web:* learningworlds.com	212-725-0436	725-7267	180
Learning Wrap-Ups Inc 1660 W Gordon Ave Ste 4 ....Layton UT 84041 *TF:* 800-992-4966 ■ *Web:* learningwrapups.com	801-497-0050	497-0063	243
LearningWare Inc 700 Raymond Ave ....Saint Paul MN 55114 *TF:* 800-457-5661 ■ *Web:* www.learningware.com	612-904-6878	904-1781	178-1
LearnKey Inc 35 N Main ....Saint George UT 84770 *TF:* 800-865-0165 ■ *Web:* www.learnkey.com	800-865-0165		514
LearnSpectrum 9912 Georgetown Pke Ste D203..............Great Falls VA 22066 *TF:* 888-682-9485 ■ *Web:* www.learnspectrum.com	703-757-8200	757-8202	317
LearnWell 2 Main St Ste 2A...................Plymouth MA 02360 *Web:* learnwelleducation.com	508-732-9101	732-9717	148
Lease Crutcher Lewis 2200 Western Ave Ste 500 ....Seattle WA 98121 **Fax Area Code:* 202 ■ *Web:* lewisbuilds.com	206-622-0500	622-6451*	186
Lease Harbor LLC 3350 W Salt Creek Ln Ste 100 ....Arlington Heights IL 60005 *Web:* leaseharbor.com	312-494-9470		177
Lease Plan USA 1165 Sanctuary Pkwy ....Alpharetta GA 30009 *TF:* 877-645-3750 ■ *Web:* www.leaseplan.com	877-645-3750		289
LeaseQ Inc 1 Burlington Woods Dr Ste 200 ....Burlington MA 01803 *TF:* 888-688-4519 ■ *Web:* www.leaseq.com	781-281-2436		393
Leasing Associates Inc 12600 N Featherwood Dr Ste 400...............Houston TX 77034 *TF:* 800-449-4807 ■ *Web:* www.theleasingcompany.com	832-300-1300	300-1317	289
Leasing Technologies Intl 221 Danbury Rd ....Wilton CT 06897 *Web:* www.ltileasing.com	203-563-1100	563-1112	264-1
Leason Ellis LLP 1 Barker Ave 5th Fl ....White Plains NY 10601 **Fax Area Code:* 914 ■ *Web:* www.leasonellis.com	212-532-4900	288-0023*	428
Leath Correctional Institution 2809 Airport Rd ....Greenwood SC 29649 **Fax Area Code:* 803 ■ *Web:* doc.sc.gov	864-229-5709	896-1766*	213
Leather Bros Inc 1314 Nabholz Ave ....Conway AR 72034 *TF:* 800-442-5522 ■ *Web:* www.leatherbrothers.com	501-329-9471	329-9820	432
Leather Creations Inc 2692 Peachtree Sq ....Atlanta GA 30360 *Web:* www.leathercreationsfurniture.com	678-584-1000		321
Leather Specialty Co, The 1088 Business Ln............................Naples FL 34110	239-333-1000		453
Leathercraft 102 Section House Rd ....Conover NC 28613 *TF:* 800-627-1561 ■ *Web:* www.leathercraft-furniture.com	800-627-1561	627-1562	319-2
Leatherman Tool Group Inc 12106 NE Ainsworth Cir......................Portland OR 97220 *TF:* 800-847-8665 ■ *Web:* www.leatherman.com	503-253-7826	253-7830	758
Leatherock International Inc 5285 Lovelock St ....San Diego CA 92110 *TF:* 800-466-6667 ■ *Web:* leatherock.com	619-299-7625		432
Leavcon II Inc 108 American Ave ....Lansing KS 66043 *Web:* www.leavcon.com	913-351-1430	351-1597	183
Leave No Trace Center for Outdoor Ethics Inc 1830 17th St..............................Boulder CO 80302 *TF:* 800-332-4100 ■ *Web:* lnt.org	303-442-8222		48-23

	Phone	Fax	Class
Leavell Insurance 117 E Broadway...............Hobbs NM 88240 *Web:* www.leavellinsurance.com	575-393-2550		390
Leavenworth Convention & Visitors Bureau 100 N Fifth St Rm 104 ....Leavenworth KS 66048 *Web:* www.visitleavenworthks.com	913-758-2948		206
Leavenworth County 300 Walnut St Ste 106 ....Leavenworth KS 66048 *TF:* 855-893-9533 ■ *Web:* www.leavenworthcounty.gov	913-684-0421		338
Leavenworth Public Library 417 Spruce St..........................Leavenworth KS 66048 *Web:* leavenworthpubliclibrary.org	913-682-5666	682-1248	434-3
Leavenworth Times 422 Seneca............Leavenworth KS 66048 *Web:* www.leavenworthtimes.com	913-682-0305		532-2
Leavenworth-Jefferson Electric Co-opeartive Inc 507 N Union St............................McLouth KS 66054 *TF:* 888-796-6111 ■ *Web:* www.ljec.coop	888-796-6111		245
Leavenworth-Lansing Area Chamber of Commerce 518 Shawnee St ....Leavenworth KS 66048 *Web:* www.llchamber.com	913-682-4112	682-8170	139
Leavitt Corp, The 100 Santilli Hwy...............Everett MA 02149 *Web:* teddie.com	617-389-2600	387-9085	296-28
Leavitt Group Enterprises 216 S 200 W.............................Cedar City UT 84720 *TF:* 800-264-8085 ■ *Web:* leavitt.com	435-586-6553	586-1510	390
Leavitt Machinery & Rentals Inc 24389 Fraser Hwy.............................Langley BC V2Z2L3 *TF:* 877-850-6499 ■ *Web:* www.leavittmachinery.com	604-607-4450		358
Lebanese Taverna 719 S President St ....Baltimore MD 21202 *Web:* lebanesetaverna.com	410-244-5533		671
Lebanon 866 UN Plz Rm 531-533 ....New York NY 10017 *Web:* www.lebanonun.com	212-355-5460	838-2819	784
Lebanon *Consulate General* 9 E 76th St................New York NY 10021 *Web:* www.nylebcons.org	212-744-7905	794-1510	257
Embassy 2560 28th St NW ....Washington DC 20008 *Web:* www.lebanonembassyus.org	202-939-6300		257
LeBaron Area Chamber of Commerce 186 N Adams St ....Lebanon MO 65536 *TF:* 888-588-5710 ■ *Web:* lebanonmissouri.com	417-588-3256	588-3251	139
Lebanon Building Supply Co 225 N 10th St..............................Lebanon PA 17046 *Web:* www.lebanonbuildingsupplyco.com	717-272-4649	272-1628	191-3
Lebanon Correctional Institution 3791 SR-63 ....Lebanon OH 45036 *Web:* drc.ohio.gov	513-932-1211	932-1320	213
Lebanon County 400 S Eigth St.................Lebanon PA 17042 *Web:* www.lebcounty.org	717-274-2801	274-8094	338
Lebanon Daily News 718 Poplar St ....Lebanon PA 17042 *TF:* 800-457-5929 ■ *Web:* www.ldnews.com	717-272-5611	274-1608	532-2
Lebanon Express 90 E Grant....................Lebanon OR 97355 *Web:* www.lebanon-express.com	541-258-3151	259-3569	532-2
Lebanon High School 700 Holbrook Ave ....Lebanon OH 45036 *Web:* www.lebanonschools.org	513-934-5770	932-5906	685
Lebanon National Cemetery 20 Hwy 208.........Lebanon KY 40033 *Web:* www.cem.va.gov	270-692-3390	692-0018	136
Lebanon Public Library 101 S Broadway.........Lebanon OH 45036 *Web:* lebanonlibrary.org	513-932-2665		434-3
Lebanon Publishing Company Inc 402 N Cumberland St........................Lebanon TN 37087 *Web:* www.lebanondemocrat.com	615-444-3952		532-3
Lebanon Seaboard Corp 1600 E Cumberland St ....Lebanon PA 17042 *TF:* 800-233-0628 ■ *Web:* lebsea.com	717-273-1685		280
Lebanon Valley Chamber of Commerce 604 Cumberland St..........................Lebanon PA 17042 *Web:* www.lvchamber.org	717-273-3727	273-7940	139
Lebanon Valley College 101 N College Ave ....Annville PA 17003 *TF:* 866-582-4236 ■ *Web:* www.lvc.edu	717-867-6181	867-6026	166
Lebanon-Wilson County Chamber of Commerce 149 Public Sq..............................Lebanon TN 37087 *Web:* www.lebanonwilsontnchamber.org	615-444-5503		139
Lebanon-Wilson County Public Library 108 S Hatton Ave ....Lebanon TN 37087	615-444-0632		434-3
LeBaron Bonney Co 6 Chestnut St ....Amesbury MA 01913 *TF:* 800-221-5408 ■ *Web:* www.lebaronbonney.com	800-221-5408		34
Lebco Graphics Inc 31400 IH-10 W..............Boerne TX 78006 *TF:* 800-725-3226 ■ *Web:* www.lebcographics.com	210-698-3062	698-0103	627
LeBeouf Brothers Towing LLC 124 Dry Dock Rd ....Bourg LA 70343 *Web:* www.lebeouftowing.com	985-594-6691	594-5253	465
Leblon 106 S Holden Rd ....Greensboro NC 27407 *Web:* www.leblonsteakhouse.com	336-294-2605		671
Lebowitz & Mzhen LLC 9 Park Center Ct Ste 220 ....Owings Mills MD 21117 *TF:* 800-654-1949 ■ *Web:* marylandinjurylawyer.net	410-654-3600	654-3601	41
Lebowitz Gould Design Inc 150 W 30th St Ste 1202 ....New York NY 10001 *Web:* lgd-inc.com	212-695-5700		344
Lebus International Inc 215 Industrial Dr..........................Longview TX 75602 *Web:* lebus-intl.com	903-758-5521	757-7782	198
LEC (Lincoln Electric Co-opeartive Inc) 500 Osloski Rd PO Box 628....................Eureka MT 59917 *TF:* 800-442-2994 ■ *Web:* www.lincolnelectric.coop	406-889-3301	889-3874	245
LEC Environmental Consultants Inc 384 Lowell St Ste 101.......................Wakefield MA 01880 *Web:* www.lecenvironmental.com	781-245-2500	245-6677	192
Lec Inc 110 Excell Dr ....Pearl MS 39208 *TF:* 800-439-8535 ■ *Web:* www.lecinc.com	601-939-8535	939-9427	261
Lecanto Veterinary Hospital 1250 S Lecanto Hwy.........................Lecanto FL 34461 *Web:* lecantovethospital.com	352-270-8819		794
LeCesse Development Corp 650 S Northlake Blvd Ste 450..........Altamonte Springs FL 32701 *Web:* www.lecesse.com	407-645-5575	645-0553	653
LeChase Construction Services LLC (LC) 205 Indigo Creek Dr........................Rochester NY 14626 *TF:* 888-953-2427 ■ *Web:* www.lechase.com	585-254-3510	254-3871	186

	Phone	Fax	Class
Lechler Inc 445 Kautz Rd . . . . . Saint Charles IL 60174 **Fax Area Code: 800* ■ *TF:* 800-777-2926 ■ *Web:* www.lechlerusa.com	630-377-6611	444-7069*	487
Lechner Realty Group Inc 13421 Manchester Rd. . . . . . Saint Louis MO 63131 *Web:* www.lechnerrealty.com	314-909-8100	909-8105	652
Leco Corp 3000 Lakeview Ave . . . . . Saint Joseph MI 49085 *TF:* 800-292-6141 ■ *Web:* leco.com	269-985-5496	982-8977	419
Lecole Culinaire 9811 S Forty Dr . . . . . Saint Louis MO 63124 *TF:* 866-205-2521 ■ *Web:* www.lecole.edu	314-587-2433		167-3
Leconte Wealth Management LLC 703 William Blount Dr . . . . . Maryville TN 37801 *TF:* 888-236-6630 ■ *Web:* lecontewealth.com	865-379-8200		401
Lecoq Cuisine Corp 35 Union Ave . . . . . Bridgeport CT 06607 *Web:* lecoqcuisine.com	203-334-1010	334-1800	297-11
LeCroy Corp 700 Chestnut Ridge Rd. . . . . . Chestnut Ridge NY 10977 *NASDAQ: LCRY* ■ *TF:* 800-553-2769 ■ *Web:* teledynelecroy.com	845-425-2000	425-8967	248
Lectra USA Inc 889 Franklin Rd SE Bldg 100 . . . . . Marietta GA 30067 *Web:* www.lectra.com	770-422-8050		180
Lectronix Inc 5858 Enterprise Dr. . . . . . Lansing MI 48911 *Web:* www.lectronixinc.com	517-492-1900		494
Lectrosonics Inc PO Box 15900. . . . . . Rio Rancho NM 87174 *TF:* 800-821-1121 ■ *Web:* www.lectrosonics.com	505-892-4501	892-6243	52
LED Supply Co 12340 W Cedar Dr. . . . . . Lakewood CO 80228 *TF:* 877-595-4769 ■ *Web:* ledsupplyco.com	877-595-4769		196
Leda Corp 7080 Kearny Dr . . . . . Huntington Beach CA 92648 *Web:* www.ledacorp.net	714-841-7821	842-3683	625
Ledalite 9087A 198 St . . . . . Langley BC V1M3B2 *TF:* 800-665-5332 ■ *Web:* www.signify.com	604-888-6811	888-2003	439
Ledding Library 10660 SE 21st Ave . . . . . Milwaukie OR 97222 *TF:* 800-701-8560 ■ *Web:* www.milwaukieoregon.gov	503-786-7580	659-9497	434-3
LEDdynamics Inc 44 Hull St. . . . . . Randolph VT 05060 *Web:* www.leddynamics.com	802-728-4533	728-3800	362
LedEngin Inc 3350 Scott Blvd Bldg 9. . . . . . Santa Clara CA 95054 *Web:* www.ledengin.com	408-492-0620		696
Lederle Machine Co 830 Jefferson St . . . . . Pacific MO 63069 *TF:* 800-433-2106 ■ *Web:* www.lederle.com	636-271-7200	271-7020	514
Ledge Light Technologies Inc 88D Howard St Ste D . . . . . New London CT 06320 *Web:* www.ledgelight.com	860-444-0138	444-0274	180
Ledger Systems Inc 865 Laurel St . . . . . San Carlos CA 94070 *Web:* www.ledgersys.com	650-592-6211		175
Ledger, The 300 W Lime St . . . . . Lakeland FL 33815 *TF:* 888-431-7323 ■ *Web:* www.theledger.com	863-802-7000		532-2
Ledges State Park 1515 P Ave. . . . . . Madrid IA 50156 *Web:* www.iowadnr.gov	515-432-1852		565
LEDO Pizza System Inc 2001 Tidewater Colony Dr . . . . . Annapolis MD 21401 *Web:* www.ledopizza.com	410-721-6887		670
Ledoux & Company Inc 359 Alfred Ave . . . . . Teaneck NJ 07666 *Web:* ledouxandcompany.com	201-837-7160	837-1235	743
Ledtronics Inc 23105 Kashiwa Ct . . . . . Torrance CA 90505 *TF:* 800-579-4875 ■ *Web:* www.led.net	310-534-1505	534-1424	437
LeDuc & Dexter Plumbing 2833A Dowd Dr . . . . . Santa Rosa CA 95406 *Web:* www.leducanddexterplumbing.com	707-575-1500		610
Ledwell & Son Enterprises 3300 Waco St. . . . . . Texarkana TX 75501 *TF:* 888-533-9355 ■ *Web:* www.ledwell.com	903-838-6531	831-2719	779
Ledyard National Bank 320 Main St . . . . . Norwich VT 05055 *Web:* www.ledyardbank.com	802-649-2050	649-2060	70
Lee & Associates Commercial Real Estate Services Inc 13181 Crossroads Pkwy N Ste 300 . . . . . City of Industry CA 91746 *Web:* www.lee-associates.com	562-699-7500		652
Lee & Cates Glass Inc 5355 Shawland Rd . . . . . Jacksonville FL 32254 *TF:* 888-844-1989 ■ *Web:* www.leeandcatesglass.com	904-358-8555		189-6
Lee & Hayes PLLC 601 W Riverside Ave Ste 1400 . . . . . Spokane WA 99201 *Web:* www.leehayes.com	509-324-9256		428
Lee & Low Books Inc 95 Madison Ave Ste 1205. . . . . . New York NY 10016 *Web:* www.leeandlow.com	212-779-4400		95
Lee Air Company Inc 7545 Wheatland Ave. . . . . . Sun Valley CA 91352 *Web:* www.leeairinc.com	818-767-0777		24
Lee Arrendale State Prison 2023 Gainesville Hwy . . . . . Alto GA 30510 *Web:* dcor.state.ga.us	706-776-4700		213
Lee Barbara (Rep D - CA) 2470 Rayburn House Office Bldg . . . . . Washington DC 20515 *Web:* lee.house.gov	202-225-2661	225-9817	342-2
Lee Brass Co 1800 Golden Springs Rd . . . . . Anniston AL 36207 *TF:* 800-876-1811 ■ *Web:* www.leebrass.com	800-876-1811	876-1800	308
Lee Brick & Tile Co 3704 Hawkins Ave PO Box 1027 . . . . . Sanford NC 27330 *TF:* 800-672-7559 ■ *Web:* www.leebrickonline.com	919-774-4800	774-7557	150
Lee Bros Foodservice Inc 660 E Gish Rd. . . . . . San Jose CA 95112 *Web:* www.leebros.com	408-275-0700	275-0416	299
Lee Builder Mart Inc 1000 N Horner Blvd . . . . . Sanford NC 27330 *TF:* 800-849-7544 ■ *Web:* www.leebuildermart.com	919-775-5555	774-9561	364
Lee Co 2 Pellitaug Rd PO Box 424 . . . . . Westbrook CT 06498 *TF:* 800-533-7584 ■ *Web:* www.theleeco.com	860-399-6281	399-7058	789
Lee College 200 Lee Dr PO Box 818 . . . . . Baytown TX 77520 *TF:* 800-621-8724 ■ *Web:* www.lee.edu	281-427-5611		162
Lee Company Inc 4057 Rural Plains Cir . . . . . Franklin TN 37064 *Web:* www.leecompany.com	615-567-1000		189-10
Lee Company Inc 27 S 12th St . . . . . Terre Haute IN 47807 *Web:* leecompanyinc.com	812-235-8155	235-3587	320
Lee Construction Co 633 Eagleton Downs Dr . . . . . Pineville NC 28134 *Web:* www.leecarolinas.com	704-588-5272	588-1535	188-4

	Phone	Fax	Class
Lee Correctional Institution 990 Wisacky Hwy . . . . . Bishopville SC 29010 *Web:* www.doc.sc.gov	803-428-2800	896-1766	213
Lee County PO Box G. . . . . . Beattyville KY 41311 *Web:* www.leecounty.ky.gov	606-464-4100	464-4145	338
Lee County 112 E Second St PO Box 329 . . . . . Dixon IL 61021 *Web:* leecountyil.com	815-288-3309	288-6492	338
Lee County 933 Ave H . . . . . Fort Madison IA 52627 *TF:* 800-458-6672 ■ *Web:* www.leecounty.org	319-372-6557	372-8200	338
Lee County PO Box 398 . . . . . Fort Myers FL 33902 *Web:* www.leegov.com	239-533-2236	485-2262	338
Lee County PO Box 419 . . . . . Giddings TX 78942 *Web:* www.co.lee.tx.us	979-542-3684	542-2623	338
Lee County 102 Starksville Ave N. . . . . . Leesburg GA 31763 *Web:* www.lee.ga.us	229-759-6000	759-6050	338
Lee County 15 E Chestnut St . . . . . Marianna AR 72360 *Web:* leecounty.arkansas.gov	870-295-7715		338
Lee County 7992 Villanow Dr. . . . . . Sanford NC 27332 *Web:* leecountync.gov	919-718-4605		338
Lee County 510 N Commerce St . . . . . Tupelo MS 38804 *TF:* 800-773-8477 ■ *Web:* www.leecosheriff.com	662-841-9040	841-9044	338
Lee County Visitors & Convention Bureau 2201 Second St Ste 600 . . . . . Fort Myers FL 33901 *TF:* 800-237-6444 ■ *Web:* www.fortmyers-sanibel.com	239-338-3500	334-1106	206
Lee Dan Communications Inc 155 Adams Ave. . . . . . Hauppauge NY 11788 *TF:* 800-231-1414 ■ *Web:* www.leedan.com	631-231-1414	231-1498	392
Lee Delauter & Sons Inc 12037 Wolfsville Rd . . . . . Myersville MD 21773 *Web:* leedelauter.com	301-293-2648		204
Lee Electric Inc 309-11 51st St . . . . . West New York NJ 07093 *TF:* 800-433-3417 ■ *Web:* www.leeelectric.com	201-866-3656	866-0735	425
Lee Engineering Supply Company Inc 6200 Humphreys St Ste J . . . . . Harahan LA 70123 *Web:* www.leeengineeringsupply.com	504-733-3333	734-8114	770
Lee Enterprises Inc 201 N Harrison St Ste 600 . . . . . Davenport IA 52801 *NYSE: LEE* ■ *Web:* lee.net	563-383-2100		637-8
Lee Industries Inc 50 W Pine St. . . . . . Philipsburg PA 16866 *Web:* www.leeind.com	814-342-0461	342-5660	386
Lee James & Associates Nine Wedge Way. . . . . . Littleton CO 80123 **Fax Area Code: 303* ■ *TF:* 877-738-9140 ■ *Web:* www.leejames.com	877-738-9140	738-1009*	261
Lee Jeans 9001 W 67th St . . . . . Merriam KS 66202 *TF:* 800-453-3348 ■ *Web:* www.lee.com	800-453-3348		155-11
Lee Kennedy Company Inc 122 Quincy Shore Dr . . . . . Quincy MA 02171 *Web:* leekennedy.com	617-825-6930		186
Lee Kum Kee 14841 Don Julian Rd . . . . . City of Industry CA 91746 *TF:* 800-654-5082 ■ *Web:* corporate.lkk.com	626-709-1888		296-19
Lee L. Dopkin 2100 W Cold Spring Ln . . . . . Baltimore MD 21209 *Web:* leedopkin.com	410-466-3500	466-8715	612
Lee Lewis Construction Inc 7810 Orlando Ave. . . . . . Lubbock TX 79423 *Web:* www.leelewis.com	806-797-8400	797-8492	186
Lee M. Smith & Assoc 929 Harrison Ave Ste 300. . . . . . Columbus OH 43215 *Web:* leesmithlaw.com	614-464-1626		41
Lee Michaels Fine Jewelry 7560 Corporate Blvd. . . . . . Baton Rouge LA 70809 *Web:* www.lmfj.com	225-926-4644	926-9600	410
Lee Mike (Sen R - UT) 361A Russell Senate Office Bldg. . . . . . Washington DC 20510 *Web:* www.lee.senate.gov	202-224-5444		342-2
Lee Myles AutoCare + Transmissions Group 920 Penn Ave . . . . . Wyomissing PA 19610 *TF:* 800-533-6953 ■ *Web:* www.leemyles.com	800-533-6953		62-6
Lee Oil Company Inc 1655 Bypass 35 . . . . . Alvin TX 77511 *Web:* www.leeoilalvin.com	281-331-3445		581
Lee Plastics Inc 102 Pratts Jct Rd . . . . . Sterling MA 01564 *Web:* www.leeplastics.com	978-422-7611	422-8808	604
Lee Printing Company Inc 3904 Leeland St . . . . . Houston TX 77003 *Web:* www.leeprintingco.com	713-227-5566	227-2811	627
Lee Products Co 800 E 80th St. . . . . . Bloomington MN 55420 *TF:* 800-989-3544 ■ *Web:* www.leeproducts.com	952-854-3544	854-7177	534
Lee Publications Inc 6113 State Hwy 5 . . . . . Palatine Bridge NY 13428 *TF:* 800-836-2888 ■ *Web:* www.leepub.com	518-673-3237	673-3245	637-8
Lee Resources International Inc 104 Maxwell Ave Ste 223 . . . . . Greenwood SC 29646 *TF:* 800-277-7888 ■ *Web:* www.leeresources.com	800-277-7888		631
Lee Richardson Zoo 312 E Finnup Dr . . . . . Garden City KS 67846 *Web:* leerichardsonzoo.org	620-276-1250	276-1259	823
Lee Silsby Compounding Pharmacy 3216 Silsby Rd. . . . . . Cleveland Heights OH 44118 *Web:* www.leesilsby.com	216-321-4300		237
Lee Spring Company Inc 140 58th St Unit 3C . . . . . Brooklyn NY 11220 *TF:* 800-110-2500 ■ *Web:* www.leespring.com	718-236-2222	236-3919	719
Lee State Natural Area 487 Loop Rd. . . . . . Bishopville SC 29010 *Web:* southcarolinaparks.com	803-428-5307		565
Lee State Prison 153 Pinewood Rd . . . . . Leesburg GA 31763 *Web:* dcor.state.ga.us	229-759-6453	759-3065	213
Lee Strasberg Theatre & Film Institute, The 7936 Santa Monica Blvd. . . . . . West Hollywood CA 90046 *Web:* strasberg.edu	323-650-7777	650-7770	166
Lee Supply Corp 6610 Guion Rd. . . . . . Indianapolis IN 46268 *TF:* 800-873-1103 ■ *Web:* www.leesupplycorp.com	317-290-2500		612
Lee Susie (Rep D - NV) 522 Cannon House Office Bldg. . . . . . Washington DC 20515 *Web:* www.susielee.house.gov	202-225-3252		342-2
Lee University 1120 N Ocoee St . . . . . Cleveland TN 37311 *Web:* www.leeuniversity.edu	423-614-8000	614-8533	166

Name / Address	City	State	Zip	Phone	Fax	Class
Lee Veterinary Clinic Pc 484 Bachelor Rd *Web:* leevetclinic.com	Atmore	AL	36502	251-368-8668		794
Lee's Grinding Inc 15620 Foltz Pky *Web:* www.leesgrinding.com	Strongsville	OH	44149	440-572-4610	572-2411	454
Lee's Marketplace Inc 555 E 1400 N Ste 110 *Web:* leesmarketplace.com	Logan	UT	84341	435-755-5100		297-8
Lee's Morvillo Group 160 Niantic Ave *TF:* 800-821-1700 ■ *Web:* www.leesmfg.com	Providence	RI	02907	401-353-1740		407
Lee's Ready-Mix & Trucking Inc PO Box 496	North Vernon	IN	47265	812-346-9767		135
Lee's Summit Chamber of Commerce 220 SE Main St *TF:* 888-816-5757 ■ *Web:* www.lschamber.com	Lee's Summit	MO	64063	816-524-2424	524-5246	139
Leeann Rasmuson & Associates Inc 370 W Line St *Web:* bishoprealestate.com	Bishop	CA	93514	760-873-4264	873-4875	652
Leebaw Manufacturing Company Inc PO Box 553 *TF:* 800-841-8083 ■ *Web:* www.leebaw.com	Canfield	OH	44406	800-841-8083		470
Leeber Limited USA 115 Pencader Dr *Web:* leeber.com	Newark	DE	19702	302-733-0991		411
Leech Lake Area Chamber of Commerce 205 Minnesota Ave E *TF:* 800-833-1118 ■ *Web:* leech-lake.com	Walker	MN	56484	218-547-1313	547-1338	139
Leech Tishman Fuscaldo & Lampl LLC 525 William Penn Pl 28th Fl *Web:* www.leechtishman.com	Pittsburgh	PA	15219	412-261-1600		445
Leech Tool & Die Works 13144 Dickson Rd PO Box 748 *Web:* www.leechind.com	Meadville	PA	16335	814-336-2141	337-0354	757
Leeco Steel LLC 1011 Warrenville Rd Ste 500 *TF:* 800-621-4366 ■ *Web:* www.leecosteel.com	Lisle	IL	60532	630-427-2100		791
Leed - Himmel Industries Inc 75 Leeder Hill Dr *TF:* 800-243-6566 ■ *Web:* leed-himmel.com	Hamden	CT	06517	203-287-6662		362
Leed Selling Tools Corp 9700 Hwy 57 *TF:* 855-687-5333 ■ *Web:* www.leedsamples.com	Evansville	IN	47725	812-867-4340		86
Leeds Consulting Group LLC 1381 Bellewood Ln *Web:* www.leedscg.com	Freeland	WA	98249	360-331-5745		196
Leedy Manufacturing Co 210 Hall St SW *Web:* www.leedymfg.com	Grand Rapids	MI	49507	616-245-0517	245-3888	709
Lee-Fendall House Museum 614 Oronoco St *Web:* www.leefendallhouse.org	Alexandria	VA	22314	703-548-1789		520
Leelanau County 8527 E Government Center Dr *TF:* 866-256-9711 ■ *Web:* www.leelanau.cc	Suttons Bay	MI	49682	231-256-9824	256-0174	338
Leelanau Fruit Co 2900 SW Bay Shore Dr *TF:* 800-431-0718 ■ *Web:* leelanaufruit.com	Suttons Bay	MI	49682	231-271-3514	271-4367	296-21
Leelanau School 1 Old Homestead Rd *Web:* leelanau.org	Glen Arbor	MI	49636	231-334-5800	334-5898	622
Leelanau State Park 15310 N Lighthouse Pt Rd *Web:* www.michigan.org	Northport	MI	49670	231-386-5422		565
LeeMAH Electronics Inc 155 S Hill Dr *Web:* www.leemah.com	Brisbane	CA	94005	415-394-1288	433-2560	253
Leer LP 206 Leer St *TF:* 800-766-5337 ■ *Web:* www.leerinc.com	New Lisbon	WI	53950	608-562-7100	562-6022	664
Lees Supermarket 796 Main Rd *Web:* www.leesmarket.com	Westport	MA	02790	508-636-3348		345
Leesburg Animal Park 19270 James Monroe Hwy *Web:* www.leesburganimalpark.com	Leesburg	VA	20175	703-433-0002		31
Leesburg Public Library 100 E Main St *Web:* www.leesburgflorida.gov	Leesburg	FL	34748	352-728-9790		434-3
Lees-McRae College 191 Main St W *TF:* 800-280-4562 ■ *Web:* www.lmc.edu	Banner Elk	NC	28604	828-898-5241		166
Leesta Industries Ltd 8 Plateau *Web:* www.leesta.com	Pointe-Claire	QC	H9R5W2	514-694-3930	694-3935	21
Leesville Animal Hospital 9309 Leesville Rd *Web:* leesvilleanimalhospital.com	Raleigh	NC	27613	919-870-7000		794
Leesville Lumber Company Inc PO Box 320 *Web:* leesvillelumber.com	Leesville	LA	71496	337-238-1387	239-3984	683
Leesylvania State Park 2001 Daniel K Ludwig Dr *Web:* www.dcr.virginia.gov	Woodbridge	VA	22191	703-730-8205		565
Leete Kosto & Wizner LLC 999 Asylum Ave Ste 202 *Web:* lkwvisa.com	Hartford	CT	06105	860-249-8100	727-9184	428
Leevers Foods 501 Main St *Web:* www.leeversfoods.com	Cavalier	ND	58220	701-265-4011		345
Leevers Supermarkets Inc 2195 N Hwy 83 **Fax Area Code:* 720 ■ *Web:* www.leevers.com	Franktown	CO	80116	303-814-8646	343-2196*	345
Leewens Corp 630 Seventh Ave PO Box 2549 *Web:* www.leewens.com	Kirkland	WA	98033	425-827-7667		291
Leff Electronics Inc (LE) 455 N Center Ave *TF:* 800-245-4200 ■ *Web:* www.leff.com	New Stanton	PA	15672	724-925-3001	925-3022	246
Leffler Accountancy Corp 3757 Green Vista Dr Ste 490	Encino	CA	91436	818-501-1181		2
Leffler Energy Inc 15 Mt Joy St *TF:* 800-984-1411 ■ *Web:* www.lefflerenergy.com	Mount Joy	PA	17552	800-984-1411		579
LeFiell Manufacturing Co 13700 Firestone Blvd *TF:* 800-451-5971 ■ *Web:* www.lefiell.com	Santa Fe Springs	CA	90670	800-451-5971	373-3361	490

Name / Address	City	State	Zip	Phone	Fax	Class
Lefler Engineering Inc 1651 Second St *Web:* leflerengineering.com	San Rafael	CA	94901	415-456-4220	456-1248	261
LeFleur's Bluff State Park 2140 Riverside Dr *TF:* 800-237-6278 ■ *Web:* www.mdwfp.com	Jackson	MS	39202	601-987-3923		565
Left Bank 511 Rhode Island St *Web:* www.leftbankrestaurant.com	Buffalo	NY	14213	716-882-3509		671
Left Bank 377 Santana Row *Web:* www.leftbank.com	San Jose	CA	95128	408-984-3500	984-0300	671
Left Bank Books 399 N Euclid Ave *Web:* www.left-bank.com	Saint Louis	MO	63108	314-367-6731	367-3256	95
Left Bank Wine Co 4910 Triangle St *Web:* www.leftbankwine.com	McFarland	WI	53558	608-838-8400		443
Legacies LLC 51 W Fourth St *Web:* livewellwinona.org	Winona	MN	55987	507-474-9110		363
Legacy Bank 1580 E Cheyenne Mtn Blvd *TF:* 866-627-0800 ■ *Web:* www.elegacybank.com	Colorado Springs	CO	80906	719-579-9150		70
Legacy Bank of Florida 2300 Glades Rd Ste 140W *Web:* legacybankfl.com	Boca Raton	FL	33431	561-347-1970		70
Legacy Cabinets Inc 285 Legacy Blvd *Web:* www.legacycabinetsllc.com	Eastaboga	AL	36260	256-831-4888		319-2
Legacy Capital LLC 433 Metairie Rd Ste 405 *Web:* www.legacycapital.com	Metairie	LA	70005	504-837-3450	837-3488	194
Legacy Classic Furniture Inc 2575 Penny Rd *Web:* www.legacyclassic.com	High Point	NC	27265	336-449-4600		321
Legacy Electronics Inc 1220 N Dakota St PO Box 348 *TF:* 888-466-3853 ■ *Web:* www.legacyelectronics.com	Canton	SD	57013	949-498-9600		174
Legacy Engineering LLC 18662 Macarthur Blvd Ste 457 *Web:* www.legacyeng.com	Irvine	CA	92612	805-418-9862		631
Legacy Golf Resort 6808 S 32nd St *TF:* 866-729-7182 ■ *Web:* www.shellhospitality.com	Phoenix	AZ	85042	602-305-5500		669
Legacy grain Coop 402 N Walnut St PO Box 80 *Web:* www.legacygrain.com	Stonington	IL	62567	217-325-3211		10-5
Legacy Health 1919 NW Lovejoy St *Web:* www.legacyhealth.org	Portland	OR	97209	503-415-5600		353
Legacy Learning Systems Inc 2510 8th Ave S 2nd Fl *TF:* 866-683-6027 ■ *Web:* www.learnandmaster.com	Nashville	TN	37204	615-515-3605		637-2
Legacy Maintenance Services 2475 Scoto Harper Dr *Web:* lmsoh.com	Columbus	OH	43204	614-473-8400		104
Legacy Partners 1610 16th Ave S *Web:* www.legacy-fp.com	Nashville	TN	37212	615-292-5351		194
Legacy Partners Inc 4000 E Third Ave Ste 600 *Web:* legacypartners.com	Foster City	CA	94404	650-571-2250		390
Legacy Pharmaceutical Packaging LLC 13333 Lakefront Dr *Web:* www.legacypharmasolutions.com	Earth City	MO	63045	314-813-1555		583
Legacy Publishing Group 75 Green St *TF:* 800-322-3866 ■ *Web:* www.shoplegacy.com	Clinton	MA	01510	800-322-3866		130
Legacy Real Estate Partners LLC 18801 N Thompson Peak Pkwy Ste 100 *Web:* legacyrealestatepartners.com	Scottsdale	AZ	85255	480-515-0148		652
Legacy Station Ltd 4153 Lawrenceville Hwy Ste 12 *Web:* legacystation.com	Lilburn	GA	30047	770-339-7780		761
Legacy Tax Group 1088 Bishop St Ste 508 *Web:* legacytaxgroup.com	Honolulu	HI	96813	808-533-2272		2
Legacy Venture 180 Lytton Ave *Web:* www.legacyventure.com	Palo Alto	CA	94301	650-324-5980	324-5982	792
Legacy Ventures 300 Marietta St NW Ste 304 *Web:* lvmgt.com	Atlanta	GA	30313	404-222-9100	222-9090	653
Legacy Wealth Management Inc 1715 Aaron Brenner Dr Ste 301 *TF:* 888-326-8554 ■ *Web:* www.legacywealth.com	Memphis	TN	38120	901-758-9006	758-9007	690
Legal & General America Inc 3275 Bennett Creek Ave *TF:* 800-638-8428 ■ *Web:* www.lgamerica.com	Frederick	MD	21704	301-279-4800	294-6960	360-4
Legal Aid Bureau Inc 500 E Lexington St *TF:* 800-666-8330 ■ *Web:* www.mdlab.org	Baltimore	MD	21202	410-951-7777	269-8916	428
Legal Aid Chicago 120 S LaSalle St Ste 900 *Web:* www.legalaidchicago.org	Chicago	IL	60603	312-341-1070	341-1041	434-3
Legal Aid Foundation of Los Angeles 1550 W Eighth St *Web:* lafla.org	Los Angeles	CA	90017	323-801-7991	801-7945	428
Legal Aid of West Virginia Inc 922 Quarrier St 4th Fl *TF:* 866-255-4370 ■ *Web:* www.lawv.net	Charleston	WV	25301	304-343-4481	345-5934	445
Legal Aid of Wyoming Inc 1813 Carey Ave *TF:* 877-432-9955 ■ *Web:* lawyoming.org	Cheyenne	WY	82001	307-432-0807	432-0808	41
Legal Aid Society of Palm Beach County Inc 423 Fern St Ste 200 *TF:* 800-403-9353 ■ *Web:* www.legalaidpbc.org	West Palm Beach	FL	33401	561-655-8944		428
Legal Aid Society of San Mateo County, The 330 Twin Dolphin Dr Ste 123 *Web:* www.legalaidsmc.org	Redwood City	CA	94065	650-558-0915		428
Legal Club of America Corp 7771 W Oakland Park Blvd Ste 217 *TF:* 800-316-5387 ■ *Web:* www.legalclub.com	Sunrise	FL	33351	954-377-0222		463
Legal Cost Control Inc (LCC) 8 Kings Hwy W Ste C *TF:* 800-493-7345 ■ *Web:* legalcost.com	Haddonfield	NJ	08033	856-216-0800	216-1736	445
Legal Data Resources Inc 2816 W Summerdale Ave *Web:* www.ldrsearch.com	Chicago	IL	60625	773-561-2468		635

	Phone	Fax	Class
Legal Directories Publishing Company Inc 1313 Oates Dr . . . Mesquite TX 75150 *Web:* legaldirectories.com	214-321-3238		5
Legal Directory Inc 4276 Lomac St . . . Montgomery AL 36106 *TF:* 800-448-0461 ■ *Web:* www.creditunionatty.com	334-265-5365	271-5815	637-10
Legal Interpreting Services Inc 81 Willougyb St Ste 602 . . . Brooklyn NY 11201 *Web:* lissol.com	718-237-8919	749-0113	768
Legal Resources Inc 2877 Guardian Ln Ste 101 . . . Virginia Beach VA 23452 *TF:* 800-728-5768 ■ *Web:* www.legalresources.com	757-498-1220	498-4114	260
Legal Sea Foods 26 Park Plz . . . Boston MA 02116 *Web:* www.legalseafoods.com	617-426-4444		671
Legal Search 510 E 85th St Apt 9f . . . New York NY 10028 *Web:* www.legalsearchusa.com	212-472-3000		260
Legal Services Corp 3333 K St NW 3rd Fl . . . Washington DC 20007 *Web:* www.lsc.gov	202-295-1500	337-6797	340-20
LegalEase Inc 205 E 42nd St 20th Fl . . . New York NY 10017 **Fax Area Code:* 888 ■ *TF:* 800-393-1277 ■ *Web:* www.legaleaseinc.com	212-393-9070	580-4761*	635
LegaLees Corp 556 E 1400 S . . . Orem UT 84097 *TF:* 800-806-1998 ■ *Web:* www.legalees.com	801-802-9020	802-9157	41
Legend Data Systems Inc 18024 72nd Ave S . . . Kent WA 98032 *TF:* 866-371-1670 ■ *Web:* www.legendid.com	425-251-1670		45
Legend Energy Services LLC 5801 Broadway Extn Ste 210 . . . Oklahoma City OK 73118 *Web:* www.legendenergyservices.com	405-600-1264	608-8851	536
Legend Financial Advisors Inc 5700 Corporate Dr Ste 350 . . . Pittsburgh PA 15237 *TF:* 888-236-5960 ■ *Web:* www.legend-financial.com	412-635-9210	635-9213	401
Legend Power Systems Inc 1480 Frances St . . . Vancouver BC V5L1Y9 *TF:* 866-772-8797 ■ *Web:* legendpower.com	604-420-1500	420-1533	767
Legend Seeds Inc PO Box 241 . . . De Smet SD 57231 *TF:* 800-678-3346 ■ *Web:* legendseeds.net	605-854-3346	854-3135	276
Legend Technical Services of Arizona Inc 17031 N 25th Ave . . . Phoenix AZ 85023 *Web:* www.legend-group.com	602-324-6100	324-6101	194
Legendary LLC 4471 Legendary Dr . . . Destin FL 32541 *Web:* legendaryinc.com	850-337-8000		360-3
Legendary Marketing 3729 S Lecanto Hwy . . . Lecanto FL 34461 *TF:* 800-827-1663 ■ *Web:* legendarymarketing.com	352-527-3553		195
Legendary Publications 23923 County Rd 29 . . . Sleepy Eye MN 56085 *Web:* www.theorphantrain.com	507-766-6239		637-2
Legendary Whitetails 820 Enterprise Dr . . . Slinger WI 53086 *TF:* 800-875-9453 ■ *Web:* www.deergear.com	800-875-9453		361
Legends Furniture Inc 10300 W Buckeye Rd . . . Tolleson AZ 85353 *Web:* legendsfurniture.com	623-931-6500	939-9486	321
Legends Theater 1600 W Hwy 76 . . . Branson MO 65616 *TF:* 800-374-7469 ■ *Web:* www.legendsinconcert.com	702-253-1333		572
Leger, The Research Intelligence Group 507 Pl d'Armes Ste 700 . . . Montreal QC H2Y2W8 *Web:* leger360.com	514-982-2464		466
Legere Group Ltd PO Box 1527 . . . Avon CT 06001 *Web:* www.legeregroup.com	860-674-0392	674-0469	115
Legg Company Inc 325 E Tenth St . . . Halstead KS 67056 **Fax Area Code:* 316 ■ *TF:* 800-835-1003 ■ *Web:* www.leggbelting.com	800-835-1003	835-3218*	370
Legg Mason Inc (LMI) 100 International Dr . . . Baltimore MD 21202 *NYSE:* LM ■ *TF:* 800-822-5544 ■ *Web:* www.leggmason.com	800-221-3627		690
Leggett & Platt Inc 1 Leggett Rd PO Box 757 . . . Carthage MO 64836 *NYSE:* LEG ■ *TF:* 800-888-4569 ■ *Web:* www.leggett.com	417-358-8131	358-6996	719
Legion Lighting Company Inc 221 Glenmore Ave . . . Brooklyn NY 11207 *TF:* 800-453-4466 ■ *Web:* www.legionlighting.com	718-498-1770	498-0128	439
Legion of Valor Museum 2425 Fresno St . . . Fresno CA 93721 *Web:* legionofvalor.org	559-498-0510		520
Legion State Park 635 Legion State Park Rd . . . Louisville MS 39339 *Web:* www.mdwfp.com	662-773-8323		565
Legislative Assembly of Alberta 10800-97th Ave 216 Legislature Bldg . . . Edmonton AB T5K2B6 *Web:* www.assembly.ab.ca	780-427-2473	427-6016	434-3
Legler Systems Co 23 Charles Hill Rd . . . Orinda CA 94563 *Web:* www.legler.com	925-254-1264		179
LEGO Systems Inc 555 Taylor Rd . . . Enfield CT 06082 *TF:* 877-518-5346 ■ *Web:* www.lego.com	860-749-2291		762
LEGOLAND California 1 Legoland Dr . . . Carlsbad CA 92008 *TF:* 877-534-6526 ■ *Web:* www.legoland.com	888-690-5346		32
Legrand Johnson Construction Co 1000 S Main St . . . Logan UT 84321 *Web:* www.kilgorecompanies.com	435-752-2001		182
Lehan Drugs Inc 1407 S Fourth St . . . Dekalb IL 60115 *Web:* lehandrugs.com	815-758-0911		237
Lehigh - Northampton Airport Authority 3311 Airport Rd . . . Allentown PA 18109 *TF:* 800-359-5842 ■ *Web:* www.flyabe.com	800-359-5842		27
Lehigh Career & Technical Institute 4500 Education Park Dr . . . Schnecksville PA 18078 *Web:* www.lcti.org	610-799-2300	799-1808	668
Lehigh County 455 W Hamilton St . . . Allentown PA 18101 *Web:* www.lccpa.org	610-782-3000		338
Lehigh County Museum 432 W Walnut St . . . Allentown PA 18102 *Web:* www.lchs.museum	610-435-1074		520
Lehigh Engineering LLC 200 Mahantongo St . . . Pottsville PA 17901 *Web:* www.lehighengineer.com	570-628-2300	622-2612	261
Lehigh Fluid Power Inc 1413 Rt 179 . . . Lambertville NJ 08530 *TF:* 800-257-9515 ■ *Web:* lehighfluidpower.com	800-257-9515		641
Lehigh Hanson *Edmonton Cement Plant and Terminal* 12640 Inland Way . . . Edmonton AB T5V1K2 *TF:* 800-252-9304 ■ *Web:* www.lehighhanson.com	780-420-2500	420-2550	135
Lehigh Heavy Forge Corp 275 Emery St . . . Bethlehem PA 18015 *Web:* lhforge.com	610-332-8100	332-8101	483
Lehigh University Press (LUP) Christmas-Saucon Hall 14 E Packer Ave . . . Bethlehem PA 18015 *Web:* lupress.cas2.lehigh.edu	610-758-3933		637-2
Lehigh Valley Cooperative Telephone Assn (LVCTA) 9090 Taylor Rd . . . Lehigh IA 50557 *Web:* www.lvcta.net	515-359-2211		224
Lehigh Valley Dairy Farms 880 Allentown Rd . . . Lansdale PA 19446 *Web:* www.lehighvalleydairyfarms.com	215-855-8205		296-27
Lehigh Valley Health Network 700 E Broad St . . . Hazleton PA 18201 *Web:* www.lvhn.org	570-501-4000		374-3
Lehigh Valley Plastics Inc 187 N Commerce Way . . . Bethlehem PA 18017 *TF:* 800-354-5344 ■ *Web:* www.lehighvalleyplastics.com	484-893-5500	893-5511	604
Lehigh Valley Technologies Inc 514 N 12th St . . . Allentown PA 18102 *Web:* www.lvtechinc.com	610-782-9780		583
Lehigh Valley Visitor Ctr 840 Hamilton St Ste 200 . . . Allentown PA 18101 *Web:* www.discoverlehighvalley.com	610-882-9200		206
Lehman College 250 Bedford Pk Blvd W . . . Bronx NY 10468 *Web:* www.lehman.cuny.edu	718-960-8000	960-8712	166
Lehman Hardware & Appliances Inc 4779 Kidron Rd . . . Dalton OH 44618 *TF:* 888-438-5346 ■ *Web:* www.lehmans.com	800-438-5346		393
Lehmann, Ullman & Barclay 2908 Clairmont Ave . . . Birmingham AL 35205 *Web:* lub.com	205-439-6500	254-8016	2
Lehman-Roberts Co 1111 Wilson St . . . Memphis TN 38106 *Web:* www.lehmanroberts.com	901-774-4000	774-4028	188-4
Lehr Construction Company Inc 2115 Frederick Ave . . . Saint Joseph MO 64501 *Web:* www.lehrconstruction.com	816-232-4431		186
Lehr Middlebrooks & Vreeland PC 2021 Third Ave N . . . Birmingham AL 35203 *Web:* lehrmiddlebrooks.com	205-326-3002		428
Lehrer & Madden Inc 10 Union St . . . Natick MA 01760 *TF:* 877-534-6233 ■ *Web:* lehrermadden.com	508-650-1202	655-8999	390
LEI (Ladd Engineering Inc) 1127 Brookside Dr . . . Lebanon IN 46052 *TF:* 877-437-6145 ■ *Web:* www.laddengr.com	765-482-9219	482-9224	261
Leica Camera AG 1 Pearl Ct . . . Allendale NJ 07401 **Fax Area Code:* 201 ■ *TF:* 800-222-0118 ■ *Web:* en.leica-camera.com	800-222-0118	995-1686*	544
Leica Microsystems Inc 1700 Leider Ln . . . Buffalo Grove IL 60089 *TF:* 800-248-0123 ■ *Web:* www.leica-microsystems.com	800-248-0123		743
Leichtman Research Group Inc (LRG) 567 Bay Rd . . . Durham NH 03824 *Web:* www.leichtmanresearch.com	603-397-5400		194
Leick Furniture Inc 2219 S 19th St . . . Sheboygan WI 53081 *Web:* www.leickhome.com	920-451-4060		321
Leidenheimer Baking Co 1501 Simon Bolivar Ave . . . New Orleans LA 70113 *TF:* 800-259-9099 ■ *Web:* www.leidenheimer.com	504-525-1575	525-1596	296-1
Leigh Baldwin & Company LLC 112 Albany St . . . Cazenovia NY 13035 *TF:* 800-659-8044 ■ *Web:* www.leighbaldwin.com	315-734-1410		690
Leigh Fibers Inc 1101 Syphrit Rd . . . Wellford SC 29385 *Web:* www.leighfibers.com	864-439-4111	439-4116	745-8
Leigh Yawkey Woodson Art Museum 700 N 12th St . . . Wausau WI 54403 *Web:* www.lywam.org	715-845-7010	845-7103	637-2
Leighton Group Inc 17781 Cowan St . . . Irvine CA 92614 *Web:* www.leightongroup.com	949-250-1421		261
Leighton State Bank 900 Washington St PO Box 6 . . . Pella IA 50219 *Web:* leightonbank.com	641-628-1566		70
Leila Arboretum Society 928 W Michigan Ave . . . Battle Creek MI 49037 *Web:* www.leilaarboretumsociety.org	269-969-0270	969-0616	97
Leimkuehler Inc 4625 Detroit Ave . . . Cleveland OH 44102 *Web:* www.leimkuehlerinc.com	216-651-7788	651-4057	45
Leininger and Short 909 W Holt Blvd . . . Ontario CA 91762 *Web:* www.leiningerandshort.com	909-986-2793		755
Leinoff & Lemos PA 7301 SW 57 Ct Ste 545 . . . South Miami FL 33143 *Web:* llpa.com	305-661-1556		41
Leis By Ron Inc 851 Mapunapuna St Bay 3 . . . Honolulu HI 96819 *Web:* leisbyron.net	808-838-1455		293
Leiss Tool & Die Co 801 N Pleasant Ave . . . Somerset PA 15501 *Web:* www.leiss.com	814-444-1444	445-3456	454
Leisure & Recreation Concepts Inc 2151 Ft Worth Ave . . . Dallas TX 75211 *Web:* www.larcinc.com	214-942-4474		195
Leisure Chateau Care & Rehabilitation Ctr 962 River Ave . . . Lakewood NJ 08701 *Web:* leisurechateau.com	732-370-8600		371
Leisure Hotels LLC *Leisure Hotel Corp* 8725 Rosehill Rd Ste 300 . . . Lenexa KS 66215 *Web:* www.leisurehotel.com	913-905-1460		379
Leisure Living Management Inc 3196 Kraft Ave SE Ste 200 . . . Grand Rapids MI 49512 *Web:* leisure-living.com	616-464-1564	464-2470	371
Leisure Pro 42 W 18th St . . . New York NY 10011 *TF:* 800-637-6880 ■ *Web:* www.leisurepro.com	212-645-1234		711
Leisure Sports Inc 4670 Willow Rd Ste 100 . . . Pleasanton CA 94588 *Web:* www.leisuresportsinc.com	925-600-1966	600-1144	379

				Phone	Fax	Class
Leisure Systems Inc 502 TechneCenter Dr Ste D *TF:* 866-928-9644 ■ *Web:* www.jellystonefranchise.com	Milford	OH	45150	513-831-2100	576-8670	121
Leisure World of Maryland 3701 Rossmoor Blvd *Web:* leisureworldmaryland.com	Silver Spring	MD	20906	301-598-1000		652
Leisure World Pool & Hearth Inc 406 E 16th Ave *Web:* www.leisureworldkc.com	Kansas City	MO	64116	816-221-1731	221-1726	361
Leitner Williams Dooley & Napolitan PLLC 200 W M L King Blvd Ste 500 *TF:* 800-421-0979 ■ *Web:* www.leitnerfirm.com	Chattanooga	TN	37402	423-265-0214		445
Leitz Music Company Inc 508 Harrison Ave *Web:* leitzmusic.com	Panama City	FL	32401	850-769-0111		526
LeJeune Steel Co 118 W 60th St *Web:* www.lejeunesteel.com	Minneapolis	MN	55419	612-861-3321	861-2724	480
LEK Consulting 28 State St 16th Fl *TF:* 800-929-4535 ■ *Web:* www.lek.com	Boston	MA	02109	617-951-9500	951-9392	194
Lek Technology Consultants Inc 12788 Gillard Rd *Web:* lekcomp.com	Winter Garden	FL	34787	407-877-6505		180
Lek's Taste of Thailand 428 Planters Rd	Montgomery	AL	36109	334-244-8994		671
LEKTRO Inc 1190 SE Flightline Dr *TF:* 800-535-8767 ■ *Web:* www.lektro.com	Warrenton	OR	97146	503-861-2288		22
Leland Little Auctions Ltd 620 Cornerstone Ct *Web:* lelandlittle.com	Hillsborough	NC	27278	919-644-1243		366
Leland Management Inc 6972 Lake Gloria Blvd *Web:* lelandmgt.com	Orlando	FL	32809	407-447-9955		463
Leland Paper Company Inc 10 Leland Dr *TF:* 888-753-5263 ■ *Web:* www.lelandpaper.com	Glens Falls	NY	12801	518-792-0949	792-7966	553
Leland Stanford Mansion State Historic Park 800 N St *Web:* www.parks.ca.gov	Sacramento	CA	95814	916-324-0575		565
Leland, The 400 Bagley St *Web:* theleland.net	Detroit	MI	48226	313-962-2300		379
Lellyett & Rogers Services Company LLC 1717 Lebanon Pk *Web:* www.landrco.com	Nashville	TN	37210	615-316-0780		627
Lemaire 101 W Franklin St *Web:* www.lemairerestaurant.com	Richmond	VA	23220	804-649-4629	649-4400	671
LeMaitre Vascular Inc 63 Second Ave *Web:* www.lemaitre.com	Burlington	MA	01803	781-221-2266		476
Leman Machine Co 1049 S Railroad Ave *Web:* www.lemanmachine.com	Portage	PA	15946	814-736-9696	736-8101	480
Leman USA Inc 1860 Renaissance Blvd *Web:* us.leman.com	Sturtevant	WI	53177	262-884-4700	884-4690	311
LeMar Industries Corp 2070 NE 60th Ave *Web:* www.lemarindustries.com	Des Moines	IA	50313	515-266-7264	266-0274	492
Lematic Inc 2410 W Main St *Web:* lematic.com	Jackson	MI	49203	517-787-3301		362
Lemco Mills Inc 766 Koury Dr	Burlington	NC	27215	336-226-5548		155-10
Lemco Tool Corp 1850 Metzger Ave *TF:* 800-233-8713 ■ *Web:* www.lemco-tool.com	Cogan Station	PA	17728	570-494-0620	494-0860	454
LeMessurier Consultants 1380 Soldiers Field Rd *Web:* www.lemessurier.com	Boston	MA	02135	617-868-1200		261
Lemhi County 206 Courthouse Dr *Web:* www.lemhicountyidaho.org	Salmon	ID	83467	208-756-2861	756-2046	338
Lemhi Ventures Inc 315 E Lake St Ste 304 *Web:* lemhiventures.com	Wayzata	MN	55391	952-908-9680		760
Lemieux Bedard Communications Inc 2665 King W Ste 315 *TF:* 800-823-0850 ■ *Web:* www.lemieuxbedard.com	Sherbrooke	QC	J1L2G5	819-823-0850	823-1484	224
Lemko Corp 1515 E Woodfield Rd Ste 630 *Web:* www.lemkocorp.com	Schaumburg	IL	60173	630-948-3025	948-3030	177
Lemoine Multinational Technologies Inc 3170 Martin Rd *Web:* lemoinetechnologies.com	Walled Lake	MI	48390	248-960-5989	960-4644	173-1
Lemon Creek Correctional Ctr 2000 Lemon Creek Rd *Web:* doc.alaska.gov	Juneau	AK	99801	907-465-6200	465-6207	213
Lemon Grass 238 W Jefferson St *Web:* www.lemongrasscny.com	Syracuse	NY	13202	315-475-1111		671
Lemon Grass 601 Munroe St *Web:* www.lemongrassrestaurant.com	Sacramento	CA	95825	916-486-4891		671
Lemon Grass 331 Elgin St *Web:* www.ottawalemongrass.com	Ottawa	ON	K2P1M5	613-233-5000		671
Lemon Grass Restaurant, The 212 Fourth Ave W *Web:* www.thelemongrassrestaurants.com	Olympia	WA	98501	360-705-1832		671
Lemon Peak 500 W Putnam Ave Ste 400 *TF:* 888-253-7348 ■ *Web:* www.lemonpeak.com	Greenwich	CT	06830	888-253-7348		5
Lemonade Inc 5 Crosby St *TF:* 844-733-8666 ■ *Web:* www.lemonade.com	New York	NY	10013	844-733-8666		390
Lemonaid Health 150 Spear St Ste 350 *Web:* www.lemonaid.com	San Francisco	CA	94105	415-926-5818		48-17
Lemongrass 641 N High St *Web:* www.lemongrassfusion.com	Columbus	OH	43215	614-224-1414	221-2535	671
Lemongrass Thai Cuisine 106 N Main St *Web:* www.lemongrassthai.net	Greenville	SC	29601	864-241-9988		671
LemonStand eCommerce Inc 2416 Main St Ste 126 *TF:* 855-332-0555 ■ *Web:* www.lemonstandapp.com	Vancouver	BC	V5T3E2	604-398-4188		224
Lemont High School 800 Porter St *Web:* www.lhs210.net	Lemont	IL	60439	630-257-5838		685
Lena's Artistic Beauty College 1140 W 87th St *Web:* www.lenasbeautyschool.com	Chicago	IL	60620	773-994-5257	723-0820	167-3
Lenape Forged Products Corp 1334 Lenape Rd *Web:* www.lenapeforge.com	West Chester	PA	19382	610-793-5090	793-3070	483
Lenape Resources Inc 9489 Alexander Rd *Web:* www.lenaperesources.com	Alexander	NY	14005	585-344-1200	344-3283	536
Lenape Tech 2215 Chaplin Ave *Web:* www.lenape.k12.pa.us	Ford City	PA	16226	724-763-7116	763-9888	167-3
Lenard Tool & Machine Inc 4480 S Nicholson Ave *Web:* www.ltmmold.com	Saint Francis	WI	53235	414-483-7620	483-4348	757
Lenawee County 301 N Main St Old Courthouse Second Fl *Web:* www.lenawee.mi.us	Adrian	MI	49221	517-264-4599	264-4790	338
Lenawee County Library 4459 W US 223 *Web:* www.lenawee.lib.mi.us	Adrian	MI	49221	517-263-1011		434-3
Lenawee Economic Development Corp 5285 W US Hwy 223 *Web:* www.lenaweenow.org	Adrian	MI	49221	517-265-5141		139
Len-Co Lumber Corp 1445 Seneca St *TF:* 800-258-4585 ■ *Web:* www.lencobuffalo.com	Buffalo	NY	14210	716-822-0243	822-1821	364
Lencore Acoustics Corp 1 Crossways Park Dr W *Web:* lencore.com	Woodbury	NY	11797	516-682-9292		52
Lend Lease Corp 200 Park Ave 9th Fl *Web:* www.lendlease.com	New York	NY	10166	212-592-6800	592-6988	186
Lenderlive Network Inc 710 S Ash St Ste 200 **Fax Area Code:* 303 ■ *TF:* 800-891-2281 ■ *Web:* www.lenderlive.com	Glendale	CO	80246	800-891-2281	226-8154*	393
LendingTree Inc 11115 Rushmore Dr *Web:* www.lendingtree.com	Charlotte	NC	28277	704-541-5351	541-1824	509
Lenel System International Inc 1212 Pittsford-Victor Rd *Web:* www.lenel.com	Pittsford	NY	14534	585-248-9720	248-9185	178-12
Lenexa Convention & Visitors Bureau 11180 Lackman Rd *Web:* www.lenexa.org	Lenexa	KS	66219	913-888-1414	888-3770	206
Lenexpo Inc 1293 Mtn View Alviso Rd Ste A *Web:* atlona.com	Sunnyvale	CA	94089	408-962-0515		253
Lennertson Sample Co 101 Industrial Dr *TF:* 800-231-1129 ■ *Web:* www.lennertsonsample.com	Hermann	MO	65041	800-231-1129		86
Lenning & Company Inc 13924 Seal Beach Blvd Ste C *TF:* 800-200-4829 ■ *Web:* www.lenning.com	Seal Beach	CA	90740	562-594-9729		2
Lennon Telephone Co 3095 Sheridan Rd *TF:* 888-204-1077 ■ *Web:* www.lentel.com	Lennon	MI	48449	810-621-3301	621-9600	224
Lennon Weinberg Inc 514 W 25th St *Web:* www.lennonweinberg.com	New York	NY	10001	212-941-0012	929-3265	42
Lennox Employees Credit Union 1004 E Main St *TF:* 844-675-9559 ■ *Web:* lennoxecu.com	Marshalltown	IA	50158	641-754-4501	754-4505	219
Lennox Industries Inc 2100 Lake Pk Blvd *TF:* 800-953-6669 ■ *Web:* www.lennox.com	Richardson	TX	75080	800-953-6669		15
Lennox International Inc 2140 Lake Pk Blvd *NYSE:* LII ■ *Web:* www.lennoxinternational.com	Richardson	TX	75080	972-497-5000	497-5292	15
Lenny's Franchisor LLC 8295 Tournament Dr Ste 200 *Web:* www.lennys.com	Memphis	TN	38125	901-753-4002		360-3
Lenoir City Public Library 100 W Broadway *Web:* www.lenoircitytn.gov	Lenoir City	TN	37771	865-986-3210		434-3
Lenoir Community College 231 Hwy 58 S PO Box 188 *TF:* 866-866-2362 ■ *Web:* www.lenoircc.edu	Kinston	NC	28502	252-527-6223	233-6879	162
Lenoir County 130 S Queen St PO Box 3289 *Web:* www.co.lenoir.nc.us	Kinston	NC	28502	252-559-6450	559-6454	338
Lenoir County Public School (LCPS) 2017 W Vernon Ave PO Box 729 *Web:* www.lcpsnc.org	Kinston	NC	28504	252-527-1109	527-6884	685
Lenoir Empire Furniture 1625 Cherokee Rd *Web:* www.lenoirempirefurniture.com	Johnson City	TN	37604	423-929-7283	929-7040	320
Lenoir Mirror Company Inc 401 Kincaid St *TF:* 800-438-8204 ■ *Web:* www.lenoirmirror.com	Lenoir	NC	28645	828-728-3271	728-5010	332
Lenoir-Rhyne University PO Box 7164 *TF:* 800-277-5721 ■ *Web:* www.lr.edu	Hickory	NC	28601	828-328-7300	328-7378	166
Lenox Advisors Inc 530 Fifth Ave *Web:* www.lenoxadvisors.com	New York	NY	10036	212-536-8700	536-6014	401
Lenox Corp PO Box 2006 *TF:* 800-223-4311 ■ *Web:* www.lenox.com	Bristol	PA	19007	800-223-4311		730
Lenox Group LLC, The 3384 Peachtree Rd N E Ste 300 *Web:* lenoxgroupllc.com	Atlanta	GA	30326	404-419-1660		690
Lenox Hill Radiology 61 E 77th St *Web:* www.radnet.com	New York	NY	10075	212-772-3111		415
Lenox Hotel 61 Exeter St *TF:* 800-225-7676 ■ *Web:* www.lenoxhotel.com	Boston	MA	02116	617-536-5300	267-1237	379
Lenox Hotel & Suites 140 N St *Web:* lenoxhotelandsuites.com	Buffalo	NY	14201	716-884-1700		379
Lenox Wealth Management Inc 8044 Montgomery Rd Ste 170 *Web:* www.fundalifeyoulove.com	Cincinnati	OH	45236	513-618-7080		401
LENSAR Inc 2800 Discovery Dr *TF:* 888-536-7271 ■ *Web:* www.lensar.com	Orlando	FL	32826	888-536-7271		475
LensCrafters Inc 4000 Luxottica Pl *TF:* 877-753-6727 ■ *Web:* www.lenscrafters.com	Mason	OH	45040	513-765-4321		543
Lensic Performing Arts Ctr 211 W San Francisco St *Web:* www.lensic.org	Santa Fe	NM	87501	505-988-7050	988-4370	572

Company / Address	City	State	ZIP	Phone	Fax	Class
Lenstec Inc 1765 Commerce Ave N *Web:* www.lenstec.com	Saint Petersburg	FL	33716	727-571-2272		544
LensVector 6203 San Ignacio Ave Ste 110 *Web:* www.lensvector.com	San Jose	CA	95119	669-247-5095		542
Lentol, Violet, Kienitz & Co 2981 Blue Jacket Ct *Web:* lvk-cpa.com	Lima	OH	45806	419-999-2000		2
Lentros Engineering Inc 280 Eliot St *Web:* www.lentros.com	Ashland	MA	01721	508-881-1240		454
Lentz Associates Inc 150 E Sprague Rd *Web:* era-lentz.com	Broadview Heights	OH	44147	440-842-7171		652
Lentz Milling Co 2045 N 11th St *TF:* 800-523-8132 ■ *Web:* www.lentzmilling.com	Reading	PA	19604	800-523-8132		805
Lenze 630 Douglas St *TF:* 800-217-9100 ■ *Web:* www.lenze.com	Uxbridge	MA	01569	508-278-9100		709
Lenzi Martin Communications 701 Hayes Ave *Web:* lenzimartin.com	Oak Park	IL	60302	708-848-8404		636
Leo A Daly 8600 Indian Hills Dr *Web:* www.leoadaly.com	Omaha	NE	68114	402-391-8111		261
Leo Castelli Gallery 18 E 77th St *Web:* www.castelligallery.com	New York	NY	10075	212-249-4470		42
Leo Events 265 S Front St *Web:* leoevents.com	Memphis	TN	38103	901-766-1836		184
Leo Pharma Inc 123 Commerce Valley Dr E Ste 400 *TF:* 800-668-7234 ■ *Web:* www.leo-pharma.ca	Thornhill	ON	L3T7W8	905-886-9822	886-6622	85
Leo Wolleman Inc 31 S St Ste 4-N-3 *TF:* 800-223-5667 ■ *Web:* www.leowolleman.com	Mount Vernon	NY	10550	212-840-1881	869-4216	411
Leo's Jewelry & Gifts Inc 34900 W Michigan Ave *Web:* leosjeweler.com	Wayne	MI	48184	734-721-4311		410
Leo's Ristorante 11 Leo Turo Wy *Web:* www.leosristorante.net	Worcester	MA	01604	508-753-9490		671
Leola Village Inn & Suites 38 Deborah Dr *TF:* 877-669-5094 ■ *Web:* www.theinnatleolavillage.com	Leola	PA	17540	717-656-7002	656-7648	379
Leominster Animal Hospital Inc 129 New Lancaster Rd *Web:* leominsteranimalhospital.com	Leominster	MA	01453	978-534-0936		794
Leominster Credit Union 20 Adams St *TF:* 800-649-4646 ■ *Web:* leominstercu.com	Leominster	MA	01453	978-537-8021		219
Leominster Public Library 30 West St *Web:* www.leominsterlibrary.org	Leominster	MA	01453	978-534-7522		434-3
Leominster State Forest 90 Fitchburg Rd Rt 31 *Web:* www.mass.gov	Westminster	MA	01473	978-874-2303		565
Leon County PO Box 98 *Web:* www.co.leon.tx.us	Centerville	TX	75833	903-536-2352	536-7581	338
Leon County Public Library System 200 W Park Ave *Web:* www.cms.leoncountyfl.gov	Tallahassee	FL	32301	850-606-2665	606-2601	434-3
Leon County Schools (LCS) 2757 W Pensacola St *Web:* www.leonschools.net	Tallahassee	FL	32304	850-487-7100		685
Leon D. DeMatteis Construction 820 Elmont Rd *Web:* www.dematteisorg.com	Elmont	NY	11003	516-285-5500		186
Leon Farmer & Co 100 Rail Ridge Rd *Web:* leonfarmer.com	Athens	GA	30607	706-353-1166		81-1
Leon Max Inc 3100 New York Dr *TF:* 888-334-4629	Pasadena	CA	91107	888-334-4629		155-21
Leon Studio One School of Hair Design 5385 Main St *Web:* www.leonstudioone.com	Williamsville	NY	14221	716-631-3878		685
Leon's Beauty School Inc 1305 Colisem Blvd *Web:* www.leonsbeauty.com	Greensboro	NC	27403	336-274-4601	370-9107	685
Leon's Texas Cuisine Co 2100 Redbud Blvd *TF:* 800-527-1243 ■ *Web:* www.texascuisine.com	McKinney	TX	75069	972-529-5050		296-36
Leona Group LLC 2125 University Pk Dr *Web:* www.leonagroup.com	Okemos	MI	48864	517-333-9030		242
Leonard 5275 Boul Wilfrid-Hamel *TF:* 800-561-2982 ■ *Web:* leonardagenceweb.com	Quebec City	QC	G2E5M7	418-780-1706		396
Leonard H. Shapiro, Esquire 10220 S Dolfield Rd Ste 203 *Web:* marylanddwiattorney.com	Owings Mills	MD	21117	410-363-3311		41
Leonard Holding Co 2001 S Laredo St *Web:* www.leonardhc.com	San Antonio	TX	78207	210-532-3241		473
Leonard Legal Group LLC 165 Washington St *Web:* leonardlawyers.com	Morristown	NJ	07960	973-984-1414		41
Leonard Masonry Inc 5925 Fee Fee Rd *Web:* www.leonardmasonry.com	Hazelwood	MO	63042	314-731-5500	731-3366	189-7
Leonard Mountain Inc PO Box 67 *TF:* 800-822-7700 ■ *Web:* www.leonardmountain.com	Leonard	OK	74043	918-366-2800	366-0335	296-20
Leonard Paper Co 725 N Haven St **Fax Area Code:* 410 ■ *TF:* 800-327-5547 ■ *Web:* www.leonardpaper.com	Baltimore	MD	21205	800-327-5547	563-0249*	559
Leonard S. Fiore Inc 5506 Sixth Ave Rear *Web:* www.lsfiore.com	Altoona	PA	16602	814-946-3686	946-5288	186
Leonard T. Jernigan, Jr. PA 3105 Glenwood Ave Ste 300 *TF:* 888-877-3956 ■ *Web:* jernlaw.com	Raleigh	NC	27612	919-833-0299		41
Leonard Valve Co 1360 Elmwood Ave *Web:* www.leonardvalve.com	Cranston	RI	02910	401-461-1200	941-5310	789
Leonard's Bakery Ltd 933 Kapahulu Ave *Web:* www.leonardshawaii.com	Honolulu	HI	96816	808-737-5591	732-2133	68
Leonard's Express Inc 6070 Collett Rd W *TF:* 866-924-8140 ■ *Web:* www.leonardsexpress.com	Farmington	NY	14425	585-924-8140	924-0508	780
Leonardo DRS 2345 Crystal Dr Ste 1000 *Web:* www.leonardodrs.com	Arlington	VA	22202	703-416-8000		248
Leonardo State Marina 102 Concord Ave *Web:* www.state.nj.us	Leonardo	NJ	07737	732-291-1333		565
Leonardo's 706 706 W University Ave *Web:* www.leonardosgainesville.com	Gainesville	FL	32601	352-378-2001		671
Leone Advertising 2024 Santa Cruz Ave *Web:* leonead.com	Menlo Park	CA	94025	650-854-5895		7
Leone Mcdonnell & Roberts PA CPA 5 Nelson St *Web:* www.lmrpa.com	Dover	NH	03820	603-749-2700		2
Leone, Throwe Teller & Nagle 33 Connecticut Blvd *Web:* lttnlaw.com	East Hartford	CT	06108	860-528-2145		41
Leonhard Insurance Agency Inc 5065 N Hwy 94 *Web:* leonhardins.com	Saint Charles	MO	63301	636-250-4155		390
Leoni Wiring Systems Inc 3100 N Campbell Ave Ste 101 *Web:* www.leoni.com	Tucson	AZ	85719	520-741-0895	741-0864	813
Leonie 1545 Crossways Blvd Ste 250 **Fax Area Code:* 703 ■ *Web:* www.leoniegroup.com	Chesapeake	VA	23320	757-777-3608	940-9120*	5
Leonis Partners 230 Park Ave *Web:* leonispartners.com	New York	NY	10169	212-804-8815		528
Leonoro's Spaghetti House 1507 Washington St E *Web:* leonorosspaghettihouse.com	Charleston	WV	25311	304-343-1851		671
Leopardo Companies Inc 5200 Prairie Stone Pkwy *Web:* www.leopardo.com	Hoffman Estates	IL	60192	847-783-3000	783-3001	186
Leopold Brothers Furniture Co 8147 Brecksville Rd *Web:* leopoldsfurniture.com	Brecksville	OH	44141	440-526-2400		321
Leopold Ketel & Partners 118 SW 1st Ave *Web:* www.leoketel.com	Portland	OR	97204	503-295-1918		7
Lepel Corp W227 N937 Westmound Dr *TF:* 800-548-8520 ■ *Web:* lepel.com	Waukesha	WI	53186	631-586-3300	586-3232	318
Lepercq de Neuflize & Co 156 W 56th St Ste 1204 *Web:* www.lepercq.com	New York	NY	10019	212-698-0700		690
LePoidevin Marketing 245 S Executive Dr Ste 365 *Web:* www.lepoidevinmarketing.com	Brookfield	WI	53005	262-754-9550	754-9554	7
Leppo Inc 176 W Ave *Web:* www.leppos.com	Tallmadge	OH	44278	330-633-3999		264-3
Leprino Foods Co 1830 W 38th Ave *Web:* leprinofoods.com	Denver	CO	80211	303-480-2600		296-5
Leprohon 6171 Boul Bourque *Web:* www.leprohon.com	Sherbrooke	QC	J1N1H2	819-563-2454		610
LERA (Leslie E. Robertson Associates) 40 Wall St 23rd Fl *Web:* www.lera.com	New York	NY	10005	212-750-9000	750-9002	194
Lerch Bates Inc 9780 S Meridian Blvd Ste 450 *TF:* 800-409-5471 ■ *Web:* www.lerchbates.com	Englewood	CO	80122	303-795-7956		261
Lerch Vinci & Higgins 17-17 SR-208 *Web:* www.lvhcpa.com	Fair Lawn	NJ	07410	201-791-7100	791-3035	2
Lereta LLC 1123 Parkview Dr *TF:* 800-537-3821 ■ *Web:* www.lereta.com	Covina	CA	91724	800-537-3821		652
Lerman Senter PLLC 2001 L St NW Ste 400 *Web:* www.lermansenter.com	Washington	DC	20036	202-429-8970	293-7783	428
Lerner David Littenberg Krumholz & Mentlik 600 South Ave W *TF:* 800-870-0008 ■ *Web:* www.lernerdavid.com	Westfield	NJ	07090	908-654-5000		428
Lerner Enterprises 2000 Tower Oaks Blvd 8th Fl *Web:* lerner.com	Rockville	MD	20852	301-284-6000	692-2626	652
Lerner Publishing Group 1251 Washington Ave N *TF:* 800-328-4929 ■ *Web:* www.lernerbooks.com	Minneapolis	MN	55401	800-328-4929	332-1132	637-2
Lerner Research Institute 9500 Euclid Ave *Web:* www.lerner.ccf.org	Cleveland	OH	44195	216-444-3900	444-3279	668
Lerner, Sampson & Rothfuss A Legal Professional Assn 120 E Fourth St *Web:* www.lsrlaw.com	Cincinnati	OH	45202	513-241-3100		428
Lernia Training Solutions 3603 Winding Way *Web:* lernia-ts.com	Newtown Square	PA	19073	610-356-1792		138
Leroy & Clarkson 211 Centre St Rm 5l *Web:* www.leroyandclarkson.com	New York	NY	10013	212-431-9291		344
Leroy Percy State Park 1400 Hwy 12 W *Web:* www.mdwfp.com	Hollandale	MS	38748	662-827-5436		565
Leroy Springs and Co 2201 Old Nation Rd *Web:* www.leroysprings.com	Fort Mill	SC	29715	803-547-1000		239
Le-Ru Telephone Co 555 Carter St *TF:* 888-394-4772 ■ *Web:* www.leru.net	Stella	MO	64867	417-628-3844		224
LES (Loyd's Electric Supply Inc) 838 Stonetree Dr *TF:* 800-492-4030 ■ *Web:* www.loydselectric.com	Branson	MO	65616	417-334-2171	334-6635	246
LES (Licensing Executives Society) 11130 Sunrise Valley Dr Ste 350 *Web:* www.lesusacanada.org	Reston	VA	20191	703-836-3106	836-3107	49-18
Les Boulangers Associes Inc 18842 13th Pl S *TF:* 800-522-1185 ■ *Web:* www.lba-inc.com	Seatac	WA	98148	206-241-9343	433-2844	296-2

Name / Address	City	State	ZIP	Phone	Fax	Class
Les Entreprises Energie Cardio 300-1040 Blvd Michele-Bohec Ste 120 *TF:* 877-363-7443 ■ *Web:* www.energiecardio.com	Blainville	QC	J7C5E2	450-979-3613		354
Les Entreprises JF Faucher 1100 St-Jean Rd *Web:* www.botanix.com	La Prairie	QC	J5R2L5	450-659-2222		183
Les Folies 2552 Riva Rd *Web:* www.lesfoliesbrasserie.com	Annapolis	MD	21401	410-573-0970		671
Les Mars Hotel 27 North St *Web:* www.hotellesmars.com	Healdsburg	CA	95448	707-433-4211	433-4611	379
Les Nomades 222 E Ontario St *Web:* www.lesnomades.net	Chicago	IL	60611	312-649-9010	649-0608	671
Les Stanford Chevrolet Inc 21730 Michigan Ave *TF:* 800-836-0972 ■ *Web:* www.lesstanfordchevrolet.com	Dearborn	MI	48124	800-836-0972		57
Les Stumpf Ford 3030 W College Ave *TF:* 855-864-8134 ■ *Web:* www.stumpfford.com	Appleton	WI	54914	920-731-5212		57
Les Suites Hotel Ottawa 130 Besserer St *TF:* 866-682-0879 ■ *Web:* www.les-suites.com	Ottawa	ON	K1N9M9	613-232-2000	232-1242	379
Les Trois Petits Cochons Inc 4223 First Ave 2nd Fl *TF:* 800-537-7283 ■ *Web:* 3pigs.com	Brooklyn	NY	11232	212-219-1230	941-9726	296-26
Les Wilkins & Associates Inc 6850 35th Ave NE *TF:* 800-426-6634 ■ *Web:* www.leswilkins.com	Seattle	WA	98115	206-522-0908	522-5292	475
Les Wilson Inc 205 Industrial Ave *Web:* www.leswilsoninc.com	Carmi	IL	62821	618-382-4667		540
Lesaffre Yeast Corp 7475 W Main St *TF:* 800-770-2714 ■ *Web:* lesaffreyeast.com	Milwaukee	WI	53214	414-615-3300		296-42
LeSaint Logistics 868 W Crossroads Pkwy *TF:* 877-566-9375 ■ *Web:* www.lesaint.com	Romeoville	IL	60446	630-243-5950		449
Lescarden Inc 420 Lexington Ave Ste 212 *Web:* www.catrix.com	New York	NY	10170	212-687-1050		85
LESCO (Lesco Distributing) 1203 E Industrial Dr *Web:* www.lescodistributing.com	Orange City	FL	32763	386-775-7244	775-1146	246
Lesco Design & Manufacturing Company Inc 1120 Ft Pickens Rd *Web:* lescodesign.com	LaGrange	KY	40031	502-222-7101	222-1429	261
Lesco Distributing (LESCO) 1203 E Industrial Dr *Web:* www.lescodistributing.com	Orange City	FL	32763	386-775-7244	775-1146	246
Lescure Company Inc 2301 Arnold Industrial Way Ste C *Web:* lescurecompany.com	Concord	CA	94520	925-283-2528	283-1630	610
Leshkowitz Law PLLC 45 Broadway Ste 3010 *Web:* leshkowitzlaw.com	New York	NY	10006	212-248-0880	248-0999	41
Leshner & Associates Inc 47 N Lockwood Rd *Web:* www.leshnerlabs.com	Elkton	MD	21921	410-964-0311		192
Lesic & Camper Communications 172 E State St Ste 410 *Web:* lesiccamper.com	Columbus	OH	43215	614-224-0658		224
Lesko Debbie (Rep R - AZ) 1113 Longworth House Office Bldg *Web:* lesko.house.gov	Washington	DC	20515	202-225-4576		342-2
Lesko Enterprises Inc 21 Euclid St *Web:* www.leskoenterprises.com	Albion	PA	16401	814-756-4030	756-5260	604
Lesley University 29 Everett St *TF:* 800-999-1959 ■ *Web:* lesley.edu	Cambridge	MA	02138	617-868-9600		166
Leslie Controls Inc 12501 Telecom Dr *TF:* 800-323-8366 ■ *Web:* www.lesliecontrols.com	Tampa	FL	33637	813-978-1000	978-0984	789
Leslie County PO Box 619 *Web:* www.lesliecounty.ky.gov	Hyden	KY	41749	606-672-3200	672-7373	338
Leslie E. Robertson Associates (LERA) 40 Wall St 23rd Fl *Web:* www.lera.com	New York	NY	10005	212-750-9000	750-9002	194
Leslie Lewis & Assoc 247 Spring St *Web:* www.leslielewisdesign.com	Jeffersonville	IN	47130	812-282-6606		393
Leslie Science & Nature Ctr 1831 Traver Rd *Web:* www.lesliesnc.org	Ann Arbor	MI	48105	734-997-1553	997-1072	520
Leslie Tonkonow Artworks & Projects 535 W 22nd St 6th Fl *Web:* www.tonkonow.com	New York	NY	10011	212-255-8450		42
Lesman Instrument Co 135 Bernice Dr *TF:* 800-953-7626 ■ *Web:* www.lesman.com	Bensenville	IL	60106	630-595-8400	595-2386	386
Leson Chevrolet Company Inc 1501 Westbank Express *TF:* 877-496-2420 ■ *Web:* www.lesonauto.com	Harvey	LA	70058	504-366-4381		516
Lesperance & Martineau 1440 Ste-Catherine W Bureau 700 *TF:* 888-273-8387 ■ *Web:* l-m.ca	Montreal	QC	H3G1R8	514-861-4831	392-9112	428
Lesser Lutrey Pasquesi & Howe LLP 191 E Deerpath Ste 300 *Web:* llphlegal.com	Lake Forest	IL	60045	847-295-8800	295-8886	41
Lessing-Flynn Adv Co 3106 Ingersoll Ave *Web:* www.lessingflynn.com	Des Moines	IA	50312	515-274-9271		4
Lessonly Inc 1129 E 16th St *Web:* www.lessonly.com	Indianapolis	IN	46202	317-469-9194		39
Lessors Inc 1056 Gemini Rd *TF:* 800-233-1865 ■ *Web:* www.lessorsinc.com	Eagan	MN	55121	651-454-1202	452-9510	780
Lestelle & Lestelle Aplc 3421 N Causeway Blvd Ste 602 *Web:* lestellelaw.com	Metairie	LA	70002	504-828-1224		41
Lester Building Systems LLC 1111 Second Ave S *TF:* 800-826-4439 ■ *Web:* www.lesterbuildings.com	Lester Prairie	MN	55354	320-395-2531		106
Lester Catalog Co 9850 Hillview Rd *Web:* www.waiglobal.com	Newcastle	CA	95658	530-823-0063		530
Lester Group, The 101 E Commonwealth Blvd *Web:* www.lestergroup.com	Martinsville	VA	24115	276-632-2195		752
Lester Inc 19 Business Pk Dr *TF:* 800-999-5265 ■ *Web:* www.lesterusa.com	Branford	CT	06405	203-488-5265	483-0408	737
Lester Lampert Corporate 7 E Huron St *Web:* lesterlampert.com	Chicago	IL	60611	312-944-6888		410
Lester Lithograph Inc 1128 N Gilbert St **Fax Area Code:* 714 ■ *TF:* 800-794-0858 ■ *Web:* www.castlepress.com	Anaheim	CA	92801	800-794-0858	535-2362*	627
Lester R. Summers Inc 40 Garden Spot Rd Ste 100 *Web:* www.summerstrucking.com	Ephrata	PA	17522	717-733-6556	733-3065	780
Lester Sales Company Inc 4312 W Minnesota St *TF:* 888-963-6270 ■ *Web:* www.lestersalesco.com	Indianapolis	IN	46241	317-244-7811	248-2369	246
Let's Play 8300 S County Line Rd *Web:* www.letsplaysoccer.com	Oklahoma City	OK	73169	405-261-6076	261-0328	181
Letcher County 156 Main St Ste 107 *Web:* www.letchercounty.ky.gov	Whitesburg	KY	41858	606-633-2129	633-7105	338
Letchworth State Park 1 Letchworth State Pk *Web:* parks.ny.gov	Castile	NY	14427	585-493-3600		565
Letco Medical Inc 1316 Commerce Dr NW *TF:* 800-239-5288 ■ *Web:* www.letcomedical.com	Decatur	AL	35601	800-239-5288		583
Lethbridge Chamber of Commerce 200 Commerce House 529 - 6th St S *Web:* www.lethbridgechamber.com	Lethbridge	AB	T1J2E1	403-327-1586	327-1001	137
Lethbridge Herald 504 Seventh St S *Web:* lethbridgeherald.com	Lethbridge	AB	T1J2H1	403-328-4411	328-4536	532-1
Lethbridge Public Library 810 5 Ave S *Web:* www.lethlib.ca	Lethbridge	AB	T1J4C4	403-380-7310		435
Letica Corp 52585 Dequindre Rd *TF:* 800-538-4221 ■ *Web:* www.letica.com	Rochester	MI	48307	248-652-0557		548
LeTip International Inc 4838 E Baseline Rd Ste 123 *TF:* 800-255-3847 ■ *Web:* www.letip.com	Mesa	AZ	85206	480-264-4600		393
Letnan Industries Inc 6520 Arrow Dr *Web:* www.letnanind.com	Sterling Heights	MI	48314	586-726-1155		247
Letourneau Federal Credit Union 2301 S High St *Web:* www.etpcu.org	Longview	TX	75602	903-234-3480		219
LeTourneau University 2100 S Mobberly Ave *TF:* 800-759-8811 ■ *Web:* www.letu.edu	Longview	TX	75602	903-233-3000	233-4301	166
Lets Get Checked 330 W 38th St Ste 405 *Web:* www.letsgetchecked.com	New York	NY	10018	929-376-0056		353
Lets Talk Business Network 54 W 39th At Avenue of the Americas *Web:* ltbn.com	New York	NY	10018	212-742-1553		78
Letsos Co 8435 Westglen Dr PO Box 36927 *Web:* www.letsos.com	Houston	TX	77063	713-783-3200	972-7880	186
Letter Arts Review 1833 Sping Garden St *TF:* 800-369-9598 ■ *Web:* www.johnnealbooks.com	Greensboro	NC	27403	336-272-6139	272-9015	637-9
Lettich & Zipay 2500 W End Ave Ste 10 *Web:* lettichandzipay.com	Pottsville	PA	17901	570-622-8761		2
Lettire Construction Corp 334-336 E 110th St *Web:* www.lettire.com	New York	NY	10029	212-996-6640	534-1421	186
Leucadia State Beach 948 Neptune Ave *Web:* www.parks.ca.gov	Encinitas	CA	92024	760-633-2740		565
Leunig's Bistro 115 Church St *Web:* www.leunigsbistro.com	Burlington	VT	05401	802-863-3759		671
Leupold & Stevens Inc 14400 NW Greenbrier Pkwy *TF:* 800-538-7653 ■ *Web:* www.leupold.com	Beaverton	OR	97006	800-538-7653		544
Leuthold Group, The 150 S 5th St Ste 1700 *TF:* 800-273-6886 ■ *Web:* funds.leutholdgroup.com	Minneapolis	MN	55402	612-332-1567		194
Levasseur Dier & Associates Pc 3233 Coolidge Hwy *Web:* ldalaw.com	Berkley	MI	48072	248-586-1200		428
Level 3 Post 2901 W Alameda Ave *Web:* www.level3post.com	Burbank	CA	91505	818-840-7200		512
Level Agency 235 Fort Pitt Blvd *TF:* 877-733-8625 ■ *Web:* www.level.agency	Pittsburgh	PA	15222	877-733-8625		5
Level II Inc 555 Andover Pk W Ste 110 *TF:* 888-232-9609 ■ *Web:* www.leveltwo.com	Tukwila	WA	98188	206-575-7682	575-7981	463
Levelfieldcom Inc 11675 Jollyville Rd Ste 207 *Web:* www.levelfield.com	Austin	TX	78759	512-401-9200		177
Levementum LLC 55 N Arizona Pl Ste 203 *Web:* www.levementum.com	Chandler	AZ	85225	480-320-2500		196
Levene Gouldin & Thompson LLP 450 Plaza Dr *Web:* www.lgtlegal.com	Vestal	NY	13850	607-763-9200	763-9211	445
Levenger 420 S Congress Ave *TF:* 800-544-0880 ■ *Web:* www.levenger.com	Delray Beach	FL	33445	561-276-2436	243-3629	459
Leventhal Law Group PC 45 Main St Ste 528 *Web:* llg.nyc	Brooklyn	NY	11201	718-556-9600		41
Lever 155 5th St 6th Fl *Web:* lever.co	San Francisco	CA	94103	415-458-2731		178-1
Lever Interactive Inc 701 Warrenville Rd Ste 200 *Web:* www.leverinteractive.com	Lisle	IL	60532	630-435-6400	435-6404	195
Leverage2Market Associates Inc 274 Redwood Shores Pky 544 *Web:* www.leverage2market.com	Redwood City	CA	94065	650-281-4854	453-3661	194

				Phone	Fax	Class
Levert Personnel Resources Inc 17 Frood Rd *TF:* 800-461-5934 ■ *Web:* www.levert.ca	Sudbury	ON	P3C4Y9	705-525-8367		260
Leverx Inc 800 W El Camino Real Ste 180 *Web:* leverx.com	Mountain View	CA	94040	650-625-8347		177
Levi Jackson State Park 998 Levi Jackson Mill Rd *Web:* parks.ky.gov	London	KY	40744	606-330-2130		565
Levi Ray & Shoup Inc 2401 W Monroe St *Web:* www.lrs.com	Springfield	IL	62704	217-793-3800	787-3286	178-1
Levi Strauss & Co 1155 Battery St *Web:* www.levistrauss.com	San Francisco	CA	94111	415-501-6000	501-7112	155-11
Leviathan Corp 55 Washington St Ste 457 *TF:* 855-687-8721 ■ *Web:* www.leviathancorp.com	Brooklyn	NY	11201	855-687-8721		386
LEVICK LLC 1900 M St NW *Web:* levick.com	Washington	DC	20036	202-973-1300		636
Levin Andy (Rep D - MI) 228 Cannon House Office Bldg. *Web:* www.andylevin.house.gov	Washington	DC	20515	202-225-4961		342-2
Levin Furniture Co 5280 Rt 30 *TF:* 844-600-1795 ■ *Web:* www.levinfurniture.com	Greensburg	PA	15601	724-834-3550		321
Levin Group Inc 10 New Plant Ct. *Web:* levingroup.com	Owings Mills	MD	21117	410-654-1234		463
Levin Mike (Rep D - CA) 1626 Longworth House Office Bldg *Web:* www.mikelevin.house.gov	Washington	DC	20515	202-225-3906		342-2
Levine & Blit PLLC 350 Fifth Ave 40th Fl *TF:* 866-254-8529 ■ *Web:* levineblit.com	New York	NY	10118	866-254-8529		41
Levine & Levine PLLC 2 Jefferson Plz Ste 100 *Web:* levinelevinelaw.com	Poughkeepsie	NY	12601	845-452-2350		41
Levine Blaszak Block & Boothby LLP 2001 L St NW Ste 900 *Web:* www.lb3law.com	Washington	DC	20036	202-857-2550		428
Levine Builders 42-09 235th St *Web:* www.levinebuilders.com	Douglaston	NY	11363	212-400-9292		186
Levine Jacobs & Company LLC 333 Eisenhower Pkwy *Web:* ljcpa.com	Livingston	NJ	07039	973-992-9400		2
Levine Law LLC 4500 Cherry Creek S Dr Ste 400 *Web:* mydenveraccidentlawfirm.com	Denver	CO	80246	303-333-8000		41
Levine Leichtman Capital Partners (LLCP) 335 N Maple Dr Ste 130 *Web:* www.llcp.com	Beverly Hills	CA	90210	310-275-5335	275-1441	690
Levine Museum of the New South 200 E Seventh St *Web:* www.museumofthenewsouth.org	Charlotte	NC	28202	704-333-1887	333-1896	520
Levinson Axelrod 2 Lincoln Ct *Web:* www.njlawyers.com	Edison	NJ	08820	732-440-3089		445
Levinson Institute Inc 28 Main St Ste 100 *TF:* 800-290-5735 ■ *Web:* levinsonandco.com	Jaffrey	NH	03452	603-532-4700	532-4750	765
Levittown Beauty Academy 8919 New Falls Rd *Web:* www.levittownbeautyacademy.com	Levittown	PA	19054	215-943-0298		167-3
Levitt-Safety Ltd 2872 Bristol Cir. *TF:* 888-453-8488 ■ *Web:* www.levitt-safety.com	Oakville	ON	L6H5T5	905-829-3299	829-2919	419
Levolor Inc 5775 Glenridge Dr Bldg A *TF:* 800-752-9677 ■ *Web:* www.levolor.com	Atlanta	GA	30328	800-752-9677		87
Levy Affiliated Holdings LLC 201 Wilshire Blvd 2nd Fl *Web:* www.levyaffiliated.com	Santa Monica	CA	90401	310-883-7900	917-1101	528
Levy County 355 S Ct St *Web:* www.levycounty.org	Bronson	FL	32621	352-486-5218	486-5167	338
Levy Craig Law Firm 4520 Main St Ste 1600 *Web:* levycraig.com	Kansas City	MO	64111	816-474-8181	471-2186	41
Levy Diamond Bello & Associates LLC 260 Quarry Rd Unit D *Web:* ldbassociates.com	Milford	CT	06461	203-876-1000		317
Levy Economics Institute of Bard College Bard College Blithewood Rd *Web:* www.levyinstitute.org	Annandale-on-Hudson	NY	12504	845-758-7700	758-1149	634
Levy Leff & Defrank P C 129 Church St Ste 712 *Web:* levyleffdefrank.com	New Haven	CT	06510	203-777-6887		41
Levy Restaurants 980 N Michigan Ave. *Web:* www.levyrestaurants.com	Chicago	IL	60611	312-664-8200		670
Levy, Mosse & Co 11400 W Olympic Blvd Ste 330 *Web:* levymosse.com	Los Angeles	CA	90064	310-473-2773	473-7550	2
Lew A. Cummings Company Inc 4 Peters Brook Dr PO Box 16495 *TF:* 800-647-0035 ■ *Web:* www.cummingsprinting.com	Hooksett	NH	03106	800-647-0035		627
Lew Edwards Group, The 5454 Broadway *Web:* lewedwardsgroup.com	Oakland	CA	94618	510-594-0224		196
Lew Electric Fittings Co 371 Randy Rd **Fax Area Code:* 708 ■ *Web:* www.lewelectric.com	Carol Stream	IL	60188	630-665-2075	345-6490*	816
Lew Jan Textile Corp 366 Veterans Memorial Hwy **Fax Area Code:* 631 ■ *TF:* 800-899-0531 ■ *Web:* www.lewjan.com	Commack	NY	11725	800-899-0531	543-0561*	594
LEWA Inc 132 Hopping Brook Rd *Web:* www.lewa-inc.com	Holliston	MA	01746	508-429-7403		641
Lewan Technology 1400 S Colorado Blvd *TF:* 888-539-2611 ■ *Web:* www.lewan.com	Denver	CO	80222	303-759-5440		225
LEWCO Inc 706 Lane St *Web:* www.lewcoinc.com	Sandusky	OH	44870	419-625-4014		207
Lewcott Corp 86 Providence Rd *TF:* 800-225-7725 ■ *Web:* barrday.com	Millbury	MA	01527	508-865-1791	865-0302	605-2
Lewellen Accountancy Corp 23521 Paseo De Valencia 205	Laguna Hills	CA	92653	949-859-4644		2
Lewer Agency Inc 4534 Wornall Rd **Fax Area Code:* 816 ■ *TF:* 800-821-7715 ■ *Web:* www.lewer.com	Kansas City	MO	64111	800-821-7715	561-6840*	390
Lewes Historical Society 110 Shipcarpenter St *Web:* www.historiclewes.org	Lewes	DE	19958	302-645-7670	645-2375	520
Lewin Group 3130 Fairview Pk Dr Ste 800 *TF:* 877-227-5042 ■ *Web:* www.lewin.com	Falls Church	VA	22042	703-269-5500	269-5501	194
Lewis & Clark Bank 1900 Mcloughlin Blvd Ste 67 *Web:* lewisandclarkbank.com	Oregon City	OR	97045	503-212-3200	212-3199	70
Lewis & Clark Caverns State Park PO Box 489 *Web:* stateparks.mt.gov	Whitehall	MT	59759	406-287-3541		565
Lewis & Clark College 0615 SW Palatine Hill Rd *TF:* 800-444-4111 ■ *Web:* www.lclark.edu	Portland	OR	97219	503-768-7040	768-7055	166
Lewis & Clark County 316 N Park Ave Rm142 *Web:* www.lccountymt.gov	Helena	MT	59623	406-447-8369		338
Lewis & Clark Library 120 S Last Chance Gulch *Web:* www.lclibrary.org	Helena	MT	59601	406-447-1690	447-1687	434-3
Lewis & Clark National Historic Trail Interpretive Ctr 4201 Giant Springs Rd *Web:* www.fs.usda.gov	Great Falls	MT	59405	406-727-8733	453-6157	50-5
Lewis & Clark State Historic Site 1 Lewis & Clark Trl *Web:* www.campdubois.com	Hartford	IL	62048	618-251-5811		50-3
Lewis & Clark State Park 21914 Pk Loop *Web:* www.lewisandclarktrail.com	Onawa	IA	51040	712-423-2829		565
Lewis & Clark State Park 801 Lake Crest Blvd *Web:* mostateparks.com	Rushville	MO	64484	816-579-5564		565
Lewis & Clark State Park 4583 Jackson Hwy *Web:* www.parks.state.wa.us	Winlock	WA	98596	360-864-2643		565
Lewis & Clark State Recreation Area 54731 897 Rd *Web:* outdoornebraska.gov	Crofton	NE	68730	402-388-4169		565
Lewis & Clark Trail Heritage Foundation 4201 Giant Springs Rd *TF:* 888-701-3434 ■ *Web:* www.lewisandclark.org	Great Falls	MT	59405	406-454-1234		48-23
Lewis & Clark Trail State Park 36149 Hwy 12 *Web:* parks.state.wa.us	Dayton	WA	99328	509-337-6457		565
Lewis & Company PC 3804 Poplar Hill Rd Ste B	Chesapeake	VA	23321	757-638-4566		2
Lewis & Ellis Inc 2929 N Central Expy Ste 200 *Web:* lewisellis.com	Richardson	TX	75080	972-850-0850		196
Lewis & Knopf CPAs PC 5206 Gateway Centre Ste 100 *TF:* 877-244-1787 ■ *Web:* www.lewis-knopf.com	Flint	MI	48507	810-238-4617		2
Lewis & Michael Inc 1827 Woodman Dr *TF:* 800-543-3524 ■ *Web:* atlaslm.com	Dayton	OH	45420	800-543-3524		186
Lewis & Raulerson Inc 1759 State St *Web:* lewisandraulerson.com	Waycross	GA	31501	912-283-5951	283-8281	316
Lewis & Van Vleet 18660 SW Boones Ferry Rd *Web:* lvvi.com	Tualatin	OR	97062	503-885-8605		261
Lewis Advertising Inc 1050 Country Club Rd *Web:* www.lewisadvertising.com	Rocky Mount	NC	27804	252-443-5131		7
Lewis Bakeries Inc 500 N Fulton Ave *Web:* lewisbakeries.net	Evansville	IN	47710	812-425-4642		296-1
Lewis Bear Co 6120 Enterprise Dr. *Web:* lewisbearcompany.com	Pensacola	FL	32505	850-434-8612		81-1
Lewis Brisbois Bisgaard & Smith LLP 221 N Figueroa St Ste 1200 *Web:* lewisbrisbois.com	Los Angeles	CA	90012	213-250-1800	250-7900	428
Lewis Builders Inc 54 Sawyer Ave *Web:* www.lewisbuilders.com	Atkinson	NH	03811	603-362-5333	362-4936	187
Lewis Chrysler 4440 N Vine St *TF:* 888-758-8221 ■ *Web:* www.lewischryslerdodgejeepofhays.com	Hays	KS	67601	888-758-8221		57
Lewis Communications Inc 2030 First Ave N *Web:* www.lewiscommunications.com	Birmingham	AL	35203	205-980-0774		4
Lewis Contractors 55 Gwynns Mill Ct *Web:* lewis-contractors.com	Owings Mills	MD	21117	410-356-4200		186
Lewis Corp 15136 W Hunziker Rd *Web:* www.lcorp.com	Pocatello	ID	83202	208-238-1202		697
Lewis County 351 NW North St *Web:* lewiscountywa.gov	Chehalis	WA	98532	360-740-1192		338
Lewis County 100 E Lafayette *Web:* www.lewiscountymo.org	Monticello	MO	63457	573-767-5205	767-8245	338
Lewis County 112 Second St PO Box 129 *TF:* 800-230-5740 ■ *Web:* lewiscountyclerk.ky.gov	Vanceburg	KY	41179	606-796-3062	796-0822	338
Lewis County 499 US Hwy 33 E Ste 102 *TF:* 800-296-7329 ■ *Web:* www.stonewallcountry.com	Weston	WV	26452	304-269-7328		338
Economic Development 31 Smith Ave *Web:* www.lewiscountytn.com	Hohenwald	TN	38462	931-796-6012	796-6020	338
Lewis County Chamber of Commerce 7576 S State St *TF:* 800-724-0242 ■ *Web:* www.adirondackstughill.com	Lowville	NY	13367	315-376-2213	376-0326	139
Lewis County Court House 7660 N State St *Web:* www.lewiscounty.org	Lowville	NY	13367	315-377-2000	376-3768	338
Lewis County Herald Publishing Co 187 Main St *TF:* 800-572-2685 ■ *Web:* www.lewiscountyherald.com	Vanceburg	KY	41179	606-796-2331	796-3110	532-2
Lewis County Rural Electric Co-op 18256 Hwy 16 PO Box 68 *TF:* 888-454-4485 ■ *Web:* www.lewiscountyrec.org	Lewistown	MO	63452	573-215-4000		245

	Phone	Fax	Class
Lewis Critter Gitter 25 W Frnt St S Thomasville AL 36784 *Web:* lewiscrittergitter.com	334-636-4530		577
Lewis Direct Marketing 325 E Oliver St Baltimore MD 21202 *TF:* 800-533-5394 ■ *Web:* www.lewisdirect.com	410-539-5100	685-5144	5
Lewis Drug Inc 4409 E 26th St Sioux Falls SD 57103 *Web:* www.lewisdrug.com	605-367-2710	367-2876	237
Lewis Electric Supply Company Inc 1306 Second St PO Box 2237 Muscle Shoals AL 35662 *TF:* 800-239-0681 ■ *Web:* www.lesupply.com	256-383-0681		246
Lewis Fire Protection Inc 423 W Industrial Ct. Villa Rica GA 30180 *Web:* lewisfire.com	770-459-3636	459-5159	189-10
Lewis Ford Sales Inc 3373 N College Ave PO Box 8430 Fayetteville AR 72703 *Web:* www.lewiscars.com	479-442-5301		57
Lewis Ginter Botanical Garden 1800 Lakeside Ave Richmond VA 23228 *Web:* www.lewisginter.org	804-262-9887	262-6329	97
Lewis Group 283 G St Chula Vista CA 91902 *Web:* thelewisgroupinc.com	619-470-9110		652
Lewis Industrial Supply Co 3307 N 6th St Harrisburg PA 17110 *TF:* 800-929-2400 ■ *Web:* www.lewisindustrialsupply.com	717-234-2409	233-4380	454
Lewis John (Rep D - GA) 300 Cannon House Office Bldg. Washington DC 20515 *Web:* johnlewis.house.gov	202-225-3801		342-2
Lewis Kappes 1 American Sq Ste 2500 Indianapolis IN 46282 *Web:* www.lewis-kappes.com	317-639-1210	639-4882	428
Lewis Legal News Inc 1701 E Cedar St Ste 111 Olathe KS 66062 *Web:* thelegalrecord.net	913-780-5790		532-3
Lewis Manufacturing Co 3601 S Byers Ave Oklahoma City OK 73129 **Fax Area Code:* 405 ■ *TF:* 888-398-4719 ■ *Web:* www.lewismfg.com	888-398-4719	632-8608*	523
Lewis Marine Supply Company Inc 220 SW 32nd St Fort Lauderdale FL 33315 *TF:* 800-327-3792 ■ *Web:* www.lewismarine.com	954-523-4371	523-1934	770
Lewis Media Partners LLC 500 Libbie Ave Ste 2-C Richmond VA 23226 *Web:* lewismediapartners.com	804-741-7115		5
Lewis Military Museum PO Box 331001 Lewis-McChord WA 98433 *Web:* lewisarmymuseum.com	253-967-7206		520
Lewis Newspapers Inc 111 E Main Pilot Point TX 76258 *Web:* www.postsignal.com	940-686-2169	686-2437	532-2
Lewis O. Flom Lansing Public Library 2750 Indiana Ave Lansing IL 60438 *Web:* www.lansingpl.org	708-474-2447	474-9466	434-3
Lewis O. Unglesby, Attorney LLC 246 Napoleon St. Baton Rouge LA 70802 *Web:* unglesbylaw.com	225-387-0120		41
Lewis Rice 600 Washington Ave Ste 2500 Saint Louis MO 63101 *Web:* www.lewisrice.com	314-444-7600		445
Lewis Roca Rothgerber LLP 201 E Washington St Ste 1200 Phoenix AZ 85004 *Web:* www.lrrc.com	602-262-5311	262-5747	41
Lewis S. Mills High School 24 Lyon Rd Burlington CT 06013 *Web:* www.region10ct.org	860-673-0423	673-9128	685
Lewis Steel Works Inc 613 S Main St Wrens GA 30833 *TF:* 800-521-5239 ■ *Web:* www.lewissteelworks.com	706-547-6561		91
Lewis Transport Inc 506 Burkesville St. Columbia KY 42728 **Fax Area Code:* 270 ■ *TF:* 800-982-0363 ■ *Web:* www.lewistransportinc.com	800-982-0363	384-5749*	780
Lewis Tree Service Inc 300 Lucius Gordon Dr West Henrietta NY 14586 *TF:* 800-333-1593 ■ *Web:* lewistree.com	585-436-3208	235-5864	776
Lewis University 1 University Pkwy Romeoville IL 60446 *TF:* 800-897-9000 ■ *Web:* www.lewisu.edu	815-838-0500	836-5002	166
Lewis Wagner LLP 501 Indiana Ave Ste 200 Indianapolis IN 46202 *TF:* 800-237-0505 ■ *Web:* www.lewiswagner.com	317-237-0500	630-2790	428
Lewis Yockey & Brown Inc 505 N Main St Bloomington IL 61701 *Web:* www.lybinc.com	309-829-2552		727
Lewisburg Printing Co 170 Woodside Ave PO Box 2608 Lewisburg TN 37091 *TF:* 800-559-1526 ■ *Web:* www.lpcink.com	800-559-1526		627
Lewis-Clark State College 500 Eighth Ave Lewiston ID 83501 *TF:* 800-933-5272 ■ *Web:* www.lcsc.edu	208-792-5272	792-2210	166
Lewiston Livestock Market Inc 3200 E Main Lewiston ID 83501 *TF:* 800-473-3406 ■ *Web:* Www.lewistonlivestock.com	208-743-5506	746-4442	446
Lewiston Morning Tribune 505 Capital St. Lewiston ID 83501 *TF:* 800-745-9411 ■ *Web:* lmtribune.com	208-743-9411	746-1185	532-2
Lewiston Municipal Federal Credit Union 291 Pine St. Lewiston ME 04240 *Web:* lewistoncu.com	207-783-3991		219
Lewiston Public Library 200 Lisbon St. Lewiston ME 04240 *Web:* lplonline.org	207-513-3004		434-3
Lewiston Sales Inc 21241 Dutchmans Crossing Rd Lewiston MN 55952 *TF:* 800-732-6334 ■ *Web:* www.lewistonsales.com	507-523-2112	523-2400	446
Lewiston Veterinary Clinic 421 22nd St N Lewiston ID 83501 *Web:* lewistonvet.vetstreet.com	208-743-6553	743-4564	794
Lewiston Wholesale Flowers 2937 Magnolia St Ste 202 Lewiston ID 83501 *Web:* www.lwflowers.com	208-503-9200		293
Lewistown Florist Store 129 S Main St Ste 200 Lewistown PA 17044 *Web:* www.lewistownflorist.com	717-248-9683		292
Lewistown Livestock Auction PO Box 1190 Lewistown MT 59457 *TF:* 866-538-9413 ■ *Web:* www.laauctionco.com	866-538-9413		446
Lewistown News-Argus, The 521 W Main St PO Box 900 Lewistown MT 59457 *TF:* 800-879-5627 ■ *Web:* www.lewistownnews.com	406-535-3401	535-3405	532-3
Lewisville Chamber of Commerce 551 N Valley Pkwy Lewisville TX 75067 *Web:* www.lewisvillechamber.org	972-436-9571	436-5949	139
Lewisville Public Library 1197 W Main St Lewisville TX 75067 *Web:* www.cityoflewisville.com	972-219-3570	219-5094	434-3
LeWiz Communications Inc 1376 N Fourth St Ste 300 San Jose CA 95112 *Web:* www.lewiz.com	408-432-6248		246
Lewnes' Steakhouse 401 Fourth St Annapolis MD 21403 *Web:* www.lewnessteakhouse.com	410-263-1617		671
Lex La-Ray Technical Ctr 2323 High School Dr Lexington MO 64067 *Web:* www.lexlaray.com	660-259-2264	259-6262	167-3
Lexair Inc 2025 Mercer Rd Lexington KY 40511 *Web:* www.lexairinc.com	859-255-5001	255-6656	128
LexaMed Ltd 705 Front St Toledo OH 43605 *TF:* 888-232-5227 ■ *Web:* lexamed.net	419-693-5307	691-0418	463
Lexar Media Inc 47300 Bayside Pkwy Fremont CA 94538 *TF:* 877-747-4031 ■ *Web:* www.lexar.com	408-933-1088		288
LexCentral 5443 W 70th Pl Bedford Park IL 60638 *Web:* lexcentral.net	708-594-9200	594-5233	492
Lexel Corp 532 Broadhollow Rd Ste 125 Melville NY 11747 *TF:* 877-772-4111 ■ *Web:* www.lexel.com	631-501-0700	501-1930	518
Lexel Imaging Systems Inc 510 Henry Clay Blvd. Lexington KY 40505 *Web:* www.lexelimaging.com	859-721-1600	243-5555	253
LexiCode 100 Executive Center Dr Ste 101 Columbia SC 29210 **Fax Area Code:* 248 ■ *TF:* 800-448-2633 ■ *Web:* www.lexicode.com	800-448-2633	524-7522*	194
Lexicon Branding Inc 30 Liberty Ship Way Ste 3360 Sausalito CA 94965 *Web:* www.lexiconbranding.com	415-332-1811		195
Lexicon Bridge Publishers 202 Bridge St Ithaca NY 14850 *Web:* www.lexiconbridge.com	607-277-3981		637-10
Lexicon Inc 8900 Fourche Dam Pk Little Rock AR 72206 *TF:* 800-925-4565 ■ *Web:* www.lexicon-inc.com	501-490-4200		480
Lexicon International Corp 1400A Adams Rd Bensalem PA 19020 *TF:* 800-448-8201 ■ *Web:* www.lexicon-int.com	215-639-8220		387
Lexicon Marketing Inc 6380 Wilshire Blvd Ste 1400 Los Angeles CA 90048	323-782-7400		737
Lexicon Pharmaceuticals Inc 8800 Technology Forest Pl The Woodlands TX 77381 *NASDAQ: LXRX* ■ *TF:* 855-828-4651 ■ *Web:* www.lexpharma.com	281-863-3000		85
Lexinet Corp, The 701 N Union St. Council Grove KS 66846 *TF:* 800-767-1577 ■ *Web:* www.lexinetcorporation.com	620-767-7000		5
Lexington Ballet Co (LBC) 161 N Mill St Lexington KY 40507 *Web:* www.lexingtonballet.org	859-233-3925		573-1
Lexington Building Supply Company Inc 1077 Eastland Dr Lexington KY 40505	859-254-8834		499
Lexington Chamber of Commerce 1875 Massachusetts Ave Lexington MA 02420 *Web:* www.lexingtonchamber.org	781-862-2480		139
Lexington Chamber of Commerce 311 W Main St Lexington SC 29072 *Web:* www.lexingtonsc.org	803-359-6113	359-0634	139
Lexington City Schools 1010 Fair St Lexington NC 27292 *Web:* www.lexcs.org	336-242-1527	249-3206	685
Lexington Engineering Associates 2 Moore Cir Bedford MA 01730 *Web:* www.lexingtonengineering.com	781-862-1115		194
Lexington Financial 42855 Garfield Rd Ste 109 Clinton Township MI 48038 *Web:* lexington-financial.com	586-226-9800		690
Lexington Furniture Company Inc, The 3024 Blake James Dr Lexington KY 40509 *Web:* www.lexfurniture.com	859-254-4412		321
Lexington Health Care Ctr 17 Cornelia Dr Lexington NC 27292 *Web:* www.mfa.net	336-242-1349		354
Lexington Herald-Leader 100 Midland Ave. Lexington KY 40508 *Web:* www.kentucky.com	859-231-3100		532-2
Lexington Historical Society (LHS) 13 Depot Sq Lexington MA 02420 *Web:* www.lexingtonhistory.org	781-862-1703		48-13
Lexington Home Brands 1300 National Hwy Thomasville NC 27360 *TF:* 800-333-4300 ■ *Web:* lexington.com	336-474-5300		319-2
Lexington (Independent City) 300 E Washington St Lexington VA 24450 *Web:* lexingtonva.gov	540-462-3700	463-5310	338
Lexington Insurance Company Inc 99 High St 2nd Fl Boston MA 02110 *Web:* www.lexingtoninsurance.com	617-330-1100		391-4
Lexington Livestock Market Inc 300 Plum Creek Pkwy. Lexington NE 68850 *Web:* www.lexlivestock.com	308-324-4663	324-5803	446
Lexington Manufacturing Inc 1330 115th Ave NW Minneapolis MN 55448 *Web:* www.lexingtonmfg.com	763-754-9055		820
Lexington Market 400 W Lexington St. Baltimore MD 21201 *Web:* lexingtonmarket.com	410-685-6169		460
Lexington Medical Ctr 2720 Sunset Blvd West Columbia SC 29169 *Web:* www.lexmed.com	803-791-2000		374-3
Lexington New York City, The 511 Lexington Ave 48th St New York NY 10017 *Web:* www.lexingtonhotelnyc.com	212-755-4400		707

Name / Address	City	State	Zip	Phone	Fax	Class
Lexington Opera House 401 W Short St *Web:* www.lexingtonoperahouse.com	Lexington	KY	40507	859-233-4567	253-2718	572
Lexington Philharmonic 161 N Mill St *TF:* 888-494-4226 ■ *Web:* www.lexphil.org	Lexington	KY	40507	859-233-4226	233-7896	573-3
Lexington Public Library 140 E Main St *Web:* www.lexpublib.org	Lexington	KY	40507	859-231-5504	231-5598	434-3
Lexington Public Library District 207 S Cedar St *Web:* www.lexington.lib.il.us	Lexington	IL	61753	309-365-7801		434-3
Lexington Realty Trust Inc 1 Penn Plz Ste 4015 *Web:* www.lxp.com	New York	NY	10119	212-692-7200	594-6600	654
Lexington School District 4 607 E Fifth St *Web:* www.lex4.org	Swansea	SC	29160	803-490-7000	399-7960	685
Lexington Technologies in 99 Rome St *Web:* lexingtontech.net	Farmingdale	NY	11735	631-755-8660		261
Lexington Theological Seminary 230 Lexington Green Cir Ste 300 *TF:* 866-296-6087 ■ *Web:* www.lextheo.edu	Lexington	KY	40503	859-252-0361	281-6042	167-3
Lexington VA Health Care System 1101 Veterans Dr *Web:* www.lexington.va.gov	Lexington	KY	40502	859-233-4511		391-3
Lexington Visitors Ctr 401 W Main St *TF:* 800-845-3959 ■ *Web:* www.visitlex.com	Lexington	KY	40507	859-233-7299	254-4555	206
Lexington Wealth Management 12 Waltham St *Web:* www.lexingtonwealth.com	Lexington	MA	02421	781-860-7745	862-4392	401
Lexington, The 1096 Grand Ave *Web:* thelexmn.com	Saint Paul	MN	55105	763-548-2297		671
Lexipol LLC 6B Liberty Ste 200 *TF:* 844-312-9500 ■ *Web:* www.lexipol.com	Aliso Viejo	CA	92656	949-484-4444		194
Lexis Nexis InterAction 2000 Clearwater Dr Ste 100 *TF:* 800-180-7126 ■ *Web:* www.lexisnexis.co.in	Oak Brook	IL	60523	800-180-7126		178-1
LexisNexis 1801 Varsity Dr *TF:* 800-543-6862 ■ *Web:* www.lexisnexis.com	Raleigh	NC	27606	800-543-6862		457-5
LexisNexis Matthew Bender 744 Broad St *TF:* 800-252-9257 ■ *Web:* www.lexisnexis.com	Newark	NJ	07102	973-820-2000		637-2
LexJet Corp 1680 Fruitville Rd 3rd Fl *TF:* 800-453-9538 ■ *Web:* www.lexjet.com	Sarasota	FL	34236	941-330-1210		628
Lexmark Carpet Mills Inc 285 Kraft Dr *TF:* 800-871-3211 ■ *Web:* www.lexmarkcarpet.com	Dalton	GA	30721	800-871-3211		131
Lexmark International Inc 740 W New Cir Rd *NYSE:* LXK ■ *TF:* 800-539-6275 ■ *Web:* www.lexmark.com	Lexington	KY	40550	859-232-2000		173-6
Lextant Corp 250 S High St Ste 600 *Web:* www.lextant.com	Columbus	OH	43215	614-228-9711		180
Lextech Inc 202 Wilson Downing Rd *Web:* lextechky.com	Lexington	KY	40517	859-278-9230	278-1843	180
Lexus of Memphis Inc 2600 Ridgeway Rd *Web:* www.lexusofmemphis.com	Memphis	TN	38119	901-362-8833		57
Lexy Pacific Corp 611 Vaqueros Ave *Web:* www.lexypacific.com	Sunnyvale	CA	94085	408-331-8818	331-8830	174
Leyman Manufacturing Corp 10335 Wayne Ave *TF:* 866-539-6261 ■ *Web:* www.leymanlift.com	Cincinnati	OH	45215	513-891-6210	891-4901	112
LFA (Lupus Foundation of America Inc) 2000 L St NW Ste 410 *TF:* 800-558-0121 ■ *Web:* www.lupus.org	Washington	DC	20036	202-349-1155	349-1156	48-17
LFA (Lawson-Fisher Associates PC) 525 W Washington Ave *Web:* lawson-fisher.com	South Bend	IN	46601	574-234-3167		261
LFCU (Lockheed Federal Credit Union) 2340 Hollywood Way *TF:* 800-328-5328 ■ *Web:* www.logixbanking.com	Burbank	CA	91505	818-565-2020		219
LFI Inc 271 US Hwy 46 Ste C101 *Web:* lfiincorporated.com	Fairfield	NJ	07004	973-882-0550		297-8
LFP Inc 8484 Wilshire Blvd Ste 900 *Web:* hustler.com	Beverly Hills	CA	90211	323-651-5400		637-9
LG Barcus & Sons Inc 1430 State Ave *TF:* 800-255-0180 ■ *Web:* www.barcus.com	Kansas City	KS	66102	913-621-1100	621-3288	188-2
LG Electronics USA Inc 1000 Sylvan Ave *TF:* 800-243-0000 ■ *Web:* www.lg.com	Englewood Cliffs	NJ	07632	201-816-2000		173-4
LG Everist Inc 300 S Phillips Ave Ste 200 *TF:* 800-843-7992 ■ *Web:* www.lgeverist.com	Sioux Falls	SD	57117	605-334-5000	334-3656	503-4
LG2 Environmental Solutions Inc 10475 Fortune Pkwy Ste 201 *TF:* 800-435-0072 ■ *Web:* www.lg2es.com	Jacksonville	FL	32256	904-288-8631	262-8637	652
LGA Engineering 399 N St *Web:* www.lgaengineering.com	Duxbury	MA	02332	781-837-6300	837-6344	194
LGB & Associates Inc 332 W Lee Hwy PMB 307 *Web:* www.lgb-inc.com	Warrenton	VA	20186	703-359-6950		177
LGH (Lakeshore General Hospital) 160 Stillview Ste 1249 *Web:* fondationlakeshore.ca	Pointe-Claire	QC	H9R2Y2	514-630-2081	630-2873	374-2
LGH (Lowell General Hospital) 295 Varnum Ave *TF:* 800-544-2424 ■ *Web:* www.lowellgeneral.org	Lowell	MA	01854	978-937-6000	937-6869	374-3
LGHA (Lake George Historical Assn) 290 Canada St *Web:* www.lakegeorgehistorical.org	Lake George	NY	12845	518-668-5044		49-19
LGL Group Inc, The 2525 Shader Rd *NYSE:* LGL ■ *Web:* www.lglgroup.com	Orlando	FL	32804	407-298-2000		185
LGPL (Los Gatos Public Library) 110 E Main St *Web:* www.losgatosca.gov	Los Gatos	CA	95030	408-354-8600	354-0578	434-3
LGR (Los Gatos Research Inc) 3055 Orchard Dr *Web:* www.lgrinc.com	San Jose	CA	95134	650-965-7772	965-7074	256
LGS Technologies LP 2950 W Wintergreen Rd *Web:* www.lgstechnologies.com	Lancaster	TX	75134	972-224-9201		326
LGWM (Lloyd Gray Whitehead Monroe) 880 Montclair Rd Ste 100 *TF:* 800-967-7299 ■ *Web:* lgwmlaw.com	Birmingham	AL	35213	205-967-8822	967-2380	428
LH Computer Services 12296 Wiles Rd *Web:* www.lhcomp.com	Tamarac	FL	33321	954-752-5805		175
LH Lacy Company Ltd 1880 Crown Dr Ste 1200 *Web:* www.lhlacy.com	Dallas	TX	75234	214-357-0146	350-0662	188-4
LHA (Louisiana Hospital Assn) 9521 Brookline Ave *Web:* www.lhaonline.org	Baton Rouge	LA	70809	225-928-0026	923-1004	48-13
LHB Inc 21 W Superior St Ste 500 *Web:* www.lhbcorp.com	Duluth	MN	55802	218-727-8446	727-8456	261
LHC (NYU Langone Hospitals) 150 55th St *Web:* www.lutheranhealthcare.org	Brooklyn	NY	11220	718-630-7000	630-8653	374-3
LHC Group Inc 901 Hugh Wallis Rd S *NASDAQ:* LHCG ■ *TF:* 866-542-4768 ■ *Web:* www.lhcgroup.com	LaFayette	LA	70508	337-289-8188		363
LHCSD (La Habra City School District) 500 N Walnut St *Web:* www.lahabraschools.org	La Habra	CA	90631	562-690-2305	690-4154	186
LHM Technologies Inc 446 Rowtree Dairy Rd *Web:* www.lhmtech.com	Woodbridge	ON	L4L8H2	905-856-2466		454
LHotel Montreal 262 St Jacques St W *TF:* 877-553-0019 ■ *Web:* www.lhotelmontreal.com	Old Montreal	QC	H2Y1N1	514-985-0019	985-0059	379
LHR Hospitality 1793 Buerkle Cir *Web:* lhrhospitality.com	Saint Paul	MN	55110	651-340-1880		377
LHR Services & Equipment Incorporated lc-disc 4200 Fm 1128 Rd *Web:* www.lhrservices.com	Pearland	TX	77581	713-943-2321		608
LHR Technologies Inc 4930 Allen Genoa Rd Ste D *Web:* www.carvewright.com	Pasadena	TX	77504	713-473-6572		173-1
LHS (Lexington Historical Society) 13 Depot Sq *Web:* www.lexingtonhistory.org	Lexington	MA	02420	781-862-1703		48-13
LHS Productions Inc 260 Union St *Web:* www.videobankdigital.com	Northvale	NJ	07647	201-767-2002		177
LHSD (Laurel Highlands School District) 304 Bailey Ave *Web:* laurelhighlandssd.wixsite.com	Uniontown	PA	15401	724-437-4741	437-5653	685
LHTC (Laurel Highland Total Communications Inc) 4157 Main St *Web:* lhtcbroadband.com	Stahlstown	PA	15687	724-593-2411		224
LHUCA (Louise Hopkins Underwood Center for the Arts) 511 Ave K *Web:* lhuca.org	Lubbock	TX	79401	806-762-8606		50-2
LHV Power Corp 10221 Buena Vista Ave *Web:* www.lhvpower.com	Santee	CA	92071	619-258-7700		253
LHWH Advertising & PR 3005 Hwy 17 N Bypass *Web:* www.lhwhadvertising.com	Myrtle Beach	SC	29577	843-448-1123		7
Li Cor Inc PO Box 4425 *TF:* 800-447-3576 ■ *Web:* www.licor.com	Lincoln	NE	68504	402-467-3576	467-2819	419
Li'l Porgy's Bar-B-Q 1917 W Springfield Ave *Web:* www.lilporgysbbq.com	Champaign	IL	61821	217-398-8575		671
LIA (Laser Institute of America) 13501 Ingenuity Dr Ste 128 *TF:* 800-345-2737 ■ *Web:* www.lia.org	Orlando	FL	32826	407-380-1553	380-5588	49-19
Lia Auto Group, The 1258 Central Ave *TF:* 855-212-7985 ■ *Web:* www.liacars.com	Albany	NY	12205	855-212-7985		57
Lia Schorr Institute 57 W 57th St No 1409 *Web:* www.liaschorrinstitute.com	New York	NY	10019	212-486-9541		167-3
Liacouras Ctr 1776 N Broad St *TF:* 800-298-4200 ■ *Web:* www.liacourascenter.com	Philadelphia	PA	19121	215-204-2400		572
Liaison Committee on Medical Education (LCME) 330 N Wabash Ave Ste 39300 *Web:* lcme.org	Chicago	IL	60611	312-464-4933		48-1
Liaison Creative + Marketing 4302 Airport Blvd *TF:* 877-323-0550 ■ *Web:* liaisoncreative.com	Austin	TX	78722	512-323-0550		260
Libbey Inc 300 Madison Ave PO Box 10060 *NYSE:* LBY ■ *TF:* 888-794-8469 ■ *Web:* libbey.com	Toledo	OH	43699	419-325-2100		334
Libby Hill Seafood Restaurants Inc 3920 Cotswold Ave *Web:* libbyhill.com	Greensboro	NC	27410	336-294-0505		670
Libby Hoopes PC 399 Boylston St *Web:* libbyhoopes.com	Boston	MA	02116	617-338-9300		41
Libby Laboratories Inc 1700 Sixth St *Web:* www.libbylabs.com	Berkeley	CA	94710	510-527-5400	527-8687	479
Libby Perszyk Kathman Holdings Inc (LPK) 19 Garfield Pl *Web:* www.lpk.com	Cincinnati	OH	45202	513-241-6401		195
Liberal Area Chamber of Commerce PO Box 676 *Web:* www.liberalkschamber.com	Liberal	KS	67905	620-624-3855	624-8851	139
Liberal New Iron & Metal LLC 426 SW Ave *Web:* www.liberalnewironandmetal.com	Liberal	KS	67901	620-624-5663		492
Liberal Party of Canada 350 Albert St Ste 920 *TF:* 888-542-3725 ■ *Web:* www.liberal.ca	Ottawa	ON	K1P6M8	888-542-3725		615
Liberal R-II School District 104 N Payne *Web:* www.liberal.k12.mo.us	Liberal	MO	64762	417-843-2125	843-2403	685
Liberia *Embassy* 5201 16th St NW *Web:* www.liberianembassyus.org	Washington	DC	20011	202-723-0437	723-0436	257

Name / Address	City	State	ZIP	Phone	Fax	Class
Libertarian Party 2600 Virginia Ave NW Ste 200 *TF:* 800-735-1776 ■ *Web:* www.lp.org	Washington	DC	20037	202-333-0008	333-0072	616
Libertel Associates 283 Swanson Dr. **Fax Area Code:* 731 ■ *TF:* 800-748-8535 ■ *Web:* www.libertelassociates.com	Dresden	TN	38225	800-748-8535	364-2719*	246
Liberty Advisor Group LLC 30 S Wacker Dr. *Web:* www.libertyadvisorgroup.com	Chicago	IL	60606	312-869-9707		466
Liberty Bank 315 Main St *TF:* 800-622-6732 ■ *Web:* www.liberty-bank.com	Middletown	CT	06457	888-570-0773		70
Liberty Bank & Trust Co PO Box 60131 *TF:* 800-883-3943 ■ *Web:* www.libertybank.net	New Orleans	LA	70160	504-240-5100		70
Liberty Bell Equipment Corp 3201 S 76th St *TF:* 800-541-5827 ■ *Web:* www.medcotool.com	Philadelphia	PA	19153	215-492-6700		200
Liberty Bell Steak Co 3457 Janney St. *Web:* www.libertybellsteak.com	Philadelphia	PA	19134	215-537-4797	537-1256	297-9
Liberty Bottle Co 2900 Sutherland Dr *Web:* libertybottles.com	Union Gap	WA	98903	509-834-6500		124
Liberty Brass Turning Company Inc 1200 Shames Dr. *TF:* 800-345-5939 ■ *Web:* www.libertybrass.com	Westbury	NY	11590	718-784-2911	784-2038	621
Liberty Capital Bank 5055 Keller Springs Rd Ste 120 *Web:* libertycapital.bank	Addison	TX	75001	469-375-6600	375-6565	70
Liberty Carton Co 870 Louisiana Ave *Web:* www.libertycarton.com	Golden Valley	MN	55426	763-540-9600		100
Liberty Casting Company LLC 550 S Liberty Rd. *Web:* www.libertycasting.com	Delaware	OH	43015	740-363-1941		492
Liberty Coating Company LLC 21 S Steel Rd *Web:* www.libertycoating.com	Morrisville	PA	19067	215-736-1111		481
Liberty Communications Business Office 413 N Calhoun St. *Web:* www.libertycommunications.com	West Liberty	IA	52776	319-627-2145		387
Liberty Correctional Institution 11064 NW Dempsey Barron Rd *Web:* dc.state.fl.us	Bristol	FL	32321	850-643-9400	643-9412	213
Liberty County 11493 Summers Rd PO Box 523 *Web:* www.libertycountyflorida.com	Bristol	FL	32321	850-643-2359		338
Liberty County 1923 Sam Houston St. *Web:* www.co.liberty.tx.us	Liberty	TX	77575	936-336-4600		338
Liberty County Combined Chamber of Commerce & CVB 208 E Court St *Web:* libertycounty.org	Hinesville	GA	31313	912-368-4445		139
Liberty County Georgia 112 N Main St *Web:* www.libertycountyga.com	Hinesville	GA	31310	912-876-2164		338
Liberty Diversified International Inc 5600 Hwy 169 N. *TF:* 800-421-1270 ■ *Web:* www.libertydiversified.com	New Hope	MN	55428	763-536-6600	536-6685	360-3
Liberty Drug & Surgical Inc 195 Main St *TF:* 877-816-0111 ■ *Web:* www.libertydrug.com	Chatham	NJ	07928	973-635-6200	635-6208	237
Liberty Falls State Recreation Site 3700 Airport Way *Web:* www.dnr.alaska.gov	Fairbanks	AK	99709	907-823-2265		565
Liberty for Trading Agencies PO Box 833 *Web:* www.libertyfta.com	Hazel Park	MI	48030	586-939-2554		169
Liberty Forge Inc 1507 Fort Worth St PO Box 1210 *TF:* 800-231-2377 ■ *Web:* libertyforgeinc.com	Liberty	TX	77575	936-336-5785	336-2740	483
Liberty Fund Inc 8335 Allison Pt Trial Ste 300 *TF:* 800-955-8335 ■ *Web:* www.libertyfund.org	Indianapolis	IN	46250	317-842-0880	579-6060	305
Liberty Furniture Industries 6021 Greensboro Dr. *TF:* 800-275-2223 ■ *Web:* www.mylibertyfurniture.com	Atlanta	GA	30336	800-275-2223		319-1
Liberty Glass & Metal Industries Inc 339 Riverside Dr. *Web:* www.lgminc.net	North Grosvenordale	CT	06255	860-923-3623		234
Liberty Global Inc 1550 Wewatta St Ste 1000 *NASDAQ: LBTYA* ■ *Web:* www.libertyglobal.com	Denver	CO	80202	303-220-6600		736
Liberty Group LLC 411 30th St 2nd Fl. *TF:* 888-588-5818 ■ *Web:* www.libertygroupllc.com	Oakland	CA	94609	510-658-1880	658-1886	690
Liberty Hall Historic Site 202 Wilkinson St *Web:* libertyhall.org	Frankfort	KY	40601	502-227-2560		50-3
Liberty Hardware Manufacturing Corp 140 Business Pk Dr *TF:* 800-652-7277 ■ *Web:* www.libertyhardware.com	Winston-Salem	NC	27107	336-769-4077		350
Liberty Home Equity Solutions Inc 10951 White Rock Rd Ste 200 *TF:* 800-218-1415 ■ *Web:* libertyhomeequity.com	Rancho Cordova	CA	95670	916-636-0183		509
Liberty Hospital 2525 Glenn Hendren Dr *TF:* 800-344-3829 ■ *Web:* www.libertyhospital.org	Liberty	MO	64068	816-781-7200	781-7550	374-3
Liberty Hotel, The 215 Charles St *Web:* libertyhotel.com	Boston	MA	02114	617-224-4000		378
Liberty House 76 Audrey Zapp Dr *Web:* libertyhouserestaurant.com	Jersey City	NJ	07305	201-395-0300		671
Liberty Independent School District 1600 Grand Ave *Web:* www.libertyisd.net	Liberty	TX	77575	936-336-7213	336-2283	685
Liberty Industries Inc 130 E Cemetery Rd. *Web:* libertytrailers.com	Fillmore	IN	46128	765-246-4031		779
Liberty Maritime Corp 1979 Marcus Ave Ste 200. *Web:* libertygl.com	Lake Success	NY	11042	516-488-8800	488-8806	313
Liberty Media Holding Corp 12300 Liberty Blvd *Web:* www.libertymedia.com	Englewood	CO	80112	720-875-5400		360-3
Liberty Molds Inc 8631 Portage Indus Dr *Web:* libertymolds.com	Portage	MI	49024	269-327-0997	327-1697	757
Liberty Moving & Storage Inc 350 Moreland Rd *TF:* 800-640-4487 ■ *Web:* www.libertymoving.com	Commack	NY	11725	631-234-3000		780
Liberty Mutual Group 175 Berkeley St. *TF:* 800-426-9898 ■ *Web:* www.libertymutual.com	Boston	MA	02116	617-357-9500		391-4
Liberty Natural Products Inc 20949 S Harris Rd *TF:* 800-289-8427 ■ *Web:* www.libertynatural.com	Oregon City	OR	97045	503-631-4488	631-2424	238
Liberty Oak Restaurant & Bar 100-D W Washington St. *Web:* libertyoakrestaurant.com	Greensboro	NC	27401	336-273-7057		671
Liberty Personnel Services 410 Feheley Dr *Web:* www.libertyjobs.com	King of Prussia	PA	19406	610-941-2424		631
Liberty Pioneer Energy Source Inc 1411 East 840 North. *Web:* www.libertypioneer.com	Orem	UT	84097	801-224-4771	224-1593	540
Liberty Pumps Inc 7000 Apple Tree Ave *TF:* 800-543-2550 ■ *Web:* www.libertypumps.com	Bergen	NY	14416	585-494-1817		641
Liberty Safe & Security Products Inc 1199 W Utah Ave *TF:* 800-247-5625 ■ *Web:* www.libertysafe.com	Payson	UT	84651	801-925-1000	465-2712	487
Liberty Savings Bank FSB 3435 Airborne Rd Ste B *TF:* 800-436-6300 ■ *Web:* www.libertysavingsbank.com	Wilmington	OH	45177	800-436-6300		70
Liberty Savings Federal Credit Union 666 Newark Ave *Web:* lsfcu.org	Jersey City	NJ	07306	201-659-3900		219
Liberty Science Ctr Liberty State Pk 222 Jersey City Blvd *Web:* lsc.org	Jersey City	NJ	07305	201-200-1000		520
Liberty Staffing USA LLC One Scenic Central Bldg 1 N Scenic Hwy Ste 109 *Web:* www.libertystaffingusa.com	Lake Wales	FL	33853	863-456-4949		260
Liberty State Park 200Morris Pesin Dr *Web:* www.njparksandforests.org	Jersey City	NJ	07305	201-915-3440	915-3408	565
Liberty Steel Products Inc 11650 Mahoning Ave *Web:* www.libertysteelproducts.com	North Jackson	OH	44451	330-538-2236	538-0833	492
Liberty Tax Service Inc 1716 Corporate Landing Pkwy *TF:* 800-790-3863 ■ *Web:* www.libertytax.com	Virginia Beach	VA	23454	757-493-8855	493-0169	734
Liberty Throwing Company Inc Pringle St & Zerby Ave	Kingston	PA	18704	570-287-1114	283-3531	745-9
Liberty Tobacco 7341 Clairemont Mesa Blvd *TF:* 877-255-4237 ■ *Web:* www.libertytobacco.com	San Diego	CA	92111	858-292-1772		756
Liberty Tool Inc 44404 Phoenix Dr. *Web:* www.liberty-tool.com	Sterling Heights	MI	48314	586-726-2449	726-1377	455
Liberty Toyota Scion 4397 Rt 130 S *TF:* 888-809-7798 ■ *Web:* www.libertytoyota.com	Burlington	NJ	08016	609-386-6300		516
Liberty Transportation & Storage Company Inc 50 Industrial Rd *TF:* 800-524-0567 ■ *Web:* thelibertygroupcompany.com	Berkeley Heights	NJ	07922	908-964-8390		311
Liberty Travel Inc 69 Spring St. *TF:* 888-271-1584 ■ *Web:* www.libertytravel.com	Ramsey	NJ	07446	201-934-3643		771
Liberty Trust & Savings Bank 502 Eighth Ave *Web:* mylibertytrust.com	Durant	IA	52747	563-785-4441		70
Liberty University 1971 University Blvd **Fax Area Code:* 800 ■ *TF:* 800-543-5317 ■ *Web:* www.liberty.edu	Lynchburg	VA	24502	434-582-2000	542-2311*	166
Liberty Vegetable Oil Co 15306 S Carmenita Rd *Web:* www.libertyvegetableoil.com	Santa Fe Springs	CA	90670	562-921-3567		297-8
Liberty Wood Products 874 Iotla Church Rd *Web:* libertywoodproducts.net	Franklin	NC	28734	828-524-7958	369-7652	819
Liberty Woods International Inc (LWI) 1903 Wright Pl Ste 360 *TF:* 800-367-7054 ■ *Web:* www.libertywoods.com	Carlsbad	CA	92008	760-438-8030	438-8018	191-3
Liberty-Dayton Area Chamber of Commerce 1801 Trinity St *Web:* www.libertydaytonchamber.com	Liberty	TX	77575	936-336-5736	336-1159	139
Liberty-Eylau Independent School District 2901 Leopard Dr. *Web:* www.leisd.net	Texarkana	TX	75501	903-832-1535	838-9444	685
Libertyone Credit Union 2221 E Lamar Blvd Ste 110 *Web:* libertyonecu.com	Arlington	TX	76006	214-413-5588		219
Liberty-Pittsburgh Systems Inc 3498 Grand Ave *Web:* www.golps.com	Pittsburgh	PA	15225	877-577-2345		110
Libertyville Bank & Trust Co 507 N Milwaukee Ave *TF:* 866-564-7330 ■ *Web:* www.libertyvillebank.com	Libertyville	IL	60048	847-367-6800		70
Libertyville Chevrolet Inc 1001 S Milwaukee Ave *TF:* 877-520-1807 ■ *Web:* www.libertyvillechevrolet.com	Libertyville	IL	60048	847-362-1400		516
Libertyville District 70 1381 W Lake St *Web:* www.d70schools.org	Libertyville	IL	60048	847-362-9695	362-3003	685
Libertyville Financial Group Ltd 900 Technology Way Ste 130 *Web:* inspirionwealth.com	Libertyville	IL	60048	847-918-9100		690
Libertyville Savings Bank 2000 W Jefferson *Web:* lsbia.bank	Fairfield	IA	52556	641-472-9839		70
Libman Co 220 N Sheldon St *TF:* 877-818-3380 ■ *Web:* libman.com	Arcola	IL	61910	217-268-4200	268-4168	103

Name / Address	City	State	ZIP	Phone	Fax	Class
Libra Industries Inc 7770 Div Dr	Mentor	OH	44060	440-974-7770		625
Web: www.libraindustries.com						
Libra Technical Center (LTC)						
200 Centennial Ave Ste 140	Piscataway	NJ	08854	732-667-5626	667-5572	743
TF: 855-441-5200 ■ *Web:* www.libratechnicalcenter.com						
Librairie Paragraphe Bookstore						
2220 McGill College Ave	Montreal	QC	H3A3P9	514-845-5811		95
Web: www.paragraphbooks.com						
Libraries of Middlesex Automation Consortium						
27 Mayfield Ave	Edison	NJ	08837	732-750-2525		434-3
Web: www.lmxac.org						
Library & Archives Canada						
550 de la Cite Blvd	Gatineau	QC	K1A0N4	613-995-6274		434
Web: www.collectionscanada.ca						
Library Binding Service (LBS)						
1801 Thompson Ave	Des Moines	IA	50316	515-262-3191	262-4091*	92
**Fax Area Code:* 800 ■ *TF:* 800-247-5323 ■ *Web:* www.lbsbind.com						
Library Company of Philadelphia						
1314 Locust St	Philadelphia	PA	19107	215-546-3181	546-5167	434-4
Web: librarycompany.org						
Library Corp, The (TLC) 1 Research Pk	Inwood	WV	25428	304-229-0100	229-0295	178-1
TF: 800-325-7759 ■ *Web:* www.tlcdelivers.com						
Library Hotel 299 Madison Ave	New York	NY	10017	212-983-4500		379
Web: libraryhotel.com						
Library of Congress						
101 Independence Ave SE	Washington	DC	20540	202-707-5000		434-3
Web: www.loc.gov						
National Library Service for the Blind & Physically Handicapped						
1291 Taylor St NW	Washington	DC	20542	202-707-5100	707-0712	342
TF: 888-657-7323 ■ *Web:* www.loc.gov						
Library of Hattiesburg Petal & Forrest County						
329 Hardy St	Hattiesburg	MS	39401	601-582-4461		434-3
Web: hattlibrary.org						
Library of Michigan, The						
702 W Kalamazoo St PO Box 30007	Lansing	MI	48909	517-335-0488		434-5
TF: 800-726-7323 ■ *Web:* www.michigan.gov						
Library of Rush University						
Rush University Medical Ctr						
600 S Paulina St Ste 571	Chicago	IL	60612	312-942-5950		434-1
Web: rushu.libguides.com						
Library of Virginia 800 E Broad St	Richmond	VA	23219	804-692-3500	692-3594	434-5
Web: www.lva.virginia.gov						
Library Reproduction Service						
19146 Van Ness Ave	Torrance	CA	90501	800-255-5002	354-2601*	626
**Fax Area Code:* 310 ■ *TF:* 800-255-5002 ■ *Web:* largeprintschoolbooks.com						
Library System of Lebanon County						
125 N 7th St	Lebanon	PA	17046	717-273-7624	273-2719	434-3
Web: www.lclibs.org						
Library Systems & Services L L C						
6235 River Crest Ste S	Riverside	CA	92507	800-638-8725		434-3
TF: 800-638-8725 ■ *Web:* www.lsslibraries.com						
Liburdi Engineering Ltd 400 Hwy 6 N	Dundas	ON	L9H7K4	905-689-0734		454
TF: 800-991-2100 ■ *Web:* www.liburdi.com						
LIC (Lafayette Instrument Company Inc)						
3700 Sagamore Pky N	Lafayette	IN	47903	765-423-1505	423-4111	472
TF: 800-428-7545 ■ *Web:* www.lafayetteinstrument.com						
Liccardi Ford Inc 1615 Rt 22 W	Watchung	NJ	07069	908-561-7500		57
Web: liccardi.com						
Licensing Executives Society (LES)						
11130 Sunrise Valley Dr Ste 350	Reston	VA	20191	703-836-3106	836-3107	49-18
Web: www.lesusacanada.org						
Licher Direct Mail Inc 980 Seco St	Pasadena	CA	91103	626-795-3333		5
Web: www.licherdm.com						
Lichte Insurance Agency Inc						
149 W Main St	Reedsburg	WI	53959	608-524-3113		390
Web: lichteinsurance.com						
Lichtenwald-Johnston Iron Works Corp						
7840 Lehigh St	Morton Grove	IL	60053	847-966-1100	966-1159	480
Web: lichtenwald-johnston.com						
Lichtman & Rosenblum PLLC						
1666 Connecticut Ave NW Ste 500	Washington	DC	20009	202-986-1666	986-1665	41
Web: lrimmlaw.com						
Lick Observatory						
7281 Mt Hamilton Rd	Mount Hamilton	CA	95140	408-274-5061		598
TF: 800-866-1131 ■ *Web:* www.ucolick.org						
Licking County Chamber of Commerce						
50 W Locust St	Newark	OH	43055	740-345-9757	345-5141	139
Web: www.lickingcountychamber.com						
Licking Memorial Hospital						
1320 W Main St	Newark	OH	43055	220-564-4000		374-3
Web: www.lmhealth.org						
Licking Valley Oil Inc						
8160 US Hwy 27 N PO Box 246	Butler	KY	41006	859-472-7111	472-7112	579
TF: 800-899-9449 ■ *Web:* www.lvoinc.com						
Licking Valley Rural Electric Co-opeartive Corp						
271 Main St	West Liberty	KY	41472	606-743-3179	743-2415	245
TF: 800-596-6530 ■ *Web:* lvrecc.com						
Liconix Industries Inc						
78-35 Springfield Blvd	Oakland Gardens	NY	11364	718-217-7900	468-6900	625
Web: www.liconix-usa.com						
LICT Corp 401 Theodore Fremd Ave	Rye	NY	10580	914-921-8821	921-6410	736
Web: lictcorp.com						
Liddle & Dubin Pc 975 E Jefferson Ave	Detroit	MI	48207	313-392-0015		41
Web: ldclassaction.com						
Liddle & Robinson LLP						
800 Third Ave 8th Fl	New York	NY	10022	212-687-8500	687-1505	428
Web: liddlerobinson.com						
LiDestri 815 Whitney Rd W	Fairport	NY	14450	585-377-7700	377-8150	296-20
Web: www.lidestrifoodanddrink.com						
Lidia's Italy 1400 Smallman St	Pittsburgh	PA	15222	412-552-0150		671
Web: lidias-pittsburgh.com						
Lidia's Kansas City 101 W 22nd St	Kansas City	MO	64108	816-221-3722		671
Web: www.lidias-kc.com						
Lido Beach Resort						
700 Ben Franklin Dr	Sarasota	FL	34236	941-388-2161		707
TF: 800-441-2113 ■ *Web:* www.lidobeachresort.com						
LidoChem Inc 20 Village Ct	Hazlet	NJ	07730	732-888-8000	264-2751	146
Web: www.lidochem.com						
Lieber Correctional Institution						
136 Wilborn Ave	Ridgeville	SC	29472	843-875-3332		213
Web: www.doc.sc.gov						
Lieberman Group LLC, The						
223 NW Second St Ste 300	Evansville	IN	47708	812-434-6600		179
Web: www.ltnow.com						
Lieberman Research						
98 Cutter Mill Rd	Great Neck	NY	11021	516-829-8880		466
Web: www.liebermanresearch.com						
Lieberman, Ryan & Forest LLC						
141 W End Ave	Somerville	NJ	08876	908-231-8844		41
Web: liryfo.com						
Liebherr USA Co						
4100 Chestnut Ave	Newport News	VA	23607	757-928-8732	928-8701	779
Web: www.liebherr.com						
Liebovich Steel & Aluminum Co						
2116 Preston St	Rockford	IL	61102	815-987-3200	987-9865	723
TF: 800-892-2981 ■ *Web:* www.liebovichsteel.com						
Liechtenstein Embassy						
2900 K St NW Ste 602B	Washington	DC	20007	202-331-0590	331-3221	257
Web: www.liechtensteinusa.org						
Lied Discovery Children's Museum						
360 Promenade Pl	Las Vegas	NV	89106	702-382-3445	382-0592	521
Web: www.discoverykidslv.org						
Lied Lodge & Conference Ctr						
2700 Sylvan Rd	Nebraska City	NE	68410	402-873-8733		205
Web: www.liedlodge.org						
Liese Lumber Company Inc						
319 E Main St	Belleville	IL	62220	618-234-0105		364
Web: www.lieselumber.com						
Lieu Ted (Rep D - CA)						
403 Cannon House Office Bldg	Washington	DC	20515	202-225-3976		342-2
Web: lieu.house.gov						
Life 97.3 1101 E Central Entrance	Duluth	MN	55811	218-722-6700		645-50
TF: 888-720-9730 ■ *Web:* life973.com						
Life Advantages LLC						
600 First Ave N Ste 307	Saint Petersburg	FL	33701	727-381-9446		260
Web: www.lifeadvantages.com						
Life Alert's Encino						
16027 Ventura Blvd Ste 400	Encino	CA	91436	800-920-3410		575
TF: 800-920-3410 ■ *Web:* www.lifealertencino.com						
Life Baptist Church						
2720 Harristown Rd PO Box 1236	Saint Stephen	SC	29479	843-567-4773		48-20
Web: lifebaptistsc.org						
Life Brokerage Financial Group						
2360 Boy Scout Rd	Clearwater	FL	33763	800-965-5234		690
TF: 800-965-5234 ■ *Web:* lbfg.net						
Life Care Centers of America						
3570 Keith St NW	Cleveland	TN	37312	423-472-9585	476-5974	451
Web: lcca.com						
Life Changing Radio 8 Lawrence Rd	Derry	NH	03038	603-437-9337	831-7964*	645-171
**Fax Area Code:* 508 ■ *Web:* www.lifechangingradio.com						
Life Cycle Engineering Inc						
4360 Corporate Rd	North Charleston	SC	29405	843-744-7110		261
TF: 800-556-9589 ■ *Web:* www.lce.com						
Life Equity LLC						
Canal Place Bldg 17 530 S Main St Ste 1731	Akron	OH	44311	330-655-7500	342-7782	796
Web: lifeequity.com						
Life Flight Network LLC						
22285 Yellow Gate Ln NE	Aurora	OR	97002	503-678-4364		13
TF: 800-232-0911 ■ *Web:* www.lifeflight.org						
Life Inc 2609 Royall Ave	Goldsboro	NC	27534	919-778-1900	778-1911	48-15
Web: www.lifeincorporated.com						
Life Insurance Company of Alabama						
302 Broad St	Gadsden	AL	35901	256-543-2022		391-2
TF: 800-226-2371 ■ *Web:* www.licoa.com						
Life Insurance Company of Boston and New York						
120 Royall St	Canton	MA	02021	800-669-2668	821-4976*	796
**Fax Area Code:* 781 ■ *TF:* 800-669-2668 ■ *Web:* www.lifeofboston.com						
Life Insurance Company of Louisiana						
207 Texas St	Shreveport	LA	71166	318-221-0646	221-0795	796
Web: www.lifeofla.com						
Life Lessons PO Box 382346	Cambridge	MA	02238	617-576-2546		637-2
TF: 877-646-3925 ■ *Web:* www.mindwalks.com						
Life of Learning Foundation						
459 Galice Rd	Merlin	OR	97532	541-476-1200		48-20
Web: www.guyfinley.org						
Life Options Health Services Inc						
4001 W Devon Ave Ste 409	Chicago	IL	60646	773-628-7499	647-1394	363
Web: www.lohealthservices.com						
Life Outreach Intl 1801 W Euless Blvd	Euless	TX	76040	817-267-4211		48-20
Web: lifetoday.org						
Life Pacific College						
1100 W Covina Blvd	San Dimas	CA	91773	909-599-5433		161
TF: 877-886-5433 ■ *Web:* www.lifepacific.edu						
Life Packaging Technology LLC						
2751 Tern Cir Ste A	Costa Mesa	CA	92626	949-395-8145	751-5027*	393
**Fax Area Code:* 714 ■ *Web:* www.lifepackagingtechnology.com						
Life Products Solutions Group LLC						
7900 SW 57th Ave Ste 23	Miami	FL	33143	305-668-8780	668-8323	463
TF: 866-772-2370 ■ *Web:* www.lpsgroup.com						
Life Saver Pool Fence Systems Inc						
1085 SW 15th Ave Bldg E-3	Delray Beach	FL	33444	561-272-8242	272-8289	73
TF: 800-282-3836 ■ *Web:* www.poolfence.com						
Life Science Publishing						
520 S 850 E Unit C6	Lehi	UT	84043	800-336-6308		95
TF: 800-336-6308 ■ *Web:* www.discoverlsp.com						
Life Sciences Greenhouse						
225 Market St Ste 500	Harrisburg	PA	17101	717-635-2100		792
Web: www.lsgpa.com						
Life Settlement Solutions Inc						
9201 Spectrum Center Blvd Ste 105	San Diego	CA	92123	858-576-8067	576-9329	796
TF: 800-762-3387 ■ *Web:* www.lss-corp.com						
Life Style Staffing						
6765 W Greenfield Ave	Milwaukee	WI	53214	414-475-0090		721
Web: www.lifestylestaffing.com						
Life Trust LLC 330 Madison Ave 6th Fl	New York	NY	10017	212-653-0840	653-0844	796
Web: www.life-trust.net						

Name / Address	City	State	ZIP	Phone	Fax	Class
Life University 1269 Barclay Cir *TF:* 800-543-3203 ■ *Web:* www.life.edu	Marietta	GA	30060	770-426-2884		166
Life's Resources Inc (LRI) 114 E Main St *Web:* www.lifes.org	Addison	MI	49220	517-547-7494	547-5444	637-2
Life's WORC 1501 Franklin Ave PO Box 8165 *Web:* www.lifesworc.org	Garden City	NY	11530	516-741-9000	741-5560	48-15
Life-Assist Inc 11277 Sunrise Park Dr *TF:* 800-824-6016 ■ *Web:* www.life-assist.com	Rancho Cordova	CA	95742	800-824-6016		475
LifeBanc 4775 Richmond Rd *TF:* 888-558-5433 ■ *Web:* www.lifebanc.org	Cleveland	OH	44128	216-751-4204		545
Lifebridge Health 2401 W Belvedere Ave *Web:* www.lifebridgehealth.org	Baltimore	MD	21215	410-601-9355		354
Lifecare Alliance 1699 W Mound St *Web:* www.lifecarealliance.org	Columbus	OH	43223	614-278-3130		363
LifeCenter Plus 5133 Darrow Rd *Web:* www.lifecenterplus.com	Hudson	OH	44236	330-655-2377		354
Lifechurch-tv 4600 E Second St *Web:* www.life.church	Edmond	OK	73034	405-478-5433		48-20
Lifecircle Enterprises 3106 Zachary St *Web:* www.lifecircleent.com	Burlington	IA	52601	319-759-5800		637-2
LifeCore Biomedical LLC 3515 Lyman Blvd *TF:* 800-348-4368 ■ *Web:* www.lifecore.com	Chaska	MN	55318	952-368-4300	368-3411	85
LifeCourse Associates Inc 9080 Eaton Park Rd *TF:* 866-537-4999 ■ *Web:* www.lifecourse.com	Great Falls	VA	22066	866-537-4999		193
LifeFone 16 Yellowstone Ave *TF:* 888-687-0451 ■ *Web:* www.lifefone.com	White Plains	NY	10607	888-687-0451		575
Lifeforce USA 495 Raleigh Ave *Fax Area Code: 800 ■ *TF:* 800-531-4877 ■ *Web:* lifeforce.net	El Cajon	CA	92020	858-218-3200	809-8208*	345
LifeLabs Inc 3680 Gilmore Way *TF:* 844-453-5504 ■ *Web:* www.lifelabs.com	Burnaby	BC	V5G4V8	844-453-5504		418
LifeLearn Inc 367 Woodlawn Rd W Unit 9 *TF:* 800-375-7994 ■ *Web:* www.lifelearn.com	Guelph	ON	N1H7K9	519-767-5043		242
Lifeline Data Centers LLC 401 N Shadeland Ave *Web:* lifelinedatacenters.com	Indianapolis	IN	46219	317-423-2591		225
Lifeline Foods 2811 S 11th St Rd *Web:* www.lifeline-foods.com	Saint Joseph	MO	64503	816-279-1651		144
Lifeline Home Care LLC 15 E Park Blvd *Web:* lifelinehomecarellc.com	Villa Park	IL	60181	630-359-4666	501-0554	363
Lifeline Medical Associates LLC 99 Cherry Hill Rd Ste 220 *TF:* 800-845-2785 ■ *Web:* lma-llc.com	Parsippany	NJ	07054	800-845-2785		374-3
Lifeline of Ohio 770 Kinnear Rd Ste 200 *TF:* 800-525-5667 ■ *Web:* lifelineofohio.org	Columbus	OH	43212	614-291-5667	291-0660	545
Lifeline Scientific Inc 1 Pierce Pl Ste 475W *Web:* www.lifeline-scientific.com	Itasca	IL	60143	847-294-0300		250
Lifeline Theatre 6912 N Glenwood Ave *Web:* www.lifelinetheatre.com	Chicago	IL	60626	773-761-4477	761-4582	572
Lifelink Foundation Inc 9661 Delaney Creek Blvd *TF:* 800-262-5775 ■ *Web:* www.lifelinkfoundation.org	Tampa	FL	33619	813-253-2640		363
LifeLink Home Health Care Services Inc 11885 12 Mile Rd Ste 100B *TF:* 866-583-5433 ■ *Web:* www.lifelinkhomehealthcare.com	Warren	MI	48093	586-558-9112	558-9113	363
LifeLink Tissue Bank 9661 Delaney Creek Blvd *TF:* 800-683-2400 ■ *Web:* www.lifelinktissuebank.org	Tampa	FL	33619	813-886-8111	886-1851	545
Lifeloc Technologies Inc 12441 W 49th Ave *TF:* 800-722-4817 ■ *Web:* www.lifeloc.com	Wheat Ridge	CO	80033	303-431-9500		407
Lifelong Medical Care Inc PO Box 11247 *Web:* www.lifelongmedical.org	Berkeley	CA	94712	510-981-4100		374-3
LifeNet 1864 Concert Dr *TF:* 800-847-7831 ■ *Web:* www.lifenethealth.org	Virginia Beach	VA	23453	800-847-7831		545
Lifenet Inc 6225 St Michaels Dr *TF:* 800-832-6395 ■ *Web:* www.lifenetems.org	Texarkana	TX	75503	903-832-8531		30
Lifepath Hospice 3010 W Azeele St *TF:* 800-209-2200 ■ *Web:* www.chaptershealth.org	Tampa	FL	33609	813-877-2200		371
LifePics Inc 5777 Central Ave Ste 120 *Web:* www.lifepics.com	Boulder	CO	80301	303-413-9500		225
LifePlans Inc 51 Sawyer Rd Ste 340 *Web:* www.lifeplansinc.com	Waltham	MA	02453	781-893-7600	647-3552	194
LifePoint Health 330 Seven Springs Way *NASDAQ: LPNT* ■ *Web:* www.lifepointhealth.net	Brentwood	TN	37027	615-920-7000		353
Lifeport Inc 1610 Heritage St *Web:* www.lifeport.com	Woodland	WA	98674	360-225-1212	225-1214	256
LifeRhythm PO Box 806 *Web:* www.liferhythm.com	Mendocino	CA	95460	707-937-2309	633-0195	95
LifeRing Secular Recovery 1440 Broadway Ste 312 *Fax Area Code: 510 ■ *TF:* 800-811-4142 ■ *Web:* lifering.org	Oakland	CA	94612	970-227-6650	763-1513*	48-21
LifeSafe Services LLC 5971 Powers Ave Ste 108 *TF:* 888-767-0050 ■ *Web:* www.lifesafeservices.com	Jacksonville	FL	32217	888-767-0050		194
LifeSafer 4290 Glendale Milford Rd *Web:* www.lifesafer.com	Blue Ash	OH	45242	513-651-9560	651-9563	407
Lifescan Canada Ltd 210-4321 Still Creek Dr *TF:* 800-663-5521 ■ *Web:* www.onetouch.ca	Burnaby	BC	V5C6S7	604-293-1619		476
LifeScan Inc 1000 Gibraltar Dr *Web:* www.lifescan.com	Milpitas	CA	95035	408-263-9789		231
LifeScan Inc 965 Chesterbrook Blvd *TF:* 800-227-8862 ■ *Web:* www.lifescan.com	Wayne	PA	19087	800-227-8862		476
LifeScan Laboratory Inc 5255 W Golf *TF:* 800-270-0037 ■ *Web:* lifescanlab.com	Skokie	IL	60077	800-270-0037		415
LifeSensors Inc 271 Great Vly Pkwy Ste 100 *Web:* lifesensors.com	Malvern	PA	19355	610-644-8845	644-8616	668
LifeServe Blood Ctr 431 E Locust St *TF:* 800-287-4903 ■ *Web:* www.lifeservebloodcenter.org	Des Moines	IA	50309	800-287-4903		89
LifeShare Blood Centers 8910 Linwood Ave *TF:* 800-256-4483 ■ *Web:* www.lifeshare.org	Shreveport	LA	71106	318-222-7770		89
LifeShare of the Carolinas 1200 Ridgefield Blvd Ste 150 *Web:* www.lifesharecarolinas.org	Asheville	NC	28806	828-665-4729		269
LifeShare Technologies LLC 2177 Intelliplex Dr Ste 150 *Web:* www.lifesharetech.com	Shelbyville	IN	46176	317-825-0320		387
LifeShare Transplant Donor Services of Oklahoma 4705 NW Expy *TF:* 888-580-5680 ■ *Web:* www.lifeshareoklahoma.org	Oklahoma City	OK	73132	405-840-5551	840-9748	545
Lifesharing 7436 Mission Valley Rd *TF:* 888-423-6667 ■ *Web:* www.lifesharing.org	San Diego	CA	92108	619-543-7225	543-0017	545
Lifeshield National Insurance Co 5701 N Shartel 1st Fl *Web:* www.lifeshieldnational.com	Oklahoma City	OK	73118	405-236-2640		390
LifeSize Communications Inc 1601 S Mopac Expwy Ste 100 *TF:* 877-543-3749 ■ *Web:* www.lifesize.com	Austin	TX	78746	512-347-9300	347-9301	52
Lifesize Entertainment & Releasing 194 Elmwood Dr Ste 2 *Web:* lifesizeentertainment.com	Parsippany	NJ	07054	973-884-4884		511
LifeSkill Institute Inc PO Box 302 *TF:* 800-570-4009 ■ *Web:* www.lifeskillinstitute.org	Wilmington	NC	28402	910-262-2680		637-2
LifeSource Blood Services 2764 Aurora Ave *Web:* www.lifesource.org	Naperville	IL	60540	877-543-3768		89
LifeSouth Community Blood Centers 4039 Newberry Rd *Fax Area Code: 352 ■ *TF:* 888-795-2707 ■ *Web:* lifesouth.org	Gainesville	FL	32607	888-795-2707	224-1650*	89
Lifespace Communities Inc 4201 Corporate Dr *Web:* www.lifespacecommunities.com	West Des Moines	IA	50266	515-288-5805		672
Lifespire 1 Whitehall St 9th Fl *Web:* www.lifespire.org	New York	NY	10118	212-741-0100	320-0407	48-17
Lifespring Inc 460 Spring St *TF:* 800-456-2117 ■ *Web:* www.lifespringhealthsystems.org	Jeffersonville	IN	47130	812-280-2080		353
Lifestar Response 3710 Commerce Dr Ste 1006 *Web:* lifestar-response.net	Halethorpe	MD	21227	301-596-2800		30
Lifestream Inc PO Box 50487 *Web:* www.lifestreaminc.com	New Bedford	MA	02745	508-993-1991		48-15
Lifestyle Enterprises Inc 529 Townsend Ave *Web:* www.lifestyle-datong.com	High Point	NC	27263	336-882-7900	882-9122	321
Lifetech Resources LLC 9540 Cozycroft Ave *Web:* www.lifetechresources.com	Chatsworth	CA	91311	818-885-1199		297-8
Lifetime Brands Inc 1000 Steward Ave *NASDAQ: LCUT* ■ *TF:* 800-252-3390 ■ *Web:* www.lifetimebrands.com	Garden City	NY	11530	516-683-6000		486
Lifetime Cabinet 601 Kellam Rd *Web:* www.lifetimecabinets.com	Dublin	GA	31021	478-275-7457		115
Lifetime Care 3111 Winton Rd S *TF:* 800-724-1410 ■ *Web:* www.lifetimecare.org	Rochester	NY	14623	585-214-1000		363
Lifetime Nut Covers Inc 720 320th St *Web:* lifetimenutcovers.com	Britt	IA	50423	641-565-3566		697
Lifetime Pharmacy 23080 Alessandro Blvd Ste 212 *Web:* www.lifetimepharmacyca.com	Moreno Valley	CA	92553	951-656-7171	656-6363	237
Lifetime Products Inc Freeport Ctr Bldg D-11 PO Box 160010 *TF:* 800-242-3865 ■ *Web:* www.lifetime.com	Clearfield	UT	84016	801-776-1532		710
Lifetime Recovery 10290 Southton Rd *Web:* www.lifetimerecoverytx.org	San Antonio	TX	78223	210-633-0201		726
Lifeway Foods Inc 6431 W Oakton St *NASDAQ: LWAY* ■ *Web:* lifewaykefir.com	Morton Grove	IL	60053	847-967-1010	967-6558	296-27
Lifewings 9198 Crestwyn Hills Dr *TF:* 800-290-9314 ■ *Web:* www.saferpatients.com	Memphis	TN	38125	800-290-9314		463
LifeWIRE Corp 130 King St W Ste 1900 *TF:* 888-738-4260 ■ *Web:* www.lifewiregroup.com	Toronto	ON	M5X1E3	888-738-4260	738-8981	177
LifeWise Health Plan of Oregon PO Box 327 *TF:* 800-596-3440 ■ *Web:* www.lifewiseor.com	Seattle	WA	98111	800-596-3440		391-3
Lifewise Health Plan of Washington 7001 220th St SW Bldg 1 *TF:* 800-842-5357 ■ *Web:* www.lifewisewa.com	Mountlake Terrace	WA	98043	800-842-5357		391-3
Lifeyield LLC 175 Federal St 7th Fl *Web:* www.lifeyield.com	Boston	MA	02110	617-502-5660	502-5701	178-1
Lift Agency Inc 3250 Bloor St W E Tower Ste 600 *Web:* www.getlift.com	Toronto	ON	M8X2X9	888-207-0438		195
Lift Technologies Inc 7040 S Hwy 11 *Web:* www.lift-tek.com	Westminster	SC	29693	864-647-1119	647-5406	358
Lift-All Company Inc 1909 McFarland Dr *TF:* 800-909-1964 ■ *Web:* www.lift-all.com	Landisville	PA	17538	717-898-6615	898-1215	470
Liftech Equipment Cos 6847 Ellicott Dr *TF:* 877-543-8324 ■ *Web:* www.liftech.com	East Syracuse	NY	13057	315-463-7333	463-6971	385
Liftoff 555 Bryant St Ste 133 *Web:* liftoff.io	Palo Alto	CA	94301	650-453-8305		178-1
Liftoff LLC 1667 Patrice Cir *Web:* www.liftofflearning.com	Crofton	MD	21114	410-419-1591		177
Liftone 440 E Westinghouse Blvd *TF:* 855-543-8663 ■ *Web:* www.liftone.net	Charlotte	NC	28273	855-543-8663		470
Liftow 3150 American Dr *Fax Area Code: 905 ■ *TF:* 800-387-3140 ■ *Web:* www.liftow.com	Toronto	ON	L4V1B4	866-465-4386	677-1429*	358

Name / Address	Phone	Fax	Class
Lifts West Condominium Resort Hotel PO Box 330 .... Red River NM 87558 *TF:* 800-221-1859 ■ *Web:* www.liftswest.com	505-754-2778	754-6617	669
Ligand Pharmaceuticals Inc 11085 N Torrey Pines Rd Ste 300 .... La Jolla CA 92037 *NASDAQ: LGND* ■ *Web:* www.ligand.com	858-550-7500	550-7506	582
Light 103.9 FM, The 8001-101 Creedmoor Rd .... Raleigh NC 27613 *TF:* 877-310-9665 ■ *Web:* thelightnc.com	919-848-9736		645-128
Light Brigade Inc, The 837 Industry Dr .... Tukwila WA 98188 *Web:* www.lightbrigade.com	206-575-0404		577
Light Engines LLC 29 Library Ln S .... Sturbridge MA 01566	508-347-0111		253
Light for Life Foundation Intl PO Box 644 .... Westminster CO 80036 *Web:* yellowribbon.org	303-429-3530	426-4496	48-17
Light Horse Tavern 199 Washington St .... Jersey City NJ 07302 *Web:* www.lighthorsetavern.com	201-946-2028	946-2029	671
Light Impressions 100 Carlson Rd .... Rochester NY 14610 **Fax Area Code:* 866 ■ *TF:* 800-975-6429 ■ *Web:* www.lightimpressionsdirect.com	844-659-3477	592-8642*	628
Light Lines Inc 3337 Rauch St .... Houston TX 77029 *Web:* lightlines.net	713-673-7502		362
Light Metals Corp 2740 Prairie St SW .... Wyoming MI 49519 *TF:* 888-363-8257 ■ *Web:* www.light-metals.com	616-538-3030	538-2713	485
Light of Christ Rcssd 16 9301 19th Ave .... North Battleford SK S9A3N5 *Web:* www.loccsd.ca	306-445-6158		685
Light Publications Hope Artiste Village 1005 Main St .... Pawtucket RI 02860 *Web:* lightpublications.com	401-484-0228		637-2
Light Radio, The 140 Main St .... Essex Junction VT 05452 *TF:* 866-878-8885 ■ *Web:* www.thelightradio.net	866-878-8885		647
Lightbourn Equipment Co 13655 Welch Rd .... Dallas TX 75244 *TF:* 800-729-3131 ■ *Web:* www.lightbournequipment.com	972-233-5151	661-0738	61
LightBridge Hospice 6155 Cornerstone Ct E Ste 220 .... San Diego CA 92121 *Web:* www.lightbridgehospice.com	858-458-2992	458-3655	371
Lightburn 325 E Chicago St Ste 301 .... Milwaukee WI 53202 *Web:* lightburn.co	414-347-1866		180
Lightech Fiberoptic Inc 1987 Adams Ave .... San Leandro CA 94577 *Web:* www.lightech.net	510-567-8700		253
LightEdge Solutions Inc 215 Tenth St Ste 1000 .... Des Moines IA 50309 *TF:* 877-771-3343 ■ *Web:* www.lightedge.com	515-471-1000	471-1112	808
Lightel Technologies Inc 2210 Lind Ave SW Ste 100 .... Renton WA 98057 *Web:* lightel.com	425-277-8000	277-5280	696
Lightfoot Capital Partners GP LLC 725 Fifth Ave 19th Fl .... New York NY 10022 *Web:* www.lightfootcapital.com	212-993-1280	993-1299	360-3
Lightfoot, Franklin & White LLC The Clark Bldg 400 20th St N .... Birmingham AL 35203 *Web:* www.lightfootlaw.com	205-581-0700		428
Lighthouse 531 Roselane St Ste 320 .... Marietta GA 30060 *Web:* insidelighthouse.com	770-590-4897		261
Lighthouse ArtCenter Gallery 373 Tequesta Dr .... Tequesta FL 33469 *Web:* www.lighthousearts.org	561-746-3101		50-2
Lighthouse Club Hotel 56st in the Bay .... Ocean City MD 21842 *TF:* 888-371-5400 ■ *Web:* www.fagers.com	410-524-5400	524-3928	379
Lighthouse Compliance Solutions 500 President Clinton Ave .... Little Rock AR 72201 *TF:* 888-233-6287 ■ *Web:* www.lighthousecompliance.com	501-658-8883		178-1
Lighthouse Computer Services Inc 6 Blackstone Valley Pl Ste 205 .... Lincoln RI 02865 *TF:* 888-542-8030 ■ *Web:* www.lighthousecs.com	401-334-0799		180
Lighthouse Electric Cooperative Inc 703 A Hwy 70 E .... Floydada TX 79235 *Web:* www.lighthouse.coop	806-983-2814	983-2804	245
Lighthouse Healthcare Inc 11734 Bowman Green Dr .... Reston VA 20190 *TF:* 888-975-0506 ■ *Web:* lhihome.com	703-828-6500		363
Lighthouse Hospice 200 Lake Dr E Ste 205 .... Cherry Hill NJ 08002 **Fax Area Code:* 856 ■ *TF:* 888-467-7423 ■ *Web:* www.lighthousehospice.net	888-467-7423	414-1313*	371
Lighthouse Imaging LLC 765 Roosevelt Trl Ste 9 .... Windham ME 04062 *Web:* www.lighthouseoptics.com	207-893-8233	893-8245	544
Lighthouse Investment Partners LLC 3801 PGA Blvd Ste 500 .... Palm Beach Gardens FL 33410 *Web:* www.lighthousepartners.com	561-741-0820		401
Lighthouse Lodge & Cottages 1150 Lighthouse Ave .... Pacific Grove CA 93950 *TF:* 800-858-1249 ■ *Web:* www.lighthouselodgecottages.com	831-655-2111		379
Lighthouse Networks Inc 400 Nathan Ellis Hwy .... Mashpee MA 02649 *Web:* lighthouse-networks.com	508-477-4767		180
Lighthouse People, The 517 Thornhill Rd .... Fort Walton Beach FL 32547 *Web:* www.thelighthousepeople.com	850-862-4069		637-2
Lighthouse Travel & Tours 1556 Halford Ave Ste 230 .... Santa Clara CA 95051 *Web:* www.lighthouse-tours.com	408-260-5802		463
Lighting Quotient, The 114 Boston Post Rd .... West Haven CT 06516 *Web:* www.thelightingquotient.com	203-931-4455	931-4464	439
Lighting Retrofit Services Inc 234 Ballardville St .... Wilmington MA 01887 *Web:* lrs-lighting.com	978-988-7800		362
Lighting Services 2 Holt Dr .... Stony Point NY 10980 *TF:* 800-999-9574 ■ *Web:* www.lightingservicesinc.com	845-942-2800	942-2177	439
Lighting Technology Services Inc 2801 Catherine Way .... Santa Ana CA 92705 *TF:* 888-587-7782 ■ *Web:* ltsinc.net	949-428-5040	428-5044	104
Lighting Zone Inc 17354 Hawthorne Blvd .... Torrance CA 90504 *TF:* 877-548-3149 ■ *Web:* dreamonlighting.com	310-921-9495	921-3567	362
Light-Life Foods Inc 153 Industrial Blvd .... Turners Falls MA 01376 *Web:* lightlife.com	413-774-9000		123
Lightner Electronics Inc 1771 Beaver Dam Rd .... Claysburg PA 16625 *TF:* 866-239-3888 ■ *Web:* www.lightnerelectronics.com	814-239-8323		186
Lightner Museum, The 75 King St .... Saint Augustine FL 32084 *Web:* www.lightnermuseum.org	904-824-2874		520
Lightner Property Group Inc 612 Howard St Ste 390 .... San Francisco CA 94105 *Web:* lightnergroup.com	415-267-2900		652
Lightning 100 1310 Clinton St Ste 215 .... Nashville TN 37203 *Web:* lightning100.com	615-242-5600	296-9039	645-106
Lightning Energy Services LLC 104 Heliport Loop Rd .... Bridgeport WV 26330 *Web:* lightningenergy.com	304-933-3544	933-3416	536
Lightning Strike & Electric Shock Survivors International Inc (LSESSI) PO Box 1156 .... Jacksonville NC 28541 *Web:* www.lightning-strike.org	910-346-4708		48-21
Lightning Transportation Inc 16820 Blake Rd .... Hagerstown MD 21740 *TF:* 800-233-0624 ■ *Web:* lightningtrans.com	301-582-5700	582-5898	780
Lightopia LLC 3323 Hyland Ave Ste E2 .... Costa Mesa CA 92626 *TF:* 877-559-7516 ■ *Web:* www.lightopiaonline.com	949-715-5575	715-5577	35
LightPath Technologies Inc 2603 Challenger Tech Ct Ste 100 .... Orlando FL 32826 *NASDAQ: LPTH* ■ *Web:* www.lightpath.com	407-382-4003	382-4007	544
Lightriver Technologies 2150 John Glenn Dre Ste 200 .... Concord CA 94520 *TF:* 888-544-4825 ■ *Web:* lightriver.com	925-363-9000	363-9001	681
Lights of America 611 Reyes Dr .... Walnut CA 91789 *TF:* 800-321-8100 ■ *Web:* www.lightsofamerica.com	800-321-8100		439
LightSand Communications Inc 101 E Pk Blvd Ste 600 .... Plano TX 75074 *Web:* lightsand.com	972-516-3740	516-3741	176
Lightship Wealth Strategies Inc 2344 Washington St 2nd Fl .... Newton Lower Falls MA 02462 *Web:* lightshipwealth.com	617-581-6100		390
Lightspeed Aviation Inc 6135 Jean Rd .... Lake Oswego OR 97035 *TF:* 800-332-2421 ■ *Web:* www.lightspeedaviation.com	503-968-3113		647
Lightspeed Venture Partners 2200 Sand Hill Rd Ste 100 .... Menlo Park CA 94025 *Web:* lsvp.com	650-234-8300	234-8333	792
Lightstone Group, The 460 Park Ave Ste 1300 .... New York NY 10022 *Web:* www.lightstonegroup.com	212-616-9969		652
Lightware Inc 1329 W Byers Pl .... Denver CO 80223 *TF:* 800-455-6556 ■ *Web:* www.lightwareinc.com	303-744-0202	722-4545	453
Lightwave Management Resources 4707 140th Ave N 316 .... Clearwater FL 33762 *TF:* 877-507-0983 ■ *Web:* www.golightwave.com	727-507-0983	507-9862	177
Lightwaves 2020 Inc 1323 Great Mall Dr .... Milpitas CA 95035 *Web:* www.lightwaves2020.com	408-503-8888		668
Lightway Industries 28435 Industry Dr .... Valencia CA 91355 *Web:* www.lightwayind.com	661-257-0286	257-0201	439
Lignite Energy Council 1016 E Owens Ave .... Bismarck ND 58502 *TF:* 800-932-7117 ■ *Web:* lignite.com	701-258-7117		138
Lignumvitae Key Botanical State Park 77200 Overseas Hwy .... Islamorada FL 33036 *Web:* www.floridastateparks.org	305-664-2540		565
Ligon Industries LLC 1927 First Ave N 5th Fl .... Birmingham AL 35203 *Web:* www.ligonindustries.com	205-322-3302	322-3188	386
Ligon Oil Company Inc 803 Cabe St .... Malvern AR 72104 *Web:* www.ligonoil.com	501-332-3271	337-9591	579
Lil Ray's 500A Courthouse Rd .... Gulfport MS 39507 *Web:* lilraysrestaurant.com	228-896-9601		671
Lil' Angels Photography 6831 Crumpler Blvd .... Olive Branch MS 38654 *Web:* www.lilangelsphoto.com	662-890-9103		310
Lil' Drug Store Products Inc 1201 Continental Pl NE .... Cedar Rapids IA 52402 *TF:* 800-553-5022 ■ *Web:* www.lildrugstore.com	800-553-5022		238
Lilette 3637 Magazine St .... New Orleans LA 70115 *Web:* www.liletterestaurant.com	504-895-1636		671
Liliuokalani Trust 1100 Alakea St Ste 1100 .... Honolulu HI 96813 *Web:* www.onipaa.org	808-203-6150	203-6151	305
Lilja Corp 229 Rickenbacker Cir .... Livermore CA 94551 *Web:* www.liljacorp.com	925-455-2300		256
Lilja Precision Rifle Barrel 81 Lower Lynch Creek Rd .... Plains MT 59859 *Web:* riflebarrels.com	406-826-3084	826-3083	807
Lilker Associates Consulting Engineers PC 1001 Avenue of the Americas 9th Fl .... New York NY 10018 *Web:* www.lilker.com	212-695-1000		261
Lillard Wise & Szygenda PLLC 13760 Noel Rd Ste 1150 .... Dallas TX 75240 *Web:* lwsattorneys.com	214-739-2000		41
Lillenas Publishing Co PO Box 419527 .... Kansas City MO 64141 **Fax Area Code:* 816 ■ *TF:* 800-363-2122 ■ *Web:* www.lillenas.com	800-363-2122	412-8390*	637-10
Lilleys' Landing Resort 367 River Ln .... Branson MO 65616 *TF:* 866-545-5397 ■ *Web:* www.lilleyslanding.com	417-334-6380	334-6311	669
Lillian & Albert Small Jewish Museum 701 Third St NW .... Washington DC 20001 *Web:* www.loc.gov	202-789-0900	789-0485	520

Name	Address	City	State	ZIP	Phone	Fax	Class	Other
Lillian August Designs Inc	32 Knight St	Norwalk	CT	06851	203-847-3314		361	*Web:* www.lillianaugust.com
Lilling & Company LLP	2 Seaview Blvd Ste 200	Port Washington	NY	11050	516-829-1099		2	*Web:* lillingcpa.com
Lilly Endowment Inc	2801 N Meridian St	Indianapolis	IN	46208	317-924-5471		305	*Web:* www.lillyendowment.org
Lilly Ventures	115 W Washington St	Indianapolis	IN	46204	317-429-0140		792	*Web:* lillyventures.com
Lilly's Bistro	1147 Bardstown Rd	Louisville	KY	40204	502-451-0447		671	*Web:* lillysbistro.com
Lily Bay State Park	13 Myrle's Way	Greenville	ME	04441	207-695-2700		565	*Web:* www.maine.gov
Lily Transportation Corp	145 Rosemary St	Needham	MA	02494	800-248-5459		778	*TF:* 800-248-5459 ■ *Web:* lily.com
Lima Memorial Hospital	1001 Bellefontaine Ave	Lima	OH	45804	419-228-3335	226-5013	374-3	*TF:* 877-362-5672 ■ *Web:* www.limamemorial.org
Lima News	3515 Elida Rd	Lima	OH	45807	419-223-1010	229-2926	532-2	*TF:* 800-686-9924 ■ *Web:* www.limaohio.com
Lima Public Library	650 W Market St	Lima	OH	45801	419-228-5113		434-3	*Web:* www.limalibrary.com
Lima/Allen County Chamber of Commerce	144 S Main St Ste 100	Lima	OH	45801	419-222-6045	229-0266	139	*TF:* 800-233-5462 ■ *Web:* limachamber.com
Lima/Allen County Convention & Visitors Bureau	144 S Main St Ste 101	Lima	OH	45801	419-222-6075		206	*TF:* 888-222-6075 ■ *Web:* www.visitgreaterlima.com
Limbach	175 Titus Ave Ste 100	Warrington	PA	18976	215-488-9700	488-9699	189-10	*Web:* www.limbachinc.com
Limberlost Press	17 Canyon Trl	Boise	ID	83716	208-344-2120		637-10	*Web:* www.limberlostpress.com
Lime Brokerage LLC	625 Broadway 12th Fl	New York	NY	10012	212-824-5000		690	*Web:* www.limebrokerage.com
Lime City Manufacturing Co	1470 Etna Ave	Huntington	IN	46750	260-356-6826		489	*Web:* www.limecitymfg.com
Lime Instruments LLC	1187 Brittmoore Rd	Houston	TX	77043	713-781-1883	678-7221	201	*Web:* limeinst.com
Lime Kiln Point State Park	1567 Westside Rd	Friday Harbor	WA	98250	360-378-2044		565	*Web:* parks.state.wa.us
Lime Rock Park	60 White Hollow Rd	Lakeville	CT	06039	860-435-5000	435-5010	515	*TF:* 800-722-3577 ■ *Web:* limerock.com
Lime Street Cafe	951 S Durkin Dr	Springfield	IL	62704	217-793-1905		671	
Limekiln State Park	63025 CA-1	Big Sur	CA	93920	805-434-1996		565	*Web:* www.parks.ca.gov
Limelight Theatre	11 Old Mission Ave	Saint Augustine	FL	32084	904-825-1164	825-4662	572	*Web:* limelight-theatre.org
Limerick Machine Company Inc	81 Central Ave	Limerick	ME	04048	207-793-2288	793-2014	454	*Web:* www.limerickmachine.com
Limerick Traditional Public House	7304 MacLeod Trail SE	Calgary	AB	T2H0L9	403-252-9190	252-9174	671	*Web:* calgarysbestpubs.com
Limestone College	1115 College Dr	Gaffney	SC	29340	864-489-7151		166	*TF:* 800-795-7151 ■ *Web:* www.limestone.edu
Limestone County Archives	102 W Washington St	Athens	AL	35611	256-233-6404		434-3	*Web:* limestonearchives.com
Limestone County School District	300 S Jefferson St	Athens	AL	35611	256-232-5353	233-6461	685	*Web:* www.lcsk12.org
Limited Papers Ltd	67 34th St 4th Fl	Brooklyn	NY	11232	718-499-5481	499-5735	553	*TF:* 800-797-7022 ■ *Web:* www.limitedpapers.com
Limon Dance Co	466 W 152nd St 2nd Fl	New York	NY	10031	212-777-3353	777-4764	573-1	*Web:* www.limon.nyc
Limoneira Co	1141 Cummings Rd	Santa Paula	CA	93060	805-525-5541	525-8211	315-2	*NASDAQ: LMNR* ■ *Web:* limoneira.com
Limpert Bros Inc	202 NW Blvd	Vineland	NJ	08362	856-691-1353	794-8968	296-15	*TF:* 800-691-1353 ■ *Web:* www.limpertbrothers.com
LIMRA International Inc	300 Day Hill Rd	Windsor	CT	06095	860-688-3358	298-9555	49-9	*TF:* 800-235-4672 ■ *Web:* www.limra.com
Lin Engineering Inc	16245 Vineyard Blvd	Morgan Hill	CA	95037	408-919-0200		256	*Web:* www.linengineering.com
Linak US Inc	2200 Stanley Gault Pkwy	Louisville	KY	40223	502-253-5595	253-5596	223	*Web:* www.linak-us.com
Linamar Corp	287 Speedvale Ave W	Guelph	ON	N1H1C5	519-836-7550	824-8479	60	*TSX: LNR* ■ *Web:* www.linamar.com
Linbeck Group LLC	3900 Essex Ln Ste 1200	Houston	TX	77027	713-621-2350		186	*Web:* www.linbeck.com
Linc Services Mid-Atlantic LLC	3711 Saunders Ave	Richmond	VA	23227	804-254-5790		152	*Web:* www.lincservice.com
Linch Capital LLC	3384 Peachtree Rd NW Ste 450	Atlanta	GA	30326	404-334-7047		691	*Web:* www.linchcapital.com
Linchris Hotel Corp	269 Hanover St	Hanover	MA	02339	781-826-8824	826-2411	463	*Web:* www.linchris.com
Lincluden Investment Management	201 City Centre Dr Ste 201	Mississauga	ON	L5B2T4	844-373-4240		528	*TF:* 800-532-7071 ■ *Web:* www.lincluden.com
Lincoln Agency LLC, The	504 S Service Rd E Ste 2	Ruston	LA	71270	318-255-2913	251-0204	390	*Web:* lincolnagency.com
Lincoln Airport	2400 W Adams St	Lincoln	NE	68524	402-458-2400	458-2490	27	*TF:* 877-228-1327 ■ *Web:* www.lincolnairport.com
Lincoln Boyhood National Memorial	2916 E S St PO Box 1816	Lincoln City	IN	47552	812-937-4541	937-9929	564	*Web:* www.nps.gov
Lincoln Builders Inc	1809 Northpointe Ste 201	Ruston	LA	71270	318-255-3822	251-0114	186	*Web:* www.lincolnbuilders.com
Lincoln Center Shops	374 Lincoln Centre	Stockton	CA	95207	209-477-4868		460	*Web:* lincolncentershops.com
Lincoln Center Theater	150 W 65th St	New York	NY	10023	800-432-7250		749	*TF:* 800-432-7250 ■ *Web:* www.lct.org
Lincoln Chamber of Commerce	1128 Lincoln Mall Ste 100	Lincoln	NE	68508	402-436-2350		139	*Web:* www.lcoc.com
Lincoln Children's Museum	1420 P St	Lincoln	NE	68508	402-477-4000	477-2004	521	*Web:* www.lincolnchildrensmuseum.org
Lincoln Children's Zoo	1222 S 27th St	Lincoln	NE	68502	402-475-6741	475-6742	823	*Web:* www.lincolnzoo.org
Lincoln Christian College Seminary	100 Campus View Dr	Lincoln	IL	62656	217-732-3168		167-3	*TF:* 888-522-5228 ■ *Web:* lincolnchristian.edu
Lincoln City Hall	555 S Tenth St	Lincoln	NE	68508	402-441-7515	441-6533	337	*Web:* www.lincoln.ne.gov
Lincoln City Libraries	136 S 14th St	Lincoln	NE	68508	402-441-8500		434-3	*Web:* www.lincolnlibraries.org
Lincoln City Visitor & Convention Bureau	801 SW Hwy 101 Ste 401	Lincoln City	OR	97367	541-996-1274	994-2408	206	*TF:* 800-452-2151 ■ *Web:* www.oregoncoast.org
Lincoln College	300 Keokuk St	Lincoln	IL	62656	217-732-3155	732-8859	162	*TF:* 800-569-0556 ■ *Web:* lincolncollege.edu
Lincoln College of Technology	11194 E 45th Ave	Denver	CO	80239	303-722-5724		800	*TF:* 800-254-0547 ■ *Web:* www.lincolntech.edu
Lincoln Community Playhouse	2500 S 56th St	Lincoln	NE	68506	402-489-7529		572	*Web:* www.lincolnplayhouse.com
Lincoln Construction Inc	4790 Shuster Rd	Columbus	OH	43214	614-457-6015	457-0180	186	*Web:* www.lincolnconstruction.com
Lincoln Contracting & Equipment Company Inc	2478 Lincoln Hwy	Stoystown	PA	15563	814-629-6641		480	*TF:* 800-229-5205 ■ *Web:* www.lincolncontracting.com
Lincoln Contractors Supply Inc	11111 W Hayes Ave	Milwaukee	WI	53227	414-541-1327		358	*TF:* 800-242-1255 ■ *Web:* www.shoplcsonline.com
Lincoln Controls Inc	55 W 39th St Rm 201	New York	NY	10018	212-545-7705		400	*Web:* www.lincolncontrolsinc.com
Lincoln Convention & Visitors Bureau	3 Landmark Ctr 1128 Lincoln Mall Ste 100	Lincoln	NE	68508	402-434-5335	436-2360	206	*TF:* 800-423-8212 ■ *Web:* www.lincoln.org
Lincoln Correctional Ctr	1098 1350th St PO Box 549	Lincoln	IL	62656	217-735-5411	735-5381	213	*Web:* www2.illinois.gov
Lincoln Correctional Ctr	3216 W Van Dorn St PO Box 22800	Lincoln	NE	68522	402-471-2861		213	*Web:* www.corrections.nebraska.gov
Lincoln County	104 N Main St Ste 110	Canton	SD	57013	605-764-2581	764-0134	338	*Web:* www.lincolncountysd.org
Lincoln County	PO Box 711	Carrizozo	NM	88301	575-648-2385	648-2576	338	*Web:* www.lincolncountynm.gov
Lincoln County	450 Logan St	Davenport	WA	99122	509-725-1401	725-5045	338	*Web:* www.co.lincoln.wa.us
Lincoln County	112 Main St S	Fayetteville	TN	37334	931-433-3045	433-9304	338	*Web:* lincolncountytngov.com
Lincoln County	103 Third Ave PO Box 67	Hugo	CO	80821	719-743-2444	743-2524	338	*TF:* 866-652-0111 ■ *Web:* www.lincolncountyco.us
Lincoln County WY	925 Sage Ave	Kemmerer	WY	83101	307-877-9056	877-3101	338	*TF:* 800-442-9001 ■ *Web:* lcwy.org
Lincoln County	512 California Ave	Libby	MT	59923	406-293-7781	293-8577	338	*Web:* www.lincolncountymt.us
Lincoln County	216 E Lincoln Ave	Lincoln	KS	67455	785-524-4757	524-5008	338	*Web:* www.lincolncoks.com
Lincoln County	210 Humphrey St PO Box 340	Lincolnton	GA	30817	706-359-4444	359-4729	338	*Web:* www.lincolncountyga.com
Lincoln County	115 W Main St	Lincolnton	NC	28092	704-736-8471		338	*Web:* www.co.lincoln.nc.us
Lincoln County	1110 E Main St	Merrill	WI	54452	715-536-6200		338	*Web:* www.co.lincoln.wi.us
Lincoln County	225 W Olive St Rm 201	Newport	OR	97365	541-265-4131	265-4950	338	*Web:* www.co.lincoln.or.us
Lincoln County	301 N Jeffers St	North Platte	NE	69101	308-534-4350	535-3527	338	*TF:* 800-831-4573 ■ *Web:* www.co.lincoln.ne.us
Lincoln County	111 W 'B' St Ste C	Shoshone	ID	83352	208-886-7641	886-2798	338	*Web:* lincolncountyid.us
Lincoln County	102 E Main St	Stanford	KY	40484	606-365-2534	365-4514	338	*Web:* www.lincolnky.com
Lincoln County	201 Main St	Troy	MO	63379	636-528-6300	528-4340	338	*Web:* www.lincolncountycollector.com
Lincoln County	32 High St PO Box 249	Wiscasset	ME	04578	207-882-6311	882-4320	338	*Web:* www.lincolncountymaine.me
Lincoln County Courthouse	PO Box 373	Hamlin	WV	25523	304-824-7990	824-2012	338	*TF:* 800-859-7375 ■ *Web:* lincolncountywv.org
Lincoln County Courthouse	319 N Rebecca St PO Box 29	Ivanhoe	MN	56142	507-694-1000	694-1198	338	*Web:* www.co.lincoln.mn.us
Lincoln Electric Co	22801 St Clair Ave	Cleveland	OH	44117	216-481-8100	486-1751	811	*TF:* 888-935-3878 ■ *Web:* www.lincolnelectric.com
Lincoln Electric Co-opeartive Inc (LEC)	500 Osloski Rd PO Box 628	Eureka	MT	59917	406-889-3301	889-3874	245	*TF:* 800-442-2994 ■ *Web:* www.lincolnelectric.coop
Lincoln Equities Group LLC	1 Meadowlands Plz Ste 803	East Rutherford	NJ	07073	201-460-3440		652	*Web:* lincolnequities.com

Name / Address	City	State	ZIP	Phone	Fax	Class
Lincoln Financial Services Inc 7878 Wadsworth Blvd Ste 300 — *Web:* lfsinc.net	Arvada	CO	80003	303-425-8890		390
Lincoln FSB 1101 North St. — *TF:* 800-333-2158 ■ *Web:* www.lincolnfed.com	Lincoln	NE	68508	402-474-1400	474-1585	71
Lincoln General Insurance Co 3501 Concord Rd — *TF:* 800-876-3350 ■ *Web:* www.lincolngeneral.com	York	PA	17402	717-757-0000		390
Lincoln Heritage Life Insurance Co 4343 E Camelback Rd Ste 400 — **Fax Area Code:* 602 ■ *TF:* 800-438-7180 ■ *Web:* www.lhlic.com	Phoenix	AZ	85018	888-881-7391	840-0969*	391-2
Lincoln Heritage Public Library 105 N Wallace St — *Web:* www.lincolnheritage.lib.in.us	Dale	IN	47523	812-937-7170		434-3
Lincoln Highway Assn 136 N Elm St — *Web:* www.lincolnhighwayassoc.org	Franklin Grove	IL	61031	815-456-3030		48-23
Lincoln Hills School W4380 Copper Lake Rd — *Web:* www.doc.wi.gov	Irma	WI	54442	715-536-8386		412
Lincoln Home National Historic Site 413 S Eigth St. — *Web:* www.nps.gov	Springfield	IL	62701	217-492-4241		564
Lincoln Homestead State Park 5079 Lincoln Park Rd — *Web:* parks.ky.gov	Springfield	KY	40069	859-336-7461		565
Lincoln Industrial Corp 5148 N Hanley Rd. — **Fax Area Code:* 800 ■ *Web:* www.lincolnindustrial.com	Saint Louis	MO	63134	314-679-4200	424-5359*	386
Lincoln Journal-Star 926 P St — *TF:* 800-742-7315 ■ *Web:* www.journalstar.com	Lincoln	NE	68508	402-475-4200	473-7291	532-2
Lincoln Laboratory Massachusetts Institute of Technology 244 Wood St — *Web:* www.ll.mit.edu	Lexington	MA	02421	781-981-5500		668
Lincoln Land Community College 5250 Shepherd Rd PO Box 19256 — *TF:* 800-727-4161 ■ *Web:* www.llcc.edu	Springfield	IL	62794	217-786-2200		162
Lincoln Library 326 S Seventh St — *Web:* www.lincolnlibrary.info	Springfield	IL	62701	217-753-4900		434-3
Lincoln Machine Inc 6401 Cornhusker Hwy — *Web:* www.lincolnmachine.com	Lincoln	NE	68507	402-434-9140	434-9160	454
Lincoln Manufacturing Inc 31209 FM 2978 Rd. — *Web:* www.lincolnmanufacturing.com	Magnolia	TX	77354	713-514-0059		539
Lincoln Memorial Garden & Nature Ctr 2301 E Lake Shore Dr. — *Web:* www.lincolnmemorialgarden.org	Springfield	IL	62712	217-529-1111		50-5
Lincoln Memorial Shrine 125 W Vine St. — *Web:* www.lincolnshrine.org	Redlands	CA	92373	909-798-7632		50-4
Lincoln Memorial University 6965 Cumberland Gap Pkwy — *TF:* 800-325-0900 ■ *Web:* www.lmunet.edu	Harrogate	TN	37752	423-869-3611		166
Lincoln Military Housing 98 San Jacinto Rd. — *Web:* lincolnmilitary.com	Oceanside	CA	92058	760-430-5000		655
Lincoln Motor Co PO Box 6248 — *TF:* 800-521-4140 ■ *Web:* www.lincoln.com	Dearborn	MI	48126	800-521-4140		59
Lincoln National Corp (LNC) 150 N Radnor-Chester Rd. — *NYSE:* LNC ■ **Fax Area Code:* 215 ■ *TF:* 877-275-5462 ■ *Web:* www.lfg.com	Radnor	PA	19087	866-533-3410	448-3962*	360-4
Lincoln Packing Co 7 Industrial Rd — *Web:* www.lincolnpackingllc.com	Cranston	RI	02920	401-943-0878	943-7603	296-26
Lincoln Parish Clerk of Court PO Box 924 — *Web:* lpso.lincolnparish.org	Ruston	LA	71273	318-251-5130	255-6004	338
Lincoln Parish Library 910 N Trenton St. — *Web:* www.mylpl.org	Ruston	LA	71270	318-251-5030		434-3
Lincoln Park Chamber of Commerce 1925 N Clybourn Ste 301 — *Web:* www.lincolnparkchamber.com	Chicago	IL	60614	773-880-5200	880-0266	139
Lincoln Park Historical Society and Museum 1335 Southfield Rd. — *Web:* www.lphistorical.org	Lincoln Park	MI	48146	313-386-3137		520
Lincoln Park Hospital 550 W Webster Ave.	Chicago	IL	60614	773-883-2000		374-3
Lincoln Park Zoo 2001 N Clark St PO Box 14903 — *Web:* www.lpzoo.org	Chicago	IL	60614	312-742-2000	742-2299	823
Lincoln Property Co 2000 McKinney Ave Ste 1000. — *Web:* www.lpc.com	Dallas	TX	75201	214-740-3300		655
Lincoln Provision Inc 824 W 38th Pl — *Web:* www.lincolnprovision.com	Chicago	IL	60609	773-254-2400		297-6
Lincoln Public Schools PO Box 82889 — *Web:* www.lps.org	Lincoln	NE	68510	402-436-1610		685
Lincoln Publishing Company Inc 5460 Pinecrest Dr. — **Fax Area Code:* 716 ■ *TF:* 800-431-5768 ■ *Web:* www.lincolnpublishing.com	Lockport	NY	14094	800-431-5768	478-0059*	637-2
Lincoln Rock State Park 13253 SR-2 — *Web:* parks.state.wa.us	East Wenatchee	WA	98802	509-884-8702		565
Lincoln Shoe Polish c/o Maxton & Company 3130 20th St Ste 175 — *Web:* www.lincolnshoepolish.com	San Francisco	CA	94110	408-732-5121		151
Lincoln State Park Hwy 162 PO Box 216 — *TF:* 877-478-3657 ■ *Web:* www.in.gov	Lincoln City	IN	47552	812-937-1902		565
Lincoln Surgery Center LLC 11960 Lioness Way Ste 120 — *Web:* lincolnsurgerycenter.com	Parker	CO	80134	720-542-6700		374-3
Lincoln Telephone Co 111 Stemple Pass Rd — *Web:* www.linctel.net	Lincoln	MT	59639	406-362-4216		224
Lincoln Tomb 1500 Monument Ave — *Web:* www.lincolntomb.org	Springfield	IL	62702	217-782-2717		50-4
Lincoln Trail State Park 16985 E 1350th Rd — *Web:* www.dnr.illinois.gov	Marshall	IL	62441	217-826-2222		565
Lincoln Unified School District 2010 W Swain Rd — *Web:* www.lusd.net	Stockton	CA	95207	209-953-8700	951-5195	685
Lincoln University 820 Chestnut St — *TF:* 800-521-5052 ■ *Web:* www.lincolnu.edu	Jefferson City	MO	65101	573-681-5000	681-5889	166
Lincoln University 1570 Old Baltimore Pk PO Box 179 — *TF:* 800-790-0191 ■ *Web:* www.lincoln.edu	Lincoln	PA	19352	484-365-8000	365-8109	166
Lincoln University 401 15th St. — *TF:* 888-810-9998 ■ *Web:* www.lincolnuca.edu	Oakland	CA	94612	510-628-8010	628-8012	166
Lincoln Way Community Bank 1000 E Lincoln Hwy — *Web:* lwcbank.com	New Lenox	IL	60451	815-462-4300		70
Lincoln Wood Products Inc 1400 W Taylor St PO Box 375 — *TF:* 800-967-2461 ■ *Web:* www.lincolnwindows.com	Merrill	WI	54452	715-536-2461	536-7090	236
Lincoln Woods State Park 2 Manchester Print Works Rd — *Web:* www.riparks.com	Lincoln	RI	02865	401-723-7892	724-7951	565
Lincoln's New Salem State Historic Site 15588 History Ln — *Web:* www.lincolnsnewsalem.com	Petersburg	IL	62675	217-632-4000	632-4010	520
Lincoln's Symphony Orchestra 233 S 13th St Ste 1702 — *Web:* lincolnsymphony.com	Lincoln	NE	68508	402-476-2211		573-3
Lincolnshire Management Inc 780 Third Ave 40th Fl — *Web:* www.lincolnshiremgmt.com	New York	NY	10017	212-319-3633	755-5457	690
Lincolnton-Lincoln County Chamber of Commerce 101 E Main St — *TF:* 800-222-1167 ■ *Web:* www.lincolnchambernc.org	Lincolnton	NC	28092	704-735-3096	735-5449	130
Lincolnville Telephone Co 133 Back Meadow Rd — *Web:* www.lintelco.net	Nobleboro	ME	04555	207-563-9911		116
Lincoln-Way Central High School 1801 E Lincoln Hwy — *Web:* www.lw210.org	New Lenox	IL	60451	815-462-2100		685
Lincus Inc 8950 S 52nd St Ste 415 — *TF:* 877-525-8898 ■ *Web:* www.lincusenergy.com	Tempe	AZ	85284	480-598-8441		261
Lind Jensen Sullivan & Peterson 901 S Marquette Ave. — *Web:* www.lindjensen.com	Minneapolis	MN	55402	612-333-3637		428
Lind Marine Inc 300 E D St. — *Web:* www.lindmarine.com	Petaluma	CA	94952	707-762-7251	762-2129	447
Linda Hall Library 5109 Cherry St — *TF:* 800-662-1545 ■ *Web:* www.lindahall.org	Kansas City	MO	64110	816-363-4600	926-8790	434-3
Linda Layman Agency Ltd 3546 E 51st St. — *Web:* www.lindalaymanagency.com	Tulsa	OK	74135	918-744-0888	744-1802	167-3
Linda Roth 1217 S 40th Ave — *TF:* 888-909-7765 ■ *Web:* lindarothinsurance.com	Yakima	WA	98908	509-248-7765	248-7767	390
Linda Suzzanne Griffin PA 1455 Court St — *Web:* helpwithestateplanning.com	Clearwater	FL	33756	727-449-9800	446-2748	41
Linda's La Cantina 4721 E Colonial Dr. — *Web:* www.lindaslacantina.com	Orlando	FL	32803	407-894-4491	894-6415	671
Lindal Cedar Homes Inc 4300 S 104th Pl — *TF:* 800-426-0536 ■ *Web:* lindal.com	Seattle	WA	98178	206-725-0900	725-1615	106
Lindamar Industries (Manufacturing Plant) 1603 Commerce Way — *TF:* 800-235-1811 ■ *Web:* www.columbiapkg.com	Paso Robles	CA	93446	805-237-1910		362
Lindar Corp 7789 Hastings Rd — *Web:* lindarcorp.com	Baxter	MN	56425	218-829-3457		596
Lindblad Construction Co 717 E Cass St — *Web:* lindbladconstruction.com	Joliet	IL	60432	815-726-6251	723-4907	189-3
Lindblad Expeditions 96 Morton St 9th Fl — **Fax Area Code:* 212 ■ *TF:* 800-397-3348 ■ *Web:* www.expeditions.com	New York	NY	10014	800-397-3348	265-3770*	760
Linde Group 6550 Vallejo St Ste 201 — *Web:* www.lindegroup.com	Emeryville	CA	94608	510-705-8910	705-8911	180
Linde Hydraulics Corp 5089 W Western Reserve Rd. — *Web:* www.linde-hydraulics.com	Canfield	OH	44406	330-533-6801		470
Lindeberg & Assoc 12191 W 64th Ave Ste 200 — *Web:* la-cpas.com	Arvada	CO	80004	303-424-0314	424-0391	2
Lindeblad Piano Restoration 101 Us 46 — *TF:* 888-587-4266 ■ *Web:* www.lindebladpiano.com	Pine Brook	NJ	07058	888-587-4266		527
Linden Bulk Transportation Company Inc 4200 Tremley Pt Rd. — *Web:* www.odysseylogistics.com	Linden	NJ	07036	908-862-3883		780
Linden Hall School for Girls 212 E Main St. — *TF:* 800-258-5778 ■ *Web:* www.lindenhall.org	Lititz	PA	17543	717-626-8512	627-1384	622
Linden Kildare 205 Kildare Rd. — *Web:* www.lkcisd.net	Linden	TX	75563	903-756-7071		685
Linden Lab 945 Battery St — *TF:* 800-294-1067 ■ *Web:* www.lindenlab.com	San Francisco	CA	94111	415-243-9000		636
Linden Public Library 31 E Henry St — *Web:* www.lindenpl.org	Linden	NJ	07036	908-298-3830		434-3
Linden Publishing 2006 S Mary St. — *TF:* 800-345-4447 ■ *Web:* www.woodworkerslibrary.com	Fresno	CA	93721	559-233-6633	233-6933	637-2
Linden Row Inn 100 E Franklin St. — *TF:* 800-348-7424 ■ *Web:* www.lindenrowinn.com	Richmond	VA	23219	804-783-7000	648-7504	379
Linden Warehouse & Distribution Company Inc 1300 Lower Rd — *TF:* 800-333-2855 ■ *Web:* www.lindenwarehouse.com	Linden	NJ	07036	908-862-1400	862-7539	780
Lindenmeyr Munroe 14 Research Pkwy. — *TF:* 800-842-8480 ■ *Web:* lindenmeyrmunroe.com	Wallingford	CT	06492	800-842-8480	890-3115	553

Name / Address	City	State	Zip	Phone	Fax	Class
Lindenmeyr Munroe Central Central National-Gottesman Inc 3 Manhattanville Rd *TF:* 800-221-3042 ■ *Web:* www.cng-inc.com	Purchase	NY	10577	800-221-3042		553
Lindenwood University 209 S Kings Hwy *TF:* 877-615-8212 ■ *Web:* www.lindenwood.edu	Saint Charles	MO	63301	636-949-2000		166
Linder & Associates Inc 840 N Main St PO Box 1202 *Web:* www.linderandassociates.com	Wichita	KS	67203	316-265-1616	265-8097	189-4
Linder Assoc 7 E 14th St Apt 817 *Web:* www.srlinder.com	New York	NY	10003	212-645-7598		193
Linder Equipment Co 311 E Kern St *Web:* linderequipment.com	Tulare	CA	93274	559-685-5000		274
Linder Farm Network 255 Cedardale Dr SE *Web:* www.linderfarmnetwork.com	Owatonna	MN	55060	507-444-9224	444-9080	647
Lindey's 169 E Beck St *Web:* www.lindeys.com	Columbus	OH	43206	614-228-4343		671
Lindey's Prime Steak House 3600 N Snelling Ave *TF:* 866-491-0538 ■ *Web:* www.theplaceforsteak.com	Arden Hills	MN	55112	651-633-9813		671
Lindi Skin 408 E 4th St Ste 302 *TF:* 800-380-4704 ■ *Web:* www.lindiskin.com	Bridgeport	PA	19405	610-649-3900		582
Lindner Aviation 2504 340th St *TF:* 800-383-3104 ■ *Web:* www.lindneraviation.com	Keokuk	IA	52632	319-524-6203	524-8448	167-3
LINDO Systems Inc 1415 N Dayton St *TF:* 800-441-2378 ■ *Web:* www.lindo.com	Chicago	IL	60622	312-988-7422	988-9065	178-5
Lindon Engineering Services Inc 350 Missouri Ave Ste 201 *Web:* lindonengineering.com	Jeffersonville	IN	47130	812-282-1250	282-1350	261
Lindquist Machine Corp 610 Baeten Rd *Web:* www.lmc-corp.com	Green Bay	WI	54304	920-713-4100	499-8482	454
Lindquist Steels Inc 1050 Woodend Rd **Fax Area Code:* 203 ■ *TF:* 800-243-9637 ■ *Web:* www.lindquiststeels.com	Stratford	CT	06615	800-243-9637	386-0132*	492
Lindquist Von Husen & Joyce LLP 301 Howard St Ste 850 *Web:* lvhj.com	San Francisco	CA	94105	415-957-9999	957-1629	2
Lindsay Cadillac Co 1525 Kenwood Ave *Web:* www.lindsaycars.com	Alexandria	VA	22302	703-647-8600		57
Lindsay Foods Inc 2211 W National Ave *TF:* 800-856-3895 ■ *Web:* www.lindsayfoods.com	Milwaukee	WI	53204	800-856-3895		297-9
Lindsay Hill Design 529 Main St Ste 345 *Web:* www.lindsayhilldesign.com	Charlestown	MA	02129	617-886-0255		344
Lindsay Manufacturing Inc PO Box 1708 *TF:* 800-546-3729 ■ *Web:* www.lindsaymfg.com	Ponca City	OK	74602	580-762-2457	762-9547	788
Lindsay Precast Inc 6845 Erie Ave NW **Fax Area Code:* 330 ■ *TF:* 800-837-7788 ■ *Web:* www.lindsayprecast.com	Canal Fulton	OH	44614	800-837-7788	854-6664*	183
Lindsay Stone & Briggs Inc 1 S Pinckney St Ste 500	Madison	WI	53703	608-251-7070	251-8989	4
Lindsay Wildlife Museum 1931 First Ave *Web:* lindsaywildlife.org	Walnut Creek	CA	94597	925-627-2920		520
Lindsay Windows LLC 1995 Commerce Ln *Web:* lindsaywindows.com	North Mankato	MN	56003	507-625-4278		499
Lindsey & Company Inc 484 Boston Post Rd *Web:* www.lindseycompany.com	Darien	CT	06820	203-655-1590		260
Lindsey Hopkins Technical College 750 NW 20 St Rm D106 *Web:* www.lindseyhopkins.edu	Miami	FL	33127	305-324-6070		167-3
Lindsey Office Furnishings 2223 1st Ave N *Web:* www.lindseyof.com	Birmingham	AL	35203	205-251-9088		321
Lindsey Software 500 President Clinton Ave Ste 401 *TF:* 800-890-7058 ■ *Web:* www.lindseysoftware.com	Searcy	AR	72201	501-268-5324	268-1198	174
Lindsey Wilson College 210 Lindsey Wilson St *TF:* 800-264-0138 ■ *Web:* www.lindsey.edu	Columbia	KY	42728	270-384-2126	384-8591	166
Lindsey-Cooper Refrigeration School Inc 815 S Beltline Rd *TF:* 800-338-2709 ■ *Web:* www.lindseycooperschool.com	Irving	TX	75060	972-790-7404		685
Lindstrand Balloons USA 11440 Dandar St *Web:* www.lindstrand.com	Galena	IL	61036	815-777-6006	777-6004	28
Lindstrom Sorenson & Associates LLP 3815 N Mulford Rd *Web:* www.lsallp.com	Rockford	IL	61114	815-282-1288	282-1612	2
Lindt & Sprungli USA 1 Fine Chocolate Pl *TF:* 877-695-4638 ■ *Web:* www.lindtusa.com	Stratham	NH	03885	877-695-4638		296-8
Lindy Property Management 309 York Rd Ste 211 *Web:* www.lindyproperty.com	Jenkintown	PA	19046	215-886-8030	543-7546	652
Line 6 26580 Agoura Rd *Web:* line6.com	Calabasas	CA	91302	818-575-3600	575-3601	52
Lineage Capital LLC 399 Boylston St Ste 450 *Web:* www.lineagecap.com	Boston	MA	02116	617-778-0660		401
Lineage Cell Therapeutics Inc 2173 Salk Ave Ste 200 *Web:* lineagecell.com	Carlsbad	CA	92008	442-287-8963		85
Lineagen Inc 2677 E Parleys Way *Web:* www.lineagen.com	Salt Lake City	UT	84109	801-931-6200		668
Linear Industries Ltd 1850 Enterprise Way *TF:* 800-821-2875 ■ *Web:* www.linearindustries.com	Monrovia	CA	91016	626-303-1130	303-2035	385
Linear Laboratories 42025 Osgood Rd *TF:* 800-536-0262 ■ *Web:* www.linearlabs.com	Fremont	CA	94539	510-226-0488	226-1112	201
Linear Pump Corp 1331 E Waterford Ave *Web:* www.linearpumpcorp.com	Saint Francis	WI	53235	414-374-3332		641
Linebach - Funkhouser Inc 114 Fairfax Ave *Web:* www.linebachfunkhouser.com	Louisville	KY	40207	502-895-5009	895-4005	261
Linebaugh Public Library 105 W Vine St *Web:* www.rclstn.org	Murfreesboro	TN	37130	615-893-4131	848-5038	434-3
Linedata Services Inc 260 Franklin St *Web:* www.linedata.com	Boston	MA	02110	617-912-4700		180
Linemark Printing Inc 501 Prince Georges Blvd *Web:* www.linemark.com	Upper Marlboro	MD	20774	301-925-9000	925-8943	627
Linemaster Switch Corp 29 Plaine Hill Rd **Fax Area Code:* 800 ■ *Web:* www.linemaster.com	Woodstock	CT	06281	860-974-1000	974-3668*	485
Linen Chest Inc 4455 Autoroute Des Laurentides *TF:* 800-363-3832 ■ *Web:* www.linenchest.com	Laval	QC	H7L5X8	514-341-7077		364
Linens of the Week 713 Lamont St NW *Web:* www.linensoftheweek.com	Washington	DC	20010	202-291-9200		442
Liner Products LLC 1468 W Hospital Rd *Web:* linerproducts.com	Paoli	IN	47454	812-723-0244		601
LineStar Services Inc 5391 Bay Oaks Dr *TF:* 800-790-3758 ■ *Web:* linestar.com	Pasadena	TX	77505	281-422-4989		538
Linetec 725 S 75th Ave *TF:* 888-717-1472 ■ *Web:* www.linetec.com	Wausau	WI	54401	715-843-4100		480
Linfield College 900 SE Baker St *TF:* 800-640-2287 ■ *Web:* www.linfield.edu	McMinnville	OR	97128	503-883-2213	883-2472	166
Linfield Hunter & Junius 3608 18th St 200 *Web:* www.lhjunius.com	Metairie	LA	70002	504-833-5300		261
Ling Shen Ching Tze Temple 17012 NE 40th Ct *Web:* tbsseattle.org	Redmond	WA	98052	425-882-0916		50-1
Linger Peterson & Shrum 575 E Locust Ave Ste 308 *Web:* www.lingercpa.com	Fresno	CA	93720	559-438-8740		2
Lingo Inc 7901 Jones Branch Dr Ste 900 *TF:* 888-546-4699 ■ *Web:* www.lingo.com	McLean	VA	22102	800-393-7881		387
Lingo Manufacturing Co 7400 Industrial Rd *TF:* 800-354-9771 ■ *Web:* www.lingomfg.com	Florence	KY	41042	859-371-2662	371-0283	233
Lingo Media Corp 151 Bloor St W Ste 703 *TF:* 866-927-7011 ■ *Web:* lingomedia.com	Toronto	ON	M5S1S4	416-927-7000		242
Lingua Language Ctr 111 E Las Olas Blvd *TF:* 888-654-6482 ■ *Web:* www.linguaschool.com	Fort Lauderdale	FL	33301	954-577-9955		423
Linguagraphics 194 Park Pl *Web:* www.linguagraphics.com	Brooklyn	NY	11238	718-789-2782		196
Lingualinx Language Solutions Inc 433 River St *Web:* lingualinx.com	Troy	NY	12180	518-388-9000		768
LinguaText Ltd 103 Walker Way *Web:* www.linguatextltd.com	Newark	DE	19711	302-453-8695		637-2
Linguistic Analysis PO Box 2237 *Web:* www.linguisticanalysis.com	Vashon Island	WA	98070	206-567-4373	567-5711	637-9
Linguistic Society of America (LSA) 1325 18th St NW Ste 211 *TF:* 800-726-0479 ■ *Web:* www.linguisticsociety.org	Washington	DC	20036	202-835-1714	835-1717	48-11
Linguistics Systems Inc 201 Broadway *TF:* 877-654-5006 ■ *Web:* www.linguist.com	Cambridge	MA	02139	617-528-7410		768
Linium 187 Wolf Rd Ste 302 *Web:* www.liniumrecruiting.com	Albany	NY	12205	518-689-3140		260
Link America Inc 3002 Century Dr *TF:* 800-318-4955 ■ *Web:* www.linkam.com	Rowlett	TX	75088	800-318-4955		224
Link Computer Corporation Inc PO Box 250 *Web:* www.linkcorp.com	Bellwood	PA	16617	814-742-7700		176
Link Electronics Inc 2137 Rust Ave *TF:* 800-776-4411 ■ *Web:* linkelectronics.com	Cape Girardeau	MO	63703	573-334-4433		116
Link Engineering Company Inc 43855 Plymouth Oaks Blvd *Web:* www.linkeng.com	Plymouth	MI	48170	734-453-0800		472
Link Insurance Agency Inc 111 Fifth Ave *Web:* marklink.us	Pelham	NY	10803	914-712-3680		390
Link Manufacturing Ltd 223 15th St NE *TF:* 800-222-6283 ■ *Web:* www.linkmfg.com	Sioux Center	IA	51250	712-722-4874	722-4876	59
Link Medical Computing Inc 1208 B VFW Pkwy Ste 203 *TF:* 888-893-0900 ■ *Web:* www.linkmed.com	Boston	MA	02132	617-676-6165	676-6170	180
Link Solutions Inc 8251 Greensboro Dr 8th Fl *Web:* www.linksol-inc.com	McLean	VA	22102	703-707-6256		624
Link Staffing Services Inc 1800 Bering Dr Ste 800 *TF:* 888-929-5465 ■ *Web:* www.linkstaffing.com	Houston	TX	77057	713-784-4400		734
Link Technologies 9505 Hillwood Dr Ste 150 *TF:* 888-367-5549 ■ *Web:* www.linktechconsulting.com	Las Vegas	NV	89134	702-233-8703	233-8053	261
Linkage Credit Union 4527 Speight Ave *TF:* 800-791-2525 ■ *Web:* linkagecu.com	Waco	TX	76711	254-754-1168	754-7768	219
Link-Belt Construction Equipment Co 2651 Palumbo Dr *Web:* www.linkbelt.com	Lexington	KY	40509	859-263-5200		190
Link-Burns Manufacturing Company Inc 253 American Way *TF:* 800-457-4358 ■ *Web:* linkburns.com	Voorhees	NJ	08043	800-457-4358		697
Linkedin Corp 2029 Stierlin Ct *Web:* www.linkedin.com	Mountain View	CA	94043	650-687-3600		736

Name / Address	City	State	ZIP	Phone	Fax	Class
Linkex Inc 1621 Hutton Dr Ste 140	Dallas	TX	75006	866-289-9838		311
Web: www.linkex.us						
Linkfield & Cross Agency Inc						
1600 E Beltline NE Ste 211	Grand Rapids	MI	49525	616-447-2777		390
Web: linkfieldcross.com						
Linkous Construction Company Inc						
1661 Aaron Brenner Dr Ste 207	Memphis	TN	38120	901-754-0700	754-0302	360-2
Web: www.linkousconstruction.com						
Links Magazine PO Box 7628	Hilton Head Island	SC	29928	843-842-6200	842-6233	457-20
Web: www.linksmagazine.com						
Links Medical Products Inc						
9247 Research Dr	Irvine	CA	92618	949-753-0001		476
TF: 888-425-1149 ■ *Web:* linksmed.com						
Link-Systems International Inc						
4515 George Rd Ste 340	Tampa	FL	33634	813-674-0660	674-0040	177
Web: www.link-systems.com						
LinkUp 430 1st Ave N Ste 790	Minneapolis	MN	55401	866-359-9360		260
Web: www.linkup.com						
Linkus Enterprises Inc						
5595 W San Madele Ave	Fresno	CA	93722	559-256-6600		681
TF: 888-854-6587 ■ *Web:* linkuscorp.com						
Linn County 935 Second St SW	Cedar Rapids	IA	52404	319-892-5000	892-5009	338
Web: www.linncounty.org						
Linn County 108 N High St	Linn	MO	64653	660-895-5417	895-5527	338
Web: marcelinemo.us						
Linn County 306 Main St PO Box 350	Mound City	KS	66056	913-795-2660	795-2004	338
Web: www.linncountyks.com						
Linn County Historical Society						
716 Oakland Rd NE Ste 103	Pleasanton	KS	66075	319-362-1501		637-2
Web: historycenter.org						
Linn County Leader						
314 N Main St PO Box 40	Brookfield	MO	64628	660-258-7237		532-2
Web: www.linncountyleader.com						
Linn County Rural Electric Co-op						
5695 Rec Dr	Marion	IA	52302	319-377-1587		245
TF: 888-271-6250 ■ *Web:* www.linncountyrec.com						
Linn Gear Co 100 N Eigth St PO Box 397	Lebanon	OR	97355	541-259-1211	259-1299	620
TF: 800-547-2471 ■ *Web:* www.linngear.com						
Linn Run State Park PO Box 50	Rector	PA	15677	724-238-6623		565
Web: www.dcnr.pa.gov						
Linn-Benton Community College						
6500 Pacific Blvd SW	Albany	OR	97321	541-917-4999		162
Web: www.linnbenton.edu						
Linnell, Choate & Webber LLP						
83 Pleasant St	Auburn	ME	04210	207-784-4563		41
Web: lcwlaw.com						
Linnie's Thai Cuisine 3908 E 24th Ave	Spokane	WA	99201	509-838-0626		671
Web: linniesthai.wordpress.com						
Linnihan Foy Adv						
615 First Ave NE Ste 320	Minneapolis	MN	55413	612-331-3586	238-3000	4
Web: linnihanfoy.com						
Linon Home Dcor Products Inc						
22 Jericho Tpke	Mineola	NY	11501	516-699-1000		362
Web: www.linon.com						
Linowes & Blocher LLP						
7200 Wisconsin Ave Ste 800	Bethesda	MD	20814	301-654-0504	654-2801	428
Web: www.linowes-law.com						
LINQ Services						
1200 Steuart St Unit C3	Baltimore	MD	21230	800-421-5467		387
TF: 800-421-5467 ■ *Web:* www.linqservices.com						
Linscomb & Williams Inc						
1400 Post Oak Blvd Ste 1000	Houston	TX	77056	713-840-1000		401
TF: 800-960-1200 ■ *Web:* www.linscomb-williams.com						
Linseis Inc 109 N Gold Dr	Robbinsville	NJ	08691	609-223-2070	223-2074	248
Web: www.linseis.com						
Linsly School 60 Knox Ln	Wheeling	WV	26003	304-233-3200	234-4014	622
TF: 866-648-1893 ■ *Web:* www.linsly.org						
LinTech Global Inc						
34119 W 12 Mile Rd Ste 200	Farmington Hills	MI	48331	248-553-8037	736-9017*	180
**Fax Area Code:* 866 ■ *Web:* lintechglobal.com						
Lintern Corp 8685 Stn St	Mentor	OH	44060	440-255-9333	255-6427	14
TF: 800-321-3638 ■ *Web:* www.lintern.com						
Linville Caverns Inc 19929 US 221 N	Marion	NC	28752	800-419-0540	756-4171*	50-5
**Fax Area Code:* 828 ■ *TF:* 800-419-0540 ■ *Web:* www.linvillecaverns.com						
Linwood Spiritual Ctr 50 Linwood Rd	Rhinebeck	NY	12572	845-876-4178	876-1920	673
Web: www.linwoodspiritual.com						
Linx Industries Inc						
2600 Airline Blvd	Portsmouth	VA	23701	800-797-7476		697
TF: 800-797-7476 ■ *Web:* www.li-hvac.com						
Linx Partners LLC						
100 Galleria Pkwy Ste 1150	Atlanta	GA	30339	770-818-0335		403
Web: linxpartners.com						
Linxus Credit Union						
1405 W Lane Rd Ste A	Machesney Park	IL	61115	815-282-8711		219
Web: linxuscu.org						
Linxx Global Solutions Inc						
272 Bendix Rd Ste 220	Virginia Beach	VA	23452	757-222-0300	965-9806	393
Web: linxxglobal.com						
Linzer Products Corp						
248 Wyandanch Ave	West Babylon	NY	11704	800-221-0787		103
Web: www.linzerproducts.com						
Linzer Truck Lines Inc PO Box 138	Bertram	TX	78605	866-982-4242	234-8185*	780
**Fax Area Code:* 512 ■ *TF:* 866-982-4242 ■ *Web:* linzertrucklines.com						
Lion Apparel Inc 7200 Poe Ave Ste 400	Dayton	OH	45414	937-898-1949		155-19
TF: 800-548-6614 ■ *Web:* www.lionprotects.com						
Lion Brand Yarn Co 135 Kero Rd	Carlstadt	NJ	07072	212-243-8995		745-9
TF: 800-795-5466 ■ *Web:* www.lionbrand.com						
Lion Brewery, The						
700 N Pennsylvania Ave	Wilkes-Barre	PA	18705	570-823-8801		102
Web: www.lionbrewery.com						
Lion Bros Company Inc						
300 Red Brook Blvd	Owings Mills	MD	21117	800-365-6543		258
TF: 800-365-6543 ■ *Web:* www.lionbrothers.com						
Lion Chemical Partners						
535 Madison Ave 4th Fl	New York	NY	10022	212-355-5500		405
Web: www.lionchemicalpartners.com						
Lion Country Safari						
2003 Lion Country Safari Rd	Loxahatchee	FL	33470	561-793-1084	793-9603	823
Web: www.lioncountrysafari.com						
Lion Inc						
318 W Half Day Rd Ste 314	Buffalo Grove	IL	60089	872-228-5466		509
TF: 800-867-6320 ■ *Web:* lioninc.us						
Lion Investigation Academy						
434 Clearfield St	Bethlehem	PA	18017	877-747-2466		167-3
TF: 877-747-2466 ■ *Web:* www.lia.amdetective.us						
Lion Raisins 9500 De Wolf Ave	Selma	CA	93662	559-834-6677	834-6622	315-5
Web: www.lionraisins.com						
Lion Rex Ata Inc						
818-A E Franklin St	Centerville	OH	45459	937-436-1400		2
Web: lionrexata.com						
Lion Ribbon 2015 W Front St	Berwick	PA	18603	800-551-5466		292
TF: 800-551-5466 ■ *Web:* www.lionribbon.com						
Lion Supermarket 1710 Tully Rd	San Jose	CA	95122	408-238-4451		345
Web: www.lionsupermarket.com						
Lion World Travel 33 Kern Rd	Toronto	ON	M3B1S9	800-387-2706		774
TF: 800-387-2706 ■ *Web:* www.lionworldtravel.com						
Lionakis Beaumont Design Group Inc						
1919 19th St	Sacramento	CA	95811	916-558-1900		261
Web: www.lionakis.com						
Lionbridge Technologies Inc						
1050 Winter St Ste 2300	Waltham	MA	02451	781-434-6000	434-6034	768
NASDAQ: LIOX ■ *TF:* 866-267-0437 ■ *Web:* lionbridge.com						
Lionel com LLC 26750 23 Mile Rd	Chesterfield	MI	48051	586-949-4100		762
TF: 800-454-6635 ■ *Web:* www.lionel.com						
Lionetti Associates LLC						
450 S Front St	Elizabeth	NJ	07202	800-734-0910	820-8412*	580
**Fax Area Code:* 908 ■ *TF:* 800-734-0910 ■ *Web:* lorcopetroleum.com						
Lions Clubs Intl 300 West 22nd St	Oak Brook	IL	60523	630-571-5466		378
Web: www.lionsclubs.org						
Lions Eye Bank for Long Island						
900 Franklin Ave	Valley Stream	NY	11580	516-256-6990	256-6661	269
Web: www.lebli.org						
Lions Eye Bank of Nebraska Inc						
University of Nebraska Medical Ctr						
985541 Nebraska Medical Ctr	Omaha	NE	68198	402-559-4039		269
TF: 800-225-7244 ■ *Web:* eyebanknebraska.org						
Lions Eye Bank of Wisconsin						
2401 American Ln	Madison	WI	53704	608-233-2354		269
TF: 877-233-2354 ■ *Web:* lebw.org						
Lions Foundation of Manitoba & Northwestern Ontario Inc						
320 Sherbrook St	Winnipeg	MB	R3B2W6	204-772-1899	943-6823	269
TF: 800-552-6820 ■ *Web:* eyebankmanitoba.com						
Lions Gate Entertainment Inc						
2700 Colorado Ave Ste 200	Santa Monica	CA	90404	310-449-9200		514
Web: www.lionsgate.com						
Lions Gift of Sight						
1000 Westgate Dr Ste 260	Saint Paul	MN	55114	612-624-0446		269
TF: 866-887-4448 ■ *Web:* lionsgiftofsight.umn.edu						
Lions Medical Eye Bank & Research Center of Eastern Virginia						
600 Gresham Dr	Norfolk	VA	23507	800-453-6059	388-3744*	269
**Fax Area Code:* 757 ■ *TF:* 800-453-6059 ■ *Web:* www.lionseyebank.org						
Lionshare Leadership Group Inc						
7065 Moores Ln Ste 200	Brentwood	TN	37027	615-377-4688		463
Web: www.lionshare.org						
Lionshare Marketing Inc						
7830 Barton St	Overland Park	KS	66214	913-631-8400		195
TF: 800-928-0712 ■ *Web:* www.lionsharemarketing.com						
Lipan Telephone Company Inc (LTC)						
109 N Kickapoo St	Lipan	TX	76462	254-646-2211		224
Web: www.lipan.net						
Lipari Foods LLC 26661 Bunert Rd	Warren	MI	48089	586-447-3500		297-11
Web: liparifoods.com						
Liphart Steel Company Inc						
3308 Rosedale Ave	Richmond	VA	23230	804-355-7481	355-0948	480
Web: www.liphartsteel.com						
LiphaTech Inc 3600 W Elm St	Milwaukee	WI	53209	414-351-1476	247-8166	85
TF: 888-331-7900 ■ *Web:* www.liphatech.com						
Lipinski Daniel (Rep D - IL)						
2346 Rayburn House Office Bldg	Washington	DC	20515	202-225-5701	225-1012	342-2
Web: lipinski.house.gov						
Lipinski Landscape & Irrigation Contractors Inc						
100 Sharp Rd	Marlton	NJ	08053	800-644-6035		422
TF: 800-644-6035 ■ *Web:* www.meritservicesolutions.com						
Lipman Hearne Inc						
200 S Michigan Ave Ste 1600	Chicago	IL	60604	312-356-8000		317
Web: www.lipmanhearne.com						
Lipman, Frizzell & Mitchell						
6240 Old Dobbin Ln Ste 140	Columbia	MD	21045	410-423-2300		653
Web: lfmvalue.com						
Lippa Associates Inc						
3633 Camino Del Rio S 207	San Diego	CA	92108	619-283-2581		734
Lipparelli & Associates Inc 517 Idaho St	Elko	NV	89801	775-738-7131		390
Web: www.progressive.com						
Lipper International Inc						
235 Washington St	Wallingford	CT	06492	203-269-8588	284-8637	730
TF: 800-243-3129 ■ *Web:* www.lipperinternational.com						
Lippert Bros Inc						
2211 E I-44 Service Rd PO Box 17450	Oklahoma City	OK	73136	405-478-3580	478-3301	186
Web: www.lippertbros.com						
Lippes Mathias Wexler Friedman LLP						
665 Main St Ste 300	Buffalo	NY	14203	716-853-5100		428
Web: www.lippes.com						
Lippin Group						
11601 Wilshire Blvd Ste 1900	Los Angeles	CA	90025	323-965-1990		317
Web: www.lippingroup.com						
Lippincott 499 Park Ave	New York	NY	10022	212-521-0000		4
Web: www.lippincott.com						
Lippincott & Peto Inc						
1741 Akron-Peninsula Rd	Akron	OH	44313	330-864-2122	864-5298	637-2
Web: www.rubberworld.com						
Lippincott Marine 3420 Main St	Grasonville	MD	21638	410-827-9300	827-9303	697
Web: www.lippincottmarina.com						
Lippincott Williams & Wilkins						
530 Walnut St	Philadelphia	PA	19106	215-521-8300	521-8902	637-2
Web: shop.lww.com						
Lippmann-Milwaukee Inc						
3271 E Van Norman Ave	Cudahy	WI	53110	800-648-0486		190
TF: 800-648-0486 ■ *Web:* lippmann-milwaukee.com						

				Phone	Fax	Class
Lipschultz, Levin & Gray LLC 425 Huehl Rd Bldg 7 *Web:* thethinkers.com	Northbrook	IL	60062	847-205-5452		2
Lipscomb County PO Box 70 *Web:* www.co.lipscomb.tx.us	Lipscomb	TX	79056	806-862-3091	862-3004	338
Lipscomb Insurance Group 750 N St Paul St Ste 1400 *Web:* lipscombinsurance.com	Dallas	TX	75201	214-420-5200		390
Lipscomb University 3901 Granny White Pk *TF:* 800-333-4358 ■ *Web:* www.lipscomb.edu	Nashville	TN	37204	615-966-1000	966-1804	166
Lipson, Neilson, Cole, Seltzer & Garin PC 3910 Telegraph Rd Ste 200 *Web:* www.lipsonneilson.com	Bloomfield Hills	MI	48302	248-593-5000		428
Lipten Company LLC 28033 Center Oaks Ct **Fax Area Code:* 248 ■ *TF:* 800-860-0790 ■ *Web:* www.lipten.com	Wixom	MI	48393	800-860-0790	374-8906*	385
Lipton Energy 458 S St *TF:* 877-443-9191 ■ *Web:* liptonenergy.com	Pittsfield	MA	01201	413-443-9191		580
Lipton Law Center Pc 18930 W 10 Mile Rd *Web:* www.liptonlaw.com	Southfield	MI	48075	248-557-1688		428
Liquent Inc 101 Gibraltar Rd *Web:* www.parexel.com	Horsham	PA	19044	215-347-1800	328-4360	178-11
Liquid Adv Inc 138 Eucalyptus Dr *Web:* liquidadvertising.com	El Segundo	CA	90245	310-450-2653		4
Liquid Agency Inc 448 S Market St *Web:* www.liquidagency.com	San Jose	CA	95113	408-850-8800		195
Liquid Controls LLC 105 Albrecht Dr *Web:* www.lcmeter.com	Lake Bluff	IL	60044	847-295-1050		201
Liquid Measurement Systems 141 Morse Dr PO Box 2070 *Web:* liquidmeasurement.com	Georgia	VT	05468	802-528-8100	528-8131	529
Liquid Networx Inc PO Box 780099 *TF:* 866-547-8439 ■ *Web:* liquidnetworx.com	San Antonio	TX	78278	866-547-8439		196
Liquid Packaging Solutions 3999 E Hupp Rd Bldg R43 *Web:* www.liquidpackagingsolution.com	La Porte	IN	46350	219-393-3600		547
Liquid Solids Control Inc PO Box 259 *Web:* liquidsolidscontrol.com	Upton	MA	01568	508-529-3339	529-6591	385
Liquid Transport Corp 8470 Allison Pt Blvd Ste 400 *TF:* 800-942-3175 ■ *Web:* www.liquidtransport.com	Indianapolis	IN	46250	317-841-4200	841-8259	780
Liquid Waste Technology 1750 Madison Ave *Web:* www.mudcatdredge.com	New Richmond	WI	54017	715-246-2888		190
LiquidFrameworks Inc 24 E Greenway Plz *Web:* www.liquidframeworks.com	Houston	TX	77046	713-552-9250		177
Liquidhub Inc 500 E Swedesford Rd Ste 300 *Web:* www.liquidhub.com	Wayne	PA	19087	610-688-6531		194
Liquidia Technologies Inc 419 Davis Dr Ste 100 *Web:* liquidia.com	Morrisville	NC	27560	919-328-4400		194
Liquidity Services Inc 1920 L St NW 6th Fl *NASDAQ: LQDT* ■ *TF:* 800-310-4604 ■ *Web:* www.liquidityservices.com	Washington	DC	20036	202-467-6868	467-5475	51
Liquidmetal Coatings Enterprises 6942 FM 1960 Rd E PMB 190 *Web:* www.liquidmetal-coatings.com	Humble	TX	77346	281-359-1283	359-1185	481
Liquidmetal Technologies Inc (LQMT) 30452 Esperanza *OTC: LQMT* ■ *Web:* www.liquidmetal.com	Rancho Santa Margarita	CA	92688	949-635-2100	635-2188	482
Liquidnet Holdings Inc 498 Seventh Ave 15th Fl *Web:* www.liquidnet.com	New York	NY	10018	646-674-2000	674-2003	405
Liquiflo Equipment Co 443 N Ave *Web:* www.liquiflo.com	Garwood	NJ	07027	908-518-0777	518-1847	641
Liquor Barn Inc 4301 Towne Center Dr *Web:* liquorbarn.com	Louisville	KY	40241	502-426-4222		443
Liquor Mart Inc 1750 15th St *TF:* 800-597-4440 ■ *Web:* www.liquormart.com	Boulder	CO	80302	303-449-3374		443
LiRo Group 3 Aerial Way *Web:* www.liro.com	Syosset	NY	11791	516-938-5476	937-5421	261
LIRS (Lutheran Immigration & Refugee Service) 700 Light St *Web:* www.lirs.org	Baltimore	MD	21230	410-230-2700	230-2890	48-5
Lirtzman Nehls LLC 2595 Canyon Blvd Ste 200 *Web:* packarddierking.com	Boulder	CO	80302	303-447-0450		41
Lisa Davis Associates (LDA) 33 Bradford St *Web:* www.davisplanning.com	Concord	MA	01742	978-254-6287		194
Lisa Hall Insurance Agency Inc 117 Irvine St *Web:* lisahallinsurance.com	Galena	IL	61036	815-777-2697		390
Lisa Haver Wain Insurance Agency Inc 139 Main St *Web:* lisahaverwain.com	Dundee	MI	48131	734-529-2394		390
Lisa Nickels Insurance Agency Inc 995 W Glade Rd *Web:* lisanickelsinsurance.com	Hurst	TX	76054	817-318-8900		390
Lisanti Capital Growth LLC 28 Liberty St *Web:* dinosaurlisanti.com	New York	NY	10020	212-792-6990		411
Lisega Inc 370 E Dumplin Valley Rd *Web:* www.lisega.de	Kodak	TN	37764	423-625-2000		295
LISI LLC 1600 W Hillsdale Blvd Ste 201 *TF:* 800-930-5190 ■ *Web:* www.lisibroker.com	San Mateo	CA	94402	866-570-5474		390
Liskow & Lewis 701 Poydras St Ste 5000 *Web:* www.liskow.com	New Orleans	LA	70139	504-581-7979		428
Lisle Corp 813 E Main St *Web:* www.lislecorp.com	Clarinda	IA	51632	712-542-5101	542-6591	758
Lisle Library District 777 Front St *Web:* www.lislelibrary.org	Lisle	IL	60532	630-971-1675	971-1701	434-3
Lisle Park District 1825 Short St *TF:* 800-526-0854 ■ *Web:* www.lisleparkdistrict.org	Lisle	IL	60532	630-964-3410		31
Lismore Cooperative Telephone Co 230 S 3rd Ave *Web:* www.lismoretel.com	Lismore	MN	56155	507-472-8748		224
List Industries Inc 401 Jim Moran Blvd *TF:* 800-776-1342 ■ *Web:* www.listindustries.com	Deerfield Beach	FL	33442	954-429-9155	428-3843	319-3
Lista International Corp 106 Lowland St *TF:* 800-722-3020 ■ *Web:* www.listaintl.com	Holliston	MA	01746	508-429-1350	429-0711	286
Listel Hotel, The 1300 Robson St *TF:* 800-663-5491 ■ *Web:* www.thelistelhotel.com	Vancouver	BC	V6E1C5	604-684-8461	684-7092	379
ListEngage 5 Edgell Rd Ste 20 *Web:* www.listengage.com	Framingham	MA	01701	508-935-2275	935-2276	225
ListenUp Audiobooks 514 Flat Shoals Ave SE *Web:* listenupaudiobooks.com	Atlanta	GA	30316	678-733-9487		637-10
Listo Pencil Corp 1925 Union St *TF:* 800-547-8648 ■ *Web:* www.listo.com	Alameda	CA	94501	510-522-2910		571
Liston Manufacturing Inc 421 Payne Ave *Web:* www.listonmfg.com	North Tonawanda	NY	14120	716-695-2111	695-0443	620
Litaliano Restaurant, The 701 Barksdale Blvd *Web:* litalianorestaurant.webs.com	Bossier City	LA	71111	318-747-7777		671
Litchfield Beach & Golf Resort 14276 Ocean Hwy *TF:* 888-734-8228 ■ *Web:* www.litchfieldbeach.com	Pawleys Island	SC	29585	843-237-3000	237-3282	669
Litchfield County PO Box 396 *Web:* www.litchfieldcty.com	Washington Depot	CT	06794	860-868-7313		338
Litchfield National Bank 316 N State St *Web:* www.ibanklnb.com	Litchfield	IL	62056	217-324-6161		70
Litchfield Park Recreation 100 N Old Litchfield Rd *Web:* www.litchfield-park.org	Litchfield Park	AZ	85340	623-935-9040		354
Litchfield Plantation 216 Hwy 17	Pawleys Island	SC	29585	843-543-3146		379
Litchfield Special Risks Inc 7016 Orizaba *Web:* lsrinc.org	El Paso	TX	79912	915-533-1111		390
Litco International Inc 1 Litco Dr PO Box 150 *TF:* 800-236-1903 ■ *Web:* www.litco.com	Vienna	OH	44473	330-539-5433	539-5388	551
Lite Access Technologies 20678 Duncan Way Unit 5 *TF:* 800-252-0893 ■ *Web:* liteaccess.com	Langley	BC	V3A7A3	604-247-4704		696
Lite Energy 780 Salaberry *Web:* www.liteenergy.com	Laval	QC	H7S1H3	450-668-9620	668-9625	439
Lite Metals Co 700 N Walnut St *Web:* www.litemetals.com	Ravenna	OH	44266	330-296-6110		492
LiteCure LLC 250 Corporate Blvd Ste B *TF:* 877-627-3858 ■ *Web:* www.litecure.com	Newark	DE	19702	877-627-3858		250
Litehouse Inc 1109 N Ella Ave *TF:* 800-669-3169 ■ *Web:* www.litehousefoods.com	Sandpoint	ID	83864	800-669-3169		296-19
Litelab Corp 251 Elm St *TF:* 800-238-4120 ■ *Web:* www.litelab.com	Buffalo	NY	14203	716-856-4491		362
Lite-On Trading USA Inc 720 S Hillview Dr *Web:* www.us.liteon.com	Milpitas	CA	95035	408-946-4873	941-4597	173-4
Liter's Quarry Inc 5918 Haunz Ln *Web:* www.litersinc.com	Louisville	KY	40241	502-241-7637	241-9410	503-6
Litera Corp 550 W Jackson Blvd Ste 200 *Web:* www.litera.com	Chicago	IL	60661	630-598-1100		177
Literacy Council of Alaska (LCA) 517 Gaffney Rd *Web:* www.literacycouncilofalaska.org	Fairbanks	AK	99701	907-456-6212	456-4302	48-6
Literacy Council of Tyler 1530 Loop 323 SSW Rm 120 *Web:* www.lcotyler.org	Tyler	TX	75711	903-533-0330	533-1801	242
Literacy KC 211 W Armour Blvd 3rd Fl *Web:* literacykc.org	Kansas City	MO	64111	816-333-9332	444-6628	148
Litetronics International Inc 4101 W 123rd St *TF:* 800-860-3392 ■ *Web:* www.litetronics.com	Alsip	IL	60803	708-389-8000	371-0627	437
Lithgow Public Library 45 Winthrop St *Web:* www.lithgow.lib.me.us	Augusta	ME	04330	207-626-2415		434-3
Lithia Motors Inc 360 E Jackson St *NYSE: LAD* ■ *TF:* 866-318-9660 ■ *Web:* www.lithia.com	Medford	OR	97501	866-318-9660		57
Litho Technical Services Inc 1600 W 92nd St *Web:* www.lithotechusa.com	Bloomington	MN	55431	952-888-7945		687
Lithographix Inc 12250 Crenshaw Blvd **Fax Area Code:* 310 ■ *Web:* www.lithographix.com	Hawthorne	CA	90250	323-770-1000	706-6574*	627
Litholink Corp 2250 W Campbell Park Dr *TF:* 800-338-4333 ■ *Web:* www.litholink.com	Chicago	IL	60612	312-243-0600		415
Lith-O-Roll Corp 9521 Telstar Ave *TF:* 800-423-4176 ■ *Web:* www.lithoroll.com	El Monte	CA	91731	626-579-0340		454
Lithotone Inc 1313 W Hively Ave *TF:* 800-654-5671 ■ *Web:* www.lithotone.com	Elkhart	IN	46517	574-294-5521		627
Lithtex Northwest 2000 Kentucky St *Web:* www.lithtexnw.com	Bellingham	WA	98229	360-676-1977	676-1895	627
Lithtex Printing Solutions Inc 6770 NW Century Blvd *Web:* www.lithtex.com	Hillsboro	OR	97124	503-641-5367		627
Lithuania *Consulate General* 420 Fifth Ave 3rd Fl *Web:* ny.mfa.lt	New York	NY	10018	212-354-7840	354-7911	257
Embassy 2622 16th St NW *Web:* www.usa.mfa.lt	Washington	DC	20009	202-234-5860	328-0466	257
Lithuanian Museum/Archives of Canada 2105 Stavebank Rd *Web:* www.klb.org	Mississauga	ON	L5C1T3	416-533-3292		520

Name	Address	City	State	ZIP	Phone	Fax	Class	Other
Litigation Insights Inc	9393 W 110th St Ste 400	Overland Park	KS	66210	913-339-9885		41	Web: litigationinsights.com
Litigation Solution Inc (LSI)	5995 Greenwood Plz Blvd Ste 160	Greenwood Village	CO	80111	303-820-2000		627	TF: 888-767-7088 ■ Web: www.lsilegal.com
Lititz Mutual Insurance Co	2 N Broad St PO Box 900	Lititz	PA	17543	717-626-4751	626-0970	391-4	TF: 800-626-4751 ■ Web: www.lititzmutual.com
Litman Gregory Asset Management LLC	100 Larkspur Landing Cir Ste 204	Larkspur	CA	94939	415-461-8999		401	Web: lgam.com
Litman Gregory Research Inc	100 Larkspur Landing Cir Ste 204	Larkspur	CA	94939	925-254-8999		401	TF: 800-960-0188 ■ Web: litmangregory.com
Litronic	17861 Cartwright Rd	Irvine	CA	92614	949-851-1085		178-12	Web: www.litronic.com
Littau Harvester Inc	855 Rogue Ave	Stayton	OR	97383	503-769-5953		274	TF: 866-262-2495 ■ Web: www.littauharvester.com
Littelfuse Inc	8755 W Higgins Rd Ste 500	Chicago	IL	60631	773-628-1000		729	NASDAQ: LFUS ■ TF: 800-227-0029 ■ Web: www.littelfuse.com
Littell LLC	1211 Tower Rd	Schaumburg	IL	60173	630-622-4700	622-4747	492	TF: 800-548-8355 ■ Web: www.littell.com
Littfin Lumber Co	555 Baker Ave W	Winsted	MN	55395	320-485-3861		448	Web: www.littfintruss.com
Little America Hotel & Resort Cheyenne	2800 W Lincolnway	Cheyenne	WY	82009	307-775-8400	775-8425	379	TF: 800-445-6945 ■ Web: www.cheyenne.littleamerica.com
Little America Hotel & Towers Salt Lake City	555 S Main St	Salt Lake City	UT	84101	801-258-6568		379	TF: 800-453-9450 ■ Web: saltlake.littleamerica.com
Little America Hotel Flagstaff	2515 E Butler Ave	Flagstaff	AZ	86004	928-779-7900	779-7983	379	TF: 800-352-4386 ■ Web: flagstaff.littleamerica.com
Little Apple Technologies	112 S Broadway	Manhattan	MT	59741	406-281-3174		226	Web: www.littleappletech.com
Little Bay Lobster Co	158 Shattack Way	Newington	NH	03801	603-431-3170	431-3496	297-5	Web: www.littlebaylobster.com
Little Bear Inn	1700 Little Bear Rd	Cheyenne	WY	82009	307-634-3684		671	Web: littlebearinn.com
Little Beaver State Park	1402 Grandview Rd	Beaver	WV	25813	304-763-2494		565	Web: wvstateparks.com
Little Big Horn College	8645 S Weaver Dr PO Box 370	Crow Agency	MT	59022	406-638-3100	638-3169	165	Web: www.lbhc.edu
Little Bighorn Battlefield National Monument	PO Box 39	Crow Agency	MT	59022	406-638-3216	638-2623	564	Web: www.nps.gov
Little Brick House	621 St Clair St	Vandalia	IL	62471	618-283-4866		637-2	Web: www.vandaliaillinois.com
Little Buffalo State Park	1579 State Park Rd	Newport	PA	17074	717-567-9255		565	Web: www.dcnr.pa.gov
Little Caesars Inc	2211 Woodward Ave	Detroit	MI	48201	313-983-6000		670	TF: 800-722-3727 ■ Web: www.littlecaesars.com
Little Caesars Pizza	2524 Third Line	Oakville	ON	L6M4Y7	905-825-0199		610	Web: littlecaesars.ca
Little Creek Casino Resort	91 W SR-108	Shelton	WA	98584	360-427-7711		669	TF: 800-667-7711 ■ Web: www.little-creek.com
Little Cypress-Mauriceville Cisd Inc	6500 FM 1130	Orange	TX	77632	409-883-2232	883-3509	685	Web: www.lcmcisd.org
Little Door, The	8164 W 3rd St	West Hollywood	CA	90048	323-951-1210		671	Web: thelittledoorla.com
Little Dutch Boy Bakeries Inc	12349 S 970 E PO Box 240	Draper	UT	84020	801-571-3800		296-9	
Little Earth Productions	2400 Josephine St	Pittsburgh	PA	15203	412-471-0909		514	Web: www.littlearth.com
Little Enterprises Inc	31 Locust St	Ipswich	MA	01938	978-356-7422	356-1393	454	Web: www.littleenterprisesinc.com
Little Falls Granite Works	10802 Hwy 10	Little Falls	MN	56345	800-862-2417		724	TF: 800-862-2417 ■ Web: lfgranite.com
Little Flower Children & Family Services of New York	2450 N Wading River Rd	Wading River	NY	11792	631-929-6200		48-6	Web: www.littleflowerny.org
Little Friends Inc	140 N Wright St	Naperville	IL	60540	630-355-6533		685	Web: www.littlefriendsinc.org
Little General Store Inc	202 S Eisenhower Dr	Beckley	WV	25801	304-253-9592		791	Web: lgstoreswv.com
Little Gym International Inc	7500 N Dobson Rd Ste 220	Scottsdale	AZ	85256	888-228-2878		354	TF: 888-228-2878 ■ Web: www.thelittlegymfranchise.com
Little Havana	1325 Key Hwy	Baltimore	MD	21230	410-837-9903		671	Web: www.littlehavanas.com
Little India	330 E Sixth Ave	Denver	CO	80203	303-871-9777	733-7193	671	Web: www.littleindiaofdenver.com
Little Italy	2300 E 88th Ave	Anchorage	AK	99507	907-344-1515		671	Web: www.littleitalyalaska.com
Little Kids Inc	1015 Newman Ave	Seekonk	MA	02771	800-545-5437		608	TF: 800-545-5437 ■ Web: www.littlekidsinc.com
Little King Inc	14005 Q St	Omaha	NE	68137	402-896-6347		670	Web: www.littlekingsubs.com
Little League Baseball Inc	PO Box 3485	Williamsport	PA	17701	570-326-1921	326-1074	48-22	TF: 800-811-7443 ■ Web: www.littleleague.org
Little Manatee River State Park	215 Lightfoot Rd	Wimauma	FL	33598	813-671-5005		565	Web: www.floridastateparks.org
Little Manila Lumpia House	2124 Waldron Rd	Corpus Christi	TX	78418	361-937-5651		671	
Little Men Studio	32B Beeholm Rd	Redding	CT	06896	203-664-1086		344	Web: www.littlemenstudio.com
Little Miami Publishing Co	19 Water St	Milford	OH	45150	513-576-9369		194	Web: www.littlemiamibooks.com
Little Moreau Recreation Area	19150 Summerville Rd	Shadehill	SD	57638	605-374-5114		565	Web: gfp.sd.gov
Little Mountain Printing	234 E Rosebud Rd	Myerstown	PA	17067	717-933-8091	933-8017	627	Web: www.littlemountainprinting.com
Little Nell, The	675 E Durant Ave	Aspen	CO	81611	970-920-6334		379	TF: 888-843-6355 ■ Web: www.thelittlenell.com
Little Nepal	925 Cortland Ave	San Francisco	CA	94110	415-643-3881	643-8088	671	Web: littlenepalsf.com
Little Ocmulgee Electric Membership Corp	26 W Railroad Ave	Alamo	GA	30411	912-568-7171		245	TF: 800-342-1290 ■ Web: www.littleocmulgeeemc.com
Little Ocmulgee State Park & Lodge	80 Live Oak Trl	Helen	GA	31037	229-868-7474		565	Web: littleocmulgeelodge.com
Little Palm Island Resort & Spa	28500 Overseas Hwy	Little Torch Key	FL	33042	305-872-2524		669	TF: 800-343-8567 ■ Web: www.littlepalmisland.com
Little Panda	1035 N Judge Ely Blvd	Abilene	TX	79601	325-670-9393		671	Web: www.littlepandaonline.com
Little Paws Animal Clinic	1100 Eichelberger St	Hanover	PA	17331	717-633-3603	633-3604	794	Web: littlepawsanimalclinic.com
Little Pedersen Fankhauser LLP	901 Main St Ste 4110	Dallas	TX	75202	214-573-2300	573-2323	428	Web: www.lpf-law.com
Little Pee Dee State Park	1298 State Park Rd	Dillon	SC	29536	843-774-8872		565	Web: southcarolinaparks.com
Little Pine State Park	4205 Little Pine Creek Rd	Waterville	PA	17776	570-753-6000		565	Web: www.dcnr.pa.gov
Little Priest Tribal College	601 E College Dr PO Box 270	Winnebago	NE	68071	402-878-2380	878-2355	165	TF: 833-416-9010 ■ Web: www.littlepriest.edu
Little Professor Book Ctr	725 N Placentia Ave	Fullerton	CA	92831	714-996-3133		95	Web: www.fullertontextbooks.com
Little Rae's Bakery	309 S Cloverdale St Ste D-47	Seattle	WA	98108	206-658-2167		297-3	TF: 866-954-5750 ■ Web: www.littleraesbakery.com
Little Rapids Corp	2273 Larsen Rd	Green Bay	WI	54303	920-496-3040		576	Web: www.littlerapids.com
Little Red Services Inc	3900 C St Ste 701	Anchorage	AK	99503	907-349-2931	349-2750	539	Web: littleredservices.com
Little Rhein Steak House	231 S Alamo St	San Antonio	TX	78205	210-225-2111	271-9180	671	Web: littlerheinsteakhouse.com
Little River Canyon National Preserve	2141 Gault Ave N	Fort Payne	AL	35967	256-845-9605	997-9129	564	Web: www.nps.gov
Little River Electric Cooperative Inc (LRECI)	300 Cambridge St	Abbeville	SC	29620	864-366-2141		245	TF: 800-459-2141 ■ Web: www.lreci.coop
Little River State Park	3444 Little River Rd	Waterbury	VT	05676	802-244-7103		565	Web: www.vtstateparks.com
Little Rock Air Force Base	1250 Thomas Ave	Little Rock	AR	72099	501-987-1110		497-1	TF: 800-557-6815 ■ Web: www.littlerock.af.mil
Little Rock Central High School National Historic Site	2120 W Daisy L Gatson Bates Dr	Little Rock	AR	72202	501-374-1957	376-4728	564	Web: www.nps.gov
Little Rock National Cemetery	2523 Confederate Blvd	Little Rock	AR	72206	501-324-6401		136	Web: www.cem.va.gov
Little Rock Regional Chamber of Commerce	1 Chamber Plz	Little Rock	AR	72201	501-374-2001	374-6018	139	Web: www.littlerockchamber.com
Little Rock School District	810 W Markham	Little Rock	AR	72201	501-447-1000		685	Web: www.lrsd.org
Little Rock Water Reclamation Authority	11 Clearwater Dr	Little Rock	AR	72204	501-376-2903	688-1409	804	Web: www.lrwra.com
Little Rock Zoo	1 Zoo Dr	Little Rock	AR	72205	501-666-2406	666-7040	823	Web: littlerockzoo.com
Little Sahara State Park	101 Main St	Waynoka	OK	73860	580-824-1471	824-1472	565	Web: www.travelok.com
Little Saigon	1106 E Colonial Dr	Orlando	FL	32803	407-423-8539		671	Web: www.littlesaigonrestaurant.com
Little Savannah	3811 Clairmont Ave	Birmingham	AL	35222	205-591-1119		671	Web: www.birminghammenus.com
Little Theatre of Alexandria	600 Wolfe St	Alexandria	VA	22314	703-683-5778	683-1378	572	Web: www.thelittletheatre.com
Little Theatre of Norfolk	801 Claremont Ave	Norfolk	VA	23507	757-627-8551		572	Web: www.ltnonline.org
Little Tikes Co, The	2180 Barlow Rd	Hudson	OH	44236	800-321-0183		762	TF: 800-321-0183 ■ Web: www.littletikes.com
Little Tokyo	160 Spear St Fl 19	Green Bay	WI	54303	920-433-9323	433-9523	671	Web: www.greenbaysushi.com
Little Valley Homes Inc	8459 M-115	Cadillac	MI	49601	231-775-8102		505	Web: www.lvhomes.net
Littlefield Corp	PO Box 21028	Waco	TX	76702	254-741-4612		322	OTC: LTFD ■ Web: littlefield.com
Littlefield Oil Co	3403 Cavanaugh Rd	Fort Smith	AR	72908	479-646-0595		579	Web: www.littlefieldcompanies.com

Name / Address	City	State	ZIP	Phone	Fax	Class
Littlejohn & Company LLC 8 Sound Shore Dr Ste 303 *Web:* littlejohnllc.com	Greenwich	CT	06830	203-552-3500		403
Littler Mendelson PC 650 California St 20th Fl. *TF:* 888-548-8537 ■ *Web:* www.littler.com	San Francisco	CA	94108	415-433-1940	399-8490	428
Littlestown Foundry Inc 150 Charles St PO Box 69 *TF:* 800-471-0844 ■ *Web:* www.littlestownfoundry.com	Littlestown	PA	17340	717-359-4141	359-5010	308
Littleton Coin Company LLC 1309 Mt Eustis Rd **Fax Area Code:* 603 ■ *TF:* 800-645-3122 ■ *Web:* www.littletoncoin.com	Littleton	NH	03561	800-645-3122	444-0121*	50-4
Litton Engineering Laboratories 200 Litton Dr Ste 200 *TF:* 800-821-8866 ■ *Web:* www.littonengr.com	Grass Valley	CA	95945	530-273-6176		454
Litton's Market & Restaurant & Bakery 2803 Essary Dr. *Web:* www.littonsdirecttoyou.com	Knoxville	TN	37918	865-688-0429		671
Liturgical Publications Inc 2875 S James Dr *TF:* 800-950-9952 ■ *Web:* www.4lpi.com	New Berlin	WI	53151	262-785-1188		637-9
Liturgy Training Publications (LTP) 3949 S Racine Ave *TF:* 800-933-1800 ■ *Web:* www.ltp.org	Chicago	IL	60609	773-579-4900	579-4929	637-2
Litz Manufacturing Inc 48056 N Coyote Pass *Web:* litzinc.com	Phoenix	AZ	85087	623-742-0102		76
Live Auctioneers LLC 220 12th Ave 2nd Fl *TF:* 888-600-2437 ■ *Web:* www.liveauctioneers.com	New York	NY	10001	212-947-4428	947-0184	317
Live Design 605 3rd Ave **Fax Area Code:* 913 ■ *Web:* www.livedesignonline.com	New York	NY	10158	212-204-4266	514-3619*	457-9
Live Eyewear Inc 3490 Broad St. *Web:* www.cocoonseyewear.com	San Luis Obispo	CA	93401	805-782-5070		543
Live Nation Worldwide Inc 9348 Civic Centre Dr *TF:* 800-653-8000 ■ *Web:* www.livenationentertainment.com	Beverly Hills	CA	90210	800-653-8000		750
Live Oak County PO Box 280 *Web:* www.co.live-oak.tx.us	George West	TX	78022	361-449-2733	449-1616	338
Live Oak Gottesman LLC 4330 Gaines Ranch Loop Ste 100. *Web:* www.liveoak.com	Austin	TX	78735	512-472-5000	472-5066	653
Live Oak Public Libraries 2002 Bull St *Web:* www.liveoakpl.org	Savannah	GA	31401	912-652-3600	652-3638	434-3
Live Wire Net 4577 Pecos St. *TF:* 866-913-5221 ■ *Web:* www.livewirenet.com	Denver	CO	80211	303-458-5667		116
Livecareer 1 Hallidie Plz Ste 600 *TF:* 800-652-8430 ■ *Web:* www.livecareer.com	San Francisco	CA	94102	800-652-8430		396
Livelogic LLC 13601 Preston Rd *Web:* www.livelogic.net	Dallas	TX	75240	972-385-8515		463
Lively Technical Ctr 500 N Appleyard Dr *Web:* www.livelytech.com	Tallahassee	FL	32304	850-487-7555	922-3880	167-3
Livengrin Foundation 4833 Hulmeville Rd *TF:* 800-245-4746 ■ *Web:* www.livengrin.org	Bensalem	PA	19020	215-638-5200		726
LivePerson Inc 475 10th Ave 5th Fl *NASDAQ: LPSN* ■ *Web:* www.liveperson.com	New York	NY	10018	212-609-4200	609-4201	39
LiveRelay Inc 10815 Rancho Bernardo Rd Ste 300. *Web:* www.relaytv.com	San Diego	CA	92127	858-348-1710		387
Livermore Chamber of Commerce 2157 First St. *Web:* www.livermorechamber.org	Livermore	CA	94550	925-447-1606	447-1641	139
Livermore Public Library 1188 S Livermore Ave. *Web:* www.cityoflivermore.net	Livermore	CA	94550	925-373-5500		434-3
Livermore Valley Tennis Club II 2000 Arroyo Rd *Web:* www.lvtc.com	Livermore	CA	94550	925-443-7700		354
Liverpool Productions 315 Derby Ave. *TF:* 800-777-5295 ■ *Web:* www.toursandevents.com	Orange	CT	06477	203-795-4737	891-8433	637-10
Livers Bronze Co 4621 E 75th Terr *Web:* www.liversbronze.com	Kansas City	MO	64132	816-300-2828	300-0864	491
Livescribe Inc 7677 Oakport St 12th Fl. *TF:* 877-727-4239 ■ *Web:* Www.livescribe.com	Oakland	CA	94621	510-777-0071		177
Livestock Marketing Assn (LMA) 10510 N Ambassador Dr *TF:* 800-821-2048 ■ *Web:* lmaweb.com	Kansas City	MO	64153	816-891-0502	891-7108	48-2
LiveTechnology Holdings Inc 16 Sterling Lake Rd LiveTechnology Pk *Web:* www.livetechnology.com	Tuxedo Park	NY	10987	845-351-5100		180
Livewire LLC 4900 W Clay St. *Web:* www.getlivewire.com	Richmond	VA	23230	804-937-9001		180
Livewire Printing Co 310 Second St *Web:* www.livewireprinting.com	Jackson	MN	56143	507-847-3771		627
LiveWorld Inc 4340 Stevens Creek Blvd Ste 101 *TF:* 800-301-9507 ■ *Web:* www.liveworld.com	San Jose	CA	95129	800-301-9507		7
Living Assistance Services Inc 937 Haverford Rd Ste 200. *TF:* 800-365-4189 ■ *Web:* www.livingassistance.com	Bryn Mawr	PA	19010	800-365-4189		310
Living Bank PO Box 6725 *TF:* 800-528-2971 ■ *Web:* www.livingbank.org	Houston	TX	77027	713-961-9431		48-17
Living Classrooms Foundation 515 M St SE Ste 222 *Web:* livingclassrooms.org	Washington	DC	20003	202-488-0627		521
Living Color Enterprises Inc 6850 NW 12th Ave *TF:* 800-878-9511 ■ *Web:* www.livingcolor.com	Fort Lauderdale	FL	33309	954-970-9511		41
Living Desert Zoo & Gardens 47900 Portola Ave *Web:* www.livingdesert.org	Palm Desert	CA	92260	760-346-5694	568-9685	97
Living Earth Crafts 3210 Executive Ridge Dr. *TF:* 800-358-8292 ■ *Web:* www.livingearthcrafts.com	Vista	CA	92081	760-597-3605		76
Living Earth Technology Co 1901 California Crossing *Web:* www.livingearth.net	Dallas	TX	75220	972-869-4332		280
Living Faith Christian Church 19503 Business Center Dr *Web:* living.org	Northridge	CA	91324	818-709-8532		48-20
Living Faith Ministries Inc PO Box 16226 *Web:* www.livingfaithministriesinc.org	Duluth	MN	55816	218-624-7717		48-20
Living History Farms 11121 Hickman Rd. *Web:* www.lhf.org	Urbandale	IA	50322	515-278-5286		520
Living Meadows 503 Benzel Ave SW *Web:* livingmeadows.com	Madelia	MN	56062	507-642-3271		371
Living Prairie Museum 2795 Ness Ave *Web:* www.winnipeg.ca	Winnipeg	MB	R3J3S4	204-832-0167		520
Living Room Realtors Inc 1401 NE Alberta St. *Web:* www.livingroomre.com	Portland	OR	97211	503-719-5588		652
Living Spa at El Monte Sagrado 317 Kit Carson Rd *TF:* 855-846-8267 ■ *Web:* www.elmontesagrado.com	Taos	NM	87571	575-758-3502	737-2985	707
Living Spaces Furniture LLC 14501 Artesia Blvd *TF:* 877-266-7300 ■ *Web:* www.livingspaces.com	La Mirada	CA	90638	877-266-7300		321
Living Stream Ministry 2431 W La Palma Ave. *TF:* 800-549-5164 ■ *Web:* www.lsm.org	Anaheim	CA	92801	714-991-4681		637-2
Living Systems Instrumentation (LSI) St Albans *Web:* www.livingsys.com	Burlington	VT	05401	802-863-5547		250
Livingston & Haven 11529 Wilmar Blvd PO Box 7207. *Web:* www.livhaven.com	Charlotte	NC	28273	704-588-3670	504-2530	385
Livingston County 304 E Grand River Ave Ste 201. *Web:* www.livgov.com	Howell	MI	48843	517-546-0500	546-4354	338
Livingston County 112 W Madison St *Web:* www.livingstoncounty-il.org	Pontiac	IL	61764	815-844-7214		338
Livingston County 726 Blue Ridge Rd *Web:* www.livingstoncounty.ky.gov	Smithland	KY	42081	270-928-2162		338
Livingston County Chamber of Commerce 4635 Millennium Dr *TF:* 800-538-7365 ■ *Web:* fingerlakeswest.com	Geneseo	NY	14454	585-243-2222	243-4824	139
Livingston County Daily Press & Argus 323 E Grand River Ave *TF:* 888-999-1288 ■ *Web:* www.livingstondaily.com	Howell	MI	48843	517-548-2000		637-8
Livingston County Government Ctr 6 Court St. *Web:* www.livingstoncounty.us	Geneseo	NY	14454	585-243-7030	243-7045	338
Livingston Engineering, Lc 3300 S Old Us 23 *Web:* livingstoneng.com	Brighton	MI	48114	810-225-7100		261
Livingston Healtcare 320 Alpenglow Ln. *Web:* www.livingstonhealthcare.org	Livingston	MT	59047	406-222-3541	823-6499	374-3
Livingston Memorial Visiting Nurse Association Hospice 1996 Eastman Ave Ste 101. *TF:* 800-830-8881 ■ *Web:* www.lmvna.org	Ventura	CA	93003	805-642-1608	642-2320	371
Livingston Parish 20399 Government Blvd. *Web:* www.livingstonparishla.gov	Livingston	LA	70754	225-686-4400		338
Livingston Parish Chamber of Commerce 248 Veterans Blvd. *Web:* www.livingstonparishchamber.org	Denham Springs	LA	70726	225-665-8155		139
Livingston Parish Library 13986 Florida Blvd PO Box 397 *Web:* www.mylpl.info	Livingston	LA	70754	225-686-2436	686-3888	434-3
Livingston Pipe & Tube Inc 1612 Rt 4 N *TF:* 800-548-7473 ■ *Web:* www.lpt-i.com	Staunton	IL	62088	618-635-8700		492
Livingston Public Library 10 Robert H Harp Dr. *Web:* www.livingstonlibrary.org	Livingston	NJ	07039	973-992-4600		434-3
Livingston Regional Hospital 315 Oak St *Web:* mylivingstonhospital.com	Livingston	TN	38570	931-823-5611		374-3
Livingstone College 701 W Monroe St *TF:* 800-835-3435 ■ *Web:* livingstone.edu	Salisbury	NC	28144	704-216-6000	638-5426	166
Livingstone Partners LLP 443 N Clark *Web:* www.livingstonepartners.com	Chicago	IL	60654	312-670-5900		194
Livingstone's Restaurant & Pub 831 E Fern Ave *Web:* towerdistrict.org	Fresno	CA	93728	559-485-5198		671
Livongo 150 W Evelyn Ave Unit 150. *TF:* 866-435-5643 ■ *Web:* livongo.com	Mountain View	CA	94041	866-435-5643		89
Livonia Chamber of Commerce 33233 5 Mile Rd. *Web:* www.livonia.org	Livonia	MI	48154	734-427-2122	427-6055	139
Livonia Public Library *Robert and Janet Bennett Civic Center Library* 32777 Five Mile Rd *Web:* livonialibrary.info	Livonia	MI	48154	734-466-2491	458-6011	434-3
Li-Way Transfer and Storage Inc 55 Chamisa Rd. *Web:* www.li-way.com	Covington	GA	30016	770-787-8113		780
Liz Lerman Dance Exchange 7117 Maple Ave *Web:* www.danceexchange.org	Takoma Park	MD	20912	301-270-6700		573-1
Lizardos Engineering Associates PC 200 Old Country Rd Ste 670. *Web:* www.leapc.com	Mineola	NY	11501	516-484-1020	484-0926	187
Lizzadro Museum of Lapidary Art 220 Cottage Hill Ave Wilder Pk. *Web:* lizzadromuseum.org	Elmhurst	IL	60126	630-833-1616	833-1225	520
LJ Gonzer Associates Inc 14 Commerce Dr Ste 305 *Web:* www.gonzer.com	Cranford	NJ	07016	908-709-9494	709-9077	721

Name / Address	City	State	Zip	Phone	Fax	Class
LJ Kushner & Associates LLC						
36 W Main St Ste 302	Freehold	NJ	07728	732-577-8100		193
Web: ljkushner.com						
LJ Smith Co 35280 Scio-Bowerston Rd	Bowerston	OH	44695	740-269-2221	269-9047	499
Web: www.ljsmith.com						
LJB Inc 2500 Newmark Dr	Miamisburg	OH	45342	937-259-5000	259-5100	261
TF: 866-552-3536 ■ *Web:* www.ljbinc.com						
LJG Partners Inc 680 W Beech St	San Diego	CA	92101	619-232-3000		449
Web: ljg.com						
LJP (Law Journal Press)						
120 Broadway 5th Fl	New York	NY	10271	877-807-8076		637-2
TF: 877-807-8076 ■ *Web:* www.lawjournalpress.com						
LJR Engineering Inc 234 Park St	North Reading	MA	01864	978-664-8141		261
Web: ljrengineering.com						
L-K Industries Inc 6952 Lawndale	Houston	TX	77023	713-926-2623		537
Web: www.lk-ind.com						
LKG Industries Inc						
3660 Publisher's Dr	Rockford	IL	61109	815-874-2301		52
Web: www.philmore-datak.com						
LKM Industries Inc 44 Sixth Rd	Woburn	MA	01801	781-935-9210	935-4259	454
Web: lkmindustries.com						
LKQ Corp 500 W Madison St Ste 2800	Chicago	IL	60661	877-557-2677	621-1969*	61
NASDAQ: LKQX ■ **Fax Area Code:* 312 ■ *TF:* 877-557-2677 ■ *Web:* www.lkqcorp.com						
LKT Laboratories Inc						
545 Phalen Blvd	Saint Paul	MN	55130	651-644-8424	558-7329*	668
**Fax Area Code:* 888 ■ *TF:* 888-558-5227 ■ *Web:* www.lktlabs.com						
LL Johnson Distributing Co						
4700 Holly St	Denver	CO	80216	303-320-1270		429
Web: www.lljohnson.com						
LL Roberts Group						
7475 Skillman St Ste 102c	Dallas	TX	75231	214-221-6463		260
TF: 877-878-6463 ■ *Web:* www.llroberts.com						
LL Smith Trucking Inc						
711 S Railroad Ave	Riverton	WY	82501	307-856-2491		780
Llabona Law Group 1309 E Robinson St	Orlando	FL	32801	407-894-6003		41
Web: llabona.com						
Llano County						
Texas 107 W Sandstone	Llano	TX	78643	325-247-4455	247-2406	338
Web: www.co.llano.tx.us						
Llano Estacado Winery 3426 E FM 1585	Lubbock	TX	79404	806-745-2258		50-7
TF: 800-634-3854 ■ *Web:* llanowine.com						
Llano National Bank 1001 Ford St	Llano	TX	78643	325-247-5701		70
Web: www.llanonationalbank.com						
LLBL (Locke Lord Bissell & Liddell LLP)						
2200 Ross Ave Ste 2200	Dallas	TX	75201	214-740-8000		428
Web: www.lockelord.com						
LLCP (Levine Leichtman Capital Partners)						
335 N Maple Dr Ste 130	Beverly Hills	CA	90210	310-275-5335	275-1441	690
Web: www.llcp.com						
LLEC (Lyon-Lincoln Electric Co-opeartive Inc)						
205 W Hwy 14 PO Box 639	Tyler	MN	56178	507-247-5505		245
Web: www.llec.coop						
Llewellyn Worldwide Inc						
2143 Wooddale Dr	Woodbury	MN	55125	651-291-1970	291-1908	637-2
TF: 800-843-6666 ■ *Web:* www.llewellyn.com						
Llewelyn-davies Sahni International Inc						
5120 Woodway Dr Ste 8010	Houston	TX	77056	713-850-1500		186
Web: www.theldnet.com						
Lli Engineering Inc						
1501 Preble Ave Ste 300	Pittsburgh	PA	15233	412-904-4310		261
Web: lliengineering.com						
LLLI (La Leche League International Inc)						
957 N Plum Grove Rd	Schaumburg	IL	60173	847-519-7730	969-0460	48-17
TF: 800-525-3243 ■ *Web:* www.llli.org						
LLNL (Lawrence Livermore National Laboratory)						
7000 E Ave PO Box 808	Livermore	CA	94550	925-422-1100	422-1370	668
Web: www.llnl.gov						
Llorens Pharmaceuticals International Division						
7080 NW 37th Ct	Miami	FL	33147	305-716-0595		414
TF: 866-595-5598 ■ *Web:* llorenspharm.com						
Lloyd & McDaniel PLC						
11405 Park Rd Ste 200	Louisville	KY	40223	502-585-1880	585-3054	428
TF: 866-548-2486 ■ *Web:* www.lloydmc.com						
Lloyd Bilyeu McLellan Construction Company Inc (LBM)						
11421 Blankenbaker Access Dr	Louisville	KY	40299	502-452-1151	454-0291	186
Web: www.lbmconstructionco.com						
Lloyd Gray Whitehead Monroe (LGWM)						
880 Montclair Rd Ste 100	Birmingham	AL	35213	205-967-8822	967-2380	428
TF: 800-967-7299 ■ *Web:* lgwmlaw.com						
Lloyd Group Inc 263 W 38th St 7th Fl	New York	NY	10018	212-221-3320		180
Web: www.lloydgroup.com						
Lloyd Inc						
604 W Thomas Ave PO Box 130	Shenandoah	IA	51601	712-246-4000	246-5245	584
TF: 800-831-0004 ■ *Web:* www.lloydinc.com						
Lloyd Industries Inc						
231 Commerce Dr	Montgomeryville	PA	18936	215-412-4445		697
Web: firedamper.com						
Lloyd Pest Control Company Inc, The						
1331 Morena Blvd Ste 300	San Diego	CA	92110	800-223-2847		577
TF: 800-223-2847 ■ *Web:* www.lloydpest.com						
Lloyd S. Berkett Insurance Agency Inc						
11150 W Olympic Blvd Ste 1100	Los Angeles	CA	90064	310-857-5757		390
Web: berkettinsurance.com						
Lloyd'S America Inc						
25 W 53rd St Fl 14	New York	NY	10019	212-938-0110		360-3
Web: lloyds.com						
Lloyd's Florist 9216 Preston Hwy	Louisville	KY	40229	502-968-5428	964-5696	292
TF: 800-264-1825 ■ *Web:* www.lloydsflorist.net						
Lloyd's Register North America Inc						
1330 Enclave Pkwy Ste 200	Houston	TX	77077	281-675-3100		196
Web: www.lr.org						
Lloyds Inc 103 S 2nd Ave	Walla Walla	WA	99362	509-525-4110		390
Web: lloydsinsurance.net						
LLR Partners Inc						
2929 Arch St Ste 2700	Philadelphia	PA	19104	215-717-2900	717-2270	690
Web: www.llrpartners.com						
LLS (Lakeshores Library System)						
725 Cornerstone Crossing Ste C	Waterford	WI	53185	262-514-4500		434-3
Web: www.lakeshores.lib.wi.us						
LM Air Technology Inc 1467 Pinewood St	Rahway	NJ	07065	732-381-8200	381-4091	18
Web: www.lmairtech.com						
LM Capital Group LLC						
750 B St Ste 3010	San Diego	CA	92101	619-814-1401	814-1404	401
Web: www.lmcapital.com						
LMA (Livestock Marketing Assn)						
10510 N Ambassador Dr	Kansas City	MO	64153	816-891-0502	891-7108	48-2
TF: 800-821-2048 ■ *Web:* lmaweb.com						
LMA (Louisiana Municipal Assn)						
700 N 10th St	Baton Rouge	LA	70802	225-344-5001	344-3057	48-13
Web: www.lma.org						
LMC PO Box 428	Donalsonville	GA	39845	229-524-2197	524-2531	298
TF: 800-332-8232 ■ *Web:* www.lmcarter.com						
LMC (Laredo Medical Ctr)						
1700 E Saunders Ave	Laredo	TX	78041	956-796-5000		374-3
Web: www.laredomedical.com						
LMC (League of Minnesota Cities)						
145 University Ave W	Saint Paul	MN	55103	651-281-1200	281-1299	49-19
TF: 800-925-1122 ■ *Web:* www.lmc.org						
LMC Industries Inc						
100 Manufacturers Dr	Arnold	MO	63010	636-282-8080	282-7114	489
Web: www.lmcindustries.com						
LMCG Investments LLC						
200 Clarendon St 28th Fl	Boston	MA	02116	617-380-5600	380-5601	792
TF: 877-241-5191 ■ *Web:* www.lmcg.com						
LMD Agency 14409 Greenview Dr Ste 200	Laurel	MD	20708	301-498-6656		195
Web: www.lmdagency.com						
LMG Inc 2350 Investors Row	Orlando	FL	32837	407-850-0505	438-8422	264-2
TF: 888-226-3100 ■ *Web:* lmg.net						
LMH (Lawrence Memorial Hospital)						
325 Maine St	Lawrence	KS	66044	785-505-5000		374-3
TF: 800-749-4144 ■ *Web:* www.lmh.org						
LMI (Legg Mason Inc)						
100 International Dr	Baltimore	MD	21202	800-221-3627		690
NYSE: LM ■ *TF:* 800-822-5544 ■ *Web:* www.leggmason.com						
LMI (Luthier's Mercantile International Inc)						
7975 Camoron Dr Bldg 1600	Windsor	CA	95492	707-087-2020	087-2014	820
TF: 800-477-4437 ■ *Web:* www.lmii.com						
LMI Advertising 24e E Roseville Rd	Lancaster	PA	17601	717-569-8826		7
Web: lmiadvertising.com						
LMI Aerospace Inc (LMIA)						
411 Fountain Lakes Blvd	Saint Charles	MO	63301	636-946-6525	949-1576	22
NASDAQ: LMIA ■ *Web:* www.lmiaerospace.com						
LMI Landscapes Inc 1437 Halsey Way	Carrollton	TX	75007	972-446-0020		422
Web: www.lmilandscapes.com						
LMI Packaging Solutions Inc						
8911 102nd St	Pleasant Prairie	WI	53158	262-947-3300		627
Web: www.lmipackaging.com						
LMIA (LMI Aerospace Inc)						
411 Fountain Lakes Blvd	Saint Charles	MO	63301	636-946-6525	949-1576	22
NASDAQ: LMIA ■ *Web:* www.lmiaerospace.com						
LMN Architects 801 Second Ave Ste 501	Seattle	WA	98104	206-682-3460		261
Web: lmnarchitects.com						
LMS Reinforcing Steel Group Inc						
6320 148th St	Surrey	BC	V3S3C4	604-598-9930	598-9931	492
Web: www.lmsgroup.ca						
LMS Technical Services Inc						
21 Grand Ave	Farmingdale	NY	11735	631-694-2034	694-2315	175
Web: lmstech.com						
LMT Mercer Group Inc						
690 Puritan Ave	Lawrenceville	NJ	08648	609-989-0399		596
Web: lmtproducts.com						
LMT Onsrud LP 1081 S Northpoint Blvd	Waukegan	IL	60085	800-234-1560	969-5492*	386
**Fax Area Code:* 630 ■ *TF:* 800-234-1560 ■ *Web:* www.onsrud.com						
LMW Engineering Group LLC						
125 Lexington Ave	Linden	NJ	07036	908-862-7600		261
Web: www.ftcny.com						
LN Curtis & Sons 1800 Peralta St	Oakland	CA	94607	510-839-5111	839-5325	679
TF: 800-443-3556 ■ *Web:* www.lncurtis.com						
LNC (Lincoln National Corp)						
150 N Radnor-Chester Rd	Radnor	PA	19087	866-533-3410	448-3962*	360-4
NYSE: LNC ■ **Fax Area Code:* 215 ■ *TF:* 877-275-5462 ■ *Web:* www.lfg.com						
LNG Publishing Company Inc						
7389 Lee Hwy Ste 300	Falls Church	VA	22044	703-536-0800	536-0803	637-10
Web: www.lubesngreases.com						
LNI Custom Manufacturing Inc						
12536 Chadron Ave	Hawthorne	CA	90250	310-978-2000	978-4000	701
TF: 800-338-3387 ■ *Web:* www.lnisigns.com						
LNK International Inc 22 Arkay Dr	Hauppauge	NY	11788	631-435-3500		231
Web: www.lnkintl.com						
Lo Sole Mio 3001 S 32nd Ave	Omaha	NE	68105	402-345-5656		671
Web: losolemio.com						
Load King Manufacturing Co						
LK Industries 1357 W Beaver St	Jacksonville	FL	32209	904-354-8882		298
Web: www.loadking.com						
Load Rite Trailers Inc						
265 Lincoln Hwy	Fairless Hills	PA	19030	215-949-0500	949-1385	763
Web: www.loadrite.com						
Loadcraft Industries Inc						
3811 N Bridge St	Brady	TX	76825	325-597-2911		779
TF: 800-803-0183 ■ *Web:* www.loadcraft.com						
Loadmaster Derrick and Equipment						
1084 Cruse Ave	Broussard	LA	70518	337-837-5429		539
Web: www.loadmasterindustries.com						
Loadmaster Universal Rigs Inc						
6935 Brittmoore Rd	Houston	TX	77041	281-598-7240		256
Web: loadmasterur.com						
Loadstar Sensors						
48521 Warm Springs Blvd Ste 308	Fremont	CA	94539	510-274-1872	952-3700	179
Web: www.loadstarsensors.com						
Loadtest Inc 2631-D NW 41st St	Gainesville	FL	32606	352-378-3717	378-3934	189-11
TF: 800-368-1138 ■ *Web:* www.loadtest.com						
Loaf N' Jug Mini Mart 442 Keeler Pkwy	Pueblo	CO	81001	888-200-6211		204
TF: 888-200-6211 ■ *Web:* www.loafnjug.com						
Loan Science PO Box 81671	Austin	TX	78708	866-311-9450		215
TF: 866-311-9450 ■ *Web:* www.loanscience.com						
Loan Value Group LLC						
47 W River Rd Ste C	Rumson	NJ	07760	732-741-7300	741-7399	466
Web: www.loanvaluegroup.com						

				Phone	Fax	Class
loanDepot 26642 Towne Centre Dr *TF:* 888-337-6888 ■ *Web:* www.loandepot.com	Foothill Ranch	CA	92610	888-337-6888		509
Loanpal LLC 8781 Sierra College Blvd *TF:* 877-290-9991 ■ *Web:* www.loanpal.com	Roseville	CA	95661	916-290-9999		217
Loblaw Companies Ltd 1 President's Choice Cir *TF:* 888-495-5111 ■ *Web:* www.loblaw.ca	Brampton	ON	L6Y5S5	905-459-2500		345
Loblaws Inc 1100 - 60 Bloor St W *Web:* www.loblaws.ca	Toronto	ON	M4T1L7	416-960-8108		345
Loblolly Consulting LLC 1600 W 38th St Ste 322 *Web:* www.loblollyconsulting.com	Austin	TX	78731	512-320-5421	320-8584	196
Loblolly Writer's House PO Box 7438 *Web:* www.loblollywritershouse.com	Gulfport	MS	39506	228-864-1823		637-2
Lobob Laboratories Inc 1440 Atteberry Ln *Web:* www.loboblabs.com	San Jose	CA	95131	408-432-0580		543
Lobster Shop South 4015 Ruston Way *Web:* wp.lobstershop.com	Tacoma	WA	98402	253-759-2165	752-9640	671
Lobster Sports Inc 7340 Fulton Ave *TF:* 800-210-5992 ■ *Web:* www.lobstersports.com	North Hollywood	CA	91605	818-764-6000	764-6061	710
LoBue & Majdalany Management Group 572B Ruger St PO Box 29920 *TF:* 800-820-4690 ■ *Web:* www.lm-mgmt.com	San Francisco	CA	94129	415-561-6110	561-6120	47
LoBue Associates Inc 6550 S Pecos Rd Ste 116 *Web:* www.lobue.com	Las Vegas	NV	89120	702-898-6940	433-4021	463
LOC Enterprises LLC 255 E Fifth St Ste 2400 *TF:* 888-963-6320 ■ *Web:* www.loccard.com	Cincinnati	OH	45249	888-963-6320		195
Loca Luna 3519 Old Cantrell Rd *Web:* www.localuna.com	Little Rock	AR	72202	501-663-4666	664-4176	671
Local 2110 Uaw 256 W 38th St 704 *Web:* 2110uaw.org	New York	NY	10018	212-387-0220		414
Local Concept 3920 Conde St *TF:* 800-654-9243 ■ *Web:* en.localconcept.com	San Diego	CA	92110	619-295-2682	295-2984	177
Local Government Federal Credit Union 3600 Wake Forest Rd Ste Ste 2000 **Fax Area Code:* 919 ■ *Web:* www.lgfcu.org	Raleigh	NC	27603	800-344-4846	755-0193*	219
Local Investment Commission 3100 Broadway St Ste 1100 *Web:* kclinc.org	Kansas City	MO	64111	816-889-5050	889-5051	251
Local Media San Diego 6160 Cornerstone Ct E Ste 150 *Web:* www.magic925.com	San Diego	CA	92121	619-570-1925		647
Local Motion Inc 870 Kawaiahao St *Web:* www.localmotionhawaii.com	Honolulu	HI	96813	808-523-7873	526-4760	710
Local, The 931 Nicollet Mall *Web:* the-local.com	Minneapolis	MN	55402	612-904-1000	904-1005	671
Localcom 501 Silverside Rd Ste 105 *Web:* www.local.com	Wilmington	DE	19809	949-784-0800		175
LocalMemphis.com 1725 N Shelby Oaks Dr Ste 101 *Web:* www.localmemphis.com	Memphis	TN	38112	901-323-2430		741-81
Localstake 1010 Central Ave Ste C *Web:* localstake.com	Indianapolis	IN	46202	317-602-4790	602-4792	387
LocalWineEvents.com 2042 General Alexander Dr *Web:* www.localwineevents.com	Malvern	PA	19355	610-647-4888		443
Locanda Veneta 8638 W Third St *Web:* www.locandaveneta.net	Los Angeles	CA	90048	310-274-1893	274-4217	671
Locascio, Hadden & Dennis LLC 250 W 96th St Ste 350 *Web:* lhdbenefits.com	Indianapolis	IN	46260	317-705-1600		41
Locator Search 3250 Briarpark Dr Ste 400 *TF:* 877-729-0086 ■ *Web:* www.locatorsearch.com	Houston	TX	77042	877-729-0086		393
Locator Services Inc 315 S Patrick St *TF:* 800-537-1446 ■ *Web:* www.locatoronline.com	Alexandria	VA	22314	703-836-9700	836-7665	637-10
Lochard Inc 903 Wapakoneta Ave *Web:* www.lochard-inc.com	Sidney	OH	45365	937-492-8811	492-5640	610
Lochinvar Corp 300 Maddox Simpson Pkwy *TF:* 800-722-2101 ■ *Web:* www.lochinvar.com	Lebanon	TN	37090	615-889-8900	547-1000	36
Lochmead Dairy Inc 1120 Ivy St *Web:* www.lochmead.com	Junction City	OR	97448	541-998-8544	998-4667	296-27
Lochmueller Group 6200 Vogel Rd *Web:* lochgroup.com	Evansville	IN	47715	812-479-6200		256
Lochsa Engineering Inc 6345 S Jones Blvd Ste 100 *TF:* 866-606-9784 ■ *Web:* www.lochsa.com	Las Vegas	NV	89118	702-365-9312		261
Lock Haven University 401 N Fairview St *Web:* www.lockhaven.edu	Lock Haven	PA	17745	570-484-2011	484-2201	166
Lock Joint Tube Inc 515 W Ireland Rd *TF:* 800-257-6859 ■ *Web:* www.ljtube.com	South Bend	IN	46614	574-299-5326	299-3464	490
Lock Museum of America 230 Main St Rt 6 *Web:* www.lockmuseumofamerica.org	Terryville	CT	06786	860-589-6359		520
Lock Up Self Storage, The 800 Frontage Rd *Web:* www.thelockup.com	Northfield	IL	60093	847-441-7477		803-3
Lockard & Wechsler Inc 2 Bridge St Ste 200 *Web:* www.lwdirect.com	Irvington	NY	10533	914-591-6600		7
Locke Insulators Inc 2525 Insulator Dr *Web:* ngk-locke.com	Baltimore	MD	21230	410-752-8020	347-1724	249
Locke Lord Bissell & Liddell LLP (LLBL) 2200 Ross Ave Ste 2200 *Web:* www.lockelord.com	Dallas	TX	75201	214-740-8000		428
Locker's Florist 1640 S 83rd St *Web:* www.lockersflorist.com	West Allis	WI	53214	414-276-7673		292
Lockerly Arboretum 1534 Irwinton Rd *Web:* lockerly.org	Milledgeville	GA	31061	478-452-2112		97
Lockhart Cadillac Inc 9265 E 126th St *Web:* www.lockhartcadillac.com	Fishers	IN	46038	317-644-2817		57
Lockhart State Park 4179 State Park Rd *Web:* tpwd.texas.gov	Lockhart	TX	78644	512-398-3479		565
Lockheed Federal Credit Union (LFCU) 2340 Hollywood Way *TF:* 800-328-5328 ■ *Web:* www.logixbanking.com	Burbank	CA	91505	818-565-2020		219
Lockheed Martin Corp 5600 Sand Lake Rd *Web:* www.lockheedmartin.com	Orlando	FL	32819	407-356-2000		20
Lockheed Window Corp 925 S Main St PO Box 166 *TF:* 800-537-3061 ■ *Web:* commercial.lockheedwindow.com	Pascoag	RI	02859	401-568-3061	568-2273	234
Locklin Technical college 5330 Berryhill Rd *Web:* www.locklintech.com	Milton	FL	32570	850-983-5700	983-5715	167-3
Lockmasters Security Institute 2101 John C Watts Dr *TF:* 800-654-0637 ■ *Web:* www.lockmasters.com	Nicholasville	KY	40356	859-885-6041		350
Lockport Public Library Local History Room 23 East Ave 3rd Fl *Web:* www.lockportlibrary.org	Lockport	NY	14094	716-433-5935	439-0198	434-3
Locks Co 1175 NW 159 Dr *TF:* 800-288-0801 ■ *Web:* www.locksco.com	Miami Gardens	FL	33169	305-949-0700	949-3619	351
Locks Gallery 600 Washington Sq S *Web:* www.locksgallery.com	Philadelphia	PA	19106	215-629-1000	629-3868	42
Lockton Companies 444 W 47th St Ste 900 *Web:* global.lockton.com	Kansas City	MO	64112	816-960-9000	960-9099	390
Lockwood Advisors Inc 760 Moore Rd *Web:* www.pershing.com	King of Prussia	PA	19406	800-200-3033		69
Lockwood Andrews & Newnam Inc 2925 Briar Pk Dr *Web:* www.lan-inc.com	Houston	TX	77042	713-266-6900	266-2089	261
Lockwood Kessler & Bartlett Inc 1 Aerial Way *Web:* lkbinc.com	Syosset	NY	11791	516-938-0600	931-6344	261
Lockwood Law Office Pc 400 N Main Ave Ste 202 *Web:* lockwoodlaw.com	Sioux Falls	SD	57104	605-331-3643		41
Lockwood Products Inc 5615 Willow Ln **Fax Area Code:* 503 ■ *TF:* 800-423-1625 ■ *Web:* www.loc-line.com	Lake Oswego	OR	97035	800-423-1625	635-2844*	370
Lockwood-Mathews Mansion Museum 295 W Ave *Web:* www.ohwy.com	Norwalk	CT	06850	203-838-9799		520
Locus Systems Inc 146 W Beaver Creek Rd Unit 1 *TF:* 888-275-5628 ■ *Web:* locussystems.com	Richmond Hill	ON	L4B1C2	905-948-0093		180
Locust Grove Historic Home 561 Blankenbaker Ln *Web:* www.locustgrove.org	Louisville	KY	40207	502-897-9845	897-0103	50-3
Locust Lake State Park 687 Tuscarora Park Rd *Web:* www.dcnr.pa.gov	Barnesville	PA	18214	570-467-2404		565
Locust Lumber Company Inc 312 E Main St *Web:* www.locustlumber.com	Locust	NC	28097	704-888-4411	888-3419	191-3
Locust Shade Park 4701 Locust Shade Dr *Web:* www.pwcgov.org	Triangle	VA	22172	703-792-8780		564
Locust Valley Central School District 22 Horse Hollow Rd *Web:* www.lvcsd.k12.ny.us	Locust Valley	NY	11560	516-277-5000		685
Lodal Inc 620 N Hooper St PO Box 2315 *TF:* 800-435-3500 ■ *Web:* www.lodal.com	Kingsford	MI	49802	906-779-1700	779-1160	516
LoDan Electronics Inc 3311 N Kennicott Ave *TF:* 800-401-4995 ■ *Web:* www.lodanelectronics.com	Arlington Heights	IL	60004	847-398-5311		816
Lode Data Systems Inc 10609 W 159th St *TF:* 888-843-1476 ■ *Web:* www.tamretail.com	Orland Park	IL	60467	888-843-1476		180
Lodestar Research Corp 2400 Central Ave Ste P-5 *Web:* www.lodestar.com	Boulder	CO	80301	303-449-9691	449-9692	668
Lodgco Management LLC 5225 E Pickard Rd *Web:* www.lodgco.net	Mount Pleasant	MI	48858	989-773-2400		707
Lodge & Club at Ponte Vedra Beach 607 Ponte Vedra Blvd **Fax Area Code:* 904 ■ *TF:* 800-243-4304 ■ *Web:* www.pontevedra.com	Ponte Vedra Beach	FL	32082	888-839-9145	273-0210*	669
Lodge at Big Sky LLC, The 75 Sitting Bull Rd *Web:* www.lodgeatbigsky.com	Big Sky	MT	59716	406-995-7858		378
Lodge At Breckenridge, The 112 Overlook Dr *TF:* 800-736-1607 ■ *Web:* thelodgeatbreckenridge.com	Breckenridge	CO	80424	970-453-9300		379
Lodge at Desert Canyon, The 1030 Desert Canyon Blvd *TF:* 800-258-4173 ■ *Web:* desertcanyonresort.com	Orondo	WA	98843	509-784-1234		669
Lodge at Port Arrowhead, The 3080 Bagnell Dam Blvd *Web:* www.lodgeatportarrowhead.com	Lake Ozark	MO	65049	573-693-9988		669
Lodge at the Mountain Village 1850 Sidewinder Dr Ste 320 *TF:* 800-453-1360 ■ *Web:* www.visitparkcity.com	Park City	UT	84060	800-453-1360		379
Lodge at Tiburon, The 1651 Tiburon Blvd *TF:* 800-762-7770 ■ *Web:* www.lodgeattiburon.com	Tiburon	CA	94920	415-435-3133		378
Lodge At Torrey Pines, The 11480 N Torrey Pines Rd *Web:* www.lodgetorreypines.com	La Jolla	CA	92037	858-453-4420		669

Name / Address	City	State	Zip	Phone	Fax	Class
Lodge at Ventana Canyon - A Wyndham Luxury Resort 6200 N Clubhouse Ln. *TF:* 800-828-5701 ■ *Web:* www.thelodgeatventanacanyon.com	Tucson	AZ	85750	520-577-1400		669
Lodge at Woodloch 109 River Birch Ln *TF:* 866-953-8500 ■ *Web:* www.thelodgeatwoodloch.com	Hawley	PA	18428	570-685-8500		379
Lodge Casino PO Box 50 *Web:* thelodgecasino.com	Black Hawk	CO	80422	303-582-1771	582-6464	133
Lodge of Four Seasons 315 Four Seasons Dr *TF:* 888-265-5500 ■ *Web:* www.4seasonsresort.com	Lake Ozark	MO	65049	573-365-3000		669
Lodge on the Desert 306 N Alvernon Way *Web:* www.lodgeonthedesert.com	Tucson	AZ	85711	520-320-2000		379
LodgeWorks LP 8100 E 22nd St Bldg 500 *Web:* lodgeworks.com	Wichita	KS	67226	316-681-5100	681-0905	379
Lodgian Inc 3445 Peachtree Rd NE Ste 700 *NYSE: LGN*	Atlanta	GA	30319	404-364-9400	812-3102	379
Lodging Dynamics Hospitality Group LLC 5314 N River Run Dr Ste 310 *Web:* www.lodgingdynamics.com	Provo	UT	84604	801-919-3440		707
Lodging Hospitality Management Corp 111 W Port Plaza Dr Ste 500 *Web:* www.lhmc.com	Saint Louis	MO	63146	314-434-9500	434-5885	379
Lodging Media 385 Oxford Valley Rd Ste 420 *Web:* www.lodgingmagazine.com	Yardley	PA	19067	215-321-9662	321-5124	457-5
Lodi Conference & Visitors Bureau 115 S School St *TF:* 800-798-1810 ■ *Web:* www.visitlodi.com	Lodi	CA	95240	209-365-1195		206
Lodi District Chamber of Commerce 35 S School St *Web:* lodichamber.com	Lodi	CA	95240	209-367-7840	369-9344	139
Lodi Library Foundation 201 W Locust St. *Web:* www.lodilibraryfoundation.org	Lodi	CA	95240	209-333-5536		434-3
Lodi News-Sentinel 125 N Church St. *Web:* www.lodinews.com	Lodi	CA	95240	209-369-2761		532-2
Lodi Pumb & Irrigation 1301 E Armstrong Rd *TF:* 800-634-7272 ■ *Web:* www.lodiirrigation.com	Lodi	CA	95242	800-634-7272		429
Lodima Press PO Box 367 *Web:* lodima.org	Revere	PA	18953	610-847-2007		637-2
Lodolce Machine Coinc 196 Malden Tpke *Web:* www.lodolce.com	Saugerties	NY	12477	845-217-0983		567
Loeb & Loeb LLP 345 Park Ave *Web:* www.loeb.com	New York	NY	10154	212-407-4284	407-4990	2
Loeb Electric Co 1800 E Fifth Ave *Web:* www.loebelectric.com	Columbus	OH	43219	614-294-6351	294-7640	246
Loeb Enterprises LLC 712 Fifth Ave 14th Fl *Web:* www.loebenterprises.com	New York	NY	10019	646-442-5807		401
Loeb Equipment & Appraisal Co 4131 S State St. *TF:* 800-560-5632 ■ *Web:* www.loebequipment.com	Chicago	IL	60609	773-548-4131		41
Loeber Motors Inc 4255 W Touhy Ave *TF:* 888-211-4485 ■ *Web:* www.loebermotors.com	Lincolnwood	IL	60712	847-675-1000		57
Loebl Schlossman & Hackl Inc 233 N Michigan Ave Ste 3000 *Web:* www.lshdesign.com	Chicago	IL	60601	312-565-1800		186
Loebsack David (Rep D - IA) 1211 Longworth House Office Bldg *Web:* loebsack.house.gov	Washington	DC	20515	202-225-6576	226-0757	342-2
Loeffel Steel Products PO Box 2100 *Web:* www.loeffelsteel.com	Barrington	IL	60011	847-382-6770	382-2487	492
Loeffler Randall Inc 588 Broadway Ste 1203 *TF:* 888-982-8800 ■ *Web:* www.loefflerrandall.com	New York	NY	10012	212-226-8787		174
Loehmann-Blasius Chevrolet Inc 90 Scott Rd *Web:* www.blasiuschevrolet.com	Waterbury	CT	06705	203-437-4141		57
Loesel Schaaf Insurance Agency Inc 3537 W 12th St. *TF:* 877-718-9935 ■ *Web:* lsinsure.com	Erie	PA	16505	814-833-5433		390
Loewinsohn Flegle Deary Simon LLP 12377 Merit Dr Ste 900 *Web:* lfdslaw.com	Dallas	TX	75251	214-572-1700		428
Loews Corp 667 Madison Ave *Web:* loews.com	New York	NY	10065	212-521-2000		185
Loews Hotels & Co 667 Madison Ave. *TF:* 800-235-6397 ■ *Web:* www.loewshotels.com	New York	NY	10065	800-235-6397		379
Loffler Companies Inc 1101 E 78th St Ste 200 *TF:* 888-425-2801 ■ *Web:* www.loffler.com	Bloomington	MN	55420	952-925-6800		196
Lofgren Zoe (Rep D - CA) 1401 Longworth House Office Bldg *Web:* lofgren.house.gov	Washington	DC	20515	202-225-3072		342-2
Loft Communications & Events Inc 27 Atlantic Ave *Web:* loftcommunications.com	Toronto	ON	M6K3E7	416-699-5638		224
Loft Press Inc 9293 Fort Valley Rd *Web:* www.loftpress.com	Fort Valley	VA	22652	540-933-6210	933-6523	637-2
Loft Restaurant, The 201 W Orange St *Web:* www.theloftlancaster.com	Lancaster	PA	17603	717-299-0661		671
Loftin & Company Inc 1908 Gateway Blvd *Web:* www.loftinco.com	Charlotte	NC	28208	704-393-9393		627
Loftin Equipment Company Inc 12 N 45th Ave *TF:* 800-437-4376 ■ *Web:* www.loftinequip.com	Phoenix	AZ	85043	602-272-9466		536
Loftness Specialized Farm Equipment Inc 650 S Main St PO Box 337 *TF:* 800-828-7624 ■ *Web:* www.loftness.com	Hector	MN	55342	320-848-6266	848-6269	273
Lofton Label Inc 6290 Claude Way *TF:* 877-447-8118 ■ *Web:* www.loftonlabel.com	Inver Grove Heights	MN	55076	651-552-6257	457-3709	552-1
Lofts Hotel, The 55 E Nationwide Blvd *Web:* www.55lofts.com	Columbus	OH	43215	614-461-2663		379
Loftus Engineering Inc 201 S Capitol Ave Ste 310 *Web:* www.loftusengineering.com	Indianapolis	IN	46225	317-352-5822		194
Loftware Inc 249 Corporate Dr *Web:* www.loftware.com	Portsmouth	NH	03801	603-766-3630		177
Log Cabin 11 Lehoy Forest Dr *Web:* www.logcabin1933.com	Leola	PA	17540	717-626-9999		671
Log Cabin Homes Ltd PO Drawer 1457 *Web:* www.logcabinhomes.com	Rocky Mount	NC	27802	252-454-1599	977-7511	106
Log Cabin Village 2100 Log Cabin Village Ln *Web:* www.logcabinvillage.org	Fort Worth	TX	76109	817-392-5881		520
Log Haven 6451 East Milcreek Canyon *Web:* www.log-haven.com	Salt Lake City	UT	84109	801-272-8255		671
Log House Foods Inc 700 Berkshire Ln N. *Web:* www.loghousefoods.com	Plymouth	MN	55441	763-546-8395	546-7339	805
Logan Capital Management Inc 6 Coulter Ave Ste 2000 *TF:* 800-215-1100 ■ *Web:* www.logancapital.com	Ardmore	PA	19003	800-215-1100		401
Logan Clay Products Co 201 S Walnut St **Fax Area Code: 740* ■ *TF:* 800-848-2141 ■ *Web:* www.loganclaypipe.com	Logan	OH	43138	800-848-2141	385-9336*	150
Logan Corp 555 Seventh Ave *TF:* 888-853-4751 ■ *Web:* www.logancorp.com	Huntington	WV	25701	304-526-4700	526-4747	385
Logan Correctional Ctr 1096 1350th St PO Box 1000 *Web:* www2.illinois.gov	Lincoln	IL	62656	217-735-5581	735-1077	213
Logan County 117 E Columbus St *Web:* www.co.logan.oh.us	Bellefontaine	OH	43311	937-599-7283	599-7268	338
Logan County 601 Broadway St *Web:* www.logancountyil.gov	Lincoln	IL	62656	217-732-4148	732-6064	338
Logan County 300 Stratton St *Web:* www.logancounty.wv.gov	Logan	WV	25601	304-792-8626	792-8611	338
Logan County 710 W Second St *Web:* kansastreasurers.org	Oakley	KS	67748	785-671-3216	671-0065	338
Logan County 317 Main St PO Box 8 *Web:* www.stapleton-ne.com	Stapleton	NE	69163	308-636-2331		338
Logan County 315 Main St Ste 3 *Web:* www.colorado.gov	Sterling	CO	80751	970-522-1544		338
Logan County Chamber of Commerce 325 Stratton St PO Box 218 *Web:* www.logancountychamberofcommerce.com	Logan	WV	25601	304-752-1324		139
Logan County Chamber of Commerce 116 S Main St. *Web:* www.loganchamber.com	Russellville	KY	42276	270-726-2206		139
Logan County Chamber of Commerce 100 S Main St. *Web:* www.logancountyohio.com	Bellefontaine	OH	43311	937-599-5121	599-2411	139
Logan County Cooperative Power & Light Association Inc 1587 County Rd 32 N *Web:* www.logancounty.coop	Bellefontaine	OH	43311	937-592-4781	592-5746	245
Logan County District Library 220 N Main St *Web:* logancountylibraries.org	Bellefontaine	OH	43311	937-599-4189	599-5503	434-3
Logan County Oklahoma 301 E Harrison Ste 102 *Web:* logancountyok.com	Guthrie	OK	73044	405-282-0266	282-0267	338
Logan County Tourism Bureau 1555 Fifth St. *Web:* www.destinationlogancountyil.com	Lincoln	IL	62656	217-732-8687		206
Logan Insurance Agency 53 S Market St *Web:* loganinsurance.com	Logan	OH	43138	740-385-8575	385-3757	390
Logan Lavelle Hunt 11420 Bluegrass Pkwy *Web:* www.loganlavellehunt.com	Louisville	KY	40299	502-499-6880		390
Logan Library 255 N Main *Web:* library.loganutah.org	Logan	UT	84321	435-716-9123		434-3
Logan Machine Co 1405 Home Ave *Web:* www.loganmachine.com	Akron	OH	44310	330-633-6163	633-6362	454
Logan Regional Medical Ctr 20 Hospital Dr *TF:* 888-982-9144 ■ *Web:* www.loganregionalmedicalcenter.com	Logan	WV	25601	304-831-1101	831-1871	374-3
Logan Simpson Design Inc 51 W Third St Ste 450 *Web:* logansimpson.com	Tempe	AZ	85281	480-967-1343	966-9232	192
Logan Square Aluminum Supply Inc 2500 N Pulaski Rd *Web:* climateguardwindows.com	Chicago	IL	60639	773-395-2900		234
Logan Telephone Cooperative Inc 10725 Bowling Green Rd *TF:* 800-752-6007 ■ *Web:* www.logantele.com	Auburn	KY	42206	270-542-4121	542-4800	224
Logan Trucking Inc 3224 Navarre Rd SW *TF:* 800-683-0142 ■ *Web:* www.logantrucking.com	Canton	OH	44706	330-478-1404	478-6706	186
Logan's Roadhouse 4249 Balmoral Dr SW *Web:* logansroadhouse.com	Huntsville	AL	35801	256-881-0584		671
Logan's Roadhouse Inc 16132 Athens Limestone Blvd *Web:* www.locations.logansroadhouse.com	Athens	AL	35611	256-216-1880		327
LoganBritton Inc 1700 Park St Ste 111 *TF:* 800-362-4352 ■ *Web:* www.loganbritton.com	Naperville	IL	60563	800-362-4352		225
Logan-Hocking County District Library 230 E Main St. *Web:* www.hocking.lib.oh.us	Logan	OH	43138	740-385-2348	385-9093	434-3
Logansport Financial Corp 723 E Broadway *OTC: LOGN* ■ *TF:* 866-454-0112 ■ *Web:* logansportsavings.com	Logansport	IN	46947	574-722-3855	722-3857	360-2
Logansport Juvenile Correctional Facility 1118 S St Rd 25 *Web:* www.in.gov	Logansport	IN	46947	574-753-7571	732-0729	412
Logansport Machine Company Inc 1200 W Linden Ave. *Web:* www.lmcworkholding.com	Logansport	IN	46947	574-735-0225	722-6559	493

				Phone	Fax	Class
Logansport/Cass County Chamber of Commerce 311 S 5th St *Web:* web.logan-casschamber.com	Logansport	IN	46947	574-753-6388	735-0909	139
Logansport-Cass County Public Library 616 E Broadway *Web:* www.logan.lib.in.us	Logansport	IN	46947	574-753-6383	722-5889	434-3
Logapps LLC 7115 Leesburg Pke *Web:* logapps.com	Falls Church	VA	22043	703-592-6360		463
Logees Greenhouses Ltd 141 N St *TF:* 888-330-8038 ■ *Web:* www.logees.com	Danielson	CT	06239	860-774-8038		192
Logfret Inc 6801 W Side Ave *Web:* www.logfret.com	North Bergen	NJ	07047	201-817-1140		311
Loggins Logistics Inc 5706 Commerce Sq *Web:* www.logginslogistics.com	Jonesboro	AR	72401	870-932-9231	802-2190	449
Loghurst Western Reserve 3967 Boardman-Canfield Rd *Web:* www.loghurst.org	Canfield	OH	44406	330-533-4330		50-3
Logic Choice Technologies LLC 950 E Haverford Rd *Web:* logicchoice.com	Bryn Mawr	PA	19010	610-525-1236		177
Logic Devices Inc 1375 Geneva Dr *OTC: LOGC* ■ *Web:* www.logicdevices.com	Sunnyvale	CA	94089	408-542-5400	542-0080	696
Logic Solutions Inc 2929 Plymouth Rd Ste 207 *Web:* www.logicsolutions.com	Ann Arbor	MI	48105	734-930-0009		180
Logic Technologies Inc 117 Bellamy Pl *Web:* logictechnologies.com	Stockbridge	GA	30281	770-389-4964		729
Logical Images Inc 3445 Winton Pl Ste 240 *TF:* 800-357-7611 ■ *Web:* www.logicalimages.com	Rochester	NY	14623	585-427-2790		177
Logical Innovations Inc 16902 El Camino Real Ste 3C *Web:* www.logical-i2.com	Houston	TX	77058	281-990-8560	990-8484	177
Logical Maintenance Solutions 17551 Von Karman Ave *TF:* 800-240-8721 ■ *Web:* www.lmsservice.com	Irvine	CA	92614	714-549-1608	662-0491	180
Logical Net Corp 450 Duane Ave *TF:* 800-600-0638 ■ *Web:* www.logical.net	Schenectady	NY	12305	518-292-4500		387
Logical Operations Inc 3535 Winton Pl *TF:* 800-456-4677 ■ *Web:* www.logicaloperations.com	Rochester	NY	14623	585-350-7000	350-7005	393
Logical Solution Services Inc 200 Union Ave *Web:* solutionservices.us	Lakehurst	NJ	08733	732-657-7777		449
Logical Solutions Inc PO Box 7128 *Web:* www.logicalcorp.com	Wantagh	NY	11793	516-731-1314		178-1
Logical System Solutions Inc (LSSI) 1602 Baumgart *Web:* www.logical-systems.com	Normal	IL	61761	309-310-3780		393
Logicalis 1 Penn Plz 51st Fl Ste 5130 *TF:* 866-456-4422 ■ *Web:* www.us.logicalis.com	New York	NY	10119	866-456-4422		180
LogiCan Technologies Inc 150 Karl Clark Rd *Web:* www.logican.com	Edmonton	AB	T6N1E2	780-450-4400		253
LogicData 10800 E Bethany Dr Ste 400 *Web:* www.logicdata.com	Aurora	CO	80014	303-694-4400		463
Logicease Solutions Inc 111 Anza Blvd Ste 200 *TF:* 866-212-3273 ■ *Web:* www.complianceease.com	Burlingame	CA	94010	650-373-1111	373-7844	180
LogiCore Corp 345 Voyager Way NW *Web:* logicorehsv.com	Huntsville	AL	35816	256-533-5789	533-5785	63
Logicorps 35015 Automation Dr *Web:* www.logicorps.com	Clinton Township	MI	48035	586-792-9900		177
LOGIKA Corp 3717 N Ravenswood Ave *Web:* www.logika.net	Chicago	IL	60613	773-529-3482	529-3483	178-7
Logikal Solutions 3915 N 1800E Rd *Web:* www.logikalsolutions.com	Herscher	IL	60941	815-949-1593		180
Logile Inc 2600 E Southlake Blvd Ste 120 *Web:* www.logile.com	Southlake	TX	76092	972-550-6000		194
Logility Inc 470 E Paces Ferry Rd *TF:* 800-762-5207 ■ *Web:* www.logility.com	Atlanta	GA	30305	404-261-9777	264-5206	178-1
Login Consulting Services Inc 300 N Continental Blvd Ste 530 *Web:* www.loginconsult.com	El Segundo	CA	90245	310-607-9091		180
Login Inc 4003 E Speedway Blvd *Web:* www.login.com	Tucson	AZ	85712	520-618-3000		225
Logis Tech Inc 9450 Innovation Dr Ste 1 *TF:* 800-974-9771 ■ *Web:* logis-tech.com	Manassas	VA	20110	703-393-0122		472
LogiSense Corp 278 Pinebush Rd Ste 102 *Web:* www.logisense.com	Cambridge	ON	N1T1Z6	519-249-0508		177
LogiSolve LLC 600 Inwood Ave N Ste 275 **Fax Area Code:* 651 ■ *Web:* www.logisolve.com	Oakdale	MN	55128	763-383-1000	207-5067*	177
Logistic Dynamics Inc 155 Pineview Dr *TF:* 800-554-3734 ■ *Web:* www.logisticdynamics.com	Amherst	NY	14228	716-250-3477		314
Logistic Professionals Inc 1920 Pennsylvania Ave *Web:* www.logisticpros.com	Mcdonough	GA	30253	770-692-0431		478
Logistics Applications 2760 Eisenhower Ave *Web:* logapp.com	Alexandria	VA	22314	703-317-9800		271
Logistics Capital & Strategy LLC 1110 N Glebe Rd Ste 250 *Web:* www.logcapstrat.com	Arlington	VA	22201	703-276-9100		463
Logistics Plus Inc 1406 Peach St *TF:* 866-564-7587 ■ *Web:* www.logisticsplus.net	Erie	PA	16501	814-461-7600	461-7635	311
Logistics Store, The 26 Westwoods Dr *Web:* www.thelogisticsstore.com	Liberty	MO	64068	816-781-0450		314
Logitek Electronic Systems Inc 5622 Edgemoor Dr *TF:* 877-231-5870 ■ *Web:* logitekaudio.com	Houston	TX	77081	713-664-4470		647
Logitek Inc 110 Wilbur Pl *Web:* www.naii.com	Bohemia	NY	11716	631-567-1100	567-1823	253
Logiticks 17726 NE 26th St *Web:* www.logiticks.com	Redmond	WA	98052	206-787-9004		180
Logix Guru LLC 3821 Old William Penn Hwy *Web:* www.logixguru.com	Murrysville	PA	15668	724-733-4500		177
Loglan Institute Inc 1701 NE 75th St *Web:* www.loglan.org	Gainesville	FL	32641	352-378-5655		48-13
Logo Inc 117 SE Pkwy *TF:* 844-564-6432 ■ *Web:* logobrands.com	Franklin	TN	37064	844-564-6432		321
Logoly State Park PO Box 245 *Web:* www.arkansasstateparks.com	McNeil	AR	71752	870-695-3561		565
LogoNation Inc PO Box 3847 Ste 102 *TF:* 800-955-7375 ■ *Web:* www.logonation.com	Mooresville	NC	28117	800-955-7375		627
Logos Bible Software 1313 Commercial St *Web:* www.logos.com	Bellingham	WA	98225	360-527-1700		178-9
Logos Christian College 6620 Southpoint Dr S Ste 115 *TF:* 800-776-0127 ■ *Web:* www.logos.edu	Jacksonville	FL	32216	904-329-1723	527-3581	166
Logos Evangelical Seminary 9358 Telstar Ave *Web:* www.les.edu	El Monte	CA	91731	626-571-5110	571-5119	167-3
Logo-Wear Inc 717 W Freeport St *TF:* 877-251-2140 ■ *Web:* www.logowear1.com	Broken Arrow	OK	74012	918-251-2140	258-0992	155-3
Logoworks 1 State St Plz *Web:* www.logoworks.com	New York	NY	10004	747-666-5646		627
Lohmiller Real Estate 325 Walnut St *Web:* lohmillerrealestate.com	Lawrenceburg	IN	47025	812-537-1023		652
Lohr Structural Fasteners Inc (LSF) 2355 Wilson Rd *TF:* 800-782-4544 ■ *Web:* www.lohrfasteners.com	Humble	TX	77396	281-446-6766	446-7805	278
Lois Lauer Inc 1998 Orange Tree Ln *TF:* 800-786-5647 ■ *Web:* loislauer.com	Redlands	CA	92374	800-786-5647		653
Lois Pope LIFE Foundation 1720 S Ocean Blvd *Web:* www.life-edu.org	Manalapan	FL	33462	561-582-8083	582-8086	305
Loki Systems Inc 1258-13351 Commerce Pkwy *TF:* 800-378-5654 ■ *Web:* www.lokisys.com	Richmond	BC	V6V2X7	800-378-5654		179
LOKRING Technology LLC 38376 Apollo Pkwy *TF:* 800-876-2323 ■ *Web:* www.lokring.com	Willoughby	OH	44094	440-942-0880		723
Loleta Cheese Factory 252 Loleta Dr *Web:* www.artisancheesefactory.com	Loleta	CA	95551	707-733-5470		296-5
Lolita 900 Literary Rd *Web:* www.lolitarestaurant.com	Cleveland	OH	44113	216-771-5652		671
Loma 6190 Powers Ferry Rd Ste 600 *TF:* 800-275-5662 ■ *Web:* www.loma.org	Atlanta	GA	30339	770-951-1770	984-0441	49-9
Loma Linda University 11234 Anderson St *TF:* 800-872-1212 ■ *Web:* home.llu.edu	Loma Linda	CA	92354	909-558-1000		166
Loma Linda University School of Medicine 11175 Campus St *TF:* 800-422-4558 ■ *Web:* medicine.llu.edu	Loma Linda	CA	92350	909-558-4467		167-2
Lomanco Inc 2101 W Main St *TF:* 800-643-5596 ■ *Web:* www.lomanco.com	Jacksonville	AR	72076	501-982-6511	982-1258	14
Lomar Distributing 2500 Dixon St *TF:* 888-370-1724 ■ *Web:* www.hy-vee.com	Des Moines	IA	50316	515-244-3105		297-11
Lomar Machine & Tool Co 135 Main St *Web:* www.lomar.com	Horton	MI	49246	517-563-8136	563-8107	494
Lomax Companies LP, The 200 Highpoint Dr Ste 215	Chalfont	PA	18914	215-822-1550	997-9582	655
Lomax Consulting Group 1435 N Rt 9 PO Box 9 *Web:* lomaxconsulting.com	Cape May	NJ	08210	609-465-9857	465-2449	196
Lombard Area Chamber of Commerce 10 Lilac Ln *Web:* www.lombardchamber.com	Lombard	IL	60148	630-627-5040	627-5519	139
Lombard Co 4245 W 123rd St *Web:* lombardcompany.com	Alsip	IL	60803	708-389-1060	389-7120	183
Lombard Inc 1 Embarcadero Ctr Ste 320 *Web:* www.lombardinvestments.com	San Francisco	CA	94111	415-397-5900	397-5820	690
Lombardi Comprehensive Cancer Center at Georgetown University 3800 Reservoir Rd NW *Web:* lombardi.georgetown.edu	Washington	DC	20007	202-444-4000	444-7338	374-7
Lombardi Contracting Corp 7744 Formula Pl *Web:* www.lombardicontracting.com	San Diego	CA	92121	858-566-0060	566-0750	186
Lombardi Loper & Conant LLP 1999 Harrison St 26th Fl *Web:* www.llcllp.com	Oakland	CA	94612	510-433-2600		445
Lombardi Sports Inc 1600 Jackson St *Web:* www.lombardisports.com	San Francisco	CA	94109	415-771-0600		711
Lombardi's 3100 Monticello Ave Ste 325 *Web:* lombardifamilyconcepts.com	Dallas	TX	75205	214-748-5566	748-6204	671
Lombardian 929 S Main St Ste 100 *Web:* theindependentnewspapers.com	Lombard	IL	60148	630-627-7010	627-7027	532-4
Lombardo Insurance Agency 2096B Silas Deane Hwy *Web:* lombardo-ins.com	Rocky Hill	CT	06067	860-236-6064		390
Lombardo's 216 Harrisburg Ave *Web:* www.lombardosrestaurant.com	Lancaster	PA	17603	717-394-3749		671
Lombardy Hotel, The 111 E Fifth St *TF:* 833-223-5254 ■ *Web:* lombardyhotel.com	New York	NY	10022	212-753-8600	832-3170	379
Lomont In-Mold Technologies (IMT) 1516 E Mapleleaf Dr *TF:* 800-776-0380 ■ *Web:* www.lomontimt.com	Mount Pleasant	IA	52641	319-385-1528	385-1533	601
Lompoc Record, The 115 N H St *Web:* lompocrecord.com	Lompoc	CA	93436	805-736-2313		532-3
Lompoc Unified School District 1301 N A St *Web:* www.lusd.org	Lompoc	CA	93436	805-736-2371	735-8452	685
Lompoc Valley Chamber of Commerce & Visitors Bureau PO Box 626 *TF:* 800-240-0999 ■ *Web:* www.lompoc.com	Lompoc	CA	93438	805-736-4567		139

Name	Address	City	State	Zip	Phone	Fax	Class
Lon Musolf Distributing Inc	985 E Berwood Ave *Web:* musolfs.com	Vadnais Heights	MN	55110	651-484-3020		683
Lonati Law Firm PC	110 Evans Mill Dr Ste 101 *Web:* lonatilaw.com	Dallas	GA	30157	678-363-3500	363-5800	41
Loncar Associates	1104 Travis St *Web:* loncarassociates.com	Wichita Falls	TX	76301	877-239-4878		445
London Bridge Trading Company Ltd (LBT)	585 London Bridge Rd *TF:* 800-229-0207 ■ *Web:* www.lbtinc.com	Virginia Beach	VA	23454	757-498-0207	498-0059	67
London Broadcasting Company Inc	5420 LBJ Frwy Ste 1000 *Web:* www.londonbroadcastingcompany.com	Dallas	TX	75240	214-730-0151		514
London Chamber of Commerce	244 Pall Mall St Ste 101 *Web:* www.londonchamber.com	London	ON	N6A5P6	519-432-7551		137
London Church Furniture Inc	345 Sinking Creek Rd *TF:* 800-249-2230 ■ *Web:* www.londonchurchfurniture.com	London	KY	40743	800-249-2230		319-3
London City School District	380 Elm St *Web:* www.london.k12.oh.us	London	OH	43140	740-852-5700		685
London Company Investment Counsel, The	1801 Bayberry Ct Ste 301 *Web:* www.tlcadvisory.com	Richmond	VA	23226	804-775-0317	649-9447	41
London Computer Services	9140 Waterstone Blvd *TF:* 800-669-0871 ■ *Web:* www.lcs.com	Cincinnati	OH	45249	513-583-1482		179
London Correctional Institution	1580 SR 56 *Web:* drc.ohio.gov	London	OH	43140	740-852-2454	845-3399	213
London Drugs Ltd	12251 Horseshoe Way *TF:* 888-991-2299 ■ *Web:* www.londondrugs.com	Richmond	BC	V7A4X5	888-991-2299		238
London Economics International LLC	717 Atlantic Ave Ste 1A *Web:* www.londoneconomics.com	Boston	MA	02111	617-933-7200		317
London Fischer LLP	59 Maiden Ln *Web:* www.londonfischer.com	New York	NY	10038	212-972-1000	972-1030	445
London Fog	1615 Kellogg Dr *TF:* 877-588-8189 ■ *Web:* www.londonfog.com	Douglas	GA	31535	732-346-9009		155-5
London Free Press	369 York St PO Box 2280 *TF:* 866-541-6757 ■ *Web:* lfpress.com	London	ON	N6A4G1	519-679-1111	667-4528	532-1
London Health Sciences Centre Victoria Campus	800 Commissioners Rd E *Web:* www.lhsc.on.ca	London	ON	N6A5W9	519-685-8500		374-2
London Life Insurance Co	255 Dufferin Ave *TF:* 800-990-6654 ■ *Web:* www.londonlife.com	London	ON	N6A4K1	519-432-5281	435-7679	391-2
London Luxury Bedding Inc	295 Fifth Ave Ste 817 *TF:* 877-636-2100 ■ *Web:* www.londonlux.com	New Rochelle	NY	10801	914-636-2100		321
London Machinery Inc	15790 Robin's Hill Rd *TF:* 800-265-1098 ■ *Web:* www.lmi.ca	London	ON	N5V0A4	519-963-2500	659-2306	61
London Properties Ltd	6442 N Maroa Ave *Web:* www.londonproperties.com	Fresno	CA	93704	559-436-4000		652
London West Hollywood Hotel	1020 N San Vicente Blvd *TF:* 866-282-4560 ■ *Web:* www.thelondonwesthollywood.com	West Hollywood	CA	90069	866-282-4560		378
Londonderry Village	1200 Grubb Rd *Web:* www.londonderryvillage.org	Palmyra	PA	17078	717-838-5406		672
London-Laurel County Tourist Commission	140 Faith Assembly Church Rd *TF:* 800-348-0095 ■ *Web:* visitlondonky.com	London	KY	40741	606-878-6900	877-1689	206
Londrigan Potter & Randle P C	1227 S Seventh St *TF:* 866-658-3248 ■ *Web:* www.lprpc.com	Springfield	IL	62703	217-544-9823	544-9826	445
Lone Mountain Ranch	750 Lone Mtn Ranch Rd PO Box 160069 *TF:* 800-514-4644 ■ *Web:* lonemountainranch.com	Big Sky	MT	59716	406-995-4644		239
Lone Mountain Sports	39 Black Eagle Rd *Web:* www.lonemountainsports.net	Big Sky	MT	59716	406-995-4471		711
Lone Oak First Baptist Church Inc	3601 Lone Oak Rd *Web:* loneoakfbc.org	Paducah	KY	42003	270-554-1441		48-20
Lone Oak Fund LLC	11611 San Vincente Blvd Ste 640 *Web:* www.loneoakfund.com	Los Angeles	CA	90049	310-826-2888		655
Lone Oak Lodge	2221 N Fremont St *TF:* 800-283-5663 ■ *Web:* www.loneoaklodge.com	Monterey	CA	93940	831-372-4924	372-4985	379
Lone Peak Labeling	1785 S 4490 W *TF:* 800-658-8599 ■ *Web:* lonepeak.com	Salt Lake City	UT	84104	801-975-1818	975-1865	627
Lone Star Abstract & Title Company Inc	600 N Loraine *Web:* www.lonestarabstract.com	Midland	TX	79701	432-683-1818		390
Lone Star Beef Processors LP	2150 E 37th St *Web:* lonestarbeef.net	San Angelo	TX	76903	325-658-5555		473
Lone Star Behavioral Health	30903 Quinn Rd *TF:* 800-793-0725 ■ *Web:* lonestarbehavioralhealth.com	Tomball	TX	77375	281-351-6644		374-5
Lone Star Circuits	901 Hensley Ln *Web:* www.lscpcbs.com	Wylie	TX	75098	214-291-1427		625
Lone Star College System Office	5000 Research Forest Dr *Web:* www.lonestar.edu	The Woodlands	TX	77381	832-813-6500		166
Lone Star Container Corp	700 N Wildwood Dr **Fax Area Code:* 972 ■ *TF:* 800-552-6937 ■ *Web:* www.lonestarcontainer.com	Irving	TX	75061	800-552-6937	554-6081*	100
Lone Star Flight Museum	11551 Aerospace Ave *TF:* 888-359-5736 ■ *Web:* www.lonestarflight.org	Houston	TX	77034	346-708-2517		520
Lone Star Funds	2711 N Haskell Ave Ste 1700 *Web:* www.lonestarfunds.com	Dallas	TX	75204	214-754-8300		401
Lone Star Legal Aid	1415 Fannin St 17th Fl *TF:* 800-733-8394 ■ *Web:* www.lonestarlegal.org	Houston	TX	77002	713-652-0077	652-3814	428
Lone Star Lions Eye Bank	102 E Wheeler PO Box 347 *TF:* 800-977-3937 ■ *Web:* lsleb.org	Manor	TX	78653	512-457-0638	457-0658	269
Lone Star National Bank	520 E Nolana Ave Ste 110 *TF:* 800-580-0322 ■ *Web:* lonestarnationalbank.com	Mcallen	TX	78504	956-682-1722		70
Lone Star Park at Grand Prairie	1000 Lone Star Pkwy *TF:* 800-795-7223 ■ *Web:* www.lonestarpark.com	Grand Prairie	TX	75050	972-263-7223		642
Lone Star Percussion	10611 Control Pl *TF:* 866-792-0143 ■ *Web:* www.lonestarpercussion.com	Dallas	TX	75238	214-340-0835		526
Lone Star Railroad Contractors Inc	4201 S I-45 *TF:* 800-838-7225 ■ *Web:* www.lonestarrailroad.com	Ennis	TX	75119	972-878-9500		188
Lone Star Steakhouse	5055 W Pk Blvd Ste 500 *Web:* www.lonestarsteakhouse.com	Plano	TX	75093	972-295-8600		670
Lone Star Texas Grill	472 Morden Rd Ste 101 *Web:* lonestartexasgrill.com	Oakville	ON	L6K3W4	905-845-5852		670
Lone Star Title Company of El Paso	6701 N Mesa *Web:* lonestartitle.com	El Paso	TX	79912	915-545-2222		653
Lone Tree Brewing Company LLC	8200 Park Meadows Dr *Web:* lonetreebrewingco.com	Lone Tree	CO	80124	303-792-5822		102
Lone Wolf Real Estate Technologies Inc	231 Shearson Crescent Ste 310 *Web:* www.lwolf.com	Cambridge	ON	N1T1J5	519-624-1236		179
Lonely Planet Online	150 Linden St *Web:* www.lonelyplanet.com	Oakland	CA	94607	510-250-6400		773
Lonelybrand LLC	118 W Kinzie St *Web:* lonelybrand.com	Chicago	IL	60654	312-880-7506		195
Loners on Wheels (LOW)	1795 O'Kelley Rd SE *Web:* www.lonersonwheels.com	Deming	NM	88030	575-544-7303		48-23
Lonesome Dove Western Bistro	2406 N Main St *Web:* www.lonesomedovebistro.com	Fort Worth	TX	76164	817-740-8810		671
Lonesome Pine Regional Library	124 Library Rd SW *Web:* lonesomepine.boundless.ly	Wise	VA	24293	276-328-8061	328-3627	434-3
Lonestar Badge & Sign	301 Quail Run *Web:* www.lonestarbadge.com	Martindale	TX	78655	512-357-2261		366
Lonestar Resources Inc	509 Pecan Ste 200 *Web:* lonestarresources.com	Fort Worth	TX	76102	817-921-1889		536
LoneStar West Inc	RR 1 PO Box 1 Site 5 *Web:* www.lonestarwest.com	Sylvan Lake	AB	T4S1X6	403-887-2074		539
Loney & Schueller LLC	1311 50th St *Web:* loneylaw.com	West Des Moines	IA	50266	515-225-4485		41
Long & Foster Realtors	14501 George Carter Way *TF:* 800-237-8800 ■ *Web:* www.longandfoster.com	Chantilly	VA	20151	703-653-8500		652
Long & Foster Vacation Rentals	41 Maryland Ave *TF:* 800-981-8234 ■ *Web:* www.lfvacations.com	Annapolis	MD	21401	410-263-3262	263-1703	376
Long & McQuade Musical Instruments	722 Rosebank Rd *TF:* 855-588-6519 ■ *Web:* www.long-mcquade.com	Pickering	ON	L1W4B2	905-837-9785		526
Long & Silverman Publishing Inc (L&S)	800 N Rainbow Blvd Ste 208 *TF:* 888-902-2766 ■ *Web:* www.lspub.com	Las Vegas	NV	89107	702-948-5073		637-2
Long Beach Airport LGB	4100 Donald Douglas Dr *Web:* www.longbeach.gov	Long Beach	CA	90808	562-570-2600	570-2601	27
Long Beach Area Chamber of Commerce	1 World Trade Ctr Ste 1650 *Web:* www.lbchamber.com	Long Beach	CA	90831	562-436-1251	436-7099	139
Long Beach Arena	300 E Ocean Blvd *Web:* www.longbeachcc.com	Long Beach	CA	90802	562-436-3636	436-9491	720
Long Beach Chamber of Commerce	350 National Blvd *Web:* www.thelongbeachchamber.com	Long Beach	NY	11561	516-432-6000	432-0273	139
Long Beach City College	4901 E Carson St *Web:* www.lbcc.edu	Long Beach	CA	90808	562-938-4111	938-4858	162
Long Beach City Hall	333 W Ocean Blvd *Web:* www.longbeach.gov	Long Beach	CA	90802	562-570-6101	570-6789	337
Long Beach Convention & Visitors Bureau	301 E Ocean Blvd *TF:* 800-452-7829 ■ *Web:* www.visitlongbeach.com	Long Beach	CA	90802	562-436-3645	435-5653	206
Long Beach Firemen's Credit Union	2245 Argonne Ave *Web:* lbfcu.org	Long Beach	CA	90815	562-597-0351		219
Long Beach Hose & Coupling CoInc	1265 W 16th St *Web:* www.lbhose.com	Long Beach	CA	90813	562-901-2970		790
Long Beach Museum of Art	2300 E Ocean Blvd *Web:* www.lbma.org	Long Beach	CA	90803	562-439-2119	439-3587	520
Long Beach Opera	507 Pacific Ave *Web:* www.longbeachopera.org	Long Beach	CA	90802	562-432-5934	683-2109	573-2
Long Beach Playhouse	5021 E Anaheim St *Web:* www.lbplayhouse.org	Long Beach	CA	90804	562-494-1014		572
Long Beach Police Officers Assn	2865 Temple Ave *Web:* longbeach.gov	Long Beach	CA	90755	562-426-1201		414
Long Beach Public Library	200 W Broadway *Web:* www.longbeach.gov	Long Beach	CA	90802	562-570-7500	570-7408	434-3

Name / Address	City	State	Zip	Phone	Fax	Class
Long Beach Symphony Orchestra (LBSO) 249 E Ocean Blvd Ste 200 *Web:* longbeachsymphony.org	Long Beach	CA	90802	562-436-3203	491-3599	573-3
Long Beach Transit 1963 E Anaheim St *Web:* ridelbt.com	Long Beach	CA	90813	562-591-2301		108
Long Billy (Rep R - MO) 2454 Rayburn House Office Bldg *Web:* www.long.house.gov	Washington	DC	20515	202-225-6536	225-5604	342-2
Long Branch Free Public Library 328 Broadway *Web:* www.longbranchlib.org	Long Branch	NJ	07740	732-222-3900		434-3
Long Branch Nature Ctr 625 S Carlin Springs Rd *Web:* www.arlingtonva.us	Arlington	VA	22204	703-228-6535		50-5
Long Branch State Park 28615 Visitor Center Rd *Web:* mostateparks.com	Macon	MO	63552	660-773-5229		565
Long Building Technologies Inc 5001 S Zuni St *Web:* www.long.com	Littleton	CO	80120	303-975-2100		189-10
Long Business Systems Inc 10749 Pearl Rd Ste 2A *Web:* www.lbsi.com	Strongsville	OH	44136	440-846-8500		177
Long Chilton LLP 3125 Central Blvd *Web:* www.longchilton.com	Brownsville	TX	78520	956-546-1655		2
Long County 459 S McDonald St *Web:* www.longcountyboc.com	Ludowici	GA	31316	912-545-2143	545-2150	338
Long County Board of Education 468 S McDonald St PO Box 428 *Web:* longcountyps.com	Ludowici	GA	31316	912-545-2367	545-2380	685
Long Engineering Inc 2550 Heritage Ct Ste 250 *Web:* www.longeng.com	Atlanta	GA	30339	770-951-2495	951-2496	261
Long Farms Inc 1053 S Pantano Overlook *Web:* www.longfarms.net	Tucson	AZ	85710	208-869-5307		10-11
Long Hollow Ranch 71105 Holmes Rd *TF:* 877-923-1901 ■ *Web:* www.lhranch.com	Sisters	OR	97759	541-923-1901		239
Long House Reserve 133 Hands Creek Rd *Web:* www.longhouse.org	East Hampton	NY	11937	631-329-3568	329-4299	97
Long International Inc 5265 Skytrail Dr *Web:* www.long-intl.com	Littleton	CO	80123	303-972-2443		194
Long Island Advance 20 Medford Ave *Web:* www.longislandadvance.net	Patchogue	NY	11772	631-475-1000	475-1565	532-2
Long Island Assn 300 Broadhollow Rd Ste 110-W *Web:* www.longislandassociation.org	Melville	NY	11747	631-493-3000	499-2194	139
Long Island Business News Inc 2150 Smithtown Ave Ste 7 *Web:* libn.com	Ronkonkoma	NY	11779	631-737-1700		532-3
Long Island Care at Home 15 Newbridge Rd *Web:* licareathome.com	Hicksville	NY	11801	516-794-0700	794-0787	363
Long Island Children's Museum 11 Davis Ave *Web:* www.licm.org	Garden City	NY	11530	516-224-5800	302-8188	521
Long Island Community Hospital 101 Hospital Rd *Web:* licommunityhospital.org	Patchogue	NY	11772	631-654-7100		374-3
Long Island Convention & Visitors Bureau & Sports Commission 330 Motor Pkwy Ste 203 *TF:* 877-386-6654 ■ *Web:* www.discoverlongisland.com	Hauppauge	NY	11788	631-951-3900	951-3439	206
Long Island Hotels LLC 1757 Veteran'S Memorial Hwy Ste 36 *Web:* www.longislandhotelsllc.com	Islandia	NY	11749	631-234-9700	234-4700	379
Long Island MacArthur Airport 100 Arrival Ave Ste 100 *TF:* 888-542-4776 ■ *Web:* www.macarthurairport.com	Ronkonkoma	NY	11779	631-467-3300	467-3348	27
Long Island Museum of American Art History & Carriages 1200 Rt 25A *Web:* www.longislandmuseum.org	Stony Brook	NY	11790	631-751-0066	751-0353	520
Long Island Pipe Supply Inc 586 Commercial Ave *Web:* www.lipipe.com	Garden City	NY	11530	516-222-8008	222-9234	595
Long Island Power Authority 333 Earle Ovington Blvd Ste 403 *TF:* 877-275-5472 ■ *Web:* www.lipower.org	Uniondale	NY	11553	516-222-7700	222-9137	787
Long Island Press 575 Underhill Blvd Ste 210 *TF:* 800-545-6683 ■ *Web:* www.longislandpress.com	Syosset	NY	11791	516-284-3300	284-3310	532-5
Long Island State Veterans Home 100 Patriots Rd *Web:* veteranshome.stonybrookmedicine.edu	Stony Brook	NY	11790	631-444-8500		793
Long Island University *Brentwood* 100 Second Ave *Web:* www.liunet.edu	Brentwood	NY	11717	631-273-5112	273-3155	166
Brooklyn 1 University Plz *TF:* 800-548-7526 ■ *Web:* www.liu.edu	Brooklyn	NY	11201	718-488-1011	797-2399	166
Long Jewelers Inc 2965 Virginia Beach Blvd *Web:* longjewelers.net	Virginia Beach	VA	23452	757-498-1186		410
Long John Silver's Restaurants Inc 9505 Williamsburg Plz *Web:* www.ljsilvers.com	Louisville	KY	40222	502-815-6100		670
Long Key State Park PO Box 776 *Web:* www.floridastateparks.org	Long Key	FL	33001	305-664-4815		565
Long Lines LLC 501 Fourth St PO Box 67 *TF:* 866-901-5664 ■ *Web:* www.longlines.com	Sergeant Bluff	IA	51054	712-271-4000		225
Long Painting Co 21414 68th Ave S *TF:* 800-687-5664 ■ *Web:* www.longpainting.com	Kent	WA	98032	253-234-8050	234-0034	189-8
Long Point Capital Inc 26700 Woodward Ave *Web:* www.longpointcapital.com	Royal Oak	MI	48067	248-591-6000	591-6001	796
Long Point State Park - Finger Lakes 2063 Lake Rd *Web:* parks.ny.gov	Aurora	NY	13026	315-364-5637		565
Long Point State Park - Thousand Islands 7495 State Park Rd *Web:* parks.ny.gov	Three Mile Bay	NY	13693	315-649-5258		565
Long Point State Park on Lake Chautauqua 4459 Rt 430 *Web:* parks.ny.gov	Bemus Point	NY	14712	716-386-2722		565
Long Term Solutions Inc 235 W Central St *TF:* 877-443-3777 ■ *Web:* www.longtermsol.com	Natick	MA	01760	508-907-6290	907-6292	363
Long Trail Brewing Co 5520 Rt 4 *Web:* www.longtrail.com	Bridgewater Corners	VT	05035	802-672-5011	672-5012	102
Long Valley Charter School 436 Susan Dr 965 PO Box 7 *Web:* www.longvalleycs.org	Doyle	CA	96109	530-827-2395	832-5523	685
Long View Systems Corp 250-2 St SW Ste 2100 *TF:* 866-515-6900 ■ *Web:* www.longviewsystems.com	Calgary	AB	T2P0C1	403-515-6900		174
Long Wharf Theatre 222 Sargent Dr *TF:* 800-782-8497 ■ *Web:* www.longwharf.org	New Haven	CT	06511	203-787-4282	776-2287	572
Long Wholesale Distributors Inc 5173 Pioneer Rd *Web:* www.longwholesale.com	Meridian	MS	39301	601-482-3144		297-8
Longboard Restaurant & Pub 217 Main St *Web:* www.longboardpub.com	Huntington Beach	CA	92648	714-960-1896		671
Longboat Key Club 220 Sands Point Rd *TF:* 800-237-8821 ■ *Web:* www.longboatkeyclub.com	Longboat Key	FL	34228	941-383-8821		669
Longboat Observer 5570 Gulf of Mexico Dr *Web:* www.yourobserver.com	Longboat Key	FL	34228	941-383-5509	362-4808	532-4
Longbotham Furniture Co 109 W Navasota *Web:* www.longbothamfurniture.com	Groesbeck	TX	76642	254-729-3809		361
Longbottom Coffee & Tea Inc 4893 NW 235th Ave *TF:* 800-288-1271 ■ *Web:* www.longbottomcoffee.com	Hillsboro	OR	97124	503-924-4470	924-4472	805
Longbranch, The 351 S Pierre St *Web:* lbpierre.com	Pierre	SD	57501	605-224-6166		671
Longcrier & Associates CPAS LLP 100 Cross St Ste 103 *Web:* longcriercpas.com	San Luis Obispo	CA	93401	805-541-2500		2
Longfellow National Historic Site 105 Brattle St *Web:* www.nps.gov	Cambridge	MA	02138	617-876-4491		564
Longfellow-Evangeline State Historic Site 1200 N Main St *TF:* 888-677-2900 ■ *Web:* www.crt.state.la.us	Saint Martinville	LA	70582	337-394-3754		565
Longhorn BBQ 635 C St SW *Web:* thelonghornbbq.com	Auburn	WA	98001	253-804-9600	804-5493	671
Longhorn Cavern State Park PO Box 732 *TF:* 877-441-2883 ■ *Web:* longhorncaverns.com	Burnet	TX	78611	830-598-2283		565
Longhorn Imports Inc 2202 E Union Bower *TF:* 800-641-8348 ■ *Web:* longhornimports.com	Irving	TX	75061	972-721-9102	579-4890	311
Longhorn Packaging Inc 110 Pierce Ave *Web:* www.longhornpackaging.com	San Antonio	TX	78208	210-222-9686		548
Longhorn Recycling LP 5785 Fm 1346 *Web:* www.longhornrecycling.com	San Antonio	TX	78220	210-661-2341		638
LongHorn Steakhouse 1000 Darden Center Dr *TF:* 888-221-0642 ■ *Web:* www.longhornsteakhouse.com	Orlando	FL	32837	888-221-0642		670
Longhouse 1604 River Rd *Web:* www.longhousepoetry.com	Guilford	VT	05301	802-254-4242		637-2
Longistics Transportation Inc 10900 World Trade Blvd *TF:* 800-289-0082 ■ *Web:* www.longistics.com	Raleigh	NC	27617	919-872-7626	872-2883	803-1
Longley Supply Co 2018 Oleander Dr PO Box 3809 *Web:* www.longleysupplycompany.com	Wilmington	NC	28403	910-762-7793	762-9178	612
Longmont Area Chamber of Commerce 528 Main St *Web:* www.longmontchamber.org	Longmont	CO	80501	303-776-5295	776-5657	139
Longmont Public Library 409 Fourth Ave *Web:* www.longmontcolorado.gov	Longmont	CO	80501	303-651-8470		434-3
Longnecker & Assoc 11011 Jones Rd Ste 200 *Web:* www.longnecker.com	Houston	TX	77070	281-378-1350		193
Longos A. fresh tradition 8800 Huntington Rd *TF:* 800-956-6467 ■ *Web:* www.longos.com	Vaughan	ON	L4H3M6	800-956-6467		297-8
Longport Media LLC 1601 New Rd *Web:* www.longportmedia.com	Linwood	NJ	08221	609-653-1400		643
Longs Human Resource Services 19 Midtown Pk W *Web:* www.longshrs.com	Mobile	AL	36606	251-476-4080	476-4091	260
Long-Stanton Manufacturing Co 9388 Sutton Pl *Web:* www.longstanton.com	West Chester	OH	45011	513-874-8020		488
Longstreet House PO Box 730 *Web:* www.longstreethouse.com	Hightstown	NJ	08520	609-448-1501		637-2
Longsworth Law Offices LLC 7030 Pointe Inverness Way Ste 330 *Web:* www.longsworthlaw.com	Fort Wayne	IN	46804	260-436-1555		428
Longtail Publishing 176 Pleasant St *Web:* www.longtailpublishing.com	Laconia	NH	03246	603-524-1102		637-2
Longue Vue House & Gardens 7 Bamboo Rd *TF:* 800-476-9137 ■ *Web:* longuevue.com	New Orleans	LA	70124	504-488-5488	486-7015	520
Longust Distributing Inc 2432 W Birchwood Ave **Fax Area Code:* 800 ■ *TF:* 800-352-0521 ■ *Web:* www.longust.com	Mesa	AZ	85202	480-820-6244	352-0526*	361

Name / Address	City	State	ZIP	Phone	Fax	Class
Longview News-Journal 320 E Methvin St *TF:* 800-825-9799 ■ *Web:* www.news-journal.com	Longview	TX	75601	903-757-3311	757-3742	532-2
Longview Partnership 410 N Center St *Web:* www.longviewchamber.com	Longview	TX	75601	903-237-4000	237-4049	139
Longview Public Library 1600 Louisiana St *Web:* www.longviewlibrary.org	Longview	WA	98632	360-442-5300	442-5954	434-3
Longview Public Library 222 W Cotton St *Web:* www.longviewtexas.gov	Longview	TX	75601	903-237-1350		434-3
Longview Regional Medical Ctr 2901 N Fourth St *Web:* www.longviewregional.com	Longview	TX	75605	903-758-1818		374-3
Longview School District 2715 Lilac St *Web:* longviewschools.com	Longview	WA	98632	360-575-7900	575-7912	685
Longview Wealth Management LLC 15268 Boulder Pointe Rd *Web:* www.longviewwealth.com	Eden Prairie	MN	55347	952-906-1289		401
Longwall Associates Inc 212 Kendall Ave *Web:* www.longwall.com	Chilhowie	VA	24319	276-646-2004	646-3999	45
Longway Planetarium 1310 E Kearsley St *Web:* www.sloanlongway.org	Flint	MI	48503	810-237-3400	237-3417	598
Longwood Elastomers Inc 706 Green Valley Rd Ste 212 *TF:* 800-829-7231 ■ *Web:* www.longwoodindustries.com	Greensboro	NC	27408	336-272-3710		677
Longwood Foundation Inc 100 W 10th St Ste 1109 *Web:* www.longwoodfoundation.org	Wilmington	DE	19801	302-683-8200		303
Longwood Gardens 1001 Longwood Rd *Web:* longwoodgardens.org	Kennett Square	PA	19348	610-388-1000	388-5488	97
Longwood Management Corp 4032 Wilshire Blvd Ste 600 *Web:* www.longwoodmgmt.com	Los Angeles	CA	90010	213-389-6900	201-0345	363
Longwood University 201 High St *TF:* 800-281-4677 ■ *Web:* www.longwood.edu	Farmville	VA	23909	434-395-2060	395-2332	166
Lonn Manufacturing Company Inc 5450 W 84th St *Web:* lonn.net	Indianapolis	IN	46268	317-897-1440	898-4561	151
Lonoke County 5406 Hwy 70 East PO Box 870 *Web:* www.lonokecircuitclerk.com	Lonoke	AR	72086	501-676-2316	676-3014	338
Lonsdale Quay Hotel 123 Carrie Cates Ct *TF:* 800-836-6111 ■ *Web:* www.lonsdalequayhotel.com	North Vancouver	BC	V7M3K7	604-986-6111		379
Lonseal Inc 928 E 238th St *TF:* 800-832-7111 ■ *Web:* lonseal.com	Carson	CA	90745	310-830-7111	830-9986	361
Look Ahead Veterinary Services 1451 Clark Rd *Web:* www.lookaheadvet.net	Oroville	CA	95965	530-534-0722		794
Lookout Mountain Youth Services Ctr 2901 Ford St *Web:* www.colorado.gov	Golden	CO	80401	303-273-2600		412
Lookout Valley Tool & Machine Inc 2923 Gordon Rd *Web:* www.lvtminc.com	Chattanooga	TN	37419	423-825-5203		488
Loom Press (LP) PO Box 1394 *Web:* www.loompress.com	Lowell	MA	01853	978-454-4883		637-2
Loomis Agency LLC, The 17120 Dallas Pkwy Ste 200 *Web:* theloomisagency.com	Dallas	TX	75248	972-331-7000		7
Loomis Armored US Inc 2500 Citywest Blvd Ste 900 *TF:* 866-383-5069 ■ *Web:* www.loomis.us	Houston	TX	77042	713-435-6700		693
Loomis Chaffee School 4 Batchelder Rd *Web:* www.loomischaffee.org	Windsor	CT	06095	860-687-6400	298-8756	622
Loomis Co, The 850 N Park Rd PO Box 7011 *Web:* www.loomisco.com	Wyomissing	PA	19610	610-374-4040	374-6578	390
Loomis Communities 246 N Main St *TF:* 800-865-7655 ■ *Web:* www.loomiscommunities.org	South Hadley	MA	01075	413-532-5325	532-8676	672
Loomis Industries Inc 1204 Church St *Web:* www.loomisinc.com	Saint Helena	CA	94574	707-963-4111	963-3753	248
Loomis Sayles & Company Incorporated LP 1 Financial Ctr *TF:* 800-343-2029 ■ *Web:* www.loomissayles.com	Boston	MA	02111	800-633-3330		401
Loon Energy Corp 1100-700 4 Ave SW *Web:* www.loonenergy.com	Calgary	AB	T2P3J4	403-264-8877		536
Looney Ricks Kiss (LRK) 175 Toyota Plz Ste 500 *Web:* www.lrk.com	Memphis	TN	38103	901-521-1440		261
Loop Capital Markets LLC 111 W Jackson Blvd Ste 1901 *TF:* 888-294-8898 ■ *Web:* www.loopcapital.com	Chicago	IL	60604	312-913-4900		690
Loop88 1001 19th St N Ste 930 *Web:* www.loop88.com	Arlington	VA	22209	202-595-9545		5
Loop-Loc Ltd 390 Motor Pkwy *TF:* 800-562-5667 ■ *Web:* www.looploc.com	Hauppauge	NY	11788	631-582-2626	582-2636	733
LOPA (Louisiana Organ Procurement Agency) 3545 N I-10 Service Rd Ste 300 *TF:* 800-521-4483 ■ *Web:* www.lopa.org	Metairie	LA	70002	800-521-4483		545
Lopata Flegel & Company LLP 600 Mason Ridge Center Dr Ste 100 *Web:* www.lopataflegel.com	Saint Louis	MO	63141	314-514-8881	514-8872	2
Lopez Foods Inc 6016 NW 120th Ct *Web:* lopezfoods.com	Oklahoma City	OK	73162	405-603-7500		296-26
Lopez Marketing Group Inc 11169 La Quinta Pl *Web:* www.lopezgroup.com	El Paso	TX	79936	915-772-8018		7
Lopez Mchugh LLP 1123 Admiral Peary Way *TF:* 877-703-7070 ■ *Web:* lopezmchugh.com	Philadelphia	PA	19112	215-952-6910		428
Lopez Negrete Communications Inc 3336 Richmond Ave Ste 200 *Web:* www.lopeznegrete.com	Houston	TX	77098	713-877-8777		4
Lopez Research LLC 2269 Chestnut St *Web:* lopezresearch.com	San Francisco	CA	94123	415-894-5781		466
Lopez, Severt & Pratt Co 18 E Water St *Web:* www.lopezsevertpratt.com	Troy	OH	45373	937-335-5658		41
Lor Manufacturing Company Inc 7131 W Drew Rd **Fax Area Code:* 888 ■ *TF:* 866-644-8622 ■ *Web:* www.lormfg.com	Weidman	MI	48893	866-644-8622	524-6292*	203
Lorain Correctional Institution 2075 Avon Belden Rd *Web:* drc.ohio.gov	Grafton	OH	44044	440-748-1049	748-2191	213
Lorain County 225 Ct St *Web:* www.loraincounty.us	Elyria	OH	44035	440-329-5536	329-5404	338
Lorain County Automotive Systems Inc 7470 Industrial Pkwy Dr *Web:* www.camacollc.com	Lorain	OH	44053	440-960-7470		60
Lorain County Chamber of Commerce 226 Middle Ave *Web:* www.loraincountychamber.com	Elyria	OH	44035	440-328-2550	328-2557	139
Lorain County Community College 1005 N Abbe Rd *Web:* www.lorainccc.edu	Elyria	OH	44035	440-365-5222	366-4167	162
Lorain County Visitors Bureau 8025 Leavitt Rd *TF:* 800-334-1673 ■ *Web:* www.visitloraincounty.com	Amherst	OH	44001	440-984-5282		206
Lorain Public Library System 351 W Sixth St *Web:* www.lorainpubliclibrary.org	Lorain	OH	44052	440-244-1192		434-3
Loraines Academy & Spa 1012 58th St N *TF:* 888-393-5015 ■ *Web:* www.lorainesacademy.edu	Saint Petersburg	FL	33710	727-347-4247		167-3
Lorain-Medina Rural Electric Co-opeartive Inc 22898 W Rd *TF:* 800-222-5673 ■ *Web:* www.lmro.org	Wellington	OH	44090	440-647-2133	647-4870	245
Loral Space & Communications Ltd 600 Third Ave *NASDAQ:* LORL ■ *TF:* 800-368-5948 ■ *Web:* www.loral.com	New York	NY	10016	212-697-1105		529
Loram Maintenance of Way 3900 Arrowhead Dr PO Box 188 *Web:* www.loram.com	Hamel	MN	55340	763-478-6014		650
Loranger International Corp 817 Fourth Ave *Web:* www.loranger.com	Warren	PA	16365	814-723-2250	723-5391	695
Lorann Oils 4518 Aurelius Rd *TF:* 800-862-8620 ■ *Web:* www.lorannoils.com	Lansing	MI	48910	517-882-0215		345
Loras College 1450 Alta Vista St *TF:* 800-245-6727 ■ *Web:* www.loras.edu	Dubuque	IA	52001	563-588-7100	588-7119	166
Lorber Greenfield & Polito LLP 13985 Stowe Dr *Web:* www.lorberlaw.com	Poway	CA	92064	858-513-1020		428
Lord & Taylor 424 Fifth Ave *TF:* 800-223-7440 ■ *Web:* www.lordandtaylor.com	New York	NY	10018	212-391-3344		229
Lord Abbett & Co 90 Hudson St *TF:* 888-522-2388 ■ *Web:* www.lordabbett.com	Jersey City	NJ	07302	888-522-2388		401
Lord Baltimore Properties 6225 Smith Ave Ste B-100	Baltimore	MD	21209	410-415-7635	580-9250	653
Lord Corp 111 Lord Dr *TF:* 877-275-5673 ■ *Web:* www.lord.com	Cary	NC	27511	919-468-5979		3
Lord Electric Company of Puerto Rico Inc 8 Simon Madera *Web:* www.lordcg.com	San Juan	PR	00924	787-758-4040		787
Lord Elgin Hotel 100 Elgin St *TF:* 800-267-4298 ■ *Web:* lordelginhotel.ca	Ottawa	ON	K1P5K8	613-235-3333	235-3223	379
Lord Fairfax Community College *Middletown* 173 Skirmisher Ln *TF:* 800-906-5322 ■ *Web:* lfcc.edu	Middletown	VA	22645	540-868-7000	868-7005	162
Lord Nelson Hotel & Suites 1515 S Park St *TF:* 800-565-2020 ■ *Web:* www.lordnelsonhotel.com	Halifax	NS	B3J2L2	902-423-6331	423-7148	379
Lord of Life Lutheran Church Lcms 3601 W 15th St *Web:* planolutheran.com	Plano	TX	75075	972-867-5588		48-20
Lord Stanley Suites on the Park 1889 Alberni St *TF:* 888-767-7829 ■ *Web:* www.lordstanley.com	Vancouver	BC	V6G3G7	604-688-9299	688-9297	379
Lordco Parts Ltd 22866 Dewdney Trunk Rd *TF:* 877-591-1581 ■ *Web:* www.lordco.com	Maple Ridge	BC	V2X3K6	604-467-1581		57
LORE Product Design Engineering & Development Inc 36 Eglinton Ave W Ste 707 *Web:* www.designlore.com	Toronto	ON	M4R1A1	416-489-9008		261
Lore's Chocolate 34 S 7th St *Web:* www.loreschocolates.com	Philadelphia	PA	19106	215-627-8644		297-3
Loren Cook Co 2015 E Dale St *Web:* www.lorencook.com	Springfield	MO	65803	417-869-6474	862-3820	18
Loren D. Stark Company Inc 10750 Rockley Rd *Web:* ldsco.com	Houston	TX	77099	281-498-5777	879-1204	463
Lorentson Manufacturing Company Inc 1111 Rank Pky *Web:* www.lorentson.com	Kokomo	IN	46901	765-452-4425	452-7940	604
Lorenz Corp 501 E Third St **Fax Area Code:* 937 ■ *TF:* 800-444-1144 ■ *Web:* www.lorenz.com	Dayton	OH	45402	800-444-1144	223-2042*	637-7
Lorenzo State Historic Site 17 Rippleton Rd *Web:* parks.ny.gov	Cazenovia	NY	13035	315-655-3200		565
Lorenzo Walker Technical College 3702 Estey Ave *Web:* www.lwtc.edu	Naples	FL	34104	239-377-0900	377-1000	167-3
Lorenzo's Trattoria 1933 Edwards St *Web:* www.lorenzostrattoria.com	Saint Louis	MO	63110	314-773-2223		671
Loreto Publications Inc PO Box 603 *Web:* loretopubs.org	Fitzwilliam	NH	03447	603-239-6671		637-2

				Phone	Fax	Class
Loretta Paganini School of Cooking 8613 Mayfield Rd *TF:* 888-748-4063 ■ *Web:* www.lpscinc.com	Chesterland	OH	44026	440-729-1110	729-6459	685
Loretto Hospital 645 S Central Ave *Web:* www.lorettohospital.org	Chicago	IL	60644	773-626-4300		374-3
LOREX Corp 3700 Koppers St Ste 504 *TF:* 888-425-6739 ■ *Web:* www.lorextechnology.com	Baltimore	MD	21227	888-425-6739		693
Lorge & Lorge Law Firm 501 W Willow St *Web:* www.lawfirm.net	Bear Creek	WI	54922	715-752-3304		428
Lori Bonn Jewelery 106 Linden St *TF:* 877-507-4206 ■ *Web:* loribonn.com	Oakland	CA	94607	510-286-8181		410
Lori Swindell Insurance Agency 5672 Marquesas Cir *Web:* swindellinsurance.com	Sarasota	FL	34233	941-366-1476	366-1475	390
Lorin Industries 1960 S Roberts St *TF:* 800-654-1159 ■ *Web:* www.lorin.com	Muskegon	MI	49443	231-722-1631		481
Loring Ward International Ltd 3055 Olin Ave Ste 2000 *Web:* loringward.com	San Jose	CA	95128	408-260-3100		194
Loring, Wolcott & Coolidge Fiduciary Advisors LLP 230 Congress St *Web:* www.lwcotrust.com	Boston	MA	02110	617-523-6531		251
Loroco Industries Inc 5000 Creek Rd *TF:* 800-215-9474 ■ *Web:* lorocoindustries.com	Cincinnati	OH	45242	513-891-9544	891-9549	555
Lorraine Gregory Communications Inc 95 A Executive Dr *Web:* lorrainegregory.com	Edgewood	NY	11717	631-694-1500	694-1501	5
Lorraine Travel Bureau Inc 377 Alhambra Cir *TF:* 800-666-8911 ■ *Web:* www.lorrainetravel.com	Coral Gables	FL	33134	305-446-4433		771
LORT (League of Resident Theatres) 1501 Broadway Ste 1801 *Web:* lort.org	New York	NY	10036	212-944-1501		48-4
LoRusso's Cucina 3121 Watson Rd *Web:* www.lorussos.com	Saint Louis	MO	63139	314-647-6222		671
Lory State Park 708 Lodgepole Dr *Web:* cpw.state.co.us	Bellvue	CO	80512	970-493-1623	493-4104	565
Los Abrigados Resort 160 Portal Ln *TF:* 877-374-2582 ■ *Web:* www.diamondresorts.com	Sedona	AZ	86336	928-282-1777		669
Los Adaes State Historic Site 6354 Hwy 485 *Web:* crt.state.la.us	Robeline	LA	71469	318-472-9449		565
Los Alamitos Medical Ctr 3751 Katella Ave *Web:* www.losalamitosmedctr.com	Los Alamitos	CA	90720	562-598-1311		374-3
Los Alamitos Race Course 4961 Katella Ave *Web:* www.losalamitos.com	Los Alamitos	CA	90720	714-820-2800		642
Los Alamitos Unified School District 10293 Bloomfield St *Web:* www.losal.org	Los Alamitos	CA	90720	562-799-4700	799-4711	685
Los Alamos Historical Museum 1050 Bathtub Row PO Box 43 *Web:* www.losalamoshistory.org	Los Alamos	NM	87544	505-662-6272		520
Los Alamos National Laboratory (LANL) PO Box 1663 *TF:* 877-723-4101 ■ *Web:* www.lanl.gov	Los Alamos	NM	87545	505-667-7000		668
Los Alamos Technical Associates Inc 6501 Americas Pkwy NE Ste 200 *TF:* 800-952-5282 ■ *Web:* www.lata.com	Albuquerque	NM	87110	505-884-3800	880-3560	192
Los Altos Agave 3431 W Forest Home Ave *Web:* www.losaltosagavedistributor.com	Milwaukee	WI	53215	414-671-4751	671-4755	81-3
Los Altos Chamber of Commerce 321 University Ave *Web:* www.losaltoschamber.org	Los Altos	CA	94022	650-948-1455	948-6238	139
Los Altos Community Foundation 183 Hillview Ave *Web:* losaltoscf.org	Los Altos	CA	94022	650-949-5908		305
Los Altos Food Products Inc 450 N Baldwin Park Blvd *Web:* losaltosfoods.com	City of Industry	CA	91746	626-330-6555	330-6755	296-5
Los Altos School District 201 Covington Rd *Web:* www.lasdschools.org	Los Altos	CA	94024	650-947-1150		685
Los Altos Town Crier 138 Main St *Web:* www.losaltosonline.com	Los Altos	CA	94022	650-948-9000		532-4
Los Altos Veterinary Clinic 440 First St *Web:* losaltosvet.com	Los Altos	CA	94022	650-948-8287		794
Los Amigos 1926 Atlantic Ave *Web:* www.losamigosac.com	Atlantic City	NJ	08401	609-344-2293		671
Los Angeles Air Force Base Los Angeles AFB 483 N Aviation Blvd *Web:* www.losangeles.af.mil	El Segundo	CA	90245	310-653-1110		497-1
Los Angeles Area Chamber of Commerce 350 S Bixel St *Web:* www.lachamber.com	Los Angeles	CA	90017	213-580-7500	580-7511	139
Los Angeles Athletic Club 431 W Seventh St *TF:* 800-421-8777 ■ *Web:* www.laac.com	Los Angeles	CA	90014	213-625-2211	689-1194	379
Los Angeles Business Journal 5700 Wilshire Blvd Ste 170 *Web:* www.labusinessjournal.com	Los Angeles	CA	90036	323-549-5225	549-5255	457-5
Los Angeles City College 855 N Vermont Ave *Web:* www.lacitycollege.edu	Los Angeles	CA	90029	323-953-4000	953-4013	162
Los Angeles City Hall 200 N Spring St Rm 360 *Web:* www.lacity.org	Los Angeles	CA	90012	213-473-3231		337
Los Angeles Cold Storage Co 400 S Central Ave *Web:* www.lacold.com	Los Angeles	CA	90013	213-624-1831	680-4723	803-2
Los Angeles Confidential Magazine 10100 Santa Monica Blvd Ste 410 **Fax Area Code:* 310 ■ *Web:* laconfidentialmag.com	Los Angeles	CA	90067	424-253-3200	289-0444*	457-22
Los Angeles Convention & Visitors Bureau 333 S Hope St 18th Fl *Web:* www.discoverlosangeles.com	Los Angeles	CA	90071	213-624-7300		206
Los Angeles Convention Ctr 1201 S Figueroa St *Web:* www.lacclink.com	Los Angeles	CA	90015	213-741-1151		205
Los Angeles County 500 W Temple St *TF:* 888-807-2111 ■ *Web:* www.lacounty.gov	Los Angeles	CA	90012	213-974-1311		338
Los Angeles County Arboretum & Botanic Garden 301 N Baldwin Ave *Web:* www.arboretum.org	Arcadia	CA	91007	626-821-3222	445-1217	97
Los Angeles County Bar Assn (LACBA) PO Box 55020 *Web:* www.lacba.org	Los Angeles	CA	90055	213-243-1525	833-6717	49-19
Los Angeles County Fairplex 1101 W McKinley Ave *Web:* www.fairplex.com	Pomona	CA	91768	909-623-3111	865-3602	515
Los Angeles County Metropolitan Transportation Authority 1 Gateway Plz *TF:* 866-827-8646 ■ *Web:* www.metro.net	Los Angeles	CA	90012	213-922-6000		468
Los Angeles County Museum of Art 5905 Wilshire Blvd *Web:* www.lacma.org	Los Angeles	CA	90036	323-857-6000	857-6212	520
Los Angeles County Public Library 7400 E Imperial Hwy *Web:* lacountylibrary.org	Downey	CA	90242	562-940-8462	803-3032	434-3
Los Angeles Downtown News 1264 W First St *TF:* 877-338-1010 ■ *Web:* www.ladowntownnews.com	Los Angeles	CA	90026	213-481-1448	250-4617	532-4
Los Angeles Federal Credit Union PO Box 53032 *TF:* 877-695-2328 ■ *Web:* www.lafcu.org	Los Angeles	CA	90053	818-242-8640	242-5812	219
Los Angeles Galaxy 18400 Avalon Blvd *TF:* 877-342-5299 ■ *Web:* www.lagalaxy.com	Carson	CA	90746	310-630-2200	630-2250	717
Los Angeles Harbor College 1111 Figueroa Pl *Web:* www.lahc.cc.ca.us	Wilmington	CA	90744	310-233-4000	233-4223	162
Los Angeles Lighting Manufacturing Company Inc 10141 Olney St *Web:* www.lalighting.com	El Monte	CA	91731	626-454-8300		362
Los Angeles Magazine 5900 Wilshire Blvd 10th Fl *TF:* 800-876-5222 ■ *Web:* www.lamag.com	Los Angeles	CA	90036	323-801-0100	801-0105	457-22
Los Angeles Memorial Coliseum & Sports Arena 3939 S Figueroa St *Web:* www.lacoliseum.com	Los Angeles	CA	90037	213-747-7111		720
Los Angeles Mission College 13356 Eldridge Ave *TF:* 800-854-7771 ■ *Web:* www.lamission.edu	Sylmar	CA	91342	818-364-7600	364-7806	162
Los Angeles Opera 135 N Grand Ave *Web:* laopera.org	Los Angeles	CA	90012	213-972-7219	687-3490	573-2
Los Angeles Police Federal Credit Union PO Box 10188 *TF:* 877-695-2732 ■ *Web:* www.lapfcu.org	Van Nuys	CA	91410	818-787-6520		219
Los Angeles Poultry Company Inc 4816 Long Beach Ave *Web:* www.lapoultry.com	Los Angeles	CA	90058	323-232-1619	234-9777	619
Los Angeles Public Library 630 W Fifth St *Web:* www.lapl.org	Los Angeles	CA	90071	213-228-7000		434-3
Los Angeles Southwest College 1600 W Imperial Hwy *Web:* www.lasc.edu	Los Angeles	CA	90047	323-241-5225		162
Los Angeles Times 202 W First St *TF:* 800-528-4637 ■ *Web:* www.latimes.com	Los Angeles	CA	90012	877-554-4000		532-2
Los Angeles Times-Washington Post News Service Inc 1150 15th St NW *TF:* 800-627-1150 ■ *Web:* www.washingtonpost.com	Washington	DC	20071	202-334-5509		530
Los Angeles Trade Technical College 400 W Washington Blvd *Web:* www.lattc.edu	Los Angeles	CA	90015	213-763-7000	763-5386	162
Los Angeles Turf Club Inc 285 W Huntington Dr *Web:* www.santaanita.com	Arcadia	CA	91007	626-574-7223		642
Los Angeles Unified School District (LAUSD) 333 S Beaudry Ave *Web:* achieve.lausd.net	Los Angeles	CA	90017	213-241-1000		685
Los Angeles VA Clinic 351 E Temple St *Web:* www.va.gov	Los Angeles	CA	90012	213-253-5000		136
Los Angeles Valley College 5800 Fulton Ave *Web:* www.lavc.edu	Valley Glen	CA	91401	818-947-2600		162
Los Angeles Wine Co 4935 McConnell Ave Ste 8 *Web:* www.lawineco.com	Los Angeles	CA	90066	310-306-9463		443
Los Angeles Zoo & Botanical Gardens 5333 Zoo Dr *Web:* www.lazoo.org	Los Angeles	CA	90027	323-644-4200	662-9786	823
Los Arcos Mexican Grill 4120 Commercial St SE *Web:* www.losarcosmexicangrilloregon.com	Salem	OR	97302	503-581-2740		671
Los Cerritos Ctr 239 Los Cerritos Ctr *Web:* www.shoploscerritos.com	Cerritos	CA	90703	562-402-7467		460
Los Compadres Restaurant 2102 W Pensacola St *Web:* loscompadrestally.com	Tallahassee	FL	32304	850-576-8946		671
Los Compas Cafe 603 S Nevarez Ste C	Las Cruces	NM	88001	575-523-1778		671
Los Feliz Publishing PO Box 291899 *Web:* www.losfelizpublishing.com	Los Angeles	CA	90029	323-662-8260		637-2
Los Gatos Chamber of Commerce 10 Station Way *Web:* www.losgatoschamber.com	Los Gatos	CA	95030	408-354-9300	399-1594	139
Los Gatos Lodge Inc 50 Los Gatos Saratoga Rd *Web:* losgatoslodge.com	Los Gatos	CA	95032	408-354-3300		132

Name / Address	City	State	Zip	Phone	Fax	Class
Los Gatos Meadows 110 Wood Rd *Web:* covia.org	Los Gatos	CA	95030	408-354-0211	354-4193	672
Los Gatos Public Library (LGPL) 110 E Main St *Web:* www.losgatosca.gov	Los Gatos	CA	95030	408-354-8600	354-0578	434-3
Los Gatos Research Inc (LGR) 3055 Orchard Dr *Web:* www.lgrinc.com	San Jose	CA	95134	650-965-7772	965-7074	256
Los Gatos Union Elementary School District 17010 Roberts Rd *Web:* www.lgusd.org	Los Gatos	CA	95032	408-335-2000		685
Los Medanos College 2700 E Leland Rd *TF:* 800-677-6337 ■ *Web:* www.losmedanos.edu	Pittsburg	CA	94565	925-439-2181	427-1599	162
Los Molcajetes 4320 Western Center Blvd *Web:* www.losmolcajetes.com	Fort Worth	TX	76137	817-306-9000	306-9033	671
Los Olivos Mexican Patio 7328 E Second St *Web:* losolivosrestaurants.com	Scottsdale	AZ	85251	480-946-2256	946-5964	671
Los Robles Regional Medical Ctr 215 W Janss Rd *Web:* losrobleshospital.com	Thousand Oaks	CA	91360	805-497-2727		374-3
Los Tarascos 622 S College Ave *Web:* www.lostarascos.com	Fort Collins	CO	80524	970-416-0265		671
Los Tarascos on Skyland 110 Skyland Blvd *Web:* los-tarascos.com	Tuscaloosa	AL	35405	205-553-8896		671
Los Willows Inn & Spa 530 Stewart Canyon Rd *TF:* 888-731-9400 ■ *Web:* www.loswillows.com	Fallbrook	CA	92028	888-731-9400		707
Losasso Adv Inc 4853 N Ravenswood Ave *Web:* www.losasso.com	Chicago	IL	60640	773-271-2100		4
Loscalzo Enterprises Ltd 3245 Rt 112 Bldg 2 Ste 5 *Web:* loscalzoagency.com	Medford	NY	11763	631-676-7080		390
LOSFA (Louisiana Office of Student Financial Assistance) 602 N 5th St *TF:* 800-259-5626 ■ *Web:* mylosfa.la.gov	Baton Rouge	LA	70802	225-219-1012		725
LOSGH (Lady of The Sea General Hospital) 200 W 134th Pl *Web:* www.losgh.org	Cut Off	LA	70345	985-632-6401		374-3
Lost Dutchman State Park 6109 N Apache Tr *Web:* azstateparks.com	Apache Junction	AZ	85119	480-982-4485		565
Lost Horse Press 105 Lost Horse Ln *Web:* www.losthorsepress.org	Sandpoint	ID	83864	208-255-4410	255-1560	637-2
Lost Nation Theater 39 Main St *Web:* www.lostnationtheater.org	Montpelier	VT	05602	802-229-0492		573-4
Lost Planet Editorial 113 Spring St *Web:* lostplanet.com	New York	NY	10012	212-226-5678		4
Lost River Career Co-op 600 Elm St Ste 1 *Web:* www.lostrivercareercooperative.com	Paoli	IN	47454	812-723-4818		623
Lost River Caverns 726 Durham St PO Box M *TF:* 888-529-1907 ■ *Web:* www.lostcave.com	Hellertown	PA	18055	610-838-8767	838-2961	50-5
Lost River State Park 321 Pk Dr *Web:* wvstateparks.com	Mathias	WV	26812	304-897-5372		565
Lost Valley Ranch 29555 Goose Creek Rd *Web:* ranchweb.com	Sedalia	CO	80135	707-217-5205		239
Losurdo Foods Inc 20 Owens Rd *Web:* www.losurdofoods.com	Hackensack	NJ	07601	201-343-6680	343-8078	297-11
Lotek Wireless Inc 115 Pony Dr *Web:* www.lotek.com	Newmarket	ON	L3Y7B5	905-836-6680	836-6455	256
Loteria! Grill 6333 W Third St *Web:* www.loteriagrill.com	Los Angeles	CA	90036	323-930-2211		671
Loth Inc 3574 E Kemper Rd *Web:* www.lothinc.com	Cincinnati	OH	45241	513-554-4900	554-8700	320
Lotos Club, The 5 E 66th St *Web:* www.lotosclub.org	New York	NY	10065	212-737-7100		181
Lotsa Helping Hands Inc 118 N Peoria St 3rd Fl *Web:* lotsahelpinghands.com	Chicago	IL	60607	301-942-6430		387
Lotspeich Company Inc 16101 NW 54th Ave *Web:* www.lotspeich.com	Miami	FL	33014	305-624-7777		189-9
Lott Oil Company Inc 1855 Hwy 1 *Web:* lottoil.com	Natchitoches	LA	71457	318-352-2055	352-1643	581
Lotte USA Inc 5243 Wayne Rd *Web:* koalasmarch-usa.com	Battle Creek	MI	49037	269-963-6664	963-6695	296-6
Lotus Communications Corp 3301 Barham Blvd Ste 200 *Web:* www.lotuscorp.com	Los Angeles	CA	90068	323-512-2225	512-2224	643
Lotus Garden 111 E Hospitality Ln *Web:* www.lotusgardenhospitality.com	San Bernardino	CA	92408	909-381-6171		671
Lotus Garden 810 Charnelton St *Web:* lotusgardenveg.com	Eugene	OR	97401	541-344-1928		671
Lotus Hotels Inc 2525 San Pablo Dam Rd *Web:* www.lotushotels.com	San Pablo	CA	94806	925-979-5758		377
Lotus Inn 905 N Expy *Web:* lotuscafe.us	Brownsville	TX	78520	956-542-5715		671
Lotus Management Inc 6030 Hellyer Ave 150 *Web:* lotusmgmtinc.com	San Jose	CA	95138	408-912-5118		360-3
Lotus of Siam 953 E Sahara Ave *Web:* lotusofsiamlv.com	Las Vegas	NV	89104	702-735-3033		671
Lotus Press PO Box 325 *TF:* 800-824-6396 ■ *Web:* www.lotuspress.com	Twin Lakes	WI	53181	262-889-8561	889-8591	637-2
Lou & Mickey's 224 Fifth Ave *Web:* www.louandmickeys.com	San Diego	CA	92101	619-237-4900		671
Lou Bachrodt Auto Group 7070 Cherryvale N Blvd *Web:* www.bachrodt.com	Rockford	IL	61112	815-332-3000		57
Lou Reda Productions PO Box 68 *Web:* www.redafilms.com	Easton	PA	18042	610-258-2957	250-7553	514
Loudermilk Barry (Rep R - GA) 422 Cannon House Office Bldg *Web:* loudermilk.house.gov	Washington	DC	20515	202-225-2931	225-2944	342-2
Loudhouse Creative 2903 W Wyoming Ave *Web:* www.loudhousecreative.com	Burbank	CA	91505	818-643-1725		637-10
Loudon County 100 River Rd *Web:* www.loudoncounty.org	Loudon	TN	37774	865-458-5411	458-6138	338
Loudon County Chamber of Commerce (LCCC) 318 Angel Row *Web:* www.loudoncountychamberofcommerce.com	Loudon	TN	37774	865-458-2067	458-1206	139
Loudoun County 1 Harrison St SE PO Box 7000 *Web:* www.loudoun.gov	Leesburg	VA	20177	703-777-0200	777-0325	338
Loudoun County Chamber of Commerce 19301 Winmeade Dr Ste 210 *Web:* www.loudounchamber.org	Lansdowne	VA	20176	703-777-2176	777-1392	139
Loudoun County Public Library 380 Old Waterford Rd *Web:* library.loudoun.gov	Leesburg	VA	20176	703-777-0368	771-5620	434-3
Loudoun House 209 Castlewood Dr *Fax Area Code: 209 ■ *Web:* www.nps.gov	Lexington	KY	40505	859-254-7024	372-0739*	50-3
Loudoun Stairs Inc 341 N Maple Ave *Web:* www.loudounstairs.com	Purcellville	VA	20132	703-478-8800		499
Loudoun Times-Mirror 215 Depot Ct SE Ste 303 *Web:* www.loudountimes.com	Leesburg	VA	20175	703-777-1111	771-1285	532-4
Loudspeaker Components Corp 7596 US Hwy 61 S *Web:* loudspeakercomponents.com	Lancaster	WI	53813	608-723-2127	723-7775	52
Louhelen Baha'i School 3208 S State Rd *TF:* 800-894-9716 ■ *Web:* www.louhelen.org	Davison	MI	48423	810-653-5033	653-7181	673
Louie's Backyard 700 Waddell Ave *Web:* www.louiesbackyard.com	Key West	FL	33040	305-294-1061		671
Louie's Finer Meats Inc Hwy 63 N 2025 Superior Ave *Web:* louiesfinermeats.com	Cumberland	WI	54829	715-822-4728	822-3150	296-26
Louis A. Johnson Veterans Affairs Medical Ctr 1 Medical Center Dr *TF:* 800-733-0512 ■ *Web:* www.clarksburg.va.gov	Clarksburg	WV	26301	304-623-3461		374-8
Louis Allis Co 645 Lester Doss Rd *Web:* louisallis.com	Warrior	AL	35180	205-590-2986	590-1571	518
Louis Calder Memorial Library University of Miami School of Medicine R-950 PO Box 016950 *Web:* calder.med.miami.edu	Miami	FL	33101	305-243-6648	325-9670	434-1
Louis Dreyfus Co 7255 Goodlett Farms Pkwy *Web:* www.ldc.com	Cordova	TN	38016	901-383-5079		275
Louis F. Burke PC 460 Park Ave 21st Fl *Web:* lfblaw.com	New York	NY	10022	212-682-1700		41
Louis Ferre Inc 302 Fifth Ave *TF:* 800-695-1061 ■ *Web:* www.louisferre.com	New York	NY	10001	800-695-1061		348
Louis Glunz Beer Inc 7100 N Capitol Dr *Web:* www.glunzbeers.com	Lincolnwood	IL	60712	847-676-9500	675-5678	81-1
Louis Hornick & Company Inc 117 E 38th St *Web:* www.louishornick.com	New York	NY	10016	212-679-2448	779-7098	746
Louis J Rheb Candy Company Inc 3352 Wilkens Ave *TF:* 800-514-8293 ■ *Web:* rhebs.com	Baltimore	MD	21229	410-644-4321		296-8
Louis M. Gerson Company Inc 16 Commerce Blvd *TF:* 800-225-8623 ■ *Web:* www.gersonco.com	Middleboro	MA	02346	508-947-4000	947-5442	576
Louis M. Martini Winery 254 S St Helena Hwy *TF:* 800-321-9463 ■ *Web:* www.louismartini.com	Saint Helena	CA	94574	707-968-3362		80-3
Louis Maull Co, The 219 N Market St *Web:* maulls.com	Saint Louis	MO	63102	314-241-8410		296-20
Louis P. Batson Co 1 Club Rd *Fax Area Code: 864 ■ *TF:* 866-572-2876 ■ *Web:* www.lpbatson.com	Greenville	SC	29608	866-572-2876	271-4535*	385
Louis Padnos Iron & Metal Co 185 W 8th St *TF:* 800-442-3509 ■ *Web:* www.padnos.com	Holland	MI	49422	616-396-6521		686
Louis Plung & Company LLP 420 Ft Duquesne Blvd Ste 1900 *Web:* www.louisplung.com	Pittsburgh	PA	15222	412-281-8771	281-7001	2
Louis Riel School Division 900 St Mary's Rd *TF:* 800-940-3447 ■ *Web:* www.lrsd.net	Winnipeg	MB	R2M3R3	204-257-7827		685
Louis Shanks of Texas PO Box 10448 *Web:* www.louisshanksfurniture.com	Austin	TX	78757	512-451-6501	451-6520	321
Louis Stokes Cleveland Veterans Affairs Medical Ctr 10701 E Blvd *TF:* 888-838-6446 ■ *Web:* www.cleveland.va.gov	Cleveland	OH	44106	216-791-3800		374-8
Louis T. Ollesheimer & Son Inc 605 E 12 Mile Rd *Fax Area Code: 248 ■ *TF:* 800-572-5037 ■ *Web:* www.ollesheimer.com	Madison Heights	MI	48071	800-572-5037	545-6970*	191-4
Louis Tussaud's Plaza Wax Museum & Ripley's Believe It or Not! Museum 301 Alamo Plz *Web:* www.ripleys.com	San Antonio	TX	78205	210-224-9299		520
Louis Vuitton NA Inc 1 E 57th St *TF:* 866-884-8866 ■ *Web:* www.louisvuitton.com	New York	NY	10022	212-758-8877		157-6
Louis' Basque Corner 301 E Fourth St *Web:* louisbasquecorner.com	Reno	NV	89501	775-323-7203		671
Louisa County 1 Woolfolk Ave *Web:* www.louisacounty.com	Louisa	VA	23093	540-967-0401	967-3411	338
Louisa County Courthouse 117 S Main St *Web:* louisacountyia.gov	Wapello	IA	52653	319-523-4541	523-4542	338
Louisbourg Investments 1000-770 Main St *TF:* 888-608-7070 ■ *Web:* www.louisbourg.net	Moncton	NB	E1C1E7	506-853-5410	853-5457	528
Louisburg College 501 N Main St *TF:* 800-775-0208 ■ *Web:* www.louisburg.edu	Louisburg	NC	27549	919-496-2521	496-1788	162

Name / Address	City	State	Zip	Phone	Fax	Class
Louise Hopkins Underwood Center for the Arts (LHUCA) 511 Ave K *Web:* lhuca.org	Lubbock	TX	79401	806-762-8606		50-2
Louise Paris Ltd 1407 Broadway 14th Fl *Web:* www.louiseparis.com	New York	NY	10018	212-354-5411		360-3
Louisiana						
Agriculture & Forestry Dept 5825 Florida Blvd *TF:* 866-927-2476 ■ *Web:* www.ldaf.state.la.us	Baton Rouge	LA	70806	225-922-1234	922-1253	339-19
Board of Regents 1201 N Third St *Web:* regents.la.gov	Baton Rouge	LA	70802	225-342-4253	342-6926	339-19
Certified Public Accountants Board 601 Poydras St Ste 1770 *Web:* www.cpaboard.state.la.us	New Orleans	LA	70130	504-566-1244	566-1252	339-19
Consumer Protection Office 1885 N Third St *TF:* 800-351-4889 ■ *Web:* www.ag.state.la.us	Baton Rouge	LA	70802	225-326-6465	326-6499	339-19
Contractors Licensing Board 2525 Quail Dr *TF:* 800-256-1392 ■ *Web:* www.lslbc.louisiana.gov	Baton Rouge	LA	70808	225-765-2301	765-2431	339-19
Crime Victims Reparations Board PO Box 3133 *TF:* 888-684-2846 ■ *Web:* www.lcle.state.la.us	Baton Rouge	LA	70821	225-342-1749		339-19
Culture Recreation & Tourism Dept PO Box 94361 *Web:* crt.state.la.us	Baton Rouge	LA	70804	225-342-0880		339-19
Environmental Quality Dept 602 N Fifth St *TF:* 866-896-5337 ■ *Web:* www.deq.louisiana.gov	Baton Rouge	LA	70802	225-219-5337		339-19
Ethics Board 617 N Third St LaSalle Bldg Ste 10-36 *TF:* 800-842-6630 ■ *Web:* www.ethics.la.gov	Baton Rouge	LA	70802	225-219-5600	381-7271	339-19
Financial Institutions Office PO Box 94095 *TF:* 888-525-9414 ■ *Web:* www.ofi.state.la.us	Baton Rouge	LA	70804	225-925-4660	925-4548	339-19
Historic Preservation Div 1051 N Third St Capitol Annex Bldg *Web:* www.crt.state.la.us	Baton Rouge	LA	70802	225-342-8160	219-9772	339-19
Homeland Security & Emergency Preparedness Office 7667 Independence Blvd *Web:* lerc.dps.louisiana.gov	Baton Rouge	LA	70806	225-925-7500	925-7501	339-19
Insurance Dept 1702 N Third Str *TF:* 800-259-5300 ■ *Web:* www.ldi.la.gov	Baton Rouge	LA	70802	225-342-5900		339-19
Legislature 900 N Third St PO Box 94062 *TF:* 800-256-3793 ■ *Web:* www.legis.state.la.us	Baton Rouge	LA	70804	225-342-0472		339-19
Lieutenant Governor 1051 N Third St *Web:* crt.state.la.us	Baton Rouge	LA	70802	225-342-7009	342-1949	339-19
Lottery Corp 555 Laurel St *TF:* 877-770-7867 ■ *Web:* louisianalottery.com	Baton Rouge	LA	70801	225-297-2000		452
Medical Examiners Board (LSBME) 630 Camp St *Web:* www.lsbme.la.gov	New Orleans	LA	70130	504-568-6820	568-6880	339-19
Natural Resources Dept PO Box 94396 *Web:* www.dnr.louisiana.gov	Baton Rouge	LA	70804	225-342-8955	342-3442	339-19
Office of Cultural Development Division of Historic Preservation PO Box 44247 *Web:* www.crt.state.la.us	Baton Rouge	LA	70804	225-342-8180	342-8173	339-19
Office of Management & Finance Information Services 1201 N Third St *Web:* louisiana.gov	Baton Rouge	LA	70802	225-342-0770		339-19
Office of the Governor PO Box 94004 *Web:* gov.louisiana.gov	Baton Rouge	LA	70804	225-342-7015		339-19
Public Service Commission 801 N Blvd *TF:* 800-256-2397 ■ *Web:* www.lpsc.org	Baton Rouge	LA	70821	225-342-4999	342-2831	339-19
Racing Commission 320 N Carrollton Ave Ste 2-B *Web:* horseracing.louisiana.gov	New Orleans	LA	70119	504-483-4000	483-4898	712
Revenue Dept 617 N Third St PO Box 201 *TF:* 855-307-3893 ■ *Web:* www.rev.state.la.us	Baton Rouge	LA	70802	855-307-3893		339-19
Secretary of State PO Box 94125 *Web:* www.sos.la.gov	Baton Rouge	LA	70804	225-922-2880		339-19
State Parks Office PO Box 44426 *TF:* 877-226-7652 ■ *Web:* crt.state.la.us	Baton Rouge	LA	70804	225-342-8111		339-19
State Police 7919 Independence Blvd *Web:* www.lsp.org	Baton Rouge	LA	70896	225-925-6006		339-19
Supreme Court 400 Royal St Ste 1190 *Web:* www.lasc.org	New Orleans	LA	70130	504-310-2400		339-19
Tourism Office 1051 N Third Stt PO Box 94291 *Web:* crt.state.la.us	Baton Rouge	LA	70802	225-342-8100	342-1051	339-19
Veterans Affairs Dept PO Box 94095 *TF:* 877-432-8982 ■ *Web:* www.vetaffairs.la.gov	Baton Rouge	LA	70804	225-219-5000		339-19
Wildlife & Fisheries Dept 2000 Quail Dr *TF:* 800-256-2749 ■ *Web:* www.wlf.louisiana.gov	Baton Rouge	LA	70898	225-765-2800		339-19
Workforce Commission 1001 N 23rd St *Web:* www.laworks.net	Baton Rouge	LA	70802	225-342-3111	342-7960	259
Louisiana Academy of Beauty 550 E Laurel Ave *Web:* www.louisianaacademyofbeauty.net	Eunice	LA	70535	337-457-7627		167-3
Louisiana Art & Science Museum 100 S River Rd *Web:* www.lasm.org	Baton Rouge	LA	70802	225-344-5272	344-9477	520
Louisiana Association for The Blind, The 1750 Claiborne Ave *TF:* 877-913-6471 ■ *Web:* lablind.com	Shreveport	LA	71103	318-635-6471	635-8902	552-2
Louisiana Association of Business & Industry 3113 Vly Creek Dr PO Box 80258 *TF:* 888-816-5224 ■ *Web:* www.labi.org	Baton Rouge	LA	70898	225-928-5388		140
Louisiana Association of Educators 8322 One Kalais Ave *TF:* 800-256-4523 ■ *Web:* www.lae.org	Baton Rouge	LA	70809	225-343-9243	343-9272	457-8
Louisiana Banker PO Box 2871 *TF:* 888-249-3050 ■ *Web:* lba.org	Baton Rouge	LA	70821	225-387-3282	343-3159	531-1
Louisiana Baptist Children's Home Inc (LBCH) 7200 DeSiard St *Web:* www.lbch.org	Monroe	LA	71203	318-343-2244		48-15
Louisiana Chemical Equipment Company LLC 7911 Wrenwood Ste A *Web:* www.lcec.com	Baton Rouge	LA	70896	225-923-3602		144
Louisiana Children's Museum 420 Julia St *Web:* www.lcm.org	New Orleans	LA	70130	504-523-1357	529-3666	521
Louisiana Clerks of Court Assn 10202 Jefferson Hwy Bldg A *TF:* 800-256-6660 ■ *Web:* www.laclerksofcourt.org	Baton Rouge	LA	70809	225-293-1162		48-5
Louisiana College 1140 College Dr *TF:* 800-487-1906 ■ *Web:* www.lacollege.edu	Pineville	LA	71359	318-487-7011	487-7550	166
Louisiana Creole Gumbo Restaurant 2051 Gratiot Ave *Web:* detroitgumbo.com	Detroit	MI	48207	313-567-1200		671
Louisiana Culinary Institute 10550 Airline Hwy **Fax Area Code:* 225 ■ *TF:* 877-533-3198 ■ *Web:* lci.edu	Baton Rouge	LA	70816	877-533-3198	769-8792*	163
Louisiana Delta Community College 7500 Millhaven Rd *TF:* 866-500-5322 ■ *Web:* www.ladelta.edu	Monroe	LA	71203	318-345-9000		162
Louisiana Democratic Party 701 Government St *Web:* louisianademocrats.org	Baton Rouge	LA	70802	225-336-4155	336-0046	616-1
Louisiana Dental Assn 7833 Office Pk Blvd *TF:* 800-388-6642 ■ *Web:* www.ladental.org	Baton Rouge	LA	70809	225-926-1986	926-1886	227
Louisiana Dental Plan 3636 Sherwood Twr Ste 440 *TF:* 800-256-1948 ■ *Web:* louisianadentalplan.com	Baton Rouge	LA	70816	225-291-3077	291-3969	391-3
Louisiana Department of Education 1201 N 3rd St PO Box 94064 *TF:* 877-453-2721 ■ *Web:* www.louisianabelieves.com	Baton Rouge	LA	70802	877-453-2721		339-19
Louisiana Hospital Assn (LHA) 9521 Brookline Ave *Web:* www.lhaonline.org	Baton Rouge	LA	70809	225-928-0026	923-1004	48-13
Louisiana Housing Corp 2415 Quail Dr *TF:* 888-454-2001 ■ *Web:* www.lhc.la.gov	Baton Rouge	LA	70808	225-763-8700	763-8710	339-19
Louisiana Municipal Assn (LMA) 700 N 10th St *Web:* www.lma.org	Baton Rouge	LA	70802	225-344-5001	344-3057	48-13
Louisiana Office of Student Financial Assistance (LOSFA) 602 N 5th St *TF:* 800-259-5626 ■ *Web:* mylosfa.la.gov	Baton Rouge	LA	70802	225-219-1012		725
Louisiana Office Products 210 Edwards Ave *Web:* www.laop.com	Harahan	LA	70123	504-733-9650	734-2387	320
Louisiana Office Supply Co 7643 Florida Blvd *Web:* losco.com	Baton Rouge	LA	70806	225-927-1110		535
Louisiana Organ Procurement Agency (LOPA) 3545 N I-10 Service Rd Ste 300 *TF:* 800-521-4483 ■ *Web:* www.lopa.org	Metairie	LA	70002	800-521-4483		545
Louisiana Pharmacists Assn 450 Laurel St Ste 1400 *Web:* www.louisianapharmacists.com	Baton Rouge	LA	70801	225-346-6883	344-1132	585
Louisiana Philharmonic Orchestra 1010 Common St Ste 2120 *Web:* www.lpomusic.com	New Orleans	LA	70112	504-523-6530		573-3
Louisiana Plastic Industries Inc 501 Downing Pines Rd *Web:* laplastic.com	West Monroe	LA	71292	318-388-4562	387-5642	600
Louisiana Purchase Restaurant 10320 111th St NW *Web:* www.louisianapurchase.ca	Edmonton	AB	T5K1M9	780-420-6779		671
Louisiana Radio Network Inc 10500 Coursey Blvd Ste 104 *Web:* louisianaradionetwork.com	Baton Rouge	LA	70816	225-291-2727		116
Louisiana Republican Party 530 Lake Land Rd *Web:* www.lagop.com	Baton Rouge	LA	70802	225-389-4495	389-4493	616-2
Louisiana Restaurant 1708 Aliceanna St *Web:* louisianasrestaurant.com	Baltimore	MD	21231	410-327-2610		671
Louisiana Sports Hall of Fame 500 Front St *Web:* www.lasportshall.com	Natchitoches	LA	71457	318-238-4255	238-4258	522
Louisiana State Arboretum 1300 Sudie Lawton Ln *TF:* 888-677-6100 ■ *Web:* crt.state.la.us	Ville Platte	LA	70586	337-363-6289		565
Louisiana State Bar Assn (LSBA) 601 St Charles Ave *TF:* 800-421-5722 ■ *Web:* www.lsba.org	New Orleans	LA	70130	504-566-1600	566-0930	72
Louisiana State Department of Treasury 900 N 3rd St Fl 3 PO Box 44154 *Web:* www.treasury.la.gov	Baton Rouge	LA	70802	225-342-0010		339-19
Louisiana State Museum 751 Chartres St *TF:* 800-568-6968 ■ *Web:* crt.state.la.us	New Orleans	LA	70116	504-568-6968	568-4995	520
Louisiana State Nurses Assn (LSNA) 543 Spanish Town Rd *Web:* www.lsna.org	Baton Rouge	LA	70802	225-201-0993		533
Louisiana State Penitentiary 17544 Tunica Trace *Web:* doc.louisiana.gov	Angola	LA	70712	225-655-4411		213
Louisiana State University						
Alexandria 8100 US Hwy 71 S *TF:* 888-473-6417 ■ *Web:* www.lsua.edu	Alexandria	LA	71302	318-445-3672	473-6418	166

				Phone	Fax	Class
Eunice PO Box 1129	Eunice	LA	70535	337-457-7311	550-1306	162
TF: 888-367-5783 ■ *Web:* www.lsue.edu						
Shreveport 1 University Pl	Shreveport	LA	71115	318-797-5000	797-5286	166
TF: 800-229-5957 ■ *Web:* www.lsus.edu						
Louisiana State University Paul M Hebert Law Ctr						
Paul M Hebert Law Ctr	Baton Rouge	LA	70803	225-578-8646	578-8647	167-1
Web: www.law.lsu.edu						
Louisiana State University School of Medicine in New Orleans						
433 Bolivar St	New Orleans	LA	70112	504-568-6262	568-7701	167-2
Web: www.medschool.lsuhsc.edu						
Louisiana State University System						
125 E Boyd Dr	Baton Rouge	LA	70803	225-578-3357		786
Web: www.lsu.edu						
Louisiana Supreme Court						
Judicial Administrator's Office						
400 Royal St Ste 1190	New Orleans	LA	70130	504-310-2550		339-19
Web: www.lasc.org						
Louisiana Tech University						
305 Wisteria St	Ruston	LA	71272	318-257-2000	257-5943	166
Web: www.latech.edu						
Louisiana Technical College - T H Harris Campus						
332 E S St	Opelousas	LA	70570	337-943-1518	948-0243	800
Web: www.solacc.edu						
Louisiana Technical College, Margaret Surles Branch						
Hwy 883-1 PO Box 388	Lake Providence	LA	71254	318-559-0864	559-0239	167-3
TF: 888-844-8711 ■ *Web:* www.ltctallulah.com						
Louisiana Television Broadcasting						
1650 Highland Rd	Baton Rouge	LA	70802	225-336-2203		647
Web: www.wbrz.com						
Louisiana Valve Source Inc						
101 Metals Dr	Youngsville	LA	70592	337-856-9100		454
Web: lavalve.com						
Louisiana Veterinary Medical Assn						
8550 United Plaza Blvd Ste 1001	Baton Rouge	LA	70809	225-928-5862	408-4422	795
TF: 800-524-2996 ■ *Web:* lvma.org						
Louisiana War Veterans' Home						
4739 Hwy 10	Jackson	LA	70748	225-634-5265		793
Web: www.doa.la.gov						
Louisiana Wholesale Florists Inc						
151 High Meadows Blvd	LaFayette	LA	70507	337-237-6010		293
Web: louisianawholesaleflorists.com						
Louisiana-Pacific Corp						
414 Union St Ste 2000	Nashville	TN	37219	615-986-5600	986-5666	683
NYSE: LPX ■ *TF:* 888-820-0325 ■ *Web:* lpcorp.com						
Louisville & Indiana Railroad Co						
500 Willinger Ln	Jeffersonville	IN	47130	812-406-4581	288-4977	649
TF: 800-434-5472 ■ *Web:* www.anacostia.com						
Louisville & Jefferson County Convention & Visitors Bureau						
401 W Main St Ste 2300	Louisville	KY	40202	502-584-2121	584-6697	206
TF: 800-626-5646 ■ *Web:* www.gotolouisville.com						
Louisville Athletic Club LLC						
9565 Taylorsville Rd	Louisville	KY	40299	502-753-0999		354
Web: louisvilleathleticclub.com						
Louisville Ballet 315 E Main St	Louisville	KY	40202	502-583-3150	583-0006	573-1
Web: www.louisvilleballet.org						
Louisville Bedding Co						
10400 Bunsen Way	Louisville	KY	40299	502-491-3370		746
Web: www.loubed.com						
Louisville Bible College						
8013 Damascus Rd	Louisville	KY	40228	502-231-5221		166
Web: louisvillebible.net						
Louisville City Hall						
601 W Jefferson St Ste 19	Louisville	KY	40202	502-574-1100		337
Web: louisvilleky.gov						
Louisville Eccentric Observer						
607 W Main St Ste 001	Louisville	KY	40202	502-895-9770	895-9779	532-5
Web: www.leoweekly.com						
Louisville Free Public Library						
301 York St	Louisville	KY	40203	502-574-1611		434-3
Web: www.lfpl.org						
Louisville Golf Club Co						
2320 Watterson Trl	Louisville	KY	40299	502-491-5490		710
Web: www.louisvillegolf.com						
Louisville International Airport						
700 Administration Dr PO Box 9129	Louisville	KY	40209	502-368-6524	367-0199	27
Web: www.flylouisville.com						
Louisville Lamp Co						
3314 Gilmore Industrial Blvd	Louisville	KY	40213	502-964-4094		437
Web: www.louisvillelamp.com						
Louisville Lumber & Millwork						
1400 Lincoln Ave	Louisville	KY	40213	502-459-8710		499
Web: www.llmproducts.com						
Louisville Magazine						
137 W Muhammad Ali Blvd Ste 101	Louisville	KY	40202	502-625-0100		457-22
TF: 866-832-0011 ■ *Web:* www.louisville.com						
Louisville Municipal School District						
112 S Columbus Ave PO Box 909	Louisville	MS	39339	662-773-3411	773-4013	685
Web: www.louisville.k12.ms.us						
Louisville Orchestra						
323 W Broadway Ste 700	Louisville	KY	40202	502-587-8681		573-3
Web: louisvilleorchestra.org						
Louisville Palace Theatre						
625 S Fourth St	Louisville	KY	40202	502-583-4555		572
Web: www.louisvillepalace.com						
Louisville Presbyterian Theological Seminary						
1044 Alta Vista Rd	Louisville	KY	40205	502-895-3411	895-1096	167-3
TF: 800-264-1839 ■ *Web:* www.lpts.edu						
Louisville Public Media						
619 S Fourth St	Louisville	KY	40202	502-814-6500	814-6599	645-89
Web: www.louisvillepublicmedia.org						
Louisville Science Ctr						
727 W Main St	Louisville	KY	40202	502-561-6100	561-6145	520
TF: 800-591-2203 ■ *Web:* kysciencecenter.org						
Louisville Slugger Museum						
800 W Main St	Louisville	KY	40202	877-775-8443	585-1179*	522
**Fax Area Code:* 502 ■ *TF:* 877-775-8443 ■ *Web:* www.sluggermuseum.com						
Louisville State Recreation Area						
15810 Hwy 50	Louisville	NE	68037	402-234-6855		565
Web: outdoornebraska.gov						
Louisville Technical Institute						
Sullivan College of Technology & Design						
3901 Atkinson Sq Dr	Louisville	KY	40218	502-456-6509	456-2341	800
TF: 800-844-6528 ■ *Web:* sctd.edu						
Louisville Tile 4520 Bishop Ln	Louisville	KY	40218	502-371-4987		191-1
Web: www.louisville-tile.com						
Louisville Zoo 1100 Trevilian Way	Louisville	KY	40213	502-459-2181	459-2196	823
Web: www.louisvillezoo.org						
Louisville-Jefferson County						
527 W Jefferson St	Louisville	KY	40202	502-574-3427		338
Web: louisvilleky.gov						
Loup County PO Box 138	Taylor	NE	68879	308-942-6146	942-3103	338
Web: www.co.loup.ne.us						
Loup Public Power District (LPPD)						
2404 15th St PO Box 988	Columbus	NE	68602	402-564-3171	564-0970	245
TF: 866-869-2087 ■ *Web:* www.loup.com						
Lourdes College 6832 Convent Blvd	Sylvania	OH	43560	419-885-5291		166
TF: 800-878-3210 ■ *Web:* www.lourdes.edu						
Lourdes Industries Inc						
65 Hoffman Ave	Hauppauge	NY	11788	631-234-6600	234-7595	789
Web: www.lourdesinc.com						
Lourdes Medical Ctr 520 N Fourth Ave	Pasco	WA	99301	509-547-7704		374-3
TF: 800-783-0544 ■ *Web:* www.yourlourdes.com						
Lourdes-Noreen Mckeen Residence For Geriatric Care Inc						
315 S Flagler Dr	West Palm Beach	FL	33401	561-655-8544		371
Web: lourdesmckeen.org						
Loureiro Engineering Assoc						
100 Northwest Dr	Plainville	CT	06062	860-747-6181		727
Web: www.loureiro.com						
Lou-Rich Machine Tool Inc						
505 W Front St	Albert Lea	MN	56007	507-377-8910	373-7110	757
TF: 800-893-3235 ■ *Web:* www.lou-rich.com						
Lous Clinical Laboratory Inc						
635 N Grandview	Odessa	TX	79761	432-332-9421		415
Web: drug-screen.com						
Loutit District Library						
407 Columbus St	Grand Haven	MI	49417	616-842-5560	847-0570	434-3
Web: loutitlibrary.org						
Love & Quiches Desserts						
178 Hanse Ave	Freeport	NY	11520	516-623-8800		297-11
TF: 800-525-5251 ■ *Web:* www.loveandquiches.com						
Love & War In Texas 601 E Plano Pkwy	Plano	TX	75074	972-422-6201	633-1225	671
Web: www.loveandwarintexas.com						
Love Adv Inc 3550 W 12th St	Houston	TX	77008	713-552-1055		4
Web: loveadv.com						
Love Bottling Co 3200 S 24th St W	Muskogee	OK	74402	800-244-3648		297-2
TF: 800-244-3648 ■ *Web:* www.lvbeverages.com						
Love Communications						
546 South 200 West	Salt Lake City	UT	84101	801-519-8880	519-8884	636
Web: lovecomm.net						
Love County 405 W Main St Ste 203	Marietta	OK	73448	580-276-3059		338
Web: love.okcounties.org						
Love Envelopes Inc 10733 E Ute St	Tulsa	OK	74116	918-836-3535	832-9978	263
TF: 800-532-9747 ■ *Web:* www.loveenvelopes.com						
Love Heating & Air Conditioning Inc						
4115 E 10th St	Indianapolis	IN	46201	317-353-2141		610
Web: love-hvac.com						
Love Scherle & Bauer PC						
310 Grant St Ste 1020	Pittsburgh	PA	15219	412-281-8270	281-7791	2
Web: www.lovescherlebauer.com						
Love's Travel Stops						
10601 N Pennsylvania Ave	Oklahoma City	OK	73120	800-655-6837		204
TF: 800-655-6837 ■ *Web:* www.loves.com						
Lovegreen Industrial Services Inc						
2280 Sibley Ct	Eagan	MN	55122	651-890-1166	890-8370	470
TF: 800-262-8284 ■ *Web:* www.lovegreen.com						
Lovejoy Inc 2655 Wisconsin Ave	Downers Grove	IL	60515	630-852-0500	852-2120	620
Web: www.lovejoy-inc.com						
Lovejoy Tool Company Inc						
133 Main St	Springfield	VT	05156	802-885-2194	885-9511	493
TF: 800-843-8376 ■ *Web:* www.lovejoytool.com						
Lovelace Medical Ctr						
5400 Gibson Blvd SE	Albuquerque	NM	87108	505-727-8000		374-3
Web: www.lovelace.com						
Lovelace Respiratory Research Institute (LRRI)						
2425 Ridgecrest Dr SE	Albuquerque	NM	87108	505-348-9400		668
TF: 800-700-1016 ■ *Web:* lrri.org						
Loveland Chamber of Commerce						
5400 Stone Creek Cir Ste 200	Loveland	CO	80538	970-667-6311	667-5211	139
Web: www.loveland.org						
Loveland Daily Reporter-Herald						
201 E Fifth St	Loveland	CO	80537	970-669-5050		532-2
Web: www.reporterherald.com						
Loveland Ready Mix Concrete Inc						
644 N County Rd 19 E	Loveland	CO	80537	970-667-1108		182
Web: www.lrmconcrete.com						
Love-Less Ash Co 1285 E 650 S	Price	UT	84501	435-637-5885		427
TF: 800-568-3949 ■ *Web:* www.lovelessash.com						
Lovelock Correctional Ctr						
1200 Prison Rd	Lovelock	NV	89419	775-273-1300		213
Web: doc.nv.gov						
Lovely Lane Museum 2200 St Paul St	Baltimore	MD	21218	410-889-4458		520
Web: www.lovelylanemuseum.org						
Loveman Steel Corp						
5455 Perkins Rd	Bedford Heights	OH	44146	800-568-3626		492
TF: 800-568-3626 ■ *Web:* www.lovemansteel.com						
Loven Contracting Inc						
1100 S Pinnacle St	Flagstaff	AZ	86001	928-774-9040		186
Web: lovencontracting.com						
LovePop 61 Chatham St 5th Fl	Boston	MA	02109	888-687-9589		637-10
TF: 888-687-9589 ■ *Web:* www.lovepopcards.com						
Lovers Key State Park						
8700 Estero Blvd	Fort Myers Beach	FL	33931	239-463-4588	463-8851	565
Web: www.floridastateparks.org						
Lovers Lane & Co 46750 Port St	Plymouth	MI	48170	734-414-0010		157-6
TF: 888-568-3775 ■ *Web:* www.loverslane.com						
Loveshaw Corp 2206 Easton Tpke	South Canaan	PA	18459	570-937-4921		547
TF: 800-747-1586 ■ *Web:* www.loveshaw.com						

Name / Address	City	State	ZIP	Phone	Fax	Class
Lovett Schefrin Harnett Ltd 300 Centerville Rd Summit E Ste 200 *Web:* lovettlaw.com	Warwick	RI	02886	401-863-8800		41
Lovewell State Park 2446 250 Rd *Web:* www.ksoutdoors.com	Webber	KS	66970	785-753-4971		565
Loving Hands Home Care Services Inc 1777 Hamilton Ave *Web:* www.lovinghandshmcare.com	San Jose	CA	95125	408-266-8331		363
Loving Healing Press 5145 Pontiac Trl *TF:* 888-761-6268 ■ *Web:* www.lovinghealing.com	Ann Arbor	MI	48105	734-662-6864	663-6861	637-2
Loving More Magazine PO Box 1658 *Web:* www.lovemore.com	Loveland	CO	80539	970-667-5683		637-2
Lovio George Inc 681 W Forest Ave *Web:* www.loviogeorge.com	Detroit	MI	48201	313-832-2210		636
Lovitt & Touche Inc 7202 E Rosewood St Ste 200 PO Box 32702 *TF:* 800-426-2756 ■ *Web:* lovitt-touche.com	Tucson	AZ	85710	520-722-3000	722-7245	390
LOW (Loners on Wheels) 1795 O'Kelley Rd SE *Web:* www.lonersonwheels.com	Deming	NM	88030	575-544-7303		48-23
Low Cost Movers Inc 3400 Dundee Rd *TF:* 888-856-9267 ■ *Web:* www.lowcostmovers.net	Northbrook	IL	60062	888-856-9267		519
Low Cost Spay Neuter Clinic Inc 1707 E Andy Devine Ave *Web:* lowcostspayneuteraz.org	Kingman	AZ	86401	928-692-5226		794
Lowden State Park 1411 N River Rd *Web:* www2.illinois.gov	Oregon	IL	61061	815-732-6828		565
Lowe Art Museum University of Miami 1301 Stanford Dr *Web:* www.lowe.miami.edu	Coral Gables	FL	33124	305-284-3535	284-2024	520
Lowe Boats 2900 Industrial Dr *TF:* 800-641-4372 ■ *Web:* www.loweboats.com	Lebanon	MO	65536	417-532-9101		90
Lowe Electric Supply Co 1525 Forsyth St PO Box 4767 **Fax Area Code:* 478 ■ *TF:* 800-868-8661 ■ *Web:* www.loweelectric.com	Macon	GA	31208	800-868-8661	742-3374*	246
Lowe Enterprises 11777 San Vicente Blvd Ste 900 *TF:* 800-842-2252 ■ *Web:* lowe-re.com	Los Angeles	CA	90049	310-820-6661	207-1132	655
Lowe Hauptman Ham & Berner LLP 2318 Mill Rd Ste 1400 *Web:* ipfirm.com	Alexandria	VA	22314	703-684-1111	518-5499	445
Lowe Products Company Inc 777 Potomac Farms Dr *TF:* 800-430-1936 ■ *Web:* lowe-products.com	Shepherdstown	WV	25443	304-876-2546		200
Lowe's Companies Inc 1000 Lowe's Blvd *NYSE: LOW* ■ *TF:* 800-445-6937 ■ *Web:* www.lowes.com	Mooresville	NC	28117	704-758-1000		364
Lowe's Market 1804 Hall Ave *Web:* lowesmarket.com	Littlefield	TX	79339	806-385-3366		345
Lowell Academy Hairstyling Institute 136 Central St *Web:* www.lowellacademy.com	Lowell	MA	01852	978-453-3235		167-3
Lowell Correctional Institution-Women's Unit 11120 NW Gainesville Rd *Web:* dc.state.fl.us	Ocala	FL	34482	352-401-5301	401-5331	213
Lowell Five Cent Savings Bank, The 34 John St *Web:* www.lowellfive.com	Lowell	MA	01852	978-452-1300		70
Lowell General Hospital (LGH) 295 Varnum Ave *TF:* 800-544-2424 ■ *Web:* www.lowellgeneral.org	Lowell	MA	01854	978-937-6000	937-6869	374-3
Lowell Heritage State Park 160 Pawtucket Blvd *Web:* www.mass.gov	Lowell	MA	01854	978-458-8750		565
Lowell Inc 9425 83rd Ave N *Web:* lowellinc.com	Brooklyn Park	MN	55445	763-425-3355		567
Lowell Inn 102 N Second St *Web:* www.lowellinn.com	Stillwater	MN	55082	651-439-1100		379
Lowell Ledger 105 N Broadway *Web:* www.lowellbuyersguide.com	Lowell	MI	49331	616-897-9261	897-4809	532-2
Lowell Manufacturing Co 100 Integram Dr *TF:* 800-325-9660 ■ *Web:* www.lowellmfg.com	Pacific	MO	63069	636-257-3400	257-6606	52
Lowell National Historical Park 67 Kirk St *Web:* www.nps.gov	Lowell	MA	01852	978-970-5000		564
Lowell Observatory 1400 W Mars Hill Rd *Web:* lowell.edu	Flagstaff	AZ	86001	928-774-3358	774-6296	598
Lowell Sun Publishing Co 491 Dutton St *TF:* 800-359-1300 ■ *Web:* www.lowellsun.com	Lowell	MA	01854	978-458-7100	970-4600	637-8
Lowe-Martin Company Inc 400 Hunt Club Rd *TF:* 866-521-9871 ■ *Web:* www.lmgroup.com	Ottawa	ON	K1V1C1	613-741-0962		225
Lowen Corp PO Box 1528 *TF:* 800-835-2365 ■ *Web:* www.lowen.com	Hutchinson	KS	67504	620-663-2161		627
Lowenstein Associates Inc 115 E 23rd St 4th Fl *Web:* lowensteinassociates.com	New York	NY	10010	212-206-1630	727-0280	444
Lowenstein Sandler PC 65 Livingston Ave St 2 *Web:* www.lowenstein.com	Roseland	NJ	07068	973-597-2500		428
Lowenthal Alan (Rep D - CA) 108 Cannon House Office Bldg *Web:* lowenthal.house.gov	Washington	DC	20515	202-225-7924	225-7926	342-2
Lower & Kesner LLP 15910 Ventura Blvd *Web:* lowerkesner.com	Encino	CA	91436	818-933-0930	933-0933	41
Lower Brule Community College 111 Little Partisan Ln *Web:* www.lowerbrulecc.org	Lower Brule	SD	57548	605-473-9232	473-5462	162
Lower Bucks County Chamber of Commerce 409 Hood Blvd *TF:* 800-786-2234 ■ *Web:* www.lbccc.org	Fairless Hills	PA	19030	215-943-7400	943-7404	139
Lower Bucks Hospital 501 Bath Rd *Web:* www.lowerbuckshosp.com	Bristol	PA	19007	215-785-9200	785-9825	374-3
Lower Cape Fear LifeCare 1414 Physicians Dr *TF:* 800-733-1476 ■ *Web:* lifecare.org	Wilmington	NC	28401	910-796-7900	796-7901	371
Lower Columbia College 1600 Maple St PO Box 3010 *TF:* 866-900-2311 ■ *Web:* lowercolumbia.edu	Longview	WA	98632	360-442-2301	442-2379	162
Lower Columbia Longshoremens Federal Credit Union 629 14th Ave *TF:* 888-337-4404 ■ *Web:* lclfcu.org	Longview	WA	98632	360-423-2770	577-8120	219
Lower East Side Tenement Museum National Historic Site 108 Orchard St *Web:* www.tenement.org	New York	NY	10002	212-431-0233	431-0402	520
Lower East Side Visitor Ctr 54 Orchard St *Web:* les.nyc	New York	NY	10002	212-226-9010		460
Lower Fort Garry National Historic Site 5925 Hwy 9 *Web:* www.pc.gc.ca	Saint Andrews	MB	R1A4A8	204-785-6050	482-5887	563
Lower Keys Chamber of Commerce 31020 Overseas Hwy *TF:* 800-872-3722 ■ *Web:* www.lowerkeyschamber.com	Big Pine Key	FL	33043	305-872-2411	872-0752	139
Lower Keys Medical Ctr 5900 College Rd *TF:* 800-355-2470 ■ *Web:* www.lkmc.com	Key West	FL	33040	305-294-5531	294-8065	374-3
Lower Valley Energy 236 N Washington PO Box 188 *TF:* 800-882-5875 ■ *Web:* www.lvenergy.com	Afton	WY	83110	307-885-3175	885-5787	245
Lower White River Museum State Park 2009 Main St *Web:* www.arkansasstateparks.com	Des Arc	AR	72040	870-256-3711		565
Lower Yellowstone Rural Electric Association Inc 3200 W Holly St PO Box 1047 *TF:* 844-441-5627 ■ *Web:* www.lyrec.com	Sidney	MT	59270	406-488-1602	488-6524	245
Lowes Food Stores Inc 1381 Old Mill Cir Ste 200 *TF:* 800-669-5693 ■ *Web:* www.lowesfoods.com	Winston-Salem	NC	27103	336-659-0180	768-4702	345
Lowes Greenhouses & Gift Shop Inc 16540 Chillicothe Rd *Web:* lowesgreenhouse.com	Chagrin Falls	OH	44023	440-543-5123		292
Lowey Nita (Rep D - NY) 2365 Rayburn House Office Bldg *Web:* www.lowey.house.gov	Washington	DC	20515	202-225-6506	225-0546	342-2
Lowndes County 1121 Main St *Web:* lowndescountyms.com	Columbus	MS	39701	662-329-5884	241-1935	338
Lowndes County PO Box 1349 *Web:* www.lowndescounty.com	Valdosta	GA	31603	229-671-2400	245-5222	338
Lowrance Electronics Inc 12000 E Skelly Dr *TF:* 800-628-4487 ■ *Web:* www.lowrance.com	Tulsa	OK	74128	918-437-6881		529
Lowrider Magazine 1821 E Dyer Rd PO Box 420235 *TF:* 800-283-2013 ■ *Web:* www.lowrider.com	Santa Ana	CA	92705	800-283-2013		457-3
Lowry Manufacturing Co 317 Cherry St *TF:* 800-950-4792 ■ *Web:* www.lowrymfgco.com	Lowry	MN	56349	320-283-5450	283-5246	273
Lowry Mechanical Inc 111 Rosemary Ln *Web:* www.lowrymechanical.com	Laurens	SC	29360	864-984-2589	984-7168	189-10
Lowry Park Zoo 1101 W Sligh Ave *Web:* zootampa.org	Tampa	FL	33604	813-935-8552	935-9486	823
Lowville Producers Dairy Co-op 7396 Utica Blvd *Web:* www.gotgoodcheese.com	Lowville	NY	13367	315-376-3921	376-3442	297-4
Loxcreen Company Inc, The 1630 Old Dunbar Rd PO Box 4004 *TF:* 800-330-5699 ■ *Web:* www.loxcreen.com	West Columbia	SC	29172	803-822-8200	822-8547	485
Loyal Termite & Pest Control Company Inc 2610 E Parham Rd *Web:* www.loyalpest.com	Richmond	VA	23228	804-737-7777		577
Loyalist College Wallbridge-Loyalist Rd *TF:* 800-992-5866 ■ *Web:* www.loyalistcollege.com	Belleville	ON	K8N5B9	613-969-1913		162
Loyalty 360 Inc 4120 Dumont St *Web:* loyalty360.org	Cincinnati	OH	45226	513-800-0360		5
Loyalty Factor 579 Sagamore Ave Unit 109 *Web:* www.loyaltyfactor.com	Portsmouth	NH	03801	603-334-3401		196
Loyalty Methods Inc 80 Yesler Way Ste 310 *TF:* 800-693-2040 ■ *Web:* loyaltymethods.com	Seattle	WA	98104	206-512-3933		463
LoyaltyExpress Inc 53 Commerce Way *Web:* www.loyaltyexpress.com	Woburn	MA	01801	781-938-1175		195
LoyaltyPlant Inc 106 W 32nd St 2nd Fl Office 113 *TF:* 888-932-7888 ■ *Web:* loyaltyplant.com	New York	NY	10001	347-943-6134		180
Loyd Keith Friedlander Partners 18 Prospect St *Web:* www.lkfins.com	Huntington	NY	11743	631-424-2600		390
Loyd's Aviation 1601 Skyway Dr Ste 100 PO Box 80958 *TF:* 800-284-1334 ■ *Web:* www.bakersfieldjetcenter.com	Bakersfield	CA	93308	661-393-1344	393-0824	63
Loyd's Electric Supply Inc (LES) 838 Stonetree Dr *TF:* 800-492-4030 ■ *Web:* www.loydselectric.com	Branson	MO	65616	417-334-2171	334-6635	246
Loy-Lange Box Co 222 Russell Blvd *Web:* www.loylangebox.com	Saint Louis	MO	63104	314-776-4712		100
Loyola Academy 1100 Laramie *Web:* www.goramblers.org	Wilmette	IL	60091	847-256-1100	853-4512	685
Loyola College 4501 N Charles St *TF:* 800-221-9107 ■ *Web:* www.loyola.edu	Baltimore	MD	21210	410-617-5012	617-2176	166
Loyola Enterprises Inc 2984 S Lynnhaven Rd Ste 101 *TF:* 800-937-9021 ■ *Web:* www.loyola.com	Virginia Beach	VA	23452	757-498-6118	498-6110	261
Loyola Marymount Law School 919 Albany St *Web:* www.lls.edu	Los Angeles	CA	90015	213-736-1000	736-6523	167-1
Loyola Marymount University 1 LMU Dr *TF:* 800-568-4636 ■ *Web:* www.lmu.edu	Los Angeles	CA	90045	310-338-2700	338-2797	166
Loyola Paper Co 951 Lunt Ave	Elk Grove Village	IL	60007	847-956-7770		554
Loyola Press 3441 N Ashland Ave *TF:* 800-621-1008 ■ *Web:* www.loyolapress.com	Chicago	IL	60657	773-281-1818	281-0885	95

Phone Fax Class

Loyola Retreat House 161 James St Morristown NJ 07960 973-539-0740 898-9839 673
Web: www.loyola.org
Loyola University
New Orleans 6363 St Charles Ave New Orleans LA 70118 504-865-3240 865-3383 166
TF: 800-456-9652 ■ *Web:* www.loyno.edu
Loyola University Chicago
Cudahy Library 1032 W Sheridan Rd Chicago IL 60660 773-508-2632 434-6
Web: www.libraries.luc.edu
School of Law 25 E Pearson St Ste 1434 Chicago IL 60611 312-915-7181 915-7201 167-1
Web: www.luc.edu
Loyola University Medical Ctr
2160 S First Ave Maywood IL 60153 888-584-7888 374-3
TF: 888-584-7888 ■ *Web:* www.luhs.org
Loyola University New Orleans College of Law
7214 St Charles Ave CB 903 New Orleans LA 70118 504-861-5550 861-5739 167-1
Web: www.law.loyno.edu
Loysville Youth Development Ctr
10 Opportunity Dr Loysville PA 17047 717-789-3841 412
Web: www.dhs.pa.gov
Lozano Smith 7404 N Spalding Ave Fresno CA 93720 559-431-5600 428
Web: www.lozanosmith.com
Lozier Corp 6336 John J Pershing Dr Omaha NE 68110 402-457-8000 286
TF: 800-228-9882 ■ *Web:* www.lozier.com
Lozier Group 7485 Westerfield Rd Lynden WA 98264 425-635-3922 653
Web: www.loziergroup.com
Lozier's Box R Ranch
552 Willow Creek Rd PO Box 100 Cora WY 82925 307-367-4868 367-6260 239
TF: 800-822-8466 ■ *Web:* www.boxr.com
LP (Lakeland Plastics Inc)
1550 McCormick Blvd Mundelein IL 60060 847-680-1550 680-1595 599
TF: 800-454-4006 ■ *Web:* lakelandplastics.com
LP (Loom Press) PO Box 1394 Lowell MA 01853 978-454-4883 637-2
Web: www.loompress.com
LPA Designs
21 Gregory Dr Ste 140 South Burlington VT 05403 802-658-0038 407
Web: www.lpadesign.com
LPA Inc 5301 California Ave Ste 100 Irvine CA 92617 949-261-1001 260-1190 261
Web: lpadesignstudios.com
LPA Software Solutions LLC
400 Linden Oaks Ste 140 Rochester NY 14625 866-783-9900 177
TF: 866-783-9900 ■ *Web:* lpa.com
LPB Holding Company Inc
6060 Primacy Pkwy Ste 400 Memphis TN 38119 901-524-4000 524-4050 803-1
LPCH (Lucile Packard Children's Hospital)
725 Welch Rd Palo Alto CA 94304 650-497-8000 497-8968 374-1
TF: 800-995-5724 ■ *Web:* www.stanfordchildrens.org
LPCiminelli 2421 Main St Buffalo NY 14214 716-855-1200 186
Web: lpciminelli.com
Lpd Music International Corp
32575 Industrial Dr Madison Heights MI 48071 248-585-9630 526
Web: lpdmusic.com
LPD Press
925 Salamanca NW Los Ranchos de Albuquerque NM 87107 505-344-9382 345-5129 637-2
Web: www.nmsantos.com
LPGA (Ladies Professional Golf Assn)
100 International Golf Dr Daytona Beach FL 32124 386-274-6200 274-1099 48-22
Web: www.lpga.com
LPH (La Porte Hospital)
1007 Lincolnway PO Box 250 La Porte IN 46350 219-326-1234 374-3
Web: www.laportehealth.com
LPI Group 253 62 Ave SE Ste 101 Calgary AB T2H0R5 403-735-0655 224
Web: www.lpi-group.com
LPI Memphis Inc 5264 Poplar Ave Memphis TN 38119 901-761-3333 761-3334 652
Web: lpimemphis.com
LPK (Libby Perszyk Kathman Holdings Inc)
10 Garfield Pl Cincinnati OH 45202 513-241-6401 195
Web: www.lpk.com
LPL Financial 75 State St 22nd Fl Boston MA 02109 800-877-7210 690
Web: www.lpl.com
LPPD (Loup Public Power District)
2404 15th St PO Box 988 Columbus NE 68602 402-564-3171 564-0970 245
TF: 866-869-2087 ■ *Web:* www.loup.com
LPS Industries Inc 10 Caesar Pl Moonachie NJ 07074 201-438-3515 548
TF: 800-275-6577 ■ *Web:* www.lpsind.com
LPWSL (Larzelere Picou Wells Simpson Lonero LLC)
2 Lakeway Ctr 3850 N Causeway Blvd Ste 500 Metairie LA 70002 504-834-6500 834-6565 445
Web: lpwsl.com
LQM Petroleum Services Inc
1 River Rd 2nd Fl Cos Cob CT 06807 201-871-9010 579
Web: lqm.com
LQMT (Liquidmetal Technologies Inc)
30452 Esperanza Rancho Santa Margarita CA 92688 949-635-2100 635-2188 482
OTC: LQMT ■ *Web:* www.liquidmetal.com
LQP (Lac qui Parle County) 600 Sixth St Madison MN 56256 320-598-7444 598-3125 338
Web: www.lqpco.com
LR Services 602 Hayden Cir Allentown PA 18109 610-266-2500 266-3100 13
TF: 888-675-9650 ■ *Web:* lrservices.com
LRB (Hawaii Legislative Reference Bureau)
Hawaii State Capitol Honolulu HI 96813 808-587-0690 587-0699 434-3
Web: www.lrbhawaii.org
LRCC (Lakes Region Community College)
379 Belmont Rd Laconia NH 03246 603-524-3207 524-8084 162
TF: 800-357-2992 ■ *Web:* www.lrcc.edu
LRDC (Learning Research & Development Ctr)
University of Pittsburgh 3939 O'Hara St Pittsburgh PA 15260 412-624-7020 624-9149 668
Web: www.lrdc.pitt.edu
LRECI (Little River Electric Cooperative Inc)
300 Cambridge St Abbeville SC 29620 864-366-2141 245
TF: 800-459-2141 ■ *Web:* www.lreci.coop
LRF (Lymphoma Research Foundation)
115 Broadway Ste 1301 New York NY 10006 212-349-2910 349-2886 48-17
TF: 800-500-9976 ■ *Web:* www.lymphoma.org
LRG (Leichtman Research Group Inc)
567 Bay Rd Durham NH 03824 603-397-5400 194
Web: www.leichtmanresearch.com
LRG Marketing Communications Inc
48 Burd St Ste 105 Nyack NY 10960 845-358-1801 195
Web: lrgmarketing.com

Phone Fax Class

LRI (Life's Resources Inc) 114 E Main St Addison MI 49220 517-547-7494 547-5444 637-2
Web: www.lifes.org
LRK (Looney Ricks Kiss)
175 Toyota Plz Ste 500 Memphis TN 38103 901-521-1440 261
Web: www.lrk.com
LRL Associates Ltd 5430 Canotek Rd Ottawa ON K1J9G2 613-842-3434 261
TF: 877-632-5664 ■ *Web:* lrl.ca
LRP Publications
360 Hiatt Dr Palm Beach Gardens FL 33418 561-622-6520 622-2423 637-2
TF: 800-621-5463 ■ *Web:* www.lrp.com
LRRI (Lovelace Respiratory Research Institute)
2425 Ridgecrest Dr SE Albuquerque NM 87108 505-348-9400 668
TF: 800-700-1016 ■ *Web:* lrri.org
LRS Federal LLC
8221 Ritchie Hwy Ste 300 Pasadena MD 21122 410-544-3570 647-4183 261
Web: lrsfederal.com
L&S (Long & Silverman Publishing Inc)
800 N Rainbow Blvd Ste 208 Las Vegas NV 89107 702-948-5073 637-2
TF: 888-902-2766 ■ *Web:* www.lspub.com
LS Gallegos & Associates Inc
116 Inverness Dr E Ste 207 Englewood CO 80112 303-790-8474 463
Web: www.lsgallegos.com
LS Industries Inc 710 E 17th St N Wichita KS 67214 316-265-7997 265-0013 695
Web: www.lsindustries.com
LS Tractor USA LLC
6900 Corporation Pkwy Battleboro NC 27809 252-984-0700 273
Web: lstractorusa.com
LS3P Associates Ltd
205 1/2 King St Charleston SC 29401 843-577-4444 722-4789 261
Web: www.ls3p.com
LSA (Linguistic Society of America)
1325 18th St NW Ste 211 Washington DC 20036 202-835-1714 835-1717 48-11
TF: 800-726-0479 ■ *Web:* www.linguisticsociety.org
LSA Associates Inc
20 Executive Pk Ste 200 Irvine CA 92614 949-553-0666 193
Web: lsa.net
LSB Industries Inc
16 S Pennsylvania Ave Oklahoma City OK 73107 405-235-4546 235-5067 143
NYSE: LXU ■ *TF:* 800-657-4428 ■ *Web:* lsbindustries.com
LSBA (Louisiana State Bar Assn)
601 St Charles Ave New Orleans LA 70130 504-566-1600 566-0930 72
TF: 800-421-5722 ■ *Web:* www.lsba.org
LSC & LSC Digital
6 Trowbridge Dr PO Box 516 Bethel CT 06801 203-743-2600 5
Web: www.listservices.com
LSC Mail Marketing 711 Bond Ave Little Rock AR 72202 501-374-7676 374-4466 195
Web: www.lscmarketing.com
LSE Crane & Transportation
313 Westgate Rd LaFayette LA 70506 337-234-9435 234-0217 189-14
TF: 877-234-9435 ■ *Web:* www.lsecrane.com
LSESSI (Lightning Strike & Electric Shock Survivors International Inc)
PO Box 1156 Jacksonville NC 28541 910-346-4708 48-21
Web: www.lightning-strike.org
LSF (Lohr Structural Fasteners Inc)
2355 Wilson Rd Humble TX 77396 281-446-6766 446-7805 278
TF: 800-782-4544 ■ *Web:* www.lohrfasteners.com
Lsg Solutions LLC
501 E 15th St Ste 200B Edmond OK 73013 405-285-2500 631
Web: lsgsolutions.com
LSI (Lake Shore Industries Inc)
1817 Poplar St PO Box 3427 Erie PA 16508 800-458-0463 453-4293* 701
**Fax Area Code: 814* ■ *TF:* 800-458-0463 ■ *Web:* www.lsisigns.com
LSI (Litigation Solution Inc)
5995 Greenwood Plz Blvd Ste 160 Greenwood Village CO 80111 303-820-2000 627
TF: 888-767-7088 ■ *Web:* www.lsilegal.com
LSI (Living Systems Instrumentation)
St Albans Burlington VT 05401 802-863-5547 250
Web: www.livingsys.com
LSI Casework 704 W Main St Teutopolis IL 62467 763-559-4664 559-4395 599
Web: www.lsicasework.com
LSI Computer Systems Inc
1235 Walt Whitman Rd Melville NY 11747 631-271-0400 271-0405 696
Web: lsicsi.com
Lsi Controls Inc 11664 Orchard Rd Waynesboro PA 17268 717-762-2191 762-0863 201
Web: www.lsi-controls.com
LSI Industries Inc
10000 Alliance Rd Cincinnati OH 45242 513-793-3200 984-1335 439
NASDAQ: LYTS ■ *TF:* 800-436-7800 ■ *Web:* www.lsi-industries.com
LSI Wallcovering 2073 McDonald Ave New Albany IN 47150 502-458-1502 802
Web: www.versawallcovering.com
LSMVC (Lake Superior Maritime Visitor Ctr)
600 Canal Park Dr Duluth MN 55802 218-788-6430 520
Web: www.lsmma.com
LSNA (Louisiana State Nurses Assn)
543 Spanish Town Rd Baton Rouge LA 70802 225-201-0993 533
Web: www.lsna.org
LSO (Lansing Symphony Orchestra)
104 S Washington Sq Ste 300 Lansing MI 48933 517-487-5001 487-0210 573-3
Web: www.lansingsymphony.org
LSP Products Group Inc
3689 Arrowhead Dr Carson City NV 89706 800-854-3215 243-1777 608
TF: 800-854-3215 ■ *Web:* www.lspproducts.com
LSQ Funding Group LC
2600 Lucien Way Ste 100 Maitland FL 32751 800-474-7606 272
TF: 800-474-7606 ■ *Web:* www.lsq.com
LSSI (Logical System Solutions Inc)
1602 Baumgart Normal IL 61761 309-310-3780 393
Web: www.logical-systems.com
LSSU (Lake Superior State University)
650 W Easterday Ave Sault Sainte Marie MI 49783 906-632-6841 635-2111 166
Web: www.lssu.edu
LST (Leading Systems Technologies Inc)
2721 Prosperity Ave Ste 100 Fairfax VA 22031 703-204-0404 463
LSU (LSU Health Shreveport)
1501 Kings Hwy Shreveport LA 71103 318-675-5000 374-3
Web: www.lsuhs.edu
LSU Health Shreveport (LSU)
1501 Kings Hwy Shreveport LA 71103 318-675-5000 374-3
Web: www.lsuhs.edu

Phone | Fax | Class

LSWNY (Landmark Society of Western New York)
133 S Fitzhugh St ... Rochester NY 14608 585-546-7029 546-4788 48-6
Web: www.landmarksociety.org

LT Apparel Group
100 W 33rd St Ste 1012 ... New York NY 10001 212-502-6000 268-5160 155-4
Web: www.ltapparel.com

LTA (Land Trust Alliance)
1660 L St NW Ste 1100 ... Washington DC 20036 202-638-4725 638-4730 48-13
Web: www.landtrustalliance.org

LTC (Lipan Telephone Company Inc)
109 N Kickapoo St ... Lipan TX 76462 254-646-2211 224
Web: www.lipan.net

LTC (Libra Technical Center)
200 Centennial Ave Ste 140 ... Piscataway NJ 08854 732-667-5626 667-5572 743
TF: 855-441-5200 ■ *Web:* www.libratechnicalcenter.com

LTC (Laughlin Trucking Inc)
12850 NE Hendricks Rd ... Carlton OR 97111 503-852-7186 852-7056 780
TF: 800-452-9436 ■ *Web:* www.laughlintrucking.com

LTC Properties Inc
2829 Townsgate Rd Ste 350 ... Westlake Village CA 91361 805-981-8655 981-8663 654
NYSE: LTC ■ *Web:* www.ltcreit.com

LTC Roll & Engineering Co
23500 John Gorsuch Dr ... Clinton Township MI 48036 586-465-1023 482
Web: ltcroll.com

LTD Hospitality Group LLC
1564 Crossways Blvd ... Chesapeake VA 23320 757-420-0900 420-0931 378
Web: www.ltdhospitality.com

LTD Managemen
1230 Pottstown Pk Ste 6 ... Glenmoore PA 19343 610-715-3710 458-8039 194
Web: www.ltdmgmt.com

LTI Optics LLC
10850 Dover St Ste 300 ... Westminster CO 80021 720-891-0030 178-1
Web: www.ltioptics.com

LTI Power Systems
10800 Middle Ave Bldg B ... Elyria OH 44035 440-327-5050 458-8140 767
TF: 888-327-5050 ■ *Web:* ltipowersystems.com

LTI Printing Inc 518 N Centerville Rd ... Sturgis MI 49091 269-651-7574 627
TF: 800-592-6990 ■ *Web:* www.ltiprinting.com

LTI Technology Solutions
4139 S 143rd Cir ... Omaha NE 68137 402-493-3445 177
Web: www.ltisolutions.com

LTI Trucking Services Inc
411 N Tenth St Ste 500 ... Saint Louis MO 63101 800-642-7222 314
TF: 800-642-7222 ■ *Web:* www.ltitrucking.com

LTK Engineering Services Inc
100 W Butler Ave ... Ambler PA 19002 215-542-0700 434-3
Web: www.ltk.com

LTL Consultants Ltd 1 Town Center Dr ... Oley PA 19547 610-987-9290 261
Web: www.ltlconsultants.com

LTM Inc 925 E Main St Ste 66 ... Havelock NC 28532 252-444-6881 444-5782 393
Web: www.ltminc.net

LTP (Liturgy Training Publications)
3949 S Racine Ave ... Chicago IL 60609 773-579-4900 579-4929 637-2
TF: 800-933-1800 ■ *Web:* www.ltp.org

LTS (Lawrence Companies)
872 Lee Hwy Ste 100 ... Roanoke VA 24019 800-336-9626 966-4555* 780
**Fax Area Code:* 540 ■ *TF:* 800-336-9626 ■ *Web:* www.lawrencecompanies.com

Lts Lohmann Therapy Systems Corp
21 Henderson Dr ... West Caldwell NJ 07006 973-396-5345 575-5174 583
TF: 800-587-1872 ■ *Web:* www.ltslohmann.de

Lu Ross Academy 470 E Thompson Blvd ... Ventura CA 93001 805-643-5690 643-7716 167-3
Web: www.lurossacademy.com

Lu'ma Native Housing Society
2960 Nanaimo St ... Vancouver BC V5N5G3 604-876-0811 653
Web: lnhs.ca

LUA (Lumbermen's Underwriting Alliance)
1905 NW Corporate Blvd Ste 110 ... Boca Raton FL 33431 561-994-1900 391-4
TF: 800-327-0630 ■ *Web:* www.lumbermensunderwriting.com

Lubar & Co 700 N Water St Ste 1200 ... Milwaukee WI 53202 414-291-9000 291-9061 792
Web: www.lubar.com

Lubbock Avalanche-Journal 710 Ave J ... Lubbock TX 79401 806-762-8844 744-9603 532-2
TF: 800-692-4021 ■ *Web:* www.lubbockonline.com

Lubbock Chamber of Commerce
1500 Broadway Ste 101 ... Lubbock TX 79401 806-761-7000 761-7013 139
Web: www.lubbockchamber.com

Lubbock Christian University
5601 19th St ... Lubbock TX 79407 806-720-7151 720-7162 166
TF: 800-933-7601 ■ *Web:* lcu.edu

Lubbock City Hall 1625 13th St ... Lubbock TX 79401 806-775-3000 337
Web: ci.lubbock.tx.us

Lubbock Convention & Visitors Bureau
1500 Broadway St 6th Fl ... Lubbock TX 79401 806-747-5232 747-1419 206
TF: 800-692-4035 ■ *Web:* www.visitlubbock.org

Lubbock County 904 Broadway St Rm 207 ... Lubbock TX 79401 806-775-1000 775-7950 338
Web: www.co.lubbock.tx.us

Lubbock Memorial Arboretum
4111 University Ave ... Lubbock TX 79413 806-797-4520 97
Web: www.lubbockarboretum.org

Lubbock Memorial Civic Ctr
1501 MacDavis Ln ... Lubbock TX 79401 806-775-2242 775-3240 205
Web: civiclubbock.com

Lubbock National Bank 4811 50th St ... Lubbock TX 79414 806-792-1000 792-0976 70

Lubbock-Cooper ISD 16302 Loop 493 ... Lubbock TX 79423 806-863-7100 863-7130 685
Web: www.lcisd.net

Lube USA Inc 781 Congaree Rd ... Greenville SC 29607 864-297-3950 684
TF: 800-326-3765 ■ *Web:* www.lube-global.com

Luber Bros Inc 5224 Bear Creek Ct ... Irving TX 75061 972-313-2020 274
TF: 800-375-8237 ■ *Web:* www.luber.com

Luberski Inc
310 N Harbor Blvd Ste 205 ... Fullerton CA 92832 714-680-3447 297-4
TF: 800-326-3220 ■ *Web:* www.hiddenvilla.com

Lubitz Financial Group, The
9130 S Dadeland Blvd Ste 1625 ... Miami FL 33156 305-670-4440 528
Web: www.lubitzfinancial.com

Lubricating Specialties Co
8015 Paramount Blvd ... Pico Rivera CA 90660 562-776-4000 541
Web: www.lsc-online.com

Lubrication Engineers Inc
300 Bailey Ave ... Fort Worth TX 76107 817-834-6321 228-1142* 541
**Fax Area Code:* 800 ■ *TF:* 800-537-7683 ■ *Web:* www.lelubricants.com

Lubrication Technologies Inc
900 Mendelssohn Ave N ... Golden Valley MN 55427 763-545-0707 545-9256 541
TF: 800-328-5573 ■ *Web:* www.lubetech.com

Lubri-Lab Inc 1540 de Coulomb ... Boucherville QC J4B8A3 450-449-1626 449-9174 541
Web: www.lubrilab.com

Lubrizol Corp 29400 Lakeland Blvd ... Wickliffe OH 44092 440-943-4200 145
NYSE: LZ ■ *TF:* 800-380-5397 ■ *Web:* www.lubrizol.com

Luburgh Inc 4174 E Pk ... Zanesville OH 43701 740-452-3668 189-5

Luby's Inc 13111 NW Fwy Ste 600 ... Houston TX 77040 713-329-6800 670
NYSE: LUB ■ *TF:* 800-886-4600 ■ *Web:* www.lubys.com

LUC Global Label
2025 Joshua Rd ... Lafayette Hill PA 19444 610-825-3250 825-8334 413
Web: www.luxgloballabel.com

Luca 711 Grant St ... Denver CO 80203 303-832-6600 671
Web: www.lucadenver.com

Lucano 1815 E Ave ... Rochester NY 14610 585-244-3460 671
Web: www.ristorantelucano.com

Lucas
3160 George Washington Way Sigma III Bldg
Ste B ... Richland WA 99352 509-942-1080 942-1081 194
Web: www.lucasinc.com

Lucas Associates Inc
950 E Paces Ferry Rd NE Ste 2300 ... Atlanta GA 30326 404-239-5620 239-5688 721
TF: 800-515-0819 ■ *Web:* www.lucasgroup.com

Lucas Color Card
4900 N Santa Fe Ave ... Oklahoma City OK 73118 405-524-1811 344
Web: lucascolorcard.com

Lucas County 916 Braden St ... Chariton IA 50049 641-774-4411 338
Web: lucas.iowaassessors.com

Lucas County 1 Government Ctr Ste 800 ... Toledo OH 43604 419-213-4500 213-4532 338
Web: www.co.lucas.oh.us

Lucas Frank (Rep R - OK)
2405 Rayburn House Office Bldg ... Washington DC 20515 202-225-5565 225-8698 342-2
Web: www.lucas.house.gov

Lucas Horsfall Murphy & Pindroh LLP
100 E Corson St Ste 200 ... Pasadena CA 91103 626-744-5100 828-2209* 2
**Fax Area Code:* 714 ■ *Web:* www.lhmp.com

Lucas Oil Stadium
500 S Capitol Ave ... Indianapolis IN 46225 317-262-8600 720
Web: www.icclos.com

Lucas Precision LP
13020 St Clair Ave ... Cleveland OH 44108 216-451-5588 451-5174 455
TF: 800-336-1262 ■ *Web:* www.lucasprecision.com

Lucas Systems Inc
11279 Perry Hwy 4th Fl ... Wexford PA 15090 724-940-7000 177
Web: www.lucasware.com

Lucasfilm Ltd PO Box 29901 ... San Francisco CA 94129 415-623-1000 514
Web: www.lucasfilm.com

Lucasfilm Ltd
LucasArts Entertainment Div
1110 Gorgas St ... San Francisco CA 94129 410-568-3670 662-1639* 178-6
**Fax Area Code:* 415 ■ *Web:* www.starwars.com

Lucas-Milhaupt Inc
5656 S Pennsylvania Ave ... Cudahy WI 53110 414-769-6000 769-1093 485
TF: 800-558-3856 ■ *Web:* lucasmilhaupt.com

Lucca 226 Hanover St ... Boston MA 02113 617-742-9200 671
Web: www.luccaboston.com

Lucca Restaurant & Bar 1615 J St ... Sacramento CA 95814 916-669-5300 671
Web: www.luccarestaurant.com

Lucchese Boot Co 20 Zane Grey ... El Paso TX 79906 888-582-1883 301
TF: 800-637-6888 ■ *Web:* www.lucchese.com

Luce County 407 W Harrie St ... Newberry MI 49868 906-293-5531 293-5773 338
Web: www.lucecountymi.com

Luce Smith & Scott Inc
6860 W Snowville Rd Ste 110 ... Brecksville OH 44141 440-746-1700 390
Web: lucesmithscott.com

Luce, Schwab & Kase Inc 9 Gloria Ln ... Fairfield NJ 07004 973-227-4840 665
TF: 800-458-7329 ■ *Web:* www.lskair.com

Lucent Capital Inc
9454 Wilshire Blvd Ste 525 ... Beverly Hills CA 90212 310-876-8454 691
Web: www.lucentcapital.com

Lucent Medical Systems Inc
821 Kirkland Ave Ste 100 ... Kirkland WA 98033 425-822-3310 476
Web: www.lucentmedical.com

Lucero Cables Inc 193 Stauffer Blvd ... San Jose CA 95125 408-298-6001 298-6002 253
Web: www.luceromfg.com

Luci Ancora 2060 Randolph Ave ... Saint Paul MN 55105 651-698-6889 671
Web: luciancora.com

Lucia Marquand 1400 Second Ave ... Seattle WA 98101 206-624-2030 624-1821 344
Web: luciamarquand.com

Lucid Fusion Inc
17875 Von Karman Ave Ste 150 ... Irvine CA 92614 949-502-7750 7
Web: www.lucidfusion.com

Lucid Technology 1754 N Wilmot ... Chicago IL 60647 312-238-8976 180
Web: www.lucidtec.com

Lucile Packard Children's Hospital (LPCH)
725 Welch Rd ... Palo Alto CA 94304 650-497-8000 497-8968 374-1
TF: 800-995-5724 ■ *Web:* www.stanfordchildrens.org

Lucile Plane State Jail 904 FM 686 ... Dayton TX 77535 936-258-2476 257-4449 213
Web: www.tdcj.texas.gov

Lucile's Famous Creole Seasonings
2124 14th St ... Boulder CO 80302 303-442-4743 939-9848 296-37
Web: www.luciles.com

Lucille Lortel Theatre
121 Christopher St ... New York NY 10014 212-924-2817 572
Web: www.lortel.org

Lucille Roberts Women's Gym
430 89th St ... Brooklyn NY 11209 718-680-8200 354
Web: lucilleroberts.com

Lucille's Smokehouse Bar-B-Que
7411 Carson St ... Long Beach CA 90808 562-938-7427 671
Web: lucillesbbq.com

Lucille's Stateside Bistro
4700 Camp Bowie Blvd ... Fort Worth TX 76107 817-738-4761 671
Web: lucillesstatesidebistro.com

Name / Address	City	State	Zip	Phone	Fax	Class
Lucinda Hall Public Relations						
PO Box 874	Brentwood	TN	37024	615-394-7592		317
Web: www.lhpr.com						
Lucis Publishing Co						
120 Wall St 24th Fl	New York	NY	10005	212-292-0707	292-0808	637-2
Web: www.lucistrust.org						
Lucius Beebe Memorial Library						
345 Main St	Wakefield	MA	01880	781-246-6334		434-3
Web: www.wakefieldlibrary.org						
Lucix Corp 800 Avenida Acaso	Camarillo	CA	93012	805-987-3677		253
Web: www.lucix.com						
Luckett & Farley Architects Engineers & Construction Managers Inc						
737 S Third St	Louisville	KY	40202	502-585-4181		186
Web: www.luckett-farley.com						
Luckey Farmers Inc						
1200 W Main St PO Box 217	Woodville	OH	43469	419-849-2711	849-2720	276
Web: luckeyfarmers.com						
Luckie & Co 600 Luckie Dr Ste 150	Birmingham	AL	35223	205-879-2121		4
Web: www.luckie.com						
Luckman Fine Arts Complex						
5151 State University Dr	Los Angeles	CA	90032	323-343-6600		572
Web: www.luckmanarts.org						
Lucks Co, The 3003 S Pine St	Tacoma	WA	98409	253-383-4815	383-0071	296-8
TF: 800-426-9778 ■ *Web:* www.lucks.com						
Lucky Chances Casino 1700 Hillside Blvd	Colma	CA	94014	650-758-2237	758-6462	452
Web: www.luckychances.com						
Lucky Eagle Casino						
12888 188th Ave SW	Rochester	WA	98579	360-273-2000		133
TF: 800-720-1788 ■ *Web:* www.luckyeagle.com						
Lucky Fortune 1401 Lancaster Dr NE	Salem	OR	97301	503-399-9189		671
Web: www.luckyfortunechinesesalem.com						
Lucky Strike Lanes Orange						
20 City Blvd W Ste G2	Orange	CA	92868	714-937-5263		99
Web: www.luckystrikesocial.com						
Luco Mop Co 3345 Morganford Rd	Saint Louis	MO	63116	314-772-5656	772-5826	103
TF: 800-522-5826 ■ *Web:* www.lucomop.com						
Lucor Inc 790 Pershing Rd	Raleigh	NC	27608	919-828-9511		62-5
Lucques 8474 Melrose Ave	Los Angeles	CA	90069	323-655-6277		671
Web: www.lucques.com						
Lucy Corr Village						
6800 Lucy Corr Blvd	Chesterfield	VA	23832	804-748-1511	706-5572	450
Web: lucycorr.org						
Lucy Craft Laney Museum						
1116 Phillips St	Augusta	GA	30901	706-724-3576		520
Web: www.lucycraftlaneymuseum.com						
Lucy Robbins Welles Library						
95 Cedar St	Newington	CT	06111	860-665-8700	667-1255	434-3
Web: www.newingtonct.gov						
Lucy's Chinese Food						
3330 S Campbell	Springfield	MO	65807	417-882-5383		671
Web: www.lucyschinesefood.com						
Ludeca Inc 1425 NW 88th Ave	Doral	FL	33172	305-591-8935		246
Web: www.ludeca.com						
Luderman & Konst Inc						
317 Jefferson Ave	Defiance	OH	43512	419-782-7166		2
Web: ludermankonstcpas.com						
Ludington State Park PO Box 709	Ludington	MI	49431	231-843-2423		565
Web: www.michigan.org						
Ludl Electronic Products Ltd						
171 Brady Ave	Hawthorne	NY	10532	914-769-6111	769-4759	248
TF: 888-769-6111 ■ *Web:* www.ludlsemi.com						
Ludlow Composites Corp						
2100 Commerce Dr	Fremont	OH	43420	800-628-5463	332-7776*	676
**Fax Area Code:* 419 ■ *TF:* 800-628-5463 ■ *Web:* www.ludlow-comp.com						
Ludlum Measurements Inc 501 Oak St	Sweetwater	TX	79556	325-235-5494	235-4672	472
TF: 800-622-0828 ■ *Web:* www.ludlums.com						
Ludowici Roof Tile Inc						
4757 Tile Plant Rd PO Box 69	New Lexington	OH	43764	740-342-1995	342-0025	150
TF: 800-945-8453 ■ *Web:* www.ludowici.com						
Ludvik Electric Co 3900 S Teller St	Lakewood	CO	80235	303-781-9601		189-4
Web: www.ludvik.com						
Ludwig Buildings Inc						
521 Timesaver Ave	Harahan	LA	70123	504-733-6260	733-7458	105
Web: www.ludwigbuildings.com						
Ludwig Von Mises Institute						
518 W Magnolia Ave	Auburn	AL	36832	334-321-2100	321-2119	166
Web: mises.org						
Ludwigs Corner Veterinary Hospital LLC						
915 N Pottstown Pk	Chester Springs	PA	19425	610-458-8567		794
Web: ludwigscornervet.net						
Lueder Construction Co 9999 J St	Omaha	NE	68127	402-339-1000	592-4769	186
Web: www.lueder.com						
Luedtke Engineering Co 10 4th St	Frankfort	MI	49635	231-352-9631	352-7178	261
Web: www.luedtke-eng.com						
Luetkemeyer Blaine (Rep R - MO)						
2230 Rayburn House Office Bldg	Washington	DC	20515	202-225-2956	225-5712	342-2
Web: www.luetkemeyer.house.gov						
Luetzow Industries LLP						
1105 Davis Ave	South Milwaukee	WI	53172	414-762-0410	762-0943	604
Web: www.luetzowind.com						
Lufkin Daily News 300 Ellis Ave	Lufkin	TX	75904	936-632-6631	632-6655	532-2
Web: lufkindailynews.com						
Lufkin/Angelina County Chamber of Commerce						
1615 S Chestnut St	Lufkin	TX	75901	936-634-6644	634-8726	139
Web: lufkintexas.org						
Luhr Bros Inc						
250 W Sand Bank Rd PO Box 50	Columbia	IL	62236	618-281-4106	281-4288	188-5
Web: www.luhr.com						
Luhring Augustine Gallery						
531 W 24th St	New York	NY	10011	212-206-9100	206-9055	42
Web: www.luhringaugustine.com						
Luigi Vitrone's Pastabilities						
415 N Lincoln St	Wilmington	DE	19805	302-656-9822		671
Web: ljvpastabilities.com						
Luigi's 245 W Main Ave	Spokane	WA	99201	509-624-5226		671
Web: www.luigis-spokane.com						
Luigi's 947 S Tejon St	Colorado Springs	CO	80903	719-632-7339		671
Web: www.luigiscoloradosprings.com						
Luigi's 590 Broad St	Augusta	GA	30901	706-722-4056		671
Web: www.luigisinc.com						
Luigi's 2132 Davison Rd	Flint	MI	48506	810-234-9545		671
Web: www.luigissince1955.com						
Luigi's Italian Bistro						
2733 Mantiwoc Rd	Green Bay	WI	54311	920-468-4900		671
Web: www.luigisitalianbistromenu.com						
Luigi's Restaurant 1524 Valley Dr	Syracuse	NY	13207	315-492-9997		671
Web: luigisrestaurantinsyracuse.com						
Luitpold Pharmaceuticals Inc						
1 Luitpold Dr PO Box 9001	Shirley	NY	11967	631-924-4000	924-1731	584
TF: 800-645-1706 ■ *Web:* www.luitpold.com						
Lujan Ben R (Rep D - NM)						
2323 Rayburn House Office Bldg	Washington	DC	20515	202-225-6190		342-2
Web: www.lujan.house.gov						
Lukas Partners Inc 11915 P St Ste 100	Omaha	NE	68137	402-895-2552		636
Web: www.lukaspartners.com						
Luke AFB 14185 W Falcon St	Luke AFB	AZ	85309	623-856-6550		497-1
Web: www.luke.af.mil						
Luke Ortgessen Insurance Agency Inc						
5125 S Kipling Ste 207	Littleton	CO	80127	303-933-5333		390
Web: countryfinancial.com						
Luke Soules Acosta 2003 Rickety Ln Ste D	Tyler	TX	75703	903-561-4241		297-8
Lukins & Annis PS						
1600 WA Trust Financial Ctr 717 W Sprague Ave Ste 1600	Spokane	WA	99201	509-455-9555		428
Web: www.lukins.com						
Lula Westfield LLC						
451 LA 1005 PO Box 10	Paincourtville	LA	70391	985-369-6450	369-6139	296-38
Web: www.luwest.com						
Luling Independent School District						
212 E Bowie St	Luling	TX	78648	830-875-3191		685
Web: www.luling.txed.net						
Lumbee River Electric Membership Corp						
PO Box 830	Red Springs	NC	28377	910-843-4131	843-6422	245
TF: 800-683-5571 ■ *Web:* www.lumbeeriver.com						
Lumber Liquidators Inc						
1455 VFW Pkwy	West Roxbury	MA	02132	617-327-1222	750-7802*	290
**Fax Area Code:* 978 ■ *TF:* 800-227-0332 ■ *Web:* www.lumberliquidators.com						
Lumber One Avon Inc						
101 Second St NW PO Box 7	Avon	MN	56310	320-356-7342		186
Web: lumber-one.com						
Lumber River State Park						
2819 Princess Ann Rd	Orrum	NC	28369	910-628-4564		565
Web: www.ncparks.gov						
Lumber Specialties Ltd						
1700 Beltline Rd	Dyersville	IA	52040	563-875-2858		817
Web: www.lbrspec.com						
Lumberjack Building Centers						
3470 Pointe Tremble Rd	Algonac	MI	48001	810-794-4921		550
TF: 800-466-5164 ■ *Web:* www.lumber-jack.com						
Lumbermen's Merchandising Corp						
137 W Wayne Ave	Wayne	PA	19087	610-293-7000		191-3
TF: 800-218-0043 ■ *Web:* www.lmc.net						
Lumbermen's Underwriting Alliance (LUA)						
1905 NW Corporate Blvd Ste 110	Boca Raton	FL	33431	561-994-1900		391-4
TF: 800-327-0630 ■ *Web:* www.lumbermensunderwriting.com						
Lumberton Area Chamber of Commerce						
800 N Chestnut St	Lumberton	NC	28358	910-739-4750		139
Web: www.lumbertonchamber.com						
Lumberton Area Visitors Bureau						
3431 Lackey St	Lumberton	NC	28360	910-739-9999		206
TF: 800-359-6971 ■ *Web:* www.lumberton-nc.com						
Lumberton Correctional Institution						
75 Legend Rd	Lumberton	NC	28359	910-618-5574		213
Web: www.ncdps.gov						
Lumberton Honda Mitsubishi Inc						
301 Wintergreen Dr	Lumberton	NC	28358	910-739-9871		516
TF: 855-712-9438 ■ *Web:* www.lumbertonhonda.com						
Lumedx Corp 555 12th St Ste 2060	Oakland	CA	94607	800-966-0699	419-3699*	178-10
**Fax Area Code:* 510 ■ *TF:* 800-966-0699 ■ *Web:* www.lumedx.com						
Lumedyne Technologies Inc						
9275 Sky Park Ct	San Diego	CA	92123	858-560-5208		590
Lumen Legal 1025 N Campbell Rd	Royal Oak	MI	48067	248-597-0400	597-0410	721
TF: 877-933-1330 ■ *Web:* www.lumenlegal.com						
Lumen, The 6101 Hillcrest Ave	Dallas	TX	75205	214-219-2400	219-2402	379
TF: 800-908-1140 ■ *Web:* www.thelumendallas.com						
LumenAd 111 N Higgins Ave Ste 500	Missoula	MT	59802	406-552-1022		194
Web: lumenad.com						
Lumenera Corp 7 Capella Ct	Ottawa	ON	K2E8A7	613-736-4077		692
Web: www.lumenera.com						
Lumenis Ltd 2033 Gateway Pl Ste 200	San Jose	CA	95110	408-764-3000	764-3999	424
TF: 877-586-3647 ■ *Web:* www.lumenis.com						
Lumens Light & Living 2028 K St	Sacramento	CA	95811	916-444-5585		815
TF: 877-445-4486 ■ *Web:* www.lumens.com						
LumenVox LLC 3615 Kearny Villa Rd	San Diego	CA	92123	858-707-7700		177
Web: www.lumenvox.com						
Lumeta Corp 300 Atrium Dr Ste 302	Somerset	NJ	08873	732-357-3511		178-1
TF: 844-267-0864 ■ *Web:* www.lumeta.com						
Lumex Inc 290 E Helen Rd	Palatine	IL	60067	847-359-2790		253
Web: www.lumex.com						
Lumicor Inc 1400 Monster Rd SW	Renton	WA	98057	425-255-4000		610
Web: www.lumicor.com						
Lumiere 1293 Washington St	Newton	MA	02465	617-244-9199	796-9178	671
Web: lumiererestaurant.com						
Lumiere Place Casino & Hotels						
999 N 2nd St	Saint Louis	MO	63102	877-450-7711		132
TF: 877-450-7711 ■ *Web:* www.lumiereplace.com						
Lumina Foundation for Education						
30 S Meridian St Ste 700	Indianapolis	IN	46204	317-951-5300		305
TF: 800-834-5756 ■ *Web:* www.luminafoundation.org						
Lumina Power Inc 26 Ward Hill Ave	Bradford	MA	01835	978-241-8260		425
Web: luminapower.com						
Luminaire (Miami) Inc 8950 NW 33rd St	Miami	FL	33172	305-437-7975		321
Web: www.luminaire.com						
LuminaIt Energy Corp						
1320 Potrero Ave	San Francisco	CA	94110	415-641-4000		48-12
Web: luminalt.com						

Name / Address	City	State	ZIP	Phone	Fax	Class
Luminator 900 Klein Rd *TF:* 800-388-8205 ■ *Web:* www.luminator.com	Plano	TX	75074	972-424-6511	423-1540	438
Luminex Corp 12212 Technology Blvd. *NASDAQ: LMNX* ■ *TF:* 888-219-8020 ■ *Web:* www.luminexcorp.com	Austin	TX	78727	512-219-8020	219-5195	419
Luminex Software Inc 871 Marlborough Ave *TF:* 888-586-4639 ■ *Web:* www.luminex.com	Riverside	CA	92507	951-781-4100	781-4105	178-12
Luminit LLC 1850 W 205th St *Web:* www.luminitco.com	Torrance	CA	90501	310-320-1066		253
Luminite Products Corp 148 Commerce Dr *TF:* 888-545-2270 ■ *Web:* luminite.com	Bradford	PA	16701	814-817-1420		781
Lumisolution Inc 162 Av Du Sacre-Coeur *TF:* 800-463-6978 ■ *Web:* www.lumisolution.com	Quebec City	QC	G1N2W2	418-522-5693		361
Lumitex Inc 8443 Dow Cir *TF:* 800-969-5483 ■ *Web:* www.lumitex.com	Strongsville	OH	44136	440-600-3745	243-8402	729
Lumitron Inc 10503 Timberwood Cir Ste 120 *Web:* www.lumitron-ir.com	Louisville	KY	40223	502-423-7225		358
Lummus Corp 225 Bourne Blvd PO Box 929 *TF:* 800-458-6687 ■ *Web:* www.lummus.com	Savannah	GA	31408	912-447-9000	447-9250	744
Lummus Supply Co 1554 Bolton Rd NW *Web:* www.lummussupply.com	Atlanta	GA	30331	404-794-1501		191-2
Lumos & Associates Inc 308 N Curry St Ste 200 *TF:* 800-621-7155 ■ *Web:* www.lumosinc.com	Carson City	NV	89706	775-883-7077	883-7114	261
Lumos Networks 1 Lumos Plz *TF:* 800-320-6144 ■ *Web:* www.lumosnetworks.com	Waynesboro	VA	22980	800-320-6144		224
Lumpkin County 99 Courthouse Hill Ste A *Web:* www.lumpkincounty.gov	Dahlonega	GA	30533	706-864-3742	482-2697	338
Lums Pond State Park 1068 Howell School Rd *Web:* www.destateparks.com	Bear	DE	19701	302-368-6989	368-6971	565
Lumtron Technologies Inc 18014 Collins Rd *Web:* lumtron.com	Woodstock	IL	60098	815-788-0088		180
Lum-Yuen 3190 Portland Rd NE *Web:* lumyuensalem.com	Salem	OR	97303	503-581-2912	581-2903	671
Luna Community College 366 Luna Dr *TF:* 800-588-7232 ■ *Web:* luna.edu	Las Vegas	NM	87701	505-454-2500	454-2519	162
Luna County Broadcasting 1700 S Gold Ave *Web:* www.demingradio.com	Deming	NM	88031	575-546-9011	546-9342	645-141
Luna Garcia 201 San Juan Ave *Web:* www.lunagarcia.com	Venice	CA	90291	310-396-8026		730
Luna Maya 2010 Colley Ave & 21st St *Web:* www.lunamayarestaurant.com	Norfolk	VA	23517	757-622-6986		671
Luna Press PO Box 15511 Kenmore STA *Web:* www.thelunapress.com	Boston	MA	02215	617-327-8000		637-10
Luna Restaurant 5620 S Perry St *Web:* www.lunaspokane.com	Spokane	WA	99223	509-448-2383		671
Luna Vineyards Inc 2921 Silverado Trl *Web:* www.lunavineyards.com	Napa	CA	94558	707-255-5862		443
Lunan Corp 414 N Orleans St Ste 402 *Web:* www.lunancorp.com	Chicago	IL	60654	312-645-9898	646-0654	670
Lunar Cow 120 E Mill St Ste 415 *Web:* www.lunarcow.com	Akron	OH	44308	330-253-9000		180
Lunar Tool & Mold Inc 9860 York Alpha Dr *Web:* www.lunarmold.com	North Royalton	OH	44133	440-237-2141	237-8606	757
Lunarline Inc 3300 N Fairfax Dr Ste 308 *Web:* www.lunarline.com	Arlington	VA	22201	571-481-9300		225
Lunarpages Inc 1360 N Hancock St *Web:* lunarpages.com	Anaheim	CA	92807	714-521-8150		463
Lund Food Holdings Inc 4100 W 50th St *Web:* lundsandbyerlys.com	Edina	MN	55424	952-548-1400		345
Lund Industrial Group 400 E Industrial Park Rd *Web:* www.lundonline.com	Holly Springs	MS	38635	662-252-2340	252-3352	273
Lund International Holdings Inc 4325 Hamilton Mill Rd Ste 400 *TF:* 800-241-7219 ■ *Web:* www.lundinternational.com	Buford	GA	30519	800-241-7219		60
Lund's Fisheries Inc 997 Ocean Dr *Web:* www.lundsfish.com	Cape May	NJ	08204	609-884-7600	884-0664	285
Lunda Construction Company Inc 620 Gebhardt Rd PO Box 669 *Web:* www.lundaconstruction.com	Black River Falls	WI	54615	715-284-9491	284-9146	188-4
Lundbeck Canada Inc 2600 Alfred-Nobel Blvd Ste 400 *TF:* 800-586-2325 ■ *Web:* www.lundbeck.com	Saint-Laurent	QC	H4S0A9	514-844-8515	844-5495	85
Lundberg Family Farms 5370 Church St PO Box 369 *Web:* www.lundberg.com	Richvale	CA	95974	530-882-4551		296-4
Lundell Manufacturing Corp 2700 Ranchview Ln *Web:* www.lundellmfg.com	Plymouth	MN	55447	763-559-4114		326
Lundquist Consulting 111 Anza Blvd Ste 310 *Web:* www.lundquistconsulting.com	Burlingame	CA	94010	650-342-9486		196
Lundquist Institute, The 1124 W Carson St **Fax Area Code:* 310 ■ *Web:* lundquist.org	Torrance	CA	90502	424-201-3000	222-3640*	668
Lundylaw LLP 1635 Market St 19th Fl *Web:* lundylaw.com	Philadelphia	PA	19103	215-567-3000		41
Lunenburg Correctional Ctr 690 Falls Rd *Web:* vadoc.virginia.gov	Victoria	VA	23974	434-696-2045		213
Lunenburg County 11413 Courthouse Rd *Web:* www.lunenburgva.org	Lunenburg	VA	23952	434-696-2142		338
Lunseth Plumbing & Heating Co 1710 N Washington St *Web:* www.dakotafire.com	Grand Forks	ND	58203	701-772-6631		610
LUP (Lehigh University Press) Christmas-Saucon Hall 14 E Packer Ave *Web:* lupress.cas2.lehigh.edu	Bethlehem	PA	18015	610-758-3933		637-2
Lupa Osteria Romana 170 Thompson St *Web:* luparestaurant.com	New York	NY	10012	212-982-5089		671
Lupin Pharmaceuticals Inc 111 S Calvert St 21st Fl *TF:* 866-587-4617 ■ *Web:* www.lupinpharmaceuticals.com	Baltimore	MD	21202	866-587-4617	587-4627	238
Luppen & Hawley Inc 7400 14th Ave *Web:* www.luppenandhawleyinc.com	Sacramento	CA	95820	916-456-7831		610
Lupus Foundation of America Inc (LFA) 2000 L St NW Ste 410 *TF:* 800-558-0121 ■ *Web:* www.lupus.org	Washington	DC	20036	202-349-1155	349-1156	48-17
Lupus Research Alliance 275 Madison Ave 10th Fl *TF:* 800-867-1743 ■ *Web:* www.lupusresearch.org	New York	NY	10016	212-218-2840	218-2848	48-17
Luquire George Andrews Inc 4201 Congress St Ste 400 *Web:* thinklga.com	Charlotte	NC	28209	704-552-6565	552-1972	4
Luria Elaine (Rep D - VA) 534 Cannon House Office Bldg *Web:* www.luria.house.gov	Washington	DC	20515	202-225-4215		342-2
Lurleen B. Wallace Community College *Andalusia* 1000 Dannelly Blvd PO Box 1418 *Web:* www.lbwcc.edu	Andalusia	AL	36420	334-222-6591	881-2201	162
Lusardi Construction Company Inc 1570 Linda Vista Dr *Web:* www.lusardi.com	San Marcos	CA	92078	760-744-3133	744-9064	186
Luse Holdings Inc 3990 Enterprise Ct *TF:* 844-295-6709 ■ *Web:* www.luse.com	Aurora	IL	60504	630-862-2600	862-2674	189-9
Luseaux Laboratories Inc 16816 S Gramercy Pl *Web:* luseaux.com	Gardena	CA	90247	310-324-1555		151
Lush Group Inc 28 Narragansett Ave *Web:* lgisoftware.com	Jamestown	RI	02835	401-423-9111		41
Luso-Americano Newspaper 66 Union St *Web:* www.lusoamericano.com	Newark	NJ	07105	973-344-3200	344-4201	532-3
Luster Products Inc 1104 W 43rd St *TF:* 800-621-4255 ■ *Web:* www.lusterproducts.com	Chicago	IL	60609	773-579-1800	579-1912	214
Lutamar Electrical Assemblies Inc 8030 Ridgeway Ave *Web:* www.lutamar.com	Skokie	IL	60076	847-679-5400		625
Lutco Inc 677 Cambridge St *Web:* www.lutco.com	Worcester	MA	01610	508-756-6296	799-6848	75
Lute Plumbing Supply Inc 3920 US Hwy 23 *Web:* www.lutesupply.com	Portsmouth	OH	45662	740-353-7638		610
Luth Research Inc 1365 Fourth Ave *TF:* 800-465-5884 ■ *Web:* luthresearch.com	San Diego	CA	92101	800-465-5884		466
Luther Brookdale Chevrolet 6701 Brooklyn Blvd *Web:* www.brookdalechevrolet.com	Brooklyn Center	MN	55429	612-424-7337		516
Luther Burbank Home & Gardens 204 Santa Rosa Ave *Web:* www.lutherburbank.org	Santa Rosa	CA	95404	707-524-5445		97
Luther Burbank Savings 804 Fourth St *TF:* 888-205-6005 ■ *Web:* www.lutherburbanksavings.com	Santa Rosa	CA	95404	707-578-9216	581-2102	70
Luther College 700 College Dr *TF:* 800-458-8437 ■ *Web:* www.luther.edu	Decorah	IA	52101	563-387-2000	387-2159	166
Luther Consulting LLC 10435 Commerce Dr Ste 140 *TF:* 866-517-6570 ■ *Web:* lutherconsulting.com	Carmel	IN	46032	866-517-6570		196
Luther Luckett Correctional Complex Dawkins Rd PO Box 6 *TF:* 800-511-1670 ■ *Web:* www.corrections.ky.gov	LaGrange	KY	40031	502-222-0363	222-8112	213
Luther Manor 3131 Hillcrest Rd *Web:* www.luthermanor.com	Dubuque	IA	52001	563-588-1413		371
Luther Rice College & Seminary 3038 Evans Mill Rd *TF:* 800-442-1577 ■ *Web:* www.lutherrice.edu	Lithonia	GA	30038	800-442-1577		166
Luther Seminary 2481 Como Ave *TF:* 800-588-4373 ■ *Web:* www.luthersem.edu	Saint Paul	MN	55108	651-641-3456	641-3425	167-3
Lutheran Church Missouri Synod (LCMS) 1333 S Kirkwood Rd *TF:* 888-843-5267 ■ *Web:* www.lcms.org	Saint Louis	MO	63122	314-965-9000		48-20
Lutheran Church of Hope 925 Jordan Creek Pkwy *Web:* www.lutheranchurchofhope.org	West Des Moines	IA	50266	515-222-1520		48-20
Lutheran Community at Telford 12 Lutheran Home Dr *TF:* 877-343-7518 ■ *Web:* www.lctelford.org	Telford	PA	18969	215-723-9819	723-3623	672
Lutheran Home at Hollidaysburg, The 916 Hickory St *TF:* 800-400-2285 ■ *Web:* www.alsm.org	Hollidaysburg	PA	16648	814-696-4527		48-20
Lutheran Hospital of Indiana 7950 W Jefferson Blvd *TF:* 800-444-2001 ■ *Web:* www.lutheranhospital.com	Fort Wayne	IN	46804	260-435-7001		374-3
Lutheran Immigration & Refugee Service (LIRS) 700 Light St *Web:* www.lirs.org	Baltimore	MD	21230	410-230-2700	230-2890	48-5
Lutheran Life Villages 6701 S Anthony Blvd *Web:* www.lutheranlifevillages.org	Fort Wayne	IN	46816	260-557-1016	447-7369	672
Lutheran Metropolitan Ministry The Richard Sering Ctr 4515 Superior Ave **Fax Area Code:* 770 ■ *TF:* 800-917-2081 ■ *Web:* www.lutheranmetro.org	Cleveland	OH	44103	216-696-2715	396-3790*	48-20
Lutheran School of Theology at Chicago 1100 E 55th St *TF:* 800-635-1116 ■ *Web:* www.lstc.edu	Chicago	IL	60615	773-256-0700	256-0782	167-3
Lutheran SeniorLife 191 Scharberry Ln *Web:* www.lutheranseniorlife.org	Mars	PA	16046	724-776-1100		672
Lutheran Social Services 715 Falconer St *Web:* www.lutheran-jamestown.org	Jamestown	NY	14701	716-665-4905		450
Lutheran Social Services of Illinois 1001 E Touhy Ave Ste 50 *TF:* 888-671-0300 ■ *Web:* www.lssi.org	Des Plaines	IL	60018	847-635-4600		48-15

Phone | Fax | Class

Lutheran Theological Seminary
114 Seminary Crescent . . . Saskatoon SK S7N0X3 306-966-7850 966-7852 167-3
Web: www.usask.ca

Luthi Machinery Company Inc
1 Atlas Ave . . . Pueblo CO 81001 719-948-1110 948-4273 298
Web: www.luthi.com

Luthier's Mercantile International Inc (LMI)
7975 Cameron Dr Bldg 1600 . . . Windsor CA 95492 707-687-2020 687-2014 820
TF: 800-477-4437 ■ *Web:* www.lmii.com

Lutonix Inc 9409 Science Center Dr . . . New Hope MN 55428 763-445-2352 668

Lutron Electronics Company Inc
7200 Suter Rd . . . Coopersburg PA 18036 610-282-6280 282-6253 203
TF: 800-523-9466 ■ *Web:* www.lutron.com

Lutsen Resort 5700 W Hwy 61 PO Box 9 . . . Lutsen MN 55612 218-663-7212 669
TF: 800-258-8736 ■ *Web:* www.lutsenresort.com

Luttmann Precision Mold Inc
1200 W Lafayette St . . . Sturgis MI 49091 269-651-1193 604
Web: www.luttmannprecisionmold.com

Lutz & Carr 551 Fifth Ave Ste 400 . . . New York NY 10017 212-697-2299 2
Web: lutzandcarr.com

Lutz Frey Corp 1195 Ivy Dr . . . Lancaster PA 17601 717-898-6808 898-3578 189-10
TF: 800-280-6794 ■ *Web:* freylutz.com

Lutz, Daily & Brain LLC
6400 Glenwood St . . . Shawnee Mission KS 66202 913-831-0833 261
Web: www.ldbeng.com

Luurtsema Sales Inc
6672 Ctr Industrial Dr . . . Jenison MI 49428 616-669-9301 292
TF: 800-253-2052 ■ *Web:* www.luurtsema.com

Luv N' Care Ltd 3030 Aurora Ave . . . Monroe LA 71201 800-588-6227 258
TF: 800-588-6227 ■ *Web:* www.nuby.com

Luvata Appleton LLC 553 Carter Ct . . . Kimberly WI 54136 920-749-3820 749-3850 485
TF: 800-749-5510 ■ *Web:* www.luvata.com

Luverne Truck Equipment Inc
1200 Birch St . . . Brandon SD 57005 605-582-7200 60
Web: www.luvernetruck.com

Luverne Veterans Home
1300 N Kniss Ave . . . Luverne MN 56156 507-283-1100 793
Web: mn.gov

Lux Art Institute
1550 S El Camino Real . . . Encinitas CA 92024 760-436-6611 520
Web: www.luxartinstitute.org

Lux Bond & Green Inc
46 Lasalle Rd . . . West Hartford CT 06107 800-524-7336 521-8693* 410
*Fax Area Code: 860 ■ *TF:* 800-524-7336 ■ *Web:* www.lbgreen.com

Lux Scientiae Inc PO Box 326 . . . Westwood MA 02090 800-441-6612 809
TF: 800-441-6612 ■ *Web:* luxsci.com

Luxco 5050 Kemper Ave . . . Saint Louis MO 63139 314-772-2626 772-6021 81-3
Web: www.luxco.com

Luxe Bistro 47 York St . . . Ottawa ON K1N5S7 613-241-8805 671
Web: www.luxebistro.com

Luxe City Center Hotel
1020 S Figueroa St . . . Los Angeles CA 90015 213-748-1291 707
Web: luxecitycenter.com

Luxe Hotel Rodeo Drive
360 N Rodeo Dr . . . Beverly Hills CA 90210 310-273-0300 859-8730 379
Web: www.luxehotels.com

Luxe Travel Management Inc
16450 Bake Pkwy . . . Irvine CA 92618 949-336-1000 772
TF: 855-665-5900 ■ *Web:* www.luxetm.com

Luxembourg
Consulate General
1 Sansome St Ste 830 . . . San Francisco CA 94104 415-788-0816 788-0985 257
Web: www.sanfrancisco.mae.lu
Consulate General 17 Beekman Pl . . . New York NY 10022 212-888-6664 888-6116 257
Web: newyork-cg.mae.lu
Embassy 2200 Massachusetts Ave NW . . . Washington DC 20008 202-265-4171 328-8270 257
Web: www.washington.mae.lu

Luxfer Gas Cylinders
3016 Kansas Ave . . . Riverside CA 92507 951-684-5110 223
Web: www.luxfer.com

Luxo Corp 5 Westchester Plz . . . Elmsford NY 10523 914-345-0067 345-0068 439
TF: 800-222-5896 ■ *Web:* www.glamox.com

Luxon Printing Inc 375 Wegner Dr . . . West Chicago IL 60185 630-293-7710 627
Web: www.luxonprintinginc.com

Luxor Hotel 3900 Las Vegas Blvd S . . . Las Vegas NV 89119 702-262-4000 262-4404 133
TF: 800-288-1000 ■ *Web:* luxor.mgmresorts.com

Luxottica 5th Avenue Back & Forth . . . New York NY 10018 212-302-1200 253
Web: www.luxottica.com

Luxour 2245 Delany Rd . . . Waukegan IL 60087 847-244-1800 327-1698* 319-1
*Fax Area Code: 800 ■ *TF:* 800-323-4656 ■ *Web:* luxorfurn.com

Luxury Bath Technologies
1800 Industrial Dr . . . Libertyville IL 60048 800-263-9882 362
TF: 800-263-9882 ■ *Web:* www.luxurybath.com

Luxury Link LLC
5200 W Century Blvd Ste 410 . . . Los Angeles CA 90045 310-215-8060 772
TF: 888-297-3299 ■ *Web:* www.luxurylink.com

Luxury Retreats
5530 St Patrick St Ste 2210 . . . Montreal QC H4E1A8 877-993-0100 505
TF: 877-993-0100 ■ *Web:* www.luxuryretreats.com

Luzerne County 200 N River St . . . Wilkes-Barre PA 18711 570-825-1500 825-9343 338
Web: www.luzernecounty.org

Luzerne County Community College
1333 S Prospect St . . . Nanticoke PA 18634 800-377-5222 740-0238* 162
*Fax Area Code: 570 ■ *TF:* 800-377-5222 ■ *Web:* www.luzerne.edu

Luzerne Optical Laboratories Ltd
180 N Wilkes Barre Blvd . . . Wilkes-Barre PA 18702 570-822-3183 237
Web: www.luzerneoptical.com

Luzo Maxi Market 115 Church St . . . New Bedford MA 02746 508-999-1771 997-8357 297-8
TF: 800-225-8169 ■ *Web:* www.luzo.com

LVCTA (Lehigh Valley Cooperative Telephone Assn)
9090 Taylor Rd . . . Lehigh IA 50557 515-359-2211 224
Web: www.lvcta.net

LVM Systems Inc 4262 E Florian Ave . . . Mesa AZ 85206 480-633-8200 892-7016 177
Web: www.lvmsystems.com

LW Bills Co 7-9 Park St . . . Georgetown MA 01833 978-352-6660 352-6639 392
TF: 800-892-0275 ■ *Web:* www.lwbills.com

LW Rozzo Inc 17200 Pines Blvd . . . Pembroke Pines FL 33029 954-435-8501 436-6243 503-6

LWBJ
4200 University Ave Ste 410 . . . West Des Moines IA 50266 515-222-5680 222-5681 463
Web: lwbj.com

LWDH (Lake of the Woods District Hospital)
21 Sylvan St . . . Kenora ON P9N3W7 807-468-9861 468-3939 374-2
Web: www.lwdh.on.ca

LWI (Liberty Woods International Inc)
1903 Wright Pl Ste 360 . . . Carlsbad CA 92008 760-438-8030 438-8018 191-3
TF: 800-367-7054 ■ *Web:* www.libertywoods.com

LWISD (Lake Worth Independent School District)
6805 Telephone Rd . . . Lake Worth TX 76135 817-306-4200 237-2583 685
Web: www.lwisd.org

LWRC International LLC
815 Chesapeake Dr . . . Cambridge MD 21613 410-901-1348 807
Web: www.lwrci.com

LWS (Laminated Wood Systems Inc)
1327 285th Rd PO Box 386 . . . Seward NE 68434 800-949-3526 643-4374* 817
*Fax Area Code: 402 ■ *TF:* 800-949-3526 ■ *Web:* www.lwsinc.com

LWV (League of Women Voters)
1730 M St NW Ste 1000 . . . Washington DC 20036 202-429-1965 429-0854 48-7
Web: www.lwv.org

LWV (League of Women Voters of Metropolitan Tulsa)
3336 E 32nd St Ste 4 . . . Tulsa OK 74135 918-747-7933 48-13
Web: www.lwvtulsa.org

LWVMN (League of Women Voters Minnesota)
550 Rice St . . . Saint Paul MN 55103 651-224-5445 637-2
Web: www.lwvmn.org

LWVNYS (League of Women Voters of New York State)
62 Grand St . . . Albany NY 12207 518-465-4162 465-0812 615
Web: www.lwvny.org

LWVOEF (League of Women Voters of Ohio Education Fund)
17 S High St Ste 650 . . . Columbus OH 43215 614-469-1505 469-7918 637-2
TF: 800-598-6446 ■ *Web:* www.lwvohio.org

LXE Inc 125 Technology Pkwy . . . Norcross GA 30092 770-447-4224 447-4405 173-2
TF: 800-664-4593 ■ *Web:* www.honeywellaidc.com

Lyceum History Museum 301 King St . . . Alexandria VA 22314 703-838-4994 838-4997 520
Web: www.alexandriava.gov

Lyceum Kennedy French & American School
1 Cross Rd . . . Ardsley NY 10502 914-479-0722 479-0280 196
Web: lyceumkennedy.org

Lycian Stage Lighting
1144 Kings Hwy PO Box D . . . Sugar Loaf NY 10981 845-469-2285 469-5355 722
Web: www.lycian.com

Lyco Manufacturing Inc
115 Commercial Dr . . . Columbus WI 53925 920-623-4152 623-3780 697
Web: lycomfg.com

Lyco Wausau Inc 1574 Hillcrest Rd . . . Phillips WI 54555 715-845-7867 842-8228 172
Web: www.lycowausau.com

Lycoming College 700 College Pl . . . Williamsport PA 17701 570-321-4000 321-4317 166
TF: 800-345-3920 ■ *Web:* www.lycoming.edu

Lycoming Engines 652 Oliver St . . . Williamsport PA 17701 570-323-6181 529
TF: 800-258-3279 ■ *Web:* www.lycoming.com

LycoRed 377 Crane St . . . Orange NJ 07050 877-592-6733 882-0323* 479
*Fax Area Code: 973 ■ *TF:* 877-592-6733 ■ *Web:* www.lycored.com

Lycos Inc 52 Second Ave . . . Waltham MA 02451 781-370-2700 370-2991 397
Web: www.lycos.com

Lydall Inc 1 Colonial Rd . . . Manchester CT 06042 860-646-1233 646-4917 561
NYSE: LDL ■ *TF:* 800-463-8929 ■ *Web:* www.lydall.com

Lydall Thermal/Acoustical Inc
1241 Buck Shoals Rd . . . Hamptonville NC 27020 336-468-8522 468-8555 745-6
Web: www.lydallautomotive.com

Lyden Oil Company Inc
30692 Tracy Rd . . . Walbridge OH 43465 419-666-1948 579
TF: 800-362-9410 ■ *Web:* www.lydenoilcompany.com

Lydig Construction Inc
11001 E Montgomery St . . . Spokane WA 99206 509-534-0451 535-6622 186
Web: www.lydig.com

Lykes Cartage Company Inc
8606 Wall St Bldg 19 . . . Austin TX 78754 512-933-9060 314
Web: lykescartage.com

Lylab Technology Solutions Inc
526 Cumberland St . . . Lebanon PA 17042 717-279-8595 196
Web: www.lylab.net

Lyle B. Masnikoff and Associates PA
1645 Palm Beach Lakes Blvd Ste 550 . . . West Palm Beach FL 33401 561-598-7120 598-7127 41
TF: 877-817-4127 ■ *Web:* workerscompfl.net

Lyle Co
3140 Gold Camp Dr Ste 30 . . . Rancho Cordova CA 95670 916-266-7000 196
Web: www.lyleco.com

Lyles Diversified Inc 1210 W Olive Ave . . . Fresno CA 93728 559-441-1900 188-3
Web: www.lylesgroup.com

Lyles-De Grazier Co
2050 N Stemmons Fwy Ste 7943 . . . Dallas TX 75207 214-747-3558 411
Web: www.lylesjewelry.com

Lyman & Nielsen LLC
900 Oakmont Ln Ste 308 . . . Westmont IL 60559 630-575-0020 590-5042 41
Web: lymannielsen.com

Lyman Allyn Art Museum
625 Williams St . . . New London CT 06320 860-443-2545 442-1280 520
Web: www.lymanallyn.org

Lyman Lumber Co 520 Third St Ste 200 . . . Excelsior MN 55331 952-470-3600 470-3670 191-3
Web: www.lymanlumber.com

Lyman Museum & Mission House
276 Haili St . . . Hilo HI 96720 808-935-5021 969-7685 520
Web: www.lymanmuseum.org

Lyman Products Corp 475 Smith St . . . Middletown CT 06457 860-632-2020 284
TF: 800-225-9626 ■ *Web:* www.lymanproducts.com

Lyman-Richey Corp 2625 S 158th Pl . . . Omaha NE 68130 402-558-2727 557-3810 191-1
Web: www.lymanrichey.com

Lymba Corp 901 Waterfall Way Bldg 5 . . . Richardson TX 75080 972-680-0800 177
Web: www.lymba.com

Lyme Academy College of Fine Arts
84 Lyme St . . . Old Lyme CT 06371 860-434-5232 166
TF: 800-342-5864 ■ *Web:* www.newhaven.edu

Lymphoma Research Foundation (LRF)
115 Broadway Ste 1301 . . . New York NY 10006 212-349-2910 349-2886 48-17
TF: 800-500-9976 ■ *Web:* www.lymphoma.org

Name / Address	City	State	ZIP	Phone	Fax	Class
Lyna Manufacturing Inc 1125 15th St W *TF:* 800-993-4007 ■ *Web:* tirelyna.com	North Vancouver	BC	V7P1M7	604-990-0988		754
Lynair Inc 3515 Scheele Dr *Web:* www.lynair.com	Jackson	MI	49202	517-787-2240	787-4521	223
Lynbrook Glass & Architectural Metals Corp 941 Motor Pkwy *Web:* www.lynbrookglass.com	Hauppauge	NY	11788	631-582-3060	582-3974	189-6
Lynch & Karcich LLC 1000 White Horse Rd Ste 703 *Web:* lkylaw.com	Voorhees	NJ	08043	856-309-0200		41
Lynch Ford Chevrolet 410 Hwy 30 SW *Web:* www.lynchfordchevrolet.com	Mount Vernon	IA	52314	319-895-8500		57
Lynch Livestock Co 331 Third St NW *TF:* 800-468-3178 ■ *Web:* www.lynchlivestock.com	Waucoma	IA	52171	563-776-3311		446
Lynch Management Co 2165 River Blvd	Jacksonville	FL	32204	904-387-1537		57
Lynch Metals Inc 1075 Lousons Rd *TF:* 888-272-9464 ■ *Web:* lynchmetals.com	Union	NJ	07083	908-686-8401		791
Lynch Oil Company Inc 1244 E Carroll St *Web:* lynchoil.com	Kissimmee	FL	34744	407-847-5111		316
Lynch Stephen F (Rep D - MA) 2109 Rayburn House Office Bldg *Web:* lynch.house.gov	Washington	DC	20515	202-225-8273	225-3984	342-2
Lynch, Traub, Keefe & Errante A Professional Corp 52 Trumbull St *TF:* 888-692-7403 ■ *Web:* www.ltke.com	New Haven	CT	06510	203-787-0275		428
Lynch, Traub, Keefe & Errante PC 52 Trumbull St PO Box 1612 *Web:* ltke.com	New Haven	CT	06510	203-800-7343		41
Lynchburg College 1501 Lakeside Dr *TF:* 800-426-8101 ■ *Web:* www.lynchburg.edu	Lynchburg	VA	24501	434-544-8100	544-8653	166
Lynchburg Health & Rehabilitation Ctr 5615 Seminole Ave *Web:* www.mfa.net	Lynchburg	VA	24502	434-239-2657		450
Lynchburg Public Library 2315 Memorial Ave *Web:* www.lynchburgpubliclibrary.org	Lynchburg	VA	24501	434-455-6300		434-3
Lynchburg Regional Chamber of Commerce 2015 Memorial Ave *Web:* www.lynchburgregion.org	Lynchburg	VA	24501	434-845-5966	522-9592	139
Lynchburg Steel & Specialty Co 275 Francis Ave *Web:* lynchburgsteel.com	Monroe	VA	24574	434-929-0951	929-2613	723
Lynches River Electric Co-opeartive Inc 1104 W McGregor St *TF:* 800-922-3486 ■ *Web:* www.lynchesriver.com	Pageland	SC	29728	843-672-6111	672-6118	245
Lynchval Systems Worldwide Inc 13921 Park Center Rd Ste 100 *Web:* www.lynchval.com	Herndon	VA	20171	703-709-1000	709-8704	463
Lynco Flange & Fitting Inc 5114 Steadmont Dr *TF:* 800-749-5539 ■ *Web:* www.lyncoflange.com	Houston	TX	77040	713-690-0040		61
Lyncole Grounding 3547 Voyager St Ste 204 *TF:* 800-962-2610 ■ *Web:* www.lyncole.com	Torrance	CA	90503	310-214-4000	214-1114	261
Lyndacom Inc 6410 Via Real *TF:* 888-335-9632 ■ *Web:* www.lynda.com	Carpinteria	CA	93013	805-477-3900		194
Lyndale Plant Services (DDI) 301 W 92nd St *Web:* www.lyndaleplants.com	Bloomington	MN	55420	952-345-8240		293
Lynden Door Inc 2077 Main St *Web:* www.lyndendoor.com	Lynden	WA	98264	360-354-5676		499
Lynden Inc 18000 International Blvd Ste 800 *TF:* 888-596-3361 ■ *Web:* www.lynden.com	Seattle	WA	98188	206-241-8778	243-8415	311
Lynden Tribune 113 Sixth St *Web:* www.lyndentribune.com	Lynden	WA	98264	360-354-4444	354-4445	5
Lynde-Ordway Company Inc 5402 Commercial Dr *Web:* www.lynde-ordway.com	Huntington Beach	CA	92649	714-957-1311	433-2166	111
Lyndhurst 635 S Broadway *Web:* lyndhurst.org	Tarrytown	NY	10591	914-631-4481		50-3
Lyndhurst Foundation 517 E Fifth St *Web:* www.lyndhurstfoundation.org	Chattanooga	TN	37403	423-756-0767		305
Lyndon B. Johnson National Historical Park 100 Lady Bird Ln *Web:* www.nps.gov	Johnson City	TX	78636	830-868-7128		564
Lyndon B. Johnson School of Public Affairs Sid Richardson Hall Unit 3 2300 Red River St Stop E2700 *Web:* lbj.utexas.edu	Austin	TX	78712	512-471-3200		166
Lyndon B. Johnson State Park & Historic Site 199 Park Rd 52 *Web:* tpwd.texas.gov	Stonewall	TX	78671	830-644-2252		565
Lyndon Baines Johnson Memorial Grove on the Potomac Turkey Run Pk George Washington Memorial Pkwy *Web:* www.nps.gov	McLean	VA	22101	703-289-2500	289-2598	564
Lyndon Campus 1001 College Rd *TF:* 800-225-1998 ■ *Web:* www.northernvermont.edu	Lyndonville	VT	05851	802-626-6413	626-6335	166
Lyndon Group LLC 220 Newport Center Dr Ste 11-529 *Web:* www.lyndon-group.com	Newport Beach	CA	92660	949-494-7722		466
Lyndon State Bank 817 Topeka Ave *Web:* lyndonstatebank.com	Lyndon	KS	66451	785-828-4411		70
Lyndon Steel Co 1947 Union Cross Rd *Web:* www.lyndonsteel.com	Winston-Salem	NC	27107	336-785-0848		480
Lyndon Veterinary Clinic PLLC 6867 E Genesee St *Web:* lyndonvet.com	Fayetteville	NY	13066	315-445-8170		794
Lyne, Woodworth & Evarts LLP 600 Atlantic Ave Ste 2500 2nd Fl *Web:* lwelaw.com	Boston	MA	02109	617-523-6655		41
Lyn-Flex West Inc 405 Red Oak Rd PO Box 570 *Web:* www.lynflex.com	Owensville	MO	65066	573-437-4125	437-2350	301
Lyniate 3010 Gaylord Pkwy Ste 320 *Web:* www.lyniate.com	Frisco	TX	75034	214-618-7000	618-7002	177
Lynn A. Sylvester CPA PA 675 S Haywood St *Web:* www.lascpa-nc.com	Waynesville	NC	28786	828-456-6505	456-6569	2
Lynn Blueprint & Supply Company Inc 328 Old Vine St *Web:* www.lynnimaging.com	Lexington	KY	40507	859-255-1021		627
Lynn County PO Box 937 *Web:* www.co.lynn.tx.us	Tahoka	TX	79373	806-561-4750	561-4988	338
Lynn Electronics Corp 154 Railroad Dr *TF:* 800-624-2220 ■ *Web:* www.lynnelec.com	Ivyland	PA	18974	215-355-8200		253
Lynn Ladder & Scaffolding Company Inc 20 Boston St *TF:* 800-225-2510 ■ *Web:* www.lynnladder.com	Lynn	MA	01904	781-598-6010	593-2915	421
Lynn Law office PC 102 S Wabash St *Web:* lynnandstein.net	Wabash	IN	46992	260-563-8020		41
Lynn Layton Chevrolet Inc 2416 Hwy 31 S *TF:* 866-917-9502 ■ *Web:* www.lynnlaytonchevrolet.com	Decatur	AL	35601	256-274-4665		57
Lynn Manufacturing Inc 15 Marion St *Web:* www.lynnmfg.com	Lynn	MA	01905	781-593-2500	596-0430	201
Lynn Meadows Discovery Ctr 246 Dolan Ave *Web:* www.lmdc.org	Gulfport	MS	39507	228-897-6039	248-0071	521
Lynn Products Inc 2645 W 237th St *Web:* lynnprod.com	Torrance	CA	90505	310-530-5966	530-8426	814
Lynn University 3601 N Military Trl *TF:* 800-888-5966 ■ *Web:* www.lynn.edu	Boca Raton	FL	33431	561-237-7900	237-7100	166
Lynn Veterinary Hospital Inc 2111 East 900 South *Web:* lynnvet.com	Lynn	IN	47355	765-874-1777		794
Lynn Water & Sewer Commission 400 Parkland Ave *Web:* www.lynnwatersewer.org	Lynn	MA	01905	781-596-2400		192
Lynn Wood & Associates Inc 1228 Camellia Blvd Ste D *Web:* docdollar.com	LaFayette	LA	70508	337-989-2685		690
Lynn's Steakhouse 955 Dairy Ashford *Web:* www.lynnssteakhouse.com	Houston	TX	77079	281-870-0807	870-0888	671
LynnCo Supply Chain Solutions 2448 E 81st St Ste 2600 *TF:* 866-872-3264 ■ *Web:* lynnco.com	Tulsa	OK	74137	866-872-3264		314
Lynnhaven House 2040 Potters Rd *Web:* www.virginiabeachhistory.org	Virginia Beach	VA	23454	757-491-3490		50-3
Lynnhaven Mall 701 Lynnhaven Pkwy *Web:* www.lynnhavenmall.com	Virginia Beach	VA	23452	757-340-9340		460
Lynntech Inc 2501 Earl Rudder Fwy S Ste 100 *Web:* lynntech.com	College Station	TX	77845	979-764-2200		201
Lynnwood Co 8840 Elder Creek Rd Unit A *Web:* www.lynnwoodco.com	Sacramento	CA	95828	916-381-0293	381-4031	328
Lynnwood Convention Ctr 3711 196th St SW *Web:* www.lynnwoodcc.com	Lynnwood	WA	98036	425-778-7155		184
Lyntegar Electric Co-opeartive Inc PO Box 970 *TF:* 877-218-2308 ■ *Web:* lyntegar.coop	Tahoka	TX	79373	806-561-4588		245
Lynx Brand Fence Products 4330 76 Ave SE *TF:* 800-665-5969 ■ *Web:* www.lynxfence.com	Calgary	AB	T2C2J2	403-273-4821		191-1
Lynx Collaborative Care Network PO Box 2370 *Web:* lynxcare.net	Denver	CO	80201	303-670-5969		194
Lynx Computer Technologies Inc 7 Bristol Ct *TF:* 800-331-5969 ■ *Web:* lynxnet.com	Wyomissing	PA	19610	610-678-8131		180
Lynx Enterprises Inc 724B E Grantline Rd *Web:* lynxenterprises.com	Tracy	CA	95304	209-833-3400	833-3512	697
Lynx Equity Ltd 692 Queen St E Ste 205 *Web:* www.lynxequity.com	Toronto	ON	M4M1G9	416-323-3512		528
Lynx Grills Inc 5895 Rickenbacker Rd *TF:* 888-289-5969 ■ *Web:* www.lynxgrills.com	Commerce	CA	90040	323-838-1770		362
Lynx Group Inc 2746 Front St NE *Web:* www.lynxgroup.com	Salem	OR	97301	503-588-9339		627
Lynx House Press PO Box 940 *Web:* www.lynxhousepress.org	Spokane	WA	99210	509-624-4894		637-2
Lynx Media Inc 12501 Chandler Blvd Ste 202 *TF:* 800-451-5969 ■ *Web:* lynxmedia.com	Valley Village	CA	91607	818-761-5859		177
Lynx Software Technologies Inc 855 Embedded Way *TF:* 800-255-5969 ■ *Web:* www.lynx.com	San Jose	CA	95138	408-979-3900	979-3920	178-10
Lynx Studio Technology Inc 1048 Irvine Ave *Web:* www.lynxstudio.com	Newport Beach	CA	92660	949-515-8265		526
Lyon & Billard Co, The 38 Gypsy Ln *Web:* www.lyon-billard.com	Meriden	CT	06451	203-235-4487		191-3
Lyon & Healy Harps Inc 168 N Ogden Ave *TF:* 800-621-3881 ■ *Web:* lyonhealy.com	Chicago	IL	60607	312-786-1881	226-1502	527
Lyon Advertising 600 Escarpment Blvd 745 28 *Web:* www.lyonadvertising.com	Austin	TX	78749	512-480-5966		7
Lyon College 2300 Highland Rd *TF:* 800-423-2542 ■ *Web:* www.lyon.edu	Batesville	AR	72501	870-793-9813		166
Lyon County 27 S Main St *Web:* www.lyon-county.org	Yerington	NV	89447	775-577-5005	577-5200	338
Lyon County 430 Commercial St *Web:* www.lyoncounty.org	Emporia	KS	66801	620-341-4380		338

Phone | Fax | Class

Lyon County 607 W Main St. Marshall MN 56258 507-537-6722 537-6091 338
Web: www.lyonco.org

Lyon County 206 S Second Ave Rock Rapids IA 51246 712-472-8530 338
Web: www.lyoncountyiowa.com

Lyon Rural Electric Co-op
116 S Marshall St. Rock Rapids IA 51246 712-472-2506 245
TF: 800-658-3976 ■ *Web:* www.lyonrec.coop

Lyon Shipyard Inc PO Box 2180 Norfolk VA 23501 757-622-4661 698
Web: lyonshipyard.com

Lyon Veterinary Clinic
21188 Pontiac Trl South Lyon MI 48178 248-486-5600 794
Web: lyonveterinaryclinic.com

Lyon Work Space Products
420 N Main St Montgomery IL 60538 630-892-8941 892-8966 286
TF: 800-433-8488 ■ *Web:* www.lyonworkspace.com

Lyon's Mirror-Sun PO Box 59 Lyons NE 68038 402-685-5624 532-2
Web: www.enterprisepub.com

Lyondellbasell Industries Inc
1221 McKinney St Lyondellbasell Tower
Ste 700 Houston TX 77010 713-309-7200 604-3835* 787
**Fax Area Code:* 281 ■ *TF:* 800-525-7516 ■ *Web:* www.lyondellbasell.com

Lyon-Lincoln Electric Co-opeartive Inc (LLEC)
205 W Hwy 14 PO Box 639 Tyler MN 56178 507-247-5505 245
Web: www.llec.coop

Lyons & Lyons Attorneys at Law
8310 Princeton Glendale Rd West Chester OH 45069 513-777-2222 428
Web: www.lyonsandlyonslaw.com

Lyons Company Inc 308 Samson St Glasgow KY 42141 270-651-2733 697
Web: www.lyonscompany.com

Lyons Doughty & Veldhuis PC
15 Ashley Pl Ste 2b Wilmington DE 19804 302-428-1670 445
TF: 888-322-3922 ■ *Web:* www.ldvlaw.com

Lyons Magnus Inc 3158 E Hamilton Ave. Fresno CA 93702 800-344-7130 233-8249* 296-20
**Fax Area Code:* 559 ■ *TF:* 800-344-7130 ■ *Web:* www.lyonsmagnus.com

Lyons School District 103
4100 Joliet Ave. Lyons IL 60534 708-783-4100 780-9725 685
Web: www.sd103.com

Lyons Tool & Die Company Inc, The
185 Research Pkwy. Meriden CT 06450 203-238-2689 237-8769 697
TF: 800-422-9363 ■ *Web:* www.lyons.com

LyonsHR 201 S Court St Ste 700 Florence AL 35630 256-767-5900 767-7798 260
Web: www.lyonshr.com

Lyric Optical Company Wholsle
3533 Cardiff Ave. Cincinnati OH 45209 513-321-2456 544
TF: 800-543-7376 ■ *Web:* www.superoptical.com

Lyric Theatre of Oklahoma
1727 NW 16th St Oklahoma City OK 73106 405-524-9312 524-9316 573-4
Web: www.lyrictheatreokc.com

Lyster Army Health Clinic
Andrews Ave. Fort Rucker AL 36362 800-261-7193 374-4
TF: 800-261-7193 ■ *Web:* www.lyster.amedd.army.mil

Lytica Inc 308 Legget Dr Ste 200 Kanata ON K2K1Y6 613-271-1414 463
Web: www.lytica.com

Lytle Land & Cattle Co
1150 E S 11th St. Abilene TX 79604 325-677-1925 671
Web: www.lytlelandandcattle.com

Lytles Redwood Empire Beauty College
186 Wikiup Dr Santa Rosa CA 95403 707-545-8490 545-7258 167-3
Web: www.lytlesrebc.edu

LZ Truck Equipment Inc
1881 Rice St. Saint Paul MN 55113 651-488-2571 488-9857 516
TF: 800-247-1082 ■ *Web:* www.lztruckequipment.com

M

Phone | Fax | Class

M & A Advisor LLC, The
108-18 Queens Blvd 2nd Fl Forest Hills NY 11375 718-997-7900 557
Web: www.maadvisor.com

M & A Supply Company Inc
1540 Amherst Rd Knoxville TN 37909 865-584-0510 612
TF: 800-264-0820 ■ *Web:* www.masupplycompany.com

M & A Technology Inc
2045 Chenault Dr. Carrollton TX 75006 972-490-5803 174
TF: 800-225-1452 ■ *Web:* www.macomp.com

M & B Carriers Inc
16183 E Whittier Blvd. Whittier CA 90603 562-902-0161 311
Web: mbcarriers.com

M & C Saatchi LA Inc
2032-2034 Broadway Santa Monica CA 90404 310-401-6070 7
Web: mcsaatchi-la.com

M & C Specialties Co 90 James Way. Southampton PA 18966 215-322-1600 322-1620 732
TF: 800-441-6996 ■ *Web:* www.mcspecialties.com

M & G Graphics 3500 W 38th St. Chicago IL 60632 773-247-1596 627
Web: m-g-graphics.com

M & G Industries Inc
85 Broadcommon Rd Bristol RI 02809 401-253-0096 492
Web: www.m-gind.com

M & H Enterprises Inc
19450 Hwy 249 Ste 600 Houston TX 77070 281-664-7222 261
Web: mhes.com

M & H Plastics Inc 485 Brooke Rd. Winchester VA 22603 540-504-0030 504-0040 358
Web: mhplastics.com

M & I Machine Inc 5040 M 63 N Coloma MI 49038 269-849-3624 849-3626 385
Web: www.shotendtooling.com

M & J Materials Inc
7561 Gadsden Hwy. Trussville AL 35173 205-655-7451 480

M & J Transportation
3536 Nicholson Ave. Kansas City MO 64120 816-231-6733 231-7645 449
TF: 866-298-3858 ■ *Web:* www.mjtransportationkc.com

M & K CPAs PLLC
363 N Sam Houston Pkwy E Ste 650 Houston TX 77060 832-242-9950 242-9956 2
TF: 866-770-5931 ■ *Web:* www.mkacpas.com

M & L Industries Inc 1210 St Charles St Houma LA 70360 985-876-2280 872-9596 385
TF: 800-969-0068 ■ *Web:* mlind.net

Phone | Fax | Class

M & I Professional Services Inc
7667 N Ave. Lemon Grove CA 91945 619-469-1604 104
Web: www.mlproclean.com

M & L Transit Systems Inc
60 Olympia Ave. Woburn MA 01801 781-938-8646 108
Web: mltsi.com

M & L Worldwide Logistics 1 Revere Pk. Rome NY 13440 315-339-2550 339-0978 780
TF: 800-756-1331 ■ *Web:* www.mltrucking.com

M & M Designs Inc
1981 Quality Blvd. Huntsville TX 77320 800-627-0656 295-9286* 687
**Fax Area Code:* 936 ■ *TF:* 800-627-0656 ■ *Web:* www.m-mdesigns.com

M & M Industries Inc
316 Corporate Pl Chattanooga TN 37419 423-821-3302 596
Web: ultimatepail.com

M & M Innovations
7424 Blythe Island Hwy Brunswick GA 31523 912-265-7110 228
TF: 800-688-3384 ■ *Web:* www.drgeorges.com

M & M Manufacturing Co
4001 Mark IV Pkwy. Fort Worth TX 76106 817-336-2311 625-0756 697
Web: www.mmmfg.com

M & M Meat Shops Ltd
2240 Argentia Rd Ste 100. Mississauga ON L5N2K7 905-465-6325 336
TF: 800-461-0171 ■ *Web:* www.mmfoodmarket.com

M & M Pipeline Services LLC
274 Mt Moriah Rd Eupora MS 39744 662-258-7101 539
Web: www.mmpipeline.com

M & M Refrigeration Inc
412 Railroad Ave. Federalsburg MD 21632 410-754-8005 610
Web: www.mmrefrigeration.com

M & M Sales & Equipment
2639 Kermit Hwy Odessa TX 79763 800-592-4516 385
TF: 800-592-4516 ■ *Web:* www.mandmsales.net

M & M Sales Co, The 2529 E Main St Columbus OH 43209 614-231-8510 535
Web: mmsalesco.com

M & M Supply Co
901 Peach Ave PO Box 548 Duncan OK 73534 580-252-7879 252-7708 537
Web: www.mmsupply.com

M & M Transport Inc 170 St Hwy 508 Chehalis WA 98532 360-262-9383 780
Web: www.mandmtransport.com

M & M Transport Services Inc
21 Mcgrath Hwy Ste 204 Quincy MA 02169 617-769-9370 311
Web: mmtransport.com

M & P Export Management Corp
2329 Hwy 34 Manasquan NJ 08736 732-223-0160 223-6745 195
Web: www.mpexport.com

M & Q Plastic Products Inc
Earl St PO Box 180 Schuylkill Haven PA 17972 570-385-4991 385-4954 604
Web: www.mqplastics.com

M & R Consultants Corp
700 Technology Park Dr Ste 203 Billerica MA 01821 781-273-5050 177
Web: mrccsolutions.com

M & R Cos 440 Medinah Rd Roselle IL 60172 630-858-6101 858-6134 627
TF: 800-736-6431 ■ *Web:* www.mrprint.com

M & T Bank 345 Main St Buffalo NY 14203 716-842-4470 70
NYSE: MTB ■ *TF:* 800-724-2440 ■ *Web:* locations.mtb.com

M & W Transportation Company Inc
1110 Pumping Sta Rd. Nashville TN 37210 615-256-5755 393
TF: 800-251-4209 ■ *Web:* www.mwlginc.com

M & Z Carpets Inc 325 Arch St. Carlisle PA 17013 717-249-2904 290
Web: mzcarpet.com

M at Miranova 2 Miranova PL Ste 100 Columbus OH 43215 614-629-0000 221-5020 671
Web: www.matmiranova.com

M B Klein Inc
243-A Cockeysville Rd Cockeysville MD 21030 888-872-4675 761
TF: 888-872-4675 ■ *Web:* www.modeltrainstuff.com

M Block & Sons Inc
5020 W 73rd St Bedford Park IL 60638 866-654-7936 728-0022* 361
**Fax Area Code:* 708 ■ *TF:* 800-621-8845 ■ *Web:* www.mblock.com

M Booth 666 Third Ave 7th Fl. New York NY 10017 212-481-7000 636
Web: www.mbooth.com

M Box Design 9234 Deering Ave Chatsworth CA 91311 818-700-7770 180
Web: www.mboxdesign.com

M Braun Inc 14 Marin Way Stratham NH 03885 603-773-9333 773-0008 419
Web: www.mbraun.com

M C Electronics Inc 1891 Airway Dr Hollister CA 95023 831-637-1651 45
Web: mcelectronics.com

M C Steel Inc
2 Braco International Blvd. Wilder KY 41076 859-781-8600 492
Web: www.mcsteel.com

M Conley Co 1312 Fourth St SE. Canton OH 44707 330-456-8243 588-2572 559
TF: 800-362-6001 ■ *Web:* www.mconley.com

M Corp 947 Enterprise Dr Loft C Sacramento CA 95825 916-254-0355 463
Web: www.the-mcorp.com

M Davis & Sons Inc 19 Germay Dr. Wilmington DE 19804 302-998-3385 610
Web: www.mdavisinc.com

M Ecker & Co 9525 W Bryn Mawr Ave Rosemont IL 60018 847-994-6000 233-9715 189-9

M G America Inc 31 Kulick Rd Fairfield NJ 07004 973-808-8185 358
Web: www.mgamerica.com

M G Credit 5115 San Juan Ave. Jacksonville FL 32210 904-387-6503 160
Web: www.mgcredit.com

M Gibson Hotels Group
409 Montbrook Ln Knoxville TN 37919 865-539-0588 378
Web: www.mgibsonhotels.com

M Gingerich Gereaux & Assoc (MG2A)
240 N Industrial Dr. Bradley IL 60915 815-939-4921 261
Web: www.mg2a.com

M Gottfried Roofing Inc
89 Research Dr. Stamford CT 06906 203-323-8173 189-12
Web: www.mgottfried.com

M Group Consulting LLC 2 Lyon Pl White Plains NY 10601 914-644-9200 466
Web: www.mmjllp.com

M Group Inc
187 S Old Woodward Ste 200. Birmingham MI 48009 248-540-8843 540-8846 360-3
Web: www.mgroupinc.com

M Holland 400 Skokie Blvd Ste 600 Northbrook IL 60062 800-872-7370 603
TF: 800-872-7370 ■ *Web:* www.mholland.com

M J Engineering & Land Surveying
1533 Crescent Rd. Clifton Park NY 12065 518-371-0799 261
Web: mjels.com

Phone | Fax | Class

M J M Laundry Inc
5388 Hidden Steam Dr Lewisville NC 27023 336-671-9596 671
M J Nicholls Landscaping Inc
77 Gridley St Quincy MA 02169 617-471-0555 422
Web: nichollslandscaping.com
M K & Assoc
5360 Cascade Rd SE Lower Level Grand Rapids MI 49546 616-532-5006 180
Web: mkassoc.com
M K Products Inc 16882 Armstrong Ave Irvine CA 92606 949-863-1234 474-1428 811
TF: 800-787-9707 ■ *Web:* www.mkprod.com
M K Smith Chevrolet 12845 Central Ave Chino CA 91710 909-628-8961 628-6637 516
Web: www.mksmithchevrolet.com
M K Specialty Metal Fabricators
725 W Wintergreen Rd Hutchins TX 75141 972-225-6562 697
TF: 866-814-4617 ■ *Web:* www.mkspecialty.com
M L S Data Management Solutions
6115 Camp Bowie Blvd Ste 200 Fort Worth TX 76116 817-989-3800 463
Web: www.mlsc.com
M Lee Smith Publishers LLC
PO Box 5094 Brentwood TN 37024 615-373-7517 627
Web: www.mleesmith.com
M Lipsitz & Company Inc 100 Elm St Waco TX 76704 254-756-6661 752-0175 686
Web: www.mlipsitzco.com
M N S Ltd 766 Pohukaina St Honolulu HI 96813 808-591-2550 237
Web: www.abcstores.com
M Neils Engineering Inc
100 Howe Ave Sacramento CA 95825 916-923-4400 261
Web: mneilsengineering.com
M P A General Contractors
4320 Rand Ln Sacramento CA 95864 916-768-1835 283-6915 186
Web: www.mpallen.com
M R L Equipment Company Inc
PO Box 31154 Billings MT 59107 406-869-9900 896-8880 358
TF: 877-788-2907 ■ *Web:* www.markritelines.com
M Ramsey King Securities Inc
93 Tomlin Cir Burr Ridge IL 60527 630-789-0607 690
Web: mramseyking.com
M Resort LLC, The
12300 Las Vegas Blvd S Henderson NV 89044 702-797-1000 133
TF: 877-673-7678 ■ *Web:* www.themresort.com
M Robzen Inc 734 Milford Dr Kingston PA 18704 570-283-1226 331-4522 473
TF: 800-833-7808 ■ *Web:* robzenmeats.com
M Rondano Inc 49 E Ave Norwalk CT 06851 203-846-1577 846-9564 189-5
Web: www.rondano.com
M S Benbow & Associates Professional Engineering Corp
2450 Severn Ave Metairie LA 70001 504-832-2000 261
Web: www.msbenbow.com
M Squared Engineering LLC
W62n215 Washington Ave Cedarburg WI 53012 262-376-4246 261
Web: www.msquaredengineering.com
M Steinert & Sons Co 1 Columbus Ave Boston MA 02116 617-426-1900 526
TF: 877-343-0662 ■ *Web:* www.msteinert.com
M Tm Molded Products 3370 Obco Ct Dayton OH 45414 937-890-7461 361
Web: www.mtmcase-gard.com
M W Consulting Engineers LLC
222 Wall St Ste 200 Spokane WA 99201 509-838-9020 838-1123 261
Web: www.mwengineers.com
M Waterfront Grille
4300 Gulf Shore Blvd N Naples FL 34103 239-263-4421 671
Web: mwaterfrontgrille.com
M. Brown & Associates Ltd
2728 Forgue Dr Ste 100 Naperville IL 60564 630-637-8600 637-8606 390
Web: mbrownltd.com
M. C. Machine Company Inc 98 Mill St Hopedale MA 01747 508-473-3642 473-1290 350
Web: www.mcmachineinc.com
M. C. Petty & Company Inc
PO Box 1218 Hempstead TX 77445 713-223-0111 225-2644 401
Web: liquidityresources.com
M. D. M. Commercial Enterprises Inc
1102 A1a N Ste 205 Ponte Vedra Beach FL 32082 800-359-6741 241-3133* 38
**Fax Area Code:* 904 ■ *TF:* 800-359-6741 ■ *Web:* www.mdmcommercial.com
M. Gervich & Sons Inc
901 E Nevada St Marshalltown IA 50158 641-753-3359 753-3340 492
TF: 800-622-8833 ■ *Web:* www.gervich.com
M. L. Bath Company Ltd
610 Market St Shreveport LA 71101 318-221-7141 425-7117 627
Web: www.mlbath.com
M. P. Industries Inc 4939 Profit Dr Tyler TX 75707 903-561-4232 581-8823 677
Web: www.mpioiltool.com
M.A. Bongiovanni Inc PO Box 147 Syracuse NY 13205 315-475-9937 475-3620 188-10
Web: www.mabinc.net
M.B. Kahn Construction Company Inc
101 Flintlake Rd Columbia SC 29223 803-736-2950 186
Web: www.mbkahn.com
M.D. On-Line Inc 6 Century Dr Parsippany NJ 07054 973-734-9900 734-9910 178-1
TF: 888-460-4310 ■ *Web:* www.mdon-line.com
M.D. Solutions Inc
7922 Veterans Pkwy Columbus GA 31909 706-323-6201 180
Web: mdsolutions.com
M.E. Wilson Company Inc 300 W Platt St Tampa FL 33606 813-229-8021 229-2795 390
TF: 888-229-8021 ■ *Web:* www.mewilson.com
M.E.K. Interiors & Floors Inc
5510 Brittmoore Rd Houston TX 77041 281-598-6001 290
Web: mekfloors.com
M.G. Newell Corp 301 Citation Ct Greensboro NC 27409 336-393-0100 358
TF: 800-334-0231 ■ *Web:* www.mgnewell.com
M.G.I. USA Inc 3143 Skyway Cir Melbourne FL 32934 321-751-6755 751-6777 173-1
Web: www.mgi-fr.com
M.G.S. Manufacturing Inc 122 Otis St Rome NY 13441 315-337-3350 337-4502 494
Web: www.mgshall.com
M.H. Equipment Co
2001 E Hartman Rd Chillicothe IL 61523 309-579-8020 579-2510 358
TF: 877-884-8465 ■ *Web:* mhfleet.com
M.I.B. Chock LLC 1048 24th St Santa Monica CA 90403 310-829-1612 194
Web: www.mibchock.com
M.J. Harris Construction Services LLC
1 Riverchase Rdg Birmingham AL 35244 205-380-6800 380-6801 186
Web: www.mjharris.com

M.K. Chambers Co
2251 Johnson Mill Rd North Branch MI 48461 810-688-3750 688-1909 621
Web: www.mkchambers.com
M.L. Roberts Inc 8 Industrial Ln Johnston RI 02919 401-421-0600 273-4970 411
Web: www.mlroberts.com
M.R. Danielson Advertising
1464 Summit Ave Saint Paul MN 55105 651-324-5078 4
Web: www.mrdan.com
M.R. Williams Inc 235 Raleigh Rd Henderson NC 27536 252-438-8104 438-2117 345
TF: 800-733-8104 ■ *Web:* www.mrwilliams.com
M/A/R/C Research 1660 Westridge Cir Irving TX 75038 972-983-0400 983-0444 466
TF: 800-884-6272 ■ *Web:* www.marcresearch.com
M/A-COM Technology Solutions Inc
100 Chelmsford St Lowell MA 01851 978-656-2500 696
TF: 800-366-2266 ■ *Web:* www.macom.com
M/E Engineering PC 300 Trolley Blvd Rochester NY 14606 585-288-5590 288-0233 261
Web: www.meengineering.com
M/I Homes Inc 3 Easton Oval Columbus OH 43219 614-418-8000 418-8080 653
NYSE: MHO ■ *Web:* www.mihomes.com
M1 Networks Inc 6019 Mcpherson Rd Ste 4 Laredo TX 78041 956-718-1005 723-0460 175
Web: m1networks.net
M-13 Construction Inc
775 W 1200 N Ste 100 Springville UT 84663 801-489-3215 480
Web: www.m-13.com
M2 Antenna Systems Inc
4402 N Selland Ave Fresno CA 93722 559-432-8873 253
Web: www.m2inc.com
M2 Global Inc 5714 Epsilon San Antonio TX 78249 210-561-4800 561-4852 697
Web: www.m2global.com
M2 Logistics Inc 2701 Executive Dr Green Bay WI 54304 920-569-8800 463
TF: 800-391-5121 ■ *Web:* www.m2logistics.com
M2 Technology Inc
21702 Hardy Oak Ste 100 San Antonio TX 78258 210-566-3773 566-3993 178-1
TF: 800-267-1760 ■ *Web:* www.m2ti.com
M2Gen 10902 N McKinley Dr Tampa FL 33612 813-745-4261 416
Web: www.m2gen.com
M2M Data Corp
345 Inverness Dr S Ste C-320 Englewood CO 80112 303-768-0064 799-8828 177
Web: www.m2mdatacorp.com
M2M Datasmart Inc
31915 Rancho California Rd Ste 200-336 Temecula CA 92591 951-514-9792 802-6784* 387
**Fax Area Code:* 888 ■ *Web:* www.m2mdatasmart.com
M2M Strategies
33 Buford Village Way Ste 329 Buford GA 30519 678-835-9080 466
TF: 800-345-1070 ■ *Web:* www.m2mstrategies.com
M2ns Inc 6037 Frantz Rd Ste 103 Dublin OH 43017 614-798-5177 180
Web: www.m2ns.com
M2S Inc 12 Commerce Ave West Lebanon NH 03784 603-298-5509 298-5055 177
Web: www.m2s.com
M2SYS LLC
1050 Crown Pointe Pkwy Ste 850 Atlanta GA 30338 770-393-0986 400
Web: www.m2sys.com
M3 Capital Partners
150 S Wacker Dr 31st Fl Chicago IL 60606 312-499-8500 691
Web: www.m3cp.com
M3 Engineering & Technology Corp
2051 W Sunset Rd Tucson AZ 85704 520-293-1488 261
Web: m3eng.com
M3 Technology Inc 58 Sawgrass Dr Bellport NY 11713 631-205-0005 179
Web: m3-tec.com
M3 USA Corp
501 Office Center Dr Ste 410 Fort Washington PA 19034 202-293-2288 395
Web: usa.m3.com
M45 Marketing Services Inc
524 W Stephenson St Ste 100 Freeport IL 61032 815-232-2121 195
Web: www.m45.com
M5 Marketing Communications Inc
42 O'Leary Ave Saint John NL A1B4B7 709-753-5559 5
Web: m5.ca
M-5 Steel Manufacturing Inc
1450 Mirasol St Los Angeles CA 90023 323-263-9383 480
Web: www.m5steel.com
MA (Marble Arms) 420 Industrial Pk Dr Gladstone MI 49837 906-428-3710 710
Web: www.marblearms.com
MA (Monico Alloys Inc)
3039 Ana St Rancho Dominguez CA 90221 310-928-0168 928-0179 686
Web: www.monicoalloys.com
MA Angeliades Inc
5-44 47th Ave Long Island City NY 11101 718-786-5555 786-4700 186
Web: www.ma-angeliades.com
MA Engineers Inc
5160 Carroll Canyon Rd Ste 200 San Diego CA 92121 858-200-0030 261
Web: www.ma-engr.com
MA Gedney Co 2100 Stoughton Ave Chaska MN 55318 952-448-2612 448-1790 296-19
TF: 888-244-0653 ■ *Web:* www.gedneyfoods.com
MA Industries Inc
303 Dividend Dr Peachtree City GA 30269 770-487-7761 487-1482 596
TF: 800-241-8250 ■ *Web:* www.maind.com
MA Laboratories Inc
2075 N Capitol Ave San Jose CA 95132 408-941-0808 941-0909 174
TF: 855-962-5227 ■ *Web:* www.malabs.com
MA Mortenson Co 700 Meadow Ln N Minneapolis MN 55422 763-522-2100 186
Web: www.mortenson.com
MA Ogg Heating & Air Conditioning Inc
4721 Arrow Hwy Ste B Montclair CA 91763 909-624-8608 624-9326 189-10
Web: www.airconditioningcontractorca.com
MA Patout & Son Ltd
3512 J Patout Burns Rd Jeanerette LA 70544 337-276-4592 276-4247 296-38
Web: www.mapatout.com
MAA (MAAC) 6584 Poplar Ave Memphis TN 38138 866-620-1130 682-6667* 655
NYSE: MAA ■ **Fax Area Code:* 901 ■ *TF:* 866-620-1130 ■ *Web:* www.maac.com
MAA (Mathematical Association of America)
1529 18th St NW Washington DC 20036 202-387-5200 265-2384 49-19
TF: 800-331-1622 ■ *Web:* www.maa.org
MAAC (MAA) 6584 Poplar Ave Memphis TN 38138 866-620-1130 682-6667* 655
NYSE: MAA ■ **Fax Area Code:* 901 ■ *TF:* 866-620-1130 ■ *Web:* www.maac.com
MAAC Machinery Corp
590 Tower Blvd Carol Stream IL 60188 630-665-1700 111
TF: 800-588-6222 ■ *Web:* maacmachinery.com

Name / Address	City	State	ZIP	Phone	Fax	Class
Maaco LLC 8765 Jefferson Hwy Ste 700 *TF:* 800-523-1180 ■ *Web:* www.maaco.com	Charlotte	NC	28202	800-523-1180		62-4
Maahs & Vanlahr PC 3911 Old Lee Hwy Ste 43E *Web:* www.mandvcpa.com	Fairfax	VA	22030	703-691-8632	691-0363	734
Maas Bros Construction Company Inc 410 Water Tower Ct *Web:* www.maasbros.com	Watertown	WI	53094	920-261-1682		186
Maas-Hansen Steel 2435 E 37th St PO Box 58364 *Web:* www.maashansen.com	Vernon	CA	90058	323-583-6321	586-0171	492
Maas-Rowe Carillons Inc 2255 Meyers Ave **Fax Area Code: 760* ■ *TF:* 800-854-2023 ■ *Web:* www.maasrowe.com	Escondido	CA	92029	800-854-2023	747-2677*	527
Maax Corp 160 St Joseph Blvd *TF:* 888-957-7816 ■ *Web:* www.maax.com	Lachine	QC	H8S2L3	877-438-6229		610
Maax Spas Industries Corp 25605 S Arizona Ave *Web:* www.maaxspas.com	Chandler	AZ	85248	480-895-0598		610
MAB (MAB Community Services) 200 Ivy St *Web:* www.mabcommunity.org	Brookline	MA	02446	617-738-5110	738-1247	48-6
MAB Community Services (MAB) 200 Ivy St *Web:* www.mabcommunity.org	Brookline	MA	02446	617-738-5110	738-1247	48-6
Mabbett & Associates Inc 5 Alfred Cir *Web:* www.mabbett.com	Bedford	MA	01730	781-275-6050		256
Mabe Trucking Company Inc 1603 Mill Ave *Web:* www.mabetrucking.com	Eden	NC	27288	336-635-1793	635-1791	780
Mabel Bassett Correctional Ctr 29501 Kickapoo Rd *Web:* doc.ok.gov	McLoud	OK	74851	405-964-3020		213
Mabiles Corner Pharmacy 100 Gulf St *Web:* pioneer.rxlocal.com	Coushatta	LA	71019	318-932-5727	932-5630	237
Mabry House 1540 Irving Pl	Shreveport	LA	71101	318-227-1121		671
Mabuchi Motor America Corp 3001 W Big Beaver Rd Ste 328 *Web:* www.mabuchi-motor.co.jp	Troy	MI	48084	248-816-3100	816-3242	518
MabVax Therapeutics Inc 11535 Sorrento Valley Rd Ste 400 *Web:* www.mabvax.com	San Diego	CA	92121	858-259-9405		231
MAC (Monongalia Arts Ctr) 107 High St PO Box 239 *Web:* www.monartscenter.com	Morgantown	WV	26507	304-292-3325	292-3326	50-2
MAC (Macarthur Associated Consultants LLC) 25 NW 146th St *Web:* www.macokc.com	Edmond	OK	73013	405-848-2471		261
MAC (Minority Alliance Capital) 6960 Orchard Lake Rd Ste 306 *Web:* www.mac-leasing.com	West Bloomfield	MI	48322	248-855-8746	539-1397	69
MAC Cal Co 1737 Junction Ave *Web:* www.maccal.com	San Jose	CA	95112	408-452-4803	441-1440	697
MAC Federal Credit Union 541 Tenth Ave *TF:* 877-883-1253 ■ *Web:* macfcu.org	Fairbanks	AK	99701	907-456-1253		219
MAC Habee Office Environments 6435 Sunset Corporate Dr *Web:* www.machabee.com	Las Vegas	NV	89120	702-263-8800	263-8801	112
MAC Haik Chevrolet Inc 11711 Katy Fwy *Web:* www.machaikchevy.com	Houston	TX	77079	218-596-6290		57
MAC Haik Ford Inc 10333 Katy Fwy *TF:* 866-746-8950 ■ *Web:* www.machaikford.com	Houston	TX	77024	866-746-8950		57
MAC Haik Ford Jackson 6130 I-55 N *Web:* www.machaikfordjackson.com	Jackson	MS	39211	601-956-7000		57
MAC Machine & Metal Works Inc 100 N Grand Ave *TF:* 888-227-8919 ■ *Web:* www.mmmw.com	Connersville	IN	47331	888-227-8919		757
MAC Machine Company Inc 7209 Rutherford Rd *Web:* www.macmachine.com	Baltimore	MD	21244	410-944-6171		454
MAC Metal Products of Wisconsin Inc W190 N11225 Carnegie Dr *Web:* www.macmetal.com	Germantown	WI	53022	262-251-4890	251-0979	567
MAC Metal Sales Inc 1650 W Hwy 80 *Web:* www.macmetalsales.com	Somerset	KY	42503	606-678-8331		492
MAC Paper Supply Inc 9622 S Ridge Rd *TF:* 800-486-5783 ■ *Web:* www.macpaper.com	Sedgwick	KS	67135	316-772-0311		534
MAC Papers 3300 Phillips Hwy PO Box 5369 *TF:* 800-622-2968 ■ *Web:* www.macpapers.com	Jacksonville	FL	32207	904-348-3300		553
MAC Pizza Management 12633 State Hwy 30 *Web:* www.macpizzamgmt.com	College Station	TX	77802	979-695-9912		194
MAC Products Inc 60 Pennsylvania Ave *Web:* www.macproducts.net	Kearny	NJ	07032	973-344-0700	344-5368	203
MAC Tools Inc 505 N Cleveland Ave *TF:* 800-622-8665 ■ *Web:* www.mactools.com	Westerville	OH	43082	614-755-7000		758
MAC Trailer Manufacturing Inc 14599 Commerce St NE *TF:* 800-795-8454 ■ *Web:* www.mactrailer.com	Alliance	OH	44601	330-823-9900	823-0232	779
MAC Valves Inc 30569 Beck Rd *TF:* 800-622-8587 ■ *Web:* www.macvalves.com	Wixom	MI	48393	248-624-7700	624-0549	789
MAC's Antique Auto Parts 6150 Donner Rd *TF:* 800-828-1051 ■ *Web:* www.macsautoparts.com	Lockport	NY	14094	716-210-1340	210-1370	61
Mac's Convenience Stores Inc 305 Milner Ave Ste 400 4th Fl *TF:* 800-268-5574 ■ *Web:* www.macs.ca	Toronto	ON	M1B3V4	416-291-4441	291-4947	204
Macabe Associates Inc, The 110 Union St Ste 310 *Web:* www.macabe.com	Seattle	WA	98101	206-382-0924		809
Macadam Capital Partners 3 Centerpointe Dri Ste 290 *Web:* macadamcapital.com	Lake Oswego	OR	97035	503-225-0889	225-0009	194
Macadamian Technologies Inc 165 Rue Wellington *TF:* 877-779-6336 ■ *Web:* www.macadamian.com	Gatineau	QC	J8X2J3	819-772-0300		463
Macalegin Electronics LLC 800 Stockton Ave Unit 1 *Web:* macaleginelectronics.com	Fort Collins	CO	80524	307-399-6642		366
Macalester College 1600 Grand Ave *TF:* 800-231-7974 ■ *Web:* www.macalester.edu	Saint Paul	MN	55105	651-696-6357	696-6724	166
MacAllister Machinery Company Inc 7515 E 30th St *TF:* 800-382-1896 ■ *Web:* www.macallister.com	Indianapolis	IN	46219	317-545-2151	860-3310	358
Macally USA Mace Group Inc 4601 E Airport Dr *Web:* www.macally.com	Ontario	CA	91761	909-230-6888	230-6889	173-1
Macaluso's 1747 Alton Rd *Web:* macalusosmiami.com	Miami Beach	FL	33139	305-604-1811		671
MacAndrews & Forbes Holdings Inc 35 E 62nd St *Web:* www.macandrewsandforbes.com	New York	NY	10065	212-572-8600		185
Macaroni Joe's 1619 S Kentucky St Ste 1500-D *Web:* www.macaronijoes.com	Amarillo	TX	79102	806-358-8990		671
Macaroni's 9315 Old Bustleton Ave *Web:* www.macaronis.net	Philadelphia	PA	19115	215-464-3040		671
Macarthur Associated Consultants LLC (MAC) 25 NW 146th St *Web:* www.macokc.com	Edmond	OK	73013	405-848-2471		261
MacArthur Co 2400 Wycliff St *TF:* 800-777-7507 ■ *Web:* www.macarthurco.com	Saint Paul	MN	55114	651-646-2773		191-4
MacArthur Ctr 300 Monticello Ave *Web:* www.shopmacarthur.com	Norfolk	VA	23510	757-627-6000		460
MacArthur Memorial Museum, The 198 Bank St *Web:* macarthurmemorial.org	Norfolk	VA	23510	757-441-2965	441-5389	520
MacArthur Museum of Arkansas Military History 503 E Ninth St *Web:* www.littlerock.gov	Little Rock	AR	72202	501-376-4602	376-4593	520
Macatawa Bank Corp 10753 Macatawa Dr PO Box 3119 *NASDAQ: MCBC* ■ *TF:* 877-820-2265 ■ *Web:* www.macatawabank.com	Holland	MI	49424	616-820-1444	494-7644	360-2
Macaulay-Brown Inc 4021 Executive Dr *TF:* 800-432-3421 ■ *Web:* careers.macb.com	Dayton	OH	45430	937-426-3421	426-5364	261
Macayo Mexican Restaurants 12637 S 48th St *Web:* www.macayo.com	Phoenix	AZ	85044	480-598-5101		670
MacBride Museum 1124 First Ave *Web:* www.macbridemuseum.com	Whitehorse	YT	Y1A1A4	867-667-2709	633-6607	520
MACC (Murray Area Chamber of Commerce) 5250 S Commerce Dr Ste 180 *Web:* murraychamber.org	Murray	UT	84107	801-263-2632	263-8262	139
MacCabe Electric Conductors Inc 426 Stump Rd PO Box 590 *Web:* www.maccabeelectric.com	Montgomeryville	PA	18936	215-368-9420	368-9220	470
Maccabee 211 N First St Ste 425 *Web:* maccabee.com	Minneapolis	MN	55401	612-337-0087		636
Maccabi USA/Sports for Israel 1926 Arch St Ste 4R *Web:* www.maccabiusa.com	Philadelphia	PA	19103	215-561-6900	561-5470	48-22
Macco Law Group LLP 2950 Express Dr S Ste 109 *Web:* www.maccolaw.com	Islandia	NY	11749	631-479-2869		41
MacConnell & Associates PC PO Box 129 *Web:* www.macconnellandassoc.com	Morrisville	NC	27560	919-467-1239	319-6510	194
Maccorkle Lavender PLLC 300 Summers St Ste 800 *Web:* mlclaw.com	Charleston	WV	25301	304-344-5600		41
MacCormac College 29 E Madison St *TF:* 800-621-7740 ■ *Web:* maccormac.edu	Chicago	IL	60602	312-922-1884	922-4286	800
MacCurrach Golf Construction Inc 3501 Faye Rd *Web:* www.maccurrachgolf.com	Jacksonville	FL	32226	904-646-1581		188-3
Macdac Engineering 27 Quality Ave *Web:* macdac.com	Somers	CT	06071	860-749-5544	749-5373	177
Macdaniel E. Reynolds PC 3220 Southwest First Ave Ste 200 *Web:* reynoldsdefensefirm.com	Portland	OR	97239	503-223-3422		41
MacDermid Inc 245 Freight St *Web:* www.macdermid.com	Waterbury	CT	06702	203-575-5700		145
MacDon Industries Ltd 680 Moray St *Web:* www.macdon.com	Winnipeg	MB	R3J3S3	204-885-5590	832-7749	273
Macdonald Campus of McGill University 21111 Lakeshore Rd Laird Hall Rm 107 *Web:* www.mcgill.ca	Sainte Anne de Bellevue	QC	H9X3V9	514-398-7773	398-7953	800
Macdonald Devin PC 3800 Renaissance Tower 1201 Elm St *Web:* www.macdonalddevin.com	Dallas	TX	75270	214-744-3300	747-0942	428
MacDonald Garber Broadcasting Inc c/o Kerry Davis Sales Manager / General Manager 2095 US 131 *Web:* www.macdonaldgarberbroadcasting.com	Petoskey	MI	49770	231-347-8713	347-9920	647
Macdonald Realty 203 5188 Wminster Hwy *TF:* 877-278-3888 ■ *Web:* macrealty.com	Richmond	BC	V7C5S7	604-279-9822		652
MacDonald-Bedford LLC 2900 Main St Ste 200 *TF:* 877-521-4020 ■ *Web:* macdonaldbedford.com	Alameda	CA	94501	510-521-4020		186
MacDonald-Miller Facility Solutions Inc 7717 Detroit Ave SE *TF:* 800-962-5979 ■ *Web:* www.macmiller.com	Seattle	WA	98106	206-763-9400		189-10
MacDougall Correctional Institution 1153 E St S *Web:* portal.ct.gov	Suffield	CT	06080	860-627-2100	627-2144	213
MacDougall Correctional Institution 1516 Old Gilliard Rd *Web:* doc.sc.gov	Ridgeville	SC	29472	843-871-0741		213
MacDuffie School 66 School St *Web:* macduffie.org	Granby	MA	01033	413-255-0000		622

Company	Phone	Fax	Class
Mace Security International Inc 240 Gibraltar Rd Ste 220 . . . . Horsham PA 19044 *OTC: MACE* ■ *Web:* corp.mace.com	267-317-4009		692
Macedonia Brook State Park 159 Macedonia Brook Rd . . . . Kent CT 06757 *Web:* portal.ct.gov	860-927-4100		565
Macedonian Tribune Museum 124 W Wayne St Ste 204 . . . . Fort Wayne IN 46802 *Web:* www.macedonian.org	260-422-5900	422-1348	520
MacElree Harvey Ltd 17 W Miner St . . . . West Chester PA 19382 *Web:* www.macelree.com	610-436-0100		428
Macera & Jarzyna LLP 1200-427 Laurier Ave W. . . . . Ottawa ON K1R7Y2 *TF:* 800-379-6668 ■ *Web:* moffatco.com	613-238-8173		428
Macerich Co, The 401 Wilshire Blvd Ste 700 . . . . Santa Monica CA 90401 *NYSE: MAC* ■ *Web:* www.macerich.com	310-394-6000	395-2791	655
MacEwan College 10700 104 Ave NW. . . . . Edmonton AB T5J4S2 *TF:* 888-497-4622 ■ *Web:* www.macewan.ca	888-497-4622		162
MacEwan University PO Box 1796 . . . . Edmonton AB T5J2P2 *Web:* www.macewan.ca	780-497-5040	497-5001	800
MacEwen Petroleum Inc 18 Adelaide St PO Box 100. . . . . Maxville ON K0C1T0 *TF:* 800-267-7175 ■ *Web:* macewen.ca	800-267-7175		579
Macey's Inc 7850 S 1300 E. . . . . Sandy UT 84094 *Web:* www.maceys.com	801-255-4888		345
MacFarms of Hawaii LLC 89-406 Mamalahoa Hwy. . . . . Captain Cook HI 96704 *Web:* www.macfarms.com	808-328-2435		10-10
MACFS (Mid-America College of Funeral Science) 3111 Hamburg Pk. . . . . Jeffersonville IN 47130 *Web:* www.mid-america.edu	812-288-8878	288-5942	800
Mach Industrial Group 6119 Fulton St . . . . Houston TX 77022 *Web:* www.machindustrialgroup.com	713-695-6000		595
Machaon Diagnostics Inc 3023 Summit St . . . . Oakland CA 94609 *TF:* 800-566-3462 ■ *Web:* www.machaondiagnostics.com	510-839-5600		418
MaCher Inc 1518 Abbot Kinney Blvd . . . . Venice CA 90291 *Web:* www.macher.com	310-581-5222		636
Machias Savings Bank PO Box 318 . . . . Machias ME 04654 *TF:* 800-982-7179 ■ *Web:* www.machiassavings.bank	207-255-3347		70
Machine and Process Design Inc 820 Mckinley St . . . . Anoka MN 55303 *TF:* 877-224-0653 ■ *Web:* www.mpd-inc.com	763-427-9991		261
Machine Center Inc 4344 Bridgeton Indus Dr . . . . Bridgeton MO 63044 *Web:* www.machinecenter.com	314-739-3181	739-5367	454
Machine Maintenance Inc 2300 Cassens Dr . . . . Fenton MO 63026 *TF:* 800-325-3322 ■ *Web:* www.lubyequipment.com	636-343-9970		190
Machine Products Corp 5660 Webster St. . . . . Dayton OH 45414 *Web:* www.mpcdayton.com	937-890-6600	890-1916	454
Machine Service Inc 1000 Ashwaubenon St . . . . Green Bay WI 54304 *TF:* 800-677-8711 ■ *Web:* www.machineservice.com	920-339-3000	339-3001	61
Machine Shop Service Inc 202 Venture Blvd . . . . Houma LA 70360 *Web:* www.msshouma.com	985-876-6630		454
Machine Specialties Inc (MSI) 6511 Franz Warner Pkwy . . . . Whitsett NC 27377 *Web:* www.machspec.com	336-603-1919	603-1921	621
Machine Specialty & Manufacturing Inc 215 Rousseau Rd . . . . Youngsville LA 70592 *TF:* 800-256-1292 ■ *Web:* www.msmmfg.com	337-837-0020	837-0062	483
Machine Tool Engineering Inc 2916 Hwy 18 . . . . Charles City IA 50616 *Web:* www.gomte.com	641-228-4524		454
Machined Metals Manufacturing Inc 1450 Jarvis Ave . . . . Elk Grove Village IL 60007 *Web:* machinedmetalsmfg.com	847-364-6116	364-6134	454
Machined Products Co 82 Pitney Rd. . . . . Lancaster PA 17602 *Web:* www.mpco.net	717-299-3757	299-3750	455
Machinery & Equipment Company Inc 3401 Bayshore Blvd . . . . Brisbane CA 94005 *TF:* 800-227-4544 ■ *Web:* www.machineryandequipment.com	415-467-3400		358
Machinery Dealers National Assn (MDNA) 315 S Patrick St . . . . Alexandria VA 22314 *TF:* 800-872-7807 ■ *Web:* www.mdna.org	703-836-9300	836-9303	49-18
Machinery Movers & Erectors 1622 Commerce Rd . . . . Richmond VA 23224 *Web:* machmovers.com	804-271-5125	271-6836	311
Machinery Sales Co 17253 Chestnut St . . . . City of Industry CA 91748 *TF:* 800-588-8111 ■ *Web:* www.mchysales.com	626-581-9211	581-9277	385
Machinery Sales Company Inc 120 Webster Ave. . . . . Memphis TN 38126 *TF:* 800-932-8376 ■ *Web:* machinery-sales.com	901-527-8671	526-2339	821
Machinery Systems Inc 614 E State Pkwy . . . . Schaumburg IL 60173 *Web:* www.machsys.com	847-882-8085	882-2894	385
Machining Concepts Inc W188 N 12050 Maple Rd . . . . Germantown WI 53022 *Web:* www.machiningconcepts.com	262-735-8100	415-8120	454
Machining Time Savers Inc 1338 S State College Pkwy. . . . . Anaheim CA 92806 *Web:* www.mtscnc.com	714-635-7373	635-3268	358
Machinists Inc 7600 5th Ave S. . . . . Seattle WA 98108 *Web:* www.machinistsinc.com	206-763-0990		454
Machtronics Incorporated of Spooner WI 1100 Roundhouse Rd. . . . . Spooner WI 54801 *TF:* 888-552-0835 ■ *Web:* machtronicinc.com	715-635-3220	635-4718	629
MACI (Michigan Automotive Compressor Inc) 2400 N Dearing Rd . . . . Parma MI 49269 *Web:* www.michauto.com	517-796-3200		172
Macie Publishing Co 13 E Main St . . . . Mendham NJ 07945 **Fax Area Code:* 973 ■ *TF:* 888-697-1333 ■ *Web:* www.maciepublishing.com	888-697-1333	983-1415*	527
Macina Bose Copeland & Associates Inc 1035 Central Pkwy N . . . . San Antonio TX 78232 *Web:* www.mbcengineers.com	210-545-1122		261
Macintosh Engineering 2 Mill Rd Ste 100 . . . . Wilmington DE 19806 *Web:* www.macintosheng.com	302-252-9200		261
MacIntyre Associates Inc 106 W State St . . . . Kennett Square PA 19348 *Web:* www.macintyreassociates.com	610-925-5925		317
Mack & Associates Ltd 100 N La Salle St Ste 2110. . . . . Chicago IL 60602 *Web:* www.mackltd.com	312-368-0677		390
Mack Avenue Records Ii LLC 19900 Harper Ave. . . . . Harper Woods MI 48225 *Web:* www.mackavenue.com	313-640-8414		657
Mack Boring & Parts Co 2365 US Hwy 22 W . . . . Union NJ 07083 *Web:* mackboring.com	908-964-0700	964-8475	385
Mack Energy Co 1202 N Tenth St. . . . . Duncan OK 73533 *Web:* www.mackenergy.com	580-252-5580		536
Mack Engineering Corp 3215 E 26th St . . . . Minneapolis MN 55406 *Web:* www.mackengineering.com	612-721-2471	721-8774	757
Mack Hils Inc 544 North Ave. . . . . Moberly MO 65270 *Web:* mackhilsmetalfabrication.com	660-263-7444		480
Mack Industries Inc 1321 Industrial Pkwy N Ste 500 . . . . Brunswick OH 44212 *Web:* www.mackconcrete.com	330-460-7005		183
Mack Iron Works Co, The 124 Warren St. . . . . Sandusky OH 44870 *Web:* www.mackiron.com	419-626-6225	626-3362	491
Mack Manufacturing Inc 7205 Bellingrath Rd . . . . Theodore AL 36582 *Web:* mackmfg.com	251-653-9999	653-1365	190
Mack Molding Company Inc 608 Warm Brook Rd . . . . Arlington VT 05250 *Web:* www.mack.com	802-375-2511	375-0792	604
Mack Prototype Inc 424 Main St. . . . . Gardner MA 01440 *Web:* www.mackprototype.com	978-632-3700	632-3777	602
Mack Pump & Equipment Company Inc 12005 S Spaulding School Dr . . . . Plainfield IL 60585 *Web:* www.mackpump.com	815-439-2030	439-2451	358
Mack Sign Advertising 893 Main St . . . . Wakefield MA 01880 *Web:* battensign.com	617-387-1010		7
MACK Technologies Inc 27 Carlisle Rd. . . . . Westford MA 01886 *Web:* www.macktech.com	978-392-5500		179
MacKay & Somps (MSCE) 5142 Franklin Dr Ste B . . . . Pleasanton CA 94588 *Web:* www.msce.com	925-225-0690	225-0698	261
Mackay Communications Inc 3691 Trust Dr . . . . Raleigh NC 27616 **Fax Area Code:* 919 ■ *TF:* 888-798-7979 ■ *Web:* www.mackaycomm.com	281-478-6245	954-1707*	529
Mackay Envelope Co 2100 Elm St SE . . . . Minneapolis MN 55414 *TF:* 800-622-5299 ■ *Web:* mackaymitchell.com	800-622-5299		263
Mackay Manufacturing Inc 10011 E Montgomery Dr . . . . Spokane Valley WA 99206 *Web:* www.mackaymfg.com	509-922-7742	922-8308	454
Mack-Cali Realty Corp 343 Thornall St. . . . . Edison NJ 08837 *NYSE: CLI* ■ *TF:* 800-317-4445 ■ *Web:* www.mack-cali.com	732-590-1000	205-8237	655
MacKellar Associates Inc 1729 Northfield Dr . . . . Rochester Hills MI 48309 *Web:* mackellar.com	248-335-4440		96
Macken Instruments Inc 3196 Coffey Ln Ste 604 . . . . Santa Rosa CA 95403 *Web:* www.macken.com	707-566-2110	566-2119	476
Mackenthun's 851 Marketplace Dr . . . . Waconia MN 55387 *Web:* www.mackenthuns.com	952-442-2512		345
Mackenzie Eason & Assoc 3023 S University Dr Ste 230 . . . . Fort Worth TX 76109 *Web:* mackenzieeason.com	817-922-9152		363
Mackenzie Financial Corp 180 Queen St W . . . . Toronto ON M5V3K1 *TF:* 888-653-7070 ■ *Web:* www.mackenzieinvestments.com	416-922-5322	922-5660	401
Mackenzie Hughes LLP 440 S Warren St Ste 400 . . . . Syracuse NY 13202 *Web:* mackenziehughes.com	315-474-7571		41
MacKenzie's Chop House Restaurant 128 S Tejon St . . . . Colorado Springs CO 80903 *Web:* www.mackenzieschophouse.com	719-635-3536		671
MacKenzie-Childs LLC 3260 SR-90. . . . . Aurora NY 13026 *TF:* 888-665-1999 ■ *Web:* www.mackenzie-childs.com	315-364-6118		321
MacKerricher State Park 24100 MacKerricher Park Rd . . . . Fort Bragg CA 95437 *Web:* www.parks.ca.gov	707-937-5804		565
Mackevich Burke & Stanicki 1435 Raritan Rd . . . . Clark NJ 07066 *Web:* mbslawyers.com	732-388-2121		41
Mackie Consultants LLC 9575 W Higgins Rd Ste 500. . . . . Rosemont IL 60018 *Web:* mackieconsult.com	847-696-1400		727
Mackie Group 933 Bloor St W. . . . . Oshawa ON L1J5Y7 *TF:* 800-565-4646 ■ *Web:* www.mackiegroup.com	905-728-2400		314
Mackie Research Capital Corp 199 Bay St Commerce Ct W Ste 4500 . . . . Toronto ON M5L1G2 *TF:* 888-860-7606 ■ *Web:* www.mackieresearch.com	416-860-7600		401
Mackie Shea PC 20 Park Plz Ste 1118 . . . . Boston MA 02116 *Web:* mackieshea.com	617-266-5700		41
Mackin Educational Resources 3505 County Rd 42 W . . . . Burnsville MN 55306 **Fax Area Code:* 800 ■ *TF:* 800-245-9540 ■ *Web:* www.mackin.com	952-895-9540	369-5490*	434-3
Mackinac County 100 S Marley St Rm 10. . . . . Saint Ignace MI 49781 *Web:* www.mackinaccounty.net	906-643-7300	643-7302	338
Mackinac Island Butterfly 6750 Mcgulpin St. . . . . Mackinac Island MI 49757 *Web:* www.originalbutterflyhouse.com	906-847-3972		522
Mackinac Partners LLC 74 W Long Lake Rd Ste 205 . . . . Bloomfield Hills MI 48304 *Web:* www.mackinacpartners.com	248-258-6900		401

				Phone	Fax	Class
Mackinaw Area Visitors Bureau 10800 US 23 — TF: 800-666-0160 ■ Web: www.mackinawcity.com	Mackinaw City	MI	49701	231-436-5664	436-5991	206
Mackinaw River State Fish & Wildlife Area 15470 Nelson Rd — Web: www2.illinois.gov	Mackinaw	IL	61755	309-963-4969		565
Mackinaws Grill & Spirits 2925 Voyager Dr — Web: mackinaws.com	Green Bay	WI	54311	920-406-8000		671
MacKinnon Calderwood Advertising Inc 1555 Dundas St W — Web: www.mackinnoncalderwood.com	Mississauga	ON	L5C1E3	905-281-6146		7
Mackintire Insurance Agency Inc 11 W Main St — Web: www.mackintire.com	Westborough	MA	01581	508-366-6161		390
MacKissic Inc PO Box 111 — TF: 800-348-1117 ■ Web: www.mackissic.com	Parker Ford	PA	19457	610-495-7181	495-5951	429
Macklowe Properties 767 Fifth Ave — Web: www.macklowepropertie s.com	New York	NY	10153	212-265-5900	554-5895	655
Macks Prairie Wings 2335 Hwy 63 N — Web: www.mackspw.com	Stuttgart	AR	72160	870-673-6960		711
Macktown Living History 2221 Freeport Rd — Web: www.macktownlivinghistory.com	Rockton	IL	61072	815-624-4200		50-3
Macky's Bayside Bar & Grill 54th Street on the Bay — Web: mackys.com	Ocean City	MD	21842	410-723-5565		671
Mac-Lander Inc 509 E Maple — TF: 800-346-1792 ■ Web: www.mac-lander.com	Milton	IA	52570	641-656-4271	656-4225	763
MacLaren Youth Correctional Facility 2630 N Pacific Hwy — Web: www.oregon.gov	Woodburn	OR	97071	503-981-9531	982-4439	412
Maclean & Ema PA 2600 NE 14th Street Cswy — Web: maclean-ema.com	Pompano Beach	FL	33062	954-785-1900		41
Maclean's 1 Mt Pleasant Rd 11th Fl — TF: 800-268-9119 ■ Web: www.macleans.ca	Toronto	ON	M4Y2Y5	416-764-1300		457-17
MacLean-Fogg Co 1000 Allanson Rd — TF: 800-323-4536 ■ Web: www.macleanfogg.com	Mundelein	IL	60060	847-566-0010		60
MacLellan Services Inc 3120 Wall St Ste 100 — Web: www.maclellanlive.com	Lexington	KY	40513	859-219-5400	219-5438	256
MacMicro Inc 29 Williamsburg Close — Web: www.macmicro.com	Scarsdale	NY	10583	914-472-8292		396
Macmillan Piper Inc 1509 Taylor Way — Web: www.macpiper.com	Tacoma	WA	98421	253-627-3767		549
Macmillan Publishers Ltd 175 Fifth Ave — *Fax Area Code: 212 ■ TF: 800-221-7945 ■ Web: us.macmillan.com	New York	NY	10010	800-221-7945	598-9173*	637-2
Macmillan Scholz & Marks PC 900 SW Fifth Ave Ste 1800 — Web: msmlegal.com	Portland	OR	97204	503-224-2165		41
MacMillan Sobanski & Todd LLC 1 Maritime Plz 720 Water St 5th Fl — Web: mstfirm.com	Toledo	OH	43604	419-255-5900	255-9639	445
MacMunnis Inc 1840 Oak Ave Ste 300 — Web: www.macmunnis.com	Evanston	IL	60201	847-316-1100		463
MacMurray College 447 E College Ave — TF: 800-252-7485 ■ Web: www.mac.edu	Jacksonville	IL	62650	217-479-7056	291-0702	166
MacNeal Hospital 3249 S Oak Park Ave — TF: 888-622-6325 ■ Web: macnealhospital.org	Berwyn	IL	60402	708-783-9100		374-3
MacNeill Engineering Company Inc 140 Locke Dr — TF: 800-652-4267 ■ Web: champspikes.com	Marlborough	MA	01752	508-481-8830	303-4923	710
Macnica Americas Inc 380 Stevens Ave Ste 206 — *Fax Area Code: 760 ■ TF: 888-399-4937 ■ Web: www.macnica.com	Solana Beach	CA	92075	858-771-0846	452-7548*	246
MACO (Maryland Association of Counties) 169 Conduit St — Web: www.mdcounties.org	Annapolis	MD	21401	410-269-0043	268-1775	49-7
Maco Industries Inc 19051 Al Hwy 174 — Web: www.macoindustries.com	Pell City	AL	35125	205-338-7341	338-4536	821
Macomb Area Chamber of Commerce & Downtown Development Corp 214 N Lafayette St — Web: www.macombareachamber.com	Macomb	IL	61455	309-837-4855	837-4857	139
Macomb Area Convention & Visitors Bureau, The 201 S Lafayette — Web: www.visitforgottonia.com	Macomb	IL	61455	309-833-1315	833-3575	206
Macomb Community College *South* 14500 E 12-Mile Rd — TF: 866-622-6621 ■ Web: www.macomb.edu	Warren	MI	48088	586-445-7000	445-7140	162
Macomb Correctional Facility 34625 26th Mile Rd — Web: www.michigan.gov	New Haven	MI	48048	586-749-4900		213
Macomb County 40 N Main St — Web: www.macombgov.org	Mount Clemens	MI	48043	586-469-5120		338
Macomb County 1 S Main — Web: living.macombgov.org	Mount Clemens	MI	48043	586-469-7001		434-3
Macomb County Chamber of Commerce 28 1st St — Web: macombcountychamber.com	Mount Clemens	MI	48043	586-493-7600	493-7602	139
Macomb Daily 100 Macomb Daily Dr — Web: www.macombdaily.com	Mount Clemens	MI	48043	586-469-4510		532-2
Macomb Group Inc, The 6600 E 15 Mile Rd — TF: 888-756-4110 ■ Web: www.macombgroup.com	Sterling Heights	MI	48312	586-274-4100	274-4125	492
Macomb Mall 32233 Gratiot Ave — Web: www.shopmacombmall.com	Roseville	MI	48066	586-293-7800		460
Macomb Reservation State Park 201 Campsite Rd — Web: parks.ny.gov	Schuyler Falls	NY	12985	518-643-9952		565
Macomb School District 323 W Washington St — Web: www.macomb185.org	Macomb	IL	61455	309-833-4161	836-2133	685
Macon Cigar & Tobacco Company Inc 575 12th St — Web: www.mctweb.com	Macon	GA	31201	478-743-2236	744-0903	756
Macon City Hall 700 Poplar St — Web: www.maconbibb.us	Macon	GA	31201	478-751-7400		337
Macon County 5700 W Main St Rm 104 — Web: www.maconcountyga.gov	Decatur	IL	62523	217-424-1305		338
Macon County 5 W Main St — Web: www.maconnc.org	Franklin	NC	28734	828-349-2025	349-2400	338
Macon County 201 County Courthouse — Web: www.maconcountytn.gov	LaFayette	TN	37083	615-666-2363	666-5323	338
Macon County 28890 US Highway 63 Ste D — TF: 800-981-9409 ■ Web: www.maconcounty.org	Macon	MO	63552	660-676-0578		338
Macon County Courthouse 101 E Northside St — Web: alabama.travel	Tuskegee	AL	36083	334-727-5120		338
Macon County History Museum (MCHM) 5580 N Fork Rd — Web: www.mchmdecatur.org	Decatur	IL	62521	217-422-4919		520
Macon County Nursing Home District 701 Sunset Hills Dr — Web: www.lochhaven.com	Macon	MO	63552	660-385-3113		371
Macon County R-1 School District 702 N Missouri St — Web: www.macon.k12.mo.us	Macon	MO	63552	660-385-5719	385-7179	242
Macon Electric Co-op 31571 Bus Hwy 36 E PO Box 157 — TF: 800-553-6901 ■ Web: www.maconelectric.com	Macon	MO	63552	660-385-3157	385-3334	245
Macon Little Theater 4220 Forsyth Rd — Web: www.maconlittletheatre.org	Macon	GA	31210	478-471-7529		572
Macon Mall 3661 Eisenhower Pkwy — Web: www.maconmall.com	Macon	GA	31206	478-741-4496		460
Macon Resources Inc 2121 Hubbard Ave — TF: 844-876-5623 ■ Web: maconresources.org	Decatur	IL	62526	217-875-1910		488
Macon Supply Inc 2730 Gabel Rd — TF: 800-835-1114 ■ Web: maconsupply.net	Billings	MT	59101	406-245-5107	245-5260	191-4
Macon Symphony Orchestra 328 Poplar St — Web: www.maconsymphony.com	Macon	GA	31201	478-301-5300		573-3
Macon Systems Inc PO Box 1388 — Web: www.maconsys.com	Colorado Springs	CO	80901	719-520-1555		225
Macon Water Authority 790 Second St PO Box 108 — Web: www.maconwater.org	Macon	GA	31202	478-464-5600	741-9146	806
Macon-Bibb County Convention/Visitors Bureau 450 Martin Luther King Jr Blvd — TF: 800-768-3401 ■ Web: www.maconga.org	Macon	GA	31201	478-743-1074	745-2022	206
Macoser Inc 2747 Interstate St — Web: www.macoserwood.com	Charlotte	NC	28208	704-392-0110		385
Macoupin County 201 E Main — Web: www.macoupincountyil.gov	Carlinville	IL	62626	217-854-3214	854-7361	338
Macoy Publishing and Masonic Supply Company Inc 3011 Dumbarton Rd — *Fax Area Code: 804 ■ TF: 800-637-4640 ■ Web: macoy.com	Richmond	VA	23228	800-637-4640	266-8256*	410
Macphail Center For Music - Minneapolis 501 S Second St — Web: www.macphail.org	Minneapolis	MN	55401	612-321-0100	321-9740	572
Macpherson Oil Co 100 Wilshire Ste 800 — *Fax Area Code: 661 ■ Web: www.macphersonenergy.com	Santa Monica	CA	90401	310-452-3880	393-8065*	536
MacPherson's Real Estate 18551 Aurora Ave N Ste 100 — Web: macphersonspm.com	Shoreline	WA	98133	206-546-6235		652
MacPractice Inc 233 N Eighth St Ste 300 — TF: 877-220-8418 ■ Web: www.macpractice.com	Lincoln	NE	68508	402-420-2430		174
Macquarie Infrastructure Company Inc 125 W 55th St — NYSE: MIC ■ Web: www.macquarie.com	New York	NY	10019	212-231-1000		70
Macquarium Intelligent Communications 1800 Peachtree St NW Ste 250 — Web: www.macquarium.com	Atlanta	GA	30309	404-554-4000		7
MacQue's BBQ 8101 Elder Creek Rd Ste O — Web: www.macquesbbq.com	Sacramento	CA	95824	916-381-4119		671
Macritchie Engineering Inc 197 Quincy Ave — Web: macritchie.net	Braintree	MA	02184	781-848-4464	848-2613	261
Macro Engineering & Technology Inc 199 Traders Blvd E — Web: www.macroeng.com	Mississauga	ON	L4Z2E5	905-507-9000		757
Macro Group Inc, The 1200 Washington Ave S Ste 350 — Web: www.macrogroup.net	Minneapolis	MN	55415	612-332-7880	335-3674	177
Macro International Co 78 Bunsen St — *Fax Area Code: 949 ■ TF: 888-336-3939 ■ Web: www.macrointlco.com	Irvine	CA	92618	888-336-3939	727-1488*	676
Macro Management Service 800 Navarro St — Web: macromgt.com	San Antonio	TX	78205	210-226-1047		463
Macro Plastics Inc 2250 Huntington Dr — TF: 800-845-6555 ■ Web: www.macroplastics.com	Fairfield	CA	94533	707-437-1200		596
Macro Solutions 800 Maryland Ave NE Ste 900 — Web: macrosolutions.com	Washington	DC	20002	202-618-8144		177
Macronix America Inc 680 N McCarthy Blvd — Web: www.macronix.com	Milpitas	CA	95035	408-262-8887	262-8810	696
MacroSoft Inc 2 Sylvan Way 3rd Fl — Web: www.macrosoftinc.com	Parsippany	NJ	07054	973-889-0500		195
Macrovision Inc 300 Brookside Ave Bldg 18 Ste 130 — Web: www.macrovis.com	Ambler	PA	19002	215-348-1010		7
MACS (Mobile Air Conditioning Society Worldwide) 225 S Broad St — Web: www.macsw.org	Lansdale	PA	19446	215-631-7020	631-7017	49-21
Macs at Work Inc 775 Hartford Tpke — Web: www.macsatwork.com	Shrewsbury	MA	01545	508-845-0709		179

Name / Address	City	State	Zip	Phone	Fax	Class
Macs Landing Veterinary Services PC 2716 62nd St *Web:* macslanding.com	Fennville	MI	49408	269-561-7304		794
MACTE (Montessori Accreditation Council for Teacher Education) 420 Park St **Fax Area Code: 888 ■ Web:* www.macte.org	Charlottesville	VA	22902	434-202-7793	525-8838*	48-1
Mactus Group 4034 148th Ave NE Bldg K1 *Web:* mactusgroup.com	Redmond	WA	98052	425-883-3640		393
Macuch Steel Products Inc 1527 Augusta Ave *TF:* 866-441-9545 ■ *Web:* www.macuchsteel.com	Augusta	GA	30901	706-823-2420	823-2439	480
Macula Foundation Inc 210 E 64th St *Web:* maculafoundation.org	New York	NY	10065	212-605-3777		48-17
Macwhinnie Financial Group 1035 Boyce Rd Ste 200 *Web:* macwhinniefinancial.com	Pittsburgh	PA	15241	412-564-5166		390
Macy's Inc 7 W Seventh St *Web:* macysinc.com	Cincinnati	OH	45202	513-579-7000		229
Mad 4 Marketing Inc 5255 NW 33rd Ave *Web:* www.mad4marketing.com	Fort Lauderdale	FL	33309	954-485-5448		7
Mad City Labs Inc (MCL) 2524 Todd Dr *Web:* www.madcitylabs.com	Madison	WI	53713	608-298-0855	298-9525	419
Mad Dogg Athletics Inc 2111 Narcissus Ct *TF:* 800-847-7746 ■ *Web:* spinning.com	Venice	CA	90291	310-823-7008		711
Mad Mary's Steakhouse & Saloon 110 E Dakota Ave	Pierre	SD	57501	605-224-6469		671
Mad Science Group 8360 Bougainville St Ste 201 *TF:* 800-586-5231 ■ *Web:* www.madscience.org	Montreal	QC	H4P2G1	514-344-4181	344-6695	310
Mad*Pow 27 Congress St *Web:* www.madpow.com	Portsmouth	NH	03801	603-387-8307	386-6608	393
Mada Medical Products Inc 625 Washington Ave *TF:* 800-526-6370 ■ *Web:* www.madamedical.com	Carlstadt	NJ	07072	201-460-0454	460-3509	475
Madagascar Embassy 2374 Massachusetts Ave NW *Web:* www.madagascar-embassy.org	Washington	DC	20008	202-265-5525		257
Madam Mam's 510 W 26th St *Web:* www.madammam.com	Austin	TX	78705	512-305-3955		671
Madame Claude Cafe 390 Fourth St *Web:* www.madameclaudejc.com	Jersey City	NJ	07302	201-876-8800		671
Madame Tussauds New York Inc 234 W 42nd St Times Sq *Web:* www.madametussauds.com	New York	NY	10036	212-512-9600		520
Madame Walker Theatre Ctr 617 Indiana Ave *Web:* www.thewalkertheatre.org	Indianapolis	IN	46202	317-236-2099	236-2097	572
Madan Plastics Inc 108 N Union Ave Ste 3 *TF:* 888-676-5926 ■ *Web:* madanplastics.com	Cranford	NJ	07016	908-276-8484	276-9483	596
MadCap Software Inc 7777 Fay Ave *TF:* 888-623-2271 ■ *Web:* www.madcapsoftware.com	La Jolla	CA	92037	858-320-0387	320-0338	179
MADD (Mothers Against Drunk Driving) 511 E John Carpenter Fwy Ste 700 *TF:* 877-275-6233 ■ *Web:* www.madd.org	Irving	TX	75062	877-275-6233		48-6
Madden Communications Inc 901 Mittel Dr *Web:* www.madden.com	Wood Dale	IL	60191	630-787-2200		535
Madden Manufacturing Inc PO Box 387 *TF:* 800-369-6233 ■ *Web:* www.maddenmfg.com	Elkhart	IN	46515	574-295-4292	295-7562	641
Madden's on Gull Lake 11266 Pine Beach Peninsula *TF:* 800-642-5363 ■ *Web:* www.maddens.com	Brainerd	MN	56401	800-233-2934		669
MaddenCo Inc 4847 E Virginia Ste G *Web:* www.maddenco.com	Evansville	IN	47715	812-474-6245	474-6254	225
Maddock Douglas Inc 111 Adell Pl *Web:* maddockdouglas.com	Elmhurst	IL	60126	630-279-3939		7
Maddox Foundry & Machine Works Inc 13370 SW 170th St *Web:* www.maddoxfoundry.com	Archer	FL	32618	352-495-2121	495-3962	307
Maddox Marketing Group Inc 964 Gavington Pl *TF:* 800-949-5208 ■ *Web:* www.maddoxmarketing.com	Akron	OH	44313	330-945-6232		4
Maddox Metal Works Inc 4116 Bronze Way *Web:* www.maddoxmetalworks.com	Dallas	TX	75237	214-333-2311	337-8169	697
Madeira School 8328 Georgetown Pk *Web:* www.madeira.org	McLean	VA	22102	703-556-8200		622
Madelaine Chocolate Novelties Inc 9603 Beach Ch Dr *TF:* 800-322-1505 ■ *Web:* www.madelainechocolate.com	Rockaway Beach	NY	11693	718-945-1500	318-4607	296-8
Maden Technologies 4601 N Fairfax Dr Ste 1030 *Web:* www.madentech.com	Arlington	VA	22203	703-940-3609	522-2082	180
Mader News Inc 913 Ruberta Ave *Web:* www.madernews.com	Glendale	CA	91201	818-551-5000		532-3
Mader's German Restaurant 1037 N Old World Third St *Web:* www.madersrestaurant.com	Milwaukee	WI	53203	414-271-3377		671
Madera Adult School 2037 W Cleveland Ave *Web:* www.madera.k12.ca.us	Madera	CA	93637	559-675-4425	675-4562	685
Madera Chamber of Commerce 120 NE St *TF:* 800-872-7245 ■ *Web:* www.maderachamber.com	Madera	CA	93638	559-673-3563	673-5009	139
Madera Community Hospital 1250 E Almond Ave *Web:* www.maderahospital.org	Madera	CA	93637	559-675-5555	675-5529	374-3
Madera Component Systems Inc 6323 W van Buren St *Web:* www.maderacomponents.com	Phoenix	AZ	85043	623-245-1001	936-6392	817
Madera County 200 W Fourth St *TF:* 800-427-6897 ■ *Web:* www.maderacounty.com	Madera	CA	93637	559-675-7703	673-3302	338
Made-Rite Co PO Box 3283 *Web:* www.themade-ritecompany.com	Longview	TX	75606	903-753-8604	236-9743	81-2
MadeToOrder Inc 1244-A Quarry Ln *Web:* www.madetoorder.com	Pleasanton	CA	94566	925-484-0600		7
Madewell Inc 486 Broadway *Web:* www.madewell.com	New York	NY	10013	212-226-6954		157-2
MadgeTech Inc 6 Warner Rd *TF:* 877-671-2885 ■ *Web:* www.madgetech.com	Warner	NH	03278	603-456-2011		256
Madia Insurance Agency Inc 9370 Mcknight Rd Ste 300A *Web:* madiainsurance.com	Pittsburgh	PA	15237	412-367-9200	367-9887	390
Madico Inc 64 Industrial Pkwy *TF:* 800-456-4331 ■ *Web:* www.madico.com	Woburn	MA	01801	781-935-7850	935-6841	599
Madigan, Dahl & Harlan PA 222 S Ninth St Ste 3150 *Web:* mdh-law.com	Minneapolis	MN	55402	612-604-2000	604-2599	41
Madison & Associates Inc 4108 Holly Rd *Web:* www.tdmadison.com	Virginia Beach	VA	23451	757-425-9950		260
Madison Area Chamber of Commerce 301 E Main St *TF:* 800-559-2956 ■ *Web:* www.madisonindiana.com	Madison	IN	47250	812-265-3135	265-9784	139
Madison Area Technical College 1701 Wright St *TF:* 800-322-6282 ■ *Web:* madisoncollege.edu	Madison	WI	53704	608-246-6100	246-6880	800
Madison Ballet 160 Westgate Mall *Web:* www.madisonballet.org	Madison	WI	53711	608-278-7990		573-1
Madison Cable Corp 125 Goddard Memorial Dr *TF:* 877-623-4766 ■ *Web:* www.te.com	Worcester	MA	01603	508-752-2884	752-4230	814
Madison Capital Partners Corp 500 W Madison St Ste 3890 *Web:* madison.net	Chicago	IL	60661	312-277-0156	277-0163	403
Madison Chemical Company Inc 3141 Clifty Dr *Web:* www.madchem.com	Madison	IN	47250	812-273-6000	273-6002	151
Madison Children's Museum 100 N Hamilton St *Web:* www.madisonchildrensmuseum.org	Madison	WI	53703	608-256-6445		521
Madison City Hall 210 Martin Luther King Jr Blvd Rm 403 *Web:* www.cityofmadison.com	Madison	WI	53703	608-266-4611	267-8671	337
Madison Companion Animal Hospital LLC 2658 S Seminole Trl *Web:* madisonpetvet.com	Madison	VA	22727	540-948-6876		794
Madison Concourse Hotel & Governors Club 1 W Dayton St *TF:* 800-356-8293 ■ *Web:* www.concoursehotel.com	Madison	WI	53703	608-257-6000	257-5280	379
Madison Correctional Facility 800 MSH Busstop Dr *Web:* www.in.gov	Madison	IN	47250	812-265-6154	265-2142	213
Madison Correctional Institution 382 SW MCI Way *Web:* dc.state.fl.us	Madison	FL	32340	850-973-5300		213
Madison Correctional Institution 1851 SR-56 PO Box 740 *Web:* drc.ohio.gov	London	OH	43140	740-852-9777	852-3666	213
Madison County 1106 Meridian St Ste 109 *Web:* www.madisoncty.com	Anderson	IN	46016	765-641-9419		338
Madison County 238 Fox Ln *TF:* 800-428-0584 ■ *Web:* www.madison-co.com	Canton	MS	39046	601-859-1177	859-5875	338
Madison County 157 N Main St Ste 109 PO Box 218 *Web:* www.co.madison.il.us	Edwardsville	IL	62025	618-692-6290	692-8903	338
Madison County 1 Courthouse Sq *Web:* madisoncountymo.us	Fredericktown	MO	63645	573-783-6544		338
Madison County 100 Northside Sq *Web:* madisoncountyal.gov	Huntsville	AL	35801	256-532-3492	532-6994	338
Madison County 201 Main St *Web:* madisoncogov.com	Huntsville	AR	72740	479-738-2747		338
Madison County 1 N Main St PO Box 618 *Web:* www.co.madison.oh.us	London	OH	43140	740-852-2972	845-1660	338
Madison County 182 NW College Loop PO Box 817 *TF:* 877-272-3642 ■ *Web:* www.madisonfl.org	Madison	FL	32341	850-973-2788	973-8864	338
Madison County 1313 N Main St *Web:* www.madisoncountyne.com	Madison	NE	68748	402-454-3311		338
Madison County 110 N Main St *Web:* madisonva.com	Madison	VA	22727	540-948-4455		338
Madison County PO Box 142 *Web:* www.madisoncountync.gov	Marshall	NC	28753	828-649-2531	649-0187	338
Madison County PO Box 389 *Web:* www.co.madison.id.us	Rexburg	ID	83440	208-359-6200	356-8396	338
Madison County 100 Wallace St PO Box 185 *Web:* madisoncountymt.gov	Virginia City	MT	59755	406-843-4230	843-5207	338
Madison County 138 N Ct St Bldg 4 PO Box 668 *Web:* madisoncounty.ny.gov	Wampsville	NY	13163	315-366-2261		338
Madison County 73 Jefferson St *TF:* 800-298-6119 ■ *Web:* www.madisoncounty.com	Winterset	IA	50273	515-462-1185		338
Madison County Chamber of Commerce 618 Crescent Blvd Ste 101 *Web:* www.madisoncountychamber.com	Ridgeland	MS	39157	601-605-2554	605-2260	139
Madison County County Clerk 100 E Main St Ste 105 *Web:* www.madisoncountytn.gov	Jackson	TN	38301	731-423-6022	423-6129	338
Madison County Federal Credit Union 621 E Eighth St *Web:* madcofcu.org	Anderson	IN	46012	765-644-3623		219
Madison County Healthcare System 300 Hutchings St *Web:* www.madisonhealth.com	Winterset	IA	50273	515-462-2373	462-5132	374-3
Madison County Historical Society 435 Main St *Web:* mchs1900.org	Oneida	NY	13421	315-363-4136		49-19
Madison County Record 201 Church St *Web:* www.mcrecordonline.com	Huntsville	AR	72740	479-738-2141	738-1250	532-2
Madison Credit Union 949 E Washington Ave *Web:* madisoncu.com	Madison	WI	53703	608-266-4750	266-4510	219

Name / Address	City	State	ZIP	Phone	Fax	Class
Madison Dearborn Partners LLC (MDP) 70 W Madison Ste 4600 *Web:* www.mdcp.com	Chicago	IL	60602	312-895-1000	895-1001	792
Madison Electric Co 31855 Van Dyke Ave *Web:* www.madisonelectric.com	Warren	MI	48093	586-825-0200	825-0225	246
Madison English as a Second Language School 3009 University Ave *TF:* 866-575-4240 ■ *Web:* www.mesls.org	Madison	WI	53705	608-233-9962	233-9967	685
Madison Gas & Electric Co 133 S Blair St *TF:* 800-245-1125 ■ *Web:* www.mge.com	Madison	WI	53703	608-252-7000	252-7098	787
Madison Group Inc 6551 Stage Oaks Dr Ste 1 *Web:* madisong.com	Bartlett	TN	38134	901-791-4116	791-4129	261
Madison Heights Public Library 240 W 13 Mile Rd *Web:* www.madison-heights.org	Madison Heights	MI	48071	248-588-7763		434-3
Madison Heights-Hazel Park Chamber of Commerce (MHP) 939 E 12 Mile Rd *Web:* www.madisonheightschamber.com	Madison Heights	MI	48071	248-542-5010		139
Madison Hotel 79 Madison Ave *Web:* www.madisonhotelmemphis.com	Memphis	TN	38103	901-333-1200	333-1210	379
Madison Hotel, The 1 Convent Rd *TF:* 800-526-0729 ■ *Web:* www.themadisonhotel.com	Morristown	NJ	07960	973-285-1800	540-8566	379
Madison Industries Incorporated of Georgia 1035 Iris Dr *Web:* www.madisonind.com	Conyers	GA	30094	770-483-4401	785-7967	105
Madison Investment Advisors 550 Science Dr *TF:* 800-767-0300 ■ *Web:* madisoninvestments.com	Madison	WI	53711	608-274-0300		401
Madison Local School District 1379 Grace St *Web:* www.mlsd.net	Mansfield	OH	44905	419-589-2600		685
Madison Marquette 909 Montgomery St Ste 200 *Web:* www.madisonmarquette.com	San Francisco	CA	94133	415-277-6800		655
Madison Mechanical Contracting LLC 5621 Old Frederick Rd Ste 1 *Web:* www.madisonmechanical.net	Catonsville	MD	21228	443-038-5192		610
Madison Media Institute 2702 Agriculture Dr *TF:* 800-236-4997 ■ *Web:* www.mediainstitute.edu	Madison	WI	53718	800-236-4997		167-3
Madison Metropolitan School District 545 W Dayton St *Web:* www.madison.k12.wi.us	Madison	WI	53703	608-663-1879	204-0346	685
Madison Mill Inc PO Box 90886 *Fax Area Code: 615 ■ *TF:* 800-251-2443 ■ *Web:* www.madisonmill.com	Ashland City	TN	37015	800-251-2443	269-3855*	820
Madison National Life Insurance Company Inc PO Box 5008 *TF:* 800-356-9601 ■ *Web:* www.madisonlife.com	Madison	WI	53705	608-830-2000	830-2700	391-2
Madison Park Financial Corp 155 Grand Ave Ste 950 *Web:* www.mpfcorp.com	Oakland	CA	94612	510-452-2944		655
Madison Polymeric Engineering Inc 965 W Main St *Web:* www.madpoly.com	Branford	CT	06405	203-488-4554	488-4922	601
Madison Precision Products Inc 94 E 400 N	Madison	IN	47250	812-273-4702	273-2451	308
Madison Public Library 201 W Mifflin St *Web:* www.madisonpubliclibrary.org	Madison	WI	53703	608-266-6300		434-3
Madison Rivergate Area Chamber of Commerce 301 Madison St *Web:* www.madisonrivergatechamber.com	Madison	TN	37115	615-865-5400		139
Madison School of Massage Therapy 1634 Slaughter Rd Ste C *Web:* www.madisonschoolofmassagetherapy.com	Madison	AL	35758	256-430-9756	430-9757	685
Madison Security Group Inc 31 Kirk St *Web:* www.madisonsg.com	Lowell	MA	01852	978-459-5911		693
Madison Symphony Orchestra 201 State St *Web:* www.madisonsymphony.org	Madison	WI	53703	608-257-3734	280-6192	573-3
Madison Wood Preservers Inc 216 Oak Park Rd *TF:* 844-623-9663 ■ *Web:* www.madwood.com	Madison	VA	22727	844-623-9663		818
Madison's Cafe 216 Madison St *Web:* www.madisonscafe.com	Jefferson City	MO	65101	573-634-2988		671
Madison, Mroz, Steinman & Dekleva PA 201 Third St NW Ste 1600 *Web:* madisonlaw.com	Albuquerque	NM	87102	505-242-2177		41
Madison-Kipp Corp 201 Waubesa St *TF:* 800-356-6148 ■ *Web:* www.madison-kipp.com	Madison	WI	53704	800-356-6148		308
Madison-Morgan Chamber of Commerce 118 N Main St *Web:* www.madisonga.org	Madison	GA	30650	706-438-3120		206
Madisonville Community College 2000 College Dr *TF:* 866-227-4812 ■ *Web:* madisonville.kctcs.edu	Madisonville	KY	42431	270-821-2250	824-1864	162
Madisonville Tire & Retreading Inc 48 Federal St *Web:* www.madisonvilletire.com	Madisonville	KY	42431	270-821-2954	824-3005	755
Madisonville-Hopkins County Chamber of Commerce 15 E Center St *Web:* www.hopkinscochamber.com	Madisonville	KY	42431	270-821-3435	821-9190	139
Madonna Rehabilitation Hospital 5401 S St *TF:* 800-676-5448 ■ *Web:* www.madonna.org	Lincoln	NE	68506	402-413-4409		374-6
Madonna University 36600 Schoolcraft Rd *TF:* 800-852-4951 ■ *Web:* www.madonna.edu	Livonia	MI	48150	734-432-5339	432-5424	166
Madras Pavilion 3910 Kirby Dr *Web:* madraspavilion.us	Houston	TX	77098	713-521-2617		671
Madrid Engineering Group Inc 2030 State Rd 60 E *Web:* madridengineering.com	Bartow	FL	33830	863-533-9007		261
MADROCK 1800 Teague Dr Ste 300 *Web:* www.madrock1025.com	Sherman	TX	75090	903-463-6800		647
Madsen Inc 2901 Springfield Rd *Web:* www.madseninc.com	Broomall	PA	19008	610-356-4800		115
Madsen Kneppers & Associates Inc 100 Pringle Ave Ste 340 *TF:* 800-822-6624 ■ *Web:* www.mkainc.com	Walnut Creek	CA	94596	925-934-3235		261
Madwire 3405 S Timberline Rd *TF:* 888-872-3734 ■ *Web:* www.madwiremedia.com	Fort Collins	CO	80525	855-773-8171		7
Maelstrom Press PO Box 403 *Web:* www.maelstrompress.info	Silverado	CA	92676	714-649-0651		637-10
Maersk Inc 9300 Arrowpoint Blvd *Web:* www.maerskline.com	Charlotte	NC	28273	704-571-2000		313
Maersk Line Ltd 2510 Walmer Ave Ste C *Web:* www.maersklinelimited.com	Norfolk	VA	23513	757-857-4800		313
Maestro SVP 3615 St Laurent Blvd *Web:* www.maestrosvp.com	Montreal	QC	H2X1V5	514-842-6447		671
Maestro Technologies Inc 1471 Boul Lionel Boulet *Web:* maestro.ca	Varennes	QC	J3X1P7	514-990-0864		180
MAF (Mission Aviation Fellowship) 112 N Pilatus Ln *TF:* 800-359-7623 ■ *Web:* www.maf.org	Nampa	ID	83687	208-498-0800	498-0801	48-20
Maf Industries Inc 36470 Hwy 99 *Web:* www.mafindustries.com	Traver	CA	93673	559-897-2905	897-3422	547
Mafcote Industries Inc 108 Main St *TF:* 800-526-4280 ■ *Web:* www.mafcote.com	Norwalk	CT	06851	203-847-8500	849-9177	554
MAG (Medical Association of Georgia) 1849 The Exchange Ste 200 *TF:* 800-282-0224 ■ *Web:* www.mag.org	Atlanta	GA	30339	678-303-9290	303-3732	474
Mag Instrument Inc 2001 S Hillman Ave *TF:* 800-289-6241 ■ *Web:* www.maglite.com	Ontario	CA	91761	909-947-1006	947-3116	439
Mag Management Corp 780 Ridge Lake Blvd Ste 202 *Web:* jglawfirm.com	Memphis	TN	38120	901-682-3450		41
Maga Ltd 2610 Lake Cook Rd Ste 250 *TF:* 800-533-6242 ■ *Web:* www.magaltc.com	Riverwoods	IL	60015	800-533-6242		390
Magasin Latulippe 637 Rue Saint-Vallier O *Web:* latulippe.com	Quebec City	QC	G1N1C6	418-529-0024		711
Magavern Magavern & Grimm LLP 1100 Rand Bldg *TF:* 800-366-2603 ■ *Web:* www.magavern.com	Buffalo	NY	14203	716-856-3500	856-3390	428
Magazine Publishers of AmNAerica PAC 1211 Connecticut Ave NW Ste 610 *Web:* magazine.org	Washington	DC	20036	202-296-7277	296-0343	615
Magazine Telephone Co 25 Magtel Dr *TF:* 800-478-8465 ■ *Web:* www.magtel.com	Booneville	AR	72927	479-969-2211	969-2502	224
Magazines Inc 1135 Hammond St *TF:* 800-649-9224 ■ *Web:* www.magazinesinc.com	Bangor	ME	04401	800-649-9224		96
Magbee Contractors Supply 1065 Bankhead Hwy *Web:* www.magbee.com	Winder	GA	30680	678-425-2600	425-2602	191-3
Mage LLC 831 Beacon St Ste 310 *Web:* www.mageusa.com	Newton	MA	02459	617-244-8366		463
Magee Hartman PC 444 N Cedar Lake Rd *Web:* mageehartman.com	Round Lake	IL	60073	847-546-0055		41
Magee Plastics Co 303 Brush Creek Rd *Web:* www.mageeplastics.com	Warrendale	PA	15086	724-776-2220		596
Magee Rehabilitation 1513 Race St *Web:* mageerehab.org	Philadelphia	PA	19102	215-587-3000	568-3736	374-6
Magee Resource Group LLC 620 Texas St Ste 200 *Web:* www.mageeresource.com	Shreveport	LA	71101	318-865-8411	861-3411	463
Magellan Aerospace 2320 Wedekind Dr *Web:* magellan.aero	Middletown	OH	45042	513-422-2751		22
Magellan Aerospace Corp 3160 Derry Rd E *TSE: MAL* ■ *Web:* www.magellan.aero	Mississauga	ON	L4T1A9	905-677-1889	677-5658	22
Magellan Development Group LLC 225 N Columbus Dr Ste 100 *Web:* www.magellandevelopment.com	Chicago	IL	60601	312-469-8100		653
Magellan Health Services Inc 55 Nod Rd *NASDAQ: MGLN* ■ *TF:* 800-424-4399 ■ *Web:* www.magellanhealth.com	Avon	CT	06001	860-507-1900	507-1990	462
Magellan Industrial Trading Company Inc 227 Wilson Ave *Web:* www.magellanmetals.com	South Norwalk	CT	06854	203-838-5700	838-1300	492
Magellan Midstream Partners LP 1 Williams Ctr *NYSE: MMP* ■ *TF:* 800-574-6671 ■ *Web:* www.magellanlp.com	Tulsa	OK	74172	918-574-7000		597
Magellan Search Group Inc 620 W Germantown Pk Ste 300 *Web:* magellangroup.com	Plymouth Meeting	PA	19462	610-941-0100		193
Magellan Transport Logistics 2511 St Johns Bluff Rd Ste 107 *TF:* 866-699-9394 ■ *Web:* magellantransportlogistics.com	Jacksonville	FL	32246	904-620-0311		314
Magenium Solutions LLC 535 Pennsylvania Ave Ste 103 *Web:* www.magenium.com	Glen Ellyn	IL	60137	630-786-5900		180
Magenta Corp 15160 New Ave *Web:* www.magentallc.com	Lockport	IL	60441	773-777-5050		154
Maggiano's Little Italy 205 Northpark Ctr *Web:* www.maggianos.com	Dallas	TX	75225	214-360-0707		670
Maggie L. Walker National Historic Site 3215 E Broad St *Web:* www.nps.gov	Richmond	VA	23223	804-771-2017	771-2226	564
Maggie Valley Resort & Country Club 1819 Country Club Dr *TF:* 800-438-3861 ■ *Web:* www.maggievalleyclub.com	Maggie Valley	NC	28751	800-438-3861		669
Maggie's Kitchen 636 Bridge St NW	Grand Rapids	MI	49504	616-458-8583		671
Magi Realty Inc 10010 San Pedro Ste 105 *Web:* www.magirealestate.com	San Antonio	TX	78216	210-340-5500	499-5496	652
Magic 107.3 KMJK-FM 5800 Foxridge Dr Ste 600 *Web:* www.magic1073.com	Mission	KS	66202	816-576-7107		645

Phone | Fax | Class

Magic Beans LLC 312 Harvard St Brookline MA 02446 617-383-8250 383-8299 761
TF: 866-600-2326 ■ *Web:* mbeans.com

Magic Brush Inc PO Box 16530 Portal AZ 85632 520-558-2285 637-2
Web: www.sherrycnelson.com

Magic Castle Hotel
7025 Franklin Ave Los Angeles CA 90028 323-851-0800 379
Web: magiccastlehotel.com

Magic House Saint Louis Children's Museum
516 S Kirkwood Rd Saint Louis MO 63122 314-822-8900 822-8930 521
Web: www.magichouse.org

Magic Johnson Foundation Inc
9100 Wilshire Blvd Beverly Hills CA 90212 310-246-4400 305
Web: magicjohnson.org

Magic Logix Inc
15601 Dallas Pkwy Ste 900 Dallas TX 75001 214-694-2162 195
Web: www.magiclogix.com

Magic Metals Inc 3401 Bay St Union Gap WA 98903 509-453-1690 697
Web: www.magicmetals.com

Magic Micro Inc 26055 Emery Rd Ste I Cleveland OH 44128 216-896-9870 591-1819* 459
**Fax Area Code:* 877 ■ *TF:* 800-964-2761 ■ *Web:* www.magicmicro.com

Magic Mountain Fun Centers
5890 Scarborough Blvd Columbus OH 43232 614-840-9600 863-2811 31
Web: www.magicmountainfuncenter.com

Magic Novelty Company Inc
308 Dyckman St New York NY 10034 212-304-2777 567-2809 407
Web: inv.magicnovelty.com

Magic Plastics Inc
25215 Ave Stanford Valencia CA 91355 800-369-0303 608
TF: 800-369-0303 ■ *Web:* magicplastics.com

Magic Software Enterprises Inc
24422 Avenida De La Carlota Ste 365 Laguna Hills CA 92653 949-250-1718 177
Web: magicsoftware.com

Magic Springs Theme Park & Crystal Falls Water Park
1701 E Grand Ave Hot Springs AR 71901 501-624-0100 318-5367 32
Web: www.magicsprings.com

Magic Steel Sales LLC
4242 Clay Ave SW Grand Rapids MI 49548 616-532-4071 492
Web: magicsteel.com

Magic Tilt Trailers
2161 Lions Club Rd Clearwater FL 33764 727-535-5561 779
Web: magictilt.com

Magic Valley Electric Co-opeartive Inc
1 3/4 Mile W Hwy 83 Mercedes TX 78570 866-225-5683 245
TF: 866-225-5683 ■ *Web:* magicvalley.coop

Magic Valley Newspapers
132 Fairfield St W Twin Falls ID 83301 208-733-0931 637-8
TF: 800-658-3883 ■ *Web:* www.magicvalley.com

Magic Valley Speedway
3369 N 2800 E Twin Falls ID 83301 208-734-3700 324-9616 515
Web: www.magicvalleyspeedway.com

Magid Glove & Safety Manufacturing Co
2060 N Kolmar Ave Chicago IL 60639 773-384-2070 384-6677 155-8
TF: 800-444-8010 ■ *Web:* www.magidglove.com

Magidov CPA Firm
1080 S La Cienega Blvd Ste205 Los Angeles CA 90035 310-278-5004 2
Web: magidovcpafirm.com

Magil Construction Corp
1655 Rue De Beauharnois Ouest Montreal QC H4N1J6 514-341-9899 186
Web: www.magil.com

Maginating 421 S Clay Ave Kirkwood MO 63122 314-287-6628 637-10
Web: www.maginating.com

MagiQ Technologies Inc 11 Ward St Somerville MA 02143 617-661-8300 354-9844 743
Web: www.magiqtech.com

Magis Group LLC, The
106 Brinker Rd Barrington IL 60010 847-756-4200 193
Web: www.themagisgroup.com

Magitech Corp
1500 Don Mills Rd Ste 702 Toronto ON M3B3K4 416-441-1933 179
Web: www.ezgame.com

Mag-Knight 18121 117th St SE Snohomish WA 98290 360-805-0100 805-0811 517
Web: www.mag-knight.com

Maglin Miskiv & Associates CPA'S PA
299 Cherry Hill Rd Ste 100 Parsippany NJ 07054 973-263-3300 2

Magline Inc 1205 W Cedar St Standish MI 48658 800-624-5463 879-5399* 470
**Fax Area Code:* 989 ■ *TF:* 800-624-5463 ■ *Web:* www.magliner.com

Maglio & Company Whlse Fruits
4287 N Port Washington Rd Milwaukee WI 53212 414-906-8800 260
Web: www.maglioproduce.com

Magmic 126 York St 4th Fl Ottawa ON K1N5T5 613-241-3571 225
Web: magmic.com

Magmotor Technologies Inc
10 Coppage Dr Worcester MA 01603 508-459-5991 253
Web: www.magmotor.com

Magna Chek Inc
32701 Edward Ave Madison Heights MI 48071 248-597-0089 597-0440 743
TF: 800-582-8947 ■ *Web:* www.magnachek.com

Magna Design Inc 12020 NE 26th PL Bellevue WA 98005 206-852-5282 319-1
TF: 800-426-1202 ■ *Web:* www.magnadesign.com

Magna Global USA 100 W 33rd St 9th Fl New York NY 10001 212-883-4751 6
Web: magnaglobal.com

Magna Graphics Inc PO Box 1015 Lakeland FL 33801 800-624-5442 457-4044 344
TF: 800-624-5442 ■ *Web:* www.magna-graphics.com

Magna International Inc 337 Magna Dr Aurora ON L4G7K1 905-726-2462 726-7164 60
TSE: MG ■ *Web:* www.magna.com

Magna IV 2401 Commercial Ln Little Rock AR 72206 501-376-2397 627
TF: 800-946-2462 ■ *Web:* www.magna4.com

Magna Iv Engineering Inc
96 Inverness Dr E Unit R Englewood CO 80112 800-462-3157 790-4816* 261
**Fax Area Code:* 303 ■ *TF:* 800-462-3157 ■ *Web:* magnaiv.com

Magna Machine & Tool Company Inc
3722 N Messick Rd New Castle IN 47362 765-766-5388 766-5300 454
Web: magnamachine.com

Magna Machine Co
11180 Southland Rd Cincinnati OH 45240 513-851-6900 851-6904 556
Web: www.magna-machine.com

Magna Manufacturing Inc
85 Hill Ave Fort Walton Beach FL 32548 850-243-1112 243-6406 601
TF: 888-243-1112 ■ *Web:* loboy.com

Magna Visual Inc 9400 Watson Rd Sappington MO 63126 800-843-3399 843-0000* 534
**Fax Area Code:* 314 ■ *TF:* 800-843-3399 ■ *Web:* www.magnavisual.com

Magnani & Associates Advertising Inc
200 S Michigan Ave Ste 500 Chicago IL 60604 312-957-0770 195
Web: www.magnani.com

Magnani & Buck Ltd
321 S Plymouth Ct Ste 1700 Chicago IL 60604 312-294-4800 294-4815 41
Web: magnanibuck.com

Magnatech International Inc
17 E Meadow Ave Robesonia PA 19551 610-693-8866 111
TF: 800-523-8193 ■ *Web:* magnatech-int.com

Magnatech LLC 6 Kripes Rd East Granby CT 06026 860-653-2573 653-0486 811
Web: www.magnatechllc.com

Magnatex Pumps Inc 3575 W 12th St Houston TX 77008 713-972-8666 972-8665 641
TF: 866-624-7867 ■ *Web:* magnatexpumps.com

Magnatron Inc 225 S Peters Rd Knoxville TN 37923 865-769-2622 177
Web: magnatron.com

Magnaworks Technology Inc
36 Carlough Rd Bohemia NY 11716 631-218-3431 458
Web: www.magnaworkstechnology.com

Magneco/Metrel Inc 51365 SR-154 Addison IL 60101 630-543-6660 543-1479 662
Web: www.magneco-metrel.com

Magnelink Inc 1060 NE 25th Ave Ste C Hillsboro OR 97124 503-844-6620 203
Web: www.magnelinkinc.com

Magnes Collection of Jewish Art & Life, The
2121 Allston Way Berkeley CA 94720 510-643-2526 520
Web: www.magnes.org

Magnesita Refractories Co
425 S Salem Church Rd York PA 17408 717-792-3611 663
Web: www.rhimagnesita.com

Magnesium Products of America Inc
2001 Industrial Dr (Island Cty Industrial Pk)
Eaton Rapids MI 48827 517-663-2700 821
Web: www.meridian-mag.com

Magness Livestock 105 Custer Ave SE Huron SD 57350 605-352-8759 446
TF: 800-310-8760 ■ *Web:* www.magness.info

Magness Oil Co
167 Tucker Cemetary Rd Gassville AR 72635 870-425-4353 425-6286 581
Web: magnessoil.com

Magnet Schultz of America Inc
401 Plaza Dr Westmont IL 60559 630-789-0600 203
Web: www.magnet-schultz.com

Magnet Technology Inc
1599 Kingsview Dr Lebanon OH 45036 513-932-4416 932-4502 458
Web: www.magtech.cc

Magnetech Industrial Services Inc
800 Nave Rd SE Massillon OH 44646 330-830-3500 830-3520 485
TF: 800-837-1614 ■ *Web:* www.magnetech.com

Magnetecs Corp
10524 La Cienega Blvd Inglewood CA 90304 310-670-7700 293
Web: www.magnetecs.com

MagneTek Inc
N49 W13650 Campbell Dr Menomonee Falls WI 53051 800-288-8178 298-3503 253
NASDAQ: MAG ■ *TF:* 800-288-8178 ■ *Web:* www.magnetek.com

Magneti Marelli Powertrain USA Inc
2101 Nash St Sanford NC 27330 919-776-4111 60
Web: www.magnetimarelli.com

Magnetic Analysis Corp
103 Fairview Park Dr Elmsford NY 10523 914-530-2000 703-3790 472
TF: 800-463-8622 ■ *Web:* www.mac-ndt.com

Magnetic Component Engineering Inc
2830 Lomita Blvd Torrance CA 90505 310-784-3100 458
Web: www.mceproducts.com

Magnetic Design Labs Inc
1636 E Edinger Ave Stes H & I Santa Ana CA 92705 714-558-3355 558-8125 253
Web: www.magneticdesign.com

Magnetic Inspection Laboratory Inc
1401 Greenleaf Ave Elk Grove Village IL 60007 847-437-4488 437-4538 743
Web: www.milinc.com

Magnetic Instrumentation Inc
8431 Castlewood Dr Indianapolis IN 46250 317-842-7500 849-7600 487
Web: maginst.com

Magnetic Metals Corp 1900 Hayes Ave Camden NJ 08105 856-964-7842 963-8569 481
TF: 800-257-8174 ■ *Web:* www.magneticmetals.com

Magnetic Products and Services Inc
7600 Boone Ave Ste 1 Brooklyn Park MN 55428 763-424-2700 237-3287 175
TF: 800-447-1277 ■ *Web:* www.mpsinc.org

Magnetic Products Inc
683 Town Center Dr Highland MI 48357 800-544-5930 567
TF: 800-544-5930 ■ *Web:* www.mpimagnet.com

Magnetic Springs Water Co
1917 Joyce Ave Columbus OH 43219 800-572-2990 297-8
TF: 800-572-2990 ■ *Web:* www.magneticsprings.com

Magnetrol International Inc
5300 Belmont Rd Downers Grove IL 60515 630-969-4000 969-9489 201
TF: 800-624-8765 ■ *Web:* www.magnetrol.com

Magnets Usa 817 Connecticut Ave NE Roanoke VA 24012 800-869-7562 195
TF: 800-869-7562 ■ *Web:* www.magnetsusa.com

Magnetscom 51 Pacific Ave Ste 4 Jersey City NJ 07304 866-229-8237 366
TF: 866-229-8237 ■ *Web:* www.magnets.com

Magnevolt Inc 5335 US 70 Bus Hwy W Clayton NC 27520 919-790-9686 74
Web: magnevolt.com

Magni Group Inc 390 Park St Birmingham MI 48009 248-647-4500 550
Web: magnicoatings.com

Magniflood Inc
7200 New Horizons Blvd Amityville NY 11701 631-226-1000 439
Web: www.magniflood.com

Magnifying Ctr 10086 W McNab Rd Tamarac FL 33321 954-722-1580 543
TF: 800-364-1612 ■ *Web:* www.magnifyingcenter.com

Magnitude Capital LLC
200 Park Ave 56th Fl New York NY 10166 212-915-3900 915-3901 401
Web: www.magnitudecapital.com

Magnitude Software
515 Congress Ave Ste 1510 Austin TX 78701 866-466-3849 436-0406 178-1
TF: 866-466-3849 ■ *Web:* www.magnitudesoftware.com

Magno International Lp
11014 NW 33rd St Ste 100 Doral FL 33172 305-392-4726 770
TF: 877-506-8909 ■ *Web:* www.magnointl.com

	Phone	Fax	Class
Magno Sound Inc			
729 Seventh Ave 2nd Fl . . . New York NY 10019	212-302-2505		514
Web: magnoscreening.com			
Magnolia Advanced Materials Inc			
4360 NE Expy . . . Atlanta GA 30340	770-451-2777		3
TF: 800-831-8031 ■ *Web:* magnolia-adv-mat.com			
Magnolia Brush Manufacturing Ltd			
1000 N Cedar St PO Box 932 . . . Clarksville TX 75426	903-427-2261	427-5231*	103
**Fax Area Code: 800* ■ *TF:* 800-248-2261 ■ *Web:* www.magnoliabrush.com			
Magnolia Cafe 2304 Lake Austin Blvd . . . Austin TX 78703	512-478-8645		671
Web: www.magnoliacafeaustin.com			
Magnolia Clipping Service			
298 Commerce Pk Dr Ste A . . . Ridgeland MS 39157	601-856-0911	856-3340	624
Web: magnoliaclips.com			
Magnolia College of Cosmetology			
4725 I-55 N . . . Jackson MS 39206	601-362-6940	362-7405	167-3
Web: www.mcocjackson.com			
Magnolia Consulting LLC			
5135 Blenheim Rd . . . Charlottesville VA 22902	434-984-5540		196
Web: magnoliaconsulting.org			
Magnolia Estates 1511 Dulles Dr. . . . LaFayette LA 70506	337-216-0950		371
Web: camelotseniorliving.com			
Magnolia Financial Inc			
187 W Broad St . . . Spartanburg SC 29306	864-699-8178	573-9912	272
TF: 866-573-0611 ■ *Web:* www.magfinancial.com			
Magnolia Forest Products Inc			
13252 I- 55 S PO Box 99 . . . Terry MS 39170	800-366-6374	878-2590*	191-3
**Fax Area Code: 601* ■ *TF:* 800-366-6374 ■ *Web:* www.magnoliaforest.com			
Magnolia Grange & Museum			
10111 Iron Bridge Rd PO Box 40 . . . Chesterfield VA 23832	804-796-7121	777-9643	520
Web: www.chesterfieldhistory.com			
Magnolia Hotel & Spa, The			
623 Courtney St . . . Victoria BC V8W1B8	250-381-0999	381-0988	379
TF: 877-624-6654 ■ *Web:* magnoliahotel.com			
Magnolia Hotel Dallas 1401 Commerce St . . . Dallas TX 75201	214-915-6500	253-0053	379
TF: 888-915-1110 ■ *Web:* magnoliahotels.com			
Magnolia Manor Inc 2001 S Lee St . . . Americus GA 31709	229-924-9352		450
TF: 855-540-5433 ■ *Web:* www.magnoliamanor.com			
Magnolia Metal Corp			
10675 Bedford Ave Ste 200 . . . Omaha NE 68134	402-455-8762		308
TF: 800-228-4043 ■ *Web:* magnoliabronze.com			
Magnolia Mound Plantation			
2161 Nicholson Dr . . . Baton Rouge LA 70802	225-343-4955		520
Web: brec.org			
Magnolia Pictures LLC			
49 W 27th St 7th Fl . . . New York NY 10001	212-924-6701	924-6742	748
Web: www.magpictures.com			
Magnolia Plantation & Gardens			
3550 Ashley River Rd . . . Charleston SC 29414	843-571-1266		97
TF: 800-367-3517 ■ *Web:* www.magnoliaplantation.com			
Magnolia Regional Health Ctr			
611 Alcorn Dr . . . Corinth MS 38834	662-293-1000	287-5792	374-3
Web: www.mrhc.org			
Magnolia Springs State Park			
1053 Magnolia Springs Dr . . . Millen GA 30442	478-982-1660		565
Web: gastateparks.org			
Magnolia Steel Company Inc			
PO Box 5007 . . . Meridian MS 39302	601-693-4301		480
Web: www.magnoliasteel.com			
Magnolia-Columbia County Chamber of Commerce			
211 W Main St PO Box 866 . . . Magnolia AR 71753	870-234-4352	234-9291	139
Web: www.magnoliachamber.com			
Magnotta Winery Corp 271 Chrislea Rd . . . Vaughan ON L4L8N6	905-738-9463	738-5551	80-3
TF: 800-461-9463 ■ *Web:* www.magnotta.com			
Magnum Equipment Inc			
5817 Plauche St . . . New Orleans LA 70123	800-737-6322		605
TF: 800-737-6322 ■ *Web:* www.magnumequipment.com			
Magnum Hospitality Inc			
5112 US 31 N . . . Williamsburg MI 49690	231-932-1633		360-3
Web: www.magnumhospitality.com			
Magnum Integrated Technologies Inc			
200 First Gulf Blvd . . . Brampton ON L6W4T5	905-595-1998	455-0422	674
TF: 800-830-0642 ■ *Web:* www.mit-world.com			
Magnum Machining Inc			
20959 State Hwy 6 . . . Deerwood MN 56444	218-534-3552		454
Web: www.magnummachining.com			
Magnum Magnetics Corp			
801 Masonic Park Rd . . . Marietta OH 45750	740-373-7770	373-2880	458
TF: 800-258-0991 ■ *Web:* www.magnummagnetics.com			
Magnum Photos 12 W 31st St. . . . New York NY 10001	212-929-6000	929-9325	592
Web: magnumphotos.com			
Magnum Research Inc			
12602 33rd Ave SW . . . Pillager MN 56473	218-746-4597	746-3097	711
TF: 800-772-6168 ■ *Web:* www.magnumresearch.com			
Magnum Staffing			
2500 E TC Jester Ste 250 . . . Houston TX 77008	713-658-0068	523-3621	721
Web: www.magnumstaffing.com			
Magnus Equipment 4500 Beidler Rd . . . Willoughby OH 44094	440-942-8488		358
TF: 800-456-6423 ■ *Web:* magnusequipment.com			
Magnus Mobility Systems Inc			
2805 Barranca Pkwy . . . Irvine CA 92606	714-771-2630	744-0134	350
TF: 800-858-7801 ■ *Web:* www.magnusinc.com			
Magnus Studios 905 Early St . . . Santa Fe NM 87505	505-983-0810		411
Web: www.douglasmagnus.com			
Magnus/Farley Inc			
1300 Morningside Rd PO Box 1029 . . . Fremont NE 68025	402-721-9540		650
Web: magnus-bearings.com			
Magnus-hitech Industries Inc			
1605 Lake St. . . . Melbourne FL 32901	321-724-9731		697
Web: www.magnushitech.com			
Magnuson Hotels 525 E Mission Ave . . . Spokane WA 99202	866-904-1309	744-0364*	707
**Fax Area Code: 509* ■ *TF:* 866-904-1309 ■ *Web:* www.magnusonhotels.com			
Magnussen Home Furnishings Ltd			
66 Hincks St . . . New Hamburg ON N3A2A3	877-552-5670		320
TF: 877-552-5670 ■ *Web:* www.magnussen.com			
Magnusson Klemencic Associates Inc			
1301 Fifth Ave Ste 3200 . . . Seattle WA 98101	206-292-1200		261
Web: www.mka.com			

	Phone	Fax	Class
Magoffin County			
201 E Maple St PO Box 430 . . . Salyersville KY 41465	606-349-2313		338
Web: magoffincounty.ky.gov			
Magoffin Home State Historic Site			
1120 Magoffin Ave . . . El Paso TX 79901	915-533-5147		565
Web: www.thc.texas.gov			
Magotteaux Inc			
725 Cool Springs Blvd Cool Springs III Ste 200 . . . Franklin TN 37067	615-385-3055		485
Web: www.magotteaux.com			
Magpie Publications PO Box 636 . . . Alamo CA 94507	925-838-9287	838-9287*	637-2
**Fax Area Code: 825* ■ *TF:* 800-624-7435 ■ *Web:* magpiepublications.com			
MagPortal.com PO Box 463 . . . Bryn Mawr PA 19010	610-581-7702		397
Web: www.magportal.com			
Magtech Industries Corp			
5625 Arville St Ste A . . . Las Vegas NV 89118	702-364-9998		253
TF: 888-954-4481 ■ *Web:* www.magtechind.com			
Magtrol Inc 70 Gardenville Pkwy . . . Buffalo NY 14224	716-668-5555	668-8705	620
TF: 800-828-7844 ■ *Web:* www.magtrol.com			
Maguire & Schneider LLP			
1650 Lake Shore Dr Ste 150 . . . Columbus OH 43204	614-224-1222		41
TF: 800-600-1222 ■ *Web:* msh-lawfirm.com			
Maguire Associates Inc			
555 Virginia Rd 5 Concord Farms Ste 201 . . . Concord MA 01742	978-371-1775		466
Web: www.maguireassoc.com			
Maguire Iron Inc			
1610 N Minnesota Ave . . . Sioux Falls SD 57104	605-334-9749	334-9752	480
Web: maguireiron.com			
MaguireZay 17194 Preston Rd Ste 102-143 . . . Dallas TX 75248	214-692-5002	250-4467*	463
**Fax Area Code: 972* ■ *TF:* 888-400-6929 ■ *Web:* maguirezay.com			
Magyar Bancorp Inc			
400 Somerset St . . . New Brunswick NJ 08901	732-342-7600		70
NASDAQ: MGYR ■ *Web:* www.magbank.com			
MAH (Mount Auburn Hospital)			
330 Mt Auburn St . . . Cambridge MA 02138	617-492-3500		374-3
Web: www.mountauburnhospital.org			
Mahaffey & Gore PC			
300 NE First St . . . Oklahoma City OK 73104	405-236-0478		428
Web: www.mahaffeygorelaw.com			
Mahaffey Enterprises			
3327 E Ridgeview St . . . Springfield MO 65804	417-883-9180		643
Mahaffey Theater for the Performing Arts			
400 First St S . . . Saint Petersburg FL 33701	727-892-5798	892-5897	572
Web: www.themahaffey.com			
Mahaffey's Quality Printing Inc			
355 W Pearl St . . . Jackson MS 39203	601-353-9663	960-3662	627
TF: 800-843-1135 ■ *Web:* qualityprinting.com			
Mahanoy Area School District			
1 Golden Bear Dr . . . Mahanoy City PA 17948	570-773-3443		685
Web: www.mabears.net			
Mahar Tool Supply Company Inc			
112 Williams St PO Box 1747 . . . Saginaw MI 48602	989-799-5530	799-0830	385
TF: 800-456-2427 ■ *Web:* www.mahartool.com			
Maharaja 1550 N Farwell Ave . . . Milwaukee WI 53202	414-276-2250		671
Web: www.maharajarestaurants.com			
Maharaja Restaurant			
6308 Hulen Bend Blvd . . . Fort Worth TX 76132	817-263-7156		671
Web: www.maharajadfw.com			
Maharishi University of Management			
1000 N 4th St . . . Fairfield IA 52557	641-472-1110	472-1179	166
TF: 800-369-6480 ■ *Web:* www.mum.edu			
Mahaska Bottling Co 1407 17th Ave E . . . Oskaloosa IA 52577	800-747-3481		805
TF: 800-747-3481 ■ *Web:* www.mahaska.com			
Mahaska County 106 S First St 2nd Fl . . . Oskaloosa IA 52577	641-673-7786	673-2586	338
Web: www.mahaskacounty.org			
Maher Accountancy			
1101 Fifth Ave Ste 200 . . . San Rafael CA 94901	415-459-1249		2
Web: mahercpa.com			
Maher Duessel			
DL Clark Bldg 503 Martindale St Ste 600 . . . Pittsburgh PA 15212	412-471-5500		466
Web: www.md-cpas.com			
Maher Terminals LLC 1210 Corbin St . . . Elizabeth NJ 07201	908-527-8200	436-4803	313
Web: www.maherterminals.com			
Maher, Guiley & Maher PA			
271 W Canton Ave Ste 1 PO Box 2209 . . . Winter Park FL 32789	855-338-0720		428
TF: 855-338-0720 ■ *Web:* www.maherlawfirm.com			
Mahindra USA Inc			
9020 Jackrabbit Rd Ste 600 . . . Houston TX 77095	281-449-7771	372-0357	273
TF: 877-449-7771 ■ *Web:* www.mahindrausa.com			
MAHLE Industries Inc 2020 Sanford St . . . Muskegon MI 49444	231-722-1300		128
TF: 888-255-1942 ■ *Web:* www.us.mahle.com			
Mahlum Architects Inc			
71 Columbia 4th Fl . . . Seattle WA 98104	206-441-4151	441-0478	261
Web: www.mahlum.com			
Mahogany Grille 699 Main Ave . . . Durango CO 81301	970-247-4433	259-2208	671
TF: 800-247-4431 ■ *Web:* www.strater.com			
Mahogany Prime Steak House			
4840 E 61st St . . . Tulsa OK 74136	918-494-4043		671
Web: www.mahoganyprimesteakhouse.com			
Mahomed Sales and Warehousing LLC			
8258 Zionsville Rd . . . Indianapolis IN 46268	317-472-5800	472-5801	803-1
Web: www.whse.com			
Mahoney Associates Inc			
2455 E Sunrise Blvd Ste 300 . . . Fort Lauderdale FL 33304	954-564-4300		194
TF: 800-477-7303 ■ *Web:* www.mahoneyandassociates.com			
Mahoney Group, The			
5330 N La Cholla Blvd . . . Tucson AZ 85741	520-795-8511	795-8542	390
Web: www.mahoneygroup.com			
Mahoney Institute of Neurological Sciences			
3535 Market St Mezzanine . . . Philadelphia PA 19104	215-662-2560	349-8312	668
Web: www.med.upenn.edu			
Mahoney Ulbrich Christiansen & Russ P A			
30 E Plato Blvd . . . Saint Paul MN 55107	651-227-6695		2
Web: www.mucr.com			
Mahoney's Garden Ctr			
242 Cambridge St . . . Winchester MA 01890	781-729-5900		323
Web: www.mahoneysgarden.com			
Mahoning County 120 Market St . . . Youngstown OH 44503	330-740-2104	740-2105	338
TF: 800-548-7175 ■ *Web:* www.mahoningcountyoh.gov			

	Phone	Fax	Class
Mahoning County Convention & Visitors Bureau 21 W Boardman St........................Youngstown OH 44503 *TF:* 800-447-8201 ■ *Web:* youngstownlive.com	330-740-2130	740-2144	206
Mahoning Valley Distributing Agency Inc 2556 Rush Blvd.........................Youngstown OH 44507 *TF:* 866-203-8809 ■ *Web:* www.booksnmagz.com	330-788-9661	788-9046	96
Mahopac Bank 1441 Rt 22....................Brewster NY 10509 *TF:* 866-462-2658 ■ *Web:* www.mahopacbank.com	845-278-1011		70
Mahr Inc 1144 Eddy St......................Providence RI 02905 *Web:* www.mahr.com	401-784-3100	784-3246	201
Mahuta Tool Corp N118W19137 Bunsen Dr.................Germantown WI 53022 *TF:* 888-686-4940 ■ *Web:* www.mahutatool.com	262-502-4100		757
MAI (Minuteman Aviation Inc) 5225 Hwy 10 W...........................Missoula MT 59808 *Web:* www.minutemanaviation.net	406-728-9363		63
MAI (Medical Action Industries Inc) 9120 Lockwood Blvd..................Mechanicsville VA 23116 *TF:* 800-645-7042 ■ *Web:* www.medical-action.com	800-488-8850		477
Mai Thai 750 W Idaho St........................Boise ID 83702 *Web:* www.maithaigroup.com	208-344-8424		671
Maibec Inc 202 1984 Fifth St.....................Levis QC G6W5M6 *TF:* 800-363-1930 ■ *Web:* www.maibec.com	418-659-3323	653-4354	683
Maid Brigade USA/Minimaid Canada 4 Concourse Pkwy Ste 200.....................Atlanta GA 30328 *TF:* 866-800-7470 ■ *Web:* www.maidbrigade.com	800-722-6243		152
Maida Development Co 201 S Mallory St.......Hampton VA 23663 *Web:* www.maida.com	757-723-0785	722-1194	253
MaidPro Corp 180 Canal St.....................Boston MA 02114 *Web:* www.maidpro.com	617-742-8080		310
Maid-Rite Specialty Foods LLC 105 Keystone Industrial Pk...................Dunmore PA 18512 *TF:* 800-233-4259 ■ *Web:* www.mr-specialty.com	800-233-4259		296-26
Maids Intl 9394 W Dodge Rd Ste 140.............Omaha NE 68114 *TF:* 800-843-6243 ■ *Web:* www.maids.com	402-558-8600	558-4112	152
Maidstone Hotel, The 207 Main St........East Hampton NY 11937 *Web:* www.themaidstone.com	631-324-5006		378
Maidstone State Park 5956 Maidstone Lake Rd....................Guildhall VT 05905 *Web:* vtstateparks.com	802-676-3930		565
Maier Siebel Baber 80 E Sir Francis Drake Blvd..................Larkspur CA 94939 *Web:* www.msb-realestate.com	415-591-9900		655
Mail Bag Inc 3030 Waterview Ave.............Baltimore MD 21230 **Fax Area Code:* 410 ■ *Web:* www.mailbaginc.com	301-249-7800	565-5017*	5
Mail Communications Group LLC 4100 121st St..........................Des Moines IA 50323 *Web:* www.mailcommunicationsgroup.com	515-727-7700	246-1248	627
Mail Contractors of America 3809 Roundtop Dr N.................North Little Rock AR 72117	501-280-0500		780
Mail Dispatch LLC 9710 Distribution Ave......................San Diego CA 92121 *Web:* www.maildispatch.com	858-444-2350		317
Mail Handling Inc 7550 Corporate Way......................Eden Prairie MN 55344 *Web:* www.mailhandling.com	952-975-5000		627
Mail My Prescriptions 622 Banyan Trl Ste 614....................Boca Raton FL 33431 *TF:* 800-811-2541 ■ *Web:* www.mailmyprescriptions.com	800-811-2541		582
Mail Shark 4125 New Holland Rd.............Mohnton PA 19540 *TF:* 888-457-4275 ■ *Web:* www.themailshark.com	610-621-2994		366
Mail Source Inc 111 Boardwalk.............Fall Creek WI 54742 *Web:* mailsourceinc.com	715-877-3711		5
Mail Stream Inc 125 Mason Cir Ste K...........Concord CA 94520 *Web:* www.mailstream.net	925-676-6711		627
Mail Unlimited Inc 4607 Metric Dr..........Winter Park FL 32792 *Web:* mailunlimited.com	407-657-9333		5
Mailender Inc 9500 Glades Dr................Hamilton OH 45011 *TF:* 800-998-5453 ■ *Web:* www.mailender.com	513-942-5453		690
Mailer's Choice Inc 1504 Elm Hill Pk..........................Nashville TN 37210 *Web:* www.mailerschoice.com	615-883-0070		5
Mailing Services of Pittsburgh Inc 155 Commerce Dr.........................Freedom PA 15042 *TF:* 800-876-3211 ■ *Web:* www.msp-pgh.com	724-774-3244		5
Mailing Systems Inc (MSI) 2431 Mercantile Dr Ste A..............Rancho Cordova CA 95742 *TF:* 877-577-2647 ■ *Web:* www.msimail.net	916-631-7400	631-7488	5
Mailings Unlimited 116 Riverside Industrial Pkwy..................Portland ME 04103 *TF:* 800-773-7417 ■ *Web:* www.growwithmail.com	207-347-5000		5
Maillie LLP 1521 Concord Pk Ste 301.........Wilmington DE 19803 *Web:* www.maillie.com	302-358-2371		466
Mailman Research Ctr *McLean Hospital* 115 Mill St..................Belmont MA 02478 *TF:* 800-333-0338 ■ *Web:* www.mcleanhospital.org	617-855-2000		668
Mailrite Print & Mail Inc 834 Striker Ave Ste C.....................Sacramento CA 95834 *Web:* www.mailritemail.com	916-927-6245	927-8437	5
Mailroom Service Center Inc 3075 Shattuck Rd..........................Saginaw MI 48603 *Web:* www.mailroomservicecenter.com	989-790-2166		5
Maimonides Medical Ctr (MMC) 4802 Tenth Ave...........................Brooklyn NY 11219 *Web:* www.maimonidesmed.org	718-283-6000		374-3
Main & Sky Park City 201 Heber Ave Main St......................Park City UT 84060 *Web:* www.skyparkcity.com	435-658-2500	615-6751	378
Main Auction 2912 Main St.....................Boise ID 83702 *Web:* www.mainauctioncorp.com	208-344-8314		393
Main Banc Inc 2424 Louisiana Blvd NE..................Albuquerque NM 87110 *Web:* www.mainbank.com	505-880-1700		70
Main Electric Supply Co 6700 S Main St..........................Los Angeles CA 90003 *Web:* www.mainelectricsupply.com	323-753-5131	753-7750	246
Main Industries Inc 107 E St.................Hampton VA 23661 *TF:* 800-970-7264 ■ *Web:* www.mainindustries.com	757-380-0180		313
Main Line 25 Penncraft Ave Ste 4...........Chambersburg PA 17201 *Web:* www.mix95.com	717-263-0813		643
Main Line Chamber of Commerce 175 Strafford Ave Ste 130......................Wayne PA 19087 *Web:* www.mlcc.org	610-687-6232	687-8085	139
Main Line Health 240 N Radnor Chester Rd......................Radnor PA 19087 *Web:* www.mainlinehealth.org	484-580-1200		363
Main Line Speech Consultants 626 Haverford Rd.........................Haverford PA 19041 *Web:* www.mainlinespeech.com	610-649-8255	649-2924	196
Main Line Supply Company Inc 300 NFindlay Rd............................Dayton OH 45403 *Web:* www.mainlinesupply.com	937-254-6910		358
Main Line Tire & Service 100 Robbins Rd........................Downingtown PA 19335 *Web:* unitedtire.com	610-514-3600		57
Main Moon 1502 S Raccoon Rd.............Youngstown OH 44504	330-743-1638		671
Main St Animal Hospital of Bradford Inc 839 S Main St............................Bradford MA 01835 *Web:* mainstanimalhospital.com	978-373-6460		794
Main Street Advisors LLC 205 E Main St..........................Westminster MD 21157 *Web:* www.mainstadvisors.com	410-840-9200		401
Main Street America Group, The 4601 Touchton Rd E Ste 3400.............Jacksonville FL 32246 **Fax Area Code:* 866 ■ *TF:* 800-258-5310 ■ *Web:* www.msagroup.com	877-425-2467	420-8141*	391-4
Main Street Capital Corp 1300 Post Oak Blvd........................Houston TX 77056 *NYSE: MAIN* ■ *TF:* 800-966-1559 ■ *Web:* www.mainstcapital.com	713-350-6000	350-6042	405
Main Street Chamber of Leake County Inc 103 N Pearl St P O Box 209...............Carthage MS 39051 *TF:* 800-267-0111 ■ *Web:* www.leakems.com	601-267-9231		338
Main Street Gourmet Inc 170 Muffin Ln........................Cuyahoga Falls OH 44223 *TF:* 800-678-6246 ■ *Web:* www.mainstreetgourmet.com	330-929-0000		296-2
Main Street Grill & Bar 118 Main St............................Montpelier VT 05602 *Web:* www.neci.edu	802-223-3188		671
Main Street Radiology 136-25 37th Ave..........................Flushing NY 11354 *TF:* 888-930-4674 ■ *Web:* www.mainstreetradiology.com	718-428-1500	428-2475	415
Main Street Station Hotel & Casino 200 N Main St...........................Las Vegas NV 89101 *TF:* 800-713-8933 ■ *Web:* www.mainstreetcasino.com	702-387-1896		379
Main Street Veterinary Hospital 20306 N Main St.........................Cornelius NC 28031 *Web:* mainstreetveterinary.com	704-765-1115		794
Main Street Veterinary Hospital Inc 11617 Reisterstown Rd..................Reisterstown MD 21136 *Web:* mainstvet.com	410-526-7500		794
Main-Care Energy 1 Booth Ln PO Box 11029.....................Albany NY 12211 **Fax Area Code:* 518 ■ *TF:* 800-542-5552 ■ *Web:* www.maincareenergy.com	800-542-5552	438-5991*	579
Maine			
Administrative Office of the Courts PO Box 4820............................Portland ME 04112 *Web:* courts.maine.gov	207-822-0792		339-20
Arts Commission 193 State St................Augusta ME 04330 *Web:* mainearts.maine.gov	207-287-2724	287-2725	339-20
Attorney General 6 State House Stn............Augusta ME 04333 *Web:* www.maine.gov	207-626-8800		339-20
Bureau of Financial Institutions 36 State House Sta......................Augusta ME 04333 *TF:* 800-965-5235 ■ *Web:* www.maine.gov	207-624-8570	624-8590	339-20
Chief Medical Examiner 37 State House Stn.......................Augusta ME 04333 *Web:* www.maine.gov	207-624-7180	624-7178	339-20
Child & Family Services Office 2 Anthony Ave...........................Augusta ME 04333 *Web:* www.maine.gov	207-624-7900	287-5282	339-20
Consumer Protection Unit 85 Leighton Rd..........................Augusta ME 04333 *TF:* 800-436-2131 ■ *Web:* www.maine.gov	207-287-2923	287-4667	339-20
Corrections Dept 25 Tyson Dr Third Fl 111 State House Stn......Augusta ME 04333 *Web:* www.maine.gov	207-287-2711	287-4370	339-20
Economic & Community Development Dept 111 Sewall St Burton Cross Bldg Third Fl......Augusta ME 04330 *Web:* www.maine.gov	207-624-9800		339-20
Education Dept 23 State House Stn............Augusta ME 04333 *Web:* www.maine.gov	207-624-6600	624-6700	339-20
Environmental Protection Dept 17 State House Stn......................Augusta ME 04333 *TF:* 800-452-1942 ■ *Web:* www.maine.gov	207-287-7688	287-7826	339-20
Finance Authority of Maine 5 Community Dr PO Box 949...............Augusta ME 04332 *TF:* 800-228-3734 ■ *Web:* www.famemaine.com	207-623-3263	623-0095	725
Governmental Ethics & Election Practices Com 19 Anthony Ave..........................Augusta ME 04330 *Web:* www.maine.gov	207-287-4179	287-6775	265
Governor 1 State House Stn..................Augusta ME 04333 *TF:* 855-721-5203 ■ *Web:* www.maine.gov	207-287-3531	287-1034	339-20
Historic Preservation Commission 65 State House Stn......................Augusta ME 04333 *Web:* www.maine.gov	207-287-2132		339-20
Housing Authority 353 Water St..............Augusta ME 04330 *TF:* 800-452-4668 ■ *Web:* www.mainehousing.org	207-626-4600	626-4678	339-20
Human Services Dept 109 Capitol St 11 State House Sta............Augusta ME 04333 *Web:* www.maine.gov	207-287-3707		339-20
Information Services Bureau 145 State House Stn.....................Augusta ME 04333 *Web:* www.maine.gov	207-624-8800	287-4563	339-20
Inland Fisheries & Wildlife Dept 41 State House Stn......................Augusta ME 04333 *Web:* www.maine.gov	207-287-8000	287-6395	339-20
Insurance Bureau 34 State House Stn..........Augusta ME 04333 *TF:* 800-300-5000 ■ *Web:* www.maine.gov	207-624-8475	624-8599	339-20

	Phone	Fax	Class
Legislature 115 State House Stn Augusta ME 04333 *Web:* www.maine.gov	207-624-7650	287-1621	339-20
Motor Vehicles Bureau 29 State House Stn Augusta ME 04333 *Web:* www.maine.gov	207-624-9000	624-9013	339-20
Public Utilities Commission 18 State House Stn Augusta ME 04333 *TF:* 800-437-1220 ■ *Web:* www.maine.gov	207-287-3831	287-1039	339-20
Quality Assurance & Regulations Div 28 State House Stn Augusta ME 04333 *Web:* www.maine.gov	207-287-3841	287-5576	339-20
Rehabilitation Services Bureau 150 State House Sta Augusta ME 04333 **Fax Area Code: 207* ■ *TF:* 800-698-4440 ■ *Web:* www.maine.gov	800-698-4440	287-5292*	339-20
Revenue Services 24 State House Stn Augusta ME 04333 *Web:* www.maine.gov	207-287-2076	287-3618	339-20
Secretary of State 148 State House Stn Augusta ME 04333 *Web:* www.maine.gov	207-626-8400	287-8598	339-20
Securities Div 76 Northern Ave Gardiner ME 04345 *TF:* 877-624-8551 ■ *Web:* www.maine.gov	207-624-8551	624-8590	339-20
State Government Information 26 Edison Dr Augusta ME 04330 *TF:* 888-577-6690 ■ *Web:* www.maine.gov	207-624-9494		339-20
State Police 45 Commerce Dr 42 State House Stn Augusta ME 04333 *Web:* www.maine.gov	207-626-3805		339-20
Supreme Court 205 Newbury St Rm 139 Portland ME 04101 *Web:* www.courts.maine.gov	207-822-4286		339-20
Tourism Office 59 State House Sta Augusta ME 04333 **Fax Area Code: 877* ■ *TF:* 888-624-6345 ■ *Web:* visitmaine.com	207-624-7483	624-6331*	339-20
Veterans' Services Bureau 117 State House Stn Augusta ME 04333 *Web:* www.maine.gov	207-430-6035	626-4471	339-20
Victims' Compensation Program 6 State House Sta Augusta ME 04333 *TF:* 800-903-7882 ■ *Web:* www.maine.gov	207-624-7882	624-7730	339-20
Vital Records Office 220 Capitol St Augusta ME 04333 *TF:* 888-664-9491 ■ *Web:* www.maine.gov	207-287-3181		339-20
Workers' Compensation Board 442 Civic Center Dr 27 State House Stn Ste 100 Augusta ME 04333 *TF:* 888-801-9087 ■ *Web:* www.maine.gov	207-287-3751	287-7198	339-20
Maine Association of Realtors 19 Community Dr Augusta ME 04330 *Web:* www.mainerealtors.com	207-622-7501	623-3590	656
Maine Beer Company LLC 525 US Route 1 Freeport ME 04032 *Web:* mainebeercompany.com	207-221-5711		102
Maine Biotechnology Services Inc 1037 R Forest Ave Portland ME 04103 *TF:* 800-925-9476 ■ *Web:* mainebiotechnology.com	207-797-5454	797-5595	231
Maine Board of Licensure in Medicine 161 Capitol St Augusta ME 04330 *Web:* www.maine.gov	207-287-3601	287-6590	339-20
Maine Boats, Homes & Harbors 218 S Main St Rockland ME 04841 *TF:* 800-565-4951 ■ *Web:* www.maineboats.com	207-594-8622	593-0026	637-9
Maine Bucket Co 21 Fireslate Pl Lewiston ME 04240 *TF:* 800-231-7072 ■ *Web:* mainebucket.com	207-784-6700		200
Maine Central Institute 295 Main St Pittsfield ME 04967 *Web:* www.mci-school.org	207-487-3355	487-3512	622
Maine Coast Heritage Trust 1 Bowdoin Mill Is Ste 201 Topsham ME 04086 *Web:* mcht.org	207-729-7366		804
Maine College of Art 522 Congress St Portland ME 04101 *Web:* www.meca.edu	207-775-3052	772-5069	164
Maine College of Health Professions 70 Middle St Lewiston ME 04240 *Web:* www.mchp.edu	207-795-2840	795-2849	800
Maine Correctional Ctr 17 Mallison Falls Rd Windham ME 04062 *Web:* www.maine.gov	207-893-7000	893-7001	213
Maine Course Hospitality Group Inc 15 Main St Ste 210 Freeport ME 04032 *Web:* www.mchg.com	207-865-6105		378
Maine Democratic Party PO Box 5258 Augusta ME 04332 *Web:* www.mainedems.org	207-622-6233	352-0482	616-1
Maine Dental Assn 29 Assn Dr Manchester ME 04351 *Web:* www.medental.org	207-622-7900		227
Maine Educator Magazine 35 Community Dr Augusta ME 04330 *TF:* 800-332-8529 ■ *Web:* www.centralmaine.com	207-622-5866		457-8
Maine Endwell Central School 712 Farm to Market Rd Endwell NY 13760 *Web:* www.me.stier.org	607-754-1400	754-1650	685
Maine Family Federal Credit Union 555 Sabattus St Lewiston ME 04240 *Web:* mainefamilyfcu.com	207-783-2071		219
Maine Historical Society Maine Historical Society 489 Congress St Portland ME 04101 *Web:* www.mainehistory.org	207-774-1822	775-4301	520
Maine Hospital Assn 33 Fuller Rd Augusta ME 04330 *Web:* themha.org	207-622-4794		138
Maine Instrument Flight Inc 215 Winthrop St Augusta ME 04330 *TF:* 888-643-3597 ■ *Web:* www.maineinstrumentflight.com	207-622-1211	622-7858	63
Maine International Trade Ctr 2 Portland Fish Pier Ste 204 Portland ME 04101 *Web:* www.mitc.com	207-541-7400	541-7420	78
Maine Lobster Direct 48 Union Wharf Portland ME 04101 *TF:* 800-556-2783 ■ *Web:* www.mainelobsterdirect.com	800-556-2783		297-5
Maine Machine Products Co 79 Prospect Ave PO Box 260 South Paris ME 04281 *Web:* www.precinmac.com	207-743-6344		454
Maine Mall 364 Maine Mall Rd South Portland ME 04106 *Web:* www.mainemall.com	207-774-0303		460
Maine Maritime Academy 66 Pleasant St Castine ME 04420 *TF:* 800-464-6565 ■ *Web:* www.mainemaritime.edu	207-326-4311	326-2515	166
Maine Maritime Museum 243 Washington St Bath ME 04530 *Web:* www.mainemaritimemuseum.org	207-443-1316	443-1665	520
Maine Medical Assn 30 Assn Dr Manchester ME 04351 *Web:* www.mainemed.com	207-622-3374	622-3332	474
Maine Medical Ctr (MMC) 22 Bramhall St Portland ME 04102 *TF:* 877-339-3107 ■ *Web:* mainehealth.org	207-662-0111		374-3
Maine Municipal Assn (MMA) 60 Community Dr Augusta ME 04330 *TF:* 800-452-8786 ■ *Web:* www.memun.org	207-623-8428	626-5947	48-13
Maine Narrow Gauge Railroad Museum 58 Fore St Portland ME 04101 *Web:* www.mainenarrowgauge.org	207-828-0814		520
Maine Nurse Practitioners Assn 11 Columbia St Augusta ME 04330 *Web:* www.mnpa.us	207-621-0313		533
Maine People's Alliance 27 State St Ste 44 Bangor ME 04401 *Web:* www.mainepeoplesalliance.org	207-990-0672		615
Maine Pharmacy Assn 127 Pleasant Hill Rd Scarborough ME 04074 *Web:* www.mparx.com	207-502-0825		585
Maine Plastics Inc 1817 Kenosha Rd Zion IL 60099 *TF:* 800-338-7728 ■ *Web:* www.maineplastics.com	847-379-9100		603
Maine Pointe LLC 470 Atlantic Ave 4th Fl Boston MA 02210 *Web:* www.mainepointe.com	617-273-8450		194
Maine Potato Growers Inc 261 Main St Presque Isle ME 04769 *TF:* 800-649-3358 ■ *Web:* www.mpgco-op.com	207-764-3131	764-8450	274
Maine Public Broadcasting Network 63 Texas Ave Bangor ME 04401 **Fax Area Code: 207* ■ *TF:* 800-884-1717 ■ *Web:* www.mainepublic.org	800-884-1717	942-2857*	647
Maine Republican Party 9 Higgins St Augusta ME 04330 *Web:* www.mainegop.com	207-622-6247		616-2
Maine State Ballet 348 US Rt 1 Falmouth ME 04105 *Web:* www.mainestateballet.org	207-781-7672		573-1
Maine State Bar Assn 124 State St Augusta ME 04330 *TF:* 800-475-7523 ■ *Web:* www.mainebar.org	207-622-7523	623-0083	72
Maine State Chamber of Commerce 125 Community Dr Ste 101 Augusta ME 04330 *TF:* 800-546-7866 ■ *Web:* www.mainechamber.org	207-623-4568	622-7723	140
Maine State Library 64 State House Stn Augusta ME 04333 *TF:* 800-427-8336 ■ *Web:* www.maine.gov	207-287-5600	287-5615	434-5
Maine State Museum 83 State House Sta Augusta ME 04333 *Web:* mainestatemuseum.org	207-287-2301	287-6633	520
Maine Tourism Assn (MTA) 327 Water St Hallowell ME 04347 *Web:* www.mainetourism.com	207-623-0363	623-0388	139
Maine Veterans' Homes 460 Civic Center Dr Augusta ME 04330 *TF:* 800-278-9494 ■ *Web:* mainevets.org	800-278-9494		793
Maine Veterinary Medical Assn (MVMA) 97A Exchange St Ste 305 Portland ME 04101 *TF:* 800-448-2772 ■ *Web:* netforum.avectra.com	800-448-2772		795
Maine Windjammer Cruises PO Box 617 Camden ME 04843 *TF:* 800-736-7981 ■ *Web:* www.mainewindjammercruises.com	207-236-2938	236-3229	220
Maine Wood Concepts Inc 1687 New Vineyard Rd New Vineyard ME 04956 *TF:* 800-374-6961 ■ *Web:* www.mainewoodconcepts.com	877-728-4442		820
Mainebiz 48 Free St Portland ME 04101 *Web:* www.mainebiz.biz	207-761-8379		530
MaineGeneral Medical Ctr (MGMC) *Augusta* 361 Old Belgrade Rd Augusta ME 04330 *TF:* 855-464-4463 ■ *Web:* www.mainegeneral.org	207-621-6100		374-3
Mainegov *Fort O'Brien State Historic Site* c/o Cobscook Bay State Pk 40 S Edmunds Rd Edmunds Township ME 04628 *Web:* www.maine.gov	207-726-4412		565
Mainelli Wagner & Associates Inc 6920 Van Dorn St Ste A Lincoln NE 68506 *Web:* www.mwaeng.com	402-421-1717		261
Mainetti USA 300 Mac Ln Keasbey NJ 08832 **Fax Area Code: 732* ■ *Web:* www.mainetti.com	201-215-2900	738-7210*	607
Mainland Medical Center Auxilary Inc 6801 Emmett Lowry Expy Texas City TX 77591 *Web:* mainlandmedical.com	409-938-5000		374-3
Mainland preparatory Academy 319 Newman Rd La Marque TX 77568 *Web:* mainland-classical.responsiveed.com	409-934-9100		559
Mainland Press 4340 J A Yount Farm Rd Conover NC 28613 *Web:* www.mainlandpress.com	828-464-1565	464-3721	637-2
Mainline Information Systems Inc 1700 Summit Lake Dr Tallahassee FL 32317 *TF:* 866-490-6246 ■ *Web:* www.mainline.com	850-219-5000		180
Mainline Printing Inc 3500 SW Topeka Blvd Topeka KS 66611 *Web:* mainlineprinting.com	785-233-2338		627
Mains'l Services Inc 7000 78th Ave N Brooklyn Park MN 55445 *TF:* 800-441-6525 ■ *Web:* www.mainsl.com	800-441-6525		363
Mainsail Partners 1 Front St Ste 3000 San Francisco CA 94111 *Web:* www.mainsailpartners.com	415-391-3150		360-3
Mainsaver Software LLC 10803 Thornmint Rd San Diego CA 92127 *TF:* 844-324-9190 ■ *Web:* www.mainsaver.com	858-674-8700	674-8735	179
MainScapes Inc 20400 New Hampshire Ave Brinklow MD 20862 *Web:* www.mainscapes.com	301-260-0190		776
MainSpring Inc 8 E Second St Ste 205 Frederick MD 21701 *Web:* gomainspring.com	301-948-8077		180
Mainstay 770 Paseo Camarillo Ste 120 Camarillo CA 93010 *TF:* 800-362-2605 ■ *Web:* www.mstay.com	805-484-9400	484-9428	178-1
Mainstay Publishing PO Box 293 Middletown DE 19709 *Web:* www.mainstaypublishing.com	302-223-6636		637-2

				Phone	Fax	Class
Mainstay Technologies 201 Daniel Webster Hwy. *Web:* www.mstech.com	Belmont	NH	03220	603-524-4774	556-8074	180
Mainstay Veterinary Practice L 3083 Nutley St *Web:* mainstayvet.com	Fairfax	VA	22031	703-280-4588		794
Mainstream Data Inc 375 Chipeta Way Ste B *TF:* 800-473-3332 ■ *Web:* www.mainstreamdata.com	Salt Lake City	UT	84108	801-584-2800	584-2831	387
Mainstream Engineering Corp 200 Yellow Pl *TF:* 800-866-3550 ■ *Web:* www.mainstream-engr.com	Rockledge	FL	32955	321-631-3550	631-3552	256
Mainstream Technologies Inc 325 W Capitol Ave Ste 200 *Web:* mainstream-tech.com	Little Rock	AR	72201	501-217-9490		177
Mainstreet Computers LLC 330 Charles St *TF:* 800-698-6246 ■ *Web:* mainstreetcomp.com	Belleville	MI	48111	734-699-0025		225
Mainstreet Organization of Realtors 6655 S Main *Web:* succeedwithmore.com	Downers Grove	IL	60516	630-324-8400		652
Mainstreet Ventures Inc 15 Research Dr *Web:* www.mainstreetventuresinc.com	Ann Arbor	MI	48103	734-668-6062	668-7261	670
Maintech Inc 14 Commerce Dr Ste 200 *Web:* www.maintech.com	Cranford	NJ	07016	973-330-3200		177
Maintenx 2202 N Howard Ave *TF:* 855-751-0075 ■ *Web:* maintenx.com	Tampa	FL	33607	855-751-0075		610
Mainthia Technologies Inc 7055 Engle Rd Ste 502 *Web:* www.mainthia.com	Cleveland	OH	44130	440-816-0202	816-1121	271
MaintStar 28 Hammond Unit D *TF:* 800-255-5675 ■ *Web:* www.maintstar.com	Irvine	CA	92618	949-458-7560	458-7626	261
Mairs & Power Inc 332 Minnesota St W Ste 1520 First National Bank Bldg *TF:* 800-304-7404 ■ *Web:* www.mairsandpower.com	Saint Paul	MN	55101	651-222-8478		528
Maison 140 Beverly Hills 140 Lasky Dr *Web:* www.maison140.com	Beverly Hills	CA	90212	310-281-4000		379
Maison Carlos 3010 S Dixie Hwy *Web:* www.maisoncarlos.com	West Palm Beach	FL	33405	561-659-6524		671
Maison Dupuy Hotel 1001 Toulouse St *TF:* 800-535-9177 ■ *Web:* www.maisondupuy.com	New Orleans	LA	70112	504-586-8000		379
Maison May 246 DeKalb Ave *Web:* maison-may.com	Brooklyn	NY	11205	718-789-2778		671
Maison Sapho School of Dressmaking & Design 312 W 83rd St *Web:* www.dressmaking-school.com	New York	NY	10024	212-873-9183		685
Maison Weiss 4500 I-55 N Ste 109 *Web:* maisonweiss.com	Jackson	MS	39211	601-981-4621	981-4671	157-6
Maisons Marques & Domaines USA Inc 383 Fourth St Ste 400 *Web:* mmdusa.net	Oakland	CA	94607	510-587-2000		81-3
Maitech International Inc 12603 SW Fwy Ste 552 *Web:* www.maitechinternational.com	Stafford	TX	77477	281-240-2030	240-2032	351
Maithuna Publications 324 Minister Hill Rd *Web:* www.goodideacreative.com	Wheelock	VT	05851	802-626-1154		637-2
Maitland Area Chamber of Commerce 110 N Maitland Ave *Web:* maitlandchamber.com	Maitland	FL	32751	407-644-0741	539-2529	139
Maitland Art Ctr 231 W Packwood Ave **Fax Area Code:* 888 ■ *Web:* www.artandhistory.org	Maitland	FL	32751	407-539-2181	316-5729*	50-2
Maitland Primrose Group Inc 7220 N 16th St Ste c *Web:* www.maitlandprimrose.com	Phoenix	AZ	85020	602-944-0046		514
Maitra Associates PC 27 Worlds Fair Dr *Web:* www.maitra.com	Somerset	NJ	08873	732-868-1313	868-1778	261
Maize *Maize Restaurant* 50 Pk Pl *Web:* maizerestaurant.com	Newark	NJ	07102	973-639-1200		671
Majerle's Sports Grill 24 N Second St *Web:* majerles.com	Phoenix	AZ	85004	602-253-0118		671
Majesco 412 Mt Kemble Ave Ste 110c *Web:* www.majesco.com	Morristown	NJ	07960	973-461-5200	496-9126	225
Majestic Drug Company Inc 4996 Main St Rt 42 *TF:* 800-238-0220 ■ *Web:* www.majesticdrug.com	South Fallsburg	NY	12779	845-436-0011		237
Majestic Hotel, The 528 W Brompton *TF:* 800-727-5108 ■ *Web:* majestic-chicago.com	Chicago	IL	60657	773-404-3499		379
Majestic Industries Inc 15378 Hallmark Ct *Web:* www.majesticind.net	Macomb	MI	48042	586-786-9100		697
Majestic Medical Solutions LLC 207 W Eastbank St *TF:* 866-580-9729 ■ *Web:* majesticms.com	Gonzales	LA	70737	225-677-9867		475
Majestic Metals Inc 7770 N Washington St *Web:* majesticmetals.com	Denver	CO	80229	303-288-6855	288-2880	697
Majestic Realty Co 13191 Crossroads Pkwy N 6th Fl *Web:* www.majesticrealty.com	City of Industry	CA	91746	562-692-9581	695-2329	655
Majestic Star Casino & Hotel 1 Buffington Harbor Dr *TF:* 888-225-8259 ■ *Web:* www.majesticstarcasino.com	Gary	IN	46406	888-225-8259		133
Majestic Steakhouse 931 Broadway *Web:* majestickc.com	Kansas City	MO	64105	816-221-1888		671
Majestic Steel USA 5300 Majestic Pkwy *TF:* 800-321-5590 ■ *Web:* www.majesticsteel.com	Cleveland	OH	44146	440-786-2666	786-0576	492
Majestic Theatre 1925 Elm St Ste 500 *Web:* dallasculture.org	Dallas	TX	75201	214-670-3687	670-1404	572
Majestic Theatre 4120 Woodward Ave *Web:* majesticdetroit.com	Detroit	MI	48201	313-833-9700		572
Majestic Transportation 283 Lockhaven Ste 100 *Web:* www.majestictransportation.com	Houston	TX	77073	281-869-8031	869-8039	449
Majesty Home Health Inc 18527 Roscoe Blvd *Web:* majestyhomehealthinc.com	Northridge	CA	91324	818-775-9447	775-9448	363
Majic 102.3/92.7 8515 Georgia Ave 9th Fl *Web:* mymajicdc.com	Silver Spring	MD	20910	301-306-1111	306-9540	645
Majilite Corp 1530 Broadway Rd *Web:* www.majilite.com	Dracut	MA	01826	978-441-6800	441-0835	594
Majon Intl PO Box 6059 *Web:* www.majon.com	Los Osos	CA	93412	805-270-5585		530
Major Brands Inc 6701 SW Ave **Fax Area Code:* 573 ■ *Web:* www.majorbrands.com	Saint Louis	MO	63143	314-645-1843	335-2192*	80-3
Major County Economic Development Corp 2004 Commerce St PO Box 303 *Web:* www.okmajordev.org	Fairview	OK	73737	580-227-2512		338
Major Custom Cable 281 Lotus Dr **Fax Area Code:* 573 ■ *TF:* 800-455-6224 ■ *Web:* www.majorcustomcable.com	Jackson	MO	63755	800-455-6224	243-1365*	813
Major Fulfillment Inc 13707 S Figueroa St *Web:* www.majorfulfillment.com	Los Angeles	CA	90061	310-204-1874	645-9959	5
Major Hospital 150 W Washington St *Web:* www.mymhp.org	Shelbyville	IN	46176	317-392-3211		374-3
Major Industries Inc 7120 Stewart Ave *TF:* 888-759-2678 ■ *Web:* majorskylights.com	Wausau	WI	54401	888-759-2678		697
Major League Baseball (Office of the Commissioner) 245 Park Ave 31st Fl *Web:* www.mlb.com	New York	NY	10167	212-931-7800	949-5654	713
Major League Baseball Players Assn 12 E 49th St Ste 24 *Web:* www.mlbplayers.com	New York	NY	10017	212-826-0808	752-4378	48-22
Major League Soccer (MLS) 420 Fifth Ave 7th Fl *Web:* www.mlssoccer.com	New York	NY	10018	212-450-1200		717
Major Lindsey & Africa 555 Montgomery St Ste 1500 *Web:* www.mlaglobal.com	San Francisco	CA	94111	415-956-1010	398-2425	266
Major Pharmaceutical Co 31778 Enterprise Dr *TF:* 800-616-2471 ■ *Web:* www.majorpharmaceuticals.com	Livonia	MI	48150	800-616-2471		582
Major Prime Plastics Inc 649 N Ardmore Ave *Web:* majorprime.com	Villa Park	IL	60181	630-834-9400	834-9412	600
Major Properties Real Estate 1200 W Olympic Blvd *Web:* www.majorproperties.com	Los Angeles	CA	90015	213-747-4151	749-7972	652
Major Tool & Machine Inc 1458 E 19th St *Web:* www.majortool.com	Indianapolis	IN	46218	317-636-6433	634-9420	454
Majors Plastics Inc 10117 I St *Web:* www.majorsplastics.com	Omaha	NE	68127	402-331-1660	331-9041	608
Mak Design Build Inc 430 F St Ste B *Web:* makdesignbuild.com	Davis	CA	95616	530-750-2209		186
Maka Beauty Systems 4042 W Kitty Hawk *TF:* 800-293-6252 ■ *Web:* www.makabeauty.com	Chandler	AZ	85226	480-968-7980	968-8881	77
Makai Ocean Engineering Inc 41-305 Kalanianaole Hwy *Web:* www.makai.com	Waimanalo	HI	96795	808-259-8871	854-2416	256
Makarios Consulting LLC 2900 Cir Crest Ct *Web:* makariosconsulting.com	Prospect	KY	40059	610-380-8735		196
Make It Better LLC 1150 Wilmette Ave Ste J *Web:* makeitbetter.net	Wilmette	IL	60091	847-256-4642		761
Make It Work Inc 836 Anacapa St Unit 2536 *Web:* www.makeitwork.com	Santa Barbara	CA	93101	805-705-9371		809
Make-A-Wish Foundation of America 4742 N 24th St Ste 400 *TF:* 800-722-9474 ■ *Web:* www.wish.org	Phoenix	AZ	85016	602-279-9474	279-0855	48-5
MakeMusic! Inc 7615 Golden Triangle Dr Ste M *NASDAQ: MMUS* ■ *TF:* 800-843-2066 ■ *Web:* www.makemusic.com	Eden Prairie	MN	55344	952-937-9611	937-9760	178-6
Maker's Mark Distillery Inc 3350 Burke Spring Rd *Web:* www.makersmark.com	Loretto	KY	40037	270-865-2881		80-1
Make-up Designory 65 Broadway 15th Fl *Web:* www.mud.edu	New York	NY	10006	212-925-9250	925-9254	167-3
Making Waves Education Program 3220 Blume Dr Ste 250 *Web:* making-waves.org	Richmond	CA	94806	510-237-6027	262-1559	196
Makino 7680 Innovation Way *TF:* 888-625-4661 ■ *Web:* www.makino.com	Mason	OH	45040	513-573-7200	573-7360	455
Makit Products Inc PO Box 769100 *TF:* 800-248-9443 ■ *Web:* www.makit.com	Dallas	TX	75376	972-709-1579		322
Makita Latin America Inc 10801 NW 97th St Ste 13 *Web:* www.makitalatinamerica.com	Medley	FL	33178	305-882-0522		455
Makita USA Inc 14930 Northam St *TF:* 800-462-5482 ■ *Web:* www.makitatools.com	La Mirada	CA	90638	714-522-8088	522-8133	759
Mako Medical Laboratories 8461 Garvey Dr *TF:* 844-625-6522 ■ *Web:* makomedical.com	Raleigh	NC	27616	844-625-6522		415
Makor Solutions LLC 7430 W 27th St *Web:* www.makorerp.com	Minneapolis	MN	55426	952-922-2975		196
Makoshika State Park 1301 Snyder Ave PO Box 1242 *Web:* stateparks.mt.gov	Glendive	MT	59330	406-377-6256		565
Makovsky + Co 16 E 34th St *Web:* www.makovsky.com	New York	NY	10016	212-508-9600		636
Makower Abbate Guerra Wegner Vollmer PLLC 30140 Orchard Lake Rd *Web:* maglawpllc.com	Farmington Hills	MI	48334	248-254-7600		41

Name / Address	City	State	ZIP	Phone	Fax	Class
Makowski's Real Sausage						
2710 S Poplar Ave	Chicago	IL	60608	312-842-5330		296-26
TF: 800-746-9554 ■ *Web:* www.realsausage.com						
Makoy Center Inc 5462 Center St	Hilliard	OH	43026	614-777-1211		354
Web: www.makoy.com						
Makro Technologies Inc						
4 Independence Way Ste 110	Princeton	NJ	08540	973-241-1381	241-1382	225
Web: www.makrotech.com						
Maksteel 19800 Middle Gibraltar Rd	Gibraltar	MI	48073	734-362-1144		492
Web: www.maksteel.com						
Mal Energy International Inc, The						
36 Bentley Ave	Ottawa	ON	K2E6T8	613-723-6776		463
Web: www.thermalenergy.com						
Malabar Farm State Park						
4050 Bromfield Rd	Lucas	OH	44843	419-892-2784	892-3988	565
Web: ohiodnr.gov						
Malaco Music Group Inc						
3023 W Northside Dr	Jackson	MS	39213	601-982-4522	982-4528	657
TF: 800-272-7936 ■ *Web:* www.malaco.com						
Malaga Financial Corp						
2514 Via Tejon	Palos Verdes Estates	CA	90274	310-375-9000	373-3615	360-2
OTC: MLGF ■ *Web:* www.malagabank.com						
Malaga Inn 359 Church St	Mobile	AL	36602	251-438-4701		379
TF: 800-235-1586 ■ *Web:* malagainn.com						
Malaika Corp 3010 63rd Ave	Hyattsville	MD	20785	240-235-6570		180
Web: www.malaikacorp.com						
Malarkey Consulting 1429 Shaner Dr	Pottstown	PA	19465	610-405-9423	326-0530	194
Web: www.malarkey.us						
Malarkey Roofing Products						
PO Box 17217	Portland	OR	97217	503-283-1191	289-7644	46
TF: 800-545-1191 ■ *Web:* malarkeyroofing.com						
Malaya Restaurant						
857 Collier Rd Ste 10	Atlanta	GA	30318	404-609-9991		671
Web: ordermalayarestaurant.com						
Malaysia						
Consulate General						
777 S Figueroa St Ste 600	Los Angeles	CA	90017	213-892-1238		257
Web: www.kln.gov.my						
Embassy 3516 International Ct NW	Washington	DC	20008	202-572-9700	572-9882	257
Web: www.kln.gov.my						
Malaysia Airlines						
100 N Sepulveda Blvd Ste 1710	El Segundo	CA	90245	310-535-9288		25
TF: 800-552-9264 ■ *Web:* www.malaysiaairlines.com						
Malbar Vision Ctr 409 N 78th St	Omaha	NE	68114	402-391-6600	493-4041	543
Web: malbar.com						
Malco Products Inc						
14080 State Hwy 55 NW PO Box 400	Annandale	MN	55302	320-274-8246	274-2269	758
TF: 800-328-3530 ■ *Web:* malcoproducts.com						
Malco Products Inc						
361 Fairview Ave PO Box 892	Barberton	OH	44203	330-753-0361	753-2025	151
TF: 800-253-2526 ■ *Web:* www.malcopro.com						
Malco Theatres Inc						
5851 Ridgeway Center Pkwy	Memphis	TN	38120	901-761-3480	681-2044	748
Web: www.malco.com						
Malcolm Drilling Company Inc						
3503 Breakwater Ct	Hayward	CA	94545	510-780-9181	780-9167	188-2
Web: www.malcolmdrilling.com						
Malcolm T Gilliland Inc						
405 Dividend Dr	Peachtree City	GA	30269	770-487-7942	487-7941	385
Web: www.mtgilliland.com						
Malcom Randall VAMC NF/SGVHS						
1601 SW Archer Rd	Gainesville	FL	32608	352-376-1611		374-8
TF: 800-324-8387 ■ *Web:* www.va.gov						
Maldaner's 222 S Sixth St	Springfield	IL	62701	217-522-4313		671
Web: www.maldaners.com						
MALDEF (Mexican American Legal Defense & Educational Fund)						
634 S Spring St	Los Angeles	CA	90014	213-629-2512	629-0266	48-14
Web: www.maldef.org						
Malden Chamber of Commerce						
200 Pleasant St Ste 416	Malden	MA	02148	781-322-4500	322-4866	139
Web: www.maldenchamber.org						
Malden Public Library 36 Salem St	Malden	MA	02148	781-324-0218		434-3
Web: maldenpubliclibrary.org						
Maldonado Nursery & Landscaping Inc						
16348 Nacogdoches Rd	San Antonio	TX	78247	210-599-1219	599-9736	776
Web: mnlsa.com						
Male Survivor						
350 Central Park W Ste 1H	New York	NY	10025	800-738-4181		48-17
TF: 800-738-4181 ■ *Web:* malesurvivor.org						
Malema Engineering Corp						
1060 S Rogers Cir	Boca Raton	FL	33487	561-995-0595	995-0622	201
TF: 800-637-6418 ■ *Web:* www.malema.com						
Maley & Wertz Inc						
900 E Columbia St	Evansville	IN	47711	812-425-3358		683
Web: www.maleyandwertz.com						
Malheur County 251 B St W	Vale	OR	97918	541-473-5151	473-5523	338
Web: www.malheurco.org						
Mali Embassy 2130 R St NW	Washington	DC	20008	202-332-2249	332-6603	257
Web: www.maliembassy.us						
Mali Restaurant 961 Amsterdam Ave NE	Atlanta	GA	30306	404-874-1411	874-5112	671
Web: www.malirestaurant.com						
Malibu Beach Inn						
22878 Pacific Coast Hwy	Malibu	CA	90265	800-462-5428		379
TF: 800-462-5428 ■ *Web:* www.malibubeachinn.com						
Malibu Boats 5075 Kimberly Way	Loudon	TN	37774	865-458-5478		698
Web: www.malibuboats.com						
Malibu Chamber of Commerce						
23805 Stuart Ranch Rd Ste 210	Malibu	CA	90265	310-456-9025	456-0195	139
TF: 800-442-4988 ■ *Web:* www.malibu.org						
Malibu Creek State Park						
1925 Las Virgenes Rd	Calabasas	CA	91302	818-880-0367		565
Web: www.parks.ca.gov						
Malibu Grill 106 N Walnut St	Bloomington	IN	47404	812-332-4334	333-2282	671
Web: www.malibugrill.net						
Malibu Lagoon State Beach						
23200 Pacific Coast Hwy	Malibu	CA	90265	310-457-8143		565
Web: www.parks.ca.gov						
Malibu Technologies Inc						
48700 Structural Dr	Chesterfield	MI	48051	586-598-9900		196
TF: 855-742-5086 ■ *Web:* www.malibutech.com						
Malik Real Estate Group Inc						
7450 Morro Rd	Atascadero	CA	93422	805-466-2540		652
Web: www.malikrealestate.com						
Malin Inc 15870 Midway Rd	Addison	TX	75001	972-687-1720		385
TF: 800-926-2546 ■ *Web:* www.malinusa.com						
Malin International Ship Repair & Drydock Inc						
320 77th St Pier 41	Galveston	TX	77554	409-740-3314		698
Web: www.malinshiprepair.com						
Malinowski Tom (Rep D - NJ)						
426 Cannon House Office Bldg	Washington	DC	20515	202-225-5361		342-2
Web: www.malinowski.house.gov						
Malisko Engineering Inc						
500 N Broadway Ste 1600	Saint Louis	MO	63102	720-596-4067		177
Web: malisko.com						
Malki Museum Press						
Morongo Reservation 11795 Malki Rd	Banning	CA	92220	951-849-7289	849-3549	637-2
Web: www.malkimuseum.org						
Mall at Cortana 9401 Cortana Pl	Baton Rouge	LA	70815	225-927-6747		460
Web: www.cortanamall.com						
Mall at Fairfield Commons						
2727 Fairfield Commons	Beavercreek	OH	45431	937-427-4300		460
Web: mallatfairfieldcommons.com						
Mall at Greece Ridge, The						
271 Greece Ridge Center Dr	Rochester	NY	14626	585-225-0430		460
Web: www.themallatgreeceridge.com						
Mall at Millenia 4200 Conroy Rd	Orlando	FL	32839	407-363-3555	363-6877	460
Web: www.mallatmillenia.com						
Mall at Robinson						
100 Robinson Centre Dr	Pittsburgh	PA	15205	412-788-0816	788-1156	460
Web: www.shoprobinsonmall.com						
Mall at Short Hills						
1200 Morris Tpke	Short Hills	NJ	07078	973-376-7350		460
Web: www.shopshorthills.com						
Mall at Wellington Green						
10300 W Forest Hill Blvd	Wellington	FL	33414	561-227-6900		460
Web: www.shopwellingtongreen.com						
Mall del Norte 5300 San Dario	Laredo	TX	78041	956-724-8191		460
Web: www.malldelnorte.com						
Mall of America 60 E Broadway	Bloomington	MN	55425	952-883-8810		460
Web: www.mallofamerica.com						
Mall of Louisiana						
6401 Bluebonnet Blvd	Baton Rouge	LA	70836	225-761-7228		460
Web: www.mallofIouisiana.com						
Mall Saint Matthews						
5000 Shelbyville Rd	Louisville	KY	40207	502-893-0311		460
Web: www.mallstmatthews.com						
Mall Saint Vincent						
1133 St Vincent Ave Ste 200	Shreveport	LA	71104	318-227-9880		460
Web: www.mallstvincent.com						
Mallett Group Inc, The						
5 Booth House Ln	New Milford	CT	06776	860-350-0809	350-0853	195
Web: mallettgroup.com						
Malleys Chocolates						
13400 Brookpark Rd	Cleveland	OH	44135	216-362-8700	211-0567*	296-8
**Fax Area Code:* 800 ■ *TF:* 800-275-6255 ■ *Web:* www.malleys.com						
Mallick Plumbing & Heating						
8010 Cessna Ave	Gaithersburg	MD	20879	888-805-3354		610
TF: 888-805-3354 ■ *Web:* www.mallickplumbing.com						
Mallilo & Grossman						
16309 Northern Blvd	Flushing	NY	11358	718-461-6633		428
TF: 866-593-6274 ■ *Web:* www.malliloandgrossman.com						
Mallin Casual Furniture						
1 Minson Way	Montebello	CA	90640	323-513-1041		319-4
Web: www.minson.com						
Mallin Casual Furniture						
222 Merchandise Mart Plaza Ste 1525	Chicago	IL	60654	312-836-0375		319-3
Web: www.mallinfurniture.com						
Mallof, Abruzino & Nash Marketing						
765 Kimberly Dr	Carol Stream	IL	60188	630-929-5200		7
Web: manmarketing.com						
Mallorca 2228 E Carson St	Pittsburgh	PA	15203	412-488-1818		671
Web: mallorcarestaurantpgh.com						
Mallorca 1390 W Ninth St	Cleveland	OH	44113	216-687-9494		671
Web: www.mallorcacle.com						
Mallory Capital Group LLC						
62 Deepwood Rd Ste 204	Darien	CT	06820	203-655-1571	794-7049	401
Web: www.mallorycapital.com						
Mallory Headsets Inc						
679 N Main St	West Bridgewater	MA	02379	508-586-0117		246
TF: 800-701-2289 ■ *Web:* www.malloryheadsets.com						
Mallory Safety & Supply Inc						
1040 Industrial Way PO Box 2068	Longview	WA	98632	360-636-5750		535
TF: 800-625-5679 ■ *Web:* www.malloryco.com						
Mallory Sonalert Products Inc						
4411 S High School Rd	Indianapolis	IN	46241	317-612-1000		791
Web: www.mallory-sonalert.com						
Malmark Inc 5712 Easton Rd	Plumsteadville	PA	18949	215-766-7200	766-0762	526
Web: www.malmark.com						
Malmstrom Air Force Base						
21 77th St N Bldg 500	Malmstrom AFB	MT	59402	406-731-1110	731-2759	497-1
Web: www.malmstrom.af.mil						
Malnati Organization Inc						
1326 Shermer Rd	Northbrook	IL	60062	847-562-1814		670
TF: 800-568-8646 ■ *Web:* www.loumalnatis.com						
Malnove Inc 13434 F St	Omaha	NE	68137	402-330-1100	330-2941	101
TF: 800-228-9877 ■ *Web:* www.malnove.com						
Malone College 2600 Cleveland Ave NW	Canton	OH	44709	800-521-1146	471-8149*	166
**Fax Area Code:* 330 ■ *TF:* 800-521-1146 ■ *Web:* www.malone.edu						
Malone Office Equipment						
1345 13th Ave	Columbus	GA	31901	706-322-2513		535
Web: maloneoffice.com						
Malone's						
Bluegrass Hospitality Group						
3347 Tates Creek Rd	Lexington	KY	40502	859-335-6500		671
Web: bluegrasshospitality.com						

	Phone	Fax	Class
MaloneBailey LLP 9801 Westheimer Rd Ste 1100 Houston TX 77042 *Web:* www.malonebailey.com	713-343-4286		734
Maloney & Bell General Contractors Inc 3117 Fite Cir Ste 101 Sacramento CA 95827 *Web:* www.maloneyandbell.com	916-687-8779	756-2402	186
Maloney & Kennedy PLLC 15 Dartmouth Dr Ste 203 Auburn NH 03032 *Web:* www.maloneyandkennedy.com	603-624-8819		2
Maloney & Porcelli 37 E 50th St New York NY 10022 *Web:* www.maloneyandporcelli.com	212-750-2233		671
Maloney Carolyn (Rep D - NY) 2308 Rayburn House Office Bldg Washington DC 20515 *Web:* www.maloney.house.gov	202-225-7944	225-4709	342-2
Maloney Sean Patrick (Rep D - NY) 2331 Rayburn House Office Bldg Washington DC 20515 *Web:* www.seanmaloney.house.gov	202-225-5441	225-3289	342-2
Maloney Security Inc 1055 Laurel St San Carlos CA 94070 *Web:* www.maloneysecurityinc.com	650-593-0163	593-1101	693
Maloney Technical Products 1300 E Berry St Fort Worth TX 76119 *TF:* 800-231-7236 ■ *Web:* www.maloneytech.com	817-923-3344	923-1339	596
Maloney Tool & Mold Inc 10890 Mercer Pke Meadville PA 16335 *Web:* www.maloneycos.com	814-337-8407		757
Malouf Engineering International Inc 17950 Preston Rd Ste 720 Dallas TX 75252 *Web:* www.maloufengineering.com	972-783-2578	783-2583	188-1
Malt Products Corp 88 Market St Saddle Brook NJ 07663 **Fax Area Code:* 201 ■ *TF:* 800-526-0180 ■ *Web:* www.maltproducts.com	800-526-0180	845-0028*	102
Malta *Malta Commons Business Park* 100 Saratoga Village Blvd New York NY 12020 *Web:* www.dcgdevelopment.com	212-725-2345		784
Maltby Electric Supply Company Inc 336 Seventh St San Francisco CA 94103 *TF:* 800-339-0668 ■ *Web:* maltbyelectric.com	415-863-5000	863-5011	246
Maltz Jupiter Theatre 1001 E Indiantown Rd Jupiter FL 33477 *TF:* 800-445-1666 ■ *Web:* www.jupitertheatre.org	561-743-2666	743-0107	749
Maltz Sales Company Inc 67 Green St Foxborough MA 02035 *TF:* 800-370-0439 ■ *Web:* www.maltzsales.com	508-203-2400		358
Malvern Bank National Assn 42 E Lancaster Ave Paoli PA 19301 *Web:* www.mymalvernbank.com	610-644-9400	695-3675	70
Malvern Institute 940 W King Rd Malvern PA 19355 *Web:* www.malverninstitute.com	610-647-0330		726
Malvern Panalytical Ltd 117 Flanders Rd Westborough MA 01581 *Web:* www.malvernpanalytical.com	508-768-6400	768-6403	146
Malvern Prep School 418 S Warren Ave Malvern PA 19355 *Web:* www.malvernprep.org	484-595-1100		685
Malvern Systems Inc 81 Lancaster Ave Ste 219 Malvern PA 19355 *TF:* 800-296-9642 ■ *Web:* www.malvernsys.com	800-296-9642		178-1
Malverne Union Free School District 12 301 Wicks Ln Malverne NY 11565 *Web:* www.malverne.k12.ny.us	516-887-6400		685
Malwin Electronics Corp 52 E 22nd St Paterson NJ 07514 *Web:* www.malwin.com	973-881-1500	881-7044	703
Maly Ceramic Tile Co 5353 Maly Rd Ste A Sun Prairie WI 53590 *Web:* www.malyceramictile.com	608-837-6927	837-3199	189-2
MAM Global Financial Services 16161 Ventura Blvd Encino CA 91436 *Web:* mamgfs.com	818-784-8752	784-8745	691
Mama Carolla's Old Italian Restaurant 1031 E 54th St Indianapolis IN 46220 *Web:* mamacarollas.com	317-259-9412		671
Mama DiMatteo's 34 Kennebec Pl Bar Harbor ME 04609 *Web:* www.mamadimatteos.com	207-288-3666		671
Mama Inez 390 Yellowstone Ave Pocatello ID 83201 *Web:* www.mamainezid.com	208-234-7674	234-3707	671
Mama Ricotta's 601 S Kings Dr Charlotte NC 28204 *Web:* www.mamaricottas.com	704-343-0148	377-7461	671
Mama Tosca's 9000 Ming Ave Ste K2-K3 Bakersfield CA 93311 *Web:* mamatoscas.com	661-831-1242		671
Mama's on the Half Shell 2901 O'Donnell St Baltimore MD 21224 *Web:* www.mamasmd.com	410-276-3160		671
Mama's Royal Cafe 4012 Broadway Oakland CA 94611 *Web:* mamasroyalcafeoakland.com	510-547-7600		671
MAMAC Systems Inc 8189 Century Blvd Chanhassen MN 55317 *TF:* 800-843-5116 ■ *Web:* www.mamacsys.com	952-556-4900		201
Mamasan 2800 Monroe Ave Rochester NY 14618 *Web:* www.mamasans.com	585-461-3290		671
Mamata USA LLC 2275 Cornell Ave Montgomery IL 60538 *Web:* www.mamatausa.com	630-801-2320		358
Mamco Corp 8630 Industrial Dr Franksville WI 53126 *Web:* www.mamcomotors.com	262-886-9069	886-4639	518
Mamiye Bros Inc 1385 Broadway 18th Fl New York NY 10018 *Web:* mamiye.com	212-279-4150	695-2659	155-16
Mamma 'Zu 501 S Pine St Richmond VA 23220	804-788-4205		671
Mamma DiSalvo's Italian Ristorante 1375 E Stroop Rd Dayton OH 45429 *Web:* www.mammadisalvo.com	937-299-5831	299-1752	671
Mamma Grazzi's Kitchen 25 George St Ottawa ON K1N8W5 *Web:* mammagrazzis.com	613-241-8656	241-5738	671
Mamma Luisa 673 Thames St Newport RI 02840 *Web:* mammaluisa.com	401-848-5257		671
Mamma Maria's 3 North Sq Boston MA 02113 *Web:* www.mammamaria.com	617-523-0077		671
Mamma Mia's 420 W Francis Ave Spokane WA 99205 *Web:* www.mammamiaspokane.com	509-467-7786		671
Mamma Ventura 13 Chambersburg St Gettysburg PA 17325 *Web:* mammaventuras.com	717-334-5548	334-7231	671
Mammoet USA Inc 20525 Farm-to-Market Rd 521 Rosharon TX 77583 *Web:* www.mammoet.com	281-369-2200		314
Mammoth Cave National Park 1 Mammoth Cave Pkwy PO Box 7 Mammoth Cave KY 42259 *Web:* www.nps.gov	270-758-2180		564
Mammoth Mountain Resort 10001 Minaret Rd PO Box 24 Mammoth Lakes CA 93546 *TF:* 800-626-6684 ■ *Web:* www.mammothmountain.com	760-934-2571	934-0615	669
Mammoth Spring State Park PO Box 36 Mammoth Spring AR 72554 *Web:* www.arkansasstateparks.com	870-625-7364		565
Mammoth Times, The PO Box 3929 Mammoth Lakes CA 93546 *Web:* www.mammothtimes.com	760-934-3929	934-3951	532-4
Mamoun's Falafel Restaurant 85 Howe St New Haven CT 06511 *Web:* www.mamouns.com	203-562-8444		671
Man Lift Manufacturing Co 5707 S Pennsylvania Ave Cudahy WI 53110 *Web:* manliftmfg.com	414-486-1760		190
Man Roland Inc 800 E Oak Hill Dr Westmont IL 60559 *Web:* www.manrolandsheetfed.com	630-920-2000		629
Mana Products Inc 32-02 Queens Blvd Long Island City NY 11101 *Web:* www.manaproducts.com	718-361-2550		214
Manafort Bros Inc 414 New Britain Ave Plainville CT 06062 *Web:* www.manafort.com	860-229-4853	747-4861	189-5
Managecore LLC 9875 S Franklin Dr Ste 300 Franklin WI 53132 *TF:* 844-999-3133 ■ *Web:* managecore.com	844-999-3133		180
Managed Business Solutions 12295 Oracle Blvd Ste 210 Colorado Springs CO 80921 *Web:* www.mbshome.com	719-314-3400	314-3499	180
Managed by Q Inc 161 Avenue of the Americas 11th Fl New York NY 10013 *Web:* www.managedbyq.com	212-401-1982		393
Managed Care Network Inc 1625 Buffalo Ave Niagara Falls NY 14303 *TF:* 800-285-1437 ■ *Web:* www.managedcarenetwork.com	716-285-5710	285-2618	2
Managed Care of America Inc 1910 Cochran Rd Ste 605 Pittsburgh PA 15220 *TF:* 800-922-4966 ■ *Web:* www.mcaadministrators.com	412-922-2803		390
Managed Funds Assn 600 14th St NW Ste 900 Washington DC 20005 *Web:* www.managedfunds.org	202-367-1140		533
Managed Health Network Inc 2370 Kerner Blvd Ste 300 San Rafael CA 94903 *TF:* 800-327-2133 ■ *Web:* mhn.com	800-327-2133		462
Managed HealthCare Northwest Inc 422 E Burnside St Ste 215 PO Box 4629 Portland OR 97208 *TF:* 800-648-6356 ■ *Web:* www.mhninc.com	503-413-5800	413-5801	390
Managed Maintenance Inc 301 Yamato Rd Ste 2180 Boca Raton FL 33431 *TF:* 855-810-8918 ■ *Web:* www.managedmaint.com	561-869-4399	869-4398	177
Managed Technical Services Inc 70 Bloomfield Ave Pine Brook NJ 07058 *Web:* www.mtsnj.com	973-808-2882	244-7999	180
Management & Engineering Technologies International Inc (METI) 8600 Boeing Dr El Paso TX 79925 *Web:* www.meticorp.com	915-772-4975	772-2253	463
Management Consulting Inc 1961 Diamond Springs Rd Virginia Beach VA 23455 *TF:* 888-892-0787 ■ *Web:* manconinc.com	757-460-0879	457-9337	261
Management Consulting Services 414 Wilson Ave Ste 102B Tullahoma TN 37388 *Web:* www.theknowisgroup.com	931-455-0155		393
Management Information Control Systems Inc (MICS) 2025 Ninth St Los Osos CA 93402 **Fax Area Code:* 805 ■ *TF:* 800-838-6427 ■ *Web:* www.bissoftware.com	800-838-6427	543-0373*	178-10
Management Information Tools Inc 801 2nd Ave Ste 1210 Seattle WA 98104 *TF:* 888-700-6487 ■ *Web:* www.mits.com	206-789-8313	782-8045	178-1
Management International Inc 1828 SE First Ave Fort Lauderdale FL 33316 *TF:* 800-425-1995 ■ *Web:* www.currentreviews.com	954-763-8003	762-9111	184
Management Network Group Inc 7300 College Blvd Ste 302 Overland Park KS 66210 *NASDAQ: CRTN* ■ *Web:* www.cartesian.com	913-345-9315		196
Management Performance International Inc 6836 Ashfield Dr Cincinnati OH 45242 *TF:* 800-543-6744 ■ *Web:* www.managementperformance.com	800-543-6744		194
Management Recruiters International Inc 1735 Market St Ste 200 Philadelphia PA 19103 **Fax Area Code:* 215 ■ *TF:* 800-875-4000 ■ *Web:* www.mrinetwork.com	800-875-4000	751-1760*	266
Management Science Associates Inc 6565 Penn Ave Pittsburgh PA 15206 *Web:* www.msa.com	412-362-2000	363-5598	178-12
Management Solutions Plus Inc 1300 Piccard Dr Ste LL 14 Rockville MD 20850 *Web:* www.mgmtsol.com	301-258-9210	990-9771	47
Management Technologies Inc 414 1/2 Central Ave SE Ste 4 Albuquerque NM 87102 *Web:* www.lannygoodman.com	505-884-7300		194
Manager Tools LLC 5765-F Burke Centre Pkwy Ste 152 Burke VA 22015 *Web:* www.manager-tools.com	571-336-6211		463
Managing Editor Inc 610 York Rd Ste 250 Jenkintown PA 19046 *TF:* 800-638-1214 ■ *Web:* maned.com	215-886-5662	886-5681	178-10
Manahan Group, The 222 Capitol St Ste 400 Charleston WV 25301 *Web:* manahangroup.com	304-343-2800		7
Manassas (Independent City) 9027 Center St Manassas VA 20110 *Web:* www.manassascity.org	703-257-8200	335-0042	338

Phone | Fax | Class

Manassas Park (Independent City)
1 Park Center Ct Manassas Park VA 20111 703-335-8800 335-0053 338
Web: www.cityofmanassaspark.us

Manatee Cafe
525 SR 16 Ste 106 Westgate Plz Saint Augustine FL 32084 904-826-0210 826-4080 671
Web: www.manateecafe.com

Manatee Chamber of Commerce
222 Tenth St W Bradenton FL 34205 941-748-3411 745-1877 139
Web: www.manateechamber.com

Manatee County 1112 Manatee Ave W Bradenton FL 34205 941-748-4501 338
Web: www.mymanatee.org

Manatee County Port Authority
300 Tampa Bay Way Palmetto FL 34221 941-722-6621 729-1463 618
Web: www.portmanatee.com

Manatee Memorial Hospital
206 Second St E Bradenton FL 34208 941-746-5111 745-6862 374-3
Web: www.manateememorial.com

Manatee Press PO Box 225001 San Francisco CA 94122 415-665-4829 637-2
Web: www.savethemanatee.com

Manatee Regional Juvenile Detention Ctr
1115 Manatee Ave W Bradenton FL 34205 941-741-3023 412
Web: manateeclerk.com

Manatee Springs State Park
11650 NW 115th St Chiefland FL 32626 352-493-6072 565
Web: www.floridastateparks.org

Manatee Technical College
6305 State Rd 70 E Bradenton FL 34203 941-751-7900 162
Web: manateetech.edu

Manatron Inc 510 E Milham Ave Portage MI 49002 269-567-2900 178-11
TF: 866-471-2900 ■ *Web:* tax.thomsonreuters.com

Manatt's Inc 1775 Old 6 Rd Brooklyn IA 52211 641-522-9206 522-5594 188-4
TF: 800-532-1121 ■ *Web:* www.manatts.com

Manatt, Phelps & Phillips
11355 W Olympic Blvd Los Angeles CA 90064 310-312-4000 428
Web: www.manatt.com

Manchac Consulting Group Inc
10542 S Glenstone Pl Baton Rouge LA 70810 225-448-3972 261
Web: manchacgroup.com

Manchester Area Chamber of Commerce
200 E Main St Manchester IA 52057 563-927-4141 139
Web: www.manchesteriowa.org

Manchester Capital Management LLC
3657 Main St PO Box 416 Manchester VT 05254 802-362-4410 362-1377 194
Web: www.mcmllc.com

Manchester City Hall
1 City Hall Plaza W Wing Manchester NH 03101 603-624-6455 624-6481 337
Web: www.manchesternh.gov

Manchester City Library
405 Pine St Manchester NH 03104 603-624-6550 624-6559 434-3
Web: www.manchesternh.gov

Manchester College
604 E College Ave North Manchester IN 46962 260-982-5000 982-5239 166
TF: 800-852-3648 ■ *Web:* www.manchester.edu

Manchester Community College
PO Box 1046 Manchester CT 06045 860-512-2800 512-3221 162
TF: 888-999-5545 ■ *Web:* www.manchestercc.edu

Manchester Community College
1066 Front St Manchester NH 03102 603-206-8000 668-5354 162
TF: 800-924-3445 ■ *Web:* www.mccnh.edu

Manchester Ctr
1901 E Shields Ave Ste 203 Fresno CA 93726 559-227-1901 460
Web: thenewmanchester.com

Manchester Financial Inc
2815 Townsgate Rd Ste 100 Westlake Village CA 91361 800-492-1107 401
TF: 800-492-1107 ■ *Web:* www.mfinvest.com

Manchester Grand Hyatt San Diego
1 Market Pl San Diego CA 92101 619-232-1234 378
Web: www.manchester.grand.hyatt.com

Manchester Manor Health Care Ctr
385 W Center St Manchester CT 06040 860-646-0129 450
Web: www.manchestermanorct.com

Manchester Memorial Hospital
71 Haynes St Manchester CT 06040 860-646-1222 374-3
Web: www.manchestermemorial.org

Manchester Monarchs 555 Elm St Manchester NH 03101 603-626-7825 717
Web: www.manchestermonarchs.com

Manchester Municipal Federal Credit Union
479 Main St Manchester CT 06040 860-649-7922 219
Web: mmfcu.net

Manchester State Park
44500 Kinney Ln Manchester CA 95459 707-882-2463 565
Web: www.parks.ca.gov

Manchester State Park
7767 E Hilldale Port Orchard WA 98366 360-871-4065 565
Web: www.parks.state.wa.us

Manchester Tank
1000 Corporate Center Dr Ste 300 Franklin TN 37067 615-370-3833 172
Web: www.mantank.com

Manchin Joe III (Sen D - WV)
306 Hart Senate Office Bldg Washington DC 20510 202-224-3954 228-0002 342-2
Web: www.manchin.senate.gov

Mancini Duffy 275 Seventh Ave 19th Fl New York NY 10001 212-938-1260 393
Web: www.manciniduffy.com

Mancini Foods PO Box 157 Zolfo Springs FL 33890 800-741-1778 735-1172* 296-36
**Fax Area Code:* 863 ■ *TF:* 800-741-1778 ■ *Web:* www.mancinifoods.com

Mancini Sales & Marketing
164 E 3900 S Salt Lake City UT 84107 801-266-4453 297-8
Web: www.mancinisales.com

Mancini Schreuder Kline Pc
28225 Mound Rd Warren MI 48092 586-751-3900 751-7203 41
TF: 866-319-7995 ■ *Web:* mancini-law.com

Mancini's Char House
531 Seventh St W Saint Paul MN 55102 651-224-7345 671
Web: www.mancinis.com

Mancino Burfield Edgerton
12 Roszel Rd Ste C-101 Princeton NJ 08540 609-520-8400 260
Web: www.mbels.com

Mancom Manufacturing Inc
1335 Osprey Dr Ancaster ON L9G4V5 905-304-6141 711

Mancor Industries Inc 2485 Speers Rd Oakville ON L6L2X9 905-827-3737 295
Web: www.mancor.com

Mancos State Park 42545 County Rd N Mancos CO 81328 970-533-7065 565
Web: cpw.state.co.us

Mancuso Business Development Group
56 Harvester Ave Batavia NY 14020 585-343-2800 652
Web: www.mancusogroup.com

Mancuso Cheese Co 612 Mills Rd Joliet IL 60433 815-722-2475 722-1302 296-5
Web: mancusocheese.com

Mancy's 953 Phillips Ave Toledo OH 43612 419-476-4154 671
Web: mancys.com

Manda Fine Meats 2445 Sorrel Ave Baton Rouge LA 70802 225-344-7636 344-7647 297-9
TF: 800-343-2642 ■ *Web:* www.mandafinemeats.com

Manda Machine Co
2683 Myrtle Springs Ave Dallas TX 75220 214-352-5946 351-0615 757
Web: www.mandamachine.com

Mandala Agency, The 2855 NW Crossing Dr Bend OR 97701 541-389-6344 7
Web: mandala.agency

Mandalay Bay Resort & Casino
3950 Las Vegas Blvd S Las Vegas NV 89119 702-632-7777 669
TF: 877-632-7800 ■ *Web:* www.mandalaybay.com

Mandalay Pictures
4751 Wilshire Blvd 3rd Fl Los Angeles CA 90010 323-549-4300 514
Web: www.mandalay.com

Mandalyn Academy Skin & Body Care Institute
648 E State Rd Ste B/ Ste L American Fork UT 84003 801-772-3131 772-3132 166
Web: www.mandalynacademy.com

Mandarin 8 Clipper Crt Brampton ON L6W4T9 905-451-4100 456-3411 671
Web: mandarinrestaurant.com

Mandarin Garden 2394 S Oneida St Green Bay WI 54304 920-499-4459 671
Web: mandaringardengreenbay.com

Mandarin House
675 Yellowstone Ave Ste D Pocatello ID 83201 208-233-6088 671
Web: mandarinhouseonline.com

Mandarin Kitchen
8766 Lyndale Ave S Minneapolis MN 55420 952-884-5356 671
Web: www.mandarinkitchenminneapolis.com

Mandarin Oriental Hotel Group Ltd
1330 Maryland Ave SW Washington DC 20024 202-554-8588 379
Web: www.mandarinoriental.com

Mandarin Presbyterian Church (MPC)
11844 Mandarin Rd Jacksonville FL 32223 904-680-9944 48-20
Web: www.mandarinpres.com

Mandee Shop 275 W Rte 46 Totowa NJ 07512 973-256-7080 157-6
Web: www.mandee.com

Mandel & Mandel LLP
169 E Flagler St Ste 1200 Miami FL 33131 305-374-7771 41
Web: mandel-law.com

Mandel Co 727 W Glendale Ave Ste 100 Milwaukee WI 53209 414-271-6970 627
TF: 800-888-6970 ■ *Web:* www.mandelcompany.com

Mandel Communications Inc
820 Bay Ave Ste 113 Capitola CA 95010 831-475-8202 765
TF: 800-262-6335 ■ *Web:* www.mandel.com

Mandel Ctr 8120 E Cactus Rd Ste 310 Scottsdale AZ 85260 480-734-1199 551-3363 374-5
Web: www.mandelcenter.com

Mandel Metals Inc
11400 W Addison Ave Franklin Park IL 60131 847-455-6606 492
TF: 800-962-9851 ■ *Web:* www.mandelmetals.com

Mandel Scientific 2 Admiral Pl Guelph ON N1G4N4 519-763-9292 763-2005 419
TF: 888-883-3636 ■ *Web:* www.mandel.ca

Mandel, Katz & Brosnan LLP
210 Rt 303 The Law Bldg Valley Cottage NY 10989 845-639-7800 428
Web: www.mkbllp.com

Mandell School, The 795 Columbus Ave New York NY 10025 212-222-2925 685
Web: mandellschool.org

Manders Merighi Portadin Farrell Architects LLC
1138 E Chestnut Ave Bldg 4 Vineland NJ 08360 856-696-9155 261
Web: www.mmpfa.com

Mandeville Press (MP)
3500 W Adams Blvd Los Angeles CA 90018 323-737-4055 737-5680 637-2
Web: www.mandevillepress.org

MANDEX Inc
12500 Fair Lakes Cir Ste 125 Fairfax VA 22033 703-227-0900 227-0910 180
Web: www.mandex.com

Mandil Inc 846 Elati St Denver CO 80204 303-892-5805 393
Web: mandilinc.com

Mandl School College of Allied Health
254 W 54th St New York NY 10019 212-247-3434 685
Web: www.mandl.edu

Mandli Communications
2655 Research Park Dr Fitchburg WI 53711 608-835-3500 545-2214* 180
**Fax Area Code:* 888 ■ *Web:* www.mandli.com

Mandrake Management Consultants
135 Yorkville Ave Ste 1000 Toronto ON M5R0C7 416-922-5400 193
Web: www.mandrake.ca

Manduka LLC 2250 E Maple Ave El Segundo CA 90245 310-426-1495 648-7968 361
Web: www.manduka.com

Maneki 304 Sixth Ave S Seattle WA 98104 206-622-2631 671
Web: www.manekirestaurant.com

Manetek Inc 105 Burgess Dr Broussard LA 70518 337-837-2921 837-2963 695
Web: www.manetek.com

Manex Resource Group Inc
1100 - 1199 W Hastings St Vancouver BC V6E3T5 604-684-9384 194
TF: 888-456-1112 ■ *Web:* www.manexresourcegroup.com

Manga Hotels Inc 3279 Caroga Dr Mississauga ON L4V1A3 905-672-4821 707
Web: www.mangahotels.com

Mangan & Mangan Inc
1400 Old Country Rd Ste 401 Westbury NY 11590 516-333-0600 2
Web: mmtaxes.com

Mangan Holcomb Partners
2300 Cottondale Ln Ste 300 Little Rock AR 72202 501-376-0321 4
Web: www.manganholcomb.com

Manganal Sales Co 1240 S Lincoln St Colton CA 92324 800-572-5809 824-5581* 492
**Fax Area Code:* 909 ■ *TF:* 800-572-5809 ■ *Web:* www.manganal.com

Manganaro Midatlantic LLC
52 Cummings Pk Woburn MA 01801 781-937-8880 189-9
Web: www.manganaro-ne.com

	Phone	Fax	Class
Mangia Italian Grill & Sports Bar 81 Main St . . . . . Annapolis MD 21401 *Web:* www.mangiaitaliangrill.com	410-268-1350		671
Mangia Mangia 900 Southard St . . . . . Key West FL 33040 *Web:* www.mangia-mangia.com	305-294-2469		671
Mangiamo 2000 Main St . . . . . Hilton Head Island SC 29926 *Web:* www.hhipizza.com	843-682-2444	682-3355	671
Mango Dsp Inc 83 East Ave. . . . . Norwalk CT 06851 *Web:* mangodsp.com	203-857-4008		225
Mango Salon 123 Libbie Ave. . . . . Richmond VA 23226 *Web:* mangosalon.com	804-285-2800		77
Mango Tree 217 S Reynolds Rd. . . . . Toledo OH 43615 *Web:* mangotreedining.com	419-536-2883		671
Mango's Thai Cuisine 4701 W Pk Blvd Ste 104. . . . . Plano TX 75093 *Web:* www.mangothaicuisine.com	469-666-4244		671
Mangoes Key West 700 Duval St. . . . . Key West FL 33040 *Web:* www.mangoeskeywest.com	305-294-8002		671
Mangos 1010 Spring Mill Ave Ste 200. . . . . Conshohocken PA 19428 *Web:* mangos.agency	610-296-2555		7
Mangy Moose PO Box 590 . . . . . Teton Village WY 83025 *Web:* www.mangymoose.com	307-733-4913		671
Manhasset Specialty Co 3505 Fruitvale Blvd. . . . . Yakima WA 98902 *TF:* 800-795-0965 ■ *Web:* www.manhasset-specialty.com	509-248-3810	248-3834	527
Manhattan Area Chamber of Commerce 501 Poyntz Ave. . . . . Manhattan KS 66502 *TF:* 800-759-0134 ■ *Web:* www.manhattan.org	785-776-8829	776-0679	139
Manhattan Area Technical College 3136 Dickens . . . . . Manhattan KS 66503 *TF:* 800-352-7575 ■ *Web:* www.manhattantech.edu	785-587-2800		162
Manhattan Associates Inc 2300 Windy Ridge Pkwy 10th Fl. . . . . Atlanta GA 30339 *NASDAQ: MANH* ■ *TF:* 877-756-7435 ■ *Web:* www.manh.com	770-955-7070	955-0302	178-10
Manhattan at Times Square Hotel, The 790 Seventh Ave. . . . . New York NY 10019 *TF:* 855-513-4394 ■ *Web:* www.manhattanhoteltimessquare.com	212-581-3300		378
Manhattan Beach Chamber of Commerce 425 15th St. . . . . Manhattan Beach CA 90266 *Web:* www.manhattanbeachchamber.com	310-545-5313		139
Manhattan Beach State Recreation Site Hwy 101 N . . . . . Rockaway Beach OR 97136 *Web:* oregonstateparks.org	503-368-5943		565
Manhattan Center Studios 311 W 34th St. . . . . New York NY 10001 *Web:* mc34.com	212-695-6600		572
Manhattan Chamber of Commerce 575 Fifth Ave 14th Fl . . . . . New York NY 10017 *Web:* www.manhattancc.org	212-479-7772	473-8074	139
Manhattan Christian College 1415 Anderson Ave. . . . . Manhattan KS 66502 *TF:* 877-246-4622 ■ *Web:* www.mccks.edu	785-539-3571	776-9251	161
Manhattan College 4513 Manhattan College Pkwy . . . . . Bronx NY 10471 *TF:* 855-841-2843 ■ *Web:* manhattan.edu	718-862-8000	862-8027	166
Manhattan Commission Co 8424 E Hwy 24 . . . . . Manhattan KS 66502 *TF:* 800-834-1029 ■ *Web:* www.mcclivestock.com	785-776-4815	776-0815	446
Manhattan Institute for Policy Research Inc 52 Vanderbilt Ave . . . . . New York NY 10017 *Web:* www.manhattan-institute.org	212-599-7000	599-3494	634
Manhattan Media LLC 79 Madison Ave 16th Fl . . . . . New York NY 10016 *Web:* www.manhattanmedia.com	212-268-8600		637-8
Manhattan Neighborhood Network 59th St Studios 537 W 59th St. . . . . New York NY 10019 *Web:* www.mnn.org	212-757-2670	757-1603	116
Manhattan Public Library 629 Poyntz Ave. . . . . Manhattan KS 66502 *Web:* www.mhklibrary.org	785-776-4741	776-1545	434-3
Manhattan School of Music 120 Claremont Ave . . . . . New York NY 10027 *Web:* www.msmnyc.edu	212-749-2802	749-3025	166
Manhattan Telecommunications Corp 55 Water St 32nd Fl . . . . . New York NY 10041 *TF:* 877-963-8663 ■ *Web:* www.mettel.net	212-607-2000		387
Manhattan Theatre Club Inc 311 W 43rd St 8th Fl . . . . . New York NY 10036 *Web:* www.manhattantheatreclub.com	212-399-3000	445-7329	749
Manhattan Toy 300 First Ave N Ste 200 . . . . . Minneapolis MN 55401 *TF:* 800-541-1345 ■ *Web:* www.manhattantoy.com	800-541-1345		64
Manhattanville College 2900 Purchase St . . . . . Purchase NY 10577 *TF:* 800-328-4553 ■ *Web:* www.mville.edu	914-323-5464	694-1732	166
Manheim Township School District 450 Candlewyck Rd PO Box 5134 . . . . . Lancaster PA 17601 *Web:* www.mtwp.net	717-569-8231		685
Manidokan Camp & Retreat Ctr 1600 Harpers Ferry Rd . . . . . Knoxville MD 21758 **Fax Area Code:* 410 ■ *Web:* www.bwccampsandretreats.com	301-834-7244	867-0991*	377
Manifest Solutions Corp 2035 Riverside Dr. . . . . Upper Arlington OH 43221 *Web:* manifestcorp.com	614-930-2800		177
MANifestation Inc PO Box 2024 . . . . . Asheville NC 28802 *Web:* www.avatarmeherbaba.org	704-251-2253		637-2
Manifold Capital Corp 140 Broadway 47th Fl. . . . . New York NY 10005 *NASDAQ: MANF* ■ *Web:* www.aca.com	212-375-2000	375-2100	360-3
Manildra Group USA 4210 Shawnee Mission Pkwy Ste 312A . . Shawnee Mission KS 66205 *TF:* 800-323-8435 ■ *Web:* manildrausa.com	913-362-0777	362-0052	296-23
Manire & Galla LLP 205 E 42nd St. . . . . New York NY 10017 *Web:* maniregallalaw.com	646-780-5300		41
Manischewitz Co, The 80 Ave K . . . . . Newark NJ 07105 *Web:* www.rabfoodgroup.com	201-553-1100		296-36

	Phone	Fax	Class
Manistee County Historical Museum 425 River St . . . . . Manistee MI 49660 *Web:* www.manisteemuseum.org	231-723-5531		520
Manitex Inc 3000 S Austin Ave . . . . . Georgetown TX 78626 *TF:* 877-314-3390 ■ *Web:* www.manitex.com	512-942-3000		470
Manitoba Agricultural Services Corp 525 First St S Unit 100. . . . . Brandon MB R7A7A1 *Web:* www.masc.mb.ca	204-726-6850		316
Manitoba Chamber Orchestra 393 Portage Ave Portage Pl Unit Y300 . . . . . Winnipeg MB R3B3H6 *Web:* www.themco.ca	204-783-7377	783-7383	573-3
Manitoba Chambers of Commerce, The 227 Portage Ave . . . . . Winnipeg MB R3B2A6 *TF:* 877-444-5222 ■ *Web:* www.mbchamber.mb.ca	204-948-0100	948-0110	137
Manitoba Museum 190 Rupert Ave . . . . . Winnipeg MB R3B0N2 *Web:* www.manitobamuseum.ca	204-956-2830	942-3679	520
Manitoba Sports Hall of Fame & Museum 145 Pacific Ave. . . . . Winnipeg MB R3B2Z6 *Web:* www.sportmanitoba.ca	204-925-5600		522
Manitok Energy Inc 444 7th Ave SW Ste 700. . . . . Calgary AB T2P0X8 *TF:* 877-503-5957 ■ *Web:* www.manitokenergy.com	403-984-1750	984-1749	536
Manitou Cliff Dwellings Museum 10 Cliff Rd . . . . . Manitou Springs CO 80829 *TF:* 800-354-9971 ■ *Web:* www.cliffdwellingsmuseum.com	719-685-5242		520
Manitou North America 6401 Imperial Dr. . . . . Waco TX 76712 *Web:* www.constructionequipment.com	254-799-0232		470
Manitowoc Area Visitor & Convention Bureau 4221 Calumet Ave. . . . . Manitowoc WI 54220 *TF:* 800-627-4896 ■ *Web:* www.manitowoc.info	800-627-4896		206
Manitowoc Company Inc 2400 S 44th St . . . . . Manitowoc WI 54220 *NYSE: MTW* ■ *Web:* www.manitowoccranes.com	920-684-4410		190
Manitowoc County 1010 S Eighth St 1st Fl Rm 115 . . . . . Manitowoc WI 54220 *Web:* www.co.manitowoc.wi.us	920-683-4003	683-5180	338
Manitowoc Ice 2110 S 26th St. . . . . Manitowoc WI 54220 **Fax Area Code:* 920 ■ *TF:* 800-545-5720 ■ *Web:* www.manitowocice.com	800-545-5720	683-7589*	664
Manitowoc Public Library 707 Quay St . . . . . Manitowoc WI 54220 *Web:* www.manitowoclibrary.org	920-686-3000		434-3
Manitowoc-Two Rivers Area Chamber of Commerce 1515 Memorial Dr . . . . . Manitowoc WI 54220 *TF:* 866-727-5575 ■ *Web:* chambermanitowoccounty.org	920-684-5575	684-1915	139
Manix Manufacturing Inc 1650 Loretta Ave. . . . . Feasterville-Trevose PA 19053 *Web:* www.manixmfg.com	215-953-9797	953-9399	246
Mankato Iron and Metal Inc 215 W Elm St . . . . . Mankato MN 56001 *Web:* mankatoiron.com	507-625-6489	388-9940	686
Mankato-Kasota Stone Inc 818 N Willow St . . . . . Mankato MN 56001 *Web:* www.mankato-kasota-stone.com	507-625-2746		724
Manke Lumber Company Inc 1717 Marine View Dr . . . . . Tacoma WA 98422 *TF:* 800-426-8488 ■ *Web:* www.mankelumber.com	253-572-6252	383-2489	683
Mankind Research Unlimited (MRU) 1315 Apple Ave. . . . . Silver Spring MD 20910 *Web:* mankindresearchunlimited.weebly.com	301-587-8686	585-8959	637-2
Manko Window Systems Inc 800 Hayes Dr . . . . . Manhattan KS 66502 *TF:* 877-642-1488 ■ *Web:* www.mankowindows.com	785-776-9643		480
Manley Deas & Kochalski LLC 1555 Lake Shore Dr . . . . . Columbus OH 43216 *Web:* www.mdk-llc.com	614-220-5611		428
Manley Performance Engineering 1960 Swarthmore Ave. . . . . Lakewood NJ 08701 *Web:* manleyperformance.com	732-905-3366		60
Man-Maid Cleaning Services 29 Fox Creek Dr . . . . . Rehoboth Beach DE 19971 *Web:* www.manmaidcleaning.com	302-226-5050		104
Mann & Parker Lumber Company Inc, The 335 N Constitution Ave. . . . . New Freedom PA 17349 *TF:* 800-632-9098 ■ *Web:* m-pgoldbrand.com	717-235-4834	235-5547	499
Mann Armistead & Epperson Ltd 119 Shockoe Slip . . . . . Richmond VA 23219 *Web:* www.maeltd.com	804-644-1200		401
Mann Center for the Performing Arts 5201 Parkside Ave . . . . . Philadelphia PA 19131 *Web:* manncenter.org	215-546-7900	546-9524	572
Mann Packing Co PO Box 690 . . . . . Salinas CA 93902 *TF:* 800-285-1002 ■ *Web:* www.veggiesmadeeasy.com	800-285-1002		11-1
Mann's Jewelers Inc 2945 Monroe Ave. . . . . Rochester NY 14618 *TF:* 800-828-6234 ■ *Web:* www.mannsjewelers.com	585-271-4000		410
Manna House of Prayer 323 E Fifth St . . . . . Concordia KS 66901 *Web:* mannahouse.org	785-243-4428		673
Manna Pro Corp 707 Spirit 40 Pk Dr Ste 150 . . . . . Chesterfield MO 63005 *TF:* 800-690-9908 ■ *Web:* www.mannapro.com	800-690-9908		447
Mannatech Inc 1410 Lakeside Pkwy Ste 200 . . . . . Flower Mound TX 75028 *NASDAQ: MTEX* ■ *Web:* us.mannatech.com	972-471-7400	471-8191	366
Manncorp Inc 1610 Republic Rd . . . . . Huntingdon Valley PA 19006 *Web:* www.manncorp.com	215-830-1200	830-1206	295
Manneco Inc 600 S Cottage . . . . . Independence MO 64050 *TF:* 800-397-9627 ■ *Web:* www.manneco.com	800-397-9627		45
Mannhardt Ice LLC 3209 S 32nd St. . . . . Sheboygan Falls WI 53085 *TF:* 800-423-2327 ■ *Web:* www.mannhardtice.com	920-467-1027		14
Mannik & Smith Group Inc 1800 Indian Wood Cir. . . . . Maumee OH 43537 *TF:* 888-891-6321 ■ *Web:* www.manniksmithgroup.com	419-891-2222		261
Manning & Napier Advisors Inc 290 Woodcliff Dr. . . . . Fairport NY 14450 *Web:* www.manning-napier.com	585-325-6880		401

Listing	City	State	ZIP	Phone	Fax	Class
Manning Elliott LLP 1050 W Pender St 11th Fl *Web:* manningelliott.com	Vancouver	BC	V6E3S7	604-714-3600		2
Manning Fulton & Skinner PA 3605 Glenwood Ave *Web:* www.manningfulton.com	Raleigh	NC	27612	919-787-8880		428
Manning Grain Co 4 Burress Rd *Web:* www.manninggrain.com	Fairmont	NE	68354	402-266-3701	266-2169	276
Manning Lighting 1810 N Ave PO Box 1063 *Web:* www.manningltg.com	Sheboygan	WI	53083	920-458-2184	458-2491	439
Manning Search Group 1101 St Peters Howell Rd *Web:* manningsearchgroup.com	Saint Peters	MO	63376	636-875-5080		260
Manning, Leaver, Bruder & Berberich 801 S Figueroa St Ste 1150 *Web:* manningleaver.com	Los Angeles	CA	90017	323-937-4730	937-6727	41
Mannington Mills Inc PO Box 30 *TF:* 800-356-6787 ■ *Web:* mannington.com	Salem	NJ	08079	800-241-2262		291
Mannix Architectural Window Products 345 Crooked Hill Rd *Web:* mannixwindows.com	Brentwood	NY	11717	631-231-0800	231-0571	234
Mannix Marketing Inc 11 Broad St 3rd Fl *Web:* www.mannixmarketing.com	Glens Falls	NY	12801	518-743-9424	743-0337	195
MannKind Corp 28903 N Ave Paine *NASDAQ: MNKD* ■ *Web:* www.mannkindcorp.com	Valencia	CA	91355	661-775-5300		85
Manns Bait Co 1111 State Docks Rd *TF:* 800-841-8435 ■ *Web:* www.mannsbait.com	Eufaula	AL	36027	334-687-5716		710
Manny Silverman Gallery 619 N Almont Dr *Web:* mannysilvermangallery.com	Los Angeles	CA	90069	310-659-8256	659-1001	42
Manny's Steak House 825 Marquette Ave *Web:* www.mannyssteakhouse.com	Minneapolis	MN	55403	612-339-9900	341-2373	671
Manoir du Lac Delage 40 Ave du Lac *TF:* 888-202-3242 ■ *Web:* www.lacdelage.com	Lac Delage	QC	G3C5C4	418-848-2551	848-1352	669
Manoir-Papineau National Historic Site 500 Notre-Dame *Web:* www.pc.gc.ca	Montebello	QC	J0V1L0	819-423-6965	423-6455	563
Manomet Center for Conservation Sciences 125 Manomet Point Rd PO Box 1770 *Web:* www.manomet.org	Plymouth	MA	02360	508-224-6521	224-9220	41
Manor College 700 Fox Chase Rd *Web:* manor.edu	Jenkintown	PA	19046	215-885-2360	576-6564	162
Manor House Inn 106 West St *TF:* 800-437-0088 ■ *Web:* www.barharbormanorhouse.com	Bar Harbor	ME	04609	800-437-0088		379
Manor Insurance Agency Inc 1325 S Colorado Blvd Ste 210 *Web:* manorins.com	Denver	CO	80222	303-691-9100		390
Manor Park Inc 2208 N Loop 250 W *TF:* 800-523-9898 ■ *Web:* manorparkinc.org	Midland	TX	79707	432-689-9898		672
Manor Real Estate 3270 Hampton Ave Ste 100 *Web:* www.manorrealestate.com	Saint Louis	MO	63139	314-647-6611	647-6622	652
Manor Tool & Manufacturing Co 9200 Ivanhoe St *Web:* stamping.manortool.com	Schiller Park	IL	60176	847-678-2020	678-6937	454
Manor Vail Lodge 595 E Vail Vly Dr *TF:* 800-950-8245 ■ *Web:* www.manorvail.com	Vail	CO	81657	970-476-5000		669
Manora's Thai Cuisine 1600 Folsom St *Web:* www.manorasthai.com	San Francisco	CA	94103	415-861-6224		671
Manorhouse - Assisted Living & Memory Care 706 Old Stream Rd *Web:* www.manorhouseretirement.com	Manakin Sabot	VA	23103	804-360-7777	270-7251	463
Manos Greek Restaurant & Bar 1701 Adams St *Web:* www.manosgreekrestaurant.com	Toledo	OH	43604	419-244-4479		671
Manpower Demonstration Research Corp 16 E 34th St 19th Fl *TF:* 800-221-3165 ■ *Web:* www.mdrc.org	New York	NY	10016	212-532-3200	684-0832	634
ManpowerGroup 100 Manpower Pl *NYSE: MAN* ■ *Web:* www.manpower.com	Milwaukee	WI	53212	414-961-1000		721
Manroy USA LLC 201 Lonnie E Crawford Blvd *Web:* www.manroy-usa.com	Scottsboro	AL	35769	256-259-9800		807
Mansard Commercial Properties 14 Essex St *Web:* masscommercialproperties.com	Andover	MA	01810	617-674-2043		652
Mansco Products Inc 34 Richard Rd *Web:* www.manscoproducts.com	Warminster	PA	18974	215-674-4395	674-4396	201
Mansermar Inc 2405 Satellite Blvd Ste 100 *Web:* www.mansermar.com	Duluth	GA	30096	602-993-4665		652
Mansfield Beauty Schools 200 Parkingway St *Web:* www.mansfieldbeautyschools.edu	Quincy	MA	02169	617-479-1090	479-8095	685
Mansfield Hotel, The 12 W 44th St *TF:* 844-591-5565 ■ *Web:* www.mansfieldhotel.com	New York	NY	10036	212-277-8700	764-4477	379
Mansfield Industries 1776 Harrington Memorial Rd *Web:* mansfieldec.com	Mansfield	OH	44903	419-524-1300		350
Mansfield Mirror 300 E Commercial St *Web:* www.mansfieldmirror.com	Mansfield	MO	65704	417-924-3226	924-3227	532-2
Mansfield Motorsports Speedway 400 E Crall Rd *Web:* www.mansfieldmotorspeedway.com	Mansfield	OH	44903	419-465-7223		515
Mansfield Oil Co 1025 Airport Pkwy SW *TF:* 800-695-6626 ■ *Web:* mansfield.energy	Gainesville	GA	30501	800-695-6626		539
Mansfield Plumbing Products Inc 150 E First St *TF:* 877-850-3060 ■ *Web:* www.mansfieldplumbing.com	Perrysville	OH	44864	419-938-5211	938-6234	611
Mansfield State Historic Site 15149 Hwy 175 *TF:* 888-677-6267 ■ *Web:* www.crt.state.la.us	Mansfield	LA	71052	318-872-1474		565
Mansfield University Alumni Hall *TF:* 800-577-6826 ■ *Web:* www.mansfield.edu	Mansfield	PA	16933	570-662-4000	662-4121	166
Mansfield-Richland County Public Library 43 W Third St *TF:* 877-795-2111 ■ *Web:* www.mrcpl.org	Mansfield	OH	44902	419-521-3100	525-4750	434-3
Manship House Museum 420 E Fortification St *Web:* mdah.state.ms.us	Jackson	MS	39202	601-961-4724		520
Mansion Grove House PO Box 201734 *Web:* www.mansiongrovehouse.com	Austin	TX	78720	512-366-9012		95
Mansion View Inn & Suites 529 S 4th St *TF:* 800-252-1083 ■ *Web:* www.mansionview.com	Springfield	IL	62701	217-544-7411		379
Manson Bolves PA 109 N Brush St Ste 300 *Web:* mansonbolves.com	Tampa	FL	33602	813-514-4700		41
Manson Construction Co 5209 E Marginal Way S *Web:* www.mansonconstruction.com	Seattle	WA	98134	206-762-0850	764-8590	188-5
Mansour Travel Co 8383 Wilshire Blvd Ste 350 *Web:* www.mansourtravel.com	Beverly Hills	CA	90211	310-276-2768		772
Mansur and Co 676 N Michigan Ave Ste 2930 *Web:* www.mansurco.com	Chicago	IL	60611	312-263-2400	642-6278	690
Mansur's 5720 Corporate Blvd Ste A *Web:* www.mansursontheboulevard.com	Baton Rouge	LA	70808	225-923-3366		671
Mantaline Corp 4754 E High St *Web:* www.mantaline.com	Mantua	OH	44255	330-274-2264	274-8850	677
MANTEC Inc 600 N Hartley St Ste 100 *Web:* mantec.org	York	PA	17404	717-843-5054		138
Mantec Services Inc 4400 24th Ave W *Web:* www.mantecservicesinc.com	Seattle	WA	98199	206-285-5656		599
Manteca Chamber of Commerce 183 W North St Ste 6 *Web:* manteca.org	Manteca	CA	95336	209-823-6121	239-6131	139
ManTech Advanced Systems International Inc 12015 Lee Jackson Hwy *TF:* 800-800-4857 ■ *Web:* www.mantech.com	Fairfax	VA	22033	703-218-6000		256
Mantel Machine Products Inc W141 N9350 Fountain Blvd *Web:* www.mantelmachine.com	Menomonee Falls	WI	53051	262-255-6780	255-9724	621
Mantell, Rossi & Company CPAS PC 461 Watchung Ave *Web:* mantellrossi.com	Watchung	NJ	07069	908-755-6664		2
MantelsDirect.com 217 N Seminary St *TF:* 888-493-8898 ■ *Web:* www.mantelsdirect.com	Florence	AL	35630	256-765-2171		183
Manteno High School 443 N Maple St *Web:* mhs.manteno5.org	Manteno	IL	60950	815-928-7100	468-2344	685
Manteo High School 829 Wingina St *Web:* mhs.daretolearn.org	Manteo	NC	27954	252-473-5841		685
Mantese Honigman PC 1361 E Big Beaver Rd *Web:* manteselaw.com	Troy	MI	48083	248-457-9200		41
Manth-Brownell Inc 1120 Fyler Rd *Web:* www.manth.com	Kirkville	NY	13082	315-687-7263	687-6856	621
Manti Telecommunications Co (MTCC) 34 W Union *Web:* www.manti.com	Manti	UT	84642	435-835-2929		735
Mantissa Corp 616 Pressley Rd *Web:* www.mantissacorporation.com	Charlotte	NC	28217	704-525-1749	525-6129	358
Mantle, Zimmer & Eulo LLP 4685 Macarthur Ct Ste 390 *Web:* mantlezimmer.com	Newport Beach	CA	92660	949-757-5900		41
Manton Industrial Cork Products Inc 415 Oser Ave Unit U **Fax Area Code:* 631 ■ *TF:* 800-663-1921 ■ *Web:* www.mantoncork.com	Hauppauge	NY	11788	800-663-1921	273-0038*	209
Mantra Technologies 284 S Main St Ste 700 *Web:* www.mantrasys.com	Alpharetta	GA	30009	770-456-5652		180
Mantros-Haeuser & Company Inc 1175 Post Rd E *TF:* 800-344-4229 ■ *Web:* www.mantrose.com	Westport	CT	06880	203-454-1800	227-0558	550
Mantua Manufacturing Co 7900 Northfield Rd *TF:* 800-333-8333 ■ *Web:* www.bedframes.com	Walton Hills	OH	44146	800-333-8333	929-8014	319-2
Manty & Associates PA 401 Second Ave N Ste 400 *Web:* mantylaw.com	Minneapolis	MN	55401	612-465-0990		41
Mantz Automation Inc 1630 Innovation Way *Web:* mantzautomation.com	Hartford	WI	53027	262-673-7560		697
Manual Woodworkers & Weavers Inc 3737 HoWard Gap Rd *TF:* 800-542-3139 ■ *Web:* www.manualww.com	Hendersonville	NC	28792	828-692-7333		746
Manufactured Housing Enterprises Inc 09302 St Rt 6 *TF:* 800-821-0220 ■ *Web:* www.mheinc.com	Bryan	OH	43506	419-636-4511		505
Manufactured Housing Institute (MHI) 1655 Fort Myer Dr *Web:* www.manufacturedhousing.org	Arlington	VA	22209	703-236-2300	558-0401	49-3
Manufacturers Alliance/MAPI Inc 1600 Wilson Blvd Ste 1100 *Web:* www.mapi.net	Arlington	VA	22209	703-841-9000	841-9514	49-12
Manufacturers Chemicals LLC 4325 Old Tasso Rd *Web:* synalloychemicals.com	Cleveland	TN	37320	423-476-6518		131
Manufacturers Industrial Group LLC 659 Natchez Trace Dr *Web:* www.migllc.com	Lexington	TN	38351	731-967-0001	968-3320	482
Manufacturers Supplies Co (MSC) 4220 Rider Trl N *Web:* www.mfgsup.com	Earth City	MO	63045	314-770-0880		695
Manufacturers' Lease Plans Inc 818 E Osborn Rd Ste 200	Phoenix	AZ	85014	602-944-4411	944-4417	264-1
Manufacturers' News Inc 1633 Central St *Web:* www.mni.net	Evanston	IL	60201	847-864-7000		532-3
Manufacturing & Design Technology Inc 1033a Cavalier Blvd *Web:* www.m-d-t.com	Chesapeake	VA	23323	757-485-8924		454

Name / Address	City	State	Zip	Phone	Fax	Class
Manufacturing Action Group Inc 2660 Horizon Dr SE Ste 135 — *TF:* 866-946-6244 ■ *Web:* www.magierp.com	Grand Rapids	MI	49546	616-956-5345	956-5362	178-1
Manufacturing Information System Inc 4 Maxham Meadow Way Ste 2G — *Web:* www.misysinc.com	Woodstock	VT	05091	802-457-4600		178-1
Manufacturing Jewelers & Suppliers of America Inc (MJSA) 57 John L Dietsch Sq — *TF:* 800-444-6572 ■ *Web:* www.mjsa.org	Attleboro	MA	02763	401-274-3840	274-0265	49-4
Manufacturing Support Industries Inc 2414 Northgate Dr Ste 2 — *Web:* mfg-support.com	Salisbury	MD	21801	410-334-6140		350
Manufacturing Systems Group LLC 111 Snead Dr — *Web:* www.mfgsysgroup.com	North Fort Myers	FL	33903	727-642-4677		322
Manufacturing Technology Inc (MTI) 1702 W Washington St — *Web:* www.mtiwelding.com	South Bend	IN	46628	574-233-9490	233-9489	811
Manulife Financial Corp 200 Bloor St E — *NYSE: MFC* ■ *Web:* www.manulife.com	Toronto	ON	M4W1E5	416-926-3000		360-4
Manulife Securities Inc 500-1235 N Service Rd W — *Web:* www.manulife.ca	Oakville	ON	L6M2W2	905-469-2100		691
Manus & Associates Literary Agency Inc 425 Sherman Ave Ste 200 — *Web:* www.manuslit.com	Palo Alto	CA	94306	650-470-5151	470-5159	444
Manus Group, The 5000-18 Hwy 17 S Ste 134 — **Fax Area Code:* 904 ■ *TF:* 888-735-8311 ■ *Web:* www.themanusgroup.com	Fleming Island	FL	32003	888-735-8311	264-5406*	317
Manus Products of Minnesota Inc 866 Industrial Blvd — *Web:* www.manus.net	Waconia	MN	55387	952-442-3323	442-3327	3
Manville Rubber Products Inc 1009 Kennedy Blvd — *Web:* www.manvillerubber.com	Manville	NJ	08835	908-526-9111	526-7123	676
Manx Pub, The 370 Elgin St — *Web:* manxpub.com	Ottawa	ON	K2P1N1	613-231-2070		671
ManyChat 353 Sacramento St — *Web:* manychat.com	San Francisco	CA	94111	650-644-5043		178-8
Manzama Inc 543 NW York Dr Ste 100 — *Web:* manzama.com	Bend	OR	97701	541-306-3271		5
Manzanar National Historic Site 5001 Hwy 395 PO Box 426 — *Web:* www.nps.gov	Independence	CA	93526	760-878-2194	878-2949	564
Manzella Marketing Group 5360 Genesee St Ste 203 — *Web:* manzellamarketing.com	Bowmansville	NY	14026	716-681-6565		636
Manzi Metals Inc 15293 Flight Path Dr — *TF:* 800-799-8211 ■ *Web:* www.manzimetals.com	Brooksville	FL	34604	352-799-8211		492
Manzi, Pino & Company PC 1895 Walt Whitman Rd - — *Web:* manzipinocpa.com	Melville	NY	11747	631-420-5620	420-8332	2
MAOF (Mexican-American Opportunity Foundation) 401 N Garfield Ave — *Web:* www.maof.org	Montebello	CA	90640	323-890-9600	890-9637	48-14
MAP (Maryland Art Place) 218 W Saratoga St — *Web:* www.mdartplace.org	Baltimore	MD	21201	410-962-8565		50-2
MAP (Mississippi Action For Progress Inc) 1751 Morson Rd — *TF:* 800-924-4615 ■ *Web:* www.mapheadstart.org	Jackson	MS	39209	601-923-4100		147
MAP Intl 4700 Glynco Pkwy — *TF:* 800-225-8550 ■ *Web:* www.map.org	Brunswick	GA	31525	912-265-6010	265-6170	48-5
MAPEI Corp 1144 E Newport Center Dr — *TF:* 800-426-2734 ■ *Web:* www.mapei.com	Deerfield Beach	FL	33442	954-246-8888	246-8800	3
Mapes LLC PO Box 622501 — *TF:* 866-667-5307 ■ *Web:* www.mapesllc.com	Oviedo	FL	32762	407-901-4333	477-5543	194
Mapes Panels LLC 2929 Cornhusker Hwy PO Box 80069 — *TF:* 800-228-2391 ■ *Web:* mapes.com	Lincoln	NE	68504	800-228-2391	737-6756	697
Maple City Ice Company Inc 371 Cleveland Rd — *TF:* 800-736-6091 ■ *Web:* www.maplecityice.net	Norwalk	OH	44857	419-668-2531		81-1
Maple City Rubber Co 55 Newton St — *TF:* 800-841-9434 ■ *Web:* www.maplecityrubber.com	Norwalk	OH	44857	419-668-8261	668-1275	762
Maple Direct Inc 2349 Haddonfield Rd — *Web:* www.mapledirect.com	Pennsauken Township	NJ	08110	856-488-4700		5
Maple Donuts Inc 3455 E Market St — *Web:* www.mapledonutsinc.com	York	PA	17402	717-627-5348	755-8725	261
Maple Federal Credit Union 105 Toledo Dr — *TF:* 800-304-2273 ■ *Web:* maplefcu.net	LaFayette	LA	70506	337-233-6264	233-6234	219
Maple Garden 1275 Alder St — *Web:* www.eugenemaplegarden.com	Eugene	OR	97401	541-683-8128		671
Maple Grove Farms of Vermont B&G Foods North America Inc Four Gatehall Dr — *TF:* 800-525-2540 ■ *Web:* www.maplegrove.com	Parsippany	NJ	07054	800-813-4416		296-39
Maple Grove Raceway 30 Stauffer Pk Ln — *Web:* www.maplegroveraceway.com	Mohnton	PA	19540	610-856-9200	856-1601	515
Maple Hill Auto Group 5622 W Main St — *TF:* 888-344-4042 ■ *Web:* www.maplehillauto.com	Kalamazoo	MI	49009	269-342-6600		57
Maple Hill Farm Bed & Breakfast Inn 11 Inn Rd — *TF:* 800-622-2708 ■ *Web:* www.maplebb.com	Hallowell	ME	04347	207-622-2708		379
Maple Hill Farms Inc 12 Burr Rd PO Box 767 — *Web:* mhfct.com	Bloomfield	CT	06002	860-242-9689	243-2490	296-27
Maple Island Inc 2497 7th Ave E Ste 105 — *TF:* 800-369-1022 ■ *Web:* maple-island.com	North Saint Paul	MN	55109	651-773-1000		296-10
Maple Knoll Communities Inc 11100 Springfield Pk — *Web:* www.mapleknoll.org	Cincinnati	OH	45246	513-782-2400		672
Maple Lane Nursing & Retirement Home 60 Maple Ln	Barton	VT	05822	802-754-8575		793
Maple Lawn Homes 116 S Clinton Dr — *Web:* www.maplelawnhomes.com	Eureka	IL	61530	309-431-2370		371
Maple Lawn Nursing Home 400 Seventh St — *Web:* www.maplelawn.org	Fulda	MN	56131	507-425-2571		371
Maple Leaf Farms Inc PO Box 167 — *TF:* 800-348-2812 ■ *Web:* www.mapleleaffarms.com	Leesburg	IN	46538	800-348-2812		10-8
Maple Leaf Foods Inc PO Box 61016 — *TSE: MFI* ■ *TF:* 800-268-3708 ■ *Web:* www.mapleleaf.ca	Winnipeg	MB	R3M3X8	800-268-3708		296-26
Maple Press 480 Willow Springs Ln — *Web:* www.maplepress.com	York	PA	17406	717-764-5911	764-4702	626
Maple Ridge Farms Inc 975 S Park View Cir — *Web:* mapleridge.com	Mosinee	WI	54455	715-693-4346		297-8
Maple Shade Mazda 2921 Rt 73 S — *Web:* www.msmazda.com	Maple Shade	NJ	08052	856-667-8004		516
Maple Technologies LLC 500 Craig Rd 2nd Fl — *Web:* maple-tech.com	Manalapan	NJ	07726	732-863-5523		177
Maple Valley School District 11090 Nashville Hwy — *Web:* www.mvs.k12.mi.us	Vermontville	MI	49096	517-852-9699		685
Maples Gas Company Inc PO Box 292 — *Web:* maplesgas.com	Meridian	MS	39301	601-693-5115		581
Maples Industries Inc PO Box 40 — *Web:* www.maplesrugs.com	Scottsboro	AL	35768	256-259-1327	259-2072	131
Mapleton License of Spokane LLC 60 Garden Ct Ste 300	Monterey	CA	93940	831-658-5281		49-7
Maplewood Barn Community Theatre Maplewood Barn PO Box 1704 — *Web:* www.maplewoodbarn.com	Columbia	MO	65205	573-227-2276		572
Maplewood Investment Advisors Inc 12222 Merit Dr Ste 1390 — *Web:* maplewoodinvestments.com	Dallas	TX	75251	214-739-5677	739-0166	401
Maplewood Nursing & Rehabilitation 100 Daniel Dr — *Web:* visitmaplewood.com	Webster	NY	14580	585-872-1800		371
Maplewood State Park 39721 Park Entrance Rd — *Web:* www.dnr.state.mn.us	Pelican Rapids	MN	56572	218-863-8383		565
Mapp Biopharmaceutical Inc 6160 Luck Blvd Ste C-105 — **Fax Area Code:* 800 ■ *Web:* mappbio.com	San Diego	CA	92121	858-625-0335	372-2176*	582
Mapp Construction LLC 344 Third St — *Web:* www.mappbuilt.com	Baton Rouge	LA	70801	225-757-0111		186
Mapping Analytics LLC 120 Allens Creek Rd Ste 10 — *TF:* 877-893-6490 ■ *Web:* www.mappinganalytics.com	Rochester	NY	14618	877-893-6490		195
MAPSYS Inc 920 Michigan Ave — *Web:* www.mapsysinc.com	Columbus	OH	43215	614-224-5193	224-6048	176
MAQ Software 15446 Bel-Red Rd 2nd Fl — *Web:* www.MAQSoftware.com	Redmond	WA	98052	425-526-5399		178-1
Maquoketa Caves State Park 10970 98th St — *Web:* www.iowadnr.gov	Maquoketa	IA	52060	563-652-5833	652-0061	565
Maquoketa Valley Electric Co-op 109 N Huber St — *TF:* 800-927-6068 ■ *Web:* www.mvec.coop	Anamosa	IA	52205	319-462-3542	462-3217	245
Mar Cor Purification Inc 14550 28th Ave N — *TF:* 800-633-3080 ■ *Web:* www.mcpur.com	Plymouth	MN	55447	484-991-0220	991-0230	806
MAR Inc 1803 Research Blvd Ste 204 — **Fax Area Code:* 240 ■ *Web:* www.marinc.com	Rockville	MD	20850	301-231-0100	453-9871*	261
Mar Tek Electronics Inc 510 Railroad Ave W — *Web:* www.martekmn.com	Onamia	MN	56359	320-532-4111		625
Mar West Real Estate Inc 1049 Camino Del Mar Ste 12 — *Web:* marwestcommercial.com	Del Mar	CA	92014	858-775-4917		652
Maradyne Corp 4540 W 160th St — *TF:* 800-537-7444 ■ *Web:* www.maradyne.com	Cleveland	OH	44135	216-362-0755		14
Marakon 1411 Broadway 35th Fl — *Web:* www.marakon.com	New York	NY	10018	212-520-7120		463
Marana Unified School District 6 (MUSD) 11279 W Grier Rd — *Web:* www.maranausd.org	Marana	AZ	85653	520-682-3243	682-2421	685
Maranatha Baptist Bible College 745 W Main St — *TF:* 800-622-2947 ■ *Web:* www.mbu.edu	Watertown	WI	53094	920-206-2330	261-9109	166
Maranatha Bible Camp Inc 16800 E Maranatha Rd — *Web:* maranathacamp.org	Maxwell	NE	69151	308-582-4513	582-4516	239
Maranda Insurance Agency Inc 607 W Lumsden Rd — *Web:* mariarocks.com	Brandon	FL	33511	813-661-1003		390
Marans, Weisz & Newmann LLC 29 Broadway Ste 2400 — *Web:* mwatlaw.com	New York	NY	10006	212-968-0244		41
Marantz America Inc 100 Corporate Dr — *Web:* www.marantz.com	Mahwah	NJ	07430	201-762-6500	762-6670	52
Marashlian & Donahue PLLC 1430 Spring Hill Rd Ste 401 — *Web:* commtechdatalaw.com	McLean	VA	22102	703-714-1300		41
Marathon Cheese Corp 304 E St PO Box 185 — *Web:* www.mcheese.co	Marathon	WI	54448	715-443-2211	443-3843	296-5
Marathon Coach 91333 Coburg Industrial Way — *TF:* 800-234-9991 ■ *Web:* www.marathoncoach.com	Coburg	OR	97408	541-343-9991	343-2401	62-7
Marathon County 500 Forest St — *TF:* 800-247-5645 ■ *Web:* www.co.marathon.wi.us	Wausau	WI	54403	715-261-1500	261-1515	338
Marathon County Public Library (MCPL) 300 N First St — *Web:* mcpl.us	Wausau	WI	54403	715-261-7200	261-7204	434-3
Marathon Digital Services 901 N 8th St — *TF:* 877-568-1121 ■ *Web:* www.mysmartplans.com	Kansas City	KS	66101	816-221-7881	241-5237	177

	City	State	Zip	Phone	Fax	Class
Marathon Electric Motors 100 E Randolf St PO Box 8003 *TF:* 800-616-7077 ■ *Web:* www.marathongenerators.com	Wausau	WI	54401	715-675-3311		518
Marathon Electrical Contractors Inc 614 38th St S *Web:* marathonelectrical.com	Birmingham	AL	35222	205-323-8500		189-4
Marathon Enterprises Inc 9 Smith St *TF:* 800-722-7388 ■ *Web:* sabrett.com	Englewood	NJ	07631	201-935-3330	935-5693	296-26
Marathon Equipment Co PO Box 1798 *TF:* 800-633-8974 ■ *Web:* www.marathonequipment.com	Vernon	AL	35592	205-695-9105	695-8813	386
Marathon Ethiopian Restaurant 130 Tenth St NW *Web:* www.marathonethiopianrestaurantcalgary.com	Calgary	AB	T2N1V3	403-283-6796		671
Marathon Oil Corp 5555 San Felipe St *TF:* 855-652-3067 ■ *Web:* www.marathonoil.com	Houston	TX	77056	713-629-6600	296-4490	536
Marathon Petroleum LLC PO Box 1 *TF:* 866-462-7284 ■ *Web:* www.marathonpetroleum.com	Findlay	OH	45839	419-421-2071		46
Marathon Pipe Line LLC (MPL) 539 S Main St *TF:* 800-537-6644 ■ *Web:* www.marathonpipeline.com	Findlay	OH	45840	419-421-4600		597
Marathon Press 1500 Sq Turn Blvd PO Box 407 **Fax Area Code:* 402 ■ *TF:* 800-228-0629 ■ *Web:* www.marathonpress.com	Norfolk	NE	68702	800-228-0629	371-9382*	627
Marathon Special Products 13300 Van Camp Rd PO Box 468 *Web:* www.marathonsp.com	Bowling Green	OH	43402	419-352-8441	352-0875	729
MarathonFoto 3490 Martin Hurst Rd *TF:* 800-424-3686 ■ *Web:* www.marathonfoto.com	Tallahassee	FL	32312	800-424-3686		590
MarathonNorco Aerospace Inc 8301 Imperial Dr *Web:* www.mnaerospace.com	Waco	TX	76712	254-776-0650	776-6558	621
Maravia Corporation of Idaho 602 E 45th St *TF:* 800-223-7238 ■ *Web:* www.maravia.com	Boise	ID	83714	208-322-4949	322-5016	710
Maravilla Foundation 5729 E Union Pacific Ave *Web:* maravilla.org	Commerce	CA	90022	323-869-4500	278-7788	305
Maraziti Falcon LLP 150 John F Kennedy Pkwy *Web:* mfhlaw.com	Short Hills	NJ	07078	973-912-9008		41
Mar-Bal Inc 16930 Munn Rd *Web:* www.mar-bal.com	Chagrin Falls	OH	44023	440-543-7526	543-4374	599
Marberry Cleaners & Launderers 220 John St *Web:* www.marberrycleaners.com	North Aurora	IL	60542	630-897-0011		426
Marberry Machine Co 6210 Cunningham Rd *Web:* www.marberrymachine.com	Houston	TX	77041	713-466-9666	466-4731	454
Marble Arms (MA) 420 Industrial Pk Dr *Web:* www.marblearms.com	Gladstone	MI	49837	906-428-3710		710
MARBLE Computer Inc 6416 Via De Albur Ct Ste 100 *TF:* 800-252-1400 ■ *Web:* www.marblecomputer.com	El Paso	TX	79912	915-845-0963		178-1
Marble Systems Inc 2737 Dorr Ave *Web:* www.marblesystems.com	Fairfax	VA	22031	703-204-1818	204-1888	191-1
Marblehead Lighthouse State Park *Marblehead Lighthouse Historical Society* PO Box 144 *Web:* www.marbleheadlighthouseohio.org	Marblehead	OH	43440	419-798-2094		565
Marbles Kids Museum 201 E Hargett St *Web:* www.marbleskidsmuseum.org	Raleigh	NC	27601	919-834-4040	834-3516	520
Marborg Industries 728 E Yanonali St *TF:* 800-798-1852 ■ *Web:* www.marborg.com	Santa Barbara	CA	93103	805-963-1852	962-0552	660
Marbridge Foundation Inc 2310 Bliss Spillar Rd *Web:* www.marbridge.org	Manchaca	TX	78652	512-282-1144		305
Marburg Technology Inc 304 Turquoise St *Web:* www.glidewrite.com	Milpitas	CA	95035	408-262-8400		173-1
Marburger Farm Dairy Inc 1506 Mars Evans City Rd *TF:* 800-331-1295 ■ *Web:* www.marburgerdairy.com	Evans City	PA	16033	724-538-4800	538-3250	10-3
Marburn Academy 1860 Walden Dr *Web:* marburnacademy.org	Columbus	OH	43229	614-433-0822		148
Marc A. Austin Pc 3521 N University Ave Ste 200 *Web:* austinlawpc.com	Provo	UT	84604	801-374-8925		41
Marc B. Freedman Certified Public Accountant PC 215 W 95th St *Web:* www.mbfcpa.com	New York	NY	10025	212-678-2418	932-1254	2
Marc Boogay 1584 Whispering Palm Dr *Web:* www.boogay.com	Oceanside	CA	92056	760-407-4000	407-4004	192
Marc Bouwer 141 Fulton St 2nd Fl *Web:* www.marcbouwer.com	New York	NY	10038	212-242-7510		277
Marc Jacobs Intl 72 Spring St *TF:* 877-707-6272 ■ *Web:* www.marcjacobs.com	New York	NY	10012	212-965-4000		277
Marc Publishing Co 600 Germantown Pk *TF:* 800-432-5478 ■ *Web:* www.marcpub.com	Lafayette Hill	PA	19444	610-834-8585		637-6
MARC USA 225 W Stn Sq Dr Ste 500 *Web:* www.marcusa.com	Pittsburgh	PA	15219	412-562-2000	562-2022	4
Marca Miami 3390 Mary St Ste 254 *Web:* marcamiami.com	Coconut Grove	FL	33133	305-423-8300		4
Marcari, Russotto, Spencer & Balaban PC 2443 Lynn Rd Ste 208 *Web:* www.donmarcari.com	Raleigh	NC	27612	919-787-9944		428
Marcegaglia USA Inc 1001 E Waterfront Dr *Web:* www.marcegaglia.com	Munhall	PA	15120	412-462-2185	462-6059	490
Marcel Media LLC 445 W Erie St Ste 200 *Web:* www.marceldigital.com	Chicago	IL	60654	312-255-8044		4
Marcel's 2401 Pennsylvania Ave NW *Web:* www.marcelsdc.com	Washington	DC	20037	202-296-1166		671
Marcella Restaurant 3507 Tully Rd	Modesto	CA	95356	209-577-3777		671
March Associates Inc 601 Hamburg Tpke *Web:* www.marchassociates.com	Wayne	NJ	07470	973-904-0213		186
March Consulting Associates Inc 200 201 21st St E *Web:* www.marchconsulting.com	Saskatoon	SK	S7K0B8	306-651-6330		261
March Field Air Museum 22550 Van Buren Blvd *Web:* www.marchfield.org	Riverside	CA	92518	951-902-5949		520
March of Dimes Foundation 1275 Mamaroneck Ave *TF:* 800-336-4363 ■ *Web:* www.marchofdimes.org	White Plains	NY	10605	914-428-7100		48-17
Marchant Kenny (Rep R - TX) 2304 Rayburn House Office Bldg *TF:* 866-213-3803 ■ *Web:* marchant.house.gov	Washington	DC	20515	202-225-6605	225-0074	342-2
Marchant Schmidt Inc 24 W Larsen Dr *Web:* www.marchantschmidt.com	Fond Du Lac	WI	54937	920-921-4760		492
Marche 296 E Fifth Ave *Web:* marcherestaurant.com	Eugene	OR	97401	541-342-3612		671
Marche Akhavan 6170 Rue Sherbrooke O *Web:* akhavanfood.com	Montreal	QC	H4B1L8	514-485-4887		297-8
Marcheschi Plankis & Pogore LLP 9951 W 190th St Ste A *Web:* mppcpa.com	Mokena	IL	60448	708-479-7333		2
Marchex Inc 520 Pike St Ste 2000 *NASDAQ: MCHX* ■ *TF:* 800-840-1012 ■ *Web:* www.marchex.com	Seattle	WA	98101	206-331-3300	331-3695	7
Marchman Technical College 7825 Campus Dr *Web:* www.mtec.pasco.k12.fl.us	New Port Richey	FL	34653	727-774-1700	774-1791	167-3
Marcive Inc PO Box 47508 Ste 160 *TF:* 800-531-7678 ■ *Web:* home.marcive.com	San Antonio	TX	78265	800-531-7678		434-3
Marck Industries Inc 401 Main St Ste E PO Box 912 **Fax Area Code:* 417 ■ *TF:* 877-228-2565 ■ *Web:* www.marck.net	Cassville	MO	65625	877-228-2565	847-5990*	660
Marc-michaels Interior Design Inc 850 E Palmetto Park Rd *TF:* 888-664-6272 ■ *Web:* www.marc-michaels.com	Boca Raton	FL	33432	561-362-7037		393
Marco 4581 Forsyth Rd *Web:* www.marcomacon.com	Macon	GA	31210	478-405-5660		671
Marco Beach Ocean Resort 480 S Collier Blvd *TF:* 800-715-8517 ■ *Web:* www.marcoresort.com	Marco Island	FL	34145	239-393-1400	393-1401	669
Marco Corp, The 470 Hardy Rd **Fax Area Code:* 519 ■ *TF:* 888-636-6161 ■ *Web:* www.themarcocorporation.biz	Brantford	ON	N3V6T1	888-636-6161	751-0561*	7
Marco Crane & Rigging Co 221 S 35th Ave *TF:* 800-668-2671 ■ *Web:* www.marcocrane.com	Phoenix	AZ	85009	602-272-2671	352-0413	264-3
Marco Enterprises Inc 3504 Watkins Ave *Web:* www.marcoenterprises.com	Landover Hills	MD	20785	301-773-5656	773-0422	186
Marco Global 7915 Tenth Ave S *Web:* www.marcoglobal.com	Seattle	WA	98199	206-285-3200	282-8520	698
Marco Island Chamber of Commerce 1102 N Collier Blvd *Web:* www.marcoislandchamber.org	Marco Island	FL	34145	239-394-7549		139
Marco Machine & Design Inc 7740 Whitepine Rd *Web:* www.marcomachine.com	North Chesterfield	VA	23237	804-275-5555	271-3409	454
Marco Ophthalmic Inc 11825 Central Pkwy *TF:* 800-874-5274 ■ *Web:* marco.com	Jacksonville	FL	32224	904-642-9330	642-9338	543
Marco Polo Global Restaurant 300 Liberty St SE *Web:* www.marcopolosalem.com	Salem	OR	97301	503-364-4833		671
Marco Polo Securities Inc 144 E 44th St 8th Fl *Web:* www.mpsecurities.com	New York	NY	10017	212-220-2670		690
Marco Promotional Products 2640 Commerce Dr **Fax Area Code:* 866 ■ *TF:* 877-545-9322 ■ *Web:* www.marcopromotionalproducts.com	Harrisburg	PA	17110	877-545-9322	545-5672*	9
Marco Rubber 35 Woodworkers Way *TF:* 800-775-6525 ■ *Web:* www.marcorubber.com	Seabrook	NH	03874	603-468-3600		326
Marco Sales Inc 11972 Riverwood Dr *TF:* 800-552-9237 ■ *Web:* www.marcosalesmn.com	Burnsville	MN	55337	952-854-2231	854-7552	297-9
Marco's 1085 Niagara St *Web:* marcosbuffalo.com	Buffalo	NY	14213	716-882-5539		671
Marco's Franchising LLC 5252 Monroe St *TF:* 800-262-7267 ■ *Web:* www.marcosfranchising.com	Toledo	OH	43623	419-746-6361		670
MARCOA Publishing Inc 9955 Black Mtn Rd *TF:* 800-854-2935 ■ *Web:* www.marcoa.com	San Diego	CA	92126	858-695-9600	695-9641	637-1
Marcom 540 Hauer Apple Way *Web:* www.mar-com.com	Aptos	CA	95003	707-202-7535		647
Marcom Gurus 2083 Louise Ln *Web:* marcomgurus.com	Los Altos	CA	94024	650-564-0011		195
Marcone Appliance Parts Ctr 13825 Cerritos Corporate Dr *TF:* 800-482-6022 ■ *Web:* www.marcone.com	Cerritos	CA	90703	800-482-6022		246
Marcrom's Pharmacy Inc 1277 Mcarthur St *Web:* marcromspharmacy.com	Manchester	TN	37355	931-728-1100		237
Marcum LLP 750 3rd Ave 11th Fl *TF:* 855-627-2861 ■ *Web:* www.marcumllp.com	New York	NY	10017	212-485-5500	485-5501	2
Marcus & Associates Inc 1045 Mapunapuna St *Web:* www.marcusrealty.com	Honolulu	HI	96819	808-839-7446		652
Marcus & Cinelli LLP 8416 Main St *Web:* marcuscinelli.com	Williamsville	NY	14221	716-565-3800	565-3801	41
Marcus & Pollack LLP 633 Third Ave 9th Fl *Web:* www.marcuspollack.com	New York	NY	10017	212-490-2900		428
Marcus A. Rosin PC 327 Dahlonega St Ste 102A *Web:* marcusrosin.com	Cumming	GA	30040	678-208-0339		41
Marcus Bros Textiles Inc 980 Avenue of the Americas *TF:* 800-548-8295 ■ *Web:* marcusfabrics.com	New York	NY	10018	212-354-8700		594
Marcus Center for the Performing Arts 929 N Water St *TF:* 888-612-3500 ■ *Web:* www.marcuscenter.org	Milwaukee	WI	53202	414-273-7206		572

Name / Address	City	State	ZIP	Phone	Fax	Class
Marcus Corp, The 100 E Wisconsin Ave *Web:* www.marcuscorp.com	Milwaukee	WI	53202	414-905-1000		707
Marcus Errico Emmer & Brooks PC 45 Braintree Hill Pk Ste 107 *Web:* meeb.com	Braintree	MA	02184	781-843-5000		2
Marcus Evans Inc 455 N Cityfront Plaza Dr the NBC Tower 9th Fl *Web:* www.marcusevans.com	Chicago	IL	60611	312-540-3000		387
Marcus Group Inc, The 310 Passaic Ave Ste 301 *Web:* www.marcusgroup.com	Fairfield	NJ	07004	973-890-9590		636
Marcus Hotels & Resorts 100 E Wisconsin Ave Ste 1950 *Web:* www.marcushotels.com	Milwaukee	WI	53202	414-905-1200		379
Marcus Paint Co 235 E Market St **Fax Area Code:* 502 ■ *Web:* www.marcuspaint.com	Louisville	KY	40202	866-348-1392	587-0922*	493
Marcus Productions Inc 3107 Stirling Rd Ste 204 *Web:* marcusproductions.com	Fort Lauderdale	FL	33312	954-965-5295		513
Marcus Restaurant Group 100 E Wisconsin Ave *Web:* www.marcusrestaurants.com	Milwaukee	WI	53202	414-935-5995		670
Marcus Whitman Hotel & Conference Center LLC 6 W Rose St *TF:* 866-826-9422 ■ *Web:* marcuswhitmanhotel.com	Walla Walla	WA	99362	509-525-2200		707
Marcy Correctional Facility 9000 Old River Rd PO Box 5000 *Web:* www.doccs.ny.gov	Marcy	NY	13403	315-768-1400		213
Mardel Stores Inc 7727 SW 44th St *TF:* 888-262-7335 ■ *Web:* www.mardel.com	Oklahoma City	OK	73179	888-262-7335		685
Marden's 458 Kennedy Memorial Dr *Web:* www.mardenssurplus.com	Waterville	ME	04901	207-873-6112		791
Marden-Kane Inc 575 Underhill Blvd Ste 222 *Web:* www.mardenkane.com	Syosset	NY	11791	516-365-3999		7
Mardon Control Systems Inc N169 W20901 Tower Dr *Web:* mardoncontrols.com	Jackson	WI	53037	262-677-0200		201
Mared Industries Inc 15222 Keswick St *TF:* 800-678-8006 ■ *Web:* www.ditool.com	Van Nuys	CA	91405	800-678-8006		61
Mared Mechanical Contractors Corp 4230 W Douglas Ave *Web:* maredmechanical.com	Milwaukee	WI	53209	414-536-0411		189-10
Marek Bros Co 3539 Oak Forest Dr *Web:* www.marekbros.com	Houston	TX	77018	713-681-2626	681-4614	393
Maren Engineering 111 W Taft Dr *TF:* 800-875-1038 ■ *Web:* www.marenengineering.com	South Holland	IL	60473	708-333-6250		261
Marena Studio 12W 23rd St *Web:* marenastudios.com	New York	NY	10010	212-243-3070		344
Marengo County 101 E Coats Ave *Web:* www.marengocountyal.com	Linden	AL	36748	334-295-2200	295-2081	338
Mares America Corp 1 Selleck St *TF:* 800-874-3236 ■ *Web:* www.mares.com	Norwalk	CT	06855	203-855-0631		710
Marfield Corporate Stationery 1225 E Crosby Rd Ste B1 *TF:* 877-245-9122 ■ *Web:* www.marfield.com	Carrollton	TX	75006	972-245-9122		627
Margaret E. Heggan Public Library 606 Delsea Dr *Web:* www.hegganlibrary.org	Sewell	NJ	08080	856-589-3334		434-3
Margaret Harwell Art Museum 421 N Main St *Web:* www.mham.org	Poplar Bluff	MO	63901	573-686-8002		520
Margaret Lewis Norrie State Park 9 Old Post Rd PO Box 308 *Web:* parks.ny.gov	Staatsburg	NY	12580	845-889-4646	889-8321	565
Margaret Mary Community Hospital Inc 321 Mitchell Ave PO Box 226 *TF:* 800-562-5698 ■ *Web:* www.mmhealth.org	Batesville	IN	47006	812-934-6624	934-5373	374-3
Margaret R. Pardee Memorial Hospital 800 N Justice St *Web:* www.pardeehospital.org	Hendersonville	NC	28791	828-696-1000		374-3
Margaret Reaney Memorial Library & Museum Local History Collection 19 Kingsbury Ave *Web:* www.margaretreaneylibrary.blogspot.com	Saint Johnsville	NY	13452	518-568-7822		434-3
Margaret Sanger Center Intl (MSCI) 26 Bleecker St *Web:* www.plannedparenthood.org	New York	NY	10012	212-965-7000	274-7299	48-6
Margaret Tietz Center for Nursing Care 164-11 Chapin Pkwy *Web:* www.margarettietz.org	Jamaica	NY	11432	718-298-7800		450
Margaretville Telephone Co 50 Swart St PO Box 260 *TF:* 800-586-3387 ■ *Web:* www.mtctelcom.com	Margaretville	NY	12455	845-586-3311	586-4050	647
Margaritas 390 Western Ave *Web:* www.margs.com	Augusta	ME	04330	207-622-7874		671
Margaritaville 500 Duval St *Web:* www.margaritavillekeywest.com	Key West	FL	33040	305-292-1435		671
Margate on Winnipesaukee, The 76 Lake St *Web:* www.themargate.com	Laconia	NH	03246	603-524-5210		669
Margaux Farm LLC 596 Moores Mill Rd PO Box 4220 *Web:* margauxfarm.com	Midway	KY	40347	859-846-4433	846-4486	368
Marge Carson Inc 1260 E Grand Ave *Web:* www.margecarson.com	Pomona	CA	91766	626-571-1111		319-2
Margin Edge 8315 Lee Hwy Ste 501 *TF:* 888-488-9612 ■ *Web:* www.marginedge.com	Fairfax	VA	22031	888-488-9612		178-8
MarginPoint Inc 23046 Avenida de la Carlota Ste 250 *TF:* 866-850-0500 ■ *Web:* marginpoint.com	Laguna Hills	CA	92653	866-850-0500		174
Marglen Industries Inc 1748 Ward Mtn Rd *Web:* www.marglen.us	Rome	GA	30161	706-295-5621		131
Margolin Winer & Evens LLP 400 Garden City Plz 5th Fl *Web:* www.mwellp.com	Garden City	NY	11530	516-747-2000	747-6707	2
Margolis Edelstein 170 S Independence Mall W The Curtis Ctr Ste 400E *Web:* www.margolisedelstein.com	Philadelphia	PA	19106	814-695-5064		428
Margot Cafe & Bar 1017 Woodland St *Web:* www.margotcafe.com	Nashville	TN	37206	615-227-4668		671
Margullis Luedtke & Ray 2601 N Alder St *TF:* 800-618-6445 ■ *Web:* mlr-law.com	Tacoma	WA	98407	253-752-2251	752-1071	41
Maria Collection, The 1048 N Pearl St *Web:* www.themariacollection.com	Bridgeton	NJ	08302	856-453-9523		410
Maria College 700 New Scotland Ave *Web:* mariacollege.edu	Albany	NY	12208	518-438-3111	453-1366	162
Maria Mitchell Association Aquarium 4 Vestal St *Web:* www.mariamitchell.org	Nantucket	MA	02554	508-228-9198	228-1031	40
Maria Parham Medical Ctr 566 Ruin Creek Rd PO Box 59 *Web:* www.mariaparham.com	Henderson	NC	27536	252-438-4143		374-3
Maria's New Mexican Kitchen 555 W Cordova Rd *Web:* www.marias-santafe.com	Santa Fe	NM	87505	505-983-7929		671
Marian College School of Nursing 3325 Wilshire Blvd 10th Fl *Web:* www.mariancollege.edu	Los Angeles	CA	90010	213-388-3566	487-7498	685
Marian Goodman Gallery 24 W 57th St *Web:* www.mariangoodman.com	New York	NY	10019	212-977-7160	581-5187	42
Marian Koshland Science Museum 525 E St *Web:* www.koshland-science-museum.org	Washington	DC	20001	202-334-1201		520
Marian University 3200 Cold Spring Rd *TF:* 800-772-7264 ■ *Web:* www.marian.edu	Indianapolis	IN	46222	317-955-6038	955-6401	166
Marian University 45 S National Ave *TF:* 800-262-7426 ■ *Web:* www.marianuniversity.edu	Fond du Lac	WI	54935	800-262-7426		166
Marianapolis Preparatory School 26 Chase Rd PO Box 304 *Web:* www.marianapolis.org	Thompson	CT	06277	860-923-9565	923-3730	622
Mariani Enterprises Inc 300 Rockland Rd *Web:* www.marianilandscape.com	Lake Bluff	IL	60044	847-234-2172		422
Mariani Nut Co 709 Dutton St *Web:* www.marianinut.com	Winters	CA	95694	530-662-3311	795-2681	11-1
Mariani Packing Company Inc 500 Crocker Dr *TF:* 800-231-1287 ■ *Web:* www.mariani.com	Vacaville	CA	95688	707-452-2800	452-2973	11-1
Mariani Reck Lane LLC 83 Broad St *Web:* www.marianirecklane.com	New London	CT	06320	860-443-5023	443-8897	428
Marianjoy Rehabilitation Hospital 26 W 171 Roosevelt Rd *TF:* 800-462-2366 ■ *Web:* www.marianjoy.org	Wheaton	IL	60187	630-462-4000		374-6
Marianna Industries Inc 11222 "I" St *TF:* 800-228-9060 ■ *Web:* www.mariannabeauty.com	Omaha	NE	68137	402-593-0211		231
Mariano's Mexican Cuisine 2614 Majesty Dr *Web:* www.laharanch.com	Arlington	TX	76011	817-640-5118		671
Marianopolis College 4873 Westmount Ave *Web:* www.marianopolis.edu	Westmount	QC	H3Y1X9	514-931-8792		166
Marias River Electric Co-opeartive Inc PO Box 729 *Web:* www.mariasriverec.com	Shelby	MT	59474	406-434-5575		245
Maricich Brand Communications 18201 McDurmott W Ste A *Web:* www.maricich.com	Irvine	CA	92614	949-223-6455		4
Marick Group, The 25 Catoctin Cir SE Ste 1318 *Web:* marickgroup.com	Leesburg	VA	20177	410-800-4858		809
Maricopa County 301 W Jefferson St 10th Fl *Web:* www.maricopa.gov	Phoenix	AZ	85003	602-506-3011	506-6402	338
Maricopa County Library District (MCLD) 2700 N Central Ave Ste 700 *Web:* mcldaz.org	Phoenix	AZ	85004	602-652-3000		434-3
Maricopa County Medical Society (MCMS) 326 E Coronado Rd Ste 101 *Web:* www.mcmsonline.com	Phoenix	AZ	85004	602-252-2015	256-2749	49-19
Maricopa Medical Ctr 2601 E Roosevelt St *TF:* 866-749-2876 ■ *Web:* www.mihs.org	Phoenix	AZ	85008	602-344-5011	344-0719	374-3
Marie Callender Restaurant & Bakery 27101 Puerta Real Ste 260 *TF:* 800-776-7437 ■ *Web:* www.mariecallenders.com	Mission Viejo	CA	92691	800-776-7437		670
Marie Claire Magazine 300 W 57th St 34th Fl *TF:* 800-777-3287 ■ *Web:* www.marieclaire.com	New York	NY	10019	515-282-1607		457-11
Marie Joseph Spiritual Ctr 10 Evans Rd *Web:* mariejosephspiritual.org	Biddeford	ME	04005	207-284-5671		673
Marie Livingston's Steakhouse & Saloon 2705 Apalachee Pkwy *Web:* marielivingstonsteakhouse.com	Tallahassee	FL	32301	850-562-2525		671
Marie Selby Botanical Gardens 811 S Palm Ave *Web:* selby.org	Sarasota	FL	34236	941-366-5731	366-9807	97
Maries County Court House 211 Fourth St PO Box 490 *Web:* www.mariescountymo.gov	Vienna	MO	65582	573-422-3338		338
Marietta Area Chamber of Commerce 100 Front St Ste 200 *Web:* www.mariettachamber.com	Marietta	OH	45750	740-373-5176	373-7808	139
Marietta College 215 Fifth St *TF:* 800-331-7896 ■ *Web:* www.marietta.edu	Marietta	OH	45750	740-376-4000	376-8888	166
Marietta Drapery & Window Coverings Company Inc 22 Trammel St PO Box 569 *TF:* 800-241-7974 ■ *Web:* www.mariettadrapery.com	Marietta	GA	30064	800-241-7974	824-9456	746

	Phone	Fax	Class
Marietta Hospitality 37 Huntington St Cortland NY 13045 *TF:* 800-950-7772 ■ *Web:* www.mariettahospitality.com	607-753-6746		9
Marietta Memorial Hospital 401 Matthew St. Marietta OH 45750 *TF:* 800-523-3977 ■ *Web:* mhsystem.org	740-374-1400	374-1787	374-3
Marietta National Cemetery 500 Washington Ave. Marietta GA 30060 **Fax Area Code:* 770 ■ *TF:* 866-236-8159 ■ *Web:* www.cem.va.gov	866-236-8159	479-9311*	136
Marigold Cafe 4605 Centennial Blvd Colorado Springs CO 80919 *Web:* marigoldcoloradosprings.com	719-599-4776		671
Marijuana Anonymous World Services (MAWS) 340 S Lemon Ave Ste 9420 Walnut CA 91789 *TF:* 800-766-6779 ■ *Web:* www.marijuana-anonymous.org	800-766-6779		48-21
Mariko Boutique Inc 329 Worth Ave Palm Beach Gardens FL 33480 *Web:* marikopalmbeach.com	561-655-5770		410
Marilyn Colon PA 2424 Coral Way Miami FL 33145 *Web:* marilyncolonpa.com	305-859-2424		41
Marilyn Model Agency 32 Un Sq E PH New York NY 10003 *Web:* www.marilynagency.com	212-260-6500		506
Marimba One Inc 901 O St Ste D Arcata CA 95521 *TF:* 888-990-6663 ■ *Web:* www.marimbaone.com	707-822-9570		527
Marin Academy 1600 Mission Ave San Rafael CA 94901 *Web:* www.ma.org	415-453-4550		685
Marin Charter & Tours 8 Lovell Ave San Rafael CA 94901 *Web:* marinairporter.com	415-256-8830		107
Marin Christian Academy 1370 S Novato Blvd Novato CA 94947 *Web:* marinchristian.org	415-892-5713	493-0591	148
Marin Community Foundation, The (MCF) 5 Hamilton Landing Ste 200 Novato CA 94949 *Web:* www.marincf.org	415-464-2500	464-2555	303
Marin Convention & Visitors Bureau 1 Mitchell Blvd Ste B San Rafael CA 94903 *TF:* 866-925-2060 ■ *Web:* www.visitmarin.org	415-925-2060	925-2063	206
Marin County 3501 Civic Center Dr Ste 325 San Rafael CA 94903 *TF:* 800-985-7277 ■ *Web:* www.marincounty.org	415-473-6358		338
Marin County Free Library 3501 Civic Center Dr Ste 414 San Rafael CA 94903 *Web:* www.marinlibrary.org	415-473-6058		434-3
Marin County Law Library 20 N San Pedro Rd San Rafael CA 94903 *Web:* www.marincountylawlibrary.org	415-472-3733	472-3729	434-3
Marin County's News Monthly-Free Press PO Box 31 Bolinas CA 94924 *Web:* www.coastalpost.com	415-868-1600	868-0502	637-9
Marin General Hospital 250 Bon Air Rd Greenbrae CA 94904 *TF:* 888-996-9644 ■ *Web:* www.maringeneral.org	415-925-7000	925-7317	374-3
Marin Independent Journal 150 Alameda Del Prado Novato CA 94949 *Web:* www.marinij.com	415-883-8600	883-5458	532-2
Marin Investments Ltd 700 W Georgia St Ste 3010 Vancouver BC V7Y1B6 *Web:* marin.ca	604-687-1450	681-5187	360-3
Marin Mountain Bikes Inc 265 Bel Marin Keys Blvd Novato CA 94949 *Web:* www.marinbikes.com	415-382-6000		711
Marin Suites Hotel LLC 45 Tamal Vista Blvd Corte Madera CA 94925 *TF:* 800-362-3372 ■ *Web:* www.marinsuites.com	833-827-3206		378
Marin Symphony 4340 Redwood Hwy Ste 409C San Rafael CA 94903 *Web:* marinsymphony.org	415-479-8100		573-3
Marina Care Ctr 5240 Sepulveda Blvd Culver City CA 90230 *Web:* marinacare.com	310-391-7266		371
Marina Chamber of Commerce PO Box 425 Marina CA 93933 *Web:* marinachamber.com	831-384-0155		139
Marina Civic Ctr 8 Harrison Ave Panama City FL 32401 *Web:* www.marinaciviccenter.com	850-763-4696		572
Marina Deck 306 Dorchester St. Ocean City MD 21842 *Web:* www.marinadeckrestaurant.com	410-289-4411		671
Marina Del Mar Resort & Marina 527 Caribbean Dr Key Largo FL 33037 *Web:* www.marinadelmarkeylargo.com	305-451-4107	451-1891	379
Marina Del Rey Hospital 4650 Lincoln Blvd Marina CA 90292 *TF:* 888-600-5600 ■ *Web:* www.marinahospital.com	310-823-8911		374-3
Marina del Rey Hotel 13534 Bali Way Marina CA 90292 *Web:* www.marinadelreyhotel.com	310-301-1000		707
Marina Graphic Ctr 12901 Cerise Ave Hawthorne CA 90250 *TF:* 800-974-5777 ■ *Web:* www.marinagraphics.com	310-970-1777		627
Marina Inn at Grande Dunes 8121 Amalfi Pl Myrtle Beach SC 29572 *TF:* 877-913-1333 ■ *Web:* www.marinainnatgrandedunes.com	843-913-1333	913-1334	379
Marina Power Company Inc 8456 NW 61st St Miami FL 33166 *Web:* www.marinapower.net	305-470-0037	470-0021	767
Marinco 2655 Napa Valley Corp Dr Napa CA 94558 *TF:* 800-307-6702 ■ *Web:* www.marinco.com	707-226-9600		815
Marine PO Box 5185 Des Plaines IL 60019 *TF:* 800-627-4637 ■ *Web:* www.marines.com	800-627-4637		340-7
Marine & Industrial Hydraulics Inc 329 Ctr Ave. Mamaroneck NY 10543 *Web:* www.mihtrident.com	914-698-2650	698-5629	223
Marine Bank & Trust 571 Beachland Blvd Vero Beach FL 32963 *Web:* marinebankandtrust.com	772-231-6611		70
Marine Bank of Champaign-Urbana 2434 Village Green Pl. Champaign IL 61822 *Web:* www.ibankmarine.com	217-239-0100		70
Marine Biological Laboratory (MBL) 7 MBL St Woods Hole MA 02543 *Web:* www.mbl.edu	508-548-3705	540-6902	668
Marine Corps Air Station Beaufort PO Box 55001 Beaufort SC 29904 *Web:* www.beaufort.marines.mil	843-228-7201	228-6005	497-3
Marine Corps Air Station Yuma (MCAS YUMA) Marine Corps Air Station Yuma Yuma AZ 85369 *Web:* www.mcasyuma.marines.mil	928-269-5505		497-3
Marine Corps Assn (MCA) PO Box 1775 Quantico VA 22134 *TF:* 800-336-0291 ■ *Web:* www.mca-marines.org	703-640-6161	640-0823	48-19
Marine Corps Base Quantico 3250 Catlin Ave Quantico VA 22134 *TF:* 800-268-3710 ■ *Web:* www.quantico.marines.mil	703-432-0303		497-3
Marine Corps Community Services (MCCS) 3044 Catlin Ave Quantico VA 22134 *Web:* www.usmc-mccs.org	703-784-3005		229
Marine Corps League Auxiliary INC 3619 Jefferson Davis Hwy Ste 115 Stafford VA 22554 *Web:* www.nationalmcla.org	571-477-2780		138
Marine Corps Recruit Depot San Diego 1600 Henderson Ave. San Diego CA 92145 *Web:* www.marines.mil	619-524-6719		497-3
Marine Depot 14271 Corporate Dr Garden Grove CA 92843 *TF:* 800-566-3474 ■ *Web:* www.marinedepot.com	800-566-3474		770
Marine Engineers' Beneficial Assn (MEBA) 444 N Capitol St NW Ste 800 Washington DC 20001 *Web:* www.mebaunion.org	202-638-5355	638-5369	414
Marine Equipment and Supply (MESCO) 1401 Metropolitan Ave Thorofare NJ 08086 *Web:* www.mesconet.com	856-853-8320	853-9732	770
Marine Exhaust Systems of Alabama Inc 757 Nichols Ave Fairhope AL 36532 *TF:* 800-237-3160 ■ *Web:* www.mesamarine.com	251-928-1234		454
Marine Hydraulics International Inc (MHI) 543 E Indian River Rd Norfolk VA 23523 *Web:* www.mhi-shiprepair.com	757-545-6400	545-8169	698
Marine Industrial Fabrication Inc 4912 Marina Rd New Iberia LA 70560 *Web:* www.mifinc.com	337-369-7004		698
Marine Mammal Commission 4340 E W Hwy Ste 700 Bethesda MD 20814 *Web:* www.mmc.gov	301-504-0087	504-0099	340-20
Marine Mammal Stranding Ctr 3625 Brigantine Blvd Brigantine NJ 08203 *Web:* mmsc.org	609-266-0538		520
Marine Military Academy Air Wing Inc 320 Iwo Jima Blvd Harlingen TX 78550 *Web:* www.mma-tx.org	956-423-6006		685
Marine Petroleum Trust 2911 Turtle Creek Blvd Ste 850 Dallas TX 75219 *NASDAQ: MARPS* ■ *TF:* 800-758-4672 ■ *Web:* www.marps-marine.com	800-758-4672		675
Marine Power Holding LLC 17506 Marine Power Industrial Pk Ponchatoula LA 70454 *TF:* 877-388-9555 ■ *Web:* marinepowerusa.com	985-386-2081		262
Marine Rescue Products Inc 41 Prospect Ave Middletown RI 02842 *TF:* 800-341-9500 ■ *Web:* www.marine-rescue.com	401-847-9144		770
Marine Room, The 2000 Spindrift Dr La Jolla CA 92037 *TF:* 866-644-2351 ■ *Web:* www.marineroom.com	858-459-7222	551-4673	671
Marine Safety Corp 5050 Industrial Rd Wall NJ 07719 *Web:* www.marinesafetycorporation.com	732-938-5668	938-4839	90
Marine Science Institute University of California Santa Barbara CA 93106 *Web:* www.msi.ucsb.edu	805-893-4093	893-8062	668
Marine Surf Waikiki Hotel 2415 Ala Wai Blvd Ste 1801 Honolulu HI 96815 *Web:* www.waikikiview.com	808-779-3261		379
Marine Systems Corp Seaport Ctr 70 Fargo St Boston MA 02210 *Web:* www.mscorp.net	617-542-3345	542-2461	261
Marine Systems Inc 116 Capital Blvd Houma LA 70360 *Web:* kirbycorp.com	985-223-7100		698
Marine Toys for Tots Foundation 18251 Quantico Gateway Dr Triangle VA 22172 *Web:* toysfortots.org	703-640-9433	649-2054	48-5
Marine Underwriters of America Inc 2040 N Loop 336 W Ste 225 Conroe TX 77304 *Web:* marineuw.com	936-230-5537		390
Marineland 7657 Portage Rd Niagara Falls ON L2E6X8 *Web:* www.marinelandcanada.com	905-356-9565	374-6652	32
Marineland of Florida 9600 Ocean Shore Blvd Saint Augustine FL 32080 *TF:* 877-933-3402 ■ *Web:* www.marineland.net	904-471-1111		40
Marinelife Center of Juno Beach Loggerhead Pk 14200 US Hwy 1 Juno Beach FL 33408 *TF:* 800-843-5451 ■ *Web:* www.marinelife.org	561-627-8280		40
Mariner Partners 1 Germain St 18th Fl. Saint John NB E2L4V1 *TF:* 888-240-9333 ■ *Web:* marinerpartners.com	506-642-9000		463
Mariner Wealth Advisors 1 Giralda Farms Ste 130 Madison NJ 07940 *TF:* 800-364-2468 ■ *Web:* www.marinerwealthadvisors.com	800-364-2468		194
Mariner's Inn, The 5339 Lighthouse Bay Dr Madison WI 53704 *Web:* marinersmadison.com	608-246-3120		671
Mariner's Point Resort of Cape Cod 425 Grand Ave Falmouth MA 02540 *Web:* www.marinerspointresort.com	508-457-0300		379
Mariners' Museum 100 Museum Dr. Newport News VA 23606 *TF:* 800-581-7245 ■ *Web:* www.marinersmuseum.org	757-596-2222		520
Marines Memorial Theatre 609 Sutter St. San Francisco CA 94102 *Web:* www.marinesmemorialtheatre.com	415-447-0188		572
Marinette County 1926 Hall Ave Marinette WI 54143 *Web:* www.marinettecounty.com	715-732-7406	732-7532	338
Marinette Marine Corp 3301 S Packerland Dr. De Pere WI 54115 *Web:* fincantierimarinettemarine.com	715-735-9341	735-8708	698
Marinette School District 2139 Pierce Ave Marinette WI 54143 *Web:* www.marinette.k12.wi.us	715-735-1400		685

				Phone	Fax	Class
Marino/Ware Industries Inc 400 Metuchen Rd *Web:* www.marinoware.com	South Plainfield	NJ	07080	908-757-9000		190
Marinsa Miami Corp 12250 SW 133 Ct *Web:* www.marinsa.com	Miami	FL	33186	305-252-0118		311
Marinus Pharmaceuticals Inc 21 Business Park Dr *Web:* www.marinuspharma.com	Branford	CT	06405	203-315-0566		668
Mario A. Juarez Inc 625 E Chapel St *Web:* mariojuarezattorney.com	Santa Maria	CA	93454	805-922-4553		41
Mario Industries of Virginia Inc 2490 Patterson Ave SW PO Box 3190 **Fax Area Code:* 540 ■ *TF:* 800-458-1244 ■ *Web:* www.marioindustries.com	Roanoke	VA	24016	800-458-1244	345-4813*	439
Mario's 4222 Second Ave *Web:* www.mariosdetroit.com	Detroit	MI	48201	313-832-1616		671
Mario's Italian Restaurant 13th & Main *Web:* mariosofdubuque.com	Dubuque	IA	52001	563-556-9424		671
Mario's Mexican Food & Cantina 15964 Springdale St *Web:* mariosmexicanfoodcantina.com	Huntington Beach	CA	92649	714-842-5811		671
Mario's Peruvian 5786 Melrose Ave *Web:* www.mariosperuvianseafood.com	Los Angeles	CA	90038	323-466-4181		671
Mario's Place 3646 Mission Inn Ave *Web:* www.mariosplace.com	Riverside	CA	92501	951-684-7755		671
Marion Area Chamber of Commerce 267 W Center St Ste 100 *TF:* 800-371-6688 ■ *Web:* www.marionareachamber.org	Marion	OH	43302	740-382-2181	387-7722	139
Marion Body Works Inc 211 W Ramsdell St PO Box 500 *Web:* www.marionbody.com	Marion	WI	54950	715-754-5261	754-5776	516
Marion Center Area School District PO Box 156 *Web:* www.mcasd.net	Marion Center	PA	15759	724-397-5551		685
Marion Center Bank 1271 Indian Springs Rd PO Box 130 *Web:* marioncenterbank.com	Indiana	PA	15701	724-464-2265		70
Marion Ceramics Inc PO Box 1134 *TF:* 800-845-4010 ■ *Web:* www.marionceramics.com	Marion	SC	29571	843-423-1311	423-1515	150
Marion Computer Technologies LLC 201 E Main St Centre Square Bldg *Web:* www.mctechno.com	Marion	VA	24354	276-783-6986		681
Marion County 200 Jackson St *Web:* www.marioncountywv.com	Fairmont	WV	26554	304-367-5410	366-6532	338
Marion County 130 Industrail Dr PO Box 964 *Web:* marioncountyalabama.org	Hamilton	AL	35570	205-921-3625		338
Marion County 1 Courthouse Sq PO Box 789 *Web:* marioncountytn.net	Jasper	TN	37347	423-942-2552		338
Marion County 102 W Austin St *Web:* www.co.marion.tx.us	Jefferson	TX	75657	903-665-3971		338
Marion County 214 E Main St *Web:* www.redrockarea.com	Knoxville	IA	50138	641-828-2257		338
Marion County 223 N Spalding Ave Ste 201 *Web:* www.marioncounty.ky.gov	Lebanon	KY	40033	270-692-3451	692-9487	338
Marion County 200 S Third St Ste 104 *TF:* 800-305-8851 ■ *Web:* www.marioncoks.net	Marion	KS	66861	620-382-2185	382-3420	338
Marion County 100 N Main St *Web:* www.co.marion.oh.us	Marion	OH	43302	740-223-4270		338
Marion County 2523 E Hwy 76 *Web:* www.marionsc.org	Marion	SC	29571	843-431-5059	423-8306	338
Marion County 118 Cross Creek Blvd *TF:* 800-438-4318 ■ *Web:* www.marioncountyhealthdept.org	Salem	IL	62881	618-548-3878	548-3866	338
Marion County 555 Court St NE Ste 5232 PO Box 14500 *Web:* www.co.marion.or.us	Salem	OR	97301	503-588-5225	373-4408	338
Marion County Board of Education Inc 200 Gaston Ave *Web:* www.marionboe.com	Fairmont	WV	26554	304-367-2100		685
Marion County Chamber of Commerce 110 Adams St *Web:* www.marionchamber.com	Fairmont	WV	26554	304-363-0442	363-0480	139
Marion County Development Partnership (MCDP) 412 Courthouse Sq PO Box 272 *Web:* www.mcdp.info	Columbia	MS	39429	601-736-6385	736-6392	139
Marion County Historical Society (MCHS) 169 E Church St *Web:* www.marionhistory.com	Marion	OH	43302	740-387-4255	387-0117	520
Marion County Law Library 258 W Center St *Web:* www.marionlawlibrary.org	Marion	OH	43302	740-223-4170	223-4179	434-3
Marion County Library System (MCL) 101 E Ct St *Web:* www.marioncountylibrary.org	Marion	SC	29571	843-423-8300	423-8302	434-3
Marion County Medical Ctr 2829 E Hwy 76 *Web:* muschealth.org	Mullins	SC	29574	843-431-2000		374-3
Marion County Raceway Inc 2303 Richwood-LaRue Rd *Web:* www.racemcr.com	La Rue	OH	43332	740-692-3267	499-2185	515
Marion General Hospital (MGH) 441 N Wabash Ave *Web:* www.mgh.net	Marion	IN	46952	765-660-6000	651-7351	374-3
Marion J. Mohr Memorial Library 1 Memorial Ave *Web:* www.mohrlibrary.org	Johnston	RI	02919	401-231-4980		434-3
Marion Military Institute 1101 Washington St *TF:* 800-664-1842 ■ *Web:* marionmilitary.edu	Marion	AL	36756	334-683-2322		162
Marion Mold & Tool Inc 176 Rifton Dr *Web:* www.marionmold.com	Marion	VA	24354	276-783-6101	783-6104	757
Marion National Cemetery 1700 E 38th St *Web:* www.cem.va.gov	Marion	IN	46953	765-674-0284	674-4521	136
Marion Public Library 1095 Sixth Ave *Web:* marionpubliclibrary.org	Marion	IA	52302	319-377-3412	377-0113	434-3
Marion Regional Juvenile Detention Ctr 3040 NW 10th St	Ocala	FL	34475	352-732-1450	732-1457	412
Marion Star, The 163 E Center St *Web:* www.marionstar.com	Marion	OH	43302	740-387-0400		532-2
Marion Technical College 1467 Mt Vernon Ave *Web:* www.mtc.edu	Marion	OH	43302	740-386-4176	389-6136	800
Marion'S Carpets Inc 1635 SE Grand Ave *Web:* marionscarpets.com	Portland	OR	97214	503-239-0528		290
Marion/Walthall Correctional Facility 503 S Main St *Web:* www.co.walthall.ms.us	Columbia	MS	39429	601-736-3621	736-4473	213
Marion-Grant County Chamber of Commerce 215 S Adams St *Web:* www.marionchamber.org	Marion	IN	46952	765-664-5107	668-5443	139
Marion-Grant County Convention & Visitors Bureau 1500 S Western Ave *TF:* 800-662-9474 ■ *Web:* www.showmegrantcounty.com	Marion	IN	46953	765-668-5435	668-5424	206
Mariplast North America Inc 365 Business Pkwy *Web:* www.mariplast.com	Greer	SC	29651	864-989-0560	989-0561	608
Mariposa 1450 Ala Moana Blvd *TF:* 888-888-4757 ■ *Web:* neimanmarcus.com	Honolulu	HI	96814	808-951-3420		671
Mariposa County 5100 Bullion St PO Box 784 *TF:* 800-549-6741 ■ *Web:* www.mariposacounty.org	Mariposa	CA	95338	209-966-3222	966-5147	338
Mariposa County Library 4978 10th St *Web:* www.mariposalibrary.org	Mariposa	CA	95338	209-966-2140		434-3
Mariposa Horticultural Enterprises Inc 15529 Arrow Hwy *Web:* mariposa-ca.com	Irwindale	CA	91706	626-960-0196		422
Maris West & Baker Inc 18 Northtown Dr *Web:* mwb.com	Jackson	MS	39211	601-977-9200		4
Marisco Ltd 91-607 Malakole Rd *Web:* www.marisco.net	Kapolei	HI	96707	808-682-1333		698
Marisol 5834 High Point Rd *Web:* themarisol.com	Greensboro	NC	27407	336-852-3303		671
Marist College 3399 N Rd *TF:* 800-436-5483 ■ *Web:* www.marist.edu	Poughkeepsie	NY	12601	845-575-3000	575-3215	166
Maritime Administration						
Div of Gulf Operations 500 Poydras St Ste 1223 *Web:* www.marad.dot.gov	New Orleans	LA	70130	504-589-6559		340-17
National Maritime Resource & Education Ctr (NMREC) 1200 New Jersey Ave SE *Web:* www.marad.dot.gov	Washington	DC	20590	202-366-6988		340-17
Maritime Administration Regional Offices						
Great Lakes Region PO Box 1156 *Web:* www.marad.dot.gov	Chicago	IL	60690	312-353-1032	353-1036	340-17
North Atlantic Region 1 Bowling Green Rm 418 *Web:* www.marad.dot.gov	New York	NY	10004	212-668-3330	668-3382	340-17
Western Region 1200 New Jersey Ave SE *Web:* www.marad.dot.gov	Washington	DC	20590	415-744-3125	744-2576	340-17
Maritime Antiques Inc 935 US Rte 1 *Web:* www.maritiques.com	York	ME	03909	207-363-4247	363-1416	637-2
Maritime Aquarium at Norwalk 10 N Water St *Web:* www.maritimeaquarium.org	Norwalk	CT	06854	203-852-0700	838-5416	40
Maritime Broadcasting System (MBS) 90 Lovett Lake Crt *Web:* www.mbsradio.com	Halifax	NS	B3S0H6	902-425-1225	423-2093	643
Maritime Company For Navigation, The 249 Shipyard Blvd *TF:* 800-626-4777 ■ *Web:* themaritimecompany.com	Wilmington	NC	28412	910-343-8900	343-8284	311
Maritime Energy Inc 234 Park St PO Box 485 *TF:* 800-333-4489 ■ *Web:* www.maritimeenergy.com	Rockland	ME	04841	800-333-4489		579
Maritime Helicopters 3520 Faa Rd *Web:* maritimehelicopters.com	Homer	AK	99603	907-235-7771		313
Maritime Museum of San Diego 1492 N Harbor Dr *Web:* sdmaritime.org	San Diego	CA	92101	619-234-9153	234-8345	520
Maritime Museum of the Atlantic 1675 Lower Water St *Web:* maritimemuseum.novascotia.ca	Halifax	NS	B3J1S3	902-424-7490	424-0612	520
Maritime Pacific Brewing Company Inc 1111 NW Ballard Way *Web:* maritimebrewery.com	Seattle	WA	98107	206-782-6181	782-0718	102
Maritime Paper Products Ltd 25 Borden Ave PO Box 668 *TF:* 800-565-5353 ■ *Web:* www.maritimepaper.com	Dartmouth	NS	B3B1C7	902-468-5353		554
Maritime Professional Training 1915 S Andrews Ave *TF:* 888-839-5025 ■ *Web:* www.mptusa.com	Fort Lauderdale	FL	33316	954-525-1014	764-0431	167-3
Maritime Travel Inc 202-2000 Barrington St Cogswell Tower *TF:* 800-593-3334 ■ *Web:* www.maritimetravel.ca	Halifax	NS	B3J3K1	902-420-1554		775
Maritz Inc 1375 N Hwy Dr *TF:* 877-462-7489 ■ *Web:* www.maritz.com	Fenton	MO	63099	636-827-4000		466
MaritzCX Research LLC 1355 N Hwy Dr *Web:* www.maritzcx.com	Fenton	MO	63099	385-695-2940		466
Mar-Jac Poultry Inc 1020 Aviation Blvd *Web:* www.marjacpoultry.com	Gainesville	GA	30501	770-531-5007	531-5015	619
MarJam Supply Company Inc 20 Rewe St *TF:* 800-848-8407 ■ *Web:* www.marjam.com	Brooklyn	NY	11211	718-388-6465	989-0029	364
Marjon Specialty Foods Inc 3508 Sydney Rd *Web:* marjonspecialtyfoods.com	Plant City	FL	33566	813-752-3482		345
Marjorie Kinnan Rawlings Historic State Park 18700 S County Rd 325 *Web:* www.floridastateparks.org	Cross Creek	FL	32640	352-466-3672		565
Mark A. Gallagher 1400 N Harbor Blvd Ste 515 **Fax Area Code:* 714 ■ *TF:* 800-797-8406 ■ *Web:* socaldefenselawyers.com	Fullerton	CA	92835	800-797-8406	680-9982*	41

Name / Address	City	State	ZIP	Phone	Fax	Class
Mark A. Healey 666 Savin Ave *Web:* markahealey.com	West Haven	CT	06516	203-937-6500		41
Mark A. Stephens Ltd 10018 Colesville Rd *TF:* 800-358-8001 ■ *Web:* www.mastaxpub.com	Silver Spring	MD	20901	800-358-8001		637-10
Mark Andy Inc 18081 Chesterfield Airport Rd *TF:* 800-700-6275 ■ *Web:* www.markandy.com	Chesterfield	MO	63005	636-532-4433	532-4701	629
Mark Anthony Brewing Inc 300 W Hubbard St Ste 301 *Web:* www.mabrewing.com	Chicago	IL	60654	312-202-1712		77
Mark Asset Management Corp 667 Madison Ave 9th Fl *Web:* www.markasset.com	New York	NY	10065	212-372-2500		401
Mark Bailey & Company Ltd 5335 Kietzke Ln Ste 110 *Web:* www.excelsisaccounting.com	Reno	NV	89511	775-332-4200		2
Mark C. Pope Assoc 2215 Birmingham Dr *Web:* markcpope.com	Albany	GA	31705	229-435-2473		770
Mark Cerrone Inc 2368 Maryland Ave *Web:* www.markcerrone.com	Niagara Falls	NY	14305	716-282-5244		186
Mark Chesson and Sons Inc 101 Chesson Dr *Web:* www.chessonandsons.com	Williamston	NC	27892	252-792-1566		274
Mark Chevrolet Inc 33200 Michigan Ave *Web:* www.markchevrolet.com	Wayne	MI	48184	734-629-4964		57
Mark Citsay State Farm Insurance 9455 W Russell Ste 110 *Web:* markcitsay.com	Las Vegas	NV	89148	702-363-1979		390
Mark Custom Recording Service 10815 Bodine Rd *Web:* www.markcustom.com	Clarence	NY	14031	716-759-2600	759-2329	658
Mark D. Alliod CPA PC 348 Hartford Tpke Ste 201 *Web:* markalliodcpa.com	Vernon	CT	06066	860-648-9503		2
Mark D. Alpert 1399 Washington St *Web:* alpertfinancial.com	Hanover	MA	02339	781-829-8868		2
Mark D. Dickstein Pa 2400 N University Dr Ste 206 *Web:* flahurt.com	Pembroke Pines	FL	33024	954-893-8000		41
Mark E. Koller CPA 500 Buffalo Rd *Web:* www.MarkKollerCPA.com	East Aurora	NY	14052	716-805-1040	805-1045	2
Mark Garrison Salon 108 E 60th St *Web:* markgarrisonsalon.com	New York	NY	10022	212-400-8000		77
Mark Goodman & Associates Inc 875 N Michigan Ave Ste 2710 *Web:* mgachicago.com	Chicago	IL	60611	312-280-8030		653
Mark Harris Plumbing Company Inc 1770 Gillespie Way Ste 101 *Web:* mhp-co.com	El Cajon	CA	92020	619-596-9470		610
Mark Hershey Farms Inc 479 Horseshoe Pk *TF:* 888-801-3301 ■ *Web:* www.markhersheyfarms.com	Lebanon	PA	17042	717-867-4624	867-4313	447
Mark I. Publications Inc 62-33 Woodhaven Blvd *Web:* www.qchron.com	Rego Park	NY	11374	718-205-8000	205-0150	532-2
Mark IV Capital Inc 100 Bayview Cir Ste 4500 *Web:* www.markiv.com	Newport Beach	CA	92660	949-509-1444		41
Mark Kislingbury's Academy of Court Reporting 15840 FM 529 Rd Ste 104 *Web:* www.mkcourtreporting.com	Houston	TX	77095	281-859-0791		800
Mark Knox Flowers Inc 1209 E Eighth St *TF:* [illegible] ■ *Web:* markknoxflowers.com	Odessa	TX	79761	432-332-0858		292
Mark Line Industries Inc 51687 County Rd 133 PO Box 277 *Web:* marklineindustries.com	Bristol	IN	46507	574-825-5851	825-9139	505
Mark Maker Company Inc 4157 Stafford Ave SW *Web:* www.mark-makerco.com	Grand Rapids	MI	49548	616-538-6980		467
Mark Morris Dance Group 3 Lafayette Ave *TF:* 800-957-1046 ■ *Web:* www.markmorrisdancegroup.org	Brooklyn	NY	11217	718-624-8400	624-8900	573-1
Mark Optics Inc 1424 E St Gertrude Pl *Web:* www.markoptics.com	Santa Ana	CA	92705	714-545-6684		544
Mar-K Quality Parts LLC 6625 W Wilshire Blvd *Web:* mar-k.com	Oklahoma City	OK	73132	405-721-7945	721-8906	54
Mark R. Manceri PA 1600 S Federal Hwy Ste 900 *Web:* estateprobatelitigation.com	Fort Lauderdale	FL	33308	954-491-7099		41
Mark Sand & Gravel Co 525 Kennedy Park Rd PO Box 458 *TF:* 800-427-8316 ■ *Web:* www.marksandgravel.com	Fergus Falls	MN	56537	218-736-7523	736-2647	503-4
Mark Scott Construction 2835 Contra Costa Blvd *Web:* msconstruction.com	Pleasant Hill	CA	94523	925-944-0502		378
Mark Spencer Hotel 409 SW 11th Ave *TF:* 800-548-3934 ■ *Web:* www.markspencer.com	Portland	OR	97205	503-224-3293	223-7848	379
Mark T. Raymond Agency Inc 282 Higbie La *Web:* markraymondagency.com	West Islip	NY	11795	631-661-7070		390
Mark Thomas & Company Inc 2290 N First St Ste 304 *Web:* www.markthomas.com	San Jose	CA	95131	408-453-5373		261
Mark Travel Corp 8907 N Port Washington Rd *Web:* www.marktravel.com	Milwaukee	WI	53217	414-228-7472		771
Mark Trece Inc 2001 Stockton Rd *Web:* www.marktrece.com	Joppa	MD	21085	410-879-0060	879-3438	781
Mark Twain Birthplace State Historic Site 37352 Shrine Rd *Web:* mostateparks.com	Florida	MO	65283	573-565-3449		565
Mark Twain Hotel 225 NE Adams St *TF:* 866-325-6351 ■ *Web:* www.marktwainhotel.com	Peoria	IL	61602	309-676-3600	636-6118	379
Mark Twain House & Museum 351 Farmington Ave *Web:* marktwainhouse.org	Hartford	CT	06105	860-247-0998		520
Mark Twain Rural Telephone Co 48054 State Hwy 6 E *Web:* www.marktwain.net	Hurdland	MO	63547	660-423-5211	423-5496	224
Mark Twain State Park 20057 State Park Rd *Web:* mostateparks.com	Stoutsville	MO	65283	573-565-3440		565
Mark Twain State Park & Soaring Eagles Golf Course 201 Middle Rd *Web:* parks.ny.gov	Horseheads	NY	14845	607-739-0034		565
Mark V. Williamson Company Inc 1910 N Grant St *Web:* mvwilliamson.com	Little Rock	AR	72207	501-664-7728		390
Mark Vii Equipment 5981 Tennyson St *TF:* 877-627-5844 ■ *Web:* www.markvii.net	Arvada	CO	80003	303-423-4910		427
Mark Young Construction Inc 7200 Miller Pl *Web:* markyoungconstruction.com	Frederick	CO	80504	303-776-1449	776-1729	685
Mark's Plumbing Parts 3312 Ramona Dr *TF:* 800-772-2347 ■ *Web:* www.markspp.com	Fort Worth	TX	76116	817-731-6211		612
Mark's Work Warehouse 1035 64th Ave SE Ste 30 *TF:* 800-663-6275 ■ *Web:* www.marks.com	Calgary	AB	T2H2J7	403-255-9220		157-5
Mark/Space Inc 1999 S Bascom Ave Ste 300B *Web:* www.markspace.com	Campbell	CA	95008	408-293-7299		178-7
Mark-10 Corp 11 Dixon Ave *Web:* www.mark-10.com	Copiague	NY	11726	631-842-9200		201
Mark-Age Inc PO Box 10 *Web:* www.thenewearth.org	Pioneer	TN	37847	423-784-3269		637-2
Markal Finishing Corp 400 Bostwick Ave *Web:* markalfinishing.com	Bridgeport	CT	06605	203-384-8219	336-1231	555
Mark-Costello Co, The 1145 E Dominguez St *Web:* www.mark-costello.com	Carson	CA	90746	310-637-1851	762-2330	386
Mar-Kee Group, The 26248 Equity Dr *TF:* 888-300-4629 ■ *Web:* www.markeegroup.com	Daphne	AL	36526	888-300-4629		196
Markeim-Chalmers Inc 1415 Rt 70 E Ste 500 *Web:* markeim-chalmers.com	Cherry Hill	NJ	08034	856-354-9700		652
Markel Corp 435 School Ln *Web:* markelcorporation.com	Plymouth Meeting	PA	19462	610-272-8960	270-3138	605-2
Markel Corp 4521 Highwoods Pkwy *TF:* 800-446-6671 ■ *Web:* www.markelcorp.com	Glen Allen	VA	23060	800-446-6671		391-4
Markel Specialty Commercial 4600 Cox Rd *Fax Area Code: 804 ■ *TF:* 800-416-4364 ■ *Web:* www.markelinsurance.com	Glen Allen	VA	23060	800-416-4364	527-7915*	391-4
Markem-Imaje Inc 100 Chastain Center Blvd Ste 165 *TF:* 800-267-5108 ■ *Web:* www.markem-imaje.com	Mississauga	ON	L4W2T7	800-267-5108		358
Markent Personnel Inc 121 E Conant St *Web:* www.markentpersonnel.com	Portage	WI	53901	608-742-7300		175
Marker 32 14549 Beach Blvd *Web:* marker32.com	Jacksonville	FL	32250	904-223-1534		671
Marker Seven 301 Folsom St Ste D *Web:* markerseven.com	San Francisco	CA	94105	415-447-2841	447-2860	396
Markery Law LLC 1200 G St NW Ste 800 *Web:* markerylaw.com	Washington	DC	20005	202-888-7892		41
Markesbery & Richardson Co 2368 Victory Pkwy Ste 200 *Web:* m-r-law.com	Cincinnati	OH	45206	513-961-6200		41
Market Actives LLC 8300 SW 71st Ave *Web:* www.marketactives.com	Portland	OR	97223	503-244-0166	244-1555	146
Market America Inc 1302 Pleasant Ridge Rd *TF:* 866-420-1709 ■ *Web:* www.marketamerica.com	Greensboro	NC	27409	336-605-0040	605-0041	114
Market Basket Inc, The 813 Franklin Lakes Rd *Web:* www.marketbasket.com	Franklin Lakes	NJ	07417	201-891-2000		345
Market Builder Inc, The 5135 E Ingram St *Web:* www.themarketbuilder.com	Mesa	AZ	85205	480-641-6200		396
Market Connections 82 Patton Ave Ste 710 *Web:* www.mktconnections.com	Asheville	NC	28801	828-398-5250		195
Market Contractors 10250 NE Marx St *TF:* 800-876-9133 ■ *Web:* www.marketcontractors.com	Portland	OR	97220	503-255-0977		186
Market Data Retrieval 6 Armstrong Rd *TF:* 800-333-8802 ■ *Web:* www.schooldata.com	Shelton	CT	06484	203-926-4800		5
Market Decisions Research 75 Washington Ave Ste 2C *TF:* 800-293-1538 ■ *Web:* marketdecisions.com	Portland	ME	04101	207-767-6440	767-8158	466
Market Finders Insurance Corp 9117 Leesgate Rd *TF:* 800-626-5660 ■ *Web:* mfic.com	Louisville	KY	40222	502-423-1800		390
Market Force Information LLC 6025 The Corners Pkwy Ste 200 *TF:* 800-669-9939 ■ *Web:* www.marketforce.com	Peachtree Corners	GA	30092	770-441-5366	441-5355	196
Market Grocery Co 16 Forest Pkwy Bldg K *Web:* www.marketgrocery.com	Forest Park	GA	30297	404-361-8620	361-3773	345
Market Hall Foods 5655 College Ave Ste 201 *Web:* www.rockridgemarkethall.com	Oakland	CA	94618	510-250-6000		345
Market Line Computers 317 Harrington Ave *Web:* www.marketlinecomputers.com	Closter	NJ	07624	201-768-8887	768-4335	178-1
Market Metrics Inc 101 Federal St 16th Fl *Web:* www.marketmetrics.com	Boston	MA	02110	617-376-0550	376-0004	194
Market of Choice 1475 Siskiyou Blvd *TF:* 877-901-7128 ■ *Web:* www.marketofchoice.com	Ashland	OR	97520	541-488-2773		297-8
Market One Builders Inc 1200 R St Ste 150 *Web:* www.m1b.com	Sacramento	CA	95811	916-928-7474	928-7475	186

Phone | Fax | Class

Market Optical of Bellevue LLC
235 Bellevue Sq ... Bellevue WA 98004 425-451-1184 543
Web: marketoptical.com

Market Place, The 20 Wall St ... Asheville NC 28801 828-252-4162 253-3120 671
Web: marketplace-restaurant.com

Market Resource Partners
1650 Arch St ... Philadelphia PA 19103 215-587-8800 792
Web: www.mrpfd.com

Market Scan Information Systems Inc
811 Camarillo Springs Rd Ste B ... Camarillo CA 93012 800-658-7226 178-10
TF: 800-658-7226 ■ *Web:* www.marketscan.com

Market Semiotics PO Box 1457 ... Castleton VT 05735 802-273-3800 297-8
Web: www.marketsemiotics.com

Market Square Travel LLC
13756 83rd Way N ... Maple Grove MN 55369 763-231-8870 281-2297* 772
**Fax Area Code:* 507 ■ *Web:* tvlleaders.com

Market Street Consulting Group Inc
6965 El Camino Real Ste 105599 ... Carlsbad CA 92009 760-518-2310 621-5904* 691
**Fax Area Code:* 888 ■ *Web:* www.marketstreetfs.com

Market Street Partners LLC
477 Pacific Ave ... San Francisco CA 94133 415-445-3240 401
Web: www.marketstreetpartners.com

Market Street Trust Co
80 E Market St Ste 300 ... Corning NY 14830 607-962-6876 528
Web: www.marketstreettrust.com

Market Track LLC
24 E Washington St Ste 1200 ... Chicago IL 60602 312-529-5102 529-5127 466
Web: www.markettrack.com

Market Traders Institute
400 Colonial Center Pkwy Ste 350 ... Lake Mary FL 32746 407-740-0900 528
Web: www.markettraders.com

Market Vane Corp PO Box 90490 ... Pasadena CA 91109 626-395-7436 795-7654 637-10
Web: www.marketvane.net

Market Velocity Inc
1305 Mall of Georgia Blvd Ste 190 ... Buford GA 30519 770-325-6300 925-9064 387
TF: 877-519-2899 ■ *Web:* www.marketvelocity.com

Market, The 2628 S Glenstone Ave ... Springfield MO 65804 417-889-1145 460
Web: www.the-market-1.business.site

MarketAxess Holdings Inc
299 Park Ave 10th Fl ... New York NY 10171 212-813-6000 813-6390 178-4
NASDAQ: MKTX ■ *Web:* www.marketaxess.com

MarketBridge Inc
4350 East-West Hwy 6th Fl ... Bethesda MD 20814 240-752-1800 195
Web: www.market-bridge.com

MarketCounsel LLC 61 W Palisade Ave ... Englewood NJ 07631 201-705-1200 194
Web: marketcounsel.com

Marketech 7915 Westglen Dr ... Houston TX 77063 713-667-7778 463
Web: www.marketechcorp.com

Marketechs Design Studio
3425 Woodbridge Cir ... York PA 17406 717-764-2588 764-2930 232
Web: marketechs.com

MarketFrames Group LLC
5331 SW Macadam Ave Ste 357 ... Portland OR 97239 503-892-0160 296-5942 45
Web: www.marketframes.com

Marketing Analysts Inc
2000 Sam Rittenberg Blvd Ste 3007 ... Charleston SC 29407 843-329-0163 466
Web: www.mairesearch.com

Marketing Arm, The
1999 Bryan St 18th Fl ... Dallas TX 75201 214-259-3200 259-3201 4
Web: www.themarketingarm.com

Marketing Company Inc 93 West St ... Medfield MA 02052 508-655-4300 359-7071 5
TF: 800-791-7916 ■ *Web:* www.marketco.com

Marketing Design Group
2445 Fifth Ave Ste 450 ... San Diego CA 92101 619-298-1445 7
Web: www.marketingdesigngroup.com

Marketing Directions Inc
28005 Clemens Rd ... Cleveland OH 44145 440-835-5550 4
Web: marketingdirectionsinc.com

Marketing Drive LLC
800 Connecticut Ave ... Norwalk CT 06854 203-857-6100 5
Web: www.matchmg.com

Marketing Evolution Inc
122 E 42nd St Ste 4500 ... New York NY 10168 646-651-4300 809
Web: www.marketingevolution.com

Marketing General Inc
625 N Washington St Ste 450 ... Alexandria VA 22314 703-739-1000 195
Web: www.marketinggeneral.com

Marketing Informatics
5629 Professional Cir ... Indianapolis IN 46241 317-788-4440 5
Web: www.marketinginformatics.com

Marketing Innovators International Inc
9701 W Higgins Rd ... Rosemont IL 60018 800-543-7373 696-3194* 384
**Fax Area Code:* 847 ■ *TF:* 800-543-7373 ■ *Web:* www.marketinginnovators.com

Marketing Management Group Inc
561 Seventh Ave 17th Fl ... New York NY 10018 212-768-9660 944-5860 195
Web: www.mmgus.com

Marketing Management Services LLC
PO Box 273 ... Coopersville MI 49404 616-997-7387 837-7701 194
Web: www.marketingmanagementllc.com

Marketing Resource Group Inc (MRG)
225 S Washington Sq ... Lansing MI 48933 517-372-4400 372-4045 5
TF: 800-928-2086 ■ *Web:* mrgmi.com

Marketing Results
2900 W Horizon Ridge Pkwy Ste 200 ... Henderson NV 89052 702-361-3850 195
Web: www.marketingresults.net

Marketing Werks Inc
130 E Randolph St Ste 2400 ... Chicago IL 60601 312-228-0800 228-0801 194
Web: www.marketingwerks.com

Marketing Workshop Inc
3725 Da Vinci Ct ... Norcross GA 30092 770-449-6767 466
Web: www.mwshop.com

MarketingNewAuthors.com
2910 E Eisenhower Pky ... Ann Arbor MI 48108 734-975-0028 973-9475 194
Web: marketingnewauthors.biz

MarketingProfs LLC
419 N Larchmont Blvd Ste 295 ... Los Angeles CA 90004 866-557-9625 195
TF: 866-557-9625 ■ *Web:* www.marketingprofs.com

Marketlab Inc 6850 Southbelt Dr ... Caledonia MI 49316 866-237-3722 656 2475* 475
**Fax Area Code:* 616 ■ *TF:* 866-237-3722 ■ *Web:* www.marketlab.com

MarketLauncher Inc PO Box 916582 ... Longwood FL 32791 800-901-3803 7
TF: 800-901-3803 ■ *Web:* www.marketlauncher.com

MarketLeverage LLC
5000 E Bannister Rd Mezz Fl ... Kansas City MO 64137 888-653-8372 5
TF: 888-653-8372 ■ *Web:* www.marketleverage.com

Marketocracy Inc
1208 W Magnolia Ste 236 ... Fort Worth TX 76104 877-462-4180 777-6181* 401
**Fax Area Code:* 888 ■ *TF:* 877-462-4180 ■ *Web:* www.marketocracy.com

Marketplace Mall 1 Miracle Mile Dr ... Rochester NY 14623 585-424-6220 427-2745 460
Web: www.themarketplacemall.com

Marketplace Publications
234 Silverlake Blvd ... Carle Place NY 11514 516-997-7909 997-7906 532-2
Web: www.marketplacepublications.com

Marketpointe Realty Advisors Inc
9201 Spectrum Center Blvd Ste 110 ... San Diego CA 92123 619-233-3781 653
Web: marketpointe.com

MarketPro Inc
53 Perimeter Center E Ste 200 ... Atlanta GA 30346 404-222-9992 260
Web: marketproinc.com

Marketreach Inc 12 Murphy Dr Unit D ... Nashua NH 03062 603-645-1300 194
Web: www.mreach.com

MarketResearch.com
11200 Rockville Pk Ste 504 ... Rockville MD 20852 240-747-3000 387
Web: www.marketresearch.com

Marketri LLC
1700 Market St Ste 1005 ... Philadelphia PA 19103 800-695-1356 463
TF: 800-695-1356 ■ *Web:* www.marketri.com

Marketsmith Inc 2 Wing Dr ... Cedar Knolls NJ 07927 973-889-0006 5
Web: www.marketsmithinc.com

MarketSphere Consulting
9393 W 110th St Ste 430 ... Overland Park KS 66210 816-559-0600 194
Web: www.marketsphere.com

Marketstar Corp 2475 Washington Blvd ... Ogden UT 84401 800-877-8259 721
TF: 800-877-8259 ■ *Web:* www.marketstar.com

Marketview Liquor Inc
1100 Jefferson Rd ... Rochester NY 14623 888-427-2480 443
TF: 888-427-2480 ■ *Web:* marketviewliquor.com

MarketVision Research Inc
5151 Pfeiffer Rd Ste 300 ... Cincinnati OH 45242 513-791-3100 794-3500 466
TF: 800-232-4250 ■ *Web:* www.mv-research.com

Marketware Inc
7070 Union Park Ctr Ste 300 ... Midvale UT 84047 800-777-6368 225
TF: 800-777-6368 ■ *Web:* www.marketware.com

Marketwell Inc PO Box 70 ... Tivoli NY 12583 646-435-5987 463
Web: marketwell.com

MarketWise Solutions Inc
4843 W 106th St ... Zionsville IN 46077 317-873-6976 195
Web: www.marketwisesolutions.com

Markey Edward J (Sen D - MA)
255 Dirksen Senate Office Bldg ... Washington DC 20510 202-224-2742 342-2
Web: www.markey.senate.gov

Markey Machinery Company Inc
7266 Eigth Ave S ... Seattle WA 98108 206-763-0382 770
TF: 800-637-3430 ■ *Web:* www.markeymachinery.com

Markforged Inc 480 Pleasant St ... Watertown MA 02472 866-496-1805 629
TF: 866-496-1805 ■ *Web:* markforged.com

Markham Board of Trade
80 F Centurian Dr Ste 206 ... Markham ON L3R8C1 905-474-0730 474-0685 137
Web: markhamboard.com

Markham Contracting Company Inc
22820 N 19th Ave ... Phoenix AZ 85027 623-869-9100 189-5
Web: www.markhamcontracting.com

Markham Regional Arboretum
1202 La Vista Ave ... Concord CA 94521 925-681-2968 97
Web: markhamarboretum.org

Markham Stouffville Hospital
381 Church St PO Box 1800 ... Markham ON L3P7P3 905-472-7000 374-2
Web: www.msh.on.ca

Markin Consulting LLC
120 Woodland Pond Pk 12072 87th Pl N ... Maple Grove MN 55369 763-493-3568 322-5013 194
Web: www.markinconsulting.com

Marking Services Inc
8265 N Faulkner Rd ... Milwaukee WI 53224 414-973-1331 973-1332 554
Web: www.markserv.com

Markitects Inc
107 W Lancaster Ave Ste 203 ... Wayne PA 19087 610-687-2200 195
Web: www.markitects.com

Markland Industries Inc
1111 E McFadden Ave ... Santa Ana CA 92705 714-245-2850 481
Web: www.marklandindustries.com

Markley Enterprise Inc 800 Lillian St ... Elkhart IN 46516 574-295-4195 687
Web: www.markleyent.com

Markley Motors
3401 S College Ave ... Fort Collins CO 80525 970-226-2214 57
Web: www.markleymotors.com

Markload Systems Inc 1118 N Main St ... Pearland TX 77581 281-485-8600 485-3007 203
Web: www.markload.com

MarkLogic Corp 999 Skyway Rd ... San Carlos CA 94070 650-655-2300 655-2310 178-1
TF: 877-992-8885 ■ *Web:* www.marklogic.com

Markman'S Diamond Brokers Inc
6932 Kingston Pk ... Knoxville TN 37919 865-584-0247 410
Web: markmansdiamonds.com

Markon Solutions
400 S Maple Ave Ste 230 ... Falls Church VA 22046 703-884-0030 639-0922 463
Web: markonsolutions.com

Markow Walker PA
599 Highland Colony Pkwy Ste 100 ... Ridgeland MS 39157 601-853-1911 41
Web: markowwalker.com

Markowitz & Richman
123 S Broad St Ste 2020 ... Philadelphia PA 19109 267-528-0121 790-0668* 41
**Fax Area Code:* 215 ■ *TF:* 800-590-4561 ■ *Web:* markowitzandrichman.com

Mark-Pack Inc (MP) 776 Main St ... Coopersville MI 49404 800-521-9684 559
TF: 800-521-9684 ■ *Web:* www.markpackinc.com

Markraft Cabinets Inc
2705 Castle Creek Ln ... Wilmington NC 28401 910-762-1986 762-1985 191-3
Web: www.markraft.com

Marks Brothers Inc 12265 SE 282nd Ave ... Boring OR 97009 503-663-0211 454
Web: marks-brothers.com

	Phone	Fax	Class
Marks Group P C 45 E City Ave Ste 342 .... Bala Cynwyd PA 19004 *Fax Area Code: 610 ■ TF: 888-224-0649 ■ Web: www.marksgroup.net	888-224-0649	471-0709*	196
Marks Law Group Llp, The 1120 N Town Center Dr Ste 200 .... Las Vegas NV 89144 Web: markslg.com	702-341-7870		41
Marks Metal Technology Inc 10300 SE Jennifer St .... Clackamas OR 97015 Web: www.marksmetal.com	503-656-0901		492
Marks Nelson Vohland & Campbel 7500 W 110 St Ste 110 .... Overland Park KS 66210 Web: www.marksnelsoncpa.com	913-498-9000		41
Marks Paneth & Shron LLP 685 Third Ave .... New York NY 10017 Web: www.markspaneth.com	212-503-8800		2
Marks Richardson Pc 3700 Buffalo Speedway Ste 830 .... Houston TX 77098 Web: marksrichardsonpc.com	713-942-9922	942-9590	41
Marksmen Energy Inc 368 Sunmills Dr SE .... Calgary AB T2X3H6 Web: www.marksmenenergy.com	403-265-7270		539
Marksville State Historic Site 837 ML King Dr .... Marksville LA 71351 TF: 888-253-8954 ■ Web: crt.state.la.us	318-253-8954		565
Markus Wiener Publishers Inc 231 Nassau St .... Princeton NJ 08542 Web: www.markuswiener.com	609-921-1141	921-1140	637-10
MarkWest Energy Partners LP 1515 Arapahoe St Tower 1 Ste 1600 .... Denver CO 80202 NYSE: MWE ■ TF: 800-730-8388 ■ Web: www.markwest.com	303-925-9200	290-8769	597
Markwins International Corp 22067 Ferrero Pkwy .... Walnut CA 91789 Web: www.markwinsbeauty.com	909-595-8898		214
Markwort Sporting Goods Co 1101 Research Blvd .... Saint Louis MO 63132 TF: 800-280-5555 ■ Web: www.markwort.com	314-942-1199	942-1179	711
Marky's 1000 NW 159 Dr .... Miami Gardens FL 33169 Web: www.markys.com	305-758-9288	758-8000	297
Marla Junes Clothing Co 5215 W Clearwater Ave Ste 101 .... Kennewick WA 99336 Web: www.marlajunes.com	509-820-3187		157-6
Marland Clutch 23601 Hoover Rd .... Warren MI 48089 *Fax Area Code: 877 ■ TF: 800-216-3515 ■ Web: www.marland.com	800-216-3515	216-3001*	620
Marlboro College 2582 S Rd PO Box A .... Marlboro VT 05344 TF: 800-343-0049 ■ Web: www.marlboro.edu	802-257-4333	451-7555	166
Marlboro County Library 203 Fayetteville Ave .... Bennettsville SC 29512 Web: www.edelmanpubliclibrary.org	843-479-5630	479-5645	434-3
Marlboro Wire 2403 N 24th St .... Quincy IL 62305 Web: www.marlborowire.com	217-224-7989	224-7990	73
Marlborough Hills Healthcare Ctr 121 Northboro Rd E .... Marlborough MA 01752 Web: www.athenanh.com	508-485-4040		450
Marlborough Public Library 35 W Main St .... Marlborough MA 01752 Web: www.marlborough-ma.gov	508-624-6900		434-3
Marlborough Public Schools (MPS) 17 Washington St .... Marlborough MA 01752 Web: www.mps-edu.org	508-460-3509		186
Marlborough Regional Chamber of Commerce 11 Florence St .... Marlborough MA 01752 TF: 800-508-2265 ■ Web: marlboroughchamber.org	508-485-7746	481-1819	139
Marlen International Inc 4780 NW 41st St Ste 100 .... Riverside MO 64150 *Fax Area Code: 913 ■ TF: 800-862-7536 ■ Web: marlen.com	800-862-7536	888-6440*	298
Marlette Funding LLC 1523 Concord Pke .... Wilmington DE 19803 TF: 800-711-8198 ■ Web: www.marlettefunding.com	800-711-8198		217
Marlette Regional Hospital Sleep Lab 2770 Main St .... Marlette MI 48453 Web: www.marletteregionalhospital.org	989-635-4036		374-3
Marlex Pharmaceuticals 65 Lukens Dr .... New Castle DE 19720 Web: marlexpharm.com	302-328-3355		583
Marley Engineered Products 470 Beauty Spot Rd E .... Bennettsville SC 29512 TF: 800-452-4179 ■ Web: www.marleymep.com	843-479-4006	479-8912	37
Marley Precision Inc 455 Fritz Keiper Blvd .... Battle Creek MI 49037 Web: www.marueikogyo.jp	269-963-7374		247
Marley's Island Grille 35 Office Park Rd .... Hilton Head Island SC 29928 Web: www.marleyshhi.com	843-686-5800		671
Marlin Alliance Inc 3990 Old Town Ave Ste C-205 .... San Diego CA 92110 Web: themarlinalliance.com	619-450-1717		463
Marlin Business Services Corp 300 Fellowship Rd .... Mount Laurel NJ 08054 NASDAQ: MRLN ■ TF: 888-479-9111 ■ Web: www.marlinfinance.com	888-479-9111	479-1100	264-2
Marlin Controls Inc 11011 Regency Crest Dr .... Dallas TX 75238 *Fax Area Code: 214 ■ TF: 800-788-5750 ■ Web: www.marlincontrols.com	800-788-5750	533-1011*	472
Marlin Firearms Co PO Box 1871 .... Madison NC 27025 *Fax Area Code: 336 ■ TF: 800-544-8892 ■ Web: www.marlinfirearms.com	800-544-8892	548-7801*	284
Marlin Network Inc 305 W Mill St Ste 300 .... Springfield MO 65806 Web: marlinco.com	417-885-4524		7
Marlin Steel Wire Products 2640 Merchant Dr .... Baltimore MD 21230 Web: www.marlinwire.com	410-644-7456	630-7797	490
Marlo Beauty Supply 2660 Burdette St .... Ferndale MI 48220 TF: 800-333-9499 ■ Web: www.marlobeauty.com	800-333-9499	537-2201	76
Marlo Furniture Company Inc 3300 Marlo Ln .... Forestville MD 20747 Web: www.marlofurniture.com	301-735-2000		321
Marlo Plastic Products Inc Pkwy 100 Bldg 1 Rte 66 .... Neptune City NJ 07753 Web: marloplasticproducts.com	732-792-1988		196
Marlow Industries Inc 10451 Vista Park Rd .... Dallas TX 75238 TF: 877-627-5691 ■ Web: www.marlow.com	877-627-5691		253
Marman Industries Inc 1701 Earhart .... La Verne CA 91750 Web: www.marman.com	909-392-2136	392-2140	604
Marmen 557 des Erables St .... Trois-Rivieres QC G8T8Y8 Web: www.marmeninc.com	819-379-0453		454
Marmik Oil Co 200 N Jefferson Ave .... El Dorado AR 71730 Web: marmikoil.com	870-862-8546		539
Marmol Radziner & Associates AIA 12210 Nebraska Ave .... Los Angeles CA 90025 Web: www.marmol-radziner.com	310-826-6222		321
Marmon Group LLC, The 181 W Madison St 26th Fl .... Chicago IL 60602 Web: www.marmon.com	312-372-9500	845-5305	185
Marmon/Keystone Corp PO Box 992 .... Butler PA 16003 TF: 800-544-1748 ■ Web: www.marmonkeystone.com	724-283-3000	283-0558	492
Marmone Crane Services Inc 2440 - 76 Ave PO Box 8610 .... Edmonton AB T6E6R2 Web: www.sterlingcrane.ca	780-440-4434	440-1951	23
Marmon-Herrington Co 13001 Magisterial Dr .... Louisville KY 40223 TF: 800-227-0727 ■ Web: www.marmon-herrington.com	502-253-0277		60
Marne Construction Inc 749 N Poplar St Ste 100 .... Orange CA 92868 Web: www.marneconstruction.com	714-935-0995		186
Marnell Companies LLC 222 Via Marnell Way .... Las Vegas NV 89119 Web: www.marnellcompanies.com	702-739-2000		195
Marnen Mioduszewski Bordonaro Wagner & Sinnott LLC 516 W Tenth St .... Erie PA 16502 Web: mmbwslaw.com	814-874-3460	874-3476	428
Maron Hotel & Suites 42 Lake Ave Ext .... Danbury CT 06811 Web: www.maronhotel.com	203-791-2200		379
Maron Products Inc 1301 Industrial Dr .... Mishawaka IN 46544 Web: www.maronproducts.com	574-259-1971	259-1978	488
Maroon Financial Credit Union 5525C S Ellis Ave Ste C .... Chicago IL 60637 Web: maroonfinancial.org	773-702-7179		219
Maroon Inc 1390 Jaycox Rd .... Avon OH 44011 Web: maroongroupllc.com	440-937-1000		146
Maroosh 223 Valencia Ave .... Coral Gables FL 33134 Web: www.maroosh.com	305-476-9800		671
Marotta Controls Inc 78 Boonton Ave PO Box 427 .... Montville NJ 07045 TF: 888-627-6882 ■ Web: www.marotta.com	973-334-7800		789
Marouch 4905 Santa Monica Blvd .... Los Angeles CA 90029 Web: www.hollywoodmarouch.com	323-662-9325		671
Marox Corp 373 Whitney Ave .... Holyoke MA 01040 Web: www.marox.com	413-536-1300	534-1829	621
Marpat Aviation Logan County Airport Rt 17 N .... Logan WV 25601 Web: www.marpataviation.com	304-752-0094	752-0097	167-3
Marposs Corp 3300 Cross Creek Pkwy .... Auburn Hills MI 48326 TF: 888-627-7677 ■ Web: www.marposs.com	248-370-0404	370-0991	472
Marq Packaging Systems Inc 3801 W Washington Ave .... Yakima WA 98903 TF: 800-998-4301 ■ Web: www.marq.net	509-966-4300		557
Marquardt Switches Inc 2711 US 20 .... Cazenovia NY 13035 Web: us.marquardt.com	315-655-8050	655-8042	203
Marque Millennium Capital Management LLC 850 3rd Ave 13th Fl .... New York NY 10022 Web: www.marqmil.com	212-759-6801		401
Marquee Energy Ltd 500 Fourth Ave SW Ste 1700 .... Calgary AB T2P2V6 TF: 866-405-4854 ■ Web: www.marquee-energy.com	403-384-0000		539
Marquee Fire Protection 710 W Stadium Ln .... Sacramento CA 95834 Web: www.marqueefire.com	916-641-7997	641-0775	610
MarQueen Hotel 600 Queen Anne Ave N .... Seattle WA 98109 Web: www.marqueen.com	206-282-7407	283-1499	379
Marquette 8140 Township Line Rd .... Indianapolis IN 46260 Web: www.marquetteseniorliving.org	317-875-9700		672
Marquette Adams Telephone Cooperative Inc 113 N Oxford St .... Oxford WI 53952 TF: 800-331-5619 ■ Web: www.marquetteadams.com	608-586-4111	586-5209	224
Marquette Asset Management 150 S 5th St Ste 2800 .... Minneapolis MN 55402 TF: 866-661-3770 ■ Web: marquetteam.com	612-661-3770		401
Marquette Associates Inc 180 N LaSalle St Ste 3500 .... Chicago IL 60601 Web: www.marquetteassociates.com	312-527-5500	527-9064	792
Marquette Bank 10000 W 151st St .... Orland Park IL 60462 TF: 888-254-9500 ■ Web: emarquettebank.com	708-226-8026		70
Marquette Branch Prison 1960 US Hwy 41 S .... Marquette MI 49855 Web: www.michigan.gov	906-226-6531	226-6557	213
Marquette Country Convention & Visitors Bureau 117 W Washington St .... Marquette MI 49855 TF: 800-544-4321 ■ Web: www.travelmarquettemichigan.com	906-228-7749		206
Marquette County 234 W Baraga Ave .... Marquette MI 49855 Web: www.co.marquette.mi.us	906-225-8151	225-8155	338
Marquette County 77 W Park St PO Box 129 .... Montello WI 53949 Web: www.co.marquette.wi.us	608-297-3100	297-7606	338
Marquette General Hospital 580 W College Ave .... Marquette MI 49855 Web: www.mgh.org	906-228-9440	225-3084	374-3
Marquette Partners LP 801 W Adams Ste 500 .... Chicago IL 60607 Web: www.marquettepartners.com	312-224-2400		690
Marquette Public Service Garage 919 W Baraga Ave .... Marquette MI 49855 Web: www.publicservicegarage.com	906-662-4395		57
Marquette Regional History Ctr (MRHC) 145 W Spring St .... Marquette MI 49855 Web: www.marquettecohistory.org	906-226-3571		48-13

Name / Address	Phone	Fax	Class
Marquette Savings Bank 920 Peach St. . . . . Erie PA 16501 *TF:* 866-672-3743 ■ *Web:* www.marquettesavings.bank	814-455-4481	453-5345	70
Marquette Transportation Company LLC 150 Ballard Cir . . . . . Paducah KY 42001 *TF:* 800-456-9404 ■ *Web:* www.marquettetrans.com	270-443-9404		314
Marquette University 1217 W Wisconsin Ave. . . . . Milwaukee WI 53233 *TF:* 800-222-6544 ■ *Web:* www.marquette.edu	414-288-7302	288-3764	166
Marquette University Law School 1215 W Michigan St. . . . . Milwaukee WI 53233 *Web:* law.marquette.edu	414-288-7090	288-6403	167-1
Marquette University Press (MUP) PO Box 3141 . . . . . Milwaukee WI 53201 *Web:* www.mu.edu	414-288-1564	288-7813	637-2
Marquez Bros International Inc 5801 Rue Ferrari. . . . . San Jose CA 95138 *Web:* elmexicano.net	408-960-2700	960-3213	297-8
MarquipWardUnited 1300 N Airport Rd . . . . . Phillips WI 54555 *Web:* marquipwardunited.com	715-339-2191	339-4469	556
Marquis Energy LLC 11953 Prairie Industrial Pkwy. . . . . Hennepin IL 61327 *TF:* 800-343-6258 ■ *Web:* www.marquisgrain.com	800-343-6258		580
Marquis Group, The 16201 Dodd St . . . . . Volente TX 78641 *Web:* www.marquis-group.com	512-336-8100		194
Marquis Software 1625 Summit Lake Loop Ste 105 . . . . . Tallahassee FL 32317 *Web:* www.marquisware.com	850-877-8864	877-0359	177
Marquis Spas Corp 596 Hoffman Rd . . . . . Independence OR 97351 *TF:* 800-275-0888 ■ *Web:* www.marquisspas.com	503-838-0888	838-3849	375
Marquis Who's Who 100 Connell Dr Ste 2300 . . . . . Berkeley Heights NJ 07922 *TF:* 800-473-7020 ■ *Web:* www.marquiswhoswho.com	908-673-0100		637-2
Marr & Company PC 1401 E 104th St Ste 100. . . . . Kansas City MO 64131 *Web:* marrandcompany.com	816-363-8700		2
Marra's Homecare Equipment & Supplies Inc 21087 State Hwy 12F . . . . . Watertown NY 13601 *TF:* 800-974-6277 ■ *Web:* www.marrashomecare.com	315-788-8280	785-9715	352
Marra's Pharmacy Inc 217 Remsen St . . . . . Cohoes NY 12047 *Web:* marraspharmacy.com	518-237-2110		237
Marrakech 1833 Fulton Ave. . . . . Sacramento CA 95825 *Web:* www.marrakechrestaurant.com	916-486-1944		671
Marrakech Express Inc 720 Wesley Ave Ste 10. . . . . Tarpon Springs FL 34689 *TF:* 800-940-6566 ■ *Web:* www.marrak.com	727-942-2218	937-4758	627
Marrakesh 517 S Leithgow St . . . . . Philadelphia PA 19147 *Web:* marrakesheastcoast.com	215-925-5929		671
Marriner Marketing Communications Inc 6731 Columbia Gateway Dr Ste 250. . . . . Columbia MD 21046 *Web:* www.marriner.com	410-715-1500		7
Marrinson Senior Care Residences 1601 NE 26th St. . . . . Wilton Manors FL 33305 *Web:* www.marrinson.com	954-566-8353		371
Marriott International Inc 10400 Fernwood Rd . . . . . Bethesda MD 20817 *NASDAQ: MAR* ■ *TF:* 800-450-4442 ■ *Web:* www.marriott.com	301-380-2821		379
Marriott Theatre in Lincolnshire 10 Marriott Dr. . . . . Lincolnshire IL 60069 *Web:* www.marriotttheatre.com	847-634-0200	634-7358	572
Marriott Vacation Club Intl 6649 Westwood Blvd Ste 500. . . . . Orlando FL 32821 *TF:* 800-307-7312 ■ *Web:* www.marriottvacationclub.com	407-903-6100		753
Marrone, Robinson, Frederick & Foster 111 N First St Ste 209 . . . . . Burbank CA 91502 *Web:* www.mrfflaw.net	818-841-1144	841-0746	428
Marrs Electric Inc 2358 E Skelly Dr. . . . . Tulsa OK 74128 *Web:* www.marrselectric.com	918-437-5802	438-3563	189-4
Marrs Printing Inc 860 Tucker Ln. . . . . City of Industry CA 91789 *Web:* www.marrs.com	909-594-9459	598-1016	627
Marrs Wealth Management LLC 313 Fifth St Ste 101 . . . . . Ames IA 50010 *Web:* marrswealthmanagement.com	515-233-0307		690
Mars & Co 124 Mason St. . . . . Greenwich CT 06830 *Web:* www.marsandco.com	203-629-9292	629-9432	194
Mars Agency, The 25200 Telegraph Rd . . . . . Southfield MI 48034 *Web:* www.themarsagency.com	248-936-2200		4
Mars Electric Co 6655 Beta Dr. . . . . Mayfield OH 44143 *Web:* www.mars-electric.com	440-946-2250	946-3214	246
Mars Hill College 100 Athletics St . . . . . Mars Hill NC 28754 *Web:* www.marshilllions.com	828-689-1219		166
Mars Hill Productions Inc 4711 Lexington Blvd. . . . . Missouri City TX 77459 *TF:* 800-580-6479 ■ *Web:* www.mars-hill.org	281-403-1463	403-4463	514
Mars Inc 6885 Elm St. . . . . McLean VA 22101 *Web:* www.mars.com	703-821-4900		185
Mars Stout Inc 4500 Majestic Dr . . . . . Missoula MT 59808 *TF:* 800-451-6277 ■ *Web:* www.marsstout.com	406-721-6280		737
Marsden Inc 6800 Westfield Ave . . . . . Pennsauken NJ 08110 *Web:* www.marsdeninc.com	856-663-2227	663-2137	318
Marsh & Mclennan Agency 250 Pehle Ave. . . . . Saddle Brook NJ 07663 **Fax Area Code: 866* ■ *TF:* 800-669-6330 ■ *Web:* www.mma-ne.com	800-642-0106	795-0931*	390
Marsh & McLennan Companies Inc 1166 Avenue of the Americas . . . . . New York NY 10036 *NYSE: MMC* ■ *TF:* 866-374-2662 ■ *Web:* www.mmc.com	212-345-5000		360-3
Marsh Bellofram Corp 8019 Ohio River Blvd . . . . . Newell WV 26050 *TF:* 800-727-5646 ■ *Web:* www.marshbellofram.com	304-387-1200	387-1212	201
Marsh Berry & Company Inc 28601 Chagrin Blvd Ste 400. . . . . Willoughby OH 44094 *TF:* 800-426-2774 ■ *Web:* www.marshberry.com	440-354-3230		194
Marsh Creek State Park 675 Park Rd . . . . . Downingtown PA 19335 *Web:* www.dcnr.pa.gov	610-458-5119		565
Marsh Electronics Inc 1563 S 101st St . . . . . Milwaukee WI 53214 *TF:* 800-926-2774 ■ *Web:* www.marshelectronics.com	414-475-6000	771-2847	246
Marsh Fischmann & Breyfogle LLP 8055 E Tufts Ave Ste 450 . . . . . Denver CO 80237 *Web:* www.mfblaw.com	303-770-0051		428
Marsh Furniture Co PO Box 870 . . . . . High Point NC 27261 *Web:* www.marshfurniture.com	336-884-7363	884-3553	115
Marsh Industries Inc 49680 Leona Dr . . . . . Chesterfield MI 48051 *Web:* www.marshindustries.com	586-949-9300	949-1290	326
Marsh Ridge Resort 420 University Blvd . . . . . Indianapolis IN 46202 *Web:* www.marshridge.com	233-123-3355		669
Marsh's Edge 136 Marsh's Edge Ln . . . . . Saint Simons Island GA 31522 *Web:* marshs-edge.com	912-291-2000		371
Marsha Veenstra 4807 Cascade Rd SE . . . . . Grand Rapids MI 49546 *TF:* 866-819-6631 ■ *Web:* marshaveenstra.com	616-940-2888	940-3083	390
Marshack Hays LLP 870 Roosevelt Ave . . . . . Irvine CA 92620 *Web:* marshackhays.com	949-333-7777		41
Marshad Technology Group 99 Hudson St 5th Fl . . . . . New York NY 10013 *Web:* marshad.com	917-209-3467		4
Marshal Mize Ford Inc 5348 Hwy 153 . . . . . Chattanooga TN 37415 *TF:* 888-633-5038 ■ *Web:* www.marshalmizeford.net	888-633-5038		57
Marshall & Bruce Printing Co 689 Davidson St. . . . . Nashville TN 37213 *Web:* www.marbruco.com	615-256-3661	256-6803	92
Marshall & Sterling Inc 110 Main St . . . . . Poughkeepsie NY 12601 *TF:* 800-333-3766 ■ *Web:* www.marshallsterling.com	845-454-0800	454-0880	390
Marshall & Stevens Inc 601 S Figueroa St Ste 2301 . . . . . Los Angeles CA 90017 *TF:* 800-950-9588 ■ *Web:* marshall-stevens.com	213-612-8000	612-8010	194
Marshall & Sullivan Inc 1109 First Ave Ste 200. . . . . Seattle WA 98101 *TF:* 800-735-7290 ■ *Web:* www.msinvest.com	206-621-9014		401
Marshall Air Systems 419 Peachtree Dr S. . . . . Charlotte NC 28217 *Web:* www.marshallair.com	704-525-6230	525-6229	697
Marshall Area Convention & Visitors Bureau 317 W Main St . . . . . Marshall MN 56258 *TF:* 800-581-0081 ■ *Web:* www.marshall-mn.org	507-537-2271	532-4485	206
Marshall Communications 44040 Airport View Dr Ste A. . . . . Hollywood MD 20636 *Web:* www.marshallcomm.com	571-223-2010		194
Marshall County 1101 Main St. . . . . Benton KY 42025 *Web:* www.marshallcounty.net	270-527-4750		338
Marshall County 520 J M Ash Dr. . . . . Holly Springs MS 38635 *Web:* www.marshallcoms.com	662-252-3916	252-7168	338
Marshall County 122 N Prairie St PO Box 328 . . . . . Lacon IL 61540 *Web:* www.marshallcountyillinois.com	309-246-6325	246-3667	338
Marshall County 1 E Main St . . . . . Marshalltown IA 50158 *Web:* www.co.marshall.ia.us	641-754-6355	754-6349	338
Marshall County 1201 Broadway . . . . . Marysville KS 66508 *Web:* ks-marshall.manatron.com	785-562-5361	562-5262	338
Marshall County 208 E Colvin Ave. . . . . Warren MN 56762 *Web:* www.visitnwminnesota.com	218-745-4851		338
Marshall County Chamber of Commerce 609 Jefferson Ave. . . . . Moundsville WV 26041 *Web:* www.marshallcountychamber.com	304-845-2773		139
Marshall County Correctional Facility 833 W St. . . . . Holly Springs MS 38635 *Web:* www.hollyspringsmsus.com	662-274-0225		213
Marshall County Courthouse 424 Blount Ave Ste 305 . . . . . Guntersville AL 35976 *Web:* www.marshallco.org	256-571-7701		338
Marshall County Library 109 E Gholson Ave. . . . . Holly Springs MS 38635 *Web:* www.marshall.lib.ms.us	662-252-3823	252-3066	434-3
Marshall County REMC 11299 12th Rd PO Box 250 . . . . . Plymouth IN 46563 *Web:* www.marshallremc.com	574-936-3161	935-4162	245
Marshall County Superior Court 2 211 W Madison St . . . . . Plymouth IN 46563 *Web:* www.co.marshall.in.us	574-935-8763	935-8700	338
Marshall County WV PO Box 459 . . . . . Moundsville WV 26041 *Web:* www.marshallcountywv.org	304-845-1220	845-5891	338
Marshall Dennehey Warner Coleman & Goggin 1845 Walnut St. . . . . Philadelphia PA 19103 *TF:* 800-220-3308 ■ *Web:* www.marshalldennehey.com	215-575-2600	575-0856	428
Marshall Durbin Co 2830 Commerce Blvd. . . . . Birmingham AL 35210 *TF:* 800-245-8204 ■ *Web:* www.marshalldurbin.com	205-380-3251		619
Marshall Furniture Inc 999 Anita Ave . . . . . Antioch IL 60002 *Web:* www.marshallfurniture.com	847-395-9350	395-9351	321
Marshall Gold Discovery State Historic Park 310 Back St PO Box 265. . . . . Coloma CA 95613 *Web:* www.parks.ca.gov	530-622-3470		565
Marshall Graphics Systems 210 Hill Ave . . . . . Nashville TN 37210 *Web:* marshallgraphics.com	615-399-8896	399-8898	387
Marshall Hotels & Resorts Inc 1315 S Division St . . . . . Salisbury MD 21804 *Web:* marshallhotels.com	410-749-8464	749-0679	378
Marshall ISD PO Box 43 . . . . . Marshall TX 75670 *Web:* www.marshallisd.com	903-927-8700	935-0203	685
Marshall Islands 800 2nd Ave 18th Fl . . . . . New York NY 10017 *Web:* mirror.unhabitat.org	212-983-3040		784
Marshall Islands Embassy 2433 Massachusetts Ave NW . . . . . Washington DC 20008 *Web:* www.rmiembassyus.org	202-234-5414	232-3236	257
Marshall L. Rubin, A Professional Corp 16255 Ventura Blvd Ste 840. . . . . Encino CA 91436 *Web:* rubinlaw.yolasite.com	818-379-9775		41
Marshall Long Acoustics 13636 Riverside Dr. . . . . Sherman Oaks CA 91423 *Web:* www.mlacoustics.com	818-981-8005	981-9418	189-9

				Phone	Fax	Class
Marshall Medical Center South (MMCS) 2505 US Hwy 431 *Web:* www.mmcenters.com	Boaz	AL	35957	256-593-8310		374-3
Marshall Memorial Library 110 S Diamond Ave	Deming	NM	88030	575-546-9202		434-3
Marshall Middle School 401 S Saratoga *Web:* www.marshall.k12.mn.us	Marshall	MN	56258	507-537-6938	537-6931	685
Marshall Music Co 4555 Wilson Ave SW Ste 1 *TF:* 800-242-4705 ■ *Web:* www.marshallmusicweb.com	Grandville	MI	49418	616-530-7700		526
Marshall Pierce & Co 960 N Michigan Ave *Web:* marshallpierce.com	Chicago	IL	60611	312-642-4299		411
Marshall Public Library 113 S Garfield Ave *Web:* www.marshallpl.org	Pocatello	ID	83204	208-232-1263		434-3
Marshall Public Library 300 S Alamo St *Web:* www.marshalltexas.net	Marshall	TX	75670	903-935-4465		434-3
Marshall Retail Group (MRG) 3755 W Sunset Rd *Web:* marshallretailgroup.com	Las Vegas	NV	89118	702-385-5233		157-6
Marshall Roger (Rep R - KS) 312 Cannon House Office Bldg *Web:* marshall.house.gov	Washington	DC	20515	202-225-2715		342-2
Marshall Screw Products Co 3820 Chandler Dr NE *TF:* 800-321-6727 ■ *Web:* www.marshallmfg.com	Minneapolis	MN	55421	800-321-6727		454
Marshall Square Mall 720 University Ave *Web:* www.subway.com	Syracuse	NY	13210	315-422-3234		460
Marshall State Fish & Wildlife Area 236 SR-26 *Web:* www.dnr.illinois.gov	Lacon	IL	61540	309-246-8351		565
Marshall Truss Systems Inc 200 S 11th St	Marshall	MN	56258	507-537-0581		817
Marshall University 1 John Marshall Dr *TF:* 800-642-3463 ■ *Web:* www.marshall.edu	Huntington	WV	25755	304-696-3170	696-3135	166
Marshall V. Miller & Company Pc 4929 Main St *Web:* www.millerco.com	Kansas City	MO	64112	816-561-4999	561-5999	428
Marshall, Williams & Gorham LLP 14 S Fifth St *Web:* mwglaw.com	Wilmington	NC	28401	910-763-9891		41
Marshalltown Area Chamber of Commerce 709 S Center St PO Box 1000 *Web:* www.marshalltown.org	Marshalltown	IA	50158	641-753-6645	752-8373	139
Marshalltown Co 104 S Eigth Ave *TF:* 800-888-0127 ■ *Web:* marshalltown.com	Marshalltown	IA	50158	641-753-5999	753-6341	758
Marshalltown Community College 3700 S Center St *TF:* 866-622-4748 ■ *Web:* mcc.iavalley.edu	Marshalltown	IA	50158	641-844-5708	752-8149	162
Marshalltown Public Library 105 W Boone St *Web:* www.marshalltownlibrary.org	Marshalltown	IA	50158	641-754-5738	754-5708	434-3
Marsh-Billings-Rockefeller National Historical Park 54 Elm St *Web:* www.nps.gov	Woodstock	VT	05091	802-457-3368	457-3405	564
Marshfield Animal Hospital Inc 490 Plain St *Web:* marshfieldanimal.com	Marshfield	MA	02050	781-837-5005		794
Marshfield Convention & Visitors Bureau 700 S Central Ave PO Box 868 *TF:* 800-422-4541 ■ *Web:* marshfieldchamber.com	Marshfield	WI	54449	715-384-3454	387-8925	206
Marshfield Public Library 211 E Second St *Web:* www.marshfieldlibrary.org	Marshfield	WI	54449	715-387-8494		434-3
Marson & Marson Lumber Inc 11724 Riverbend Dr *Web:* www.marsonandmarson.com	Leavenworth	WA	98826	509-548-5829		364
Marston House Museum & Gardens 3525 Seventh Ave *TF:* 800-577-6679 ■ *Web:* www.sohosandiego.org	San Diego	CA	92103	619-297-9327		50-3
Marston Keyser Associates Inc 160 Pacific Ave Ste 204 *Web:* www.keysermarston.com	San Francisco	CA	94111	415-398-3050		196
Marstons Mills Public Library 2160 Main St *Web:* www.mmpl.org	Marstons Mills	MA	02648	508-428-5175	420-5194	434-3
Marsulex Environmental Technology 200 N Seventh St Ste 1 *Web:* www.met.net	Lebanon	PA	17046	717-274-7000	274-7103	18
MARTA (Metropolitan Atlanta Rapid Transit Authority) 2424 Piedmont Rd NE *Web:* www.itsmarta.com	Atlanta	GA	30324	404-848-5000		468
Martec 105 W Adams St Ste 2900 *TF:* 888-811-5755 ■ *Web:* www.martecgroup.com	Chicago	IL	60603	312-606-9690		668
Martec Intl 529 Dowd Ave *TF:* 800-862-7832 ■ *Web:* www.martecintl.com	Elizabeth	NJ	07201	908-248-9001		770
Martec USA LLC 1201 Wallnut St	Kansas City	MO	64106	816-241-4144		583
Martech Medical Products Inc 1500 Delp Dr *Web:* www.martechmedical.com	Harleysville	PA	19438	215-256-8833	256-8837	477
MarTech Systems Inc 35 Viburnum Ct **Fax Area Code:* 509 ■ *Web:* www.martechsystems.com	Lawrenceville	NJ	08648	609-896-4457	351-5503*	194
Martel Construction Inc 1203 S Church *Web:* www.martelconstruction.com	Bozeman	MT	59715	406-586-8585	586-8646	188-3
Marten Law 1191 Second Ave Ste 2200 *Web:* www.martenlaw.com	Seattle	WA	98101	206-292-2600	292-2601	428
Marten Transport Ltd 129 Marten St *NASDAQ: MRTN* ■ *TF:* 800-395-3000 ■ *Web:* www.marten.com	Mondovi	WI	54755	715-926-4216	926-5609	780
Martenson & Eisele Inc 1377 Midway Rd *Web:* martenson-eisele.com	Menasha	WI	54952	920-731-0381		261
Martexport Inc 155 E 55th St Ste 4E *Web:* ncolindres.tripod.com	New York	NY	10022	212-935-0300	935-0437	328
Martguild Inc 8563 Rte10 Hwy 46 *TF:* 800-245-8978 ■ *Web:* www.martguild.com	New Point	IN	47263	812-663-6311	663-5530	322
Martha Jo Leslie State Veterans Affairs Board 310 Autumn Ridge Dr *Web:* www.vab.ms.gov	Kosciusko	MS	39090	662-289-7809	289-7824	793
Martha Stewart Living Magazine 601 W 26th St 9th Fl *TF:* 800-999-6518 ■ *Web:* www.marthastewart.com	New York	NY	10001	800-999-6518		457-11
Martha Washington Inn & Spa, The 150 W Main St *Web:* www.themartha.com	Abingdon	VA	24210	276-628-3161	628-8885	379
Martha's Vineyard & Nantucket Reservations 31 N Summer St *Web:* mvnres.com	Vineyard Haven	MA	02568	508-693-7200		376
Martha's Vineyard Museum 59 School St PO Box 1310 *Web:* www.mvmuseum.org	Edgartown	MA	02539	508-627-4441	627-4436	520
Martha's Vineyard Regional Transit Authority 11 A St MV Business Pk *Web:* www.vineyardtransit.com	Edgartown	MA	02539	508-693-9440	693-9953	108
Martha's Vineyard Savings Bank 78 Main St PO Box 1069 *Web:* www.mvbank.com	Edgartown	MA	02539	508-627-4266		71
Martin & Bayley Inc 1311 A W Main *TF:* 800-876-2511 ■ *Web:* www.martinandbayley.com	Carmi	IL	62821	618-382-2334		345
Martin & Jones PLLC 410 Glenwood Ave Ste 200 *Web:* martinandjones.com	Raleigh	NC	27603	919-821-0005		41
Martin & Martin CPA Ltd 1001 W Hawthorn Dr *Web:* www.mmcpasltd.com	Itasca	IL	60143	847-250-5074	250-5105	2
Martin & Whitacre Surveyors & Engineers Inc 1508 Bidwell Rd *Web:* martin-whitacre.com	Muscatine	IA	52761	563-263-7691		261
Martin Agency Inc 1 Shockoe Plz *Web:* www.martinagency.com	Richmond	VA	23219	804-698-8000	698-8001	4
Martin Allgeier & Assoc 7231 E 24th St *Web:* www.amce.com	Joplin	MO	64804	417-680-7200		186
Martin Archery 3301 E Isaacs Ave Ste B *Web:* www.martinarchery.com	Walla Walla	WA	99362	509-529-2554		710
Martin Army Community Hospital 6600 Van Aalst Blvd *TF:* 877-995-5247 ■ *Web:* www.martin.amedd.army.mil	Fort Benning	GA	31905	762-408-2604		374-4
Martin Automatic Inc 1661 Northrock Ct *Web:* www.martinauto.com	Rockford	IL	61103	815-654-4800	654-4810	203
Martin Automotive Group 12101 W Olympic Blvd *Web:* www.martinautogroup.com	Los Angeles	CA	90064	310-622-9334		57
Martin Avenue Pharmacy 1247 Rickert Dr *Web:* www.martinavenue.com	Naperville	IL	60540	630-355-6400		237
Martin Aviation 19300 Ike Jones Rd *Web:* martin-aviation.com	Santa Ana	CA	92707	714-210-2945	557-0637	24
Martin Bontempo Matacera Bartlett Inc 212 W State St *Web:* www.mbigluckshaw.com	Trenton	NJ	08608	609-392-3100		636
Martin Cabinet Inc 336 S Washington St *Web:* martincabinet.com	Plainville	CT	06062	860-747-5769	747-9595	115
Martin Capital Management LLP 131 E Franklin St Ste 14 *Web:* www.mcmadvisors.com	Elkhart	IN	46516	574-293-2077		401
Martin Chevrolet 23505 Hawthorne Blvd *Web:* www.martinchevrolet.com	Torrance	CA	90505	310-853-5846		516
Martin Communications Inc 25 W Main St *Web:* www.martincommunicationsinc.com	Shiremanstown	PA	17011	717-712-0980		7
Martin Community College 1161 Kehukee Park Rd *TF:* 800-488-4101 ■ *Web:* www.martincc.edu	Williamston	NC	27892	252-792-1521	792-0826	162
Martin County 201 Lake Ave *Web:* www.co.martin.mn.us	Fairmont	MN	56031	507-238-3211		338
Martin County PO Box 460 *Web:* www.peoplesmart.com	Inez	KY	41224	606-298-2810	298-0143	338
Martin County PO Box 1349 *Web:* www.martincountytexas.us	Stanton	TX	79782	432-756-3336	607-2992	338
Martin County 2401 SE Monterey Rd *Web:* www.martin.fl.us	Stuart	FL	34996	772-288-5400	288-5548	338
Martin County 305 E Main St PO Box 308 *Web:* www.martincountyncgov.com	Williamston	NC	27892	252-789-4300	789-4309	338
Martin County Chamber of Commerce 415 E Blvd *Web:* martincountync.com	Williamston	NC	27892	252-792-4131		139
Martin County Historical Society (MCHS) 304 E Blue Earth Ave *Web:* www.fairmont.org	Fairmont	MN	56031	507-235-5178		48-13
Martin County Travel & Tourism Authority 100 E Church St PO Box 382 *TF:* 800-776-8566 ■ *Web:* visitmartincounty.com	Williamston	NC	27892	252-792-6605		206
Martin County West High School 16 W Fifth St *Web:* martin.k12.mn.us	Sherburn	MN	56171	507-764-4661		685
Martin Creek Lake State Park 9515 CR 2181D *Web:* tpwd.texas.gov	Tatum	TX	75691	903-836-4336		565
Martin Dies Jr State Park 634 Park Rd 48 S *Web:* tpwd.texas.gov	Jasper	TX	75951	409-384-5231		565
Martin Door Manufacturing Inc 2828 South 900 West *TF:* 800-388-9310 ■ *Web:* www.martindoor.com	Salt Lake City	UT	84119	801-973-9310	688-8182	364
Martin Eagle Oil Company Inc 2700 James St *TF:* 800-316-6148 ■ *Web:* www.martineagle.com	Denton	TX	76205	940-383-2351	382-9342	579

Company / Address	Phone	Fax	Class
Martin Elfant Inc 7112 Germantown Ave Philadelphia PA 19119 *Web:* elfantpontz.com	215-844-1200		652
Martin Engineering 1 Martin Pl Neponset IL 61345 **Fax Area Code:* 309 ■ *TF:* 800-544-2947 ■ *Web:* www.martin-eng.com	800-544-2947	594-2432*	207
Martin F. White Company LPA 156 N Park Ave Warren OH 44481 *Web:* martinfwhite.com	330-394-9692		41
Martin Federal Credit Union 1727 Orlando Central Pkwy Orlando FL 32809 *Web:* midflorida.com	407-857-6328		219
Martin Furniture 2345 Britannia Blvd San Diego CA 92154 **Fax Area Code:* 619 ■ *TF:* 800-268-5669 ■ *Web:* www.martinfurniture.com	800-268-5669	671-5199*	319-1
Martin Glass Co 25 Center Plz Belleville IL 62220 *TF:* 800-325-1946 ■ *Web:* www.martinglass.net	618-277-1946		62-2
Martin Group LLC, The 477 Main St Buffalo NY 14203 *Web:* www.martingroup.co	716-853-2757		195
Martin Health System (MMHS) 200 SE Hospital Ave PO Box 9010 Stuart FL 34994 *TF:* 844-630-4968 ■ *Web:* www.martinhealth.org	772-287-5200		374-3
Martin Hild PA 555 Winderley Pl Ste 415 Maitland FL 32751 *Web:* martinhild.com	407-660-4488		41
Martin Industrial Supplies 860 E Lincoln Ave Searcy AR 72143 **Fax Area Code:* 501 ■ *TF:* 800-343-4421 ■ *Web:* www.martinindustrial.com	800-343-4421	268-1829*	146
Martin Investment Management LLC 1560 Sherman Ave Ste 1250 Evanston IL 60201 *Web:* www.martin-investments.com	847-424-9124		195
Martin Iron Works Inc 530 E Fourth St Reno NV 89512 *Web:* martinironworks.net	775-329-8631	329-9003	480
Martin J. Braun Co 6325 Erdman Ave Ste 1 Baltimore MD 21205	410-488-3990		189-10
Martin K. Eby Construction Co 2525 E 36th Cir Wichita KS 67219 *Web:* www.ebycorp.com	316-268-3500	268-3649	188-4
Martin Kilpatrick Table Tennis 4482 Technology Dr NW Wilson NC 27896 *Web:* butterflyonline.com	252-291-8202		711
Martin Law Firm 2059 N Green Acres Rd Fayetteville AR 72702 *TF:* 800-633-2160 ■ *Web:* www.martinlawpartners.com	479-442-2244	442-0134	445
Martin Luther College 1995 Luther Ct New Ulm MN 56073 *Web:* www.mlc-wels.edu	507-354-8221	354-8225	166
Martin Luther King Jr Memorial Library (MLK) 901 G St NW Washington DC 20001 *Web:* www.dclibrary.org	202-727-0321		434-3
Martin Luther King Jr National Historic Site 450 Auburn Ave NE Atlanta GA 30312 *Web:* www.nps.gov	404-331-5190	730-3112	564
Martin Management Group Inc 1048 Ashley St Ste 401 Bowling Green KY 42103 *Web:* www.martingp.com	270-783-8080		57
Martin Marietta Magnesia Specialties Inc 8140 Corporate Dr Ste 220 Baltimore MD 21236 *TF:* 800-648-7400 ■ *Web:* www.magnesiaspecialties.com	410-780-5500	780-5777	143
Martin Marietta Materials Inc 2710 Wycliff Rd Raleigh NC 27607 *NYSE: MLM* ■ *Web:* www.martinmarietta.com	919-781-4550		503-5
Martin Mechanical Design Inc 1201 25th Ave N Fargo ND 58102 *Web:* www.martinmech.com	701-293-7957	293-7381	261
Martin Memorial Library 159 E Market St York PA 17401 *Web:* www.yorklibraries.org	717-846-5300		434-3
Martin Methodist College 433 W Madison St Pulaski TN 38478 *TF:* 800-467-1273 ■ *Web:* www.martinmethodist.edu	931-363-9804		166
Martin Midstream Partners LP 4200 Stone Rd Kilgore TX 75662 *NASDAQ: MMLP* ■ *TF:* 800-256-6644 ■ *Web:* martinmidstream.com	903-983-6200		579
Martin Newby Management Corp 3310 Us Hwy 301 N Ellenton FL 34222 *Web:* newbymanagement.com	941-721-0046		652
Martin Park Nature Ctr 5000 W Memorial Rd Oklahoma City OK 73142 *Web:* okc.gov	405-297-3882		50-5
Martin Paving Co PO Box 548 Medina TN 38355 *TF:* 877-783-3962 ■ *Web:* www.martinpaving.net	731-783-3962	783-3126	188-4
Martin Petersen Company Inc 9800 55th St Kenosha WI 53144 *Web:* www.mpcmech.com	262-658-1326	658-1048	189-10
Martin Printing Company Inc 1765 Powdersville Rd Easley SC 29642 *TF:* 888-985-7330 ■ *Web:* www.martinprinting.com	864-859-4032	859-8620	627
Martin Properties Inc 372 S Eagle Rd Ste 395 Eagle ID 83616 *Web:* martinprop.com	208-841-4700		652
Martin Rosol Inc 45 Grove St New Britain CT 06053 *Web:* martinrosolsinc.com	860-223-2707	229-6690	296-26
Martin Sprocket & Gear Inc 3100 Sprocket Dr Arlington TX 76015 *Web:* www.martinsprocket.com	817-258-3000	258-3333	620
Martin Supply Co 200 Appleton Ave Sheffield AL 35660 *TF:* 800-828-8116 ■ *Web:* www.martinsupply.com	256-383-3132		385
Martin Trucking Inc PO Box M Hugoton KS 67951 *Web:* www.martintruckingks.com	620-544-4920		780
Martin University 2186 N Sherman Dr Indianapolis IN 46218 *TF:* 866-344-3114 ■ *Web:* www.martin.edu	317-543-3235		166
Martin Van Buren National Historic Site 1013 Old Post Rd Kinderhook NY 12106 *Web:* www.nps.gov	518-758-9689	758-6986	564
Martin Wheel Company Inc, The 342 W Ave PO Box 157 Tallmadge OH 44278 *TF:* 800-462-7846 ■ *Web:* www.martinwheelco.com	330-633-3278	633-3303	754
Martin Yale Industries Inc 251 Wedcor Ave Wabash IN 46992 *TF:* 800-225-5644 ■ *Web:* martinyale.com	260-563-0641	563-4575	111

Company / Address	Phone	Fax	Class
Martin's Famous Pastry Shoppe Inc 1000 Potato Roll Ln Chambersburg PA 17202 *TF:* 800-548-1200 ■ *Web:* potatorolls.com	717-263-9580		296-1
Martin's Marketplace 130 Titchenal Way Cashmere WA 98815 *Web:* www.martinsmarketplace.com	509-782-3801	782-2212	345
Martin's Point Veterinary Hospital LLC 6405 N Croatan Hwy Kitty Hawk NC 27949 *Web:* martinspointvethosp.com	252-261-2250		794
Martin's Potato Chips Inc 5847 Lincoln Hwy W PO Box 28 Thomasville PA 17364 *TF:* 800-272-4477 ■ *Web:* martinssnacks.com	717-792-3565	792-4906	296-35
Martin's Super Markets Inc 926 Erskine Plz South Bend IN 46614 *TF:* 800-910-7079 ■ *Web:* martins-supermarkets.com	574-291-3571		345
Martin, Bircher, Thompson PC 11400 98th Ave NE Ste 200 Kirkland WA 98033 *Web:* martinbirchercpa.com	425-827-3041		2
Martin, Disiere, Jefferson & Wisdom LLP 808 Travis 20th Fl Houston TX 77002 *Web:* www.mdjwlaw.com	713-632-1700	222-0101	428
Martin, Dolan & Holton Ltd 4435 Waterfront Dr Ste 200 Glen Allen VA 23060 *Web:* martindolanholtoncpas.com	804-346-9595		2
Martin, Harding & Mazzotti LLP 1222 Troy-Schenectady Rd Niskayuna NY 12309 *TF:* 800-529-1010 ■ *Web:* www.1800law1010.com	518-862-1200		428
Martin, Leigh, Laws & Fritzlen Professional Corp 1044 Main St Ste 900 Kansas City MO 64105 *Web:* www.martinleigh.com	816-221-1430		428
Martin, Shudt, Wallace, DiLorenzo & Johnson 258 Hoosick St Ste 201 Troy NY 12180 *Web:* www.martinshudt.com	518-272-6565	272-5573	428
Martin, White & Griffis Structural Engineers Inc 3501 E Speedway Blvd Ste Tucson AZ 85716 *Web:* mwgstructural.com	480-382-7370		261
Martin/F Weber Co 2727 Southampton Rd Philadelphia PA 19154 *TF:* 800-876-8076 ■ *Web:* www.weberart.com	215-677-5600	677-3336	43
Martina's Flowers & Gifts 3925 Washington Rd Augusta GA 30907 *Web:* www.martinas.com	706-863-7172		292
MartinAire Aviation LLC 4553 Glenn Curtiss Dr Addison TX 75001 *TF:* 866-557-1861 ■ *Web:* www.martinaire.com	972-349-5700	349-5750	12
Martin-Baker America Inc 423 Walters Ave Johnstown PA 15904 *Web:* martin-baker.com	814-262-9325		529
Martindale Electric Co 1375 Hird Ave Cleveland OH 44107 *TF:* 800-344-9191 ■ *Web:* www.martindaleco.com	216-521-8567	521-9476	518
Martindell Swearer Shaffer Ridenour LLP 20 Compound Dr Hutchinson KS 67502 *Web:* martindell.com	620-662-3331	662-9978	41
Martinez & Turek Inc 300 S Cedar Ave Rialto CA 92376 *Web:* www.martinezandturek.com	909-820-6800	873-3735	454
Martinez Area Chamber of Commerce 603 Marina Vista Martinez CA 94553 *Web:* www.martinezchamber.com	925-228-2345	228-2356	139
Martinez Couch & Associates LLC 1084 Cromwell Ave Rocky Hill CT 06067 *Web:* martinezcouch.com	860-436-4364		261
Martinez Law Group PC 720 S Colorado Blvd Ste 1020-S Denver CO 80246 *Web:* mlgrouppc.com	303-597-4000		41
Martinez Unified School District 921 Susana St Martinez CA 94553 *Web:* www.martinezusd.net	925-335-5800		685
Martinfederal Consulting LLC 513 Madison St SE Ste 100 Huntsville AL 35801 *TF:* 855-212-1810 ■ *Web:* martinfed.com	855-212-1810		180
Martin-Harris Construction LLC 3030 S Highland Dr Las Vegas NV 89109 *Web:* www.martinharris.com	702-385-5257	474-8257	186
Martini Akpovi Partners LLP 16830 Ventura Blvd Ste 415 Encino CA 91436 *Web:* miacpas.com	818-789-1179	789-1162	734
Martini Modern Italian 445 N High St Columbus OH 43215 *Web:* www.martinimodernitalian.com	614-224-8259	224-8780	671
Martinique Promotion Bureau 825 3rd Ave 29th Fl New York NY 10022 *Web:* martiniquepro.org	212-838-6887		775
MartinLogan Ltd 2101 Delaware St Lawrence KS 66046 *Web:* www.martinlogan.com	785-749-0133	749-5320	52
Martino-White Printing 543 N Central Ave Atlanta GA 30354 *Web:* www.martinowhite.com	404-768-8708		627
Martins Elevators Inc 13219 Maugansville Rd Hagerstown MD 21740 *Web:* www.martinselevator.com	301-733-2553		447
Martinsburg Broadcasting Inc 724 Rebecca Furnace Rd Martinsburg PA 16662 *Web:* wjsm.com	814-793-2188		741-99
Martinsburg-Berkeley County Chamber of Commerce 198 Viking Way Martinsburg WV 25401 *Web:* www.berkeleycounty.org	304-267-4841	263-4695	139
Martinsburg-Berkeley County Public Library 101 W King St Martinsburg WV 25401 *Web:* www.mbcpl.org	304-267-8933	267-9720	434-3
Martinsville (Independent City) PO Box 1112 Martinsville VA 24114 *Web:* www.martinsville-va.gov	276-403-5106	403-5280	338
Martinsville Speedway PO Box 3311 Martinsville VA 24115 *TF:* 877-722-3849 ■ *Web:* www.martinsvillespeedway.com	276-666-7200	956-2820	515
Martinsville-Henry County Chamber of Commerce 115 Broad St Martinsville VA 24112 *Web:* www.martinsville.com	276-632-6401	632-5059	139

	Phone	Fax	Class
Martin-Williams Adv 150 S Fifth St Ste 900 .... Minneapolis MN 55402 *Web:* www.martinwilliams.com	612-340-0800		4
Marton Precision Manufacturing LLC 1365 S Acacia Ave .... Fullerton CA 92831 *TF:* 800-871-2871 ■ *Web:* martoninc.com	714-808-6523	808-6524	454
Martopia Inc 3805 E Main St Ste H .... Saint Charles IL 60174 *Web:* www.martopia.com	630-587-9944		466
Martori Farms 7332 E Butherus Dr .... Scottsdale AZ 85260 *Web:* www.martorifarms.com	480-998-1444		315-4
Martrex Inc 1107 Hazeltine Blvd Ste 535 .... Chaska MN 55318 *TF:* 800-328-3627 ■ *Web:* www.martrexinc.com	952-933-5000	933-1889	276
Martronic Engineering Inc (MEI) 874 Patriot Dr Unit D .... Moorpark CA 93021 *TF:* 800-960-0808 ■ *Web:* meilaser.com	805-583-0808	583-5364	261
Marts & Lundy Inc 1200 Wall St W .... Lyndhurst NJ 07071 *TF:* 800-526-9005 ■ *Web:* www.martsandlundy.com	201-460-1660	460-0680	787
Marty Franich Ford Lincoln 550 Auto Center Dr .... Watsonville CA 95076 *TF:* 888-442-9037 ■ *Web:* www.midbayfordwatsonville.com	831-722-4181	722-1853	57
Martz First Class Coach Company Inc 4783 37th St N .... Saint Petersburg FL 33714 **Fax Area Code:* 727 ■ *TF:* 800-282-8020 ■ *Web:* www.martzfirstclass.com	800-282-8020	522-5548*	107
Martz Group 239 Old River Rd .... Wilkes-Barre PA 18702 *Web:* www.martzgroup.com	570-821-3838	821-3811	107
Martz Plumbing, Heating & Air Conditioning 216 W Fifth St .... Waynesboro PA 17268 *Web:* martzplumbing.com	717-762-6115		189-10
Martz Supply Co 5330 Pecos St .... Denver CO 80221 *TF:* 800-456-4672 ■ *Web:* www.martzsupply.com	800-456-4672		612
Marubeni America Corp 375 Lexington Ave .... New York NY 10017 *Web:* www.marubeniamerica.com	212-450-0100	450-0700	169
Marucco, Stoddard, Ferenbach & Walsh Inc 3445 Liberty Dr .... Springfield IL 62704 *Web:* www.msfw.com	217-698-3535		180
Maruhide Marine Products Inc 2145 W 17th St .... Long Beach CA 90813 *Web:* www.maruhide.us	562-435-6509	432-4692	296-14
Maruichi American Corp 11529 Greenstone Ave .... Santa Fe Springs CA 90670 *Web:* www.macsfs.com	562-903-8600		492
Maruichi Leavitt Pipe & Tube LLC 1717 W 115th St .... Chicago IL 60643 **Fax Area Code:* 773 ■ *TF:* 800-532-8488 ■ *Web:* www.maruichi-leavitt.com	800-532-8488	239-1023*	490
Maruji & Raines PS 775 S Main St Ste A .... Colville WA 99114 *Web:* www.mrcpas.com	509-684-5289		2
Maruka USA Inc 1210 NE Douglas St .... Lee's Summit MO 64086 **Fax Area Code:* 816 ■ *TF:* 800-262-7852 ■ *Web:* www.marukausa.com	800-262-7852	542-5444*	386
Marukai Wholesale Mart 2310 Kamehameha Hwy .... Honolulu HI 96819 *Web:* www.marukaihawaii.com	808-845-5051		812
Marus and Weimer Inc 190 E Washington St .... Chagrin Falls OH 44022 *Web:* www.m-winc.com	440-247-3570	247-2132	612
Maruson Technology Corp 18557 Gale Ave .... City of Industry CA 91748 *Web:* www.marusonusa.com	626-912-8388		767
Marvair 156 Seedling Dr .... Cordele GA 31015 *Web:* airxcel.com	229-273-3636	273-5154	14
Marval Industries Inc 315 Hoyt Ave .... Mamaroneck NY 10543 *Web:* www.marvalindustries.com	914-381-2400	381-2259	605-2
Marvel Abrasive Products Inc 6230 S Oak Park Ave .... Chicago IL 60638 *TF:* 800-621-0673 ■ *Web:* www.marvelabrasives.com	800-621-0673	701-0187	1
Marvel Aero International Inc 21 Rancho Cir .... Lake Forest CA 92630 *Web:* marvelaero.com	949-829-8031		771
Marvel Consultants Inc 28601 Chagrin Blvd Ste 210 .... Cleveland OH 44122 *TF:* 800-338-1257 ■ *Web:* www.marvelconsultants.com	216-292-2855	292-7207	631
Marvel Group Inc 3843 W 43rd St .... Chicago IL 60632 **Fax Area Code:* 800 ■ *TF:* 800-621-8846 ■ *Web:* www.marvelgroup.com	773-523-4804	237-0358*	319-1
Marvel Manufacturing Company Inc 3501 Marvel Dr .... Oshkosh WI 54902 *TF:* 800-472-9464 ■ *Web:* www.marvelsaws.com	920-236-7200	236-7209	682
Marvell Semiconductor Inc 5488 Marvell Ln .... Santa Clara CA 95054 *Web:* www.marvell.com	408-222-2500		176
Marvelwood School 476 Skiff Mountain Rd .... Kent CT 06757 *Web:* marvelwood.org	860-927-0047		622
Marvin & Company PC 11 British American Blvd .... Latham NY 12110 *Web:* marvincpa.com	518-785-0134		2
Marvin & Palmer Associates Inc 200 Bellevue Pky Ste 220 .... Wilmington DE 19809 *Web:* www.marvinandpalmer.com	302-573-3570	573-2545	401
Marvin Engineering Co 261 W Beach Ave .... Inglewood CA 90302 *TF:* 888-837-8297 ■ *Web:* www.marvingroup.com	310-674-5030	673-9472	807
Marvin F. Poer & Co 12720 Hillcrest Rd Ste 900 .... Dallas TX 75230 *Web:* www.mfpoer.com	972-770-1100	770-1103	194
Marvin Huffaker Consulting Inc PO Box 72643 .... Phoenix AZ 85050 *TF:* 888-690-0013 ■ *Web:* www.redjuju.com	480-988-7215	269-8773	196
Marvin K. Brown Auto Center Inc 1441 Camino Del Rio S .... San Diego CA 92108 *TF:* 877-743-0217 ■ *Web:* www.mkb.com	619-272-6867		57
Marvin M. Wurtzel & Associates Inc 5227 Espana Ave .... Boynton Beach FL 33437 *Web:* wurtzela.ipower.com	508-574-2175		196
Marvin Windows & Doors PO Box 100 .... Warroad MN 56763 *TF:* 888-537-7828 ■ *Web:* www.marvin.com	218-386-1430		236
Marvitec Corp 1475 NW 97th Ave .... Doral FL 33172 *Web:* www.marvitec.com	305-593-1475	591-9200	385
Marwit Capital 100 Bayview Cir Ste 550 .... Newport Beach CA 92660 *Web:* www.marwit.com	949-861-3636	861-3637	402
Marwood Group LLC 733 Third Ave 11th Fl .... New York NY 10017 *Web:* www.marwoodgroup.com	212-532-3651		390
Marx | Okubo Associates Inc 455 Sherman St Ste 200 .... Denver CO 80203 *Web:* www.marxokubo.com	303-861-0300		261
Marx Bros Cafe 627 W Third Ave .... Anchorage AK 99501 *Web:* www.marxcafe.com	907-278-2133	258-6279	671
Marx Foods.com 144 Western Ave W .... Seattle WA 98119 *TF:* 866-588-6279 ■ *Web:* www.marxfoods.com	206-477-1818		393
Marx Layne & Co 31420 NW Hwy .... Farmington Hills MI 48334 *Web:* www.marxlayne.com	248-855-6777		636
Mary & Elizabeth Hospital 1850 Bluegrass Ave .... Louisville KY 40215 *Web:* www.uoflhealthnetwork.org	502-361-9271	217-1050	374-3
Mary Ann's Baking Co 8371 Carbide Ct .... Sacramento CA 95828 *Web:* maryannsbaking.com	916-681-7444		296-1
Mary Baker Eddy Library, The 200 Massachusetts Ave P02-10 .... Boston MA 02115 *TF:* 888-222-3711 ■ *Web:* www.marybakereddylibrary.org	617-450-7000	450-7048	434-3
Mary Baldwin College 318 Prospect St .... Staunton VA 24401 *TF:* 800-468-2262 ■ *Web:* www.marybaldwin.edu	540-887-7019		166
Mary Cheney Library 586 Main St .... Manchester CT 06040 *Web:* library.townofmanchester.org	860-643-2471		434-3
Mary E. Koontz 235 East St .... Methuen MA 01844 *Web:* dahercompanies.com	978-688-7251		652
Mary Fisher Design LLC 1731 Emerson St .... Jacksonville FL 32207 *Web:* www.maryfisherdesign.com	904-398-3699		395
Mary Free Bed Rehabilitation Hospital 235 Wealthy St SE .... Grand Rapids MI 49503 *TF:* 800-528-8989 ■ *Web:* www.maryfreebed.com	616-840-8000		374-6
Mary G. Commander, Attorney At Law PC 5442 Tidewater Dr .... Norfolk VA 23509 *Web:* commanderlaw.com	757-533-5400		41
Mary Greeley Medical Ctr 1111 Duff Ave .... Ames IA 50010 *Web:* www.mgmc.org	515-239-2011		374-3
Mary H. Weirton Public Library 3442 Main St .... Weirton WV 26062 *TF:* 800-774-2429 ■ *Web:* www.weirton.lib.wv.us	304-797-8510	797-8526	434-3
Mary Institute & Saint Louis Country Day School 101 N Warson Rd .... Saint Louis MO 63124 *Web:* www.micds.org	314-993-5100		623
Mary Janes Solid Oak Furniture 5170 Chain of Rocks Rd .... Edwardsville IL 62025 *Web:* www.maryjanessolidoak.com	618-655-0299	655-0858	319-2
Mary Jurek Design Inc 2301 W 205th St Unit 114 .... Torrance CA 90501 *Web:* maryjurekdesign.com	310-533-1196	533-8545	393
Mary Kay Inc PO Box 799045 .... Dallas TX 75379 *TF:* 800-627-9529 ■ *Web:* www.marykay.com	972-687-6300		214
Mary Lanning Memorial Hospital 715 N St Joseph Ave .... Hastings NE 68901 *TF:* 800-269-0473 ■ *Web:* www.marylanning.org	402-463-4521		374-3
Mary Mahoney's 110 Rue Magnolia .... Biloxi MS 39530 *Web:* www.marymahoneys.com	228-374-0163		671
Mary Maxim Inc 2001 Holland Ave PO Box 5019 .... Port Huron MI 48061 *TF:* 800-962-9504 ■ *Web:* www.marymaxim.com	810-987-2000	987-5056	459
Mary Maxim Ltd 75 Scott Ave .... Paris ON N3L3G5 *TF:* 888-442-2266 ■ *Web:* www.marymaxim.ca	888-442-2266		761
Mary McLeod Bethune Council House National Historic Site 1318 Vermont Ave NW .... Washington DC 20005 *Web:* www.nps.gov	202-673-2402		564
Mary Means + Associates 3419 Pendleton Dr .... Silver Spring MD 20902 *Web:* www.marymeans.com	703-582-9165		196
Mary Pomerantz Advertising 300 Raritan Ave .... Highland Park NJ 08904 *Web:* www.marypomerantzadvertising.com	732-214-9600		7
Mary Rutan Hospital 205 E Palmer Rd .... Bellefontaine OH 43311 *Web:* www.maryrutan.org	937-592-4015	592-0207	374-7
Mary Ryan Gallery 515 W 26th St .... New York NY 10001 *Web:* maryryangallery.com	212-397-0669		42
Mary Siebert Insurance Agency LLC 520 Gravois Rd .... Fenton MO 63026 *Web:* siebertinsurance.net	636-343-4000	343-6039	390
Mary Todd Lincoln House 578 W Main St .... Lexington KY 40507 *Web:* www.mtlhouse.org	859-233-9999		50-3
Mary Washington Hospice 5012 Southpoint Pkwy .... Fredericksburg VA 22407 *TF:* 800-257-1667 ■ *Web:* www.marywashingtonhealthcare.com	540-741-1667		371
Mary-Anne Martin Fine Art 23 E 73rd St 4th Fl .... New York NY 10021 *Web:* mamfa.com	212-288-2213	861-7656	42
Maryanov Madsen Gordon & Campbell CPA 801 E Tahquitz Canyon Way Ste 200 PO Box 1826 .... Palm Springs CA 92262 *Web:* mmgccpa.com	760-320-6642	327-6854	401
Marycrest Assisted Living 2850 Columbine Rd .... Denver CO 80221 *Web:* marycrest.org	303-433-0282		673
Marycrest Manor 15475 Middlebelt Rd .... Livonia MI 48154 *Web:* www.trinityhealthseniorcommunities.org	734-427-9175		672
Marygrove College 8425 W McNichols Rd .... Detroit MI 48221 *Web:* www.marygrove.edu	313-927-1200		166
Maryhill State Park 50 Hwy 97 .... Goldendale WA 98620 *Web:* www.parks.state.wa.us	509-773-5007		565
Maryland *Administrative Office of the Courts* 580 Taylor Ave .... Annapolis MD 21401 *Web:* courts.state.md.us	410-260-1400		339-21

	Phone	Fax	Class
Aging Dept 301 W Preston St Ste 1007 .... Baltimore MD 21201 *TF:* 800-243-3425 ■ *Web:* www.aging.maryland.gov	410-767-1100	333-7943	339-21
Agriculture Dept 50 Harry S Truman Pkwy .... Annapolis MD 21401 *Web:* www.mda.maryland.gov	410-841-5700	841-5914	339-21
Assessments & Taxation Dept 301 W Preston St........................ Baltimore MD 21201 *TF:* 888-246-5941 ■ *Web:* www.dat.maryland.gov	410-767-1184		339-21
Business & Economic Development Dept 217 E Redwood St....................... Baltimore MD 21202 *Web:* commerce.maryland.gov	410-767-6300		339-21
Chief Medical Examiner 900 W Baltimore St...................... Baltimore MD 21223 *Web:* www.health.maryland.gov	410-333-3250	333-3063	339-21
Criminal Injuries Compensation Board 6776 Reisterstown Rd Ste 311B............ Baltimore MD 21215 *Web:* msa.maryland.gov	410-339-5065	764-3815	339-21
Department of Budget & Management 45 Calvert St .... Annapolis MD 21401 *TF:* 800-705-3493 ■ *Web:* www.dbm.maryland.gov	800-705-3493		339-21
Department of Housing And Community Development 7800 Harkins Rd .... Lanham MD 20706 *Web:* dhcd.maryland.gov	301-429-7400		339-21
Department of Legislative Services 90 State Cir .... Annapolis MD 21401 *Web:* msa.maryland.gov	410-946-5500		433
Department of Public Safety & Correctional Services 300 East Joppa Rd Ste 1000 .... Towson MD 21286 *Web:* www.dpscs.maryland.gov	410-339-5000		339-21
Education Dept 200 W Baltimore St........... Baltimore MD 21201 *TF:* 888-246-0016 ■ *Web:* www.marylandpublicschools.org	410-767-0100		339-21
Emergency Management Agency 5401 Rue St Lo Dr.................... Reisterstown MD 21136 *TF:* 877-636-2872 ■ *Web:* www.mema.maryland.gov	410-517-3600	517-3610	339-21
Environment Dept 1800 Washington Blvd.................... Baltimore MD 21230 *TF:* 800-633-6101 ■ *Web:* www.mde.maryland.gov	410-537-3000		339-21
Ethics Commission 45 Calvert St .... Annapolis MD 21401 *TF:* 877-669-6085 ■ *Web:* ethics.maryland.gov	410-260-7770	260-7746	265
Financial Regulation Div 500 N Calvert St Ste 402.................. Baltimore MD 21202 *TF:* 888-784-0136 ■ *Web:* www.dllr.state.md.us	410-230-6100	333-0475	339-21
General Assembly 134 Holiday Ct Ste 316 .... Annapolis MD 21401 *Web:* www.mlis.state.md.us	410-841-3766	841-3850	339-21
Health & Mental Hygiene Dept 201 W Preston St 5th Fl................... Baltimore MD 21201 *Web:* www.health.maryland.gov	410-767-6500		339-21
Higher Education Commission 839 Bestgate Rd Ste 400 .... Baltimore MD 21201 *TF:* 800-974-0203 ■ *Web:* www.mhec.state.md.us	410-260-4500	260-3200	339-21
Historical & Cultural Programs Div 909 Woodward Ln 3rd Fl................ Crownsville MD 21032 *Web:* www.marylandhistoricaltrust.net	410-514-7648	514-7678	339-21
Insurance Administration 200 St Paul Pl Ste 2700.................. Baltimore MD 21202 *TF:* 800-492-6116 ■ *Web:* www.mdinsurance.state.md.us	410-468-2000	468-2020	339-21
Labor & Industry Div 1100 N Eutaw St Rm 600................. Baltimore MD 21201 *TF:* 888-257-6674 ■ *Web:* www.dllr.state.md.us	410-767-2241	767-2986	339-21
Motor Vehicle Administration 6601 Ritchie Hwy NE................... Glen Burnie MD 21062 *TF:* 800-950-1682 ■ *Web:* www.mva.maryland.gov	410-768-7000		339-21
Parole & Probation Div 6776 Reisterstown Rd .... Baltimore MD 21215 *Web:* msa.maryland.gov	410-585-3500		339-21
Physician Quality Assurance Board 4201 Patterson Ave...................... Baltimore MD 21215 *TF:* 800-492-6836 ■ *Web:* www.mbp.state.md.us	410-764-4777	358-2252	339-21
Public Service Commission 6 St Paul St 16th Fl...................... Baltimore MD 21202 *TF:* 800-492-0474 ■ *Web:* www.psc.state.md.us	410-767-8000	333-6495	339-21
Racing Commission 300 E Towsontown Blvd.................... Towson MD 21286 *Web:* www.dllr.state.md.us	410-296-9682	296-9687	339-21
Secretary of State 16 Francis St............. Annapolis MD 21401 *TF:* 888-373-7888 ■ *Web:* www.sos.state.md.us	410-974-5521	974-5190	339-21
Securities Div 200 St Paul Pl................. Baltimore MD 21202 *TF:* 888-743-0023 ■ *Web:* www.marylandattorneygeneral.gov	410-576-6360		339-21
Social Services Administration 311 W Saratoga St....................... Baltimore MD 21201 *Web:* dhr.maryland.gov	410-767-7216		339-21
State Arts Council 175 W Ostend St Ste E.................... Baltimore MD 21230 *Web:* www.msac.org	410-767-6555	333-1062	339-21
State Athletic Commission 500 N Calvert St......................... Baltimore MD 21202 *Web:* www.dllr.state.md.us	410-230-6223	962-8480	712
State Police 1201 Reisterstown Rd .... Pikesville MD 21208 *TF:* 800-525-5555 ■ *Web:* www.mdsp.maryland.gov	410-653-4200		339-21
Tourism Development Office 401 E Pratt Str 14th Fl.................... Baltimore MD 21202 *TF:* 877-333-4455 ■ *Web:* www.visitmaryland.org	410-767-3400		339-21
Treasurer 80 Calvert St Rm 109.............. Annapolis MD 21401 *TF:* 800-974-0468 ■ *Web:* www.treasurer.state.md.us	410-260-7533		339-21
Veterans Affairs Dept 16 Francis St 4th Fl..................... Annapolis MD 21401 *Web:* veterans.maryland.gov	410-260-3838		339-21
Vital Records Div 6764-B Reisterstown Rd .... Baltimore MD 21215 *TF:* 800-832-3277 ■ *Web:* www.health.maryland.gov	410-764-3038		339-21
Workforce Development Div 1100 N Eutaw St Rm 505.................. Baltimore MD 21201 *Web:* www.dllr.state.md.us	410-767-2173	767-2986	259
Maryland & Virginia Milk Producers Cooperative Association Inc 1985 Isaac Newton Sq W .... Reston VA 20190 *TF:* 800-552-1976 ■ *Web:* www.mdvamilk.com	703-742-6000	742-7450	297-4

	Phone	Fax	Class
Maryland Art Place (MAP) 218 W Saratoga St......................... Baltimore MD 21201 *Web:* www.mdartplace.org	410-962-8565		50-2
Maryland Association of Counties (MACO) 169 Conduit St........................... Annapolis MD 21401 *Web:* www.mdcounties.org	410-269-0043	268-1775	49-7
Maryland Association of Realtors 2594 Riva Rd .... Annapolis MD 21401 *Fax Area Code: 301 ■ *TF:* 800-638-6425 ■ *Web:* www.mdrealtor.org	800-638-6425	261-8369*	656
Maryland Bartending Academy 209 New Jersey Ave NE .... Glen Burnie MD 21060 *Web:* www.marylandbartending.com	410-787-0020		800
Maryland Beachcomber 12417 Ocean Gateway Ste A-7............... Ocean City MD 21842 *Web:* www.mddcpress.com	410-213-9442		532-4
Maryland Ceramic & Steatite Company Inc PO Box 527 .... Bel Air MD 21014 *Web:* marylandceramic.com	410-838-4114	457-4333	249
Maryland Chamber of Commerce 60 W St Ste 100........................... Annapolis MD 21401 *Web:* mdchamber.org	410-269-0642	269-5247	140
Maryland Cork Company Inc 190 Triumph Industrial Park Dr Ste 190 .... Elkton MD 21921 *TF:* 800-662-2675 ■ *Web:* www.marylandcork.com	410-398-2955	392-9433	209
Maryland Correctional Enterprises (MCE) 7275 Waterloo Rd............................ Jessup MD 20794 *Web:* mce.md.gov	410-540-5454	540-5570	630
Maryland Federation of Art Cir Gallery (MFA) 18 State Cir.............................. Annapolis MD 21401 *Web:* mdfedart.com	410-268-4566		50-2
Maryland Film Festival 34 E 25th St........... Baltimore MD 21218 *Web:* mdfilmfest.com	410-752-8083		282
Maryland Hall for the Creative Arts 801 Chase St .... Annapolis MD 21401 *TF:* 866-438-3808 ■ *Web:* marylandhall.org	410-263-5544	263-5114	572
Maryland Health Enterprises Inc 3300 N Ridge Rd Ste 390.................. Ellicott City MD 21043 *Web:* www.lorienhealth.com	410-750-7500		194
Maryland Heights Chamber of Commerce 547 W Port Plz .... Saint Louis MO 63146 *Web:* www.mhcc.com	314-576-6603	576-6855	139
Maryland Historical Society 201 W Monument St......................... Baltimore MD 21201 *Web:* www.mdhs.org	410-685-3750		520
Maryland Institute College of Art 1300 W Mt Royal Ave....................... Baltimore MD 21217 *Web:* www.mica.edu	410-669-9200	225-2337	164
Maryland Library Assn (MLA) 1401 Hollins St............................ Baltimore MD 21223 *Web:* www.mdlib.org	410-947-5090	947-5089	435
Maryland Lottery 1800 Washington Blvd Ste 330 .... Baltimore MD 21230 *Web:* www.mdlottery.com	410-230-8800		452
Maryland Match Corp 605 Alluvion St .... Baltimore MD 21230 *TF:* 800-423-0013 ■ *Web:* www.marylandmatch.com	410-752-8164	752-3441	469
Maryland Municipal League 1212 W St....... Annapolis MD 21401 *TF:* 800-492-7121 ■ *Web:* www.mdmunicipal.org	410-295-9100		533
Maryland Museums Assn (MMA) c/o Historic London Town 839 Londontown Road .... Edgewater MD 21037 *Web:* www.mdmuseums.org	410-222-1919		48-13
Maryland Nurses Assn (MNA) 21 Governor's Ct Ste 195 .... Baltimore MD 21244 *Web:* www.marylandrn.org	410-944-5800		533
Maryland Pharmacists Assn 9115 Guilford Rd Ste 200.................... Columbia MD 21046 *Web:* www.marylandpharmacist.org	410-727-0746	727-2253	585
Maryland Plastics Inc 251 E Central Ave........................ Federalsburg MD 21632 *TF:* 800-544-5582 ■ *Web:* www.marylandplastics.com	410-754-5566		607
Maryland Public Interest Research Group (MARYPIRG) 3121 St Paul St Ste 26...................... Baltimore MD 21218 *Web:* marylandpirg.org	410-467-0439	366-2051	633
Maryland Public Television (MPT) 11767 Owings Mills Blvd................. Owings Mills MD 21117 *TF:* 800-223-3678 ■ *Web:* www.mpt.org	410-581-4201	581-4338	632
Maryland Renaissance Festival PO Box 315 .... Crownsville MD 21032 *TF:* 800-296-7304 ■ *Web:* www.rennfest.com	410-266-7304	573-1508	149
Maryland Republican Party PO Box 631 .... Annapolis MD 21401 *Web:* mdgop.org	443-906-3534		616-2
Maryland Science Ctr 601 Light St............ Baltimore MD 21230 *Web:* www.mdsci.org	410-685-2370	545-5974	520
Maryland State Archives 350 Rowe Blvd .... Annapolis MD 21401 *Web:* www.msa.maryland.gov	410-260-6400		339-21
Maryland State Bar Association Inc 520 W Fayette St.......................... Baltimore MD 21201 *TF:* 800-492-1964 ■ *Web:* www.msba.org	410-685-7878	685-1016	72
Maryland State Dental Assn 8901 Herrmann Dr .... Columbia MD 21045 *Web:* www.msda.com	410-964-2880	964-0583	227
Maryland State Medical Society 1211 Cathedral St.......................... Baltimore MD 21201 *TF:* 800-492-1056 ■ *Web:* www.medchi.org	410-539-0872	547-0915	474
Maryland Symphony Orchestra, The 30 W Washington St...................... Hagerstown MD 21740 *Web:* www.marylandsymphony.org	301-797-4000	797-2314	573-3
Maryland Theatre 21 S Potomac St........... Hagerstown MD 21740 *Web:* www.mdtheatre.org	301-790-3500	791-6114	572
Maryland Thermoform Corp 2717 Wilmarco Ave......................... Baltimore MD 21223 *Web:* mdthermo.com	410-947-5063		596
Maryland Transit Administration (MTA) 6 St Paul St.............................. Baltimore MD 21202 *TF:* 866-743-3682 ■ *Web:* www.mta.maryland.gov	410-539-5000	333-4810	468

Name	Address	City	State	ZIP	Phone	Fax	Class
Maryland University of Integrative Health	7750 Montpelier Rd *TF:* 800-735-2968 ■ *Web:* www.muih.edu	Laurel	MD	20723	410-888-9048	888-9239	166
Maryland Veterinary Medical Assn	PO Box 5407 *Web:* mdvma.org	Annapolis	MD	21403	410-268-1311	931-2060	795
Maryland Workers Compensation Commission	10 E Baltimore St *TF:* 800-492-0479 ■ *Web:* www.wcc.state.md.us	Baltimore	MD	21202	410-864-5100		339-21
Maryland Zoo in Baltimore	1876 Mansion House Dr *Web:* www.marylandzoo.org	Baltimore	MD	21217	410-396-7102		823
Maryland-National Capital Park and Planning Commission (M-NCPPC)	6611 Kenilworth Ave *Web:* www.mncppc.org	Riverdale	MD	20737	301-699-2255		637-2
Marylhurst University	17600 Pacific Hwy 43 PO Box 261 *TF:* 800-634-9982 ■ *Web:* www.marylhurst.edu	Marylhurst	OR	97036	503-636-8141	635-6585	166
Marymount California University	30800 Palos Verdes Dr E *Web:* www.marymountcalifornia.edu	Rancho Palos Verdes	CA	90275	310-377-5501	377-6223	786
Marymount Manhattan College	221 E 71st St *Web:* www.mmm.edu	New York	NY	10021	212-517-0400	517-0448	166
Marymount University	2807 N Glebe Rd *TF:* 800-548-7638 ■ *Web:* www.marymount.edu	Arlington	VA	22207	703-522-5600	522-0349	166
MARYPIRG (Maryland Public Interest Research Group)	3121 St Paul St Ste 26 *Web:* marylandpirg.org	Baltimore	MD	21218	410-467-0439	366-2051	633
Marysville House	153 Main St *Web:* www.marysvillehouse.com	Marysville	MT	59640	406-443-6677		671
Marysville Mutual Insurance Co	1001 Broadway *Web:* www.marysvillemutual.com	Marysville	KS	66508	785-562-2379	562-5235	391-4
Maryville College	502 E Lamar Alexander Pkwy *TF:* 800-597-2687 ■ *Web:* www.maryvillecollege.edu	Maryville	TN	37804	865-981-8000	981-8005	166
Marywood University Arboretum	2300 Adams Ave *Web:* www.marywood.edu	Scranton	PA	18509	570-348-6218		97
Marzano	516 Garfield St S *Web:* www.dinemarzano.com	Tacoma	WA	98444	253-537-4191		671
Marzolf Company Inc, The	N8705 County Rd W *Web:* www.marzolf.com	River Falls	WI	54022	715-426-5705	426-5708	455
Marzouk and Parry	1901 Pennsylvania Ave NW *Web:* www.mptechlaw.com	Washington	DC	20006	202-463-7293	955-9371	41
Marzulla Law LLC	1150 Connecticut Ave NW Ste 1050 *Web:* marzulla.com	Washington	DC	20036	202-822-6760	822-6774	41
MAS Capital Inc	2715 Coney Island Ave *TF:* 866-553-7493 ■ *Web:* www.mascapital.com	Brooklyn	NY	11235	866-553-7493		691
Masa Fujioka and Associates (MFA)	98-021 Kamehameha Hwy Ste 337 *Web:* www.masa-fujioka-associates.com	Aiea	HI	96701	808-484-5366	484-0007	192
Masami Foods Inc	5222 Tingley Ln *Web:* www.masami-foods.com	Klamath Falls	OR	97603	541-884-1735		473
Maschmeyer Concrete Company of Florida	1142 Watertower Rd *Web:* www.maschmeyer.com	Lake Park	FL	33403	561-844-9994		182
Maschoff Brennan	1389 Center Dr Ste 300 *Web:* maschoffbrennan.com	Park City	UT	84098	435-252-1360		41
Maschoff Design Engineering Inc	1325 Kenilworth Dr	Woodbury	MN	55125	651-578-3565		261
Masco Cabinetry LLC	5353 W US 223 *TF:* 866-850-8557 ■ *Web:* www.merillat.com	Adrian	MI	49221	517-263-0771	265-3325	115
Masco Corp	17450 College Pky *NYSE:* MAS ■ *TF:* 888-712-3217 ■ *Web:* www.masco.com	Livonia	MI	48152	313-274-7400	792-4177	609
Mascott Equipment Company Inc	435 NE Hancock St *TF:* 800-452-5019 ■ *Web:* mascottec.com	Portland	OR	97212	503-282-2587	288-9664	480
Maser Consulting PA	331 Newman Springs Rd Ste 203 *Web:* www.maserconsulting.com	Red Bank	NJ	07701	732-383-1950	383-1984	261
Maser's Academy of Fine Grooming	6515 NE 181st St PO Box 82344 *Web:* www.masers.com	Kenmore	WA	98028	425-485-1500		167-3
Masergy	2740 N Dallas Pkwy **Fax Area Code: 214* ■ *TF:* 866-588-5885 ■ *Web:* www.masergy.com	Plano	TX	75093	866-588-5885	442-5756*	224
Mash Studios Inc	2611 W Exposition Blvd *Web:* mashstudios.com	Los Angeles	CA	90018	310-313-4700		321
Mashamoquet Brook State Park	147 Wolf Den Dr *Web:* portal.ct.gov	Pomfret	CT	06259	860-928-6121		565
Masimo Corp	40 Parker *TF:* 800-326-4890 ■ *Web:* www.masimo.com	Irvine	CA	92618	949-297-7000		250
Mask-Off Company Inc	345 W Maple Ave PO Box 1148 *Web:* www.mask-off.com	Monrovia	CA	91016	626-359-3261	359-7160	3
Masland Carpets Inc	716 Bill Myles Dr *TF:* 800-633-0468 ■ *Web:* www.maslandcarpets.com	Saraland	AL	36571	800-633-0468		131
Maslon Edelman Borman & Brand LLP	3300 Wells Fargo Ctr 90 S Seventh St *Web:* www.maslon.com	Minneapolis	MN	55402	612-672-8200		428
Maslow Media Group Inc, The	2233 Wisconsin Ave NW Ste 400 *Web:* www.maslowmedia.com	Washington	DC	20007	202-965-1100		514
Mason & Associates LLC	11827 Canon Blvd Ste 204 *Web:* masonllc.net	Newport News	VA	23606	757-223-9898		390
Mason & Blair LLC	1762 Technology Dr Ste 206 *Web:* masonblair.com	San Jose	CA	95110	408-436-6300		260
Mason & Carter Inc	23 South St *Web:* masoncarter.com	Baltimore	MD	21202	410-539-6767		390
Mason & Hamlin Piano Co	35 Duncan St *Web:* www.masonhamlin.com	Haverhill	MA	01830	978-374-8888	374-8080	527
Mason Assocaites Inc	170 Us Rt 1 Ste 280 *Web:* www.masonassociates.com	Falmouth	ME	04105	207-347-3557		180
Mason City Area Chamber of Commerce	25 W State St *Web:* www.masoncityia.com	Mason City	IA	50401	641-423-5724	423-5725	139
Mason City Convention & Visitors Bureau	2021 Fourth St SW Hwy 122 W *TF:* 800-423-5724 ■ *Web:* visitmasoncityiowa.com	Mason City	IA	50401	641-422-1663		206
Mason City National Bank	104 W Pine St PO Box 152 *Web:* onlinebanking.masoncitynationalbank.com	Mason City	IL	62664	217-482-3246	482-3823	70
Mason City Public Library	225 2nd St SE *Web:* www.masoncity.lib.ia.us	Mason City	IA	50401	641-421-3668		434-3
Mason City Schools	211 NE St *Web:* www.masonohioschools.com	Mason	OH	45040	513-398-0474		780
Mason Contractors Association of America (MCCA) (MCAA)	1481 Merchant Dr *TF:* 800-536-2225 ■ *Web:* www.masoncontractors.org	Algonquin	IL	60102	224-678-9709	678-9714	49-3
Mason Controls	13955 Balboa Blvd *Web:* www.masoncontrols.com	Sylmar	CA	91342	818-361-3366	365-6809	504
Mason County	125 N Plum *Web:* www.masoncountyil.org	Havana	IL	62644	309-543-6661	543-2085	338
Mason County	304 E Ludington Ave *Web:* www.masoncounty.net	Ludington	MI	49431	231-843-8202	843-1972	338
Mason County	PO Box 702 *Web:* www.co.mason.tx.us	Mason	TX	76856	325-347-5253	347-6868	338
Mason County	200 Sixth St *Web:* www.masoncounty.wv.gov	Point Pleasant	WV	25550	304-675-1110	675-4982	338
Mason County	419 N Fourth St PO Box 340 *TF:* 800-833-6384 ■ *Web:* www.co.mason.wa.us	Shelton	WA	98584	360-427-9670	427-7787	338
Mason County Area Chamber of Commerce	305 Main St *Web:* www.masoncountychamber.org	Point Pleasant	WV	25550	304-675-1050	675-1601	139
Mason County Garbage & Recycling	81 E Wilburs Way PO Box 787 *TF:* 877-722-0223 ■ *Web:* www.masoncountygarbage.com	Shelton	WA	98584	360-426-8729	427-0319	660
Mason County Public Library	508 Viand St *Web:* masoncounty.lib.wv.us	Point Pleasant	WV	25550	304-675-0894	675-0895	434-3
Mason Enterprise Center - Leesburg/Loudoun	202 Church St SE *Web:* masonenterprisecenterloudoun.com	Leesburg	VA	20175	703-466-0466		393
Mason Horvath Inc	999 Canada Pl Ste 404 *Web:* masonhorvath.com	Vancouver	BC	V6C3E2	604-899-9498		774
Mason Inc	23 Amity Rd *Web:* www.mason23.com	Bethany	CT	06524	203-393-1101		5
Mason Industries Inc	350 Rabro Dr *Web:* mason-ind.com	Hauppauge	NY	11788	631-348-0282		472
Mason Jar, The	2925 W Colorado Ave *Web:* www.masonjarcolorado.com	Colorado Springs	CO	80904	719-632-4820		671
Mason Machinings Inc	1015 Jaybird Rd *Web:* www.masonmachinings.net	Morristown	TN	37814	423-586-2555	581-6616	455
Mason Manufacturing LLC	1645 N Railroad Ave *Web:* www.masonmfg.com	Decatur	IL	62524	217-422-2770		361
Mason Structural Steel Inc	7500 Northfield Rd *TF:* 800-686-1223 ■ *Web:* www.masonsteel.com	Walton Hills	OH	44146	440-439-1040		362
Mason Wells	411 E Wisconsin Ave Ste 1280 *Web:* www.masonwells.com	Milwaukee	WI	53202	414-727-6400	727-6410	402
Mason West Inc	1601 E Miraloma Ave *Web:* www.masonwest.com	Placentia	CA	92870	714-630-0701		358
Mason, Griffin & Pierson PC	101 Poor Farm Rd *Web:* www.mgplaw.com	Princeton	NJ	08540	609-921-6543		428
MasonBaronet Inc	1801 N Lamar St Ste 250 *Web:* masonbaronet.com	Dallas	TX	75202	214-954-0316		7
Mason-Dixon Historical Park	79 Buckeye Rd *Web:* www.masondixonhistoricalpark.com	Core	WV	26541	304-879-4101		50-4
Masonic	22 Masonic Ave *Web:* www.masonicare.org	Wallingford	CT	06492	203-679-5900		450
Masonic Grand Lodge Library and Museum of Texas	PO Box 446 *Web:* www.grandlodgeoftexas.org	Waco	TX	76703	254-753-7395	753-2944	434-3
Masonic Service Association of North America (MSANA)	8120 Fenton St Ste 203 *TF:* 855-476-4010 ■ *Web:* www.msana.com	Silver Spring	MD	20910	301-588-4010	608-3457	48-15
Masonic Temple Theatre	3011 West Grand Blvd *Web:* www.themasonic.com	Detroit	MI	48201	313-832-7100		572
Masonic Villages of Pennsylvania	1 Masonic Dr *Web:* www.masonicvillages.org	Elizabethtown	PA	17022	717-367-1121		793
Masonic, The	1111 California St *Web:* sfmasonic.com	San Francisco	CA	94108	415-776-7457		205
Masonite International Corp	201 N Franklin St Ste 300 *TF:* 800-895-2723 ■ *Web:* www.masonite.com	Tampa	FL	33602	813-877-2726	739-0204	236
Masonry Arts Inc	2 21st St N *Web:* www.masonryarts.com	Bessemer	AL	35020	205-428-0780	424-1931	189-7

	Phone	Fax	Class
Masonry Products Sales Inc 410 N Alexander St. . . . . New Orleans LA 70119 *Web:* www.masonryproducts.com	504-488-2647		191-1
Masonry Reinforcing Corporation of America 400 Roundtree Rd. . . . . Charlotte NC 28224 *Web:* wirebond.com	704-525-5554		480
Masonry Technology Inc 24235 Electric St . . . . Cresco IA 52136 *Web:* www.iqpowertools.com	563-547-1122		608
Maspeth Federal Savings 56-18 69th St . . . . Maspeth NY 11378 *TF:* 888-558-1300 ■ *Web:* www.maspethfederal.com	718-335-1300	446-3671	70
Masraff's 1025 S Post Oak Ln . . . . Houston TX 77056 *Web:* www.masraffs.com	713-355-1975	355-1965	671
Mass Bay Transportation Authority (MBTA) 10 Park Plz Ste 5610 . . . . Boston MA 02116 *TF:* 800-392-6100 ■ *Web:* www.mbta.com	617-222-3200		546
Mass Connections Inc 13131 E 166th St . . . . Cerritos CA 90703	562-365-0200		195
Mass Live Media 1350 Main St . . . . Springfield MA 01103 *TF:* 800-246-0855 ■ *Web:* www.masslivemedia.com	800-246-0855		6
Mass Media Inc 883 Patriot Dr. . . . . Moorpark CA 93021 *Web:* www.massmedia.com	805-531-9399		225
Mass Movement Inc 65 Green St Ste 1 . . . . Foxborough MA 02035 *Web:* www.massmovement.com	508-543-2073	543-4036	711
Mass Precision Sheetmetal Inc 2110 Oakland Rd . . . . San Jose CA 95131 *Web:* www.massprecision.com	408-954-0200		488
Massa Products Corp 280 Lincoln St . . . . Hingham MA 02043 *TF:* 800-962-7543 ■ *Web:* www.massa.com	781-749-4800		668
Massachusetts			
Attorney General 1 Ashburton Pl . . . . Boston MA 02108 *Web:* www.mass.gov	617-727-4100		339-22
Banks Div 1000 Washington St 1st Fl . . . . Boston MA 02118 *TF:* 800-495-2265 ■ *Web:* www.mass.gov	617-521-7478	956-1599	339-22
Business Development Office 136 Blackstone St 5th Fl . . . . Boston MA 02109 *Web:* www.mass.gov	617-973-8600	973-8554	339-22
Child Support Enforcement Div 51 Sleeper St 4th Fl. . . . . Boston MA 02205 *TF:* 800-332-2733 ■ *Web:* www.mass.gov	617-660-1234		339-22
Correction Dept 50 Maple St Ste 3 . . . . Milford MA 01757 *Web:* www.mass.gov	508-422-3300		339-22
Cultural Council 10 St James Ave 3rd Fl. . . . . Boston MA 02116 *Web:* www.massculturalcouncil.org	617-858-2700	727-0044	339-22
Department of Elementary & Secondary Education 350 Main St. . . . . Malden MA 02148 *Web:* www.doe.mass.edu	781-338-3000		339-22
Emergency Management Agency 400 Worcester Rd . . . . Framingham MA 01702 *Web:* www.mass.gov	508-820-2000	820-2030	339-22
Environmental Protection Dept 1 Winter St. . . . . Boston MA 02108 *Web:* www.mass.gov	617-292-5500		339-22
Executive Office of Transportation 10 Park Plz Ste 4160 . . . . Boston MA 02116 *Web:* www.mass.gov	617-973-7000	973-8031	339-22
Fish & Game Dept 251 Cswy St Ste 400 . . . . Boston MA 02114 *Web:* www.mass.gov	617-626-1500	626-1505	339-22
General Court State House Rm 174. . . . . Boston MA 02133 *Web:* malegislature.gov	617-722-2140		339-22
Governor 24 Beacon St State House Rm 280 . . . . Boston MA 02133 *TF:* 888-870-7770 ■ *Web:* www.mass.gov	617-722-1673	727-9725	339-22
Higher Education Board 1 Ashburton Pl Rm 1401 . . . . Boston MA 02108 *Web:* www.mass.edu	617-994-6950	727-6397	339-22
Housing Finance Agency 1 Beacon St. . . . . Boston MA 02108 *TF:* 800-882-1154 ■ *Web:* www.masshousing.com	617-854-1000	854-1029	339-22
Information Technology Div 200 Arlington St. . . . . Chelsea MA 02150 *Web:* www.mass.gov	617-660-5530		339-22
Insurance Div 1000 Washington St Ste 810. . . . . Boston MA 02118 *TF:* 877-563-4467 ■ *Web:* www.mass.gov	617-521-7794	753-6830	339-22
Medical Examiner 720 Albany St. . . . . Boston MA 02118 *TF:* 800-962-7877 ■ *Web:* www.mass.gov	617-267-6767	266-6763	339-22
Mental Health Dept 25 Staniford St . . . . Boston MA 02114 *TF:* 800-221-0053 ■ *Web:* www.mass.gov	617-626-8000		339-22
Parole Board 12 Mercer Rd . . . . Natick MA 01760 *TF:* 888-298-6272 ■ *Web:* www.mass.gov	508-650-4500	650-4599	339-22
Professional Licensure Div 1000 Washington St Ste 710. . . . . Boston MA 02118 *Web:* www.mass.gov	617-727-3074	727-1944	339-22
Public Health Dept 250 Washington St . . . . Boston MA 02108 *Web:* www.mass.gov	617-624-6000		339-22
Public Utilities Dept 100 Cambridge St Ste 900. . . . . Boston MA 02114 *Web:* www.mass.gov	617-626-1000	626-1181	339-22
Rehabilitation Commission 27 Wormwood St Ste 600 . . . . Boston MA 02210 *Web:* www.mass.gov	617-204-3600		339-22
Revenue Dept PO Box 7010. . . . . Boston MA 02204 *TF:* 800-392-6089 ■ *Web:* www.mass.gov	617-887-6367		339-22
Securities Div 1 Ashburton Pl 17th Fl . . . . Boston MA 02108 *TF:* 800-269-5428 ■ *Web:* www.sec.state.ma.us	617-727-3548	248-0177	339-22
Standards Div 1 Ashburton Pl Rm 1115 . . . . Boston MA 02108 *Web:* www.mass.gov	617-727-3480		339-22
State Boxing Commission 1 Ashburton Pl Rm 1301 . . . . Boston MA 02108 *Web:* www.mass.gov	617-727-3200		712
State Ethics Commission 1 Ashburton Pl Rm 619 Sixth Fl . . . . Boston MA 02108 *Web:* www.mass.gov	617-720-3300	723-5851	265
State Lottery Commission 60 Columbian St . . . . Braintree MA 02184 *Web:* www.masslottery.com	781-849-5555	849-5546	452
State Parks & Recreation Div 251 Cswy St Ste 900 . . . . Boston MA 02114 *Web:* www.mass.gov	617-626-1200	626-1351	339-22
State Police Dept 470 Worcester Rd . . . . Framingham MA 01702 *Web:* www.mass.gov	508-820-2300	820-2211	339-22
Supreme Judicial Court 1 Pemberton Sq Ste 2500 . . . . Boston MA 02108 *Web:* www.mass.gov	617-557-1000		339-22
Transitional Assistance Dept 600 Washington St . . . . Boston MA 02111 *Web:* www.mass.gov	617-748-2000		339-22
Travel & Tourism Office 136 Blackstone St 5th Fl . . . . Boston MA 02109 *TF:* 800-227-6277 ■ *Web:* www.massvacation.com	617-973-8500	973-8525	339-22
Treasurer State House Rm 227 . . . . Boston MA 02133 *Web:* www.mass.gov	617-367-6900		339-22
Veterans' Services Dept 600 Washington St 7th Fl . . . . Boston MA 02111 *Web:* www.mass.gov	617-210-5480	210-5755	339-22
Vital Records & Statistics Registry 150 Mt Vernon St 1st Fl. . . . . Dorchester MA 02125 *Web:* www.mass.gov	617-740-2600		339-22
Massachusetts Association of Realtors 333 Wyman St Ste 200. . . . . Waltham MA 02451 *TF:* 800-725-6272 ■ *Web:* www.marealtor.com	781-890-3700	890-4919	656
Massachusetts Bar Assn 20 West St . . . . Boston MA 02111 *Web:* www.mass.gov	617-338-0500		72
Massachusetts Bay Community College *Wellesley Hills* 50 Oakland St . . . . Wellesley MA 02481 *TF:* 800-233-3182 ■ *Web:* www.massbay.edu	781-239-3000	239-2561	162
Massachusetts Board of Library Commissioners 98 N Washington St . . . . Boston MA 02114 *TF:* 800-952-7403 ■ *Web:* mblc.state.ma.us	617-725-1860	725-0140	434-5
Massachusetts Capital Resource Co 420 Boylston St 5th Fl . . . . Boston MA 02116 *Web:* masscapital.com	617-536-3900		792
Massachusetts College of Art 621 Huntington Ave . . . . Boston MA 02115 *TF:* 800-834-3242 ■ *Web:* massart.edu	617-879-7222	879-7250	166
Massachusetts College of Liberal Arts 375 Church St . . . . North Adams MA 01247 *Web:* www.mcla.edu	413-662-5000	662-5179	166
Massachusetts College of Pharmacy & Health Sciences 179 Longwood Ave. . . . . Boston MA 02115 *TF:* 800-225-5506 ■ *Web:* www.mcphs.edu	617-732-2850	732-2118	166
Massachusetts Correctional Industries 50 Maple St . . . . Milford MA 01757 *Web:* www.mass.gov	508-422-1956		630
Massachusetts Correctional Institution 1 Bumps Pond Rd. . . . . South Carver MA 02366 *Web:* www.mass.gov	508-291-2441		213
Massachusetts Correctional Institution-Framingham 99 Loring Dr PO Box 9007 . . . . Framingham MA 01704 *Web:* www.mass.gov	508-532-5100		213
Massachusetts Democratic Party 11 Beacon St Ste 410 . . . . Boston MA 02108 *Web:* massdems.org	617-939-0800		616-1
Massachusetts Dental Society 2 Willow St. . . . . Southborough MA 01745 **Fax Area Code: 508* ■ *TF:* 800-342-8747 ■ *Web:* www.massdental.org	800-342-8747	480-0002*	227
Massachusetts Eye & Ear 243 Charles St . . . . Boston MA 02114 *TF:* 800-841-2900 ■ *Web:* www.masseyeandear.org	617-523-7900		374-7
Massachusetts General Hospital 55 Fruit St. . . . . Boston MA 02114 *Web:* www.massgeneral.org	617-726-2000		374-3
Massachusetts Growth Capital Corp (MGCC) 529 Main St Schrafft Ctr Ste 1M10. . . . . Charlestown MA 02129 *Web:* www.massgcc.com	617-523-6262	523-7676	792
Massachusetts Historical Society, The 1154 Boylston St . . . . Boston MA 02215 *Web:* www.masshist.org	617-646-0500	859-0074	520
Massachusetts Institute of Technology 77 Massachusetts Ave . . . . Cambridge MA 02139 *Web:* web.mit.edu	617-253-5973		166
Massachusetts Maritime Academy 101 Academy Dr. . . . . Buzzards Bay MA 02532 *TF:* 800-544-3411 ■ *Web:* www.maritime.edu	508-830-5000	830-5077	166
Massachusetts Medical Society (MMS) 860 Winter St . . . . Waltham MA 02451 *TF:* 800-322-2303 ■ *Web:* www.massmed.org	781-893-4610	893-8009	474
Massachusetts Mutual Life Insurance Co 100 Bright Meadow Blvd . . . . Enfield CT 06082 *TF:* 800-272-2216 ■ *Web:* www.massmutual.com	800-272-2216		391-2
Massachusetts National Cemetery Conery Ave. . . . . Bourne MA 02532 *Web:* www.cem.va.gov	508-563-7113	564-9946	136
Massachusetts Nurses Assn (MNA) 340 Tpke St . . . . Canton MA 02021 *TF:* 800-882-2056 ■ *Web:* www.massnurses.org	781-821-4625	821-4445	533
Massachusetts Pharmacists Assn (MPHA) 500 W Cummings Pk Ste 3475. . . . . Woburn MA 01801 *Web:* www.masspharmacists.org	781-933-1107	933-1109	585
Massachusetts Port Authority 1 Harborside Dr Ste 200S. . . . . East Boston MA 02128 *Web:* www.massport.com	617-568-7300		618
Massachusetts Public Interest Research Group (MASSPIRG) 294 Washington St Ste 500 . . . . Boston MA 02108 *Web:* masspirg.org	617-292-4800		633
Massachusetts Registry of Motor Vehicles			
Boston (Haymarket) RMV Service Center 36 Blackstone St . . . . Boston MA 02205 *Web:* www.mass.gov	617-351-4500		339-22
Massachusetts Republican State Committee 85 Merrimac St Ste 400 . . . . Boston MA 02114 *Web:* www.massgop.com	617-523-5005		616-2
Massachusetts School of Barbering 58 Ross Way. . . . . Quincy MA 02169 *Web:* www.massschoolofbarbering.com	617-770-4444		685
Massachusetts Society of CPAS 105 Chauncy St 10th Fl . . . . Boston MA 02111 *TF:* 800-392-6145 ■ *Web:* www.mscpaonline.org	617-556-4000		2

				Phone	Fax	Class
Massachusetts Symphony Orchestra Tuckerman Hall Po Box 20070 *Web:* www.masymphony.org	Worcester	MA	01602	508-754-1234		573-3
Massachusetts Veterinary Medical Assn 163Lakeside Ave *Web:* www.massvet.org	Marlborough	MA	01752	508-460-9333	460-9969	795
Massacre Rocks State Park 3592 N Pk Ln *Web:* parksandrecreation.idaho.gov	American Falls	ID	83211	208-548-2672		565
Massage Therapy Center Palo Alto 368 S California Ave *Web:* www.massagetherapypaloalto.com	Palo Alto	CA	94306	650-328-9400		167-3
Massage Therapy Institute of Colorado 1441 York St Ste 301 *Web:* www.mtic.edu	Denver	CO	80206	303-329-6345		167-3
Massage Warehouse 360 Veterans Pky Ste 115 **Fax Area Code:* 888 ■ *TF:* 800-910-9955 ■ *Web:* www.massagewarehouse.com	Bolingbrook	IL	60440	630-771-7400	674-4380*	76
Massage Works Clinic & School of Massage 201 W Jefferson St Ste A PO Box 1033 *Web:* www.massageschooloftherapy.com	Mountain View	AR	72560	870-269-6101		685
Massanutten Military Academy 614 S Main St *TF:* 877-466-6222 ■ *Web:* www.militaryschool.com	Woodstock	VA	22664	540-459-2167	459-5421	622
Massanutten Regional Library 174 S Main St *Web:* www.mrlib.org	Harrisonburg	VA	22801	540-434-4475		434-3
Massanutten Resort 1822 Resort Dr *Web:* www.massresort.com	McGaheysville	VA	22840	540-289-9441	289-6981	669
Massanutten Technical Ctr 325 Pleasant Valley Rd *Web:* www.mtcva.com	Harrisonburg	VA	22801	540-434-5962		167-3
Massaro Properties LLC 120 Delta Dr *Web:* www.massaroproperties.com	Pittsburgh	PA	15238	412-963-2800		652
Massasoit Community College 1 Massasoit Blvd *TF:* 800-434-6000 ■ *Web:* www.massasoit.edu	Brockton	MA	02302	508-588-9100	427-1255	162
Massasoit State Park Middleboro Ave *Web:* www.mass.gov	East Taunton	MA	02718	508-828-4231		565
massAV 3 Radcliff Rd *TF:* 800-423-7830 ■ *Web:* www.massav.com	Tewksbury	MA	01876	800-423-7830		232
Massey Cancer Ctr *Virginia Commonwealth University* 401 College St PO Box 980037 *TF:* 877-462-7739 ■ *Web:* www.massey.vcu.edu	Richmond	VA	23298	804-828-0450	828-8453	668
Massey Fuel Inc 40 Hollister Ave *Web:* heatingoilllc.com	Bridgeport	CT	06607	203-366-6641		316
Massey Hall 178 Victoria St *Web:* www.masseyhall.com	Toronto	ON	M5B1T7	416-872-4255		572
Massey Hauling Company Inc 2315 2nd Ave E *Web:* www.masseyhauling.com	Oneonta	AL	35121	205-625-3855	625-3857	780
Massey Services Inc 315 Groveland St E *TF:* 888-262-7739 ■ *Web:* www.masseyservices.com	Orlando	FL	32804	407-645-2500		577
Massey Theatre 735 8th Ave *Web:* www.masseytheatre.com	New Westminster	BC	V3M2R2	604-517-5900	517-5901	749
Massie Thomas (Rep R - KY) 2453 Rayburn House Office Bldg *Web:* massie.house.gov	Washington	DC	20515	202-225-3465		342-2
Massillon Area Chamber of Commerce 50 North Ave NE The First North Bldg *Web:* massillonohchamber.com	Massillon	OH	44646	330-833-3146	833-8944	139
Massillon City School District 930 17th St NE *Web:* www.massillonschools.org	Massillon	OH	44646	330-830-3900	830-6537	685
Massimo's 5200 Mowry Ave *Web:* www.massimos.com	Fremont	CA	94538	510-792-2000	792-7041	671
Massini Group 4400 SW 110th Ave Ste 200 *Web:* www.massini-group.com	Beaverton	OR	97005	503-640-9800	640-9888	195
Massive Audio 2261 S Atlantic Blvd *Web:* www.massiveaudio.com	Commerce	CA	90040	323-262-2262		57
Massive Prints Inc 2035 Vista Bella Way *Web:* www.massiveinc.com	Compton	CA	90220	310-637-9050		195
Massman Automation Designs LLC 1010 E Lake St *Web:* www.massmanllc.com	Villard	MN	56385	320-554-3611	554-2650	547
Massman Construction Co 4400 W 109th St *Web:* www.massman.net	Overland Park	KS	66211	913-291-2600	291-2601	188-5
MassMutual Ctr 1277 Main St *Web:* www.massmutualcenter.com	Springfield	MA	01103	413-787-6610	787-6645	205
Masson & Associates Inc 200 E Washington Ave Ste 200 *Web:* masson-assoc.com	Escondido	CA	92025	760-741-3570		261
Massoud Furniture Manufacturing Inc 8351 Moberly Ln *Web:* www.massoudfurniture.com	Dallas	TX	75227	214-388-8655		321
MASSPIRG (Massachusetts Public Interest Research Group) 294 Washington St Ste 500 *Web:* masspirg.org	Boston	MA	02108	617-292-4800		633
Mass-Ri Veterinary E.R. Inc 477 Milford Rd *Web:* massriveter.com	Swansea	MA	02777	508-730-1112		794
MassTech Inc 6992 Columbia Gateway Dr *Web:* apmaldi.com	Columbia	MD	21046	443-539-1758		419
MAST Biosurgery Inc 6749 Top Gun St Ste 108 *Web:* mastbio.com	San Diego	CA	92121	858-550-8050	550-8060	475
Mast Brian (Rep R - FL) 2182 Rayburn House Office Bldg *Web:* mast.house.gov	Washington	DC	20515	202-225-3026	225-8398	342-2
Mast Drug Company Inc 1910 Ross Mill Rd *Web:* www.mastdrug.com	Henderson	NC	27537	252-438-3112		237
Mast General Store Inc 3565 Hwy 194 S *TF:* 866-367-6278 ■ *Web:* www.mastgeneralstore.com	Valle Crucis	NC	28691	828-963-6511		206
Mast Trucking Inc 6471 County Rd 625 *Web:* masttruckinginc.com	Millersburg	OH	44654	330-674-8913		780
MAST Vacation Partners Inc 635 Butterfield Rd Ste 220 *Web:* www.mvptravel.com	Oakbrook Terrace	IL	60181	630-889-9817	889-9832	772
MasTec Inc 800 Douglas Rd 12th Fl *NYSE: MTZ* ■ *Web:* www.mastec.com	Coral Gables	FL	33134	305-599-1800	406-1960	188-1
Master Appliance Corp 2420 18th St *TF:* 800-558-9413 ■ *Web:* www.masterappliance.com	Racine	WI	53403	262-633-7791	633-9745	759
Master Automatic Inc 40485 Schoolcraft Rd *Web:* www.masterautomatic.com	Plymouth	MI	48170	734-414-0500		454
Master Bond Inc 154 Hobart St *Web:* www.masterbond.com	Hackensack	NJ	07601	201-343-8983		3
Master Books c/o New Leaf Publishing Group Inc 3142 Hwy 103 N *TF:* 800-999-3777 ■ *Web:* www.masterbooks.com	Green Forest	AR	72638	800-999-3777		637-2
Master Control Systems Inc 910 N Shore Dr *Web:* www.mastercontrols.com	Lake Bluff	IL	60044	847-295-1010	295-0704	201
Master Cutlery Inc 700 Penhorn Ave **Fax Area Code:* 201 ■ *TF:* 888-271-7229 ■ *Web:* www.mastercutlery.com	Secaucus	NJ	07094	888-271-7229	271-7666*	222
Master Design Co 789 SR-94 E *Web:* masterdesign.org	Fulton	KY	42041	270-838-7060		65
Master Finish Co 2020 Nelson SE *TF:* 877-590-5819 ■ *Web:* www.masterfinishco.com	Grand Rapids	MI	49510	616-942-6273	245-0039	481
Master Graphics LLC 1100 S Main St *Web:* www.mg-printing.com	Rochelle	IL	61068	815-562-5800	562-6600	627
Master Halco Inc 3010 Lyndon B Johnson Fwy Ste 800 *TF:* 800-883-8384 ■ *Web:* www.masterhalco.com	Dallas	TX	75234	972-714-7300		279
Master Klean Janitorial Inc 2149 S Clermont St *Web:* masterklean.com	Denver	CO	80222	303-753-6084	753-0565	104
Master Lock Company LLC 6744 S Howell Ave PO Box 927 *TF:* 800-464-2088 ■ *Web:* www.masterlock.com	Oak Creek	WI	53154	800-464-2088	308-9245	350
Master Machine & Tool Company Inc 5857 Jefferson Ave *Web:* www.master-machine.com	Newport News	VA	23605	757-245-6653		757
Master Magnetics Inc 747 S Gilbert St *Web:* www.magnetsource.com	Castle Rock	CO	80104	303-688-3966		295
Master Manufacturing Company Inc 4703 Ohara Dr *Web:* mastermfg.com	Evansville	IN	47711	812-425-1561	425-4320	172
Master Marine Inc 14284 Shell Belt Rd *Web:* www.mastermarineinc.com	Bayou La Batre	AL	36509	251-824-4151		698
Master Mark Plastics 210 Ampe Dr *Web:* mastermark.com	Paynesville	MN	56362	320-243-7318		429
Master Mechanical Inc 820 Greenbrier Cir Ste 11 *Web:* mastermechanical.com	Chesapeake	VA	23320	757-424-5013		698
Master Metal Products Co 495 Emory St *Web:* www.mastermetalproducts.com	San Jose	CA	95110	408-275-1210	275-0523	482
Master Package Corp, The 200 Madson St *TF:* 800-396-8425 ■ *Web:* www.masterpackage.com	Owen	WI	54460	715-229-2156	229-2689	546
Master Pitching Machine 4200 NE Birmingham Rd *TF:* 800-878-8228 ■ *Web:* www.masterpitch.com	Kansas City	MO	64117	816-452-0228	452-7581	710
Master Plastics Inc 820 Eubanks Dr *Web:* www.masterplastics.com	Vacaville	CA	95688	707-451-3168	451-3123	604
Master Precision Machining Inc 2199 Ronald St *Web:* master-precision.com	Santa Clara	CA	95050	408-727-0185		757
Master Print Inc 8401 Terminal Rd *Web:* www.master-print.com	Newington	VA	22122	703-550-9555	550-9673	627
Master Purveyors 6003 N 54th St *TF:* 800-565-6328 ■ *Web:* www.masterpurveyorsfla.com	Tampa	FL	33610	813-253-0865	253-0996	297-9
Master Recording Supply Inc 891 W 16th St *TF:* 800-860-4560 ■ *Web:* www.mrsmedia.com	Newport Beach	CA	92663	714-556-6700	556-5970	246
Master Solutions Inc 20 Wolf Bridge Rd *Web:* www.mastersi.com	Carlisle	PA	17013	717-243-6849	243-8021	207
Master Spas Inc 6927 Lincoln Pkwy *TF:* 800-860-7727 ■ *Web:* www.masterspas.com	Fort Wayne	IN	46804	260-436-9100		375
MASTER Teacher Inc, The 2600 Leadership Ln *TF:* 800-669-9633 ■ *Web:* www.masterteacher.com	Manhattan	KS	66505	800-669-9633		528
Master Tile 7350 Denny St Ste 100 *TF:* 888-647-8453 ■ *Web:* mastertile.net	Houston	TX	77040	832-467-8850	467-8899	191-1
Master Wholesale Inc 520 S Front St *TF:* 800-938-7925 ■ *Web:* www.masterwholesale.com	Seattle	WA	98108	206-767-6771		385
Master Workholding Inc 315 Burke Dr *Web:* masterworkholding.com	Morganton	NC	28655	828-437-0011	438-0069	757
Master's College 21726 Placerita Canyon Rd *TF:* 800-568-6248 ■ *Web:* www.masters.edu	Santa Clarita	CA	91321	661-259-3540	288-1037	166
Master-Bilt Products 908 Hwy 15 N *TF:* 800-647-1284 ■ *Web:* www.master-bilt.com	New Albany	MS	38652	662-534-9061	534-6049	14
MasterCard Inc 2000 Purchase St *NYSE: MA* ■ *TF:* 800-100-1087 ■ *Web:* www.mastercard.us	Purchase	NY	10577	914-249-2000		215
Masterchem Industries LLC 3135 Old Hwy M *TF:* 866-774-6371 ■ *Web:* www.kilz.com	Imperial	MO	63052	866-774-6371		550
Mastercoil Spring 4010 Albany *Web:* www.mastercoil.com	McHenry	IL	60050	815-344-0051	344-0071	719

Name / Address	City	State	ZIP	Phone	Fax	Class
Mastercool Usa Inc 1 Aspen Dr *Web:* www.mastercool.com	Randolph	NJ	07869	973-252-9119		787
MasterCraft Boat Co 100 Cherokee Cove Dr *TF:* 800-443-8774 ■ *Web:* www.mastercraft.com	Vonore	TN	37885	845-676-7876		90
Mastercraft Engineering Inc 323 Southwell Blvd *Web:* www.mastercraftengineering.com	Tifton	GA	31794	229-386-1858	386-8886	488
Mastercraft Industries Inc 777 S St *TF:* 800-835-7812 ■ *Web:* www.mastercraftusa.com	Newburgh	NY	12550	845-565-8850	565-9392	115
MasterDrive 15659 E Hinsdale Dr *Web:* www.masterdrive.com	Centennial	CO	80112	303-627-4447		507
Masterfile Corp 3 Concorde Gate 4th Fl *TF:* 800-387-9010 ■ *Web:* www.masterfile.com	Toronto	ON	M3C3N7	416-929-3000		589
MasterGraphics Inc 2979 Triverton Pike Dr *TF:* 800-873-7238 ■ *Web:* mastergraphics.com	Madison	WI	53711	608-256-4884		174
Master-Lee Energy Services Corp 1639 Clearview Dr *Web:* masterlee.com	Latrobe	PA	15650	724-539-8060		104
Masterline Design & Manufacturing 41580 Production Dr *Web:* www.masterlinedesigninc.com	Harrison Township	MI	48045	586-463-5888	463-8817	620
Masterloy Products Ltd 5663 Doncaster Rd *Web:* www.masterloy.com	Ottawa	ON	K1G3N4	613-822-1010		492
Masterman's LLP 11 C St *TF:* 800-525-3313 ■ *Web:* www.mastermans.com	Auburn	MA	01501	800-525-3313		45
Mastermind LP 2134 Queen St E *TF:* 888-388-0000 ■ *Web:* www.mastermindtoys.com	Toronto	ON	M4E1E3	416-699-3797		95
Mastermind Marketing Inc 1450 W Peachtree St *Web:* www.mastermindmarketing.com	Atlanta	GA	30309	678-420-4000		4
Masterpiece International Ltd 39 Broadway 14th Fl *Web:* masterpieceintl.com	New York	NY	10006	212-825-4800	825-7010	311
MasterPlans 1355 NW Everett St Ste 100 *TF:* 877-453-2011 ■ *Web:* www.masterplans.com	Portland	OR	97209	503-226-4400		196
Masters & Associates Insurance Inc 24 E Linden Ave *Web:* www.mastersins.com	Miamisburg	OH	45343	937-866-3361		390
Masters Academy of Central Florida Inc, The 1500 Lukas Ln *Web:* www.mastersacademy.org	Oviedo	FL	32765	407-971-2221		685
Masters Advisors Inc 480 New Holland Ave Ste 7201 *TF:* 800-571-1323 ■ *Web:* www.mastersadvisors.com	Lancaster	PA	17602	717-581-1323		463
Masters Gallery Foods Inc 328 County Hwy PP PO Box 170 *TF:* 800-236-8431 ■ *Web:* www.mastersgalleryfoods.com	Plymouth	WI	53073	920-893-8431		297-4
Masters Gallery Ltd 2115 Fourth St SW *TF:* 866-245-0616 ■ *Web:* www.mastersgalleryltd.com	Calgary	AB	T2S1W8	403-245-2064	244-1636	42
Masters Law Group PLLC 241 Madison Ave N *Web:* appeal-law.com	Bainbridge Island	WA	98110	206-780-5033		41
Masters Machine Company Inc 500 Lower Round Pond Rd *Web:* www.mastersmachine.com	Round Pond	ME	04564	207-529-5191	529-5231	493
Masters Pharmaceutical Inc 11930 Kemper Springs Dr *Web:* www.mastersrx.com	Cincinnati	OH	45240	513-354-2690		238
Masters School, The 49 Clinton Ave *Web:* www.mastersny.org	Dobbs Ferry	NY	10522	914-479-6400	693-1230	622
Masters' Supply Inc 4505 Bishop Ln *TF:* 800-388-6353 ■ *Web:* www.masterssupply.net	Louisville	KY	40218	800-388-6353		612
Masterson Company Inc 4023 W National Ave *Web:* www.mastersoncompany.com	Milwaukee	WI	53215	414-647-1132	647-1170	296-8
Mastertech Services Inc 691 Corporate Cir *Web:* www.mastertechservices.com	Golden	CO	80401	303-278-7300		260
Masterword Services International Inc 303 Stafford St *Web:* www.masterword.com	Houston	TX	77079	281-589-0810		768
Masterwork Electronics Inc 630 Martin Ave *Web:* www.masterworkelectronics.com	Rohnert Park	CA	94928	707-588-9906	588-9908	625
Masterwork Inc 19265 Powder Hill Pl NE *Web:* masterworks.com	Poulsbo	WA	98370	360-394-4300		5
Mastery Technologies Inc 41214 Bridge St *TF:* 800-258-3837 ■ *Web:* www.masterytech.com	Novi	MI	48375	800-258-3837		178-1
Mastics-moriches-shirley Community Library 407 William Floyd Pkwy *Web:* www.communitylibrary.org	Shirley	NY	11967	631-399-1511	281-4442	434-3
Mastrapasqua Asset Management Inc 104 Woodmont Blvd Ste 320 *TF:* 800-466-9055 ■ *Web:* mcapitaladv.com	Nashville	TN	37205	615-244-8400		690
Mastro Graphic Arts Inc 67 Deep Rock Rd *Web:* www.mastrographics.com	Rochester	NY	14624	585-436-7570		687
Mastro's Steakhouse 246 N Canon Dr *Web:* www.mastrosrestaurants.com	Beverly Hills	CA	90210	310-888-8782		671
Mat & Naddie's Restaurant 937 Leonidas St *Web:* www.matandnaddies.com	New Orleans	LA	70118	504-861-9600		671
MATA (Memphis Area Transit Authority) 1370 Levee Rd *Web:* www.matatransit.com	Memphis	TN	38108	901-722-7100		468
Mataco 2861 E Royalton Rd *TF:* 888-785-7810 ■ *Web:* matacoinc.net	Broadview Heights	OH	44147	440-546-8355	546-8311	455
Matador Resources Co 5400 Lyndon B Johnson Fwy Ste 1500 *Web:* www.matadorresources.com	Dallas	TX	75240	972-371-5200	371-5201	536
Matagorda County Courthouse 1700 Seventh St Rm 301 *Web:* www.co.matagorda.tx.us	Bay City	TX	77414	979-244-7605	245-3697	338
Matagorda Island Wildlife Management Area 1700 Seventh St *Web:* tpwd.texas.gov	Bay City	TX	77414	979-244-7670		565
Matan Companies LLLP 4600 Wedgewood Blvd Ste A *Web:* www.mataninc.com	Frederick	MD	21703	301-694-9200		528
Matandy Steel & Metal Products LLC 1200 Central Ave *Web:* www.matandy.com	Hamilton	OH	45011	513-844-2277		295
Matanuska Electric Association Inc (MEA) 163 E Industrial Way *Web:* www.mea.coop	Palmer	AK	99645	907-745-3231	761-9352	245
Matanuska Telephone Association Inc 1740 S Chugach St *TF:* 800-478-3211 ■ *Web:* www.mtasolutions.com	Palmer	AK	99645	907-745-3211		736
Matanuska Valley Fcu 1020 S Bailey St *Web:* mvfcu.coop	Palmer	AK	99645	907-745-4891		219
Matanuska-Susitna Borough 350 E Dahlia Ave *Web:* www.matsugov.us	Palmer	AK	99645	907-861-7801		338
Matawan-Aberdeen Chamber of Commerce 201 Broad St PO Box 522 *Web:* macocnj.com	Matawan	NJ	07747	732-290-1125		139
Match Eyewear LLC 1600 Shames Dr *TF:* 877-886-2824 ■ *Web:* www.matcheyewear.com	Westbury	NY	11590	877-886-2824		543
MatchCraft Inc 2701 Ocean Park Blvd Ste 220 *TF:* 888-502-7238 ■ *Web:* www.matchcraft.com	Santa Monica	CA	90405	310-314-3320		7
Matchless Metal Polish Co, The 840 W 49th Pl *Web:* www.matchlessmetal.com	Chicago	IL	60609	773-924-1515	924-5513	151
Matchless Plastics Inc 13225 Industrial Pk Blvd *Web:* www.matchlessplastics.com	Plymouth	MN	55441	763-557-0995	557-0625	493
Matchmd Inc 711 E Monument Ave **Fax Area Code:* 937 ■ *TF:* 866-257-5363 ■ *Web:* matchmd.com	Dayton	OH	45402	866-257-5363	291-3946*	177
Mat-Co Business Forms Inc 814 Fesslers Ln *Web:* www.matcoforms.com	Nashville	TN	37210	615-244-4404	254-8103	627
Matco Electric Corp 3913 Gates Rd *Web:* www.matcoelectric.com	Vestal	NY	13850	607-729-4921	729-0932	189-4
Matco Tools 4403 Allen Rd *TF:* 866-289-8665 ■ *Web:* www.matcotools.com	Stow	OH	44224	330-926-5332		758
Matco-Norca Inc 1944 Rt 22 PO Box 27 *TF:* 800-431-2082 ■ *Web:* www.matco-norca.com	Brewster	NY	10509	845-278-7570		610
Matcor Automotive 401 S Steele St *Web:* www.matcor-matsu.com	Ionia	MI	48846	616-527-4050		489
MATCOR Inc 101 Liberty Ln *TF:* 800-523-6692 ■ *Web:* www.matcor.com	Chalfont	PA	18914	215-348-2974	348-2699	261
Mate Inc 8910 Point Six Cir *TF:* 888-419-8181 ■ *Web:* www.matetrailers.com	Houston	TX	77095	281-855-0045		779
Mate Pcs 8480 Baltimore National Pke Ste 323 **Fax Area Code:* 443 ■ *Web:* gpmate.com	Ellicott City	MD	21043	410-244-8548	819-0997*	177
Mate Precision Tooling Inc 1295 Lund Blvd *TF:* 800-328-4492 ■ *Web:* www.mate.com	Anoka	MN	55303	763-421-0230	421-0285	757
Matec Instrument Companies Inc 56 Hudson St *Web:* www.matec.com	Northborough	MA	01532	508-393-0155		360-2
Matech Advanced Materials Development Corp 31304 Via Colinas Ste 102 *Web:* www.matech.us	Westlake Village	CA	91362	818-991-8500	991-4134	743
Matelski Lumber Co 2617 M 75 S *Web:* www.matelskilumbercompany.com	Boyne Falls	MI	49713	231-549-2780		279
Matenaer Corp 810 Schoenhaar Dr *TF:* 800-254-0873 ■ *Web:* www.matenaer.com	West Bend	WI	53090	262-338-0700		492
Mater Dei Academy 3695 Elm St *Web:* materdeiacademy.org	Whitehall	OH	43213	614-231-1984	516-0481	41
Material & Contract Services LLC 5820 Stoneridge Mall Rd Ste 217 *Web:* www.macservices.us	Pleasanton	CA	94588	925-460-0397		463
Material Fabricators Inc 33 Commerce Dr *TF:* 800-392-7567 ■ *Web:* www.materialfabricators.com	Buellton	CA	93427	805-686-5244	686-5250	326
Material Handling Equipment Distributors Assn (MHEDA) 201 US Hwy 45 *Web:* www.mheda.org	Vernon Hills	IL	60061	847-680-3500	362-6989	49-13
Material Handling Products Corp 6601 Joy Rd *TF:* 866-980-4788 ■ *Web:* mhpcorp.com	East Syracuse	NY	13057	315-437-2891		770
Material Motion Inc 203 Rio Cir *Web:* www.materialmotion.com	Decatur	GA	30030	404-237-6127		358
Material Transfer and Storage Inc 1214 Lincoln Rd **Fax Area Code:* 269 ■ *TF:* 800-836-7068 ■ *Web:* www.materialtransfer.com	Allegan	MI	49010	800-836-7068	673-4883*	454
Materials Engineer & Testing 125 Valley Ct *Web:* www.meandt.com	Oak Ridge	TN	37830	865-482-7762		743
Materials Innovation Technologies LLC 320 Rutledge Rd	Fletcher	NC	28732	828-651-9646	651-9648	791
Materials Marketing Ltd 120 W Josephine St *Web:* www.mstoneandtile.com	San Antonio	TX	78212	210-731-8453		191-1
Materials Properties Council (MPC) PO Box 201547 *Web:* www.forengineers.org	Shaker Heights	OH	44122	216-658-3847		49-19
Materials Research Society (MRS) 506 Keystone Dr *Web:* www.mrs.org	Warrendale	PA	15086	724-779-3003	779-8313	49-19
Materials Transportation Co (MTC) 1408 S Commerce PO Box 1358 *TF:* 800-433-3110 ■ *Web:* www.gomtc.com	Temple	TX	76503	254-298-2900		386
Materion Corp 6070 Parkland Blvd *NYSE:* MTRN ■ *TF:* 800-321-2076 ■ *Web:* materion.com	Mayfield Heights	OH	44124	216-486-4200	383-4091	502

Company / Address	City	State	ZIP	Phone	Fax	Class
Materion Technical Materials 5 Wellington Rd *TF:* 800-241-2523 ■ *Web:* www.materion.com	Lincoln	RI	02865	401-333-1700	333-2848	567
Math Teachers Press Inc 4850 Park Glen Rd *TF:* 800-852-2435 ■ *Web:* www.movingwithmath.com	Saint Louis Park	MN	55416	800-852-2435		196
Mathematica PO Box 2393 *Web:* www.mathematica-mpr.com	Princeton	NJ	08543	609-799-3535	799-0005	634
Mathematical Association of America (MAA) 1529 18th St NW *TF:* 800-331-1622 ■ *Web:* www.maa.org	Washington	DC	20036	202-387-5200	265-2384	49-19
Matheny Medical & Educational Ctr 65 Highland Ave *Web:* www.matheny.org	Peapack	NJ	07977	908-234-0011	719-2137	374-7
Matheny Sears Linkert & Jaime LLP 3638 American River Dr *Web:* mathenysears.com	Sacramento	CA	95864	916-978-3434	978-3430	428
Mather & Company CPAS LLC 9100 Shelbyville Rd *Web:* www.matherandcompany.com	Louisville	KY	40222	502-429-0800		2
Mather Economics LLC 1215 Hightower Trail Bldg A Ste 100 *Web:* www.mathereconomics.com	Atlanta	GA	30350	770-993-4111		196
Mather Group LLC, The Oakbrook Ter Tower One Tower Ln Ste 1820 *Web:* www.themathergroup.com	Oakbrook Terrace	IL	60181	630-537-1080		528
Matherly Mechanical Contractors LLC 1520 Ocama Blvd PO Box 30889 *Web:* www.matherlymech.com	Midwest City	OK	73140	405-737-3488		610
Matheson Tri-Gas Inc 150 Allen Rd *Web:* www.mathesongas.com	Parsippany	NJ	07054	973-257-1100		143
Matheson Trucking Inc 9785 Goethe Rd *TF:* 800-455-7678 ■ *Web:* www.mathesoninc.com	Sacramento	CA	95827	800-455-7678		780
Matheus Lumber 15800 Woodinville-Redmond Rd NE *TF:* 800-281-7501 ■ *Web:* www.matheuslumber.com	Woodinville	WA	98072	425-489-3000	822-4028	191-3
Mathew Zechman Company Inc 152 Resar Ct	Elyria	OH	44035	440-366-2442		756
Mathews & Peddibhotla Law Group Pc 39899 Balentine Dr Ste 380 *Web:* mplg.us	Newark	CA	94560	510-498-1949	225-2333	41
Mathews Associates Inc 220 Power Ct *TF:* 800-871-5262 ■ *Web:* www.maifl.com	Sanford	FL	32771	407-323-3390	323-3115	74
Mathews Bros Co 22 Perkins Rd *TF:* 800-615-2004 ■ *Web:* www.mathewsbrothers.com	Belfast	ME	04915	207-338-6490	338-6300	236
Mathews Co 500 Industrial Ave *TF:* 800-323-7045 ■ *Web:* www.mathewscompany.com	Crystal Lake	IL	60012	815-459-2210	459-5889	273
Mathews County 10622 Buckley Hall Rd PO Box 463 *Web:* www.mathewscountyva.gov	Mathews	VA	23109	804-725-2550	725-7456	338
Mathews Inc 919 River Rd *Web:* www.mathewsinc.com	Sparta	WI	54656	608-269-2728		711
Mathews Jewelers 126 Strickland Dr *Web:* www.mathewsjewelers.com	Orange	TX	77630	409-886-7233		327
Mathias Die Company Inc 391 Malden St *TF:* 800-899-3437 ■ *Web:* www.mathias-die.com	South Saint Paul	MN	55075	651-451-0105	451-1943	757
Mathiowetz Construction Co 30676 County Rd 24 *Web:* www.mathiowetzconst.com	Sleepy Eye	MN	56085	507-794-6953	794-3514	186
Mathis Bros Furniture Inc 6611 S 101st East Ave *TF:* 800-329-3434 ■ *Web:* www.mathisbrothers.com	Tulsa	OK	74133	855-294-3434		321
Mathnasium LLC 5120 W Goldleaf Cir Ste 300 *TF:* 877-601-6284 ■ *Web:* www.mathnasium.com	Los Angeles	CA	90056	888-763-2604		310
Mathtech Inc 6402 Arlington Blvd Ste 1200 *Web:* mathtechinc.com	Falls Church	VA	22042	703-875-8866	237-4231	225
Mathworks Inc 3 Apple Hill Dr *Web:* in.mathworks.com	Natick	MA	01760	508-647-7000	647-7001	178-5
Mathy Construction Company Inc 920 Tenth Ave N PO Box 189 *Web:* www.mathy.com	Onalaska	WI	54650	608-783-6411	783-4311	188-4
Mathys+Potestio 917 SW Oak St Ste 315 *Web:* mathys-potestio.com	Portland	OR	97205	503-489-7396		260
Mati Therapeutics Inc 4317 Dunning Ln *Web:* www.matitherapeutics.com	Austin	TX	78746	512-329-6360		475
Matich Corp 1596 Harry Sheppard Blvd *TF:* 800-404-4975 ■ *Web:* www.matichcorp.com	San Bernardino	CA	92408	909-382-7400		188-4
Matik Inc 33 Brook St *TF:* 800-245-1628 ■ *Web:* www.matik.com	West Hartford	CT	06110	860-232-2323		535
Matis Warfield Inc 954 Ridgebrook Rd Ste 120 *Web:* matiswarfield.com	Sparks	MD	21152	410-683-7004		261
Matis, Baum, O'Connor PC 912 Fort Duquesne Blvd *Web:* mbo-pc.com	Pittsburgh	PA	15222	412-338-4750	338-4742	41
Matlab Inc 1112 Nc Hwy 49 S *Web:* www.matlabinc.com	Asheboro	NC	27205	336-629-4161		608
MatlinPatterson Global Advisers LLC 520 Madison Ave 35 Fl *Web:* www.matlinpatterson.com	New York	NY	10022	212-651-9500		401
Matlock Adv & Public Relations 107 Luckie St *Web:* www.matlock-adpr.com	Atlanta	GA	30303	404-872-3200		4
Matmoncom 303 W Capitol Ave Ste 150 *TF:* 800-995-0442 ■ *Web:* www.matmon.com	Little Rock	AR	72201	501-375-4999		396
Matot Inc 2501 Van Buren St *TF:* 800-369-1070 ■ *Web:* www.matot.com	Bellwood	IL	60104	708-547-1888	547-1608	256
Matous Construction Ltd 8602 State Hwy 317 *Web:* www.matousconstruction.com	Belton	TX	76513	254-780-1400	780-2599	186
Matr Boomie 3007 Longhorn Blvd Ste 113 **Fax Area Code:* 734 ■ *Web:* www.handmadeexpressions.net	Austin	TX	78758	512-535-5228	348-9904*	411
Matric Group LLC 2099 Hill City Rd *Web:* www.matricgroup.com	Seneca	PA	16346	814-677-0716		393
Matrix 2 Advertising 1903 NW 97th Ave *Web:* www.matrix2advertising.com	Miami	FL	33172	305-591-7672		344
Matrix Automation Inc 340 N Main St *Web:* www.matrixautomation.com	Huron	OH	44839	419-433-4013		196
Matrix Capital Advisors LLC 200 S Wacker Dr Ste 680 *Web:* matrixcapital.com	Chicago	IL	60606	312-612-6100		401
Matrix Commercial Cleaning LLC 726 E Industrial Park Dr Unit 11 *Web:* matrixcommercialcleaning.com	Manchester	NH	03109	603-622-1430		104
Matrix Companies, The 7162 Reading Rd Ste 250 *TF:* 877-550-7973 ■ *Web:* www.matrixtpa.com	Cincinnati	OH	45237	513-351-1222		393
Matrix Composites Inc 275 Barnes Blvd *Web:* matrixcomp.com	Rockledge	FL	32955	321-633-4480	633-4490	256
Matrix Computer Solutions Inc 3001 Bridgeway Ste K314 *Web:* www.matrixcomp.net	Sausalito	CA	94965	415-331-3600		176
Matrix Controls Company Inc 330 Elizabeth Ave *Web:* www.matrixcontrols.net	Somerset	NJ	08873	732-469-5551		201
Matrix Design Group Inc 1601 Blake St Ste 200 *Web:* www.matrixdesigngroup.com	Denver	CO	80202	303-572-0200		261
Matrix Energy Services Inc 3239 Ramos Cir *TF:* 800-556-2123 ■ *Web:* matrixescorp.com	Sacramento	CA	95827	916-363-9283		256
Matrix Engineering Inc 225 Hwy 35 *Web:* matrixengineering.net	Red Bank	NJ	07701	732-747-9111		261
Matrix Engineering PLLC 112 Walter Jetton Blvd *Web:* matrixengineer.com	Paducah	KY	42001	270-442-5600		261
Matrix Fitness Systems Corp 1600 Landmark Dr *Web:* www.matrixfitness.com	Cottage Grove	WI	53527	608-839-8686		354
Matrix Hotel 10640-100 Ave *TF:* 866-465-8150 ■ *Web:* www.matrixedmonton.com	Edmonton	AB	T5J3N8	780-429-2861		379
Matrix Imaging Solutions Inc 6341 Inducon Dr *Web:* www.matriximaging.com	Sanborn	NY	14132	716-504-9700		627
Matrix Inc 266 Harristown Rd Ste 202 *Web:* www.hiredbymatrix.com	Glen Rock	NJ	07452	201-587-0777	291-8614	631
Matrix Integration LLC 417 Main St *Web:* www.matrixintegration.com	Jasper	IN	47546	812-634-1550		180
Matrix Metals LLC B 10643 W Airport Blvd Ste 100 *Web:* www.matrixmetalsllc.com	Stafford	TX	77477	281-633-4200		307
Matrix Networks 4243 SE International Way Ste C *Web:* www.mtrx.com	Portland	OR	97222	503-654-3000	513-9201	180
Matrix Partners 101 Main St 17th Fl *Web:* www.matrixpartners.com	Cambridge	MA	02142	617-494-1223		792
Matrix Product Development Inc 11 N Bird St *Web:* www.matrixpd.com	Sun Prairie	WI	53590	608-834-1661	834-6443	253
Matrix Publishing Services 36 N Highland Ave *Web:* matrix508.com	York	PA	17404	717-764-9673	764-9672	781
Matrix Realty Group LLC 2066 Ridge Rd *Web:* www.matrixrealtygroup.com	Homewood	IL	60430	708-799-3600		652
Matrix Service Co 5100 E Skelly Dr Ste 100 *NASDAQ: MTRX* ■ **Fax Area Code:* 918 ■ *TF:* 866-367-6879 ■ *Web:* www.matrixservice.com	Tulsa	OK	74135	866-367-6879	838-8810*	539
Matrix Systems Inc 1041 Byers Rd *TF:* 800-562-8749 ■ *Web:* www.matrixsys.com	Miamisburg	OH	45342	937-438-9033	438-0900	692
Matrix Technologies Inc 1760 Indian Wood Cir *TF:* 844-310-7015 ■ *Web:* matrixti.com	Maumee	OH	43537	419-897-7200	897-7214	180
Matrix Tool Inc 4976 Franklin Ave *Web:* www.matrixtoolinc.com	Fairview	PA	16415	814-474-5531		596
Matrix4 610 E Judd St *Web:* www.matrix4.com	Woodstock	IL	60098	815-338-4500		608
Matrox Electronic Systems Ltd 1055 St Regis Blvd *TF:* 800-361-1408 ■ *Web:* www.matrox.com	Dorval	QC	H9P2T4	514-822-6000	822-6363	173-5
MATRRIX Energy Technologies 250 6 Ave SW Ste 350 *Web:* www.matrrix.com	Calgary	AB	T2P3H7	403-984-5042		540
Mats Inc 37 Shuman Ave *Web:* www.matsinc.com	Stoughton	MA	02072	781-344-1536		131
Matson & Cuprill 100 E-Business Way Ste 160 *TF:* 800-944-8596 ■ *Web:* matsonandcuprill.com	Cincinnati	OH	45249	513-563-7526		390
Matson Logistics Inc 555 12th St *TF:* 800-762-8766 ■ *Web:* www.matson.com	Oakland	CA	94607	510-628-4000		449
Matson Lumber Company Inc 132 Main St *Web:* www.matsonlumber.com	Brookville	PA	15825	814-849-5334	849-3811	683
Matsu Japanese Restaurant 18035 Beach Blvd *Web:* matsusogood.com	Huntington Beach	CA	92648	714-848-4404	842-4049	671
Matsuhisa 303 E Main St *Web:* www.matsuhisarestaurants.com	Aspen	CO	81611	970-544-6628		671
Matsuhisa Beverly Hills 129 N La Cienega Blvd *Web:* matsuhisabeverlyhills.com	Beverly Hills	CA	90211	310-659-9639	659-0492	671
Matsui Doris O (Rep D - CA) 2311 Rayburn House Office Bldg *Web:* matsui.house.gov	Washington	DC	20515	202-225-7163	225-0566	342-2
Matsui International Company Inc 1501 W 178th St *TF:* 800-359-5679 ■ *Web:* matsui-color.com	Gardena	CA	90248	310-767-7812		388
Matsui Nursery Inc 1645 Old Stage Rd *TF:* 800-793-6433 ■ *Web:* www.matsuinursery.com	Salinas	CA	93908	831-422-6433	422-2387	369

Name / Address	Phone	Fax	Class
Matsuo Industries USA Inc 408 Municipal Dr ... Jefferson City TN 37760 *Web:* www.matsuousa.com	865-475-9085		54
Matsuri Restaurant 1105 S Charles St ... Baltimore MD 21230 *Web:* www.matsuri-restaurant.com	410-752-8561		671
Matsys Inc 45490 Ruritan Cir ... Sterling VA 20166 *Web:* matsys.com	703-964-0400	964-0409	261
Matt & Allen LLC 1026 St John St ... LaFayette LA 70501 *Web:* mattandallen.com	337-237-1000	232-7580	41
Matt & Molly Team LLC, The 86 Asheland Ave ... Asheville NC 28801 *Web:* themattandmollyteam.com	828-210-1697		652
Matt Blatt Inc 501 Delsea Dr N ... Glassboro NJ 08028 *TF:* 877-462-5288 ■ *Web:* www.mattblatt.com	856-881-0444		57
Matt Castrucci Auto Mall of Dayton 3013 Mall Pk Dr ... Dayton OH 45459 *TF:* 855-204-5293 ■ *Web:* www.mattcastrucciautomall.com	855-204-5293		516
Matt Construction Corp 9814 Norwalk Blvd Ste 100 ... Santa Fe Springs CA 90670 *Web:* www.mattconstruction.com	562-903-2277		196
Matt Swanson's School of Golf 6224 Theall Rd ... Houston TX 77066 *Web:* swingpure.com	713-413-4484		148
Matt's Building Materials 404 E Expy 83 ... Pharr TX 78577 *Web:* www.mattsbuildingmaterials.com	956-787-5561		191-3
Matt's in the Market 94 Pike St Ste 32 ... Seattle WA 98101 *Web:* www.mattsinthemarket.com	206-467-7909		671
Mattatuck Museum of the Mattatuck Historical Society 144 W Main St ... Waterbury CT 06702 *Web:* www.mattmuseum.org	203-753-0381	756-6283	520
Mattel Inc 333 Continental Blvd ... El Segundo CA 90245 *NASDAQ: MAT* ■ *TF:* 800-524-8697 ■ *Web:* www.mattel.com	310-252-2000		762
Mattenson & Gordon 1 Northfield Plz Ste 500 ... Northfield IL 60093 *Web:* mattensongordon.com	847-441-1900		41
Matter Communications Inc 50 Water St Mill No 3 The Tannery ... Newburyport MA 01950 *Web:* www.matternow.com	978-518-4547		463
Mattermost Inc 530 Lytton Ave Ste 201 ... Palo Alto CA 94301 *Web:* about.mattermost.com	650-866-5518		39
Mattern & Craig Inc 701 First St SW ... Roanoke VA 24016 *Web:* matternandcraig.com	540-345-9342		261
Mattersight Corp 200 W Madison St Ste 3100 ... Chicago IL 60606 **Fax Area Code:* 312 ■ *TF:* 877-235-6925 ■ *Web:* www.mattersight.com	877-235-6925	454-3501*	463
Matteuzzi & Brooker PC 10111 W 105th St ... Overland Park KS 66212 *Web:* ma2zlaw.com	913-253-2500		41
Matthew D. Kaplan Llc Attorney At Law 50 SW Pine St Ste 302 ... Portland OR 97204 *Web:* mdkaplanlaw.com	503-226-3844		41
Matthew Marks Gallery 523 W 24th St ... New York NY 10011 *Web:* www.matthewmarks.com	212-243-0200		42
Matthew's 2107 Hendricks Ave ... Jacksonville FL 32207 *Web:* matthewsrestaurant.com	904-396-9922		671
Matthews Book Co 11559 Rock Island Ct ... Maryland Heights MO 63043 *TF:* 800-633-2665 ■ *Web:* www.matthewsbooks.com	314-432-1400	432-7044	95
Matthews Carter & Boyce PC 12500 Fair Lakes Cir Ste 260 ... Fairfax VA 22033 *Web:* www.mcb-cpa.com	703-218-3600	218-1808	2
Matthews Construction Company Inc 210 First Ave S ... Conover NC 28613 *Web:* www.matthewsconstruction.com	828-464-7325	465-6747	186
Matthews Currie Ford Company Inc 130 N Tamiami Trl ... Nokomis FL 34275 *TF:* 855-491-3131 ■ *Web:* www.matthewscurrie.com	800-248-2378		57
Matthews Firm Pllc, The 2000 Bering Dr Ste 700 ... Houston TX 77057 *Web:* matthewsfirm.com	713-355-4200		41
Matthews Group Inc, The 400 Lake St ... Bryan TX 77801 *Web:* thematthewsgroup.com	979-823-3600		4
Matthews International Corp *Marking Products Div* 6515 Penn Ave ... Pittsburgh PA 15206 *TF:* 800-775-7775 ■ *Web:* matthewsmarking.com	412-665-2500	665-2550	467
Matthews Opera House 612 Main St ... Spearfish SD 57783 *Web:* www.matthewsopera.com	605-642-7973		572
Matthews Paint Co 760 Pittsburgh Dr ... Delaware OH 43015 *TF:* 800-323-6593 ■ *Web:* www.matthewspaint.com	800-323-6593	947-0377	550
Matthews Pierce & Lloyd Inc 830 Walker Rd Ste 12 ... Dover DE 19904 *TF:* 800-267-4026 ■ *Web:* mpli.net	302-678-5500		160
Matthews Studio Equipment Group 2405 W Empire Ave ... Burbank CA 91504 **Fax Area Code:* 323 ■ *TF:* 800-237-8263 ■ *Web:* www.msegrip.com	818-843-6715	849-1525*	591
Matthews-Hargreaves Chevrolet Co 2000 E12 Mile Rd ... Royal Oak MI 48067 *TF:* 877-628-5440 ■ *Web:* www.mhchevy.com	248-398-8800		516
Matthiesen & Assoc 511 Lovett Blvd ... Houston TX 77006 *Web:* matthiesenlaw.com	713-877-8522	800-8500	41
Matthijssen Inc 14 Rt 10 ... East Hanover NJ 07936 **Fax Area Code:* 973 ■ *TF:* 800-845-2200 ■ *Web:* www.mattnj.com	800-845-2200	887-2453*	175
Mattingly Lumber & Millwork Inc 410 E St ... Granite City IL 62040 *Web:* www.mattinglylumber.com	636-343-3877		191-3
Mattioni LLP 1316 Kings Hwy ... Swedesboro NJ 08085 *Web:* www.mattioni.com	856-241-9779	241-9989	428
Mattoon Precision Manufacturing Inc 2408 S 14th St ... Mattoon IL 61938 *Web:* www.mpmiusa.com	217-235-6000	235-6010	60
Mattracks Inc 202 Cleveland Ave E ... Karlstad MN 56732 *TF:* 877-436-7800 ■ *Web:* www.mattracks.co	218-436-7000		370
Mattress & More 5225 SW Blvd ... Hamburg NY 14075 *Web:* mattymattress.com	716-648-1200		362
Mattress Firm Inc 5815 Gulf Fwy ... Houston TX 77023 *Web:* www.mattressfirm.com	713 923 1090		362
Mattsco Supply Co 1111 N 161st E Ave ... Tulsa OK 74116 *TF:* 800-331-4013 ■ *Web:* www.mattsco.org	918-836-0451	836-0454	492
Mattson Technology Inc 47131 Bayside Pkwy ... Fremont CA 94538 *Web:* www.mattson.com	510-657-5900		695
Matuba 2930 McKinley Ave ... South Bend IN 46615 *Web:* matuba-japanese-bar-restaurant.business.site	574-251-0674		671
Maturango Museum 100 E Las Flores Ave ... Ridgecrest CA 93555 *Web:* www.maturango.org	760-375-6900	375-0479	637-2
Maturehealth Communications 502 Centennial Ave ... Cranford NJ 07016 *Web:* www.maturehealth.com	908-709-8080		195
Matuszko Trucking Inc 137 Damon Rd Ste B ... Northampton MA 01060 **Fax Area Code:* 413 ■ *TF:* 800-331-6880 ■ *Web:* www.matuszko.com	800-331-6880	587-5020*	780
Maude Cobb Convention Ctr 100 Grand Blvd PO Box 1952 ... Longview TX 75604 *Web:* www.longviewtexas.gov	903-237-1230		205
Maude Kerns Art Ctr 1910 E 15th Ave ... Eugene OR 97403 *Web:* www.mkartcenter.org	541-345-1571	345-6248	50-2
Maudslay State Park 74 Curzon Mill Rd ... Newburyport MA 01950 *Web:* www.mass.gov	978-465-7223		565
Maui Beach Hotel Inc 170 Kaahumanu Ave ... Kahului HI 96732 *TF:* 866-970-4168 ■ *Web:* www.mauibeachhotel.net	808-877-0051		378
Maui Community College 310 W Kaahumanu Ave ... Kahului HI 96732 *TF:* 800-479-6692 ■ *Web:* www.maui.hawaii.edu	808-984-3500	984-3660	162
Maui County 200 S High St ... Wailuku HI 96793 *TF:* 800-272-0117 ■ *Web:* www.mauicounty.gov	808-270-7748	270-7171	338
Maui County Federal Credit Union 1888 Wili Pa Loop ... Wailuku HI 96793 *Web:* mauicountyfcu.org	808-244-7968		219
Maui Divers of Hawaii 1520 Liona St ... Honolulu HI 96814 *TF:* 800-462-4454 ■ *Web:* www.mauidivers.com	808-946-7979		409
Maui Jim Inc 721 Wainee St ... Lahaina HI 96761 *TF:* 888-352-2001 ■ *Web:* www.mauijim.com	808-661-8841	661-0351	542
Maui Land & Pineapple Company Inc 200 Village Rd ... Lahaina HI 96761 *Web:* www.mauiland.com	808-877-1608	665-0641	315-4
Maui Media LLC 1215 S Kihei Rd Ste O-155 ... Kihei HI 96753 *TF:* 800-675-3290 ■ *Web:* www.mauimedia.com	808-344-4800	442-7298	637-2
Maui Memorial Medical Ctr 221 Mahalani St ... Wailuku HI 96793 *Web:* www.mauihealth.org	808-244-9056	242-2443	374-3
Maui News 100 Mahalani St ... Wailuku HI 96793 *Web:* www.mauinews.com	808-242-9087		532-2
Maui Ocean Ctr 192 Maalaea Rd ... Wailuku HI 96793 *Web:* mauioceancenter.com	808-270-7000	270-7070	40
Maui School of Therapeutic Massage 1043 Makawao Ave Ste 207 PO Box 1891 ... Makawao HI 96768 *Web:* www.massagemaui.com	808-572-2277	572-2274	685
Maui Soda & Ice Works Ltd 918 Lower Main St ... Wailuku HI 96793 *Web:* www.mauisoda.com	808-244-7951	244-4108	249
Maui Tacos International Inc 2001 Palmer Ave Ste 105 ... Larchmont NY 10538 *TF:* 866-388-3758 ■ *Web:* mauitacos.com	866-388-3758		670
Maui Time Weekly 33 N Market St Ste 201 ... Wailuku HI 96793 *Web:* mauitime.com	808-244-0777		532-5
Mauldin & Jenkins CPA LLC 200 Galleria Pkwy SE ... Atlanta GA 30339 **Fax Area Code:* 229 ■ *TF:* 800-277-0080 ■ *Web:* www.mjcpa.com	770-955-8600	446-3664*	2
Mauldin Vaught PLLC 4064 N Remington Dr ... Fayetteville AR 72703 *Web:* mauldinvaught.com	479-587-1040		734
Maule Air Inc 2099 GA Hwy 133 S ... Moultrie GA 31788 *Web:* mauleairinc.com	229-985-2045	890-2402	20
Maumee Bay Lodge & Conference Ctr 1750 Park Rd Ste 2 ... Oregon OH 43616 *Web:* www.maumeebaylodge.com	419-836-1466	836-2438	379
Maumee Bay State Park 1400 State Park Rd ... Oregon OH 43616 *Web:* ohiodnr.gov	419-836-7758	836-8711	565
Maumee Valley Fabricators 4801 Bennett Rd ... Toledo OH 43612 *Web:* www.maumeevalleyfab.com	419-476-1411	729-6134	492
Mauna Lani Bay Hotel & Bungalows 68-1400 Mauna Lani Dr ... Kamuela HI 96743 *TF:* 800-367-2323 ■ *Web:* www.maunalani.com	808-885-6622	881-7000	669
Mauna Loa Macadamia Nut Corp 16-701 Macadamia Rd ... Keaau HI 96749 *TF:* 888-628-6256 ■ *Web:* www.maunaloa.com	808-966-8618		10-10
Maupin Travel Inc 510 Daniels St ... Raleigh NC 27605 *Web:* www.maupintravel.com	919-821-2146		771
Maupintour Inc 2690 Weston Rd Ste 200 ... Weston FL 33331 **Fax Area Code:* 954 ■ *TF:* 800-255-4266 ■ *Web:* www.maupintour.com	800-255-4266	888-9082*	760
Maur Hill-Mount Academy 1000 Green St ... Atchison KS 66002 *Web:* mh-ma.com	913-367-5482	367-5096	622
Maurey Manufacturing Corp 410 Industrial Park Rd ... Holly Springs MS 38635 **Fax Area Code:* 662 ■ *TF:* 800-284-2161 ■ *Web:* www.maurey.biz	800-284-2161	252-6364*	620
Maurice Electrical Supply Co 6500A Seriff Rd ... Landover Hills MD 20785 *TF:* 866-913-0922 ■ *Web:* www.mauriceelectric.com	301-333-5990		246
Maurice K. Goddard State Park 684 Lake Wilhelm Rd ... Sandy Lake PA 16145 *Web:* www.dcnr.pa.gov	724-253-4833		565
Maurice M. Pine Free Public Library 10-01 Fair Lawn Ave ... Fair Lawn NJ 07410 *Web:* www.fairlawnlibrary.org	201-796-3400		434-3
Maurice Pincoffs Company Inc 1235 N Loop W Ste 510 ... Houston TX 77008 *Web:* www.pincoffs.com	713-681-5461	681-8521	485

	Phone	Fax	Class
Maurice Vaughan Furniture Co 610 E Stuart Dr . . . Galax VA 24333 *Web:* mauricevaughaninc.com	276-236-9781		321
Maurice Veterinary Clinic LLC 4080 Beau Rd . . . Maurice LA 70555 *Web:* mauricevet.com	337-385-2030		794
Maurice's Gourmet Barbeque 1600 Charleston Hwy . . . West Columbia SC 29171 *TF:* 800-628-7423 ■ *Web:* www.piggiepark.com	803-791-5887	791-8707	296-19
Maurices Inc 105 W Superior St . . . Duluth MN 55802 *TF:* 866-977-1542 ■ *Web:* www.maurices.com	218-727-8431	720-2102	157-4
Mauritius Embassies 1709 N St NW . . . Washington DC 20036 *Web:* www.maurinet.com	202-244-1491	966-0983	257
Mauritzon Inc 3939 W Belden Ave . . . Chicago IL 60647 *TF:* 800-621-4352 ■ *Web:* www.mauritzon.net	773-235-6000	235-1479	733
Maury Alliance 106 W Sixth St . . . Columbia TN 38401 *Web:* mauryalliance.com	931-388-2155	380-0335	139
Maury Farmers Coop 423 Westover Dr . . . Columbia TN 38401 *Web:* www.mauryfarmerscoop.com	931-388-0714		276
Maury Regional Hospital 1224 Trotwood Ave . . . Columbia TN 38401 *Web:* www.mauryregional.com	931-381-1111		374-3
Mauser Packaging Solutions 2 Tower Center Blvd . . . East Brunswick NJ 08816 *Web:* www.mausergroup.com	732-353-7101		608
Mautino Distributing Co 500 N Richards St . . . Spring Valley IL 61362	815-664-4311	664-2224	81-1
Maven Engineering Corp 15946 Derwood Rd . . . Rockville MD 20855 *Web:* www.mavencorporation.com	301-519-3400		529
Maven Group LLC, The 320 N Salem St Ste 204 . . . Apex NC 27502 *TF:* 800-343-6612 ■ *Web:* www.themavengroup.com	919-386-1010		260
Maven Wave Partners LLC 71 S Wacker Dr Ste 2040 . . . Chicago IL 60606 *Web:* www.mavenwave.com	312-878-4100		180
Maverick Auto parts 2801 N Central Ave . . . Chicago IL 60634 *Web:* maverickautopartschicago.com	773-283-6277		54
Maverick Boat Company Inc 3207 Industrial 29th St . . . Fort Pierce FL 34946 *Web:* maverickboats.com	772-465-0631	489-2168	90
Maverick Construction Corp 1 Westinghouse Plz . . . Boston MA 02136 *Web:* www.maverickcorporation.com	617-361-6700		256
Maverick County 1508 Las Quintas Blvd . . . Eagle Pass TX 78852 *Web:* co.maverick.tx.us	830-757-9201	752-1664	338
Maverick Enterprises Inc 751 E Gobbi St . . . Ukiah CA 95482 *Web:* www.maverickcaps.com	707-463-5591		297-8
Maverick Media Inc 123 W 17th St . . . Syracuse NE 68446 *Web:* www.ncnewspress.com	402-269-2135		637-8
Maverick Oilfield Services Ltd 3808 - 52 Ave PO Box 597 . . . Provost AB T0B3S0 *Web:* mavoil.com	780-753-2992		538
Maverick Technologies 265 Admiral Trost Dr . . . Columbia IL 62236 *TF:* 888-917-9109 ■ *Web:* www.mavtechglobal.com	618-281-9100		178-1
Maverick USA Inc 13301 Valentine Rd . . . North Little Rock AR 72117 **Fax Area Code:* 501 ■ *TF:* 800-289-6600 ■ *Web:* www.maverickusa.com	800-289-6600	955-4670*	780
Maverik Inc 10425 S 1300 W . . . North Salt Lake UT 84054 *TF:* 800-789-4455 ■ *Web:* loyalty.maverik.com	801-936-5573		204
Maverix Solutions Inc 1633 E Fourth St Ste 220 . . . Santa Ana CA 92701 *Web:* mavcoatmoldrelease.com	714-501-6383		177
Maveron LLC 411 First Ave S Ste 600 . . . Seattle WA 98104 *Web:* www.maveron.com	206-288-1700		792
Mavro Imaging LLC 22 Maple Tree Dr . . . Westampton NJ 08060 *Web:* www.mavroimaging.com	609-949-9010		138
Mawer Investment Management Ltd 517 - Tenth Ave S W Ste 600 . . . Calgary AB T2R0A8 *TF:* 800-889-6248 ■ *Web:* www.mawer.com	800-889-6248		528
Mawicke & Goisman SC 1509 N Prospect Ave . . . Milwaukee WI 53202 *Web:* mawickelaw.com	414-224-0600	224-9359	428
MAWS (Marijuana Anonymous World Services) 340 S Lemon Ave Ste 9420 . . . Walnut CA 91789 *TF:* 800-766-6779 ■ *Web:* www.marijuana-anonymous.org	800-766-6779		48-21
Mawson & Mawson Inc 1800 Old Lincoln Hwy PO Box 248 . . . Langhorne PA 19047 *Web:* www.mawsonandmawson.com	215-750-1100		780
Max & Erma's 3750 W Market St . . . Fairlawn OH 44333 *Web:* www.maxandermas.com	330-666-1002		671
Max Arnold & Sons LLC 702 N Main St . . . Hopkinsville KY 42240 *Web:* maxfuel.net	270-885-8488		581
Max Auto Supply Co 1101 Monroe St . . . Toledo OH 43604	419-243-7281		54
Max Credit Union 400 Eastdale Cir . . . Montgomery AL 36117 *TF:* 800-776-6776 ■ *Web:* www.mymax.com	334-260-2600		70
Max Environmental Technologies Inc 1815 Washington Rd . . . Pittsburgh PA 15241 *TF:* 800-851-7845 ■ *Web:* www.maxenvironmental.com	412-343-4900		196
Max Group Corp 17011 Green Dr . . . City of Industry CA 91745 *Web:* www.maxgroup.com	626-935-0050		174
Max International Converters Inc 2360 Dairy Rd . . . Lancaster PA 17601 *TF:* 800-233-0222 ■ *Web:* www.maxintl.com	800-233-0222		554
Max Intertrade Inc 4471 NW 36th St Ste 203 . . . Miami FL 33166 *Web:* www.maxintertradeinc.com	305-887-0837		311
Max It Group Inc 715 Rt 10 E Ste 205 . . . Randolph NJ 07869 *Web:* www.maxitgroupinc.com	973-343-2951		180
Max J. Kuney Co 120 N Ralph St PO Box 4008 . . . Spokane WA 99220 *Web:* maxkuney.com	509-535-0651	534-6828	186
Max Levy Autograph Inc 2710 Commerce Way . . . Philadelphia PA 19154 *TF:* 800-798-3675 ■ *Web:* www.maxlevy.com	800-798-3675		481
Max Machinery Inc 33A Healdsburg Ave . . . Healdsburg CA 95448 *Web:* www.maxmachinery.com	707-433-2662		495
Max Media of Arkansas LLC 2758 Hwy 64 . . . Wynne AR 72396 *Web:* www.rivervalleyradio.com	479-968-6816	968-2946	645-141
Max Restaurant Group 249 Pearl St 2nd Fl . . . Hartford CT 06103 *Web:* www.maxrestaurantgroup.com	860-522-9806	522-5705	670
Max Technical Training 4900 Pkwy Dr Ste 160 . . . Mason OH 45040 *TF:* 866-595-6863 ■ *Web:* maxtrain.com	513-322-8888		196
MAX Technologies Inc 2051 Victoria Ave . . . Saint-Lambert QC J4S1H1 *TF:* 800-361-1629 ■ *Web:* www.maxt.com	450-443-3332	443-1618	668
Max Tool Inc 119b Citation Ct . . . Birmingham AL 35209 *TF:* 800-783-6298 ■ *Web:* maxtoolinc.com	205-942-2466	942-7144	351
Max's Allegheny Tavern 537 Suismon St . . . Pittsburgh PA 15212 *Web:* www.maxsalleghenytavern.com	412-231-1899		671
Max's Grille 404 Plaza Real . . . Boca Raton FL 33432 *Web:* www.maxsgrille.com	561-368-0080		671
Max's Restaurant 313 W Broadway . . . Glendale CA 91204 *Web:* www.maxsrestaurantna.com	818-637-7751		671
Maxair Inc Wittman Regional Airport 1257 W 20th Ave . . . Oshkosh WI 54902 *TF:* 800-833-1544 ■ *Web:* www.maxair-inc.com	920-738-3020	738-3026	167-3
MaxBotix Inc 13860 Shawkia Dr . . . Brainerd MN 56401 *Web:* www.maxbotix.com	218-454-0766	454-0768	693
MaxBounty Inc PO Box 17039 . . . Ottawa ON K4A4W8 *Web:* www.maxbounty.com	613-834-3955		393
Maxcare Inc 1114 Pennsylvania NE . . . Albuquerque NM 87110 *Web:* maxcarenm.net	505-271-2433	237-0715	363
Maxcel Co, The 54 Masland Cir . . . Dallas TX 75230 *Web:* maxcel.net	972-644-0000	680-2400	304
Maxcess International Inc 222 W Memorial Rd . . . Oklahoma City OK 73114 *Web:* www.maxcessintl.com	405-755-1600	755-8425	203
Maxell Corporation of America 3 Garret Mountain Plz 3rd Fl Ste 300 . . . Woodland Park NJ 07424 **Fax Area Code:* 201 ■ *TF:* 800-533-2836 ■ *Web:* maxell-usa.com	973-653-2400	796-8790*	658
Maxey Law Office PLLC 1835 W Broadway Ave . . . Spokane WA 99201 *TF:* 800-477-7758 ■ *Web:* maxeylaw.com	509-326-0338	325-4490	41
Maxi Aids Inc 42 Executive Blvd . . . Farmingdale NY 11735 *Web:* www.maxiaids.com	631-752-0521	752-0689	475
Maxi Foods LLC 8616 California Ave . . . Riverside CA 92504 *Web:* www.maxifoodsmarkets.com	951-688-0538		297-8
Maxi Volt Corporation Inc 800 S Rusk St . . . Amarillo TX 79106 *Web:* www.maxivolt.com	806-371-0722		580
Maxijet Inc 8400 Lake Trask Rd . . . Dundee FL 33838 *Web:* www.maxijet.com	863-439-3667	439-6608	273
Maxil Technology Solutions Inc 2625 Butterfield Rd St 138S . . . Oak Brook IL 60523 *Web:* www.maxiltechnology.com	630-472-7335	929-9733	177
Maxim Crane Works 1225 Washington Pk . . . Bridgeville PA 15017 *TF:* 877-629-5438 ■ *Web:* www.cranerental.com	412-504-0200	504-0126	264-3
Maxim Group LLC 405 Lexington Ave . . . New York NY 10174 *TF:* 800-724-0761 ■ *Web:* www.maximgrp.com	212-895-3500		401
Maxim Healthcare Services 7600 Leesburg Pke West Bldg Ste 204 . . . Falls Church VA 22043 **Fax Area Code:* 855 ■ *Web:* www.maximhealthcare.com	703-533-3131	239-6134*	363
Maxim Integrated 6440 Oak Canyon Ste 100 . . . Irvine CA 92618 *Web:* www.maximintegrated.com	714-508-8800		696
Maxim Integrated 160 Rio Robles . . . San Jose CA 95134 *Web:* www.maximintegrated.com	408-601-1000		261
Maxim Partners LLC 105 E First St Ste 203 . . . Hinsdale IL 60521 *Web:* www.maximpartnersllc.com	630-206-4040		528
Maxim Technologies Inc 1607 Derwent Way . . . Delta BC V3M6K8 *TF:* 800-663-9925 ■ *Web:* www.maxim-technologies.com	800-663-9925		151
Maxima Technologies Stewart Warner 1811 Rohrerstown Rd . . . Lancaster PA 17601 *TF:* 800-676-1837 ■ *Web:* www.maximatecc.com	717-581-1000	569-7247	495
Maxime 1131 St Mary's Rd . . . Winnipeg MB R2M3T9 *Web:* www.maximesrestaurant.ca	204-257-1521		671
Maximizer Software Inc 1090 W Pender St 10th Fl . . . Vancouver BC V6E2N7 *TF:* 800-804-6299 ■ *Web:* www.maximizer.com	604-601-8000		180
Maximum Marketing Services Inc 833 W Jackson Blvd . . . Chicago IL 60607 *Web:* www.maxmarketing.com	312-226-4111		636
Maximum Potential Inc 2854 Hwy 55 Ste 150 . . . Saint Paul MN 55121 *Web:* www.maximumpotential.com	651-452-8256		463
Maximum Quality Foods Inc 3351 Tremley Pt Rd . . . Linden NJ 07036 *Web:* www.maximumqualityfoods.com	908-474-0003		299
Maximum Title & Escrow Services Inc 22021 Brookpark Rd Ste 124 . . . Fairview Park OH 44126 *Web:* maximumtitle.net	440-801-5000		653
Maximus Federal Services Inc 3750 Monroe Ave Ste 702 . . . Pittsford NY 14534 *Web:* www.medicareappeal.com	585-348-3300		449
MAXIMUS Inc 1891 Metro Center Dr . . . Reston VA 20190 *NYSE:* MMS ■ *Web:* www.maximus.com	703-251-8500	251-8240	194
Maxitrol Co 23555 Telegraph Rd PO Box 2230 . . . Southfield MI 48033 *Web:* www.maxitrol.com	248-356-1400	356-0829	201
Maxland International Inc 9457 Rush St . . . South El Monte CA 91733 *Web:* maxland.com	626-443-2443	443-4674	787

Phone | Fax | Class

MaxLinear Inc
2051 Palomar Airport Rd Ste 100 .... Carlsbad CA 92011 760-692-0711 444-8598 695
NYSE: MXL ■ *TF:* 888-505-4369 ■ *Web:* www.maxlinear.com

Maxmedia 2160 Hills Ave Bldg A .... Atlanta GA 30318 404-564-0063 5
Web: www.maxmedia.com

Maxmind Inc 14 Spring St 3rd Fl .... Waltham MA 02451 617-500-4493 177
Web: maxmind.com

Maxon Computer Inc
2640 Lavery Ct Ste A .... Newbury Park CA 91320 805-376-3333 376-3331 177
Web: www.maxon.net

Maxon Corp 201 E 18th St PO Box 2068 .... Muncie IN 47307 765-284-3304 286-8394 789
Web: maxoncorp.com

Maxon Furniture Inc 200 Oak St .... Muscatine IA 52761 800-876-4274 319-1
TF: 800-876-4274 ■ *Web:* www.maxonfurniture.com

Maxon Industries Inc
11921 Slauson Ave .... Santa Fe Springs CA 90670 562-464-0099 771-7713* 470
**Fax Area Code:* 888 ■ *TF:* 800-227-4116 ■ *Web:* www.maxonlift.com

Maxon Industries Inc 3204 W Mill Rd .... Milwaukee WI 53209 414-351-4000 351-9057 190
Web: www.maxon.com

Maxor National Pharmacy Services Corp
320 S Polk St Ste 100 .... Amarillo TX 79101 806-324-5400 324-5495 586
TF: 800-658-6146 ■ *Web:* www.maxor.com

Maxpak Total Packing
2808 New Tampa Hwy .... Lakeland FL 33815 863-682-0123 683-7895 559
Web: www.maxpak.cc

Maxs Bistro 1784 W Bullard Ave .... Fresno CA 93711 559-439-6900 439-7206 671
Web: www.maxsbistro.com

Maxson & Associates Accountancy Corp
6700 E Pacific Coast Hwy .... Long Beach CA 90803 562-594-4681 547-0924* 2
**Fax Area Code:* 714 ■ *Web:* maxson-accounting.com

Maxson Automatic Machinery Co
70 Airport Rd .... Westerly RI 02891 401-596-0162 596-1050 556
Web: www.maxsonautomatic.com

Maxsys 173 Dalhousie St .... Ottawa ON K1N7C7 613-562-9943 260
TF: 800-429-5177 ■ *Web:* maxsys.ca

Maxtec 2305 South 1070 West .... Salt Lake City UT 84119 801-266-5300 973-6090 476
TF: 800-748-5355 ■ *Web:* www.maxtec.com

Maxtex Inc 3620 Francis Cir .... Alpharetta GA 30004 770-772-6757 361
TF: 800-241-1836 ■ *Web:* www.maxtexinc.com

MaxTool 5798 Ontario Mills Pkwy .... Ontario CA 91764 909-568-2800 351
TF: 800-629-3325 ■ *Web:* www.maxtool.com

MaxTradeIn.com LLC
9102 N Meridian St Ste 450 .... Indianapolis IN 46260 317-218-3612 387
Web: maxtradein.com

Maxum LLC 1307 Tool Dr .... New Iberia LA 70560 337-364-9526 260
Web: www.maxumllc.com

Maxus Realty Trust Inc
104 Armour Rd PO Box 34729 .... North Kansas City MO 64116 816-303-4500 221-1829 655
OTC: MRTI ■ *Web:* mrti.com

MaxVal Group Inc 2251 Grant Rd .... Los Altos CA 94024 650-472-0644 226
Web: www.maxval.com

MaxVision Corp 495 Production Ave .... Madison AL 35758 256-772-3058 772-3078 173-2
TF: 800-533-5805 ■ *Web:* maxvision.com

Maxwell Air Force Base
55 Le May Plaza S .... Montgomery AL 36112 334-953-2014 497-1
TF: 877-353-6807 ■ *Web:* www.maxwell.af.mil

Maxwell Davidson Gallery
521 W 26th St .... New York NY 10001 212-759-7555 759-5824 42
Web: www.davidsongallery.com

Maxwell Electrical Services Inc
2601 N Arlington Ave .... Indianapolis IN 46218 317-546-9600 546-0205 189-4
TF: 800-406-0999 ■ *Web:* www.maxwellelectrical.com

Maxwell Geoservices
1168 Hamilton St .... Vancouver BC V6B2S2 604-678-3298 177
Web: maxwellgeoservices.com

Maxwell Hardwood Flooring
190 Wilson Mill Rd .... Monticello AR 71655 870-367-2436 367-2968 106
Web: www.maxwellhardwoodflooring.com

Maxwell Locke & Ritter LLP
401 Congress Ave Ste 1100 .... Austin TX 78701 512-370-3200 734
Web: www.mlrpc.com

Maxwell Noll 600 S Lake Ave .... Pasadena CA 91106 800-660-2466 796-5834* 428
**Fax Area Code:* 626 ■ *TF:* 800-660-2466 ■ *Web:* www.maxnoll.com

Maxwell Sensors Inc
10020 Pioneer Blvd Ste 103 .... Santa Fe Springs CA 90670 562-801-2088 801-2089 743
Web: www.maxwellsensors.com

Maxwell Silverman's Toolhouse
2 Washington Square Union Sta PO Box 702 .... Worcester MA 01613 508-755-1200 753-8217 671
Web: www.maxwellsilvermansbanquet.com

Maxwell Tools Co 328 Brightfield Dr .... Ballwin MO 63021 314-662-6510 493
TF: 866-586-7331 ■ *Web:* www.maxwelltools.com

Maxwell Welding and Machine Inc
11 Starck Dr .... Burgettstown PA 15021 724-729-3160 729-3161 480
Web: www.mwm-inc.com

Maxwelton Braes Golf Resort
7670 Hwy 57 .... Baileys Harbor WI 54202 920-421-4653 669
Web: maxweltonbraes.com

MAXXAM Inc 1330 Post Oak Blvd Ste 2000 .... Houston TX 77056 713-975-7600 185
OTC: MAXX ■ *Web:* www.charleshurwitz.com

Maxxon Corp 920 Hamel Rd PO Box 253 .... Hamel MN 55340 763-478-9600 135
Web: www.maxxon.com

MaxYield Co-op
313 Third Ave NE PO Box 49 .... West Bend IA 50597 515-887-7211 887-7291 275
TF: 800-383-0003 ■ *Web:* www.maxyieldcooperative.com

Maxymillian Technologies Inc
1801 E St .... Pittsfield MA 01201 413-499-3050 443-0511 192
Web: www.maxymillian.com

Maxzone Auto Parts 15889 Slover Ave .... Fontana CA 92337 909-822-3288 822-3399 61
Web: www.maxzone.com

May & Co 110 Monument Pl .... Vicksburg MS 39180 601-636-4762 2
Web: www.maycpa.com

May Advertising & Design Inc
724 N First St Ste 650 .... Minneapolis MN 55401 612-332-2450 4
Web: www.mayads.com

May Cocagne & King Pc
1353 E Mound Rd Ste 300 .... Decatur IL 62526 217-762-3136 2
Web: www.mckcpa.com

May Dragon 4848 Beltline Rd .... Dallas TX 75254 972-302-0998 490-5023 671
Web: www.maydragon.com

May FoodService 51 Washington Ave .... Cranston RI 02920 401-942-4221 942-2619 300
Web: www.mayfoodservice.com

May Institute Inc 41 Pacella Pk Dr .... Randolph MA 02368 781-440-0400 48-6
TF: 800-778-7601 ■ *Web:* www.mayinstitute.org

May Media Group LLC
104 Centre Blvd Ste A .... Marlton NJ 08053 856-753-3800 574-4996 637-9
Web: www.kiwimagonline.com

May Memorial Library
342 S Spring St .... Burlington NC 27215 336-229-3588 229-3592 434-3
Web: www.alamancelibraries.org

May Supply Company Inc
1775 Erickson Ave .... Harrisonburg VA 22801 540-433-2611 612
TF: 800-296-9997 ■ *Web:* maysupply.com

May Tool & Mold Company Inc
2922 Wheeling Ave .... Kansas City MO 64129 816-923-6262 923-6277 757
Web: mayinc.com

May Trucking Co 4185 Brooklake Rd .... Salem OR 97303 503-393-7030 780
TF: 800-547-9169 ■ *Web:* www.maytrucking.com

May, Adam, Gerdes & Thompson LLP
503 S Pierre St .... Pierre SD 57501 605-224-8803 428
TF: 800-636-8803 ■ *Web:* www.magt.com

Maya Overseas Foods Inc
151 Fulton Ave .... Garden City Park NY 11040 718-894-5145 894-5178 297-8
Web: www.mayafoods.com

Mayall Hurley, A Professional Corp
2453 Grand Canal Blvd .... Stockton CA 95207 209-477-3833 41
Web: mayallaw.com

Maybank Industries LLC
288 Meeting St .... Charleston SC 29401 843-278-0339 175
Web: www.maybanksystems.com

Maybelline New York
575 5th Ave PO Box 1010 .... New York NY 10017 800-944-0730 214
TF: 800-944-0730 ■ *Web:* www.maybelline.com

Mayberry Fine Art Inc
212 Mcdermot Ave .... Winnipeg MB R3B0S3 204-255-5690 42
TF: 877-871-9261 ■ *Web:* www.mayberryfineart.com

Maybury State Park 20145 Beck Rd .... Northville MI 48167 248-349-8390 565
Web: www.michigan.org

Mayco Industries LLC
18 W Oxmoor Rd .... Birmingham AL 35209 205-942-4242 945-8704 697
TF: 800-749-6061 ■ *Web:* maycoindustries.com

Mayco International LLC
42400 Merrill Rd .... Sterling Heights MI 48314 586-803-6000 60
Web: maycointernational.com

Mayer Bros Apple Products Inc
3300 Transit Rd .... West Seneca NY 14224 716-668-1787 668-2437 296-20
TF: 800-696-2928 ■ *Web:* mayerbrothers.com

Mayer Electric Supply Co
3405 Fourth Ave S .... Birmingham AL 35222 205-583-3500 246
TF: 866-637-1255 ■ *Web:* www.mayerelectric.com

Mayer Hoffman McCann PC
700 W 47th St Ste 1100 .... Kansas City MO 64112 816-945-5600 897-1280 2
TF: 877-887-1090 ■ *Web:* www.mhmcpa.com

Mayer Laboratories Inc
1950 Addison St Ste 101 .... Berkeley CA 94704 510-229-5300 743
Web: www.mayerlabs.com

Mayer Pollock Steel Corp
Industrial Hwy .... Pottstown PA 19464 610-323-5500 323-5506 686
Web: www.mayerpollock.com

Mayer Tool & Engineering Inc
1404 N Centerville Rd .... Sturgis MI 49091 269-651-1428 651-4144 757
Web: www.mayertool.com

Mayer, Shanzer, & Mayer PC
918 Maple St .... Conshohocken PA 19428 610-828-0200 2
Web: mayererp.com

Mayers & Associates Civil Engineering Inc
19 Spectrum Pointe Dr Ste 609 .... Lake Forest CA 92630 949-599-0870 261
Web: mayerscivil.com

Mayers Electric Company Inc
4004 Erie Ct .... Cincinnati OH 45227 513-272-2900 272-2904 189-4
Web: mayerselectriccompany.com

Mayers Firm LLC, The
3031 Walton Rd Ste A 330 .... Plymouth Meeting PA 19462 610-825-0300 41
Web: themayersfirm.com

Mayerson & Assoc
330 W 38th St Ste 600 .... New York NY 10018 212-265-7200 41
Web: mayerslaw.com

Mayes County 1 Court Pl .... Pryor OK 74361 918-825-2426 338
Web: mayes.okcounties.org

Mayes County Petroleum
120 W Peak Blvd .... Muskogee OK 74403 918-682-9924 682-8640 579
Web: www.mcpetro.com

Mayes Harris Realty Inc
13422 Scanlan Way .... Davidson NC 28036 704-589-8166 896-7178 652
Web: mayesharrisrealty.com

Mayes Testing Engineers Inc
20225 Cedar Valley Rd Ste 110 .... Lynnwood WA 98036 425-742-9360 745-1737 743
Web: www.mayestesting.com

Mayesh Wholesale Florist Inc
5401 W 104th St .... Los Angeles CA 90045 310-348-4921 292
TF: 888-462-9374 ■ *Web:* www.mayesh.com

Mayfair 2500 N Mayfair Rd .... Milwaukee WI 53226 414-771-1300 460
Web: www.mayfairmall.com

Mayfair Hotel 1256 W Seventh St .... Los Angeles CA 90017 213-632-1200 378
Web: www.mayfairla.com

Mayfair Hotel & Spa
3000 Florida Ave .... Coconut Grove FL 33133 305-441-0000 447-9173 379
TF: 800-433-4555 ■ *Web:* www.mayfairhotelandspa.com

Mayfield & Assoc 12452 Hwy 49 N Ste B .... Gulfport MS 39503 228-896-1555 390
TF: 866-896-1555 ■ *Web:* www.mayfieldis.com

Mayfield Fund
Quadrus Complex 2484 Sand Hill Rd .... Menlo Park CA 94025 650-854-5560 792
Web: www.mayfield.com

Mayfield Paper Co 1115 S Hill St .... San Angelo TX 76903 325-653-1444 559
TF: 800-725-1441 ■ *Web:* www.mayfieldpaper.com

Mayfield Transfer Company Inc
3200 W Lake St .... Melrose Park IL 60160 708-681-4440 681-4483 780
TF: 800-222-2959 ■ *Web:* www.mfld.net

Name / Address	Phone	Fax	Class
Mayfield-Graves County Chamber of Commerce 201 E College St ... Mayfield KY 42066 *Web:* www.mayfieldgraveschamber.com	270-247-6101		139
Mayflower Park Hotel 405 Olive Way ... Seattle WA 98101 *TF:* 800-426-5100 ■ *Web:* www.mayflowerpark.com	206-623-8700	382-6996	379
Mayflower Retirement Community 1620 Mayflower Ct ... Winter Park FL 32792 *TF:* 800-228-6518 ■ *Web:* www.themayflower.com	407-672-1620	671-6336	672
Mayflower Tours Inc 1225 Warren Ave PO Box 490 ... Downers Grove IL 60515 *TF:* 800-323-7604 ■ *Web:* www.mayflowercruisesandtours.com	630-435-8500	960-3575	760
Mayflower Transit LLC 1 Mayflower Dr ... Fenton MO 63026 *TF:* 800-325-9970 ■ *Web:* www.mayflower.com	636-305-4000		519
Mayflowers Software 44 Stoneymeade Wy ... Acton MA 01720 *Web:* www.maysoft.com	978-635-1700		178-1
Mayfran International Inc 6650 Beta Dr ... Cleveland OH 44143 *Web:* www.mayfran.com	440-461-4100	461-5565	207
Mayhall Law Firm APLC, The 724 E Boston St ... Covington LA 70433 *Web:* mayhalltaxlaw.com	985-246-1700	246-1706	41
Mayhew Steel Products Inc 199 Industrial Blvd ... Turners Falls MA 01376 *TF:* 800-872-0037 ■ *Web:* www.mayhew.com	413-863-4860	863-8464	758
Maykadeh 470 Green St ... San Francisco CA 94133 *Web:* maykadehrestaurant.com	415-362-8286		671
Mayland Community College 200 Mayland Dr PO Box 547 ... Spruce Pine NC 28777 *TF:* 800-462-9526 ■ *Web:* www.mayland.edu	828-765-7351	765-0728	162
Mayline Company LLC 619 N Commerce St PO Box 728 ... Sheboygan WI 53082 *TF:* 800-822-8037 ■ *Web:* www.mayline.com	920-457-5537	457-7388	319-1
Maymead Inc 1995 Roan Creek Rd ... Mountain City TN 37683 *Web:* www.maymead.com	423-727-2000		188-4
Maymont 2201 Shields Dr ... Richmond VA 23220 *Web:* maymont.org	804-358-7166	358-9994	520
Maynard Furniture Company Inc 725 Anderson St ... Belton SC 29627 *Web:* www.maynardshomefurnishings.com	864-338-7751		321
Maynard Inc 7175 S Mcguire St ... Fayetteville AR 72704 *Web:* www.maynardinc.us	479-443-6677	443-2810	488
Maynard Steel Casting Co 2856 S 27th St ... Milwaukee WI 53215 *Web:* www.maynardsteel.com	414-385-6500	645-7378	307
Maynards Industries Ltd 1837 Main St ... Vancouver BC V5T3B8 *Web:* www.maynards.com	604-876-6787		459
Mayo Aviation Inc 7735 S Peoria St ... Englewood CO 80112 *TF:* 800-525-0194 ■ *Web:* www.mayoaviation.com	303-790-9777		13
Mayo Civic Ctr 30 Civic Center Dr SE ... Rochester MN 55904 *TF:* 800-422-2199 ■ *Web:* mayociviccenter.com	507-328-2220	328-2221	205
Mayo Clinic Health Letter 200 First St NW ... Rochester MN 55905 *TF:* 800-291-1128 ■ *Web:* marketplace.mayoclinic.com	800-291-1128		531-8
Mayo Clinic Health System Austin 1000 First Dr NW ... Austin MN 55912 *TF:* 888-609-4065 ■ *Web:* mayoclinichealthsystem.org	507-433-7351		374-3
Mayo Clinic Hospital 5777 E Mayo Blvd ... Phoenix AZ 85054 *TF:* 888-266-0440 ■ *Web:* www.mayoclinic.org	480-342-2000		374-3
Mayo Clinic Proceedings Magazine Siebens Bldg 770 ... Rochester MN 55905 *Web:* www.mayoclinicproceedings.org	507-284-2094	284-0252	457-16
Mayo Collaborative Services Inc 3050 Superior Dr NW ... Rochester MN 55901 *TF:* 800-533-1710 ■ *Web:* www.mayomedicallaboratories.com	507-266-5700		415
Mayo Knitting Mills Inc PO Box 160 ... Tarboro NC 27886 *Web:* mayoknitting.com	252-823-3101	823-0368	155-10
Mayo Manufacturing Corp 4101 Terry St ... Texarkana TX 75501 *Web:* www.mayofurniture.com	903-838-0518	838-4531	321
Mayo Medical School 200 First St SW ... Rochester MN 55905 *Web:* www.mayo.edu	507-284-2511	284-2634	167-2
Mayport Coast Guard Base 4200 Ocean St ... Atlantic Beach FL 32233 *Web:* www.uscg.mil	904-564-7500		158
Mays Chemical Co 5611 E 71st St ... Indianapolis IN 46220 *Web:* www.mayschem.com	317-842-8722		146
Mays Meats Inc 541 E Main Ave ... Taylorsville NC 28681 *Web:* www.maysmeats.net	828-632-2034	632-7081	297-2
Maysteel 469 Hospital Dr Ste A / Ste B2 ... Gastonia NC 28054 *Web:* www.maysteel.com	704-864-1313		490
MayStreet LLC 135 W 26th St ... New York NY 10001 *Web:* maystreet.com	212-600-1639		196
Maysville Community & Technical College 1755 US 68 ... Maysville KY 41056 *Web:* maysville.kctcs.edu	606-759-7141	759-5818	162
Maytag Aircraft Corp 6145 Lehman Dr Ste 300 ... Colorado Springs CO 80918 *Web:* www.maytagaircraft.com	719-593-1600	593-8518	359
Maytag Appliances 403 W Fourth St N ... Newton IA 50208 *TF:* 800-344-1274 ■ *Web:* www.maytag.com	800-344-1274		36
Maytag Dairy Farms Inc 2282 E 8th St N ... Newton IA 50208 *Web:* www.maytagdairyfarms.com	641-792-1133		296-5
Maytex 261 Fifth Ave Ste 1701 17th Fl ... New York NY 10016 *Web:* www.maytex.com	212-684-1191		361
Mayvenn 1714 Franklin St ... Oakland CA 94607 *TF:* 888-562-7952 ■ *Web:* shop.mayvenn.com	888-562-7952		77
Mayville Engineering Company Inc 715 S St ... Mayville WI 53050 *Web:* www.mecinc.com	920-387-4500		190
Mayville Products Corp 403 Degner Ave ... Mayville WI 53050 *Web:* www.optimastantron.com	920-387-3000	387-3497	697
Mayville Savings Bank 200 S Main St ... Mayville WI 53050 *Web:* www.mayvillesavings.com	920-387-2310	387-5282	70
Mayville State University 330 Third St NE ... Mayville ND 58257 *Fax Area Code: 701 ■ *TF:* 800-437-4104 ■ *Web:* www.leightoninteractive.com	800-437-4104	788-4748*	166
Mayway Corp 1338 Mandela Pkwy ... Oakland CA 94607 *TF:* 800-262-9929 ■ *Web:* www.mayway.com	510-208-3113		297
Maywood Park 1805 N 5 Ave ... Melrose Park IL 60160 *Web:* maywoodpark.com	708-343-4800		642
Maywood Public Library 121 S Fifth Ave ... Maywood IL 60153 *Web:* www.maywoodlibrary.org	708-343-1847	343-2115	434-3
Maz Mezcal Inc 316 E 86th St ... New York NY 10028 *Web:* mazmezcal.com	212-472-1599		670
Mazaheri Law Firm PLLC 3000 W Memorial Rd Ste 230 ... Oklahoma City OK 73120 *Web:* mazaherilawfirm.com	405-414-2222		41
Mazany Office Interiors 428 Livingston Ave ... Jamestown NY 14701 *Web:* www.mazanyoffice.com	716-487-1617		320
Mazars Harel Drouin LLP 215 St Jacques Bureau 1200 ... Montreal QC H2Y1M6 *Web:* www.mazars.ca	514-845-9253		194
Mazatlan 211 N 70th St ... Lincoln NE 68505 *Web:* www.lincolnsbestmexican.com	402-464-7201		671
Mazda North American Operations 7755 Irvine Center Dr PO Box 19734 ... Irvine CA 92623 *TF:* 800-222-5500 ■ *Web:* www.mazdausa.com	800-222-5500		59
Mazda of Roswell 11185 Alpharetta Hwy ... Roswell GA 30076 *Web:* www.mazdaofroswell.com	770-594-6535		57
Mazda Publishers Inc PO Box 2603 ... Costa Mesa CA 92628 *Web:* www.mazdapublishers.com	714-751-5252	751-4805	637-2
Mazel & Company Inc 4300 W Ferdinand St ... Chicago IL 60624 *TF:* 800-525-4023 ■ *Web:* www.mazelandco.com	773-533-1600	533-9490	492
Mazie, Slater, Katz & Freeman LLC 103 Eisenhower Pkwy ... Roseland NJ 07068 *Web:* mazieslater.com	973-228-9898		41
Mazon Associates Inc 800 W Airport Fwy Ste 900 ... Irving TX 75062 *TF:* 800-442-2740 ■ *Web:* mazonfactoring.com	972-554-6967	554-0951	272
Mazonia-Braidwood State Fish & Wildlife Areas Route 53 & Huston Rd ... Braceville IL 60407 *Web:* www.dnr.illinois.gov	815-237-0063		565
Mazuma Credit Union 9300 Troost Ave ... Kansas City MO 64131 *Web:* www.mazuma.org	816-361-4194		219
Mazza 1515 S 1500 E ... Salt Lake City UT 84105 *Web:* www.mazzacafe.com	801-484-9259		671
Mazza Gallerie 5300 Wisconsin Ave NW ... Washington DC 20015 *Web:* www.mazzagallerie.com	202-966-6114		460
Mazza Vineyards 11815 E Lake Rd ... North East PA 16428 *Fax Area Code: 814 ■ *TF:* 800-796-9463 ■ *Web:* www.enjoymazza.com	800-796-9463	725-3948*	50-7
Mazzarelli's Bakery Inc 229 Central St ... Milford MA 01757 *Web:* www.mazzarellisbakery.com	508-473-1175		297-2
Mazzella Lifting Technologies 21000 Aerospace Pkwy ... Cleveland OH 44142 *TF:* 800-362-4601 ■ *Web:* www.mazzellacompanies.com	440-239-7000	239-7010	470
Mazzeo Agency 1 Bethany Rd Ste 50 ... Hazlet NJ 07730 *TF:* 800-777-0044 ■ *Web:* www.mazzeoagency.com	732-344-5154	344-5155	390
Mazzetta Co 1990 St Johns Ave ... Highland Park IL 60035 *Web:* www.mazzetta.com	847-433-1150		297-5
Mazzo Oil Co PO Box 1101 ... Garfield NJ 07026 *Web:* mazzoenergy.com	973-473-5181		316
Mazzone & Associates Inc 75 14th St NE Office Tower at the Four Seasons Ste 2800 ... Atlanta GA 30309 *Web:* www.globalmna.com	404-931-8545	574-5738	194
Mazzotta, Sherwood & Vagianelis PC 9 Washington Sq Washington Ave Ext ... Albany NY 12205 *Web:* mvattorneys.com	518-452-0941	452-0417	428
MB Bark LLC 100 Bark Mulch Dr ... Auburn ME 04210 *Fax Area Code: 207 ■ *TF:* 800-866-4991 ■ *Web:* www.mbbark.com	800-866-4991	786-0800*	200
MB Companies Inc 1615 Wisconsin Ave ... New Holstein WI 53061 *Fax Area Code: 920 ■ *TF:* 800-558-5800 ■ *Web:* www.m-bco.com	800-558-5800	898-4588*	190
MB Haynes Corp 187 Deaverview Rd ... Asheville NC 28806 *Web:* www.mbhaynes.com	828-254-6141	253-8136	189-7
MB Industries Inc 9205 Rosman Hwy ... Rosman NC 28772 *Web:* www.m-bindustries.com	828-862-4201	862-4297	744
MB Trading Futures Inc 1926 E Maple Ave ... El Segundo CA 90245 *TF:* 866-628-3001 ■ *Web:* mbtrading.com	310-647-4281		690
MB Westfield Inc 44 School St Ste 325 ... Boston MA 02108	413-568-8676		621
MBA (Military Benefit Assn) 14605 Avion Pkwy PO Box 221110 ... Chantilly VA 20153 *TF:* 800-336-0100 ■ *Web:* www.militarybenefit.org	703-968-6200	968-6423	48-19
MBA Publishing 821 Lincoln St ... Walla Walla WA 99362 *Web:* www.volunteertoday.com	509-529-0244		637-2
MBA Surety Agency Inc 207 E Capitol Ave ... Jefferson City MO 65101 *Web:* www.mobankers.com	573-636-2142		69
MBAF 1450 Brickell Ave 18th Fl ... Miami FL 33131 *TF:* 800-239-3843 ■ *Web:* mbafcpa.com	305-373-5500	373-0056	2
MBB Enterprises 3352 W Grand Ave ... Chicago IL 60651 *Web:* www.mbbmasonry.com	773-278-7100	278-7503	358
MBC (Memorial Blood Centers) 737 Pelham Blvd ... Saint Paul MN 55114 *Fax Area Code: 651 ■ *TF:* 888-448-3253 ■ *Web:* www.mbc.org	888-448-3253	332-7001*	89
MBC (McKenzie Banking Co) 676 N Main St ... McKenzie TN 38201 *Web:* foundationbank.org	731-352-2262	352-7778	70
MBC (Medical Billing Concepts Inc) 16001 Ventura Blvd Ste 135 ... Encino CA 91436 *TF:* 866-351-2852 ■ *Web:* www.medbillconcepts.com	866-351-2852		2
MBDA (Minority Business Development Agency) 1401 Constitution Ave NW ... Washington DC 20230 *TF:* 888-324-1551 ■ *Web:* www.mbda.gov	888-324-1551		340-2

Phone Fax Class

MBF Clearing Corp
225 Liberty St Ste 1020A .... New York NY 10281 212-845-5000 845-4198 691
Web: www.mbfcc.com

MBF Inc 620 Industrial Ave.................. Greensboro NC 27406 336-379-9352 272-0864 5
Web: www.infodog.com

MBFI (Miami Book Fair Intl)
300 NE Second Ave .... Miami FL 33132 305-237-3258 281
Web: www.miamibookfair.com

MBG Technologies Inc
PO Box 2024 .... Newport Beach CA 92659 949-644-0126 528
Web: www.mbgtech.com

MBH Architects 960 Atlantic Ave .... Alameda CA 94501 510-865-8663 261
Web: www.mbharch.com

MBH Engineering Systems
61 Howard Ave .... Lynnfield MA 01940 781-334-2600 334-2915 385
Web: www.mbhes.com

MBHB (McDonnell Boehnen Hulbert & Berghoff LLP)
1136 Water St......................... Port Townsend WA 98368 360-379-6514 913-2557* 445
**Fax Area Code:* 312 ■ *Web:* www.mbhb.com

MBHC (Mississippi Baptist Historical Commission)
200 S Capitol St............................. Clinton MS 39058 601-925-3434 48-20
Web: mc.libguides.com

MBI Data Systems Inc
25 Kenwood Cir Ste 16....................... Franklin MA 02038 508-541-1057 225
Web: mbidata.com

MBI Direct Mail
710 W New Hampshire Ave..................... Deland FL 32720 386-736-9998 736-1100 7
TF: 800-359-4780 ■ *Web:* www.mbidirectmail.com

MBI Inc 47 Richards Ave....................... Norwalk CT 06857 203-853-2000 459
Web: www.mbi-inc.com

MBI Intl 3815 Technology Blvd.................. Lansing MI 48910 517-337-3181 337-2122 668
Web: www.mbi.org

MBIA Inc 113 King St......................... Armonk NY 10504 914-273-4545 360-4
NYSE: MBI ■ *Web:* www.mbia.com

MBK Real Estate LLC 4 Park Plz Ste 850........... Irvine CA 92614 949-789-8300 789-9300 653
Web: mbk.com

MBK Senior Living Ltd
4 Park Plz Ste 400 .... Irvine CA 92614 949-242-1400 371
Web: www.mbkseniorliving.com

MBL (Marine Biological Laboratory)
7 MBL St .... Woods Hole MA 02543 508-548-3705 540-6902 668
Web: www.mbl.edu

MBL International Corp
4 H Constitution Way .... Woburn MA 01801 800-200-5459 194
TF: 800-200-5459 ■ *Web:* www.mblintl.com

MBM (MBM Corp) 3134 Industry Dr ...... North Charleston SC 29418 843-552-2700 552-2974 111
TF: 800-223-2508 ■ *Web:* www.mbmcorp.com

MBM Corp (MBM) 3134 Industry Dr ...... North Charleston SC 29418 843-552-2700 552-2974 111
TF: 800-223-2508 ■ *Web:* www.mbmcorp.com

MBMG (Montana Bureau of Mines and Geology)
101 Grand Ave .... Billings MT 59101 406-496-4167 496-4451 637-2
Web: www.mbmg.mtech.edu

MBMS Inc 90a John Muir Dr .... Amherst NY 14228 716-689-2000 177
Web: www.mbms.com

MBN Corp 812 Memorial Dr NW................. Calgary AB T2N3C8 403-269-2100 403
TF: 888-890-1868 ■ *Web:* www.middlefield.com

MBNA (Monument Builders of North America)
136 S Keowee St............................. Dayton OH 45402 800-233-4472 222-5794* 49-3
**Fax Area Code:* 937 ■ *TF:* 800-233-4472 ■ *Web:* www.monumentbuilders.org

MBO Partners Inc
13454 Sunrise Vly Dr Ste 300 .... Herndon VA 20171 703-793-6000 387
Web: www.mbopartners.com

Mbox Communications LLC
1319 Wisconsin Ave NW .... Washington DC 20007 202-536-4903 33
Web: www.mboxcommunications.com

MBP (McDonough Bolyard Peck Inc)
3040 Williams Dr Williams Plz 1 Ste 300.......... Fairfax VA 22031 703-641-9088 641-8965 261
TF: 800-898-9088 ■ *Web:* www.mbpce.com

MBP (Miller, Beam & Paganelli Inc)
12040 S Lakes Dr Ste 104 .... Reston VA 20191 703-506-0005 506-0009 261
Web: www.millerbp.com

MBS (Maritime Broadcasting System)
90 Lovett Lake Crt............................ Halifax NS B3S0H6 902-425-1225 423-2093 643
Web: www.mbsradio.com

MBS (Metro Appliances & More Inc)
5313 S Mingo Rd .... Tulsa OK 74145 918-622-7692 38
Web: www.metroappliancesandmore.com

MBS Textbook Exchange Inc
2711 W Ash St............................ Columbia MO 65203 573-445-2243 96
TF: 800-325-0530 ■ *Web:* www.mbsbooks.com

MBSII.Net LLC 194 Main St N................ Southbury CT 06488 888-466-2744 262-1310* 178-1
**Fax Area Code:* 203 ■ *TF:* 888-466-2744 ■ *Web:* www.mbsii.net

MBT Financial Corp 102 E Front St .... Monroe MI 48161 734-241-3431 360-2
NASDAQ: MBTF ■ *TF:* 800-321-0032 ■ *Web:* www.mbandt.com

MBTA (Mass Bay Transportation Authority)
10 Park Plz Ste 5610 .... Boston MA 02116 617-222-3200 546
TF: 800-392-6100 ■ *Web:* www.mbta.com

MBTC (Mifflinburg Bank & Trust Co)
250 E Chestnut St PO Box 186................ Mifflinburg PA 17844 570-966-1041 70
TF: 888-966-3131 ■ *Web:* www.mbtc.com

M-B-W Inc 250 Hartford Rd .... Slinger WI 53086 262-644-5234 644-5169 190
Web: www.mbw.com

MC (Music Choice)
110 Gibraltar 650 Dresher Rd Ste 200 .... Horsham PA 19044 646-459-3357 524
Web: www.musicchoice.com

MC & A Inc 615 Piikoi St Ste 1000 .... Honolulu HI 96814 808-589-5500 589-5501 771
TF: 877-589-5589 ■ *Web:* www.mcahawaii.com

MC Basset LLC PO Box 241 .... Asbury NJ 08802 908-537-6410 637-2
Web: www.mcbasset.com

MC Brady Engineering Inc
1251 S Larkin Ave.......................... Rockdale IL 60436 815-744-8900 298
Web: www.mcbradyengineering.com

MC Dixon Lumber Company Inc
605 W Washington St......................... Eufaula AL 36027 334-687-8204 687-8208 683
Web: www.dixonlumber.com

MC Flooring LLC 6800 W 47th Ter .... Shawnee KS 66203 913-362-0711 290
Web: mcflooringkc.com

MC Gill Corp 4056 Easy St.................... El Monte CA 91731 626-443-4022 350-5880 22
Web: www.thegillcorp.com

MC Group Inc 7310 N 16th St Ste 130............ Phoenix AZ 85020 602-297-2400 180
Web: itsynergy.com

MC Machinery Systems Inc
1500 Michael Dr.......................... Wood Dale IL 60191 630-860-4210 491
Web: www.mcmachinery.com

MC Pherson Plastics Inc PO Box 58............. Otsego MI 49078 269-694-9487 694-6662 608
Web: www.mcpherson-plastics.com

MC Sign Company Inc 8959 Tyler Blvd .... Mentor OH 44060 440-209-6200 701
TF: 800-627-4460 ■ *Web:* www.mcsign.com

MC Software LLC 2225 Washington Blvd .... Ogden UT 84401 801-621-3900 178-11

MC Squared Energy Services LLC
175 W Jackson Blvd Ste 240 .... Chicago IL 60604 877-622-7697 281-1279 245
TF: 877-622-7697 ■ *Web:* www.mc2energyservices.com

MC Squared Inc
17 Harbourton Ridge Dr .... Pennington NJ 08534 609-474-8100 474-8101 178-12
Web: www.mcsqd.com

MC Van Kampen Trucking Inc
5841 Clay Ave SW .... Wyoming MI 49548 800-253-8102 780
TF: 800-253-8102 ■ *Web:* www.mcvankampen.com

MC Waste Services Inc 1437 NW 13 Terr......... Miami FL 33125 305-631-0097 326-3331 660
Web: www.mcwasteservices.com

MC10 Inc 10 Maguire Rd Bldg 3 1st Fl........... Lexington MA 02421 617-234-4448 538-6641* 253
**Fax Area Code:* 781 ■ *Web:* www.mc10inc.com

Mc2 Executive Search Inc
PO Box 452 .... Washington Crossing PA 18977 215-504-5488 504-5538 193
Web: www.mc2execsearch.com

MC2 Inc
15010 W Greenfield Ave Ste 102 .... Brookfield WI 53005 414-276-2200 179
Web: www.mc2wi.com

MC2 Studios Inc
7970 Fredericksburg Rd Ste 101-348......... San Antonio TX 78229 210-824-4106 824-4633 177
Web: www.mc2studios.com

MCA (Medical Center of Aurora, The)
1501 S Potomac St........................... Aurora CO 80012 303-695-2600 374-3
Web: auroramed.com

MCA (Medical City Arlington Volunteer Auxiliary Inc)
3301 Matlock Rd .... Arlington TX 76015 682-509-6200 472-4878* 374-3
**Fax Area Code:* 817 ■ *Web:* medicalcityarlington.com

MCA (Marine Corps Assn) PO Box 1775........ Quantico VA 22134 703-640-6161 640-0823 48-19
TF: 800-336-0291 ■ *Web:* www.mca-marines.org

MCAA (Mason Contractors Association of America (MCCA))
1481 Merchant Dr......................... Algonquin IL 60102 224-678-9709 678-9714 49-3
TF: 800-536-2225 ■ *Web:* www.masoncontractors.org

MCAA (Mechanical Contractors Association of America)
1385 Piccard Dr .... Rockville MD 20850 301-869-5800 990-9690 49-3
TF: 800-556-3653 ■ *Web:* www.mcaa.org

Mcabee Construction Inc
5724 21st St............................. Tuscaloosa AL 35401 205-349-2212 758-0762 188-3
Web: www.mcabeeconstruction.com

McAbee Medical Inc 1401 6th Ave SE .... Decatur AL 35601 800-729-9817 475
TF: 800-729-9817 ■ *Web:* www.mcabeemedical.com

MCAconnect LLC
8055 E Tufts Ave Ste 1300 .... Denver CO 80237 866-662-0669 196
TF: 866-662-0669 ■ *Web:* mcaconnect.com

McAdams Ben (Rep D - UT)
130 Cannon House Office Bldg.............. Washington DC 20515 202-225-3011 342-2
Web: www.mcadams.house.gov

McAdams Graphics Inc
7200 S First St .... Oak Creek WI 53154 414-768-8080 768-8099 626
Web: mcadamsgraphics.com

McAfee & Taft A Professional Corp
211 N Robinson .... Oklahoma City OK 73102 405-235-9621 235-0439 428
TF: 800-235-9621 ■ *Web:* www.mcafeetaft.com

McAfee Inc
2821 Mission College Blvd .... Santa Clara CA 95054 408-988-3832 970-9727 178-12
TF: 888-847-8766 ■ *Web:* www.mcafee.com

McAfee Tool & Die Inc
1717 Boettler Rd......................... Uniontown OH 44685 330-896-9555 896-9549 757
Web: www.mcafeetool.com

Mcairlaid's Inc 180 Corporate Dr .... Rocky Mount VA 24151 540-352-5050 548
Web: www.mcairlaids.com

McAlester Regional Health Ctr
1 Clark Bass Blvd .... McAlester OK 74501 918-426-1800 374-3
Web: www.mrhcok.com

McAllen Chamber of Commerce
1200 Ash Ave............................. McAllen TX 78501 956-682-2871 687-2917 139
Web: mcallen.org

McAllen Memorial Library
4001 N 23rd St............................ McAllen TX 78504 956-681-3300 434-3
Web: mcallenlibrary.net

Mcallister & Quinn LLC
1030 15th St NW Ste 590W .... Washington DC 20005 202-296-2741 296-2751 41
Web: jm-aq.com

McAllister House Museum
423 N Cascade Ave.................. Colorado Springs CO 80903 719-635-7925 520
Web: www.mcallisterhouse.org

McAllister Towing & Transportation Company Inc
17 Battery Pl Ste 1200 .... New York NY 10004 212-269-3200 509-1147 465
TF: 888-764-5980 ■ *Web:* www.mcallistertowing.com

McAlpin Industries Inc
255 Hollenbeck St .... Rochester NY 14621 585-266-3060 266-8091 488
Web: www.mcalpin-ind.com

McAndrews Held & Malloy
500 W Madison St 34th Fl .... Chicago IL 60661 312-775-8000 775-8100 428
Web: www.mcandrews-ip.com

McAninch Corp 4001 Delaware Ave .... Des Moines IA 50313 515-267-2500 267-2550 189-5
Web: www.mcaninchcorp.com

MCAP Financial Corp
1140 W Pender St......................... Vancouver BC V6E4G1 604-681-8805 217
TF: 800-977-5877 ■ *Web:* www.mcap.com

Mcapitol Management Inc
1341 G St NW Ste 700 .... Washington DC 20005 202-296-5354 296-7248 393
Web: www.mcapitol.com

McArdle Laboratory for Cancer Research
University of Wisconsin Dept of Oncology 1111 Highland Ave
.... Madison WI 53705 608-262-2177 262-2824 668
Web: mcardle.oncology.wisc.edu

	Phone	Fax	Class
McArthur-Burney Falls Memorial State Park 24898 Ca Hwy 89 ... Burney CA 96013 *Web:* www.burneyfallspark.org	530-335-2777		565
MCASC (Mechanical Contractors Association of South Carolina) 1504 Morninghill Dr ... Columbia SC 29210 *Web:* www.mcasc.com	803-772-7834	731-0390	139
MCB Printing 230 Walnut Hill Ln ... Havertown PA 19083 *Web:* www.mcbprinting.com	610-446-6011	446-6013	626
McBath Lucy (Rep D - GA) 1513 Longworth House Office Bldg ... Washington DC 20515 *Web:* www.mcbath.house.gov	202-225-4501		342-2
McBee Associates Inc 997 Old Eagle School Rd ... Wayne PA 19087 *TF:* 800-767-6203 ■ *Web:* mcbeeassociates.com	610-964-9680	964-7987	194
McBooks Press Inc 520 N Meadow St ID Booth Bldg ... Ithaca NY 14850 *TF:* 888-266-5711 ■ *Web:* www.mcbooks.com	607-272-2114		637-2
McBride & Associates Inc 1633 Normandy Ct Ste A ... Lincoln NE 68512 *Web:* mcbridemanagement.com	402-476-3852		47
McBride & Son Inc 16091 Swingley Ridge Rd Ste 300 ... Chesterfield MO 63005 *Web:* www.mcbridehomes.com	636-537-2000	537-2546	187
McBride Associates LLC 1840 Plymouth St NW ... Washington DC 20012 *Web:* www.mcbrideassociates.com	202-297-6259		463
McBride Construction Resources Inc 224 Nickerson St ... Seattle WA 98109 *Web:* www.mcbrideconstruction.com	206-283-7121	284-5670	186
Mcbride Dale Associates Inc 5721 Dragon Way Ste 300 ... Cincinnati OH 45227 *Web:* mcbridedale.com	513-561-6232		261
MCC (Mini-Cassia Chamber of Commerce) 1177 Seventh St ... Heyburn ID 83336 *Web:* www.minicassiachamber.com	208-679-4793	679-4794	139
MCC (Moore Carlyle Consulting) 290 N Queen St Ste 208 ... Toronto ON M9C5L2 *Web:* mccevents.ca	416-621-6622	621-0363	317
MCC (Mennonite Central Committee) 21 S 12th St PO Box 500 ... Akron PA 17501 *TF:* 888-563-4676 ■ *Web:* mcc.org	717-859-1151	859-2171	48-5
MCC Healthcare Services Inc 9143 S Ketzie Ave ... Evergreen Park IL 60805 *Web:* mcchealthcareservices.com	708-581-7700	581-7999	450
Mcc Inc 2600 N Roemer Rd ... Appleton WI 54911 *Web:* www.mcc-inc.org	920-749-3360		182
Mcc International Inc 110 Centrifugal Ct ... Mcdonald PA 15057 *Web:* www.millercentrifugal.com	724-745-0300		308
Mccabe & Hogan PC 19 S Bothwell St Ste 200 ... Palatine IL 60067 *Web:* mccabehogan.com	847-359-6100		41
McCabe Hamilton & Renny Company Ltd (MHR) 521 Ala Moana Blvd Ste M-311 ... Honolulu HI 96813 *Web:* www.mhrhawaii.com	808-524-3255	545-3101	465
Mccabe Russell PA 8171 Maple Lawn Blvd Ste 350 ... Fulton MD 20759 *Web:* mccaberussell.com	443-812-1435		41
McCabe Software Inc 3300 N Ridge Rd ... Ellicott City MD 21043 *TF:* 800-638-6316 ■ *Web:* www.mccabe.com	410-381-3710		178-12
Mccabe's Quality Flooring 1100 S Front St ... Marquette MI 49855 *Web:* www.mccabesflooring.com	906-228-8821	228-9679	290
Mccaffery Interests Inc 875 N Michigan Ave Ste 1800 ... Chicago IL 60611 *Web:* www.mccafferyinc.com	312-944-3777		652
McCain Engineering Inc 2002 Mccain Pkwy ... Pelham AL 35124 *Web:* www.mccainengineering.com	205-663-0123	663-6823	612
McCain Foods Ltd 181 Bay St Ste 3600 ... Toronto ON M5J2T3 *TF:* 800-938-7799 ■ *Web:* www.mccain.com	416-955-1700		296-21
McCain Foods USA Inc 2275 Cabot Dr ... Lisle IL 60532 *Web:* www.mccainusafoodservice.com	630-955-0400		296-21
Mccall & Almy Inc 1 Post Office Sq Ste 2800 ... Boston MA 02109 *Web:* mccallalmy.com	617-542-4141		652
McCall & Associates Inc 3308 Country Club Rd ... Valdosta GA 31605 *Web:* mccallinc.com	229-242-2551		256
McCall Aviation 300 Deinhard Ln ... McCall ID 83638 *TF:* 800-992-6559 ■ *Web:* www.mccallaviation.com	208-634-7137	634-3917	63
Mccall Gibson Swedlund Barfoot PLLC 13100 Wortham Center Dr Ste 235 ... Houston TX 77065 *Web:* mgsbpllc.com	713-462-0341		2
McCall Handling Co 8801 Wise Ave ... Dundalk MD 21222 *TF:* 888-870-0685 ■ *Web:* www.mccallhandling.com	888-870-0685		385
McCall Oil & Chemical Corp 5480 NW Front Ave ... Portland OR 97210 *TF:* 800-622-2558 ■ *Web:* www.mccalloil.com	503-221-6400		579
McCall Patterns Magazine 120 Broadway ... New York NY 10271 *TF:* 800-782-0323 ■ *Web:* www.mccall.com	800-782-0323		457-14
McCall Service Inc 2861 College St ... Jacksonville FL 32205 *TF:* 800-342-6948 ■ *Web:* www.mccallservice.com	904-389-5561		577
McCall's Quilting 741 Corporate Cir Ste A ... Golden CO 80401 *TF:* 800-944-0736 ■ *Web:* www.quiltingdaily.com	303-215-5600		457-14
McCallie Associates Inc 3906 Raynor Pkwy Ste 200 ... Bellevue NE 68123 *Web:* www.mccallie.com	402-291-2203	291-8221	178-11
McCallie School 500 Dodds Ave ... Chattanooga TN 37404 *TF:* 800-234-2163 ■ *Web:* www.mccallie.org	423-624-8300	493-5426	622
McCallum Printing Group Inc 11755 108 Ave NW ... Edmonton AB T5H1B8 *Web:* www.mcprint.ca	780-455-8885		627
McCallum Theatre 73000 Fred Waring Dr ... Palm Desert CA 92260 *TF:* 866-889-2787 ■ *Web:* www.mccallumtheatre.com	760-340-2787	779-9445	572
Mccallum, Hoaglund, Cook & Irby LLP 905 Montgomery Hwy Ste 201 ... Vestavia Hills AL 35216 *TF:* 866-974-8145 ■ *Web:* www.mhcilaw.com	205-824-7767		428
Mccallum, Methvin & Terrell PC 2201 Arlington Ave S ... Birmingham AL 35205 *TF:* 800-210-7476 ■ *Web:* mmlaw.net	205-939-0199		41
Mccandlish & Lillard 11350 Random Hills Rd ... Fairfax VA 22030 *Web:* mccandlishlawyers.com	703-273-2288	352-4300	41
McCann Realty Partners LLC 2520-B Gaskins Rd ... Richmond VA 23238 *Web:* www.mrpapts.com	804-290-8870		652
McCann School of Business & Technology 2319 Louisville Ave ... Monroe LA 71201 *TF:* 866-865-8064 ■ *Web:* www.careertc.edu	866-865-8064		685
McCann School of Business & Technology 370 Maplewood Dr ... Hazleton PA 18202 *TF:* 866-865-8065 ■ *Web:* www.mccann.edu	570-497-8173		685
Mccann Systems LLC 290 Fernwood Ave ... Edison NJ 08837 *Web:* www.mccannsystems.com	732-346-9600		196
McCann WorldGroup Inc 622 Third Ave ... New York NY 10017 *Web:* www.mccannworldgroup.com	646-865-2000		5
McCarl's Inc 1413 Ninth Ave ... Beaver Falls PA 15010 *Web:* www.mccarl.com	724-843-5660	843-3180	189-10
McCarran International Airport 5757 Wayne Newton Blvd PO Box 11005 ... Las Vegas NV 89119 *Web:* www.mccarran.com	702-261-5211	597-9553	27
McCarter Theatre 91 University Pl ... Princeton NJ 08540 *Web:* www.mccarter.org	609-258-6500	497-0369	749
McCarthy Building Companies Inc 1341 N Rock Hill Rd ... Saint Louis MO 63124 *Web:* www.mccarthy.com	314-968-3300		186
McCarthy Improvement Company Inc 5401 Victoria Ave ... Davenport IA 52807 *Web:* www.mccarthyimprovement.com	563-359-0321		100-4
McCarthy Kevin (Rep R - CA) 2468 Rayburn House Office Bldg ... Washington DC 20515 *Web:* kevinmccarthy.house.gov	202-225-2915	225-2908	342-2
Mccarthy Print Inc 1804 Chicon St ... Austin TX 78702 *Web:* www.mccarthyprint.com	512-479-8938	494-8540	627
McCarthy Tetrault Library 1000 De la Gauchetiere St W Ste 2500 ... Montreal QC H3B0A2 *TF:* 877-244-7711 ■ *Web:* www.mccarthy.ca	514-397-4100	875-6246	434-3
McCartney Carpet 404 N Main St ... Westfield WI 53964 *Web:* www.mccartneycarpet.com	608-369-3998		131
McCarty Equipment Company Ltd 1103 Industrial Blvd ... Abilene TX 79602 *Web:* www.mccartyequipment.com	325-691-5558		386
Mccarty Law LLP 2401 E Enterprise Ave ... Appleton WI 54913 *Web:* mccartylaw.com	920-882-4070	882-7986	41
McCarty Printing Corp 246 E Seventh St ... Erie PA 16503 *Web:* www.mccartyprinting.com	814-454-6337		627
Mccarville Financial Network 104 N 27th St ... Fort Dodge IA 50501 *Web:* mccarvillefinancial.com	515-576-1731		390
Mccarys Jewelers Inc 6959 Fern Loop ... Shreveport LA 71105 *Web:* mccarys.com	318-798-3050	798-0155	410
McCaul Michael T (Rep R - TX) 2001 Rayburn House Office Bldg ... Washington DC 20515 *Web:* mccaul.house.gov	202-225-2401	225-5955	342-2
Mccauley Sound Inc 16607 Meridian E ... Puyallup WA 98375 *Web:* www.mccauleysound.com	253-848-0363		52
Mc-Caulou's Inc 3512 Mt Diablo Blvd ... LaFayette CA 94549 *Web:* mccaulous.com	925-283-3380		229
Mccausland Keen & Buckman 80 W Lancaster Ave 4th Fl ... Devon PA 19333 *Web:* mkbattorneys.com	610-341-1000		41
McClain County 121 N Second St Ste 206 PO Box 629 ... Purcell OK 73080 *Web:* www.mcclain-co-ok.us	405-527-6561		338
McClain Printing Co (MPC) 212 Main St ... Parsons WV 26287 *TF:* 800-654-7179 ■ *Web:* www.mcclainprinting.com	304-478-2881	478-4658	627
Mcclanahan & Holmes LLP 228 Sixth St SE ... Paris TX 75460 *Web:* mchcpa.net	903-784-4316		2
McClancy Seasoning Co 1 Spice Rd ... Fort Mill SC 29707 *TF:* 800-843-1968 ■ *Web:* www.mcclancy.com	803-548-2366	548-2379	345
McClard's Bar-B-Q 505 Albert Pike Rd ... Hot Springs AR 71901 *TF:* 866-622-5273 ■ *Web:* www.mcclards.com	501-623-9665		671
McClarin Plastics Inc 15 Industrial Dr ... Hanover PA 17331 *TF:* 800-233-3189 ■ *Web:* www.mcclarinplastics.com	717-637-2241		606
McClatchy Newspapers 2100 Q St ... Sacramento CA 95816 *TF:* 866-807-2200 ■ *Web:* www.mcclatchy.com	916-321-1000		637-8
Mcclean Anderson LLC 300 Ross Ave ... Schofield WI 54476 *Web:* www.mccleananderson.com	715-355-3006	359-0600	385
Mcclellan Davis LLC 508 Gibson Dr Ste 120 ... Roseville CA 95678 **Fax Area Code:* 916 ■ *TF:* 855-995-6789 ■ *Web:* salestaxhelp.com	855-995-6789	788-0989*	734
McClellan Park LLC 3140 Peacekeeper Way ... Mcclellan CA 95652 *Web:* www.mcclellanpark.com	916-965-7100		10-3
Mcclelland & Anderson LLP 1142 S Washington Ave ... Lansing MI 48910 *Web:* malansing.com	517-482-4890	482-4875	41
McClelland Oilfield Rentals Ltd 7901 99 St ... Clairmont AB T8X5B1 *TF:* 866-539-3656 ■ *Web:* www.mcclellandoilfieldrentals.com	780-539-3656		540
McClenahan Bruer 1200 NW Naito Pkwy ... Portland OR 97209 *Web:* www.mcbru.com	503-546-1000		7
McClintock Tom (Rep R - CA) 2312 Rayburn House Office Bldg ... Washington DC 20515 *Web:* mcclintock.house.gov	202-225-2511	225-5444	342-2

	Phone	Fax	Class
McClinton Chevrolet Co 1325 7th St ... Parkersburg WV 26101 *Web:* www.mcclintonchevrolet.com	304-699-2478		516
McClone Agency Inc 150 Main St Ste 300 ... Menasha WI 54952 *TF:* 800-236-1034 ■ *Web:* www.mcclone.com	920-725-3232	725-3233	390
McCloskey Motors Inc 6710 N Academy Blvd ... Colorado Springs CO 80918 *Web:* www.bigjoeauto.com	719-594-9400		57
McClung Cos 550 Commerce Ave ... Waynesboro VA 22980 *TF:* 800-942-1066 ■ *Web:* www.mcclungco.com	800-942-1066		344
McClure Co 4101 N Sixth St ... Harrisburg PA 17110 *TF:* 800-382-1319 ■ *Web:* www.mcclureco.com	717-232-9743		189-10
McClure Oil Corp 1212 W 500 S PO Box 1750 ... Marion IN 46952 *Web:* www.in.mcclureoil.net	765-674-9771	677-3223	579
McClure Telephone Co 311 S E St ... McClure OH 43534 *Web:* www.mccluretelephone.com	419-748-8008	748-8000	224
McCluskey Chevrolet Inc 9673 Kings Automall Dr ... Cincinnati OH 45249 *TF:* 855-622-5875 ■ *Web:* www.mccluskeychevrolet.com	513-761-1111		516
McCollister's Transportation Group Inc 1800 Rt 130 N ... Burlington NJ 08016 *TF:* 800-257-9595 ■ *Web:* www.mccollisters.com	609-386-0600		519
McCollum Betty (Rep D - MN) 2256 Rayburn House Office Bldg ... Washington DC 20515 *Web:* mccollum.house.gov	202-225-6631	225-1968	342-2
McComb Wholesale Paper Co 120 24th St ... McComb MS 39649 *Web:* mccombwholesale.com	601-684-5521		559
McCone County 1004 C Ave PO Box 199 ... Circle MT 59215 *Web:* mcconecountymt.com	406-485-3505	485-2689	338
McConkey 1615 Puyallup St PO Box 1690 ... Sumner WA 98390 *TF:* 800-426-8124 ■ *Web:* www.mcconkeyco.com	253-863-8111	863-5833	199
McConnaughhay Duffy Coonrad Pope & Weaver PA 1709 Hermitage Blvd Ste 200 ... Tallahassee FL 32308 *Web:* www.mcconnaughhay.com	850-222-8121		428
McConnell Air Force Base 57837 Coffeyville St Ste 271 ... McConnell AFB KS 67221 *Web:* www.mcconnell.af.mil	316-759-6100		497-1
McConnell Jones Lanier & Murphy LLP The Lakes On Post Oak 3040 Post Oak Blvd Ste 1600 ... Houston TX 77056 *Web:* mcconnelljones.com	713-968-1600		2
McConnell State Recreation Area 8800 McConnell Rd ... Ballico CA 95303 *Web:* www.parks.ca.gov	209-394-7755		565
McConnell Valdes 270 Munz Rivera Ave ... San Juan PR 00918 *Web:* www.mcvpr.com	787-759-9292		445
Mcconnell, Rothman & Company PC 175 Derby St Ste 36 ... Hingham MA 02043 *Web:* mcconnellrothman.com	781-740-5000		2
McCook Community College 1205 E Third St ... McCook NE 69001 *TF:* 800-658-4348 ■ *Web:* www.mpcc.edu	308-345-8100	345-8180	162
McCook County 130 W Essex PO Box 504 ... Salem SD 57058 *TF:* 800-231-8346 ■ *Web:* www.mccookcountysd.com	605-425-2781	425-3144	338
McCook Public Power District 1510 N Hwy 83 ... McCook NE 69001 *TF:* 800-658-4285 ■ *Web:* www.mppdonline.com	308-345-2500	345-4772	245
Mccool Carlson Green Inc 421 W First Ave Ste 300 ... Anchorage AK 99501 *Web:* mcgalaska.com	907-563-8474	563-4572	261
McCord Museum of Canadian History 690 Sherbrooke St W ... Montreal QC H3A1E9 *Web:* www.musee-mccord.qc.ca	514-398-7100	398-5045	520
Mccorkle & Johnson LLP 319 Tattnall St ... Savannah GA 31401 *Web:* mccorklejohnson.com	912-232-6000	232-4080	41
Mccormack Guyette & Associates PC 66 Grove St ... Rutland VT 05701 *Web:* www.cpa-vermont.com	802-775-3221		2
McCormack/Ellington Telecom 200 College Ave ... Ellington MO 63638 *TF:* 800-392-8111 ■ *Web:* www.mccormacksolutions.com	573-663-2000	663-2255	224
McCormick & Company Inc 18 Loveton Cir ... Sparks MD 21152 *NYSE: MKC* ■ *Web:* www.mccormickcorporation.com	410-771-7244		296-37
McCormick & Company Inc *McCormick Flavor Div* PO Box 552 ... Traverse City MI 49685 *TF:* 800-322-7742 ■ *Web:* www.mccormickforchefs.com	800-442-4733		296-37
McCormick & Schmick's 0309 SW Montgomery ... Portland OR 97201 **Fax Area Code:* 614 ■ *Web:* www.mccormickandschmicks.com	503-220-1865	476-3663*	671
Mccormick Armstrong Company Inc 1501 E Douglas ... Wichita KS 67211 *TF:* 800-733-1363 ■ *Web:* www.mcaprint.com	316-264-1363		627
McCormick Correctional Institution 386 Redemption Way ... McCormick SC 29899 *Web:* doc.sc.gov	864-443-2114		213
McCormick County 133 S Mine St Rm 201 ... McCormick SC 29835 *Web:* www.mccormickcountysc.org	864-852-2931	852-0071	338
McCormick Distilling Company Inc 1 McCormick Ln ... Weston MO 64098 *Web:* www.mccormickdistilling.com	816-640-2276		80-1
McCormick Group Inc, The 1440 Central Park Blvd Ste 207 ... Fredericksburg VA 22401 *Web:* www.mccormickgroup.com	540-786-9777		463
Mccormick Law Office PA 1200 Hosford St Ste 201 ... Hudson WI 54016 *Web:* mccormicklawoffice.com	715-386-6542	386-6592	41
McCormick Place 2301 S King Dr ... Chicago IL 60616 *TF:* 877-377-4153 ■ *Web:* mccormickplace.com	312-791-7000	791-6543	205
McCormick Refrigeration 1600 Front St ... Anniston AL 36201 *Web:* www.annistonrestaurantequipment.com	256-831-2271		665
McCormick Taylor & Associates Inc 2001 Market St 10th Fl ... Philadelphia PA 19103 *Web:* www.mccormicktaylor.com	215-592-4200		261
McCormick Theological Seminary 5460 S University Ave ... Chicago IL 60615 *TF:* 800-228-4687 ■ *Web:* www.mccormick.edu	773-947-6300	288-2612	167-3
McCormick's Creek State Park 250 McCormick's Creek Rd ... Spencer IN 47460 *Web:* www.in.gov	812-829-2235		565
McCormick's Group LLC 216 W Campus Dr ... Arlington Heights IL 60004 *TF:* 800-323-5201 ■ *Web:* www.mccormicksnet.com	847-398-8680		711
Mccormick-Klessig & Associates Ltd 522 Clermont St ... Antigo WI 54409 *Web:* mccormickklessig.com	715-627-4302		390
McCorriston Miller Mukai MacKinnon 500 Ala Moana Blvd 5 Waterfront Plz 4th Fl ... Honolulu HI 96813 *Web:* www.m4law.com	808-529-7300	524-8293	41
McCorvey Sheet Metal Works LP 8610 Wallisville Rd ... Houston TX 77029 *TF:* 800-580-7545 ■ *Web:* www.mccorvey.com	713-672-7545	672-0509	697
McCourt Construction 60 K St Ste 2 ... Boston MA 02127 *Web:* www.mccourtconstruction.com	617-269-2330	269-2313	188-4
McCourt Label Co 20 Egbert Ln ... Lewis Run PA 16738 *TF:* 800-458-2390 ■ *Web:* www.mccourtlabel.com	814-362-3851	362-4156	413
McCowan Design & Manufacturing Ltd 1760 Birchmount Rd ... Toronto ON M1P2H7 *Web:* www.mccowan.ca	416-291-7111		535
Mccown Gordon Construction LLC 422 Admiral Blvd ... Kansas City MO 64106 *TF:* 888-304-4929 ■ *Web:* www.mccowngordon.com	816-960-1111		186
McCoy & McCoy LLC 20 Church St 17th Fl ... Hartford CT 06103 *Web:* mccoymccoy.com	860-856-9283		41
McCoy Machinery Company Inc 1101 Curtis St ... Monroe NC 28111 *Web:* mccoy-usa.com	704-289-5413	283-0480	744
McCoy Miller LLC 1110 Di Dr ... Elkhart IN 46514 *Web:* mccoymiller.com	574-970-6799		59
McCoy's Building Supply 1350 IH 35 N ... San Marcos TX 78666 *Web:* www.mccoys.com	512-353-5400		364
Mc-Coy-Mills 700 W Commonwealth ... Fullerton CA 92832 *TF:* 888-434-3145 ■ *Web:* www.mccoymillsford.com	888-434-3145		516
Mccracken & Gillen LLC 1315 W 22nd St Ste 225 ... Oak Brook IL 60523 *Web:* mfgip.com	630-286-7600		41
McCracken County 300 Clarence Gaines St ... Paducah KY 42001 *Web:* www.mccrackenky.com	270-444-4769	444-4704	338
McCracken County Public Library 555 Washington St ... Paducah KY 42003 *TF:* 866-829-7532 ■ *Web:* www.mclib.net	270-442-2510		434-3
McCracken Financial Solutions Corp 8 Suburban Park Dr ... Billerica MA 01821 *Web:* www.mccrackenfs.com	978-439-9000		180
McCrady's 2 Unity Alley ... Charleston SC 29401 *Web:* mccradysrestaurant.com	843-577-0025		671
McCranie, Sistrunk, Anzelmo, Hardy, McDaniel & Welch LLC 909 Poydras St Ste 1000 ... New Orleans LA 70112 *TF:* 800-977-8810 ■ *Web:* mcsalaw.com	504-831-0946		428
Mccraw Oil Company Inc 2207 N Center St ... Bonham TX 75418 *Web:* mccrawoil.com	903-583-7481		581
McCray Lumber Co 15295 S Hwy 169 ... Olathe KS 66063 *Web:* www.mccraylumber.com	913-780-0060		191-3
McCrea Equipment Company Inc 4463 Beech Rd ... Temple Hills MD 20748 *TF:* 800-597-0091 ■ *Web:* www.mccreaway.com	800-597-0091		189-10
McCreary County Tourist Commission PO Box 699 ... Whitley City KY 42653 *Web:* www.mccrearycounty.com	606-376-3008		338
McCrometer Inc 3255 W Stetson Ave ... Hemet CA 92545 *TF:* 800-220-2279 ■ *Web:* www.mccrometer.com	951-652-6811	652-3078	201
McCrone Associates Inc 850 Pasquinelli Dr ... Westmont IL 60559 *Web:* www.mccrone.com	630-887-7100	887-7417	668
McCrone Inc 20 Ridgely Ave ... Annapolis MD 21401 *Web:* mccrone-engineering.com	410-267-8621	267-6326	261
McCrory Construction 522 Lady St ... Columbia SC 29201 *Web:* www.mccroryconstruction.com	803-799-8100	254-9800	685
MCCS (Marine Corps Community Services) 3044 Catlin Ave ... Quantico VA 22134 *Web:* www.usmc-mccs.org	703-784-3005		229
McCullagh Coffee 245 Swan St ... Buffalo NY 14204 *Web:* www.mccullaghcoffee.com	716-856-3473		296-7
McCulloch County 199 Courthouse Sq Rm 103 ... Brady TX 76825 *Web:* co.mcculloch.tx.us	325-597-0733	597-0606	338
McCullough & Assoc 1746 NE Expy PO Box 29803 ... Atlanta GA 30329 *TF:* 800-969-1606 ■ *Web:* mccanda.com	404-325-1606	329-0208	146
McCullough & Associates LLC 100 Shoreline Hwy Bldg B Ste 380 ... Mill Valley CA 94941 *Web:* www.macinv.com	415-956-8700	989-9459	401
Mccullough Industries Inc 13047 County Rd 175 ... Kenton OH 43326 *TF:* 800-245-9490 ■ *Web:* www.mcculloughind.com	800-245-9490		697
Mccullough, Goldberger & Staudt LLP 1311 Mamaroneck Ave ... White Plains NY 10605 *Web:* mcculloughgoldberger.com	914-949-6400		41
Mccullough, Perez & Assn 601 S Rancho Dr Ste A-7 ... Las Vegas NV 89106 *Web:* mcpalaw.com	702-385-7383		41
Mccune & Tsiatsos PLLC 115 W King St ... Martinsburg WV 25401 *Web:* richardmccunelawoffice.com	304-707-3143		41
McCune Foundation 3 PPG Pl Ste 400 ... Pittsburgh PA 15222 *Web:* www.mccune.org	412-644-8779	644-8059	305
Mccurdy & Candler LLC 160 Clairemont Ave Ste 550 ... Decatur GA 30030 *Web:* mccurdycandler.com	404-373-1612		41

Name / Address	City	State	ZIP	Phone	Fax	Class
McCutchen Group LLC 925 4th Ave Ste 2288 *Web:* www.mccutchengroup.com	Seattle	WA	98104	206-816-6850	816-6830	401
MCD Innovations 3303 N McDonald St *TF:* 800-804-1757 ■ *Web:* mcdinnovations.com	Mckinney	TX	75071	972-548-1850		499
McDade-Woodcock Inc 2404 Claremont Ave NE PO Box 11592 *Web:* www.mwieic.com	Albuquerque	NM	87107	505-884-0155	884-6073	203
McDanel Advanced Ceramic Technologies LLC 510 9th Ave. *Web:* www.ceramics.com	Beaver Falls	PA	15010	724-843-8300		663
McDaniel College 2 College Hill *TF:* 800-638-5005 ■ *Web:* www.mcdaniel.edu	Westminster	MD	21157	410-857-2230	857-2757	166
Mcdaniel Corp, The 6156 St Andrews Rd Ste 108 *Web:* mcdanielcorp.com	Columbia	SC	29212	803-750-4848		390
Mcdaniel Law Firm 1315 Elmwood Ave *Web:* pfmcdaniellaw.com	Columbia	SC	29201	803-771-7211		41
McDaniel Motor Co 1111 Mt Vernon Ave. *TF:* 877-362-0288 ■ *Web:* www.mcdanieltoyota.com	Marion	OH	43302	740-389-2355		516
Mcdaniel Tech Services Inc 2005 N Yellowood Ave *Web:* www.mcdanieltsi.com	Broken Arrow	OK	74012	918-294-1628		261
Mcdaniels Marketing Communications 11 Olt Ave. *TF:* 866-431-4230 ■ *Web:* mcdanielsmarketing.com	Pekin	IL	61554	309-346-4230		195
McDantim Inc 750 Shepard Way *TF:* 888-735-5607 ■ *Web:* mcdantim.com	Helena	MT	59601	406-442-5153	442-5154	789
Mcdermott & Bull Executive Search 2 Venture Ste 100 *Web:* mbsearch.com	Irvine	CA	92618	949-753-1700		260
McDermott Auto Group 655 Main St *Web:* www.mcdermottauto.com	East Haven	CT	06512	203-466-1000		516
McDermott International Inc 757 N Eldridge Pkwy *NYSE:* MDR ■ *Web:* www.mcdermott.com	Houston	TX	77079	281-870-5838		188-5
McDermott Will & Emery 444 W Lake St *Web:* www.mwe.com	Chicago	IL	60606	312-372-2000	984-7700	428
McDevitt Trucks Inc 1 Mack Ave **Fax Area Code:* 603 ■ *TF:* 800-370-6225 ■ *Web:* www.mctrucks.com	Manchester	NH	03108	800-370-6225	668-1865*	57
MCDI (Medical Care Development Intl) 8401 Colesville Rd Ste 425 *TF:* 800-427-7566 ■ *Web:* www.mcd.org	Silver Spring	MD	20910	301-562-1920	562-1921	48-5
McDiarmid Controls Inc 85579 Hwy 99 S. *Web:* www.mcdiarmidcontrols.com	Eugene	OR	97405	541-726-1677	747-9081	385
McDill Assn 5161 Soquel Dr Ste C *Web:* mcdill.com	Soquel	CA	95073	831-462-3198	462-1050	195
McDill Design 626 N Water St. *Web:* mcdilldesign.com	Milwaukee	WI	53202	414-277-8111	277-8220	344
Mcdivitt Law Firm 19 E Cimarron St *TF:* 877-846-4878 ■ *Web:* mcdivittlaw.com	Colorado Springs	CO	80903	303-426-4878		428
Mcdonald & Barnhill PA 12000 N Dale Mabry Hwy Ste 270 *Web:* mcdonaldbarnhill.com	Tampa	FL	33618	813-265-2020	200-2030	41
McDonald & Woodward Publishing Co 431 E College St. **Fax Area Code:* 740 ■ *TF:* 800-233-8787 ■ *Web:* www.mwpubco.com	Granville	OH	43023	800-233-8787	321-1141*	637-2
McDonald Carano LLP 2300 W Sahara Ave Ste 1200 *TF:* 800-872-3862 ■ *Web:* www.mcdonaldcarano.com	Las Vegas	NV	89102	702-873-4100	873-9966	41
McDonald County 602 Main St PO Box 606 *Web:* www.mcdonaldcountygov.com	Pineville	MO	64856	417-223-7523	223-2881	338
McDonald County Telephone Co PO Box 207 *Web:* www.olemac.net	Pineville	MO	64856	417-223-4313		224
McDonald Information Service Inc 215 14th St. *Web:* www.callmis.com	Jersey City	NJ	07310	201-659-2600		194
Mcdonald Kuhn PLLC 5400 Poplar Ave Ste 330 *Web:* mckuhn.com	Memphis	TN	38119	901-526-0606		41
Mcdonald Law Office Sc 200 S Main St. *Web:* mcdonald-lawoffice.com	Janesville	WI	53545	608-756-2000		41
McDonald Oil Company Inc 1700 Lukken Indus Dr W *Web:* www.mcdonaldoil.com	LaGrange	GA	30240	706-884-6191		443
McDonald Partners LLC 1301 E Ninth St Ste 3700 *TF:* 866-899-2997 ■ *Web:* www.mcdonald-partners.com	Cleveland	OH	44114	216-912-0567	912-1461	194
McDonald Technologies International Inc 2310 McDaniel Dr *Web:* www.mcdonald-tech.com	Carrollton	TX	75006	972-421-4100		625
McDonald Theatre 1010 Willamette St. *Web:* www.mcdonaldtheatre.com	Eugene	OR	97401	541-345-4442		572
McDonald Wholesale Co 2350 W Broadway St *TF:* 877-722-5503 ■ *Web:* www.mcdonaldwhsl.com	Eugene	OR	97402	541-345-8421	345-7146	297-3
McDonald's Corp 1 McDonald's Plz *NYSE:* MCD ■ *TF:* 800-244-6227 ■ *Web:* www.mcdonalds.com	Oak Brook	IL	60523	630-623-3000		670
McDonald's Restaurants of Canada Ltd PO Box 61023 *TF:* 888-424-4622 ■ *Web:* www.mcdonalds.com	Winnipeg	MB	R3M3X8	416-443-1000	446-3443	670
Mcdonald, Mccann & Metcalf LLP 15 E Fifth St *Web:* mmmsk.com	Tulsa	OK	74103	918-430-3700		41
McDonnell Boehnen Hulbert & Berghoff LLP (MBHB) 1136 Water St. **Fax Area Code:* 312 ■ *Web:* www.mbhb.com	Port Townsend	WA	98368	360-379-6514	913-2557*	445
McDonnell Investment Management LLC 18W140 Butterfield Rd Ste 1200. *Web:* www.mcdmgmt.com	Villa Park	IL	60181	630-684-8600		401
McDonough Bolyard Peck Inc (MBP) 3040 Williams Dr Williams Plz 1 Ste 300 *TF:* 800-898-9088 ■ *Web:* www.mbpce.com	Fairfax	VA	22031	703-641-9088	641-8965	261
McDonough County Voice, The 26 W Side Sq *Web:* www.mcdonoughvoice.com	Macomb	IL	61455	309-833-2114		532-2
Mcdonough Democrat Inc, The 358 E Main St. *Web:* www.themcdonoughdemocrat.com	Bushnell	IL	61422	309-772-2129	772-3994	627
McDonough Engineering Corp 5625 Schumacher Ln *Web:* www.mectx.com	Houston	TX	77057	713-975-9990		261
McDonough Manufacturing Co 2320 Melby St PO Box 510 *Web:* www.mcdonough-mfg.com	Eau Claire	WI	54702	715-834-7755	834-3968	821
McDonough Power Co-op 1210 W Jackson St. *Web:* mcdonoughpower.com	Macomb	IL	61455	309-833-2101		245
McDonough Telephone Cooperative Inc (MDTC) 210 N Coal St. *TF:* 888-640-4334 ■ *Web:* www.mdtc.net	Colchester	IL	62326	309-776-3211	776-3299	224
Mcdougall & Duval Adv 26 Millyard Ste 7 *Web:* www.mcdougallduval.com	Amesbury	MA	01913	978-388-3100		4
McDougall & Sons Inc 305 Olds Stn Rd *Web:* www.webapps.compu-tech-inc.com	Wenatchee	WA	98801	509-662-2136		315-3
McDougall Gauley 500-616 Main St *Web:* www.mcdougallgauley.com	Saskatoon	SK	S7H0J6	306-653-1212		428
McDowell & Associates Inc 21355 Hatcher Ave *Web:* www.mcdowasc.com	Ferndale	MI	48220	248-399-2066	399-2157	256
Mcdowell & Osburn PA 282 River Rd *Web:* mcdowell-osburn.com	Manchester	NH	03104	603-623-9300		41
McDowell County 60 E Court St. *Web:* www.mcdowellgov.com	Marion	NC	28752	828-652-7121		338
McDowell County Hc 31 PO Box 4361 *Web:* www.mcdowellcounty.wv.gov	Welch	WV	24801	304-436-8548	436-8572	338
McDowell County Chamber of Commerce 1170 W Tate St. *Web:* www.mcdowellchamber.com	Marion	NC	28752	828-652-4240	659-9020	139
McDowell County Schools 172 Lukin St. *Web:* mcdowell.k12.nc.us	Marion	NC	28752	828-652-4535		434-3
McDowell County Tourism Development Authority 91 S Catawba Ave. *TF:* 888-233-6111 ■ *Web:* blueridgetravelers.com	Old Fort	NC	28762	828-668-4282		206
Mcdowell Group Inc 9360 Glacier Hwy Ste 201 *Web:* www.mcdowellgroup.net	Juneau	AK	99801	907-586-6126	274-3201	195
McDowell Public Library 90 Howard St *Web:* mcdowell.lib.wv.us	Welch	WV	24801	304-436-3070	436-8079	434-3
Mcdowell Rice Smith & Buchanan PC 605 W 47th St Ste 350 *Web:* mcdowellrice.com	Kansas City	MO	64112	816-753-5400		428
McDowell Technical Community College 54 College Dr. *Web:* www.mcdowelltech.edu	Marion	NC	28752	828-652-6021	652-1014	162
McDowell-Craig Office Furniture 13146 Firestone Blvd *Web:* www.mcdowellcraig.com	Norwalk	CA	90650	714-521-7170		319-1
MCDP (Marion County Development Partnership) 412 Courthouse Sq PO Box 272. *Web:* www.mcdp.info	Columbia	MS	39429	601-736-6385	736-6392	139
MCE (Maryland Correctional Enterprises) 7275 Waterloo Rd. *Web:* mce.md.gov	Jessup	MD	20794	410-540-5454	540-5570	630
MCE (Medical Center Enterprise) 400 N Edwards St. *Web:* www.mcehospital.com	Enterprise	AL	36330	334-347-0584		374-3
MCE Technologies LLC 30 Hughes Ste 203. *TF:* 800-500-0622 ■ *Web:* www.mcetech.com	Irvine	CA	92618	949-458-0800		95
McEachin A. Donald (Rep D - VA) 314 Cannon House Office Bldg. *Web:* mceachin.house.gov	Washington	DC	20515	202-225-6365	226-1170	342-2
McEagle Properties LLC 1001 Boardwalk Springs Pl	O'Fallon	MO	63366	636-561-9300		652
McEllin Company Inc 17 Water St. *Web:* www.mcellinco.com	Waltham	MA	02451	781-647-9322	647-4740	361
Mcelrath Geyer Sandler & Fisher 1300 Bristol St N Ste 216. *Web:* www.brucesandler.com	Newport Beach	CA	92660	949-252-0252	252-9013	2
McElroy Deutsch & Mulvaney LLP PO Box 2075 *Web:* www.mdmc-law.com	Morristown	NJ	07962	973-993-8100	425-0161	428
McElroy Manufacturing Inc 833 N Fulton Ave *Web:* www.mcelroy.com	Tulsa	OK	74115	918-836-8611		454
McElroy Metal Inc 1500 Hamilton Rd. *TF:* 800-562-3576 ■ *Web:* www.mcelroymetal.com	Bossier City	LA	71111	318-747-8097	747-8657	480
McElroy Truck Lines Inc 111 80 Spur PO Box 104 *Web:* mcelroytrucklines.com	Cuba	AL	36907	205-392-5579		449
McElvaine Investment Trust, The 2187 Oak Bay Ave Ste 219 *Web:* www.valuefund.ca	Victoria	BC	V8R1G1	250-708-8345		528
Mcenearney Associates Inc 109 S Pitt St. *TF:* 877-624-9322 ■ *Web:* www.mcenearney.com	Alexandria	VA	22314	703-549-9292	717-5930	652
McEntire Produce Inc 2040 American Italian Way. *TF:* 800-845-2334 ■ *Web:* mcentireproduce.com	Columbia	SC	29209	803-799-3388	254-3540	10-11
MCESI (Mid-Coast Electric Supply Inc) 1801 Stolz St PO Box 2505 *Web:* www.mcesi.com	Victoria	TX	77901	361-575-6311	575-5515	246
MCF (Marin Community Foundation, The) 5 Hamilton Landing Ste 200. *Web:* www.marincf.org	Novato	CA	94949	415-464-2500	464-2555	303
MCF (Minnesota Council on Foundations) 800 Washington Ave N Ste 703 *Web:* www.mcf.org	Minneapolis	MN	55401	612-338-1989	337-5089	48-13

Name / Address	City	State	Zip	Phone	Fax	Class
MCF Communications Inc						
733 Turnpike St Ste 105	North Andover	MA	01845	978-687-2536	258-8850	681
Web: www.mcfcommunications.com						
MCF Systems Atlanta Inc						
4319 Tanners Church Rd	Ellenwood	GA	30294	866-315-8116		660
TF: 866-315-8116 ■ *Web:* mcfenvironmental.com						
MCF Technology Solutions LLC						
30400 Detroit Rd	Westlake	OH	44145	440-201-6050	545-5752	225
Web: www.mcftech.com						
McFarland & Company Inc						
960 NC Hwy 88 W PO Box 611	Jefferson	NC	28640	336-246-4460		637-2
TF: 800-253-2187 ■ *Web:* mcfarlandbooks.com						
McFarland Cascade						
1640 E Marc St PO Box 1496	Tacoma	WA	98421	253-572-3033	627-0764	818
TF: 800-426-8430 ■ *Web:* www.ldm.com						
McFarland Truck Lines 1304 16th Ave NE	Austin	MN	55912	507-437-6651	437-7643	780
TF: 800-643-6042 ■ *Web:* www.mcfgtl.com						
McFarlane Inc						
3473 N Washington St PO Box 12095	Grand Forks	ND	58203	701-772-9511	772-7528	697
Web: mcfarlane-e3.com						
McFarlane Manufacturing Company Inc						
PO Box 100	Sauk City	WI	53583	608-643-3321	643-2309	276
TF: 800-627-8569 ■ *Web:* www.mcfarlanes.net						
McFarling Foods Inc						
5273 Lakeview Pkwy S Dr	Indianapolis	IN	46202	800-622-9003		345
TF: 800-622-9003 ■ *Web:* www.mcfarling.com						
MCFelk Lighting and Design						
153 N Lee Ave	Yadkinville	NC	27055	877-500-4464	677-0400*	189-4
**Fax Area Code:* 336 ■ *TF:* 877-500-4464 ■ *Web:* www.mcfelklighting.com						
MCG Architecture 111 Pacifica Ste 280	Irvine	CA	92618	949-553-1117		261
Web: www.mcgarchitecture.com						
MCG Global LLC						
300 Long Beach Blvd Ste 13	Stratford	CT	06615	203-386-0615	386-0771	403
McGard LLC 3875 California Rd	Orchard Park	NY	14127	716-662-8980	662-8985	61
TF: 800-444-5847 ■ *Web:* www.mcgard.com						
McGarrah Jessee LP 121 W Fifth St	Austin	TX	78701	512-225-2524		7
Web: www.mc-j.com						
Mcgarry Bair Pc						
45 Ottawa Ave SW Ste 700	Grand Rapids	MI	49503	616-742-3500	742-1010	428
Web: www.mcgarrybair.com						
McGean-Rohco Inc 2910 Harvard Ave	Cleveland	OH	44105	216-441-4900	441-1377	145
TF: 800-932-7006 ■ *Web:* www.mcgean.com						
McGee Company Inc 1140 S Jason St	Denver	CO	80223	800-525-8888		172
TF: 800-525-8888 ■ *Web:* www.mcgeecompany.com						
McGee Creek State Park						
576-A S McGee Creek Dam Rd	Atoka	OK	74525	580-889-5822	889-7868	565
Web: www.travelok.com						
McGee Jewelers Inc 880 US 31 N	Greenwood	IN	46142	317-882-0500		410
Web: mcgeejewelers.com						
MCGG (Morrow County Grain Growers Inc)						
350 N Main St	Lexington	OR	97839	541-989-8221	989-8229	10-5
TF: 800-452-7396 ■ *Web:* www.mcgg.net						
McGhee Tyson Airport 2055 Alcoa Hwy	Alcoa	TN	37701	865-342-3000		27
Web: flyknoxville.com						
McGiffert & Associates LLC						
2814 Stillman Blvd	Tuscaloosa	AL	35401	205-759-1521	759-1524	256
Web: www.mcgiffert.com						
McGill Airflow Corp 900 Pinder Ave	Grinnell	IA	50112	641-236-1580	829-1291*	697
**Fax Area Code:* 614 ■ *Web:* www.mcgillairflow.com						
McGill Buckley Inc 2206 Anthony Ave	Ottawa	ON	K2B6V2	613-728-4199		7
Web: mcgillbuckley.com						
McGill Hose & Coupling Inc						
41 Benton Dr PO Box 408	East Longmeadow	MA	01028	413-525-3977		385
TF: 800-669-1467 ■ *Web:* www.mcgillhose.com						
McGill Maintenance Partnership Ltd						
6402 E Hwy 332	Freeport	TX	77542	979-233-5438	233-5417	454
Web: mcgillmaintenance.com						
McGill Smith Punshon Inc						
3700 Park 42 Dr Ste 190B	Cincinnati	OH	45241	513-759-0004		261
Web: mspdesign.com						
McGill University						
845 Sherbrooke St W	Montreal	QC	H3A2T5	514-398-4455	398-8939	785
Web: mcgill.ca						
Montreal Neurological Institute & Hospital						
3801 University St	Montreal	QC	H3A2B4	514-398-6644		167-3
Web: www.mcgill.ca						
McGill's 1560 E 21st St	Tulsa	OK	74114	918-742-8080		671
Web: dinemcgills.com						
McGillicuddy's Irish Pub						
28 Walnut St	Williston	VT	05495	802-857-5908		671
Web: www.mcgillicuddysirishalehouse.com						
Mcginnis Inc 502 Second St Ext	South Point	OH	45680	740-377-4391		698
Web: www.mcnational.com						
Mcginnis Lochridge & Kilgore LLP						
600 Congress Ave	Austin	TX	78701	512-495-6000	495-6093	428
Web: www.mcginnislaw.com						
McGinnis Meadows Cattle & Guest Ranch						
6220 Mcginnis Meadows Rd	Libby	MT	59923	406-293-5000		239
Web: www.mmgranch.net						
McGlaughlin Oil Co, The						
3750 E Livingston Ave	Columbus	OH	43227	614-231-2518		579
TF: 800-839-6589 ■ *Web:* www.mcglaughlinoil.com						
Mcgohan Brabender Inc 3931 S Dixie Dr	Dayton	OH	45439	937-293-1600		390
Web: www.mcgohanbrabender.com						
McGough 2737 Fairview Ave N	Saint Paul	MN	55113	651-633-5050	633-5673	186
Web: www.mcgough.com						
McGovern James (Rep D - MA)						
408 Cannon House Office Bldg	Washington	DC	20515	202-225-6101	225-5759	342-2
Web: mcgovern.house.gov						
Mcgowan Hood & Felder LLC						
1517 Hampton St	Columbia	SC	29201	803-779-0100	388-3194*	428
**Fax Area Code:* 843 ■ *TF:* 888-302-7546 ■ *Web:* www.mcgowanhood.com						
McGowen Hurst Clark & Smith PC						
1601 W Lakes Pkwy Ste 300	West Des Moines	IA	50266	515-288-3279		2
Web: www.mhcscpa.com						
McGraphics Inc 601 Hagan St	Nashville	TN	37203	615-242-8779		555
Web: www.mcgraphicsinc.com						
McGrath Auto 1548 Collins Rd NE	Cedar Rapids	IA	52402	855-495-3118		57
TF: 855-495-3118 ■ *Web:* www.mcgrathauto.com						

Name / Address	City	State	Zip	Phone	Fax	Class
McGrath Ford Hyundai BMW						
4001 1st Ave SE	Cedar Rapids	IA	52402	319-366-4000		57
TF: 855-795-7289 ■ *Web:* www.gozimmerman.com						
McGrath RentCorp						
5700 Las Positas Rd	Livermore	CA	94551	925-606-9200	453-3200	505
NASDAQ: MGRC ■ *Web:* www.mgrc.com						
McGrath's Fish House						
1036 Vly River Way	Eugene	OR	97401	541-342-6404	391-2846*	671
**Fax Area Code:* 503 ■ *Web:* www.mcgrathsfishhouse.com						
McGrath's Pub 202 Locust St	Harrisburg	PA	17101	717-232-9914		671
Web: mcgrathspub.net						
McGrath/Power Public Relations Inc						
75 E Santa Clara St 6th Fl	San Jose	CA	95113	408-727-0351		317
Web: www.mcgrathpower.com						
Mcgraw & Strickland LLC						
165 W Lucero Ave	Las Cruces	NM	88005	575-523-4321		41
Web: lawfirmnm.com						
McGraw-Hill 2 Penn Plaza 20th Fl	New York	NY	10121	646-766-2000		166
Web: www.mheducation.com						
McGraw-Hill Professional Publishing Group						
2 Penn Plz 9th Fl	New York	NY	10121	877-833-5524		637-2
TF: 877-833-5524 ■ *Web:* www.mhprofessional.com						
McGraw-Hill/Irwin						
1333 Burr Ridge Pky	Hinsdale	IL	60521	800-338-3987		637-2
TF: 800-338-3987 ■ *Web:* www.mhhe.com						
Mcgreal & Company PC 5740 W 95th St	Oak Lawn	IL	60453	708-422-8600		2
Web: mcgreal.com						
McGregor & Company LLP						
1190 Blvd NE	Orangeburg	SC	29115	803-536-1015		2
Web: mcgregorcpa.com						
McGregor Industries Inc 46 Line St	Dunmore	PA	18512	570-343-2436	343-4915	491
Web: www.mcgregorindustries.com						
McGregor Metalworking Cos						
2100 S Yellow Springs St	Springfield	OH	45506	937-325-5561	325-1957	256
Web: www.mcgregormetal.com						
McGriff Seibels & Williams Inc						
2211 Seventh Ave S	Birmingham	AL	35233	205-252-9871	581-9293	390
TF: 800-476-2211 ■ *Web:* www.mcgriff.com						
Mcgruder Group CPAS PC, The						
3925 Chain Bridge Rd Ste 302	Fairfax	VA	22030	703-273-7381		2
Web: mcgrudercpas.com						
McGuff Compounding Pharmacy Services Inc						
2921 W MacArthur Blvd Ste 142	Santa Ana	CA	92704	877-444-1133	444-1155	582
TF: 877-444-1133 ■ *Web:* www.mcguffpharmacy.com						
McGuffin Creative Group						
566 W Adams St Ste 440	Chicago	IL	60661	312-715-9812		5
Web: mcguffincg.com						
McGuire						
W194 N11481 McCormick Dr PO Box 309	Germantown	WI	53022	518-828-7652	255-9399*	470
**Fax Area Code:* 262 ■ *TF:* 800-624-8473 ■ *Web:* www.wbmcguire.com						
McGuire Cadillac Inc 910 Rt 1 N	Woodbridge	NJ	07095	866-552-4208	326-0385*	516
**Fax Area Code:* 732 ■ *TF:* 866-552-4208 ■ *Web:* www.mcguirecadillac.com						
McGuire Craddock & Strother P C						
2501 N Harwood St Ste 1800	Dallas	TX	75201	214-954-6800	954-6868	445
Web: www.mcslaw.com						
McGuire Manufacturing						
60 Grandview Ct	Cheshire	CT	06410	203-699-1801	699-1813	612
TF: 800-676-1832 ■ *Web:* www.mcguiremfg.com						
McGuire's Irish Pub						
600 E Gregory St	Pensacola	FL	32502	850-433-6789		671
Web: www.mcguiresirishpub.com						
McGuires Motor Inn						
120 S Telegraph Rd	Waterford	MI	48328	248-682-5100		378
Web: www.mcguiresmotorinn.com						
McGuireWoods LLP						
Gateway Plz 800 E Canal St	Richmond	VA	23219	804-775-1000	775-1061	428
TF: 877-712-8778 ■ *Web:* www.mcguirewoods.com						
McGuyer Homebuilders Inc (MHI)						
7676 Woodway Ste 104	Houston	TX	77063	713-952-6767	952-5637	653
Web: www.mcguyerhomebuilders.com						
MCH (Medical Center Hospital)						
500 W Fourth St	Odessa	TX	79761	432-640-6000		374-3
Web: www.medicalcenterhealthsystem.com						
MCH Inc 601 E Marshall St	Sweet Springs	MO	65351	800-776-6373	335-4157*	225
**Fax Area Code:* 660 ■ *TF:* 800-776-6373 ■ *Web:* mchdata.com						
McHale & Slavin PA						
2855 PGA Blvd	Palm Beach Gardens	FL	33410	561-625-6575		428
Web: www.mchaleslavin.com						
McHenry Area Chamber of Commerce						
1257 N Green St	McHenry	IL	60050	815-385-4300	385-9142	139
TF: 800-374-8373 ■ *Web:* mchenrychamber.com						
McHenry County 407 Main St S Rm 201	Towner	ND	58788	701-537-5724		338
Web: www.mchenrycountynd.com						
McHenry County 2200 N Seminary Ave	Woodstock	IL	60098	815-334-4000	334-8727	338
Web: www.mchenrycountyil.gov						
McHenry County College						
8900 US Hwy 14	Crystal Lake	IL	60012	815-455-3700	455-3766	162
TF: 888-977-4847 ■ *Web:* www.mchenry.edu						
McHenry Creative Services Inc						
345 Main St	Harleysville	PA	19438	877-627-0345		514
TF: 877-627-0345 ■ *Web:* www.mchenrycreative.com						
McHenry Museum 1402 'I' St	Modesto	CA	95354	209-577-5235		520
Web: www.mchenrymuseum.org						
McHenry Patrick T (Rep R - NC)						
2004 Rayburn House Office Bldg	Washington	DC	20515	202-225-2576	225-0316	342-2
Web: www.mchenry.house.gov						
McHenry Public Library District						
809 N Front St	Mchenry	IL	60050	815-385-0036		434-3
Web: mchenrylibrary.org						
McHenry Savings Bank 353 Bank Dr	McHenry	IL	60050	815-385-3000	385-4433	70
Web: www.mchenrysavings.com						
MCHM (Macon County History Museum)						
5580 N Fork Rd	Decatur	IL	62521	217-422-4919		520
Web: www.mchmdecatur.org						
McHone Industries Inc 110 Elm St	Salamanca	NY	14779	716-945-3380	945-3780	488
Web: www.mchoneind.com						
McHone Metal Fabricators Inc						
10300 County Rd 304	Terrell	TX	75160	972-524-7775	524-2777	697
Web: www.kwlkbllt.com						

	Phone	Fax	Class
MCHS (Marion County Historical Society) 169 E Church St ... Marion OH 43302 *Web:* www.marionhistory.com	740-387-4255	387-0117	520
MCHS (Milwaukee County Historical Society) 910 N Old World 3rd St ... Milwaukee WI 53203 *Web:* www.milwaukeehistory.net	414-273-8288		637-2
MCHS (Martin County Historical Society) 304 E Blue Earth Ave ... Fairmont MN 56031 *Web:* www.fairmont.org	507-235-5178		48-13
MCHS (Michigan City Historical Society) Old Lightgouse Museum 100 Heisman Harbor Rd Washington Park ... Michigan City IN 46361 *Web:* www.oldlighthousemuseum.org	219-872-6133		48-13
MCI Inc 26 First Ave N ... Waite Park MN 56387 *Web:* www.mcicarpetonewaitepark.com	320-227-4061		290
MCI Optonix LLC 2020 Contractors Rd Ste 8 ... Sedona AZ 86336 *TF:* 800-678-6649 ■ *Web:* www.mcio.com	800-678-6649		475
MCI-Cedar Junction 2405 Main St ... Walpole MA 02071 *Web:* www.mass.gov	508-660-8000		213
McIlhenny Co LA Hwy 329 ... Avery Island LA 70513 *TF:* 800-634-9599 ■ *Web:* www.tabasco.com	800-634-9599		296-19
McInnis Brothers Construction Inc 119 Pearl St ... Minden LA 71055 *TF:* 888-408-7897 ■ *Web:* www.mcinnisbrothers.com	318-377-6134	371-9156	256
McIntire Co 745 Clark Ave ... Bristol CT 06010 *TF:* 800-437-9247 ■ *Web:* www.mcintireco.com	860-585-0050	314-4500	18
Mcintosh & Associates LLC 1955 Lakeway Dr Ste 270b ... Lewisville TX 75057 *Web:* www.mcintoshassociates.com	214-488-2321		463
McIntosh County PO Box 584 ... Darien GA 31305 *Web:* georgia.gov	912-437-6671	437-6416	338
McIntosh County Board of Education 200 Pine St ... Darien GA 31305 *Web:* www.mcintosh.k12.ga.us	912-437-6645		685
McIntosh Laboratory Inc 2 Chambers St ... Binghamton NY 13903 *TF:* 800-538-6576 ■ *Web:* www.mcintoshlabs.com	607-723-3512	724-0549	52
Mcintosh Law Firm PC, The 209 Delburg St Ste 203 ... Davidson NC 28036 *Web:* mcintoshlawfirm.com	704-892-1699	892-8664	41
McIntosh Woods State Park 1200 E Lake St ... Ventura IA 50482 *Web:* www.iowadnr.gov	641-829-3847		565
McIntyre Elwell & Strammer General Contractors Inc 1645 Barber Rd ... Sarasota FL 34240 *Web:* www.mesgc.com	941-377-6800		186
Mcintyre Softwater Service 1014 N Bridge St ... Linden MI 48451 *Web:* www.sunshinewatertreatment.com	810-735-5778		190
McIver's Grant Public Library 410 W Court St ... Dyersburg TN 38024 *Web:* www.dyersburgdyercolibrary.com	731-285-5032	325-5685	434-3
Mckamish Inc 50 55th St ... Pittsburgh PA 15201 *Web:* www.mckamish.com	412-781-6262		189-10
Mckay Brothers LLC 2355 Broadway ... Oakland CA 94612 *Web:* www.mckay-brothers.com	312-948-9188		736
Mckay Derito & Co 1039 Mill Creek Dr ... Feasterville-Trevose PA 19053 *Web:* mckayderito.com	215-355-7400	322-8986	2
McKay Nursery Company Inc 750 S Monroe St PO Box 185 ... Waterloo WI 53594 *TF:* 800-236-4242 ■ *Web:* www.mckaynursery.com	920-478-2121	478-3615	323
McKay Press Inc 7600 W Wackerly St ... Midland MI 48642 *Web:* www.mckaypress.com	989-631-2360		627
McKean County 500 W Main St ... Smethport PA 16749 *TF:* 800-482-1280 ■ *Web:* www.mckeancountypa.org	814-887-5571	887-2242	338
McKee Botanical Garden 350 US 1 ... Vero Beach FL 32962 *Web:* mckeegarden.org	772-794-0601	794-0602	97
McKee Foods Corp PO Box 750 ... Collegedale TN 37315 *TF:* 800-522-4499 ■ *Web:* www.mckeefoods.com	423-238-7111		296-1
McKee Gallery 745 Fifth Ave 4th Fl ... New York NY 10151 *Web:* mckeegallery.com	212-688-5951	752-5638	42
McKee Group 940 W Sproul Rd Ste 301 ... Springfield PA 19064 *Web:* www.mckeebuilders.com	610-604-9800		653
Mckee Medical Pharmacy Inc 2350 Mckee Rd Ste A3 ... San Jose CA 95116 *Web:* mckeepharmacy.com	408-923-8871		237
McKee Wallwork Cleveland LLC 1030 18th St NW ... Albuquerque NM 87104 *TF:* 888-821-2999 ■ *Web:* www.mckeewallwork.com	888-821-2999		4
McKee, Voorhees & Sease PLC 801 Grand Ste 3200 ... Des Moines IA 50309 *Web:* www.ipmvs.com	515-288-3667	288-1338	428
McKeesport Candy Co 1101 Fifth Ave ... McKeesport PA 15132 *TF:* 888-525-7577 ■ *Web:* www.candyfavorites.com	888-525-7577		328
Mckeever Enterprises Inc *PRICE CHOPPER* 16611 E 23RD ST S ... Independence MO 64055 *Web:* www.mypricechopper.com	816-478-3095		345
Mckeil Marine Ltd 208 Hillyard St ... Hamilton ON L8L6B6 *TF:* 800-454-4780 ■ *Web:* mckeil.com	905-528-4780		313
McKelvie's 1680 Lower Water St ... Halifax NS B3J2Y3 *Web:* mckelvies.com	902-421-6161		671
McKendree College 701 College Rd ... Lebanon IL 62254 *TF:* 800-232-7228 ■ *Web:* www.mckendree.edu	618-537-4481	537-6496	166
McKendrick's Steak House 4505 Ashford Dunwoody Rd ... Atlanta GA 30346 *Web:* www.mckendricks.com	770-512-8888		671
Mckenna & Associates PC 1515 S Washington St ... Grand Forks ND 58206 *Web:* www.mckennaandassociates.net	701-772-4819		2
Mckenna Distribution & Warehousing 1260 Lkshore Rd E ... Mississauga ON L5E3B8 *TF:* 800-561-4997 ■ *Web:* www.mckennalogistics.ca	905-274-1234		205
McKenna Pro Imaging 2815 Falls Ave ... Waterloo IA 50701 *TF:* 800-238-3456 ■ *Web:* www.mckennapro.com	319-235-6265	235-1121	588
McKenna Storer 33 N LaSalle St Ste 1400 ... Chicago IL 60602 *Web:* www.mckenna-law.com	312-558-3900		428
McKenney's Inc 1056 Moreland Industrial Blvd SE ... Atlanta GA 30316 *TF:* 877-440-4204 ■ *Web:* www.mckenneys.com	404-622-5000		189-10
Mckenneys Air Conditioning Inc 2323 R St ... Bakersfield CA 93301 *Web:* mckenneysair.com	661-327-4037		610
McKenzie Area School 23292 Hwy 22 ... McKenzie TN 38201 *Web:* www.mckenziehighschool.org	731-352-2133	352-1424	685
McKenzie Banking Co (MBC) 676 N Main St ... McKenzie TN 38201 *Web:* foundationbank.org	731-352-2262	352-7778	70
McKenzie County 201 Fifth St NW ... Watford City ND 58854 *Web:* county.mckenziecounty.net	701-444-3616		338
McKenzie Electric Co-opeartive Inc PO Box 649 ... Watford City ND 58854 *TF:* 800-584-9239 ■ *Web:* www.mckenzieelectric.com	701-444-9288	444-3002	245
McKenzie Galleries and Commercial 6150 Westview Dr ... Houston TX 77055 *Web:* www.mckenziegalleries.com	713-863-1213	863-1216	344
Mckenzie Lake Lawyers LLP 140 Fullarton St Ste 1800 ... London ON N6A5P2 *TF:* 800-261-4844 ■ *Web:* www.mckenzielake.com	519-672-5666	672-2674	428
Mckenzie Property Management Inc 1966 Commonwealth Ln ... Tallahassee FL 32303 *TF:* 800-828-6495 ■ *Web:* www.mckenzietank.com	850-576-1221		780
McKenzie Valve & Machining LLC 145 Airport Rd ... McKenzie TN 38201 *Web:* www.mckenzievalve.com	731-352-5027	352-3029	789
McKenzie-Willamette Hospital 1460 G St ... Springfield OR 97477 *Web:* www.mckweb.com	541-726-4400		374-3
McKeon Door Co 44 Sawgrass Dr ... Bellport NY 11713 *TF:* 800-266-9392 ■ *Web:* www.mckeondoor.com	631-803-3000	803-3030	234
McKesson Corp 1 Post St ... San Francisco CA 94104 *NYSE: MCK* ■ *Web:* www.mckesson.com	415-983-8300		360-3
McKesson Medical Group Extended Care 8121 Tenth Ave N ... Golden Valley MN 55427 **Fax Area Code: 763* ■ *TF:* 800-328-8111 ■ *Web:* mbbnet.ahc.umn.edu	800-328-8111	595-6677*	475
McKey Perforating Company Inc 3033 S 166th St ... New Berlin WI 53151 *TF:* 800-345-7373 ■ *Web:* www.mckeyperforatedmetal.com	262-786-2700		198
McKibbon Hospitality 5315 Avion Park Dr Ste 170 ... Tampa FL 33607 *Web:* www.mckibbon.com	813-241-2399		379
McKim & Creed PA 1730 Varsity Dr Ste 500 ... Wilmington NC 28401 *Web:* www.mckimcreed.com	910-343-1048	251-8282	261
McKim Group 1185 Washington St Ste 7 ... Newton MA 02465 *Web:* www.mckimgroup.com	617-969-7772	969-7773	351
McKing Consulting Corp 2810 Old Lee Hwy Ste 300 ... Fairfax VA 22031 *Web:* www.mcking.com	703-204-2385	204-2704	196
McKinley Air Transport Inc 5430 Lauby Rd Bldg 4 ... Canton OH 44720 *TF:* 800-225-6446 ■ *Web:* mckinleyair.com	330-499-3316	499-0444	24
McKinley Capital Management LLC 3301 C St Ste 500 ... Anchorage AK 99503 *TF:* 800-563-9969 ■ *Web:* www.mckinleycapital.com	907-563-4488	561-7142	401
McKinley County 207 W Hill Ave ... Gallup NM 87301 *Web:* www.co.mckinley.nm.us	505-863-6866	863-1419	338
McKinley David (Rep R - WV) 2239 Rayburn House Office Bldg ... Washington DC 20515 *Web:* www.mckinley.house.gov	202-225-4172	225-7564	342-2
McKinley Equipment Corp 17611 Armstrong Ave ... Irvine CA 92614 *TF:* 800-770-6094 ■ *Web:* www.mckinleyequipment.com	949-261-9222		385
Mckinley Marketing Partners Inc 111 Franklin St ... Alexandria VA 22314 *Web:* mckinleymarketingpartners.com	703-836-4445		195
McKinney 318 Blackwell St ... Durham NC 27701 *Web:* mckinney.com	919-313-0802		4
Mckinney & Company Inc 100 S Railroad Ave ... Ashland VA 23005 *Web:* mckinney-usa.com	804-798-1451		261
McKinney Avenue Contemporary (The MAC) 1601 S Ervay St ... Dallas TX 75204 *Web:* the-mac.org	214-953-1212		50-2
McKinney Chamber of Commerce 2150 S Central Expy Ste 150 ... McKinney TX 75070 *Web:* www.mckinneychamber.com	972-542-0163	548-0876	139
McKinney Falls State Park 5808 McKinney Falls Pkwy ... Austin TX 78744 *Web:* tpwd.texas.gov	512-243-1643		565
Mckinney Petroleum Equipment Inc 3926 Halls Mill Rd ... Mobile AL 36693 *TF:* 800-476-7867 ■ *Web:* mckinneypetroleum.com	251-661-8800		358
Mckinneys Appliance Center Inc 6723 Martin Way E ... Olympia WA 98516 *Web:* mckinneysappliance.com	360-456-8525		35
McKinnon Body Therapy Ctr 2940 Webster St ... Oakland CA 94609 *Web:* www.mckinnonmassage.com	510-465-3488		167-3
McKinsey & Company Inc 55 E 52nd St ... New York NY 10055 *Web:* www.mckinsey.com	212-446-7000	446-8575	194
McKissock LP 218 Liberty St ... Warren PA 16365 *TF:* 800-328-2008 ■ *Web:* www.mckissock.com	814-723-6979		177
Mcknight Advisory Group Inc 1800 S Rutherford Blvd Ste 202 ... Murfreesboro TN 37130 *Web:* mcknightadvisory.com	615-895-8574		390
McKnight Foundation 710 Second St S Ste 400 ... Minneapolis MN 55401 *Web:* www.mcknight.org	612-333-4220	332-3833	305
McKnight's Long-Term Care News 900 Skokie Blvd Ste 114 ... Northbrook IL 60062 *TF:* 800-558-1703 ■ *Web:* www.mcknights.com	847-559-2884		637-9

Company / Address	City	State	Zip	Phone	Fax	Class
McKonly & Asbury LLP						
415 Fallowfield Rd	Camp Hill	PA	17011	717-761-7910		2
Web: www.macpas.com						
MCL (Marion County Library System)						
101 E Ct St	Marion	SC	29571	843-423-8300	423-8302	434-3
Web: www.marioncountylibrary.org						
MCL (Monmouth County Library)						
125 Symmes Rd	Manalapan	NJ	07726	732-431-7220		434-3
Web: www.monmouthcountylib.org						
MCL (Mercer County Library System)						
2751 Brunswick Pk	Lawrenceville	NJ	08648	609-989-6920		434-3
Web: www.mcl.org						
MCL (Morris County Library)						
30 E Hanover Ave	Whippany	NJ	07981	973-285-6930		434-3
Web: mclib.info						
MCL (Mad City Labs Inc) 2524 Todd Dr	Madison	WI	53713	608-298-0855	298-9525	419
Web: www.madcitylabs.com						
MCL Inc 501 S Woodcreek Rd	Bolingbrook	IL	60440	630-759-9500	759-5018	647
TF: 800-743-4625 ■ *Web:* www.mcl.com						
Mcl Industries Inc 1005 W Fayette St	Syracuse	NY	13204	315-422-5010	471-7119	196
Web: www.mclindustries.com						
Mclain Group LLC, The						
653 W Dickson St	Fayetteville	AR	72701	479-304-1035		653
Web: mclain-group.com						
McLain Plumbing & Electrical Service Inc						
107 Magnolia St	Philadelphia	MS	39350	601-656-6333	656-6351	610
Web: www.mclaininc.com						
McLanahan Corp 200 Wall St	Hollidaysburg	PA	16648	814-695-9807		492
Web: www.mclanahan.com						
McLane Company Inc 4747 McLane Pkwy	Temple	TX	76504	254-771-7500	771-7244	297-8
TF: 800-299-1401 ■ *Web:* www.mclaneco.com						
McLane Global						
16607 Central Green Blvd	Houston	TX	77032	281-210-3295	210-3296	297-8
Web: www.mclaneglobal.com						
McLane Livestock Transport Inc						
8498 Hwy 67 N	Poplar Bluff	MO	63901	573-785-0177	785-0212	780
Web: www.mclanetransport.com						
McLane Manufacturing Inc						
7110 E Rosecrans Ave	Paramount	CA	90723	562-633-8158		429
Web: www.mclaneedgers.com						
Mclaren & Lee 1508 Laurel St	Columbia	SC	29201	803-799-3074	252-3548	41
Web: mclarenandlee.com						
McLaren Health Care						
One McLaren Pkwy	Grand Blanc	MI	48439	866-642-2667	342-1450*	353
**Fax Area Code:* 810 ■ *TF:* 866-642-2667 ■ *Web:* www.mclaren.org						
McLaren Software Inc						
10375 Richmond Ave Ste 825	Houston	TX	77042	713-357-4710		177
Web: www.mclarensoftware.com						
McLarty Assoc						
900 17th St NW Ste 800	Washington	DC	20006	202-419-1420		463
Web: maglobal.com						
McLaughlin & Moran Inc 40 Slater Rd	Cranston	RI	02920	401-463-5454	463-3770	81-1
Web: www.mclaughlinmoran.com						
McLaughlin Body Co 2430 River Dr	Moline	IL	61265	309-762-7755	762-7807	516
Web: www.mclbody.com						
Mclaughlin Boring Systems						
2006 Perimeter Rd	Greenville	SC	29605	864-277-5870		190
TF: 800-435-9340 ■ *Web:* mclaughlinunderground.com						
McLaughlin Research Corp						
132 Johnnycake Hill Rd	Middletown	RI	02842	401-849-4010		261
TF: 800-556-7154 ■ *Web:* www.mrcds.com						
McLaughlin Youth Ctr						
2600 Providence Dr	Anchorage	AK	99508	907-261-4399	261-4308	412
Web: www.dhss.alaska.gov						
MCLD (Maricopa County Library District)						
2700 N Central Ave Ste 700	Phoenix	AZ	85004	602-652-3000		434-3
Web: mcldaz.org						
Mclean 75 Great Pond Rd	Simsbury	CT	06070	860-658-3700		793
Web: www.mcleancare.org						
McLean & Partners Wealth Management Ltd						
801 Tenth Ave S W	Calgary	AB	T2R0B4	403-234-0005		528
Web: www.cwbmcleanpartners.com						
McLean Contracting Co						
6700 McLean Way	Glen Burnie	MD	21060	410-553-6700	553-6718	188-10
TF: 800-677-1997 ■ *Web:* www.mcleancontracting.com						
McLean County						
115 E Washington St Rm 102	Bloomington	IL	61701	309-888-5190	888-5932	338
Web: www.mcleancountyil.gov						
McLean County 210 Main St PO Box 127	Calhoun	KY	42327	270-273-3213	273-9965	338
Web: www.mcleancounty.ky.gov						
McLean County 712 Fifth Ave	Washburn	ND	58577	701-462-8541	462-8212	338
Web: www.mcleancountynd.gov						
McLean County Chamber of Commerce						
2203 E Empire St	Bloomington	IL	61704	309-829-6344	827-3940	139
TF: 888-681-6561 ■ *Web:* www.mcleancochamber.org						
McLean County Museum of History						
200 N Main St	Bloomington	IL	61701	309-827-0428		48-13
Web: www.mchistory.org						
McLean Electric Co-opeartive Inc						
4031 Hwy 37 Bypass NW	Garrison	ND	58540	701-463-2291		245
TF: 800-263-4922 ■ *Web:* www.mcleanelectric.com						
Mclean Engineering Company Inc						
815 S Main St	Moultrie	GA	31776	229-985-1148		261
Web: mcleanengineering.com						
McLean Inc 3409 E Miraloma Ave	Anaheim	CA	92806	714-996-5451	996-5453	455
TF: 800-451-2424 ■ *Web:* mcleaninc.com						
Mclean Packaging Corp						
1000 Thomas Busch Memorial Hwy	Pennsauken Township	NJ	08110	856-359-2600		100
Web: www.mcleanpackaging.com						
Mclean School of Maryland Inc, The						
8224 Lochinver Ln	Potomac	MD	20854	301-299-8277		685
Web: www.mcleanschool.org						
McLellan Botanicals 2352 San Juan Rd	Aromas	CA	95004	800-467-2443	543-6836*	369
**Fax Area Code:* 415 ■ *TF:* 800-467-2443 ■ *Web:* www.taisucoamerica.com						
Mclellan Creative						
695 Mistletoe Rd Ste M2	Ashland	OR	97520	541-488-2270		195
Web: www.mclellanwritingteam.com						
McLellan Equipment Inc						
251 Shaw Rd	South San Francisco	CA	94080	800-848-8449	589-7398*	190
**Fax Area Code:* 650 ■ *TF:* 800-848-8449 ■ *Web:* www.mclellanindustries.com						
McLemore Building Maintenance Inc						
110 Fargo	Houston	TX	77006	713-528-7775	523-4341	152
TF: 800-524-0290 ■ *Web:* www.mbminc.com						
Mclendon Hardware Inc						
440 Rainier Ave S	Renton	WA	98057	425-235-3555		351
Web: www.mclendons.com						
Mclendon Veterinary Clinic Inc						
1525 University Blvd E	Tuscaloosa	AL	35404	205-553-8306		794
Web: mclendonvet.com						
McLennan Community College						
1400 College Dr	Waco	TX	76708	254-299-8000		162
Web: www.mclennan.edu						
McLennan County 501 Washington Ave	Waco	TX	76701	254-757-5078	757-5146	338
Web: www.co.mclennan.tx.us						
McLennan Ross LLP						
600 W Chambers 12220 Stony Plain Rd	Edmonton	AB	T5N3Y4	780-482-9200		428
TF: 800-567-9200 ■ *Web:* mross.com						
McLeod Cooperative Power Assn						
1231 Ford Ave N	Glencoe	MN	55336	320-864-3148	864-4850	245
TF: 800-494-6272 ■ *Web:* www.mcleodcoop.com						
McLeod County 830 11th St	Glencoe	MN	55336	320-864-5551		338
Web: www.co.mcleod.mn.us						
McLeod Express LLC 5002 Cundiff Ct	Decatur	IL	62526	800-709-3936		685
TF: 800-709-3936 ■ *Web:* mcleodexpress.com						
McLeod Hospice 1203 E Cheves St	Florence	SC	29506	843-777-2564		371
TF: 800-768-4556 ■ *Web:* www.mcleodhealth.org						
McLeod Optical Company Inc						
50 Jefferson Park Rd	Warwick	RI	02888	401-467-3000		543
TF: 800-288-5367 ■ *Web:* www.mcleodoptical.com						
McLeod Software Corporation Inc						
2550 Acton Rd PO Box 43200	Birmingham	AL	35243	205-823-5100		177
Web: www.mcleodsoftware.com						
McLoone 75 Sumner St	La Crosse	WI	54603	608-784-1260		701
TF: 800-624-6641 ■ *Web:* www.mcloone.com						
McLure Hotel, The 1200 Market St	Wheeling	WV	26003	304-232-0300		379
Web: www.mclurehotelwheeling.com						
Mclure Moving & Storage Inc						
167 Colchester Rd	Essex Junction	VT	05452	802-878-5344		311
Web: vermontmovers.com						
MCM (Municipal Capital Markets Group Inc)						
5220 Spring Valley Rd Ste 522	Dallas	TX	75244	972-386-0200		2
Web: www.municapital.com						
MCM Composites LLC 1315 S 41st St	Manitowoc	WI	54220	920-684-7800	684-1799	604
TF: 866-977-0977 ■ *Web:* www.mcmusa.net						
MCM Construction Inc						
6413 32nd St	North Highlands	CA	95660	916-334-1221		188-4
Web: www.mcmconstructioninc.com						
MCM Elegante Suites 4250 Ridgemont Dr	Abilene	TX	79606	325-698-1234	698-2771	379
TF: 888-897-9644 ■ *Web:* www.mcmelegantesuites.com						
MCM Management Corp						
35980 Woodward Ave Ste 210	Bloomfield Hills	MI	48304	248-932-9600	932-9638	667
Web: mcmmanagement.com						
MCMA (Middlebury College Museum of Art)						
Mahaney Center for the Arts						
72 Porter Field Rd	Middlebury	VT	05753	802-443-5007	443-2069	637-2
Web: museum.middlebury.edu						
Mcmahan Law Pc						
11755 Wlshre Blvd Ste 1845	Los Angeles	CA	90025	310-479-8827		41
Web: personalinjurylawusa.com						
Mcmahon & Associates PC						
10010 Calumet Ave	Munster	IN	46321	219-924-3450		2
Web: mcmahonpc.com						
Mcmahon Agency Inc, The						
901 Simpson Ave	Ocean City	NJ	08226	609-399-0060		390
Web: mcmahonagency.com						
Mcmahon Associates Inc						
425 Commerce Dr Ste 200	Fort Washington	PA	19034	215-283-9444		261
Web: mcmahonassociates.com						
Mcmahon Degulis LLP						
812 Huron Rd Ste 650	Cleveland	OH	44115	216-621-1312		41
Web: mdllp.net						
McMahon Group 1445 McMahon Dr	Neenah	WI	54956	920-751-4200	751-4284	261
Web: mcmgrp.com						
Mcmahon Group Inc						
670 Mason Ridge Center Dr Ste 220	Saint Louis	MO	63141	314-744-5040		196
Web: mcmahongroup.com						
McMahon Paper and Packaging Inc						
1810 S Anthony Blvd	Fort Wayne	IN	46803	260-422-3491		559
Web: www.mcmahonpaperandpackaging.com						
Mcmahon Publishing Group						
545 W 45th St	New York	NY	10036	212-957-5300		418
Web: www.mcmahonmed.com						
McManis & Monsalve Assoc						
100 State St Ste 103	Erie	PA	16507	814-454-4000	438-2210*	463
**Fax Area Code:* 866 ■ *Web:* www.mcmanis-monsalve.com						
McManis Faulkner						
Fairmont Plz 50 W San Fernando St 10th Fl	San Jose	CA	95113	408-279-8700		428
Web: www.mcmanislaw.com						
Mcmann-Smoot Inc 1553 Commerce Rd	Springfield	OH	45504	937-325-7048		390
TF: 800-476-1377 ■ *Web:* msrins.com						
McMaster University 1280 Main St W	Hamilton	ON	L8S4L8	905-525-9140	527-1105	785
TF: 800-238-1623 ■ *Web:* www.mcmaster.ca						
MCMC LLC 300 Crown Colony Dr Ste 203	Quincy	MA	02169	800-227-1464		317
TF: 866-401-6262 ■ *Web:* www.mcmcllc.com						
McMenamins 430 N Killingsworth	Portland	OR	97217	503-223-0109	294-0837	102
TF: 800-669-8610 ■ *Web:* www.mcmenamins.com						
Mcmillan & Smith 205 W Martin St	Raleigh	NC	27601	919-821-5124		41
Web: mspraleigh.com						
Mcmillan & Terry PA						
6101 Carnegie Blvd Ste 310	Charlotte	NC	28209	704-552-9997		428
Web: mplawcarolinas.com						
Mcmillan Education Inc 266 Beacon St	Boston	MA	02116	617-536-4319		41
Web: mcmillaneducation.com						
McMillan Electric Co 400 Best Rd	Woodville	WI	54028	715-698-2488		518
Web: www.mcmillanelectric.com						

	Phone	Fax	Class
McMillan Memorial Library 490 E Grand Ave.................... Wisconsin Rapids WI 54494 *Web:* www.mcmillanlibrary.org	715-423-1040	423-2665	434-3
McMillan Publications Inc 9968 W 70th Pl..............................Arvada CO 80004 *TF:* 800-344-1106 ■ *Web:* www.mcmillanpublications.com	303-456-4564	456-2049	637-10
Mcmillan Study Guides Inc 265 South St Ste D.................. San Luis Obispo CA 93401 *TF:* 800-821-1338 ■ *Web:* mcmguides.com	805-545-0112		96
Mcmillen Engineering Inc 115 Wayland Smith Dr.....................Uniontown PA 15401 *Web:* www.mcmilleng.com	724-439-8110		261
McMinn County 6 E Madison Ave................Athens TN 37303 *Web:* mcminncountytn.gov	423-745-4440	744-1657	338
McMinnville-Warren County Chamber of Commerce 110 S Ct Sq .... McMinnville TN 37110 *Web:* www.warrentn.com	931-473-6611	473-4741	139
MCMS (Maricopa County Medical Society) 326 E Coronado Rd Ste 101...................Phoenix AZ 85004 *Web:* www.mcmsonline.com	602-252-2015	256-2749	49-19
McMullen Oil Company Inc 11965 49th St N..........................Clearwater FL 33762 *Web:* www.mcmullenoil.com	727-573-0016		316
McMurray Fabrics Inc 105 Vann Pl...........Aberdeen NC 28315 *Web:* www.mcmurrayfabrics.com	910-944-2128	944-5616	745-4
McMurry Ready Mix Co 5684 Old W Yellowstone Hwy..................Casper WY 82604 *Web:* www.mcmurryreadymix.com	307-473-9581	235-0144	188-4
McMurry University 1400 Sayles Blvd...........Abilene TX 79697 *TF:* 800-460-2392 ■ *Web:* www.mcm.edu	325-793-3800		166
MCN Healthcare Inc 1777 S Harrison St Ste 405 ....Denver CO 80210 *TF:* 800-538-6264 ■ *Web:* www.mcnhealthcare.com	303-762-0778	762-0774	507
McNabb Telephone Co 308 W Main St ....McNabb IL 61335 *Web:* www.nabbnet.com	815-882-2201		224
Mcnabola & Associates LLC 161 N Clark St Ste 2550......................Chicago IL 60601 *Web:* personalinjurylawchicago.com	312-888-8700		41
McNair McLemore Middlebrooks & Company LLP 389 Mulberry St.............................Macon GA 31202 *Web:* mmmcpa.com	478-746-6277	987-0526	2
McNairy County 144 N 2nd St Ste 102............Selmer TN 38375 *Web:* www.mcnairycountytn.com	731-645-3241	646-1414	338
McNally Group 5445 DTC Pkwy P4.................Greenwood Village CO 80111 *Web:* www.mcnally-group.com	303-846-3035		21
McNally Industries LLC 340 W Benson Ave.........................Grantsburg WI 54840 *TF:* 800-366-1410 ■ *Web:* www.northern-pump.com	715-463-8300		641
McNally International Inc 1855 Barton St E...........................Hamilton ON L8H2Y7 *Web:* www.mcnallycorp.com	905-549-6561		188
McNally Law SC 1233 N Mayfair Rd Ste 200.................Milwaukee WI 53226 *Web:* mcpetelaw.com	414-257-3399	257-3223	41
McNally Robinson Booksellers Inc 1120 Grant Ave...........................Winnipeg MB R3M2A6 *TF:* 800-561-1833 ■ *Web:* www.mcnallyrobinson.com	204-475-0483		95
McNally Temple Associates Inc 1817 Capitol Ave .... Sacramento CA 95811 *Web:* www.mcnallytemple.com	916-447-8186		636
Mcnamara Financial Services Inc 1020 Plain St Ste 200......................Marshfield MA 02050 *Web:* mcnamarafinancial.com	781-834-2010		251
McNaughton & Gunn Inc 960 Woodland Dr .... Saline MI 48176 **Fax Area Code:* 800 ■ *Web:* www.mcnaughton-gunn.com	734-429-5411	677-2665*	626
McNaughton-McKay Electric Company Inc 1357 E Lincoln Ave...................Madison Heights MI 48071 *Web:* www.mc-mc.com	248-399-7500	399-6828	246
MCNB Bank & Trust Co PO Box 549 ....Welch WV 24801 *TF:* 800-532-9553 ■ *Web:* www.mcnbbanks.com	304-436-4112		70
MCNC Inc 3021 E Cornwallis Rd PO Box 12889 .... Research Triangle Park NC 27709 *Web:* www.mcnc.org	919-248-1900		387
McNeal Enterprises Inc 2031 Ringwood Ave .... San Jose CA 95131 *TF:* 800-562-6325 ■ *Web:* www.mcnealplasticmachining.com	408-922-7290	922-7299	602
Mcneal, Schick, Archibald & Biro Company LPA 123 W Prospect Ave Ste 250 ....Cleveland OH 44115 *Web:* msablaw.com	216-621-9870		41
McNear Brick & Block 1 McNear Brickyard Rd PO Box 151380........San Rafael CA 94901 *TF:* 888-442-6811 ■ *Web:* www.mcnear.com	415-453-7702	453-3141	150
McNease Convention Ctr 500 Rio Concho Dr....................... San Angelo TX 76903 *Web:* www.cosatx.us	325-653-9577		205
McNeece Brothers Oil Company Inc 691 E Heil Ave ....El Centro CA 92243 *Web:* www.mcneecebros.com	760-352-4721		579
McNeely Pigott & Fox (MP&F) 611 Commerce St Ste 3000 ....Nashville TN 37203 *TF:* 800-818-6953 ■ *Web:* www.mpf.com	615-259-4000	259-4040	636
McNees Wallace & Nurick LLC 125 N Washington Ave...................... Scranton PA 18503 *Web:* www.mcneeslaw.com	570-209-7220	871-4595	428
McNeese State University 4205 Ryan St .... Lake Charles LA 70609 **Fax Area Code:* 337 ■ *TF:* 800-622-3352 ■ *Web:* www.mcneese.edu	800-622-3352	475-5151*	166
McNeil & NRM Inc 96 E Crosier St................Akron OH 44311 *TF:* 800-669-2525 ■ *Web:* www.mcneilnrm.com	330-253-2525	253-7022	386
Mcneilepappas PC 7500 W 110th St Ste 110................ Overland Park KS 66210 *Web:* cmplaw.net	913-491-4050	491-9318	41
Mcneills Appliance 104 W Oak St...............Denton TX 76201 *Web:* www.mcneillsappliance.com	940-382-6932		35
McNeilus Truck & Manufacturing Inc 524 E Hwy St PO Box 70 ....Dodge Center MN 55927 *TF:* 888-686-7278 ■ *Web:* www.mcneiluscompanies.com	507-374-6321	374-6394	516
Mcnerney & Associates Inc 440 Northland Blvd........................ Cincinnati OH 45240 *Web:* www.pjmcnerney.com	513-825-5547		627
McNerney Jerry (Rep D - CA) 2265 Rayburn House Office Bldg ....Washington DC 20515 *Web:* mcnerney.house.gov	202-225-1947	225-4060	342-2
McNichols Co 9401 Corporate Lake Dr............ Tampa FL 33634 **Fax Area Code:* 813 ■ *TF:* 877-884-4653 ■ *Web:* www.mcnichols.com	877-884-4653	243-1888*	492
McNinch House 511 N Church St.............. Charlotte NC 28202 *Web:* mcninchhouserestaurant.com	704-332-6159		671
McNulty's Tea & Coffee Company Inc 109 Christopher St.........................New York NY 10014 *TF:* 800-356-5200 ■ *Web:* mcnultys.com	212-242-5351		159
MCO Transport Inc 3301 Hwy 421 N .... Wilmington NC 28402 *Web:* www.mcotransport.com	910-343-8372		780
M-CON Products Inc 2150 Richardson Side Rd........................Carp ON K0A1L0 *TF:* 800-267-5515 ■ *Web:* mconproducts.com	613-831-1736	831-2048	183
MCP (MediaTech Capital Partners LLC) 70 E 55th St 21st Fl ....New York NY 10022 *Web:* www.mediatechcapital.com	212-759-3022	534-5328	360-3
MCP Computer Products Inc 1565 Creek St Ste 103 ....San Marcos CA 92078 **Fax Area Code:* 800 ■ *TF:* 800-255-8607 ■ *Web:* www.mcpgov.com	760-471-5383	886-1192*	174
MCP Industries Inc *Mission Clay Products Div* 708 S Temescal St Ste 101 ....Corona CA 92879 *Web:* mcpind.com	951-736-1881		150
Mcphail Animal Hospital Inc 2 Jenkins Ct...............................Mauldin SC 29662 *Web:* mcphailah.com	864-288-7618		794
McPherson College 1600 E Euclid........... McPherson KS 67460 *TF:* 800-365-7402 ■ *Web:* www.mcpherson.edu	620-242-0400	241-8443	166
McPherson Companies Inc, The 5051 Cardinal St...........................Trussville AL 35173 *TF:* 888-802-7500 ■ *Web:* www.mcphersonoil.com	205-661-4400		581
McPherson Concrete Storage Systems Inc 110 N Augustus St .... Mcpherson KS 67460 *Web:* www.mcphersonconcrete.com	620-241-4382		188
McPherson County 117 N Maple .... McPherson KS 67460 *Web:* www.mcphersoncountyks.us	620-241-8149	241-5484	338
Mcpherson Design Group PC 6371 Center Dr Ste 100 ....Norfolk VA 23502 *Web:* mcphersondesigngroup.com	757-965-2000		261
McPherson Publishing Co PO Box 21266 ....Oklahoma City OK 73156 *TF:* 800-657-5962 ■ *Web:* www.mcpubco.com	405-752-9400		637-10
McPherson Sentinel 301 S Main............ McPherson KS 67460 *Web:* www.mcphersonsentinel.com	620-241-2422		532-2
McPhie Cabinetry 435 E Main St............. Bozeman MT 59715 *Web:* www.mcphiecabinetry.com	406-586-1708		321
MCPL (Marathon County Public Library) 300 N First St.............................Wausau WI 54403 *Web:* mcpl.us	715-261-7200	261-7204	434-3
McQ Inc 1551 Forbes St..................Fredericksburg VA 22405 *TF:* 866-373-2374 ■ *Web:* www.mcqinc.com	540-371-1358		256
McQuade & Bannigan Inc 1300 Stark St........... Utica NY 13502 *Web:* www.mqb.com	315-724-7119		358
MCR American Pharmaceuticals Inc 16255 Aviation Loop.......................Brooksville FL 34604 *Web:* www.mcramerican.com	352-754-8587	754-8507	231
MCR Health (MCRHS) *Edgar H Price Jr Children and Family Healthcare Ctr* 12271 US Hwy 301 ....Parrish FL 34219 *Web:* mcr.health	941-776-4050	776-4057	374-3
MCR LLC 2010 Corporate Rdq Ste 350............ McLean VA 22102 *Web:* www.mcri.com	703-506-4600	506-8601	261
MCR Safety 5321 E Shelby Dr................. Memphis TN 38118 **Fax Area Code:* 800 ■ *TF:* 800-955-6887 ■ *Web:* www.mcrsafety.com	901-795-5810	999-3908*	155-8
MCR Technologies 285 Newburyport Tpke.........Rowley MA 01969 *Web:* www.mcrtechnologies.com	781-245-6644		535
McRae Industries Inc PO Box 1239 ....Mount Gilead NC 27306 *Web:* www.mcraeindustries.com	910-439-6147	439-4190	185
MCRD Parris Island 283 Blvd de France...................... Parris Island SC 29905 *Web:* www.mcrdpi.marines.mil	843-228-2111		497-3
MCREL (Mid-Continent Research for Education & Learning) 4601 DTC Blvd Ste 500 ....Denver CO 80237 *Web:* www.mcrel.org	303-337-0990	337-3005	668
MCRHS (MCR Health) *Edgar H Price Jr Children and Family Healthcare Ctr* 12271 US Hwy 301 ....Parrish FL 34219 *Web:* mcr.health	941-776-4050	776-4057	374-3
Mcruer & & Associates CPAS 1251 NW Briarcliff Pkwy Ste 100 .... Kansas City MO 64116 *Web:* www.kccpa.com	816-741-7882		2
MCS (Metropolitan Construction Services LLC) 2901 Butterfield Rd........................ Oak Brook IL 60523 *Web:* www.metroconstructionllc.com	630-691-7200	691-7234	685
MCS Advertising 4110 Progress Blvd Ste 1c ....Peru IL 61354 *Web:* mcsadv.com	815-224-3011		261
MCS Family of Companies 818 S Beltline Hwy E ....Scottsbluff NE 69361 *Web:* mcsfamilyofcompanies.com	308-635-1926		261
MCS Financial Advisors 360 E Tenth Ave Ste 200......................Eugene OR 97401 *Web:* mcsfa.com	541-345-7023		401
MCS Healthcare Public Relations 110 Allen Rd Ste 303 .... Basking Ridge NJ 07921 *Web:* www.mcspr.com	908-234-9900	470-4490	636
MCS Referral & Resources Inc 6101 Gentry Ln...........................Baltimore MD 21210 *TF:* 800-526-7234 ■ *Web:* www.mcsrr.org	410-889-6666	889-4944	48-17
McSally Martha (Sen R - AZ) 404 Russell Senate Office Bldg..............Washington DC 20510 *Web:* www.mcsally.senate.gov	202-224-2235		342-2
MCSD Studio 5623 E Washington St Ste 7................Indianapolis IN 46219 *Web:* mcsdstudio.com	317-926-0773		657

Name / Address	City	State	Zip	Phone	Fax	Class
McShan Lumber Company Inc PO Box 27 *TF:* 800-882-3712 ■ *Web:* www.mcshanlumber.com	McShan	AL	35471	205-375-6277	375-2773	752
Mcshane Firm LLC, The 3601 Vartan Way 2nd Fl *Web:* themcshanefirm.com	Harrisburg	PA	17110	717-657-3900	657-2060	41
Mcspadden Development Corp 548 Nautical Dr Ste 201 *Web:* mcspaddenhomes.com	Lake Wylie	SC	29710	704-825-7324		652
McStain Neighborhoods 7100 N Broadway Ste 5-H *Web:* www.mcstain.com	Denver	CO	80221	303-494-5900		653
Mcswain & Company PS 612 Woodland Sq Loop SE Ste 300 *TF:* 800-282-1301 ■ *Web:* www.mcswaincpa.net	Lacey	WA	98503	360-357-9304		2
Mcswain Engineering Inc 3320 Mclemore Dr *Web:* mcswain-eng.com	Pensacola	FL	32514	850-484-0506	484-0508	261
McSweeney & Associates A Professional Corp 350 Crown Point Cir Ste 200 *Web:* mcsweeneyandassociates.com	Grass Valley	CA	95945	530-272-5555		2
Mcsweeney & Ricci Insurance Agency Inc 420 Washington St *TF:* 844-501-1359 ■ *Web:* mcsweeneyricci.com	Braintree	MA	02184	781-848-8600		390
MCT Industries Inc 500 Tierra Montana Loop *TF:* 800-876-8651 ■ *Web:* www.mct-ind.com	Bernalillo	NM	87004	505-345-8651	867-2255	779
McTeague Higbee Case Cohen Whitney & Toker PA 4 Union Pk PO Box 5000 *TF:* 800-482-0958 ■ *Web:* www.me-law.com	Topsham	ME	04086	207-725-5581		428
Mctech Inc 10821 Red Run Blvd PO Box 1438 *TF:* 866-535-2040 ■ *Web:* mctech-inc.com	Owings Mills	MD	21117	866-535-2040		180
Mctish Kunkel & Assoc 3500 Winchester Rd *Web:* mctish.com	Allentown	PA	18104	610-841-2700		261
Mc-U Sports 822 W Jefferson St *TF:* 800-632-6651 ■ *Web:* www.mcusports.com	Boise	ID	83702	208-342-7734		711
MCUA (Middlesex County Utilities Authority Inc) 2571 Main St PO Box 159 *Web:* www.mcua.com	Sayreville	NJ	08872	732-721-3800	721-0206	787
Mcube Investment Technologies Inc 5600 Tennyson Pkwy Ste 355 *Web:* www.mcubeit.com	Plano	TX	75024	214-550-0460		796
McVay Drilling Co 401 E Bender St *Web:* www.mcvaydrilling.com	Hobbs	NM	88241	575-397-3311	393-7455	540
MCVB (Merced Conference & Visitors Bureau) 710 W 16th St *TF:* 800-446-5353 ■ *Web:* visitmerced.travel	Merced	CA	95340	209-384-2791		206
McVean Trading & Investments LLC 850 Ridge Lake Blvd Ste One *TF:* 800-374-1937 ■ *Web:* www.mcvean.com	Memphis	TN	38120	901-761-8400		791
Mcveigh & Mangum Engineering Inc 9133 Rg Skinner Pkwy *Web:* www.mcveighmangum.com	Jacksonville	FL	32256	904-483-5200		261
McVeigh Associates Ltd 275 Dixon Ave *TF:* 800-726-5655 ■ *Web:* www.mcveigh.com	Amityville	NY	11701	631-789-8833		196
McWane Inc 2900 Hwy 280 Ste 300 *TF:* 800-634-4746 ■ *Web:* www.mcwane.com	Birmingham	AL	35223	205-414-3100	414-3170	595
McWane Science Ctr 200 19th St N *Web:* www.mcwane.org	Birmingham	AL	35203	205-714-8300	714-8400	520
Mcwhirter Realty Partners LLC Formerly Mcwhirter Realty Corp 300 Galleria Pkwy Ste 300 *Web:* mcwrealty.com	Atlanta	GA	30339	770-955-2000		652
McWilliams Forge Company Inc 387 Franklin Ave *Web:* www.mcwilliamsforge.com	Rockaway	NJ	07866	973-627-0200	625-9316	483
Mcx Inc 2811 Broadmore St Ste 301 *TF:* 800-835-5356 ■ *Web:* www.mcxinc.com	Klamath Falls	OR	97603	541-884-4004	884-4114	813
MD & E Clarity 5805 State Bridge Rd Ste G-371 *Web:* www.mdeclarity.com	Johns Creek	GA	30092	678-291-9690		317
MD Anderson Cancer Ctr 1515 Holcombe Blvd *TF:* 800-889-2094 ■ *Web:* www.mdanderson.org	Houston	TX	77030	713-792-2121		374-7
MD Atkinson Company Inc 1401 19th St Ste 400 *Web:* www.mdatkinson.com	Bakersfield	CA	93301	661-334-4800	334-4811	652
MD Building Products Inc 4041 N Santa Fe Ave *TF:* 800-654-8454 ■ *Web:* www.mdteam.com	Oklahoma City	OK	73118	800-654-8454		234
MD Financial Management 1870 Alta Vista Dr *TF:* 800-267-4022 ■ *Web:* mdm.ca	Ottawa	ON	K1G6R7	613-731-4552		528
MD Helicopters Inc 4555 E Mcdowell Rd *Web:* www.mdhelicopters.com	Mesa	AZ	85215	480-346-6300		25
MD Management Inc 5201 Johnson Dr Ste 100 *Web:* www.mdmgt.com	Mission	KS	66205	913-831-2996	384-2996	652
MD Pharmacy LLC 4101 13th Ave S *TF:* 844-409-3674 ■ *Web:* m-dpharmacy.com	Fargo	ND	58103	701-364-5690		237
MD Sass Investor Services Inc 55 W 46th St 28th Fl *Web:* www.mdsass.com	New York	NY	10036	212-730-2000	764-0381	401
MDA (Muscular Dystrophy Assn) 3300 E Sunrise Dr *TF:* 800-572-1717 ■ *Web:* www.mda.org	Tucson	AZ	85718	520-529-2000		48-17
MDA Engineering Inc 1415 Holland Rd *Web:* mdaengr.com	Maumee	OH	43537	419-893-3141		261
MDA Geospatial Services Intl 13800 Commerce Pkwy *Web:* www.mdacorporation.com	Richmond	BC	V6V2J3	604-244-0400		393
MDA Information Systems LLC 820 W Diamond Ave Ste 300 *Web:* www.mdaus.com	Gaithersburg	MD	20878	240-833-8200	833-8201	261
MDA Leadership Consulting 225 S Sixth St *Web:* www.mdaleadership.com	Minneapolis	MN	55402	612-332-8182		463
MDAH (Mississippi Department of Archives & History) 200 N St *Web:* www.mdah.ms.gov	Jackson	MS	39201	601-576-6876	576-6964	520
MDC Inc 2547 Progress Rd *TF:* 800-395-9405 ■ *Web:* www.mcd.net	Madison	WI	53716	608-221-3422		555
MDC Systems Inc 37 N Valley Rd 3 Sta Sq Ste 100 *Web:* www.mdcsystems.com	Paoli	PA	19301	610-640-9600		186
M-DCPS (Miami-Dade County Public Schools) 1450 NE Second Ave *TF:* 800-955-5504 ■ *Web:* www.dadeschools.net	Miami	FL	33132	305-995-1000		685
MDE International Inc 4033 S Center Rd *Web:* www.mdeintl.com	Burton	MI	48519	810-743-5980	743-5987	743
MDH Law Group LLC 1001 Bannock St Ste 135 *Web:* mdhlawgroup.com	Denver	CO	80204	720-737-0140	533-2022	41
MDI (Molecular Devices Inc) 1311 Orleans Dr *TF:* 800-635-5577 ■ *Web:* www.moleculardevices.com	Sunnyvale	CA	94089	408-747-1700	747-3601	419
MDI Achieve 10900 Hampshire Ave S Ste 100 *TF:* 800-869-1322 ■ *Web:* www.matrixcare.com	Bloomington	MN	55438	952-995-9800	995-9735	178-10
MDI Imaging & Mail LLC 21955 Cascades Pkwy *Web:* mdimail.biz	Sterling	VA	20166	703-433-1200		7
MDI Worldwide 38271 W 12-Mile Rd *TF:* 800-228-8925 ■ *Web:* www.mdiworldwide.com	Farmington Hills	MI	48331	248-553-1900	488-5700	233
MDIC Investment Advisory Service LLC 116 Kraft Ave Ste 8 *Web:* www.mdicinc.com	Bronxville	NY	10708	914-793-4095		251
MDL Enterprise Inc 9888 SW Fwy *TF:* 800-879-0840 ■ *Web:* www.mdlent.com	Houston	TX	77074	713-771-6350		180
MDM Distributors PO Box 10 **Fax Area Code:* 618 ■ *TF:* 800-289-6361 ■ *Web:* www.mdmdistributors.com	Energy	IL	62933	800-289-6361	988-8864*	559
MDM Inc 3135 Tuttle Rd *Web:* www.mdmincorporated.com	Archdale	NC	27263	336-861-6666	861-1999	744
MDM Office Systems Inc 35 Sheridan St NW *Web:* mdmstandardofficesolutions.com	Washington	DC	20011	202-829-4820		535
MDM Publications 3151 Airway Ave Ste C-3 *Web:* www.socalnewhomes.com	Costa Mesa	CA	92626	714-751-5813	755-5500	637-10
MDM Services Inc 1055 Kathleen Rd *Web:* mdmservices.com	Lakeland	FL	33805	863-646-9130		261
MDNA (Machinery Dealers National Assn) 315 S Patrick St *TF:* 800-872-7807 ■ *Web:* www.mdna.org	Alexandria	VA	22314	703-836-9300	836-9303	49-18
MDP (Madison Dearborn Partners LLC) 70 W Madison Ste 4600 *Web:* www.mdcp.com	Chicago	IL	60602	312-895-1000	895-1001	792
MDPL (Mechanicville District Public Library) 190 N Main St *Web:* meclib.sals.edu	Mechanicville	NY	12118	518-664-4646	664-8641	434-3
MDR Associates Inc 6486 Little Falls Dr *Web:* mdrnet.com	San Jose	CA	95120	408-927-8302		809
MDR Fitness Corp 14101 NW Fourth St *TF:* 800-637-8227 ■ *Web:* www.mdr.com	Sunrise	FL	33325	954-845-9500		354
MDRT (Million Dollar Round Table) 325 W Touhy Ave *Web:* www.mdrt.org	Park Ridge	IL	60068	847-692-6378	518-8921	49-9
MDS (Mennonite Disaster Service) 583 Airport Rd *TF:* 800-241-8111 ■ *Web:* mds.mennonite.net	Lititz	PA	17543	717-735-3536		48-5
MDS Aero Support Corp 1220 Old Innes Rd Ste 200 *Web:* mdsaero.com	Ottawa	ON	K1B3V3	613-744-7257		256
MDS Builders Inc 301 NW Crawford Blvd Ste 201 **Fax Area Code:* 561 ■ *TF:* 844-637-2845 ■ *Web:* www.mdsbuilders.com	Boca Raton	FL	33432	844-637-2845	241-7939*	186
MDSL 1410 Broadway Ste 2101 *Web:* www.mdsl.com	New York	NY	10018	212-201-6199		387
MDT Home Health Care Agency 8672 SW 40th St Ste 200 *Web:* www.mdthomehealth.com	Miami	FL	33155	305-644-2100	644-2910	363
MDTA (Miami-Dade Transit) 701 NW First Ct **Fax Area Code:* 786 ■ *Web:* www.miamidade.gov	Miami	FL	33136	305-468-5402	469-5580*	468
MDTC (McDonough Telephone Cooperative Inc) 210 N Coal St *TF:* 888-640-4334 ■ *Web:* www.mdtc.net	Colchester	IL	62326	309-776-3211	776-3299	224
MDU (Montana-Dakota Utilities Co) 400 N Fourth St *TF:* 800-638-3278 ■ *Web:* www.montana-dakota.com	Bismarck	ND	58501	701-222-7900		787
MDU Resources Group Inc 1200 W Century Ave PO Box 5650 *NYSE:* MDU ■ *TF:* 866-760-4852 ■ *Web:* www.mdu.com	Bismarck	ND	58506	701-530-1000		185
MDX Medical Inc 160 Chubb Ave Ste 301 *TF:* 866-325-8972 ■ *Web:* www.vitals.com	Lyndhurst	NJ	07071	201-842-0760	438-4555	363
M-E Engineers Inc 10055 W 43rd Ave *Web:* me-engineers.com	Wheat Ridge	CO	80033	303-421-6655		261
ME Tile 447 Atlas Dr *TF:* 888-348-8453 ■ *Web:* www.metile.com	Nashville	TN	37211	888-348-8462		751
MEA (Matanuska Electric Association Inc) 163 E Industrial Way *Web:* www.mea.coop	Palmer	AK	99645	907-745-3231	761-9352	245
MEA Advisors LLC Ste 300 420 Lexington Ave Graybar Bldg *Web:* www.meaadvisorsllc.com	New York	NY	10170	212-249-2239		70
MEA Energy Assn 7825 Telegraph Rd *TF:* 800-542-6096 ■ *Web:* www.meaenergy.org	Bloomington	MN	55438	651-289-9600		78
Mea Inc 1365 Ackermanville Rd *Web:* meaincpa.com	Bangor	PA	18013	610-599-5127		261
MEA Voice Magazine 1216 Kendale Blvd PO Box 2573 **Fax Area Code:* 517 ■ *TF:* 800-292-1934 ■ *Web:* www.mea.org	East Lansing	MI	48826	800-292-1934	337-5414*	457-8

Name / Address	City	State	ZIP	Phone	Fax	Class
Mead & Hunt Inc 6501 Watts Rd *Web:* meadhunt.com	Madison	WI	53719	608-273-6380		261
Mead Clark Lumber Co 2667 Dowd Dr PO Box 529 *TF:* 800-585-9663 ■ *Web:* www.meadclark.com	Santa Rosa	CA	95407	707-576-3333	523-0350	191-3
Mead Jewelers Inc 1309 13th St *Web:* www.meadjewelers.com	Woodward	OK	73801	580-256-6373		410
Mead Johnson Nutritionals 2701 Patriot Blvd 4th Fl *TF:* 800-231-5469 ■ *Web:* www.meadjohnson.com	Glenview	IL	60026	847-832-2420		296-10
Mead Metals Inc 555 Cardigan Rd *TF:* 800-992-1484 ■ *Web:* www.meadmetals.com	Saint Paul	MN	55126	651-484-1400		492
Mead O'brien Inc 1429 Atlantic Ave *TF:* 800-892-2769 ■ *Web:* www.meadobrien.com	North Kansas City	MO	64116	816-471-3993		112
Mead Public Library 710 N Eigth St *TF:* 800-441-4563 ■ *Web:* meadpl.org	Sheboygan	WI	53081	920-459-3400	459-0204	434-3
Mead School District 2323 E Farwell Rd *Web:* www.mead354.org	Mead	WA	99021	509-465-6000	465-6020	685
Meade Auto Group 45001 Northpointe Blvd *Web:* www.meadelexus.com	Utica	MI	48315	586-726-7900		57
Meade County 516 Hillcrest Dr *Web:* kentucky.gov	Brandenburg	KY	40108	270-422-3967		338
Meade County 200 N Fowler PO Box 278 *Web:* www.meadeco.org	Meade	KS	67864	620-873-8700	873-8713	338
Meade County 1300 Sherman St Ste 126 *Web:* www.meadecounty.org	Sturgis	SD	57785	605-347-2356	720-6619	338
Meade County Rural Electric Co-opeartive Corp 1351 Kentucky 79 *Web:* www.mcrecc.com	Brandenburg	KY	40108	270-422-2162	422-4705	245
Meade Instruments Corp 27 Hubble *TF:* 800-626-3233 ■ *Web:* www.meade.com	Irvine	CA	92618	949-451-1450	451-1460	544
Meade Law Office PC 3106 N Main St *Web:* meadelawpc.com	Canton	IL	61520	309-647-6301		41
Meade State Park 13051 V Rd *Web:* www.stateparks.com	Meade	KS	67864	620-873-2572		565
Meaden Precision Machined Products Co 16W210 83rd St *Web:* meaden.com	Burr Ridge	IL	60527	630-655-0888		621
Meador Staffing Services Inc 722A Fairmont Pkwy *TF:* 800-332-3310 ■ *Web:* www.meador.com	Pasadena	TX	77504	713-941-0616		260
Meadow Burke LLC 531 S US Hwy 301 *Web:* meadowburke.com	Tampa	FL	33619	813-248-1944		191-1
Meadow Farms Sausage Co 6215 S Western Ave *Web:* www.meadowfarmssausage.com	Los Angeles	CA	90047	323-752-2300		296-26
Meadow Green Nursing & Rehabilitation Ctr 45 Woburn St *Web:* www.meadowgreenrehabandnursing.com	Waltham	MA	02452	781-899-8600		450
Meadow Grove Federal Credit Union 210 Main St *TF:* 866-634-2911 ■ *Web:* www.Meadowgrovefcu.Org	Meadow Grove	NE	68752	402-634-2911		532-2
Meadow Lake Resort 100 St Andrews Dr *TF:* 800-321-4653 ■ *Web:* www.meadowlake.com	Columbia Falls	MT	59912	406-892-8700		669
Meadow Valley Corp 3800 N Central Ave Ste 460 *Web:* www.meadowvalley.com	Phoenix	AZ	85012	602-437-5400		188-4
Meadow View Nursing Ctr 1404 Hay St *Web:* meadowview.net	Berlin	PA	15530	814-267-4212		371
Meadow Wind Health Care Center Inc 300 23rd St NE *Web:* www.meadowwind.net	Massillon	OH	44646	330-833-2026	481-1250	371
Meadow, The 3731 N Mississippi Ave *TF:* 800-300-4033 ■ *Web:* themeadow.com	Portland	OR	97227	503-974-8349		297-2
Meadowbrook Inventions Inc 260 Mine Brook Rd *Web:* meadowbrookglitter.com	Bernardsville	NJ	07924	908-766-0606	766-6878	43
Meadowbrook Machine & Tool Inc PO Box 685 *Web:* www.mmtcnc.com	Toccoa	GA	30577	706-779-3327	779-5870	190
Meadowlands Bindery Inc 146 W Commercial Ave *Web:* www.meadowlandsbindery.com	Moonachie	NJ	07074	201-935-6161	935-9014	92
Meadowlands Exposition Ctr 355 Plaza Dr *Web:* mecexpo.com	Secaucus	NJ	07094	201-330-7773	330-1172	205
Meadowlands Racing & Entertainment 1 Racetrack Dr *Web:* www.meadowlandsracetrack.com	East Rutherford	NJ	07073	201 843 2446		642
Meadowlands Regional Chamber of Commerce 201 Rt 17 *Web:* www.meadowlands.org	Rutherford	NJ	07070	201-939-0707	939-0522	139
Meadowlark Botanical Gardens 9750 Meadowlark Gardens Ct *Web:* www.novaparks.com	Vienna	VA	22182	703-255-3631		97
Meadowmere Resort 74 Main St *TF:* 800-633-8718 ■ *Web:* www.meadowmere.com	Ogunquit	ME	03907	207-646-9661		378
Meadowood 3205 Skippack Pk PO Box 670 *Web:* www.meadowood.net	Worcester	PA	19490	610-584-1000	584-3645	672
Meadowood Napa Valley 900 Meadowood Ln **Fax Area Code:* 707 ■ *TF:* 800-458-8080 ■ *Web:* www.meadowood.com	Saint Helena	CA	94574	877-963-3646	963-3532*	669
Meadowridge School 12224 240 St *Web:* www.meadowridge.bc.ca	Maple Ridge	BC	V4R1N1	604-467-4444		685
Meadows & Ohly LLC 275 Scientific Dr Ste 1000 *Web:* www.meadowsandohly.com	Peachtree Corners	GA	30092	678-282-0220		205
Meadows Farms Inc 43054 John Mosby Hwy *Web:* meadowsfarms.com	Chantilly	VA	20152	703-327-3940		323
Meadows Field Airport 3701 Wings Way Ste 300 *Web:* www.meadowsfield.com	Bakersfield	CA	93308	661-391-1800	391-1801	27
Meadows Foundation Inc 3003 Swiss Ave *TF:* 800-826-9431 ■ *Web:* www.mfi.org	Dallas	TX	75204	214-826-9431	827-7042	305
Meadows Mills Inc 1352 W D St *TF:* 800-626-2282 ■ *Web:* www.meadowsmills.com	North Wilkesboro	NC	28659	336-838-2282	667-6501	190
Meadows Museum 5900 Bishop Blvd *Web:* www.meadowsmuseumdallas.org	Dallas	TX	75205	214-768-2516	768-1688	520
Meadows Office Interiors 885 Third Ave 29th Fl *TF:* 800-337-6671 ■ *Web:* meadowsofficeinteriors.com	New York	NY	10022	212-741-0333	741-0334	319-3
Meadows Psychiatric Ctr 132 The Meadows Dr *TF:* 800-641-7529 ■ *Web:* www.themeadows.net	Centre Hall	PA	16828	814-364-2161		374-5
Meadows Racetrack 210 Racetrack Rd *TF:* 877-824-5050 ■ *Web:* www.meadowsgaming.com	Washington	PA	15301	724-225-9300		642
Meadows Regional Medical Ctr (MRMC) 1 Meadows Pkwy *TF:* 800-382-4023 ■ *Web:* meadowshealth.com	Vidalia	GA	30474	912-535-5555		374-3
Meadows Urquhart Acree & Cook LLP 1802 Bayberry Ct Ste 102 *Web:* www.muacllp.com	Richmond	VA	23226	804-249-5786	249-5781	734
Meadowview Regional Medical Ctr (MRMC) 989 Medical Pk Dr *Web:* www.meadowviewregional.com	Maysville	KY	41056	606-759-5311		374-3
Meadville Lombard Theological School (MLTS) 610 S Michigan Ave **Fax Area Code:* 312 ■ *TF:* 800-848-0979 ■ *Web:* www.meadville.edu	Chicago	IL	60605	773-256-3000	327-7002*	167-3
Meadville Medical Ctr (MMC) 751 Liberty St *TF:* 800-254-5164 ■ *Web:* www.mmchs.org	Meadville	PA	16335	814-333-5000		374-3
Meadville New Products Inc 15850 Conneaut Lake Rd *Web:* www.meadvillenewproducts.com	Meadville	PA	16335	814-336-2174	337-1315	604
Meadville Tribune 947 Federal Ct *TF:* 800-879-0006 ■ *Web:* www.meadvilletribune.com	Meadville	PA	16335	814-724-6370	724-8755	532-2
Meadville-Western Crawford County Chamber of Commerce 908 Diamond Pk *Web:* www.meadvillechamber.com	Meadville	PA	16335	814-337-8030	337-8022	139
MEAG Power 1470 Riveredge Pkwy NW *TF:* 800-333-0324 ■ *Web:* www.meagpower.org	Atlanta	GA	30328	770-563-0300		787
Meaher State Park 5200 Battleship Pkwy *Web:* www.alapark.com	Spanish Fort	AL	36577	251-626-5529		565
Mealey's Furniture Inc 908 W St Rd *Web:* www.mealeysfurniture.com	Warminster	PA	18974	215-672-1333		321
Meals on Wheels Incorporated of Tarrant County 5740 Airport Fwy *Web:* mealsonwheels.org	Haltom City	TX	76117	817-336-0912		305
Meaningful Day Services Inc 225 S School St *Web:* meaningfuldays.com	Brownsburg	IN	46112	317-858-8630		363
Means Industries Inc 3715 E Washington Rd *Web:* www.meansindustries.com	Saginaw	MI	48601	989-754-1433	754-1103	489
Mears Group Inc 4500 N Mission Rd *Web:* www.mears.net	Rosebush	MI	48878	989-433-2929		188-10
Mears Transportation Group 324 W Gore St *Web:* www.mearstransportation.com	Orlando	FL	32806	407-422-4561	422-6923	441
Mearthane Products Corp 16 W Industrial Dr *TF:* 888-883-8391 ■ *Web:* www.mearthane.com	Cranston	RI	02921	401-946-4400	943-8210	596
Mease Manor Retirement Living 700 Mease Plz *Web:* www.measemanor.com	Dunedin	FL	34698	727-738-3000		672
Measurabl 707 Broadway *Web:* www.measurabl.com	San Diego	CA	92101	619-719-1716		178-1
Measurement Group LLC, The 5757 Uplander Way Ste 200 *Web:* themeasurementgroup.com	Culver City	CA	90230	310-216-1800		196
Measurement Systems Intl 230 W Coleman St *Web:* www.msiscales.com	Rice Lake	WI	54868	715-234-9171		770
Measurement Technology Group Inc 1310 Emerald Rd *Web:* www.redsealmeasurement.com	Greenwood	SC	29646	864-223-1212		407
Measurement Technology Northwest Inc 4211 24th Ave W *Web:* www.mtnw-usa.com	Seattle	WA	98199	206-634-1308		201
Measurements Technology Inc 600 Kirk Rd Ste B *Web:* tensiletestmachines.com	Marietta	GA	30060	770-587-2222		173-2
Meat & Potatoes 649 Penn Ave *Web:* meatandpotatoespgh.com	Pittsburgh	PA	15222	412-325-7007		671
Meat Handler Co 1030 Beech St *Web:* www.meathandler.com	Cleveland	WI	53015	920-693-3141	693-8772	177
MEB Management services 1215 E Missouri Ave *Web:* www.mebapts.com	Phoenix	AZ	85014	602-279-5515		652
MEB Manufacturing 3410 Everett Ave *Web:* www.mebmfg.net	Everett	WA	98201	425-259-6074		454
MEBA (Marine Engineers' Beneficial Assn) 444 N Capitol St NW Ste 800 *Web:* www.mebaunion.org	Washington	DC	20001	202-638-5355	638-5369	414
MEC Dynamics Corp 90 Rose Orchard Way *Web:* www.mecdynamics.com	San Jose	CA	95125	408-428-9721		743
MECA Electronics Inc 459 E Main St *TF:* 866-444-6322 ■ *Web:* www.e-meca.com	Denville	NJ	07834	973-625-0661	625-9277	253
MECA Sportswear 1120 Townline Rd **Fax Area Code:* 608 ■ *TF:* 800-729-6322 ■ *Web:* www.mecasportswear.com	Tomah	WI	54660	800-729-6322	374-6405*	155-5
Mecanica Solutions Inc 10000 Blvd Henri-Bourassa Ouest *TF:* 800-567-4223 ■ *Web:* www.mecanicasolutions.com	Montreal	QC	H4S1R5	514-340-1818	340-1891	261
Meccanica Nova Corp 33341 Dequindre Ste A *Web:* novagrinders.com	Troy	MI	48083	248-588-2900		261
Mecco Partners LLC 290 Executive Dr Ste 200 *Web:* www.mecco.com	Cranberry Township	PA	16066	724-779-9555		467
Meccon Industries Inc 2703 Bernice Rd *Web:* www.meccon.com	Lansing	IL	60438	708-474-8300	474-9550	189-10

Company / Address	City	State	Zip	Phone	Fax	Class
Mecham Co, The 4107 S Forest Meadows *Web:* mechamcompany.com	Spokane	WA	99206	509-922-0535		41
Mechancial Service Corp 41 S Jefferson Rd *Web:* mscnj.com	Whippany	NJ	07981	973-884-5000		189-10
Mechanical Construction Company LLC 3330 N Causeway Blvd Ste 400	Metairie	LA	70002	504-833-8291		189-10
Mechanical Contractor 3965 Old Getwell Rd *Web:* www.msystemscompany.com	Memphis	TN	38133	901-730-4799		186
Mechanical Contractors Association of America (MCAA) 1385 Piccard Dr *TF:* 800-556-3653 ■ *Web:* www.mcaa.org	Rockville	MD	20850	301-869-5800	990-9690	49-3
Mechanical Contractors Association of South Carolina (MCASC) 1504 Morninghill Dr *Web:* www.mcasc.com	Columbia	SC	29210	803-772-7834	731-0390	139
Mechanical Design Systems Inc 6302 Aaron Ln *Web:* www.mds-hvac.com	Clinton	MD	20735	301-877-9600		610
Mechanical Designs of Virginia Inc 25582 Jeb Stuart Hwy *Fax Area Code: 540 ■ *Web:* www.mechanicaldesigns.com	Stuart	VA	24171	276-694-7442	694-7088*	454
Mechanical Elastomerics Inc 3264 Coral Rd *TF:* 800-262-3241 ■ *Web:* www.meibelts.com	Malvern	OH	44644	330-863-1014	863-2265	370
Mechanical Equipment Company Inc 68375 Compass Way E *Web:* www.meco.com	Mandeville	LA	70471	985-249-5500	249-7762	806
Mechanical Equipment Company Inc (MECO) 1301 Industrial Dr *Web:* www.mechequip.com	Matthews	NC	28105	704-847-2100	847-2349	612
Mechanical Products Co 1112 N Garfield St *Web:* www.mechprod.com	Lombard	IL	60148	630-953-4100		729
Mechanical Rubber Products Corp 77 Forester Ave *Web:* mechanicalrubber.com	Warwick	NY	10990	845-986-2271		677
Mechanical Servants Inc 2755 Thomas St *TF:* 800-351-2000 ■ *Web:* www.cvalet.com	Melrose Park	IL	60160	800-351-2000		238
Mechanical Services Inc 400 Presumpscot St *TF:* 844-840-8233 ■ *Web:* www.mechanicalservices.com	Portland	ME	04103	207-774-1531		610
Mechanical Systems of Dayton 4401 Springfield St *TF:* 800-254-9455 ■ *Web:* msdinc.net	Dayton	OH	45431	937-254-3235	254-4295	610
Mechanics Bank 1026 E Grand Ave *TF:* 800-942-6222 ■ *Web:* www.mechanicsbank.com	Arroyo Grande	CA	93420	805-473-7710		70
Mechanics Bank Arena Theater & Convention Ctr 1001 Truxtun Ave *Web:* www.rabobankarena.com	Bakersfield	CA	93301	661-852-7300	861-9904	205
Mechanics Hall 321 Main St *Web:* www.mechanicshall.org	Worcester	MA	01608	508-752-5608	754-8442	572
Mechanics Savings Bank 100 Minot Ave PO Box 400 *TF:* 877-886-1020 ■ *Web:* www.mechanicssavings.com	Auburn	ME	04210	207-786-5700	786-5709	70
Mechanicsburg Area School District (Inc) 100 E Elmwood Ave 2nd Fl *Web:* www.mbgsd.org	Mechanicsburg	PA	17055	717-691-4500		685
Mechanicsville Local 6400 Mechanicsville Tpke *TF:* 800-468-3382 ■ *Web:* www.richmond.com	Mechanicsville	VA	23111	804-746-1235	730-0476	532-4
Mechanicville District Public Library (MDPL) 190 N Main St *Web:* meclib.sals.edu	Mechanicville	NY	12118	518-664-4646	664-8641	434-3
Mechatronics Inc 8152 304th Ave SE PO Box 5012 *Web:* www.mechatronics.com	Preston	WA	98050	425-222-5900		75
Mech-Tronics Corp 1635 N 25th Ave *Web:* www.mech-tronics.com	Melrose Park	IL	60160	708-344-9823	344-0067	697
Mecklenburg County 393 Washington St PO Box 530 *Web:* www.mecklenburgva.com	Boydton	VA	23917	434-738-6191	738-6861	338
Mecklenburg Electric Co-op 11633 Hwy Ninety Two *TF:* 800-989-4161 ■ *Web:* www.meckelec.org	Chase City	VA	23924	434-372-6100		245
Meckley Services Inc 9704 Gunston Cove Rd Ste E *TF:* 877-632-5539 ■ *Web:* www.meckleyservices.com	Lorton	VA	22079	703-333-2040	333-2042	610
Meckley's Limestone Products Inc 1543 SR-225 *Web:* www.meckleys.com	Herndon	PA	17830	570-758-3011	758-2400	503-5
Meclabs LLC 1300 Marsh Landing Pkwy Ste 106 *TF:* 800-517-5531 ■ *Web:* www.meclabs.com	Jacksonville Beach	FL	32250	800-517-5531		138
MECO (Mechanical Equipment Company Inc) 1301 Industrial Dr *Web:* www.mechequip.com	Matthews	NC	28105	704-847-2100	847-2349	612
Meco Corp 1500 Industrial Rd *Fax Area Code: 423 ■ *TF:* 800-251-7558 ■ *Web:* www.meco.net	Greeneville	TN	37745	800-251-7558	639-1055*	319-3
MECO Engineering Company Inc 3120 Palmyra Rd *Web:* www.mecoengineering.com	Hannibal	MO	63401	573-221-4048	221-4377	261
Mecor Inc 1567 Elmhurst Rd *Web:* www.mecor.net	Elk Grove Village	IL	60007	847-690-0777	690-0778	358
Mecosta County 400 Elm St *Web:* www.mecostacounty.org	Big Rapids	MI	49307	231-796-2505	592-0121	338
Mecosta County Area Chamber of Commerce 127 S State St *Web:* www.mecostacounty.com	Big Rapids	MI	49307	231-796-7649	796-1625	139
Mecosta-Osceola Intermediate School District 15760 190th Ave *Web:* www.moisd.org	Big Rapids	MI	49307	231-796-3543		685
MECS Inc 14522 S Outer 40 Rd *Web:* www.mecsglobal.com	Chesterfield	MO	63017	314-275-5700	275-5701	188-7
MecSoft Corp 18019 Sky Park Cir Ste KL *Web:* mecsoft.com	Irvine	CA	92614	949-654-8163	654-8164	225
Mectron Engineering Company Inc 400 S Industrial Dr *Web:* www.mectron.net	Saline	MI	48176	734-944-8777	944-8778	419
Mecx Inc 8864 Interchange Dr *Web:* mecx.net	Houston	TX	77054	713-585-7000		261
Med 4 Home Inc 10800 N Congress Ave *Web:* www.med4home.com	Kansas City	MO	64153	816-801-7400		475
Med Associates Inc 166 Industrial Park Rd *Web:* www.med-associates.com	Fairfax	VT	05454	802-527-2343	524-2110	419
Med Fusion 2501 S State Hwy 121 Business Ste 1100 *TF:* 855-500-8535 ■ *Web:* www.medfusionservices.com	Lewisville	TX	75067	972-966-7000	966-7227	415
Med Legal Source Inc 1746 S Victoria Ave Ste F-326 *Web:* www.medlegalsource.com	Ventura	CA	93003	805-729-1968		196
Med Pro Health Care Staffing 5608 Princeton Ave *Web:* www.medprostaffing.com	Columbus	GA	31904	706-322-7085		193
Med Shield Inc 2424 E 55th St *TF:* 800-272-5454 ■ *Web:* medshield.com	Indianapolis	IN	46220	317-613-3700		160
Med Shop Total Care Inc 470 E Loop 281 *TF:* 800-867-6762 ■ *Web:* medshoptotalcare.com	Longview	TX	75605	903-234-0080		237
Meda Ltd 1575 Lauzon Rd *TF:* 888-518-6332 ■ *Web:* www.medagroup.com	Windsor	ON	N8S3N4	519-944-7221		256
MedaCheck LLC 602 Main St Ste 401 *Web:* www.medacheck.com	Cincinnati	OH	45202	513-488-1111		475
Medaglia & Company Inc 26 E Pearl St *Web:* medagliaco.com	Nashua	NH	03060	603-889-4411		2
Medaille College 18 Agassiz Cir *TF:* 800-292-1582 ■ *Web:* www.medaille.edu	Buffalo	NY	14214	716-880-2200	880-2007	166
Medaire Inc 14901 N Scottsdale Rd Ste 200 *Web:* www.medaire.com	Phoenix	AZ	85016	480-333-3700		477
Medalcraft Mint Inc, The 2660 W Mason St *Fax Area Code: 800 ■ *TF:* 888-940-1776 ■ *Web:* medalcraftusa.com	Green Bay	WI	54303	888-940-1776	428-6468*	488
Medallion Bank 22232 17th Ave SE Ste 308 *Fax Area Code: 888 ■ *TF:* 888-833-8570 ■ *Web:* www.medallionbank.com	Bothell	WA	98021	425-368-9200	868-4410*	217
Medallion Cabinetry One Medallion Way *TF:* 800-543-4074 ■ *Web:* www.medallioncabinetry.com	Waconia	MN	55378	800-476-4181		115
Medallion Financial Corp 437 Madison Ave 38th Fl *NASDAQ: MFIN* ■ *TF:* 877-633-2554 ■ *Web:* www.medallion.com	New York	NY	10022	212-328-2100	328-2121	216
Medallion Industries Inc 3221 NW Yeon Ave *Web:* www.medallionindustries.com	Portland	OR	97210	503-221-0170		499
Medallion Laboratories 1 General Mills Blvd *TF:* 800-245-5615 ■ *Web:* www.medallionlabs.com	Minneapolis	MN	55427	763-764-4453	764-4010	192
Medallion Wealth Management 2605 Nicholson Rd Ste 2103 *Web:* medallion-wealth.com	Sewickley	PA	15143	724-934-8600		41
MedAltus 9053 Robins Nest Way Ste B *TF:* 800-393-3848 ■ *Web:* medaltus.com	Summerville	SC	29486	800-393-3848		395
Medarray Inc 3915 Research Park Dr *Web:* www.permselect.com	Ann Arbor	MI	48108	734-769-1066		476
Medart Marine 124 Manufacturers Dr *Fax Area Code: 888 ■ *Web:* www.medartmarine.com	Arnold	MO	63010	636-282-2300	510-3100*	385
Med-Assist School of Hawaii 345 Queen St Ste 400 *Web:* www.mash.edu	Honolulu	HI	96813	808-524-3363		685
MedAvail Technologies Inc 6665 Millcreek Dr Unit No 1 *TF:* 877-830-0826 ■ *Web:* medavail.com	Mississauga	ON	L5N5M4	905-812-0023	812-0402	475
MedAvante-ProPhase Inc 100 American Metro Blvd Ste 201 *Web:* www.medavante.com	Hamilton Township	NJ	08619	609-528-9400	528-9405	582
Medbuy Corp 4056 Meadowbrook Dr Unit 135 *Web:* www.medbuy.ca	London	ON	N6L1E4	519-652-1688		317
Medcare Products Inc 151 Cliff Rd E Ste 10 *TF:* 800-695-4479 ■ *Web:* www.medcarelifts.com	Burnsville	MN	55337	952-894-7076		475
Medcare Supply Inc 4300 Geary Blvd *Web:* medcaremart.com	San Francisco	CA	94118	818-923-6963		475
MedChi Insurance Agency Inc 1204 Maryland Ave *TF:* 800-543-1262 ■ *Web:* www.medchiagency.com	Baltimore	MD	21201	410-539-6642	752-5421	390
Medco Enterprises Inc 3530 Wayne Ave	Bronx	NY	10467	718-655-1700		463
Medco Services Inc 7037 Madison Pk Ste 450 *Fax Area Code: 256 ■ *TF:* 866-661-5739 ■ *Web:* www.extendedearlyout.com	Huntsville	AL	35806	866-661-5739	971-1516*	160
Medcom Inc 6060 Phyllis Dr *Fax Area Code: 714 ■ *TF:* 800-541-0253 ■ *Web:* www.medcomrn.com	Cypress	CA	90630	800-877-1443	891-3140*	33
Medcor Inc 4805 W Prime Pkwy *Web:* www.medcor.com	McHenry	IL	60050	815-363-9500	363-9696	463
Medcore IPA 2609 E Hammer Ln *Web:* medcoreipa.com	Stockton	CA	95210	209-320-2650	320-2644	391-3
MedCost Benefit Services LLC 165 Kimel Park Dr *Fax Area Code: 336 ■ *TF:* 800-433-9178 ■ *Web:* www.medcost.com	Winston-Salem	NC	27114	800-795-1023	970-2139*	390
Medcure 18111 NE Sandy Blvd *TF:* 866-560-2525 ■ *Web:* medcure.org	Portland	OR	97230	503-257-9100	257-9101	363
MEDecision Inc 550 E Swedesford Rd Ste 220 *Web:* www.medecision.com	Wayne	PA	19087	610-540-0202	540-0270	178-10
Medeco Security Locks Inc 3625 Alleghany Dr *Fax Area Code: 800 ■ *Web:* www.medeco.com	Salem	VA	24153	540-380-5000	421-6615*	350
Medefis Inc 10826 Old Mill Rd Suitte 101 *Web:* www.medefis.com	Omaha	NE	68154	402-393-6333		463

	Phone	Fax	Class
Medegen Medical Products LLC 360 Motor Pkwy Ste 800 .... Hauppauge NY 11788 *TF:* 800-511-6298 ■ *Web:* www.medegenmed.com	800-511-6298		476
MED-EL Corp 2511 Old Cornwalls Rd Ste 100................ Durham NC 27713 *TF:* 888-633-3524 ■ *Web:* www.medel.com	919-572-2222	484-9229	475
Medela Inc 1101 Corporate Dr................. Mchenry IL 60050 *TF:* 800-435-8316 ■ *Web:* www.medela.us	815-363-1166		684
MedeliaCommunications LLC 2029 Taft St.............................. Hollywood FL 33020	954-922-0846		195
Medelis Inc 30 Burton Hills Blvd Ste 500 .... Nashville TN 37215 *Web:* www.medelis.com	615-297-6105	385-7055	743
Medely 1315 3rd St .... Santa Monica CA 90401 *TF:* 888-858-7660 ■ *Web:* medely.com	888-858-7660		39
Medexcel USA Inc 484 Temple Hill Rd...................... New Windsor NY 12553 *TF:* 800-563-6384 ■ *Web:* www.medexcelusa.com	845-565-3700		463
MedExpert International Inc 1300 Hancock St .... Redwood City CA 94063 *TF:* 800-999-1999 ■ *Web:* www.medexpert.com	650-326-6000		194
Medflow Inc 14045 Ballantyne Corporate Pl Ste 300 .... Charlotte NC 28277 *TF:* 844-366-5129 ■ *Web:* www.eyecareleaders.com	704-750-5927		179
Medford Care Ctr 185 Tuckerton Rd............ Medford NJ 08055 *Web:* www.medfordcare.com	856-983-8500		371
Medford Chamber of Commerce 1 Shipyard Way Ste 302 .... Medford MA 02155 *Web:* medfordchamberma.com	781-396-1277		139
Medford Leas 1 Medford Leas Way.............. Medford NJ 08055 *TF:* 800-331-4302 ■ *Web:* www.medfordleas.org	609-654-3000		672
Medford Mail Tribune PO Box 1108 .... Medford OR 97501 *Web:* www.mailtribune.com	541-776-4411	858-5126	532-2
Medford Public Library 111 High St............ Medford MA 02155 *Web:* www.medfordlibrary.org	781-395-7950	391-2261	434-3
Medford Township Board of Education 137 Hartford Rd Ste 1........................ Medford NJ 08055 *Web:* medford.k12.nj.us	609-654-6416	654-7436	685
Medford Veterinary Clinic SC 898 S Gibson .... Medford WI 54451 *Web:* medfordvet.com	715-748-2341		794
Medgar Evers College 1650 Bedford Ave.......................... Brooklyn NY 11225 *Web:* www.mec.cuny.edu	718-270-4900		166
MedGyn Products Inc 100 W Industrial Rd .... Addison IL 60101 *TF:* 800-451-9667 ■ *Web:* www.medgyn.com	630-627-4105		608
Media America Inc PO Box 682268............. Franklin TN 37068 *Web:* www.copingmag.com	615-790-2400		637-9
Media Breakaway LLC 1490 W 121st Ave Ste 201 .... Westminster CO 80234 *Web:* www.mediabreakaway.com	303-464-8164	464-8218	194
Media Brokers International Inc 555 N Point Ctr E Ste 700.................. Alpharetta GA 30022 *TF:* 866-514-1620 ■ *Web:* www.media-brokers.com	866-514-1620		6
Media Buying Services Inc 4545 E Shea Blvd Ste 162 .... Phoenix AZ 85028 *TF:* 888-996-2232 ■ *Web:* www.mediabuyingservices.com	602-996-2232		4
Media Communications Inc 1212 Communication Cr .... Virginia Beach VA 23455 *TF:* 800-324-9452	800-324-9452		463
Media Consultants Inc 3908 E Valley Ct............................ Raleigh NC 27606 *Web:* www.mediaconsultants.com	919-821-2190		192
Media Convergence Group Inc 904 Elm St Ste 208......................... Columbia MO 65201 *Web:* www.newsy.com	573-442-4557		387
Media Cybernetics Inc 4340 E W Hwy Ste 400...................... Bethesda MD 20814 *TF:* 800-263-2088 ■ *Web:* www.mediacy.com	301-495-3305	495-5964	178-10
Media Excel Inc 8834 N Capital of Texas Hwy Ste 230............ Austin TX 78759 *Web:* www.mediaexcel.com	512-502-0034	502-0119	177
Media Financial Management Assn (MFM) 550 W Frontage Rd Ste 3600 .... Northfield IL 60093 *Web:* www.mediafinance.org	847-716-7000	716-7004	49-14
Media Flex Inc PO Box 1107 .... Champlain NY 12919 **Fax Area Code:* 514 ■ *TF:* 877-331-1022 ■ *Web:* www.mediaflex.net	518-298-3330	336-8217*	177
Media Fusion Inc 4951 Century St............ Huntsville AL 35816 *Web:* www.fusiononline.com	256-532-3874	704-0404	7
Media Imagery 7905 Browning Rd Ste 218......... Pennsauken Township NJ 08109 *Web:* www.mediaimagery.com	856-317-0990		514
Media Inc PO Box 496......................... Media PA 19063 *TF:* 800-523-0118 ■ *Web:* www.mediaincorporated.com	610-565-2844	565-3614	393
Media Information Services Inc (MIC) 350 5th Ave Ste 4200 .... New York NY 10118 *Web:* welcome.misnyc.com	212-329-2200		393
Media Law Resource Ctr (MLRC) 266 W 37th St 20th Fl........................ New York NY 10018 *Web:* www.medialaw.org	212-337-0200	337-9893	49-10
Media Loft Inc 615 First Ave NE Ste 100 .... Minneapolis MN 55413 *Web:* medialoft.com	612-375-1086		514
Media Logic USA LLC 59 Wolf Rd .... Albany NY 12205 *TF:* 866-353-3011 ■ *Web:* www.medialogic.com	518-456-3015	456-4279	4
Media Services 500 S Sepulveda Blvd 4th Fl................ Los Angeles CA 90049 *TF:* 800-738-0409 ■ *Web:* www.media-services.com	310-440-9600		570
Media Services Group 14614 N Kierland Blvd Ste 270............... Scottsdale AZ 85254 *Web:* www.msgl.com	602-674-5800	674-5874	514
Media Space Solutions 5600 Rowland Rd Ste 170 .... Minnetonka MN 55343 **Fax Area Code:* 612 ■ *TF:* 888-672-2100 ■ *Web:* www.mediaspacesolutions.com	888-672-2100	454-2848*	6
Media Storm 99 Washington St........... South Norwalk CT 06854 *Web:* www.mediastorm.biz	203-852-8001		4
Media Supply Inc 208 Philips Rd................. Exton PA 19341 *Web:* mediasupply.com	610-884-4400		535
Media Tech Inc 12999 E Adam Aircraft Cir Ste 250............ Englewood CO 80112 *Web:* www.mediatech1.com	303-741-6878		177
Media Temple 6060 Center Dr 5th Fl .... Los Angeles CA 90045 **Fax Area Code:* 310 ■ *TF:* 877-578-4000 ■ *Web:* mediatemple.net	877-578-4000	564-2007*	395
Media Two Interactive LLC 112 S Blount St Ste 200 .... Raleigh NC 27601 *Web:* www.mediatwo.net	919-553-1246		4
Media Watch PO Box 618 .... Santa Cruz CA 95061 *TF:* 800-631-6355 ■ *Web:* www.mediawatch.com	831-423-6355		48-8
Media Works Ltd 1425 Clarkview Rd Ste 500................... Baltimore MD 21209 *Web:* www.medialtd.com	443-470-4400		6
Media/Professional Insurance Inc 1201 Walnut Ste 1800 .... Kansas City MO 64106 *TF:* 866-282-0565 ■ *Web:* www.axiscapital.com	816-471-6118	471-6119	391-5
Media3 Technologies LLC N River Commerce Pk 33 Riverside Dr .... Pembroke MA 02359 *TF:* 800-903-9327 ■ *Web:* www.media3.net	781-826-1213	826-1513	808
Mediabidscom Inc 448 Main St................ Winsted CT 06098 **Fax Area Code:* 860 ■ *TF:* 800-545-1135 ■ *Web:* www.mediabids.com	800-545-1135	379-9617*	7
MediaBrains Inc 9015 Strada Stell Ct Ste 203.................... Naples FL 34109 *TF:* 866-627-2467 ■ *Web:* www.mediabrains.com	239-594-3200	594-3207	395
MediaChoice LLC 3701 Bee Caves Rd .... Austin TX 78746 *TF:* 888-567-2424 ■ *Web:* www.mediachoice.com	512-693-9905	693-9904	8
Mediacom Communications Corp 1 Mediacom Way .... Chester NY 10918 *TF:* 855-633-4226 ■ *Web:* www.onmediaadsales.com	855-633-4226		5
Mediafour Corp 1101 5th St .... West Des Moines IA 50265 *Web:* www.mediafour.com	515-225-7409	225-6370	178-12
Mediagrif Interactive Technologies Inc 1111 St-Charles St W E Tower Ste 255......... Longueuil QC J4K5G4 *TSE: MDF* ■ *TF:* 877-677-9088 ■ *Web:* www.mediagrif.com	450-449-0102	449-8725	178-1
Medialets Inc 80 8th Ave .... New York NY 10011 **Fax Area Code:* 646	212-300-5670	569-3199*	387
Media-Max Inc 5316 Lycoming Mall Dr .... Montoursville PA 17754 *Web:* www.mediamaxinc.net	570-368-7633		4
MediaNet Inc 305 Madison Ave .... New York NY 10165 *Web:* www.medianet-ny.com	212-599-5173		194
MediaNews Group Inc 101 W Colfax Ave .... Denver CO 80202 *Web:* www.digitalfirstmedia.com	303-954-6360		637-8
MediaPost Communications 15 E 32nd St.............................. New York NY 10016 *Web:* www.mediapost.com	212-204-2000	204-2038	637-10
MediaPro Inc 20021 120th Ave NE Ste 102 .... Bothell WA 98011 *TF:* 800-726-6951 ■ *Web:* www.mediapro.com	425-483-4700		180
Mediapro US 7331 NW 74th St .... Miami FL 33166 *Web:* mediaprous.tv	305-357-6000		514
Mediaspot Inc 1550 Bayside Dr .... Corona del Mar CA 92625 *Web:* mediaspot.com	949-721-0500		6
Mediassociates Inc 75 Glen Rd............. Sandy Hook CT 06482 *Web:* www.mediassociates.com	203-797-9500	797-1400	7
MediaTech Capital Partners LLC (MCP) 70 E 55th St 21st Fl .... New York NY 10022 *Web:* www.mediatechcapital.com	212-759-3022	534-5328	360-3
Mediatech Institute of Austin 4719 S Congress Ave .... Austin TX 78745 *Web:* mediatech.edu	512-447-2002		162
MediaTek USA Inc 120 Presidential Way .... Woburn MA 01801 *TF:* 855-376-3291 ■ *Web:* www.mediatek.com	781-503-8000	503-8302	360-3
Mediation Institute of Tulsa 1408 S Denver Ave............................. Tulsa OK 74119 *Web:* www.mediationinstitute.net	918-877-1427		167-3
MediaTracks Communications 2250 E Devon Ave Ste 150 .... Des Plaines IL 60018 *Web:* mediatracks.com	847-299-9500		646
MediBase Group Inc, The 3205 S Cherokee Ln Ste 110 .... Woodstock GA 30188 *TF:* 800-499-6781 ■ *Web:* www.medibase.com	770-422-4287	422-9142	194
Medic Publishing Co 30535 SE 84th Pl Ste 8....................... Preston WA 98050 *Web:* www.medicpublishingco.com	425-222-0844	222-0845	637-2
Medic Rescue 313 Bridge St.................... Beaver PA 15009 *Web:* www.medicrescue.org	724-728-3620		30
MEDICA 401 Carlson Pkwy .... Minnetonka MN 55305 *TF:* 800-952-3455 ■ *Web:* www.medica.com	866-317-1169		391-3
Medica Corp 5 Oak Park Dr .... Bedford MA 01730 *TF:* 800-777-5983 ■ *Web:* www.medicacorp.com	781-275-4892		476
Medical Action Industries Inc (MAI) 9120 Lockwood Blvd .... Mechanicsville VA 23116 *TF:* 800-645-7042 ■ *Web:* www.medical-action.com	800-488-8850		477
Medical Associates Healthcare 4333 Edgewood Road NE .... Elkader IA 52043 *TF:* 800-648-6868 ■ *Web:* www.mahealthcare.com	563-245-1717		543
Medical Association of Georgia (MAG) 1849 The Exchange Ste 200 .... Atlanta GA 30339 *TF:* 800-282-0224 ■ *Web:* www.mag.org	678-303-9290	303-3732	474
Medical Benefits Mutual Life Insurance Co 1975 Tamarack Rd .... Newark OH 43058 *TF:* 800-423-3151 ■ *Web:* www.medben.com	740-522-8425		391-3
Medical Billing Concepts Inc (MBC) 16001 Ventura Blvd Ste 135.................... Encino CA 91436 *TF:* 866-351-2852 ■ *Web:* www.medbillconcepts.com	866-351-2852		2
Medical Billing Unlimited Inc 5959 Gateway Blvd W Ste 120 .... El Paso TX 79925 *TF:* 888-311-1716 ■ *Web:* www.mbuinc.com	915-779-1716	779-1754	2
Medical Care Development Intl (MCDI) 8401 Colesville Rd Ste 425 .... Silver Spring MD 20910 *TF:* 800-427-7566 ■ *Web:* www.mcd.org	301-562-1920	562-1921	48-5
Medical Careers Institute Cobblestone Village 901 W Park Ave .... Ocean City NJ 07712 *Web:* www.mcinj.edu	732-695-1190		167-3
Medical Center Enterprise (MCE) 400 N Edwards St......................... Enterprise AL 36330 *Web:* www.mcehospital.com	334-347-0584		374-3

Name / Address	Phone	Fax	Class
Medical Center for Federal Prisoners Springfield			
1900 W Sunshine St. . . . Springfield MO 65807	417-862-7041	837-1717	212
Web: www.bop.gov			
Medical Center Hospital (MCH)			
500 W Fourth St . . . . Odessa TX 79761	432-640-6000		374-3
Web: www.medicalcenterhealthsystem.com			
Medical Center of Aurora, The (MCA)			
1501 S Potomac St. . . . Aurora CO 80012	303-695-2600		374-3
Web: auroramed.com			
Medical Center of South Arkansas			
700 W Grove St . . . . El Dorado AR 71730	870-863-2000	863-5442	374-3
TF: 800-285-1131 ■ *Web:* www.themedcenter.net			
Medical Center of Southeast Texas, The			
2555 Jimmy Johnson Blvd . . . . Port Arthur TX 77640	409-724-7389		374-3
Web: www.medicalcentersetexas.org			
Medical Center Pharmacy			
805 S Long Dr . . . . Rockingham NC 28379	910-997-4471		237
Web: medicalcenterpharmacy.com			
Medical Center Pharmacy Inc			
1050 E S Temple. . . . Salt Lake City UT 84102	801-350-4791		237
Web: medcenterpharm.com			
Medical Center Pharmacy of Cherryville Inc			
607 E Academy St. . . . Cherryville NC 28021	704-435-3263		237
Web: mcpcherryville.com			
Medical City Arlington Volunteer Auxiliary Inc (MCA)			
3301 Matlock Rd . . . . Arlington TX 76015	682-509-6200	472-4878*	374-3
**Fax Area Code:* 817 ■ *Web:* medicalcityarlington.com			
Medical City Las Colinas			
6800 N MacArthur Blvd . . . . Irving TX 75039	972-969-2000	969-2080	374-3
Web: medicalcitylascolinas.com			
Medical City Mckinney Volunteer Auxiliary			
4500 Medical Center Dr . . . . McKinney TX 75069	972-547-8000		374-3
Web: www.medicalcitymckinney.com			
Medical city plano 3901 W 15th St. . . . Plano TX 75075	972-596-6800		374-3
Web: medicalcityplano.com			
Medical Clinic of North Texas			
4300 City Point Dr . . . . North Richland Hills TX 76180	817-514-5200		374-2
Web: www.mcnt.com			
Medical Coaches Inc 399 County Hwy 58. . . . Oneonta NY 13820	607-432-1333	432-8190	516
Web: www.medcoach.com			
Medical Coding Academy			
PO Box 120325 . . . . East Haven CT 06512	203-848-0496		167-3
Web: www.medicalcodingacademy.net			
Medical College of Wisconsin			
8701 Watertown Plank Rd. . . . Milwaukee WI 53226	414-955-8296	456-6506	167-2
Web: www.mcw.edu			
Medical Communications Media Inc			
17 Blacksmith Rd Ste 100. . . . Newtown PA 18940	267-364-0556	364-0567	194
Web: www.cmecorner.com			
Medical Components Inc			
1499 Delp Dr . . . . Harleysville PA 19438	215-256-4201		476
Web: www.medcompnet.com			
Medical Cost Management Corp			
105 W Adams St Ste 2200 . . . . Chicago IL 60603	312-236-2694		363
TF: 800-367-9938 ■ *Web:* www.medicalcost.com			
Medical Ctr Compounding Pharmacy & Health Ctr			
2401 N Ocoee St. . . . Cleveland TN 37311	423-476-5548		237
TF: 877-753-9555 ■ *Web:* www.medicalcenterrx.com			
Medical Ctr, The 250 Park St. . . . Bowling Green KY 42101	270-780-2660		374-3
Web: www.mcbg.org			
Medical Depot Inc			
99 Seaview Blvd . . . . Port Washington NY 11050	516-998-4600	998-4601	477
TF: 877-224-0946 ■ *Web:* www.drivemedical.com			
Medical Designs LLC			
6709 S Minnesota Ave Ste 04. . . . Sioux Falls SD 05710	888-276-7271		476
Web: medicaldesignsllc.com			
Medical Device Assistance Inc			
7117 N 3rd St. . . . Phoenix AZ 85020	602-354-8491	354-8696	192
Web: www.mdassist.com			
Medical Diagnostic Laboratories LLC			
2439 Kuser Rd . . . . Hamilton Township NJ 08690	609-570-1000		418
TF: 877-269-0090 ■ *Web:* www.mdlab.com			
Medical Education Technologies Inc (METI)			
6300 Edgelake Dr . . . . Sarasota FL 34240	941-377-5562		250
TF: 866-462-7920 ■ *Web:* caehealthcare.com			
Medical Energy Inc			
8806 Paul Starr Dr . . . . Pensacola FL 32514	800-786-0137	469-1746*	250
**Fax Area Code:* 850 ■ *TF:* 800-786-0137 ■ *Web:* www.medicalenergy.com			
Medical Extrusion Technologies Inc			
26608 Pierce Cir. . . . Murrieta CA 92562	951-698-4346		596
TF: 800-618-4346 ■ *Web:* www.medicalextrusion.com			
Medical Eye Services Inc			
345 Baker St E . . . . Costa Mesa CA 92626	714-619-4660		390
TF: 800-877-6372 ■ *Web:* www.mesvision.com			
Medical Facilities of America			
2917 Penn Forest Blvd . . . . Roanoke VA 24018	540-989-3618		418
TF: 866-614-9771 ■ *Web:* www.mfa.net			
Medical Graphics Corp			
350 Oak Grove Pkwy. . . . Saint Paul MN 55127	651-484-4874	379-8227	250
NASDAQ: ANGN ■ *TF:* 800-950-5597 ■ *Web:* mgcdiagnostics.com			
Medical Group Management Assn (MGMA)			
104 Inverness Terr E. . . . Englewood CO 80112	303-799-1111		49-8
Web: www.mgma.com			
Medical Home Ctr			
13800 Arizona St Ste 202. . . . Westminster CA 92683	866-560-9999		363
TF: 866-560-9999 ■ *Web:* medhomecenter.com			
Medical Imaging Technologies (MTI)			
875 Valley St. . . . Colorado Springs CO 80915	800-541-5306		475
TF: 800-541-5306 ■ *Web:* www.medicalimagingtech.com			
Medical Indicators			
16 Thomas J Rhodes Industrial Dr . . . . Hamilton Township NJ 08619	609-737-1600	587-8635	475
Web: medicalindicators.com			
Medical Informatics Engineering Inc (MIE)			
6302 Constitution Dr . . . . Fort Wayne IN 46804	260-459-6270		180
Web: www.mieweb.com			
Medical Information Technology Inc			
1 Meditech Cir . . . . Westwood MA 02090	781-821-3000	821-2199	178-10
Web: ehr.meditech.com			
Medical Instrument Development Laboratories Inc			
557 McCormick St . . . . San Leandro CA 94577	510-357-3952		415
TF: 800-929-5227 ■ *Web:* www.midlabs.com			
Medical International Technology Inc			
1872 Beaulac Ville Saint-Laurent . . . . Montreal QC H4R2E7	514-339-9355		476
Web: www.mitneedlefree.com			
Medical Lette, The 1000 Main St . . . . New Rochelle NY 10801	914-235-0500		434-3
Web: secure.medicalletter.org			
Medical Library Assn (MLA)			
65 E Wacker Pl Ste 1900 . . . . Chicago IL 60601	312-419-9094	419-8950	49-11
TF: 800-523-1850 ■ *Web:* www.mlanet.org			
Medical Management Specialists			
4100 Embassy Dr SE Ste 200. . . . Grand Rapids MI 49546	616-975-1845		2
TF: 888-707-2684 ■ *Web:* www.mms.med.pro			
Medical Marketing Inc PO Box 547478 . . . . Orlando FL 32854	407-843-8871	650-3886	352
Web: www.medicalmarketinginc.com			
Medical Metrics Inc			
2121 Sage Rd Ste 300 . . . . Houston TX 77056	713-850-7500		363
Web: www.medicalmetrics.com			
Medical Mutual Group			
700 Spring Forest Rd . . . . Raleigh NC 27609	919-872-7117	878-7550	391-5
TF: 800-662-7917 ■ *Web:* www.medicalmutualgroup.com			
Medical Mutual Insurance Company of Maine			
1 City Ctr PO Box 15275 . . . . Portland ME 04112	207-775-2791	523-8300	391-5
TF: 800-942-2791 ■ *Web:* www.medicalmutual.com			
Medical Mutual Liability Insurance Society of Maryland			
225 International Cir PO Box 8016. . . . Hunt Valley MD 21030	410-785-0050	785-2631	391-5
TF: 800-492-0193 ■ *Web:* www.medicalmutualofmd.com			
Medical Mutual of Ohio			
2060 E 9th St . . . . Cleveland OH 44115	216-687-7000	687-6585	391-3
TF: 800-700-2583 ■ *Web:* www.medmutual.com			
Medical Park Pharmacy Inc			
301 Penny Ln . . . . Morehead City NC 28557	252-726-0777	726-6497	237
Web: www.medicalparkpharmacy.net			
Medical Physics Publishing Corp (MPP)			
4513 Vernon Blvd. . . . Madison WI 53705	608-262-4021	265-2121	637-2
TF: 800-442-5778 ■ *Web:* www.medicalphysics.org			
Medical Practice Partners			
29 Naek Rd Ste 5 . . . . Vernon Rockville CT 06066	860-872-2289		734
Web: www.medicalpracticepartners.com			
Medical Products Laboratories Inc			
9990 Global Rd. . . . Philadelphia PA 19115	215-677-2700	677-7736	582
TF: 800-523-0191 ■ *Web:* www.mplusa.com			
Medical Properties Trust Inc			
1000 Urban Center Dr Ste 501 . . . . Birmingham AL 35242	205-969-3755		654
NYSE: MPW ■ *Web:* www.medicalpropertiestrust.com			
Medical Protective Co 5814 Reed Rd. . . . Fort Wayne IN 46835	260-485-9622	398-6726*	391-5
**Fax Area Code:* 800 ■ *TF:* 800-463-3776 ■ *Web:* www.medpro.com			
Medical Risk Managers Inc			
1170 Ellington Rd. . . . South Windsor CT 06074	800-732-3248		390
TF: 800-732-3248 ■ *Web:* www.mrmstoploss.com			
Medical Security Card Company LLC			
4911 E Broadway Blvd . . . . Tucson AZ 85711	520-888-8070		393
TF: 800-347-5985 ■ *Web:* www.medicalsecuritycard.com			
Medical Services of America Inc (MSA)			
171 Monroe Ln. . . . Lexington SC 29072	803-957-0500		363
TF: 800-845-5850 ■ *Web:* www.msa-corp.com			
Medical Society of Virginia			
2924 Emerywood Pkwy Ste 300 . . . . Richmond VA 23294	800-746-6768	355-6189*	474
**Fax Area Code:* 804 ■ *TF:* 800-746-6768 ■ *Web:* www.msv.org			
Medical Specialties Distributors LLC (MSD)			
800 Technology Center Dr . . . . Stoughton MA 02072	800-967-6400	491-2665*	475
**Fax Area Code:* 866 ■ *TF:* 800-967-6400 ■ *Web:* msdonline.com			
Medical Specialties Managers Inc			
One City Blvd W Ste 1100 . . . . Orange CA 92868	714-571-5000	571-5055	196
Web: www.msmnet.com			
Medical Staffing Associates Inc			
6731 Whittier Ave 3rd Fl. . . . McLean VA 22101	800-235-5105	893-7358*	721
**Fax Area Code:* 703 ■ *TF:* 800-235-5105 ■ *Web:* www.medstaffer.com			
Medical Strategic Planning Inc			
5 Shelbern Dr . . . . Lincroft NJ 07738	732-219-5090		463
Web: www.medsp.com			
Medical Systems Support Inc			
4000 Eagle Point Corporate Dr. . . . Birmingham AL 35242	205-314-5775	258-4877*	177
**Fax Area Code:* 866 ■ *Web:* www.mssus.com			
Medical Team Inc, The			
45 NE Loop 410 Ste 800. . . . San Antonio TX 78216	210-227-9000	224-7224	363
TF: 800-700-1001 ■ *Web:* www.medicalteam.com			
Medical Teams Intl (MTI) PO Box 10 . . . . Portland OR 97207	503-624-1000	624-1001	48-5
TF: 800-959-4325 ■ *Web:* www.medicalteams.org			
Medical Technology Stock Letter			
PO Box 40460 . . . . Berkeley CA 94704	510-843-1857	843-0901	401
Web: www.bioinvest.com			
Medical Training College			
10525 Plaza Americana Dr . . . . Baton Rouge LA 70816	225-926-5820	928-9795	167-3
Web: www.mtcbr.com			
Medical Treatment Systems Inc			
6300 Westgate Rd Ste A . . . . Raleigh NC 27617	800-951-9050		475
TF: 800-951-9050 ■ *Web:* mtxs.com			
Medical University of South Carolina (MUSC)			
Blood & Marrow Transplant Program			
171 Ashley Ave Ste 424. . . . Charleston SC 29425	843-792-9300		769
Web: academicdepartments.musc.edu			
Medical University of South Carolina Children's Hospital			
165 Ashley Ave. . . . Charleston SC 29425	843-792-1414		374-1
Web: www.musckids.org			
MedicAlert Foundation Intl			
5226 Pirrone Ct . . . . Salida CA 95368	800-432-5378	669-2495*	48-17
**Fax Area Code:* 209 ■ *TF:* 800-432-5378 ■ *Web:* www.medicalert.org			
Medicalodges Inc 201 W Eighth St . . . . Coffeyville KS 67337	800-782-0120		793
TF: 800-782-0120 ■ *Web:* www.medicalodges.com			
MedicaMetrix Inc 600 Suffolk St 2nd Fl . . . . Lowell MA 01854	617-694-1713		475
Web: www.medicametrix.com			
Medicap Pharmacy 2105 W Davis St e A . . . . Conroe TX 77304	936-494-4002		237
Web: conroe.medicap.com			
MediCapture Inc			
580 W Germantown Pk Ste 103 . . . . Plymouth Meeting PA 19462	610-238-0700		475
Web: www.medicapture.com			

Phone | Fax | Class

Medicare Payment Advisory Comm
601 New Jersey Ave NW ... Washington DC 20001 202-220-3700 434-3
Web: www.medpac.gov

Medicare Rights Ctr (MRC)
266 W 37th St 3rd Fl ... New York NY 10018 212-869-3850 869-3532 48-17
TF: 800-333-4114 ■ *Web:* www.medicarerights.org

Medicat LLC
303 Perimeter Ctr N Ste 320 ... Atlanta GA 30346 404-252-2295 252-2298 179
TF: 866-633-4053 ■ *Web:* medicat.com

Medicatech USA Inc 50 Maxwell Ave ... Irvine CA 92618 949-679-2881 476
TF: 800-817-5030 ■ *Web:* www.medicatechusa.com

Medicine Hat & District Chamber of Commerce
413 Sixth Ave SE ... Medicine Hat AB T1A2S7 403-527-5214 527-5182 137
Web: business.medicinehatchamber.com

Medicine Lodge Memorial Hospital
710 N Walnut St ... Medicine Lodge KS 67104 620-886-3771 371
Web: www.mlmh.net

Medicine Lodge State Archaeological Site
4800 Co Rd 52 ... Hyattville WY 82428 307-469-2234 565
Web: wyoparks.state.wy.us

Medicine Rocks State Park
PO Box 1630 ... Miles City MT 59301 406-232-0900 565
Web: www.stateparks.com

Medicine Shoppe Pharmacy, The
542 S Eufaula Ave ... Eufaula AL 36027 334-687-0021 237

Medicines Co 8 Sylvan Way ... Parsippany NJ 07054 973-290-6000 656-9898 85
NASDAQ: MDCO ■ *TF:* 800-388-1183 ■ *Web:* www.themedicinescompany.com

Medicis Pharmaceutical Corp
7720 N Dobson Rd ... Scottsdale AZ 85256 602-808-8800 582
TF: 866-246-8245 ■ *Web:* www.valeant.com

Medicity Inc
3600 Mansell Rd Ste 400 ... Alpharetta GA 30022 888-830-1022 174
TF: 888-830-1022 ■ *Web:* www.medicity.com

Medico Industries Inc
1500 Hwy 315 ... Wilkes-Barre PA 18702 570-825-7711 824-1169 264-3
TF: 800-633-0027 ■ *Web:* www.medicoind.com

Medicomp Inc 600 Atlantis Rd ... Melbourne FL 32904 800-234-3278 639
TF: 800-234-3278 ■ *Web:* medicompinc.com

Medicount Management Inc
10361 Spartan Dr ... Cincinnati OH 45215 513-772-4465 41
TF: 800-962-1484 ■ *Web:* medicount.com

MedicTalk Software Inc
12935 Alcosta Blvd Ste 3497 ... San Ramon CA 94583 877-270-8255 178-1
TF: 877-270-8255 ■ *Web:* www.medictalk.com

Medicus Healthcare Solutions LLC
22 Roulston Rd Ste 5 ... Windham NH 03087 855-301-0563 193
TF: 855-301-0563 ■ *Web:* medicushcs.com

Medicx Media Solutions
10799 N 90th St Ste 200 ... Scottsdale AZ 85260 480-614-0060 614-0160 5
Web: www.medicxmedia.com

Mediderm Laboratories
1267 Willis St Ste 200 ... Redding CA 96001 424-338-6442 231
Web: www.medidermstore.com

Medieval Academy of America, The
17 Dunster St Ste 202 ... Cambridge MA 02138 617-491-1622 492-3303 48-11
Web: www.medievalacademy.org

Medifast Inc 11445 Cronhill Dr ... Owings Mills MD 21117 800-209-0878 296-11
NYSE: MED ■ *TF:* 800-209-0878 ■ *Web:* www.medifast1.com

MediGene Inc
10650 Scripps Ranch Blvd Ste 206 ... San Diego CA 92131 858-586-2240 85
Web: www.medigene.com

Medigroup Services Corp
100 Chesterfield Business Pkwy Ste 200 ... Chesterfield MO 63005 636-947-7555 475
Web: www.medigroup.com

MediLodge Group, The
64500 Van Dyke ... Washington MI 48095 586-752-5008 194
Web: medilodge.com

MedImpact Healthcare Systems Inc
10680 Treena St Ste 500 ... San Diego CA 92131 858-566-2727 586
TF: 800-788-2949 ■ *Web:* www.medimpact.com

Medin Corp 11 Jackson Rd ... Totowa NJ 07512 973-779-2400 779-2463 476
TF: 800-922-0476 ■ *Web:* www.medin.com

Medina County 1100 16th St ... Hondo TX 78861 830-741-6000 741-6015 338
Web: www.medinacountytexas.org

Medina County District Library
210 S Broadway ... Medina OH 44256 330-725-0588 725-2053 434-3
Web: www.mcdl.info

Medina Electric Co-opeartive Inc
PO Box 370 ... Hondo TX 78861 866-632-3532 426-2796* 245
**Fax Area Code:* 830 ■ *TF:* 866-632-3532 ■ *Web:* www.medinaec.org

Medine Environmental Engineering LLC (MEE)
900 Valley Ln ... Boulder CO 80302 303-449-2409 192
Web: www.medinellc.com

MedInformatix Inc
5777 W Century Blvd Ste 1700 ... Los Angeles CA 90045 310-348-7367 174
Web: www.medinformatix.com

Medi-Nuclear Corporation Inc
4610 Littlejohn St ... Baldwin Park CA 91706 626-960-9822 476
TF: 800-321-5981 ■ *Web:* www.medinuclear.com

Mediostream Inc
4962 El Cmno Real 201 ... Los Altos CA 94022 650-625-8900 658
Web: www.mediostream.com

Med-I-Pant Inc 9100 Ray Lawson Blvd ... Montreal QC H1J1K8 514-356-1224 476
TF: 866-448-9175 ■ *Web:* www.mipinc.com

Mediplay Inc 526 Pylon Dr ... Raleigh NC 27606 919-341-8582 195
Web: mediplay.com

MediRevv Inc 2600 University Pkwy ... Coralville IA 52241 888-665-6310 196
TF: 888-665-6310 ■ *Web:* www.medirevv.com

Medisolv Inc
10420 Little Patuxent Pkwy Ste 400 ... Columbia MD 21044 443-539-0505 196
Web: medisolv.com

Medisys for Physicians Inc
7201 Halcyon Summit Dr ... Montgomery AL 36117 334-277-6201 631-8292* 179
**Fax Area Code:* 205 ■ *Web:* www.medisysinc.com

Meditech Communications Inc
533 Phalen Blvd ... Saint Paul MN 55130 651-636-7350 636-7460 514
TF: 877-848-7350 ■ *Web:* www.gomeditech.com

Phone | Fax | Class

Mediteranno Restaurant
2900 S State St ... Ann Arbor MI 48108 734-332-9700 671
Web: mediterrano.com

Mediterranean Bistro 1712 N 120th St ... Omaha NE 68154 402-493-3080 671
Web: www.medbistro.com

Mediterranean Grill 42 S Park Ave ... Helena MT 59601 406-495-1212 671
Web: www.mediterraneangrillhelena.com

Mediterranean Gyros Products Inc
1102 38th Ave ... Long Island City NY 11101 718-786-3399 786-8518 297-2
Web: www.mediterraneanpita.com

Mediterranean Inn
425 Queen Anne Ave N ... Seattle WA 98109 206-428-4700 379
Web: www.mediterranean-inn.com

Mediterranean Shipping Company (USA) Inc
420 Fifth Ave 37th St 8th Fl ... New York NY 10018 212-764-4800 770
Web: www.msc.com

Mediterraneo 1970 Main St ... Sarasota FL 34236 941-365-4122 671
Web: www.mediterraneorest.com

Mediu LLC 106 Stover Dr ... Delaware OH 43015 614-885-2100 177
Web: mediu.com

Medium Blue Search Engine Marketing
3365 Piedmont Rd NE St 1400 2nd Fl ... Atlanta GA 30305 678-536-8336 463
TF: 866-436-2583 ■ *Web:* www.mediumblue.com

MediUSA 6481 Franz Warner Pkwy ... Whitsett NC 27377 800-633-6334 156
TF: 800-633-6334 ■ *Web:* www.mediusa.com

Medivance Inc
321 S Taylor Ave Ste 200 ... Louisville CO 80027 303-926-1917 476
Web: www.medivance.com

MediVista Media LLC
1100 Spring St Ste 750 ... Atlanta GA 30309 404-817-7767 708
Web: www.everwell.com

Medix 222 S Riverside Plz Ste 2120 ... Chicago IL 60606 866-446-3349 260
TF: 866-446-3349 ■ *Web:* www.medixteam.com

Medix Specialty Vehicles Inc
3008 Mobile Dr ... Elkhart IN 46514 574-266-0911 59
TF: 888-988-4090 ■ *Web:* www.medixambulance.com

Medizone International Inc
4000 Bridgeway Ste 401 ... Sausalito CA 94965 415-331-0303 477
Web: www.medizoneint.com

MedjetAssist
3500 Colonnade Pkwy Ste 500 PO Box 43099 ... Birmingham AL 35243 205-595-6626 595-6658 30
TF: 800-527-7478 ■ *Web:* medjetassist.com

Medkare Pharmacy LLC
8540 Blue Ridge Blvd ... Kansas City MO 64138 816-353-3314 237
Web: medkarepharmacy.com

MedLearn Media Inc
445 Minnesota St Ste 514 ... Saint Paul MN 55101 800-252-1578 196
TF: 800-252-1578 ■ *Web:* www.medlearnmedia.com

Medler Electric Co 2155 Redman Dr ... Alma MI 48801 989-463-1108 463-4522 249
TF: 800-229-5740 ■ *Web:* medlerelectric.com

Medler Ferro Woodhouse & Mills PLLC
8201 Greensboro Dr ... McLean VA 22102 703-712-8531 41
Web: medlerferro.com

Medley 220 Humboldt Ct ... Sunnyvale CA 94089 408-745-5555 5
Web: www.medley.com

Medley Material Handling Company Inc
4201 Will Rogers Pkwy ... Oklahoma City OK 73108 405-946-3453 358
Web: www.medleycompany.com

Medley Steel & Supply Inc
9925 NW 116th Way ... Medley FL 33178 305-863-7480 492
Web: www.medleysteel.com

Medline Industries Inc 1 Medline Pl ... Mundelein IL 60060 847-949-5500 643-3295 576
TF: 800-633-5463 ■ *Web:* www.medline.com

MedlinePlus
US National Library of Medicine 8600 Rockville Pk
... Bethesda MD 20894 888-346-3656 356
TF: 888-346-3656 ■ *Web:* medlineplus.gov

Medlink Corp
10393 San Diego Mission Rd Ste 120 ... San Diego CA 92108 619-640-4660 194
TF: 800-452-2400 ■ *Web:* www.medlink.com

Medmart Inc 10780 Reading Rd ... Cincinnati OH 45241 513-733-8100 196
TF: 888-260-4430 ■ *Web:* medmartonline.com

MedMaster Inc PO Box 640028 ... Miami FL 33164 954-962-8414 962-4508 637-2
TF: 800-335-3480 ■ *Web:* www.medmaster.net

MedMatica Consulting Assoc
18 Barrington Ln ... Chester Springs PA 19425 610-827-1356 194
Web: www.medmatica.com

Mednovus Inc 664 Hymettus Ave ... Leucadia CA 92024 760-390-1410 476
Web: www.mednovus.com

Medoc Mountain State Park
1541 Medoc State Park Rd ... Hollister NC 27844 252-586-6588 565
Web: www.ncparks.gov

MEDomics LLC 426 N San Gabriel Ave ... Azusa CA 91702 626-804-3645 415
Web: www.medomics.me

Medone Surgical Inc 670 Tallevast Rd ... Sarasota FL 34243 941-359-3129 476
TF: 866-633-6631 ■ *Web:* www.medone.com

Medpace Medical Device Inc
3787 95th Ave NE Ste 100 ... Circle Pines MN 55014 612-234-8500 743
Web: www.medpace.com

MedPlus Inc 4690 Pkwy Dr ... Mason OH 45040 513-229-5500 229-5505 178-10
TF: 800-444-6235 ■ *Web:* questdiagnostics.com

Med-Plus Medical Supplies PO Box 1242 ... Monsey NY 10952 718-222-4416 419
TF: 888-433-2300 ■ *Web:* www.medexsupply.com

Medplus Pharmacy LLC
5130 Duke St Ste 2 ... Alexandria VA 22304 703-751-1111 751-1199 237
Web: mplusrx.com

MedPoint Digital Inc
909 Davis St Ste 500 ... Evanston IL 60201 847-869-4700 4
TF: 800-409-5932 ■ *Web:* www.medpt.com

Medpoint Search PO Box 812582 ... Boca Raton FL 33481 713-524-4443 260
Web: medpointsearch.com

Medquest Associates Inc
3480 Preston Ridge Rd Ste 600 ... Alpharetta GA 30005 678-992-7200 383
Web: www.mqimaging.com

MEDRelief 8502 Tybor Dr ... Houston TX 77074 713-270-4836 596-9770 363
TF: 800-342-6704 ■ *Web:* www.medrelief.com

MedReview Inc
1 Seaport Plz 199 Water St 27th Fl ... New York NY 10038 212-897-6000 897-6062 533
Web: www.medreview.us

	Phone	Fax	Class
Med-RT 27758 Santa Margarita Pkwy . . . . Mission Viejo CA 92691 *Web:* www.med-rt.com	949-502-2800		393
MedRx Inc 1200 Starkey Rd Ste 105 . . . . Largo FL 33771 *TF:* 888-392-1234 ■ *Web:* www.medrx-usa.com	727-584-9600		476
MedSafe 4200 Underwood Rd . . . . La Porte TX 77571 *TF:* 800-330-9240 ■ *Web:* www.gosafe.com	281-476-5392	476-5394	475
MedShape Inc 1575 Northside Dr NW Ste 440 . . . . Atlanta GA 30318 *TF:* 877-343-7016 ■ *Web:* www.medshape.com	877-343-7016		477
MedSignals Corp 462 E High St . . . . Lexington KY 40507 *Web:* www.medsignals.com	781-555-0191		475
Medsphere Systems Corp 1903 Wright Pl Ste 120 . . . . Carlsbad CA 92008 *Web:* www.medsphere.com	760-692-3700	683-3701	178-1
MedStar Health 10980 Grantchester Way. Columbia MD 21044 *TF:* 877-772-6505 ■ *Web:* www.medstarhealth.org	410-772-6500		353
MedStudy Corp 1455 Quail Lake Loop Ste 100 . . . . Colorado Springs CO 80906 **Fax Area Code:* 719 ■ *TF:* 800-841-0547 ■ *Web:* www.medstudy.com	800-841-0547	520-5973*	637-2
MedSupply 5850 E Shields Ave Ste 105. . . . . Fresno CA 93727 *TF:* 800-889-9081 ■ *Web:* www.gomedsupply.net	559-292-1540		475
Med-Tech Resource Inc 29485 Airport Rd . . . . Eugene OR 97402 *TF:* 888-627-7779 ■ *Web:* www.mtrsuperstore.com	888-627-7779		525
MedTelcom Inc 353 Third Ave Ste 190. . . . . New York NY 10010 *Web:* www.medtel.com	212-777-7722		224
MedTera Solutions 40 W 37th St Ste 1203 . . . . New York NY 10018 *Web:* www.medterasolutions.com	212-488-2130		5
MEDTOX Diagnostics Inc 1238 Anthony Rd . . . . Burlington NC 27215 **Fax Area Code:* 651 ■ *TF:* 800-334-1116 ■ *Web:* www.medtox.com	336-226-6311	286-6222*	231
Medtronic Inc 710 Medtronic Pkwy NE . . . . Minneapolis MN 55432 *NYSE:* MDT ■ *TF:* 800-328-2518 ■ *Web:* www.medtronic.com	763-514-4000	514-4879	250
Medtronic MiniMed Inc 18000 Devonshire St . . . . Northridge CA 91325 *TF:* 800-646-4633 ■ *Web:* www.medtronicdiabetes.com	800-646-4633		477
Medullan Inc 240 Elm St 2nd Fl . . . . Somerville MA 02144 *Web:* www.medullan.com	617-547-0273		180
Meduri Farms Inc 12375 Smithfield Rd . . . . Dallas OR 97338 *Web:* medurifarms.com	503-623-0308	623-0726	296-19
Medusind 6115 Camp Bowie Ste 260. . . . . Fort Worth TX 76116 **Fax Area Code:* 866 ■ *TF:* 877-741-4573 ■ *Web:* www.medusind.com	817-570-5102	899-7771*	371
MedValue Offshore Solutions Inc 1415 W 22nd St Tower Fl Regency Towers . . . . . . Oak Brook IL 60523 *Web:* www.medvaluebpo.com	630-299-7370		624
Medvantx Inc 4655 Executive Dr Ste 230 . . . . San Diego CA 92121 *TF:* 866-744-0621 ■ *Web:* www.medvantx.com	866-526-1206		721
Medve Group Inc 1411 W Walnut Hill Ln . . . . Irving TX 75038 *Web:* medve.com	972-827-2292	827-2290	652
Medved Autoplex 11001 W I-70 Frontage Rd N . . . . Wheat Ridge CO 80033 *Web:* www.medved.com	303-421-0100		57
Medway Country Manor 115 Holliston St . . . . Medway MA 02053 *Web:* www.medwaymanor.com	508-533-6634		793
Medway Plastics Corp 2250 Cherry Industrial Cir . . . . Long Beach CA 90805 *Web:* medwayplastics.com	562-630-1175	630-3379	596
Medweb 667 Folsom St . . . . San Francisco CA 94107 *Web:* www.medweb.com	415-541-9980		194
Medwork Instruments Inc 13023 NE Hwy 99 Ste 7-3 . . . . Vancouver WA 98686 **Fax Area Code:* 888 ■ *TF:* 800-323-9790 ■ *Web:* www.medexamtools.com	360-574-3927	523-2128*	475
MedX Health Corp 1495 Bonhill Rd Unit 1. . . . . Mississauga ON L5T1M2 *Web:* www.medxhealth.com	905-670-4428		250
Med-X International Inc 20 Foster St . . . . Bergenfield NJ 07621 *Web:* www.med-x.com	201-387-8556	387-8499	475
MEE (Medine Environmental Engineering LLC) 900 Valley Ln . . . . Boulder CO 80302 *Web:* www.medinellc.com	303-449-2409		192
Mee Industries Inc 16021 Adelante St . . . . Irwindale CA 91702 *TF:* 800-732-5364 ■ *Web:* www.meefog.com	626-359-4550		14
Meeco Inc 250 Titus Ave . . . . Warrington PA 18976 *Web:* www.meeco.com	215-343-6600	343-4194	201
Meeder Equipment Co 12323 Sixth St . . . . Rancho Cucamonga CA 91739 *TF:* 800-423-3711 ■ *Web:* www.meeder.com	909-463-0600	463-0102	357
Meehleis Modular Buildings Inc 1303 E Lodi Ave . . . . Lodi CA 95240 *Web:* meehleis.com	209-334-4637	334-4726	186
Meeker Cooperative Light & Power Assn 1725 E US Hwy 12 PO Box 68 . . . . Litchfield MN 55355 *Web:* www.meeker.coop	320-693-3231	693-2980	245
Meeker County 325 N Sibley Ave . . . . Litchfield MN 55355 *Web:* www.co.meeker.mn.us	320-693-5200	693-5294	338
Meeker Mansion 312 Spring St . . . . Puyallup WA 98372 *Web:* meekermansion.org	253-848-1770		520
Meeks PO Box 1746 . . . . Springfield MO 65801 *Web:* www.meeks.com	417-521-2801		236
Meeks Gregory W (Rep D - NY) 2310 Rayburn House Office Bldg . . . . Washington DC 20515 *Web:* www.meeks.house.gov	202-225-3461	226-4169	342-2
Meeks Lithographing Co 6913 E 13th St . . . . Tulsa OK 74112 *Web:* www.meeksgroup.com	918-836-0900		627
Meeman-Shelby Forest State Park 910 Riddick Rd . . . . Millington TN 38053 *Web:* www.state.tn.us	901-876-5201		565
Meers Engineering Inc 3444 N 1st St Ste 200. . . . . Abilene TX 79603 *Web:* www.meersengineering.com	325-691-1200	691-1206	261
Mees Distributors Inc 1541 W Fork Ave . . . . Cincinnati OH 45223 *Web:* www.meesdistributors.com	513-541-2311	541-4831	191-1
Mees Tile & Marble Inc 4536 Poplar Level Rd . . . . Louisville KY 40213 *Web:* www.meestile.com	502-969-5858	969-3838	191-1
Meet Minneapolis 250 Marquette Ave Ste 1300. . . . . Minneapolis MN 55401 *Web:* www.minneapolis.org	612-767-8000		206
Meeting Alliance 14 Main St . . . . Robbinsville NJ 08691 *Web:* www.meetingalliance.com	609-208-1908		184
Meeting Connection Inc, The 6373 Meadow Glen Dr N . . . . Westerville OH 43082 *TF:* 800-398-2568 ■ *Web:* www.the-meeting-connection.com	614-898-9361		184
Meeting House, The 5885 Robert Oliver Pl . . . . Columbia MD 21045 *Web:* themeetinghouse.org	410-730-4090		720
Meeting Incentive Experts 61 W 15th St Ste 301 . . . . Chicago IL 60605 *Web:* www.miexperts.com	312-842-3600		463
Meeting Masters Inc 6619 McCambell Cluster . . . . Centreville VA 20120 *Web:* meetingmastersinc.com	703-266-0016	383-1215	196
Meeting Matters Inc 11 Dougal Ln . . . . East Northport NY 11731 *Web:* www.meeting-matters.com	631-368-2082		463
Meeting Professionals Intl (MPI) 2711 Lyndon B Johnson Fwy Ste 600. . . . . Dallas TX 75234 *TF:* 866-318-2743 ■ *Web:* www.mpiweb.org	972-702-3053	702-3065	49-12
Meeting Services Unlimited 135 S Mitthoeffer Rd. . . . . Indianapolis IN 46229 *Web:* www.meetingservicesunlimited.com	317-841-7171		184
Meeting Street Inn 173 Meeting St . . . . Charleston SC 29401 *TF:* 800-842-8022 ■ *Web:* www.meetingstreetinn.com	843-723-1882		379
Meeting Systems Inc 600 N Curtis Rd Ste 170. . . . . Boise ID 83706 *Web:* www.meetingsystems.com	208-288-0290		463
MeetingOne Corp 501 S Cherry St One Cherry Ctr Ste 1000 . . . . Denver CO 80246 *TF:* 888-523-9194 ■ *Web:* www.meetingone.com	303-623-2530	623-1294	387
Meetings & Events Intl 1314 Burch Dr . . . . Evansville IN 47725 *TF:* 800-378-1601 ■ *Web:* www.meintl.com	800-378-1601		463
Meetings & Incentives 10520 Seven Mile Rd . . . . Caledonia WI 53108 *Web:* www.meetings-incentives.com	262-835-3553	835-6866	376
MeetMe Inc 100 Union Sq Dr . . . . New Hope PA 18938 *Web:* www.meetme.com	215-862-1162		395
MEFA (Mixed Emotions Fine Art Inc) 95 Tuam St . . . . Houston TX 77006 *Web:* www.mixedemotions.com	713-861-9666		520
Mefferts One Stop 404 W Main St . . . . Waunakee WI 53597 *TF:* 888-255-2300 ■ *Web:* www.meffertoil.com	608-850-3835	849-6170	579
Meg Brown Home Furnishings Inc 5491 US Hwy 158. . . . . Advance NC 27006 *Web:* megbrownhome.com	336-998-7277		321
MEG Energy Corp 600 - 3 Ave SW . . . . Calgary AB T2P0R3 *TF:* 800-661-9675 ■ *Web:* www.megenergy.com	403-770-0446	264-1711	536
Mega Care 1883 Whitney Mesa Dr. . . . . Henderson NV 89014 *TF:* 888-883-6342 ■ *Web:* megacare.com	626-382-9492		793
Mega Circuit Inc 1040 S Westgate St. . . . . Addison IL 60101 *Web:* www.megacircuit.com	630-629-1800	629-2080	625
Mega Force Staffing Services Inc 1001 Hay St . . . . Fayetteville NC 28305 *Web:* www.megaforce.com	910-484-5313		260
Mega Goods Inc 26308 Spirit Ct. . . . . Santa Clarita CA 91350 **Fax Area Code:* 323 ■ *TF:* 800-788-7618 ■ *Web:* megagoods.com	800-788-7618	234-3211*	246
Mega Group Inc 720-1st Ave N. . . . . Saskatoon SK S7K6R9 *TF:* 800-265-9030 ■ *Web:* www.megagroup.ca	306-242-7366		41
Megabyte Minute 250 Mt Lebanon Blvd Ste 320 . . . . Pittsburgh PA 15234 *Web:* www.megabyteminute.com	412-531-4270		645-141
MegaFab PO Box 457. . . . . Hutchinson KS 67504 *TF:* 800-338-5471 ■ *Web:* piranhafab.com	620-663-1127		456
Megaplexus Corp 214 California St . . . . Newton MA 02458 *Web:* www.megaplexus.com	617-244-4405		196
Mega-Pro International Inc 251 W Hilton Dr . . . . Saint George UT 84770 *TF:* 800-541-9469 ■ *Web:* www.mega-pro.com	435-673-1001	673-1007	799
Megaputer Intelligence 1600 W Bloomfield Rd Ste E. . . . . Bloomington IN 47403 *Web:* www.megaputer.com	812-330-0110		178-10
Megastar Financial Corp 1080 Cherokee St . . . . Denver CO 80204 *Web:* www.megastarfinancial.com	303-321-8800		401
Megatech Corp 525 Woburn St. . . . . Tewksbury MA 01876 *Web:* www.megatechcorp.com	978-937-9600		766
Mega-Tech Services LLC 11118 Manor View Dr. . . . . Mechanicsville VA 23116 *Web:* mega-techservices.biz	804-789-1577	789-1578	261
Megger 4271 Bronze Way . . . . Dallas TX 75237 *TF:* 800-723-2861 ■ *Web:* megger.com	214-333-3201	331-7399	248
Meggitt Safety Systems Inc 891 Devon Ct . . . . Simi Valley CA 93063 *Web:* meggitt.com	805-584-4100		283
Meggitt Training Systems Inc 296 Brogdon Rd . . . . Suwanee GA 30024 *TF:* 800-813-9046 ■ *Web:* meggitttrainingsystems.com	678-288-1090	288-1515	703
Meguiar's Inc 17991 Mitchell S . . . . Irvine CA 92614 **Fax Area Code:* 949 ■ *TF:* 800-347-5700 ■ *Web:* www.meguiars.com	800-347-5700	752-5784*	151
Meharry Medical College Library 1005 DB Todd Blvd. . . . . Nashville TN 37208 *Web:* www.mmc.edu	615-327-6318	327-5555	434-1
Meherrin Agricultural & Chemical Company Inc 413 Main St . . . . Severn NC 27877 *TF:* 800-775-0333 ■ *Web:* meherrinag.com	800-775-0333		276
Mehlhop & Vogt 1330 21st St Ste 102 . . . . Sacramento CA 95811 *Web:* injuredworkerhelp.com	916-930-9675	930-0786	41
Mehling & Associates Inc 9846 Hwy 31 E. . . . . Tyler TX 75705 *Web:* www.athomehealth.org	903-592-8001		363

Name / Address	City	State	ZIP	Phone	Fax	Class
Mehlville School District 3120 Lemay Ferry Rd *Web:* www.mehlvilleschooldistrict.com	Saint Louis	MO	63125	314-467-5000		186
Mehron Inc 100 Red Schoolhouse Rd Ste C2 *TF:* 800-332-9955 ■ *Web:* www.mehron.com	Chestnut Ridge	NY	10977	845-426-1700	426-1515	237
Mehta Tech Inc 208 N 12th Ave *Web:* www.mehtatech.com	Eldridge	IA	52748	563-285-9151	285-7576	639
MEI (Martronic Engineering Inc) 874 Patriot Dr Unit D *TF:* 800-960-0808 ■ *Web:* meilaser.com	Moorpark	CA	93021	805-583-0808	583-5364	261
Mei Ji Sushi 454 River Ave *Web:* www.meiji-sushi-wpg.com	Winnipeg	MB	R3L0C6	204-284-3996		671
MEI Real Estate Services 5757 W Century Blvd Ste 605 *Web:* www.meirealty.com	Los Angeles	CA	90045	310-258-0444		652
MEI Technologies Inc 18050 Saturn Ln Ste 300 *Web:* www.meitechinc.com	Houston	TX	77058	281-283-6200		261
Meier Enterprises Inc 12 W Kennewick Ave *TF:* 800-239-7589 ■ *Web:* meierinc.com	Kennewick	WA	99336	509-735-1589		261
Meier Supply Company Inc 275 Corporate Pkwy *TF:* 800-418-3216 ■ *Web:* www.meiersupply.com	Conklin	NY	13748	845-733-5666		610
Meier Tool & Engineering Inc 875 Lund Blvd *Web:* meiertool.com	Anoka	MN	55303	763-427-6275		488
Meier's Wine Cellars 6955 Plainfield Rd *TF:* 800-229-9813 ■ *Web:* www.meierswinecellars.com	Cincinnati	OH	45236	513-891-2900	891-6370	80-3
Meigs County *Economic Development Office* 238 W Main St *Web:* www.meigscountyohio.com	Pomeroy	OH	45769	740-992-3034	992-7942	338
Meijer Inc 2929 Walker Ave NW *TF:* 800-543-3704 ■ *Web:* www.meijer.com	Grand Rapids	MI	49544	616-453-6711		345
Meiji Corp 660 Fargo Ave *Web:* www.meijicorp.com	Elk Grove Village	IL	60007	847-364-9333		60
Meisel 2019 McKenzie Dr *TF:* 800-527-5186 ■ *Web:* www.meisel.com	Carrollton	TX	75006	214-688-4950		588
Meisner & Associates Pc 30200 Telegraph Rd Ste 467 *Web:* meisner-law.com	Bingham Farms	MI	48025	248-644-4433		428
Meisner Electric Inc 220 NE 1st St *Web:* www.mei.cc	Delray Beach	FL	33444	561-278-8362	278-8397	189-4
Meissner Tierney Fisher & Nichols SC 111 E Kilbourn Ave 19th Fl *Web:* www.mtfn.com	Milwaukee	WI	53202	414-273-1300		428
Meister Media Worldwide 37733 Euclid Ave *TF:* 800-572-7740 ■ *Web:* www.meistermedia.com	Willoughby	OH	44094	440-942-2000	942-0662	637-9
Meister Seelig & Fein LLP 125 Park Ave 7th Fl *Web:* www.meisterseelig.com	New York	NY	10017	212-655-3500		445
Meister Sports Management Ltd 770 Lake Cook Rd Ste 300 *Web:* barrymeister.com	Deerfield	IL	60015	847-559-8420		41
MEJ Personal Business Services Inc 245 E 116th St *TF:* 866-418-3836 ■ *Web:* www.mejpbs.com	New York	NY	10029	212-426-6017		113
Mekanika Inc 1501 SE Decker Ave Ste 107 *Web:* www.mekanika.com	Stuart	FL	34994	561-210-5671	892-8202	177
Mekanism Inc 570 Pacific Ave 3rd Fl *Web:* mekanism.com	San Francisco	CA	94133	415-908-4000		7
Meketa Investment Group 100 Lowder Brook Dr Ste 1100 *Web:* www.meketagroup.com	Westwood	MA	02090	781-471-3500		796
Mekong 6004 W Broad St *Web:* mekongisforbeerlovers.com	Richmond	VA	23230	804-288-8929		671
Mekong 637 Somerset St W *Web:* www.mekong.ca	Ottawa	ON	K1R5K3	613-237-7717		671
Mel Bay Publications Inc 1734 Gilsinn Ln *TF:* 800-863-5229 ■ *Web:* www.melbay.com	Fenton	MO	63026	636-257-3970	257-5062	637-2
Mel Chemicals Inc 500 Brbrtown Pt Breeze Rd *Web:* www.zrchem.com	Flemington	NJ	08822	908-782-5800	782-7768	146
Mel Fisher Maritime Museum 200 Greene St *Web:* www.melfisher.org	Key West	FL	33040	305-294-2633		520
Mel Foster Company Inc 5850 Opus Pkwy Ste 120 *Web:* www.melfoster.com	Minnetonka	MN	55343	952-941-9790	944-0634	360-3
Mel Rapton Inc 3630 Fulton Ave *TF:* 800-529-3053 ■ *Web:* www.melraptonhonda.com	Sacramento	CA	95821	916-482-5400		516
Mel Trotter Ministries 363 E State St *Web:* www.meltrotter.org	Belding	MI	48809	616-794-9844		48-20
Mel Wheeler Inc 3934 Electric Rd *Web:* melwheelerinc.com	Roanoke	VA	24018	540-774-9200		643
Melaleuca Inc 3910 S Yellowstone Hwy **Fax Area Code:* 888 ■ *TF:* 800-282-3000 ■ *Web:* www.melaleuca.com	Idaho Falls	ID	83402	208-522-0700	528-2090*	366
Melancon Pharmacy Inc 730 Veterans Dr *Web:* melanconpharmacy.com	Carencro	LA	70520	337-896-8434		237
Melanson Company Inc, The 353 West St PO Box 523 *Web:* www.melanson.com	Keene	NH	03431	603-352-4232	352-5375	697
Melanson Heath & Company PC 102 Perimeter Rd *TF:* 800-282-2440 ■ *Web:* melansonheath.com	Nashua	NH	03063	603-882-1111		2
Melbourne Greyhound Park 1100 N Wickham Rd *Web:* mgpark.com	Melbourne	FL	32935	321-259-9800		642
Melbourne Regional Chamber of East Central Florida 1005 E Strawbridge Ave *Web:* melbourneregionalchamber.com	Melbourne	FL	32901	321-724-5400	725-2093	206
Melder & Melder PC 2304 E Eleven Mile Rd *Web:* melderandmelder.com	Royal Oak	MI	48067	248-541-3400		41
Mele & Co 2007 Beechgrove Pl *TF:* 800-635-6353 ■ *Web:* www.melejewelrybox.com	Utica	NY	13501	315-733-4600	733-3183	200
MELE Associates Inc 11 Taft Ct Ste 101 *Web:* www.meleassociates.com	Rockville	MD	20850	240-453-6990		463
Mele Printing Company LLC 619 N Tyler St *Web:* www.meleprinting.com	Covington	LA	70433	985-893-9522		113
Melges Boatworks Inc PO Box 1 *Web:* www.melges.com	Zenda	WI	53195	262-275-1110	275-8012	90
Meli-Melo 362 Greenwich Ave *Web:* www.melimelogreenwich.com	Greenwich	CT	06830	203-629-6153	861-9359	671
Melin Tool Co 5565 Venture Dr Unit C **Fax Area Code:* 800 ■ *TF:* 800-521-1078 ■ *Web:* www.endmill.com	Cleveland	OH	44130	216-362-4200	521-1558*	493
Melissa & Doug 50 Washington St *Web:* www.melissaanddoug.com	Norwalk	CT	06854	203-838-6400	855-5582	94
Melissa B. Brisman, Esq. LLC 1 Paragon Dr Ste 160 *Web:* reproductivelawyer.com	Montvale	NJ	07645	201-505-0099	505-0097	41
Melissa DATA Corp 22382 Avenida Empresa *TF:* 800-635-4772 ■ *Web:* www.melissa.com	Rancho Santa Margarita	CA	92688	949-858-3000		225
Melissa's/World Variety Produce Inc 5325 S Soto St *TF:* 800-588-0151 ■ *Web:* www.melissas.com	Vernon	CA	90058	800-588-0151		297-7
Melisse 1104 Wilshire Blvd *Web:* www.melisse.com	Santa Monica	CA	90401	310-395-0881		671
Melitta Canada Inc 50 Ronson Dr Unit 150 *TF:* 800-565-4882 ■ *Web:* www.melitta.ca	Toronto	ON	M9W1B3	800-565-4882		296-7
Melitta USA Inc 13925 58th St N *Web:* www.melitta.com	Clearwater	FL	33760	727-535-2111		548
Mel-Kay Electric Company Inc 1511 N Garvin St *Web:* www.mel-kayelectric.com	Evansville	IN	47711	812-423-1128		787
Mellano & Co 766 Wall St *Web:* www.mellano.com	Los Angeles	CA	90014	213-622-0796		292
Mellen Company Inc, The 40 Chenell Dr *Web:* www.mellencompany.com	Concord	NH	03301	603-228-2929	228-5727	420
Melling Tool Co 2620 Saradan St PO Box 1188 *Web:* www.melling.com	Jackson	MI	49204	517-787-8172	787-5304	60
Mellon Investments Corp 50 Fremont St Ste 3900 *Web:* www.mellon.com	San Francisco	CA	94105	415-546-6056	777-5699	401
Mellor Engineering Inc 887 N 100 E Ste 1 *Web:* www.mellorengineering.com	Lehi	UT	84043	801-768-0658		261
Mellott Manufacturing Co 13156 Long Ln *Web:* www.mellottmfg.com	Mercersburg	PA	17236	717-369-3125		454
Melloy Nissan 7707 Lomas Blvd NE *TF:* 877-206-4809 ■ *Web:* www.melloynissan.com	Albuquerque	NM	87110	505-545-6420		57
Mellwood Arts & Entertainment Ctr 1860 Mellwood Ave *Web:* www.mellwoodartcenter.com	Louisville	KY	40206	502-895-3650		50-6
Melnor Inc 109 Tyson Dr **Fax Area Code:* 888 ■ *TF:* 877-283-0697 ■ *Web:* www.melnor.com	Winchester	VA	22603	540-722-5600	411-2500*	429
Meloon Foundries Inc 1841 Lemoyne Ave *Web:* www.meloon.com	Syracuse	NY	13208	315-454-3231	454-8559	492
Melrose Cafe & Bar 730 17th Ave SW *Web:* melrosecalgary.com	Calgary	AB	T2S0B7	403-984-3577		671
Melrose Chamber of Commerce 1 W Foster St *Web:* melrosechamber.org	Melrose	MA	02176	781-665-3033		139
Melrose Farm Service Inc 308 Mill St *Web:* www.melrosefarmservice.com	Melrose	WI	54642	608-488-6661		276
Melrose Hotel Washington DC, The 2430 Pennsylvania Ave NW *TF:* 800-635-7673 ■ *Web:* www.melrosehoteldc.com	Washington	DC	20037	202-955-6400		378
Melrose Industries PLC 1180 Peachtree St NE Ste 2450 *Web:* www.melroseplc.net	Atlanta	GA	30309	404-941-2100		723
Melrose Public Library 69 W Emerson St *Web:* www.melrosepubliclibrary.org	Melrose	MA	02176	781-665-2313		434-3
Melting Pot Restaurants Inc 8810 Twin Lakes Blvd *TF:* 800-783-0867 ■ *Web:* www.meltingpot.com	Tampa	FL	33614	813-881-0055		670
Melting Pot Restaurants Inc, The 2045 S Hurstbourne Pkwy *Web:* meltingpot.com	Louisville	KY	40220	502-491-4762		671
Meltmedia 2120 E Rio Salado Pkwy Ste 201 *Web:* meltmedia.com	Tempe	AZ	85281	602-340-9440		196
Melton Machine & Control Co 6350 Bluff Rd *Web:* meltonmachine.com	Washington	MO	63090	636-239-7765		811
Melton Truck Lines Inc 808 N 161 E Ave *Web:* www.meltontruck.com	Tulsa	OK	74116	918-270-9451		780
Meltzer, Lippe, Goldstein & Breitstone LLP 190 Willis Ave *Web:* www.meltzerlippe.com	Mineola	NY	11501	516-747-0300		428
Melville Publications PO Box 2036 *TF:* 888-248-6608 ■ *Web:* www.boomeranglove.com	Santa Maria	CA	93457	805-937-6608	937-1452	637-2
Melvindale-Northern Allen Park Public Schools 18530 Prospect St *Web:* www.melnapschools.com	Melvindale	MI	48122	313-389-3300		685
Melwood Horticultural Training Center In 5606 Dower House Rd *Web:* www.melwood.org	Upper Marlboro	MD	20772	301-599-8000		260

Name / Address	Phone	Fax	Class
MEMA (Motor & Equipment Manufacturers Assn) 79 TW Alexander Dr 4501 Research Commons Ste 200 ... Research Triangle Park NC 27709 *Web:* www.mema.org	919-549-4800		49-21
Member One Federal Credit Union 202 Fourth NE ... Roanoke VA 24016 *TF:* 800-666-8811 ■ *Web:* www.memberonefcu.com	540-982-8811		219
Member Preferred Federal Credit Union 340 S Blue Mound Rd Ste 342 ... Saginaw TX 76131 *Web:* memberpreferredfcu.com	817-222-2288		219
memberplanet 23224 Crenshaw Blvd ... Torrance CA 90505 *TF:* 888-298-8845 ■ *Web:* www.memberplanet.com	888-298-8845		387
Members 1st of Nj Fcu 37 W Landis Ave ... Vineland NJ 08360 *Web:* membersonenj.org	856-696-0767		219
Members Community Credit Union 159 Colorado St ... Muscatine IA 52761 *Web:* memberscommunitycu.org	563-264-7210		219
Members Credit Union 2098 Frontis Plaza Blvd ... Winston-Salem NC 27103 *TF:* 800-951-8000 ■ *Web:* memcu.com	336-748-4800		219
Members Trust Co 14025 Riveredge Dr Ste 280 ... Tampa FL 33637 *Web:* memberstrust.com	813-631-9191		70
Membersfirst Credit Union of Florida 251 W Garden St ... Pensacola FL 32502 *Web:* membersfirstfl.org	850-434-2211		219
MembersFirst Inc 321 Commonwealth Rd ... Wayland MA 01778 *Web:* www.membersfirst.com	508-653-3399	974-8121	177
Membership Consultants 3868 Russell Blvd ... Saint Louis MO 63110 *Web:* www.membership-consultants.com	314-771-4664	771-2759	194
Membersown Credit Union 1391 S 33rd St ... Lincoln NE 68510 *Web:* membersowncu.org	402-436-5365		219
Membrane Technology & Research Inc 1360 Willow Rd Ste 103 ... Menlo Park CA 94025 *Web:* www.mtrinc.com	650-328-2228	328-6580	668
MEMC Pasadena Inc 501 Pearl Dr ... Saint Peters MO 63376 *Web:* www.memc.com	636-474-5000		696
MEMdata LLC 1601 Sebesta ... College Station TX 77845 *Web:* www.memdata.com	979-695-1950		194
Memering Motorplex Inc 1949 Hart St ... Vincennes IN 47591 *Web:* www.memeringmotorplex.com	812-882-5367		57
Memocast Inc PO Box 321198 ... Los Gatos CA 95032 *Web:* www.memocast.com	415-673-5122		514
Memoir Network, The 95 Gould Rd ... Lisbon Falls ME 04252 *Web:* thememoirnetwork.com	207-353-5454		637-2
Memorial Art Gallery of the University of Rochester 500 University Ave ... Rochester NY 14607 *Web:* www.mag.rochester.edu	585-276-8900		520
Memorial Blood Centers (MBC) 737 Pelham Blvd ... Saint Paul MN 55114 **Fax Area Code:* 651 ■ *TF:* 888-448-3253 ■ *Web:* www.mbc.org	888-448-3253	332-7001*	89
Memorial City Mall 303 Memorial City ... Houston TX 77024 *Web:* www.memorialcity.com	713-464-8640		460
Memorial Credit Union 6800 Longview Rd ... Chattanooga TN 37421 *Web:* memorialcreditunion.com	423-855-1770		219
Memorial Hall Library 2 N Main St ... Andover MA 01810 *Web:* www.mhl.org	978-623-8400		434-3
Memorial Health University Medical Ctr 4700 Waters Ave ... Savannah GA 31404 *Web:* www.memorialhealth.com	912-350-8000		374-3
Memorial Healthcare Ctr 826 W King St ... Owosso MI 48867 *TF:* 800-206-8706 ■ *Web:* www.memorialhealthcare.org	800-206-8706		374-3
Memorial Home Services- Hospice 720 N Bond St ... Springfield IL 62702 *TF:* 800-582-8667 ■ *Web:* www.memorialhomeservices.com	217-788-4663		363
Memorial Hospital 4500 Memorial Dr ... Belleville IL 62226 *Web:* www.memhosp.com	618-233-7750		374-3
Memorial Hospital 2525 Desales Ave ... Chattanooga TN 37404 *Web:* www.memorial.org	423-495-2525		374-3
Memorial Hospital & Health Care Ctr 800 W Ninth St ... Jasper IN 47546 *TF:* 800-852-7279 ■ *Web:* www.mhhcc.org	812-996-2345		374-3
Memorial Hospital at Gulfport 4500 13th St ... Gulfport MS 39501 *Web:* www.gulfportmemorial.com	228-867-4000	867-4137	374-3
Memorial Hospital of Carbondale 405 W Jackson St ... Carbondale IL 62902 *TF:* 800-457-1393 ■ *Web:* www.sih.net	618-549-0721	529-0449	374-3
Memorial Hospital of Rhode Island (MHRI) 111 Brewster St ... Pawtucket RI 02860 *TF:* 800-647-4362 ■ *Web:* www.mhri.org	401-729-2000		374-3
Memorial Hospital of Salem County 310 Woodstown Rd ... Salem NJ 08079 *Web:* www.mhschealth.com	856-935-1000		374-3
Memorial Hospital of Sweetwater County 1200 College Dr ... Rock Springs WY 82901 *Web:* www.sweetwatermemorial.com	307-362-3711		374-3
Memorial Hospital of Tampa 2901 W Swann Ave ... Tampa FL 33609 *Web:* memorialhospitaltampa.com	813-873-6400		374-3
Memorial Hospital Pembroke (MHP) 7800 Sheridan St ... Pembroke Pines FL 33024 *Web:* www.mhs.net	954-962-9650		374-3
Memorial Lake State Park 18 Boundary Rd ... Grantville PA 17028 *Web:* www.dcnr.pa.gov	717-865-6470		565
Memorial Medical Ctr 1086 Franklin St ... Johnstown PA 15905 *TF:* 800-441-2555 ■ *Web:* www.conemaugh.org	814-534-9000		374-3
Memorial Medical Ctr 2450 S Telshor Blvd ... Las Cruces NM 88011 *Web:* www.mmclc.org	575-522-8641		374-3
Memorial Medical Ctr 701 N First St ... Springfield IL 62781 *Web:* www.memorialmedical.com	217-788-3000		374-3
Memorial Medical Ctr 1615 Maple Ln ... Ashland WI 54806 *TF:* 888-868-9292 ■ *Web:* ashlandmmc.com	715-685-5500	685-7504	374-3
Memorial MRI & Diagnostic 1241 Campbell Rd ... Houston TX 77055 *Web:* memorialdiagnostic.com	713-461-3399	461-1969	383
Memorial Sloan-Kettering Cancer Ctr 1275 York Ave ... New York NY 10065 *TF:* 800-525-2225 ■ *Web:* www.mskcc.org	212-639-2000		374-7
Memorial Veterinary Hospital Inc 1534 Scranton Carbondale Hwy ... Scranton PA 18508 *Web:* memorialveterinaryhospital.com	570-483-1930		794
Memorial White Rose Home Health and Hospice 1412 6th Ave ... York PA 17403 *Web:* www.memorialwhiterose.com	717-843-5091	849-5630	363
MemorialCare 17360 Brookhurst St ... Fountain Valley CA 92708 *Web:* www.memorialcare.org	714-377-2900		374-3
MemoryMinder Journals Inc PO Box 23108 ... Eugene OR 97402 *TF:* 800-888-3392 ■ *Web:* www.memoryminder.com	541-342-2300	935-1106	637-9
Memphis 201 N Broadway ... Santa Ana CA 92701 *Web:* memphiscafe.com	714-432-7685		671
Memphis Area Association of Realtors 6393 Poplar Ave ... Memphis TN 38119 *Web:* maar.org	901-685-2100		653
Memphis Area Transit Authority (MATA) 1370 Levee Rd ... Memphis TN 38108 *Web:* www.matatransit.com	901-722-7100		468
Memphis Botanic Garden 750 Cherry Rd ... Memphis TN 38117 *Web:* www.memphisbotanicgarden.com	901-636-4100	682-1561	97
Memphis Brooks Museum of Art 1934 Poplar Ave Overton Pk ... Memphis TN 38104 *Web:* www.brooksmuseum.org	901-544-6200	725-4071	520
Memphis City Hall 125 N Main St ... Memphis TN 38103 *Web:* www.cityofmemphis.org	901-576-6500		337
Memphis College of Art 1930 Poplar Ave ... Memphis TN 38104 *TF:* 800-727-1088 ■ *Web:* www.mca.edu	901-272-5100	272-5158	164
Memphis Convention & Visitors Bureau 47 Union Ave ... Memphis TN 38103 *TF:* 888-633-9099 ■ *Web:* www.memphistravel.com	901-543-5300	543-5350	206
Memphis Cotton Exchange, The 65 Union Ave Mezzanine ... Memphis TN 38103 *Web:* memphiscottonmuseum.org	901-531-7826		520
Memphis Flyer 460 Tennessee St ... Memphis TN 38103 *TF:* 877-292-3804 ■ *Web:* www.memphisflyer.com	901-521-9000	521-0129	532-5
Memphis International Airport 2491 Winchester Rd Ste 113 ... Memphis TN 38116 *Web:* www.flymemphis.com	901-922-8000	922-8099	27
Memphis Light Gas & Water (MLGW) 220 S Main St ... Memphis TN 38103 *Web:* www.mlgw.com	901-528-4011		787
Memphis National Cemetery 3568 Townes Ave ... Memphis TN 38122 *Web:* www.cem.va.gov	901-386-8311	382-0750	136
Memphis Rock 'n' Soul Museum 191 Beale St ... Memphis TN 38103 *Web:* www.memphisrocknsoul.org	901-205-2533	205-2534	520
Memphis Symphony Orchestra 610 Goodman St ... Memphis TN 38111 *Web:* memphissymphony.org	901-537-2525	537-2550	573-3
Memphis Theological Seminary 168 E Pkwy S ... Memphis TN 38104 *Web:* memphisseminary.edu	901-458-8232	452-4051	167-3
Memphis Zoo 2000 Prentiss Pl ... Memphis TN 38112 *Web:* www.memphiszoo.org	901-333-6500	333-6501	823
Memry Corp 3 Berkshire Blvd ... Bethel CT 06801 *TF:* 866-466-3679 ■ *Web:* www.memry.com	203-739-1100		485
MEMS Optical Inc 205 Import Cir ... Huntsville AL 35806 *Web:* www.jenoptik.us	256-859-1886		542
Memsic Inc 1 Tech Dr Ste 325 ... Andover MA 01810 *Web:* www.memsic.com	978-738-0900		696
MEMStaff Inc 8 Pine St ... Newburyport MA 01950 *Web:* www.memstaff.com	617-996-9263		226
Men Against Destruction Defending Against Drugs & Social Disorder Inc 3026 Fourth Ave S ... Minneapolis MN 55408 *Web:* www.maddads.com	612-822-0802	253-0663	48-6
Men's Journal LLC 1290 Avenue of the Americas ... New York NY 10104 *Web:* www.mensjournal.com	212-484-1616	767-8204	457-11
Men's Wearhouse Inc 6380 Rogerdale Rd ... Houston TX 77072 *NYSE: TLRD* ■ *TF:* 877-986-9669 ■ *Web:* www.menswearhouse.com	281-776-7038		157-3
Mena Regional Health System 311 Morrow St N ... Mena AR 71953 *TF:* 800-394-6185 ■ *Web:* menaregional.com	479-394-6100		363
Mena Tours & Travel 5209 N Clark St ... Chicago IL 60640 *TF:* 800-937-6362 ■ *Web:* www.mena.travel	773-275-2125	275-9927	377
Menara 41 E Gish Rd ... San Jose CA 95112 *Web:* www.menara41.com	408-453-1983		671
Menard Correctional Ctr 711 Kaskaskia St ... Menard IL 62259 *Web:* www.illinois.gov	618-826-5071		213
Menard County 102 S Seventh St PO Box 465 ... Petersburg IL 62675 *Web:* www.menardcountyil.com	217-632-3201		338
Menard County Texas PO Box 1038 ... Menard TX 76859 *Web:* www.co.menard.tx.us	325-396-4682	396-2047	338
Menard Electric Co-op 14300 State Hwy 97 PO Box 200 ... Petersburg IL 62675 *TF:* 800-872-1203 ■ *Web:* www.menard.com	217-632-7746		245
Menard Electronics Inc 6451 Choctaw Dr ... Baton Rouge LA 70805 *TF:* 800-272-3003 ■ *Web:* www.menardelectronics.com	800-272-3003		246
Menard Inc 5101 Menard Dr ... Eau Claire WI 54703 *Web:* www.menards.com	715-876-5911	876-2868	364
Menardi 1 Maxwell Dr ... Trenton SC 29847 **Fax Area Code:* 803 ■ *TF:* 800-321-3218 ■ *Web:* menardifilters.com	800-321-3218	663-4029*	67

Name / Address	City	State	ZIP	Phone	Fax	Class
Menas Realty Co 4990 Mission Blvd *Web:* www.menas.com	San Diego	CA	92109	858-270-7870		652
Menasha Corp 1645 Bergstrom Rd *TF:* 800-558-5073 ■ *Web:* www.menasha.com	Neenah	WI	54956	920-751-1000		100
Menasha Public Library 440 First St *Web:* www.menashalibrary.org	Menasha	WI	54952	920-967-3690	967-5159	434-3
Menasha Utilities 321 Milwaukee St PO Box 340 *Web:* www.menashautilities.com	Menasha	WI	54952	920-967-3400	967-3441	787
MENC: NA for Music Education 1806 Robert Fulton Dr *TF:* 800-336-3768 ■ *Web:* nafme.org	Reston	VA	20191	703-860-4000	860-1531	49-5
Menches Tool & Die Inc 30995 San Benito St *Web:* www.menches.com	Hayward	CA	94544	510-476-1160		697
Menda 3651 Walnut Ave *Web:* www.mendapump.com	Chino	CA	91710	909-627-2453	627-7449	45
Mended Hearts Inc, The 8150 N Central Expy M2248 *TF:* 888-432-7899 ■ *Web:* mendedhearts.org	Dallas	TX	75206	214-296-9252	295-9552	48-17
Mendenfreiman LLP 5565 Glenridge Connector NE Ste 850 *Web:* mendenfreiman.com	Atlanta	GA	30342	770-379-1450		41
Mendenhall Homeplace 603 W Main St *Web:* www.mendenhallhomeplace.com	Jamestown	NC	27282	336-454-3819		50-3
Mendes & Mount LLP 750 Seventh Ave *Web:* www.mendes.com	New York	NY	10019	212-261-8000		428
Mendocino Beacon 450 N Franklin St *Web:* www.mendocinobeacon.com	Fort Bragg	CA	95437	707-964-5642	964-0424	532-2
Mendocino Brewing Co 1901 Antler Rd *Web:* www.mendobrew.com	Ukiah	CA	95482	707-462-1697	462-1699	102
Mendocino Coast Botanical Gardens 18220 N Hwy 1 *Web:* www.gardenbythesea.org	Fort Bragg	CA	95437	707-964-4352	964-3114	97
Mendocino Coast Chamber of Commerce 217 S Main St PO Box 1141 *Web:* mendocinocoast.com	Fort Bragg	CA	95437	707-961-6300		139
Mendocino Coast District Hospital 700 River Dr *Web:* www.mcdh.org	Fort Bragg	CA	95437	707-961-1234		374-3
Mendocino College 1000 Hensley Creek Rd *Web:* www.mendocino.edu	Ukiah	CA	95482	707-468-3000	468-3430	162
Mendocino County 501 Low Gap Rd Rm 1060 *Web:* www.mendocinocounty.org	Ukiah	CA	95482	707-234-6800	463-4257	338
Mendocino Hotel & Garden Suites 45080 Main St *Web:* www.mendocinohotel.com	Mendocino	CA	95460	707-937-0511		379
Mendocino Redwood Company LLC 850 Kunzler Ranch Rd *Web:* www.hrcllc.com	Ukiah	CA	95482	707-463-5110		752
Mendocino Sea Vegetable Co PO Box 455 *Web:* www.seaweed.net	Philo	CA	95466	707-895-2996	895-3270	297-7
Mendocino Wine Co 501 Parducci Rd *TF:* 800-362-9463 ■ *Web:* www.mendocinowineco.com	Ukiah	CA	95482	707-463-5350	462-7260	80-3
Mendocino Woodlands State Park 39350 Little Lake Rd *Web:* www.parks.ca.gov	Mendocino	CA	95460	707-937-5755		565
Mendon Truck Leasing & Rental 362 Kingsland Ave *TF:* 877-636-3661 ■ *Web:* www.mendonleasing.com	Brooklyn	NY	11236	718-209-9886		778
Mendota Insurance Co PO Box 64586 **Fax Area Code:* 866 ■ *TF:* 800-422-0792 ■ *Web:* www.mendota-insurance.com	Saint Paul	MN	55164	651-468-2910	385-0553*	391-4
Mendota Mental Health Institute 301 Troy Dr *TF:* 800-323-8942 ■ *Web:* www.dhs.wisconsin.gov	Madison	WI	53704	608-301-1000	301-1358	374-5
Mendoza Ribas Farinas & Assn 6265 Executive Blvd *Web:* www.engineerunion.org	Rockville	MD	20852	301-468-8882		261
Me-n-Ed's Pizzeria 7025 N W Ave *Web:* www.meneds.com	Fresno	CA	93711	559-436-0563		670
Menendez Robert (Sen D - NJ) 528 Hart Senate Office Bldg *Web:* www.menendez.senate.gov	Washington	DC	20510	202-224-4744	228-2197	342-2
Meng Grace (Rep D - NY) 2209 Rayburn House Office Bldg *Web:* www.meng.house.gov	Washington	DC	20515	202-225-2601	225-1589	342-2
Mengel Metzger Barr & Company LLP 100 Chestnut St Ste 1200 *Web:* mengelmetzgerbarr.com	Rochester	NY	14604	585-423-1860		734
Menger Hotel 204 Alamo Plz *TF:* 800-345-9285 ■ *Web:* www.mengerhotel.com	San Antonio	TX	78205	210-223-4361	228-0022	379
Mengis Capital Management Inc 1 SW Columbia St Ste 780 *TF:* 877-916-0780 ■ *Web:* www.mengiscapital.com	Portland	OR	97258	503-916-0776	916-0781	401
Menifee County Clerk 12 Main St PO Box 123 *Web:* www.menifeecountyclerk.com	Frenchburg	KY	40322	606-768-3512	768-6738	338
Menifee Valley Chamber of Commerce 29683 New Hub Dr Ste C *Web:* www.menifeevalleychamber.com	Menifee	CA	92586	951-672-1991		139
Menil Collection 1533 Sul Ross St *Web:* www.menil.org	Houston	TX	77006	713-525-9400		520
Menke Jackson Beyer LLP 807 N 39th Ave *Web:* mjbe.com	Yakima	WA	98902	509-575-0313		41
Menke Marking Devices 13253 Alondra Blvd *TF:* 800-231-6023 ■ *Web:* www.menkemarking.com	Santa Fe Springs	CA	90670	562-921-1380	921-1184	467
Menk-USA LLC 2207 Enterprise Dr *Web:* menk-usa.com	Sterling	IL	61081	815-626-9730	626-9740	567
Menlo College 1000 El Camino Real *TF:* 800-556-3656 ■ *Web:* www.menlo.edu	Atherton	CA	94027	650-543-3753	543-4496	166
Menlo Engineering Associates I 261 Cleveland Ave *Web:* menloeng.com	Highland Park	NJ	08904	732-846-8585		261
Menlo Innovations LLC 505 E Liberty LL500 *Web:* www.menloinnovations.com	Ann Arbor	MI	48104	734-665-1847		180
Menlo Park Chamber of Commerce 1100 Merrill St *Web:* menloparkchamber.com	Menlo Park	CA	94025	650-325-2818	325-0920	139
Menlo Park Public Library 800 Alma St *Web:* www.menlopark.org	Menlo Park	CA	94025	650-330-2500	327-7030	434-3
Menlo Scientific Ltd 5161 Rain Cloud Dr *Web:* www.menloscientific.com	Richmond	CA	94803	510-758-9014		196
Menlo Technologies 4675 Stevens Creek Blvd Ste 230 *Web:* menlo-technologies.com	Santa Clara	CA	95051	408-736-8100		180
Menlo Ventures 2884 Sand Hill Rd Ste 100 *Web:* www.menlovc.com	Menlo Park	CA	94025	650-854-8540	854-7059	792
Mennel Milling Co 128 W Crocker St *TF:* 800-688-8151 ■ *Web:* mennel.com	Fostoria	OH	44830	419-435-8151		296-23
Mennello Museum of American Art 900 E Princeton St *Web:* www.mennellomuseum.org	Orlando	FL	32803	407-246-4278	246-4329	520
Mennen Medical Corp 290 Andrews Rd *Web:* www.mennenmedical.com	Feasterville-Trevose	PA	19053	215-259-1020		250
Mennie's Machine Co (MMC) 10549 Mennie Ln PO Box 110 *Web:* www.mennies.com	Mark	IL	61340	815-339-2226	339-6550	621
Menninger Clinic 12301 Main St *TF:* 800-351-9058 ■ *Web:* www.menningerclinic.com	Houston	TX	77035	713-275-5000	275-5107	374-5
Menno Village 2075 Scotland Ave *Web:* mennohaven.org	Chambersburg	PA	17201	717-262-2373		672
Mennonite Brethren Biblical Seminary 4824 E Butler Ave *TF:* 800-251-6227 ■ *Web:* www.fresno.edu	Fresno	CA	93727	559-453-2000		167-3
Mennonite Central Committee (MCC) 21 S 12th St PO Box 500 *TF:* 888-563-4676 ■ *Web:* mcc.org	Akron	PA	17501	717-859-1151	859-2171	48-5
Mennonite Disaster Service (MDS) 583 Airport Rd *TF:* 800-241-8111 ■ *Web:* mds.mennonite.net	Lititz	PA	17543	717-735-3536		48-5
Mennonite Economic Development Associates of Canada 155 Frobisher Dr Ste I-106 *Web:* www.meda.org	Waterloo	ON	N2V2E1	519-725-1633		393
Mennonite Friendship Communities 600 W Blanchard Rd *Web:* www.mennofriend.com	South Hutchinson	KS	67505	620-663-7175	663-4221	672
Mennonite Historians of Eastern Pennsylvania (MHEP) 565 Yoder Rd *Web:* www.mhep.org	Harleysville	PA	19438	215-256-3020		520
Mennonite Home 1520 Harrisburg Pk *Web:* www.mennonitehome.org	Lancaster	PA	17601	717-393-1301		48-15
Mennonite Village 5353 Columbus St SE *TF:* 800-211-2713 ■ *Web:* mennonitevillage.org	Albany	OR	97322	541-928-7232	917-1399	672
Menominee County 839 Tenth Ave *TF:* 800-236-0242 ■ *Web:* www.menomineecounty.com	Menominee	MI	49858	906-863-9968	863-8839	338
Menominee Hotel N277 Hwy 47/55 PO Box 760 *TF:* 800-343-7778 ■ *Web:* www.menomineecasinoresort.com	Keshena	WI	54135	800-343-7778		378
Menominee Tribal Enterprises PO Box 10 *Web:* www.mtewood.com	Neopit	WI	54150	715-756-2311		683
Menomonee Falls Chamber of Commerce N91 W17271 *Web:* www.fallschamber.com	Menomonee Falls	WI	53051	262-251-2430	251-0969	139
Menomonee Falls Public Library W156 N8436 Pilgrim Rd *Web:* www.menomoneefallslibrary.org	Menomonee Falls	WI	53051	262-532-8900	532-8939	434-3
Menomonie Public Library 600 Wolske Bay Rd *Web:* menomonielibrary.org	Menomonie	WI	54751	715-232-2164	232-2324	434-3
Menorah Medical Ctr 5721 W 119th St *Web:* www.menorahmedicalcenter.com	Overland Park	KS	66209	913-498-6000		374-3
Menshen Packaging USA Inc 21 Industrial Pk *Web:* www.menshenusa.com	Waldwick	NJ	07463	201-445-7436		557
Mensor Corp 201 Barnes Dr *Web:* www.mensor.com	San Marcos	TX	78666	512-396-4200	396-1820	201
Mental Floss Publications PO Box 11571 *Web:* www.terrybraverman.com	Marina del Rey	CA	90295	310-397-6543		637-2
Mental Health America (MHA) 2000 N Beauregard St 6th Fl *TF:* 800-969-6642 ■ *Web:* www.mentalhealthamerica.net	Alexandria	VA	22311	703-684-7722	684-5968	48-17
Mental Health America of Franklin County (MHAFC) 2323 W 5th Ave Ste 160 *Web:* mhafc.org	Columbus	OH	43204	614-221-1441	221-1491	48-6
Mental Health America of Hawaii 1136 Union Mall Ste 510 *Web:* mentalhealthhawaii.org	Honolulu	HI	96813	808-521-1846		48-6
Mental Health Institute 2277 Iowa Ave *Web:* independenceia.com	Independence	IA	50644	319-334-2583		374-5
Mental Models Inc PO Box 225 *Web:* mentalmodels.com	Elk	CA	95432	415-789-6684		177
Mentholatum Company Inc 707 Sterling Dr *TF:* 800-688-7660 ■ *Web:* www.mentholatum.com	Orchard Park	NY	14127	716-677-2500		582
Mentis 3 Columbus Cir 15th Fl **Fax Area Code:* 612 ■ *TF:* 800-267-0858 ■ *Web:* www.mentisoftware.com	New York	NY	10019	212-203-4365	465-4873*	387
Mentis Group 8330 Lyndon B Johnson Fwy Ste 450 *Web:* www.mentis-group.com	Dallas	TX	75243	214-691-7800		180
Mentor Chamber of Commerce 6972 Spinach Dr *Web:* mentorchamber.org	Mentor	OH	44060	440-255-1616	255-1717	139
Mentor Graphics Corp 8005 SW Boeckman Rd *NASDAQ:* MENT ■ *TF:* 800-592-2210 ■ *Web:* www.mentor.com	Wilsonville	OR	97070	503-685-7000	685-1204	178-5

Phone | Fax | Class

MENTOR Network, The
313 Congress St 5th Fl. Boston MA 02210 617-790-4800 790-4848 462
TF: 800-388-5150 ■ *Web:* www.thementornetwork.com

Mentor Public Schools 6451 Center St. Mentor OH 44060 440-255-4444 255-4622 685
Web: www.mentorschools.net

MENTOR/National Mentoring Partnership
201 South St Ste 615 Boston MA 02111 703-224-2200 226-2581 48-6
TF: 877-333-2464 ■ *Web:* www.mentoring.org

Mentus
4660 La Jolla Village Dr Ste 100 San Diego CA 92122 858-455-5500 344
Web: mentus.com

Menucha Publishers Inc 1235 38th St Brooklyn NY 11218 718-232-0856 637-2
TF: 855-636-8242 ■ *Web:* www.menuchapublishers.com

Menzner Lumber & Supply Co
PO Box 217 Marathon WI 54448 800-257-1284 443-3798* 499
**Fax Area Code:* 715 ■ *TF:* 800-257-1284 ■ *Web:* www.menznerhardwoods.com

MEP (Mongrel Empire Press)
133 24th Ave NW Ste 103 Norman OK 73069 405-459-0042 596-1484* 637-2
**Fax Area Code:* 866 ■ *Web:* www.mongrelempire.org

MEP Assoc 2720 Arbor Ct Eau Claire WI 54701 715-832-5680 186
Web: www.mepassociates.com

MEP Consulting Engineers Inc
2928 Story Rd W Ste A Irving TX 75038 972-870-9060 186
Web: www.mepce.com

Mep Engineering Inc 6402 S Troy Cr Centennial CO 80111 303-936-1633 261
Web: mep-eng.com

MEP Engineering PC 65 Nassau Ave Islip NY 11751 631-587-1999 261
Web: mepengineeringpc.com

Mepkin Abbey Botanical Garden
1098 Mepkin Abbey Rd Moncks Corner SC 29461 843-761-8509 761-6719 97
Web: www.mepkinabbey.org

Meramec Group Inc 338 Ramsey St Sullivan MO 63080 573-468-3101 301
Web: www.meramec.com

Meramec State Park 115 Meramec Pk Dr Sullivan MO 63080 573-468-6072 565
Web: mostateparks.com

Meramec Valley Bank
199 Clarkson Rd Ellisville MO 63011 636-230-3500 230-3191 70
Web: www.meramecvalleybank.com

Meramec Valley R-3 School District
126 N Payne St Pacific MO 63069 636-271-1400 271-1406 685
Web: www.mvr3.k12.mo.us

Mercadien Group
3625 Quakerbridge Rd Ste D Hamilton Township NJ 08619 609-689-9700 689-9720 401
Web: www.mercadien.com

Mercado Latino Inc
245 Baldwin Park Blvd City of Industry CA 91746 626-333-6862 805
Web: www.mercadolatinoinc.com

Mercana Growth Partners
390 Bay St Ste 1706 Toronto ON M5H2Y2 416-947-1300 70
Web: www.mercanagrowth.com

Mercantile Bank
200 N 33rd St PO Box 3455 Quincy IL 62305 217-223-7300 223-1980 360-2
TF: 800-405-6372 ■ *Web:* www.mercantilebk.com

Mercantile Bank Corp
310 Leonard St NW Grand Rapids MI 49504 616-406-3000 360-2
NASDAQ: MBWM ■ *Web:* www.mercbank.com

Mercato 111 Market St NW Olympia WA 98501 360-528-3663 671
Web: www.mercatoristorante.com

Mercator Asset Management LP
1314 E Las Olas Blvd Ste 1233 Fort Lauderdale FL 33301 561-361-1079 690
Web: www.mercatorasset.com

Mercatus Energy Advisors LLC
5100 Westheimer Rd Ste 200 Houston TX 77056 713-970-1003 463
Web: www.mercatusenergy.com

Merce Cunningham Dance Co
130 W 56th St Ste 707 New York NY 10019 212-255-8240 573-1
Web: www.mercecunningham.org

Merced College 3600 M St Merced CA 95348 209-384-6000 384-6339 162
Web: www.mccd.edu

Merced Conference & Visitors Bureau (MCVB)
710 W 16th St Merced CA 95340 209-384-2791 206
TF: 800-446-5353 ■ *Web:* visitmerced.travel

Merced County 2222 M St Merced CA 95340 209-385-7434 385-7375 338
Web: www.co.merced.ca.us

Merced Irrigation District PO Box 2288 Merced CA 95344 209-722-5761 722-6421 186
Web: mercedirwmp.org

Merced Sun-Star 3033 N G St Merced CA 95340 209-722-1511 532-2
Web: www.mercedsunstar.com

Merced Transportation Co
300 Grogan Ave Merced CA 95341 209-384-2575 108

Mercedes Restaurants Inc
2402 W Nebraska Ave Peoria IL 61604 309-676-6443 670
Web: mercedesrestaurants.com

Mercedes Textiles Ltd
5838 Cypihot St Ville Saint Laurent QC H4S1Y5 514-335-4337 335-9633 678
Web: www.mercedestextiles.com

Mercedes-Benz Canada Inc
98 Vanderhoof Ave Toronto ON M4G4C9 800-387-0100 57
TF: 800-387-0100 ■ *Web:* www.mercedes-benz.ca

Mercedes-Benz Financial Services USA LLC
PO Box 685 Roanoke TX 76262 800-654-6222 267-6745* 217
**Fax Area Code:* 877 ■ *TF:* 800-654-6222 ■ *Web:* www.mbfs.com

Mercedes-Benz of Caldwell
1230 Bloomfield Ave Fairfield NJ 07004 973-227-3600 57
TF: 877-821-1469 ■ *Web:* www.mbofcaldwell.com

Mercedes-Benz of Cincinnati
8727 Montgomery Rd Cincinnati OH 45236 513-984-9000 516
Web: www.mbcincy.com

Mercedes-Benz of Ft. Pierce
4500 S US Hwy 1 Fort Pierce FL 34982 888-593-1866 57
TF: 888-593-1866 ■ *Web:* www.mercedesbenzofftpierce.com

Mercedes-Benz of San Francisco
500 Eigth St San Francisco CA 94103 415-673-2000 57
TF: 877-554-6016 ■ *Web:* www.sfbenz.com

Mercedes-Benz of Seattle
2025 Airport Way S Seattle WA 98134 206-467-9999 57
TF: 855-263-5688 ■ *Web:* www.mbseattle.com

Mercedes-Benz of Virginia Beach
4949 Virginia Beach Blvd Virginia Beach VA 23462 757-499-3771 57
Web: www.mercedesbenzofvirginiabeach.com

Mercedes-Benz of White Plains
50 Bank St White Plains NY 10606 914-750-4120 57
Web: www.mbwhiteplains.com

Mercedes-Benz Superdome
PO Box 52439 New Orleans LA 70152 504-587-3663 720
TF: 800-756-7074 ■ *Web:* www.mbsuperdome.com

Mercedes-Benz US. International Inc
1 Mercedes Dr Vance AL 35490 205-507-2252 59
TF: 888-286-8762 ■ *Web:* www.mbusi.com

Mercedes-Benz USA LLC 1 Mercedes Dr Montvale NJ 07645 800-367-6372 59
TF: 800-367-6372 ■ *Web:* www.mbusa.com

Mercedes-Benz USA LLC
11850 Bel-Red Rd Bellevue WA 98005 425-249-7391 516
Web: www.mercedesbenzofbellevue.com

Mercedes-Benz USA LLC
4500 Stevens Creek Blvd San Jose CA 95129 408-641-4610 57
Web: www.mbofstevenscreek.com

Mercer Arboretum & Botanic Gardens
22306 Aldine Westfield Rd Humble TX 77338 281-443-8731 97
Web: www.hcp4.net

Mercer Canyons Inc 46 Sonova Rd Prosser WA 99350 509-894-4773 894-4965 10-4
Web: mercercanyons.com

Mercer Construction Company Inc
42690 Rio Nedo Way Ste D Temecula CA 92590 951-296-0111 186
Web: www.mercerconstruction.com

Mercer County 100 S E Third St Aledo IL 61231 309-582-2138 582-7022 338
Web: www.mercercountyil.org

Mercer County 220 W Livingston St Ste 1 Celina OH 45822 419-586-3289 586-1699 338
TF: 800-686-1093 ■ *Web:* www.mercercountyohio.org

Mercer County
207 W Lexington St PO Box 426 Harrodsburg KY 40330 859-734-2365 338
Web: mercercounty.ky.gov

Mercer County 109 Courthouse Mercer PA 16137 724-662-3800 662-2096 338
Web: www.mcc.co.mercer.pa.us

Mercer County
621 Commerce St PO Box 4088 Bluefield WV 24701 304-325-8438 324-8483 338
TF: 800-221-3206 ■ *Web:* visitmercercounty.com

Mercer County PO Box 39 Stanton ND 58571 800-441-2649 338
TF: 800-441-2649 ■ *Web:* www.mercercountynd.com

Mercer County PO Box 8068 Trenton NJ 08650 609-989-6468 338
Web: www.nj.gov

Mercer County Community College
PO Box B Trenton NJ 08690 609-586-4800 162
Web: www.mccc.edu

Mercer County Joint Township Community Hospital
800 W Main St Coldwater OH 45828 419-678-2341 374-3
TF: 888-844-2341 ■ *Web:* www.mercer-health.com

Mercer County Library System (MCL)
2751 Brunswick Pk Lawrenceville NJ 08648 609-989-6920 434-3
Web: www.mcl.org

Mercer County State Bancorp Inc
3279 S Main St Sandy Lake PA 16145 724-376-7015 780
Web: www.mcsbank.bank

Mercer Engineering & Research
135 Osigian Blvd Warner Robins GA 31088 478-953-6800 138
TF: 877-650-6372 ■ *Web:* www.merc-mercer.org

Mercer Forge Corp 200 Brown St Mercer PA 16137 724-662-2750 662-5642 483
Web: www.nfco.com

Mercer Global Advisors Inc
1801 E Cabrillo Blvd Santa Barbara CA 93108 800-898-4642 401
TF: 800-898-4642 ■ *Web:* www.merceradvisors.com

Mercer Intl
14900 Interurban Ave S Ste 282 Seattle WA 98168 604-684-1099 638
TF: 866-816-3254 ■ *Web:* mercerint.com

Mercer Island Reporter
7845 SE 30th St Mercer Island WA 98040 206-232-1215 532-2
Web: www.mi-reporter.com

Mercer Machine Company Inc
1421 S Holt Rd Indianapolis IN 46241 317-241-9903 241-5726 454
Web: www.mercermachine.net

Mercer Morgan
8350 E Raintree Dr Ste 140 Scottsdale AZ 85260 480-281-1833 260
Web: mercermorgan.com

Mercer Rubber Co 350 Rabro Dr Hauppauge NY 11788 631-582-1524 348-0279 370
Web: mercer-rubber.com

Mercer Transportation Co
1128 W Main St Louisville KY 40203 502-584-2301 780
TF: 800-626-5375 ■ *Web:* mercer-trans.com

Mercer Trucking Company Inc
1414 N Fancher Spokane Valley WA 99212 800-541-3529 534-5153* 780
**Fax Area Code:* 509 ■ *TF:* 800-541-3529 ■ *Web:* www.mercertrucking.com

Mercer University 1400 Coleman Ave Macon GA 31207 478-301-2650 166
TF: 800-637-2378 ■ *Web:* www.mercer.edu

Mercer University
Jack Tarver Library
1501 Mercer University Dr Macon GA 31207 478-301-2961 301-2252 434-6
Web: libraries.mercer.edu

Mercer University Press
1501 Mercer University Dr Macon GA 31207 478-301-2880 301-2585 637-2
TF: 866-895-1472 ■ *Web:* www.mupress.org

Mercer Wrecking Recycling Corp
1519 Calhoun St Trenton NJ 08638 609-393-6775 189-16
Web: mercergroup.com

Mercersburg Academy
300 E Seminary St Mercersburg PA 17236 717-328-6173 622
TF: 800-588-2550 ■ *Web:* www.mercersburg.edu

Mercersburg Printing
9964 Buchanan Trl W Mercersburg PA 17236 717-328-3902 627
TF: 800-955-3902 ■ *Web:* www.mercersburg.net

Merch-A-Mart Wholesale
717-B Atando Ave Charlotte NC 28206 704-335-8868 335-8869 361
Web: www.merchamartwholesale.com

Merchant & Evans Inc
308 Connecticut Dr Burlington NJ 08016 609-387-3033 480
TF: 800-257-6215 ■ *Web:* www.zlprib.com

Company	Phone	Fax	Class
Merchant & Gould 3200 IDS Ctr 80 S Eighth St................Minneapolis MN 55402 *Web:* www.merchantgould.com	612-332-5300		428
Merchant Energy Partners LLC 10901 W Toller Dr Ste 200....................Littleton CO 80127 **Fax Area Code:* 303 ■ *Web:* mehllc.com	720-351-4000	861-5701*	538
Merchant Financial Group 1441 Broadway 22nd Fl.....................New York NY 10018 *TF:* 800-970-9997 ■ *Web:* www.merchantfinancial.com	212-840-7575	869-1752	272
Merchant Law Group LLP 2401 Saskatchewan Dr Saskatchewan Dr Plz.......Regina SK S4P4H8 *TF:* 888-567-7777 ■ *Web:* www.merchantlaw.com	306-359-7777		41
Merchant One Inc 524 Arthur Godfrey Rd 3rd Fl.............Miami Beach FL 33140 *TF:* 800-910-8375 ■ *Web:* www.merchantone.com	800-610-4189		217
Merchants & Medical Credit Corporation Inc 6324 Taylor Dr................................Flint MI 48507 *TF:* 800-562-0273 ■ *Web:* www.mermed.com	810-239-3030		160
Merchants Auto 1278 Hooksett Rd.............Hooksett NH 03106 *Web:* www.merchantsauto.cars	603-669-4100		57
Merchants Bank of Bangor 1250 Braden Blvd.............................Easton PA 18040 *Web:* www.bankatfidelity.com	484-548-6095		70
Merchants Building Maintenance 606 Monterey Pass Rd..................Monterey Park CA 91754 *TF:* 800-560-6700 ■ *Web:* mbmonline.com	800-560-6700		104
Merchants Co 1100 Edwards St PO Box 1351..............Hattiesburg MS 39401 *TF:* 800-844-3663 ■ *Web:* merchantsfoodservice.com	601-583-4351	582-5333	297-8
Merchants Credit Bureau 955 Green St.........Augusta GA 30901 *TF:* 800-426-5265 ■ *Web:* www.mcbusa.com	706-823-6200	823-6253	218
Merchants Grocery Co 800 Maddox Dr PO Box 1268.................Culpeper VA 22701 *TF:* 877-897-9893 ■ *Web:* merchants-grocery.com	540-825-0786	825-9016	345
Merchants Insurance Group 250 Main St........Buffalo NY 14202 **Fax Area Code:* 716 ■ *TF:* 800-462-1077 ■ *Web:* www.merchantsgroup.com	800-462-1077	849-3246*	391-4
Merchants Metals 211 Perimeter Center Pkwy Ste 250..............Atlanta GA 30346 *Web:* www.merchantsmetals.com	770-741-0300		279
Merchants Overseas Inc 41 Bassett St.............................Providence RI 02903 *Web:* www.merchantsoverseas.com	401-331-5603		411
Merchants Paper Co 4625 SE 24th Ave..........Portland OR 97202 *TF:* 800-605-6301 ■ *Web:* merchantspaper.com	503-235-2171		557
Merck & Company Inc 2000 Galloping Hill Rd.....................Kenilworth NJ 07033 *NYSE: MRK* ■ *TF:* 800-444-2080 ■ *Web:* www.merck.com	908-740-4000		582
Merco Inc 1117 Rt 31 S.........................Lebanon NJ 08833 *Web:* www.mercoinc.com	908-730-8622	730-6472	188-4
Mercom Capital Group LLC 4611 Bee Caves Rd Ste 303....................Austin TX 78746 *Web:* mercomcapital.com	512-215-4452		796
Mercom Inc 313 Commerce Dr............Pawleys Island SC 29585 *TF:* 877-223-8330 ■ *Web:* mercomcorp.com	843-979-9957		180
Merco-Savory Inc 1111 N Hadley Rd.........Fort Wayne IN 46804 *TF:* 800-547-2513 ■ *Web:* www.mercoproducts.com	260-459-8200	436-0735	298
Mercury Air Group Inc 2780 Skypark Dr............................Torrance CA 90505 *Web:* www.mercuryairgroup.com	310-827-5778	827-8921	24
Mercury Aircraft Inc 17 Wheeler Ave.......................Hammondsport NY 14840 *Web:* www.mercurycorp.com	607-569-4200	569-4306	697
Mercury Casualty Co 555 W Imperial Hwy..........Brea CA 92821 **Fax Area Code:* 323 ■ *Web:* www.mercuryinsurance.com	714-671-6600	857-7116*	391-4
Mercury Communication Partners 13414 Watertown Plank Rd..................Elm Grove WI 53122 *Web:* www.mercuryww.com	262-782-4637		7
Mercury Communication Services Inc 3333 Earhart Dr Ste 250....................Carrollton TX 75006 *Web:* www.mercurycom.com	214-637-4900	637-4905	224
Mercury Displacement Industries Inc 25028 Us 12 E..........................Edwardsburg MI 49112 *Web:* www.mdius.com	269-663-8574	663-2924	203
Mercury Intl 19 Alice Agnew Dr....................North Attleboro MA 02763 *Web:* www.mercuryfootwear.com	508-699-9000		301
Mercury Investment Group 40 S Main St Ste 1530.......................Memphis TN 38103 *Web:* www.mercuryprop.com	901-327-2788	521-4201	401
Mercury Lighting Products Company Inc 20 Audrey Pl.................................Fairfield NJ 07004 *TF:* 800-637-2584 ■ *Web:* www.mercltg.com	973-244-9444	244-9522	439
Mercury Luggage Manufacturing Co 12276 San Jose Blvd Ste 618...............Jacksonville FL 32223 *Web:* www.mercuryluggage.com	904-482-0091	733-9671	453
Mercury Machining Company Inc 1085 W Gimble St..........................Pensacola FL 32502 *TF:* 800-852-5086 ■ *Web:* www.mercurymachining.com	850-433-5017	433-1076	454
Mercury Mambo 1107 S Eighth St...............Austin TX 78704 *Web:* mercurymambo.com	512-447-4440		344
Mercury Marine Ltd 8698 Escarpment Way........Milton ON L9T0M1	905-636-4700		690
Mercury Medical 11300 49th St N............Clearwater FL 33762 *TF:* 800-237-6418 ■ *Web:* www.mercurymed.com	727-573-0088	571-3922	476
Mercury Paper Inc 495 Radio Sta Rd..........Strasburg VA 22657 *Web:* www.mercurypaper.com	540-465-7700		557
Mercury Pen Company Inc 245 Eastline Rd.............................Ballston NY 12019 *Web:* www.mercurypen.com	518-899-9653	899-9657	571
Mercury Plastics Inc 15760 Madison Rd.......................Middlefield OH 44062 *Web:* www.mercury-plastics.com	440-632-5281		326
Mercury Press Inc 1910 S Nicklas Ave.....................Oklahoma City OK 73128 *TF:* 800-423-5984 ■ *Web:* www.mercury.press.com	405-682-3468		627
Mercury Public Affairs 200 Varick St Ste 600......................New York NY 10014 *TF:* 800-325-4151 ■ *Web:* www.mercuryllc.com	212-681-1380		636
Mercury Publishing Services Inc 1300 Piccard Dr Ste 100.....................Rockville MD 20850 *TF:* 800-634-9409 ■ *Web:* www.mercurypubs.com	240-631-1000	631-1378	637-9
Mercury Systems Inc 50 Minuteman Rd.........Andover MA 01810 *NASDAQ: MRCY* ■ *TF:* 866-627-6951 ■ *Web:* www.mrcy.com	978-256-1300		735
Mercury Tool and Machine Inc 7420 Karl May Dr.............................Waco TX 76708 *Web:* www.mercurytool.com	254-752-1639	752-2559	454
Mercury Tube Products 3211 W Bear Creek Dr.....................Englewood CO 80110 *Web:* www.merctube.com	303-761-1835	781-7307	490
Mercury Wire Products Inc 1 Mercury Dr..............................Spencer MA 01562 *Web:* www.mercurywire.com	508-885-6363		813
Mercury Wireless LLC 2825 SE California Ave........................Topeka KS 66605 *TF:* 800-354-4915 ■ *Web:* www.mercurywireless.com	800-354-4915		736
Mercury Z. 1150 SE Maynard Rd...................Cary NC 27511 *Web:* www.mercuryz.com	919-439-5000		196
Mercury, The 24 N Hanover St................Pottstown PA 19464 *Web:* www.pottsmerc.com	610-323-3000		532-2
Mercury, The 11909 Preston Rd Ste 1418..........Dallas TX 75240 *Web:* www.themercurydallas.com	972-960-7774	960-7988	671
Mercy 615 S New Ballas Rd.................Saint Louis MO 63141 *Web:* www.mercy.net	314-251-6000		374-3
Mercy by the Sea 167 Neck Rd................Madison CT 06443 *Web:* www.mercybythesea.org	203-245-0401	245-8718	673
Mercy Care Plan 4350 E Cotton Center Blvd Bldg D..............Phoenix AZ 85040 *TF:* 800-602-1982 ■ *Web:* www.mercycareplan.com	602-263-3000		391-3
Mercy Career & Technical High School 2900 W Hunting Park Ave.................Philadelphia PA 19129 *Web:* www.mercycte.org	215-226-1225	228-6337	685
Mercy College 555 Broadway...............Dobbs Ferry NY 10522 *TF:* 800-637-2969 ■ *Web:* www.mercy.edu	914-674-7600	674-7382	166
Mercy College of Ohio 2221 Madison Ave........Toledo OH 43604 *Web:* www.mercycollege.edu	419-251-1313		507
Mercy Ctr 520 W Buena Ventura St..............Colorado Springs CO 80907 *Web:* www.mercycenter.com	719-633-2302		673
Mercy Flights Inc 2020 Milligan Way...........Medford OR 97504 *TF:* 800-903-9000 ■ *Web:* www.mercyflights.com	541-858-2600		30
Mercy Health 1701 Mercy Health Pl...........Cincinnati OH 45237 *Web:* www.mercy.com	513-956-3729		356
Mercy Health *Muskegon Campus* 1500 E Sherman Blvd.....Muskegon MI 49444 *TF:* 800-368-4125 ■ *Web:* www.mercyhealth.com	231-672-2000		374-3
Mercy Health Arena 955 4th St..............Muskegon MI 49440 *Web:* mercyhealtharena.com	231-726-2400		720
Mercy Home Care & Medical Supplies Inc 1706 E 35th St.............................Brooklyn NY 11223 *Web:* www.mercymedsupplies.com	718-376-3131		690
Mercy Hospital 3663 S Miami Ave...............Miami FL 33133 *Web:* mercymiami.com	305-854-4400		374-3
Mercy Hospital & Medical Ctr (MHMC) 2525 S Michigan Ave........................Chicago IL 60616 *Web:* www.mercy-chicago.org	312-567-2000		374-3
Mercy Hospital & Trauma Ctr 1000 Mineral Point Ave....................Janesville WI 53548 *TF:* 800-756-4147 ■ *Web:* www.mercyhealthsystem.com	608-756-6000		374-3
Mercy Hospital Cadillac 400 Hobart St..............................Cadillac MI 49601 *Web:* www.munsonhealthcare.org	231-876-7473		374-3
Mercy Housing Inc 1999 Broadway Ste 1000......................Denver CO 80202 *TF:* 866-338-0557 ■ *Web:* www.mercyhousing.org	303-830-3300		187
Mercy Iowa City 500 E Market St............Iowa City IA 52245 *TF:* 800-637-2942 ■ *Web:* www.mercyiowacity.org	319-339-0300	339-3788	374-3
Mercy Medical Center South 638 S Bluff Blvd............................Clinton IA 52732 *Web:* www.mercyclinton.com	563-244-5555		374-3
Mercy Medical Ctr 1000 N Village Ave...................Rockville Centre NY 11570 *Web:* mercymedicalcenter.chsli.org	516-705-2525		374-3
Mercy Medical Ctr 701 Tenth St SE........................Cedar Rapids IA 52403 *Web:* www.mercycare.org	319-398-6011		374-3
Mercy Medical Ctr 1320 Mercy Dr NW...........Canton OH 44708 *TF:* 800-223-8662 ■ *Web:* www.cantonmercy.org	330-489-1000		374-3
Mercy Memorial Hospital (MMH) 718 N Macomb St...........................Monroe MI 48162 *Web:* www.mercymemorial.org	734-240-8400		374-3
Mercy St Anne Hospital 3404 W Sylvania Ave.........................Toledo OH 43623 *Web:* www.mercyweb.org	419-407-2663		374-3
Mercy Surgical Dressing Group Inc 4 Zesta Dr................................Pittsburgh PA 15205 *Web:* mercyscb.com	412-788-5200		475
MercyCare Insurance Company Inc 580 N Washington St PO Box 550............Janesville WI 53547 *TF:* 800-895-2421 ■ *Web:* mercycarehealthplans.com	608-752-3431		390
Mercyhurst College 501 E 38th St...............Erie PA 16546 *TF:* 800-825-1926 ■ *Web:* www.mercyhurst.edu	814-824-2202	824-3634	166
Mercyhurst University-Northeast 16 W Division St.........................North East PA 16428 *Web:* www.northeast.mercyhurst.edu	814-824-2000		786
MercyOne Des Moines Medical Ctr 1111 6th Ave............................Des Moines IA 50314 *TF:* 800-637-2993 ■ *Web:* www.mercyone.org	515-247-3121		374-3
Mercy-USA for Aid & Development Inc (M-USA) 44450 Pinetree Dr Ste 201...................Plymouth MI 48170 *TF:* 800-556-3729 ■ *Web:* mercyusa.org	734-454-0011	454-0303	48-5
Meredith & Jeannie Ray Cancer Ctr 255 N 30th St...............................Laramie WY 82072 *TF:* 800-854-1115 ■ *Web:* www.ivinsonhospital.org	307-742-7586	742-0286	374-3
Meredith College 3800 Hillsborough St.........Raleigh NC 27607 *TF:* 800-637-3348 ■ *Web:* meredith.edu	919-760-8600	760-8330	166
Meredith Corp 1716 Locust St..............Des Moines IA 50309 *NYSE: MDP* ■ *TF:* 800-950-3829 ■ *Web:* www.meredith.com	515-284-3000		637-9

Name	Address	City	State	ZIP	Phone	Fax	Class
Meredith Enterprises Inc	3000 Sand Hill Rd Bldg 2 Ste 120 *Web:* www.meredithreit.com	Menlo Park	CA	94025	650-233-7140		654
Meredith Long & Co	2323 San Felipe *Web:* www.meredithlonggallery.com	Houston	TX	77019	713-523-6671	523-2355	42
Meredith Manor International Equestrian Ctr	147 Saddle Ln *TF:* 800-679-2603 ■ *Web:* www.meredithmanor.edu	Waverly	WV	26184	304-679-3128	679-3793	167-3
Meredith O'Donnell Fine Furniture	1751 Post Oak Blvd *Web:* www.meredithodonnell.com	Houston	TX	77056	713-526-7332		321
Meredith Village Savings Bank (MVSB)	24 SR-25 PO Box 177 *TF:* 800-922-6872 ■ *Web:* www.mvsb.com	Meredith	NH	03253	603-279-7986	279-5710	70
Meredith-Webb Printing Company Inc	334 N Main St *Web:* www.meredithwebb.com	Burlington	NC	27217	336-228-8378		627
Mereen-Johnson Machine Co	4401 Lyndale Ave N *TF:* 888-465-7297 ■ *Web:* www.mereen-johnson.com	Minneapolis	MN	55412	612-529-7791	529-0120	821
Merfish Pipe & Supply Co	PO Box 15879 *TF:* 800-869-5731 ■ *Web:* www.merfish.com	Houston	TX	77220	713-869-5731	867-0738	492
Mergenet Solutions Inc	1701 W Hillsboro Blvd Ste 303 *TF:* 888-956-2526 ■ *Web:* www.mergenetsolutions.com	Deerfield Beach	FL	33442	561-208-3770	253-2573	475
Mergenthaler Transfer & Storage	1414 N Montana Ave *TF:* 800-826-5463 ■ *Web:* www.mergenthaler.net	Helena	MT	59601	406-442-9470	442-4340	780
Mergon Corp	5350 Old Pearman Dairy Rd *Web:* www.mergon.com	Anderson	SC	29625	864-222-0422		596
Meriam Process Technologies Inc	10920 Madison Ave *TF:* 800-817-7849 ■ *Web:* www.meriam.com	Cleveland	OH	44102	216-281-1100	281-0228	407
Mericle Commercial Real Estate Services	100 Baltimore Dr *Web:* www.mericle.com	Wilkes-Barre	PA	18702	570-823-1100	823-0300	655
Mericon Industries Inc	8819 N Pioneer Rd *TF:* 800-242-6464 ■ *Web:* mericonindustries.com	Peoria	IL	61615	309-693-2150		583
Meriden Manufacturing Inc	PO Box 694 *Web:* www.meridenmfg.com	Meriden	CT	06450	203-237-7481	235-3146	488
Meriden Public Library	105 Miller St *Web:* meridenlibrary.org	Meriden	CT	06450	203-238-2344	238-3647	434-3
Meridian Aerospace Group Ltd	3109 Buena Vista Rd *Web:* www.airunion.us	Winston-Salem	NC	27103	336-765-5560	765-5577	770
Meridian Associates Inc	1 E Erie St Ste 240 *Web:* www.meridianai.com	Chicago	IL	60611	312-335-8050		196
Meridian Auto Parts	10211 Pacific Mesa Blvd Ste 404 *TF:* 800-874-1974 ■ *Web:* www.meridianautoparts.com	San Diego	CA	92121	800-874-1974		54
Meridian Bioscience Inc	3471 River Hills Dr *NASDAQ: VIVO* ■ *TF:* 800-543-1980 ■ *Web:* www.meridianbioscience.com	Cincinnati	OH	45244	513-271-3700	272-5421	231
Meridian Capital LLC	1809 Seventh Ave Ste 1330 *Web:* meridianllc.com	Seattle	WA	98101	206-623-4000	623-8221	690
Meridian Chamber of Commerce	215 E Franklin Rd *Web:* meridianchamber.org	Meridian	ID	83642	208-888-2817	888-2682	139
Meridian Community College	910 Hwy 19 N *TF:* 800-622-8431 ■ *Web:* www.meridiancc.edu	Meridian	MS	39307	601-483-8241	484-8635	162
Meridian Display & Merchandising Inc	162 York Ave E *TF:* 800-786-2501 ■ *Web:* meridiandisplay.com	Saint Paul	MN	55117	800-786-2501		5
Meridian Equity Partners Inc	40 Wall St Ste 1704 *Web:* meptraders.com	New York	NY	10005	212-500-6650	742-8535	690
Meridian Graphics Inc	2652 Dow Ave *Web:* www.mglitho.com	Tustin	CA	92780	949-833-3500		627
Meridian Institute	105 Village Pl *Web:* www.merid.org	Dillon	CO	80435	970-513-8340		196
Meridian Investment Partners	400 Galleria Pkwy Ste 1500 *Web:* investmeridian.com	Atlanta	GA	30339	404-585-5946		690
Meridian Life Science Inc	5171 Wilfong Rd *Web:* meridianlifescience.com	Memphis	TN	38134	901-382-8716	333-8223	582
Meridian Mall	1982 W Grand River Ave *Web:* www.meridianmall.com	Okemos	MI	48864	517-349-2031		460
Meridian Mattress Factory Inc	200 Rubush Rd *Web:* www.meridianmattress.com	Meridian	MS	39301	601-693-3875		471
Meridian Medical Technologies Inc	6350 Stevens Forest Rd Ste 301 *TF:* 800-638-8093 ■ *Web:* www.meridianmeds.com	Columbia	MD	21046	443-259-7800	259-7801	476
Meridian Mobile Home Park Spaces & Rentals	1801 Meridian St Ofc 18 *Web:* www.mobilehome.net	Nashville	TN	37207	615-227-1159		505
Meridian One Corp	5775 General Washington Dr *TF:* 800-636-2377 ■ *Web:* www.meridianone.com	Alexandria	VA	22312	800-636-2377		195
Meridian Plaza Vacation	1410 48th Ave Ext N *TF:* 888-590-0801 ■ *Web:* meridianplaza.vacations	Myrtle Beach	SC	29577	843-626-4734	497-5717	379
Meridian Precision Inc	80 Roberts Rd *Web:* www.meridianprecision.com	Pine Grove	PA	17963	570-345-6600	345-6604	604
Meridian Press	PO Box 21567 *Web:* www.meridianpress.com	Oklahoma City	OK	73156	405-751-2342	752-9373	637-2
Meridian Products	124 Earland Dr Bldg 2 *TF:* 888-423-2804 ■ *Web:* www.meridianproduct.com	New Holland	PA	17557	717-355-7700		115
Meridian Specialty Yarns Inc	312 Colombo St SW *Web:* www.msyg.com	Valdese	NC	28690	828-874-2151	874-3780	745-9
Meridian Star Inc	814 22nd Ave *TF:* 800-232-2525 ■ *Web:* www.meridianstar.com	Meridian	MS	39301	601-693-1551	485-1275	637-8
Meridian State Park	173 Park Rd 7 *Web:* tpwd.texas.gov	Meridian	TX	76665	254-435-2536		565
Meridian Surveys Ltd	355 16th St W *TF:* 866-934-1818 ■ *Web:* meridiansurveys.ca	Prince Albert	SK	S6V3V6	306-764-9229		466
Meridian Technology Group Inc	12909 SW 68th Pkwy Ste 100 *TF:* 800-755-1038 ■ *Web:* www.meridiangroup.com	Portland	OR	97223	503-697-1600		177
Meridian Title Corp	202 S Michigan St *TF:* 800-777-1574 ■ *Web:* www.meridiantitle.com	South Bend	IN	46601	800-777-1574		391-6
Meridian West Consultants LLC	745 E Knoll Ct *Web:* www.meridian-west.com	Draper	UT	84020	801-542-7082		261
Meridian/Lauderdale County Tourism Bureau	212 Constitution Ave *TF:* 888-868-7720 ■ *Web:* www.visitmeridian.com	Meridian	MS	39301	601-482-8001	486-4988	206
Meridican Incentive Consultants	16 Esna Park Dr Ste 103 *Web:* meridican.com	Markham	ON	L3R5X1	905-477-7700		772
MeringCarson	1700 I St 2nd Fl *Web:* www.meringcarson.com	Sacramento	CA	95811	916-441-0571		7
Merion Publications Inc	2900 Horizon Dr **Fax Area Code:* 610 ■ *TF:* 800-355-1088 ■ *Web:* www.advanceweb.com	King of Prussia	PA	19406	484-804-4888	278-1425*	637-9
Merisant Co	125 S Wacker Dr Ste 3150 *Web:* www.merisant.com	Chicago	IL	60606	312-840-6000		296-38
Meristem LLP	601 Carlson Pkwy Ste 800 *Web:* www.meristemfw.com	Minnetonka	MN	55305	952-835-2577		41
Merit Accounting & Financial Services	2201 Broadway *Web:* www.meritaf.com	North Bend	OR	97459	541-756-2252	756-1784	401
Merit Aluminum Corp	2480 Railroad St *Web:* www.frontier-aluminum.com	Corona	CA	92880	951-735-1770		492
Merit Brass Co	1 Merit Dr *Web:* www.meritbrass.com	Cleveland	OH	44143	216-261-9800		595
Merit Electric Company Inc	6520 125th Ave N *Web:* www.meritelectricco.com	Largo	FL	33773	727-536-5945	536-9014	189-4
Merit Electrical Inc	17723 Airline Hwy *Web:* www.meritelectrical.com	Prairieville	LA	70769	225-673-8850	673-8838	189-4
Merit Gage Inc	St Louis Pk 3954 Meadowbrook Rd *Web:* www.meritgage.com	Minneapolis	MN	55426	952-935-0113		454
Merit Health Biloxi	150 Reynoir St *Web:* www.merithealthbiloxi.com	Biloxi	MS	39530	228-432-1571		374-3
Merit Health Central	1850 Chadwick Dr *TF:* 844-462-3627 ■ *Web:* www.merithealthcentral.com	Jackson	MS	39204	601-376-1000		374-3
Merit Health Rankin	350 Crossgates Blvd *Web:* www.merithealthrankin.com	Brandon	MS	39042	601-825-2811		374-3
Merit Health River Region	2100 Hwy 61 N *Web:* www.merithealthriverregion.com	Vicksburg	MS	39183	601-883-5000		374-3
Merit Health Wesley	5001 Hardy St *Web:* www.merithealthwesley.com	Hattiesburg	MS	39402	601-268-8000		374-3
Merit Marketing & Communications	2420 Avery Dr *Web:* meritmarketinginc.com	Troy	MI	48085	248-250-9343	250-9344	195
Merit Marketing Inc	5773 Arrowhead Dr Ste 204 *Web:* www.meritmarketing.com	Virginia Beach	VA	23462	757-437-2616		156
Merit Medical Systems Inc	1600 W Merit Pkwy *NASDAQ: MMSI* ■ *TF:* 800-356-3748 ■ *Web:* www.merit.com	South Jordan	UT	84095	801-253-1600	253-1652	476
Merit Network Inc	1000 Oakbrook Dr Ste 200 *Web:* www.merit.edu	Ann Arbor	MI	48104	734-764-9430	527-5790	171
Merit Software	121 W 27 St Ste 603 **Fax Area Code:* 646 ■ *TF:* 800-753-6488 ■ *Web:* www.meritsoftware.com	New York	NY	10001	212-675-8567	351-0423*	178-1
Merit Solutions Inc	1749 S Naperville Rd Ste 200 *Web:* www.meritsolutions.com	Wheaton	IL	60189	630-614-7133		196
Merit Systems Protection Board (MSPB)	1615 M St NW *TF:* 800-209-8960 ■ *Web:* www.mspb.gov	Washington	DC	20036	202-653-7200	653-7130	340-20
New York Field Office	26 Federal Plz Rm 3137-A *Web:* www.mspb.gov	New York	NY	10278	212-264-9372	264-1417	340-20
Merit Systems Protection Board Regional Offices (MSPB)							
Atlanta Region	401 W Peachtree St NW 10th Fl *Web:* www.mspb.gov	Atlanta	GA	30308	404-730-2751	730-2767	340-20
Central Region	230 S Dearborn St 31st Fl *TF:* 800-424-9121 ■ *Web:* www.mspb.gov	Chicago	IL	60604	312-353-2923	886-4231	340-20
Denver Field Office	165 S Union Blvd Ste 318 *Web:* www.mspb.gov	Lakewood	CO	80228	303-969-5101	969-5109	340-20
Northeastern Region	1601 Market St Ste 1700 *Web:* www.mspb.gov	Philadelphia	PA	19103	215-597-9960	597-3456	340-20
Western Region	201 Mission St Ste 2310 *Web:* www.mspb.gov	San Francisco	CA	94105	415-904-6772	904-0580	340-20
Merit Travel Group Inc	111 Peter St *TF:* 866-341-1777 ■ *Web:* www.merit.ca	Toronto	ON	M5V2H1	416-364-3775		771
Merit USA	620 Clark Ave **Fax Area Code:* 925 ■ *TF:* 800-445-6374 ■ *Web:* www.meritsteel.com	Pittsburg	CA	94565	800-445-6374	427-6427*	492
Meritage Homes Corp	17851 N 85th St Ste 300 *NYSE: MTH* ■ *Web:* www.meritagehomes.com	Scottsdale	AZ	85255	480-515-8100		653
Meritage Hospitality Group Inc	45 Ottawa SW Ste 600 *OTC: MHGU* ■ *Web:* www.meritagehospitality.com	Grand Rapids	MI	49525	616-776-2600		670

Name / Address	City	State	ZIP	Phone	Fax	Class
Meritage Midstream Services LLC 1331 Seventeenth St Ste 1100 — *Web:* www.meritagemidstream.com	Denver	CO	80202	303-551-8150		539
Meritage Portfolio Management Inc 7500 College Blvd Ste 1212 — *Web:* www.meritageportfolio.com	Overland Park	KS	66210	913-345-7000		401
MeriTec Services Inc 4440 S Piedras Dr Ste 140 — *Web:* www.meritecservices.com	San Antonio	TX	78228	210-694-4635	694-4633	225
Meritech Inc 4577 Hinckley Industrial Pkwy — *TF:* 888-505-6567 ■ *Web:* www.meritechinc.com	Cleveland	OH	44109	216-459-8333		179
Meritide Inc 2685 Patton Rd — *Web:* www.meritide.com	Saint Paul	MN	55113	651-255-7300		809
Meritool LLC PO Box 148 — *Web:* www.meritool.com	Salamanca	NY	14779	716-699-6005	699-6337	759
Merits Health Products Inc 4245 Evans Ave — *TF:* 800-963-7487 ■ *Web:* www.meritshealth.com	Fort Myers	FL	33901	800-963-7487		477
Merittech LLC 6700 Kirkville Rd Ste 105	East Syracuse	NY	13057	315-234-4545		180
Meritus Health 11116 Medical Campus Rd — *Web:* www.meritushealth.com	Hagerstown	MD	21742	301-790-8000		374-3
Meriwest Credit Union PO Box 530953 — **Fax Area Code:* 408 ■ *TF:* 877-637-4937 ■ *Web:* www.meriwest.com	San Jose	CA	95153	877-637-4937	363-3330*	219
Meriwether Capital LLC 30 Rockefeller Plz Rm 5600 — *Web:* www.meriwethercapital.net	New York	NY	10112	212-649-5890		41
Meriwether County 17234 Roosevelt Hwy Bldg B — *Web:* meriwethercountyga.gov	Greenville	GA	30222	706-672-1314	672-9544	338
Meriwether County Schools 2100 Gaston St PO Box 70 — *Web:* www.mcssga.org	Greenville	GA	30222	706-672-4297		685
Meriwether Godsey Inc 4944 Old Boonsboro Rd — *Web:* www.merig.com	Lynchburg	VA	24503	434-384-3663		77
Meriwether Publishing Ltd (MP) 885 Elkton Dr — *Web:* www.meriwether.com	Colorado Springs	CO	80907	719-594-9916		637-2
Merix Financial 56 Temperance St Ste 400 — *TF:* 877-637-4911 ■ *Web:* www.merixfinancial.com	Toronto	ON	M5H3V5	877-637-4911		509
Merkaz Bnos Business School & Career Institute 2115 Benson Ave — *Web:* www.mbs-career.org	Brooklyn	NY	11214	718-234-4000	234-4475	685
Merkel Brothers Inc 205 S Main St — *Web:* merkelfurniture.com	Chelsea	MI	48118	734-475-8621		321
Merkle Group Inc 7001 Columbia Gateway Dr — *Web:* www.merkleinc.com	Columbia	MD	21046	443-542-4000	542-4758	636
Merkle-Korff Industries Inc 25 NW Pt Blvd Ste 900 — *Web:* www.merkle-korff.com	Elk Grove Village	IL	60007	847-439-3760	439-3963	518
Merkley & Partners 200 Varick St — *Web:* www.merkleyandpartners.com	New York	NY	10014	212-805-7500		4
Merkley Jeff (Sen D - OR) 313 Hart Senate Office Bldg — *Web:* www.merkley.senate.gov	Washington	DC	20510	202-224-3753	228-3997	342-2
Merl Inc 1777 N Colony Rd — *Web:* www.merlinc.net	Meriden	CT	06450	203-237-8811	237-0265	247
Merle Boes Inc 11372 E Lakewood Blvd — *TF:* 800-545-0706 ■ *Web:* www.merleboes.com	Holland	MI	49424	616-392-7036		579
Merle Hay Mall 3800 Merle Hay Rd — *Web:* www.merlehaymall.com	Des Moines	IA	50310	515-276-8551	276-9227	460
Merle Norman Cosmetics Inc 9130 Bellanca Ave — *TF:* 800-421-6648 ■ *Web:* www.merlenorman.com	Los Angeles	CA	90045	310-641-3000		214
Merle's Automotive Supply Inc 33 W University Blvd — *Web:* www.merlesauto.com	Tucson	AZ	85705	520-622-3526	746-1417	54
Merlex Stucco Co 2911 N Orange-Olive Rd — *Web:* www.merlex.com	Orange	CA	92865	714-637-1700	637-4865	500
Merlin 3815 E Main St Ste D — *TF:* 800-652-9900 ■ *Web:* www.merlins.com	Saint Charles	IL	60174	630-513-8200		310
Merlin Law Group PA 777 S Harbour Island Blvd — *TF:* 877-449-4700 ■ *Web:* www.merlinlawgroup.com	Tampa	FL	33602	813-229-1000	229-3692	41
Merlin Petroleum Company Inc 235 Post Rd W — *Web:* www.merlinpetroleum.com	Westport	CT	06880	203-227-3200	227-3910	539
Merlino Foods 4100 Fourth Ave S — *Web:* www.merlino.com	Seattle	WA	98134	206-723-4700		138
MerlinOne Inc 17 Whitney Rd — *Web:* merlinone.com	Quincy	MA	02169	617-328-6645		226
Merlo on Maple 16 W Maple St — *Web:* www.merlochicago.com	Chicago	IL	60610	312-335-8200	335-8205	671
Merlot Marketing 4430 Duckhorn Dr — *Web:* www.merlotmarketing.com	Sacramento	CA	95834	916-285-9835		7
Merman Law Firm PC, The 743 W 18th St — *Web:* mermanlawfirm.com	Houston	TX	77008	713-351-0679		41
Mermet Lake State Fish & Wildlife Area 1812 Grinnell Rd — *Web:* www.dnr.illinois.gov	Belknap	IL	62908	618-524-5577		565
Merrell University of Beauty Arts & Science 1101 Southwest Blvd — *TF:* 855-227-1161 ■ *Web:* www.merrelluniversity.edu	Jefferson City	MO	65109	573-635-5780	636-6117	786
Merriam Press 133 Elm St Apt 3R — *Web:* www.merriam-press.com	Bennington	VT	05201	802-447-0313		637-2
Merriam-Webster Inc 47 Federal St PO Box 281 — *Web:* www.merriam-webster.com	Springfield	MA	01105	413-734-3134	731-5979	637-2
Merrick & Co 2450 S Peoria St — *TF:* 800-544-1714 ■ *Web:* www.merrick.com	Aurora	CO	80014	303-751-0741	751-2581	261
Merrick Engineering Inc 1275 Quarry St — *Web:* www.merrickengineering.com	Corona	CA	92879	951-737-6040		608
Merrick House 907 Coral Way — *Web:* coralgables.com	Coral Gables	FL	33134	305-460-5361	460-5371	50-3
Merrick Industries Inc 10 Arthur Dr — *TF:* 800-345-8440 ■ *Web:* www.merrick-inc.com	Lynn Haven	FL	32444	850-265-3611	265-9768	684
Merrick Inn, The 1074 Merrick Dr — *Web:* www.themerrickinn.com	Lexington	KY	40502	859-269-5417		671
Merrick Machine Co 104 S Apollo St — **Fax Area Code:* 308 ■ *TF:* 800-568-7423 ■ *Web:* www.merrickmachine.com	Alda	NE	68810	800-568-7423	384-8326*	759
Merrick State Park S2965 Sr 35 — *Web:* dnr.wi.gov	Fountain City	WI	54629	608-687-4936		565
Merrick Towle Associates Inc 5801-F Ammendale Rd — *Web:* www.merricktowle.com	Beltsville	MD	20705	301-974-6000		5
Merrick's Inc 2415 Parview Rd PO Box 620307 — *TF:* 800-637-7425 ■ *Web:* www.merricks.com	Middleton	WI	53562	608-831-3440	836-8943	447
Merrifield Consulting Group Inc, The 104 York Pl — *Web:* www.merrifield.com	Chapel Hill	NC	27517	919-933-7474	933-7454	194
Merrigan, Brandt, Ostenso & Cambre PA 25 9th Ave N — *Web:* www.merriganlaw.com	Hopkins	MN	55343	952-933-2390		428
Merrill and Ring Inc (MR) 813 E 8th St — *Web:* www.merrillring.com	Port Angeles	WA	98362	360-452-2367	452-2015	191-3
Merrill Area Chamber of Commerce 705 N Center Ave — *Web:* www.merrillchamber.org	Merrill	WI	54452	715-536-9474	539-2043	139
Merrill Auditorium 20 Myrtle St — *Web:* www.porttix.com	Portland	ME	04101	207-842-0800	842-0810	572
Merrill Corp 1 Merrill Cir — *TF:* 800-688-4400 ■ *Web:* www.merrillcorp.com	Saint Paul	MN	55108	651-646-4501		627
Merrill Distributing Inc 1301 N Memorial Dr — *TF:* 800-289-6232 ■ *Web:* www.merrilldistributing.com	Merrill	WI	54452	800-289-6232		345
Merrill Manufacturing Co 315 Flindt Dr — *Web:* www.merrillmfg.com	Storm Lake	IA	50588	712-732-2760		789
Merrill Manufacturing Corp 236 S Genesee St — *Web:* www.merrill-mfg.com	Merrill	WI	54452	715-536-5533	536-5590	811
Merrill Steel Inc 900 Alderson St — *Web:* www.merrillsteel.com	Schofield	WI	54476	715-355-8924		480
Merrill's Packaging Inc 1529 Rollins Rd — *TF:* 800-284-5910 ■ *Web:* merrills.com	Burlingame	CA	94010	800-284-5910		596
Merrillville Beauty College 48 W 67th Pl — *Web:* www.merrillvillebeautycollege.com	Merrillville	IN	46410	219-769-2232	769-2220	167-3
Merrimac Tile & Stone 8 Merrill Industrial Dr Unit 2 — *Web:* www.merrimactile.com	Hampton	NH	03842	603-432-2544	432-0853	191-1
Merrimack College 315 Tpke St — *Web:* www.merrimack.edu	North Andover	MA	01845	978-837-5000	837-5133	166
Merrimack Films 530 Concord Ave — *Web:* www.merrimack-films.com	Belmont	MA	02478	617-489-4729		514
Merrimack Repertory Theatre 132 Warren St — *Web:* www.mrt.org	Lowell	MA	01852	978-654-7550	654-7575	749
Merrimack Valley Chamber of Commerce 264 Essex St — *Web:* merrimackvalleychamber.com	Lawrence	MA	01840	978-686-0900	794-9953	139
Merrimack Valley Distributing Co 50 Prince St — *Web:* www.mvdc.com	Danvers	MA	01923	978-777-2213	774-7487	81-1
Merrimack Valley Hospice 360 Merrimack St Bldg 9 — **Fax Area Code:* 978 ■ *TF:* 800-933-5593 ■ *Web:* www.homehealthfoundation.org	Lawrence	MA	01843	800-933-5593	552-4401*	371
Merrion Group LLC 210 Elmer St — *Web:* www.merriongroup.net	Westfield	NJ	07090	908-654-0033		690
Merrion Oil & Gas 610 Reilly Ave — *Web:* www.merrion.bz	Farmington	NM	87401	505-324-5300		536
Merrithew Corp 2200 Yonge St Ste 500 — *TF:* 800-910-0001 ■ *Web:* www.merrithew.com	Toronto	ON	M4S2C6	416-482-4050		787
Merritt Capital Management Inc 30 Western Ave Harbor Rm — *Web:* www.merrittcapitalmanagement.com	Gloucester	MA	01930	978-282-0035	282-0013	401
Merritt College 12500 Campus Dr — *Web:* www.merritt.edu	Oakland	CA	94619	510-531-4911		162
Merritt Environmental Consulting Corp 77 Arkay Dr — *Web:* merrittec.com	Hauppauge	NY	11788	631-617-6200	617-6201	261
Merritt Federal Credit Union 3 Danbury Rd — *Web:* merrittfcu.org	Wilton	CT	06897	203-210-7585	210-7587	219
Merritt Hawkins 8840 Cypress Waters Blvd Ste 300 — *TF:* 866-675-3755 ■ *Web:* www.merritthawkins.com	Dallas	TX	75019	800-876-0500		260
Merritt Properties LLC 2066 Lord Baltimore Dr — *Web:* www.merrittproperties.com	Baltimore	MD	21244	410-298-2600	298-9644	655
Merritt Technical Associates Inc 114 St Johns Rd — *Web:* www.merritt-tech.com	Wilton	CT	06897	203-834-0010	762-1347	225
Merritt Trailers 9339 Brighton Rd — **Fax Area Code:* 303 ■ *TF:* 800-634-3036 ■ *Web:* www.merritt-trailers.com	Henderson	CO	80640	800-634-3036	288-6127*	779
Merritt's Boat & Engine Works Inc 2931 NE 16th St — *Web:* www.merrittboat.com	Pompano Beach	FL	33062	954-943-6250		90
Merriweather Post Pavilion (MPP) 10475 Little Patuxent Pkwy — *TF:* 877-435-9849 ■ *Web:* www.merriweathermusic.com	Columbia	MD	21044	410-715-5550	715-5560	572
Merry Lane Press 265 Post Ave Ste 280 — *Web:* www.halpern-group.com	Westbury	NY	11590	516-338-5100	338-5129	637-2
Merry Maids 1661 Shelby Oaks Dr N Ste 108 — **Fax Area Code:* 901 ■ *TF:* 800-798-8000 ■ *Web:* www.merrymaids.com	Memphis	TN	38125	800-798-8000	597-8140*	152

Name / Address	City	State	ZIP	Phone	Fax	Class
Merry Rama Insurance 4236 County Hwy 18 *Web:* www.cattlexchange.com	Delhi	NY	13753	607-746-2226	746-2911	391-1
Merry X-Ray Corp 4909 Murphy Canyon Rd Ste 120 *TF:* 800-635-9729 ■ *Web:* www.merryxray.com	San Diego	CA	92123	800-635-9729		475
Merryfield School of Pet Grooming 5040 NE 13th Ave *TF:* 800-361-4548 ■ *Web:* www.merryfieldschool.com	Fort Lauderdale	FL	33334	954-771-4030	493-8916	685
Mersana Therapeutics Inc 840 Memorial Dr *Web:* www.mersana.com	Cambridge	MA	02139	617-498-0020		668
Merschman Seeds Inc 103 Ave D *TF:* 800-848-7333 ■ *Web:* www.merschmanseeds.com	West Point	IA	52656	319-837-6111	837-6104	276
Mersen Inc 374 Merrimac St *TF:* 800-388-5428 ■ *Web:* www.mersen.us	Newburyport	MA	01950	978-462-6662	462-7934	729
Mershon Ctr 1501 Neil Ave *Web:* mershoncenter.osu.edu	Columbus	OH	43201	614-292-1681	292-2407	634
Mersoft Corp 7007 College Blvd Ste 450 *Web:* www.mersoft.com	Overland Park	KS	66211	913-871-6200		177
Mert's Heart & Soul 214 N College St *Web:* www.uptown2go.com	Charlotte	NC	28202	704-342-4222		671
Mertz Manufacturing Inc 1701 N Waverly St *Web:* www.mertzok.com	Ponca City	OK	74601	580-762-5646	767-8411	273
Meruelo Construction 9550 Firestone Blvd Ste 105 *Web:* merueloenterprises.com	Downey	CA	90241	562-745-2300		787
Mervis Diamond Importers 1900 Mervis Way *TF:* 800-437-5683 ■ *Web:* www.mervisdiamond.com	Tysons	VA	22182	703-448-9000		410
Mervis Industries Inc 3295 E Main St *TF:* 800-637-3016 ■ *Web:* www.mervis.com	Danville	IL	61834	217-442-5300	477-9245	686
MERX Networks Inc 6 Antares Dr Phase II Unit 103 *TF:* 800-964-6379 ■ *Web:* www.merx.com	Ottawa	ON	K2E8A9	613-727-4900		387
Merz Agency Inc, The 4412 SW Barbur Blvd Ste 240 *TF:* 800-440-5433 ■ *Web:* merzagency.com	Portland	OR	97239	503-228-9595		390
Merz Group, The 1570 Mcdaniel Dr *TF:* 800-600-9900 ■ *Web:* merzbranding.com	West Chester	PA	19380	610-429-3160		7
Mesa Arizona Temple 101 S LeSueur *TF:* 855-537-4357 ■ *Web:* www.churchofjesuschrist.org	Mesa	AZ	85204	480-833-1211		50-1
Mesa Arts Ctr 1 E Main St PO Box 1466 *Web:* www.mesaartscenter.com	Mesa	AZ	85201	480-644-6501	644-6503	50-2
Mesa Associates Inc PO Box 196 *Web:* www.mesainc.com	Madison	AL	35758	256-258-2100	258-2103	261
Mesa Chamber of Commerce 165 N Centennial Way *Web:* www.mesachamber.org	Mesa	AZ	85201	480-969-1307	827-0727	139
Mesa City Hall PO Box 1466 *TF:* 866-406-9659 ■ *Web:* www.mesaaz.gov	Mesa	AZ	85211	480-644-2221	644-2821	337
Mesa Community College 1833 W Southern Ave *TF:* 866-532-4983 ■ *Web:* www.mesacc.edu	Mesa	AZ	85202	480-461-7000		162
Mesa Convention Ctr 263 N Center St *Web:* www.mesaaz.gov	Mesa	AZ	85201	480-644-2178	644-2617	205
Mesa County PO Box 20000 *Web:* www.mesacounty.us	Grand Junction	CO	81502	970-244-1800	256-1588	338
Mesa Equipment & Supply Co 7100 Second St NW *Web:* www.mesaequipment.com	Albuquerque	NM	87107	505-345-0284		358
Mesa Fully Formed Inc 1111 S Sirrine *Web:* www.mffinc.com	Mesa	AZ	85210	480-834-9331		115
Mesa Grande School Elementary School 9172 Third Ave *Web:* www.mesagrandeelementary.org	Hesperia	CA	92345	760-244-3709		685
Mesa Historical Museum 51 E Main St PO Box 582 *Web:* www.valleyhistoryinc.com	Mesa	AZ	85201	480-835-2286		520
Mesa Industries Inc 1726 S Magnolia Ave *Web:* www.mesaetp.com	Monrovia	CA	91016	626-359-9361	359-7985	326
Mesa Laboratories Inc 12100 W Sixth Ave *NASDAQ: MLAB* ■ *TF:* 800-992-6372 ■ *Web:* mesalabs.com	Lakewood	CO	80228	303-987-8000	987-8989	475
Mesa Mechanical Inc 3514 Pinemont Dr *TF:* 800-405-9018 ■ *Web:* www.mesamechanical.com	Houston	TX	77018	713-681-5300	681-6675	610
Mesa Products Inc 4445 S 74th E Ave *TF:* 888-800-6372 ■ *Web:* www.mesaproducts.com	Tulsa	OK	74145	918-627-3188	627-2676	690
Mesa Public Library 64 E First St *Web:* www.mesalibrary.org	Mesa	AZ	85201	480-644-3100		434-3
Mesa Systems Inc 2275 South 900 West *TF:* 800-523-4656 ■ *Web:* www.mesasystemsinc.com	Salt Lake City	UT	84119	800-523-4656		360-2
Mesa Ventures 85 Fifth Ave 6th Fl *Web:* www.mesa.vc	New York	NY	10003	212-792-3950		792
Mesa Verde Museum Assn (MVMA) PO Box 38 *Web:* www.mesaverde.org	Mesa Verde National Park	CO	81330	970-529-4445	529-4446	637-2
Mesabi Range Community & Technical College 1100 Industrial Pk Dr PO Box 648 *TF:* 800-657-3860 ■ *Web:* www.mr.mnscu.edu	Eveleth	MN	55734	218-741-3095	744-7466	162
Mesalands Community College 911 S Tenth St *Web:* www.mesalands.edu	Tucumcari	NM	88401	575-461-4413		162
Mesch, Clark & Rothschild PC 259 N Meyer Ave *Web:* www.mcrazlaw.com	Tucson	AZ	85701	520-624-8886		428
MESCO (Marine Equipment and Supply) 1401 Metropolitan Ave *Web:* www.mesconet.com	Thorofare	NJ	08086	856-853-8320	853-9732	770
Mesco Building Solutions 5244 Bear Creek Ct *TF:* 800-556-3726 ■ *Web:* www.mescobuildingsolutions.com	Irving	TX	75061	214-687-9999	687-9736	105
Mesco Inc 986 N Maple St *Web:* www.mescosc.com	Simpsonville	SC	29681	864-228-6372	228-6329	248
MESDA (Museum of Early Southern Decorative Arts) 924 S Main St *Web:* www.mesda.org	Winston-Salem	NC	27101	336-721-7360		520
Mesh Dynamics Inc 2953 Bunker Hill Ln Ste 400 *Web:* meshdynamics.com	Santa Clara	CA	95054	408-373-7700		647
Mesh Systems LLC 12400 N Meridian St Ste 175 *Web:* www.mesh-systems.com	Carmel	IN	46032	317-661-4800		387
Meshbesher & Spence Ltd 1616 Park Ave S *Web:* meshbesher.com	Minneapolis	MN	55404	612-339-9121		41
Mesilla Valley Hospice Inc 299 E Montana Ave *Web:* mvhospice.org	Las Cruces	NM	88005	575-523-4700		363
Mesilla Valley Mall 700 S Telshor Blvd *Web:* www.mesillavalleymall.com	Las Cruces	NM	88011	575-521-4409		460
Mesirow Financial Inc 350 N Clark St *TF:* 800-453-0600 ■ *Web:* www.mesirowfinancial.com	Chicago	IL	60654	312-595-6000	595-4246	690
Mesker Park Zoo 1545 Mesker Pk Dr *Web:* www.meskerparkzoo.com	Evansville	IN	47720	812-435-6143	435-6140	823
Mesko Glass & Mirror Company Inc 801 Wyoming Ave *TF:* 800-982-4055 ■ *Web:* mesko.com	Scranton	PA	18509	570-346-0777		330
Meskwaki Bingo Hotel Casino 1504 305th St *TF:* 800-728-4263 ■ *Web:* www.meskwaki.com	Tama	IA	52339	800-728-4263		133
Mesorah Publications Ltd 4401 2nd Ave *TF:* 800-637-6724 ■ *Web:* www.artscroll.com	Brooklyn	NY	11232	718-921-9000	680-1875	637-2
Mesotec Inc 4705 Boul de Portland *Web:* mesotec.ca	Sherbrooke	QC	J1L0H3	819-822-2777	822-4117	21
Mesquite Chamber of Commerce 617 N Ebrite St *Web:* www.mesquitechamber.com	Mesquite	TX	75149	972-285-0211	285-3535	139
Mesquite Championship Rodeo Inc 1818 Rodeo Dr *Web:* www.mesquiterodeo.com	Mesquite	TX	75149	972-285-8777		671
Mesquite Credit Union 1510 N Galloway Ave *Web:* mesquitecu.org	Mesquite	TX	75149	972-285-8951	289-6801	219
Mesquite Public Library 300 W Grubb Dr *TF:* 877-631-5278 ■ *Web:* www.cityofmesquite.com	Mesquite	TX	75149	972-216-6220	216-6740	434-3
Mesquite Specialty Hospital 1024 N Galloway Ave *Web:* www.msh.ernesthealth.com	Mesquite	TX	75149	972-216-2300	216-2485	374-3
Messa & Associates PC 123 S 22nd St *Web:* www.messalaw.com	Philadelphia	PA	19103	215-568-3500		428
MessageBank LLC 260 Madison Ave 16th Fl *TF:* 800-989-8001 ■ *Web:* www.messagebank.com	New York	NY	10016	212-333-9300		387
MessageSolution Inc 1851 McCarthy Blvd Ste 105 *Web:* www.messagesolution.com	Milpitas	CA	95035	408-383-0100		225
Messaging Architects 180 Peel St Ste 333 *TF:* 866-497-0101 ■ *Web:* www.netmail.com	Montreal	QC	H3C2G7	514-392-9220		179
Messaging Solutions LLC 29563 Usonia Dr *Web:* www.messagingsolutions.com	Spring	TX	77386	281-852-1301		435
Messe Frankfurt Inc 3200 Windy Hill Rd Ste 500 *Web:* us.messefrankfurt.com	Atlanta	GA	30339	770-984-8016	984-8023	822
Messenger Molding Inc 7854 White Fir St *Web:* www.messengermolding.com	Reno	NV	89523	775-747-7006	747-2609	604
Messenger, The 713 Central Ave *TF:* 800-622-6613 ■ *Web:* www.messengernews.net	Fort Dodge	IA	50501	515-573-2141	574-4529	532-2
Messenger, The PO Box 727 *Web:* www.troymessenger.com	Troy	AL	36081	334-566-4270		532-2
Messenger-Inquirer 1401 Fredrica St *TF:* 800-633-2008 ■ *Web:* www.messenger-inquirer.com	Owensboro	KY	42301	270-926-0123	686-7868	532-2
Messer Construction Co 5158 Fishwick Dr *Web:* www.messer.com	Cincinnati	OH	45216	513-242-1541	242-6467	186
Messerli & Kramer PA 1400 Fifth St Towers 100 S Fifth St *Web:* messerlikramer.com	Minneapolis	MN	55402	612-672-3600	672-3777	428
Messiah College PO Box 3005 *TF:* 800-233-4220 ■ *Web:* www.messiah.edu	Grantham	PA	17027	717-691-6000	796-5374	166
Messiah Lutheran Church 303 Rt- 101 PO Box 488 *Web:* www.messiahnh.org	Amherst	NH	03031	603-673-2011		48-20
Messiah Village 100 Mt Allen Dr *Web:* www.messiahlifeways.org	Mechanicsburg	PA	17055	717-790-8232		48-20
Mesta Electronics Inc 11020 Parker Dr *TF:* 800-535-6798 ■ *Web:* www.mesta.com	North Huntingdon	PA	15642	412-754-3000		767
Mestek Inc 260 N Elm St *Web:* www.mestek.com	Westfield	MA	01085	413-568-9571		14
Mestel & Company Inc 575 Madison Ave Ste 3000 *Web:* www.mestel.com	New York	NY	10022	646-356-0500	356-0545	266
Education Trust PO Box 30198 *TF:* 800-638-4543 ■ *Web:* www.michigan.gov	Lansing	MI	48909	517-335-4767	373-6967	725
Met One Instruments Inc 1600 Washington Blvd *Web:* metone.com	Grants Pass	OR	97526	541-471-7111		407
Met Tran Federal Credit Union 2150 W 18th 215 *Web:* mettranfcu.org	Houston	TX	77008	713-861-4780		219
Met Weld International LLC 5727 Ostrander Rd *Web:* www.metweldintl.com	Altamont	NY	12009	518-765-2318		454
Meta Environmental Inc 1000 Truck Hill Rd *Web:* metaenv.com	Fairport	NY	14450	585-364-0728		261

				Phone	Fax	Class
META Manufacturing Corp 8901 Blue Ash Rd *Web:* metamfg.com	Cincinnati	OH	45242	513-793-6382	793-6390	757
Meta Solutions Inc 63 Grove St *Web:* www.metasol.com	Somerville	NJ	08876	908-791-1900		196
Meta5 Inc 122 W Main St *TF:* 866-638-2555 ■ *Web:* www.meta5.us	Babylon	NY	11702	631-587-6800		393
Metabo Corp 1231 Wilson Dr *Web:* www.metabo.com	West Chester	PA	19380	610-436-5900		350
Metabolic Maintenance 601 N Larch St PO Box 940 *Fax Area Code: 541 ■ *TF:* 800-772-7873 ■ *Web:* www.metabolicmaintenance.com	Sisters	OR	97759	800-772-7873	549-3299*	345
Metabolon Inc 617 Davis Dr Ste 100 *Web:* www.metabolon.com	Morrisville	NC	27560	919-572-1711	572-1721	668
Metacred Inc 6841 Elm St Ste 300 *Web:* metacred.com	McLean	VA	22101	703-327-2733		78
MetaDesign North America 615 Battery St 6th Fl *Web:* en.metadesign.com	San Francisco	CA	94111	415-627-0790		7
Metadyne Inc Fox Chase Dr PO Box 328 *Web:* www.towandametadyne.com	Towanda	PA	18848	570-265-6963		567
Metafile Information Systems Inc 3428 Lakeridge Pl NW *TF:* 800-638-2445 ■ *Web:* www.metaviewer.com	Rochester	MN	55901	507-286-9232	286-9065	178-11
Metairie Bank & Trust Co 3344 Metairie Rd *Web:* www.metairiebank.com	Metairie	LA	70001	504-834-6330		70
Metairie Park Country Day School Alumni Assn 300 Park Rd *Web:* www.mpcds.com	Metairie	LA	70005	504-837-5204		685
Metal & Wire Products Co 1065 Salem Pkwy *Web:* www.metalandwire.com	Salem	OH	44460	330-332-9448		492
Metal Arts Finishing Inc 1001 S Lake St *Web:* www.metalartsfinishing.com	Aurora	IL	60506	630-892-6744		481
Metal by the Foot Inc 3600 E Truman Rd *Web:* www.metalbythefoot.com	Kansas City	MO	64127	816-241-5550	241-7707	492
Metal Cladding Inc 230 S Niagara St *Fax Area Code: 716 ■ *TF:* 800-432-5513 ■ *Web:* www.metalcladding.com	Lockport	NY	14094	800-432-5513	439-4010*	481
Metal Coatings Corp 3700 Dunvale Rd *Web:* www.metcoat.com	Houston	TX	77063	713-977-0123	977-0824	481
Metal ComponentsLLC 3281 Roger B Chaffee Memorial Blvd SE *Web:* metalcomp.us	Grand Rapids	MI	49548	616-252-1900		488
Metal Craft Machine & Engineering Inc 13760 Business Center Dr *Web:* www.metal-craft.com	Elk River	MN	55330	763-441-1855		454
Metal Culverts Inc 2107 Rear Missouri Blvd *Web:* metalculverts.com	Jefferson City	MO	65109	573-636-7312		295
Metal Cutting Corp 89 Commerce Rd *TF:* 800-783-6382 ■ *Web:* metalcutting.com	Cedar Grove	NJ	07009	973-239-1100	239-6651	455
Metal Depot 1509 S Bluff Rd *Web:* www.starscrap.com	Montebello	CA	90640	714-994-3450	994-0480	492
Metal Exchange Corp 111 W Port Plaza Dr Ste 350 *Web:* metalexchangecorp.com	Saint Louis	MO	63146	314-434-3500		686
Metal Fabricating Corp 10408 Berea Rd *Web:* www.metalfabricatingcorp.com	Cleveland	OH	44102	216-631-2480	631-2453	482
Metal Flow Corp 11694 James St *Web:* www.metalflow.com	Holland	MI	49424	616-392-7976	392-5814	488
Metal Form Manufacturing Co 5960 W Washington St *Fax Area Code: 866 ■ *Web:* www.mfmca.com	Phoenix	AZ	85043	602-233-1211	233-2033*	37
Metal Forming & Coining Corp (MFC) 1007 Illinois Ave *Web:* www.mfccorp.com	Maumee	OH	43537	419-893-8748		483
Metal Forms Corp 3334 N Booth St *Web:* www.metalforms.com	Milwaukee	WI	53212	414-964-4550		697
Metal Goods Manufacturing Company Inc 309 W Hensley Blvd *Web:* www.metalgoodsmfg.com	Bartlesville	OK	74003	918-336-4282	336-8993	420
Metal Improvement Company LLC 80 Rt 4 E Ste 310 *Web:* cwst.com	Paramus	NJ	07652	201-843-7800	843-3460	484
Metal Management Mississippi Inc 304 W Bankhead St *Web:* www.simsmm.com	New Albany	MS	38652	662-534-3004		660
Metal Marketplace Intl (MMI) 718 Sansom St *TF:* 800-523-9191 ■ *Web:* www.metalmarketplace.com	Philadelphia	PA	19106	215-592-8777	592-8195	411
Metal Master Sales Corp 1159 N Main St *Web:* www.metalmaster.com	Glendale Heights	IL	60139	630-858-4750		256
Metal Masters Inc 3825 Crater Lake Hwy *TF:* 800-866-9437 ■ *Web:* www.metalmasters-inc.com	Medford	OR	97504	541-779-1049		186
Metal Powder Industries Federation (MPIF) 105 College Rd E *Web:* www.mpif.org	Princeton	NJ	08540	609-452-7700	987-8523	49-13
Metal Seal & Products Inc 4323 Hamann Pkwy *Web:* www.metalseal.com	Willoughby	OH	44094	440-946-8500		247
Metal Specialties Inc 300 Rodman Rd *Web:* www.metal-specialties.com	Auburn	ME	04210	207-786-4268	783-1958	493
Metal Standard Corp 286 Hedcor St *Web:* metalstandard.com	Holland	MI	49423	616-396-6356		697
Metal Store, The 5454 Dunham Rd *Web:* www.themetalstore.com	Maple Heights	OH	44137	216-663-0458		492
Metal Supermarkets IP Inc 520 Abilene Dr 2nd Fl *TF:* 866-867-9344 ■ *Web:* www.metalsupermarkets.com	Mississauga	ON	L5T2H7	905-362-8226		492
Metal Suppliers Online LLC (MSO) 35 Gigante Dr *TF:* 800-380-1470 ■ *Web:* www.metalsuppliersonline.com	Hampstead	NH	03841	603-329-0101	329-0171	492

				Phone	Fax	Class
Metal Tech Company Inc 10877 Rockwall Rd *Web:* www.metaltechcompany.com	Dallas	TX	75238	214-253-2332	253-2335	492
Metal Technologies of Murfreesboro Inc 314 W Broad St *Web:* www.metaltechnc.com	Murfreesboro	NC	27855	252-398-4041		757
Metal Textiles 970 New Durham Rd *Web:* www.metaltextiles.com	Edison	NJ	08818	732-287-0800	287-8546	688
Metal Trades Inc PO Box 129 *Web:* www.metaltrades.com	Hollywood	SC	29449	843-889-6441	889-2818	697
Metal Works Manufacturing Co 2501 W Dixon Blvd *Web:* www.metalworksmfg.com	Shelby	NC	28152	704-482-1399	482-2327	480
Metalcare Group Inc PO Box 6549 *Web:* metalcare.com	Fort McMurray	AB	T9H5N4	780-715-1889		195
Metalcraft Enterprises Inc 202 Industrial Dr *Fax Area Code: 573 ■ *TF:* 800-325-0890 ■ *Web:* www.metalcraft.com	New Haven	MO	63068	800-325-0890	237-2330*	91
Metalcraft of Mayville Inc 1000 Metalcraft Dr *Web:* www.mtlcraft.com	Mayville	WI	53050	920-387-3150		492
Metalcraft Technologies Inc 526 N Aviation Way *Web:* www.metalcraft.net	Cedar City	UT	84721	435-586-3871	586-0289	697
Metal-Era Inc 1600 Airport Rd *TF:* 800-558-2162 ■ *Web:* www.metalera.com	Waukesha	WI	53188	800-558-2162		697
Metalex Corp 700 Liberty Dr *TF:* 877-667-8634 ■ *Web:* industrial.metlx.com	Libertyville	IL	60048	847-362-5400	362-5434	723
Metalex Manufacturing Inc 5750 Cornell Rd *Web:* www.metalexmfg.com	Cincinnati	OH	45242	513-489-0507	489-1020	454
Metal-Fab Inc 3025 May St *TF:* 800-835-2830 ■ *Web:* www.mtlfab.com	Wichita	KS	67213	316-943-2351	943-2717	697
Metalfab Inc Prices Switch Rd Po Box 9 *Web:* www.metalfabinc.com	Vernon	NJ	07462	973-764-2000	764-0272	697
Metalforms Manufacturing Inc 7218 Garth St *Web:* metalformsltd.com	Beaumont	TX	77705	409-842-1626	842-1503	91
Metalico Annaco Inc 943 Hazel St *TF:* 800-966-1499 ■ *Web:* www.metalico.com	Akron	OH	44305	330-376-1400	376-9696	686
Metalink Technologies Inc 417 Wayne Ave PO Box 1124 *TF:* 888-999-8002 ■ *Web:* www.metalink.net	Defiance	OH	43512	419-782-3472		224
Metalist International Inc 1159 S Pennsylvania Ave *Web:* www.metalist.com	Lansing	MI	48912	517-371-2940	371-3027	483
Metallics Inc W7274 County Hwy Z PO Box 99 *Web:* www.metallics.net	Onalaska	WI	54650	608-781-5200	781-2254	702
Metallized Carbon Corp 19 S Water St *Web:* www.metcar.com	Ossining	NY	10562	914-941-3738		620
Metalloid Southwest 1829 Norman Dr *Web:* www.metalloidcorp.com	Jacksonville	TX	75766	903-589-3933		579
Metallurgical Products Co 810 Lincoln Ave PO Box 598 *Web:* www.metprodco.com	West Chester	PA	19381	610-696-6770	430-8431	485
Metallurgical Technologies Incorporated PA 160 Bevan Dr *Web:* met-tech.com	Mooresville	NC	28115	704-663-5108		415
Metal-Matic Inc 629 2nd St Se *Fax Area Code: 612 ■ *TF:* 800-328-5494 ■ *Web:* www.metal-matic.com	Minneapolis	MN	55414	800-328-5494	392-3399*	490
MetaLogix Inc 9789 Charlotte Hwy Ste 400-142 *Web:* www.metalogixinc.com	Fort Mill	SC	29707	704-543-1616		177
Metalor Electrotechnics 1003 Corporate Ln *Web:* www.metalor.com	Export	PA	15632	724-733-8332	733-8341	815
MetaLPlate Galvanizing LP 1120 39th St N *Web:* www.metalplate.com	Birmingham	AL	35234	205-595-4700	595-7800	481
Metals Service Center Institute (MSCI) 4201 Euclid Ave *TF:* 800-634-2358 ■ *Web:* www.msci.org	Rolling Meadows	IL	60008	847-485-3000	485-3001	49-18
Metals Technology Corp 120 N Schmale Rd *Web:* www.metalstechnology.com	Carol Stream	IL	60188	630-221-2500		484
Metalsco Inc 1828 Craig Rd *Web:* www.metalsco.com	Saint Louis	MO	63146	314-997-5200	997-5921	686
Metaltech Inc 206 Prospect Ave	Kirkwood	MO	63122	314-965-4550		697
Metal-Tech Inc 265 Airport Rd *TF:* 800-234-7077 ■ *Web:* www.metaltech-de.com	New Castle	DE	19720	302-322-7770	322-7953	454
Metal-Tech Partners 2103 R St *Web:* www.mtpartners.com	Geneva	NE	68361	402-759-7000	759-7001	735
Metaltech Service Center Inc 9915 Monroe *TF:* 800-644-1204 ■ *Web:* www.metaltechsc.com	Houston	TX	77075	713-991-5100		492
Metal-Tronics Inc 126 Merrimack St *Web:* www.metaltronics.com	Lawrence	MA	01843	978-659-6960		488
Metalwerx Inc 50 Guinan St *Web:* metalwerx.com	Waltham	MA	02451	781-891-3854	891-3811	411
Metalworking Group Inc 9070 Pippin Rd *TF:* 800-476-9409 ■ *Web:* www.metalworkinggroup.com	Cincinnati	OH	45251	513-521-4114	521-2816	487
Metalworking Lubricants Co 25 W Silverdome Industrial Pk *TF:* 800-394-5494 ■ *Web:* www.metalworkinglubricants.com	Pontiac	MI	48342	248-332-3500	332-4959	541
Metalworks 902 E Fourth St *Web:* metalworks1.com	Ludington	MI	49431	231-845-5136	845-1043	697
Metalworx Inc 340 Deming Way *Web:* www.metalworxinc.com	Summerville	SC	29483	843-402-0999	402-0270	697
MetaMetrics Inc 1000 Park Forty Plaza Dr Ste 120 *Web:* lexile.com	Durham	NC	27713	919-547-3400		242
Metamora-Hadley Recreation Area 3871 Herd Rd *Fax Area Code: 810 ■ *Web:* www.michigan.org	Metamora	MI	48455	800-447-2757	797-4387*	565
Metaops Inc 30425 Munger Dr *Web:* metaops.com	Livonia	MI	48154	734-425-1455		396

Phone | Fax | Class

MetaOption LLC
574 Newark Ave Ste 210 — Jersey City NJ 07306 — 201-377-3150 — 196
Web: www.metaoption.com

MetaResponse Group Inc
700 W Hillsboro Blvd Ste 4-107 — Deerfield Beach FL 33441 — 954-360-0644 — 5
Web: www.metaresponse.com

Metasense Inc
403 Commerce Ln Ste 5 — West Berlin NJ 08091 — 856-873-9950 — 225
TF: 866-875-6382 ■ *Web:* www.metasenseusa.com

Metasys Technologies
3460 Summit Ridge Pkwy — Duluth GA 30096 — 678-218-1593 — 218-1601 — 260
Web: metasysinc.com

Metasystems Inc
13700 State Rd Ste 1 — North Royalton OH 44133 — 440-526-1454 — 463
TF: 800-788-5253 ■ *Web:* www.metasystems.com

Metcalfe County PO Box 42 — Edmonton KY 42129 — 270-432-4821 — 338
Web: www.metcalfecountyclerk.com

Metcalfe Group Inc, The
30405 Solon Rd Unit 5 — Solon OH 44139 — 440-349-5995 — 349-5997 — 393
Web: www.metcalfegroup.com

Metcalfe Realty & Auction Company Inc
100 Castle Ridge Dr — Edmonton KY 42129 — 270-432-7355 — 652
Web: www.metcalferealty.net

Metcam Inc 305 Tidwell Cir — Alpharetta GA 30004 — 770-475-9633 — 442-3425 — 697
TF: 888-394-9633 ■ *Web:* www.metcam.com

Met-Chem Canada Inc
555 Blvd Rene-Levesque Ouest 3e Etage — Montreal QC H2Z1B1 — 514-288-5211 — 261
Web: www.met-chem.com

Metco Industries Inc
1241 Brusselles St — Saint Marys PA 15857 — 814-781-3630 — 487
Web: www.metcopm.com

Metco Landscape Inc 2200 Rifle St — Aurora CO 80011 — 303-421-3100 — 776
Web: metcolandscape.com

Metcom Inc PO Box 49065 — Cookeville TN 38506 — 931-526-8412 — 526-1092 — 488
Web: www.metcomusa.com

Met-Con Cos 15760 Acorn Trl — Faribault MN 55021 — 507-332-2266 — 332-8742 — 186
Web: www.met-con.com

Met-Con Inc 465 Canaveral Groves Blvd — Cocoa FL 32926 — 321-632-4880 — 639-0158 — 480
Web: www.metconinc.com

Metcut Research Inc
3980 Rosslyn Dr — Cincinnati OH 45209 — 513-271-5100 — 271-9511 — 743
TF: 877-847-1985 ■ *Web:* www.metcut.com

Metem Corp 700 Parsippany Rd — Parsippany NJ 07054 — 973-887-6635 — 887-1755 — 386
Web: www.metem.com

Meteor Crater & Museum of Astrogeology
Exit 233 off I-40 — Winslow AZ 86047 — 800-289-5898 — 289-2598* — 520
**Fax Area Code:* 928 ■ *TF:* 800-289-5898 ■ *Web:* www.meteorcrater.com

Meteor Express Inc PO Box 248 — Scottsboro AL 35768 — 256-218-3000 — 449
Web: www.meteorx.com

Meteorcomm LLC 1201 SW Seventh St — Renton WA 98057 — 253-872-2521 — 872-7662 — 224
Web: www.meteorcomm.com

Meters Inc 137 Wansley Dr — Cartersville GA 30121 — 770-386-0080 — 386-6640 — 695
TF: 866-386-0080 ■ *Web:* www.metersinc.com

Metex Inc 789 Don Mills Rd Ste 218 — North York ON M3C1T5 — 416-203-8388 — 764
TF: 866-817-8137 ■ *Web:* www.metex.com

Metglas Inc 440 Allied Dr — Conway SC 29526 — 843-349-7319 — 485
TF: 800-581-7654 ■ *Web:* metglas.com

Methane Specialists
621 Via Alondra Ste 611 — Camarillo CA 93012 — 805-987-5356 — 987-3968 — 261
Web: www.methanespecialists.com

Methanex Corp
1800 Waterfront Centre 200 Burrard St — Vancouver BC V6C3M1 — 604-661-2600 — 661-2676 — 144
TSX: MX ■ *TF:* 800-661-8851 ■ *Web:* www.methanex.com

Methapharm Inc
11772 W Sample Rd — Coral Springs FL 33065 — 954-341-0795 — 238
TF: 800-287-7686 ■ *Web:* methapharm.com

Method Inc 1741 Technology Dr — San Jose CA 95110 — 415-901-6300 — 7
Web: www.method.com

Method Studios
3401 Exposition Blvd — Santa Monica CA 90404 — 310-434-6500 — 393
Web: www.methodstudios.com

Methode Electronics Inc
7401 W Wilson Ave — Chicago IL 60706 — 708-867-6777 — 867-6999 — 253
NYSE: MEI ■ *TF:* 877-316-7700 ■ *Web:* www.methode.com

Methodist Charlton Medical Ctr
3500 W Wheatland Rd — Dallas TX 75237 — 214-947-7777 — 374-3
Web: www.methodisthealthsystem.org

Methodist ElderCare Services
5155 N High St — Columbus OH 43214 — 614-396-4990 — 436-6012 — 672
TF: 855-636-2225 ■ *Web:* www.wesleyridge.com

Methodist Healthcare Inc
1265 Union Ave — Memphis TN 38104 — 901-516-7000 — 353
Web: www.methodisthealth.org

Methodist Healthcare Ministries of South Texas Inc
4507 Medical Dr — San Antonio TX 78229 — 210-692-0234 — 614-7563 — 353
TF: 800-959-6673 ■ *Web:* www.mhm.org

Methodist Hospital 1305 N Elm St — Henderson KY 42420 — 270-827-7700 — 374-3
TF: 800-241-8322 ■ *Web:* www.methodisthospital.net

Methodist Hospital 600 Grant St — Gary IN 46402 — 219-886-4000 — 374-3
TF: 888-909-3627 ■ *Web:* www.methodisthospitals.org

Methodist Hospital
1701 N Senate Blvd PO Box 1367 — Indianapolis IN 46202 — 317-962-2000 — 962-0304 — 374-3
TF: 800-899-8448 ■ *Web:* iuhealth.org

Methodist Hospital
2301 S Broad St — Philadelphia PA 19148 — 215-952-9000 — 374-3
Web: hospitals.jefferson.edu

Methodist Hospital of Chicago (MHC)
5025 N Paulina St — Chicago IL 60640 — 773-271-9040 — 374-3
Web: www.methodistchicago.org

Methodist Hospital of Southern California
300 W Huntington Dr — Arcadia CA 91007 — 626-898-8000 — 374-3
TF: 888-388-2838 ■ *Web:* www.methodisthospital.org

Methodist Hospital System, The
6445 Main St Ste 2500 — Houston TX 77030 — 713-790-3333 — 374-3
Web: www.houstonmethodist.org

Methodist Medical Center of Oak Ridge
990 Oak Ridge Tpke — Oak Ridge TN 37831 — 865-835-1000 — 374-3
Web: www.mmcoakridge.com

Methodist Rehabilitation Ctr
1350 E Woodrow Wilson Dr — Jackson MS 39216 — 601-981-2611 — 374-6
TF: 800-223-6672 ■ *Web:* www.methodistonline.org

Methodist Retirement Communities
1440 Lake Front Cir Ste 110 — The Woodlands TX 77380 — 281-363-2600 — 371
Web: www.mrcaff.org

Methodist Senior Services
300 Airline Rd — Columbus MS 39702 — 662-327-6716 — 482-5567* — 672
**Fax Area Code:* 601 ■ *Web:* www.mss.org

Methodist Theological School in Ohio
3081 Columbus Pk — Delaware OH 43015 — 740-363-1146 — 362-3135 — 167-3
TF: 800-333-6876 ■ *Web:* www.mtso.edu

Methodist University
5400 Ramsey St — Fayetteville NC 28311 — 910-630-7000 — 630-7285 — 166
TF: 800-488-7110 ■ *Web:* www.methodist.edu

Methods and Equipment Associates
31731 Glendale St — Livonia MI 48150 — 734-293-0660 — 293-0663 — 385
Web: www.methods-equipment.com

Methods Machine Tools Inc
65 Union Ave — Sudbury MA 01776 — 978-443-5388 — 358
TF: 877-668-4262 ■ *Web:* www.methodsmachine.com

Meth-Wick Community
1224 13th St NW — Cedar Rapids IA 52405 — 319-365-9171 — 672
Web: www.methwick.org

METI (Management & Engineering Technologies International Inc)
8600 Boeing Dr — El Paso TX 79925 — 915-772-4975 — 772-2253 — 463
Web: www.meticorp.com

METI (Medical Education Technologies Inc)
6300 Edgelake Dr — Sarasota FL 34240 — 941-377-5562 — 250
TF: 866-462-7920 ■ *Web:* caehealthcare.com

Metier Law Firm LLC
4828 S College Ave — Fort Collins CO 80525 — 833-228-6596 — 41
Web: metierlaw.com

Metis Communications Inc
294 Washington St Ste 607 — Boston MA 02108 — 617-236-0500 — 636
Web: www.metiscomm.com

Metis Strategy LLC
6900 Wisconsin Ave Ste 300 — Bethesda MD 20815 — 301-893-4610 — 463
Web: www.metisstrategy.com

Met-L-Flo Inc
720 Heartland Dr Unit S — Sugar Grove IL 60554 — 630-409-9860 — 463
Web: www.metlflo.com

MetLife Foundation
27-01 Queens Plz N — Long Island City NY 11101 — 800-638-5433 — 304
TF: 800-638-5433 ■ *Web:* www.metlife.com

MetlSaw 2950 Bay Vista Ct — Benicia CA 94510 — 707-746-6200 — 746-5085 — 455
Web: www.metlsaw.com

Metl-Span LLC
1720 Lakepointe Dr Ste 101 — Lewisville TX 75057 — 972-221-6656 — 420-9382 — 105
TF: 877-585-9969 ■ *Web:* www.metlspan.com

Met-L-Tec LLC 7310 Express Rd — Temperance MI 48182 — 734-847-7004 — 757
Web: www.met-l-tec.com

MetoKote Corp 1340 Neubrecht Rd — Lima OH 45801 — 419-996-7800 — 996-7801 — 481
TF: 866-806-4018 ■ *Web:* www.ppgcoatingsservices.com

Metompkin Bay Oyster Co
101-105 Eleventh St PO Box 671 — Crisfield MD 21817 — 410-968-0660 — 968-0670 — 296-14
Web: www.metompkinseafood.com

Metpar Corp 95 State St — Westbury NY 11590 — 516-333-2600 — 333-2618 — 286
Web: www.metpar.com

Metplas Inc 3 Acee Dr — Natrona Heights PA 15065 — 724-295-1900 — 295-3055 — 599
TF: 800-827-1900 ■ *Web:* www.metplas.com

Metra Electronics Corp
460 Walker St — Holly Hill FL 32117 — 386-257-1186 — 255-3965 — 52
TF: 800-221-0932 ■ *Web:* www.metraonline.com

MetraPark 308 Sixth Ave N — Billings MT 59101 — 406-256-2400 — 205
TF: 800-366-8538 ■ *Web:* www.metrapark.com

Metrex Research Corp
1717 W Collins Ave — Orange CA 92867 — 800-841-1428 — 228
TF: 800-841-1428 ■ *Web:* www.metrex.com

Metric Machining Co
1425 S Vineyard Ave — Ontario CA 91761 — 909-947-9222 — 923-1796 — 621
Web: www.metricorp.com

Metric Manufacturing Company Inc
1001 Foreman St — Lowell MI 49331 — 616-897-5959 — 897-4138 — 454
Web: www.metricmfg.com

Metric Products 4630 Leahy St — Culver City CA 90232 — 310-815-9000 — 838-0241 — 34
Web: www.metric-products.com

Metric Stream Inc
2479 E Bayshore Rd Ste 260 — Palo Alto CA 94303 — 650-620-2900 — 565-8542 — 178-7
Web: www.metricstream.com

Metrican Stamping LLC
101 Warren G Medley Dr — Dickson TN 37055 — 615-446-1018 — 489
Web: metrican.com

Metrics Contract Services
1240 Sugg Pkwy — Greenville NC 27834 — 252-752-3800 — 758-8522 — 668
Web: www.metricscontractservices.com

Metriguard Inc 2465 NE Hopkins Ct — Pullman WA 99163 — 509-332-0554 — 332-0485 — 248
Web: www.metriguard.com

MetriTech Inc 4106 Fieldstone Rd — Champaign IL 61826 — 217-398-4868 — 94
TF: 800-747-4868 ■ *Web:* www.metritech.com

Metrix Instrument Co
8824 Fallbrook Dr — Houston TX 77064 — 281-940-1802 — 559-9417* — 472
**Fax Area Code:* 713 ■ *TF:* 800-638-7494 ■ *Web:* www.metrixvibration.com

Metrix Marketing Inc
40 Wildbriar Rd — Rochester NY 14623 — 585-334-0890 — 195
Web: www.metrix-marketing.com

Metro - Sales Inc 1640 E 78th St — Minneapolis MN 55423 — 612-861-4000 — 866-8069 — 112
TF: 800-862-7414 ■ *Web:* www.metrosales.com

Metro 1 120 NE 27 St Ste 200 — Miami FL 33137 — 305-571-9991 — 571-9661 — 224
Web: www.metro1.com

Metro Alloys Inc 1024 Sampler Way — Atlanta GA 30344 — 404-753-6063 — 695
Web: www.metroalloysinc.com

Metro Appliances & More Inc (MBS)
5313 S Mingo Rd — Tulsa OK 74145 — 918-622-7692 — 38
Web: www.metroappliancesandmore.com

Metro Atlanta Chamber of Commerce
191 Peachtree St NE Ste 3400 — Atlanta GA 30303 — 404-880-9000 — 139
Web: www.metroatlantachamber.com

Name / Address	City	State	ZIP	Phone	Fax	Class
Metro Aviation Inc 1214 Hawn Ave PO Box 7008 *Web:* www.metroaviation.com	Shreveport	LA	71137	318-222-5529	222-0503	30
Metro Bay Associates Inc 3090 Charles Ave *Web:* www.metrobayassociatesinc.com	Clearwater	FL	33765	727-442-1225		652
Metro Business Systems 2950 Kaverton Rd *Web:* www.mbs-copiers.com	District Heights	MD	20747	301-967-8758		535
Metro Business Systems Inc 11 Largo Dr S *TF:* 800-551-8225 ■ *Web:* metropc.com	Stamford	CT	06907	203-967-3435	967-2591	179
Metro Coast Insurance Services LLC 23456 Madero Rd Ste 240 *Web:* metrocoastinsurance.com	Mission Viejo	CA	92691	949-238-6399		390
Metro Creative Graphics Inc 519 Eigth Ave *TF:* 800-223-1600 ■ *Web:* www.mcg.metrocreativeconnection.com	New York	NY	10018	212-947-5100		344
Metro Development Group 2502 N Rocky Point Dr Ste 1050 *Web:* metrodevelopmentgroup.com	Tampa	FL	33607	813-288-8078		653
Metro ECSU 2 Pine Tree Dr Ste 101 *Web:* www.metroecsu.org	Arden Hills	MN	55112	612-638-1500		242
Metro Express Transportation Services Inc 875 Fee Fee Rd *TF:* 800-805-0073 ■ *Web:* www.metroexpressinc.com	Maryland Heights	MO	63043	314-993-1511	993-8707	311
Metro Fabricating 1650 Tech Dr *TF:* 800-551-7936 ■ *Web:* www.metrofab.com	Bay City	MI	48706	989-667-8100		729
Metro Flag 30 E 21st St 2nd Fl **Fax Area Code: 973* ■ *Web:* nationalflag.com	New York	NY	10010	212-462-4000	366-0956*	287
Metro Ford Inc 9000 NW Seventh Ave *Web:* www.metrofordmiami.com	Miami	FL	33150	305-751-9711		57
Metro Group Inc 3150 W 900 S *Web:* metrogroup.com	Salt Lake City	UT	84104	801-590-3000		660
Metro Health Hospital 5900 Byron Center Ave *TF:* 800-968-0051 ■ *Web:* metrohealth.net	Wyoming	MI	49519	616-252-7200	252-0630	374-3
Metro Jackson Convention & Visitors Bureau 111 E Capitol St Ste 102 *TF:* 800-354-7695 ■ *Web:* www.visitjackson.com	Jackson	MS	39201	601-960-1891	960-1827	206
Metro Machine & Engineering Corp 8001 Wallace Rd *Web:* www.metromachine.com	Eden Prairie	MN	55344	952-937-2800	937-2374	547
Metro Machine Works 11977 Harrison Rd *Web:* www.metromachineworks.net	Romulus	MI	48174	734-941-4571	941-4820	21
Metro Mailing Service Inc 4251 Gateway Park Blvd *Web:* mmsmail.com	Sacramento	CA	95834	916-928-0801		5
Metro Materials Inc 2174 E Person Ave *Web:* www.metromaterials.com	Memphis	TN	38114	901-324-3894	452-9592	182
Metro Metals Northwest Inc 5611 NE Columbia Blvd *TF:* 800-610-5680 ■ *Web:* www.metrometalsnw.com	Portland	OR	97218	503-287-8861	287-5569	686
Metro Mold & Design Inc 20600 County Rd 81 *Web:* www.metromold.com	Rogers	MN	55374	763-428-8310		757
Metro Moulded Parts Inc 11610 Jay St Nw **Fax Area Code: 877* ■ *TF:* 800-878-2237 ■ *Web:* www.metrommp.com	Minneapolis	MN	55448	800-878-2237	399-2562*	676
Metro North Chamber of Commerce 1870 W 122nd Ave Ste 300 *Web:* www.metronorthchamber.com	Westminster	CO	80234	303-288-1000	227-1050	139
Metro Packaging & Imaging Inc 5 Haul Rd *Web:* www.metro-pi.com	Wayne	NJ	07470	973-709-9100		557
Metro Park Warehouses Inc 6920 Executive Dr *Web:* www.metroparkwarehouses.com	Kansas City	MO	64120	816-231-0777	231-7797	803-1
Metro Parks 1069 W Main St *Web:* www.metroparks.net	Westerville	OH	43081	614-891-0700		564
Metro Parks 4702 19th St *Web:* www.metroparkstacoma.org	Tacoma	WA	98405	253-305-1030		303
Metro Pavia Health System MaraMar Plaza Bldg Avenida San Patricio Ste 960 *TF:* 888-882-0882 ■ *Web:* metropavia.com	Guaynabo	PR	00968	787-620-9770		363
Metro Phoenix Bank 4686 E Van Buran Ste 150 *Web:* metrophoenixbank.com	Phoenix	AZ	85008	602-346-1800		70
Metro Pictures 519 W 24th St *Web:* www.metropictures.com	New York	NY	10011	212-206-7100	337-0070	42
Metro Santa Cruz 550 S First St *Web:* www.metroactive.com	San Jose	CA	95113	408-298-8500		532-5
Metro South Chamber of Commerce 60 School St *TF:* 877-777-4414 ■ *Web:* www.metrosouthchamber.com	Brockton	MA	02301	508-586-0500	587-1340	139
Metro South Medical Ctr 12935 S Gregory St *Web:* www.metrosouthmedicalcenter.com	Blue Island	IL	60406	708-597-2000		374-3
Metro Storage LLC 13528 Boulton Blvd *Web:* www.metrostorage.com	Lake Forest	IL	60045	847-235-8900		803-3
Metro Teleproductions Inc 2425 L St NW Ste 224 *Web:* www.mtitv.com	Washington	DC	20037	301-608-9077	608-9078	514
Metro Times 733 St Antoine St *Web:* www.metrotimes.com	Detroit	MI	48226	313-961-4060	961-6598	532-5
Metro Toronto Convention Ctr 255 Front St W *TF:* 800-422-7969 ■ *Web:* www.mtccc.com	Toronto	ON	M5V2W6	416-585-8000	585-8262	205
Metro Transit 560 Sixth Ave N *TF:* 855-340-0035 ■ *Web:* www.metrotransit.org	Minneapolis	MN	55411	612-349-7400		468
Metro Travel & Tours 9298 Central Ave NE Ste 222 *Web:* www.metrotravel.biz	Minneapolis	MN	55434	763-784-0560	784-2934	772
Metro Truck Body Inc 240 Citation Cir *Web:* www.metrotruckbody.com	Corona	CA	92878	310-532-5570	532-0754	516
Metro Video Systems Inc 1220 E Imperial Ave *Web:* metrovideosystems.com	El Segundo	CA	90245	310-640-9250	640-9347	35

Name / Address	City	State	ZIP	Phone	Fax	Class
Metro Waste Authority 300 E Locust St Ste 100 *Web:* www.mwatoday.com	Des Moines	IA	50309	515-244-0021	244-9477	804
Metro Web Corp 5901 Tonnelle Ave *Web:* www.metrowebnj.com	North Bergen	NJ	07047	201-553-0700		627
Metro West Ambulance Service Inc 5475 NE Dawson Creek Dr *Web:* metrowest.fm	Hillsboro	OR	97124	503-648-6656		30
Metro West Chamber of Commerce 1671 Worcester Rd Ste 201 *Web:* www.metrowest.org	Framingham	MA	01701	508-879-5600	875-9325	139
Metro Wine Bar & Bistro 6418 N Western Ave *Web:* www.metrowinebar.com	Oklahoma City	OK	73116	405-840-9463		671
Metro Wire & Cable Co 6636 Metropolitan Pkwy *TF:* 800-633-1432 ■ *Web:* www.metrowire.net	Sterling Heights	MI	48312	586-264-3050	264-7390	246
Metro-Can Construction Ltd 10470 152 St Ste 520 *Web:* www.metrocan.com	Surrey	BC	V3R0Y3	604-583-1174		261
Metroclean Commercial Building Services Inc 9000 SW Fwy Ste 412 *Web:* www.metrocleanonline.com	Houston	TX	77074	713-255-0100		104
Metrocrest Chamber of Commerce 2550 Midway Rd Ste 240 *Web:* www.metrocrestchamber.com	Carrollton	TX	75006	469-587-0420	587-0428	139
Metro-Goldwyn-Mayer Studios Inc (MGM) 245 N Beverly Dr *Web:* mgm.com	Beverly Hills	CA	90210	310-449-3000		514
MetroHartford Alliance 31 Pratt St 5th Fl *Web:* www.metrohartford.com	Hartford	CT	06103	860-525-4451	293-2592	139
MetroHealth Medical Ctr 2500 MetroHealth Dr *Web:* www.metrohealth.org	Cleveland	OH	44109	216-778-7800		374-3
Metroland Magazine 100 State St	Albany	NY	12207	518-463-2500		532-5
Metroland Media Group Ltd 3125 Wolfedale Rd *Web:* metroland.com	Mississauga	ON	L5C1W1	905-281-5656		532-3
Metrolaser Inc 22941 Mill Creek Dr *Web:* www.metrolaserinc.com	Laguna Hills	CA	92653	949-553-0688	553-0495	419
Metrolina Greenhouses Inc 16400 Huntersville-Concord Rd *TF:* 800-543-3915 ■ *Web:* www.metrolinagreenhouses.com	Huntersville	NC	28078	704-875-1371	875-6741	369
Metrolina Steel Inc 11330 Vanstory Dr *Web:* www.metrolinasteel.com	Charlotte	NC	28273	704-598-7007		492
MetroList Services Inc 1164 W National Dr Ste 60 *Web:* www.metrolistmls.com	Sacramento	CA	95834	916-922-7584		656
Metro-Med Inc 1701 N San Fernando Blvd *TF:* 800-660-2590 ■ *Web:* www.metromed.com	Burbank	CA	91504	818-840-9090		45
Metromobile Communications 1140 Old County Rd Ste A *TF:* 800-383-2929 ■ *Web:* www.metromobile.com	Belmont	CA	94002	650-367-1992	832-1943	38
Metromont Corp PO Box 2486 *TF:* 844-882-4015 ■ *Web:* www.metromont.com	Greenville	SC	29602	844-882-4015		183
Metron Technology Inc 1401 Walnut St Ste 060 *Web:* www.metrontechnology.com	Boulder	CO	80302	303-449-8000	443-0949	385
Metronet 1619 Dayton Ave Ste 314 *Web:* www.metrolibraries.net	Saint Paul	MN	55104	651-646-0475	649-3169	434-3
Metropark Communications Inc 10405 Baur Blvd Ste A *TF:* 877-900-6856 ■ *Web:* www.metropark.com	Saint Louis	MO	63132	314-439-1900	439-1313	38
Metroplex Hospital 2201 S Clear Creek Rd *TF:* 800-926-7664 ■ *Web:* www.mplex.org	Killeen	TX	76549	254-526-7523	526-3483	374-3
Metropole Products Inc 2040 Jefferson Davis Hwy *Web:* www.metropoleproducts.com	Stafford	VA	22554	540-659-2132	659-2133	647
Metropolis Cafe 584 Tremont St *Web:* www.metropolisboston.com	Boston	MA	02118	617-247-2931		671
Metropolis Coffee Co 1039 W Granville Ave *Web:* metropoliscoffee.com	Chicago	IL	60660	773-764-0400		297-8
Metropolis Magazine 205 Lexington Ave 17th Fl *Web:* www.metropolismag.com	New York	NY	10016	212-627-9977		457-2
Metropolitan Abstract Corp 1 Old Country Rd *Web:* metropolitanabstract.com	Carle Place	NY	11514	516-741-5474		653
Metropolitan Alloys Corp 17385 Ryan Rd *Web:* www.metroalloys.com	Detroit	MI	48212	313-366-4443	366-9698	492
Metropolitan Atlanta Rapid Transit Authority (MARTA) 2424 Piedmont Rd NE *Web:* www.itsmarta.com	Atlanta	GA	30324	404-848-5000		468
Metropolitan Ceramics 1201 Millerton St SE *TF:* 800-325-3945 ■ *Web:* www.metroceramics.com	Canton	OH	44707	800-325-3945		751
Metropolitan Club Inc 1 E 60th St *Web:* metropolitanclubnyc.org	New York	NY	10022	212-838-7400	755-6849	378
Metropolitan College of New York 431 Canal St *Web:* www.mcny.edu	New York	NY	10013	212-343-1234	625-2072	166
Metropolitan Communication Services Inc 914 Palmetto Ave *TF:* 800-725-0025 ■ *Web:* www.metropolitancomm.com	Melbourne	FL	32901	321-723-9300	984-8278	393
Metropolitan Communications 309 Commerce Dr Ste 100 *Web:* www.mcsradio.com	Exton	PA	19341	610-363-5858		647
Metropolitan Community College PO Box 3777 *TF:* 800-228-9553 ■ *Web:* mccneb.edu	Omaha	NE	68103	531-622-2400		162

Phone | Fax | Class

Metropolitan Construction Services LLC (MCS)
2901 Butterfield Rd . . . Oak Brook IL 60523 630-691-7200 691-7234 685
Web: www.metroconstructionllc.com

Metropolitan Correctional Ctr
Chicago 71 W Van Buren St . . . Chicago IL 60605 312-322-0567 322-1120 212
Web: www.bop.gov
New York 150 Pk Row . . . New York NY 10007 646-836-6300 836-7751 212
Web: www.bop.gov

Metropolitan Glass Inc (MGI)
6400 Franklin St . . . Denver CO 80229 303-853-4527 288-4000 186
Web: metroglass.com

Metropolitan Grill
2931 E Battlefield . . . Springfield MO 65804 417-889-4951 671
Web: metropolitan-grill.com

Metropolitan Grill 820 Second Ave . . . Seattle WA 98104 206-624-3287 671
Web: www.themetropolitangrill.com

Metropolitan Halifax Chamber of Commerce
656 Windmill Rd Ste 200 . . . Dartmouth NS B3B1B8 902-468-7111 468-7333 137
Web: halifaxchamber.com

Metropolitan Hotel Vancouver
645 Howe St . . . Vancouver BC V6C2Y9 604-687-1122 379
Web: www.metropolitan.com

Metropolitan Institute of Design
200 Oak Dr . . . Syosset NY 11791 516-845-4033 364-7726 167-3
Web: www.met-design.com

Metropolitan Insurance Service Consultants Inc
5550 N Elston Ave . . . Chicago IL 60630 773-631-9595 390
Web: xmetropolitan.com

Metropolitan L Federal Credit Union
949 S Ridgeland Ave . . . Oak Park IL 60304 708-386-9272 386-9088 219
Web: metlfcu.com

Metropolitan Methodist Hospital
1310 McCullough Ave . . . San Antonio TX 78212 210-757-2200 374-3
TF: 800-553-6321 ■ *Web:* sahealth.com

Metropolitan Milwaukee Association of Commerce
756 N Milwaukee St . . . Milwaukee WI 53202 414-287-4100 271-7753 139
TF: 855-729-1300 ■ *Web:* www.mmac.org

Metropolitan Nashville Airport Authority
1 Terminal Dr Ste 501 . . . Nashville TN 37214 615-275-1675 27
Web: www.flynashville.com

Metropolitan Nashville Public Schools (MNPS)
2601 Bransford Ave . . . Nashville TN 37204 615-259-8531 214-8890 685
Web: www.mnps.org

Metropolitan Opera
30 Lincoln Center Plz . . . New York NY 10023 212-799-3100 573-2
Web: www.metopera.org

Metropolitan Plant & Flower Exchange
2125 Fletcher Ave . . . Fort Lee NJ 07024 201-944-1050 292
TF: 800-638-7613 ■ *Web:* www.metroplantexchange.com

Metropolitan Poultry & Seafood Co
1920 Stanford Ct . . . Landover Hills MD 20785 301-772-0060 772-1013 297-10
TF: 800-522-0060 ■ *Web:* www.metropoultry.com

Metropolitan School District of Wayne Township
1220 S High School Rd . . . Indianapolis IN 46241 317-988-8600 243-5744 685
Web: district.wayne.k12.in.us

Metropolitan Services Credit Union
475 Etna St Ste 10 . . . Saint Paul MN 55106 651-602-8105 602-8844 219
Web: mymscu.org

Metropolitan State College of Denver
890 Auraria Pkwy Ste 160 . . . Denver CO 80204 303-556-3991 778-5845* 166
**Fax Area Code:* 720 ■ *Web:* msudenver.edu

Metropolitan State Hospital
11401 Bloomfield Ave . . . Norwalk CA 90650 562-863-7011 374-5
Web: dsh.ca.gov

Metropolitan State University
700 E Seventh St . . . Saint Paul MN 55106 651-793-1300 793-1310 166
TF: 888-234-2690 ■ *Web:* www.metrostate.edu

Metropolitan Steel Industries Inc
601 Fritztown Rd . . . Reading PA 19608 610-678-6411 480
Web: www.metropolitan-steel.com

Metropolitan Theaters Corp
8727 W Third St . . . Los Angeles CA 90048 310-858-2800 748
Web: www.metrotheatres.com

Metropolitan Tickets Inc
531 N Grand Blvd . . . Saint Louis MO 63103 314-534-1111 775
Web: www.metrotix.com

Metropolitan Transit Authority of Harris County
1900 Maine . . . Houston TX 77002 713-658-0854 739-4096 468
Web: www.ridemetro.org

Metropolitan Vacuum Cleaner Company Inc
5 Raritan Rd . . . Oakland NJ 07436 845-357-1600 357-1640 788
TF: 800-822-1602 ■ *Web:* www.metrovacworld.com

Metropolitan Washington Airports Authority
1 Aviation Cir . . . Washington DC 20001 703-417-8000 27
Web: www.mwaa.com

Metropower 798 21st Ave . . . Albany GA 31701 229-432-7345 189-4
TF: 800-332-7345 ■ *Web:* www.metropower.com

MetroStage 1201 N Royal St . . . Alexandria VA 22314 703-548-9044 548-9089 572
TF: 800-494-8497 ■ *Web:* www.metrostage.org

MetroStar Systems Inc
1856 Old Reston Ave Ste 100 . . . Reston VA 20190 703-481-9581 177
Web: www.metrostarsystems.com

Metrovision Production Group LLC
130 Commerce Rd . . . Carlstadt NJ 07072 212-989-1515 738
TF: 800-242-2424 ■ *Web:* metrovision.tv

MetroWest Daily News
33 New York Ave . . . Framingham MA 01701 508-626-4412 626-4400 532-2
TF: 800-624-7355 ■ *Web:* www.metrowestdailynews.com

Metrowest Veterinary Associates Inc
207 E Main St . . . Milford MA 01757 508-478-7300 794
Web: mvavet.com

Metrus Group Inc 953 Rt 202 . . . Somerville NJ 08876 908-231-1900 463
Web: metrus.com

Met-scan Canada Ltd 30 Kern Rd Ste 104 . . . Toronto ON M3B1T1 416-391-2200 261
Web: met-scan.com

Metsch Refractories Inc
12413 Ohio River Blvd . . . Chester WV 26034 304-387-1067 387-0555 249
Web: www.metschinc.com

Phone | Fax | Class

Metso Corp 44 Bowditch Dr Ste 1545 . . . Shrewsbury MA 01545 508-852-0200 789
Web: www.metso.com

Metson Marine Inc
2060 Knoll Dr Ste 100 . . . Ventura CA 93003 805-658-2628 667
Web: www.metsonmarine.com

Metterra Hotel on Whyte
10454 82nd Ave . . . Edmonton AB T6E4Z7 780-465-8150 379
Web: www.metterra.com

Mettler Electronics Corp
1333 S Claudina St . . . Anaheim CA 92805 714-533-2221 635-7539 477
TF: 800-854-9305 ■ *Web:* www.mettlerelectronics.com

Mettler-Toledo International Inc
1900 Polaris Pkwy . . . Columbus OH 43240 614-438-4511 419
Web: www.mt.com

Metton America Inc
2727 Miller Cut-Off Rd . . . La Porte TX 77571 281-479-8078 479-4906 605-2
Web: www.metton.com

Metz Beverage Company Inc
376 W Heald St . . . Sheridan WY 82801 307-674-4818 81-2

Metzgar Conveyor Company Inc
901 Metzgar Dr NW . . . Comstock Park MI 49321 616-784-0930 784-4100 207
TF: 888-266-8390 ■ *Web:* www.metzgarconveyors.com

Metzger + Willard Inc
8600 Hidden River Pkwy Ste 550 . . . Tampa FL 33637 813-977-6005 261
Web: metzgerwillard.com

Metzger's German Restaurant
305 N Zeeb Rd . . . Ann Arbor MI 48103 734-668-8987 671
Web: www.metzgers.net

Meurer Research Inc 16133 W 45th Dr . . . Golden CO 80403 303-279-8373 279-8429 806
Web: www.meurerresearch.com

Meuser Daniel (Rep R - PA)
326 Cannon House Office Bldg . . . Washington DC 20515 202-225-6511 342-2
Web: www.meuser.house.gov

Meux Home Museum 1007 R St . . . Fresno CA 93721 559-233-8007 520
Web: meuxhomemuseum.org

Mevion Medical Systems Inc
300 Foster Sreet . . . Littleton MA 01460 978-540-1500 540-1501 723
TF: 855-463-8466 ■ *Web:* www.mevion.com

Mewbourne Oil Co PO Box 7698 . . . Tyler TX 75711 903-561-2900 561-1045 536
Web: mewbourne.net

Mews Restaurant & Cafe
429 Commercial St . . . Provincetown MA 02657 508-487-1500 487-3700 671
Web: mews.com

Mexco Energy Corp
214 W Texas Ave Ste 1101 PO Box 10502 . . . Midland TX 79701 432-682-1119 682-1123 536
NYSE: MXC ■ *Web:* www.mexcoenergy.com

MexGrocercom LLC
4060 Morena Blvd Ste C . . . San Diego CA 92117 858-270-0577 387
TF: 844-639-4762 ■ *Web:* www.mexgrocer.com

Mexicali Blues 2933 Wilson Blvd . . . Arlington VA 22201 703-812-9352 671
Web: www.mexicali-blues.com

Mexican American Legal Defense & Educational Fund (MALDEF)
634 S Spring St . . . Los Angeles CA 90014 213-629-2512 629-0266 48-14
Web: www.maldef.org

Mexican Museum
Fort Mason Ctr 2 Marina Blvd Bldg D . . . San Francisco CA 94123 415-202-9700 520
Web: www.mexicanmuseum.org

Mexican Post 3100 Naamans Rd . . . Wilmington DE 19810 302-478-3939 478-5599 671
Web: www.mexicanpost.com

Mexican Restaurants Inc
12000 Aerospace Ave Ste 400 . . . Houston TX 77034 713-943-7574 300-5859* 670
OTC: CASA ■ **Fax Area Code:* 832

Mexican Village 814 Main Ave . . . Fargo ND 58103 701-293-0120 671
Web: www.mexicanvillage.com

Mexican-American Opportunity Foundation (MAOF)
401 N Garfield Ave . . . Montebello CA 90640 323-890-9600 890-9637 48-14
Web: www.maof.org

Mexic-Arte Museum 419 Congress Ave . . . Austin TX 78701 512-480-9373 520
Web: www.mexic-artemuseum.org

Mexico 3810 Ventor Ave . . . Atlantic City NJ 08401 609-344-0366 671
Web: www.mexicorestaurantbar.com

Mexico
Consulate General 127 Navarro St . . . San Antonio TX 78205 210-227-9145 257
Web: consulmex.sre.gob.mx
Consulate General 800 Brazos St Ste 330 . . . Austin TX 78701 512-380-1030 478-8008 257
Web: consulmex.sre.gob.mxaustin
Consulate General
910 E San Antonio Ave . . . El Paso TX 79901 915-533-8555 532-7163 257
Web: www.sre.gob.mx
Consulate General 27 E 39th St . . . New York NY 10016 212-217-6400 257
Web: www.consulmexny.org
Consulate General of Mexico in Nogales
PO Box 1729 . . . Nogales AZ 85621 520-364-3142 287-3175 257
Web: www.gob.mx
Consulate of Mexico
5350 Leesdale Dr Ste 100 . . . Denver CO 80246 303-331-1110 331-0169 257
Web: consulmex.sre.gob.mxdenver
Embassy 1911 Pennsylvania Ave NW . . . Washington DC 20006 202-728-1600 257
Web: embamex.sre.gob.mx

Mexico Ledger, The 300 N Washington . . . Mexico MO 65265 573-581-1111 581-2029 532-2
Web: www.mexicoledger.com

Mexico Lindo 3635 Dutch Village Rd . . . Halifax NS B3N2S4 902-445-0996 671
Web: mexicolindo.ca

Mexico Plastics Company Inc
2000 W Blvd St . . . Mexico MO 65265 573-581-4128 581-8711 66
Web: www.continentalproducts.com

Mexico Tourism Board
4507 San Jacinto St . . . Houston TX 77004 713-772-2581 775
Web: www.visitmexico.com

Meydenbauer Ctr 11100 NE Sixth St . . . Bellevue WA 98004 425-637-1020 637-0166 205
Web: www.meydenbauer.com

Meyenberg PO Box 934 . . . Turlock CA 95381 800-891-4628 668-4977* 296-10
**Fax Area Code:* 209 ■ *TF:* 800-891-4628 ■ *Web:* meyenberg.com

Meyer & Najem Inc
11787 Lantern Rd Ste 100 . . . Fishers IN 46038 317-577-0007 577-0286 186
TF: 888-578-5131 ■ *Web:* www.meyer-najem.com

Meyer Associates Inc 14 7th Ave N . . . Saint Cloud MN 56303 320-259-4000 737

Company	Phone	Fax	Class
Meyer Brothers Building Company Inc 800 E 101st Terr Ste 120 Kansas City MO 64131 *Web:* www.meyerbro.com	816-246-4800		104
Meyer Corp 1 Meyer Pl Vallejo CA 94590 *TF:* 800-888-3883 ■ *Web:* www.meyer.com	707-551-2800	551-2953	486
Meyer Crest Ltd 725 Folger Ave Berkeley CA 94710 *Web:* www.meyercrest.com	510-845-1077		379
Meyer Gallery 225 Canyon Rd Ste 14 Santa Fe NM 87501 *TF:* 800-779-7387 ■ *Web:* www.meyergalleries.com	505-983-1434	988-5170	42
Meyer Jabara Hotels 1601 Belvedere Rd Ste 407 S West Palm Beach FL 33406 *Web:* www.meyerjabarahotels.com	561-689-6602	689-4363	379
Meyer Manufacturing Corp County Hwy A W 574 W Center Ave PO Box 405 Dorchester WI 54425 *Web:* meyermfg.com	715-654-5132		273
Meyer May House 450 Madison Ave SE Grand Rapids MI 49503 *Web:* meyermayhouse.steelcase.com	616-246-4821		50-3
Meyer Memorial Trust 425 NW Tenth Ave Ste 400 Portland OR 97209 *Web:* mmt.org	503-228-5512		305
Meyer Plastics Inc 5167 E 65th St Indianapolis IN 46220 *TF:* 800-968-4131 ■ *Web:* www.meyerplastics.com	317-259-4131		602
Meyer Products LLC 18513 Euclid Ave Cleveland OH 44112 *Web:* www.meyerproducts.com	216-486-1313	486-1321	190
Meyer Sound Laboratories Inc 2832 San Pablo Ave Berkeley CA 94702 *TF:* 866-773-1096 ■ *Web:* meyersound.com	510-486-1166	486-8356	52
Meyer Tool Inc 3055 Colerain Ave Cincinnati OH 45225 *Web:* www.meyertool.com	513-853-4400		454
Meyer Truck Equipment 196 W State Rd 56 Jasper IN 47546 *Web:* www.meyertruckeq.com	812-695-3451		516
Meyer Unkovic & Scott LLP 535 Smithfield St Ste 1300 Pittsburgh PA 15222 *Web:* muslaw.com	412-456-2800	456-2864	428
Meyercord Revenue Inc 475 Village Dr Carol Stream IL 60188 *Web:* meyercord.com	630-682-6200		627
Meyers Fozi & Dwork LLP 1808 Aston Ave Ste 100 Carlsbad CA 92008 *Web:* meyersfozi.com	760-444-0039		41
Meyers Printing Companies Inc, The 7277 Boone Ave N Minneapolis MN 55428 *Web:* www.meyers.com	763-533-9730		627
Meyocks Group Inc, The 6800 Lake Dr Ste 150 West Des Moines IA 50266 *Web:* www.meyocks.com	515-225-1200		7
Meziere Enterprises Inc 220 S Hale Ave Escondido CA 92029 *TF:* 800-208-1755 ■ *Web:* www.meziere.com	760-746-3273		481
Mezzanotte Bistro 50 Murray St Ottawa ON K1N9M5 *Web:* www.mezzanottebistro.com	613-562-3978		671
MF Digital 155 Sherwood Ave East Farmingdale NY 11735 *TF:* 800-645-8461 ■ *Web:* www.mfdigital.com	631-249-9393	249-9273	240
MFA (Maryland Federation of Art Cir Gallery) 18 State Cir Annapolis MD 21401 *Web:* mdfedart.com	410-268-4566		50-2
MFA (Masa Fujioka and Associates) 98-021 Kamehameha Hwy Ste 337 Aiea HI 96701 *Web:* www.masa-fujioka-associates.com	808-484-5366	484-0007	192
MFA Financial Inc 350 Park Ave 20th Fl New York NY 10022 *Web:* www.mfafinancial.com	212-207-6400	207-6420	654
MFA Inc 201 Ray Young Dr Columbia MO 65201 *Web:* mfa-inc.com	573-874-5111		276
MFA Oil Co 1 Ray Young Dr PO Box 519 Columbia MO 65201 *TF:* 800-366-0200 ■ *Web:* www.mfaoil.com	573-442-0171		581
MFA Publications 465 Huntington Ave Boston MA 02115 *Web:* www.mfashop.com	617-369-4285		637-2
MFC (Metal Forming & Coining Corp) 1007 Illinois Ave Maumee OH 43537 *Web:* www.mfccorp.com	419-893-8748		483
MFJ Enterprises Inc 300 Industrial Park Rd Starkville MS 39759 *TF:* 800-647-1800 ■ *Web:* www.mfjenterprises.com	662-323-5869	323-6551	647
MFLEX (Multi-Fineline Electronix Inc) 8659 Research Dr Irvine CA 92618 *NASDAQ: MFLX* ■ *Web:* www.mflex.com	949-453-6800		253
MFM (Media Financial Management Assn) 550 W Frontage Rd Ste 3600 Northfield IL 60093 *Web:* www.mediafinance.org	847-716-7000	716-7004	49-14
MFour Mobile Research Inc 19800 MacArthur Blvd Ste 700 Irvine CA 92612 *Web:* mfour.com	714-754-1234		224
MFR Consultants Inc 128 Chestnut St Philadelphia PA 19106 *Web:* mfrconsultants.com	215-238-9270	238-9733	195
MFS (Monadnock Family Services) 64 Main St Keene NH 03431 *Web:* www.mfs.org	603-357-4400		726
MFS Investment Management 111 Huntington Ave Boston MA 02199 *TF:* 800-637-8255 ■ *Web:* www.mfs.com	617-954-5000	954-6621	401
MFX Solutions Inc 1050 17th St NW Ste 550 Washington DC 20036 *Web:* www.mfxsolutions.com	202-527-9947		401
MG Design Associates Corp 8778 100th St Pleasant Prairie WI 53158 *Web:* www.mgdesign.com	262-947-8890		232
MG Machining 1505 Industrial Ave Bedford IA 50833 *Web:* www.mgmachining.com	712-523-2840	523-2959	493
MG Mechanical Contracting Inc 1513 Lamb Rd Woodstock IL 60098 *Web:* www.mgmechanical.com	815-334-9450		610
MG Oil Inc 1180 Creek Dr Rapid City SD 57703 *TF:* 800-333-5173 ■ *Web:* mgoil.com	605-342-0527	341-1899	579
MG Scientific Inc 8500 107th St Pleasant Prairie WI 53158 *TF:* 800-343-8338 ■ *Web:* www.mgscientific.com	262-947-7000		535
MG2A (M Gingerich Gereaux & Assoc) 240 N Industrial Dr Bradley IL 60915 *Web:* www.mg2a.com	815-939-4921		261
MGA Entertainment Inc 16300 Roscoe Blvd Ste 150 Van Nuys CA 91406 *TF:* 800-222-4685 ■ *Web:* www.mgae.com	818-894-2525		761
MGBW (Mitchell Gold & Bob Williams Co) 135 One Comfortable Pl Taylorsville NC 28681 *TF:* 800-789-5401 ■ *Web:* www.mgbwhome.com	828-632-9200	632-2693	319-2
MGCC (Massachusetts Growth Capital Corp) 529 Main St Schrafft Ctr Ste 1M10 Charlestown MA 02129 *Web:* www.massgcc.com	617-523-6262	523-7676	792
MGCCI (Morton Grove Chamber of Commerce and Industry) 6101 Capulina Ave Morton Grove IL 60053 *Web:* www.mgcci.org	847-965-0330	965-0349	139
MGE (Mohegan Gaming & Entertainment) 1 Mohegan Sun Blvd Uncasville CT 06382 *TF:* 888-777-7922 ■ *Web:* mohegangaming.com	888-226-7711		322
MGE Engineering Inc 7415 Greenhaven Dr Sacramento CA 95831 *Web:* www.mgeeng.com	916-421-1000		261
MGH (Marion General Hospital) 441 N Wabash Ave Marion IN 46952 *Web:* www.mgh.net	765-660-6000	651-7351	374-3
MGH Adv Inc 100 Painters Mill Rd Ste 600 Owings Mills MD 21117 *Web:* www.mghus.com	410-902-5000		4
MGH Institute of Health Professions Inc 36 First Ave Boston MA 02129 *Web:* www.mghihp.edu	617-726-2947		166
MGI (Metropolitan Glass Inc) 6400 Franklin St Denver CO 80229 *Web:* metroglass.com	303-853-4527	288-4000	186
MGM (Metro-Goldwyn-Mayer Studios Inc) 245 N Beverly Dr Beverly Hills CA 90210 *Web:* mgm.com	310-449-3000		514
MGM Grand Detroit 1777 3rd St Detroit MI 48226 *TF:* 877-888-2121 ■ *Web:* www.mgmgranddetroit.com	313-465-1400		133
MGM Hotels Bellagio Hotel & Casino 3600 S Las Vegas Blvd Las Vegas NV 89109 *TF:* 855-788-6775 ■ *Web:* www.mgmresorts.com	855-788-6775		379
MGM Industries Inc 287 Freehill Rd Hendersonville TN 37075 *TF:* 800-476-5584 ■ *Web:* www.mgmindustries.com	615-824-6572		390
MGM Resorts Intl 3770 Las Vegas Blvd S Las Vegas NV 89109 *TF:* 800-311-8999 ■ *Web:* parkmgm.mgmresorts.com	702-730-7777	730-7200	669
MGM Transformer Co 5701 Smithway St Commerce CA 90040 *TF:* 800-423-4366 ■ *Web:* www.mgmtransformer.com	323-726-0888	726-8224	767
MGMA (Medical Group Management Assn) 104 Inverness Terr E Englewood CO 80112 *Web:* www.mgma.com	303-799-1111		49-8
MGMC (MaineGeneral Medical Ctr) *Augusta* 361 Old Belgrade Rd Augusta ME 04330 *TF:* 855-464-4463 ■ *Web:* www.mainegeneral.org	207-621-6100		374-3
MGP (Museum of the Great Plains) 601 NW Ferris Ave Lawton OK 73507 *Web:* www.discovermgp.org	580-581-3460		637-2
MGP Ingredients Inc 100 Commercial St PO Box 130 Atchison KS 66002 *NASDAQ: MGPI* ■ *TF:* 800-255-0302 ■ *Web:* www.mgpingredients.com	913-367-1480	367-0192	296-23
MGQ & Associates Inc 3104 N Armenia Ave Ste 4 Tampa FL 33607 *Web:* www.mgqassociates.com	813-877-8895		186
MGS Inc 178 Muddy Creek Church Rd Denver PA 17517 **Fax Area Code:* 717 ■ *TF:* 800-952-4228 ■ *Web:* www.mgsincorporated.com	800-952-4228	336-0514*	91
MGS Machine Corp 9900 85th Ave N Maple Grove MN 55369 *Web:* www.mgsmachine.com	763-425-8808		547
MGS Services LLC 18775 N Frederick Ave Ste 205 Gaithersburg MD 20879 *TF:* 877-647-4255 ■ *Web:* www.mgsservices.com	301-330-9793	330-9792	539
MGT of America Consulting LLC 516 N Adams St Tallahassee FL 32301 *Web:* www.mgtconsulting.com	850-386-3191	385-4501	194
MH (Milford Hospital) 300 Seaside Ave Milford CT 06460 *Web:* www.milfordhospital.org	203-876-4000	876-4220	374-3
MH (Michael Halebian & Company Inc) 557 Washington Ave Carlstadt NJ 07072 **Fax Area Code:* 201 ■ *TF:* 800-631-4115 ■ *Web:* www.michaelhalebian.com	800-631-4115	460-1138*	290
MH EBY 1194 Main St PO Box 127 Blue Ball PA 17506 *TF:* 800-292-4752 ■ *Web:* www.mheby.com	717-354-4971	355-2114	516
MH Engineering Co 16075 Vineyard Blvd Morgan Hill CA 95037 *Web:* mhengineering.com	408-779-7381		261
MH Professional Engineering PLLC 5 Corporate Dr Clifton Park NY 12065 *Web:* mhproengineering.com	518-280-6522		261
MHA (Mental Health America) 2000 N Beauregard St 6th Fl Alexandria VA 22311 *TF:* 800-969-6642 ■ *Web:* www.mentalhealthamerica.net	703-684-7722	684-5968	48-17
MHA an Association of Montana Health Care Providers 2625 Winne Ave Helena MT 59601 *TF:* 800-351-3551 ■ *Web:* mtha.org	406-442-1911		533
MHAFC (Mental Health America of Franklin County) 2323 W 5th Ave Ste 160 Columbus OH 43204 *Web:* mhafc.org	614-221-1441	221-1491	48-6
Mhart Express Inc PO Box 192 Hope IN 47246 *TF:* 800-457-7441 ■ *Web:* www.mhartexpress.com	812-546-5010	546-0404	780
MHC (Methodist Hospital of Chicago) 5025 N Paulina St Chicago IL 60640 *Web:* www.methodistchicago.org	773-271-9040		374-3
MHC (Michigan Humanities Council) 119 Pere Marquette Ste 3B Lansing MI 48912 *Web:* www.michiganhumanities.org	517-372-7770	372-0027	48-13

Name / Address	City	State	ZIP	Phone	Fax	Class
MHC Engineers Inc 150 Eighth St *Web:* mhcengr.com	San Francisco	CA	94103	415-512-7141	512-7120	261
MHC Kenworth 1524 N Corrington Ave *TF:* 888-259-4826 ■ *Web:* mhc.com	Kansas City	MO	64120	816-483-7035		778
MHD Enterprises 9715 Burnet Rd Ste 125 *Web:* www.mhdenterprises.com	Austin	TX	78758	512-992-2565		449
Mhd-Rockland Inc 2111 Baldwin Ave Ste 8 **Fax Area Code:* 443 ■ *Web:* www.mhdrockland.com	Crofton	MD	21114	410-451-0969	292-4093*	20
MHEDA (Material Handling Equipment Distributors Assn) 201 US Hwy 45 *Web:* www.mheda.org	Vernon Hills	IL	60061	847-680-3500	362-6989	49-13
Mhelpdesk Inc 3040 Williams Dr Ste 550 *TF:* 888-558-6275 ■ *Web:* mhelpdesk.com	Fairfax	VA	22031	888-558-6275		180
MHEP (Mennonite Historians of Eastern Pennsylvania) 565 Yoder Rd *Web:* www.mhep.org	Harleysville	PA	19438	215-256-3020		520
MHF Inc 2328 Evans City Rd *Web:* mhftrans.com	Zelienople	PA	16063	724-452-3900		311
MHG (MHG Hotels) 1220 Brookville Way *Web:* www.mhghotelsllc.com	Indianapolis	IN	46239	317-356-4000	356-4004	463
MHG Hotels (MHG) 1220 Brookville Way *Web:* www.mhghotelsllc.com	Indianapolis	IN	46239	317-356-4000	356-4004	463
MHI (Manufactured Housing Institute) 1655 Fort Myer Dr *Web:* www.manufacturedhousing.org	Arlington	VA	22209	703-236-2300	558-0401	49-3
MHI (Marine Hydraulics International Inc) 543 E Indian River Rd *Web:* www.mhi-shiprepair.com	Norfolk	VA	23523	757-545-6400	545-8169	698
MHI (McGuyer Homebuilders Inc) 7676 Woodway Ste 104 *Web:* www.mcguyerhomebuilders.com	Houston	TX	77063	713-952-6767	952-5637	653
MHM Services Inc 1593 Spring Hill Rd Ste 600 *TF:* 800-416-3649 ■ *Web:* www.mhm-services.com	Vienna	VA	22182	703-749-4600	749-4604	463
MHMC (Mercy Hospital & Medical Ctr) 2525 S Michigan Ave *Web:* www.mercy-chicago.org	Chicago	IL	60616	312-567-2000		374-3
MHP (Madison Heights-Hazel Park Chamber of Commerce) 939 E 12 Mile Rd *Web:* www.madisonheightschamber.com	Madison Heights	MI	48071	248-542-5010		139
MHP (Memorial Hospital Pembroke) 7800 Sheridan St *Web:* www.mhs.net	Pembroke Pines	FL	33024	954-962-9650		374-3
MHPS (Mitsubishi Hitachi Power Systems Americas Inc) 400 Colonial Center Pkwy **Fax Area Code:* 140 ■ *TF:* 800-445-9723 ■ *Web:* amer.mhps.com	Lake Mary	FL	32746	407-688-6100	768-8648*	536
MHR (McCabe Hamilton & Renny Company Ltd) 521 Ala Moana Blvd Ste M-311 *Web:* www.mhrhawaii.com	Honolulu	HI	96813	808-524-3255	545-3101	465
MHRI (Memorial Hospital of Rhode Island) 111 Brewster St *TF:* 800-647-4362 ■ *Web:* www.mhri.org	Pawtucket	RI	02860	401-729-2000		374-3
MHTC (Mount Horeb Telephone Co) 200 E Main St *Web:* www.mhtc.net	Mount Horeb	WI	53572	608-437-5551	437-8898	224
mHUB 965 W Chicago Ave *Web:* mhubchicago.com	Chicago	IL	60642	312-248-8701		393
MHW Ltd 1129 Northern Blvd Ste 312 *Web:* mhwltd.com	Manhasset	NY	11030	516-869-9170		80-3
Mi Casita Mexican Grill 3600 Bonney Rd *Web:* www.micasitamexicangrill.com	Virginia Beach	VA	23452	757-463-3819		671
Mi Nidito Restaurant 1813 S 4th Ave *Web:* www.miniditorestaurant.com	Tucson	AZ	85713	520-622-5081		671
Mi Pueblo Mexican Restaurant 2419 W Jefferson Blvd *Web:* mipueblofortwayne.com	Fort Wayne	IN	46802	260-432-6462		671
Mi Ranchito Cafe 425 S Center St *Web:* mi-ranchito-cafe.local-cafes.com	Stockton	CA	95203	209-946-9257		671
Mi Tierra Mexican Restaurant 27 Mellichamp Dr Unit 101 *Web:* www.mitierrabluffton.com	Bluffton	SC	29910	843-757-7200		671
MI Windows & Doors LLC 650 W Market St *Web:* miwindows.com	Gratz	PA	17030	717-365-3300		234
Mi9 Retail 12000 Biscayne Blvd Ste 600 *TF:* 888-326-8579 ■ *Web:* mi9retail.com	Miami	FL	33181	786-577-3200		177
Miami Ad School 1414 Van Ness Ave *Web:* www.miamiadschool.com	San Francisco	CA	94109	305-538-3193		685
Miami Ad School Portfolio Ctr 125 Bennett St *Web:* www.portfoliocenter.edu	Atlanta	GA	30309	404-351-5055		167-3
Miami Air International Inc 5000 NW 36 St Ste 307 *Web:* www.miamiair.com	Miami	FL	33122	305-876-3600		13
Miami Beach Botanical Garden 2000 Convention Center Dr *Web:* www.mbgarden.org	Miami Beach	FL	33139	305-673-7256		97
Miami Beach Chamber of Commerce 1920 Meridian Ave *TF:* 800-501-0401 ■ *Web:* www.miamibeachchamber.com	Miami Beach	FL	33139	305-674-1300	538-4336	139
Miami Beach Convention Ctr 1901 Convention Center Dr **Fax Area Code:* 305 ■ *Web:* www.miamibeachconvention.com	Miami Beach	FL	33139	786-276-2600	673-7435*	205
Miami Beef Company Inc 4870 NW 157th St *TF:* 888-551-2333 ■ *Web:* www.miamibeef.com	Miami Lakes	FL	33014	305-621-3252	620-4562	297-6
Miami Book Fair Intl (MBFI) 300 NE Second Ave *Web:* www.miamibookfair.com	Miami	FL	33132	305-237-3258		281
Miami Children's Hospital 3100 SW 62nd Ave *TF:* 800-432-6837 ■ *Web:* www.nicklauschildrens.org	Miami	FL	33155	305-666-6511	663-8466	374-1
Miami Children's Museum 980 MacArthur Cswy *Web:* www.miamichildrensmuseum.org	Miami	FL	33132	305-373-5437		521
Miami City Ballet 2200 Liberty Ave *TF:* 877-929-7010 ■ *Web:* www.miamicityballet.org	Miami Beach	FL	33139	305-929-7000		573-1
Miami City Hall 3500 Pan American Dr *Web:* www.ci.miami.fl.us	Miami	FL	33133	305-416-2037	250-5410	337
Miami Corp, The 720 Anderson Ferry Rd *TF:* 800-543-0448 ■ *Web:* www.miamicorp.com	Cincinnati	OH	45238	513-451-6700		594
Miami Correctional Facility 3038 W 850 S *TF:* 800-451-6028 ■ *Web:* www.in.gov	Bunker Hill	IN	46914	765-689-8920	689-7479	213
Miami County 201 S Pearl St Ste 102 *Web:* www.miamicountyks.org	Paola	KS	66071	913-294-3976	294-9544	338
Miami County 25 N Broadway *Web:* miamicountyin.gov	Peru	IN	46970	765-472-3901	472-1778	338
Miami County 201 W Main St *Web:* www.co.miami.oh.us	Troy	OH	45373	937-335-1920	440-3530	338
Miami County Chamber of Commerce 13 E Main St *TF:* 800-521-9945 ■ *Web:* www.miamicochamber.com	Peru	IN	46970	765-472-1923	472-7099	139
Miami Dade College *Kendall* 11011 SW 104th St *Web:* www.mdc.edu	Miami	FL	33176	305-237-2767		162
Miami Direct Inc 3470 NW 82nd Ave Ste 650 *Web:* www.gbm.net	Doral	FL	33122	305-597-3998		317
Miami Dolphins 7500 SW 30th St *Web:* www.miamidolphins.com	Davie	FL	33314	305-943-8000		715-3
Miami Federal Credit Union 51 SW 1st Ave Ste 604 *Web:* miamifcu.org	Miami	FL	33130	305-377-1017		219
Miami Film Festival 300 NE Second Ave *Web:* miamifilmfestival.com	Miami	FL	33132	305-237-3456		282
Miami Heart Institute 4770 Biscayne Blvd Ste 500 *Web:* www.msmc.com	Miami Beach	FL	33140	305-672-1111		374-7
Miami Industrial Trucks Inc 2830 E River Rd *Web:* www.mitlift.com	Dayton	OH	45439	937-293-4194		358
Miami Innovation Center for Entrepreneurship 1951 NW 7th Ave Ste 600 *TF:* 800-384-3730 ■ *Web:* www.startup-miami.com	Miami	FL	33136	305-782-7887		48-13
Miami International Airport 4200 NW 36th St 4th Fl *TF:* 800-825-5642 ■ *Web:* www.miami-airport.com	Miami	FL	33166	305-876-7000	876-8077	27
Miami International Airport Hotel NW 20th St & Le Jeune Rd *TF:* 800-327-1276 ■ *Web:* usmia2.webhotel.microsdc.us	Miami	FL	33122	305-871-4100	871-0800	379
Miami Jacobs Career College 150 Gay St *TF:* 866-865-8067 ■ *Web:* www.miamijacobs.edu	Columbus	OH	43215	614-360-9320		167-3
Miami Law LLC 150 SE 2nd Ave Ste 1000 10th Fl *TF:* 866-438-6574 ■ *Web:* www.themiamilaw.com	Miami	FL	33131	305-590-8909	415-9920	41
Miami Machine Corp 4251 Riverside Dr *Web:* www.miamimachine.com	Overpeck	OH	45055	513-863-6707		821
Miami Nation Enterprises 3531 P St NW *Web:* www.mn-e.com	Miami	OK	74354	918-541-2100	542-3967	615
Miami New Times 2800 Biscayne Blvd *Web:* www.miaminewtimes.com	Miami	FL	33137	305-576-8000	571-7677	532-5
Miami Parking System 190 NE Third St *Web:* www.miamiparking.com	Miami	FL	33132	305-373-6789		562
Miami Project to Cure Paralysis Lois Pope LIFE Ctr 1095 NW 14th Terr *Web:* www.themiamiproject.org	Miami	FL	33136	305-243-6001	243-6017	668
Miami Seaquarium 4400 Rickenbacker Cswy *Web:* www.miamiseaquarium.com	Miami	FL	33149	305-361-5705	361-6077	40
Miami Symphony Orchestra, The (MISO) 3900 N Miami Ave Ste 307 *Web:* themiso.org	Miami	FL	33127	305-275-5666		573-3
Miami Tape Inc 6200 W 21st Ct *TF:* 866-642-6482 ■ *Web:* www.miami-tape.com	Hialeah	FL	33016	305-558-9211		657
Miami Today 2000 S Dixie Hwy Ste 100 *Web:* www.miamitodaynews.com	Miami	FL	33133	305-358-2663	358-4811	532-4
Miami University 501 E High St *TF:* 866-426-4643 ■ *Web:* miamioh.edu	Oxford	OH	45056	513-529-3600	529-1550	166
Middletown 4200 N University Blvd *Web:* www.mid.muohio.edu	Middletown	OH	45042	513-727-3200		166
Miami University Press Miami University 356 Bachelor Hall *Web:* www.orgs.muohio.edu	Oxford	OH	45056	513-529-2602		637-2
Miami Valley Child Development Centers 215 Horace St *Web:* mvcdc.org	Dayton	OH	45402	937-226-5664		148
Miami Valley Family Care Ctr 922 W Riverview Ave *Web:* cssmv.org	Dayton	OH	45402	937-223-7217		726
Miami Valley Hospital 1 Wyoming St *TF:* 800-544-0630 ■ *Web:* www.miamivalleyhospital.org	Dayton	OH	45409	937-208-8000		374-3
Miami Valley Steel Service Inc 201 Fox Dr *Web:* www.miamivalleysteel.com	Piqua	OH	45356	937-773-7127		492
Miami-Cass County Rural Electric Membership Corp 3086 W 100 N PO Box 168 *TF:* 800-844-6668 ■ *Web:* mcremc.coop	Peru	IN	46970	765-473-6668		245
Miami-Dade Chamber of Commerce 100 S Biscayne Blvd 3rd Fl *Web:* m-dcc.org	Miami	FL	33131	305-751-8648	758-3839	139
Miami-Dade County 111 NW First St Ste 220 *Web:* www.miamidade.gov	Miami	FL	33128	305-375-5218		338
Miami-Dade County Auditorium 2901 W Flagler St *Web:* www.miamidadecountyauditorium.org	Miami	FL	33135	305-547-5414		572

Name / Address	City	State	ZIP	Phone	Fax	Class
Miami-Dade County Public Schools (M-DCPS) 1450 NE Second Ave *TF:* 800-955-5504 ■ *Web:* www.dadeschools.net	Miami	FL	33132	305-995-1000		685
Miami-Dade Transit (MDTA) 701 NW First Ct. **Fax Area Code:* 786 ■ *Web:* www.miamidade.gov	Miami	FL	33136	305-468-5402	469-5580*	468
MIAT College of Technology 2955 S Haggerty Rd *TF:* 800-447-1310 ■ *Web:* www.miat.edu	Canton	MI	48188	800-447-1310		167-3
MIB Inc 50 Braintree Hill Pk *Web:* www.mib.com	Braintree	MA	02184	781-751-6000		225
Miba Coatings US LLC 5045 N State Rte 60 *Web:* www.miba.com	Mcconnelsville	OH	43756	740-962-4242		247
Mibor Realtor Association Inc 1912 N Meridian St *Web:* mibor.com	Indianapolis	IN	46202	317-956-1912		653
MIBRO Group 111 Sinnott Rd. *TF:* 866-941-9006 ■ *Web:* mibro.com	Toronto	ON	M1L4S6	416-285-9000		758
MIC (Micro Instrument Corp) 1199 Emerson St PO Box 60619 *TF:* 800-200-3150 ■ *Web:* www.microinst.com	Rochester	NY	14606	585-458-3150		454
MIC (Motorcycle Industry Council) 2 Jenner St Ste 150 *Web:* www.mic.org	Irvine	CA	92618	949-727-4211	727-3313	49-21
MIC (Media Information Services Inc) 350 5th Ave Ste 4200 *Web:* welcome.misnyc.com	New York	NY	10118	212-329-2200		393
Mic Industries Inc 11911 Freedom Dr *Web:* www.micindustries.com	Reston	VA	20190	703-318-1900		190
Mic Mac Mall 21 MicMac Blvd *TF:* 800-998-6844 ■ *Web:* www.micmacmall.com	Dartmouth	NS	B3A4N3	902-463-5891	469-5268	460
MIC Services Insurance 170 Kinnelon Rd Ste 26 *Web:* micinsurance.com	Kinnelon	NJ	07405	973-492-2828		390
MICA (Mortgage Insurance Companies of America) 1101 17th St NW Ste 700 *Web:* www.usmi.org	Washington	DC	20036	202-280-1820		49-9
Mica Corp 5750 N Riverside Dr *Web:* www.micacorporation.com	Fort Worth	TX	76137	817-847-6121	847-6831	188-4
Micanopy Historical Society Library and Archives 607 Cholakka Blvd *Web:* www.afn.org	Micanopy	FL	32667	352-466-3848		434-3
Micato Safaris 15 W 26th St 11th Fl *TF:* 800-642-2861 ■ *Web:* www.micato.com	New York	NY	10010	212-545-7111	545-8297	760
Mice Groups Inc, The 1730 S Amphlett Blvd Ste 100 *Web:* www.micegroups.com	San Mateo	CA	94402	650-655-4800		193
Miceli Dairy Products 2721 E 90th St *Web:* www.miceli-dairy.com	Cleveland	OH	44104	216-791-6222		296-5
Michael A. Starr Insurance Inc 1113B Kennebec Dr *Web:* insurewithstarr.com	Chambersburg	PA	17201	717-263-1752		390
Michael Allen Co 9 Old Kings Hwy S *Web:* www.michaelallencompany.com	Darien	CT	06820	203-662-5100		195
Michael Angelo's Gourmet Foods Inc 200 Michael Angelo Way *TF:* 877-482-5426 ■ *Web:* www.michaelangelos.com	Austin	TX	78728	512-218-3500		296-36
Michael Anthony's Cucina Italiana 37 New Orleans Rd Ste L *Web:* www.michael-anthonys.com	Hilton Head Island	SC	29928	843-785-6272		671
Michael B. Cohen & Assoc 12201 Merit Dr Ste 230 *Web:* dallaselderlawyer.com	Dallas	TX	75251	214-720-0102		41
Michael B. Feinman 69 Park St *Web:* feinmanlaw.com	Andover	MA	01810	978-475-0080		41
Michael Best & Friedrich LLP 100 E Wisconsin Ave Ste 3300 *Web:* www.michaelbest.com	Milwaukee	WI	53202	414-271-6560		41
Michael Bossy Group 252 James St *TF:* 888-522-2231 ■ *Web:* www.bnggroup.ca	Delhi	ON	N4B2B2	519-582-1260		2
Michael Brandman Assoc 220 Commerce Ste 200 *TF:* 888-826-5814 ■ *Web:* www.firstcarbonsolutions.com	Irvine	CA	92602	714-508-4100		196
Michael C. Carlos Museum 571 S Kilgo St *Web:* www.carlos.emory.edu	Atlanta	GA	30322	404-727-4282	727-4292	520
Michael C. Kim & Assoc 19 S Lasalle St Ste 303 *Web:* mkimlaw.com	Chicago	IL	60603	312-419-4000		41
Michael Critchley & Assoc 75 Livingston Ave *Web:* critchleylaw.com	Roseland	NJ	07068	973-422-9200		41
Michael D. Hooker 25 Main St Ste 439 *Web:* elderlawservice.com	Northampton	MA	01060	413-582-0200		41
Michael D. Lyman 3703 Hunter Valley Dr *Web:* www.policeexpert.net	Columbia	MO	65203	573-268-4224		196
Michael D. Mannis & Assoc 180 N Wacker Dr Ste 201 *Web:* mannis.com	Chicago	IL	60606	312-704-4300		41
Michael D. Tannenbaum 2161 Palm Beach Lakes Blvd Ste 304 *Web:* mdtlawoffice.com	West Palm Beach	FL	33409	561-471-1406	683-7551	41
Michael Day Enterprises PO Box 151 *Web:* www.mdayinc.com	Wadsworth	OH	44282	330-335-5100		605-2
Michael F. Evers Fund Raising 252 2nd St *Web:* drumlish.wordpress.com	Hoboken	NJ	07030	201-659-5700		192
Michael Foods Inc 301 Carlson Pkwy Ste 400 *TF:* 800-328-5474 ■ *Web:* michaelfoods.com	Minnetonka	MN	55305	952-258-4000		619
Michael G. Berger 250 Park Ave 20th Fl *Web:* mgberger.com	New York	NY	10177	212-983-6000		41
Michael G. Malaier *Chapter 13 Trustee* 2122 Commerce St *Web:* chapter13tacoma.org	Tacoma	WA	98402	253-572-6600		41
Michael Gibson Gallery 157 Carling St *TF:* 866-644-2766 ■ *Web:* gibsongallery.com	London	ON	N6A1H5	519-439-0451		42
Michael Graham 813 Gravel Pk *Web:* mgrahaminsurance.com	Collegeville	PA	19426	610-287-6161	287-0727	390
Michael Halebian & Company Inc (MH) 557 Washington Ave **Fax Area Code:* 201 ■ *TF:* 800-631-4115 ■ *Web:* www.michaelhalebian.com	Carlstadt	NJ	07072	800-631-4115	460-1138*	290
Michael I. Flores Pc 12 Main St PO Box 1056 *Web:* miflorespc.com	Orleans	MA	02653	508-240-1115		41
Michael J. Bloom PC 100 N Stone Ave Ste 701 *Web:* michaeljbloom.net	Tucson	AZ	85701	520-882-9904		41
Michael J. Fox Foundation for Parkinson's Research Grand Central Stn PO Box 4777 *TF:* 800-708-7644 ■ *Web:* www.michaeljfox.org	New York	NY	10163	800-708-7644		305
Michael J. Liccar & Co 231 S La Salle St *TF:* 800-922-6604 ■ *Web:* www.liccar.com	Chicago	IL	60604	312-922-6600	922-0315	2
Michael J. O'Connor & Associates LLC 608 W Oak St *TF:* 800-518-4529 ■ *Web:* www.oconnorlaw.com	Frackville	PA	17931	570-874-3300		445
Michael K. Allen & Assoc 810 Sycamore St 5th Fl *Web:* mkallenlaw.com	Cincinnati	OH	45202	513-823-4224	914-4901	41
Michael Kors 11 W 42nd St *Web:* www.michaelkors.com	New York	NY	10036	212-201-8100		277
Michael Lewis Co 8900 W 50th St *Web:* www.mlco.com	McCook	IL	60525	708-688-2200	688-2880	86
Michael P. Bush 1293 Broad St *Web:* michaelbushinsurance.com	Bloomfield	NJ	07003	973-338-6420		390
Michael P. Callahan Insurance Agency Inc 5372 N Milwaukee Ave *Web:* callahanagency.com	Chicago	IL	60630	773-775-1880		390
Michael P. Mazza LLC 686 Crescent Blvd *Web:* mazzallc.com	Glen Ellyn	IL	60137	630-858-5071		41
Michael R. Rubenstein & Assoc 12527 New Brittany Blvd *TF:* 888-616-1222 ■ *Web:* www.mrubensteincpa.com	Fort Myers	FL	33907	239-489-4443		2
Michael Raiser Associates Inc 500 Valley Rd Ste 106 *Web:* teammra.com	Wayne	NJ	07470	973-305-0011		463
Michael Ramey & Associates Inc PO Box 744 *TF:* 800-321-0505 ■ *Web:* www.rameypi.com	Danville	CA	94526	800-321-0505		400
Michael Rosenfeld Gallery 100 Eleventh Ave *Web:* www.michaelrosenfeldart.com	New York	NY	10011	212-247-0082	247-0402	42
Michael Simon Inc 250 W 39th St Ste 202 *Web:* www.michaelsimon.com	New York	NY	10018	212-382-1910		157-4
Michael Taylor Collections Inc 12020 Woodruff Ave Ste E **Fax Area Code:* 415 ■ *Web:* www.michaeltaylordesigns.com	Downey	CA	90241	323-838-7810	934-9404*	321
Michael W. Middleton PC (MWMPC) 3330 Longmire Dr *Web:* mwmpc.com	College Station	TX	77845	979-695-2726	695-2754	787
Michael Weining Inc 124 Crosslake Park Dr PO Box 3158 *TF:* 877-548-0929 ■ *Web:* www.weinigusa.com	Mooresville	NC	28117	704-799-0100	799-7400	821
Michael Werner Gallery 4 E 77th St *Web:* michaelwerner.com	New York	NY	10075	212-988-1623	988-1774	42
Michael's 9777 Las Vegas Blvd S *TF:* 866-796-7111 ■ *Web:* southpointcasino.com	Las Vegas	NV	89183	702-796-7111		671
Michael's 532 Margaret St *Web:* www.michaelskeywest.com	Key West	FL	33040	305-295-1300		671
Michael'S Appliances Sales & Service Inc 585 E Main St *Web:* michaelsappliance.com	Middletown	NY	10940	845-342-0369		35
Michael's New York 24 W 55th St *Web:* www.michaelsnewyork.com	New York	NY	10019	212-767-0555		671
Michael's on East 1212 E Ave S *Web:* bestfood.com	Sarasota	FL	34239	941-366-0007		671
Michael's Transportation Service Inc 140 Yolano Dr *TF:* 800-295-2448 ■ *Web:* bustransportation.com	Vallejo	CA	94589	707-643-2099	643-1906	109
Michael's Volkswagen of Bellevue 15000 SE Eastgate Way *TF:* 888-480-5424 ■ *Web:* www.michaelsvolkswagen.com	Bellevue	WA	98007	425-641-2002		57
Michael-David Winery 4580 W Hwy 12 *Web:* michaeldavidwinery.com	Lodi	CA	95242	209-368-7384	368-5801	50-7
Michaelmas Press PO Box 702 *Web:* www.michaelmaspress.com	Amesbury	MA	01913	978-388-7066	388-6031	637-2
Michaels Creative Jewelry 4843 E Ray Rd *Web:* michaelscreative.com	Phoenix	AZ	85044	480-598-0306		410
Michaels Group Homes 1 Marions Way *Web:* www.michaelsgroup.com	Mechanicville	NY	12118	518-899-6311		187
Michaels Stores Inc 8000 Bent Branch Dr *TF:* 800-642-4235 ■ *Web:* www.michaels.com	Irving	TX	75063	800-642-4235		45
Michalik & Daniels Inc 934 Western Ave *Web:* www.eztaxtime.com	Pittsburgh	PA	15233	412-322-2662	322-0513	2
Michaud Cooley Erickson & Associates Inc 333 S 7Th St Ste 1200 *Web:* www.michaudcooley.com	Minneapolis	MN	55402	612-339-4941	339-8354	261
Michbi Doors Inc 175 Marine St *TF:* 800-854-4541 ■ *Web:* www.michbidoors.com	Farmingdale	NY	11735	631-231-9050		499
Michel Soskine Inc 900 Park Ave *Web:* www.soskine.com	New York	NY	10075	212-988-2050		637-2
Michel's 2895 Kalakaua Ave Colony Surf Hotel *Web:* www.michelshawaii.com	Honolulu	HI	96815	808-923-6552	926-6063	671
Micheletti Inc 111 N Market St Ste 705 *Web:* michelettinsurance.com	San Jose	CA	95113	408-292-4900		390

Phone | Fax | Class

Michelin Canada Inc
2500 Blvd Daniel-Johnson Ste 500 ... Laval QC H7L3K8 888-871-4444 755
TF: 888-871-4444 ■ *Web:* www.michelin.ca
Michelin North America Inc
1 Parkway S PO Box 19001 ... Greenville SC 29615 864-458-5000 458-6359 754
TF: 866-866-6605 ■ *Web:* www.michelin.com
Michelina's 3241 E Shea Blvd ... Phoenix AZ 85028 602-996-8977 671
Web: www.michelinasrestaurant.com
Michell Consulting Group
8240 NW 52nd Terr Ste 410 ... Doral FL 33166 305-592-5433 196
TF: 800-442-5011 ■ *Web:* www.michellgroup.com
Michelle Raber Agency
696 US Route 1 ... Scarborough ME 04074 207-883-0111 652
Web: michelleraber.com
Michelman Inc 9080 Shell Rd ... Cincinnati OH 45236 513-793-7766 793-2504 550
TF: 800-333-1723 ■ *Web:* www.michelman.com
Michels Corp 817 W Main St ... Brownsville WI 53006 920-583-3132 583-3429 188-10
TF: 877-297-8663 ■ *Web:* www.michels.us
Michel-Schlumberger Partners LP
4155 Wine Creek Rd ... Healdsburg CA 95448 707-433-7427 80-3
TF: 800-447-3060 ■ *Web:* www.michelschlumberger.com
Michelson Laboratories Inc
6280 Chalet Dr ... Commerce CA 90040 562-928-0553 743
Web: michelsonlab.com
Michener Institute for Applied
222 St Patrick St ... Toronto ON M5T1V4 416-596-3101 685
TF: 800-387-9066 ■ *Web:* michener.ca
Michiana Beauty College
7321 Heritage Square Dr Ste 160 ... Granger IN 46530 574-271-1542 167-3
Web: www.tcbeautycollege.com
Michiana Business Publications Inc
7729 Westfield Dr ... Fort Wayne IN 46825 260-497-0433 497-0822 637-9
Web: www.businesspeople.com
Michiana Health Information Network LLC
220 W Colfax Ave Ste 300 ... South Bend IN 46601 574-968-1001 624
TF: 800-814-6446 ■ *Web:* www.mhin.org
Michigan
Aging Services Office
201 N Washington Sq Ste 920 ... Lansing MI 48933 517-323-3687 323-4569 339-23
Web: www.leadingagemi.org
Arts & Cultural Affairs Council
300 N Washington Sq ... Lansing MI 48913 517-241-3972 339-23
Web: www.michigan.gov
Attorney General 525 W Ottawa St ... Lansing MI 48909 517-335-7431 373-3042 339-23
Web: www.michigan.gov
Career Education & Workforce Programs
Victor Office Ctr 201 N Washington Sq ... Lansing MI 48913 517-335-5858 339-23
TF: 888-253-6855 ■ *Web:* www.michigan.gov
Charles Mears State Park
400 W Lowell St ... Pentwater MI 49449 231-869-2051 565
Web: www.michigan.org
Civil Rights Dept
110 W Michigan Ave
Capitol Tower Bldg Ste 800 ... Lansing MI 48933 517-335-3164 339-23
Web: www.michigan.gov
Civil Service Dept
400 S Pine St Capitol Commons Ctr
PO Box 30002 ... Lansing MI 48909 517-373-3030 373-7690 339-23
TF: 800-788-1766 ■ *Web:* www.michigan.gov
Community Health Dept
201 Townsend St Capitol View Bldg ... Lansing MI 48913 517-373-3740 339-23
Web: www.michigan.gov
Consumer Protection Div PO Box 30213 ... Lansing MI 48909 877-765-8388 241-3771* 339-23
**Fax Area Code:* 517 ■ *TF:* 877-765-8388 ■ *Web:* www.michigan.gov
Crime Victims Services Commission
320 S Walnut St Garden Level Lewis Cass Bldg . Lansing MI 48933 517-373-7373 373-2439 339-23
TF: 877-251-7373 ■ *Web:* www.michigan.gov
Department of Natural Resources
PO Box 30028 ... Lansing MI 48909 517-284-6367 339-23
Web: www.michigan.gov
Driver & Vehicle Bureau
7064 Crowner Dr ... Lansing MI 48918 517-322-1097 339-23
Web: www.michigan.gov
Education Dept
608 W Allegan St PO Box 30008 ... Lansing MI 48909 517-373-3324 339-23
Web: www.michigan.gov
Education Trust PO Box 30198 ... Lansing MI 48909 517-335-4767 373-6967 725
TF: 800-638-4543 ■ *Web:* www.michigan.gov
eLibrary Information
702 W Kalamazoo St PO Box 30007 ... Lansing MI 48909 517-335-2582 339-23
TF: 877-479-0021 ■ *Web:* www.michigan.gov
Environmental Quality Dept
3423 N Logan St ... Lansing MI 48906 517-373-7917 339-23
Web: www.michigan.gov
Financial & Insurance Regulation
530 W Allegan St ... Lansing MI 48909 517-373-0220 339-23
TF: 877-999-6442 ■ *Web:* www.michigan.gov
Gaming Control Board
3062 W Grand Blvd Ste L-700 ... Detroit MI 48202 313-456-4100 456-4200 339-23
Web: www.michigan.gov
Island Lake Recreation Area
12950 E Grand River Ave ... Brighton MI 48116 810-229-7067 565
Web: www.michigan.gov
Labor & Economic Growth Dept
611 W Ottawa St ... Lansing MI 48933 517-335-1980 373-2129 339-23
Web: www.michigan.gov
Lieutenant Governor PO Box 30013 ... Lansing MI 48909 517-373-3400 339-23
Web: www.michigan.gov
Management & Budget Dept
320 S Walnut St PO Box 30026 ... Lansing MI 48909 517-241-5545 373-7268 339-23
Web: www.michigan.gov
Military & Veterans Affairs Dept
3411 N ML King Blvd ... Lansing MI 48906 517-481-8000 339-23
Web: www.michigan.gov
North Higgins Lake State Park
11747 N Higgins Lake Dr ... Roscommon MI 48653 989-821-6125 565
TF: 800-447-2757 ■ *Web:* www.michigan.org
Parks & Recreation Div PO Box 30257 ... Lansing MI 48909 517-284-7275 339-23
Web: www.michigan.gov
Public Service Commission
7109 W Saginaw Hwy ... Lansing MI 48917 517-241-6180 284-8304 339-23
Web: www.michigan.gov
Secretary of State
430 W Allegan St 4th Fl ... Lansing MI 48918 517-373-2510 339-23
Web: www.michigan.gov
State Court Administrator
500 E Michigan Ave Ste 200 ... Lansing MI 48823 517-373-0130 373-7517 339-23
Web: courts.mi.gov
State Housing Development Authority
PO Box 30044 ... Lansing MI 48909 866-466-7328 335-4797* 339-23
**Fax Area Code:* 517 ■ *TF:* 866-466-7328 ■ *Web:* www.michigan.gov
State Lottery
101 E Hillsdale St PO Box 30023 ... Lansing MI 48909 517-335-5756 335-5644 452
TF: 844-887-6836 ■ *Web:* www.michigan.gov
State Police Dept 7150 Harrison Dr ... Dimondale MI 48821 517-332-2521 339-23
Web: www.michigan.gov
Student Financial Services Bureau
430 W Allegan Austin Bldg ... Lansing MI 48922 888-447-2687 725
TF: 888-447-2687 ■ *Web:* www.michigan.gov
Supreme Court 925 W Ottawa St ... Lansing MI 48909 517-373-0120 339-23
Web: www.courts.mi.gov
Transportation Dept PO Box 30050 ... Lansing MI 48909 313-549-0575 339-23
Web: www.michigan.gov
Travel Michigan 300 N Washington Sq ... Lansing MI 48913 517-335-4590 339-23
Web: www.michigan.org
Treasurer 430 W Allegan St ... Lansing MI 48922 517-636-5260 339-23
Web: www.michigan.gov
Unemployment Insurance Agency
3024 W Grand Blvd Ste 11-500 ... Detroit MI 48202 313-456-2733 339-23
Web: www.michigan.gov
Wildlife Div PO Box 30444 4th Fl ... Lansing MI 48909 517-284-9453 339-23
Web: www.michigan.gov
Workers Compensation Agency
2501 Woodlake Cir ... Okemos MI 48864 517-284-8902 339-23
TF: 888-396-5041 ■ *Web:* www.michigan.gov
Michigan Arc Products Corp
2040 Austin Dr ... Troy MI 48083 248-740-8066 358
Web: www.micharc.com
Michigan Association of Insurance Agents
1141 Centennial Way ... Lansing MI 48917 517-323-9473 138
Web: www.michagent.org
Michigan Association of Realtors
720 N Washington Ave ... Lansing MI 48906 517-372-8890 334-5568 656
TF: 800-454-7842 ■ *Web:* www.mirealtors.com
Michigan Auto Title Service
300 Church St ... Mount Clemens MI 48043 586-532-8150 532-8533 652
Web: mi-autotitle.com
Michigan Automotive Compressor Inc (MACI)
2400 N Dearing Rd ... Parma MI 49269 517-796-3200 172
Web: www.michauto.com
Michigan Bankers Assn 507 S Grand Ave ... Lansing MI 48933 517-485-3600 138
TF: 800-368-7764 ■ *Web:* www.mibankers.com
Michigan Barber School Inc
8990 Grand River Ave ... Detroit MI 48204 313-894-2300 685
Web: www.michiganbarberschool.org
Michigan Blueberry Growers Assn
4726 County Rd 215 ... Grand Junction MI 49056 269-434-6791 315-1
Web: www.blueberries.com
Michigan Boating Industries Assn
32398 5 Mile Rd ... Livonia MI 48154 734-261-0123 533
Web: www.mbia.org
Michigan Bulb Co PO Box 4180 ... Lawrenceburg IN 47025 513-354-1498 354-1499 323
Web: www.michiganbulb.com
Michigan Chamber of Commerce
600 S Walnut St ... Lansing MI 48933 517-371-2100 371-7224 140
TF: 800-748-0266 ■ *Web:* www.michamber.com
Michigan Chandelier Company Inc
20855 Telegraph Rd ... Southfield MI 48033 248-353-0510 353-0973 246
Web: www.michand.com
Michigan City Area Chamber of Commerce
200 E Michigan Blvd ... Michigan City IN 46360 219-874-6221 873-1204 139
Web: mcachamber.com
Michigan City Historical Society (MCHS)
Old Lightgouse Museum
100 Heisman Harbor Rd Washington Park ... Michigan City IN 46361 219-872-6133 48-13
Web: www.oldlighthousemuseum.org
Michigan College of Beauty
1020 S Monroe St ... Monroe MI 48161 734-241-8877 167-3
TF: 877-456-6623 ■ *Web:* www.michigancollegebeauty.com
Michigan College of Beauty Pivot Point Career Ctr
3498 Rochester Rd ... Troy MI 48083 248-528-0303 528-2432 167-3
Web: www.michigancollegeofbeautytroy.com
Michigan Democratic Party
606 Townsend St ... Lansing MI 48933 517-371-5410 371-2056 616-1
Web: michigandems.com
Michigan Dental Assn
3657 Okemos Rd Ste 200 ... Okemos MI 48864 517-372-9070 372-0008 227
TF: 800-589-2632 ■ *Web:* www.smilemichigan.com
Michigan Department of corrections (RMI)
Michigan Reformatory 1342 W Main ... Ionia MI 48846 616-527-2500 213
Web: www.michigan.gov
Michigan Design Ctr 1700 Stutz Dr ... Troy MI 48084 248-649-4772 393
Web: www.michigandesign.com
Michigan Drill Corporation North
1863 Larch Wood ... Troy MI 48083 248-689-5050 454
Web: www.michigandrill.com
Michigan Economic Development Corp
300 N Washington Sq ... Lansing MI 48913 888-522-0103 230
TF: 888-522-0103 ■ *Web:* www.michiganbusiness.org
Michigan Extruded Aluminum Corp
205 Watts Rd PO Box 1109 ... Jackson MI 49203 517-764-5400 492
Web: www.michiganextruded.com
Michigan Fluid Power Inc
4556 Spartan Industrial Dr SW ... Grandville MI 49418 616-538-5700 538-0888 386
TF: 800-635-0289 ■ *Web:* www.mifp.com
Michigan Freeze Pack Co 835 S Griswold ... Hart MI 49420 231-873-2175 297-7
Web: www.michiganfreezepack.com

Name / Address	City	State	Zip	Phone	Fax	Class
Michigan Historical Museum 702 W Kalamazoo St *Web:* www.michigan.gov	Lansing	MI	48915	517-373-3559	241-3647	520
Michigan Humanities Council (MHC) 119 Pere Marquette Ste 3B *Web:* www.michiganhumanities.org	Lansing	MI	48912	517-372-7770	372-0027	48-13
Michigan Instruments Inc 4717 Talon Ct SE *TF:* 800-530-9939 ■ *Web:* www.michiganinstruments.com	Grand Rapids	MI	49512	616-554-9696	554-3067	476
Michigan Insurance Co 1700 E Beltline NE Ste 100 PO Box 152120 *TF:* 888-606-6426 ■ *Web:* www.michiganinsurance.com	Grand Rapids	MI	49515	888-606-6426		390
Michigan International Speedway 12626 US 12 *TF:* 800-354-1010 ■ *Web:* www.mispeedway.com	Brooklyn	MI	49230	517-592-6666		515
Michigan Language Ctr (MLC) 715 E Huron St Ste 1W *Web:* www.englishclasses.com	Ann Arbor	MI	48104	734-663-9415	663-9623	423
Michigan League for Public Policy (MLPP) 1223 Turner St Ste G-1 *Web:* www.mlpp.org	Lansing	MI	48906	517-487-5436	371-4546	48-13
Michigan Legacy Credit Union 22855 Gibraltar Rd *Fax Area Code: 248 ■ *TF:* 800-552-8643 ■ *Web:* michiganlegacycu.org	Flat Rock	MI	48134	734-379-9125	451-5071*	219
Michigan Legal Services (MLS) 2727 2nd Ave *Web:* www.milegalservices.org	Detroit	MI	48201	313-964-4130	964-1192	637-2
Michigan Library Assn (MLA) 3410 Belle Chase Way Ste 100 *Web:* www.milibraries.org	Lansing	MI	48911	517-394-2774	394-2675	637-2
Michigan Manufacturers Assn 620 S Capitol Ave *Web:* mimfg.org	Lansing	MI	48933	517-372-5900		49-13
Michigan Manufacturing Technology Ctr 47911 Halyard Dr *Fax Area Code: 734 ■ *TF:* 888-414-6682 ■ *Web:* www.the-center.org	Plymouth	MI	48170	888-414-6682	451-4201*	668
Michigan Maple Block Co 1420 Standish Ave *Web:* www.butcherblock.com	Petoskey	MI	49770	231-347-4170		820
Michigan Masonic Home 1200 Wright Ave *TF:* 800-321-9357 ■ *Web:* www.masonicpathways.com	Alma	MI	48801	989-463-3141		672
Michigan Milk Producers Assn 41310 Bridge St *Web:* www.mimilk.com	Novi	MI	48375	248-474-6672	474-0924	296-27
Michigan Millers Mutual Insurance Co 2425 E Grand River Ave PO Box 30060 *TF:* 800-888-1914 ■ *Web:* www.mimillers.com	Lansing	MI	48912	800-888-1914		391-4
Michigan Montessori Teacher Education Ctr 4860 Midland Ave *Web:* www.montessoriedu.com	Waterford	MI	48329	248-674-3800		167-3
Michigan Municipal League 1675 Green Rd PO Box 1487 *TF:* 800-653-2483 ■ *Web:* www.mml.org	Ann Arbor	MI	48105	734-662-3246	662-8083	48-5
Michigan Nature Assn (MNA) 2310 Science Pky Ste 100 *TF:* 866-223-2231 ■ *Web:* www.michigannature.org	Okemos	MI	48864	866-223-2231		49-19
Michigan Nurses Assn (MNA) 2310 Jolly Oak Rd *Web:* www.minurses.org	Okemos	MI	48864	517-349-5640	349-5818	533
Michigan Organic Food and Farm Alliance (MOFFA) PO Box 26102 *Web:* www.moffa.net	Lansing	MI	48909	248-262-6826		48-13
Michigan Paving & Materials Co 1100 Market Ave SW *Web:* www.michiganpaving.com	Grand Rapids	MI	49503	616 459-9545		188-4
Michigan Pharmacists Assn 408 Kalamazoo Plz *Web:* www.michiganpharmacists.org	Lansing	MI	48933	517-484-1466	484-4893	585
Michigan Production Machining Inc 16700 23 Mile Rd *Web:* www.michpro.com	Macomb	MI	48044	586-228-9700	228-7347	454
Michigan Public Media 535 W William St Ste 110 *TF:* 866-203-1136 ■ *Web:* www.michiganradio.org	Ann Arbor	MI	48103	734-764-9210	647-3488	632
Michigan Republican State Committee 520 Seymour Ave *Web:* www.migop.org	Lansing	MI	48933	517-487-5413		616-2
Michigan School of Canine Cosmetology 5915 S Cedar St *Web:* www.k9grooming.com	Lansing	MI	48911	517-393-6311	393-5611	685
Michigan Schools & Government Credit Union 40400 Garfield Rd *TF:* 866-674-2848 ■ *Web:* www.msgcu.org	Clinton Township	MI	48038	586-263-8800		219
Michigan Society of Association Executives 1350 Haslett Rd *Web:* www.msae.org	East Lansing	MI	48823	517-332-6723		533
Michigan Space Grant Consortium University of Michigan 2455 Hayward St *Web:* www.mispacegrant.org	Ann Arbor	MI	48109	734-764-9508	763-6904	167-3
Michigan Spline Gage Company Inc 1626 E 9 Mile Rd *Web:* www.michiganspline.com	Hazel Park	MI	48030	248-544-7303	544-7420	493
Michigan Spring & Stamping LLC 2700 Wickham Dr *Web:* www.msands.com	Muskegon	MI	49441	231-755-1691	755-3449	719
Michigan Stadium University of Michigan 1201 S Main St *TF:* 866-296-6849 ■ *Web:* mgoblue.com	Ann Arbor	MI	48104	734-647-2583	764-3221	720
Michigan State Industries 5656 S Cedar St *Web:* www.michigan.gov	Lansing	MI	48909	517-373-4277		630
Michigan State Medical Society 120 W Saginaw St *TF:* 800-482-4881 ■ *Web:* msms.org	East Lansing	MI	48823	517-337-1351	337-2490	474
Michigan State University 250 Hannah Admin Bldg *TF:* 800-500-1554 ■ *Web:* msu.edu	East Lansing	MI	48824	517-355-1855		166

Name / Address	City	State	Zip	Phone	Fax	Class
Michigan State University College of Human Medicine 15 Michigan St NE *Web:* humanmedicine.msu.edu	Grand Rapids	MI	49503	616-233-1678	234-2625	167-2
Michigan State University College of Law 368 Law College Bldg *Web:* www.law.msu.edu	East Lansing	MI	48824	517-432-6810	432-0098	167-1
Michigan State University Library 366 W Circle Dr *Web:* lib.msu.edu	East Lansing	MI	48824	517-353-8700	432-1191	434-6
Michigan State University Museum 409 W Cir Dr *Web:* museum.msu.edu	East Lansing	MI	48824	517-355-2370	432-2846	520
Michigan State University Press 1405 S Harrison Rd Ste 110 *Web:* msupress.org	East Lansing	MI	48823	517-355-9543	432-2611	637-4
Michigan State Utility Workers Council 4815 Lansing Rd *Web:* uwua.net	Charlotte	MI	48813	517-645-4555		414
Michigan Sugar Company Inc 2600 S Euclid Ave *TF:* 877-417-8427 ■ *Web:* www.michigansugar.com	Bay City	MI	48706	989-686-0161	671-3719	296-38
Michigan Technological University 1400 Townsend Dr *TF:* 888-688-1885 ■ *Web:* www.mtu.edu	Houghton	MI	49931	906-487-2335	487-2125	166
Michigan Theater 603 E Liberty St *Web:* www.michtheater.org	Ann Arbor	MI	48104	734-668-8397	668-7136	572
Michigan Theological Seminary 41550 E Ann Arbor Trl *TF:* 800-356-6639 ■ *Web:* www.moody.edu	Plymouth	MI	48170	734-207-9581	207-9582	167-3
Michigan Tractor and Machinery Co 24800 Novi Rd *Web:* www.michigancat.com	Novi	MI	48375	248-349-4800	349-4791	358
Michigan United Conservation Clubs 2101 Wood St *TF:* 800-777-6720 ■ *Web:* www.mucc.org	Lansing	MI	48912	517-371-1041		457-22
Michigan Veterinary Medical Assn (MVMA) 2144 Commonc Pkwy *Web:* michvma.org	Okemos	MI	48864	517-347-4710	347-4666	795
Michigan Wheel Corp 1501 Buchanan Ave SW *TF:* 800-369-4335 ■ *Web:* www.miwheel.com	Grand Rapids	MI	49507	616-452-6941	247-0227	386
Michigan Women Forward 105 W Allegan St Ste 100 *Web:* www.michiganwomenshalloffame.org	Lansing	MI	48933	517-484-1880	372-0170	520
Michigan's Adventure Inc 4750 Whitehall Rd *Web:* www.miadventure.com	Muskegon	MI	49445	231-766-3377	766-3804	31
Michles & Booth PA 501 Brent Ln *TF:* 800-438-3606 ■ *Web:* michlesbooth.com	Pensacola	FL	32503	850-438-4848		41
Michoud Assembly Facility 13800 Old Gentilly Rd *Web:* mafspace.msfc.nasa.gov	New Orleans	LA	70129	504-257-3311		504
Mick Law PC 816 S 169th St *Web:* micklawpc.com	Omaha	NE	68118	402-504-1710		41
Micke Grove Zoo 11793 N Micke Grove Rd *Web:* www.sjgov.org	Lodi	CA	95240	209-953-8840	331-7271	823
Mickelson, Jacobs & Bozek LLC 433 S Main St Ste 323 *Web:* mjblawct.com	West Hartford	CT	06110	860-561-5511		41
Mickey & Mooch PO Box 1366 *Web:* www.mickeyandmooch.com	Mount Pleasant	SC	29465	843-388-0002	971-8909	671
Mickey Casanova & Sack 1735-28th St	Bakersfield	CA	93301	661-325-9451		2
Mickey Mantle's Steakhouse 7 Mickey Mantle Dr *Web:* mickeymantlesteakhouse.com	Oklahoma City	OK	73104	405-272-0777	232-7111	671
Mickey Thompson Tires 4600 Prosper Dr *TF:* 800-222-9092 ■ *Web:* www.mickeythompsontires.com	Stow	OH	44224	330-928-9092		754
Mickey Truck Bodies Inc 1305 Trinity Ave *TF:* 800-334-9061 ■ *Web:* www.mickeybody.com	High Point	NC	27261	336-882-6806		779
Mickey's Bar-B-Q Catering and Custom Smoking 1622 Park Ave *Web:* www.mickeysbbqsauce.com	Hot Springs	AR	71901	501-624-1247		671
Mickey's Linen 4601 W Addison St *Fax Area Code: 773 ■ *TF:* 800-545-7511 ■ *Web:* www.mickeyslinen.com	Chicago	IL	60641	800-545-7511	545-9111*	442
Mickle Wagner Coleman Inc 3434 Country Club Ave *Web:* www.mwc-engr.com	Fort Smith	AR	72903	479-649-8484		261
Mico Inc 1911 Lee Blvd *TF:* 800-477-6426 ■ *Web:* www.mico.com	North Mankato	MN	56003	507-625-6426	625-3212	386
Mico Industries Inc 2929 32nd St *Web:* micoindustries.com	Kentwood	MI	49512	616-245-6426	245-2661	61
MiCocina 509 Main St *Web:* www.micocinarestaurants.com	Fort Worth	TX	76102	214-217-3000		671
Micor Industries Inc 1314 A State Docks Rd *Web:* www.micorind.com	Decatur	AL	35601	256-560-0770		621
Mi-Corp 4601 Creekstone Dr Ste 180 *Fax Area Code: 866 ■ *TF:* 888-621-6230 ■ *Web:* www.mi-corporation.com	Durham	NC	27703	919-485-4819	610-1942*	177
Micrgraphics Printing Inc 2637 Emerson Blvd *TF:* 888-464-2701 ■ *Web:* www.micrgraphics.com	Muskegon	MI	49441	231-733-3165	739-2329	627
Micro 100 Tool Corp 1410 E Pine Ave *TF:* 800-421-8065 ■ *Web:* www.micro100.com	Meridian	ID	83642	208-888-7310	888-2106	493
Micro Abrasives Corp 720 Southampton Rd *Web:* www.microgrit.com	Westfield	MA	01085	413-562-3641	562-7409	1
Micro Care Corp 595 John Downey Dr *TF:* 800-638-0125 ■ *Web:* www.microcare.com	New Britain	CT	06051	860-827-0626	827-8105	151
Micro Circuit Inc 1225 W National Ave *Web:* www.microcircuitsinc.com	Addison	IL	60101	630-628-5760	628-5769	625
Micro Com Systems Ltd 8527 Eastlake Dr *Web:* www.microcomsys.com	Burnaby	BC	V5A4T7	604-872-6771		496
Micro Connectors Inc 2700 Mccone Ave *TF:* 800-333-2113 ■ *Web:* www.microconnectors.com	Hayward	CA	94545	510-266-0299	266-0289	173-1

Company	City	State	Zip	Phone	Fax	Class
Micro Control Co 7956 Main St NE *TF:* 800-328-9923 ■ *Web:* www.microcontrol.com	Minneapolis	MN	55432	763-786-8750		248
Micro Craft Inc 207 Big Springs Ave *Web:* www.microcraft.aero	Tullahoma	TN	37388	931-455-2617	455-7060	20
Micro Electronics Corp 3375 Scott Blvd Ste 222 *Web:* www.microelectr.com.hk	Santa Clara	CA	95054	408-988-1101	988-7626	246
Micro Electronics Inc 4119 Leap Rd *Web:* www.microcenter.com	Hilliard	OH	43026	614-850-3000		173-2
Micro Encoder Inc 11533 NE 118th St *Web:* www.microen.com	Kirkland	WA	98034	425-821-3906		668
Micro Express Inc 8 Hammond Dr Ste 105 **Fax Area Code:* 949 ■ *TF:* 800-989-9900 ■ *Web:* www.microexpress.net	Irvine	CA	92618	800-989-9900	269-3070*	173-2
Micro Force Inc 505 Jericho Tpke *TF:* 800-589-6614 ■ *Web:* www.micro-force.com	Huntington Station	NY	11746	631-421-1030		180
Micro Instrument Corp (MIC) 1199 Emerson St PO Box 60619 *TF:* 800-200-3150 ■ *Web:* www.microinst.com	Rochester	NY	14606	585-458-3150		454
Micro Lithography Inc 1257 Elko Dr *Web:* www.mliusa.com	Sunnyvale	CA	94089	408-747-1769	747-1978	201
Micro Machine Company LLC 2429 N Burdick *Web:* www.micromachineco.com	Kalamazoo	MI	49007	269-388-2440		454
Micro Matic USA Inc 10726 N Second St *TF:* 866-291-5756 ■ *Web:* www.micromatic.com	Machesney Park	IL	61115	815-968-7557	968-0363	664
Micro Mold Plastics Inc 2314 Ludelle St *Web:* www.micromoldplastics.com	Fort Worth	TX	76105	817-536-0930	536-2868	604
Micro Powders Inc 580 White Plains Rd *Web:* www.micropowders.com	Tarrytown	NY	10591	914-793-4058	472-7098	145
Micro Precision Calibration Inc 22835 Industrial Pl *TF:* 866-683-7837 ■ *Web:* www.microprecision.com	Grass Valley	CA	95949	530-268-1860	268-1203	743
Micro Precision Inc 1102 Windham Rd *Web:* www.microprecisiongroup.com	South Windham	CT	06266	860-423-8334		454
Micro Stamping Corp 140 Belmont Dr *Web:* www.microstamping.com	Somerset	NJ	08873	732-302-0800	302-0436	488
Micro Strategies Inc 1140 Parsippany Blvd **Fax Area Code:* 973 ■ *TF:* 888-467-6588 ■ *Web:* microstrat.com	Parsippany	NJ	07054	888-467-6588	625-5130*	177
Micro Surface Engineer Inc 1550 E Slauson Ave *Web:* www.baltecballs.com	Los Angeles	CA	90011	323-582-7348		485
Micro Surface Finishing Products Inc 1217 W Third St *TF:* 800-225-3006 ■ *Web:* micro-surface.com	Wilton	IA	52778	563-732-3240		1
Micro Systems Engineering Inc 6024 SW Jean Rd *Web:* www.mst.com	Lake Oswego	OR	97035	503-744-8500	744-8001	696
Micro Tech Manufacturing Inc 100 Grand St *Web:* www.microtechmfginc.com	Worcester	MA	01610	508-752-5212	754-2415	454
Micro Technology Concepts (MTC) 17837 Rowland St *Web:* www.mtcusa.com	City of Industry	CA	91748	626-839-6800	839-6899	174
Micro/Sys Inc 3730 Pk Pl *Web:* www.embeddedsys.com	Montrose	CA	91020	818-244-4600	244-4246	173-2
MicroAire Surgical Instruments Inc 3590 Grand Forks Blvd *TF:* 800-722-0822 ■ *Web:* www.microaire.com	Charlottesville	VA	22911	800-722-0822		476
Microalloying International Inc 9977 W Sam Houston Pkwy N Ste 140 *Web:* www.microalloying.com	Houston	TX	77064	281-664-0150	664-0153	463
MicroAutomation Inc 5870 Trinity Pky Ste 600 *TF:* 800-817-2771 ■ *Web:* www.microautomation.com	Centreville	VA	20120	800-817-2771		180
Microbac Laboratories Inc 101 Bellevue Rd Ste 301 *Web:* www.microbac.com	Pittsburgh	PA	15229	412-459-1060		743
Microbest Inc 670 Captain Neville Dr *Web:* www.microbest.com	Waterbury	CT	06705	203-597-0355		621
Microbial Insights Inc 10515 Research Dr *Web:* microbe.com	Knoxville	TN	37932	865-573-8188		743
MicroBilt Corp 1640 Airport Rd Ste 115 *TF:* 800-884-4747 ■ *Web:* www.microbilt.com	Kennesaw	GA	30144	800-884-4747		178-10
Microbiologics Inc 200 Cooper Ave N *TF:* 800-599-2847 ■ *Web:* www.microbiologics.com	Saint Cloud	MN	56303	320-253-1640	253-6250	231
MicroBiz Corp 655 Oak Grove Ave Ste 493 *TF:* 800-937-2289 ■ *Web:* microbiz.com	Menlo Park	CA	94026	702-749-5353		178-1
Microboard Processing Inc 36 Cogwheel Ln *Web:* www.microboard.com	Seymour	CT	06483	203-881-4300		625
Microboards Technology LLC 8150 Mallory Ct *TF:* 800-646-8881 ■ *Web:* www.microboards.com	Chanhassen	MN	55317	952-556-1600	556-1620	173-8
Microbrush International Ltd 1376 Cheyenne Ave *TF:* 866-866-8698 ■ *Web:* microbrush.com	Grafton	WI	53024	262-375-4011	375-2777	228
Microcast Technologies Corp (MTC) 1611 W Elizabeth Ave *Web:* www.mtcnj.com	Linden	NJ	07036	908-523-9503	523-0910	481
Microchip Technology Inc 2355 W Chandler Blvd *NASDAQ: MCHP* ■ *Web:* www.microchip.com	Chandler	AZ	85224	480-792-7200	899-9210	696
Microcomputer Applications Inc 777 S Wadsworth Blvd Bldg 4-220 *TF:* 800-453-9565 ■ *Web:* www.keylok.com	Lakewood	CO	80226	303-801-0338		637-10
Microcredit Summit 440 First St NW Ste 460 *Web:* www.microcreditsummit.org	Washington	DC	20001	202-637-9600		533
Microdea Inc 85 Enterprise Blvd Ste 407 *Web:* www.microdea.com	Markham	ON	L6G0B5	905-881-6071		179
Microdesk Inc 10 Tara Blvd Ste 420 *TF:* 800-336-3375 ■ *Web:* www.microdesk.com	Nashua	NH	03062	603-657-3800	888-3407	180
Microdynamics Group 1400 Shore Rd *Web:* microdg.com	Naperville	IL	60563	630-527-8400	527-8440	393
Microdyne Plastics Inc 1901 E Cooley Dr *Web:* microdyneplastics.com	Colton	CA	92324	909-503-4010		608
Micro-Fab 7081 Swedetown Rd *TF:* 800-221-1397 ■ *Web:* www.micro-fab.com	Theodore	AL	36590	251-653-9186	653-6639	194
Microfibres Inc 1 Moshassuck St PO Box 1208 *Web:* www.microfibres.com	Pawtucket	RI	02862	401-725-4883	722-8520	745-7
Microflex Inc 1800 N US Hwy 1 *Web:* www.microflexinc.com	Ormond Beach	FL	32174	386-677-8100		295
Microfluidics International Corp 90 Glacier Dr Ste 1000 *TF:* 800-370-5452 ■ *Web:* www.microfluidicscorp.com	Westwood	MA	02090	617-969-5452	965-1213	298
Microgauge Inc 7350 Kensington Rd *Web:* www.muellerindustriesipd.com	Brighton	MI	48116	248-446-3720		454
MicroGroup Inc 7 Industrial Park Rd *TF:* 800-255-8823 ■ *Web:* www.microgroup.com	Medway	MA	02053	508-533-4925	533-5691	595
Micro-Hybrid Dimensions Inc 2161 E 5th St *Web:* www.micro-hybrid.com	Tempe	AZ	85281	480-731-3131	784-1604	696
Microintegration Inc 460 Stull St Ste 200 *Web:* microintegration.net	South Bend	IN	46601	574-256-6777		177
Microland Electronics Corp 1883 Ringwood Ave *TF:* 800-632-1688 ■ *Web:* www.microlandusa.com	San Jose	CA	95131	408-441-1688	441-1767	174
Microlap Technologies Inc 213 1st St Nw *TF:* 800-382-2496 ■ *Web:* www.microlap.com	Rolla	ND	58367	701-477-3193	477-6579	407
Microlife USA Inc 1617 Gulf to Bay Blvd Second Fl Ste B *TF:* 888-314-2599 ■ *Web:* www.microlifeusa.com	Clearwater	FL	33755	727-451-0484		476
Microline Surgical Inc 50 Dunham Rd Ste 1500 *Web:* www.microlinesurgical.com	Beverly	MA	01915	978-922-9810		476
MicroLink Devices Inc 6457 W Howard St *Web:* www.mldevices.com	Niles	IL	60714	847-588-3001		696
Microlog Corp 401 Professional Dr Ste 125 *Web:* www.mlog.com	Gaithersburg	MD	20879	301-540-5500		735
MicroLumen Inc 1 Microlumen Way *TF:* 800-968-9014 ■ *Web:* www.microlumen.com	Oldsmar	FL	34677	813-886-1200		476
Microlynx Systems Ltd 1925 18 Ave NE Ste 107 *TF:* 866-835-4332 ■ *Web:* www.microlynxsystems.com	Calgary	AB	T2E7T8	403-275-7346		261
MicroMass Communications Inc 100 Regency Forest Dr Ste 400 *Web:* www.micromass.com	Cary	NC	27518	919-851-3182		178-11
Micromatic LLC 525 Berne St *TF:* 800-333-5752 ■ *Web:* www.micromaticllc.com	Berne	IN	46711	260-589-2136	589-8966	223
Micromatic Screw Products Inc 825 Carroll Ave *Web:* www.microspi.com	Jackson	MI	49202	517-787-3666	787-6397	621
Micromatic Spring & Stamping Company Inc 45 N Church St *Web:* www.micromaticspring.com	Addison	IL	60101	847-671-6600	671-3452	719
Micro-Matics Corp 8050 Ranchers Rd *Web:* micro-matics.com	Fridley	MN	55432	763-780-2700	780-2706	621
microMEDIA Imaging Systems Inc 300-2 Rte 17 S Ste 4 **Fax Area Code:* 516 ■ *Web:* www.imagingservices.com	Lodi	NJ	07644	973-685-5164	355-0316*	496
Micromeritics Instrument Corp 4356 Communications Dr *TF:* 800-229-5052 ■ *Web:* www.micromeritics.com	Norcross	GA	30093	770-662-3636	662-3696	419
Micrometals Inc 5615 E La Palma Ave *TF:* 800-356-5977 ■ *Web:* www.micrometals.com	Anaheim	CA	92807	714-970-9400		767
MicroMetl Corp 3035 N Shadeland Ave Ste 300 *TF:* 800-662-4822 ■ *Web:* www.micrometl.com	Indianapolis	IN	46226	800-662-4822		664
Micromex Inc 1625 S Euclid Ave *Web:* www.micromex.com	Tucson	AZ	85713	520-748-0101		253
MicroMod Automation Inc 75 Town Centre Dr *TF:* 800-480-1975 ■ *Web:* www.micmod.com	Rochester	NY	14623	585-321-9200		201
Micron Business Products Inc 2998 Syene Rd *Web:* www.micronbp.com	Madison	WI	53713	608-274-2099		179
Micron Industries Corp 1211 22nd St Ste 200 *TF:* 800-664-4660 ■ *Web:* www.micronpower.com	Oak Brook	IL	60523	630-516-1222		45
Micron Laser Technology Inc 22750 NW Wagon Way *Web:* micronlaser.com	Hillsboro	OR	97124	503-439-9000	439-3365	625
Micron Optics Inc 1852 Century Pl NE *Web:* www.micronoptics.com	Atlanta	GA	30345	404-325-0005		407
Micron Technology Inc 8000 S Federal Way *NASDAQ: MU* ■ *TF:* 888-363-2589 ■ *Web:* www.micron.com	Boise	ID	83707	208-368-4000	368-4617	625
Micronesia 300 E 42nd St Ste 1600 *TF:* 800-469-4828 ■ *Web:* www.fsmgov.org	New York	NY	10017	212-697-8370	697-8295	784
Micronesia *Consulate* 1725 North St NW *TF:* 877-730-9753 ■ *Web:* www.fsmembassydc.org	Washington	DC	20036	202-223-4383	223-4391	257
Micronics Inc 8463 154th Ave NE Bldg G *Web:* www.micronics.net	Redmond	WA	98052	425-895-9197		743
Micropac Industries Inc 905 E Walnut St *OTC: MPAD* ■ *Web:* www.micropac.com	Garland	TX	75040	972-272-3571	487-6918	696
Micropace EP Inc 3205 W Warner Ave *Web:* www.micropaceep.com	Santa Ana	CA	92704	714-258-7025	258-7280	476
MicroPact 12901 Worldgate Dr Ste 800 *TF:* 866-346-9492 ■ *Web:* www.micropact.com	Herndon	VA	20170	703-709-6110	709-6118	177

	Phone	Fax	Class
Micropaleontology Press 6530 Kissena Blvd . . . . . Flushing NY 11367 *Web:* www.micropress.org	718-570-0505	570-0506	637-9
Microphase Corp 587 Connecticut Ave. . . . . Norwalk CT 06854 *Web:* www.microphase.com	203-866-8000	538-5597	735
Microphoto Inc 30499 Edison Dr . . . . . Roseville MI 48066 *Web:* www.microphoto.net	586-772-1999	772-9691	386
Micro-Poise Measurment Systems LLC 555 Mondial Pkwy . . . . . Streetsboro OH 44241 *TF:* 800-428-3812 ■ *Web:* www.micropoise.com	330-541-9100	541-9111	386
Micro-Precision Technologies Inc 10 Manor Pky Ste C . . . . . Salem NH 03079 *Web:* www.micropt.com	603-893-7600	893-9110	696
MicroPRINT 335 Bear Hill Rd. . . . . Waltham MA 02451 *Web:* www.mprint.com	781-890-7500	890-7541	627
Microprocessor Report 355 Chesley Ave. . . . . Mountain View CA 94040 **Fax Area Code:* 650 ■ *TF:* 800-413-2881 ■ *Web:* www.linleygroup.com	408-270-3772	745-1490*	531-3
Micro-Processor Services Inc 92 Stone Hurst Ln. . . . . Dix Hills NY 11746 *Web:* www.mpsinc.com	631-499-4461	499-4727	177
Micropulse Inc 5865 E State Rd 14 . . . . . Columbia City IN 46725 *TF:* 888-625-3304 ■ *Web:* www.micropulseinc.com	260-625-3304		476
Micropump Inc 1402 NE 136th Ave. . . . . Vancouver WA 98684 *TF:* 800-222-9565 ■ *Web:* www.micropump.com	360-253-2008	253-8294	641
MicroRam Electronics Inc 222 Dunbar Ct . . . . . Oldsmar FL 34677 *TF:* 800-642-7671 ■ *Web:* www.microram.com	813-854-5500		246
Microscope Publications 2820 S Michigan Ave . . . . . Chicago IL 60616 *Web:* www.mcri.org	312-842-7100	842-1078	637-2
Microsemi Corp 2381 Morse Ave . . . . . Irvine CA 92614 *NASDAQ: MSCC* ■ *TF:* 800-713-4113 ■ *Web:* www.microsemi.com	949-221-7100	756-0308	696
MicroSense LLC 205 Industrial Ave E . . . . . Lowell MA 01852 *Web:* www.microsense.net	978-843-7670	856-3375	407
Microserve 276 Fifth Ave Ste 1011 . . . . . New York NY 10001 *Web:* mserve.com	212-683-2811		808
Microsmarts LLC 600 Holiday Plaza Dr Ste 545 . . . . . Matteson IL 60443 *Web:* microsmartsllc.com	708-748-7558		177
Microsoft Corp 1 Microsoft Way. . . . . Redmond WA 98052 *NASDAQ: MSFT* ■ *TF:* 800-642-7676 ■ *Web:* www.microsoft.com	425-882-8080	936-7329	178-1
Microsoft Great Plains Business Solutions 200 E Hardin St . . . . . Findlay OH 45840	419-424-0422		178-1
Microsolve Consulting Inc 190 E Fifth Ave Ste 2 . . . . . Naperville IL 60564 *Web:* www.microsolve.net	630-440-8173	563-0816	194
Microsonic Systems Inc 76 Bonaventura Dr . . . . . San Jose CA 95134 *TF:* 866-404-4898 ■ *Web:* www.microsonics.com	408-844-4980		419
Microspace Communications Corp 3100 Highwoods Blvd Ste 120 . . . . . Raleigh NC 27604 *Web:* microspace.com	919-850-4500	850-4518	681
Microspace Instruments Inc 4751 Wilburton Dr . . . . . Dallas TX 75227 *Web:* www.mspace.com	214-388-0461	388-9370	322
Microspecialties Inc 430 Smith St . . . . . Middletown CT 06457 *Web:* www.microspecialties.com	203-874-1832		542
Micross Components 7725 N Orange Blossom Trl . . . . . Orlando FL 32810 *TF:* 855-426-6766 ■ *Web:* www.micross.com	407-298-7100	290-0164	696
Micro-Star Int'l Company Ltd 901 Canada Ct . . . . . City of Industry CA 91748 *TF:* 888-447-6564 ■ *Web:* msicomputer.com	888-447-6564		625
Microstore Inc 601 S Elmwood Ave . . . . . Le Sueur MN 56058 *TF:* 800-962-8885 ■ *Web:* www.1stpads.com	507-665-3284	665-2604	173-1
MicroStrategy Inc 1850 Towers Crescent Plz. . . . . Tysons VA 22182 *NASDAQ: MSTR* ■ *TF:* 888-266-0321 ■ *Web:* www.microstrategy.com	703-848-8600	848-8610	178-11
Microsurgical Technology Inc 8415 154th Ave NE. . . . . Redmond WA 98052 *TF:* 888-279-3323 ■ *Web:* www.microsurgical.com	425-556-0544		476
Microtech Computers Inc 4921 Legends Dr . . . . . Lawrence KS 66049 *Web:* www.microtechcomp.com	785-841-9513		173-2
Microtechnologies Inc 128 Garden St. . . . . Farmington CT 06032 *Web:* www.temperatureguard.com	860-516-1549		201
Microtek Inc 2070 Westover Rd . . . . . Chicopee MA 01022 *Web:* www.microtek-cables.com	413-593-1025	593-6216	253
Microthermics Inc 3216-B Wellington Ct. . . . . Raleigh NC 27615 *TF:* 800-466-2369 ■ *Web:* microthermics.com	919-878-8045	878-8032	296
Microthought Network 3810 Murrell Rd Ste 201 . . . . . Viera FL 32955 *Web:* www.microthought.com	321-622-3309		224
Microtrac Inc 215 Keystone Dr. . . . . Montgomeryville PA 18936 *Web:* www.microtrac.com	888-643-5880		419
Micro-Tronics Inc 2905 S Potter Dr . . . . . Tempe AZ 85282 *Web:* www.micro-tronics.com	602-437-8995	431-9480	454
MicroVention Inc 1311 Valencia Ave . . . . . Tustin CA 92780 *TF:* 800-990-8368 ■ *Web:* www.microvention.com	714-247-8000		477
MicroVision Development Inc 5541 Fermi Ct Ste 120 . . . . . Carlsbad CA 92008 *TF:* 800-998-4555 ■ *Web:* www.mvd.com	760-438-7781	438-7406	178-8
Microvision Inc 6244 185th Ave NE Ste 100 . . . . . Redmond WA 98052 *NASDAQ: MVIS* ■ *Web:* www.microvision.com	425-882-6600		544
Microvolt Labs Inc 1543 Brandywyn Ln . . . . . Buffalo Grove IL 60089 *TF:* 877-746-4364 ■ *Web:* www.microvolt.com	847-809-5340		194
MicroVote General Corp 6366 Guilford Ave. . . . . Indianapolis IN 46220 *TF:* 800-257-4901 ■ *Web:* www.microvote.com	317-257-4900		801
Micro-Vu Corp 7909 Conde Ln . . . . . Windsor CA 95492 *Web:* www.microvu.com	707-838-6272		493

	Phone	Fax	Class
Microwave Applications Group 3030 Industrial Pkwy . . . . . Santa Maria CA 93455 *Web:* magsmx.com	805-928-5711	925-5903	700
Microwave Devices Inc 240 N Forsythe St. . . . . Franklin IN 46131 *Web:* www.mwdevices.com	317-736-8833	736-8382	253
Microwave Engineering Corp 1551 Osgood St . . . . . North Andover MA 01845 *Web:* microwaveeng.com	978-685-2776	975-4363	253
Microwave Filter Company Inc 6743 Kinne St. . . . . East Syracuse NY 13057 *TF:* 800-448-1666 ■ *Web:* www.microwavefilter.com	315-438-4700		253
Microwave Networks Inc 4000 Greenbriar . . . . . Stafford TX 77477 *Web:* www.microwavenetworks.com	281-263-6500		647
Microwave Technology Inc 4268 Solar Way . . . . . Fremont CA 94538 *Web:* www.mwtinc.com	510-651-6700	952-4000	696
Microway Inc 12 Richards Rd . . . . . Plymouth MA 02360 *Web:* www.microway.com	508-746-7341	746-4678	173-2
Microwest Software Systems Inc 10981 San Diego Mson Rd Ste 210 . . . . . San Diego CA 92108 *TF:* 800-969-9699 ■ *Web:* www.microwestsoftware.com	619-280-0440		180
Microworks 359 Kent St Ste 301 . . . . . Ottawa ON K2P0R6 *Web:* www.microworks.ca	613-232-3859		180
MICS (Management Information Control Systems Inc) 2025 Ninth St . . . . . Los Osos CA 93402 **Fax Area Code:* 805 ■ *TF:* 800-838-6427 ■ *Web:* www.bissoftware.com	800-838-6427	543-0373*	178-10
Micucci Grocery Company Inc 45 India St . . . . . Portland ME 04103 *Web:* micuccigrocery.com	207-775-1854		345
Mid America Appliance Parts Ctr 5065 American Way . . . . . Memphis TN 38115 *TF:* 800-332-1945 ■ *Web:* www.midamericaparts.com	901-332-1414	398-6187	38
Mid America Computer Corp PO Box 700 . . . . . Blair NE 68008 *TF:* 800-622-2502 ■ *Web:* maccnet.com	402-426-6222	533-5369	225
Mid America Machine Inc 92 Pioneer Industrial Dr . . . . . Mayfield KY 42066 *Web:* www.midamericamachine.com	270-247-6909	247-6996	454
Mid America Motorworks 17082 N US Hwy 45 PO Box 1368 . . . . . Effingham IL 62401 *TF:* 866-350-4543 ■ *Web:* www.mamotorworks.com	217-540-4200	540-4800	61
Mid American Growers Inc 14240 Greenhouse Ave. . . . . Granville IL 61326	815-339-6831		369
Mid American Products Inc 1623 Wildwood Ave . . . . . Jackson MI 49202 *Web:* www.deplastics.com	517-789-8116		596
Mid Atlantic Center for The Arts 1048 Washington St. . . . . Cape May NJ 08204 *TF:* 800-275-4278 ■ *Web:* www.capemaymac.org	609-884-5404		520
Mid Atlantic Printers Ltd 503 Third St . . . . . Altavista VA 24517 *TF:* 888-231-3175 ■ *Web:* www.mapl.net	434-369-6633		532-3
Mid Atlantic Rf Systems Inc 105 E Jarrettsville Rd . . . . . Forest Hill MD 21050 *Web:* www.midatlanticrf.com	410-893-2430		253
Mid City Steel Fabricating Inc 115 Buchner Pl. . . . . La Crosse WI 54603 *TF:* 877-742-0770 ■ *Web:* www.mid-citysteel.com	608-782-0770		492
Mid Coast Hospital 123 Medical Center Dr . . . . . Brunswick ME 04011 *Web:* www.midcoasthealth.com	207-373-6000	721-1230	374-3
Mid Columbia Lumber & Box Company Inc 380 NW Adler. . . . . Madras OR 97741 *Web:* mid-columbialumber.com	541-475-7241		683
Mid Florida Tech 2900 W Oak Ridge Rd. . . . . Orlando FL 32809 *Web:* www.orangetechcollege.net	407-251-0047		107-0
Mid Iowa Insurance Associates Incorporated of Lake Cit 110 N Illinois St . . . . . Lake City IA 51449 *Web:* insuranceiniowa.com	712-464-3144		390
Mid Michigan Community College (MMCC) 1375 S Clare Ave . . . . . Harrison MI 48625 *Web:* www.midmich.edu	989-386-6622	386-6613	162
Mid Oaks Investments 750 Lake Cook Rd Ste 460 . . . . . Buffalo Grove IL 60089 *Web:* www.midoaks.com	847-215-3475	215-3421	792
Mid Ohio Energy Co-opeartive Inc 555 W Franklin St. . . . . Kenton OH 43326 *TF:* 888-382-6732 ■ *Web:* www.midohioenergy.com	419-673-7289	673-8388	245
Mid Ohio Regional Planning Commission 111 Liberty St Ste 100 . . . . . Columbus OH 43215 *Web:* www.morpc.org	614-228-2663	228-1904	463
Mid Pacific Testing & Inspection Inc 94-547 Ukee St Ste 200 . . . . . Waipahu HI 96797 *Web:* midpacifictesting.com	808-676-2720	676-2769	794
Mid Penn Bancorp Inc 349 Union St. . . . . Millersburg PA 17061 *NASDAQ: MPB* ■ *Web:* midpennbank.com	717-692-2133		360-2
Mid Pines Inn & Golf Club 1010 Midland Rd . . . . . Southern Pines NC 28387 *TF:* 800-747-7272 ■ *Web:* www.pineneedleslodge.com	910-692-2114	692-5349	669
Mid Rivers Mall 1600 Mid Rivers Mall . . . . . Saint Peters MO 63376 *Web:* www.shopmidriversmall.com	636-970-2610		460
Mid Seven Transportation Co 2323 Delaware Ave. . . . . Des Moines IA 50317 *Web:* www.mid7.com	515-266-5181		780
Mid South Lumber Inc 6595 Marshall Blvd PO Box 1185. . . . . Lithonia GA 30058 *TF:* 800-759-3076 ■ *Web:* www.mid-southlumber.com	770-482-4800	484-8888	683
Mid South Sales Inc 243 County Rd 414. . . . . Jonesboro AR 72404 *Web:* midsouthsales.com	870-933-6457	933-0446	579
Mid South Steel Inc 15 Welborn St . . . . . Pelham AL 35124 *Web:* www.midsouthsteelinc.com	205-663-1750		492
Mid State Sales Inc 1101 Gahanna Pkwy . . . . . Columbus OH 43230 *TF:* 800-421-7051 ■ *Web:* www.midstate-sales.com	614-864-1811		755
Mid State Trading Co 2525 Trenton Ave . . . . . Williamsport PA 17701	570-326-9431		686

Name / Address	City	State	ZIP	Phone	Fax	Class
Mid States Concession Supply 1026 Burlington Dr. *TF:* 800-227-4929 ■ *Web:* www.msconcession.com	Muncie	IN	47302	765-289-5505		297-3
Mid Valley Agricultural Services Inc 16401 E Hwy 26 PO Box 593 *Web:* www.midvalleyag.com	Linden	CA	95236	209-931-7600	931-0747	10-4
Mid Valley Chamber of Commerce 7120 Hayvenhurst Ave Ste 114 *Web:* www.sanfernandovalleychamber.com	Van Nuys	CA	91406	818-989-0300	989-3836	139
Mid Valley Industries 1151 Delanglade St *Web:* mvii.com	Kaukauna	WI	54130	920-759-0314		454
Mid Valley School District 52 Underwood Rd. *Web:* www.mvsd.us	Throop	PA	18512	570-307-1150		186
Mid West Products Inc PO Box 301 *Web:* www.lambertmfg.com	Phillipsburg	OH	45354	937-337-3641	337-0755	429
Mid Yellowstone Elec Co-opeartive Inc (MYEC) 203 Elliott PO Box 386 *Web:* www.myec.coop	Hysham	MT	59038	406-342-5521		245
Mid-AM Building Supply Inc 1615 Omar Bradley Dr PO Box 645 *TF:* 800-892-5850 ■ *Web:* www.midambuilding.com	Moberly	MO	65270	800-892-5850	299-7892	191-3
Midamar Corp PO Box 218 *TF:* 800-362-3711 ■ *Web:* www.midamar.com	Cedar Rapids	IA	52406	319-362-3711	362-4111	297-9
Mid-America Ag Network 1632 S Maize Rd *Web:* www.midamericaagnetwork.com	Wichita	KS	67209	316-721-8484	721-8276	647
Mid-America Cabinet Inc 20980 Marion Lee Rd *Web:* www.midamericacabinets.com	Gentry	AR	72734	479-736-2671	736-8086	115
Mid-America Christian University 3500 SW 119th St *TF:* 888-888-2341 ■ *Web:* www.macu.edu	Oklahoma City	OK	73170	405-691-3800	692-3165	166
Mid-America College of Funeral Science (MACFS) 3111 Hamburg Pk. *Web:* www.mid-america.edu	Jeffersonville	IN	47130	812-288-8878	288-5942	800
Mid-America Festivals Inc 1244 Canterbury Rd S Ste 306 *Web:* www.renaissancefest.com	Shakopee	MN	55379	952-445-7361	445-7380	239
Midamerica Hotels Corp 105 S Mt Auburn Rd. *TF:* 888-866-4326 ■ *Web:* www.midamcorp.com	Cape Girardeau	MO	63703	573-334-0546		378
Mid-America Lumbermens Assn (MLA) 638 W 39th St. *TF:* 800-747-6529 ■ *Web:* themla.com	Kansas City	MO	64111	816-561-5323	561-1249	139
Mid-America Machining Inc 11530 Brooklyn Rd. *Web:* www.mid-americamachining.com	Brooklyn	MI	49230	517-592-8988		454
Mid-America Manufacturing Inc 1300 S B Ave *Web:* www.midamericamfg.com	Nevada	IA	50201	515-382-3113	382-4142	454
Mid-America Merchandising Inc 204 W Third St *TF:* 800-333-6737 ■ *Web:* www.mmipromo.com	Kansas City	MO	64105	816-471-5600	842-0952	9
Midamerica National Bancshares 100 W Elm St *TF:* 877-647-5050 ■ *Web:* www.midnatbank.com	Canton	IL	61520	309-647-5000	647-8551	70
MidAmerica Nazarene University 2030 E College Way *TF:* 800-800-8887 ■ *Web:* mnu.edu	Olathe	KS	66062	913-782-3750	971-3481	166
Mid-America Precision Products LLC 1927 W 4th St. *Web:* www.midampp.com	Joplin	MO	64801	417-623-2285		234
Mid-America Publishing Corp 9 Second St NW *TF:* 800-558-1244 ■ *Web:* www.hamptonchronicle.com	Hampton	IA	50441	641-456-2585	456-2587	637-8
Mid-America Radio Group 1639 Burton Ln. *Web:* www.wcbk.com	Martinsville	IN	46151	765-342-3394	342-5020	643
Mid-America Reformed Seminary 229 Seminary Dr. *TF:* 888-440-6277 ■ *Web:* www.midamerica.edu	Dyer	IN	46311	219-864-2400	864-2410	167-3
Mid-America Rehabilitation Hospital 5701 W 110th St. *Web:* midamericarehabhospital.com	Overland Park	KS	66211	913-491-2400	338-3762	374-6
Mid-America Risk Managers Inc 5036 S 136th St *Web:* marm.net	Omaha	NE	68137	402-894-2666		390
Mid-America Science Museum 500 Mid-America Blvd *Web:* midamericamuseum.org	Hot Springs	AR	71913	501-767-3461		520
Mid-America Tile 1650 Howard St *TF:* 800-325-5679 ■ *Web:* www.midamericatile.com	Elk Grove Village	IL	60007	847-439-3110		191-1
Mid-America Transplant Services (MTS) 1110 Highlands Plaza Dr E Ste 100 *TF:* 888-376-4854 ■ *Web:* www.midamericatransplant.org	Saint Louis	MO	63110	314-735-8200		545
Mid-American Coaches Inc 4530 Hwy 47 *TF:* 866-944-8687 ■ *Web:* www.mid-americancoaches.com	Washington	MO	63090	866-944-8687		760
Mid-American Elevator Company Inc 820 N Wolcott Ave *Web:* www.mid-americanelevator.com	Chicago	IL	60622	773-486-6900	486-2438	189-1
MidAmerican Energy Holdings Co 500 E Court Ave PO Box 657 *TF:* 888-427-5632 ■ *Web:* www.midamericanenergy.com	Des Moines	IA	50303	888-427-5632		360-5
Midas Hospitality LLC 1804 Borman Cir Dr Ste 100 *Web:* www.midashospitality.com	Saint Louis	MO	63146	314-692-0100	692-0103	378
Midas International Corp 823 Donald Ross Rd. *Fax Area Code: 630 ■ *TF:* 800-621-8545 ■ *Web:* www.midas.com	Juno Beach	FL	33408	800-621-8545	438-3015*	62-3
Mid-Atlantic Christian University 715 N Poindexter St *TF:* 866-996-6228 ■ *Web:* www.macuniversity.edu	Elizabeth City	NC	27909	252-334-2000	334-2071	161
Mid-Atlantic Clearing House Association Inc, The 1344 Ashton Rd Ste 202 *Web:* www.macha.org	Hanover	MD	21076	410-859-0090	859-3452	507
Mid-Atlantic Diamond Ventures 1801 Liacouras Walk *Web:* www.fox.temple.edu	Philadelphia	PA	19122	215-204-3082		734
Mid-Atlantic PenFed Realty Berkshire Hathaway HomeServices 3050 Chain Bridge Rd *TF:* 866-225-5778 ■ *Web:* penfedrealty.com	Fairfax	VA	22030	703-691-7653	691-7662	655
MidCap Advisors LLC 675 3rd Ave 28th Fl *Web:* www.midcapadvisors.com	New York	NY	10017	212-722-5683	722-6861	390
Mid-Carolina Electric Co-opeartive Inc PO Box 669 *TF:* 888-813-8000 ■ *Web:* www.mcecoop.com	Lexington	SC	29071	803-749-6555		245
Mid-Carolina Steel & Recycling Company Inc 7425 Fairfield Rd *Web:* mid-carolinasteel.com	Columbia	SC	29203	803-786-9888		480
Mid-Cities Barber College 2345 SW 3rd St Ste 101 *Web:* www.mcbc.edu	Grand Prairie	TX	75051	972-642-1892	642-8198	167-3
Mid-City Electrical Construction 1099 Sullivant Ave *Web:* www.midcityelectric.com	Columbus	OH	43223	614-221-5153		189-4
Mid-City Motor World 4800 N Hwy 101 *Web:* www.midcitymotorworld.com	Eureka	CA	95503	707-443-4871		57
Mid-City Precision Inc 7430 Oxford St *Web:* www.mid-cityprecision.com	Minneapolis	MN	55426	952-933-2501	933-4363	454
Mid-City Transit Corp 518 SR-17M *Web:* www.midcitytransit.com	Middletown	NY	10940	845-343-4702	343-7717	108
Midco Connections Inc 4901 E 26th St *Web:* www.midcoconnections.com	Sioux Falls	SD	57110	605-330-4125		393
MIDCO Intl PO Box 8440 *Web:* www.midcointernational.com	Waco	TX	76714	254-709-6438	399-9052	523
MidCoast Capital 259 N Radnor-Chester Rd Radnor Ct Ste 210 *Web:* www.midcoastcapital.com	Radnor	PA	19087	610-687-8580	971-2154	792
Mid-Coast Electric Supply Inc (MCESI) 1801 Stolz St PO Box 2505 *Web:* www.mcesi.com	Victoria	TX	77901	361-575-6311	575-5515	246
Mid-Columbia Bus Co PO Box 1108 *Web:* midcobus.com	Pendleton	OR	97801	541-278-1444		109
Mid-Columbia Libraries 405 S Dayton St *Web:* www.midcolumbialibraries.org	Kennewick	WA	99336	509-586-3156		434-3
Midcom Data Technologies Inc 33493 W 14 Mile Rd Ste 150 *TF:* 800-643-2664 ■ *Web:* midcomdata.com	Farmington Hills	MI	48331	248-661-0100	661-3920	246
MIDCON Data Services Inc 401 W 33rd St *Web:* www.midcondata.com	Edmond	OK	73013	405-478-1234		539
Mid-Con Energy Partners LP 2501 N Harwood St Ste 2410 *Web:* www.midconenergypartners.com	Dallas	TX	75201	918-743-7575		536
Midcontinent Airport 2173 Air Cargo Rd *TF:* 800-628-6800 ■ *Web:* www.flywichita.com	Wichita	KS	67209	316-946-4700		27
Midcontinent Communications PO Box 5010 *TF:* 800-888-1300 ■ *Web:* www.midco.com	Sioux Falls	SD	57117	605-274-9810		116
Mid-Continent Engineering Inc 405 35th Ave NE *Web:* www.mid-continent.com	Minneapolis	MN	55418	612-781-0260	782-1320	697
Mid-Continent Group 1437 S Boulder Ave STE 200 PO Box 1409 *TF:* 800-722-4994 ■ *Web:* www.mcg-ins.com	Tulsa	OK	74119	918-587-7221		391-4
Mid-Continent Public Library 15616 E 24 Hwy *Web:* www.mymcpl.org	Independence	MO	64050	816-836-5200	521-7253	434-3
Mid-Continent Research for Education & Learning (MCREL) 4601 DTC Blvd Ste 500 *Web:* www.mcrel.org	Denver	CO	80237	303-337-0990	337-3005	668
Mid-Continent Safety 8225 E 35th St N *Web:* www.midsafe.com	Wichita	KS	67226	316-522-0900		679
Mid-Continent University 99 Powell Rd E *TF:* 888-628-4723 ■ *Web:* www.midcontinent.edu	Mayfield	KY	42066	270-247-8521	247-3115	166
Mid-Continental Restoration Company Inc 401 E Hudson Rd PO Box 429 *TF:* 800-835-3700 ■ *Web:* www.midcontinental.com	Fort Scott	KS	66701	620-223-3700	223-5052	189-7
MidCountry Financial Corp 30 Patewood Dr Ste 160 *Web:* www.midcountryfinancial.com	Greenville	SC	29615	478-746-8222		360-2
Mid-Del Technology Ctr 1621 Maple Dr *Web:* www.middeltech.com	Midwest City	OK	73110	405-739-1707	739-1716	167-3
Mid-Delta Health Systems Inc 405 N Hayden St. *TF:* 800-543-9055 ■ *Web:* www.middelta.com	Belzoni	MS	39038	662-563-1021		371
Middle Atlantic Products Inc 300 Fairfield Rd *TF:* 888-766-9770 ■ *Web:* www.middleatlantic.com	Fairfield	NJ	07004	973-839-1011	839-1976	697
Middle Bucks Institute of Technology, The 2740 York Rd *Web:* www.mbit.org	Jamison	PA	18929	215-343-2480	343-8626	167-3
Middle Country Public Library 101 Eastwood Blvd. *Web:* www.mcplibrary.org	Centereach	NY	11720	631-585-9393		434-3
Middle Georgia College 1100 Second St SE *TF:* 800-548-4221 ■ *Web:* mga.edu	Cochran	GA	31014	478-934-6221		162
Middle Georgia Electric Membership Corp 600 Tippettville Rd *TF:* 800-342-0144 ■ *Web:* mgemc.com	Vienna	GA	31092	229-268-2671		245
Middle Georgia Regional Airport 1000 Terminal Dr Ste 100 *Web:* www.iflymacon.com	Macon	GA	31216	478-788-3760		27
Middle River Aircraft Systems (MRAS) 103 Chesapeake Park Plz *TF:* 877-432-3272 ■ *Web:* www.mras-usa.com	Baltimore	MD	21220	410-682-1500	682-1230	22

	Phone	Fax	Class
Middle States Commission on Higher Education 3624 Market St .... Philadelphia PA 19104 *Fax Area Code: 215 ■ Web: www.msche.org	267-284-5000	662-5501*	49-5
Middle Tennessee Electric Membership Corp 555 New Salem Hwy .... Murfreesboro TN 37129 TF: 877-777-9020 ■ Web: www.mtemc.com	877-777-9020		245
Middle Tennessee Mental Health Institute 221 Stewarts Ferry Pk .... Nashville TN 37214 Web: www.tn.gov	615-902-7400	741-8953	374-5
Middle Tennessee Natural Gas Utility District (MTNG) 1036 W Broad St PO Box 670 .... Smithville TN 37166 TF: 800-880-6373 ■ Web: www.mtng.com	615-597-4300	597-6331	787
Middle Tennessee State University 1301 E Main St .... Murfreesboro TN 37132 TF: 800-533-6878 ■ Web: www.mtsu.edu	615-898-2300	898-5478	166
Middlebridge Marketing Inc 1525 Old Louisquisset Pk Ste 105-C .... Lincoln RI 02865 Web: middlebridgemarketing.com	401-728-0040		4
Middlebury College 131 S Main St .... Middlebury VT 05753 TF: 877-214-3330 ■ Web: www.middlebury.edu	802-443-3000	443-2056	166
Middlebury College Museum of Art (MCMA) Mahaney Center for the Arts 72 Porter Field Rd .... Middlebury VT 05753 Web: museum.middlebury.edu	802-443-5007	443-2069	637-2
Middlebury Community Schools 57853 Northridge Dr .... Middlebury IN 46540 Web: www.mcsin-k12.org	574-825-9425		685
Middlebury Hardwood Products Inc 101 Joan Dr PO Box 1429 .... Middlebury IN 46540 Web: mhpi.us	574-825-9524		499
Middlebury National Corp PO Box 189 .... Middlebury VT 05753 OTC: MDVT ■ TF: 877-508-8455 ■ Web: nbmvt.com	802-388-4982		70
Middleby Corp 1400 Toastmaster Dr .... Elgin IL 60120 NASDAQ: MIDD ■ TF: 800-331-5842 ■ Web: www.middleby.com	847-741-3300	741-0015	298
Middlefield Plastics Inc 15235 Burton Windsor Rd .... Middlefield OH 44062 Web: www.middlefieldplastics.com	440-834-4638		608
Middlesboro Coca-Cola Bottling Works Inc 1324 Cumberland Ave .... Middlesboro KY 40965 TF: 800-442-0102 ■ Web: www.mccbw.com	877-692-4679		80-2
Middlesboro Independent School 220 N 20th St .... Middlesboro KY 40965 Web: www.mboro.k12.ky.us	606-242-8800	242-8805	780
Middlesex Community College 590 Springs Rd .... Bedford MA 01730 *Fax Area Code: 781 ■ TF: 800-818-3434 ■ Web: www.middlesex.mass.edu	978-656-3370	280-3603*	162
Middlesex Community College 100 Training Hill Rd .... Middletown CT 06457 TF: 800-818-5501 ■ Web: mxcc.edu	860-343-5800	344-7488	162
Middlesex County *Middlesex Judicial District including Superior Court* 1 Court St .... Middletown CT 06457 Web: www.jud.ct.gov	860-343-6400	343-6423	338
Middlesex County Animal Hospital LLC 330 Boston Rd .... North Billerica MA 01862 Web: mcahwebsite.com	978-600-0444		794
Middlesex County Chamber of Commerce 393 Main St .... Middletown CT 06457 Web: www.middlesexchamber.com	860-347-6924	346-1043	139
Middlesex County College 2600 Woodbridge Ave PO Box 3050 .... Edison NJ 08818 Web: middlesexcc.edu	732-548-6000		162
Middlesex County Educational Service Commission 1660 Stelton Rd .... Piscataway NJ 08854 Web: www.escnj.us	732-777-9848		685
Middlesex County Regional Chamber of Commerce 109 Church St .... New Brunswick NJ 08901 Web: www.mcrcc.org	732-745-8090	745-8098	139
Middlesex County Utilities Authority Inc (MCUA) 2571 Main St PO Box 159 .... Sayreville NJ 08872 Web: www.mcua.com	732-721-3800	721-0206	787
Middlesex County Vocational & Technical High Schools PO Box 1070 .... East Brunswick NJ 08816 Web: www.mcvts.net	732-257-3300		685
Middlesex Gases & Technologies Inc 292 Second St PO Box 490249 .... Everett MA 02149 TF: 800-649-6704 ■ Web: www.middlesexgases.com	617-387-5050		791
Middlesex Hospital 28 Crescent St .... Middletown CT 06457 TF: 800-548-2394 ■ Web: middlesexhospital.org	860-358-6000	358-2626	374-3
Middlesex Mutual Assurance Co 213 Ct St PO Box 891 .... Middletown CT 06457 TF: 800-622-3780 ■ Web: www.middleoak.com	800-622-3780		391-4
Middlesex Research Manufacturing Company Inc 27 Apsley St .... Hudson MA 01749 TF: 800-424-5188 ■ Web: www.middlesexresearch.com	978-562-3697	562-7446	745-2
Middlesex Savings Bank 120 Flanders Rd .... Westborough MA 01581 TF: 877-463-6287 ■ Web: www.middlesexbank.com	508-653-0300		70
Middlesex School 1400 Lowell Rd .... Concord MA 01742 Web: www.mxschool.edu	978-369-2550	287-4759	622
Middlesex West Chamber of Commerce 179 Great Rd Ste 104B .... Acton MA 01720 Web: mwcoc.com	978-263-0010		139
Middleton & Co 186 Halsey Rd .... Newton NJ 07860 Web: middletonins.com	973-383-5525		390
Middleton & Company Inc 600 Atlantic Ave 18th Fl .... Boston MA 02210 TF: 800-357-5101 ■ Web: www.middletonco.com	617-357-5101		41
Middleton & Reutlinger 401 S Fourth St Ste 2600 .... Louisville KY 40202 Web: www.middletonlaw.com	502-584-1135	561-0442	445
Middleton Cross Plains Area School District 7106 S Ave .... Middleton WI 53562 Web: mcpasd.k12.wi.us	608-829-9000		685
Middleton Place 4300 Ashley River Rd .... Charleston SC 29414 TF: 800-782-3608 ■ Web: www.middletonplace.org	843-556-6020	766-4460	671

	Phone	Fax	Class
Middleton Public Library 7425 Hubbard Ave .... Middleton WI 53562 Web: www.midlibrary.org	608-831-5564	836-5724	434-3
Middleton Village Nursing & Rehabilitation Ctr 6201 Elmwood Ave .... Middleton WI 53562 Web: villaatmiddletonvillage.com	608-831-8300		450
Middletown & Hummelstown Rr Co 136 Brown St .... Middletown PA 17057 Web: www.mhrailroad.com	717-944-4435		649
Middletown Animal Hospital Inc 1330 Hwy 35 .... Middletown NJ 07748 Web: middletownvet.com	732-671-1503		794
Middletown City School 1516 First Ave .... Middletown OH 45044 Web: www.middletowncityschools.com	513-423-0781	420-4579	685
Middletown Convention-Visitors 1500 Central Ave .... Middletown OH 45042	513-422-3030		206
Middletown Public Library 125 S Broad St .... Middletown OH 45044 Web: www.midpointelibrary.org	513-424-1251		434-3
Middletown Township Library 55 New Monmouth Rd .... Middletown NJ 07748 Web: www.mtpl.org	732-671-3700	671-5839	434-3
Middleville Tool & Die Co 1900 Patterson .... Middleville MI 49333 Web: mtd-inc.com	269-795-3646	795-7460	488
Middough Inc 1901 E 13th St .... Cleveland OH 44114 Web: www.middough.com	216-367-6000	367-6020	261
Mide Technology Corp 475 Wildwood Ave .... Woburn MA 01801 Web: www.mide.com	781-306-0609		261
Mid-East Career & Technology Centers 400 Richards Rd .... Zanesville OH 43701 TF: 800-551-1548 ■ Web: www.mid-east.k12.oh.us	740-454-0101	454-0731	685
MidFirst Bank PO Box 76149 .... Oklahoma City OK 73147 TF: 888-643-3477 ■ Web: www.midfirst.com	405-767-7000	840-0862	70
Midhattan Woodworking Corp 3130 Bordentown Ave .... Old Bridge NJ 08857 Web: www.midhattan.com	732-727-3020		499
Mid-Hudson Civic Ctr 14 Civic Center Plz .... Poughkeepsie NY 12601 Web: www.midhudsonciviccenter.org	845-454-5800		572
Mid-Hudson Library System 103 Market St .... Poughkeepsie NY 12601 Web: www.midhudson.org	845-471-6060	454-5940	434-3
MidHudson Regional Hospital 241 N Rd .... Poughkeepsie NY 12601 Web: www.midhudsonregional.org	845-483-5000		374-3
Midi Inc 125 Sandy Dr .... Newark DE 19713 Web: www.midi-inc.com	302-824-4736		476
Midian Electronic Comm Systems 2302 E 22nd St .... Tucson AZ 85713 TF: 800-643-4267 ■ Web: www.midians.com	520-884-7981		647
MIDIOR Consulting Inc 22 Putnam Ave .... Cambridge MA 02139 Web: www.midior.com	617-864-8813		463
MIDJersey Chamber of Commerce 423 Riverview Plz .... Trenton NJ 08611 Web: midjerseychamber.org	609-689-9960	394-6829	139
Mid-Kansas Co-op (MKC) PO Box D .... Moundridge KS 67107 TF: 800-864-4428 ■ Web: www.mkcoop.com	800-864-4428		48-2
Midkiff, Muncie & Ross PC 300 Arboretum Pl Ste 420 .... Richmond VA 23236 Web: www.midkifflaw.com	804-560-9600	560-5997	428
Mid-Lakes Distributing Inc 1029 W Adams St .... Chicago IL 60607 TF: 888-733-2700 ■ Web: www.mid-lakes.com	312-733-1033	733-1721	612
Midland Area *Chamber of Commerce* 300 Rodd St Ste 101 .... Midland MI 48640 TF: 800-999-3199 ■ Web: www.macc.org	989-839-9901	835-3701	139
Midland Area Community Foundation 76 Ashman Cir .... Midland MI 48640 Web: www.midlandfoundation.org	989-839-9661		305
Midland Asphalt Materials Inc 640 Young St .... Tonawanda NY 14150 Web: www.midlandasphalt.com	716-692-0730	692-0613	46
Midland by AMC, The 1228 Main St .... Kansas City MO 64105 Web: www.arvestbanktheatre.com	816-283-9900		572
Midland Center for the Arts Inc 1801 W St Andrews Rd .... Midland MI 48640 TF: 800-523-7649 ■ Web: www.mcfta.org	989-631-5930	631-7890	520
Midland Chamber of Commerce 303 W Wall St Ste 200 .... Midland TX 79701 TF: 800-624-6435 ■ Web: www.midlandtxchamber.com	432-683-3381	686-3556	139
Midland College 3600 N Garfield St .... Midland TX 79705 TF: 800-474-7164 ■ Web: www.midland.edu	432-685-4500	685-6480	162
Midland Community Healthcare Services 801 E Florida Ave .... Midland TX 79701 Web: midlandchs.org	432-699-3817		463
Midland County 220 W Ellsworth St .... Midland MI 48640 Web: co.midland.mi.us	989-832-6739	832-6680	338
Midland County 500 N Loraine St .... Midland TX 79701 Web: www.co.midland.tx.us	432-688-4401	688-4926	338
Midland Credit Union 2891 106th St .... Urbandale IA 50322 TF: 866-508-2693 ■ Web: midlandcu.org	515-278-1994	278-0209	219
Midland Daily News 124 McDonald St .... Midland MI 48640 TF: 877-411-2762 ■ Web: www.ourmidland.com	989-835-7171	835-6991	532-2
Midland Engineering 52369 SR 933 N .... South Bend IN 46637 Web: midlandengineering.com	574-272-0200	272-7400	189-12
Midland Hospice Care 200 SW Frazier Cir .... Topeka KS 66606 TF: 800-491-3691 ■ Web: www.midlandcareconnection.org	785-232-2044	232-5567	371
Midland Implement Company Inc 402 Daniel St .... Billings MT 59101 *Fax Area Code: 406 ■ TF: 800-677-6426 ■ Web: www.midlandimplement.com	800-677-6426	252-5772*	274
Midland Independent School District 615 W Missouri Ave .... Midland TX 79701 Web: www.midlandisd.net	432-240-1000		685

Phone | Fax | Class

Midland Industries Inc
1424 N Halsted St.......Chicago IL 60642 312-664-7300 664-7371 485
TF: 800-662-8228 ■ *Web:* Www.midlandindustries.com

Midland Information Resources Co
5440 Corporate Pk Dr.......Davenport IA 52807 563-359-3696 359-1333 627
TF: 800-232-3696 ■ *Web:* www.elandersamericas.com

Midland International Air & Space Port
9506 Laforce Blvd PO Box 60305.......Midland TX 79706 432-560-2200 27
TF: 800-973-2867 ■ *Web:* www.flymaf.com

Midland Iron & Steel Corp
3301 Fourth Ave.......Moline IL 61265 309-764-6723 764-6729 686
Web: midlanddavis.com

Midland Machinery Company Inc
101 Cranbrook Ext.......Tonawanda NY 14150 716-692-1200 190
Web: www.midlandmachinery.com

Midland Manufacturing
101 E County Line Rd.......Monroe IA 50170 641-259-2625 259-3216 98
Web: www.midlandmfgco.com

Midland Memorial Hospital
400 Rosalind Redfern Grover Pkwy.......Midland TX 79701 432-221-1111 374-3
TF: 800-833-2916 ■ *Web:* www.midlandhealth.org

Midland Metal Products 1200 W 37th St.......Chicago IL 60609 773-927-5700 927-1456 454
Web: www.midlandmetalproducts.com

Midland Mortgage Co
999 NW Grand Blvd Ste 100.......Oklahoma City OK 73118 800-654-4566 767-5500* 509
**Fax Area Code:* 405 ■ *TF:* 800-654-4566 ■ *Web:* www.mymidlandmortgage.com

Midland National Bank 527 Main St.......Newton KS 67114 316-283-1700 283-3813 70
TF: 800-810-9457 ■ *Web:* www.midland.bank

Midland National Life Insurance Co
1 Sammons Plz.......Sioux Falls SD 57193 605-335-5700 335-3621 391-2
TF: 800-923-3223 ■ *Web:* www.midlandnational.com

Midland Packaging & Display Inc
3545 Nicholson Rd.......Franksville WI 53126 262-886-8851 886-4581 100
Web: midlandpkg.com

Midland Paper 101 E Palatine Rd.......Wheeling IL 60090 847-777-2700 777-2552 553
TF: 800-323-8522 ■ *Web:* www.midlandpaper.com

Midland Power Co-op
1005 E Lincolnway PO Box 420.......Jefferson IA 50129 515-386-4111 386-2385 245
TF: 800-833-8876 ■ *Web:* www.midlandpower.coop

Midland Precision Machining Inc
4043 W Kitty Hawk Ste 1.......Chandler AZ 85226 480-777-5720 493
Web: www.midlandprecision.com

Midland Radio Corp
5900 Parretta Dr.......Kansas City MO 64120 816-241-8500 241-5713 35
Web: midlandusa.com

Midland Reporter-Telegram PO Box 1650.......Midland TX 79702 432-682-5311 570-7650 532-2
TF: 800-542-3952 ■ *Web:* www.mrt.com

Midland School
5100 Figueroa Mtn Rd PO Box 8.......Los Olivos CA 93441 805-688-5114 686-2470 622
Web: midland-school.org

Midland Stamping & Fabricating
9521 W Ainslie St.......Schiller Park IL 60176 847-678-7573 488
Web: midlandsf.com

Midland University 900 N Clarkson St.......Fremont NE 68025 402-721-5480 941-6513 166
Web: www.midlandu.edu

Midland Wholesale Blinds
12601 NE 148th ST.......Liberty MO 64068 913-642-4100 361
Web: www.midlandwholesaleblinds.com

Midland's Choice 8420 W Dodge Ste 210.......Omaha NE 68114 402-390-8233 390-8239 391-3
TF: 800-605-8259 ■ *Web:* www.midlandschoice.com

Midlands Business Journal
1324 S 119th St.......Omaha NE 68144 402-330-1760 758-9315 457-5
Web: www.mbj.com

Midlands Millroom Supply Inc
1911 36th St NE.......Canton OH 44705 330-453-9100 453-6644 677
Web: www.midlandsmillroom.com

Midlands Technical College
PO Box 2408.......Columbia SC 29202 803-732-5211 790-7524 162
TF: 800-922-8038 ■ *Web:* www.midlandstech.edu

Midlantic Marketing
117 Commons Ct.......Chadds Ford PA 19317 610-361-0500 195
Web: www.midches.com

Midlothian Public Library
14701 Kenton Ave.......Midlothian IL 60445 708-535-2027 535-2053 435
Web: www.midlothianlibrary.org

Mid-Maine Chamber of Commerce
50 Elm St.......Waterville ME 04901 207-873-3315 877-0087 139
Web: www.midmainechamber.com

Midmarch Arts Press 300 Riverside Dr.......New York NY 10025 212-666-6990 865-5509 637-2
Web: www.midmarchartsbooks.org

MidMark Capital 177 Madison Ave.......Morristown NJ 07960 973-971-9960 401
Web: www.midmarkcapital.com

Midmark Corp 60 Vista Dr.......Versailles OH 45380 937-526-3662 476
TF: 800-643-6275 ■ *Web:* www.midmark.com

MidMichigan Health 4000 Wellness Dr.......Midland MI 48670 989-839-3000 48-17
Web: www.midmichigan.org

Mid-Michigan Home Health Care Inc
1020 Professional Dr Bldg A Ste 5.......Flint MI 48532 810-732-9528 732-9548 363
TF: 877-732-9528 ■ *Web:* midmichiganhc.com

Mid-Michigan Industries Inc (MMI)
2426 Pkwy Dr.......Mount Pleasant MI 48858 989-773-6918 193
Web: www.mmionline.com

MIDMRKT Suite
5409 Overseas Hwy Ste 295.......Marathon FL 33050 786-361-0454 393
Web: midmrkt.com

Midnight Call Ministries Inc
4694 Platt Springs Rd.......Columbia SC 29228 803-755-0733 755-6002 637-2
TF: 800-845-2420 ■ *Web:* www.midnightcall.com

Midnight Media Group Inc (MMGI)
45 E Willow St.......Millburn NJ 07041 973-379-5959 514
Web: www.mmgi.tv

Midnight Oil 3800 W Vanowen St.......Burbank CA 91505 818-295-6100 344
Web: www.moagency.com

Midnight Rose Hotel & Casino
256 E Bennett Ave.......Cripple Creek CO 80813 800-635-5825 133
TF: 800-635-5825 ■ *Web:* www.triplecrowncasinos.com

Midnight Sun Adventure Travel
1027 Pandora Ave.......Victoria BC V8V3P6 250 480 0400 760
TF: 800-255-5057 ■ *Web:* www.midnightsuntravel.com

Mid-Ohio Sports Car Course
7721 Steam Corners Rd PO Box 3108.......Lexington OH 44904 419-884-4000 515
Web: midohio.com

Midori Lashes & Skin Care PC
4839 NE Martin Luther King Blvd Ste 202.......Portland OR 97211 503-282-2777 77
Web: midorilashes.com

Mid-Pacific Institute 2445 Kaala St.......Honolulu HI 96822 808-973-5000 622
Web: www.midpac.edu

Mid-Park Inc 1021 Salt River Rd.......Leitchfield KY 42754 270-259-3152 488
TF: 800-259-3559 ■ *Web:* www.mid-park.com

MidPenn Legal Services
213 A N Front St.......Harrisburg PA 17101 717-234-0492 428
Web: www.midpenn.org

Mid-Plains Rural Telephone Cooperative Inc (MPRTC)
300 411 N Hale St.......Tulia TX 79088 806-668-4420 668-4444 681
TF: 888-817-2052 ■ *Web:* www.midplains.coop

Midpoint National 1263 SW Blvd.......Kansas City KS 66103 913-362-7400 463
Web: www.midpt.com

Midrange Software Inc
12716 Riverside Dr.......Studio City CA 91607 818-762-8539 178-10

Midrange Solutions Inc
20 Hillside Ave.......Springfield NJ 07081 973-912-7050 196
TF: 800-882-4008 ■ *Web:* www.midrangeusa.com

Midrex Technologies
2725 Water Ridge Pkwy Ste 100.......Charlotte NC 28217 704-373-1600 373-1611 261
Web: www.midrex.com

Mid-South Appliance Parts Inc
7501 Enmar Dr.......Little Rock AR 72209 501-565-1597 38
Web: www.midsouthparts.com

MidSouth Bancorp Inc
102 Versailles Blvd.......LaFayette LA 70501 337-237-8343 360-2
NYSE: MSL ■ *TF:* 800-213-2265 ■ *Web:* www.midsouthbank.com

Mid-South Building Supply Inc
7940 Woodruff Ct.......Springfield VA 22151 703-321-8500 321-9308 191-3
TF: 800-284-9111 ■ *Web:* www.msbs.net

Mid-South Community College
2000 W Broadway.......West Memphis AR 72301 870-733-6722 733-6719 162
TF: 866-733-6722 ■ *Web:* www.asumidsouth.edu

Mid-South Engineering Co
1658 Malvern Ave.......Hot Springs AR 71901 501-321-2276 256
Web: www.mseco.com

Mid-south Health Systems
2707 Browns Ln.......Jonesboro AR 72401 870-972-4000 972-4968 726
TF: 800-356-3035 ■ *Web:* www.mshs.org

Mid-South Industrial Automation
2295B W Broad St.......Cookeville TN 38501 931-526-6742 526-8823 806
TF: 866-611-6742 ■ *Web:* www.msautomation.com

Mid-South Wire Company Inc
1070 Visco Dr.......Nashville TN 37210 615-743-2850 256-5836 813
TF: 800-714-7800 ■ *Web:* www.midsouthwire.com

Midstate Aviation Inc
1207 E Bowers Rd.......Ellensburg WA 98926 509-962-7850 167-3
Web: www.midstateaviation.net

Midstate College 411 W Northmoor Rd.......Peoria IL 61614 309-692-4092 692-3893 800
TF: 800-251-4299 ■ *Web:* www.midstate.edu

Midstate Construction Corp
1180 Holm Rd.......Petaluma CA 94954 707-762-3200 762-0700 186
Web: www.midstateconstruction.com

Mid-State Contracting LLC
2001 County Hwy U PO Box 1425.......Wausau WI 54402 715-675-2388 675-6971 189-10
Web: www.midstatecontracting.com

Mid-State Correctional Facility
PO Box 216.......Marcy NY 13403 315-768-8581 213
Web: www.prisontalk.com

Mid-State Distributing Co
2600 Bell Ave.......Des Moines IA 50321 800-798-2568 246
TF: 800-798-2568 ■ *Web:* www.midstatedistributing.com

Midstate Electric Co-opeartive Inc
16755 Finley Butte Rd.......La Pine OR 97739 541-536-2126 536-1423 245
TF: 800-722-7219 ■ *Web:* www.midstateelectric.coop

Mid-State Equipment Inc
W 1115 Bristol Rd.......Columbus WI 53925 920-623-4020 623-4500 274
TF: 877-677-4020 ■ *Web:* www.midstateequipment.com

Midstate Financial Corp
1 E Main St.......Brownsburg IN 46112 317-852-2268 852-1559 70

Mid-State Machine & Fabricating Corp
2730 Mine & Mill Rd.......Lakeland FL 33801 844-785-4180 295
TF: 844-785-4180 ■ *Web:* www.midstatefl.com

Midstate Manufacturing Company Inc
750 W 3rd St.......Galesburg IL 61401 309-342-9555 342-7940 454
Web: www.steelwld.com

Mid-State Petroleum Inc
4192 Mendenhall Oaks Pkwy.......High Point NC 27265 336-841-3000 581
Web: www.mid-statepetroleum.com

Midstate Steel Inc
2001 Jeffersonville Rd.......Macon GA 31217 478-741-1550 480
Web: www.midstatesteel.com

Mid-States Bolt & Screw Co
4126 Somers Dr.......Burton MI 48529 800-482-0867 744-3798* 278
**Fax Area Code:* 810 ■ *TF:* 800-482-0867 ■ *Web:* www.midstatesbolt.com

Mid-States Packaging Inc
12163 State Rte 274.......Lewistown OH 43333 937-843-3243 843-4378 547
Web: www.midstatespackaging.com

Mid-States Paint & Chemical Co
9315 Watson Industrial Pa.......Saint Louis MO 63126 314-961-6464 961-6243 550
Web: www.midstatespaint.com

Mid-States Supply Co
1716 Guinotte Ave.......Kansas City MO 64120 816-842-4290 842-3630 612
TF: 800-825-1410 ■ *Web:* www.midcoonline.com

Mid-Tech Services Inc
2348 S Linn Ave.......New Hampton IA 50659 641-394-4756 366
Web: midtechservices.com

MIDTEL 103 Cliff St.......Middleburgh NY 12122 518-827-5211 827-7600 116
TF: 877-827-5211 ■ *Web:* www.midtel.com

Midtex Oil LP 3455 IH 35 S.......New Braunfels TX 78132 830-328-4374 324
Web: www.midtexoil.com

Midtown Cafe 102 19th Ave S.......Nashville TN 37203 615-320-7176 671
Web: www.midtowncafe.com

Name / Address	City	State	ZIP	Phone	Fax	Class
Midtown Cafe & Dessertery 151 S Stratford Rd *Web:* www.midtowncafews.com	Winston-Salem	NC	27104	336-724-9800	724-9830	671
Midtown Educational Foundation 718 S Loomis St *Web:* www.midtown-metro.org	Chicago	IL	60607	312-738-8300		242
Midtown Electric Supply Corp 157 W 18th St *Web:* www.midtownelectric.com	New York	NY	10011	212-255-3388	255-3177	246
Midtown Hotel 220 Huntington Ave *TF:* 800-343-1177 ■ *Web:* www.midtownhotel.com	Boston	MA	02115	617-262-1000	262-8739	379
Midtown Kia 4747 S Yale Ave *Web:* www.midtownkia.com	Tulsa	OK	74135	918-622-3160		57
Mid-valley Distributors Inc 3886 E Jensen Ave *Web:* www.mvdinc.com	Fresno	CA	93725	559-485-2660		619
Midvalley Federal Credit Union 2687 West 7800 South *TF:* 877-992-8663 ■ *Web:* amucu.org	West Jordan	UT	84088	801-359-9600	569-1206	219
Midway Auto Supply Inc 1101 S Hampton Rd *Web:* www.midwayautosupply.com	Dallas	TX	75208	214-943-4341		54
Midway College 512 E Stephens St **Fax Area Code:* 859 ■ *TF:* 800-952-4122 ■ *Web:* www.midway.edu	Midway	KY	40347	800-952-4122	846-5787*	166
Midway Dental Supply Inc 701 N Michigan St *TF:* 800-474-6111 ■ *Web:* www.midwaydental.com	Lakeville	IN	46536	574-784-2533		475
Midway Displays Inc 6554 S Austin Ave *Web:* www.midwaydisplays.com	Bedford Park	IL	60638	708-563-2323		8
Midway Grinding Inc 1451 Lunt Ave *Web:* www.midwaygrinding.com	Elk Grove Village	IL	60007	847-439-7424		454
Midway Industrial Supply Inc 51 Wurz Ave *Web:* www.midway.ws	Utica	NY	13502	315-797-6660		385
Midway Mall 3343 Midway Mall *Web:* www.midwaymallshopping.com	Elyria	OH	44035	440-324-6610		460
Midway Manufacturing Inc 400 Winchester Ave *TF:* 888-659-3631 ■ *Web:* www.midwaymfg.com	Kinsley	KS	67547	620-659-3631	659-2674	223
Midway Oil Co PO Box 4540 *Web:* www.midwayoil.com	Rock Island	IL	61201	309-788-4549	788-5083	579
Midway Products Group Inc 1 Lyman Hoyt Dr *Web:* www.midwayproducts.com	Monroe	MI	48161	734-241-7242	384-0811	489
Midway Speedway 20377 Silver Dr *Web:* www.lebanonmidwayspeedway.com	Lebanon	MO	65536	417-588-4430		515
Midway Structural Pipe and Supply Inc 1611 Clara St *Web:* midwaysupply.com	Jackson	MI	49203	517-787-1350	787-4537	612
Midway Village Museum 6799 Guilford Rd *Web:* www.midwayvillage.com	Rockford	IL	61107	815-397-9112	397-9156	520
Midway-Paris Beauty School 54-40 Myrtle Ave *Web:* www.midwayparis.com	Ridgewood	NY	11385	718-418-2790	418-2730	685
Midwest Acoust-A-Fiber Inc 759 Pittsburgh Dr *Web:* www.mwaaf.com	Delaware	OH	43015	740-369-3624		247
Midwest Action Cycle Inc 251 Host Dr *Web:* www.midwestactioncycle.com	Lake Geneva	WI	53147	262-249-0600	249-0608	61
Midwest Aero Support Inc 1303 Turret Dr *Web:* www.midwestaerosupport.com	Machesney Park	IL	61115	815-398-9202		443
Midwest Ambulance Service of Iowa 2535 106th St *Web:* www.midwestambulance.com	Des Moines	IA	50322	515-222-2222		30
Midwest America Federal Credit Union 1104 Medical Pk Dr *TF:* 800-348-4738 ■ *Web:* www.mwafcu.org	Fort Wayne	IN	46825	260-482-3334		219
Midwest Automotive Inc 1065 Lee St *Web:* www.midwestautomotiveinc.com	Des Plaines	IL	60016	847-827-8400		54
Midwest Bank 105 E Soo St PO Box 40 *TF:* 877-365-5155 ■ *Web:* www.midwestbank.net	Parkers Prairie	MN	56361	218-338-6054	338-5070	70
Midwest Bio-systems Inc 28933 35 E St *TF:* 877-649-2114 ■ *Web:* midwestbiosystems.com	Tampico	IL	61283	815-438-7200		429
Midwest Book Review 278 Orchard Dr *Web:* www.midwestbookreview.com	Oregon	WI	53575	608-835-7937		637-10
Midwest Canvas Corp 4635 W Lake St *TF:* 800-433-4701 ■ *Web:* www.midwestcanvas.com	Chicago	IL	60644	773-287-4400	854-2017	733
Midwest Cast Stone Inc 1610 State Ave *Web:* midwestcaststone.com	Kansas City	KS	66102	913-371-3300		183
Midwest City Chamber of Commerce 5905 Trosper Rd *Web:* www.midwestcityok.com	Midwest City	OK	73110	405-733-3801		139
Midwest College of Oriental Medicine 6232 Bankers Rd *TF:* 800-593-2320 ■ *Web:* www.acupuncture.edu	Racine	WI	53403	262-554-2010	554-7475	167-3
Midwest Commercial Interiors 987 SW Temple *Web:* www.midwestcommercialinteriors.com	Salt Lake City	UT	84101	801-359-7681		319-1
Midwest Communications Inc 904 Grand Ave *Web:* mwcradio.com	Wausau	WI	54403	715-842-1437	842-7061	643
Midwest Consulting Group 5605 N MacArthur Blvd Ste 1000 *Web:* www.mcginfo.com	Irving	TX	75038	972-910-9200		463
Midwest Continental Inc 33941 Frelon Dr *Web:* www.midwestcontinental.com	Sioux City	IA	51108	712-239-1613	239-1616	780
Midwest Control Products Corp 590 E Main St *Web:* www.midwestcontrol.com	Bushnell	IL	61422	309-772-3163	772-2266	620
Midwest Cooling Towers 1156 E Hwy 19 *Web:* midwesttowers.com	Chickasha	OK	73018	405-224-4622	224-4625	14
Midwest Corp 1716 Locust St *Web:* www.midwestliving.com	Des Moines	IA	50309	515-247-2982		457-22
Midwest Corporate Aviation 3512 N Webb Rd *TF:* 800-435-9622 ■ *Web:* www.midwestaviation.com	Wichita	KS	67226	316-636-9700	636-9747	63
Midwest Dental Equipment Services & Supplies 2700 Commerce St **Fax Area Code:* 888 ■ *TF:* 800-766-2025 ■ *Web:* www.mwdental.com	Wichita Falls	TX	76301	800-766-2025	551-3514*	228
Midwest Designer Supply Inc N30 W22377 Green Rd Ste C *TF:* 888-523-2611 ■ *Web:* midwestdesignersupply.com	Waukesha	WI	53186	888-523-2611		361
Midwest Direct 2222 W 110th St *TF:* 800-686-6666 ■ *Web:* www.mw-direct.com	Cleveland	OH	44102	216-251-2500		7
Midwest Drywall Company Inc 1351 S Reca Ct *Web:* www.mwdw.com	Wichita	KS	67209	316-722-9559	722-9682	189-9
Midwest Elastomers Inc 700 Industrial Dr PO Box 412 *TF:* 877-786-3539 ■ *Web:* www.midwestelastomers.com	Wapakoneta	OH	45895	419-738-8844		605-3
Midwest Electric Co-opeartive Corp 104 Washington Ave *TF:* 800-451-3691 ■ *Web:* www.midwestecc.com	Grant	NE	69140	308-352-4356	352-4957	245
Midwest Electric Inc 6029 County Rd 33A *TF:* 800-962-3830 ■ *Web:* www.midwestrec.com	Saint Marys	OH	45885	419-394-4110	394-8333	245
Midwest Employers Casualty Co 14755 N Outer 40 Dr Ste 300 *TF:* 877-975-2667 ■ *Web:* www.mwecc.com	Chesterfield	MO	63017	636-449-7000		391-4
Midwest Energy & Communications 60590 Decatur Rd *TF:* 800-492-5989 ■ *Web:* teammidwest.com	Cassopolis	MI	49031	800-492-5989		245
Midwest Energy Inc 1330 Canterbury Dr **Fax Area Code:* 785 ■ *TF:* 800-222-3121 ■ *Web:* www.mwenergy.com	Hays	KS	67601	800-222-3121	625-1494*	245
Midwest Express Inc 11590 Township Rd 157 *Web:* www.midwestexpressgroup.com	East Liberty	OH	43319	937-642-0335		54
Mid-West Fabricating Co 313 N Johns St *Web:* www.midwestfab.com	Amanda	OH	43102	740-969-4411	969-4433	113
Mid-West Family PO Box 9425 *TF:* 800-225-5636 ■ *Web:* midwestfamily.com	Minneapolis	MN	55440	800-225-5636		390
Midwest Family Broadcasting 2453 E Elm St *Web:* www.mwfmarketing.fm	Springfield	MO	65802	417-886-5677	886-2155	643
Midwest Fasteners Inc 450 Richard St *TF:* 800-852-8352 ■ *Web:* www.midwestfasteners.com	Miamisburg	OH	45342	937-866-0463	866-4174	350
Midwest Federal Savings & Loan Association of St Joseph 1901 Frederick Ave	Saint Joseph	MO	64501	816-233-5148		70
Midwest Feeders Inc 5013 13 Rd *Web:* www.midwest-feeders.com	Ingalls	KS	67853	620-335-5790	335-5636	10-1
Midwest Filtration LLC 9775 International Blvd *Web:* www.midwestfiltration.com	Cincinnati	OH	45246	513-874-6510	874-7913	386
Midwest Financial Networks LLC 1615 S Ingram Mill Rd Bldg C *Web:* mfncuso.com	Springfield	MO	65804	417-851-1818		219
Midwest Financial Solutions Inc 7100 Northland Cir Ste 408 *Web:* www.midwestfinancialsolutions.com	Brooklyn Park	MN	55428	763-535-1562		390
Midwest Folding Products Inc 1414 S Western Ave *TF:* 000 021 4710 ■ *Web:* www.midwestfolding.com	Chicago	IL	60608	312-666-3366	666-2606	319-3
Mid-West Forge Corp 200 Public Square Ste 2800 *Web:* www.mid-westforge.com	Cleveland	OH	44110	216-481-3030	481-7288	483
Midwest Grinding Company Inc 7725 W Twr Ave *Web:* www.midwestgrindinginc.com	Milwaukee	WI	53223	414-354-4440	354-1386	454
Midwest Gun & Supply Inc 16 E Peoria	Paola	KS	66071	913-557-4867		711
Midwest Hardwood Corp 9540 83rd Ave N *Web:* www.midwesthardwood.com	Maple Grove	MN	55369	763-425-8700	391-6740	683
Midwest Helicopter Airways Inc 525 Executive Dr *TF:* 800-323-7609 ■ *Web:* www.midwesthelicopters.com	Willowbrook	IL	60527	630-325-7860	325-3313	359
MIDWEST Homes for Pets 3142 S Cowan Rd PO Box 1031 *TF:* 800-428-8560 ■ *Web:* www.midwesthomes4pets.com	Muncie	IN	47302	765-289-3355	289-6524	578
Midwest Horseshoeing School 1398 Horse Farm Rd **Fax Area Code:* 888 ■ *Web:* www.midwesthorseshoeingschool.com	Divernon	IL	62530	217-697-4899	505-5786*	685
Mid-West Industrial Chemical Co 1509 Sublette Ave *Web:* www.vangrip.com	Saint Louis	MO	63110	314-781-5831	781-7603	3
Midwest Industrial Metal Fabrication Inc 281 Thurman Poe Way *Web:* midwestimf.com	Huntington	IN	46750	260-356-5262	356-5336	567
Midwest Industries Inc 122 E State Hwy 175 *TF:* 800-859-3028 ■ *Web:* www.shorelandr.com	Ida Grove	IA	51445	712-364-3365	364-3361	763
Midwest Institute For Clinical Research Inc 8803 N Meridian St *Web:* micr.com	Indianapolis	IN	46260	317-705-7050		743
Midwest International Standard Products Inc 105 Stover Rd *Web:* www.midwestmagic.com	Charlevoix	MI	49720	231-547-4000	547-9453	18
Midwest Janitorial Service 2831 Falls Ave *TF:* 800-747-6167 ■ *Web:* midwestjanitorialservice.com	Waterloo	IA	50701	319-233-6787		104
Midwest Laboratories Inc 13611 B St *Web:* midwestlabs.com	Omaha	NE	68144	402-334-7770		743
Midwest Library Service Inc 11443 St Charles Rock Rd *TF:* 800-325-8833 ■ *Web:* www.midwestls.com	Bridgeton	MO	63044	314-739-3100	739-1326	96

Name / Address	City	State	ZIP	Phone	Fax	Class
Midwest Livestock Systems Inc 3600 N 6th St *Web:* www.midwestlivestock.com	Beatrice	NE	68310	402-223-5281		446
Midwest Manufacturing Inc 5311 Kane Rd *TF:* 800-826-7126 ■ *Web:* www.midwestmanufacturing.com	Eau Claire	WI	54703	715-876-5555		815
Midwest Manufacturing Resources Inc 1993 Case Pkwy N *TF:* 800-874-0160 ■ *Web:* www.hfomidwest.com	Twinsburg	OH	44087	330-405-4227		791
Mid-West Marketing 91 Mill Hill Rd *Web:* mwmktg.espwebsite.com	Bloomsdale	MO	63627	573-483-2577		366
Midwest Materials Inc 3687 Shepard Rd *Web:* www.midwestmaterials.com	Perry	OH	44081	440-259-5200		492
Midwest Mechanical Group 801 Parkview Blvd *TF:* 800-214-3680 ■ *Web:* www.midwestmech.com	Lombard	IL	60148	630-850-2300	655-0730	189-10
Midwest Medical Equipment Inc 9117 W Belden Ave *Web:* www.medequip.com	Franklin Park	IL	60131	847-288-9900	288-9902	475
Midwest Metal Products 111 Mariner Dr *Web:* www.anglerings.com	Michigan City	IN	46361	219-879-8566		482
Midwest Metal Products Co 2100 W Mt Pleasant Rd *TF:* 888-741-1044 ■ *Web:* midwestmetal.com	Muncie	IN	47302	888-741-1044		480
Midwest Minerals Inc 709 N Locust St PO Box 412 *Web:* www.midwestminerals.com	Pittsburg	KS	66762	620-231-8120	235-0840	503-5
Midwest Motor Express Inc 5015 E Main Ave *TF:* 800-741-4097 ■ *Web:* www.mmeinc.com	Bismarck	ND	58502	701-223-1880	224-1405	780
Midwest Mountaineering Inc 309 Cedar Ave S *Web:* www.midwestmtn.com	Minneapolis	MN	55454	612-339-3433		711
Midwest Paper Group 540 Prospect St **Fax Area Code:* 800 ■ *Web:* www.appletoncoated.com	Combined Locks	WI	54113	888-488-6742	991-1542*	557
Midwest Patterns Inc 4901 N 12th St *Web:* www.midwestpatterns.com	Quincy	IL	62305	217-228-6900	228-6906	567
Midwest Plan Service 122 Davidson Hall ISU *TF:* 800-562-3618 ■ *Web:* www-mwps.sws.iastate.edu	Ames	IA	50011	515-294-4337	294-9589	637-2
Midwest Plastic Engineering Inc 1501 Progress St *Web:* www.midwestplastic.com	Sturgis	MI	49091	269-651-5223	651-1798	604
Midwest Plastics Company Inc 1690 E 5th St *Web:* www.midwestplasticscompany.com	Cherryvale	KS	67335	620-336-3611	336-3671	604
Midwest Pro Painting Inc 12845 Farmington Rd *TF:* 800-860-6757 ■ *Web:* www.mpp-inc.com	Livonia	MI	48150	734-427-1040	427-0209	189-8
Midwest Products & Engineering Inc 10597 W Glenbrook Ct *Web:* www.mpe-inc.com	Milwaukee	WI	53224	414-355-0310		198
Midwest Products Company Inc 400 S Indiana St *TF:* 800-348-3497 ■ *Web:* midwestproducts.com	Hobart	IN	46342	219-942-1134	947-2347	762
Midwest Products Finishing Company Inc 6194 Section Rd *Web:* www.midwestecoat.com	Ottawa Lake	MI	49267	734-856-5200	856-7267	481
Midwest Quality Gloves Inc 835 Industrial Rd *TF:* 800-821-3028 ■ *Web:* midwestglove.com	Chillicothe	MO	64601	660-646-2165	646-6933	155-8
Midwest Railcar Repair Inc 25965 482nd Ave *Web:* mwrail.com	Brandon	SD	57005	605-582-8300		366
Midwest Reliability Organization 380 St Peter St Ste 800 *Web:* www.midwestreliability.org	Saint Paul	MN	55102	651-855-1760		533
Midwest Renewable Energy Assn (MREA) 7558 Deer Rd *Web:* www.midwestrenew.org	Custer	WI	54423	715-592-6595		139
Midwest Research Institute (MRI) 425 Volker Blvd *Web:* www.mriglobal.org	Kansas City	MO	64110	816-753-7600		668
Midwest Risk Management Services Inc 5502 Walsh Ln Ste 103 *TF:* 800-440-7475 ■ *Web:* midwestrisk.net	Rogers	AR	72758	479-271-7475	271-7141	390
Midwest Sales & Service Inc 917 S Chapin St *TF:* 800-772-7262 ■ *Web:* mwss-inc.com	South Bend	IN	46601	574-287-3365		38
Midwest School of Massage 6550 S 84th St Ste 400 *Web:* www.midwestschoolofmassage.com	Omaha	NE	68127	402-331-8383		685
Midwest Screw Products Inc 34700 Lakeland Blvd *Web:* www.midwestllc.com	Eastlake	OH	44095	440-951-2333	951-2336	621
Midwest Sealing Products Inc 1001 Commerce Ct **Fax Area Code:* 877 ■ *TF:* 877-686-8320 ■ *Web:* www.midwestsealingproducts.com	Buffalo Grove	IL	60089	847-459-2202	686-9050*	326
Midwest Specialized Transportation Inc 4515 Hwy 63 N PO Box 6418 *TF:* 800-927-8007 ■ *Web:* www.midspec.com	Rochester	MN	55906	507-288-5649		449
Midwest Sports Supply Inc 11613 Reading Rd *TF:* 800-334-4580 ■ *Web:* www.midwestsports.com	Cincinnati	OH	45241	513-956-4900		711
Mid-West Spring & Stamping Co 1404 Joliet Rd Unit C *TF:* 800-619-0909 ■ *Web:* mwspring.com	Romeoville	IL	60446	630-739-3800		719
Midwest Steel & Equipment Company Inc 9825 Moers Rd *Web:* www.midwest-steel.com	Houston	TX	77075	713-991-7843	991-4745	189-16
Mid-West Steel Building Co 7301 Fairview *TF:* 800-777-9378 ■ *Web:* www.mid-weststeel.com	Houston	TX	77041	713-466-7788		105
Midwest Steel Inc 2525 E Grand Blvd *Web:* www.midweststeel.com	Detroit	MI	48211	313-873-2220	873-2222	189-14
Midwest Steeplejacks Inc 133 W Main Ave Ste 201 *Web:* www.midweststeeplejacks.com	West Fargo	ND	58078	701-241-7040	298-8485	480
Midwest Studios 5742 N Post Rd *Web:* www.midweststudios.com	Indianapolis	IN	46216	317-257-5131		514
Midwest Supplies 5825 Excelsior Blvd *Web:* www.midwestsupplies.com	Saint Louis Park	MN	55416	952-562-5300		298
Midwest Supply and Distributing 828 19th Ave NE *TF:* 800-397-6972 ■ *Web:* www.mws-d.com	Saint Joseph	MN	56374	320-363-4700	363-4798	276
Midwest Systems 5911 Hall St *TF:* 800-383-6281 ■ *Web:* www.mwsystems.com	Saint Louis	MO	63147	314-389-6280	389-9443	779
Midwest Technical Institute 2731 Farmers Market Rd *TF:* 888-976-5171 ■ *Web:* www.midwesttech.edu	Springfield	IL	62707	217-527-8324		167-3
Midwest Telemark International Inc 112 Main St W	Mohall	ND	58761	701-756-6483		393
Mid-West Terminal Warehouse Company Inc 1700 Universal Ave *Web:* www.mwtco.com	Kansas City	MO	64120	816-231-8811	231-0020	803-1
Midwest Tile 200 W Industrial Lake Dr *TF:* 888-818-6864 ■ *Web:* midwesttile.com	Lincoln	NE	68528	402-476-2542	476-7891	191-1
Midwest Tile & Concrete Products Inc 4309 Webster Rd *TF:* 800-359-4701 ■ *Web:* www.midwesttile.net	Woodburn	IN	46797	260-749-5173	493-2477	183
Midwest Tool & Cutlery Company Inc 1210 Progress St PO Box 160 *TF:* 800-782-4659 ■ *Web:* midwestsnips.com	Sturgis	MI	49091	269-651-7964	651-4412	222
Midwest Tool & Engineering Co 112 Webster St *Web:* www.themidwesttool.com	Dayton	OH	45402	937-224-0756	224-0757	757
Midwest Trading Horticultural Supplies Inc 48w805 Il Rt 64 *Web:* www.midwest-trading.com	Maple Park	IL	60151	630-365-1990	365-3818	292
Midwest Transmission Center Inc 40312 County 8 Blvd *Web:* www.midwesttrans.com	Zumbrota	MN	55992	507-824-2487		62-6
Midwest Truck & Auto Parts Inc 1001 W Exchange *TF:* 800-934-2727 ■ *Web:* www.midwesttruck.com	Chicago	IL	60609	773-247-3400	579-3788	61
Mid-West Truckers Association Inc 2727 N Dirksen Pkwy *Web:* mid-westtruckers.com	Springfield	IL	62702	217-525-0310	525-0342	49-21
Midwest Venture Alliance (MVA) 7829 E Rockhill St Ste 307 *Web:* www.midwestventure.com	Wichita	KS	67206	316-651-5900		393
Midwest Vision Centers Inc 2824 W Division St Division Place Shopping Ctr *Web:* www.midwestvisioncenters.com	Saint Cloud	MN	56301	320-253-2020	251-6886	542
Midwest Walnut 1914 Tostevin *TF:* 800-592-5688 ■ *Web:* www.midwestwalnut.com	Council Bluffs	IA	51503	712-325-9191		448
Midwest Wire Products Inc PO Box 770 *TF:* 800-445-0225 ■ *Web:* www.wireforming.com	Sturgeon Bay	WI	54235	920-743-6591	743-3777	488
Midwestern Baptist Theological Seminary 5001 N Oak Trafficway *TF:* 800-944-6287 ■ *Web:* www.mbts.edu	Kansas City	MO	64118	816-414-3700		167-3
Midwestern Dental Plans Inc 5050 Schaefer Rd *TF:* 800-544-6374 ■ *Web:* www.midwesterndentalplansinc.com	Dearborn	MI	48126	313-582-0150		390
Midwestern Industries Inc 915 Oberlin Rd SW *TF:* 877-474-9464 ■ *Web:* midwesternind.com	Massillon	OH	44647	330-837-4203	837-4210	190
Midwestern Intermediate Unit Iv 453 Maple St *TF:* 800-942-8035 ■ *Web:* www.miu4.org	Grove City	PA	16127	724-458-6700	458-5083	685
Midwestern Manufacturing Company Inc 2119 S Union Ave *Web:* sidebooms.com	Tulsa	OK	74107	918-858-4200		537
Midwestern Rail Association Archives 123 Main St PO Box 48 *Web:* www.wpgrailwaymuseum.com	Winnipeg	MB	R3C1A3	204-942-4632		434-3
Midwestern Regional Medical Ctr (MRMC) 2520 Elisha Ave *TF:* 800-615-3055 ■ *Web:* www.cancercenter.com	Zion	IL	60099	847-872-4561		374-7
Midwestern State University 3410 Taft Blvd *TF:* 800-842-1922 ■ *Web:* mwsu.edu	Wichita Falls	TX	76308	940-397-4000	397-4672	166
Midwestern University Library Downers Grove Campus 555 31st St *Web:* library.midwestern.edu	Downers Grove	IL	60515	630-515-6200		434-3
MidWestOne Bank 102 S Clinton St PO Box 1700 *NASDAQ: MOFG* ■ *TF:* 866-802-9128 ■ *Web:* www.midwestone.bank	Iowa City	IA	52240	319-356-5800		360-2
Midwood Ambulance & Oxygen Service Inc 2593 W 13th St *Web:* www.midwoodambulance.com	Brooklyn	NY	11223	718-645-1000		30
Mid-York Library System 1600 Lincoln Ave *Web:* www.catalog.midyork.org	Utica	NY	13502	315-735-8328		434-3
Mid-York Press Inc, The 2808 State Hwy 80 *Web:* www.midyorkpress.com	Sherburne	NY	13460	607-674-4491	674-4088	554
MIE (Medical Informatics Engineering Inc) 6302 Constitution Dr *Web:* www.mieweb.com	Fort Wayne	IN	46804	260-459-6270		180
Miele Inc 9 Independence Way *TF:* 800-843-7231 ■ *Web:* www.miele.com	Princeton	NJ	08540	609-419-9898	419-4298	36
Mierendorf & Company PC 4639 W River Dr NE *Web:* miercpa.com	Comstock Park	MI	49321	616-784-4445		2
Miers Insurance Inc 2222 S 12th St *Web:* www.miersinsurance.com	Allentown	PA	18103	610-797-7900		390
Mifflin County 20 N Wayne St *Web:* www.co.mifflin.pa.us	Lewistown	PA	17044	717-248-6733	248-3695	338

Name	Address	City	State	ZIP	Phone	Fax	Class	Notes
Mifflin County School District	201 Eigth St	Lewistown	PA	17044	717-248-0148		685	Web: www.mcsdk12.org
Mifflinburg Bank & Trust Co (MBTC)	250 E Chestnut St PO Box 186	Mifflinburg	PA	17844	570-966-1041		70	TF: 888-966-3131 ■ Web: www.mbtc.com
Mig Communications	800 Hearst Ave	Berkeley	CA	94710	510-845-7549		224	Web: www.migcom.com
Mighty Distributing System of America Inc	650 Engineering Dr	Norcross	GA	30092	770-448-3900	446-8627	61	TF: 800-829-3900 ■ Web: www.mightyautoparts.com
Mighty Eighth Air Force Museum	175 Bourne Ave	Pooler	GA	31322	912-748-8888	748-0209	520	Web: www.mightyeighth.org
Mighty Way Books	PO Box 6176	Somerset	NJ	08875	732-951-8715		637-2	Web: www.mightywaybooks.com
Migis Hotel Group	400 Commercial St Ste 304	Portland	ME	04103	207-899-3860		378	Web: migishotelgroup.com
Mignanelli & Associates Ltd	10 Weybosset St Ste 400	Providence	RI	02903	401-455-3500		41	Web: mignanelli.com
Mignano Tree Care Inc	1127 Se Second St	Boynton Beach	FL	33435	561-738-2850		422	Web: mignanotreecare.com
Migrant Legal Action Program (MLAP)	1001 Connecticut Ave NW Ste 915	Washington	DC	20036	202-775-7780		48-8	Web: www.mlap.org
Migration & Refugee Services	US Conference of Catholic Bishops 3211 Fourth St NE	Washington	DC	20017	202-541-3200		48-5	Web: www.usccb.org
Migration Policy Institute (MPI)	1400 16th St NW Ste 300	Washington	DC	20036	202-266-1940	266-1900	637-10	Web: www.migrationpolicy.org
Migratory Bird Conservation Commission	5275 Leesburg Pk	Falls Church	VA	22041	800-344-9453		340-20	TF: 800-344-9453 ■ Web: www.fws.gov
MI-GSO PCUBED	1340 Eisenhower Pl	Ann Arbor	MI	48108	734-741-7770	741-1343	194	TF: 877-728-2331 ■ Web: www.migso-pcubed.com
Migu Press Inc	260 Ivyland Rd	Warminster	PA	18974	215-957-9763		627	Web: www.migupress.com
Mihlfeld & Associates Inc	2841 E Division St	Springfield	MO	65803	417-831-6727		311	Web: www.mihlfeld.com
MII (Mitcham Industries Inc)	8141 Hwy 75 S PO Box 1175	Huntsville	TX	77340	936-291-2277	295-1922	264-3	NASDAQ: MIND ■ Web: www.mitchamindustries.com
MII Amo at Enchantment Resort	525 Boynton Canyon Rd	Sedona	AZ	86336	928-203-8500		707	TF: 888-749-2137 ■ Web: www.miiamo.com
Mijac Alarm	9339 Charles Smith Ave Ste 100	Rancho Cucamonga	CA	91730	909-982-7612		693	TF: 800-982-7612 ■ Web: www.mijacalarm.com
Mi-Jack Products Inc	3111 W 167th St	Hazel Crest	IL	60429	708-596-5200		190	Web: www.mi-jack.com
Mika Meyers PLC	900 Monroe Ave NW	Grand Rapids	MI	49503	616-632-8000		445	Web: www.mikameyers.com
Mikado Japanese Restaurant	148 S Illinois St	Indianapolis	IN	46225	317-972-4180		671	Web: indymikado.com
Mikado Ryotei	9033 Research Blvd	Austin	TX	78758	512-833-8188		671	Web: mikadoaustin.com
MIKAL Salon & Spa Software	4382 Mt Carmel Tobasco	Cincinnati	OH	45244	513-528-5100	528-8264	177	TF: 800-448-5420 ■ Web: www.mikal-salon-software.com
Mikan Associates Consulting	141 W Jackson Blvd Ste 1520	Chicago	IL	60604	847-613-6010		463	Web: www.mikanassociates.com
Mikart Inc	1750 Chattahoochee Ave NW	Atlanta	GA	30318	404-351-4510	350-0432	582	Web: www.mikart.com
Mikasa Sports Usa	556 Vanguard Way Unit D	Brea	CA	92821	800-854-6927	854-6960	711	TF: 800-854-6927 ■ Web: mikasasports.com
Mikata Japanese Steakhouse	5300 Sidney Simons Blvd	Columbus	GA	31904	706-327-5100		671	Web: www.mikatajapanesesteakhouse.com
Mikato Japanese Steak House	1092 S Ponce de Leon Blvd	Saint Augustine	FL	32084	904-824-7064		671	Web: www.mymikato.com
Mike Alexander Dies Inc	1134 W Kentucky St	Louisville	KY	40210	502-515-2777	515-3949	757	Web: www.madies.com
Mike Anderson's Seafood	1031 W Lee Dr	Baton Rouge	LA	70820	225-766-7823		671	Web: www.mikeandersons.com
Mike Balter Mallets	15 E Palatine Rd Ste 116	Prospect Heights	IL	60070	847-541-5777	541-5785	523	Web: www.mikebalter.com
Mike Calvert Toyota Inc	2333 S Loop W	Houston	TX	77054	713-558-8100		57	TF: 844-862-8395 ■ Web: www.mikecalverttoyota.com
Mike Castrucci Ford Sales Inc	1020 SR-28	Milford	OH	45150	513-248-1402		516	Web: www.mikecastrucciford.com
Mike Collins & Associates Inc	6048 Century Oaks Dr	Chattanooga	TN	37416	423-892-8899		175	TF: 800-347-6950 ■ Web: www.mcollins.com
Mike Davis & Associates Inc	15505 Long Vista Dr Ste 200	Austin	TX	78728	512-836-8442		344	TF: 888-836-8442 ■ Web: www.imagecraftexhibits.com
Mike Ditka's Restaurants	100 E Chestnut St	Chicago	IL	60611	312-587-8989		671	Web: www.ditkasrestaurants.com
Mike Donelson CPA PC	14550 Torrey Chase Blvd Ste 270	Houston	TX	77014	281-537-8202		2	Web: mikedonelsoncpa.com
Mike Durfee State Prison	1412 Wood St	Springfield	SD	57062	605-369-2201	369-2813	213	Web: doc.sd.gov
Mike Ferry Organization, The	7220 S Cimarron Rd Ste 300	Las Vegas	NV	89113	702-982-6260		260	TF: 800-448-0647 ■ Web: www.mikeferry.com
Mike Kelly Law Group LLC	500 Taylor St Ste 400	Columbia	SC	29201	803-726-0123	252-7145	428	TF: 866-692-0123 ■ Web: www.mklawgroup.com
Mike Murach & Associates Inc	4340 N Knoll	Fresno	CA	93722	559-440-9071	440-0963	637-2	TF: 800-221-5528 ■ Web: www.murach.com
Mike Noonan Insurance Financial Services	6106 Covington Rd Ste 110	Fort Wayne	IN	46804	260-969-0783		390	Web: mikenoonan.net
Mike Preis Inc	39 Lower Main St PO Box 280	Callicoon	NY	12723	845-887-4210	887-5162	390	Web: mikepreis.com
Mike Reed Chevrolet	1559 E Oglethorpe	Hinesville	GA	31313	877-228-3943		57	TF: 877-228-3943 ■ Web: mikereedchevy.com
Mike Roess Gold Head Branch State Park	6239 SR 21	Keystone Heights	FL	32656	352-473-4701		565	Web: www.floridastateparks.org
Mike Rose's Auto Body Inc	2260 Via de Marcardos	Concord	CA	94520	925-689-1739	689-0991	62-4	TF: 855-340-1739 ■ Web: mikesautobody.com
Mike Savoie Chevrolet	1900 W Maple PO Box 520	Troy	MI	48099	248-566-6523		57	Web: www.mikesavoie.com
Mike Shannon's	871 S Arbor Vitae Ste 101	Edwardsville	IL	62025	618-655-9911		671	Web: www.mikeshannonsgrill.com
Mike Thomas & Associates Inc	9601 Coldwater Rd	Fort Wayne	IN	46825	260-489-2000		652	Web: mikethomasrealtor.com
Mike's Famous Harley-Davidson of Groton	951 Bank St	New London	CT	06320	860-574-9200		520	Web: www.mikesfamous.com
Miken Sales Inc	539 S Mission Rd	Los Angeles	CA	90033	323-266-2560	266-2580	157-6	Web: mikenclothing.com
Mikes Pharmacy Inc	211 W Washington Ave	Myerstown	PA	17067	717-866-7547		237	Web: medicineshoppe.com
Mike-Sell's Potato Chip Co	333 Leo St PO Box 115	Dayton	OH	45404	937-228-9400	461-5707	296-35	TF: 800-257-4742 ■ Web: mikesells.com
Miki Japanese Restaurant	106 S First St	Ann Arbor	MI	48104	734-665-8226		671	Web: www.mikiannarbor.com
Miki Sangyo (USA) Inc	400 Interpace Pky	Parsippany	NJ	07054	973-263-4111	263-1325	146	Web: www.mikisangyo.com
Mikimoto (America) Company Ltd	730 Fifth Ave	New York	NY	10019	844-341-0579		411	TF: 844-341-0579 ■ Web: www.mikimotoamerica.com
Mikimoto's	1212 Washington St	Wilmington	DE	19801	302-656-8638		671	Web: mikimotos.com
MikiSushi	180 Leveland Ave Ste 5	Modesto	CA	95350	209-524-3555		671	Web: www.mikisushi.net
Mikita & Roccanova Ltd	1301 Hwy 36 Bldg 1	Hazlet	NJ	07730	732-705-3363		41	Web: mr-laws.com
Mikro Systems Inc	1180 Seminole Trl Ste 220	Charlottesville	VA	22901	434-244-6480		261	Web: www.mikrosystems.com
MikroPul LLC	4433 Chesapeake Dr	Charlotte	NC	28216	704-398-7906		18	Web: www.mikropul.com
Mikros Engineering Inc	8755 Wyoming Ave N	Brooklyn Park	MN	55445	763-424-4642		261	TF: 800-394-5499 ■ Web: www.mikros.com
Mikros Systems Corp	707 Alexander Rd Ste 208	Princeton	NJ	08540	609-987-1513		529	Web: www.mikrossystems.com
Mikuni American Corp	8910 Mikuni Ave	Northridge	CA	91324	818-885-1242	993-6877	60	Web: www.mikuni.com
Mil Corp	4000 Mitchellville Rd	Bowie	MD	20716	301-805-8500	805-8505	177	Web: www.milcorp.com
Mila Displays Inc	1315 Broadway Ste 108	Hewlett Neck	NY	11557	516-791-2643		154	TF: 800-295-6452 ■ Web: www.miladisplays.com
Mila's European Bakery Inc	239 N Main St	Thiensville	WI	53092	262-242-1404		297-2	Web: www.milasbakery.com
Milaeger's Inc	4838 Douglas Ave	Racine	WI	53402	262-639-2040	681-6192	323	TF: 800-669-1229 ■ Web: www.milaegers.com
Milam County	107 W Main St	Cameron	TX	76520	254-697-7049	697-7055	338	TF: 800-299-2437 ■ Web: www.milamcounty.net
Milam's Market	11 N Royal Poinciana Blvd Ste 100	Miami Springs	FL	33166	305-884-4870	884-5590	345	Web: www.milamsmarkets.com
Milan Engineering Inc	2102 NE 3rd St	Winter Park	FL	32792	407-678-2055		186	
Milan Express Company Inc	1091 Kefauver Dr	Milan	TN	38358	800-231-7303		780	TF: 800-231-7303 ■ Web: www.milanexpress.com
Milan Hill State Park	427 Milan Hill Rd	Milan	NH	03588	603-449-2429		565	Web: www.nhstateparks.org
Milan Institute & Milan Institute of Cosmetology	75-030 Gerald Ford Dr Ste 203	Palm Desert	CA	92211	888-207-9460		668	TF: 888-207-9460 ■ Web: www.milaninstitute.edu
Milan Salami Company Inc	1155 67th St	Oakland	CA	94608	510-654-7055		296-26	
Milan Tool Corp	8989 Brookpark Rd	Cleveland	OH	44129	216-661-1078	661-6946	350	Web: milantool.com
Milano & Wanat LLC	471 E Main St	Branford	CT	06405	203-315-7000		41	Web: mwllc.com

Name / Address	Phone	Fax	Class
Milano Restaurants Intl 6729 N Palm Ave Ste 200 .... Fresno CA 93704 *Web:* www.milano-ri.com	559-432-0399	432-0398	670
Milara Inc 49 Maple St. .... Milford MA 01757 *TF:* 877-572-0006 ■ *Web:* www.milarasmt.com	508-533-5322	422-9933	494
Milbank Manufacturing Company Inc 4801 Deramus Ave .... Kansas City MO 64120 *Web:* milbankworks.com	816-483-5314	483-6357	697
Milbank Tweed Hadley & McCloy LLP 1 Chase Manhattan Plz. .... New York NY 10005 *Web:* www.milbank.com	212-530-5000	530-5219	428
Milbar Hydro-Test Inc 651 Aero Dr .... Shreveport LA 71107 *TF:* 800-259-8210 ■ *Web:* www.milbarhydro-test.com	318-227-8210	222-2558	539
Milber Makris Plousadis & Seiden LLP 709 Westchester Ave Ste 300 .... White Plains NY 10604 *Web:* milbermakris.com	914-681-8700	681-8709	445
Milco Industries Inc 550 E Fifth St .... Bloomsburg PA 17815 *Web:* milcotextile.com	570-784-0400		155-15
Milco Manufacturing Co 2147 E 10-Mile Rd .... Warren MI 48091 *Web:* www.milcomfg.com	586-755-7320	755-7442	811
Mildred Elley Business School 100 West St .... Pittsfield MA 01201 *TF:* 888-291-4574 ■ *Web:* www.mildred-elley.edu	413-499-8618	442-2269	685
Mildred Independent School District 5475 S US Hwy 287 .... Corsicana TX 75109 *Web:* www.mildredisd.org	903-872-6505	872-1341	685
Mildred's Big City Food 3445 W University Ave .... Gainesville FL 32607 *Web:* mildredsbigcityfood.com	352-371-1711		671
Mile High Press Ltd PO Box 460880 .... Aurora CO 80046 *Web:* www.milehighpress.com	303-885-2207		637-2
Mile High Racing & Entertainment/Mile High 10750 E Iliff Ave .... Aurora CO 80014 *Web:* www.mihiracing.com	303-751-5918		642
Mile High Shooting Accessories LLC 3731 Monarch St .... Erie CO 80516 *TF:* 877-871-9990 ■ *Web:* www.milehighshooting.com	303-255-9999		807
Mile High United Way Inc 2505 18th St .... Denver CO 80211 *Web:* www.unitedwaydenver.org	303-433-8383	455-6462	48-15
Mile Marker International Inc 2121 Blount Rd. .... Pompano Beach FL 33069 *TF:* 800-886-8647 ■ *Web:* milemarker.com	800-886-8647		61
Milender White Construction Co 12655 W 54th Dr .... Arvada CO 80002 *Web:* www.milenderwhite.com	303-216-0420		186
Miles & More PO Box 946 .... Santa Clarita CA 91380 **Fax Area Code:* 661 ■ *TF:* 800-581-6400 ■ *Web:* www.miles-and-more.com	800-581-6400	244-4950*	26
Miles & Stockbridge P C 100 Light St .... Baltimore MD 21202 *Web:* www.milesstockbridge.com	410-727-6464		445
Miles Chemical Co 12801 Rangoon St. .... Arleta CA 91331 *Web:* www.mileschemical.com	818-504-3355		146
Miles City Livestock Commission 337 I-94 Bus Loop .... Miles City MT 59301 *Web:* www.milescitylivestock.net	406-234-1790		446
Miles College 5500 Myron Massey Blvd. .... Fairfield AL 35064 *TF:* 800-445-0708 ■ *Web:* www.miles.edu	205-929-1000	929-1627	166
Miles Community College 2715 Dickinson St .... Miles City MT 59301 *TF:* 800-541-9281 ■ *Web:* www.milescc.edu	406-874-6100	874-6283	162
Miles Hansford & Tallant LLC 202 Tribble Gap Rd Ste 200 .... Cumming GA 30040 *Web:* mhtlegal.com	770-781-4100	781-9191	41
Miles Kimball Co 250 City Ctr Bldg .... Oshkosh WI 54906 *TF:* 855-202-7394 ■ *Web:* www.mileskimball.com	855-202-7394		459
Miles LeHane Companies Inc The Glenfiddich House 205 N King St .... Leesburg VA 20176 *Web:* www.mileslehane.com	703-777-3370	777-3375	194
Miles Media Group LLLP 6751 Professional Pkwy W Ste 200 .... Sarasota FL 34240 *TF:* 800-683-0010 ■ *Web:* www.milespartnership.com	941-342-2300		637-9
Miles Sand & Gravel Company Inc 400 Valley Ave NE. .... Puyallup WA 98372 *Web:* miles.rocks	253-833-3705	833-3746	503-4
Miles Technologies Inc 300 W Rt 38 .... Moorestown NJ 08057 *TF:* 800-496-8001 ■ *Web:* www.milestechnologies.com	856-439-0999		180
MilesTek Corp 1506 I-35 W .... Denton TX 76207 *TF:* 800-958-5173 ■ *Web:* www.milestek.com	940-484-9400		194
Milestone 300 International Blvd .... Clarksville TN 37040 *Web:* www.milestonetiles.com	931-645-5100		751
Milestone Hospitality Management LLC 729 E Pratt St Ste 800. .... Baltimore MD 21202 *Web:* www.milestonehotels.com	561-981-8828	981-8827	653
Milestone Scientific Inc 220 S Orange Ave. .... Livingston NJ 07039 *OTC:* MLSS ■ *TF:* 800-862-1125 ■ *Web:* www.milestonescientific.com	973-535-2717	535-2829	477
Milestone Technologies Inc 3101 Skyway Ct .... Fremont CA 94539 *TF:* 877-651-2454 ■ *Web:* www.milestonepowered.com	877-651-2454		393
Milestone Venture Partners 551 Madison Ave 7th Fl .... New York NY 10022 *Web:* www.activatevp.com	212-223-7400		792
Milford Area Chamber of Commerce 258 Main St .... Milford MA 01757 *Web:* milfordchamber.org	508-473-6700		139
Milford Bank 33 Broad St .... Milford CT 06460 *TF:* 800-340-4862 ■ *Web:* www.milfordbank.com	203-783-5700		70
Milford Chamber of Commerce 5 Broad St. .... Milford CT 06460 *Web:* www.milfordct.com	203-878-0681	876-8517	139
Milford Daily News Co 197 Main St. .... Milford MA 01757 *Web:* www.milforddailynews.com	508-634-7522	634-7514	637-8
Milford Exempted Village School District 1039 St Rt 28 .... Milford OH 45150 *Web:* www.milfordschools.org	513-831-9690	831-3208	685
Milford Federal Savings & Loan Assn 246 Main St .... Milford MA 01757 *TF:* 800-478-6990 ■ *Web:* www.milfordfederal.com	508-634-2500		71
Milford Historical Society 124 E Commerce St .... Milford MI 48381 *Web:* www.milfordhistory.org	248-685-7308		520
Milford Hospital (MH) 300 Seaside Ave. .... Milford CT 06460 *Web:* www.milfordhospital.org	203-876-4000	876-4220	374-3
Milford Mirror 1000 Bridgeport Ave .... Shelton CT 06484 *Web:* www.milfordmirror.com	203-402-2315		532-4
Milford National Bank & Trust Co, The 300 E Main St. .... Milford MA 01757 *Web:* www.milfordnationalonline.com	508-634-4100		70
Milford Printers 22 Whitney Dr Park 50 Near Cintas .... Milford OH 45150 *Web:* www.milfordprinters.com	513-831-6630	248-7606	627
Milford Public Library 57 New Haven Ave .... Milford CT 06460 *Web:* www.ci.milford.ct.us	203-783-3290		434-3
Milford Regional Medical Ctr 14 Prospect St .... Milford MA 01757 *Web:* www.milfordregional.org	508-473-1190		374-3
Milford State Park 3612 State Park Rd .... Milford KS 66514 *Web:* www.ksoutdoors.com	785-238-3014		565
Milford Town Library 80 Spruce St .... Milford MA 01757 *Web:* www.milfordtownlibrary.org	508-473-2145		434-3
Milford-Miami Township Chamber of Commerce 745 Center St Ste 302. .... Milford OH 45150 *TF:* 800-837-3200 ■ *Web:* www.milfordmiamitownship.com	513-831-2411	831-3547	139
Milgo Industrial Inc 68 Lombardy St. .... Brooklyn NY 11222 *Web:* www.milgo-bufkin.com	718-388-6476	963-0614	491
Milgro Nursery LLC 1085 Victoria Ave .... Oxnard CA 93030 *Web:* www.milgro.com	805-985-0855		292
Milhouse Engineering & Construction Inc 60 E Van Buren St Ste 1501 .... Chicago IL 60605 *Web:* milhouseinc.com	312-987-0061		261
Milian & Swain Associates Inc 2025 SW 32nd Ave. .... Miami FL 33145 *Web:* www.milianswain.com	305-441-0123		261
Milieu Landscaping 48 E Hintz Rd. .... Wheeling IL 60090 *Web:* milieuland.com	847-465-1160		317
Milio's Sandwiches 901 Deming Way Ste 202 .... Madison WI 53717 *Web:* milios.com	608-662-3000	662-3001	670
Military & Aerospace Electronics Magazine PO Box 3425 .... Northbrook IL 60065 *Web:* www.militaryaerospace.com	847-559-7330	763-9607	457-12
Military Advantage 55 Second St Ste 300 .... San Francisco CA 94105 *Web:* www.military.com	415-820-3434	820-0552	171
Military Benefit Assn (MBA) 14605 Avion Pkwy PO Box 221110 .... Chantilly VA 20153 *TF:* 800-336-0100 ■ *Web:* www.militarybenefit.org	703-968-6200	968-6423	48-19
Military Officers Association of America (MOAA) 201 N Washington St .... Alexandria VA 22314 *TF:* 800-234-6622 ■ *Web:* www.moaa.org	800-234-6622		48-19
Military Sales & Service Co 5301 S Westmoreland Rd .... Dallas TX 75237 *Web:* mssco.com	214-330-4621		195
Military/Info Publishing PO Box 41211 .... Plymouth MN 55441 *Web:* www.military-info.com	763-533-8627		637-2
Milk Products LLC PO Box 150 .... Chilton WI 53014 *TF:* 800-657-0793 ■ *Web:* www.milkproductsinc.com	920-849-2348	849-9014	296-10
Milk Specialties Co 7500 Flying Cloud Dr Ste 500 .... Eden Prairie MN 55344 *TF:* 800-323-4274 ■ *Web:* www.milkspecialties.com	952-942-7310		447
Milkco Inc 220 Deaverview Rd. .... Asheville NC 28806 *TF:* 800-842-8021 ■ *Web:* www.milkco.com	828-254-9560		296-27
Milken Community High School 15800 Zeldins Way .... Los Angeles CA 90049 *Web:* www.milkenschool.org	310-440-3500	471-5139	685
Milken Family Foundation 1250 Fourth St .... Santa Monica CA 90401 *Web:* www.mff.org	310-570-4800	570-4801	305
Milkshake Media LP 2210 S Congress Ave. .... Austin TX 78704 *Web:* www.hellomilkshake.com	512-474-7777		344
Milkweed Editions Open Book Bldg 1011 Washington Ave S Ste 300 .... Minneapolis MN 55415 *TF:* 800-520-6455 ■ *Web:* www.milkweed.org	612-332-3192		637-9
Mill & Timber Products Ltd 12745- 116th Ave. .... Surrey BC V3V7H9 *Web:* www.millandtimber.com	604-580-2781		683
Mill Creek Carpet & Tile Co 6845 E 41st St .... Tulsa OK 74145 *Web:* www.millcreekcarpet.com	918-621-4000		290
Mill Creek Community Assn 15524 Country Club Dr .... Mill Creek WA 98012 *Web:* mcca.info	425-316-3344		653
Mill Creek Mall 496 Mill Creek Mall. .... Erie PA 16565 *TF:* 800-615-3535 ■ *Web:* www.millcreekmall.net	814-868-9000	864-1193	460
Mill Falls 312 Daniel Webster Hwy. .... Meredith NH 03253 **Fax Area Code:* 603 ■ *TF:* 844-745-2931 ■ *Web:* www.millfalls.com	844-745-2931	279-6797*	379
Mill Hill Historic Park & Museum 2 E Wall St .... Norwalk CT 06851 *Web:* www.norwalkhistoricalsociety.org	203-846-0525		50-3
Mill Masters Inc 39 Mill Masters Dr. .... Jackson TN 38305 *Web:* www.millmasters.com	731-668-5558	668-2477	91
Mill Mountain Theatre 1 Market Sq .... Roanoke VA 24011 *Web:* www.millmountain.org	540-342-5730		572
Mill Neck Manor School for The Deaf 40 Frost Mill Rd .... Mill Neck NY 11765 *Web:* millneck.org	516-922-4100		768
Mill Power Inc 3141 SW High Desert Dr .... Prineville OR 97754 *Web:* www.millpower.com	541-447-1100	447-1101	207
Mill Ridge Farm 2800 Bowman Mill Rd .... Lexington KY 40513 *Web:* www.millridge.com	859-231-0606	255-6010	368

	Phone	Fax	Class
Mill River Lumber Ltd 2639 Middle Rd .... Clarendon VT 05759 *Web:* www.millriverlumber.com	802-775-0032		683
Mill Run Tours 424 Madison Ave 12th Fl .... New York NY 10017 *TF:* 855-645-5868 ■ *Web:* www.millrun.com	212-486-9840	223-8129	16
Mill Steel Co 5116 36th St SE .... Grand Rapids MI 49512 **Fax Area Code:* 616 ■ *TF:* 800-247-6455 ■ *Web:* www.millsteel.com	800-247-6455	977-9411*	723
Mill Street Inn 75 Mill St .... Newport RI 02840 *TF:* 800-392-1316 ■ *Web:* www.millstreetinn.com	401-849-9500	848-5131	379
Mill Valley Film Festival (MVFF) 1001 Lootens Pl Ste 220 .... San Rafael CA 94901 *Web:* www.mvff.com	415-383-5256	383-8606	282
Mill Valley Public Library 375 Throckmorton Ave .... Mill Valley CA 94941 *Web:* www.millvalleylibrary.org	415-389-4292	388-8929	434-3
Mill's Tavern 101 N Main St .... Providence RI 02903 *Web:* www.millstavernrestaurant.com	401-272-3331		671
Millard County 50 South Main .... Fillmore UT 84631 *Web:* millardcounty.com	435-743-5227		338
Millard Lumber Inc 12900 I St .... Omaha NE 68145 *TF:* 800-228-9260 ■ *Web:* millardlumber.com	402-896-2800	896-2865	191-3
Millard Manufacturing Corp 10602 Olive St .... La Vista NE 68128 *TF:* 800-662-4263 ■ *Web:* www.millardmfg.com	402-331-8010		207
Millard, Rouse & Rosebrugh LLP 96 Nelson St .... Brantford ON N3T5N3 *Web:* millards.com	519-863-3557		2
Millbrook 36865 Schoolcraft Rd .... Livonia MI 48150 *Web:* www.millbrook.us	734-432-9334		261
Millbrook Benefits & Insurance Services LLC 270 Benton Dr E Longmeadow .... Springfield MA 01028 *Web:* millbrookbenefits.com	413-886-0008		390
Millbrook Capital Management Inc 570 Lexington Ave 46th Fl .... New York NY 10022 *Web:* www.millcap.com	212-586-4333		401
Millbrook School 131 Millbrook School Rd .... Millbrook NY 12545 *Web:* www.millbrook.org	845-677-8261	677-1265	622
Millburn Township New Jersey Board Education 434 Millburn Ave .... Millburn NJ 07041 *Web:* www.millburn.org	973-376-3600		685
Millburn Veterinary Hospital 147 Millburn Ave .... Millburn NJ 07041 *TF:* 800-365-8295 ■ *Web:* www.millburnvet.com	973-467-1700		794
Millcraft Investments 95 W Beau St Ste 600 .... Washington PA 15301 *Web:* millcraftideas.com	724-229-8800		190
Millcraft Paper Co 58 Grant Ave .... Cleveland OH 44105 *TF:* 800-860-2482 ■ *Web:* www.millcraft.com	216-441-5500		553
Mille Fabricating 1270 Niagara St .... Buffalo NY 14213 **Fax Area Code:* 716 ■ *TF:* 888-645-5332 ■ *Web:* www.millefab.com	888-645-5332	362-8963*	480
Mille Lacs Band of Ojibwe 43408 Oodena Dr .... Onamia MN 56359 *TF:* 800-709-6445 ■ *Web:* millelacsband.com	320-532-4181	532-7505	132
Mille Lacs County 635 Second St SE .... Milaca MN 56353 *Web:* www.co.mille-lacs.mn.us	320-983-8308		338
Mille Lacs Electric Co-op PO Box 230 .... Aitkin MN 56431 *TF:* 800-450-2191 ■ *Web:* www.mlecmn.net	218-927-2191	927-6822	245
Mille Lacs Health System 200 Elm St N .... Onamia MN 56359 *TF:* 877-535-3154 ■ *Web:* www.mlhealth.org	320-532-3154		374-3
Mille Lacs Kathio State Park 15066 Kathio State Park Rd .... Onamia MN 56359 *Web:* www.dnr.state.mn.us	320-532-3523		565
Milledgeville-Baldwin Convention & Visitors Bureau, The 200 W Hancock St .... Milledgeville GA 31061 *TF:* 800-653-1804 ■ *Web:* www.visitmilledgeville.org	478-452-4687	453-4440	206
Milledgeville-Baldwin County Chamber of Commerce 130 S Jefferson St .... Milledgeville GA 31061 *Web:* milledgevillega.com	478-453-9311		139
Millenia Products Group 1345 Norwood Ave .... Itasca IL 60143 *TF:* 800-822-0092 ■ *Web:* www.dwyerproducts.com	630-741-7900	458-1271	36
Millenium Aviation 2365 Bernville Rd .... Reading PA 19605 *TF:* 800-366-9419 ■ *Web:* majets.com	610-372-4728	374-7580	63
Millenium Challenge Corp 1099 14th St NW Ste 700 .... Washington DC 20005 *Web:* www.mcc.gov	202-521-3600		340-20
Millenium Home Health Care Inc 370 Reed Rd Ste 319 .... Broomall PA 19008 *Web:* www.mhomehealth.com	610-543-4126		363
Millenium Products Inc 6346 Heron Pkwy .... Clarkston MI 48346 *TF:* 888-901-7430 ■ *Web:* milleniumproducts.net	888-901-7430		183
Millennia Consulting 3530 N Damen Ave Ste 1000 .... Chicago IL 60618 *Web:* www.consultmillennia.com	312-922-9920		194
Millennia Holdings Inc 3731 Wilshire Blvd Ste 900 .... Los Angeles CA 90010 *Web:* mhiholdings.com	213-252-1230		363
Millennium 580 Geary St .... San Francisco CA 94102 *Web:* www.millenniumrestaurant.com	415-345-3900		671
Millennium Airship Inc Bremerton National Airport PO Box 1972 .... Belfair WA 98528 *Web:* www.millenniumairship.com	360-674-2488	674-2494	28
Millennium Dental Technologies Inc 10945 South St Ste 104-A .... Cerritos CA 90703 *TF:* 888-638-5262 ■ *Web:* www.lanap.com	562-860-2908		250
Millennium Die Group Inc 2022 Bridge St .... Three Rivers MA 01080 *Web:* www.millenniumdie.com	413-283-3500	283-5400	757
Millennium Forge Inc 990 W Ormsby Ave .... Louisville KY 40210 *Web:* www.millenniumforge.com	502-635-3350	635-3028	483
Millennium Hotels & Resorts 1345 28th St .... Boulder CO 80302 *Web:* www.millenniumhotels.com	303-779-2000		379
Millennium Industrial Tires LLC 433 Lane Dr .... Florence AL 35630 *TF:* 800-421-1180 ■ *Web:* www.millenniumtire.com	256-764-2900		754
Millennium Line X & Truck Accessories 905 N Raceway Rd .... Indianapolis IN 46234 *Web:* www.millenniumlinings.com	317-209-8000	209-8039	54
Millennium Management LLC 666 Fifth Ave .... New York NY 10103 *Web:* www.mlp.com	212-841-4100		690
Millennium Marking Co 2600 Greenleaf Ave .... Elk Grove Village IL 60007 **Fax Area Code:* 800 ■ *TF:* 800-453-5362 ■ *Web:* www.millmarking.com	847-806-1750	453-5366*	534
Millennium Pharmaceuticals Inc 40 Lansdowne St .... Cambridge MA 02139 *Web:* www.takedaoncology.com	617-679-7000	374-7788	85
Millennium Respiratory Services 30 Troy Rd .... Whippany NJ 07981 *TF:* 800-269-9436 ■ *Web:* www.millenniumrespiratory.com	973-463-1880	463-1886	363
Miller & Associates Consulting Engineers PC 1111 Central Ave .... Kearney NE 68847 *Web:* miller-engineers.com	308-234-6456		261
Miller & Chevalier Chartered 655 15th St NW Ste 900 .... Washington DC 20005 *Web:* www.millerchevalier.com	202-626-5800	626-5801	428
Miller & Company CPA PC 265 Racine Dr Ste 203 .... Wilmington NC 28403 *Web:* millercocpas.com	910-452-5260		2
Miller & Company LLC 9700 W Higgins Rd Ste 1000 .... Rosemont IL 60018 *TF:* 800-727-9847 ■ *Web:* www.millerandco.com	847-696-2400	696-2419	500
Miller & Company LLP 21700 Oxnard St Ste 1250 .... Woodland Hills CA 91367 *Web:* millerandcollp.com	818-449-7920		2
Miller & Company Plc 900 S Shackleford Rd Ste 100 .... Little Rock AR 72211 *Web:* millercocpas.net	501-221-3343		2
Miller & Holmes Inc 2311 O'Neil Rd .... Hudson WI 54016 *Web:* mhgas.com	715-377-1730		204
Miller & Hurt Financial Group 182 Barton Blvd .... Rockledge FL 32955 *Web:* millerandhurt.com	321-632-2996		690
Miller & Long Concrete Construction Inc 7101 Wisconsin Ave .... Bethesda MD 20814 *Web:* www.millerandlong.com	301-657-8000	657-8610	189-3
Miller & Luring Company LPA 314 W Main St .... Troy OH 45373 *TF:* 800-381-9680 ■ *Web:* www.millerluring.com	937-339-2627		428
Miller & Martin PLLC 832 Georgia Ave Volunteer Bldg Ste 1000 .... Chattanooga TN 37402 *Web:* www.millermartin.com	423-756-6600		428
Miller & Miller Accountancy Corp 1320 E Shaw Ave Ste 167 .... Fresno CA 93710 *Web:* www.millermillerpc.com	559-225-6211	222-9635	2
Miller & Olson LLP 20 Park Rd Ste E .... Burlingame CA 94010 *Web:* www.millerpoliticallaw.com	650-401-8735	401-8739	428
Miller & Smith Cos 8401 Greensboro Dr Ste 450 .... McLean VA 22102 *Web:* www.millerandsmithcompanies.com	703-821-2500		653
Miller & Wagner LLP 2210 NW Flanders St .... Portland OR 97210 *Web:* miller-wagner.com	503-299-6116	299-6106	41
Miller Advertising Agency Inc 220 W 42nd St 12th Fl .... New York NY 10036 *Web:* www.milleraa.com	212-929-2200		4
Miller and Lents Ltd 2 Houston Ctr 909 Fannin St Ste 1300 .... Houston TX 77010 *Web:* www.millerandlents.com	713-651-9455	654-9914	194
Miller Bonded Inc 4538 Mcleod Rd NE .... Albuquerque NM 87109 *Web:* millerbonded.com	505-881-0220	881-0867	610
Miller Brooks Inc 11712 N Michigan Rd .... Zionsville IN 46077 *Web:* www.millerbrooks.com	317-873-8100		4
Miller Brothers Contractors Inc 990 Cattleman Rd .... Sarasota FL 34232 *Web:* www.millerbrosinc.com	941-371-4162		183
Miller Buettner & Parrott Inc 1515 S Meridian Rd .... Rockford IL 61102	815-986-0059		390
Miller Canfield Paddock & Stone PLC 150 W Jefferson Ste 2500 .... Detroit MI 48226 *Web:* www.millercanfield.com	313-963-6420	496-7500	428
Miller Carol (Rep R - WV) 1605 Longworth House Office Bldg .... Washington DC 20515 *Web:* www.miller.house.gov	202-225-3452		342-2
Miller Chemical & Fertilizer Corp 120 Radio Rd PO Box 333 .... Hanover PA 17331 *TF:* 800-233-2040 ■ *Web:* www.millerchemical.com	717-632-8921		280
Miller Consolidated Industries Inc 2221 Arbor Blvd .... Dayton OH 45439 *TF:* 800-589-4133 ■ *Web:* www.millerconsolidated.com	937-294-2681		484
Miller Consulting Group LLC 4100 Monument Corner Dr Ste 450 .... Fairfax VA 22030 *Web:* mcg-cpa.com	703-591-9280	591-1941	2
Miller Cooper & Company Ltd 1751 Lake Cook Rd Ste 400 .... Deerfield IL 60015 *Web:* millercooper.com	847-205-5000	205-1400	2
Miller County 2001 Hwy 52 .... Tuscumbia MO 65082 *Web:* millercountymissouri.org	573-369-2359	369-2350	338
Miller Edge Inc 300 N Jennersville Rd .... West Grove PA 19390 *Web:* www.milleredge.com	610-869-4422	869-4423	425
Miller Electric Co 2251 Rosselle St .... Jacksonville FL 32204 *TF:* 800-554-4761 ■ *Web:* www.mecojax.com	904-388-8000	389-8653	189-4
Miller Energy Inc 3200 S Clinton Ave .... South Plainfield NJ 07080 *TF:* 800-631-5454 ■ *Web:* www.millerenergy.com	908-755-6700		789
Miller Engineering Co 1616 S Main St .... Rockford IL 61102 *Web:* mecogroup.com	815-963-4878		189-10

Name / Address	City	State	Zip	Phone	Fax	Class
Miller Engineers & Associates Inc 601 Main St *Web:* millerengineersinc.com	Franklin	LA	70538	337-828-1950		261
Miller Engineers & Scientists 5308 S 12th St *TF:* 800-969-7013 ■ *Web:* www.startwithmiller.com	Sheboygan	WI	53081	920-458-6164		261
Miller Environmental Services Inc 401 Navigation Blvd *TF:* 800-929-7227 ■ *Web:* www.millerenviro.com	Corpus Christi	TX	78408	361-289-9800		63
Miller Excavating Inc 3741 Stagecoach Trl N *Web:* www.millerexc.com	Stillwater	MN	55082	651-439-1637	351-7210	189-5
Miller Fireworks 501 Glengary Rd *Web:* www.millerfireworks.com	Holland	OH	43528	419-865-7329	866-7107	45
Miller Formless Company Inc 1805 Dot St *Web:* www.millerformless.com	McHenry	IL	60050	815-385-7700	385-2494	190
Miller Giangrande LLP 915 W Imperial Hwy *Web:* www.mngcpa.com	Brea	CA	92821	714-494-2200		2
Miller Grossbard Advisors LLP 2204 Louisiana 2nd Fl *Web:* mgallp.com	Houston	TX	77002	713-622-3960		734
Miller Group, The 7025 N Scottsdale Rd Ste 235 *TF:* 800-264-1870 ■ *Web:* www.themillergroup.net	Scottsdale	AZ	85253	602-225-0505	225-9024	194
Miller Heiman Group 10509 Professional Cir Ste 100 *Web:* www.millerheimangroup.com	Reno	NV	89521	775-827-4411	827-5517	195
Miller Industries Inc 8503 Hilltop Dr *NYSE: MLR* ■ *TF:* 800-292-0330 ■ *Web:* www.millerind.com	Ooltewah	TN	37363	423-238-4171	238-5371	516
Miller International Inc *Rocky Mountain Clothing Co* 8500 Zuni St *Web:* www.rockymountainclothing.com	Denver	CO	80260	303-428-5696		155-20
Miller Johnson Snell & Cummiskey PLC 250 Monroe Ave NW Ste 800 PO Box 306 *Web:* millerjohnson.com	Grand Rapids	MI	49503	616-831-1700	831-1701	428
Miller Jordan Middle School 700 N McCullough *Web:* mjms.sbcisd.net	San Benito	TX	78586	956-361-6650		685
Miller Kaplan Arase & Company LLP 4123 Lankershim Blvd *Web:* www.millerkaplan.com	North Hollywood	CA	91602	818-769-2010		2
Miller Law Firm Pc, The 950 W University Dr Ste 300 *Web:* millerlawpc.com	Rochester	MI	48307	248-841-2200		428
Miller Machine & Tool Company Inc 201 Precision Dr *Web:* www.millermachinetool.com	Winchester	VA	22603	540-662-6512	665-0704	454
Miller Machinery & Supply Co 127 NE 27th St *Web:* millermachineryandsupply.net	Miami	FL	33137	305-573-1300		274
Miller Mechanical Specialties Inc (MMS) 510 Murphy St *Web:* www.mmsinconline.com	Des Moines	IA	50309	515-243-4287	243-7313	385
Miller Memorial Community Inc 360 Broad St *Web:* www.millercommunity.org	Meriden	CT	06450	203-237-8815		450
Miller Metals 2400 Bond St *Web:* www.millermetals.com	University Park	IL	60484	708-534-7200		492
Miller Morton Caillat & Nevis LLP 2001 W Gateway Pl Ste 220 W *Web:* www.millermorton.com	San Jose	CA	95110	408-292-1765		445
Miller Motorcars Inc 342 W Putnam Ave *TF:* 800-721-8781 ■ *Web:* www.millermotorcars.com	Greenwich	CT	06830	203-629-3890		57
Miller Nash LLP 3400 US Bancorp Tower *Web:* www.millernash.com	Portland	OR	97204	503-224-5858		428
Miller Newlin & Company PC 12941 I-45 N Ste 200 *Web:* miller-newlin.com	Houston	TX	77060	281-873-6600		2
Miller Oil Co 1000 E City Hall Ave *Web:* gotomillers.com	Norfolk	VA	23504	757-623-6600	625-0528	579
Miller Outdoor Theatre 6000 Hermann Pk Dr **Fax Area Code:* 713 ■ *Web:* www.milleroutdoortheatre.com	Houston	TX	77030	281-823-9103	942-0863*	572
Miller Pacific Engineering Group 504 Redwood Blvd Ste 220 *Web:* www.millerpac.com	Novato	CA	94947	415-382-3444		261
Miller Packing Co PO Box 1390 *TF:* 800-624-2328 ■ *Web:* www.millerhotdogs.com	Lodi	CA	95241	800-624-2328		296-26
Miller Paint Company Inc 12812 NE Whitaker Way *Web:* www.millerpaint.com	Portland	OR	97230	503-255-0190	255-0192	550
Miller Pipeline Corp 8850 Crawfordsville Rd *TF:* 800-428-3742 ■ *Web:* www.millerpipeline.com	Indianapolis	IN	46234	317-293-0278	293-8502	188-10
Miller Real Estate Investments LLC 6900 E Belleview Ave Ste 300 *Web:* www.millerre.com	Greenwood Village	CO	80111	303-799-6300	996-6361	654
Miller Saint Nazianz Inc 511 E Main St *TF:* 800-247-5557 ■ *Web:* www.millerstn.com	Saint Nazianz	WI	54232	920-773-2121	773-1200	273
Miller Sales & Engineering Inc 3801 N Hwy Dr *Web:* www.anm-equipment.com	Tucson	AZ	85705	520-888-2605	888-5984	358
Miller School 1000 Samuel Miller Loop *Web:* millerschoolofalbemarle.org	Charlottesville	VA	22903	434-823-4805	823-6617	622
Miller Scott & Holbrook 122 Touro St *Web:* millerscott.com	Newport	RI	02840	401-847-7500		41
Miller Shingle Company Inc 20820 Gun Club Rd *TF:* 866-612-1086 ■ *Web:* www.millershingle.com	Granite Falls	WA	98252	360-691-7727	691-7151	448
Miller Staffing 2525 Rt 130 Bldg A *Web:* www.millerstaffing.com	Cranbury	NJ	08512	609-395-1800		260
Miller State Park 13 Miller Park Rd *Web:* www.nhstateparks.org	Peterborough	NH	03458	603-924-3672		565
Miller Stratvert PA 500 Marquette Ave NW Ste 1100 *TF:* 800-424-7585 ■ *Web:* mstlaw.com	Albuquerque	NM	87125	505-842-1950	243-4408	428
Miller Studio 734 Fair Ave NW *TF:* 800-332-0050 ■ *Web:* miller-studio.com	New Philadelphia	OH	44663	330-339-1100		500
Miller Supply Inc 29902 Avenida de las Banderas *TF:* 888-240-9237 ■ *Web:* www.millersupplyinc.com	Rancho Santa Margarita	CA	92688	888-240-9237		553
Miller Systems Inc 175 Portland St 5th Fl *Web:* www.millersystems.com	Boston	MA	02114	617-266-4200		113
Miller Technical Services (MTS) 47801 W Anchor Ct *Web:* www.mtsmedicalmfg.com	Plymouth	MI	48170	734-738-1970	738-1975	492
Miller Thomson LLP Scotia Plz 40 King St W Ste 5800 *TF:* 888-762-5559 ■ *Web:* www.millerthomson.com	Toronto	ON	M5H3S1	416-595-8500		41
Miller Transfer 3833 SR-183 *TF:* 800-669-6877 ■ *Web:* www.millertransfer.com	Rootstown	OH	44272	800-669-6877		207
Miller Transporters Inc 5500 Hwy 80 W *TF:* 800-645-5378 ■ *Web:* www.millert.com	Jackson	MS	39209	601-922-8331	923-2535	780
Miller Travel Services Inc 4380 W 12th St *TF:* 800-989-8747 ■ *Web:* www.millertravel.com	Erie	PA	16505	814-833-8888		771
Miller Valentine Group 137 N Main St Ste 600 *TF:* 877-684-7687 ■ *Web:* mvg.com	Dayton	OH	45402	937-293-0900	299-1564	655
Miller Wire Works Inc 7429 Georgia Rd *Web:* www.millerwireworks.com	Birmingham	AL	35212	205-592-0341	592-3725	73
Miller Zell 6100 Fulton Industrial Blvd SW *Web:* www.millerzell.com	Atlanta	GA	30336	404-691-7400	699-2189	393
Miller's Health Systems 1690 S County Farm Rd *Web:* www.millershealthsystems.com	Warsaw	IN	46580	574-267-7211		793
Miller's Honey Company Inc 3000 SW Temple *Web:* www.millerhoney.com	Salt Lake City	UT	84115	801-486-8479	486-8494	296-24
Miller's Print & Mail Inc 1147 Sweitzer Ave *Web:* www.millersprintandmail.com	Akron	OH	44301	330-434-9200		5
Miller, Beam & Paganelli Inc (MBP) 12040 S Lakes Dr Ste 104 *Web:* www.millerbp.com	Reston	VA	20191	703-506-0005	506-0009	261
Miller, Mannix, Schachner & Hafner LLC 15 W Notre Dame St *Web:* millermannix.com	Glens Falls	NY	12801	518-793-6611		41
Miller, Monson, Peshel, Polacek & Hoshaw 501 W Broadway Ste 700 *Web:* mmpph.com	San Diego	CA	92101	619-239-7777	238-8808	41
Millerbernd Manufacturing Co 622 Sixth St S *Web:* www.millerberndmfg.com	Winsted	MN	55395	320-485-2111	485-4420	723
Miller-Bradford & Risberg Inc W250 N6851 Hwy 164 *TF:* 800-242-3115 ■ *Web:* www.miller-bradford.com	Sussex	WI	53089	262-246-5700	246-5719	358
Miller-Davis Co 1029 Portage St *Web:* www.miller-davis.com	Kalamazoo	MI	49001	269-345-3561		186
Miller-Eads Company Inc 4125 N Keystone Ave *Web:* www.miller-eads.com	Indianapolis	IN	46205	317-495-6700		787
Miller-Green Financial Services 600 Travis St Ste 5900 *Web:* www.miller-green.com	Houston	TX	77002	281-364-9100	364-9101	401
Miller-Keystone Blood Ctr 1465 Vly Center Pkwy *TF:* 800-444-4272 ■ *Web:* www.hcsc.org	Bethlehem	PA	18017	610-691-5850		89
Miller-Leaman 800 Orange Ave *TF:* 800-881-0320 ■ *Web:* www.millerleaman.com	Daytona Beach	FL	32114	386-248-0500		697
Miller-Lewis Benefit Consultants 121 E Sixth Ave *Web:* www.miller-lewis.com	Lancaster	OH	43130	740-654-4055	687-2236	390
Miller-Motte Technical College 1011 Creekside Ln *Web:* www.miller-motte.edu	Lynchburg	VA	24502	434-329-3192		167-3
Millers Forge Inc 1411 Capital Ave *Web:* www.millersforge.com	Plano	TX	75074	972-422-2145	881-0639	222
Millersburg Electric Inc 996 S Washington St *Web:* millersburgelectric.com	Millersburg	OH	44654	330-674-3806		35
Miller-Stephenson Chemical Co 55 Backus Ave *TF:* 800-992-2424 ■ *Web:* www.miller-stephenson.com	Danbury	CT	06810	203-743-4447	791-8702	145
Millerstown Veterinary Associates PC 807 Sunbury Path *Web:* millerstownvets.com	Millerstown	PA	17062	717-589-3111		794
Millersville University of Pennsylvania PO Box 1002 *TF:* 800-682-3648 ■ *Web:* www.millersville.edu	Millersville	PA	17551	717-872-3011	871-2147	166
Millersylvania State Park 12405 Tilley Rd S *Web:* www.parks.wa.gov	Olympia	WA	98512	360-753-1519		565
Miller-Thomas-Gyekis Inc 3341 Stafford St	Pittsburgh	PA	15204	412-331-4610		189-12
Millerton Lake State Recreation Area 5290 Millerton Rd *Web:* www.parks.ca.gov	Friant	CA	93626	559-822-2332		565
Millet Learning Ctr 3660 Southfield Dr *Web:* www.sisd.cc	Saginaw	MI	48601	989-777-2520		685
Millet the Printer Inc 1000 S Ervay St *Web:* www.millettheprinter.com	Dallas	TX	75201	214-741-3602		627

				Phone	Fax	Class
Millford Farm 377 Weisenberger Mill Rd PO Box 4351	Midway	KY	40347	859-846-4705	846-4226	368
Web: www.millford.com						
Millhopper Veterinary Medical Ctr 4209 NW 37th Pl	Gainesville	FL	32606	352-373-8055	373-1310	794
Web: millhoppervet.com						
Millicent Library 45 Center St	Fairhaven	MA	02719	508-992-5342	993-7288	434-3
Web: www.millicentlibrary.org						
Millie & Severson Inc 3601 Serpentine Dr	Los Alamitos	CA	90720	562-493-3611		186
Web: www.mandsinc.com						
Millie's 2603 E Main St	Richmond	VA	23223	804-643-5512	648-4321	671
Web: www.milliesdiner.com						
Milligan & Higgins Maple Ave PO Box 506	Johnstown	NY	12095	518-762-4638	762-7039	296-22
Web: www.milligan1868.com						
Milligan College 130 Richardson Rd	Milligan College	TN	37682	423-461-8730		166
TF: 800-262-8337 ■ *Web:* www.milligan.edu						
Milligan Pusateri Company LPA 4684 Douglas Cir NW	Canton	OH	44718	330-526-0764		41
Web: milliganpusateri.com						
Milliken & Co 920 Milliken Rd	Spartanburg	SC	29303	864-503-2020	503-2100	745-1
Web: www.milliken.com						
Milliken & Co *KEX Div* 924 Milliken Rd	Spartanburg	SC	29303	864-503-2505	880-5358*	131
**Fax Area Code:* 706 ■ *Web:* www.millikencarpet.com						
Millikin University 1184 W Main St	Decatur	IL	62522	217-424-6211		166
TF: 800-373-7733 ■ *Web:* millikin.edu						
Milliman USA 1301 Fifth Ave Ste 3800	Seattle	WA	98101	206-624-7940	340-1380	194
TF: 866-767-1212 ■ *Web:* in.milliman.com						
Milliner & Associates LLC 4181 E 96th St Ste 120	Indianapolis	IN	46240	317-218-1195		260
Web: www.millinerandassoc.com						
Million Air 4300 Westgrove Dr	Addison	TX	75001	972-248-1600	733-5803	63
TF: 800-248-1602 ■ *Web:* www.millionair.com						
Million Dollar Baby 841 Washington Blvd	Montebello	CA	90640	323-728-9988		319-2
Web: www.milliondollarbaby.com						
Million Dollar Round Table (MDRT) 325 W Touhy Ave	Park Ridge	IL	60068	847-692-6378	518-8921	49-9
Web: www.mdrt.org						
Milliron Auto Parts 76 N Mulberry St	Mansfield	OH	44903	419-747-4566	747-1539	61
TF: 800-747-4566 ■ *Web:* millironautoparts.com						
Millis Transfer Inc PO Box 550	Black River Falls	WI	54615	715-284-4384		780
TF: 800-937-0880 ■ *Web:* www.millistransfer.com						
Millman Search Group Inc 9902 Reisterstown Rd Ste 310	Owings Mills	MD	21117	410-902-6600		95
Web: www.millmansearch.com						
Mill-Max Manufacturing Corp 190 Pine Hollow Rd	Oyster Bay	NY	11771	516-922-6000	922-9253	815
TF: 800-333-4237 ■ *Web:* www.mill-max.com						
Millogic Ltd 89 Cambridge St	Burlington	MA	01803	339-234-5700		261
Web: millogic.com						
Mill-Rite Woodworking Company Inc 6401 47th St N	Pinellas Park	FL	33781	727-527-7808		499
Web: www.mill-rite.com						
Millrock *River Run Commercial* 4660 Early Rd	Mount Crawford	VA	22841	540-437-3458		286
Web: www.millrock.com						
Mill-Rose Co 7995 Tyler Blvd	Mentor	OH	44060	440-255-9171	255-5039	103
TF: 800-321-3533 ■ *Web:* www.millrose.com						
Millry Communications 30433 Hwy 17	Millry	AL	36558	251-846-2911		224
TF: 888-227-5710 ■ *Web:* www.millry.net						
Mills & Mills Agency Inc 35 Old Ridgefield Rd	Wilton	CT	06897	203-762-8373	761-8555	390
Web: millsandmillsinsurance.com						
Mills & Partners Inc 8235 Forsyth Blvd Ste 300	Saint Louis	MO	63105	314-727-1701	862-7401	792
Web: www.mills-partners.com						
Mills College 5000 MacArthur Blvd	Oakland	CA	94613	510-430-2135	430-3314	166
TF: 877-746-4557 ■ *Web:* www.mills.edu						
Mills County 418 Sharp St	Glenwood	IA	51534	712-527-4880		338
Web: www.millscoia.us						
Mills County PO Box 646	Goldthwaite	TX	76844	325-648-2711	648-3251	338
Web: www.co.mills.tx.us						
Mills House Hotel 115 Meeting St	Charleston	SC	29401	843-577-2400		379
Web: www.millshouse.com						
Mills Iron Works Inc 14834 Maple Ave	Gardena	CA	90248	323-321-6520	532-0476*	595
**Fax Area Code:* 310 ■ *TF:* 800-421-2281 ■ *Web:* www.millsiron.com						
Mills, Potoczak & Co 27600 Chagrin Blvd Ste 200	Cleveland	OH	44122	216-464-7481	464-7581	2
Web: mpccpa.com						
Millsap Fuel Distributors Ltd 905 Ave P S	Saskatoon	SK	S7M2X3	306-244-7916		580
TF: 800-667-9767 ■ *Web:* www.millsapfuels.ca						
Millsaps College 1701 N State St	Jackson	MS	39210	601-974-1000	974-1059	166
TF: 800-352-1050 ■ *Web:* www.millsaps.edu						
Mills-James Inc 3545 Fishinger Blvd	Hilliard	OH	43026	614-777-9933		514
Web: www.millsjames.com						
Mills-Shellhammer-Puetz & Associates Inc 117 Pierce St Ste 200	Sioux City	IA	51101	712-258-2580	258-2184	390
Web: mspinsurance.com						
Millstone Medical Outsourcing LLC 580 Commerce Dr	Fall River	MA	02720	508-679-8384	679-8414	195
Web: millstonemedical.com						
Millstream Area Credit Union 1007 W Ave	Findlay	OH	45840	419-422-5626		219
Web: millstreamcu.com						
Mills-Wilson-George Inc (MWG) 1847 Vanderhorn Dr	Memphis	TN	38134	901-373-5100	373-5155	665
Web: www.millswilsongeorge.com						
Milltech Manufacturing Co 537 Easy St	Garland	TX	75042	972-276-1786		454
Web: www.milltechmfg.com						
Milluzzo & Company PC 182 Kelsey St	Newington	CT	06111	860-667-9991		2
Millville Chamber of Commerce 4 City Pk Dr	Millville	NJ	08332	856-825-2600	825-5333	139
Web: www.millville-nj.com						
Millwood Inc 33 Stiles Ln	North Haven	CT	06473	203-248-7902		200
Web: www.millwoodinc.com						
Millwood State Park 1564 Hwy 32 E	Ashdown	AR	71822	870-898-2800		565
Web: www.arkansasstateparks.com						
Milman Labuda Law Group PLLC 3000 Marcus Ave	New Hyde Park	NY	11042	516-328-8899		41
Web: milmanlabuda.com						
Milne Fruit Products Inc 804 Bennett Ave	Prosser	WA	99350	509-786-2611	786-1724	296-21
Web: www.milnefruit.com						
Milne Public Library 1095 Main St	Williamstown	MA	01267	413-458-5369	458-3085	434-3
Web: www.milnelibrary.org						
Milner Technologies Inc 5125 Peachtree Industrial Blvd	Norcross	GA	30092	770-734-5300		178-1
TF: 800-592-3766 ■ *Web:* www.milnertechnologies.com						
Milnot Co 105 Washington Ave	Seneca	MO	64865	417-776-2243		619
Web: www.milnot.com						
Milo McIver State Park 24101 SE Entrance Rd	Estacada	OR	97023	503-630-7150		565
Web: oregonstateparks.org						
Milos 5357 du Parc Ave	Montreal	QC	H2V4G9	514-272-3522		671
Web: milos.ca						
Mil-Pac Technology Inc 1672 Main St Ste 254	Ramona	CA	92065	760-788-3030		177
Web: milpac.com						
Milport Enterprises Inc 2829 S Fifth Ct	Milwaukee	WI	53207	414-769-7350		146
Web: www.milport.com						
Milrose Consultants Inc 498 Seventh Ave	New York	NY	10018	212-643-4545	643-4859	365
Web: www.milrose.com						
Milsco Manufacturing Co 1301 W Canal St	Milwaukee	WI	53233	414-354-0500	354-0508	689
Web: www.milsco.com						
Miltenyi Biotec Inc 2303 Lindbergh St	Auburn	CA	95602	530-888-8871	888-8925	743
TF: 866-811-4466 ■ *Web:* www.miltenyibiotec.com						
Miltex Inc 589 Davies Dr	York	PA	17402	717-840-9335		228
TF: 866-854-8400 ■ *Web:* www.miltex.com						
Milton & Hattie Kutz Home Inc, The 704 River Rd	Wilmington	DE	19809	302-764-7000	764-2224	371
Web: kutzhome.org						
Milton Academy 170 Centre St	Milton	MA	02186	617-898-1798		622
Web: www.milton.edu						
Milton CAT 30 Industrial Dr	Londonderry	NH	03053	603-665-4500		358
TF: 800-473-5298 ■ *Web:* www.miltoncat.com						
Milton Chamber of Commerce 251 Main St E Ste 104	Milton	ON	L9T1P1	905-878-0581	878-4972	137
Web: www.miltonchamber.ca						
Milton H. Erickson Foundation Press 2632 E Thomas Rd Ste 200	Phoenix	AZ	85016	602-956-6196	956-0519	637-2
Web: www.erickson-foundation.org						
Milton Hershey School 801 Spartan Ln PO Box 830	Hershey	PA	17033	717-520-2100	520-2117	622
TF: 800-322-3248 ■ *Web:* www.mhskids.org						
Milton Industries Inc 4500 W Cortland	Chicago	IL	60639	855-464-6458		153
TF: 855-464-6458 ■ *Web:* www.miltonindustries.com						
Milton Martin Toyota 3150 Milton Martin Toyota Way	Gainesville	GA	30507	770-532-4355		57
Web: www.miltonmartintoyota.com						
Milton Public Library 476 Canton Ave	Milton	MA	02186	617-698-5757		434-3
Web: www.miltonlibrary.org						
Milton Roy USA 201 Ivyland Rd	Ivyland	PA	18974	215-441-0800	441-8620	640
Web: www.miltonroy.com						
Milton State Park Bridge Ave	Sunbury	PA	17801	570-988-5557		565
Web: www.dcnr.pa.gov						
Milton Transportation Inc 5505 SR-405 PO Box 355	Milton	PA	17847	570-742-8774	742-2856	780
Milton Veterinary Services LLC 745 Mcewan Ln	Milton	WI	53563	608-868-4715		794
Web: miltonveterinaryclinic.com						
Miltons Inc 250 Granite St	Braintree	MA	02184	781-848-1880		157-3
TF: 888-645-8667 ■ *Web:* www.miltons.com						
Miltonvale Record 22 W Spruce	Miltonvale	KS	67466	785-427-2211		532-2
Web: www.miltonvaleks.com						
MILVETS Systems Technology Inc 11825 High Tech Ave Ste 150	Orlando	FL	32817	407-207-2242	207-6356	180
Web: www.milvets.com						
Milwaukee Academy of Science 2000 W Kilbourn Ave	Milwaukee	WI	53233	414-933-0302		165
Web: www.milwaukeeacademyofscience.org						
Milwaukee Area Technical College 700 W State St	Milwaukee	WI	53233	414-297-6600	297-6496	800
TF: 866-211-3380 ■ *Web:* www.matc.edu						
Milwaukee Art Museum 700 N Art Museum Dr	Milwaukee	WI	53202	414-224-3200	271-7588	520
TF: 877-638-7620 ■ *Web:* www.mam.org						
Milwaukee Athletic Club 758 N Broadway	Milwaukee	WI	53202	414-273-5080	273-4133	354
Web: www.macwi.org						
Milwaukee Ballet 504 W National Ave	Milwaukee	WI	53204	414-643-7677	649-4066	573-1
Web: www.milwaukeeballet.org						
Milwaukee Bearing & Machining Inc W134N5235 Campbell Dr	Menomonee Falls	WI	53051	262-783-1100		757
Web: www.milwaukeebearing.com						
Milwaukee Brewers Miller Pk 1 Brewers Way	Milwaukee	WI	53214	414-902-4400	902-4588	713
Web: milwaukee.brewers.mlb.com						
Milwaukee Cabinetry 1168 N 50th Pl	Milwaukee	WI	53208	414-771-1960	771-3638	362
Web: www.milwaukeecabinetry.com						
Milwaukee Catholic Home 2330 & 2462 N Prospect Ave	Milwaukee	WI	53211	414-224-9700	224-1666	672
Web: www.milwaukeecatholichome.org						
Milwaukee Chamber Theatre Broadway Theatre Ctr 158 N Broadway	Milwaukee	WI	53202	414-276-8842	277-4477	572
Web: www.chamber-theatre.com						

Name / Address	City	State	Zip	Phone	Fax	Class
Milwaukee Chop House 633 N 5th St *Web:* chophouse411.com	Milwaukee	WI	53203	414-226-2467		671
Milwaukee City Hall 200 E Wells St *Web:* www.city.milwaukee.gov	Milwaukee	WI	53202	414-286-2200	286-3191	337
Milwaukee Coast Guard Base 2420 S Lincoln Memorial Dr *TF:* 866-772-8724 ■ *Web:* www.uscg.mil	Milwaukee	WI	53207	414-747-7100	747-7108	158
Milwaukee County 901 N Ninth St *TF:* 877-652-6377 ■ *Web:* county.milwaukee.gov	Milwaukee	WI	53233	414-278-4143	223-1379	338
Milwaukee County Historical Society (MCHS) 910 N Old World 3rd St *Web:* www.milwaukeehistory.net	Milwaukee	WI	53203	414-273-8288		637-2
Milwaukee County Mental Health Complex 9455 Watertown Plank Rd *Web:* www.county.milwaukee.gov	Milwaukee	WI	53226	414-257-6995		374-5
Milwaukee County Transit System 1942 N 17th St *Web:* www.ridemcts.com	Milwaukee	WI	53205	414-343-1700	343-1787	468
Milwaukee Courier, The 2003 W Capitol Dr *Web:* milwaukeecourieronline.com	Milwaukee	WI	53206	414-449-4860	906-5383	532-4
Milwaukee Electric Tool Corp 13135 W Lisbon Rd **Fax Area Code:* 800 ■ *TF:* 800-729-3878 ■ *Web:* www.milwaukeetool.com	Brookfield	WI	53005	262-783-8586	638-9582*	759
Milwaukee Gear Co 5150 N Port Washington Rd *Web:* www.regalpts.com	Milwaukee	WI	53217	414-962-3532	962-2774	709
Milwaukee Institute of Art & Design 273 E Erie St *TF:* 888-749-6423 ■ *Web:* www.miad.edu	Milwaukee	WI	53202	414-276-7889	291-8077	166
Milwaukee Jewish Federation Inc 1360 N Prospect Ave *Web:* milwaukeejewish.org	Milwaukee	WI	53202	414-390-5700		522
Milwaukee Magazine 126 N Jefferson St Ste 100 *TF:* 800-662-4818 ■ *Web:* www.milwaukeemag.com	Milwaukee	WI	53202	414-273-1101		457-22
Milwaukee Malleable & Grey Iron Works 2773 S 29th St *Web:* www.milwtool.com	Milwaukee	WI	53201	414-645-0200		307
Milwaukee Protestant Home For The Aged 2505 E Bradford Ave *Web:* eastcastleplace.com	Milwaukee	WI	53211	414-219-1398		371
Milwaukee Public Library 814 W Wisconsin Ave *TF:* 866-947-7363 ■ *Web:* www.mpl.org	Milwaukee	WI	53233	414-286-3000	286-2798	434-3
Milwaukee Public Museum 800 W Wells St *Web:* www.mpm.edu	Milwaukee	WI	53233	414-278-2728		520
Milwaukee Public Schools 5225 W Vliet St *Web:* www.mps.milwaukee.k12.wi.us	Milwaukee	WI	53208	414-475-8393	475-8722	685
Milwaukee Repertory Theater 108 E Wells St *Web:* www.milwaukeerep.com	Milwaukee	WI	53202	414-224-1761	224-9097	573-4
Milwaukee Rescue Mission 830 N 19th St *Web:* www.milmission.org	Milwaukee	WI	53233	414-344-2211	344-6972	764
Milwaukee School of Engineering 1025 N Broadway *TF:* 800-332-6763 ■ *Web:* www.msoe.edu	Milwaukee	WI	53202	414-277-7300	277-7475	166
Milwaukee Symphony Orchestra 1101 N Market St Ste 100 *TF:* 888-367-8101 ■ *Web:* www.mso.org	Milwaukee	WI	53202	414-291-7605		573-3
Milwaukee Valve Company Inc 16550 W Stratton Dr *TF:* 800-348-6544 ■ *Web:* www.milwaukeevalve.com	New Berlin	WI	53151	262-432-2800	432-2801	789
Milwaukee Wave LLC 510 W Kilbourn Ave *Web:* www.milwaukeewave.com	Milwaukee	WI	53203	414-224-9283	224-9290	717
Milwhite Inc 5487 S Padre Island Hwy *TF:* 800-442-0082 ■ *Web:* www.milwhite.com	Brownsville	TX	78521	956-547-1970	547-1999	503-2
Milyli Inc 415 N Sangamon St *Web:* milyli.com	Chicago	IL	60642	312-265-0136		138
Mimaki USA Inc 150 Satellite Blvd NE Ste A *TF:* 888-530-3988 ■ *Web:* www.mimakiusa.com	Suwanee	GA	30024	888-530-3988		174
MIMC (Mobile Infirmary Medical Ctr) 5 Mobile Infirmary Cir *Web:* www.infirmaryhealth.org	Mobile	AL	36607	251-435-2400		374-3
MiMedx Group Inc 1775 W Oak Commons Ct NE *TF:* 888-543-1917 ■ *Web:* mimedx.com	Marietta	GA	30062	888-543-1917		476
Mimi's Cafe 7450 W Bell Rd *Web:* www.mimiscafe.com	Glendale	AZ	85308	623-979-4500		671
Mimic Technologies Inc 811 First Ave Ste 408 *TF:* 800-918-1670 ■ *Web:* mimicsimulation.com	Seattle	WA	98104	800-918-1670		177
MIMICS Inc 319 Washington St Ste 501 *Web:* www.mimics.com	Portland	OR	97204	505-332-9220	332-3148	177
Mimosa Grill 327 S Tryon St *Web:* www.harpersgroup.com	Charlotte	NC	28202	704-343-0700		671
Minco Manufacturing Inc 855 Aeroplaza Dr *Web:* www.mincomfg.com	Colorado Springs	CO	80916	719-550-1223	550-1390	591
Minco Products Inc 7300 Commerce Ln NE *Web:* www.minco.com	Minneapolis	MN	55432	763-571-3121	571-0927	201
Minco Tool & Mold Co 5690 Webster St *Web:* www.mincogroup.com	Dayton	OH	45414	937-890-7905	890-0543	604
Mind Drivers LLC 381 Brinton Lake Rd	Thornton	PA	19373	610-361-2000		196
Mind Gym 475 Park Ave S FL 2 *Web:* themindgym.com	New York	NY	10016	646-649-4333		242
Mind Matters Jury Consulting 1420 5th Ave Ste 2200 *Web:* www.mmjury.com	Seattle	WA	98101	206-274-5300		194
Mind Your Business Inc (MYB) 305 Eighth Ave E *TF:* 888-869-2462 ■ *Web:* www.mybinc.com	Hendersonville	NC	28792	888-869-2462		260
MINDBODY Inc 4051 Broad St Ste 220 *TF:* 877-755-4279 ■ *Web:* www.mindbodyonline.com	Sn Luis Obisp	CA	93401	877-755-4279		396
MindEdge Inc 271 Waverley Oaks Rd *Web:* mindedge.com	Waltham	MA	02452	781-250-1805		397
Minden Medical Ctr 1 Medical Plz *Web:* www.mindenmedicalcenter.com	Minden	LA	71055	318-377-2321		374-3
Mindex Technologies Inc 3495 Winton Pl *Web:* www.mindex.com	Rochester	NY	14623	585-424-3590	424-3809	177
Mindfinders Inc 1200 18th St NW Ste 550 *Web:* www.themindfinders.com	Washington	DC	20036	202-400-2602		177
Mindgrub Technologies LLC 1215 E Fort Ave Ste 200 *TF:* 855-646-3472 ■ *Web:* www.mindgrub.com	Baltimore	MD	21230	410-988-2444		4
Mindgruve Inc 1018 Eight Ave *Web:* mindgruve.com	San Diego	CA	92101	619-757-1325		624
Mindjet Corp 1160 Battery St E 4th Fl *TF:* 877-646-3538 ■ *Web:* www.mindjet.com	San Francisco	CA	94111	415-229-4200	229-4201	178-12
Mindlance 1095 Morris Ave 4th Fl Ste 101A **Fax Area Code:* 201 ■ *TF:* 877-965-2623 ■ *Web:* www.mindlance.com	Hoboken	NJ	07030	877-965-2623	386-0553*	194
MindPlay Educational Software 5151 E Broadway Blvd Ste 1403 *TF:* 800-221-7911 ■ *Web:* mindplay.com	Tucson	AZ	85711	520-888-1800	888-7904	178-3
Mindpower Inc 337 Georgia Ave SE *Web:* mindpowerinc.com	Atlanta	GA	30312	404-581-1991		7
Mindray DS USA Inc 800 MacArthur Blvd *TF:* 800-288-2121 ■ *Web:* www.mindraynorthamerica.com	Mahwah	NJ	07430	201-995-8000		476
Minds Eye Entertainment Ltd 402 Dewdney Ave *Web:* mindseyepictures.com	Regina	SK	S4N6E3	306-359-7618		514
Mindseeker 20130 Lakeview Center Plz **Fax Area Code:* 703 ■ *Web:* www.mindseeker.com	Ashburn	VA	20147	571-313-5950	738-7030*	260
MindShare 498 Seventh Ave *Web:* www.mindshareworld.com	New York	NY	10018	212-297-7000		4
Mindsight 2001 Butterfield Rd Ste 250 *Web:* www.gomindsight.com	Downers Grove	IL	60515	630-981-5000		177
MindSnacks Inc 1479 Folsom St *Web:* www.mindsnacks.com	San Francisco	CA	94103	415-400-4626		387
MindSpark International Inc 1205 Peachtree Pkwy Ste 1204 *TF:* 888-820-3616 ■ *Web:* www.mindsparkit.com	Cumming	GA	30041	888-820-3616		196
Mindstorm Communications Group Inc 10316 Feld Farm Ln Ste 200 *Web:* www.gomindstorm.com	Charlotte	NC	28210	704-331-0870		4
Mindstream LLC 2872 NE 25th Ct **Fax Area Code:* 866 ■ *Web:* mindstreamstudio.com	Fort Lauderdale	FL	33305	954-594-2601	990-5622*	463
Mindteck Inc 1828 Good Hope Rd Ste 201 *Web:* www.mindteck.com	Enola	PA	17025	717-732-2211	732-2927	177
MindTouch Inc 101 W Broadway Ste 1500 *Web:* mindtouch.com	San Diego	CA	92101	619-795-8459		177
Mindways Software Inc 3001 S Lamar Blvd Ste 302 *Web:* qct.com	Austin	TX	78704	512-912-0871		476
Mindwrap Inc 492 Blackwell Rd Ste 202 *Web:* www.mindwrap.com	Warrenton	VA	20186	540-347-2552	347-2556	180
Mine & Mill Industrial Supply Company Inc 2500 S Combee Rd *TF:* 800-282-8489 ■ *Web:* www.minemill.com	Lakeland	FL	33801	863-665-5601		186
Mine Development Assoc 210 S Rock Blvd *Web:* www.mda.com	Reno	NV	89502	775-856-5700		261
Mine Kill State Park PO Box 923 Rt 30 *Web:* parks.ny.gov	North Blenheim	NY	12131	518-827-6111		565
Mine Safety & Health Administration *Metal & Non-Metal Mine Safety & Health Office* 1100 Wilson Blvd *Web:* www.msha.gov	Arlington	VA	22209	202-693-9600		340-15
National Mine Health & Safety Academy 1301 Airport Rd *Web:* www.msha.gov	Beaver	WV	25813	304-256-3257	256-3368	340-15
MineAfrica Inc 769 Euclid Ave *Web:* www.mineafrica.com	Toronto	ON	M6G2V3	416-588-7749		5
Miner County Park Ave & Main St 401 N Main St 2nd Fl PO Box 86 *Web:* www.minercountysd.org	Howard	SD	57349	605-772-4671	772-4203	338
Miner Enterprises Inc 1200 E State St *TF:* 888-822-5334 ■ *Web:* www.minerent.com	Geneva	IL	60134	630-232-3000	232-3055	650
Miner'S Inc 5065 Miller Trunk Hwy *Web:* www.superonefoods.com	Hermantown	MN	55811	218-729-5882		345
Miner, Barnhill & Galland PC 325 N LaSalle St Ste 350 *Web:* www.lawmbg.com	Chicago	IL	60654	312-751-1170	751-0438	428
Mineral Area College 5270 Frat River Rd PO Box 1000 *Web:* www.mineralarea.edu	Park Hills	MO	63601	573-431-4593	518-2166	162
Mineral County PO Box 150 *Web:* www.courtswv.gov	Keyser	WV	26726	304-788-5150	788-4100	338
Mineral Daily News Tribune Inc 21 Shamrock Dr *Web:* www.newstribune.info	Keyser	WV	26726	304-788-3333		637-8
Mineral Labs Inc 309 Pkwy Dr *Web:* minerallabs.com	Salyersville	KY	41465	606-349-6145		743
Mineral Mound State Park 48 Finch Ln *Web:* parks.ky.gov	Eddyville	KY	42038	270-388-3673		565
Mineral Resources Intl 2720 Wadman Dr *TF:* 800-731-7866 ■ *Web:* www.mineralresourcesint.com	Ogden	UT	84401	801-731-7040	731-7985	297-8
Mineral Wells Area Chamber of Commerce 511 E Hubbard St *TF:* 800-252-6989 ■ *Web:* www.mineralwellstx.com	Mineral Wells	TX	76067	940-325-2557	328-0850	139

Listing	City	State	ZIP	Phone	Fax	Class
Mineralogical Record Inc, The 4631 Paseo Tubutama *Web:* www.minrec.org	Tucson	AZ	85750	520-299-5274		637-2
Minerals Management Service 1849 C St NW *Web:* www.doi.gov	Washington	DC	20240	202-208-5308	208-7242	340-13
Minerals Metals & Materials Society, The (TMS) 5700 Corporate Dr Ste 750 *Web:* www.tms.org	Pittsburgh	PA	15237	724-776-9000	776-3770	49-13
Minerals Research Inc 4620 S Coach Dr	Tucson	AZ	85714	520-748-9362		191-1
Minerals Technologies Inc 405 Lexington Ave *Web:* www.mineralstech.com	New York	NY	10174	212-878-1800		663
MineralTree Inc 125 Cambridgepark Dr *Web:* mineraltree.com	Cambridge	MA	02140	617-299-3399		177
Miner-Dederick Construction LLP 1532 Peden St	Houston	TX	77006	713-529-3001		360-2
Minergy Corp 1512 S Commercial St *Web:* www.minergy.com	Neenah	WI	54956	920-727-1919		660
Minerva & D'agostino PC 107 S Central Ave *Web:* mindaglaw.com	Valley Stream	NY	11580	516-872-7400		428
Minerva Networks Inc 2150 Gold St *TF:* 800-806-9594 ■ *Web:* www.minervanetworks.com	Alviso	CA	95002	408-567-9400	567-0747	647
Minerva's 2111 N Lacrosse St *Web:* www.minervas.net	Rapid City	SD	57701	605-394-9505		671
Mines of Spain State Recreation Area 8991 Bellevue Hts *Web:* www.iowadnr.gov	Dubuque	IA	52003	563-556-0620	556-8474	565
Mines Press Inc, The 231 Croton Ave *TF:* 800-447-6788 ■ *Web:* www.minespress.com	Cortlandt Manor	NY	10567	800-447-6788		627
Minford Telephone Co 10717 State Rte 139 *Web:* www.falcon1.net	Minford	OH	45653	740-820-2151	820-2222	224
Ming Wah Restaurant LLC 1618 W 3rd Ave	Spokane	WA	99201	509-455-9474		671
Ming's 2330 S Carson St *Web:* www.officialmobilesite.com	Carson City	NV	89701	775-887-8878		671
Ming's Cuisine 2496 Rocky Ridge Rd *Web:* mingsmenu.com	Birmingham	AL	35242	205-991-3803		671
Mingan Archipelago National Park Reserve of Canada 1340 de la Digue St *Web:* www.pc.gc.ca	Havre-Saint-Pierre	QC	G0G1P0	418-538-3331	538-3595	563
Mingei International Museum of Folk Art 1439 El Prado *Web:* mingei.org	San Diego	CA	92101	619-239-0003	239-0605	520
Mingo County PO Box 1197 *Web:* www.mingocountywv.com	Williamson	WV	25661	304-235-0330	235-0565	338
Mingo Manufacturing Inc 8091 N 115th E Ave *Web:* www.mingomanufacturing.com	Owasso	OK	74055	918-272-1151		537
Mings Garden Chinese Restaurant 1741 Eastern Blvd *Web:* www.mingsgarden-al.com	Montgomery	AL	36117	334-277-8188		671
Minhas Craft Brewery 1208 14th Ave *TF:* 800-233-7205 ■ *Web:* www.minhasbrewery.com	Monroe	WI	53566	800-233-7205		102
Miniature Museum of Greater Saint Louis 4746 Gravois Ave *Web:* miniaturemuseum.org	Saint Louis	MO	63116	314-832-7790		520
Miniature Precision Components Inc 820 Wisconsin St *Web:* www.mpc-inc.com	Walworth	WI	53184	262-275-5791	275-6346	599
Mini-Cassia Chamber of Commerce (MCC) 1177 Seventh St *Web:* www.minicassiachamber.com	Heyburn	ID	83336	208-679-4793	679-4794	139
Mini-Circuits 13 Neptune Ave *TF:* 800-654-7949 ■ *Web:* www.minicircuits.com	Brooklyn	NY	11235	718-934-4500	332-4661	696
Minidoka County 715 G St *Web:* www.minidoka.id.us	Rupert	ID	83350	208-436-7180	436-0737	338
Minidoka National Historic Site PO Box 570 *Web:* www.nps.gov	Hagerman	ID	83332	208-933-4127	837-4857	564
Minier Financial Inc 101 S Main	Minier	IL	61759	309-392-2623	392-2504	70
Mining Journal PO Box 430 *Web:* www.miningjournal.net	Marquette	MI	49855	906-228-2500	228-2617	532-2
Minisink Valley Central School District PO Box 217 Rte 6 *Web:* www.minisink.com	Slate Hill	NY	10973	845-355-5100	355-5205	685
MiniSoft Inc 1024 1st St *TF:* 800-682-0200 ■ *Web:* www.minisoft.com	Snohomish	WA	98290	360-568-6602	568-2923	177
Ministry of Foreign Affairs Republic of Indonesia 325 E 38th St *Web:* www.indonesiamission-ny.org	New York	NY	10016	212-972-8333		784
Ministry of Foreign Affairs Singapore 318 E 48th St *Web:* www.mfa.gov.sg	New York	NY	10017	212-223-3331	826-5028	784
Ministry of Tourism of Dominican Republic 848 Brickell Ave *TF:* 888-358-9594 ■ *Web:* www.godominicanrepublic.com	Miami	FL	33131	305-358-2899		775
Ministry Partners Investment Company LLC 915 W Imperial Hwy Ste 120 *Web:* www.ministrypartners.org	Brea	CA	92821	714-671-5720		217
Minitab Inc Quality Plz 1829 Pine Hall Rd *TF:* 800-448-3555 ■ *Web:* www.minitab.com	State College	PA	16801	814-238-3280		178-10
Minka Group 1151 W Bradford Ct *TF:* 800-221-7977 ■ *Web:* www.minkagroup.net	Corona	CA	92882	951-735-9220		439
Minkin Chandler Corp 15400 Oakwood Dr *Web:* minkinchandler.weebly.com	Romulus	MI	48174	734-229-9200		686
Minn-Dak Farmers Cooperative Inc 7525 Red River Rd *Web:* www.mdf.coop	Wahpeton	ND	58075	701-642-8411		296-37
Minn-Dak Growers Ltd 4034 40th Ave N PO Box 13276 *Web:* www.minndak.com	Grand Forks	ND	58208	701-746-7453	780-9050	10-5
Minneapolis Business College 1711 W County Rd B Ste 100 F *TF:* 800-279-5200 ■ *Web:* www.minneapolisbusinesscollege.edu	Roseville	MN	55113	651-636-7406		167-3
Minneapolis City Hall 350 S 5th St *Web:* www.ci.minneapolis.mn.us	Minneapolis	MN	55415	612-673-2244	673-3940	337
Minneapolis College of Art & Design 2501 Stevens Ave *TF:* 800-874-6223 ■ *Web:* mcad.edu	Minneapolis	MN	55404	612-874-3760	874-3701	164
Minneapolis Community & Technical College 1501 Hennepin Ave *TF:* 800-247-0911 ■ *Web:* www.minneapolis.edu	Minneapolis	MN	55403	612-659-6200	659-6210	162
Minneapolis Convention Ctr 1301 Second Ave S *TF:* 800-438-5547 ■ *Web:* minneapolis.org	Minneapolis	MN	55403	612-335-6000	335-6757	205
Minneapolis Foundation 80 S 8th St 800 IDS Ctr Ste 800 *TF:* 866-305-0543 ■ *Web:* www.minneapolisfoundation.org	Minneapolis	MN	55402	612-672-3878	672-3846	303
Minneapolis Glass Company Inc 14600 28th Ave N *Web:* www.minneapolisglass.com	Plymouth	MN	55447	763-559-0635	559-8816	191-2
Minneapolis Grain Exchange 400 S Fourth St 130 Grain Exchange Bldg *TF:* 800-827-4746 ■ *Web:* www.mgex.com	Minneapolis	MN	55415	612-321-7101	339-1155	691
Minneapolis Institute of Arts 2400 Third Ave S *TF:* 888-642-2787 ■ *Web:* new.artsmia.org	Minneapolis	MN	55404	612-297-3131	870-3004	520
Minneapolis Northwest 6200 Shingle Creek Pkwy Ste 130 *TF:* 800-541-4364 ■ *Web:* www.minneapolisnorthwest.com	Brooklyn Center	MN	55430	763-852-7500		206
Minneapolis Public Schools 3345 Chicago Ave *TF:* 800-543-7709 ■ *Web:* www.mpls.k12.mn.us	Minneapolis	MN	55407	612-668-0000	668-0525	685
Minneapolis Regional Chamber of Commerce 81 S Ninth St Ste 200 *Web:* www.mplschamber.com	Minneapolis	MN	55402	612-370-9100	370-9195	139
Minneapolis School of Flower Design 2265 W County Rd Ste C *Web:* www.flowerschool101.com	Roseville	MN	55113	414-617-7162		685
Minneapolis/St Paul City Pages 401 N Third St Ste 550 *TF:* 844-387-6962 ■ *Web:* www.citypages.com	Minneapolis	MN	55401	612-375-1015	372-3737	532-5
Minneapolis/St Paul International Film Festival 125 SE Main St Ste 341 *Web:* www.mspfilm.org	Minneapolis	MN	55414	612-331-7563		282
Minneapolis-Saint Paul Magazine 220 S Sixth St Ste 500 *TF:* 800-999-5589 ■ *Web:* www.mspmag.com	Minneapolis	MN	55402	612-339-7571	339-5806	457-22
Minnehaha Academy 4200 W River Pkwy *Web:* www.minnehahaacademy.net	Minneapolis	MN	55406	612-729-8321		685
Minnehaha County 415 N Dakota Ave *Web:* www.minnehahacounty.org	Sioux Falls	SD	57104	605-367-4206	367-8314	338
Minneopa State Park 54497 Gadwall Rd *Web:* www.dnr.state.mn.us	Mankato	MN	56001	507-386-3910		565
Minneota Mascot 210 N Jefferson *Web:* www.minneotamascot.com	Minneota	MN	56264	507-872-6492	872-6840	532-2
Minnequa Works Credit Union 1549 E Abriendo Ave *TF:* 888-346-2733 ■ *Web:* mymwcu.com	Pueblo	CO	81004	719-544-6928		219
Minnesota						
Aging Board 540 Cedar St *TF:* 800-882-6262 ■ *Web:* www.mnaging.org	Saint Paul	MN	55155	651-431-2500		339-24
Arts Board 540 Fairview Ave N Ste 304 *TF:* 800-866-2787 ■ *Web:* www.arts.state.mn.us	Saint Paul	MN	55101	651-215-1600	215-1602	339-24
Attorney General 445 Minnesota St Ste 1400 *Web:* www.ag.state.mn.us	Saint Paul	MN	55101	651-296-3353		339-24
Campaign Finance & Public Disclosure Board 190 Centennial Office Bldg 658 Cedar St *TF:* 800-657-3889 ■ *Web:* cfb.mn.gov	Saint Paul	MN	55155	651-539-1180	296-1722	265
Commerce Dept 876 7th St E Ste 500 *TF:* 800-657-3602 ■ *Web:* mmd.admin.state.mn.us	Saint Paul	MN	55101	651-539-1500		339-24
Department of Education 1500 Hwy 36 W *Web:* education.state.mn.us	Roseville	MN	55113	651-582-8200		339-24
Department of Public Safety 444 Minnesota St *TF:* 800-657-3787 ■ *Web:* www.dps.mn.gov	Saint Paul	MN	55101	651-201-7000		339-24
Employment & Economic Development Dept (DEED) 332 Minnesota St Ste E200 *TF:* 800-657-3858 ■ *Web:* mn.gov	Saint Paul	MN	55101	651-259-7114		339-24
Governor 130 State Capitol 75 Rev Dr Martin Luther King Jr Blvd *TF:* 800-657-3717 ■ *Web:* www.mn.gov	Saint Paul	MN	55155	651-201-3400	797-1850	339-24
Health Dept 625 Robert St N *TF:* 888-345-0823 ■ *Web:* www.health.state.mn.us	Saint Paul	MN	55164	651-201-4545	201-4606	339-24
House of Representatives 645 State Office Bldg *Web:* www.house.leg.state.mn.us	Saint Paul	MN	55155	651-296-2146		433
Housing Finance Authority 400 Sibley St Ste 300 *TF:* 800-657-3769 ■ *Web:* mnhousing.gov	Saint Paul	MN	55101	651-296-7608		339-24
Labor & Industry Dept 443 Lafayette Rd N *TF:* 800-342-5354 ■ *Web:* www.doli.state.mn.us	Saint Paul	MN	55155	651-284-5005	284-5727	339-24
Legislature 211 State Capitol *TF:* 888-234-1112 ■ *Web:* www.leg.state.mn.us	Saint Paul	MN	55155	651-296-2314	296-1326	339-24
Medical Practice Board 2829 University Ave SE Ste 500 *TF:* 800-657-3709 ■ *Web:* mn.gov	Minneapolis	MN	55414	612-617-2130	617-2166	339-24
Natural Resources Dept 500 Lafayette Rd *Web:* www.dnr.state.mn.us	Saint Paul	MN	55155	651-296-6157		339-24
Office of Enterprise Technology 658 Cedar St *Web:* www.mbbnet.umn.edu	Saint Paul	MN	55155	651-296-3985		339-24

	Phone	Fax	Class
Office of Higher Education 1450 Energy Pk Dr Ste 350 Saint Paul MN 55108 *TF:* 800-657-3866 ■ *Web:* www.ohe.state.mn.us	651-642-0567	642-0675	725
Public Utilities Commission 121 Seventh Pl E Ste 350 Saint Paul MN 55101 *TF:* 800-657-3782 ■ *Web:* mn.gov	651-296-7124		339-24
Revenue Dept 600 N Roberts St. Saint Paul MN 55101 *TF:* 800-657-3666 ■ *Web:* www.revenue.state.mn.us	651-556-3000		339-24
Secretary of State 100 Rev Dr Martin Luther King Jr Blvd Ste 100 Saint Paul MN 55103 *TF:* 866-723-3035 ■ *Web:* www.sos.state.mn.us	651-201-1342	215-0682	339-24
State Court Administrator 25 Rev Dr Martin Luther King Jr Blvd Rm 135 Saint Paul MN 55155 *Web:* www.mncourts.gov	651-296-2474	297-5636	339-24
State Lottery 2645 Long Lake Rd. Roseville MN 55113 *Web:* www.mnlottery.com	651-635-8273		452
Supreme Court 401 Robert St N Ste 150 Saint Paul MN 55155	651-297-1000		339-24
Transportation Dept 395 John Ireland Blvd Saint Paul MN 55155 *TF:* 800-657-3774 ■ *Web:* www.dot.state.mn.us	651-296-3000		339-24
Veterans Affairs Dept 20 W 12th St Rm 206 Saint Paul MN 55155 *Web:* mn.gov	651-296-2562		339-24
Weights & Measures Div 14305 Southcross Dr W Ste 500 Burnsville MN 55306 *Web:* mn.gov	651-539-1555		339-24
Minnesota Association of Realtors 5750 Lincoln Dr Minneapolis MN 55436 *TF:* 800-862-6097 ■ *Web:* www.mnrealtor.com	952-935-8313		656
Minnesota Ballet 301 W First St Ste 800 Duluth MN 55802 *Web:* www.minnesotaballet.org	218-529-3742	529-3744	573-1
Minnesota Chamber of Commerce 400 Robert St N Ste 1500 Saint Paul MN 55101 *TF:* 800-821-2230 ■ *Web:* www.mnchamber.com	651-292-4650	292-4656	140
Minnesota Chemical Co 3750 Dunlap St N Arden Hills MN 55112 *TF:* 800-328-5689 ■ *Web:* minnesotachemical.com	651-646-7521	649-1101	427
Minnesota Children's Museum 10 W Seventh St Saint Paul MN 55102 *Web:* mcm.org	651-225-6000	225-6006	521
Minnesota Christian Broadcasters Inc PO Box 409 Pequot Lakes MN 56472 *TF:* 866-568-4422 ■ *Web:* theword.mn	218-568-4422		645-141
Minnesota Commercial Association of Real Estate 6600 France Ave Ste 485 Edina MN 55435 *Web:* mncar.org	952-908-1780		653
Minnesota Commercial Railway 508 Cleveland Ave N. Saint Paul MN 55114 *Web:* mnnr.net	651-632-9033	646-8337	651
Minnesota Correctional Facility-Fairbault 1101 Linden Ln Faribault MN 55021 *Web:* www.doc.state.mn.us	507-334-0700		213
Minnesota Correctional Facility-Lino Lakes 7525 Fourth Ave. Lino Lakes MN 55014 *Web:* mn.gov	651-717-6100		213
Minnesota Correctional Facility-Moose Lake 1000 Lake Shore Dr Moose Lake MN 55767 *Web:* mn.gov	218-485-5000		213
Minnesota Correctional Facility-Rush City 7600 - 525th St Rush City MN 55069 *Web:* www.mn.gov	320-358-0400		213
Minnesota Correctional Facility-Stillwater 970 Picket St Bayport MN 55003 *Web:* mn.gov	651-351-3600		213
Minnesota Council on Foundations (MCF) 800 Washington Ave N Ste 703 Minneapolis MN 55401 *Web:* www.mcf.org	612-338-1989	337-5089	48-13
Minnesota Dance Theatre 528 Hennepin Ave 6th Fl Minneapolis MN 55403 *Web:* mndance.org	612-338-0627		573-1
Minnesota Dehydrated Vegetables Inc 915 Omland Ave. Fosston MN 56542 *Web:* www.mdvcorp.com	218-435-1997	435-6770	296-18
Minnesota Dental Assn 1335 Industrial Blvd Ste 200 Minneapolis MN 55413 *TF:* 800-950-3368 ■ *Web:* www.mndental.org	612-767-8400	767-8500	227
Minnesota Department of Corrections 1450 Energy Park Dr Ste 200 Saint Paul MN 55108 *Web:* www.mn.gov	651-361-7200		339-24
Minnesota Discovery Ctr 1005 Discovery Dr Chisholm MN 55719 *TF:* 800-372-6437 ■ *Web:* www.mndiscoverycenter.com	218-254-7959	254-7971	520
Minnesota Diversified Products Inc 9091 County Rd 50. Rockford MN 55373 *Web:* www.diversifoam.com	763-477-5854	477-5863	601
Minnesota Educator Magazine 41 Sherburne Ave. Saint Paul MN 55103 *TF:* 800-652-9073 ■ *Web:* www.educationminnesota.org	651-227-9541	292-4802	457-8
Minnesota Electric Technology Inc 1507 1st Ave. Mankato MN 56001 *TF:* 800-373-3166 ■ *Web:* www.metmotors.com	507-625-6117	625-1485	518
Minnesota Elevator Inc 19336 607th Ave. Mankato MN 56001 *TF:* 800-450-3060 ■ *Web:* www.meielevatorsolutions.com	507-245-3060	245-3956	256
Minnesota Eye Consultants PA 710 E 24th St Ste 100. Minneapolis MN 55404 *TF:* 800-526-7632 ■ *Web:* www.mneye.com	612-813-3600	813-3601	798
Minnesota Home Improvements 8850 Ridgewood Ct Saint Joseph MN 56374 *TF:* 888-363-3305 ■ *Web:* www.mnhomeimprovements.com	320-363-4435	363-4405	191-4
Minnesota judicial branch 25 Rev Dr Martin Luther King Jr Blvd. Saint Paul MN 55155 *Web:* www.mncourts.gov	651-297-7650		341
Minnesota Knitting Mills 1450 Mendota Heights Rd Saint Paul MN 55120 *Web:* www.mnknit.com	651-452-2240		745-4
Minnesota Landscape Arboretum 3675 Arboretum Dr. Chaska MN 55318 *Web:* www.arboretum.umn.edu	952-443-1400	443-2521	97
Minnesota Lawyers Mutual Insurance Co 333 S Seventh St Ste 2200. Minneapolis MN 55402 *TF:* 800-422-1370 ■ *Web:* www.mlmins.com	800-422-1370	305-1510	390
Minnesota Library Assn (MLA) 400 S Fourth St Ste 754E Minneapolis MN 55415 *Web:* www.mnlibraryassociation.org	612-294-6549		435
Minnesota Medical Assn 1300 Godward St NE Ste 2500 Minneapolis MN 55413 *Web:* www.mnmed.org	612-378-1875		474
Minnesota Multi Housing Services Inc 1600 W 82nd St Ste 110. Bloomington MN 55431 *Web:* www.mmha.com	952-854-8500		138
Minnesota News Network PO Box 26216 Minneapolis MN 55426 *Web:* www.minnesotanewsnetwork.com	952-545-6660	545-6669	647
Minnesota Nurses Assn (MNA) 345 Randolph Ave Ste 200 Saint Paul MN 55102 *TF:* 800-536-4662 ■ *Web:* mnnurses.org	651-414-2800		533
Minnesota Opera 620 N 1st St Minneapolis MN 55401 *Web:* www.mnopera.org	612-333-2700	333-0869	573-2
Minnesota Orchestra Orchestra Hall 1111 Nicollet Mall. Minneapolis MN 55403 *TF:* 800-292-4141 ■ *Web:* www.minnesotaorchestra.org	612-371-5600	371-7170	573-3
Minnesota Pharmacists Assn (MPHA) 1000 Westgate Dr Ste 252 Saint Paul MN 55114 **Fax Area Code:* 650 ■ *TF:* 800-451-8349 ■ *Web:* www.mpha.org	651-697-1771	290-2266*	585
Minnesota Physician Publishing Inc 2812 E 26th St Minneapolis MN 55406 *Web:* www.mppub.com	612-728-8600	728-8601	637-2
Minnesota Power 30 W Superior St. Duluth MN 55802 *TF:* 800-228-4966 ■ *Web:* www.mnpower.com	218-722-2625	720-2795	787
Minnesota Public Radio (MPR) 480 Cedar St. Saint Paul MN 55101 *TF:* 800-228-7123 ■ *Web:* www.mpr.org	651-290-1212		632
Minnesota Public Television Assn 2723 N Walnut St Bloomington IN 47401 *Web:* www.spirit95fm.com	812-335-9500	335-8880	647
Minnesota Rubber & Plastics 1100 Xenium Ln N Minneapolis MN 55441 *TF:* 800-927-1422 ■ *Web:* mnrubber.com	952-927-1400	927-1470	604
Minnesota Rusco Inc 5558 Smetana Dr Minneapolis MN 55401 *Web:* minnesotarusco.com	952-935-9669		191-3
Minnesota School of Bartending Inc 2426 University Ave Saint Paul MN 55114 *Web:* www.mnschoolofbartending.com	651-645-1252		685
Minnesota School of Cosmetology 1750 Weir Dr No 3 Woodbury MN 55125 *TF:* 877-477-4840 ■ *Web:* www.msccollege.edu	651-287-2180		685
Minnesota School of Horseshoeing 6250 Riverdale Dr NW Ramsey MN 55303 *TF:* 800-257-5850 ■ *Web:* www.mnschoolofhorseshoeing.com	763-427-5850	427-3395	685
Minnesota State Bar Assn 600 Nicollet Mall Ste 380. Minneapolis MN 55402 *TF:* 800-882-6722 ■ *Web:* www.mnbar.org	612-333-1183	333-4927	72
Minnesota State Community & Technical College *Detroit Lakes* 900 Hwy 34 E. Detroit Lakes MN 56501 *TF:* 877-450-3322 ■ *Web:* www.minnesota.edu	218-846-3700	846-3794	162
Minnesota State University *Mankato* 122 Taylor Ctr. Mankato MN 56001 *Web:* mankato.mnsu.edu	507-389-1822	389-1511	166
Minnesota State University Mankato *Memorial Library* 601 Maywood Ave PO Box 8419 Mankato MN 56002 *TF:* 800-722-0544 ■ *Web:* www.lib.mnsu.edu	507-389-5952	389-5155	434-6
Minnesota Supply Company Inc 6470 Flying Cloud Dr. Eden Prairie MN 55344 *TF:* 800-869-1028 ■ *Web:* www.mnsupply.com	952-828-7300	828-7301	385
Minnesota Tool & Die Works Inc 6220 Mckinley St NW. Ramsey MN 55303 *Web:* www.mtdwi.com	763-323-0145	323-0625	757
Minnesota Transportation Museum 193 E Pennsylvania Ave Saint Paul MN 55130 *Web:* transportationmuseum.org	651-228-0263		520
Minnesota Valley Cooperative Light & Power Assn 501 S First St Montevideo MN 56265 *TF:* 800-247-5051 ■ *Web:* www.mnvalleyrec.com	320-269-2163	269-2302	245
Minnesota Valley Electric Co-op 125 Minnesota Vly Electric Dr PO Box 77024. Jordan MN 55352 *TF:* 800-282-6832 ■ *Web:* www.mvec.net	952-492-2313	492-8281	245
Minnesota Valley State Recreation Area 19825 Park Blvd. Jordan MN 55352 *Web:* www.dnr.state.mn.us	651-259-5774		565
Minnesota Veterans Home-Fergus Falls 1821 N Park St Fergus Falls MN 56537 *TF:* 877-838-4633 ■ *Web:* mn.gov	218-736-0400	739-7686	793
Minnesota Veterans Home-Minneapolis 5101 Minnehaha Ave S. Minneapolis MN 55417 *TF:* 877-838-6757 ■ *Web:* mn.gov	612-548-5700	548-5732	793
Minnesota Veterans Home-Silver Bay 56 Outer Dr. Silver Bay MN 55614 *TF:* 877-729-8387 ■ *Web:* mn.gov	218-353-8700	226-6336	793
Minnesota Veterinary Medical Assn 101 Bridgepoint Way Ste 100. South Saint Paul MN 55075 *Web:* www.mvma.org	651-645-7533	645-7539	795
Minnesota Vikings 9520 Viking Dr Eden Prairie MN 55344 *Web:* www.vikings.com	952-828-6500		715-3
Minnesota Visiting Nurse Agency 2000 Summer St. Minneapolis MN 55413 *Web:* www.mvna.org	612-617-4600	617-4782	363
Minnesota West Community & Technical College 1450 Collegeway Worthington MN 56187 *TF:* 800-657-3966 ■ *Web:* www.mnwest.edu	507-372-3400	372-5803	162
Minnesota Wing Commemorative Air Force Museum 310 Airport Rd Hanger 3. South Saint Paul MN 55075 *Web:* www.cafmn.org	651-455-6942		520

Name / Address	City	State	Zip	Phone	Fax	Class
Minnesota Wire & Cable Co 1835 Energy Park Dr *TF:* 800-258-6922 ■ *Web:* mnwire.com	Saint Paul	MN	55108	651-642-1800		815
Minnesota Womens Press Inc 771 Raymond Ave *Web:* www.womenspress.com	Saint Paul	MN	55114	651-646-3968		532-3
Minnesota Zoo 13000 Zoo Blvd *TF:* 800-366-7811 ■ *Web:* mnzoo.org	Apple Valley	MN	55124	952-431-9200	431-9300	823
Minnesuing Acres 8084 E Minnesuing Acres Dr *Web:* www.minnesuingacres.com	Lake Nebagamon	WI	54849	715-374-2262	374-2118	317
Minnetonka Public School Service Ctr 5621 County Rd 101 *Web:* www.minnetonkaschools.org	Minnetonka	MN	55345	952-401-5000	401-5093	685
Minnetronix Inc 1635 Energy Park Dr *Web:* www.minnetronix.com	Saint Paul	MN	55108	651-917-4060		261
Minnewaska Area High School 25122 State Hwy 28 *Web:* www.minnewaska.k12.mn.us	Glenwood	MN	56334	320-239-4820		685
Minnkota Windows Inc 2324 Main Ave W *Web:* www.minnkotawindows.com	West Fargo	ND	58078	701-282-7025	282-7435	234
Minnotte Contracting Corp 1 Minnotte Sq *Web:* minnotte.com	Pittsburgh	PA	15220	412-922-1633	922-5051	307
Minnow Project a Creative Lab 815 O St Ste 3 *Web:* www.minnowproject.com	Lincoln	NE	68508	402-475-3322		4
Minnpar LLC 5273 Program Ave *TF:* 800-889-3382 ■ *Web:* www.minnpar.com	Mounds View	MN	55112	612-379-0606		61
Minntech Corp 14605 28th Ave N *TF:* 800-328-3345 ■ *Web:* www.medivators.com	Minneapolis	MN	55447	763-553-3300	553-3387	476
Minnwest Bank 14820 Hwy 7 *Web:* www.minnwest.com	Minnetonka	MN	55345	952-230-9800	230-9810	360-3
Minor Heron Press 512 Camino San Miguel *Web:* www.minorheron.org	Taos	NM	87571	505-758-1029		637-2
Minor League Baseball 9550 16th St N *Web:* www.milb.com	Saint Petersburg	FL	33716	727-822-6937	821-5819	48-22
Minor Rubber Company Inc 49 Ackerman St *TF:* 800-433-6886 ■ *Web:* www.minorrubber.com	Bloomfield	NJ	07003	973-338-6800	893-1399	677
Minor Tire & Wheel Company Inc 3512 6th Ave SE *TF:* 800-633-3936 ■ *Web:* www.visionwheel.com	Decatur	AL	35603	256-353-4957		54
Minority Alliance Capital (MAC) 6960 Orchard Lake Rd Ste 306 *Web:* www.mac-leasing.com	West Bloomfield	MI	48322	248-855-8746	539-1397	69
Minority Business Development Agency (MBDA) 1401 Constitution Ave NW *TF:* 888-324-1551 ■ *Web:* www.mbda.gov	Washington	DC	20230	888-324-1551		340-2
Minority Business Development Agency Regional Offices *Atlanta Region* 75 Fifth St NW Ste 300 *Web:* www.mbda.gov	Atlanta	GA	30308	404-894-2096		340-2
Chicago Region 105 W Adams St Ste 2300 *Web:* www.mbda.gov	Chicago	IL	60603	312-353-0182		340-2
New York Region 48 Wall St Ste 10 Fifth Fl *Web:* www.mbda.gov	New York	NY	10005	917-830-2920		340-2
Minot Air Force Base 201 Summit Dr *Web:* www.minot.af.mil	Minot	ND	58705	701-723-6212		497-1
Minot Area Chamber of Commerce 1020 20th Ave SW *Web:* www.minotchamber.org	Minot	ND	58701	701-852-6000	838-2488	139
Minot Convention & Visitors Bureau 1020 S Broadway *TF:* 800-264-2626 ■ *Web:* visitminot.org	Minot	ND	58701	701-857-8206	857-8228	206
Minot Daily News 301 Fourth St SE *TF:* 800-735-3119 ■ *Web:* www.minotdailynews.com	Minot	ND	58702	701-857-1900		532-2
Minot Public Library 516 Second Ave SW *TF:* 800-843-9948 ■ *Web:* www.minotlibrary.org	Minot	ND	58701	701-852-1045	852-2595	434-3
Minot Public Schools 215 2nd St SE *Web:* www.minot.k12.nd.us	Minot	ND	58701	701-857-4400	857-4432	685
Minot State University 500 University Ave W *TF:* 800-777-0750 ■ *Web:* www.minotstateu.edu	Minot	ND	58707	701-858-3000	858-3888	166
MinoTech Engineering Inc JRD Technology Ctr 242 Sturbridge Rd *Web:* www.minotecheng.com	Charlton	MA	01507	978-474-8034		466
Minova USA Inc 150 Carley Ct *TF:* 800-626-2948 ■ *Web:* www.minovaglobal.com	Georgetown	KY	40324	502-863-6800	863-6805	605-2
Minskoff Theatre 200 W 45th St *TF:* 800-714-8452 ■ *Web:* broadwaydirect.com	New York	NY	10036	212-869-0550		747
Minster Bank 95 W Fourth St *Web:* www.minsterbank.com	Minster	OH	45865	419-628-2351		70
Minster Machine Co 240 W Fifth St PO Box 120 *Web:* www.minster.com	Minster	OH	45865	419-628-2331	628-3517	456
Mint Magazine Inc 6960 Bonneval Rd Ste 102 *TF:* 888-620-3877 ■ *Web:* mintmag.com	Jacksonville	FL	32216	904-281-8800		5
Mint Museum of Art 2730 Randolph Rd *Web:* www.mintmuseum.org	Charlotte	NC	28207	704-337-2000	337-2101	520
Mint Turbines LLC 2915 N State Hwy 99 *Web:* www.mintturbines.com	Stroud	OK	74079	918-968-9561		21
Minter Field Air Museum 401 Vultee St PO Box 445 *Web:* www.minterfieldairmuseum.com	Shafter	CA	93263	661-393-0291		520
Minterbrook Oyster Co 12002 114th St Kp N Ct *Web:* www.minterbrookoyster.com	Gig Harbor	WA	98329	253-857-5251	857-5521	296-14
Mintie Corp 1114 San Fernando Rd *TF:* 800-964-6843 ■ *Web:* www.mintie.com	Los Angeles	CA	90065	323-225-4111		35
Minto Rentals In Ottawa 185 Lyons St N *TF:* 800-267-3377 ■ *Web:* www.minto.com	Ottawa	ON	K1R7Y4	613-232-2200	232-6962	379
Minton Door Co 1150 Elko Dr *Web:* www.mintondoor.com	Sunnyvale	CA	94089	408-744-1790		191-3

Name / Address	City	State	Zip	Phone	Fax	Class
Mintz & Gold Esq 600 Third Ave 25th Fl *Web:* mintzandgold.com	New York	NY	10016	212-696-1231		41
Mintz & Hoke Inc 40 Tower Ln *Web:* www.mintz-hoke.com	Avon	CT	06001	860-678-0473		7
Mintz Levin Cohn Ferris Glovsky & Popeo PC 1 Financial Ctr *Web:* www.mintz.com	Boston	MA	02111	617-542-6000	542-2241	428
Minus Forty Technologies Corp 30 Armstrong Ave *TF:* 800-800-5706 ■ *Web:* www.minusforty.com	Georgetown	ON	L7G4R9	905-702-1441		665
Minute Man National Historical Park 174 Liberty St *Web:* www.nps.gov	Concord	MA	01742	978-369-6993		564
Minute Men Staffing Services 3740 Carnegie Ave *TF:* 877-873-8856 ■ *Web:* www.minutemeninc.com	Cleveland	OH	44115	216-426-9675	426-2246	721
Minuteman Aviation Inc (MAI) 5225 Hwy 10 W *Web:* www.minutemanaviation.net	Missoula	MT	59808	406-728-9363		63
Minuteman Group Inc 35 Bedford St Ste 2 *TF:* 800-861-7493 ■ *Web:* www.minuteman-group.com	Lexington	MA	02420	781-861-7493	863-8810	177
Minuteman International Inc 14N845 US Rte 20 *TF:* 800-323-9420 ■ *Web:* minutemanintl.com	Pingree Grove	IL	60140	847-264-5400	683-5207	386
Minuteman Missile National Historic Site 21280 SD Hwy 240 *Web:* www.nps.gov	Philip	SD	57567	605-433-5552	433-5558	564
Minuteman Press International Inc 61 Executive Blvd *TF:* 800-645-3006 ■ *Web:* www.minutemanpress.com	Farmingdale	NY	11735	631-249-1370	249-5618	310
Minuteman Regional High School 758 Marrett Rd *Web:* www.minuteman.org	Lexington	MA	02421	781-861-6500		685
Minuteman Senior Services 26 Crosby Dr *Web:* www.minutemansenior.org	Bedford	MA	01730	781-272-7177		672
Minuteman Trucks Inc 2181 Providence Hwy *TF:* 800-231-8458 ■ *Web:* www.minutemantrucks.com	Walpole	MA	02081	508-668-3112		780
Minvalco Inc 3340 Gorham Ave *TF:* 800-642-9090 ■ *Web:* minvalco.com	Minneapolis	MN	55426	952-920-0131		612
Minwax Co 10 Mountainview Rd *TF:* 800-523-9299 ■ *Web:* www.minwax.com	Upper Saddle River	NJ	07458	800-523-9299		550
MinXray Inc 3611 Commercial Ave *TF:* 800-221-2245 ■ *Web:* www.minxray.com	Northbrook	IL	60062	847-564-0323		475
Mio Sushi 2271 NW Johnson St *Web:* www.miosushi.com	Portland	OR	97210	503-221-1469		671
MIQ Logistics LLC 11501 Outlook St Ste 500 *TF:* 877-246-4909 ■ *Web:* www.miq.com	Overland Park	KS	66211	913-696-7100	696-7501	449
Mira Godard Gallery 22 Hazelton Ave *Web:* www.godardgallery.com	Toronto	ON	M5R2E2	416-964-8197	964-5912	42
Mira Monte Inn & Suites 69 Mt Desert St *Fax Area Code: 207 ■ *TF:* 800-553-5109 ■ *Web:* miramonte.com	Bar Harbor	ME	04609	800-553-5109	288-3115*	379
Mira Vista Diagnostics 4705 Decatur Blvd *TF:* 866-647-2847 ■ *Web:* miravistalabs.com	Indianapolis	IN	46241	317-856-2681	856-3685	743
Mirabeau Park Hotel 1100 N Sullivan Rd *Web:* www.mirabeauparkhotel.com	Spokane Valley	WA	99037	509-924-9000		379
Mirabito Fuel Group Inc 40 Ct St PO Box 5306 *TF:* 800-934-9480 ■ *Web:* www.mirabito.com	Binghamton	NY	13002	607-352-2800	581-5130	316
Miracapo Pizza Co 2323 Pratt Blvd *Web:* miracapopizza.com	Elk Grove Village	IL	60007	847-631-3500		296-36
Miracell Botanicals 921 North 1420 West *Web:* www.miracell.com	Orem	UT	84057	801-434-8165		77
Miracle Healthcare 4322 N Hamilton Rd *TF:* 844-560-7775 ■ *Web:* www.miraclehealthcare.com	Gahanna	OH	43230	614-237-7702	235-5383	363
Miracle Method US Corp 4310 Arrowswest Dr *TF:* 800-444-8827 ■ *Web:* www.miraclemethod.com	Colorado Springs	CO	80907	719-594-9196	594-9282	189-11
Miracle Mile Shops at Planet Hollywood 3663 Las Vegas Blvd S *Web:* www.miraclemileshopslv.com	Las Vegas	NV	89109	702-366-0502		50-6
Miracle Pruzan & Pruzan PC 1000 Second Ave Ste 1550 *Web:* miraclelaw.com	Seattle	WA	98104	206-624-8830		41
Miracle Recreation Equipment Co 878 Hwy 60 *TF:* 800-523-4202 ■ *Web:* www.miracle-recreation.com	Monett	MO	65708	417-235-6917		346
Miracle-Ear Inc 5000 Cheshire Pkwy N *TF:* 800-464-8002 ■ *Web:* www.miracle-ear.com	Minneapolis	MN	55446	800-464-8002		477
Miracles Can Happen Inc 1600 Church Ave	Brooklyn	NY	11226	718-693-3400		260
Miraco PO Box 686 *TF:* 800-541-7866 ■ *Web:* www.miraco.com	Grinnell	IA	50112	641-236-5822	236-3341	276
Miraco Inc 102 Maple St *Web:* www.miracoinc.com	Manchester	NH	03103	603-665-9449		359
MiraCosta College *San Elijo* 3333 Manchester Ave Rm 407 *TF:* 888-201-8480 ■ *Web:* www.miracosta.edu	Cardiff-By-The-Sea	CA	92007	760-757-2121	634-7875	162
Mirage Productions Inc 111 Spring St *Web:* www.mirageproductions.com	Newton	NJ	07860	973-300-9477		514
Mirage, The 3400 Las Vegas Blvd S *TF:* 800-627-6667 ■ *Web:* www.mirage.com	Las Vegas	NV	89109	702-791-7111	791-7414	669
Miragee Corp 2512 Merriwood Dr *Web:* www.miragee.com	Louisville	KY	40299	502-266-8768		180
Miragen Therapeutics Inc 6200 Lookout Rd Ste 100 *Web:* www.miragen.com	Boulder	CO	80301	720-643-5200		231

Name / Address	City	State	ZIP	Phone	Fax	Class
Mirai Sushi 2020 W Div St. *Web:* www.miraisushi.com	Chicago	IL	60622	773-862-8500		671
Miramar Hospitality 1100 Lincoln Ave Ste 265 *Web:* www.miramarhospitality.com	Los Altos	CA	94022	408-297-5202	297-5225	196
Miramar-Pembroke Pines Regional Chamber of Commerce 9001-B Pembroke Rd *Web:* www.miramarpembrokepines.org	Pembroke Pines	FL	33025	954-432-9808	432-9193	139
Miramax Film NY LLC 1901 Avenue of the Stars Ste 2000 *Web:* www.miramax.com	Los Angeles	CA	90067	310-409-4321		514
Miramichi Chamber of Commerce 120 Newcastle Blvd Ste 2 PO Box 342 *Web:* www.miramichichamber.com	Miramichi	NB	E1N3A7	506-622-5522		137
Miramont Castle Museum 9 Capitol Hill Ave *TF:* 888-685-1011 ■ *Web:* www.miramontcastle.org	Manitou Springs	CO	80829	719-685-1011	685-1985	520
Miramonte Resort & Spa 45000 Indian Wells Ln *TF:* 800-237-2926 ■ *Web:* www.miramonteresort.com	Indian Wells	CA	92210	760-341-2200		669
Miratek Corporation Inc 8201 Lockheed Dr Ste 218 *Web:* miratek.us	El Paso	TX	79925	915-772-2852		194
Miratel Solutions Inc 2501 Steeles Ave W *TF:* 866-647-2835 ■ *Web:* www.miratelinc.com	North York	ON	M3J2P1	416-650-7850		737
Mirau, Edwards, Cannon, Lewin & Tooke Attorneys at Law 1806 Orange Tree Ln Ste C *Web:* mechlaw.com	Redlands	CA	92374	909-793-0200		41
Miraval AZ Resort & Spa 5000 E Via Estancia Miraval **Fax Area Code:* 520 ■ *TF:* 800-232-3969 ■ *Web:* www.miravalresorts.com	Tucson	AZ	85739	800-232-3969	825-5163*	706
Mirbeau Inn & Spa 851 W Genesee St *TF:* 877-647-2328 ■ *Web:* www.mirbeau.com	Skaneateles	NY	13152	315-685-5006		379
Mircom 25 Interchange Way *TF:* 888-660-4655 ■ *Web:* www.mircom.com	Vaughan	ON	L4K5W3	905-660-4655	660-4113	693
Mirealsource Inc 920 E Long Lake Rd Ste 100A *Web:* mirealsource.com	Troy	MI	48085	248-247-1040		653
Miria Systems Inc 2570 Blvd of the Generals Ste 222 *Web:* miriasystems.com	Norristown	PA	19403	484-446-3300		177
Miriam Hospital, The 164 Summit Ave *Web:* www.miriamhospital.org	Providence	RI	02906	401-793-2500		374-3
Miriam Shiell Fine Art Ltd 16-A Hazelton Ave *Web:* www.miriamshiell.com	Toronto	ON	M5R2E2	416-925-2461	925-2471	42
Mirick O'Connell Demaillie & Lougee LLP 100 Front St *Web:* www.mirickoconnell.com	Worcester	MA	01608	508-791-8500	791-8502	428
Mirixa Corp 11600 Sunrise Vly Dr Ste 100 *TF:* 866-218-6649 ■ *Web:* www.mirixa.com	Reston	VA	20191	703-683-1955		612
Miro 201 Spear St Ste 1100 *Web:* miro.com	San Francisco	CA	94105	415-669-8098		242
Miro Consulting Inc 167 Main St *Web:* www.miroconsulting.com	Woodbridge	NJ	07095	732-738-8511	738-8466	393
Miro Spanish Grille 12239 N Community House Rd *Web:* www.mirospanishgrille.com	Charlotte	NC	28277	704-540-7374		671
Miron Construction Company Inc 1471 McMahon Dr *Web:* miron-construction.com	Neenah	WI	54956	920-969-7000	969-7393	186
Mirror Image Internet Inc 2 Highwood Dr	Tewksbury	MA	01876	781-376-1100	376-1110	178-7
Mirror Lake Inn Resort & Spa 77 Mirror Lake Dr *Web:* www.mirrorlakeinn.com	Lake Placid	NY	12946	518-523-2544	523-2871	707
Mirror Lake State Park E10320 Fern Dell Rd *Web:* dnr.wi.gov	Baraboo	WI	53913	608-254-2333		565
Mirror Show Management Inc 855 Hard Rd *Web:* www.mirrorshow.com	Webster	NY	14580	585-232-4020		184
Mirrorball Group LLC 134 W 25th St *Web:* www.mirrorball.com	New York	NY	10001	212-604-9988		636
Mirrotek International LLC 90 Dayton Ave *TF:* 888-659-3030 ■ *Web:* www.mirrotek.com	Passaic	NJ	07055	973-472-1400		544
Mirum 500 rue St-Jacques Ste 1420 *Web:* www.mirumagency.com	Montreal	QC	H2Y2G3	514-987-9992		7
Mirus International Inc 31 Sun Pac Blvd *TF:* 888-866-4787 ■ *Web:* www.mirusinternational.com	Brampton	ON	L6S5P6	905-494-1120		767
MIRUS Restaurant Solutions 820 Gessner Rd Ste 1600 *TF:* 866-647-8748 ■ *Web:* www.mirus.com	Houston	TX	77024	713-468-7300		196
MIS (Modern Information Systems Inc) 817 First Ave N *TF:* 800-841-1084 ■ *Web:* www.moderninformation.com	Grand Forks	ND	58203	701-772-4844	772-1266	112
MIS Inc 222 W Highland Dr *TF:* 866-506-7006 ■ *Web:* www.mis-inc.net	Lakeland	FL	33813	863-669-1100	669-1005	196
MIS Training Institute LLC 153 Cordaville Rd Ste 200 *Web:* www.misti.com	Southborough	MA	01772	508-879-7999		177
Misa Metal Fabricating Inc 7101 International Dr *Web:* www.misametalfab.com	Louisville	KY	40258	502-933-5555		480
MISA Metal Processing of Tennessee Inc 104 Western Dr *Web:* www.misa.com	Portland	TN	37148	615-325-5454		690
Misaki Japanese Steak House 8207 Kingston Pk *Web:* www.misakiknoxville.com	Knoxville	TN	37919	865-691-3121		671
Misaki Seafood & Steak House of Japan Inc 3104 Bristol Hwy Ste C	Johnson City	TN	37601	423-282-5451		671
Misaki Sushi 379 W Main St *Web:* www.misakisushi.com	Hyannis	MA	02601	508-771-3771		671
Misco Home & Garden 100 S Washington Ave *Web:* www.miscohomeandgarden.com	Dunellen	NJ	08812	732-752-7500		292
Mise En Place 442 W Kennedy Blvd *Web:* www.miseonline.com	Tampa	FL	33606	813-254-5373		671
Misericordia Nursing & Rehabilitation Ctr 998 S Russell St *Web:* mn-rc.org	York	PA	17402	717-755-1964		371
Misericordia University 301 Lake St *TF:* 866-262-6363 ■ *Web:* www.misericordia.edu	Dallas	PA	18612	570-674-6400	675-2441	166
Mishaels Electrolysis Ctr 5825 Glenridge Dr NE Bldg 1 Ste 103 *Web:* mecatlanta.com	Atlanta	GA	30328	404-843-9993		77
Mishawaka-Penn-Harris Public Library Indiana 209 Lincoln Way E *TF:* 800-622-4970 ■ *Web:* mphpl.org	Mishawaka	IN	46544	574-259-5277		435
Miskelly Furniture 101 Airport Rd *TF:* 888-939-6288 ■ *Web:* www.miskellys.com	Jackson	MS	39208	601-939-6288		321
MISO (Miami Symphony Orchestra, The) 3900 N Miami Ave Ste 307 *Web:* themiso.org	Miami	FL	33127	305-275-5666		573-3
Misonix Inc 1938 New Hwy *TF:* 800-694-9612 ■ *Web:* www.misonix.com	Farmingdale	NY	11735	631-694-9555		250
MISource Inc 11940 Sheldon Rd *Web:* www.misource.com	Tampa	FL	33626	813-286-9888		260
Miss Elaine Inc 8430 Valcour Ave *TF:* 800-458-1422 ■ *Web:* www.misselaine.com	Saint Louis	MO	63123	314-631-1900		155-15
Miss Foundation PO Box 5333 *Web:* missfoundation.org	Peoria	AZ	85385	623-979-1000		48-21
Miss Hall's School 492 Holmes Rd *Web:* www.misshalls.org	Pittsfield	MA	01201	413-443-6401		622
Miss Porter's School 60 Main St *Web:* www.porters.org	Farmington	CT	06032	860-409-3530		622
Miss Universe LP 1370 Avenue of the Americas 16th Fl *Web:* www.missuniverse.com	New York	NY	10019	212-373-4999	315-5378	181
Missaukee County 111 S Canal PO Box 800 *Web:* www.missaukee.org	Lake City	MI	49651	231-839-4967	839-3684	338
MISSCO Contract Sales 2001 Airport Rd Ste 102 PO Box 321400 *Web:* www.missco.com	Flowood	MS	39232	601-987-8600	487-2800	320
Missio Seminary 200 N Main St *Web:* missio.edu	Hatfield	PA	19440	215-368-5000		167-3
Mission Ambulance 1055 E Third St *TF:* 800-899-9100 ■ *Web:* missionambulance.com	Corona	CA	92879	800-899-9100		30
Mission Aviation Fellowship (MAF) 112 N Pilatus Ln *TF:* 800-359-7623 ■ *Web:* www.maf.org	Nampa	ID	83687	208-498-0800	498-0801	48-20
Mission Basilica San Diego de Alcala 10818 San Diego Mission Rd *Web:* www.missionsandiego.org	San Diego	CA	92108	619-283-7319	283-7762	520
Mission Bell Manufacturing Inc 16100 Jacqueline Ct *Web:* www.missionbell.com	Morgan Hill	CA	95037	408-778-2036		499
Mission Benefits 753 E El Camino Real Ste C *Web:* missionbenefits.com	Sunnyvale	CA	94087	408-419-2600	419-2601	193
Mission Bicycles Inc 766 Valencia St *Web:* www.missionbicycle.com	San Francisco	CA	94110	415-683-6166		711
Mission Chamber of Commerce 202 W Tom Landry St *TF:* 800-827-8298 ■ *Web:* www.missionchamber.com	Mission	TX	78572	956-585-2727		139
Mission City Federal Credit Union 1391 Franklin St *TF:* 888-361-1894 ■ *Web:* www.missioncityfcu.org	Santa Clara	CA	95050	408-244-5818	244-9390	219
Mission College 3000 Mission College Blvd *Web:* missioncollege.edu	Santa Clara	CA	95054	408-855-5007	980-8980	162
Mission Creative 140 E Ninth St *Web:* www.missioncreative.biz	Dubuque	IA	52001	563-583-0853		7
Mission Critical Technologies Inc 2041 Rosecrans Ave	El Segundo	CA	90245	310-246-4455		177
Mission Cultural Center for Latino Arts 2868 Mission St *Web:* missionculturalcenter.org	San Francisco	CA	94110	415-643-2785	648-0933	50-2
Mission Dolores 3321 16th St *Web:* www.missiondolores.org	San Francisco	CA	94114	415-621-8203		50-1
Mission Essential Personnel LLC 4343 Easton Commons Ste 100 *TF:* 888-542-3447 ■ *Web:* www.missionessential.com	Columbus	OH	43219	614-416-2345		766
Mission Federal Credit Union PO Box 919023 *TF:* 800-500-6328 ■ *Web:* www.missionfed.com	San Diego	CA	92191	858-524-2850		219
Mission Foods 1159 Cottonwood Ln Ste 200 **Fax Area Code:* 972 ■ *TF:* 800-443-7994 ■ *Web:* www.missionfoodservice.com	Irving	TX	75038	214-208-7010	232-5229*	296-35
Mission Golf Cars 18865 Redland Rd *TF:* 800-324-7868 ■ *Web:* www.missiongolfcars.com	San Antonio	TX	78259	210-545-7868		57
Mission Health 509 Biltmore Ave *Web:* www.missionhealth.org	Asheville	NC	28801	828-213-1111		374-3
Mission Hospice & Home Care 1670 S Amphlett Blvd Ste 300 *Web:* www.missionhospice.org	San Mateo	CA	94402	650-554-1000	554-1001	371
Mission Houses Museum 553 S King St *Web:* missionhouses.org	Honolulu	HI	96813	808-447-3910	545-2280	520
Mission Inn 3649 Mission Inn Ave *TF:* 800-843-7755 ■ *Web:* www.missioninn.com	Riverside	CA	92501	951-784-0300	683-1342	379
Mission Inn Museum 3696 Main St *Web:* missioninnmuseum.org	Riverside	CA	92501	951-788-9556	341-6574	520
Mission Inn Resort & Club 10400 County Rd 48 *TF:* 800-874-9053 ■ *Web:* missioninnresort.com	Howey in the Hills	FL	34737	352-324-3101		669

Name / Address	City	State	ZIP	Phone	Fax	Class
Mission Janitorial & Abrasive Supplies 9292 Activity Rd TF: 800-733-1748 ■ Web: www.missionjanitorial.com	San Diego	CA	92126	858-566-6700	271-5079	482
Mission Laboratories 2433 Birkdale St Web: www.missionlabs.net	Los Angeles	CA	90031	323-223-1405	223-9968	151
Mission Landscape Services Inc 536 E Dyer Rd TF: 800-545-9963 ■ Web: www.missionlandscape.com	Santa Ana	CA	92707	714-545-9962	668-0119	422
Mission Mill Museum 1313 Mill St SE Ste 200 Web: www.willametteheritage.org	Salem	OR	97301	503-585-7012		50-3
Mission Mortgage of Texas Inc 901 S Mopac Expwy Barton Oaks V Ste 120 Web: www.missionmortgage.com	Austin	TX	78746	512-328-0400	328-0472	509
Mission Mountain Winery 82420 Us Hwy 93 Web: www.missionmountainwinery.com	Dayton	MT	59914	406-849-5524		80-3
Mission Petroleum Carriers Inc 8450 Mosley TF: 800-737-9911 ■ Web: www.mipe.com	Houston	TX	77075	713-943-8250		468
Mission Pharmacal PO Box 786099 TF: 800-531-3333 ■ Web: www.missionpharmacal.com	San Antonio	TX	78278	210-696-8400	696-6010	582
Mission Point Mackinac Island 1 Lakeshore Dr TF: 800-833-7711 ■ Web: www.missionpoint.com	Mackinac Island	MI	49757	231-331-3419		669
Mission Pools of Escondido 755 W Grand Ave Web: www.missionpools.com	Escondido	CA	92025	760-743-2605		728
Mission Produce Inc 2500 Vineyard Ave Ste 300 Web: www.worldsfinestavocados.com	Oxnard	CA	93036	805-981-3650		315-4
Mission Regional Chamber of Commerce 34033 Lougheed Hwy Web: www.missionchamber.bc.ca	Mission	BC	V2V5X8	604-826-6914	826-5916	137
Mission Regional Medical Ctr 900 S Bryan Rd Web: www.missionrmc.org	Mission	TX	78572	956-323-9000		374-3
Mission Rubber Co 1660 Leeson Web: missionrubber.com	Corona	CA	92879	951-736-1343		677
Mission San Fernando Rey De Espana 15151 San Fernando Mission Blvd Web: www.missiontour.org	Mission Hills	CA	91345	818-361-0186		50-1
Mission San Jose 2202 Roosevelt Ave Web: www.nps.gov	San Antonio	TX	78210	210-932-1001		50-1
Mission San Luis Apalachee 2100 W Tennessee St Web: www.missionsanluis.org	Tallahassee	FL	32304	850-245-6406	488-6186	50-3
Mission Search 2203 N Lois Ave Ste 1225 TF: 877-479-1545 ■ Web: missionsearch.com	Tampa	FL	33607	877-479-1545		193
Mission Stucco Company Inc 7751 E 70th St Web: missionstucco.net	Paramount	CA	90723	562-634-1400	634-4440	500
Mission Tejas State Park 120 State Park Rd 44 Web: tpwd.texas.gov	Grapeland	TX	75844	936-687-2394		565
Mission Trail Waste Systems 1060 Richard Ave Web: www.missiontrail.com	Santa Clara	CA	95050	408-727-5365		427
Mission Valley Ford Truck Sales Inc 780 E Brokaw Rd TF: 888-284-7471 ■ Web: missionvalleykubota.com	San Jose	CA	95112	408-933-2300	436-0313	57
Mission Ventures 9255 Towne Center Dr Ste 350 Web: missionventures.com	San Diego	CA	92121	858-350-2100		792
Mission Wealth 1123 Chapala St 3rd Fl TF: 888-642-7221 ■ Web: missionwealth.com	Santa Barbara	CA	93101	805-882-2360		401
Mission, The 304 E Onondaga St Web: www.themissionrestaurant.com	Syracuse	NY	13202	315-475-7344		671
Mission1st Group Inc Princeton Forrestal Village 155 Village Blvd Ste 203 Web: www.mission1st.com	Princeton	NJ	08540	609-520-1900		463
Missionary Oblates 327 Oblate Dr Web: www.oblatemissions.com	San Antonio	TX	78216	210-349-1475		148
Mississauga Board of Trade 701-77 City Centre Dr 7th Fl West Twr Web: www.mbot.com	Mississauga	ON	L5B1M5	905-273-6151	273-4937	137
Mississinewa Lake 4673 S 625 E Web: www.in.gov	Peru	IN	46970	765-473-6528		565
Mississippi						
Archives & History Dept 200 N St PO Box 571 Web: www.mdah.ms.gov	Jackson	MS	39201	601-576-6850		339-25
Banking & Consumer Finance Dept PO Box 12129 TF: 800-844-2499 ■ Web: www.dbcf.state.ms.us	Jackson	MS	39236	601-321-6901	321-6933	339-25
Contractors Board 2679 Crane Ridge Dr Ste C TF: 800-880-6161 ■ Web: msboc.us	Jackson	MS	39216	601-354-6161	354-6715	339-25
Dept of Human Service 200 S Lamar St TF: 800-345-6347 ■ Web: www.mdhs.ms.gov	Jackson	MS	39201	601-359-4500		339-25
Development Authority 501 NW St TF: 800-360-3323 ■ Web: www.mississippi.org	Jackson	MS	39201	601-359-3449	359-2832	339-25
Education Dept PO Box 771 Web: mdek12.org	Jackson	MS	39205	601-359-3513		339-25
Emergency Management Agency 1 Mema Dr PO Box 5644 TF: 800-222-6362 ■ Web: www.msema.org	Pearl	MS	39288	601-407-4408	933-6800	339-25
Employment Security Commission 1235 Echelon Pkwy PO Box 1699 TF: 888-844-3577 ■ Web: www.mdes.ms.gov	Jackson	MS	39215	601-321-6000	321-6004	259
Environmental Quality Dept 515 E Amite St TF: 888-786-0661 ■ Web: www.mdeq.ms.gov	Jackson	MS	39201	601-961-5611	961-5171	339-25
Ethics Commission 660 N St Ste 100-C Web: www.ethics.state.ms.us	Jackson	MS	39202	601-359-1285	359-1292	265
Finance & Administration Dept 501 NW St Woolfolk Bldg Ste 1301 Web: www.dfa.ms.gov	Jackson	MS	39201	601-359-3402	359-2405	339-25
Health Dept PO Box 1700 Web: www.msdh.state.ms.us	Jackson	MS	39215	601-576-7400		339-25
Higher Learning Institutions Board of Trustees 3825 Ridgewood Rd Web: www.ihl.state.ms.us	Jackson	MS	39211	601-432-6198	432-6972	339-25
Information Technology Services Dept 3771 Eastwood Dr Web: www.its.ms.gov	Jackson	MS	39211	601-432-8000	713-6380	339-25
Insurance Dept PO Box 79 TF: 800-562-2957 ■ Web: www.mid.ms.gov	Jackson	MS	39201	601-359-3569		339-25
Legislature PO Box 1018 Web: billstatus.ls.state.ms.us	Jackson	MS	39215	601-359-3770		339-25
Medical Licensure Board 1867 Crane Ridge Dr Ste 200-B Web: www.msbml.ms.gov	Jackson	MS	39216	601-987-3079	987-4159	339-25
Motor Vehicle Commission 1755 Lelia Dr Ste 200 Web: www.mmvc.ms.gov	Jackson	MS	39216	601-987-3995	987-3997	339-25
Parole Board 633 N State St Web: www.mdoc.ms.gov	Jackson	MS	39202	601-576-3520	576-3528	339-25
Public Accountancy Board (MSBPA) 2310 Hwy 80 W Ste 1202 Web: www.msbpa.ms.gov	Jackson	MS	39202	601-354-7320	354-7290	339-25
Public Service Commission PO Box 1174 Web: www.psc.state.ms.us	Jackson	MS	39215	601-961-5434	961-5469	339-25
Real Estate Commission 4780 I-55 N LeFleur's Bluff Tower Ste 300 Web: www.mrec.state.ms.us	Jackson	MS	39211	601-321-6970	321-6955	339-25
Rehabilitation Services Dept 1281 Hwy 51 PO Box 1698 TF: 800-443-1000 ■ Web: www.mdrs.ms.gov	Madison	MS	39110	800-443-1000		339-25
Securities Div 401 Mississippi St Web: www.sos.ms.gov	Jackson	MS	39201	601-359-1334	359-9070	339-25
State Medical Examiner PO Box 958 Web: www.dps.state.ms.us	Jackson	MS	39205	601-987-1212		339-25
Treasury Dept PO Box 138 Web: www.treasurerlynnfitch.ms.gov	Jackson	MS	39205	601-359-3600	359-2001	339-25
Veterans Affairs Board (MSVAB) PO Box 5947 Web: www.vab.ms.gov	Pearl	MS	39288	601-576-4850	576-4868	339-25
Wildlife Fisheries & Parks Dept 1505 Eastover Dr Web: www.mdwfp.com	Jackson	MS	39211	601-432-2400		339-25
Worker's Compensation Commission 1428 Lakeland Dr TF: 866-473-6922 ■ Web: mwcc.ms.gov	Jackson	MS	39216	601-987-4200		339-25
Mississippi Action For Progress Inc (MAP) 1751 Morson Rd TF: 800-924-4615 ■ Web: www.mapheadstart.org	Jackson	MS	39209	601-923-4100		147
Mississippi Agricultural and Forestry Experiment Station 190 Bost N Web: mafes.msstate.edu	Mississippi State	MS	39762	662-325-3005	325-3001	668
Mississippi Agriculture & Forestry Museum/National Agricultural Aviation Museum 1150 Lakeland Dr TF: 800-844-8687 ■ Web: www.mdac.ms.gov	Jackson	MS	39216	601-432-4500	982-4292	520
Mississippi Arts Commission 501 N West St Woolfolk Bldg Ste 1101A Web: arts.ms.gov	Jackson	MS	39201	601-359-6030	359-6008	50-2
Mississippi Association of Realtors 4274 Lakeland Dr PO Box 321000 TF: 800-747-1103 ■ Web: msrealtors.org	Jackson	MS	39232	601-932-9325	932-0382	656
Mississippi Automated Resource Information System 3825 Ridgewood Rd Web: www.maris.state.ms.us	Jackson	MS	39211	601-432-6128	432-6893	387
Mississippi Baptist Historical Commission (MBHC) 200 S Capitol St Web: mc.libguides.com	Clinton	MS	39058	601-925-3434		48-20
Mississippi Bar 643 N State St TF: 800-682-6423 ■ Web: www.msbar.org	Jackson	MS	39202	601-948-4471	355-8635	72
Mississippi Blood Services 115 Tree St TF: 888-902-5663 ■ Web: www.msblood.com	Flowood	MS	39232	601-981-3232		89
Mississippi Business Journal 200 N Congress St Web: www.msbusiness.com	Jackson	MS	39201	601-364-1000	364-1007	457-5
Mississippi Coast Coliseum & Convention Ctr 2350 Beach Blvd TF: 800-726-2781 ■ Web: www.mscoastcoliseum.com	Biloxi	MS	39531	228-594-3700	594-3812	205
Mississippi College 200 S Capitol St TF: 800-738-1236 ■ Web: www.mc.edu	Clinton	MS	39056	601-925-3000		166
Mississippi College School of Law 151 E Griffith St Web: www.law.mc.edu	Jackson	MS	39201	601-925-7100		167-1
Mississippi County 200 N Main St Web: www.misscomo.net	Charleston	MO	63834	573-683-2146	683-6071	338
Mississippi County Electric Co-op 510 N Broadway St TF: 800-439-4563 ■ Web: www.mceci.com	Blytheville	AR	72315	870-763-4563		245
Mississippi Credit Union League Inc 1400 Lakeover Rd Ste 200 Web: mscua.com	Jackson	MS	39213	601-981-4552		219
Mississippi Delta Community College PO Box 668 Web: www.msdelta.edu	Moorhead	MS	38761	662-246-6322		162
Mississippi Dental Assn 439 B Katherine Dr Web: www.msdental.org	Flowood	MS	39232	601-664-9691	664-9796	227
Mississippi Department of Agriculture & Commerce 121 North Jefferson St TF: 800-551-1830 ■ Web: www.mdac.ms.gov	Jackson	MS	39201	601-359-1100	354-6290	339-25
Mississippi Department of Archives & History (MDAH) 200 N St Web: www.mdah.ms.gov	Jackson	MS	39201	601-576-6876	576-6964	520

Listing	Phone	Fax	Class
Mississippi Department of Corrections			
Issaquena County Regional Correctional Facility 301 N Lamar St .... Jackson MS 39201 **Fax Area Code:* 662 ■ *Web:* www.mdoc.ms.gov	601-359-5600	873-2956*	213
Winston-Choctaw County Regional Correctional Facility PO Drawer 1437 .... Louisville MS 39339 *Web:* www.mdoc.ms.gov	662-773-2528	773-4989	213
Mississippi Economic Council PO Box 23276 .... Jackson MS 39225 *TF:* 800-748-7626 ■ *Web:* www.msmec.com	601-969-0022	353-0247	140
Mississippi Export Railroad Co 4519 McInnis Ave .... Moss Point MS 39563 *Web:* www.mserr.com	228-475-3322	475-3337	648
Mississippi Gulf Coast Chamber of Commerce 11975-E Seaway Rd .... Gulfport MS 39503 *Web:* mscoastchamber.com	228-604-0014	604-0105	139
Mississippi Gulf Coast Community College 51 Main St PO Box 548 .... Perkinston MS 39573 *TF:* 866-735-1122 ■ *Web:* www.mgccc.edu	601-928-5211	928-6345	162
Mississippi Home Corp *Home Corp* 735 Riverside Dr .... Jackson MS 39202 *Web:* www.mshomecorp.com	601-718-4642	718-4647	339-25
Mississippi Library Commission (MLC) 3881 Eastwood Dr .... Jackson MS 39211 *TF:* 800-647-7542 ■ *Web:* www.mlc.lib.ms.us	601-432-4111		434-3
Mississippi Lions Eye Bank 431 Katherine Dr .... Flowood MS 39232 *Web:* www.mslionseyebank.org	601-420-5739		269
Mississippi Magazine 5 Lakeland Cir .... Jackson MS 39216 *Web:* www.mismag.com	601-982-8418	982-8447	457-22
Mississippi Market Natural Foods Coop 1500 W Seventh St .... Saint Paul MN 55102 *Web:* msmarket.coop	651-690-0507		345
Mississippi Municipal League (MML) 600 E Amite St Ste 104 .... Jackson MS 39201 *TF:* 800-325-7641 ■ *Web:* www.mmlonline.com	601-353-5854	353-6980	48-13
Mississippi Museum of Art 380 S Lamar St .... Jackson MS 39201 *TF:* 866-843-9278 ■ *Web:* www.msmuseumart.org	601-960-1515	960-1505	520
Mississippi Museum of Natural Science 2148 Riverside Dr .... Jackson MS 39202 *TF:* 800-467-2757 ■ *Web:* www.mdwfp.com	601-576-6000	354-7227	520
Mississippi Music Inc 222 N Main St .... Hattiesburg MS 39401 *TF:* 800-844-5821 ■ *Web:* mississippimusic.net	800-844-5821		525
Mississippi National River & Recreation Area 111 E Kellogg Blvd Ste 105 .... Saint Paul MN 55101 *Web:* www.nps.gov	651-290-4160	290-3214	564
Mississippi Nurses Assn (MNA) 31 Woodgreen Pl .... Madison MS 39110 *Web:* www.msnurses.org	601-898-0670	898-0190	533
Mississippi Opera PO Box 1551 .... Jackson MS 39215 *Web:* www.msopera.org	601-960-2300		573-2
Mississippi Palisades State Park 16327A IL Rt 84 .... Savanna IL 61074 *Web:* www.dnr.illinois.gov	815-273-2731		565
Mississippi Petrified Forest 124 Forest Park Rd .... Flora MS 39071 *Web:* www.mspetrifiedforest.com	601-879-8189		50-5
Mississippi Pharmacists Assn 341 Edgewood Terr Dr .... Jackson MS 39206 *Web:* mspharm.org	601-981-0416		585
Mississippi Polymers Inc 2733 S Harper Rd .... Corinth MS 38834 *TF:* 800-339-9440 ■ *Web:* www.mississippipolymers.com	662-287-1401	287-9752	600
Mississippi Prison Industries Corp (MPIC) 663 N State St .... Jackson MS 39202 *Web:* mpic.net	601-969-5760	969-5765	630
Mississippi Products Inc 2457 Valley St .... Jackson MS 39204 *TF:* 800-748-3106 ■ *Web:* www.msprodinc.com	601-502-1481	502-1484	475
Mississippi Public Broadcasting 3825 Ridgewood Rd .... Jackson MS 39211 *TF:* 800-850-4406 ■ *Web:* mpbonline.org	601-432-6565	432-6311	645-75
Mississippi Republican Party 415 Yazoo St PO Box 60 .... Jackson MS 39201 *Web:* www.msgop.org	601-948-5191	354-0972	616-2
Mississippi River Museum 22 N Front St Ste 960 .... Memphis TN 38103 *TF:* 800-507-6507 ■ *Web:* www.mudisland.com	901-576-7241	576-6666	520
Mississippi River State Fish & Wildlife Area 17836 State Hwy 100 N .... Grafton IL 62037 *Web:* www.dnr.illinois.gov	618-376-3303		565
Mississippi Sports Hall of Fame & Museum 1152 Lakeland Dr .... Jackson MS 39216 *TF:* 800-280-3263 ■ *Web:* msfame.com	601-982-8264		522
Mississippi State Hospital PO Box 157A .... Whitfield MS 39193 *Web:* www.msh.state.ms.us	601-351-8000		374-5
Mississippi State Port Authority at Gulfport 2510 14th St Ste 1450 .... Gulfport MS 39501 *TF:* 877-881-4367 ■ *Web:* shipmspa.com	228-865-4300	865-4335	618
Mississippi State University PO Box 6305 .... Mississippi State MS 39762 *Web:* www.msstate.edu	662-325-2323	325-7360	166
Mississippi State Veterans Home 120 Veterans Dr .... Oxford MS 38655 *Web:* caremississippi.org	662-236-7641		793
Mississippi Symphony Orchestra 201 E Pascagoula St .... Jackson MS 39201 *Web:* www.msorchestra.com	601-960-1565	960-1564	573-3
Mississippi Tank & Manufacturing Co 3000 W Seventh St .... Hattiesburg MS 39401 *Web:* mstank.com	601-264-1800	264-0769	91
Mississippi University for Women 1100 College St MUW-1613 .... Columbus MS 39701 *TF:* 877-462-8439 ■ *Web:* web3.muw.edu	662-329-7350	241-7481	166

Listing	Phone	Fax	Class
Mississippi Valley Equipment Company Inc 1198 Pershall Rd .... Saint Louis MO 63137 *TF:* 800-325-8001 ■ *Web:* www.mve-stl.com	314-869-8600	869-6862	358
Mississippi Valley Forest Products PO Box 1250 .... Dubuque IA 52004 *TF:* 800-533-2107 ■ *Web:* www.hartbrand.com	608-568-7290	568-3884	191-3
Mississippi Valley State University 14000 Hwy 82 .... Itta Bena MS 38941 *TF:* 800-844-6885 ■ *Web:* www.mvsu.edu	662-254-9041	254-3759	166
Mississippi Valley Title Services Co 1022 Highland Colony Pkwy Ste 200 .... Ridgeland MS 39157 *TF:* 800-647-2124 ■ *Web:* mvt.com	601-969-0222	969-2215	391-6
Mississippi Veterans Memorial Stadium 2531 N State St .... Jackson MS 39216 *Web:* www.ms-veteransstadium.com	601-354-6021	354-6019	720
Mississippi Welders Supply Co 5150 W Sixth St .... Winona MN 55987 *Web:* www.mwsco.com	507-454-5231		386
Missoula Area Chamber of Commerce 825 E Front St .... Missoula MT 59802 *Web:* www.missoulachamber.com	406-543-6623		139
Missoula Electric Co-opeartive Inc 1700 West Broadway .... Missoula MT 59808 *TF:* 800-352-5200 ■ *Web:* www.missoulaelectric.com	406-541-4433	541-6318	245
Missoula Public Library 301 E Main St .... Missoula MT 59802 *Web:* www.missoula.lib.mt.us	406-721-2665	728-5900	434-3
Missoulian PO Box 8029 .... Missoula MT 59807 *TF:* 800-366-7102 ■ *Web:* www.missoulian.com	406-523-5200	523-5294	532-2
Missouri			
Agriculture Dept 1616 Missouri Blvd PO Box 630 .... Jefferson City MO 65102 *Web:* mda.mo.gov	573-751-4211	751-1784	339-26
Arts Council 815 Olive St Ste 16 .... Saint Louis MO 63101 *TF:* 866-407-4752 ■ *Web:* www.missouriartscouncil.org	314-340-6845	340-7215	339-26
Attorney General 207 W High St PO Box 899 .... Jefferson City MO 65102 *TF:* 800-392-8222 ■ *Web:* www.ago.mo.gov	573-751-3321	751-0774	339-26
Child Support Enforcement Div 205 Jefferson St 1st Fl .... Jefferson City MO 65103 *TF:* 800-859-7999 ■ *Web:* dss.mo.gov	573-522-8024		339-26
Conservation Dept 2901 W Truman Blvd .... Jefferson City MO 65109 *Web:* mdc.mo.gov	573-751-4115	751-4467	339-26
Corrections Dept PO Box 236 .... Jefferson City MO 65102 *Web:* doc.mo.gov	573-522-1118		339-26
Crime Victims' Compensation Unit PO Box 1589 .... Jefferson City MO 65102 *Web:* dps.mo.gov	573-526-6006		339-26
Department of Corrections Medical Services Section Division of Offender Rehabilitative Services PO Box 236 .... Jefferson City MO 65102 *Web:* doc.mo.gov	573-751-6663		630
Department of Elementary & Secondary Education 205 Jefferson St PO Box 480 .... Jefferson City MO 65101 *Web:* dese.mo.gov	573-751-4212		339-26
Economic Development Dept 301 W High St Ste 720 .... Jefferson City MO 65101 *TF:* 866-506-0251 ■ *Web:* www.ded.mo.gov	573-522-4173	522-9462	339-26
Emergency Management Agency 2302 Militia Dr PO Box 116 .... Jefferson City MO 65102 *Web:* sema.dps.mo.gov	573-526-9100	634-7966	339-26
Family Services Div PO Box 2320 .... Jefferson City MO 65102 *Web:* dss.mo.gov	573-751-3221		339-26
Finance Div Truman State Office Bldg Rm 630 .... Jefferson City MO 65102 *TF:* 888-246-7225 ■ *Web:* finance.mo.gov	573-751-3242	751-9192	339-26
General Assembly State Capitol .... Jefferson City MO 65101 *Web:* www.moga.mo.gov	573-751-4633		339-26
Healing Arts Board 3605 Missouri Blvd PO Box 4 .... Jefferson City MO 65102 *Web:* www.pr.mo.gov	573-751-0098	751-3166	339-26
Health & Senior Services Dept 912 Wildwood PO Box 570 .... Jefferson City MO 65102 *TF:* 888-497-4564 ■ *Web:* health.mo.gov	573-751-6400	751-6010	339-26
Higher Education Dept 301 W High St .... Jefferson City MO 65101 *TF:* 800-473-6757 ■ *Web:* dhe.mo.gov	573-751-2361	751-6635	339-26
Housing Development Commission 3435 Broadway .... Kansas City MO 64111 *Web:* www.mhdc.com	816-759-6600	759-6828	339-26
Insurance Dept 301 W High St Rm 530 .... Jefferson City MO 65101 *TF:* 800-726-7390 ■ *Web:* insurance.mo.gov	573-751-4126	751-1165	339-26
Labor & Industrial Relations Dept 421 E Dunklin St PO Box 504 .... Jefferson City MO 65102 *Web:* labor.mo.gov	573-751-2461	751-7806	339-26
Lieutenant Governor State Capitol Bldg Rm 224 .... Jefferson City MO 65101 *Web:* ltgov.mo.gov	573-751-4727	751-9422	339-26
Lottery 1823 Southridge Dr PO Box 1603 .... Jefferson City MO 65109 *TF:* 888-238-7633 ■ *Web:* www.molottery.com	573-751-4050	751-5188	452
Motor Vehicles & Drivers Licensing Div 301 W High St Ste 370 .... Jefferson City MO 65101 *Web:* dor.mo.gov	573-751-3505	751-2195	339-26
Natural Resources Dept 1101 Riverside Dr .... Jefferson City MO 65101 *TF:* 800-361-4827 ■ *Web:* dnr.mo.gov	573-751-3443		339-26
Professional Registration Div 3605 Missouri Blvd PO Box 1335 .... Jefferson City MO 65102 *Web:* www.pr.mo.gov	573-751-0293		339-26
Public Service Commission 200 Madison St PO Box 360 .... Jefferson City MO 65102 *TF:* 800-819-3180 ■ *Web:* psc.mo.gov	573-751-3234		339-26
Real Estate Commission 3605 Missouri Blvd PO Box 1339 .... Jefferson City MO 65102 *TF:* 800-735-2466 ■ *Web:* www.pr.mo.gov	573-751-2628	751-2777	339-26

				Phone	Fax	Class
Revenue Dept 301 W High St *Web:* dor.mo.gov	Jefferson City	MO	65101	573-526-3669		339-26
Secretary of State PO Box 778 *Web:* www.sos.mo.gov	Jefferson City	MO	65102	573-751-4936		339-26
Securities Div 600 W Main St Rm 229 PO Box 1276 *TF:* 800-721-7996 ■ *Web:* s1.sos.mo.gov	Jefferson City	MO	65102	573-751-4136		339-26
Social Services Dept Broadway State Office Bldg *Web:* dss.mo.gov	Jefferson City	MO	65102	573-751-4815	751-3203	339-26
State Courts Administrator 2112 Industrial Dr *Web:* www.courts.mo.gov	Jefferson City	MO	65109	573-751-4377		339-26
State Highway Patrol 1510 E Elm St *Web:* www.mshp.dps.missouri.gov	Jefferson City	MO	65101	573-751-3313	751-9419	339-26
State Parks Div PO Box 176 *Web:* mostateparks.com	Jefferson City	MO	65102	573-751-2479		339-26
Tourism Div PO Box 1055 *TF:* 800-519-2100 ■ *Web:* www.visitmo.com	Jefferson City	MO	65102	573-751-4133	751-5160	339-26
Transportation Dept 105 W Capitol Ave PO Box 270 *TF:* 888-275-6636 ■ *Web:* www.modot.org	Jefferson City	MO	65102	573-751-2551	751-6555	339-26
Treasurer PO Box 210 *Web:* treasurer.mo.gov	Jefferson City	MO	65102	573-751-8533	751-0343	339-26
Veterans Commission 205 Jefferson St 12th Fl Jefferson Bldg PO Drawer 147 *TF:* 866-838-4636 ■ *Web:* mvc.dps.mo.gov	Jefferson City	MO	65102	573-751-3779		339-26
Vital Records Bureau 930 Wildwood PO Box 570 *Web:* www.sos.mo.gov	Jefferson City	MO	65102	573-751-6387		339-26
Vocational & Adult Education Div 3024 Dupont Cir PO Box 480 *TF:* 877-222-8963 ■ *Web:* dese.mo.gov	Jefferson City	MO	65109	573-751-3251	751-1441	339-26
Workers Compensation Div PO Box 58 *TF:* 800-775-2667 ■ *Web:* labor.mo.gov	Jefferson City	MO	65102	573-751-4231	751-2012	339-26
Missouri Afl-Cio 227 Jefferson St *Web:* moaflcio.org	Jefferson City	MO	65101	573-634-2115		414
Missouri Association of Realtors 2601 Bernadette Pl *TF:* 800-403-0101 ■ *Web:* www.missourirealtor.org	Columbia	MO	65203	573-445-8400	445-7865	656
Missouri Athletic Club 405 Washington Ave *Web:* www.mac-stl.org	Saint Louis	MO	63102	314-231-7220		354
Missouri Baptist Hospital of Sullivan 751 Sappington Bridge Rd *TF:* 800-939-2273 ■ *Web:* www.missouribaptistsullivan.org	Sullivan	MO	63080	573-468-4186	860-2696	374-3
Missouri Baptist Medical Ctr 3015 N Ballas Rd *TF:* 800-392-0936 ■ *Web:* www.missouribaptist.org	Saint Louis	MO	63131	314-996-5000		374-3
Missouri Bar, The 326 Monroe St PO Box 119 *TF:* 888-253-6013 ■ *Web:* www.mobar.org	Jefferson City	MO	65102	573-635-4128	635-2811	72
Missouri Chamber of Commerce 428 E Capitol Ave *Web:* mochamber.com	Jefferson City	MO	65101	573-634-3511	634-8855	140
Missouri Delta Medical Ctr 1008 N Main St *Web:* www.missouridelta.com	Sikeston	MO	63801	573-471-1600		374-3
Missouri Democratic Party 300 St James St Ste 104 *Web:* missouridemocrats.org	Columbia	MO	65201	573-777-1364	441-0601	616-1
Missouri Dental Assn 3340 American Ave *TF:* 800-688-1907 ■ *Web:* www.modental.org	Jefferson City	MO	65109	573-634-3436	635-0764	227
Missouri Department of Mental Health 1706 E Elm St *TF:* 800-364-9687 ■ *Web:* www.dmh.mo.gov	Jefferson City	MO	65101	573-751-4122	751-8224	339-26
Missouri Department of Public Safety Veterans Commission 1600 S Hickory *Web:* mvc.dps.mo.gov	Mount Vernon	MO	65712	417-466-7103	466-4040	793
Missouri Eastern Correctional Ctr 18701 Old Hwy 66 *Web:* www.mo.gov	Pacific	MO	63069	636-257-3322	257-5296	213
Missouri Enterprise 900 Innovation Dr Ste 300 *TF:* 800-956-2682 ■ *Web:* www.missourienterprise.org	Rolla	MO	65401	800-956-2682		195
Missouri Fox Trotting Horse Breed Association Inc PO Box 1027 *Web:* www.mfthba.com	Ava	MO	65608	417-683-2468	683-6144	48-3
Missouri Gas Energy 3420 Broadway *TF:* 800-582-1234 ■ *Web:* www.missourigasenergy.com	Kansas City	MO	64111	816-360-5500		787
Missouri General Insurance Agency Inc 1227 Fern Ridge Pkwy *Web:* missourigeneral.com	Saint Louis	MO	63141	314-432-6464		390
Missouri Headwaters State Park 1585 Trident Rd *Web:* stateparks.mt.gov	Three Forks	MT	59752	406-285-3610		565
Missouri History Museum 5700 Lindell Blvd PO Box 11940 *TF:* 800-610-2094 ■ *Web:* www.mohistory.org	Saint Louis	MO	63112	314-746-4599		520
Missouri Home Therapy 11636 W Florissant Ave *Web:* www.missourihometherapy.com	Florissant	MO	63033	314-246-0137	524-3959	726
Missouri Lawyers Media 319 N Fourth St *Web:* www.molawyersmedia.com	Saint Louis	MO	63102	314-421-1880	421-0436	637-8
Missouri Metals LLC 9970 Page Boulvard *Web:* www.missourimetals.com	Saint Louis	MO	63132	314-222-7100		697
Missouri Mines State Historic Site 4000 Missouri 32 *Web:* mostateparks.com	Park Hills	MO	63601	573-431-6226		565
Missouri Municipal League 1727 Southridge Dr *Web:* www.mocities.site-ym.com	Jefferson City	MO	65109	573-635-9134		533
Missouri National Recreational River 508 E Second St *Web:* www.nps.gov	Yankton	SD	57078	605-665-0209	665-4183	564
Missouri Net 505 Hobbs Rd *Web:* www.missourinet.com	Jefferson City	MO	65109	573-893-2829	893-8094	647
Missouri Petroleum Products Co 1620 Woodson Rd *TF:* 800-633-8253 ■ *Web:* www.missouripetroleum.com	Saint Louis	MO	63114	314-219-7305	991-9624	191-4
Missouri Pharmacy Assn 211 E Capitol Ave *TF:* 800-468-4672 ■ *Web:* www.morx.com	Jefferson City	MO	65101	573-636-7522	636-7485	585
Missouri Pressed Metals Inc 1200 E Boonville St *Web:* www.mo-press.com	Sedalia	MO	65302	660-827-3460	826-1570	620
Missouri Protection & Advocacy Services 925 S Country Club Dr *TF:* 800-392-8667 ■ *Web:* moadvocacy.org	Jefferson City	MO	65109	573-659-0678	659-0677	41
Missouri Refractories Company Inc 1198 Mason Cir *Web:* www.refractories.net	Pevely	MO	63070	636-479-7770		751
Missouri River Regional Library 214 Adams St *Web:* www.mrrl.org	Jefferson City	MO	65101	573-634-2464	634-7028	434-3
Missouri School Boards Assn 2100 I-70 Dr SW *TF:* 800-221-6722 ■ *Web:* www.mosba.org	Columbia	MO	65203	573-445-9920		685
Missouri Slope Lutheran Care Center Foundation 2425 Hillview Ave *Web:* www.mslcc.com	Bismarck	ND	58501	701-223-9407		48-20
Missouri Southern State University 3950 Newman Rd *TF:* 866-818-6778 ■ *Web:* www.mssu.edu	Joplin	MO	64801	417-625-9300	659-4429	166
Missouri Sports Hall of Fame 3861 E Stan Musial Dr *TF:* 800-498-5678 ■ *Web:* www.mosportshalloffame.com	Springfield	MO	65809	417-889-3100	889-2761	522
Missouri State Employees' Retirement System 907 Wildwood Dr *TF:* 800-827-1063 ■ *Web:* www.mosers.org	Jefferson City	MO	65109	573-632-6100		528
Missouri State Library 600 W Main St *Web:* www.sos.mo.gov	Jefferson City	MO	65101	573-751-3615		434-5
Missouri State Museum 201 W Capitol *Web:* mostateparks.com	Jefferson City	MO	65101	573-751-2854		520
Missouri State Park *Saint Francois State Park* 8920 US Hwy 67 N *Web:* www.mostateparks.com	Bonne Terre	MO	63628	573-358-2173		565
Missouri State Teachers Assn 407 S Sixth St *TF:* 800-392-0532 ■ *Web:* www.msta.org	Columbia	MO	65201	573-442-3127		457-8
Missouri State University (MSU) 901 S National Ave *TF:* 800-492-7900 ■ *Web:* www.missouristate.edu	Springfield	MO	65897	417-836-5000	836-6334	166
Missouri Theatre 203 S Ninth St *Web:* concertseries.missouri.edu	Columbia	MO	65211	573-882-3781		572
Missouri Tie LLC 8324 Hwy 72 *Web:* www.missouritie.com	Bunker	MO	63629	573-689-2040	689-2120	683
Missouri University of Science & Technology *Rolla* 1870 Miner Cir *TF:* 800-522-0938 ■ *Web:* www.mst.edu	Rolla	MO	65409	573-341-4111	341-4082	166
Missouri Valley College 500 E College St *TF:* 800-999-8219 ■ *Web:* www.moval.edu	Marshall	MO	65340	660-831-4000	831-4233	166
Missouri Valley Times-enterprise Inc 513 E Erie St PO Box 159 *Web:* www.dcpostgazette.com	Missouri Valley	IA	51555	712-642-2791		532-3
Missouri Veterans Home-Cape Girardeau 2400 Veterans Memorial Dr *TF:* 800-392-0210 ■ *Web:* www.mo.gov	Cape Girardeau	MO	63701	573-290-5870	290-5909	793
Missouri Veterans Home-Saint James 620 N Jefferson St *Web:* www.nasvh.org	Saint James	MO	65559	573-265-3271		793
Missouri Veterans Home-Saint Louis 10600 Lewis & Clark Blvd *Web:* mvc.dps.mo.gov	Saint Louis	MO	63136	314-340-6389	340-6379	793
Missouri Veterinary Medical Assn 2500 Country Club Dr *Web:* www.movma.org	Jefferson City	MO	65109	573-636-8612	659-7175	795
Missouri Welding Institute 3300 N Industrial Pkwy PO Box 445 **Fax Area Code:* 417 ■ *TF:* 800-667-5885 ■ *Web:* www.mwi.ws	Nevada	MO	64772	800-667-5885	667-5885*	167-3
Missouri Western State University 4525 Downs Dr *TF:* 800-662-7041 ■ *Web:* www.missouriwestern.edu	Saint Joseph	MO	64507	816-271-4266	271-5833	166
Missourian Publishing Co 14 W Main St *TF:* 888-239-7701 ■ *Web:* www.emissourian.com	Washington	MO	63090	636-239-7701	239-0915	637-8
Missy Herron Insurance Agency 6701 W 12th St Ste 7A *Web:* missyherron.com	Little Rock	AR	72204	501-664-3400		390
Mist Mobility Integrated Systems Technology Inc 3 Iber Rd *Web:* www.mmist.ca	Ottawa	ON	K2S1E6	613-723-0403	723-8925	21
Mister A's Restaurant 2550 Fifth Ave 12th Fl *Web:* www.asrestaurant.com	San Diego	CA	92103	619-239-1377	239-1379	671
Mister Car Wash 3101 E Speedway Blvd *TF:* 866-254-3229 ■ *Web:* mistercarwash.com	Tucson	AZ	85716	520-327-5656		62-1
Mister Kleen Maintenance Company Inc 7302 Beulah St *Web:* www.misterkleen.com	Alexandria	VA	22315	703-719-6900		104
Mister Safety Shoes Inc 2300 Finch Ave W Unit 6 *TF:* 800-707-0051 ■ *Web:* mistersafetyshoes.com	North York	ON	M9M2Y3	416-746-3001	748-8791	358
Mister Transmission 9555 Yonge St Ste 204 *TF:* 800-373-8432 ■ *Web:* www.mistertransmission.com	Richmond Hill	ON	L4C9M5	905-884-1511	884-4727	62-6

Name / Address	City	State	Zip	Phone	Fax	Class
Mistletoe State Park 3723 Mistletoe Rd *Web:* gastateparks.org	Appling	GA	30802	706-541-0321		565
Mistral 223 Columbus Ave *Web:* mistralbistro.com	Boston	MA	02116	617-867-9300	351-2601	671
Misty Harbor & Barefoot Beach Resort 118 Weirs Rd *TF:* 800-336-4789 ■ *Web:* www.mistyharbor.com	Gilford	NH	03249	603-293-4500		379
Misty River Consulting (MRC) EP938 Hillside St *Web:* www.mistyriver.com	Stratford	WI	54484	715-687-8818		196
Misty's Steakhouse & Brewery 200 N 11th St *Web:* www.mistyslincoln.com	Lincoln	NE	68508	402-476-7766		671
MIT Group Inc 5090 Dorsey Hall Dr *Web:* www.xpertechs.com	Ellicott City	MD	21042	410-884-4357	884-4107	178-1
MIT List Visual Arts Ctr 20 Ames St Bldg E15 Atrium Level *Web:* listart.mit.edu	Cambridge	MA	02139	617-253-4680	258-7265	637-2
MIT Media Laboratory 77 Massachusetts Ave E14/E15 *Web:* www.media.mit.edu	Cambridge	MA	02139	617-253-5960	258-6264	668
MIT Press, The 1 Rogers St *TF:* 800-405-1619 ■ *Web:* www.mitpress.mit.edu	Cambridge	MA	02142	617-253-5646	253-1709	637-4
Mit Professionals Inc 523 Lovett Blvd *Web:* www.mitprof.com	Houston	TX	77006	713-934-9700		196
MIT Technology Review Magazine 1 Main St *Web:* www.technologyreview.com	Cambridge	MA	02142	617-475-8000		457-19
MiTAC Digital Corp 279 E Arrow Hgwy Ste 201 *Web:* magellangps.com	San Dimas	CA	91773	408-615-5100	615-3905	647
MITAGS 1729 Alaskan Way S *TF:* 888-893-7829 ■ *Web:* www.mitags.org	Seattle	WA	98134	206-441-2880	441-2995	167-3
Mitaja Corp 8115 Maple Lawn Blvd *Web:* www.mitajacorp.com	Fulton	MD	20759	301-965-2395		193
Mitch Grissim & Assoc 325 Union St *Web:* mitchgrissim.com	Nashville	TN	37201	615-255-9999		41
Mitcham Industries Inc (MII) 8141 Hwy 75 S PO Box 1175 *NASDAQ: MIND* ■ *Web:* www.mitchamindustries.com	Huntsville	TX	77340	936-291-2277	295-1922	264-3
Mitchco International Inc 4801 Sherburn Ln *Web:* www.mitchcointernational.com	Louisville	KY	40207	502-896-9653	896-2989	670
Mitchell & Titus LLP 1 Battery Park Plz 27th Fl *Web:* www.mitchelltitus.com	New York	NY	10004	212-709-4500	709-4680	401
Mitchell 1 14145 Danielson St *TF:* 888-724-6742 ■ *Web:* www.mitchell1.com	Poway	CA	92064	888-724-6742		637-11
Mitchell Aircraft 1160 Alexander Ct *Web:* mitchellair.com	Cary	IL	60013	847-516-3773		770
Mitchell Associates Inc 1 Avenue of the Arts *Web:* www.mitchellai.com	Wilmington	DE	19801	302-594-9400		344
Mitchell Bank 1039 W Mitchell St *Web:* www.mitchellbank.com	Milwaukee	WI	53204	414-645-0600		70
Mitchell Block Theme, The 173 McDermot Ave *Web:* www.trevisirestaurant.com	Winnipeg	MB	R3B0S1	204-949-9032		671
Mitchell C. Zwaik Esq. & Associates PC 5014 Express Dr S *Web:* zwaik.com	Ronkonkoma	NY	11779	631-588-4040		41
Mitchell College 437 Pequot Ave *TF:* 800-443-2811 ■ *Web:* www.mitchell.edu	New London	CT	06320	860-701-5000	444-1209	166
Mitchell Community College 500 W Broad St *Web:* mitchellcc.edu	Statesville	NC	28677	704-878-3200	878-0872	162
Mitchell Company Inc, The 41 W I-65 Service Rd N *Web:* www.mitchellcompany.com	Mobile	AL	36608	251-380-2929	345-1264	653
Mitchell County 26 Crimson Laurel Cir Ste 5 *Web:* www.mitchellcounty.org	Bakersville	NC	28705	828-688-2139	688-4443	338
Mitchell County PO Box 190 *Web:* www.mcks.org	Beloit	KS	67420	785-738-3652	738-5524	338
Mitchell County 26 N Ct St PO Box 187 *TF:* 800-427-2457 ■ *Web:* www.mitchellcountyga.net	Camilla	GA	31730	229-336-2000	336-2003	338
Mitchell Day Law Firm PLLC 618 Crescent Blvd Ste 203 *Web:* mitchellday.com	Ridgeland	MS	39157	601-707-4036	213-4116	41
Mitchell Electric Membership Corp 475 Cairo Rd *TF:* 800-479-6034 ■ *Web:* mitchellemc.com	Camilla	GA	31730	229-336-5221	336-7088	245
Mitchell Electronics Inc 1005 E State St Ste 5 *Web:* www.mitchell-electronics.com	Athens	OH	45701	740-594-8532	594-8533	253
Mitchell Elementary School 14429 Condon Ave *Web:* www.lawndale.k12.ca.us	Lawndale	CA	90260	310-676-6140		685
Mitchell Enterprises Inc 300 N Coit Ste 1525 *Web:* www.mitchellent.com	Richardson	TX	75080	972-239-0063	239-7472	186
Mitchell Fuel Company Inc 1209 Sullivan Ave *Web:* www.mitchellfuel.com	South Windsor	CT	06074	860-644-2561	644-4683	316
Mitchell Furniture Systems Inc 1700 W St Paul Ave *TF:* 800-290-5960 ■ *Web:* www.mitchell-tables.com	Milwaukee	WI	53233	800-290-5960		319-3
Mitchell Gallery of Flight 5300 S Howell Ave *Web:* www.mitchellgallery.org	Milwaukee	WI	53207	414-747-4503	747-4525	520
Mitchell Gold & Bob Williams Co (MGBW) 135 One Comfortable Pl *TF:* 800-789-5401 ■ *Web:* www.mgbwhome.com	Taylorsville	NC	28681	828-632-9200	632-2693	319-2
Mitchell Golf Equipment Co 954 Senate Dr *TF:* 800-437-1314 ■ *Web:* www.mitchellgolf.com	Dayton	OH	45459	937-436-1314		711

Name / Address	City	State	Zip	Phone	Fax	Class
Mitchell Group The Consltnt 1816 11th St NW *Web:* the-mitchellgroup.com	Washington	DC	20001	202-745-1919		195
Mitchell Humphrey and Co 1285 Fern Ridge Pky *TF:* 800-237-0028 ■ *Web:* www.mitchellhumphrey.com	Saint Louis	MO	63141	314-991-2440	991-5288	178-1
Mitchell Industrial Tire Co 2915 Eigth Ave *TF:* 800-251-7226 ■ *Web:* www.mitco.com	Chattanooga	TN	37407	423-698-4442	697-7143	754
Mitchell Institute, The 75 Washington Ave Ste 2E *TF:* 888-220-7209 ■ *Web:* mitchellinstitute.org	Portland	ME	04101	207-773-7700	773-1133	305
Mitchell International Inc 6220 Greenwich Dr *TF:* 866-428-8679 ■ *Web:* www.mitchell.com	San Diego	CA	92122	858-368-7000		637-11
Mitchell Machine Inc 224 Hancock St *Web:* www.mitchellmachine.com	Springfield	MA	01109	413-739-9693	781-2250	556
Mitchell Martin Inc 307 W 38th St Ste 1305 **Fax Area Code:* 646 ■ *Web:* www.mitchellmartin.com	New York	NY	10018	212-943-1404	355-0229*	631
Mitchell Metal Products Inc 19250 Hwy 12 E PO Box 789 *TF:* 800-258-6137 ■ *Web:* www.mitchellmetal.net	Kosciusko	MS	39090	662-289-7110	289-7112	697
Mitchell Paul (Rep R - MI) 211 Cannon House Office Bldg *Web:* mitchell.house.gov	Washington	DC	20515	202-225-2106	226-1169	342-2
Mitchell Plumbing & Heating Company Inc 801 N Rowley St 1328	Mitchell	SD	57301	605-996-7583		189-10
Mitchell Rubber Products Inc 10220 San Sevaine Way *TF:* 800-453-7526 ■ *Web:* mitchellrubber.com	Mira Loma	CA	91752	800-453-7526		676
Mitchell Selling Dynamics 1360 Puritan Ave *TF:* 800-328-9696 ■ *Web:* www.mitchellsell.com	Birmingham	MI	48009	248-644-8092		463
Mitchell State Park 6093 E M-115	Cadillac	MI	49601	231-775-7911		565
Mitchell Supreme Fuel Co 532 Freeman St *TF:* 800-832-7090 ■ *Web:* supremeenergyinc.com	Orange	NJ	07050	973-678-1800	672-0148	316
Mitchell Technical Institute 1800 E Spruce St **Fax Area Code:* 605 ■ *TF:* 800-684-1969 ■ *Web:* www.mitchelltech.edu	Mitchell	SD	57301	800-684-1969	995-3083*	162
Mitchell Williams Selig Gates & Woodyard PLLC 425 W Capitol Ave Ste 1800 *Web:* mitchellwilliamslaw.com	Little Rock	AR	72201	501-688-8800	688-8807	428
Mitchell's Fish Market 1245 Olentangy River Rd *Web:* www.mitchellsfishmarket.com	Columbus	OH	43212	614-291-3474		671
Mitchell's Ocean Club 4002 Easton Stn *Web:* www.ocean-prime.com	Columbus	OH	43219	614-416-2582	416-2800	671
Mitchell's Steakhouse 45 N Third St *Web:* www.mitchellssteakhouse.com	Columbus	OH	43215	614-621-2333		671
Mitchell, Lewis & Staver Co 9935 SW Commerce Cir *TF:* 866-748-8077 ■ *Web:* www.mitchellewis.com	Wilsonville	OR	97070	866-748-8077		641
Mitchell-Iness & Nash Gallery 1018 Madison Ave *Web:* www.miandn.com	New York	NY	10075	212-744-7400	744-7401	42
Mitchells Family of Stores 270 Main St *Web:* shop.mitchellstores.com	Huntington	NY	11743	631-423-1660		157-3
Mitchells Salon & Day Spa 5901 E Galbraith Rd *Web:* mitchellssalon.com	Cincinnati	OH	45236	513-793-0900		77
Mitchell-wayne Technologies 2901 Third Ave N *Web:* www.mitchellwaynetech.com	Birmingham	AL	35203	205-313-7500		180
MITECH Trading PO Box 101039 *Web:* www.mitechtrading.com	Palm Bay	FL	32910	321-674-9377	608-2389	44
Mitee-bite Products Inc PO Box 430 *TF:* 800-543-3580 ■ *Web:* www.miteebite.com	Center Ossipee	NH	03814	603-539-4538	539-2183	454
MiTek Canada Inc 100 Industrial Rd **Fax Area Code:* 905 ■ *TF:* 800-268-3434 ■ *Web:* www.mitek.ca	Bradford	ON	L3Z3G7	800-268-3434	952-2901*	491
MiTek Industries Inc 16023 Swingley Ridge Rd *TF:* 800-325-8075 ■ *Web:* www.mii.com	Chesterfield	MO	63017	314-434-1200	434-5343	91
Mitek Systems Inc 600 B St Ste 100 *Web:* www.miteksystems.com	San Diego	CA	92101	619-269-6800	269-6801	178-8
Mitel Networks Corp 350 Legget Dr *TF:* 800-722-1301 ■ *Web:* www.mitel.com	Kanata	ON	K2K2W7	613-592-2122		735
Mitem Corp 640 Menlo Ave *TF:* 800-648-3660 ■ *Web:* www.mitem.com	Menlo Park	CA	94025	650-323-1500	323-1511	178-12
MITIMCo Private Equity 238 Main St Ste 200 *Web:* www.mitimco.org	Cambridge	MA	02142	617-253-4900		528
Mi-T-M Corp 8650 Enterprise Dr *Web:* www.mitm.com	Peosta	IA	52068	563-556-7484		198
Mitographers Inc, The 4720 Fourth Ave N *Web:* mito.com	Sioux Falls	SD	57104	605-336-1818		687
MITRE Corp 202 Burlington Rd *Web:* www.mitre.org	Bedford	MA	01730	781-271-2000		668
Mitronics Products Inc 239 Morristown Rd *Web:* mitronicsproducts.com	Gillette	NJ	07933	908-647-5006		249
Mitsu Sato Hair Academy 9062 Metcalf Ave *Web:* www.mitsusatohairacademy.com	Overland Park	KS	66212	913-341-7286		167-3
Mitsuba Bardstown Inc 901 Withrow Ct *Web:* www.americanmitsuba.com	Bardstown	KY	40004	502-348-3100		60
Mitsubishi Caterpillar Forklift America Inc 2121 W Sam Houston Pkwy N *Web:* www.mcfa.com	Houston	TX	77043	713-365-1000		470
Mitsubishi Chemical Advanced Materials Inc 2120 Fairmont Ave PO Box 14235 *TF:* 800-366-0300 ■ *Web:* www.mcam.com	Reading	PA	19612	610-320-6600	320-6638	602

Company / Address	City	State	Zip	Phone	Fax	Class
Mitsubishi Chemical Holdings America Inc (MCHA) 401 Volvo Pkwy *Web:* www.mitsubishichemicalholdings.com	Chesapeake	VA	23320	757-382-5750		234
Mitsubishi Corp 2800-200 Granville St *Web:* www.mitsubishicorp.com	Vancouver	BC	V6C1G6	604-654-8000	654-8222	59
Mitsubishi Digital Electronics America Inc 9351 Jeronimo Rd *TF:* 800-332-2119 ■ *Web:* www.mitsubishi-tv.com	Irvine	CA	92618	949-465-6000		52
Mitsubishi Electric Automotive America Inc 4773 Bethany Rd *Web:* www.meaa-mea.com	Mason	OH	45040	513-398-2220	398-1121	247
Mitsubishi Electric Power Products Inc Thorn Hill Industrial Pk 530 Keystone Dr *TF:* 800-887-7830 ■ *Web:* www.meppi.com	Warrendale	PA	15086	724-772-2555		729
Mitsubishi Heavy Industries Ltd 20 E Greenway Plz Ste 830 *Web:* www.mhi.com	Houston	TX	77046	346-308-8800		698
Mitsubishi Hitachi Power Systems Americas Inc (MHPS) 400 Colonial Center Pkwy **Fax Area Code:* 140 ■ *TF:* 800-445-9723 ■ *Web:* amer.mhps.com	Lake Mary	FL	32746	407-688-6100	768-8648*	536
Mitsubishi Motors North America Inc PO Box 6400 *TF:* 855-298-2559 ■ *Web:* www.mitsubishicars.com	Cypress	CA	90630	855-298-2559		59
Mitsubishi Polycrystalline Silicon America Corp 7800 Mitsubishi Ln *Web:* www.mpsac.com	Theodore	AL	36582	251-443-6440		144
Mitsubishi Polyester Film LLC 2001 Hood Rd *TF:* 800-334-1934 ■ *Web:* www.m-petfilm.com	Greer	SC	29650	864-879-5000	879-5006	600
Mitsui & Company (USA) Inc 200 Park Ave. *Web:* www.mitsui.com	New York	NY	10166	212-878-4000	878-4800	449
Mitsui Chemicals America Inc 800 Westchester Ave Ste 306 *Web:* www.mitsuichemicals.com	Rye Brook	NY	10573	914-253-0777	253-0790	144
Mitsui Foods Intl 35 Maple St *Web:* www.mitsuifoods.com	Norwood	NJ	07648	201-750-0500	750-0150	297-11
Mitsui Fudosan America Inc 1251 Avenue of the Americas Ste 800 *Web:* www.mfamerica.com	New York	NY	10020	212-403-5600		652
Mitsumi Electronics Corp 40000 Grand River Ave Ste 200 *Web:* mitsumi.com	Novi	MI	48375	248-426-8448		173-8
Mitsven Surfboards 1157 Cushman Ave *Web:* mitsvensurfboards.com	San Diego	CA	92110	619-299-7873		710
Mittelasen LLC 85 Exchange St 4th Fl PO Box 427 *Web:* mittelasen.com	Portland	ME	04101	207-775-3101		41
Mitternight Boiler Works Inc 5301 Hwy 43 N PO Box 489 *Web:* mitternight.com	Satsuma	AL	36572	251-675-2550	675-0921	91
Mittler Corp 10 Cooperative Way *TF:* 800-467-2464 ■ *Web:* www.mittlerbros.com	Wright City	MO	63390	636-745-7757		454
Mity-Lite Inc 1301 W 400 N *TF:* 800-909-8034 ■ *Web:* mitylite.com	Orem	UT	84057	801-224-0589	224-6191	319-3
Miura International Americas Inc 2200 Steven B Smith Blvd *Web:* www.miuraz.co.jp	Rockmart	GA	30153	678-685-0929	685-0930	91
Mivatek International Inc 48460 Kato Rd *Web:* mivatek.com	Fremont	CA	94538	510-490-6999		177
MIX 2020 Pennsylvania Ave NW Ste 353 *Web:* www.themix.org	Washington	DC	20006	202-659-9094		530
MIX 100.7 345 SW Cyber Dr No 101 *Web:* backyardbend.com	Bend	OR	97702	541-389-3333		647
MIX 101.5 WRAL-FM 3100 Highwoods Blvd Ste 140 *Web:* www.wralfm.com	Raleigh	NC	27604	919-890-6101	890-6146	645-128
MIX 103.1 301 Arctic Slope Ave Ste 200 *Web:* www.kmxs.com	Anchorage	AK	99518	907-349-7103		645-7
Mix 106.1 WMXU-FM 105 Fifth St N Ste 400 *Web:* www.mymix1061.com	Columbus	MS	39701	662-327-1183	241-4821	645
MIX 108 14 E Central Entrance *Web:* mix108.com	Duluth	MN	55811	218-727-4500		645-50
MIX 93.1 1331 Main St 4th Fl *TF:* 866-999-7200 ■ *Web:* mix931.iheart.com	Springfield	MA	01103	413-293-9393		645-6
Mix 95.7FM 125 Ottawa Ave NW Ste 350 *Web:* www.mix957gr.com	Grand Rapids	MI	49503	616-451-4800		645-63
Mix 96 3535 E Kimberly Rd. *Web:* mix96online.iheart.com	Davenport	IA	52807	563-344-7000		647
Mix 96.9 8402 Memorial Pkwy SW. *Web:* www.mix969huntsville.com	Huntsville	AL	35802	256-489-4969	885-9796	645-73
Mix 97-3 1015 Main St. *Web:* mix973wheeling.iheart.com	Wheeling	WV	26003	304-232-1170		645-172
Mix 99.5 WJBR 812 Philadelphia Pk Ste A *TF:* 888-995-9527 ■ *Web:* www.wjbr.com	Wilmington	DE	19809	302-765-1160		645-174
Mix Pacific Rim 1001 E University Ave. *Web:* themixpacificrim.com	Las Cruces	NM	88001	575-532-2042		671
Mix Software Inc 1203 Berkeley Dr *TF:* 800-333-0330 ■ *Web:* www.mixsoftware.com	Richardson	TX	75081	972-231-0949		178-2
Mixcor Aggregates Inc 6303 43 St. *Web:* www.mixcor.ca	Leduc	AB	T9E0G8	780-986-6721		191-1
Mixed Emotions Fine Art Inc (MEFA) 95 Tuam St. *Web:* www.mixedemotions.com	Houston	TX	77006	713-861-9666		520
Mixer Systems Inc 190 Simmons Ave *TF:* 800-756-4937 ■ *Web:* www.mixersystems.com	Pewaukee	WI	53072	262-691-3100		190
Mixmax Inc 512 2nd St *Web:* mixmax.com	San Francisco	CA	94107	415-938-9296		178-1
Mixology Wine Institute 77 W Broad St *Web:* mixologywine.com	Bethlehem	PA	18018	610-814-2900		800
Mixtec Group 9829 Blue Larkspur Ln *Web:* mixtec.net	Monterey	CA	93940	831-373-7077		41
Miya's Sushi 68 Howe St. *Web:* www.miyassushi.com	New Haven	CT	06511	203-777-9760		671
Miyabi 9732 N Kings Hwy. *Web:* www.miyabi.life	Myrtle Beach	SC	29572	843-449-9294		671
Miyako 227 N Second St *Web:* www.pasushi.net	Harrisburg	PA	17101	717-234-3250		671
Miyako Hotel Los Angeles 328 E 1st St *TF:* 800-228-6596 ■ *Web:* www.miyakoinn.com	Los Angeles	CA	90012	213-617-2000	617-2700	379
Miz Zips Cafe 2924 E Rt 66 *Web:* lodel.com	Flagstaff	AZ	86004	928-526-0104		671
Mize CPAS Inc 534 S Kansas Ave Ste 700 *TF:* 800-234-5573 ■ *Web:* www.mizehouser.com	Topeka	KS	66603	785-233-0536	233-1078	178-7
Mizel Museum of Judaica 400 S Kearney St *Web:* mizelmuseum.org	Denver	CO	80224	303-394-9993		520
Mizkan Americas Inc 1661 Feehanville Dr Ste 300. *TF:* 800-323-4358 ■ *Web:* www.mizkan.com	Mount Prospect	IL	60056	847-590-0059		296-41
Mizpah Precision Manufacturing 11522 Bartlett Ave. *Web:* www.mizpahprecision.com	Mizpah	MN	56660	218-897-5922	897-5905	128
Mizuho America Inc 133 Brimbal Ave *Web:* www.mizuho.publishpath.com	Beverly	MA	01915	978-921-1718		476
Mizuho OSI Inc 30031 Ahern Ave *TF:* 800-777-4674 ■ *Web:* www.mizuhosi.com	Union City	CA	94587	510-429-1500		475
Mizuho Securities USA 320 Park Ave 12th Fl *Web:* www.mizuhoamericas.com	New York	NY	10022	212-209-9300		690
Mizuna 214 N Howard St *Web:* www.mizuna.com	Spokane	WA	99201	509-747-2004		671
Mizuna 225 E Seventh Ave *Web:* www.mizunadenver.com	Denver	CO	80203	303-832-4778		671
Mizuno USA 4925 Avalon Ridge Pkwy *TF:* 800-966-1211 ■ *Web:* www.mizunousa.com	Norcross	GA	30071	770-441-5553		710
Mizzen Marketing Resources LLC 8195 Bramble Creek Ct. *Web:* www.mizzenmarketing.com	Mansfield	TX	76063	817-477-1991		195
Mizzou Aviation Joplin Regional Airport PO Box 1446 *Web:* www.mizzouaviation.com	Joplin	MO	64802	417-623-1331	782-6283	167-3
MJ Altman Companies Inc 205 S Magnolia Ave *TF:* 800-927-2655 ■ *Web:* mjaltman.com	Ocala	FL	34471	352-732-1112		160
MJ Celco Inc 3900 Wesley Terr *Web:* www.mjcelco.com	Schiller Park	IL	60176	847-671-1900		488
MJ Electric Inc PO Box 686 *Web:* www.mjelectric.com	Iron Mountain	MI	49801	906-774-8000	779-4217	189-4
MJ Insurance Inc 9225 Priority Way W Dr *Web:* www.mjinsurance.com	Indianapolis	IN	46240	317-805-7500	805-7515	390
MJ Manufacturing Co 2441 E Bristol Rd *Web:* www.mjmanufacturingco.com	Burton	MI	48529	810-744-3840	743-6460	550
MJ Mechanical Services Inc 2040 Military Rd. *Web:* www.mjmechanical.com	Tonawanda	NY	14150	716-874-9200		189-10
MJ Murdock Charitable Trust 703 Broadway St Ste 710 *Web:* murdocktrust.org	Vancouver	WA	98660	360-694-8415		305
MJ Partners Inc 1433 43rd Ave *Web:* www.mjpartnersinc.com	Kenosha	WI	53144	262-553-9696		177
MJ Soffe Co 1 Soffe Dr *TF:* 888-257-8673 ■ *Web:* www.soffe.com	Fayetteville	NC	28312	888-257-8673		155-1
MJJ Brilliant 902 Broadway 18th Fl *Web:* www.mjjbrilliant.com	New York	NY	10010	212-353-2326		411
MJL Enterprises LLC 2748 Sonic Dr *TF:* 888-621-0789 ■ *Web:* www.mjl-enterprises.com	Virginia Beach	VA	23453	757-963-8740		350
MJM Creative Services Inc 636 Eleventh Ave The Chocolate Factory *Web:* www.mjmcreative.com	New York	NY	10036	212-924-7070		232
MJM Electric Co-opeartive Inc (MJMEC) 264 NE St PO Box 80 *TF:* 800-648-4729 ■ *Web:* www.mjmec.coop	Carlinville	IL	62626	217-854-3137	854-3918	245
Mjm Manufacturing Inc 5205 NW 161st St *Web:* www.mjmmfg.com	Miami Lakes	FL	33014	305-620-2020	625-3342	697
MJMEC (MJM Electric Co-opeartive Inc) 264 NE St PO Box 80 *TF:* 800-648-4729 ■ *Web:* www.mjmec.coop	Carlinville	IL	62626	217-854-3137	854-3918	245
MJQ Music Inc c/o Hal Leonard Corp 7777 W Bluemound Rd *Web:* www.mjqmusic.com	Milwaukee	WI	53213	414-774-3630	774-3259	525
MJS Advertising Marketing Consulting LLC 301 Yamato Rd Ste 4100 *Web:* mjsadvertising.com	Boca Raton	FL	33431	561-443-0440		7
MJS Publishing Group (MJSPG) PO Box 505 **Fax Area Code:* 847 ■ *Web:* www.mjspub.com	Monte Vista	CO	81144	719-852-2547	745-0219*	637-2
MJSA (Manufacturing Jewelers & Suppliers of America Inc) 57 John L Dietsch Sq *TF:* 800-444-6572 ■ *Web:* www.mjsa.org	Attleboro	MA	02763	401-274-3840	274-0265	49-4
MJSPG (MJS Publishing Group) PO Box 505 **Fax Area Code:* 847 ■ *Web:* www.mjspub.com	Monte Vista	CO	81144	719-852-2547	745-0219*	637-2
MK Diamond Products Inc 1315 Storm Pkwy *TF:* 800-421-5830 ■ *Web:* www.mkdiamond.com	Torrance	CA	90501	310-539-5221	539-5158	682
MK Hansen Co PO Box 2066 *Web:* www.mkhansen.com	Wenatchee	WA	98807	509-884-1396		202
MK Morse Co 1101 11th St SE *TF:* 800-733-3377 ■ *Web:* www.mkmorse.com	Canton	OH	44707	330-453-8187	453-1111	682
MK Partners Inc 5709 Cahuenga Blvd *Web:* mkpartners.com	North Hollywood	CA	91601	818-760-8285		177
MKC (Mid-Kansas Co-op) PO Box D *TF:* 800-864-4428 ■ *Web:* www.mkcoop.com	Moundridge	KS	67107	800-864-4428		48-2

	Phone	Fax	Class
MKC Beauty Academy 3603 Seneca Ave .... Los Angeles CA 90039 *TF:* 877-798-1785 ■ *Web:* www.mkcbeautyacademy.com	877-798-1785		167-3
MKEC Engineering Consultants Inc 411 N Webb Rd. .... Wichita KS 67206 *Web:* www.mkec.com	316-684-9600		261
MKM Partners LLC 300 First Stamford Pl E 4th Fl. .... Stamford CT 06902 *Web:* www.mkmpartners.com	203-861-9060		690
MKP communications Inc 5 E 16th St 3rd Fl .... New York NY 10003 *Web:* mkpteam.com	212-983-5700		463
MKS Instruments Inc 2 Tech Dr Ste 201 .... Andover MA 01810 *TF:* 800-428-9401 ■ *Web:* www.mksinst.com	978-645-5500	557-5100	201
MKT Manufacturing Inc 1198 Pershall Rd .... Saint Louis MO 63137 *Web:* www.mktpileman.net	314-388-2254		190
MKTG Inc 32 Avenue of the Americas 20th Fl .... New York NY 10013 *OTC:* CMKG ■ *Web:* www.mktg.com	212-366-3400		4
ML McDonald LLC 50 Oakland St PO Box 315 .... Watertown MA 02471 *TF:* 800-733-6243 ■ *Web:* www.mlmcdonald.com	617-923-0900	926-8418	189-8
MLA (Music Library Assn) 8551 Research Way Ste 180 .... Middleton WI 53562 *Web:* www.musiclibraryassoc.org	608-836-5825	831-8200	49-11
MLA (Maryland Library Assn) 1401 Hollins St. .... Baltimore MD 21223 *Web:* www.mdlib.org	410-947-5090	947-5089	435
MLA (Minnesota Library Assn) 400 S Fourth St Ste 754E .... Minneapolis MN 55415 *Web:* www.mnlibraryassociation.org	612-294-6549		435
MLA (Medical Library Assn) 65 E Wacker Pl Ste 1900 .... Chicago IL 60601 *TF:* 800-523-1850 ■ *Web:* www.mlanet.org	312-419-9094	419-8950	49-11
MLA (Modern Language Assn) 26 Broadway 3rd Fl. .... New York NY 10004 *TF:* 800-323-4900 ■ *Web:* www.mla.org	646-576-5000	458-0030	49-5
MLA (Mid-America Lumbermens Assn) 638 W 39th St. .... Kansas City MO 64111 *TF:* 800-747-6529 ■ *Web:* themla.com	816-561-5323	561-1249	139
MLA (Michigan Library Assn) 3410 Belle Chase Way Ste 100. .... Lansing MI 48911 *Web:* www.milibraries.org	517-394-2774	394-2675	637-2
MLA General Contractor Inc PO Box 624 .... Fallbrook CA 92088 *Web:* www.mlacontractor.com	760-723-0210	723-3297	169
MLAP (Migrant Legal Action Program) 1001 Connecticut Ave NW Ste 915. .... Washington DC 20036 *Web:* www.mlap.org	202-775-7780		48-8
MLB Advertising 182 N Franklin St .... Wilkes-Barre PA 18701 *Web:* www.mlbadvertising.agency	570-824-1500		5
MLC (Michigan Language Ctr) 715 E Huron St Ste 1W. .... Ann Arbor MI 48104 *Web:* www.englishclasses.com	734-663-9415	663-9623	423
MLC (Mississippi Library Commission) 3881 Eastwood Dr .... Jackson MS 39211 *TF:* 800-647-7542 ■ *Web:* www.mlc.lib.ms.us	601-432-4111		434-3
MLGW (Memphis Light Gas & Water) 220 S Main St. .... Memphis TN 38103 *Web:* www.mlgw.com	901-528-4011		787
MLive Media Group 169 Monroe Ave Ste 100 .... Grand Rapids MI 49503 *TF:* 800-878-1400 ■ *Web:* www.mlivemediagroup.com	800-878-1400		532-2
MLK (Martin Luther King Jr Memorial Library) 901 G St NW. .... Washington DC 20001 *Web:* www.dclibrary.org	202-727-0321		434-3
MLMIA (Multi-Level Marketing International Assn) 119 Stanford Ct .... Irvine CA 92612 *Web:* www.mlmia.com	949-854-0484		49-18
Mlnarik Law Group Inc 2930 Bowers Ave .... Santa Clara CA 95051 *Web:* mlnariklaw.com	408-919-0088		41
MLP Seating Corp 2125 Lively Blvd. .... Elk Grove Village IL 60007 *TF:* 800-723-3030 ■ *Web:* www.mlpseating.com	847-956-1700	956-1776	319-3
MLPP (Michigan League for Public Policy) 1223 Turner St Ste G-1 .... Lansing MI 48906 *Web:* www.mlpp.org	517-487-5436	371-4546	48-13
MLQ Attorney Services 2000 River Edge Pkwy Ste 885. .... Atlanta GA 30328 *TF:* 800-446-8794 ■ *Web:* www.mlqattorneyservices.com	770-984-7007		635
MLRC (Media Law Resource Ctr) 266 W 37th St 20th Fl. .... New York NY 10018 *Web:* www.medialaw.org	212-337-0200	337-9893	49-10
MLS (Major League Soccer) 420 Fifth Ave 7th Fl .... New York NY 10018 *Web:* www.mlssoccer.com	212-450-1200		717
MLS (Michigan Legal Services) 2727 2nd Ave .... Detroit MI 48201 *Web:* www.milegalservices.org	313-964-4130	964-1192	637-2
MLS Property Information Network Inc 904 Hartford Tpke. .... Shrewsbury MA 01545 *TF:* 800-695-3000 ■ *Web:* www.mlspin.com	508-845-1011		656
MLTS (Meadville Lombard Theological School) 610 S Michigan Ave .... Chicago IL 60605 **Fax Area Code:* 312 ■ *TF:* 800-848-0979 ■ *Web:* www.meadville.edu	773-256-3000	327-7002*	167-3
MM (Moderation Management Network Inc) 22 W 27th St. .... New York NY 10001 *TF:* 888-557-7217 ■ *Web:* www.moderation.org	212-871-0974	867-1555	48-21
MM (Morgan Meredith Inc) 4299 Mount Vernon Rd SE. .... Cedar Rapids IA 52403 *TF:* 800-228-9241 ■ *Web:* www.labelmaker.com	319-362-9615		770
MM Comfort Systems 18103 NE 68th St. .... Redmond WA 98052 *TF:* 800-835-0291 ■ *Web:* www.mmcomfortsystems.com	425-881-7920	558-0582	189-10
MM Fowler Inc 4220 Neal Rd .... Durham NC 27705 *Web:* familyfareconveniencestores.com	919-309-2925	309-9924	324
MM Smith Storage Warehouse Inc 601 Hillsboro St. .... Fayetteville NC 28301 *Web:* www.mmsmithstorage.com	910-483-4186	483-5453	803-1
MM Systems Corp 50 MM Way .... Pendergrass GA 30567 *TF:* 800-241-3460 ■ *Web:* www.mmsystemscorp.com	706-824-7500	824-7501	234
MMA (Maine Municipal Assn) 60 Community Dr. .... Augusta ME 04330 *TF:* 800-452-8786 ■ *Web:* www.memun.org	207-623-8428	626-5947	48-13
MMA (Maryland Museums Assn) c/o Historic London Town 839 Londontown Road .... Edgewater MD 21037 *Web:* www.mdmuseums.org	410-222-1919		48-13
MMA Capital Management LLC (MMAC) 3600 O'Donnell St Ste 600 .... Baltimore MD 21224 *OTC:* MMAC ■ *TF:* 855-650-6932 ■ *Web:* www.mmacapitalmanagement.com	443-263-2900		509
MMA Creative Inc 705 North Dixie Ave Ste 201. .... Cookeville TN 38501 *TF:* 800-499-2332 ■ *Web:* www.mmacreative.com	931-528-8852	520-3833	7
MMAC (MMA Capital Management LLC) 3600 O'Donnell St Ste 600 .... Baltimore MD 21224 *OTC:* MMAC ■ *TF:* 855-650-6932 ■ *Web:* www.mmacapitalmanagement.com	443-263-2900		509
Mmar Medical Group Inc 9619 Yupondale Dr. .... Houston TX 77080 *TF:* 800-662-7633 ■ *Web:* www.mmarmedical.com	713-465-2003	465-2818	475
MMBC Computer Service Inc 11134 Downs Rd .... Pineville NC 28134 *Web:* www.mbcservice.com	704-525-7590	525-7592	685
MMC (Maimonides Medical Ctr) 4802 Tenth Ave. .... Brooklyn NY 11219 *Web:* www.maimonidesmed.org	718-283-6000		374-3
MMC (Maine Medical Ctr) 22 Bramhall St .... Portland ME 04102 *TF:* 877-339-3107 ■ *Web:* mainehealth.org	207-662-0111		374-3
MMC (Mennie's Machine Co) 10549 Mennie Ln PO Box 110 .... Mark IL 61340 *Web:* www.mennies.com	815-339-2226	339-6550	621
MMC (Meadville Medical Ctr) 751 Liberty St. .... Meadville PA 16335 *TF:* 800-254-5164 ■ *Web:* www.mmchs.org	814-333-5000		374-3
MMC Corp 10955 Lowell Ste 350. .... Overland Park KS 66210 *Web:* mmccorp.com	913-469-0101		189-10
MMC Group LP 105 Decker Ct Ste 1100 .... Irving TX 75062 *TF:* 800-779-2505 ■ *Web:* www.mmcgrp.com	972-893-0100	573-3428	194
MMC Materials Inc 133 New Ragsdale Rd. ...... Madison MS 39110 *Web:* www.mmcmaterials.com	601-898-4000		182
MMC Metrology Lab Inc 4989 Cleveland St .... Virginia Beach VA 23462 *TF:* 800-288-1662 ■ *Web:* www.mmcmetlab.com	757-456-2220	473-2204	385
MMCC (Mid Michigan Community College) 1375 S Clare Ave .... Harrison MI 48625 *Web:* www.midmich.edu	989-386-6622	386-6613	162
MMCS (Marshall Medical Center South) 2505 US Hwy 431. .... Boaz AL 35957 *Web:* www.mmcenters.com	256-593-8310		374-3
MMDesign Business Solutions 216 Jones Rd .... Los Gatos CA 95030 *TF:* 888-885-0205 ■ *Web:* mmdbiz.com	888-885-0205	422-0186	177
MME Consulting Inc 4714 Duckhorn Dr .... Sacramento CA 95834 *Web:* mmeconsulting.com	916-419-1102		180
MMF Industries 1111 S Wheeling Rd .... Wheeling IL 60090 *TF:* 800-323-8181 ■ *Web:* www.mmfind.com	800-323-8181		692
MMG Corporate Communication Inc 515 W Loveland Ave. .... Loveland OH 45140 *Web:* www.mmgonline.com	513-677-8787		514
MMG Insurance Co 44 Maysville St PO Box 729. .... Presque Isle ME 04769 **Fax Area Code:* 207 ■ *TF:* 800-343-0533 ■ *Web:* www.mmgins.com	800-343-0533	764-4622*	390
MMG Partners 1605 John St Ste 203A .... Fort Lee NJ 07024 **Fax Area Code:* 212 ■ *Web:* www.mmgpartners.com	774-234-6647	709-9403*	463
MMG Ventures LP 826 E Baltimore St .... Baltimore MD 21202 *TF:* 800-248-1960 ■ *Web:* mmgcapitalgroup.com	410-333-2548		403
MMG Worldwide 4601 Madison Ave. .... Kansas City MO 64112 *Web:* www.mmgyglobal.com	816-472-5988		4
MMGI (Midnight Media Group Inc) 45 E Willow St .... Millburn NJ 07041 *Web:* www.mmgi.tv	973-379-5959		514
MMH (Mercy Memorial Hospital) 718 N Macomb St. .... Monroe MI 48162 *Web:* www.mercymemorial.org	734-240-8400		374-3
MMHS (Martin Health System) 200 SE Hospital Ave PO Box 9010 .... Stuart FL 34994 *TF:* 844-630-4968 ■ *Web:* www.martinhealth.org	772-287-5200		374-3
MMI (Metal Marketplace Intl) 718 Sansom St. .... Philadelphia PA 19106 *TF:* 800-523-9191 ■ *Web:* www.metalmarketplace.com	215-592-8777	592-8195	411
MMI (Mid-Michigan Industries Inc) 2426 Pkwy Dr. .... Mount Pleasant MI 48858 *Web:* www.mmionline.com	989-773-6918		193
MMI Engineered Solutions Inc 1715 Woodland Dr .... Saline MI 48176 *TF:* 800-825-2566 ■ *Web:* www.moldedmaterials.com	800-825-2566		455
MMI Engineering 1111 Broadway 6th Fl. .... Oakland CA 94607 *Web:* www.mmiengineering.com	510-836-3002		256
MMI Hotel Group 1000 Red Fern Pl .... Flowood MS 39232 *Web:* mmihospitality.com	601-936-3666		379
MMI Services Inc 4042 Patton Way .... Bakersfield CA 93308 *TF:* 800-595-9369 ■ *Web:* mmi-services.com	661-589-9366	589-2080	539
MMIC Group 7701 France Ave S Ste 500. .... Minneapolis MN 55435 **Fax Area Code:* 952 ■ *TF:* 800-328-5532 ■ *Web:* www.mmicgroup.com	800-328-5532	838-6808*	177
MML (Mississippi Municipal League) 600 E Amite St Ste 104. .... Jackson MS 39201 *TF:* 800-325-7641 ■ *Web:* www.mmlonline.com	601-353-5854	353-6980	48-13
MML Diagnostics Packaging Inc 1625 NW Sundial Rd .... Troutdale OR 97060 *Web:* www.mmldiagnostics.com	503-666-8398	666-8510	85
MML Investors Services Inc 1295 State St .... Springfield MA 01111 *TF:* 888-697-8687 ■ *Web:* www.massmutual.com	888-697-8687		390

				Phone	Fax	Class
MMLJ Inc 5711 Schurmier Rd *TF:* 800-727-5707 ■ *Web:* www.mmlj.com	Houston	TX	77048	713-869-2227	868-8041	386
MMR Group Inc 15961 Airline Hwy *TF:* 800-880-5090 ■ *Web:* www.mmrgrp.com	Baton Rouge	LA	70817	225-756-5090	753-7012	189-4
MMS (Massachusetts Medical Society) 860 Winter St *TF:* 800-322-2303 ■ *Web:* www.massmed.org	Waltham	MA	02451	781-893-4610	893-8009	474
MMS (Miller Mechanical Specialties Inc) 510 Murphy St *Web:* www.mmsinconline.com	Des Moines	IA	50309	515-243-4287	243-7313	385
MMS Education 1 Summit Sq 1717 Langhorne-Newtown Rd Ste 301 **Fax Area Code:* 215 ■ *TF:* 866-395-3193 ■ *Web:* www.mmseducation.com	Langhorne	PA	19047	800-523-5948	579-8589*	393
MN Designs Inc 307 Industrial Dr **Fax Area Code:* 877 ■ *TF:* 866-663-3746 ■ *Web:* www.mndesignsinc.com	Lexington	SC	29072	803-996-6633	438-8465*	45
MN Health Insurance Network 12280 Nicollet Ave Ste 104 *TF:* 866-664-4638 ■ *Web:* mnhealthnetwork.com	Burnsville	MN	55337	952-224-0123		390
MNA (Maryland Nurses Assn) 21 Governor's Ct Ste 195 *Web:* www.marylandrn.org	Baltimore	MD	21244	410-944-5800		533
MNA (Massachusetts Nurses Assn) 340 Tpke St *TF:* 800-882-2056 ■ *Web:* www.massnurses.org	Canton	MA	02021	781-821-4625	821-4445	533
MNA (Michigan Nurses Assn) 2310 Jolly Oak Rd *Web:* www.minurses.org	Okemos	MI	48864	517-349-5640	349-5818	533
MNA (Minnesota Nurses Assn) 345 Randolph Ave Ste 200 *TF:* 800-536-4662 ■ *Web:* mnnurses.org	Saint Paul	MN	55102	651-414-2800		533
MNA (Mississippi Nurses Assn) 31 Woodgreen Pl *Web:* www.msnurses.org	Madison	MS	39110	601-898-0670	898-0190	533
MNA (Montana Nurses Assn) 20 Old Montana State Hwy *Web:* www.mtnurses.org	Montana City	MT	59634	406-442-6710	442-1841	533
MNA (Michigan Nature Assn) 2310 Science Pky Ste 100 *TF:* 866-223-2231 ■ *Web:* www.michigannature.org	Okemos	MI	48864	866-223-2231		49-19
M-NCPPC (Maryland-National Capital Park and Planning Commission) 6611 Kenilworth Ave *Web:* www.mncppc.org	Riverdale	MD	20737	301-699-2255		637-2
Mnemonics Inc 3900 Dow Rd *Web:* www.mnemonicsinc.com	Melbourne	FL	32934	321-254-7300		22
MNJ Technologies Direct Inc 1025 E Busch Pky **Fax Area Code:* 847 ■ *TF:* 800-870-4340 ■ *Web:* www.mnjtech.com	Buffalo Grove	IL	60089	800-870-4340	634-0702*	225
MNMP (Museum of New Mexico Press) 725 Camino Lejo *Web:* www.mnmpress.org	Santa Fe	NM	87505	505-476-1160		637-2
MNOP Ltd 4737 Habersham Rdg *Web:* www.mnopltd.com	Lilburn	GA	30047	770-972-5430		178-1
MNP LLP 400-10104 103 Ave 7th Fl *Web:* www.mnp.ca	Calgary	AB	T2P2X6	403-444-0150		2
MNPS (Metropolitan Nashville Public Schools) 2601 Bransford Ave *Web:* www.mnps.org	Nashville	TN	37204	615-259-8531	214-8890	685
MNS Financial Management LLC 6216 Whiskey Creek Dr Ste A *Web:* marquiswealthgroup.com	Fort Myers	FL	33919	239-454-1117		2
Mnuchin Gallery LLC 45 E 78th St *Web:* mnuchingallery.com	New York	NY	10021	212-861-0020		42
MNX Solutions 123 W First St Ste D *TF:* 888-877-7118 ■ *Web:* mnxsolutions.com	Monroe	MI	48161	888-877-7118		225
M-O Federal Credit Union 1730 Dakota Ave S *Web:* m-ofcu.com	Huron	SD	57350	605-353-9977		219
Mo's Restaurant 1116 White St *Web:* www.mosrestaurantfl.com	Key West	FL	33040	305-296-8955		671
Mo's Restaurants 657 SW Bay Blvd *Web:* www.moschowder.com	Newport	OR	97365	541-265-7512	265-9323	670
MOA (Museum of the Americas) 2500 NW 79th Ave Ste 104 *Web:* www.museumamericas.org	Doral	FL	33122	305-599-8089		520
MOAA (Military Officers Association of America) 201 N Washington St *TF:* 800-234-6622 ■ *Web:* www.moaa.org	Alexandria	VA	22314	800-234-6622		48-19
Moag & Company LLC 323 W Camden St Ste 400 *Web:* www.moagandcompany.com	Baltimore	MD	21201	410-230-0105	230-0547	690
Moai Technologies Inc 550 William Pitt Way *TF:* 800-814-1548 ■ *Web:* www.moai.com	Pittsburgh	PA	15222	412-454-5550	454-5555	178-7
Moapa Valley Telephone Co (MVT) 183 S Anderson St *TF:* 800-227-2600 ■ *Web:* www.mvtel.com	Overton	NV	89040	702-397-2601		224
Mob Media Inc 27042 Towne Centre Dr Ste 260 *Web:* www.mobmedia.com	Foothill Ranch	CA	92610	949-222-0220		4
Moberg Research Inc 224 S Maple St *Web:* www.moberg.com	Ambler	PA	19002	215-283-0860		476
Moberly Area Community College 101 College Ave *TF:* 800-622-2070 ■ *Web:* www.macc.edu	Moberly	MO	65270	660-263-4110	263-2406	162
Moberly Correctional Ctr 5201 S Morley *Web:* doc.mo.gov	Moberly	MO	65270	660-263-3778		213
Moberly Monitor Index 218 N Williams *Web:* www.moberlymonitor.com	Moberly	MO	65270	660-263-4123		532-3
Mobi PCS Inc 1467 S King St Ste B *Web:* mobipcs.com	Honolulu	HI	96814	808-723-1111		387
Mobile Air Conditioning Society Worldwide (MACS) 225 S Broad St *Web:* www.macsw.org	Lansdale	PA	19446	215-631-7020	631-7017	49-21
Mobile Air Transport Inc 12 Runway Ave *TF:* 800-342-4110 ■ *Web:* mobileairtrans.com	Latham	NY	12110	518-783-5111		780

				Phone	Fax	Class
Mobile Area Chamber of Commerce 451 Government St *TF:* 800-422-6951 ■ *Web:* www.mobilechamber.com	Mobile	AL	36602	251-433-6951	432-1143	139
Mobile Area Education Foundation 605 Bel Air Blvd Ste 400 *Web:* www.maef.net	Mobile	AL	36606	251-476-0002		305
Mobile Aspects Inc 3700 S Water St Ste 310 *TF:* 800-921-7343 ■ *Web:* www.mobileaspects.com	Pittsburgh	PA	15203	412-325-1690	325-1685	387
Mobile Botanical Gardens 5151 Museum Dr *Web:* www.mobilebotanicalgardens.org	Mobile	AL	36608	251-342-0555		97
Mobile City Hall 205 Government St *TF:* 800-957-3676 ■ *Web:* www.cityofmobile.org	Mobile	AL	36602	251-208-7411	208-7576	337
Mobile Climate Control Corp 17103 State Rd 4 E *Web:* www.mcc-hvac.com	Goshen	IN	46528	574-534-1516	533-4452	14
Mobile Communication of Gwinnett Inc 2241 Tucker Industrial Rd *TF:* 800-749-7170 ■ *Web:* www.callmc.com	Tucker	GA	30084	770-963-3748		246
Mobile Communications America MCA 510 S Pike E *Web:* callmc.com	Sumter	SC	29150	803-773-9743		647
Mobile Concepts by Scotty Inc 480 Bessemer Rd *Web:* mobileconcepts.com	Mount Pleasant	PA	15666	724-542-7640		59
Mobile County 205 Government St *Web:* www.mobilecountyal.gov	Mobile	AL	36644	251-574-5077		338
Mobile County Public Schools 1 Magnum Pass PO Box 180069 *Web:* www.mcpss.com	Mobile	AL	36618	251-221-4000	221-4545	685
Mobile Demand LC 1501 Boyson Square Dr Ste 101 *Web:* ruggedtabletpc.com	Hiawatha	IA	52233	319-363-4121		180
Mobile Electric Power Solutions Inc 2623 National Cir *Web:* www.meps.com	Garland	TX	75041	972-864-1015	271-0635	518
Mobile Fixture & Equipment Company Inc 1155 Montlimar Dr *TF:* 800-345-6458 ■ *Web:* www.mobilefixture.com	Mobile	AL	36609	251-342-0455		406
Mobile Id Solutions Inc 1574 N Batavia St Ste 1 *Web:* mobileidsolutions.com	Orange	CA	92867	714-922-1134		761
Mobile Infirmary Medical Ctr (MIMC) 5 Mobile Infirmary Cir *Web:* www.infirmaryhealth.org	Mobile	AL	36607	251-435-2400		374-3
Mobile Life Support Services Inc 3188 US Rt 9w *TF:* 800-209-8815 ■ *Web:* www.mobilelife.com	New Windsor	NY	12553	845-562-4368		30
Mobile Medical International Corp 2176 Portland St Ste 4 PO Box 672 *TF:* 800-692-5205 ■ *Web:* mmicmedical.com	Saint Johnsbury	VT	05819	802-748-2322	748-2323	475
Mobile Museum of Art 4850 Museum Dr *Web:* www.mobilemuseumofart.com	Mobile	AL	36608	251-208-5200		520
Mobile National Cemetery 1202 Virginia St **Fax Area Code:* 850 ■ *Web:* www.cem.va.gov	Mobile	AL	36604	251-690-2858	453-4635*	136
Mobile Office Acquisition Corp 9155 Harrison Park Ct *Web:* www.pacvan.com	Indianapolis	IN	46216	317-489-5771	489-9971	256
Mobile One Courier Services Inc 1619 Diamond Springs Rd Ste C *Web:* mobileonecourier.com	Virginia Beach	VA	23455	757-622-9500		314
Mobile Opera Inc 257 Dauphin St *Web:* www.mobileopera.org	Mobile	AL	36602	251-432-6772	431-7613	573-2
Mobile Paint 4775 Hamilton Blvd *TF:* 800-621-6952 ■ *Web:* mobilepaint.com	Theodore	AL	36582	251-443-6110	408-0410	550
Mobile Parts Inc 2472 Evans Rd PO Box 327 *TF:* 800-461-4055 ■ *Web:* www.mobileparts.com	Val Caron	ON	P3N1P5	705-897-4955		358
Mobile Posse Inc 1010 N Glebe Rd Ste 200 *Web:* www.mobileposse.com	McLean	VA	22101	703-348-4084		196
Mobile Public Library 701 Government St *TF:* 877-322-8228 ■ *Web:* www.mobilepubliclibrary.org	Mobile	AL	36602	251-208-7073		434-3
Mobile Regional Airport 8400 Airport Blvd *TF:* 800-357-5373 ■ *Web:* www.mobairport.com	Mobile	AL	36608	251-633-4510	639-7437	27
Mobile Smith 5400 Trinity Rd Ste 208 *TF:* 855-516-2413 ■ *Web:* www.mobilesmith.com	Raleigh	NC	27607	855-516-2413		39
Mobile Symphony PO Box 3127 *Web:* mobilesymphony.org	Mobile	AL	36652	251-432-2010		573-3
Mobile Video Services Ltd 1620 I St NW Ste 1000 *Web:* www.mobilevideo.net	Washington	DC	20006	202-331-8882		194
Mobilis Technologies LLC 12337 Jones Ste 480 *Web:* mobilistech.com	Houston	TX	77070	281-807-3533		180
Mobility Center Inc 6693 Dixie Hwy *TF:* 866-361-7559 ■ *Web:* www.myamigo.com	Bridgeport	MI	48722	989-777-0910		480
Mobiquity Networks Inc 35 Torrington Ln *Web:* www.mobiquitynetworks.com	Shoreham	NY	11786	516-246-9422		195
Mobisante Inc 8201 164th Ave NE Ste 200 *Web:* www.mobisante.com	Redmond	WA	98052	425-605-0600		723
Mobius Executive Leadership 177 Worcester St *Web:* www.mobiusleadership.com	Wellesley	MA	02481	781-237-1362		138
Mobivity Inc 58 W Buffalo Ste 200 *TF:* 877-282-7660 ■ *Web:* www.mobivity.com	Chandler	AZ	85225	877-282-7660		5
Mobotrex Inc 109 W 55th St *Web:* www.mobotrex.com	Davenport	IA	52806	563-323-0009	323-8256	770
Mobridge Regional Hospital Inc PO Box 580 *Web:* www.mobridgehospital.org	Mobridge	SD	57601	605-845-3692	845-8239	374-3
Mobridge Tribune 1413 E Grand Xing *TF:* 800-594-9418 ■ *Web:* www.mobridgetribune.com	Mobridge	SD	57601	605-845-3646		532-3

Company	City	State	Zip	Phone	Fax	Class
MoCA Westport 51 Riverside Ave *Web:* mocawestport.org	Westport	CT	06880	203-222-7070	222-7999	50-2
MOCAP Inc 409 Pkwy Dr *TF:* 800-633-6775 ■ *Web:* www.mocap.com	Park Hills	MO	63601	314-543-4000	543-4111	608
MoCaro Industries Inc 2201 Mocaro Dr *Web:* www.mocaro.com	Statesville	NC	28677	704-878-6645	873-6139	745-4
Moccasin Bend Mental Health Institute 100 Moccasin Bend Rd *TF:* 800-560-5767 ■ *Web:* www.tn.gov	Chattanooga	TN	37405	423-265-2271	785-3333	374-5
Moccasin Creek State Park 3655 Hwy 197 *Web:* gastateparks.org	Clarkesville	GA	30523	706-947-3194		565
Moceri & Company PC 45100 Sterritt St *Web:* moceri-cpa.com	Utica	MI	48317	586-254-2010		2
Moceri Development Corp 3005 University Dr *Web:* www.moceri.com	Auburn Hills	MI	48326	248-340-9400		653
Mock Plumbing & Mechanical Inc PO Box 22456 *Web:* www.mocksavannah.com	Savannah	GA	31403	912-232-1104	232-6284	189-10
Mock, Roos & Associates Inc 5720 Corporate Way *Web:* mockroos.com	West Palm Beach	FL	33407	561-683-3113		261
Mockler Beverage Co 11811 Reiger Rd *Web:* www.mocklerbeverage.com	Baton Rouge	LA	70809	225-408-4283		297-8
Mocon Inc 7500 Mendelssohn Ave N *NASDAQ: MOCO* ■ *Web:* www.mocon.com	Minneapolis	MN	55428	763-493-6370	493-6358	201
Mocse Federal Credit Union 3600 Coffee Rd *Web:* mocse.org	Modesto	CA	95355	209-572-3600		219
Moctezuma's 4102 S 56th St *Web:* www.moctezumas.com	Tacoma	WA	98409	253-474-5593		671
Mod Tech Industries Inc 1523 Industrial Dr *Web:* www.modtechindustries.com	Shawano	WI	54166	715-524-4510	524-3202	454
Mod43 Inc 414 Lenox Dr *Web:* www.mod43.com	Canton	MI	48187	734-416-1009		225
Moda Health Plan Inc 601 SW 2nd Ave *TF:* 877-605-3229 ■ *Web:* www.modahealth.com	Portland	OR	97240	503-243-3962		391-3
Moda Hotel 900 Seymour St *TF:* 877-683-5522 ■ *Web:* www.modahotel.ca	Vancouver	BC	V6B3L9	604-683-4251	683-0611	379
MODAEXPRESS 900 Secaucus Rd *Web:* modaexpress.com	Secaucus	NJ	07094	201-325-8808	325-8868	34
Modagrafics Inc 5300 Newport Dr *TF:* 800-860-3169 ■ *Web:* www.modagrafics.com	Rolling Meadows	IL	60008	847-392-3980		687
Modal Shop Inc, The 1776 Mentor Ave *TF:* 800-860-4867 ■ *Web:* www.modalshop.com	Cincinnati	OH	45212	513-351-9919		419
Mode Analytics 208 Utah St Ste 400 *Web:* mode.com	San Francisco	CA	94103	650-993-9125		788
Modea Corp 117 Washington St SW *Web:* www.modea.com	Blacksburg	VA	24060	540-552-3210		7
Model Airplane News 88 Danbury Rd Ste 1A *Web:* www.modelairplanenews.com	Wilton	CT	06897	802-846-9410		457-14
Model Cleaners Uniforms & Apparel LLC 100 Third St *Web:* modeluniforms.com	Charleroi	PA	15022	724-489-9553		426
Model College of Hair Design 201 8th Ave S *TF:* 800-450-3300 ■ *Web:* www.mcohd.com	Saint Cloud	MN	56301	320-253-4222	259-4731	167-3
Model Coverall Service Inc 100 28th St SE *TF:* 800-968-6491 ■ *Web:* www.modelcoverall.com	Grand Rapids	MI	49548	616-241-6491	241-0677	442
Model Rectifier Corp 80 Newfield Ave *Web:* www.modelrectifier.com	Edison	NJ	08837	732-225-2100		762
Modell's Sporting Goods 498 Seventh Ave 20th Fl *TF:* 800-275-6633 ■ *Web:* www.modells.com	New York	NY	10018	800-275-6633		157-5
Models & Images 8918 W 21 St N Ste 200 *Web:* www.modelsandimages.com	Wichita	KS	67205	316-612-9070	612-9073	50-1
Moderation Management Network Inc (MM) 22 W 27th St *TF:* 888-557-7217 ■ *Web:* www.moderation.org	New York	NY	10001	212-871-0974	867-1555	48-21
Modern Abrasive Corp PO Box 219 *Web:* modernabrasive.com	Spring Grove	IL	60081	815-675-2352	675-2822	1
Modern Aire Manufacturing Corp 7319 Lankershim Blvd *Web:* modernaire.com	North Hollywood	CA	91605	818-765-9870		198
Modern American Safety Training-mast 841 Alton Ave *Web:* mastohio.com	Columbus	OH	43219	614-252-0565		507
Modern Art Museum of Fort Worth 3200 Darnell St *TF:* 866-824-5566 ■ *Web:* www.themodern.org	Fort Worth	TX	76107	817-738-9215		520
Modern Automation Inc 134 Tennsco Dr *TF:* 800-921-9705 ■ *Web:* www.modernautomation.com	Dickson	TN	37055	615-446-1990		358
Modern Bank NA 250 W 55th St 15th Fl *Web:* modernbank.com	New York	NY	10019	212-323-1100		70
Modern Beauty Academy 699 S C St *Web:* www.modernbeautyacademy.org	Oxnard	CA	93030	805-483-4994	486-7394	167-3
Modern Building Systems Inc 9493 Porter Rd SE *TF:* 800-682-1422 ■ *Web:* www.modernbuildingsystems.com	Aumsville	OR	97325	503-749-4949	749-4950	106
Modern Business Associates Inc 9455 Koger Blvd Ste 200 *TF:* 888-622-6460 ■ *Web:* www.mbahro.com	Saint Petersburg	FL	33702	888-622-6460		631
Modern Cafe 337 13th Ave NE *Web:* www.moderncafeminneapolis.com	Minneapolis	MN	55413	612-378-9882		671
Modern Chevrolet of Winston-Salem 5955 University Pkwy *TF:* 888-306-0825 ■ *Web:* www.modernchevy.com	Winston-Salem	NC	27105	877-399-2830		57
Modern Comfort Systems Inc 100 Airport Dr *Web:* moderncomfortsystems.com	Westminster	MD	21157	410-876-2200		697
Modern Concrete Inc 1770 Sharps Access *Web:* www.modernconcrete.net	Elko	NV	89801	775-753-5100	738-9199	189-3
Modern Controls Inc 7 Bellecor Dr *Web:* www.moderncontrols.com	New Castle	DE	19720	302-325-6800		610
Modern Corp 4746 Model City Rd *TF:* 800-662-0012 ■ *Web:* www.moderncorporation.com	Model City	NY	14107	716-754-8226		804
Modern Dental Laboratory USA 500 Stephenson Hwy Ste 100 **Fax Area Code: 248* ■ *TF:* 877-711-8778 ■ *Web:* moderndentalusa.com	Troy	MI	48083	877-711-8778	307-0420*	415
Modern Dispersions Inc 78 Marguerite Ave *Web:* www.moderndispersions.com	Leominster	MA	01453	978-534-3370	537-6065	605-2
Modern Distributors Inc 817 W Columbia St *TF:* 800-880-5543 ■ *Web:* www.teammodern.com	Somerset	KY	42501	606-679-1178		756
Modern Drop Forge Co 13810 S Western Ave *Web:* www.modernforge.com	Blue Island	IL	60406	708-388-1806	597-3633	483
Modern Earth 449 Provencher Blvd *TF:* 866-766-7640 ■ *Web:* www.modernearth.net	Winnipeg	MB	R2J0B8	204-885-2469		225
Modern Equipment Company Inc 6161 Abbott Dr PO Box 12278 *Web:* www.meco-omaha.com	Omaha	NE	68110	402-341-4939	346-9550	567
Modern Exploration Inc 4900 Texoma Pkwy *Web:* www.modernexploration.com	Sherman	TX	75090	903-893-1129		536
Modern Group Ltd 2501 Durham Rd *TF:* 800-223-3827 ■ *Web:* moderngroup.com	Bristol	PA	19007	215-943-9100	943-4978	385
Modern Group Ltd 1655 Louisiana St *TF:* 800-231-8198 ■ *Web:* www.modernusa.com	Beaumont	TX	77701	409-833-2665		273
Modern Hardware Inc 1500 Kalamazoo Ave SE *Web:* modernhardware.com	Grand Rapids	MI	49507	616-241-2655		351
MODERN Honolulu, The 1775 Ala Moana Blvd *TF:* 855-599-9604 ■ *Web:* www.themodernhonolulu.com	Honolulu	HI	96815	808-943-5800	943-5841	707
Modern Ice Equipment & Supply Co 5709 Harrison Ave **Fax Area Code: 513* ■ *TF:* 800-543-1581 ■ *Web:* www.modernice.com	Cincinnati	OH	45248	800-543-1581	367-5762*	665
Modern Industries Inc 613 W 11th St *TF:* 844-603-6105 ■ *Web:* modernind.com	Erie	PA	16501	814-455-8061	453-4382	484
Modern Information Systems Inc (MIS) 817 First Ave N *TF:* 800-841-1084 ■ *Web:* www.moderninformation.com	Grand Forks	ND	58203	701-772-4844	772-1266	112
Modern Institute of Reflexology 4086 Youngfield St *TF:* 800-533-1837 ■ *Web:* www.reflexologyinstitute.com	Wheat Ridge	CO	80033	303-237-1562	237-1606	167-3
Modern Language Assn (MLA) 26 Broadway 3rd Fl *TF:* 800-323-4900 ■ *Web:* www.mla.org	New York	NY	10004	646-576-5000	458-0030	49-5
Modern Litho 5111 Southwest Ave *TF:* 800-456-5867 ■ *Web:* www.modernlitho.com	Saint Louis	MO	63110	314-781-6505	781-0551	627
Modern Machine & Engineering Corp 9380 Winnetka Ave N *TF:* 800-443-5117 ■ *Web:* www.mmeincmn.com	Brooklyn Park	MN	55445	612-781-3347	781-0030	621
Modern Machine & Tool Company Inc 11844 Jefferson Ave *TF:* 800-482-1835 ■ *Web:* www.mmtool.com	Newport News	VA	23606	757-873-1212		407
Modern Machinery Company Inc 2842 Rand Rd *TF:* 800-589-1444 ■ *Web:* modernmachinerycompany.com	Indianapolis	IN	46241	317-791-8290		366
Modern Machinery of Beaverton Inc 3031 Guernsey Rd *Web:* www.modernmachineinc.com	Beaverton	MI	48612	989-435-9071	435-3940	695
Modern Management Inc 253 Commerce Dr Ste 105 *TF:* 800-323-1331 ■ *Web:* www.modernmanagement.com	Grayslake	IL	60030	847-945-7400		193
Modern Marketing Partners 1220 Iroquois Ave Ste 210 *Web:* www.modernmarketingpartners.com	Naperville	IL	60563	630-868-5060		7
Modern Office Methods Inc 4747 Lake Forest Dr *TF:* 800-345-3888 ■ *Web:* www.momnet.com	Cincinnati	OH	45242	513-791-0909		366
Modern Parking Inc 303 S Union Ave 1st Fl *Web:* www.modernparking.com	Los Angeles	CA	90017	213-482-8400		562
Modern Plastics Inc 88 Long Hill Cross Rd *Web:* www.modernplastics.com	Shelton	CT	06484	203-333-3128		601
Modern Polymers Inc 901 W Academy St *Web:* www.modernpolymers.com	Cherryville	NC	28021	704-435-5825	435-2063	601
Modern Press Inc 1 Colonie St *TF:* 888-728-8861 ■ *Web:* www.modernpress.com	Albany	NY	12207	518-434-2921	434-2954	627
Modern Print Shop 508 Cortlandt St *Web:* modernprintshop.com	Houston	TX	77007	713-861-7262		627
Modern Process Equipment Inc 3125 S Kolin Ave *Web:* www.mpechicago.com	Chicago	IL	60623	773-254-3929		300
Modern Signs Press Inc 10443 Los Alamitos Blvd *Web:* www.modernsignspress.com	Los Alamitos	CA	90720	562-596-8548	795-6614	637-2
Modern Technology Solutions Inc (MTSI) 5285 Shawnee Rd Ste 400 *Web:* www.mtsi-va.com	Alexandria	VA	22312	703-564-3800		261
Modern Track Machinery 1415 Davis Rd *Web:* www.geismar-mtm.com	Elgin	IL	60123	847-697-7510		770
Modern Transportation Service Inc 2605 Nicholson Rd Ste 2301 *Web:* moderntrans.com	Sewickley	PA	15143	412-489-4800		449
Modern Welding Company Inc 2880 New Hartford Rd *TF:* 800-922-1932 ■ *Web:* www.modweldco.com	Owensboro	KY	42303	270-685-4400	684-6972	91
Modern Wireless Inc 1163 N Patt St *TF:* 800-474-9724 ■ *Web:* www.modernwirelessusa.com	Anaheim	CA	92801	714-535-6399		736
Modern Woodcrafts LLC Farmington Industrial Pk 72 NW Dr *Web:* www.modernwoodcrafts.com	Plainville	CT	06062	860-677-7371		286

Phone | Fax | Class

Modern Woodmen of America
1701 First Ave. .... Rock Island IL 61201 800-447-9811 793-5547* 391-2
Fax Area Code: 309 ■ *TF:* 800-447-9811 ■ *Web:* www.modernwoodmen.org

Moderna Therapeutics Inc
320 Bent St. .... Cambridge MA 02141 617-714-6500 231
Web: www.modernatx.com

Moderne Glass Company Inc
1000 Industrial Blvd .... Aliquippa PA 15001 800-645-5131 330
TF: 800-645-5131 ■ *Web:* glassamerica.com

Moderne Hotel, The 243 W 55th St .... New York NY 10019 212-397-6767 397-8787 379
TF: 855-779-7040 ■ *Web:* modernehotelnyc.com

Modernfold Inc 215 W New Rd .... Greenfield IN 46140 800-869-9685 410-5016* 286
Fax Area Code: 866 ■ *TF:* 800-869-9685 ■ *Web:* www.modernfold.com

Modernism Inc
685 Market St Ste 290 .... San Francisco CA 94105 415-541-0461 541-0425 42
Web: www.modernisminc.com

Modernism Magazine 199 George St. .... Lambertville NJ 08530 609-397-4104 457-2
Web: www.ragoarts.com

ModernThink LLC 4519 Weldin Rd .... Wilmington DE 19803 302-764-4477 195
Web: www.modernthink.com

Modesto & Empire Traction Co
530 11th St. .... Modesto CA 95354 209-524-4631 529-0336 648
Web: metrr.com

Modesto Bee 1325 H St. .... Modesto CA 95354 209-578-2000 578-2207 532-2
TF: 800-776-4233 ■ *Web:* www.modbee.com

Modesto Centre Plaza 1000 L St. .... Modesto CA 95354 209-577-6444 544-6729 205
Web: www.modestogov.com

Modesto Chamber of Commerce 1114 J St. .... Modesto CA 95354 209-577-5757 577-2673 139
Web: www.modchamber.org

Modesto City Schools 426 Locust St. .... Modesto CA 95351 209-574-1500 685
TF: 800-942-3767 ■ *Web:* www.mcs4kids.com

Modesto Convention & Visitors Bureau
1150 Ninth St Ste C .... Modesto CA 95354 209-526-5588 526-5586 206
TF: 888-640-8467 ■ *Web:* www.visitmodesto.com

Modesto Junior College
435 College Ave .... Modesto CA 95350 209-575-6550 575-6859 162
Web: www.mjc.edu

Modesto Symphony Orchestra
911 13th St. .... Modesto CA 95354 209-523-4156 523-0201 573-3
TF: 877-488-3380 ■ *Web:* www.modestosymphony.org

Modified Plastics Inc
1240 E Glenwood Pl .... Santa Ana CA 92707 714-546-4667 546-0401 604
Web: www.modifiedplastics.com

Modine Manufacturing Co
1500 De Koven Ave. .... Racine WI 53403 262-636-1200 636-1424 15
NYSE: MOD ■ *TF:* 800-828-4328 ■ *Web:* www.modine.com

Modineer Co 2190 Industrial Dr. .... Niles MI 49120 269-683-2550 489
Web: www.modineer.com

Modis Inc 10 Bay St 7th Fl .... Toronto ON M5J2R8 904-360-2300 360-2110 463
TF: 800-842-5907 ■ *Web:* www.modis.com

Modjeski & Masters Inc
100 Sterling Pkwy Ste 302 .... Mechanicsburg PA 17050 717-790-9565 790-9564 261
TF: 888-663-5375 ■ *Web:* www.modjeski.com

Modo Inc 20325 NW Von Neumann Dr. .... Beaverton OR 97006 800-685-8784 475
TF: 800-685-8784 ■ *Web:* www.modocarts.com

MOD-PAC Corp 1801 Elmwood Ave .... Buffalo NY 14207 716-873-0640 873-6008 101
NASDAQ: MPAC ■ *TF:* 866-216-6193 ■ *Web:* www.modpac.com

Modrall Sperling Roehl Harris & Sisk PA
PO Box 2168 .... Albuquerque NM 87103 505-848-1800 428
Web: www.modrall.com

Modtech Holdings Inc
1660 Chicago Ave Ste M-21 .... Riverside CA 92507 951-686-3633 106
Web: www.modtech.com

Modulant Inc 15305 Dallas Pkwy Ste 300 .... Addison TX 75001 972-378-6677 177
TF: 800-470-3575 ■ *Web:* www.modulant.com

Modular Communications Systems
13309 Saticoy St .... North Hollywood CA 91605 818-764-1333 647
Web: moducom.com

Modular Components National Inc
105 E Jarrettsville Rd PO Box 453 .... Forest Hill MD 21050 410-879-6553 625
Web: www.modularcomp.com

Modular Connections LLC
1090 Industrial Blvd .... Bessemer AL 35022 205-980-4565 186
TF: 877-903-6335 ■ *Web:* modularconnections.com

Modular Devices Inc 1 Roned Rd .... Shirley NY 11967 631-345-3100 345-3106 696
Web: www.mdipower.com

Modular Genius Inc 1201 S Mountain Rd .... Joppa MD 21085 410-676-3424 186
TF: 888-420-1113 ■ *Web:* www.modulargenius.com

Modular Mining Systems
3289 E Hemisphere Loop .... Tucson AZ 85706 520-746-9127 454
Web: www.modularmining.com

Modular Process Control LLC
11477 Olde Cabin Rd Ste 300 .... Saint Louis MO 63141 636-536-1000 715-3400* 463
Fax Area Code: 314 ■ *Web:* www.mpcenergyllc.com

Modular Systems Inc 169 Park St .... Fruitport MI 49415 231-865-3167 865-6101 286
Web: www.mod-eez.com

Moduline Industries Canada Ltd
1421 Brier Park Crescent NW .... Medicine Hat AB T1C1T8 403-527-1555 505
Web: www.moduline.ca

Modulis Inc 6250 Blvd Monk .... Montreal QC H4E3H7 514-284-2020 224
Web: www.modulis.com

Modumetal Inc 1443 Northlake Way .... Seattle WA 98103 877-632-4242 770-7338* 308
Fax Area Code: 206 ■ *TF:* 877-632-4242 ■ *Web:* www.modumetal.com

Modus Furniture Intl
5410 McConnell Ave .... Los Angeles CA 90066 310-827-2129 827-7972 361
Web: www.modusfurniture.com

Modus Group LLC, The
555 Nishnabe Trail .... Rossville KS 66533 785-584-6261 261
Web: modus-llc.com

Moe's Books 2476 Telegraph Ave .... Berkeley CA 94704 510-849-2087 95
Web: www.moesbooks.com

Moe's Southwest Grill
6401 E Lloyd Expy .... Evansville IN 47715 812-491-6637 671
Web: www.moes.com

Moelis & Company LLC
399 Park Ave 5th Fl .... New York NY 10022 212-883-3800 69
Web: www.moelis.com

Moeller Fine Art Ltd 35 E 64th St .... New York NY 10065 212-644-2133 644-2134 42
Web: www.moellerfineart.com

Moeller Manufacturing Company Inc
Aircraft Div 30100 Beck Rd .... Wixom MI 48393 248-960-3999 960-1593 21
TF: 800-321-8010 ■ *Web:* www.moelleraircraft.com

Moen Inc 25300 Al Moen Dr .... North Olmsted OH 44070 440-962-2000 848-6636* 609
Fax Area Code: 800 ■ *TF:* 800-289-6636 ■ *Web:* www.moen.com

Moet Hennessy USA 85 10th Ave .... New York NY 10011 212-251-8200 81-3
Web: www1.mhusa.com

MOFFA (Michigan Organic Food and Farm Alliance)
PO Box 26102 .... Lansing MI 48909 248-262-6826 48-13
Web: www.moffa.net

Moffat County 221 W Victory Way .... Craig CO 81625 970-824-9104 824-0351 338
Web: www.colorado.gov

Moffatt & Nichol Engineers
3780 Kilroy Airport Way Ste 750 .... Long Beach CA 90806 562-590-6500 590-6512 261
TF: 888-399-6609 ■ *Web:* www.moffattnichol.com

Moffatt Thomas Barrett Rock & Fields Chartered
101 S Capitol Blvd 10th Fl .... Boise ID 83702 208-345-2000 428
Web: www.moffatt.com

MoffettNathanson LLC
600 Madison Ave 17th Fl .... New York NY 10022 212-519-0020 401
Web: www.moffettnathanson.com

Moffitt Corporation Inc
1351 13th Ave S Ste 130 .... Jacksonville Beach FL 32250 904-241-9944 256
TF: 800-474-3267 ■ *Web:* www.moffittcorp.com

Mogas Industries 14330 E Hardy Rd .... Houston TX 77039 281-449-0291 789
Web: www.mogas.com

Mogg Inc 3650 Woodhead Dr. .... Northbrook IL 60062 847-498-0700 498-1258 591
Web: www.moogs3.com

MOGL Loyalty Services Inc
9645 Scranton Rd Ste 110 .... San Diego CA 92121 888-664-5669 387
TF: 888-664-5669 ■ *Web:* www.mogl.com

Mohair Council of America
233 W Twohig Rd .... San Angelo TX 76903 325-655-3161 48-2
TF: 800-583-3161 ■ *Web:* www.mohairusa.com

Mohan Group, The
2345 Stanfield Rd .... Mississauga ON L4Y3Y3 416-255-2500 5
Web: www.mohangroup.com

Mohave Community College
North Mohave PO Box 980 .... Colorado City AZ 86021 928-875-2799 875-2831 162
TF: 800-678-3992 ■ *Web:* www.mohave.edu

Mohave County Fair Association, The
2600 Fairgrounds Blvd .... Kingman AZ 86401 928-753-2636 642
Web: mcfafairgrounds.org

Mohave Educational Services Cooperative Inc
625 E Beale St .... Kingman AZ 86401 928-753-6945 434-3
TF: 800-742-2437 ■ *Web:* www.mesc.org

Mohave Mental Health Clinic Inc
1743 Sycamore Ave .... Kingman AZ 86409 928-757-8111 726
Web: www.mmhc-inc.org

Mohawk College 135 Fennell Ave W .... Hamilton ON L9C0E5 905-575-1212 162
Web: www.mohawkcollege.ca

Mohawk Council of Akwesasne
PO Box 579 .... Akwesasne QC H0M1A0 613-575-2250 685
Web: www.akwesasne.ca

Mohawk Dairy 260 Forest Ave. .... Amsterdam NY 12010 518-842-4942 297-4
Web: www.mohawkdairy.com

Mohawk Fine Papers Inc 465 Saratoga St .... Cohoes NY 12047 518-237-1740 237-7394 552-2
TF: 800-843-6455 ■ *Web:* www.mohawkconnects.com

Mohawk Industries Inc
Lees Carpets Div
160 S Industrial Blvd .... Calhoun GA 30701 706-629-7721 131
TF: 800-241-4494 ■ *Web:* www.mohawkind.com

Mohawk Machinery Inc
10601 Glendale Rd .... Cincinnati OH 45215 513-771-1952 771-5120 385
TF: 800-543-7696 ■ *Web:* www.mohawkmachinery.com

Mohawk Metal Co 30011 Leghorn Ln .... Eugene OR 97402 541-744-3838 744-8956 567
TF: 855-548-7467 ■ *Web:* www.mohawkmetal.com

Mohawk Trail State Forest
Cold River Rd .... Charlemont MA 01339 413-339-5504 565
Web: www.mass.gov

Mohawk Valley Chamber of Commerce
520 Seneca St Ste 102 .... Utica NY 13502 315-724-3151 724-3177 139
Web: www.greateruticachamber.org

Mohawk Valley Community College
1101 Sherman Dr .... Utica NY 13501 315-792-5400 792-5527 162
TF: 800-733-6822 ■ *Web:* www.mvcc.edu

Mohawk Valley Library System
858 Duanesburg Rd .... Schenectady NY 12306 518-355-2010 863-6922 434-3
Web: www.mvls.info

Mohawk Valley Psychiatric Ctr
1400 Noyes St .... Utica NY 13502 315-738-3800 738-4414 374-5
Web: omh.ny.gov

Mohegan Gaming & Entertainment (MGE)
1 Mohegan Sun Blvd .... Uncasville CT 06382 888-226-7711 322
TF: 888-777-7922 ■ *Web:* mohegangaming.com

Mohl Fur Company Inc
270 Broadway Rm 1212 .... New York NY 10007 212-736-7676 629-4832 155-7

Mohonk Mountain House
1000 Mtn Rest Rd .... New Paltz NY 12561 845-255-1000 669
TF: 855-883-3798 ■ *Web:* www.mohonk.com

Mohr & Associates Inc
1324 N Hearne Ave Ste 301 .... Shreveport LA 71107 318-686-7190 261
Web: www.mohrandassoc.com

Mohr Corp PO Box 1600 .... Brighton MI 48114 810-225-9494 225-4634 458
TF: 800-223-6647 ■ *Web:* www.mohrcorp.com

Mohr Davidow Ventures
777 Mariners Island Blvd Ste 550 .... San Mateo CA 94404 650-854-7236 792
Web: www.mdv.com

Mohr Power Solar Inc 1452 Pomona Rd .... Corona CA 92882 951-736-2000 610
TF: 800-637-6527 ■ *Web:* www.mohrpower.com

Moishe's 6333 W Third St .... Los Angeles CA 90036 323-936-4998 671
Web: www.moishes-la.com

Moishes Steakhouse
3961 St Laurent Blvd .... Montreal QC H2W1Y4 514-845-3509 671
Web: moishes.ca

Moja Inc
7000 Infantry Ridge Rd Ste 104 .... Manassas VA 20109 703-369-4339 225
Web: www.moja.net

Company	City	State	Zip	Phone	Fax	Class
Mojave A. Desert Resort 73721 Shadow Mtn Dr *TF:* 800-391-1104 ■ *Web:* resortmojave.com	Palm Desert	CA	92260	760-346-6121	674-9072	379
Mojave Copy & Printing Inc 12402 Industrial Blvd *Web:* www.mojavecopy.com	Victorville	CA	92395	760-241-7898		627
Mojave Electric Inc 3755 W Hacienda Ave *Web:* mojaveelectric.com	Las Vegas	NV	89118	702-798-2970		189-4
Mojave National Preserve 2701 Barstow Rd *Web:* www.nps.gov	Barstow	CA	92311	760-252-6100		564
Mojio Inc 1080 Howe St 9th Fl *TF:* 855-556-6546 ■ *Web:* www.moj.io	Vancouver	BC	V6Z2T1	855-556-6546		224
Mojix Inc 11075 Santa Monica Blvd Ste 350 *TF:* 877-886-6549 ■ *Web:* www.mojix.com	Los Angeles	CA	90025	310-479-9021		194
Mojo Interactive Corp 1060 Woodcock Rd Ste 128 *Web:* www.mojointeractive.com	Orlando	FL	32803	407-206-0700		177
Mojo Tech LLC 56 Exchange Ter Ste 210 *TF:* 855-665-6832 ■ *Web:* mojotech.com	Providence	RI	02903	855-665-6832		177
Mokan Dial Inc 112 S Broadway *TF:* 800-758-1715 ■ *Web:* mokandial.net	Louisburg	KS	66053	913-837-2219	837-5108	224
MOL (America) Inc 700 E Butterfield Rd Ste 150 *Web:* www.molpower.com	Lombard	IL	60148	630-812-3700		312
Mol Belting Systems Inc 2532 Waldorf Ct NW *Web:* www.molbelting.com	Grand Rapids	MI	49544	616-453-2484	453-2008	370
Molalla Communications Co-op 211 Robbins St PO Box 360 *TF:* 800-332-2344 ■ *Web:* www.molalla.com	Molalla	OR	97038	503-829-1100	829-7781	736
Mold Base Industries Inc 7501 Derry St **Fax Area Code:* 717 ■ *TF:* 800-241-6656 ■ *Web:* www.moldbase.com	Harrisburg	PA	17111	800-241-6656	564-2250*	757
Mold Craft Inc 200 Stillwater Rd PO Box 458 *Web:* mold-craft.com	Willernie	MN	55090	651-426-3216	426-9472	604
Mold in Graphic Systems 999 SR-89A *Web:* www.moldingraphics.com	Clarkdale	AZ	86324	928-634-8838		627
Mold-A-Matic Corp 147 River St **Fax Area Code:* 607 ■ *TF:* 866-886-2626 ■ *Web:* www.mamco-molding.com	Oneonta	NY	13820	866-886-2626	432-7861*	757
Moldamatic LLC 29 Noeland Ave *Web:* moldamatic.com	Penndel	PA	19047	215-757-4819		608
Molded Acoustical Products of Easton Inc 3 Danforth Dr *Web:* mapeaston.com	Easton	PA	18045	610-253-7135	253-1664	389
Molded Devices Inc 6918 Ed Perkic St *TF:* 800-211-9897 ■ *Web:* www.moldeddevices.com	Riverside	CA	92504	951-509-6918		608
Molded Fiber Glass Cos 2925 MFG Pl PO Box 675 *TF:* 800-860-0196 ■ *Web:* www.moldedfiberglass.com	Ashtabula	OH	44005	440-997-5851	994-5162	604
Molded Fiber Glass Tray Co 6175 US Hwy 6 *TF:* 800-458-6050 ■ *Web:* www.mfgtray.com	Linesville	PA	16424	814-683-4500	683-4504	199
Molded Plastic Industries Inc 2382 Jarco Dr *Web:* www.moldedplastic.com	Holt	MI	48842	517-694-7434	694-6620	470
Molded Products Inc 21920 E 96th St *Web:* www.moldedproductsinc.com	Broken Arrow	OK	74014	918-254-9061	254-9645	676
Molded Rubber & Plastic Corp 13161 W Glendale Ave *Web:* www.mrpcorp.com	Butler	WI	53007	262-781-7122	781-5353	677
Moldex 823 Bessemer St *Web:* www.moldexcorp.com	Meadville	PA	16335	814-337-3190		604
Moldex Metric Inc 10111 W Jefferson Blvd *TF:* 800-421-0668 ■ *Web:* www.moldex.com	Culver City	CA	90232	310-837-6500	837-9563	576
Molding Corporation of America 10349 Norris Ave *TF:* 800-423-2747 ■ *Web:* www.moldingcorp.com	Pacoima	CA	91331	818-890-7877	890-7885	604
Moldmaster Engineering Inc 187 Newell St *Web:* www.moldmaster.com	Pittsfield	MA	01201	413-443-4406	443-5713	604
Mold-Rite Plastics LLC 1 Plant St *TF:* 800-432-5277 ■ *Web:* www.mrpcap.com	Plattsburgh	NY	12901	518-561-1812		608
Moldtech Inc 1900 Commerce Pkwy *Web:* moldtechrubber.com	Lancaster	NY	14086	716-685-3344		677
Mole Hollow Candles Ltd 208 Charlton Rd Rt 20 PO Box 223 **Fax Area Code:* 888 ■ *TF:* 800-445-6653 ■ *Web:* molehollowcandles.com	Sturbridge	MA	01566	800-445-6653	998-9292*	327
Mole Lake Casino Lodge & Conference Ctr 3084 State Hwy 55 *TF:* 800-236-9466 ■ *Web:* www.molelakecasino.com	Crandon	WI	54520	715-478-3200		452
Mole Publishing Co 333 Gandhi Way *TF:* 800-328-8790 ■ *Web:* www.undergroundhousing.com	Bonners Ferry	ID	83805	208-267-7349		637-2
Molecular Devices Inc (MDI) 1311 Orleans Dr *TF:* 800-635-5577 ■ *Web:* www.moleculardevices.com	Sunnyvale	CA	94089	408-747-1700	747-3601	419
Molecular Imaging Services Inc 10 Whitaker Ct *TF:* 866-937-8855 ■ *Web:* www.mismedical.com	Bear	DE	19701	866-937-8855		415
Molecular Pathology Laboratory Network Inc 250 E Broadway *TF:* 800-932-2943 ■ *Web:* www.mplnet.com	Maryville	TN	37804	865-380-9746	380-9191	417
Moleculera Labs LLC 755 Research Pkwy Ste 410 *Web:* www.moleculeralabs.com	Oklahoma City	OK	73104	405-239-5250		415
Moler Barber School 4864 Central Ave NE *Web:* www.molerbarberschool.com	Hilltop	MN	55421	763-710-9093	951-3582	685
Moler Beauty Academies 5951 Boymel Dr *Web:* www.molerhollywood.com	Fairfield	OH	45014	513-874-5116	874-5102	214
Mole-Richardson Company Inc 937 N Sycamore Ave *Web:* www.mole.com	Hollywood	CA	90038	323-851-0111	851-5593	439
Molex Inc 2222 Wellington Ct *TF:* 800-786-6539 ■ *Web:* www.molex.com	Lisle	IL	60532	630-969-4550	969-1352	253
Molin Concrete Products Co 415 Lilac St *TF:* 800-336-6546 ■ *Web:* www.molin.com	Lino Lakes	MN	55014	651-786-7722	786-0229	183
Molina Healthcare Inc 200 Oceangate Ste 100 *NYSE: MOH* ■ *TF:* 888-562-5442 ■ *Web:* www.molinahealthcare.com	Long Beach	CA	90802	562-435-3666		391-3
Molina's Ranch Restaurant 4090 E Eigth Ave *Web:* www.molinasranchrestaurant.com	Hialeah	FL	33013	305-693-4440		671
Moline Dispatch Publishing Co 1720 Fifth Ave *TF:* 800-660-2472 ■ *Web:* qconline.com	Moline	IL	61265	309-757-5041	797-0317	637-8
Moline Forge Inc 4101 Fourth Ave *Web:* www.molineforge.com	Moline	IL	61265	309-762-5506		483
Moline Machinery LLC 114 S Central Ave *TF:* 800-767-5734 ■ *Web:* www.moline.com	Duluth	MN	55807	800-767-5734		362
Molle Toyota Inc 601 W 103rd St *TF:* 888-510-7705 ■ *Web:* www.molletoyota.com	Kansas City	MO	64114	816-942-5200		57
Mollenberg-Betz Inc 300 Scott St *Web:* mollenbergbetz.com	Buffalo	NY	14204	716-614-7473		189-10
Mollenhauer Group 919 W Glenoaks *Web:* mollenhauergroup.com	Glendale	CA	91202	213-624-2661		261
Moller International Inc 1222 Research Park Dr *Web:* www.moller.com	Davis	CA	95618	530-756-5086		20
Mollidgewock State Park 1437 Berlin Rd *Web:* www.nhstateparks.org	Errol	NH	03579	603-482-3373		565
Mollie's La Casita Mexican Restaurant 2006 Madison Ave *Web:* www.mollyslacasita.com	Memphis	TN	38104	901-726-1873		671
Molloy College 1000 Hempstead Ave *TF:* 888-466-5569 ■ *Web:* www.molloy.edu	Rockville Centre	NY	11571	516-678-5000		166
Mollusk Surf Shop LLC 4500 Irving St *Web:* mollusksurfshop.com	San Francisco	CA	94122	415-564-6300		711
Molly Brannigans 31 N Second St *Web:* www.mollybrannigans.com	Harrisburg	PA	17101	717-260-9242		671
Molly Brown House 1340 Pennsylvania St *Web:* mollybrown.org	Denver	CO	80203	303-832-4092		520
Molly Murphy 1541 Ocean Ave Ste 200 *Web:* www.jury-trialconsultant.com	Santa Monica	CA	90401	310-458-7720		196
Molly Pitcher Inn, The 88 Riverside Ave *Web:* www.themollypitcher.com	Red Bank	NJ	07701	732-203-5187		379
Molly Stark State Park 705 Rt 9 E *Web:* www.vtstateparks.com	Wilmington	VT	05363	802-464-5460		565
Molly's House 430 SE Osceola St *Web:* www.mollyshouse.org	Stuart	FL	34994	772-223-6659	223-9990	372
Molo Companies Inc 123 Southern Ave *TF:* 877-983-3761 ■ *Web:* www.molocompanies.com	Dubuque	IA	52003	563-557-7540		581
Molo Solutions 120 N Racine Ave *Web:* shipmolo.com	Chicago	IL	60607	847-306-3557		311
Molod, Spitz & Desantis PC 1430 Broadway *Web:* molodspitz.com	New York	NY	10018	212-869-3200		41
Molok North America Ltd 152 Harry Bye Blvd PO Box 693 *TF:* 877-558-5576 ■ *Web:* molokna.com	Mount Forest	ON	N0G2L0	519-323-9909		38
Molon Motor & Coil Corp 300 N Ridge Ave *TF:* 800-526-6867 ■ *Web:* www.molon.com	Arlington Heights	IL	60005	847-253-6000		518
Moloney Securities 13537 Barrett Pkwy Dr Ste 300 *TF:* 800-628-6002 ■ *Web:* www.moseco.com	Manchester	MO	63021	314-909-0600	909-0606	390
Molpus Co, The 502 Vly View Dr PO Box 59 *TF:* 800-535-5434 ■ *Web:* www.molpus.com	Philadelphia	MS	39350	601-656-3373	656-4947	817
Molson Coors Brewing Co 1225 17th St Ste 3200 *NYSE: TAP* ■ *TF:* 800-645-5376 ■ *Web:* www.molsoncoors.com	Denver	CO	80202	303-927-2337		102
Mom & Dad's 3421 Bannerman Rd Ste 104 *Web:* www.momanddadstally.com	Tallahassee	FL	32312	850-877-4518		671
Mom Innovations 8017 Fite Rd *Web:* www.mominnovations.com	Pearland	TX	77584	713-817-1998		157-1
Momar Inc 1830 Ellsworth Industrial Dr **Fax Area Code:* 800 ■ *TF:* 800-556-3967 ■ *Web:* www.momar.com	Atlanta	GA	30318	404-355-4580	849-5684*	145
Moment Design 13 Crosby St 6th Fl *Web:* www.momentdesign.com	New York	NY	10013	212-625-9744		180
Moment Magazine 4115 Wisconsin Ave NW Ste 10 *TF:* 800-777-1005 ■ *Web:* www.momentmag.com	Washington	DC	20016	202-363-6422		457-18
Momenta Pharmaceuticals Inc 675 W Kendall St *NASDAQ: MNTA* ■ *Web:* www.momentapharma.com	Cambridge	MA	02142	617-491-9700		85
Momentive 180 E Broad St *Web:* www.momentive.com	Columbus	OH	43215	614-225-2223		3
Momentum Bmw Ltd 10002 SW Fwy *TF:* 800-731-8114 ■ *Web:* www.momentumbmw.net	Houston	TX	77074	855-645-6452		516
Momentum Capital Partners 5535 Airport Fwy *Web:* mocappartners.com	Haltom City	TX	76117	817-920-7599		225
Momentum Efficient Engineering Solutions 12651 Briar Forest Ste 350 *Web:* momentumtx.com	Houston	TX	77007	281-741-1998	741-2068	186
Momentum For Mental Health 438 N White Rd *Web:* www.momentumformentalhealth.org	San Jose	CA	95127	408-254-6828		726
Momentum Healthware Inc 308-131 Provencher Blvd *Web:* www.momentumhealthware.com	Winnipeg	MB	R2H0G2	204-231-3836		179

Name / Address	City	State	ZIP	Phone	Fax	Class
Momentum Inc 1520 Fourth Ave Ste 300	Seattle	WA	98101	206-267-1900		226
Web: www.momentumbuilds.com						
Momentum Manufacturing Group LLC						
210 Pierce Rd PO Box 54	Saint Johnsbury	VT	05819	802-748-5007	748-0067	697
Web: www.mmg1982.com						
Momentum Systems Inc						
2332 Galiano St Ste 8	Coral Gables	FL	33134	856-727-0777		178-7
Web: www.momentumsystems.com.au						
Momentum Technologies Inc (MTI)						
4400 Easton Common Way Ste 125	Columbus	OH	43219	330-896-5900	896-9943	603
Momentum Technologies LLC						
PO Box 460813	Glendale	CO	80246	303-229-4841	705-2031*	387
**Fax Area Code:* 408 ■ *Web:* www.mtt.com						
Momentum Worldwide						
250 Hudson St 2nd Fl	New York	NY	10013	646-638-5400		4
Web: www.momentumww.com						
Momo Automotive Accessories Inc						
1161 N Knollwood Cir	Anaheim	CA	92801	949-380-7556	380-7256	54
TF: 800-749-6666 ■ *Web:* www.momo.com						
Momocho Mod Mex 1835 Fulton Rd	Cleveland	OH	44113	216-694-2122		671
Web: www.momocho.com						
Mon Ami Gabi 2300 N Lincoln Pk W	Chicago	IL	60614	773-348-8886		671
Web: www.monamigabi.com						
Mon Cheri Bridals LLC						
1018 Whitehead Rd Extn	Trenton	NJ	08638	609-530-1900		594
Web: moncheribridals.com						
Mon Health Medical Ctr						
1200 JD Anderson Dr	Morgantown	WV	26505	304-598-1200		374-3
Web: mongeneral.com						
Mona 216 S Brand Blvd	Glendale	CA	91204	818-696-2149		520
Web: www.neonmona.org						
Mona Electric Group Inc						
7915 Malcolm Rd	Clinton	MD	20735	301-868-8400		189-4
Web: www.getmona.com						
Mona Lisa Ristorante Italiano						
1697 Corydon Ave	Winnipeg	MB	R3N0K4	204-488-3687		671
Web: www.monalisarestaurant.ca						
Monacelli Press LLC, The						
6 W 18th St Ste 2C	New York	NY	10011	212-229-9925		637-2
Web: www.monacellipress.com						
Monache High School						
960 N Newcomb St	Porterville	CA	93257	559-782-7150	781-3377	685
Web: mhs.portervilleschools.org						
Monaco Coach Corp 1031 US 224 E	Decatur	IN	46733	877-466-6226		120
TF: 877-466-6226 ■ *Web:* www.monacocoach.com						
Monaco Enterprises Inc						
14820 E Sprague Ave PO Box 14129	Spokane	WA	99216	509-926-6277	924-4980	678
Web: www.monaco.com						
Monaco Government Tourist Office						
565 Fifth Ave 23rd Fl	New York	NY	10017	212-286-3330		775
TF: 800-753-9696 ■ *Web:* www.visitmonaco.com						
Monadnock Family Services (MFS) 64 Main St	Keene	NH	03431	603-357-4400		726
Web: www.mfs.org						
Monadnock Ledger, The						
20 Grove St	Peterborough	NH	03458	603-924-7172	924-3681	532-2
TF: 800-621-9152 ■ *Web:* www.ledgertranscript.com						
Monadnock Paper Mills Inc						
117 Antrim Rd	Bennington	NH	03442	603-588-3311	588-3158	557
TF: 800-221-2159 ■ *Web:* mpm.com						
Monadnock State Park 116 Poole Rd	Jaffrey	NH	03452	603-532-8862		565
Web: www.nhstateparks.org						
Monaghan Medical Corp						
5 Latour Ave Ste 1600	Plattsburgh	NY	12901	800-833-9653		477
TF: 800-833-9653 ■ *Web:* www.monaghanmed.com						
Monahans Sandhills State Park						
PO Box 1738	Monahans	TX	79756	432-943-2092		565
Web: tpwd.texas.gov						
Monarch Brands 5601 Paschall Ave	Philadelphia	PA	19143	800-333-7247		76
TF: 800-333-7247 ■ *Web:* www.monarchbrands.com						
Monarch Capital Management Inc						
127 W Berry St Ste 402	Fort Wayne	IN	46802	260-422-2765		401
TF: 800-893-3547 ■ *Web:* www.monarchcapitalmgmt.com						
Monarch Casino & Resort Inc						
3800 S Virginia St	Reno	NV	89502	775-335-4600	332-9171	669
NASDAQ: MCRI ■ *Web:* www.monarchcasino.com						
Monarch Cement Co						
449 1200 St PO Box 1000	Humboldt	KS	66748	620-473-2222	473-2447	135
OTC: MCEM ■ *Web:* www.monarchcement.com						
Monarch Construction Company Inc						
1654 Sherman Ave PO Box 12249	Cincinnati	OH	45212	513-351-6900	351-0979	186
Web: www.monarchconstruction.cc						
Monarch Dental 14400 N Dallas Pky	Dallas	TX	75254	214-222-9798		194
Web: www.monarchdental.com						
Monarch Hotel & Conference Ctr						
12566 SE 93rd Ave	Clackamas	OR	97015	503-652-1515	652-7509	379
TF: 800-492-8700 ■ *Web:* www.monarchhotel.cc						
Monarch Industries Inc 99 Main St	Warren	RI	02885	401-247-5200		309
Web: www.monarchinc.com						
Monarch Instrument Inc 15 Columbia Dr	Amherst	NH	03031	603-883-3390		201
Web: monarchinstrument.com						
Monarch Lathes						
615 N Oaks Ave PO Box 4609	Sidney	OH	45365	937-492-4111	492-7958	455
TF: 800-543-7666 ■ *Web:* www.monarchlathe.com						
Monarch Litho Inc 1501 Date St	Montebello	CA	90640	323-727-0300	720-1169	627
Web: monarchlitho.com						
Monarch LLC 7050 N 76th St	Milwaukee	WI	53223	414-353-8820	353-8832	480
Web: www.monarchcorp.com						
Monarch Machine & Tool Company Inc						
410 S Oregon Bay	Pasco	WA	99301	509-547-7753		480
Web: monarchmachineandtool.com						
Monarch Medical Imaging Equipment Inc						
101 Ellis St	Staten Island	NY	10307	718-317-0124		475
Web: www.monarchmedical.com						
Monarch Molding Inc PO Box 279	Council Grove	KS	66846	620-767-5115	767-6500	604
TF: 888-767-5116 ■ *Web:* www.monarchmoldinginc.com						
Monarch Mountain 123 North F St	Salida	CO	81201	719-530-5000		377
Web: www.skimonarch.com						
Monarch Plastics Inc 1205 65th St	Kenosha	WI	53143	262-652-4444	652-3561	601
Web: www.mcorptechnologies.com						
Monarch Recovery Management Inc						
3260 Tillman Dr Ste 75	Bensalem	PA	19020	215-281-7500	642-3864	160
TF: 800-220-0605 ■ *Web:* monarchrm.com						
Monarch Steel Company Inc						
4650 Johnston Pky	Cleveland	OH	44128	216-587-8000	587-8010	492
TF: 800-288-7835 ■ *Web:* www.monarchsteel.com						
Monarch Textile Rental Services Inc						
2810 Foundation Dr	South Bend	IN	46628	574-233-9433		258
TF: 800-589-9434 ■ *Web:* www.monarchlinen.com						
Monastery of Saint Gertrude						
465 Keuterville Rd	Cottonwood	ID	83522	208-962-3224	962-7212	673
Web: www.stgertrudes.org						
Monceaux Buller & Associates LLC						
610 Desoto St	Alexandria	LA	71301	318-442-8465		261
Web: monceauxbuller.com						
Moncla Marine LLC 2107 Carmel Dr	LaFayette	LA	70501	337-456-8799		536
Web: www.moncla.com						
Moncove Lake State Park						
695 Moncove Lake Access Rd	Gap Mills	WV	24941	304-772-3450		565
Web: wvstateparks.com						
Moncton Flight College						
1719 Champlain St	Dieppe	NB	E1A7P5	506-857-3080		23
TF: 800-760-4632 ■ *Web:* www.mfc.nb.ca						
Moncton Hospital, The						
135 MacBeath Ave	Moncton	NB	E1C6Z8	506-857-5111	857-5545	374-2
Web: horizonnb.ca						
Moncton Museum 20 Mountain Rd	Moncton	NB	E1C2J8	506-856-4383		522
TF: 800-363-4558 ■ *Web:* www.moncton.ca						
Monday Magazine 818 Broughton St	Victoria	BC	V8W1E4	250-382-6183		532-5
Web: www.mondaymag.com						
Monday Morning Inc						
726 Rte 202 S Ste 320-341	Bridgewater	NJ	08807	908-526-4884	668-4558	148
Web: www.mondayam.com						
Mondial International Corp						
101 Secor Ln PO Box 8369	Pelham Manor	NY	10803	914-738-7411	738-7521	360-3
Web: mondialgroup.com						
Mondorf & Fenwick PLLC						
523 Columbia Dr	Johnson City	NY	13790	607-797-4339		2
Web: mfcpas.com						
Mondre Energy Inc						
1800 John F Kennedy Blvd Ste 1504	Philadelphia	PA	19103	215-988-0577	988-0579	192
Web: www.mondreenergy.com						
Mondrian Hotel						
8440 Sunset Blvd	West Hollywood	CA	90069	323-650-8999	650-5215	379
TF: 800-525-8029 ■ *Web:* www.morganshotelgroup.com						
Monebo Technologies Inc						
1800 Barton Creek Blvd	Austin	TX	78735	512-732-0235	732-0285	475
Web: www.monebo.com						
Monell Chemical Senses Ctr						
3500 Market St	Philadelphia	PA	19104	267-519-4700	519-4805	668
Web: www.monell.org						
Moneris 3300 Bloor St W	Toronto	ON	M8X2X2	416-734-1000		215
Web: www.moneris.com						
Monett Motor Speedway 685 Chapell Dr	Monett	MO	65708	417-737-1806		515
Web: monettmotorspeedway.myracepass.com						
Monetta Financial Services Inc						
1776A S Naperville Rd Ste 100	Wheaton	IL	60189	630-462-9800		528
TF: 800-241-9772 ■ *Web:* monetta.com						
Monex Deposit Co 4910 Birch St	Newport Beach	CA	92660	800-997-7859		411
TF: 800-997-7859 ■ *Web:* www.monex.com						
Money Concepts International Inc						
11440 N Jog Rd	Palm Beach Gardens	FL	33418	561-472-2000		690
Web: www.moneyconcepts.com						
Money Federal Credit Union						
100 Madison St	Syracuse	NY	13202	315-671-4000	671-4030	219
Web: moneyfcu.org						
Money Mailer LLC						
12131 Western Ave	Garden Grove	CA	92841	714-889-3800		5
Web: www.moneymailer.com						
Money Market Directories Inc						
401 E Market St Ste Es	Charlottesville	VA	22902	434-977-1450	979-9962	195
Money Movers Inc PO Box 241	Sebastopol	CA	95473	707-829-5577		251
TF: 800-861-5029 ■ *Web:* moneymovers.com						
Money Tree Software Ltd						
2430 NW Professional Dr	Corvallis	OR	97330	541-754-3701	738-6522	177
TF: 877-421-9815 ■ *Web:* www.moneytree.com						
MoneyGram International Inc						
2828 N Harwood 1st Fl	Dallas	TX	75201	800-666-3947		69
NASDAQ: MGI ■ *TF:* 800-666-3947 ■ *Web:* www.secure.moneygram.com						
Moneytree Inc 6720 Ft Dent Way Ste 230	Seattle	WA	98188	206-246-3500	248-3400	69
TF: 877-613-6669 ■ *Web:* www.moneytreeinc.com						
Mongolia Embassy 2833 M St NW	Washington	DC	20007	202-333-7117	298-9227	257
Web: mongolianembassy.us						
Mongolian Grill						
1415 N Lacrosse St Ste 1	Rapid City	SD	57701	605-388-3187		671
Web: mongoliangrill.com						
Mongrel Empire Press (MEP)						
133 24th Ave NW Ste 103	Norman	OK	73069	405-459-0042	596-1484*	637-2
**Fax Area Code:* 866 ■ *Web:* www.mongrelempire.org						
Monheit Law PC 1368 Barrowdale Rd	Rydal	PA	19046	866-761-1385		41
TF: 866-761-1385 ■ *Web:* monheit.com						
Monic Fly Lines						
2400 Central Ave Unit D	Boulder	CO	80301	303-530-3050		208
Web: monic.com						
Monica + Andy 2052 N Halsted St	Chicago	IL	60614	312-600-8530		459
Web: www.monicaandandy.com						
Monical Pizza Corp 530 N Kinzie Ave	Bradley	IL	60915	815-937-1890	937-9828	670
Web: www.monicals.com						
Monico Alloys Inc (MA)						
3039 Ana St	Rancho Dominguez	CA	90221	310-928-0168	928-0179	686
Web: www.monicoalloys.com						
Monigle Associates Inc 150 Adams St	Denver	CO	80206	303-388-9358		5
Web: www.monigle.com						
Monin Inc 2100 Range Rd	Clearwater	FL	33765	855-352-8671		297-8
TF: 855-352-8671 ■ *Web:* www.monin.com						
Moniteau County 200 E Main St	California	MO	65018	573-796-2213		338
Web: www.moniteau.net						

				Phone	Fax	Class
Monitor Clipper Partners LLC 116 Huntington Ave 9th Fl *Web:* www.monitorclipper.com	Boston	MA	02116	617-638-1100		401
Monitor Dynamics Inc 12500 Network Dr Ste 303 *TF:* 866-435-7634 ■ *Web:* www.mdisecure.com	San Antonio	TX	78249	210-477-5400	477-5401	692
Monitor Elevator Products 125 Ricefield Ln *Web:* www.mcontrols.com	Hauppauge	NY	11788	631-543-4334		256
Monitor, The 1400 E Nolana Loop *TF:* 800-366-4343 ■ *Web:* www.themonitor.com	Mcallen	TX	78504	956-683-4000	683-4401	532-2
Monitor, The 16311 Goodes Bridge Rd *Web:* www.ameliamonitor.com	Amelia Court House	VA	23002	804-561-3655	561-2065	532-2
Monitoring Association, The 7918 Jones Branch Dr Ste 510 *Web:* tma.us	McLean	VA	22102	703-242-4670	242-4675	49-3
Monjunis 7601 Youree Dr *Web:* www.monjunis.com	Shreveport	LA	71101	318-227-0847		671
Monkee Business Fanzine 2770 S Broad St *Web:* www.monkees.net	Trenton	NJ	08610	609-888-4567		637-10
Monkey Jungle 14805 SW 216th St *Web:* www.monkeyjungle.com	Miami	FL	33170	305-235-1611		823
Monkon Sushi & Bar 394 University Ave *Web:* www.monkonsushi.com	Saint Paul	MN	55103	651-495-1678		671
Monmouth Battlefield State Park 347 Freehold-Englishtown Rd *Web:* www.njparksandforests.org	Manalapan	NJ	07726	732-462-9616		565
Monmouth College 700 E Broadway *TF:* 888-827-8268 ■ *Web:* www.ou.monmouthcollege.edu	Monmouth	IL	61462	309-457-2235	457-2141	166
Monmouth County 1 E Main St *Web:* www.co.monmouth.nj.us	Freehold	NJ	07728	732-431-7324	409-7566	338
Monmouth County Library (MCL) 125 Symmes Rd *Web:* www.monmouthcountylib.org	Manalapan	NJ	07726	732-431-7220		434-3
Monmouth Historic Inn & Gardens 1358 John A Quitman Blvd *TF:* 800-828-4531 ■ *Web:* www.monmouthhistoricinn.com	Natchez	MS	39120	601-442-5852	446-7762	379
Monmouth Park Racetrack 175 Oceanport Ave *Web:* www.monmouthpark.com	Oceanport	NJ	07757	732-222-5100	571-5226	642
Monmouth Real Estate Investment Corp (MREIC) 3499 Rt 9 N Ste 3C *NYSE: MNR* ■ *Web:* www.mreic.reit	Freehold	NJ	07728	732-577-9996		655
Monmouth Telecom 10 Drs James Parker Blvd Ste 110 *TF:* 877-666-6688 ■ *Web:* www.monmouth.com	Red Bank	NJ	07701	732-704-1000	704-1180	224
Monmouth University 400 Cedar Ave *TF:* 800-543-9671 ■ *Web:* www.monmouth.edu	West Long Branch	NJ	07764	732-571-3456	263-5166	166
Mono County PO Box 237 *Web:* monocounty.ca.gov	Bridgeport	CA	93517	760-932-5530	932-5531	338
Mono Lake Tufa State Reserve US Hwy 395 *Web:* www.parks.ca.gov	Lee Vining	CA	93541	760-647-6331		565
Monobind Inc 100 N Pt Dr *Web:* www.monobind.com	Lake Forest	CA	92630	949-951-2665	951-3539	231
Monocacy National Battlefield 5201 Urbana Pk *Web:* www.nps.gov	Frederick	MD	21704	301-662-3515		564
Monoflo International Inc 882 Baker Ln *Web:* miworldwide.com	Winchester	VA	22603	540-665-0010		596
Monogram Aerospace Fasteners 3423 S Garfield Ave *Web:* www.monogramaerospace.com	Los Angeles	CA	90040	323-722-4760	721-1851	278
Monogram Ctr 437 Amboy Ave *Web:* www.monogramcenter.com	Perth Amboy	NJ	08861	732-442-1800		258
Monograms 5301 S Federal Cir *TF:* 866-270-9841 ■ *Web:* monograms.com	Littleton	CO	80123	866-270-9841		760
Monolithic Power Systems Inc (MPS) 6409 Guadalupe Mines Rd *NASDAQ: MPWR* ■ *Web:* www.monolithicpower.com	San Jose	CA	95120	408-826-0600		696
Monon Telephone Company Inc 311 N Market St *TF:* 800-531-7121 ■ *Web:* www.monontelephone.com	Monon	IN	47959	219-253-6601	253-7500	224
Monona County 610 Iowa Ave *Web:* www.mononacounty.org	Onawa	IA	51040	712-423-2491		338
Monona Plumbing & Fire Protection Inc 3126 Watford Way *Web:* www.mononapfp.com	Madison	WI	53713	608-273-4556	273-8492	610
Monona Terrace Community & Convention Ctr 1 John Nolen Dr *Web:* www.mononaterrace.com	Madison	WI	53703	608-261-4000	261-4049	205
Monongahela Animal Hospital 321 Hazelkirk Rd *Web:* monongahelavet.com	Monongahela	PA	15063	724-258-8406		794
Monongahela Valley Hospital 1163 Country Club Rd *Web:* www.monvalleyhospital.com	Monongahela	PA	15063	724-258-1000	258-1830	374-3
Monongalia Arts Ctr (MAC) 107 High St PO Box 239 *Web:* www.monartscenter.com	Morgantown	WV	26507	304-292-3325	292-3326	50-2
Monongalia County 243 High St Courthouse Rm 123 *Web:* www.co.monongalia.wv.us	Morgantown	WV	26505	304-291-7230		338
MonoSol LLC 707 E 80th Pl Ste 301 *TF:* 800-237-9552 ■ *Web:* www.monosol.com	Merrillville	IN	46410	800-237-9552		601
Monroe Ambulance 1669 Lyell Ave *Web:* www.monroeambulance.com	Rochester	NY	01669	585-232-9000		30
Monroe Chamber of Commerce 212 Walnut St Ste 100 *TF:* 888-677-5200 ■ *Web:* www.monroe.org	Monroe	LA	71201	318-323-3461	322-7594	139
Monroe Chamber of Commerce & Industry 1505 Ninth St *Web:* monroechamber.org	Monroe	WI	53566	608-325-7648	328-2241	139
Monroe Clinic Hospital 515 22nd Ave *TF:* 800-338-0568 ■ *Web:* www.monroeclinic.org	Monroe	WI	53566	608-324-2000		374-3
Monroe College 2501 Jerome Ave *TF:* 800-556-6676 ■ *Web:* www.monroecollege.edu	Bronx	NY	10468	718-933-6700	364-3552	800
Monroe Community College 1000 E Henrietta Rd *Web:* www.monroecc.edu	Rochester	NY	14623	585-292-2000	292-3860	162
Monroe Community Hospital 435 E Henrietta Rd *Web:* www.monroehosp.org	Rochester	NY	14620	585-760-6500		374-7
Monroe County 124 W Commerce St *TF:* 800-457-5351 ■ *Web:* www.gomonroe.org	Aberdeen	MS	39730	662-369-6488	369-6489	338
Monroe County 10 Benton Ave E *Web:* www.monroecoia.us	Albia	IA	52531	641-932-2180		338
Monroe County 38 W Main St PO Box 189 *TF:* 800-282-5852 ■ *Web:* www.monroecoga.org	Forsyth	GA	31029	478-994-7000	994-7294	338
Monroe County 1100 Simonton St *Web:* www.monroecounty-fl.gov	Key West	FL	33040	305-294-4641		338
Monroe County 103 College St S Ste 1 *Web:* www.monroetn.com	Madisonville	TN	37354	423-442-2220	442-9542	338
Monroe County 106 E First St *TF:* 800-401-6402 ■ *Web:* co.monroe.mi.us	Monroe	MI	48161	734-240-7020	240-7045	338
Monroe County PO Box 8 *Web:* www.monroecountyal.com	Monroeville	AL	36461	251-743-4107	575-7934	338
Monroe County 300 N Main Rm 101 *Web:* www.monroecountycollector.com	Paris	MO	65275	660-327-4320	327-5063	338
Monroe County 202 S K St *Web:* www.co.monroe.wi.us	Sparta	WI	54656	608-269-8710	269-8958	338
Monroe County 216 Main St PO Box 350 *Web:* www.monroecountywv.net	Union	WV	24983	304-772-3096	772-4191	338
Monroe County 100 S Main St *Web:* monroecountyil.gov	Waterloo	IL	62298	618-939-8681		338
Monroe County 101 N Main St Rm 12 *Web:* www.monroecountyohio.net	Woodsfield	OH	43793	740-472-5181	472-2526	338
Monroe County Chamber of Commerce 1645 N Dixie Hwy Ste 20 *TF:* 855-386-1280 ■ *Web:* www.monroecountychamber.com	Monroe	MI	48162	734-384-3366	384-3367	139
Monroe County Chamber of Commerce 520 Cook St Ste A *Web:* www.monroecountychamber.org	Madisonville	TN	37354	423-442-4588	442-9016	139
Monroe County Community College 1555 S Raisinville Rd *TF:* 877-937-6222 ■ *Web:* www.monroeccc.edu	Monroe	MI	48161	734-242-7300	242-9711	162
Monroe County Electric Power Assn 50408 Greenbriar Rd PO Box 300 *TF:* 866-656-2962 ■ *Web:* www.monroecountyelectric.com	Amory	MS	38821	662-256-2962		245
Monroe County History Ctr 202 E Sixth St *Web:* monroehistory.org	Bloomington	IN	47408	812-332-2517	355-5593	520
Monroe County Intermediate School District 1101 S Raisinville Rd *Web:* www.monroeisd.us	Monroe	MI	48161	734-242-5799		685
Monroe County Library System 3700 S Custer Rd *TF:* 800-462-2050 ■ *Web:* www.monroe.lib.mi.us	Monroe	MI	48161	734-241-5277	241-4722	434-3
Monroe County Public Library 303 E Kirkwood Ave *Web:* mcpl.info	Bloomington	IN	47408	812-349-3050	349-3051	434-3
Monroe County Public Library System 700 Fleming St *Web:* www.keyslibraries.org	Key West	FL	33040	305-292-3595	295-3626	434-3
Monroe County Title Inc 139 N Court St PO Box 458 *Web:* monroe-title.com	Sparta	WI	54656	608-269-6781	269-6455	653
Monroe County Tourist Development Council 1201 White St Ste 102 *TF:* 800-242-5229 ■ *Web:* fla-keys.com	Key West	FL	33040	305-296-1552		206
Monroe County Water Authority 475 Norris Dr PO Box 10999 *TF:* 866-426-6292 ■ *Web:* www.mcwa.com	Rochester	NY	14610	585-442-2000	442-0220	787
Monroe Energy LLC 4101 Post Rd *Web:* www.monroe-energy.com	Trainer	PA	19061	610-364-8000		579
Monroe Environmental Corp 810 W Front St *TF:* 800-992-7707 ■ *Web:* www.monroeenvironmental.com	Monroe	MI	48161	734-242-7654	242-5275	386
Monroe Evening News 20 W First St *Web:* www.monroenews.com	Monroe	MI	48161	734-242-1100		532-2
Monroe Financial Partners Inc 100 N Riverside Plz Ste 1620 *TF:* 800-766-5560 ■ *Web:* www.monroefp.com	Chicago	IL	60606	312-327-2530		194
Monroe Fluid Technology Inc 36 Draffin Rd *TF:* 800-828-6351 ■ *Web:* www.monroefluid.com	Hilton	NY	14468	585-392-3434	392-2691	145
Monroe Hardware Co 101 N Sutherland Ave *TF:* 800-222-1974 ■ *Web:* www.monroehardware.com	Monroe	NC	28110	704-289-3121	289-2838	351
Monroe Home Care Shoppe Inc 474 N Telegraph *Web:* www.sobakshomemedical.com	Monroe	MI	48162	734-241-7875	241-7469	264-4
Monroe Lake 4850 S State Rd 446 *Web:* www.in.gov	Bloomington	IN	47401	812-837-9546		565
Monroe Oil Co 519 E Franklin St *TF:* 800-452-2717 ■ *Web:* www.monroeoilco.com	Monroe	NC	28112	704-289-5438		324
Monroe Road Animal Hospital PA 3736 Monroe Rd *Web:* mrahonline.com	Charlotte	NC	28205	704-333-3336		794
Monroe School Transportation 970 Emerson St *Web:* monroeschooltrans.com	Rochester	NY	14606	585-458-3230	458-9159	109
Monroe Shine & Company Inc 222 E Market St *Web:* www.monroeshine.com	New Albany	IN	47150	812-945-2311		2
Monroe Table Co 316 N Walnut St *TF:* 844-822-5370 ■ *Web:* www.monroetable.com	Salamanca	NY	14779	716-945-7700	945-7707	319-3
Monroe Township Free Public Library 713 Marsha Ave *Web:* www.monroetpl.org	Williamstown	NJ	08094	856-629-1212		434-3

Name / Address	City	State	Zip	Phone	Fax	Class
Monroe Tractor & Implement Company Inc 1001 Lehigh Stn Rd *TF:* 866-683-5338 ■ *Web:* www.monroetractor.com	Henrietta	NY	14467	585-334-3867	334-0001	358
Monroe Truck Equipment Inc 1051 W Seventh St *TF:* 800-356-8134 ■ *Web:* www.monroetruck.com	Monroe	WI	53566	608-328-8127	328-4278	516
Monroeville Area Chamber of Commerce 4268 Northern Pk *TF:* 800-527-8941 ■ *Web:* www.monroevillechamber.com	Monroeville	PA	15146	412-856-0622	856-1030	139
Monroeville Mall 200 Mall Blvd *Web:* www.monroevillemall.com	Monroeville	PA	15146	412-243-8511		460
Monroe-West Monroe Convention & Visitors Bureau 601 Constitution Dr PO Box 1436 *TF:* 800-843-1872 ■ *Web:* www.monroe-westmonroe.org	West Monroe	LA	71292	318-387-5691	324-1752	206
Monrovia Chamber of Commerce 620 S Myrtle Ave *TF:* 800-755-1515 ■ *Web:* www.monroviacc.com	Monrovia	CA	91016	626-358-1159	357-6036	139
Monrovia Public Library 321 S Myrtle Ave *Web:* www.cityofmonrovia.org	Monrovia	CA	91016	626-256-8274	256-8255	434-3
Monrovia Unified School District 325 E Huntington Dr *Web:* www.monroviaschools.net	Monrovia	CA	91016	626-471-2000		685
Monsieur Touton Selections Ltd 129 W 27th St 9th Fl *TF:* 800-366-6987 ■ *Web:* www.mtouton.com	New York	NY	10001	212-255-0674	255-2628	80-3
Monson Lake State Park 1690 15th St Ne *Web:* www.dnr.state.mn.us	Sunburg	MN	56289	320-366-3797		565
Monsoon Capital LLC 4720 Montgomery Ln Ste 410 *Web:* www.monsooncapital.com	Bethesda	MD	20814	301-222-8000		194
Monsoon Solutions Inc 2405 140th Ave NE Ste A-115 *Web:* msoon.com	Bellevue	WA	98005	425-378-8081		261
Monster Cable Products Inc 455 Valley Dr *TF:* 877-800-8989 ■ *Web:* www.monsterstore.com	Brisbane	CA	94005	415-840-2000		52
Monster Energy Corp 550 Monica Cir Ste 201 *TF:* 800-426-7367 ■ *Web:* monsterbevcorp.com	Corona	CA	92880	800-426-7367		805
Monster Lead Group LLC 10461 Mill Run Cir Ste 1050 *TF:* 855-717-0952 ■ *Web:* monsterleadgroup.com	Owings Mills	MD	21117	410-504-6584		653
MonsterMedia LLC 949 S Ave B *Web:* www.monstermediayuma.com	Yuma	AZ	85364	928-782-4321		645-141
Monstermoving.com 19232 Beach Blvd *TF:* 800-380-1756 ■ *Web:* monstermovingandstorage.com	Huntington Beach	CA	92648	714-380-7721		519
Mont Clare-Elmwood Park Chamber of Commerce 11 Conti Pkwy *Web:* www.grandchamber.org	Elmwood Park	IL	60707	708-456-8000	456-8680	139
Mont Eagle Mills Inc 804 W Main St *Web:* www.monteaglemills.com	Oblong	IL	62449	618-592-4211		275
Montachusett Regional Vocational Technical School 1050 Westminster St *TF:* 800-853-6689 ■ *Web:* www.montytech.net	Fitchburg	MA	01420	978-345-9200	348-1176	800
Montage Inc 3636 16th St *Web:* www.montageinc.com	Washington	DC	20010	202-332-0186	232-2153	186
Montage Resort & Spa 30801 S Coast Hwy *TF:* 866-271-6953 ■ *Web:* www.montagehotels.com	Laguna Beach	CA	92651	949-715-6000		669
Montagna Klein Camden LLP 425 Monticello Ave *Web:* montagnalaw.com	Norfolk	VA	23510	757-622-8100		41
Montague County PO Box 77 *Web:* www.co.montague.tx.us	Montague	TX	76251	940-894-2461	894-3110	338
Montagulaw PC 1120 Avenue of the Americas 4th Fl *Web:* montagulaw.com	New York	NY	10036	212-996-1287		41
Montalbano Group, The 15400 Knoll Trail Dr Ste 102 *Web:* www.cardealeradagency.com	Dallas	TX	75248	214-484-3705	484-6159	4
Montalbano Lumber Company Inc 1309 Houston Ave *Web:* www.montalbanolumber.com	Houston	TX	77007	713-228-9011	228-8222	364
Montalvan's Sales Inc 2225 S Castle Harbour Pl *Web:* montalvans.com	Ontario	CA	91761	909-930-5670		345
Montana						
Arts Council PO Box 202201 *TF:* 800-282-3092 ■ *Web:* www.art.mt.gov	Helena	MT	59620	406-444-6430	444-6548	339-27
Attorney General 215 N Sanders St *Web:* www.dojmt.gov	Helena	MT	59601	406-444-2026	444-3549	339-27
Banking & Financial Institutions Div 301 S Park Ste 316 PO Box 200546 *TF:* 800-914-8423 ■ *Web:* banking.mt.gov	Helena	MT	59620	406-841-2920	841-2930	339-27
Chief Plenty Coups State Park 1 Edgar/Pryor Rd *Web:* www.fwp.mt.gov	Pryor	MT	59066	406-252-1289		565
Child & Family Services Div PO Box 8005 *TF:* 866-820-5437 ■ *Web:* dphhs.mt.gov	Helena	MT	59604	406-841-2400	841-2487	339-27
Commerce Dept 301 S Park Ave PO Box 200501 *TF:* 800-761-6264 ■ *Web:* www.commerce.mt.gov	Helena	MT	59601	406-841-2700	841-2701	339-27
Commissioner of Political Practices 1205 Eigth Ave PO Box 202401 *Web:* www.politicalpractices.mt.gov	Helena	MT	59620	406-444-2942	444-1643	265
Community Development Div 301 S Park Ave PO Box 200523 *Web:* www.comdev.mt.gov	Helena	MT	59620	406-841-2770	841-2771	339-27
Corrections Dept 5 S Last Chance Gulch PO Box 201301 *Web:* www.cor.mt.gov	Helena	MT	59620	406-444-3930	444-4920	339-27
Court Administration 301 South Pk PO Box 203005 *TF:* 800-624-3270 ■ *Web:* montanacourts.org	Helena	MT	59620	406-841-2950	444-5705	339-27
Department of Labor & Industry - Business Standard 301 S Pk PO Box 200513 *Web:* www.bsd.dli.mt.gov	Helena	MT	59620	406-841-2300		339-27
Environmental Quality Dept 1520 E Sixth Ave PO Box 200901 *Web:* deq.mt.gov	Helena	MT	59620	406-444-2544	444-4386	339-27
Forensic Science Div 2679 Palmer St *Web:* dojmt.gov	Missoula	MT	59808	406-728-4970	549-1067	339-27
Healthcare Licensing Bureau 301 S Park Ave PO Box 200513 *Web:* bsd.dli.mt.gov	Helena	MT	59620	406-841-2303		339-27
Highway Patrol Div 2550 Prospect Ave *Web:* dojmt.gov	Helena	MT	59620	406-444-3780	444-4169	339-27
Housing Div PO Box 200528 *Web:* www.housing.mt.gov	Helena	MT	59620	406-841-2840	841-2841	339-27
Information Technology Services Div 125 N Roberts St PO Box 200113 *TF:* 800-628-4917 ■ *Web:* sitsd.mt.gov	Helena	MT	59620	406-444-2511	444-2701	339-27
Insurance Div 1315 E Lockey *Web:* uid.dli.mt.gov	Helena	MT	59604	406-444-3783	444-0629	339-27
Labor & Industry Dept PO Box 1728 *Web:* www.dli.mt.gov	Helena	MT	59624	406-444-2840	444-1394	339-27
Legislative Services 1301 E Sixth Ave PO Box 201706 *Web:* leg.mt.gov	Helena	MT	59620	406-444-3064	444-3036	433
Montana Fish Wildlife & Parks 1420 E 6thAve c/o Helena Area Resource Ofc PO Box 200701 *Web:* www.stateparks.mt.gov	Helena	MT	59620	406-444-3750		339-27
Motor Vehicle Div 302 N Roberts St PO Box 201430 *Web:* dojmt.gov	Helena	MT	59620	406-444-3933		339-27
Natural Resources & Conservation Dept 1539 Eleventh Ave *Web:* www.dnrc.mt.gov	Helena	MT	59601	406-444-2074	444-2684	339-27
Public Education Board 40 N Last Chance Gulch PO Box 200601 *Web:* bpe.mt.gov	Helena	MT	59620	406-444-6576	444-0847	339-27
Public Health & Human Services Dept 111 N Sanders St Rm 6 *Web:* mt.gov	Helena	MT	59604	406-444-5622	444-1970	339-27
Public Service Commission 1701 Prospect Ave PO Box 202601 *TF:* 800-646-6150 ■ *Web:* www.psc.mt.gov	Helena	MT	59620	406-444-6199	444-7618	339-27
Revenue Dept 125 N Roberts St PO Box 5805 *TF:* 866-859-2254 ■ *Web:* mtrevenue.gov	Helena	MT	59604	406-444-6900	444-3696	339-27
Secretary of State 1301 E 6th Ave PO Box 202801 *Web:* www.sos.mt.gov	Helena	MT	59601	406-444-2034	444-3976	339-27
State Auditor Office 840 Helena Ave *TF:* 800-332-6148 ■ *Web:* csimt.gov	Helena	MT	59601	406-444-2040	444-3497	339-27
State Government Information PO Box 200113 *Web:* www.mt.gov	Helena	MT	59620	406-444-2000	444-2701	339-27
State Legislature PO Box 201706 *Web:* www.leg.mt.gov	Helena	MT	59620	406-444-3060	444-3036	339-27
Supreme Court Justice Bldg 215 N Sanders St Rm 323 *Web:* courts.mt.gov	Helena	MT	59620	406-444-3858	444-5705	339-27
Transportation Dept 2701 Prospect Ave PO Box 201001 *Web:* www.mdt.mt.gov	Helena	MT	59620	406-444-6200		339-27
Veterans Home 400 Veterans Dr *TF:* 888-270-7532 ■ *Web:* dphhs.mt.gov	Columbia Falls	MT	59912	406-892-3256	892-0256	793
Vital Records Bureau 111 N Sanders St Rm 6 PO Box 4210 *Web:* dphhs.mt.gov	Helena	MT	59604	406-444-4228		339-27
Weights & Measures Program PO Box 200516 *Web:* www.bsd.dli.mt.gov	Helena	MT	59620	406-443-8065	443-8163	339-27
Worker's Compensation Ct 1625 11th Ave PO Box 537 *Web:* www.wcc.dli.mt.gov	Helena	MT	59624	406-444-7794	444-7798	339-27
Montana Academy of Salons 501 2nd St S *Web:* www.montanabeautyschool.com	Great Falls	MT	59405	406-205-3363		167-3
Montana Association of Realtors 1 S Montana Ave Ste M1 *TF:* 800-477-1864 ■ *Web:* www.montanarealtors.org	Helena	MT	59601	406-443-4032	443-4220	656
Montana Brewing Co 113 N 28th St *Web:* montanabrewingcompany.com	Billings	MT	59101	406-252-9200		671
Montana Bureau of Mines and Geology (MBMG) 101 Grand Ave *Web:* www.mbmg.mtech.edu	Billings	MT	59101	406-496-4167	496-4451	637-2
Montana Chamber of Commerce 900 Gibbon St PO Box 1730 *TF:* 888-442-6668 ■ *Web:* www.montanachamber.com	Helena	MT	59624	406-442-2405	442-2409	140
Montana Club 24 W Sixth Ave *Web:* montanaclub.coop	Helena	MT	59601	406-442-5980		671
Montana Coffee Traders Inc 5810 Hwy 93 S *TF:* 800-345-5282 ■ *Web:* www.coffeetraders.com	Whitefish	MT	59937	406-862-7650	862-7680	159
Montana Construction Corporation Inc 80 Contant Ave *Web:* www.montanaconstructioninc.com	Lodi	NJ	07644	973-478-5200	478-7604	188-10
Montana Credit Unions League 101 N Rodney St *Web:* montanacreditunions.coop	Helena	MT	59601	406-442-9081		219
Montana Democratic Party PO Box 802 *Web:* www.montanademocrats.org	Helena	MT	59624	406-442-9520		616-1
Montana Dental Assn 17 1/2 S Last Chance Gulch PO Box 1154 *TF:* 800-257-4988 ■ *Web:* www.mtdental.com	Helena	MT	59624	406-443-2061	443-1546	227
Montana Department of Labor & Industry Workforce Services Division 1315 E Lockey PO Box 1728 *Web:* wsd.dli.mt.gov	Helena	MT	59604	406-444-2648	444-3037	259

Name / Address	City	State	Zip	Phone	Fax	Class
Montana Exploration Corp 555 4th Ave SW Ste 810 *Web:* www.montanaexplorationcorp.com	Calgary	AB	T2P3E7	403-265-9091		536
Montana Historical Society 225 N Roberts St *Web:* www.helenamt.com	Helena	MT	59601	406-444-2694		339-27
Montana Idaho Log & Timber 1069 US Hwy 93 N *Web:* www.mtidlog.com	Victor	MT	59875	406-961-3092		106
Montana Leather Company Inc 2015 1st Ave N *TF:* 800-527-0227 ■ *Web:* www.montanaleather.com	Billings	MT	59103	406-245-1660	245-4109	76
Montana Livestock Ag Credit Inc 420 N California *TF:* 800-332-3405 ■ *Web:* ag-credit.com	Helena	MT	59601	406-442-3740		217
Montana Lottery 2525 N Montana Ave *Web:* www.montanalottery.com	Helena	MT	59601	406-444-5825	444-5830	452
Montana Medical Assn 2021 11th Ave Ste 1 *TF:* 877-443-4000 ■ *Web:* www.mmaoffice.org	Helena	MT	59601	406-443-4000	443-4042	474
Montana Nurses Assn (MNA) 20 Old Montana State Hwy *Web:* www.mtnurses.org	Montana City	MT	59634	406-442-6710	442-1841	533
Montana Propane Inc 3440 Centennial Dr *Web:* montanapropane.com	Helena	MT	59601	406-449-6177		316
Montana Public Radio University of Montana 32 Campus Dr *TF:* 800-325-1565 ■ *Web:* www.mtpr.org	Missoula	MT	59812	406-243-4931	243-3299	632
Montana Rail Link Inc 101 International Way *TF:* 800-338-4750 ■ *Web:* www.montanarail.com	Missoula	MT	59808	406-523-1500	523-1493	648
Montana Republican Party PO Box 935 *Web:* www.mtgop.org	Helena	MT	59624	406-442-6469		616-2
Montana River Outfitters 923 10th Ave N *Web:* www.montanariveroutfitters.com	Great Falls	MT	59401	406-761-1677		760
Montana Standard 25 W Granite St *TF:* 800-877-1074 ■ *Web:* www.mtstandard.com	Butte	MT	59701	406-496-5500	496-5551	532-2
Montana State Fair 400 Third St NW *Web:* www.goexpopark.com	Great Falls	MT	59404	406-727-8900	452-8955	642
Montana State Library (MSL) 1515 E 6th Ave *Web:* home.msl.mt.gov	Helena	MT	59620	406-444-3115		434-5
Montana State Parks 3201 Spurgin Rd FWP Reg 2 Ofc *Web:* stateparks.mt.gov	Missoula	MT	59804	406-444-3818		565
Montana State Prison 400 Conley Lake Rd *TF:* 888-739-9122 ■ *Web:* www.cor.mt.gov	Deer Lodge	MT	59722	406-846-1320		213
Montana State University						
Billings 1500 University Dr *TF:* 800-565-6782 ■ *Web:* www.msubillings.edu	Billings	MT	59101	406-657-2011	657-2302	166
Bozeman 1401 W Lincoln St *TF:* 888-678-2287 ■ *Web:* www.montana.edu	Bozeman	MT	59717	406-994-3621	994-7360	166
Library Centennial Mall PO Box 173320 *Web:* www.lib.montana.edu	Bozeman	MT	59717	406-994-3171	994-2851	434-6
Montana Sulphur & Chemical Co 627 Exxonmobil Rd *Web:* montanasulphur.com	Billings	MT	59101	406-252-9324		145
Montana Tech of the University of Montana 1300 W Park St *TF:* 800-445-8324 ■ *Web:* mtech.edu	Butte	MT	59701	406-496-4101	496-4710	166
Montana Telecommunications Assn (MTA) 208 N Montana Ave Ste 105 *Web:* www.telecomassn.org	Helena	MT	59601	406-442-4316	442-8243	139
Montana Tire Distr Inc 421 N 13th St *Web:* www.montanatiredistributors.net	Billings	MT	59101	406-259-9877	259-9738	755
Montana University System 560 N Park Ave 4th Fl *Web:* www.mus.edu	Helena	MT	59601	406-449-9157		786
Montana Veterinary Medical Assn PO Box 6322 *Web:* www.mtvma.org	Helena	MT	59604	406-447-4259		795
Montana Wilderness Assn (MWA) 80 S Warren St *Web:* wildmontana.org	Helena	MT	59601	406-443-7350	443-0750	48-13
Montana Women's Prison 701 S 27th St *Web:* mt.gov	Billings	MT	59101	406-247-5100	247-5161	213
Montana World Trade Ctr Gallagher Business Bldg Ste 257 *Web:* www.mwtc.org	Missoula	MT	59812	406-243-6982		822
Montana-Dakota Utilities Co (MDU) 400 N Fourth St *TF:* 800-638-3278 ■ *Web:* www.montana-dakota.com	Bismarck	ND	58501	701-222-7900		787
Montara State Beach c/o Santa Cruz District Ofc 303 Big Trees Park Rd *Web:* www.parks.ca.gov	Felton	CA	95018	650-726-8819		565
Montauk Point State Park 2000 Montauk Hwy *Web:* parks.ny.gov	Montauk	NY	11954	631-668-3781		565
Montauk State Park 345 County Rd 6670 *Web:* mostateparks.com	Salem	MO	65560	573-548-2201		565
MontaVista Software Inc 2929 Patrick Henry Dr *Web:* www.mvista.com	Santa Clara	CA	95054	408-572-8000	572-8005	174
Montcalm Community College 2800 College Dr *Web:* www.montcalm.edu	Sidney	MI	48885	989-328-2111	328-2950	162
Montcalm County PO Box 368 *Web:* montcalm.org	Stanton	MI	48888	989-831-7339		338
Montclair Art Museum 3 S Mtn Ave *Web:* montclairartmuseum.org	Montclair	NJ	07042	973-746-5555	746-0536	520
Montclair Chamber of Commerce 5000 San Bernadino St *Web:* www.montclairchamber.com	Montclair	CA	91763	909-624-4569	625-2009	139
Montclair Kimberley Academy, The 201 Valley Rd *Web:* www.mka.org	Montclair	NJ	07042	973-746-9800		164
Montclair Plaza 5060 Montclair Plaza Ln *Web:* montclairplace.com	Montclair	CA	91763	909-626-2442		460
Montclair Public Library 50 S Fullerton Ave *Web:* www.montclairlibrary.org	Montclair	NJ	07042	973-744-0500		435
Montclair State University 1 Normal Ave *TF:* 800-331-9205 ■ *Web:* www.montclair.edu	Montclair	NJ	07043	973-655-4000	655-7700	166
Montclair Stationery Inc 612 Valley Rd *Web:* montclairstationery.com	Upper Montclair	NJ	07043	973-509-8345		534
Monte Carlo Inn-Airport Suites 7035 Edwards Blvd *TF:* 800-363-6400 ■ *Web:* www.montecarloinns.com	Mississauga	ON	L5T2H8	905-564-8500	564-8400	379
Monte L. Bean Life Science Museum 645 E 1430 N *Web:* mlbean.byu.edu	Provo	UT	84602	801-422-5050	422-0093	520
Monte Package Company Inc 3752 Riverside Rd *TF:* 800-653-2807 ■ *Web:* shop.montepkg.com	Riverside	MI	49084	269-849-1722	849-0185	200
Monte R. Lee & Co 525 Central Park Dr Ste 300 *Web:* www.mrleng.com	Oklahoma City	OK	73105	405-842-2405	848-8018	261
Monte Sano State Park 5105 Nolen Ave *Web:* www.alapark.com	Huntsville	AL	35801	256-534-3757	539-7069	565
Monte Vista Christian School 2 School Way *Web:* www.mvcs.org	Watsonville	CA	95076	831-722-8178	722-6003	622
Monte Vista High School Keynoters 3131 Stone Valley Blvd *Web:* www.mvkeynoters.org	Danville	CA	94526	925-552-5530	743-1744	685
Montebello Brands Inc 1919 Willow Spring Ave	Baltimore	MD	21222	410-282-8800	282-8809	80-1
Montebello Chamber of Commerce 109 N 19th St *Web:* www.montebellochamber.org	Montebello	CA	90640	323-721-1153	721-7946	139
Montebello Container Corp 13220 Molette St *Web:* www.montcc.com	Santa Fe Springs	CA	90670	562-404-6221		100
Montebello Unified School District (MUSD) 123 S Montebello Blvd *Web:* www.montebello.k12.ca.us	Montebello	CA	90640	323-887-7900		685
Montecito Bank & Trust 1000 State St *Web:* montecito.bank	Santa Barbara	CA	93101	805-963-7511		70
Montecito Inn Inc 1295 Coast Village Rd *TF:* 800-843-2017 ■ *Web:* www.montecitoinn.com	Santa Barbara	CA	93108	805-969-7854		707
Montecito Water District (MWD) 583 San Ysidro Rd *Web:* www.montecitowater.com	Montecito	CA	93108	805-969-2271		192
Montefiore Medical Ctr 111 E 210th St *Web:* www.montefiore.org	Bronx	NY	10467	718-920-4321		374-3
MonteLago Village Resort 30 Strada di Villaggio *Web:* thevillagelakelasvegas.com	Henderson	NV	89011	702-564-4700		655
Montello Heel Manufacturing Inc 13 Emerson Ave *Web:* www.montelloheel.com	Brockton	MA	02301	508-586-0603		301
Montello Inc 6106 E 32nd Pl Ste 100 **Fax Area Code:* 918 ■ *TF:* 800-331-4628 ■ *Web:* www.montelloinc.com	Tulsa	OK	74135	800-331-4628	665-1480*	145
Montemayor Press PO Box 546 *Web:* www.montemayorpress.com	Montpelier	VT	05601	802-552-0750		637-2
Montereau Inc 6800 S Granite Ave *TF:* 888-795-1122 ■ *Web:* www.montereau.net	Tulsa	OK	74136	918-495-1500		672
Monterey Adult School 1295 La Salle Ave *Web:* www.mas.mpusd.net	Seaside	CA	93955	831-392-3565		685
Monterey Bay Aquarium 886 Cannery Row *Web:* www.montereybayaquarium.org	Monterey	CA	93940	831-648-4800		40
Monterey Bay Inn 242 Cannery Row *TF:* 800-424-6242 ■ *Web:* www.montereybayinn.com	Monterey	CA	93940	831-373-6242	655-8174	379
Monterey Bay Nursery Inc 748 San Miguel Canyon Rd *Web:* www.montereybaynsy.com	Watsonville	CA	95077	831-724-6361	724-8903	293
Monterey Boats 1579 SW 18th St *Web:* www.montereyboats.com	Williston	FL	32696	352-528-2628	529-2628	90
Monterey Conference Ctr 1 Portola Plz *TF:* 800-742-8091 ■ *Web:* montereyconferencecenter.com	Monterey	CA	93940	831-646-3388	646-3777	205
Monterey County 168 W Alisal St *TF:* 800-994-9662 ■ *Web:* www.co.monterey.ca.us	Salinas	CA	93901	831-755-5115	757-5792	338
Monterey County Convention & Visitors Bureau PO Box 1770 **Fax Area Code:* 831 ■ *TF:* 888-221-1010 ■ *Web:* www.seemonterey.com	Monterey	CA	93942	888-221-1010	648-5373*	206
Monterey County Herald 2200 Garden Rd *TF:* 800-688-1808 ■ *Web:* www.montereyherald.com	Monterey	CA	93940	831-372-3311	372-8401	532-2
Monterey County Weekly 668 Williams Ave *Web:* www.montereycountyweekly.com	Seaside	CA	93955	831-394-5656	394-2909	532-5
Monterey Financial Services LLC 4095 Avenida De La Plata *TF:* 800-456-2225 ■ *Web:* www.montereyfinancial.com	Oceanside	CA	92056	760-639-3500	639-3501	393
Monterey Hotel 406 Alvarado St *Web:* www.montereyhotel.com	Monterey	CA	93940	831-375-3184	373-2899	379
Monterey Jet Center LLC 300 Skypark Dr *Web:* www.montereyjetcenter.com	Monterey	CA	93940	831-373-0100		63
Monterey Maritime & History Museum 5 Custom House Plz *Web:* montereyhistory.org	Monterey	CA	93940	831-372-2608		520

	Phone	Fax	Class
Monterey Mechanical Co 8275 San Leandro St .... Oakland CA 94621 *Web:* www.montmech.com	510-632-3173	632-0732	189-10
Monterey Mills Inc 1725 E Delavan Dr .... Janesville WI 53546 *TF:* 800-255-9665 ■ *Web:* www.montereymills.com	608-754-2866		745-4
Monterey Museum of Art 559 Pacific St .... Monterey CA 93940 *Web:* www.montereyart.org	831-372-5477	372-5680	520
Monterey Mushrooms Inc 260 Westgate Dr .... Watsonville CA 95076 *TF:* 800-333-6874 ■ *Web:* www.montereymushrooms.com	831-763-5300	763-2300	10-7
Monterey Pasta Co 2315 Moore Ave .... Fullerton CA 92833 *TF:* 800-588-7782 ■ *Web:* www.montereygourmetfoods.com	800-588-7782		296-31
Monterey Peninsula Airport 200 Fred Kane Dr Ste 200 .... Monterey CA 93940 *Web:* www.montereyairport.com	831-648-7000	373-2625	27
Monterey Peninsula Artists/Paradigm 404 W Franklin St .... Monterey CA 93940 *Web:* www.paradigmagency.com	831-375-4889		731
Monterey Peninsula Chamber of Commerce 243 El Dorado St Ste 200 .... Monterey CA 93940 *Web:* www.montereychamber.com	831-648-5350	649-3502	139
Monterey Peninsula College 980 Fremont St .... Monterey CA 93940 *TF:* 877-663-5433 ■ *Web:* www.mpc.edu	831-646-4000	646-4015	162
Monterey Plaza Hotel & Spa 400 Cannery Row .... Monterey CA 93940 *TF:* 877-862-7552 ■ *Web:* montereyplazahotel.com	877-862-7552		379
Monterey Regional Waste Management District (MRWMD) 14201 Del Monte Blvd .... Marina CA 93933 *Web:* www.mrwmd.org	831-384-5313	384-3567	660
Monterey State Historic Park 20 Custom House Plz .... Monterey CA 93940 *Web:* www.parks.ca.gov	831-649-2907		565
Monterey Technologies Inc 1790 Sun Peak Dr Ste A203 .... Park City UT 84098 *Web:* montereytechnologies.com	435-659-3711		466
Monterey-Salinas Transit (MST) 19 Upper Ragsdale Dr Ste 200 .... Monterey CA 93940 *TF:* 888-678-2871 ■ *Web:* mst.org	888-678-2871		468
Monteris Medical Inc 14755 27th Ave N Ste C .... Plymouth MN 55447 *TF:* 866-799-7655 ■ *Web:* www.monteris.com	866-799-7655		475
Monterrey 3724 Battleground Ave .... Greensboro NC 27410 *Web:* monterrey29.com	336-282-5588		671
Montesquieu Winery 8929 Aero Dr Ste F .... San Diego CA 92123 *TF:* 877-705-5669 ■ *Web:* montesquieu.com	877-705-5669		636
Montessori Academy at Spring Valley 36605 Pacific Hwy S .... Federal Way WA 98003 *Web:* www.springvalley.org	253-874-0563		167-3
Montessori Accreditation Council for Teacher Education (MACTE) 420 Park St .... Charlottesville VA 22902 **Fax Area Code:* 888 ■ *Web:* www.macte.org	434-202-7793	525-8838*	48-1
Montessori Center for Teacher Education 4544 Pocahontas Ave .... San Diego CA 92117 *Web:* www.montessoricenterforteachereducation.org	858-270-9350		167-3
Montessori on the Lake 23311 Muirlands Blvd .... Lake Forest CA 92630 *Web:* www.montessorionthelake.com	949-855-5630	855-5633	167-3
Montessori Schools of Snohomish County 1804 Puget Dr .... Everett WA 98203 *Web:* www.mymssc.com	425-355-1311		685
Montessori Teacher Education Institute - Houston 6012 Maple .... Houston TX 77074 *Web:* www.mtei-houston.org	713-774-6952		167-3
Montessori Teacher Preparation of Washington 23807 98th Ave S .... Kent WA 98031 *Web:* www.montessoriplus.org	253-859-2262	859-1737	167-3
Montezuma Castle National Monument 527 S Main St .... Camp Verde AZ 86322 *Web:* www.nps.gov	928-567-5276	567-3597	564
Montezuma County 109 W Main St .... Cortez CO 81321 *Web:* www.montezumacounty.org	970-565-8317	565-3420	338
Montfort Hospital 713 Montreal Rd .... Ottawa ON K1K0T2 *TF:* 866-670-4621 ■ *Web:* hopitalmontfort.com	613-746-4621	748-4914	374-2
Montfort Publications 26 S Saxon Ave .... Bay Shore NY 11706 *Web:* www.montfortpublications.com	631-665-0726		96
Montgomery Advertiser 425 Molton St .... Montgomery AL 36104 *TF:* 877-424-0007 ■ *Web:* www.montgomeryadvertiser.com	334-262-1611		532-2
Montgomery Air Freight 4820 Westport Blvd .... Montgomery AL 36108 *TF:* 800-392-1589 ■ *Web:* www.mgmair.com	334-281-9157	281-1987	780
Montgomery Amatuzio Chase Bell Jones LLP 4100 E Mississippi Ave Ste 1600 .... Denver CO 80246 *Web:* madc-law.com	303-592-6600	592-6666	41
Montgomery Area Chamber of Commerce 41 Commerce St PO Box 79 .... Montgomery AL 36104 *Web:* www.montgomerychamber.com	334-834-5200	265-4745	139
Montgomery Area Chamber of Commerce Convention & Visitor Bureau 300 Water St .... Montgomery AL 36104 *TF:* 800-240-9452 ■ *Web:* www.visitingmontgomery.com	334-261-1100		206
Montgomery Aviation 4525 Selma Hwy ...... Montgomery AL 36108 *Web:* www.montgomeryaviation.com	334-288-7334	288-7337	63
Montgomery Ballet 2101 E Blvd Ste 223 .... Montgomery AL 36117 *Web:* www.montgomeryballet.org	334-409-0522		573-1
Montgomery Bank 1 Montgomery Bank Plz PO Box 948 .... Sikeston MO 63801 *TF:* 800-455-2275 ■ *Web:* www.montgomerybank.com	573-471-2275		70
Montgomery Bell State Resort Park 1020 Jackson Hill Rd .... Burns TN 37029 *TF:* 800-250-8613 ■ *Web:* www.state.tn.us	615-797-9052		565
Montgomery Botanical Ctr 11901 Old Cutler Rd .... Miami FL 33156 *Web:* www.montgomerybotanical.org	305-667-3800	661-5984	97
Montgomery Carpets Inc 3202 Brady St .... Davenport IA 52803 *Web:* waynemontgomeryfloors.com	563-322-5976		290
Montgomery City Hall 103 N Perry St .... Montgomery AL 36104 *Web:* www.montgomeryal.gov	334-625-4400		337
Montgomery City-County Public Library 245 High St .... Montgomery AL 36104 *Web:* www.mccpl.lib.al.us	334-240-4999	240-4980	434-3
Montgomery College Rockville 51 Mannakee St .... Rockville MD 20850 *Web:* www.montgomerycollege.edu	240-567-5063		162
Montgomery Communications Inc 222 W 6th St .... Junction City KS 66441 *Web:* www.dailyu.com	785-762-5000		532-3
Montgomery Community College Foundation Inc 1011 Page St .... Troy NC 27371 *Web:* www.montgomery.edu	910-576-6222		434-3
Montgomery County 755 Roanoke St Ste 2E .... Christiansburg VA 24073 *Web:* www.montva.com	540-382-6954	382-6943	338
Montgomery County 1 Millennium Plz .... Clarksville TN 37040 *Web:* mcgtn.org	931-648-8482	553-5160	338
Montgomery County 20 Park St .... Fonda NY 12068 *Web:* www.co.montgomery.ny.us	518-853-4304	853-8220	338
Montgomery County 101 S Lawrence St PO Box 1667 .... Montgomery AL 36102 *Web:* www.mc-ala.org	334-832-1210	832-2533	338
Montgomery County 723 N Sturgeon St .... Montgomery City MO 63361 *Web:* www.montgomerycitymo.org	573-564-3160	564-3802	338
Montgomery County 44 W Main St .... Mount Sterling KY 40353 *Web:* montgomerycounty.ky.gov	859-498-8707	498-1040	338
Montgomery County 310 W Broad St PO Box 295 .... Mount Vernon GA 30445 *Web:* www.montgomerycountyga.gov	912-583-2363	583-2026	338
Montgomery County PO Box 311 .... Norristown PA 19404 *Web:* www.montcopa.org	610-278-3346	278-5188	338
Montgomery County 105 Coolbaugh St .... Red Oak IA 51566 *Web:* www.montgomerycountyiowa.com	712-623-3180	623-6540	338
Montgomery County 101 Monroe St .... Rockville MD 20850 *Web:* www.montgomerycountymd.gov	240-777-0311	777-2517	338
Montgomery County 203 W Main St .... Troy NC 27371 *Web:* montgomery.ces.ncsu.edu	910-576-6011	576-2635	338
Montgomery County Chamber of Commerce 1520 N Franklin St .... Christiansburg VA 24073 *Web:* montgomerycc.org	540-382-3020		139
Montgomery County Chamber of Commerce 51 Monroe St Ste 1800 .... Rockville MD 20850 *Web:* www.montgomerycountychamber.com	301-738-0015	738-8792	139
Montgomery County Community College *Pottstown* 101 College Dr .... Pottstown PA 19464 *Web:* www.mc3.edu	610-718-1800	718-1999	162
Montgomery County Intermediate Unit 23 2 W Lafayette St .... Norristown PA 19401 *Web:* www.mciu.org	610-755-9400		193
Montgomery County Library 104 I-45 N .... Conroe TX 77301 *Web:* www.countylibrary.org	936-442-7712	788-8398	434-3
Montgomery County Mississippi Genealogy & History Network PO Box 71 .... Winona MS 38967 *Web:* www.montgomery.msghn.org	662-283-2333		338
Montgomery County Visitors & Convention Bureau 218 E Pike St .... Crawfordsville IN 47933 *TF:* 800-866-3973 ■ *Web:* www.visitmoco.com	765-362-5200		206
Montgomery County-Norristown Public Library 1001 Powell St .... Norristown PA 19401 *Web:* mnl.mclinc.org	610-278-5100	277-0344	434-3
Montgomery Gallery 406 Jackson St .... San Francisco CA 94111 *Web:* montgomerygallery.com	415-788-8300	788-5469	42
Montgomery Hospice 1355 Piccard Dr Ste 100 .... Rockville MD 20850 *Web:* www.montgomeryhospice.org	301-921-4400	921-4433	371
Montgomery Hospital 1301 Powell St .... Norristown PA 19401 *Web:* www.montgomeryhospital.org	610-270-2000		374-3
Montgomery Independent 141 Market Pl .... Montgomery AL 36117 *Web:* www.al.com	334-265-7323		532-4
Montgomery Industries International Inc 2017 Thelma St .... Jacksonville FL 32206 *Web:* www.montgomeryindustries.com	904-355-4055	355-0401	273
Montgomery Inn 9440 Montgomery Rd ...... Montgomery OH 45242 *Web:* www.montgomeryinn.com	513-791-3482		671
Montgomery Investment Management Inc 6229 Executive Blvd .... Rockville MD 20852 *Web:* www.miminvest.com	301-897-9700		690
Montgomery Little & Soran PC 5445 Dtc Pkwy Ste 800 .... Greenwood Village CO 80111 *Web:* www.montgomerylittle.com	303-773-8100	220-0412	428
Montgomery Martin Contractors LLC 8245 Tournament Dr Ste 300 .... Memphis TN 38125 *Web:* www.montgomerymartin.com	901-374-9400	374-9402	186
Montgomery Museum of Fine Arts 1 Museum Dr PO Box 230819 .... Montgomery AL 36117 *Web:* mmfa.org	334-625-4333	240-4384	520
Montgomery Public Schools 307 S Decatur St .... Montgomery AL 36104 *Web:* www.mps.k12.al.us	334-223-6700	269-3076	685
Montgomery Regional Airport 4445 Selma Hwy .... Montgomery AL 36108 *Web:* www.flymgm.com	334-281-5040	281-5041	27
Montgomery Street Antique Mall 2601 Montgomery St .... Fort Worth TX 76107 *Web:* www.montgomerystreetantiques.com	817-735-9685		460
Montgomery Truss & Panel Inc 803 W Main St .... Grove City PA 16127 **Fax Area Code:* 724 ■ *TF:* 800-942-8010 ■ *Web:* montgomerytruss.com	800-942-8010	458-0765*	817

Name / Address	City	State	ZIP	Phone	Fax	Class
Montgomery Zoo 2301 Coliseum Pkwy *Web:* www.montgomeryzoo.com	Montgomery	AL	36110	334-240-4900	240-4916	823
Montgomery-Floyd Regional Library 125 Sheltman St *Web:* www.mfrl.org	Christiansburg	VA	24073	540-382-6965	382-6964	434-3
Montgomerys Furniture Inc 747 S Washington Ave *Web:* montgomerys.com	Madison	SD	57042	605-256-4000		321
Monti Inc 4510 Reading Rd *Web:* www.monti-inc.com	Cincinnati	OH	45229	513-761-7775	948-6858	816
Monticello 2976 Cove Terr Ste 107 *TF:* 800-243-0743 ■ *Web:* home.monticello.org	Charlottesville	VA	22903	434-984-9822		50-3
Monticello Central School 237 Forestburgh Rd *Web:* www.monticelloschools.net	Monticello	NY	12701	845-794-7700	794-7710	685
Monticello Corp, The PO Box 190645 **Fax Area Code:* 815 ■ *TF:* 866-701-1561 ■ *Web:* thepapertiger.com	Atlanta	GA	31119	404-478-6413	331-5270*	7
Monticello Nursing & Rehabilitation Ctr 500 Pinehaven Dr *Web:* www.monticellocampus.com	Monticello	IA	52310	319-465-5415	465-3205	450
Monticello Spring Corp 3137 Freeman Rd PO Box 705 *Web:* www.monticellospring.com	Monticello	IN	47960	574-583-8090	583-9299	719
Montie Roland 2106 Jerimouth Dr *Web:* www.montie.com	Apex	NC	27502	919-412-0559		196
Montien Thai Restaurant 63 Stuart St *Web:* montienthaiboston.com	Boston	MA	02116	617-338-5600		671
Montini Catholic High School 19w070 16th St *Web:* www.montini.org	Lombard	IL	60148	630-627-6930		685
Montisa 323 Acorn St *TF:* 800-875-6836 ■ *Web:* hellomontisa.com	Plainwell	MI	49080	269-924-0730	685-9195	319-1
Montlake Capital 1200 Fifth Ave Ste 1800 *Web:* www.montlakecapital.com	Seattle	WA	98101	206-956-0898	956-0863	792
Mont-Laurier Chamber of Commerce 385 Rue Du Pont 2E Etage *Web:* www.ccmont-laurier.com	Mont-Laurier	QC	J9L3G9	819-623-3642	623-5220	137
Montlick & Associates PC 17 Executive Park Dr Ste 300 *TF:* 800-529-6333 ■ *Web:* www.montlick.com	Atlanta	GA	30329	404-529-6333	965-1977	428
Montmarte 327 Seventh St SE *Web:* montmartredc.com	Washington	DC	20003	202-544-1244		671
Montmorency County PO Box 789 *TF:* 877-742-7576 ■ *Web:* montmorencycountymichigan.us	Atlanta	MI	49709	989-785-8022	785-8023	338
Montopolis Supply Co 255 US Hwy 183 S *Web:* www.montopolissupplyco.com	Austin	TX	78741	512-385-3270	385-1160	191-4
Montour County Courthouse 253 Mill St *TF:* 800-632-9063 ■ *Web:* www.montourco.org	Danville	PA	17821	570-271-3010	271-3089	338
Montowese Health & Rehabilitation Center Inc 163 Quinnipiac Ave *Web:* www.montowesehealth.com	North Haven	CT	06473	203-624-3303		450
Montoya Group LLC 650 S 4th Ave *Web:* montoyagroup.com	Yuma	AZ	85364	928-782-1648		390
Montpelier City Hall 39 Main St *Web:* montpelier-vt.org	Montpelier	VT	05602	802-223-9502	223-9519	337
Montpelier Glove Company Inc 129 N Main St *TF:* 800-645-3931 ■ *Web:* www.montpeliergsp.com	Montpelier	IN	47359	765-728-2481		155-8
Montreal Alouettes 1260 Boul Robert-Bourassa Ste 100 *Web:* www.montrealalouettes.com	Montreal	QC	H3B3B9	514-787-2525	871-2277	715-2
Montreal Beach Resort 1025 Beach Ave *TF:* 800-525-7011 ■ *Web:* www.montrealbeachresort.com	Cape May	NJ	08204	609-884-7011		669
Montreal Botanical Garden 4581 Rue Sherbrooke Est *Web:* ville.montreal.qc.ca	Montreal	QC	H1X2B2	514-872-1400		97
Montreal Exchange 1800 - 1190 Ave des Canadiens-de-Montreal PO Box 37 *TF:* 800-361-5353 ■ *Web:* www.m-x.ca	Montreal	QC	H3B0G7	514-871-2424	871-3514	691
Montreal Heart Institute 5000 Belanger St E *TF:* 855-922-6387 ■ *Web:* www.icm-mhi.org	Montreal	QC	H1T1C8	514-376-3330	593-2540	374-2
Montreal Holocaust Memorial Ctr 5151 Ch de la Cote-Sainte-Catherine *Web:* www.museeholocauste.ca	Montreal	QC	H3W1M6	514-345-2605	344-2651	520
Montreal Intl 380 Saint-Antoine St W Ste 8000 *Web:* www.montrealinternational.com	Montreal	QC	H2Y3X7	514-987-8191		463
Montreal Port Authority 2100 Pierre-Dupuy Ave Wing 1 Port of Montreal Bldg *Web:* www.port-montreal.com	Montreal	QC	H3C3R5	514-283-7011	283-0829	618
Montreat College 310 Gaither Cir PO Box 1267 *TF:* 800-622-6968 ■ *Web:* www.montreat.edu	Montreat	NC	28757	828-669-8012		166
Montrio 414 Calle Principal *Web:* www.montrio.com	Monterey	CA	93940	831-648-8880		671
Montrose County 161 S Townsend *Web:* www.co.montrose.co.us	Montrose	CO	81401	970-249-3362	249-7761	338
Montrose County School District Re-1j Inc PO Box 10000 *Web:* www.mcsd.org	Montrose	CO	81402	970-249-7726	249-7173	685
Montrose Environmental Group Inc *Curtis & Tompkins Ltd* 1 Park Plz Ste 1000 *Web:* montrose-env.com	Irvine	CA	92614	949-988-3500		743
Montrose Historical & Telephone Pioneer Museum 144 E Hickory St *Web:* montrosemuseum.org	Montrose	MI	48457	810-639-6644		520
Montrose Visitor Ctr 107 S Cascade Ave *TF:* 855-497-8558 ■ *Web:* www.visitmontrose.com	Montrose	CO	81401	970-497-8558		206
Montrose West Hollywood 900 Hammond St *TF:* 800-776-0666 ■ *Web:* www.montrosewesthollywood.com	West Hollywood	CA	90069	310-855-1115	657-9192	379
Montrusco Bolton Investments Inc 1501 McGill College Ave Ste 1200 *Web:* www.montruscobolton.com	Montreal	QC	H3A3M8	514-842-6464		528
Montserrat College of Art 23 Essex St *TF:* 800-836-0487 ■ *Web:* www.montserrat.edu	Beverly	MA	01915	978-921-4242	921-4241	166
Montserrat Jesuit Retreat House 600 N Shady Shores Dr PO Box 1390 *Web:* www.montserratretreat.org	Lake Dallas	TX	75065	940-321-6020	321-6040	673
Montverde Academy 17235 Seventh St *Web:* www.montverde.org	Montverde	FL	34756	407-469-2561	469-3711	622
Monument Builders of North America (MBNA) 136 S Keowee St **Fax Area Code:* 937 ■ *TF:* 800-233-4472 ■ *Web:* www.monumentbuilders.org	Dayton	OH	45402	800-233-4472	222-5794*	49-3
Monument Consulting LLC 1800 Summit Ave *Web:* www.monumentconsulting.com	Richmond	VA	23230	804-622-9992		463
Monument Hill & Kreische Brewery State Historic Sites 414 State Loop 92 *Web:* tpwd.texas.gov	LaGrange	TX	78945	979-968-5658		565
Mood Media Corp 1703 W Fifth St Ste 600 *Web:* us.moodmedia.com	Austin	TX	78703	512-380-8500		195
Moody Air Force Base 4343 George St Bldg 904 *TF:* 888-732-7302 ■ *Web:* www.moody.af.mil	Moody AFB	GA	31699	229-257-3395	257-3114	497-1
Moody Aldrich Partners LLC 18 Sewall St *Web:* www.moodyaldrich.com	Marblehead	MA	01945	781-639-2750	639-2751	401
Moody Dunbar Inc PO Box 6048 *TF:* 800-251-8202 ■ *Web:* www.moodydunbar.com	Johnson City	TN	37602	423-952-0100	952-0289	296-20
Moody Famiglietti & Andronico LLP 1 Highwood Dr *Web:* www.mfa-cpa.com	Tewksbury	MA	01876	978-557-5300		734
Moody Foundation 2302 Post Office St Ste 704 *TF:* 866-742-1133 ■ *Web:* moodyf.org	Galveston	TX	77550	409-797-1500		305
Moody Gardens Convention Ctr 7 Hope Blvd *TF:* 888-388-8484 ■ *Web:* www.moodygardenshotel.com	Galveston	TX	77554	409-741-8484		205
Moody Global Ministries 820 N LaSalle Dr *Web:* www.moodyglobal.org	Chicago	IL	60610	312-329-4000		644
Moody Medical Library 914 Market St **Fax Area Code:* 832 ■ *TF:* 866-235-5223 ■ *Web:* library.utmb.edu	Galveston	TX	77555	409-772-2372	202-2689*	434-1
Moody Nolan Inc 300 Spruce St Ste 300 *Web:* moodynolan.com	Columbus	OH	43215	614-461-4664		261
Moody Rambin Interests 3003 W Alabama St *Web:* www.moodyrambin.com	Houston	TX	77098	713-271-5900		655
Moody's Corp 250 Greenwich St 7 World Trade Ctr *NYSE: MCO* ■ *Web:* www.moodys.com	New York	NY	10007	212-553-0300		401
Moody's of Dayton Inc 4359 Infirmary Rd *Web:* www.moodysofdayton.com	Miamisburg	OH	45342	937-859-4482		537
Moody-Price LLC 18320 Petroleum Dr **Fax Area Code:* 225 ■ *TF:* 800-272-9832 ■ *Web:* moodyprice.com	Baton Rouge	LA	70809	800-272-9832	763-6005*	386
Moog Animatics 3200 Patrick Henry Dr *TF:* 888-356-0357 ■ *Web:* www.animatics.com	Santa Clara	CA	95054	408-748-8721		225
Moog Flo-Tork 1701 N Main St PO Box 68 *Web:* www.flotork.com	Orrville	OH	44667	330-682-0010	683-6857	223
Moog Inc Jamison Rd *NYSE: MOG.A* ■ *TF:* 800-336-2112 ■ *Web:* www.moog.com	East Aurora	NY	14052	716-652-2000	687-4457	203
Moog Music Inc 160 Broadway St *Web:* www.moogmusic.com	Asheville	NC	28801	828-251-0090		526
Moolenaar John (Rep R - MI) 117 Cannon House Office Bldg *Web:* moolenaar.house.gov	Washington	DC	20515	202-225-3561	225-9679	342-2
Moon Distributors Inc 2800 Vance St *Web:* moondist.com	Little Rock	AR	72206	501-604-6666		81-1
Moon Lake Electric Association Inc 800 W Hwy 40 PO Box 278 *Web:* www.mleainc.com	Roosevelt	UT	84066	435-722-5400		245
Moon Valley Nurseries 14025 N 7th St *Web:* www.moonvalleynurseries.com	Phoenix	AZ	85022	602-938-6666		276
Moon's Drug Store Inc 132 Main St *Web:* moonsdrugstore.com	Westminster	SC	29693	864-647-5941	647-2906	237
Moondance Press 4830 Dawson Dr Dept W *Web:* www.blessingway.net	Ann Arbor	MI	48103	734-426-1641		637-2
Mooney & Thomas PC 2111 Plum St Ste 150 *Web:* mooneythomas.com	Aurora	IL	60506	630-844-5272	844-0058	2
Mooney Aircraft Corp 165 Al Mooney Rd *TF:* 800-456-3033 ■ *Web:* www.mooney.com	Kerrville	TX	78028	800-456-3033		20
Mooney Alex (Rep R - WV) 2440 Rayburn House Office Bldg *Web:* www.mooney.house.gov	Washington	DC	20515	202-225-2711	225-7856	342-2
Mooney Farms 1220 Fortress St *Web:* www.bellasunluci.com	Chico	CA	95973	530-899-2661	899-7746	11-1
Mooney General Paper Co 1451 Chestnut Ave PO Box 3800 *TF:* 800-882-8846 ■ *Web:* www.mooneygeneral.com	Hillside	NJ	07205	973-926-3800	926-0425	547
Mooney, Green, Saindon, Murphy & Welch 1920 L St NW Ste 400 *Web:* mooneygreen.com	Washington	DC	20036	202-783-0010		41
Moon-matz Ltd 2902 S Sheridan Way Ste 300 *Web:* moon-matz.com	Oakville	ON	L6J7L6	905-274-7556	274-5382	261
Moonshine Patio Bar & Grill 303 Red River St *Web:* moonshinegrill.com	Austin	TX	78701	512-236-9599		671
Moonstone Hotel Properties Inc 2905 Burton Dr *TF:* 800-966-6490 ■ *Web:* www.moonstonehotels.com	Cambria	CA	93428	805-927-4200	927-4016	707

Name / Address	City	State	Zip	Phone	Fax	Class
Moonstruck Chocolate Co 6600 N Baltimore Ave *TF:* 800-557-6666 ■ *Web:* www.moonstruckchocolate.com	Portland	OR	97203	503-247-3448		296-8
Moontress Press PO Box 477 *Web:* www.moontress.com	Marquette	MI	49855	906-228-6181		637-2
Moonworks 1137 Park East Dr *TF:* 800-975-6666 ■ *Web:* www.moonworkshome.com	Woonsocket	RI	02895	800-975-6666		752
Moore & Bruggink Inc 2020 Monroe Ave *Web:* www.mbce.com	Grand Rapids	MI	49505	616-363-9801	363-2480	261
Moore & Lee LLP 1751 Pinnacle Dr Ste 1100 *Web:* mooreandlee.com	McLean	VA	22102	703-506-2050		41
Moore & Neidenthal Inc 3034 N Wooster Ave PO Box 468 *TF:* 866-364-7774 ■ *Web:* www.mnpinnacle.com	Dover	OH	44622	330-364-7774		2
Moore & Scarry Advertising Inc 12601 Westlinks Dr Ste 7 *Web:* www.mooreandscarry.com	Fort Myers	FL	33913	239-689-4000		7
Moore & Van Allen PLLC 100 N Tryon St Ste 4700 *Web:* www.mvalaw.com	Charlotte	NC	28202	704-331-1000	331-1159	41
Moore Aviation Inc Beaver County Airport 7 Piper St *Web:* www.mooreaviation.com	Beaver Falls	PA	15010	724-843-4800	843-4831	167-3
Moore Bass Consulting Inc 805 N Gadsden St *Web:* www.moorebass.com	Tallahassee	FL	32303	850-222-5678		261
Moore Brothers Inc 84622 US Hwy 81 *Web:* moorebrothers.net	Norfolk	NE	68701	402-371-8100		780
Moore Carlyle Consulting (MCC) 290 N Queen St Ste 208 *Web:* mccevents.ca	Toronto	ON	M9C5L2	416-621-6622	621-0363	317
Moore Chamber of Commerce 305 W Main St *Web:* www.moorechamber.com	Moore	OK	73160	405-794-3400	794-8555	139
Moore College of Art & Design 20th St & the Pkwy *TF:* 800-523-2025 ■ *Web:* moore.edu	Philadelphia	PA	19103	215-965-4000	568-0017	166
Moore Communications Group Inc 2011 Delta Blvd *Web:* themooreagency.com	Tallahassee	FL	32303	850-224-0174		7
Moore Computing LLP 317 N 11th St Ste 200 *Web:* www.moorecomputing.com	Saint Louis	MO	63101	314-621-5585		180
Moore County PO Box 905 *Web:* www.moorecountync.gov	Carthage	NC	28327	910-947-6363	947-1874	338
Moore County 715 S Dumas Ave Rm 202 *Web:* co.moore.tx.us	Dumas	TX	79029	806-935-5588	935-9004	338
Moore County 196 Main St PO Box 206 *Web:* www.lynchburgtn.com	Lynchburg	TN	37352	931-759-7346		338
Moore County Chamber of Commerce 10677 Hwy 15-501 *Web:* www.moorecountychamber.com	Southern Pines	NC	28387	910-692-3926	692-0619	139
Moore Erection LP 19921 Fm 2252 *Web:* www.melpsteel.com	Garden Ridge	TX	78266	210-648-7461		723
Moore Group, The 407 W Bute St *Web:* www.themooregroup.com	Norfolk	VA	23510	757-627-1015	627-8951	764
Moore Gwen (Rep D - WI) 2252 Rayburn House Office Bldg *Web:* www.gwenmoore.house.gov	Washington	DC	20515	202-225-4572		342-2
Moore Haven Correctional Facility Moore Haven Correctional Facility PO Box 69 *Web:* dc.state.fl.us	Moore Haven	FL	33471	863-946-2420	946-3437	213
Moore Industries International Inc 16650 Schoenborn St *TF:* 800-999-2900 ■ *Web:* www.miinet.com	North Hills	CA	91343	818-894-7111	891-2816	201
Moore Ingram Johnson & Steele LLP Emerson Overlook 326 Roswell Rd *Web:* www.mijs.com	Marietta	GA	30060	770-429-1499		428
Moore J. & Co 118 Naylon Ave *Web:* jmoore.com	Livingston	NJ	07039	973-992-6970		189-10
Moore Landrey LLP 905 Orleans St *TF:* 800-706-4442 ■ *Web:* moorelandrey.com	Beaumont	TX	77701	409-835-3891	835-2707	41
Moore Lane Veterinary Hospital 30 Moore Ln *Web:* www.yellowstonevalleyvet.com	Billings	MT	59101	406-252-4159		794
Moore Law Firm, The 1060 Nimitzview Dr Ste 200 *Web:* moorelaw.com	Cincinnati	OH	45230	513-494-6941		41
Moore Marketing LLC 608 Kings Hwy W *Web:* www.mooremarketingonline.com	Southport	CT	06890	203-610-1934		466
Moore Memorial Public Library 1701 Ninth Ave N *Web:* www.texascity-library.org	Texas City	TX	77590	409-643-5975	948-1106	434-3
Moore Norman Technology Center - Franklin Road Campus 4701 12th Ave NW *Web:* www.mntc.edu	Norman	OK	73069	405-364-5763	360-9989	167-3
Moore Reichl & Baker P C 11200 Wheimer Ste 410 *Web:* mrbcpas.com	Houston	TX	77042	281-558-9800		2
Moore Staffing Services 184 Pleasant Vly St *Web:* moorestaffing.com	Methuen	MA	01844	978-682-4994	794-1935	260
Moore State Park 1 Sawmill Rd *TF:* 800-437-5922 ■ *Web:* www.mass.gov	Paxton	MA	01612	508-792-3969		565
Moore Stephens Lovelace PA 255 S Orange Ave Ste 600 *TF:* 800-683-5401 ■ *Web:* www.mslcpa.com	Orlando	FL	32801	407-740-5400	740-0012	2
Moore Supply Co 200 N Loop 336 W *Web:* www.mooresupply.com	Conroe	TX	77301	936-756-4445	441-8468	612
Moore Tool Company Inc 800 Union Ave *Web:* mooretool.com	Bridgeport	CT	06607	203-366-3224	367-0418	360-3
Moore Twining Associates Inc 2527 Fresno St *Web:* www.mooretwining.com	Fresno	CA	93721	559-268-7021	268-7126	743
Moore, Schulman & Moore, Apc 12636 High Bluff Dr Ste 200 *Web:* msmfamilylaw.com	San Diego	CA	92130	858-492-7968		41
MooreCo Inc 2885 Lorraine Ave **Fax Area Code: 866* ■ *Web:* moorecoinc.com	Temple	TX	76501	800-749-2258	888-7483*	286
Moores Creek National Battlefield 40 Patriots Hall Dr *Web:* www.nps.gov	Currie	NC	28435	910-283-5591	283-5351	564
Moores Electrical & Mechanical PO Box 119 *TF:* 888-722-2712 ■ *Web:* www.mooreselectric.com	Altavista	VA	24517	434-369-4374	369-7402	186
Mooresville Graded School District 305 N Main St *Web:* www.mgsd.k12.nc.us	Mooresville	NC	28115	704-658-2530	663-3005	685
Mooresville Public Library 220 W Harrison St *Web:* www.mooresvillelib.org	Mooresville	IN	46158	317-831-7323	831-7383	434-3
Mooresville-South Iredell Chamber of Commerce 149 E Iredell Ave *TF:* 800-764-7113 ■ *Web:* www.mooresvillenc.org	Mooresville	NC	28115	704-664-3898	664-2549	139
Moorfeed Corp 4162 N EMS Blvd *Web:* moorfeed.com	Greenfield	IN	46140	317-545-7171	375-1906	273
Mooring, The Sayer's Wharf *Web:* www.mooringrestaurant.com	Newport	RI	02840	401-846-2260		671
Moorings Park 132 Moorings Park Dr *TF:* 866-802-4302 ■ *Web:* www.mooringspark.org	Naples	FL	34105	239-643-9111		672
Moorpark Chamber of Commerce 18 E High St *Web:* www.moorparkchamber.com	Moorpark	CA	93021	805-529-0322	529-5304	139
Moorpark College 7075 Campus Rd *Web:* www.moorparkcollege.edu	Moorpark	CA	93021	805-378-1400		162
Moors & Cabot Inc 111 Devonshire St *TF:* 800-426-0501 ■ *Web:* www.moorscabot.com	Boston	MA	02109	800-426-0501		405
Moose Cafe 570 Brevard Rd *Web:* www.eatatthemoosecafe.com	Asheville	NC	28806	828-255-0920		671
Moose International Inc 155 S International Dr *TF:* 800-668-5901 ■ *Web:* www.mooseintl.org	Mooseheart	IL	60539	630-966-2211		48-15
Moose Jaw & District Chamber of Commerce 88 Saskatchewan St E *Web:* www.mjchamber.com	Moose Jaw	SK	S6H0V4	306-692-6414		137
Moose Jaw Museum & Art Gallery 461 Langdon Crescent *Web:* www.mjmag.ca	Moose Jaw	SK	S6H0X6	306-692-4471	694-8016	520
Moose Lake State Park 4252 County Rd 137 *Web:* www.dnr.state.mn.us	Moose Lake	MN	55767	218-460-7001		565
Moose Point State Park 310 W Main St *Web:* www.maine.gov	Searsport	ME	04974	207-548-2882		565
Moose School Productions PO Box 960 *TF:* 800-676-5480 ■ *Web:* www.peteralsop.com	Topanga	CA	90290	310-455-2318		525
Moose Travel Network 192 Spadina Ave Unit 408 *TF:* 888-244-6673 ■ *Web:* moosenetwork.com	Toronto	ON	M5T2C2	604-297-0255	297-0228	760
Moosylvania Marketin LC 7303 Marietta Ave *Web:* moosylvania.com	Saint Louis	MO	63143	314-644-7900		195
Moot House 2626 S College Ave *Web:* themoothouse.com	Fort Collins	CO	80525	970-226-2121		671
MOPS Intl 2370 S Trenton Way *TF:* 888-910-6677 ■ *Web:* www.mops.org	Denver	CO	80231	303-733-5353	733-5770	48-6
Moquin Press Inc 555 Harbor Blvd *Web:* moquinpress.com	Belmont	CA	94002	650-592-0575		627
Morabito Baking Company Inc 757 Kohn St *TF:* 800-525-7747 ■ *Web:* www.morabitobaking.com	Norristown	PA	19401	610-275-5419	275-0358	290-1
Moraine Hills State Park 1510 S River Rd *Web:* www.dnr.illinois.gov	McHenry	IL	60051	815-385-1624		565
Moraine Park Technical College 235 N National Ave *TF:* 800-472-4554 ■ *Web:* www.morainepark.edu	Fond du Lac	WI	54935	920-922-8611	924-3421	800
Moraine State Park 225 Pleasant Valley Rd *Web:* www.dcnr.pa.gov	Portersville	PA	16051	724-368-8811		565
Moraine Valley Community College 9000 W College Pkwy *Web:* www.morainevalley.edu	Palos Hills	IL	60465	708-974-4300		162
Moraine View State Recreation Area 27374 Moraine View Park Rd *Web:* www.dnr.illinois.gov	Le Roy	IL	61752	309-724-8032		565
Morales Group Inc 5628 W 74th St *Web:* moralesgroup.net	Indianapolis	IN	46278	317-472-7600		260
Moran Environmental Recovery LLC 75-D York Ave *TF:* 888-233-5338 ■ *Web:* www.moranenvironmental.com	Randolph	MA	02368	781-815-1100	815-1102	192
Moran Jerry (Sen R - KS) 521 Dirksen Senate Office Bldg *Web:* www.moran.senate.gov	Washington	DC	20510	202-224-6521	228-6966	342-2
Moran Printing Inc 5425 Florida Blvd *TF:* 800-211-8335 ■ *Web:* emprint.com	Baton Rouge	LA	70806	225-923-2550		626
Moran Refrigeration Inc 820 S Wayne St PO Box 188 *Web:* moranrefrigeration.com	Saint Marys	OH	45885	419-394-2351		35
Moran State Park 3572 Olga Rd *Web:* www.parks.wa.gov	Olga	WA	98279	360-376-2326		565
Moran Technology Consulting LLC 1215 Hamilton Ln Ste 200 *TF:* 888-699-4440 ■ *Web:* www.morantechnology.com	Naperville	IL	60540	888-699-4440		196
Moran Towing Corp 50 Locust Ave *Web:* www.morantug.com	New Canaan	CT	06840	203-442-2800		478
Moran's 4020 Compton Ave *Web:* www.moransgroundbeef.com	Los Angeles	CA	90011	323-585-0068		473
Mora-San Miguel Electric Co-op Hwy 518 Main St *TF:* 800-421-6773 ■ *Web:* www.morasanmiguel.coop	Mora	NM	87732	575-387-2205	387-5975	245

Name / Address	City	State	Zip	Phone	Fax	Class
Morasch Meats Inc 4050 NE 158th Ave *Web:* moraschmeats.com	Portland	OR	97230	503-257-9821		345
Moravek Biochemicals Inc 577 Mercury Ln *TF:* 888-723-2436 ■ *Web:* www.moravek.com	Brea	CA	92821	714-990-2018		143
Moravian Archives, The 41 W Locust St *Web:* www.moravianchurcharchives.org	Bethlehem	PA	18018	610-866-3255	866-9210	434-3
Moravian College 1200 Main St *TF:* 800-441-3191 ■ *Web:* www.moravian.edu	Bethlehem	PA	18018	610-861-1300	625-7930	166
Moravian Florist & Garden Center Inc 2286 Richmond Rd *Web:* moravianflorist.com	Staten Island	NY	10306	718-351-4440		292
Moravian Hall Square 175 W N St *Web:* www.moravian.com	Nazareth	PA	18064	610-746-1000	746-1023	672
Moravian Manor Communities 300 W Lemon St	Lititz	PA	17543	717-626-0214		672
Moravian Theological Seminary 1200 Main St *TF:* 800-843-6541 ■ *Web:* www.moravianseminary.edu	Bethlehem	PA	18018	610-861-1516	861-1569	167-3
Moravian Village of Bethlehem 526 Wood St *Web:* www.moravianvillage.com	Bethlehem	PA	18018	610-625-4885		672
Morbark Inc 8507 S Winn Rd *TF:* 800-831-0042 ■ *Web:* www.morbark.com	Winn	MI	48896	989-866-2381		448
Morcom International Inc 3656 Centerview Dr Unit 1 *Web:* www.morcom.com	Chantilly	VA	20151	703-263-9305	263-9308	647
Morcon Construction Company Inc 5151 Industrial Blvd NE *Web:* www.morcon.com	Fridley	MN	55421	763-546-6066	546-3129	186
Mordecai Historic Park 1 Mimosa St *Web:* www.raleighnc.gov	Raleigh	NC	27604	919-996-4364		50-3
Mordine & Company Dance Theatre 1016 N Dearborn St *Web:* www.mordine.org	Chicago	IL	60610	847-687-3782		573-1
More Effective Consulting LLC 10 Chestnut Cir *Web:* www.moreeffective.com	Mont Vernon	NH	03057	603-801-3923		196
More Hawaii for Less 11 Ash Tree Ln *TF:* 800-967-6687 ■ *Web:* www.hawaii4less.com	Irvine	CA	92612	949-724-5050		771
More Media Group 1427 Goodman Ave *Web:* www.moremediagroup.com	Redondo Beach	CA	90278	310-991-9798		7
More Space Place Inc 5040 140th Ave N *TF:* 888-731-3051 ■ *Web:* www.morespaceplace.com	Clearwater	FL	33760	888-731-3051		361
Moreau Lake State Park 605 Old Saratoga Rd *Web:* parks.ny.gov	Gansevoort	NY	12831	518-793-0511		565
Moreau-Grand Electric Co-opeartive Inc 405 Ninth St *TF:* 800-952-3158 ■ *Web:* www.mge.coop	Timber Lake	SD	57656	605-865-3511		245
MoreDirect Inc 1001 Yamato Rd Ste 200 *TF:* 800-800-5555 ■ *Web:* www.moredirect.com	Boca Raton	FL	33431	561-237-3300		196
Morehead Community Federal Credit Union 503 W Main St *Web:* moreheadcommunity.com	Morehead	KY	40351	606-784-2201		219
Morehead Memorial Hospital 117 E King's Hwy *TF:* 800-291-4020 ■ *Web:* www.uncrockingham.org	Eden	NC	27288	336-623-9711	623-7660	374-3
Morehead Planetarium 250 E Franklin St The University of North Carolina at Chapel Hill CB 3480 *Web:* moreheadplanetarium.org	Chapel Hill	NC	27599	919-962-1236	962-1238	598
Morehead State University 100 Admissions Ctr *TF:* 800-585-6781 ■ *Web:* www.moreheadstate.edu	Morehead	KY	40351	606-783-2000	783-5038	166
Morehouse 760 Epperson Dr *Web:* www.morehousefoods.com	City of Industry	CA	91748	626-854-1655	854-1656	296-19
Morehouse College 830 Westview Dr SW *Web:* www.morehouse.edu	Atlanta	GA	30314	404-681-2800	572-3668	166
Morehouse Instrument Co 1742 6th Ave *Web:* www.mhforce.com	York	PA	17403	717-843-0081	846-4193	248
Morehouse School of Medicine 720 Westview Dr SW *Web:* www.msm.edu	Atlanta	GA	30310	404-752-1500	752-1512	167-2
Morehouse-COWLES 13930 Magnolia Ave *Web:* www.morehousecowles.com	Chino	CA	91710	909-627-7222		111
Moreland Altobelli Associates LLC 2450 Commerce Ave Ste 100 *Web:* www.maai.net	Duluth	GA	30096	770-263-5945	263-0166	261
Moreland Assoc 2532 Santa Clara Ave Ste 413 *Web:* www.morelandassoc.com	Alameda	CA	94501	510-833-7308		463
Moreland Plaza Pharmacy Inc 827 W Moreland Blvd *Web:* morelandplazapharmacy.com	Waukesha	WI	53188	262-542-4488	650-4040	237
Morell Engineering 711 Hobbs St E *Web:* www.morellengineering.com	Athens	AL	35611	256-867-4957		261
Morelle Joseph (Rep D - NY) 1317 Longworth House Office Bldg *Web:* www.morelle.house.gov	Washington	DC	20515	202-225-3615		342-2
Morelli Law Firm PLLC 777 Third Ave *TF:* 877-751-9800 ■ *Web:* morellilaw.com	New York	NY	10017	212-751-9800	751-0046	41
Morely Library 184 Phelps St *Web:* www.morleylibrary.org	Painesville	OH	44077	440-352-3383		434-3
Moreman, Moore & Company Inc 820 Jordan St Ste 400 *Web:* moremanmoore.com	Shreveport	LA	71101	318-424-9160		390
Moreno Valley Chamber of Commerce 12625 Frederick St *Web:* www.movalchamber.org	Moreno Valley	CA	92553	951-697-4404		139
Moreno Valley Mall 22500 Town Cir *Web:* www.morenovalleymall.com	Moreno Valley	CA	92553	951-653-1177		460
Moresatile Global Mktng LLC 4110 Milano Way *Web:* www.moresatile.com	Oceanside	CA	92057	760-757-7676		193
Moresource Inc 401 Vandiver Dr *Web:* moresource-inc.com	Columbia	MO	65202	573-443-1234		631
Morette Company Inc 2503 N 12th Ave *Web:* www.moretteco.com	Pensacola	FL	32503	850-432-4084	434-5005	186
Morey Corp 100 Morey Dr *Web:* www.moreycorp.com	Woodridge	IL	60517	630-754-2300		253
Morey's Piers & Raging Waters Waterparks 3501 Boardwalk *Web:* www.moreyspiers.com	Wildwood	NJ	08260	609-729-3700		32
Morey's Seafood International LLC 1218 Hwy 10 S *TF:* 800-808-3474 ■ *Web:* www.moreys.com	Motley	MN	56466	218-352-6345		296-14
Morga-Gallacher Inc 8707 Millergrove Dr *TF:* 877-647-6279 ■ *Web:* www.morgan-gallacher.com	Santa Fe Springs	CA	90670	877-647-6279		151
Morgan & Akins PLLC 2000 Richard Jones Rd Ste 260 *Web:* morganakins.com	Nashville	TN	37215	615-829-5995		41
Morgan & Myers N 16 W 23233 Stone Ridge Dr Ste 200 *Web:* www.morganmyers.com	Waukesha	WI	53188	262-650-7260		636
Morgan Adhesives Co 4560 Darrow Rd *TF:* 866-262-2822 ■ *Web:* www.mactac.com	Stow	OH	44224	330-688-1111	688-2540	3
Morgan Advanced Materials 251 Forrester Dr *Web:* www.morgantechnicalceramics.com	Greenville	SC	29607	864-458-7700		411
Morgan Bronze Products Inc 340 E Il Rte 22 *TF:* 800-445-9970 ■ *Web:* www.morganbronze.com	Lake Zurich	IL	60047	847-526-6000	438-6600	454
Morgan Community College 920 Barlow Rd *TF:* 800-622-0216 ■ *Web:* www.morgancc.edu	Fort Morgan	CO	80701	970-542-3100		162
Morgan Corp 111 Morgan Way PO Box 588 *TF:* 800-666-7426 ■ *Web:* www.morgancorp.com	Morgantown	PA	19543	800-666-7426		516
Morgan County 77 Fairfax St Rm 102 *Web:* morgancountywv.gov	Berkeley Springs	WV	25411	304-258-8547	258-8545	338
Morgan County PO Box 668 *Web:* www.co.morgan.al.us	Decatur	AL	35602	256-351-4730	351-4738	338
Morgan County 231 Ensign St PO Box 1399 *Web:* www.colorado.gov	Fort Morgan	CO	80701	970-542-3521	542-3520	338
Morgan County 300 W State St *Web:* www.morgancounty-il.com	Jacksonville	IL	62651	217-243-8581	243-8368	338
Morgan County 150 E Washington St *Web:* www.morganga.org	Madison	GA	30650	706-342-0725	343-6450	338
Morgan County 180 S Main St *TF:* 800-382-9467 ■ *Web:* www.morgancounty.in.gov	Martinsville	IN	46151	765-342-1007	342-1111	338
Morgan County 358 E Main St *Web:* www.morgan.lib.oh.us	McConnelsville	OH	43756	740-962-2533	962-3316	338
Morgan County PO Box 886 *Web:* www.morgan-county.net	Morgan	UT	84050	801-845-4011	829-6176	338
Morgan County 100 E Newton St *Web:* www.morgan-county.org	Versailles	MO	65084	573-378-5436	378-5991	338
Morgan County 415 N Kingston St *Web:* www.morgancountytn.gov	Wartburg	TN	37887	423-346-6288		338
Morgan County 450 Prestonsburg St *Web:* www.morgancounty.ky.gov	West Liberty	KY	41472	606-743-3949	743-2111	338
Morgan County Rural Electric Assn 20169 US Hwy 34 *TF:* 877-495-6487 ■ *Web:* www.mcrea.org	Fort Morgan	CO	80701	970-867-5688	867-3277	245
Morgan County Schools 1325 Pt Mallard Pkwy *Web:* www.morgank12.org	Decatur	AL	35601	256-353-6442		685
Morgan Creek Capital Management LLC 301 W Barbee Chapel Rd Ste 200 *Web:* www.morgancreekcap.com	Chapel Hill	NC	27517	919-933-4004	933-4048	194
Morgan Dempsey Capital Management LLC 111 Heritage Reserve Ste 200 *Web:* www.morgandempsey.com	Menomonee Falls	WI	53051	414-319-1080	319-1087	401
Morgan Distributing Inc 3425 N 22nd St *TF:* 800-800-6625 ■ *Web:* www.mdilubes.com	Decatur	IL	62526	217-877-3570		579
Morgan Distribution Inc 4930 Old Maumee Rd *TF:* 800-482-3903 ■ *Web:* www.morgandist.com	Fort Wayne	IN	46803	800-482-3903		802
Morgan Fabrics Corp 4265 Exchange Ave *Web:* www.morganfabrics.com	Los Angeles	CA	90058	323-583-9981	923-2352	413
Morgan Foods Inc 90 W Morgan St *TF:* 888-430-1780 ■ *Web:* www.morganfoods.com	Austin	IN	47102	812-794-1170		296-20
Morgan Group Inc 5606 S Rice Ave *Web:* www.morgangroup.com	Houston	TX	77081	713-361-7200	361-7299	187
Morgan Hill Chamber of Commerce 17485 Monterey St Ste 105 *TF:* 866-287-5709 ■ *Web:* www.morganhill.org	Morgan Hill	CA	95037	408-779-9444	779-5405	139
Morgan Hill Plastics Inc 8118 Arroyo Cir *Web:* morganhillplastics.net	Gilroy	CA	95020	408-842-1322	842-1335	602
Morgan Hunter Cos 7600 W 110th St *TF:* 800-917-6447 ■ *Web:* www.morganhunter.com	Overland Park	KS	66210	913-491-3434		260
Morgan Industries Inc 3311 E 59th St *Web:* www.morganindustriesinc.com	Long Beach	CA	90805	562-634-4074		695
Morgan Jacoby Thurn Boyle & Associates PA 700 20th St *Web:* www.mjtbcpa.com	Vero Beach	FL	32960	772-562-4158	563-2024	734
Morgan Levine Dolan PC 18 E 41st St 6th Fl *Web:* morganlevinelaw.com	New York	NY	10017	212-785-5115		41
Morgan Lewis & Bockius LLP 1701 Market St *TF:* 866-963-7137 ■ *Web:* www.morganlewis.com	Philadelphia	PA	19103	215-963-5000	963-5001	428
Morgan Library & Museum, The 225 Madison Ave *Web:* www.themorgan.org	New York	NY	10016	212-685-0008	481-3484	520

Phone | Fax | Class

Morgan Linen Service Inc
145 Broadway Menands Albany NY 12204 518-465-3337 426-1106 442
Web: www.linenservicealbany.com

Morgan Lumber Company Inc PO Box 25 Red Oak VA 23964 434-735-8151 683
Web: www.morganlumber.com

Morgan Marketing & Communications
21 Davis Hill Rd Weston CT 06883 203-255-4686 195
Web: morganmarketcomm.com

Morgan Meighen & Associates Ltd
10 Toronto St Toronto ON M5C2B7 416-366-2931 528
Web: www.mmainvestments.com

Morgan Meredith Inc (MM)
4299 Mount Vernon Rd SE Cedar Rapids IA 52403 319-362-9615 770
TF: 800-228-9241 ■ *Web:* www.labelmaker.com

Morgan Olson 1801 S Nottawa Rd Sturgis MI 49091 800-624-9005 516
TF: 800-624-9005 ■ *Web:* morganolson.com

Morgan Park Academy 2153 W 111th St Chicago IL 60643 773-881-6700 148
Web: www.morganparkacademy.org

Morgan Printers Inc
4120 Bayswater Rd Winterville NC 28590 252-355-5588 756-2559 627
Web: www.morganprinters.com

Morgan Printing Inc 402 Hill Ave Grafton ND 58237 701-352-0640 627
Web: morganprinting.com

Morgan Properties
500 W University Pkwy Baltimore MD 21210 443-529-0185 671
Web: www.morgan-properties.com

Morgan Recreational Supply Inc
6013 Denny Dr Farmington NY 14425 800-836-5300 924-4410* 770
*Fax Area Code: 585 ■ *TF:* 800-836-5300 ■ *Web:* www.morganrec.com

Morgan Run Natural Environment Area
Benrose Ln Westminster MD 21157 410-461-5005 565
Web: www.dnr.maryland.gov

Morgan RV Resorts LLC
PO Box 480 Ste 201 Saratoga Springs NY 12866 518-615-0552 121

Morgan Schaffer Systems Inc
8300 Rue Saint-Patrick Bureau 150 LaSalle Montreal QC H8N2H1 514-739-1967 739-0434 743
TF: 855-861-1967 ■ *Web:* www.morganschaffer.com

Morgan Scientific Inc 151 Essex St Haverhill MA 01832 978-521-4440 476
TF: 800-525-5002 ■ *Web:* www.morgansci.com

Morgan Services Inc
323 N Michigan Ave Chicago IL 60601 877-546-3601 442
TF: 888-966-7426 ■ *Web:* www.morganservices.com

Morgan Stanley 1585 Broadway New York NY 10036 212-761-4000 690
NYSE: MS ■ *TF:* 800-223-2440 ■ *Web:* www.morganstanley.com

Morgan State University
1700 E Cold Spring Ln Baltimore MD 21251 443-885-3333 885-8260 166
TF: 800-319-4678 ■ *Web:* morgan.edu

Morgan USA
1651 N Glenville Dr Ste 214 Richardson TX 75081 972-864-7341 106
Web: morganusa.com

Morgan Verkamp LLC
35 E Seventh St Ste 600 Cincinnati OH 45202 513-651-4400 41
Web: morganverkamp.com

Morgan's Foods Inc
4829 Galaxy Pkwy Ste S Cleveland OH 44128 216-359-9000 670
Web: www.morgansfoods.com

MorganFranklin Consulting
7900 Tysons One Pl Ste 300 McLean VA 22102 703-564-7525 180
Web: www.morganfranklin.com

Morgan-Keller Inc
70 Thomas Johnson Dr Ste 200 Frederick MD 21702 301-663-0626 261
Web: www.morgankeller.com

Morganti Group Inc
100 Mill Plain Rd 4th Fl Danbury CT 06811 203-743-2675 830-4478 186
Web: www.morganti.com

Morganton Honda 1600 Burkemont Ave Morganton NC 28655 828-437-3181 57
Web: www.morgantonhonda.com

Morgantown Area Chamber of Commerce
265 Spruce St Morgantown WV 26508 304-292-3311 296-6619 139
TF: 800-618-2525 ■ *Web:* www.morgantownchamber.org

Morgantown Beauty College
276 Walnut St Morgantown WV 26505 304-292-8475 167-3
Web: www.morgantownbeautycollege.com

Morgantown City Hall 389 Spruce St Morgantown WV 26505 304-284-7405 337
Web: www.morgantownwv.gov

Morgantown Municipal Airport
100 Hartfield Rd Morgantown WV 26505 304-291-5867 27
Web: www.morgantownairport.com

Morgantown Printing & Binding LLC
915 Greenbag Rd Morgantown WV 26508 304-292-3368 627
TF: 888-292-0001 ■ *Web:* morgantownprintingandbinding.com

Morgantown Public Library System
373 Spruce St Morgantown WV 26505 304-291-7425 291-7437 434-3
Web: www.mympls.org

Morgenstern & Herd PA
2002 N Lois Ave Ste 150 Tampa FL 33607 813-597-3000 540-8029 41
Web: morgensternandherd.com

Morgenstern Devoesick PLLC
1080 Pittsford Victor Rd Ste 200 Pittsford NY 14534 585-672-5500 41
Web: morgdevo.com

Morgenstern Phifer & Messina
101 E Kennedy Blvd Ste 1480 Tampa FL 33602 813-222-8888 2
Web: mpmpa.com

Morgenthaler 3200 Alpine Rd Portola CA 94028 650-388-7600 388-7601 792
Web: www.morgenthaler.com

Morgood Tools Inc 940 Millstead Way Rochester NY 14624 585-436-2426 455
Web: www.morgood.com

Mor-Gran-Sou Electric Co-opeartive Inc
202 Sixth Ave W Flasher ND 58535 701-597-3301 245
TF: 800-750-8212 ■ *Web:* www.morgransou.com

Morguard Investments Ltd
55 City Centre Dr Ste 800 Mississauga ON L5B1M3 905-281-3800 653
Web: www.morguard.com

Mori Sushi 11500 W Pico Blvd Los Angeles CA 90064 310-479-3939 671
Web: www.morisushi.org

Moriah School of Engelwood
53 S Woodland St Englewood NJ 07631 201-567-0208 685
Web: www.moriahschool.org

Moriah Shock Incarceration Correctional Facility
75 Burhart Ln PO Box 999 Mineville NY 12956 518-942-7561 213
Web: www.doccs.ny.gov

Moriarty/Fox Inc
20 N Wacker Dr Ste 2410 Chicago IL 60606 312-332-4600 372-8440 194
Web: www.moriartyfox.com

Morihara Lau & Fong LLP, A Limited Liability Law Partnership
841 Bishop St Ste 400 Honolulu HI 96813 808-526-2888 41
Web: moriharagroup.com

Morikami Museum & Japanese Gardens
4000 Morikami Park Rd Delray Beach FL 33446 561-495-0233 520
Web: morikami.org

Morimoto 723 Chestnut St Philadelphia PA 19106 215-413-9070 671
Web: morimotorestaurant.com

Morin Brick Co PO Box 1510 Auburn ME 04210 207-784-9375 784-2013 150
Web: www.morinbrick.com

Moritani America Inc
300 Park Blvd Ste 320 Itasca IL 60143 630-250-9898 385
Web: www.moritaniusa.com

Moritomo 32 Ft Eddy Rd Concord NH 03301 603-224-8363 671
Web: www.moritomonh.com

Moritz Embroidery Works Inc, The
Pocono Mountain Business Park 405 Industrial Park Dr
PO Box 187 Mount Pocono PA 18344 800-533-4183 839-3031* 258
*Fax Area Code: 570 ■ *TF:* 800-533-4183 ■ *Web:* www.moritzembroidery.com

Morken Transport Storage Inc
1247 Andover Blvd NE Ham Lake MN 55304 763-434-2930 311
Web: morkencompanies.net

Morlan & Associates Inc
6625 McVey Blvd Columbus OH 43235 614-889-6152 767
Web: www.flex-core.com

Morley 100 High Grove Blvd Glendale Heights IL 60139 847-639-4646 639-4723 527
TF: 800-284-5172 ■ *Web:* www.morleypedals.com

Morley 4800 Rosebud Ln Newburgh IN 47630 812-464-9585 464-2514 261
Web: morleycorp.com

Morley Candy Makers Inc
23770 Hall Rd Clinton Township MI 48036 800-651-7263 296-8
TF: 800-651-7263 ■ *Web:* www.sanderscandy.com

Morley Companies Inc 1 Morley Plz Saginaw MI 48603 989-791-2550 426-6753* 775
*Fax Area Code: 800 ■ *TF:* 800-336-5554 ■ *Web:* www.morleycompanies.com

Morley Financial Services Inc
1300 SW Fifth Ave Ste 3300 Portland OR 97201 503-484-9300 401
TF: 800-548-4806 ■ *Web:* www.morley.com

Morley Sales Company Inc 119 N 2nd St Geneva IL 60134 630-845-8750 845-8749 297-5

Morley-Murphy Co
200 S Washington St Ste 305 Green Bay WI 54301 920-499-3171 499-9409 612
TF: 877-499-3171 ■ *Web:* www.morley-murphycompany.com

Mormon Station State Historic Park
PO Box 302 Genoa NV 89411 775-782-2590 565
Web: parks.nv.gov

Morning Breeze Inc 950 N Lkview Dr Greensburg IN 47240 812-662-7778 793
Web: www.exceptionallivingcenters.com

Morning Call PO Box 1260 Allentown PA 18105 610-217-7644 820-6693 532-2
TF: 800-666-5492 ■ *Web:* www.mcall.com

Morning Consult 729 15th St NW Washington DC 20005 202-506-1957 177
Web: morningconsult.com

Morning Glory Cafe 450 Willamette St Eugene OR 97401 541-687-0709 671
Web: morninggloryeugene.squarespace.com

Morning Glory Diner
10 E Flizwater St Philadelphia PA 19146 215-413-3999 671
Web: www.themorningglorydiner.com

Morning Journal 1657 Broadway Ave Lorain OH 44052 440-245-6901 532-2
TF: 888-757-0727 ■ *Web:* www.morningjournal.com

Morning News 310 S Dargan St Florence SC 29506 843-317-6397 317-7292 532-2
Web: www.scnow.com

Morning News of Northwest Arkansas
2560 N Lowell Rd Springdale AR 72764 479-751-6200 872-5055 532-2
Web: www.nwaonline.com

Morning Star Packing Co
13448 Volta Rd Los Banos CA 93635 209-827-7847 826-5086 296-20
Web: www.morningstarco.com

Morningside College
1501 Morningside Ave Sioux City IA 51106 712-274-5000 274-5101 166
TF: 800-831-0806 ■ *Web:* www.morningside.edu

Morningside Equities Group Inc
223 W Erie St 3rd Fl Chicago IL 60654 312-280-7770 653
Web: morningsideusa.com

Morningside Ministries
700 Babcock Rd San Antonio TX 78201 210-734-1000 48-20
Web: www.mmliving.org

Morningside of Fullerton
800 Morningside Dr Fullerton CA 92835 714-256-8000 672
TF: 800-803-7597 ■ *Web:* www.morningsideoffullerton.com

Morningstar Inc 22 W Washington St Chicago IL 60602 312-696-6000 696-6009 401
NASDAQ: MORN ■ *TF:* 800-735-0700 ■ *Web:* www.corporate.morningstar.com

Morningstar Press PO Box 156 Cambria CA 93428 805-927-2542 637-2
Web: www.loveshealingenergy.org

Mornington Communications Co-operative Ltd
16 Mill St E Milverton ON N0K1M0 519-595-8331 224
TF: 800-250-8750 ■ *Web:* www.mornington.ca

Moro Bay State Park 6071 US Hwy 600 Jersey AR 71651 870-463-8555 565
Web: www.arkansasstateparks.com

Moroch Partners 3625 N Hall St Ste 1100 Dallas TX 75219 214-520-9700 4
Web: www.moroch.com

Morongo Casino Resort & Spa
49500 Seminole Dr Cabazon CA 92230 951-849-3080 669
TF: 800-252-4499 ■ *Web:* www.morongocasinoresort.com

Moroso Performance Products Inc
80 Carter Dr Guilford CT 06437 203-453-5200 453-6906 489
Web: www.moroso.com

MORPAC (Mortgage Bankers Association PAC)
1919 M St NW Washington DC 20036 202-557-2700 615
Web: www.mba.org

Morphix Business Consulting
PO Box 5217 Stn A Calgary AB T2H1X3 403-520-7710 196
TF: 866-680-2503 ■ *Web:* www.morphix.biz

MorphoTrak Inc
5515 E La Palma Ave Ste 100 Anaheim CA 92807 714-238-2000 238-2049 84
TF: 800-346-2674 ■ *Web:* usa.morpho.com

Name	Phone	Fax	Class
MorphoTrust USA Inc 296 Concord Rd .... Billerica MA 01821 *Web:* www.morphotrust.com	978-215-2400		692
Morrell Inc 333 Bald Mtn Rd .... Auburn Hills MI 48326 *Web:* www.morrell-group.com	248-373-1600	373-0612	386
Morrill County 606 L St PO Box 10............ Bridgeport NE 69336 *Web:* www.morrillcountyne.gov	308-262-0860	262-1469	338
Morrill Memorial Library 33 Walpole St PO Box 220................... Norwood MA 02062 *Web:* www.norwoodlibrary.org	781-769-0200		434-3
Morrill Public Library 431 Oregon St .... Hiawatha KS 66434 *Web:* www.hiawathalibrary.org	785-742-3831	742-2054	434-3
Morrilton Packing Company Inc 51 Blue Diamond Dr........................ Morrilton AR 72110 *TF:* 800-264-2475 ■ *Web:* petitjeanmeats.com	501-354-2474	354-2283	473
Morris & Associates Inc 803 Morris Dr .... Garner NC 27529 *Web:* www.morris-associates.com	919-582-9200	582-9100	664
Morris & Broms LLC 900 Wellington Ave......................... Cranston RI 02910 *Web:* www.morrisandbroms.com	401-781-3134	461-4460	567
Morris & Dickson Company Ltd 410 Kay Ln.............................. Shreveport LA 71115 *TF:* 800-388-3833 ■ *Web:* www.morrisdickson.com	318-797-7900		238
Morris & Gwendolyn Cafritz Foundation 1825 K St NW Ste 1400................... Washington DC 20006 *Web:* www.cafritzfoundation.org	202-223-3100	296-7567	305
Morris & Mcdaniel Incorporated Consultants 117 S St Asaph St......................... Alexandria VA 22314 *Web:* www.morrisandmcdaniel.com	703-836-3600		195
Morris & Morris PC 32 Kearney Rd .... Needham MA 02494 *Web:* mmpc-cpa.com	781-455-6900		2
Morris Arboretum of the University of Pennsylvania 100 E NW Ave.......................... Philadelphia PA 19118 *Web:* www.morrisarboretum.org	215-247-5777		97
Morris Artists Management LLC 818 19th Ave S............................ Nashville TN 37203 *Web:* www.dalemorrismgt.com	615-327-3400		226
Morris Bean & Co 777 E Hyde Rd.......... Yellow Springs OH 45387 *Web:* www.morrisbean.com	937-767-7301		492
Morris Cerullo World Evangelism 3545 Aero Ct Frnt......................... San Diego CA 92123 *TF:* 866-756-4200 ■ *Web:* mcwe.com	866-756-4200		48-20
Morris College 100 W College St .... Sumter SC 29150 *TF:* 866-853-1345 ■ *Web:* www.morris.edu	803-934-3200	773-8241	166
Morris Costumes 4300 Monroe Rd............. Charlotte NC 28205 *Web:* morriscostumes.com	704-333-4653	348-3032	155-6
Morris County 501 W Main St............. Council Grove KS 66846 *Web:* www.morriscountyks.org	620-767-5533	767-7717	338
Morris County 500 Broadnax St.............. Daingerfield TX 75638 *Web:* www.co.morris.tx.us	903-645-3911	645-5729	338
Morris County 10 Court St PO Box 900................... Morristown NJ 07960 *Web:* morriscountynj.gov	973-285-6000		338
Morris County Chamber of Commerce 325 Columbia Tpke Ste 101.............. Florham Park NJ 07932 *Web:* www.morrischamber.org	973-539-3882		139
Morris County Library (MCL) 30 E Hanover Ave......................... Whippany NJ 07981 *Web:* mclib.info	973-285-6930		434-3
Morris Coupling Co 2240 W 15th St................ Erie PA 16505 *TF:* 800-426-1579 ■ *Web:* www.morriscoupling.com	814-459-1741	453-5155	490
Morris Duffy Alonso & Faley 2 Rector St 22nd Fl......................... New York NY 10006 *Web:* mdafny.com	212-766-1888	766-3252	428
Morris Engineering Inc 515 Warrenville Rd............................ Lisle IL 60532 *Web:* ecivil1.com	630-271-0770	271-0774	261
Morris Furniture Company Inc 2377 Commerce Center Dr.................... Fairborn OH 45324 *Web:* www.morrisathome.com	937-439-0900		321
Morris Group Inc 910 Day Hill Rd............... Windsor CT 06095 *Fax Area Code: 860 ■ *Web:* www.morrisgroupinc.com	205-871-3500	687-3476*	186
Morris Herald-News 1804 N Division St .... Morris IL 60450 *TF:* 800-397-9397 ■ *Web:* www.morrisherald-news.com	815-942-3221		532-3
Morris Hospital 150 W High St.................. Morris IL 60450 *Web:* www.morrishospital.org	815-942-2932		374-3
Morris Industries Inc 777 Rt 23 .... Pompton Plains NJ 07444 *TF:* 800-835-0777 ■ *Web:* www.morrispipe.com	973-835-6600	835-1245	537
Morris Inn University of Notre Dame 130 Morris Inn ...... Notre Dame IN 46556 *Web:* morrisinn.nd.edu	574-631-2000		379
Morris J. Golombeck Inc 960 Franklin Ave........................... Brooklyn NY 11225 *Web:* www.golombeckspice.com	718-284-3505	693-1941	297-11
Morris K. Udall Foundation 130 S Scott Ave .... Tucson AZ 85701 *Web:* www.udall.gov	520-901-8500	670-5530	340-20
Morris Machine Company Inc 6480 S Belmont .... Indianapolis IN 46217 *Web:* www.morrismachine.com	317-788-0371		454
Morris Material Handling Inc 315 W Forest Hill Ave....................... Oak Creek WI 53154 *TF:* 800-933-3001 ■ *Web:* www.morriscranes.com	414-764-6200	570-2779	470
Morris Minor Registry North America 318 Hampton Pk.......................... Westerville OH 43081 *Web:* www.morrisminor.us	614-899-2394		637-10
Morris Multimedia Inc 27 Abercorn St .... Savannah GA 31401 *Web:* www.morrismultimedia.com	912-233-1281	232-4639	637-8
Morris Murdock LLC 515 South 700 East Ste 1B............... Salt Lake City UT 84102 *TF:* 800-944-8018 ■ *Web:* www.morrismurdock.com	801-483-6441		772
Morris Museum 6 Normandy Heights Rd .... Morristown NJ 07960 *Web:* morrismuseum.org	973-971-3700		520
Morris Museum of Art 1 Tenth St.............. Augusta GA 30901 *Web:* www.themorris.org	706-724-7501	724-7612	520
Morris Performing Arts Ctr 211 N Michigan St .... South Bend IN 46601 *Web:* www.morriscenter.org	574-235-9190		572
Morris Printing Group 3212 Hwy 30 E........... Kearney NE 68847 *Web:* www.morriscookbooks.com	308-236-7888		627
Morris Products Inc 53 Carey Rd............ Queensbury NY 12804 *TF:* 888-777-6678 ■ *Web:* www.morrisproducts.com	518-743-0523		787
Morris School District 31 Hazel St .... Morristown NJ 07960 *Web:* www.morrisschooldistrict.org	973-292-2300		685
Morris School District 54 54 White Oak Dr................................ Morris IL 60450 *Web:* www.morris54.org	815-942-0056	942-0240	780
Morris Tile Distributors Inc (MTD) 9132 Gaither Rd .... Gaithersburg MD 20877 *Web:* morristile.com	301-670-4222	590-0792	191-1
Morris Tile Distributors Inc (MTD) 2525 Kenilworth Ave.......................... Tuxedo MD 20781 *Web:* www.morristile.com	301-773-7000	386-2261	191-1
Morris Wilson PC Eight Tower Bridge 161 Washington St Ste 900............................ Conshohocken PA 19428 *Web:* morriswilson.com	610-825-0500		41
Morris-Depew Associates Inc 2914 Cleveland Ave .... Fort Myers FL 33901 *TF:* 866-337-7341 ■ *Web:* morris-depew.com	239-337-3993	337-3994	653
Morrisette Paper Company Inc 5925 Summit Ave..................... Browns Summit NC 27214 *Web:* morrisette.com	336-375-1515		553
Morris-Jumel Mansion 65 Jumel Terr at 160th St .... New York NY 10032 *Web:* www.morrisjumel.org	212-923-8008		520
Morrison & Foerster LLP 425 Market St......................... San Francisco CA 94105 *Web:* www.mofo.com	415-268-7000	268-7522	428
Morrison Agency Inc, The 3365 Piedmont Rd Tower Walk at Tower Pl Ste 1400 .... Atlanta GA 30305 *Web:* morrison.agency	404-233-3405	261-8384	195
Morrison Berkshire Inc 865 S Church St........................ North Adams MA 01247 *Web:* www.morrisonberkshire.com	413-663-6501	663-6522	744
Morrison Bros Co 570 E Seventh St .... Dubuque IA 52001 *TF:* 800-553-4840 ■ *Web:* www.morbros.com	563-583-5701	583-5028	537
Morrison Cohen LLP 909 3rd Ave............. New York NY 10022 *Web:* www.mcsw.com	212-735-8600	735-8708	41
Morrison Communities, The 6 Ter St......... Whitefield NH 03598 *Web:* themorrison.org	603-837-2541	837-3878	793
Morrison Construction Co 1834 Summer St.......................... Hammond IN 46320 *Web:* www.mcco.com	219-932-5036	933-7302	189-10
Morrison Container Handling Solutions 335 W 194th St........................... Glenwood IL 60425 *Web:* morrison-chs.com	708-756-6660	756-6620	454
Morrison Correctional Institution 1573 McDonald Church Rd PO Box 169 .... Hoffman NC 28347 *Web:* www.ncdps.gov	910-281-3161		412
Morrison County 213-1st Ave SE .... Little Falls MN 56345 *TF:* 866-401-1111 ■ *Web:* www.co.morrison.mn.us	320-632-2941		338
Morrison County Record 216 SE First St .... Little Falls MN 56345 *TF:* 888-637-2345 ■ *Web:* www.hometownsource.com	320-632-2345	632-2348	532-4
Morrison Express Corporation USA 18900 8th Ave S Ste 700 .... El Segundo CA 90245 *Web:* www.morrisonexpress.com	310-322-8999	322-6688	311
Morrison Hershfield Group Inc 125 Commerce Valley Dr W Ste 300........... Markham ON L3T7W4 *TF:* 888-649-4730 ■ *Web:* morrisonhershfield.com	416-499-3110		261
Morrison House 116 S Alfred St .... Alexandria VA 22314 *Web:* morrisonhouse.com	703-838-8000		671
Morrison Industrial Equipment Co 1825 Monroe NW....................... Grand Rapids MI 49505 *Web:* www.morrison-ind.com	616-447-3800	361-0885	57
Morrison Institute of Technology 701 Portland Ave .... Morrison IL 61270 *Web:* www.morrisontech.edu	815-772-7218	772-7584	800
Morrison Karsten Group 528 B St............ Santa Rosa CA 95401 *Web:* mkgrp.com	707-575-9416		652
Morrison Mahoney LLP 250 Summer St .... Boston MA 02210 *Web:* www.morrisonmahoney.com	617-439-7500	439-7590	428
Morrison Management Specialists Inc 5801 Peachtree Dunwoody Rd .... Atlanta GA 30342 *Fax Area Code: 404 ■ *TF:* 800-225-4368 ■ *Web:* www.greatstartshere.com	800-225-4368	845-3333*	299
Morrison Milling Co 319 E Prairie St............. Denton TX 76201 *TF:* 800-531-7912 ■ *Web:* morrisonmilling.com	940-387-6111		296-23
Morrison Scott Alan Law Offices of PA 141 W Patrick St Ste 300 .... Frederick MD 21701 *TF:* 866-220-5185 ■ *Web:* www.samlawoffice.com	301-694-6262		428
Morrison Sund PLLC 5125 County Rd 101 Ste 200 .... Minnetonka MN 55345 *Web:* morrisonsund.com	952-975-0050		41
Morrison Supply Company - Abilene Inc 311 E Vickery Blvd .... Fort Worth TX 76104 *Fax Area Code: 817 ■ *TF:* 877-709-2227 ■ *Web:* www.morsco.com	877-709-2227	877-4942*	612
Morrison Terrebonne Lumber Center LLC 605 Barataria Ave .... Houma LA 70360 *Web:* www.morrisonterrebonne.com	985-879-1597		361
Morrison Textile Machinery Co 6044 Lancaster Hwy .... Fort Lawn SC 29714 *Web:* www.morrisontexmach.com	803-872-4401		744
Morrison Weighing Systems Inc 7605 50th St.................................. Milan IL 61264 *Web:* www.morrisonweighing.com	309-799-7311	799-7313	684
Morrison, Frost, Olsen, Irvine & Schartz LLP 323 Poyntz Ave Ste 204 .... Manhattan KS 66502 *TF:* 800-316-2324 ■ *Web:* mfoilaw.com	785-776-9208		41
Morrison, Sherwood, Wilson & Deola, Pllp 401 N Last Chance Gulch...................... Helena MT 59601 *Web:* mswdlaw.com	406-442-3261		41
Morrison-Clark Historic Inn & Restaurant 1010 Massachusetts Ave NW .... Washington DC 20001 *Web:* www.morrisonclark.com	202-898-1200		379

Name / Address	Phone	Fax	Class
Morrison-Knudsen Nature Ctr 600 S Walnut St ... Boise ID 83712 *Web:* www.idfg.idaho.gov	208-334-2225		50-5
Morrison-Maierle 1 Engineering Pl ... Helena MT 59602 *Web:* www.m-m.net	406-442-3050		261
Morrison-Rockwood State Park 18750 Lake Rd ... Morrison IL 61270 *Web:* www2.illinois.gov	815-772-4708		565
Morrissey Family Businesses Inc 5919 Spring Creek Rd ... Rockford IL 61114 *Web:* www.morrisseyfamily.com	815-282-4600		734
Morrissey Hospitality Companies Inc 345 St Peter St Ste 2000 ... Saint Paul MN 55102 *Web:* www.morrisseyhospitality.com	651-221-0815		707
Morrissey Inc 9304 Bryant Ave S ... Bloomington MN 55420 *Web:* morrisseyinc.com	952-888-4675		488
Morrisson-Reeves Public Library 80 N Sixth St ... Richmond IN 47374 *Web:* mrlinfo.org	765-966-8291	962-1318	434-3
Morristown Area Chamber of Commerce 825 W First N St ... Morristown TN 37814 *Web:* www.morristownchamber.com	423-586-6382	586-6576	139
Morristown Drivers Service Inc 1111 Gateway Service Park Rd ... Morristown TN 37813 *Web:* www.mdstrucking.com	423-581-6048	581-9696	780
Morristown National Historical Park 30 Washington Pl ... Morristown NJ 07960 *Web:* www.nps.gov	973-539-2016	451-9212	564
Morristown Utility Systems PO Box 667 ... Morristown TN 37815 *Web:* www.morristownutilities.org	423-586-4121	587-6590	787
Morristown-Hamblen Public Library 417 W Main St ... Morristown TN 37814 *Web:* www.morristownhamblenlibrary.org	423-586-6410	587-6226	434-3
Morris-Union Jointure Commission 340 Central Ave ... New Providence NJ 07974 *Web:* www.mujc.org	908-464-7625	464-1244	685
Morrisville State College 80 Eaton St PO Box 901 ... Morrisville NY 13408 *TF:* 800-258-0111 ■ *Web:* www.morrisville.edu	315-684-6000	684-6427	166
Morrow Control & Supply Co 810 Marion Motley Ave NE ... Canton OH 44705 *TF:* 800-362-9830 ■ *Web:* www.morrowcontrol.com	330-452-9791		612
Morrow County 100 Ct St PO Box 788 ... Heppner OR 97836 *Web:* www.co.morrow.or.us	541-676-9061	676-9876	338
Morrow County 80 N Walnut St Ste A ... Mount Gilead OH 43338 *Web:* www.morrowcounty.info	419-947-4085		338
Morrow County Chamber of Commerce 9 1/2 W High St PO Box 174 ... Mount Gilead OH 43338 *Web:* morrowchamber.org	419-946-2821		139
Morrow County Grain Growers Inc (MCGG) 350 N Main St ... Lexington OR 97839 *TF:* 800-452-7396 ■ *Web:* www.mcgg.net	541-989-8221	989-8229	10-5
Morrow Enterprises 17725 82nd Rd N ... Loxahatchee FL 33470 *Web:* www.morrowent.com	561-793-5532	791-0775	328
Morrow Equipment Company LLC 3218 Pringle Rd SE PO Box 3306 ... Salem OR 97302 *Web:* www.morrow.com	503-585-5721	363-1172	264-3
Morrow Mountain State Park 49104 Morrow Mtn Rd ... Albemarle NC 28001 *Web:* www.ncparks.gov	704-982-4402		565
Morrow Realty Company Inc (MRC) 809 22nd Ave ... Tuscaloosa AL 35401 *Web:* www.morrowrealty.com	205-759-5781	391-0031	652
Morrow Romine & Pearson Pc Atty 122 S Hull St ... Montgomery AL 36104 *Web:* www.mrplaw.com	334-262-7707		445
Morrow-Meadows Corp 231 Benton Ct ... City of Industry CA 91789 *Web:* www.morrow-meadows.com	909-598-7700	598-3907	189-4
Morse & Edwards LLC 191 Cleveland Ave Sw ... Atlanta GA 30315 *Web:* morseandedwardslaw.com	404-762-1100		41
Morse Electric Inc 500 W S St ... Freeport IL 61032 *Web:* www.themorsegroup.com	815-266-4200	266-8900	189-4
Morse Industries Inc 25811 74th Ave S ... Kent WA 98032 *TF:* 800-325-7513 ■ *Web:* morseindustries.com	800-325-7513		697
Morse Institute Library 14 E Central St ... Natick MA 01760 *Web:* morseinstitute.org	508-647-6520		434-3
Morse Operations Inc 3790 W Blue Heron Blvd ... Riviera Beach FL 33404 *TF:* 800-755-2593 ■ *Web:* www.edmorsehonda.com	800-755-2593		516
Morse, Barnes-Brown & Pendleton PC CityPoint 230 3rd Ave 4th Fl ... Waltham MA 02451 *Web:* www.mbbp.com	781-622-5930	622-5933	428
MorseLife Inc 4847 Fred Gladstone Dr ... West Palm Beach FL 33417 *Web:* morselife.org	561-471-5111		371
Morstan General Agency Inc 600 Community Dr PO Box 4500 ... Manhasset NY 11030 *Web:* www.morstan.com	516-488-4747		390
Mort Crim Communications Inc 155 W Congress Ste 501 ... Detroit MI 48226 *Web:* mccicorp.com	313-481-4700		514
Mortara Instrument Inc 7865 N 86th St ... Milwaukee WI 53224 *TF:* 800-231-7437 ■ *Web:* www.mortara.com	414-354-1600	354-4760	250
Mortech Inc 5960 S 57th St ... Lincoln NE 68516 *TF:* 855-298-9327 ■ *Web:* www.mortech.com	402-441-4647	420-6549	178-1
Mortech Manufacturing Inc 411 N Aerojet Ave ... Azusa CA 91702 *TF:* 800-410-0100 ■ *Web:* mortechmfg.com	626-334-1471		406
Mortgage Bankers Association PAC (MORPAC) 1919 M St NW ... Washington DC 20036 *Web:* www.mba.org	202-557-2700		615
Mortgage Banking Solutions Frost Bank Tower 401 Congress Ave Ste 1540 ... Austin TX 78701 *TF:* 800-476-0853 ■ *Web:* www.mbs-team.com	512-977-9900		463
Mortgage Builder 24370 NW Hwy ... Southfield MI 48075 *TF:* 800-850-8060 ■ *Web:* www.mortgagebuilder.com	800-850-8060		178-10
Mortgage Guaranty Insurance Corp 270 E Kilbourn Ave ... Milwaukee WI 53202 *TF:* 800-558-9900 ■ *Web:* mgic.com	414-347-6480		391-5
Mortgage Insurance Companies of America (MICA) 1101 17th St NW Ste 700 ... Washington DC 20036 *Web:* www.usmi.org	202-280-1820		49-9
Mortgage Intelligence Inc 5770 Hurontario St Ste 600 ... Mississauga ON L5R3G5 *TF:* 888-468-4734 ■ *Web:* www.mortgageintelligence.ca	905-283-3600		217
Mortgage Investors Group 8320 E Walker Springs Ln ... Knoxville TN 37923 *TF:* 800-489-8910 ■ *Web:* migonline.com	865-691-8910	691-7714	509
Mortgage Recovery Law Group Llp (Mrlg) 700 N Brand Blvd Ste 830 ... Glendale CA 91203 *Web:* themrlg.com	818-630-7900		41
Mortgageflex Systems Inc 25 N Market St ... Jacksonville FL 32202 *TF:* 800-326-3539 ■ *Web:* www.mortgageflex.com	904-356-2490		177
Morton Arboretum 4100 Illinois Rt 53 ... Lisle IL 60532 *Web:* www.mortonarb.org	630-968-0074		97
Morton Buildings Inc 252 W Adams St PO Box 399 ... Morton IL 61550 **Fax Area Code:* 309 ■ *TF:* 800-447-7436 ■ *Web:* mortonbuildings.com	800-447-7436	263-6341*	105
Morton Capital Management 27200 Agoura Rd Ste 200 ... Calabasas CA 91301 *Web:* mortoncapital.com	818-222-4727	222-8457	401
Morton College 3801 S Central Ave ... Cicero IL 60804 *Web:* www.morton.edu	708-656-8000	656-9592	162
Morton Community Bank 721 W Jackson St ... Morton IL 61550 *Web:* www.hometownbanks.com	309-266-5337		70
Morton Consulting LLC 4701 Cox Rd ... Glen Allen VA 23060 *Web:* themortonway.com	804-290-4272		194
Morton County PO Box 1116 ... Elkhart KS 67950 *Web:* www.mtcoks.com	620-697-2157	697-2159	338
Morton County 210 2nd Ave NW ... Mandan ND 58554 *Web:* www.co.morton.nd.us	701-667-3300		338
Morton Grove Chamber of Commerce and Industry (MGCCI) 6101 Capulina Ave ... Morton Grove IL 60053 *Web:* www.mgcci.org	847-965-0330	965-0349	139
Morton Grove Pharmaceuticals Inc 6451 Main St ... Morton Grove IL 60053 **Fax Area Code:* 973 ■ *TF:* 800-346-6854 ■ *Web:* www.wockhardtusa.com	847-967-5600	257-4978*	583
Morton Grove Public Library 6140 Lincoln Ave ... Morton Grove IL 60053 *Web:* www.mgpl.org	847-965-4220	965-7903	434-3
Morton High School 500 Champion Dr ... Morton TX 79346 *Web:* www.mortonisd.net	806-266-5505		685
Morton Hospital & Medical Ctr 88 Washington St ... Taunton MA 02780 *Web:* www.mortonhospital.org	508-828-7000		374-3
Morton Industries LLC 70 Commerce Dr ... Morton IL 61550 *Web:* www.mortonind.com	309-263-2590		482
Morton Machining & Manufacturing Co 701 Flint Ave ... Morton IL 61550 *Web:* www.mortonmachining.com	309-266-6551		454
Morton Salt Inc 123 N Wacker Dr ... Chicago IL 60606 *TF:* 800-725-8847 ■ *Web:* www.mortonsalt.com	312-807-2000		680
Morton's The Steakhouse 1050 N State St ... Chicago IL 60610 *Web:* www.mortons.com	312-266-4820		671
Morven Museum & Gardens 55 Stockton St ... Princeton NJ 08540 *Web:* morven.org	609-924-8144		97
Morvillo Abramowitz Grand Iason & Anello PC 565 5th Ave ... New York NY 10017 *Web:* www.maglaw.com	212-856-9600	856-9494	41
Mosaic Business Solutions LLC 6766 Racetrack Rd Ste 217 ... Bowie MD 20715	301-464-2665		570
Mosaic Company Inc, The 555 S Renton Village Pl ... Renton WA 98057 *Web:* themosaiccompany.com	425-254-1724		260
Mosaic Energy Ltd 606-4th St SW Ste 900 ... Calgary AB T2P1T1 *TF:* 888-221-4420 ■ *Web:* mosaicenergy.ca	403-699-7650		539
Mosaic Event Management Inc 67 Haight St ... San Francisco CA 94102 *Web:* www.mosaicevents.com	415-908-2650		196
Mosaic Hotel 125 S Spalding Dr ... Beverly Hills CA 90212 *TF:* 800-463-4466 ■ *Web:* mosaichotel.com	310-278-0303		379
Mosaic Records 425 Fairfield Ave Ste 421 ... Stamford CT 06902 *Web:* www.mosaicrecords.com	203-327-7111	323-3526	657
Moschip Semiconductor Technology USA 840 N Hillview Dr ... Milpitas CA 95035 *Web:* moschip.com	408-737-7141	737-7708	696
Moscone Ctr 747 Howard St ... San Francisco CA 94103 *Web:* www.moscone.com	415-974-4000	974-4073	205
Moscot 108 Orchard St ... New York NY 10002 *TF:* 866-667-2687 ■ *Web:* moscot.com	212-477-3796		543
Moscow Chamber of Commerce 411 S Main St ... Moscow ID 83843 *TF:* 866-770-2020 ■ *Web:* www.moscowchamber.com	208-882-1800		139
Moscow on the Hill 371 Selby Ave ... Saint Paul MN 55102 *Web:* www.moscowonthehill.com	651-291-1236		671
Moscowitz & Moscowitz PA 201 Alhambra Cir Ste 1200 ... Miami FL 33134 *Web:* moscowitz.com	305-379-8300		41
Mosdos Press 1508 Warrensville Center Rd ... Cleveland Heights OH 44121 *Web:* www.mosdospress.com	216-291-4158		637-2
Mosebach Manufacturing Co 1417 Mclaughlin Run Rd ... Pittsburgh PA 15241 *Web:* www.mosebachresistors.com	412-220-0200	220-0236	203

Name / Address	Phone	Fax	Class
Moseley Architects PC 3200 Norfolk St Richmond VA 23230 *Web:* www.moseleyarchitects.com	804-794-7555	355-5690	186
Moseley Associates Inc 82 Coromar Dr Santa Barbara CA 93117 *Web:* www.moseleysb.com	805-968-9621	685-9638	647
Moseley Corp, The 31 Hayward St Franklin MA 02038 *Web:* www.moseleycorp.com	508-520-4004		463
Moseley Technical Services Inc 7500 S Memorial Pkwy Ste 215-R Huntsville AL 35802 *Web:* www.moseleytechnical.com	256-880-0446	880-0936	261
Moseo Corp 2722 Elake Ave E Seattle WA 98102 *TF:* 800-741-0926 ■ *Web:* www.seniorhomes.com	800-741-0926		387
Moser Corp 601 N 13th St Rogers AR 72756 *TF:* 800-632-4564 ■ *Web:* www.mosercorporation.com	479-636-3481		321
Moses Greeley Parker Memorial Library 28 Arlington St Dracut MA 01826 *Web:* www.dracutlibrary.org	978-454-5474	454-9120	434-3
Moses Inc 106 E Buchanan St Phoenix AZ 85004 *Web:* mosesinc.com	602-417-1301		4
Moses Lake Area Chamber of Commerce 324 S Pioneer Way Moses Lake WA 98837 *TF:* 800-992-6234 ■ *Web:* www.moseslake.com	509-765-7888		139
Moses Lake Industries Inc 8248 Randolph Rd NE Moses Lake WA 98837 *Web:* www.mlindustries.com	509-762-5336	762-5981	145
Moses Lake Steel Supply Inc 1502 W Broadway Moses Lake WA 98837 *TF:* 800-765-1741 ■ *Web:* www.moseslakesteel.com	509-765-1741	766-2496	492
Moshannon Valley Economic Development Partnership 200 Shady Ln Philipsburg PA 16866 *Web:* www.mvedp.org	814-342-2260	342-2878	139
Mosher Co 15 Exchange St Chicopee MA 01014 *Web:* www.mocomfg.com	413-598-8341		1
Mosholu Parkway Nursing & Rehabilitation Ctr 3356 Perry Ave Bronx NY 10467 *Web:* www.mosholucares.com	718-655-3568	881-4422	450
Mosier & Associates CPAS Inc 180 E Spring Valley Pk Ste B Centerville OH 45458 *Web:* mosiercpas.com	937-291-2600		2
Mosites Rubber Company Inc PO Box 2115 Fort Worth TX 76113 *Web:* www.mositesrubber.com	817-335-3451	870-1564	676
Mosquito Lake State Park 1439 SR-305 Cortland OH 44410 *Web:* parks.ohiodnr.gov	330-637-2856		565
Moss Adams LLP 999 Third Ave Ste 2800 Seattle WA 98104 *Web:* www.mossadams.com	206-302-6500		2
Moss Construction Management 2101 N Andrews Ave Fort Lauderdale FL 33311 *Web:* mosscm.com	954-524-5678		610
Moss Inc PO Box 189 Pasadena MD 21123 *TF:* 800-932-6677 ■ *Web:* www.mosssubstrates.com	410-768-3442	768-3971	231
Moss Insurance Group PO Box 220 Siloam Springs AR 72761 *Web:* mossins.com	479-524-5111	524-8943	390
Moss Landing State Beach c/o Monterey District Ofc 2211 Garden Rd Monterey CA 93940 *Web:* www.parks.ca.gov	831-384-7695	647-6239	565
Moss Mansion 914 Div St Billings MT 59101 *Web:* www.mossmansion.com	406-256-5100		50-3
Moss Precision Inc 3200 Arden Rd Hayward CA 94545 *Web:* www.mossprecision.com	510-785-2235		454
Moss Supply Company Inc 5001 N Graham St Charlotte NC 28269 *TF:* 800-438-0770 ■ *Web:* www.mosssupply.com	704-596-8717	598-9012	234
Mossberg & Company Inc 301 E Sample St South Bend IN 46601 *TF:* 800-428-3340 ■ *Web:* www.mossbergco.com	574-289-9253		626
Mossberg Industries Inc 204 N Second St Garrett IN 46738 *Web:* www.mossbergind.com	260-357-5141	357-5144	601
Mossbrook & Hicks Insurance Agency Inc 19 N Main St Cape May NJ 08210 *Web:* mossbrookhicks.com	609-465-7121		390
Mosser Construction 122 S Wilson Ave Fremont OH 43420 *Web:* www.mosserconstruction.com	419-334-3801	332-1534	186
Mosser Cos 308 Jessie St San Francisco CA 94103 *Web:* www.mosserco.com	415-284-9000		463
Mosser Hotel 54 Fourth St San Francisco CA 94103 *TF:* 800-227-3804 ■ *Web:* www.themosser.com	415-986-4400		379
Mossman's Southwest 3610 Wible Rd Bakersfield CA 93309 *Web:* www.mossmanscatering.com	661-832-5130	832-4783	671
MossWarner 33332 Valle Rd Ste 200 San Juan Capistrano CA 92675 *Web:* mosswarner.com	949-429-2266		7
Mossy Motors Inc 1331 S Broad St New Orleans LA 70125 *Web:* www.mossymotors.com	504-822-2050		57
Mosteller & Assoc 2433 Morgantown Rd Ste 100 Reading PA 19607 *Web:* www.mostellerhr.com	610-779-3870	779-7954	195
MoSys Inc 3301 Olcott St Santa Clara CA 95054 *Web:* www.mosys.com	408-418-7500		696
Motan Inc 320 N Acorn St Plainwell MI 49080 *Web:* www.motan-colortronic.com	269-685-1050	685-1059	207
Mote Marine Laboratory 1600 Ken Thompson Pkwy Sarasota FL 34236 *Web:* mote.org	941-388-4441	388-4312	668
Mother Bethel AME Church 419 S Sixth St Philadelphia PA 19147 *Web:* www.motherbethel.org	215-925-0616	925-1402	50-1
Mother Frances Hospital 800 E Dawson St Tyler TX 75701 *Web:* www.tmfhc.org	903-593-8441		374-3
Mother Jones Magazine 222 Sutter St Ste 600 San Francisco CA 94108 *TF:* 800-438-6656 ■ *Web:* www.motherjones.com	415-321-1700	321-1701	457-17
Mother Murphy's Labs Inc 2826 S Elm St PO Box 16846 Greensboro NC 27416 *TF:* 800-849-1277 ■ *Web:* www.mothermurphys.com	336-273-1737	273-2615	296-15
Mother Neff State Park 1680 Texas 236 Hwy Moody TX 76557 *Web:* tpwd.texas.gov	254-853-2389		565
Mother of Good Counsel Home 6825 Natural Bridge Rd Saint Louis MO 63121 *Web:* mogch.org	314-383-4765		672
Mother Tongue Ink 4815 NE 47th Ave Wolf Creek OR 97497 *TF:* 877-693-6666 ■ *Web:* www.wemoon.ws	541-956-6052		637-2
Mother's 33 Virginia Pl Buffalo NY 14202 *Web:* www.mothersbuffalo.com	716-882-2989		671
Mother's Bistro & Bar 212 SW Stark St Portland OR 97204 *Web:* www.mothersbistro.com	503-464-1122		671
Mother's Market & Kitchen 1890 Newport Blvd Costa Mesa CA 92627 *TF:* 800-595-6667 ■ *Web:* www.mothersmarket.com	949-631-4741		345
Mother's Polishes Waxes & Cleaners 5456 Industrial Dr Huntington Beach CA 92649 *Web:* www.mothers.com	714-891-3364	893-1827	151
Motherbaby Press PO Box 2672 Eugene OR 97402 *Web:* www.midwiferytoday.com	541-344-7438	344-1422	637-2
Motherhood Maternity 456 N Fifth St Philadelphia PA 19123 *Web:* www.motherhood.com	215-873-2200	625-3843	157-6
MotherMassage PO Box 150337 Brooklyn NY 11215 *Web:* www.mothermassage.net	718-832-6575		167-3
Mothers Against Drunk Driving (MADD) 511 E John Carpenter Fwy Ste 700 Irving TX 75062 *TF:* 877-275-6233 ■ *Web:* www.madd.org	877-275-6233		48-6
Mothers Supporting Daughters with Breast Cancer (MSDBC) 25235 Fox Chase Dr Chestertown MD 21620 *Web:* www.mothersdaughters.org	410-778-1982	778-1411	48-17
Moti Mahal 1805 14 St SW Calgary AB T2T3T1 *Web:* motimahal.ca	403-228-9990		671
Motio Inc 7161 Bishop Rd Ste 200 Plano TX 75024 *TF:* 877-362-8708 ■ *Web:* motio.com	877-362-8708		177
Motion Agency, The 233 N Michigan Ave Ste 3000 Chicago IL 60601 *Web:* agencyinmotion.com	312-565-0044		4
Motion Analysis Corp 3617 Wwind Blvd Santa Rosa CA 95403 *Web:* www.motionanalysis.com	707-579-6500		639
Motion Composites 160 Armand-Majeau Sud Saint-Roch-de-l'Achigan QC J0K3H0 *Web:* www.motioncomposites.com	450-588-6555		477
Motion Control Engineering Inc 11380 White Rock Rd Rancho Cordova CA 95742 *TF:* 800-444-7442 ■ *Web:* www.mceinc.com	916-463-9200		256
Motion Dynamics Corp 5625 Airline Rd Fruitport MI 49415 *Web:* www.motiondc.com	231-865-7400	865-7401	492
Motion Envelope Inc 1455 Terre Colony Ct Dallas TX 75212 *Web:* i3plasticcards.com	214-634-2131		263
Motion Fitness LLC 1400 W Northwest Hwy Palatine IL 60067 *Web:* www.motionfitness.com	847-963-8969		711
Motion Machine Co 524 Mccormick Dr Lapeer MI 48446 *Web:* www.motionmach.com	810-664-9901	664-4377	454
Motion Message Inc 20 Frontier Trl Ste 201 Manorville NY 11949 *TF:* 800-323-4777 ■ *Web:* www.cbd-shack.com	631-924-9500		9
Motion Picture & Television Fund 23388 Mulholland Dr Woodland Hills CA 91364 *TF:* 855-760-6783 ■ *Web:* www.mptf.com	855-760-6783		48-4
Motion Picture Assn (MPA) 15301 Ventura Blvd Bldg E Sherman Oaks CA 91403 *Web:* www.mpaa.org	818-995-6600		48-4
Motion Recruitment Partners 131 Clarendon St 3rd Fl Boston MA 02116 *Web:* www.motionrecruitment.com	617-585-6500		721
Motion Specialties Inc 106-2517 Bowen Rd Calgary AB V9T3L2 *Web:* motionspecialties.com	403-247-2222		45
Motion Systems Corp 600 Industrial Way W Eatontown NJ 07724 *Web:* www.actuator.com	732-222-1800	389-9191	223
Motion Tech Automation Inc 7166 4th St N Saint Paul MN 55128 *Web:* www.motiontech.com	651-730-9010	730-9039	815
MotionDSP Inc 700 Airport Blvd Ste 270 Burlingame CA 94010 *Web:* www.motiondsp.com	650-288-1164		174
MotionMasters Inc 2288 Roxalana Rd Dunbar WV 25064 *Web:* www.motionmasters.com	304-345-8800	345-8809	514
MotionPoint Corp Lyons Technology Ctr 4661 Johnson Rd Ste 14 Coconut Creek FL 33073 *Web:* www.motionpoint.com	954-421-0890		768
Motionsoft Inc 1451 Rockville Pke Ste 500 Rockville MD 20852 *TF:* 800-829-4321 ■ *Web:* www.motionsoft.net	800-829-4321		178-1
Mo-Tires Ltd 2830 5 Ave N Lethbridge AB T1H0P1 *TF:* 800-774-3888 ■ *Web:* www.mo-tires.com	403-329-4533		393
Motista Inc 1777 Borel Pl Ste 500 San Mateo CA 94402 *Web:* www.motista.com	650-204-7976		387
Motiva Enterprises LLC 700 Milam St Houston TX 77002 *Web:* www.motiva.com	713-277-8000		580
MotivAction LLC 16355 36th Ave N Ste 100 Minneapolis MN 55446 *Web:* www.motivaction.com	763-412-3000		384
Motivating Graphics Inc 3100 Eagle Pkwy Fort Worth TX 76177 *Web:* www.motivatinggraphics.com	817-491-4788		627
Motivation Through Incentives Inc 10400 W 103 St Ste 10 Overland Park KS 66214 *TF:* 800-826-3464 ■ *Web:* www.mtievents.com	913-438-2600		384
Motive 2901 Blake St Ste 180 Denver CO 80205 *Web:* thinkmotive.com	303-302-2100		195

Listing	Phone	Fax	Class
Motive Entertainment Inc 28128 Pacific Coast Hwy Ste 95 Westlake Village CA 91362 *Web:* www.motivemarketing.biz	805-778-1930		5
Motive Equipment Inc 8300 W Sleske Ct Milwaukee WI 53223 *Web:* www.motiveequipment.com	414-446-3379		650
Motivos PO Box 34391 Philadelphia PA 19101 *Web:* www.motivosmag.com	267-283-1733		637-9
Motley County 701 Dundee Ave PO Box 715 Matador TX 79244 *Web:* www.motleycountytexas.us	806-347-2234	347-2692	338
Motley Fool Inc 2000 Duke St 4th Fl Alexandria VA 22314 *TF:* 800-292-7677 ■ *Web:* www.fool.com	703-838-3665	254-1999	404
Motlow State Community College PO Box 8500 Lynchburg TN 37352 *TF:* 800-654-4877 ■ *Web:* www.mscc.edu	931-393-1544		162
Moto Japanese Restaurant 2607 N Roan St Johnson City TN 37601 *Web:* www.motojc.com	423-282-6686		671
Motor & Equipment Manufacturers Assn (MEMA) 79 TW Alexander Dr 4501 Research Commons Ste 200 Research Triangle Park NC 27709 *Web:* www.mema.org	919-549-4800		49-21
Motor Appliance Corp 601 International Ave Washington DC 20004 *TF:* 800-622-3406 ■ *Web:* www.macmc.com	636-231-6100	532-4609	518
Motor City Computer 1610 E Highwood Dr Pontiac MI 48340 *Web:* www.motorcitycomputer.com	248-454-2000		393
Motor City Electric Co 9440 Grinnell St Detroit MI 48213 *Web:* www.mceco.com	313-921-5300	921-5310	189-4
Motor Coach Industries Intl 1700 E Golf Rd Ste 300 Schaumburg IL 60173 *Web:* www.mcicoach.com	847-285-2000		516
Motor Inn of Knoxville 1705 N Lincoln Knoxville IA 50138 *Web:* www.motorinnautogroup.com	641-842-3200		57
Motor Racing Network (MRN) 555 MRN Dr Concord NC 28027 *Web:* www.mrn.com	704-262-6700	262-6811	78
Motor Service Inc 130 Byassee Dr Hazelwood MO 63042 *TF:* 800-966-5080 ■ *Web:* www.motorserviceinc.net	314-731-4111	731-1213	186
Motor Specialty Inc 2801 Lathrop Ave Racine WI 53405 *Web:* www.motorspecialty.com	262-632-2794	632-8899	518
Motor State Distributing 8300 Lane Dr Watervliet MI 49098 *Web:* www.motorstate.com	269-463-4113		54
Motor Supply Company Bistro 920 Gervais St Columbia SC 29201 *Web:* www.motorsupplycobistro.com	803-256-6687		671
Motor Trend Magazine 6420 Wilshire Blvd 7th Fl Los Angeles CA 90048 *TF:* 800-800-6848 ■ *Web:* www.motortrend.com	323-782-2000	782-2355	457-3
Motor Works Inc 1026 N Haven St Spokane WA 99202 *Web:* www.motorworksengines.com	509-535-9240		60
Motorcar Parts & Accessories 2929 California St Torrance CA 90503 *TF:* 800-890-9988 ■ *Web:* www.motorcarparts.com	310-212-7910	212-7581	247
Motorcars Intl 3015 E Cairo St Springfield MO 65802 *TF:* 866-970-6800 ■ *Web:* www.motorcars-intl.com	417-831-9999	831-9995	57
Motorcycle Consumer News Magazine 3 Burroughs Irvine CA 92618 *TF:* 888-333-0354 ■ *Web:* www.mcnews.com	888-333-0354		457-3
Motorcycle Industry Council (MIC) 2 Jenner St Ste 150 Irvine CA 92618 *Web:* www.mic.org	949-727-4211	727-3313	49-21
Motorcycle Mechanics Institute 9751 Delegates Dr Orlando FL 32837 *TF:* 800-342-9253 ■ *Web:* www.uti.edu	800-342-9253		167-3
MotorHome Magazine 2750 Park View Ct Ste 240 Oxnard CA 93036 *TF:* 800-678-1201 ■ *Web:* www.motorhome.com	800-848-6247		457-22
Motoring Technical Training Institute 1241 Fall River Ave Seekonk MA 02771 *TF:* 866-454-6884 ■ *Web:* www.mtti.edu	508-336-6611	336-8887	167-3
Motorists Insurance Group 471 E Broad St Columbus OH 43215 *TF:* 800-876-6642 ■ *Web:* www.motoristsinsurancegroup.com	866-839-1372		391-2
Motorlease Corp 1506 New Britain Ave Farmington CT 06032 *TF:* 800-243-0182 ■ *Web:* motorlease.com	860-677-9711	674-8677	289
Motorola Foundation 1303 E Algonquin Rd Schaumburg IL 60196 *Web:* www.motorola.com	847-576-5000		304
Motor-Services Hugo Stamp Inc 3190 SW Fourth Ave Fort Lauderdale FL 33315 *TF:* 800-622-6747 ■ *Web:* www.mshs.com	954-763-3660		757
Motorsports Hall of Fame of America (MSHFA) 1801 W International Speedway Blvd Daytona Beach FL 32114 *Web:* www.mshf.com	248-349-7223		522
Motovan Corp 1391 Guy Lussac Boucherville QC J4B7K1 *TF:* 800-363-0808 ■ *Web:* www.motovan.com	450-449-3903		517
Motown Museum 2648 W Grand Blvd Detroit MI 48208 *Web:* www.motownmuseum.org	313-875-2264	875-2267	520
Motrec Inc 200 Rue Des PME St Sherbrooke QC J1C0R2 *Web:* www.motrec.com	819-846-2010		711
Mo-Trim Inc 240 Steubenville Ave Cambridge OH 43725 *Web:* www.motrim.net	740-432-2098		429
Motson Graphics Inc 1717 Bethlehem Pk Flourtown PA 19031 *TF:* 800-972-1986 ■ *Web:* www.motson.com	215-233-0500	233-5014	687
Mott Corp 84 Spring Ln Farmington CT 06032 *TF:* 800-289-6688 ■ *Web:* mottcorp.com	860-747-6333		476
Mott's LLP PO Box 869077 Plano TX 75086 *TF:* 800-426-4891 ■ *Web:* www.motts.com	800-426-4891		296-20
MOTU Inc 1280 Massachusetts Ave Cambridge MA 02138 *Web:* www.motu.com	617-576-2760	576-3609	178-9
Mouat Company Inc, The 1950 Stonegate Dr Ste 150 Birmingham AL 35242 *Web:* mouat.com	205-951-1815	951-3759	261
Moulton Logistics Management 7850 Ruffner Ave Van Nuys CA 91406 *TF:* 800-808-3304 ■ *Web:* www.moultonlogistics.com	800-808-3304		194
Moulton Seth (Rep D - MA) 1127 Longworth House Office Bldg Washington DC 20515 *Web:* moulton.house.gov	202-225-8020	225-5915	342-2
Moultrie Feeders 150 Industrial Rd Alabaster AL 35007 *TF:* 800-653-3334 ■ *Web:* www.moultriefeeders.com	205-664-6700		710
Moultrie News 134 Columbus St Charleston SC 29403 *Web:* www.moultrienews.com	843-958-7489		532-4
Moultrie Observer 25 N Main St Moultrie GA 31768 *Web:* www.moultrieobserver.com	229-985-4545	985-4548	532-2
Moultrie-Colquitt County Chamber of Commerce 116 First Ave SE Moultrie GA 31768 *TF:* 888-408-4748 ■ *Web:* www.moultriechamber.com	229-985-2131		139
Moulures M. Warnet Inc 105 rue Claude-Audy Saint-Jerome QC J5L1Z6 *Web:* www.mwarnet.com	450-438-8447	437-3679	752
Mound City National Cemetery 141 State Hwy 37 Mound City IL 62963 *Web:* www.cem.va.gov	618-748-9107	748-9108	136
Mound Correctional Facility 17601 Mound Rd Detroit MI 48212 *Web:* www.michigan.gov	313-368-8300	368-8972	213
Mound Technologies Inc 25 Mound Pk Dr Springboro OH 45066 *Web:* www.moundtechnologies.com	937-748-2937	748-9763	480
Mounds State Park 4306 Mounds Rd Anderson IN 46017 *Web:* www.in.gov	765-642-6627		565
Mount Airy News 319 N Renfro St Mount Airy NC 27030 *Web:* www.mtairynews.com	336-786-4141	789-2816	532-2
Mount Allison University 62 York St Sackville NB E4L1E2 *TF:* 866-890-6318 ■ *Web:* www.mta.ca	506-364-2269	364-2272	785
Mount Aloysius College 7373 Admiral Perry Hwy Cresson PA 16630 *TF:* 888-823-2220 ■ *Web:* www.mtaloy.edu	814-886-6383	886-6441	166
Mount Angel Seminary 1 Abbey Dr Saint Benedict OR 97373 *TF:* 800-845-8272 ■ *Web:* www.mountangelabbey.org	503-845-3951		167-3
Mount Arlington Public Library 333 Howard Blvd Mount Arlington NJ 07856 *Web:* mountarlingtonlibrary.org	973-398-1516		434-3
Mount Auburn Hospital (MAH) 330 Mt Auburn St Cambridge MA 02138 *Web:* www.mountauburnhospital.org	617-492-3500		374-3
Mount Bachelor Village Resort & Conference Ctr 19717 Mt Bachelor Dr Bend OR 97702 **Fax Area Code:* 541 ■ *TF:* 800-547-5204 ■ *Web:* mtbachelorvillage.com	888-691-3069	388-7401*	669
Mount Blue State Park 297 Center Hill Rd PO Box 610 Weld ME 04285 *Web:* www.maine.gov	207-585-2261		565
Mount Calvary Retreat House 505 E Los Olivos Santa Barbara CA 93105 *Web:* mount-calvary.org	805-682-4117		673
Mount Carmel Ctr 4600 W Davis St Dallas TX 75211 *Web:* mountcarmelcenter.org	214-331-6224		673
Mount Carmel Health System 6150 East Broad St Columbus OH 43213 *Web:* www.mountcarmelhealth.com	614-546-4000		353
Mount Carmel Public Utility Co 316 Market St Po Box 220 Mount Carmel IL 62863 *TF:* 877-262-7036 ■ *Web:* mtcpu.com	618-262-5151		787
Mount Clare Museum House Carroll Pk 1500 Washington Blvd Baltimore MD 21230 *Web:* www.mountclare.org	410-837-3262	837-0251	520
Mount Dora Farms 16398 Jacinto Ft Blvd Houston TX 77015 *Web:* www.mountdorafarms.com	713-821-7439		315-4
Mount Greylock State Reservation 30 Rockwell Rd Lanesborough MA 01237 *Web:* www.mass.gov	413-499-4262		565
Mount Holyoke College 50 College St South Hadley MA 01075 *TF:* 800-642-4483 ■ *Web:* www.mtholyoke.edu	413-538-2000	538-2409	166
Mount Hood Community College 26000 SE Stark St Gresham OR 97030 *Web:* www.mhcc.edu	503-491-6422	491-7388	162
Mount Horeb Telephone Co (MHTC) 200 E Main St Mount Horeb WI 53572 *Web:* www.mhtc.net	608-437-5551	437-8898	224
Mount Ida College 777 Dedham St Newton Center MA 02459 *Web:* www.mountida.edu	617-928-4500	928-4507	166
Mount Jefferson State Natural Area 1481 Mt Jefferson State Park Rd West Jefferson NC 28694 *Web:* www.ncparks.gov	336-246-9653		565
Mount Joy Wire Corp 1000 E Main St Mount Joy PA 17552 *TF:* 800-321-2305 ■ *Web:* www.mjwire.com	717-653-1461		813
Mount Juliet *Chamber of Commerce* 2055 N Mt Juliet Rd Ste 200 Mount Juliet TN 37122 *Web:* www.mjchamber.org	615-758-3478	754-8595	139
Mount Kearsarge Indian Museum 18 Highlawn Rd PO Box 142 Warner NH 03278 *Web:* www.indianmuseum.org	603-456-2600		520
Mount Laurel Library 100 Walt Whitman Ave Mount Laurel NJ 08054 *TF:* 888-576-5529 ■ *Web:* www.mtlaurel.lib.nj.us	856-234-7319	234-6916	434-3
Mount Magazine State Park 16878 Hwy 309 S Paris AR 72855 *Web:* www.arkansasstateparks.com	479-963-8502		565
Mount Marty College 1105 W Eigth St Yankton SD 57078 *TF:* 800-658-4552 ■ *Web:* www.mtmc.edu	605-668-1545	668-1508	166
Mount Mary College 2900 N Menomonee River Pkwy Milwaukee WI 53222 *TF:* 800-321-6265 ■ *Web:* mtmary.edu	414-256-1219	256-0180	166

Name	Address	City	State	ZIP	Phone	Fax	Class
Mount Mercy College	1330 Elmhurst Dr NE *TF:* 800-248-4504 ■ *Web:* mtmercy.edu	Cedar Rapids	IA	52402	319-368-6460	861-2390	166
Mount Miguel Covenant Village	325 Kempton St *TF:* 877-321-4895 ■ *Web:* www.mountmiguelcovenantvillage.org	Spring Valley	CA	91977	619-479-4790		672
Mount Mitchell State Park	2388 State Hwy 128 *Web:* www.ncparks.gov	Burnsville	NC	28714	828-675-4611		565
Mount Nebo State Park	16728 W State Hwy 155 *Web:* www.arkansasstateparks.com	Dardanelle	AR	72834	479-229-3655		565
Mount Nittany Medical Ctr	1800 E Park Ave *TF:* 866-686-6171 ■ *Web:* www.mountnittany.org	State College	PA	16803	814-231-7000		374-3
Mount Olive Area Chamber of Commerce	123 N Center St *TF:* 800-424-8802 ■ *Web:* www.moachamber.com	Mount Olive	NC	28365	919-658-3113		139
Mount Olive Area Chamber of Commerce	PO Box 192 *Web:* www.mountolivechambernj.com	Budd Lake	NJ	07828	908-509-1774		139
Mount Olive College	634 Henderson St *TF:* 800-653-0854 ■ *Web:* umo.edu	Mount Olive	NC	28365	919-658-2502	658-9816	166
Mount Olivet Careview Home	5517 Lyndale Ave S *Web:* www.mtolivethomes.org	Minneapolis	MN	55419	612-827-5677		371
Mount Philo State Park	5425 Mt Philo Rd *Web:* www.vtstateparks.com	Charlotte	VT	05445	802-425-2390		565
Mount Pisgah Arboretum	34901 Frank Parrish Rd *Web:* mountpisgaharboretum.org	Eugene	OR	97405	541-747-1504	741-4904	97
Mount Pisgah State Park	28 Entrance Rd *Web:* www.dcnr.pa.gov	Troy	PA	16947	570-297-2734		565
Mount Pleasant Public Library NY	350 Bedford Rd *Web:* www.mountpleasantlibrary.org	Pleasantville	NY	10570	914-769-0548		434-3
Mount Pleasant-Titus County Chamber of Commerce	1604 N Jefferson Ave *Web:* www.mtpleasanttx.com	Mount Pleasant	TX	75455	903-572-8567	572-0613	139
Mount Prospect Chamber of Commerce	662 E NW Hwy *Web:* www.mountprospectchamber.org	Mount Prospect	IL	60056	847-398-6616	398-6780	139
Mount Prospect Public Library	10 S Emerson St *Web:* mppl.org	Mount Prospect	IL	60056	847-253-5675		434-3
Mount Rainier National Park	55210 238th Ave E *Web:* www.nps.gov	Ashford	WA	98304	360-569-2211		564
Mount Regis Ctr	125 Knotbreak Rd *TF:* 866-302-6609 ■ *Web:* www.mtregis.com	Salem	VA	24153	877-217-3447		726
Mount Revelstoke National Park of Canada	PO Box 350 *TF:* 866-787-6221 ■ *Web:* www.pc.gc.ca	Revelstoke	BC	V0E2S0	250-837-7500	837-7536	563
Mount Royal College	4825 Mt Royal Gate SW *Web:* www.mtroyal.ca	Calgary	AB	T3E6K6	403-974-8646		785
Mount Royal Printing Company Inc	6310 Blair Hill Ln *Web:* mtroyalprinting.com	Baltimore	MD	21209	410-296-1117		627
Mount Rushmore National Memorial	13000 Hwy 244 Bldg 31 Ste 1 *Web:* www.nps.gov	Keystone	SD	57751	605-574-2523		564
Mount Rushmore Society	711 N Creek Dr *TF:* 800-699-3142 ■ *Web:* www.mountrushmoresociety.com	Rapid City	SD	57703	605-341-8883	341-0433	48-13
Mount Saint Helens National Volcanic Monument	42218 NE Yale Bridge Rd *Web:* www.fs.usda.gov	Amboy	WA	98601	360-449-7800	449-7801	50-5
Mount Saint Joseph Hospital	3080 Prince Edward St *Web:* www.providencehealthcare.org	Vancouver	BC	V5T3N4	604-874-1141		374-2
Mount Saint Mary College	330 Powell Ave *TF:* 888-937-6762 ■ *Web:* www.msmc.edu	Newburgh	NY	12550	845-569-3248	562-6762	166
Mount Saint Mary' s University	12001 Chalon Rd *Web:* www.msmu.edu	Los Angeles	CA	90049	310-954-4000	954-4259	166
Mount Saint Mary's University	16300 Old Emmitsburg Rd *TF:* 800-448-4347 ■ *Web:* www.msmary.edu	Emmitsburg	MD	21727	301-447-5214	447-5860	166
Mount Saint Mary's University Doheny	10 Chester Pl *Web:* www.bkstr.com	Los Angeles	CA	90007	613-562-5353		162
Mount Saint Michael Academy	4300 Murdock Ave *Web:* mtstmichael.org	Bronx	NY	10466	718-515-6400	994-7729	685
Mount Saint Vincent University	166 Bedford Hwy *TF:* 877-733-6788 ■ *Web:* www.msvu.ca	Halifax	NS	B3M2J6	902-457-6117	457-6498	785
Mount San Jacinto College	1499 N State St *TF:* 800-624-5561 ■ *Web:* www.msjc.edu	San Jacinto	CA	92583	951-487-6752	654-6738	162
Mount Shasta Resort	1000 Siskiyou Lake Blvd *TF:* 800-958-3363 ■ *Web:* www.mountshastaresort.com	Mount Shasta	CA	96067	530-926-3030	926-0333	669
Mount Sinai Hospital	600 University Ave *Web:* www.mountsinai.on.ca	Toronto	ON	M5G1X5	416-596-4200	586-4807	374-2
Mount Sinai Hospital Medical Center of Chicago	California Ave 15th St *TF:* 877-448-7848 ■ *Web:* www.sinai.org	Chicago	IL	60608	773-542-2000		374-3
Mount Sinai Medical Ctr, The	1 Gustave L Levy Pl *TF:* 800-637-4624 ■ *Web:* www.mountsinai.org	New York	NY	10029	212-241-6500	731-3418	374-3
Mount Sinai Memorial Park	5950 Forest Lawn Dr *TF:* 800-600-0076 ■ *Web:* mountsinaiparks.org	Los Angeles	CA	90068	323-469-6000		510
Mount St Helena Brewing Co	21167 Calistoga St *Web:* sainthelenabrewery.com	Middletown	CA	95461	707-987-3361		102
Mount St Louis Moonstone Ski Resort Ltd	24 Mt St Louis Rd W Rr 4 *Web:* www.skicanada.org	Coldwater	ON	L0K1E0	905-856-4754		377
Mount Sugarloaf State Reservation	300 Sugarloaf St *Web:* www.mass.gov	South Deerfield	MA	01373	413-665-2928		565
Mount Tom State Reservation	125 Resv Rd *Web:* www.mass.gov	Holyoke	MA	01040	413-534-1186		565
Mount Union College	1972 Clark Ave *TF:* 800-334-6682 ■ *Web:* www.mountunion.edu	Alliance	OH	44601	330-823-2590	823-5097	166
Mount Vernon & Knox County Public Library	201 N Mulberry St *Web:* www.knox.net	Mount Vernon	OH	43050	740-392-2665	397-3866	434-3
Mount Vernon Chamber of Commerce	66 Mt Vernon Ave *TF:* 888-868-2269 ■ *Web:* www.mvccny.com	Mount Vernon	NY	10550	914-775-8127	699-0139	139
Mount Vernon City School Dist 80	2710 N St *Web:* www.mtv80.org	Mount Vernon	IL	62864	618-244-8080		449
Mount Vernon Hospital	12 N Seventh Ave *Web:* www.montefiorehealthsystem.org	Mount Vernon	NY	10550	914-664-8000		374-3
Mount Vernon Hotel Museum & Garden	421 E 61st St *Web:* www.mvhm.org	New York	NY	10065	212-838-6878	838-7390	520
Mount Vernon Mills Inc	503 S Main St PO Box 100 *Web:* www.mvmills.com	Mauldin	SC	29662	864-688-7100		745-1
Mount Vernon Nazarene University	800 Martinsburg Rd *TF:* 800-766-8206 ■ *Web:* mvnu.edu	Mount Vernon	OH	43050	740-392-6868		166
Mount Vernon Public Library	28 S First Ave *Web:* mountvernonpubliclibrary.org	Mount Vernon	NY	10550	914-668-1840		434-3
Mount Vernon-Lee *Chamber of Commerce*	7686 Richmond Hwy Ste 203 A *Web:* www.mtvernon-leechamber.org	Alexandria	VA	22306	703-360-6925	360-6928	139
Mount View Hotel & Spa	1457 Lincoln Ave *TF:* 800-816-6877 ■ *Web:* mountviewhotel.com	Calistoga	CA	94515	707-942-6877	942-6904	379
Mount View Youth Services Ctr	7862 W Mansfield Pkwy *Web:* www.colorado.gov	Denver	CO	80235	303-987-4502		412
Mount Wachusett Community College	444 Green St *Web:* mwcc.edu	Gardner	MA	01440	978-632-6600	630-9554	162
Mount Washington Hotel & Resort	310 Mt Washington Hotel Rd *TF:* 800-314-1752 ■ *Web:* www.brettonwoods.com	Bretton Woods	NH	03575	603-278-1000		669
Mount Washington Pediatric Hospital	1708 W Rogers Ave *Web:* www.mwph.org	Baltimore	MD	21209	410-578-8600		374-1
Mount Yale Capital Group LLC	8000 Norman Center Dr Ste 630 *Web:* www.mtyale.com	Minneapolis	MN	55437	952-897-5390		194
Mountain Air Conditioning & Heating Corp	735 S Broadway *Web:* www.mountain.ac	Hicksville	NY	11801	516-935-0149		189-10
Mountain America Credit Union	PO Box 9001 *TF:* 800-748-4302 ■ *Web:* www.macu.com	West Jordan	UT	84084	801-325-6228		219
Mountain Cablevision Inc	4930 Jonathan Creek Rd *TF:* 866-571-8671 ■ *Web:* www.cbvnol.com	Waynesville	NC	28785	828-926-2288	377-0006	116
Mountain Cascade Inc	555 Exchange Ct PO Box 5050 *Web:* mountaincascade.com	Livermore	CA	94550	925-373-8370	373-0179	188-10
Mountain Cement Co	5 Sand Creek Rd *Web:* www.mountaincement.com	Laramie	WY	82070	307-745-4879	742-4534	135
Mountain Creek Resort	200 Rt 94 *Web:* www.mountaincreek.com	Vernon	NJ	07462	973-827-3900		669
Mountain Democrat	1360 Broadway *Web:* www.mtdemocrat.com	Placerville	CA	95667	530-622-1255		532-3
Mountain Electric Co-opeartive Inc	PO Box 180 *TF:* 800-638-3788 ■ *Web:* www.mountainelectric.com	Mountain City	TN	37683	423-727-1800	727-1822	245
Mountain Empire Community College	3441 Mtn Empire Rd *TF:* 800-981-0600 ■ *Web:* www.me.cc.va.us	Big Stone Gap	VA	24219	276-523-2400	523-9699	162
Mountain Empire Family Medicine	31115 Hwy 94 *Web:* www.mtnhealth.org	Campo	CA	91906	619-445-6200		354
Mountain Empire Unified School District	3291 Buckman Springs Rd *Web:* www.meusd.k12.ca.us	Pine Valley	CA	91962	619-473-9022		685
Mountain Enterprise, The	PO Box 610 *Web:* www.mountainenterprise.com	Frazier Park	CA	93225	805-245-3794	245-5620	532-2
Mountain Equipment Co-op	149 W Fourth Ave *TF:* 800-722-1960 ■ *Web:* www.mec.ca	Vancouver	BC	V5Y4A6	604-707-3300		711
Mountain Fresh Supermarket	2203 SR-118 *Web:* www.shursavemarkets.com	Hunlock Creek	PA	18621	570-477-2988		345
Mountain Gear Inc	6021 E Mansfield *TF:* 800-829-2009 ■ *Web:* mountaingear.com	Spokane Valley	WA	99212	800-829-2009		711
Mountain Glass Arts Inc	191 Lyman St Ste 400 *TF:* 800-310-8588 ■ *Web:* mountainglass.com	Asheville	NC	28801	828-225-5599		327
Mountain Haus	292 E Meadow Dr *TF:* 800-237-0922 ■ *Web:* mountainhaus.com	Vail	CO	81657	970-476-2434	476-3007	379

Name / Address	City	State	ZIP	Phone	Fax	Class
Mountain Health Arena 1 Civic Center Plz *Web:* www.mountainhealtharena.com	Huntington	WV	25701	304-696-5990		720
Mountain High Resort 24510 State Hwy 2 *TF:* 888-754-7878 ■ *Web:* www.mthigh.com	Wrightwood	CA	92397	888-754-7878		132
Mountain Home Air Force Base 90 HOPE DR *TF:* 855-366-0140 ■ *Web:* www.mountainhome.af.mil	Mountain Home	ID	83648	208-828-6800		497-1
Mountain Home Area Chamber of Commerce 1023 Hwy 62 *TF:* 800-822-3536 ■ *Web:* enjoymountainhome.com	Mountain Home	AR	72653	870-425-5111	425-4446	139
Mountain Home National Cemetery 53 Memorial Ave *Web:* www.cem.va.gov	Mountain Home	TN	37684	423-979-3535	979-3521	136
Mountain Home News 195 S Third E St PO Box 1330 *Web:* www.mountainhomenews.com	Mountain Home	ID	83647	208-587-3331	587-9205	637-8
Mountain King PO Box 14532 *TF:* 800-395-2004 ■ *Web:* www.mtnking.com	Houston	TX	77221	800-395-2004		10-11
Mountain Lake Hotel 115 Hotel Cir *Web:* www.mtnlakelodge.com	Pembroke	VA	24136	540-626-7121	626-7172	379
Mountain Lake Press 24 D St *Web:* www.mountainlakepress.com	Mountain Lake Park	MD	21550	301-501-5151		637-2
Mountain Laurel 81 Treetops Cir *TF:* 888-243-9300 ■ *Web:* www.mountainlaurelresorts.com	White Haven	PA	18661	570-443-8411		669
Mountain Light Photography Inc 106 S Main St *Web:* www.mountainlight.com	Bishop	CA	93514	760-873-7700		593
Mountain Lion Foundation PO Box 1896 *TF:* 800-319-7621 ■ *Web:* www.mountainlion.org	Sacramento	CA	95812	916-442-2666		48-3
Mountain Lion Inc PO Box 799 *Web:* www.publishersmarketplace.com	Pennington	NJ	08534	609-730-1665	730-1286	94
Mountain Lodge at Telluride 457 Mtn Village Blvd *TF:* 866-368-6867 ■ *Web:* www.mountainlodgetelluride.com	Telluride	CO	81435	970-369-5000	369-4317	669
Mountain Ltd 19 Yarmouth Dr Ste 301 *TF:* 800-322-8627 ■ *Web:* www.mountainltd.com	New Gloucester	ME	04260	207-688-6200	688-6212	631
Mountain Machine Works 2589 Hotel Rd *Web:* www.mountainmachineworks.com	Auburn	ME	04210	207-783-6680	783-8055	454
Mountain Manor of Paintsville 1025 Euclid Ave *Web:* mountainmanorofpaintsville.com	Paintsville	KY	41240	606-789-5808		371
Mountain Manor Treatment Ctr 3800 Frederick Ave *Web:* www.mountainmanor.org	Baltimore	MD	21229	800-446-8833		726
Mountain Measurement Inc PO Box 86736 *TF:* 800-261-6227 ■ *Web:* www.mountainmeasurement.com	Portland	OR	97286	503-284-1288		637-10
Mountain Messenger 122 N Court St *Web:* www.mountainmessenger.com	Lewisburg	WV	24901	304-647-5724		637-9
Mountain Mission School 1760 Edgewater Dr *Web:* mmskids.org	Grundy	VA	24614	276-935-2954		685
Mountain N' Air Books PO Box 12540 *TF:* 800-446-9696 ■ *Web:* www.mountain-n-air.com	La Crescenta	CA	91214	818-248-9345		637-2
Mountain Pacific Bank 3732 Broadway *Web:* mountainpacificbank.com	Everett	WA	98201	425-263-3500		70
Mountain Parks Electric Inc 321 W Agate Ave *TF:* 877-887-3378 ■ *Web:* www.mpei.com	Granby	CO	80446	970-887-3378	887-3996	245
Mountain Peak Music 2700 Woodlands Village Blvd Ste 300-124 *Web:* www.mountainpeakmusic.com	Flagstaff	AZ	86001	928-266-9582	773-9201	637-2
Mountain Plains Equity Group Inc 2101 Overland Ave *Web:* mpequity.com	Billings	MT	59102	406-254-1677	869-8693	653
Mountain Province Diamonds Inc 161 Bay St Ste 2315 *TSX: MPVD* ■ *Web:* www.mountainprovince.com	Toronto	ON	M5J2S1	416-361-3562	603-8565	503-3
Mountain Research LLC 825 25th St *TF:* 800-837-4674 ■ *Web:* www.mountainresearch.com	Altoona	PA	16601	814-949-2034		743
Mountain Sales and Service Inc 6759 E 50th Ave *TF:* 800-847-2557 ■ *Web:* www.mtnsales.com	Commerce City	CO	80022	303-289-5558	286-7054	665
Mountain Sky Guest Ranch PO Box 1219 *TF:* 800-548-3392 ■ *Web:* www.mountainsky.com	Emigrant	MT	59027	406 333-4911		239
Mountain State Insurance Agency Inc 1206 Kanawha Blvd E *Web:* mountainstateinsurance.com	Charleston	WV	25301	304-720-2000		390
Mountain States Constructors Inc 3601 Pan American Rd NE *Web:* msconstructors.com	Albuquerque	NM	87107	505-292-0108		188-4
Mountain States Pipe & Supply Co 111 W Las Vegas St *TF:* 800-777-7173 ■ *Web:* msps.com	Colorado Springs	CO	80903	719-634-5555	634-5551	612
Mountain States Supply Inc 1505 W 130 S *Web:* www.mountainlandsupply.com	Salt Lake City	UT	84115	801-484-8885		612
Mountain Supply Co 2101 Mullan Rd *TF:* 800-821-1646 ■ *Web:* www.mountainsupply.com	Missoula	MT	59808	406-543-8255		612
Mountain Telephone Co 405 Main St *TF:* 800-939-3121 ■ *Web:* www.mrtc.com	West Liberty	KY	41472	606-743-3121		387
Mountain Thunder Lodge 50 Mountain Dr *TF:* 888-400-9590 ■ *Web:* www.breckresorts.com	Breckenridge	CO	80424	970-547-5650		652
Mountain Times PO Box 1815 *Web:* www.wataugademocrat.com	Boone	NC	28607	828-264-6397	262-0282	532-4
Mountain Tools 225 Crossroads Blvd PO Box 222295 *TF:* 800-510-2514 ■ *Web:* www.mtntools.com	Carmel By The Sea	CA	93923	831-620-0911	620-0977	711
Mountain Top Arboretum Rt 23C Maude Adams Rd PO Box 379 *Web:* www.mtarboretum.org	Tannersville	NY	12485	518-589-3903		97
Mountain Travel Sobek 1266 66th St Ste 4 *TF:* 888-831-7526 ■ *Web:* www.mtsobek.com	Emeryville	CA	94608	888-831-7526		760
Mountain V Oil & Gas Inc PO Box 470 *Web:* mountainvoilandgas.com	Bridgeport	WV	26330	304-842-6320	842-0016	536
Mountain Valley Bank 317 Davis Ave *TF:* 800-555-3503 ■ *Web:* www.mountainvalleybank.com	Elkins	WV	26241	304-637-2265	637-2270	70
Mountain Valley Farms & Lumber Inc 1240 Nawakwa Rd *Web:* www.mtvalleyfarms.com	Biglerville	PA	17307	717-677-6166	677-9283	551
Mountain Valley Spring Co 150 Central Ave *Web:* www.mountainvalleyspring.com	Hot Springs	AR	71901	501-624-1635		805
Mountain View Electric Association Inc 1655 Fifth St PO Box 1600 *TF:* 800-388-9881 ■ *Web:* www.mvea.coop	Limon	CO	80828	719-775-2861	775-9513	245
Mountain View Hospital 1000 E 100 N *TF:* 877-865-9738 ■ *Web:* mvhpayson.com	Payson	UT	84651	801-465-7000		374-3
Mountain View Management Inc 847 East 500 North *Web:* mvmrentals.com	Orem	UT	84097	801-224-4846		653
Mountain View Public Library 585 Franklin St *Web:* www.mountainview.gov	Mountain View	CA	94041	650-903-6335	962-0438	434-3
Mountain View School District (MVSD) 3320 Gilman Rd *Web:* www.mtviewschools.com	El Monte	CA	91732	626-652-4000		685
Mountain View Tire & Auto Service Inc 8548 Utica Ave *TF:* 877-688-4737 ■ *Web:* www.mountainviewtire.com	Rancho Cucamonga	CA	91730	877-688-4737		755
Mountain View Youth Development Ctr 809 Peal Ln	Dandridge	TN	37725	865-397-0174		412
Mountain Villas 9525 W Skyline Pkwy *TF:* 866-688-4552 ■ *Web:* www.mtvillas.com	Duluth	MN	55810	866-688-4552		379
Mountain West Bank 125 Ironwood Dr 1715 W Kathleen Ave *TF:* 800-641-5401 ■ *Web:* www.mountainwest-bank.com	Coeur d'Alene	ID	83814	208-765-0284		70
Mountain Wings Inc 120 Selig Dr *Web:* www.mountainwings.com	Atlanta	GA	30336	404-696-2480		387
Mountain Xpress 2 Wall St *Web:* mountainx.com	Asheville	NC	28801	828-251-1333	251-1311	532-5
Mountain/Service Distributors 40 Lake St *Web:* www.mtnservice.com	South Fallsburg	NY	12779	845-434-5674	434-0059	297-8
Mountaineer Capital LP 305 Washington st W *Web:* www.mountaineercapital.com	Charleston	WV	25302	304-347-7519	347-0072	792
Mountaineer Inn 3343 Mountain Rd *Web:* stowemountaineerinn.com	Stowe	VT	05672	802-253-7525		378
Mountaineers Books 1001 SW Klickitat Way Ste 201 *TF:* 800-553-4453 ■ *Web:* www.mountaineersbooks.org	Seattle	WA	98134	206-223-6303	223-6306	637-2
Mountaineers, The 7700 Sand Pt Way NE *TF:* 800-573-8484 ■ *Web:* www.mountaineers.org	Seattle	WA	98115	206-521-6000	523-6763	48-23
Mountainland Supply Co 1505 W 130 S *Web:* www.mtncom.net	Orem	UT	84058	801-224-6050		612
Mountainside Fitness 9745 W Happy Valley Rd *TF:* 866-686-3488 ■ *Web:* www.mountainsidefitness.com	Peoria	AZ	85383	866-686-3488		354
MountainView Hospital 3100 N Tenaya Way *Web:* mountainview-hospital.com	Las Vegas	NV	89128	702-962-5021		374-3
MountainView Regional Medical Ctr 4311 E Lohman Ave *Web:* www.mountainviewregional.com	Las Cruces	NM	88001	575-556-7600	556-7619	374-3
Mountaire Farms 17269 NC Hwy 71 N *Web:* mountaire.com	Lumber Bridge	NC	28357	910-843-5942		619
Mountaire Farms PO Box 1320 *TF:* 877-887-1490 ■ *Web:* www.mountaire.com	Millsboro	DE	19966	302-934-1100		619
Mountrail County Mountrail McKenzie 18 2nd Ave Se Po Box 39 *Web:* www.co.mountrail.nd.us	Stanley	ND	58784	701-628-2925	628-3175	338
Mountrail-Williams Electric Co-op 218 58th St W PO Box 1346 *TF:* 800-279-2667 ■ *Web:* www.mwec.com	Williston	ND	58802	701-577-3765	577-3777	245
Mounts Botanical Garden 531 N Military Trl *Web:* www.mounts.org	West Palm Beach	FL	33415	561-233-1757		97
Mountwest Community & Technical College 1 Mountwest Way *TF:* 866-676-5533 ■ *Web:* www.mctc.edu	Huntington	WV	25701	304-710-3140	696-2608	165
Mountz Inc 1080 N 11th St *Web:* www.mountztorque.com	San Jose	CA	95112	408-292-2214		350
Mousehouse Cheesehaus Inc 4494 Lake Cir *Web:* mousehousecheese.com	Windsor	WI	53598	608-846-4455		327
Mouser Custom Cabinetry 2112 N Hwy 31 W *TF:* 800-345-7537 ■ *Web:* www.mousercc.com	Elizabethtown	KY	42701	270-737-7477		115
Mouser Electronics Corp 1000 N Main St *Web:* www.mouser.in	Mansfield	TX	76063	817-804-3888	804-3899	246
Mousetail Landing State Park 3 Campground Rd *Web:* www.state.tn.us	Linden	TN	37096	731-847-0841		565
Movado Group Inc 650 From Rd Ste 375 *NYSE: MOV* ■ *Web:* www.movadogroupinc.com	Paramus	NJ	07652	201-267-8000		153
Move Networks Inc 796 E Utah Vly Dr 1st Fl	American Fork	UT	84003	801-756-5805		5
Movie Colony Hotel 726 N Indian Canyon Dr *Web:* www.moviecolonyhotel.com	Palm Springs	CA	92262	760-320-6340	320-1640	379
Moviecraft Home Video PO Box 438 *Web:* www.moviecraft.com	Orland Park	IL	60462	708-460-9082	460-9099	514
Movieland Wax Museum of the Stars 4848 Clifton Hill *Web:* www.cliftonhill.com	Niagara Falls	ON	L2G3N4	905-358-3676		520

Company	Address	City	State	Zip	Phone	Fax	Class
Movies Unlimited Inc	3015 Darnell Rd *Web:* www.moviesunlimited.com	Philadelphia	PA	19154	630-919-2192		459
MovieTicketscom Inc	2255 Glades Rd Ste 100E *Web:* www.movietickets.com	Boca Raton	FL	33431	310-954-0478		41
Moving Media	3150 18th St Ste 241 *Web:* www.movingmedia.com	San Francisco	CA	94110	415-777-1759		344
Moving Off Campus LLC	10 S Brentwood Blvd Ste 200 *Web:* www.movingoffcampus.com	Clayton	MO	63105	314-367-2456		5
Moving Parts Press	10699 Empire Grade *Web:* www.movingpartspress.com	Santa Cruz	CA	95060	831-427-2271	458-2810	637-2
Moving Right Along Service Inc	101-21 101st St *Web:* www.movingrightalong.com	Ozone Park	NY	11416	718-738-2468	738-2661	780
Movius	4450 River Green Pkwy Ste 300 *Web:* moviuscorp.com	Duluth	GA	30096	770-283-1000		735
Mowat Mackie & Anderson LLP	1999 Harrison St Ste 1500 *Web:* www.mowat.com	Oakland	CA	94612	510-893-1120		2
Mower Boston's One-Stop B2B Marketing Agency	134 Rumford Ave Ste 307 *TF:* 800-553-6477 ■ *Web:* www.hbagency.com	Newton	MA	02466	781-818-4201		4
Mowery Consulting Group	200 S Lawrence St *Web:* www.moweryconsulting.com	Montgomery	AL	36104	334-207-9906		194
Moxie Hair Salon	2649 Lyndale Ave S *Web:* www.moxiesalon.com	Minneapolis	MN	55408	612-813-0330		77
Moxie Interactive Inc	384 Northyards Blvd NW Ste 300 *Web:* www.moxieusa.com	Atlanta	GA	30313	678-916-4500		4
Moxie Java International LLC	4990 W Chinden Blvd *Web:* moxiejava.com	Boise	ID	83714	208-322-7773		159
Moxie Pictures	18 E 16th St 4th Fl *Web:* moxiepictures.com	New York	NY	10003	212-807-6901		362
Moximed Inc	26460 Corporate Ave Ste 100 *Web:* www.moximed.com	Hayward	CA	94545	510-887-3300		477
Moxley, Moxley & Olson Inc	19550 S Harlem Ave Unit 1 *Web:* mmocpa.com	Frankfort	IL	60423	708-342-4400		2
Moxtek Inc	452 W 1260 N *Web:* www.moxtek.com	Orem	UT	84057	801-225-0930	221-1121	544
Moye's Pharmacy	4467 N Henry Blvd *Web:* moyespharmacy.com	Stockbridge	GA	30281	770-474-0704		237
Moyer & Son Inc	113 E Reliance Rd *TF:* 866-669-3747 ■ *Web:* emoyer.com	Souderton	PA	18964	215-799-2000		447
Moyer Aviation Inc	Pocono Mountains Airport 2780 Memorial Blvd *TF:* 800-321-5890 ■ *Web:* www.moyeraviation.com	Tobyhanna	PA	18466	570-839-7161	839-7162	167-3
Moyer Ford Sales Inc	10111 State Hwy 59 S *Web:* www.moyerfordsales.com	Foley	AL	36535	251-943-1661		57
Moyer Group	3690 N Peachtree Rd Ste 100 *TF:* 844-377-1514 ■ *Web:* www.moyergroup.com	Chamblee	GA	30341	404-229-1127		180
Moyer Law PC	51 Jefferson Blvd *Web:* moyerdivorcelaw.com	Warwick	RI	02888	401-461-7800		41
Moyno Inc	1895 W Jefferson St *TF:* 877-486-6966 ■ *Web:* www.moyno.com	Springfield	OH	45506	937-327-3111	327-3177	641
Mozambique Embassy	1525 New Hampshire Ave NW *TF:* 888-810-4054 ■ *Web:* www.embamoc-usa.org	Washington	DC	20036	888-810-4054		257
Mozingo Liquors Inc	120 S 6th St	Hartsville	SC	29550	843-332-6554		443
Moznaim Publishing Corp	4304 12th Ave *Web:* www.moznaim.com	Brooklyn	NY	11219	718-438-7680	438-1305	637-2
Mozzetti Inc	3350 Scott Blvd Bldg 24 *Web:* mozzetti.com	Santa Clara	CA	95054	408-248-2612	248-4007	2
MP (Meriwether Publishing Ltd)	885 Elkton Dr *Web:* www.meriwether.com	Colorado Springs	CO	80907	719-594-9916		637-2
MP (Mark-Pack Inc)	776 Main St *TF:* 800-521-9684 ■ *Web:* www.markpackinc.com	Coopersville	MI	49404	800-521-9684		559
MP (Mandeville Press)	3500 W Adams Blvd *Web:* www.mandevillepress.org	Los Angeles	CA	90018	323-737-4055	737-5680	637-2
MP Associates Inc	1721 Boxelder St Ste 107 *Web:* www.mpassociates.com	Louisville	CO	80027	303-530-4562	530-4334	184
MP Biomedicals LLC	3 Hutton Center Dr Ste 100 *TF:* 800-633-1352 ■ *Web:* www.mpbio.com	Santa Ana	CA	92707	949-833-2500		477
MP Components	8499 Centre Indus Dr SW *Web:* www.mpcomponents.net	Byron Center	MI	49315	616-878-9710	878-9709	567
MP Environmental Services Inc	3400 Manor St **Fax Area Code:* 661 ■ *TF:* 800-458-3036 ■ *Web:* www.mpenviro.com	Bakersfield	CA	93308	800-458-3036	393-0508*	780
MP Global Products	2500 Old Hadar Rd PO Box 2283 **Fax Area Code:* 402 ■ *TF:* 888-379-9695 ■ *Web:* www.mpglobalproducts.com	Norfolk	NE	68702	888-379-9695	379-9737*	386
MP Husky Corp	204 Old Piedmont Hwy PO Box 16749 *TF:* 800-277-4810 ■ *Web:* www.mphusky.com	Greenville	SC	29605	864-234-4800	234-4822	816
MP Metal Products Inc	W1250 Elmwood Ave *TF:* 800-824-6744 ■ *Web:* mpmetals.com	Ixonia	WI	53036	920-261-9650	261-9652	482
MP Pumps Inc	34800 Bennett Dr *TF:* 800-563-8006 ■ *Web:* www.mppumps.com	Fraser	MI	48026	586-293-8240	293-8469	641
MP2 Energy Texas LLC	21 Waterway Ave Ste 450 *Web:* www.mp2energy.com	The Woodlands	TX	77380	832-510-1030		466
MPA (Motion Picture Assn)	15301 Ventura Blvd Bldg E *Web:* www.mpaa.org	Sherman Oaks	CA	91403	818-995-6600		48-4
MPA (Association of Magazine Media, The)	757 Third Ave 11th Fl *TF:* 800-234-3368 ■ *Web:* www.magazine.org	New York	NY	10017	212-872-3700	888-4217	49-16
MPA Media	5406 Bolsa Ave *TF:* 800-324-7758 ■ *Web:* www.mpamedia.com	Huntington Beach	CA	92649	800-324-7758		463
Mpathix Inc	87 Skyway Ave Ste 200 *Web:* www.mpathix.com	Toronto	ON	M9W6R3	416-849-4210		387
MPBS Industries	2820 E Washington Blvd *TF:* 800-421-6265 ■ *Web:* www.mpbs.com	Los Angeles	CA	90023	323-268-8514	386-4058	385
MPC (MPC Theatre Co)	980 Fremont St *Web:* www.mpctheatreco.com	Monterey	CA	93940	831-646-4213		572
MPC (Materials Properties Council)	PO Box 201547 *Web:* www.forengineers.org	Shaker Heights	OH	44122	216-658-3847		49-19
MPC (Mandarin Presbyterian Church)	11844 Mandarin Rd *Web:* www.mandarinpres.com	Jacksonville	FL	32223	904-680-9944		48-20
MPC (McClain Printing Co)	212 Main St *TF:* 800-654-7179 ■ *Web:* www.mcclainprinting.com	Parsons	WV	26287	304-478-2881	478-4658	627
MPC Promotions	4300 Produce Rd PO Box 34336 **Fax Area Code:* 888 ■ *TF:* 800-331-0989 ■ *Web:* www.mpcpromotions.com	Louisville	KY	40232	502-451-4900	451-8475*	155-9
MPC Theatre Co (MPC)	980 Fremont St *Web:* www.mpctheatreco.com	Monterey	CA	93940	831-646-4213		572
MPCA	10635 Santa Monica Blvd *Web:* www.mpcafilm.com	Los Angeles	CA	90025	310-319-9500	319-9501	514
MPD Inc	316 E Ninth St *TF:* 866-225-5673 ■ *Web:* www.mpdinc.com	Owensboro	KY	42303	270-685-6200		419
MPE Engineering Ltd	6715 - 8 St NE Ste 320 *Web:* www.mpe.ca	Calgary	AB	T2E7H7	403-250-1362	250-1518	261
Mpell Solutions LLC	3142 Tiger Run Ct Ste 108 *TF:* 800-450-1575 ■ *Web:* mpellsolutions.com	Carlsbad	CA	92010	760-727-9600	727-9614	195
MP&F (McNeely Pigott & Fox)	611 Commerce St Ste 3000 *TF:* 800-818-6953 ■ *Web:* www.mpf.com	Nashville	TN	37203	615-259-4000	259-4040	636
MPHA (Massachusetts Pharmacists Assn)	500 W Cummings Pk Ste 3475 *Web:* www.masspharmacists.org	Woburn	MA	01801	781-933-1107	933-1109	585
MPHA (Minnesota Pharmacists Assn)	1000 Westgate Dr Ste 252 **Fax Area Code:* 650 ■ *TF:* 800-451-8349 ■ *Web:* www.mpha.org	Saint Paul	MN	55114	651-697-1771	290-2266*	585
Mphasis Corp	460 Park Ave S Rm 1101 *Web:* www.mphasis.com	New York	NY	10016	212-686-6655	686-2422	179
MPI (Meeting Professionals Intl)	2711 Lyndon B Johnson Fwy Ste 600 *TF:* 866-318-2743 ■ *Web:* www.mpiweb.org	Dallas	TX	75234	972-702-3053	702-3065	49-12
MPI (Migration Policy Institute)	1400 16th St NW Ste 300 *Web:* www.migrationpolicy.org	Washington	DC	20036	202-266-1940	266-1900	637-10
MPI Group LLC, The	319 N Hills Rd *Web:* www.metalproductsinc.com	Corbin	KY	40701	606-523-0461		295
MPI Label Systems Inc	450 Courtney Rd *TF:* 800-423-0442 ■ *Web:* www.mpilabels.com	Sebring	OH	44672	330-938-2134	938-9878	413
MPI Media Group	16101 108th Ave *TF:* 800-323-0442 ■ *Web:* mpimedia.com	Orland Park	IL	60467	800-323-0442		511
MPI Technologies	37 East St *TF:* 888-674-8088 ■ *Web:* www.mpirelease.com	Winchester	MA	01890	781-729-8300	729-9093	600
MPIC (Mississippi Prison Industries Corp)	663 N State St *Web:* mpic.net	Jackson	MS	39202	601-969-5760	969-5765	630
MPIF (Metal Powder Industries Federation)	105 College Rd E *Web:* www.mpif.org	Princeton	NJ	08540	609-452-7700	987-8523	49-13
MPL (Marathon Pipe Line LLC)	539 S Main St *TF:* 800-537-6644 ■ *Web:* www.marathonpipeline.com	Findlay	OH	45840	419-421-4600		597
MPM Capital Offices	200 Clarendon St 54th Fl *Web:* www.mpmcapital.com	Boston	MA	02116	617-425-9200		792
MPM Medical Inc	2301 Crown Ct *TF:* 800-232-5512 ■ *Web:* www.mpmmedicalinc.com	Irving	TX	75038	972-893-4000		476
mPower Software Services LLC	115 Pheasant Run Ste 110 *Web:* www.mpowerss.com	Newtown	PA	18940	215-497-9730		19
MPP (Merriweather Post Pavilion)	10475 Little Patuxent Pkwy *TF:* 877-435-9849 ■ *Web:* www.merriweathermusic.com	Columbia	MD	21044	410-715-5550	715-5560	572
MPP (Medical Physics Publishing Corp)	4513 Vernon Blvd *TF:* 800-442-5778 ■ *Web:* www.medicalphysics.org	Madison	WI	53705	608-262-4021	265-2121	637-2
MPR (Minnesota Public Radio)	480 Cedar St *TF:* 800-228-7123 ■ *Web:* www.mpr.org	Saint Paul	MN	55101	651-290-1212		632
Mpress Inc	4100 Howard Ave *Web:* www.mpressnow.com	New Orleans	LA	70125	504-524-8248		5
MPRTC (Mid-Plains Rural Telephone Cooperative Inc)	300 411 N Hale St *TF:* 888-817-2052 ■ *Web:* www.midplains.coop	Tulia	TX	79088	806-668-4420	668-4444	681
MPS (Monolithic Power Systems Inc)	6409 Guadalupe Mines Rd *NASDAQ: MPWR* ■ *Web:* www.monolithicpower.com	San Jose	CA	95120	408-826-0600		696
MPS (Marlborough Public Schools)	17 Washington St *Web:* www.mps-edu.org	Marlborough	MA	01752	508-460-3509		186
MPS Group Inc	2920 Scotten St **Fax Area Code:* 248 ■ *Web:* www.mpsgrp.com	Detroit	MI	48210	313-841-7588	489-0653*	192
MPS LORIA Financial Planners LLC	7500 S County Line Rd *Web:* www.mpsloria.com	Burr Ridge	IL	60527	630-887-4404		401

	Phone	Fax	Class
MPT (Maryland Public Television) 11767 Owings Mills Blvd .... Owings Mills MD 21117 *TF:* 800-223-3678 ■ *Web:* www.mpt.org	410-581-4201	581-4338	632
Mpw Engineering LLC 110 W 7th St Ste 600 .... Tulsa OK 74119 *Web:* mpwengineering.com	918-582-4088		261
MPW Industrial Services Group Inc 9711 Lancaster Ro SE .... Hebron OH 43025 *TF:* 800-827-8790 ■ *Web:* www.mpwservices.com	740-929-1614	928-8140	152
MPX Geophysics Ltd 45 Cranfield Rd Unit 16 .... Toronto ON M4B3H6 *Web:* www.mpxgeo.com	905-947-1782		536
MR (Merrill and Ring Inc) 813 E 8th St .... Port Angeles WA 98362 *Web:* www.merrillring.com	360-452-2367	452-2015	191-3
MR Appliance Corp 304 E Church Ave .... Killeen TX 76541 *TF:* 888-998-2011 ■ *Web:* www.mrappliance.com	888-998-2011		310
Mr B's Bistro 201 Royal St .... New Orleans LA 70130 *Web:* www.mrbsbistro.com	504-523-2078	521-8304	671
Mr Button Products Inc 7840 Rockville Rd .... Indianapolis IN 46214 *TF:* 800-777-0111 ■ *Web:* www.mrbutton.com	800-777-0111		627
Mr Crane Inc 647 N Hariton St .... Orange CA 92868 *TF:* 800-598-3465 ■ *Web:* www.mrcrane.com	714-633-2100		190
MR Diamonds Inc 66 W 47th St Window 1A .... New York NY 10036 *Web:* www.mr-diamond-usa.com	212-869-7202	869-0470	411
Mr Floor LLC 3828 Oakton St .... Skokie IL 60076 *Web:* mrfloor.com	847-674-7500		290
Mr Friendly's New Southern Cafe 2001 Greene St .... Columbia SC 29205 *Web:* www.mrfriendlys.com	803-254-7828	621-9070	671
Mr Goodcents Franchise Systems Inc 8997 Commerce Dr .... De Soto KS 66018 *TF:* 800-648-2368 ■ *Web:* goodcentssubs.com	800-648-2368		670
Mr Greek 1670 Pass Rd Ste H .... Biloxi MS 39531 *Web:* www.mrgreekbiloxi.com	228-432-7888		671
Mr Handyman International LLC 3948 Ranchero Dr .... Ann Arbor MI 48108 *TF:* 855-632-2126 ■ *Web:* www.mrhandyman.com	855-632-2126		310
Mr Jim's Pizza Inc *Franchise Service Ctr* 2521 Pepperwood St .... Farmers Branch TX 75234 *TF:* 800-583-5960 ■ *Web:* mrjims.pizza	972-267-5467		670
Mr John's School of Cosmetology Esthetics & Nails 1745 E Eldorado .... Decatur IL 62521 *Web:* www.mrjohns.com	217-423-8173	423-9506	685
MR Label Inc 5018 Gray Rd .... Cincinnati OH 45232 *Web:* www.mrlabelco.com	513-681-2088		627
Mr Leon's School of Hair Design 618 S Main St .... Moscow ID 83843 *Web:* www.mrleons.com	208-882-2923		685
Mr Maintenance Inc 5123 Pearl St .... Schiller Park IL 60176 *Web:* mrmaintinc.com	847-233-7088		653
Mr Powdrell's Barbeque House 11301 Central Ave NE .... Albuquerque NM 87123 *Web:* www.bbqandsoulfoodabq.com	505-298-6766		671
MR Rooter Corp 1010 N University Parks Dr .... Waco TX 76707 *TF:* 855-982-2028 ■ *Web:* www.mrrooter.com	254-340-1321	745-2501	189-10
M-R Sign Company Inc 1706 First Ave N .... Fergus Falls MN 56537 *TF:* 800-231-5564 ■ *Web:* www.mrsigncompany.com	218-736-5681	736-4070	701
MRAS (Middle River Aircraft Systems) 103 Chesapeake Park Plz .... Baltimore MD 21220 *TF:* 877-432-3272 ■ *Web:* www.mras-usa.com	410-682-1500	682-1230	22
Mrasek & Associates PC 6193 Miller Rd .... Swartz Creek MI 48473 *Web:* www.mrasekcpa.com	810-635-2409	630-8921	2
MRAZ, Amerine & Associates Inc 1120 13th St Ste K .... Modesto CA 95354 *Web:* www.mrazamerine.com	209-593-5870		528
MRB Partners Inc 2001 Boul Robert-Bourassa Ste 810 .... Montreal QC H3A2A6 *Web:* www.mrbpartners.com	514-558-1515		401
MRC (Medicare Rights Ctr) 266 W 37th St 3rd Fl .... New York NY 10018 *TF:* 800-333-4114 ■ *Web:* www.medicarerights.org	212-869-3850	869-3532	48-17
MRC (Morrow Realty Company Inc) 809 22nd Ave .... Tuscaloosa AL 35401 *Web:* www.morrowrealty.com	205-759-5781	391-0031	652
MRC (Misty River Consulting) EP938 Hillside St .... Stratford WI 54484 *Web:* www.mistyriver.com	715-687-8818		196
MRC Global Inc 2 Houston Ctr .... Houston TX 77010 *TF:* 877-294-7574 ■ *Web:* www.mrcglobal.com	877-294-7574		787
MRC Polymers Inc 3307 S Lawndale Ave .... Chicago IL 60623 *Web:* www.mrcpolymers.com	815-221-6400		605-2
MRCE (Mueser Rutledge Consulting Engineers) 14 Penn Plz 225 W 34th St .... New York NY 10122 *Web:* mrce.com	917-339-9300		261
MrClean Car Wash 2567 E West Conn SW .... Austell GA 30106 *Web:* www.mrcleancarwash.com	770-222-5811		62-1
MrCopy Inc 5657 Copley Dr .... San Diego CA 92111 *Web:* www.mrc360.com	858-573-6300		196
MREA (Midwest Renewable Energy Assn) 7558 Deer Rd .... Custer WI 54423 *Web:* www.midwestrenew.org	715-592-6595		139
MREIC (Monmouth Real Estate Investment Corp) 3499 Rt 9 N Ste 3C .... Freehold NJ 07728 *NYSE:* MNR ■ *Web:* www.mreic.reit	732-577-9996		655
MRG (Marketing Resource Group Inc) 225 S Washington Sq .... Lansing MI 48933 *TF:* 800-928-2086 ■ *Web:* mrgmi.com	517-372-4400	372-4045	5
MRG (Marshall Retail Group) 3755 W Sunset Rd .... Las Vegas NV 89118 *Web:* marshallretailgroup.com	702-385-5233		157-6
MRG Document Technologies 717 N Harwood St Ste 1600 .... Dallas TX 75201 *TF:* 800-688-7335 ■ *Web:* www.mrgdocs.com	214-220-6300	220-2785	387
MRHC (Marquette Regional History Ctr) 145 W Spring St .... Marquette MI 49855 *Web:* www.marquettecohistory.org	906-226-3571		48-13
MRI (Midwest Research Institute) 425 Volker Blvd .... Kansas City MO 64110 *Web:* www.mriglobal.org	816-753-7600		668
MRI Group 2100 Harrisburg Pk .... Lancaster PA 17601 *TF:* 888-674-1377 ■ *Web:* www.mrigroup.com	717-291-1016		415
MRI Technologies 17047 El Camino Real Ste 200 .... Houston TX 77058 *Web:* mricompany.com	281-786-2004		175
MRL Agency Ii Corp 1010 Northern Blvd .... Great Neck NY 11021 *TF:* 800-945-7461 ■ *Web:* mrlagency.com	516-487-4000		390
MRM Industries Inc 1655 Industrial Dr .... Owosso MI 48867 *Web:* www.mrmindustries.com	989-723-7443	725-2328	605-2
MRM//McCANN 622 3rd Ave .... New York NY 10017 *Web:* mrm-mccann.com	646-865-6230		4
MRMC (Midwestern Regional Medical Ctr) 2520 Elisha Ave .... Zion IL 60099 *TF:* 800-615-3055 ■ *Web:* www.cancercenter.com	847-872-4561		374-7
MRMC (Meadows Regional Medical Ctr) 1 Meadows Pkwy .... Vidalia GA 30474 *TF:* 800-382-4023 ■ *Web:* meadowshealth.com	912-535-5555		374-3
MRMC (Meadowview Regional Medical Ctr) 989 Medical Pk Dr .... Maysville KY 41056 *Web:* www.meadowviewregional.com	606-759-5311		374-3
MRN (Motor Racing Network) 555 MRN Dr ...... Concord NC 28027 *Web:* www.mrn.com	704-262-6700	262-6811	78
MRS (Materials Research Society) 506 Keystone Dr .... Warrendale PA 15086 *Web:* www.mrs.org	724-779-3003	779-8313	49-19
Mrs Clark's Foods 740 SE Dalbey Dr .... Ankeny IA 50021 *TF:* 800-736-5674 ■ *Web:* www.mrsclarks.com	515-299-6400		296-21
Mrs Gerrys Kitchen Inc 2110 Y H Hanson Ave .... Albert Lea MN 56007 *Web:* www.mrsgerrys.com	507-373-6384		123
Mrs Grissom's Salads Inc 2500 Bransford Ave .... Nashville TN 37204 *Web:* www.mrsgrissoms.com	615-255-4137	251-9763	296-37
MRS Homecare Inc 1497 Kennedy Rd .... Tifton GA 31794 *TF:* 800-342-6666 ■ *Web:* www.mrshomecare.com	229-382-2002		475
Mrs Nelsons Library Service 1650 W Orange Grove Ave .... Pomona CA 91768 *TF:* 800-875-9911 ■ *Web:* www.mrsnelsons.com	909-865-8550		95
Mrs Ressler's Food Products Co 5501 Tabor Ave .... Philadelphia PA 19120 *Web:* www.ressler.com	215-744-4700	744-4750	296-26
Mrs Robino's Restaurant 520 N Union St .... Wilmington DE 19801 *Web:* www.mrsrobinos.com	302-652-9223		671
Mrs Stratton's Salads Inc 380 Industrial Ln .... Birmingham AL 35211 *Web:* www.mrsstrattons.com	205-940-9640		297-8
MRS Systems Inc 19000 33rd Ave W Ste 130 .... Lynnwood WA 98036 **Fax Area Code:* 206 ■ *TF:* 800-253-4827 ■ *Web:* www.mrsys.com	800-253-4827	633-6038*	177
MRU (Mankind Research Unlimited) 1315 Apple Ave .... Silver Spring MD 20910 *Web:* mankindresearchunlimited.woobly.com	301-587-8686	585-8959	637-2
MRU Instruments Inc 18838 - S Memorial Dr Ste 103 .... Humble TX 77338 *Web:* www.mru-instruments.com	713-426-3260		407
MRWMD (Monterey Regional Waste Management District) 14201 Del Monte Blvd .... Marina CA 93933 *Web:* www.mrwmd.org	831-384-5313	384-3567	660
MS Aerospace Inc 13928 Balboa Blvd .... Sylmar CA 91342 *Web:* www.msaerospace.com	818-833-9095	833-9525	278
MS Bubbles Inc 2731 S Alameda St .... Los Angeles CA 90058 **Fax Area Code:* 213 ■ *Web:* www.msbubbles.com	323-544-0300	239-9709*	155-3
MS Consultants Inc 333 E Federal St .... Youngstown OH 44503 *Web:* www.msconsultants.com	330-744-5321		261
MS Dallas Reprographics Inc 2300 Reagan St .... Dallas TX 75219 *Web:* www.msdallas.com	214-521-7000		113
MS Fitness Magazine PO Box 2490 .... White City OR 97503 *Web:* www.msfitness.com	541-830-0400		457-13
MS Foundation for Women 12 MetroTech Ctr 26th Fl .... Brooklyn NY 11201 *Web:* forwomen.org	212-742-2300	742-1653	48-24
MS Govern 424 S Woods Mill Rd Ste 310 .... Chesterfield MO 63017 *TF:* 855-574-9261 ■ *Web:* www.msgovern.com	314-802-5158		177
MS Howells & Co 20555 N Pima Rd Ste 100 .... Scottsdale AZ 85255 *Web:* mshowells.com	480-563-2000	563-2001	690
MS Nonwovens Inc 275 Industrial Dr .... Pontotoc MS 38863 *Web:* www.shinih.com.tw	662-489-4100	489-4848	146
MS of A Dent-All Plans Inc PO Box 1418 .... Tomball TX 77377 *TF:* 866-362-1517 ■ *Web:* www.firstdentalchoice.com	281-351-2484		391-3
MS Roberts Academy of Beauty Culture Inc 552 Mannheim Rd .... Hillside IL 60162 *Web:* www.msroberts-academy.com	708-649-9088		167-3
MS Rubber Co 715 E McDowell Rd .... Jackson MS 39204 *TF:* 800-748-9083 ■ *Web:* www.msrubber.com	601-948-2575	360-1703	695
MS Supply and Home Health Co 618 Ware Blvd .... Tampa FL 33619 *TF:* 800-680-3722 ■ *Web:* www.mssupplycompany.com	813-621-2001	621-2480	475
MS Technology Inc 137 Union Valley Rd .... Oak Ridge TN 37830 *Web:* mstechnology.com	865-483-0895		261
MS Willett Inc 220 Cockeysville Rd .... Cockeysville MD 21030 *Web:* www.mswillett.com	410-771-0460	771-6972	757

	Phone	Fax	Class
MSA (Medical Services of America Inc) 171 Monroe Ln. . . . . Lexington SC 29072 *TF:* 800-845-5850 ■ *Web:* www.msa-corp.com	803-957-0500		363
MSA Aircraft Products Inc 10000 Iota Dr. . . . . San Antonio TX 78217 *TF:* 800-695-1212 ■ *Web:* www.msaaircraft.com	210-590-6100		22
MSA architecture + design 360 22nd St Ste 800. . . . . Oakland CA 94612 *Web:* www.msasf.com	415-541-0977		393
MSA Consulting Inc 34200 Bob Hope Dr . . . . . Rancho Mirage CA 92270 *Web:* www.msaconsultinginc.com	760-320-9811		261
MSA Professional Services Inc 1230 South Blvd. . . . . Baraboo WI 53913 *TF:* 800-362-4505 ■ *Web:* www.msa-ps.com	608-356-2771		261
MSA Security 9 Murray St 2nd Fl . . . . . New York NY 10007 *Web:* www.msasecurity.net	212-509-1336	608-3895	692
MSANA (Masonic Service Association of North America) 8120 Fenton St Ste 203 . . . . . Silver Spring MD 20910 *TF:* 855-476-4010 ■ *Web:* www.msana.com	301-588-4010	608-3457	48-15
MSB Fairway Capital Partners 1800 St James Pl Ste 450. . . . . Houston TX 77056 *Web:* www.msfairway.com	713-622-9961		691
MSC (Murray Supply Co) 260 Olive St . . . . . Winston-Salem NC 27103 *Web:* murraysupply.com	336-765-9480	245-0686	612
MSC (Manufacturers Supplies Co) 4220 Rider Trl N . . . . . Earth City MO 63045 *Web:* www.mfgsup.com	314-770-0880		695
MSC Cruises USA Inc 6750 N Andrews Ave Ste 100 . . . . . Fort Lauderdale FL 33309 *Web:* www.msccruisesusa.com	954-772-6262		220
MSC Filtration Technologies 198 Freshwater Blvd. . . . . Enfield CT 06082 *TF:* 800-237-7359 ■ *Web:* www.mscfiltertech.com	860-745-7475	745-7477	806
MSC Industrial Direct Co 75 Maxess Rd. . . . . Melville NY 11747 *NYSE: MSM* ■ *TF:* 800-645-7270 ■ *Web:* www.mscdirect.com	800-645-7270	255-5067	385
MSCE (MacKay & Somps) 5142 Franklin Dr Ste B. . . . . Pleasanton CA 94588 *Web:* www.msce.com	925-225-0690	225-0698	261
MSCI (Metals Service Center Institute) 4201 Euclid Ave . . . . . Rolling Meadows IL 60008 *TF:* 800-634-2358 ■ *Web:* www.msci.org	847-485-3000	485-3001	49-18
MSCI (Margaret Sanger Center Intl) 26 Bleecker St. . . . . New York NY 10012 *Web:* www.plannedparenthood.org	212-965-7000	274-7299	48-6
MSCSoftware Corp 4675 MacArthur Crt . . . . . Newport Beach CA 92660 *Web:* www.mscsoftware.com	714-540-8900	784-4056	178-5
MSD (Medical Specialties Distributors LLC) 800 Technology Center Dr . . . . . Stoughton MA 02072 **Fax Area Code: 866* ■ *TF:* 800-967-6400 ■ *Web:* msdonline.com	800-967-6400	491-2665*	475
MSD Capital LP 645 5th Ave 21st Fl . . . . . New York NY 10022 *Web:* www.msdcapital.com	212-303-1650		690
MSDBC (Mothers Supporting Daughters with Breast Cancer) 25235 Fox Chase Dr. . . . . Chestertown MD 21620 *Web:* www.mothersdaughters.org	410-778-1982	778-1411	48-17
MSDSonline 222 Merchandise Mart Plz Ste 1750. . . . . Chicago IL 60654 *TF:* 888-362-2007 ■ *Web:* www.msdsonline.com	312-881-2000		49-5
MSE Express America Inc 2700 Delta Ln. . . . . Elk Grove Village IL 60007 *Web:* www.tasexpress.com	847-238-2600		311
MSF (Multiple Sclerosis Foundation) 6520 N Andrews Ave. . . . . Fort Lauderdale FL 33309 *TF:* 800-225-6495 ■ *Web:* msfocus.org	954-776-6805		48-17
MSF Electric Inc 10455 Fountaingate Dr. . . . . Stafford TX 77477 *Web:* www.msfelectric.com	281-494-4700	494-4707	189-4
MSHFA (Motorsports Hall of Fame of America) 1801 W International Speedway Blvd . . . . . Daytona Beach FL 32114 *Web:* www.mshf.com	248-349-7223		522
MSI (Machine Specialties Inc) 6511 Franz Warner Pkwy . . . . . Whitsett NC 27377 *Web:* www.machspec.com	336-603-1919	603-1921	621
MSI (Mailing Systems Inc) 2431 Mercantile Dr Ste A. . . . . Rancho Cordova CA 95742 *TF:* 877-577-2647 ■ *Web:* www.msimail.net	916-631-7400	631-7488	5
MSI Benefits Group Inc 245 Townpark Dr Ste 100. . . . . Kennesaw GA 30144 *TF:* 800-580-1629 ■ *Web:* Www.msibg.com	770-425-1231	425-4722	390
MSI Data Systems 10033 N Port Washington Rd. . . . . Mequon WI 53092 *Web:* www.msidata.com	262-241-7800		177
MSI General Corp PO Box 7 . . . . . Oconomowoc WI 53066 *Web:* msigeneral.com	262-367-3661		803-1
MSI International Inc 710 Morgan Falls Rd . . . . . Sandy Springs GA 30350 *TF:* 800-927-0919	610-265-2000	265-2213	266
MSI Inventory Service Corp PO Box 320129 . . . . . Flowood MS 39232 *TF:* 800-820-1460 ■ *Web:* www.msi-inv.com	601-939-0130	939-0061	399
MSI Tec Inc 8925 E Nichols Ave . . . . . Centennial CO 80112 *TF:* 866-397-7388 ■ *Web:* www.msitec.com	720-875-9835		180
MSI Transducers Corp 543 Great Rd . . . . . Littleton MA 01460 *Web:* www.matsysinc.com	978-486-0404		253
Msights Inc 9935 Rea Rd Ste D-301 . . . . . Charlotte NC 28277 *TF:* 877-267-4448 ■ *Web:* www.msights.com	877-267-4448		809
MSK Precision Products Inc 10101 NW 67th St . . . . . Tamarac FL 33321 *TF:* 800-992-5018 ■ *Web:* www.mskprecision.com	954-776-0770	776-3780	621
MSL (Montana State Library) 1515 E 6th Ave. . . . . Helena MT 59620 *Web:* home.msl.mt.gov	406-444-3115		434-5
MSL Group 1675 Broadway 29th Fl . . . . . New York NY 10019 *Web:* northamerica.mslgroup.com	646-500-7600		636
MSM Industries Inc 802 Swan Dr . . . . . Smyrna TN 37167 *TF:* 800-648-6648 ■ *Web:* www.msmind.com	615-355-4355	355-6874	676
MSO (Metal Suppliers Online LLC) 35 Gigante Dr. . . . . Hampstead NH 03841 *TF:* 800-380-1470 ■ *Web:* www.metalsuppliersonline.com	603-329-0101	329-0171	492
MSP Corp 5910 Rice Creek Pkwy Ste 300. . . . . Shoreview MN 55126 *Web:* Www.tsi.com	651-287-8100	287-8140	407
MSPB (Merit Systems Protection Board) 1615 M St NW . . . . . Washington DC 20036 *TF:* 800-209-8960 ■ *Web:* www.mspb.gov	202-653-7200	653-7130	340-20
MSPB (Merit Systems Protection Board Regional Offices) *Atlanta Region* 401 W Peachtree St NW 10th Fl. . . . . Atlanta GA 30308 *Web:* www.mspb.gov	404-730-2751	730-2767	340-20
MSPCA Animal Shelter 1577 Falmouth Rd . . . . . Centerville MA 02632 *Web:* www.mspca.org	508-775-0940		794
MSPTA 1715 Abbey Rd Ste B . . . . . East Lansing MI 48823 *Web:* www.mspta.net	517-336-7782		414
MSR Communications 832 Sansome St 2nd Fl . . . . . San Francisco CA 94111 *TF:* 866-247-6172 ■ *Web:* www.msrcommunications.com	415-989-9000		636
MSR Wholesale Balloons 19009 16th Ave S. . . . . Seattle WA 98188 *TF:* 800-984-1159 ■ *Web:* www.msrballoons.com	206-523-1010	523-1037	328
MSRB (Municipal Securities Rulemaking Board) 1900 Duke St Ste 600. . . . . Alexandria VA 22314 *Web:* www.msrb.org	703-797-6600	797-6700	49-2
MSS Services Inc 14200 Schaeffer Rd . . . . . Germantown MD 20874 *Web:* mssserv.com	301-528-5531	528-5559	463
MSS Technologies Inc 1555 E Orangewood Ave. . . . . Phoenix AZ 85020 *TF:* 800-694-1302 ■ *Web:* mssbta.com	602-387-2100		180
MSSC U.S. Inc 102 Bill Bryan Blvd. . . . . Hopkinsville KY 42240 *Web:* www.msscna.com	270-887-3000		718
MST (Monterey-Salinas Transit) 19 Upper Ragsdale Dr Ste 200 . . . . . Monterey CA 93940 *TF:* 888-678-2871 ■ *Web:* mst.org	888-678-2871		468
MST Steel Corp 24417 Groesbeck Hwy. . . . . Warren MI 48089 *Web:* www.mststeel.com	586-773-5460		399
MSU (Missouri State University) 901 S National Ave. . . . . Springfield MO 65897 *TF:* 800-492-7900 ■ *Web:* www.missouristate.edu	417-836-5000	836-6334	166
MSU-DOE Plant Research Laboratory 612 Wilson Rd . . . . . East Lansing MI 48824 *Web:* prl.natsci.msu.edu	517-353-2270	353-9168	668
Msys Inc 140 Iowa Ln Ste 201 . . . . . Cary NC 27511 *Web:* www.msysinc.com	919-454-5604		193
MT & L Card Products & Fulfillment Services 2911 Kraft Dr . . . . . Nashville TN 37204 *Web:* www.mtlcard.com	615-254-9471	244-6063	627
Mt Diablo Adult Education 1266 San Carlos Ave . . . . . Concord CA 94518 *Web:* www.mdae-mdusd-ca.schoolloop.com	925-685-7340		167-3
Mt Hood Equity 4800 SW Meadows Rd Ste 300 . . . . . Lake Oswego OR 97035	503-639-0915		194
Mt Konocti Growers Inc 2550 Big Valley Rd. . . . . Kelseyville CA 95451 *Web:* mtkonoctiwines.com	707-279-4213		315-3
Mt Lebanon School District 7 Horsman Dr. . . . . Pittsburgh PA 15228 *Web:* www.mtlsd.org	412-344-2000	344-2047	685
Mt Mckinley Animal Hospital 425 Harold Bentley Ave. . . . . Fairbanks AK 99701 *TF:* 888-755-6104 ■ *Web:* mmahak.com	907-452-6104		794
MT McKinley Bank 500 Fourth Ave . . . . . Fairbanks AK 99701 *TF:* 888-515-1774 ■ *Web:* mtmckinleybank.com	907-452-1751	451-3501	70
Mt Pleasant Central School District 825 Westlake Dr . . . . . Thornwood NY 10594 *Web:* www.mtplcsd.org	914-769-5500	769-3733	685
Mt San Antonio College 1100 N Grand Ave. . . . . Walnut CA 91789 *Web:* www.mtsac.edu	909-274-4027		162
Mt Shasta Spring Water Company Inc 1878 Twin View Blvd. . . . . Redding CA 96003 *TF:* 800-922-6227 ■ *Web:* www.mtshastaspringwater.com	530-246-8800		366
Mt Vernon illinois 1100 Main St . . . . . Mount Vernon IL 62864 *Web:* www.mtvernon.com	618-242-5000	244-0746	206
Mt. Carmel Stabilization Group Inc 1611 College Dr. . . . . Mount Carmel IL 62863 *Web:* www.mtcsg.com	618-262-5118	263-4084	188-4
Mt. Eden Floral Co 2124 Bering Dr . . . . . San Jose CA 95131 *Web:* www.mteden.com	408-213-5777		293
MTA (Maryland Transit Administration) 6 St Paul St. . . . . Baltimore MD 21202 *TF:* 866-743-3682 ■ *Web:* www.mta.maryland.gov	410-539-5000	333-4810	468
MTA (Montana Telecommunications Assn) 208 N Montana Ave Ste 105. . . . . Helena MT 59601 *Web:* www.telecomassn.org	406-442-4316	442-8243	139
MTA (Maine Tourism Assn) 327 Water St . . . . . Hallowell ME 04347 *Web:* www.mainetourism.com	207-623-0363	623-0388	139
MTA Today Magazine 20 Ashburton Pl . . . . . Boston MA 02108 *TF:* 800-392-6175 ■ *Web:* massteacher.org	617-878-8000	742-7046	457-8
MTAS (Municipal Technical Advisory Service) 1610 University Ave . . . . . Knoxville TN 37921 *Web:* www.mtas.tennessee.edu	865-974-0411	974-0423	637-10
MTC (Micro Technology Concepts) 17837 Rowland St . . . . . City of Industry CA 91748 *Web:* www.mtcusa.com	626-839-6800	839-6899	174
MTC (Microcast Technologies Corp) 1611 W Elizabeth Ave. . . . . Linden NJ 07036 *Web:* www.mtcnj.com	908-523-9503	523-0910	481
MTC (Materials Transportation Co) 1408 S Commerce PO Box 1358 . . . . . Temple TX 76503 *TF:* 800-433-3110 ■ *Web:* www.gomtc.com	254-298-2900		386
MTC Logistics 4851 Holabird Ave. . . . . Baltimore MD 21224 *Web:* mtccold.com	410-342-9300	522-1163	803-2

Name / Address	City	State	Zip	Phone	Fax	Class
MTCC (Manti Telecommunications Co)						
34 W Union	Manti	UT	84642	435-835-2929		735
Web: www.manti.com						
MTD (Morris Tile Distributors Inc)						
9132 Gaither Rd	Gaithersburg	MD	20877	301-670-4222	590-0792	191-1
Web: morristile.com						
MTD (Morris Tile Distributors Inc)						
2525 Kenilworth Ave.	Tuxedo	MD	20781	301-773-7000	386-2261	191-1
Web: www.morristile.com						
MTD Corp 41 Otis St	West Babylon	NY	11704	631-491-3905		321
Web: mtdwoodwork.com						
MTD Products Inc 5965 Grafton Rd	Valley City	OH	44280	330-225-2600		429
TF: 800-800-7310 ■ *Web:* www.mtdproducts.com						
MTE Consultants Inc						
520 Bingemans Centre Dr	Kitchener	ON	N2B3X9	519-743-6500		196
Web: www.mte85.com						
MTE Corp PO Box 9013	Menomonee Falls	WI	53051	800-455-4683	253-8222*	767
**Fax Area Code:* 262 ■ *TF:* 800-455-4683 ■ *Web:* www.mtecorp.com						
Mte Hydraulics 4701 Kishwaukee St	Rockford	IL	61109	815-397-4701	399-5528	640
Web: mtehydraulics.com						
M-Tec Systems Inc						
1329 E Kemper Rd Ste 4222	Cincinnati	OH	45246	513-742-3100	893-1651*	180
**Fax Area Code:* 888 ■ *Web:* www.mtecsystems.com						
Mtech Mechanical Technologies Group Inc						
12300 Pecos St	Westminster	CO	80234	303-650-4000		610
Web: www.mtechg.com						
mThink 3053 Fillmore St Ste 325	San Francisco	CA	94123	415-420-0835		4
Web: mthink.com						
MTI (Momentum Technologies Inc)						
4400 Easton Common Way Ste 125	Columbus	OH	43219	330-896-5900	896-9943	603
MTI (Manufacturing Technology Inc)						
1702 W Washington St	South Bend	IN	46628	574-233-9490	233-9489	811
Web: www.mtiwelding.com						
MTI (Medical Teams Intl) PO Box 10	Portland	OR	97207	503-624-1000	624-1001	48-5
TF: 800-959-4325 ■ *Web:* www.medicalteams.org						
MTI (Medical Imaging Technologies)						
875 Valley St	Colorado Springs	CO	80915	800-541-5306		475
TF: 800-541-5306 ■ *Web:* www.medicalimagingtech.com						
MTI America						
1350 S Powerline Rd Ste 200	Pompano Beach	FL	33069	800-553-2155		393
TF: 800-553-2155 ■ *Web:* www.mtiamerica.com						
MTI Business College of Stockton						
6006 N El Dorado St	Stockton	CA	95207	209-957-3030		167-3
TF: 888-302-2009 ■ *Web:* www.mtistockton.com						
MTI College 5221 Madison Ave	Sacramento	CA	95841	916-339-1500		167-3
Web: www.mticollege.edu						
MTI Electronics Inc						
W133 N5139 Campbell Dr	Menomonee Falls	WI	53051	262-783-6080		625
Web: www.mtielectronics.com						
MTI Instruments Inc						
325 Washington Ave Ext	Albany	NY	12205	518-218-2550		407
TF: 800-342-2203 ■ *Web:* www.mtiinstruments.com						
MTI Systems Inc						
1111 Elm St Ste 6	West Springfield	MA	01089	413-733-1972	739-9250	178-12
TF: 800-644-4318 ■ *Web:* www.mtisystems.com						
MTI-Milliren Technologies Inc						
2 New Pasture Rd	Newburyport	MA	01950	978-465-6064		253
Web: www.mti-milliren.com						
MTM Association for Standards & Research						
1111 E Touhy Ave Ste 280	Des Plaines	IL	60018	844-686-1951	299-3509*	49-19
**Fax Area Code:* 847 ■ *TF:* 844-300-5355 ■ *Web:* www.mtm.org						
MTM Publishing Inc						
435 W 23rd St Ste 8C	New York	NY	10011	212-242-6930	242-6906	94
Web: www.mtmpublishing.com						
MTM Recognition Corp						
3201 SE 29th St	Oklahoma City	OK	73115	405-670-4545	672-1308	409
TF: 877-686-7464 ■ *Web:* mtmrecognition.com						
MTM Technologies Inc						
4 High Ridge Pk Ste 102	Stamford	CT	06905	203-975-3700		176
NASDAQ: MTMC ■ *Web:* www.mtm.com						
MTNA (Music Teachers NA)						
441 Vine St Ste 3100	Cincinnati	OH	45202	513-421-1420	421-2503	49-5
TF: 888-512-5278 ■ *Web:* www.mtna.org						
MTNG (Middle Tennessee Natural Gas Utility District)						
1036 W Broad St PO Box 670	Smithville	TN	37166	615-597-4300	597-6331	787
TF: 800-880-6373 ■ *Web:* www.mtng.com						
MTO (Munger, Tolles & Olson LLP)						
355 S Grand Ave 35th Fl	Los Angeles	CA	90071	213-683-9100		41
Web: www.mto.com						
MTPB (Tourism Malaysia)						
120 E 56th St Ste 810	New York	NY	10022	212-754-1113	754-1116	775
Web: www.malaysia.travel						
MTR Family Law PLLC 205 23rd Ave N	Nashville	TN	37203	615-341-0070		41
Web: mtrfamilylaw.com						
MtronPTI 1703 E Hwy 50	Yankton	SD	57078	605-665-9321		253
TF: 800-762-8800 ■ *Web:* www.mtronpti.com						
MTS (Mid-America Transplant Services)						
1110 Highlands Plaza Dr E Ste 100	Saint Louis	MO	63110	314-735-8200		545
TF: 888-376-4854 ■ *Web:* www.midamericatransplant.org						
MTS (MTS Safety Products Inc) PO Box 204	Golden	MS	38847	800-647-8168	329-9687	576
TF: 800-647-8168 ■ *Web:* www.mts-safety.com						
MTS (Musical Theatre Southwest)						
6320 Domingo Rd NE Ste B	Albuquerque	NM	87108	505-265-9119		573-2
Web: www.musicaltheatresw.com						
MTS (Miller Technical Services)						
47801 W Anchor Ct	Plymouth	MI	48170	734-738-1970	738-1975	492
Web: www.mtsmedicalmfg.com						
MTS Ambulance 2431 Greenup Ave	Ashland	KY	41101	606-324-3286		30
TF: 800-598-3458 ■ *Web:* www.mtsambulance.com						
MTS Broadcasting LC						
2500 Mullinix Mill Rd	Mt Airy	MD	21771	410-228-4800		647
Web: www.mtslive.com						
MTS Consulting LLC 7444 Long Ave	Skokie	IL	60077	847-675-6666		734
Web: www.mtsconsulting.com						
MTS Safety Products Inc (MTS) PO Box 204	Golden	MS	38847	800-647-8168	329-9687	576
TF: 800-647-8168 ■ *Web:* www.mts-safety.com						
MTS Seating Inc 7100 Industrial Dr	Temperance	MI	48182	734-847-3875	329-0687*	319-1
**Fax Area Code:* 800 ■ *Web:* www.mtsseating.com						
MTS Systems Corp						
14000 Technology Dr	Eden Prairie	MN	55344	952-937-4000	937-4515	472
NASDAQ: MTSC ■ *TF:* 800-328-2255 ■ *Web:* www.mts.com						
MTSI (Modern Technology Solutions Inc)						
5285 Shawnee Rd Ste 400	Alexandria	VA	22312	703-564-3800		261
Web: www.mtsi-va.com						
MTSI Inc 212 E Rowland St	Covina	CA	91723	714-257-1144	257-1654	647
Web: www.mtsiinc.com						
MTT-S (IEEE Microwave Theory & Techniques Society)						
5829 Bellanca Dr	Elkridge	MD	21075	410-796-5866		49-19
TF: 800-678-4333 ■ *Web:* www.mtt.org						
MTU Aero Engines North America Inc						
795 Brook St Bldg 5	Rocky Hill	CT	06067	860-258-9700	258-9797	21
Web: www.mtu.de						
MTU Onsite Energy Corp 100 Power Dr	Mankato	MN	56001	507-625-7973	625-2968	518
TF: 800-325-5450 ■ *Web:* www.mtuonsiteenergy.com						
MTV Networks 1515 Broadway	New York	NY	10036	212-258-8000	258-8146	740
Web: www.mtv.com						
Mtw Solutions LLC						
3236 W Edgewood Dr Ste D	Jefferson City	MO	65109	573-893-7997	893-6636	180
Web: www.mtwsolutions.com						
Mu Lan 824 Juniper St NE	Atlanta	GA	30308	404-877-5797		671
Web: mulanatlanta.net						
Mu Net Inc 442 Marrett Rd Ste 9	Lexington	MA	02421	781-861-8644		625
Web: munet.com						
Mu Phi Epsilon						
1611 County Rd B W Ste 320	Saint Paul	MN	55113	888-259-1471		48-11
TF: 888-259-1471 ■ *Web:* muphiepsilon.site-ym.com						
Mucarsel-Powell Debbie (Rep D - FL)						
114 Cannon House Office Bldg	Washington	DC	20515	202-225-2778		342-2
Web: www.mucarsel-powell.house.gov						
Mud Hole Custom Tackle Inc 400 Kane Ct	Oviedo	FL	32765	407-447-7637		711
TF: 866-790-7637 ■ *Web:* www.mudhole.com						
Mud Puddle Inc 36 W 25th St	New York	NY	10010	212-647-9168	495-0749*	637-2
**Fax Area Code:* 206 ■ *Web:* www.mudpuddleinc.com						
Mudd Advertising						
915 Technology Pkwy	Cedar Falls	IA	50613	877-321-4992		6
TF: 877-321-4992 ■ *Web:* mudd.com						
Mudiam Inc 7100 Regency Sq Blvd	Houston	TX	77036	713-484-7266		225
TF: 888-306-2062 ■ *Web:* www.mudiaminc.com						
Mueller Brass Co 2199 Lapeer Ave	Port Huron	MI	48060	810-987-7770	794-1214*	485
**Fax Area Code:* 616 ■ *TF:* 800-553-3336 ■ *Web:* muellerindustriesipd.com						
Mueller Co PO Box 671	Decatur	IL	62522	217-423-4471	425-7537	789
TF: 800-423-1323 ■ *Web:* www.muellerflo.com						
Mueller Gages Co 318 Agostino Rd	San Gabriel	CA	91776	626-287-2911	286-8693	493
Web: www.mueller-gages.com						
Mueller Graphic Supply Inc						
11475 W Thdore Trcker Way	Milwaukee	WI	53214	414-475-0990	475-0454	386
Web: www.muellergraphics.com						
Mueller Inc 1913 Hutchins Ave	Ballinger	TX	76821	325-365-3555	365-8181	105
TF: 877-268-3553 ■ *Web:* www.muellerinc.com						
Mueller Industries Inc						
8285 Tournament Dr Ste 150	Memphis	TN	38125	901-753-3200	753-3251	485
NYSE: MLI ■ *TF:* 800-348-8464 ■ *Web:* www.muellerindustries.com						
Mueller Law Office, The 404 W 7th St	Austin	TX	78701	512-478-1236		41
Web: themuellerlawoffice.com						
Mueller Metals LLC						
2152 Schwartz Rd	San Angelo	TX	76904	866-651-6702		492
TF: 866-651-6702 ■ *Web:* muellermetals.com						
Mueller Prost PC						
7733 Forsyth Blvd Ste 1200	Saint Louis	MO	63105	314-862-2070	862-1549	2
TF: 800-649-4838 ■ *Web:* www.muellerprost.com						
Mueller Recreational Products Inc						
4825 S 16th St	Lincoln	NE	68512	402-423-8888		711
TF: 800-925-7665 ■ *Web:* www.muellers.com						
Mueller Refrigeration LLC						
121 Rogers St	Hartsville	TN	37074	615-374-2124	374-2080	789
Web: www.muellerrefrigeration.com						
Mueller Sports Medicine Inc						
1 Quench Dr	Prairie Du Sac	WI	53578	608-643-8530	643-2568	582
TF: 800-356-9522 ■ *Web:* www.muellersportsmed.com						
Mueller State Park						
21045 Hwy 67 S Po Box 39	Divide	CO	80814	719-687-2366	687-6867	565
Web: cpw.state.co.us						
Mueller Steam Specialty						
1491 NC Hwy 20 W	Saint Pauls	NC	28384	910-865-8241	865-8245	386
TF: 800-334-6259 ■ *Web:* www.muellersteam.com						
Mueller-Yurgae Assoc 1055 SE 28th St	Grimes	IA	50111	515-986-0491	986-0492	297-8
Web: www.mueller-yurgae.com						
Muermann Engineering LLC 116 Fremont St	Kiel	WI	53042	920-894-7800		261
Web: www.me-pe.com						
Mueser Rutledge Consulting Engineers (MRCE)						
14 Penn Plz 225 W 34th St	New York	NY	10122	917-339-9300		261
Web: mrce.com						
Muhammad Ali Ctr 144 N Sixth St	Louisville	KY	40202	502-584-9254	589-4905	520
Web: www.alicenter.org						
Muhlenberg College 2400 Chew St	Allentown	PA	18104	484-664-3100	664-3234	166
Web: www.muhlenberg.edu						
Muhlenberg County PO Box 137	Greenville	KY	42345	270-338-2520	338-6116	338
Web: www.muhlenbergcounty.ky.gov						
Mui Scientific 145 Traders Blvd E	Mississauga	ON	L4Z3L3	905-890-5525		476
TF: 800-303-6611 ■ *Web:* muiscientific.com						
Muir Enterprises Inc						
3575 West 900 South PO Box 26775	Salt Lake City	UT	84104	801-363-7695	322-1640	297-7
TF: 877-268-2002 ■ *Web:* www.coppercanyonfarms.com						
Muir Woods National Monument						
1 Muir Woods Rd	Mill Valley	CA	94941	415-388-2596	389-6957	564
Web: www.nps.gov						
Mukwonago Animal Hospital SC						
1065 N Rochester St	Mukwonago	WI	53149	262-363-4557		794
Web: mukwonagoanimalhospital.com						
Mulberry Metal Products Inc						
2199 Stanley Terr	Union	NJ	07083	908-688-8850	688-7294	816
Web: www.mulberrymetal.com						
Mulberry Tree Press						
10 Sun Valley Ct	Northport	NY	11768	631-754-0408		637-2
Web: mulberrytreepress.com						

Company	Phone	Fax	Class
Mulch Unlimited Inc 8369 Richfood Rd, Mechanicsville VA 23116 *Web:* mulchunlimited.com	804-730-4166		422
Mule Creek State Prison 4001 Hwy 104, Ione CA 95640 *Web:* cdcr.ca.gov	209-274-4911		213
Mule Lighting Inc 46 Baker St, Providence RI 02905 *TF:* 800-556-7690 ■ *Web:* www.mulelighting.com	401-941-4446	941-2929	439
Mules and More Inc PO Box 460, Bland MO 65014 *Web:* www.mulesandmore.com	573-646-3934	646-3407	637-9
Muleshoe Journal 201 W Ave C, Muleshoe TX 79347 *Web:* www.muleshoejournal.com	806-272-4536	272-3567	532-2
Mulgrew Aircraft Components Inc 1810 S Shamrock Ave, Monrovia CA 91016 *Web:* www.mulgrewaircraft.com	626-256-1375		454
Mulherin, Rehfeldt & Varchetto PC 211 S Wheaton Ave Ste 200, Wheaton IL 60187 *Web:* www.mrvlaw.com	630-653-9300	653-9316	428
Mulhern Belting Inc 148 Bauer Dr, Oakland NJ 07436 *TF:* 800-253-6300 ■ *Web:* www.mulhernbelting.com	201-337-6540		370
Mull Group Inc 1025 Main St, Wheeling WV 26003 *Web:* www.mullgroup.com	304-232-2520		492
Mullan Enterprises Inc 2330 W Joppa Rd Ste 210, Lutherville Timonium MD 21093 *Web:* www.mullancontr.com	410-494-9200		655
Mullaney Engineering Inc 4937 G - Green Valley Rd, Monrovia MD 21770 *Web:* mullengr.com	301-921-0115		261
Mullaney's Harp & Fiddle 2329 Penn Ave, Pittsburgh PA 15222 *Web:* www.harpandfiddle.com	412-642-6622		671
Mullen 40 Broad St, Boston MA 02109 *Web:* us.mullenlowe.com	617-226-9000	226-9100	4
Mullen & Filippi LLP 1601 Response Rd Ste 300, Sacramento CA 95815 *Web:* www.mulfil.com	916-442-4503		428
Mullen Circle Brand Inc 3514 W Touhy Ave, Skokie IL 60076 *Web:* mullenoil.com	847-676-1880	676-3748	541
Mullen Guitar Company Inc 11906 County Rd Mm, Flagler CO 80815 *Web:* mullenguitars.com	970-664-2518		526
Muller Engineering Company Inc 777 S Wadsworth Blvd, Lakewood CO 80226 *Web:* www.mullereng.com	303-988-4939		261
Muller Inc 2800 Grant Ave, Philadelphia PA 19114 *Web:* mullerbev.com	215-676-7575		81-1
Muller Martini 456 Wheeler Rd, Hauppauge NY 11788 *TF:* 888-268-5537 ■ *Web:* www.mullermartini.com	631-582-4343		547
Muller Media Conversions Inc 21 Locust St, Manhasset NY 11030 *Web:* mullermedia.com	516-833-3067		396
Muller Muller Richmond Harms Myers & Sgroi Atty 33233 Woodward Ave, Birmingham MI 48009 *Web:* mullerfirm.com	248-645-2440		428
Muller Systems Corp 926 Juliana Dr, Woodstock ON N4V1B9 *TF:* 800-668-6954 ■ *Web:* www.mullersys.com	519-421-1800		180
Mullin Hoard & Brown LLP Amarillo National Plz Two 500 S Taylor Lobby Box Ste 213, Amarillo TX 79101 *Web:* mullinhoard.com	806-372-5050	372-5086	428
Mullin Markwayne (Rep R - OK) 2421 Rayburn House Office Bldg, Washington DC 20515 *Web:* www.mullin.house.gov	202-225-2701	225-3038	342-2
Mullins Ctr University of Massachusetts 200 Commonwealth Ave, Amherst MA 01003 *Web:* www.mullinscenter.com	413-545-3001		720
Mullins Food Products Inc 2200 S 25th Ave, Broadview IL 60155 *Web:* www.mullinsfood.com	708-344-3224	344-0153	296-20
MultAlloy Inc 8511 Monroe St, Houston TX 77061 *TF:* 800-568-9551 ■ *Web:* multalloy.com	800-568-9551		492
Multi Dimensional Integration 39 E Forrest Ave, Shrewsbury PA 17361 *Web:* www.mdiadvantage.com	717-227-1800		180
Multi Products Company Inc 5301 21st St, Racine WI 53406 *TF:* 877-444-1011 ■ *Web:* www.multiproducts.com	262-554-3700	554-3711	595
MultiCam Inc 1025 W Royal Ln DFW Airport, Dallas TX 75261 *Web:* www.multicam.com	972-929-4070	929-4071	455
MultiCare Deaconess Hospital 800 W 5th Ave, Spokane WA 99204 *Web:* www.deaconessspokane.com	509-458-5800		374-3
MultiCare Health System 315 Martin Luther King Jr Way PO Box 5299, Tacoma WA 98405 *Web:* www.multicare.org	253-403-1126		353
Multichannel News 28 E 28th St 12th Fl, New York NY 10016 **Fax Area Code:* 917 ■ *TF:* 888-343-5563 ■ *Web:* www.multichannel.com	888-343-5563	281-4704*	457-9
Multicim Technologies Inc 16 Westminster Ave N Ste 306C, Montreal West QC H4X1Z1 *Web:* www.multicim.com	514-633-6401		180
Multicoat Corp 23331 Antonio Pkwy, Rancho Santa Margarita CA 92688 **Fax Area Code:* 949 ■ *TF:* 877-685-8426 ■ *Web:* www.multicoat.com	877-685-8426	888-2555*	500
Multi-Color Corp 4053 Clough Woods Dr, Batavia OH 45103 *NASDAQ: LABL* ■ *Web:* www.multicolorcorp.com	513-381-1480	381-2240	413
Multicom Inc 1076 Florida Central Pkwy, Longwood FL 32750 *TF:* 800-423-2594 ■ *Web:* www.multicominc.com	407-331-7779		116
Multicorp Inc 69 W Main St, Westminster MD 21157 *TF:* 800-876-2063 ■ *Web:* www.multicorpfranchising.com	410-876-5000	876-5003	104
Multicraft Inc 4701 Lakeside Ave, Cleveland OH 44114 *Web:* www.multicraftink.com	216-432-5656	432-5757	385
Multi-Craft Plastics Inc 7298 SW Tech Center Dr, Tigard OR 97223 *TF:* 800-488-9030 ■ *Web:* www.multicraftplastics.com	503-352-0970	352-0980	603
Multi-Cultural Center of Sioux Falls 515 N Main Ave, Sioux Falls SD 57104 *Web:* www.sfmcc.org	605-367-7401	367-7404	50-2
Multicultural Foodservice & Hospitality Alliance 1144 Narragansett Blvd, Providence RI 02905 *Web:* www.mfha.net	401-461-6342		78
Multicultural Marketing Resources Inc 101 Fifth Ave Ste 10B, New York NY 10003 *Web:* www.multicultural.com	212-242-3351	691-5969	317
Multidev Technologies Inc 999 de Maisonneuve W Ste 1100, Montreal QC H3A3L4 *Web:* chaindrive.com	514-337-6465		180
Multi-Electric Manufacturing Inc 4223-43 W Lake St, Chicago IL 60624 *Web:* www.multielectric.com	773-722-1900	722-5694	439
Multi-fab Products LLC N90 W14507 Commerce Dr, Menomonee Falls WI 53051 *Web:* www.multi-fab.com	262-502-1707		207
Multifeeder Technology Inc 4821 White Bear Pkwy, Saint Paul MN 55110 *Web:* multifeeder.com	651-407-3100	407-3199	757
Multifilm Packaging Corp 1040 N McLean Blvd, Elgin IL 60123 *Web:* multifilm.com	847-695-7600		548
Multi-Fineline Electronix Inc (MFLEX) 8659 Research Dr, Irvine CA 92618 *NASDAQ: MFLX* ■ *Web:* www.mflex.com	949-453-6800		253
Multigon Industries 525 Executive Blvd, Elmsford NY 10523 *TF:* 800-289-6858 ■ *Web:* www.multigon.com	914-376-5200	376-6111	186
Multi-Level Marketing International Assn (MLMIA) 119 Stanford Ct, Irvine CA 92612 *Web:* www.mlmia.com	949-854-0484		49-18
MultiLing Corp 180 N University Ave 6th Fl, Provo UT 84601 *TF:* 888-960-7827 ■ *Web:* www.multiling.com	801-377-2000	377-7085	196
MultiLingual Solutions Inc 6110 Executive Blvd Ste 325, Rockville MD 20852 **Fax Area Code:* 301 ■ *TF:* 800-815-1964 ■ *Web:* www.mlsolutions.com	800-815-1964	424-7331*	194
Multilink Inc 580 Ternes Ln, Elyria OH 44035 *Web:* multi-link.net	440-366-6966		567
Multimatic Products Inc 390 Oser Ave, Hauppauge NY 11788 *TF:* 800-767-7633 ■ *Web:* www.multimaticproducts.com	631-231-1515	231-1625	621
Multi-Media Communications Inc 190 Adams Ave, Hauppauge NY 11788 *TF:* 800-689-6929 ■ *Web:* www.mmc.net	631-669-2100	669-6455	681
Multi-metal & Manufacturing Company Inc 1500 E I-30, Rockwall TX 75087 *Web:* www.multi-metal.com	972-771-1376		697
Multi-Pak 180 Atlantic St, Hackensack NJ 07601	201-342-7474		36
Multipet International Inc 245 W Commercial Ave, Moonachie NJ 07074 *TF:* 800-900-6738 ■ *Web:* www.multipet.com	201-438-6600	438-2990	578
Multiplan Inc 115 5th Ave, New York NY 10003 *Web:* www.ihplan.com	212-780-2000		390
Multi-Plastics Inc 7770 N Central Dr, Lewis Center OH 43035 *Web:* www.multi-plastics.com	740-548-4894	548-5177	603
Multiple Media Inc 465 McGill St Office 1000, Montreal QC H2Y2H1 *TF:* 866-790-6626 ■ *Web:* www.multiplemedia.com	514-276-7660		180
Multiple Path Communications 5709 Gardendale Dr Ste C, Houston TX 77092 *TF:* 800-753-9994 ■ *Web:* www.multiplepath.com	713-735-5100		681
Multiple Sclerosis Foundation (MSF) 6520 N Andrews Ave, Fort Lauderdale FL 33309 *TF:* 800-225-6495 ■ *Web:* msfocus.org	954-776-6805		48-17
Multiple Ventilation Products Inc 63 Old Main Plz, Saint Albans WV 25177 *Web:* www.mvphvac.net	304-720-8686	727-8687	189-10
Multiples of America 2000 Mallory Ln Ste 130-600, Franklin TN 37067 *Web:* www.multiplesofamerica.org	248-231-4480		48-6
Multi-Precision Detail Inc 2635 Paldan Dr, Auburn Hills MI 48326 *Web:* multi-precision.com	248-373-3330	373-7241	757
Multiquip Inc 18910 Wilmington Ave, Carson CA 90746 *TF:* 800-421-1244 ■ *Web:* www.multiquip.com	310-537-3700	537-3927	385
Multiseal Inc 4320 Hitch Peters Rd, Evansville IN 47711 *Web:* www.multiseal-usa.com	812-428-3422	428-3432	3
Multiservice Management Co 994 Old Eagle School Rd Ste 1019, Wayne PA 19087 *Web:* mmco1.com	610-971-4850		47
Multi-shifter Inc 11110 Park Charlotte Blvd, Charlotte NC 28278 *TF:* 800-457-4472 ■ *Web:* multi-shifter.com	704-588-9611		358
Multi-Shot LLC 3335 Pollok Dr, Conroe TX 77303 **Fax Area Code:* 817 ■ *TF:* 844-643-6737 ■ *Web:* msenergyservices.com	936-442-2500	568-1499*	539
Multisoft Corp 1723 SE 47th Terr, Cape Coral FL 33904 *TF:* 888-415-0554 ■ *Web:* www.multisoft.com	239-945-6433		177
Multisorb Technologies Inc 325 Harlem Rd, Buffalo NY 14224 *Web:* www.multisorb.com	716-824-8900	824-4128	145
Multistack LLC 1065 Maple Ave, Sparta WI 54656 *Web:* www.multistack.com	608-366-2400		14
Multi-State Lottery Assn 4400 Nw Urbandale Dr, Urbandale IA 50322 *Web:* www.musl.com	515-453-1400	453-1420	452
Multistate Tax Commission 444 N Capitol St NW Ste 425, Washington DC 20001 *Web:* www.mtc.gov	202-624-8699		734
Multitech Industries Inc 350 Village Dr, Carol Stream IL 60188 *Web:* www.multitechind.com	630-784-9200		729
Multi-Tech Industries Inc 64 S Main St, Marlboro NJ 07746 *Web:* www.multi-tech-industries.com	732-431-0550	409-6695	816

Phone | Fax | Class

Multi-Tech Systems
2205 Woodale Dr .... Mounds View MN 55112 763-785-3500 785-9874 173-3
TF: 800-328-9717 ■ *Web:* www.multitech.com

Multi-Wing America Inc
15030 Brkshire Indus Pky .... Middlefield OH 44062 440-834-9400 834-0449 18
TF: 800-311-8465 ■ *Web:* www.multi-wing.net

Multnomah Athletic Club
1849 SW Salmon St .... Portland OR 97205 503-223-6251 354
Web: themac.com

Multnomah Bar Assn
620 SW Fifth Ave Ste 1220 .... Portland OR 97204 503-222-3275 533
Web: mbabar.org

Multnomah County Library
801 SW Tenth Ave .... Portland OR 97205 503-988-5123 434-3
Web: www.multcolib.org

Multnomah University
8435 NE Glisan St .... Portland OR 97220 503-255-0332 254-1268 167-3
TF: 800-275-4672 ■ *Web:* www.multnomah.edu

Mulvaney Kahan & Barry
401 W A St 1st Fl .... San Diego CA 92101 619-238-1010 445
Web: www.mulvaneybarry.com

Mulvey, Cornell & Mulvey PA
378 Islington St .... Portsmouth NH 03801 603-431-1333 41
Web: newhampshireinjuryfirm.com

Mulzer Crushed Stone Inc
534 Mozart St PO Box 249 .... Tell City IN 47586 812-547-7921 547-6757 503-5
Web: www.mulzer.com

Mumford Micro Systems PO Box 156 .... Green Bank WV 24944 805-687-5116 253
Web: www.bmumford.com

Mummers Museum 1100 S Second St .... Philadelphia PA 19147 215-336-3050 520
Web: www.mummersmuseum.com

Muncaps LLP
2901 Douglas Blvd Ste 290 .... Roseville CA 95661 916-774-4208 774-4230 2
Web: www.muncpas.com

Muncie Area Career Ctr 2500 N Elgin St .... Muncie IN 47303 765-747-5250 747-5455 167-3
Web: www.muncie.k12.in.us

Muncie Children's Museum 515 S High St .... Muncie IN 47306 765-286-1660 521
Web: munciemuseum.com

Muncie Novelty Company Inc
9610 N State Rd 67 .... Muncie IN 47308 800-428-8640 428-8640* 781
**Fax Area Code:* 888 ■ *TF:* 800-428-8640 ■ *Web:* www.muncienovelty.com

Muncie Power Products Inc
201 E Jackson St .... Muncie IN 47305 765-284-7721 770
TF: 800-367-7867 ■ *Web:* www.munciepower.com

Muncie Star-Press 345 S High St .... Muncie IN 47305 765-213-5700 532-2
TF: 800-783-7827 ■ *Web:* www.thestarpress.com

Muncie Symphony Orchestra
2000 W University Ave Ste Ac112 .... Muncie IN 47306 765-285-5531 285-9128 573-3
Web: www.munciesymphony.org

Muncie Visitors Bureau
3700 S Madison St .... Muncie IN 47302 765-284-2700 284-3002 206
TF: 800-568-6862 ■ *Web:* www.visitmuncie.org

Muncie-Delaware County Chamber of Commerce
401 S High St .... Muncie IN 47305 765-288-6681 751-9151 139
TF: 800-336-1373 ■ *Web:* www.muncie.com

Munck Wilson Mandala LLP
600 Banner Pl Tower 12770 Coit Rd .... Dallas TX 75251 972-628-3600 428
Web: www.munckwilson.com

Mundelein Park & Recreation District
1401 N Midlothian Rd .... Mundelein IL 60060 847-566-0650 31
Web: mundeleinparks.org

Mundy Contract Maintenance Inc
11150 S Wilcrest .... Houston TX 77099 281-530-8711 260
Web: www.mundycos.com

Munger, Tolles & Olson LLP (MTO)
355 S Grand Ave 35th Fl .... Los Angeles CA 90071 213-683-9100 41
Web: www.mto.com

Municipal Art Gallery 839 N State St .... Jackson MS 39202 601-960-1582 960-2066 50-2
Web: www.jacksonms.gov

Municipal Capital Markets Group Inc (MCM)
5220 Spring Valley Rd Ste 522 .... Dallas TX 75244 972-386-0200 2
Web: www.municapital.com

Municipal Credit Union PO Box 3205 .... New York NY 10007 212-693-4900 219
TF: 866-512-6109 ■ *Web:* www.nymcu.org

Municipal Employees Credit Union
8812 S Walker Ave .... Oklahoma City OK 73139 405-813-5550 219
TF: 800-281-4016 ■ *Web:* mecuokc.org

Municipal Infrastructure Group Ltd, The
8800 Dufferin St Ste 200 .... Vaughan ON L4K0C5 905-738-5700 261
Web: tmig.ca

Municipal Securities Rulemaking Board (MSRB)
1900 Duke St Ste 600 .... Alexandria VA 22314 703-797-6600 797-6700 49-2
Web: www.msrb.org

Municipal Technical Advisory Service (MTAS)
1610 University Ave .... Knoxville TN 37921 865-974-0411 974-0423 637-10
Web: www.mtas.tennessee.edu

Munilla Construction Management LLC
6201 SW 70th St 2nd Fl .... Miami FL 33143 305-541-0000 541-9771 186
Web: www.mcm-us.com

MuniServices LLC
7625 N Palm Ave Ste 108 .... Fresno CA 93711 800-800-8181 312-2920* 734
**Fax Area Code:* 559 ■ *TF:* 800-800-8181 ■ *Web:* www.muniservices.com

Muniz & Associates Inc
601 Bayshore Blvd Ste 645 .... Tampa FL 33606 813-258-0033 258-1702 390
Web: munizandassociates.com

Munn Rabot 33 W 17th St .... New York NY 10011 212-727-3900 604-9804 7
Web: www.munnrabot.com

Munot Plastics Inc 2935 W 17th St .... Erie PA 16505 814-580-9920 601
Web: www.munotplastics.com

Munoz Engineering & Land Surveying PC
505 Eighth Ave 21st Fl .... New York NY 10018 212-967-6588 268-9464 261
Web: munozeng.com

Munro Crafts 3954 12 Mile Rd .... Berkley MI 48072 248-544-1590 411
Web: munrocrafts.com

Munsch Hardt Kopf & Harr PC
500 N Akard St Ste 3800 .... Dallas TX 75201 214-855-7500 855-7584 428
Web: www.munsch.com

Munsee Meats Inc 1701 W Kilgore Ave .... Muncie IN 47304 765-288-3645 282-8076 297-9
Web: www.munseemeats.com

Munson's Candy Kitchen Inc
174 Hop River Rd .... Bolton CT 06043 860-649-4332 649-7209 296-8
TF: 888-686-7667 ■ *Web:* www.munsonschocolates.com

Munson-Williams-Proctor Arts Institute
310 Genesee St .... Utica NY 13502 315-797-0000 797-5608 520
Web: www.mwpai.org

Munters Corp
210 Sixth St PO Box 6428 .... Fort Myers FL 33907 239-936-1555 278-8790 14
TF: 800-843-5360 ■ *Web:* www.munters.com

Muntz Industries Inc 710 Twr Rd .... Mundelein IL 60060 847-949-8280 949-8284 385
Web: www.muntzind.com

MUP (Marquette University Press)
PO Box 3141 .... Milwaukee WI 53201 414-288-1564 288-7813 637-2
Web: www.mu.edu

Murata Electronics North America Inc
2200 Lake Pk Dr .... Smyrna GA 30080 770-436-1300 436-3030 253
TF: 800-704-6079 ■ *Web:* www.murata.com

Murata Machinery Ltd
3301 E Plano Pky Ste 100 .... Plano TX 75074 469-429-3300 429-3311 246
TF: 800-347-3296 ■ *Web:* www.muratec.com

Murata Machinery USA Inc
2120 Queen City Dr .... Charlotte NC 28208 800-428-8469 392-6541* 456
**Fax Area Code:* 704 ■ *TF:* 800-428-8469 ■ *Web:* www.muratec-usa.com

Murata Manufacturing Company Ltd
4441 Sigma Rd .... Dallas TX 75244 972-233-2903 246
Web: wireless.murata.com

Murdoch Marketing
217 E 24th St Ste 220 .... Holland MI 49423 616-392-4893 195
Web: www.murdochmarketing.com

Murdock Industrial Supply 1111 E 1st .... Wichita KS 67214 316-262-4476 263-8100 246
TF: 800-876-6867 ■ *Web:* www.mcos.com

Murdock Webbing Company Inc
27 Foundry St .... Central Falls RI 02863 401-724-3000 722-9730 745-5
Web: www.murdockwebbing.com

Murex Petroleum Corp
363 N Sam Houston Pkwy E Ste 200 .... Houston TX 77060 281-590-3313 538
Web: murexpetroleum.com

Murfee Meadows Inc
120 Office Park Dr Ste 100 .... Birmingham AL 35223 205-871-9515 871-9519 463
TF: 800-600-0947 ■ *Web:* www.murfeemeadows.com

Murfin Drilling Company Inc
250 N Water St Ste 300 .... Wichita KS 67202 316-267-3241 267-6004 540
Web: www.murfindrilling.com

Muriel's 801 Chartres St .... New Orleans LA 70116 504-568-1885 568-9795 671
Web: muriels.com

Murkowski Lisa (Sen R - AK)
522 Hart Senate Office Bldg .... Washington DC 20510 202-224-6665 224-5301 342-2
Web: www.murkowski.senate.gov

Murnane Building Contractors Inc
104 Sharron Ave .... Plattsburgh NY 12901 518-561-4010 186
Web: www.murnanebuilding.com

Murnane Paper Corp
345 W Fischer Farm Rd .... Elmhurst IL 60126 630-530-8222 530-8325 553
TF: 855-632-8191 ■ *Web:* www.murnanepaper.com

Murphy & Decker PC 730 17th St Ste 925 .... Denver CO 80202 303-468-5980 41
Web: murphydecker.com

Murphy & Grantland PA
4406-B Forest Dr PO Box 6648 .... Columbia SC 29206 803-782-4100 782-4140 428
Web: www.murphygrantland.com

Murphy & McGonigle
4870 Sadler Rd Ste 301 .... Glen Allen VA 23060 804-762-5320 428
Web: www.mmlawus.com

Murphy & Miller Inc 600 W Taylor St .... Chicago IL 60607 312-427-8900 427-0324 189-10
Web: www.murphymiller.com

Murphy & Murphy CPA LLC
108 La Grange Ave .... La Plata MD 20646 301-637-6453 609-7510 2
Web: murphycpallc.com

Murphy & Nolan Inc
340 Peat St PO Box 6689 .... Syracuse NY 13217 315-474-8203 474-8208 492
TF: 866-900-6385 ■ *Web:* www.murphynolan.com

Murphy & Prachthauser SC
330 E Kilbourn Ave Ste 1200 .... Milwaukee WI 53202 414-271-1011 41
TF: 888-271-1022 ■ *Web:* murphyprachthauser.com

Murphy & Sons Inc 9148 Corporate Dr .... Southaven MS 38671 662-393-3130 393-8111 186
Web: www.murphyandsons.com

Murphy Christopher (Sen D - CT)
136 Hart Senate Office Bldg .... Washington DC 20510 202-224-4041 224-9750 342-2
Web: www.murphy.senate.gov

Murphy Co 455 W Broad St .... Columbus OH 43215 614-221-7731 221-6991 393
Web: www.murphycompany.com

Murphy Company Mechanical Contractors & Engineers
1233 N Price Rd .... Saint Louis MO 63132 314-997-6600 189-10
Web: www.murphynet.com

Murphy Door, The 2380 S 1900 W .... West Haven UT 84401 888-458-5911 321
TF: 888-458-5911 ■ *Web:* www.themurphydoor.com

Murphy Industries 1650 Cascade Dr .... Marion OH 43302 740-387-7890 225
Web: www.murphyind.com

Murphy Insurance Agency Inc
5767 Harrison Ave .... Cincinnati OH 45248 513-574-3700 390
Web: murphyinsagency.com

Murphy Marine Services Inc
701 Christiana Ave .... Wilmington DE 19801 302-571-4700 571-4702 465
Web: www.murphymarine.com

Murphy Mckay & Associates Inc
3468 Mt Diablo Blvd Ste B108 .... LaFayette CA 94549 925-283-9555 175
Web: www.murphymckay.com

Murphy Oil Corp 200 Peach St .... El Dorado AR 71730 870-862-6411 875-7675 580
TF: 888-289-9314 ■ *Web:* www.murphyoilcorp.com

Murphy Plywood Co 2350 Prairie Rd .... Eugene OR 97402 541-461-4545 461-4547 613
TF: 888-461-4545 ■ *Web:* www.murphyplywood.com

Murphy Road Animal Hospital PA
6114 Murphy Rd .... Sachse TX 75048 972-496-4126 794
Web: murphyroadah.com

Murphy Stephanie (Rep D - FL)
1710 Longworth House Office Bldg .... Washington DC 20515 202-225-4035 342-2
Web: www.murphy.house.gov

Murphy Sullivan Kronk
275 College St .... Burlington VT 05401 802-861-7000 428
Web: www.mskvt.com

	Phone	Fax	Class
Murphy Tractor and Equipment Co 5375 N Deere Rd ... Park City KS 67219 *TF:* 800-262-0139 ■ *Web:* www.murphytractor.com	316-945-1015	942-3087	274
Murphy Wall Products International Inc 2032 N Commerce ... Fort Worth TX 76164 *TF:* 800-446-7124 ■ *Web:* www.murphywallproducts.com	817-429-6500	626-0821	183
Murphy Warehouse Co 701 24th Ave SE ... Minneapolis MN 55414 *Web:* www.murphywarehouse.com	612-623-1200	623-9108	803-1
Murphy's Grand Irish Pub 713 King St ... Alexandria VA 22314 *Web:* www.murphyspub.com	703-548-1717	739-4583	671
Murphy, Hesse, Toomey & Lehane LLP Crown Colony Plz 300 Crown Colony Dr Ste 410 ... Quincy MA 02169 *TF:* 888-841-4850 ■ *Web:* www.mhtl.com	617-479-5000	479-6469	428
MurphyEpson Inc 1650 Watermark Dr Ste 210 ... Columbus OH 43215 *Web:* murphyepson.com	614-221-2885	221-2889	636
Murphy-Harpst 740 Fletcher St ... Cedartown GA 30125 *Web:* murphyharpst.org	770-748-1500		226
Murray & Heister Inc 10101-H Bacon Dr ... Beltsville MD 20705 *Web:* mhprint.com	301-937-5980		534
Murray & Murray 301 Main St Ste 810 ... Baton Rouge LA 70801 *Web:* murraylaw.net	225-925-1110		41
Murray & Zuckerman Inc 128 Erie Blvd ... Schenectady NY 12305 *Web:* mandzinc.com	518-382-5483	382-7904	390
Murray Area Chamber of Commerce (MACC) 5250 S Commerce Dr Ste 180 ... Murray UT 84107 *Web:* murraychamber.org	801-263-2632	263-8262	139
Murray Bank, The 405 S 12th St ... Murray KY 42071 *TF:* 877-965-1122 ■ *Web:* www.themurraybank.com	270-753-5626		70
Murray Co 1215 Fern Ridge Pkwy Ste 213 ... Saint Louis MO 63141 *TF:* 888-323-5560 ■ *Web:* www.murray-company.com	314-576-2818	434-5780	685
Murray Corp 260 Schilling Cir ... Hunt Valley MD 21031 *Web:* www.murraycorp.com	410-771-0380	771-5576	350
Murray County PO Box 1129 ... Chatsworth GA 30705 *Web:* www.murraycountyga.org	706-695-2413	695-8721	338
Murray County 2500 28th St ... Slayton MN 56172 *Web:* murraycountymn.com	507-836-6148	836-8904	338
Murray Devine & Company Inc 1650 Arch St Ste 2700 ... Philadelphia PA 19103 *Web:* www.murraydevine.com	215-977-8700	977-8181	401
Murray Guard Inc 58 Murray Guard Dr ... Jackson TN 38305 *TF:* 800-238-3830 ■ *Web:* www.murrayguard.com	731-668-3400	664-1343	693
Murray Hill Veterinary Assoc 179 South St ... New Providence NJ 07974 *Web:* murrayhillvet.com	908-464-0664	464-4920	794
Murray Kaizer Dental Laboratory 24 Spring Ln ... Farmington CT 06032 *Web:* www.murraykaizer.com	860-677-7700		415
Murray Law Offices PA 4214 Mayfair St Ste A ... Myrtle Beach SC 29577 *Web:* murraylawofficespa.com	843-286-2000		41
Murray Patty (Sen D - WA) 154 Russell Senate Office Bldg ... Washington DC 20510 *TF:* 866-481-9186 ■ *Web:* www.murray.senate.gov	202-224-2621	224-0238	342-2
Murray Sheet Metal Company Inc 3112 Seventh St ... Parkersburg WV 26104 *TF:* 800-464-8801 ■ *Web:* www.murraysheetmetal.com	304-422-5431	428-4623	697
Murray State College 1 Murray Campus ... Tishomingo OK 73460 *TF:* 800-342-0698 ■ *Web:* www.mscok.edu	580-371-2371	371-9844	162
Murray State University 102 Curris Ctr ... Murray KY 42071 *TF:* 800-272-4678 ■ *Web:* www.murraystate.edu	270-809-3741	809-3780	166
Murray Supply Co (MSC) 260 Olive St ... Winston-Salem NC 27103 *Web:* murraysupply.com	336-765-9480	245-0686	612
Murray's 26 S Sixth St ... Minneapolis MN 55402 *Web:* www.murraysrestaurant.com	612-339-0909		671
Murray, Morin & Herman PA 255 Alhambra Cir Ste 750 ... Coral Gables FL 33134 *Web:* mmhlaw.com	305-441-1180		41
Murray, Plumb & Murray 75 Pearl St ... Portland ME 04101 *Web:* www.mpmlaw.com	207-773-5651		428
Murray-Calloway County Hospital 803 Poplar St ... Murray KY 42071 *Web:* www.murrayhospital.org	270-762-1100	767-3600	374-3
Murrays Ford Inc 3007 Blinker Pkwy ... DuBois PA 15801 *TF:* 800-371-6601 ■ *Web:* www.murraysford.net	800-371-6601		516
Murrey International Inc 14150 S Figueroa St ... Los Angeles CA 90061 *TF:* 800-421-1022 ■ *Web:* murreybowling.com	310-532-6091		710
Murrieta Chamber of Commerce 25125 Madison Ave Ste 108 ... Murrieta CA 92562 *Web:* www.murrietachamber.org	951-677-7916	677-9976	139
Murrieta Day Spa Inc 41885 Ivy St ... Murrieta CA 92562 *Web:* mdayspa.com	951-677-8111		77
Murrows Transfer Inc PO Box 4095 ... High Point NC 27263 *TF:* 800-669-2928 ■ *Web:* www.murrows.com	336-475-6101	475-1240	780
Murry's 3107 Green Meadows Way ... Columbia MO 65203 *Web:* murrysrestaurant.net	573-442-4969		671
Mursix Corp 2401 N Executive Park Dr ... Yorktown IN 47396 *Web:* www.mursix.com	765-282-2221		488
Murty Pharmaceuticals Inc 518 Codell Dr ... Lexington KY 40509 *Web:* www.mpirx.com	859-266-2446		582
Murzan Inc 2909 Langford Rd ... Norcross GA 30071 *Web:* www.murzan.com	770-448-0583	448-0967	641
M-USA (Mercy-USA for Aid & Development Inc) 44450 Pinetree Dr Ste 201 ... Plymouth MI 48170 *TF:* 800-556-3729 ■ *Web:* mercyusa.org	734-454-0011	454-0303	48-5
Musashi 10110 Johnston Rd ... Charlotte NC 28210 *Web:* www.musashi-nc.com	704-543-5181		671
Musashi's Japanese Steakhouse 4315 N Western ... Oklahoma City OK 73118 *Web:* www.musashis.com	405-602-5623	602-5574	671
Musashino Sushi Dokoro 3407 Greystone Dr ... Austin TX 78731 *Web:* www.musashinosushi.com	512-795-8593		671
MUSC (Medical University of South Carolina) *Blood & Marrow Transplant Program* 171 Ashley Ave Ste 424 ... Charleston SC 29425 *Web:* academicdepartments.musc.edu	843-792-9300		769
Muscarelle Museum of Art PO Box 8795 ... Williamsburg VA 23187 *Web:* muscarelle.org	757-221-2700	221-2711	520
Muscatine County 401 E Third St ... Muscatine IA 52761 *Web:* www.co.muscatine.ia.us	563-263-5821	263-7248	338
Muscatine Journal 301 E 3rd St ... Muscatine IA 52761 *TF:* 866-880-2108 ■ *Web:* www.muscatinejournal.com	563-262-0559	262-8042	532-2
Muscle & Fitness Hers Magazine 21100 Erwin St ... Woodland Hills CA 91367 *TF:* 800-340-8954 ■ *Web:* www.muscleandfitness.com	800-340-8954		457-13
Muscle Shoals Broadcasting 1570 Woodmont Dr ... Tuscumbia AL 35674 *Web:* www.wzzaradio.com	256-381-1862		645-141
Muscle Shoals City School District 3200 S Wilson Dam Rd ... Muscle Shoals AL 35661 *Web:* www.mscs.k12.al.us	256-389-2600	389-2605	449
Musco Sports Lighting LLC 100 First Ave W PO Box 808 ... Oskaloosa IA 52577 *TF:* 800-825-6020 ■ *Web:* www.musco.com	641-673-0411	673-4852	439
Muscular Dystrophy Assn (MDA) 3300 E Sunrise Dr ... Tucson AZ 85718 *TF:* 800-572-1717 ■ *Web:* www.mda.org	520-529-2000		48-17
Musculoskeletal Transplant Foundation 125 May St Ste 300 ... Edison NJ 08837 *TF:* 800-946-9008 ■ *Web:* www.mtfbiologics.org	732-661-0202	661-2298	545
MUSD (Montebello Unified School District) 123 S Montebello Blvd ... Montebello CA 90640 *Web:* www.montebello.k12.ca.us	323-887-7900		685
MUSD (Marana Unified School District 6) 11279 W Grier Rd ... Marana AZ 85653 *Web:* www.maranausd.org	520-682-3243	682-2421	685
Muse Communications Inc 9543 Culver Blvd 2nd Fl ... Culver City CA 90232 **Fax Area Code:* 323 ■ *Web:* www.museusa.com	310-945-4100	954-9260*	4
Muse Concrete Contractors Inc 8599 Commercial Way ... Redding CA 96002 *Web:* www.museconcrete.com	530-226-5151		186
Muse Entertainment Enterprises Inc 3451 Rue St-Jacques ... Montreal QC H4C1H1 *Web:* www.muse.ca	514-866-6873		514
Muse, The 130 W 46th St ... New York NY 10036 *TF:* 877-692-6873 ■ *Web:* www.themusehotel.com	212-485-2400	485-2789	379
Musee de la Civilisation 85 Rue Dalhousie St ... Quebec City QC G1K8R2 *TF:* 866-710-8031 ■ *Web:* www.mcq.org	418-643-2158		520
Musee Des Beaux-Arts De Montreal 1380 Sherbrooke St W ... Montreal QC H3G1J5 *Web:* www.mbam.qc.ca	514-285-2000		520
Museo de las Americas 861 Santa Fe Dr ... Denver CO 80204 *Web:* www.museo.org	303-571-4401	607-9761	520
Museo del Barrio 1230 Fifth Ave ... New York NY 10029 *Web:* www.elmuseo.org	212-831-7272		520
Museo Italo-Americano Fort Mason Ctr Bldg C ... San Francisco CA 94123 *Web:* museoitaloamericano.org	415-673-2200	673-2292	520
Museum & Library of confederate 15 Boyce Ave ... Greenville SC 29601 *Web:* confederatemuseumandlibrary.org	864-421-9039		520
Museum Facsimiles 117 Fourth St ... Pittsfield MA 01201 *TF:* 877-499-0020 ■ *Web:* www.museumfacsimiles.com	413-499-0020		130
Museum of African American History 46 Joy St ... Boston MA 02114 *Web:* maah.org	617-725-0022	720-5225	520
Museum of American Financial History 48 Wall St ... New York NY 10005 *Web:* www.moaf.org	212-908-4110	908-4601	520
Museum of American Illustration 128 E 63rd St ... New York NY 10065 *Web:* www.societyillustrators.org	212-838-2560	838-2561	520
Museum of American Railroad, The 8004 N Dallas Pkwy ... Frisco TX 75034 *Web:* www.museumoftheamericanrailroad.org	214-428-0101	426-1937	520
Museum of Anthropology 115 Business Loop 70 W Rm 2002 ... Columbia MO 65211 *Web:* anthromuseum.missouri.edu	573-882-3573		520
Museum of Anthropology Wake Forest University ... Winston-Salem NC 27109 *TF:* 888-925-3622 ■ *Web:* moa.wfu.edu	336-758-5282	758-5116	520
Museum of Appalachia 2819 Andersonville Hwy ... Clinton TN 37716 *Web:* www.museumofappalachia.org	865-494-7680	494-8957	520
Museum of Art & Archaeology 1 Pickard Hall ... Columbia MO 65211 *TF:* 866-447-9821 ■ *Web:* maa.missouri.edu	573-882-3591	884-4039	520
Museum of Art Fort Collins 201 S College Ave ... Fort Collins CO 80524 *Web:* moafc.org	970-482-2787		520
Museum of Arts & Design 2 Columbus Cir ... New York NY 10019 *Web:* madmuseum.org	212-299-7777		520
Museum of Arts & Sciences 352 S Nova Rd ... Daytona Beach FL 32114 *TF:* 866-439-4769 ■ *Web:* www.moas.org	386-255-0285		520
Museum of Arts & Sciences 4182 Forsyth Rd ... Macon GA 31210 *Web:* www.masmacon.org	478-477-3232	477-3251	520
Museum of Aviation PO Box 2460 ... Warner Robins GA 31099 *Web:* www.museumofaviation.org	478-926-6870		520

				Phone	Fax	Class
Museum of Boulder 1206 Euclid Ave *Web:* www.museumofboulder.org	Boulder	CO	80302	303-449-3464	938-8322	520
Museum of Children's Art 1625 Clay Ste 100 *Web:* www.mocha.org	Oakland	CA	94612	510-465-8770		521
Museum of Church History & Art 45 NW Temple St *Web:* history.lds.org	Salt Lake City	UT	84150	801-240-3310	240-5342	520
Museum of Contemporary Art 220 E Chicago Ave *Web:* www.mcachicago.org	Chicago	IL	60611	312-280-2660		520
Museum of Contemporary Art 250 S Grand Ave *Web:* www.moca.org	Los Angeles	CA	90012	213-621-2766	620-8674	520
Museum of Contemporary Art Cleveland 11400 Euclid Ave *Web:* www.mocacleveland.org	Cleveland	OH	44106	216-421-8671	421-0737	520
Museum of Contemporary Art Denver 1485 Delgany *Web:* mcadenver.org	Denver	CO	80202	303-298-7554		520
Museum of Contemporary Art Inc 770 NE 125th St Joan Lehman Bldg *Web:* mocanomi.org	North Miami	FL	33161	305-893-6211		520
Museum of Contemporary Art San Diego 700 Prospect St *Web:* www.mcasd.org	La Jolla	CA	92037	858-454-3541		520
Museum of Contemporary Photography 600 S Michigan Ave Columbia College *Web:* www.mocp.org	Chicago	IL	60605	312-663-5554	369-8067	520
Museum of Darien 45 Old King's Hwy *Web:* museumofdarien.org	Darien	CT	06820	203-655-9233	861-9720	50-3
Museum of Design Atlanta 1315 Peachtree St NE *Web:* www.museumofdesign.org	Atlanta	GA	30309	404-979-6455		520
Museum of Early Southern Decorative Arts (MESDA) 924 S Main St *Web:* www.mesda.org	Winston-Salem	NC	27101	336-721-7360		520
Museum of Fine Arts 255 Beach Dr NE *Web:* mfastpete.org	Saint Petersburg	FL	33701	727-896-2667	894-4638	520
Museum of Fine Arts Boston 465 Huntington Ave *Web:* www.mfa.org	Boston	MA	02115	617-267-9300		520
Museum of Flight, The 9404 E Marginal Way S *Web:* www.museumofflight.org	Seattle	WA	98108	206-764-5700	764-5707	520
Museum of Florida History 500 S Bronough St *Web:* www.museumoffloridahistory.com	Tallahassee	FL	32399	850-245-6400	245-6433	520
Museum of Geology *South Dakota School of Mines & Technology* 501 E St Joseph St *TF:* 800-544-8162 ■ *Web:* www.sdsmt.edu	Rapid City	SD	57701	605-394-2467	394-6131	520
Museum of Glass 1801 Dock St *Web:* www.museumofglass.org	Tacoma	WA	98402	253-284-4750		520
Museum of Health & Medical Science 1515 Herman Dr *Web:* www.thehealthmuseum.org	Houston	TX	77004	713-521-1515	526-1434	520
Museum of History & Art 1100 Orange Ave *TF:* 866-599-7242 ■ *Web:* coronadohistory.org	Coronado	CA	92118	619-435-7242	435-8504	520
Museum of History & Industry 860 Terry Ave N *Web:* www.mohai.org	Seattle	WA	98109	206-324-1126		520
Museum of Indian Arts & Culture 710 Camino Lejo PO Box 2087 *Web:* www.miaclab.org	Santa Fe	NM	87501	505-476-1250	476-1330	520
Museum of International Folk Art 706 Camino Lejo *Web:* www.internationalfolkart.org	Santa Fe	NM	87505	505-476-1200	476-1300	520
Museum of Jewish Heritage 36 Battery Pl *Web:* mjhnyc.org	New York	NY	10280	646-437-4202		520
Museum of Jurassic Technology 9341 Venice Blvd *Web:* www.mjt.org	Culver City	CA	90232	310-836-6131	287-2267	520
Museum of Latin American Art 628 Alamitos Ave *Web:* molaa.org	Long Beach	CA	90802	562-437-1689		520
Museum of Life+Science 433 Murray Ave *Web:* www.lifeandscience.org	Durham	NC	27704	919-220-5429	220-5575	520
Museum of Local History 190 Anza St *Web:* museumoflocalhistory.org	Fremont	CA	94539	510-623-7907		520
Museum of Making Music 5790 Armada Dr *Web:* www.museumofmakingmusic.org	Carlsbad	CA	92008	760-438-5996		520
Museum of Modern Art 11 W 53rd St *Web:* www.moma.org	New York	NY	10019	212-708-9400		520
Museum of Nature & Science 2201 N Field St *Web:* www.perotmuseum.org	Dallas	TX	75201	214-428-5555		520
Museum of Nebraska History 15th & P St PO Box 82554 *TF:* 800-833-6747 ■ *Web:* history.nebraska.gov	Lincoln	NE	68508	402-471-4754	471-3314	520
Museum of New Mexico Press (MNMP) 725 Camino Lejo *Web:* www.mnmpress.org	Santa Fe	NM	87505	505-476-1160		637-2
Museum of Newport History at the Brick Market 82 Touro St *Web:* newporthistory.org	Newport	RI	02840	401-841-8770	846-1853	520
Museum of North Idaho 115 NW Blvd PO Box 812 *TF:* 800-344-4867 ■ *Web:* www.museumni.org	Coeur d'Alene	ID	83816	208-664-3448		520
Museum of Northern Arizona 3101 N Ft Valley Rd *Web:* www.musnaz.org	Flagstaff	AZ	86001	928-774-5213	774-1229	520
Museum of Photographic Arts 1649 El Prado *Web:* mopa.org	San Diego	CA	92101	619-238-7559	238-8777	520
Museum of Russian Art 5500 Stevens Ave S *Web:* tmora.org	Minneapolis	MN	55419	612-821-9045		520
Museum of Science & History of Jacksonville 1025 Museum Cir *Web:* www.themosh.org	Jacksonville	FL	32207	904-396-6674		520
Museum of Science & Industry 5700 S Lake Shore Dr *TF:* 800-468-6674 ■ *Web:* www.msichicago.org	Chicago	IL	60637	773-684-1414		520
Museum of Science & Industry 4801 E Fowler Ave *TF:* 800-995-6674 ■ *Web:* www.mosi.org	Tampa	FL	33617	813-987-6000	987-6310	520
Museum of Science & Technology 500 S Franklin St *Web:* www.most.org	Syracuse	NY	13202	315-425-9068		520
Museum of Sex 233 Fifth Ave Rm 3b *Web:* www.museumofsex.com	New York	NY	10016	212-689-6337		520
Museum of Southern History 4304 Herschel St *Web:* www.scv-kirby-smith.org	Jacksonville	FL	32210	904-294-7358		520
Museum of Spanish Colonial Art 750 Camino Lejo PO Box 5378 *Web:* spanishcolonial.org	Santa Fe	NM	87502	505-982-2226	982-4585	520
Museum of Texas Tech University 3301 Fourth St *Web:* www.depts.ttu.edu	Lubbock	TX	79409	806-742-2442	742-1136	520
Museum of the Americas (MOA) 2500 NW 79th Ave Ste 104 *Web:* www.museumamericas.org	Doral	FL	33122	305-599-8089		520
Museum of the City of New York 1220 Fifth Ave *Web:* www.mcny.org	New York	NY	10029	212-534-1672		520
Museum of the Grand Prairie 950 N Lombard Rt 47 *Web:* www.museumofthegrandprairie.org	Mahomet	IL	61853	217-586-3360		520
Museum of the Great Plains (MGP) 601 NW Ferris Ave *Web:* www.discovermgp.org	Lawton	OK	73507	580-581-3460		637-2
Museum of the Mountain Man 700 E Hennick St *TF:* 877-686-6266 ■ *Web:* www.pinedaleonline.com	Pinedale	WY	82941	307-367-4101	367-6768	520
Museum of the Moving Image 3601 35th Ave *Web:* www.movingimage.us	Astoria	NY	11106	718-777-6800		520
Museum of the National Center of Afro-American Artists (NCAAA) 300 Walnut Ave *Web:* www.ncaaa.org	Roxbury	MA	02119	617-442-8614		520
Museum of the Rockies 600 W Kagy Blvd *Web:* www.museumoftherockies.org	Bozeman	MT	59717	406-994-1998	994-2682	520
Museum of the Southern Jewish Experience PO Box 16528 *Web:* www.isjl.org	Jackson	MS	39236	601-362-6357	366-6293	520
Museum of Tolerance 1399 S Roxbury Dr *TF:* 800-900-9036 ■ *Web:* www.wiesenthal.com	Los Angeles	CA	90035	310-553-8403		520
Museum of Vancouver 1100 Chestnut St Vanier Pk *Web:* museumofvancouver.ca	Vancouver	BC	V6J3J9	604-736-4431	736-5417	520
Museum of World Treasures 835 E First St *TF:* 888-700-1311 ■ *Web:* worldtreasures.org	Wichita	KS	67202	316-263-1311		520
Museum of Yachting Fort Adams State Pk *Web:* iyrs.edu	Newport	RI	02840	401-848-5777		520
Museum Outdoor Arts MOA 1000 Englewood Pkwy *Web:* www.moaonline.org	Englewood	CO	80110	303-806-0444		520
Museum Store Products Inc 430 Sandshore Rd Ste 4 5 *Web:* www.museumstoreproducts.com	Hackettstown	NJ	07840	908-852-2078		522
Museums at 18th & Vine 1616 E 18th St *Web:* americanjazzmuseum.org	Kansas City	MO	64108	816-474-8463		520
Museums of Oglebay Institute 1330 National Rd *TF:* 800-624-6988 ■ *Web:* www.oionline.com	Wheeling	WV	26003	304-242-7272		520
Musgrave Pencil Company Inc 701 W Lane St *TF:* 800-736-2450 ■ *Web:* www.pencils.net	Shelbyville	TN	37160	931-684-3611	685-1049	571
Musgrove Mill State Historic Site 398 State Park Rd *Web:* southcarolinaparks.com	Clinton	SC	29325	864-938-0100		565
Mushroom Co, The 902 Woods Rd *Web:* www.themushroomcompany.com	Cambridge	MD	21613	410-221-8971	221-8952	296-20
Music & Arts Centers Inc 4626 Wedgewood Blvd *TF:* 888-731-5396 ■ *Web:* www.musicarts.com	Frederick	MD	21703	301-620-4040	620-0462	526
Music Box Dinner Playhouse 196 Hughes St *Web:* www.musicbox.org	Swoyersville	PA	18704	570-283-2195		572
Music Celebrations Intl 1440 S Priest Dr Ste 102 *TF:* 800-395-2036 ■ *Web:* musiccelebrations.com	Tempe	AZ	85281	800-395-2036		772
Music Center Inc 1540 Haight St *Web:* haightashburymusic.com	San Francisco	CA	94117	415-863-7327	863-1384	526
Music Center of Los Angeles County 135 N Grand Ave *Web:* www.musiccenter.org	Los Angeles	CA	90012	213-972-7211		572
Music Choice (MC) 110 Gibraltar 650 Dresher Rd Ste 200 *Web:* www.musicchoice.com	Horsham	PA	19044	646-459-3357		524
Music Connection Inc 3441 Ocean View Blvd *Web:* www.musicconnection.com	Glendale	CA	91208	818-995-0101		637-9
Music Conservatory of Westchester 216 Central Ave *Web:* www.musicconservatory.org	White Plains	NY	10606	914-761-3900	761-4576	167-3
Music Exchange 1501 N Main St *Web:* muex.com	Walnut Creek	CA	94596	925-933-6310	933-6355	526

	Phone	Fax	Class
Music for All 39 W Jackson Pl Ste 150 ... Indianapolis IN 46225 *Web:* www.musicforall.org	317-636-2263	524-6200	48-11
Music Hall at Fair Park 909 First Ave ... Dallas TX 75210 *Web:* www.liveatthemusichall.com	214-565-1116	565-0071	572
Music Hall Center for the Performing Arts 350 Madison ... Detroit MI 48226 *Web:* www.musichall.org	313-887-8500	887-8502	572
Music Institute of Chicago - Lincolnshire Lutheran Church of the Holy Spirit 30 Riverwoods Rd ... Lincolnshire IL 60069 *Web:* www.musicinst.org	847-905-1500	295-1341	167-3
Music Library Assn (MLA) 8551 Research Way Ste 180 ... Middleton WI 53562 *Web:* www.musiclibraryassoc.org	608-836-5825	831-8200	49-11
Music of the Baroque 111 N Wabash Ave Ste 810 ... Chicago IL 60602 *TF:* 800-595-4849 ■ *Web:* www.baroque.org	312-551-1414	551-1444	573-3
Music People Inc 154 Woodlawn Rd Ste C ... Berlin CT 06037 **Fax Area Code:* 860 ■ *TF:* 800-289-8889 ■ *Web:* www.musicpeopleinc.com	800-289-8889	828-1353*	246
Music Road Resort Inc 303 Henderson Chapel Rd ... Pigeon Forge TN 37863 *TF:* 844-993-9644 ■ *Web:* www.musicroadresort.com	844-993-9644		707
Music Teachers NA (MTNA) 441 Vine St Ste 3100 ... Cincinnati OH 45202 *TF:* 888-512-5278 ■ *Web:* www.mtna.org	513-421-1420	421-2503	49-5
Music Theatre of Wichita 225 W Douglas Ste 202 ... Wichita KS 67202 *Web:* www.mtwichita.org	316-265-3253	265-8708	573-4
Music Works Publications 1250 Ollie St ... Stephenville TX 76401 *Web:* www.musicworkspublications.com	254-592-4454		637-10
Musical Theatre Southwest (MTS) 6320 Domingo Rd NE Ste B ... Albuquerque NM 87108 *Web:* www.musicaltheatresw.com	505-265-9119		573-2
Musician's Friend Inc PO Box 7479 ... Westlake Village CA 91359 **Fax Area Code:* 818 ■ *TF:* 800-449-9128 ■ *Web:* www.musiciansfriend.com	801-501-8110	735-7547*	526
Musicians Institute 6752 Hollywood Blvd ... Hollywood CA 90028 *TF:* 800-255-7529 ■ *Web:* www.mi.edu	323-462-1384	462-1575	167-3
Musicians On Call Inc 39 W 32nd St Ste 1103 ... New York NY 10001 *Web:* www.musiciansoncall.org	212-741-2709		720
Musiciansbuycom Inc 7830 Byron Dr Ste 1 ... West Palm Beach FL 33404 *TF:* 877-778-7845 ■ *Web:* www.musiciansbuy.com	561-842-4246	840-9032	526
Musick Peeler & Garrett LLP 1 Wilshire Blvd Ste 2000 ... Los Angeles CA 90017 *Web:* www.musickpeeler.com	213-629-7600		428
Musicol Recording 780 Oakland Park Ave ... Columbus OH 43224 *TF:* 800-240-5963 ■ *Web:* www.musicolrecording.com	614-267-3133		658
Musictoday LLC 5391 Three Notch'd Rd ... Crozet VA 22932 *TF:* 800-927-7821 ■ *Web:* www.musictoday.com	434-244-7200		225
Musiker Discovery Programs Inc 1326 Old Northern Blvd ... Roslyn NY 11576 *Web:* www.summerdiscovery.com	516-621-3939	625-3438	760
Muska Electric Co 1985 Oakcrest Ave ... Roseville MN 55113 *TF:* 800-694-0884 ■ *Web:* www.muskaelectric.com	651-636-5820		189-4
Muskallonge Lake State Park 29881 Co Rd 407 ... Newberry MI 49868 *Web:* www.dnr.state.mi.us	906-658-3338		565
Muskegon Area Chamber of Commerce 380 W Western Ste 202 ... Muskegon MI 49440 *Web:* www.muskegon.org	231-722-3751	728-7251	139
Muskegon Area District Library 4845 Airline Rd ... Muskegon MI 49444 *TF:* 877-569-4801 ■ *Web:* www.madl.org	231-737-6248	737-6307	434-3
Muskegon Community College 221 S Quarterline Rd ... Muskegon MI 49442 *TF:* 866-711-4622 ■ *Web:* www.muskegoncc.edu	231-773-9131	777-0471	162
Muskegon Correctional Facility 2400 S Sheridan Dr ... Muskegon MI 49442 *Web:* www.michigan.gov	231-773-3201		213
Muskegon County 990 Terrace St ... Muskegon MI 49442 *Web:* www.co.muskegon.mi.us	231-724-6520	724-6673	338
Muskegon County Convention & Visitors Bureau 610 W Western Ave ... Muskegon MI 49440 *TF:* 800-250-9283 ■ *Web:* visitmuskegon.org	231-724-3100	724-1398	206
Muskegon State Park 3560 Memorial Dr ... North Muskegon MI 49445 *Web:* www.michigan.org	231-744-3480		565
Muskingum College 163 Stormont St ... New Concord OH 43762 *TF:* 800-752-6082 ■ *Web:* www.muskingum.edu	740-826-8211	826-8100	166
Muskingum County Library System 220 N Fifth St ... Zanesville OH 43701 *Web:* www.muskingumlibrary.org	740-453-0391	455-6357	434-3
Muskingum Valley Area Chamber of Commerce PO Box 837 ... Beverly OH 45715 *Web:* www.mvacc.com	740-984-8259		139
Muskogee County 229 W Okmulgee Ave ... Muskogee OK 74401 *TF:* 800-444-1187 ■ *Web:* www.cityofmuskogee.com	918-682-6602		338
Muskogee Daily Phoenix 214 Wall St ... Muskogee OK 74401 *Web:* www.muskogeephoenix.com	918-684-2828	684-2865	532-2
Muslim Community Association of Ann Arbor and Vicinity 2301 Plymouth Rd ... Ann Arbor MI 48105 *Web:* www.mca-a2.org	734-665-6772		48-20
Musselman & Hall Contractors LLC 4922 Blue Banks Ave ... Kansas City MO 64130 *Web:* www.musselmanandhall.com	816-861-1234	861-1237	189-3
Musselman Hotels LLC 2912 Eastpoint Pkwy ... Louisville KY 40223 *Web:* musselmanhotels.com	502-426-3006		194
Musselshell County 506 Main St ... Roundup MT 59072 *Web:* musselshellcounty.org	406-323-1104		338
Musser Forests Inc 1880 Rte 119 Hwy N ... Indiana PA 15701 *TF:* 800-643-8319 ■ *Web:* www.musserforests.com	724-465-5685	465-9893	293
Musser Lumber Company Inc 200 Shoal Ridge Dr ... Rural Retreat VA 24368 *Web:* www.musserlumber.com	276-686-5113	686-5169	191-3
Musser Public Library 304 Iowa Ave ... Muscatine IA 52761 *Web:* musserpubliclibrary.org	563-263-3065		434-3
Musson Theatrical Inc 890 Walsh Ave ... Santa Clara CA 95050 *TF:* 800-843-2837 ■ *Web:* www.musson.com	408-986-0210	986-9552	722
Mustang Dynamometer 2300 Pinnacle Pkwy ... Twinsburg OH 44087 *TF:* 888-468-7826 ■ *Web:* mustangdyne.com	330-963-5400	425-3310	472
Mustang Fuel Corp 9800 N Oklahoma Ave ... Oklahoma City OK 73114 *TF:* 800-332-9400 ■ *Web:* www.mustangfuel.com	405-748-9400		538
Mustang Gas Compression LLC 2500 Woodbine Dr ... Kilgore TX 75662 *Web:* mustangcompression.com	903-218-4161	984-3781	538
Mustang Island State Park 17047 State Hwy 361 ... Port Aransas TX 78373 *Web:* tpwd.texas.gov	361-749-5246		565
Mustang Rental Services Inc 15907 E Fwy ... Channelview TX 77530 *Web:* www.mustangcat.com	281-452-7368		264-3
Mustang Technical Consultants 3405 Tyrone Dr ... Austin TX 78759 *Web:* www.mustangtech.com	512-636-8255		194
Mustang Tractor & Equipment Co 12800 NW Fwy ... Houston TX 77040 *TF:* 800-256-1001 ■ *Web:* www.mustangcatused.com	832-500-3674		358
Mustard Seed 4750 N Div ... Spokane WA 99207 *Web:* www.mustardseedweb.com	509-483-1500		671
Mustel Research Group Ltd 1505 W Second Ave Ste 402 ... Vancouver BC V6H3Y4 *TF:* 888-733-4213 ■ *Web:* mustelgroup.com	604-733-4213		466
Mutare Healthcare Inc 2325 Hicks Rd ... Rolling Meadows IL 60008 *TF:* 855-782-3890 ■ *Web:* www.mutare.com	847-496-9000		177
Muth Electric Inc 1717 N Sanborn PO Box 1400 ... Mitchell SD 57301 *TF:* 800-888-1597 ■ *Web:* www.muthelectric.com	605-996-3983	996-2203	189-4
Mutiny Hotel 2951 S Bayshore Dr ... Miami FL 33133 *TF:* 888-868-8469 ■ *Web:* www.providentresorts.com	305-441-2100	441-2822	379
Mutoh America Inc 2602 S 47th St Ste 102 ... Phoenix AZ 85034 *TF:* 800-996-8864 ■ *Web:* www.mutoh.com	480-968-7772	968-7990	173-6
Mutual Beneficial Association Inc 1301 Lancaster Ave Ste 102 ... Berwyn PA 19312 *TF:* 800-456-0402 ■ *Web:* www.mutualbeneficial.com	800-456-0402		48-6
Mutual Benefit Group 409 Penn St PO Box 577 ... Huntingdon PA 16652 *TF:* 800-283-3531 ■ *Web:* www.mutualbenefitgroup.com	814-643-3000		528
Mutual Engraving Company Inc 511 Hempstead Ave ... West Hempstead NY 11552 *Web:* www.mutualengraving.com	516-486-2996		627
Mutual Industries Inc 707 W Grange St ... Philadelphia PA 19120 *TF:* 800-523-0888 ■ *Web:* www.mutualindustries.com	215-927-6000	927-3388	745-3
Mutual Insurance Associates Inc 1575 Baldy Ave ... Pocatello ID 83201 *Web:* mutualid.com	208-237-9696		390
Mutual Insurance Company of Arizona 2602 EThomas Rd Po Box 33180 ... Phoenix AZ 85016 *TF:* 800-352-0402 ■ *Web:* www.mica-insurance.com	602-956-5276	468-1710	391-2
Mutual Liquid Gas & Equipment Company Inc 17117 S Broadway St ... Gardena CA 90248 *TF:* 800-633-3574 ■ *Web:* www.mutualpropane.com	800-633-3574		316
Mutual Materials Co 605 119th Ave NE ... Bellevue WA 98005 *TF:* 888-688-8250 ■ *Web:* www.mutualmaterials.com	425-452-2363		150
Mutual Mobile Inc 206 E Ninth St Ste 1400 ... Austin TX 78701 *TF:* 800-208-3563 ■ *Web:* mutualmobile.com	800-208-3563		177
Mutual of America Life Insurance Co 320 Park Ave ... New York NY 10022 *TF:* 800-468-3785 ■ *Web:* www.mutualofamerica.com	212-224-1600		391-2
Mutual of Enumclaw Insurance Co 1460 Wells St ... Enumclaw WA 98022 *TF:* 800-366-5551 ■ *Web:* www.mutualofenumclaw.com	360-825-2591	825-6885	391-4
Mutual of Omaha Bank 3333 Farnam St ... Omaha NE 68131 *TF:* 866-351-5646 ■ *Web:* www.mutualofomahabank.com	877-471-7896		70
Mutual of Omaha Co 3300 Mutual of Omaha Plz ... Omaha NE 68175 *TF:* 800-775-6000 ■ *Web:* www.mutualofomaha.com	800-228-2499		360-4
Mutual Sales Inc 2 Corporate Park Dr ... Derry NH 03038 *TF:* 800-486-9469 ■ *Web:* www.mutualsales.com	603-421-0110	421-0550	328
Mutual Savings Credit Union Inc 2040 Valleydale Rd ... Birmingham AL 35244 *Web:* www.mutualsavings.org	205-682-1100		219
Mutual Trading Company Ltd 431 Crocker St ... Los Angeles CA 90013 *Web:* lamtc.com	213-626-9458	626-5130	297-11
Mutual Trust Life Insurance Co 1200 Jorie Blvd ... Oak Brook IL 60522 **Fax Area Code:* 630 ■ *TF:* 800-323-7320 ■ *Web:* www.mutualtrust.com	800-323-7320	990-7083*	391-2
Mutual Wheel Company Inc 2345 Fourth Ave ... Moline IL 61265 *TF:* 800-798-6926 ■ *Web:* www.mutualwheel.com	309-757-1200	757-1241	61
Muza Metal Products Corp 606 E Murdock Ave ... Oshkosh WI 54901 *Web:* www.muzametal.com	920-236-3535	236-3520	487
Muzi Motors Inc 557 Highland Ave ... Needham MA 02494 *TF:* 800-296-9440 ■ *Web:* www.muzimotors.com	800-296-9440		57
Muzinich & Company Inc 450 Park Ave ... New York NY 10022 *Web:* www.muzinich.com	212-888-3413		690
Mv Printing Solutions Inc 23531 Ridge Rt Dr Ste A ... Laguna Hills CA 92653 *Web:* mvprintsolutions.com	949-598-9610		627
MV Transportation Inc 5910 N Central Expy Ste 1145 ... Dallas TX 75206 *Web:* www.mvtransit.com	972-391-4000		468

Name / Address	City	State	ZIP	Phone	Fax	Class
MVA (Midwest Venture Alliance) 7829 E Rockhill St Ste 307 *Web:* www.midwestventure.com	Wichita	KS	67206	316-651-5900		393
MVA Engineering Group Ltd 246 Waterloo St *Web:* www.mva.on.ca	London	ON	N6B2N4	519-668-4698		256
MVC Capital Inc 287 Bowman Ave 2nd Fl *NYSE: MVC* ■ *Web:* www.mvccapital.com	Purchase	NY	10577	914-701-0310	701-0315	792
MVFF (Mill Valley Film Festival) 1001 Lootens Pl Ste 220 *Web:* www.mvff.com	San Rafael	CA	94901	415-383-5256	383-8606	282
MVI Administrators Inc 1011 Camino Del Rio S Ste 300 *TF:* 800-927-8380 ■ *Web:* www.mviadmin.com	San Diego	CA	92108	619-260-2660		390
MVI HomeCare 4891 Belmont Ave *TF:* 800-449-4684 ■ *Web:* www.mvihomecare.com	Youngstown	OH	44505	330-759-9487		363
MVM Inc 44620 Guilford Dr *Web:* www.mvminc.com	Ashburn	VA	20147	571-223-4500	223-4474	693
MVM Products LLC 940 Calle Amanecer Ste K *Web:* www.ink-jet.com	San Clemente	CA	92673	949-366-1470		591
MVMA (Maine Veterinary Medical Assn) 97A Exchange St Ste 305 *TF:* 800-448-2772 ■ *Web:* netforum.avectra.com	Portland	ME	04101	800-448-2772		795
MVMA (Michigan Veterinary Medical Assn) 2144 Commons Pkwy *Web:* michvma.org	Okemos	MI	48864	517-347-4710	347-4666	795
MVMA (Mesa Verde Museum Assn) PO Box 38 *Web:* www.mesaverde.org	Mesa Verde National Park	CO	81330	970-529-4445	529-4446	637-2
MVNP 745 Fort St Ste 900 *Web:* www.mvnp.com	Honolulu	HI	96813	808-536-0881		7
MVP Global Logistics 580 Chelsea St Ste 212 *Web:* forglobal.com	East Boston	MA	02128	617-569-6300		311
MVP Health Care 625 State St *TF:* 800-777-4793 ■ *Web:* www.mvphealthcare.com	Schenectady	NY	12305	518-370-4793	370-0830	391-3
MVP Sports Spot 3701 32nd St SE *Web:* msasportsspot.com	Grand Rapids	MI	49512	616-464-1000		717
MVP Trading Company Inc 1 Garvies Point Rd Bldg 1 **Fax Area Code: 240* ■ *Web:* www.mvptrading.com	Glen Cove	NY	11542	516-204-7793	331-7101*	328
MVS Group 1086 Goffle Rd *TF:* 800-619-9989 ■ *Web:* mvsusa.com	Hawthorne	NJ	07506	201-447-1505		387
MVS Inc 1150 18th St NW Ste 325 *Web:* www.mvsconsulting.com	Washington	DC	20036	202-722-7981	722-7982	463
MVSB (Meredith Village Savings Bank) 24 SR-25 PO Box 177 *TF:* 800-922-6872 ■ *Web:* www.mvsb.com	Meredith	NH	03253	603-279-7986	279-5710	70
MVSD (Mountain View School District) 3320 Gilman Rd *Web:* www.mtviewschools.com	El Monte	CA	91732	626-652-4000		685
MVT (Moapa Valley Telephone Co) 183 S Anderson St *TF:* 800-227-2600 ■ *Web:* www.mvtel.com	Overton	NV	89040	702-397-2601		224
MW Bevins Co 9903 E 54th St *Web:* bevinsco.com	Tulsa	OK	74146	918-627-1273	627-1294	758
MW Davis Dumas & Associates Inc 2720 Third Ave S *Web:* www.mwdda.com	Birmingham	AL	35233	205-252-0246	251-8506	261
MW Industries Inc 2400 Farrell *Web:* www.mw-ind.com	Houston	TX	77073	281-233-0448		567
MW Mcwong International Inc 1921 Arena Blvd *Web:* www.mcwonginc.com	Sacramento	CA	95834	916-371-8080		350
MW Sewall & Co 259 Front St *Web:* mwsewall.com	Bath	ME	04530	207-442-7994		579
MWA (Mystery Writers of America Inc) 1140 Broadway Ste 1507 *Web:* www.mysterywriters.org	New York	NY	10001	212-888-8171	888-8107	48-4
MWA (Montana Wilderness Assn) 80 S Warren St *Web:* wildmontana.org	Helena	MT	59601	406-443-7350	443-0750	48-13
M-Wave Inc 100 High Grove Blvd *Web:* www.mwav.com	Glendale Heights	IL	60139	630-318-1900		625
MWD (Montecito Water District) 583 San Ysidro Rd *Web:* www.montecitowater.com	Montecito	CA	93108	805-969-2271		192
MWG (Mills-Wilson-George Inc) 1847 Vanderhorn Dr *Web:* www.millswilsongeorge.com	Memphis	TN	38134	901-373-5100	373-5155	665
MWH Global Inc 380 Interlocken Cres Ste 200 *TF:* 866-257-5984 ■ *Web:* www.mwhglobal.com	Broomfield	CO	80021	303-533-1900		192
MWI Inc 1269 Brighton Henrietta Townline Rd *TF:* 855-222-4230 ■ *Web:* www.mwi.com	Rochester	NY	14623	855-222-4230		127
MWI Pumps 33 NW Eller St *TF:* 800-296-7004 ■ *Web:* www.mwicorp.com	Deerfield Beach	FL	33441	954-426-1500	426-1582	641
MWL Engineering Corp 6825 SW 81st St *Web:* mwleng.com	Miami	FL	33143	305-661-3357		261
MWMPC (Michael W. Middleton PC) 3330 Longmire Dr *Web:* mwmpc.com	College Station	TX	77845	979-695-2726	695-2754	787
MWP Blue Ridge Building Supply 5221 Rockfish Gap Tpke *Web:* mwpblueridgebuildingsupply.com	Charlottesville	VA	22903	434-823-1387		290
MWS Enterprises Inc 5869 Forest Creek Dr	East Amherst	NY	14051	716-689-0600		297-8
MX Consulting Services Inc 544 Paramount Dr *Web:* www.mxcsi.com	Raynham	MA	02767	508-821-5855	823-0290	196
MX Group, The 7020 High Grove Blvd **Fax Area Code: 630* ■ *TF:* 800-827-0170 ■ *Web:* www.themxgroup.com	Burr Ridge	IL	60527	800-827-0170	654-0302*	194
MXI Environmental Services LLC 26319 Old Trail Rd *Web:* mxiinc.com	Abingdon	VA	24210	276-628-6636	628-4435	196
MXL Industries Inc 1764 Rohrerstown Rd *TF:* 800-233-0159 ■ *Web:* www.mxl-industries.com	Lancaster	PA	17601	717-569-8711	569-8716	604
MXN Corp 1025 Rose Creek Dr Ste 620 *Web:* www.mxncorp.com	Woodstock	GA	30189	770-926-1884		196
My Alarm Center LLC 3803 W Chester Pk Ste 100 *TF:* 866-484-4800 ■ *Web:* myalarmcenter.com	Newtown Square	PA	19073	866-484-4800		693
My Cleaning Service Inc 2701 Cresmont Ave *Web:* www.mycleaningservice.com	Baltimore	MD	21211	410-889-0505		104
My Healthcare Federal Credit Union 4720 NW 39th Ave *Web:* myhcfcu.org	Gainesville	FL	32606	352-333-4760		219
My Jewish Discovery Place Children's Museum 6501 W Sunrise Blvd *Web:* www.sorefjcc.org	Plantation	FL	33313	954-792-6700	792-4839	520
My Lethbridge Now 220 3rd Ave S Ste 400 *Web:* www.mylethbridgenews.com	Lethbridge	AB	T1J0G9	403-388-2910	388-4648	647
My Museum 425 Washington St *Web:* mymuseum.org	Monterey	CA	93940	831-649-6444		521
My Old Kentucky Home State Park 501 E Stephen Foster Ave *Web:* parks.ky.gov	Bardstown	KY	40004	502-348-3502		565
My Praise ATL 102.5 101 Marietta St 12th Fl *Web:* mypraiseatl.com	Atlanta	GA	30303	404-765-9750		645-11
My Receptionist 800 Wisconsin St Ste 410 *TF:* 800-686-0162 ■ *Web:* www.myreceptionist.com	Eau Claire	WI	54703	800-686-0162		737
My Service Depot 8774 Cotter St *TF:* 888-518-0818 ■ *Web:* www.smartservice.com	Lewis Center	OH	43035	888-518-0818		764
My Table Magazine 1733 Harold St *Web:* www.my-table.com	Houston	TX	77098	713-529-5500		637-9
My Thai 2029 Coulter Dr *Web:* www.mythaiamarillo.com	Amarillo	TX	79106	806-355-9541		671
My Town Media Inc 412 N Locust St *Web:* mytown-media.com	Pittsburg	KS	66762	620-232-5993		645-141
My Web Times 110 W Jefferson St *Web:* www.mywebtimes.com	Ottawa	IL	61350	815-433-1060	433-1639	532-2
Myakka River State Park 13208 SR 72 *Web:* www.floridastateparks.org	Sarasota	FL	34241	941-361-6511	361-6501	565
Myat Inc 360 Franklin Tpke *Web:* www.myat.com	Mahwah	NJ	07430	201-684-0100		645-11
Myatt & Bell PC 10300 SW Greenburg Rd Ste 500 *Web:* myattandbell.com	Portland	OR	97223	503-641-6262		41
MYB (Mind Your Business Inc) 305 Eighth Ave E *TF:* 888-869-2462 ■ *Web:* www.mybinc.com	Hendersonville	NC	28792	888-869-2462		260
MyClean Inc 247 W 35th St Ste 9R *TF:* 855-692-5326 ■ *Web:* www.myclean.com	New York	NY	10001	855-692-5326		192
Myco Trailers LLC 2703 29th Ave E *Web:* www.mycotrailers.com	Bradenton	FL	34208	941-748-2397		120
MYCON General Contractors Inc 17311 Dallas Pkwy Ste 300 *Web:* www.mycon.com	Dallas	TX	75248	972-529-2444		186
MyCorporation Business Services Inc 26025 Mureau Rd Ste 120 *TF:* 877-692-6772 ■ *Web:* www.mycorporation.com	Calabasas	CA	91302	877-692-6772		387
Mydax Inc 12260 Shale Ridge Ln *TF:* 800-732-2284 ■ *Web:* www.mydax.com	Auburn	CA	95602	530-888-6662	888-0962	14
MYEC (Mid Yellowstone Elec Co-opeartive Inc) 203 Elliott PO Box 386 *Web:* www.myec.coop	Hysham	MT	59038	406-342-5521		245
Myelotec Inc 4000 Northfield Way Ste 900 *Web:* www.myelotec.com	Roswell	GA	30076	770-664-4656		476
Myers 2200 Monroe St *Web:* myersbps.com	York	PA	17404	717-792-2500	792-5115	191-2
Myers & Company Architectural Metals 555 Basalt Ave *Web:* www.myersandco.com	Basalt	CO	81621	970-927-4761		492
Myers Brothers of Kansas City Inc 1210 W 28th St *TF:* 800-264-2404 ■ *Web:* www.myersbrotherskc.com	Kansas City	MO	64108	816-931-5501		54
Myers Container Corp 8435 NE Killingsworth *TF:* 800-406-9377 ■ *Web:* www.myerscontainer.com	Portland	OR	97220	503-501-5830	501-5831	198
Myers Engineering Consulting 13911 Quail Pointe Dr *Web:* mecokc.com	Oklahoma City	OK	73134	405-755-5325	755-5373	261
Myers Engineering Inc 8376 Salt Lake Ave *TF:* 877-652-4767 ■ *Web:* myersmixers.com	Bell	CA	90201	323-560-4723	771-7789	298
Myers Industries Inc 1293 S Main St *NYSE: MYE* ■ *Web:* www.myersindustries.com	Akron	OH	44301	330-253-5592	761-6156	199
Myers Power Products Inc 2950 E Philadelphia St *Web:* www.myerspowerproducts.com	Ontario	CA	91761	909-923-1800		767
Myers White LLC 66280 Pancoast Rd	Belmont	OH	43718	740-695-1350		41
Myers, Oliver & Price PC 1401 Central Ave NW Ste B *Web:* moplaw.com	Albuquerque	NM	87104	505-247-9080		428
Myers, Widders, Gibson, Jones & Feingold LLP 5425 Everglades St *Web:* www.mwgjlaw.com	Ventura	CA	93003	805-644-7188		428
Myers-Holum Inc 244 Madison Ave Ste 217 *Web:* myersholum.com	New York	NY	10016	212-753-5353		177
Myerson Agency Inc, The 11835 W Olympic Blvd Ste 465E *Web:* Www.myersonwealth.com	Los Angeles	CA	90064	424-363-0300		390
MyEvent com Inc 221 de la Commune St W Ste 305 *TF:* 877-769-3836 ■ *Web:* myevent.com	Montreal	QC	H2Y2C9	514-282-7747		396
MyEyeDr Inc 401 Maple Ave W *Web:* www.myeyedr.com	Vienna	VA	22180	703-938-5544		544

Name	Address	City	State	Zip	Phone	Fax	Class	Other
MyFreightWorld	7133 W 95th St Ste 205	Overland Park	KS	66212	877-549-9438		393	TF: 877-549-9438 ■ Web: myfreightworld.com
Myhre Equine Clinic PLLC	100 Ten Rod Rd	Rochester	NH	03867	603-335-4777		794	Web: myhreequine.com
Mylan	1000 Mylan Blvd	Canonsburg	PA	15317	724-514-1800		582	TF: 800-527-4278 ■ Web: www.mylan.com
Mylan Pharmaceuticals ULC	85 Advance Rd	Etobicoke	ON	M8Z2S6	416-236-2631		583	TF: 800-575-1379 ■ Web: www.mylan.ca
Myles Standish Monument State Reservation	Crescent St	Duxbury	MA	02332	508-747-5360		565	Web: www.mass.gov
Myles Standish State Forest	Cranberry Rd	South Carver	MA	02366	508-866-2526		565	Web: www.mass.gov
MyLLCcom Inc	1910 Thomes Ave	Cheyenne	WY	82001	888-886-9552		463	TF: 888-886-9552 ■ Web: www.myllc.com
Mynah Technologies	504 Trade Center Blvd	Chesterfield	MO	63005	636-728-2000		177	Web: www.mynah.com
Mynelle Gardens	4736 Clinton Blvd	Jackson	MS	39209	601-960-1894	960-1576	97	Web: www.jacksonms.gov
MyNewPlace	343 Sansome St Ste 700	San Francisco	CA	94104	415-348-2009		387	Web: www.mynewplace.com
Myoderm	48 E Main St	Norristown	PA	19401	610-233-3300	233-3301	238	Web: www.myoderm.com
Myomo Inc	Myomo Inc One Broadway 14th Fl	Cambridge	MA	02142	617-996-9058		477	TF: 877-736-9666 ■ Web: www.myomo.com
Myotherapy College of Utah	334B Bugatti Dr	Salt Lake City	UT	84115	801-484-7624		167-3	TF: 888-809-9274 ■ Web: www.myotherapycollege.com
Myotherapy Institute	4001 Pioneer Woods Dr	Lincoln	NE	68506	402-421-7410		167-3	Web: www.myotherapy.edu
Myotronics-noromed Inc	5870 S 194th St	Kent	WA	98032	206-243-4214		228	TF: 800-426-0316 ■ Web: www.myotronics.com
MyPath Support Services	1746 Executive Dr	Oconomowoc	WI	53066	262-569-5515	569-3160	463	Web: www.mypathcompanies.com
MYR Group inc	1701 W Golf Rd Ste 1012	Rolling Meadows	IL	60008	847-290-1891	290-1892	189-4	TF: 800-360-1321 ■ Web: myrgroup.com
Myra Museum	2405 Belmont Rd	Grand Forks	ND	58201	701-775-2216		520	Web: www.grandforkshistory.com
Myre-Big Island State Park	19499 780th Ave	Albert Lea	MN	56007	507-668-7060	379-3405	565	Web: www.dnr.state.mn.us
Myres & Assoc	1 Greenway Plz Ste 450	Houston	TX	77046	713-622-1600		41	Web: thehoustondivorcefirm.com
Myriad Botanical Gardens/Crystal Bridge Tropical Conservatory	301 W Reno Ave	Oklahoma City	OK	73102	405-445-7080		97	Web: oklahomacitybotanicalgardens.com
Myriad Computer Solutions Inc	7225A Bryan Dairy Rd	Largo	FL	33777	727-541-6000		174	
Myriad Genetics Inc	320 Wakara Way	Salt Lake City	UT	84108	801-584-3600	584-3640	85	NASDAQ: MYGN ■ TF: 800-469-7423 ■ Web: myriad.com
Myriad RBM	3300 Duval Rd	Austin	TX	78759	512-835-8026	835-4687	582	TF: 866-726-6277 ■ Web: myriadrbm.com
Myriad Restaurant Group Inc	249 W Broadway	New York	NY	10013	212-219-9500	219-2380	670	Web: www.myriadrestaurantgroup.com
Myrmidon Corp	10555 W Little York Rd	Houston	TX	77041	713-880-0044	880-4720	697	TF: 800-880-0771 ■ Web: www.myrmcorp.com
Myrmo & Sons Inc	3600 Franklin Blvd	Eugene	OR	97403	541-747-4565		454	Web: www.myrmo.com
Myron Corp	205 Maywood Ave	Maywood	NJ	07607	877-803-3358		9	TF: 877-803-3358 ■ Web: www.myron.com
Myrtle Beach Area Chamber of Commerce	1200 N Oak St	Myrtle Beach	SC	29577	843-626-7444		139	TF: 800-356-3016 ■ Web: www.visitmyrtlebeach.com
Myrtle Beach Convention Ctr	2101 N Oak St	Myrtle Beach	SC	29577	843-918-5000		205	Web: www.sheratonmyrtlebeach.com
Myrtle Beach Herald	3364 Huger St	Myrtle Beach	SC	29577	843-626-3131		532-4	
Myrtle Beach Hotels LLC	2102-B Cromley Cir	Myrtle Beach	SC	29577	843-692-9977		377	Web: myrtlebeachhotels.net
Myrtle Beach International Airport	1100 Jetport Rd	Myrtle Beach	SC	29577	843-448-1589	626-9096	27	TF: 800-778-4838 ■ Web: www.flymyrtlebeach.com
Myrtle Beach Resort Vacations	5905 S Kings Hwy PO Box 3936	Myrtle Beach	SC	29578	843-238-1559	238-2424	669	TF: 888-627-3767 ■ Web: www.myrtle-beach-resort.com
Myrtle Beach Speedway	455 Hospitality Ln	Myrtle Beach	SC	29579	843-236-0500		515	Web: www.myrtlebeachspeedway.com
Myrtle Beach State Park	4401 S Kings Hwy	Myrtle Beach	SC	29575	843-238-5325		565	Web: southcarolinaparks.com
Myrtle Waves Water Park	3000 Tenth Ave N Ext	Myrtle Beach	SC	29577	843-913-9260		32	Web: www.myrtlewaves.com
Mysterious Bookshop, The	58 Warren St	New York	NY	10007	212-587-1011	587-1126	637-2	Web: www.mysteriousbookshop.com
Mystery Writers of America Inc (MWA)	1140 Broadway Ste 1507	New York	NY	10001	212-888-8171	888-8107	48-4	Web: www.mysterywriters.org
Mystic Aquarium & Institute for Exploration	55 Coogan Blvd	Mystic	CT	06355	860-572-5955	572-5960	40	Web: www.mysticaquarium.org
Mystic Lake Casino Hotel	2400 Mystic Lake Blvd	Prior Lake	MN	55372	866-832-6402		133	TF: 800-262-7799 ■ Web: www.mysticlake.com
Mystic Rose Books	PO Box 1036/Sms	Fairfield	CT	06825	203-371-6912	371-4843	637-2	Web: www.mysticrose.com
Mystic Sea Resort	2105 S Ocean Blvd	Myrtle Beach	SC	29577	843-448-8446		669	TF: 800-443-7050 ■ Web: www.mysticsea.com
Mystic Seaport -- The Museum of America & the Sea	75 Greenmanville Ave PO Box 6000	Mystic	CT	06355	860-572-0711	572-5395	520	TF: 888-973-2767 ■ Web: www.mysticseaport.org
Mystic Stamp Co	9700 Mill St	Camden	NY	13316	315-245-2690	385-4919*	459	*Fax Area Code: 800 ■ TF: 866-660-7147 ■ Web: www.mysticstamp.com
Mystic Valley Wheel Works Inc	480 Trapelo Rd	Belmont	MA	02478	617-489-3577		711	Web: wheelworks.com
MySuburbanLife.com	1101 W 31st St Ste 100	Downers Grove	IL	60515	630-368-1100	969-0228	532-4	Web: www.mysuburbanlife.com
MySupplyChainGroup LLC	2700 Corporate Dr Ste 200	Birmingham	AL	35242	205-706-4300		449	Web: www.mysupplychaingroup.com
My-T Acres Inc	8127 Lewiston Rd	Batavia	NY	14020	585-343-1026		10-11	Web: mytacres.com
Myt Home Health Care Inc	1349 El Prado Ave	Torrance	CA	90501	800-464-3258		363	TF: 800-464-3258 ■ Web: mobilitycare.com
MYTA Technologies	7979 Old Georgetown Rd Ste 800	Bethesda	MD	20814	301-656-6982	656-3782	196	Web: www.myta.com
Mytech Partners Inc	300 Second St NW	New Brighton	MN	55112	612-659-9800		180	Web: www.mytech.com
MYTecSoft Inc	1225 Laurel St Ste 401	Columbia	SC	29201	803-244-0255		196	Web: www.mytecsoft.com
Mythics Inc	4525 Main St Ste 1500	Virginia Beach	VA	23462	757-412-4362	412-1060	174	TF: 866-698-4427 ■ Web: www.mythics.com
Mytina Inc	842 Foothill Blvd	La Canada Flintridge	CA	91011	818-507-0077		652	
Mytrex Inc	10321 S Beckstead Ln	South Jordan	UT	84095	801-571-4121		476	Web: rescuealert.com
MyUSACorporationcom Inc	1 Radisson Plz Ste 800	New Rochelle	NY	10801	877-330-2677		317	TF: 877-330-2677 ■ Web: www.myusacorporation.com
MZA Associates Corp	2021 Girard Blvd SE Ste 150	Albuquerque	NM	87106	505-245-9970		544	Web: www.mza.com
Mzinga	10 Mall Rd	Burlington	MA	01803	888-694-6428		194	TF: 888-694-6428 ■ Web: mzinga.com

N

Name	Address	City	State	Zip	Phone	Fax	Class	Other
N & B Team Consulting Inc	3625 NW 82nd Ave Ste 207	Doral	FL	33166	305-514-2404		196	Web: nbteamconsulting.com
N & K Technology Inc	80 Las Colinas Ln	San Jose	CA	95119	408-513-3800		696	Web: www.nandk.com
N & N Supply Co	5909-17 Ditman St	Philadelphia	PA	19135	215-535-7068	535-7363	364	Web: www.nnsupply.net
N & S Supply of Fishkill Inc	205 Old Rt 9	Fishkill	NY	12524	845-896-6291		612	Web: www.nssupply.com
N & S Tractor Co	600 S Hwy 59	Merced	CA	95341	209-383-5888		274	Web: www.nstractor.com
N Barton & Associates Inc	3629 Old Capital Trail Rd	Marshallton	DE	19808	302-998-5272		567	Web: www.nbartoninc.com
N Cell Systems Inc	1907 E Wayzata Blvd	Wayzata	MN	55391	952-746-5125		180	Web: www.ncell.com
N E Florida Educational Consortium	3841 Reid St	Palatka	FL	32177	386-329-3800		685	TF: 800-227-6036 ■ Web: www.nefec.org
N E W Credit Union	301 Jackson St	Oconto Falls	WI	54154	920-848-2793		219	TF: 800-924-1250 ■ Web: newcu.org
N J R Corp	125 Nicholson Ln	San Jose	CA	95134	408-321-0200	232-6060	695	Web: www.njr.com
N K Bhandari, Consulting Engineers PC (NKB)	1005 W Fayette St Ste 500	Syracuse	NY	13204	315-428-1177	428-9822	261	Web: www.nkbpc.com
N L Fisher Supervision & Engineering	522 - 11th Ave SW 2nd Fl	Calgary	AB	T2R0C8	403-266-7478		538	Web: nlfisher.com
N O A Medical Industries Inc	801 Terry Ln	Washington	MO	63090	636-239-7600		321	Web: www.noamedical.com
N R S I	179 Lafayette Dr	Syosset	NY	11791	516-921-5500		242	TF: 800-331-3117 ■ Web: nrsi.com
N Tepperman Ltd	2595 Ouellette Ave	Windsor	ON	N8X4V8	519-969-9700		321	TF: 800-265-5062 ■ Web: teppermans.com
N W Electric Power Co-op	PO Box 565	Cameron	MO	64429	816-632-2121	632-3114	245	Web: www.nwepc.com
N Wasserstrom & Sons Inc	2300 Lockbourne Rd	Columbus	OH	43207	614-228-5550		300	TF: 800-444-4697 ■ Web: www.wasserstrom.com
N'DIGO | Hartman Publishing Group	1006 S Michigan Ave Ste 200	Chicago	IL	60605	312-822-0202		532-3	Web: ndigo.com
N'Ware Technologies Inc	2885 01e Rue	Saint-Georges	QC	G6A0C5	418-227-4292	227-1861	180	TF: 800-270-9420 ■ Web: www.nwaretech.com

				Phone	Fax	Class
N. A. Chaderjian Youth Correctional Facility 7650 S Newcastle Rd PO Box 213014 *Web:* www.cdcr.ca.gov	Stockton	CA	95215	209-944-6400		412
N. C. Center for Nonprofit Organizations Inc 5800 Faringdon Pl *Web:* www.ncnonprofits.org	Raleigh	NC	27609	919-790-1555		138
N. Chasen and Son Inc 2924 W Marshall St *Web:* www.nchasen.com	Richmond	VA	23230	804-353-4563		189-8
N.A. Cohen Group Inc 15720 Ventura Blvd Ste 500 *Web:* nacohengroup.com	Encino	CA	91436	818-461-1420		261
N.A.Williams Co 2900 A Paces Ferry Rd *Web:* www.nawilliams.com	Atlanta	GA	30339	770-433-2282		195
N.B. Liebman 4705 Carlisle Pk *Web:* www.nbliebman.com	Mechanicsburg	PA	17050	717-761-4550		321
N.B.C. Truck Equipment Inc 28130 Groesbeck Hwy *TF:* 800-778-8207 ■ *Web:* www.nbctruckequip.com	Roseville	MI	48066	586-774-4900	772-1280	61
N.E.T. & Die Inc 24 Foster St *Web:* www.netdieinc.com	Fulton	NY	13069	315-592-4311	598-1232	454
N.E.T. Inc 5651 Palmer Way Ste C *TF:* 800-888-4638 ■ *Web:* www.netmindbody.com	Carlsbad	CA	92010	760-929-5980		85
N.M. Knight Company Inc 1001 S 2nd St *Web:* nmknight.com	Millville	NJ	08332	856-327-4855	825-9142	201
N9ne Steakhouse 4321 W Flamingo Rd *Web:* www.palms.com	Las Vegas	NV	89103	702-942-7777		671
NA (Norris Associates) 2534 Murrell Rd *Web:* www.norris-associates.com	Santa Barbara	CA	93109	805-962-7703	456-2169	194
NA Degerstrom Inc 3303 N Sullivan Rd *Web:* www.nadinc.com	Spokane	WA	99216	509-928-3333	927-2010	502
NA for Home Care & Hospice (NAHC) 228 Seventh St SE *Web:* www.nahc.org	Washington	DC	20003	202-547-7424	547-3540	49-8
NA for the Advancement of Colored People (NAACP) 4805 Mt Hope Dr *TF:* 877-622-2798 ■ *Web:* www.naacp.org	Baltimore	MD	21215	410-580-5777		48-8
Na Go Ya 4921 Brainerd Rd *Web:* www.nagoyatn.com	Chattanooga	TN	37411	423-899-9252		671
NA of Colleges & Employers (NACE) 62 Highland Ave *TF:* 800-544-5272 ■ *Web:* www.naceweb.org	Bethlehem	PA	18017	610-868-1421		49-5
NA of Collegiate Directors of Athletics (NACDA) 24651 Detroit Rd *TF:* 877-887-2261 ■ *Web:* www.nacda.com	Westlake	OH	44145	440-892-4000	892-4007	48-22
NA of Convenience Stores (NACS) 1600 Duke St 7th Fl *TF:* 800-966-6227 ■ *Web:* www.convenience.org	Alexandria	VA	22314	703-684-3600	836-4564	49-18
NA of Independent Colleges & Universities (NAICU) 1025 Connecticut Ave NW Ste 700 *Web:* www.naicu.edu	Washington	DC	20036	202-785-8866		49-5
NA of Insurance & Financial Advisors (NAIFA) 2901 Telestar Ct *Web:* www.naifa.org	Falls Church	VA	22042	703-770-8100		49-9
NA of Nurse Practitioners in Women's Health 505 C St NE *Web:* www.npwh.org	Washington	DC	20002	202-543-9693	543-9858	49-8
NA of Professional Employer Organizations (NAPEO) 707 N St Asaph St *Web:* www.napeo.org	Alexandria	VA	22314	703-836-0466	836-0976	49-12
NA of Television Program Executives (NATPE) 5757 Wilshire Blvd PH 10 *Web:* www.natpe.com	Los Angeles	CA	90036	310-453-4440	453-5258	49-14
NA of Women in Construction (NAWIC) 327 S Adams St *TF:* 800-552-3506 ■ *Web:* www.nawic.org	Fort Worth	TX	76104	817-877-5551	877-0324	49-3
NA World Services Inc 19737 Nordhoff Pl *Web:* www.na.org	Chatsworth	CA	91311	818-773-9999	700-0700	393
NAA (Natural Areas Assn) PO Box 594 *Web:* www.naturalareas.org	Ligonier	PA	15658	724-995-8466		48-13
NAA (National Apartment Assn) 4300 Wilson Blvd Ste 400 *TF:* 800-632-3007 ■ *Web:* www.naahq.org	Arlington	VA	22203	703-518-6141	248-9440	49-17
NAA (National Auctioneers Assn) 8880 Ballentine St *TF:* 877-657-1990 ■ *Web:* www.auctioneers.org	Overland Park	KS	66214	913-541-8084	894-5281	49-18
NAAA (National Agricultural Aviation Assn) 1005 E St SE *Web:* www.agaviation.org	Washington	DC	20003	202-546-5722	546-5726	48-2
NAAA (National Auto Auction Assn) 5320 Spectrum Dr Ste D *TF:* 800-232-5411 ■ *Web:* www.naaa.com	Frederick	MD	21703	301-696-0400	631-1359	49-18
NAAB (National Association of Animal Breeders) 8413 Excelsior Dr Ste 140 *Web:* www.naab-css.org	Madison	WI	53717	608-827-0277	827-1535	11-2
NAAB (National Architectural Accrediting Board) 1735 New York Ave NW *Web:* www.naab.org	Washington	DC	20006	202-783-2007	783-2822	48-1
NAACLS (National Accrediting Agency for Clinical Laboratory Sciences) 5600 N River Rd Ste 720 *Web:* www.naacls.org	Rosemont	IL	60018	773-714-8880	714-8886	48-1
NAACP (NA for the Advancement of Colored People) 4805 Mt Hope Dr *TF:* 877-622-2798 ■ *Web:* www.naacp.org	Baltimore	MD	21215	410-580-5777		48-8
NAADAC PAC 44 Canal Center Plz Ste 301 *TF:* 800-377-1136 ■ *Web:* www.naadac.org	Alexandria	VA	22314	703-741-7686	741-7698	615
NAAF (National Alopecia Areata Foundation) 14 Mitchell Blvd *Web:* www.naaf.org	San Rafael	CA	94903	415-472-3780	472-5343	48-17
NAB (National Association of Broadcasters) 1771 N St NW *Web:* www.nab.org	Washington	DC	20036	202-429-5300		49-14
NAB Construction Corp 112-20 14th Ave *Web:* www.nabconstruction.com	College Point	NY	11356	718-762-0001	961-3789	188-4
NABC (North American Blueberry Council) 1847 Iron Pt Rd Ste 100 *Web:* www.blueberry.org	Folsom	CA	95630	916-983-0111	983-9370	48-2
NABC (New Age Bible and Philosophy Ctr) 1139 Lincoln Blvd *Web:* newagebible.tripod.com	Santa Monica	CA	90403	310-395-4346		637-2
NABCA (National Alcohol Beverage Control Assn) 2900 S Quincy St Ste 800 *Web:* www.nabca.org	Alexandria	VA	22206	703-578-4200	820-3551	49-7
Nabco Entrances Inc S82W18717 Gemini Dr *TF:* 888-679-3319 ■ *Web:* www.nabcoentrances.com	Muskego	WI	53150	877-622-2694		480
Nabco Systems LLC 171 Hillpointe Dr Ste 303 *Web:* www.nabcoinc.com	Canonsburg	PA	15317	724-746-9617	746-9709	693
Nabeel's Cafe 1706 Oxmoor Rd *Web:* www.nabeels.com	Homewood	AL	35209	205-879-9292		671
Nabet 700-M Unifor 100 Lombard St Ste 203 *TF:* 800-889-9487 ■ *Web:* nabet700.com	Toronto	ON	M5C1M3	416-536-4827	536-0859	397
NABET-CWA 501 Third St NW *Web:* www.nabetcwa.org	Washington	DC	20001	202-434-1254	434-1426	414
Nabholz Construction Corp 612 Garland St *Web:* www.nabholz.com	Conway	AR	72033	501-505-5800		186
Nabors Alaska Drilling Inc 2525 C St Ste 200 *Web:* www.nabors.com	Anchorage	AK	99503	907-263-6000	563-3734	540
Nabors Industries Ltd 515 W Greens Rd Ste 1200 *TF:* 800-422-2066 ■ *Web:* nabors.com	Houston	TX	77067	281-874-0035	872-5205	540
Nabtesco Aerospace Inc 17770 NE 78th Pl *TF:* 888-867-1243 ■ *Web:* www.nabtescoaero.com	Redmond	WA	98052	425-602-8400	602-8408	529
NAC (National Automobile Club) 1151 E Hillsdale Blvd Ste E *TF:* 800-622-2136 ■ *Web:* www.nacroadservice.com	Foster City	CA	94404	800-622-2136		53
NAC (National Audio Company Inc) 309 E Water St *Web:* www.nationalaudiocompany.com	Springfield	MO	65806	417-863-1925	863-7825	238
NAC Group Inc 1790 Commerce Ave N *TF:* 866-651-2901 ■ *Web:* www.nacsemi.com	Saint Petersburg	FL	33716	727-828-0187	828-0155	246
NACA (National Air Carrier Assn) 1735 N Lynn St Ste 105 *Web:* www.naca.cc	Arlington	VA	22209	703-358-8060	358-8070	49-21
NACAC (North American Council on Adoptable Children) 970 Raymond Ave Ste 106 *TF:* 877-823-2237 ■ *Web:* www.nacac.org	Saint Paul	MN	55114	651-644-3036	644-9848	48-6
Nacarato Volvo Truck 519 New Paul Rd *TF:* 888-392-8486 ■ *Web:* www.nacaratotrucks.com	La Vergne	TN	37086	888-392-8486		516
NACAS (National Association of College Auxiliary Services) 3 Boar's Head Ln Ste B *Web:* nacas.org	Charlottesville	VA	22903	434-245-8425	245-8453	49-5
NACB (Native American Community Board) PO Box 572 *Web:* www.nativeshop.org	Lake Andes	SD	57356	605-487-7072	487-7964	48-7
NACB Group Corp 10 Starwood Dr *TF:* 800-370-2737 ■ *Web:* www.ncabgroup.com	Hampstead	NH	03841	603-329-4551		246
NACC (Norwegian-American Chamber of Commerce Southwest Chapter) 5219 Pine Arbor Dr *Web:* www.nacchouston.org	Houston	TX	77066	281-537-6879	587-9284	138
NACCAS (National Accrediting Commission of Cosmetology Arts & Sciences) 3015 Colvin St *TF:* 877-212-5752 ■ *Web:* www.naccas.org	Alexandria	VA	22314	703-600-7600	379-2200	48-1
NACCC (National Association of Congregational Christian Churches) 8473 S Howell Ave *TF:* 800-262-1620 ■ *Web:* www.naccc.org	Oak Creek	WI	53154	414-764-1620	764-0319	48-20
NACCO Industries Inc 5875 Landerbrook Dr Ste 220 *NYSE: NC* ■ *TF:* 877-756-5118 ■ *Web:* nacco.com	Cleveland	OH	44124	440-229-5151		185
NACD (National Association of Conservation Districts NACD) 509 Capitol Ct Ne *Web:* www.nacdnet.org	Washington	DC	20002	202-547-6223	547-6450	49-7
NACDA (NA of Collegiate Directors of Athletics) 24651 Detroit Rd *TF:* 877-887-2261 ■ *Web:* www.nacda.com	Westlake	OH	44145	440-892-4000	892-4007	48-22
NACDA (Collegiate Directories Inc) PO Box 450640 *TF:* 800-426-2232 ■ *Web:* www.collegiatedirectories.com	Cleveland	OH	44145	440-835-1172	835-8835	637-2
NACDS (National Association of Chain Drug Stores) 413 N Lee St *TF:* 800-678-6223 ■ *Web:* www.nacds.org	Alexandria	VA	22314	703-549-3001	836-4869	49-18
NACE (NA of Colleges & Employers) 62 Highland Ave *TF:* 800-544-5272 ■ *Web:* www.naceweb.org	Bethlehem	PA	18017	610-868-1421		49-5
NACE (National Association for Catering & Events) 10440 Little Patuxent Pkwy Ste 300 *Web:* www.nace.net	Columbia	MD	21046	410-290-5410	630-5768	49-6
NACE International: Corrosion Society 1440 S Creek Dr *TF:* 800-797-6223 ■ *Web:* www.nace.org	Houston	TX	77084	281-228-6200	228-6300	49-13
Nacel Open Door Inc 380 Jackson St Ste 200 *Web:* www.nacelopendoor.org	Saint Paul	MN	55101	651-686-0080		148
NACFAM (National Council for Advanced Mfg) 2025 M St NW Ste 800 *Web:* www.nacfam.org	Washington	DC	20036	202-367-1247	429-2422	49-12
NACHA - Electronic Payments Assn 2550 Wasser Terr Ste 400 *TF:* 800-487-9180 ■ *Web:* www.nacha.org	Herndon	VA	20171	703-561-1100	787-0996	49-2
NACHER Corp, The 111 E Angus Dr *Web:* www.nacher.net	Youngsville	LA	70592	337-856-9144		667
Nachi America Inc 715 Pushville Rd *TF:* 888-340-2747 ■ *Web:* www.nachiamerica.com	Greenwood	IN	46143	317-530-1001	530-1011	75
Nachi Robotic Systems Inc 22285 Roethel Dr *Web:* www.nachirobotics.com	Novi	MI	48375	248-305-6545	305-6542	385

Company	Address	City	State	Zip	Phone	Fax	Class	TF / Web
Nachi Technology Inc	713 Pushville Rd/700 N	Greenwood	IN	46143	317-535-5000		247	Web: www.nachitech.com
Nacho Mama's	2907 O'donnell St	Baltimore	MD	21224	410-675-0898		671	Web: www.nachomamasmd.com
Na-Churs/Alpine Solutions	421 Leader St	Marion	OH	43302	740-382-5701	383-2615	280	TF: 800-622-4877 ■ Web: www.nachurs.com
NACM Connect	3005 Tollview Dr	Rolling Meadows	IL	60008	847-483-6400	253-6685	138	TF: 800-935-6226 ■ Web: www.nacmconnect.org
NACM Gulf States	10887 S Wilcrest Dr	Houston	TX	77099	281-228-6100		218	TF: 866-252-6226 ■ Web: www.nacmgs.org
NACO Industries Inc	2100 Main St	Logan	UT	84341	435-753-8020	752-7041	601	TF: 800-445-4151 ■ Web: www.nacopvc.com
Nacogdoches Convention & Visitors Bureau	200 E Main St	Nacogdoches	TX	75961	936-564-7351		206	TF: 888-564-7351 ■ Web: www.visitnacogdoches.org
Nacogdoches County	101 W Main St Ste 230	Nacogdoches	TX	75961	936-560-7789	560-7809	338	Web: www.co.nacogdoches.tx.us
Nacogdoches County Chamber of Commerce	2516 N St	Nacogdoches	TX	75965	936-560-5533	560-3920	139	Web: www.nacogdoches.org
Nacogdoches Medical Ctr	4920 NE Stallings Dr	Nacogdoches	TX	75965	936-569-9481		374-3	TF: 866-898-8446 ■ Web: www.nacmedicalcenter.com
Nacogdoches Memorial Hospital	1204 N Mound St	Nacogdoches	TX	75961	936-564-4611	568-8588	374-3	Web: nacmem.org
Nacogdoches Public Library	1112 N St	Nacogdoches	TX	75961	936-559-2970		434-3	Web: www.ci.nacogdoches.tx.us
NACS (National Association of College Stores)	500 E Lorain St	Oberlin	OH	44074	440-775-7777	775-4769	49-18	TF: 800-622-7498 ■ Web: www.nacs.org
NACS (NA of Convenience Stores)	1600 Duke St 7th Fl	Alexandria	VA	22314	703-684-3600	836-4564	49-18	TF: 800-966-6227 ■ Web: www.convenience.org
NACWA (National Association of Clean Water Agencies)	1816 Jefferson Pl NW	Washington	DC	20036	202-833-2672	833-4657	49-7	TF: 888-267-9505 ■ Web: www.nacwa.org
NADAguides	3186 K Airway Ave	Costa Mesa	CA	92626	800-966-6232		387	TF: 800-966-6232 ■ Web: www.nadaguides.com
NADCA (North American Die Casting Assn)	3250 N Arlington Hts Rd Ste 101	Arlington Heights	IL	60004	847-279-0001	279-0002	49-13	Web: diecasting.org
Nadel Architects	1990 S Bundy Dr Ste 400	Los Angeles	CA	90025	310-826-2100		261	Web: www.nadelarc.com
NADF (National Adrenal Diseases Foundation)	505 Northern Blvd	Great Neck	NY	11021	847-726-9010		48-17	Web: www.nadf.us
Nadim's Downtown Mediterranean Grill	1390 Main St	Springfield	MA	01103	413-737-7373		671	Web: www.nadims.com
Nadine International Inc	2325 Skymark Ave	Mississauga	ON	L4W5A9	905-602-1850	602-1853	261	Web: www.nadineintl.on.ca
Nading Mechanical Inc	11673 N County Rd 775 E	Hope	IN	47246	812-546-6111		610	Web: nadingmechanicalinc.com
Nadler Jerrold (Rep D - NY)	2132 Rayburn House Office Bldg	Washington	DC	20515	202-225-5635	225-6923	342-2	Web: www.nadler.house.gov
NADP (National Association of Dental Plans)	12700 Pk Central Dr Ste 400	Dallas	TX	75251	972-458-6998	458-2258	49-9	Web: www.nadp.org
Nady Systems Inc	6701 Shellmound St	Emeryville	CA	94608	510-652-2411	652-5075	52	Web: www.nady.com
NAEA (National Art Education Assn)	1806 Robert Fulton Dr	Reston	VA	20191	703-860-8000	860-2960	49-5	TF: 800-299-8321 ■ Web: www.arteducators.org
NAED (National Association of Electrical Distributors)	1181 Corporate Lake Dr	Saint Louis	MO	63132	314-991-9000	991-3060	49-18	TF: 888-791-2512 ■ Web: www.naed.org
NAEIR	560 McClure St	Galesburg	IL	61401	309-343-0704		48-5	TF: 800-562-0955 ■ Web: www.naeir.org
NAES Corp	1180 NW Maple St Ste 200	Issaquah	WA	98027	425-961-4700		245	Web: www.naes.com
NAESP (National Association of Elementary School Principals)	1615 Duke St	Alexandria	VA	22314	703-684-3345	548-6021	49-5	TF: 800-386-2377 ■ Web: www.naesp.org
NAF (National Abortion Federation)	1755 Massachusetts Ave NW	Washington	DC	20036	202-667-5881	667-5890	49-8	TF: 800-772-9100 ■ Web: prochoice.org
NAF (National Acupuncture Foundation)	PO Box 137	Chaplin	CT	06235	860-455-4424		637-2	Web: www.nationalacupuncturefoundation.org
NAFCU (National Association of Federally-Insured Credit Unions)	3138 Tenth St N	Arlington	VA	22201	703-522-4770	524-1082	49-2	TF: 800-336-4644 ■ Web: www.nafcu.org
NAFEM (North American Association of Food Equipment Manufacturers)	161 N Clark St Ste 2020	Chicago	IL	60601	312-821-0201	821-0202	49-13	TF: 888-493-5961 ■ Web: www.nafem.org
Naffs	3301C SR-66 Ste 205	Neptune City	NJ	07753	732-922-3218		138	Web: www.naffs.org
Nafis & Young Engineers Inc	1355 Middletown Ave	Northford	CT	06472	203-484-2793	484-7343	261	Web: nafisandyoung.com
NAFSA: Association of International Educators	1307 New York Ave NW 8th Fl	Washington	DC	20005	202-737-3699	737-3657	49-5	Web: www.nafsa.org
NAFWB (National Association of Free Will Baptists Inc)	5233 Mt View Rd	Antioch	TN	37013	615-731-6812	731-0771	48-20	TF: 877-767-7659 ■ Web: www.nafwb.org
Naga Ctr	4423 NE Tillamook St	Portland	OR	97213	503-473-4268		167-3	Web: www.nagacenter.org
Nagase America Holdings Inc	546 Fifth Ave 16th Fl	New York	NY	10036	212-703-1340		146	Web: nagaseamerica.com
Nagel Agency Inc	215 W Sioux Ave	Pierre	SD	57501	605-224-4662	224-8530	390	TF: 800-807-4662 ■ Web: nagelagency.com
Nagel Chase Inc	2323 Delaney Rd	Gurnee	IL	60031	800-323-4552		350	TF: 800-323-4552 ■ Web: paysoncasters.com
Nagel Gun & Sports Shop	6201 San Pedro Ave	San Antonio	TX	78216	210-342-5420		711	Web: nagelsguns.net
Nagel Paper Inc	6437 W Lennon Rd	Swartz Creek	MI	48473	810-644-7043	644-7215	559	TF: 800-292-3654 ■ Web: www.nagelpaper.com
Nagelbush Mechanical Inc	1800 NW 49th St Ste 110	Fort Lauderdale	FL	33309	954-736-3000	748-7881	189-10	Web: www.nagelbush.com
NAGGL (National Association of Government Guaranteed Lenders)	215 E Ninth Ave	Stillwater	OK	74074	405-377-4022	377-3931	49-2	Web: www.naggl.org
Nagle & Assoc	380 Knollwood St Ste 320	Winston-Salem	NC	27103	336-723-4500		428	TF: 800-411-1583 ■ Web: www.naglefirm.com
Nagle & Zaller PC	7226 Lee Deforest Dr Ste 102	Columbia	MD	21046	410-740-8100		41	Web: naglezaller.com
Nagle Paving Co	39525 W 13 Mile Rd 300	Novi	MI	48377	248-553-0600	553-0669	188-4	Web: www.naglepaving.com
Nagle Pumps Inc	1249 Center Ave	Chicago Heights	IL	60411	708-754-2940	754-2944	641	Web: www.naglepumps.com
Nagoya Japanese Restaurant	1155 W Arbrook Blvd	Arlington	TX	76015	817-466-3688	466-3684	671	Web: www.txnagoya.com
Nags Head Art Inc	2500 Maritime Woods Dr	Manteo	NC	27954	252-475-9891	246-7014*	637-2	*Fax Area Code: 800 ■ TF: 800-541-2722
Nagy & Croniser CPA'S LLP	5564 Woodlawn Ave	Lowville	NY	13367	315-376-6518		2	
Nahan Printing Inc	7000 Saukview Dr PO Box 697	Saint Cloud	MN	56302	320-251-7611	259-1378	627	Web: www.nahan.com
NAHB Research Ctr	400 Prince Georges Blvd	Upper Marlboro	MD	20774	301-249-4000	430-6180	668	TF: 800-638-8556 ■ Web: www.homeinnovation.com
NAHC (NA for Home Care & Hospice)	228 Seventh St SE	Washington	DC	20003	202-547-7424	547-3540	49-8	Web: www.nahc.org
Nahon, Saharovich & Trotz PLC	488 S Menhenhall Rd	Memphis	TN	38117	901-683-7000		428	TF: 800-529-4004 ■ Web: www.nstlaw.com
Nai Hunneman	303 Congress St	Boston	MA	02210	617-457-3400		652	Web: www.naihunneman.com
NAI Southern Real Estate Inc	4201 Congress St Ste 170	Charlotte	NC	28209	704-375-1000	375-2384	652	Web: www.srenc.com
NAI/Merin Hunter Codman Inc	1601 Forum Pl Ste 700	West Palm Beach	FL	33401	561-471-8000	640-7855	652	Web: www.mhcreal.com
NAIA (National Association of Intercollegiate Athletics)	1200 Grand Blvd	Kansas City	MO	64106	816-595-8000	595-8200	48-22	Web: www.naia.org
NAICS (North American Industry Classification System)	US Census Bureau 4600 Silver Hill Rd	Washington	DC	20233	301-763-4636		340-2	TF: 800-923-8282 ■ Web: www.census.gov
NAICU (NA of Independent Colleges & Universities)	1025 Connecticut Ave NW Ste 700	Washington	DC	20036	202-785-8866		49-5	Web: www.naicu.edu
NAIFA (NA of Insurance & Financial Advisors)	2901 Telestar Ct	Falls Church	VA	22042	703-770-8100		49-9	Web: www.naifa.org
NAIGSO-AA (Native American Indian General Service Office of Alcoholics Anonymous)	PO Box 838	Rogersville	AL	35652	951-927-2626		48-21	Web: www.naigso-aa.org
NAIHC (National American Indian Housing Council)	122 C S NW Ste 350	Washington	DC	20001	202-789-1754	789-1758	49-7	TF: 800-284-9165 ■ Web: www.naihc.net
Naik Consulting Group p C	200 Metroplex Dr Ste 403	Edison	NJ	08817	732-777-0030		261	Web: naikgroup.com
NAIL	63 Eddy St	Providence	RI	02903	401-331-6245		7	Web: www.nail.cc
Nail Emporium	1221 N Lakeview Ave	Anaheim	CA	92807	714-779-9889		76	Web: www.nailemporium.com
Nail Mckinney Professional Assn	110 Madison St	Tupelo	MS	38802	662-842-6475		2	Web: nmcpa.com
Nailor Industries Inc	98 Toryork Rd	Toronto	ON	M9L1X6	416-744-3300	744-3360	610	Web: nailor.com
NAIMA (North American Insulation Manufacturers Assn)	44 Canal Center Plz Ste 310	Alexandria	VA	22314	703-684-0084	684-0427	49-3	Web: insulationinstitute.org
Naimies Beauty Center Inc	12640 Riverside Dr	Valley Village	CA	91607	818-655-9933		77	Web: www.naimies.com
Naismith Memorial Basketball Hall of Fame	1000 Hall of Fame Ave	Springfield	MA	01105	413-781-6500		522	TF: 877-446-6752 ■ Web: www.hoophall.com
Najafi Companies LLC	2525 E Camelback Rd	Phoenix	AZ	85016	602-476-0600		360-3	Web: najafi.com
Najarian Furniture Company Inc	265 N Euclid Ave	Pasadena	CA	91101	888-781-3088		320	TF: 888-781-3088 ■ Web: www.najarianfurniture.com
Nakama Japanese Steakhouse	1611 E Carson St	Pittsburgh	PA	15203	412-381-6000	381-6643	671	Web: www.eatatnakama.com
Nakanishi Dental Laboratory Inc	2959 Northup Way	Bellevue	WA	98004	425-822-2245		415	TF: 800-735-7231 ■ Web: www.nakanishidentallab.com

	Phone	Fax	Class
Nakase Brothers Wholesale Nursery 9441 Krepp Dr ... Huntington Beach CA 92646 *TF:* 800-747-4388 ■ *Web:* www.nakasebros.com	949-855-4388		292
Nakato 1776 Cheshire Bridge Rd NE ... Atlanta GA 30324 *Web:* nakatorestaurant.com	404-873-6582	874-7897	671
Naked Oyster Bistro & Raw Bar 410 Main St ... Hyannis MA 02601 *Web:* www.nakedoyster.com	508-778-6500		671
Nakisa Inc 733 Cathcart ... Montreal QC H3B1M6 *Web:* www.nakisa.com	514-228-2000		177
NAKIVO Inc 4894 Sparks Blvd ... Sparks NV 89436 *Web:* www.nakivo.com	702-605-4495		178-8
Naknek Electric Association Inc 1 School Rd ... Naknek AK 99633 *Web:* naknekelectric.com	907-246-4261		245
NAL 10416 Investment Cir ... Rancho Cordova CA 95670 *TF:* 800-774-9555 ■ *Web:* nal1.com	916-361-0555		192
NAL Group 241 Main St 5th Fl ... Buffalo NY 14203 *Web:* www.installs.com	716-854-1994		681
NALC (National Association of Letter Carriers) 100 Indiana Ave NW ... Washington DC 20001 *TF:* 800-424-5186 ■ *Web:* www.nalc.org	202-393-4695	737-1540	414
Nalco Co 1601 W Diehl Rd ... Naperville IL 60563 *TF:* 800-288-0879 ■ *Web:* www.ecolab.com	630-305-1000	305-2900	145
NALF (North American Limousin Foundation) 6 Inverness Ct E Ste 260 ... Englewood CO 80112 *TF:* 888-320-8747 ■ *Web:* nalf.org	303-220-1693	220-1884	48-2
Nalley Lexus Smyrna 2750 Cobb Pkwy SE ... Smyrna GA 30080 *TF:* 877-454-4206 ■ *Web:* www.nalleylexussmyrna.com	877-454-4206		57
Nalpro Business Solutions LLC Brier Hill Ct Bldg C ... East Brunswick NJ 08816 *TF:* 888-693-6800 ■ *Web:* www.nalpro.com	732-390-1400		178-1
NALS - Association for Legal Professionals 8159 E 41st St ... Tulsa OK 74145 *Web:* www.nals.org	918-582-5188	582-5907	49-10
NAM (National Arbitration & Mediation) 990 Stewart Ave 1st Fl ... Garden City NY 11530 **Fax Area Code:* 516 ■ *TF:* 800-358-2550 ■ *Web:* www.namadr.com	800-358-2550	794-8518*	41
NAMA (National Automatic Merchandising Assn) 20 N Wacker Dr Ste 3500 ... Chicago IL 60606 *Web:* www.namanow.org	312-346-0370	704-4140	49-18
NAMA (North American Millers Assn) 600 Maryland Ave SW Ste 825-W ... Washington DC 20024 *Web:* www.namamillers.org	202-484-2200	488-7416	49-6
NAMA (National Agri-Marketing Assn) 11020 King St Ste 205 ... Overland Park KS 66210 *Web:* nama.org	913-491-6500	491-6502	49-18
Nama Sushi Bar 506 S Gay St ... Knoxville TN 37902 **Fax Area Code:* 615 ■ *Web:* namasushibar.com	865-633-8539	739-5819*	671
Namaste Indian Cuisine 6300 NE 117th Ave ... Vancouver WA 98662 *Web:* www.hstrial-namasteindiac.homestead.com	360-891-5857	891-5906	671
Namco Manufacturing Inc 1651 Blalock Rd ... Houston TX 77080 **Fax Area Code:* 713 ■ *TF:* 800-634-5816 ■ *Web:* www.namcomfg.com	800-634-5816	932-7605*	806
NAMCP 4435 Waterfront Dr Ste 101 ... Glen Allen VA 23060 *Web:* namcp.org	804-527-1905	747-5316	49-8
Name Brands Inc 7215 S Memorial Dr ... Tulsa OK 74133 *Web:* www.halfofhalf.com	918-307-0289		157-2
Name Maker Inc 4450 Commerce Cir PO Box 43821 ... Atlanta GA 30336 *TF:* 800-241-2890 ■ *Web:* www.namemaker.com	404-691-2237	691-7711	745-5
Namecheap Inc 11400 W Olympic Blvd Ste 200 ... Los Angeles CA 90064 *Web:* www.namecheap.com	310-259-3259		224
Namecom LLC 414 14th St Ste 200 ... Denver CO 80202 *Web:* www.name.com	720-249-2374	235-0091	396
Nameplate & Panel Technology 387 Gundersen Dr ... Carol Stream IL 60188 *TF:* 800-833-8397 ■ *Web:* www.nptec.com	630-690-9360		627
Namgis First Nation 49 Atli St PO Box 210 ... Alert Bay BC V0N1A0 *TF:* 888-962-6447 ■ *Web:* www.namgis.bc.ca	250-974-5556		138
NAMI (National Alliance on Mental Illness) 3803 N Fairfax Dr Ste 100 ... Arlington VA 22203 *TF:* 800-950-6264 ■ *Web:* nami.org	703-524-7600	524-9094	48-17
NAMI Connecticut (NAMI-CT) 576 Farmington Ave ... Hartford CT 06105 *TF:* 800-215-3021 ■ *Web:* www.namict.org	860-882-0236	882-0240	48-6
Nami Sushi 251 N First Ave Ste 100 ... Minneapolis MN 55401 *Web:* www.menusearch.net	612-333-1999		671
NAMI-CT (NAMI Connecticut) 576 Farmington Ave ... Hartford CT 06105 *TF:* 800-215-3021 ■ *Web:* www.namict.org	860-882-0236	882-0240	48-6
NAMM 5790 Armada Dr ... Carlsbad CA 92008 *TF:* 800-767-6266 ■ *Web:* www.namm.org	760-438-8001	438-7327	49-18
Nammo Inc 2000 N 14th St Ste 250 ... Arlington VA 22201 *Web:* www.nammo.com	703-524-6100		268
Nampa Chamber of Commerce 315 11th Ave S ... Nampa ID 83651 *Web:* www.nampa.com	208-466-4641	466-4677	139
Nampa Public Library (NPL) 215 12th Ave S ... Nampa ID 83651 *Web:* www.nampalibrary.org	208-468-5800		434-3
NAMS (North American Menopause Society, The) 5900 Landerbrook Dr Ste 390 ... Mayfield Heights OH 44124 *Web:* www.menopause.org	440-442-7550	442-2660	49-8
NAMTI Spa 2120 West Hwy 89A ... Sedona AZ 86336 *Web:* www.namti.com	928-282-7737		167-3
Nan Thai 1350 Spring St NW ... Atlanta GA 30309 *Web:* www.nanfinedining.com	404-870-9933	870-9955	671
NANA Regional Corp 909 W 9th Ave ... Anchorage AK 99501 *TF:* 800-478-2000 ■ *Web:* nana-dev.com	907-265-4100	265-4123	194
NANA Regional Corporation Inc 1001 E Benson Blvd ... Kotzebue AK 99752 *TF:* 800-478-3301 ■ *Web:* www.nana.com	907-442-3301		539
Nana Wall Systems Inc 707 Redwood Hwy ... Mill Valley CA 94941 *TF:* 800-873-5673 ■ *Web:* www.nanawall.com	415-383-3148		499
Nana's 2514 University Dr ... Durham NC 27707 *Web:* www.nanasdurham.com	919-493-8545	403-8487	671
Nanaimo Port Authority 104 Front St PO Box 131 ... Nanaimo BC V9R5H7 *Web:* www.npa.ca	250-753-4146	753-4899	618
Nanavati Consulting Inc 505 Sidehill Dr ... Bel Air MD 21015 *Web:* www.nanavaticonsulting.com	410-421-5184		396
Nance County Nebraska 209 Esther St Po Box 837 ... Fullerton NE 68638 *Web:* www.co.nance.ne.us	308-536-2675	536-2742	338
Nance International Inc 2915 Milam St ... Beaumont TX 77701 *TF:* 877-626-2322 ■ *Web:* nanceinternational.com	409-838-6127		664
Nancy Carol Roberts Memorial Library 100 Martin Luther King Junior Pkwy ... Brenham TX 77833 *Web:* cityofbrenham.org	979-337-7201		434-3
Nancy Chang 372 Chandler St ... Worcester MA 01602 *Web:* nancychang.com	508-752-8899	798-6688	671
Nancy Hoffman Gallery 520 W 27th St ... New York NY 10001 *Web:* www.nancyhoffmangallery.com	212-966-6676	334-5078	42
Nancy Wolfe-Smith Insurance Agency Inc 1797 N University Dr ... Plantation FL 33322 *Web:* nancywolfesmith.com	954-358-2886		390
Nancy Z. Bender Insurance Agency Inc 31 Milk St ... Boston MA 02109 *Web:* nancybenderinsurance.com	617-367-4900		390
Nancy's Homemade Fudge Inc 2684 Jeb Stuart Hwy ... Meadows of Dan VA 24120 *Web:* www.nancyshomemadefudge.com	276-952-2112	952-1042	296-8
Nancy's Pizza 7929 W 171st St ... Tinley Park IL 60477 *Web:* www.nancyspizza.com	708-614-6100		670
Nanka Seimen Co 3030 Leonis Blvd ... Vernon CA 90058 *Web:* nankaseimen.com	323-585-9967	585-9969	296-31
NANN (National Association of Neonatal Nurses) 8735 W Higgins Rd Ste 300 ... Chicago IL 60631 *TF:* 800-451-3795 ■ *Web:* www.nann.org	847-375-3660	375-6491	49-8
Nanney & Son Inc 205 Air Depot Rd E ... Glencoe AL 35905 *Web:* nsicnc.com	256-492-2910	492-2917	493
Nannicola Inc 2750 Salt Springs Rd ... Youngstown OH 44509 *TF:* 800-837-2789 ■ *Web:* www.nannicola.com	800-837-2789		44
Nannis & Associates Inc 505 E Main St ... Buford GA 30519 **Fax Area Code:* 678 ■ *Web:* www.nannis.com	770-614-6114	765-7966*	261
NanOasis Technologies Inc 4677 Meade St Ste 210 ... Richmond CA 94804 *Web:* www.nanoasisinc.fogcitydesign.com	510-215-0186	215-0188	612
Nanocopoeia LLC 1246 W University Ave Ste 463 ... Saint Paul MN 55104 *Web:* nanocopoeia.com	651-209-1184	209-1187	231
Nanohmics Inc 6201 E Oltorf St ... Austin TX 78741 *Web:* www.nanohmics.com	512-389-9990		261
Nanolab Technologies Inc 1708 McCarthy Blvd ... Milpitas CA 95035 *Web:* www.nanolabtechnologies.com	408-433-3320		743
Nanonation Inc 301 S 13th St Ste 700 ... Lincoln NE 68508 *Web:* nanonation.net	402-323-6266		177
Nanophase Technologies Corp 1319 Marquette Dr ... Romeoville IL 60446 *OTC:* NANX ■ *Web:* nanophase.com	630-771-6700	771-0825	145
Nanoscience Instruments Inc 10008 S 51st St Ste 110 ... Phoenix AZ 85044 *Web:* nanoscience.com	480-758-5400		366
NanoScreen 4401 Piggly Wiggly Dr Ste 1000 ... North Charleston SC 29405 *TF:* 800-684-2191 ■ *Web:* www.automatedliquidhandlers.com	843-881-8841		582
Nanosyn 3100 Central Expy ... Santa Clara CA 95051 *Web:* nanosyn.com	408-987-2000	987-2001	743
Nanotechnology Research & Education Ctr (NREC) 4202 E Fowler Ave ... Tampa FL 33620 *Web:* www.nrec.usf.edu	813-974-3780	974-3610	743
Nanotechnology Research Ctr *Georgia Institute of Technology* 791 Atlantic Dr ... Atlanta GA 30332 *Web:* www.ien.gatech.edu	404-894-5100		668
Nanovea 6 Morgan Ste 156 ... Irvine CA 92618 *Web:* nanovea.com	949-461-9292		407
Nanowave Technologies Inc 425 Horner Ave ... Etobicoke ON M8W4W3 *Web:* www.nanowavetech.com	416-252-5602	252-7077	647
Nansemond Insurance Agency Inc 453 W Washington St ... Suffolk VA 23434 *Web:* nansemondins.com	757-539-3421		390
Nantahala Outdoor Ctr (NOC) 13077 Hwy 19 W ... Bryson City NC 28713 *Web:* www.noc.com	828-488-2175	488-2498	239
NantEnergy Inc 8455 N 90th St Ste 4 ... Scottsdale AZ 85258 *Web:* nantenergy.com	480-966-0242		74
Nanticoke Memorial Hospital 801 Middleford Rd ... Seaford DE 19973 *Web:* www.nanticoke.org	302-629-6611		374-3
Nantucket Accommodations 1 Macys Ln ... Nantucket MA 02554 *TF:* 866-743-3330 ■ *Web:* nantucketaccommodations.com	508-228-9559	901-4032	376
Nantucket Bank 104 Pleasant St ... Nantucket MA 02554 *TF:* 800-533-9313 ■ *Web:* www.nantucketbank.com	508-228-0580		70
Nantucket County 16 Broad St ... Nantucket MA 02554 *Web:* www.nantucket-ma.gov	508-228-7216	325-5313	338
Nantucket Historical Assn 15 Broad St PO Box 1016 ... Nantucket MA 02554 *Web:* www.nha.org	508-228-1894		48-5
Nantucket Looms LLC 51 Main St ... Nantucket MA 02554 *Web:* nantucketlooms.com	508-228-1908		362
Nantze Springs Inc PO Box 1273 ... Dothan AL 36301 *Web:* nantzesprings.com	334-794-4218		297-11
Nanuet Public Library 149 Church St ... Nanuet NY 10954 *Web:* nanuetpubliclibrary.org	845-623-4281		435
Nanz & Kraft Florists Inc 141 Breckenridge Ln ... Louisville KY 40207 *TF:* 800-897-6551 ■ *Web:* www.nanzandkraft.com	502-897-6551	897-2082	292

				Phone	Fax	Class
NAO Inc 1284 E Sedgley Ave TF: 800-523-3495 ■ Web: www.nao.com	Philadelphia	PA	19134	215-743-5300	743-3018	18
Naos Graphics Inc 103 Edgevale Rd Web: www.naosgraphics.com	Baltimore	MD	21210	410-435-0031	435-1849	130
NAP (National Association of Parliamentarians) 213 S Main St TF: 888-627-2929 ■ Web: www.parliamentarians.org	Independence	MO	64050	816-833-3892	833-3893	49-12
NAP Windows & Doors Ltd 2150 Enterprise Way TF: 888-762-5311 ■ Web: www.napwindows.com	Kelowna	BC	V1Y6H7	250-762-5343		601
NAPA (National Automotive Parts Assn) 2999 Circle 75 Pkwy Web: genpt.com	Atlanta	GA	30339	770-953-1700		61
Napa Chamber of Commerce 1556 1st St Ste 104 Web: www.napachamber.com	Napa	CA	94559	707-226-7455		139
Napa County 1195 Third St Ste 310 Web: www.countyofnapa.org	Napa	CA	94559	707-253-4421	253-4176	338
Napa Jet Ctr 2030 Airport Rd TF: 800-229-6272 ■ Web: www.napajetcenter.com	Napa	CA	94558	707-224-0887	257-7770	167-3
Napa Printing 630 Airpark Rd Ste D Web: www.napaprinting.com	Napa	CA	94558	707-257-6555	257-3295	627
Napa Recycling & Waste Services (NRWS) 820 Levitin Way PO Box 239 Web: www.naparecycling.com	Napa	CA	94559	707-256-3500	256-3565	804
Napa River Inn 500 Main St TF: 877-251-8500 ■ Web: www.napariverinn.com	Napa	CA	94559	707-251-8500		379
Napa State Hospital 2100 Napa-Vallejo Hwy TF: 866-327-4762 ■ Web: www.dsh.ca.gov	Napa	CA	94558	707-253-5000	253-5513	374-5
NAPA Transportation Inc 4800 E Trindle Rd Web: www.napatran.com	Mechanicsburg	PA	17050	717-920-9840		780
Napa Valley Aloft Inc 6525 Washington St Web: www.nvaloft.com	Yountville	CA	94599	707-944-4400	944-4406	13
Napa Valley Balloon Inc 4086 Byway E TF: 800-253-2224 ■ Web: www.napavalleyballoons.com	Napa	CA	94558	707-944-0228		239
Napa Valley College 2277 Napa-Vallejo Hwy TF: 800-826-1077 ■ Web: www.napavalley.edu	Napa	CA	94558	707-256-7000	253-3064	162
Napa Valley Conference & Visitors Bureau 600 Main St TF: 855-847-6272 ■ Web: www.visitnapavalley.com	Napa	CA	94559	707-251-5895		206
Napa Valley Register 1615 Second St TF: 877-433-5056 ■ Web: napavalleyregister.com	Napa	CA	94559	707-226-3711		532-2
Napa Wealth Management Inc 1836 Second St Web: napawealth.com	Napa	CA	94559	707-252-1343		690
Napaba 1612 K St NW Ste 1400 Web: www.napaba.org	Washington	DC	20006	202-775-9555	775-9333	533
NAPAC Inc 229 Southbridge St Web: www.napacinc.com	Worcester	MA	01608	508-363-4411		609
NAPCO (North American Publishing Co) 1500 Springarden St 12th Fl TF: 800-627-2689 ■ Web: www.napco.com	Philadelphia	PA	19130	215-238-5300	238-5457	637-9
NAPCO 2400 Cantrell Rd Ste 116 Web: www.napcolr.com	Little Rock	AR	72202	501-374-5884		559
NAPCO Inc 120 Trojan Ave TF: 800-854-8621 ■ Web: www.napcousa.com	Sparta	NC	28675	800-854-8621		86
NAPCO International Inc 11055 Excelsior Blvd Web: www.napcointl.com	Hopkins	MN	55343	952-931-2400	931-2402	807
NAPCO Precast LLC 6949 Low Bid Ln Web: www.napcosa.com	San Antonio	TX	78250	210-509-9100	509-9111	183
NAPCO Security Systems Inc 333 Bayview Ave NASDAQ: NSSC ■ TF: 800-645-9445 ■ Web: www.napcosecurity.com	Amityville	NY	11701	631-842-9400	842-9137	692
Napco Steel Inc 1800 Arthur Dr TF: 800-292-8010 ■ Web: www.napcosteel.com	West Chicago	IL	60185	630-293-1900	293-0881	492
NAPEO (NA of Professional Employer Organizations) 707 N St Asaph St Web: www.napeo.org	Alexandria	VA	22314	703-836-0466	836-0976	49-12
Naperville Area Chamber of Commerce 55 S Main St Ste 351 Web: www.naperville.net	Naperville	IL	60540	630-355-4141	355-8335	139
Naperville Public Libraries 200 W Jefferson Ave Web: www.naperville-lib.org	Naperville	IL	60540	630-961-4100		434-3
NAPF (Nuclear Age Peace Foundation) 1622 Anacapa St Web: www.wagingpeace.org	Santa Barbara	CA	93101	805-965-3443	568-0466	48-5
NaphCare Inc 2090 Columbiana Rd Ste 4000 TF: 800-834-2420 ■ Web: www.naphcare.com	Birmingham	AL	35216	205-536-8400	536-8401	352
Napi Inc 2154 W Northwest Hwy Ste 212 Web: www.napiinc.com	Dallas	TX	75220	972-401-7488		4
Napili Kai Beach Club 5900 Honoapiilani Rd TF: 800-367-5030 ■ Web: www.napilikai.com	Lahaina	HI	96761	808-669-6271	669-5740	669
Naples Bay Resort 1500 Fifth Ave S TF: 866-605-1199 ■ Web: naplesbayresort.com	Naples	FL	34102	239-530-1199		669
Naples Beach Hotel & Golf Club 851 Gulf Shore Blvd N TF: 800-237-7600 ■ Web: www.naplesbeachhotel.com	Naples	FL	34102	239-261-2222	261-7380	669
Naples Botanical Garden 4820 Bayshore Dr TF: 877-433-1874 ■ Web: www.naplesgarden.org	Naples	FL	34112	239-643-7275	649-7306	97
Naples Daily News 1100 Immokalee Rd TF: 800-404-7343 ■ Web: www.naplesnews.com	Naples	FL	34110	239-213-6000		532-2
Naples Grande Beach Resort 475 Seagate Dr TF: 844-993-9576 ■ Web: www.naplesgrande.com	Naples	FL	34103	239-227-2182		379
Naples Italian Restaurant 5500 Kingston Pk Web: naplesitalianrestaurant.net	Knoxville	TN	37919	865-584-5033		671
Naples Lumber & Supply Company Inc 3828 Radio Rd Web: www.napleslumber.com	Naples	FL	34104	239-643-7000		364
Naples Municipal Airport 160 Aviation Dr N Web: www.flynaples.com	Naples	FL	34104	239-643-0733	643-4084	27
Naples/Fort Myers Greyhound Track 10601 Bonita Beach Rd Web: www.naplesfortmyersdogs.com	Bonita Springs	FL	34135	239-992-2411		642
Napleton Hyundai Glenview 1620 Waukegan Rd Web: www.napletonhyundaiglenview.com	Glenview	IL	60025	847-558-7801		516
Napo Pharmaceuticals Inc 201 Mission St Ste 2375 TF: 844-722-8256 ■ Web: www.napopharma.com	San Francisco	CA	94105	415-963-9938		582
Napoleon/Henry County Chamber of Commerce 611 N Perry St TF: 800-322-6849 ■ Web: henrycountychamber.org	Napoleon	OH	43545	419-592-1786	592-4945	139
Napoli Italian Restaurant 24960 Redlands Blvd Web: www.napolilomalinda.com	Loma Linda	CA	92354	909-796-3770	478-7756	671
Napolitano Grace (Rep D - CA) 1610 Longworth House Office Bldg Web: napolitano.house.gov	Washington	DC	20515	202-225-5256	225-0027	342-2
Napp Technologies LLC 401 Hackensack Ave Web: www.napptech.com	Hackensack	NJ	07601	201-843-4664	843-4737	582
Nappi Distributors 615 Main St Web: www.nappidistributors.com	Gorham	ME	04038	207-887-8200		186
Naprotek Inc 90 Rose Orchard Way Web: www.naprotek.com	San Jose	CA	95134	408-830-5000	830-5050	625
NAPS (North American Production Sharing Inc) 517 S Cedros Ave TF: 800-551-8581 ■ Web: www.napsintl.com	Solana Beach	CA	92075	858-794-7947		194
NARA (National Archives & Records Administration) 8601 Adelphi Rd *Fax Area Code: 301 ■ TF: 866-272-6272 ■ Web: www.archives.gov	College Park	MD	20740	866-272-6272	837-0483*	340-20
Nara Sushi 1115 Independence Blvd Ste 104 Web: www.narasushi.com	Virginia Beach	VA	23455	757-456-5111	490-0109	671
NARAL Pro-Choice America 1156 15th St NW Ste 700 Web: www.prochoiceamerica.org	Washington	DC	20005	202-973-3000	973-3096	48-8
NARBHA (Northern Arizona Regional Behavioral Health Authority Inc) 1300 S Yale St TF: 877-923-1400 ■ Web: www.narbha.org	Flagstaff	AZ	86001	928-774-7128		49-15
Narcolepsy Network Inc PO Box 2178 Ste A212 TF: 888-292-6522 ■ Web: narcolepsynetwork.org	Lynnwood	WA	98036	401-667-2523	633-6567	48-17
Narda-MITEQ 100 Davids Dr Web: nardamiteq.com	Hauppauge	NY	11788	631-436-7400	436-7430	253
Nardella Inc 6700 Essington Ave Ste G4-G6 TF: 800-486-1980 ■ Web: www.nardellainc.com	Philadelphia	PA	19153	215-336-1558	336-5757	297-7
Nardin Academy 135 Cleveland Ave Web: www.nardin.org	Buffalo	NY	14222	716-881-6262		148
Nardini Fire Equipment Company Inc 405 County Rd E W TF: 888-627-3464 ■ Web: nardinifire.com	Saint Paul	MN	55126	651-483-6631	483-6945	679
Nardone Bros Baking Company Inc 420 New Commerce Blvd TF: 800-822-5320 ■ Web: nardonebros.com	Wilkes-Barre	PA	18706	570-823-0141	823-2581	296-36
Nareit 1875 'I' St NW Ste 600 TF: 800-362-7348 ■ Web: www.reit.com	Washington	DC	20006	202-739-9400	739-9401	615
NAREL (National Air & Radiation Environmental Laboratory) 540 S Morris Ave Web: www.epa.gov	Montgomery	AL	36115	334-270-3401	270-3454	743
NARF (Native American Rights Fund) 1506 Broadway TF: 888-280-0726 ■ Web: www.narf.org	Boulder	CO	80302	303-447-8760	443-7776	49-10
NARH (North Adams Regional Hospital) 71 Hospital Ave Web: www.nbhealth.org	North Adams	MA	01247	413-664-5000		374-3
NARIC (National Rehabilitation Information Ctr) 8400 Corporate Dr Ste 500 TF: 800-346-2742 ■ Web: www.naric.com	Landover Hills	MD	20785	301-459-5900	459-4263	48-17
Narita Trading Company Inc 24 Park Ave Web: www.naritatrading.com	Clifton	NJ	07014	973-777-2288	777-3288	290
NARM (North Alabama Railroad Museum Inc) 694 Chase Rd NE Web: northalabamarailroadmuseum.com	Huntsville	AL	35811	256-851-6276		520
Naropa University 2130 Arapahoe Ave TF: 800-772-6951 ■ Web: www.naropa.edu	Boulder	CO	80302	303-444-0202	546-3536	166
Narragansett Bay Commission 1 Service Rd Web: www.narrabay.com	Providence	RI	02905	401-461-8848		539
Narragansett Improvement Co 223 Allens Ave Web: www.nicori.com	Providence	RI	02903	401-331-7420	351-6444	653
Narricot Industries LP 1556 Montgomery St	South Hill	VA	23970	215-322-3900		745-5
Narrow Fabric Industries Corp 701 Reading Ave TF: 877-523-6373 ■ Web: www.readingeagle.com	Reading	PA	19611	610-376-2891		745-5
Narrow Gate Foundation 242 Dry Prong Rd Web: narrowgate.org	Williamsport	TN	38487	931-583-0633		305
NARSA (National Automotive Radiator Service Assn) 3000 Village Run Rd Ste 103 221 Web: www.narsa.org	Wexford	PA	15090	724-799-8415	799-8416	49-21
Nartron Corp 5000 N US 131 Web: www.nartron.com	Reed City	MI	49677	231-832-5525	832-3876	248
NAS (National Audubon Society) 225 Varick St TF: 800-274-4201 ■ Web: www.audubon.org	New York	NY	10014	212-979-3000	979-3188	48-13
NAS Recruitment Communications 9700 Rockside Rd Ste 170 TF: 866-627-7327 ■ Web: www.nasrecruitment.com	Cleveland	OH	44125	216-503-9001		4

Name / Address	City	State	ZIP	Phone	Fax	Class
NASA Pennsylvania Space Grant Consortium, The 2217 Earth-Engineering Sciences Bldg *Web:* sites.psu.edu	University Park	PA	16802	814-863-7688	863-9563	167-3
NASA TV 300 E St SW ste 1J20 *Web:* www.nasa.gov	Washington	DC	20546	202-358-0000	358-4338	740
NASAA (North American Securities Administrators Assn) 750 First St NE Ste 1140 *Web:* www.nasaa.org	Washington	DC	20002	202-737-0900	783-3571	49-2
NASAA (National Assembly of State Arts Agencies) 1029 Vermont Ave NW 2nd Fl. *Web:* nasaa-arts.org	Washington	DC	20005	202-347-6352	737-0526	49-7
NASB (North American Savings Bank) 12520 S 71 Hwy *TF:* 800-677-6272 ■ *Web:* www.nasb.com	Grandview	MO	64030	816-765-2200		70
NASBE (National Association of State Boards of Education) 333 John Carlyle St Ste 530 *TF:* 800-899-6693 ■ *Web:* www.nasbe.org	Alexandria	VA	22314	703-684-4000		49-5
NASBP (National Association of Surety Bond Producers) 1140 19th St NW Ste 800 *Web:* www.nasbp.org	Washington	DC	20036	202-686-3700	686-3656	49-9
NASCAR (National Association for Stock Car Auto Racing Inc) 1801 W International Speedway Blvd *Web:* www.nascar.com	Daytona Beach	FL	32114	704-348-7131		48-22
NASCAR Hall of Fame 400 E Martin Luther King Jr Blvd *TF:* 888-902-6463 ■ *Web:* www.nascarhall.com	Charlotte	NC	28202	704-654-4400		522
NASCAR SpeedPark 1545 Pkwy *Web:* nascarspeedpark.com	Sevierville	TN	37862	865-908-5500		32
Nasco Aircraft Brake Inc 13300 Estrella Ave *Web:* www.nascoaircraft.com	Gardena	CA	90248	310-532-4430	532-6014	22
NASCO International Inc 901 Janesville Ave *TF:* 800-558-9595 ■ *Web:* www.enasco.com	Fort Atkinson	WI	53538	920-563-2446	563-8296	459
Nasdaq Stock Market Inc 165 Broadway *Web:* www.nasdaq.com	New York	NY	10006	212-401-8700		691
NASFAA (National Association of Student Financial Aid Administrators) 1801 Pennsylvania Avenue NW Ste 850 *Web:* www.nasfaa.org	Washington	DC	20006	202-785-0453	785-1487	49-5
Nash Academy 857 Lane Allen Rd. *TF:* 888-491-2064 ■ *Web:* www.nashacademy.com	Lexington	KY	40504	859-277-7217	277-1977	167-3
Nash Brick Co 532 Nash Brick Rd *Web:* www.nashbrick.com	Enfield	NC	27823	252-443-4965	446-7398	751
Nash Chevrolet Co 630 Scenic Hwy *Web:* www.nashchevy.com	Lawrenceville	GA	30046	770-822-6678		516
Nash Community College PO Box 7488 *Web:* www.nashcc.edu	Rocky Mount	NC	27804	252-443-4011		162
Nash Correctional Institution 2869 US 64 Alt PO Box 600 *Web:* www.ncdps.gov	Nashville	NC	27856	252-459-4455	459-7728	213
Nash County 120 W Washington St Ste 3072 *Web:* www.co.nash.nc.us	Nashville	NC	27856	252-459-9800	459-9817	338
Nash Entertainment 1438 N Gower St Ste 35 *Web:* www.nashentertainment.com	Los Angeles	CA	90028	323-993-7384		514
Nash Produce Co 6160 S N Carolina 58 *TF:* 800-334-3032 ■ *Web:* www.nashproduce.com	Nashville	NC	27856	800-334-3032		10-11
Nashbar 6103 State Rte 446 *TF:* 800-627-4227 ■ *Web:* www.nashbar.com	Canfield	OH	44406	800-627-4227		459
Nasher Sculpture Ctr 2001 Flora St *Web:* www.nashersculpturecenter.org	Dallas	TX	75201	214-242-5100	242-5155	50-2
Nashoba Regional School District 50 Mechanic St. *Web:* www.nrsd.net	Bolton	MA	01740	978-779-0539		685
Nashoba Valley Chamber of Commerce 2 Shaker Rd Ste B200 *Web:* www.nvcoc.com	Shirley	MA	01464	978-425-5761	425-5764	139
Nashotah House 2777 Mission Rd *Web:* www.nashotah.edu	Nashotah	WI	53058	262-646-6500	646-6504	167-3
Nashua Community College 505 Amherst St. *Web:* www.nashuacc.edu	Nashua	NH	03063	603-578-8900	882-8690	162
Nashua Homes of Idaho Inc PO Box 170008 *TF:* 855-766-0222 ■ *Web:* www.nashuabuilders.com	Boise	ID	83717	208-345-0222		505
Nashua Public Library 2 Court St *Web:* www.nashualibrary.org	Nashua	NH	03060	603-589-4600	594-3457	434-3
Nashville & Davidson County Metropolitan City Hall 100 Metropolitan Courthouse *Web:* www.nashville.gov	Nashville	TN	37201	615-862-6000	862-6040	337
Nashville Ballet 3630 Redmon St. *Web:* www.nashvilleballet.com	Nashville	TN	37209	615-297-2966	297-9972	573-1
Nashville Chamber of Commerce 211 Commerce St Ste 100 *Web:* www.nashvillechamber.com	Nashville	TN	37201	615-743-3000		139
Nashville Convention & Visitors Bureau (NCVB) 150 Fourth Ave N Ste G250 *TF:* 800-657-6910 ■ *Web:* www.visitmusiccity.com	Nashville	TN	37219	615-259-4730	259-4126	206
Nashville Convention Ctr 201 Fifth Ave S *Web:* www.nashvilleconventionctr.com	Nashville	TN	37203	615-742-2000		205
Nashville Dental Inc 1229 Northgate Business Pkwy *Web:* nashvilledental.com	Madison	TN	37115	615-868-3911		475
Nashville Display 306 Hartmann Dr *TF:* 800-251-1150 ■ *Web:* www.nashvilledisplay.com	Lebanon	TN	37087	615-743-2900		233
Nashville Film Festival 161 Rains Ave. *Web:* nashvillefilmfestival.org	Nashville	TN	37203	615-742-2500		282
Nashville General Hospital 1818 Albion St *Web:* www.nashville.gov	Nashville	TN	37208	615-341-4000	341-4493	374-3
Nashville Jet 635 Hangar Ln *Web:* www.nashvillejetcharters.com	Nashville	TN	37217	615-933-7894		13
Nashville Municipal Auditorium 417 Fourth Ave N *Web:* www.nashville.gov	Nashville	TN	37201	615-862-6390	862-6394	572
Nashville National Cemetery 1420 Gallatin Rd S *Web:* www.cem.va.gov	Madison	TN	37115	615-860-0086	860-8691	136
Nashville Office Interiors 1621 Church St *TF:* 877-342-0294 ■ *Web:* noifurniture.com	Nashville	TN	37203	615-329-1811		321
Nashville Public Library 615 Church St *Web:* library.nashville.org	Nashville	TN	37219	615-862-5800		434-3
Nashville Ready Mix Inc 605 Cowan St *Web:* www.nashvillereadymix.net	Nashville	TN	37207	615-256-2071		135
Nashville Rescue Mission 639 Lafayette St *Web:* www.nashvillerescuemission.org	Nashville	TN	37203	615-255-2475		48-20
Nashville Rubber & Gasket Company Inc 1900 Elm Tree Dr *Web:* nashvillerubber.com	Nashville	TN	37210	615-883-0030		791
Nashville Scene 210 12th Ave S Ste 100 *Web:* www.nashvillescene.com	Nashville	TN	37203	615-244-7989		532-5
Nashville Shores Holdings LLC 4001 Bell Rd. *Web:* www.nashvilleshores.com	Hermitage	TN	37076	615-889-7050		360-3
Nashville State Community College (NSCC) 120 White Bridge Rd. *TF:* 800-272-7363 ■ *Web:* www.nscc.edu	Nashville	TN	37209	615-353-3333	353-3243	800
Nashville Steel Co 7211 Centennial Blvd *Web:* www.nashvillesteel.com	Nashville	TN	37209	615-350-7933		492
Nashville Tempered Glass Corp 1860 Air Ln Dr *Web:* www.ntglass.com	Nashville	TN	37210	615-889-6350		330
Nashville Wire Products Manufacturing Co 199 Polk Ave. *TF:* 800-448-2125 ■ *Web:* www.nashvillewire.com	Nashville	TN	37210	615-743-2500		73
Nashville Zoo 3777 Nolensville Rd *Web:* www.nashvillezoo.org	Nashville	TN	37211	615-833-1534	333-0728	823
Nasiff Assoc 841-1 County Rt 37 *TF:* 866-627-4332 ■ *Web:* nasiff.com	Central Square	NY	13036	315-676-2346		476
Nasland Engineering 4740 Rufner St. *Web:* nasland.com	San Diego	CA	92111	858-292-7770		261
NASMHPD (National Association of State Mental Health Program Directors) 66 Canal Center Plz Ste 302 *Web:* www.nasmhpd.org	Alexandria	VA	22314	703-739-9333	548-9517	49-7
Nason, Yeager, Gerson, White & Lioce PA 3001 PGA Blvd Ste 305 *Web:* nasonyeager.com	Palm Beach Gardens	FL	33410	561-686-3307	686-5442	428
NASS (North American Spine Society) 7075 Veterans Blvd. *Web:* www.spine.org	Burr Ridge	IL	60527	630-230-3600		49-8
NASS (North American Substation Services LLC) 190 N Westmonte Dr. *Web:* www.nassusa.com	Altamonte Springs	FL	32714	407-788-3717	788-3767	767
Nassal Co, The 415 W Kaley St. *Web:* www.nassal.com	Orlando	FL	32806	407-648-0400	648-0841	106
Nassau Community College 1 Education Dr *Web:* www.ncc.edu	Garden City	NY	11530	516-572-7500	572-9743	162
Nassau County 416 Centre St *TF:* 888-615-1308 ■ *Web:* www.nassauflpa.com	Fernandina Beach	FL	32034	904-491-7300	491-3629	338
Nassau County School District 1201 Atlantic Ave *Web:* www.nassau.k12.fl.us	Fernandina Beach	FL	32034	904-491-9900		685
Nassau Financial Federal Credit Union 1325 Franklin Ave Ste 500 *TF:* 800-216-2328 ■ *Web:* www.nassaufinancial.org	Garden City	NY	11530	516-742-4900		219
Nassau Inn, The 10 Palmer Sq *Web:* www.nassauinn.com	Princeton	NJ	08542	609-921-7500	921-9385	379
Nassau Regional Off Track Betting Corp 220 Fulton Ave. *Web:* secure.nassauotb.com	Hempstead	NY	11550	516-572-2800		452
Nassau Tool Works Inc 34 Lamar St *Web:* www.airindustriesgroup.com	West Babylon	NY	11704	631-643-5000		454
Nassau University Medical Ctr 2201 Hempstead Tpke *Web:* www.numc.edu	East Meadow	NY	11554	516-572-0123		374-3
Nassau Valley Vineyards 32165 Winery Way *TF:* 800-425-2355 ■ *Web:* www.nassauvalley.com	Lewes	DE	19958	302-645-9463	645-6666	50-7
Nassau Veterans Memorial Coliseum 1255 Hempstead Tpke *Web:* www.nycblive.com	Uniondale	NY	11553	516-231-4848	794-9389	720
NASSCO-Norfolk 200 Ligon St. *Web:* www.nassconorfolk.com	Norfolk	VA	23501	757-543-6801	494-0430	698
Nasseo Inc 13660 N 94th Dr D-7 *TF:* 866-207-8919 ■ *Web:* nasseo.com	Peoria	AZ	85381	866-207-8919		228
Nastos Construction Inc 1421 Kenilworth Ave NE *Web:* www.nastos.com	Washington	DC	20019	202-398-5500	398-5501	186
Nas-Tra Automotive Industries Inc 3 Sidney Ct. *TF:* 800-662-7872 ■ *Web:* www.nastra.com	Lindenhurst	NY	11757	631-225-1225		60
Nasuti & Hinkle 8101-A Glenbrook Rd *Web:* nasuti.com	Bethesda	MD	20814	301-222-0010		4
NASW News 750 First St NE Ste 700 *TF:* 800-227-3590 ■ *Web:* www.naswpress.org	Washington	DC	20002	202-408-8600	336-8312	457-16
Nat Klarsfeld Inc 18 E 48th St *Web:* klarsfeldjewelry.com	New York	NY	10017	212-245-5300		410
NATA (National Air Transportation Assn) 4226 King St. *TF:* 800-808-6282 ■ *Web:* www.nata.aero	Alexandria	VA	22302	703-845-9000	845-8176	49-21

Name / Address	City	State	Zip	Phone	Fax	Class
NATA (National Athletic Trainers Assn) 2952 N Stemmons Fwy Ste 200 *TF:* 800-879-6282 ■ *Web:* www.nata.org	Dallas	TX	75247	214-637-6282	637-2206	48-22
Natalia's 201 N Macon St *Web:* www.natalias.net	Macon	GA	31210	478-741-1380		671
NatAlliance Securities 111 Congress Ave Ste 800 *Web:* www.natalliance.com	Austin	TX	78701	512-609-1700	609-1650	690
Nataraj Books Inc 7967 Twist Ln *Web:* www.natarajbooks.com	Springfield	VA	22153	703-455-4996	455-4001	96
NATCA (National Air Traffic Controllers Assn) 1325 Massachusetts Ave NW *TF:* 800-266-0895 ■ *Web:* natca.org	Washington	DC	20005	202-628-5451	628-5767	414
Natchez Convention & Visitors Bureau 640 S Canal St *TF:* 800-647-6724 ■ *Web:* www.visitnatchez.org	Natchez	MS	39120	601-446-6345		206
Natchez Democrat Inc 503 N Canal St *Web:* www.natchezdemocrat.com	Natchez	MS	39120	601-442-9101		532-2
Natchez National Cemetery 41 Cemetery Rd *Web:* www.cem.va.gov	Natchez	MS	39120	601-445-4981	445-8815	136
Natchez National Historical Park 1 Melrose Montebello Pkwy *Web:* www.nps.gov	Natchez	MS	39120	601-446-5790	442-9516	564
Natchez State Park 230-B Wickcliff Rd *Web:* www.mdwfp.com	Natchez	MS	39120	601-442-2658		565
Natchez Trace National Scenic Trail 2680 Natchez Trace Pkwy *TF:* 800-305-7417 ■ *Web:* www.nps.gov	Tupelo	MS	38804	662-680-4025		564
Natchez Trace State Park 24845 Natchez Trace Rd *Web:* www.state.tn.us	Wildersville	TN	38388	731-968-3742		565
Natchez-Adams County *Chamber of Commerce* 211 Main St *Web:* www.natchezchamber.com	Natchez	MS	39120	601-445-4611	445-9361	139
Natchitoches Area Chamber of Commerce 780 Front St Ste 101 *TF:* 877-646-6689 ■ *Web:* www.natchitocheschamber.com	Natchitoches	LA	71457	318-352-6894		139
Natchitoches Parish 200 Church St Rm 210 *Web:* www.npgov.org	Natchitoches	LA	71457	318-352-2714		338
Natchitoches Regional Medical Ctr 501 Keyser Ave *TF:* 888-728-8383 ■ *Web:* www.nrmchospital.org	Natchitoches	LA	71457	318-214-4200		374-3
Natco 346 W Cerritos Ave *Web:* www.natcoglobal.com	Glendale	CA	91204	818-409-0019		258
NATCO (NATCO Communications Inc) 301 E Main St *TF:* 800-775-6682 ■ *Web:* www.natconet.com	Flippin	AR	72634	870-453-8800	453-3835	224
NATCO Communications Inc (NATCO) 301 E Main St *TF:* 800-775-6682 ■ *Web:* www.natconet.com	Flippin	AR	72634	870-453-8800	453-3835	224
Natco Home Corporate 155 Brookside Ave *TF:* 800-828-8906 ■ *Web:* www.natcohome.com	West Warwick	RI	02893	401-828-0300		131
NAT-COM Inc 2622 Audubon Rd *Web:* www.nat-com.com	Eagleville	PA	19403	610-666-7947		188-1
NATE (National Association of Tower Erectors) 8 Second St SE *TF:* 888-882-5865 ■ *Web:* natehome.com	Watertown	SD	57201	605-882-5865	886-5184	49-3
Natel 907 W Burlington Ave *Web:* natel.net	Fairfield	IA	52556	641-469-6220	472-6624	225
Nathan Adelson Hospice 4141 Swenson St *Web:* www.nah.org	Las Vegas	NV	89119	702-733-0320		371
Nathan Bedford Forrest State Park 1825 Pilot Knob Rd *Web:* www.state.tn.us	Eva	TN	38333	731-584-6356		565
Nathan Boone Homestead State Historic Site 7850 N State Hwy V *Web:* mostateparks.com	Ash Grove	MO	65604	417-751-3266		565
Nathan Cummings Foundation 475 Tenth Ave 14th Fl *Web:* www.nathancummings.org	New York	NY	10018	212-787-7300		305
Nathan D. Maier Consulting Engineers Inc 8080 Park Ln Two North Pk Ste 600 *Web:* www.ndmce.com	Dallas	TX	75231	214-739-4741		261
Nathan Inc 1777 N Kent St Ste 1400 *Web:* www.nathaninc.com	Arlington	VA	22209	703-516-7700	351-6162	194
Nathan Littauer Hospital & Nursing Home 99 E State St *Web:* www.nlh.org	Gloversville	NY	12078	518-773-5505		371
Nathan S. Kline Institute for Psychiatric Research 140 Old Orangeburg Rd *Web:* www.rfmh.org	Orangeburg	NY	10962	845-398-5500		668
Nathan Segal and Company Inc 4635 SW Fwy Ste 350 **Fax Area Code:* 713 ■ *TF:* 800-969-3333 ■ *Web:* www.nathansegal.com	Houston	TX	77027	800-969-3333	963-0738*	276
Nathan Sommers Jacobs PC 2800 Post Oak Blvd 61st Fl *Web:* www.nathansommers.com	Houston	TX	77056	713-960-0303	892-4800	41
Nathan's Famous Inc 1 Jericho Plz 2nd Fl- Wing A *NASDAQ: NATH* ■ *Web:* nathansfamous.com	Jericho	NY	11753	516-338-8500	338-7220	670
Natick Junior Redmen 15 West St *Web:* www.natickma.gov	Natick	MA	01760	508-653-9900		717
Natick Mall Natick Mall Level 2 near Wegmans *Web:* www.natickmall.com	Natick	MA	01760	508-655-4800		460
Nation Consulting LLC 5027 W N Ave *Web:* www.nationconsulting.com	Milwaukee	WI	53208	414-344-1733		196
Nation Magazine 33 Irving Pl *TF:* 800-333-8536 ■ *Web:* www.thenation.com	New York	NY	10003	212-209-5400	982-9000	457-17
Nation of Islam 7351 S Stony Is *Web:* www.noi.org	Chicago	IL	60649	773-324-6000		48-20
National 4-H Council 7100 Connecticut Ave *Web:* 4-h.org	Chevy Chase	MD	20815	301-961-2800		459
National Able Network Inc 567 W Lake St Ste 1150 *TF:* 855-994-8300 ■ *Web:* www.nationalable.org	Chicago	IL	60661	312-994-4200	994-4201	260
National Abortion Federation (NAF) 1755 Massachusetts Ave NW *TF:* 800-772-9100 ■ *Web:* prochoice.org	Washington	DC	20036	202-667-5881	667-5890	49-8
National Academies of Sciences Engineering Medicine 500 5th St NW *TF:* 800-624-6242 ■ *Web:* www.nationalacademies.org	Washington	DC	20001	202-334-2000	334-2158	49-19
National Academy Museum of Art 1083 Fifth Ave *Web:* www.nationalacademy.org	New York	NY	10128	212-369-4880		520
National Academy of Education 500 Fifth St NW *Web:* naeducation.org	Washington	DC	20001	202-334-1947	334-2350	49-5
National Academy of Engineering 500 Fifth St NW *Web:* www.nae.edu	Washington	DC	20001	202-334-2431	334-2290	49-19
National Academy of Public Administration 1600 K St Ste 400 *Web:* www.napawash.org	Washington	DC	20006	202-347-3190	393-0993	49-7
National Academy of Television Arts & Sciences 450 Park Ave S 3rd Fl *Web:* emmyonline.com	New York	NY	10016	212-586-8424	246-8129	48-4
National Academy Press 500 Fifth St NW *Web:* www.nap.edu	Washington	DC	20001	202-334-3313	334-2451	637-2
National Accrediting Agency for Clinical Laboratory Sciences (NAACLS) 5600 N River Rd Ste 720 *Web:* www.naacls.org	Rosemont	IL	60018	773-714-8880	714-8886	48-1
National Accrediting Commission of Cosmetology Arts & Sciences (NACCAS) 3015 Colvin St *TF:* 877-212-5752 ■ *Web:* www.naccas.org	Alexandria	VA	22314	703-600-7600	379-2200	48-1
National Acoustics Inc 13-06 43rd Ave *Web:* nationalacoustics.com	Long Island City	NY	11101	212-695-1252	695-4539	189-9
National Active & Retired Federal Employees Assn 606 N Washington St *TF:* 800-627-3394 ■ *Web:* www.narfe.org	Alexandria	VA	22314	703-838-7760	838-7785	615
National Acupuncture Foundation (NAF) PO Box 137 *Web:* www.nationalacupuncturefoundation.org	Chaplin	CT	06235	860-455-4424		637-2
National Adoption Ctr 1500 Walnut St Ste 701 *Web:* www.adopt.org	Philadelphia	PA	19102	215-735-9988	735-9410	48-6
National Adrenal Diseases Foundation (NADF) 505 Northern Blvd *Web:* www.nadf.us	Great Neck	NY	11021	847-726-9010		48-17
National Aeronautic Assn Hanger 7 Ste 202 *TF:* 800-644-9777 ■ *Web:* naa.aero	Washington	DC	20001	703-416-4888	416-4877	48-22
National Agricultural Aviation Assn (NAAA) 1005 E St SE *Web:* www.agaviation.org	Washington	DC	20003	202-546-5722	546-5726	48-2
National Agricultural Center & Hall of Fame 630 N 126th St *Web:* www.aghalloffame.com	Bonner Springs	KS	66012	913-721-1075		520
National Agricultural Library 10301 Baltimore Ave *TF:* 800-633-7701 ■ *Web:* www.nal.usda.gov	Beltsville	MD	20705	301-504-5755		340-1
National Agri-Marketing Assn (NAMA) 11020 King St Ste 205 *Web:* nama.org	Overland Park	KS	66210	913-491-6500	491-6502	49-18
National Air & Radiation Environmental Laboratory (NAREL) 540 S Morris Ave *Web:* www.epa.gov	Montgomery	AL	36115	334-270-3401	270-3454	743
National Air & Space Museum (Smithsonian Institution) Independence Ave & Sixth St SW *Web:* airandspace.si.edu	Washington	DC	20560	202-633-2214		520
National Air Carrier Assn (NACA) 1735 N Lynn St Ste 105 *Web:* www.naca.cc	Arlington	VA	22209	703-358-8060	358-8070	49-21
National Air Traffic Controllers Assn (NATCA) 1325 Massachusetts Ave NW *TF:* 800-266-0895 ■ *Web:* natca.org	Washington	DC	20005	202-628-5451	628-5767	414
National Air Transportation Assn (NATA) 4226 King St *TF:* 800-808-6282 ■ *Web:* www.nata.aero	Alexandria	VA	22302	703-845-9000	845-8176	49-21
National Air Vibrator Co, The 11929 Brittmoore Park Dr *Web:* www.navco.us	Houston	TX	77041	832-467-3636	467-3800	190
National Alcohol Beverage Control Assn (NABCA) 2900 S Quincy St Ste 800 *Web:* www.nabca.org	Alexandria	VA	22206	703-578-4200	820-3551	49-7
National Alliance for Caregiving 4720 Montgomery Ln Ste 205 *Web:* www.caregiving.org	Bethesda	MD	20814	301-718-8444	652-7711	48-6
National Alliance for Hispanic Health 1501 16th St NW *TF:* 866-783-2645 ■ *Web:* www.healthyamericas.org	Washington	DC	20036	866-783-2645		48-17
National Alliance for Youth Sports 2050 Vista Pkwy *TF:* 800-729-2057 ■ *Web:* www.nays.org	West Palm Beach	FL	33411	561-684-1141	684-2546	48-22
National Alliance of Medical Auditing Specialists 10401 Kingston Pke *Web:* namas.co	Knoxville	TN	37922	865-531-0722		2
National Alliance of Postal & Federal Employees 1628 11th St NW *TF:* 800-222-8733 ■ *Web:* www.napfe.com	Washington	DC	20001	202-939-6325	939-6389	414
National Alliance of Preservation Commissions PO Box 1011 *Web:* napcommissions.org	Virginia Beach	VA	23451	757-802-4141		48-13
National Alliance on Mental Illness (NAMI) 3803 N Fairfax Dr Ste 100 *TF:* 800-950-6264 ■ *Web:* nami.org	Arlington	VA	22203	703-524-7600	524-9094	48-17
National Alliance to End Homelessness 1518 K St NW 2nd Fl *Web:* endhomelessness.org	Washington	DC	20005	202-638-1526	638-4664	48-5

Phone | Fax | Class

National Alopecia Areata Foundation (NAAF)
14 Mitchell Blvd .... San Rafael CA 94903 415-472-3780 472-5343 48-17
Web: www.naaf.org

National Alumni Association of Concordia College- Selma Inc, The
1804 Green St .... Selma AL 36701 334-874-5700 166
Web: www.ccal.edu

National American Indian Housing Council (NAIHC)
122 C S NW Ste 350 .... Washington DC 20001 202-789-1754 789-1758 49-7
TF: 800-284-9165 ■ *Web:* www.naihc.net

National American University
5301 Mt Rushmore Rd .... Rapid City SD 57701 605-394-4800 394-4871 166
TF: 800-843-8892 ■ *Web:* www.national.edu

National Amputation Foundation
40 Church St .... Malverne NY 11565 516-887-3600 48-17
Web: www.nationalamputation.org

National Amusements Inc
846 University Ave .... Norwood MA 02062 781-461-1600 748
Web: www.showcasecinemas.com

National Animal Care & Control Assn
101 N Church St Ste C .... Olathe KS 66061 913-768-1319 48-3
Web: nacanet.site-ym.com

National Anti-Vivisection Society (NAVS)
53 W Jackson Blvd Ste 1552 .... Chicago IL 60604 312-427-6065 427-6524 48-3
TF: 800-888-6287 ■ *Web:* www.navs.org

National Apartment Assn (NAA)
4300 Wilson Blvd Ste 400 .... Arlington VA 22203 703-518-6141 248-9440 49-17
TF: 800-632-3007 ■ *Web:* www.naahq.org

National Aquarium in Baltimore
501 E Pratt St .... Baltimore MD 21202 410-576-3800 576-8641 40
TF: 800-628-9944 ■ *Web:* www.aqua.org

National Arbitration & Mediation (NAM)
990 Stewart Ave 1st Fl .... Garden City NY 11530 800-358-2550 794-8518* 41
**Fax Area Code:* 516 ■ *TF:* 800-358-2550 ■ *Web:* www.namadr.com

National Arbor Day Foundation
100 Arbor Ave .... Nebraska City NE 68410 402-474-5655 474-0820 48-13
TF: 888-448-7337 ■ *Web:* www.arborday.org

National Architectural Accrediting Board (NAAB)
1735 New York Ave NW .... Washington DC 20006 202-783-2007 783-2822 48-1
Web: www.naab.org

National Archives & Records Administration (NARA)
8601 Adelphi Rd .... College Park MD 20740 866-272-6272 837-0483* 340-20
**Fax Area Code:* 301 ■ *TF:* 866-272-6272 ■ *Web:* www.archives.gov
Office of the Federal Register
7 G St NW Ste A-734 .... Washington DC 20401 202-435-7495 340-20
TF: 877-684-6448 ■ *Web:* www.archives.gov

National Archives & Records Administration Regional Offices
Central Plains Region
400 W Pershing Rd .... Kansas City MO 64108 816-268-8000 340-20
Web: www.archives.gov
Great Lakes Region 7358 S Pulaski Rd .... Chicago IL 60629 773-948-9001 948-9050 340-20
Web: www.archives.gov
Mid-Atlantic Region
900 Market St .... Philadelphia PA 19107 215-597-3000 340-20
Web: www.archives.gov
Northeast Region 380 Trapelo Rd .... Waltham MA 02452 781-663-0144 663-0154 340-20
TF: 866-406-2379 ■ *Web:* www.archives.gov
Pacific Alaska Region
6125 Sand Pt Way NE .... Seattle WA 98115 206-336-5115 336-5112 340-20
TF: 866-325-7208 ■ *Web:* www.archives.gov
Pacific Region 1000 Commodore Dr .... San Bruno CA 94066 650-238-3501 238-3510 340-20
TF: 800-234-8861 ■ *Web:* www.archives.gov
Southeast Region 5780 Jonesboro Rd .... Morrow GA 30260 770-968-2100 968-2547 340-20
TF: 800-447-1830 ■ *Web:* www.archives.gov
Southwest Region
1400 John Burgess Dr .... Fort Worth TX 76140 817-551-2051 340-20
Web: www.archives.gov

National Art Education Assn (NAEA)
1806 Robert Fulton Dr .... Reston VA 20191 703-860-8000 860-2960 49-5
TF: 800-299-8321 ■ *Web:* www.arteducators.org

National Art Materials Trade Assn
20200 Zion Ave .... Cornelius NC 28031 704-892-6244 892-6247 49-18
TF: 800-349-1039 ■ *Web:* www.namta.org

National Art Shop
509 S National Ave .... Springfield MO 65802 417-866-3743 866-3748 45
Web: nationalartshop.com

National Artcraft Supply Co
300 Campus Dr .... Aurora OH 44202 330-562-3500 562-3507 43
TF: 888-937-2723 ■ *Web:* www.nationalartcraft.com

National Assembly of State Arts Agencies (NASAA)
1029 Vermont Ave NW 2nd Fl .... Washington DC 20005 202-347-6352 737-0526 49-7
Web: nasaa-arts.org

National Association for Catering & Events (NACE)
10440 Little Patuxent Pkwy Ste 300 .... Columbia MD 21046 410-290-5410 630-5768 49-6
Web: www.nace.net

National Association for Stock Car Auto Racing Inc (NASCAR)
1801 W International Speedway Blvd .... Daytona Beach FL 32114 704-348-7131 48-22
Web: www.nascar.com

National Association of Animal Breeders (NAAB)
8413 Excelsior Dr Ste 140 .... Madison WI 53717 608-827-0277 827-1535 11-2
Web: www.naab-css.org

National Association of Broadcasters (NAB)
1771 N St NW .... Washington DC 20036 202-429-5300 49-14
Web: www.nab.org

National Association of Chain Drug Stores (NACDS)
413 N Lee St .... Alexandria VA 22314 703-549-3001 836-4869 49-18
TF: 800-678-6223 ■ *Web:* www.nacds.org

National Association of Clean Water Agencies (NACWA)
1816 Jefferson Pl NW .... Washington DC 20036 202-833-2672 833-4657 49-7
TF: 888-267-9505 ■ *Web:* www.nacwa.org

National Association of College Auxiliary Services (NACAS)
3 Boar's Head Ln Ste B .... Charlottesville VA 22903 434-245-8425 245-8453 49-5
Web: nacas.org

National Association of College Stores (NACS)
500 E Lorain St .... Oberlin OH 44074 440-775-7777 775-4769 49-18
TF: 800-622-7498 ■ *Web:* www.nacs.org

National Association of Congregational Christian Churches (NACCC)
8473 S Howell Ave .... Oak Creek WI 53154 414-764-1620 764-0319 48-20
TF: 800-262-1620 ■ *Web:* www.naccc.org

National Association of Conservation Districts NACD (NACD)
509 Capitol Ct Ne .... Washington DC 20002 202-547-6223 547-6450 49-7
Web: www.nacdnet.org

National Association of Credit Management
8840 Columbia 100 Pkwy .... Columbia MD 21045 410-740-5560 740-5574 457-5
TF: 800-955-8815 ■ *Web:* www.nacm.org

National Association of Dental Plans (NADP)
12700 Pk Central Dr Ste 400 .... Dallas TX 75251 972-458-6998 458-2258 49-9
Web: www.nadp.org

National Association of Electrical Distributors (NAED)
1181 Corporate Lake Dr .... Saint Louis MO 63132 314-991-9000 991-3060 49-18
TF: 888-791-2512 ■ *Web:* www.naed.org

National Association of Elementary School Principals (NAESP)
1615 Duke St .... Alexandria VA 22314 703-684-3345 548-6021 49-5
TF: 800-386-2377 ■ *Web:* www.naesp.org

National Association of Federal Retirees
865 Shefford Rd .... Ottawa ON K1J1H9 613-745-2559 745-5457 138
TF: 855-304-4700 ■ *Web:* www.federalretirees.ca

National Association of Federally-Insured Credit Unions (NAFCU)
3138 Tenth St N .... Arlington VA 22201 703-522-4770 524-1082 49-2
TF: 800-336-4644 ■ *Web:* www.nafcu.org

National Association of Free Will Baptists Inc (NAFWB)
5233 Mt View Rd .... Antioch TN 37013 615-731-6812 731-0771 48-20
TF: 877-767-7659 ■ *Web:* www.nafwb.org

National Association of Government Guaranteed Lenders (NAGGL)
215 E Ninth Ave .... Stillwater OK 74074 405-377-4022 377-3931 49-2
Web: www.naggl.org

National Association of Home Builders PAC
1201 15th St NW .... Washington DC 20005 800-368-5242 266-8400* 615
**Fax Area Code:* 202 ■ *TF:* 800-368-5242 ■ *Web:* www.nahb.org

National Association of Housing & Redevelopment Officials
1300 Ogden St .... Washington DC 20001 202-289-3500 289-8181 457-5
TF: 877-866-2476 ■ *Web:* www.nahro.org

National Association of Intercollegiate Athletics (NAIA)
1200 Grand Blvd .... Kansas City MO 64106 816-595-8000 595-8200 48-22
Web: www.naia.org

National Association of Letter Carriers (NALC)
100 Indiana Ave NW .... Washington DC 20001 202-393-4695 737-1540 414
TF: 800-424-5186 ■ *Web:* www.nalc.org

National Association of Neonatal Nurses (NANN)
8735 W Higgins Rd Ste 300 .... Chicago IL 60631 847-375-3660 375-6491 49-8
TF: 800-451-3795 ■ *Web:* www.nann.org

National Association of Parliamentarians (NAP)
213 S Main St .... Independence MO 64050 816-833-3892 833-3893 49-12
TF: 888-627-2929 ■ *Web:* www.parliamentarians.org

National Association of REALTORS
430 N Michigan Ave .... Chicago IL 60611 800-874-6500 49-17
TF: 800-874-6500 ■ *Web:* www.nar.realtor

National Association of State Boards of Education (NASBE)
333 John Carlyle St Ste 530 .... Alexandria VA 22314 703-684-4000 49-5
TF: 800-899-6693 ■ *Web:* www.nasbe.org

National Association of State Mental Health Program Directors (NASMHPD)
66 Canal Center Plz Ste 302 .... Alexandria VA 22314 703-739-9333 548-9517 49-7
Web: www.nasmhpd.org

National Association of Student Financial Aid Administrators (NASFAA)
1801 Pennsylvania Avenue NW Ste 850 .... Washington DC 20006 202-785-0453 785-1487 49-5
Web: www.nasfaa.org

National Association of Surety Bond Producers (NASBP)
1140 19th St NW Ste 800 .... Washington DC 20036 202-686-3700 686-3656 49-9
Web: www.nasbp.org

National Association of Theatre Owners (NATO)
1705 N St NW .... Washington DC 20036 202-962-0054 962-0370 48-4
Web: www.natoonline.org

National Association of Tower Erectors (NATE)
8 Second St SE .... Watertown SD 57201 605-882-5865 886-5184 49-3
TF: 888-882-5865 ■ *Web:* natehome.com

National Athletic Trainers Assn (NATA)
2952 N Stemmons Fwy Ste 200 .... Dallas TX 75247 214-637-6282 637-2206 48-22
TF: 800-879-6282 ■ *Web:* www.nata.org

National Auctioneers Assn (NAA)
8880 Ballentine St .... Overland Park KS 66214 913-541-8084 894-5281 49-18
TF: 877-657-1990 ■ *Web:* www.auctioneers.org

National Audio Company Inc (NAC)
309 E Water St .... Springfield MO 65806 417-863-1925 863-7825 238
Web: www.nationalaudiocompany.com

National Audubon Society (NAS)
225 Varick St .... New York NY 10014 212-979-3000 979-3188 48-13
TF: 800-274-4201 ■ *Web:* www.audubon.org

National Australia Bank Americas
245 Park Ave 28th Fl .... New York NY 10167 212-916-9500 70
TF: 866-706-0509 ■ *Web:* www.nab.com.au

National Auto Auction Assn (NAAA)
5320 Spectrum Dr Ste D .... Frederick MD 21703 301-696-0400 631-1359 49-18
TF: 800-232-5411 ■ *Web:* www.naaa.com

National Auto Sound Inc
11001 E Hwy 40 .... Independence MO 64055 816-356-8700 35
Web: nationalautosound.com

National Auto Stores Inc
2512 Quakertown Rd .... Pennsburg PA 18073 215-679-2300 57
Web: www.nationalautostores.com

National Automatic Merchandising Assn (NAMA)
20 N Wacker Dr Ste 3500 .... Chicago IL 60606 312-346-0370 704-4140 49-18
Web: www.namanow.org

National Automatic Sprinkler Industries
8000 Corporate Dr .... Landover Hills MD 20785 301-577-1700 429-4709 189-13
TF: 800-638-2603 ■ *Web:* www.nasifund.org

National Automobile Club (NAC)
1151 E Hillsdale Blvd Ste E .... Foster City CA 94404 800-622-2136 53
TF: 800-622-2136 ■ *Web:* www.nacroadservice.com

National Automobile Museum 10 S Lake St .... Reno NV 89501 775-333-9300 333-9309 520
Web: www.automuseum.org

National Automotive Parts Assn (NAPA)
2999 Circle 75 Pkwy .... Atlanta GA 30339 770-953-1700 61
Web: genpt.com

National Automotive Radiator Service Assn (NARSA)
3000 Village Run Rd Ste 103 221 .... Wexford PA 15090 724-799-8415 799-8416 49-21
Web: www.narsa.org

Phone | Fax | Class

National Aviation Academy
150 Hanscom Dr. Bedford MA 01730 727-535-8727 274-8490* 800
Fax Area Code: 781 ■ *TF:* 800-659-2080 ■ *Web:* www.naa.edu

National Ballet 1816 Margaret Ave. Annapolis MD 21401 301-218-9822 686-7040 573-1
Web: www.nationalballet.com

National Ballet of Canada
Walter Carsen Centre for the National Ballet of Ca 470 Queens Quay W
Toronto ON M5V3K4 416-345-9686 345-8323 573-1
Web: www.national.ballet.ca

National Balloon Museum
1601 N Jefferson Way PO Box 149 Indianola IA 50125 515-961-3714 520
Web: www.nationalballoonmuseum.com

National Band Saw Co
25322 Ave Stanford Valencia CA 91355 661-294-9552 294-9554 759
Web: www.nbsparts.com

National Bank of Arizona
6001 N 24th St Phoenix AZ 85016 602-235-6000 70
TF: 800-655-7622 ■ *Web:* www.nbarizona.com

National Bank of Blacksburg
PO Box 90002 Blacksburg VA 24062 800-552-4123 951-6337* 70
Fax Area Code: 540 ■ *TF:* 800-552-4123 ■ *Web:* nbbank.com

National Bank, The 852 Middle Rd Bettendorf IA 52722 563-344-3935 823-3350 70
TF: 877-321-4347 ■ *Web:* www.bankwithtriumph.com

National Bankcard Systems Inc
5725 W Hwy 290 Ste 105 Austin TX 78735 800-550-7892 255
Web: enbs.com

National Bankshares Inc
101 Hubbard St Blacksburg VA 24060 540-951-6300 360-2
NASDAQ: NKSH ■ *Web:* www.nationalbankshares.com

National Banner Company Inc
11938 Harry Hines Blvd Dallas TX 75234 972-241-2131 287

National Baptist Convention of America International Inc
1000 S Fourth St Louisville KY 40203 844-610-6222 48-20
TF: 844-610-6222 ■ *Web:* www.nbcainc.com

National Baptist Convention USA Inc
1700 Baptist World Center Dr. Nashville TN 37207 615-228-6292 262-3917 48-20
TF: 866-531-3054 ■ *Web:* www.nationalbaptist.com

National Bar Assn (NBA)
1816 12th St NW 4th Fl Washington DC 20009 202-842-3900 289-6170 49-10
Web: nationalbar.org

National Barn Co 818 N Broadway Portland TN 37148 615-325-2700 106
Web: www.nationalbarn.com

National Baseball Hall of Fame & Museum
25 Main St Cooperstown NY 13326 607-547-7200 547-2044 522
TF: 888-425-5633 ■ *Web:* baseballhall.org

National Basketball Players Assn (NBPA)
1133 Avenue of Americas New York NY 10036 212-655-0880 655-0881 48-22
TF: 800-955-6272 ■ *Web:* nbpa.com

National Bearing Co 1596 Manheim Pk. Lancaster PA 17604 717-569-0485 569-1605 75
Web: www.nationalbearings.com

National Beauty Culturists' League Inc, The (NBCL)
25 Logan Cir Nw. Washington DC 20005 202-332-2695 49-4
Web: www.nbcl.info

National Beef Packing Company LLC
12200 Ambassador Dr Ste 500 PO Box 20046 Kansas City MO 64163 800-449-2333 473
TF: 800-449-2333 ■ *Web:* www.nationalbeef.com

National Beer Wholesalers Assn (NBWA)
1101 King St Ste 600 Alexandria VA 22314 703-683-4300 683-8965 49-6
TF: 800-300-6417 ■ *Web:* www.nbwa.org

National Benevolent Assn (NBA)
733 Union Blvd Ste 300 Saint Louis MO 63108 314-993-9000 349-1379 48-5
TF: 866-262-2669 ■ *Web:* www.nbacares.org

National Beverage Screen Printers Inc
12000 Main St Williston SC 29853 803-266-5272 266-5301 9
Web: www.nbsinc.net

National Bicycle Dealers Assn (NBDA)
777 W 19th St Ste O Costa Mesa CA 92627 949-722-6909 49-4
Web: nbda.com

National Billiard Manufacturing Co
3315 Eugenia Ave. Covington KY 41015 859-431-4129 431-4179 710
TF: 800-543-0880 ■ *Web:* www.nationalbilliard.com

National Biodynamics Laboratory
University of New Orleans College of Engineering
2000 Lakeshore Dr. New Orleans LA 70148 888-514-4275 280-7413* 668
Fax Area Code: 504 ■ *TF:* 888-514-4275 ■ *Web:* new.uno.edu

National Black MBA Assn (NBMBAA)
400 W Peachtree St NW Ste 203 Atlanta GA 30308 404-260-5444 49-12
Web: www.nbmbaa.org

National Board for Certified Counselors Inc
3 Terrace Way Ste D Greensboro NC 27403 336-547-0607 21
Web: www.nbcc.org

National Board of Boiler & Pressure Vessel Inspectors
1055 Crupper Ave. Columbus OH 43229 614-888-8320 847-1147 49-7
TF: 877-682-8772 ■ *Web:* www.nationalboard.org

National Board of Medical Examiners (NBME)
3750 Market St. Philadelphia PA 19104 215-590-9500 49-8
Web: www.nbme.org

National Border Patrol Museum
4315 Woodrow Bean Transmountain Rd El Paso TX 79924 915-759-6060 759-0992 520
TF: 877-276-8738 ■ *Web:* borderpatrolmuseum.com

National Braille Press Inc
88 St Stephen St. Boston MA 02115 617-266-6160 437-0456 637-2
TF: 888-965-8965 ■ *Web:* www.nbp.org

National Breast Cancer Coalition (NBCC)
1010 Vermont Ave NW Ste 900. Washington DC 20005 202-296-7477 265-6854 48-17
TF: 800-622-2838 ■ *Web:* www.breastcancerdeadline2020.org

National Builders Hardware Co
1019 SE Tenth Ave Portland OR 97214 503-233-5381 351
Web: nbhco.com

National Building Museum
401 F St NW Washington DC 20001 202-272-2448 520
Web: www.nbm.org

National Bulk Equipment
12838 Stainless Dr. Holland MI 49424 616-399-2220 454
Web: www.nbe-inc.com

National Bureau of Asian Research (NBR)
George F. Russell Jr Hall
1414 NE 42nd St Ste 300 Seattle WA 98105 206-632-7370 632-7487 637-10
Web: www.nbr.org

National Bureau of Economic Research
1050 Massachusetts Ave Cambridge MA 02138 617-868-3900 868-2742 668
TF: 800-621-8476 ■ *Web:* www.nber.org

National Business Assn (NBA)
5151 Beltline Rd Ste 1150 Dallas TX 75254 972-458-0900 960-9149 49-12
TF: 800-456-0440 ■ *Web:* www.nationalbusiness.org

National Business Aviation Assn (NBAA)
1200 18th St NW Ste 400 Washington DC 20036 202-783-9000 331-8364 49-21
TF: 800-394-6222 ■ *Web:* www.nbaa.org

National Business Education Assn (NBEA)
1914 Assn Dr Reston VA 20191 703-860-8300 620-4483 49-5
Web: www.nbea.org

National Business Furniture Inc
735 N Water St Ste 440 Milwaukee WI 53202 800-558-1010 320
TF: 800-558-1010 ■ *Web:* www.nationalbusinessfurniture.com

National Business Services Budget Store Inc (NBS)
11-D El Paso Natl Bank El Paso TX 79901 915-544-1271 351-0170 319-1

National Businesswomen's Leadership Assn
PO Box 419107 Kansas City MO 64141 800-258-7246 432-0824* 765
Fax Area Code: 913 ■ *TF:* 800-258-7246 ■ *Web:* www.nationalseminarstraining.com

National Cable & Telecommunications Assn (NCTA)
25 Massachusetts Ave NW Ste 100 Washington DC 20001 202-222-2300 49-14
Web: www.ncta.com

National Cancer Institute at Frederick
Bldg 427 Rm 1 PO Box B Frederick MD 21702 301-846-1108 846-1494 668
Web: www.ncifrederick.cancer.gov

National Cancer Registrars Assn (NCRA)
1340 Braddock Pl Ste 203 Alexandria VA 22314 703-299-6640 299-6620 48-17
Web: www.ncra-usa.org

National Capital Companies LLC
7910 Woodmont Ave Ste 1250 Bethesda MD 20814 240-988-1296 657-0856* 690
Fax Area Code: 301 ■ *Web:* www.nationalcapital-dc.com

National Capital Planning Commission
401 Ninth St NW N Lobby Ste 500 Washington DC 20004 202-482-7200 482-7272 340-20
Web: www.ncpc.gov

National Capital Regional Office
1100 Ohio Dr SW Washington DC 20242 202-619-7054 340-13
Web: www.nps.gov

National Captioning Institute (NCI)
3725 Concorde Pkwy Ste 100 Chantilly VA 20151 703-917-7600 917-9853 632
TF: 800-825-6758 ■ *Web:* www.ncicap.org

National Car Mart Inc
9255 Brookpark Rd. Cleveland OH 44129 216-505-1750 57
Web: www.nationalcarmart.com

National Career Education
11080 White Rock Rd Ste 100 Rancho Cordova CA 95670 800-915-3593 642-1159* 167-3
Fax Area Code: 916 ■ *TF:* 800-915-3593 ■ *Web:* www.nceschool.com

National Cargo Bureau Inc (NCB)
180 Maiden Ln Ste 903 New York NY 10038 212-785-8300 785-8333 49-21
Web: www.natcargo.org

National Carriers Inc 1501 E Eigth St Liberal KS 67901 620-624-1621 780
TF: 800-835-9180 ■ *Web:* www.nationalcarriers.com

National Carton & Coating Co
1439 Lavelle Dr Xenia OH 45385 937-372-8001 372-9809 561
TF: 800-800-6221 ■ *Web:* www.nationalcarton.com

National CASA Assn (CASA)
100 W Harrison St N Tower Ste 500 Seattle WA 98119 206-270-0072 270-0078 48-6
TF: 800-628-3233 ■ *Web:* www.casaforchildren.org

National Cathedral School
3612 Woodley Rd NW. Washington DC 20016 202-537-6300 537-5743 623
Web: www.ncs.cathedral.org

National Catholic Educational Assn (NCEA)
1005 N Glebe Rd Ste 525 Arlington VA 22201 571-257-0010 243-0025* 49-5
Fax Area Code: 703 ■ *TF:* 800-711-6232 ■ *Web:* ncea.org

National Catholic Reporter Publishing Co
115 E Armour Blvd Kansas City MO 64111 816-531-0538 968-2292 637-9
Web: www.ncronline.org

National Cattlemen's Beef Assn (NCBA)
9110 E Nichols Ave Ste 300 Centennial CO 80112 303-694-0305 694-2851 48-2
TF: 866-233-3872 ■ *Web:* www.beefusa.org

National Caucus & Center on Black Aged Inc (NCBA)
1220 L St NW Ste 800 Washington DC 20005 202-637-8400 347-0895 48-6
Web: www.ncba-aged.org

National Cemetery Administration
810 Vermont Ave NW Washington DC 20420 202-632-8035 340-19
Web: www.cem.va.gov

National Center for Agricultural Utilization Research
USDA/ARS 1815 N University St Peoria IL 61604 309-685-4011 681-6686 668
Web: www.ars.usda.gov

National Center for Atmospheric Research (NCAR)
3090 Center Green Dr. Boulder CO 80301 303-497-1000 668
Web: ncar.ucar.edu

National Center for Bicycling & Walking (NCBW)
8120 Woodmont Ave Ste 520 Bethesda MD 20814 301-656-4220 656-4225 48-22
Web: www.bikewalk.org

National Center for Children in Poverty (NCCP)
215 W 125th St 3rd Fl New York NY 10027 646-284-9600 284-9623 48-6
Web: www.nccp.org

National Center for Children's Illustrated Literature Museum
102 Cedar St. Abilene TX 79601 325-673-4586 520
Web: www.nccil.org

National Center for Drug Free Sport, The
2537 Madison Ave Kansas City MO 64108 816-474-8655 474-8658 415
Web: www.drugfreesport.com

National Center for Ecological Analysis & Synthesis (NCEAS)
735 State St Ste 300 Santa Barbara CA 93101 805-892-2500 892-2510 668
Web: www.nceas.ucsb.edu

National Center for Education Statistics
1990 K St NW Washington DC 20006 202-502-7300 502-7466 340-8
Web: nces.ed.gov

National Center for Employee Development (NCED)
2701 E Imhoff Rd Norman OK 73071 405-366-4420 366-4319 377
TF: 866-438-6233 ■ *Web:* www.nced.com

National Center for Employee Ownership (NCEO)
1629 Telegraph Ave Ste 200 Oakland CA 94612 510-208-1300 272-9510 48-10
Web: www.nceo.org

National Center for Family Literacy (NCFL)
325 W Main St Ste 300 Louisville KY 40202 502-584-1133 584-0172 48-11
Web: familieslearning.org

Name / Address	City	State	ZIP	Phone	Fax	Class
National Center for Genetic Resources Preservation (NCGRP) 1111 S Mason St *Web:* www.ars.usda.gov	Fort Collins	CO	80521	970-495-3200	221-1427	668
National Center for Genome Resources 2935 Rodeo Pk Dr E *TF:* 800-450-4854 ■ *Web:* www.ncgr.org	Santa Fe	NM	87505	505-982-7840	995-4461	668
National Center for Homeopathy (NCH) 1120 Rte 73 Ste 200 **Fax Area Code:* 856 ■ *Web:* www.homeopathycenter.org	Mount Laurel	NJ	08054	703-548-7790	439-0525*	48-17
National Center for Juvenile Justice (NCJJ) 3700 S Water St Ste 200 *TF:* 800-851-3420 ■ *Web:* ncjj.org	Pittsburgh	PA	15203	412-227-6950	227-6955	48-8
National Center for Manufacturing Sciences (NCMS) 3025 Boardwalk *TF:* 800-222-6267 ■ *Web:* www.ncms.org	Ann Arbor	MI	48108	734-995-3457	995-1150	668
National Center for Missing & Exploited Children (NCMEC) 333 John Carlyle St Ste 125 *Web:* www.missingkids.com	Alexandria	VA	22314	703-224-2150	274-2200	48-6
National Center for Public Policy Research (NCPPR) 501 Capitol Ct NE Ste 200 *Web:* nationalcenter.org	Washington	DC	20002	202-543-4110	543-5975	634
National Center for Retirement Benefits Inc 666 Dundee Rd Ste 1200 **Fax Area Code:* 847 ■ *TF:* 800-666-1000 ■ *Web:* www.ncrb.com	Northbrook	IL	60062	800-666-1000	564-4944*	193
National Center for State Courts (NCSC) 300 Newport Ave *TF:* 800-616-6164 ■ *Web:* www.ncsc.org	Williamsburg	VA	23185	757-259-1525	220-0449	49-7
National Center for Supercomputing Applications University of Illinois Urbana-Champaign 1205 W Clark St Rm 1008 MC-257 *Web:* www.ncsa.illinois.edu	Urbana	IL	61801	217-244-0072	244-8195	668
National Center for Victims of Crime, The 2000 M St NW Ste 480 *TF:* 800-394-2255 ■ *Web:* www.victimsofcrime.org	Washington	DC	20036	202-467-8700	467-8701	48-8
National Center on Institutions & Alternatives 7222 Ambassador Rd **Fax Area Code:* 410 ■ *Web:* www.ncianet.org	Baltimore	MD	21244	443-780-1300	597-9656*	634
National Certification Commission for Acupuncture & Oriental Medicine (NCCAOM) 2025 M St NW Ste 800 *TF:* 888-381-1140 ■ *Web:* www.nccaom.org	Washington	DC	20036	202-381-1140	381-1141	48-1
National Chemical Laboratories Inc 401 N Tenth St *TF:* 800-628-2436 ■ *Web:* www.nclonline.com	Philadelphia	PA	19123	215-922-1200	922-5517	151
National Chemicals Inc 105 Liberty St PO Box 32 **Fax Area Code:* 877 ■ *TF:* 800-533-0027 ■ *Web:* www.nationalchemicals.com	Winona	MN	55987	507-454-5640	858-4141*	151
National Chicken Council 1152 15th St NW Ste 430 *Web:* www.chickencheck.in	Washington	DC	20005	202-296-2622		48-2
National Child Care Assn (NCCA) 1325 G St NW Ste 500 *TF:* 866-536-1945 ■ *Web:* www.nccanet.org	Washington	DC	20005	866-536-1945		48-6
National Child Support Enforcement Assn (NCSEA) 1760 Old Meadow Rd Ste 500 *Web:* www.ncsea.org	McLean	VA	22102	703-506-2880		48-6
National Children's Advocacy Ctr (NCAC) 210 Pratt Ave *Web:* www.nationalcac.org	Huntsville	AL	35801	256-533-5437		48-5
National Children's Center Inc 6200 Second St NW *Web:* www.nccinc.org	Washington	DC	20011	202-722-2300		685
National Christmas Tree Assn (NCTA) 16020 Swingley Ridge Rd Ste 300 **Fax Area Code:* 636 ■ *TF:* 800-975-5920 ■ *Web:* www.realchristmastrees.org	Chesterfield	MO	63017	800-975-5920	449-5051*	48-2
National Church Supply Co, The PO Box 269 *TF:* 800-627-9900 ■ *Web:* www.ncssolutions.org	Chester	WV	26034	304-387-5200		263
National Citizens' Coalition for Nursing Home Reform (NCCNHR) *National Consumer Voice for Quality Long-Term Care* 1828 L St NW Ste 801 *TF:* 866-992-3668 ■ *Web:* theconsumervoice.org	Washington	DC	20036	202-332-2275	332-2949	48-17
National City Chamber of Commerce 901 National City Blvd *Web:* www.nationalcitychamber.org	National City	CA	91950	619-477-9339	477-5018	139
National City Public Library 1401 National City Blvd *Web:* www.nationalcityca.gov	National City	CA	91950	619-470-5800		434-3
National Civic League (NCL) 190 E Ninth Ave Ste 200 **Fax Area Code:* 888 ■ *Web:* www.nationalcivicleague.org	Denver	CO	80206	303-571-4343	314-6053*	48-7
National Civil Rights Museum 450 Mulberry St *Web:* www.civilrightsmuseum.org	Memphis	TN	38103	901-521-9699		520
National Civil War Naval Museum 1002 Victory Dr *Web:* www.portcolumbus.org	Columbus	GA	31901	706-327-9798		520
National Cleaners Assn 252 W 29th St *TF:* 800-888-1622 ■ *Web:* www.nca-i.com	New York	NY	10001	212-967-3002	967-2240	49-4
National Clothesline Magazine 801 Easton Rd Ste 2 *Web:* www.natclo.com	Willow Grove	PA	19090	215-830-8467	830-8490	457-21
National Club Assn (NCA) 1201 15th St NW Ste 450 *TF:* 800-625-6221 ■ *Web:* www.nationalclub.org	Washington	DC	20005	202-822-9822	822-9808	48-23
National Coalition Against Censorship (NCAC) 19 Fulton St Ste 407 *Web:* www.ncac.org	New York	NY	10038	212-807-6222	807-6245	48-8
National Coalition Against Domestic Violence (NCADV) 600 Grant Ste 750 *Web:* www.ncadv.org	Denver	CO	80203	303-839-1852	831-9251	48-6
National Coalition for Cancer Survivorship (NCCS) 8455 Colesville Rd Ste 930 *TF:* 877-622-7937 ■ *Web:* www.canceradvocacy.org	Silver Spring	MD	20910	877-622-7937		48-17
National Coalition for the Homeless (NCH) 2201 P St NW *Web:* www.nationalhomeless.org	Washington	DC	20037	202-462-4822	462-4823	48-5
National Coalition of Black Meeting Planners (NCBMP) 1800 Diagonal Rd **Fax Area Code:* 301 ■ *Web:* www.ncbmp.com	Alexandria	VA	22314	571-366-1779	588-0011*	49-12
National Coalition of Girls' Schools (NCGS) PO Box 5729 *Web:* www.ncgs.org	Charlottesville	VA	22905	434-205-4496		49-5
National Coalition on Health Care 1120 G St NW Ste 810 *Web:* nchc.org	Washington	DC	20005	202-638-7151		48-17
National Coalition to Abolish the Death Penalty (NCADP) 1620 L St Ste 250 *Web:* www.ncadp.org	Washington	DC	20036	202-331-4090		48-8
National Coatings Inc 3520 Rennie School Rd *Web:* www.nationalcoatings.biz	Traverse City	MI	49685	231-943-2557		481
National Coffee Association of USA Inc (NCA) 45 Broadway Ste 1140 *Web:* www.ncausa.org	New York	NY	10006	212-766-4007	766-5815	49-6
National College of Business & Technology 7627 Ewing Blvd *Web:* www.national-college.edu	Florence	KY	41042	859-525-6510		800
National Collegiate Athletic Assn (NCAA) 700 W Washington St PO Box 6222 *Web:* www.ncaa.org	Indianapolis	IN	46206	317-917-6222	917-6888	48-22
National Commission Assn 2501 Exchange Ave Ste 102 *TF:* 800-999-8998 ■ *Web:* www.nationallivestock.com	Oklahoma City	OK	73108	405-232-3128		446
National Commission on Certification of Physician Assistants (NCCPA) 12000 Findley Rd Ste 100 *Web:* www.nccpa.net	Johns Creek	GA	30097	678-417-8100	417-8135	48-1
National Committee for Employer Support of the Guard & Reserve (ESGR) 1555 Wilson Blvd Ste 319 *TF:* 800-336-4590 ■ *Web:* www.esgr.mil	Arlington	VA	22209	800-336-4590		48-19
National Committee for Quality Assurance (NCQA) 1100 13th St *TF:* 888-275-7585 ■ *Web:* www.ncqa.org	Washington	DC	20005	202-955-3500	955-3599	48-10
National Committee for Responsive Philanthropy (NCRP) 1900 L St NW Ste 825 *Web:* www.ncrp.org	Washington	DC	20036	202-387-9177	332-5084	48-5
National Committee to Preserve Social Security & Medicare (NCPSSM) 10 G St NE Ste 600 *TF:* 800-966-1935 ■ *Web:* www.ncpssm.org	Washington	DC	20002	202-216-0420		48-7
National Communication Assn (NCA) 1765 N St NW *Web:* www.natcom.org	Washington	DC	20036	202-464-4622	464-4600	49-5
National Community Action Foundation (NCAF) PO Box 78214 *Web:* www.ncaf.org	Washington	DC	20013	202-842-2092	842-2095	48-7
National Community Pharmacists Assn (NCPA) 100 Daingerfield Rd *TF:* 800-544-7447 ■ *Web:* www.ncpanet.org	Alexandria	VA	22314	703-683-8200	683-3619	49-8
National Community Renaissance of California 9421 Haven Ave *Web:* nationalcore.org	Rancho Cucamonga	CA	91730	909-483-2444	483-2448	49-3
National Concrete Masonry Assn 13750 Sunrise Vly Dr *TF:* 877-343-6268 ■ *Web:* ncma.org	Herndon	VA	20171	703-713-1900	713-1910	49-3
National Coney Island Inc 27947 Groesback Hwy *Web:* www.nationalconeyisland.com	Roseville	MI	48066	586-771-7744		670
National Confectioners Assn (NCA) 1101 30th St NW Ste 200 *Web:* www.candyusa.com	Washington	DC	20007	202-534-1440	337-0637	49-6
National Conference of Diocesan Vocation Directors (NCDVD) 440 W Neck Road *Web:* ncdvd.org	Huntington	NY	11743	631-645-8210	812-0249	48-20
National Conference of Firemen & Oilers NCFO 1212 Bath Ave Fl F&O *Web:* www.ncfo.org	Ashland	KY	41101	606-324-3445	326-7039	414
National Conference of State Historic Preservation Officers 444 N Capitol St NW Ste 342 *Web:* ncshpo.org	Washington	DC	20001	202-624-5465		49-7
National Conference of State Legislatures 7700 E First Pl *TF:* 800-659-2656 ■ *Web:* www.ncsl.org	Denver	CO	80230	303-364-7700	364-7800	49-7
National Conference on Citizenship (NCOC) 1900 L St NW Ste 450 *Web:* ncoc.org	Washington	DC	20036	202-601-7096		48-8
National Congress of American Indians (NCAI) 1516 P St NW *TF:* 800-388-2227 ■ *Web:* www.ncai.org	Washington	DC	20005	202-466-7767	466-7797	48-14
National Congress of Neighborhood Women 249 Manhattan Ave *Web:* neighborhoodwomen.org	Brooklyn	NY	11211	718-388-8915		48-24
National Conservatory of Dramatic Arts 1556 Wisconsin Ave NW *Web:* www.theconservatory.org	Washington	DC	20007	202-333-2202		167-3
National Constitution Ctr Independence Mall 525 Arch St *Web:* constitutioncenter.org	Philadelphia	PA	19106	215-409-6600	409-6650	520
National Construction Rentals Inc 15319 Chatsworth St *TF:* 800-352-5675 ■ *Web:* www.rentnational.com	Mission Hills	CA	91345	800-352-5675	896-8411	264-3
National Consumer Law Ctr (NCLC) 7 Winthrop Sq *Web:* www.nclc.org	Boston	MA	02110	617-542-8010	542-8028	48-8
National Consumers League (NCL) 1701 K St NW Ste 1200 *Web:* www.nclnet.org	Washington	DC	20006	202-835-3323	835-0747	48-10
National Contract Management Assn (NCMA) 21740 Beaumeade Cir Ste 125 **Fax Area Code:* 703 ■ *TF:* 800-344-8096 ■ *Web:* www.ncmahq.org	Ashburn	VA	20147	571-382-0082	448-0939*	49-12
National Co-operative Directory 3381 Royalton Turnpike Rd *Web:* www.nationalco-opdirectory.com	South Royalton	VT	05068	802-763-2368		637-10
National Copper & Smelting Company Inc 3333 Stanwood Blvd *Web:* www.nationaltube.com	Huntsville	AL	35811	256-859-4510		492
National Corn Growers Assn (NCGA) 632 Cepi Dr *Web:* www.ncga.com	Chesterfield	MO	63005	636-733-9004	733-9005	48-2

	Phone	Fax	Class
National Corporate Housing 8400 E Crescent Pkwy Ste 300 Greenwood Village CO 80111 *Web:* www.nationalcorporatehousing.com	703-464-5700		376
National Corrugated Steel Pipe Assn (NCSPA) 14070 Proton Rd Ste 100 Dallas TX 75244 *Web:* ncspa.org	972-850-1907		49-3
National Corvette Museum 350 Corvette Dr Bowling Green KY 42101 *TF:* 800-538-3883 ■ *Web:* www.corvettemuseum.org	270-781-7973	781-5286	520
National Cotton Council of America 7193 Goodlett Farms Pkwy Cordova TN 38016 *Web:* www.cotton.org	901-274-9030	725-0510	532-2
National Council for Accreditation of Teacher Education (NCATE) 2010 Massachusetts Ave NW Ste 500 Washington DC 20036 *Web:* www.ncate.org	202-466-7496	296-6620	48-1
National Council for Adoption (NCFA) 225 N Washington St Alexandria VA 22314 *Web:* www.adoptioncouncil.org	703-299-6633	299-6004	48-6
National Council for Advanced Mfg (NACFAM) 2025 M St NW Ste 800 Washington DC 20036 *Web:* www.nacfam.org	202-367-1247	429-2422	49-12
National Council for Prescription Drug Programs (NCPDP) 9240 E Raintree Dr Scottsdale AZ 85260 *Web:* www.ncpdp.org	480-477-1000	767-1042	49-9
National Council for the Social Studies (NCSS) 8555 16th St Ste 500 Silver Spring MD 20910 *TF:* 800-683-0812 ■ *Web:* socialstudies.org	301-588-1800	588-2049	49-5
National Council for the Traditional Arts (NCTA) 8757 Georgia Ave Ste 450 Silver Spring MD 20910 *Web:* ncta-usa.org	301-565-0654		48-4
National Council for Therapeutic Recreation Certification (NCTRC) 7 Elmwood Dr New City NY 10956 *Web:* www.nctrc.org	845-639-1439	639-1471	49-15
National Council of Architectural Registration Boards (NCARB) 1801 K St NW Ste 700-K Washington DC 20006 *Web:* www.ncarb.org	202-783-6500	783-0290	49-7
National Council of Examiners for Engineering & Surveying (NCEES) 280 Seneca Creek Rd Seneca SC 29678 *TF:* 800-250-3196 ■ *Web:* ncees.org	864-654-6824		49-3
National Council of Farmer Co-ops (NCFC) 50 F St NW Ste 900 Washington DC 20001 *TF:* 800-344-2626 ■ *Web:* ncfc.org	202-626-8700	626-8722	48-2
National Council of Jewish Women (NCJW) 475 Riverside Dr Ste 1901 New York NY 10115 *Web:* www.ncjw.org	212-645-4048	645-7466	48-24
National Council of Jewish Women New York 241 W 72nd St New York NY 10023 *Web:* www.ncjwny.org	212-687-5030	799-7283	48-20
National Council of Juvenile & Family Court Judges (NCJFCJ) Univ of Nevada PO Box 8970 Reno NV 89507 *TF:* 800-527-3223 ■ *Web:* www.ncjfcj.org	775-784-6012	784-6628	49-10
National Council of Negro Women Inc (NCNW) 633 Pennsylvania Ave NW Washington DC 20004 *Web:* www.ncnw.org	202-737-0120	737-0476	48-24
National Council of State Boards of Nursing (NCSBN) 111 E Wacker Dr Ste 2900 Chicago IL 60601 *TF:* 866-293-9600 ■ *Web:* www.policies.ncsbn.org	312-525-3600	279-1032	49-8
National Council of State Housing Agencies (NCSHA) 444 N Capitol St NW Ste 438 Washington DC 20001 *TF:* 800-475-2098 ■ *Web:* www.ncsha.org	202-624-7710	624-5899	49-7
National Council of Supervisors of Mathematics (NCSM) 2851 S Parker Rd Ste 1210 Aurora CO 80014 *Web:* www.mathedleadership.org	303-317-6595	200-7099	49-5
National Council of Teachers of English (NCTE) 1111 W Kenyon Rd Urbana IL 61801 *TF:* 877-369-6283 ■ *Web:* www.ncte.org	217-328-3870	328-0977	49-5
National Council of Teachers of Mathematics (NCTM) 1906 Assn Dr Reston VA 20191 *TF:* 800-235-7566 ■ *Web:* www.nctm.org	703-620-9840	476-2970	49-5
National Council of Textile Organizations (NCTO) 1701 K St NW Ste 625 Washington DC 20006 *TF:* 800-238-7192 ■ *Web:* www.ncto.org	202-822-8028	822-8029	49-13
National Council on Crime & Delinquency (NCCD) 1970 Broadway Ste 500 Oakland CA 94612 *TF:* 800-306-6223 ■ *Web:* www.nccdglobal.org	510-208-0500	208-0511	48-8
National Council on Disability (NCD) 1331 F St NW Ste 850 Washington DC 20004 *Web:* ncd.gov	202-272-2004	272-2022	340-20
National Council on Economic Education (NCEE) 122 E 42nd St Ste 2600 New York NY 10168 *TF:* 800-338-1192 ■ *Web:* www.councilforeconed.org	212-730-7007	730-1793	49-5
National Council on Family Relations (NCFR) 1201 W River Pkwy Ste 200 Minneapolis MN 55454 *TF:* 888-781-9331 ■ *Web:* www.ncfr.org	888-781-9331		48-6
National Council on Problem Gambling Inc 730 11th St NW Ste 601 Washington DC 20001 *Web:* www.ncpgambling.org	202-547-9204	547-9206	49-8
National Council on Public History (NCPH) 425 University Blvd 127 Cavanaugh Hall Indianapolis IN 46202 *Web:* www.ncph.org	317-274-2716	278-5230	48-7
National Council on the Aging (NCOA) 1901 L St NW 4th Fl Washington DC 20036 **Fax Area Code: 202* ■ *Web:* www.ncoa.org	571-527-3900	479-0735*	48-6
National Counterintelligence & Security Ctr, The LX/ICC-B Washington DC 20511 *Web:* www.dni.gov	703-733-8600		340-20
National Court Reporters Assn (NCRA) 8224 Old Courthouse Rd Vienna VA 22182 *TF:* 800-272-6272 ■ *Web:* www.ncra.org	703-556-6272	556-6291	49-10
National Cowboy & Western Heritage Museum 1700 NE 63rd St Oklahoma City OK 73111 *Web:* www.nationalcowboymuseum.org	405-478-2250	478-4714	520
National Cowgirl Museum & Hall of Fame 1720 Gendy St Fort Worth TX 76107 *Web:* www.cowgirl.net	817-336-4475	336-2470	520
National CPA Health Care Advisors Assn (HCAA) 1801 W End Ave Ste 800 Nashville TN 37203 *TF:* 800-231-2524 ■ *Web:* hcaa.com	615-373-9880	377-7092	49-1
National Cred-A-Chek Inc 3770 Fourth Ave San Diego CA 92103 *TF:* 800-421-2168 ■ *Web:* nccreports.com	619-296-0900	296-9115	225
National Credit Adjusters LLC 327 W 4th Ave Hutchinson KS 67501 **Fax Area Code: 620* ■ *TF:* 888-768-0674 ■ *Web:* ncaks.worldsecuresystems.com	888-768-0674	664-5947*	361
National Credit Union Admin 580 Westlake Park Blvd Ste 150 Houston TX 77079 *Web:* bpfcu.org	281-870-8000		219
National Credit Union Administration 1775 Duke St Alexandria VA 22314 *TF:* 800-827-9650 ■ *Web:* www.ncua.gov	703-518-6300	518-6319	340-20
National Credit Union Administration Regional Offices			
Region 3 7000 Central Pkwy Ste 1600 Atlanta GA 30328 *Web:* www.ncua.gov	678-443-3000	443-3020	340-20
Region 4 4807 Spicewood Springs Rd Ste 5200 Austin TX 78759 *Web:* www.ncua.gov	512-342-5600	342-5620	340-20
Region 5 1230 W Washington St Ste 301 Tempe AZ 85281 *Web:* ncua.gov	602-302-6000	302-6024	340-20
National Crime Prevention Council (NCPC) 2345 Crystal Dr Ste 500 Arlington VA 22202 **Fax Area Code: 202* ■ *TF:* 800-627-2911 ■ *Web:* www.ncpc.org	443-292-4565	296-1356*	48-8
National Criminal Justice Reference Service PO Box 6000 Rockville MD 20849 **Fax Area Code: 301* ■ *Web:* www.ncjrs.gov	202-836-6998	240-5830*	340-14
National Crop Insurance Services (NCIS) 8900 Indian Creek Pkwy Ste 600 Overland Park KS 66210 *TF:* 800-951-6247 ■ *Web:* www.ag-risk.org	913-685-2767	685-3080	48-2
National Customs Brokers & Forwarders Association of America Inc (NCBFAA) 1200 18th St NW Ste 901 Washington DC 20036 *Web:* www.ncbfaa.org	202-466-0222	466-0226	49-21
National Cutting Horse Assn (NCHA) 260 Bailey Ave Fort Worth TX 76107 *Web:* www.nchacutting.com	817-244-6188	244-2015	48-3
National Cycle Inc 2200 S Maywood Dr PO Box 158 Maywood IL 60153 *TF:* 877-972-7336 ■ *Web:* www.nationalcycle.com	708-343-0400	343-0625	517
National Czech & Slovak Museum & Library 87 16th Ave SW Cedar Rapids IA 52404 *Web:* www.ncsml.org	319-362-8500	363-2209	520
National Dairy Council (NDC) 10255 W Higgins Rd Ste 900 Rosemont IL 60018 *Web:* www.nationaldairycouncil.org	847-627-3790		48-2
National Dairy Herd Improvement Association Inc 421 S 9 Mound Rd PO Box 930399 Verona WI 53593 *Web:* www.dhia.org	608-848-6455	848-7675	11-2
National Defense Industrial Assn (NDIA) 2111 Wilson Blvd Ste 400 Arlington VA 22201 *Web:* www.ndia.org	703-522-1820	522-1885	48-19
National Defense University Fort McNair 300 Fifth Ave SW Washington DC 20319 *Web:* www.ndu.edu	202-685-4700		340-3
National Delivery Systems Inc 8700 Robert Fulton Dr Columbia MD 21046 *Web:* www.national-delivery.com	410-312-4770	312-4775	546
National Diagnostics Inc 305 Patton Dr Atlanta GA 30336 *TF:* 800-526-3867 ■ *Web:* www.nationaldiagnostics.com	404-699-2121	699-2077	231
National Disaster Search Dog Foundation 6800 Wheeler Canyon Rd Ojai CA 93023 *TF:* 888-459-4376 ■ *Web:* searchdogfoundation.org	805-646-1015		48-3
National Discount Cruise Co 1401 N Cedar Crest Blvd Ste 110 Allentown PA 18104 *TF:* 800-788-8108 ■ *Web:* www.nationaldiscountcruise.com	800-788-8108		771
National Disease Research Interchange (NDRI) 1628 John F Kennedy Blvd 8 Penn Ctr Eighth Fl Philadelphia PA 19103 *TF:* 800-222-6374 ■ *Web:* ndriresource.org	215-557-7361		269
National Distributors Leasing 1517 Avco Blvd Sellersburg IN 47172 *Web:* www.drive4ndl.com	812-246-6306		449
National Domestic Violence Hotline (NDVH) PO Box 161810 Austin TX 78716 *Web:* www.thehotline.org	512-794-1133		48-6
National Door Industries Inc 6310 Airport Fwy Fort Worth TX 76117 *Web:* www.natdoor.com	817-834-7300		596
National Down Syndrome Congress (NDSC) 30 Mansell Ct Ste 108 Roswell GA 30076 *TF:* 800-232-6372 ■ *Web:* www.ndsccenter.org	770-604-9500	604-9898	48-17
National Down Syndrome Society (NDSS) 666 Broadway 8th Fl New York NY 10012 **Fax Area Code: 212* ■ *TF:* 800-221-4602 ■ *Web:* www.ndss.org	800-221-4602	979-2873*	48-17
National Drug Intelligence Ctr 319 Washington St 5th Fl Johnstown PA 15901 *Web:* www.justice.gov	814-532-4601	532-4690	340-14
National Eating Disorders Assn 200 W 41st St Ste 1203 New York NY 10036 *Web:* www.nationaleatingdisorders.org	212-575-6200	575-1650	48-17
National Economic Research Associates Inc 1166 Avenue of the Americas 29th Fl New York NY 10036 *Web:* www.nera.com	914-448-4000	448-4040	194
National Education Assn (NEA) 1201 16th St NW Washington DC 20036 *TF:* 888-552-0624 ■ *Web:* www.nea.org	202-833-4000	822-7974	49-5
National Educational Telecommunications Assn (NETA) 939 S Stadium Rd Columbia SC 29201 *Web:* www.netaonline.org	803-799-5517	771-4831	632
National Electrical Carbon 251 Forrester Dr Greenville SC 29607 **Fax Area Code: 408* ■ *TF:* 800-471-7842 ■ *Web:* www.ndt.org	864-284-9728	280-7706*	127
National Electrical Contractors Assn (NECA) 3 Bethesda Metro Ctr Ste 1100 Bethesda MD 20814 *TF:* 800-214-0585 ■ *Web:* www.necanet.org	301-657-3110	215-4500	49-3
National Electrical Manufacturers Assn (NEMA) 1300 N 17th St Ste 1752 Rosslyn VA 22209 *TF:* 800-699-9277 ■ *Web:* www.nema.org	703-841-3200	841-5900	49-13

	Phone	Fax	Class
National Electrical Manufacturers Representatives Assn (NEMRA) 28 Deer St Ste 302 .... Portsmouth NH 03801 *Fax Area Code: 603 ■ TF: 800-446-3672 ■ Web: www.nemra.org	914-524-8650	319-1667*	49-18
National Electronic Alloys Inc 3 Fir Ct .... Oakland NJ 07436 Web: www.nealloys.com	201-337-9400	337-9698	492
National Electronic Attachment Inc (NEA) 100 Ashford Ctr N Ste 300 .... Dunwoody GA 30338 *Fax Area Code: 770 ■ TF: 800-782-5150 ■ Web: www.nea-fast.com	800-782-5150	441-3204*	390
National Electronics Service Dealers Assn (NESDA) 3608 Pershing Ave .... Fort Worth TX 76107 Web: nesda.wildapricot.org	817-921-9061	921-3741	49-18
National Electrostatics Corp 7540 Graber Rd .... Middleton WI 53562 Web: www.pelletron.com	608-831-7600		250
National Elevator Industry Inc 1677 County Rd 64 PO Box 838 .... Salem NY 12865 Web: www.neii.org	518-854-3100	854-3257	49-3
National Emblem Inc 3925 E Vernon St PO Box 15680 .... Long Beach CA 90815 TF: 800-877-6185 ■ Web: www.nationalemblem.com	310-515-5055	515-5966	258
National Employee Assistance Services Inc N 17 W 24100 Riverwood Dr Ste 300 .... Waukesha WI 53188 TF: 800-634-6433 ■ Web: www.empathia.com	262-574-2500		462
National Employment Lawyers Assn (NELA) 417 Montgomery St 4th Fl .... San Francisco CA 94104 Web: www.nela.org	415-296-7629	677-9445	49-10
National Endowment for Democracy (NED) 1025 F St NW Ste 800 .... Washington DC 20004 Web: www.ned.org	202-378-9700	378-9407	48-7
National Endowment for Financial Education (NEFE) 1331 17th St Ste 1200 .... Denver CO 80202 Web: www.nefe.org	303-741-6333		48-10
National Endowment for the Arts 400 7th St SW .... Washington DC 20506 Web: www.arts.gov	202-682-5400		572
National Endowment for the Humanities (NEH) 400 Seventh St SW .... Washington DC 20506 TF: 800-634-1121 ■ Web: www.neh.gov	202-606-8400		340-20
National Energy Research Scientific Computing Ctr (NERSC) Lawrence Berkeley National Laboratory .... Berkeley CA 94720 TF: 800-666-3772 ■ Web: www.nersc.gov	510-486-5849	486-4300	668
National Energy Technology Laboratory (NETL) 3610 Collins Ferry Rd .... Morgantown WV 26505 TF: 800-432-8330 ■ Web: netl.doe.gov	304-285-4764		668
National Entertainment Network LLC 325 Interlocken Pkwy B .... Broomfield CO 80021	303-444-2559		55
National Environmental Balancing Bureau (NEBB) 8575 Grovemont Cir .... Gaithersburg MD 20877 TF: 866-497-4447 ■ Web: www.nebb.org	301-977-3698	977-9589	49-19
National Environmental Health Assn (NEHA) 720 S Colorado Blvd Ste 1000-N .... Denver CO 80246 TF: 866-956-2258 ■ Web: www.neha.org	303-756-9090	691-9490	49-7
National Environmental Safety & Health Training Assn (NESHTA) 584 Main St .... South Portland ME 04106 Web: www.neshta.org	207-771-9020		49-5
National Environmental Satellite Data & Information Service 1335 East-West Hwy .... Silver Spring MD 20910 Web: www.nesdis.noaa.gov	301-713-3578	713-1249	340-2
National Environmental Satellite Data & Information Service *National Climatic Data Ctr* 151 Patton Ave Rm 120 .... Asheville NC 28801 Web: www.ncdc.noaa.gov	828-271-4800	271-4876	340-2
National Coastal Data Development Ctr Bldg 1100 Ste 101 .... Stennis Space Center MS 39529 TF: 866-732-2382 ■ Web: www.ncddc.noaa.gov	228-688-2936	688 2010	340-2
National Geophysical Data Ctr E/GC 325 Broadway .... Boulder CO 80305 Web: www.ngdc.noaa.gov	303-497-6826	497-6513	340-2
National Equity Project 1720 Broadway 4th Fl .... Oakland CA 94612 Web: nationalequityproject.org	510-208-0160		242
National Events Inc 501 Baily Rd .... Yeadon PA 19050 Web: nationaleventservices.com	610-284-3000		760
National Excelsior Co 1999 N Ruby St .... Melrose Park IL 60160 TF: 855-373-9235 ■ Web: www.excelsiorhvac.com	708-343-4225	681-0041	595
National Exchange Bank & Trust 130 S Main St PO Box 988 .... Fond Du Lac WI 54936 TF: 877-921-7700 ■ Web: nebat.com	920-921-7700		70
National Exchange Club 3050 W Central Ave .... Toledo OH 43606 TF: 800-924-2643 ■ Web: www.nationalexchangeclub.org	419-535-3232	535-1989	48-15
National Exposure Research Laboratory 109 TW Alexander Dr Rm D310-G .... Durham NC 27709 Web: www.epa.gov	919-541-2777		668
National Eye Institute Information 31 Center Dr MSC 2510 .... Bethesda MD 20892 Web: www.nei.nih.gov	301-496-5248		668
National Fabtronix Inc 28800 Hesperian Blvd .... Hayward CA 94545 Web: www.natfab.com	510-785-3135	785-1253	697
National Fallen Firefighters Foundation PO Box 498 .... Emmitsburg MD 21727 TF: 800-223-9708 ■ Web: www.firehero.org	301-447-1365	447-1645	48-19
National Family Care Life Insurance Co 13530 Inwood Rd Farmers Br .... Dallas TX 75244 *Fax Area Code: 972 ■ TF: 800-527-0996 ■ Web: www.nfclife.com	800-527-0996	788-1156*	796
National Family Caregivers Assn (NFCA) 1150 Connecticut Ave NW Ste 501 .... Washington DC 20036 TF: 800-896-3650 ■ Web: caregiveraction.org	202-454-3970		48-6
National Family Farm Coalition (NFFC) 110 Maryland Ave NE Ste 307 .... Washington DC 20002 Web: www.nffc.net	202-543-5675	543-0978	48-2
National Farm Toy Museum 1110 16th Ave SE .... Dyersville IA 52040 Web: www.nationalfarmtoymuseum.com	563-875-2727		520
National Farmers Organization (NFO) 528 Billy Sunday Rd Ste 100 PO Box 2508 .... Ames IA 50010 TF: 800-247-2110 ■ Web: www.nfo.org	515-292-2000	292-7106	48-2
National Farmers Union News (NFU) 20 F St NW Ste 300 .... Washington DC 20001 TF: 800-442-8277 ■ Web: nfu.org	202-554-1600	554-1654	531-13
National Federation of Community Broadcasters (NFCB) PO Box 11270 .... Denver CO 80211 Web: nfcb.org	970-279-3411		49-14
National Federation of Families for Children's Mental Health (NFFCMH) 12320 Parklawn Dr .... Rockville MD 20852 Web: www.ffcmh.org	240-403-1901	403-1909	49-15
National Federation of Republican Women (NFRW) 124 N Alfred St .... Alexandria VA 22314 TF: 800-373-9688 ■ Web: www.nfrw.org	703-548-9688	548-9836	48-7
National Federation of the Blind (NFB) 1800 Johnson St .... Baltimore MD 21230 TF: 800-392-5671 ■ Web: nfb.org	410-659-9314	685-5653	48-17
National Fence Systems Inc 1033 Rt One .... Avenel NJ 07001 TF: 800-211-2444 ■ Web: www.nationalfencesystems.com	732-636-5600		186
National FFA Organization 6060 FFA Dr .... Indianapolis IN 46268 TF: 800-772-0939 ■ Web: www.ffa.org	317-802-6060	802-6061	48-2
National Fiber Technology LLC 15 Union St .... Lawrence MA 01840 TF: 800-842-2751 ■ Web: www.nftech.com	978-686-2964		348
National Field Service Corp (NFS) 162 Orange Ave .... Suffern NY 10901 Web: nfsco.com	845-368-1600	368-1989	736
National Film Board of Canada Stn Centre-Ville PO Box 6100 .... Montreal QC H3C3H5 TF: 800-267-7710 ■ Web: www.nfb.ca	514-283-9000		513
National Filter Media Corp 691 North 400 West .... Salt Lake City UT 84103 TF: 800-777-4248 ■ Web: www.nfm-filter.com	801-363-6736	531-1293	18
National Financial Partners Corp (NFP) 340 Madison Ave 20th Fl .... New York NY 10173 NYSE: NFP ■ Web: www.nfp.com	212-301-4000	301-4001	401
National Fingerprint Inc 6999 Dolan Rd .... Glouster OH 45732 TF: 888-823-7873 ■ Web: www.nationalfingerprint.com	740-767-3853		692
National Fire & Marine Insurance Co 3024 Harney St .... Omaha NE 68131 TF: 866-720-7861 ■ Web: www.nationalindemnity.com	402-916-3000	916-3030	391-4
National Fire Protection Assn (NFPA) 1 Batterymarch Pk .... Quincy MA 02169 TF: 800-344-3555 ■ Web: www.nfpa.org	617-770-3000	770-0700	48-17
National Fire Sprinkler Assn (NFSA) 40 Jon Barrett Rd .... Patterson NY 12563 Web: nfsa.org	845-878-4200	878-4215	49-3
National Fish & Wildlife Foundation 1133 15th St NW Ste 1100 .... Washington DC 20005 Web: www.nfwf.org	202-857-0166	857-0162	48-13
National Fisherman Magazine 121 Free St .... Portland ME 04101 TF: 800-959-5073 ■ Web: www.nationalfisherman.com	207-842-5608	842-5603	457-21
National Flange & Fitting Co 955 Dairy Ashford Rd STE 100 .... Houston TX 77079	713-688-2515		483
National Flavors Inc 3680 Stadium Park Way .... Kalamazoo MI 49009 TF: 800-525-2431 ■ Web: www.nationalflavors.com	800-525-2431		297-8
National Floral Supply Inc 3825 Leonardtown Rd Ste 4 .... Waldorf MD 20601 TF: 800-932-2772 ■ Web: www.flowersonbase.com	301-932-7600		292
National Fluid Power Assn (NFPA) 3333 N Mayfair Rd Ste 211 .... Milwaukee WI 53222 Web: www.nfpa.com	414-778-3344	778-3361	49-13
National Food Equipment and Supplies (NFE) 3186 Old Farm Ln .... Walled Lake MI 48390 TF: 800-345-5872 ■ Web: www.nationalfoodequipment.com	248-960-7292	960-0774	300
National Football League Players (NFLPA) 1133 20th St NW .... Washington DC 20036 TF: 800-372-2000 ■ Web: www.nflpa.com	800-372-2000		48-22
National Foreign Trade Council (NFTC) 1625 K St NW Ste 200 .... Washington DC 20006 Web: www.nftc.org	202-887-0278	452-8160	49-18
National Forest Foundation 27 Ft Missoula Rd Bldg 27 Ste 3 .... Missoula MT 59804 Web: www.nationalforests.org	406-542-2805	542-2810	48-13
National Forest Recreation Assn (NFRA) PO Box 488 .... Woodlake CA 93286 TF: 800-272-7238 ■ Web: nfra.org	559-564-2365	564-2048	48-23
National Forum for Black Public Administrators (NFBPA) 777 N Capitol St NE Ste 807 .... Washington DC 20002 Web: www.nfbpa.org	202-408-9300	408-8558	49-7
National Foundation for Cancer Research (NFCR) 4600 E W Hwy Ste 525 .... Bethesda MD 20814 *Fax Area Code: 301 ■ TF: 800-321-2873 ■ Web: www.nfcr.org	800-321-2873	654-5824*	305
National Foundation for Infectious Diseases (NFID) 4733 Bethesda Ave Ste 750 .... Bethesda MD 20814 Web: www.nfid.org	301-656-0003	907-0878	49-8
National Franchise Sales 1601 Dove St Ste 150 .... Newport Beach CA 92660 Web: www.nationalfranchisesales.com	949-428-0480		317
National Franchisee Association Inc 1701 Barrett Lakes Blvd Ste 180 .... Kennesaw GA 30144 Web: nfabk.org	678-797-5160	797-5170	360-3
National Fraternity of Kappa Delta Rho (KDR) 331 S Main St .... Greensburg PA 15601 TF: 800-536-5371 ■ Web: www.kdr.com	724-838-7100	838-7101	48-16
National Freedom of Information Coalition 344 Hearnes Ctr .... Columbia MO 65211 TF: 866-682-6663 ■ Web: www.nfoic.org	573-882-4856		48-8
National Freshwater Fishing Hall of Fame & Museum 10360 Hall of Fame Dr .... Hayward WI 54843 Web: www.freshwater-fishing.org	715-634-4440		522
National Frozen & Refrigerated Foods Assn (NFRA) 4755 Linglestown Rd Ste 300 .... Harrisburg PA 17112 Web: www.nfraweb.org	717-657-8601	657-9862	49-6

	Phone	Fax	Class
National Frozen Foods Corp 1600 Fairview Ave E Ste 200 .... Seattle WA 98102 *Web:* www.nffc.com	206-322-8900	322-4458	296-21
National Fruit Flavor Company Inc 935 Edwards Ave .... New Orleans LA 70123 *Web:* www.nationalfruitflavor.com	504-733-6757		345
National Fruit Product Company Inc 701 Fairmont Ave .... Winchester VA 22601 *TF:* 800-655-4022 ■ *Web:* whitehousefoods.com	540-662-3401		315-3
National Fuel Resources Inc 165 Lawrence Bell Dr Ste 120 .... Williamsville NY 14221 *TF:* 800-839-9993 ■ *Web:* www.nfrinc.com	716-630-6778	630-6798	787
National Fulfillment Services 105 Commerce Dr .... Aston PA 19014 **Fax Area Code:* 610 ■ *TF:* 800-637-1306 ■ *Web:* www.nfsrv.com	800-637-1306	586-3232*	225
National Funeral Directors & Morticians Assn (NFDMA) 6290 Shannon Pkwy .... Union City GA 30291 *TF:* 800-434-0958 ■ *Web:* www.nfdma.com	770-969-0064		49-4
National Funeral Directors Assn (NFDA) 13625 Bishop's Dr .... Brookfield WI 53005 *TF:* 800-228-6332 ■ *Web:* www.nfda.org	262-789-1880	789-6977	49-4
National Furniture Liquidators I LLC (NFL) 2865 Log Cabin Dr .... Atlanta GA 30339 *Web:* www.nflinc.com	404-872-7280		321
National Futures Assn (NFA) 300 S Riverside Plz Ste 1800 .... Chicago IL 60606 *Web:* www.nfa.futures.org	312-781-1300	781-1467	49-2
National Gallery of Art 6th St & Constitution Ave NW .... Washington DC 20565 *TF:* 800-697-9350 ■ *Web:* www.nga.gov	202-737-4215		520
National Garden 100 Maryland Ave .... Washington DC 20001 *Web:* www.usbg.gov	202-225-8333		97
National Garden Clubs Inc (NGC) 4401 Magnolia Ave .... Saint Louis MO 63110 *TF:* 800-550-6007 ■ *Web:* www.gardenclub.org	314-776-7574	776-5108	48-18
National Gardening Assn (NGA) 1100 Dorset St .... South Burlington VT 05403 *TF:* 800-538-7476 ■ *Web:* garden.org	802-863-5251	864-6889	48-18
National Gaucher Foundation (NGF) 5410 Edson Ln Ste 220 .... Rockville MD 20852 *TF:* 800-504-3189 ■ *Web:* www.gaucherdisease.org	800-504-3189		48-17
National Gay & Lesbian Task Force (NGLTF) 1325 Massachusetts Ave NW Ste 600 .... Washington DC 20005 *Web:* www.thetaskforce.org	202-393-5177	393-2241	48-8
National Genealogical Society (NGS) 3108 Columbia Pk Ste 300 .... Arlington VA 22204 *TF:* 800-473-0060 ■ *Web:* www.ngsgenealogy.org	703-525-0050	525-0052	48-18
National Genetics Institute 2440 S Blvd .... Los Angeles CA 90064 *TF:* 800-352-7788 ■ *Web:* www.ngi.com	310-996-0036		418
National Geographic Maps 212 Beaver Brook Canyon Rd .... Evergreen CO 80439 **Fax Area Code:* 800 ■ *TF:* 800-962-1643 ■ *Web:* www.natgeomaps.com	303-670-3457	626-8676*	637-10
National Geographic Society 1145 17th St NW .... Washington DC 20036 *Web:* www.nationalgeographic.com	202-857-7700		49-19
National Gift Card Corp 300 Millennium Dr .... Crystal Lake IL 60012 *TF:* 888-472-8747 ■ *Web:* ngc-group.com	888-472-8747		366
National Glass & Metal Company Inc 1424 Easton Rd Ste 400 .... Horsham PA 19044 *Web:* www.ngmco.com	215-938-8880	938-7028	189-6
National Glass Ltd 5744 198th St .... Langley BC V3A7J2 *TF:* 800-663-8168 ■ *Web:* nationalglass.ca	604-530-2311	530-4662	361
National Golf Course Owners Assn (NGCOA) 291 Seven Farms Dr 2nd Fl .... Charleston SC 29492 *TF:* 800-933-4262 ■ *Web:* www.ngcoa.org	843-881-9956	881-9958	48-23
National Golf Foundation (NGF) 1150 S US Hwy 1 Ste 401 .... Jupiter FL 33477 *TF:* 800-733-6006 ■ *Web:* www.ngf.org	561-744-6006	744-6107	48-22
National Governors Assn (NGA) 444 N Capitol St NW Ste 267 .... Washington DC 20001 *Web:* www.nga.org	202-624-5300	624-5313	49-7
National Graduate School of Quality Management, The 186 Jones Rd .... Falmouth MA 02540 *TF:* 800-838-2580 ■ *Web:* ngs.edu	800-838-2580		166
National Grange 1616 H St NW .... Washington DC 20006 *TF:* 888-447-2643 ■ *Web:* www.nationalgrange.org	202-628-3507	347-1091	48-2
National Grange Mutual Insurance Co 55 West St .... Keene NH 03431 *Web:* msagroup.com	603-352-4000		391-4
National Grape Cooperative Association Inc 2 S Portage St .... Westfield NY 14787 *Web:* www.ncfc.org	716-326-5200		315-5
National Graphics Inc 248 Branford Rd .... North Branford CT 06471 *Web:* natgraphics.com	203-481-2351	483-0256	627
National Great Blacks in Wax Museum 1601-03 E N Ave .... Baltimore MD 21213 *Web:* www.greatblacksinwax.org	410-563-3404		520
National Greyhound Assn (NGA) 729 Old US 40 .... Abilene KS 67410 *TF:* 800-366-1471 ■ *Web:* www.ngagreyhounds.com	785-263-4660	263-4689	48-22
National Grid USA Service Company Inc 25 Research Dr .... Westborough MA 01582 *TF:* 800-548-8000 ■ *Web:* www.nationalgridus.com	508-389-2000		360-5
National Grocers Assn (NGA) 1005 N Glebe Rd Ste 250 .... Arlington VA 22201 *Web:* www.nationalgrocers.org	703-516-0700	516-0115	49-6
National Ground Water Assn (NGWA) 601 Dempsey Rd .... Westerville OH 43081 *TF:* 800-551-7379 ■ *Web:* www.ngwa.org	614-898-7791	898-7786	48-12
National Guard Educational Foundation (NGAUS) 1 Massachusetts Ave NW .... Washington DC 20001 *TF:* 888-226-4287 ■ *Web:* www.ngaus.org	202-789-0031	682-9358	48-19
National Guard Products Inc 4985 E Raines Rd .... Memphis TN 38118 *TF:* 800-647-7874 ■ *Web:* www.ngp.com	800-647-7874	255-7874	234
National Guardian Life Insurance Co (NGL) 2 E Gilman St .... Madison WI 53703 **Fax Area Code:* 608 ■ *TF:* 800-548-2962 ■ *Web:* www.nglic.com	800-548-2962	257-3940*	391-2
National Guild for Community Arts Education 520 Eighth Ave Ste 302 .... New York NY 10018 **Fax Area Code:* 216 ■ *TF:* 800-441-1414 ■ *Web:* www.nationalguild.org	212-268-3337	916-3563*	49-5
National Gypsum Co 2001 Rexford Rd .... Charlotte NC 28211 **Fax Area Code:* 800 ■ *TF:* 800-628-4662 ■ *Web:* nationalgypsum.com	704-365-7300	329-6421*	347
National Hansen's Disease Program (NHDP) 1770 Physicians Pk Dr .... Baton Rouge LA 70816 *TF:* 800-221-9393 ■ *Web:* www.hrsa.gov	800-221-9393		668
National Hardwood Lumber Assn (NHLA) 6830 Raleigh-LaGrange Rd .... Memphis TN 38134 *TF:* 800-933-0318 ■ *Web:* nhla.com	901-377-1818	382-6419	49-3
National Head Start Assn (NHSA) 1651 Prince St .... Alexandria VA 22314 *TF:* 866-677-8724 ■ *Web:* www.nhsa.org	703-739-0875	739-0878	48-11
National Headache Foundation (NHF) 820 N Orleans St Ste 217 .... Chicago IL 60610 *Web:* headaches.org	312-274-2650	640-9049	48-17
National Health Council (NHC) 1730 M St NW Ste 500 .... Washington DC 20036 *Web:* www.nationalhealthcouncil.org	202-785-3910	785-5923	48-17
National Health Investors Inc 222 Robert Rose Dr .... Murfreesboro TN 37129 *NYSE:* NHI ■ *TF:* 800-942-5909 ■ *Web:* www.nhireit.com	615-890-9100		654
National HealthCare Corp 100 E Vine St PO Box 1398 .... Murfreesboro TN 37133 *NYSE:* NHC ■ *Web:* nhccare.com	615-890-2020	890-0123	451
National Hearing Conservation Assn (NHCA) 3030 W 81st Ave .... Westminster CO 80031 *Web:* www.hearingconservation.org	303-224-9022	458-0002	48-17
National Heavy Equipment Operators School 188 College Dr .... Orange Park FL 32065 *TF:* 800-488-7364 ■ *Web:* www.earthmoverschool.com	904-272-4000	272-6702	685
National Hemophilia Foundation (NHF) 7 Penn Plz Ste 1204 .... New York NY 10001 *TF:* 800-424-2634 ■ *Web:* www.hemophilia.org	212-328-3700	328-3777	48-17
National Heritage Academies 3850 Broadmoor Ave SE Ste 201 .... Grand Rapids MI 49512 *TF:* 877-223-6402 ■ *Web:* www.nhaschools.com	877-223-6402		242
National High Magnetic Field Laboratory (NHMFL) 1800 E Paul Dirac Dr .... Tallahassee FL 32310 *Web:* nationalmaglab.org	850-644-0311		668
National Highway Traffic Safety Administration *National Center for Statistics & Analysis* 1200 New Jersey Ave SE .... Washington DC 20590 *TF:* 800-934-8517 ■ *Web:* www.nhtsa.gov	202-366-2555	366-7078	340-17
National Highway Traffic Safety Administration *Vehicle Research & Test Ctr* 10820 SR 347 PO Box B37 .... East Liberty OH 43319 *TF:* 800-262-8309 ■ *Web:* www.nhtsa.gov	937-666-4511		340-17
Region 1 1200 New Jersey Ave SE West Bldg .... Cambridge MA 02142 *Web:* www.nhtsa.gov	617-494-3427	494-3646	340-17
NHTSA Region 2 222 Mamaroneck Ave Ste 204 .... White Plains NY 10605 *Web:* www.nhtsa.gov	914-682-6162	682-6239	340-17
NHTSA Region 3 1200 New Jersey Ave SE West Bldg .... Washington DC 20590 **Fax Area Code:* 410 ■ *TF:* 888-327-4236 ■ *Web:* www.nhtsa.gov	888-327-4236	962-2770*	340-17
NHTSA Region 4 61 Forsyth St SW .... Atlanta GA 30303 *Web:* www.nhtsa.gov	404-562-3739	562-3763	340-17
NHTSA Region 5 1200 New Jersey Ave SE .... Washington DC 20590 *Web:* www.nhtsa.gov	708-503-8822	503-8991	340-17
NHTSA Region 6 819 Taylor St Rm 8A38 .... Fort Worth TX 76102 *Web:* www.nhtsa.gov	817-978-3653	978-8339	340-17
NHTSA Region 7 901 Locust St Rm 466 .... Kansas City MO 64106 *Web:* www.nhtsa.gov	816-329-3900	329-3910	340-17
NHTSA Region 8 12300 W Dakota Ave Ste 140 .... Lakewood CO 80228 *Web:* www.nhtsa.gov	720-963-3100	963-3124	340-17
NHTSA Region 9 201 Mission St Ste 2230 .... San Francisco CA 94105 *Web:* www.nhtsa.gov	415-744-3089	744-2532	340-17
National Highway Traffic Safety Administration Regional Offices *NHTSA Region 10* 915 Second Ave Ste 3140 .... Seattle WA 98174 *Web:* www.nhtsa.gov	206-220-7640	220-7651	340-17
National Hispanic Council on Aging (NHCOA) 2201 12th St NW Ste 101 .... Washington DC 20009 *Web:* www.nhcoa.org	202-347-9733	347-9735	48-6
National Hispanic Cultural Ctr 1701 Fourth St SW .... Albuquerque NM 87102 *Web:* www.nhccnm.org	505-246-2261	246-2613	50-2
National Hispanic Institute (NHI) 472 FM 1966 Rd .... Maxwell TX 78656 *Web:* www.nationalhispanicinstitute.org	512-357-6137		48-14
National Hispanic University 14271 Story Rd .... San Jose CA 95127 *TF:* 877-762-9801 ■ *Web:* www.nhu.edu	408-254-6900	254-1369	166
National HME Inc 7451 Airport Fwy .... Richland Hills TX 76118 *Web:* www.nationalhme.com	817-332-4433		475
National Hockey League (NHL) 1185 Avenue of the Americas .... New York NY 10036 *Web:* www.nhl.com	212-789-2000	789-2020	716
National Holistic Institute 5900 Doyle St .... Emeryville CA 94608 *TF:* 800-315-3552 ■ *Web:* www.nhi.edu	510-547-6442		167-3
National Home Infusion Assn (NHIA) 100 Daingerfield Rd .... Alexandria VA 22314 *Web:* www.nhia.org	703-549-3740	683-1484	49-8
National Honor Society (NHS) 1904 Assn Dr .... Reston VA 20191 *TF:* 800-253-7746 ■ *Web:* www.nhs.us	703-860-0200	476-5432	48-11

Name / Address	City	State	ZIP	Phone	Fax	Class
National Hospice & Palliative Care Organization (NHPCO) 1700 Diagonal Rd Ste 625 *TF:* 800-658-8898 ■ *Web:* www.nhpco.org	Alexandria	VA	22314	703-837-1500	837-1233	49-8
National Hotel 1677 Collins Ave *TF:* 800-327-8370 ■ *Web:* nationalhotel.com	Miami Beach	FL	33139	305-532-2311	534-1426	379
National House Check 950 W Bannock St Ste 950 *Web:* housecheckboise.com	Boise	ID	83702	208-495-0826		113
National Housing & Rehabilitation Assn (NH&RA) 1400 16th St NW Ste 420 *Web:* www.housingonline.com	Washington	DC	20036	202-939-1750	265-4435	49-17
National Housing Conference (NHC) 1801 K St NW Ste M-100 *Web:* www.nhc.org	Washington	DC	20006	202-466-2121	466-2122	49-3
National Humanities Alliance (NHA) 21 Dupont Cir NW Ste 800 *Web:* www.nhalliance.org	Washington	DC	20036	202-296-4994	872-0884	48-4
National HVAC Service Ltd 100 Bradford Rd Ste 120 *Web:* www.nationalhvacservice.com	Wexford	PA	15090	724-935-9390		189-10
National Immigration Forum 50 F St NW Ste 300 *Web:* www.immigrationforum.org	Washington	DC	20001	202-347-0040	347-0058	48-8
National Immigration Project of the National Lawyers Guild Inc (NIPNLG) 14 Beacon St Ste 602 *Web:* www.nationalimmigrationproject.org	Boston	MA	02108	617-227-9727	227-5495	393
National Independent Automobile Dealers Assn (NIADA) 2521 Brown Blvd *TF:* 800-682-3837 ■ *Web:* www.niada.com	Arlington	TX	76006	817-640-3838	649-5866	49-18
National Independent Flag Dealers Assn (NIFDA) 7984 S Chicago Ave *TF:* 800-356-4085 ■ *Web:* www.nifda.net	Chicago	IL	60617	773-768-8076	768-3138	49-18
National Indian Gaming Assn (NIGA) 224 Second St SE *Web:* www.indiangaming.org	Washington	DC	20003	202-546-7711	546-1755	48-23
National Indian Gaming Commission 1441 L St NW Ste 9100 *Web:* www.nigc.gov	Washington	DC	20005	202-632-7003	632-7066	340-20
National Industrial Lumber Co 1 Chicago Ave **Fax Area Code:* 412 ■ *TF:* 800-289-9352 ■ *Web:* www.nilco.net	Elizabeth	PA	15037	800-289-9352	384-3955*	191-3
National Infantry Museum 1775 Legacy Way *Web:* www.nationalinfantrymuseum.org	Columbus	GA	31903	706-685-5800	545-5158	520
National Information Standards Organization (NISO) 3600 Clipper Mill Rd Ste 302 **Fax Area Code:* 410 ■ *TF:* 877-375-2160 ■ *Web:* www.niso.org	Baltimore	MD	21211	301-654-2512	685-5278*	49-16
National Institute for Fitness & Sport Inc, The 250 University Blvd *Web:* www.nifs.org	Indianapolis	IN	46202	317-274-3432		354
National Institute for Literacy (NIFL) 1775 'I' St NW Ste 730 *TF:* 800-228-8813 ■ *Web:* lincs.ed.gov	Washington	DC	20006	202-233-2025	233-2050	340-8
National Institute for Women in Trades Technology & Science (IWITTS) 1150 Ballena Blvd Ste 102 *Web:* www.iwitts.org	Alameda	CA	94501	510-749-0200	749-0500	49-19
National Institute of Building Sciences (NIBS) 1090 Vermont Ave NW Ste 700 *Web:* www.nibs.org	Washington	DC	20005	202-289-7800	289-1092	49-3
National Institute of Child Health & Human Development (NICHD) 31 Center Dr Bldg 31 Rm 2A32 *TF:* 800-370-2943 ■ *Web:* www.nih.gov	Bethesda	MD	20892	800-370-2943		668
National Institute of Food & Agriculture 1400 Independence Ave SW Ste 2201 *Web:* nifa.usda.gov	Washington	DC	20250	202-401-4952	720-6486	340-1
National Institute of Governmental Purchasing Inc (NIGP) 151 Spring St *TF:* 800-367-6447 ■ *Web:* www.nigp.org	Herndon	VA	20170	703-736-8900	736-2818	49-7
National Institute of Standards & Technology (NIST) 100 Bureau Dr Sp 1070 *Web:* www.nist.gov	Gaithersburg	MD	20899	301-975-6478		340-2
National Institutes of Biomedical Imaging & Bioengineering 6707 Democracy Blvd Ste 202 *Web:* www.nibib.nih.gov	Bethesda	MD	20892	301-496-8859		340-10
National Institutes of Health (NIH) 9000 Rockville Pk *TF:* 800-411-1222 ■ *Web:* www.nih.gov	Bethesda	MD	20892	301-496-4000		340-10
National Institutes of Health						
Center for Scientific Review 6701 Rockledge Dr MSC 7950 *TF:* 800-438-4380 ■ *Web:* www.nih.gov	Bethesda	MD	20892	301-435-1111		340-10
Clinical Ctr 10 Center Dr *Web:* www.cc.nih.gov	Bethesda	MD	20892	301-496-2563	402-2984	340-10
National Cancer Institute 9609 Medical Center Dr BG 9609 MSC 9760 *TF:* 800-422-6237 ■ *Web:* www.cancer.gov	Bethesda	MD	20892	301-435-3848		668
National Center on Minority Health & Health Disparities 6707 Democracy Blvd Ste 800 *Web:* www.nimhd.nih.gov	Bethesda	MD	20892	301-402-1366	480-4049	340-10
National Heart Lung & Blood Institute (NHLBI) 31 Center Dr Bldg 31 *Web:* www.nhlbi.nih.gov	Bethesda	MD	20892	301-496-5166		340-10
National Human Genome Research Institute 9000 Rockville Pk 31 Center Dr MSC 2152 Bldg 31 Rm 4B09 *Web:* www.genome.gov	Bethesda	MD	20892	301-402-0911	402-2218	668
National Institute of Arthritis & Musculoskeletal 1 AMS Cir *TF:* 877-226-4267 ■ *Web:* www.niams.nih.gov	Bethesda	MD	20892	301-495-4484	718-6366	340-10
National Institute of Dental & Craniofacial Research 9000 Rockville Pk *Web:* www.nidcr.nih.gov	Bethesda	MD	20892	301-594-6578	402-2185	668
National Institute of Diabetes & Digestive & Kidney Diseases 31 Center Dr MSC 2560 *Web:* www.niddk.nih.gov	Bethesda	MD	20892	301-496-3583		340-10
National Institute of Environmental Health Science PO Box 12233 *Web:* www.niehs.nih.gov	Research Triangle Park	NC	27709	919-541-3201	541-2260	340-10
National Institute of General Medical Sciences 45 Center Dr MSC 6200 *Web:* www.nigms.nih.gov	Bethesda	MD	20892	301-496-7301		340-10
National Institute of Mental Health 6001 Executive Blvd Rm 6200 MSC 9663 *Web:* www.nimh.nih.gov	Bethesda	MD	20892	301-443-4513	443-4279	340-10
National Institute of Neurological Disorders & Stroke PO Box 5801 *TF:* 800-352-9424 ■ *Web:* www.ninds.nih.gov	Bethesda	MD	20824	301-496-5751		340-10
National Institute of Nursing Research 31 Center Dr Rm 5B03 *Web:* www.ninr.nih.gov	Bethesda	MD	20892	301-496-0207	480-4969	668
National Institute on Aging 31 Center Dr Bldg 31 MSC 2292 Rm 5C27 *Web:* www.nia.nih.gov	Bethesda	MD	20892	301-496-1752	496-1072	340-10
National Institute on Alcohol Abuse & Alcoholism 5635 Fishers Ln MSC 9304 *Web:* www.niaaa.nih.gov	Bethesda	MD	20892	301-443-3885	443-7043	340-10
National Institute on Deafness & Other Communication Disorders, The 31 Center Dr MSC 2320 *TF:* 800-241-1044 ■ *Web:* www.nidcd.nih.gov	Bethesda	MD	20892	301-496-7243	402-0018	668
National Institute on Drug Abuse 6001 Executive Blvd Rm 4123 *Web:* www.drugabuse.gov	Bethesda	MD	20892	301-443-6480		340-10
National Library of Medicine 8600 Rockville Pk *Web:* www.nlm.nih.gov	Bethesda	MD	20894	301-594-5983	402-1384	340-10
Office of Communications & Public Liaison 31 Center Dr Bldg 1 Rm 344 *Web:* www.nih.gov	Bethesda	MD	20892	301-451-7636	496-0017	340-10
Office of Dietary Supplements 6100 Executive Blvd MSC 7517 Rm 3B01 *Web:* ods.od.nih.gov	Bethesda	MD	20892	301-435-2920	480-1845	340-10
Office of Rare Diseases 6701 Democracy Blvd Ste 1001 *TF:* 800-942-6825 ■ *Web:* rarediseases.info.nih.gov	Bethesda	MD	20892	301-402-4336	480-9655	340-10
National Instrument LLC 4119 Fordleigh Rd *TF:* 866-258-1914 ■ *Web:* www.filamatic.com	Baltimore	MD	21215	410-764-0900	764-7719	547
National Instruments Corp 11500 N Mopac Expy *NASDAQ: NATI* ■ *TF:* 800-433-3488 ■ *Web:* www.ni.com	Austin	TX	78759	512-683-0100	683-8411	178-5
National Insulation Assn (NIA) 99 Canal Center Plz Ste 222 *TF:* 877-968-7642 ■ *Web:* insulation.org	Alexandria	VA	22314	703-549-4838		49-3
National Insurance Brokerage of NY Inc 175 Oval Dr *Web:* nibony.com	Islandia	NY	11749	631-273-4242	273-8990	390
National Insurance Crime Bureau (NICB) 1111 E Touhy Ave Ste 400 *TF:* 800-447-6282 ■ *Web:* www.nicb.org	Des Plaines	IL	60018	847-544-7002		49-9
National Interagency Fire Ctr 3833 S Development Ave *TF:* 877-471-2262 ■ *Web:* www.nifc.gov	Boise	ID	83705	208-387-5512		340-13
National Interstate Corp 3250 I- Dr *NASDAQ: NATL* ■ *TF:* 800-929-1500 ■ *Web:* www.nationalinterstate.com	Richfield	OH	44286	330-659-8900	659-8901	391-4
National Intramural-Recreational Sports Assn (NIRSA) 4185 SW Research Way *Web:* www.nirsa.net	Corvallis	OR	97333	541-766-8211	766-8284	48-22
National Investor Relations Institute (NIRI) 225 Reinekers Ln Ste 560 *Web:* www.niri.org	Alexandria	VA	22314	703-562-7700	562-7701	49-2
National Italian American Sports Hall of Fame 1431 W Taylor St *Web:* www.niashf.org	Chicago	IL	60607	312-226-5566		522
National Jet Company Inc 10 Cupler Dr *TF:* 800-272-1930 ■ *Web:* www.najet.com	Cumberland	MD	21502	301-729-2300	729-4298	455
National Jets 3495 SW Ninth Ave *TF:* 800-327-3710 ■ *Web:* www.nationaljets.com	Fort Lauderdale	FL	33315	954-359-9900	359-0064	63
National Jewish Medical & Research Ctr 1400 Jackson St *TF:* 877-225-5654 ■ *Web:* www.nationaljewish.org	Denver	CO	80206	303-388-4461		374-7
National Jurist Magazine 7670 Opportunity Rd Ste 105 *Web:* www.nationaljurist.com	San Diego	CA	92111	858-300-3200		457-15
National Kappa Kappa Iota Inc 1875 E 15th St *TF:* 800-678-0389 ■ *Web:* www.nationalkappakappaiota.org	Tulsa	OK	74104	918-744-0389	744-0578	48-16
National Kidney Foundation (NKF) 30 E 33rd St *TF:* 800-622-9010 ■ *Web:* www.kidney.org	New York	NY	10016	212-889-2210		48-17
National Kitchen & Bath Assn (NKBA) 687 Willow Grove St **Fax Area Code:* 908 ■ *TF:* 800-843-6522 ■ *Web:* nkba.org	Hackettstown	NJ	07840	800-843-6522	852-1695*	49-3
National Labor Relations Board (NLRB) 1099 14th St NW *Web:* www.nlrb.gov	Washington	DC	20570	202-273-1991		340-20
Region 1 10 Causeway St 6th Fl *TF:* 866-667-6572 ■ *Web:* www.nlrb.gov	Boston	MA	02222	617-565-6700	565-6725	340-20
Region 2 26 Federal Plz Rm 3614 *Web:* www.nlrb.gov	New York	NY	10278	212-264-0300	264-2450	340-20
Region 3 130 S Elmwood Ave Niagara Ctr Bldg Ste 630 *Web:* www.nlrb.gov	Buffalo	NY	14202	716-551-4931	551-4972	340-20
Region 4 615 Chestnut St 7th Fl *Web:* www.nlrb.gov	Philadelphia	PA	19106	215-597-7601	597-7658	340-20
Region 5 103 S Gay St 8th Fl *Web:* www.nlrb.gov	Baltimore	MD	21202	410-962-2822	962-2198	340-20
Region 6 1000 Liberty Ave Rm 904 *Web:* www.nlrb.gov	Pittsburgh	PA	15222	412-395-4400	395-5986	340-20
Region 7 477 Michigan Ave Rm 300 *Web:* www.nlrb.gov	Detroit	MI	48226	313-226-3200	226-2090	340-20
Region 8 1240 E Ninth St Rm 1695 *Web:* www.nlrb.gov	Cleveland	OH	44199	216-522-3715	522-2418	340-20
Region 9 550 Main St Rm 3003 *Web:* www.nlrb.gov	Cincinnati	OH	45202	513-684-3686	684-3946	340-20

Name / Address	City	State	ZIP	Phone	Fax	Class
National Labor Relations Board Regional Offices						
Region 10 233 Peachtree St NE Ste 1000	Atlanta	GA	30303	404-331-2896	331-2858	340-20
Web: www.nlrb.gov						
Region 11 4035 University Pkwy Ste 200	Winston-Salem	NC	27106	336-631-5201	631-5210	340-20
Web: www.nlrb.gov						
Region 12 201 E Kennedy Blvd Ste 530	Tampa	FL	33602	813-228-2641	228-2874	340-20
Web: www.nlrb.gov						
Region 15 1515 Poydras St Rm 610	New Orleans	LA	70112	504-589-6361	589-4069	340-20
Web: www.nlrb.gov						
Region 16 819 Taylor St Rm 8A24	Fort Worth	TX	76102	817-978-2921	978-2928	340-20
Web: www.nlrb.gov						
Region 17 8600 Farley St Ste 100	Overland Park	KS	66212	913-967-3000	967-3010	340-20
Web: www.nlrb.gov						
Region 18 330 Second Ave S Ste 790	Minneapolis	MN	55401	612-348-1757	348-1785	340-20
Web: www.nlrb.gov						
Region 19 915 Second Ave Rm 2948	Seattle	WA	98174	206-220-6300	220-6305	340-20
Web: www.nlrb.gov						
Region 21 888 S Figueroa St 9th Fl	Los Angeles	CA	90017	213-894-5200	894-2778	340-20
Web: www.nlrb.gov						
Region 22 20 Washington Pl 5th Fl	Newark	NJ	07102	973-645-2100	645-3852	340-20
Web: www.nlrb.gov						
Region 24 525 FD Roosevelt Ave Ste 1002	San Juan	PR	00918	787-766-5347	766-5478	340-20
Web: www.nlrb.gov						
Region 25 575 N Pennsylvania St Minton-Capehart Federal Bldg Ste 238	Indianapolis	IN	46204	317-226-7381	226-5103	340-20
Web: www.nlrb.gov						
Region 26 80 Monroe Ave Ste 350	Memphis	TN	38103	901-544-0018	544-0008	340-20
Web: www.nlrb.gov						
Region 27 1961 Stout St Ste 13-103	Denver	CO	80294	303-844-3551	844-6249	340-20
Web: www.nlrb.gov						
Region 28 2600 N Central Ave Ste 1800	Phoenix	AZ	85004	602-640-2160	640-2178	340-20
Web: www.nlrb.gov						
Region 29 1 Metrotech Ctr 15th Fl	Brooklyn	NY	11201	718-330-7713	330-7579	340-20
Web: www.nlrb.gov						
Region 30 1015 Half St SE	Washington	DC	20570	202-273-1000		340-20
TF: 844-762-6572 ■ *Web:* www.nlrb.gov						
Region 31 11150 W Olympic Blvd Ste 700	Los Angeles	CA	90064	310-235-7352	235-7420	340-20
Web: www.nlrb.gov						
Region 32 1301 Clay St Rm 300N	Oakland	CA	94612	510-637-3300	637-3315	340-20
Web: www.nlrb.gov						
Region 34 450 Main St	Hartford	CT	06103	860-240-3522	240-3564	340-20
Web: nlrb.gov						
National Ladies Auxiliary Jewish War Veterans of USA Inc						
1811 R St NW	Washington	DC	20009	202-667-9061		520
Web: www.jwv.org						
National Laser Institute						
16601 N 90th St	Scottsdale	AZ	85260	800-982-6817		167-3
TF: 800-982-6817 ■ *Web:* www.nationallaserinstitute.com						
National Latino Education Institute						
2011 W Pershing Rd	Chicago	IL	60609	773-247-0707		533
Web: www.nlei.org						
National Law Library Inc						
4301 Windfern Rd Ste 200	Houston	TX	77041	877-484-7529		434-3
TF: 877-484-7529 ■ *Web:* www.itislaw.com						
National League for Nursing (NLN)						
61 Broadway 33rd Fl	New York	NY	10006	212-363-5555	812-0391	49-8
TF: 800-669-1656 ■ *Web:* www.nln.org						
National League of American Pen Women Inc (NLAPW)						
1300 17th St NW	Washington	DC	20036	202-785-1997	452-8868	48-4
Web: www.nlapw.org						
National League of Cities (NLC)						
660 N Capitol St NW	Washington	DC	20001	877-827-2385		49-7
TF: 877-827-2385 ■ *Web:* www.nlc.org						
National League of Families of American Prisoners & Missing in Southeast Asia						
5673 Columbia Pk Ste 100	Falls Church	VA	22041	703-465-7432		48-19
Web: www.pow-miafamilies.org						
National Legal Aid & Defender Assn (NLADA)						
1140 Connecticut Ave NW Ste 900	Washington	DC	20036	202-452-0620	872-1031	49-10
TF: 800-725-4513 ■ *Web:* www.nlada.org						
National Liberty Museum						
321 Chestnut St	Philadelphia	PA	19106	215-925-2800		520
Web: www.libertymuseum.org						
National Library of Medicine						
Lister Hill National Center for Biomedical Communications 8600 Rockville Pk	Bethesda	MD	20894	301-496-4441		340-10
Web: www.lhncbc.nlm.nih.gov						
National Lift Truck Inc						
3333 Mt Prospect Rd	Franklin Park	IL	60131	800-469-6420		111
TF: 800-469-6420 ■ *Web:* nlt.com						
National Lighting Company Inc						
522 Cortlandt St	Belleville	NJ	07109	973-751-1600	751-4931	439
Web: www.natltg.com						
National Little Britches Rodeo Assn (NLBRA)						
5050 Edison Ave Ste 105	Colorado Springs	CO	80915	719-389-0333	578-1367	48-22
TF: 800-763-3694 ■ *Web:* www.nlbra.com						
National Luggage Dealers Assn (NLDA)						
1817 Elmdale Ave	Glenview	IL	60026	847-998-6869	998-6884	49-18
TF: 800-411-0705 ■ *Web:* www.nlda.com						
National Lumber 71 Maple St	Mansfield	MA	02048	508-339-8020	339-4518	364
Web: www.national-lumber.com						
National Lumber & Building Material Dealers Assn (NLBMDA)						
2001 K St NW 3rd Fl	Washington	DC	20006	202-367-1169		49-18
Web: www.dealer.org						
National Machinery LLC						
161 Greenfield St	Tiffin	OH	44883	419-447-5211	443-2379	456
Web: www.nationalmachinery.com						
National Magnetic Sensors Inc						
141 Summer St	Plantsville	CT	06479	860-621-6816		250
Web: www.nationalmagnetic.com						
National Magnetics Group Inc						
1210 Win Dr	Bethlehem	PA	18017	610-867-7600	867-0200	458
Web: www.magneticsgroup.com						
National Mail Graphics Corp						
300 Old Mill Ln	Exton	PA	19341	610-524-1600		627
Web: nmgcorp.com						
National Mail Order Association LLC (NMOA)						
2807 Polk St NE	Minneapolis	MN	55418	612-788-1673	788-1147	49-18
TF: 800-992-1377 ■ *Web:* www.nmoa.org						
National Management Assn (NMA)						
2210 Arbor Blvd	Dayton	OH	45439	937-294-0421		49-12
Web: nma1.org						
National Manufacturing Company Inc						
12 River Rd	Chatham	NJ	07928	973-635-8846	635-7810	254
Web: www.natlmfg.com						
National Marfan Foundation (NMF)						
22 Manhasset Ave	Port Washington	NY	11050	516-883-8712	883-8040	48-17
TF: 800-862-7326 ■ *Web:* www.marfan.org						
National Marine Electronics Assn (NMEA)						
692 Ritchie Hwy Ste 104	Severna Park	MD	21146	410-975-9425	975-9450	49-13
TF: 800-808-6632 ■ *Web:* www.nmea.org						
National Marine Fisheries Service Regional Offices						
Alaska Regional Office 709 W 9th St Rm 420 PO Box 21668	Juneau	AK	99802	907-586-7221	586-7249	340-2
Web: www.fisheries.noaa.gov						
Greater Atlantic Region 55 Great Republic Dr	Gloucester	MA	01930	978-281-9300	281-9333	340-2
Web: www.fisheries.noaa.gov						
Northwest Region 7600 Sand Pt Way NE	Seattle	WA	98115	206-526-6150	526-6426	340-2
Web: www.fisheries.noaa.gov						
Southwest Region 501 W Ocean Blvd Ste 1200	Long Beach	CA	90802	562-388-7346		340-2
Web: www.fisheries.noaa.gov						
National Marine Manufacturers Assn (NMMA)						
200 E Randolph Dr Ste 5100	Chicago	IL	60601	312-946-6200	946-0388	49-21
Web: www.nmma.org						
National Marine Representatives Assn (NMRA)						
PO Box 360	Gurnee	IL	60031	847-662-3167	336-7126	49-18
TF: 800-890-3819 ■ *Web:* www.nmraonline.org						
National Marine Sanctuary Foundation						
8601 Georgia Ave Ste 510	Silver Spring	MD	20910	301-608-3040	608-3044	48-13
Web: marinesanctuary.org						
National Marine Underwriters Inc						
888 Bestgate Rd Ste 105	Annapolis	MD	21401	800-262-8467	639-9577*	391-4
**Fax Area Code:* 866 ■ *TF:* 800-262-8467 ■ *Web:* www.nmu.com						
National Marrow Donor Program (NMDP)						
500 N Fifth St	Minneapolis	MN	55401	800-627-7692		48-17
TF: 800-627-7692 ■ *Web:* bethematch.org						
National Material LP						
1965 Pratt Blvd	Elk Grove Village	IL	60007	847-284-8464		492
Web: www.nmlp.com						
National Medal of Honor Museum of Military History						
PO Box 11467	Chattanooga	TN	37401	423-877-2525		520
Web: www.mohm.org						
National Media Services Inc						
613 N Commerce Ave	Front Royal	VA	22630	540-635-4181		514
Web: www.nationalmediaservices.com						
National Mediation Board						
1301 K St NW Ste 250 E	Washington	DC	20005	202-692-5000		340-20
Web: www.nmb.gov						
National Medical Assn (NMA)						
8403 Colesville Rd Ste 920	Silver Spring	MD	20910	202-347-1895	347-0722	49-8
TF: 800-662-0554 ■ *Web:* www.nmanet.org						
National Memorial Cemetery of Arizona						
23029 N Cave Creek Rd	Phoenix	AZ	85024	480-513-3600	513-1412	136
Web: www.cem.va.gov						
National Mental Health Information Ctr						
PO Box 42557	Washington	DC	20015	800-487-4889	747-5470*	340-10
**Fax Area Code:* 240 ■ *TF:* 800-487-4889 ■ *Web:* www.samhsa.gov						
National Merit Scholarship Corp						
1560 Sherman Ave Ste 200	Evanston	IL	60201	847-866-5100		725
Web: www.nationalmerit.org						
National Metal Fabricators						
2395 Greenleaf Ave	Elk Grove Village	IL	60007	847-439-5321	439-4774	697
TF: 800-323-8849 ■ *Web:* www.thefabricator.com						
National Metalwares Inc						
900 N Russell Ave	Aurora	IL	60506	630-892-9000		490
Web: www.nationalmetalwares.com						
National Middle School Assn (NMSA)						
4151 Executive Pkwy Ste 300	Westerville	OH	43081	614-895-4730	895-4750	49-5
TF: 800-528-6672 ■ *Web:* www.amle.org						
National Milk Producers Federation (NMPF)						
2101 Wilson Blvd Ste 400	Arlington	VA	22201	703-243-6111	841-9328	49-6
Web: www.nmpf.org						
National Millwork						
1177 W Blue Heron Blvd Ste B-106	West Palm Beach	FL	33404	561-848-5556		191-3
Web: nationalmillworkinc.com						
National Mining Assn (NMA)						
101 Constitution Ave NW Ste 500-E	Washington	DC	20001	202-463-2600	463-2666	48-12
Web: nma.org						
National Minority Supplier Development Council (NMSDC)						
1359 Broadway 10th Fl	New York	NY	10018	212-944-2430	719-9611	49-18
TF: 800-843-4898 ■ *Web:* www.nmsdc.org						
National Mississippi River Museum & Aquarium						
350 E Third St	Dubuque	IA	52001	563-557-9545		520
TF: 800-226-3369 ■ *Web:* www.mississippirivermuseum.com						
National Model Railroad Assn (NMRA)						
4121 Cromwell Rd	Chattanooga	TN	37421	423-892-2846	899-4869	48-18
TF: 800-654-2256 ■ *Web:* nmra.org						
National Molded Products Inc						
147 Kenwood St	Elyria	OH	44035	440-365-3400	365-2900	604
Web: www.nationalmoldedproduct.com						
National Monitoring Ctr						
26800 Aliso Viejo Pkwy Ste 250	Aliso Viejo	CA	92656	800-662-1711		693
TF: 800-662-1711 ■ *Web:* www.nmccentral.com						
National Motor Club of America Inc (NMC)						
130 E John Carpenter Fwy	Irving	TX	75062	800-523-4582		53
TF: 800-523-4582 ■ *Web:* nmc.com						
National Motor Freight Traffic Assn (NMFTA)						
1001 N Fairfax St Ste 600	Alexandria	VA	22314	703-838-1810	683-6296	49-21
TF: 866-411-6632 ■ *Web:* www.nmfta.org						
National Motorists Assn (NMA)						
402 W Second St	Waunakee	WI	53597	608 840 6000		49-21
TF: 800-882-2785 ■ *Web:* www.motorists.org						

Organization	City	State	ZIP	Phone	Fax	Class
National Multi Housing Council (NMHC) 1850 M St NW Ste 540 *Web:* www.nmhc.org	Washington	DC	20036	202-974-2300	775-0112	49-17
National Multiple Sclerosis Society 733 Third Ave 3rd Fl *Web:* www.nationalmssociety.org	New York	NY	10017	212-986-3240	986-7981	48-17
National Museum of American History (Smithsonian Institution) (NMAH) 12th St & Constitution Ave NW *Web:* americanhistory.si.edu	Washington	DC	20560	202-633-3270		520
National Museum of American Illustration 492 Bellevue Ave *Web:* americanillustration.org	Newport	RI	02840	401-851-8949	851-8974	520
National Museum of American Jewish History 101 S Independence Mall E *Web:* www.nmajh.org	Philadelphia	PA	19106	215-923-3811	923-0763	520
National Museum of American Jewish Military History (JWV-NMI) 1811 R St NW *Web:* nmajmh.org	Washington	DC	20009	202-265-6280		520
National Museum of Dentistry 31 S Greene St *Web:* www.dental.umaryland.edu	Baltimore	MD	21201	410-706-0600	706-8313	520
National Museum of Funeral History 415 Barren Springs Dr *Web:* www.nmfh.org	Houston	TX	77090	281-876-3063		520
National Museum of Health & Medicine 2500 Linden Ln *Web:* www.medicalmuseum.mil	Silver Spring	MD	20910	301-319-3300		520
National Museum of Mexican Art 1852 W 19th St *Web:* www.nationalmuseumofmexicanart.org	Chicago	IL	60608	312-738-1503	738-9740	520
National Museum of Naval Aviation 1750 Radford Blvd Ste C *TF:* 800-247-6289 ■ *Web:* www.navalaviationmuseum.org	Pensacola	FL	32508	850-452-3604	452-3296	520
National Museum of Nuclear Science & History 601 Eubank Blvd SE *Web:* www.nuclearmuseum.org	Albuquerque	NM	87123	505-245-2137		520
National Museum of Polo & Hall of Fame 9011 Lake Worth Rd *Web:* www.polomuseum.com	Lake Worth	FL	33467	561-969-3210	964-8299	522
National Museum of Racing & Hall of Fame 191 Union Ave *TF:* 800-562-5394 ■ *Web:* www.racingmuseum.org	Saratoga Springs	NY	12866	518-584-0400	584-4574	522
National Museum of Roller Skating 4730 S St *Web:* www.rollerskatingmuseum.com	Lincoln	NE	68506	402-483-7551	483-1465	520
National Museum of the American Indian (Smithsonian Institution) 1 Bowling Green *TF:* 800-242-6624 ■ *Web:* Www.americanindian.si.edu	New York	NY	10004	212-514-3700		520
National Museum of the Marine Corps 18900 Jefferson Davis Hwy *Web:* www.usmcmuseum.org	Triangle	VA	22172	703-649-2369		520
National Museum of the Pacific War 340 E Main St *Web:* www.pacificwarmuseum.org	Fredericksburg	TX	78624	830-997-8600		434-3
National Museum of the United States Air Force 1100 Spaatz St *Web:* www.nationalmuseum.af.mil	Dayton	OH	45433	937-255-3286		520
National Museum of Wildlife Art 2820 Rungius Rd PO Box 6825 *TF:* 800-313-9553 ■ *Web:* www.wildlifeart.org	Jackson	WY	83002	307-733-5771		520
National Museum of Women in the Arts 1250 New York Ave NW *TF:* 866-875-4627 ■ *Web:* nmwa.org	Washington	DC	20005	202-783-5000	393-3234	520
National Music Museum 414 E Clark St *Web:* orgs.usd.edu	Vermillion	SD	57069	605-677-5306		520
National Music Publishers' Assn (NMPA) 975 F St NW Ste 375 *Web:* www.nmpa.org	Washington	DC	20004	202-393-6672		48-4
National Mutual Benefit 6522 Grand Teton Plz *TF:* 800-779-1936 ■ *Web:* www.nmblife.org	Madison	WI	53719	608-833-1936		391-2
National Nail Corp 2964 Clydon SW *Web:* www.nationalnail.com	Wyoming	MI	49519	616-538-8000		234
National NeedleArts Assn, The (TNNA) 1100-H Brandywine Blvd *TF:* 800-889-8662 ■ *Web:* www.tnna.org	Zanesville	OH	43701	740-455-6773	452-2552	48-18
National Network for Youth, The 741 Eigth St SE *Web:* www.nn4youth.org	Washington	DC	20003	202-783-7949	783-7955	48-6
National Newspaper Assn (NNA) PO Box 7540 **Fax Area Code:* 573 ■ *TF:* 800-829-4662 ■ *Web:* www.nnaweb.org	Columbia	MO	65205	217-241-1400	777-4985*	49-14
National Niemann-Pick Disease Foundation Inc (NNPDF) 401 Madison Ave Ste B PO Box 49 *TF:* 877-287-3672 ■ *Web:* nnpdf.org	Fort Atkinson	WI	53538	920-563-0930		48-17
National Night Out (NATW) PO Box 303 **Fax Area Code:* 610 ■ *TF:* 800-648-3688 ■ *Web:* natw.org	Wynnewood	PA	19096	800-648-3688	649-5456*	48-7
National Nonwovens PO Box 150 *TF:* 800-333-3469 ■ *Web:* www.nationalnonwovens.com	Easthampton	MA	01027	413-527-3445	527-9570	745-6
National Notary Assn (NNA) 9350 DeSoto Ave *TF:* 800-876-6827 ■ *Web:* www.nationalnotary.org	Chatsworth	CA	91313	800-876-6827		49-12
National Nuclear Security Administration (NNSA) 1000 Independence Ave SW *Web:* www.energy.gov	Washington	DC	20585	202-586-5000	586-4892	340-9
National Ocean Industries Assn (NOIA) 1120 G St NW Ste 900 *TF:* 800-558-9994 ■ *Web:* www.noia.org	Washington	DC	20005	202-347-6900	347-8650	48-12
National Ocean Service 1305 East-West Hwy *Web:* oceanservice.noaa.gov	Silver Spring	MD	20910	301-713-3074	713-4269	340-2
National Odd Shoe Exchange PO Box 1120 *Web:* www.oddshoe.org	Chandler	AZ	85244	480-892-3484		48-17
National Office Furniture 1205 Kimball Blvd **Fax Area Code:* 812 ■ *TF:* 800-482-1717 ■ *Web:* www.nationalofficefurniture.com	Jasper	IN	47546	800-482-1717	482-8800*	319-1
National Office Systems Inc 6804 Virginia Manor Rd Ste 400 **Fax Area Code:* 240 ■ *TF:* 800-840-6264 ■ *Web:* nosinc.com	Beltsville	MD	20705	301-840-6264	264-8335*	610
National Oil & Gas Inc 409 N Main St *TF:* 800-322-8454 ■ *Web:* natloil.com	Bluffton	IN	46714	260-824-2220	824-2223	579
National Oilseed Processors Assn 1300 L St Nw Ste 1020 *Web:* www.nopa.org	Washington	DC	20005	202-842-0463	842-9126	48-2
National Older Worker Career Ctr 3811 N Fairfax Dr Ste 900 *Web:* www.nowcc.org	Arlington	VA	22203	703-558-4200		260
National Onion Assn (NOA) 822 Seventh St Ste 510 *Web:* www.onions-usa.org	Greeley	CO	80631	970-353-5895	353-5897	48-2
National Optical Astronomy Observatory 950 N Cherry Ave *TF:* 888-809-4012 ■ *Web:* www.noao.edu	Tucson	AZ	85719	520-318-8000	318-8360	668
National Oral Health Information Clearinghouse 1 NOHIC Way *TF:* 866-232-4528 ■ *Web:* www.nidcr.nih.gov	Bethesda	MD	20892	301-496-4261		48-17
National Orange Show Events Ctr 689 SE St *Web:* www.nosevents.com	San Bernardino	CA	92408	909-888-6788		515
National Organization for Albinism & Hypopigmentation (NOAH) PO Box 959 *TF:* 800-648-2310 ■ *Web:* www.albinism.org	East Hampstead	NH	03826	603-887-2310		48-17
National Organization for Rare Disorders (NORD) 55 Kenosia Ave *Web:* rarediseases.org	Danbury	CT	06810	203-744-0100	798-2291	48-17
National Organization for the Reform of Marijuana Laws (NORML) 1420 K Street NW Ste 350 *TF:* 888-420-8932 ■ *Web:* www.norml.org	Washington	DC	20006	202-483-5500	483-0057	48-8
National Organization for Victim Assistance (NOVA) 510 King St Ste 424 *TF:* 800-879-6682 ■ *Web:* www.trynova.org	Alexandria	VA	22314	703-535-6682	535-5500	48-8
National Organization for Women (NOW) 1100 H St NW 3rd Fl *TF:* 855-212-0212 ■ *Web:* now.org	Washington	DC	20005	202-628-8669		48-24
National Organization of Black Law Enforcement Executives (NOBLE) 4609 Pinecrest Office Pk Dr Ste F *Web:* noblenational.org	Alexandria	VA	22312	703-658-1529	658-9479	49-7
National Organization of Circumcision Information Resource Centers (NOCIRC) PO Box 2512 *TF:* 800-727-8622 ■ *Web:* www.nocirc.org	San Anselmo	CA	94979	415-488-9883	488-9660	48-17
National Organization of Industrial Trade Unions 148-06 Hillside Ave *Web:* www.noitu.org	Jamaica	NY	11435	718-291-3434	526-2920	414
National Organization on Disability (NOD) 77 Water St Ste 204 *Web:* www.nod.org	New York	NY	10005	646-505-1191		48-17
National Ornamental Metal Museum 374 Metal Museum Dr *Web:* www.metalmuseum.org	Memphis	TN	38106	901-774-6380		520
National Osteoporosis Foundation (NOF) 251 18th St S Ste 630 *TF:* 800-231-4222 ■ *Web:* www.nof.org	Arlington	VA	22202	202-223-2226	223-2237	48-17
National Outdoor Leadership School (NOLS) 284 Lincoln St **Fax Area Code:* 307 ■ *TF:* 800-710-6657 ■ *Web:* www.nols.edu	Lander	WY	82520	800-710-6657	332-1220*	685
National Ovarian Cancer Coalition (NOCC) 2501 Oak Lawn Ave Ste 435 **Fax Area Code:* 214 ■ *TF:* 888-682-7426 ■ *Web:* www.ovarian.org	Dallas	TX	75219	888-682-7426	273-4201*	48-17
National Paint & Coatings Assn (NPCA) 1500 Rhode Island Ave NW *Web:* www.paint.org	Washington	DC	20005	202-462-6272	462-8549	49-13
National Paper & Sanitary Supply 2511 S 156th Cir *TF:* 800-647-2737 ■ *Web:* catalog.nationalew.com	Omaha	NE	68130	402-330-5507	330-4109	559
National Paralegal College 717 E Maryland Ave **Fax Area Code:* 212 ■ *TF:* 800-371-6105 ■ *Web:* www.nationalparalegal.edu	Phoenix	AZ	85014	845-371-9101	918-1565*	167-3
National Park Aquarium 209 Central Ave *Web:* nationalparkaquarium.org	Hot Springs	AR	71901	501-624-3474		40
National Park Community College 101 College Dr *Web:* np.edu	Hot Springs	AR	71913	501-760-4222		162
National Park Foundation (NPF) 1201 Eye St NW Ste 550-B *Web:* www.nationalparks.org	Washington	DC	20005	202-354-6460		48-13
National Park Medical Ctr 1910 Malvern Ave *Web:* www.nationalparkmedical.com	Hot Springs	AR	71901	501-321-1000		374-3
National Park Service *National Register of Historic Places* 1849 C St NW PO Box 7228 *Web:* www.nps.gov	Washington	DC	20240	202-354-2211	371-6447	340-13
National Park Service Regional Offices *Alaska Region* 240 W Fifth Ave *Web:* www.nps.gov	Anchorage	AK	99501	907-644-3510	644-3816	340-13
National Park Service Regional Offices Intermountain Region 12795 W Alameda Pkwy *Web:* www.nps.gov	Denver	CO	80225	303-969-2500		340-13
National Park Service Regional Offices NortheastRegion 200 Chestnut St *Web:* www.nps.gov	Philadelphia	PA	19106	215-597-7013	597-0815	340-13
National Park Service Regional Offices Southeast Region 100 Alabama St SW 1924 Bldg. *Web:* www.nps.gov	Atlanta	GA	30303	404-507-5600		340-13
National Park Trust (NPT) 401 E Jefferson St Ste 207 *Web:* www.parktrust.org	Rockville	MD	20850	301-279-7275	279-7211	48-13
National Parking Assn (NPA) 1112 16th St NW Ste 840 *TF:* 800-647-7275 ■ *Web:* www.weareparking.org	Washington	DC	20036	202-296-4336	296-3102	49-3
National Parks Conservation Assn (NPCA) 1300 19th St NW Ste 300 *TF:* 800-628-7275 ■ *Web:* www.npca.org	Washington	DC	20036	202-223-6722		48-13

	Phone	Fax	Class
National Partitions 10300 Goldenfern Ln .... Knoxville TN 37931 *TF:* 800-996-7266 ■ *Web:* www.nationalpartitions.com	865-670-2100		286
National Partnership for Women & Families 1875 Connecticut Ave NW Ste 650........... Washington DC 20009 *Web:* www.nationalpartnership.org	202-986-2600	986-2539	48-24
National Payroll Resources Inc 428 S Gilbert Rd Ste 104 .... Gilbert AZ 85296 *Web:* npspecialists.com	480-924-7569		570
National Peace Corporation Assn (NPCA) 1825 Connecticut Ave NW Ste 800........... Washington DC 20036 *TF:* 800-336-1616 ■ *Web:* www.peacecorpsconnect.org	202-293-7728	293-7554	48-5
National Pen Corp (NPC) 12121 Scripps Summit Dr .... San Diego CA 92131 *TF:* 888-672-7370 ■ *Web:* www.pens.com	888-672-7370		9
National Personal Training Institute 4305 Beverly St .... Colorado Springs CO 80918 *TF:* 877-215-2643 ■ *Web:* www.niche.com	719-599-4190		668
National Personal Training Institute 525 Riverside Ave......................... Lyndhurst NJ 07071 *TF:* 800-960-6294 ■ *Web:* www.nptifitness.com	800-960-6294		668
National Personal Training Institute (Orlando) Winter Park Business Ctr 809 S Orlando Ave Ste K.................................. Winter Park FL 32789 *Web:* nptiflorida.edu	407-772-0057		167-3
National Personal Training Institute (San Francisco Area) 7100 Village Pkwy .... Dublin CA 94568 *TF:* 800-460-0933 ■ *Web:* nationalpti.org	703-582-1556		167-3
National Pest Management Association Inc (NPMA) 10460 N St................................. Fairfax VA 22030 *TF:* 800-678-6722 ■ *Web:* www.pestworld.org	703-352-6762	352-3031	49-4
National Pesticide Information Ctr (NPIC) 333 Weniger Hall .... Corvallis OR 97331 **Fax Area Code:* 541 ■ *TF:* 800-858-7378 ■ *Web:* www.npic.orst.edu	800-858-7378	737-0761*	48-17
National Pharmaceutical Council (NPC) 1894 Preston White Dr........................ Reston VA 20191 *Web:* www.npcnow.org	703-620-6390	476-0904	49-8
National Philharmonic 5301 Tuckerman Ln .... North Bethesda MD 20852 *Web:* www.nationalphilharmonic.org	301-493-9283	493-9284	573-3
National Pipe & Plastics Inc 3421 Old Vestal Rd................................ Vestal NY 13850 **Fax Area Code:* 607 ■ *TF:* 800-836-4350 ■ *Web:* www.nationalpipe.com	800-836-4350	729-6130*	596
National Planning Holdings Inc 401 Wilshire Blvd Ste 1100 .... Santa Monica CA 90401 *TF:* 888-711-6720 ■ *Web:* www.natplan.com	310-899-7900		401
National Plastek Inc 7050 Dutton Industrial Park Dr.................. Dutton MI 49316 *Web:* www.plastek.com	616-698-9559	698-7370	596
National Plastics Color Inc 100 W Industrial St...................... Valley Center KS 67147 *Web:* www.nationalplasticscolor.com	316-755-1273	755-0614	605-2
National Polish-American Sports Hall of Fame 2975 E Maple .... Troy MI 48083 *Web:* www.polishsportshof.com	313-407-3300		522
National Pools of Roanoke 3112 Melrose Ave........................... Roanoke VA 24017 *TF:* 800-926-7665 ■ *Web:* www.nationalpools.com	540-345-7665	343-5240	189-11
National Pork Producers Council (NPPC) 122 C St NW Ste 875.................... Washington DC 20001 *TF:* 800-952-4629 ■ *Web:* www.nppc.org	202-347-3600	347-5265	49-6
National Postal Museum (Smithsonian Institution) 2 Massachusetts Ave NE.................. Washington DC 20002 *Web:* postalmuseum.si.edu	202-633-5555	633-9393	520
National Precast Concrete Assn (NPCA) 10333 N Meridian St Ste 272.............. Indianapolis IN 46290 *TF:* 800-366-7731 ■ *Web:* precast.org	317-571-9500	571-0041	49-3
National Presidential Wax Museum 609 Hwy 16A .... Keystone SD 57751 *Web:* www.blackhillsbadlands.com	605-666-4455		520
National Press Club (NPC) 529 14th St NW .... Washington DC 20045 *Web:* www.press.org	202-662-7500	662-7569	49-14
National Press Foundation (NPF) 1211 Connecticut Ave NW Ste 310........... Washington DC 20036 *Web:* nationalpress.org	202-663-7280		49-16
National Press Photographers Assn (NPPA) 3200 Croasdaile Dr Ste 306.................. Durham NC 27705 *Web:* nppa.org	919-237-1782	383-7261	49-14
National Presto Industries Inc 3925 N Hastings Way...................... Eau Claire WI 54703 *NYSE: NPK* ■ *TF:* 800-877-0441 ■ *Web:* www.gopresto.com	715-839-2121		37
National Printing & Packaging 9801 Walford Ave.......................... Cleveland OH 44102 *Web:* nppco.info	216-486-9400		603
National Printing Converters Inc 18 S Murphy Ave .... Brazil IN 47834 *TF:* 800-877-6724 ■ *Web:* www.npclabels.com	800-877-6724		413
National Private Truck Council (NPTC) 950 N Glebe Rd Ste 2300.................... Arlington VA 22203 *Web:* www.nptc.org	703-683-1300	683-1217	49-21
National Professional Resources Inc 1455 Rail Head Blvd Ste 6..................... Naples FL 34110 *TF:* 800-453-7461 ■ *Web:* www.nprinc.com	914-937-8879	937-9327	637-10
National Propane Gas Assn (NPGA) 1899 L St NW Ste 350 .... Washington DC 20036 *TF:* 800-328-1111 ■ *Web:* www.npga.org	202-466-7200	466-7205	48-12
National Property Inspections 9375 Burt St Ste 201 .... Omaha NE 68114 *TF:* 800-333-9807 ■ *Web:* www.npiweb.com	800-333-9807		652
National Property Inspections Inc (NPI) 9375 Burt St Ste 201 .... Omaha NE 68114 *Web:* npifranchise.com	402-917-0778		365
National Psoriasis Foundation (NPF) 6600 SW 92nd Ave Ste 300 .... Portland OR 97223 *TF:* 800-723-9166 ■ *Web:* www.psoriasis.org	503-244-7404	245-0626	48-17
National Psychological Association for Psychoanalysis (NPAP) 40 W 13th St............................. New York NY 10011 *Web:* npap.org	212-924-7440	989-7543	49-15
National PTA 1250 N Pitt St.................. Alexandria VA 22314 *TF:* 800-307-4782 ■ *Web:* www.pta.org	703-518-1200		305
National Public Finance Guarantee Corp 1 Manhattanville Rd Ste 301.................. Armonk NY 10504 *Web:* www.nationalpfg.com	914-765-3333		391-5
National Public Radio (NPR) 635 Massachusetts Ave NW .... Washington DC 20001 *TF:* 800-989-8255 ■ *Web:* www.npr.org	202-513-3232	513-3329	632
National Publisher Services LLC 43 Oak Hills Rd.............................. Edison NJ 08820 *Web:* npsmediagroup.com	732-548-1667		393
National Pump Company LLC 7706 N 71st Ave........................... Glendale AZ 85303 *TF:* 800-966-5240 ■ *Web:* www.nationalpumpcompany.com	623-979-3560	979-2177	641
National Quality Assurance - US.A. Inc 4 Post Office Sq .... Acton MA 01720 *Web:* www.nqa.com	978-635-9256		463
National Quilt Museum, The 215 Jefferson St .... Paducah KY 42001 *Web:* www.quiltmuseum.org	270-442-8856	442-5448	520
National Radio Astronomy Observatory (NRAO) 520 Edgemont Rd...................... Charlottesville VA 22903 *Web:* public.nrao.edu	434-296-0211	296-0278	668
National Railroad Museum 2285 S Broadway St....................... Green Bay WI 54304 *Web:* nationalrrmuseum.org	920-437-7623		520
National Railroad Passenger Corp 60 Massachusetts Ave NE.................. Washington DC 20002 *Web:* www.amtrak.com	202-906-3741		649
National Railway Equipment Co (NREC) 14400 Robey St .... Dixmoor IL 60426 *TF:* 800-253-2905 ■ *Web:* www.nre.com	708-388-6002		650
National Raisin Co PO Box 219 .... Fowler CA 93625 *Web:* www.nationalraisin.com	559-834-5981	834-1055	315-5
National Readerboard Supply Inc PO Box 430 .... Poncha Springs CO 81242 *TF:* 888-489-5222 ■ *Web:* www.nationalreaderboard.com	888-489-5222		9
National Ready Mixed Concrete Assn (NRMCA) 900 Spring St........................ Silver Spring MD 20910 *TF:* 888-846-7622 ■ *Web:* www.nrmca.org	301-587-1400	585-4219	49-3
National Real Estate Investor Magazine 6151 Powers Ferry Rd NW Ste 200.............. Atlanta GA 30339 **Fax Area Code:* 770 ■ *TF:* 800-633-1546 ■ *Web:* www.nreionline.com	800-633-1546	618-0348*	457-5
National Realty & Development Corp 3 Manhattanville Rd .... Purchase NY 10577 *TF:* 800-932-7368 ■ *Web:* www.nrdc.com	914-694-4444	694-5448	655
National Recreation & Park Assn 22377 Belmont Ridge Rd .... Ashburn VA 20148 **Fax Area Code:* 703 ■ *TF:* 800-626-6772 ■ *Web:* www.nrpa.org	800-626-6772	858-0794*	48-23
National Refrigerants Inc 11401 Roosevelt Blvd.................... Philadelphia PA 19154 *TF:* 800-262-0012 ■ *Web:* www.refrigerants.com	215-698-6620	698-7466	146
National Register Publishing Direct 430 Mountain Ave Ste 403............. New Providence NJ 07974 **Fax Area Code:* 908 ■ *TF:* 844-592-4197 ■ *Web:* www.nrpdirect.com	844-592-4197	608-3012*	637-2
National Rehabilitation Assn (NRA) 633 S Washington St .... Alexandria VA 22314 *TF:* 888-258-4295 ■ *Web:* www.nationalrehab.org	703-836-0850	836-0848	48-17
National Rehabilitation Information Ctr (NARIC) 8400 Corporate Dr Ste 500.............. Landover Hills MD 20785 *TF:* 800-346-2742 ■ *Web:* www.naric.com	301-459-5900	459-4263	48-17
National Reining Horse Assn (NRHA) 3021 W Reno Ave..................... Oklahoma City OK 73107 *Web:* Www.nrha.com	405-946-7400	946-8425	48-3
National Religious Broadcasters (NRB) 660 N Capitol St NW Ste 210............... Washington DC 20001 *Web:* www.nrb.org	202-543-0073	543-2649	49-14
National Renal Administrators Assn (NRAA) 100 N 20th St Ste 200 .... Philadelphia PA 19103 *Web:* www.nraa.org	215-320-4655		49-8
National Renderers Association Inc (NRA) 500 Montgomery St Ste 310................. Alexandria VA 22314 **Fax Area Code:* 571 ■ *TF:* 800-366-2563 ■ *Web:* www.nationalrenderers.org	703-683-0155	970-2279*	48-2
National Renewable Energy Laboratory (NREL) 15013 Denver West Pkwy..................... Golden CO 80401 *Web:* www.nrel.gov	303-275-3000		668
National Research Corp 1245 Q St............. Lincoln NE 68508 *NASDAQ: NRCI* ■ *Web:* nrchealth.com	402-475-2525	475-9061	466
National Research Labs Inc (NRL) 650 Haines Ave NW .... Albuquerque NM 87102 *Web:* www.nrl1.dreamhosters.com	505-243-1757	243-5194	625
National Resource Center for Family Centered Practice (NRCFCP) 2662 Crosspark Road....................... Coralville IA 52241 *Web:* clas.uiowa.edu	319-335-4965		637-2
National Resource Center on Domestic Violence (NRCDV) 6400 Flank Dr Ste 1300 .... Harrisburg PA 17112 **Fax Area Code:* 717 ■ *TF:* 800-799-7233 ■ *Web:* www.nrcdv.org	800-799-7233	545-9456*	48-6
National Resource Center on Native American Aging (NRCNAA) 1301 N Columbia Rd Ste E231 PO Box 9037 . . . Grand Forks ND 58202 *TF:* 800-896-7628 ■ *Web:* www.nrcnaa.org	701-777-3720	777-6779	48-6
National Resource Center on Nutrition Physical Activity & Aging Florida International Univ OE 200................ Miami FL 33199 *Web:* nutrition.fiu.edu	305-348-1517	348-1518	48-6
National Restaurant Assn (NRA) 2055 L St NW Ste 700 .... Washington DC 20036 *TF:* 800-424-5156 ■ *Web:* www.restaurant.org	202-331-5900		49-6
National Restorations LLC 2821 Emerywood Pkwy Ste 100.............. Richmond VA 23294 *TF:* 877-884-9446 ■ *Web:* nationalrestore.com	877-884-9446		390
National Retail Federation (NRF) 1101 New York Ave NW .... Washington DC 20005 *TF:* 800-673-4692 ■ *Web:* nrf.com	202-783-7971	737-2849	49-18
National Retail Hardware Assn (NRHA) 136 N Delaware St Ste 200................ Indianapolis IN 46204 **Fax Area Code:* 317 ■ *TF:* 800-772-4424 ■ *Web:* www.nrha.org	800-772-4424	328-4354*	49-18
National Review 19 W 44th St Ste 1701......... New York NY 10036 *Web:* www.nationalreview.com	212-679-7330		457-17

Name / Address	City	State	Zip	Phone	Fax	Class
National Reye's Syndrome Foundation (NRSF)						
426 N Lewis St	Bryan	OH	43506	419-924-9000	924-9999	48-17
TF: 800-233-7393 ■ *Web:* www.reyessyndrome.org						
National Right to Life Committee Inc (NRLC)						
512 Tenth St NW	Washington	DC	20004	202-626-8800	737-9189	48-8
Web: www.nrlc.org						
National Right to Work Committee (NRTWC)						
8001 Braddock Rd Ste 500	Springfield	VA	22160	800-325-7892	321-9319*	49-12
**Fax Area Code:* 703 ■ *TF:* 800-325-7892 ■ *Web:* nrtwc.org						
National Rivet & Manufacturing Co						
21 E Jefferson St	Waupun	WI	53963	920-324-5511	324-3388	278
TF: 888-324-5511 ■ *Web:* www.nationalrivet.com						
National Roofing Contractors Assn (NRCA)						
10255 W Higgins Rd Ste 600	Rosemont	IL	60018	847-299-9070	299-1183	49-3
TF: 800-323-9545 ■ *Web:* www.nrca.net						
National Rosacea Society (NRS)						
196 James St	Barrington	IL	60010	888-662-5874		48-17
TF: 888-662-5874 ■ *Web:* www.rosacea.org						
National Runaway Switchboard (NRS)						
3141 N Lincoln Ave	Chicago	IL	60657	773-880-9860	929-5150	48-6
TF: 800-786-2929 ■ *Web:* www.1800runaway.org						
National Rural Letter Carriers' Assn						
1630 Duke St	Alexandria	VA	22314	703-684-5545		414
Web: www.nrlca.org						
National Rural Utilities Co-opeartive Finance Corp						
2201 Co-op Way	Herndon	VA	20171	703-709-6700		509
TF: 800-424-2954 ■ *Web:* www.nrucfc.coop						
National Rural Water Assn (NRWA)						
2915 S 13th St	Duncan	OK	73533	580-252-0629	255-4476	48-12
Web: nrwa.org						
National Safety Apparel Inc (NSA)						
15825 Industrial Pkwy	Cleveland	OH	44135	800-553-0672	941-1130*	576
**Fax Area Code:* 216 ■ *TF:* 800-553-0672 ■ *Web:* www.thinknsa.com						
National Safety Commission (TNSC)						
1102 A1A N No 107	Ponte Vedra Beach	FL	32082	800-729-1997		423
TF: 800-729-1997 ■ *Web:* www.nationalsafetycommission.com						
National Safety Council (NSC)						
1121 Spring Lake Dr	Itasca	IL	60143	630-285-1121	285-1315	48-17
TF: 800-621-7615 ■ *Web:* www.nsc.org						
National Salon Resources Inc						
3109 Louisiana Ave N	Minneapolis	MN	55427	800-622-0003	577-2512	76
TF: 800-622-0003 ■ *Web:* www.nationalsalon.com						
National School Boards Assn (NSBA)						
1680 Duke St	Alexandria	VA	22314	703-838-6722	683-7590	49-5
Web: www.nsba.org						
National School District						
1500 N Ave	National City	CA	91950	619-336-7500	336-7521	685
Web: www.nsd.us						
National School Products						
1523 Old Niles Ferry Rd	Maryville	TN	37803	865-984-3960	289-3960*	243
**Fax Area Code:* 800 ■ *TF:* 800-627-9393 ■ *Web:* www.nationalschoolproducts.com						
National School Public Relations Assn (NSPRA)						
15948 Derwood Rd	Rockville	MD	20855	301-519-0496	519-0494	49-5
Web: www.nspra.org						
National School Supply & Equipment Assn (NSSEA)						
8380 Colesville Rd Ste 250	Silver Spring	MD	20910	301-495-0240	495-3330	49-18
TF: 800-395-5550 ■ *Web:* edmarket.org						
National Science Foundation (NSF)						
4201 Wilson Blvd	Arlington	VA	22230	703-292-5111	292-9232	340-20
Web: nsf.gov						
National Science Teachers Assn (NSTA)						
1840 Wilson Blvd	Arlington	VA	22201	703-243-7100	243-7177	49-5
TF: 800-722-6782 ■ *Web:* www.nsta.org						
National Sea Grant Program						
1315 East-West Hwy	Silver Spring	MD	20910	301-734-1066	713-0799	340-2
Web: seagrant.noaa.gov						
National Search Assoc						
2035 Corte del Nogal Ste 100	Carlsbad	CA	92011	760-431-1115	683-3044	266
Web: www.nsasearch.com						
National Seating Co 200 National Dr	Vonore	TN	37885	423-884-6651		247
Web: www.nsm-seating.com						
National Securities Corp						
410 Park Ave 14th Fl	New York	NY	10022	212-417-8000		690
TF: 800-742-7730 ■ *Web:* www.nationalsecurities.com						
National Security Agency						
9800 Savage Rd	Fort Meade	MD	20755	301-688-6311		340-3
Web: www.nsa.gov						
National Security Council (NSC)						
White House 1600 Pennsylvania Ave	Washington	DC	20500	202-456-1414		340
Web: www.whitehouse.gov						
National Security Systems Inc (NSS)						
1261 S Lyon St Ste 402	Santa Ana	CA	92705	800-457-1999		692
TF: 800-457-1999 ■ *Web:* www.nationalsecuritysystems.net						
National Sedimentation Laboratory						
598 McElroy Dr PO Box 1157	Oxford	MS	38655	662-232-2924	281-5706	668
Web: www.ars.usda.gov						
National Senior Golf Assn (NSGA)						
200 Perrine Rd Ste 201	Old Bridge	NJ	08857	800-282-6772	525-9590*	48-22
**Fax Area Code:* 732 ■ *TF:* 800-282-6772 ■ *Web:* www.nationalseniorgolf.com						
National Services Group Inc						
1682 Langley Ave	Irvine	CA	92614	800-394-6000		189-8
TF: 800-394-6000 ■ *Web:* www.nationalservicesgroup.com						
National Severe Storms Laboratory (NSSL)						
120 David L Boren Blvd	Norman	OK	73072	405-325-6907		668
Web: www.nssl.noaa.gov						
National Sheet Metal Machines Inc						
PO Box 72	Smartt	TN	37378	931-668-3643	668-3177	456
Web: www.national-1.com						
National Sheriffs' Assn (NSA)						
1450 Duke St	Alexandria	VA	22314	703-836-7827	683-6541	49-7
TF: 800-424-7827 ■ *Web:* www.sheriffs.org						
National Shoe Retailers Assn (NSRA)						
7386 N La Cholla Blvd	Tucson	AZ	85741	520-209-1710		49-18
TF: 800-673-8446 ■ *Web:* www.nsra.org						
National Shooting Sports Foundation (NSSF)						
11 Mile Hill Rd	Newtown	CT	06470	203-426-1320	426-1087	48-22
Web: www.nssf.org						
National Shrine of Our Lady of Lebanon, The						
2759 N Lipkey Rd	North Jackson	OH	44451	330-538-3351	538-0455	50-1
Web: www.nationalshrineofourladyoflebanonshrine.com						
National Shrine of Our Lady of the Snows						
442 S De Mazenod Dr	Belleville	IL	62223	618-397-6700	398-6549	50-1
TF: 800-682-2879 ■ *Web:* snows.org						
National Sign Corp						
1255 Westlake Ave N	Seattle	WA	98109	206-282-0700		701
Web: www.nationalsigncorp.com						
National Sintered Alloys Inc (NSA)						
Heritage Pk Rt 145 PO Box 332	Clinton	CT	06413	860-669-8653	669-5428	482
Web: www.nationalsintered.com						
National Ski Areas Assn (NSAA)						
133 S Van Gordon St Ste 300	Lakewood	CO	80228	303-987-1111	986-2345	48-23
Web: www.nsaa.org						
National Ski Patrol System Inc (NSP)						
133 S Van Gordon St Ste 100	Lakewood	CO	80228	303-988-1111		49-7
Web: www.nsp.org						
National Sleep Foundation (NSF)						
1522 K St NW Ste 500	Washington	DC	20005	202-347-3471	347-3472	48-17
Web: sleepfoundation.org						
National Slovak Society of the USA (NSS)						
351 Vly Brook Rd	McMurray	PA	15317	724-731-0094	731-0145	48-14
TF: 800-488-1890 ■ *Web:* www.nsslife.org						
National Small Business Assn (NSBA)						
1156 15th St NW Ste 1100	Washington	DC	20005	800-345-6728	872-8543*	49-12
**Fax Area Code:* 202 ■ *TF:* 800-345-6728 ■ *Web:* www.nsba.biz						
National Soaring Museum						
51 Soaring Hill Dr	Elmira	NY	14903	607-734-3128	732-6745	522
Web: www.soaringmuseum.org						
National Soccer Coaches Association of America (NSCAA)						
800 Ann Ave	Kansas City	KS	66101	913-362-1747	362-3439	48-22
TF: 800-458-0678 ■ *Web:* unitedsoccercoaches.org						
National Society of Accountants (NSA)						
1010 N Fairfax St	Alexandria	VA	22314	703-549-6400	549-2984	49-1
TF: 800-966-6679 ■ *Web:* www.nsacct.org						
National Society of Black Physicists (NSBP)						
3033 Wilson Blvd Ste 700	Arlington	VA	22201	703-647-4176		49-19
Web: www.nsbp.org						
National Society of Compliance Professionals (NSCP)						
22 Kent Rd	Cornwall Bridge	CT	06754	860-672-0843	672-3005	49-12
Web: nscp.org						
National Society of Genetic Counselors (NSGC)						
330 N Wabash Ave Ste 2000	Chicago	IL	60611	312-321-6834	673-6972	48-17
Web: www.nsgc.org						
National Society of Professional Engineers (NSPE)						
1420 King St	Alexandria	VA	22314	888-285-6773	836-4875*	49-19
**Fax Area Code:* 703 ■ *TF:* 888-285-6773 ■ *Web:* www.nspe.org						
National Soil Erosion Research Laboratory						
275 S Russell St	West Lafayette	IN	47907	765-494-8689	494-5948	668
Web: www.ars.usda.gov						
National Space Biomedical Research Institute						
6500 Main St Ste 910	Houston	TX	77030	713-798-7412	798-7413	167-3
Web: www.nsbri.org						
National Speakers Assn (NSA)						
1500 S Priest Dr	Tempe	AZ	85281	480-968-2552	968-0911	48-4
Web: www.nsaspeaker.org						
National Speakers Bureau						
1177 W Broadway Ste 300	Vancouver	BC	V6H1G3	604-734-3663		708
TF: 800-661-4110 ■ *Web:* www.nsb.com						
National Speakers Bureau Inc						
14047 W Petronalla Dr Ste 102	Libertyville	IL	60048	847-295-1122		708
TF: 800-323-9442 ■ *Web:* www.nationalspeakers.com						
National Specialty Alloys LLC						
18250 Keith Harrow Blvd	Houston	TX	77084	281-345-2115	345-1133	492
TF: 800-847-5653 ■ *Web:* www.nsalloys.com						
National Speech & Debate Association's (NFL)						
125 Watson St PO Box 38	Ripon	WI	54971	920-748-6206	748-9478	48-11
Web: www.speechanddebate.org						
National Spiritual Assembly of the Baha'is of the United States						
1233 Central St	Evanston	IL	60201	847-733-3400		48-20
Web: www.bahai.us						
National Sporting Goods Assn (NSGA)						
1601 Feehanville Dr Ste 300	Mount Prospect	IL	60056	847-296-6742	391-9827	49-4
TF: 800-815-5422 ■ *Web:* www.nsga.org						
National Sporting Library & Museum (NSLM)						
PO Box 1335	Middleburg	VA	20118	540-687-6542	687-8540	434-3
Web: www.nationalsporting.org						
National Sports Academy						
821 Mirror Lake Dr	Lake Placid	NY	12946	518-523-3460	523-3488	622
Web: www.nationalsportsacademy.com						
National Sports Center Foundation						
1700 105th Ave NE	Minneapolis	MN	55449	763-785-5600	785-5699	711
Web: www.nscsports.org						
National Sprint Car Hall of Fame & Museum						
1 Sprint Capital Pl	Knoxville	IA	50138	641-842-6176	842-6177	522
TF: 800-874-4488 ■ *Web:* www.sprintcarhof.com						
National Staff Development Council (NSDC)						
504 S Locust St	Oxford	OH	45056	513-523-6029	523-0638	49-5
TF: 800-727-7288 ■ *Web:* learningforward.org						
National Standard Company Lake St Plant						
1631 Lake St	Niles	MI	49120	269-683-8100		182
Web: www.nationalstandard.com						
National Standard Parts Associates Inc						
4400 Mobile Hwy	Pensacola	FL	32506	850-456-5771		815
TF: 800-874-6813 ■ *Web:* www.nspa.com						
National States Insurance						
1830 Craig Park Ct	Saint Louis	MO	63146	314-878-0101		390
Web: www.nstates.com						
National Steak Processors Inc						
301 E 5th Ave	Owasso	OK	74055	918-274-8787		296-26
Web: www.nationalsteak.com						
National Steinbeck Ctr 1 Main St	Salinas	CA	93901	831-775-4721	796-3828	520
Web: www.steinbeck.org						
National Stock Sign Co						
1040 El Dorado Ave	Santa Cruz	CA	95062	800-462-7726	476-1734*	701
**Fax Area Code:* 831 ■ *TF:* 800-462-7726 ■ *Web:* nationalstocksign.com						

Name / Address	City	State	Zip	Phone	Fax	Class
National Stone Sand & Gravel Assn (NSSGA) 1605 King St. *TF:* 800-342-1415 ■ *Web:* www.nssga.org	Alexandria	VA	22314	703-525-8788	525-7782	49-3
National Stores Inc 15001 S Figueroa St. *Web:* www.fallasstores.net	Gardena	CA	90248	310-324-9962		157-2
National Strand Products Inc 12611 Cain Cir *TF:* 800-455-2475 ■ *Web:* www.nationalstrand.com	Houston	TX	77015	800-455-2475		767
National Strength & Conditioning Assn (NSCA) 1885 Bob Johnson Dr. *TF:* 800-815-6826 ■ *Web:* www.nsca.com	Colorado Springs	CO	80906	719-632-6722	632-6367	48-22
National Stroke Assn (NSA) 9707 E Easter Ln. **Fax Area Code:* 303 ■ *TF:* 800-787-6537 ■ *Web:* www.stroke.org	Centennial	CO	80112	800-787-6537	649-1328*	48-17
National Student Nurses Assn (NSNA) 45 Main St Ste 606. *Web:* www.nsna.org	Brooklyn	NY	11201	718-210-0705	210-0710	49-8
National Stuttering Assn (NSA) 119 W 40th St 14th Fl. *TF:* 800-937-8888 ■ *Web:* westutter.org	New York	NY	10018	212-944-4050	944-8244	48-17
National Summer Learning Assn 575 S Charles St Ste 310 *Web:* www.summerlearning.org	Baltimore	MD	21201	410-856-1370		244
National Sunflower Association PAC 2401 46th Ave SE Ste 206 *TF:* 888-718-7033 ■ *Web:* www.sunflowernsa.com	Mandan	ND	58554	701-328-5100	328-5101	615
National Super Service Company Inc 3115 Frenchman Rd *TF:* 800-677-1663 ■ *Web:* www.nss.com	Toledo	OH	43607	419-531-2121	531-3761	386
National Swine Registry 2639 Yeager Rd *Web:* www.nationalswine.com	West Lafayette	IN	47906	765-463-3594		138
National System of Garage Ventilation Inc 714 N Church St PO Box 1186 *TF:* 800-728-8368 ■ *Web:* www.nsgv.com	Decatur	IL	62525	217-423-7314	422-5387	15
National Tank Truck Carriers Inc 950 N Glebe Rd Ste 520 *TF:* 800-228-9290 ■ *Web:* www.tanktruck.org	Arlington	VA	22203	703-838-1960		49-21
National Tax Search LLC 130 S Jefferson St Ste 300 *TF:* 888-627-5494 ■ *Web:* nts.nationaltaxsearch.com	Chicago	IL	60661	312-233-6440	233-6450	734
National Taxpayers Union (NTU) 108 N Alfred St. *Web:* www.ntu.org	Alexandria	VA	22314	703-683-5700	683-5722	48-7
National Tay-Sachs & Allied Diseases Assn (NTSAD) 2001 Beacon St Ste 204 *TF:* 800-906-8723 ■ *Web:* ntsad.org	Brighton	MA	02135	617-277-4463	277-0134	48-17
National Technical Information Service (NTIS) 5301 Shawnee Rd. *TF:* 800-363-2068 ■ *Web:* www.ntis.gov	Alexandria	VA	22312	703-605-6060	605-6880	197
National Technical Information Service (NTIS) 5285 Port Royal Rd. *TF:* 800-553-6847 ■ *Web:* www.ntis.gov	Springfield	VA	22161	703-605-6000	605-6900	668
National Technical Systems Inc (NTS) 2125 E Katella Ave Ste 250. *NASDAQ: NTSC* ■ *TF:* 800-879-9225 ■ *Web:* www.nts.com	Anaheim	CA	92806	818-591-0776	591-0899	743
National Technologies Inc 7641 S Tenth St *Web:* www.nationaltechnologies.com	Oak Creek	WI	53154	414-571-1000	571-1010	621
National Technology Group Inc 1180 Lincoln Ave Unit 8 *Web:* nattechinc.com	Holbrook	NY	11741	646-701-7477		180
National Technology Inc 1101 Carnegie St *Web:* nationaltech.com	Rolling Meadows	IL	60008	847-506-1300	506-1340	625
National Telecommunications & Information Administration (NTIA) 1401 Constitution Ave NW *Web:* www.ntia.doc.gov	Washington	DC	20230	202-482-7002		340-2
National Telecommunications Cooperative Assn (NTCA) 4121 Wilson Blvd Ste 1000 *Web:* www.ntca.org	Arlington	VA	22203	703-351-2000	351-2001	49-20
National Textile Association Inc (NTA) 6 Beacon St Ste 1125	Boston	MA	02111	617-542-8220		49-13
National Theatre 1321 Pennsylvania Ave NW *Web:* Www.thenationaldc.com	Washington	DC	20004	202-628-6161		572
National Theatre of the Deaf (NTD) 139 N Main St *Web:* www.ntd.org	West Hartford	CT	06107	860-236-4193		573-4
National Thoroughbred Racing Assn (NTRA) 2525 Harrodsburg Rd Ste 510 *TF:* 800-792-6872 ■ *Web:* www.ntra.com	Lexington	KY	40504	800-792-6872		48-22
National Tire & Wheel 5 Garden Ct. *TF:* 800-847-3287 ■ *Web:* www.ntwonline.com	Wheeling	WV	26003	800-847-3287		57
National Tobacco Company LP 5201 Interchange Way *TF:* 800-579-0975 ■ *Web:* zigzag.com	Louisville	KY	40229	502-778-4421		756
National Tool & Manufacturing Co 563 Rock Rd. *Web:* www.ntm.com	East Dundee	IL	60118	908-276-1600		757
National Tool Warehouse 221 W Fourth St Ste 4 *TF:* 866-358-1919 ■ *Web:* www.nationaltoolwarehouse.com	Carthage	MO	64836	417-358-1919		247
National Tooling & Machining Assn (NTMA) 6363 Oak Tree Blvd. **Fax Area Code:* 301 ■ *TF:* 800-248-6862 ■ *Web:* www.ntma.org	Independence	OH	44131	800-248-6862	248-7104*	49-13
National Tour Assn (NTA) 546 E Main St. *TF:* 800-682-8886 ■ *Web:* ntaonline.com	Lexington	KY	40508	859-226-4444	226-4404	48-23
National Toxicology Program (NTP) PO Box 12233 *Web:* ntp.niehs.nih.gov	Research Triangle Park	NC	27709	919-541-0530	541-3687	668
National Tractor Pullers Assn (NTPA) 6155-B Huntley Rd. *Web:* www.ntpapull.com	Columbus	OH	43229	614-436-1761	436-0964	48-22
National Trade Productions Inc 313 S Patrick St *TF:* 800 687-7469 ■ *Web:* www.ntpshow.com	Alexandria	VA	22314	703-683-8500	836-4486	184
National Transportation Safety Board (NTSB) 490 L'Enfant Plz SW *Web:* www.ntsb.gov	Washington	DC	20594	202-314-6000		340-20
National Travel Systems LP 4314 S Loop 289 Ste 300. *TF:* 866-537-8740 ■ *Web:* www.nationaltravelsystems.com	Lubbock	TX	79413	806-794-3336	794-6893	772
National Treasury Employees Union 1750 H St NW. *Web:* www.nteu.org	Washington	DC	20006	202-572-5500	572-5643	414
National Truck Equipment Assn (NTEA) 37400 Hills Tech Dr *TF:* 800-441-6832 ■ *Web:* www.ntea.com	Farmington Hills	MI	48331	248-489-7090	489-8590	49-21
National Truck Leasing System 2651 Warrenville Rd Ste 560 **Fax Area Code:* 630 ■ *TF:* 800-729-6857 ■ *Web:* www.nationalease.com	Downers Grove	IL	60515	800-729-6857	953-0040*	778
National Trust for Canada, The 190 Bronson Ave *TF:* 866-964-1066 ■ *Web:* www.nationaltrustcanada.ca	Ottawa	ON	K1R6H4	613-237-1066	237-5987	48-13
National Trust for Historic Preservation 1785 Massachusetts Ave NW *Web:* savingplaces.org	Washington	DC	20036	202-588-6000	588-6038	48-13
National Tube Supply Co 925 Central Ave *TF:* 800-229-6872 ■ *Web:* www.nationaltubesupply.com	University Park	IL	60466	800-229-6872		492
National Turkey Federation (NTF) 1225 New York Ave NW Ste 400. *TF:* 866-536-7593 ■ *Web:* www.eatturkey.com	Washington	DC	20005	202-898-0100	898-0203	48-2
National U.S. - Chamber of Commerce 1201 15th St NW Ste 200. *Web:* www.nusacc.org	Washington	DC	20005	202-289-5920		140
National Underground Railroad Freedom Ctr 50 E Freedom Way *Web:* www.freedomcenter.org	Cincinnati	OH	45202	513-333-7739		520
National Undersea Research Center for the Caribbean *Perry Institute for Marine Science Caribbean Marine Research Ctr* 5356 Main St Rte 100 Ste 1 PO Box 435 *Web:* www.perryinstitute.org	Waitsfield	VT	05673	802-496-2700		668
National Underwriter Co 4157 Olympic Blvd Ste 225 *TF:* 800-543-0874 ■ *Web:* www.nationalunderwriter.com	Erlanger	KY	41018	800-543-0874	874-1916	637-2
National Union of Healthcare Workers 5801 Christie Ave Ste 525 *Web:* nuhw.org	Emeryville	CA	94608	510-834-2009		414
National United PO Box 779. *TF:* 877-628-2265 ■ *Web:* www.nationalunited.com	Gatesville	TX	76528	254-865-2211	865-8916	70
National University 11255 N Torrey Pines Rd *TF:* 800-628-8648 ■ *Web:* www.nu.edu	La Jolla	CA	92037	858-642-8000		166
National University of Health Sciences 200 E Roosevelt Rd. *TF:* 800-826-6285 ■ *Web:* www.nuhs.edu	Lombard	IL	60148	630-629-9664	889-6554	166
National Urban League 80 Pine St 9th Fl. **Fax Area Code:* 844 ■ *Web:* nul.iamempowered.com	New York	NY	10005	212-558-5301	506-0503*	48-8
National Urban Technology Ctr 25 Broadway 9th Fl. *TF:* 800-998-3212 ■ *Web:* www.urbantech.org	New York	NY	10004	212-528-7350	528-7355	48-6
National Vaccine Information Ctr (NVIC) 407 Church St Ste H. *Web:* www.nvic.org	Vienna	VA	22180	703-938-0342	938-5768	48-17
National Van Lines Inc 2800 W Roosevelt Rd *TF:* 877-590-2810 ■ *Web:* www.nationalvanlines.com	Broadview	IL	60155	708-450-2900	450-9320	519
National Venture Capital Assn (NVCA) 25 Massachusetts Ave NW Ste 730 *Web:* nvca.org	Washington	DC	20001	703-524-2549	524-3940	615
National Veterinary Associates Inc 29229 Canwood St Ste 100 *TF:* 888-767-7755 ■ *Web:* www.nva.com	Agoura Hills	CA	91301	805-777-7722		794
National Vinegar Co 1750 S Brentwood Blvd Ste 351 *Web:* www.natvin.com	Saint Louis	MO	63144	314-962-4111	962-4115	296-37
National Vinyl LLC 7 Coburn St *Web:* www.nvpwindows.com	Chicopee	MA	01013	413-420-0548		236
National Vision Inc 2435 Commerce Ave Bldg 2200 *Web:* www.nationalvision.com	Duluth	GA	30096	770-822-3600		543
National Volunteer Fire Council (NVFC) 7852 Walker Dr Ste 450 *Web:* www.nvfc.org	Greenbelt	MD	20770	202-887-5291		49-4
National Watch & Clock Museum 514 Poplar St *Web:* nawcc.org	Columbia	PA	17512	717-684-8261	684-0878	520
National Water Purifiers Inc 1065 E 14th St *Web:* www.nationalwaterpurifiers.com	Hialeah	FL	33010	305-887-7065	887-6209	806
National Water Resources Assn (NWRA) 3800 Fairfax Dr Ste 4 **Fax Area Code:* 928 ■ *Web:* www.nwra.org	Arlington	VA	22203	703-524-1544	343-9483*	48-12
National Waterways Conference Inc (NWC) 1100 N Glebe Rd Ste 1010 *TF:* 866-371-1390 ■ *Web:* waterways.org	Arlington	VA	22201	703-224-8007		49-21
National Weather Service (NWS) 1325 East-West Hwy. *Web:* www.weather.gov	Silver Spring	MD	20910	301-427-9855		340-2
National Weather Service *Alaska Region* 222 W 7th Ave Ste 23 Rm 517. *Web:* www.weather.gov	Anchorage	AK	99513	907-271-5088	271-3711	340-2
National Hurricane Ctr 11691 SW 17th St. *Web:* www.nhc.noaa.gov	Miami	FL	33165	305-229-4470	553-1264	340-2
National Weather Service Regional Offices *Central Region* 7220 NW 101st Terr *Web:* www.weather.gov	Kansas City	MO	64153	816-891-7734		340-2
Eastern Region 630 Johnson Ave *Web:* www.weather.gov	Bohemia	NY	11716	631-244-0100		340-2
Southern Region 819 Taylor St Rm 10A06 *Web:* www.weather.gov	Fort Worth	TX	76102	817 978-1000		340-2

				Phone	Fax	Class
Western Region 125 S State St *Web:* www.weather.gov	Salt Lake City	UT	84138	801-524-5133	524-5270	340-2
National Welding Inspection School 16380 Hwy 290 W *Web:* www.nationalwelding.com	Burton	TX	77835	979-289-9000		685
National Wellness Institute (NWI) 1300 College Ct PO Box 827 *Web:* www.nationalwellness.org	Stevens Point	WI	54481	715-342-2969	342-2979	48-17
National Western Life Insurance Co 850 E Anderson Ln *NASDAQ: NWLI* ■ *TF:* 800-531-5442 ■ *Web:* www.nationalwesternlife.com	Austin	TX	78752	512-836-1010	719-0104	391-2
National Wetlands Research Ctr 700 Cajundome Blvd *Web:* www.usgs.gov	LaFayette	LA	70506	337-266-8500		668
National Wholesale Company Inc 400 National Blvd **Fax Area Code:* 336 ■ *TF:* 800-480-4673 ■ *Web:* www.shopnational.com	Lexington	NC	27294	800-480-4673	249-9326*	459
National WIC Assn (NWA) 2001 S St NW Ste 580 *TF:* 866-782-6246 ■ *Web:* www.nwica.org	Washington	DC	20009	202-232-5492	387-5281	48-6
National Wild Turkey Federation (NWTF) 770 Augusta Rd PO Box 530 *TF:* 800-843-6983 ■ *Web:* www.nwtf.org	Edgefield	SC	29824	803-637-3106	637-0034	48-3
National Wildlife Federation 11100 Wildlife Center Dr *TF:* 800-822-9919 ■ *Web:* www.nwf.org	Reston	VA	20190	800-822-9919		457-6
National Wildlife Federation (NWF) 11100 Wildlife Center Dr *Web:* nwf.org	Reston	VA	20190	703-438-6000	438-3570	48-3
National Wildlife Refuge Assn (NWRA) 1001 Connecticut Ave Nw Ste 905 *Web:* www.refugeassociation.org	Washington	DC	20036	202-417-3803		48-13
National Wildlife Research Ctr 4101 LaPorte Ave *Web:* www.aphis.usda.gov	Fort Collins	CO	80521	970-266-6000	266-6032	668
National Wine & Spirits Inc PO Box 2187 *Web:* www.nwscorp.com	Indianapolis	IN	46206	317-602-6644	602-6720	81-3
National Wire & Cable Corp 136 N San Fernando Rd *Web:* www.nationalwire.com	Los Angeles	CA	90031	323-225-5611	225-4630	814
National Wire Fabric 701 Arkansas St **Fax Area Code:* 870 ■ *TF:* 800-643-1558 ■ *Web:* www.next-wire.com	Star City	AR	71667	800-643-1558	628-3700*	688
National Wireless Inc 221 Pine St *Web:* www.nationalwireless.com	Florence	MA	01062	413-586-5111	586-4422	253
National Woman's Party 144 Constitution Ave NE *Web:* nationalwomansparty.org	Washington	DC	20002	202-546-1210	546-3997	48-24
National Women's Hall of Fame 76 Fall St PO Box 335 *Web:* www.womenofthehall.org	Seneca Falls	NY	13148	315-568-8060	568-2976	520
National Women's Law Ctr (NWLC) 11 Dupont Cir NW Ste 800 *Web:* nwlc.org	Washington	DC	20036	202-588-5180		48-24
National Women's Political Caucus (NWPC) PO Box 65010 *Web:* www.nwpc.org	Washington	DC	20035	202-785-1100		48-7
National Wood Flooring Assn (NWFA) 111 Chesterfield Industrial Blvd *TF:* 800-422-4556 ■ *Web:* www.woodfloors.org	Chesterfield	MO	63005	636-519-9663		49-3
National Wooden Pallet & Container Assn (NWPCA) 1421 Prince St Ste 340 *Web:* www.palletcentral.com	Alexandria	VA	22314	703-519-6104	519-4720	49-13
National Woodland Owners Association Inc (NWOA) 374 Maple Ave E Ste 310 *TF:* 800-476-8733	Vienna	VA	22180	703-255-2700		48-2
National World War I Museum 100 W 26th St *Web:* www.theworldwar.org	Kansas City	MO	64108	816-888-8100		520
National Wrecking Co 2441 N Leavitt St *Web:* www.nationalwrecking.com	Chicago	IL	60647	773-384-2800	384-0403	189-16
National Writers Union (NWU) 256 W 38th St Ste 703 *Web:* nwu.org	New York	NY	10018	212-254-0279	254-0673	414
National Zoological Park (Smithsonian Institution) 3001 Connecticut Ave NW *Web:* nationalzoo.si.edu	Washington	DC	20008	202-633-4888		823
National/AZON 1148 Rochester Rd *TF:* 800-325-5939 ■ *Web:* azon.com	Troy	MI	48083	800-260-0839		552-1
National-Louis University 1000 Capitol Dr *TF:* 800-443-5522 ■ *Web:* www.nl.edu	Wheeling	IL	60090	847-947-5718	465-5730	166
NationJob Inc 920 Morgan St Ste T **Fax Area Code:* 515 ■ *TF:* 800-292-7731 ■ *Web:* www.nationjob.com	Des Moines	IA	50309	800-292-7731	243-5384*	260
Nations Financial Group Inc 4000 River Ridge Dr NE PO Box 908 *TF:* 800-351-2471 ■ *Web:* www.nationsfg.com	Cedar Rapids	IA	52406	319-393-9541		691
Nations Foodservice Inc 11090 San Pablo Ave Ste 200 *Web:* www.nationsrestaurants.com	El Cerrito	CA	94530	510-237-1952		670
Nationwide Advertising Specialty Co 854 Angliana Ave *TF:* 800-683-5697 ■ *Web:* www.promoplace.com	Lexington	KY	40508	859-252-7485	402-2341	9
Nationwide Arena 200 W Nationwide Blvd *Web:* www.nationwidearena.com	Columbus	OH	43215	614-246-2000		720
Nationwide Children's Hospital 700 Children's Dr *TF:* 800-881-7385 ■ *Web:* www.nationwidechildrens.org	Columbus	OH	43205	614-722-2700	722-2716	668
Nationwide Credit Inc (NCI) PO Box 14581 **Fax Area Code:* 770 ■ *TF:* 800-456-4729 ■ *Web:* www.ncirm.com	Des Moines	IA	50306	800-456-4729	612-7335*	160
Nationwide Custom Homes 1100 Rives Rd **Fax Area Code:* 276 ■ *TF:* 800-216-7001 ■ *Web:* www.nationwide-homes.com	Martinsville	VA	24115	800-216-7001	632-1181*	106
Nationwide Glove Company Inc 925 Bauman Ln	Harrisburg	IL	62946	618-252-6303		155-8
Nationwide Graphics Inc 2007 River Oaks Blvd	Houston	TX	77019	713-961-4700	961-4701	627
Nationwide Home Health Care Inc 26645 W 12 Mile Rd Ste 212 *Web:* www.nwhci.com	Southfield	MI	48034	248-595-8134	595-8136	363
Nationwide Intelligence PO Box 1922 *Web:* www.nationwideintelligence.com	Saginaw	MI	48605	989-793-0123		771
Nationwide Life & Annuity Insurance Co 1 Nationwide Pl *TF:* 800-882-2822 ■ *Web:* www.nationwide.com	Columbus	OH	43215	855-473-6410		391-2
Nationwide Life and Annuity Insurance Co 1 Nationwide Plaza 1-11-401 *TF:* 800-321-6064 ■ *Web:* www.nationwidefinancial.com	Columbus	OH	43215	800-321-6064		796
Nationwide Lift Trucks Inc 3900 N 28th Terr *TF:* 800-327-4431 ■ *Web:* www.toyotanlt.com	Hollywood	FL	33020	954-922-4645		57
Nationwide Medical Waste Management Inc 1018 NW 132nd Ave *Web:* nationwidemedicalwaste.com	Sunrise	FL	33323	954-835-5166		686
Nationwide Property & Appraisal Services LLC 10 Foster Ave Ste 3c *Web:* onestopappraisals.com	Gibbsboro	NJ	08026	856-258-6977	385-7065	652
Nationwide Title Clearing Inc 2100 Alternate 19 N *Web:* www.nationwidetitleclearing.com	Palm Harbor	FL	34683	727-771-4000		217
Nationwide Transportation Inc 4601 S 70th Cir *TF:* 800-688-0437 ■ *Web:* www.ntwdtrans.com	Omaha	NE	68117	402-592-2924		780
Nationwide Truck Brokers Inc (NTB) 4203 Roger B Chaffee Memorial Blvd SE Ste 2 *TF:* 800-446-0682 ■ *Web:* www.ntbtrk.com	Grand Rapids	MI	49548	616-878-5554	878-5569	780
Nationwide Uniform Corp 235 Shepherdsville Rd *Web:* flyingcross.com	Hodgenville	KY	42748	270-358-4173		155-19
Nationwide Van Lines Inc 1421 NW 65th Ave *TF:* 800-310-0056 ■ *Web:* www.nationwidevanlines.com	Plantation	FL	33313	954-585-3945	585-3970	519
Nationwide Vision Center Inc 220 N Mckemy Ave *TF:* 800-393-2273 ■ *Web:* www.nationwidevision.com	Chandler	AZ	85226	480-961-1865		543
Native American Community Board (NACB) PO Box 572 *Web:* www.nativeshop.org	Lake Andes	SD	57356	605-487-7072	487-7964	48-7
Native American Indian General Service Office of Alcoholics Anonymous (NAIGSO-AA) PO Box 838 *Web:* www.naigso-aa.org	Rogersville	AL	35652	951-927-2626		48-21
Native American Rights Fund (NARF) 1506 Broadway *TF:* 888-280-0726 ■ *Web:* www.narf.org	Boulder	CO	80302	303-447-8760	443-7776	49-10
Native American Times PO Box 411 *Web:* www.nativetimes.com	Tahlequah	OK	74465	918-708-5838		637-8
Native Environmental LLC 2435 E University Dr *Web:* nativeaz.com	Phoenix	AZ	85034	602-254-0122	254-0144	192
Native Eyewear Inc 1114 Neon Forest Cir Unit 5 *TF:* 888-776-2848 ■ *Web:* nativeyewear.com	Longmont	CO	80504	888-776-2848		543
Native Grounds Nursery & Landscape Co 1172 S Mt Shasta Blvd *Web:* www.nativegrounds.org	Mount Shasta	CA	96067	530-926-0555		323
Native Instruments North America Inc 6725 Sunset Blvd 5th Fl *TF:* 866-556-6487 ■ *Web:* www.native-instruments.com	Los Angeles	CA	90028	323-467-5260	372-3676	527
Native Intelligence Inc PO Box 144 *Web:* www.nativeintelligence.com	Glenelg	MD	21737	410-531-1396		194
Native Plant Center at Westchester Community College 75 Grasslands Rd *Web:* www.sunywcc.edu	Valhalla	NY	10595	914-606-7870	606-6143	97
Native Plant Trust 180 Hemenway Rd *Web:* www.nativeplanttrust.org	Framingham	MA	01701	508-877-7630	877-3658	48-13
Native Pride 11359 Rt 20 *TF:* 800-619-8618 ■ *Web:* nativepride.com	Irving	NY	14081	716-934-5130		324
Native Seeds-search 3584 E River Rd *Web:* www.nativeseeds.org	Tucson	AZ	85718	520-622-0830		196
Native Voices Books 415 Farm Rd PO Box 99 *TF:* 888-260-8458 ■ *Web:* nativevoicesbooks.com	Summertown	TN	38483	931-964-3571	964-3518	637-2
Native West Press (NWP) PO Box 12227 *Web:* www.nativewestpress.com	Prescott	AZ	86304	928-771-8376		637-2
NativeX LLC 1900 Medical Arts Ave S *Web:* www.nativex.com	Sartell	MN	56377	320-257-7500		736
Natividad Medical Ctr (NMC) 1441 Constitution Blvd *Web:* www.natividad.com	Salinas	CA	93906	831-755-4111		374-3
Natixis Global Asset Management One Financial Ctr *Web:* www.natixis.com	Boston	MA	02111	617-482-2450	482-1985	47
Natixis Investment Managers LP 399 Boylston St *Web:* www.im.natixis.com	Boston	MA	02116	617-449-2100	247-1447	401
Natixis Securities Americas LLC 1251 Avenue of the Americas *Web:* www.blr.natixis.com	New York	NY	10020	212-891-6100		690
Natl Elevator Industrial Educational Program 11 Larsen Way *TF:* 800-228-8220 ■ *Web:* www.neiep.org	Attleboro	MA	02763	508-699-2200		196
NATO (National Association of Theatre Owners) 1705 N St NW *Web:* www.natoonline.org	Washington	DC	20036	202-962-0054	962-0370	48-4
Natoli Engineering Company Inc 28 Research Park Cir *Web:* www.natoli.com	Saint Charles	MO	63304	636-926-8900	926-8910	695
NATPE (NA of Television Program Executives) 5757 Wilshire Blvd PH 10 *Web:* www.natpe.com	Los Angeles	CA	90036	310-453-4440	453-5258	49-14
Natrol Inc 21411 Prairie St *TF:* 800-262-8765 ■ *Web:* www.natrol.com	Chatsworth	CA	91311	800-262-8765		799

Name / Address	City	State	ZIP	Phone	Fax	Class
Natrona County 200 North Ctr. *Web:* www.natronacounty-wy.gov	Casper	WY	82601	307-235-9200		338
Natrona County International Airport 8500 Airport Pkwy *Web:* www.iflycasper.com	Casper	WY	82604	307-472-6688	472-1805	27
Natrona County Public Library 307 E Second St *Web:* www.natronacountylibrary.org	Casper	WY	82601	307-237-4935	266-3734	434-3
NATSO Inc 1737 King St Ste 200 *TF:* 800-956-9160 ■ *Web:* www.natso.com	Alexandria	VA	22314	703-549-2100	684-4525	49-21
Natura *Plant Interscapes Inc* 6436 Babcock Rd. *Web:* naturahq.com	San Antonio	TX	78249	888-284-2257		292
Naturade 2030 Main St Ste 630 **Fax Area Code:* 714 ■ *TF:* 800-421-1830 ■ *Web:* www.naturade.com	Irvine	CA	92614	800-421-1830	935-9837*	799
Natural Alternatives International Inc 1185 Linda Vista Dr *NASDAQ: NAII* ■ *TF:* 800-848-2646 ■ *Web:* www.nai-online.com	San Marcos	CA	92078	760-744-7340	744-9589	799
Natural Areas Assn (NAA) PO Box 594 *Web:* www.naturalareas.org	Ligonier	PA	15658	724-995-8466		48-13
Natural Balance Nutrition 2131 Capitol Ave Ste 206 *Web:* www.gonaturalbalance.com	Sacramento	CA	95816	530-383-9705		582
Natural Bridge Caverns Caverns Rd 26495 Natural Bridge *Web:* naturalbridgecaverns.com	San Antonio	TX	78266	210-651-6101	651-6144	50-5
Natural Bridge State Park McCauley Rd PO Box 1757 *Web:* www.mass.gov	North Adams	MA	01247	413-663-6392		565
Natural Bridge State Resort Park 2135 Natural Bridge Rd *TF:* 800-325-1710 ■ *Web:* parks.ky.gov	Slade	KY	40376	800-325-1710		565
Natural Bridge Wildlife Ranch 26515 Natural Bridge Caverns Rd. *Web:* www.wildliferanchtexas.com	San Antonio	TX	78266	830-438-7400		823
Natural Bridges National Monument HC 60 PO Box 1 *Web:* www.nps.gov	Lake Powell	UT	84533	435-692-1234		564
Natural Bridges State Beach 2531 W Cliff Dr. *Web:* www.parks.ca.gov	Santa Cruz	CA	95060	831-423-4609		565
Natural Capitalism Solutions Inc 11823 N 75th St *Web:* natcapsolutions.org	Longmont	CO	80503	720-684-6580		804
Natural Casing Co 410 E Railroad St *Web:* naturalcasingco.com	Peshtigo	WI	54157	715-582-3736	582-3931	296-26
Natural Factors Nutritional Products Ltd 1550 United Blvd **Fax Area Code:* 800 ■ *TF:* 800-663-8900 ■ *Web:* naturalfactors.com	Coquitlam	BC	V3K6Y2	604-777-1757	663-2115*	799
Natural Gas Services Group Inc (NGSG) 508 W Wall Ste 550 *AMEX: NGS* ■ *Web:* www.ngsgi.com	Midland	TX	79701	432-262-2700	262-2701	537
Natural Gas Supply Assn (NGSA) 805 15th St NW Ste 510 *Web:* www.ngsa.org	Washington	DC	20005	202-326-9300	326-9330	48-12
Natural Gourmet Institute 48 W 21st St 2nd Fl *Web:* www.naturalgourmetinstitute.com	New York	NY	10010	212-645-5170		167-3
Natural Habitat Adventures PO Box 3065 *TF:* 800-543-8917 ■ *Web:* www.nathab.com	Boulder	CO	80307	303-449-3711	449-3712	760
Natural Hazards Ctr University of Colorado 483 UCB. *Web:* hazards.colorado.edu	Boulder	CO	80309	303-492-6818	492-2151	668
Natural Healing College 446 E Vine St *Web:* naturalhealingcollege.com	Stockton	CA	95202	209-390-8076		764
Natural Healthy Concepts 310 N Westhill Blvd *TF:* 866-505-7501 ■ *Web:* www.nhc.com	Appleton	WI	54914	920-968-2350		345
Natural History Magazine 105 W Hwy 54 Ste 265 **Fax Area Code:* 919 ■ *Web:* www.naturalhistorymag.com	Durham	NC	27713	646-356-6500	933-1867*	457-19
Natural History Museum of Los Angeles County 900 Exposition Blvd *Web:* www.nhm.org	Los Angeles	CA	90007	213-763-3466		520
Natural Lands Trust Inc 1031 Palmers Mill Rd. *Web:* natlands.org	Media	PA	19063	610-353-5587		564
Natural Life Pet Products Inc 205 E 29th St	Pittsburg	KS	66762	620-230-0888		578
Natural Marketing Institute Inc, The 272 Ruth Rd *Web:* www.nmisolutions.com	Harleysville	PA	19438	215-513-7300		637-9
Natural Medicines 3120 W March Ln *Web:* naturalmedicines.therapeuticresearch.com	Stockton	CA	95219	209-472-2244	472-2249	479
Natural Organics Inc 548 Broadhollow Rd *TF:* 800-645-9500 ■ *Web:* naturesplus.com	Melville	NY	11747	631-293-0030		799
Natural Products Consulting Institute 8 Cobblestone Ln *Web:* www.naturalconsulting.com	Andover	MA	01810	978-975-9902	975-4502	196
Natural Products Insider 2020 N Central Ave Ste 400 *Web:* www.naturalproductsinsider.com	Phoenix	AZ	85004	480-281-6713		457-21
Natural Resource Ecology Laboratory Colorado State University *Web:* www.nrel.colostate.edu	Fort Collins	CO	80523	970-491-6056	491-1965	668
Natural Resource Partners LP 1201 Louisiana St Ste 3400 *NYSE: NRP* ■ *TF:* 888-334-7102 ■ *Web:* nrplp.com	Houston	TX	77002	713-751-7507		501
Natural Resources Conservation Service 1400 Independence Ave SW Rm 5105A *Web:* www.nrcs.usda.gov	Washington	DC	20250	202-720-7246	720-7690	340-1
Natural Resources Defense Council (NRDC) 40 W 20th St 11th Fl. *Web:* www.nrdc.org	New York	NY	10011	212-727-2700	727-1773	48-13
Natural Resources Research Institute (NRRI) *University of Minnesota Duluth* 5013 Miller Trunk Hwy. *TF:* 800-234-0054 ■ *Web:* www.nrri.umn.edu	Duluth	MN	55811	218-788-2694	720-4219	668
Natural Stone Institute 28901 Clemens Rd Ste 100 *Web:* www.naturalstoneinstitute.org	Cleveland	OH	44145	440-250-9222	250-9223	49-3
Natural Structures 2005 Tenth St. *Web:* www.naturalstructures.com	Baker City	OR	97814	541-523-0224		106
NaturaLawn of America Inc 1 E Church St **Fax Area Code:* 301 ■ *TF:* 800-989-5444 ■ *Web:* naturalawn.com	Frederick	MD	21701	800-989-5444	846-0320*	577
Naturally Vitamins 4404 E Elwood St. **Fax Area Code:* 480 ■ *TF:* 800-899-4499 ■ *Web:* naturally.com	Phoenix	AZ	85040	800-899-4499	991-0551*	799
NaturalPoint Inc 33872 SE Eastgate Cir *Web:* www.naturalpoint.com	Corvallis	OR	97333	541-753-6645		173-1
Nature 529 14th St NW 968 National Press Bldg *TF:* 800-524-0384 ■ *Web:* www.nature.com	Washington	DC	20045	202-737-2355	628-1609	457-19
Nature Conservancy 4245 N Fairfax Dr Ste 100 *TF:* 800-628-6860 ■ *Web:* www.nature.org	Arlington	VA	22203	703-841-5300	841-1283	48-13
Nature Conservancy of Canada 36 Eglinton Ave W Ste 400 *TF:* 800-465-8005 ■ *Web:* www.natureconservancy.ca	Toronto	ON	M4R1A1	416-932-3202	932-3208	48-13
Nature's Trees Inc 550 Bedford Rd. *TF:* 800-341-8733 ■ *Web:* www.savatree.com	Bedford Hills	NY	10507	914-241-4999		776
Nature's Value Inc 468 Mill Rd *Web:* www.naturesvalue.com	Coram	NY	11727	631-846-2500		582
Nature's Way 825 Challenger Dr *TF:* 800-783-2286 ■ *Web:* www.naturesway.com	Green Bay	WI	54311	920-469-1313	469-4444	799
NatureBridge 28 Geary St Ste 650 *Web:* naturebridge.org	San Francisco	CA	94108	415-992-4700		148
Naturemaker Inc 6225 El Camino Real Ste 110 *TF:* 800-872-1889 ■ *Web:* naturemaker.com	Carlsbad	CA	92009	800-872-1889		422
Natureworks LLC 15305 Minnetonka Blvd *Web:* www.natureworksllc.com	Minnetonka	MN	55345	952-562-3400		596
Naturex Inc 375 Huyler St *Web:* www.naturex.com	South Hackensack	NJ	07606	201-440-5000		479
Naturipe Berry Growers 1611 Bunker Hill Way *Web:* www.naturipeberrygrowers.com	Salinas	CA	93906	831-722-2430		315-1
Naturopathica East Hampton 74 Montauk Hwy. *Web:* www.naturopathica.com	East Hampton	NY	11937	631-329-2525		354
Naturwood Home Furnishings Inc 2711 Mercantile Dr. *Web:* www.naturwood.com	Rancho Cordova	CA	95742	916-638-2424		361
Natus Medical Inc 1501 Industrial Rd *NASDAQ: BABY* ■ *TF:* 800-255-3901 ■ *Web:* www.natus.com	San Carlos	CA	94070	650-802-0400	802-0401	250
NATW (National Night Out) PO Box 303 **Fax Area Code:* 610 ■ *TF:* 800-648-3688 ■ *Web:* natw.org	Wynnewood	PA	19096	800-648-3688	649-5456*	48-7
Naugatuck Valley Community College 750 Chase Pkwy *Web:* www.nv.edu	Waterbury	CT	06708	203-575-8000		162
Naulty, Scaricamazza & Mc Devitt LLC 1617 John F Kennedy Blvd *Web:* naulty.com	Philadelphia	PA	19103	215-568-5116		41
Nauman Smith Shissler & Hall LLP 200 N Third St 1st Fl *Web:* www.nssh.com	Harrisburg	PA	17101	717-236-3010	234-1925	428
Nautel Ltd 10089 Peggy'S Cove Rd *TF:* 877-662-8835 ■ *Web:* www.nautel.com	Hacketts Cove	NS	B3Z3J4	902-823-3900		647
Nautic Partners LLC 50 Kennedy Plz 12th Fl. *Web:* nautic.com	Providence	RI	02903	401-278-6770	278-6387	792
Nautica Retail USA Inc 40 W 57th St *TF:* 866-376-4184 ■ *Web:* www.nautica.com	New York	NY	10019	866-376-4184		155-12
Nautical Furnishings Inc 60 NW 60th St *Web:* nauticalfurnishings.com	Fort Lauderdale	FL	33309	954-771-1100	771-1211	362
Nauticon Imaging Systems Inc 15878 Gaither Dr *Web:* www.nauticon.com	Gaithersburg	MD	20877	301-279-0123		177
NAUTICUS the National Maritime Ctr 1 Waterside Dr *TF:* 800-664-1080 ■ *Web:* nauticus.org	Norfolk	VA	23510	757-664-1000	623-1287	520
Nau-Ti-Gal 5360 Westport Rd. *Web:* nautigal.com	Madison	WI	53704	608-246-3130		671
Nautilus Entertainment Design 1010 Turquoise St Ste 215 *Web:* www.n-e-d.com	San Diego	CA	92109	858-456-6395		354
Nautilus Group, The 15305 Dallas Pkwy *Web:* thenautilusgroup.com	Addison	TX	75001	972-720-6600		466
Nautilus Inc 17750 SE Sixth Way *NYSE: NLS* ■ **Fax Area Code:* 360 ■ *TF:* 800-628-8458 ■ *Web:* www.nautilusinc.com	Vancouver	WA	98683	800-628-8458	694-7755*	267
Nautilus Insurance Group LLC 7233 E Butherus Dr *TF:* 800-842-8972 ■ *Web:* www.nautilusagents.com	Scottsdale	AZ	85260	480-281-0930		391-4
Nautilus Plus Inc 3550 1e Rue *TF:* 800-363-6763 ■ *Web:* www.nautilusplus.com	Siege Social	QC	J3Y8Y5	514-666-5814		706
Nauvoo State Park 980 S Bluff St. *Web:* www.dnr.illinois.gov	Nauvoo	IL	62354	217-453-2512		565
Nav Canada 77 Metcalfe St PO Box 3411 Stn D *TF:* 800-876-4693 ■ *Web:* www.navcanada.ca	Ottawa	ON	K1P5L6	613-563-5588	563-3426	19
NAV Canada Training & Conference Ctr 1950 Montreal Rd. *TF:* 877-832-6416 ■ *Web:* www.navcentre.ca	Cornwall	ON	K6H6L2	613-936-5800		377
Navagate Inc 130 W 42nd St Ste 1100 *Web:* www.navagate.com	New York	NY	10036	646-918-5280	918-5290	178-1

	Phone	Fax	Class
Navajo Agricultural Products Industry 10086 NM Rd Hwy 371 .... Farmington NM 87499 *TF:* 844-295-6002 ■ *Web:* www.navajopride.com	505-566-2600	960-9458	10-11
Navajo County 100 E Code Talkers Dr PO Box 668 .... Holbrook AZ 86025 *Web:* www.navajocountyaz.gov	928-524-4000	524-4261	338
Navajo Express Inc 1400 W 64 Ave .... Denver CO 80221 *TF:* 800-525-1969 ■ *Web:* www.navajoexpress.com	303-287-3800		780
Navajo Nation Oil & Gas Co (NNOGC) 50 Narbono Cir W...................... Saint Michaels AZ 86511 *Web:* www.nnogc.net	928-871-4880		536
Navajo National Monument 564 off of US Hwy 160 .... Tonalea AZ 86044 *Web:* www.nps.gov	928-672-2700	672-2703	564
Navajo Technical College PO Box 849 .... Crownpoint NM 87313 *Web:* www.navajotech.edu	505-786-4100	786-5644	165
Naval Air Station Fallon 4755 Pasture Rd............................. Fallon NV 89496	775-426-2880		497-4
Naval Air Systems Command 47123 Buse Rd Bldg 2272 Ste 075......... Patuxent River MD 20670 *Web:* www.navair.navy.mil	301-757-1487		340-6
Naval Electronics Inc 7028 W Waters Ave Ste 393 .... Tampa FL 33634 *Web:* www.naval.com	813-885-6091	885-3601	681
Naval Enlisted Reserve Assn (NERA) 6703 Farragut Ave....................... Falls Church VA 22042 *TF:* 800-776-9020 ■ *Web:* www.nera.org	800-776-9020		48-19
Naval Health Research Ctr (NHRC) 140 Sylvester Rd.......................... San Diego CA 92152 *Web:* www.med.navy.mil	619-553-8400	553-9389	668
Naval Research Laboratory (NRL) 4555 Overlook Ave SW.................... Washington DC 20375 *Web:* www.nrl.navy.mil	202-767-3200		668
Naval Reserve Assn (NRA) 1619 King St....... Alexandria VA 22314 **Fax Area Code:* 866 ■ *TF:* 877-628-9411 ■ *Web:* ausn.org	703-548-5800	683-3647*	48-19
Naval Sea Systems Command 1333 Isaac Hull Ave SE Washington Navy Yard .... Washington DC 20376 *TF:* 800-356-8464 ■ *Web:* www.navsea.navy.mil	202-781-0000		340-6
Naval Station Newport 1250 Hacker St Ste 1250 .... Newport RI 02841 *Web:* www.navymwrnewport.com	401-841-2232		497-4
Naval War College Museum 686 Cushing Rd .... Newport RI 02841 *Web:* usnwc.edu	401-841-4052		520
NavalTees LLC 22665 Van Wert Ln .... Leonardtown MD 20650 *Web:* www.navychief.com	301-475-0437		459
Navarre Beach Realty 8305 Navarre Pkwy.......................... Navarre FL 32566 *Web:* navarrebeachrealty.com	850-936-0700		652
Navarro College 3200 W Seventh Ave.......... Corsicana TX 75110 *TF:* 800-628-2776 ■ *Web:* www.navarrocollege.edu	903-874-6501	875-7353	162
Navarro County PO Box 423................. Corsicana TX 75151 *Web:* www.co.navarro.tx.us	903-654-3040	654-3097	338
Navarro County Electric Co-opeartive Inc 3800 Texas 22 PO Box 616................ Corsicana TX 75110 *TF:* 800-771-9095 ■ *Web:* navarroec.com	903-874-7411		245
Navarro Discount Pharmacy 9400 NW 104 St............................. Medley FL 33178 **Fax Area Code:* 305 ■ *TF:* 866-628-2776 ■ *Web:* www.navarro.com	786-245-8524	633-7555*	237
Navarro Regional Hospital (NRH) 3201 W Hwy 22 .... Corsicana TX 75110 *Web:* www.navarrohospital.com	903-654-6800		374-3
Navarro Research & Engineering Inc 1020 Commerce Park Dr .... Oak Ridge TN 37830 *TF:* 866-681-5265 ■ *Web:* www.navarro-inc.com	865-220-9650	220-9651	192
Navasota Valley Electric Co-opeartive Inc 2281 E US Hwy 79 PO Box 848 .... Franklin TX 77856 *TF:* 800-443-9462 ■ *Web:* www.navasotavalley.com	979-828-3232	828-5563	245
NAVBLUE 295 Hagey Blvd Ste 200 .... Waterloo ON N2L6R5 *Web:* www.navblue.aero	519-747-1170	747-1003	178-10
NavCom Defense Electronics Inc 9129 Stellar Ct.............................. Corona CA 92883 *Web:* www.navcom.com	951-268-9230		529
NavCom Technology Inc 20780 Madrona Ave.......................... Torrance CA 90503 *Web:* www.navcomtech.com	310-381-2000		196
Navcor Inc 700 W Georgia St Ste 980 .... Vancouver BC V7Y1B6 *Web:* www.navcor.com	604-688-9090		314
Nave Communications Co 8215 Dorsey Run Rd.......................... Jessup MD 20794 *Web:* www.ncctel.com	301-725-6283		246
Navellier Securities Corp 1 E Liberty St Ste 504.......................... Reno NV 89501 *TF:* 800-887-8671 ■ *Web:* navellier.com	775-785-2300		401
Navhouse Corp 10 Loring Dr.................. Bolton ON L7E1J9 *TF:* 877-628-6667 ■ *Web:* www.navhouse.com	905-857-8102	857-8104	21
Naviant Inc 201 Prairie Heights Dr................ Verona WI 53593 *TF:* 888-686-4624 ■ *Web:* naviant.com	888-686-4624		631
Navicent Health 777 Hemlock St .... Macon GA 31201 *TF:* 844-350-4968 ■ *Web:* www.navicenthealth.org	478-633-1000		374-3
Navigant Cymetrix Corp 2875 Michelle Dr Ste 250....................... Irvine CA 92606 *Web:* www.navigantcymetrix.com	714-361-6800		196
Navigate Power 2211 N Elston Ste 208 .... Chicago IL 60614 *TF:* 888-601-1789 ■ *Web:* navigatepower.com	888-601-1789		463
Navigation Capital Partners Inc 1175 Peachtree St NE 10th Fl................... Atlanta GA 30361 *Web:* www.navigationcapital.com	404-264-9180	264-9305	792
Navigator Development Group Inc 116 S Main St............................ Enterprise AL 36330 *Web:* www.ndgi.com	334-347-7612		449
Navigator Energy Services 2626 Cole Ave Ste 900........................ Dallas TX 75204 *TF:* 888-991-1162 ■ *Web:* www.navigatorenergyservices.com	214-880-6000		538
Navigator Management Partners LLC 1400 Goodale Blvd Ste 100 .... Columbus OH 43212 *Web:* www.navmp.com	614-796-0090	796-0089	463
Navigators of Canada 11 St Johns Dr.............. Arva ON N0M1C0 *TF:* 866-202-6287 ■ *Web:* www.navigators.ca	519-660-8300		48-20
Navigators, The 3820 N 30th St PO Box 6000 .... Colorado Springs CO 80934 *TF:* 866-568-7827 ■ *Web:* www.navigators.org	719-598-1212	260-0479	48-20
Navii Salon Spa 316 E US Hwy 30 .... Schererville IN 46375 *Web:* navii.com	219-865-6515		77
Navin, Haffty & Associates LLC 1900 W Park Dr Ste 180.................. Westborough MA 01581 *TF:* 888-837-1300 ■ *Web:* www.navinhaffty.com	781-871-6770	878-8703	463
Navinta LLC 1499 Lower Ferry Rd .... Ewing NJ 08618 *Web:* www.navinta.com	609-883-1135	883-1137	582
Navis Pack & Ship Centers 12742 E Caley Ave Ste 2 A.................. Centennial CO 80111 **Fax Area Code:* 303 ■ *TF:* 800-344-3528 ■ *Web:* www.gonavis.com	800-344-3528	741-6653*	113
NaviSite Inc 400 Minuteman Rd .... Andover MA 01810 *TF:* 888-298-8222 ■ *Web:* www.navisite.com	978-628-8300	688-8100	225
Navitaire LLC 333 S Seventh St Ste 1700................ Minneapolis MN 55402 *TF:* 877-216-6787 ■ *Web:* navitaire.com	612-317-7000	317-7005	194
Navitar Inc 200 Commerce Dr................. Rochester NY 14623 *TF:* 800-828-6778 ■ *Web:* navitar.com	585-359-4000	359-4999	591
Navix Diagnostix Inc 100 Myles Standish Blvd .... Taunton MA 02780 *Web:* www.navixdiagnostix.com	508-880-3700		415
Navmar Applied Sciences Corp 65 W Street Rd Bldg C .... Warminster PA 18974 *TF:* 833-668-6272 ■ *Web:* www.nasc.com	215-675-4900		256
Navone Engineering Inc 1103 Enterprise St .... Stockton CA 95204 *Web:* www.davidnavone.com	209-465-6139		52
Navopache Electric Co-opeartive Inc 1878 W White Mtn Blvd .... Lakeside AZ 85929 *TF:* 800-543-6324 ■ *Web:* www.navopache.org	928-368-5118	368-6038	245
Navpoint Internet 600 Bethlehem Pke .... Erdenheim PA 19038 *Web:* www.navpoint.com	215-836-4600		180
NAV3 (National Anti-Vivisection Society) 53 W Jackson Blvd Ste 1552 .... Chicago IL 60604 *TF:* 800-888-6287 ■ *Web:* www.navs.org	312-427-6065	427-6524	48-3
Navtech Seminars & Gps Supply 5501 Backlick Rd Ste 230................... Springfield VA 22151 *TF:* 800-628-0885 ■ *Web:* www.navtechgps.com	703-256-8900		463
Navy Brand Manufacturing 3670 Scarlet Oak Blvd .... Saint Louis MO 63122 *Web:* www.navybrand.com	636-861-5500		76
Navy Exchange Service Command (NEXCOM) 3280 Virginia Beach Blvd .... Virginia Beach VA 23452 *TF:* 800-628-3924 ■ *Web:* www.mynavyexchange.com	757-502-7404		791
Navy League of the US 2300 Wilson Blvd Ste 200 .... Arlington VA 22201 *TF:* 800-356-5760 ■ *Web:* www.navyleague.org	703-528-1775	528-2333	48-19
Navy Lodge Pensacola Naval Air Station Bldg 3875................................ Pensacola FL 32508 *Web:* www.navy-lodge.com	850-456-8676		497-4
Navy Personnel Command (NPC) 5720 Integrity Dr......................... Millington TN 38055 **Fax Area Code:* 901 ■ *TF:* 866-827-5672 ■ *Web:* www.public.navy.mil	866-827-5672	874-2615*	340-6
Navy Pier 600 E Grand Ave..................... Chicago IL 60611 *Web:* navypier.org	312-595-7437		205
Navy-Marine Corps Relief Society (NMCRS) 875 N Randolph St Ste 225 .... Arlington VA 22203 *TF:* 800-654-8364 ■ *Web:* www.nmcrs.org	703-696-4904	696-0144	48-19
NAW (NAW National Association of Wholesaler-Distributors) 1325 G St NW Ste 1000.................. Washington DC 20005 *Web:* www.naw.org	202-872-0885	785-0586	49-18
NAW National Association of Wholesaler-Distributors (NAW) 1325 G St NW Ste 1000.................. Washington DC 20005 *Web:* www.naw.org	202-872-0885	785-0586	49-18
Nawab Indian Cuisine 204 Monticello Ave..................... Williamsburg VA 23185 *Web:* www.nawabonline.com	757-565-3200		671
Nawab Indian Cuisine 129 S Stratford Rd .... Winston-Salem NC 27104 *Web:* www.nawabindiancuisine.com	336-725-3949		671
NAWIC (NA of Women in Construction) 327 S Adams St .... Fort Worth TX 76104 *TF:* 800-552-3506 ■ *Web:* www.nawic.org	817-877-5551	877-0324	49-3
Naxos of America Inc 1810 Columbia Ave .... Franklin TN 37064 *TF:* 877-629-6723 ■ *Web:* www.naxos.com	615-771-9393	771-6747	657
Naya Restaurant 1057 2nd Ave .... New York NY 10022 *Web:* www.nayarestaurants.com	212-319-7777		671
Naylor LLC 5950 NW First Pl .... Gainesville FL 32607 *TF:* 800-369-6220 ■ *Web:* www.naylor.com	800-369-6220		7
Naylor Pipe Co 1230 E 92nd St................. Chicago IL 60619 *Web:* www.naylorpipe.com	773-721-9400	721-9494	490
Nazarene Theological Seminary 1700 E Meyer Blvd .... Kansas City MO 64131 **Fax Area Code:* 816 ■ *TF:* 800-831-3011 ■ *Web:* www.nts.edu	800-831-3011	268-5500*	167-3
Nazareth College of Rochester 4245 E Ave .... Rochester NY 14618 *TF:* 800-860-6942 ■ *Web:* www.naz.edu	585-389-2525		166
Nazareth Hospital 2601 Holme Ave .... Philadelphia PA 19152 *Web:* www.mercyhealth.org	215-335-6000	335-7740	374-3
Nazcare Inc 599 White Spar Rd................. Prescott AZ 86303 *TF:* 877-756-4090 ■ *Web:* www.nazcare.org	928-442-9205		138
Nazdar 8501 Hedge Ln Terr.................... Shawnee KS 66227 *TF:* 800-767-9942 ■ *Web:* www.nazdar.com	913-422-1888	422-2296	388
NBA (National Business Assn) 5151 Beltline Rd Ste 1150 .... Dallas TX 75254 *TF:* 800-456-0440 ■ *Web:* www.nationalbusiness.org	972-458-0900	960-9149	49-12
NBA (Niles Bolton Associates Inc) 3060 Peachtree Rd NW Ste 600 .... Atlanta GA 30305 *Web:* www.nilesbolton.com	404-365-7600		261
NBA (National Benevolent Assn) 733 Union Blvd Ste 300 .... Saint Louis MO 63108 *TF:* 866-262-2669 ■ *Web:* www.nbacares.org	314-993-9000	349-1379	48-5

Phone | Fax | Class

NBA (National Bar Assn)
1816 12th St NW 4th Fl .... Washington DC 20009 202-842-3900 289-6170 49-10
Web: nationalbar.org

NBA Media Ventures LLC
201 E Jefferson St .... Phoenix AZ 85004 602-379-7856 379-7990 714-1
Web: www.nba.com

NBAA (National Business Aviation Assn)
1200 18th St NW Ste 400 .... Washington DC 20036 202-783-9000 331-8364 49-21
TF: 800-394-6222 ■ *Web:* www.nbaa.org

NBBJ 223 Yale Ave N .... Seattle WA 98109 206-223-5555 261
Web: www.nbbj.com

NBC 26 1391 N Rd .... Green Bay WI 54313 920-494-2626 490-2500 741-55
TF: 800-800-6619 ■ *Web:* www.nbc26.com

NBC (Ny) Employees Federal Credit Union
1221 Avenue of the Americas Ste C2 .... New York NY 10020 212-332-2610 219
Web: www.xcelfcu.org

NBC Universal Inc 30 Rockefeller Plz .... New York NY 10112 212-664-4444 360-3
Web: www.nbcuniversal.com

NBC Universal Media LLC
9680 Granite Ridge Dr .... San Diego CA 92101 619-231-3939 741-119
Web: www.nbcsandiego.com

NBC15 615 Forward Dr .... Madison WI 53711 608-274-1515 271-5194 741-80
Web: www.nbc15.com

NBC4 Columbus
3165 Olentangy River Rd .... Columbus OH 43202 614-263-4444 263-0166 741-35
TF: 888-812-9801 ■ *Web:* www.nbc4i.com

NBCC (National Breast Cancer Coalition)
1010 Vermont Ave NW Ste 900 .... Washington DC 20005 202-296-7477 265-6854 48-17
TF: 800-622-2838 ■ *Web:* www.breastcancerdeadline2020.org

NBCL (National Beauty Culturists' League Inc, The)
25 Logan Cir Nw .... Washington DC 20005 202-332-2695 49-4
Web: www.nbcl.info

Nbcot 1 Bank St Ste 300 .... Gaithersburg MD 20878 301-990-7979 138
TF: 800-967-1139 ■ *Web:* www.nbcot.org

NBCVB (North of Boston Convention & Visitors Bureau)
I-95 Southbound Exit 60 PO Box 5193 .... Salisbury MA 01952 978-465-6555 206
Web: northofboston.org

NBDA (National Bicycle Dealers Assn)
777 W 19th St Ste O .... Costa Mesa CA 92627 949-722-6909 49-4
Web: nbda.com

NBEA (National Business Education Assn)
1914 Assn Dr .... Reston VA 20191 703-860-8300 620-4483 49-5
Web: www.nbea.org

NBFPL (New Bedford Free Public Library)
613 Pleasant St .... New Bedford MA 02740 508-991-6275 991-6368 434-3
Web: www.newbedford-ma.gov

NBM Publishing
40 Exchange Pl Ste 1308 .... New York NY 10005 212-643-5407 643-1545 637-2
TF: 800-886-1223 ■ *Web:* www.nbmpub.com

NBMBAA (National Black MBA Assn)
400 W Peachtree St NW Ste 203 .... Atlanta GA 30308 404-260-5444 49-12
Web: www.nbmbaa.org

NBMDA (North American Building Material Distribution Assn)
330 N Wabash Ave Ste 2000 .... Chicago IL 60611 312-321-6845 644-0310 49-18
TF: 888-747-7862 ■ *Web:* www.nbmda.org

NBME (National Board of Medical Examiners)
3750 Market St .... Philadelphia PA 19104 215-590-9500 49-8
Web: www.nbme.org

NBN Infusions 2 Pin Oak Ln Ste 250 .... Cherry Hill NJ 08003 856-669-0217 424-8913 475
TF: 800-253-9111 ■ *Web:* www.nbninfusions.com

NBPA (National Basketball Players Assn)
1133 Avenue of Americas .... New York NY 10036 212-655-0880 655-0881 48-22
TF: 800-955-6272 ■ *Web:* nbpa.com

NBR (National Bureau of Asian Research)
George F. Russell Jr Hall
1414 NE 42nd St Ste 300 .... Seattle WA 98105 206-632-7370 632-7487 637-10
Web: www.nbr.org

NBS (National Business Services Budget Store Inc)
11-D El Paso Natl Bank .... El Paso TX 79901 915-544-1271 351-0170 319-1

NBS Corp 3100 E Slauson Ave .... Vernon CA 90058 323-923-1627 351
Web: www.nbsfasteners.com

NBS Technologies Inc
703 Evans Ave Ste 402 .... Toronto ON M9C5E9 416-621-1911 41
Web: www.nbstech.com

NBT Bancorp Inc 52 S Broad St .... Norwich NY 13815 607-337-2265 360-2
NASDAQ: NBTB ■ *TF:* 800-628-2265 ■ *Web:* www.nbtbancorp.com

NBT Bank NA PO Box 351 .... Norwich NY 13815 607-334-2178 70
Web: www.nbtbank.com

NBT Solutions LLC
480 Congress St 3rd Fl .... Portland ME 04101 617-202-3088 180
Web: www.nbtsolutions.com

NBWA (National Beer Wholesalers Assn)
1101 King St Ste 600 .... Alexandria VA 22314 703-683-4300 683-8965 49-6
TF: 800-300-6417 ■ *Web:* www.nbwa.org

NC Chamber
701 Corporate Center Dr Ste 400 .... Raleigh NC 27607 919-836-1400 836-1425 140
Web: ncchamber.com

NC Dynamics Inc (NCDI) 3401 E 69th St .... Long Beach CA 90805 562-634-7392 634-6220 454
Web: www.ncdynamics.com

NC Machinery Co 17025 W Valley Hwy .... Tukwila WA 98188 800-562-4735 385
TF: 800-562-4735 ■ *Web:* www.ncmachinery.com

NCA (National Club Assn)
1201 15th St NW Ste 450 .... Washington DC 20005 202-822-9822 822-9808 48-23
TF: 800-625-6221 ■ *Web:* www.nationalclub.org

NCA (National Coffee Association of USA Inc)
45 Broadway Ste 1140 .... New York NY 10006 212-766-4007 766-5815 49-6
Web: www.ncausa.org

NCA (National Confectioners Assn)
1101 30th St NW Ste 200 .... Washington DC 20007 202-534-1440 337-0637 49-6
Web: www.candyusa.com

NCA (National Communication Assn)
1765 N St NW .... Washington DC 20036 202-464-4622 464-4600 49-5
Web: www.natcom.org

NCA Architects PA
1306 Rio Grande Blvd NW .... Albuquerque NM 87104 505-255-6400 261
Web: www.nca-architects.com

NCA Partners Inc
1200 Westlake Ave N Ste 600 .... Seattle WA 98109 206-689-5615 689-5614 403
Web: www.nwcap.com

NCAA (National Collegiate Athletic Assn)
700 W Washington St PO Box 6222 .... Indianapolis IN 46206 317-917-6222 917-6888 48-22
Web: www.ncaa.org

NCAAA (Museum of the National Center of Afro-American Artists)
300 Walnut Ave .... Roxbury MA 02119 617-442-8614 520
Web: www.ncaaa.org

NCAC (National Coalition Against Censorship)
19 Fulton St Ste 407 .... New York NY 10038 212-807-6222 807-6245 48-8
Web: www.ncac.org

NCAC (National Children's Advocacy Ctr)
210 Pratt Ave .... Huntsville AL 35801 256-533-5437 48-5
Web: www.nationalcac.org

NCACASI (North Central Association Commission on Accreditation & School Improvement)
9115 Westside Pkwy .... Alpharetta GA 30009 888-413-3669 48-1
TF: 888-413-3669 ■ *Web:* www.advanc-ed.org

NCADP (National Coalition to Abolish the Death Penalty)
1620 L St Ste 250 .... Washington DC 20036 202-331-4090 48-8
Web: www.ncadp.org

NCADV (National Coalition Against Domestic Violence)
600 Grant Ste 750 .... Denver CO 80203 303-839-1852 831-9251 48-6
Web: www.ncadv.org

NCAE News Bulletin PO Box 27347 .... Raleigh NC 27611 919-832-3000 829-1626 457-8
TF: 800-662-7924 ■ *Web:* www.ncae.org

NCAF (National Community Action Foundation)
PO Box 78214 .... Washington DC 20013 202-842-2092 842-2095 48-7
Web: www.ncaf.org

NCAI (National Congress of American Indians)
1516 P St NW .... Washington DC 20005 202-466-7767 466-7797 48-14
TF: 800-388-2227 ■ *Web:* www.ncai.org

NCAR (National Center for Atmospheric Research)
3090 Center Green Dr .... Boulder CO 80301 303-497-1000 668
Web: ncar.ucar.edu

NCARB (National Council of Architectural Registration Boards)
1801 K St NW Ste 700-K .... Washington DC 20006 202-783-6500 783-0290 49-7
Web: www.ncarb.org

NCATE (National Council for Accreditation of Teacher Education)
2010 Massachusetts Ave NW Ste 500 .... Washington DC 20036 202-466-7496 296-6620 48-1
Web: www.ncate.org

NCB (National Cargo Bureau Inc)
180 Maiden Ln Ste 903 .... New York NY 10038 212-785-8300 785-8333 49-21
Web: www.natcargo.org

NCBA (National Cattlemen's Beef Assn)
9110 E Nichols Ave Ste 300 .... Centennial CO 80112 303-694-0305 694-2851 48-2
TF: 866-233-3872 ■ *Web:* www.beefusa.org

NCBA (National Caucus & Center on Black Aged Inc)
1220 L St NW Ste 800 .... Washington DC 20005 202-637-8400 347-0895 48-6
Web: www.ncba-aged.org

NCBC (North Carolina Biotechnology Ctr)
15 T.W. Alexander Dr .... Research Triangle Park NC 27709 919-541-9366 990-9544 668
Web: www.ncbiotech.org

NCBFAA (National Customs Brokers & Forwarders Association of America Inc)
1200 18th St NW Ste 901 .... Washington DC 20036 202-466-0222 466-0226 49-21
Web: www.ncbfaa.org

NCBMP (National Coalition of Black Meeting Planners)
1800 Diagonal Rd .... Alexandria VA 22314 571-366-1779 588-0011* 49-12
**Fax Area Code:* 301 ■ *Web:* www.ncbmp.com

NCBW (National Center for Bicycling & Walking)
8120 Woodmont Ave Ste 520 .... Bethesda MD 20814 301-656-4220 656-4225 48-22
Web: www.bikewalk.org

NCC Automated Systems Inc
255 Schoolhouse Rd .... Souderton PA 18964 215-721-1900 721-0633 207
Web: www.nccas.com

NCCA (National Child Care Assn)
1325 G St NW Ste 500 .... Washington DC 20005 866-536-1945 48-6
TF: 866-536-1945 ■ *Web:* www.nccanet.org

NCCAOM (National Certification Commission for Acupuncture & Oriental Medicine)
2025 M St NW Ste 800 .... Washington DC 20036 202-381-1140 381-1141 48-1
TF: 888-381-1140 ■ *Web:* www.nccaom.org

NCCD (National Council on Crime & Delinquency)
1970 Broadway Ste 500 .... Oakland CA 94612 510-208-0500 208-0511 48-8
TF: 800-306-6223 ■ *Web:* www.nccdglobal.org

NCCI Holdings Inc
901 Peninsula Corporate Cir .... Boca Raton FL 33487 561-893-1000 893-1191 390
TF: 800-622-4123 ■ *Web:* www.ncci.com

NCCNHR (National Citizens' Coalition for Nursing Home Reform)
National Consumer Voice for Quality Long-Term Care
1828 L St NW Ste 801 .... Washington DC 20036 202-332-2275 332-2949 48-17
TF: 866-992-3668 ■ *Web:* theconsumervoice.org

NCCP (National Center for Children in Poverty)
215 W 125th St 3rd Fl .... New York NY 10027 646-284-9600 284-9623 48-6
Web: www.nccp.org

NCCPA (National Commission on Certification of Physician Assistants)
12000 Findley Rd Ste 100 .... Johns Creek GA 30097 678-417-8100 417-8135 48-1
Web: www.nccpa.net

NCCRC (Northern California Carpenters Regional Council)
2102 Almaden Rd Ste 125 .... San Jose CA 95125 408-445-3000 445-5868 474
Web: www.nccrc.org

NCCS (National Coalition for Cancer Survivorship)
8455 Colesville Rd Ste 930 .... Silver Spring MD 20910 877-622-7937 48-17
TF: 877-622-7937 ■ *Web:* www.canceradvocacy.org

NCD (National Council on Disability)
1331 F St NW Ste 850 .... Washington DC 20004 202-272-2004 272-2022 340-20
Web: ncd.gov

NCD Corp 33801 Curtis Blvd Ste 100 .... Eastlake OH 44095 440-953-4488 475
Web: www.ncdcorp.com

NCDA & CS Raleigh Farmers Market
1201 Agriculture St .... Raleigh NC 27603 919-733-7417 460
Web: www.ncagr.gov

NCDI (NC Dynamics Inc) 3401 E 69th St .... Long Beach CA 90805 562-634-7392 634-6220 454
Web: www.ncdynamics.com

NCDVD (National Conference of Diocesan Vocation Directors)
440 W Neck Road .... Huntington NY 11743 631-645-8210 812-0249 48-20
Web: ncdvd.org

NCEA (National Catholic Educational Assn)
1005 N Glebe Rd Ste 525 .... Arlington VA 22201 571-257-0010 243-0025* 49-5
**Fax Area Code:* 703 ■ *TF:* 800-711-6232 ■ *Web:* ncea.org

NCEAS (National Center for Ecological Analysis & Synthesis)
735 State St Ste 300 .... Santa Barbara CA 93101 805-892-2500 892-2510 668
Web: www.nceas.ucsb.edu

Name / Address	Phone	Fax	Class
NCECA 4845 Pearl East Cir Ste 101 .... Boulder CO 80301 *Web:* nceca.net	303-828-2811		184
NCED (National Center for Employee Development) 2701 E Imhoff Rd .... Norman OK 73071 *TF:* 866-438-6233 ■ *Web:* www.nced.com	405-366-4420	366-4319	377
NCEE (National Council on Economic Education) 122 E 42nd St Ste 2600 .... New York NY 10168 *TF:* 800-338-1192 ■ *Web:* www.councilforeconed.org	212-730-7007	730-1793	49-5
NCEES (National Council of Examiners for Engineering & Surveying) 280 Seneca Creek Rd .... Seneca SC 29678 *TF:* 800-250-3196 ■ *Web:* ncees.org	864-654-6824		49-3
NCEO (National Center for Employee Ownership) 1629 Telegraph Ave Ste 200 .... Oakland CA 94612 *Web:* www.nceo.org	510-208-1300	272-9510	48-10
NCFA (National Council for Adoption) 225 N Washington St .... Alexandria VA 22314 *Web:* www.adoptioncouncil.org	703-299-6633	299-6004	48-6
NCFBMIC (North Carolina Farm Bureau Mutual Insurance Co) PO Box 27427 .... Raleigh NC 27611 *TF:* 800-584-1143 ■ *Web:* www.ncfbins.com	919-782-1705		391-4
NCFC (National Council of Farmer Co-ops) 50 F St NW Ste 900 .... Washington DC 20001 *TF:* 800-344-2626 ■ *Web:* ncfc.org	202-626-8700	626-8722	48-2
NCFI Polyurethanes 1515 Carter St .... Mount Airy NC 27030 *TF:* 800-346-8229 ■ *Web:* ncfi.com	336-789-9161	789-9586	191-4
NCFL (National Center for Family Literacy) 325 W Main St Ste 300 .... Louisville KY 40202 *Web:* familieslearning.org	502-584-1133	584-0172	48-11
NCFR (National Council on Family Relations) 1201 W River Pkwy Ste 200 .... Minneapolis MN 55454 *TF:* 888-781-9331 ■ *Web:* www.ncfr.org	888-781-9331		48-6
NCFS (New Century FS Inc) 1017 Ogan Ave ...... Grinnell IA 50112 *TF:* 888-488-3737 ■ *Web:* www.newcenturyfs.com	641-236-3117	236-5363	274
NCG (Northern California Grantmakers) 160 Spear St Ste 360 .... San Francisco CA 94105 *TF:* 877-624-2755 ■ *Web:* www.ncg.org	415-777-4111	777-1714	48-13
NCGA (National Corn Growers Assn) 632 Cepi Dr .... Chesterfield MO 63005 *Web:* www.ncga.com	636-733-9004	733-9005	48-2
NCGRP (National Center for Genetic Resources Preservation) 1111 S Mason St .... Fort Collins CO 80521 *Web:* www.ars.usda.gov	970-495-3200	221-1427	668
NCGS (National Coalition of Girls' Schools) PO Box 5729 .... Charlottesville VA 22905 *Web:* www.ncgs.org	434-205-4496		49-5
NCH (National Coalition for the Homeless) 2201 P St NW .... Washington DC 20037 *Web:* www.nationalhomeless.org	202-462-4822	462-4823	48-5
NCH (National Center for Homeopathy) 1120 Rte 73 Ste 200 .... Mount Laurel NJ 08054 **Fax Area Code:* 856 ■ *Web:* www.homeopathycenter.org	703-548-7790	439-0525*	48-17
NCH Corp 2727 Chemsearch Blvd .... Irving TX 75062 *TF:* 800-527-9919 ■ *Web:* www.nch.com	972-438-0211		151
NCH Healthcare System 350 Seventh St N .... Naples FL 34102 *Web:* nchmd.org	239-624-5000		374-3
NCHA (National Cutting Horse Assn) 260 Bailey Ave .... Fort Worth TX 76107 *Web:* www.nchacutting.com	817-244-6188	244-2015	48-3
NCHC (New Castle-Henry County Public Library) 376 S 15th St .... New Castle IN 47362 *Web:* www.nchcpl.org	765-529-0362		434-3
Ncheng LLP CPA 40 Wall St Ste 3222 32nd Fl .... New York NY 10005 *Web:* ncheng.com	212-785-0100	785-9168	2
NCHS (New Canaan Historical Society) 13 Oenoke Ridge Rd .... New Canaan CT 06840 *Web:* www.nchistory.org	203-966-1776	972-5917	48-6
NCHS (New Castle Historical Society) Horace Greeley House 100 King St .... Chappaqua NY 10514 *Web:* www.newcastlehs.org	914-238-4666	238-1296	48-13
NCI (Nissan Canada Inc) 5290 Orbitor Dr .... Mississauga ON L4W4Z5 **Fax Area Code:* 905 ■ *TF:* 800-387-0122 ■ *Web:* www.nissan.ca	800-387-0122	629-6553*	59
NCI (Nationwide Credit Inc) PO Box 14581 .... Des Moines IA 50306 **Fax Area Code:* 770 ■ *TF:* 800-456-4729 ■ *Web:* www.ncirm.com	800-456-4729	612-7335*	160
NCI (National Captioning Institute) 3725 Concorde Pkwy Ste 100 .... Chantilly VA 20151 *TF:* 800-825-6758 ■ *Web:* www.ncicap.org	703-917-7600	917-9853	632
NCI Datacom 626 Okoma Dr .... Omak WA 98841 *Web:* ncidata.com	509-826-0300		225
NCI Inc 11730 Plaza America Dr .... Reston VA 20190 *NASDAQ:* NCIT ■ *TF:* 800-274-9694 ■ *Web:* www.nciinc.com	703-707-6900	707-6901	180
NCI Technologies Inc 636 Cure-Boivin Blvd .... Boisbriand QC J7G2A7 *Web:* www.ncitech.ca	450-434-7222		407
NCIC (NCIC Inmate Communications) 607 E Whaley St .... Longview TX 75601 *Web:* www.ncic.com	903-757-4455		736
NCIC Capital Fund 900 Kettering Twr .... Dayton OH 45423 *Web:* www.ncicfund.com	937-222-4422	222-1323	792
NCIC Inmate Communications (NCIC) 607 E Whaley St .... Longview TX 75601 *Web:* www.ncic.com	903-757-4455		736
NCircle Entertainment 30 Corporate Pk Ste 207 .... Irvine CA 92606 *TF:* 800-814-4459 ■ *Web:* www.ncircleentertainment.com	949-225-1170		511
NCIS (National Crop Insurance Services) 8900 Indian Creek Pkwy Ste 600 .... Overland Park KS 66210 *TF:* 800-951-6247 ■ *Web:* www.ag-risk.org	913-685-2767	685-3080	48-2
NCJFCJ (National Council of Juvenile & Family Court Judges) Univ of Nevada PO Box 8970 .... Reno NV 89507 *TF:* 800-527-3223 ■ *Web:* www.ncjfcj.org	775-784-6012	784-6628	49-10
NCJJ (National Center for Juvenile Justice) 3700 S Water St Ste 200 .... Pittsburgh PA 15203 *TF:* 800-851-3420 ■ *Web:* ncjj.org	412-227-6950	227-6955	48-8
NCJW (National Council of Jewish Women) 475 Riverside Dr Ste 1901 .... New York NY 10115 *Web:* www.ncjw.org	212-645-4048	645-7466	48-24
NCL (National Civic League) 190 E Ninth Ave Ste 200 .... Denver CO 80206 **Fax Area Code:* 888 ■ *Web:* www.nationalcivicleague.org	303-571-4343	314-6053*	48-7
NCL (National Consumers League) 1701 K St NW Ste 1200 .... Washington DC 20006 *Web:* www.nclnet.org	202-835-3323	835-0747	48-10
NCLA (North Carolina Library Assn) 1811 Capital Blvd .... Raleigh NC 27604 *TF:* 888-977-3143 ■ *Web:* www.nclaonline.org	919-839-6252	839-6253	435
NCLC (National Consumer Law Ctr) 7 Winthrop Sq .... Boston MA 02110 *Web:* www.nclc.org	617-542-8010	542-8028	48-8
NCMA (National Contract Management Assn) 21740 Beaumeade Cir Ste 125 .... Ashburn VA 20147 **Fax Area Code:* 703 ■ *TF:* 800-344-8096 ■ *Web:* www.ncmahq.org	571-382-0082	448-0939*	49-12
NCMA (North Carolina Museum of Art) 2110 Blue Ridge Rd .... Raleigh NC 27607 *Web:* www.ncartmuseum.org	919-839-6262	733-8034	520
NCMEC (National Center for Missing & Exploited Children) 333 John Carlyle St Ste 125 .... Alexandria VA 22314 *Web:* www.missingkids.com	703-224-2150	274-2200	48-6
NCMIC Insurance Co 14001 University Ave .... Clive IA 50325 *TF:* 800-769-2000 ■ *Web:* www.ncmic.com	800-247-8043	996-2642	391-5
NCMS (National Center for Manufacturing Sciences) 3025 Boardwalk .... Ann Arbor MI 48108 *TF:* 800-222-6267 ■ *Web:* www.ncms.org	734-995-3457	995-1150	668
NCNA (North Carolina Nurses Assn) 103 Enterprise St PO Box 12025 .... Raleigh NC 27605 *TF:* 800-626-2153 ■ *Web:* ncnurses.org	919-821-4250	829-5807	533
NCNW (National Council of Negro Women Inc) 633 Pennsylvania Ave NW .... Washington DC 20004 *Web:* www.ncnw.org	202-737-0120	737-0476	48-24
NCOA (National Council on the Aging) 1901 L St NW 4th Fl .... Washington DC 20036 **Fax Area Code:* 202 ■ *Web:* www.ncoa.org	571-527-3900	479-0735*	48-6
NCOA (Non Commissioned Officers Assn) 9330 Corporate Dr Ste 708 .... Selma TX 78154 *TF:* 800-662-2620 ■ *Web:* www.ncoausa.org	210-653-6161	637-3337	48-19
NCOC (National Conference on Citizenship) 1900 L St NW Ste 450 .... Washington DC 20036 *Web:* ncoc.org	202-601-7096		48-8
NCompass International Inc 8223 Santa Monica Blvd .... West Hollywood CA 90046 *Web:* www.ncompassonline.com	323-785-1700		195
NCP (New City Press) 202 Comforter Blvd .... Hyde Park NY 12538 **Fax Area Code:* 416 ■ *TF:* 877-756-7374 ■ *Web:* www.newcitypress.com	845-229-0335	291-1378*	637-2
NCP Solutions 5200 E Lake Blvd .... Birmingham AL 35217 *Web:* www.ncpsolutions.com	205-849-5200		110
NCPA (National Community Pharmacists Assn) 100 Daingerfield Rd .... Alexandria VA 22314 *TF:* 800-544-7447 ■ *Web:* www.ncpanet.org	703-683-8200	683-3619	49-8
NCPC (National Crime Prevention Council) 2345 Crystal Dr Ste 500 .... Arlington VA 22202 **Fax Area Code:* 202 ■ *TF:* 800-627-2911 ■ *Web:* www.ncpc.org	443-292-4565	296-1356*	48-8
NCPDP (National Council for Prescription Drug Programs) 9240 E Raintree Dr .... Scottsdale AZ 85260 *Web:* www.ncpdp.org	480-477-1000	767-1042	49-9
NCPH (National Council on Public History) 425 University Blvd 127 Cavanaugh Hall ...... Indianapolis IN 46202 *Web:* www.ncph.org	317-274-2716	278-5230	48-7
NCPIRG (North Carolina Public Interest Research Group) 19 W Hargett St Ste 405 .... Raleigh NC 27601 *Web:* ncpirg.org	919-833-2070		633
NCPPR (National Center for Public Policy Research) 501 Capitol Ct NE Ste 200 .... Washington DC 20002 *Web:* nationalcenter.org	202-543-4110	543-5975	634
NCPSSM (National Committee to Preserve Social Security & Medicare) 10 G St NE Ste 600 .... Washington DC 20002 *TF:* 800-966-1935 ■ *Web:* www.ncpssm.org	202-216-0420		48-7
NCQA (National Committee for Quality Assurance) 1100 13th St .... Washington DC 20005 *TF:* 888-275-7585 ■ *Web:* www.ncqa.org	202-955-3500	955-3599	48-10
NCRA (National Cancer Registrars Assn) 1340 Braddock Pl Ste 203 .... Alexandria VA 22314 *Web:* www.ncra-usa.org	703-299-6640	299-6620	48-17
NCRA (National Court Reporters Assn) 8224 Old Courthouse Rd .... Vienna VA 22182 *TF:* 800-272-6272 ■ *Web:* www.ncra.org	703-556-6272	556-6291	49-10
NCRP (National Committee for Responsive Philanthropy) 1900 L St NW Ste 825 .... Washington DC 20036 *Web:* www.ncrp.org	202-387-9177	332-5084	48-5
NCS (Nina Construction Supply) 4102 E Superior Ave .... Phoenix AZ 85040 *Web:* www.ninaconstructionsupply.com	602-437-5760	437-5765	364
NCS Global 32 Innovation Dr .... Rochester NH 03867 *TF:* 800-711-6010 ■ *Web:* Www.ncsglobalinc.com	603-926-4300		174
NCS Multistage LLC 19450 State Hwy 249 Ste 200 .... Houston TX 77070 *Web:* www.ncsmultistage.com	281-453-2222	652-5846	538
NCS Subsea Inc 3928 Bluebonnet Dr .... Stafford TX 77477 *Web:* www.ncs-subsea.com	281-491-3123		41
NCSBN (National Council of State Boards of Nursing) 111 E Wacker Dr Ste 2900 .... Chicago IL 60601 *TF:* 866-293-9600 ■ *Web:* www.policies.ncsbn.org	312-525-3600	279-1032	49-8
NCSC (National Center for State Courts) 300 Newport Ave .... Williamsburg VA 23185 *TF:* 800-616-6164 ■ *Web:* www.ncsc.org	757-259-1525	220-0449	49-7
NCSD (Niskayuna Central School District) 1239 Van Antwerp Rd .... Schenectady NY 12309 *TF:* 866-893-6337 ■ *Web:* www.niskayunaschools.org	518-377-4666	377-4074	685
NCSEA (National Child Support Enforcement Assn) 1760 Old Meadow Rd Ste 500 .... McLean VA 22102 *Web:* www.ncsea.org	703-506-2880		48-6
NCSEAA (North Carolina State Education Assistance Authority) 2917 Highwoods Blvd .... Research Triangle Park NC 27709 *TF:* 800-700-1775 ■ *Web:* www.ncseaa.edu	919-549-8614	549-8481	725

Name / Address	City	State	Zip	Phone	Fax	Class
NCSG Crane & Heavy Haul Services Ltd 11466 Winterburn Rd *Web:* www.ncsg.com	Edmonton	AB	T5S2Y3	780-455-1075		23
NCSHA (National Council of State Housing Agencies) 444 N Capitol St NW Ste 438 *TF:* 800-475-2098 ■ *Web:* www.ncsha.org	Washington	DC	20001	202-624-7710	624-5899	49-7
NCSM (National Council of Supervisors of Mathematics) 2851 S Parker Rd Ste 1210 *Web:* www.mathedleadership.org	Aurora	CO	80014	303-317-6595	200-7099	49-5
NCSPA (National Corrugated Steel Pipe Assn) 14070 Proton Rd Ste 100 *Web:* ncspa.org	Dallas	TX	75244	972-850-1907		49-3
NCSS (National Council for the Social Studies) 8555 16th St Ste 500 *TF:* 800-683-0812 ■ *Web:* socialstudies.org	Silver Spring	MD	20910	301-588-1800	588-2049	49-5
NCTA (National Council for the Traditional Arts) 8757 Georgia Ave Ste 450 *Web:* ncta-usa.org	Silver Spring	MD	20910	301-565-0654		48-4
NCTA (National Cable & Telecommunications Assn) 25 Massachusetts Ave NW Ste 100 *Web:* www.ncta.com	Washington	DC	20001	202-222-2300		49-14
NCTA (National Christmas Tree Assn) 16020 Swingley Ridge Rd Ste 300 **Fax Area Code:* 636 ■ *TF:* 800-975-5920 ■ *Web:* www.realchristmastrees.org	Chesterfield	MO	63017	800-975-5920	449-5051*	48-2
NCTD (North County Transit District) 810 Mission Rd *Web:* www.gonctd.com	Oceanside	CA	92054	760-966-6500	967-2001	468
NCTE (National Council of Teachers of English) 1111 W Kenyon Rd *TF:* 877-369-6283 ■ *Web:* www.ncte.org	Urbana	IL	61801	217-328-3870	328-0977	49-5
NCTM (National Council of Teachers of Mathematics) 1906 Assn Dr *TF:* 800-235-7566 ■ *Web:* www.nctm.org	Reston	VA	20191	703-620-9840	476-2970	49-5
NCTO (National Council of Textile Organizations) 1701 K St NW Ste 625 *TF:* 800-238-7192 ■ *Web:* www.ncto.org	Washington	DC	20006	202-822-8028	822-8029	49-13
NCTRC (National Council for Therapeutic Recreation Certification) 7 Elmwood Dr *Web:* www.nctrc.org	New City	NY	10956	845-639-1439	639-1471	49-15
NCVB (Nashville Convention & Visitors Bureau) 150 Fourth Ave N Ste G250 *TF:* 800-657-6910 ■ *Web:* www.visitmusiccity.com	Nashville	TN	37219	615-259-4730	259-4126	206
NCVMA (North Carolina Veterinary Medical Assn) 1611 Jones Franklin Rd Ste 108 *TF:* 800-446-2862 ■ *Web:* www.ciclt.net	Raleigh	NC	27606	919-851-5850	851-5859	795
NCX Inc 70 E Beaver Creek Rd Unit 2 *Web:* www.ncxinc.com	Richmond Hill	ON	L4B3B2	905-370-7060		179
ND Graphic Product Ltd 55 Interchange Way Unit 1 *TF:* 800-811-0194 ■ *Web:* www.ndgraphics.com	Concord	ON	L4K5W3	416-663-6416		627
ND Industries Inc 1000 N Crooks Rd *TF:* 800-471-5000 ■ *Web:* www.ndindustries.com	Clawson	MI	48017	248-288-0000	288-0022	481
NDA (AMOA-National Dart Assn) 10070 W 190th Pl **Fax Area Code:* 708 ■ *TF:* 800-808-9884 ■ *Web:* www.ndadarts.com	Mokena	IL	60448	800-808-9884	226-1310*	48-22
NDA Partners LLC 40 Commerce Ln Ste D *Web:* www.ndapartners.com	Rochelle	VA	22738	540-738-2550	738-2494	463
NDAA 1400 Crystal D Ste 330 *Web:* www.ndaa.org	Arlington	VA	22202	703-549-9222	836-3195	49-7
NDC (National Dairy Council) 10255 W Higgins Rd Ste 900 *Web:* www.nationaldairycouncil.org	Rosemont	IL	60018	847-627-3790		48-2
NDC (New Dimension Controls Inc) 80 Sand Island Access Rd Ste 200 *Web:* www.ndchawaii.com	Honolulu	HI	96819	808-847-7992	847-6992	112
NDC Infrared Engineering 5314 N Irwindale Ave *TF:* 800-866-4733 ■ *Web:* www.ndc.com	Irwindale	CA	91706	626-960-3300	939-3870	201
NDC LLC 6312 S 27th St Ste 202 *Web:* www.ndcllc.com	Oak Creek	WI	53154	414-761-2040	761-3576	655
NDD Medical Technologies Inc 300 Brickton Sq Ste 604 *Web:* www.nddmed.com	Andover	MA	01810	978-470-0923		475
Ndex Systems Inc 500 Saint-Jacques St Ste 400 *Web:* www.ndexsystems.com	Montreal	QC	H2Y1S1	514-288-0908		177
NDH Medical Inc 11001 Roosevelt Blvd N Ste 800 *Web:* www.ndhmedical.com	Saint Petersburg	FL	33716	727-570-2293		476
NDIA (National Defense Industrial Assn) 2111 Wilson Blvd Ste 400 *Web:* www.ndia.org	Arlington	VA	22201	703-522-1820	522-1885	48-19
N-Dimension Solutions Inc 9030 Leslie St Ste 300 *TF:* 866-837-8884 ■ *Web:* www.n-dimension.com	Richmond Hill	ON	L4B1G2	866-837-8884		225
NDK Foods Inc 7512 Scout Ave *Web:* www.ndk-foods.sbcontract.com	Bell	CA	90201	562-927-9598	806-7059	297-8
NDLC (North Dakota League of Cities) 410 E Front Ave *TF:* 800-472-2692 ■ *Web:* www.ndlc.org	Bismarck	ND	58504	701-223-3518	223-5174	48-6
NDMA (North Dakota Medical Assn) 1622 I- Ave *Web:* www.ndmed.org	Bismarck	ND	58503	701-223-9475	223-9476	474
NDP (Neathawk Dubuque & Packett) 2912 W Leigh St *TF:* 800-847-2674 ■ *Web:* www.ndp.agency	Richmond	VA	23230	804-783-8140		4
NDPHA (North Dakota Pharmacists Assn) 1641 Capitol Way *Web:* www.nodakpharmacy.net	Bismarck	ND	58501	701-258-4968	258-9312	585
NDRI (National Disease Research Interchange) 1628 John F Kennedy Blvd 8 Penn Ctr Eighth Fl *TF:* 800-222-6374 ■ *Web:* ndriresource.org	Philadelphia	PA	19103	215-557-7361		269
NDS Surgical Imaging LLC 5750 Hellyer Ave *TF:* 866-637-5237 ■ *Web:* www.ndssi.com	San Jose	CA	95138	408-776-0085		743
NDSC (National Down Syndrome Congress) 30 Mansell Ct Ste 108 *TF:* 800-232-6372 ■ *Web:* www.ndsccenter.org	Roswell	GA	30076	770-604-9500	604-9898	48-17
NDSE (Network Data Security Experts Inc) 521 Branchway Rd *TF:* 877-440-6373 ■ *Web:* www.ndse.net	North Chesterfield	VA	23236	877-440-6373		177
NDSL (North Dakota State Library) 604 E Blvd Ave *TF:* 800-472-2104 ■ *Web:* www.library.nd.gov	Bismarck	ND	58505	701-328-4622	328-2040	434-5
NDSS (National Down Syndrome Society) 666 Broadway 8th Fl **Fax Area Code:* 212 ■ *TF:* 800-221-4602 ■ *Web:* www.ndss.org	New York	NY	10012	800-221-4602	979-2873*	48-17
NDSU Foundation 1241 University Dr N *TF:* 800-279-8971 ■ *Web:* www.ndsufoundation.com	Fargo	ND	58102	701-231-6800		671
NDT International Inc 711 S Creek Rd *Web:* www.ndtint.com	West Chester	PA	19382	610-793-1700	793-1702	472
NDVH (National Domestic Violence Hotline) PO Box 161810 *Web:* www.thehotline.org	Austin	TX	78716	512-794-1133		48-6
NDX Stern Empire 1805 W 34th St *TF:* 800-229-0214 ■ *Web:* nationaldentex.com	Houston	TX	77018	713-688-1301	688-0267	228
NE Finch Co 1925 S Darst St *Web:* nefinch.com	Peoria	IL	61607	309-671-1444	671-1449	780
NEA (National Education Assn) 1201 16th St NW *TF:* 888-552-0624 ■ *Web:* www.nea.org	Washington	DC	20036	202-833-4000	822-7974	49-5
NEA (National Electronic Attachment Inc) 100 Ashford Ctr N Ste 300 **Fax Area Code:* 770 ■ *TF:* 800-782-5150 ■ *Web:* www.nea-fast.com	Dunwoody	GA	30338	800-782-5150	441-3204*	390
Neal & Harwell PLC 1201 Demonbreun St Ste 1000 *Web:* www.nealharwell.com	Nashville	TN	37203	615-244-1713	726-0573	428
Neal Advertising LLC 153 Andover St Ste 201 *Web:* nealadv.com	Danvers	MA	01923	978-774-4444		7
Neal Analytics LLC 3240 Eastlake Ave E Ste 104 *Web:* nealanalytics.com	Seattle	WA	98102	206-286-9200		466
Neal Electri Corp 13250 Kirkham Way *Web:* www.nealelectric.com	Poway	CA	92064	858-513-2525	513-9488	787
Neal Insurance Agency Inc 101 W Mulbury *Web:* neal-insurance.com	Angleton	TX	77515	979-849-5779		390
Neal Mast & Son Incorporated Greenhouses 1780 4 Mile Rd NW *Web:* www.nealmastgreenhouses.com	Grand Rapids	MI	49544	616-784-3323		192
Neal Publications Inc 127 W Indiana Ave *Web:* www.nealpublications.com	Perrysburg	OH	43551	419-874-4787	874-1182	180
Neal Richard E (Rep D - MA) 2309 Rayburn House Office Bldg *Web:* neal.house.gov	Washington	DC	20515	202-225-5601	225-8112	342-2
Neal Systems Inc 122 Terry Dr *Web:* www.nealsystems.com	Newtown	PA	18940	215-968-7577		138
Neany Inc 44010 Commerce Ave Ste A *Web:* www.neanyinc.com	Hollywood	MD	20636	301-373-8700	373-6405	256
Neapco Inc 6735 Haggerty Rd *TF:* 800-821-2374 ■ *Web:* www.neapco.com	Belleville	MI	48111	734-447-1380	423-1003	60
Near East Foundation 110 Fayette St Ste 710 *Web:* www.neareast.org	Syracuse	NY	13202	315-428-8670		48-5
Near North Business Machines 86 West Rd *TF:* 800-522-3836 ■ *Web:* www.nearnorthbusiness.com	Huntsville	ON	P1H1M1	705-787-0517	787-0554	321
Near Space Systems Inc 2375 Telstar Dr Ste 115 *Web:* www.globalnearspace.com	Colorado Springs	CO	80920	719-685-8108	685-8133	21
Near-Cal Corp 512 Chaney St *TF:* 800-969-3578 ■ *Web:* www.nearcal.com	Lake Elsinore	CA	92530	951-245-5400		186
Nearly Me Technologies PO Box 21475 *TF:* 800-887-3370 ■ *Web:* www.tgtransforms.com	Waco	TX	76702	254-662-1752		477
Nearman Maynard Vallez 205 Brandywine Blvd Ste 200 *TF:* 800-288-0293 ■ *Web:* www.nearman.com	Fayetteville	GA	30214	800-288-0293		2
NearSpace Corp (NSC) 5755 Long Prairie Rd *Web:* nsc.aero	Tillamook	OR	97141	503-842-1990	842-1923	177
Neas Inc 43 Krupp Dr *Web:* www.neair.com	Williston	VT	05495	802-864-3800		189-10
NEASC (New England Association of Schools & Colleges) 209 Burlington Rd *Web:* www.neasc.org	Bedford	MA	01730	781-271-0022	541-5400	48-1
Nease Lagana Eden & Culley Inc 2100 Riveredge Pkwy *Web:* nlec.com	Atlanta	GA	30328	770-956-1800		390
Neasi-Weber Intl 25115 Avenue Stanford Ste B230 *Web:* www.nwintl.com	Valencia	CA	91355	818-895-6900		178-1
Neat Oh Intl 790 W Frontage Rd Ste 303 *Web:* neat-oh.com	Northfield	IL	60093	847-441-4290		41
Neathawk Dubuque & Packett (NDP) 2912 W Leigh St *TF:* 800-847-2674 ■ *Web:* www.ndp.agency	Richmond	VA	23230	804-783-8140		4
NEATO Products LLC 37 E Steel Rd *TF:* 800-984-9800 ■ *Web:* www.neato.com	Milford	CT	06460	203-466-5170		179
NEBB (National Environmental Balancing Bureau) 8575 Grovemont Cir *TF:* 866-497-4447 ■ *Web:* www.nebb.org	Gaithersburg	MD	20877	301-977-3698	977-9589	49-19
NEBCO Inc 1815 Y St PO Box 80268 *Web:* www.nebraskaash.com	Lincoln	NE	68501	402-434-1212		390
NEBHE (New England Board of Higher Education) 45 Temple Pl *Web:* www.nebhe.org	Boston	MA	02111	617-357-9620	338-1577	423
Nebo Agency Inc 197 E 100 N Ste 100	Payson	UT	84651	801-465-2535		652

	City	State	ZIP	Phone	Fax	Class
Nebraska						
Accountability & Disclosure Commission State Capitol 11th Fl *Web:* nadc.nebraska.gov	Lincoln	NE	68509	402-471-2522		265
Aging Div 301 Centennial Mall S. *Web:* www.dhhs.ne.gov	Lincoln	NE	68509	402-471-2306		339-28
Agriculture Dept 301 Centennial Mall S PO Box 94947 **Fax Area Code: 402* ■ *TF:* 800-422-6692 ■ *Web:* www.nda.nebraska.gov	Lincoln	NE	68509	800-422-6692	471-6876*	339-28
Arts Council 1004 Farnam St. *TF:* 800-341-4067 ■ *Web:* www.artscouncil.nebraska.gov	Omaha	NE	68102	402-595-2122		339-28
Attorney General 2115 State Capitol *TF:* 800-727-6432 ■ *Web:* ago.nebraska.gov	Lincoln	NE	68509	402-471-2683	471-3297	339-28
Banking & Finance Dept (NDBF) 1526 K St Ste 300 *Web:* ndbf.nebraska.gov	Lincoln	NE	68508	402-471-2171		339-28
Child Support Enforcement Div PO Box 94728 *TF:* 877-631-9973 ■ *Web:* www.dhhs.ne.gov	Lincoln	NE	68509	877-631-9973		339-28
Coordinating Commission for Postsecondary 1135 M St Ste 220. *Web:* www.ccpe.state.ne.us	Lincoln	NE	68508	402-471-2847	471-2886	725
Correctional Ctr for Women 1107 Recharge Rd *Web:* corrections.nebraska.gov	York	NE	68467	402-362-3317	362-3892	213
Correctional Services Dept PO Box 94661 *Web:* corrections.nebraska.gov	Lincoln	NE	68509	402-471-2654		339-28
Crime Victim Reparations Programs 301 Centennial Mall S PO Box 94946 *Web:* ncc.nebraska.gov	Lincoln	NE	68509	402-471-2194	471-2837	339-28
Economic Development Dept 301 Centennial Mall S *TF:* 800-426-6505 ■ *Web:* opportunity.nebraska.gov	Lincoln	NE	68509	402-471-3111	471-3778	339-28
Education Dept 301 Centennial Mall S PO Box 94987 *Web:* www.education.ne.gov	Lincoln	NE	68509	402-471-4825	471-0117	339-28
Emergency Management Agency 2433 NW 24th St *TF:* 877-297-2368 ■ *Web:* nema.nebraska.gov	Lincoln	NE	68524	402-471-7421	471-7433	339-28
Game & Parks Commission 2200 N 33rd St *Web:* outdoornebraska.gov	Lincoln	NE	68503	402-471-0641	471-5528	339-28
Governor PO Box 94848 *Web:* governor.nebraska.gov	Lincoln	NE	68509	402-471-2244	471-6031	339-28
Health & Human Services Dept 301 Centennial Mall S *TF:* 800-430-3244 ■ *Web:* www.dhhs.ne.gov	Lincoln	NE	68509	402-471-3121		339-28
Historical Society 131 Centennial Mall N *Web:* nebraskahistory.org	Lincoln	NE	68508	402-471-4782	471-3100	339-28
Insurance Dept 941 O St Ste 400. *TF:* 877-564-7323 ■ *Web:* doi.nebraska.gov	Lincoln	NE	68508	402-471-2201		339-28
Investment Finance Authority 1230 'O' St Ste 200 *TF:* 800-204-6432 ■ *Web:* www.nifa.org	Lincoln	NE	68508	402-434-3900	434-3921	339-28
Lieutenant Governor PO Box 94848. **Fax Area Code: 402* ■ *TF:* 800-747-8177 ■ *Web:* governor.nebraska.gov	Lincoln	NE	68508	800-747-8177	471-6031*	339-28
Motor Vehicles Dept 301 Centennial Mall S. *Web:* dmv.nebraska.gov	Lincoln	NE	68509	402-471-3918	471-8694	339-28
Natural Resources Dept 301 Centennial Mall S. *Web:* das.nebraska.gov	Lincoln	NE	68508	402-471-2363	471-6575	339-28
Parole Board PO Box 94754 *Web:* parole.nebraska.gov	Lincoln	NE	68509	402-471-2156		339-28
Polk County PO Box 276. *Web:* polkcounty.nebraska.gov	Osceola	NE	68651	402-747-5431	747-2656	338
Power Review Board 301 Centennial Mall S PO Box 94713 *Web:* powerreview.nebraska.gov	Lincoln	NE	68509	402-471-2301	471-3715	339-28
Public Accountancy Board 1526 K St Ste 410 *TF:* 800-564-6111 ■ *Web:* nbpa.nebraska.gov	Lincoln	NE	68508	402-471-3595	471-4484	339-28
Public Service Commission 1200 North St Ste 402 *TF:* 800-526-0017 ■ *Web:* psc.nebraska.gov	Lincoln	NE	68508	402-471-3101	471-0254	339-28
Real Estate Commission 1200 N St Ste 402 PO Box 94667 *Web:* www.nrec.ne.gov	Lincoln	NE	68509	402-471-2004	471-4492	339-28
Revenue Dept 301 Centennial Mall S PO Box 94818 *TF:* 800-742-7474 ■ *Web:* revenue.nebraska.gov	Lincoln	NE	68509	402-471-5729	471-5608	339-28
Secretary of State 1445 K St Ste 2300. *Web:* sos.ne.gov	Lincoln	NE	68508	402-471-2554	471-3237	339-28
State Court Administrator 1213 State Capitol 1445 K St PO Box 98910. *Web:* supremecourt.nebraska.gov	Lincoln	NE	68509	402-471-3730	471-2197	339-28
State Patrol 1600 Hwy 2 *Web:* statepatrol.nebraska.gov	Lincoln	NE	68509	402-471-4545		339-28
State Penitentiary 4201 S 14th St *Web:* corrections.nebraska.gov	Lincoln	NE	68502	402-471-3161		213
State Racing Commission 5903 Walker Ave *Web:* nebraskaracingcommission.com	Lincoln	NE	68507	402-471-4155		712
Supreme Court 1445 K St State Capitol Bldg *Web:* supremecourt.nebraska.gov	Lincoln	NE	68509	402-471-3731	471-3100	339-28
Teacher Certification Office PO Box 94987 *Web:* www.teaching-certification.com	Lincoln	NE	68509	402-471-2295		339-28
Travel & Tourism Div 301 Centennial Mall S. *TF:* 877-632-7275 ■ *Web:* visitnebraska.com	Lincoln	NE	68509	402-471-3796	471-3026	339-28
Treasurer 5000 N 57th St PO Box 94788. *Web:* treasurer.nebraska.gov	Lincoln	NE	68509	402-471-2455	471-4390	339-28
Veterans' Affairs Dept 301 Centennial Mall S 1st Fl PO Box 95083 *TF:* 877-420-7990 ■ *Web:* veterans.nebraska.gov	Lincoln	NE	68509	402-471-2458	471-2491	339-28

	City	State	ZIP	Phone	Fax	Class
Vital Statistics Div 1033 "O" St Ste 130 *Web:* www.dhhs.ne.gov	Lincoln	NE	68509	402-471-2871		339-28
Vocational Rehabilitation Services Div 301 Centennial Mall S. *Web:* www.vr.nebraska.gov	Lincoln	NE	68509	402-471-3231	471-6309	339-28
Weights & Measures Div 301 Centennial Mall S PO Box 94947 *Web:* www.nda.nebraska.gov	Lincoln	NE	68509	402-471-2341		339-28
Workforce Development - Dept of Labor 1111 O St Ste 205 *TF:* 800-833-7352 ■ *Web:* dol.nebraska.gov	Lincoln	NE	68508	402-441-1660	441-6038	259
Nebraska Bankers Association Inc 233 S 13th St Ste 700. *TF:* 800-593-3881 ■ *Web:* www.nebankers.org	Lincoln	NE	68508	402-474-1555		138
Nebraska Beef Council 1319 Central Ave *TF:* 800-421-5326 ■ *Web:* www.nebeef.org	Kearney	NE	68848	308-236-7551		138
Nebraska Book Co 4700 S 19th St *TF:* 800-869-0366 ■ *Web:* www.nebook.com	Lincoln	NE	68512	402-421-7300		96
Nebraska Chamber of Commerce & Industry 3 Landmark Centre Ste 302 1128 Lincoln Mall PO Box 95128 *Web:* www.nechamber.net	Lincoln	NE	68508	402-474-4422	474-5681	140
Nebraska Christian College Foundation 12550 S 114th St *Web:* www.ncchristian.edu	Papillion	NE	68046	402-935-9400		303
Nebraska City Chamber of Commerce 806 1st Ave. *Web:* www.gonebraskacity.com	Nebraska City	NE	68410	402-873-6654		140
Nebraska City Middle School 1700 14th Ave. *Web:* www.nebcityps.org	Nebraska City	NE	68410	402-873-6033	873-6030	685
Nebraska College of Technical Agriculture 404 E 7th *TF:* 800-328-7847 ■ *Web:* ncta.unl.edu	Curtis	NE	69025	308-367-4124	367-5203	800
Nebraska Community Blood Bank 100 N 84th St *TF:* 877-486-9414 ■ *Web:* www.ncbb.org	Lincoln	NE	68505	402-486-9414	486-9429	89
Nebraska Dental Assn 7160 S 29th St Ste 1. *Web:* www.nedental.org	Lincoln	NE	68516	402-476-1704	476-2641	227
Nebraska Department of Environment and Energy *Environmental Quality Dept* PO Box 98922 *TF:* 877-253-2603 ■ *Web:* www.deq.state.ne.us	Lincoln	NE	68509	402-471-2186	471-2909	339-28
Nebraska Farm Bureau Federation 5225 S 16th St *TF:* 800-742-4016 ■ *Web:* www.nefb.org	Lincoln	NE	68512	402-421-4400		138
Nebraska Furniture Mart Inc 700 S 72nd St. *TF:* 800-336-9136 ■ *Web:* www.nfm.com	Omaha	NE	68114	402-397-6100		321
Nebraska Grain & Feed Assn (NGF) 4600 Valley Rd Ste 416 *Web:* www.negfa.org	Lincoln	NE	68510	402-476-6174	476-3401	192
Nebraska House 983285 Nebraska Medical Ctr *TF:* 800-401-4444 ■ *Web:* www.nebraskamed.com	Omaha	NE	68198	402-559-5000	559-3434	372
Nebraska Humane Society Foundation 8929 Ft St. *Web:* www.nehumanesociety.org	Omaha	NE	68134	402-444-7800		305
Nebraska Indian Community College PO Box 428 *TF:* 844-440-6422 ■ *Web:* www.thenicc.edu	Macy	NE	68039	402-837-5078	837-4183	165
Nebraska Industries Corp 447 E Walnut St *Web:* www.nebraska.gov	Wauseon	OH	43567	419-335-6010		489
Nebraska Iowa Supply Company Inc 1160 Lincoln St PO Box 368 *TF:* 800-248-4410 ■ *Web:* www.neiasupply.com	Blair	NE	68008	402-426-2171		316
Nebraska Jewish Historical Museum 333 S 132nd St. *Web:* www.nebraskajhs.com	Omaha	NE	68154	402-334-6441		520
Nebraska Lottery 137 Nw 17th St PO Box 95145. *TF:* 800-587-5200 ■ *Web:* www.nelottery.com	Lincoln	NE	68509	402-471-6100	471-6108	452
Nebraska Machinery Company Inc 3501 S Jeffers St *TF:* 800-494-9560 ■ *Web:* www.nmc-corp.com	North Platte	NE	69101	308-532-3100		385
Nebraska Medical Assn 1045 Lincoln Mall *TF:* 800-684-9380 ■ *Web:* www.nebmed.org	Lincoln	NE	68508	402-474-4472	474-2198	474
Nebraska Nurses' Assn (NNA) 1407 13th Ave. *TF:* 888-885-7025 ■ *Web:* www.nebraskanurses.org	Kearney	NE	68845	888-885-7025		533
Nebraska Pharmacists Assn 6221 S 58th St Ste A *Web:* www.npharm.org	Lincoln	NE	68516	402-420-1500	420-1406	585
Nebraska Plastics Inc PO Box 45 *TF:* 800-445-2887 ■ *Web:* www.countryestate.com	Cozad	NE	69130	308-784-2500		596
Nebraska Public Power District 1414 15th St PO Box 499 *TF:* 877-275-6773 ■ *Web:* www.nppd.com	Columbus	NE	68602	402-564-8561		245
Nebraska Realtors Assn 800 S 13th St Ste 200. *TF:* 800-777-5231 ■ *Web:* www.nebraskarealtors.com	Lincoln	NE	68508	402-323-6500	323-6501	656
Nebraska Republican Party 1610 N St. *Web:* nadc.nebraska.gov	Lincoln	NE	68508	402-475-2122		616-2
Nebraska Scientific 3823 Leavenworth St *TF:* 800-228-7117 ■ *Web:* www.nebraskascientific.com	Omaha	NE	68105	402-346-7214	346-2216	166
Nebraska State Bar Assn 635 S 14th St Ste 200. *TF:* 800-927-0117 ■ *Web:* www.nebar.com	Lincoln	NE	68501	402-475-7091	475-7098	72
Nebraska State College System 1327 H St Ste 200 *Web:* www.nscs.edu	Lincoln	NE	68508	402-471-2505	471-2669	786
Nebraska Statewide Arboretum UNL Keim Hall 102 PO Box 830964. *Web:* plantnebraska.org	Lincoln	NE	68583	402-472-2971		97

Name / Address	City	State	Zip	Phone	Fax	Class
Nebraska Student Loan Program Inc 1300 O St *TF:* 800-735-8778 ■ *Web:* www.nslp.org	Lincoln	NE	68508	402-475-8686		242
Nebraska Synod Evangelical Lutheran Church in America 4980 S 118th St Ste D *Web:* nebraskasynod.org	Omaha	NE	68137	402-896-5311		48-20
Nebraska Veterinary Medical Assn PO Box 637 *Web:* www.nvma.org	Hastings	NE	68902	402-463-4704		795
Nebraska Wesleyan University 5000 St Paul Ave *TF:* 800-541-3818 ■ *Web:* www.nebrwesleyan.edu	Lincoln	NE	68504	800-541-3818		166
NEC (Nueces Electric Co-op) 14353 Cooperative Ave *TF:* 800-632-9288 ■ *Web:* nueceselectric.org	Robstown	TX	78380	361-387-2581		245
NEC America Inc 6555 N State Hwy 161 *TF:* 866-632-3226 ■ *Web:* www.necam.com	Irving	TX	75039	214-262-2000		735
NEC Laboratories America Inc 4 Independence Way *Web:* www.nec-labs.com	Princeton	NJ	08540	609-520-1555		668
NECA (National Electrical Contractors Assn) 3 Bethesda Metro Ctr Ste 1100 *TF:* 800-214-0585 ■ *Web:* www.necanet.org	Bethesda	MD	20814	301-657-3110	215-4500	49-3
Necando Solutions Inc 1080 Cote du Beaver Hall bureau 1804 *TF:* 888-984-6269 ■ *Web:* necando.com	Montreal	QC	H2Z1S8	514-360-4000		196
Necco 178 Private Dr *TF:* 866-996-3226 ■ *Web:* www.necco.org	South Point	OH	45680	513-771-9600		766
NECi Superior Enzymes 334 Hecla St *TF:* 888-648-7283 ■ *Web:* www.nitrate.com	Lake Linden	MI	49945	906-296-1000		231
Neckerman Agency, The 6200 Mineral Point Rd *TF:* 888-860-2686 ■ *Web:* neckerman.com	Madison	WI	53705	608-238-2686		390
NECN (New England Cable News) 160 Wells Ave *Web:* www.necn.com	Newton	MA	02459	617-630-5000		740
NECSI Knowledge Press 24 Mt. Auburn St *Web:* www.knowledgetoday.org	Cambridge	MA	02138	617-547-4100		637-9
Nectar Restaurant 1000 Delta Ave *Web:* tastenectar.com	Cincinnati	OH	45208	513-929-0525		671
NED (National Endowment for Democracy) 1025 F St NW Ste 800 *Web:* www.ned.org	Washington	DC	20004	202-378-9700	378-9407	48-7
Ned Clyde Construction Inc 159 Mason Cir *Web:* www.nedclydeconstruction.com	Concord	CA	94520	925-246-8164		188-3
NED Corp 31 Town Forest Rd **Fax Area Code: 508* ■ *TF:* 800-343-6086 ■ *Web:* www.nedkut.com	Oxford	MA	01540	800-343-6086	799-2796*	493
Nedco Electronics 594 American Way *TF:* 800-605-2323 ■ *Web:* www.nedcoelectronics.com	Payson	UT	84651	800-624-2771	605-3836	246
Nedco Supply Inc 4200 W Spring Mtn Rd *Web:* www.nedco.com	Las Vegas	NV	89102	702-367-0400	362-8365	246
Nederlander Organizatio Inc, The 1501 Broadwy 14th Fl *Web:* www.nederlander.com	New York	NY	10036	212-840-5577		181
Nedland Industries Inc 315 Railrd St *Web:* www.nedland.com	Ridgeland	WI	54763	715-949-1982	949-1983	806
NEDMA (New England Direct Marketing Association Inc) 396 Washington St Ste 387 *Web:* www.nedma.com	Wellesley	MA	02481	781-237-1366		138
Needham & Company Inc 445 Park Ave *TF:* 800-903-3268 ■ *Web:* www.needhamco.com	New York	NY	10022	212-371-8300	751-1450	690
Needham Funds 445 Park Ave *Web:* www.needhamfunds.com	New York	NY	10022	212-705-0404	705-0455	792
Needham Public Library 1139 Highland Ave *Web:* www.needhamma.gov	Needham	MA	02494	781-455-7559		434-3
Needle In A Haystack Inc 6911 Preston Rd *Web:* needleinahaystack.biz	Dallas	TX	75205	214-528-2850		535
Needles & Associates LLC 350 Interlocken Blvd *TF:* 877-430-4225 ■ *Web:* needles-audit.com	Broomfield	CO	80021	303-430-4225		2
NeedleTech Products Inc 452 John L Dietsch Blvd *Web:* needletech.com	North Attleboro	MA	02763	508-431-4000		791
Neefus-Stype Agency Inc 711 Union Ave *Web:* nsainsure.com	Aquebogue	NY	11931	631-722-3500		390
Neelco Industries Inc 420 Shearer Blvd *TF:* 800-247-8946 ■ *Web:* www.neelco.biz	Cocoa	FL	32922	321-631-4338	632-5711	273
Neeley Forestry Service Inc 915 Pickett St *Web:* neeleyforestryservice.com	Camden	AR	71701	870-836-5981		302
Neel-Schaffer Inc 125 S Congress St Ste 1100 *Web:* www.neel-schaffer.com	Jackson	MS	39201	601-948-3178	948-3071	261
Neeltran Inc 71 Pickett District Rd *Web:* www.neeltran.com	New Milford	CT	06776	860-350-5964	350-5024	767
Neenah Paper Inc 3460 Preston Ridge Rd Ste 600 *NYSE: NP* ■ *TF:* 800-344-5287 ■ *Web:* www.neenah.com	Alpharetta	GA	30005	678-566-6500		552-2
Neenah Public Library 240 E Wisconsin Ave PO Box 569 *Web:* www.neenahlibrary.org	Neenah	WI	54957	920-886-6315		434-3
Neenan Co 3325 S Timberline Rd Ste 100 *Web:* www.neenan.com	Fort Collins	CO	80525	970-493-8747	493-5869	186
Neese Personnel 2709 NW 39th Expy *Web:* workwithneese.com	Oklahoma City	OK	73112	405-942-8551		260
NEFE (National Endowment for Financial Education) 1331 17th St Ste 1200 *Web:* www.nefe.org	Denver	CO	80202	303-741-6333		48-10
Neff Co 112 Main St *TF:* 800-448-8373 ■ *Web:* www.neffcoag.com	Avon	IL	61415	309-465-3184	465-7517	274
Neff Engineering Co *Neff Group Distributors Inc* 7114 Innovation Blvd *Web:* neffautomation.com	Fort Wayne	IN	46818	260-489-6007		261
Neff Press Inc 6510 Page Ave *TF:* 800-325-8612 ■ *Web:* www.neffpress.com	Saint Louis	MO	63133	314-854-1200	725-2230	456
Neff-Perkins Co 16080 Industrial Pkwy *Web:* neff-perkins.com	Middlefield	OH	44062	440-632-1658	632-1206	677
Neffs Bancorp Inc 5629 Rt 873 PO Box 10 *OTC: NEFB* ■ *Web:* www.neffsnatl.com	Neffs	PA	18065	610-767-3875	767-1890	70
Negative Capability Press 62 Ridgelawn Dr E *Web:* www.negativecapabilitypress.org	Mobile	AL	36608	251-591-2922		637-2
Negative Population Growth (NPG) 2861 Duke St Ste 36 *Web:* www.npg.org	Alexandria	VA	22314	703-370-9510	370-9514	48-13
Neglia Appraisals Inc 7711 13th Ave *Web:* neglia.com	Brooklyn	NY	11228	718-331-2122		653
Negotiatus Corp 260 W 39th St 15th Fl *Web:* www.negotiatus.com	New York	NY	10018	646-665-7383		178-8
Negro Leagues Baseball Museum 1616 E 18th St *Web:* www.nlbm.com	Kansas City	MO	64108	816-221-1920	221-8424	522
Neguse Joe (Rep D - CO) 1419 Longworth House Office Bldg *Web:* www.neguse.house.gov	Washington	DC	20515	202-225-2161		342-2
NEH (National Endowment for the Humanities) 400 Seventh St SW *TF:* 800-634-1121 ■ *Web:* www.neh.gov	Washington	DC	20506	202-606-8400		340-20
NEHA (National Environmental Health Assn) 720 S Colorado Blvd Ste 1000-N *TF:* 866-956-2258 ■ *Web:* www.neha.org	Denver	CO	80246	303-756-9090	691-9490	49-7
NEHACA (New Hampshire Campground Owners Assn) PO Box 1074 *Web:* www.ucampnh.com	Epsom	NH	03234	603-736-5540		637-10
Nehalem Bay State Park 9500 Sandpiper Ln PO Box 366 *Web:* oregonstateparks.org	Nehalem	OR	97131	503-368-5154		565
Nehmen-Kodner Inc 12542 New Woodland Ct *Web:* n-kcreative.com	Saint Louis	MO	63146	314-548-6001		4
Nehring Electric Works Inc 1005 E Locust St *TF:* 800-435-4481 ■ *Web:* www.nehringwire.com	DeKalb	IL	60115	815-756-2741	756-7048	814
NEI (Nuclear Energy Institute) 1776 'I' St NW Ste 400 *Web:* www.nei.org	Washington	DC	20006	202-739-8000	785-4019	48-12
NEI (Nesbitt Engineering Inc) 227 N Upper St *Web:* nei-ky.com	Lexington	KY	40507	859-233-3111	259-2717	261
NEI Global Relocation Inc 2707 N 118th St *TF:* 800-533-7353 ■ *Web:* www.neirelo.com	Omaha	NE	68164	402-397-8486		393
NEI Treatment Systems LLC 3530 Wilshire Blvd Ste 1130 *Web:* www.nei-marine.com	Los Angeles	CA	90010	213-383-5855		475
NEI Turner Media Group 400 Broad St Unit D *Web:* ntmediagroup.com	Lake Geneva	WI	53147	262-729-4471		196
Neibart Group 20 Jay St Ste 820 *Web:* www.neibartgroup.com	Brooklyn	NY	11201	718-875-2300		636
Neider & Boucher S C 401 Charmany Dr *Web:* neiderboucher.com	Madison	WI	53705	608-661-4500		445
Neighbor To Family Inc 200 S Ridgewood Ave *Web:* www.neighbortofamily.org	Daytona Beach	FL	32114	386-523-1440		48-15
Neighborcare Health 2101 E Yesler Way *Web:* neighborcare.org	Seattle	WA	98122	206-461-7801		237
Neighborhood Housing Services of New Haven Inc 333 Sherman Ave *Web:* nhsofnewhaven.org	New Haven	CT	06510	203-562-0598	772-2876	653
Neighborhood National Bank 3511 National Ave *Web:* www.mynnb.com	San Diego	CA	92113	619-239-3360		70
Neighborhood Playhouse School of the Theatre 340 E 54th St *Web:* www.neighborhoodplayhouse.org	New York	NY	10022	212-688-3770	906-9051	685
Neighborhood Service Organization 882 Oakman Blvd Ste C *Web:* nso-mi.org	Detroit	MI	48238	313-961-4890		48-5
Neighbors Federal Credit Union PO Box 2831 *TF:* 866-819-2178 ■ *Web:* www.neighborsfcu.org	Baton Rouge	LA	70821	225-819-2178	819-8923	219
Neighbors Magazine 1324 Chippenham Dr *Web:* theneighborsmagazine.com	Baton Rouge	LA	70808	225-767-8549		457-1
NeighborWorks America 999 N Capitol St NE Ste 900 *Web:* www.neighborworks.org	Washington	DC	20002	202-760-4000	376-2600	48-10
Neil A. Kjos Music Co 4382 Jutland Dr *TF:* 800-854-1592 ■ *Web:* www.kjos.com	San Diego	CA	92117	858-270-9800	270-3507	637-10
Neil Enterprises Inc 450 E Bunker Ct *TF:* 800-621-5584 ■ *Web:* www.neilenterprises.com	Vernon Hills	IL	60061	847-549-7627		608
Neil F. Lampson Inc 607 E Columbia Dr *Web:* www.lampsoncrane.com	Kennewick	WA	99336	509-586-0411	586-0825	264-3
Neil Locke & Assoc 550 E Devon Ave Ste 130 *Web:* www.neillocke.com	Itasca	IL	60143	630-285-9085		378
Neil Medical Group Inc 2545 Jetport Rd *TF:* 800-735-9111 ■ *Web:* www.neilmedical.com	Kinston	NC	28504	800-735-9111		238
Neil O. Anderson & Associates Inc 902 Industrial Way	Lodi	CA	95240	209-367-3701		261

Name / Address	City	State	ZIP	Phone	Fax	Class
Neill Aircraft Co 1260 W 15th St *Web:* www.neillaircraft.com	Long Beach	CA	90813	562-432-7981	491-0483	22
Neill-Cochran House Museum 2310 San Gabriel St *Web:* www.nchmuseum.org	Austin	TX	78705	512-478-2335		50-3
Neilson Associates Inc 42 Blue Stone Dr *Web:* www.neilsonassociates.com	Greenville	DE	19807	610-793-0883		463
Neilson Beauty College Inc 1312 S Abbott Ave	Hillsboro	TX	76645	214-946-0458		167-3
Neiman Bros Company Inc 3322 W Newport Ave *Web:* www.neimanbrothers.com	Chicago	IL	60618	773-463-3000	463-3181	297-11
Neiman Funds Management LLC 6631 Main St *TF:* 877-385-2720 ■ *Web:* www.neimanfunds.com	Williamsville	NY	14221	877-385-2720		401
Neiman Marcus Group Inc 1618 Main St *Web:* www.neimanmarcuscareers.com	Dallas	TX	75201	214-743-7618		229
Neiman Reed Lumber Co 7875 Willis Ave. *Web:* www.neimanreed.com	Panorama City	CA	91402	818-781-3466		191-3
Neitclem Wholesale Insurance Brokerage Inc 7442 N Figueroa St. *Web:* neitclem.com	Los Angeles	CA	90041	323-258-2600		390
Neko Industries Inc 3017 Douglas Blvd Ste 300 *Web:* www.nekoind.com	Roseville	CA	95661	916-774-7125		196
Nekoosa Port Edwards State Bank 405 Market St PO Box 9 *Web:* npesb.com	Nekoosa	WI	54457	715-886-3104		70
Nektar Therapeutics 455 Mission Bay Blvd S *NASDAQ: NKTR* ■ *TF:* 855-482-6587 ■ *Web:* www.nektar.com	San Francisco	CA	94158	415-482-5300	339-5300	85
Nel Frequency Controls Inc 357 Beloit St. *Web:* www.nelfc.com	Burlington	WI	53105	262-763-3591	763-2881	253
NELA (National Employment Lawyers Assn) 417 Montgomery St 4th Fl *Web:* www.nela.org	San Francisco	CA	94104	415-296-7629	677-9445	49-10
NELCO Inc 3 Gill St Unit D *TF:* 800-635-2613 ■ *Web:* www.nelcoworldwide.com	Woburn	MA	01801	781-933-1940	933-4763	477
Nelda C. & H. J. Lutcher Stark Foundation, The 601 Green Ave *Web:* starkfoundation.org	Orange	TX	77630	409-883-3513	883-3530	303
Nell's 6804 E Green Lake Way N *Web:* www.nellsrestaurant.com	Seattle	WA	98115	206-524-4044	527-8101	671
Nella Consulting Inc 755 Milwaukee Ave. *Web:* nellatax.com	Glenview	IL	60025	847-486-4112		2
Nella's Nursing Home Inc 200 Whiteman Ave	Elkins	WV	26241	304-636-2033		371
Nellie Mae Education Foundation 1250 Hancock St Ste 701N. *TF:* 877-635-5436 ■ *Web:* nmefoundation.org	Quincy	MA	02169	781-348-4200	348-4299	305
Nellis Air Force Base 4430 Grissom Ave Ste 107 *Web:* www.nellis.af.mil	Nellis AFB	NV	89191	702-652-2750	652-9838	497-1
Nellis Management Corp 2940 104th St. *Web:* www.nellismanagement.com	Urbandale	IA	50322	515-252-1742		463
Nello Corp 1201 S Sheridan St PO Box 1960. *TF:* 800-806-3556 ■ *Web:* nelloinc.com	South Bend	IN	46619	574-288-3632	288-5860	480
Nelnet Inc PO Box 8256. *NYSE: NNI* ■ *TF:* 888-486-4722 ■ *Web:* www.nelnet.com	Lincoln	NE	68501	888-486-4722		217
Nelrod Co 3109 Lubbock Ave *TF:* 866-448-0961 ■ *Web:* www.nelrod.com	Fort Worth	TX	76109	817-922-9000		196
Nelsen Steel & Wire LP 9400 W Belmont Ave *Web:* www.nelsensteel.com	Franklin Park	IL	60131	847-671-9700		492
NELSON & Associates Interior Design & Space Planning Inc 100 S Independence Mall W Ste 500 *Web:* www.nelsononline.com	Philadelphia	PA	19106	215-925-6562		256
Nelson & Company Inc 3914 Beach Blvd. *Web:* ncjax.com	Jacksonville	FL	32207	407-365-6631		315-2
Nelson & Gilmore 1604 Aviation Blvd *Web:* www.nelsongilmore.com	Redondo Beach	CA	90278	310-376-0296		7
Nelson & Hammons 705 Milam St *TF:* 800-619-6444 ■ *Web:* nelsonhammons.com	Shreveport	LA	71101	318-227-2401		41
Nelson & Kennard 2180 Harvard St Ste 160. *TF:* 866-920-2295 ■ *Web:* nelson-kennard.com	Sacramento	CA	95815	916-920-2295		428
Nelson A. Rockefeller Institute of Government 411 State St *Web:* rockinst.org	Albany	NY	12203	518-443-5522	443-5788	634
Nelson Architectural Engineers Inc 2740 Dallas Pky Ste 220. *TF:* 877-850-8765 ■ *Web:* www.nelsonforensics.com	Plano	TX	75093	469-429-9000	326-5200	192
Nelson Co 4517 N Point Blvd *Web:* www.nelsoncompany.com	Baltimore	MD	21219	410-477-3000		551
Nelson County 113 E Steven Foster St *Web:* nelsoncountyclerk.com	Bardstown	KY	40004	502-348-1820	348-1822	338
Nelson County 210 B Ave W Ste 203. *TF:* 800-472-2286 ■ *Web:* www.nelsonco.org	Lakota	ND	58344	701-247-2462		338
Nelson County 84 Courthouse Sq PO Box 336. *TF:* 888-662-9400 ■ *Web:* www.nelsoncounty-va.gov	Lovingston	VA	22949	434-263-7000	263-7004	338
Nelson Dewey State Park PO Box 658 *Web:* dnr.wi.gov	Cassville	WI	53806	608-725-5374		565
Nelson Electric Supply Company Inc 926 State St *TF:* 800-806-3576 ■ *Web:* www.nelson-electric.com	Racine	WI	53404	262-635-5050	637-2465	246
Nelson Hardwood Lumber Co 305 E Frederick St *Web:* www.nelsonhardwoods.com	Prairie du Chien	WI	53821	608-326-8456		683
Nelson Ink 330 Second St N. *TF:* 800-644-9311 ■ *Web:* nelsonink.com	Middle River	MN	56737	218-222-3831		195
Nelson Jit Packaging Supplies Inc 4022 W Turney Ave Ste 3 *TF:* 800-939-3647 ■ *Web:* www.nelsonjit.com	Phoenix	AZ	85019	623-939-3365		557
Nelson Law Group LLC 8777 Purdue Rd Ste 310. *Web:* nelsonlawgroupllc.com	Indianapolis	IN	46268	317-755-0661		41
Nelson Mullins Riley & Scarborough LLP 1320 Main St 17th Fl *TF:* 800-237-2000 ■ *Web:* www.nelsonmullins.com	Columbia	SC	29201	803-799-2000	256-7500	428
Nelson Museum of the West 1714 Carey Ave. *Web:* www.nelsonmuseum.com	Cheyenne	WY	82001	307-635-7670		520
Nelson Numeric Inc 11201 Hampshire Ave S *Web:* www.nelsonnumeric.com	Bloomington	MN	55438	952-829-7337	829-0596	454
Nelson Packaging Company Inc 1801 Reservoir Rd *TF:* 888-229-3471	Lima	OH	45805	419-229-3471		88
Nelson Public Library 201 Cathedral Manor *Web:* www.nelsoncopublib.org	Bardstown	KY	40004	502-348-3714	348-5578	435
Nelson Publishing 2500 Tamiami Trl N. **Fax Area Code:* 941 ■ *TF:* 800-226-6113 ■ *Web:* www.nelsonpub.com	Nokomis	FL	34275	800-226-6113	966-2590*	637-9
Nelson Research 130 School St *Web:* www.mchipguru.com	Webster	MA	01570	508-943-1075		196
Nelson Roberts Investment Advisors LLC 1950 University Ave Ste 202. *Web:* www.nelsonroberts.com	East Palo Alto	CA	94303	650-322-4000		401
Nelson Schmidt Inc 600 E Wisconsin Ave *Web:* nelsonschmidt.com	Milwaukee	WI	53202	414-224-0210		7
Nelson Technology Associates Inc 1051 Hill Meadow Pl *Web:* nelsontech.com	Danville	CA	94526	925-855-3610		177
Nelson Tree Service LLC 3300 Ofc Park Dr *TF:* 800-522-4311 ■ *Web:* www.nelsontree.com	Dayton	OH	45439	937-294-1313		776
Nelson Westerberg Inc 1500 Arthur Ave *TF:* 800-245-2080 ■ *Web:* www.nelsonwesterberg.com	Elk Grove Village	IL	60007	847-437-2080		519
Nelson White Systems Inc 8725-A Loch Raven Blvd *TF:* 800-296-7555 ■ *Web:* www.nelsonwhite.com	Baltimore	MD	21286	410-668-9628	668-9629	45
Nelson's Plumbing & Electric Inc 25269 US Hwy 12. *Web:* nelsonsplumbing.net	Tomah	WI	54660	608-372-5469		610
Nelson, Tietz & Hoye Inc 81 S Ninth St Ste 330. *Web:* www.nth-inc.com	Minneapolis	MN	55402	612-344-1500		463
Nelson-Atkins Museum of Art 4525 Oak St *Web:* www.nelson-atkins.org	Kansas City	MO	64111	816-751-1278		520
Nelson-Jameson Inc 2400 E Fifth St PO Box 647 *TF:* 800-826-8302 ■ *Web:* nelsonjameson.com	Marshfield	WI	54449	715-387-1151	387-8746	385
Neltner Billing & Consulting Services 6463 Taylor Mill Rd *TF:* 888-635-8637 ■ *Web:* neltnerbilling.com	Independence	KY	41051	888-635-8637		196
NEMA (National Electrical Manufacturers Assn) 1300 N 17th St Ste 1752 *TF:* 800-699-9277 ■ *Web:* www.nema.org	Rosslyn	VA	22209	703-841-3200	841-5900	49-13
Nemacolin Woodlands Resort & Spa 1001 Lafayette Dr *TF:* 800-422-2736 ■ *Web:* www.nemacolin.com	Farmington	PA	15437	724-329-7500		669
Nemaha County 607 Nemaha *TF:* 800-259-2829 ■ *Web:* ks-nemaha.manatron.com	Seneca	KS	[illegible]	[illegible]	[illegible]	[illegible]
Nemco Food Equipment Ltd 301 Meuse Argonne *TF:* 800-782-6761 ■ *Web:* nemcofoodequip.com	Hicksville	OH	43526	419-542-7751		296
Nemetschek North America 7150 Riverwood Dr. *TF:* 888-646-4223 ■ *Web:* www.vectorworks.net	Columbia	MD	21046	410-290-5114	290-8050	178-8
NEMF World Transport 1-71 N Ave E. *TF:* 800-847-2728 ■ *Web:* www.nemf.com	Elizabeth	NJ	07201	908-965-0100	965-0795	519
Nemi Publishing Inc 553 Wilton Rd. **Fax Area Code:* 207 ■ *TF:* 800-698-4801 ■ *Web:* www.franklinprinting.com	Farmington	ME	04938	800-698-4801	778-4734*	627
Nemo Restaurant 100 Collins Ave *Web:* www.mylesrestaurantgroup.com	Miami Beach	FL	33139	305-532-4550		671
Nemo Tile Co 17702 Jamaica Ave *Web:* www.nemotile.com	Jamaica	NY	11432	718-291-5969		191-1
NEMRA (National Electrical Manufacturers Representatives Assn) 28 Deer St Ste 302 **Fax Area Code:* 603 ■ *TF:* 800-446-3672 ■ *Web:* www.nemra.org	Portsmouth	NH	03801	914-524-8650	319-1667*	49-18
Nemschoff Inc 909 N Eigth St. **Fax Area Code:* 920 ■ *TF:* 800-203-8916 ■ *Web:* www.nemschoff.com	Sheboygan	WI	53081	800-203-8916	459-1234*	319-3
Nenni & Assoc 340 W Exchange St. **Fax Area Code:* 630 ■ *Web:* www.nenniandassoc.com	Sycamore	IL	60178	815-899-9421	555-1234*	196
NENPA (New England Newspaper & Press Assn) Barletta Hall 370 Common St 3rd Fl Ste 319 *Web:* www.nenpa.com	Dedham	MA	02026	718-320-8050	320-8055	139
Neo Code Software Ltd 425 Carrall St Ste 540 *Web:* www.neocode.com	Vancouver	BC	V6B6E3	604-638-0668		396
Neo Corp 289 Silkwood Dr *TF:* 800-822-1247 ■ *Web:* neocorporation.com	Canton	NC	28716	800-822-1247		192
Neo Fabrics Inc 5650 Hayne Blvd. *Web:* www.neofabrics.com	New Orleans	LA	70186	504-241-4020	241-4738	594
Neo Marketing LLC PO Box 8198. **Fax Area Code:* 866 ■ *Web:* www.neomarketingonline.com	Canton	OH	44711	330-933-1843	861-5648*	5
Neo Products Corp 99 Record Dr *Web:* www.neoproducts.com	Henderson	TN	38340	731-989-5113		567
Neo Tech Inc 9340 Owensmouth Ave. *TF:* 800-590-5774 ■ *Web:* www.neotech.com	Chatsworth	CA	91311	818-734-6500		625
Neo-Asia Restaurant 6602 Glenwood Ave. *Web:* www.neoasiaraleigh.com	Raleigh	NC	27612	919-783-8383		670
NeoCom Solutions Inc 10064 Main St. *Web:* www.neocom.biz	Woodstock	GA	30188	678-238-1818	238-1820	186

	Phone	Fax	Class
Neodesha Plastics Inc 1206 Worley Dr Twin Twin Rivers . . . . . Neodesha KS 66757 *Web:* www.neodeshaplasticsinc.com	620-325-3096	325-3098	604
Neogard Div Jones-blair Co 2728 Empire Central St. . . . . . Dallas TX 75235 *TF:* 800-492-9400 ■ *Web:* www.jones-blair.com	214-353-1600		550
Neogen Corp 620 Lesher Pl. . . . . . Lansing MI 48912 *NASDAQ: NEOG* ■ *TF:* 800-234-5333 ■ *Web:* www.neogen.com	517-372-9200	372-2006	231
NeoGenomics Inc 12701 Commonwealth Dr Ste 9 . . . . . Fort Myers FL 33913 *TF:* 866-776-5907 ■ *Web:* neogenomics.com	941-923-1949		418
NeoLife International LLC 3500 Gateway Blvd . . . . . Fremont CA 94538 **Fax Area Code:* 510 ■ *TF:* 800-432-5842 ■ *Web:* www.neolife.com	800-432-5842	440-2818*	366
NeoMed Inc 100 Londonderry Ct Ste 112. . . . . Woodstock GA 30188 *Web:* www.neomedinc.com	770-516-2225	516-2448	475
NeoMPS Inc 9395 Cabot Dr . . . . . San Diego CA 92126 *TF:* 800-654-5592 ■ *Web:* www.neomps.com	858-408-0808	408-0799	85
Neon Co, The 858 Dekalb Ave NE . . . . . Atlanta GA 30307 *Web:* www.theneoncompany.com	404-873-6366		300
NeoPhotonics Corp 2911 Zanker Rd. . . . . San Jose CA 95134 *Web:* www.neophotonics.com	408-232-9200		696
Neopost Incorporated Canada 150 Steelcase Rd W . . . . . Markham ON L3R3J9 **Fax Area Code:* 905 ■ *TF:* 800-636-7678 ■ *Web:* www.neopost.ca	800-636-7678	475-7699*	111
Neoptix Inc 1415 Frank-Carrel Ste 220. . . . . Quebec City QC G1N4N7 *Web:* www.neoptix.com	418-687-2500		544
NEORig 100 N Fm 3083 Rd E . . . . . Conroe TX 77303 *Web:* neo-rig.com	936-539-5030		697
Neoris Inc 703 Waterford Way Ste 700. . . . . Miami FL 33126 *Web:* www.neoris.com	305-728-6000		177
Neos LLC 20 Church St. . . . . Hartford CT 06103 *Web:* www.neosllc.com	860-519-5601		196
Neos Therapeutics 2940 N Hwy 360 Ste 400 . . . . . Grand Prairie TX 75050 *TF:* 844-375-8324 ■ *Web:* www.neostx.com	972-408-1300	408-1143	582
Neosho Area Chamber of Commerce 216 W Spring St. . . . . . Neosho MO 64850 *Web:* neoshocc.com	417-451-1925	451-8097	139
Neosho Beauty College 116 N Wood St . . . . . Neosho MO 64850 *Web:* www.neoshobeautycollege.com	417-451-7216	451-8849	167-3
Neosho County 100 S Main St Rm 101 PO Box 176 . . . . . Erie KS 66733 *Web:* www.neoshocountyks.org	620-244-3858	244-3860	338
Neosho County Community College 800 W 14th St. . . . . . Chanute KS 66720 *TF:* 800-729-6222 ■ *Web:* www.neosho.edu	620-431-2820	431-0082	162
Neosho Trompler Inc 580 S Industrial Dr S-1. . . . . Hartland WI 53029 *Web:* neoshotrompler.com	262-367-5600		454
NeoTech Incubator 6751 Columbia Gateway Dr Ste 500. . . . . Columbia MD 21046 *Web:* www.hceda.org	410-313-6550		463
Neotech Products Inc 28430 Witherspoon Pkwy. . . . . Valencia CA 91355 **Fax Area Code:* 800 ■ *TF:* 800-966-0500 ■ *Web:* www.neotechproducts.com	661-775-7466	966-0585*	476
Neotelis Inc 4802 Verdun St Ste 1. . . . . Montreal QC H4G1N1 *Web:* www.neotelis.com	514-281-1211		196
NeoTract Inc 4155 Hopyard Rd . . . . . Pleasanton CA 94588 *Web:* www.neotract.com	925-401-0700	401-0699	475
Neotropix Inc 351 Phoenixville Pk. . . . . Malvern PA 19355 *Web:* www.neotropix.com	501-342-5194		743
Neovasc Inc 13700 Mayfield Pl Ste 2135. . . . . Richmond BC V6V2E4 *Web:* www.neovasc.com	604-270-4344		476
Neoventa Medical Inc 226 Lowell St. . . . . Wilmington MA 01887 *Web:* www.neoventa.com	978-657-7750		475
Neovest Inc 1145 S 800 E. . . . . Orem UT 84097 *Web:* www.neovest.com	801-373-2775		178-1
NEP (North-Eastern Pennsylvania Telephone Co) 720 Main St . . . . . Forest City PA 18421 *TF:* 866-785-3131 ■ *Web:* www.nep.net	570-785-3131	785-9299	224
NEP Electronics Inc 805 Mittel Dr. . . . . Wood Dale IL 60191 *TF:* 800-284-7470 ■ *Web:* www.nepelectronics.com	630-595-8500	595-8706	246
NEPC LLC 255 State St . . . . . Boston MA 02109 *Web:* www.nepc.com	617-374-1300	374-1313	401
Nephron Pharmaceuticals Corp 4500 12th St Ext. . . . . West Columbia SC 29172 *TF:* 800-443-4313 ■ *Web:* www.nephronpharm.com	803-569-2800	509-6034	583
Nephros Inc 41 Grand Ave. . . . . River Edge NJ 07661 *OTC: NEPH* ■ *Web:* www.nephros.com	201-343-5202	343-5207	476
Neponset Valley Chamber of Commerce 520 Providence Hwy Ste 4 . . . . . Norwood MA 02062 *Web:* www.nrrchamber.com	781-769-1126	769-0808	139
Neptec Design Group Ltd 302 Legget Dr Ste 202 . . . . . Kanata ON K2K1Y5 *Web:* neptec.com	613-599-7602		21
Neptune Public Library 25 Neptune Blvd. . . . . Neptune City NJ 07753 *Web:* www.neptunepubliclibrary.org	732-775-8241	774-1132	434-3
Neptune Society 4312 Woodman Ave 3rd Fl. . . . . Sherman Oaks CA 91423 *TF:* 888-637-8863 ■ *Web:* www.neptunesociety.com	888-637-8863		510
Neptune-Benson Inc 6 Jefferson Dr. . . . . Coventry RI 02816 *TF:* 800-832-8002 ■ *Web:* www.evoqua.com	401-821-2200		641
NEPW Logistics Inc 118 Quarry Rd . . . . . Auburn ME 04210 *Web:* www.nepw.com	207-333-3345		314
NERA (Naval Enlisted Reserve Assn) 6703 Farragut Ave. . . . . Falls Church VA 22042 *TF:* 800-776-9020 ■ *Web:* www.nera.org	800-776-9020		48-19
NERAC Inc 1 Technology Dr . . . . . Tolland CT 06084 *Web:* www.nerac.com	860-872-7000		387
NERC (North American Electric Reliability Council) 1325 G St NW Ste 600. . . . . Washington DC 20005 *Web:* www.nerc.com	609-452-8060	452-9550	48-12
Nercon 600 S Commercial St . . . . . Neenah WI 54956 *Web:* www.nerconconveyors.com	920-233-3268	233-3159	207
NERD (Nerd Gas Company LLC) 441 Landmark Dr PO Box 3003 . . . . . Casper WY 82602 *Web:* www.nerdgas.com	307-234-0583	234-4631	536
Nerd Gas Company LLC (NERD) 441 Landmark Dr PO Box 3003 . . . . . Casper WY 82602 *Web:* www.nerdgas.com	307-234-0583	234-4631	536
Nerdery, The 9555 James Ave S Ste 245. . . . . Bloomington MN 55431 *TF:* 877-664-6373 ■ *Web:* nerdery.com	877-664-6373		177
Nerel Corp 7085 W 38th Ave . . . . . Wheat Ridge CO 80033 *Web:* wheatridgecyclery.com	303-424-3221		711
NERSC (National Energy Research Scientific Computing Ctr) Lawrence Berkeley National Laboratory . . . . . Berkeley CA 94720 *TF:* 800-666-3772 ■ *Web:* www.nersc.gov	510-486-5849	486-4300	668
Nerstrand-Big Woods State Park 9700 170th St E . . . . . Nerstrand MN 55053 *Web:* www.dnr.state.mn.us	507-384-6140		565
NES Associates LLC 6400 Beulah St Ste 300 . . . . . Alexandria VA 22310 *Web:* www.nesassociates.com	703-224-2600		180
NES Health 39 Main St. . . . . Tiburon CA 94920 *TF:* 800-394-6376 ■ *Web:* www.neshealth-care.com	800-394-6376		30
Nesbitt Contracting Company Inc 100 S Price Rd . . . . . Tempe AZ 85281 *Web:* www.nesbitts.com	480-894-2831	423-7680	188-4
Nesbitt Engineering Inc (NEI) 227 N Upper St. . . . . Lexington KY 40507 *Web:* nei-ky.com	859-233-3111	259-2717	261
NESC Staffing Corp 150 Mirona Rd . . . . . Portsmouth NH 03801 *TF:* 800-562-3463 ■ *Web:* www.nesc.com	800-562-3463		721
Nesco 2344 S Green St. . . . . Tupelo MS 38801 *Web:* nescoelectric.com	662-840-4750	842-3139	23
Nesco Inc 6140 Parkland Blvd . . . . . Cleveland OH 44124 *Web:* nescoresource.com	440-461-6000	449-3111	185
Nesco Rentals (UELC) 6714 Pointe Inverness Way Ste 220. . . . . Fort Wayne IN 46804 *TF:* 800-252-0043 ■ *Web:* nescorentals.com	260-824-6340	824-6350	470
Nesco/American Harvest 1700 Monroe St PO Box 237 . . . . . Two Rivers WI 54241 *TF:* 800-288-4545 ■ *Web:* www.nesco.com	920-793-1368	793-1086	37
Nescopeck State Park 1137 Honey Hole Rd. . . . . Drums PA 18222 *Web:* www.dcnr.pa.gov	570-403-2006		565
NESDA (National Electronics Service Dealers Assn) 3608 Pershing Ave . . . . . Fort Worth TX 76107 *Web:* nesda.wildapricot.org	817-921-9061	921-3741	49-18
Neset Consulting Service Inc 6844 Hwy 40 . . . . . Tioga ND 58852 *Web:* nesetconsulting.com	701-664-1492		463
NESFA (New England Science Fiction Association Inc) PO Box 809 . . . . . Framingham MA 01701 *Web:* www.nesfa.org	617-625-2311	776-3243	637-2
Neshaminy Constructors Inc 1839 Bustleton Pk . . . . . Feasterville-Trevose PA 19053 *Web:* www.nci3.com	215-322-2700	322-0603	194
Neshoba County 401 Beacon St Ste 201. . . . . Philadelphia MS 39350 *Web:* www.neshobacounty.net	601-656-6281	650-3280	338
NESHTA (National Environmental Safety & Health Training Assn) 584 Main St . . . . . South Portland ME 04106 *Web:* www.neshta.org	207-771-9020		49-5
NESN (New England Sports Network) 480 Arsenal St Bldg 1. . . . . Watertown MA 02472 *Web:* nesn.com	617-536-9233	536-7814	740
Nespelem Valley Electric Co-opeartive Inc 1009 F St . . . . . Nespelem WA 99155 *Web:* www.nvec.org	509-634-4571	634-8138	245
Nesser Consulting Group Ltd 495 S High St Ste 170 . . . . . Columbus OH 43215 *Web:* www.nesserconsulting.com	614-221-1934	220-8794	192
NeST Technologies Corp 44901 Falcon Pl Ste 116 . . . . . Sterling VA 20166 *Web:* www.nesttech.com	703-653-1100		225
Nestech Machine Systems Inc 223 Commerce St. . . . . Hinesburg VT 05461 *Web:* www.nesms.com	802-482-4575	482-4579	547
NestFamily 1461 S Beltline Rd Ste 500 . . . . . Coppell TX 75019 *TF:* 800-634-4298 ■ *Web:* www.nestlearning.com	972-402-7100		33
Nestle Purina PetCare Co Checkerboard Sq . . . . . Saint Louis MO 63102 *TF:* 800-778-7462 ■ *Web:* www.purina.com	314-982-1000		578
Nestle USA Inc 800 N Brand Blvd . . . . . Glendale CA 91203 *Web:* www.nestle.com	818-549-6000		296-8
Nestle Waters North America 105 Pennsylvania Ave. . . . . Framingham MA 01701 *Web:* www.nestle-watersna.com	508-935-3500		805
Nest-One Solutions LLC 3796 Thornbrooke Ct . . . . . Duluth GA 30097 *TF:* 800-790-1640 ■ *Web:* nestone.jetcam.net	816-215-8014		366
Nestor Sales LLC 7337 Bryan Dairy Rd. . . . . Largo FL 33777 *Web:* www.nestorsales.com	727-544-6114	544-6211	758
Net Effect Technologies 426 E Duarte Rd . . . . . Monrovia CA 91016 *Web:* neteffecttech.com	626-930-0101		177
Net Element Inc 3363 NE 163rd St Ste 705 . . . . . North Miami Beach FL 33160 **Fax Area Code:* 786 ■ *Web:* www.netelement.com	305-507-8808	272-0696*	255
Net Endeavor Inc 982 S Main St. . . . . Pleasant Grove UT 84062 *Web:* net-endeavor.com	801-796-5582		177
Net Impact LLC, The 16690 Swingley Ridge Rd Ste 165. . . . . Chesterfield MO 63017 *Web:* www.thenetimpact.com	636-532-4424		195
Net Lease Capital Advisors 10 Tara Blvd . . . . . Nashua NH 03062 *Web:* www.netleasecapital.com	603-598-9500		652
Net (net) Inc 217 E 24th St Ste 010. . . . . Holland MI 49423 *Web:* www.netnetweb.com	616-546-3100		463
NET Radio 1800 N 33rd St . . . . . Lincoln NE 68503 *TF:* 800-868-1868 ■ *Web:* www.netnebraska.org	800-868-1868		741-74

	City	State	ZIP	Phone	Fax	Class
Net Results 308 W Blvd N *TF:* 888-470-2456 ■ *Web:* www.netresults.org	Columbia	MO	65203	888-470-2456		637-9
Net Solutions Technology Ctr 38 Sams Point Rd *Web:* www.easierway.com	Beaufort	SC	29907	843-525-6469	521-0955	225
Net Source Inc 6021 S Syracuse Way Ste 103 *Web:* www.netsourcesecure.com	Greenwood Village	CO	80111	303-948-3360		196
Net Theory Inc 64 Fulton St Ste 603 *Web:* www.nettheory.com	New York	NY	10038	212-868-5950		463
Net Wizards Inc 90 S Spruce Ave Ste S **Fax Area Code:* 877 ■ *TF:* 866-346-3894 ■ *Web:* www.netwiz.net	San Francisco	CA	94102	650-737-5470	837-1427*	387
Net World Technology Corp 65 S College St *Web:* networldtechnology.com	Carlisle	PA	17013	717-249-7232		196
Net2Phone Inc 520 Broad St *TF:* 800-386-6438 ■ *Web:* www.net2phone.com	Newark	NJ	07102	866-978-8260		736
Net32 Inc 250 Towne Village Dr *TF:* 800-517-1997 ■ *Web:* www.net32.com	Cary	NC	27513	919-468-1177		228
NETA (National Educational Telecommunications Assn) 939 S Stadium Rd *Web:* www.netaonline.org	Columbia	SC	29201	803-799-5517	771-4831	632
Neta Scientific Inc 4206 Sylon Blvd *TF:* 800-343-6015 ■ *Web:* www.netascientific.com	Hainesport	NJ	08036	800-343-6015		475
NetAbstraction Inc 3901 Centerview Dr Ste F *Web:* netabstraction.com	Chantilly	VA	20151	703-870-7481		41
Netblaze Systems Inc 1299 Newell Hill Pl Ste 202 *Web:* netblaze.biz	Walnut Creek	CA	94596	925-932-1765		180
Netbriefings Inc 421 Wabasha St N 2nd Fl *TF:* 866-225-1532 ■ *Web:* www.netbriefings.com	Saint Paul	MN	55102	651-225-1532	225-1533	681
NETC (New England Tropical Conservatory) 413 US Rt 7S PO Box 4715 *Web:* oneworldconservationcenter.org	Bennington	VT	05201	802-447-7419		97
Netcarrier Inc 4000 N Cannon Ave *TF:* 888-575-4754 ■ *Web:* www.netcarrier.com	Lansdale	PA	19446	215-257-4917		681
Netcellent System Inc 4030 Valley Blvd *TF:* 888-595-3818 ■ *Web:* elliott.com	Walnut	CA	91789	909-598-9019		177
NetCenergy Corp 231 Elm St *Web:* www.netcenergy.com	Warwick	RI	02888	401-921-3100		393
NetCenter Technologies 2536 Main Ave W *Web:* www.netcentertech.com	West Fargo	ND	58078	701-235-8100		180
Netcetera Consulting Inc 205 - 828 Harbourside Dr *Web:* www.netcetera.ca	North Vancouver	BC	V7P3R9	604-980-2700		177
Netchannel Inc PO Box 10442	Albuquerque	NM	87114	505-843-8282		131
Netchex 1155 Hwy 190 E Service Rd Ste 2 *Web:* www.netchexonline.com	Covington	LA	70433	985-220-1410	220-1415	260
Netcom 77 E Crossville Rd Ste 201 *Web:* netcom-inc.com	Roswell	GA	30075	770-642-5555		180
Netcom Inc 599 S Wheeling Rd *Web:* www.netcominc.com	Wheeling	IL	60090	847-537-6300	537-2700	253
Netcom Systems Inc 200 Metroplex Dr *Web:* www.netcom-sys.com	Edison	NJ	08817	732-393-6100		225
Netcom Technologies Inc 313 N Berry St *Web:* netcomtechnologies.net	Brea	CA	92821	714-256-9229		111
netCOMPONENTS Inc 4800 N Federal Hwy Ste 303A *Web:* www.netcomponents.com	Boca Raton	FL	33431	561-274-6780	274-6796	253
Netcong Elementary School 26 College Rd *Web:* www.netcongschool.org	Netcong	NJ	07857	973-347-0020	347-3676	685
Netcracker Technology Corp University Ofc Pk III 95 Sawyer Rd *TF:* 800-477-5785 ■ *Web:* www.netcracker.com	Waltham	MA	02453	781-419-3300	419-3301	463
Netessentials Inc 705 Eighth St Ste 1000 *TF:* 877-899-6387 ■ *Web:* netess.net	Wichita Falls	TX	76301	940-767-6387		180
Netfast Communications Inc 989 Avenue of the Americas 4th Fl *TF:* 888-678-6383 ■ *Web:* www.netfast.com	New York	NY	10018	212-792-5200		224
Netfira 4900 Hopyard Rd Ste 100 *Web:* www.netfira.com	Pleasanton	CA	94588	925-468-4178		177
NetFlix Inc 100 Winchester Cir *NASDAQ: NFLX* ■ *TF:* 866-579-7293 ■ *Web:* www.netflix.com	Los Gatos	CA	95032	408-540-3700		797
NetForecast Inc 1818 Library St Ste 500 **Fax Area Code:* 978 ■ *Web:* www.netforecast.com	Reston	VA	20190	434-252-2055	746-7038*	196
Netfronts Web Hosting 459 N 300 W Ste 16 *TF:* 800-675-4622 ■ *Web:* netfronts.com	Kaysville	UT	84037	801-497-0878		396
Netgain Information Systems Co 128 W Columbus Ave *TF:* 855-651-7001 ■ *Web:* www.netgainis.com	Bellefontaine	OH	43311	937-593-7177	593-4282	180
NetGain Motors Inc 800 S State St Ste 4 *Web:* www.go-ev.com	Lockport	IL	60441	630-243-9100		518
Netgain Networks Inc 8378 Attica Dr *TF:* 855-667-2364 ■ *Web:* netgainnetworks.com	Riverside	CA	92508	951-656-0194		179
NetGain Technology LLC 720 W St Germain St **Fax Area Code:* 320 ■ *TF:* 877-797-4700 ■ *Web:* netgaincloud.com	Saint Cloud	MN	56301	877-797-4700	251-5030*	177
netGuru Inc 1240 N Van Buren St Ste 104 *Web:* netguru.com	Anaheim	CA	92807	714-638-4878	414-0200	178-10
Nethawk Interactive Inc 1255 Park Ave Ste D *Web:* www.nethawk.net	Emeryville	CA	94608	510-595-2220		195
Netherland Rubber Co 2931 Exon Ave **Fax Area Code:* 513 ■ *TF:* 800-582-1877 ■ *Web:* www.netherlandrubber.com	Cincinnati	OH	45241	800-582-1877	733-1096*	326
Netherlands *Consulate General* 303 E Wacker Dr Ste 2600 *Web:* www.netherlandsworldwide.nl	Chicago	IL	60601	312-780-1314	856-9218	257
Embassy 4200 Linnean Ave NW *TF:* 877-388-2443 ■ *Web:* Www.nlintheusa.com	Washington	DC	20008	877-388-2443		257
Netherlands Board of Tourism & Conventions 215 Park Ave S **Fax Area Code:* 212 ■ *Web:* www.holland.com	New York	NY	10003	646-618-0818	370-9507*	775
Netherlands Chamber of Commerce 267 5th Ave *Web:* netherlands.org	New York	NY	10016	212-265-6460		138
Netimpact Strategies Inc 7600 Leesburg Pike W Bldg Ste 140 *Web:* www.netimpactstrategies.com	Falls Church	VA	22043	703-559-3280		809
Netivot Hatorah 18 Atkinson Ave *Web:* www.netivot.com	Thornhill	ON	L4J8C8	905-771-1234		685
Netkrom Technologies Inc 2134 NW 99th Ave *Web:* www.netkrom.com	Miami	FL	33172	305-418-2232	418-9266	224
NETL (National Energy Technology Laboratory) 3610 Collins Ferry Rd *TF:* 800-432-8330 ■ *Web:* netl.doe.gov	Morgantown	WV	26505	304-285-4764		668
Netlan Technology Ctr 1430 Broadway 13th Fl **Fax Area Code:* 212 ■ *Web:* netlan.com	New York	NY	10018	917-281-5663	730-4411*	765
NetLine Corp 750 University Ave Ste 200 *Web:* www.netline.com	Los Gatos	CA	95032	408-340-2200		224
Netlink Software Group America Inc 999 Tech Row *TF:* 800-485-4462 ■ *Web:* www.netlink.com	Madison Heights	MI	48071	800-485-4462		196
Netlink Systems Inc 5959 Shallowford Rd PO Box 23054 *Web:* www.netlink-systems.com	Chattanooga	TN	37421	423-855-0065		177
Netlist Inc 175 Technology Ste 150 *Web:* www.netlist.com	Irvine	CA	92618	949-435-0025	435-0031	696
Netlogix Inc 48 Court St *Web:* www.netlogix.com	Westfield	MA	01085	413-568-2777		180
Netmarkcom 3135 E 17th St Ste B *TF:* 800-935-5133 ■ *Web:* www.netmark.com	Ammon	ID	83406	208-522-1016	621-0227	195
Netmd Business 38935 Ann Arbor Rd *Web:* netmdbusiness.com	Livonia	MI	48150	734-032-0175	805-0400	303
NetMotion Inc 701 N 34th St Ste 250 *TF:* 877-818-7626 ■ *Web:* www.netmotionsoftware.com	Seattle	WA	98103	206-691-5500	691-5501	178-1
NetMotion Inc 4160 Technology Dr *Web:* www.netmotion.com	Fremont	CA	94538	510-578-2808	743-4130	385
NetNation Communications Inc 550 Burrard St Ste 200 *TF:* 888-277-0000 ■ *Web:* www.netnation.com	Vancouver	BC	V6C2B5	604-688-8946	688-8934	808
NetNumber Inc Wannalancit Technology Ctr Ste 307 *Web:* www.netnumber.com	Lowell	MA	01854	978-848-2820		178-1
Neto Sausage Company Inc Cross St Coleman 288 Brokaw Rd *Web:* www.netosausage.com	Santa Clara	CA	95050	408-296-0818	296-0538	296-26
Netology LLC 1200 Summer St Ste 302 *Web:* www.netologyllc.com	Stamford	CT	06905	203-975-9630		177
Netorian LLC 210 Research Blvd Ste 160 *TF:* 844-638-6742 ■ *Web:* netorian.com	Aberdeen	MD	21001	844-638-6742		180
Netplanner Systems Inc 3145 Northwoods Pkwy Ste 800 *TF:* 800-795-1975 ■ *Web:* www.netplanner.com	Norcross	GA	30071	770-662-5482		176
Netpop Research LLC 322 Cortland Ave *Web:* netpop.com	San Francisco	CA	94110	415-647-1007		466
NetQuest Corp 523 Fellowship Rd Ste 205 *Web:* www.netquestcorp.com	Mount Laurel	NJ	08054	856-866-0505		225
NetRate Systems Inc 3493 Woods Edge Dr *Web:* www.netrate.com	Okemos	MI	48864	877-790-1114		180
Netriplex LLC PO Box 2288 *TF:* 800-619-8801 ■ *Web:* www.netriplex.com	Skyland	NC	28776	800-619-8801		180
Netrition Inc 25 Corporate Cir Ste 118 *TF:* 888-817-2411 ■ *Web:* www.netrition.com	Albany	NY	12203	518-464-0765	456-9673	355
Netropole 5630 NE Martin Luther King Jr *Web:* www.portlandmanagedservices.com	Portland	OR	97211	503-241-3499		463
NetScout Systems Inc 310 Littleton Rd *NASDAQ: NTCT* ■ *TF:* 800-357-7666 ■ *Web:* www.netscout.com	Westford	MA	01886	978-614-4000	614-4004	178-7
Netsertive Inc 2400 Perimeter Park Dr Ste 100 *TF:* 800-940-4351 ■ *Web:* www.netsertive.com	Morrisville	NC	27560	800-940-4351		195
Netserve365 LLC 1000 Cliffmine Rd Ste 520 *TF:* 844-462-4625 ■ *Web:* magna5global.com	Pittsburgh	PA	15275	844-462-4625		180
Netsmart Technologies Inc 3500 Sunrise Hwy Ste D-122 *TF:* 800-421-7503 ■ *Web:* www.ntst.com	Great River	NY	11739	631-968-2000		178-11
Netsol Technologies Inc 23975 Park Sorrento Ste 250 *NASDAQ: NTWK* ■ *Web:* www.netsoltech.com	Calabasas	CA	91302	818-222-9195	222-9197	178-10
Netsource Technology Inc 951 Calle Negocio *TF:* 800-598-6381 ■ *Web:* www.nstechnology.com	San Clemente	CA	92673	949-713-0800	713-0600	246
Netspeed Learning Solutions 6245 36th Ave NE *TF:* 877-517-5271 ■ *Web:* netspeedlearning.com	Seattle	WA	98115	206-517-5271		194
NetStandard Inc 2000 Merriam Ln *Web:* www.netstandard.com	Kansas City	KS	66106	913-262-3888		180
Netsville Inc 72 Cascade Dr *TF:* 888-638-7845 ■ *Web:* www.netsville.com	Rochester	NY	14614	585-232-5670	232-4512	189-4
Netswitch 400 Oyster Point Blvd Ste 228 *Web:* www.netswitch.net	South San Francisco	CA	94080	415-566-6228		387
Nettech LLC 1851 Hudson Cir *Web:* nettech.net	Monroe	LA	71201	318-387-0001		180
Nettempo Inc 1501 Mariposa St Ste 318 *Web:* www.nettempo.com	San Francisco	CA	94107	415-992-4900	992-4910	177

Company	City	State	ZIP	Phone	Fax	Class
Net-Temps Inc 55 Middlesex St Ste 220 *TF:* 800-307-0062 ■ *Web:* www.net-temps.com	North Chelmsford	MA	01863	978-251-7272	251-7250	260
Nettlinx Inc 1400 Kennedy Blvd. *Web:* www.nettlinxinc.com	Union City	NJ	07087	201-330-9394	643-2477	393
Nettwerk 575 W Eighth Ave 5th Fl *Web:* www.nettwerk.com	Vancouver	BC	V5Z0C4	604-654-2929	654-1993	731
Netuno USA Inc 511 SE 5 Ave Ste 103/104 *Web:* netunousa.com	Fort Lauderdale	FL	33301	305-513-0904	513-3904	296-14
Neturen USA Inc 15335 Endeavor Dr Ste 105 *Web:* www.k-neturen.co.jp	Noblesville	IN	46060	317-674-8371	674-8372	318
Netvantage Inc 6510 Hamilton Ave Ste 1 *Web:* www.netvantageinc.com	Cincinnati	OH	45224	513-729-0207		251
NetVillagecom LLC 342 Main St. *Web:* www.netvillage.com	Laurel	MD	20707	301-498-7797	498-8110	178-7
NetVoyage Corp 2500 W Executive Pkwy Ste 350 *Web:* www.netdocuments.com	Lehi	UT	84043	801-226-6882		180
Netway Solutions Inc 240 Palomino Dr *Web:* www.netwaysolutions.com	Salisbury	NC	28146	704-637-6155		180
Netwize Inc 702 Confluence Ave *Web:* www.netwize.com	Salt Lake City	UT	84123	801-747-3200		180
Netwolves Corp 4710 Eisenhower Blvd Ste E-8 *TF:* 855-638-9658 ■ *Web:* www.netwolves.com	Tampa	FL	33634	855-638-9658		736
Netwood Communications 10736 Jefferson Blvd Ste 670 *Web:* netwood.net	Culver City	CA	90230	310-442-1530	496-0712	396
Network 1 Financial Securities Inc 2 Bridge Ave Ste 241 *TF:* 800-886-7007 ■ *Web:* network1.com	Red Bank	NJ	07701	732-758-9001	758-6671	690
Network 2000 LLC 2100 N Nimitz Hwy *Web:* www.network2000-hi.com	Honolulu	HI	96819	808-848-0000		180
Network America 200 104th Ave Ste 324 *TF:* 877-624-8311 ■ *Web:* naisolutions.com	Treasure Island	FL	33706	877-624-8311		180
Network America 1029 13th St. *Web:* www.networkam.net	Bedford	IN	47421	812-277-1499		224
Network Appliance Inc 495 E Java Dr. *NASDAQ: NTAP* ■ *TF:* 800-443-4537 ■ *Web:* www.netapp.com	Sunnyvale	CA	94089	408-822-6000		176
Network Computing Magazine 600 Community Dr *Web:* www.networkcomputing.com	Manhasset	NY	11030	516-562-5000		457-7
Network Data Security Experts Inc (NDSE) 521 Branchway Rd *TF:* 877-440-6373 ■ *Web:* www.ndse.net	North Chesterfield	VA	23236	877-440-6373		177
Network Data Systems Inc 50 E Commerce Dr Ste 120 *Web:* www.network-data.com	Schaumburg	IL	60173	847-385-6700		180
Network Depot LLC 12040 S Lakes Dr Ste 202 *Web:* www.networkdepot.com	Reston	VA	20191	703-810-3960	852-7187	179
Network Designs Integration Services 103 Hammond Ave *Web:* network-designs.com	Fremont	CA	94539	510-249-9549	249-9545	196
Network Directions Inc PO Box 511466 *Web:* www.net-directions.com	Milwaukee	WI	53203	414-587-8546		180
Network Earth Inc 2501 Alida St **Fax Area Code:* 866 ■ *TF:* 888-201-5160 ■ *Web:* www.netearth.com	Oakland	CA	94602	888-201-5160	445-9307*	224
Network Experts 260 S Beverly Dr Ste 325 *Web:* www.networkexperts.la	Beverly Hills	CA	90212	310-275-1911		175
Network Frontiers LLC 244 Lafayette Cir. *Web:* www.unifiedcompliance.com	LaFayette	CA	94549	510-962-5192		196
Network Global Logistics (NGL) 320 Interlocken Pkwy Ste 100 *TF:* 866-938-1870 ■ *Web:* www.nglog.com	Broomfield	CO	80021	866-938-1870		546
Network Innovations Inc 4424 Manilla Rd SE *TF:* 888-466-2772 ■ *Web:* www.networkinv.com	Calgary	AB	T2G4B7	403-287-5000		194
Network Integration Specialists Inc (NIS) 1600 Mountain Rd *Web:* www.netintegration.net	Glen Allen	VA	23060	804-264-9339	726-8242	180
NetWork Kansas PO Box 877 *TF:* 877-521-8600 ■ *Web:* www.networkkansas.com	Andover	KS	67002	877-521-8600		393
Network Magic Unlimited 2999 Overland Ave Ste 210 *Web:* www.netmagicu.com	Los Angeles	CA	90064	310-449-1411	449-1470	225
Network Medical Management Inc 1668 S Garfield Ave 2nd Fl *TF:* 877-282-8272 ■ *Web:* www.nmm.cc	Alhambra	CA	91801	626-282-0288		463
Network Paper & Packaging Ltd 19100 Airport Way Units 301-302 *Web:* www.netpak.net	Pitt Meadows	BC	V3Y0E2	604-458-2000	458-2003	96
Network Performance Inc 85 Green Mtn Dr *TF:* 800-639-6091 ■ *Web:* www.npi.net	South Burlington	VT	05403	802-859-0808		180
Network Planet Inc 468 N Camden Dr Ste 200 *Web:* www.networkplanetinc.com	Beverly Hills	CA	90210	310-552-5325		196
Network Programs Inc 1430 Broad Way *Web:* www.networkprograms.com	New York	NY	10018	212-575-7800	944-1434	225
Network Security Partners LLC 1401 Forum Way Ste 100 *Web:* slpowers.com	West Palm Beach	FL	33401	561-835-8351		180
Network Services Co (NSC) 1100 E Woodfield Rd *Web:* www.networkdistribution.com	Schaumburg	IL	60173	847-803-4888	803-0482	196
Network Services LLC 2065 Kensington Ave *Web:* ns-wny.com	Amherst	NY	14226	716-839-5309	839-5301	736
Network Solutions International Inc 2629 Main St *Web:* www.networksolutionsintl.com	Santa Monica	CA	90405	310-314-7325	494-5733	180
Network Solutions LLC 13861 Sunrise Valley Dr Ste 300 *TF:* 800-361-5712 ■ *Web:* www.networksolutions.com	Herndon	VA	20171	703-668-4600		396
Network Synergy Corp 126 Monroe Tpke *Web:* www.netsynergy.com	Trumbull	CT	06611	203-261-2201		180
Network Tallahassee PO Box 12035 *TF:* 866-586-1598 ■ *Web:* www.ntifl.com	Tallahassee	FL	32317	850-671-4007	224-7286	180
Network Telephone Services Inc 21135 Erwin St *Web:* www.nts.net	Woodland Hills	CA	91367	818-992-4300		252
NetworkElites Services Inc 17400 N Dallas Pkwy Ste 120 *Web:* www.networkelites.com	Dallas	TX	75287	972-235-3114		393
Networking Concepts Inc 9881 Broken Land Pkwy Ste 402 *Web:* www.networkingconcepts.com	Columbia	MD	21046	410-381-0100	381-0101	177
NetworkOmni 4353 Park Ter Dr **Fax Area Code:* 805 ■ *TF:* 800-543-4244 ■ *Web:* www.networkomni.com	Westlake Village	CA	91361	818-706-7890	367-7800*	393
Networks & More Inc 24 Highland Bnd Box 178 *Web:* www.networksandmore.com	Island Heights	NJ	08732	732-929-1485		180
Networks Electronic Co 9750 De Soto Ave *Web:* www.networkselectronic.com	Chatsworth	CA	91311	818-341-0440	718-7133	203
Networks Made Simple LLC 64 Confederate Way *Web:* www.networksmadesimple.net	Stafford	VA	22554	540-657-5360		175
Networks of Florida 25 W Avery St *TF:* 800-368-2315 ■ *Web:* www.nof.com	Pensacola	FL	32501	850-434-8600	434-8609	180
Networld Inc 300 Lanidex Plz Ste 1 *TF:* 800-992-3411 ■ *Web:* www.networldinc.com	Parsippany	NJ	07054	973-884-7474		760
Networld Media Group LLC 13100 Eastpoint Park Blvd Ste 100 *TF:* 877-441-7545 ■ *Web:* networldmediagroup.com	Louisville	KY	40223	502-241-7545		393
NetWorth Services Inc 3333 E Camelback Rd Ste 260 *Web:* www.networthservices.com	Phoenix	AZ	85018	602-222-6380		224
Netwoven Inc 3837 Stone Pointe Way *Web:* www.netwoven.com	Pleasanton	CA	94588	925-931-9390		180
Netxar Technologies Ponce St Ste 17 *Web:* www.netxar.co	San Juan	PR	00917	787-765-0058	756-5362	261
NetXperts Inc 1777 Botelho Dr Ste 102 *TF:* 888-271-9367 ■ *Web:* netxperts.com	Walnut Creek	CA	94596	925-806-0800		180
NetXposure Inc 735 SW First Ave 3rd Fl *Web:* www.netx.net	Portland	OR	97204	503-499-4342		180
Netxusa Inc 231 Beverly Rd *Web:* www.netxusa.com	Greenville	SC	29609	864-271-9868		180
Netzel Grigsby Associates Inc 9696 Culver Blvd Ste 105 *Web:* www.netzelgrigsby.com	Culver City	CA	90232	310-836-7624	836-9357	317
Netzer Metalcraft 1600 W 41st St *Web:* www.netzermetalcraftinc.com	Baltimore	MD	21211	410-467-9762	467-3584	454
NetZero Inc 21301 Burbank Blvd *TF:* 800-638-9376 ■ *Web:* www.netzero.net	Woodland Hills	CA	91367	818-287-3000		398
Netzsch 119 Pickering Way *Web:* www.pumps.netzsch.com	Exton	PA	19341	610-363-8010	363-0971	386
Neuber Environmental Services Inc 42 Ridge Rd *Web:* www.neuberenv.com	Phoenixville	PA	19460	610-933-4332		63
Neuberger Berman Funds PO Box 8403 *TF:* 800-877-9700 ■ *Web:* www.nb.com	Boston	MA	02266	212-476-8800		528
Neuberger Museum of Art Purchase College Suny 735 Anderson Hill Rd *Web:* www.neuberger.org	Purchase	NY	10577	914-251-6100	251-6101	520
Neuberger Quinn Gielen Rubin Gibber PA 1 South St 27th Fl. *Web:* www.nqgrg.com	Baltimore	MD	21202	410-332-8522		428
Neubert Millwork Co 200 S Front St *Web:* www.neubertmillwork.com	Saint Peter	MN	56082	507-387-1105	387-1068	499
NeuCo Inc 12 Post Office Sq 4th Fl *Web:* www.neuco.net	Boston	MA	02109	617-587-3100		225
Neudesic LLC 8105 Irvine Center Dr *TF:* 800-805-1805 ■ *Web:* www.neudesic.com	Irvine	CA	92618	949-754-4500		177
Neudorfer Engineers Inc 5516 First Ave S *Web:* neudorferengineers.com	Seattle	WA	98108	206-621-1810		261
Neuger Communications Group Inc 25 Bridge Sq. *Web:* www.neuger.com	Northfield	MN	55057	507-664-0700		449
Neuhoff Corp 146 Sota Dr *Web:* www.neuhoffmedia.com	Jupiter	FL	33458	561-745-2122		647
Neuisys LLC 3702-B Alliance Dr Ste 212 *TF:* 877-299-9052	Greensboro	NC	27407	877-299-9052	299-9051	743
Neuma Technology Inc 5450 Canotek Rd Ste 51 *Web:* www.neuma.com	Ottawa	ON	K1J9G3	613-749-9450		179
Neumade Products Corp 30-40 Pecks Ln Ste 40	Newtown	CT	06470	203-270-1100		591
Neuman & Neuman Real Estate Inc 516 Fifth Ave. *TF:* 800-221-2210 ■ *Web:* sellsandiego.com	San Diego	CA	92101	800-221-2210		652
Neumann Brothers Inc 1435 Ohio St. *Web:* www.neumannbros.com	Des Moines	IA	50314	515-243-0156	243-0165	186
Neumann College 1 Neumann Dr *TF:* 800-963-8626 ■ *Web:* www.neumann.edu	Aston	PA	19014	610-459-0905	361-5265	166
Neumayer Equipment Company Inc 5060 Arsenal St *TF:* 800-843-4563 ■ *Web:* neumayerequipment.com	Saint Louis	MO	63139	314-772-4501	772-2311	386
Neumedicines Inc 10426 Helendale Ave *Web:* www.neumedicines.com	Tujunga	CA	91042	626-844-3800		668

Name / Address	City	State	Zip	Phone	Fax	Class
Neumeier Engineering Inc 22610 88th Ave S *Web:* www.neumeier1.com	Kent	WA	98031	253-854-3635		454
Neundorfer Inc 4590 Hamann Pkwy *TF:* 800-863-4288 ■ *Web:* www.neundorfer.com	Willoughby	OH	44094	440-942-8990		261
Neuro Kinetics Inc 128 Gamma Dr *Web:* www.neuro-kinetics.com	Pittsburgh	PA	15238	412-963-6649		475
Neuro Logic Systems Inc 451 Constitution Ave *Web:* nlsdisplays.com	Camarillo	CA	93012	805-389-5435		180
Neurocrine Biosciences Inc 12790 El Camino Rl *NASDAQ: NBIX* ■ *TF:* 877-641-3461 ■ *Web:* www.neurocrine.com	San Diego	CA	92130	858-617-7600	617-7602	85
NeuroGenetic Pharmaceuticals Inc PO Box 2007 *Web:* neurogeneticpharmaceuticals.com	Rancho Santa Fe	CA	92067	858-735-5892		231
NeuroMetrix 62 Fourth Ave *NASDAQ: NURO* ■ *TF:* 888-786-7287 ■ *Web:* www.neurometrix.com	Waltham	MA	02451	781-890-9989	890-1556	250
Neuromonics Inc PO Box 351886 *TF:* 866-606-3876 ■ *Web:* neuromonics.com	Westminster	CO	80035	866-606-3876		250
Neuronetrix Inc 1044 E Chestnut St *Web:* www.cognision.com	Louisville	KY	40204	502-561-9040		743
NeuroPace Inc 455 N Bernardo Ave *TF:* 866-726-3876 ■ *Web:* www.neuropace.com	Mountain View	CA	94043	866-726-3876		475
Neuroptics Inc 23041 Avenida De La Carlota Ste 100 *Web:* neuroptics.com	Laguna Hills	CA	92612	949-250-9792	250-9796	476
Neuros Medical Inc 35010 Chardon Rd Ste 210 *TF:* 888-978-1745 ■ *Web:* www.neurosmedical.com	Willoughby Hills	OH	44094	440-951-2565	951-1470	476
Neuroscience Curriculum 115 Mason Farm Rd CB 7250 *TF:* 800-862-4938 ■ *Web:* www.med.unc.edu	Chapel Hill	NC	27599	919-843-8536	966-1050	668
NeuroScience Inc 373 280th St *TF:* 888-342-7272 ■ *Web:* www.neuroscienceinc.com	Osceola	WI	54020	715-294-2144		418
Neurosky Inc 125 S Market St Ste 900 *Web:* neurosky.com	San Jose	CA	95113	408-200-6675		606
Neurosource 1050 N State St	Chicago	IL	60610	312-496-3307		7
Neuro-Tec Inc 975 Cobb Pl Blvd Ste 301 *TF:* 800-554-3407 ■ *Web:* www.neurotec.net	Kennesaw	GA	30144	800-554-3407		475
Neurotech Pharmaceuticals Inc 900 Highland Corporate Dr *Web:* www.neurotechusa.com	Cumberland	RI	02864	401-333-3880		668
Neurotez Inc 991 Hwy 22 Ste 200 A *Web:* neurotez.com	Bridgewater	NJ	08807	908-998-1340		668
NeuroVentures Capital LLC 427 Park St	Charlottesville	VA	22902	434-297-1000		792
Neuse Correctional Institution 701 Stevens Mill Rd *Web:* www.ncdps.gov	Goldsboro	NC	27530	919-734-5580		213
NeuStar Inc 21575 Ridgetop Cir *TF:* 855-638-2677 ■ *Web:* www.home.neustar	Sterling	VA	20166	571-434-5400		47
Neustel Law Offices Ltd 2534 University Dr S Ste 4 *Web:* neustel.com	Fargo	ND	58103	701-281-8822		41
Neusys Inc PO Box 366 *Web:* www.neusysinc.com	Aurora	IN	47001	812-926-1828		178-1
Neutral Posture Inc 3904 N Texas Ave *TF:* 800-446-3746 ■ *Web:* neutralposture.com	Bryan	TX	77803	979-778-0502	778-0408	319-1
Neutrogena Corp 5760 W 96th St *TF:* 800-582-4048 ■ *Web:* www.neutrogena.com	Los Angeles	CA	90045	310-642-1150		214
Neutron Inc 220 Reese Rd *Web:* www.neutronusa.com	State College	PA	16801	814-237-0902		196
Neutron Motorsports 13435 S Main St *TF:* 888-327-4981 ■ *Web:* www.neutronmotorsports.com	Los Angeles	CA	90061	310-327-4981	327-5078	61
Neutron Products Inc 22301 Mt Ephraim Rd *Web:* neutronprod.com	Dickerson	MD	20842	301-349-5001	349-2433	146
Neutronix-Quintel (NXQ) 385 Woodview Ave *Web:* neutronixinc.com	Morgan Hill	CA	95037	408-776-5190	776-1039	695
Nevada						
Accountancy Board 1325 Airmotive Way Ste 220 *Web:* www.nvaccountancy.com	Reno	NV	89502	775-786-0231	786-0234	339-29
Administrative Office of the Courts 201 S Carson St Ste 250 *Web:* nvcourts.gov	Carson City	NV	89701	775-684-1700		339-29
Aging Services Div 1860 E Sahara Ave *Web:* adsd.nv.gov	Las Vegas	NV	89104	702-486-3545	486-3572	339-29
Arts Council 716 N Carson St Ste A *Web:* nvculture.org	Carson City	NV	89701	775-687-6680		339-29
Attorney General 100 N Carson St *Web:* ag.nv.gov	Carson City	NV	89701	775-684-1100	684-1108	339-29
Bill Status 401 S Carson St *TF:* 800-978-2878 ■ *Web:* www.leg.state.nv.us	Carson City	NV	89701	775-684-6827		433
Business & Industry Dept 555 E Washington Ave Ste 4900 *Web:* www.business.nv.gov	Las Vegas	NV	89101	702-486-2750		339-29
Child & Family Services Div 4126 Technology Way 3rd Fl *Web:* dcfs.nv.gov	Carson City	NV	89706	775-684-4400	684-4455	339-29
Child Support Enforcement Office 300 E Second St Ste 1200 *TF:* 800-992-0900 ■ *Web:* dwss.nv.gov	Reno	NV	89501	775-448-5150	448-5199	339-29
Commission on Ethics 704 W Nye Ln Ste 204 *Web:* ethics.nv.gov	Carson City	NV	89703	775-687-5469	687-1279	265
Conservation & Natural Resources Dept 901 S Stewart St Ste 1003 *Web:* www.dcnr.nv.gov	Carson City	NV	89701	775-684-2700	684-2715	339-29
Corrections Dept 5500 Snyder Ave Bldg 17 *Web:* www.doc.nv.gov	Carson City	NV	89702	775-887-3285		339-29
Dept of Employment Training & Rehabilitation 500 E 3rd St *Web:* www.nvdetr.org	Carson City	NV	89713	775-684-3911	684-3908	259
Economic Development Commission 808 W Nye Ln *TF:* 800-336-1600 ■ *Web:* www.diversifynevada.com	Carson City	NV	89703	775-687-9900	687-9924	339-29
Education Dept 700 E Fifth St *Web:* www.doe.nv.gov	Carson City	NV	89701	775-687-9200	687-9101	339-29
Emergency Management Div 2478 Fairview Dr *TF:* 888-363-4735 ■ *Web:* dem.nv.gov	Carson City	NV	89701	775-687-0400		339-29
Environmental Protection Div 901 S Stewart St Ste 4001 *Web:* ndep.nv.gov	Carson City	NV	89701	775-687-4670	687-5856	339-29
Gaming Commission 1919 College Pkwy PO Box 8003 *TF:* 800-326-6868 ■ *Web:* gaming.nv.gov	Carson City	NV	89706	775-684-7750	687-5817	339-29
Health Div 4150 Technology Way *Web:* dpbh.nv.gov	Carson City	NV	89706	775-684-4200	684-4211	339-29
Historic Preservation Office 901 S Stewart St Ste 5004 *Web:* shpo.nv.gov	Carson City	NV	89701	775-684-3448		339-29
Human Resources Dept 4126 Technology Way Ste 100 *Web:* dhhs.nv.gov	Carson City	NV	89706	775-684-4000	684-4010	339-29
Information Technology Dept 100 N Stewart St Ste 100 *Web:* it.nv.gov	Carson City	NV	89701	775-684-5800		339-29
Insurance Div 1818 E College Pkwy Ste 103 *TF:* 888-872-3234 ■ *Web:* doi.nv.gov	Carson City	NV	89706	775-687-0700	687-0787	339-29
Lieutenant Governor 101 N Carson St Ste 2 *Web:* www.ltgov.nv.gov	Carson City	NV	89701	775-684-7111	684-7110	339-29
Medical Examiners Board 1105 Terminal Way Ste 301 *Web:* www.medboard.nv.gov	Reno	NV	89502	775-688-2559	688-2321	339-29
Motor Vehicles Dept 555 Wright Way *Web:* www.dmvnv.com	Carson City	NV	89711	775-684-4368		339-29
Parole & Probation Div 1445 Old Hot Springs Rd Ste 104 *Web:* dps.nv.gov	Carson City	NV	89706	775-684-2600		339-29
Postsecondary Education Commission 8778 S Maryland Pkwy Ste 115 *Web:* cpe.nv.gov	Las Vegas	NV	89123	702-486-7330	486-7340	339-29
Public Safety Dept 555 Wright Way *Web:* dps.nv.gov	Carson City	NV	89711	775-684-4808	684-4809	339-29
Public Utilities Commission 1150 E William St *Web:* puc.nv.gov	Carson City	NV	89701	775-684-6101	684-6110	339-29
Real Estate Div 2501 E Sahara Ave Ste 102 *Web:* red.nv.gov	Las Vegas	NV	89104	702-486-4033	486-4275	339-29
Rehabilitation Div 1370 S Curry St *Web:* detr.state.nv.us	Carson City	NV	89703	775-684-4040		339-29
Secretary of State 101 N Carson St Ste 3 *Web:* www.nvsos.gov	Carson City	NV	89701	775-684-5708	684-5725	339-29
State Athletic Commission 3300 W Sahara Ave Ste 450 *Web:* boxing.nv.gov	Las Vegas	NV	89102	702-486-2575	486-2577	712
State Parks Div 901 S Stewart St 5th Fl *Web:* www.parks.nv.gov	Carson City	NV	89701	775-684-2770	684-2777	339-29
Supreme Court 201 S Carson St Ste 201 *Web:* nvcourts.gov	Carson City	NV	89701	775-684-1600	684-1601	339-29
System of Higher Education 2601 Enterprise Rd *Web:* www.nevada.edu	Reno	NV	89512	775-784-4901	784-1127	339-29
Taxation Dept 1550 E College Pkwy Ste 115 *TF:* 866-962-3707 ■ *Web:* tax.nv.gov	Carson City	NV	89706	775-684-2000	684-2020	339-29
Transportation Dept 1263 S Stewart St *Web:* www.nevadadot.com	Carson City	NV	89712	775-888-7000	888-7115	339-29
Treasurer 101 N Carson St Ste 4 *Web:* nevadatreasurer.gov	Carson City	NV	89701	775-684-5600	684-5781	339-29
Veterans Services Office 5460 Reno Corporate Dr Ste 131 *Web:* veterans.nv.gov	Reno	NV	89511	775-321-4880	688-1656	339-29
Vital Statistics Office 4150 Technology Way Ste 104 *Web:* dpbh.nv.gov	Carson City	NV	89706	775-684-4162	684-4156	339-29
Weights & Measures Bureau 2150 Frazier Ave *Web:* agri.nv.gov	Sparks	NV	89431	775-353-3782	353-3798	339-29
Welfare Div 2533 N Carson St *Web:* dwss.nv.gov	Carson City	NV	89706	775-684-0800	684-0844	339-29
Nevada Appeal 580 Mallory Way *Web:* www.nevadaappeal.com	Carson City	NV	89701	775-882-2111	423-9696	532-2
Nevada Area Vocational School 811 W Hickory St *Web:* www.nevada.k12.mo.us	Nevada	MO	64772	417-448-2000	448-2006	764
Nevada Association of Realtors 760 Margrave Dr Ste 200 *TF:* 800-748-5526 ■ *Web:* www.nvar.org	Reno	NV	89502	775-829-5911	829-5915	656
Nevada Auto Mall Inc 2501 E Austin Blvd *Web:* www.nevadaautomall.net	Nevada	MO	64772	417-667-3385		57
Nevada Automotive Test Ctr 605 Ft Churchill Rd *Web:* www.natc-ht.com	Silver Springs	NV	89429	775-629-2000		60
Nevada Ballet Theatre 1651 Inner Cir *Web:* nevadaballet.org	Las Vegas	NV	89134	702-243-2623	804-0365	573-1

Name / Address	City	State	ZIP	Phone	Fax	Class
Nevada Career Institute 3231 N Decatur Blvd Ste 119 *Web:* www.nevadacareerinstitute.com	Las Vegas	NV	89130	702-893-3300		167-3
Nevada Contract Carpet 6840 W Patrick Ln *Web:* nevadacontractcarpet.abbeycarpet.com	Las Vegas	NV	89118	702-362-3033		362
Nevada County 950 Maidu Ave *Web:* www.mynevadacounty.com	Nevada City	CA	95959	530-265-1218		338
Nevada County Depot & Museum 403 W First St S PO Box 592 *Web:* www.depotmuseum.org	Prescott	AR	71857	870-887-5821		338
Nevada Crystal Premium LLC 6185 S Vly View Blvd *Web:* www.nevadacrystalpremium.com	Las Vegas	NV	89118	702-892-0535		196
Nevada Dental Assn 8863 W Flamingo Rd Ste 102 *TF:* 800-962-6710 ■ *Web:* www.nvda.org	Las Vegas	NV	89147	702-255-4211	255-3302	227
Nevada Disability Advocacy & Law Ctr 2820 W Charleston Blvd Ste 11 *TF:* 888-349-3843 ■ *Web:* www.ndalc.org	Las Vegas	NV	89102	702-257-8150		428
Nevada Donor Network Inc 2055 E Sahara Ave *TF:* 855-683-6667 ■ *Web:* www.nvdonor.org	Las Vegas	NV	89104	702-796-9600	796-4225	545
Nevada Film Office (NFO) 6655 W Sahara Ste C106 *TF:* 877-638-3456 ■ *Web:* www.nevadafilm.com	Las Vegas	NV	89146	702-486-2711	486-2712	514
Nevada Gold & Casinos Inc 133 E Warm Springs Rd Ste 102 *NYSE: UWN* ■ *Web:* nevadagold.com	Las Vegas	NV	89119	702-685-1000	685-1265	132
Nevada Hay Growers Inc (NHGA) 41 S Hwy 339 *Web:* www.nevadahaygrowers.com	Yerington	NV	89447	775-463-2325	463-4320	276
Nevada Heat Treating Inc 12 Industrial Pkwy Unit C *Web:* www.californiabrazing.com	Carson City	NV	89706	775-246-1040		484
Nevada Historical Society (NHS) 1650 N Virginia St *Web:* www.nvdtca.org	Reno	NV	89503	775-688-1190		49-19
Nevada Irrigation District (NID) 1036 W Main St *Web:* nidwater.com	Grass Valley	CA	95945	530-273-6185		787
Nevada Magazine 401 N Carson St Ste 100 *TF:* 855-729-7117 ■ *Web:* www.nevadamagazine.com	Carson City	NV	89701	775-687-0647	687-6159	457-22
Nevada Museum of Art 160 W Liberty St *Web:* www.nevadaart.org	Reno	NV	89501	775-329-3333	329-1541	520
Nevada Office Machines Inc 1885 Vassar St *Web:* www.nevadaofficemachines.com	Reno	NV	89502	775-329-2870		112
Nevada Power Co 6226 W Sahara Ave *NYSE: NVE* ■ *TF:* 800-331-3103 ■ *Web:* www.nvenergy.com	Las Vegas	NV	89146	702-402-5555		787
Nevada Property 1 LLC 3708 Las Vegas Blvd S *TF:* 877-551-7778 ■ *Web:* www.cosmopolitanlasvegas.com	Las Vegas	NV	89109	702-698-7000	314-3980	132
Nevada Public Radio Corp 1289 S Torrey Pines Dr *TF:* 888-258-9895 ■ *Web:* www.knpr.org	Las Vegas	NV	89146	702-258-9895	258-5646	647
Nevada Republican Party 2810 W Charleston Ste 69 *Web:* nevadagop.org	Las Vegas	NV	89102	702-586-2000	258-9186	616-2
Nevada State Bank PO Box 990 *TF:* 800-727-4743 ■ *Web:* www.nsbank.com	Las Vegas	NV	89125	702-383-0009		70
Nevada State Library & Archives (NSLA) 100 N Stewart St *TF:* 800-922-2880 ■ *Web:* www.nsla.libguides.com	Carson City	NV	89701	775-684-3360	684-3311	434-5
Nevada State Medical Assn (NSMA) 3700 Barron Way *Web:* nvdoctors.org	Reno	NV	89511	775-825-6788		474
Nevada State Museum 600 N Carson St *Web:* www.nvculture.org	Carson City	NV	89701	775-687-4810	687-4168	520
Nevada State Railroad Museum 2180 S Carson St *Web:* www.nsrm-friends.org	Carson City	NV	89701	775-687-6953		520
Nevada Veterinary Medical Assn PO Box 34420 *Web:* www.nevadavma.org	Reno	NV	89533	775-324-5344		795
Nevco Inc 301 E Harris Ave *TF:* 800-851-4040 ■ *Web:* www.nevco.com	Greenville	IL	62246	618-664-0360		9
Nevers Industries Inc 14125 21st Ave N *TF:* 800-258-5591 ■ *Web:* www.nevers.com	Minneapolis	MN	55447	763-210-4206		320
Neville Chemical Co 2800 Neville Rd *TF:* 877-704-4200 ■ *Web:* www.nevchem.com	Pittsburgh	PA	15225	412-331-4200	771-0226	605-2
Neville Public Museum of Brown County 210 Museum Pl *Web:* www.nevillepublicmuseum.org	Green Bay	WI	54303	920-448-4460	448-4458	520
Nevis Networks Inc 295 Bernardo Ave *Web:* www.nevisnetworks.com	Mountain View	CA	94043	650-254-2500		693
Nevo Technologies Inc 26 Church St *Web:* www.nevo.com	Cambridge	MA	02138	617-354-6386		180
Nevron Plastics Inc 124 Ballard St *Web:* www.nevronplastics.com	Saugus	MA	01906	781-233-1310	231-3242	480
New & Neville Real Estate Services Inc 900 SW 13th Ave Ste 100 *Web:* newneville.com	Portland	OR	97205	503-241-1222		653
New Accountant Magazine 3525 W Peterson Ave T10 *Web:* www.newaccountantusa.com	Chicago	IL	60659	773-866-9900	866-9881	457-5
New Age Bible and Philosophy Ctr (NABC) 1139 Lincoln Blvd *Web:* newagebible.tripod.com	Santa Monica	CA	90403	310-395-4346		637-2
New Age Distributing Inc 1400 E 28th St *Web:* 7upnewage.com	Little Rock	AR	72206	501-374-5015		297-2
New Age Electronics 420 S 10th Ave *Web:* www.naenet.net	Sterling	CO	80751	970-522-2763		175
New Age Electronics Inc 21950 Arnold Center Rd Ste 100 *TF:* 800-234-0300 ■ *Web:* www.synnexcorp.com	Carson	CA	90810	310-549-0000		174
New Age Fastening Systems Inc 11 Enterprise Ct *TF:* 888-889-3833 ■ *Web:* newagestudwelding.com	Sewell	NJ	08080	856-218-8301	218-8305	480
New Age Industrial Corporation Inc 16788 E Hwy 36 *TF:* 800-255-0104 ■ *Web:* www.newageindustrial.com	Norton	KS	67654	785-877-5121		317
New Age Metal Fabricating Company Inc 26 Daniel Rd *Web:* www.namf.com	Fairfield	NJ	07004	973-227-9107		697
New Age Protection Inc 6551 Loisdale Ct Ste 801 *Web:* www.new-age-inc.com	Springfield	VA	22150	703-924-3057	924-3541	463
New Age Technologies 819 W Main St Ste 200 *Web:* www.newat.com	Louisville	KY	40203	502-412-6681		180
New Albany National Cemetery 1943 Ekin Ave *Web:* www.cem.va.gov	New Albany	IN	47150	502-893-3852	893-6612	136
New Albany-Floyd County Public Library 180 W Spring St *Web:* Www.floydlibrary.org	New Albany	IN	47150	812-944-8464		434-3
New Albin Savings Bank 118 Main St NE PO Box 8 *TF:* 888-689-1898 ■ *Web:* newalbinsavingsbank.com	New Albin	IA	52160	563-544-4214	544-4215	70
New Amber Indian Restaurant 3505 Birney Ave *Web:* www.newamberindian.com	Moosic	PA	18507	570-344-7100		671
New America Foundation 1899 L St NW *Web:* www.newamerica.org	Washington	DC	20036	202-986-2700	986-3696	634
New Amsterdam Entertainment Inc 142 W 44th St PH-2 *Web:* newamsterdamnyc.com	New York	NY	10036	212-997-1930		513
New Angle Media 535 W Thomas Rd *Web:* www.newanglemedia.com	Phoenix	AZ	85013	602-840-5530		195
New Atlantean Press PO Box 9638 *Web:* www.thinktwice.com	Santa Fe	NM	87504	505-983-1856		637-2
New Auto Toy Store, The 929 SW 8th St *Web:* www.thenewautotoystore.com	Pompano Beach	FL	33069	954-379-2886		57
New Balance Athletic Shoe Inc Brighton Landing 20 Guest St *TF:* 800-595-9138 ■ *Web:* www.newbalance.com	Brighton	MA	02135	617-783-4000	787-9355	301
New Beacon Hospice 201 Office Park Dr Ste 100 *Web:* www.newbeacon.org	Birmingham	AL	35223	205-939-8799		793
New Bedford Free Public Library (NBFPL) 613 Pleasant St *Web:* www.newbedford-ma.gov	New Bedford	MA	02740	508-991-6275	991-6368	434-3
New Bedford Harbor Development Commission 52 Fisherman S Wharf PO Box 50899 *Web:* www.portofnewbedford.org	New Bedford	MA	02745	508-961-3000	979-1517	618
New Bedford Management Corp 210 E 23rd St 5th Fl *Web:* www.nbmgmt.com	New York	NY	10010	212-674-6123	532-0248	652
New Bedford Whaling Museum 18 Johnny Cake Hill *TF:* 800-453-5040 ■ *Web:* www.whalingmuseum.org	New Bedford	MA	02740	508-997-0046		520
New Bedford Whaling National Historical Park 33 William St *Web:* www.nps.gov	New Bedford	MA	02740	508-996-4095	984-1250	564
New Beginning College of Cosmetology L L C 421 Martling Rd *Web:* www.nbccosmetology.com	Albertville	AL	35951	256-878-6430		77
New Belgium Brewing Co 500 Linden St *TF:* 888-598-9552 ■ *Web:* www.newbelgium.com	Fort Collins	CO	80524	970-221-0524		102
New Benefits Ltd 14240 Proton Rd *TF:* 800-800-8304 ■ *Web:* newbenefits.com	Dallas	TX	75244	972-404-8192	991-5218	194
New Berlin Plastics Inc 5725 S Westridge Dr *TF:* 800-270-3502 ■ *Web:* nbplastics.com	New Berlin	WI	53151	262-784-3120		596
New Berlin Public Library 15105 Library Ln *Web:* www.newberlinlibrary.org	New Berlin	WI	53151	262-785-4980		434-3
New Bern Area Chamber of Commerce 316 S Front St *Web:* www.newbernchamber.com	New Bern	NC	28560	252-637-3111	637-7541	139
New Bern National Cemetery 1711 National Ave *Web:* www.cem.va.gov	New Bern	NC	28560	252-637-2912	637-7145	136
New Bern-Craven County Public Library 400 Johnson St *Web:* newbern.cpclib.org	New Bern	NC	28560	252-638-7800	638-7817	434-3
New Boston Rtm Inc 19155 Shook Rd *Web:* newbostonrtm.com	New Boston	MI	48164	734-753-9956	753-9221	608
New Braunfels Public Library 700 E Common St *TF:* 800-434-8013 ■ *Web:* www.nbtexas.org	New Braunfels	TX	78130	830-221-4300	608-2151	434-3
New Bridge Medical Ctr 230 E Ridgewood Ave *TF:* 800-730-2762 ■ *Web:* www.newbridgehealth.org	Paramus	NJ	07652	201-967-4000		374-3
New Brighton Area School District 3225 43rd St *Web:* www.nbasd.org	New Brighton	PA	15066	724-843-1795	843-6144	685
New Britain General Campus 100 Grand St *Web:* thocc.org	New Britain	CT	06050	860-224-5011		374-3
New Britain Herald 1 Liberty Sq 3rd Fl PO Box 1090 *Web:* www.newbritainherald.com	New Britain	CT	06050	860-225-4601	225-2611	532-2
New Britain Museum of American Art 56 Lexington St *Web:* www.nbmaa.org	New Britain	CT	06052	860-229-0257	229-3445	520

Name / Address	City	State	ZIP	Phone	Fax	Class
New Britain Stadium 230 John Karbonic Way S Main St New Britain Stadiu Web: www.nbbees.com	New Britain	CT	06051	860-226-2337		713
New Brunswick Museum 1 Market Sq. TF: 888-268-9595 ■ Web: www.nbm-mnb.ca	Saint John	NB	E2L4Z6	506-643-2300	643-6081	520
New Brunswick Sports Hall of Fame 503 Queen St Web: nbsportshalloffame.com	Fredericton	NB	E3B5H1	506-453-3747	459-0481	522
New Brunswick Theological Seminary 35 Seminary Pl Web: www.nbts.edu	New Brunswick	NJ	08901	732-247-5241	249-5412	167-3
New Buck Corp 200 Ethan Allen Dr Web: buckstove.com	Spruce Pine	NC	28777	828-765-6144	765-0462	357
New Canaan Historical Society (NCHS) 13 Oenoke Ridge Rd Web: www.nchistory.org	New Canaan	CT	06840	203-966-1776	972-5917	48-6
New Canaan Library 151 Main St. Web: newcanaanlibrary.org	New Canaan	CT	06840	203-594-5000		434-3
New Canaan Nature Ctr 144 Oenoke Rdg Web: newcanaannature.org	New Canaan	CT	06840	203-966-9577	966-6536	50-5
New Castle Bellco Federal Credit Union 1011 Wilmington Ave Web: newcastlebellco.com	New Castle	PA	16101	724-654-8485	654-3837	219
New Castle Community y 20 W Washington St Web: www.lawcoymca.org	New Castle	PA	16101	724-658-4766		354
New Castle Correctional Facility 1000 Van Nuys Rd Web: www.in.gov	New Castle	IN	47362	765-593-0111		213
New Castle County 87 Read's Way Web: www.nccde.org	New Castle	DE	19720	302-395-5555		338
New Castle County Detention Ctr 963 Centre Rd. TF: 800-969-4357 ■ Web: kids.delaware.gov	Wilmington	DE	19805	302-633-3100	995-8393	412
New Castle Historical Society (NCHS) Horace Greeley House 100 King St. Web: www.newcastlehs.org	Chappaqua	NY	10514	914-238-4666	238-1296	48-13
New Castle Hotels & Resorts 2 Corporate Dr Web: newcastlehotels.com	Shelton	CT	06484	203-925-8370		379
New Castle News PO Box 60 Web: www.ncnewsonline.com	New Castle	PA	16103	724-654-6651	654-5976	532-2
New Castle-Henry County Public Library (NCHC) 376 S 15th St Web: www.nchcpl.org	New Castle	IN	47362	765-529-0362		434-3
New Center Community Mental Health Services 2051 W Grand Blvd Web: www.newcentercmhs.org	Detroit	MI	48208	313-961-3200		353
New Century Bank 700 W Cumberland St Web: www.selectbank.com	Dunn	NC	28334	910-892-7080		70
New Century Capital Partners Inc 1510 11th St Ste 203 Web: www.newcenturycap.com	Santa Monica	CA	90401	310-451-9073		690
New Century Education Foundation PO Box 43052 TF: 866-326-1133 ■ Web: www.newcenturyeducation.org	Upper Montclair	NJ	07043	866-326-1133		178-11
New Century Federal Credit Union 291 Springfield Ave Web: newcenturyfcu.org	Joliet	IL	60435	815-741-1847		219
New Century FS Inc (NCFS) 1017 Ogan Ave TF: 888-488-3737 ■ Web: www.newcenturyfs.com	Grinnell	IA	50112	641-236-3117	236-5363	274
New Century Pharmaceuticals Inc 895 Martin Rd. Web: www.newcenturypharm.com	Huntsville	AL	35824	256-461-0024		231
New Century Press Inc 310 First Ave. TF: 800-621-0801 ■ Web: www.ncppub.com	Rock Rapids	IA	51246	712-472-2525		532-3
New Choices Inc 2501 18th St Ste 201 TF: 888-355-5502 ■ Web: www.newchoicesinc.com	Bettendorf	IA	52722	563-355-5502		363
New City Communications 770 N Halsted St Ste 303 Web: newcityfilm.com	Chicago	IL	60642	312-243-8786		532-5
New City Inc 21 SE 1st Ave 4th Fl Web: www.newcityinc.com	Miami	FL	33131	305-371-4188	377-3118	411
New City Media Inc 301 S Main St Ste 207 Web: www.insidenewcity.com	Blacksburg	VA	24060	540-552-1320		396
New City Press (NCP) 202 Comforter Blvd *Fax Area Code: 416 ■ TF: 877-756-7374 ■ Web: www.newcitypress.com	Hyde Park	NY	12538	845-229-0335	291-1378*	637-2
New College of Florida 5800 Bay Shore Rd Web: www.ncf.edu	Sarasota	FL	34243	941-487-5000	487-5010	166
New Concept Technology 320 Busser Rd PO Box 0297 Web: www.newconcepttech.com	Emigsville	PA	17318	717-741-0840		602
New Conservatory Theatre Ctr 25 Van Ness Ave Web: www.nctcsf.org	San Francisco	CA	94102	415-861-4914	861-6988	572
New Constructs LLC 5110 Maryland Way Ste 350 Web: www.newconstructs.com	Brentwood	TN	37027	615-377-0443		401
NEW Co-opeartive Inc 2626 First Ave S TF: 800-362-2233 ■ Web: www.newcoop.com	Fort Dodge	IA	50501	515-955-2040		275
New Country 99.1 600 Main St. *Fax Area Code: 970 ■ TF: 800-500-2599 ■ Web: k99.com	Windsor	CO	80550	800-500-2599	686-7491*	645
New Country Motor Car Group 3002 Rt 50 Web: www.newcountry.com	Saratoga Springs	NY	12866	518-584-7700		57
New Covenant Fellowship Church 18901 Waring Stn Rd Web: www.fellowshipusa.com	Germantown	MD	20874	301-444-3100		48-20
New Current Water & Land LLC 652 W Cromwell Ave Ste 101 Web: newcurrentwater.com	Fresno	CA	93711	559-449-1111		653
New Data Systems Inc 19 Claremont Ln Web: www.catstoday.com	Suffern	NY	10901	845-357-7744		178-1
New Day Associates PO Box 6412 Web: www.lindennewday.com	Monroe Township	NJ	08831	609-655-3667		196
New Day Marketing 923 Olive St Web: newdaymarketing.com	Santa Barbara	CA	93101	805-965-7833		7
New Dimension Controls Inc (NDC) 80 Sand Island Access Rd Ste 200 Web: www.ndchawaii.com	Honolulu	HI	96819	808-847-7992	847-6992	112
New Dimensions Precision Machining Inc 6614 S Union Rd Web: www.newdims.com	Union	IL	60180	815-923-8300		454
New Dimensions Publishing 11248 N 11th St TF: 800-736-7367 ■ Web: www.thedream.com	Phoenix	AZ	85020	602-861-2631	944-1235	637-10
New Dimensions Radio Broadcasting Network PO Box 7847 Web: newdimensions.org	Santa Rosa	CA	95407	707-468-5215		646
New Dimensions Research Corp 260 Spagnoli Rd TF: 800-637-8870 ■ Web: www.ndrc.com	Melville	NY	11747	631-694-1356	694-6097	233
New Directions Behavioral Health LLC 6100 Sprint Pkwy Ste 200 *Fax Area Code: 913 ■ TF: 800-624-5544 ■ Web: www.ndbh.com	Overland Park	KS	66211	800-624-5544	982-8401*	462
New Directions Inc 30800 Chagrin Blvd Web: Www.newdirections.co	Cleveland	OH	44124	216-591-0324	591-1243	726
New Dominion Insurance Agency Inc 4320 Fulton Dr NW TF: 888-493-8655 ■ Web: newdominiongroup.com	Canton	OH	44718	888-493-8655		390
New Dominion LLC 1307 S Boulder Ave Ste 400 Web: www.newdominion.net	Tulsa	OK	74119	918-587-6242		536
New Echota State Historic Site 1211 Chatsworth Hwy NE Web: gastateparks.org	Calhoun	GA	30701	706-624-1321		565
New Edge Networks 3000 Columbia House Blvd Ste 106 TF: 877-725-3343 ■ Web: www.newedgenetworks.com	Vancouver	WA	98661	360-693-9009		398
New Energy Distributing Inc 601 6th Ave NW TF: 800-218-4947 ■ Web: www.woodstoves-fireplaces.com	Dyersville	IA	52040	800-218-4947		612
New Engel Publishing PO Box 356 Web: www.newengelpublishing.com	Export	PA	15632	724-327-7379	327-8878	637-2
New England Airlines Inc 56 Airport Rd TF: 800-243-2460 ■ Web: blockislandsairline.com	Westerly	RI	02891	401-596-2460		25
New England Aquarium 1 Central Wharf Web: www.neaq.org	Boston	MA	02110	617-973-5200		40
New England Association of Schools & Colleges (NEASC) 209 Burlington Rd Web: www.neasc.org	Bedford	MA	01730	781-271-0022	541-5400	48-1
New England Baptist Hospital 125 Parker Hill Ave TF: 855-370-6324 ■ Web: www.nebh.org	Boston	MA	02120	617-754-5000	734-7804	374-3
New England Bible College & Grace Evangelical Seminary 879 Sawyer St. Web: www.nebc.edu	South Portland	ME	04106	207-947-1665		166
New England Board of Higher Education (NEBHE) 45 Temple Pl Web: www.nebhe.org	Boston	MA	02111	617-357-9620	338-1577	423
New England Book Service Inc 7000 Vt Rte 17 W TF: 800-356-5772 ■ Web: www.nebooks.com	Addison	VT	05491	802-759-3000	759-3220	96
New England Cable News (NECN) 160 Wells Ave Web: www.necn.com	Newton	MA	02459	617-630-5000		740
New England Capital Partners 1 Gateway Ctr Ste 405 Web: www.necapitalpartners.com	Newton	MA	02458	617-964-7300	964-7301	690
New England Coffee Co 100 Charles St TF: 800-225-3537 ■ Web: www.newenglandcoffee.com	Malden	MA	02148	800-225-3537		296-7
New England College 98 Bridge St TF: 800-521-7642 ■ Web: www.nec.edu	Henniker	NH	03242	603-428-2223		166
New England College of Business & Finance 10 High St Ste 204 Web: www.necb.edu	Boston	MA	02110	617-951-2350	951-2533	800
New England Computer Services Inc 322 E Main St 3rd Fl *Fax Area Code: 203 ■ TF: 800-766-6327 ■ Web: necs.com	Branford	CT	06405	475-221-8200	208-0889*	178-10
New England Conservatory 290 Huntington Ave TF: 800-841-8371 ■ Web: necmusic.edu	Boston	MA	02115	617-585-1100		166
New England Construction Company Inc 293 Bourne Ave Web: www.neconstruction.com	Rumford	RI	02916	401-434-0112		261
New England Council Inc 98 N Washington St Ste 201 Web: newenglandcouncil.com	Boston	MA	02114	617-723-4009	723-3943	140
New England Decks & Floors Inc 13 Cedar St Web: nedecksandfloors.com	Milford	MA	01757	508-473-4641		290
New England Development 1 Wells Ave Web: www.nedevelopment.com	Newton	MA	02459	617-965-8700	243-7085	655
New England Die Cutting Inc 96 Milk St Web: www.nedc.com	Methuen	MA	01844	978-686-6332	374-9912	326
New England Direct Marketing Association Inc (NEDMA) 396 Washington St Ste 387 Web: www.nedma.com	Wellesley	MA	02481	781-237-1366		138
New England Donor Services 60 First Ave. TF: 800-446-6362 ■ Web: neds.org	Waltham	MA	02451	800-446-6362		545
New England Employee Benefits Co 15 Chenell Dr Web: www.neebco.com	Concord	NH	03301	603-228-1133	225-1960	390

Name / Address	City	State	ZIP	Phone	Fax	Class
New England Federal Credit Union PO Box 527 — *TF:* 800-400-8790 ■ *Web:* www.nefcu.com	Williston	VT	05495	802-879-8790		219
New England Foam Products LLC 760 Windsor St — *Web:* www.newenglandfoam.com	Hartford	CT	06120	860-524-0121	522-5830	676
New England Garage Door 15 Campanelli Cir — *TF:* 800-676-7734 ■ *Web:* www.wayne-dalton.com	Canton	MA	02021	781-821-2737		499
New England Historic Genealogical Society 99 -101 Newbury St — *TF:* 888-296-3447 ■ *Web:* www.americanancestors.org	Boston	MA	02116	888-296-3447		434-3
New England Homes 270 Ocean Rd — *TF:* 800-800-8831 ■ *Web:* www.newenglandhomes.net	Greenland	NH	03840	603-436-8830	431-8540	106
New England Industrial Truck Inc 195 Wildwood Ave — *Web:* www.neit.com	Woburn	MA	01801	781-935-9105		385
New England Institute of Technology 2500 Post Rd — *TF:* 800-736-7744 ■ *Web:* www.neit.edu	Warwick	RI	02886	401-467-7744		800
New England Journal of Medicine 10 Shattuck St — *TF:* 800-843-6356 ■ *Web:* www.nejm.org	Boston	MA	02115	617-734-9800	739-9864	457-16
New England Keyboard Inc 1 Princeton Rd — *Web:* www.newenglandkeyboard.com	Fitchburg	MA	01420	978-345-8332	345-4329	56
New England Life Flight Inc Robins St Hangar 1727 Hanscom Air Force Base — *TF:* 800-233-8998 ■ *Web:* www.bostonmedflight.org	Bedford	MA	01730	781-863-2213	863-2791	13
New England Machinery Inc 2820 62nd Ave E — *Web:* www.neminc.com	Bradenton	FL	34203	941-755-5550	751-6281	547
New England Medical Insurance Agency LLC 11 Summer St — *TF:* 800-443-4977 ■ *Web:* Www.nemia.com	Chelmsford	MA	01824	978-256-7400	256-6580	390
New England Miniature Ball Corp 163 Greenwood Rd W PO Box 585 — *Web:* nemb.com	Norfolk	CT	06058	860-542-5543	542-5058	485
New England Mobile Book Fair 241 Needham St — *Web:* www.nebookfair.com	Newton	MA	02464	617-527-5817		95
New England Natural Bakers 74 Fairview St E — *TF:* 800-910-2884 ■ *Web:* www.newenglandnaturalbakers.com	Greenfield	MA	01301	413-772-2239	772-2936	296-4
New England Newspaper & Press Assn (NENPA) Barletta Hall 370 Common St 3rd Fl Ste 319 — *Web:* www.nenpa.com	Dedham	MA	02026	718-320-8050	320-8055	139
New England Paper Tube Co 200 Conant St — *Web:* new-england-paper-tube-co.business.site	Pawtucket	RI	02860	401-725-2610		125
New England Peace Pagoda, The 100 Cave Hill Rd — *Web:* newenglandpeacepagoda.org	Leverett	MA	01054	413-367-2202		50-1
New England Press Inc PO Box 575 — *Web:* www.nepressvt.com	Shelburne	VT	05482	802-863-2520	863-1510	637-2
New England Propane Company Inc 162 Grassy Plain St — *Web:* newenglandpropane.com	Bethel	CT	06801	203-792-7654		316
New England Public Radio 1525 Main St — *Web:* www.nepm.org	Springfield	MA	01103	413-735-6600		645
New England Rehabilitation Hospital of Portland 335 Brighton Ave — *Web:* nerhp.com	Portland	ME	04102	207-775-4000	662-8446	374-6
New England Revolution Gillette Stadium 1 Patriot Pl — *TF:* 877-438-7387 ■ *Web:* www.revolutionsoccer.net	Foxborough	MA	02035	877-438-7387		717
New England School of English Inc, The 36 John F Kennedy St — *Web:* nese.edu	Cambridge	MA	02138	617-864-7170	864-7282	423
New England School of Law 154 Stuart St — *Web:* www.nesl.edu	Boston	MA	02116	617-451-0010		167-1
New England Science Fiction Association Inc (NESFA) PO Box 809 — *Web:* www.nesfa.org	Framingham	MA	01701	617-625-2311	776-3243	637-2
New England Security Inc 10 Industrial Dr — *Web:* newenglandsecurityinc.com	Westerly	RI	02891	401-596-0660		692
New England Sports Network (NESN) 480 Arsenal St Bldg 1 — *Web:* nesn.com	Watertown	MA	02472	617-536-9233	536-7814	740
New England Systems & Software Inc 33 Holly Ln — *Web:* www.nessnetworks.com	Lake George	NY	12845	518-377-4057		177
New England Tropical Conservatory (NETC) 413 US Rt 7S PO Box 4715 — *Web:* oneworldconservationcenter.org	Bennington	VT	05201	802-447-7419		97
New England Ultimate Finishing 709 Main St — *TF:* 800-543-5665 ■ *Web:* www.nefinishing.com	Holyoke	MA	01040	800-543-5665		560
New England Union Company Inc 107 Hay St — *TF:* 800-843-7501 ■ *Web:* www.newenglandunion.com	West Warwick	RI	02893	401-821-0800	821-9731	595
New England Wood Pellet LLC 141 Old Sharon Rd — *TF:* 877-981-9663 ■ *Web:* www.pelletheat.com	Jaffrey	NH	03452	877-981-9663		819
New England Woodcraft Inc 481 North St PO Box 165 — *Web:* newenglandwoodcraft.com	Forest Dale	VT	05745	802-247-8211	247-8042	319-2
New Enterprise Associates 2855 Sand Hill Rd — *Web:* www.nea.com	Menlo Park	CA	94025	650-854-9499	854-9397	792
New Enterprise Rural Electric Co-opeartive Inc 3596 Brumbaugh Rd — *TF:* 800-270-3177 ■ *Web:* www.newenterpriserec.com	New Enterprise	PA	16664	814-766-3221	766-3319	245
New Enterprise Stone & Lime Company Inc 3912 Brumbaugh Rd — **Fax Area Code:* 610 ■ *Web:* www.nesl.com	New Enterprise	PA	16664	814-766-2211	867-1886*	503-5
New Era Building Systems Inc 451 Southern Ave — *Web:* www.neweramodulars.com	Strattanville	PA	16258	814-764-5581		505
New Era Cap Company Inc 160 Delaware Ave — *TF:* 877-215-2748 ■ *Web:* www.neweracap.com	Buffalo	NY	14202	716-604-9000		155-9
New Era Factory Outlet 63 Orchard St — *TF:* 800-875-4959 ■ *Web:* www.newdresssuits.com	New York	NY	10002	800-875-4959		459
New Era Ohio LLC 520 W Mulberry St — *Web:* www.neweraohio.com	Bryan	OH	43506	419-633-1616	633-1232	454
New Era Optical Co 5575 N Lynch Ave — *Web:* www.neweraopt.com	Chicago	IL	60630	773-725-9600		237
New Era Portfolio 2101 E St Elmo Rd Ste 110 — *TF:* 877-321-3200 ■ *Web:* www.newerahd.com	Austin	TX	78744	512-928-3200		627
New Era Restaurant 10 Massillon Rd — *Web:* www.thenewerarestaurant.com	Akron	OH	44312	330-784-0087		671
New Europe Books 54 Arnold St — *Web:* www.neweuropebooks.com	Williamstown	MA	01267	413-685-1972		637-2
New Fairfield Free Public Library 2 Brush Hill Rd — *TF:* 877-227-7487 ■ *Web:* www.newfairfieldlibrary.org	New Fairfield	CT	06812	203-312-5679	312-5685	434-3
New Forums Press Inc (NFP) 1018 S Lewis St — *TF:* 800-606-3766 ■ *Web:* www.newforums.com	Stillwater	OK	74074	405-372-6158	377-2237	637-2
New Frontier Bank 1771 Zumbehl Rd — *Web:* www.newfb.com	Saint Charles	MO	63303	636-940-8740	940-0451	70
New Generation Mechanical 1133 Empire Central Dr — *Web:* www.newgenm.com	Dallas	TX	75247	972-830-9900	830-9993	610
New Generation Research Inc 225 Friend St Ste 801 — *TF:* 800-468-3810 ■ *Web:* www.turnarounds.com	Boston	MA	02114	617-573-9550	573-9554	637-2
New Generation Sushi 493 Bloor St W — *Web:* www.newgenerationsushi.ca	Toronto	ON	M5S1Y2	416-963-8861		671
New Glarus Woods State Park (NGWSP) W5446 County Hwy NN — *Web:* dnr.wi.gov	New Glarus	WI	53574	608-527-2335		565
New Global Publishing 2310 SE Bordeaux Ct — *TF:* 877-456-8422 ■ *Web:* www.newglobalpublishing.com	Port Saint Lucie	FL	34952	772-335-1271		637-2
New Gold Inc 666 Burrard St Ste 3110 — *NYSE:* NGD ■ *Web:* www.newgold.com	Vancouver	BC	V6C2X8	604-696-4100		502
New Hampshire						
Accountancy Board 244 N Main St Ste 1 — *Web:* www.oplc.nh.gov	Concord	NH	03301	603-271-2219		339-30
Agriculture Markets & Food Dept PO Box 2042 — *Web:* www.agriculture.nh.gov	Concord	NH	03302	603-271-3551	271-1109	339-30
Arts Council 19 Pillsbury St 1st Fl — *Web:* www.nh.gov	Concord	NH	03301	603-271-2789	271-3584	339-30
Attorney General 33 Capitol St — *Web:* www.nh.gov	Concord	NH	03301	603-271-3658		339-30
Banking Dept 95 Pleasant St — *TF:* 800-437-5991 ■ *Web:* www.nh.gov	Concord	NH	03301	603-271-3561	271-1090	339-30
Board of Medicine 121 S Fruit St — *Web:* www.oplc.nh.gov	Concord	NH	03301	603-271-2152	271-6702	339-30
Bureau of Elderly & Adult Services (BEAS) 129 Pleasant St — *Web:* www.dhhs.nh.gov	Concord	NH	03301	603-271-9203	271-4643	339-30
Chief Medical Examiner 246 Pleasant St Ste 218 — *Web:* www.doj.nh.gov	Concord	NH	03301	603-271-1235	271-6308	339-30
Child Support Services 129 Pleasant St — *TF:* 800-852-3345 ■ *Web:* www.dhhs.nh.gov	Concord	NH	03301	603-271-4427	271-4787	339-30
Children Youth & Families Div 129 Pleasant St 4th Fl — *Web:* www.dhhs.nh.gov	Concord	NH	03301	603-271-4451	271-4729	339-30
Consumer Protection & Antitrust Bureau 33 Capitol St — *Web:* www.doj.nh.gov	Concord	NH	03301	603-271-3643	271-2110	339-30
Corrections Dept 105 Pleasant St PO Box 1806 — *Web:* www.nh.gov	Concord	NH	03302	603-271-5600	271-5643	339-30
Division of Vital Records Administration 71 S Fruit St — *Web:* www.sos.nh.gov	Concord	NH	03301	603-271-4650	271-3447	339-30
Education Dept 101 Pleasant St — *Web:* www.education.nh.gov	Concord	NH	03301	603-271-3494	271-1953	339-30
Emergency Management Office 33 Hazen Dr — *Web:* www.nh.gov	Concord	NH	03305	603-271-2231	223-3609	339-30
Employment Security 32 S Main St — *TF:* 800-852-3400 ■ *Web:* www.nh.gov	Concord	NH	03301	603-224-3311	228-4145	259
Environmental Services Dept 29 Hazen Dr PO Box 95 — *TF:* 866-429-9278 ■ *Web:* www.des.nh.gov	Concord	NH	03301	603-271-3503		339-30
Fish & Game Dept 11 Hazen Dr — *Web:* www.wildlife.state.nh.us	Concord	NH	03301	603-271-3421	271-5829	339-30
General Court 244 N Main St Ste 1 — *Web:* gencourt.state.nh.us	Concord	NH	03301	603-271-2154		339-30
Historical Resources Div 19 Pillsbury St 2nd Fl — *Web:* www.nh.gov	Concord	NH	03301	603-271-3483	271-3433	339-30
Housing Finance Authority 32 Constitution Dr — *TF:* 800-439-7247 ■ *Web:* www.nhhfa.org	Bedford	NH	03110	603-472-8623	472-8729	339-30
Insurance Dept 21 S Fruit St Ste 14 — *Web:* www.nh.gov	Concord	NH	03301	603-271-2261	271-1406	339-30
Joint Board of Licensure & Certification 107 N Main St State House Rm 207 — *Web:* www.nh.gov	Concord	NH	03301	603-271-1463		339-30
Lottery Commission 14 Integra Dr — *TF:* 800-852-3324 ■ *Web:* www.nhlottery.com	Concord	NH	03301	603-271-3391	271-1160	452

				Phone	Fax	Class
Motor Vehicles Div 23 Hazen Dr	Concord	NH	03305	603-227-4000		339-30
Web: www.nh.gov						
Public Utilities Commission						
21 S Fruit St Ste 10	Concord	NH	03301	603-271-2431	271-3878	339-30
TF: 800-852-3793 ■ *Web:* www.puc.state.nh.us						
Resources & Economic Development Dept						
PO Box 1856	Concord	NH	03302	603-271-2411	271-2629	339-30
Web: www.dred.state.nh.us						
Revenue Administration Dept						
109 Pleasant St	Concord	NH	03301	603-230-5000	230-5945	339-30
Web: www.revenue.nh.gov						
Secretary of State						
107 N Main St Ste 204	Concord	NH	03301	603-271-3242	271-6316	339-30
Web: sos.nh.gov						
State Government Information						
64 South St	Concord	NH	03301	603-271-1110		339-30
Web: www.nh.gov						
State Office of Veterans Services						
275 Chestnut St Rm 517	Manchester	NH	03101	603-624-9230	624-9236	339-30
Web: www.nh.gov						
State Police Div 33 Hazen Dr	Concord	NH	03305	603-223-8813		339-30
Web: www.nh.gov						
Supreme Court 1 Charles Doe Dr	Concord	NH	03301	603-271-2646		339-30
Web: www.courts.state.nh.us						
Transportation Dept PO Box 483	Concord	NH	03302	603-271-3734	271-3914	339-30
Web: www.nh.gov						
Treasury Dept 25 Capitol St Rm 121	Concord	NH	03301	603-271-2621	271-3922	339-30
TF: 800-791-0920 ■ *Web:* www.nh.gov						
Victims' Assistance Commission						
33 Capitol St	Concord	NH	03301	603-271-1284	223-6291	339-30
TF: 800-300-4500 ■ *Web:* www.nh.gov						
Vocational Rehabilitation Office						
21 S Fruit St Ste 20	Concord	NH	03301	603-271-3471	271-7095	339-30
TF: 800-299-1647 ■ *Web:* www.education.nh.gov						
Weights & Measures Bureau PO Box 2042	Concord	NH	03302	603-271-3685	271-1109	339-30
Web: www.agriculture.nh.gov						
New Hampshire Association of Realtors						
115A Airport Rd	Concord	NH	03301	603-225-5549	228-0385	656
Web: www.nhar.org						
New Hampshire Ball Bearings Inc						
175 Jaffrey Rd	Peterborough	NH	03458	603-924-3311	924-4419	75
Web: nhbb.com						
New Hampshire Bar Assn						
2 Pillsbury St Ste 300	Concord	NH	03301	603-224-6942	224-2910	72
Web: www.nhbar.org						
New Hampshire Bindery Inc 81 Dow Rd	Bow	NH	03304	603-224-0441	225-4552	92
Web: www.nhbindery.com						
New Hampshire Campground Owners Assn (NEHACA)						
PO Box 1074	Epsom	NH	03234	603-736-5540		637-10
Web: www.ucampnh.com						
New Hampshire Democratic Party						
105 N State St	Concord	NH	03301	603-225-6899		616-1
Web: nhdp.org						
New Hampshire Dental Society						
23 S State St	Concord	NH	03301	603-225-5961	226-4880	227
TF: 800-244-5961 ■ *Web:* www.nhds.org						
New Hampshire Distributors Inc						
65 Regional Dr	Concord	NH	03301	603-224-9991		81-1
TF: 800-519-9770 ■ *Web:* nhdist.com						
New Hampshire Educator Magazine						
9 S Spring St	Concord	NH	03301	603-224-7751	224-2648	457-8
TF: 866-556-3264 ■ *Web:* neanh.org						
New Hampshire Electric Co-op						
579 Tenney Mtn Hwy	Plymouth	NH	03264	603-536-1800	536-8682	245
TF: 800-698-2007 ■ *Web:* www.nhec.com						
New Hampshire Film Festival						
28 Chestnut St	Portsmouth	NH	03801	603-436-2400		282
Web: nhfilmfestival.com						
New Hampshire Historical Society						
30 Park St	Concord	NH	03301	603-228-6688		520
Web: www.nhhistory.org						
New Hampshire Hospital 36 Clinton St	Concord	NH	03301	603-271-5200	271-5395	374-5
TF: 800-735-2964 ■ *Web:* www.dhhs.nh.gov						
New Hampshire Institute of Art						
148 Concord St	Manchester	NH	03104	603-623-0313		520
TF: 866-241-4918 ■ *Web:* www.nhia.edu						
New Hampshire Medical Society						
7 N State St	Concord	NH	03301	800-564-1909	226-2432*	474
**Fax Area Code:* 603 ■ *TF:* 800-564-1909 ■ *Web:* www.nhms.org						
New Hampshire Plastics Inc						
1 Bouchard St	Manchester	NH	03103	800-258-3036	622-4888*	600
**Fax Area Code:* 603 ■ *TF:* 800-258-3036 ■ *Web:* www.nhplastics.com						
New Hampshire Public Broadcasting						
268 Mast Rd	Durham	NH	03824	603-868-1100		647
Web: www.nhpbs.org						
New Hampshire Public Interest Research Group (NHPIRG)						
75 S Main St Unit 7- 626	Concord	NH	03301	603-637-4758		633
Web: nhpirg.org						
New Hampshire Republican State Committee						
10 Water St	Concord	NH	03301	603-225-9341	225-7498	616-2
Web: www.nh.gop						
New Hampshire Society for Technology in Education (NHSTE)						
46 Donovan St Ste 3	Concord	NH	03301	866-753-4479		48-13
TF: 866-753-4479 ■ *Web:* www.nhste.org						
New Hampshire State Library						
20 Park St	Concord	NH	03301	603-271-2144	271-2205	434-5
TF: 800-639-5290 ■ *Web:* www.nh.gov						
New Hampshire State Parks						
Echo Lake State Park						
68 Echo Lake Rd	North Conway	NH	03860	603-356-2672		565
Web: www.nhstateparks.org						
New Hampshire State Port Authority						
555 Market St	Portsmouth	NH	03801	603-436-8500		618
Web: www.portsmouthnh.com						
New Hampshire State Prison						
281 N State St PO Box 14	Concord	NH	03302	603-271-1801		213
Web: www.nh.gov						
New Hampshire Veterans Home						
139 Winter St	Tilton	NH	03276	603-527-4400	527-4402	793
Web: www.nh.gov						
New Hampton Nursing & Rehabilitation Ctr						
703 S Fourth Ave	New Hampton	IA	50659	641-394-4153		450
Web: www.nhnrc.com						
New Hampton School 70 Main St	New Hampton	NH	03256	603-677-3400		622
Web: www.newhampton.org						
New Hanover Correctional Ctr						
330 Division Dr	Wilmington	NC	28401	910-251-2666	251-2670	213
Web: www.ncdps.gov						
New Hanover County Public Library						
201 Chestnut St	Wilmington	NC	28401	910-798-6301	798-6312	434-3
Web: library.nhcgov.com						
New Haven Ballet 70 Audubon St	New Haven	CT	06510	203-782-9038	785-0088	573-1
Web: newhavenballet.org						
New Haven Body Inc (NHB)						
89 Stoddard Ave	North Haven	CT	06473	203-248-6388	281-0060	61
Web: www.newhavenbody.com						
New Haven City Hall 165 Church St	New Haven	CT	06510	203-946-8200	946-7683	337
Web: www.newhavenct.gov						
New Haven Correctional Ctr						
245 Whalley Ave	New Haven	CT	06511	203-974-4111	974-4167	213
Web: www.portal.ct.gov						
New Haven Free Public Library						
133 Elm St	New Haven	CT	06510	203-946-8130	946-8140	434-3
Web: www.newhavenct.gov						
New Haven Hotel 229 George St	New Haven	CT	06510	203-498-3100	498-0911	379
TF: 800-644-6835 ■ *Web:* www.newhavenhotel.com						
New Haven Legal Assistance Association Inc						
426 State St	New Haven	CT	06510	203-946-4811		428
Web: nhlegal.org						
New Haven Masonry and Building						
355 James St	New Haven	CT	06513	203-562-6657		191-1
Web: www.newhavenmasonrysupplies.com						
New Haven Premier Suites Hotel						
3 Long Wharf Dr	New Haven	CT	06511	203-777-5337	777-2808	379
Web: www.newhavenvillagesuites.com						
New Haven Register 40 Sargent Dr	New Haven	CT	06511	203-789-5200		532-2
TF: 888-969-0949 ■ *Web:* www.nhregister.com						
New Haven Symphony Orchestra						
4 Hamilton St	New Haven	CT	06511	203-865-0831	865-0845	573-3
Web: newhavensymphony.org						
New Haven Terminal Inc						
100 Waterfront St	New Haven	CT	06512	203-468-0805	469-6374	465
Web: www.nhterminal.com						
New Haven Unified School District						
34200 Alvarado Niles Rd	Union City	CA	94587	510-471-1100		685
Web: www.mynhusd.org						
New Heights Restaurant						
2317 Calvert St NW	Washington	DC	20008	202-234-4110		671
Web: www.newheightsrestaurant.com						
New High Glass Inc 12713 SW 125th Ave	Miami	FL	33186	305-232-0840		331
Web: www.newhigh.com						
New Holland Church Furniture						
313 Prospect St PO Box 217	New Holland	PA	17557	800-648-9663	354-2481*	319-3
**Fax Area Code:* 717 ■ *TF:* 800-648-9663 ■ *Web:* www.newhollandwood.com						
New Holland Engineering						
43 E Front St	New Holland	OH	43145	740-495-5200		261
TF: 800-734-8155 ■ *Web:* gutterhangers.net						
New Home Trends Inc 4314 148th St SE	Bothell	WA	98012	425-742-8040		466
Web: www.newhometrends.com						
New Hope Housing Inc						
8407-E Richmond Hwy	Alexandria	VA	22309	703-799-2293		48-20
Web: www.newhopehousing.org						
New Hope Publishers						
100 Missionary Ridge	Birmingham	AL	35242	866 266-8399		637-9
TF: 866-266-8399 ■ *Web:* www.newhopepublishers.com						
New Horizon Kids Quest Inc						
3405 Annapolis Ln N Ste 100	Plymouth	MN	55447	800-941-1007	383-6101*	148
**Fax Area Code:* 763 ■ *TF:* 800-941-1007 ■ *Web:* www.kidsquest.com						
New Horizon Publishers						
8325 Broadway Ste 202, Box 227	Pearland	TX	77584	281-489-9640	489-5044	637-2
Web: www.newhorizonpublishers.com						
New Horizons Baking Company Inc						
211 Woodlawn Ave	Norwalk	OH	44857	419-663-6432		68
Web: www.genesisbaking.com						
New Horizons Computer Learning Centers Inc						
100 Four Falls Corporate Ctr						
Ste 408	West Conshohocken	PA	19428	888-236-3625		764
TF: 888-236-3625 ■ *Web:* www.newhorizons.com						
New Horizons Computer Learning Centers of Albuquerque Inc						
4775 Indian School Rd NE	Albuquerque	NM	87110	505-830-7100		167-3
Web: www.nhalbuquerque.com						
New Horizons Diagnostics Corp						
1450 S Rolling Rd	Baltimore	MD	21227	443-543-5755	543-5749	231
Web: www.nhdiag.com						
New Horizons Picture Corp						
11600 San Vicente Blvd	Los Angeles	CA	90049	310-820-6733		514
Web: www.newhorizonspictures.com						
New Horizons RV Corp						
2401 Lacy Dr	Junction City	KS	66441	785-238-7575		120
TF: 800-235-3140 ■ *Web:* www.horizonsrv.com						
New ICM 220 Sam Bishkin	El Campo	TX	77437	979-578-0543	578-0503	155-4
TF: 800-987-9008 ■ *Web:* newicm.com						
New Idea Engineering Inc						
2784 Homestead Rd Ste 173	Santa Clara	CA	95051	408-446-3460		194
Web: www.ideaeng.com						
New Incite						
1197 E Los Angeles Ave Ste 302	Simi Valley	CA	93065	818-347-4248		194
Web: www.newincite.com						
New Issues Poetry & Prose						
W Michigan University 1903 W Michigan Ave	Kalamazoo	MI	49008	269-387-8185		637-10
Web: newissuespress.com						
New Jersey						
Administrative Office of the Courts						
25 Market St PO Box 37	Trenton	NJ	08625	609-984-0275	984-6968	339-31
Web: Www.njcourts.gov						

Name / Address	City	State	ZIP	Phone	Fax	Class
Agriculture Dept PO Box 330 *Web:* www.state.nj.us	Trenton	NJ	08625	609-671-6400	292-3978	339-31
Arts Council PO Box 307 *Web:* www.nj.gov	Trenton	NJ	08625	609-292-6130		339-31
Attorney General 25 Market St 8th Fl *Web:* www.state.nj.us	Trenton	NJ	08625	609-292-4925	292-3508	339-31
Banking & Insurance Dept 20 W State St PO Box 325 *TF:* 800-446-7467 ■ *Web:* www.state.nj.us	Trenton	NJ	08625	609-292-7272	984-5273	339-31
Bill Status State House Annex PO Box 068 *TF:* 800-792-8630 ■ *Web:* www.njleg.state.nj.us	Trenton	NJ	08625	609-292-4840		433
Board of Public Utilities 44 S Clinton Ave *TF:* 800-624-0241 ■ *Web:* www.state.nj.us	Newark	NJ	07102	800-624-0241		339-31
Child Support Office 175 S Broad St PO Box 8068 *TF:* 877-655-4371 ■ *Web:* www.njchildsupport.org	Trenton	NJ	08650	877-655-4371		339-31
Commerce Economic Growth & Tourism Commission 20 W State St PO Box 820 *Web:* www.state.nj.us	Trenton	NJ	08625	609-777-0885		339-31
Consumer Affairs Div 124 Halsey St *TF:* 800-242-5846 ■ *Web:* www.njconsumeraffairs.gov	Newark	NJ	07102	973-504-6200	273-8035	339-31
Economic Development Authority PO Box 990 *Web:* www.njeda.com	Trenton	NJ	08625	609-858-6700		339-31
Education Dept PO Box 500 *TF:* 877-900-6960 ■ *Web:* www.state.nj.us	Trenton	NJ	08625	609-376-3999		339-31
Environmental Protection Dept 401 E State St PO Box 402 *Web:* www.state.nj.us	Trenton	NJ	08625	609-292-2885	292-7695	339-31
Ethical Standards Commission 28 W State St 8th Fl PO Box 082 *TF:* 888-223-1355 ■ *Web:* www.state.nj.us	Trenton	NJ	08625	609-292-8700	633-9252	265
Fish Game & Wildlife Div PO Box 400 *Web:* www.state.nj.us	Trenton	NJ	08625	609-292-2965	984-1414	339-31
Health & Senior Services Dept PO Box 360 *Web:* www.state.nj.us	Trenton	NJ	08625	609-292-7837		339-31
Higher Education Commission 20 W State St 4th Fl PO Box 542 *Web:* www.state.nj.us	Trenton	NJ	08625	609-292-4310	292-7225	339-31
Higher Education Student Assistance Authority 4 Quakerbridge Plz PO Box 540 *TF:* 800-792-8670 ■ *Web:* www.hesaa.org	Trenton	NJ	08625	609-584-4480		725
Historical Commission PO Box 305 *Web:* www.state.nj.us	Trenton	NJ	08625	609-292-6062	633-8168	339-31
Housing & Mortgage Finance Agency 637 S Clinton Ave *Web:* www.state.nj.us	Trenton	NJ	08611	609-278-7400		339-31
Human Services Dept 222 S Warren St PO Box 700 *Web:* www.state.nj.us	Trenton	NJ	08625	609-341-2399	292-3824	339-31
Labor & Workforce Development Dept 1 John Fitch Plz 3rd Fl PO Box 110 *Web:* lwd.state.nj.us	Trenton	NJ	08625	609-292-2305	695-1174	339-31
Lottery 1333 Brunswick Avenue Cir *Web:* www.state.nj.us	Trenton	NJ	08648	609-392-1234	599-5935	452
Military & Veterans' Affairs Dept 101 Eggert Crossing Rd *TF:* 800-624-0508 ■ *Web:* www.state.nj.us	Lawrenceville	NJ	08648	609-530-4600		339-31
Motor Vehicle Commission PO Box 160 *Web:* www.state.nj.us	Trenton	NJ	08666	609-292-6500		339-31
Office of Information Technology PO Box 212 *Web:* www.state.nj.us	Trenton	NJ	08625	609-633-8975	633-0090	339-31
Parks & Forestry Div PO Box 404 *Web:* www.state.nj.us	Trenton	NJ	08625	609-984-0370		339-31
Parole Board PO Box 862 *Web:* www.state.nj.us	Trenton	NJ	08625	609-292-4257	943-4769	339-31
Securities Bureau 153 Halsey St 6th Fl *TF:* 866-446-8378 ■ *Web:* www.state.nj.us	Newark	NJ	07102	973-648-3333		339-31
State Athletic Control Board 25 Market St 1st Fl W Wing *Web:* www.state.nj.us	Trenton	NJ	08625	609-292-7677	292-3756	712
State Medical Examiner PO Box 094 *Web:* www.me.nj.gov	Trenton	NJ	08625	609-984-4883		339-31
State Police PO Box 7068 *Web:* www.state.nj.us	West Trenton	NJ	08628	609-963-6962		339-31
State Prison PO Box 861 *Web:* www.state.nj.us	Trenton	NJ	08625	609-292-9700		213
Supreme Court PO Box 037 *Web:* www.judiciary.state.nj.us	Trenton	NJ	08625	609-421-6100	292-6564	339-31
Transportation Dept 1035 Parkway Ave PO Box 600 *Web:* www.state.nj.us	Trenton	NJ	08625	609-530-2000		339-31
Travel & Tourism Div PO Box 460 *TF:* 800-847-4865 ■ *Web:* www.visitnj.org	Trenton	NJ	08625	609-599-6540		339-31
Treasurer PO Box 002 *Web:* www.state.nj.us	Trenton	NJ	08625	609-292-6748		339-31
Victims of Crime Compensation Board 50 Pk Pl *TF:* 877-658-2221 ■ *Web:* www.nj.gov	Newark	NJ	07102	973-648-2107	648-3937	339-31
Vital Statistics Bureau 140 E Front St *Web:* www.state.nj.us	Trenton	NJ	08608	609-586-9316		339-31
Vocational Rehabilitation Services Div (DVRS) 1 John Fitch Way PO Box 110 *Web:* jobs4jersey.com	Trenton	NJ	08625	609-292-5987	292-8347	339-31
Weights & Measures Office 1261 Rte 1&9 S *Web:* www.njconsumeraffairs.gov	Avenel	NJ	07001	732-815-4840	382-5298	339-31
Workers' Compensation Div PO Box 381 *Web:* www.lwd.dol.state.nj.us	Trenton	NJ	08625	609-292-2515	633-7783	339-31
Workforce New Jersey 1 John Fitch Plz PO Box 110 *Web:* nj.gov	Trenton	NJ	08625	609-633-6400	695-1174	259
New Jersey Association of Museums (NJAM) c/o Montclair Art Museum 3 S Mountain Ave *Web:* www.njmuseums.org	Montclair	NJ	07042	732-703-6526		637-2
New Jersey Association of Osteopathic Physicians & Surgeons 666 Plainsboro Rd Ste 365 *Web:* www.njosteo.com	Plainsboro	NJ	08536	732-940-9000	940-8899	138
New Jersey Ballet Co 15 Microlab Rd *Web:* www.njballet.org	Livingston	NJ	07039	973-597-9600	597-9442	573-1
New Jersey Business Forms Manufacturing Co 55 W Sheffield Ave *TF:* 800-466-6523 ■ *Web:* www.njbf.com	Englewood	NJ	07631	201-569-4500		110
New Jersey Business Magazine 310 Passaic Ave *Web:* www.njbmagazine.com	Fairfield	NJ	07004	973-882-5004	882-4648	457-5
New Jersey City University 2039 JFK Blvd *TF:* 888-441-6528 ■ *Web:* www.njcu.edu	Jersey City	NJ	07305	201-200-2000	200-2044	166
New Jersey Coalition of Automotive Retailers 856 River Rd *Web:* www.njcar.org	Trenton	NJ	08628	609-883-5056		533
New Jersey Convention & Exposition Ctr 97 Sunfield Ave *Web:* www.njexpocenter.com	Edison	NJ	08837	732-417-1400	417-1414	205
New Jersey Democratic State Committee 194-196 W State St *Web:* www.njdems.org	Trenton	NJ	08608	609-392-3367	396-4778	616-1
New Jersey Dental Assn 1 Dental Plz PO Box 6020 *Web:* www.njda.org	North Brunswick	NJ	08902	732-821-9400	821-1082	227
New Jersey Firemen's Home 565 Lathrop Ave *Web:* www.njfh.org	Boonton	NJ	07005	973-334-0024		672
New Jersey Herald 2 Spring St *TF:* 800-424-3725 ■ *Web:* www.njherald.com	Newton	NJ	07860	973-383-1500	383-8477	532-2
New Jersey Historical Society Museum 52 Pk Pl *Web:* www.jerseyhistory.org	Newark	NJ	07102	973-596-8500	596-6957	520
New Jersey Institute of Technology 323 Dr MLK Jr Blvd *Web:* www.njit.edu	Newark	NJ	07102	973-596-3000	596-3461	166
New Jersey Legal Copy Inc 501 King Ave *TF:* 800-426-7965 ■ *Web:* njlone.com	Cherry Hill	NJ	08002	856-910-0202		113
New Jersey Library Assn (NJLA) PO Box 1534 *Web:* njla.org	Trenton	NJ	08607	609-394-8032	394-8164	435
New Jersey Machine Inc 56 Etna Rd *TF:* 800-432-2990 ■ *Web:* www.njmpackaging.com	Lebanon	NH	03766	603-448-0300	448-4810	547
New Jersey Manufacturers Insurance Co 301 Sullivan Way *Web:* www.njm.com	West Trenton	NJ	08628	609-883-1300		391-4
New Jersey Medical School 185 S Orange Ave *Web:* njms.rutgers.edu	Newark	NJ	07103	973-972-4631	972-7986	167-2
New Jersey Medical Society 2 Princess Rd *TF:* 800-706-7893 ■ *Web:* www.msnj.org	Lawrenceville	NJ	08648	609-896-1766		474
New Jersey Monthly Magazine 55 Pk Pl PO Box 920 *TF:* 888-419-0419 ■ *Web:* njmonthly.com	Morristown	NJ	07963	973-539-8230	538-2953	457-22
New Jersey On-Line LLC 30 Journal Sq Ste 500 *Web:* www.nj.com	Jersey City	NJ	07306	201-459-2800		531-11
New Jersey Performing Arts Ctr 1 Center St *TF:* 888-466-5722 ■ *Web:* www.njpac.org	Newark	NJ	07102	973-642-8989		572
New Jersey Pharmacists Assn 760 Alexander Rd PO Box 1 *Web:* njpharmacists.org	Princeton	NJ	08543	609-275-4246	275-4066	585
New Jersey Principals & Supervisors Assn 12 Centre Dr *Web:* njpsa.org	Monroe Township	NJ	08831	609-860-1200		474
New Jersey Realtors 10 Hamilton Ave **Fax Area Code:* 732 ■ *Web:* www.njrealtor.com	Trenton	NJ	08611	609-341-7100	494-4723*	656
New Jersey Self-Help Group Clearinghouse 673 Morris Ave Ste 100 **Fax Area Code:* 973 ■ *TF:* 800-367-6274 ■ *Web:* www.njgroups.org	Springfield	NJ	07081	800-367-6274	218-0636*	637-10
New Jersey State Bar Assn One Constitution Square *Web:* www.tcms.njsba.com	New Brunswick	NJ	08901	732-249-5000	249-2815	72
New Jersey State Chamber of Commerce 216 W State St *Web:* www.njchamber.com	Trenton	NJ	08608	609-989-7888	989-9696	140
New Jersey State Museum 205 W State St *Web:* www.state.nj.us	Trenton	NJ	08625	609-292-6464	292-7636	520
New Jersey State Nurses Assn (NJSNA) 1479 Pennington Rd *TF:* 800-662-0108 ■ *Web:* njsna.org	Trenton	NJ	08618	609-883-5335	883-5343	533
New Jersey State Veteran's Memorial Home 132 Evergreen Rd PO Box 3013 *Web:* www.nj.gov	Edison	NJ	08818	732-452-4100		793
New Jersey Symphony Orchestra 60 Pk Pl Ste 900 *Web:* www.njsymphony.org	Newark	NJ	07102	973-624-3713	624-0477	573-3
New Jersey Transit Corp 1 Penn Plz E *Web:* www.njtransit.com	Newark	NJ	07105	973-491-7000		468
New Jersey Veterinary Medical Assn 390 Amwell Rd Ste 402 *Web:* www.njvma.org	Hillsborough	NJ	08844	908-281-0918	450-1286	795
New Jersey Water Supply Authority Inc 1851 SR-31 *Web:* www.njwsa.org	Clinton	NJ	08809	908-638-6121		539
New Kent County 12001 Courthouse Cir PO Box 98 *Web:* www.co.new-kent.va.us	New Kent	VA	23124	804-966-9520	966-9528	338
New Knowledge Library (NKL) PO Box 1724 *TF:* 800-938-3891 ■ *Web:* newknowledgelibrary.org	Boulder	CO	80304	800-938-3891		637-2

Name / Address	City	State	ZIP	Phone	Fax	Class
New Landmark, The 5801 Duke St *Web:* thenewlandmark.com	Alexandria	VA	22304	703-354-8405		460
New Leaders Inc 30 W 26th St 10th Fl *Web:* www.newleaders.org	New York	NY	10010	646-792-1070		305
New Leaf Community Markets 1101 Pacific Ave Ste 333 *Web:* www.newleaf.com	Santa Cruz	CA	95060	831-466-9060		345
New Leaf Market Inc 1235 Apalachee Pkwy *Web:* newleafmarket.coop	Tallahassee	FL	32301	850-942-2557		345
New Leaf Paper LLC 510 16th St Ste 520 *Web:* newleafpaper.com	Oakland	CA	94612	415-291-9210		554
New Leaf Publishing Group PO Box 726 *Web:* www.nlpg.com	Green Forest	AR	72638	870-438-5288		637-3
New Lenox Community Park District 1 Manor Dr *Web:* www.newlenoxparks.org	New Lenox	IL	60451	815-485-3584		31
New Lenox School District 122 (NLSD) 102 S Cedar Rd *Web:* www2.nlsd122.org	New Lenox	IL	60451	815-485-2169		685
New Letters University of Missouri-Kansas City University House *Web:* www.newletters.org	Kansas City	MO	64110	816-235-1168	235-2611	637-2
New Life Camp 701 Mayhew Rd *Web:* newlifecamp.org	Rose City	MI	48654	989-685-2949		239
New Life Evangelistic Center Inc 1411 Locust St *TF:* 800-242-3276 ■ *Web:* www.newlifeevangelisticcenter.org	Saint Louis	MO	63103	314-421-3020		48-20
New Life Foundation PO Box 2230 *Web:* www.anewlife.org	Pine	AZ	85544	928-476-3224	476-4743	637-2
New Life Industries Inc 140 Chappells Dairy Rd *TF:* 800-443-9523 ■ *Web:* www.newlifeshopper.com	Somerset	KY	42503	606-679-3616		687
New Life Ministries Inc 330 Wellington Ave *Web:* www.newlifeministries.org	Rochester	NY	14619	585-436-0085	436-9142	48-20
New Life Service Co 39 W Fifth St *Web:* www.nlsco.com	Eureka	CA	95501	707-444-8222		186
New Life Styles Inc 4144 N Central Expy Ste 1000 *Web:* newlifestyles.com	Dallas	TX	75204	214-824-0022		5
New Living PO Box 1519 *TF:* 800-639-5484 ■ *Web:* www.newliving.com	Stony Brook	NY	11790	631-751-8819		637-9
New London Nursing & Rehabilitation Ctr 1611 W Lakes Pkwy *Web:* www.careinitiatives.org	West Des Moines	IA	50266	319-367-5753		450
New Market Skills Ctr 7299 New Market St SW *Web:* www.newmarketskills.org	Tumwater	WA	98501	360-570-4500		167-3
New Mather Metals Inc 46855 Magellan Dr *Web:* www.nhkinternational.com	Novi	MI	48377	248-926-0111		247
New Mee Fung 350 Booth St *Web:* newmeefung.com	Ottawa	ON	K1R7K1	613-567-8228		671
New Method Steel Stamps Inc 31313 Kendall Ave *TF:* 800-582-0199 ■ *Web:* www.newmethod.org	Fraser	MI	48026	586-293-0200	296-1900	467
New Mexico						
Administrative Office of the Courts 237 Don Gaspar St *Web:* www.nmcourts.gov	Santa Fe	NM	87501	505-827-4800	827-4824	339-32
Aging Agency 2550 Cerrillos Rd PO Box 27118 *TF:* 800-432-2080 ■ *Web:* www.nmaging.state.nm.us	Santa Fe	NM	87505	505-476-4799	476-4836	339-32
Arts Div 407 Galisteo St Ste 270 *TF:* 800-879-4278 ■ *Web:* www.nmarts.org	Santa Fe	NM	87501	505-827-6490	827-6043	339-32
Attorney General 408 Galisteo St *TF:* 844-255-9210 ■ *Web:* www.nmag.gov	Santa Fe	NM	87501	505-490-4060	490-4883	339-32
Consumer Protection Div 408 Galisteo St Villagra Bldg PO Box 1508 *Web:* www.nmag.gov	Santa Fe	NM	87501	505-827-6000	490-4883	339-32
Corrections Dept (NMCD) 4337 NM 14 PO Box 27116 *Web:* cd.nm.gov	Santa Fe	NM	87502	505-827-8645	827-8533	339-32
Crime Victims Reparation Commission 6200 Uptown Blvd Ste 210 *TF:* 800-306-6262 ■ *Web:* www.cvrc.state.nm.us	Albuquerque	NM	87110	505-841-9432	841-9437	339-32
Department of Information Technology 715 Alta Vista St PO Box 22550 *Web:* www.doit.state.nm.us	Santa Fe	NM	87505	505-827-2121		339-32
Department of Veterans Services 5201 Eagle Rock Ave North E *Web:* nmdvs.org	Albuquerque	NM	87113	505-383-2417	383-2413	339-32
Dept of Workforce Solutions 501 Mountain Rd NE PO Box 1928 *Web:* www.dws.state.nm.us	Albuquerque	NM	87102	505-843-1900	843-1990	339-32
Economic Development Dept PO Box 20003 *TF:* 800-374-3061 ■ *Web:* gonm.biz	Santa Fe	NM	87504	505-827-0300	827-0328	339-32
Education Dept 300 Don Gaspar St *Web:* sde.state.nm.us	Santa Fe	NM	87501	505-827-1436		339-32
Energy Minerals & Natural Resources Dept 1644 Saint Michaels Dr	Santa Fe	NM	87505	505-476-3200		339-32
Environment Dept 1190 St Francis Dr Ste N4050 *TF:* 800-219-6157 ■ *Web:* nmenv.state.nm.us	Santa Fe	NM	87505	505-827-2855		339-32
Finance & Administration Dept 407 Galisteo St *Web:* www.nmdfa.state.nm.us	Santa Fe	NM	87501	505-827-4985	827-4984	339-32
Health Dept 1190 S St Francis Dr Ste N-4100 *Web:* nmhealth.org	Santa Fe	NM	87505	505-827-2613	827-2530	339-32
Higher Education Dept 2048 Galisteo St *TF:* 800-279-9777 ■ *Web:* www.hed.state.nm.us	Santa Fe	NM	87505	505-476-8400		339-32
Historic Preservation Div Bataan Memorial Bldg 407 Galisteo St Ste 236 *Web:* www.nmhistoricpreservation.org	Santa Fe	NM	87501	505-827-6320	827-6338	339-32
Human Services Dept (NMHSD) PO Box 2348 *TF:* 888-997-2583 ■ *Web:* www.hsd.state.nm.us	Santa Fe	NM	87504	505-827-3100	827-3185	339-32
Legislative Council Services 490 Old Santa Fe Trl Ste 411 *Web:* www.nmlegis.gov	Santa Fe	NM	87501	505-986-4600	986-4680	433
Lieutenant Governor 490 Old Santa Fe Trl Rm 417 *Web:* www.ltgov.state.nm.us	Santa Fe	NM	87501	505-476-2250	476-2257	339-32
Lottery 4511 Osuna Rd NE *Web:* www.nmlottery.com	Albuquerque	NM	87109	505-342-7600	342-7511	452
Medical Board 2538 Camino Entrada Bldg 400 Ste 102 *Web:* www.nmmb.state.nm.us	Santa Fe	NM	87505	505-476-7220	476-7237	339-32
Mortgage Finance Authority 344 Fourth St SW *TF:* 800-444-6880 ■ *Web:* www.housingnm.org	Albuquerque	NM	87102	505-843-6880	243-3289	339-32
Professional (Educator) Licensure Unit 300 Don Gaspar St Jerry Apodaca Education Bldg *Web:* webnew.ped.state.nm.us	Santa Fe	NM	87501	505-827-6581		339-32
Public Regulation Commission 1120 Paseo De Peralta PO Box 1269 *Web:* www.nmprc.state.nm.us	Santa Fe	NM	87504	505-827-4084		339-32
Racing Commission 4900 Alameda Blvd NE *Web:* www.nmrc.state.nm.us	Albuquerque	NM	87113	505-222-0700	222-0713	712
Secretary of State 325 Don Gaspar Ste 300 *Web:* www.sos.state.nm.us	Santa Fe	NM	87503	505-827-3600	827-8081	339-32
Standards & Consumers Services Div MSC 3170 PO Box 30005 *Web:* www.nmda.nmsu.edu	Las Cruces	NM	88003	575-646-1616	646-2361	339-32
State Legislature 490 Old Santa Fe Trl *Web:* www.nmlegis.gov	Santa Fe	NM	87501	505-986-4751		339-32
Supreme Court 237 Don Gaspar Ave Rm 104 PO Box 848 *Web:* supremecourt.nmcourts.gov	Santa Fe	NM	87501	505-827-4860	827-4178	339-32
Taxation & Revenue Dept 1100 S St Francis Dr *TF:* 866-285-2996 ■ *Web:* www.tax.newmexico.gov	Santa Fe	NM	87504	505-827-0700	827-2505	339-32
Tourism Dept 491 Old Santa Fe Trl *Web:* www.newmexico.org	Santa Fe	NM	87501	505-827-7400		339-32
Treasurer 2055 S Pacheco St Ste 100&200 *Web:* www.nmsto.gov	Santa Fe	NM	87505	505-955-1120		339-32
Vocational Rehabilitation Div 2935 Rodeo Park Dr E *TF:* 800-224-7005 ■ *Web:* www.dvrgetsjobs.com	Santa Fe	NM	87505	505-954-8500	954-8562	339-32
Workers' Compensation Admin 2410 Center Ave SE PO Box 27198 *TF:* 800-255-7965 ■ *Web:* workerscomp.nm.gov	Albuquerque	NM	87125	505-841-6000		339-32
New Mexico Association of Commerce & Industry (ACI) 2201 Buena Vista Dr SE Ste 410 *Web:* www.nmaci.org	Albuquerque	NM	87106	505-842-0644		140
New Mexico Behavioral Health Institute 3695 Hot Springs Blvd *TF:* 800-446-5970 ■ *Web:* nmhealth.org	Las Vegas	NM	87701	505-454-2100	454-5172	374-5
New Mexico Coalition for Literacy (NMCL) 1219 Luisa St Unit 2 *TF:* 800-233-7587 ■ *Web:* newmexicoliteracy.org	Santa Fe	NM	87505	505-982-3997	982-4095	48-13
New Mexico Democratic Party (DPNM) 8214 Second St NW Ste A *Web:* www.dpnm.net	Albuquerque	NM	87114	505-830-3650		616-1
New Mexico Dental Assn 9201 Montgomery Blvd NE Ste 601 *TF:* 888-787-1722 ■ *Web:* www.nmdental.org	Albuquerque	NM	87111	505-294-1368	294-9958	227
New Mexico Department of Game & Fish *Department of Game & Fish* 1 Wildlife Way *TF:* 888-248-6866 ■ *Web:* www.wildlife.state.nm.us	Santa Fe	NM	87507	505-476-8000	476-8116	339-32
New Mexico Department of Transportation *Highway & Transportation Dept (NMDOT)* 1120 Cerrillos Rd Po Box 1149 *TF:* 800-432-4269 ■ *Web:* www.dot.state.nm.us	Santa Fe	NM	87504	505-795-1401		339-32
New Mexico Energy Library Inc (NMEL) 312 N Main St *Web:* nmel.org	Roswell	NM	88202	575-622-1711		434-3
New Mexico Energy, Minerals and Natural Resources Dept *State Parks Div* 1220 S St Francis Dr *TF:* 888-667-2757 ■ *Web:* www.emnrd.state.nm.us	Santa Fe	NM	87505	505-476-3355		339-32
New Mexico Environmental Law Ctr 1405 Luisa St Ste 5 *Web:* nmelc.org	Santa Fe	NM	87505	505-989-9022	989-3769	41
New Mexico Farm & Ranch Heritage Museum 4100 Dripping Springs Rd *Web:* www.nmfarmandranchmuseum.org	Las Cruces	NM	88011	575-522-4100	522-3085	520
New Mexico Highlands University PO Box 9000 *TF:* 877-850-9064 ■ *Web:* www.nmhu.edu	Las Vegas	NM	87701	505-425-7511	454-3552	166
New Mexico Holocaust & Intolerance Museum & Study Ctr 616 Central Ave SW *Web:* www.nmholocaustmuseum.org	Albuquerque	NM	87102	505-247-0606		520
New Mexico Institute of Mining & Technology (NMT) 801 Leroy Pl *TF:* 800-428-8324 ■ *Web:* www.nmt.edu	Socorro	NM	87801	505-835-5434		166
New Mexico Junior College 1 Thunderbird Cir *TF:* 800-657-6260 ■ *Web:* www.nmjc.edu	Hobbs	NM	88240	505-392-4510		162
New Mexico Legal Aid Inc 301 Gold Ave SW *TF:* 866-416-1922 ■ *Web:* www.newmexicolegalaid.org	Albuquerque	NM	87102	505-243-7871		445

Phone | Fax | Class

New Mexico Lions Eye Bank
2501 Yale Blvd SE Ste 100 ... Albuquerque NM 87106 | 505-266-3937 | | 269
TF: 888-616-3937 ■ *Web:* www.nmleb.org

New Mexico Medical Society (NMMS)
316 Osuna Rd NE Ste 501 ... Albuquerque NM 87107 | 505-828-0237 | 828-0336 | 474
TF: 800-748-1596 ■ *Web:* www.nmms.org

New Mexico Military Museum, The
1050 Old Pecos Trl ... Santa Fe NM 87505 | 505-474-1670 | | 520
Web: www.newmexicomilitarymuseum.com

New Mexico Museum of Art
107 W Palace Ave ... Santa Fe NM 87501 | 505-476-5072 | 476-5076 | 520
TF: 877-567-7380 ■ *Web:* www.nmartmuseum.org

New Mexico Museum of Natural History & Science
1801 Mtn Rd NW ... Albuquerque NM 87104 | 505-841-2800 | | 520
Web: www.nmnaturalhistory.org

New Mexico Museum of Space History
Top of Hwy 2001 ... Alamogordo NM 88311 | 575-437-2840 | 434-2245 | 520
TF: 877-333-6589 ■ *Web:* www.nmspacemuseum.org

New Mexico Mutual
5201 Balloon Fiesta Parkway Ne ... Albuquerque NM 87113 | 505-345-7260 | 345-0656 | 391-4
TF: 800-788-8851 ■ *Web:* www.newmexicomutual.com

New Mexico Pharmacists Assn (NMPHA)
2716 San Pedro Dr NE Ste C ... Albuquerque NM 87110 | 505-265-8729 | | 585
Web: www.nmpharmacy.org

New Mexico Public Interest Research Group (NMPIRG)
PO Box 40173 ... Albuquerque NM 87196 | 505-254-1244 | | 633
Web: nmpirg.org

New Mexico Regulation & Licensing Dept
Regulation & Licensing Dept
2550 Cerrillos Rd Toney Anaya Bldg ... Santa Fe NM 87505 | 505-476-4500 | 476-4511 | 339-32
Web: www.rld.state.nm.us

New Mexico State Fair
300 San Pedro NE ... Albuquerque NM 87108 | 505-222-9700 | | 642
Web: www.exponm.com

New Mexico State Investment Council
41 Plaza la Prensa ... Santa Fe NM 87507 | 505-476-9500 | 424-2510 | 401
Web: www.sic.state.nm.us

New Mexico State University (NMSU)
MSC-3A PO Box 30001 ... Las Cruces NM 88003 | 575-646-3121 | 646-6330 | 166
TF: 800-662-6678 ■ *Web:* nmsu.edu

New Mexico State University
Alamogordo (NMSU-A)
2400 N Scenic Dr ... Alamogordo NM 88310 | 575-439-3600 | 439-3760 | 162
Web: www.nmsua.edu
Carlsbad 1500 University Dr ... Carlsbad NM 88220 | 575-234-9200 | | 162
TF: 888-888-2199 ■ *Web:* carlsbad.nmsu.edu
Grants 1500 Third St ... Grants NM 87020 | 505-287-6678 | 287-2329 | 162
Web: www.grants.nmsu.edu

New Mexico State University Museum
1280 E University Ave ... Las Cruces NM 88003 | 575-646-5161 | | 520
Web: univmuseum.nmsu.edu

New Mexico State Veterans Ctr
992 S Broadway St ... Truth or Consequences NM 87901 | 575-894-4200 | 894-4270 | 793
TF: 800-964-3976 ■ *Web:* nmhealth.org

New Mexico Veterans Memorial
1100 Louisiana Blvd SE ... Albuquerque NM 87108 | 505-256-2042 | | 50-4
Web: nmvetsmemorial.org

New Mexico Veterinary Medical Assn
60 Placitas Trls Rd ... Placitas NM 87043 | 505-867-6373 | 771-8963 | 795
Web: www.nmvma.org

New Millenium Directories
1630 S Galena Ave ... Freeport IL 61032 | 815-233-5797 | | 4
Web: www.bigprintphonebook.com

New Millenium Home Health
6031 Cleveland Ave ... Columbus OH 43231 | 614-882-7782 | | 363
Web: nmilleniumhomehealth.com

New Millennium Inc 953 E Libra Dr ... Tempe AZ 85283 | 602-761-0254 | | 177
Web: newmillinc.com

New Moon Girls Magazine PO Box 161287 ... Duluth MN 55816 | 218-878-9673 | | 457-6
TF: 800-381-4743 ■ *Web:* newmoon.com

New Museum of Contemporary Art
235 Bowery ... New York NY 10002 | 212-219-1222 | | 520
Web: www.newmuseum.org

New Objective Inc 2 Constitution Way ... Woburn MA 01801 | 781-933-9560 | | 419
TF: 888-220-2998 ■ *Web:* www.newobjective.com

New Omni Bank NA 1235 S Garfield Ave ... Alhambra CA 91801 | 626-284-5555 | | 70
Web: newomnibank.com

New Orange Hills 5017 E Chapman Ave ... Orange CA 92869 | 714-997-7090 | 997-4631 | 450
Web: www.neworangehills.com

New Orleans Baptist Theological Seminary
3939 Gentilly Blvd ... New Orleans LA 70126 | 504-282-4455 | 816-8023 | 167-3
TF: 800-662-8701 ■ *Web:* www.nobts.edu

New Orleans Chamber of Commerce
1515 Poydras St Ste 1010 ... New Orleans LA 70112 | 504-799-4260 | 799-4259 | 139
Web: www.neworleanschamber.org

New Orleans City Business
111 Veterans Memorial Blvd Ste 1440 ... Metairie LA 70005 | 504-834-9292 | 832-3550 | 457-5
Web: neworleanscitybusiness.com

New Orleans City Hall
1300 Perdido St ... New Orleans LA 70112 | 504-658-4000 | | 337
TF: 800-256-2748 ■ *Web:* nola.gov

New Orleans Cold Storage & Warehouse Company Inc (NOCS)
3411 Jourdan Rd ... New Orleans LA 70126 | 504-944-4400 | | 803-2
Web: www.nocs.com

New Orleans Film Festival
900 Camp St ... New Orleans LA 70130 | 504-309-6633 | 309-0923 | 282
Web: neworleansfilmsociety.org

New Orleans Firemens Federal Credit Union
PO Box 689 ... Metairie LA 70004 | 504-889-9090 | 889-9082 | 219
TF: 800-647-1689 ■ *Web:* www.noffcu.org

New Orleans Magazine
110 Veterans Blvd Ste 123 ... Metairie LA 70005 | 504-828-1380 | 828-1385 | 457-22
TF: 877-221-3512 ■ *Web:* www.myneworleans.com

New Orleans Metropolitan Convention & Visitors Bureau
2020 St Charles Ave ... New Orleans LA 70130 | 800-672-6124 | 566-5046* | 206
**Fax Area Code:* 504 ■ *TF:* 800-672-6124 ■ *Web:* www.neworleans.com

New Orleans Museum of Art (NOMA)
1 Collins C Diboll Cir City Pk ... New Orleans LA 70124 | 504-658-4100 | 658-4199 | 520
Web: www.noma.org

New Orleans Pharmacy Museum
514 Chartres St ... New Orleans LA 70130 | 504-565-8027 | | 520
Web: www.pharmacymuseum.org

New Orleans Saints 5800 Airline Dr ... Metairie LA 70003 | 504-733-0255 | | 715-3
Web: www.neworleanssaints.com

New Orleans-Birmingham Psychoanalytic Ctr
3624 Coliseum St ... New Orleans LA 70115 | 504-899-5815 | 899-5886 | 49-19
Web: www.nobpc.org

New Otani Kaimana Beach Hotel
2863 Kalakaua Ave ... Honolulu HI 96815 | 808-923-1555 | 922-9404 | 379
TF: 800-356-8264 ■ *Web:* www.kaimana.com

New Papyrus Publishing Co (NP)
548 Cedar Creek Dr ... Athens GA 30605 | 706-546-6740 | | 637-2
Web: www.genealogyresources.org

New Paris Telephone Inc (NPT)
19066 Market St ... New Paris IN 46553 | 574-831-2176 | 831-7125 | 224
Web: www.nptel.com

New Park 385 New Park Ave ... Hartford CT 06106 | 860-232-1565 | | 671
Web: www.newparkauto.com

New Peking 540 Westport Rd ... Kansas City MO 64111 | 816-531-6969 | 531-9188 | 671
Web: newpekingkansas.com

New Penn Motor Express Inc
625 S Fifth Ave ... Lebanon PA 17042 | 717-274-2521 | 274-5593 | 780
TF: 800-285-5000 ■ *Web:* www.newpenn.com

New Peoples Bankshares Inc
67 Commerce Dr ... Honaker VA 24260 | 276-873-7000 | | 70
Web: www.npbankshares.com

New Perspective Senior Living
5900 Clearwater Dr Ste 500 ... Minnetonka MN 55343 | 952-746-3630 | | 793
TF: 866-986-0215 ■ *Web:* npseniorliving.com

New Philadelphia City School District (NPCS)
248 Front Ave SW ... New Philadelphia OH 44663 | 330-364-0600 | 364-9310 | 186
Web: www.npschools.org

New Pig Corp 1 Pork Ave ... Tipton PA 16684 | 814-684-0101 | 621-7447* | 151
**Fax Area Code:* 800 ■ *TF:* 800-468-4647 ■ *Web:* www.newpig.com

New Piper Aircraft Inc
2926 Piper Dr ... Vero Beach FL 32960 | 772-567-4361 | | 20
Web: www.piper.com

New Pittsburg Veterinary Clinic Inc
1436 W Old Lincoln Way ... Wooster OH 44691 | 330-264-7787 | 262-5251 | 794
TF: 800-262-9509 ■ *Web:* newpittsburgvetclinic.com

New Pond Village 180 Main St ... Walpole MA 02081 | 508-660-1555 | 668-8893 | 672
Web: www.brightviewseniorliving.com

New Press 120 Wall St 31st Fl ... New York NY 10005 | 212-629-8802 | 629-8617 | 637-2
Web: www.thenewpress.com

New Process Fibre Co
12655 N 1st St Greenwood ... Greenwood DE 19950 | 800-497-4520 | 349-5730* | 454
**Fax Area Code:* 302 ■ *TF:* 800-497-4520 ■ *Web:* www.newprocess.com

New Process Steel Corp
1322 N Post Oak ... Houston TX 77055 | 713-686-9631 | 316-1128 | 492
TF: 800-392-4989 ■ *Web:* www.nps.cc

New Product Insights Inc
433 Ward Pkwy ... Kansas City MO 64112 | 816-582-8700 | | 195
Web: www.npinpi.com

New Products Corp
448 N Shore Dr ... Benton Harbor MI 49022 | 269-925-2161 | | 308
TF: 800-790-0252 ■ *Web:* www.newproductscorp.com

New Professions Technical Institute
4000 W Flagler St ... Miami FL 33134 | 305-461-2223 | 461-3029 | 167-3
Web: www.npti.com

New Pros Data Inc
155 Hidden Ravines Dr ... Powell OH 43065 | 740-201-0410 | | 387
TF: 800-837-5478 ■ *Web:* newpros.com

New Readers Press 101 Wyoming St ... Syracuse NY 13204 | 800-448-8878 | 894-2100* | 637-2
**Fax Area Code:* 866 ■ *TF:* 800-448-8878 ■ *Web:* www.newreaderspress.com

New Repertory Theatre
200 Dexter Ave ... Watertown MA 02472 | 617-923-7060 | | 749
Web: www.newrep.org

New Republic, The
1620 L St NW Ste 300C ... Washington DC 20036 | 202-508-4444 | | 457-17
TF: 800-827-1289 ■ *Web:* newrepublic.com

New Richmond Industries Inc
905 N Knowles Ave ... New Richmond WI 54017 | 715-246-6571 | 246-6574 | 253
Web: www.nr-inc.com

New River Community College
5251 College Dr ... Dublin VA 24084 | 540-674-3600 | 674-3642 | 162
TF: 866-462-6722 ■ *Web:* www.nr.edu

New River Electrical Corp
PO Box 70 ... Cloverdale VA 24077 | 540-966-1650 | 966-1699 | 188-10
Web: www.newriverelectrical.com

New River Press 645 Fairmount St ... Woonsocket RI 02895 | 800-273-1941 | 356-0913* | 637-2
**Fax Area Code:* 401 ■ *TF:* 800-273-1941 ■ *Web:* www.newriverpress.com

New River State Park
358 New River State Park Rd ... Laurel Springs NC 28644 | 336-982-2587 | | 565
Web: www.ncparks.gov

New River West Correctional Institution
7819 NW 228th St ... Raiford FL 32026 | 904-368-3000 | 368-2732 | 213
Web: dc.state.fl.us

New Rivers Restaurant 7 Steeple St ... Providence RI 02903 | 401-751-0350 | | 671
Web: www.newriversrestaurant.com

New Riverside Ochre Co
75 Old River Rd SE ... Cartersville GA 30120 | 770-382-4568 | | 503-1
TF: 800-248-0176 ■ *Web:* www.nroonline.com

New Roc City 29 LeCount Pl ... New Rochelle NY 10801 | 914-637-7575 | | 50-6
Web: www.funfuziononline.com

New rue21 LLC 800 Commonwealth Dr ... Warrendale PA 15086 | 724-776-9780 | 741-9020 | 157-6
NASDAQ: RUE ■ *TF:* 866-533-4783 ■ *Web:* www.rue21.com

New Sabina Industries Inc
12555 E US Rt 22 & 23 ... Sabina OH 45169 | 937-584-2433 | 584-2476 | 60
Web: www.nippon-seiki.co.jp

New Saigon 375 S Federal Blvd Unit 104 ... Denver CO 80219 | 303-936-4954 | | 671
Web: newsaigon.com

New Scale Technologies Inc
121 Victor Heights Pkwy ... Victor NY 14564 | 585-924-4450 | | 544
Web: www.newscaletech.com

New Scenic Cafe 5461 N Shore Dr ... Duluth MN 55804 | 218-525-6274 | | 671
Web: newsceniccafe.com

New School 66 W 12th St ... New York NY 10011 | 212-229-5600 | | 166
Web: www.newschool.edu

	Phone	Fax	Class
New School Center for Media, The 7 Harriman Campus Rd Albany NY 12206 *Web:* www.newschoolalbany.edu	518-438-7682		685
New School of American Music 309 Wall St Chico CA 95928 *Web:* www.pianofun.com	530-342-7401	342-7402	423
New Seabury Resort 20 Red Brook Rd Mashpee MA 02649 *TF:* 877-687-3228 ■ *Web:* www.newseabury.com	508-539-8200		669
New Seasons Market 7300 SW Beaverton Hwy Portland OR 97225 *Web:* www.newseasonsmarket.com	503-292-6838		327
New South Kitchen & Bar 8140 Providence Rd- 300 Charlotte NC 28277 *Web:* www.newsouthkitchen.com	704-541-9990	541-1163	671
New Stage Theatre 1100 Carlisle St Jackson MS 39202 *Web:* www.newstagetheatre.com	601-948-3429	948-3538	573-4
New Standard Corp 74 Commerce Way York PA 17406 *Web:* www.newstandard.com	717-757-9450	757-2312	488
New System Laundry LLC 432 NE Tenth Ave Portland OR 97232 *TF:* 800-958-6920 ■ *Web:* newsystemlaundry.com	503-232-8181		426
New Tang Dynasty-TV 229 W 28th St Ste 700 New York NY 10001 *Web:* www.ntd.tv	212-736-8535	736-8536	647
New Target Inc 815 N Royal St Ste 100 Alexandria VA 22314 *Web:* www.newtarget.com	703-548-3433		180
New Tech Global (NTG) 1030 Regional Park Dr Houston TX 77060 *Web:* www.ntglobal.com	281-951-4330	951-8719	261
New Tech Industries Inc 7911 44th Ave W Mukilteo WA 98275 *Web:* www.newtechind.com	425-778-1200	743-3566	454
New Tech Machinery 1300 40th St Denver CO 80205 *Web:* newtechmachinery.com	303-294-0538	294-9407	190
New Tech Network 1260 Main St Ste 100 Napa CA 94559 *TF:* 800-856-7038 ■ *Web:* newtechnetwork.org	707-253-6951		138
New Tech Packaging Inc 2718 Pershing Ave Memphis TN 38112 *Web:* www.newtechpackaging.com	901-498-5570		549
New Tech Solutions Inc 4179 Business Center Dr Fremont CA 94538 *Web:* www.newtechsolutions.com	510-353-4070	353-4076	179
New Tech Systems 4601 N FM 1788 Midland TX 79707 *Web:* www.newtechsystems.com	432-561-5393	561-5395	537
New Technologies Inc 4380 Baldwin Rd Holly MI 48442 *Web:* www.newtechnologiesinc.com	810-694-5426	694-1183	180
New Technology Publishing Inc 53 N Central St Peabody MA 01960 *Fax Area Code: 978 ■ *TF:* 800-672-7632 ■ *Web:* www.healthyresources.com	800-672-7632	818-6212*	637-2
New Times Broward Palm Beach 16 NE Fourth St Fort Lauderdale FL 33301 *Web:* www.browardpalmbeach.com	954-233-1600	233-1521	532-5
New Trier Township High School District 203 7 Happ Rd Northfield IL 60093 *Web:* www.newtrier.k12.il.us	847-446-7000	784-7500	685
New Tripoli Bank 6748 Madison St New Tripoli PA 18066 *Web:* newtripolibank.net	610-298-8811		70
New Tyler Barber College 1221 Bishop Lindsey Ave North Little Rock AR 72114 *Web:* www.newtylerbarbercollege.com	501-375-0377	375-1241	167-3
New Ulm 27 N Minnesota St New Ulm MN 56073 *OTC:* NULM ■ *TF:* 888-873-6853 ■ *Web:* www.nuvera.net	507-354-4111	354-1982	736
New Valley LLC 4400 Biscayne Blvd Miami FL 33137 *Web:* www.newvalleyre.com	305-579-8000		653
New Venture Partners LLC PO Box 881 New Providence NJ 07974 *Web:* www.nvpllc.com	908-464-0900	655-9142	792
New Video Group Inc 902 Broadway 9th Fl New York NY 10010 *Web:* www.newvideo.com	212-206-8600		626
New Vision Display Inc 1430 Blue Oaks Blvd Ste 100 Roseville CA 95747 *Web:* newvisiondisplay.com	916-462-8913		180
New Visions Communications Inc 6755 Manlius Center Rd E East Syracuse NY 13057 *Web:* www.nvplc.com	315-472-6300	552-9913	387
New Vista Nursing & Rehabilitation Ctr 8647 Fenwick St Sunland CA 91040 *Web:* www.newvistanursing.com	818-352-1421		793
New Vitality 260 Smith St Farmingdale NY 11735 *TF:* 888-997-2941 ■ *Web:* www.newvitality.com	888-271-7599		791
New Washington State Bank 402 E Main St PO Box 10 New Washington IN 47162 *TF:* 800-883-0131 ■ *Web:* www.newwashbank.com	812-293-3321	293-3072	70
New Wave Enviro Products Inc PO Box 4146 Greenwood Village CO 80111 *TF:* 800-592-8371 ■ *Web:* www.newwaveenviro.com	800-592-8371		612
New Wave Industries Inc 135 Day St Newington CT 06111 *Web:* www.newwaveindustries.com	860-953-9283	953-1218	180
New Wave Travel 1075 Bay St Toronto ON M5S2B1 *TF:* 800-463-1512 ■ *Web:* www.newwavetravel.net	416-928-3113		772
New Way Air Bearings Inc 50 McDonald Blvd Aston PA 19014 *Web:* www.newwayairbearings.com	610-494-6700		480
New Ways to Work Inc 103 Morris St Ste A Sebastopol CA 95472 *Web:* www.newwaystowork.org	707-824-4000	824-4410	48-24
New West Energy Services Inc 435 - Fourth Ave SW Ste 500 Calgary AB T2P3A8 *TF:* 888-977-2327 ■ *Web:* www.newwestenergyservices.com	403-984-9798		539
New West Medical Inc 2971 Churn Creek Rd Redding CA 96002 *TF:* 866-376-5864 ■ *Web:* newwestmedical.com	530-221-5864		363
New West Symphony 2100 E Thousand Oaks Blvd Ste D Thousand Oaks CA 91362 *TF:* 866-776-8400 ■ *Web:* www.newwestsymphony.org	805-497-5800	497-5839	573-3
New West Technologies Inc 4606 SE Division St Portland OR 97206 *TF:* 800-466-7839 ■ *Web:* www.newestech.com	503-235-4656		225
New Westminster Chamber 201 - 309 Sixth St New Westminster BC V3L3A7 *Web:* www.newwestchamber.com	604-521-7781		137
New Win Publishing Inc 9682 Telstar Ave Ste 110 El Monte CA 91731 *Web:* www.newwinpublishing.com	626-448-3448	602-3817	637-2
New Windsor Cantonment State Historic Site 374 Temple Hill Rd Rt 300 Vails Gate NY 12584 *Web:* parks.ny.gov	845-561-1765		565
New World Aviation Inc 987 Postal Rd Allentown PA 18109 *TF:* 877-359-0100 ■ *Web:* www.newworldaviation.com	610-231-9555		13
New World Educational Ctr 5818 N Seventh St Phoenix AZ 85014 *Web:* www.nweccharter.com	602-238-9577	238-9210	242
New World Graphics Inc 2500 Baynard Blvd Wilmington DE 19802 *Web:* www.nwginc.com	610-623-0404		344
New World Group Inc 500 County Ave Secaucus NJ 07094 *Web:* www.newworldgroup.com	201-770-1404		627
New World Imports Inc 160 Athens Way Nashville TN 37228 *TF:* 800-329-1903 ■ *Web:* www.newworldimports.com	615-329-1906		535
New World Library 14 Pamaron Way Novato CA 94949 *TF:* 800-972-6657 ■ *Web:* www.newworldlibrary.com	415-884-2100	884-2199	637-3
New World Machining Inc 2799 Aiello Dr San Jose CA 95111 *Fax Area Code: 844 ■ *Web:* www.newworldmachining.com	408-227-3810	272-5214*	454
New World Medical Inc 10763 Edison Ct Rancho Cucamonga CA 91730 *Web:* www.newworldmedical.com	909-466-4304		476
New World Publications 1861 Cornell Rd Jacksonville FL 32207 *TF:* 800-737-6550 ■ *Web:* www.fishid.com	904-737-6558		637-2
New World Sales Inc 207 Union St Hackensack NJ 07601 *Fax Area Code: 201 ■ *TF:* 800-237-8901 ■ *Web:* www.newworldsales.com	800-237-8901	488-1804*	156
New World Symphony 500 17th St Miami Beach FL 33139 *TF:* 800-597-3331 ■ *Web:* www.nws.edu	305-673-3330	673-6749	573-3
New World Tortilla 696 Pine St Burlington VT 05401 *Web:* www.newworldtortilla.com	802-865-1058		671
New Year Designs 3150 18th St Ste 306 San Francisco CA 94110 *Web:* www.newyeardesigns.com	415-370-6460	282-7020	130
New Year Tech Inc 12330 Pinecrest Rd Ste 100 Reston VA 20191 *Web:* www.nyt1.net	703-564-0290	564-0296	178-12
New York			
Aging Office 2 Empire State Plz Albany NY 12223 *TF:* 800-342-9871 ■ *Web:* aging.ny.gov	800-342-9871		339-33
Arts Council 300 Park Ave S 10th Fl New York NY 10010 *Web:* www.arts.ny.gov	212-459-8800		339-33
Athletic Commission 123 William St 20th Fl New York NY 10038 *TF:* 866-269-3769 ■ *Web:* www.dos.ny.gov	212-417-5700	417-4987	712
Banking Dept 1 State St New York NY 10004 *TF:* 877-226-5697 ■ *Web:* dfs.ny.gov	800-342-3736		339-33
Bill Status 202 Legislative Office Bldg Albany NY 12248 *TF:* 800-342-9860 ■ *Web:* www.assembly.state.ny.us	518-455-4218		433
Children & Family Services Office 52 Washington St Rensselaer NY 12144 *TF:* 866-505-7233 ■ *Web:* www.ocfs.ny.gov	518-473-7793	486-7550	339-33
Correctional Services Dept 1220 Washington Ave Bldg 2 Albany NY 12226 *Web:* www.doccs.ny.gov	518-457-8126		339-33
Crime Victims Board AE Smith Bldg 80 S Swan St 2nd Fl Albany NY 12210 *TF:* 800-247-8035 ■ *Web:* ovs.ny.gov	518-457-8727	457-8658	339-33
Department of Information Technology & Telecommunications 2 Metro Tech Ctr 5th Fl Brooklyn NY 11201 *Web:* www1.nyc.gov	212-788-6600		339-33
Division of Consumer Protection 5 Empire State Plz Ste 2101 Albany NY 12223 *Web:* www.dos.ny.gov	518-474-8583	486-3936	339-33
Education Dept 89 Washington Ave Albany NY 12234 *Web:* www.nysed.gov	518-474-3852		339-33
Emergency Management Office (OEM) 1220 Washington Ave Bldg 22 Ste 101 Albany NY 12226 *Web:* www.dhses.ny.gov	518-292-2200	322-4990	339-33
Empire State Development 30 S Pearl St 7th Fl Albany NY 12245 *TF:* 800-782-8369 ■ *Web:* esd.ny.gov	518-292-5100	292-5812	339-33
Environmental Conservation Dept 625 Broadway Albany NY 12144 *Web:* www.dec.ny.gov	518-891-0235		339-33
Health Dept Empire State Plz Corning Tower Albany NY 12237 *TF:* 866-881-2809 ■ *Web:* www.health.ny.gov	866-881-2809		339-33
Higher Education Services Corp 99 Washington Ave Albany NY 12210 *TF:* 888-697-4372 ■ *Web:* www.hesc.ny.gov	518-473-1574	474-2839	725
Housing Finance Agency 641 Lexington Ave New York NY 10022 *TF:* 866-275-3427 ■ *Web:* www.nyshcr.org	212-688-4000	872-0789	339-33
Insurance Dept 1 Commerce Plz Albany NY 12260 *Web:* dfs.ny.gov	518-474-6600		339-33
Investor Protection & Securities Bureau 120 Broadway 23rd Fl New York NY 10271 *Web:* ag.ny.gov	212-416-8222	416-8816	339-33
Labor Dept WA Harriman Campus Bldg 12 Albany NY 12240 *TF:* 888-469-7365 ■ *Web:* www.labor.ny.gov	518-457-9000		259
Lieutenant Governor NYS State Capitol Bldg Albany NY 12224 *Web:* www.governor.ny.gov	518-474-8390		339-33

Name / Address	City	State	Zip	Phone	Fax	Class
Lower Manhattan Development Corp						
1 Liberty Plz 20th Fl	New York	NY	10006	212-962-2300	962-2431	339-33
Web: www.renewnyc.com						
Mental Health Office 44 Holland Ave	Albany	NY	12229	800-597-8481		339-33
TF: 800-597-8481 ■ *Web:* omh.ny.gov						
Military & Naval Affairs Div						
330 Old Niskayuna Rd	Latham	NY	12110	518-786-4786	786-4649	339-33
TF: 877-715-7817 ■ *Web:* dmna.ny.gov						
Motor Vehicles Dept 224-260 S Pearl St	Albany	NY	12228	518-473-5595		339-33
Web: dmv.ny.gov						
Office of Court Admin						
4 ESP Ste 2001 Empire State Plz	Albany	NY	12223	212-428-2100		339-33
TF: 800-430-8457 ■ *Web:* www.courts.state.ny.us						
Office of the Professions						
89 Washington Ave	Albany	NY	12234	518-474-3817	474-3004	339-33
TF: 800-442-8106 ■ *Web:* www.op.nysed.gov						
Parole Div 97 Central Ave	Albany	NY	12206	518-473-9400		339-33
Web: www.doccs.ny.gov						
Power Authority 30 S Pearl St 10th Fl	Albany	NY	12207	518-433-6700		339-33
Web: www.nypa.gov						
Public Service Commission						
90 Church St	New York	NY	10007	518-474-7080	474-0421	339-33
Web: www.dps.ny.gov						
Secretary of State 99 Washington Ave	Albany	NY	12210	518-473-2492	473-6648	339-33
TF: 800-697-1220 ■ *Web:* www.dos.ny.gov						
State Comptroller 110 State St 15th Fl	Albany	NY	12236	518-474-4044	473-8940	339-33
TF: 877-697-2837 ■ *Web:* www.osc.state.ny.us						
State Police Div						
1220 Washington Ave Bldg 22	Albany	NY	12226	518-783-3211		339-33
Web: Www.joinstatepolice.ny.gov						
Taxation & Finance Dept						
WA Harriman Campus	Albany	NY	12227	518-457-5431		339-33
Web: www.tax.ny.gov						
Temporary & Disability Assistance Office						
40 N Pearl St 16th Fl	Albany	NY	12243	518-473-1090		339-33
TF: 800-342-3009 ■ *Web:* www.otda.ny.gov						
Transportation Dept 50 Wolf Rd	Albany	NY	12205	518-457-7082	485-5217	339-33
Web: www.dot.ny.gov						
Veterans' Affairs Div 1323 Rt 52	Carmel	NY	10512	845-808-1500		339-33
Web: veterans.ny.gov						
Vital Records Office 800 N Pearl St	Menands	NY	12204	800-541-2831		339-33
TF: 800-541-2831 ■ *Web:* www.health.ny.gov						
Vocational & Educational Services for Individuals						
1 Commerce Plz Rm 1609	Albany	NY	12234	518-730-0041	486-4683	339-33
Web: www.acces.nysed.gov						
Workers' Compensation Board						
PO Box 5205	Binghamton	NY	13902	518-402-6070	402-0113	339-33
TF: 877-632-4996 ■ *Web:* www.wcb.ny.gov						
New York & Co 330 W 34th St	New York	NY	10001	800-961-9906		157-6
TF: 800-961-9906 ■ *Web:* www.nyandcompany.com						
New York Academy of Medicine (NYAM)						
1216 Fifth Ave	New York	NY	10029	212-822-7200		49-19
Web: www.nyam.org						
New York Academy of Sciences						
250 Greenwich St 40th Fl	New York	NY	10007	212-298-8600	298-3650	49-19
TF: 800-843-6927 ■ *Web:* www.nyas.org						
New York AMA Communication Services Inc						
234 5th Ave	New York	NY	10001	212-849-2752	202-7920	637-10
Web: www.greenbook.org						
New York Apple Association Inc						
7645 Main St PO Box 350	Fishers	NY	14453	585-924-2171		414
Web: www.nyapplecountry.com						
New York Arm Wrestling Assn (NYAWA)						
PO Box 670952	Flushing	NY	11367	718-544-4592	261-8111	48-22
Web: www.nycarms.com						
New York Audio Productions						
344 W 38th St 6th Fl	New York	NY	10018	212-244-1114	243-7210	514
Web: www.nyaudio.com						
New York Banker 99 Park Ave 4th Fl	New York	NY	10016	212-297-1600	297-1683	531-1
TF: 800-346-3860 ■ *Web:* nyba.com						
New York Barbells 160 Home St	Elmira	NY	14904	800-446-1833	733-1010*	267
**Fax Area Code:* 607 ■ *TF:* 800-446-1833 ■ *Web:* www.newyorkbarbells.com						
New York Blood Ctr 310 E 67th St	New York	NY	10065	646-456-4281		89
TF: 800-688-0900 ■ *Web:* www.nybloodcenter.org						
New York Blower Co 7660 Quincy St	Willowbrook	IL	60527	630-794-5700	794-5776	18
TF: 800-208-7918 ■ *Web:* www.nyb.com						
New York Career Institute 11 Park Pl	New York	NY	10007	212-962-0002	385-7574	800
Web: www.nyci.edu						
New York Celebrity Assistants (NYCA)						
459 Columbus Ave	New York	NY	10024	212-803-5444		49-12
Web: www.nycelebrityassistants.com						
New York Central Mutual Fire Insurance Co (NYCM)						
1899 Central Plz E	Edmeston	NY	13335	800-234-6926	965-2712*	391-4
**Fax Area Code:* 607 ■ *TF:* 800-234-6926 ■ *Web:* www.nycm.com						
New York City Ballet Inc						
David H Koch Theater 20 Lincoln Ctr	New York	NY	10023	212-870-5656		573-1
Web: www.nycballet.com						
New York City Children's Center-Queens Campus (NYCCC)						
74-03 Commonwealth Blvd	Bellerose	NY	11426	718-264-4500	740-0968	374-1
Web: omh.ny.gov						
New York City College of Technology						
300 Jay St	Brooklyn	NY	11201	718-260-5000	260-5504	166
TF: 855-492-3633 ■ *Web:* www.citytech.cuny.edu						
New York City Ctr 130 W 56th St	New York	NY	10019	212-247-0430	246-9778	572
Web: www.nycitycenter.org						
New York City Department of Education						
65 Ct St	Brooklyn	NY	11201	718-935-4000		685
Web: www.schools.nyc.gov						
New York City Fire Museum						
278 Spring St	New York	NY	10013	212-691-1303	352-3117	520
Web: www.nycfiremuseum.org						
New York City Hall City Hall Pk	New York	NY	10007	212-639-9675		337
Web: www.nyc.gov						
New York City Health & Hospitals Corp						
125 Worth St	New York	NY	10013	212-788-3339		353
Web: www.nychealthandhospitals.org						
New York City Housing Development Corp						
110 William St	New York	NY	10038	212-227-5500		217
TF: 866-703-9549 ■ *Web:* www.nychdc.com						
New York City Partnership & Chamber of Commerce Inc						
1 Battery Park Plz 5th Fl	New York	NY	10004	212-493-7400	344-3344	139
Web: www.pfnyc.org						
New York Community Bank						
615 Merrick Ave	Westbury	NY	11590	877-786-6560		70
TF: 877-786-6560 ■ *Web:* www.mynycb.com						
New York Community Hospital						
2525 Kings Hwy	Brooklyn	NY	11229	718-692-5300		374-3
Web: nych.com						
New York Community Trust						
909 Third Ave 22nd Fl	New York	NY	10022	212-686-0010	532-8528	303
Web: www.nycommunitytrust.org						
New York Correctional Industries						
550 Broadway	Albany	NY	12204	518-436-6321	436-6007	630
TF: 800-436-6321 ■ *Web:* www.corcraft.org						
New York County Lawyers Assn						
14 Vesey St	New York	NY	10007	212-267-6646		533
TF: 800-255-0569 ■ *Web:* www.nycla.org						
New York Daily News 4 New York Plaza	New York	NY	10004	212-210-2100		532-2
Web: www.nydailynews.com						
New York Eye & Ear Infirmary						
310 E 14th St	New York	NY	10003	212-979-4000		374-7
TF: 800-522-4582 ■ *Web:* www.nyee.edu						
New York Foundation for the Arts (NYFA)						
20 Jay St 7th Fl	Brooklyn	NY	11201	212-366-6900	366-1778	572
Web: www.nyfa.org						
New York Giants						
1925 Giants Dr	East Rutherford	NJ	07073	201-935-8111		715-3
Web: www.giants.com						
New York Global Group Inc						
55 Broad St	New York	NY	10004	212-566-0499		401
Web: www.nyggroup.com						
New York Golf Ctr 131 W 35th St	New York	NY	10001	212-564-2255		711
Web: www.nygolfcenter.com						
New York Graphic Society Ltd						
129 Glover Ave	Norwalk	CT	06850	203-661-2400		637-10
TF: 800-221-1032 ■ *Web:* www.nygs.com						
New York Hall of Science						
47-01 111th St	Queens	NY	11368	718-699-0005		520
Web: nysci.org						
New York Health Care Inc						
33 W Hawthorne Ave 3rd Fl	Valley Stream	NY	11580	718-375-6700	488-9700	363
OTC: BBAL ■ *TF:* 877-350-6942 ■ *Web:* nyhc.com						
New York Historical Society						
170 Central Pk W	New York	NY	10024	212-873-3400	874-8706	520
Web: www.nyhistory.org						
New York Home Health Care Equipment						
30 Hopper St	Westbury	NY	11590	516-333-2473		475
Web: www.nyhhc.com						
New York Hotel Trades 707 Eighth Ave	New York	NY	10036	212-245-8100		132
Web: www.hotelworkers.org						
New York Imaging Service Inc						
1 D Alfonso Rd	Newburgh	NY	12550	845-561-6947	561-2266	416
Web: www.nyimagingservice.org						
New York Institute of Finance (NYIF)						
160 Broadway 15th Fl	New York	NY	10038	347-842-2501		423
Web: www.nyif.com						
New York Institute of Technology						
New York Institute of Technology Northern Blvd						
PO Box 8000	Old Westbury	NY	11568	516-686-1000		166
TF: 800-345-6948 ■ *Web:* www.nyit.edu						
New York International Raceway Park						
2011 New Rd	Leicester	NY	14481	585-382-3030		515
Web: empiredragway.com						
New York Jets LLC 1 Jets Dr	Florham Park	NJ	07932	973-549-4800		713
Web: www.newyorkjets.com						
New York Junior Tennis League Inc						
5812 Queens Blvd Ste 1	Woodside	NY	11377	347-417-8100		354
Web: www.nyjtl.org						
New York Law School 185 W Broadway	New York	NY	10013	212-431-2100	966-1522	167-1
Web: www.nyls.edu						
New York Library Assn (NYLA)						
6021 State Farm Rd	Guilderland	NY	12084	518-432-6952	427-1697	435
TF: 800-252-6952 ■ *Web:* www.nyla.org						
New York Life Foundation						
51 Madison Ave	New York	NY	10010	212-576-7341		304
Web: www.newyorklife.com						
New York Life Insurance & Annuity Corp						
51 Madison Ave	New York	NY	10010	212-576-7000		391-2
TF: 800-598-2019 ■ *Web:* www.nylinvestments.com						
New York Magazine 75 Varick St	New York	NY	10013	212-508-0700		457-22
TF: 800-678-0900 ■ *Web:* www.nymag.com						
New York Medical Associates						
635 Madison Ave 3rd Fl	New York	NY	10022	212-439-6690	249-6856	374-3
Web: www.nymamed.com						
New York Medical College						
40 Sunshine Cottage Rd	Valhalla	NY	10595	914-594-4507		167-2
Web: www.nymc.edu						
New York Military Academy						
78 Academy Ave	Cornwall-on-Hudson	NY	12520	845-534-3710		622
Web: www.nyma.org						
New York Mortgage Trust Inc (NYMT)						
52 Vanderbilt Ave Ste 403	New York	NY	10017	212-792-0107		654
NASDAQ: NYMT ■ *Web:* www.nymtrust.com						
New York New York Hotel & Casino						
3790 Las Vegas Blvd S	Las Vegas	NV	89109	702-740-6969	740-6700	133
TF: 800-689-1797 ■ *Web:* www.newyorknewyork.com						
New York Paint & Hardware						
1593 2nd Ave	New York	NY	10028	212-734-6900		351
Web: www.nypaintandhardware.com						
New York Palace Hotel						
455 Madison Ave 50th St	New York	NY	10022	212-888-7000	303-6000	379
TF: 800-697-2522 ■ *Web:* www.lottenypalace.com						
New York Philharmonic						
10 Lincoln Center Plz	New York	NY	10023	212-875-5900	875-5717	573-3
Web: nyphil.org						
New York Pops 333 W 52nd St Ste 900	New York	NY	10019	212-765-7677	315-3199	573-3
Web: www.newyorkpops.org						

Name / Address	City	State	ZIP	Phone	Fax	Class
New York Post 1211 Avenue of the Americas *TF:* 800-552-7678 ■ *Web:* nypost.com	New York	NY	10036	212-930-8000		532-2
New York Power Authority (NYPA) 123 Main St PO Box 10 B *Web:* www.nypa.gov	White Plains	NY	10601	914-681-6200		787
New York Presbyterian Hospital 525 E 68th St *TF:* 888-694-5700 ■ *Web:* www.nyp.org	New York	NY	10021	212-746-5454	746-4293	374-3
New York Prime 2350 Executive Center Dr NW *Web:* newyorkprime.com	Boca Raton	FL	33431	561-998-3881		671
New York Private Bank & Trust FSB 200 Bellevue Pkwy Ste 500 *Web:* www.nyptrust.com	Wilmington	DE	19809	302-792-4737		70
New York Professional Nurses Union (NYPNU) 241 E 75th St *Web:* www.nypnu.org	New York	NY	10021	212-988-5565		533
New York Prosecutors Training Institute 150 State St 5th Fl *Web:* www.nypti.org	Albany	NY	12210	518-432-1100		428
New York Red Bulls 600 Cape May St *TF:* 877-727-6223 ■ *Web:* www.newyorkredbulls.com	Harrison	NJ	07029	877-727-6223		717
New York Replacement Parts Corp 1462 Lexington Ave *TF:* 800-228-4718 ■ *Web:* www.nyrpcorp.com	New York	NY	10128	800-228-4718		612
New York Republican State Committee 315 State St *Web:* nygop.org	Albany	NY	12210	518-462-2601	449-7443	616-2
New York Review of Books 435 Hudson St 3rd Fl *TF:* 800-354-0050 ■ *Web:* www.nybooks.com	New York	NY	10014	212-757-8070	333-5374	457-11
New York Road Runners Club 320 W 57th St *Web:* www.nyrr.org	New York	NY	10019	212-860-4455		305
New York School of Interior Design 170 E 70th St *TF:* 800-336-9743 ■ *Web:* www.nysid.edu	New York	NY	10021	212-472-1500	472-3800	166
New York Sports Club 217 Broadway - City Hall *Web:* www.newyorksportsclubs.com	New York	NY	10106	212-791-9555		714-1
New York State Association of Realtors 130 Washington Ave *Web:* www.nysar.com	Albany	NY	12210	518-463-0300	462-5474	656
New York State Bar Assn 1 Elk St *TF:* 800-342-3661 ■ *Web:* www.nysba.org	Albany	NY	12207	518-463-3200	487-5517	72
New York State Bridge Authority PO Box 1010 *Web:* www.nysba.state.ny.us	Highland Falls	NY	12528	845-691-7245	691-3560	271
New York State Canal Corp 200 Southern Blvd PO Box 189 *TF:* 800-422-6254 ■ *Web:* www.canals.ny.gov	Albany	NY	12201	518-449-6000		465
New York State Dental Assn 20 Corporate Woods Blvd Ste 602 *TF:* 800-255-2100 ■ *Web:* www.nysdental.org	Albany	NY	12211	518-465-0044	465-3219	227
New York State Medical Society 865 Merrick Ave PO Box 5404 *TF:* 800-523-4405 ■ *Web:* www.mssny.org	Westbury	NY	11590	516-488-6100	488-1267	474
New York State Nurses Assn (NYSNA) 11 Cornell Rd *Web:* www.nysna.org	Latham	NY	12110	518-782-9400		533
New York State Office of Court Administration 25 Beaver St *Web:* www.nycourts.gov	New York	NY	10004	212-428-2700		340-14
New York State Veterans Home at Oxford 4207 New York 220 *Web:* Www.apps.health.ny.gov	Oxford	NY	13830	607-843-3100		793
New York State Veterans' Home at St Albans 178-50 Linden Blvd *Web:* veterans.ny.gov	Jamaica	NY	11434	718-990-0353		793
New York State Veterans' Home, Batavia 220 Richmond Ave *Web:* Www.apps.health.ny.gov	Batavia	NY	14020	585-345-2000		793
New York State Veterinary Medical Society 300 Great Oaks Blvd Ste 314 *TF:* 800-876-9867 ■ *Web:* www.nysvms.org	Albany	NY	12203	518-869-7867	869-7868	795
New York Susquehanna & Western Railway Corp (NYSW) 1 Railroad Ave *TF:* 800-366-6979 ■ *Web:* www.nysw.com	Cooperstown	NY	13326	607-547-2555	547-9834	648
New York Teacher Magazine 800 Troy-Schenectady Rd *TF:* 800-342-9810 ■ *Web:* www.nysut.org	Latham	NY	12110	518-213-6000	213-6415	457-8
New York Theatre Ballet 30 E 31st St *Web:* nytb.org	New York	NY	10016	212-679-0401	679-8171	573-1
New York Theological Seminary 475 Riverside Dr Ste 500 *Web:* www.nyts.edu	New York	NY	10115	212-870-1211	870-1236	167-3
New York Times 620 Eigth Ave *Web:* www.nytco.com	New York	NY	10018	212-556-1234		532-2
New York Transit Museum 99 Schermerhorn St *Web:* www.nytransitmuseum.org	Brooklyn	NY	11201	718-694-1600	694-5556	520
New York Twist Drill Inc (NYTD) 5368 E Rockton Rd *Web:* www.newyorktwistdrill.com	South Beloit	IL	61080	800-543-0972		455
New York University 70 Washington Sq S *Web:* www.nyu.edu	New York	NY	10012	212-998-1212		167-3
New York University Federal Credit Union 726 Broadway Ste 110 **Fax Area Code:* 347 ■ *TF:* 855-226-1712 ■ *Web:* nyufcu.com	New York	NY	10003	212-995-3171	602-4751*	219
New York University Press (NYUP) 838 Broadway 3rd Fl *TF:* 800-996-6987 ■ *Web:* nyupress.org	New York	NY	10003	212-998-2575	995-3833	637-2
New York University School of Law (NYU) 40 Washington Sq S *Web:* www.law.nyu.edu	New York	NY	10012	212-998-6100	995-4527	167-1
New York Women in Film & Television 6 E 39th St Ste 1200 *Web:* www.nywift.org	New York	NY	10016	212-679-0870		138
New York's Hotel Pennsylvania 401 Seventh Ave *TF:* 800-223-8585 ■ *Web:* www.hotelpenn.com	New York	NY	10001	212-736-5000	502-8712	379
New Yorker 48 W Market St Ste 250 *Web:* newyorkerslc.com	Salt Lake City	UT	84101	801-363-0166		671
New Yorker Hotel 481 Eigth Ave *Web:* www.newyorkerhotel.com	New York	NY	10001	212-971-0101		379
New York-New Jersey Trail Conference 600 Ramapo Valley Rd *Web:* www.nynjtc.org	Mahwah	NJ	07430	201-512-9348		239
New Zealand *Consulate General* 2425 Olympic Blvd Ste 600-E *Web:* www.mfat.govt.nz	Santa Monica	CA	90404	310-566-6555	566-6556	257
Embassy 37 Observatory Cir NW *TF:* 866-639-9325 ■ *Web:* www.mfat.govt.nz	Washington	DC	20008	202-328-4800	667-5277	257
New Zealand Tourism Board 501 Santa Monica Blvd Ste 300 *Web:* www.newzealand.com	Santa Monica	CA	90401	310-395-7480	395-5453	775
New:Team SoftWare Inc (NTS) PO Box 254807 *Web:* www.go2nts.com	Sacramento	CA	95865	415-461-8086		178-1
NewAge Industries Inc 145 James Way *TF:* 800-506-3924 ■ *Web:* www.newageindustries.com	Southampton	PA	18966	215-526-2300	526-2190	370
Newage Testing Instruments Inc 820 Pennsylvania Blvd *Web:* www.hardnesstesters.com	Feasterville-Trevose	PA	19053	215-355-6900		407
NewAgeSys Inc 231 Clarksville Rd Ste 200 *TF:* 888-863-9243 ■ *Web:* www.newagesys.com	Princeton Junction	NJ	08550	609-919-9800	919-9830	180
Newark Business Training Institute 346 Mt Prospect Ave *Web:* www.northwardcenter.org	Newark	NJ	07104	973-268-8900	481-6071	167-3
Newark Chamber of Commerce 37101 Newark Blvd *TF:* 844-245-8925 ■ *Web:* newark-chamber.com	Newark	CA	94560	510-578-4500		139
Newark Liberty International Airport 3 Brewster Rd *TF:* 888-397-4636 ■ *Web:* www.panynj.gov	Newark	NJ	07114	973-961-6000		27
Newark Museum 49 Washington St *TF:* 888-370-6765 ■ *Web:* www.newarkmuseumart.org	Newark	NJ	07102	973-596-6550	642-0459	520
Newark Public Library 101 W Main St *Web:* www.newarklibrary.info	Newark	OH	43055	740-349-5500		434-3
Newark Regional Business Partnership 744 Broad St 26th Fl *Web:* www.newarkrbp.org	Newark	NJ	07102	973-522-0099	824-6587	139
Newark Symphony Hall 1030 Broad St *Web:* www.newarksymphonyhall.org	Newark	NJ	07102	973-643-8014		572
Newark Toyota 230 E Cleveland Ave *Web:* www.newarktoyotaworld.com	Newark	DE	19711	302-368-6262		57
Newark Trade Digital Graphics 177 Oakwood Ave *Web:* www.newarktrade.com	Orange	NJ	07050	973-674-3727		627
Neway Flow Control Inc 9757 Stafford Centre Dr *Web:* www.newayvalve.com	Stafford	TX	77477	281-969-5500	969-5900	789
Neway Packaging Corp 1973 E Via Arado *TF:* 800-456-3929 ■ *Web:* www.newaypackaging.com	Rancho Dominguez	CA	90220	310-898-3400		96
Newaygo County 1087 Newell St *Web:* www.countyofnewaygo.com	White Cloud	MI	49349	231-689-7200	689-7205	338
Newaygo State Park 2793 Beech St *Web:* www.michigan.org	Newaygo	MI	49337	231-856-4452		565
Newberg School District 29 Jt 714 E Sixth St *Web:* www.newberg.k12.or.us	Newberg	OR	97132	503-554-5000	538-4374	685
Newberry Area Tourism Assn, The PO Box 308 *TF:* 800-832-5216 ■ *Web:* www.newberrytourism.com	Newberry	MI	49868	906-293-5562		206
Newberry College 2100 College St *TF:* 800-845-4955 ■ *Web:* www.newberry.edu	Newberry	SC	29108	803-276-5010	321-5138	166
Newberry Correctional Facility 13747 E County Rd 428 *Web:* www.michigan.gov	Newberry	MI	49868	906-293-6200		213
Newberry County 1226 College St PO Box 156 *Web:* www.newberrycounty.net	Newberry	SC	29108	803-321-2042	321-2102	338
Newberry County Chamber of Commerce 1209 Caldwell St PO Box 396 *Web:* www.newberrycountychamber.com	Newberry	SC	29108	803-276-4274	276-4373	139
Newberry Electric Co-opeartive Inc 882 Wilson Rd *TF:* 800-479-8838 ■ *Web:* www.nec.coop	Newberry	SC	29108	803-276-1121		245
Newberry Group Inc 2510 Old Hwy 94 S Ste 200 *Web:* newberrygroup.com	Saint Charles	MO	63303	636-928-9944	928-8899	180
Newbold Corp 450 Weaver St *TF:* 800-552-3282 ■ *Web:* www.newboldcorp.com	Rocky Mount	VA	24151	540-489-4400	489-4417	111
newBrandAnalytics Inc 1250 23rd St NW Ste 450 *Web:* www.newbrandanalytics.com	Washington	DC	20037	202-800-7850		195
Newbridge Securities Corp 1451 W Cypress Creek Rd Ste 300 *TF:* 877-447-9625 ■ *Web:* www.newbridgefinancial.com	Fort Lauderdale	FL	33309	954-278-8135		690
Newbrook Insurance Agency Inc 14 Roosevelt Ave *Web:* newbrookins.com	Port Jefferson	NY	11776	631-473-7059		390
Newbury College 129 Fisher Ave *Web:* www.newbury.edu	Brookline	MA	02445	617-730-7000	731-9618	166
Newbury Comics Inc 5 Guest St *Web:* www.newbury.com	Brighton	MA	02135	617-254-1666		525
Newburyport Five Cents Savings Bank Inc, The 63 State St PO Box 350 *Web:* www.newburyportbank.com	Newburyport	MA	01950	978-462-3136		70

Phone Fax Class

Newby Pridgen Sartip & Masel LLC
4593 Oleander Dr . . . Myrtle Beach SC 29577 843-449-9417 449-9419 445
TF: 800-858-5592 ■ *Web:* www.newbylaw.com

Newby Rubber Inc
320 Industrial St . . . Bakersfield CA 93307 661-327-5137 327-8058 676
Web: www.newbyrubber.com

Newcastle Place Inc
12600 N Port Washington Rd . . . Mequon WI 53092 262-387-8800 371
Web: www.newcastleplacelcs.com

NewCloud Networks
160 Inverness Dr W . . . Englewood CO 80112 855-255-5001 387
TF: 855-255-5001 ■ *Web:* newcloudnetworks.com

Newcomb & Boyd
303 Peachtree Center Ave NE Ste 525 . . . Atlanta GA 30303 404-730-8400 730-8401 261
Web: www.newcomb-boyd.com

Newcomb Broadcasting Corp
161-B Hillwood Ave . . . Falls Church VA 22046 719-532-1220 645-141
Web: www.wfax.com

Newcomb Spring Corp 235 Spring St . . . Southington CT 06489 860-621-0111 621-7048 719
TF: 888-579-3051 ■ *Web:* newcombspring.com

NewComLink Inc
3900 N Capital of Texas Hwy Ste 150 . . . Austin TX 78746 888-988-0603 253
TF: 888-988-0603 ■ *Web:* vyze.com

Newcon Optik 105 Sparks Ave . . . Toronto ON M2H2S5 416-663-6963 663-9065 529
Web: www.newcon-optik.com

Newcut Inc 434 E Union St . . . Newark NY 14513 315-331-7680 331-0313 481
Web: www.newcut.com

Newdea Inc
6400 So Fiddlers Green Cir
Ste 1970 . . . Greenwood Village CO 80111 720-249-3030 196
TF: 877-412-4829 ■ *Web:* www.newdea.com

NewDominion Bank
1111 Metropolitan Ave Ste 500 . . . Charlotte NC 28204 704-943-5700 70
TF: 800-592-6248 ■ *Web:* newdominionbank.com

Newegg Inc 16839 E Gale Ave . . . City of Industry CA 91745 626-271-9700 179
TF: 800-390-1119 ■ *Web:* www.newegg.com

Newell Brands 221 River St . . . Hoboken NJ 07030 201-610-6600 185
NYSE: NWL ■ *Web:* www.newellbrands.com

Newell Coach Corp 3900 N Main St . . . Miami OK 74354 918-542-3344 542-2028 120
TF: 888-363-9355 ■ *Web:* www.newellcoach.com

Newell Paper Co 1212 Grand Ave . . . Meridian MS 39301 800-844-8894 483-4900* 553
**Fax Area Code:* 601 ■ *TF:* 800-844-8894 ■ *Web:* meridian.newellpaper.com

Newell Rubbermaid Inc
Irwin Tools Div
8935 Northpointe Executive Dr . . . Huntersville NC 28078 704-987-4555 758
TF: 800-866-5740 ■ *Web:* www.irwin.com

Newfield Exploration Co
24 Waterway Ave Ste 900 . . . The Woodlands TX 77380 281-847-6000 405-4242 536
NYSE: NFX ■ *TF:* 866-902-0562 ■ *Web:* newfield.com

Newfield National Bank 18 SW Blvd . . . Newfield NJ 08344 856-692-3440 697-3114 70
TF: 800-690-3440 ■ *Web:* www.newfieldnationalbank.bank

Newfields 4000 Michigan Rd . . . Indianapolis IN 46208 317-923-1331 931-1978 97
Web: Www.discovernewfields.org

Newforma Inc 1750 Elm St . . . Manchester NH 03104 603-625-6212 248-6145 177
TF: 877-875-8252 ■ *Web:* www.newforma.com

Newgard Development Group Inc
1300 Brickell Bay Dr Ste 400 . . . Miami FL 33131 305-938-5707 653
Web: newgardgroup.com

Newgate Mall 36th St & Wall Ave . . . Ogden UT 84405 801-621-1161 460
Web: www.newgatemall.com

Newgen Software Inc
1364 Beverly Rd Ste 300 . . . McLean VA 22101 703-749-2855 177
Web: www.newgensoft.com

NewGround Resources Inc
15450 S Outer Forty Dr Ste 300 . . . Chesterfield MO 63017 636-898-8100 186
Web: www.newground.com

Newhall Klein Inc 6109 W Kl Ave . . . Kalamazoo MI 49009 269-544-0844 344
TF: 866-639-4255 ■ *Web:* newhallklein.com

Newhall Land
25124 Springfield Ct Ste 300 . . . Valencia CA 91355 661-255-4000 653
Web: valencia.com

Newhouse & Creager LLP
23801 Calabasas Rd Ste 2037 . . . Calabasas CA 91302 818-222-5600 855-8082 41
Web: newhouseandcreager.com

Newhouse Dan (Rep R - WA)
1414 Longworth House Office Bldg . . . Washington DC 20515 202-225-5816 225-3251 342-2
Web: www.newhouse.house.gov

Newhouse Manufacturing Company Inc
1048 NW 6th St . . . Redmond OR 97756 541-548-1055 548-4144 273
TF: 800-587-1055 ■ *Web:* www.newhouse-mfg.com

Newins Bay Shore Ford Inc
219 W Main St . . . Bay Shore NY 11706 631-665-1300 57
Web: www.newinsbayshoreford.com

Newjac Inc 415 S Grant St . . . Lebanon IN 46052 765-483-2190 697
TF: 800-827-3259 ■ *Web:* www.newjac.com

Newland 4790 Eastgate Mall Ste 150 . . . San Diego CA 92121 858-455-7503 455-5368 652
Web: www.newlandco.com

Newlands Systems Inc
D 31087 Peardonville Rd . . . Abbotsford BC V2T6Y7 604-855-4890 80-3
TF: 877-855-4890 ■ *Web:* nsibrew.com

NewLife Radio 100 S Hill St Ste 100 . . . Griffin GA 30223 770-229-2020 645-11
Web: newliferadio.com

NewLine Communications
831 Lincoln Ave Unit 15 . . . West Chester PA 19380 610-692-3616 692-6468 328
Web: newlinecom.com

NewlineNoosh Inc
625 Ellis St Ste 300 . . . Mountain View CA 94043 650-637-6000 965-1377 178-1
TF: 888-286-6674 ■ *Web:* noosh.com

Newly Weds Foods Inc
4140 W Fullerton Ave . . . Chicago IL 60639 773-489-7000 296-37
TF: 800-621-7521 ■ *Web:* newlywedsfoods.com

New-Mac Electric Co-opeartive Inc
12105 E Hwy 86 . . . Neosho MO 64850 417-451-1515 245
TF: 800-322-3849 ■ *Web:* www.newmac.com

Newman & Company Inc
6101 Tacony St . . . Philadelphia PA 19135 215-333-8700 332-8586 561
TF: 800-523-3256 ■ *Web:* newmanpaperboard.com

Newman & Simpson LLP 32 Mercer St . . . Hackensack NJ 07601 201-487-0200 41
Web: newmansimpson.com

Newman Grace Inc
6133 Fallbrook Ave . . . Woodland Hills CA 91367 818-713-1678 4
Web: www.newmangrace.com

Newman Regional Health
1201 W 12th Ave . . . Emporia KS 66801 620-343-6800 374-3
Web: www.newmanrh.org

Newman Sanitary Gasket Company Inc
964 W Main St . . . Lebanon OH 45036 513-932-7379 326
Web: www.newmangasket.com

Newman Signs Inc 1606 6th Ave SW . . . Jamestown ND 58401 701-252-1970 252-7325 8
TF: 800-337-9770 ■ *Web:* www.newmansigns.com

Newman Technology Inc 100 Cairns Rd . . . Mansfield OH 44903 419-525-1856 247
Web: www.newmantech.com

Newman Theological College (NTC)
10012-84 St . . . Edmonton AB T6A0B2 780-392-2450 462-4013 167-3
TF: 844-392-2450 ■ *Web:* www.newman.edu

Newman University 3100 McCormick Ave . . . Wichita KS 67213 316-942-4291 942-4483 166
TF: 877-639-6268 ■ *Web:* www.newmanu.edu

Newman's Own Inc 246 Post Rd E . . . Westport CT 06880 203-222-0136 227-5630 296-19
Web: www.newmansown.com

Newman, Mathis, Brady & Spedale, APLC
433 Metairie Rd Ste 600 . . . Metairie LA 70005 504-837-9040 41
Web: newmanmathis.com

NewmanPR 2140 S Dixie Hwy Ste 203 . . . Miami FL 33133 305-461-3300 317
Web: www.newmanpr.com

Newmans Valve LLC
4655 Wright Rd Ste 250 . . . Stafford TX 77477 832-944-5930 944-5929 385
Web: www.newmansvalves.com

Newmar Corp 355 Delaware St . . . Nappanee IN 46550 574-773-7791 120
TF: 800-731-8300 ■ *Web:* www.newmarcorp.com

Newmar Window Manufacturing Inc
7630 Airport Rd . . . Mississauga ON L4T4G6 905-672-1233 672-1076 235
TF: 800-263-5634 ■ *Web:* www.newmar.com

Newmark Grubb Knight Frank
1800 Larimer St . . . Denver CO 80202 303-892-1111 652
Web: www.ngkf.com

Newmark Learning LLC
145 Huguenot St . . . New Rochelle NY 10801 877-280-0375 637-2
TF: 877-280-0375 ■ *Web:* www.newmarklearning.com

Newmarket Chamber of Commerce
470 Davis Dr . . . Newmarket ON L3Y2P3 905-898-5900 137
Web: www.newmarketchamber.ca

Newmarket Public Library
438 Park Ave . . . Newmarket ON L3Y1W1 905-953-5110 42
Web: www.newmarketpl.ca

Newmeyer & Dillion LLP
895 Dove St 5th Fl . . . Newport Beach CA 92660 949-854-7000 428
Web: www.newmeyeranddillion.com

Newmont Goldcorp
6363 S Fiddler's Green Cir Ste 800 . . . Greenwood Village CO 80111 303-863-7414 837-5837 503-1
Web: www.newmontgoldcorp.com

Newnan-Coweta Chamber of Commerce
23 Bullsboro Dr . . . Newnan GA 30263 770-253-2270 253-2271 139
Web: www.newnancowetachamber.org

NewPages PO Box 1580 . . . Bay City MI 48706 989-671-0081 95
Web: www.newpages.com

Newpark Mall 2086 Newpark Mall . . . Newark CA 94560 510-794-5523 460
Web: www.newparkmall.com

Newpark Mats & Integrated Services LLC
2700 Research Forest Dr Ste 100 . . . The Woodlands TX 77381 281-362-6800 539
TF: 877-628-7623 ■ *Web:* www.newpark.com

Newport Animal Hospital Inc
333 Valley Rd . . . Middletown RI 02842 401-849-3400 794
Web: newportanimalhospital.com

Newport Aquarium 1 Aquarium Way . . . Newport KY 41071 800-406-3474 261-5888* 40
**Fax Area Code:* 859 ■ *TF:* 800-406-3474 ■ *Web:* www.newportaquarium.com

Newport Art Museum 76 Bellevue Ave . . . Newport RI 02840 401-848-8200 848-8205 520
Web: www.newportartmuseum.org

Newport Asia LLC
601 California St Ste 1168 . . . San Francisco CA 94108 415-677-8620 401
Web: www.newportasiallc.com

Newport Avenue Market
1121 NW Newport Ave . . . Bend OR 97701 541-382-3940 345
Web: newportavemarket.com

Newport Bay Club & Hotel
337 Thames St PO Box 1440 . . . Newport RI 02840 401-849-8600 379
Web: www.newportbayclub.com

Newport Beach Chamber of Commerce
690 Newport Center Dr . . . Newport Beach CA 92660 949-729-4400 729-4417 139
Web: www.newportbeach.com

Newport Beach Conference & Visitors Bureau
1200 Newport Center Dr Ste 120 . . . Newport Beach CA 92660 949-719-6100 206
TF: 800-216-1598 ■ *Web:* www.visitnewportbeach.com

Newport Beach Hotel & Suites
1 Wave Ave . . . Middletown RI 02842 401-846-0310 847-2621 379
TF: 800-655-1778 ■ *Web:* www.newportbeachhotelandsuites.com

Newport Beachside Hotel & Resort
16701 Collins Ave . . . North Miami Beach FL 33160 305-949-1300 379
TF: 800-327-5476 ■ *Web:* www.newportbeachsideresort.com

Newport Capital Group LLC
12 Broad St 5th Fl . . . Red Bank NJ 07701 732-741-8400 579
Web: www.newportcapitalgroup.com

Newport CH International LLC
1100 W Town & Country Rd Ste 1388 . . . Orange CA 92868 714-572-8881 690
Web: newportch.com

Newport City Hall 43 Broadway . . . Newport RI 02840 401-845-5300 845-2510 337
Web: www.cityofnewport.com

Newport County 45 Washington Sq . . . Newport RI 02840 401-841-8330 846-1673 338
Web: www.courts.ri.gov

Newport County Chamber of Commerce
513 Broadway . . . Newport RI 02840 401-847-1608 140
Web: www.newportchamber.com

Newport County Convention & Visitors Bureau
23 America's Cup Ave . . . Newport RI 02840 401-849-8048 206
Web: www.discovernewport.org

Newport Creamery LLC
35 Sockanossel Cross Rd 100 Hillside Rd . . . Cranston RI 02920 401-944-3397 296-25
Web: www.newportcreamery.com

Phone | Fax | Class

Newport Creative Communications Inc
33 Railroad Ave Ste 1 Duxbury MA 02332 781-934-0586 463
Web: www.newportcreative.com

Newport Daily News 272 Valley Rd Middletown RI 02842 401-849-3300 849-3306 532-2
Web: www.newportri.com

Newport Diversified Inc
4695 MacArthur Ct Ste 1420 Newport Beach CA 92660 949-851-1355 851-6304 322
Web: nd-inc.com

Newport Electronics Inc
2229 S Yale St Santa Ana CA 92704 203-968-7315 546-3022* 248
**Fax Area Code:* 714 ■ *TF:* 800-639-7678 ■ *Web:* www.newportinc.com

Newport Group Inc
1350 Treat Blvd Ste 300 Walnut Creek CA 94597 925-328-4540 690
Web: www.newportgroup.com

Newport Harbor Hotel & Marina
49 America's Cup Ave Newport RI 02840 401-847-9000 849-6380 379
TF: 800-955-2558 ■ *Web:* www.newporthotel.com

Newport Hospital (NH) 167 Point St Providence RI 02903 401-793-8808 374-3
Web: www.newporthospital.org

Newport Integrated Behavioral Healthcare
1810 Moseri Rd Decatur GA 30032 404-289-8223 289-8224* 374-5
**Fax Area Code:* 208 ■ *Web:* www.nibhinc.com

Newport Layton Home Fashions Inc
8515 N Columbia Blvd Portland OR 97203 503-283-4864 283-4895 746
Web: www.newportlayton.com

Newport News Tourism Development Office
702 Town Center Dr Newport News VA 23606 757-926-1400 926-1441 206
Web: www.newport-news.org

Newport News/Williamsburg International Airport
900 Bland Blvd Ste G Newport News VA 23602 757-877-0221 27
Web: flyphf.com

Newport on the Levee
1 Levee Way Ste 1113 Newport KY 41071 859-291-0550 291-7020 50-6
Web: www.newportonthelevee.com

Newport Partners LLC
3760 Tanglewood Ln Davidsonville MD 21035 301-889-0017 743
TF: 866-302-0017 ■ *Web:* newportpartnersllc.com

Newport Plain Talk 145 E Broadway Newport TN 37821 423-623-6171 532-2
Web: www.newportplaintalk.com

Newport Public Library 300 Spring St Newport RI 02840 401-847-8720 842-0841 434-3
Web: www.newportlibraryri.org

Newport Real Estate Services Inc (NRES)
2280 University Dr Ste 101 Newport Beach CA 92660 714-850-0085 194
Web: www.nres.net

Newport Seafood Grill 1717 Freeway Ct Salem OR 97303 503-315-7100 670
Web: newportseafoodgrill.com

Newport Shipyard 1 Washington St Newport RI 02840 401-846-6000 846-6001 698
Web: www.newportshipyard.com

Newport State Park
475 County Rd NP Ellison Bay WI 54210 920-854-2500 854-1914 565
Web: dnr.wi.gov

Newport Stationers Inc
17681 Mitchell N Irvine CA 92614 949-863-1200 852-8970 535
Web: www.newportstationers.com

Newport Strategic Search Inc
175 Calle Magdalena Encinitas CA 92024 760-274-0100 260
Web: www.newportsearch.com

Newport Utilities PO Box 519 Newport TN 37822 423-625-2800 245
Web: www.newportutilities.com

Newport/Cocke County Chamber of Commerce
433-B Prospect Ave Newport TN 37821 423-623-7201 139
Web: www.newportcockecountychamber.com

Newport-West Data Services Inc
18120 Bollinger Canyon Rd Bldg 2 Ste A San Ramon CA 94583 925-855-1131 177
Web: www.nwds.com

NewRetirement LLC
100 Pine St Ste 590 San Francisco CA 94111 415-738-2435 530
TF: 866-441-0246 ■ *Web:* www.newretirement.com

News & Advance PO Box 10129 Lynchburg VA 24506 434-385-5555 385-5538 532-2
TF: 800-275-8830 ■ *Web:* www.newsadvance.com

News & Observer 215 S McDowell St Raleigh NC 27602 919-829-4500 829-4529 532-2
TF: 800-522-4205 ■ *Web:* www.newsobserver.com

News & Record 200 E Market St Greensboro NC 27401 336-373-7000 532-2
TF: 800-553-6880 ■ *Web:* www.greensboro.com

News America Marketing
1185 Avenue of the Americas 27 New York NY 10036 212-782-8000 575-5845 5
TF: 800-462-0852 ■ *Web:* www.newsamerica.com

News Cafe 800 Ocean Dr Miami Beach FL 33139 305-538-6397 538-7817 671
Web: www.newscafe.com

News Center Maine One Congress Sq Portland ME 04101 207-828-6666 532-2
TF: 800-464-1213 ■ *Web:* www.newscentermaine.com

News Corp
1211 Avenue of the Americas New York NY 10036 212-416-3400 637-9
NASDAQ: NWSA ■ *Web:* newscorp.com

News Generation Inc
7508 Wisconsin Ave Ste 300 Bethesda MD 20814 301-664-6448 466
Web: www.newsgeneration.com

News Herald, The 301 Collett St Morganton NC 28655 828-437-2161 437-5372 532-2
Web: www.morganton.com

News Journal 70 W Fourth St Mansfield OH 44903 419-522-3311 532-2
TF: 877-424-0216 ■ *Web:* www.mansfieldnewsjournal.com

News Journal 950 W Basin Rd New Castle DE 19720 302-324-2500 324-5509 532-2
TF: 800-235-9100 ■ *Web:* www.delawareonline.com

News Leader 11 N Central Ave Staunton VA 24401 540-885-7281 532-2
TF: 800-793-2459 ■ *Web:* www.newsleader.com

News Media Guild
131 W 33rd St 14th Fl New York NY 10001 212-869-9290 840-0687 414
Web: www.newsmediaguild.org

News Publishing Co
1126 Mills St PO Box 286 Black Earth WI 53515 608-767-3655 637-8
Web: www.newspubinc.com

News Radio 1000 KTOK
1900 NW Expy Ste 1000 Oklahoma City OK 73118 405-841-0200 645-112
Web: ktok.iheart.com

News Radio 105 5 WERC
600 Beacon Pky W Ste 400 Birmingham AL 35209 205-439-9600 439-8390 643
TF: 877-811-3369 ■ *Web:* www.wercfm.com

News Radio 1410 WDOV
1575 McKee Rd Ste 206 Dover DE 19904 302-678-5300 645-174
Web: wdov.iheart.com

News Radio 610
70 Foundry St Ste 300 Manchester NH 03102 603-625-6915 645-93
Web: wgiram.iheart.com

News Radio 920 AM & 104.7 FM
75 Oxford St Ste 301 Providence RI 02905 866-920-9455 645-127
TF: 866-920-9455 ■ *Web:* newsradiori.iheart.com

News Radio710 555 Broadcast Dr Mobile AL 36606 251-450-0100 645-100
Web: newsradio710.iheart.com

News Reporter 1227 S Madison St Whiteville NC 28472 910-642-4104 642-1856 532-2
Web: nrcolumbus.com

News Talk 1490 6555 Carnegie Ave Cleveland OH 44103 216-579-1111 645-36
Web: newstalkcleveland.com

News Tribune, The 1950 S State St Tacoma WA 98405 253-597-8742 532-2
Web: www.thenewstribune.com

News/Talk 95.1 & 790 KFYO
4413 82nd St Ste 300 Lubbock TX 79424 806-798-7078 645-90
TF: 800-687-0790 ■ *Web:* kfyo.com

Newsbank Inc
5801 Pelican Bay Blvd Ste 600 Naples FL 34108 800-762-8182 263-3004* 387
**Fax Area Code:* 239 ■ *TF:* 800-243-7694 ■ *Web:* www.newsbank.com

News-banner Publications Inc
125 N Johnson St Bluffton IN 46714 260-824-0224 532-3
TF: 800-579-7476 ■ *Web:* news-banner.com

Newsday Inc 235 Pinelawn Rd Melville NY 11747 631-843-4050 843-2065 532-2
TF: 888-280-4719 ■ *Web:* www.newsday.com

Newsela Inc 620 8th Ave 21st Fl New York NY 10018 855-711-0118 788
TF: 855-711-0118 ■ *Web:* newsela.com

News-Enterprise 408 W Dixie Ave Elizabethtown KY 42701 270-769-1200 769-6965 532-2
Web: www.thenewsenterprise.com

Newser LLC 1395 Brickell Ave Ste 800 Miami FL 33131 305-967-6319 772
Web: www.newser.com

Newseum Inc
555 Pennsylvania Ave NW Washington DC 20001 202-292-6100 520
Web: www.newseum.org

News-Gazette Inc, The 15 Main St Champaign IL 61820 217-359-6500 351-5374 532-2
TF: 800-660-7323 ■ *Web:* www.news-gazette.com

News-Herald 501 W 11th St Panama City FL 32401 850-747-5050 532-2
Web: www.newsherald.com

News-Herald 7085 Mentor Ave Willoughby OH 44094 440-951-0000 975-2293 532-2
TF: 800-947-2737 ■ *Web:* www.news-herald.com

News-Herald, The
1 Heritage Dr Ste 100 Southgate MI 48195 734-246-0800 246-2727 637-8
TF: 888-361-6769 ■ *Web:* www.thenewsherald.com

Newslink Group LLC 6910 NW 12th St Miami FL 33126 305-594-5754 95
Web: newslinkgroup.net

Newsome Development & Investments Inc
1421 Oread West St Ste B Lawrence KS 66049 785-331-4644 653
Web: newsomedevelopment.com

Newsome House Museum & Cultural Ctr
2803 Oak Ave Newport News VA 23607 757-247-2360 926-6754 520
Web: www.newsomehouse.org

Newsome O'Donnell LLC
200 Campus Dr Ste 205 Florham Park NJ 07932 973-692-6500 41
Web: newsomeodonnell.com

Newsouth Capital Management Inc
999 S Shady Grove Rd Ste 501 Memphis TN 38120 901-761-5561 401
Web: www.newsouthcapital.com

Newspaper Guild-Communications Workers of America, The
501 Third St NW 6th Fl Washington DC 20001 202-434-7177 414
Web: www.newsguild.org

Newspaper Media Alliance
4401 Wilson Blvd Ste 900 Arlington VA 22203 571-366-1000 366-1195 49-14
Web: www.newsmediaalliance.org

NewSpring Capital
555 E Lancaster Ave 3rd Fl Radnor PA 19087 610-567-2380 567-2388 792
Web: www.newspringcapital.com

NewsRadio 790 WAEB
1541 Alta Dr Sunburst Office Bldg 4th Fl Whitehall PA 18052 610-434-1742 645
Web: 790waeb.iheart.com

NewsRadio WKCY
207 University Blvd Harrisonburg VA 22801 540-434-1777 432-9968 647
Web: newsradiowkcy.iheart.com

News-Sentinel 600 W Main St Fort Wayne IN 46802 260-461-8519 461-8817 532-2
TF: 800-324-0505 ■ *Web:* www.news-sentinel.com

News-Star 411 N Fourth St Monroe LA 71201 318-322-5161 532-2
Web: www.thenewsstar.com

News-Times 333 Main St Danbury CT 06810 203-730-0457 792-8730 532-2
TF: 877-542-6057 ■ *Web:* www.newstimes.com

Newstream Enterprises LLC
1925 E Chestnut Expy Springfield MO 65802 417-831-3112 61
Web: www.newstreaming.com

News-Tribune 426 Second St LaSalle IL 61301 815-224-3200 224-6443 532-2
TF: 800-892-6452 ■ *Web:* www.newstrib.com

Newsweek Magazine 7 Hanover Sq New York NY 10004 800-631-1040 457-17
TF: 800-631-1040 ■ *Web:* www.newsweek.com

Newt Global Consulting
1300 W Walnut Hill Ln Ste 230 Irving TX 75038 972-887-3159 177
Web: newtglobal.com

Newtec America Inc (NTA)
1055 Washington Blvd Stamford CT 06901 203-323-0042 323-8406 392
Web: www.newtec.be

Newtek Business Services Corp
1981 Marcus Ave Ste 130 Lake Success NY 11042 212-356-9500 792
NASDAQ: NEWT ■ *Web:* www.newtekone.com

NewTek Inc 5131 Beckwith Blvd San Antonio TX 78249 800-368-5441 370-8001* 178-8
**Fax Area Code:* 210 ■ *TF:* 800-862-7837 ■ *Web:* www.newtek.com

Newtex Industries Inc
8050 Victor Mendon Rd Victor NY 14564 585-924-9135 924-4645 745-3
TF: 800-836-1001 ■ *Web:* www.newtex.com

Newton & Associates Inc
1806 Rocky River Rd Charlotte NC 28213 704-597-4384 194
Web: www.newtonandassociates.com

Newton Convention & Visitor Bureau
201 E 6th St Newton IA 50208 316-284-3642 206
TF: 800-798-0299 ■ *Web:* tonewton.com

Name / Address	City	State	Zip	Phone	Fax	Class
Newton Correctional Facility 307 S 60th Ave W *Web:* www.doc.iowa.gov	Newton	IA	50208	641-792-7552		213
Newton County 1124 Clark St *Web:* www.co.newton.ga.us	Covington	GA	30014	678-625-1202		338
Newton County PO Box 68 *Web:* www.newtoncountyms.net	Decatur	MS	39327	601-635-2368		338
Newton County PO Box 312 *Web:* www.newtoncountysheriff.org	Jasper	AR	72641	870-446-5124		338
Newton County 201 N Third St *TF:* 888-663-9866 ■ *Web:* www.newtoncounty.in.gov	Kentland	IN	47951	219-474-6081		338
Newton County 115 Ct St PO Box 484 *Web:* www.co.newton.tx.us	Newton	TX	75966	409-379-5527	379-9049	338
Newton County Chamber of Commerce 2101 Clark St *Web:* www.gocovington.com	Covington	GA	30014	770-786-7510		139
Newton Crouch Inc 890 E Solomon St *Web:* www.newtoncrouch.com	Griffin	GA	30223	770-227-1234	229-5604	273
Newton Distributing Company Inc 245 W Central St *TF:* 877-837-7745 ■ *Web:* newtondistributing.com	Natick	MA	01760	617-969-4002	969-4071	612
Newton Falls Fine Paper Company LLC 875 County Rd 60	Newton Falls	NY	13666	315-848-3321		557
Newton Free Library 330 Homer St *Web:* newtonfreelibrary.net	Newton Center	MA	02459	617-796-1360		434-3
Newton Group Inc, The (TNG) 623 N 19th Ave E **Fax Area Code: 800* ■ *TF:* 800-232-5729 ■ *Web:* www.newtonpro.com	Newton	IA	50208	641-792-9962	809-8287*	542
Newton Hills State Park 28767 482nd Ave *Web:* gfp.sd.gov	Canton	SD	57013	605-987-2263		565
Newton History Museum Library 527 Washington St *Web:* www.historicnewton.org	Newton	MA	02458	617-796-1450	552-7228	434-3
Newton Independent School District 720 Rusk St *Web:* www.newtonisd.net	Newton	TX	75966	409-379-8137	379-2189	780
Newton Instrument Company Inc 111 E A St *Web:* www.enewton.com	Butner	NC	27509	919-575-6426		246
Newton Lake State Fish & Wildlife Area 3490 E 500th Ave *Web:* www.dnr.illinois.gov	Newton	IL	62448	618-783-3478		565
Newton Manufacturing Co 854 Angliana Ave *TF:* 855-754-8123 ■ *Web:* www.newtonmanufacturing.com	Lexington	KY	40508	641-316-0500	323-3100	9
Newton Media Associates Inc 824 Greenbrier Pkwy Ste 200 *Web:* www.newtonmedia.com	Chesapeake	VA	23320	757-547-5400		6
Newton One 131 Continental Dr *Web:* newtononeadvisors.com	Newark	DE	19713	302-731-1326		390
Newton Public Library (NPL) 100 N Third Ave W PO Box 746 *Web:* www.newtongov.org	Newton	IA	50208	641-792-4108	791-0729	434-3
Newton-Conover City Sch Dist 605 N Ashe Ave *Web:* www.newton-conover.org	Newton	NC	28658	828-464-3191		685
Newton-Needham Chamber of Commerce 281 Needham St *Web:* www.nnchamber.com	Newton	MA	02464	617-244-5300		139
Newton-Wellesley Hospital 2014 Washington St *Web:* www.nwh.org	Newton	MA	02462	617-243-6000		374-3
Newtown Savings Bank Foundation Inc 39 Main St *TF:* 800-461-0672 ■ *Web:* www.nsbonline.com	Newtown	CT	06470	203-426-2563		70
Newtron Group, The 8183 W El Cajon Dr *Web:* www.thenewtrongroup.com	Baton Rouge	LA	70815	225-927-8921		189-4
Newtype Inc 447 Rte 10 E Ste 14 *Web:* www.newtypeinc.com	Randolph	NJ	07869	973-361-6000	361-6005	781
NEWW Packaging & Display 205 School St *Web:* www.newwpkg.com	Gardner	MA	01440	978-632-3600	630-1513	100
NewWave Technologies Inc 4635 Wedgewood Blvd Ste 107 *TF:* 800-536-5222 ■ *Web:* www.newwavetech.com	Frederick	MD	21703	301-624-5300		174
Newyork state *Kring Point State Park* 25950 Kring Pt Rd *Web:* parks.ny.gov	Redwood	NY	13679	315-482-2444		565
Newzones Gallery of Contemporary Art 730 11th Ave SW *Web:* www.newzones.com	Calgary	AB	T2R0E4	403-266-1972		42
Nex 21 LLC 880 Montclair Rd Ste 450 *Web:* www.nex21.com	Birmingham	AL	35213	205-520-9916		195
Nex Transport Inc 13900 SR-287 *Web:* www.nextransportinc.com	East Liberty	OH	43319	937-642-8333	642-8375	314
Nexant Inc 44 S Broadway 5th Fl *Web:* www.nexant.com	White Plains	NY	10601	914-609-0300	533-3160	194
NexBank Securities Inc 2515 McKinney Ave Ste 1100 *TF:* 800-827-4818 ■ *Web:* www.nexbank.com	Dallas	TX	75201	972-763-4000		690
Nexcelle LLC 30 Merchant St MD W28 Princeton Hill *Web:* nexcelle.com	Cincinnati	OH	45246	513-552-6659		21
Nexcessnet LLC 21700 Melrose Ave *TF:* 866-639-2377 ■ *Web:* www.nexcess.net	Southfield	MI	48075	866-639-2377		225
NEXCOM (Navy Exchange Service Command) 3280 Virginia Beach Blvd *TF:* 800-628-3924 ■ *Web:* www.mynavyexchange.com	Virginia Beach	VA	23452	757-502-7404		791
nexDimension Technology Solutions LLC PO Box 921221 *TF:* 877-586-2650 ■ *Web:* www.nexdimension.net	Norcross	GA	30010	770-475-1575	475-1576	225
Nexdine LLC 905B S Main St Ste 203 *Web:* www.nexdine.com	Mansfield	MA	02048	978-674-8464		670
Nexelis 645 Elliott Ave W Ste 300 *Web:* nexelis.com	Seattle	WA	98119	206-298-0068		231
Nexelus 1430 Broadway *Web:* www.nexelus.net	New York	NY	10018	646-558-1950		180
Nexen Group Inc 560 Oak Grove Pkwy *TF:* 800-843-7445 ■ *Web:* www.nexengroup.com	Vadnais Heights	MN	55127	651-484-5900	286-1099	386
Nexenta Systems Inc 455 El Camino Real *Web:* nexenta.com	Santa Clara	CA	95050	408-791-3300		177
Nexeo Solutions LLC 3 Waterway Square Pl Ste 1000 *Web:* www.nexeosolutions.com	The Woodlands	TX	77380	281-297-0700		146
Nexgen Pharma Inc 46 Corporate Pk Ste 100 *Web:* www.nexgenpharma.com	Irvine	CA	92606	949-863-0340		583
NexGenix Pharmaceuticals 152 W 57th St	New York	NY	10019	212-974-3006		231
Nexio Group Inc 2050 de Bleury St Ste 500 *TF:* 888-798-3707 ■ *Web:* nexio.com	Montreal	QC	H3A2J5	514-798-3707	284-9002	631
Nexion 6565 N MacArthur Blvd Ste 400 *TF:* 800-949-6410 ■ *Web:* Www.nexion.com	Irving	TX	75038	408-280-6410	271-2039	772
Nexion Health Inc 6937 Warfield Ave *Web:* www.nexion-health.com	Sykesville	MD	21784	410-552-4800		371
Nexius Inc 825 Market St Ste 250 *Web:* www.nexius.com	Allen	TX	75013	703-650-7777		736
Nexlan 28 W N St *Web:* nexlan.com	Danville	IL	61832	217-431-7236	477-5731	177
Nexogy 2121 Ponce de leon Blvd Ste 200 *TF:* 866-639-6492 ■ *Web:* www.nexogy.com	Coral Gables	FL	33134	866-639-6492		387
Nexonia Inc 2 St Clair Ave E Ste 750 *TF:* 800-291-4829 ■ *Web:* www.nexonia.com	Toronto	ON	M4T2T5	416-480-0688		396
Nexpay 5121 N Mccoll Rd *Web:* www.nexpay.us	Mcallen	TX	78504	956-994-1800		570
Nexsales Corp 20660 Stevens Creek Blvd Ste 129 *Web:* www.nexsales.com	Cupertino	CA	95014	408-831-3800	831-3700	195
Nexsen Pruet LLC 1230 Main St Ste 700 *Web:* www.nexsenpruet.com	Columbia	SC	29201	803-771-8900		445
Next Breath LLC 1450 S Rolling Rd *Web:* nextbreath.net	Baltimore	MD	21227	410-455-5904		743
Next Day Flyers 8000 Haskell Ave *TF:* 855-898-9870 ■ *Web:* www.nextdayflyers.com	Van Nuys	CA	91406	855-898-9870		5
Next Eon Com 40 Meriam St *Web:* www.nexteon.com	Wakefield	MA	01880	781-231-3200		180
NEXT Financial Holdings Inc 2500 Wilcrest Dr Ste 620 *TF:* 877-876-6398 ■ *Web:* www.nextfinancialholdings.com	Houston	TX	77042	877-876-6398		690
Next Generation Energy LLC 75 Waneka Pkwy *Web:* www.ngeus.com	LaFayette	CO	80026	303-665-2000		612
Next Generation Films Inc 230 Industrial Dr *TF:* 800-884-8150 ■ *Web:* www.nextgenfilms.com	Lexington	OH	44904	419-884-8150	884-8162	600
Next Generation Press PO Box 603252 *Web:* www.nextgenerationpress.org	Providence	RI	02906	401-247-7665	245-6428	637-2
Next Insurance 409 Sherman Ave *TF:* 855-222-5919 ■ *Web:* www.next-insurance.com	Palo Alto	CA	94306	855-222-5919		391-2
Next IT Corp 12809 E Mirabeau Pkwy *Web:* www.nextit.com	Spokane Valley	WA	99216	509-242-0767		809
Next Level Commercial Cleaning 9420 Lazy Ln Ste A16 *Web:* nextlevelcc.net	Tampa	FL	33614	813-514-0985		104
Next Level Games Inc 208 Robson St 3rd Fl *Web:* www.nextlevelgames.com	Vancouver	BC	V6B6A1	604-484-6111	484-6112	761
Next Level Purchasing 1315 Coraopolis Heights Rd Ste 2002 *Web:* www.nextlevelpurchasing.com	Moon Township	PA	15108	412-294-1990	294-1992	764
Next Level Security Systems Inc 6353 Corte Del Abeto Ste 102 *Web:* nlss.com	Carlsbad	CA	92011	760-444-1410	444-1414	693
Next Level Solutions LLC 1025 Connecticut Ave Ste 1000/1012 *Web:* next-level-solutions.com	Washington	DC	20036	202-625-4343	857-9799	196
Next Marketing Inc 2820 Peterson Pl *Web:* www.nextmarketing.com	Norcross	GA	30071	770-225-2200		195
Next Model Management 15 Watts St 6th Fl *Web:* www.nextmanagement.com	New York	NY	10013	212-925-5100	925-5931	506
Next Net Media LLC 4801 Gulf Blvd Ste 334 *TF:* 800-737-5820 ■ *Web:* nextnetmedia.com	Saint Pete Beach	FL	33706	800-737-5820		387
Next Page Inc 8300 NE Underground Dr Pillar 122 *TF:* 800-660-0108 ■ *Web:* gonextpage.com	Kansas City	MO	64161	816-459-8404	459-8407	627
Next Phase Consultancy Inc, The PO Box 2975 *Web:* medintellibase.com	Redmond	WA	98073	425-869-8724		194
Next Plumbing Supply 1839 Old Okeechobee Rd *Web:* www.nextps.com	West Palm Beach	FL	33409	561-689-9060		38
NEXT Precision Marketing 10400 Yellow Circle Dr Ste 500 *Web:* nextprecisionmarketing.com	Minnetonka	MN	55343	952-443-6400		4
Next Step Partners 1730 Vallejo St Apt 5 *Web:* nextsteppartners.com	San Francisco	CA	94123	415-762-0148		196
Next Steps Marketing 1 Polk St 2nd Fl *Web:* www.nextstepsmarketing.com	San Francisco	CA	94102	415-773-1841	773-1122	195
Next View Software Inc 1401 N Batavia St Ste 104 *Web:* nextviewsoftware.com	Orange	CA	92867	714-288-0363	538-3812	178-1
Nextaff LLC 6842 W121st Crt *TF:* 800-581-6398 ■ *Web:* www.nextaff.com	Overland Park	KS	66210	913-562-5656	562-5657	734

	Phone	Fax	Class
NexTagcom Inc 555 Twin Dolphin Dr Ste 370, Redwood City CA 94065 *Web:* www.nextag.com	650-645-4700	341-3779	51
NexTalk Inc 448 E Winchester St Ste 100, Murray UT 84107 *TF:* 855-715-0110 ■ *Web:* www.nextalk.com	801-274-6001	274-6002	225
Nextant Aerospace LLC 355 Richmond Rd, Cleveland OH 44143 *Web:* www.nextantaerospace.com	216-261-9000		21
NextBio 475 El Camino Real Ste 100, Santa Clara CA 95050 *Web:* www.nextbio.com	408-861-3610	861-3630	387
NextEra Energy Resources LLC 700 Universe Blvd PO Box 14000, Juno Beach FL 33408 *Web:* www.nexteraenergyresources.com	561-691-7171		787
NextGate Solutions Inc 3579 E Foothill Blvd Ste 587, Pasadena CA 91107 *Web:* www.nextgate.com	626-376-4100		180
NextGen Consulting Inc (NGCI) 1420 N Capitol St NW, Washington DC 20002 *Web:* ngciglobal.com	202-527-9595		194
NextGen Healthcare Inc 18111 Von Karman Ave Ste 700, Irvine CA 92612 *NASDAQ: QSII* ■ *TF:* 800-888-7955 ■ *Web:* investor.nextgen.com	949-255-2600	255-2605	178-10
Nextgen Information Services Inc 3660 S Geyer Rd Ste 340, Saint Louis MO 63127 *Web:* nextgen-is.com	314-588-1212		721
Nexthome Inc 4309 Hacienda Dr Ste 110, Pleasanton CA 94588 *TF:* 855-925-6398 ■ *Web:* nexthome.com	855-925-6398		653
Nextiva 8800 E Chaparral Rd Ste 300, Scottsdale AZ 85250 *TF:* 800-799-0600 ■ *Web:* www.nextiva.com	800-983-4289		387
NextMark Inc 33 S Main St 3rd Fl, Hanover NH 03755 *Web:* www.nextmark.com	603-643-1307	643-1652	194
NextPharma Technologies Inc 5340 Eastgate Mall, San Diego CA 92121 *Web:* www.nextpharma.com	858-450-3123		582
NextPhase Medical Devices LLC 88 Airport Dr, Rochester NH 03867 *Web:* nextphasemed.com	603-332-8900		415
Nextpoint Inc 4043 N Ravenswood Ave, Chicago IL 60613 *TF:* 888-929-6398 ■ *Web:* www.nextpoint.com	773-929-4000		177
Nextran Corp 1986 W Beaver St, Jacksonville FL 32209 *TF:* 800-347-6225 ■ *Web:* nextranusa.com	904-354-3721	354-3807	57
Nextrials Inc 5000 Executive Pky Ste 540, San Ramon CA 94583 *Web:* www.nextrials.com	925-355-3000	355-3005	466
NextRidge Inc 12 Elmwood Rd, Albany NY 12204 *Web:* nextridgeinc.com	518-292-6505		196
Nextrio LLC 4803 E Fifth St, Tucson AZ 85711 *Web:* www.nextrio.com	520-545-7100		196
NextServices Inc 500 E Eisenhower Pkwy Ste 130, Ann Arbor MI 48108 *TF:* 866-362-6398 ■ *Web:* www.nextservices.com	734-677-7700		463
Nextus Inc 101 Halmar Cove, Georgetown TX 78628 *Web:* www.nextus.com	512-869-1018	869-2621	625
Nextware Technologies 233 Wilshire Blvd Ste 400, Santa Monica CA 90401 *Web:* www.nextwaretech.com	310-955-9919		177
Nexus Business Solutions 1516 Long Rd, Kalamazoo MI 49007 *Web:* nexusbusiness.com	269-373-1500		194
Nexus Corp 10983 Leroy Dr, Northglenn CO 80233 *TF:* 800-228-9639 ■ *Web:* www.nexuscorp.com	303-457-9199		106
Nexus Engineering Inc 1400 Lone Palm Ave, Modesto CA 95351 *Web:* nexusengineering.net	209-572-7399		256
Nexus Inc 50 Sunnyside Ave, Stamford CT 06902 *Web:* www.nexus.com	203-327-7300	324-7623	815
Nexus Technologies Inc 11 National Ave, Fletcher NC 28732 *Web:* www.nexus-tech.net	828-681-2844	681-2823	261
Nexus Valve Inc 9982 E 121st St, Fishers IN 46037 *TF:* 888-900-0947 ■ *Web:* www.nexusvalve.com	317-257-6050		612
nexVortex Inc 510 Spring St Ste 250, Herndon VA 20170 *TF:* 855-639-8888 ■ *Web:* www.nexvortex.com	855-639-8888		387
Nexxa Industries Ltd 1-4380 76 Ave SE, Calgary AB T2C2J2 *Web:* nexxaindustries.com	403-720-1996		757
Nexxtworks Inc 30798 US Hwy 19 N, Palm Harbor FL 34684 *TF:* 888-533-8353 ■ *Web:* www.nexxtworks.com	888-533-8353		387
Nexxus Marketing Group LLC, The 85 Sam Fonzo Dr, Beverly MA 01915 *Web:* thenexxusgroup.com	978-993-7044		225
Ney Oil Company Inc 145 S Water St, Ney OH 43549 *TF:* 800-962-9839 ■ *Web:* neyoil.com	419-658-2324	658-2723	324
Neyenesch Printers Inc 2750 Kettner Blvd, San Diego CA 92101 *Web:* www.neyenesch.com	619-297-2281		627
Neyer Properties Inc 2135 Dana Ave Ste 200, Cincinnati OH 45207 *Web:* www.neyer1.com	513-563-7555	563-4288	652
Neyra Industries 10700 Evendale Dr, Cincinnati OH 45241 *TF:* 800-543-7077 ■ *Web:* www.neyra.com	513-733-1000		46
NEZ Perce County 1230 Main St PO Box 896, Lewiston ID 83501 *Web:* www.co.nezperce.id.us	208-799-3020	799-3070	338
NEZ Perce County Historical Society & Museum 0306 3rd St, Lewiston ID 83501 *Web:* www.nezpercecountymuseum.com	208-743-2535		520
NEZ Perce National Historical Park 39063 US Hwy 95, Spalding ID 83540 *TF:* 800-537-7962 ■ *Web:* www.nps.gov	208-843-2261	843-7003	564
NFA (National Futures Assn) 300 S Riverside Plz Ste 1800, Chicago IL 60606 *Web:* www.nfa.futures.org	312-781-1300	781-1467	49-2
NFA Group Inc 900 RR 620 S Ste C101-155, Austin TX 78734 *Web:* www.buydrm.com	512-377-1340		809
N-Fab Inc 14925 Stuebner Airline Rd Ste 207, Houston TX 77069 *Web:* n-fab.com	281-880-6322		697
NFB (National Federation of the Blind) 1800 Johnson St, Baltimore MD 21230 *TF:* 800-392-5671 ■ *Web:* nfb.org	410-659-9314	685-5653	48-17
NFBPA (National Forum for Black Public Administrators) 777 N Capitol St NE Ste 807, Washington DC 20002 *Web:* www.nfbpa.org	202-408-9300	408-8558	49-7
NFC Global LLC 200 Lakeside Dr Ste 250, Horsham PA 19044 *Web:* www.nfcglobal.com	215-657-0800		463
NFCA (National Family Caregivers Assn) 1150 Connecticut Ave NW Ste 501, Washington DC 20036 *TF:* 800-896-3650 ■ *Web:* caregiveraction.org	202-454-3970		48-6
NFCB (National Federation of Community Broadcasters) PO Box 11270, Denver CO 80211 *Web:* nfcb.org	970-279-3411		49-14
NFCR (National Foundation for Cancer Research) 4600 E W Hwy Ste 525, Bethesda MD 20814 **Fax Area Code:* 301 ■ *TF:* 800-321-2873 ■ *Web:* www.nfcr.org	800-321-2873	654-5824*	305
NFDA (National Funeral Directors Assn) 13625 Bishop's Dr, Brookfield WI 53005 *TF:* 800-228-6332 ■ *Web:* www.nfda.org	262-789-1880	789-6977	49-4
NFDMA (National Funeral Directors & Morticians Assn) 6290 Shannon Pkwy, Union City GA 30291 *TF:* 800-434-0958 ■ *Web:* www.nfdma.com	770-969-0064		49-4
NFE (National Food Equipment and Supplies) 3186 Old Farm Ln, Walled Lake MI 48390 *TF:* 800-345-5872 ■ *Web:* www.nationalfoodequipment.com	248-960-7292	960-0774	300
NFFC (National Family Farm Coalition) 110 Maryland Ave NE Ste 307, Washington DC 20002 *Web:* www.nffc.net	202-543-5675	543-0978	48-2
NFFCMH (National Federation of Families for Children's Mental Health) 12320 Parklawn Dr, Rockville MD 20852 *Web:* www.ffcmh.org	240-403-1901	403-1909	49-15
NFI (NFI Industries) 1515 Burnt Mill Rd, Cherry Hill NJ 08003 *TF:* 877-634-3777 ■ *Web:* www.nfiindustries.com	877-634-3777		449
NFI Inc 2885 S Main St, Harrisonburg VA 22801 *TF:* 800-433-1987 ■ *Web:* www.harrisonburghonda.com	540-433-1467		57
NFI Industries (NFI) 1515 Burnt Mill Rd, Cherry Hill NJ 08003 *TF:* 877-634-3777 ■ *Web:* www.nfiindustries.com	877-634-3777		449
NFID (National Foundation for Infectious Diseases) 4733 Bethesda Ave Ste 750, Bethesda MD 20814 *Web:* www.nfid.org	301-656-0003	907-0878	49-8
NFL (National Furniture Liquidators I LLC) 2865 Log Cabin Dr, Atlanta GA 30339 *Web:* www.nflinc.com	404-872-7280		321
NFL (National Speech & Debate Association's) 125 Watson St PO Box 38, Ripon WI 54971 *Web:* www.speechanddebate.org	920-748-6206	748-9478	48-11
NFL Network 345 Park Ave, New York NY 10154 *Web:* www.nfl.com	212-450-2000		740
NFLPA (National Football League Players) 1133 20th St NW, Washington DC 20036 *TF:* 800-372-2000 ■ *Web:* www.nflpa.com	800-372-2000		48-22
NFM Welding Engineers 577 Oberlin Rd SW, Massillon OH 44647 *Web:* www.nfm.net	330-837-3868		456
NFO (National Farmers Organization) 528 Billy Sunday Rd Ste 100 PO Box 2508, Ames IA 50010 *TF:* 800-247-2110 ■ *Web:* www.nfo.org	515-292-2000	292-7106	48-2
NFO (Nevada Film Office) 6655 W Sahara Ste C106, Las Vegas NV 89146 *TF:* 877-638-3456 ■ *Web:* www.nevadafilm.com	702-486-2711	486-2712	514
Nfocus Consulting Inc 1594 Hubbard Dr, Lancaster OH 43130 *TF:* 800-675-5809 ■ *Web:* www.nfocus.com	740-654-5809		196
NFP (National Financial Partners Corp) 340 Madison Ave 20th Fl, New York NY 10173 *NYSE: NFP* ■ *Web:* www.nfp.com	212-301-4000	301-4001	401
NFP (New Forums Press Inc) 1018 S Lewis St, Stillwater OK 74074 *TF:* 800-606-3766 ■ *Web:* www.newforums.com	405-372-6158	377-2237	637-2
NFP Corp 8000 Ctrview Pkwy Ste 525, Cordova TN 38018 *TF:* 844-553-7872 ■ *Web:* executivebenefits.nfp.com	844-553-7872		463
NFPA (National Fire Protection Assn) 1 Batterymarch Pk, Quincy MA 02169 *TF:* 800-344-3555 ■ *Web:* www.nfpa.org	617-770-3000	770-0700	48-17
NFPA (National Fluid Power Assn) 3333 N Mayfair Rd Ste 211, Milwaukee WI 53222 *Web:* www.nfpa.com	414-778-3344	778-3361	49-13
NFR (North Fork Ranch) 55395 Hwy 285 PO Box B, Shawnee CO 80475 *TF:* 800-843-7895 ■ *Web:* www.northforkranch.com	303-838-9873	838-1549	239
NFR (North Fork Radiology PC) 1333 Roanoke Ave, Riverhead NY 11901 *Web:* www.northforkrad.com	631-727-2755		374-3
NFRA (National Frozen & Refrigerated Foods Assn) 4755 Linglestown Rd Ste 300, Harrisburg PA 17112 *Web:* www.nfraweb.org	717-657-8601	657-9862	49-6
NFRA (National Forest Recreation Assn) PO Box 488, Woodlake CA 93286 *TF:* 800-272-7238 ■ *Web:* nfra.org	559-564-2365	564-2048	48-23
Nfra Inc 77 E Thomas Rd Ste 200, Phoenix AZ 85012 *Web:* www.nfrainc.us	602-277-0967		261
NFRW (National Federation of Republican Women) 124 N Alfred St, Alexandria VA 22314 *TF:* 800-373-9688 ■ *Web:* www.nfrw.org	703-548-9688	548-9836	48-7
NFS (National Field Service Corp) 162 Orange Ave, Suffern NY 10901 *Web:* nfsco.com	845-368-1600	368-1989	736
NFSA (National Fire Sprinkler Assn) 40 Jon Barrett Rd, Patterson NY 12563 *Web:* nfsa.org	845-878-4200	878-4215	49-3
NFTC (National Foreign Trade Council) 1625 K St NW Ste 200, Washington DC 20006 *Web:* www.nftc.org	202-887-0278	452-8160	49-18
NFU (National Farmers Union News) 20 F St NW Ste 300, Washington DC 20001 *TF:* 800-442-8277 ■ *Web:* nfu.org	202-554-1600	554-1654	531-13

				Phone	Fax	Class
NG Purvis Farms Inc 2504 Spies Rd	Robbins	NC	27325	910-948-2297		10-6
NGA (National Gardening Assn)						
1100 Dorset St	South Burlington	VT	05403	802-863-5251	864-6889	48-18
TF: 800-538-7476 ■ *Web:* garden.org						
NGA (National Governors Assn)						
444 N Capitol St NW Ste 267	Washington	DC	20001	202-624-5300	624-5313	49-7
Web: www.nga.org						
NGA (National Greyhound Assn)						
729 Old US 40	Abilene	KS	67410	785-263-4660	263-4689	48-22
TF: 800-366-1471 ■ *Web:* www.ngagreyhounds.com						
NGA (National Grocers Assn)						
1005 N Glebe Rd Ste 250	Arlington	VA	22201	703-516-0700	516-0115	49-6
Web: www.nationalgrocers.org						
NGAUS (National Guard Educational Foundation)						
1 Massachusetts Ave NW	Washington	DC	20001	202-789-0031	682-9358	48-19
TF: 888-226-4287 ■ *Web:* www.ngaus.org						
NGC (National Garden Clubs Inc)						
4401 Magnolia Ave	Saint Louis	MO	63110	314-776-7574	776-5108	48-18
TF: 800-550-6007 ■ *Web:* www.gardenclub.org						
NGC Inc PO Box 608	Narragansett	RI	02882	401-789-2200		297-5
Web: www.towndock.com						
NGCI (NextGen Consulting Inc)						
1420 N Capitol St NW	Washington	DC	20002	202-527-9595		194
Web: ngciglobal.com						
NGCOA (National Golf Course Owners Assn)						
291 Seven Farms Dr 2nd Fl	Charleston	SC	29492	843-881-9956	881-9958	48-23
TF: 800-933-4262 ■ *Web:* www.ngcoa.org						
NGEN Partners LLC 733 Third Ave	New York	NY	10017	212-450-9700		792
Web: ngenpartners.com						
NGF (National Gaucher Foundation)						
5410 Edson Ln Ste 220	Rockville	MD	20852	800-504-3189		48-17
TF: 800-504-3189 ■ *Web:* www.gaucherdisease.org						
NGF (National Golf Foundation)						
1150 S US Hwy 1 Ste 401	Jupiter	FL	33477	561-744-6006	744-6107	48-22
TF: 800-733-6006 ■ *Web:* www.ngf.org						
NGF (Nebraska Grain & Feed Assn)						
4600 Valley Rd Ste 416	Lincoln	NE	68510	402-476-6174	476-3401	192
Web: www.negfa.org						
NGInstruments Inc 4643 N State Rd 15	Warsaw	IN	46582	574-268-2112		757
Web: www.nginstruments.com						
NGK Ceramics USA Inc						
119 Mazeppa Rd	Mooresville	NC	28115	704-664-7000		60
Web: www.ngkceramics.com						
NGK Metals Corp 917 Hwy 11 S	Sweetwater	TN	37874	423-337-5500	645-2328*	308
**Fax Area Code:* 877 ■ *TF:* 800-523-8268 ■ *Web:* www.ngkmetals.com						
NGK Spark Plugs Inc 46929 Magellan	Wixom	MI	48393	248-926-6900		247
TF: 877-473-6767 ■ *Web:* www.ngksparkplugs.com						
NGK-locke Polymer Insulators Inc						
1609 Diamond Springs Rd	Virginia Beach	VA	23455	757-460-3649	460-3550	816
Web: www.ngk-polymer.com						
NGL (National Guardian Life Insurance Co)						
2 E Gilman St	Madison	WI	53703	800-548-2962	257-3940*	391-2
**Fax Area Code:* 608 ■ *TF:* 800-548-2962 ■ *Web:* www.nglic.com						
NGL (Network Global Logistics)						
320 Interlocken Pkwy Ste 100	Broomfield	CO	80021	866-938-1870		546
TF: 866-938-1870 ■ *Web:* www.nglog.com						
NGLTF (National Gay & Lesbian Task Force)						
1325 Massachusetts Ave NW Ste 600	Washington	DC	20005	202-393-5177	393-2241	48-8
Web: www.thetaskforce.org						
NGM Biopharmaceuticals Inc						
333 Oyster Point Blvd	South San Francisco	CA	94080	650-243-5555		668
Web: www.ngmbio.com						
NGP Energy Capital Management						
5221 N O'Connor Blvd Ste 1100	Irving	TX	75039	972-432-1440		401
Web: ngpenergycapital.com						
nGroup 1184 Springmaid Ave Ste 104	Fort Mill	SC	29708	877-202-9677		260
TF: 877-202-9677 ■ *Web:* www.ngroup.biz						
NGS (National Genealogical Society)						
3108 Columbia Pk Ste 300	Arlington	VA	22204	703-525-0050	525-0052	48-18
TF: 800-473-0060 ■ *Web:* www.ngsgenealogy.org						
NGSA (Natural Gas Supply Assn)						
805 15th St NW Ste 510	Washington	DC	20005	202-326-9300	326-9330	48-12
Web: www.ngsa.org						
NGSG (Natural Gas Services Group Inc)						
508 W Wall Ste 550	Midland	TX	79701	432-262-2700	262-2701	537
AMEX: NGS ■ *Web:* www.ngsgi.com						
Nguoi Dan PO Box 2674	Costa Mesa	CA	92628	714-549-3443		532-2
Web: www.nguoidan.com						
Nguoi Viet News 14771 Moran St	Westminster	CA	92683	714-892-9414	894-1381	532-2
Web: www.nguoi-viet.com						
Nguyen Law Firm PLC, The						
100 Arbor Oak Dr Ste 206	Ashland	VA	23005	804-788-7070		41
Web: nhnlawfirm.com						
NGWA (National Ground Water Assn)						
601 Dempsey Rd	Westerville	OH	43081	614-898-7791	898-7786	48-12
TF: 800-551-7379 ■ *Web:* www.ngwa.org						
NGWSP (New Glarus Woods State Park)						
W5446 County Hwy NN	New Glarus	WI	53574	608-527-2335		565
Web: dnr.wi.gov						
NH (Newport Hospital) 167 Point St	Providence	RI	02903	401-793-8808		374-3
Web: www.newporthospital.org						
NH Collection New York Madison Avenue						
22 E 38th St	New York	NY	10016	212-802-0600	447-0747	379
TF: 888-726-0528 ■ *Web:* www.nh-hotels.com						
NH Department of Natural & Cultural Resources						
Mount Sunapee State Park						
86 Beach Access Rd	Newbury	NH	03255	603-763-5561		565
Web: www.nhstateparks.org						
NH Research Inc 16601 Hale Ave	Irvine	CA	92606	949-474-3900	474-7062	248
Web: nhresearch.com						
NH Yates & Company Inc						
117 Church Ln Ste C	Cockeysville	MD	21030	800-878-8181	667-9201*	641
**Fax Area Code:* 888 ■ *TF:* 800-878-8181 ■ *Web:* nhyates.com						
NHA (National Humanities Alliance)						
21 Dupont Cir NW Ste 800	Washington	DC	20036	202-296-4994	872-0884	48-4
Web: www.nhalliance.org						
NHB (New Haven Body Inc)						
89 Stoddard Ave	North Haven	CT	06473	203-248-6388	281-0060	61
Web: www.newhavenbody.com						

				Phone	Fax	Class
NHC (National Housing Conference)						
1801 K St NW Ste M-100	Washington	DC	20006	202-466-2121	466-2122	49-3
Web: www.nhc.org						
NHC (National Health Council)						
1730 M St NW Ste 500	Washington	DC	20036	202-785-3910	785-5923	48-17
Web: www.nationalhealthcouncil.org						
Nhc Financial Services Ann Arbor						
3145 Packard Rd	Ann Arbor	MI	48108	734-677-3200	677-3202	734
Web: nhcfinancial.com						
NHCA (National Hearing Conservation Assn)						
3030 W 81st Ave	Westminster	CO	80031	303-224-9022	458-0002	48-17
Web: www.hearingconservation.org						
NHCOA (National Hispanic Council on Aging)						
2201 12th St NW Ste 101	Washington	DC	20009	202-347-9733	347-9735	48-6
Web: www.nhcoa.org						
NHDP (National Hansen's Disease Program)						
1770 Physicians Pk Dr	Baton Rouge	LA	70816	800-221-9393		668
TF: 800-221-9393 ■ *Web:* www.hrsa.gov						
Employment Security 32 S Main St	Concord	NH	03301	603-224-3311	228-4145	259
TF: 800-852-3400 ■ *Web:* www.nh.gov						
NHF (National Headache Foundation)						
820 N Orleans St Ste 217	Chicago	IL	60610	312-274-2650	640-9049	48-17
Web: headaches.org						
NHF (National Hemophilia Foundation)						
7 Penn Plz Ste 1204	New York	NY	10001	212-328-3700	328-3777	48-17
TF: 800-424-2634 ■ *Web:* www.hemophilia.org						
NHGA (Nevada Hay Growers Inc)						
41 S Hwy 339	Yerington	NV	89447	775-463-2325	463-4320	276
Web: www.nevadahaygrowers.com						
NHI (National Hispanic Institute)						
472 FM 1966 Rd	Maxwell	TX	78656	512-357-6137		48-14
Web: www.nationalhispanicinstitute.org						
NHIA (National Home Infusion Assn)						
100 Daingerfield Rd	Alexandria	VA	22314	703-549-3740	683-1484	49-8
Web: www.nhia.org						
NHK Laboratories Inc						
12230 E Florience Ave	Santa Fe Springs	CA	90670	562-944-5400		479
TF: 866-645-5227 ■ *Web:* www.nhklabs.com						
NHK Seating of America Inc						
2298 W State Rd 28	Frankfort	IN	46041	765-659-4781	659-5591	60
Web: www.nhkseating.com						
NHL (National Hockey League)						
1185 Avenue of the Americas	New York	NY	10036	212-789-2000	789-2020	716
Web: www.nhl.com						
NHLA (National Hardwood Lumber Assn)						
6830 Raleigh-LaGrange Rd	Memphis	TN	38134	901-377-1818	382-6419	49-3
TF: 800-933-0318 ■ *Web:* nhla.com						
NHMFL (National High Magnetic Field Laboratory)						
1800 E Paul Dirac Dr	Tallahassee	FL	32310	850-644-0311		668
Web: nationalmaglab.org						
NHPCO (National Hospice & Palliative Care Organization)						
1700 Diagonal Rd Ste 625	Alexandria	VA	22314	703-837-1500	837-1233	49-8
TF: 800-658-8898 ■ *Web:* www.nhpco.org						
NHPIRG (New Hampshire Public Interest Research Group)						
75 S Main St Unit 7- 626	Concord	NH	03301	603-637-4758		633
Web: nhpirg.org						
NH&RA (National Housing & Rehabilitation Assn)						
1400 16th St NW Ste 420	Washington	DC	20036	202-939-1750	265-4435	49-17
Web: www.housingonline.com						
NHRC (Naval Health Research Ctr)						
140 Sylvester Rd	San Diego	CA	92152	619-553-8400	553-9389	668
Web: www.med.navy.mil						
NHS (National Honor Society) 1904 Assn Dr	Reston	VA	20191	703-860-0200	476-5432	48-11
TF: 800-253-7746 ■ *Web:* www.nhs.us						
NHS (Nevada Historical Society)						
1650 N Virginia St	Reno	NV	89503	775-688-1190		49-19
Web: www.nvdtca.org						
NHSA (National Head Start Assn)						
1651 Prince St	Alexandria	VA	22314	703-739-0875	739-0878	48-11
TF: 866-677-8724 ■ *Web:* www.nhsa.org						
NHSTE (New Hampshire Society for Technology in Education)						
46 Donovan St Ste 3	Concord	NH	03301	866-753-4479		48-13
TF: 866-753-4479 ■ *Web:* www.nhste.org						
NHT Global Inc						
609 Deep Valley Dr Ste 395	Rolling Hills Estates	CA	90274	972-241-6525	541-0880*	459
**Fax Area Code:* 310 ■ *Web:* nhtglobal.com						
NHTI Concord's Community College						
31 College Dr	Concord	NH	03301	603-271-6484	271-7139	162
TF: 800-247-0179 ■ *Web:* www.nhti.edu						
Region 1						
1200 New Jersey Ave SE West Bldg	Cambridge	MA	02142	617-494-3427	494-3646	340-17
Web: www.nhtsa.gov						
NIA (National Insulation Assn)						
99 Canal Center Plz Ste 222	Alexandria	VA	22314	703-549-4838		49-3
TF: 877-968-7642 ■ *Web:* insulation.org						
Niacet Corp 400 47th St	Niagara Falls	NY	14304	716-285-1474	285-1497	144
TF: 800-828-1207 ■ *Web:* www.niacet.com						
NIADA (National Independent Automobile Dealers Assn)						
2521 Brown Blvd	Arlington	TX	76006	817-640-3838	649-5866	49-18
TF: 800-682-3837 ■ *Web:* www.niada.com						
Niagara College Canada						
100 Niagara College Blvd	Welland	ON	L3C7L3	905-735-2211		162
Web: www.niagaracollege.ca						
Niagara Conservation Corp						
45 Horsehill Rd	Cedar Knolls	NJ	07927	800-831-8383		612
TF: 800-831-8383 ■ *Web:* www.niagaraconservation.com						
Niagara Corp 667 Madison Ave	New York	NY	10065	212-317-1000	317-1001	723
TF: 877-289-2277 ■ *Web:* www.niagaralasalle.com						
Niagara County PO Box 461	Lockport	NY	14095	716-439-7022	439-7066	338
Web: www.niagaracounty.com						
Niagara County Community College						
3111 Saunders Settlement Rd	Sanborn	NY	14132	716-614-6222	614-6820	162
TF: 800-875-6269 ■ *Web:* www.niagaracc.suny.edu						
Niagara Cutter Inc 2805 Bellingham Dr	Troy	MI	48083	248-528-5220		493
TF: 800-832-8326 ■ *Web:* www.niagaracutter.com						
Niagara Duty Free Shop						
5726 Falls Ave	Niagara Falls	ON	L2G7T5	905-374-3700		241
TF: 877-642-4337 ■ *Web:* www.niagaradutyfree.com						

Name / Address	City	State	ZIP	Phone	Fax	Class
Niagara Falls Canada Chamber of Commerce 4056 Dorchester Rd *Web:* www.niagarafallschamber.com	Niagara Falls	ON	L2E6M9	905-374-3666	374-2972	137
Niagara Falls Memorial Medical Ctr 621 Tenth St *Web:* www.nfmmc.org	Niagara Falls	NY	14302	716-278-4000		374-3
Niagara Falls Public Library 1425 Main St *TF:* 800-773-4264 ■ *Web:* www.niagarafallspubliclib.org	Niagara Falls	NY	14305	716-286-4894	286-4885	434-3
Niagara Falls Review 4424 Queen St *Web:* www.niagarafallsreview.ca	Niagara Falls	ON	L2R2L3	905-358-5711		532-1
Niagara Falls State Park PO Box 1132 *Web:* www.niagarafallsstatepark.com	Niagara Falls	NY	14303	716-278-1796		565
Niagara Fresh Fruit Co 5796 Wilson Burt Rd *Web:* niagarafreshfruit.com	Burt	NY	14028	716-778-7631	778-8768	685
Niagara Frontier Transportation Authority 181 Ellicott St *Web:* www.nfta.com	Buffalo	NY	14203	716-855-7300		468
Niagara Gazette 473 Third St *Web:* www.niagara-gazette.com	Niagara Falls	NY	14301	716-282-2311	286-3895	532-2
Niagara Helicopters Ltd 3731 Victoria Ave *TF:* 800-281-8034 ■ *Web:* www.niagarahelicopters.com	Niagara Falls	ON	L2E6V5	905-357-5672		292
Niagara Hospice 4675 Sunset Dr *Web:* www.niagarahospice.org	Lockport	NY	14094	716-439-4417		371
Niagara Parks Botanical Gardens 7400 Portage Rd PO Box 150 *TF:* 877-642-7275 ■ *Web:* www.niagaraparks.com	Niagara Falls	ON	L2E6T2	877-642-7275		97
Niagara Sheets LLC 7393 Shawnee Rd *Web:* niagarasheets.com	North Tonawanda	NY	14120	716-799-8310		100
Niagara Tourism & Convention Corp 10 Rainbow Blvd *TF:* 877-325-5787 ■ *Web:* www.niagarafallsusa.com	Niagara Falls	NY	14303	716-282-8992	285-0809	206
Niagara Transformer Corp 1747 Dale Rd *TF:* 800-817-5652 ■ *Web:* www.niagaratransformer.com	Buffalo	NY	14225	716-896-6500	896-8871	767
Niagara Tying Service Inc 176 Dingens St **Fax Area Code:* 716 ■ *TF:* 800-568-9464 ■ *Web:* www.niagaratyingservice.com	Buffalo	NY	14206	800-568-9464	825-0542*	296-26
Niagara University 5795 Lewiston Rd PO Box 2011 *TF:* 800-778-3450 ■ *Web:* www.niagara.edu	Niagara	NY	14109	716-285-1212	286-8710	166
Niagara USA Chamber of Commerce 6311 Inducon Corporate Dr Ste 2 *Web:* niagarachamber.org	Sanborn	NY	14132	716-285-9141	285-0941	139
Nialis Law Group, A Professional Law Corp 500 N State College Blvd Ste 1200 *Web:* nialislaw.com	Orange	CA	92868	714-634-8001		41
Niantic Inc 1 Ferry Bldg Ste 200 *Web:* nianticlabs.com	San Francisco	CA	94111	415-570-8871		39
Nibbi Brothers General Contractors 1000 Brannan St Ste 102 *Web:* www.nibbi.com	San Francisco	CA	94103	415-863-1820	863-1150	186
NIBS (National Institute of Building Sciences) 1090 Vermont Ave NW Ste 700 *Web:* www.nibs.org	Washington	DC	20005	202-289-7800	289-1092	49-3
NIC (North-American Interfraternity Conference) 865 W Carmel Dr Ste 116 *Web:* nicfraternity.org	Carmel	IN	46032	317-872-1112		48-11
NIC Inc 25501 W Valley Pkwy Ste 300 *NASDAQ: EGOV* ■ **Fax Area Code:* 913 ■ *TF:* 877-234-3468 ■ *Web:* www.egov.com	Olathe	KS	66061	877-234-3468	498-3472*	178-10
Nicaboyne Inc 7215 Bannockburn Cir *TF:* 866-442-9100 ■ *Web:* www.nicaboyne.com	Lakewood	IL	60014	866-442-9100		328
Nicaragua *Consulate General* 8989 Westheimer St *Web:* www.consuladodenicaragua.com	Houston	TX	77063	713-789-2762	789-3164	257
Nicasa 31979 N Fish Lake Rd *Web:* nicasa.org	Round Lake	IL	60073	847-546-6450	546-6760	726
NICB (National Insurance Crime Bureau) 1111 E Touhy Ave Ste 400 *TF:* 800-447-6282 ■ *Web:* www.nicb.org	Des Plaines	IL	60018	847-544-7002		49-9
NiceLabel Americas Inc 933 N Mayfair Rd Ste 320 *Web:* www.nicelabel.com	Wauwatosa	WI	53226	262-784-2456	784-2495	177
Nice-Pak Products Inc 2 Nice-Pak Pk *TF:* 800-444-6725 ■ *Web:* www.nicepak.com	Orangeburg	NY	10962	845-365-1700		558
Niceville-Valparaiso Chamber of Commerce 1055 E John Sims Pkwy *TF:* 800-729-9226 ■ *Web:* www.nicevillechamber.com	Niceville	FL	32578	850-678-2323	678-2602	139
NICHD (National Institute of Child Health & Human Development) 31 Center Dr Bldg 31 Rm 2A32 *TF:* 800-370-2943 ■ *Web:* www.nih.gov	Bethesda	MD	20892	800-370-2943		668
Niche Modern Home 1901 Hwy 190 Ste 3 *Web:* nichemodernhome.biz	Mandeville	LA	70448	985-624-4045		321
Nichidai USA Corp 15630 E State Rte 12 Unit 4 *Web:* www.nichidai.jp	Findlay	OH	45840	419-423-7511	423-7512	723
Nichirin Tennessee Inc 1620 Old Belfast Rd *Web:* www.nichirincanada.com	Lewisburg	TN	37091	931-359-5709		370
Nichirin-Flex USA Inc 9600 Plaza Cir *Web:* www.nichirin.co.jp	El Paso	TX	79927	915-859-1199	859-2977	60
Nicholas & Associates Inc 1001 Feehanville Dr *Web:* www.nicholasquality.com	Mount Prospect	IL	60056	847-394-6200	394-6205	186
Nicholas and Co 5520 W Harold Gatty Dr *TF:* 800-873-3663 ■ *Web:* www.nicholasandco.com	Salt Lake City	UT	84116	801-531-1100		297-2
Nicholas County 1639 Old Paris Rd *Web:* www.carlisle-nicholascounty.org	Carlisle	KY	40311	859-289-3730		338
Commission 700 Main St Ste 1 *TF:* 800-327-5405 ■ *Web:* www.nicholascountywv.org	Summersville	WV	26651	304-872-7830	872-7863	338
Nicholas E. Subashi Company LPA 50 Chestnut St Ste 230 *Web:* swohiolaw.com	Dayton	OH	45440	937-427-8800		41
Nicholas Family of Funds 615 E Michigan St *TF:* 800-544-6547 ■ *Web:* www.nicholasfunds.com	Milwaukee	WI	53202	414-765-4124		528
Nicholas Financial Inc 2454 McMullen Booth Rd *NASDAQ: NICK* ■ *TF:* 800-237-2721 ■ *Web:* nicholasfinancial.com	Clearwater	FL	33759	727-726-0763	726-2140	217
Nicholas Laboratories LLC 15 Enterprise Ste 550	Aliso Viejo	CA	92656	949-448-4360		415
Nicholas Roerich Museum 319 W 107th St *Web:* www.roerich.org	New York	NY	10025	212-864-7752	864-7704	637-2
Nicholls State University 906 E 1st St *Web:* www.nicholls.edu	Thibodaux	LA	70301	985-446-0561		166
Nichols PO Box 291 *TF:* 800-442-0213 ■ *Web:* enichols.com	Muskegon	MI	49443	231-799-2120	799-3550	559
Nichols & Stone 1 Stickley Dr PO Box 480 *Web:* www.nichols-stone.com	Manlius	NY	13104	315-682-1554		319-2
Nichols Accounting Group PC, The 230 N Oregon St *Web:* www.nicholsaccounting.com	Ontario	OR	97914	541-881-1433		2
Nichols Bros Boat Builders Inc 5400 Cameron Rd *Web:* www.nicholsboats.com	Freeland	WA	98249	360-331-5500	331-7484	698
Nichols Career Center Program of Practical Nursing 315 E Dunklin St *Web:* www.jcschools.us	Jefferson City	MO	65101	573-659-3100	659-3154	167-3
Nichols College 129 Center Rd **Fax Area Code:* 508 ■ *TF:* 800-470-3379 ■ *Web:* www.nichols.edu	Dudley	MA	01571	800-470-3379	943-9885*	166
Nichols Hills Publishing Company Inc PO Box 20340 *Web:* www.okcfriday.com	Oklahoma City	OK	73156	405-755-3311		532-2
Nichols House Museum 55 Mt Vernon St *Web:* www.nicholshousemuseum.org	Boston	MA	02108	617-227-6993		520
Nichols Jackson Dillard Hager & Smith LLP 500 N Akard St 1800 Ross Twr *Web:* www.njdhs.com	Dallas	TX	75201	214-965-9900	965-0010	41
Nichols Portland 2400 Congress St *Web:* nicholsportland.com	Portland	ME	04102	207-774-6121	774-3601	223
Nichols Research Inc 333 W El Camino Real Ste 130 *Web:* nicholsresearch.com	Sunnyvale	CA	94087	408-773-8200		466
Nichols Tillage Tools Inc 312 Hereford Ave *Web:* www.nicholstillagetools.com	Sterling	CO	80751	970-522-9756		488
Nichols Zauzig Sandler Pc 12660 Lake Ridge Dr *Web:* nzslaw.com	Lake Ridge	VA	22192	703-492-4200		41
Nicholson Companies Inc, The 819 W Little Creek Rd *Web:* thenicholsoncompanies.com	Norfolk	VA	23505	757-423-3281		652
Nicholson Construction Co 2400 Ansys Dr Ste 303 *Web:* www.nicholsonconstruction.com	Canonsburg	PA	15317	412-221-4500		189-5
Nicholson Foundation, The 60 Park Pl 18th Fl *Web:* thenicholsonfoundation.org	Newark	NJ	07102	973-242-6237		360-3
Nicholson Manufacturing Ltd 9896 Galaran Rd *TF:* 888-656-3131 ■ *Web:* www.debarking.com	Sidney	BC	V8L3S6	250-656-3131		683
Nicholson Revell LLP 4137 Columbia Rd *Web:* nicholsonrevell.com	Augusta	GA	30907	706-722-8784		41
Nicholson Terminal & Dock Co 360 E Great Lakes *Web:* www.nicholson-terminal.com	Ecorse	MI	48229	313-842-4300	843-1091	465
Nicholson's Tavern & Pub 625 Walnut St *Web:* www.tavernrestaurantgroup.com	Cincinnati	OH	45202	513-564-9111		671
Nicholville Telephone Company Inc (NTC) 3330 State Hwy 11B *Web:* www.nicholville.com	Nicholville	NY	12965	315-328-4411	328-4902	224
Nici Law Firm PL 1185 Immokalee Rd Ste 110 *Web:* nicilawfirm.com	Naples	FL	34110	239-449-6150		41
Nick & Sam's Grill 3008 Maple Ave *Web:* nick-sams.com	Dallas	TX	75201	214-871-7444	871-7663	671
Nick Alexander Imports Inc 6333 S Alameda St *Web:* www.alexanderbmw.com	Los Angeles	CA	90001	323-583-1901		57
Nick Crivelli Chevrolet Inc 294 State Ave *Web:* www.nickcrivelli.com	Beaver	PA	15009	724-987-5000		57
Nick Harris Detective Academy 5900 Sepulveda Blvd Ste 301 *TF:* 800-245-9007 ■ *Web:* www.nickharrisdetective.com	Van Nuys	CA	91411	818-343-6611		167-3
Nick Miller & Associates Insurance Agency Inc 6834 Caine Rd *Web:* allinsurance4u.com	Columbus	OH	43235	614-889-0701		390
Nick Strimbu Inc 3500 Parkway Rd *TF:* 800-446-8785 ■ *Web:* www.nickstrimbu.com	Brookfield	OH	44403	330-448-4046	448-4106	780
Nick Varner (NV) PO Box 1309 **Fax Area Code:* 270 ■ *TF:* 800-626-8408 ■ *Web:* www.nickvarner.com	Owensboro	KY	42302	800-626-8408	686-7833*	710
Nick's 3496 N Ocean Blvd *Web:* nicksitalianonline.com	Fort Lauderdale	FL	33308	954-563-6441		671
Nick's English Hut 423 E Kirkwood Ave *Web:* www.nicksenglishhut.com	Bloomington	IN	47408	812-332-4040		671
Nick's on Broadway 500 Broadway *Web:* www.nicksonbroadway.com	Providence	RI	02909	401-421-0286		671
Nick's Original House of Ribs 14410 Coastal Hwy *Web:* nickshouseofribs.com	Ocean City	MD	21842	410-250-1984		671
Nickates Stained Glass Supplies Inc 175 Main St *Web:* www.nickates.com	Avon	MA	02322	508-580-1220		189-6

	Phone	Fax	Class
Nickell Moulding Company Inc 3015 Mobile Dr ... Elkhart IN 46515 *TF:* 800-838-2151 ■ *Web:* www.nickellmoulding.com	574-264-3129		499
Nickelodeon 1515 Broadway ... New York NY 10036 *Web:* www.nick.com	212-258-7500	258-7705	740
Nickelodeon Suites Resort 14500 Continental Gateway ... Orlando FL 32821 *Web:* www.nickhotel.com	407-387-5437	387-1489	669
Nickers International Ltd PO Box 50066 ... Staten Island NY 10305 **Fax Area Code:* 718 ■ *TF:* 800-642-5377 ■ *Web:* www.nickersinternational.com	800-642-5377	448-6298*	799
Nickerson Business Supplies 876A Lebanon St ... Monroe OH 45050 *TF:* 888-385-9922 ■ *Web:* www.nickbiz.com	513-539-6600		321
Nickerson Company Inc 2301 W Indiana Ave ... Salt Lake City UT 84104 *TF:* 800-584-6973 ■ *Web:* www.nicopumps.com	801-973-8888		385
Nickerson Corp 11 Moffitt Blvd PO Box 5751 ... Bay Shore NY 11706 *Web:* www.nickersoncorp.com	631-666-0200	666-2667	320
Nickerson Lumber Co 15 Main St ... Orleans MA 02653 *Web:* www.midcape.net	508-255-0200		364
Nickerson State Park 3488 Main St ... Brewster MA 02631 *Web:* www.mass.gov	508-896-3491		565
Nickerson-Remick 95 Brewster St ... Portsmouth NH 03801 *TF:* 800-524-1342 ■ *Web:* www.nickerson-remick.com	603-436-2946	436-2595	189-9
Nickey Petroleum Company Inc 925 S Lkview Ave ... Placentia CA 92870 *Web:* nickeypetroleum.com	714-547-4123		581
Nicklaus Design 11780 US Hwy 1 Ste 500 ... North Palm Beach FL 33408 *Web:* www.nicklaus.com	561-227-0300	227-0548	710
Nicklos Drilling Co 2229 San Felipe Ste 1401 ... Houston TX 77019 *Web:* nicklosdrilling.com	713-224-5959		540
Nickson Industries Inc 336 Woodford Ave ... Plainville CT 06062 *TF:* 800-243-0126 ■ *Web:* www.nickson.com	860-747-1671	747-1678	247
Nick-Stone 969 2nd St SE ... Charlottesville VA 22902 *Web:* www.nick-stone.com	434-284-2840		180
NICL Laboratories 306 Era Dr ... Northbrook IL 60062 *Web:* www.nicl.com	847-509-9779		415
Nicodemus National Historic Site 304 Washington Ave ... Bogue KS 67625 *Web:* www.nps.gov	785-839-4233	839-4325	564
Nicol Scales 7239 Envoy Ct ... Dallas TX 75247 *TF:* 800-225-8181 ■ *Web:* nicolscales.com	214-428-8181	428-8127	639
Nicola Valley Institute of Technology 4355 Mathissi Pl ... Burnaby BC V5G4S8 *TF:* 877-682-3300 ■ *Web:* www.nvit.ca	604-602-9555		165
Nicola Wealth Management Ltd 1508 W Broadway 5th Fl ... Vancouver BC V6J1W8 *Web:* www.nicolawealth.com	604-739-6450		796
Nicola's 1420 Sycamore St ... Cincinnati OH 45202 *Web:* nicolasotr.com	513-721-6200		671
Nicolaysen Art Museum 400 E Collins Dr ... Casper WY 82601 *Web:* www.thenic.org	307-235-5247		520
Nicolet College 5364 College Dr ... Rhinelander WI 54501 *TF:* 800-544-3039 ■ *Web:* www.nicoletcollege.edu	715-365-4410		167-3
Nicolet Plastics Inc 16685 State Rd 32 ... Mountain WI 54149 *Web:* www.nicoletplastics.com	715-276-4200		596
Nicolini Paradise Ferretti 114 Old Country Rd ... Mineola NY 11501 *Web:* npfslaw.com	516-741-6355		41
Nicolinni's 1912 S Raccoon Rd ... Youngstown OH 44515 *Web:* nicolinnis.com	330-799-9999		671
Nicolino's Italian Restaurant 2544 Executive Dr ... Indianapolis IN 46241 *Web:* www.nicolinositalian.com	317-381-6146	381-6170	671
Nicollet County 501 S Minnesota Ave ... Saint Peter MN 56082 *Web:* www.co.nicollet.mn.us	507-931-6800	931-9220	338
Nicollet Island Inn 95 Merriam St ... Minneapolis MN 55401 *Web:* www.nicolletislandinn.com	612-331-1800	331-6528	671
Nicolson Porter & List Inc 1300 W Higgins Rd ... Park Ridge IL 60068 *Web:* www.nplchicago.com	847-698-7400	698-5167	652
Nicomm LLC 2235 Gateway Dr ... Sycamore IL 60178	815-758-0661		196
Nicor Gas 1844 Ferry Rd ... Naperville IL 60563 **Fax Area Code:* 630 ■ *TF:* 888-642-6748 ■ *Web:* www.nicorgas.com	888-642-6748	983-6755*	787
Nicosia Creative Expresso Ltd 330 5th Ave ... New York NY 10001 *Web:* www.niceltd.com	212-515-6600		344
Nicros Inc 845 Phalen Blvd ... Saint Paul MN 55106 *TF:* 800-699-1975 ■ *Web:* nicros.com	651-778-1975		711
NID (Nevada Irrigation District) 1036 W Main St ... Grass Valley CA 95945 *Web:* nidwater.com	530-273-6185		787
Nida Corp 300 S John Rodes Blvd ... Melbourne FL 32904 *TF:* 800-327-6432 ■ *Web:* www.nida.com	321-727-2265	727-2655	703
National Institute on Deafness & Other Communication Disorders, The 31 Center Dr MSC 2320 ... Bethesda MD 20892 *TF:* 800-241-1044 ■ *Web:* www.nidcd.nih.gov	301-496-7243	402-0018	668
Nidec America Corp 50 Braintree Hill Pk Ste 110 ... Braintree MA 02184 *Web:* www.nidec.com	781-848-0970	380-3634	518
Nidec Avtron Automation Corp 7555 E Pleasant Valley Rd Bldg 100 ... Independence OH 44131 *Web:* www.nidec-avtron.com	216-642-1230		407
Nidec Motor Corp 8050 W Florissant Ave ... Saint Louis MO 63136 *TF:* 888-637-7333 ■ *Web:* acim.nidec.com	888-637-7333		518
Nidek Inc 47651 Westinghouse Dr ... Fremont CA 94539 *TF:* 800-223-9044 ■ *Web:* usa.nidek.com	510-226-5700		475
Nidus Partners LP 1005 N Warson Rd Ste 401 ... Saint Louis MO 63132 *Web:* niduspartners.com	314-812-8080		196
Niebur Golf Inc 1230 Tenderfoot Hill Rd Ste 250 ... Colorado Springs CO 80906 *Web:* nieburdevelopment.com	719-527-0313		188-3
Niederauer Inc 1976 W San Carlos St ... San Jose CA 95128 *Web:* www.westernappliance.com	408-297-2440		35
Niederman, Stanzel & Lindsey PLLC 55 W Webster St ... Manchester NH 03104 *Web:* nslnh.com	603-668-5960		41
Niedner, Bodeux, Carmichael, Huff, Lenox & Pashos LLP 131 Jefferson St ... Saint Charles MO 63301 *TF:* 888-572-2192 ■ *Web:* www.niednerlaw.com	636-949-9300		428
NIEFERT Certified Solutions LLC 5850 Oberlin Dr ... San Diego CA 92121 *Web:* www.niefert.com	858-450-9092		809
Nielsen Business Media 770 Broadway ... New York NY 10003 *Web:* www.nielsen.com	646-654-4500		637-2
Nielsen Dodge Chrysler Jeep Ram 175 Rt 10 E ... East Hanover NJ 07936 *TF:* 877-312-2140 ■ *Web:* www.nielsendodgechryslerjeepram.com	973-884-2100		57
Nielsen Law Group Pc 1490 S Price Rd Ste 301 ... Chandler AZ 85286 *Web:* nielsenlawgroup.net	480-888-7111		41
Nielsen, Merksamer, Parrinello, Gross & Leoni LLP 2350 Kerner Blvd Ste 250 ... San Rafael CA 94901 *Web:* www.nmgovlaw.com	415-389-6800	388-6874	428
Nielsen-Massey Vanillas Inc 1550 S Shields Dr ... Waukegan IL 60085 *TF:* 800-525-7873 ■ *Web:* www.nielsenmassey.com	847-578-1550	578-1570	296-15
Nieman Printing Inc 10615 Newkirk St Ste 100 ... Dallas TX 75220 *Web:* www.niemanprinting.com	972-506-7400	869-3632	627
Niermann Weeks Company Inc 760 Generals Hwy ... Millersville MD 21108 *Web:* www.niermannweeks.com	410-923-0123	923-0647	393
Nietzke & Faupel PC 7274 Hartley St ... Pigeon MI 48755 *Web:* www.nfcpa.com	989-453-3122		2
Nifco America Corp 8015 Dove Pkwy ... Canal Winchester OH 43110 *Web:* www.nifcousa.com	614-836-3808		596
NIFDA (National Independent Flag Dealers Assn) 7984 S Chicago Ave ... Chicago IL 60617 *TF:* 800-356-4085 ■ *Web:* www.nifda.net	773-768-8076	768-3138	49-18
NIFL (National Institute for Literacy) 1775 'I' St NW Ste 730 ... Washington DC 20006 *TF:* 800-228-8813 ■ *Web:* lincs.ed.gov	202-233-2025	233-2050	340-8
Nift Networks Inc 101 Huntington Ave ... Boston MA 02199 *Web:* www.gonift.com	617-506-9310		395
Nifty After Fifty LLC 1501 E Orangethorpe Ave Ste 180 ... Fullerton CA 92831 *TF:* 855-236-4389 ■ *Web:* www.niftyafterfifty.com	714-823-4400		354
NIGA (National Indian Gaming Assn) 224 Second St SE ... Washington DC 20003 *Web:* www.indiangaming.org	202-546-7711	546-1755	48-23
Niger Embassy 2204 R St NW ... Washington DC 20008 *Web:* www.embassyofniger.org	202-483-4224	483-3169	257
Nigeria			
Consulate General 828 Second Ave ... New York NY 10017 *Web:* www.nigeriahouse.com	212-850-2200	687-1476	257
Embassy 3519 International Ct NW ... Washington DC 20008 *Web:* www.nigeriaembassyusa.org	202-986-8400		257
Night Optics USA Inc 15182 Triton Ln Ste 101 ... Huntington Beach CA 92649 *TF:* 800-306-4448 ■ *Web:* www.nightoptics.com	800-306-4448		542
Nightforce Optics 336 Hazen Ln ... Orofino ID 83544 *Web:* www.nightforceoptics.com	208-476-9814	476-9817	544
Nightingale-Conant Corp 6245 W Howard St ... Niles IL 60714 *TF:* 800-557-1660 ■ *Web:* www.nightingale.com	800-557-1660		513
Nightlinger, Colavita & Volpa PA 991 S Black Horse Pk ... Williamstown NJ 08094 *Web:* www.colavita.net	856-629-1040	728-2245	2
NightOwl Discovery Inc 1000 Parkers Lake Rd ... Wayzata MN 55391 *Web:* Www.nightowlglobal.com	612-337-0448		627
NIGP (National Institute of Governmental Purchasing Inc) 151 Spring St ... Herndon VA 20170 *TF:* 800-367-6447 ■ *Web:* www.nigp.org	703-736-8900	736-2818	49-7
NIH (National Institutes of Health) 9000 Rockville Pk ... Bethesda MD 20892 *TF:* 800-411-1222 ■ *Web:* www.nih.gov	301-496-4000		340-10
NIH Osteoporosis & Related Bone Diseases-National Resource Ctr 2 AMS Cir ... Bethesda MD 20892 *TF:* 800-624-2663 ■ *Web:* www.niams.nih.gov	202-223-0344	293-2356	340-10
NIH Research & Consulting LLC 5645 Coral Ridge Dr Ste 316 ... Coral Springs FL 33076 *Web:* nihresearch.com	954-753-7747		466
Nihon Kohden America Inc 90 Icon ... Foothill Ranch CA 92610 *TF:* 800-325-0283 ■ *Web:* us.nihonkohden.com	949-580-1555	580-1550	475
NII Holdings Inc 12110 Sunset Hills Rd Ste 600 ... Reston VA 20190 *NASDAQ: NIHD* ■ *Web:* www.nii.com	703-390-5100		736
Niigon Machines Ltd 372 New Enterprise Way ... Vaughan ON L4H0S8 *Web:* www.niigonmachines.com	905-265-0277		261
Nike Inc 1 Bowerman Dr ... Beaverton OR 97005 *NYSE: NKE* ■ *TF:* 800-344-6453 ■ *Web:* www.nike.com	503-671-6453	646-6926	301
Niki's West 233 Finley Ave W ... Birmingham AL 35204 *Web:* nikiswest.com	205-252-5751	252-8163	671
Nikitova LLC 203 N Lasalle Ste 2100 ... Chicago IL 60601	773-913-8015		514
Nikka Yuko Japanese Garden PO Box 751 ... Lethbridge AB T1J3Z6 *Web:* www.nikkayuko.com	403-328-3511	328-0511	97
Nikkei Credit Union 18425 S Western Ave 2nd Fl ... Gardena CA 90248 *TF:* 866-464-5534 ■ *Web:* nikkeicu.org	310-324-1544		219
Nikkei MC Aluminum America Inc 6875 S Inwood Dr ... Columbus IN 47201 *Web:* www.nmaluminum.net	812-342-1141		492

	Phone	Fax	Class
Nikki America Inc 9616 S Franklin Dr .... Franklin WI 53132 *Web:* www.nikkinet.co.jp	414-448-0094		128
Nikki Beach 1 Ocean Dr S Beach .... Miami Beach FL 33139 *Web:* miami-beach.nikkibeach.com	305-538-1231		671
Nikkiso Cryo Inc 4661 Eaker St .... North Las Vegas NV 89081 *Web:* nikkisocryo.com	702-643-4900	643-0391	743
Nikko 325 Arlington Ave Ste 108 .... Charlotte NC 28203 *Web:* www.nikkosushibar.net	704-209-9023		671
Niko Resources Ltd 205-5th Ave SW Ste 1500 .... Calgary AB T2P2V7 *TSE:* NKO ■ *Web:* www.nikoresources.com	403-262-1020		536
Nikolai's Roof 255 Courtland St NE .... Atlanta GA 30303 *Web:* www.nikolaisroof.com	404-221-6362		671
Nikolaus and Hohenadel 212 N Queen St .... Lancaster PA 17603 *Web:* www.n-hlaw.com	717-299-3726	299-1811	41
Nik-O-Lok Co 3130 N Mitthoeffer Rd .... Indianapolis IN 46235 *TF:* 800-428-4348 ■ *Web:* www.nikolok.com	317-899-6955	899-6977	350
Nikon Inc 1300 Walt Whitman Rd .... Melville NY 11747 *TF:* 800-645-6687 ■ *Web:* www.nikonusa.com	631-547-4200	547-0299	591
Nikon Precision Inc 1399 Shoreway Rd .... Belmont CA 94002 *Web:* www.nikon.com	650-508-4674		696
Niles Audio Corp 1969 Kellog Ave .... Carlsbad CA 92008 *TF:* 800-289-4434 ■ *Web:* www.nilesaudio.com	760-710-0992		253
Niles Barton & Wilmer LLP 111 S Calvert St Ste 1400 .... Baltimore MD 21202 *Web:* www.nilesbarton.com	410-783-6300	783-6363	428
Niles Bolton Associates Inc (NBA) 3060 Peachtree Rd NW Ste 600 .... Atlanta GA 30305 *Web:* www.nilesbolton.com	404-365-7600		261
Niles Chamber of Commerce 8060 Oakton St .... Niles IL 60714 *Web:* www.nileschamber.com	847-268-8180	268-8186	139
Niles Community School 2120 20th Pl .... Niles MI 49120 *Web:* www.nilesschools.org	269-683-0732	684-9532	685
Niles Manufacturing & Finishing Inc 465 Walnut St .... Niles OH 44446 *Web:* www.nilesmfg.com	330-544-0402	544-8018	488
Niles Precision Co PO Box 548 .... Niles MI 49120 *Web:* www.nilesprecision.com	269-683-0585	683-7762	21
Niles Sparkle Market Inc 140 N Main St .... Niles OH 44446 *Web:* sparklemarket.com	330-544-3478		345
Nilfisk-Advance America Inc 740 Hemlock Rd Ste 100 .... Morgantown PA 19543 **Fax Area Code:* 610 ■ *TF:* 800-645-3475 ■ *Web:* www.nilfiskcfm.com	800-645-3475	647-6427*	38
Nilfisk-Advance Inc 14600 21st Ave N .... Plymouth MN 55447 *TF:* 800-989-2235 ■ *Web:* www.nilfisk.com	800-989-2235	989-6566	386
Nimbix LLC 800 E Campbell Ste 241 .... Richardson TX 75081 *TF:* 866-307-0819 ■ *Web:* www.nimbix.net	866-307-0819		809
Nimbleuser 1100 Pittsford-Victor Rd .... Pittsford NY 14534 *Web:* www.nimbleuser.com	585-586-4750		177
Nimbus Design 2363 Broadway St .... Redwood City CA 94063 *Web:* www.nimbusdesign.com	650-365-7568		225
Nimensky Gallinson & Buren PA CPAs 316 Eisenhower Pkwy .... Livingston NJ 07039 *Web:* www.ngbcpa.com	973-533-9200		2
Nimo's Sushi Bar & Japanese 921 E Harmony Rd Ste 104 .... Fort Collins CO 80525 *Web:* www.nimossushi.com	970-221-1040		671
Nims & Assoc 1445 Technology Ln Ste A8 .... Petaluma CA 94954 *TF:* 877-454-3200 ■ *Web:* www.nimsassociates.com	707-781-6300		177
Nina Construction Supply (NCS) 4102 E Superior Ave .... Phoenix AZ 85040 *Web:* www.ninaconstructionsupply.com	602-437-5760	437-5705	304
Nina's Ristorante 8801 Lead Mine Rd .... Raleigh NC 27615 *Web:* ninasrestaurant.com	919-845-1122		671
Nine Dragons Restaurant 4615 23rd Ave S .... Fargo ND 58104 *Web:* 9dragonsrestaurant.com	701-232-2411		671
Nine Eagles State Park 23678 Dale Miller Rd .... Davis City IA 50065 *Web:* www.iowadnr.gov	641-442-2855	442-2856	565
Nine Energy Service 2001 Kirby Dr Ste 200 .... Houston TX 77019 *TF:* 800-953-3777 ■ *Web:* nineenergyservice.com	281-730-5100	605-1318	536
Nine Health Services Inc 1139 Delaware St .... Denver CO 80204 *TF:* 800-332-3078 ■ *Web:* www.9healthfair.org	303-698-4455		636
Nine Quarter Cir Ranch 5000 Taylor Fork Rd .... Gallatin Gateway MT 59730 *Web:* www.ninequartercircle.com	406-995-4276		239
Nine Star Enterprises Inc 730 I St .... Anchorage AK 99501 *TF:* 800-478-7587 ■ *Web:* ninestar.org	907-279-7827		260
Nines Hotel, The 525 SW Morrison .... Portland OR 97204 *TF:* 877-229-9995 ■ *Web:* www.thenines.com	877-229-9995		41
NineSigma Inc 23611 Chagrin Blvd Ste 320 .... Cleveland OH 44122 *Web:* www.ninesigma.com	216-295-4800		466
Ninety Six National Historic Site 1103 Hwy 248 .... Ninety Six SC 29666 *Web:* www.nps.gov	864-543-4068	543-2058	564
Ninety-Nine Restaurant & Pubs 291 Mishawum Rd .... Woburn MA 01801 *Web:* www.99restaurants.com	781-935-7210		670
Ninety-Nines Inc 4300 Amelia Earhart Rd .... Oklahoma City OK 73159 *TF:* 800-994-1929 ■ *Web:* www.ninety-nines.org	405-685-7969	685-7985	48-24
Ning Interactive Inc 1906 El Camino Real .... Menlo Park CA 94027 *TF:* 855-233-6436 ■ *Web:* www.ning.com	855-233-6436		395
Ninja 8433 Oak St .... New Orleans LA 70118 *Web:* www.ninjasushineworleans.com	504-866-1119		671
NinjaTrader LLC 1236 Clarkson St .... Denver CO 80218 *Web:* ninjatrader.com	312-423-2234		809
Nino Salvaggio International Marketplace 27900 Harper Ave .... Saint Clair Shores MI 48081 *Web:* www.ninosalvaggio.com	586-778-3650		345
Nino's 1931 Chesire Bridge Rd .... Atlanta GA 30324 *Web:* ninosatlanta.com	404-874-6505		671
Nino's Vincent's Grappino di Nino 2817 W Dallas St .... Houston TX 77019 *Web:* ninos-vincents.com	713-522-5120		671
Nintendo of America Inc 4820 150th Ave NE .... Redmond WA 98052 *TF:* 800-255-3700 ■ *Web:* www.nintendo.com	425-882-2040	882-3585	762
Nintex USA LLC 10800 NE Eighth St Ste 400 .... Bellevue WA 98004 *TF:* 877-462-5667 ■ *Web:* www.nintex.com	425-324-2400		180
NinthDecimal Inc 150 Post St Ste 500 .... San Francisco CA 94108 *Web:* www.ninthdecimal.com	415-821-8600		174
Ninyo & Moore 5710 Ruffin Rd .... San Diego CA 92123 *TF:* 800-427-0401 ■ *Web:* www.ninyoandmoore.com	858-576-1000		261
Niobrara County 424 S Elm St PO Box 420 .... Lusk WY 82225 *Web:* www.niobraracounty.org	307-334-2736		338
Niobrara National Scenic River 214 W US Hwy 20 PO Box 319 .... Valentine NE 69201 *Web:* www.nps.gov	402-376-1901	376-1949	564
Niobrara State Park 89261 522 Ave .... Niobrara NE 68760 *Web:* www.stateparks.com	402-857-3373		565
Niobrara Valley Electric Membership Corp 427 N Fourth St .... O'Neill NE 68763 *Web:* www.nvemc.org	402-336-2803	336-4858	245
NIP Group Inc 900 Rt 9 N .... Woodbridge NJ 07095 **Fax Area Code:* 732 ■ *TF:* 800-446-7647 ■ *Web:* www.nipgroup.com	800-446-7647	791-1630*	390
NIPCO (Northwest Iowa Power Co-op) 31002 County Rd C38 PO Box 240 .... Le Mars IA 51031 *Web:* www.nipco.coop	712-546-4141		245
Nipissing University 100 College Dr PO Box 5002 .... North Bay ON P1B8L7 *TF:* 800-655-5154 ■ *Web:* www.nipissingu.ca	705-474-3450	495-1772	785
NIPNLG (National Immigration Project of the National Lawyers Guild Inc) 14 Beacon St Ste 602 .... Boston MA 02108 *Web:* www.nationalimmigrationproject.org	617-227-9727	227-5495	393
Nippon Express USA Inc 24-01 44th Rd 14th Fl .... Long Island City NY 11101 *Web:* nipponexpressusa.com	212-758-6100	758-2595	311
Nippon Kodo Inc 2771 Plaza Del Amo Ste 805 .... Torrance CA 90503 *TF:* 888-775-5487 ■ *Web:* www.nipponkodo.com	310-320-8881		787
Nippon Paper Industries (NPI) 3001 Industrial Way .... Longview WA 98632 *Web:* www.nipponpapergroup.com	360-636-6400	423-1514	553
Nippon Sharyo USA Inc 2340 S Arlington Heights Rd Ste 605 .... Arlington Heights IL 60005 *Web:* www.nipponsharyousa.com	847-228-2700	228-5530	194
Nippon Steel USA Inc 1251 Avenue of the Americas Ste 2320 .... New York NY 10020 *Web:* www.nssmc.com	212-486-7150	593-3049	492
Nipro Medical Corp 3150 NW 107th Ave .... Miami FL 33172 *Web:* www.nipro.com	305-599-7174	592-4621	475
NIR Roof Care Inc 12191 Regency Pkwy .... Huntley IL 60142 *TF:* 800-221-7663 ■ *Web:* www.nir.com	847-669-3444	669-3173	189-12
Nirenstein, Horowitz & Associates PC 191 Post Rd W .... Westport CT 06880 *Web:* preserveyourestate.net	860-548-1000	761-1070	428
NIRI (National Investor Relations Institute) 225 Reinekers Ln Ste 560 .... Alexandria VA 22314 *Web:* www.niri.org	703-562-7700	562-7701	49-2
NIRS (Nuclear Information & Resource Service) 6930 Carroll Ave Ste 340 .... Takoma Park MD 20912 *Web:* www.nirs.org	301-270-6477	270-4291	48-8
NIRSA (National Intramural-Recreational Sports Assn) 4185 SW Research Way .... Corvallis OR 97333 *Web:* www.nirsa.net	541-766-8211	766-8284	48-22
Nirvana Systems Inc 9111 Jollyville Rd Ste 275 .... Austin TX 78731 *TF:* 800-880-0338 ■ *Web:* www.omnitrader.com	512-345-2545		177
NIS (Network Integration Specialists Inc) 1600 Mountain Rd .... Glen Allen VA 23060 *Web:* www.netintegration.net	804-264-9339	726-8242	180
NIS Inc 12995 Thomas Creek Rd .... Reno NV 89511 *Web:* nissoftware.net	775-852-0640		178-2
Nisbet Oil Co PO Box 35367 .... Charlotte NC 28235 *Web:* nisbetoil.com	704-332-7755	377-1607	579
Nisen & Elliott LLC 200 W Adams St Ste 2500 .... Chicago IL 60606 *Web:* www.nisen.com	312-346-7800		428
NISH 8401 Old Courthouse Rd .... Vienna VA 22182 *TF:* 888-411-8424 ■ *Web:* www.sourceamerica.org	888-411-8424		48-17
Nishikawa of America Inc 39555 Orchard Hill Place Dr Ste 320 .... Novi MI 48375 *Web:* www.nishikawa-rbr.co.jp	248-596-5959	596-6520	676
Nishiki Sushi 1501 16th St .... Sacramento CA 95814 *Web:* nishikisushi.com	916-446-3629		671
Nishnabotna Valley Rural Electric Co-op 1317 Chatburn Ave .... Harlan IA 51537 *TF:* 800-234-5122 ■ *Web:* www.nvrec.com	712-755-2166		245
Nisivoccia & Company LLP 200 Valley Rd Ste 300 .... Mount Arlington NJ 07856 *Web:* nisivoccia.com	973-328-1825	298-8501	2
Niskayuna Central School District (NCSD) 1239 Van Antwerp Rd .... Schenectady NY 12309 *TF:* 866-893-6337 ■ *Web:* www.niskayunaschools.org	518-377-4666	377-4074	685
NISO (National Information Standards Organization) 3600 Clipper Mill Rd Ste 302 .... Baltimore MD 21211 **Fax Area Code:* 410 ■ *TF:* 877-375-2160 ■ *Web:* www.niso.org	301-654-2512	685-5278*	49-16
Nisqually Reach Nature Ctr (NRNC) 4949 D'Milluhr Rd NE .... Olympia WA 98516 *Web:* www.nisquallyestuary.org	360-459-0387		50-5
Nissan Canada Inc (NCI) 5290 Orbitor Dr .... Mississauga ON L4W4Z5 **Fax Area Code:* 905 ■ *TF:* 800-387-0122 ■ *Web:* www.nissan.ca	800-387-0122	629-6553*	59

	Phone	Fax	Class
Nissan Motor Corp			
USA Infiniti Div 1 Nissan Way................. Franklin TN 37067	800-662-6200		59
TF: 800-662-6200 ■ *Web:* www.infinitiusa.com			
Nissan North America Inc			
25 Vantage Way .... Nashville TN 37228	800-647-7261	629-9742*	59
**Fax Area Code:* 905 ■ *TF:* 800-647-7261 ■ *Web:* www.nissanusa.com			
Nissan of Atlantic City			
6021 Black Horse Pk .... Egg Harbor Township NJ 08234	609-383-6100		57
Web: www.nissanofatlanticcity.com			
Nissan Stadium 1 Titans Way .... Nashville TN 37213	615-565-4300		720
Web: www.tennesseetitans.com			
Nissei America Inc 1480 N Hancock St......... Anaheim CA 92807	714-693-3000		111
TF: 800-693-3231 ■ *Web:* www.nisseiamerica.com			
Nissen & Company Inc			
9508 Rush St .... South El Monte CA 91733	626-579-5666	579-0628	191-3
Web: www.nissenco.com			
Nissen Chemitec America 350 E High St........ London OH 43140	740-852-3200	852-4547	608
Web: nissenchemitec.com			
Nissequogue River State Park			
799 St Johnland Rd .... Kings Park NY 11754	631-269-4927		565
Web: parks.ny.gov			
Nissha Medical Technologies			
814 Airport Way .... Sandpoint ID 83864	800-893-6361		250
TF: 800-201-3958 ■ *Web:* dm.nisshamedical.com			
Nisshin Steel Co			
1701 Golf Rd			
Continental Tower 3 Ste 1004...........Rolling Meadows IL 60008	847-290-5100	290-0826	723
Web: www.nisshin-steel.co.jp			
Nissho Electronics USA Corp			
226 Airport Pkwy .... San Jose CA 95110	408-969-9700	969-9701	178-10
Web: www.nelco.com			
Nissin Brake Ohio Inc			
1901 Industrial Dr............................Findlay OH 45839	419-425-6725		247
Web: www.nissinbrake.com			
Nissin Foods USA Company Inc			
2001 W Rosecrans Ave.......................Gardena CA 90249	310-327-8478	515-3751	296-31
Web: nissinfoods.com			
Nissin Precision North America Inc			
375 Union Blvd...........................Englewood OH 45322	937-836-1910		483
Web: nissinoh.com			
NIST (National Institute of Standards & Technology)			
100 Bureau Dr Sp 1070 .... Gaithersburg MD 20899	301-975-6478		340-2
Web: www.nist.gov			
Nistica Inc 745 Rt 202-206 .... Bridgewater NJ 08807	908-707-9500		116
Web: www.nistica.com			
NITCO (Northwestern Indiana Telephone Co)			
205 N Washington St ....Hebron IN 46341	219-996-2981		224
Web: www.nitco.com			
Nitek Laser Inc 305 Rt du Port ....Nicolet QC J3T1R7	819-293-4887		757
Web: www.niteklaser.com			
Nitel Inc 1101 W Lake St 6th Fl ....Chicago IL 60607	888-450-2100		224
TF: 888-450-2100 ■ *Web:* www.nitelusa.com			
Nitelines USA Inc			
2180 Satellite Blvd Ste 400..................... Duluth GA 30097	844-661-9120		393
TF: 844-661-9120 ■ *Web:* nitelinesusa.com			
Nitrex Metal Inc			
3474 Poirier Blvd ....Saint-Laurent QC H4R2J5	514-335-7191	335-4160	484
TF: 877-335-7191 ■ *Web:* www.nitrex.com			
Nitro Electric Services 4300 First Ave .... Nitro WV 25143	304-204-1500	204-1350	189-10
Web: nitro-electric.com			
Nitrous Express Inc			
5411 Seymour Hwy .... Wichita Falls TX 76310	940-767-7694		57
TF: 888-463-2781 ■ *Web:* www.nitrousexpress.com			
Nitta Casings Inc			
141 Southside Ave .... Bridgewater NJ 08807	908-218-4400	725-2835	298
TF: 800-526-3970 ■ *Web:* www.nittacasings.com			
Nitta Corporation of America			
7605 Nitta Dr .... Suwanee GA 30024	770-497-0212		385
Web: www.nitta.com			
Nitta Gelatin Inc			
598 Airport Blvd Ste 900 ....Morrisville NC 27560	919-238-3300	238-3222	296-22
Web: www.nitta-gelatin.com			
Nittany Beverage Co			
139 N Patterson St ....State College PA 16801	814-238-3031		81-1
Web: www.nittanybeverage.com			
Nittany Oil Company Inc			
1540 Martin St.........................State College PA 16803	814-237-4859		581
TF: 800-870-2140 ■ *Web:* www.nittanyenergy.com			
Nittany Valley Offset			
Nittany Vly Offset 1015 Benner Pk ....State College PA 16801	814-238-3071	238-3051	532-3
Web: www.nittanyvalley.com			
Nitterhouse Concrete Products Inc			
2655 Molly Pitcher Hwy.................Chambersburg PA 17201	717-267-4505	267-4518	183
Web: www.nitterhouse.com			
Nitto Denko Automotive Ohio Inc			
1620 S Main St...............................Piqua OH 45356	937-773-4820	773-9760	54
Web: www.nitto.com			
Nitto Denko Avecia Inc			
125 Fortune Blvd ....Milford MA 01757	508-532-2500		144
Web: www.avecia.com			
Nityo Infotech Corporation Inc			
2652 Hidden Valley Dr Ste 303............... Pittsburgh PA 15241	412-226-5546	941-1068*	180
**Fax Area Code:* 724 ■ *Web:* www.nityo.com			
Nitze-Stagen & Company Inc			
2401 Utah Ave S Ste 305 .... Seattle WA 98134	206-467-0420	467-0423	403
Web: nitze-stagen.com			
Niven 955 Kimberly Dr .... Carol Stream IL 60188	630-580-6000		195
Web: www.niven.net			
Niven Family Wine Estates			
4915 Orcutt Rd .... San Luis Obispo CA 93401	805-597-8200		315-5
Web: nivenfamilywines.com			
Niwot Networks Inc 721 9th Ave .... Longmont CO 80501	303-772-8664		178-1
TF: 800-657-3278 ■ *Web:* www.gigabytex.com			
Nixon Consulting Inc PO Box 440............ Chatham IL 62629	217-483-7717	483-7733	196
TF: 888-541-9560 ■ *Web:* www.nixonconsulting.com			
Nixon Gear Inc 1750 Milton Ave .... Syracuse NY 13209	315-488-0100	488-0196	709
Web: gearmotions.com			
Nixon Law Firm PLLC 105 Main St........... Whitesboro NY 13492	315-736-6787		41
Web: nixonlegal.com			
Nixon-Egli Equipment Company Inc			
2044 S Vineyard Ave..........................Ontario CA 91761	909-930-1822		358
Web: www.nixon-egli.com			
Niyamit Inc			
2201 Cooperative Way Ste 600.................Herndon VA 20171	703-788-6590	880-7181	809
Web: www.niyamit.com			
Nizhoni Health Systems LLC			
5 Middlesex Ave..........................Somerville MA 02145	800-915-3211		363
TF: 800-915-3211 ■ *Web:* nizhonihealth.com			
NJAM (New Jersey Association of Museums)			
c/o Montclair Art Museum 3 S Mountain Ave.....Montclair NJ 07042	732-703-6526		637-2
Web: www.njmuseums.org			
NJBG/Skylands Association Inc			
PO Box 302 .... Ringwood NJ 07456	973-962-9534	962-1553	97
Web: www.njbg.org			
NJCAA 1631 Mesa Ave .... Colorado Springs CO 80906	719-590-9788	590-7324	48-22
Web: www.njcaa.org			
NJEA Review 180 W State St....................Trenton NJ 08607	609-599-4561	392-6321	457-8
Web: www.njea.org			
NJHCS (East Orange Campus of the VA New Jersey Health Care System)			
385 Tremont Ave.........................East Orange NJ 07018	844-872-4681	456-1414*	374-8
**Fax Area Code:* 202 ■ *TF:* 844-872-4681 ■ *Web:* www.usa.gov			
NJLA (New Jersey Library Assn)			
PO Box 1534 .... Trenton NJ 08607	609-394-8032	394-8164	435
Web: njla.org			
Office of Information Technology			
PO Box 212............................. Trenton NJ 08625	609-633-8975	633-0090	339-31
Web: www.state.nj.us			
NJSNA (New Jersey State Nurses Assn)			
1479 Pennington Rd......................... Trenton NJ 08618	609-883-5335	883-5343	533
TF: 800-662-0108 ■ *Web:* njsna.org			
N-K Manufacturing Technologies			
1134 Freeman Ave SW...................Grand Rapids MI 49503	616-248-3200	248-3246	608
Web: www.nkmfgtech.com			
NK Parts Industry Incorporated Main Facility			
777 S Kuther Rd.............................Sidney OH 45365	937-498-4651		88
Web: www.nkparts.com			
NKB (N K Bhandari, Consulting Engineers PC)			
1005 W Fayette St Ste 500 .... Syracuse NY 13204	315-428-1177	428-9822	261
Web: www.nkbpc.com			
NKBA (National Kitchen & Bath Assn)			
687 Willow Grove St.....................Hackettstown NJ 07840	800-843-6522	852-1695*	49-3
**Fax Area Code:* 908 ■ *TF:* 800-843-6522 ■ *Web:* nkba.org			
NKC of America Inc 1584 E Brooks Rd.......... Memphis TN 38116	901-396-6334	396-2339	207
Web: www.nkc-soltech.com			
NKF (National Kidney Foundation)			
30 E 33rd St ....New York NY 10016	212-889-2210		48-17
TF: 800-622-9010 ■ *Web:* www.kidney.org			
NKL (New Knowledge Library) PO Box 1724..... Boulder CO 80304	800-938-3891		637-2
TF: 800-938-3891 ■ *Web:* newknowledgelibrary.org			
NKP Medical Marketing Inc			
8939 S Sepulveda Blvd Ste 320.............Los Angeles CA 90045	866-539-2201		195
TF: 866-539-2201 ■ *Web:* www.nkpmedical.com			
NKS Distributors Inc			
399 Churchmans Rd.......................New Castle DE 19720	302-322-1811		81-3
NKTelco Inc			
301 W South St PO Box 219..............New Knoxville OH 45871	419-753-5000	629-1424	224
TF: 888-658-3526 ■ *Web:* www.nktelco.com			
NKYCVB (Northern Kentucky Convention & Visitors Bureau)			
50 E RiverCenter Blvd Ste 200 .... Covington KY 41011	859-261-4677	261-5135	206
TF: 877-659-8474 ■ *Web:* www.meetnky.com			
NL Industries			
16801 Greenspoint Park Dr ....Houston TX 77060	281-423-3300		143
NYSE: NL ■ *TF:* 800-866-5600 ■ *Web:* www.nl-ind.com			
NLA (Northwest Learning Associates Inc)			
12 Water St............................... Hingham MA 02043	520-881-0877	626-4751*	637-2
**Fax Area Code:* 781 ■ *Web:* www.nlabooks.com			
NLADA (National Legal Aid & Defender Assn)			
1140 Connecticut Ave NW Ste 900...........Washington DC 20036	202-452-0620	872-1031	49-10
TF: 800-725-4513 ■ *Web:* www.nlada.org			
NLAPW (National League of American Pen Women Inc)			
1300 17th St NW ....Washington DC 20036	202-785-1997	452-8868	48-4
Web: www.nlapw.org			
NLBMDA (National Lumber & Building Material Dealers Assn)			
2001 K St NW 3rd Fl......................Washington DC 20006	202-367-1169		49-18
Web: www.dealer.org			
NLBRA (National Little Britches Rodeo Assn)			
5050 Edison Ave Ste 105 .... Colorado Springs CO 80915	719-389-0333	578-1367	48-22
TF: 800-763-3694 ■ *Web:* www.nlbra.com			
NLC (National League of Cities)			
660 N Capitol St NW ....Washington DC 20001	877-827-2385		49-7
TF: 877-827-2385 ■ *Web:* www.nlc.org			
NLC Products Inc PO Box 8300 .... Little Rock AR 72222	800-648-5483		711
TF: 800-648-5483 ■ *Web:* www.huntsmart.com			
NLDA (National Luggage Dealers Assn)			
1817 Elmdale Ave.......................... Glenview IL 60026	847-998-6869	998-6884	49-18
TF: 800-411-0705 ■ *Web:* www.nlda.com			
NLN (National League for Nursing)			
61 Broadway 33rd Fl........................New York NY 10006	212-363-5555	812-0391	49-8
TF: 800-669-1656 ■ *Web:* www.nln.org			
NLP Enterprises Inc PO Box 349 ....Owings Mills MD 21117	410-356-7500	356-7525	189-8
Web: www.nlpentinc.com			
NLRB (National Labor Relations Board)			
1099 14th St NW ....Washington DC 20570	202-273-1991		340-20
Web: www.nlrb.gov			
Region 16 819 Taylor St Rm 8A24............ Fort Worth TX 76102	817-978-2921	978-2928	340-20
Web: www.nlrb.gov			
NLS (Non-Linear Systems)			
4561-F Mission Gorge Pl................... San Diego CA 92120	619-521-2161	521-2169	248
Web: www.nonlinearsystems.com			
NLSD (New Lenox School District 122)			
102 S Cedar Rd ....New Lenox IL 60451	815-485-2169		685
Web: www2.nlsd122.org			
NMA (National Motorists Assn)			
402 W Second St .... Waunakee WI 53597	608-849-6000		49-21
TF: 800-882-2785 ■ *Web:* www.motorists.org			
NMA (National Medical Assn)			
8403 Colesville Rd Ste 920 .... Silver Spring MD 20910	202-347-1895	347-0722	49-8
TF: 800-662-0554 ■ *Web:* www.nmanet.org			

	Phone	Fax	Class
NMA (National Mining Assn) 101 Constitution Ave NW Ste 500-E .... Washington DC 20001 *Web:* nma.org	202-463-2600	463-2666	48-12
NMA (National Management Assn) 2210 Arbor Blvd .... Dayton OH 45439 *Web:* nma1.org	937-294-0421		49-12
NMAH (National Museum of American History (Smithsonian Institution)) 12th St & Constitution Ave NW .... Washington DC 20560 *Web:* americanhistory.si.edu	202-633-3270		520
NMB Technologies Corp 9730 Independence Ave .... Chatsworth CA 91311 *Web:* www.nmbtc.com	818-341-3355	341-8207	173-1
NMC (National Motor Club of America Inc) 130 E John Carpenter Fwy .... Irving TX 75062 *TF:* 800-523-4582 ■ *Web:* nmc.com	800-523-4582		53
NMC (Natividad Medical Ctr) 1441 Constitution Blvd .... Salinas CA 93906 *Web:* www.natividad.com	831-755-4111		374-3
NMCC (Northern Maine Community College) 33 Edgemont Dr .... Presque Isle ME 04769 *TF:* 800-535-6682 ■ *Web:* www.nmcc.edu	207-768-2700	768-2848	800
NMCL (New Mexico Coalition for Literacy) 1219 Luisa St Unit 2 .... Santa Fe NM 87505 *TF:* 800-233-7587 ■ *Web:* newmexicoliteracy.org	505-982-3997	982-4095	48-13
NMCRS (Navy-Marine Corps Relief Society) 875 N Randolph St Ste 225 .... Arlington VA 22203 *TF:* 800-654-8364 ■ *Web:* www.nmcrs.org	703-696-4904	696-0144	48-19
NMC-Wollard Inc 2021 Truax Blvd .... Eau Claire WI 54703 *TF:* 800-656-6867 ■ *Web:* www.nmc-wollard.com	715-835-3151	835-6625	470
NMDP (National Marrow Donor Program) 500 N Fifth St .... Minneapolis MN 55401 *TF:* 800-627-7692 ■ *Web:* bethematch.org	800-627-7692		48-17
NMEA (National Marine Electronics Assn) 692 Ritchie Hwy Ste 104 .... Severna Park MD 21146 *TF:* 800-808-6632 ■ *Web:* www.nmea.org	410-975-9425	975-9450	49-13
NMEL (New Mexico Energy Library Inc) 312 N Main St .... Roswell NM 88202 *Web:* nmel.org	575-622-1711		431-3
NMF (National Marfan Foundation) 22 Manhasset Ave .... Port Washington NY 11050 *TF:* 800-862-7326 ■ *Web:* www.marfan.org	516-883-8712	883-8040	48-17
NMFTA (National Motor Freight Traffic Assn) 1001 N Fairfax St Ste 600 .... Alexandria VA 22314 *TF:* 866-411-6632 ■ *Web:* www.nmfta.org	703-838-1810	683-6296	49-21
NMG Aerospace 4880 Hudson Dr .... Stow OH 44224 *Web:* www.nmgaerospace.com	330-688-6494		22
NMHC (National Multi Housing Council) 1850 M St NW Ste 540 .... Washington DC 20036 *Web:* www.nmhc.org	202-974-2300	775-0112	49-17
NMI (Northeast-Midwest Institute) 50 F St NW Ste 950 .... Washington DC 20001 *Web:* www.nemw.org	202-544-5200		634
NMI Industrial Holdings Inc 8503 Weyand Ave .... Sacramento CA 95828 *Web:* www.nmiindustrial.com	916-635-7030		492
NMMA (National Marine Manufacturers Assn) 200 E Randolph Dr Ste 5100 .... Chicago IL 60601 *Web:* www.nmma.org	312-946-6200	946-0388	49-21
NMMS (New Mexico Medical Society) 316 Osuna Rd NE Ste 501 .... Albuquerque NM 87107 *TF:* 800-748-1596 ■ *Web:* www.nmms.org	505-828-0237	828-0336	474
NMOA (National Mail Order Association LLC) 2807 Polk St NE .... Minneapolis MN 55418 *TF:* 800-992-1377 ■ *Web:* www.nmoa.org	612-788-1673	788-1147	49-18
NMotion 151 N 8th St Ste 517 .... Lincoln NE 68508 *Web:* www.nmotion.co	402-875-4166		393
NMPA (National Music Publishers' Assn) 975 F St NW Ste 375 .... Washington DC 20004 *Web:* www.nmpa.org	202-393-6672		48-4
NMPF (National Milk Producers Federation) 2101 Wilson Blvd Ste 400 .... Arlington VA 22201 *Web:* www.nmpf.org	703-243-6111	841-9328	49-6
NMPHA (New Mexico Pharmacists Assn) 2716 San Pedro Dr NE Ste C .... Albuquerque NM 87110 *Web:* www.nmpharmacy.org	505-265-8729		585
NMPIRG (New Mexico Public Interest Research Group) PO Box 40173 .... Albuquerque NM 87196 *Web:* nmpirg.org	505-254-1244		633
NMPRC (Northwest Missouri Psychiatric Rehabilitation Ctr) 3505 Frederick .... Saint Joseph MO 64506 *Web:* www.dmh.mo.gov	816-387-2300		374-5
NMRA (National Marine Representatives Assn) PO Box 360 .... Gurnee IL 60031 *TF:* 800-890-3819 ■ *Web:* www.nmraonline.org	847-662-3167	336-7126	49-18
NMRA (National Model Railroad Assn) 4121 Cromwell Rd .... Chattanooga TN 37421 *TF:* 800-654-2256 ■ *Web:* nmra.org	423-892-2846	899-4869	48-18
NMS Capital Advisors LLC 433 N Camden Dr 4th Fl .... Beverly Hills CA 90210 *TF:* 800-716-2080 ■ *Web:* nmsadvisors.com	800-716-2080		691
NMS Labs 3701 Welsh Rd .... Willow Grove PA 19090 *TF:* 800-522-6671 ■ *Web:* www.nmslabs.com	215-657-4900	657-2972	418
NMSA (National Middle School Assn) 4151 Executive Pkwy Ste 300 .... Westerville OH 43081 *TF:* 800-528-6672 ■ *Web:* www.amle.org	614-895-4730	895-4750	49-5
NMSDC (National Minority Supplier Development Council) 1359 Broadway 10th Fl .... New York NY 10018 *TF:* 800-843-4898 ■ *Web:* www.nmsdc.org	212-944-2430	719-9611	49-18
NMSU (New Mexico State University) MSC-3A PO Box 30001 .... Las Cruces NM 88003 *TF:* 800-662-6678 ■ *Web:* nmsu.edu	575-646-3121	646-6330	166
NMT (New Mexico Institute of Mining & Technology) 801 Leroy Pl .... Socorro NM 87801 *TF:* 800-428-8324 ■ *Web:* www.nmt.edu	505-835-5434		166
NMT (Northern Machine Tool Co) 761 Alberta Ave .... Muskegon MI 49441 *Web:* www.nmtdie.com	231-755-1603	759-7917	757
NMT Corp 2004 Kramer St .... La Crosse WI 54603 *TF:* 800-236-0850 ■ *Web:* www.nmt.com	608-781-0850	781-3883	180
NN Inc 2000 Waters Edge Dr .... Johnson City TN 37604 *NASDAQ: NNBR* ■ *TF:* 877-888-0002 ■ *Web:* www.nninc.com	423-434-8300	743-8870	485
NNA (Nebraska Nurses' Assn) 1407 13th Ave .... Kearney NE 68845 *TF:* 888-885-7025 ■ *Web:* www.nebraskanurses.org	888-885-7025		533
NNA (National Newspaper Assn) PO Box 7540 .... Columbia MO 65205 **Fax Area Code:* 573 ■ *TF:* 800-829-4662 ■ *Web:* www.nnaweb.org	217-241-1400	777-4985*	49-14
NNA (National Notary Assn) 9350 DeSoto Ave .... Chatsworth CA 91313 *TF:* 800-876-6827 ■ *Web:* www.nationalnotary.org	800-876-6827		49-12
NNM Peterson Manufacturing Co 24133 W 143rd St .... Plainfield IL 60544 *TF:* 800-826-9086 ■ *Web:* www.peterson-mfg.com	815-436-9201	436-2863	286
NNOGC (Navajo Nation Oil & Gas Co) 50 Narbono Cir W .... Saint Michaels AZ 86511 *Web:* www.nnogc.net	928-871-4880		536
NNPDF (National Niemann-Pick Disease Foundation Inc) 401 Madison Ave Ste B PO Box 49 .... Fort Atkinson WI 53538 *TF:* 877-287-3672 ■ *Web:* nnpdf.org	920-563-0930		48-17
NNR Global Logistics USA Inc 450 E Devon Ave Ste 260 .... Itasca IL 60143 *Web:* www.nnrglobal.com	630-773-1490		449
NNSA (National Nuclear Security Administration) 1000 Independence Ave SW .... Washington DC 20585 *Web:* www.energy.gov	202-586-5000	586-4892	340-9
NNT Corp 1320 Norwood Ave .... Itasca IL 60143 *TF:* 800-556-9999 ■ *Web:* www.nntcorp.com	630-875-9600		455
NNTC (Northeast Nebraska Telephone Co) 110 E Elk St .... Jackson NE 68743 **Fax Area Code:* 402 ■ *TF:* 888-397-4321 ■ *Web:* www.nntc.net	888-397-4321	632-4770*	224
No 9 PARK 9 Park St .... Boston MA 02108 *Web:* www.no9park.com	617-742-9991		671
No Fault Sports Products 2101 Briarglen Dr .... Houston TX 77027 *TF:* 800-462-7766 ■ *Web:* nofaultsports.com	713-683-7101		711
No Good Entertainment Inc 9903 Santa Monica Blvd .... Beverly Hills CA 90212 *Web:* www.ngtv.com	310-556-8600	556-8655	116
No Ordinary Moments Inc 16742 Gothard St Ste 115 .... Huntington Beach CA 92647 *Web:* www.noordinarymoments.com	714-848-3800		363
No Other Place Like Home 100 E Linton Blvd Ste 143 A .... Delray Beach FL 33483 *Web:* www.noplh.com	561-819-1313	819-1315	363
No Peace Without Justice (NPWJ) 866 United Nations Plz Ste 408 .... New York NY 10017 *Web:* www.npwj.org	212-980-1031		48-8
No Starch Press Inc 38 Ringold St .... San Francisco CA 94103 *TF:* 800-420-7240 ■ *Web:* nostarch.com	415-863-9900	863-9950	637-2
NOA (National Onion Assn) 822 Seventh St Ste 510 .... Greeley CO 80631 *Web:* www.onions-usa.org	970-353-5895	353-5897	48-2
NOAA Fisheries 1315 EW Hwy .... Silver Spring MD 20910 *Web:* www.fisheries.noaa.gov	508-495-2000	495-2258	668
NOAA Fisheries Pacific Islands Regional Office 1601 Kapiolani Blvd Rm 1110 .... Honolulu HI 96814 *TF:* 888-256-9840 ■ *Web:* www.nepa.noaa.gov	808-944-2200		340-2
NOAA's Undersea Research Program (NURC) University of N Carolina at Wilmington .... Silver Spring MD 20910 **Fax Area Code:* 301 ■ *Web:* research.noaa.gov	910-962-2440	713-1967*	668
NOAH (National Organization for Albinism & Hypopigmentation) PO Box 959 .... East Hampstead NH 03826 *TF:* 800-648-2310 ■ *Web:* www.albinism.org	603-887-2310		48-17
Noah Technologies Corporation of Texas 1 Noah Pk .... San Antonio TX 78249 *Web:* noahtech.com	210-691-2000		143
Noah Webster House 227 S Main St .... West Hartford CT 06107 *Web:* noahwebsterhouse.org	860-521-5362	521-4036	520
Noah's Animal Hospitals 5510 Millersville Rd .... Indianapolis IN 46226 *Web:* www.noahshospitals.com	317-253-1327		794
Noah's Ark Animal Hospital 422 N Euclid St .... Fullerton CA 92832 *Web:* www.noahsarkfullerton.com	714-525-2202		794
Noamex Inc 625 Wortman Ave .... Brooklyn NY 11208 *TF:* 800-640-5917 ■ *Web:* www.noamex.com	718-342-2278	342-2258	156
Noarus Auto Group 6701 Center Dr W Ste 925 .... Los Angeles CA 90045 *Web:* www.noarus.com	310-258-0920		57
Nobel Automotive Tennessee LLC 190 County Home Rd .... Paris TN 38242 *Web:* www.nobel-automotive.com	731-641-8198		370
Nobel Biocare USA Inc 22715 Savi Ranch Pkwy .... Yorba Linda CA 92887 *TF:* 800-993-8100 ■ *Web:* www.nobelbiocare.com	714-282-4800	998-9236	228
Nobel Systems Inc 436 E Vanderbilt Way .... San Bernardino CA 92408 *Web:* www.nobel-systems.com	909-890-5611		180
NobelBiz Inc 1545 Faraday Ave .... Carlsbad CA 92008 *TF:* 800-975-2844 ■ *Web:* nobelbiz.com	760-405-0105		736
NobelClad 5405 Spine Rd .... Boulder CO 80301 *NASDAQ: BOOM* ■ *TF:* 800-821-2666 ■ *Web:* www.nobelclad.com	303-665-5700	604-1897	482
Nobility Homes Inc 3741 SW Seventh St .... Ocala FL 34474 *OTC: NOBH* ■ *TF:* 800-476-6624 ■ *Web:* www.nobilityhomes.com	352-732-5157	732-4203	505
Nobis Engineering Inc 18 Chenell Dr .... Concord NH 03301 *Web:* nobiseng.com	603-224-4182		261
NOBLE (National Organization of Black Law Enforcement Executives) 4609 Pinecrest Office Pk Dr Ste F .... Alexandria VA 22312 *Web:* noblenational.org	703-658-1529	658-9479	49-7
Noble & Cooley Co 42 Water St .... Granville MA 01034 *Web:* www.noblecooley.com	413-357-6321	357-6314	527
Noble & Greenough School 10 Campus Dr .... Dedham MA 02026 *Web:* www.nobles.edu	781-326-3700		685

	Phone	Fax	Class
Noble Bank & Trust NA 1509 Quintard Ave .... Anniston AL 36202 *Web:* www.noblebank.com	256-741-1800	741-1818	70
Noble Corp 13135 S Dairy Ashford Rd Ste 800.......... Sugar Land TX 77478 *NYSE: NE* ■ *TF:* 877-285-4162 ■ *Web:* www.noblecorp.com	281-276-6100	491-2092	540
Noble County 101 N Orange St .... Albion IN 46701 *Web:* www.nobleco.org	260-636-2736	636-4000	338
Noble County 300 Courthouse Dr Ste 1.......... Perry OK 73077 *Web:* www.noblecountyok.com	580-336-2771	336-4010	338
Noble Energy Inc 100 Glenborough Dr Ste 100 .... Houston TX 77067 *NYSE: NBL* ■ *TF:* 800-220-5824 ■ *Web:* www.nblenergy.com	281-872-3100	872-3111	536
Noble Fields School of Real Estate 870 Market St Ste 623 .... San Francisco CA 94102 *TF:* 800-806-6253 ■ *Web:* www.noblefields.com	415-608-1388	594-0082	685
Noble Horizons 17 Cobble Rd .... Salisbury CT 06068 *Web:* noblehorizons.org	860-435-9851	435-0636	450
Noble House Hotels & Resorts 600 Sixth St S.......... Kirkland WA 98033 *TF:* 877-662-5387 ■ *Web:* www.noblehousehotels.com	425-827-8737	827-6707	379
Noble Investment Group Ltd 2000 Monarch Tower 3424 Peachtree Rd NE .... Atlanta GA 30326 *Web:* www.nobleinvestment.com	404-419-1000		378
Noble Oil Services Inc 5617 Clyde Rhyne Dr .... Sanford NC 27330 *Web:* www.nobleoil.com	919-774-8180		541
Noble REMC 300 Weber Rd PO Box 137 .... Albion IN 46701 *TF:* 800-933-7362 ■ *Web:* www.nobleremc.com	800-933-7362		245
Noble Roman's Pizza Inc 1 Virginia Ave Ste 300 .... Indianapolis IN 46204 *TF:* 800-585-0669 ■ *Web:* www.nobleromans.com	800-585-0669		670
Noble Rot 1111 E Burnside 4th Fl .... Portland OR 97214 *Web:* www.noblerotpdx.com	503-233-1999		671
Noble Royalties Inc (NRI) 15303 N Dallas Pkwy Ste 1350.......... Addison TX 75001 *TF:* 888-346-6253 ■ *Web:* www.nobleroyalties.com	972-720-1888		538
Noble Technologies Corp 2020 Noble Dr .... Wooster OH 44691 *TF:* 877-401-6340 ■ *Web:* www.nobletek.com	330-287-1500		261
Noble USA Inc 5450 Meadowbrook Indus Ct .... Rolling Meadows IL 60008 *Web:* www.nobleusa.com	847-364-6038	364-6045	253
Nobles Co-opeartive Electric 22636 US Hwy 59 PO Box 788.......... Worthington MN 56187 *TF:* 800-776-0517 ■ *Web:* www.noblesce.coop	507-372-7331	372-5148	245
Nobles County 1530 Airport Rd.......... Worthington MN 56187 *Web:* www.co.nobles.mn.us	507-295-5200		338
Noblesville Chamber of Commerce 601 Conner St .... Noblesville IN 46060 *Web:* www.noblesvillechamber.com	317-773-0086		139
NobleWorks Inc 500 Paterson Plank Rd .... Union NJ 07087 *TF:* 800-346-6253 ■ *Web:* www.nobleworkscards.com	201-420-0095		130
Noblis 3150 Fairview Pk Dr S .... Falls Church VA 22042 *Web:* noblis.org	703-610-2000		668
Noblitt Group Pllc, The 8800 N Gainey Center Dr Ste 279.......... Scottsdale AZ 85258 *Web:* ngtechlaw.com	480-994-9888	994-9025	41
Nobu Restaurants 207 Fifth Ave.......... San Diego CA 92101 *Web:* www.noburestaurants.com	619-814-4124		671
Nobu Restaurants 40 W 57th St.......... New York NY 10019 *Web:* noburestaurants.com	212-757-3000	757-6330	671
Nobu's 8643 Olive Blvd.......... Saint Louis MO 63132 *Web:* www.nobusushistl.com	314-997-2303		671
NOC (Nantahala Outdoor Ctr) 13077 Hwy 19 W .... Bryson City NC 28713 *Web:* www.noc.com	828-488-2175	488-2498	239
NOCC (National Ovarian Cancer Coalition) 2501 Oak Lawn Ave Ste 435.......... Dallas TX 75219 **Fax Area Code:* 214 ■ *TF:* 888-682-7426 ■ *Web:* www.ovarian.org	888-682-7426	273-4201*	48-17
NOCIRC (National Organization of Circumcision Information Resource Centers) PO Box 2512 .... San Anselmo CA 94979 *TF:* 800-727-8622 ■ *Web:* www.nocirc.org	415-488-9883	488-9660	48-17
Nockamixon State Park 1542 Mtn View Dr.......... Quakertown PA 18951 *Web:* www.dcnr.pa.gov	215-529-7300		565
NOCO Energy Corp 2440 Sheridan Dr.......... Tonawanda NY 14150 *TF:* 800-500-6626 ■ *Web:* www.noco.com	716-833-6626	832-1312	579
NOCS (New Orleans Cold Storage & Warehouse Company Inc) 3411 Jourdan Rd .... New Orleans LA 70126 *Web:* www.nocs.com	504-944-4400		803-2
Noction Inc 1294 Lawrence Sta Rd .... Sunnyvale CA 94089 *Web:* www.noction.com	650-618-9823		231
NOD (National Organization on Disability) 77 Water St Ste 204 .... New York NY 10005 *Web:* www.nod.org	646-505-1191		48-17
Nodak Electric Co-opeartive Inc 4000 32nd Ave S .... Grand Forks ND 58201 *TF:* 800-732-4373 ■ *Web:* www.nodakelectric.com	701-746-4461		245
Nodaway County 403 N Market.......... Maryville MO 64468 *Web:* www.nodawaycountymo.us	660-582-2251		338
Nodus Technologies Inc 2099 S State College Blvd Ste 250.......... Anaheim CA 92806 *Web:* www.nodus.com	909-482-4701		177
Noelle Spa-beauty & Wellness 1100 High Ridge Rd.......... Stamford CT 06905 *Web:* www.noelle.com	203-322-3445		77
Noel-Smyser Engineering Corp 4005 Industrial Blvd.......... Indianapolis IN 46254 *Web:* www.noel-smyser.com	317-293-2215		21
Noevir USA Inc 1095 Main St .... Irvine CA 92614 *TF:* 800-872-8817 ■ *Web:* www.noevirusa.com	949-660-1111	660-7168	366
NOF (National Osteoporosis Foundation) 251 18th St S Ste 630.......... Arlington VA 22202 *TF:* 800-231-4222 ■ *Web:* www.nof.org	202-223-2226	223-2237	48-17
NOF Metal Coatings NA 275 Industrial Pkwy .... Chardon OH 44024 *Web:* www.metal-coatings.com	440-285-2231	285-5009	481
Nofa-ny Certified Organic LLC 840 Upper Front St.......... Binghamton NY 13905 *TF:* 800-853-2676 ■ *Web:* www.nofany.org	607-724-9851		138
Noftz Sheet Metal 2737 Penn Ave .... Pittsburgh PA 15222 *Web:* www.noftz.com	412-471-1983	471-0512	697
Nogalas-Rochlin Public Library 518 N Grand Ave.......... Nogales AZ 85621 *Web:* www.nogalesaz.gov	520-285-5717	287-4823	434-3
Nogales Investors Management LLC 9229 W Sunset Blvd Ste 900 .... Los Angeles CA 90069	310-276-7439	276-7405	401
Nogales-Santa Cruz County Chamber of Commerce 123 W Kino Pk .... Nogales AZ 85621 *TF:* 800-508-7624 ■ *Web:* thenogaleschamber.com	520-287-3685		139
Noguska LLC 741 Countyline St.......... Fostoria OH 44830 *Web:* www.noguska.com	419-435-0404		175
NOHS (North Oaks Health System) PO Box 2668 .... Hammond LA 70404 *Web:* www.northoaks.org	985-345-2700		374-3
NOIA (National Ocean Industries Assn) 1120 G St NW Ste 900 .... Washington DC 20005 *TF:* 800-558-9994 ■ *Web:* www.noia.org	202-347-6900	347-8650	48-12
Nokia Inc 200 S Mathilda Ave .... Sunnyvale CA 94086 *NYSE: NOK* ■ *Web:* www.nokia.com	408-737-0900		735
Nokomis Learning Ctr 5153 Marsh Rd.......... Okemos MI 48864 *Web:* www.nokomis.org	517-349-5777		50-2
Nokomis Regional High School 266 Williams Rd.......... Newport ME 04953 *Web:* www.rsu19.org	207-368-4354	368-2192	685
Nolan & Heller LLP 80 State St 11th Fl.......... Albany NY 12207 *Web:* Www.nhkllp.com	518-449-3300		428
Nolan & Shafer PLC 40 Concord Ave.......... Muskegon MI 49442 *Web:* wemakeitright.com	231-722-2444		41
Nolan Co 1016 Ninth St SW .... Canton OH 44707 *TF:* 800-297-1383 ■ *Web:* nolancompany.com	330-453-7922	453-7449	650
Nolan County 100 E Third St .... Sweetwater TX 79556 *Web:* www.co.nolan.tx.us	325-235-2263	236-9416	338
Nolde Forest Environmental Education Ctr 2910 New Holland Rd.......... Reading PA 19607 *Web:* www.dcnr.pa.gov	610-796-3699		565
Noldus Information Technology Inc 1503 Edwards Ferry Rd NE Ste 201 .... Leesburg VA 20176 *TF:* 800-355-9541 ■ *Web:* www.noldus.com	703-771-0440		177
Noleen J6 Technologies 12180 Ridgecrest Rd Ste 230.......... Victorville CA 92395 *Web:* www.noleenj6.com	760-955-8757		61
Nolensville Veterinary Hospital 7204 Nolensville Rd .... Nolensville TN 37135 *Web:* nolensvillevet.com	615-776-5499		794
Nolin Lake State Park 2998 Brier Creek Rd .... Mammoth Cave KY 42259 *Web:* parks.ky.gov	270-286-4240		565
Nolin Rural Electric Co-opeartive Corp 411 Ring Rd .... Elizabethtown KY 42701 *TF:* 888-637-4247 ■ *Web:* www.nolinrecc.com	270-765-6153		245
Nollenberger Capital Partners Inc 101 California St Ste 3100 .... San Francisco CA 94111 *Web:* www.nollenbergercapital.com	415-402-6000	402-6099	690
Nolo Press Occidental 501 Mission St Ste 2 .... Santa Cruz CA 95060 *TF:* 800-464-5502 ■ *Web:* www.nolotech.com	831-466-9922	466-9927	637-2
Nolocom 950 Parker St.......... Berkeley CA 94710 *TF:* 800-728-3555 ■ *Web:* www.nolo.com	800-728-3555	645-0895	178-9
NOLS (National Outdoor Leadership School) 284 Lincoln St .... Lander WY 82520 **Fax Area Code:* 307 ■ *TF:* 800-710-6657 ■ *Web:* www.nols.edu	800-710-6657	332-1220*	685
Nolte Precise Manufacturing Inc 6850 Colerain Ave .... Cincinnati OH 45239 *Web:* www.nolteprecise.com	513-923-3100		757
Nolte State Park 36921 Veazie Cumberland Rd.......... Enumclaw WA 98022 *Web:* www.parks.wa.gov	360-825-4646		565
Nol-tec Systems Inc 425 Apollo Dr .... Lino Lakes MN 55014 *Web:* www.nol-tec.com	651-780-8600	780-4400	207
Noltex LLC 12220 Strang Rd.......... La Porte TX 77571 *Web:* www.noltexllc.com	281-842-5000		601
NOMA (New Orleans Museum of Art) 1 Collins C Diboll Cir City Pk.......... New Orleans LA 70124 *Web:* www.noma.org	504-658-4100	658-4199	520
Nomad Health 335 Madison Ave 6th Fl.......... New York NY 10017 *TF:* 866-656-6623 ■ *Web:* nomadhealth.com	866-656-6623		260
Nomad Press PO Box 484 .... Fort Collins CO 80522 *Web:* www.nomad-press.com	970-226-3690		637-2
Nomad Technology Group LLC 1315 Read St Unit C.......... Evansville IN 47710 *Web:* nomadtechgroup.com	812-618-4032		631
Nomadic Display Capitol Inc 5617 Industrial Dr.......... Springfield VA 22151 *TF:* 800-336-5019 ■ *Web:* www.nomadicdisplay.com	800-336-5019		317
Nomadix Inc 30851 Agoura Rd Ste 102.......... Agoura Hills CA 91301 *Web:* www.nomadix.com	818-597-1500		177
Nomanco Inc 501 Nmc Dr.......... Zebulon NC 27597 *TF:* 800-345-7279 ■ *Web:* www.nomaco.com	919-269-6500		319-1
NOMC (North Okaloosa Medical Ctr) 151 E Redstone Ave .... Crestview FL 32539 *Web:* www.northokaloosa.com	850-689-8100		374-3
Nome Convention & Visitors Bureau 301 Front St.......... Nome AK 99762 *Web:* www.visitnomealaska.com	907-443-6555	443-5832	206
Nome Youth Facility 804 E Fourth St.......... Nome AK 99762 *TF:* 800-770-5650 ■ *Web:* www.dhss.alaska.gov	907-443-5434	443-7295	412
Nomerel LLC 8147 E 63rd Pl Ste 101.......... Tulsa OK 74133 *Web:* www.nomerel.com	918-770-4099		261
Nomura Securities International Inc 2 World Financial Ctr Bldg B .... New York NY 10281 *Web:* www.nomura.com	212-667-9300		690
Non Commissioned Officers Assn (NCOA) 9330 Corporate Dr Ste 708.......... Selma TX 78154 *TF:* 800-662-2620 ■ *Web:* www.ncoausa.org	210-653-6161	637-3337	48-19

Name / Address	City	State	Zip	Phone	Fax	Class
Nonesuch Records 3300 Warner Blvd *Web:* www.nonesuch.com	Burbank	CA	91505	818-846-9090		657
Nonfiction Studios Inc 450 318 - 11th Ave SE *Web:* www.nonfiction.ca	Calgary	AB	T2G0Y2	403-686-8887		224
Nonin Medical Inc 13700 First Ave N. *Web:* www.nonin.com	Plymouth	MN	55441	763-553-9968		477
Noninvasive Medical Technologies Inc 6412 S Arville St. *TF:* 888-466-8552 ■ *Web:* www.nmtinc.org	Las Vegas	NV	89118	702-614-3360		463
Non-Linear Systems (NLS) 4561-F Mission Gorge Pl *Web:* www.nonlinearsystems.com	San Diego	CA	92120	619-521-2161	521-2169	248
Nonna's Italian American Cafe 306 S Ave *Web:* www.nonnascafe.net	Springfield	MO	65806	417-831-1222		671
Nonpareil Corp 40 N 400 W	Blackfoot	ID	83221	208-785-5880	785-3656	296-18
NoodleHead Network, The 10 Colbert St *TF:* 800-639-5680 ■ *Web:* www.noodlehead.com	Essex Junction	VT	05452	802-862-8675	764-5848	328
Noodles & Co 520 Zang St. *Web:* www.noodles.com	Broomfield	CO	80021	720-214-1900		670
Nook Industries 4950 E 49th St *TF:* 800-321-7800 ■ *Web:* www.nookindustries.com	Cleveland	OH	44125	216-271-7900	271-7020	620
Noon Hour Food Products Inc 215 N Des Plaines *Web:* noonhourfoods.com	Chicago	IL	60661	312-382-1177		296-13
Noonan Energy Corp 86 Robbins Rd *Web:* noonanenergy.com	Springfield	MA	01104	413-734-7396		316
Noone & Associates Inc 3 Crossgate Dr *Web:* www.nooneappraisals.com	Mechanicsburg	PA	17050	717-458-0482		393
Nooter Construction Co 1500 S Second St. *Web:* nooterconstruction.com	Saint Louis	MO	63104	314-421-7600		186
Nor Service Inc 215 S State Ave *Web:* www.normaplewood.com	Freeport	IL	61032	815-232-8379	232-4108	454
Nora Lighting Inc 6505 Gayhart St *Fax Area Code:* 800 ■ *TF:* 800-686-6672 ■ *Web:* www.noralighting.com	Commerce	CA	90040	323-767-2600	500-9955*	246
Nora Restaurant 2132 Florida Ave NW *Web:* www.noras.com	Washington	DC	20008	202-462-5143		671
Norair Engineering Corp 337 Brightseat Rd Ste 200 *Web:* www.norairengineering.com	Landover Hills	MD	20785	301-499-2202		188
Noralco Corp 1920 Lincoln Rd. *Web:* www.noralco.com	Pittsburgh	PA	15235	412-361-6678	361-6535	189-16
NORAM Engineering & Constructors Ltd 200 Granville St Ste 1800. *Web:* www.noram-eng.com	Vancouver	BC	V6C1S4	604-681-2030		261
Noramco Inc 1440 Olympic Dr. *Web:* www.noramco.com	Athens	GA	30601	706-353-4400		582
Norandex Building Materials Distribution Inc 1 ABC Pkwy *TF:* 800-528-0942 ■ *Web:* www.norandex.com	Beloit	WI	53511	800-528-0942		191-4
Nor-Arc Steel Fabricators 331567 Hwy 11 *Web:* www.norarc.com	Earlton	ON	P0J1E0	705-563-2656		757
Norauto Inc 1161 Route 111 E. *Web:* www.norautonissan.com	Amos	QC	J9T1N2	819-732-6637		57
Noraxon USA Inc 15770 N Greenway-Hayden Loop Ste 100 *TF:* 800-364-8985 ■ *Web:* www.noraxon.com	Scottsdale	AZ	85260	480-443-3413		475
Norben Import Corp 99 S Newman St. *Web:* www.larksilk.com	Hackensack	NJ	07601	201-487-0855		293
Norberg-ies 4237 S 74th E Ave *TF:* 800-739-9145 ■ *Web:* www.nema7.com	Tulsa	OK	74145	918-665-6888	663-8015	729
Norbest Inc 306 W 300 S PO Box 890. *Web:* www.norbest.com	Moroni	UT	84646	435-436-8211		447
Norbest Inc PO Box 890. *Fax Area Code:* 888 ■ *TF:* 800-453-5327 ■ *Web:* norbest.com	Moroni	UT	84646	800-453-5327	597-5416*	297-10
Norbridge Inc 30 Monument Sq Ste 155 *Web:* norbridgeinc.com	Concord	MA	01742	978-369-2944		463
Nor-Cal Beverage Company Inc 2286 Stone Blvd *TF:* 800-331-2059 ■ *Web:* www.ncbev.com	West Sacramento	CA	95691	916-372-0600		81-2
Nor-Cal Controls Inc 1952 Concourse Dr *TF:* 800-233-2013 ■ *Web:* www.norcal4air.com	San Jose	CA	95131	408-435-0400		419
Norcal Gold Inc 5200 Sunrise Blvd Ste 5 *Web:* remaxgold.com	Fair Oaks	CA	95628	916-536-7600	536-7620	652
Nor-Cal Metal Fabricators 1121 Third St *Web:* www.nc-mf.com	Oakland	CA	94607	510-833-7157	208-2838	482
Norcal Mutual Insurance Company Inc 575 Market St Ste 1000 *TF:* 800-652-1051 ■ *Web:* www.norcal-group.com	San Francisco	CA	94105	855-882-3412		391-5
Norcal Printing Inc 70 Dorman Ave Ste 3 *Web:* www.norcalprinting.com	San Francisco	CA	94124	415-282-8856	282-1008	627
Nor-Cal Products Inc 1967 S Oregon St *TF:* 800-824-4166 ■ *Web:* www.n-c.com	Yreka	CA	96097	530-842-4457	842-9130	595
Norcal Rental Group LLC 318 Stealth Ct. *TF:* 800-649-6629 ■ *Web:* www.crescorent.com	Livermore	CA	94551	925-961-0130		264-3
Norchem Corp 5649 Alhambra Ave *TF:* 800-442-4360 ■ *Web:* norchemcorp.com	Los Angeles	CA	90032	323-221-0221	227-8733	111
Norco Inc 1125 W Amity Rd *Web:* www.norco-inc.com	Boise	ID	83705	208-336-1643	782-0457	358
Norco Injection Molding Inc 14325 Monte Vista Ave. *Web:* www.norco.biz	Chino	CA	91710	909-393-4000	393-7800	604
Norco Products Furniture Mfrs 4985 Blue Mtn Rd. *TF:* 800-662-2300 ■ *Web:* www.norcoproducts.com	Missoula	MT	59804	406-251-3800		321
Norcon Communications Inc 510 Burnside Ave *Web:* www.norconcommunications.com	Inwood	NY	11096	516-239-0300	239-8915	52
Norcon Corp 5600 Municipal St. *Web:* www.norconcorp.com	Schofield	WI	54476	715-359-5808		186
Norcon Industries Inc 5412 E Calle Cerrito *Web:* www.norconindustries.net	Guadalupe	AZ	85283	480-839-2324		321
Norcostco Inc 825 Rhode Island Ave S *Web:* www.norcostco.com	Minneapolis	MN	55426	763-544-0601		45
Nor-Cote International Inc 506 Lafayette Ave *TF:* 800-488-9180 ■ *Web:* www.norcote.com	Crawfordsville	IN	47933	765-362-9180	364-5408	388
Norcraft cabinetry 950 Blue Gentian Rd Ste 200 *Fax Area Code:* 651 ■ *TF:* 866-802-7892 ■ *Web:* www.norcraftcabinetry.com	Eagan	MN	55121	866-802-7892	234-3398*	115
Norcross Corp 255 Newtonville Ave. *Web:* www.viscosity.com	Newton	MA	02458	586-336-0700		201
Norcross Donald (Rep D - NJ) 2437 Rayburn House Office Bldg *Web:* www.norcross.house.gov	Washington	DC	20515	202-225-6501		342-2
NORD (National Organization for Rare Disorders) 55 Kenosia Ave *Web:* rarediseases.org	Danbury	CT	06810	203-744-0100	798-2291	48-17
NORD Drivesystems 800 Nord Dr *TF:* 888-314-6673 ■ *Web:* www.nord.com	Waunakee	WI	53597	888-314-6673		54
Nordaas American Homes Company Inc 10091 State Hwy 22 *TF:* 800-658-7076 ■ *Web:* nordaashomes.com	Minnesota Lake	MN	56068	507-462-3331	462-3211	187
NORDAM Group 6911 N Whirlpool Dr *Web:* www.nordam.com	Tulsa	OK	74117	918-878-4000	878-4808	22
Nordberg Hammack Kolp & Cash PS 2737 77th Ave SE Ste 213 *Web:* nhkc-cpa.com	Bellevue	WA	98005	425-450-9995		2
Nordco Inc 245 W Forest Hill Ave *TF:* 800-445-9258 ■ *Web:* www.nordco.com	Oak Creek	WI	53154	414-766-2180	766-2379	190
Nordia Inc 3020 Jacques-Bureau 2nd Fl *TF:* 866-858-4367 ■ *Web:* www.nordia.ca	Laval	QC	H7P6G2	514-415-7088		737
Nordic Heritage Museum 2655 NW Market St *Web:* nordicmuseum.org	Seattle	WA	98107	206-789-5707		520
Nordic Semiconductor Inc 1250 Oakmead Pky Ste 210 *Web:* www.nordicsemi.com	Sunnyvale	CA	94085	408-437-7751	437-7756	246
Nordic Ware 5005 Hwy 7 *TF:* 877-466-7342 ■ *Web:* www.nordicware.com	Minneapolis	MN	55416	952-920-2888	924-8561	486
Nordion 447 March Rd *NYSE:* NDZ ■ *TF:* 800-465-3666 ■ *Web:* www.nordion.com	Ottawa	ON	K2K1X8	613-592-2790	592-6937	85
Nordis Technologies Inc 4401 NW 124th Ave *TF:* 800-208-1169 ■ *Web:* www.nordistechnologies.com	Coral Springs	FL	33065	954-323-5500		195
Nordisk Systems Inc 6400 SE Lake Rd Ste 450 *TF:* 800-676-2777 ■ *Web:* www.nordisksystems.com	Milwaukie	OR	97222	503-353-7555		196
Nordmin Engineering Ltd 160 Logan Ave *Web:* www.nordmin.com	Thunder Bay	ON	P7A6R1	807-683-1730		261
Nordoff-Robbins Music Therapy 82 Washington Sq E *Web:* steinhardt.nyu.edu	New York	NY	10003	212-998-5162		726
Nordon Inc 1 Cabot Blvd E *TF:* 800-544-0400 ■ *Web:* www.nordoninc.com	Langhorne	PA	19047	215-504-4700		111
Nordonia Hills School District 9370 Olde 8 Rd *Web:* www.nordoniaschools.org	Northfield	OH	44067	330-467-0580	468-0152	685
Nordson Corp 28601 Clemens Rd *NASDAQ:* NDSN ■ *TF:* 800-321-2881 ■ *Web:* www.nordson.com	Westlake	OH	44145	440-892-1580	892-9507	386
Nordson MEDICAL 3325 S Timberline Rd *Fax Area Code:* 970 ■ *TF:* 888-404-5837 ■ *Web:* www.nordsonmedical.com	Fort Collins	CO	80525	888-404-5837	223-0953*	608
Nordstrom Audco Inc 1511 Jefferson St *TF:* 800-225-6989 ■ *Web:* www.flowserve.nordstromaudco.com	Sulphur Springs	TX	75482	903-885-4691	439-3411	789
Nordstrong Equipment Ltd 5 Chester Ave *TF:* 800-387-9145 ■ *Web:* www.nordstrongequipment.com	Winnipeg	MB	R2L1W5	204-667-1553		207
Norduyn Inc 6200 Henri-Bourassa W. *Web:* www.norduyn.com	Montreal	QC	H4R1C3	514-334-3210	334-2989	57
Nordyne Inc 8000 Phoenix Pkwy *Web:* www.nortekhvac.com	O'Fallon	MO	63368	636-561-7300		14
Noregon Systems Inc 7009 Albert Pick Rd *TF:* 855-889-5776 ■ *Web:* www.noregon.com	Greensboro	NC	27409	855-889-5776		809
Nor-Ell Inc 851 Hubbard Ave *TF:* 877-276-4075 ■ *Web:* www.nor-ell.com	Saint Paul	MN	55104	651-487-1441	488-1626	481
Norfolk & Dedham Group 222 Ames St. *TF:* 800-688-1825 ■ *Web:* www.ndgroup.com	Dedham	MA	02027	800-688-1825		390
Norfolk Academy 1585 Wesleyan Dr *Web:* www.norfolkacademy.org	Norfolk	VA	23502	757-461-6236		685
Norfolk Botanical Garden 6700 Azalea Garden Rd. *Web:* norfolkbotanicalgarden.org	Norfolk	VA	23518	757-441-5830		97
Norfolk Collegiate School 7336 Granby St. *Web:* www.norfolkcollegiate.org	Norfolk	VA	23505	757-480-2885		685
Norfolk Convention & Visitors Bureau 232 E Main St. *TF:* 800-368-3097 ■ *Web:* www.visitnorfolk.com	Norfolk	VA	23510	757-664-6620	622-3663	206
Norfolk County 614 High St *Web:* www.norfolkcounty.org	Dedham	MA	02026	781-461-6105	326-6480	338
Norfolk Daily News 525 Norfolk Ave *Web:* www.norfolkdailynews.com	Norfolk	NE	68701	402-371-1020		532-2
Norfolk Dredging Co 110 Centervilless Tpke N *Web:* www.norfolkdredging.com	Chesapeake	VA	23320	757-547-9391	547-2833	186
Norfolk General Hospital 365 W St. *Web:* www.ngh.on.ca	Simcoe	ON	N3Y1T7	519-426-0750	428-2946	374-2
Norfolk (Independent City) 999 Waterside Dr Ste 2430 *Web:* www.norfolk.gov	Norfolk	VA	23510	757-664-4242	664-4239	338

Name / Address	Phone	Fax	Class
Norfolk International Airport 2200 Norview Ave. Norfolk VA 23518 *Web:* www.norfolkairport.com	757-857-3351	857-3265	27
Norfolk Iron and Metal Co 3001 N Victory Rd Norfolk NE 68702 *TF:* 800-228-8100 ■ *Web:* www.norfolkiron.com	402-371-1810	371-8635	492
Norfolk Public Library 139 Main St. Norfolk MA 02056 *Web:* norfolkpl.org	508-528-3380	528-6417	434-3
Norfolk Public Library 235 E Plume St Norfolk VA 23510 *Web:* www.norfolkpubliclibrary.org	757-664-7323		434-3
Norfolk Public Schools 800 E City Hall Ave. Norfolk VA 23510 *TF:* 800-846-4464 ■ *Web:* www.npsk12.com	757-670-3945	628-3820	685
Norfolk Scope Arena 201 E Brambleton Ave. Norfolk VA 23510 *Web:* www.sevenvenues.com	757-664-6464	664-6990	720
Norfolk Southern Corp 3 Commercial Pl Norfolk VA 23510 *NYSE: NSC* ■ **Fax Area Code:* 757 ■ *TF:* 800-635-5768 ■ *Web:* www.nscorp.com	855-667-3655	629-2361*	468
Norfolk State University 700 Park Ave Norfolk VA 23504 *TF:* 800-274-1821 ■ *Web:* www.nsu.edu	757-823-8600	823-2078	166
Norfolk Veterans Home 600 E Benjamin Ave Norfolk NE 68701 *Web:* www.nebraska.gov	402-370-3330	370-3190	793
Norgen Biotek Corp 3430 Schmon Pkwy Thorold ON L2V4Y6 **Fax Area Code:* 905 ■ *TF:* 866-667-4362 ■ *Web:* norgenbiotek.com	866-667-4362	227-1061*	418
Norgren 5400 S Delaware St. Littleton CO 80120 **Fax Area Code:* 303 ■ *TF:* 800-514-0129 ■ *Web:* www.imi-precision.com	800-284-0026	795-9487*	790
Noridian Healthcare Solutions LLC 900 42th St S PO Box 6055 Fargo ND 58103 *TF:* 800-633-4227 ■ *Web:* noridiansolutions.com	800-633-4227		390
Norinchukin Bank, The 245 Park Ave 21st Fl. New York NY 10167 *Web:* nochubank.or.jp	212-697-1717	697-5754	70
Noritsu Technical Services 6900 Noritsu Ave Buena Park CA 90620 *TF:* 888-435-7448 ■ *Web:* www.noritsu.com	714-521-9040		393
Norkfolk 309 N 5th St. Norfolk NE 68701 *Web:* www.ci.norfolk.ne.us	402-844-2000		206
Norkol Incorporated & Converting 11650 W Grand Ave Northlake IL 60164 *Web:* www.norkol.com	708-531-1000	531-0030	557
Nor-Lake Inc 727 Second St PO Box 248 Hudson WI 54016 *TF:* 800-388-5253 ■ *Web:* www.norlake.com	715-386-2323	386-6149	664
Norlake Manufacturing Co 39301 Taylor Pkwy North Ridgeville OH 44039 *Web:* www.norlakemfg.com	440-353-3200	353-3232	767
Nor-Lea General Hospital Inc 1600 N Main Ave Lovington NM 88260 *Web:* www.nor-lea.org	575-396-6611		374-3
Norlen Inc 900 Grossman Dr Schofield WI 54476 *TF:* 800-648-6594 ■ *Web:* www.norlen.com	715-359-0506		480
Norlift of Oregon Inc 7373 SE Milwaukie Expy Portland OR 97222 *TF:* 800-452-0050 ■ *Web:* norliftor.com	503-659-5438		770
Norm Reeves Superstore 18900 Studebaker Rd Cerritos CA 90703 *TF:* 888-318-5001 ■ *Web:* www.normreeves.com	888-318-5001		57
Norm's Refrigeration & Ice Equipment Inc 1175 N Knollwood Cir Anaheim CA 92801 *TF:* 800-933-4423 ■ *Web:* normsrefrigeration.com	714-236-3600		665
Norma Kamali 11 W 56th St New York NY 10019 *Web:* www.normakamali.com	212-957-9797		277
Normac Inc 93 Industrial Dr. Hendersonville NC 28739 *Web:* normac.com	828-209-9000	209-9001	455
Normal Public Library 206 W College Normal IL 61761 *Web:* www.normalpl.org	309-452-1757	452-5312	434-3
Norman Bros Produce Inc 7621 SW 87th Ave Miami FL 33173 *Web:* normanbrothers.com	305-274-9363	596-4541	345
Norman Convention & Visitors Bureau 309 E Main St. Norman OK 73069 *TF:* 800-767-7260 ■ *Web:* www.visitnorman.com	405-366-8095		206
Norman County 16 3rd Ave E. Ada MN 56510 *Web:* www.co.norman.mn.us	218-784-5471	784-4531	338
Norman E. Matteoni, A Professional Corp 848 The Alameda San Jose CA 95126 *Web:* matteoni.com	408-293-4300		41
Norman Fox & Co 14970 Don Julian RD City of Industry CA 91744 *TF:* 800-632-1777 ■ *Web:* www.norfoxchem.com	323-973-4900	973-4874	145
Norman Frede Chevrolet Co 16801 Feather Craft Ln Houston TX 77058 *TF:* 888-307-1703 ■ *Web:* www.fredechevrolet.com	281-486-2200		57
Norman Hecht Research Inc 20 Crossways Park Dr N Ste 400 Woodbury NY 11797 *Web:* www.normanhechtresearch.com	516-496-8866	496-8165	466
Norman Howard School 275 Pinnacle Rd Rochester NY 14623 *Web:* www.normanhoward.org	585-334-8010		685
Norman Jones Enlow & Co 226 N 5th St Ste 500 Columbus OH 43215	614-228-4000	231-5404	2
Norman Maine Publishing LLC PO Box 1401 Rapid City SD 57709 *Web:* www.normanmaineplays.com	605-791-0186		637-10
Norman Noble Inc 5507 Avion Park Dr. Highland Heights OH 44143 *TF:* 800-474-4322 ■ *Web:* www.normannoble.net	800-474-4322		583
Norman Ralph (Rep R - SC) 319 Cannon House Office Bldg. Washington DC 20515 *Web:* norman.house.gov	202-225-5501	225-0464	342-2
Norman Regional Hospital 901 N Porter St. Norman OK 73071 *Web:* www.normanregional.com	405-307-1700		374-3
Norman Scott Company Inc 126 29th St Dr SE Cedar Rapids IA 52403 *Web:* www.in-tolerance.com	319-363-8561	363-2106	192
Norman Shatz Company USA 3570 St Rd Bensalem PA 19020 *TF:* 800-292-0292 ■ *Web:* www.shatzusa.com	800-292-0292		711
Norman Technologies LLC 630 Davidson Gateway Dr Ste 250 Davidson NC 28036 *Web:* webnt.azurewebsites.net	704-896-8816		177
Norman Tool Inc 15415 Old State Rd Evansville IN 47725 *Web:* www.normantool.com	812-867-3496		106
Norman Transcript, The 215 E Comanche St PO Box 1058 Norman OK 73070 *Web:* www.normantranscript.com	405-321-1800	366-3516	532-2
Norman W. Marcoux CPA Inc 788 University Ave Sacramento CA 95825 *Web:* www.marcouxcpa.com	916-927-7772	927-7779	2
Norman W. Paschall Company Inc 1 Paschall Rd PO Box 2100 Peachtree City GA 30269 *Web:* www.paschall.com	770-487-7945	487-0840	745-8
Norman W. Pullen Inc 220 Maine Mall Rd Ste 4 Mall Plz South Portland ME 04106 *Web:* www.mainegoldandsilver.net	207-772-2211	772-7881	411
Norman Y. Mineta San Jose International Airport 1701 Airport Blvd Ste B-1130. San Jose CA 95110 *Web:* www.flysanjose.com	408-392-3600	441-4591	27
Norman, Hanson & DeTroy 415 Congress St POB 4600 Portland ME 04112 *Web:* www.nhdlaw.com	207-774-7000	775-0806	41
Norman, Wood, Kendrick & Turner 1130 22nd St S Ridge Park Pl Ste 3000 Birmingham AL 35205 *Web:* nwkt.com	205-328-6643		428
Normand's 11639 A Jasper Ave Edmonton AB T5K0M9 *Web:* www.normands.com	780-482-2600		671
Normandale Community College 9700 France Ave S Bloomington MN 55431 *TF:* 866-880-8740 ■ *Web:* www.normandale.edu	952-358-8200		162
Normandeau Associates Inc 25 Nashua Rd Bedford NH 03110 *Web:* www.normandeau.com	603-472-5191	472-7052	192
Normandy Farms Estates 9000 Twin Silo Dr Blue Bell PA 19422 *Web:* www.normandyfarm.com	215-616-8500		672
Normandy Hotel, The 2118 Wyoming Ave NW Washington DC 20008 *Web:* www.doylecollection.com	202-483-1350		377
Normandy School District 3855 Lcas Hunt Rd Saint Louis MO 63121 *Web:* www.normandysc.org	314-493-0400	493-0414	685
NormaTec 480 Pleasant St Watertown MA 02472 *TF:* 800-335-0960 ■ *Web:* www.normatec.net	857-304-4558		476
NorMed PO Box 3644 Seattle WA 98124 **Fax Area Code:* 206 ■ *TF:* 800-288-8200 ■ *Web:* www.normed.com	800-288-8200	242-3315*	477
NORML (National Organization for the Reform of Marijuana Laws) 1420 K Street NW Ste 350 Washington DC 20006 *TF:* 888-420-8932 ■ *Web:* www.norml.org	202-483-5500	483-0057	48-8
Noro-Moseley Partners 3284 Northside Pkwy NW Ste 525 Atlanta GA 30327 *Web:* www.noromoseley.com	404-233-1966		792
Norotos Inc 201 E Alton Ave Santa Ana CA 92707 *Web:* www.norotos.com	714-662-3113	662-7950	454
NORPAC Foods Inc 930 W Washington St Stayton OR 97383 *TF:* 800-733-9311 ■ *Web:* norpac.com	503-769-6361		296-21
Norplex Inc 111 3rd St NW Bldg C Auburn WA 98001 *Web:* www.norplexinc.com	253-735-3431	735-5056	604
Norpro Inc 2215 Merrill Creek Pkwy. Everett WA 98203 *Web:* wholesale.norpro.com	425-261-1000		486
Norquay Technology Inc 800 W Front St PO Box 468 Chester PA 19013 *Web:* www.norquaytech.com	610-874-4330	874-3575	144
NorQuest College Learner Centre Library 10215 108th St. Edmonton AB T5J1L6 *Web:* www.library.norquest.ca	780-664-6070		434-3
Norquist Salvage Corp 2151 Professional Dr Ste 200. Roseville CA 95661 *Web:* thrifttown.com	916-787-1070		791
Norred & Associates Inc 1003 Virginia Ave Ste 200 Atlanta GA 30354 *TF:* 800-962-6363 ■ *Web:* www.norred.com	404-761-5058	761-1152	693
Norrick Petroleum Inc 3919 E McGalliard Rd. Muncie IN 47303 *TF:* 800-473-1931 ■ *Web:* norrick.co	765-284-7374	284-7399	579
Norridge Health Care & Rehabilitation Ctr 7001 W Cullom Ave Norridge IL 60706 *Web:* norridgegardens.com	708-457-0700		450
Norris Associates (NA) 2534 Murrell Rd. Santa Barbara CA 93109 *Web:* www.norris-associates.com	805-962-7703	456-2169	194
Norris Cylinder Co 4818 W Loop 281 Longview TX 75603 *TF:* 800-527-8418 ■ *Web:* www.norriscylinder.com	903-757-7633	237-7654	223
Norris Dam State Resort Park 125 Village Green Cir Rocky Top TN 37769 *Web:* www.tnstateparks.com	865-426-7461		565
Norris Ford 901 Merritt Blvd. Baltimore MD 21222 *TF:* 888-205-0310 ■ *Web:* www.norrisford.com	410-285-0200		57
Norris Injury Lawyers 10 Old Montgomery Hwy Birmingham AL 35209 *TF:* 800-477-7510 ■ *Web:* www.norrisinjurylawyers.com	800-477-7510		445
Norris Medical Library University of S California 2003 Zonal Ave Los Angeles CA 90089 *Web:* www.libraries.usc.edu	323-442-1111	221-1235	434-1
Norris Precision Manufacturing Inc 4680 110th Ave N. Clearwater FL 33762 *Web:* www.norrisprecision.com	727-572-6330	572-6216	21
Norris Public Power District 3111 Progressive Rd PO Box 69. Seward NE 68434 *Web:* norrisppd.com	402-643-2951	646-4695	245
Norris School District 6940 Calloway Dr. Bakersfield CA 93312 *Web:* www.norris.k12.ca.us	661-387-7000	399-9750	188-5
Norris, McLaughlin & Marcus PA 400 Crossing Blvd 8th Fl Bridgewater NJ 08807 *Web:* www.nmmlaw.com	908-722-0700		428

Name / Address	City	State	ZIP	Phone	Fax	Class
Norris, Perne & French LLP 40 Pearl St N W Ste 300 *TF:* 800-748-0544 ■ *Web:* norrisperne.com	Grand Rapids	MI	49503	616-459-3421	459-5369	528
Norriseal 11122 W Little York Rd *Web:* norrisealwellmark.com	Houston	TX	77041	713-466-3552	896-7386	537
Norristown Farm Park 2500 Upper Farm Rd *Web:* www.dcnr.pa.gov	Norristown	PA	19403	610-270-0215		565
Norristown State Hospital 1001 Sterigere St *Web:* www.dhs.pa.gov	Norristown	PA	19401	610-313-1000		374-5
Norsan Group 2445 Meadowbrook Pkwy PO Box 957058 **Fax Area Code:* 770 ■ *Web:* norsan.net	Duluth	GA	30096	678-242-1640	414-0617*	670
Norsat International Inc 110-4020 Viking Way *TSX: NII* ■ *TF:* 800-644-4562 ■ *Web:* www.norsat.com	Richmond	BC	V6V2L4	604-821-2800	821-2801	735
Norsco Inc 1816 Ackley Cir *Web:* www.norscoinc.com	Oakdale	CA	95361	209-845-2327	845-2329	454
Norscot Group Inc 1000 W Donges Bay Rd *TF:* 800-653-3313 ■ *Web:* www.norscot.com	Mequon	WI	53092	262-241-3313	241-4904	9
Norshield Corp 3232 Mobile Hwy *TF:* 855-859-3716 ■ *Web:* www.norshield.net	Montgomery	AL	36108	334-551-0650		350
Nor-Son Inc 7900 Hastings Rd *Web:* www.nor-son.com	Baxter	MN	56425	218-828-1722		186
NorSouth 2000 RiverEdge Pkwy Ste 450 *Web:* www.onestreetres.com	Atlanta	GA	30328	770-850-8280	850-8230	186
Norstone Financial Corp 130 King St W The Exchange Twr Ste 1800 *Web:* www.norstonecorp.com	Toronto	ON	M5XIE3	416-357-4107		528
Nortech Engineering Inc 15 Commerce Way Ste 1003 *Web:* www.norteng.com	Norton	MA	02766	508-285-7831	285-7861	173-2
Nortech Systems Inc 7550 Meridian Cir N Ste 150 *NASDAQ: NSYS* ■ *TF:* 800-237-9576 ■ *Web:* www.nortechsys.com	Maple Grove	MN	55369	952-345-2244		253
Nortek Inc 5000 Success Dr *NASDAQ: NTK* ■ *TF:* 800-422-4328 ■ *Web:* www.nortek.com	Providence	RI	02903	800-422-4328		15
Nortek Security & Control LLC 1950 Camino Vida Roble Ste 150 *TF:* 800-421-1587 ■ *Web:* www.nortekcontrol.com	Carlsbad	CA	92008	760-438-7000	931-1340	692
North Adams Common Nursing Home 175 Franklin St *Web:* northadamscommons.org	North Adams	MA	01247	413-664-4041	664-8447	450
North Adams Regional Hospital (NARH) 71 Hospital Ave *Web:* www.nbhealth.org	North Adams	MA	01247	413-664-5000		374-3
North Africa Journal, The 66 W Flagler St 12th Fl Ste 1204-A *Web:* north-africa.com	Miami	FL	33130	508-471-3899		387
North Alabama Electric Co-op 41103 US Hwy 72 *TF:* 800-572-2900 ■ *Web:* www.naecoop.com	Stevenson	AL	35772	256-437-2281		245
North Alabama Railroad Museum Inc (NARM) 694 Chase Rd NE *Web:* northalabamarailroadmuseum.com	Huntsville	AL	35811	256-851-6276		520
North American Forest Products Inc 27263 May St *Web:* www.nafpinc.com	Edwardsburg	MI	49112	269-663-8500		683
North America's Building Trades Unions 815 16th St NW Ste 600 *Web:* nabtu.org	Washington	DC	20006	202-347-1461	628-0724	49-3
North American Arms Inc 2150 S 950 E *TF:* 800-821-5783 ■ *Web:* www.naaminis.com	Provo	UT	84606	801-374-9990		807
North American Association of Food Equipment Manufacturers (NAFEM) 161 N Clark St Ste 2020 *TF:* 888-493-5961 ■ *Web:* www.nafem.org	Chicago	IL	60601	312-821-0201	821-0202	49-13
North American Benefits Co 20 Valley Stream Pkwy Ste 310 *TF:* 800-537-4565 ■ *Web:* nabenefits.com	Malvern	PA	19355	610-995-0169	995-0181	390
North American Blueberry Council (NABC) 1847 Iron Pt Rd Ste 100 *Web:* www.blueberry.org	Folsom	CA	95630	916-983-0111	983-9370	48-2
North American Building Material Distribution Assn (NBMDA) 330 N Wabash Ave Ste 2000 *TF:* 888-747-7862 ■ *Web:* www.nbmda.org	Chicago	IL	60611	312-321-6845	644-0310	49-18
North American Cable Equipment Inc 1085 Andrew Dr Ste A *Web:* www.northamericancable.com	West Chester	PA	19380	610-428-1921		256
North American Clutch Corp 4360 N Green Bay Ave *Web:* www.noramclutch.com	Milwaukee	WI	53209	414-267-4000	267-4024	620
North American Coal Corp 5340 Legacy Dr Bldg I Ste 300 *Web:* www.nacoal.com	Plano	TX	75024	972-448-5400	387-1031	501
North American Container Corp 1811 W Oak Pkwy Ste D *TF:* 800-929-0610 ■ *Web:* www.nacontainer.com	Marietta	GA	30062	770-431-4858	431-6957	100
North American Council on Adoptable Children (NACAC) 970 Raymond Ave Ste 106 *TF:* 877-823-2237 ■ *Web:* www.nacac.org	Saint Paul	MN	55114	651-644-3036	644-9848	48-6
North American Development Bank 203 S St Mary'S Ste 300 *Web:* www.nadb.org	San Antonio	TX	78205	210-231-8000		70
North American Die Casting Assn (NADCA) 3250 N Arlington Hts Rd Ste 101 *Web:* diecasting.org	Arlington Heights	IL	60004	847-279-0001	279-0002	49-13
North American Electric Reliability Council (NERC) 1325 G St NW Ste 600 *Web:* www.nerc.com	Washington	DC	20005	609-452-8060	452-9550	48-12
North American Filter Corp 200 W Shore Blvd *Web:* www.nafcoinc.com	Newark	NY	14513	315-331-7000		14
North American Fire Hose 910 E Noble Way *Web:* www.northamericanfirehose.com	Santa Maria	CA	93454	805-922-7076	922-0086	678
North American Industries Inc 80 Holton St *TF:* 800-847-8470 ■ *Web:* www.naicranes.com	Woburn	MA	01801	781-897-4100	729-3343	470
North American Industry Classification System (NAICS) US Census Bureau 4600 Silver Hill Rd *TF:* 800-923-8282 ■ *Web:* www.census.gov	Washington	DC	20233	301-763-4636		340-2
North American Insulation Manufacturers Assn (NAIMA) 44 Canal Center Plz Ste 310 *Web:* insulationinstitute.org	Alexandria	VA	22314	703-684-0084	684-0427	49-3
North American Insurance Co 2721 N Central Ave *TF:* 800-308-2318 ■ *Web:* www.nains.com	Phoenix	AZ	85004	800-308-2318		391-4
North American Lighting Inc 2275 S Main St *Web:* www.nal.com	Paris	IL	61944	217-465-6600		438
North American Limousin Foundation (NALF) 6 Inverness Ct E Ste 260 *TF:* 888-320-8747 ■ *Web:* nalf.org	Englewood	CO	80112	303-220-1693	220-1884	48-2
North American Manufacturing Company Ltd 4455 E 71st St *Web:* combustion.fivesgroup.com	Cleveland	OH	44105	216-271-6000	641-7852	357
North American Meat Institute 1150 Connecticut Ave NW 12th Fl *Web:* www.meatinstitute.org	Washington	DC	20036	202-587-4200	587-4300	615
North American Medical Corp 1649 Sands Pl SE Ste A *Web:* www.namcorporation.com	Marietta	GA	30067	770-541-0012		475
North American Menopause Society, The (NAMS) 5900 Landerbrook Dr Ste 390 *Web:* www.menopause.org	Mayfield Heights	OH	44124	440-442-7550	442-2660	49-8
North American Millers Assn (NAMA) 600 Maryland Ave SW Ste 825-W *Web:* www.namamillers.org	Washington	DC	20024	202-484-2200	488-7416	49-6
North American Mission Board SBC 4200 N Pt Pkwy *TF:* 800-634-2462 ■ *Web:* www.namb.net	Alpharetta	GA	30022	770-410-6000		48-5
North American Network Inc 5335 Wisconsin Ave NW *Web:* www.radiospace.com	Washington	DC	20015	202-243-0592	243-0594	646
North American Palladium Ltd 1 University Ave Ste 1601 *TSX: PDL* ■ *TF:* 888-360-7590 ■ *Web:* www.napalladium.com	Toronto	ON	M5J2P1	416-360-7590	360-7709	502
North American Pipe Corp 2801 Post Oak Blvd Ste 600 *TF:* 855-624-7473 ■ *Web:* Www.napcopipe.com	Houston	TX	77056	713-840-7473	552-0087	596
North American Plywood Corp 12343 Hawkins St *TF:* 800-421-1372 ■ *Web:* naply.com	Santa Fe Springs	CA	90670	562-941-7575		613
North American Production Sharing Inc (NAPS) 517 S Cedros Ave *TF:* 800-551-8581 ■ *Web:* www.napsintl.com	Solana Beach	CA	92075	858-794-7947		194
North American Publishing Co (NAPCO) 1500 Springarden St 12th Fl *TF:* 800-627-2689 ■ *Web:* www.napco.com	Philadelphia	PA	19130	215-238-5300	238-5457	637-9
North American Rescue LLC 35 Tedwall Ct *TF:* 888-689-6277 ■ *Web:* www.narescue.com	Greer	SC	29650	888-689-6277		475
North American Roofing Services Inc 41 Dogwood Rd **Fax Area Code:* 828 ■ *TF:* 800-551-5602 ■ *Web:* naroofing.com	Asheville	NC	28806	800-551-5602	687-1230*	189-12
North American Savings Bank (NASB) 12520 S 71 Hwy *TF:* 800-677-6272 ■ *Web:* www.nasb.com	Grandview	MO	64030	816-765-2200		70
North American Science Associates Inc 6750 Wales Rd *TF:* 866-666-9455 ■ *Web:* www.namsa.com	Northwood	OH	43619	419-666-9455	662-4386	668
North American Securities Administrators Assn (NASAA) 750 First St NE Ste 1140 *Web:* www.nasaa.org	Washington	DC	20002	202-737-0900	783-3571	49-2
North American Security 4138 E Ponce De Leon Ave *TF:* 800-625-6251 ■ *Web:* www.nasecurity.com	Clarkston	GA	30021	404-294-7222	294-0242	392
North American Specialty Glass 2175 Kumry Rd PO Box 70 *TF:* 888-785-5962 ■ *Web:* naspecialtyglass.com	Trumbauersville	PA	18970	215-536-0333	536-6872	332
North American Specialty Insurance Co 650 Elm St 6th Fl *TF:* 800-542-9200 ■ *Web:* www.swissre.com	Manchester	NH	03101	603-644-6600		391-4
North American Spine Society (NASS) 7075 Veterans Blvd *Web:* www.spine.org	Burr Ridge	IL	60527	630-230-3600		49-8
North American Stainless Inc 6870 Hwy 42 E *TF:* 800-499-7833 ■ *Web:* www.northamericanstainless.com	Ghent	KY	41045	502-347-6000	347-6001	360-3
North American Steel Co 18300 Miles Ave *TF:* 800-321-9310 ■ *Web:* www.northamerican-steel.com	Cleveland	OH	44128	216-475-7300	475-6143	492
North American Substation Services LLC (NASS) 190 N Westmonte Dr *Web:* www.nassusa.com	Altamonte Springs	FL	32714	407-788-3717	788-3767	767
North American Tanning Corp 248 W 35th St Ste 505 *Web:* www.natanning.com	New York	NY	10001	212-643-1702	967-0068	432
North American Title Co 1855 Gateway Blvd Ste 600 *Web:* www.nat.com	Concord	CA	94520	925-935-5599	933-4851	391-6
North American Tool Corp 215 Elmwood Ave **Fax Area Code:* 800 ■ *TF:* 800-872-8277 ■ *Web:* www.natool.com	South Beloit	IL	61080	815-389-2300	872-3299*	493
North American Tungsten Corporation Ltd c/o Alvarez & Marsal Canada Inc 400 Burrard St Ste 1680 *Web:* www.natungsten.com	Vancouver	BC	V6C3A6	604-638-7440	638-7441	502
North American Van Lines Inc 5001 US Hwy 30 W *TF:* 800-348-2111 ■ *Web:* www.northamerican.com	Fort Wayne	IN	46818	260-429-2511		219
North Arkansas College 1515 Pioneer Dr *TF:* 800-679-6622 ■ *Web:* www.northark.edu	Harrison	AR	72601	870-743-3000	391-3339	162
North Arkansas Electric Co-opeartive Inc 225 S Main St *TF:* 844-335-4461 ■ *Web:* www.naeci.com	Salem	AR	72576	870-895-3221	895-6279	245

Name / Address	City	State	Zip	Phone	Fax	Class
North Arkansas Regional Medical Ctr						
620 N Willow St	Harrison	AR	72601	870-414-4000		374-3
Web: www.narmc.com						
North Atlantic 29 Pippy Pl	Saint John	NL	A1B3X2	709-463-8811	579-5087	536
TF: 877-635-3645 ■ *Web:* northatlantic.ca						
North Atlantic Books						
2526 Martin Luther King Jr Way	Berkeley	CA	94704	510-549-4270	549-4276	637-2
TF: 800-733-3000 ■ *Web:* www.northatlanticbooks.com						
North Atlantic Capital						
2 City Ctr 5th Fl	Portland	ME	04101	207-772-4470	772-3257	792
Web: www.northatlanticcapital.com						
North Atlantic Communications						
48 S Mall	Plainview	NY	11803	516-756-9000		224
TF: 866-572-9838 ■ *Web:* www.nactelligence.com						
North Atlantic Corp						
1255 Grand Army Hwy	Somerset	MA	02726	800-543-5403		499
TF: 800-543-5403 ■ *Web:* www.northatlanticcorp.com						
North Atlantic Publishing Systems Inc						
66 Commonwealth Ave	Concord	MA	01742	978-371-8989	371-5678	178-1
Web: www.napsys.com						
North Augusta Chamber of Commerce						
406 W Ave	North Augusta	SC	29841	803-279-2323	279-0003	139
Web: www.northaugustachamber.org						
North Augusta Star, The						
406 W Ave	North Augusta	SC	29841	803-279-2793	278-4070	532-4
Web: www.northaugustastar.com						
North Baldwin Chamber of Commerce						
301 McMeans Ave	Bay Minette	AL	36507	251-937-5665	937-5670	139
TF: 800-634-8104 ■ *Web:* www.northbaldwinchamber.com						
North Bay & District Chamber of Commerce						
205 Main St E	North Bay	ON	P1B1B2	705-472-8480	472-8027	137
TF: 888-249-8998 ■ *Web:* nbdcc.ca						
North Bay Bohemian 847 Fifth St	Santa Rosa	CA	95404	707-527-1200	527-1288	532-5
Web: www.bohemian.com						
North Bay Insurance Brokers Inc						
25 Mcdonell St PO Box Nb	Sonoma	CA	95476	800-335-5112		390
TF: 800-335-5112 ■ *Web:* northbayinsurance.com						
North Bay Nissan Inc						
1250 Auto Center Dr	Petaluma	CA	94952	707-769-7700		57
TF: 855-540-5697 ■ *Web:* www.northbaynissan.com						
North Bay Produce Inc						
PO Box 549	Traverse City	MI	49685	800-678-1941	946-1902*	297-7
**Fax Area Code:* 231 ■ *TF:* 800-678-1941 ■ *Web:* northbayproduce.com						
North Bay Regional Health Ctr						
50 College Dr PO Box 2500	North Bay	ON	P1B5A4	705-474-8600		374-2
Web: www.nbrhc.on.ca						
North Beach Pizza Inc						
1462 Grant Ave	San Francisco	CA	94133	415-433-2444		670
Web: www.northbeachpizza.com						
North Bend State Park						
202 N Bend Park Rd	Cairo	WV	26337	304-643-2931		565
Web: wvstateparks.com						
North Bennet Street School						
150 North St	Boston	MA	02109	617-227-0155	227-9292	685
Web: www.nbss.edu						
North Bergen Free Public Library						
8411 Bergenline Ave	North Bergen	NJ	07047	201-869-4715	868-0968	434-3
Web: www.nbpl.org						
North Berman & Beebe						
1200 New Hampshire Ave NW Ste 725	Washington	DC	20036	202-371-1100	371-5527	428
Web: www.northberman.com						
North Boros Veterinary Hospital Inc						
2255 Babcock Blvd	Pittsburgh	PA	15237	412-821-5600	821-3416	794
Web: northborosvet.com						
North Bridge Venture Partners						
950 Winter St Ste 4600	Waltham	MA	02451	781-290-0004	290-0999	792
Web: www.northbridge.com						
North Brunswick Library						
880 Hermann Rd	North Brunswick	NJ	08902	732-246-3545	246-1341	434-3
Web: northbrunswicklibrary.org						
North By Northwest 903 W Broadway Ave	Spokane	WA	99201	509-324-2949		514
Web: nxnw.net						
North Canton Area Chamber of Commerce						
121 S Main St	North Canton	OH	44720	330-499-5100	499-7181	139
Web: www.northcantonchamber.org						
North Carolina						
Administrative Office of the Courts						
901 Corporate Center Dr	Raleigh	NC	27607	919-890-1000		339-34
Web: www.nccourts.org						
Aging & Adult Service Div						
2101 Mail Service Ctr	Raleigh	NC	27699	919-855-3400		339-34
Web: www.ncdhhs.gov						
Arts Council 4632 Mail Service Ctr	Raleigh	NC	27699	919-807-6500	807-6532	339-34
Web: www.ncarts.org						
Attorney General 114 W Edenton St	Raleigh	NC	27603	919-716-6400	716-6750	339-34
Web: www.ncdoj.com						
Banking Commission 316 W Edenton St	Raleigh	NC	27603	919-733-3016	733-6918	339-34
Web: www.nccob.gov						
Child Support Enforcement Section						
PO Box 20800	Raleigh	NC	27619	252-789-5225		339-34
Web: www.ncdhhs.gov						
Commerce Dept 301 N Wilmington St	Raleigh	NC	27601	919-814-4600		339-34
TF: 800-562-6333 ■ *Web:* www.nccommerce.com						
Community College System						
200 W Jones St	Raleigh	NC	27603	919-807-7100	807-7165	339-34
Web: www.nccommunitycolleges.edu						
Correction Dept						
214 W Jones St 4201 MSC	Raleigh	NC	27699	919-716-3700	716-3794	339-34
Web: www.doc.state.nc.us						
Cultural Resources Dept						
109 E Jones St	Raleigh	NC	27601	919-807-7385		339-34
Web: www.ncdcr.gov						
Department of Military & Veterans Affairs						
413 N Salisbury S	Raleigh	NC	27603	844-624-8387	807-4260*	339-34
**Fax Area Code:* 919 ■ *TF:* 844-624-8387 ■ *Web:* www.milvets.nc.gov						
Department of Public Safety						
4201 Mail Service Ctr	Raleigh	NC	27699	919-825-2500		339-34
Web: www.ncdps.gov						

Name / Address	City	State	Zip	Phone	Fax	Class
Employment Security Commission						
700 Wade Ave PO Box 25903	Raleigh	NC	27605	919-707-1010	733-9420	259
TF: 888-737-0259 ■ *Web:* www.des.nc.gov						
Ethics Board 6624 Old Wake Forest Rd	Raleigh	NC	27601	919-814-3600	715-1644	265
Web: ethics.ncsbe.gov						
Governor 116 W Jones St	Raleigh	NC	27603	919-807-4499		339-34
Web: governor.nc.gov						
Housing Finance Agency 3508 Bush St	Raleigh	NC	27609	919-877-5700	877-5701	339-34
TF: 800-393-0988 ■ *Web:* www.nchfa.com						
Information Technology Services Office (ITS)						
PO Box 17209	Raleigh	NC	27619	919-754-6000		339-34
TF: 800-722-3946 ■ *Web:* it.nc.gov						
Insurance Dept 1201 MSC	Raleigh	NC	27699	919-807-6075	733-4264	339-34
TF: 888-680-7684 ■ *Web:* www.ncdoi.com						
Labor Dept 1101 Mail Service Ctr	Raleigh	NC	27699	919-807-2796		339-34
TF: 800-625-2267 ■ *Web:* www.labor.nc.gov						
Lieutenant Governor 310 N Blount St	Raleigh	NC	27601	919-733-7350	733-6595	339-34
Web: ltgov.nc.gov						
Marine Fisheries Div						
3441 Arendell St	Morehead City	NC	28557	252-726-7021		339-34
TF: 800-682-2632 ■ *Web:* www.ncfisheries.net						
Mental Health Developmental Disabilities & Substance						
2001 Mail Service Ctr	Raleigh	NC	27699	919-855-4800		339-34
Web: www.ncdhhs.gov						
Motor Vehicles Div 1100 New Bern Ave	Raleigh	NC	27699	919-715-7000	733-6948	339-34
Web: www.ncdot.gov						
Parks & Recreation Div						
121 W Jones St NRC Bldg Second Fl	Raleigh	NC	27603	919-707-9338		339-34
Web: www.ncparks.gov						
Parole Commission 4222 MSC	Raleigh	NC	27699	919-716-3010	716-3987	339-34
Web: www.ncdps.gov						
Real Estate Commission 1313 Navajo Dr	Raleigh	NC	27609	919-875-3700	877-4221	339-34
Web: www.ncrec.gov						
Revenue Dept 4701 Atlantic Ave Ste 118	Raleigh	NC	27604	919-707-0880	850-2954	339-34
Web: www.ncdor.gov						
Securities Div PO Box 29622	Raleigh	NC	27626	919-814-5400	807-2183	339-34
TF: 800-688-4507 ■ *Web:* www.sosnc.gov						
Social Services Div						
2001 Mail Service Ctr	Raleigh	NC	27699	919-733-3055		339-34
Web: www.ncdhhs.gov						
Standards Div 2 W Edenton St	Raleigh	NC	27699	919-707-3225	715-0524	339-34
Web: www.ncagr.gov						
State Highway Patrol						
512 N Salisbury St	Raleigh	NC	27604	919-733-7952	733-1189	339-34
Web: www.ncdps.gov						
State Personnel Office 116 W Jones St	Raleigh	NC	27603	919-807-4800	733-0653	339-34
Web: oshr.nc.gov						
State Ports Authority						
2202 Burnett Blvd PO Box 9002	Wilmington	NC	28402	910-763-1621		618
Web: ncports.com						
State Treasurer 3200 Atlantic Ave	Raleigh	NC	27604	919-814-4000		339-34
Web: www.nctreasurer.com						
Supreme Court 2 E Morgan St	Raleigh	NC	27601	919-831-5700		339-34
Web: www.nccourts.gov						
Transportation Dept 1 S Wilmington St	Raleigh	NC	27611	877-368-4968	715-7000*	339-34
**Fax Area Code:* 919 ■ *TF:* 877-368-4968 ■ *Web:* www.ncdot.gov						
Utilities Commission						
4325 Mail Service Ctr Dobbs Bldg	Raleigh	NC	27699	919-733-7328	733-7300	339-34
TF: 866-380-9816 ■ *Web:* www.ncuc.commerce.state.nc.us						
Victims Compensation Services Div						
311 Colleton Rd	Raleigh	NC	27699	919-733-7974		339-34
TF: 800-826-6200 ■ *Web:* www.nccrimecontrol.org						
Vital Records Unit 311 Colleton Rd	Raleigh	NC	27603	919-733-3000	733-1511	339-34
Vocational Rehabilitation Services Div						
2801 MSC	Raleigh	NC	27699	919-334-1044	733-7968	339-34
TF: 800-689-9090 ■ *Web:* www.ncdhhs.gov						
North Carolina A & T State University						
1601 E Market St	Greensboro	NC	27411	336-334-7946	334-7478	166
TF: 800-443-8964 ■ *Web:* www.ncat.edu						
North Carolina Aquarium at Fort Fisher						
900 Loggerhead Rd	Kure Beach	NC	28449	910-772-0500	458-6812	40
Web: www.ncaquariums.com						
North Carolina Arboretum						
100 Frederick Law Olmsted Way	Asheville	NC	28806	828-665-2492	665-2371	97
Web: www.ncarboretum.org						
North Carolina Association of Pharmacists						
1101 Slater Rd Ste 110	Durham	NC	27703	919-967-2237	439-1649*	585
**Fax Area Code:* 984 ■ *Web:* www.ncpharmacists.org						
North Carolina Association of Realtors Inc						
4511 Weybridge Ln	Greensboro	NC	27407	336-294-1415	299-7872	656
TF: 800-443-9956 ■ *Web:* www.ncrealtors.org						
North Carolina Auto Racing Hall of Fame						
Lakeside Pk 119 Knob Hill Rd	Mooresville	NC	28117	704-663-5331		522
Web: ncarhof.com						
North Carolina Biotechnology Ctr (NCBC)						
15 T.W. Alexander Dr	Research Triangle Park	NC	27709	919-541-9366	990-9544	668
Web: www.ncbiotech.org						
North Carolina Botanical Garden						
University of North Carolina at Chapel Hill, The						
100 Old Mason Farm Rd	Chapel Hill	NC	27599	919-962-0522	962-3531	97
Web: ncbg.unc.edu						
North Carolina Central University						
1801 Fayetteville St	Durham	NC	27707	919-530-6100	530-7625	166
Web: www.nccu.edu						
North Carolina Correctional Institution for Women						
1034 Bragg St	Raleigh	NC	27610	919-733-4340		213
Web: www.ncdps.gov						
North Carolina Democratic Party						
220 Hillsborough St	Raleigh	NC	27603	919-821-2777		616-1
Web: www.ncdp.org						
North Carolina Dental Society						
1600 Evans Rd	Cary	NC	27513	919-677-1396	677-1397	227
TF: 800-662-8754 ■ *Web:* www.ncdental.org						
North Carolina Department of Public Instruction						
Public Instruction Dept						
301 N Wilmington St	Raleigh	NC	27601	984-236-2100	807-3445*	339-34
**Fax Area Code:* 919 ■ *Web:* www.dpi.nc.gov						

Name / Address	City	State	Zip	Phone	Fax	Class
North Carolina Department of Public Safety						
Hyde Correctional Institution						
620 Prison Rd	Fairfield	NC	27826	252-926-1810	926-2306	213
Web: www.ncdps.gov						
North Carolina Eye Bank Inc						
3900 Westpoint Blvd Ste F	Winston-Salem	NC	27103	800-552-9956	499-0123*	269
**Fax Area Code:* 336 ■ *TF:* 800-552-9956 ■ *Web:* www.miraclesinsight.org						
North Carolina Farm Bureau Mutual Insurance Co (NCFBMIC)						
PO Box 27427	Raleigh	NC	27611	919-782-1705		391-4
TF: 800-584-1143 ■ *Web:* www.ncfbins.com						
North Carolina General Assembly						
General Assembly 16 W Jones St	Raleigh	NC	27601	919-733-4111		339-34
Web: www.ncleg.gov						
North Carolina Granite Corp						
151 Granite Quarry Trl PO Box 151	Mount Airy	NC	27030	336-786-5141	719-2623	724
TF: 800-227-6242 ■ *Web:* www.ncgranite.com						
North Carolina High Country Host						
1700 Blowing Rock Rd	Boone	NC	28607	828-264-1299	265-0550	206
TF: 800-438-7500 ■ *Web:* highcountryhost.com						
North Carolina Historic Sites						
Dobbs Bldg 430 North Salisbury St Ste 2050	Raleigh	NC	27603	919-814-7150		337
Web: www.historicsites.nc.gov						
North Carolina Library Assn (NCLA)						
1811 Capital Blvd	Raleigh	NC	27604	919-839-6252	839-6253	435
TF: 888-977-3143 ■ *Web:* www.nclaonline.org						
North Carolina Manufacturing Inc						
100 Industry Ct	Goldsboro	NC	27530	919-734-1115	734-1267	454
Web: www.ncmfginc.com						
North Carolina Medical Society						
222 N Person St	Raleigh	NC	27601	919-833-3836	833-2023	474
TF: 800-722-1350 ■ *Web:* www.ncmedsoc.org						
North Carolina Museum of Art (NCMA)						
2110 Blue Ridge Rd	Raleigh	NC	27607	919-839-6262	733-8034	520
Web: www.ncartmuseum.org						
North Carolina Museum of Natural Sciences						
11 W Jones St	Raleigh	NC	27601	919-707-9800	733-1573	520
Web: www.naturalsciences.org						
North Carolina Mutual Life Insurance Co						
411 W Chapel Hill St	Durham	NC	27701	800-626-1899		391-2
TF: 800-626-1899 ■ *Web:* www.ncmutuallife.com						
North Carolina Mutual Wholesale Drug Co						
816 Ellis Rd	Durham	NC	27703	919-596-2151		238
TF: 800-800-8551 ■ *Web:* www.mutualdrugcompany.com						
North Carolina News Network						
3012 Highwoods Blvd Ste 201	Raleigh	NC	27605	800-849-6266		647
TF: 800-849-6266 ■ *Web:* www.ncnn.com						
North Carolina Nurses Assn (NCNA)						
103 Enterprise St PO Box 12025	Raleigh	NC	27605	919-821-4250	829-5807	533
TF: 800-626-2153 ■ *Web:* ncnurses.org						
North Carolina Public Interest Research Group (NCPIRG)						
19 W Hargett St Ste 405	Raleigh	NC	27601	919-833-2070		633
Web: ncpirg.org						
North Carolina Railroad Co						
2809 Highwoods Blvd	Raleigh	NC	27604	919-954-7601		711
TF: 800-232-0144 ■ *Web:* www.ncrr.com						
North Carolina Republican Party						
1506 Hillsborough St	Raleigh	NC	27605	919-828-6423		616-2
Web: www.nc.gop						
North Carolina School of the Arts						
1533 S Main St	Winston-Salem	NC	27127	336-770-3399	770-1497	164
Web: www.uncsa.edu						
North Carolina Sports Hall of Fame						
NC Museum of History 5 E Edenton St	Raleigh	NC	27601	919-814-7000	733-8655	522
TF: 877-627-6724 ■ *Web:* www.ncdcr.gov						
North Carolina State Bar						
217 E Edenton St PO Box 25996	Raleigh	NC	27601	919-828-4620	821-9168	72
TF: 800-662-7407 ■ *Web:* www.ncbar.gov						
North Carolina State Education Assistance Authority (NCSEAA)						
2917 Highwoods Blvd	Research Triangle Park	NC	27709	919-549-8614	549-8481	725
TF: 800-700-1775 ■ *Web:* www.ncseaa.edu						
North Carolina State University - College of Education - Media Ctr						
400 Poe Hall	Raleigh	NC	27695	919-515-1784	515-6978	434-3
Web: www.test.ced.ncsu.edu						
North Carolina State University Libraries						
PO Box 7111	Raleigh	NC	27695	919-515-2843	515-3628	434-6
TF: 877-601-0590 ■ *Web:* www.lib.ncsu.edu						
North Carolina Symphony						
3700 Glenwood Ave Ste 130	Raleigh	NC	27612	919-733-2750	733-9920	573-3
Web: www.ncsymphony.org						
North Carolina Tennis Hall of Fame						
2709 Henry St	Greensboro	NC	27405	336-852-8577	852-7334	522
Web: www.nctennis.com						
North Carolina Theatre 1 E South St	Raleigh	NC	27601	919-831-6941	831-6951	573-4
Web: nctheatre.com						
North Carolina Veterinary Medical Assn (NCVMA)						
1611 Jones Franklin Rd Ste 108	Raleigh	NC	27606	919-851-5850	851-5859	795
TF: 800-446-2862 ■ *Web:* www.ciclt.net						
North Carolina Wesleyan College						
3400 N Wesleyan Blvd	Rocky Mount	NC	27804	252-985-5100	985-5295	166
TF: 800-488-6292 ■ *Web:* ncwc.edu						
North Carolina Zoological Park						
4401 Zoo Pkwy	Asheboro	NC	27205	336-879-7000		823
Web: www.nczoo.org						
North Cascades National Park						
810 SR 20	Sedro-Woolley	WA	98284	360-856-5700		564
Web: www.nps.gov						
North Central Agricultural Research Laboratory						
2923 Medary Ave	Brookings	SD	57006	605-693-3241	693-5240	668
Web: www.ars.usda.gov						
North Central Association Commission on Accreditation & School Improvement (NCACASI)						
9115 Westside Pkwy	Alpharetta	GA	30009	888-413-3669		48-1
TF: 888-413-3669 ■ *Web:* www.advanc-ed.org						
North Central Association Higher Learning Commission						
230 S LaSalle St	Chicago	IL	60604	312-263-0456	263-7462	49-5
TF: 800-621-7440 ■ *Web:* www.hlcommission.org						
North Central Bronx Hospital						
3424 Kossuth Ave	Bronx	NY	10467	718-519-5000		374-3
TF: 877-207-2134 ■ *Web:* www.nyc.gov						
North Central College						
30 N Brainard St	Naperville	IL	60540	630-637-5800	637-5819	166
TF: 800-411-1861 ■ *Web:* www.northcentralcollege.edu						
North Central Correctional Institution at Gardner						
500 Colony Rd	Gardner	MA	01440	978-630-6000		213
Web: www.mass.gov						
North Central Door Co						
900 Carr Lake Rd PO Box 575	Bemidji	MN	56601	218-751-6962	751-8935	234
TF: 800-677-8431 ■ *Web:* www.northcentraldoor.com						
North Central Electric Co-opeartive Inc						
538 11th St W	Bottineau	ND	58318	701-228-2202	228-2592	245
TF: 800-247-1197 ■ *Web:* www.nceci.com						
North Central Electric Co-opeartive Inc						
13978 E County Rd 56	Attica	OH	44807	419-426-3072	426-1245	245
TF: 800-426-3072 ■ *Web:* www.ncelec.org						
North Central Massachusetts Chamber of Commerce						
860 S St	Fitchburg	MA	01420	978-353-7600	353-4896	139
Web: www.northcentralmass.com						
North Central Michigan College						
1515 Howard St	Petoskey	MI	49770	231-348-6605		162
TF: 888-298-6605 ■ *Web:* www.ncmich.edu						
North Central Missouri College						
1301 Main St	Trenton	MO	64683	660-359-3948	359-2211	162
Web: www.ncmissouri.edu						
North Central Pennsylvania Regional Planning & Development Commission						
651 Montmorenci Rd	Ridgway	PA	15853	814-773-3162	772-7045	194
TF: 800-942-9467 ■ *Web:* www.ncentral.com						
North Central Public Power District						
1409 Main St PO Box 90	Creighton	NE	68729	402-358-5112	358-5129	245
TF: 800-578-1060 ■ *Web:* ncppd.com						
North Central Regional Library						
16 N Columbia St	Wenatchee	WA	98801	509-663-1117		434-3
Web: www.ncrl.org						
North Central State College						
2441 Kenwood Cir	Mansfield	OH	44906	419-755-4800	755-4750	800
TF: 888-755-4899 ■ *Web:* www.ncstatecollege.edu						
North Central Telephone Co-opeartive Corp						
PO Box 70	LaFayette	TN	37083	615-666-2151		736
Web: www.nctc.com						
North Central Texas College						
1525 W California St	Gainesville	TX	76240	940-668-7731	665-7075	162
Web: www.nctc.edu						
North Central University						
910 Elliot Ave S	Minneapolis	MN	55404	612-343-4460	343-4146	166
TF: 800-289-6222 ■ *Web:* www.northcentral.edu						
North Ch Area Chamber of Commerce						
13301 E Fwy Ste 100	Houston	TX	77015	713-450-3600	450-0700	139
Web: www.northchannelarea.com						
North Channel Capital Management Group						
5550 S 59th St Ste 26	Lincoln	NE	68516	402-421-6500	421-6505	463
TF: 877-421-6501 ■ *Web:* northchannelcapital.wfadv.com						
North Charles Street Design Organization						
222 W Saratoga St	Baltimore	MD	21201	410-539-4040		4
Web: www.ncsdo.com						
North Charleston Coliseum & Convention Ctr						
5001 Coliseum Dr	North Charleston	SC	29418	843-529-5000	529-5010	720
Web: www.northcharlestoncoliseumpac.com						
North Chicago Public Library						
2100 Argonne Dr	North Chicago	IL	60064	847-689-0125	689-9117	434-3
Web: ncplibrary.org						
North China 6090 Far Hills Ave	Centerville	OH	45459	937-433-6837		671
Web: www.northchinacenterville.com						
North China Garden 2303 Sixth Ave	Tacoma	WA	98403	253-572-5106		671
Web: northchinagardentacoma.com						
North Clackamas County Chamber of Commerce						
7740 SE Harmony Rd	Milwaukie	OR	97222	503-654-7777		139
Web: www.yourchamber.com						
North Coast Air 4645 W 12th St	Erie	PA	16505	814-836-9220	836-9901	63
Web: www.ncair.com						
North Coast Brewing Company Inc						
455 N Main St	Fort Bragg	CA	95437	707-964-2739		102
Web: www.northcoastbrewing.com						
North Coast College, The						
11724 Detroit Ave	Lakewood	OH	44107	800-473-4350	221-2311*	164
**Fax Area Code:* 216 ■ *TF:* 800-473-4350 ■ *Web:* www.thencc.edu						
North Coast Container Corp						
8806 Crane Ave	Cleveland	OH	44105	216-441-6214	441-6239	198
Web: www.ncc-corp.com						
North Coast Co-opeartive Inc 811 I St	Arcata	CA	95521	707-822-5947		297-8
Web: www.northcoast.coop						
North Country Business Products Inc						
1112 S Railroad St SE	Bemidji	MN	56601	800-937-4140	755-6039*	320
**Fax Area Code:* 218 ■ *TF:* 800-937-4140 ■ *Web:* www.ncbpinc.com						
North Country Community College						
23 Santanoni Ave	Saranac Lake	NY	12983	518-891-2915		162
TF: 888-879-6222 ■ *Web:* www.nccc.edu						
North Country Engineering Inc						
106 John Taplin Rd	Derby	VT	05829	802-766-5396		454
Web: www.northcountryeng.com						
North Country Estates Inc						
5427 Shady Ave	Lowville	NY	13367	315-376-7131		390
Web: nce-schaab.com						
North Country Federal Credit Union Inc						
69 Swift St Ste 100	South Burlington	VT	05403	802-657-6847		219
Web: www.northcountry.org						
North Country Library System						
22072 CR 190	Watertown	NY	13601	315-782-5540	782-6883	434-3
Web: web.ncls.org						
North Country Press 126 Main St	Unity	ME	04988	207-948-2208		637-2
Web: www.northcountrypress.com						
North Country School						
4382 Cascade Rd	Lake Placid	NY	12946	518-523-9329	523-4858	622
Web: www.northcountryschool.org						
North Country Trail Assn 229 E Main St	Lowell	MI	49331	616-897-5987	897-6605	48-23
TF: 866-445-3628 ■ *Web:* northcountrytrail.org						
North County Health Services						
150 Valpreda Rd	San Marcos	CA	92069	760-736-6767		374-3
Web: www.nchs-health.org						

Name / Address	Phone	Fax	Class
North County Transit District (NCTD) 810 Mission Rd, Oceanside CA 92054 *Web:* www.gonctd.com	760-966-6500	967-2001	468
North Dade Regional Chamber of Commerce 2761 N 29th Ave, Hollywood FL 33020 *Web:* www.thechamber.cc	305-690-9123	690-9124	139
North Dakota			
Accountancy Board 2701 S Columbia Rd Ste D, Grand Forks ND 58201 **Fax Area Code:* 701 ■ *TF:* 800-532-5904 ■ *Web:* ndsba.aci-dev.com	800-532-5904	775-7430*	339-35
Aging Services Div 1237 W Divide Ave Ste 6, Bismarck ND 58501 *TF:* 855-462-5465 ■ *Web:* www.nd.gov	701-328-4649	328-8744	339-35
Agriculture Dept 600 E Blvd Ave Dept 602, Bismarck ND 58505 *TF:* 800-242-7535 ■ *Web:* www.nd.gov	701-328-2231	328-4567	339-35
Attorney General 600 E Blvd Ave Dept 125, Bismarck ND 58505 *Web:* www.attorneygeneral.nd.gov	701-328-2210		339-35
Consumer Protection Div 1709 N 19th St Ste 3, Bismarck ND 58503 *TF:* 800-472-2600 ■ *Web:* www.ag.state.nd.us	701-328-3404		339-35
Corrections & Rehabilitation Dept 3100 Railroad Ave PO Box 1898, Bismarck ND 58502 *Web:* www.nd.gov	701-328-6390	328-6651	339-35
Court Administrator Office 600 E Blvd Ave State Capitol, Bismarck ND 58505 *Web:* www.ndcourts.gov	701-328-2341	328-2092	339-35
Economic Development & Finance Div 1600 E Century Ave Ste 2 PO Box 2057, Bismarck ND 58503 *Web:* www.business.nd.gov	701-328-5300		339-35
Education Standards & Practices Board 2718 Gateway Ave Ste 204, Bismarck ND 58503 *Web:* www.nd.gov	701-328-9641	328-9647	339-35
Emergency Management Div Fraine Barracks Ln Bldg 35, Bismarck ND 58504 *Web:* www.des.nd.gov	701-328-8100	328-8181	339-35
Financial Institutions Dept 2000 Schafer St Ste G, Bismarck ND 58501 *Web:* www.nd.gov	701-328-9933	328-0290	339-35
Game & Fish Dept 100 N Bismarck Expy, Bismarck ND 58501 *TF:* 800-406-6409 ■ *Web:* gf.nd.gov	701-328-6300	328-6352	339-35
Health Dept 600 E Blvd Ave Dept 301, Bismarck ND 58505 *Web:* www.ndhealth.gov	701-328-2372	328-4727	339-35
Highway Patrol 600 E Blvd Ave Dept 504, Bismarck ND 58505 *Web:* www.nd.gov	701-328-8020	328-1717	339-35
Historical Society 612 E Blvd Ave, Bismarck ND 58505 *Web:* www.nd.gov	701-328-2666		339-35
Housing Finance Agency 2624 Vermont Ave PO Box 1535, Bismarck ND 58502 *TF:* 800-292-8621 ■ *Web:* www.ndhfa.org	701-328-8080	328-8090	339-35
Indian Affairs Commission 600 E Blvd Ave 1st Fl Judicial Wing-Rm 117, Bismarck ND 58505 *Web:* www.indianaffairs.nd.gov	701-328-2428	328-1537	339-35
Information Technology Dept 4201 Normandy St, Bismarck ND 58503 **Fax Area Code:* 877 ■ *Web:* www.nd.gov	701-328-3190	328-4470*	339-35
Labor & Human Rights Dept 600 E Blvd Ave Dept 406, Bismarck ND 58505 *TF:* 800-582-8032 ■ *Web:* www.nd.gov	701-328-2660	328-2031	339-35
Legislative Assembly State Capitol 600 E Blvd Ave Ste 160, Bismarck ND 58505 *Web:* www.legis.nd.gov	701-328-2916	328-3615	339-35
Medical Examiners Board 4204 Boulder Ridge Rd, Bismarck ND 58501 *Web:* www.ndbom.org	701-328-6500	328-6505	339-35
Office of Governor 600 E Blvd Ave, Bismarck ND 58505 *Web:* www.governor.nd.gov	701-328-2200	328-2205	339-35
Parks & Recreation Dept 1600 E Century Ave Ste 3 PO Box 5594, Bismarck ND 58506 *TF:* 800-366-6888 ■ *Web:* www.parkrec.nd.gov	701-328-5357	328-5363	339-35
Parole & Probation Div 3100 E Railroad Ave PO Box 1898, Bismarck ND 58502 *Web:* www.nd.gov	701-328-6100	328-6651	339-35
Public Instruction Dept 600 E Blvd Ave Dept 201, Bismarck ND 58505 *Web:* www.nd.gov	701-328-8979	328-2461	339-35
Racing Commission 500 N Ninth St, Bismarck ND 58501 *Web:* racingcommission.nd.gov	701-328-4633	328-4280	712
Real Estate Commission 1110 College Dr Ste 207, Bismarck ND 58501 *Web:* www.realestatend.org	701-328-9749	328-9750	339-35
Secretary of State 600 E Blvd Ave Dept 108, Bismarck ND 58505 *TF:* 800-352-0867 ■ *Web:* www.nd.gov	701-328-2900	328-2992	339-35
Securities Dept 600 E Blvd Ave State Capitol 5th Fl, Bismarck ND 58505 *TF:* 800-297-5124 ■ *Web:* www.nd.gov	701-328-2910	328-2946	339-35
State Government Information 600 E Blvd Ave Dept 130 4th Fl, Bismarck ND 58505 *Web:* www.nd.gov	701-328-2471		339-35
Supreme Court 600 E Blvd Ave Dept 180, Bismarck ND 58505 *Web:* www.ndcourts.gov	701-328-4216	328-2092	339-35
Tax Dept 600 E Blvd Ave, Bismarck ND 58505 *TF:* 800-638-2901 ■ *Web:* www.nd.gov	701-328-2310	328-3700	339-35
Testing & Safety Div 600 E Blvd Dept 408, Bismarck ND 58505 *TF:* 877-245-6685 ■ *Web:* www.psc.nd.gov	701-328-2400	328-2410	339-35
Tourism Div 1600 E Century Ave Ste 2, Bismarck ND 58502 *TF:* 800-435-5663 ■ *Web:* www.ndtourism.com	701-328-2525		339-35
Transportation Dept 608 E Blvd Ave, Bismarck ND 58505 *TF:* 855-637-6237 ■ *Web:* www.dot.nd.gov	701-328-2500		339-35
Treasurer 600 E Blvd Ave Dept 120, Bismarck ND 58505 *Web:* www.nd.gov	701-328-2643	328-3002	339-35
University System 600 E Blvd Ave Dept 215, Bismarck ND 58505 *TF:* 866-457-6387 ■ *Web:* www.ndus.edu	701-328-2960	328-2961	339-35
Veterans Affairs Dept 4201 38th St SW Ste 104 PO Box 9003, Fargo ND 58104 *TF:* 866-634-8387 ■ *Web:* www.nd.gov	701-239-7165	239-7166	339-35
Vocational Rehabilitation Div 1237 W Divide Ave Ste 2, Bismarck ND 58501 *TF:* 888-862-7342 ■ *Web:* www.nd.gov	701-328-8800		339-35
Workers Compensation 1600 E Century Ave Ste 1, Bismarck ND 58503 *TF:* 800-777-5033 ■ *Web:* www.workforcesafety.com	701-328-3800	328-3820	339-35
North Dakota Association of Realtors 318 W Apollo Ave, Bismarck ND 58503 *TF:* 800-279-2361 ■ *Web:* www.ndrealtors.com	701-355-1010	258-7211	656
North Dakota Chamber of Commerce PO Box 2639, Bismarck ND 58502 *Web:* www.ndchamber.com	701-222-0929	222-1611	140
North Dakota Democratic Party 1902 E Divide Ave, Bismarck ND 58501 *Web:* www.demnpl.com	701-255-0460		616-1
North Dakota Dental Assn 1720 Burnt Boat Dr Ste 201, Bismarck ND 58503 *TF:* 800-444-1330 ■ *Web:* www.smilenorthdakota.org	701-223-8870	892-7068	227
North Dakota League of Cities (NDLC) 410 E Front Ave, Bismarck ND 58504 *TF:* 800-472-2692 ■ *Web:* www.ndlc.org	701-223-3518	223-5174	48-6
North Dakota Medical Assn (NDMA) 1622 I- Ave, Bismarck ND 58503 *Web:* www.ndmed.org	701-223-9475	223-9476	474
North Dakota Mill & Elevator 1823 Mill Rd, Grand Forks ND 58203 *TF:* 800-538-7721 ■ *Web:* www.ndmill.com	701-795-7000		296-23
North Dakota Museum of Art 261Centennial Dr S-7305, Grand Forks ND 58202 *Web:* www.ndmoa.com	701-777-4195	777-4425	520
North Dakota Pharmacists Assn (NDPHA) 1641 Capitol Way, Bismarck ND 58501 *Web:* www.nodakpharmacy.net	701-258-4968	258-9312	585
North Dakota State College of Science 800 Sixth St N, Wahpeton ND 58076 *TF:* 800-342-4325 ■ *Web:* www.ndscs.edu	701-671-2401	671-2201	162
North Dakota State Hospital 2605 Cir Dr, Jamestown ND 58401 *Web:* www.nd.gov	701-253-3650	253-3999	374-5
North Dakota State Library (NDSL) 604 E Blvd Ave, Bismarck ND 58505 *TF:* 800-472-2104 ■ *Web:* www.library.nd.gov	701-328-4622	328-2040	434-5
North Dakota State University 12th Ave N, Fargo ND 58105 *TF:* 800-726-1724 ■ *Web:* www.ndsu.edu	701-231-7932	231-2085	572
North Dakota Veterans Home 1600 Veterans Dr, Lisbon ND 58054 *Web:* www.nd.gov	701-683-6500	683-6550	793
North Dakota Veterinary Medical Assn PO Box 1231, Bismarck ND 58502 *Web:* www.ndvma.com	701-221-7740		795
North Dallas Chamber of Commerce 10707 Preston Rd, Dallas TX 75230 *Web:* ndcc.org	214-368-6485	691-5584	139
North Delta Planning & Development District 220 Power Dr, Batesville MS 38606 *TF:* 800-844-2433 ■ *Web:* www.ndpdd.com	662-561-4100	561-4112	78
North East Machine & Tool Co 320 W 7th St, Janesville IA 50647 *Web:* www.nemachine.com	319-987-2003	987-2253	454
North East MS EPA 10 PR 2050, Oxford MS 38655 *TF:* 877-234-6331 ■ *Web:* www.nemepa.org	662-234-6331		245
North Eastern Institute of Whole Health School of Massage Therapy 22 Bridge St, Manchester NH 03101 *Web:* www.neiwh.com	603-623-5018	623-4689	685
North Essex Chamber of Commerce 26 Park St Ste 2062, Montclair NJ 07042 *Web:* www.northessexchamber.com	973-226-5500	783-4407	139
North European Oil Royalty Trust 43 W Front St Ste 19A, Red Bank NJ 07701 *NYSE: NRT* ■ *Web:* www.neort.com	732-741-4008	741-3140	675
North Face, The 14450 Doolittle Dr, San Leandro CA 94577 *TF:* 855-500-8639 ■ *Web:* www.thenorthface.com	877-992-0111		710
North Florida College Foundation Inc 325 NW Turner Davis Dr, Madison FL 32340 *TF:* 866-937-6322 ■ *Web:* nfcc.edu	850-973-2288		162
North Florida Lincoln Mercury 4620 Southside Blvd, Jacksonville FL 32216 *TF:* 888-457-1949 ■ *Web:* www.northfloridalincoln.com	877-941-1435		516
North Florida Shipyards Inc 2060 E Adams St, Jacksonville FL 32202 *Web:* northfloridashipyards.com	904-354-3278		698
North Florida Technical College 609 N Orange St, Starke FL 32091 *Web:* nftc.edu	904-966-6764	966-6786	167-3
North Fork Radiology PC (NFR) 1333 Roanoke Ave, Riverhead NY 11901 *Web:* www.northforkrad.com	631-727-2755		374-3
North Fork Ranch (NFR) 55395 Hwy 285 PO Box B, Shawnee CO 80475 *TF:* 800-843-7895 ■ *Web:* www.northforkranch.com	303-838-9873	838-1549	239
North Fort Myers Chamber of Commerce 2787 N Tamiami Trl Unit 10, North Fort Myers FL 33903 *Web:* nfmchamber.org	239-997-9111		139
North Forty Resort LLC 3765 Mt Hwy 40 W, Columbia Falls MT 59912 *TF:* 800-562-8734 ■ *Web:* northfortyresort.com	406-862-7740		379
North Galveston County Chamber of Commerce 218 FM 517 W, Dickinson TX 77539 *Web:* www.northgalvestoncountychamber.com	281-534-4380	534-4389	139
North Georgia Brick Company Inc 2405 Oak St W, Cumming GA 30041 *Web:* www.ngabrick.com	770-886-6555		191-1

	Phone	Fax	Class
North Georgia Electric Membership Corp 1850 Cleveland Hwy .... Dalton GA 30721 *Web:* www.ngemc.com	706-259-9441		245
North Greenville University 7801 N Tigerville Rd PO Box 1892 .... Tigerville SC 29688 *TF:* 800-468-6642 ■ *Web:* www.ngu.edu	864-977-7000	977-7177	166
North Growth Management Ltd One Bentall Ctr 505 Burrard St Ste 830 .... Vancouver BC V7X1M4 *Web:* www.northgrowth.com	604-688-5440		528
North Hampton State Beach 27 Ocean Blvd .... North Hampton NH 03862 *Web:* www.nhstateparks.org	603-227-8722		565
North Haven Gardens Inc 7700 Northaven Rd .... Dallas TX 75230 *Web:* www.nhg.com	214-363-5316		323
North Hennepin Community College 7411 85th Ave N .... Brooklyn Park MN 55445 *TF:* 800-818-0395 ■ *Web:* www.nhcc.edu	763-488-0391	424-0929	162
North Hero State Park 3803 Lakeview Dr .... North Hero VT 05474 *Web:* www.vtstateparks.com	802-372-8727		565
North Highland Co, The 3333 Piedmont Rd NE Ste 1000 .... Atlanta GA 30305 *Web:* www.northhighland.com	404-233-1015	233-4930	721
North Hill Ventures 535 Boylston St 6th Fl .... Boston MA 02116 *Web:* www.northhillventures.com	617-835-9719		792
North Hunterdon-Voorhees Regional High School District 1445 SR- 31 .... Annandale NJ 08801 *Web:* www.nhvweb.net	908-735-2846	735-6447	685
North Idaho College 1000 W Garden Ave .... Coeur d'Alene ID 83814 *TF:* 877-404-4536 ■ *Web:* www.nic.edu	208-769-3300	769-3399	162
North Idaho Correctional Institution 236 Radar Rd .... Cottonwood ID 83522 *Web:* www.idoc.idaho.gov	208-962-3276		213
North Iowa Area Community College 500 College Dr .... Mason City IA 50401 *TF:* 888-466-4222 ■ *Web:* www.niacc.edu	641-423-1264	422-4385	162
North Island College 2300 Ryan Rd .... Courtenay BC V9N8N6 *TF:* 800-715-0914 ■ *Web:* www.nic.bc.ca	250-334-5000	334-5018	166
North Island Credit Union 5898 Copley Dr .... San Diego CA 92111 *TF:* 800-334-8788 ■ *Web:* northisland.ccu.com	800-334-8788		219
North Itasca Electric Co-opeartive Inc 301 Main Ave PO Box 227 .... Bigfork MN 56628 *TF:* 800-762-4048 ■ *Web:* www.northitascaelectric.com	218-743-3131	743-3644	245
North Jersey Regional Chamber of Commerce 547 Union Blvd .... Totowa NJ 07512 *Web:* www.northjerseychamber.org	973-470-9300	470-9245	139
North Kansas City Hospital 2800 Clay Edwards Dr .... North Kansas City MO 64116 *Web:* www.nkch.org	816-691-2000		374-3
North Kingstown Chamber of Commerce 8045 Post Rd .... North Kingstown RI 02852 *Web:* www.northkingstown.com	401-295-5566	295-5582	139
North Lake College 5001 N MacArthur Blvd .... Irving TX 75038 *Web:* www.northlakecollege.edu	972-273-3480	273-3112	162
North Las Vegas Animal Hospital 6910 S Cimarron Rd Ste 240 .... North Las Vegas NV 89113 *Web:* huntco.com	702-642-5353		794
North Lawrence Career Ctr 258 BNL Dr .... Bedford IN 47421 *Web:* www.nlcs.k12.in.us	812-279-3561	275-1578	167-3
North Light Color 5008 Hillsboro Ave N .... New Hope MN 55428 *TF:* 866-922-4700 ■ *Web:* northlightcolor.com	763-531-8222	531-8224	386
North Los Angel County Regional Ctr 9200 Oakdale Ave Ste 100 .... Chatsworth CA 91311 *TF:* 800-430-4263 ■ *Web:* www.nlacrc.org	818-778-1900	756-6140	363
North Love Christian School 5301 E Riverside Blvd .... Rockford IL 61114 *Web:* northlove.org	815-877-6021		685
North Maine Woods Inc 92 Main St PO Box 425 .... Ashland ME 04732 *Web:* northmainewoods.org	207-435-6213		752
North Market 59 Spruce St .... Columbus OH 43215 *Web:* www.northmarket.com	614-463-9664		460
North Mason School District Inc 71 E Campus Dr .... Belfair WA 98528 *Web:* www.nmsd.wednet.edu	360-277-2300		685
North Memorial Health 3300 Oakdale Ave N .... Robbinsdale MN 55422 *Web:* www.northmemorial.com	763-520-5200		374-3
North Memorial Home Health & Hospice 3500 France Ave N Ste 101 .... Robbinsdale MN 55422 *Web:* northmemorial.com	763-581-8181		371
North Meridian Title & Escrow LLC 701 N Chelan .... Wenatchee WA 98801 *Web:* northmeridiantitle.com	509-662-4721		653
North Miami Beach Chamber of Commerce 16901 NE 19th Ave .... North Miami Beach FL 33162 *Web:* www.nmbchamber.com	305-944-8500	944-8191	139
North Miami Beach Public Library 1601 NE 164th St .... North Miami Beach FL 33162 *Web:* nmblib.weebly.com	305-948-2970	787-6007	434-3
North Miami Beach/Julius Littman Performing Arts Theater 17011 NE 19th Ave .... North Miami Beach FL 33162 *Web:* www.littmantheater.com	305-948-2957		572
North Miami Public Library 776 NE 125 St .... North Miami FL 33161 *Web:* northmiamifl.gov	305-891-5535	892-0843	434-3
North Mississippi Medical Ctr 830 S Gloster St .... Tupelo MS 38801 *TF:* 800-882-6274 ■ *Web:* www.nmhs.net	662-377-3000		374-3
North Monterey County Unified School District 8142 Moss Landing Rd .... Moss Landing CA 95039 *Web:* www.nmcusd.org	831-633-3343	633-5189	685
North Museum of Nature & Science 400 College Ave .... Lancaster PA 17603 *Web:* northmuseum.org	717-358-3941	358-4504	520
North Oaks Health System (NOHS) PO Box 2668 .... Hammond LA 70404 *Web:* www.northoaks.org	985-345-2700		374-3
North of Boston Convention & Visitors Bureau (NBCVB) I-95 Southbound Exit 60 PO Box 5193 .... Salisbury MA 01952 *Web:* northofboston.org	978-465-6555		206
North of Boston Library Exchange 42A Cherry Hill Dr .... Danvers MA 01923 *Web:* www.noblenet.org	978-777-8844		434-3
North Okaloosa Medical Ctr (NOMC) 151 E Redstone Ave .... Crestview FL 32539 *Web:* www.northokaloosa.com	850-689-8100		374-3
North Oklahoma County Mental Health Ctr 2617 General Pershing Blvd .... Oklahoma City OK 73107 *Web:* www.northcare.com	405-858-2700		726
North Olmsted Chamber of Commerce 5871 Canterbury Rd .... North Olmsted OH 44070 *Web:* www.nolmstedchamber.org	440-777-3368	777-9361	139
North Olympic Peninsula Visitor & Convention Bureau 618 S Peabody Ste F PO Box 670 .... Port Angeles WA 98362 *TF:* 800-942-4042 ■ *Web:* www.olympicpeninsula.org	360-452-8552	452-7383	206
North Ontario Library Service 334 Regent St .... Sudbury ON P3C4E2 *TF:* 800 461 6348 ■ *Web:* olsn.ca	705-675-6467	675-2285	436
North Orange County Escrow Corp 1370 Brea Blvd Ste 110 .... Fullerton CA 92835 *Web:* www.nocescrow.com	714-526-5400	526-1744	652
North Pacific Corp 5612 Lake Washington Blvd NE .... Kirkland WA 98033 *Web:* www.npc-usa.com	425-822-1001	822-1004	285
North Pacific Management 1905 SE Tenth Ave .... Portland OR 97214 *Web:* www.northp.com	503-425-1500		652
North Park Lincoln 9207 San Pedro St .... San Antonio TX 78216 *TF:* 888-474-4845 ■ *Web:* www.nplincoln.com	210-341-8841		57
North Park Transportation Co 5150 Columbine St .... Denver CO 80216 *Web:* www.nopk.com	303-295-0300	295-6244	780
North Park University 3225 W Foster Ave .... Chicago IL 60625 *TF:* 800-888-6728 ■ *Web:* www.northpark.edu	773-244-5500		166
North Plains Electric Co-opeartive Inc 14585 Hwy 83 N PO Box 1008 .... Perryton TX 79070 *TF:* 800-272-5482 ■ *Web:* www.npec.org	806-435-5482		245
North Platte & Lincoln County Visitors Bureau 101 Halligan Dr .... North Platte NE 69101 *TF:* 800-955-4528 ■ *Web:* visitnorthplatte.com	308-532-4729		206
North Platte Area Chamber & Development 502 S Dewey St .... North Platte NE 69101 *Web:* www.nparea.com	308-532-4966	532-4827	139
North Platte Public Library 120 W Fourth St .... North Platte NE 69101 *Web:* www.ci.north-platte.ne.us	308-535-8036	535-8296	434-3
North Point Recreation Area 38180 297th St .... Lake Andes SD 57356 *Web:* gfp.sd.gov	605-487-7046		565
North Pointe Realty Services 1404 Race St Ste 200 .... Cincinnati OH 45202 *Web:* northpointegroup.com	513-579-1850		653
North Pond 2610 N Cannon Dr .... Chicago IL 60614 *Web:* www.northpondrestaurant.com	773-477-5845		671
North Quabbin Chamber of Commerce 251 Exchange St .... Athol MA 01331 *Web:* northquabbinchamber.com	978-249-3849		139
North Richland Hills Public Library 9015 Grand Ave .... North Richland Hills TX 76180 *Web:* www.library.nrhtx.com	817-427-6800	427-6808	434-3
North Ridgeville Visitors Bureau 34845 Lorain Rd .... North Ridgeville OH 44039 *TF:* 800-334-5910 ■ *Web:* www.nrchamber.com	440-327-3737	327-1474	206
North River Boats Inc 1750 Green Siding Rd .... Roseburg OR 97471 *TF:* 800-413-6351 ■ *Web:* www.northriverboats.com	541-673-2438		698
North Rose-Wolcott Central School District 6188 W Port Bay Rd .... Wolcott NY 14590 *Web:* www.nrwcs.org	315-594-3141	594-2352	685
North Royalton Chamber of Commerce 13737 State Rd .... North Royalton OH 44133 *Web:* www.nroyaltonchamber.com	440-237-6180	237-6181	139
North Sails Group LLC 125 Old Gate Ln .... Milford CT 06460 *Web:* www.northsails.com	203-877-7621		733
North Salem Elementary School 140 Zion Hill Rd .... Salem NH 03079 *Web:* www.sau57.org	603-893-7062		186
North San Antonio Chamber of Commerce 12930 Country Pkwy .... San Antonio TX 78216 *TF:* 877-495-5888 ■ *Web:* www.northsachamber.com	210-344-4848	525-8207	139
North Sanpete School District Inc 390 E 700 S .... Mount Pleasant UT 84647 *Web:* www.nsh.nsanpete.org	435-462-2452	462-3112	685
North Santiam School District 29 J 1155 N Third Ave .... Stayton OR 97383 *Web:* www.nsantiam.k12.or.us	503-769-6924	769-3578	685
North Schuylkill School District 15 Academy Ln .... Ashland PA 17921 *Web:* www.northschuylkill.net	570-874-0466	874-3334	685
North Seattle Community College 9600 College Way N .... Seattle WA 98103 *TF:* 866-427-4747 ■ *Web:* northseattle.edu	206-934-3600		162
North Shore Animal Hospital of Racine Inc 4630 Douglas Ave .... Racine WI 53402 *Web:* northshoreanimalhospital.com	262-639-7500		794
North Shore Bank FSB 15700 W Bluemound Rd .... Brookfield WI 53005 *TF:* 800-236-4672 ■ *Web:* www.northshorebank.com	877-672-2265		70

Name / Address	City	State	ZIP	Phone	Fax	Class
North Shore Center for the Performing Arts in Skokie 9501 N Skokie Blvd *Web:* www.northshorecenter.org	Skokie	IL	60077	847-679-9501		572
North Shore Chamber of Commerce 5 Cherry Hill Dr Ste 100 *Web:* www.northshorechamber.org	Danvers	MA	01923	978-774-8565	774-3418	139
North Shore Circuit Design LLP 2201 N Lamar Blvd Ste 200 *Web:* www.nshore.com	Austin	TX	78705	512-448-1114	448-1415	393
North Shore Communications Group Inc 85 Eastern Ave Ph Ste 107 *Web:* www.northshorecommunications.com	Gloucester	MA	01930	617-967-1227		116
North Shore Community College 1 Ferncroft Rd *Web:* www.northshore.edu	Danvers	MA	01923	978-762-4000		162
North Shore Country Club 1340 Glenview Rd *Web:* www.north-shorecc.org	Glenview	IL	60025	847-729-1200		711
North Shore Country Day School 310 Green Bay Rd *Web:* www.nscds.org	Winnetka	IL	60093	847-446-0674		623
North Shore Elder Services Inc 300 Rosewood Dr Ste 200 *Web:* nselder.org	Danvers	MA	01923	781-715-6608		48-17
North Shore Gas Co 3001 Grand Ave *TF:* 866-556-6004 ■ *Web:* accel.northshoregasdelivery.com	Waukegan	IL	60085	866-556-6004		787
North Shore Laboratories Corp 40 Endicott St *TF:* 800-888-9021 ■ *Web:* www.safetyseal.com	Peabody	MA	01960	978-531-3044	532-3509	60
North Shore Medical Ctr 1100 NW 95th St *TF:* 800-984-3434 ■ *Web:* www.northshoremedical.com	Miami	FL	33150	305-835-6000		374-3
North Shore Medical Ctr 81 Highland Ave *TF:* 877-379-5522 ■ *Web:* northshorephysicians.org	Salem	MA	01970	978-741-1200		374-3
North Shore School District 112 (NSSD) 1936 Green Bay Rd *Web:* www.nssd112.org	Highland Park	IL	60035	224-765-3000		685
North Shore Steel 1566 Miles St *Web:* www.nssco.com	Houston	TX	77015	713-980-5800		492
North Shore Trust & Savings 700 S Lewis Ave *Web:* www.northshoretrust.com	Waukegan	IL	60085	847-336-4430	336-4438	70
North Shore Window Solutions LLC 239 S Main St *Web:* nswsformarvin.com	Middleton	MA	01949	978-762-0007		362
North Side Bank & Trust Co, The 4125 Hamilton Ave *Web:* nsbt.net	Cincinnati	OH	45223	513-542-7800	541-6941	70
North Side Chamber of Commerce 809 Middle St *Web:* www.northsidechamberofcommerce.com	Pittsburgh	PA	15212	412-231-6500		139
North Sky Capital 33 S Sixth St Ste 4646 *Web:* northskycapital.com	Minneapolis	MN	55402	612-435-7150	435-7151	528
North Slope Borough PO Box 69 *TF:* 800-478-0267 ■ *Web:* www.north-slope.org	Barrow	AK	99723	907-852-2611	852-0229	338
North South Supply Inc 686 Third Pl *TF:* 800-940-3810 ■ *Web:* northsouth.net	Vero Beach	FL	32962	772-569-3810	567-3834	610
North Star Agency Inc 3663 Pontchartrain Dr *Web:* www.northstaragency.biz	Slidell	LA	70458	985-643-7977	643-7945	390
North Star Asset Management Inc 59 Racine St Ste A *Web:* northstarinvestments.com	Menasha	WI	54952	920-729-7900		690
North Star Auto Electric Inc 105 Main St *TF:* 800-659-8163 ■ *Web:* www.northstarautoelectric.com	Macedon	NY	14502	315-986-4451	986-9219	62-5
North Star BlueScope Steel LLC 6767 County Rd **Fax Area Code:* 888 ■ *Web:* nsbsl.com	Delta	OH	43515	419-822-2210	822-2113*	492
North Star Combustion Inc 3443 W Mill Rd *Web:* www.northstarcombustion.com	Milwaukee	WI	53209	414-352-2700	352-2702	357
North Star Conditioning 1890 Woodlane Dr *TF:* 800-972-0135 ■ *Web:* www.northstarwater.com	Woodbury	MN	55125	800-972-0135	531-7427	612
North Star Electric Co-op 441 State Hwy 172 NW PO Box 719 *TF:* 888-634-2202 ■ *Web:* northstarelectric.coop	Baudette	MN	56623	218-634-2202	634-2203	245
North Star Glove Co 2916 S Steele St *TF:* 800-423-1616 ■ *Web:* www.northstarglove.com	Tacoma	WA	98409	253-627-7107	627-0597	155-8
North Star Intellectual Properties 1120 Connecticut Ave NW Ste 304 *Web:* nsiplaw.com	Washington	DC	20036	202-429-0020		41
North Star Lighting Inc 2150 Parkes Dr *TF:* 800-229-4330 ■ *Web:* www.northstarlightingsite.com	Broadview	IL	60155	708-681-4330	681-4006	439
North Star Mall 7400 San Pedro Ave *TF:* 800-866-6511 ■ *Web:* www.northstarmall.com	San Antonio	TX	78216	210-340-6627		460
North Star Orthodontics Inc 218 Industrial Park Rd W *TF:* 800-346-0011 ■ *Web:* www.northstardental.com	Park Rapids	MN	56470	218-732-9503	255-9001	228
North Star Propellers Inc 3781 Dalbergia St	San Diego	CA	92113	619-239-8309	239-4610	480
North Star Resource Group Inc 2701 University Ave SE N Star Professional Ctr *TF:* 800-820-4205 ■ *Web:* www.northstarfinancial.com	Minneapolis	MN	55414	612-617-6000		390
North Star Terminal & Stevedore Company LLC 790 Ocean Dock Rd *TF:* 833-318-6737 ■ *Web:* northstarak.com	Anchorage	AK	99501	907-272-7537	272-8927	465
North State Bank Inc 6204 Falls of Neuse Rd *TF:* 877-357-2265 ■ *Web:* www.northstatebank.com	Raleigh	NC	27609	919-787-9696		360-2
North State Communications 111 N Main St *TF:* 866-542-5900 ■ *Web:* northstate.net	High Point	NC	27261	336-886-3600		736
North State Steel Inc 1010 W Gum Rd *Web:* northstatesteel.com	Greenville	NC	27834	252-830-8884	830-9451	480
North States Industries Inc 1507 92nd Ln NE *TF:* 800-848-8421 ■ *Web:* northstatesind.com	Blaine	MN	55449	763-486-1756	486-1763	578
North Sterling State Park 24005 CR 330 *Web:* cpw.state.co.us	Sterling	CO	80751	970-522-3657		565
North Suburban Chamber of Commerce 76-R Winn St Ste 3D *Web:* www.northsuburbanchamber.com	Woburn	MA	01801	781-272-0207		139
North Texas Health Care Laundry Cooperative Assn 1080 Post Paddock *Web:* nthcl.org	Grand Prairie	TX	75050	469-916-1150		426
North Texas Mountain Valley Water Corp 2109 Luna Rd Ste 100 *Web:* waterevent.com	Carrollton	TX	75006	972-488-8100		366
North Texas Telephone Co (NTTC) 519 Main St *Web:* www.northtextel.net	Byers	TX	76357	940-529-6123		225
North Toledo Bend State Park 2907 N Toledo Park Rd *TF:* 888-677-6400 ■ *Web:* crt.state.la.us	Zwolle	LA	71486	318-645-4715		565
North Town Mall 4750 N Division St *Web:* www.northtownmall.com	Spokane	WA	99207	509-482-0209		460
North Valley Bank 9001 N Washington St *TF:* 833-541-1712 ■ *Web:* nvbank.bank	Thornton	CO	80229	303-452-5500		70
North Vancouver Chamber of Commerce 124 W First St Ste 102 *Web:* www.nvchamber.ca	North Vancouver	BC	V7M3N3	604-987-4488	987-8272	137
North Vernon Industry Corp 3750 Fourth St *Web:* www.nvic-cwt.com	North Vernon	IN	47265	812-346-8772	346-9181	596
North Western Electric Co-opeartive Inc 04125 SR-576 PO Box 391 *TF:* 800-647-6932 ■ *Web:* www.nwec.com	Bryan	OH	43506	419-636-5051	636-0194	245
North Wind Inc 1425 Higham St *Web:* northwindgrp.com	Idaho Falls	ID	83402	208-528-8718		192
North Winds Investigations Inc 119 S Second St PO Box 1654 *TF:* 800-530-4514 ■ *Web:* napps.org	Rogers	AR	72756	479-925-1612	878-5989	400
North York General Hospital (NYGH) 4001 Leslie St *Web:* www.nygh.on.ca	North York	ON	M2K1E1	416-756-6000		374-2
North-American Interfraternity Conference (NIC) 865 W Carmel Dr Ste 116 *Web:* nicfraternity.org	Carmel	IN	46032	317-872-1112		48-11
Northampton Community College 3835 Green Pond Rd *TF:* 877-543-0998 ■ *Web:* northampton.edu	Bethlehem	PA	18020	610-861-5300	861-4560	162
Northampton County 669 Washington St *Web:* www.northamptoncounty.org	Easton	PA	18042	610-559-6700		338
Northampton County 16404 Courthouse Rd PO Box 36 *Web:* www.co.northampton.va.us	Eastville	VA	23347	757-678-0465	678-5410	338
Northampton County PO Box 808 *Web:* www.northamptonnc.com	Jackson	NC	27845	252-534-2501	534-1166	338
Northampton County School District 701 N Church St PO Box 158 *Web:* www.northampton.k12.nc.us	Jackson	NC	27845	252-534-1371	534-4631	685
Northborough Free Library 34 Main St *Web:* northboroughlibrary.org	Northborough	MA	01532	508-393-5025	393-5027	434-3
Northbridge Financial Corp 105 Adelaide St W Ste 700 *TF:* 855-620-6262 ■ *Web:* www.nbfc.com	Toronto	ON	M5H1P9	416-350-4400		360-2
Northbrook Chamber of Commerce & Industry 2002 Walters Ave *Web:* northbrookchamber.org	Northbrook	IL	60062	847-498-5555	498-5510	139
Northbrook Court 1515 Lake Cook Rd *Web:* www.northbrookcourt.com	Northbrook	IL	60062	847-498-8161		460
Northbrook Park District 545 Academy Dr *Web:* www.nbparks.org	Northbrook	IL	60062	847-291-2960		31
Northbrook Public Library 1201 Cedar Ln *Web:* www.northbrook.info	Northbrook	IL	60062	847-272-6224	498-0440	434-3
Northcentral Technical College 1000 W Campus Dr *TF:* 888-682-7144 ■ *Web:* www.ntc.edu	Wausau	WI	54401	715-675-3331	675-9776	800
Northco Real Estate Services LLC 5353 Wayzata Blvd Ste 400 *Web:* northco.com	Minneapolis	MN	55416	952-820-1600		652
NorthCoast Asset Management LLC 1 Greenwich Office Pk *TF:* 800-274-5448 ■ *Web:* www.northcoastam.com	Greenwich	CT	06831	203-532-7000		401
Northcoast Behavioral Healthcare System 1756 Sagamore Rd PO Box 678003 **Fax Area Code:* 330 ■ *TF:* 800-557-5512 ■ *Web:* mha.ohio.gov	Northfield	OH	44067	800-557-5512	467-2420*	374-5
Northcountry Federal Credit Union 69 Swift St *TF:* 800-660-3258 ■ *Web:* northcountry.org	South Burlington	VT	05403	800-660-3258		219
Northcrest Medical Ctr 100 Northcrest Dr *Web:* www.northcrest.com	Springfield	TN	37172	615-384-2411		374-3
Northdale Rehabilitation Ctr 3030 W Bearss Ave *Web:* northdalerehab.com	Tampa	FL	33618	813-968-8777	961-5189	450
Northeast Air Solutions Inc 3 Lopez Rd *Web:* air-eng.com	Wilmington	MA	01887	978-988-2000		492
Northeast Airmotive Inc 1011 Westbrook St *TF:* 877-354-7881 ■ *Web:* northeastair.com	Portland	ME	04102	207-774-6318		63
Northeast Alabama Community College PO Box 159 *TF:* 800-548-2546 ■ *Web:* www.nacc.edu	Rainsville	AL	35986	256-228-6001	228-6861	162

Phone | Fax | Class

Northeast Alabama Regional Medical Ctr
400 E Tenth St. Anniston AL 36207 256-235-5121 374-3
Web: www.rmccares.org

Northeast Bancorp 500 Canal St Lewiston ME 04240 207-786-3245 360-2
NASDAQ: NBN ■ *TF:* 800-284-5989 ■ *Web:* www.northeastbank.com

Northeast Bank 77 Broadway St NE Minneapolis MN 55413 612-379-8811 362-3262 70
Web: www.nebankmn.com

Northeast Battery & Alternator Inc
240 Washington St Auburn MA 01501 508-832-2700 832-2706 61
TF: 800-441-8824 ■ *Web:* northeastbattery.com

Northeast Broadcasting Corp
288 S River Rd Bedford NH 03110 603-668-6400 643
Web: www.whiteparkbroadcasting.com

Northeast Building Products Corp
4280 Aramingo Ave Philadelphia PA 19124 215-535-7110 288-9880 234
Web: nbpwindows.com

Northeast Civil Solutions Inc
381 Payne Rd Scarborough ME 04074 207-883-1000 883-1001 727
Web: www.northeastcivilsolutions.com

Northeast Community College
801 E Benjamin Ave PO Box 469 Norfolk NE 68702 402-371-2020 844-7396 162
TF: 800-348-9033 ■ *Web:* www.northeast.edu

Northeast Correctional Complex
5249 Hwy 67 W PO Box 5000 Mountain City TN 37683 423-727-7387 727-5415 213
Web: www.tn.gov

Northeast Correctional Ctr
13698 County Rd 46 Bowling Green MO 63334 573-324-9975 213
Web: www.mo.gov

Northeast Florida Telephone Company Inc
130 N Fourth St Macclenny FL 32063 904-259-2261 387
TF: 800-416-6707 ■ *Web:* www.nefcom.net

Northeast Group Inc, The
129 Morgan Dr Norwood MA 02062 781-352-1400 352-1450 36
Web: www.northeastgroup.com

Northeast Guidance Ctr
2900 Conner Ave Bldg A Detroit MI 48215 313-308-1400 726
TF: 844-202-9932 ■ *Web:* www.neguidance.org

Northeast Illinois Regional Commuter Railroad Corp
547 W Jackson Blvd Chicago IL 60661 312-322-6777 468
Web: www.metrarail.com

Northeast Innovations Inc PO Box 120 Concord NH 03302 603-226-4000 229-0434 735
Web: www.neinnovations.com

Northeast Iowa Community College
Calmar 1625 Hwy 150 S PO Box 400 Calmar IA 52132 563-562-3263 562-4369 162
TF: 800-728-2256 ■ *Web:* www.nicc.edu

Northeast Kingdom Sales Inc PO Box 550 Barton VT 05822 802-525-3997 446
Web: neksales.wordpress.com

Northeast Lakeview College
1201 Kitty Hawk Rd Universal City TX 78148 210-486-5000 165
Web: alamo.edu

Northeast Louisiana Power Co-opeartive Inc
1411 Landis St Winnsboro LA 71295 318-435-4523 435-3887 245
Web: nelpco.coop

Northeast Manufacturing Inc
300 Highpoint Ave Portsmouth RI 02871 401-683-2075 625
Web: www.northeastmanufacturing.com

Northeast Med-Equip 1101 Main St Honesdale PA 18431 570-253-7700 237
Web: www.stephenspharmacy.net

Northeast Metropolitan Regional Vocational School
100 Hemlock Rd Wakefield MA 01880 781-246-0810 246-4919 800
Web: www.northeastmetrotech.com

Northeast Mississippi Community College
101 Cunningham Blvd Booneville MS 38829 662-728-7751 720-7405 162
TF: 800-555-2154 ■ *Web:* www.nemcc.edu

Northeast Missouri Electric Power Co-op
3705 Business 61 PO Box 101 Palmyra MO 63461 573-769-2107 245
Web: www.northeast-power.coop

Northeast Mold & Plastics
137 National Dr Glastonbury CT 06033 860-633-7099 596
Web: www.nemold.com

Northeast Nebraska Telephone Co (NNTC)
110 E Elk St Jackson NE 68743 888-397-4321 632-4770* 224
**Fax Area Code:* 402 ■ *TF:* 888-397-4321 ■ *Web:* www.nntc.net

Northeast Ohio Medical University
4209 St Rt 44 PO Box 95 Rootstown OH 44272 800-686-2511 167-2
TF: 800-686-2511 ■ *Web:* www.neomed.edu

Northeast Oklahoma Electric Co-opeartive Inc
27039 S 4440 Rd Vinita OK 74301 918-256-6405 256-9380 245
TF: 800-256-6405 ■ *Web:* www.neelectric.com

Northeast Organic Farming Association of Connecticut
126 Derby Ave Derby CT 06418 203-308-2584 49-19
Web: www.ctnofa.org

Northeast Pharmacy Service Corp
1661 Worcester Rd Ste 405 Framingham MA 01701 508-875-1866 237
Web: northeastpharmacy.com

Northeast Planning Associates Inc
43 Constitution Dr Bedford NH 03110 603-471-0900 390
Web: jonpharrison.com

Northeast Plastics Inc
5 Del Carmine St Wakefield MA 01880 781-245-5512 604
Web: www.neplastics.com

Northeast Rehabilitation Hospital
70 Butler St. Salem NH 03079 603-893-2900 374-6
TF: 888-950-9939 ■ *Web:* www.northeastrehab.com

Northeast Remsco Construction Inc
1333 Campus Pkwy Wall Township NJ 07753 732-557-6100 736-8900 188-7
TF: 800-879-8204 ■ *Web:* www.northeastremsco.com

Northeast Safe-T Solutions Inc
3 Commercial Ln Unit A Londonderry NH 03053 603-434-7009 290
Web: neflooringsolutions.com

Northeast Sales Distributing Inc
840 Ronald Wood Rd Winder GA 30680 678-963-7700 81-3
Web: nesdi.com

Northeast Software Services Inc
70 Princeton St North Chelmsford MA 01863 978-251-2800 251-2528 174
Web: www.nesw.com

Northeast State Technical Community College
PO Box 246 Blountville TN 37617 423-323-3191 323-0217 800
TF: 800-836-7822 ■ *Web:* www.northeaststate.edu

Northeast Tarrant Chamber of Commerce
5001 Denton Hwy Haltom City TX 76117 817-281-9376 281-9379 139
Web: www.netarrant.org

Northeast Technical Institute
51 US Route 1 Ste K Scarborough ME 04074 207-883-5130 883-6048 167-3
TF: 800-447-1151 ■ *Web:* www.ntinow.edu

Northeast Technology Center - Afton Oklahoma
19901 South Hwy 69 Afton OK 74331 918-257-8324 257-4342 167-3
Web: www.netech.edu

Northeast Texas Community College
1735 Chapel Hill Rd Mount Pleasant TX 75455 903-572-1911 572-6712 162
TF: 800-870-0142 ■ *Web:* www.ntcc.edu

Northeast Times
2 Executive Campus Ste 400 Cherry Hill NJ 08002 215-354-3000 288-7433* 532-4
**Fax Area Code:* 856 ■ *Web:* www.northeasttimes.com

Northeast Towers 199 Brickyard Rd Farmington CT 06032 860-677-1999 480
Web: northeasttowers.com

Northeast Underwater Research, Technology & Education Ctr (NURTEC)
University of Connecticut at Avery Pt 1080 Shennecossett Rd
Groton CT 06340 860-405-9121 668
Web: www.nurtec.uconn.edu

Northeast Valley Health Corp
1172 N Maclay Ave San Fernando CA 91340 818-898-1388 365-4031 374-3
TF: 800-313-4942 ■ *Web:* nevhc.org

Northeast Veterans Business Resource Ctr
PO Box 52113 Boston MA 02205 617-938-3933 463
Web: www.nevbrc.org

Northeast Veterinary Referral & Emergency Hospital
242 S River St Plains PA 18705 570-208-8844 794
Web: northeast-vet.com

Northeast Water Solutions Inc
567 S County Trail Ste 116 Exeter RI 02822 401-667-7463 261
Web: nwsi.net

Northeast Wisconsin Technical College
PO Box 19042 Green Bay WI 54307 920-498-5400 800
TF: 800-422-6982 ■ *Web:* www.nwtc.edu

Northeast Wyoming Board of Cooperative Educational Services Boces
410 N Miller Ave Gillette WY 82716 307-682-0231 605
Web: www.newboces.com

Northeastern Connecticut Chamber of Commerce
210 Westcott Rd Danielson CT 06239 860-774-8001 774-4299 139
Web: nectchamber.com

Northeastern Illinois University
5500 N St Louis Ave Chicago IL 60625 773-442-4540 442-4020 166
Web: www.neiu.edu

Northeastern Junior College
100 College Ave Sterling CO 80751 970-521-6600 522-4664 162
TF: 800-626-4637 ■ *Web:* www.njc.edu

Northeastern Log Homes Inc
10 Ames Rd Kenduskeag ME 04450 207-884-7000 884-3000 106
TF: 800-624-2797 ■ *Web:* www.northeasternlog.com

Northeastern Nevada Museum 1515 Idaho St Elko NV 89801 775-738-3418 520
Web: www.museumelko.org

Northeastern Oklahoma A & M College
200 I St NE Miami OK 74354 918-542-8441 162
Web: www.neo.edu

Northeastern PA Carton & Finishing Company Inc
4820 Birney Ave US Rt 11 Moosic PA 18507 570-457-7711 554
Web: www.nepacartons.com

Northeastern Pennsylvania Philharmonic
4101 Birney Ave Moosic PA 18507 570-341-1568 573-3
Web: nepaphil.org

North-Eastern Pennsylvania Telephone Co (NEP)
720 Main St Forest City PA 18421 570-785-3131 785-9299 224
TF: 866-785-3131 ■ *Web:* www.nep.net

Northeastern REMC
4901 E Pk 30 Dr Columbia City IN 46725 260-244-6111 625-3407 245
Web: www.nremc.com

Northeastern Seminary at Roberts Wesleyan College
2265 Westside Dr Rochester NY 14624 585-594-6800 166
Web: www.nes.edu

Northeastern State University
Broken Arrow 3100 E New Orleans Broken Arrow OK 74014 918-449-6000 449-6190 166
Web: www.nsuba.edu
John Vaughan Library
711 N Grand Ave Tahlequah OK 74464 918-444-3278 458-2197 434-6
Web: library.nsuok.edu
Muskogee 2400 W Shawnee Muskogee OK 74401 918-683-0040 458-2106 166
TF: 800-722-9614 ■ *Web:* www.nsuok.edu

Northeastern Supply Inc
8323 Pulaski Hwy Baltimore MD 21237 410-574-0010 574-3315 612
TF: 877-637-8775 ■ *Web:* northeastern.com

Northeastern Technical College
1201 Chesterfield Hwy Cheraw SC 29520 843-921-6900 537-6148 162
TF: 800-921-7399 ■ *Web:* www.netc.edu

Northeastern University
360 Huntington Ave Boston MA 02115 617-373-5992 373-8780 166
TF: 855-476-3391 ■ *Web:* www.northeastern.edu

Northeastern Water Jet Inc
4 Willow St Amsterdam NY 12010 518-843-4988 843-2399 493
TF: 888-444-7648 ■ *Web:* www.newj.com

Northeastern Wisconsin Zoo
4378 Reforestation Rd Green Bay WI 54313 920-434-7841 823
Web: newzoo.org

Northeast-Midwest Institute (NMI)
50 F St NW Ste 950 Washington DC 20001 202-544-5200 634
Web: www.nemw.org

Northeern Kentucky Convention Ctr
1 W River Center Blvd Covington KY 41011 859-261-1500 232
Web: www.nkycc.com

Northern 3625 Cincinnati Ave Rocklin CA 95765 916-543-4000 246
TF: 855-388-7422 ■ *Web:* www.northernvideo.com

Northern Alberta Institute of Technology
11762 106 St NW Edmonton AB T5G2R1 780-471-6248 507
TF: 877-333-6248 ■ *Web:* www.nait.ca

Northern Arizona Regional Behavioral Health Authority Inc (NARBHA)
1300 S Yale St Flagstaff AZ 86001 928-774-7128 49-15
TF: 877-923-1400 ■ *Web:* www.narbha.org

Name / Address	City	State	ZIP	Phone	Fax	Class
Northern Arizona University PO Box 4084 *TF:* 888-628-2968 ■ *Web:* nau.edu	Flagstaff	AZ	86011	928-523-5511	523-6023	166
Northern Arizona VA Health Care System 500 Hwy 89 N *TF:* 800-949-1005 ■ *Web:* www.prescott.va.gov	Prescott	AZ	86301	928-445-4860		374-8
Northern Burlington County School District 160 Mansfield Rd E *Web:* www.nburlington.com	Columbus	NJ	08022	609-298-3900		685
Northern Business Products Inc 2326 W Superior St *TF:* 800-647-8775 ■ *Web:* www.ecinteractiveplus.com	Duluth	MN	55816	218-726-0167	726-1023	535
Northern California Carpenters Regional Council (NCCRC) 2102 Almaden Rd Ste 125 *Web:* www.nccrc.org	San Jose	CA	95125	408-445-3000	445-5868	474
Northern California Community Blood Bank 2524 Harrison Ave *Web:* www.nccbb.org	Eureka	CA	95501	707-443-8004	443-8007	89
Northern California Grantmakers (NCG) 160 Spear St Ste 360 *TF:* 877-624-2755 ■ *Web:* www.ncg.org	San Francisco	CA	94105	415-777-4111	777-1714	48-13
Northern California Laborers Apprenticeship Program 1001 Westside Dr *Web:* www.norcalaborers.org	San Ramon	CA	94583	925-828-2513		414
Northern California National Bank 1717 Mangrove Ave *Web:* norcalbank.com	Chico	CA	95926	530-879-5900		70
Northern California World Trade Ctr 1 Capitol Mall Ste 700 *TF:* 855-667-2259 ■ *Web:* www.norcalwtc.org	Sacramento	CA	95814	916-447-9827		822
Northern Chemical Co 6110 NW Grand Ave *TF:* 800-279-1477 ■ *Web:* www.northernchemical.com	Glendale	AZ	85301	623-937-1668		76
Northern Colorado Credit Union 2901 S 27th Ave *Web:* nococu.org	Greeley	CO	80631	970-330-3900		219
Northern Concrete Pipe Inc 401 Kelton St *Web:* www.ncp-inc.com	Bay City	MI	48706	989-892-3545		183
Northern Contours Inc 1355 Mendota Heights Rd Ste 100 *TF:* 866-344-8132 ■ *Web:* www.northerncontours.com	Mendota Heights	MN	55120	651-695-1698	695-1714	115
Northern Correctional Institution 287 Bilton Rd *Web:* portal.ct.gov	Somers	CT	06071	860-763-8600		213
Northern Data Systems Inc 362 US Rt One PO Box 66738 *TF:* 800-649-7754 ■ *Web:* www.ndsys.com	Falmouth	ME	04105	207-781-3236	781-3226	180
Northern Digital 4701 Corporate Ct *Web:* ndi.us	Bakersfield	CA	93311	661-322-6044		261
Northern Digital Inc 103 Randall Dr *TF:* 877-634-6340 ■ *Web:* www.ndigital.com	Waterloo	ON	N2V1C5	519-884-5142		407
Northern Eagle Beverage Co 600 16th St *Web:* northerneaglebeverage.com	Carlstadt	NJ	07072	201-531-7100	531-7145	297-8
Northern Electric Co-opeartive Inc 39456 133nd St *TF:* 800-529-0310 ■ *Web:* www.northernelectric.coop	Bath	SD	57427	605-225-0310	225-1684	245
Northern Engraving Corp 803 S Black River St *Web:* www.norcorp.com	Sparta	WI	54656	608-269-6911	366-3725	481
Northern Essex Community College 100 Elliott St *Web:* www.necc.mass.edu	Haverhill	MA	01830	978-556-3000	556-3729	162
Northern Exposure Greeting Cards 2194 Northpoint Pkwy *TF:* 800-237-3524 ■ *Web:* www.necards.com	Santa Rosa	CA	95407	800-237-3524		130
Northern Extrusion Tooling 905 W 19th St *Web:* www.northernextrusiontooling.com	Yankton	SD	57078	605-665-3603		456
Northern Factory Sales Inc PO Box 660 *TF:* 800-328-8900 ■ *Web:* www.northernradiator.com	Willmar	MN	56201	320-235-2288		61
Northern Fruit Co 220 Second St NE *Web:* www.northernfruit.com	East Wenatchee	WA	98802	509-884-6651	884-1990	11-1
Northern Gulf Trading Group 164 St Francis St Ste 205 *Web:* www.ngtg.net	Mobile	AL	36602	251-432-0757		539
Northern Hearing Services 111 S 13th Ave *Web:* www.northernhearingservices.net	Alpena	MI	49707	989-354-4289	340-2446	352
Northern Highland - American Legion State Forest 4125 County Hwy M *Web:* dnr.wi.gov	Boulder Junction	WI	54512	715-385-2727	385-2752	565
Northern Hospital of Surry County 830 Rockford St *Web:* www.northernhospital.com	Mount Airy	NC	27030	336-719-7000		374-3
Northern Illinois University 1425 W Lincoln Hwy *TF:* 800-892-3050 ■ *Web:* www.niu.edu	DeKalb	IL	60115	815-753-1000	753-8312	166
Northern Illinois University Press 2280 Bethany Rd *Web:* www.niupress.niu.edu	DeKalb	IL	60115	815-753-1075	753-1845	637-2
Northern Improvement Co 4000 12th Ave NW *Web:* www.northernimprovement.com	Fargo	ND	58108	701-277-1225	277-1516	188-4
Northern Indiana Commuter Transportation District 33 E US Hwy 12 *Web:* www.mysouthshoreline.com	Chesterton	IN	46304	219-926-5744	929-4438	468
Northern Industrial Sales Ltd 3526 Opie Cres *TF:* 800-668-3317 ■ *Web:* www.northernindustrialsales.ca	Prince George	BC	V2N2P9	250-562-4435		386
Northern Institute of Cosmetology 669 Broadway *Web:* www.nicosmetology.com	Lorain	OH	44052	440-244-4282	244-2049	167-3
Northern Institutional Funds 801 S Canal St C5S **Fax Area Code:* 312 ■ *TF:* 800-637-1380 ■ *Web:* www.northerntrust.com	Chicago	IL	60607	800-637-1380	557-0411*	528
Northern Inyo Hospital 150 Pioneer Ln *Web:* www.nih.org	Bishop	CA	93514	760-873-5811	873-6734	374-3
Northern Iron & Machine 867 Forest St *Web:* www.northernim.com	Saint Paul	MN	55106	651-778-3300	778-1321	307
Northern Jet Management 5500 44th St SE *TF:* 800-462-7709 ■ *Web:* northernjet.net	Grand Rapids	MI	49512	616-336-4800		23
Northern Kane County Chamber of Commerce 20 S Grove St Ste 101 *Web:* www.nkcchamber.com	Carpentersville	IL	60110	847-426-8565		139
Northern Kentucky Chamber of Commerce 300 Buttermilk Pk Ste 330 *Web:* www.nkychamber.com	Fort Mitchell	KY	41017	859-578-8800	578-8802	139
Northern Kentucky Childrens Law Center Inc 1002 Russell St *Web:* childrenslawky.org	Covington	KY	41011	859-431-3313		41
Northern Kentucky Convention & Visitors Bureau (NKYCVB) 50 E RiverCenter Blvd Ste 200 *TF:* 877-659-8474 ■ *Web:* www.meetnky.com	Covington	KY	41011	859-261-4677	261-5135	206
Northern Kentucky Educators Federal Credit Union 2805 Alexandria Way *Web:* nkefcu.org	Highland Heights	KY	41076	859-441-3405	442-1204	219
Northern Kentucky University 617 Lucas Administration Ctr, Nunn Dr *TF:* 800-637-9948 ■ *Web:* www.nku.edu	Highland Heights	KY	41099	859-572-5220	572-6665	166
Northern Kentucky Water District 2835 Crescent Springs Rd *TF:* 800-772-4636 ■ *Web:* www.nkywater.org	Erlanger	KY	41018	859-578-9898	578-5456	787
Northern Lakes College Library Bag 3000 *TF:* 866-652-3456 ■ *Web:* www.northernlakescollege.libguides.com	Grouard	AB	T0G1C0	780-849-8670		434-3
Northern Lakes Cooperative Inc 15877 US Hwy 63 S *Web:* nlcoop.com	Hayward	WI	54843	715-634-3211		345
Northern Lakes Vet Supply LLC 413 S Fourth St PO Box 366 *Web:* northernlakesvet.com	Abbotsford	WI	54405	715-223-4700		794
Northern Leasing Systems Inc 419 E Main St Ste 102 **Fax Area Code:* 800 ■ *TF:* 866-781-0440 ■ *Web:* www.northernleasing.com	Middletown	NY	10940	866-781-0440	342-7172*	216
Northern Lights College 11401 - Eigth St *Web:* www.nlc.bc.ca	Dawson Creek	BC	V1G4G2	250-782-5251		166
Northern Lights Credit Union 218 Dells Rd *Web:* northernlightscu.com	Littleton	NH	03561	603-444-9964		219
Northern Lights Enterprises Inc 3474 Andover Rd *TF:* 800-836-8797 ■ *Web:* northernlightscandles.com	Wellsville	NY	14895	585-593-1200		364
Northern Lights Inc 4420 14th Ave NW *TF:* 800-762-0165 ■ *Web:* www.northern-lights.com	Seattle	WA	98107	206-789-3880	782-5455	262
Northern Lights Inc 421 Cherry St PO Box 269 **Fax Area Code:* 866 ■ *TF:* 800-326-9594 ■ *Web:* www.nli.coop	Sagle	ID	83860	208-263-5141	665-4837*	245
Northern Local School District 8700 Sheridan Dr *Web:* www.nlsd.k12.oh.us	Thornville	OH	43076	740-743-1303	743-3301	685
Northern Louisiana Medical Ctr 401 E Vaughn St *Web:* www.northernlouisianamedicalcenter.com	Ruston	LA	71270	318-254-2100		374-3
Northern Machine Tool Co (NMT) 761 Alberta Ave *Web:* www.nmtdie.com	Muskegon	MI	49441	231-755-1603	759-7917	757
Northern Maine Community College (NMCC) 33 Edgemont Dr *TF:* 800-535-6682 ■ *Web:* www.nmcc.edu	Presque Isle	ME	04769	207-768-2700	768-2848	800
Northern Management Services Inc 607 Church St *Web:* www.nmsinc.com	Sandpoint	ID	83864	208-263-1363		194
Northern Manufacturing Company Inc 150 N Lake Winds Pkwy *Web:* www.northernmfg.com	Oak Harbor	OH	43449	419-898-2821	898-4470	697
Northern Metal Fab Inc 510 Vandeberg St *Web:* www.nmfinc.com	Baldwin	WI	54002	715-684-3535	684-3639	492
Northern Metal Recycling LLC 2800 Pacific St N *Web:* www.northernmetalrecycling.com	Minneapolis	MN	55411	612-529-9221		686
Northern Michigan Review Inc 319 State St *Web:* www.petoskeynews.com	Petoskey	MI	49770	231-347-2544		532-3
Northern Michigan University 1401 Presque Isle Ave *TF:* 800-682-9797 ■ *Web:* www.nmu.edu	Marquette	MI	49855	906-227-2650	227-1747	166
Northern Natural Gas Co 1111 S 103rd St *TF:* 877-654-0646 ■ *Web:* www.northernnaturalgas.com	Omaha	NE	68124	402-398-7000	398-7006	325
Northern Neck Electric Co-opeartive Inc 85 St Johns St PO Box 288 *TF:* 800-243-2860 ■ *Web:* www.nnec.coop	Warsaw	VA	22572	804-333-3621		245
Northern Nevada Correctional Ctr 1721 Snyder Dr PO Box 7000 *Web:* doc.nv.gov	Carson City	NV	89702	775-887-9297		213
Northern Nevada Medical Ctr 2375 E Prater Way *Web:* www.nnmc.com	Sparks	NV	89434	775-331-7000		374-3
Northern New Hampshire Correctional Facility 138 E Milan Rd *Web:* www.nh.gov	Berlin	NH	03570	603-752-2906	752-0405	213
Northern New Mexico College 921 Paseo de Onate *Web:* nnmc.edu	Espanola	NM	87532	505-747-2100	747-5449	162
Northern New York Library Network 6721 US Hwy 11 *TF:* 877-833-1674 ■ *Web:* nnyln.org	Potsdam	NY	13676	315-265-1119		434-3
Northern News 8 Duncan Ave *Web:* www.northernnews.ca	Kirkland Lake	ON	P2N3L4	705-567-5321		532-1

Company	Address	City	State	ZIP	Phone	Fax	Class	Details
Northern Oak Capital Management Inc	555 E Wells St Ste 1625	Milwaukee	WI	53202	414-278-0590		194	*Web:* northern-oak.com
Northern Ohio Lumber & Timber Co, The	2850 W 3rd St	Cleveland	OH	44113	216-771-4080	771-4793	191-3	*Web:* www.noltco.com
Northern Ohio Printing Inc	4721 Hinckley Indus Pkwy	Cleveland	OH	44109	216-398-0000		627	*TF:* 800-407-7284 ■ *Web:* www.nohioprint.com
Northern Oil & Gas Inc	315 Manitoba Ave Ste 200	Wayzata	MN	55391	952-476-9800	476-9801	538	*NYSE: NOG* ■ *Web:* www.northernoil.com
Northern Oklahoma College	1220 E Grand St PO Box 310	Tonkawa	OK	74653	580-628-6200	628-6371	162	*TF:* 800-522-0188 ■ *Web:* www.noc.edu
Northern Pines on Crescent Lake Bed & Breakfast Plus	31 Big Pine Rd	Raymond	ME	04071	207-655-7624		706	*Web:* www.norpines.com
Northern Pipe Products Inc	1302 39th St N	Fargo	ND	58102	701-282-7655		601	*Web:* www.northernpipe.com
Northern Plains Electric Co-op	1515 W Main St	Carrington	ND	58421	800-882-2500		245	*TF:* 800-882-2500 ■ *Web:* www.nplains.com
Northern Prairie Polymers LLC	20015 176th St	Big Lake	MN	55309	763-262-3456	559-2411	676	*Web:* www.imr-inc.com
Northern Prairie Wildlife Research Ctr	8711 37th St SE	Jamestown	ND	58401	701-253-5500	253-5553	668	*Web:* www.npwrc.usgs.gov
Northern Precision Plastics Inc	6553 Revlon Dr	Belvidere	IL	61008	815-544-8099	544-6313	604	*Web:* www.northernprecisionplastics.com
Northern Precision Products Inc	4790 N Mackinaw Trl	Leroy	MI	49655	231-768-4435	768-4243	454	*Web:* www.northernprecisionproducts.com
Northern Pride Communications Inc	20 Ctr Park Rd	Topsham	ME	04086	207-798-5540		480	*Web:* northernpridecommunications.com
Northern Pride Inc	401 Conley Ave S	Thief River Falls	MN	56701	218-681-1201	681-7183	619	*Web:* www.northernprideinc.com
Northern Pulp Nova Scotia Corp	PO Box 549	New Glasgow	NS	B2H5C6	902-752-8461		638	*Web:* www.paperexcellence.com
Northern Quest Resort & Casino	100 N Hayford Rd	Airway Heights	WA	99001	877-871-6772		133	*TF:* 877-871-6772 ■ *Web:* www.northernquest.com
Northern Research Station	11 Campus Blvd Ste 200	Newtown Square	PA	19073	610-557-4017	557-4095	668	*Web:* www.fs.usda.gov
Northern Response International Ltd	50 Staples Ave Richmond Hill	Toronto	ON	L4B0A7	905-737-6698		195	*TF:* 866-584-1694 ■ *Web:* www.northernresponse.com
Northern Rhode Island Chamber of Commerce	6 Blackstone Vly Pl Ste 402 Second Fl	Lincoln	RI	02865	401-334-1000	334-1009	139	*Web:* www.nrichamber.com
Northern Rio Arriba Electric Co-op	1135 Camino Escondido PO Box 217	Chama	NM	87520	575-756-2181		245	*Web:* www.noraelectric.org
Northern Rockies Lodge	Mile 462 Alaska Hwy	Muncho Lake	BC	V0C1Z0	250-776-3481		707	*TF:* 800-663-5269 ■ *Web:* www.northernrockieslodge.com
Northern Screw Machine Company Inc	300 Atwater St	Saint Paul	MN	55117	651-488-2568		621	*Web:* northernscrew.homestead.com
Northern Seminary	660 E Butterfield Rd	Lombard	IL	60148	630-620-2180	620-2190	167-3	*Web:* www.seminary.edu
Northern Skies Federal Credit Union	1001 E Benson Blvd	Anchorage	AK	99508	907-561-1407		219	*Web:* northernskiesfcu.org
Northern Stamping Corp	6600 Chapek Pkwy	Cleveland	OH	44125	216-883-8888		488	*Web:* northernstamping.com
Northern Star Broadcasting LLC	3250 Racquet Club Dr	Traverse City	MI	49684	231-922-4981		643	*Web:* www.nsbroadcasting.com
Northern State Correctional Facility	2559 Glen Rd	Newport	VT	05855	802-334-3364	334-3367	213	*Web:* www.vermont.gov
Northern State University	1200 S Jay St	Aberdeen	SD	57401	800-678-5330	626-2587*	166	**Fax Area Code:* 605 ■ *TF:* 800-678-5330 ■ *Web:* www.northern.edu
Northern States Financial Corp	1601 N Lewis Ave	Waukegan	IL	60085	847-775-8200		360-2	*OTC: NSFC* ■ *TF:* 800-339-4432 ■ *Web:* www.norstatesbank.com
Northern States Metals Co	3207 Innovation Pl	Youngstown	OH	44509	800-689-0666		361	*TF:* 800-689-0666 ■ *Web:* extrusions.com
Northern States Power St Paul	825 Rice St	Saint Paul	MN	55117	651-229-2221		219	*Web:* mynspcu.org
Northern Sun	2916 E Lake St	Minneapolis	MN	55406	800-258-8579		328	*TF:* 800-258-8579 ■ *Web:* www.northernsun.com
Northern Technologies International Corp (NTIC)	4201 Woodland Rd PO Box 69	Circle Pines	MN	55014	763-225-6600	225-6645	145	*NASDAQ: NTIC* ■ *TF:* 800-328-2433 ■ *Web:* www.ntic.com
Northern Telephone and Data (NTD)	300 N Koeller St	Oshkosh	WI	54902	920-426-9192		224	*Web:* www.ntd.net
Northern Telephone Co	13448 County Rd 25	Wawina	MN	55736	218-488-6565	488-6509	224	*Web:* www.northerntelephone.net
Northern Tier Career Ctr	120 Career Center Ln	Towanda	PA	18848	570-265-8111	265-3002	167-3	*Web:* www.ntccschool.org
Northern Tool & Equipment Co	2800 Southcross Dr W	Burnsville	MN	55306	952-894-9510	894-1020	364	*TF:* 800-222-5381 ■ *Web:* www.northerntool.com
Northern Valley Federal Credit Union	3030 Demers Ave	Grand Forks	ND	58201	701-772-7922	772-5076	219	*TF:* 800-901-2628 ■ *Web:* northernvalleyfcu.com
Northern Virginia Community College	*Alexandria* 5000 Dawes Ave	Alexandria	VA	22311	703-845-6200	845-6046	162	*TF:* 855-259-1019 ■ *Web:* www.nvcc.edu
Northern Virginia Electric Co-op	PO Box 2710	Manassas	VA	20108	703-335-0500		245	*TF:* 888-335-0500 ■ *Web:* www.novec.com
Northern Virginia Regional Park Authority	5400 Ox Rd	Fairfax Station	VA	22039	703-352-5900		565	*Web:* www.novaparks.com
Northern Wasco County People's Utility District	2345 River Rd	The Dalles	OR	97058	541-296-2226		245	*Web:* www.nwascopud.org
Northern Watch	324 Main Ave N	Thief River Falls	MN	56701	218-681-4450	681-4455	532-4	*Web:* trftimes.com
Northern Waters Library Service	3200 E Lakeshore Dr	Ashland	WI	54806	715-682-2365		434-3	*TF:* 800-228-5684 ■ *Web:* www.nwls.lib.wi.us
Northern Westchester Hospital	400 E Main St	Mount Kisco	NY	10549	914-666-1200		374-3	*TF:* 877-469-4362 ■ *Web:* nwhc.net
Northern Wholesale Supply Inc	6800 Otter Lake Rd Ste 2	Lino Lakes	MN	55038	651-429-1515	429-5757	711	*Web:* shop.northernwholesale.com
Northfield an Oldcastle Co	N59 W14909 Bobolink Ave	Menomonee Falls	WI	53051	262-338-5700		183	*Web:* www.northfieldblock.com
Northfield Lines Inc	1034 Gemini Rd	Eagan	MN	55121	651-203-8888	242-5660	107	*TF:* 888-670-8068 ■ *Web:* northfieldlines.com
Northfield Mount Hermon School	1 Lamplighter Way	Gill	MA	01354	413-498-3227	498-3152	622	*TF:* 866-664-4483 ■ *Web:* www.nmhschool.org
Northfield Park Racetrack	10705 Northfield Rd PO Box 374	Northfield	OH	44067	330-467-4101		642	*Web:* mgmnorthfieldpark.mgmresorts.com
Northfield Retirement Community	900 Cannon Vly Dr	Northfield	MN	55057	507-645-9511	664-3490	48-20	*Web:* www.northfieldretirement.org
Northfield Savings Bank (NSB)	PO Box 7180	Barre	VT	05641	800-672-2274		70	*TF:* 800-672-2274 ■ *Web:* www.nsbvt.com
Northfork Electric Co-op	301 E Main PO Box 400	Sayre	OK	73662	580-928-3366	928-3105	245	*Web:* www.nfecoop.com
Northgate Gonzalez Market	1201 N Magnolia Ave	Anaheim	CA	92801	714-778-3784	778-3295	345	*Web:* www.northgatemarket.com
Northgate Mall	9501 Colerain Ave	Cincinnati	OH	45251	513-385-7065		460	*Web:* www.mynorthgatemall.com
Northlake Engineering Inc	8320 193rd Ave	Bristol	WI	53104	262-857-9600	857-6819	767	*Web:* standexelectronics.com
Northlake Shipyard Inc	1441 N Northlake Way	Seattle	WA	98103	206-632-1441	632-8628	698	*Web:* www.northlakeshipyard.com
Northland Auto & Truck Accessories	1106 S 29th St W	Billings	MT	59102	406-245-0595		54	*TF:* 800-736-5302 ■ *Web:* northlandautomotive.com
Northland Career Ctr	1801 Branch St	Platte City	MO	64079	816-858-5505	858-3278	167-3	*Web:* www.northlandcareercenter.com
Northland Chevrolet	1420 Ogden Ave	Superior	WI	54880	877-247-7097		57	*TF:* 877-247-7097 ■ *Web:* www.northlandchevrolet.com
Northland College	1411 Ellis Ave	Ashland	WI	54806	715-682-1224		166	*TF:* 800-753-1840 ■ *Web:* www.northland.edu
Northland Community & Technical College	1101 US Hwy 1 E	Thief River Falls	MN	56701	218-681-0701	681-0774	162	*TF:* 800-959-6282 ■ *Web:* www.northlandcollege.edu
Northland Community Credit Union	6604 N Oak Trafficway	Gladstone	MO	64118	816-452-8375		219	*Web:* northlandccu.org
Northland CPAS SC	1634 N Stevens St	Rhinelander	WI	54501	715-362-2222		2	*Web:* northlandcpas.com
Northland Fishing Tackle LLC	1001 Naylor Dr SE	Bemidji	MN	56601	218-751-6723		711	*Web:* www.northlandtackle.com
Northland Furniture Co	681 SE Glenwood	Bend	OR	97702	800-497-7591		321	*TF:* 800-497-7591 ■ *Web:* www.northlandfurniture.com
Northland Insurance Co	385 Washington St	Saint Paul	MN	55102	800-237-9334	310-4949*	391-4	**Fax Area Code:* 651 ■ *TF:* 800-237-9334 ■ *Web:* www.northlandins.com
Northland Machine Inc	35234 US Hwy 2	Grand Rapids	MN	55744	218-328-6479		757	*Web:* www.northlandmachine.com
Northland Motor Technologies	2268 Fairview Blvd	Fairview	TN	37062	800-793-4793	799-3199*	518	**Fax Area Code:* 615 ■ *TF:* 800-793-4793 ■ *Web:* www.sfeg.com
Northland Pioneer College	PO Box 610	Holbrook	AZ	86025	928-532-6111		162	*TF:* 800-266-7845 ■ *Web:* www.npc.edu
Northland Plastics Inc	1420 S 16th St PO Box 290	Sheboygan	WI	53081	800-776-7163	458-4881*	600	**Fax Area Code:* 920 ■ *TF:* 800-776-7163 ■ *Web:* www.northlandplastics.com
Northland Press	PO Box 145	Outing	MN	56662	218-792-5842	792-5844	532-2	*Web:* www.northlandpress.com
Northland Process Piping Inc	1662 320th Ave	Isle	MN	56342	320-679-2119		595	*Web:* www.nppmn.com
Northland Products Co	1000 Rainbow Dr	Waterloo	IA	50701	319-234-5585		541	
Northland Properties Corp	310 1755 W Broadway	Vancouver	BC	V6J1Y2	604-730-6610	730-4645	379	*TF:* 866-378-8866 ■ *Web:* northland.ca

Name / Address	Phone	Fax	Class
Northland Public Library 300 Cumberland Rd ... Pittsburgh PA 15237 *Web:* www.northlandlibrary.org	412-366-8100		434-3
Northland Regional Chamber of Commerce 634 NW Englewood Rd ... Kansas City MO 64118 *Web:* www.northlandchamber.com	816-455-9911	455-9933	139
Northland Securities Inc 150 S Fifth St Ste 3300 ... Minneapolis MN 55402 *TF:* 800-851-2920 ■ *Web:* www.northlandsecurities.com	612-851-5900		401
Northland Telecommunications Corp 101 Stewart St Ste 700 ... Seattle WA 98101 *Web:* www.yournorthland.com	206-621-1351		116
Northland Trucking Inc 1515 S 22nd Ave ... Phoenix AZ 85009 *TF:* 800-214-5564 ■ *Web:* www.northlandtrucking.com	602-254-0007	254-0455	780
Northleaf Capital Partners 79 Wellington St W 6th Fl PO Box 120 ... Toronto ON M5K1N9 *TF:* 866-964-4141 ■ *Web:* www.northleafcapital.com	866-964-4141		792
Northlich 720 E Pete Rose Way ... Cincinnati OH 45202 *Web:* www.northlich.com	513-421-8840		4
Northlight Theatre 9501 Skokie Blvd ... Skokie IL 60077 *Web:* northlight.org	847-673-6300	679-1879	749
NorthMarq Capital Inc 3500 W American Blvd Ste 500 ... Bloomington MN 55431 *Web:* www.northmarq.com	952-356-0100	356-0097	655
Northmont Area Chamber of Commerce 9 W National Rd PO Box 62 ... Englewood OH 45322 *Web:* www.northmontchamber.com	937-836-2550	836-2485	139
NorthPark Ctr 8687 N Central Expy ... Dallas TX 75225 *Web:* www.northparkcenter.com	214-744-6664		460
Northpoint Mall 1000 N Pt Cir ... Alpharetta GA 30022 *Web:* www.northpointmall.com	770-740-9273		460
Northridge Chamber of Commerce 18860 Nordhoff St Ste 204B ... Northridge CA 91324 *Web:* northridgechamber.org	818-349-5676		139
Northridge Community Credit Union 283 Kennedy Memorial Dr PO Box 200 ... Hoyt Lakes MN 55750 *TF:* 877-672-2848 ■ *Web:* nrccu.org	218-471-2121	225-3308	219
Northridge Fashion Ctr 9301 Tampa Ave ... Northridge CA 91324 *Web:* www.northridgefashioncenter.com	818-885-9700		460
Northridge Mall 796 Northridge Mall ... Salinas CA 93906 *Web:* www.shop-northridge-mall.com	831-449-7226		460
Northrim BanCorp Inc 3111 C St ... Anchorage AK 99503 *NASDAQ: NRIM* ■ *TF:* 800-478-3311 ■ *Web:* www.northrim.com	907-562-0062		70
Northrop Grumman Corp *Military Aircraft Systems Div* 1 Hornet Way ... El Segundo CA 90245 *Web:* www.northropgrumman.com	310-332-1000		20
Northrop Rice Advanced Institute of Technology 8880 Telephone Rd ... Houston TX 77061 **Fax Area Code:* 512 ■ *Web:* www.nrait.edu	713-644-6616	828-6860*	167-3
Northrup Schlueter, A Professional Law Corp 31365 Oak Crest Dr Ste 250 ... Westlake Village CA 91361 *Web:* nsplc.com	818-707-2600		41
Northshire Information Inc 4869 Main St ... Manchester Center VT 05255 *TF:* 800-437-3700 ■ *Web:* www.northshire.com	802-362-2200	362-1233	95
Northshore Dental Assisting Academy 6610 NE 181st St Ste 1 ... Kenmore WA 98028 *Web:* www.northshoredentalacademy.com	425-408-9400		167-3
Northshore Driving Academy 265 W Causeway Approach ... Mandeville LA 70448 *Web:* www.northshoredrivingacademy.com	985-626-5825		167-3
Northshore Technical Community College - Florida Parishes 7067 Hwy 10 PO Box 1300 ... Greensburg LA 70441 *TF:* 800-827-9750 ■ *Web:* www.northshorecollege.edu	225-222-4251	222-6064	162
Northside Health Care 700 Hutchins Ave ... Gadsden AL 35901 *Web:* northsidehealthcare.com	256-543-7101		450
Northside Hospital 1000 Johnson Ferry Rd NE ... Atlanta GA 30342 *Web:* www.northside.com	404-851-8000	851-6010	374-3
Northside Hospital Medical Staff Fund Inc 6000 49th St N ... Saint Petersburg FL 33709 *TF:* 800-733-0483 ■ *Web:* northsidehospital.com	727-521-4411	521-5007	374-3
Northside Millwork Inc 301 Millstone Dr ... Hillsborough NC 27278 *Web:* www.northsidemillwork.com	919-732-6100		499
Northside Oxygen & Medical Equipment - Zanesville 702 Wabash Ave ... Zanesville OH 43701 *TF:* 800-624-2922 ■ *Web:* www.northsideoxygen.com	740-453-0693	453-0748	363
Northspan Group Inc, The 221 W First St ... Duluth MN 55802 *TF:* 800-232-0707 ■ *Web:* ardc.org	218-722-5545		196
NorthSpring Capital Partners 100 Pinebush Rd ... Cambridge ON N1R8J8 *Web:* northspringcapitalpartners.com	519-721-7144		528
Northstar Battery Co 4000 Continental Way ... Springfield MO 65803 *Web:* www.northstarbattery.com	417-575-8200		74
Northstar Broadband LLC 3660 E Covington Ave Ste C ... Post Falls ID 83854 *Web:* www.northstarbroadband.net	208-262-9394		681
Northstar Ceramic Trading LLC 14500 E Beltwood Pkwy ... Dallas TX 75244 *Web:* www.northstarceramics.com	972-392-3800	392-3808	761
Northstar Cruises PO Box 248 ... Essex Fells NJ 07021 *TF:* 800-249-9360 ■ *Web:* www.northstarcruises.com	800-249-9360		771
Northstar Equipment Inc 1341 W 1st St ... Cheney WA 99004 *TF:* 800-231-7896 ■ *Web:* www.northstarequipment.com	509-235-9200	235-9203	695
Northstar Fire Protection 875 Blue Gentian Rd ... Eagan MN 55121 *Web:* www.northstarfire.com	651-456-9111		595
Northstar Industries LLC 126 Merrimack St ... Methuen MA 01844 *Web:* www.northstarindustries.com	978-975-5500		256
Northstar Investment Advisors LLC 700 17th St Ste 2350 ... Denver CO 80202 *TF:* 800-204-6199 ■ *Web:* northstarinvest.com	303-832-2300		528
Northstar Machine & Tool Company Inc 4212 Enterprise Cir ... Duluth MN 55811 *Web:* www.northstaraerospace.com	218-720-2920		454
NorthStar Management Partners LLC 4 Bellows Rd ... Westborough MA 01581 *Web:* www.northstarmp.com	508-870-5501		463
Northstar Metal Products Inc 591 Mitchell Rd ... Glendale Heights IL 60139 *TF:* 866-446-2590 ■ *Web:* www.northstarmetal.com	866-446-2590		697
NorthStar Moving Corp 9120 Mason Ave ... Chatsworth CA 91311 *TF:* 800-275-7767 ■ *Web:* www.northstarmoving.com	818-727-0128		519
NorthStar Realty Finance Corp 399 Park Ave 18th Fl ... New York NY 10022 *Web:* www.clns.com	212-547-2600		654
Northstar Steel and Aluminum Inc 205 Bouchard St ... Manchester NH 03103 *TF:* 800-258-3515 ■ *Web:* www.nstarmetals.com	603-668-3600	668-6773	492
Northstar Technology Corp Ada Technology Pk 32-C Mauchly ... Irvine CA 92618 *Web:* www.northstar-technology.com	949-788-0738	788-0657	186
Northstar Travel Media LLC 100 Lighting Way ... Secaucus NJ 07094 *Web:* www.northstartravelgroup.com	201-902-2000		637-9
Northstar-at-Tahoe Hwy 267 & Northstar Dr ... Truckee CA 96160 *TF:* 800-466-6784 ■ *Web:* www.northstarcalifornia.com	800-466-6784		669
Northtown Automotive Companies Inc 1135 Millersport Hwy ... Amherst NY 14226 *Web:* www.northtownauto.com	716-614-7000		57
Northtown Products Inc 5202 Argosy Ave ... Huntington Beach CA 92649 *TF:* 800-972-7274 ■ *Web:* www.northtowncompany.com	714-897-0700		541
Northumberland County 72 Monument Pl PO Box 129 ... Heathsville VA 22473 *Web:* www.co.northumberland.va.us	804-580-7666	580-7053	338
Northumberland County 201 Market St 2nd Fl ... Sunbury PA 17801 *TF:* 800-692-4332 ■ *Web:* www.norrycopa.net	570-988-4167	988-4497	338
Northview Public School 4451 Hunsberger NE ... Grand Rapids MI 49525 *Web:* nvps.net	616-363-4857	361-3494	685
Northview Stallion Station 55 Northern Dancer Dr ... Chesapeake City MD 21915 *Web:* www.northviewstallions.com	410-885-2855		368
Northville Downs 301 S Center St ... Northville MI 48167 *TF:* 888-349-7100 ■ *Web:* www.northvilledowns.com	248-349-1000	348-8955	642
Northville Industries Corp 225 Broad Hollow Rd PO Box 2937 ... Melville NY 11747 *Web:* www.northville.com	631-293-4700		579
Northville Watch and Clock Shop 132 W Dunlap St ... Northville MI 48167 *Web:* www.northvilleclock.com	248-349-4938		410
Northway 8 Golf Shop Inc 1519 Crescent Rd ... Clifton Park NY 12065 *Web:* northway8golf.com	518-371-3141		711
Northway Communications Inc 105 E Oak St ... Wausau WI 54401 *Web:* www.northwaycom.com	715-842-0841	848-1413	647
Northway Industries Inc 434 Paxtonville Rd PO Box 277 ... Middleburg PA 17842 *Web:* www.northwayind.com	570-837-1564	837-1575	286
Northway Toyota 727 New Loudon Rd ... Latham NY 12110 *TF:* 877-800-5098 ■ *Web:* www.northwaytoyota.com	877-800-5098		57
Northwell Health 701 N Broadway ... Sleepy Hollow NY 10591 *Web:* phelps.northwell.edu	914-366-3000		374-3
Northwell Health *North Shore University Hospital* 300 Community Dr 9 Tower Large Conference Rm ... Manhasset NY 11030 **Fax Area Code:* 516 ■ *TF:* 888-321-3627 ■ *Web:* www.northwell.edu	888-214-4065	734-8836*	769
Northwest 100 Liberty St PO Box 128 ... Warren PA 16365 *TF:* 877-672-5678 ■ *Web:* www.northwest.bank	814-726-2140		70
Northwest Administrators Inc 2323 Eastlake Ave E ... Seattle WA 98102 *TF:* 877-304-6702 ■ *Web:* www.nwadmin.com	206-329-4900	726-3209	390
Northwest Aluminum 50 Paxman Rd Unit 17 ... Etobicoke ON M9C1B7 *Web:* nwaluminum.com	647-952-5023		492
Northwest Arctic Borough PO Box 1110 ... Kotzebue AK 99752 *TF:* 800-478-1110 ■ *Web:* www.nwabor.org	907-442-2500	442-2930	338
Northwest Area Foundation 60 Plato Blvd E Ste 400 ... Saint Paul MN 55107 *Web:* www.nwaf.org	651-224-9635	225-7701	303
NorthWest Arkansas Community College 1 College Dr ... Bentonville AR 72712 *TF:* 800-995-6922 ■ *Web:* www.nwacc.edu	479-636-9222	619-2229	162
Northwest Arkansas Regional Airport 1 Airport Blvd Ste 100 ... Bentonville AR 72712 *Web:* www.flyxna.com	479-205-1000	205-1001	27
Northwest Art Glass 9003 151st Ave NE ... Redmond WA 98052 *TF:* 800-888-9444 ■ *Web:* www.nwartglass.com	425-861-9600	861-9300	189-6
Northwest Bank & Trust Co 100 E Kimberly Rd ... Davenport IA 52806 *Web:* www.northwestbank.com	563-388-2511		690
Northwest Butane 1515 W Belt Line Rd Ste 100 ... Carrollton TX 75006 *TF:* 800-274-6121 ■ *Web:* northwestpropane.com	972-247-6121		316
Northwest Cabinet Works 453 Ash Rd ... Kalispell MT 59901 *Web:* www.nwcabinetworks.com	406-752-8383		115
Northwest Chamber of Commerce 8944 St Charles Rock Rd 3rd Fl ... Saint Louis MO 63114 *Web:* northwestchamber.com	314-291-2131	291-2153	139
Northwest Chevrolet 35108 92nd Ave S ... McKenna WA 98558 *TF:* 855-216-5183 ■ *Web:* www.northwestchevrolet.com	855-234-9884		57

				Phone	Fax	Class
Northwest College 231 W Sixth St *TF:* 800-560-4692 ■ *Web:* nwc.edu	Powell	WY	82435	307-754-6000	754-6249	162
North-West College 134 W Holt Ave *TF:* 888-408-4211 ■ *Web:* www.nw.edu	Pomona	CA	91768	909-236-7106		166
Northwest Commission on Colleges & Universities (NWCCU) 8060 165th Ave NE Ste 100 *Web:* www.nwccu.org	Redmond	WA	98052	425-558-4224		48-1
Northwest Communications Coop 111 Railroad Ave PO Box 38 *TF:* 800-245-5884 ■ *Web:* www.nccray.com	Ray	ND	58849	701-568-3331		387
Northwest Community Bank 86 Main St *TF:* 800-455-6668 ■ *Web:* www.nwcommunitybank.com	Winsted	CT	06098	860-379-7561		70
Northwest Community Hospital 800 W Central Rd *Web:* www.nch.org	Arlington Heights	IL	60005	847-618-1000		374-3
Northwest Correctional Complex 960 SR 212 *Web:* www.tn.gov	Tiptonville	TN	38079	731-253-5000	253-5150	213
Northwest Credit Union Assn 18000 International Blvd Ste 350 *TF:* 800-995-9064 ■ *Web:* nwcua.org	Seatac	WA	98188	800-995-9064		219
Northwest Dairy Forwarding Co 1305 159th Ave NE *Web:* www.tcemedia.net	Ham Lake	MN	55304	763-434-6654	434-6708	780
Northwest Data Service LLC 1169 Hilltop Pkwy Unit 105 *Web:* www.northwestdata.com	Steamboat Springs	CO	80487	970-879-0734		809
Northwest Data Solutions LLC 2627 C St *Web:* www.nwds-ak.com	Anchorage	AK	99503	907-227-1676		177
Northwest Designs Ink Inc 13456 SE 27th Pl Ste 200 **Fax Area Code:* 877 ■ *TF:* 800-925-9327 ■ *Web:* nwd.ink	Bellevue	WA	98005	800-925-9327	925-9327*	157-5
Northwest Door Inc 19000 Canyon Rd E *TF:* 800-522-2264 ■ *Web:* www.northwestdoor.com	Puyallup	WA	98375	253-375-0700	375-0800	499
Northwest Elder Law Group PLLC 2150 N 107th St Ste 501 *Web:* new.nwelderlaw.com	Seattle	WA	98133	206-937-6102	830-9326	41
Northwest Financial Services Inc 9333 N Meridian St Ste 300 *Web:* www.northwestfinancial.net	Indianapolis	IN	46260	317-844-0448		401
Northwest Fisheries Science Ctr 2725 Montlake Blvd E *Web:* www.nwfsc.noaa.gov	Seattle	WA	98112	206-860-3200	860-3217	668
Northwest Florida Ballet 310 Perry Ave SE *Web:* nfballet.org	Fort Walton Beach	FL	32548	850-664-7787		573-1
Northwest Florida Blood Ctr 2209 N Ninth Ave *Web:* www.oneblood.org	Pensacola	FL	32503	850-434-2535	432-8941	89
Northwest Florida Daily News 2 Eglin Pkwy NE *Web:* www.nwfdailynews.com	Fort Walton Beach	FL	32549	850-863-1111	863-7834	532-2
Northwest Florida State College 100 College Blvd *Web:* www.nwfsc.edu	Niceville	FL	32578	850-678-5111		162
Northwest Fuel Systems Inc 115 Industry Ct *Web:* nwestco.com	Kalispell	MT	59901	406-755-4343		579
Northwest Georgia Regional Hospital 705 N Div St *Web:* www.ngoc.com	Rome	GA	30165	706-295-6011		374-5
Northwest Georgia Regional Library 310 Cappes St *Web:* ngrl.org	Dalton	GA	30720	706-876-1360		434-3
Northwest Georgia Trade & Convention Ctr 2211 Dug Gap Battle Rd *TF:* 800-824-7469 ■ *Web:* daltonconventioncenter.com	Dalton	GA	30720	706-272-7676	278-5811	205
Northwest Grain Growers Inc 850 N Fourth Ave *TF:* 800-994-4290 ■ *Web:* www.nwgrgr.com	Walla Walla	WA	99362	509-525-6510	529-6050	275
Northwest Graphic Supply Co (NW) 4200 E Lake St *TF:* 800-544-7022 ■ *Web:* www.nwgraphic.com	Minneapolis	MN	55406	612-729-7361	729-6647	328
Northwest Grille 5115 NW 39th Ave *Web:* www.northwestgrille.com	Gainesville	FL	32606	352-376-0500		671
Northwest Healthcare 6200 N La Cholla Blvd *Web:* www.healthiertucson.com	Tucson	AZ	85741	520-742-9000		374-3
Northwest Herald Inc PO Box 250 *TF:* 800-589-8910 ■ *Web:* www.nwherald.com	Crystal Lake	IL	60039	815-459-4040	459-5640	637-8
Northwest Hills at Davenport 3801 N Capital of Texas Hwy G200 *Web:* www.shopnorthwesthills.com	Austin	TX	78746	512-329-8667	329-5495	238
Northwest Home Health - Russellville 711 Hospital Dr NE *Web:* www.russellvillehospital.com	Russellville	AL	35653	256-331-0006	331-0046	363
Northwest Hospital & Medical Ctr 1550 N 115th St *TF:* 877-694-4677 ■ *Web:* www.uwmedicine.org	Seattle	WA	98133	206-364-0500		374-3
Northwest HVAC/R Association & Training Ctr 204 E Nora Ave *TF:* 800-786-3148 ■ *Web:* www.inwhvac.org	Spokane	WA	99207	509-747-8810	747-8845	48-5
Northwest Hydraulic Consultants 12787 Gateway Dr S *Web:* nhcweb.com	Seattle	WA	98168	206-241-6000		261
Northwest Indian College 2522 Kwina Rd *TF:* 866-676-2772 ■ *Web:* www.nwic.edu	Bellingham	WA	98226	360-676-2772	392-4333	165
Northwest Installations Inc 1903 Blanchard Ave *Web:* www.nwiimi.com	Findlay	OH	45840	419-423-5738		189-1
Northwest Insurance Network Inc 515 N State St Ste 2100 *Web:* www.northwestinsurance.com	Chicago	IL	60654	312-427-1777		390
Northwest Iowa Community College 603 W Park St *TF:* 800-352-4907 ■ *Web:* nwicc.edu	Sheldon	IA	51201	712-324-5061	324-4136	162
Northwest Iowa Power Co-op (NIPCO) 31002 County Rd C38 PO Box 240 *Web:* www.nipco.coop	Le Mars	IA	51031	712-546-4141		245
Northwest Kansas Technical College 1209 Harrison St *TF:* 800-316-4127 ■ *Web:* www.nwktc.edu	Goodland	KS	67735	785-890-3641		167-3
Northwest Labs of Seattle 241 S Holden St *Web:* www.nwlabs1896.com	Seattle	WA	98108	206-763-6252	763-3949	743
Northwest Learning Associates Inc (NLA) 12 Water St **Fax Area Code:* 781 ■ *Web:* www.nlabooks.com	Hingham	MA	02043	520-881-0877	626-4751*	637-2
Northwest Local School District (NWLSD) 3240 Banning Rd *Web:* www.nwlsd.org	Cincinnati	OH	45239	513-923-1000	923-3644	685
Northwest Louisiana Federal Credit Union 7070 Jewella Ave *TF:* 800-372-5438 ■ *Web:* nwlafcu.org	Shreveport	LA	71108	318-686-5438	682-3867	219
Northwest Machining & Manufacturing Inc 1957 E Lanark St *Web:* www.nwmachandmfg.com	Meridian	ID	83642	208-888-5334	888-0917	454
Northwest Manor Health Care Ctr 6440 W 34th St *Web:* northwesthealthcare.net	Indianapolis	IN	46224	317-293-4930		450
Northwest Manufacturing & Distribution Inc 2050 Main St *Web:* www.thermo-lay.com	Billings	MT	59105	406-259-9525	245-7222	806
Northwest Medical Ctr 609 W Maple Ave *TF:* 800-734-2024 ■ *Web:* www.northwesthealth.com	Springdale	AR	72764	479-751-5711		374-3
Northwest Mississippi Community College 4975 Hwy 51 N *Web:* www.northwestms.edu	Senatobia	MS	38668	662-562-3200		162
Northwest Mississippi Regional Medical Ctr 1970 Hospital Dr *TF:* 800-582-2233 ■ *Web:* www.merithealthnorthwestms.com	Clarksdale	MS	38614	662-627-3211		374-3
Northwest Missouri Psychiatric Rehabilitation Ctr (NMPRC) 3505 Frederick *Web:* www.dmh.mo.gov	Saint Joseph	MO	64506	816-387-2300		374-5
Northwest Missouri State University 800 University Dr *TF:* 800-633-1175 ■ *Web:* www.nwmissouri.edu	Maryville	MO	64468	660-562-1148	562-1821	166
Northwest Museum of Arts & Culture 2316 W First Ave *Web:* www.northwestmuseum.org	Spokane	WA	99201	509-456-3931	363-5303	520
Northwest Nannies Institute 3 Monroe Pkwy Ste P 129 *Web:* www.nwnanny.com	Lake Oswego	OR	97035	503-245-5288	245-7617	167-3
Northwest Natural Gas Co 220 NW Second Ave *NYSE: NWN* ■ *TF:* 800-422-4012 ■ *Web:* www.nwnatural.com	Portland	OR	97209	503-226-4211		787
Northwest Nazarene University 623 Holly St *TF:* 877-668-4968 ■ *Web:* www.nnu.edu	Nampa	ID	83686	208-467-8011	467-8645	166
Northwest Outlet 1814 Belknap St *TF:* 800-569-8142 ■ *Web:* www.northwestoutlet.com	Superior	WI	54880	715-392-9838		711
Northwest Pennsylvania's Great Outdoors Visitors Bureau 2801 Maplevale Rd *TF:* 800-348-9393 ■ *Web:* www.visitpago.com	Brookville	PA	15825	814-849-5197	849-1969	206
Northwest Pet Hospital PA 3701 Williams Dr *Web:* northwestpethospital.com	Georgetown	TX	78628	512-863-9200	868-9615	794
Northwest Pipe Co 12005 N Burgard *NASDAQ: NWPX* ■ *TF:* 800-989-9631 ■ *Web:* www.nwpipe.com	Portland	OR	97203	503-285-1400		490
Northwest Pipe Fittings Inc 1725 Majestic Ln *TF:* 800-937-4737 ■ *Web:* www.northwestpipe.com	Billings	MT	59102	406-252-0142	248-8072	612
Northwest Pipeline LLC 295 Chipeta Way *Web:* www.northwest.williams.com	Salt Lake City	UT	84108	801-584-7048		325
Northwest Plus Credit Union 2821 Hewitt Ave *Web:* nwpluscu.com	Everett	WA	98201	425-297-1000	297-1070	219
Northwest Precision Fabricators 3660 Second St *Web:* www.nwprecision.com	Hubbard	OR	97032	503-557-1951	557-3355	697
Northwest Prescriptions 1536 N 115th St Ste 100 *Web:* www.nwprescriptions.com	Seattle	WA	98133	206-365-2255	368-1128	475
Northwest Print Strategies Inc 8175 SW Nimbus Ave *TF:* 800-648-5156 ■ *Web:* www.nwpsi.com	Beaverton	OR	97008	800-648-5156		589
Northwest R-1 School District 2843 Community Ln *Web:* www.northwestschools.net	High Ridge	MO	63049	636-677-3473	677-5480	685
Northwest Research Associates Inc 4118 148th Ave Ne *Web:* www.nwra.com	Redmond	WA	98052	425-556-9055	556-9099	668
Northwest Respiratory Services 716 Prior Ave N **Fax Area Code:* 651 ■ *TF:* 800-232-0706 ■ *Web:* www.nwrespiratory.com	Saint Paul	MN	55104	800-232-0706	603-8723*	264-4
Northwest Rural Public Power District 5613 State Hwy 87 PO Box 249 *TF:* 800-847-0492 ■ *Web:* www.nrppd.com	Hay Springs	NE	69347	308-638-4445	638-4448	245
Northwest School 1415 Summit Ave *Web:* www.northwestschool.org	Seattle	WA	98122	206-682-7309	328-1776	622
Northwest Software Inc 1800 NW 169th Pl Ste B150 *Web:* www.nwsi.com	Beaverton	OR	97006	503-629-5947		260
Northwest Stamping Inc 86365 College View Rd *Web:* www.nwstamping.com	Eugene	OR	97405	541-747-4269	747-1169	488
Northwest State Community College 22600 SR-34 *Web:* northweststate.edu	Archbold	OH	43502	419-267-5511	267-3688	800
Northwest State Correctional Facility 3649 Lower Newton Rd *Web:* www.doc.vermont.gov	Swanton	VT	05488	802-524-6771	527-7534	213

	Phone	Fax	Class
Northwest Steel & Pipe Inc 4802 S Proctor St.......... Tacoma WA 98409 *TF:* 800-326-1328 ■ *Web:* www.nwsteel.net	253-473-8888		492
Northwest Swiss-Matic LLC 8400 89th Ave N.......... Minneapolis MN 55445 *Web:* www.nwswissmatic.com	763-544-4222	544-6873	621
Northwest Technical College Practical Nursing Program 905 Grant Ave SE.......... Bemidji MN 56601 *TF:* 800-942-8324 ■ *Web:* www.ntcmn.edu	218-333-6600	333-6694	167-3
Northwest Technical Institute 709 S Old Missouri Rd.......... Springdale AR 72765 *Web:* www.nwti.edu	479-751-8824		167-3
Northwest Technical School 1515 S Munn.......... Maryville MO 64468 *Web:* www.nts.maryville.k12.mo.us	660-562-3022	562-2010	685
Northwest Technology Ctr 1801 11th St.......... Alva OK 73717 *Web:* www.nwtech.edu	580-327-0344	327-5467	230
Northwest Territories Chamber of Commerce 4802 - 50th Ave Unit 13.......... Yellowknife NT X1A1C4 *Web:* nwtchamber.com	867-920-9505	873-4174	137
Northwest Texas Hospital 1501 S Coulter.......... Amarillo TX 79106 *TF:* 800-887-1114 ■ *Web:* www.nwths.com	806-354-1000		374-3
Northwest Tool & Machine Inc 1014 Hurst Rd.......... Jackson MI 49201 *Web:* www.nwtool.biz	517-750-1332	750-2232	757
Northwest Trek Wildlife Park 11610 Trek Dr E.......... Eatonville WA 98328 *Web:* www.nwtrek.org	360-832-6117	832-6118	823
Northwest Uav Propulsion Systems 11160 SW Durham Ln Ste 1.......... McMinnville OR 97128 *Web:* www.nwuav.com	503-434-6845		21
Northwest University 5520 108th Ave NE.......... Kirkland WA 98033 *TF:* 800-669-3781 ■ *Web:* www.northwestu.edu	425-822-8266	889-5224	166
Northwest Washington Fair Assn 1775 Front St.......... Lynden WA 98264 *Web:* www.nwwafair.com	360-354-4111		720
Northwest Wholesale Inc 1567 N Wenatchee Ave.......... Wenatchee WA 98801 *TF:* 800-874-6607 ■ *Web:* www.nwwinc.com	509-662-2141	663-4540	276
Northwestern Bank 202 N Bridge St PO Box 49.......... Chippewa Falls WI 54729 *Web:* www.northwesternbank.com	715-723-4461	723-0586	70
Northwestern California University School of Law 2151 River Plaza Dr Ste 306.......... Sacramento CA 95833 *Web:* www.nwculaw.edu	916-480-9470	920-9475	685
Northwestern College 101 Seventh St SW.......... Orange City IA 51041 *TF:* 800-747-4757 ■ *Web:* nwciowa.edu	712-707-7000	707-7164	166
Northwestern College 3003 Snelling Ave N.......... Saint Paul MN 55113 *TF:* 800-692-4020 ■ *Web:* www.unwsp.edu	651-631-5100	631-5680	166
Northwestern College Chicago Campus 4829 N Lipps Ave.......... Chicago IL 60630 *TF:* 888-205-2283 ■ *Web:* nc.edu	773-777-4220		800
Northwestern Connecticut Community College Park Pl E.......... Winsted CT 06098 *Web:* www.nwcc.edu	860-738-6300	738-6437	162
Northwestern Counseling & Support Services Inc 107 Fisher Pond Rd.......... Saint Albans VT 05478 *TF:* 800-834-7793 ■ *Web:* www.ncssinc.org	802-524-6554		353
Northwestern Electric Coop 2925 William Ave PO Box 2707.......... Woodward OK 73801 *TF:* 800-375-7423 ■ *Web:* www.nwecok.coop	580-256-7425	254-2858	245
NorthWestern Energy Library 600 Market St W.......... Huron SD 57350 *TF:* 800-245-6977 ■ *Web:* www.northwesternenergy.com	800-245-6977		434-3
Northwestern Engineering Co 314 Founders Park Dr.......... Rapid City SD 57709 *Web:* www.nwemanagement.com	605-394-3310	341-2558	261
Northwestern Flavors LLC 120 N Aurora St.......... West Chicago IL 60185	630-231-0489		296-15
Northwestern Illinois Assn 245 W Exchange St Ste 4.......... Sycamore IL 60178 *Web:* www.thenia.org	815-895-9227	895-2971	48-11
Northwestern Indiana Telephone Co (NITCO) 205 N Washington St.......... Hebron IN 46341 *Web:* www.nitco.com	219-996-2981		224
Northwestern Industries Inc 2500 W Jameson St.......... Seattle WA 98199 *TF:* 800-426-2771 ■ *Web:* www.nwiglass.com	206-285-3140	285-3603	329
Northwestern Lehigh Sch Dist 6493 Rt 309.......... New Tripoli PA 18066 *Web:* www.nwlehighsd.org	610-298-8661		685
Northwestern Meat Inc 2100 NW 23rd St.......... Miami FL 33142 *Web:* www.numeat.com	305-633-8112	633-6907	297-9
Northwestern Memorial Hospital 251 E Huron St.......... Chicago IL 60611 *Web:* www.nm.org	312-926-2000		769
Northwestern Michigan College 1701 E Front St.......... Traverse City MI 49686 *TF:* 800-748-0566 ■ *Web:* www.nmc.edu	231-995-1000	995-1339	162
Northwestern Mutual Investment Services LLC 611 E Wisconsin Ave Ste 300.......... Milwaukee WI 53202 *TF:* 866-664-7737 ■ *Web:* www.northwesternmutual.com	866-664-7737		401
Northwestern Ohio Security Systems Inc 121 E High St.......... Lima OH 45801 *TF:* 800-833-6416 ■ *Web:* nwoss.com	419-227-1655		693
Northwestern Oklahoma State University 709 Oklahoma Blvd.......... Alva OK 73717 *Web:* www.nwosu.edu	580-327-1700	327-8699	166
Northwestern Ontario Sports Hall of Fame 219 May St S.......... Thunder Bay ON P7E1B5 *Web:* www.nwosportshalloffame.com	807-622-2852	622-2736	522
Northwestern Polytechnic University 47671 Westinghouse Dr.......... Fremont CA 94539 *TF:* 877-878-8883 ■ *Web:* www.npu.edu	510-592-9688	657-8975	166

	Phone	Fax	Class
Northwestern Products Inc 721 Industrial Park Rd.......... Ashland WI 54806	715-685-9500		328
Northwestern Publishing House N16W23379 Stone Ridge Dr.......... Waukesha WI 53188 *TF:* 800-662-6022 ■ *Web:* online.nph.net	800-662-6022		637-3
Northwestern Rural Electric Cooperative Association Inc 22534 State Hwy 86 PO Box 207.......... Cambridge Springs PA 16403 *Web:* northwesternrec.coop	814-398-8064		245
Northwestern State University 175 Sam Sibley Dr.......... Natchitoches LA 71497 *TF:* 800-767-8115 ■ *Web:* www.nsula.edu	318-357-4078	357-4660	166
Northwestern State University Watson Memorial Library 913 University Pkwy.......... Natchitoches LA 71497 *TF:* 888-540-9657 ■ *Web:* library.nsula.edu	318-357-4477	357-4470	434-6
Northwestern Technological Institute 24567 Northwestern Hwy.......... Southfield MI 48075 *TF:* 877-531-8324 ■ *Web:* www.northwesterntech.edu	248-358-4006		167-3
Northwestern Tire Co 1200 Glenwood Ave.......... Minneapolis MN 55405 *Web:* www.northwesterntire.net	612-377-4900	377-7742	755
Northwestern Tools Inc 3130 Valleywood Dr.......... Dayton OH 45429 *TF:* 800-236-3956 ■ *Web:* www.northwesterntools.com	937-298-9994	298-3715	757
Northwestern University 1801 Hinman Ave.......... Evanston IL 60208 *Web:* www.northwestern.edu	847-491-7271	467-2331	166
Northwestern University Feinberg School of Medicine 303 E Chicago Ave.......... Chicago IL 60611 *Web:* www.feinberg.northwestern.edu	312-503-8649		167-2
Northwestern University Library 1970 Campus Dr.......... Evanston IL 60208 *Web:* www.library.northwestern.edu	847-491-7658	491-8306	434-6
Northwestern University School of Law 375 E Chicago Ave.......... Chicago IL 60611 *Web:* www.law.northwestern.edu	312-503-3100	503-0178	167-1
Northwest-Shoals Community College *Phil Campbell* 2080 College Rd.......... Phil Campbell AL 35581 *TF:* 800-645-8967 ■ *Web:* www.nwscc.edu	256-331-6200	331-6272	162
Northwood Family Office LP 130 King St W Ste 2250.......... Toronto ON M5X1C8 *Web:* www.northwoodfamilyoffice.com	416-502-1245		401
Northwood Manufacturing Inc 59948 Downs Rd.......... La Grande OR 97850 *Web:* northwoodmfg.com	541-962-6274		505
Northwood Meadows State Park 755 First NH Tpke.......... Northwood NH 03261 *Web:* www.nhstateparks.org	603-485-1031		565
Northwood School 92 Northwood Rd.......... Lake Placid NY 12946 *Web:* www.northwoodschool.org	518-523-3357		622
Northwood University *Texas* 1114 W FM 1382.......... Cedar Hill TX 75104 *TF:* 800-927-9663 ■ *Web:* www.northwood.edu	800-622-9000		166
Northwood Ventures 485 Underhill Blvd.......... Syosset NY 11791 *Web:* www.northwoodventures.com	516-364-5544	364-0879	792
Northwoods Credit Union 1702 Ave B.......... Cloquet MN 55720 *TF:* 888-458-0975 ■ *Web:* northwoodscu.org	218-879-4181		219
Northwoods Mall 2150 Northwoods Blvd.......... North Charleston SC 29406 *Web:* www.shopnorthwoodsmall.com	843-797-3062		460
Norton Animal Hospital Inc 147 W Main St.......... Norton MA 02766 *Web:* nortonanimalhospital.com	508-285-9822		794
Norton Audubon Hospital 1 Audubon Plaza Dr.......... Louisville KY 40217 *Web:* nortonhealthcare.com	502-636-7111		374-3
Norton Collar Lund Lilley PLLC 7701 Six Forks Rd Ste 100.......... Raleigh NC 27615 *Web:* ncllcpa.com	919-841-1000	841-1001	2
Norton County 105 S Kansas Ave.......... Norton KS 67654 *Web:* nortoncounty.org	785-877-5710		338
Norton Ditto Company Inc 2425 W Alabama St.......... Houston TX 77098 *Web:* www.nortonditto.com	713-688-9800		157-3
Norton Eleanor Holmes (Rep D - DC) 2136 Rayburn House Office Bldg.......... Washington DC 20515 *Web:* www.norton.house.gov	202-225-8050	225-3002	342-2
Norton Healthcare 200 E Chestnut St.......... Louisville KY 40202 *Web:* www.nortonhealthcare.com	502-583-1697		353
Norton (Independent City) 618 Virginia Ave PO Box 618.......... Norton VA 24273 *Web:* www.nortonva.org	276-679-1160	679-3510	338
Norton Museum of Art 1451 S Olive Ave.......... West Palm Beach FL 33401 *Web:* www.norton.org	561-832-5196		520
Norton Outdoor Advertising 5280 Kennedy Ave.......... Cincinnati OH 45213 *Web:* www.norton-outdoor.com	513-631-4864		8
Norton Packaging Inc 20670 Cosair Blvd.......... Hayward CA 94545 *Web:* www.nortonpackaging.com	510-786-1922		198
Norton Rose Fulbright US LLP 1301 McKinney St Ste 5100.......... Houston TX 77010 *Web:* www.nortonrosefulbright.com	713-651-5208		428
Norton Sandblasting Equipment 1006 Executive Blvd.......... Chesapeake VA 23320 *TF:* 800-366-4341 ■ *Web:* www.nortonsandblasting.com	757-548-4842		1
Norton Simon Museum 411 W Colorado Blvd.......... Pasadena CA 91105 *Web:* www.nortonsimon.org	626-449-6840	796-4978	520
Norton's Flowers & Gifts 2900 Washtenaw Ave.......... Ypsilanti MI 48197 *TF:* 800-682-8667 ■ *Web:* www.nortonsflowers.com	734-434-2700		292
Norva Plastics Inc 3911 Killam Ave.......... Norfolk VA 23508 *Web:* www.norvaplastics.com	757-622-9281	623-2859	599
Norvado 43705 US Hwy 63.......... Cable WI 54821 *TF:* 800-250-8927 ■ *Web:* www.norvado.com	715-798-3303	798 3044	224

Name / Address	City	State	Zip	Phone	Fax	Class
Norvanco International Inc 4301 W Vly Hwy Ste 100 *Web:* www.norvanco.com	Sumner	WA	98390	253-987-4031	987-4015	311
Norwalk Chamber of Commerce 12040 Foster Rd *Web:* www.norwalkchamber.com	Norwalk	CA	90650	562-864-7785	864-8539	139
Norwalk Community College 188 Richards Ave *Web:* norwalk.edu	Norwalk	CT	06854	203-857-7000	857-3335	162
Norwalk Compressor Co 1650 Stratford Ave **Fax Area Code:* 203 ■ *TF:* 800-556-5001 ■ *Web:* www.norwalkcompressor.com	Stratford	CT	06615	800-556-5001	386-1300*	172
Norwalk Concert Hall 125 E Ave *Web:* www.norwalkct.org	Norwalk	CT	06851	203-854-7900	854-7939	572
Norwalk Concrete Industries Inc 80 Commerce Dr *TF:* 800-733-3624 ■ *Web:* www.nciprecast.com	Norwalk	OH	44857	419-668-8167		183
Norwalk Furniture Corp 100 Furniture Pkwy *Web:* www.norwalkfurniture.com	Norwalk	OH	44857	419-744-3200		319-2
Norwalk Hospital 34 Maple St *TF:* 844-476-7455 ■ *Web:* www.norwalkhospital.org	Norwalk	CT	06856	203-852-2000	920-1672	374-3
Norwalk Powdered Metals Inc (NPM) 30 Moffitt St *Web:* www.norwalkpm.com	Stratford	CT	06615	203-338-8000	338-8011	485
Norwalk Precast Molds Inc 205 Industrial Pky *Web:* www.norwalkprecastmolds.com	Norwalk	OH	44857	419-668-1639	668-9156	757
Norwalk Public Library 1 Belden Ave *TF:* 800-382-9463 ■ *Web:* www.norwalkpl.org	Norwalk	CT	06850	203-899-2780	866-7982	434-3
Norwalk Transit District (NTD) 275 Wilson Ave *Web:* www.norwalktransit.com	Norwalk	CT	06854	203-852-0000	299-5166	468
Norwalk-Wilbert Vault Co 425 Harral Ave *TF:* 800-826-9406 ■ *Web:* www.norwalkwilbert.com	Bridgeport	CT	06604	203-366-5678		134
Norway						
Consulate General 825 Third Ave 38th Fl *Web:* www.norway.no	New York	NY	10022	646-430-7500	430-7599	257
Consulate General 3410 W Dallas St Ste 100 *Web:* www.norway.no	Houston	TX	77019	713-620-4200	620-4290	257
Norway Savings Bank 261 Main St *TF:* 888-725-2207 ■ *Web:* www.norwaysavings.bank	Norway	ME	04268	207-743-7986	743-5377	70
Norwegian American Genealogical Center and Naeseth Library 415 W Main St *Web:* www.nagcnl.org	Madison	WI	53703	608-255-2224	255-6842	434-3
Norwegian-American Chamber of Commerce Inc, The 450 Lexington Ave 4th Fl *Web:* www.naccusa.org	New York	NY	10017	646-883-1760		138
Norwegian-American Chamber of Commerce Southwest Chapter (NACC) 5219 Pine Arbor Dr *Web:* www.nacchouston.org	Houston	TX	77066	281-537-6879	587-9284	138
Norwegian-American Historical Association Archives 1510 St Olaf Ave *Web:* www.naha.stolaf.edu	Northfield	MN	55057	507-786-3229		434-3
Norwegian-American Hospital 1044 N Francisco St *TF:* 877-624-9333 ■ *Web:* www.nahospital.org	Chicago	IL	60622	773-292-8200		374-3
Norwell Knoll Nursing Home *Royal Norwell Nursing & Rehabilitation Center* 329 Washington St *Web:* www.royalhealthgroup.com	Norwell	MA	02061	781-659-4901		371
Norwell Manufacturing Inc 82 Stevens St *TF:* 800-822-2831 ■ *Web:* www.norwellinc.com	East Taunton	MA	02718	508-823-1751	823-9431	439
Norwesco Inc 4365 Steiner St *TF:* 800-328-3420 ■ *Web:* www.norwesco.com	Saint Bonifacius	MN	55375	952-446-1945		596
Norwesco Industries (1983) Ltd 6908L - Sixth St SE *Web:* www.norwesco.ab.ca	Calgary	AB	T2H2K4	403-258-3883		111
Norwest Equity Partners 80 S Eigth St Ste 3600 *Web:* www.nep.com	Minneapolis	MN	55402	612-215-1600		792
Norwest Venture Partners 525 University Ave Ste 800 *Web:* www.nvp.com	Palo Alto	CA	94301	650-321-8000		792
Norwich Art School of the Norwich Free Academy 305 Broadway *Web:* www.nfaschool.org	Norwich	CT	06360	860-887-2505		685
Norwich Bulletin 66 Franklin St *Web:* www.norwichbulletin.com	Norwich	CT	06360	860-887-9211		532-2
Norwich Clinical Research Associates Ltd 74 E Main St *Web:* www.ncra.com	Norwich	NY	13815	607-334-5850		743
Norwich Partners LLC 10 Morgan Dr Ste 1 *Web:* www.norwichpartners.com	Lebanon	NH	03766	603-643-2206		378
Norwich Pharma Services 6826 State Hwy 12 *Web:* www.norwichpharma.com	Norwich	NY	13815	607-335-3000		743
Norwich University 158 Harmon Dr *TF:* 800-468-6679 ■ *Web:* www.norwich.edu	Northfield	VT	05663	802-485-2001	485-2032	166
Norwin Chamber of Commerce 321 Main St *TF:* 800-377-3539 ■ *Web:* www.norwinchamber.com	Irwin	PA	15642	724-863-0888	863-5133	139
Norwin School District 281 Mcmahon Dr *Web:* www.norwinsd.org	Irwin	PA	15642	724-861-3000	863-9467	685
Norwin Teachers Federal Credit Union 183 Clay Pk *Web:* norwinteachersfcu.org	North Huntingdon	PA	15642	724-864-7469	864-9230	219
Norwin Technologies Corp 193 Salem St *Web:* norwintechnologies.com	Boston	MA	02113	617-858-8231		196
Norwood Builders Inc 7458 N Harlem Ave *Web:* www.norwoodbuilders.com	Chicago	IL	60631	847-655-7700	655-7701	653
Norwood Co 375 Technology Dr *Web:* www.norwoodco.com	Malvern	PA	19355	610-240-4400	240-4499	186
Norwood Furniture 216 N Gilbert Rd *Web:* www.norwoodfurniture.com	Gilbert	AZ	85234	480-892-0174		321
Norwood Hardware & Supply Company Inc 2906 Glendale Milford Rd *Web:* www.norwoodhardware.com	Cincinnati	OH	45241	513-733-1175		351
Norwood Hotel 112 Marion St *TF:* 888-888-1878 ■ *Web:* www.norwood-hotel.com	Winnipeg	MB	R2H0T1	204-233-4475	231-1910	379
Norwood Marking Systems 1 Research Park Dr *TF:* 800-722-1125 ■ *Web:* www.itwnorwood.com	Saint Charles	MO	63304	636-300-2000		467
Norwood Promotional Products Inc 14421 Myerlake Cir *Web:* www.norwood.com	Clearwater	FL	33760	727-538-3527		9
Nosco Inc 1100 Venture Ct Ste 100 *Web:* www.nosco.com	Carrollton	TX	75006	972-478-6400		393
Noshok Inc 1010 W Bagley Rd *Web:* www.noshok.com	Berea	OH	44017	440-243-0888	243-3472	201
Nosich & Ganz Attorney At Law 75 Valencia Ave Ste 1100 *Web:* ngattorneys.com	Coral Gables	FL	33134	305-442-4800		41
Nossack Fine Meats Ltd 7240 Johnstone Dr Ste 100 *Web:* nossack.com	Red Deer	AB	T4P3Y6	403-346-5006		296-26
Nossaman LLP 777 S Figueroa St 34th Fl *Web:* www.nossaman.com	Los Angeles	CA	90017	213-612-7800	612-7801	41
Nossi College of Art 590 Cheron Rd *TF:* 888-986-2787 ■ *Web:* nossi.edu	Madison	TN	37115	615-514-2787		166
Not Just Snacks 833 Hope St *Web:* www.letseat.at	Providence	RI	02906	401-831-1150		671
Not Rocket Science Inc 251 Hwy 21 *Web:* www.notrs.com	Madisonville	LA	70447	985-845-2334		177
Not Sold Separately 2 Friends Ave *Web:* www.notsoldseparately.com	Medford	NJ	08055	856-727-8200		180
Notaro & Michalos PC 100 Dutch Hill Rd **Fax Area Code:* 212 ■ *Web:* www.notaromichalos.com	Orangeburg	NY	10962	845-359-7700	278-8687*	428
Notary of South Baton Rouge LLC 12590 Perkins Rd Ste A *Web:* notaryofsouthbr.com	Baton Rouge	LA	70810	225-767-5756		41
NotePage Inc PO Box 296 *Web:* www.notepage.net	Hanover	MA	02339	781-829-0500	829-0419	525
Nothing But NET 615 N 48th St Ste 2015 *Web:* nothingbutnet.com	Phoenix	AZ	85008	480-222-6020	222-6021	179
Nothing Shocking LLC 513 S Dudley St *Web:* www.mojotone.com	Burgaw	NC	28425	910-259-7291		527
Notions Marketing Corp 1500 Buchanan Ave SW *TF:* 800-748-0250 ■ *Web:* www.notionsmarketing.com	Grand Rapids	MI	49507	616-243-8424	243-8055	195
Notkin Hawaii Inc 738 Kaheka St Ste 301 *Web:* www.notkinhi.com	Honolulu	HI	96814	808-941-6600		261
Noto's Old World Italian 6600 28th St SE *Web:* www.notosoldworld.com	Grand Rapids	MI	49546	616-493-6686		671
Notoco Industries LLC 10380 Airline Hwy *TF:* 866-684-4134 ■ *Web:* notocoind.com	Baton Rouge	LA	70816	225-292-1303		362
Notre Dame College 4545 College Rd *TF:* 877-632-6446 ■ *Web:* www.notredamecollege.edu	South Euclid	OH	44121	877-632-6446		166
Notre Dame de Namur University 1500 Ralston Ave *TF:* 800-263-0545 ■ *Web:* www.ndnu.edu	Belmont	CA	94002	650-508-3600	508-3426	166
Notre Dame Law School University of Notre Dame 1329 Biolchini Hall *Web:* law.nd.edu	Notre Dame	IN	46556	574-631-6627	631-4197	167-1
Notre Dame of Maryland University 4701 N Charles St *Web:* www.ndm.edu	Baltimore	MD	21210	410-435-0100	532-6287	166
Notre Dame Seminary 2901 S Carrollton Ave *Web:* nds.edu	New Orleans	LA	70118	504-866-7426	866-3119	167-3
Nottage & Ward LLP 10 N Dearborn Ste 1100 *Web:* nottageandward.com	Chicago	IL	60602	312-332-2915	332-3075	41
Nottingham 116 S Franklin St *Web:* www.ncfunds.com	Rocky Mount	NC	27804	252-972-9922		401
Nottingham Advisors Inc 100 Corporate Pky Ste 338 *Web:* www.nottinghamadvisors.com	Amherst	NY	14226	716-633-3800	633-3810	401
Nottoway Correctional Ctr 2892 Schutt Rd PO Box 488 *Web:* vadoc.virginia.gov	Burkeville	VA	23922	434-767-5543		213
Nottoway County PO Box 989 *Web:* nottoway.org	Nottoway	VA	23955	434-645-8696	645-8667	338
Nottoway Plantation 31025 Louisiana Hwy 1 *TF:* 866-527-6884 ■ *Web:* www.nottoway.com	White Castle	LA	70788	225-545-2730	545-8632	520
Notubes 202 Daniel Zenker Dr *Web:* www.notubes.com	Big Flats	NY	14814	607-562-2877		711
Notus Career Management 5 Centerpointe Dr Ste 400 *TF:* 800-431-1990 ■ *Web:* getnotus.com	Lake Oswego	OR	97035	503-443-1113		41
Nourtek Services Corp 100 Decker Ct Ste 191 *TF:* 877-668-7835 ■ *Web:* www.nourtek.com	Irving	TX	75062	972-717-2700	717-2800	225
Nouveau Gallery 2146 Albert St *Web:* www.nouveaugallery.com	Regina	SK	S4P2T9	306-569-9279		42
NOVA (National Organization for Victim Assistance) 510 King St Ste 424 *TF:* 800-879-6682 ■ *Web:* www.trynova.org	Alexandria	VA	22314	703-535-6682	535-5500	48-8
Nova Academy of Cosmetology 5979 Bandel Rd NW *Web:* www.nova-academy.com	Rochester	MN	55901	507-280-6910		167-3

Company / Address	City	State	Zip	Phone	Fax	Class
Nova Biologicals Inc 1775 N Loop 336 E Ste 4 *TF:* 800-282-5416 ■ *Web:* www.novatx.com	Conroe	TX	77301	800-282-5416		743
Nova Biomedical Corp 200 Prospect St *TF:* 800-458-5813 ■ *Web:* www.novabio.us	Waltham	MA	02454	781-894-0800	894-5915	419
Nova Chemicals Corp 1000 Seventh Ave SW PO Box 2518 *TF:* 800-561-6682 ■ *Web:* www.novachem.com	Calgary	AB	T2P5C6	403-750-3600	269-7410	605-2
Nova Corp 70 W King St *Web:* nova-dine.com	Chambersburg	PA	17201	717-262-9725		196
Nova Creative Group Inc 7812 McEwen Rd Ste 300 *Web:* novacreative.com	Dayton	OH	45459	937-434-9200		7
Nova Development Corp 23801 Calabasas Rd Ste 1018 *Web:* www.novadevelopment.com	Calabasas	CA	91302	818-591-9600		177
Nova Electronics USA Inc 152 S Brent Cir *Web:* www.novaelectronicsusa.com	Walnut	CA	91789	909-598-0787		438
Nova Express Millennium Inc 105 - 14271 Knox Way *TF:* 877-566-6839 ■ *Web:* www.novex.ca	Richmond	BC	V6V2Z4	604-278-1935		317
Nova Fisheries 2532 Yale Ave E *TF:* 888-458-6682 ■ *Web:* www.novafish.com	Seattle	WA	98102	206-781-2000	781-9011	285
Nova Fitness Equipment 4511 S 119th Cir *TF:* 800-949-6682 ■ *Web:* novafitnessequipment.com	Omaha	NE	68137	402-343-0552		711
Nova Group Inc 185 Devlin Rd *Web:* www.novagrp.com	Napa	CA	94558	707-257-3200	265-1199	261
Nova Home Care LLC 24543 Indoplex Cir Ste 100 *TF:* 877-763-7816 ■ *Web:* www.novahh.com	Farmington Hills	MI	48335	248-549-9800	549-9832	363
Nova Internet Services Inc PO Box 703696 *Web:* www.novaone.net	Dallas	TX	75370	214-904-9600		398
Nova Libra Inc 8609 W Bryn Mawr Ave Ste 208 *TF:* 866-724-1807 ■ *Web:* novalibra.com	Chicago	IL	60631	773-714-1441		177
Nova Medical Products 1470 Beachey Pl *TF:* 800-557-6682 ■ *Web:* www.novajoy.com	Carson	CA	90746	800-557-6682		475
Nova Networks Inc 1700 Woodward Dr Ste 100 *Web:* novanetworks.com	Ottawa	ON	K2C3R8	613-726-5001		525
Nova of California 6323 Maywood Ave *TF:* 800-835-6682 ■ *Web:* www.novaofcalifornia.com	Huntington Park	CA	90255	323-277-6266	277-6270	35
Nova Partners Inc 201 Moffett Blvd *Web:* www.novapartners.com	Mountain View	CA	94043	650-324-5324	324-5327	196
Nova Pole International Inc 2579 188 St *TF:* 866-874-8889 ■ *Web:* www.novapole.com	Surrey	BC	V3Z2A1	604-881-0090	881-0008	261
Nova Polymers Inc 2650 Eastside Park Rd *TF:* 800-226-5143 ■ *Web:* www.novapolymers.net	Evansville	IN	47715	812-476-0339	476-0592	605-2
Nova Power Solutions 23020 Eaglewood Ct Ste 100 *TF:* 800-999-6682 ■ *Web:* novapower.com	Sterling	VA	20166	800-999-6682		767
Nova Scientific Inc 10 Picker Rd *Web:* www.novascientific.com	Sturbridge	MA	01566	508-347-7679		535
Nova Scotia Department of Tourism & Culture 8 Water Str PO Box 667 *TF:* 800-565-0000 ■ *Web:* www.novascotia.com	Windsor	NS	B0N2T0	902-798-6700	798-6610	774
Nova Scotia Health Authority 5788 University Ave *TF:* 888-429-8167 ■ *Web:* www.nshealth.ca	Halifax	NS	B3H1V7	902-429-8167		545
Nova Scotia Museum of Industry 147 N Foord St *Web:* museumofindustry.novascotia.ca	Stellarton	NS	B0K1S0	902-755-5425	755-7045	520
Nova Scotia Museum of Natural History 1747 Summer St *Web:* naturalhistory.novascotia.ca	Halifax	NS	B3H3A6	902-424-7353	424-0560	520
Nova Scotia Pension Agency 1949 Upper Water St Ste 400 Fourth Fl *Web:* www.novascotiapension.ca	Halifax	NS	B3J3N3	902-424-5070		528
Nova Scotia Power Inc PO Box 910 *TF:* 800-428-6230 ■ *Web:* www.nspower.ca	Halifax	NS	B3J2W5	902-428-6230	428-6108	787
Nova Solutions Inc 421 Industrial Ave **Fax Area Code:* 800 ■ *TF:* 800-730-6682 ■ *Web:* www.novadesk.com	Effingham	IL	62401	217-342-7070	940-6682*	319-1
Nova Southeastern University 3301 College Ave *TF:* 800-541-6682 ■ *Web:* www.nova.edu	Fort Lauderdale	FL	33314	954-262-8000	262-3811	166
Nova Southeastern University Shepard Broad Law Ctr 3305 College Ave *TF:* 800-986-6529 ■ *Web:* www.law.nova.edu	Fort Lauderdale	FL	33314	954-262-6100	262-3844	167-1
Nova Technology Corp 29 Magnolia Ave *Web:* www.novatechcorp.com	Manchester	MA	01944	978-525-3066		476
Nova Telephone Co 255 Township Rd 791 *Web:* www.novatelephone.com	Nova	OH	44859	419-652-3571		224
Nova Tours & Travel Inc 504 Vine St *TF:* 800-543-6682 ■ *Web:* www.novatours.com	Liverpool	NY	13090	800-543-6682		775
NovaBone Products LLC 1551 Atlantic Blvd Ste 105 *Web:* novabone.com	Jacksonville	FL	32207	904-807-0140	807-0141	476
Novacel Inc 21 3rd St *TF:* 877-668-2235 ■ *Web:* www.novacel.world	Palmer	MA	01069	413-283-3468	283-3964	548
Novacentrix Corp 200-B Parker Dr Ste 580 *Web:* www.novacentrix.com	Austin	TX	78728	512-491-9500	491-0002	253
Novaces LLC Poydras Ctr 650 Poydras St Ste 2320 *Web:* www.novaces.com	New Orleans	LA	70130	504-544-6888		225
Novacoast Inc 1505 Chapala St *TF:* 800-949-9933 ■ *Web:* www.novacoast.com	Santa Barbara	CA	93101	800-949-9933		180
Novacro Machining Inc 380 Dewitt Rd *Web:* novacro.com	Stoney Creek	ON	L8E2T2	905-664-2721		454
Novaflex Hose Inc 449 Trollingwood Rd *Web:* www.novaflex.com	Haw River	NC	27258	336-578-2161	578-5554	370
NovaFund Advisors 17 Old Kings Hwy S *Web:* www.novafundadvisors.com	Darien	CT	06820	203-831-0111	604-9584	70
Novagard Solutions Inc 5109 Hamilton Ave *TF:* 800-380-0138 ■ *Web:* www.novagard.com	Cleveland	OH	44114	216-881-8111	881-6977	326
NovaGold Resources Inc 789 W Pender St Ste 720 *NYSE: NG* ■ *TF:* 866-669-6277 ■ *Web:* www.novagold.com	Vancouver	BC	V6C1H2	604-669-6227	669-6272	502
Novak Biddle Venture Partners PO Box 341877 *Web:* www.novakbiddle.com	Bethesda	MD	20814	240-497-1910	223-0255	792
Novak Law Office PC 280 Adams St *Web:* lawyermanchesterct.com	Manchester	CT	06042	860-257-1980		41
Novalab 2350 Power St *TF:* 800-474-6682 ■ *Web:* www.novadent.com	Drummondville	QC	J2C7Z4	819-474-2580	474-7055	228
NovaLogic Inc 27489 Agoura Rd *Web:* www.novalogic.com	Agoura Hills	CA	91301	818-880-1997	865-6405	178-6
NovaMed Corp 30 Nutmeg Dr *TF:* 800-518-6682 ■ *Web:* www.novamedcorp.com	Trumbull	CT	06611	203-380-6682	380-8992	45
Novani 900 Kearny St Ste 388 *Web:* www.novani.com	San Francisco	CA	94133	415-731-1111		177
Novanis 3161 W White Oaks Dr Ste 100 *Web:* www.novanis.com	Springfield	IL	62704	217-698-0999		180
Novant Health Inc 3333 Silas Creek Pkwy *Web:* www.novanthealth.org	Winston-Salem	NC	27103	336-718-5000		353
Novant Health UVA Health System 501 Sunset Ln *Web:* www.novanthealthuva.org	Culpeper	VA	22701	540-829-4100		353
Novar Controls Corp 6060 Rockside Woods Blvd Ste 400 **Fax Area Code:* 216 ■ *TF:* 800-348-1235 ■ *Web:* www.novar.com	Cleveland	OH	44131	800-348-1235	682-1614*	202
Novarad Corp 752 E 1180 S Ste 200 *TF:* 877-668-2723 ■ *Web:* www.novarad.net	American Fork	UT	84003	801-642-1001		174
Novare Capital Management 521 E Morehead St The Morehead Bldg Ste 510 *TF:* 877-334-3698 ■ *Web:* novarecapital.com	Charlotte	NC	28202	704-334-3698		528
Novaria Group Inc 6300 Ridglea Pl Ste 916 *TF:* 855-381-3800 ■ *Web:* www.novariagroup.com	Fort Worth	TX	76116	817-381-3810		21
Novartis Institutes For Biomedical Research Inc 250 Massachusetts Ave *Web:* www.novartis.com	Cambridge	MA	02139	617-871-8000		583
Novartis Pharmaceuticals Canada Inc 385 Boul Bouchard *TF:* 800-465-2244 ■ *Web:* www.novartis.ca	Dorval	QC	H9S1A9	514-631-6775		582
Novasel & Schwarte Investments Inc 3170 US Rte 50 Ste 10 **Fax Area Code:* 888 ■ *TF:* 800-442-5052 ■ *Web:* www.whmtahoe.com	South Lake Tahoe	CA	96150	530-577-5050	878-8990*	690
Novasep Inc 23 Creek Cir *Web:* www.novasep.com	Boothwyn	PA	19061	610-494-0447	494-1988	145
Novaspect Inc 1124 Tower Rd *TF:* 877-509-8020 ■ *Web:* www.novaspect.com	Schaumburg	IL	60173	847-956-8020	885-8200	203
Novastar Financial Inc 2114 Central Ste 600 *Web:* www.novationcompanies.com	Kansas City	MO	64108	816-237-7000		654
Novastar Solutions Com LLC 35200 Plymouth Rd *Web:* www.novastar.net	Livonia	MI	48150	734-453-8003		175
NovaStor Corp 29209 Canwood St *Web:* www.novastor.com	Agoura Hills	CA	91301	805-579-6700	579-6710	178-12
Novatec Inc 222 Thomas Ave *TF:* 800-237-8379 ■ *Web:* www.novatec.com	Baltimore	MD	21225	410-789-4811	789-4638	318
Novatech 4106 Charlotte Ave **Fax Area Code:* 888 ■ *TF:* 800-264-0637 ■ *Web:* www.novatech.net	Nashville	TN	37209	800-264-0637	264-2985*	535
Novatech Group Inc 1401 Nobel St *TF:* 844-986-8001 ■ *Web:* www.groupenovatech.com	Sainte-Julie	QC	J3E1Z4	844-986-8001		330
Novatech LLC 1720 Molasses Way *Web:* www.novatechweb.com	Quakertown	PA	18951	484-812-6000	812-6004	202
Novatek Communications Inc 500 Helendale Rd Ste 280 *Web:* www.novatekcom.com	Rochester	NY	14609	585-482-4070		463
Novation Credit Union 500 Imperial Ave N *Web:* novation.org	Oakdale	MN	55128	651-739-8080		219
Novato Chamber of Commerce 807 DeLong Ave *TF:* 800-897-1164 ■ *Web:* www.novatochamber.com	Novato	CA	94945	415-897-1164	898-9097	139
NovaTract Surgical Inc 170 Ft Path Rd Ste 13 *Web:* www.novatract.com	Madison	CT	06443	203-687-4290		250
Novavax 20 Firstfield Rd *NASDAQ: NVAX* ■ *Web:* www.novavax.com	Gaithersburg	MD	20878	240-268-2000		85
NovaVision Inc 3651 FAU Blvd Ste 300 *Web:* www.novavision.com	Boca Raton	FL	33487	561-558-2000		476
Novco Inc 11090 173rd Ave NW *TF:* 800-894-7981 ■ *Web:* www.novco.net	Elk River	MN	55330	763-441-0047	441-4550	780
Noveda Technologies Inc 1200 US Hwy 22 E Ste 2000 *TF:* 888-233-7448 ■ *Web:* www.noveda.com	Bridgewater	NJ	08807	908-534-8855	458-9190	536
Novel Iron Works Inc 250 Ocean Rd *Web:* www.noveliron.com	Greenland	NH	03840	603-436-7950	436-1403	480
Novelaire Technologies LLC 10132 Mammoth Ave *TF:* 800-762-1320 ■ *Web:* www.novelaire.com	Baton Rouge	LA	70814	225-924-0427	930-0340	14
Novelis North America 3560 Lenox Rd Ste 2000 *Web:* www.novelis.com	Atlanta	GA	30326	404-760-4000		485
Novell Design Studio 2100 Felver Ct **Fax Area Code:* 908 ■ *TF:* 888-668-3551 ■ *Web:* www.novelldesignstudio.com	Rahway	NJ	07065	732-428-8300	245-5090*	409
Novelty Inc 351 W Muskegon Dr *Web:* www.noveltyinc.com	Greenfield	IN	46140	317-462-3121		345

Name / Address	City	State	Zip	Phone	Fax	Class
Noven Pharmaceuticals Inc 11960 SW 144th St *TF:* 800-455-8070 ■ *Web:* www.noven.com	Miami	FL	33186	305-253-5099	251-1887	582
Noventi Ventures 8100 Jarvis Ave Ste 110 *Web:* noventi.net	Newark	CA	94560	650-325-6699	325-7799	792
Noventri 20940 Twin springs Dr *TF:* 800-359-1858 ■ *Web:* www.noventri.com	Smithsburg	MD	21783	301-790-0103	790-0173	9
Noveo Technologies Inc 9655 A Ignace St *TF:* 877-314-2044 ■ *Web:* noveo.ca	Brossard	QC	J4Y2P3	450-444-2044		610
Novex Software Developments Inc 8743 Commercial St **Fax Area Code:* 902 ■ *TF:* 888-542-1813 ■ *Web:* n25c.com	New Minas	NS	B4N3C4	888-542-1813	542-1842*	177
Novi Chamber of Commerce, The 41875 W 11 Mile Rd Ste 201 *TF:* 888-440-7325 ■ *Web:* www.novichamber.com	Novi	MI	48375	248-349-3743	349-9719	139
Novi Precision Products Inc 11777 Grand River Ave *Web:* www.noviprecision.com	Brighton	MI	48116	810-227-1024	227-6160	207
Novi Public Library 45255 W 10 Mile Rd *Web:* www.novilibrary.org	Novi	MI	48375	248-349-0720	349-6520	434-3
Novigo 247 N San Mateo Dr *Web:* www.novigo.com	San Mateo	CA	94401	650-249-3200		196
NOVIPRO Inc 2055 Peel St Ste 701 *TF:* 866-726-5353 ■ *Web:* novipro.com	Montreal	QC	H3A1V4	514-744-5353		180
Novitas Capital 435 Devon Pk Dr *Web:* www.novitascapital.com	Wayne	PA	19087	610-293-4075	254-4240	405
Novix Network Specialists 2000 W Main St *Web:* www.novixinc.com	Saint Charles	IL	60174	630-443-0036		180
Novo Nordisk Pharmaceuticals Inc 800 Scudders Mill Rd *TF:* 800-727-6500 ■ *Web:* www.novonordisk-us.com	Plainsboro	NJ	08536	609-987-5800		582
Novo Solutions Inc 516 S Independence Blvd *TF:* 888-316-4559 ■ *Web:* novosolutions.com	Virginia Beach	VA	23452	757-687-6590		180
Novocol Pharmaceutical of Canada Inc 25 Wolseley Ct *Web:* www.septodont.ca	Cambridge	ON	N1R6X3	519-623-4800		231
Novogradac & Company LLP 246 First St 5th Fl *Web:* www.novoco.com	San Francisco	CA	94105	415-356-8000	356-8001	2
Novolex 101 E Carolina Ave *TF:* 800-845-6051 ■ *Web:* www.novolex.com	Hartsville	SC	29550	843-857-4800		548
Novologic 279 W Crogan St *Web:* novologic.com	Lawrenceville	GA	30046	770-277-1030		463
Novopath Inc 32 Jefferson Plz *Web:* novopath.com	Princeton	NJ	08540	732-329-3209		177
Novosci 2021 Airport Rd *TF:* 800-854-0567 ■ *Web:* www.novosci.us	Conroe	TX	77301	281-363-4949		476
Novosoft Inc 3803 Mt Bonnel Rd *Web:* www.novosoft.us	Austin	TX	78731	512-454-1140		177
Novotech Technologies Corp 57 Iber Rd Unit 2 *TF:* 800-268-8628 ■ *Web:* novotech.com	Ottawa	ON	K2S1E7	613-280-1900		196
Novotechnik U.S. Inc 155 Northboro Rd *TF:* 800-667-7492 ■ *Web:* www.novotechnik.com	Southborough	MA	01772	508-485-2244	485-2430	248
Novozymes Inc 1445 Drew Ave *Web:* www.novozymes.com	Davis	CA	95618	530-757-8100	758-0317	466
Novus Development Co 20 Allen Ave Ste 400 *Web:* novusdev.com	Webster Groves	MO	63119	314-968-0842		653
Novus Inc 655 Calle Cubitas *TF:* 888-530-4546 ■ *Web:* www.novushoes.com	Guaynabo	PR	00969	787-272-4546	272-4500	301
Novus Law LLC 8770 W Bryn Mawr Ave *Web:* novuslaw.com	Chicago	IL	60631	773-632-5900		445
Novus LLC 338 Commerce Dr *Web:* www.novusllc.com	Fairfield	CT	06825	203-331-1112		179
Novus Technologies Inc 2401 Industrial Blvd *Web:* www.novus-technologies.com	Opelika	AL	36801	334-749-6300	749-6886	208
Novus Wood Group 5900 Haynesworth Ln *Web:* www.novuswoodgroup.com	Houston	TX	77034	281-922-1474		686
NOVX Systems Inc 9133 Leslie St Ste 200 *Web:* www.novxsystems.com	Richmond Hill	ON	L4B4N1	647-946-8924		743
NOW (National Organization for Women) 1100 H St NW 3rd Fl *TF:* 855-212-0212 ■ *Web:* now.org	Washington	DC	20005	202-628-8669		48-24
NOW 97.9 257 East 200 South Ste 400 *Web:* www.kbzn.com	Salt Lake City	UT	84111	801-364-9836	364-8068	645-139
Now Courier Inc PO Box 6066 **Fax Area Code:* 317 ■ *TF:* 800-543-6066 ■ *Web:* nowcourier.com	Indianapolis	IN	46206	800-543-6066	638-5750*	459
Now Inc 7402 N Eldridge Pkwy *TF:* 800-228-2893 ■ *Web:* www.distributionnow.com	Houston	TX	77041	281-823-4700		539
Now Magazine 192 Spadina Ave *Web:* nowtoronto.com	Toronto	ON	M5T2C2	416-364-1300	364-1166	532-5
Now Solutions Inc 101 W Renner Rd Ste 300 *TF:* 833-436-7284 ■ *Web:* www.nowsolutions.com	Richardson	TX	75082	833-436-7284		177
Nowak Assoc 6 Wembley Ct *Web:* www.nowakagency.com	Albany	NY	12205	518-452-4200	452-4204	4
Nowalsky & Gothard, Apllc 1420 Veterans Blvd *Web:* nbglaw.com	Metairie	LA	70005	504-832-1984		41
Nowata County Courthouse 229 N Maple St *Web:* nowataok.gov	Nowata	OK	74048	918-273-0175		338
Nowata Printing Co 3901 E Mustard Way *Web:* nowataprinting.com	Springfield	MO	65803	417-864-0932		627
Nowcom Corp 4751 Wilshire Blvd Ste 115 *Web:* www.nowcom.com	Los Angeles	CA	90010	323-692-4040		180
NowDocs International Inc 1985 Lookout Dr *TF:* 888-669-3627 ■ *Web:* www.nowforms.nowdocs.com	North Mankato	MN	56003	888-669-3627		177
Nox-Crete Inc 1444 S 20th St *TF:* 800-669-2738 ■ *Web:* www.nox-crete.com	Omaha	NE	68108	402-341-2080	341-9752	145
Noxent Inc 6400 Boul Taschereau Bureau 220 *TF:* 800-268-4364 ■ *Web:* www.noxent.com	Brossard	QC	J4W3J2	450-926-0662	926-0264	196
Noxubee County 198 Washington St PO Box 308 *TF:* 800-487-0165 ■ *Web:* noxubeealliance.com	Macon	MS	39341	662-726-4456		338
Noyes Museum of Art 733 Lily Lake Rd *TF:* 855-894-8698 ■ *Web:* www.noyesmuseum.org	Oceanville	NJ	08231	609-652-8848		520
NP (New Papyrus Publishing Co) 548 Cedar Creek Dr *Web:* www.genealogyresources.org	Athens	GA	30605	706-546-6740		637-2
NP Dodge Real Estate 8701 W Dodge Rd Ste 300 *TF:* 800-642-5008 ■ *Web:* www.npdodge.com	Omaha	NE	68114	402-255-5099		652
NP Systems Inc 2153 Richmond Ave Ste 101 *TF:* 800-273-6889 ■ *Web:* www.npsystems.com	Staten Island	NY	10314	718-477-5600	799-1461	178-1
NPA (National Parking Assn) 1112 16th St NW Ste 840 *TF:* 800-647-7275 ■ *Web:* www.weareparking.org	Washington	DC	20036	202-296-4336	296-3102	49-3
NPA Computers Inc 751 Coates Ave *Web:* npacomputers.com	Holbrook	NY	11741	631-467-2500		175
NPAP (National Psychological Association for Psychoanalysis) 40 W 13th St *Web:* npap.org	New York	NY	10011	212-924-7440	989-7543	49-15
nParallel LLC 13120 County Rd 6 *Web:* www.nparallel.com	Minneapolis	MN	55441	763-231-4804		195
NPAworldwide 1680 Viewpond Dr SE *Web:* npaworldwide.com	Grand Rapids	MI	49508	616-455-6555		193
NPC (Navy Personnel Command) 5720 Integrity Dr **Fax Area Code:* 901 ■ *TF:* 866-827-5672 ■ *Web:* www.public.navy.mil	Millington	TN	38055	866-827-5672	874-2615*	340-6
NPC (National Press Club) 529 14th St NW *Web:* www.press.org	Washington	DC	20045	202-662-7500	662-7569	49-14
NPC (National Pharmaceutical Council) 1894 Preston White Dr *Web:* www.npcnow.org	Reston	VA	20191	703-620-6390	476-0904	49-8
NPC (National Pen Corp) 12121 Scripps Summit Dr *TF:* 888-672-7370 ■ *Web:* www.pens.com	San Diego	CA	92131	888-672-7370		9
NPC Imaging 1041 Crestview Dr *Web:* www.npcimaging.com	San Carlos	CA	94070	650-593-3238		637-2
NPC Inc 13710 Dunnings Hwy *TF:* 800-847-5757 ■ *Web:* www.npcweb.com	Claysburg	PA	16625	814-239-8787		627
NPC International Inc 7300 W 129th St *TF:* 866-299-1148 ■ *Web:* www.npcinternational.com	Overland Park	KS	66213	913-327-5555	327-5850	670
NPC Processing Inc 97 Executive Dr **Fax Area Code:* 802 ■ *TF:* 800-925-7007 ■ *Web:* www.npcprocessing.com	Shelburne	VT	05482	800-925-7007	660-0565*	619
NPCA (National Precast Concrete Assn) 10333 N Meridian St Ste 272 *TF:* 800-366-7731 ■ *Web:* precast.org	Indianapolis	IN	46290	317-571-9500	571-0041	49-3
NPCA (National Paint & Coatings Assn) 1500 Rhode Island Ave NW *Web:* www.paint.org	Washington	DC	20005	202-462-6272	462-8549	49-13
NPCA (National Parks Conservation Assn) 1300 19th St NW Ste 300 *TF:* 800-628-7275 ■ *Web:* www.npca.org	Washington	DC	20036	202-223-6722		48-13
NPCA (National Peace Corporation Assn) 1825 Connecticut Ave NW Ste 800 *TF:* 800-336-1616 ■ *Web:* www.peacecorpsconnect.org	Washington	DC	20036	202-293-7728	293-7554	48-5
NPCS (New Philadelphia City School District) 248 Front Ave SW *Web:* www.npschools.org	New Philadelphia	OH	44663	330-364-0600	364-9310	186
NPD Group Inc 900 W Shore Rd *TF:* 866-444-1411 ■ *Web:* www.npd.com	Port Washington	NY	11050	516-625-0700		466
Nperspective LLC 5971 Brick Ct Ste 100-B *Web:* www.nperspective.net	Winter Park	FL	32792	407-679-7600		2
NPES: Association for Suppliers of Printing Publishing & Converting Technologies 1899 Preston White Dr *TF:* 866-381-9839 ■ *Web:* www.npes.org	Reston	VA	20191	703-264-7200	620-0994	49-16
NPF (National Park Foundation) 1201 Eye St NW Ste 550-B *Web:* www.nationalparks.org	Washington	DC	20005	202-354-6460		48-13
NPF (National Psoriasis Foundation) 6600 SW 92nd Ave Ste 300 *TF:* 800-723-9166 ■ *Web:* www.psoriasis.org	Portland	OR	97223	503-244-7404	245-0626	48-17
NPF (National Press Foundation) 1211 Connecticut Ave NW Ste 310 *Web:* nationalpress.org	Washington	DC	20036	202-663-7280		49-16
NPG (Negative Population Growth) 2861 Duke St Ste 36 *Web:* www.npg.org	Alexandria	VA	22314	703-370-9510	370-9514	48-13
NPGA (National Propane Gas Assn) 1899 L St NW Ste 350 *TF:* 800-328-1111 ■ *Web:* www.npga.org	Washington	DC	20036	202-466-7200	466-7205	48-12
NPI (National Property Inspections Inc) 9375 Burt St Ste 201 *Web:* npifranchise.com	Omaha	NE	68114	402-917-0778		365
NPI (Nippon Paper Industries) 3001 Industrial Way *Web:* www.nipponpapergroup.com	Longview	WA	98632	360-636-6400	423-1514	553
NPIC (National Pesticide Information Ctr) 333 Weniger Hall **Fax Area Code:* 541 ■ *TF:* 800-858-7378 ■ *Web:* www.npic.orst.edu	Corvallis	OR	97331	800-858-7378	737-0761*	48-17
NPK Construction Equipment Inc 7550 Independence Dr *TF:* 800-225-4379 ■ *Web:* www.npkce.com	Walton Hills	OH	44146	440-232-7900	232-4382	358
NPL (Nampa Public Library) 215 12th Ave S *Web:* www.nampalibrary.org	Nampa	ID	83651	208-468-5800		434-3

	Phone	Fax	Class
NPL (Newton Public Library) 100 N Third Ave W PO Box 746 .... Newton IA 50208 *Web:* www.newtongov.org	641-792-4108	791-0729	434-3
NPM (Norwalk Powdered Metals Inc) 30 Moffitt St .... Stratford CT 06615 *Web:* www.norwalkpm.com	203-338-8000	338-8011	485
NPM Inc 1999 Harrison St Ste 1150 .... Oakland CA 94612 *Web:* www.npmjs.com	510-858-7608		196
NPMA (National Pest Management Association Inc) 10460 N St .... Fairfax VA 22030 *TF:* 800-678-6722 ■ *Web:* www.pestworld.org	703-352-6762	352-3031	49-4
NPower 3 Metrotech Ctr Mezzanine .... Brooklyn NY 11201 *Web:* www.npower.org	212-564-7010	564-7009	506
NPP Books PO Box 750004 .... Arlington MA 02476 *Web:* www.nppbooks.com	781-254-7502		637-2
NPPA (National Press Photographers Assn) 3200 Croasdaile Dr Ste 306 .... Durham NC 27705 *Web:* nppa.org	919-237-1782	383-7261	49-14
NPPC (National Pork Producers Council) 122 C St NW Ste 875 .... Washington DC 20001 *TF:* 800-952-4629 ■ *Web:* www.nppc.org	202-347-3600	347-5265	49-6
NPR (National Public Radio) 635 Massachusetts Ave NW .... Washington DC 20001 *TF:* 800-989-8255 ■ *Web:* www.npr.org	202-513-3232	513-3329	632
NPR Illinois 91.9 UIS University of Illinois at Springfield 1 University Plz WUIS-130 .... Springfield IL 62703 *TF:* 866-206-9847 ■ *Web:* nprillinois.org	217-206-9847		645-152
NPR of America Inc 680 Wilson Pky .... Bardstown KY 40004 *Web:* www.npr.co.jp	502-350-9270	350-9271	262
NPSS (IEEE Nuclear & Plasma Sciences Society) 445 Hoes Ln .... Piscataway NJ 08854 *Web:* ieee-npss.org	732-981-0060		49-19
NPT (National Park Trust) 401 E Jefferson St Ste 207 .... Rockville MD 20850 *Web:* www.parktrust.org	301-279-7275	279-7211	48-13
NPT (New Paris Telephone Inc) 19066 Market St .... New Paris IN 46553 *Web:* www.nptel.com	574-831-2176	831-7125	224
NPTA Alliance 330 N Wabash Ave Ste 2000 .... Chicago IL 60611 *TF:* 800-355-6782 ■ *Web:* www.gonpta.com	312-321-4092		49-18
NPTC (National Private Truck Council) 950 N Glebe Rd Ste 2300 .... Arlington VA 22203 *Web:* www.nptc.org	703-683-1300	683-1217	49-21
NPWJ (No Peace Without Justice) 866 United Nations Plz Ste 408 .... New York NY 10017 *Web:* www.npwj.org	212-980-1031		48-8
nQueue 7890 S Hardy Dr Ste 105 .... Tempe AZ 85284 *TF:* 800-299-5933 ■ *Web:* www.nqueue.com	800-299-5933		180
NR Systems Inc 165 E 500 S .... River Heights UT 84321 *Web:* www.natrescon.com	435-752-4200	752-1691	196
NRA (National Rehabilitation Assn) 633 S Washington St .... Alexandria VA 22314 *TF:* 888-258-4295 ■ *Web:* www.nationalrehab.org	703-836-0850	836-0848	48-17
NRA (National Renderers Association Inc) 500 Montgomery St Ste 310 .... Alexandria VA 22314 **Fax Area Code:* 571 ■ *TF:* 800-366-2563 ■ *Web:* www.nationalrenderers.org	703-683-0155	970-2279*	48-2
NRA (National Restaurant Assn) 2055 L St NW Ste 700 .... Washington DC 20036 *TF:* 800-424-5156 ■ *Web:* www.restaurant.org	202-331-5900		49-6
NRA (Naval Reserve Assn) 1619 King St .... Alexandria VA 22314 **Fax Area Code:* 866 ■ *TF:* 877-628-9411 ■ *Web:* ausn.org	703-548-5800	683-3647*	48-19
NRA National Firearms Museum, The 11250 Waples Mill Rd .... Fairfax VA 22030 *Web:* www.nramuseum.org	703-267-1600		520
NRAA (National Renal Administrators Assn) 100 N 20th St Ste 200 .... Philadelphia PA 19103 *Web:* www.nraa.org	215-320-4655		49-8
NRAO (National Radio Astronomy Observatory) 520 Edgemont Rd .... Charlottesville VA 22903 *Web:* public.nrao.edu	434-296-0211	296-0278	668
NRB (National Religious Broadcasters) 660 N Capitol St NW Ste 210 .... Washington DC 20001 *Web:* www.nrb.org	202-543-0073	543-2649	49-14
NRB Inc 115 S Service Rd W .... Grimsby ON L3M4G3 *Web:* www.nrb-inc.com	905-945-9622		186
NRC Realty & Capital Advisors LLC 363 W Erie St Ste 300 E .... Chicago IL 60654 *Web:* www.nrc.com	312-278-6800		652
NRCA (National Roofing Contractors Assn) 10255 W Higgins Rd Ste 600 .... Rosemont IL 60018 *TF:* 800-323-9545 ■ *Web:* www.nrca.net	847-299-9070	299-1183	49-3
Nrccua 3651 NE Ralph Powell Rd .... Lee's Summit MO 64064 *TF:* 800-876-1117 ■ *Web:* encoura.org	816-525-2201		205
NRCDV (National Resource Center on Domestic Violence) 6400 Flank Dr Ste 1300 .... Harrisburg PA 17112 **Fax Area Code:* 717 ■ *TF:* 800-799-7233 ■ *Web:* www.nrcdv.org	800-799-7233	545-9456*	48-6
NRCFCP (National Resource Center for Family Centered Practice) 2662 Crosspark Road .... Coralville IA 52241 *Web:* clas.uiowa.edu	319-335-4965		637-2
NRCNAA (National Resource Center on Native American Aging) 1301 N Columbia Rd Ste E231 PO Box 9037 ... Grand Forks ND 58202 *TF:* 800-896-7628 ■ *Web:* www.nrcnaa.org	701-777-3720	777-6779	48-6
NRD LLC 2937 Alt Blvd PO Box 310 .... Grand Island NY 14072 *TF:* 800-525-8076 ■ *Web:* nrdstaticcontrol.com	716-773-7634	773-7744	201
NRDC (Natural Resources Defense Council) 40 W 20th St 11th Fl .... New York NY 10011 *Web:* www.nrdc.org	212-727-2700	727-1773	48-13
NREC (Nanotechnology Research & Education Ctr) 4202 E Fowler Ave .... Tampa FL 33620 *Web:* www.nrec.usf.edu	813-974-3780	974-3610	743
NREC (National Railway Equipment Co) 14400 Robey St .... Dixmoor IL 60426 *TF:* 800-253-2905 ■ *Web:* www.nre.com	708-388-6002		650
NREC Power Systems 5222 Hwy 311 .... Houma LA 70360 *TF:* 800-851-6732 ■ *Web:* www.nrecps.com	985-872-5480		262
NREL (National Renewable Energy Laboratory) 15013 Denver West Pkwy .... Golden CO 80401 *Web:* www.nrel.gov	303-275-3000		668
NRES (Newport Real Estate Services Inc) 2280 University Dr Ste 101 .... Newport Beach CA 92660 *Web:* www.nres.net	714-850-0085		194
NRF (National Retail Federation) 1101 New York Ave NW .... Washington DC 20005 *TF:* 800-673-4692 ■ *Web:* nrf.com	202-783-7971	737-2849	49-18
NRG Energy Inc 211 Carnegie Ctr .... Princeton NJ 08540 *NYSE: NRG* ■ *Web:* www.nrg.com	609-524-4500	524-4501	787
NRG Media 2875 Mt Vernon Rd SE .... Cedar Rapids IA 52403 *Web:* www.nrgmedia.com	319-862-0300		643
NRH (Navarro Regional Hospital) 3201 W Hwy 22 .... Corsicana TX 75110 *Web:* www.navarrohospital.com	903-654-6800		374-3
NRHA (National Reining Horse Assn) 3021 W Reno Ave .... Oklahoma City OK 73107 *Web:* Www.nrha.com	405-946-7400	946-8425	48-3
NRHA (National Retail Hardware Assn) 136 N Delaware St Ste 200 .... Indianapolis IN 46204 **Fax Area Code:* 317 ■ *TF:* 800-772-4424 ■ *Web:* www.nrha.org	800-772-4424	328-4354*	49-18
NRI (Noble Royalties Inc) 15303 N Dallas Pkwy Ste 1350 .... Addison TX 75001 *TF:* 888-346-6253 ■ *Web:* www.nobleroyalties.com	972-720-1888		538
NRI Electronics Inc 3651 Thurston Ave .... Anoka MN 55303 *TF:* 866-627-9572 ■ *Web:* www.nrielectronics.com	763-427-9572		625
NRL (Naval Research Laboratory) 4555 Overlook Ave SW .... Washington DC 20375 *Web:* www.nrl.navy.mil	202-767-3200		668
NRL (National Research Labs Inc) 650 Haines Ave NW .... Albuquerque NM 87102 *Web:* www.nrl1.dreamhosters.com	505-243-1757	243-5194	625
NRLC (National Right to Life Committee Inc) 512 Tenth St NW .... Washington DC 20004 *Web:* www.nrlc.org	202-626-8800	737-9189	48-8
NRMCA (National Ready Mixed Concrete Assn) 900 Spring St .... Silver Spring MD 20910 *TF:* 888-846-7622 ■ *Web:* www.nrmca.org	301-587-1400	585-4219	49-3
NRNC (Nisqually Reach Nature Ctr) 4949 D'Milluhr Rd NE .... Olympia WA 98516 *Web:* www.nisquallyestuary.org	360-459-0387		50-5
NRRI (Natural Resources Research Institute) *University of Minnesota Duluth* 5013 Miller Trunk Hwy .... Duluth MN 55811 *TF:* 800-234-0054 ■ *Web:* www.nrri.umn.edu	218-788-2694	720-4219	668
National Recreation Reservation Service PO Box 140 .... Ballston NY 12020 *Web:* www.recreation.gov	518-885-3639		773
NRS (National Runaway Switchboard) 3141 N Lincoln Ave .... Chicago IL 60657 *TF:* 800-786-2929 ■ *Web:* www.1800runaway.org	773-880-9860	929-5150	48-6
NRS (National Rosacea Society) 196 James St .... Barrington IL 60010 *TF:* 888-662-5874 ■ *Web:* www.rosacea.org	888-662-5874		48-17
NRSF (National Reye's Syndrome Foundation) 426 N Lewis St .... Bryan OH 43506 *TF:* 800-233-7393 ■ *Web:* www.reyessyndrome.org	419-924-9000	924-9999	48-17
Nrtodaycom 345 NE Winchester St .... Roseburg OR 97470 *Web:* www.nrtoday.com	541-672-3321	673-5994	532-2
NRTWC (National Right to Work Committee) 8001 Braddock Rd Ste 500 .... Springfield VA 22160 **Fax Area Code:* 703 ■ *TF:* 800-325-7892 ■ *Web:* nrtwc.org	800-325-7892	321-9319*	49-12
NRV Inc N8155 American St .... Ixonia WI 53036 *TF:* 800-558-0002 ■ *Web:* nrvmilk.com	920-261-7000	261-1685	447
NRWA (National Rural Water Assn) 2915 S 13th St .... Duncan OK 73533 *Web:* nrwa.org	580-252-0629	255-4476	48-12
NRWS (Napa Recycling & Waste Services) 820 Levitin Way PO Box 239 .... Napa CA 94559 *Web:* www.naparecycling.com	707-256-3500	256-3565	804
NSA (National Stroke Assn) 9707 E Easter Ln .... Centennial CO 80112 **Fax Area Code:* 303 ■ *TF:* 800-787-6537 ■ *Web:* www.stroke.org	800-787-6537	649-1328*	48-17
NSA (National Safety Apparel Inc) 15825 Industrial Pkwy .... Cleveland OH 44135 **Fax Area Code:* 216 ■ *TF:* 800-553-0672 ■ *Web:* www.thinknsa.com	800-553-0672	941-1130*	576
NSA (National Stuttering Assn) 119 W 40th St 14th Fl .... New York NY 10018 *TF:* 800-937-8888 ■ *Web:* westutter.org	212-944-4050	944-8244	48-17
NSA (National Sheriffs' Assn) 1450 Duke St .... Alexandria VA 22314 *TF:* 800-424-7827 ■ *Web:* www.sheriffs.org	703-836-7827	683-6541	49-7
NSA (National Sintered Alloys Inc) Heritage Pk Rt 145 PO Box 332 .... Clinton CT 06413 *Web:* www.nationalsintered.com	860-669-8653	669-5428	482
NSA (National Society of Accountants) 1010 N Fairfax St .... Alexandria VA 22314 *TF:* 800-966-6679 ■ *Web:* www.nsacct.org	703-549-6400	549-2984	49-1
NSA (National Speakers Assn) 1500 S Priest Dr .... Tempe AZ 85281 *Web:* www.nsaspeaker.org	480-968-2552	968-0911	48-4
NSA Media 3025 Highland Pkwy Ste 700 .... Downers Grove IL 60515 *Web:* www.nsamedia.com	630-729-7500		532-3
NSAA (National Ski Areas Assn) 133 S Van Gordon St Ste 300 .... Lakewood CO 80228 *Web:* www.nsaa.org	303-987-1111	986-2345	48-23
NSB (Northfield Savings Bank) PO Box 7180 .... Barre VT 05641 *TF:* 800-672-2274 ■ *Web:* www.nsbvt.com	800-672-2274		70
NSBA (National School Boards Assn) 1680 Duke St .... Alexandria VA 22314 *Web:* www.nsba.org	703-838-6722	683-7590	49-5
NSBA (National Small Business Assn) 1156 15th St NW Ste 1100 .... Washington DC 20005 **Fax Area Code:* 202 ■ *TF:* 800-345-6728 ■ *Web:* www.nsba.biz	800-345-6728	872-8543*	49-12
NSBP (National Society of Black Physicists) 3033 Wilson Blvd Ste 700 .... Arlington VA 22201 *Web:* www.nsbp.org	703-647-4176		49-19

Name	Address	City	State	ZIP	Phone	Fax	Class
NSC (National Safety Council)	1121 Spring Lake Dr *TF:* 800-621-7615 ■ *Web:* www.nsc.org	Itasca	IL	60143	630-285-1121	285-1315	48-17
NSC (National Security Council)	White House 1600 Pennsylvania Ave *Web:* www.whitehouse.gov	Washington	DC	20500	202-456-1414		340
NSC (NearSpace Corp)	5755 Long Prairie Rd *Web:* nsc.aero	Tillamook	OR	97141	503-842-1990	842-1923	177
NSC (Network Services Co)	1100 E Woodfield Rd *Web:* www.networkdistribution.com	Schaumburg	IL	60173	847-803-4888	803-0482	196
NSC Communications	6820 Power Line Dr *TF:* 800-543-1584 ■ *Web:* nsccom.com	Florence	KY	41042	859-727-6640		647
NSCA (National Strength & Conditioning Assn)	1885 Bob Johnson Dr *TF:* 800-815-6826 ■ *Web:* www.nsca.com	Colorado Springs	CO	80906	719-632-6722	632-6367	48-22
NSCAA (National Soccer Coaches Association of America)	800 Ann Ave *TF:* 800-458-0678 ■ *Web:* unitedsoccercoaches.org	Kansas City	KS	66101	913-362-1747	362-3439	48-22
NSCAD University	5163 Duke St *Web:* nscad.ca	Halifax	NS	B3J3J6	902-444-9600	425-2420	785
NSCC (Nashville State Community College)	120 White Bridge Rd *TF:* 800-272-7363 ■ *Web:* www.nscc.edu	Nashville	TN	37209	615-353-3333	353-3243	800
NSCIA (United Spinal Assn)	75-20 Astoria Blvd Ste 120 *TF:* 800-962-9629 ■ *Web:* unitedspinal.org	East Elmhurst	NY	11370	718-803-3782	803-0414	48-17
NSCP (National Society of Compliance Professionals)	22 Kent Rd *Web:* nscp.org	Cornwall Bridge	CT	06754	860-672-0843	672-3005	49-12
NSDC (National Staff Development Council)	504 S Locust St *TF:* 800-727-7288 ■ *Web:* learningforward.org	Oxford	OH	45056	513-523-6029	523-0638	49-5
NSEA Voice Magazine	605 S 14th St Ste 200 *TF:* 800-742-0047 ■ *Web:* www.nsea.org	Lincoln	NE	68508	402-475-7611	475-2630	457-8
NSF (National Sleep Foundation)	1522 K St NW Ste 500 *Web:* sleepfoundation.org	Washington	DC	20005	202-347-3471	347-3472	48-17
NSF (National Science Foundation)	4201 Wilson Blvd *Web:* nsf.gov	Arlington	VA	22230	703-292-5111	292-9232	340-20
NSF Intl	789 N Dixboro Rd PO Box 130140 *TF:* 800-673-6275 ■ *Web:* www.nsf.org	Ann Arbor	MI	48105	734-769-8010	769-0109	48-17
NSGA (National Senior Golf Assn)	200 Perrine Rd Ste 201 *Fax Area Code: 732 ■ *TF:* 800-282-6772 ■ *Web:* www.nationalseniorgolf.com	Old Bridge	NJ	08857	800-282-6772	525-9590*	48-22
NSGA (National Sporting Goods Assn)	1601 Feehanville Dr Ste 300 *TF:* 800-815-5422 ■ *Web:* www.nsga.org	Mount Prospect	IL	60056	847-296-6742	391-9827	49-4
NSGC (National Society of Genetic Counselors)	330 N Wabash Ave Ste 2000 *Web:* www.nsgc.org	Chicago	IL	60611	312-321-6834	673-6972	48-17
NSI Nursing Solutions Inc	2055 E State St *Web:* nsinursingsolutions.com	East Petersburg	PA	17520	717-560-3863	560-9111	371
Nsight	450 Security Blvd *Web:* www.nsight.com	Green Bay	WI	54313	920-617-7000		387
NSK America Corp	1800 Global Pkwy *TF:* 800-585-4675 ■ *Web:* www.nskamericacorp.com	Hoffman Estates	IL	60192	847-843-7664		491
Nsk Americas	4200 Goss Rd *TF:* 800-675-9930 ■ *Web:* www.csgnetwork.com	Ann Arbor	MI	48105	800-675-9930		75
NSK Canada Inc	5585 Mcadam Rd *Web:* www.nskamericas.com	Mississauga	ON	L4Z1N4	905-890-0740		472
NSK-AKS Precision Ball Co	1100A N First St *Web:* www.aksball-us.com	Clarinda	IA	51632	712-695-2915	695-2907	75
NSL Analytical	4450 Cranwood Pkwy *TF:* 877-560-3943 ■ *Web:* www.nslanalytical.com	Cleveland	OH	44128	877-560-3992		743
NSLA (Nevada State Library & Archives)	100 N Stewart St *TF:* 800-922-2880 ■ *Web:* www.nsla.libguides.com	Carson City	NV	89701	775-684-3360	684-3311	434-5
NSLM (National Sporting Library & Museum)	PO Box 1335 *Web:* www.nationalsporting.org	Middleburg	VA	20118	540-687-6542	687-8540	434-3
NSM Insurance Group Inc	555 N Ln Ste 6060 *TF:* 800-970-9778 ■ *Web:* nsminc.com	Conshohocken	PA	19428	610-941-9877		390
NSMA (Nevada State Medical Assn)	3700 Barron Way *Web:* nvdoctors.org	Reno	NV	89511	775-825-6788		474
NSNA (National Student Nurses Assn)	45 Main St Ste 606 *Web:* www.nsna.org	Brooklyn	NY	11201	718-210-0705	210-0710	49-8
NSO Press Inc	1921 E 68th Ave *Web:* www.nsopress.com	Denver	CO	80229	303-227-1400		687
NSP (National Ski Patrol System Inc)	133 S Van Gordon St Ste 100 *Web:* www.nsp.org	Lakewood	CO	80228	303-988-1111		49-7
NSPE (National Society of Professional Engineers)	1420 King St *Fax Area Code: 703 ■ *TF:* 888-285-6773 ■ *Web:* www.nspe.org	Alexandria	VA	22314	888-285-6773	836-4875*	49-19
NSPRA (National School Public Relations Assn)	15948 Derwood Rd *Web:* www.nspra.org	Rockville	MD	20855	301-519-0496	519-0494	49-5
NSRA (National Shoe Retailers Assn)	7386 N La Cholla Blvd *TF:* 800-673-8446 ■ *Web:* www.nsra.org	Tucson	AZ	85741	520-209-1710		49-18
NSS (National Slovak Society of the USA)	351 Vly Brook Rd *TF:* 800-488-1890 ■ *Web:* www.nsslife.org	McMurray	PA	15317	724-731-0094	731-0145	48-14
NSS (National Security Systems Inc)	1261 S Lyon St Ste 402 *TF:* 800-457-1999 ■ *Web:* www.nationalsecuritysystems.net	Santa Ana	CA	92705	800-457-1999		692
NSSD (North Shore School District 112)	1936 Green Bay Rd *Web:* www.nssd112.org	Highland Park	IL	60035	224-765-3000		685
NSSEA (National School Supply & Equipment Assn)	8380 Colesville Rd Ste 250 *TF:* 800-395-5550 ■ *Web:* edmarket.org	Silver Spring	MD	20910	301-495-0240	495-3330	49-18
NSSF (National Shooting Sports Foundation)	11 Mile Hill Rd *Web:* www.nssf.org	Newtown	CT	06470	203-426-1320	426-1087	48-22
NSSGA (National Stone Sand & Gravel Assn)	1605 King St *TF:* 800-342-1415 ■ *Web:* www.nssga.org	Alexandria	VA	22314	703-525-8788	525-7782	49-3
NSSL (National Severe Storms Laboratory)	120 David L Boren Blvd *Web:* www.nssl.noaa.gov	Norman	OK	73072	405-325-6907		668
NSTA (National Science Teachers Assn)	1840 Wilson Blvd *TF:* 800-722-6782 ■ *Web:* www.nsta.org	Arlington	VA	22201	703-243-7100	243-7177	49-5
NSTAR Global Services Inc	120 Partlo St *TF:* 877-678-2766 ■ *Web:* nstarglobalservices.com	Garner	NC	27529	877-678-2766		260
NTA (National Textile Association Inc)	6 Beacon St Ste 1125	Boston	MA	02111	617-542-8220		49-13
NTA (National Tour Assn)	546 E Main St *TF:* 800-682-8886 ■ *Web:* ntaonline.com	Lexington	KY	40508	859-226-4444	226-4404	48-23
NTA (Newtec America Inc)	1055 Washington Blvd *Web:* www.newtec.be	Stamford	CT	06901	203-323-0042	323-8406	392
NTA Graphics South Inc	501 Republic Cir *TF:* 888-798-2123 ■ *Web:* www.ntagraphics.com	Birmingham	AL	35214	205-798-2123		627
Ntara Inc	2214 E Fairview Ave *Web:* ntara.com	Johnson City	TN	37601	423-926-8272		7
NTB (Nationwide Truck Brokers Inc)	4203 Roger B Chaffee Memorial Blvd SE Ste 2 *TF:* 800-446-0682 ■ *Web:* www.ntbtrk.com	Grand Rapids	MI	49548	616-878-5554	878-5569	780
NTB Associates Inc	525 Louisiana Ave *Web:* ntbainc.com	Shreveport	LA	71101	318-226-9199		538
NTB Financial Corp	9540 S Maroon Cir Ste 250 *Web:* www.ntbinc.com	Centennial	CO	80112	303-825-1825	825-3789	690
NTC (Newman Theological College)	10012-84 St *TF:* 844-392-2450 ■ *Web:* www.newman.edu	Edmonton	AB	T6A0B2	780-392-2450	462-4013	167-3
NTC (Nicholville Telephone Company Inc)	3330 State Hwy 11B *Web:* www.nicholville.com	Nicholville	NY	12965	315-328-4411	328-4902	224
NTCA (National Telecommunications Cooperative Assn)	4121 Wilson Blvd Ste 1000 *Web:* www.ntca.org	Arlington	VA	22203	703-351-2000	351-2001	49-20
NTD (Norwalk Transit District)	275 Wilson Ave *Web:* www.norwalktransit.com	Norwalk	CT	06854	203-852-0000	299-5166	468
NTD (National Theatre of the Deaf)	139 N Main St *Web:* www.ntd.org	West Hartford	CT	06107	860-236-4193		573-4
NTD (Northern Telephone and Data)	300 N Koeller St *Web:* www.ntd.net	Oshkosh	WI	54902	920-426-9192		224
NTE Aviation Ltd	1800 Waters Ridge Dr Ste 400 *Web:* www.nteaviation.com	Lewisville	TX	75057	972-353-3933	353-3923	770
NTEA (National Truck Equipment Assn)	37400 Hills Tech Dr *TF:* 800-441-6832 ■ *Web:* www.ntea.com	Farmington Hills	MI	48331	248-489-7090	489-8590	49-21
Ntegrity Networks	2017 Curtis St *Web:* ntegritynetworks.com	Denver	CO	80205	720-943-8700		180
Ntelligent Networks Inc	5303 S Florida Ave *Web:* www.ntelligentnetworks.com	Lakeland	FL	33813	863-802-9675		393
NTF (National Turkey Federation)	1225 New York Ave NW Ste 400 *TF:* 866-536-7593 ■ *Web:* www.eatturkey.com	Washington	DC	20005	202-898-0100	898-0203	48-2
NTG (New Tech Global)	1030 Regional Park Dr *Web:* www.ntglobal.com	Houston	TX	77060	281-951-4330	951-8719	261
NTG Clarity Networks Inc	2820 Fourteenth Ave Ste 202 *TF:* 800-838-7894 ■ *Web:* ntgclarity.com	Markham	ON	L3R0S9	905-305-1325		224
NTH Consultants Ltd	41780 6 Mile Rd *Web:* www.nthconsultants.com	Northville	MI	48168	248-553-6300	324-5179	256
NTH Degree Financial Solutions	1500 Noyes St *Web:* www.nthdegreefinancial.com	Evanston	IL	60201	847-328-0907		194
NTH Generation Computing Inc	17055 Camino San Bernardo *TF:* 800-548-1883 ■ *Web:* nth.com	San Diego	CA	92127	858-451-2383		180
NTH Power Technologies Inc	555 Mission St Ste 3300 *Web:* www.nthpower.com	San Francisco	CA	94105	415-983-9983		792
NTIA (National Telecommunications & Information Administration)	1401 Constitution Ave NW *Web:* www.ntia.doc.gov	Washington	DC	20230	202-482-7002		340-2
NTIC (Northern Technologies International Corp)	4201 Woodland Rd PO Box 69 *NASDAQ: NTIC* ■ *TF:* 800-328-2433 ■ *Web:* www.ntic.com	Circle Pines	MN	55014	763-225-6600	225-6645	145
N-Tier Solutions Inc	2596 Landmark Dr *Web:* www.n-tiersolutions.com	Winston-Salem	NC	27103	336-765-3500		260
NTIS (National Technical Information Service)	5301 Shawnee Rd *TF:* 800-363-2068 ■ *Web:* www.ntis.gov	Alexandria	VA	22312	703-605-6060	605-6880	197
NTIS (National Technical Information Service)	5285 Port Royal Rd *TF:* 800-553-6847 ■ *Web:* www.ntis.gov	Springfield	VA	22161	703-605-6000	605-6900	668

Name / Address	City	State	Zip	Phone	Fax	Class
NTL Institute						
1875 Connecticut Ave NW 10th Fl	Washington	DC	20009	202-280-2057		765
Web: www.ntl.org						
NTMA (National Tooling & Machining Assn)						
6363 Oak Tree Blvd.	Independence	OH	44131	800-248-6862	248-7104*	49-13
**Fax Area Code:* 301 ■ *TF:* 800-248-6862 ■ *Web:* www.ntma.org						
NTN Bearing Corporation of America						
1600 E Bishop Ct	Mount Prospect	IL	60056	847-298-7500	699-9744	620
TF: 800-323-2358 ■ *Web:* www.ntnamericas.com						
NTN Drive Shaft Inc						
8251 S International Dr.	Columbus	IN	47201	812-342-7000	342-1155*	620
**Fax Area Code:* 821 ■ *Web:* www.ntnamericas.com						
NTN-Bower Corp 707 N Bower Rd.	Macomb	IL	61455	309-837-0440		621
Web: www.ntnbower.com						
NTP (National Toxicology Program)						
PO Box 12233	Research Triangle Park	NC	27709	919-541-0530	541-3687	668
Web: ntp.niehs.nih.gov						
NTPA (National Tractor Pullers Assn)						
6155-B Huntley Rd	Columbus	OH	43229	614-436-1761	436-0964	48-22
Web: www.ntpapull.com						
NTP-STAG 19801 SW 72nd Ave Ste 300	Tualatin	OR	97062	800-521-9999		61
TF: 800-242-6987 ■ *Web:* www.ntpstag.com						
NTRA (National Thoroughbred Racing Assn)						
2525 Harrodsburg Rd Ste 510	Lexington	KY	40504	800-792-6872		48-22
TF: 800-792-6872 ■ *Web:* www.ntra.com						
NTS (National Technical Systems Inc)						
2125 E Katella Ave Ste 250	Anaheim	CA	92806	818-591-0776	591-0899	743
NASDAQ: NTSC ■ *TF:* 800-879-9225 ■ *Web:* www.nts.com						
NTS 526 Chestnut St	Virginia	MN	55792	218-741-4290		192
Web: www.netechnical.com						
NTS (New:Team SoftWare Inc)						
PO Box 254807	Sacramento	CA	95865	415-461-8086		178-1
Web: www.go2nts.com						
NTS Communications Inc 1220 Broadway	Lubbock	TX	79401	800-658-2150	788-3381*	186
**Fax Area Code:* 806 ■ *TF:* 800-658-2150 ■ *Web:* www.vexusfiber.com						
NTS Development Co						
500 North Hurstbourne Pkwy Ste 400	Louisville	KY	40222	502-426-4800		15
Web: www.ntsdevelopment.com						
NTSAD (National Tay-Sachs & Allied Diseases Assn)						
2001 Beacon St Ste 204	Brighton	MA	02135	617-277-4463	277-0134	48-17
TF: 800-906-8723 ■ *Web:* ntsad.org						
NTSB (National Transportation Safety Board)						
490 L'Enfant Plz SW	Washington	DC	20594	202-314-6000		340-20
Web: www.ntsb.gov						
NTT Associates Inc						
16205 Old Frederick Rd	Mount Airy	MD	21771	410-442-2031		653
Web: nttsurveyors.com						
NTT DATA Inc 100 City Sq	Boston	MA	02129	800-745-3263		180
TF: 800-745-3263 ■ *Web:* www.us.nttdata.com						
NTT DoCoMo USA Inc						
757 3rd Ave 16th Fl	New York	NY	10017	888-362-6661		736
TF: 888-362-6661 ■ *Web:* www.docomo-usa.com						
NTT Electronics Corp						
250 Pehle Ave Ste 706	Saddle Brook	NJ	07663	201-556-1770	556-1771	253
Web: www.ntt-electronics.com						
NTTC (North Texas Telephone Co)						
519 Main St	Byers	TX	76357	940-529-6123		225
Web: www.northtextel.net						
NTU (National Taxpayers Union)						
108 N Alfred St	Alexandria	VA	22314	703-683-5700	683-5722	48-7
Web: www.ntu.org						
NTV International Corp						
645 Fifth Ave Ste 303	New York	NY	10022	212-660-6900	660-6998	514
Web: www.ntvic.com						
Nu Aire Inc 2100 Fernbrook Ln	Plymouth	MN	55447	763-553-1270		420
TF: 800-328-3352 ■ *Web:* www.nuaire.com						
Nu Hotel 85 Smith St	Brooklyn	NY	11201	718-852-8585	852-8558	378
Web: www.nuhotelbrooklyn.com						
Nu Image Marketing 1271 N Tustin Ave.	Anaheim	CA	92807	714-575-8947		195
Web: nimarketing.com						
NU Laboratories Inc						
312 Old Allerton Rd	Annandale	NJ	08801	908-713-9300	713-9001	743
Web: www.nulabs.com						
Nu Promo 11697 Chesterdale Rd	Cincinnati	OH	45246	513-782-0168		522
Web: 74585.asisupplier.com						
Nu Van Technology Inc 2155 Hwy 1187	Mansfield	TX	76063	817-477-1734		779
Nuance Communications Inc						
1 Wayside Rd	Burlington	MA	01803	781-565-5000		178-7
NASDAQ: NUAN ■ *TF:* 800-654-1187 ■ *Web:* www.nuance.com						
NuAxis Innovations						
8603 Westwood Center Dr Ste 300	Vienna	VA	22182	703-481-7400	935-5523	177
Web: nuaxis.com						
Nubble Site Solutions Inc						
26 Brickyard Ct	York	ME	03909	207-351-8251		727
Web: nubblesitesolutions.com						
Nubenco Medical 1 Kalisa Way	Paramus	NJ	07652	201-967-9000		476
TF: 800-633-1322 ■ *Web:* nubenco.com						
Nubian Images Publishing						
PO Box 1462	Brentwood	CA	94513	925-634-7627		637-2
Web: www.vickiward.net						
NUCA of Florida						
113 E College Ave Ste 200	Tallahassee	FL	32301	850-514-5183		139
Web: www.nucaflorida.org						
Nucara Pharmacy 209 E San Marnan Dr	Waterloo	IA	50702	319-236-8891		237
TF: 800-359-2357 ■ *Web:* www.nucara.com						
NuCare Pharmaceuticals Inc						
622 W Katella Ave.	Orange	CA	92867	888-482-9545		583
TF: 888-482-9545 ■ *Web:* www.nucarerx.com						
Nu-Cast Inc 29 Grenier Field Rd.	Londonderry	NH	03053	603-432-1600		308
Web: www.nu-cast.com						
Nuclear Age Peace Foundation (NAPF)						
1622 Anacapa St.	Santa Barbara	CA	93101	805-965-3443	568-0466	48-5
Web: www.wagingpeace.org						
Nuclear Energy Institute (NEI)						
1776 'I' St NW Ste 400	Washington	DC	20006	202-739-8000	785-4019	48-12
Web: www.nei.org						
Nuclear Fuel Services Inc						
1205 Banner Hill Rd	Erwin	TN	37650	423-743-9141		143
Web: www.nuclearfuelservices.com						
Nuclear Information & Resource Service (NIRS)						
6930 Carroll Ave Ste 340	Takoma Park	MD	20912	301-270-6477	270-4291	48-8
Web: www.nirs.org						
US NRC Region II						
245 Peachtree Center Ave NE Ste 1200	Atlanta	GA	30303	404-562-4400	562-4900	340-20
TF: 800-577-8510 ■ *Web:* www.nrc.gov						
Nuclear Regulatory Commission Regional Offices						
Region 1						
2100 Renaissance Blvd	King of Prussia	PA	19406	610-337-5000		340-20
TF: 800-432-1156 ■ *Web:* www.nrc.gov						
Region 3 2443 Warrenville Rd Ste 210	Lisle	IL	60532	630-829-9500	515-1078	340-20
TF: 800-522-3025 ■ *Web:* www.nrc.gov						
Region 4 1600 E Lamar Blvd	Arlington	TX	76011	817-860-8100		340-20
TF: 800-952-9677 ■ *Web:* www.nrc.gov						
Nuclear Waste Technical Review Board (NWTRB)						
2300 Clarendon Blvd Ste 1300	Arlington	VA	22201	703-235-4473	235-4495	340-20
Web: www.nwtrb.gov						
NuCo2 Inc 2800 SE Marketplace	Stuart	FL	34997	772-221-1754	781-3500	146
TF: 800-472-2855 ■ *Web:* www.nuco2.com						
Nu-Concepts 1737 S Vineyard Ave	Ontario	CA	91761	909-930-6244		322
TF: 800-334-1065 ■ *Web:* www.nuconcepts.com						
Nucor Corp 1915 Rexford Rd	Charlotte	NC	28211	704-366-7000	362-4208	480
NYSE: NUE ■ *TF:* 800-294-1322 ■ *Web:* www.nucor.com						
Nucor Corp						
Vulcraft Div 1501 W Darlington St.	Florence	SC	29501	888-000-0000	662-3132*	480
**Fax Area Code:* 843 ■ *TF:* 888-000-0000 ■ *Web:* www.vulcraft.com						
Nucor Steel Berkeley 1455 Hagan Ave	Huger	SC	29450	843-336-6000		723
Web: www.nucorsteel.com						
Nucor Steel Marion Inc 912 Cheney Ave.	Marion	OH	43302	740-383-4011		492
TF: 800-333-4011 ■ *Web:* www.nucorhighway.com						
Nucor-Yamato Steel Co						
5929 E State Hwy 18	Blytheville	AR	72315	870-762-5500	762-1130	723
TF: 800-289-6977 ■ *Web:* www.nucoryamato.com						
Nucraft Furniture Co						
5151 W River Dr	Comstock Park	MI	49321	616-784-6016		321
TF: 877-682-7238 ■ *Web:* www.nucraft.com						
Nucro-Technics						
2000 Ellesmere Rd Unit 16	Scarborough	ON	M1H2W4	416-438-6727	438-3463	85
Web: www.nucro-technics.com						
NucSafe Inc 601 Oak Ridge Tpke	Oak Ridge	TN	37830	865-220-5050	220-5090	419
Web: www.nucsafe.com						
Nu-Di Corp 12730 Triskett Rd	Cleveland	OH	44111	216-251-9070		248
Web: www.nu-di.com						
Nudo Products Inc 1500 Taylor Ave	Springfield	IL	62703	217-528-5636	528-8722	751
TF: 800-826-4132 ■ *Web:* www.nudo.com						
Nueces County 901 Leopard St.	Corpus Christi	TX	78401	361-888-0111		338
Web: www.nuecesco.com						
Nueces Electric Co-op (NEC)						
14353 Cooperative Ave.	Robstown	TX	78380	361-387-2581		245
TF: 800-632-9288 ■ *Web:* nueceselectric.org						
Nueces Farm Ctr 4587 US-77 Business	Robstown	TX	78380	361-387-1572	387-0453	274
Web: www.nuecesfarmcenter.net						
Nuesoft Technologies Inc						
1685 Terrell Mill Rd	Marietta	GA	30067	678-303-1140		177
Web: www.nuemd.com						
Nueta Hidatsa Sahnish College						
301 College Dr PO Box 490	New Town	ND	58763	701-627-4738		167-3
Web: www.nhsc.edu						
Nuevo Laredo 1495 Chattahoochee Ave.	Atlanta	GA	30318	404-352-9009		671
Web: www.nuevolaredocantina.com						
NuFACTOR Inc						
41093 County Center Dr Ste B	Temecula	CA	92591	951-296-2516		237
TF: 800-323-6832 ■ *Web:* www.nufactor.com						
Nugent Sand Co 1833 River Rd	Louisville	KY	40206	502-584-0158		503-4
Web: www.nugentsand.com						
Nugget Markets 157 Main St	Woodland	CA	95695	530-662-5479		345
Web: www.nuggetmarket.com						
Nugget, The 259 Worthington St W	North Bay	ON	P1B3B5	705-472-3200	472-1438	532-1
Web: www.nugget.ca						
NuGrowth Solutions						
4181 ArlingGate Plz	Columbus	OH	43228	800-966-3051	388-5811*	195
**Fax Area Code:* 614 ■ *TF:* 800-966-3051 ■ *Web:* nugrowth.com						
Nuherbs co 14722 Wicks Blvd	San Leandro	CA	94577	800-233-4307		297-8
TF: 800-233-4307 ■ *Web:* www.nuherbs.com						
Nu-Hope Laboratories Inc						
12640 Branford St	Pacoima	CA	91331	818-899-7711		477
TF: 800-899-5017 ■ *Web:* www.nu-hope.com						
Nujak Development Inc						
714 N Massachusetts Ave.	Lakeland	FL	33801	863-686-1565	683-7874	186
TF: 888-685-2526 ■ *Web:* nujak.com						
Nuka Research & Planning Group LLC						
1451 N Boone Ln	Seldovia	AK	99663	907-234-7821		192
Web: nukaresearch.com						
Nukitchens LLC 132 Water St	Norwalk	CT	06854	203-831-9000		362
Web: nukitchens.com						
Nulab Inc 2180 Calumet St.	Clearwater	FL	33765	727-446-1126		231
Web: www.nulabinc.com						
Nulaid Foods Inc 200 W Fifth St	Ripon	CA	95366	209-599-2121	599-5220	297-10
TF: 800-788-8871 ■ *Web:* www.nulaid.com						
Nulayer Inc 72 Fraser Ave Ste 201	Toronto	ON	M6K3J7	416-840-4384		463
Web: www.nulayer.com						
Nu-Life Environmental Inc PO Box 1527	Easley	SC	29641	864-855-5155		385
TF: 800-654-1752 ■ *Web:* nulifeenv.com						
Nu-Lite Electrical Wholesalers						
850 Edwards Ave	Harahan	LA	70123	504-733-3300	736-1617	246
TF: 800-256-1603 ■ *Web:* www.nulite.com						
Nulton Diagnostic & Treatment Center PC						
214 College Pk	Johnstown	PA	15904	814-262-0025	266-2880	726
TF: 888-918-5465 ■ *Web:* nulton.com						
Numark Brands LLC						
105 Fieldcrest Ave Ste 502A	Edison	NJ	08837	800-214-2379		582
TF: 800-338-8079 ■ *Web:* www.numarkbrands.com						
Numatic Engineering Inc						
7915 Ajay Dr	Sun Valley	CA	91352	818-768-1200		358
Web: www.numaticengineering.com						
NumbersOnly Inc						
1520 State Hwy 130 N Ste 201	North Brunswick	NJ	08902	732-940-0033	940-0055	631
Web: numbersonly.com						

Company / Address	City	State	ZIP	Phone	Fax	Class
NuMedics Inc 6950 SW Hampton Rd Ste 221 — *Web:* www.numedics.com	Tigard	OR	97223	503-597-3861		174
Numeric Computer Systems Inc 275 Oser Ave — *Web:* www.ncssuite.com	Hauppauge	NY	11788	631-486-9000		180
Numeric Technologies Inc 4200 Cantera Dr — *Web:* www.ntsiinc.com	Warrenville	IL	60555	630-955-9060	604-2006	177
Numerica Credit Union 14610 E Sprague — *Web:* www.numericacu.com	Spokane	WA	99216	509-535-7613		219
Numerical Concepts Inc 4040 1st Pky — *Web:* www.numericalconcepts.com	Terre Haute	IN	47804	812-466-5261	466-1663	189-14
Numerical Control Computer Sciences 2600 Michelson Dr Ste 1700 — *Web:* www.nccs.com	Irvine	CA	92612	949-852-3664	553-1911	178-5
Numerical Control Support Inc 21945 W 83rd St — *TF:* 888-441-3501 ■ *Web:* ncsmanufacturing.com	Shawnee Mission	KS	66227	913-441-3500	441-3298	454
Numerical Precision 2200 Foster Ave — *Web:* www.numericalprecision.com	Wheeling	IL	60090	847-394-3610	394-3962	454
Numeridex Inc 632 S Wheeling Rd — *TF:* 800-323-7737 ■ *Web:* www.numeridex.com	Wheeling	IL	60090	847-541-8840	541-8392	112
Numero Uno Web Solutions Inc 3300 Hwy 7 Ste 908 — *TF:* 855-736-9778 ■ *Web:* www.numerounoweb.com	Concord	ON	L4K4M3	905-669-1708		5
Numo Manufacturing Co 1072 E Hwy 175 — *Web:* www.numomfg.com	Kaufman	TX	75142	972-962-5400		9
Numonics Corp 101 Commerce Dr PO Box 1005 — *TF:* 800-523-6716 ■ *Web:* interactivewhiteboards.com	Montgomeryville	PA	18936	215-362-2766	361-0167	173-1
Numotion 126 Airport Rd — *TF:* 877-856-9154 ■ *Web:* www.numotion.com	Scott City	MO	63780	573-334-0600		475
Nunes Devin (Rep R - CA) 1013 Longworth House Office Bldg Ste 1013 — *Web:* nunes.house.gov	Washington	DC	20515	202-225-2523	225-3404	342-2
Nunhems USA Inc 1200 Anderson Corner Rd — *TF:* 800-733-9505 ■ *Web:* www.nunhemsusa.com	Parma	ID	83660	208-674-4000	674-4090	694
Nunn-Bush Shoe Company Inc 333 W Estabrook Blvd — *TF:* 866-484-3718 ■ *Web:* www.nunnbush.com	Glendale	WI	53212	866-484-3718		301
Nunnery-Freeman Inc PO Box 332 — *Web:* kookrite.com	Henderson	NC	27536	252-438-3149	438-5346	806
Nuo Therapeutics Inc 207A Perry Pkwy Ste 1 — *OTC:* NUOT ■ *TF:* 866-298-6633 ■ *Web:* www.nuot.com	Gaithersburg	MD	20877	866-298-6633		85
Nupla Corp 11912 Sheldon St — *TF:* 800-872-7661 ■ *Web:* www.nuplacorp.com	Sun Valley	CA	91352	818-768-6800		610
NURC (NOAA's Undersea Research Program) University of N Carolina at Wilmington — *Fax Area Code:* 301 ■ *Web:* research.noaa.gov	Silver Spring	MD	20910	910-962-2440	713-1967*	668
Nuro 1300 Terra Bella Ave Ste 200 — *Web:* nuro.ai	Mountain View	CA	94043	650-476-2687		113
Nurol Corp 1531 Marietta Blvd NW — *TF:* 800-390-6623 ■ *Web:* nurolpos.com	Atlanta	GA	30318	404-352-3587		88
Nurse Assist Inc 3400 N Cross Blvd — *TF:* 800-649-6800 ■ *Web:* stericaresolutions.com	Fort Worth	TX	76137	800-649-6800		475
Nurse On Call Inc 100 E Vine St Ste 1400 — *TF:* 855-350-3800 ■ *Web:* www.nurseoncall.com	Brentwood	TN	37027	855-350-3800		363
Nurse Staffing LLC 1700 Rt 23 N Ste 100 — *Web:* www.nursesapply.com	Wayne	NJ	07470	973-709-1009		193
Nursecom 1721 Moon Lake Blvd Ste 540 — *TF:* 800-866-0919 ■ *Web:* www.nurse.com	Hoffman Estates	IL	60169	800-866-0919		457-16
Nursefinders Inc 12400 High Bluff Dr — *TF:* 800-445-0459 ■ *Web:* www.nursefinders.com	San Diego	CA	92130	877-214-4105		721
Nursery Supplies Inc 1415 Orchard Dr — *Web:* www.nurserysupplies.com	Chambersburg	PA	17201	717-263-7780		596
Nurserymen's Exchange 2651 N Cabrillo Hwy — *TF:* 800-227-5229 ■ *Web:* www.rocketfarms.com	Half Moon Bay	CA	94019	650-726-6361	712-4290	369
Nurses Care Inc-Cincinnati 9200 Montgomery Rd — *Web:* www.nursescareinc.com	Cincinnati	OH	45242	513-791-0233		363
Nursing Ctr 323 Norristown Rd Ste 200 — *TF:* 800-346-7844 ■ *Web:* www.nursingcenter.com	Ambler	PA	19002	800-787-8985		397
Nursing Enterprises Inc 5101 Wisconsin Ave NW Ste 250 — *Web:* www.healthcare4ppl.com	Washington	DC	20016	202-526-2400		363
Nursing Personnel Homecare Inc 175 S Ninth St — *Web:* www.nursingpersonnelhomecare.com	Brooklyn	NY	11211	718-218-8991		371
Nursing Services 4 You Corp 13205 SW 137 Ave Ste 221 — *Web:* www.nursingservices4you.com	Miami	FL	33186	305-259-6771	259-6778	363
NURTEC (Northeast Underwater Research, Technology & Education Ctr) University of Connecticut at Avery Pt 1080 Shennecossett Rd — *Web:* www.nurtec.uconn.edu	Groton	CT	06340	860-405-9121		668
Nurx 1125 Mission St 2nd Fl — *TF:* 800-321-6879 ■ *Web:* www.nurx.com	San Francisco	CA	94103	800-321-6879		582
NUS Consulting Group 1 Maynard Dr — *Web:* www.nusconsulting.com	Park Ridge	NJ	07656	201-391-4300	391-8158	196
Nushagak Electric & Telephone Co-opeartive Inc 557 Kenny Wren Rd — *TF:* 800-478-5296 ■ *Web:* www.nushtel.com	Dillingham	AK	99576	907-842-5251	842-2799	245
NuSpectra Multimedia Inc 3000F Danville Blvd Ste 122 — *TF:* 877-726-8458 ■ *Web:* www.nuspectra.com	Alamo	CA	94507	925-406-4474		177
Nusphere Corp 6015 S Virginia St Ste E 154 — *Web:* www.nusphere.com	Reno	NV	89502	408-416-5353		178-1
Nussbaum Trucking Inc 210 S East St — *TF:* 800-322-7305 ■ *Web:* www.nussbaum.com	Hudson	IL	61748	309-452-4426		780
Nussbaumer & Clarke Inc 3556 Lake Shore Rd Ste 500 — *Web:* nussclarke.com	Buffalo	NY	14219	716-827-8000		261
Nu-Star Inc 1425 Stagecoach Rd — *Web:* nustarinc.com	Shakopee	MN	55379	952-445-8295		54
NuStar Terminal Canada Partnership 4090 Port Malcolm Rd — *Web:* nustarenergy.com	Point Tupper	NS	B9A1Z5	902-625-1711	625-3098	581
NuStep Inc 5111 Venture Dr Ste 1 — *TF:* 800-322-2209 ■ *Web:* www.nustep.com	Ann Arbor	MI	48108	734-769-3939	769-8180	710
Nutcracker Publishing Co 5209 Dutch Elm Dr — *Web:* www.nutcrackerpublishing.com	Apex	NC	27539	919-924-2058		637-2
NuTEC Manufacturing 908 Garnet Ct — *Web:* www.nutecmfg.com	New Lenox	IL	60451	815-722-2800		296
Nu-Tec Tooling Company Inc 13115 SR-405 — *Web:* www.nutectool.com	Watsontown	PA	17777	570-538-2571		249
NuTech Energy Alliance Ltd 7702 FM 1960 E Ste 300 — *Web:* www.nutechenergy.com	Humble	TX	77346	281-812-4030		727
NuTech Inc 1301 Clinic Dr — *Web:* www.nutechrx.com	Tyler	TX	75701	903-592-8115		231
Nutech Information Systems 1010 Summer St Ste 406 — *Web:* www.nutechsoft.com	Stamford	CT	06905	203-961-8911		180
Nutechs LLC 6785 Telegraph Rd Ste 350 — *Web:* www.nutechs.com	Bloomfield Hills	MI	48301	248-593-5700		180
Nutfield Technology Inc 1 Wall St Ste 115 — *Web:* nutfieldtech.com	Hudson	NH	03051	603-893-6200		407
Nutherm International Inc 501 S 11th St — *Web:* www.nutherm.com	Mount Vernon	IL	62864	618-244-6000	244-6641	729
Nutley Chamber of Commerce 366 Passaic Ave — *Web:* nutleychamber.com	Nutley	NJ	07110	973-667-5300		139
Nutley Park Shop-Rite Inc 437 Franklin Ave — *Web:* www.shop.shoprite.com	Nutley	NJ	07110	973-235-1213		345
Nutman Company USA Inc, The 1319 Hwy 175 — *Web:* www.nutman.com	Hubertus	WI	53033	262-628-4771	628-4773	241
Nutonian Inc 125 Summer St Ste 1000 — *Web:* nutonian.com	Boston	MA	02110	617-702-5540		177
Nutra Food Ingredients LLC 4683 50th St SE — *Web:* nutrafoodingredients.com	Kentwood	MI	49512	616-656-9928		311
Nutra Pharma Corp 12538 W Atlantic Blvd — *Web:* www.nutrapharma.com	Coral Springs	FL	33071	954-509-0911		479
Nutra-Blend Inc 3200 Second St — *TF:* 800-657-5657 ■ *Web:* www.nutrablend.net	Neosho	MO	64850	800-657-5657		584
Nutraceutical International Corp 1400 Kearns Blvd — *TF:* 800-669-8877 ■ *Web:* www.nutraceutical.com	Park City	UT	84060	435-655-6000		799
Nutraceutics Corp 2900 Brannon Ave — *Web:* www.nutraceutics.com	Saint Louis	MO	63139	314-664-4639		231
Nutraceutix Inc 9625 153rd Ave NE — *Web:* nutraceutix.com	Redmond	WA	98052	425-883-9518		479
Nutramax Laboratories Inc 2208 Lakeside Blvd — *TF:* 888-886-6442 ■ *Web:* www.nutramaxlabs.com	Edgewood	MD	21040	410-776-4000		214
nuTravel Technology Solutions LLC 181 Westchester Ave Ste 302 — *Web:* www.nutravel.com	Port Chester	NY	10573	914-848-4566		180
Nutri Pet Research Inc 227 Hwy 33 E — *Web:* www.nuprosupplements.com	Manalapan	NJ	07726	732-786-8822		237
NutriCorp Intl 4025 Rhodes Dr — *TF:* 888-446-8874 ■ *Web:* www.nutricorp.com	Windsor	ON	N8W5B5	519-974-8178		743
Nutrifaster Inc 209 S Bennett St — *TF:* 800-800-2641 ■ *Web:* www.nutrifaster.com	Seattle	WA	98108	206-767-5054	762-2209	98
Nutri-Force Nutrition 14620 NW 60th Ave — *Fax Area Code:* 305 ■ *TF:* 800-455-3696 ■ *Web:* www.nutriforce.com	Miami Lakes	FL	33014	800-455-3696	629-9994*	238
Nutrilawn Inc 1040 Martin Grove Rd Ste 25 — *Web:* www.nutrilawn.com	Etobicoke	ON	M9W4W4	647-496-2710		577
NutriScience Innovations LLC 2450 Reservoir Ave — *Web:* nutriscienceusa.com	Trumbull	CT	06611	203-372-8877		479
NutriSystem Inc 600 Office Center Dr — *NASDAQ:* NTRI ■ *TF:* 800-585-5483 ■ *Web:* www.nutrisystem.com	Fort Washington	PA	19034	215-706-5300		810
Nutrition 21 Inc 1 Manhattanville Rd — *Web:* nutrition21.com	Purchase	NY	10577	914-701-4500	696-0860	479
Nutrition Formulators Inc 10407 N Commerce Pkwy — *Web:* www.nutritionformulators.com	Miramar	FL	33025	954-272-2220		345
Nutrition House Inc 125 Loring St — *Web:* myamarket.com	Manchester	NH	03103	603-668-2650		345
Nutrition Management Services Co 2071 Kimberton Rd — *Web:* www.nmsc.com	Kimberton	PA	19442	610-935-8287		299
Nuts & Volts Magazine 430 Princeland Ct — *TF:* 800-783-4624 ■ *Web:* www.nutsvolts.com	Corona	CA	92879	951-371-8497	371-3052	457-14
Nuttall Gear LLC 2221 Niagra Falls Blvd — *TF:* 800-724-6710 ■ *Web:* www.nuttallgear.com	Niagara Falls	NY	14304	716-298-4100	298-4101	709
Nuvantage Insurance Corp 1542 S Wickham Rd — *Web:* nuvantageinsurance.com	West Melbourne	FL	32904	321-253-9000		390
NuVasive Inc 7475 Lusk Blvd — *NASDAQ:* NUVA ■ *TF:* 800-475-9131 ■ *Web:* www.nuvasive.com	San Diego	CA	92121	858-909-1800		476

	Phone	Fax	Class
Nuveen Investments Inc 333 W Wacker Dr . . . Chicago IL 60606 *TF:* 800-257-8787 ■ *Web:* www.nuveen.com	312-917-7700		690
Nuventive LLC 9800B McKnight Rd Ste 255 . . . Pittsburgh PA 15237 *TF:* 877-366-8700 ■ *Web:* www.nuventive.com	412-847-0280	847-0285	179
Nuvera Fuel Cells LLC 129 Concord Rd Bldg 1 . . . Billerica MA 01821 *Web:* www.nuvera.com	617-245-7500	245-7511	579
NuView Life Sciences Inc 1389 Center Dr Ste 250 . . . Park City UT 84098 *TF:* 888-902-7779 ■ *Web:* nuviewlifesciences.com	435-647-9758		743
NuVision Engineering Inc 2403 Sidney St Ste 700 . . . Pittsburgh PA 15203 *TF:* 888-748-8232 ■ *Web:* nuvisionengineering.com	412-586-1810		256
NuVista Energy Ltd 525 Eighth Ave SW Ste 2500 . . . Calgary AB T2P1G1 *Web:* www.nuvistaenergy.com	403-538-8500	538-8505	536
Nuvite Chemical Compounds Corp 85 Jetson Ln. . . . Central Islip NY 11722 **Fax Area Code:* 718 ■ *TF:* 800-394-8351 ■ *Web:* nuvitechemical.com	800-394-8351	383-0008*	151
NUVO Newsweekly 3951 N Meridian St Ste 200 . . . Indianapolis IN 46208 *Web:* www.nuvo.net	317-254-2400		532-5
Nuvue Business Solutions 3061 Berks Way Ste 102 . . . Raleigh NC 27614 **Fax Area Code:* 888 ■ *TF:* 800-688-8310 ■ *Web:* nuvue.com	919-562-5599	863-9611*	196
NuVue Therapeutics Inc 11135 Sedgefield Rd . . . Fairfax VA 22030 *Web:* www.nuvuetherapeutics.com	703-591-1691		476
Nu-Wa Industries Inc 3701 Johnson Rd . . . Chanute KS 66720 *TF:* 800-835-0676 ■ *Web:* www.nuwa.com	620-431-2088		120
NuWare Technology Corporation Inc 100 Wood Ave S Ste 122 . . . Iselin NJ 08830 *Web:* www.nuware.com	732-494-0550		180
NuWave Technology Partners LLC 5268 Azo Ct . . . Kalamazoo MI 49048 *Web:* www.nuwavepartners.com	269-342-4400		179
Nu-Way 2 Access Way. . . . Bloomington IL 61704 *TF:* 800-232-9243 ■ *Web:* www.nuway.com	800-232-9243		780
NuWay Burgers 3441 E Harry . . . Wichita KS 67218 *Web:* www.nuwayburgers.com	316-684-6132		671
Nu-Way Concrete Forms Inc 4190 Hofmeister Ave. . . . Saint Louis MO 63125 *TF:* 800-542-1214 ■ *Web:* www.nuwayinc.com	314-544-1214	544-1656	191-1
Nu-Way Industries Inc 555 Howard Ave . . . Des Plaines IL 60018 *TF:* 888-488-5631 ■ *Web:* www.nuwayindustries.com	847-298-7710	635-8650	697
Nu-Way Kitchen and Bath 5227 Auburn Rd . . . Utica MI 48317 *TF:* 866-924-2284 ■ *Web:* www.nuwaysupply.com	866-924-2284		612
Nu-Way Printing Co 306 SE 8th Ave. . . . Portland OR 97215 *Web:* www.nuwayprinting.com	503-232-7151	238-0645	627
Nu-Way Torches Inc PO Box 14565 . . . Minneapolis MN 55414 *Web:* www.nuwaytorches.com	651-488-5811	488-1411	758
NuWay-K & H Cooperative PO Box Q . . . Trimont MN 56176 *TF:* 800-445-4118 ■ *Web:* www.nuway-kandh.com	800-445-4118		276
Nu-Wool Company Inc 2472 Port Sheldon Rd . . . Jenison MI 49428 *TF:* 800-748-0128 ■ *Web:* www.nuwool.com	616-669-0100	669-2370	389
Nu-Yale Cleaners 6300 Hwy 62 . . . Jeffersonville IN 47130 *TF:* 888-644-7400 ■ *Web:* www.nuyale.com	812-285-7400	285-7421	426
Nuyen, Tomtishen & Aoun PC 2001 Commonwealth Blvd Ste 300. . . . Ann Arbor MI 48105 *Web:* ntalaw.com	734-372-4100		41
Nuzoo Media Inc 606 W 18th St Apt 3 . . . Chicago IL 60616 *Web:* www.nuzoo.com	312-421-2129		7
Nuzzo & Roberts LLC 1 Town Ctr . . . Cheshire CT 06410 *Web:* www.nuzzo-roberts.com	203-250-2000	250-3131	428
NV (Nick Varner) PO Box 1309 . . . Owensboro KY 42302 **Fax Area Code:* 270 ■ *TF:* 800-626-8408 ■ *Web:* www.nickvarner.com	800-626-8408	686-7833*	710
NV Heathorn Co 1155 Beecher St . . . San Leandro CA 94577 *Web:* www.nvheathorn.com	510-569-9100	569-9106	189-10
NV5 2525 Natomas Pk Dr Ste 300 . . . Sacramento CA 95833 *TF:* 877-311-4180 ■ *Web:* www.nv5.com	916-641-9100	641-9222	261
NVC Logistics Group Inc 1 Pond Rd . . . Rockleigh NJ 07647 *TF:* 800-526-0207 ■ *Web:* www.nvclogistics.com	800-526-0207		311
NVCA (National Venture Capital Assn) 25 Massachusetts Ave NW Ste 730 . . . Washington DC 20001 *Web:* nvca.org	703-524-2549	524-3940	615
NVE Corp 11409 Vly View Rd . . . Eden Prairie MN 55344 *NASDAQ: NVEC* ■ *TF:* 800-467-7141 ■ *Web:* www.nve.com	952-829-9217	996-1600	696
NVE Pharmaceuticals 15 Whitehall Rd . . . Andover NJ 07821 *Web:* www.stacker2.com	973-786-7868		360-3
nVent 7433 Harwin Dr. . . . Houston TX 77036 *TF:* 800-545-6258 ■ *Web:* raychem.nvent.com	800-545-6258		201
NVFC (National Volunteer Fire Council) 7852 Walker Dr Ste 450 . . . Greenbelt MD 20770 *Web:* www.nvfc.org	202-887-5291		49-4
NVIC (National Vaccine Information Ctr) 407 Church St Ste H. . . . Vienna VA 22180 *Web:* www.nvic.org	703-938-0342	938-5768	48-17
NVIDIA Corp 2701 San Tomas Expy . . . Santa Clara CA 95050 *NASDAQ: NVDA* ■ *Web:* www.nvidia.com	408-486-2000	486-2200	625
N-Viro International Corp 2254 Centennial Rd . . . Toledo OH 43617 *OTC: NVIC* ■ *Web:* www.nviro.com	419-535-6374		804
Nvision Networking Inc 7450 N Thornydale Rd . . . Tucson AZ 85741 *TF:* 855-494-6943 ■ *Web:* nvisionnet.com	855-494-6943		180
NVision Solutions Inc 88360 Diamondhead Dr E. . . . Diamondhead MS 39525 *Web:* www.nvisionsolutions.com	228-222-5900	222-5904	809
NVMS Inc 9255 Center St Ste 200 . . . Manassas VA 20110 *Web:* www.nvms.com	703-361-6262		226
NVR Inc 11700 Plaza America Dr Ste 500. . . . Reston VA 20190 *NYSE: NVR* ■ *TF:* 877-550-7926 ■ *Web:* nvrinc.com	703-956-4000		187
NVT Phybridge 3495 Laird Rd Ste 12 . . . Mississauga ON L5L5S5 *TF:* 888 901-3633 ■ *Web:* www.nvtphybridge.com	905-901-3633		247
NW (Northwest Graphic Supply Co) 4200 E Lake St . . . Minneapolis MN 55406 *TF:* 800-544-7022 ■ *Web:* www.nwgraphic.com	612-729-7361	729-6647	328
NW Sign Industries Inc 360 Crider Ave . . . Moorestown NJ 08057 *Web:* www.nwsignindustries.com	856-802-1677	802-0412	701
NWA (National WIC Assn) 2001 S St NW Ste 580 . . . Washington DC 20009 *TF:* 866-782-6246 ■ *Web:* www.nwica.org	202-232-5492	387-5281	48-6
NWC (National Waterways Conference Inc) 1100 N Glebe Rd Ste 1010. . . . Arlington VA 22201 *TF:* 866-371-1390 ■ *Web:* waterways.org	703-224-8007		49-21
NWCCU (Northwest Commission on Colleges & Universities) 8060 165th Ave NE Ste 100 . . . Redmond WA 98052 *Web:* www.nwccu.org	425-558-4224		48-1
NWF (National Wildlife Federation) 11100 Wildlife Center Dr . . . Reston VA 20190 *Web:* nwf.org	703-438-6000	438-3570	48-3
NWFA (National Wood Flooring Assn) 111 Chesterfield Industrial Blvd . . . Chesterfield MO 63005 *TF:* 800-422-4556 ■ *Web:* www.woodfloors.org	636-519-9663		49-3
NWI (National Wellness Institute) 1300 College Ct PO Box 827 . . . Stevens Point WI 54481 *Web:* www.nationalwellness.org	715-342-2969	342-2979	48-17
NWL Transformers Inc 312 Rising Sun Rd . . . Bordentown NJ 08505 *TF:* 800-742-5695 ■ *Web:* www.nwl.com	609-298-7300	298-1982	253
NWLC (National Women's Law Ctr) 11 Dupont Cir NW Ste 800. . . . Washington DC 20036 *Web:* nwlc.org	202-588-5180		48-24
NWLSD (Northwest Local School District) 3240 Banning Rd . . . Cincinnati OH 45239 *Web:* www.nwlsd.org	513-923-1000	923-3644	685
NWOA (National Woodland Owners Association Inc) 374 Maple Ave E Ste 310 . . . Vienna VA 22180 *TF:* 800-476-8733	703-255-2700		48-2
NWP (Native West Press) PO Box 12227 . . . Prescott AZ 86304 *Web:* www.nativewestpress.com	928-771-8376		637-2
NWPC (National Women's Political Caucus) PO Box 65010 . . . Washington DC 20035 *Web:* www.nwpc.org	202-785-1100		48-7
NWPCA (National Wooden Pallet & Container Assn) 1421 Prince St Ste 340. . . . Alexandria VA 22314 *Web:* www.palletcentral.com	703-519-6104	519-4720	49-13
NWRA (National Water Resources Assn) 3800 Fairfax Dr Ste 4 . . . Arlington VA 22203 **Fax Area Code:* 928 ■ *Web:* www.nwra.org	703-524-1544	343-9483*	48-12
NWRA (National Wildlife Refuge Assn) 1001 Connecticut Ave Nw Ste 905 . . . Washington DC 20036 *Web:* www.refugeassociation.org	202-417-3803		48-13
NWS (National Weather Service) 1325 East-West Hwy. . . . Silver Spring MD 20910 *Web:* www.weather.gov	301-427-9855		340-2
NWT Tourism PO Box 610 . . . Yellowknife NT X1A2N5 *TF:* 800-661-0788 ■ *Web:* spectacularnwt.com	867-873-7200	873-4059	774
NWTF (National Wild Turkey Federation) 770 Augusta Rd PO Box 530 . . . Edgefield SC 29824 *TF:* 800-843-6983 ■ *Web:* www.nwtf.org	803-637-3106	637-0034	48-3
NWTRB (Nuclear Waste Technical Review Board) 2300 Clarendon Blvd Ste 1300. . . . Arlington VA 22201 *Web:* www.nwtrb.gov	703-235-4473	235-4495	340-20
NWU (National Writers Union) 256 W 38th St Ste 703 . . . New York NY 10018 *Web:* nwu.org	212-254-0279	254-0673	414
NXC Imaging 2118 4th Ave S. . . . Minneapolis MN 55404 *TF:* 800-328-5016 ■ *Web:* www.nxc-imaging.com	800-328-5016	666-9729	475
NXQ (Neutronix-Quintel) 385 Woodview Ave . . . Morgan Hill CA 95037 *Web:* neutronixinc.com	408-776-5190	776-1039	695
Nxrev Inc 39500 Stevenson Pl Ste 108. . . . Fremont CA 94539 *Web:* nxrev.com	408-986-0200		366
NxStage Medical Inc 350 Merrimack St . . . Lawrence MA 01843 *NASDAQ: NXTM* ■ *TF:* 866-697-8243 ■ *Web:* www.nxstage.com	978-687-4700		476
NXT Bank 320 Third St SE . . . Cedar Rapids IA 52401 *Web:* nxtbank.net	319-438-6621		70
NXT Energy Solutions Inc 3320 17th Ave SW Ste 302. . . . Calgary AB T3E0B4 *Web:* www.nxtenergy.com	403-264-7020		537
NY1 75 Ninth Ave. . . . New York NY 10011 *Web:* www.ny1.com	212-379-3311		530
Nyack Beach State Park 698 N Broadway . . . Upper Nyack NY 10960 *Web:* parks.ny.gov	845-358-1316		565
Nyack College 1 S Blvd. . . . Nyack NY 10960 *TF:* 800-336-9225 ■ *Web:* www.nyack.edu	845-358-1710	358-3047	166
Nyack Hospital 160 N Midland Ave. . . . Nyack NY 10960 *Web:* www.montefiorenyack.org	845-348-2000	348-2160	374-3
Nyacol Nano Technologies Inc 211 Megunko Rd . . . Ashland MA 01721 *Web:* www.nyacol.com	508-881-2220	881-1855	143
Nyala Publishing 1250 W Addison St. . . . Chicago IL 60613 *TF:* 800-288-0141 ■ *Web:* www.nyalapublishing.com	773-883-9818	883-9836	637-2
NYAM (New York Academy of Medicine) 1216 Fifth Ave. . . . New York NY 10029 *Web:* www.nyam.org	212-822-7200		49-19
Nyatex Chemical Co 2112 Industrial . . . Howell MI 48843 *Web:* www.nyatex.com	517-546-4046		3
NYAWA (New York Arm Wrestling Assn) PO Box 670952 . . . Flushing NY 11367 *Web:* www.nycarms.com	718-544-4592	261-8111	48-22
NYBDC (Pursuit) 50 Beaver St Ste 500 . . . Albany NY 12207 *TF:* 800-923-2504 ■ *Web:* www.nybdc.com	518-463-2268	463-0240	216
NYC & Co 810 Seventh Ave 3rd Fl . . . New York NY 10019 *TF:* 800-887-9103 ■ *Web:* www.nycgo.com	800-887-9103		206
NYCA (New York Celebrity Assistants) 459 Columbus Ave . . . New York NY 10024 *Web:* www.nycelebrityassistants.com	212-803-5444		49-12

Name / Address	City	State	ZIP	Phone	Fax	Class
NYCCC (New York City Children's Center-Queens Campus) 74-03 Commonwealth Blvd *Web:* omh.ny.gov	Bellerose	NY	11426	718-264-4500	740-0968	374-1
NYCM (New York Central Mutual Fire Insurance Co) 1899 Central Plz E **Fax Area Code:* 607 ■ *TF:* 800-234-6926 ■ *Web:* www.nycm.com	Edmeston	NY	13335	800-234-6926	965-2712*	391-4
NYDJ Apparel LLC 5401 S Soto St *TF:* 800-407-6001 ■ *Web:* www.nydj.com	Vernon	CA	90058	323-581-9040		157-6
NYE County PO Box 1031 *Web:* www.co.nye.nv.us	Tonopah	NV	89049	775-482-8127	482-8133	338
NYE Health Services 2230 N Somers Ave *Web:* nyehealthservices.com	Fremont	NE	68025	402-753-1400		371
NYE Lubricants Inc 12 Howland Rd *Web:* www.nyelubricants.com	Fairhaven	MA	02719	508-996-6721	997-5285	541
Nyecom Plainview Telephone Co 112 S Main St *Web:* www.plvwtelco.net	Plainview	NE	68769	402-582-4242	582-3300	224
NYFA (New York Foundation for the Arts) 20 Jay St 7th Fl *Web:* www.nyfa.org	Brooklyn	NY	11201	212-366-6900	366-1778	572
NYGH (North York General Hospital) 4001 Leslie St *Web:* www.nygh.on.ca	North York	ON	M2K1E1	416-756-6000		374-2
Nyhus Communications LLC 720 Third Ave 1st Fl *Web:* nyhus.com	Seattle	WA	98104	206-323-3733		636
NYIF (New York Institute of Finance) 160 Broadway 15th Fl *Web:* www.nyif.com	New York	NY	10038	347-842-2501		423
Nyingma Institute 1815 Highland Pl *Web:* nyingmainstitute.com	Berkeley	CA	94709	510-809-1000		423
NYLA (New York Library Assn) 6021 State Farm Rd *TF:* 800-252-6952 ■ *Web:* www.nyla.org	Guilderland	NY	12084	518-432-6952	427-1697	435
Nyle Systems LLC 12 Stevens Rd *TF:* 800-777-6953 ■ *Web:* www.nyle.com	Brewer	ME	04412	207-989-4335	989-1101	300
Nylok Corp 15260 Hallmark Dr *TF:* 800-826-5161 ■ *Web:* nylok.com	Macomb	MI	48042	580-780-0100	700-0590	3
Nylon 110 Greene St Ste 600 *Web:* nylon.com	New York	NY	10012	212-226-6454		457-11
Nylon Corporation of America 333 Sundial Ave *TF:* 800-851-2001 ■ *Web:* www.nycoa.net	Manchester	NH	03103	603-627-5150		605-1
Nylon Technology 350 Seventh Ave 10th Fl *Web:* www.nylontechnology.com	New York	NY	10001	212-691-1134		177
Nyloncraft Inc 616 W McKinley Ave *Web:* www.nyloncraft.com	Mishawaka	IN	46545	574-256-1521	255-3278	604
Nylube Products Company LLC 2299 Star Ct *Web:* www.nylube.com	Rochester Hills	MI	48309	248-852-6500	852-6505	439
NYMT (New York Mortgage Trust Inc) 52 Vanderbilt Ave Ste 403 *NASDAQ:* NYMT ■ *Web:* www.nymtrust.com	New York	NY	10017	212-792-0107		654
NYP Corp 805 E Grand St *TF:* 800-524-1052 ■ *Web:* nyp-corp.com	Elizabeth	NJ	07201	908-351-6550	351-0108	67
NYPA (New York Power Authority) 123 Main St PO Box 10 B *Web:* www.nypa.gov	White Plains	NY	10601	914-681-6200		787
NYPIRG 9 Murray St *TF:* 800-566-5020 ■ *Web:* www.nypirg.org	New York	NY	10007	212-349-6460	349-1366	633
NYPNU (New York Professional Nurses Union) 241 E 75th St *Web:* www.nypnu.org	New York	NY	10021	212-988-5565		533
Nypro Inc 101 Union St *Web:* www.jabil.com	Clinton	MA	01510	978 366 0721		596
Nypromold Inc 144 Pleasant St *Web:* www.nypromold.com	Clinton	MA	01510	978-365-4547	365-4548	757
Nyrstar Clarksville 1800 Zinc Plant Rd *Web:* www.nyrstar.com	Clarksville	TN	37041	931-552-4200	552-0471	485
NYS Office of Parks Recreation & Historic Preservation 625 Broadway *Web:* www.parks.ny.gov	Albany	NY	12207	518-474-0456		565
NYSCO Products Inc 2350 Lafayette Ave *Web:* www.nysco.com	Bronx	NY	10473	718-792-9000	792-7732	125
NYSE Arce 115 Samsone St *TF:* 877-729-7291 ■ *Web:* www.nyse.com	San Francisco	CA	94104	877-729-7291		691
NYSNA (New York State Nurses Assn) 11 Cornell Rd *Web:* www.nysna.org	Latham	NY	12110	518-782-9400		533
Nystrom 4501 W 62nd St	Indianapolis	IN	46268	317-612-3901		637-1
Nystrom Inc 9300 73rd Ave N **Fax Area Code:* 800 ■ *TF:* 800-547-2635 ■ *Web:* www.nystrom.com	Minneapolis	MN	55428	763-488-9200	317-8770*	234
NYSW (New York Susquehanna & Western Railway Corp) 1 Railroad Ave *TF:* 800-366-6979 ■ *Web:* www.nysw.com	Cooperstown	NY	13326	607-547-2555	547-9834	648
NYTD (New York Twist Drill Inc) 5368 E Rockton Rd *Web:* www.newyorktwistdrill.com	South Beloit	IL	61080	800-543-0972		455
NYU (New York University School of Law) 40 Washington Sq S *Web:* www.law.nyu.edu	New York	NY	10012	212-998-6100	995-4527	167-1
NYU Alumni Assn 25 W 4th St 4th Fl *Web:* go.alumni.nyu.edu	New York	NY	10012	212-998-6912		305
NYU Langone Hospitals (LHC) 150 55th St *Web:* www.lutheranhealthcare.org	Brooklyn	NY	11220	718-630-7000	630-8653	374-3
NYU Langone Medical Ctr 550 First Ave *Web:* med.nyu.edu	New York	NY	10016	212-263-7300		374-3
NYU Winthrop Hospital 259 1st St *Web:* www.winthrop.org	Mineola	NY	11501	516-663-0333	663-2946	374-3
NYUP (New York University Press) 838 Broadway 3rd Fl *TF:* 800-996-6987 ■ *Web:* nyupress.org	New York	NY	10003	212-998-2575	995-3833	637-2
NYX Inc 36111 Schoolcraft Rd *Web:* www.nyxinc.com	Livonia	MI	48150	734-462-2385	464-4830	604

O

Name / Address	City	State	ZIP	Phone	Fax	Class
O & F Machine Products Company Inc 3020 W 20th St PO Box 1363 *Web:* www.ofmachine.com	Joplin	MO	64802	417-623-7476	623-4736	454
O & G Industries Inc 112 Wall St *Web:* www.ogind.com	Torrington	CT	06790	860-489-9261		186
O & M Industries Inc 5901 Ericson Way *Web:* www.omindustries.com	Arcata	CA	95521	707-822-8800		610
O & P Edge, The 11154 Huron St Ste 104 *TF:* 866-613-0257 ■ *Web:* opedge.com	Northglenn	CO	80234	303-255-0843	255-0844	305
O & R Precision Grinding Inc 5315 W 900 S *Web:* www.orprecision.com	Geneva	IN	46740	260-368-9394		757
O and I Transport Inc 14301 Prospect St *TF:* 800-270-0020 ■ *Web:* www.oitransport.com	Dearborn	MI	48126	313-945-1530		780
O Bee Credit Union 3900 Cleveland Ave SE *TF:* 800-642-4014 ■ *Web:* obee.com	Tumwater	WA	98501	360-943-0740		219
O Berk Co 3 Milltown Ct *TF:* 800-631-7392 ■ *Web:* www.oberk.com	Union	NJ	07083	800-631-7392		385
O Brien & Dekker 100 N Third *Web:* obriendekker.com	LaFayette	IN	47901	765-742-9027		41
O Dell Corp 13833 Indian Mound Rd *Web:* www.odellcorp.com	Ware Shoals	SC	29692	864-861-2222	861-3171	361
O E C Graphics Inc 555 W Waukau Ave PO Box 2443 *TF:* 800-388-7770 ■ *Web:* www.oecgraphics.com	Oshkosh	WI	54902	920-235-7770	235-2252	481
O H Anderson Elementary School 666 Warner Ave S *Web:* www.ohanderson.mahtomedi.k12.mn.us	Saint Paul	MN	55115	651-407-2300	407-2325	685
O Henry Hotel 624 Green Valley Rd *Web:* ohenryhotel.com	Greensboro	NC	27408	336-854-2000	854-2223	379
O Hotel 819 S Flower St *Web:* ohotelgroup.com	Los Angeles	CA	90017	213-623-9904		379
O Keller Tool Engineering Co 12701 Inkster Rd *Web:* www.okeller.com	Livonia	MI	48150	734-425-4500		757
O Lee Turner CPA LLC 2711 Middleburg Dr Ste 209B *Web:* lturnercpa.com	Columbia	SC	29204	803-256-1162		2
O M Jones Inc PO Box 4375 *Web:* www.micro-tronics.net	Sonora	CA	95370	209-532-1008	532-1009	253
O M V Medical Inc 6940 Carroll Ave *Web:* www.omvmedical.com	Takoma Park	MD	20912	301-270-9212	270-9335	194
O Neill's Chevrolet & Buick Inc 5 W Main St *TF:* 844-315-0960 ■ *Web:* www.oneillschevybuick.com	Avon	CT	06001	844-315-0960		57
O P Solutions Inc 350 First Ave Ste MG *Web:* www.pattsy.com	New York	NY	10010	212-979-1000		177
O S F Flavors Inc 40 Baker Hollow Rd *Web:* osfflavors.com	Windsor	CT	06095	860-298-8350		297-11
O S U Center for Health Sciences 1111 W 17th St *TF:* 800-677-1972 ■ *Web:* health.okstate.edu	Tulsa	OK	74107	918-582-1972		165
O Ya Restaurant 9 E St Pl *Web:* o-ya.restaurant	Boston	MA	02111	617-654-9900		671
O'Bannon Woods State Park 7234 Old Forest Rd SW *Web:* www.in.gov	Corydon	IN	47112	812-738-8232		565
O'Brien & Company Inc 710 Second Ave Ste 925 *Web:* www.obrienandco.com	Seattle	WA	98104	206-621-8626		194
O'Brien & Gere Engineers Inc 3214 Charles B Root Wynd Ste 130 *Web:* www.obg.com	Syracuse	NY	13202	315-956-6100	463-7554	261
O'Brien County 160 S Hayes Ave *Web:* www.obriencounty.com	Primghar	IA	51245	712-957-1313	928-3536	338
O'Brien Dental Lab Inc 4311 SW Research Way *TF:* 800-445-5941 ■ *Web:* obriendentallab.com	Corvallis	OR	97333	541-754-1238		415
O'Brien Energy Co 425 Ashley Ridge Blvd Ste 300 *Web:* www.obrienenergyco.com	Shreveport	LA	71106	318-865-8568		536
O'Brien Firm Pc 325 Chestnut St Ste 1320 *Web:* obfirm.com	Philadelphia	PA	19106	267-758-6029		41
O'Brien Intl 14615 NE 91st St *TF:* 800-662-7436 ■ *Web:* obrien.com	Redmond	WA	98052	425-881-5900		710
O'Brien Steel Service Co 1700 N E Adams St *TF:* 800-322-4450 ■ *Web:* www.obriensteel.com	Peoria	IL	61603	309-671-5800		480
O'Brien's Aveda Institute 1475 Shelburne Rd *Web:* www.obriensavedainstitute.org	South Burlington	VT	05403	802-658-9591	860-0230	167-3
O'Brien's Oyster Bar & Restaurant 113 Main St *Web:* www.obriensoysterbar.com	Annapolis	MD	21401	410-268-6288	267-7767	671
O'Brien, Tanski & Young LLP 500 Enterprise Dr 4th Fl Wing B *Web:* www.otylaw.com	Hartford	CT	06067	860-525-2700		428
O'Charley's Inc 3038 Sidco Dr *NASDAQ:* CHUX ■ *Web:* ocharleys.com	Nashville	TN	37204	615-256-8500		670
O'Connell & Associates Consulting Engineers LLC 1394 County Hwy 283 S *Web:* oconnellengineers.com	Santa Rosa Beach	FL	32459	850-403-4555	213-3199	261
O'Connell & Hval Llp 401(K) Plan 8555 SW Apple Way Ste 300 *Web:* hagenoconnell.com	Portland	OR	97225	503-227-2900		41
O'Connell Electric Co 830 Phillips Rd *TF:* 800-343-2176 ■ *Web:* www.oconnellelectric.com	Victor	NY	14564	585-924-2176	924-4973	189-4

Name / Address	City	State	ZIP	Phone	Fax	Class
O'Connell Oil Associates Inc 545 Merrill Rd *TF:* 800-464-4894 ■ *Web:* www.oconnelloil.com	Pittsfield	MA	01201	413-499-4800	499-6072	324
O'Connell Robertson & Associates Inc 811 Barton Springs Rd Ste 900 *Web:* www.oconnellrobertson.com	Austin	TX	78704	512-478-7286		261
O'Connor & Drew PC 25 Braintree Hill Office Pk *Web:* www.ocd.com	Braintree	MA	02184	617-471-1120		2
O'connor Company Inc 16910 W 116th St *TF:* 888-800-3540 ■ *Web:* www.oconnor-hvac.com	Lenexa	KS	66219	913-894-8788		41
O'Connor Constructors Inc 45 Industrial Dr **Fax Area Code:* 781 ■ *Web:* www.ocgaronconst.com	Canton	MA	02021	617-364-9000	828-8248*	186
O'Connor Group Inc, The 10 Stearns Rd *Web:* www.theoconnorgroup.com	Bedford	MA	01730	781-275-2423		463
O'Connor Hospital 2105 Forest Ave *Web:* oconnor.verity.org	San Jose	CA	95128	408-947-2500		374-3
O'Connor Insurance Agency 12101 Olive Blvd *Web:* www.oconnor-ins.com	Saint Louis	MO	63141	314-434-0038		390
O'Connor Sales Inc 16107 Piuma Ave *Web:* www.oconnorsales.net	Cerritos	CA	90703	562-403-3848	403-3858	612
O'Connor Thompson Mcdonough Klotsche LLP 2500 Venture Oaks Way Ste 150 *Web:* otmklaw.com	Sacramento	CA	95833	916-993-4540		41
O'Connor Woods 3400 Wagner Heights Rd *TF:* 800-957-3308 ■ *Web:* www.oconnorwoods.org	Stockton	CA	95209	209-956-3400		672
O'Connor's Restaurant & Bar 1160 W Boylston St *Web:* www.oconnorsrestaurant.com	Worcester	MA	01606	508-853-0789	853-2879	671
O'Currance Teleservices Inc 11747 S Lonepeak Pkwy Ste 100 *Web:* www.ocurrance.com	Draper	UT	84020	801-736-0500		393
O'day Consultants Inc 2710 Loker Ave W Ste 100 *Web:* www.odayconsultants.com	Carlsbad	CA	92010	760-931-7700		261
O'Day Equipment Inc 1301 40th St NW *TF:* 800-654-6329 ■ *Web:* www.odayequipment.com	Fargo	ND	58102	701-282-9260		639
O'Doherty's Irish Grill 525 W Spokane Falls Blvd *Web:* www.odohertyspub.com	Spokane	WA	99201	509-747-0322		671
O'donnell Lee Mccowan & Phillips LLC 112 Silver St *Web:* www.odonnellandlee.com	Waterville	ME	04901	207-872-0112		428
O'Fallon Chamber of Commerce 2145 Bryan Vly Commercial Dr *TF:* 800-349-1897 ■ *Web:* www.ofallonchamber.org	O'Fallon	MO	63366	636-240-1818		139
O'Gara Coach Company LLC 8833 W Olympic Blvd *TF:* 888-291-5533 ■ *Web:* www.ogaracoach.com	Beverly Hills	CA	90211	877-588-8862		57
O'Gara Group, The 9113 Le St Dr *Web:* www.ogaragroup.com	Fairfield	OH	45014	513-338-0660	338-0692	693
O'Halleran Tom (Rep D - AZ) 324 Cannon House Office Bldg *Web:* ohalleran.house.gov	Washington	DC	20515	202-225-3361		342-2
O'halloran International Inc 3311 Adventureland Dr *TF:* 800-800-6503 ■ *Web:* www.trivistacompanies.com	Altoona	IA	50009	515-967-3300	967-0206	770
O'Hara Gallery 595 Madison Ave *Web:* www.johg.com	New York	NY	10022	212-644-3533		42
O'Harrow Construction Co 4575 Ann Arbor Rd *Web:* www.oharrow.net	Jackson	MI	49202	517-764-4770	764-5564	186
O'kane Consultants Inc 112 Research Dr *Web:* www.okc-sk.com	Saskatoon	SK	S7N3R3	306-955-0702		261
O'Keefe Drilling Co 2000 4 Mile Rd *TF:* 800-745-5554 ■ *Web:* okeefedrilling.com	Butte	MT	59701	406-494-3310		656
O'keefe Elevator Company Inc 1402 Jones St *TF:* 800-369-6317 ■ *Web:* www.okeefe-elevator.com	Omaha	NE	68102	402-345-4056		358
O'Keefe Firm Company LPA, The 7385 Far Hills Ave *Web:* gomedmalohio.com	Dayton	OH	45459	937-643-0600	586-9495	41
O'Keeffe's Inc 325 Newhall St *TF:* 888-653-3333 ■ *Web:* www.okeeffes.com	San Francisco	CA	94124	415-822-4222		234
O'Leary Paint 300 E Oakland Ave *TF:* 800-477-2066 ■ *Web:* www.olearypaint.com	Lansing	MI	48906	517-487-2066	487-1680	550
O'Leary's Seafood Restaurant 310 Third St *Web:* www.olearysseafood.com	Annapolis	MD	21403	410-263-0884		671
O'Leno State Park 410 SE Oleno Park Rd *Web:* www.floridastateparks.org	High Springs	FL	32643	386-454-1853		565
O'Malley & Berberich CPAS PC 8535 E Hartford Dr Ste 108 *Web:* omalleycpas.com	Scottsdale	AZ	85255	480-778-1751		2
O'Malley & Harvey LLP 400 Fifth Ave Ste 310 *Web:* omalleyharvey.com	Waltham	MA	02451	617-357-5544		41
O'Malley Hansen Communications 180 N Wacker Dr Ste 400 *Web:* omalleyhansen.com	Chicago	IL	60606	312-377-0630		636
O'Melveny & Myers LLP 400 S Hope St 18th Fl *Web:* www.omm.com	Los Angeles	CA	90071	213-430-6000		428
O'More College of Design 423 S Margin St *Web:* www.omorecollege.edu	Franklin	TN	37064	615-794-4254		166
O'Neal Construction Inc 525 W William *Web:* www.onealconstruction.com	Ann Arbor	MI	48103	734-769-0770		186
O'Neal Consulting 7557 Rambler Rd Ste 420 *Web:* www.onealconsulting.com	Dallas	TX	75204	214-202-6151		194
O'Neal Inc 10 Falcon Crest Dr *Web:* www.onealinc.com	Greenville	SC	29607	864-298-2000	298-2200	261
O'Neal Steel Inc 744 41st St N *TF:* 800-861-8272 ■ *Web:* www.onealsteel.com	Birmingham	AL	35222	205-599-8000		492
O'Neil & Associates Inc 495 Byers Rd *Web:* www.oneil.com	Miamisburg	OH	45342	937-865-0800	865-5858	637-10
O'Neil Data Systems Inc 12655 Beatrice St *Web:* www.oneildigitalsolutions.com	Los Angeles	CA	90066	310-448-6400		225
O'Neil Printing Inc 366 N 2nd Ave *Web:* oneilprint.com	Phoenix	AZ	85003	602-258-7789		627
O'Neil Software Inc 11 Cushing Ste 100 *Web:* www.oneilsoft.com	Irvine	CA	92618	949-458-1234		180
O'Neill & Associates LLC 617 646 1000 Thirty-One New Chardon St *TF:* 866-989-4321 ■ *Web:* www.oneillandassoc.com	Boston	MA	02114	617-646-1000		194
O'Neill Hotels & Resorts Ltd 810 - 925 W Georgia St *Web:* oneillhotels.com	Vancouver	BC	V6C3L2	604-684-0444		379
O'Neill Properties Group LP 2701 Renaissance Blvd 4th Fl *Web:* mlpventures.com	King of Prussia	PA	19406	610-239-6100		652
O'Neill Wetsuits USA 1071 41st Ave *TF:* 800-213-6444 ■ *Web:* us.oneill.com	Santa Cruz	CA	95063	831-475-7500	475-0544	710
O'Reilly & Associates Inc 1005 Gravenstein Hwy N *TF:* 800-998-9938 ■ *Web:* www.oreilly.com	Sebastopol	CA	95472	707-829-0515	829-0104	637-11
O'Reilly Auto Parts 233 S Patterson *NASDAQ: ORLY* ■ *TF:* 888-327-7153 ■ *Web:* www.oreillyauto.com	Springfield	MO	65802	417-862-6708		54
O'reilly Public Relations 3403 Tenth St Ste 110 *Web:* oprusa.com	Riverside	CA	92501	951-781-2240		636
O'Reilly Rancilio PC Sterling Town Ctr 12900 Hall Rd Ste 350 *TF:* 800-708-3528 ■ *Web:* www.orlaw.com	Sterling Heights	MI	48313	586-726-1000		428
O'Reilly Talbot & Okun Associates Inc 293 Bridge St *Web:* oto-env.com	Springfield	MA	01103	413-788-6222		261
O'Rielly Chevrolet 6160 E Broadway Blvd *Web:* www.orielly.com	Tucson	AZ	85711	520-829-4400		57
O'riordan Bethel Law Firm LLP, The 1314 19th St NW *Web:* oriordanbethel.com	Washington	DC	20036	202-822-1720	822-1721	428
O'Rorke's Family Eatery 44 Steinwehr Ave *Web:* www.ororkes.com	Gettysburg	PA	17325	717-334-2333		671
O'Rourke Petroleum Inc 223 McCarty Dr **Fax Area Code:* 817 ■ *TF:* 800-683-1331 ■ *Web:* www.orpp.com	Houston	TX	77029	713-672-4500	553-0508*	316
O'Rourke Sales Co 3885 Elmore Ave Ste 100 *TF:* 877-599-6548 ■ *Web:* www.orourkesales.com	Davenport	IA	52807	563-823-1501	823-1534	38
O'Rourke Wrecking Co 660 Lunken Pk Dr *TF:* 800-354-9850 ■ *Web:* www.orourkewrecking.com	Cincinnati	OH	45226	513-871-1400	871-1313	189-16
O'Ryan Group Inc 4010 Pilot Ste 108 *TF:* 800-253-0750 ■ *Web:* www.oryangroup.com	Memphis	TN	38118	901-794-4610		701
O'steen's Restaurant 205 Anastasia Blvd *Web:* www.osteensrestaurant.com	Saint Augustine	FL	32080	904-829-6974		671
O'sullivan Films Inc 1944 Valley Ave *TF:* 800-336-9882 ■ *Web:* www.continental-industry.com	Winchester	VA	22601	540-667-6666		600
O.K. Distributing Company Inc 522 14th Ave W *Web:* www.okdistributingco.com	Williston	ND	58802	701-572-9161		756
O.K. Tire Store 3546 M-40 *Web:* www.oktirestores.net	Hamilton	MI	49419	269-751-7323		755
O.S. Earth Inc 800 Village Walk Ste 156 *TF:* 800-220-4263 ■ *Web:* www.osearth.com	Guilford	CT	06437	800-220-4263		178-1
01 Communications Inc 4359 Town Center Blvd Ste 217 *TF:* 888-444-1111 ■ *Web:* www.o1.com	El Dorado Hills	CA	95762	888-444-1111		736
02Micro International Ltd 3118 Patrick Henry Dr *NASDAQ: OIIM* ■ *Web:* www.o2micro.com	Santa Clara	CA	95054	408-987-5920		696
OA (Overeaters Anonymous Inc) PO Box 44020 *TF:* 866-505-4966 ■ *Web:* oa.org	Rio Rancho	NM	87174	505-891-2664	891-4320	48-21
OAA (Opticians Association of America) 3740 Canada Rd *Web:* oaa.org	Lakeland	TN	38002	901-388-2423	388-2348	49-8
OAAA (Outdoor Adv Association of America Inc) 1850 M St NW Ste 1040 *Web:* oaaa.org	Washington	DC	20036	202-833-5566	833-1522	615
OABA (Outdoor Amusement Business Association Inc) 1035 S Semoran Blvd Ste 1045A **Fax Area Code:* 952 ■ *TF:* 800-517-6222 ■ *Web:* oaba.org	Winter Park	FL	32792	407-848-4958	300-2419*	615
OAG Worldwide 3025 Highland Pkwy Ste 200 **Fax Area Code:* 630 ■ *TF:* 800-342-5624 ■ *Web:* www.oag.com	Downers Grove	IL	60515	800-342-5624	515-3933*	637-10
OAGI (Open Applications Group Inc) PO Box 4897 **Fax Area Code:* 801 ■ *Web:* oagi.org	Marietta	GA	30061	404-402-1962	740-0100*	49-13
OAH (Organization of American Historians) 112 N Bryan Ave *Web:* www.oah.org	Bloomington	IN	47408	812-855-7311	855-0696	49-5
Oahe Downstream Recreation Area 20439 Marina Loop Rd *Web:* gfp.sd.gov	Fort Pierre	SD	57532	605-223-7722		565
Oahe Electric Co-opeartive Inc 102 S Cranford St PO Box 216 *TF:* 800-640-6243 ■ *Web:* www.oaheelectric.com	Blunt	SD	57522	605-962-6243	962-6306	245
Oahu Federal Credit Union 2219 Pauoa Rd *Web:* oahufcu.org	Honolulu	HI	96813	808-521-6727		219

Name / Address	City	State	ZIP	Phone	Fax	Class
Oahu Publications Inc 500 Ala Moana Blvd Ste 7-500 *TF:* 800-372-8347 ■ *Web:* www.oahupublications.com	Honolulu	HI	96813	808-529-4700		532-3
Oahu Transit Services 811 Middle St *Web:* www.thebus.org	Honolulu	HI	96819	808-848-4500	848-4419	468
OAI Corp 4545 W Hillsborough Ave *TF:* 800-783-9187 ■ *Web:* www.oaicorp.com	Tampa	FL	33614	813-888-8796		344
Oak Associates Funds c/o Ultimus Fund Solutions 225 Pictoria Dr PO Box 46707 *TF:* 888-462-5386 ■ *Web:* www.oakfunds.com	Cincinnati	OH	45246	888-462-5386		528
Oak Bay Technologies Inc PO Box 65494 *Web:* www.oakbay.com	Port Ludlow	WA	98365	360-437-0718		647
Oak Brook Care 2013 Midwest Rd *Web:* oakbrookcare.com	Oak Brook	IL	60523	630-495-0220		793
Oak Brook Golf Club 1200 Oak Brook Rd *Web:* www.oak-brook.org	Oak Brook	IL	60523	630-990-4233		393
Oak Brook Hills Marriott Resort 3500 Midwest Rd *Web:* www3.hilton.com	Oak Brook	IL	60523	630-850-5555		377
Oak Brook Mechanical Services Inc 961 S Rt 83 *Web:* omshvac.com	Elmhurst	IL	60126	630-941-3555	941-0294	189-10
Oak Cliff Bible Fellowship 1808 W Camp Wisdom Rd *Web:* www.ocbfchurch.org	Dallas	TX	75232	214-672-9100		48-20
Oak Cliff Chamber of Commerce 1001 N Bishop Ave *Web:* oakcliffchamber.org	Dallas	TX	75208	214-943-4567	943-4582	139
Oak Cliff Office Supply 1876 Lone Star Dr *Web:* www.ocopexpress.com	Dallas	TX	75212	214-943-7421		535
Oak Creek Energy Systems Inc 500 La Terraza Blvd *Web:* www.oces.com	Escondido	CA	92025	760-975-0910		194
Oak Creek-Franklin Joint School District 7630 S Tenth St *Web:* www.ocfsd.org	Oak Creek	WI	53154	414-768-5880		685
Oak Crest DeKalb Area Retirement Ctr 2944 Greenwood Acres Dr *Web:* www.oakcrestdekalb.org	DeKalb	IL	60115	815-756-8461		672
Oak Forest - Crestwood Area Chamber of Commerce 15440 S Central *Web:* oc-chamber.org	Oak Forest	IL	60452	708-687-4600		139
Oak Forest Hospital of Cook County 15900 S Cicero Ave *Web:* cookcountyhealth.org	Oak Forest	IL	60452	708-633-4293		374-7
Oak Grove School 220 W Lomita Ave *Web:* oakgroveschool.org	Ojai	CA	93023	805-646-8236	646-6509	622
Oak Grove Technologies LLC 4131 Parklake Ave Ste 100 *Web:* www.oakgrovetech.com	Raleigh	NC	27612	919-278-2225	845-1785	463
Oak Hall Inc 6150 Poplar Ave Ste 146 *TF:* 844-625-4255 ■ *Web:* www.oakhall.com	Memphis	TN	38119	901-761-3580		157-4
Oak Hall Industries 840 Union St *TF:* 800-223-0429 ■ *Web:* www.oakhalli.com	Salem	VA	24153	540-387-0000	387-2034	155-14
Oak Harbor Chamber of Commerce 32630 SR 20 *Web:* www.oakharborchamber.com	Oak Harbor	WA	98277	360-675-3755	679-1624	139
Oak Harbor Freight Lines Inc 1339 W Valley Hwy N PO Box 1469 *Web:* www.oakh.com	Auburn	WA	98071	253-288-8300	288-8301	314
Oak Hill Academy 2635 Oak Hill Rd *Web:* www.oak hill.net	Mouth of Wilson	VA	24363	276-579-2619		622
Oak Hill Capital Partners 263 Tresser Blvd One Stamford Plz, Flr 15 *Web:* www.oakhillcapital.com	Stamford	CT	06901	203-328-1600		792
Oak Hill Technology Inc 19690 Ranch Rd 12 *Web:* www.oakhilltech.com	Driftwood	TX	78619	512-842-1000		180
Oak Hills Christian College 1600 Oak Hills Rd SW *TF:* 888-751-8670 ■ *Web:* www.oakhills.edu	Bemidji	MN	56601	218-751-8670	751-8825	161
Oak Hotels Inc 2424 SR- 52 *Web:* www.oakhotels.com	Hopewell Junction	NY	12533	845-223-3603		707
Oak Island Resort & Conference Ctr 36 Treasure Dr *TF:* 800-565-5075 ■ *Web:* www.oakislandresort.ca	Western Shore	NS	B0J3M0	902-627-2600	627-2020	669
Oak Knoll Animal Hospital Ltd 3113 41st St *Web:* www.oakknollanimalhospital.com	Moline	IL	61265	309-762-9474		794
Oak Knoll Press 310 Delaware St *TF:* 800-996-2556 ■ *Web:* www.oakknoll.com	New Castle	DE	19720	302-328-7232	328-7274	637-2
Oak Lawn Chamber of Commerce 5120 Museum Dr *Web:* www.oaklawnchamber.com	Oak Lawn	IL	60453	708-424-8300		139
Oak Lawn Park District 9400 S Kenton Ave *Web:* www.olparks.com	Oak Lawn	IL	60453	708-857-2222		31
Oak Lawn Public Library 9427 Raymond Ave *Web:* www.olpl.org	Oak Lawn	IL	60453	708-422-4990	422-5061	434-3
Oak Meadows Elementary School 28600 Poinsettia St *Web:* www.menifeeusd.org	Murrieta	CA	92563	951-246-4210		685
Oak Mountain State Park 200 Terrace Dr *Web:* www.alapark.com	Pelham	AL	35124	205-620-2520	620-2531	565
Oak Park Area Convention & Visitors Bureau 1118 Westgate *TF:* 888-625-7275 ■ *Web:* www.visitoakpark.com	Oak Park	IL	60301	708-524-7800	524-7473	206
Oak Park Mall 11149 W 95th St *Web:* www.thenewoakparkmall.com	Overland Park	KS	66214	913-888-4400		460
Oak Park Park District 218 Madison *Web:* www.pdop.org	Oak Park	IL	60302	708-383-0002		31
Oak Park Public Library 834 Lake St *Web:* www.oppl.org	Oak Park	IL	60301	708-383-8200		434-3
Oak Park School District (OPSD) 13900 Granzon *Web:* www.oakparkschools.org	Oak Park	MI	48237	248-336-7700	336-7738	360-2
Oak Park-River Forest Chamber of Commerce PO Box 4554 *Web:* www.oprfchamber.org	Oak Park	IL	60304	708-613-0550		139
Oak Plantation Resort & Suites Condominium Assn 4090 Enchanted Oaks Cir *TF:* 888-411-4141 ■ *Web:* oakplantationresort.com	Kissimmee	FL	34741	888-411-4141		378
Oak Printing Co, The 19540 Progress Dr *TF:* 800-419-3316 ■ *Web:* www.oakprintingco.com	Strongsville	OH	44149	440-238-3316	238-9339	627
Oak Products Inc 504 Wade St *Web:* www.oakpresses.com	Sturgis	MI	49091	269-651-8513	659-4625	456
Oak Ridge Chamber of Commerce 1400 Oak Ridge Tpke *Web:* www.oakridgechamber.org	Oak Ridge	TN	37830	865-483-1321	483-1678	139
Oak Ridge Farms Inc 2940 N 925 E *Web:* www.oakridgefarmsinc.com	Logansport	IN	46947	574-664-2952		276
Oak Ridge Financial 701 Xenia Ave S Golden Hills Office Ctr Ste 100 *Web:* www.oakridgefinancial.com	Golden Valley	MN	55416	763-923-2200		405
Oak Ridge Hotel & Conference Ctr 1 Oak Ridge Dr *TF:* 877-874-6772 ■ *Web:* www.oakridgeminneapolis.com	Chaska	MN	55318	952-368-3100	368-1488	377
Oak Ridge National Laboratory (ORNL) PO Box 2008 *Web:* www.ornl.gov	Oak Ridge	TN	37831	865-576-9219	574-0595	668
Oak Ridge Public Library 1401 Oak Ridge Tpke *Web:* www.oakridgetn.gov	Oak Ridge	TN	37830	865-425-3455		434-3
Oak Ridge Tool - Engineering Inc 1000 Clearview Ct *Web:* www.ortool.com	Oak Ridge	TN	37830	865-482-1061	482-3368	454
Oak Ridge Winery 6100 E Victor Rd *Web:* www.oakridgewinery.com	Lodi	CA	95240	209-369-4769		50-7
Oak Room 138 St James Ave *Web:* www.oaklongbarkitchen.com	Boston	MA	02116	617-585-7222		671
Oak Street Hair Group Inc 125 Oak St *Web:* oakstreethairgroup.com	Birmingham	AL	35213	205-879-3222		77
Oak Tree Systems Inc 694 Frnt St *Web:* oaktree-systems.com	Lovingston	VA	22949	434-263-6700		809
Oak Valley Community Bank 125 N 3rd Ave *Web:* www.ovcb.com	Oakdale	CA	95361	209-848-1929		70
Oak View Mall 3001 S 144th St *Web:* www.oakviewmall.com	Omaha	NE	68144	402-330-3332		460
OakBend Medical Ctr 1705 Jackson St *Web:* www.oakbendmedcenter.org	Richmond	TX	77469	281-341-3000	341-3056	374-3
OakBrook Investments LLC 2300 Cabot Dr Ste 300 *Web:* www.oakbrookinvest.com	Lisle	IL	60532	630-271-0100		528
Oakbrook Shopping Ctr 100 Oakbrook Ctr *Web:* www.oakbrookcenter.com	Oak Brook	IL	60523	630-573-0700		460
Oakdale Electric Co-op PO Box 128 *TF:* 800-241-2468 ■ *Web:* www.oakdalerec.com	Oakdale	WI	54649	608-372-4131		245
Oakdale Precision Inc 7022 Sixth St N *Web:* oakdaleprecision.com	Oakdale	MN	55128	651-730-7700		757
Oakdale Theatre 10 Marshall St *Web:* www.oakdale.com	Wallingford	CT	06492	203-269-8721		572
Oakes Motor Sports 1210 S 7th St *Web:* www.oakesmotorsports.com	Oakes	ND	58474	701-742-2936		736
Oakgrove Construction Inc 6900 Seneca St *Web:* www.oakgroveconst.com	Elma	NY	14059	716-652-2200	655-3919	188-4
Oakhill Correctional Institution 5212 County Hwy M *Web:* www.doc.wi.gov	Oregon	WI	53575	608-835-3101	835-6090	213
Oakhurst Area Chamber of Commerce 49074 Civic Cir *Web:* oakhurstchamber.com	Oakhurst	CA	93644	559-683-7766		139
Oakhurst Dairy 364 Forest Ave *TF:* 800-482-0718 ■ *Web:* www.oakhurstdairy.com	Portland	ME	04101	207-772-7468	874-0714	296-27
Oakland Arena and RingCentral Coliseum 7000 Coliseum Way *Web:* www.theoaklandarena.com	Oakland	CA	94621	510-569-2121		720
Oakland Asian Cultural Ctr 388 Ninth St Ste 290 *Web:* oacc.cc	Oakland	CA	94607	510-637-0455	637-0459	50-2
Oakland Aviation Museum 8252 Earhart Rd *Web:* www.oaklandaviationmuseum.org	Oakland	CA	94621	510-638-7100		520
Oakland Ballet Co 2201 Broadway Ste LL17 *Web:* oaklandballet.org	Oakland	CA	94612	510-893-3132		573-1
Oakland Care Center Inc 20 Breakneck Rd *Web:* oaklandrehabhc.com	Oakland	NJ	07436	201-337-3300		371
Oakland City Hall 1 Frank H Ogawa Plz *TF:* 800-834-3773 ■ *Web:* www.oaklandca.gov	Oakland	CA	94612	510-615-5566		337
Oakland City University 138 N Lucretia St *TF:* 800-737-5125 ■ *Web:* www.oak.edu	Oakland City	IN	47660	812-749-4781	749-1433	166
Oakland Community College 2480 Opdyke Rd *Web:* oaklandcc.edu	Bloomfield Hills	MI	48304	248-341-2000	233-2828	162
Oakland Consulting Group Inc 9501 Sheridan St Ste 200 *Web:* www.ocg-inc.com	Lanham	MD	20706	301-577-4111		180
Oakland Convention & Visitors Bureau 481 Water St *TF:* 800-862-2543 ■ *Web:* www.visitoakland.com	Oakland	CA	94607	510-839-9000		206
Oakland Elementary School 2415 Brockton Ave *Web:* www.royaloakschools.org	Royal Oak	MI	48067	248-542-4406		685
Oakland House 7801 Genesta Ave *Web:* www.oaklandhousemuseum.org	Saint Louis	MO	63123	314-352-5654		50-3

Name / Address	Phone	Fax	Class
Oakland Metropolitan Chamber of Commerce 475 14th St Ste 100 ... Oakland CA 94612 *Web:* www.oaklandchamber.com	510-874-4800	839-8817	139
Oakland Museum of California 1000 Oak St ... Oakland CA 94607 *TF:* 888-625-6873 ■ *Web:* www.museumca.org	510-238-2200		520
Oakland Nursery Inc 1156 Oakland Park Ave ... Columbus OH 43224 *Web:* www.oaklandnursery.com	614-268-3511	917-1023	323
Oakland Packaging & Supply 3200 Regatta Blvd Unit F ... Richmond CA 94804 *TF:* 800-237-3103 ■ *Web:* www.oakpackaging.com	510-307-4242	307-4252	557
Oakland Press 2125 Butterfield Dr Ste 102N ... Troy MI 48084 *TF:* 888-977-3677 ■ *Web:* www.theoaklandpress.com	248-332-8181		637-8
Oakland Public Library 125 14th St ... Oakland CA 94612 *Web:* www.oaklandlibrary.org	510-238-3144	238-2232	434-3
Oakland Raiders, The 1220 Harbor Bay Pkwy ... Alameda CA 94502 *TF:* 800-724-3377 ■ *Web:* raiders.com	510-864-5000	864-5134	715-3
Oakland Schools Inc 2111 Pontiac Lake Rd ... Waterford MI 48328 *Web:* www.oakland.k12.mi.us	248-209-2000	209-2206	685
Oakland Unified School District 1000 Broadway Ste 680 ... Oakland CA 94607 *TF:* 888-604-4636 ■ *Web:* www.ousd.org	510-879-8200		685
Oakland University 2200 Squirrel Rd ... Rochester MI 48309 *TF:* 800-625-8648 ■ *Web:* www.oakland.edu	248-370-2100	370-4462	166
Oakland University Art Gallery Oakland University 208 Wilson Hall ... Rochester MI 48309 *Web:* www.ouartgallery.org	248-370-3005	370-4208	50-2
Oakland Zoo 9777 Golf Links Rd ... Oakland CA 94605 *Web:* www.oaklandzoo.org	510-632-9525		823
Oaklawn Park 2705 Central Ave ... Hot Springs AR 71901 *TF:* 800-625-5296 ■ *Web:* www.oaklawn.com	501-623-4411	624-4950	642
Oaklawn Psychiatric Center Inc 330 Lakeview Dr ... Goshen IN 46527 *TF:* 800-282-0809 ■ *Web:* www.oaklawn.org	574-533-1234		726
Oakley Inc 1 Icon ... Foothill Ranch CA 92610 *TF:* 800-403-7449 ■ *Web:* www.oakley.com	949-672-6925		542
Oakley Industries Inc 35166 Automation Dr ... Clinton Township MI 48035 *Web:* www.oakley-ind.com	586-792-1261	792-1332	489
Oakley Transport Inc 101 ABC Rd ... Lake Wales FL 33859 *TF:* 800-969-8265 ■ *Web:* www.oakleytransport.com	863-638-1435		449
Oakley's Bistro 1464 W 86th St ... Indianapolis IN 46260 *Web:* www.oakleysbistro.com	317-824-1231	824-0938	671
Oakley-Lindsay Ctr 300 Civic Center Plz ... Quincy IL 62301 *Web:* www.oakleylindsaycenter.com	217-223-1000	223-1330	205
Oakmark Family of Funds 330 W Nineth St ... Kansas City MO 64105 *TF:* 800-625-6275 ■ *Web:* www.oakmark.com	617-483-8327		528
Oakridge Equine Hospital PC 6675 E Waterloo Rd ... Edmond OK 73034 *Web:* oakridgevet.com	405-359-5002	359-2869	794
Oakridge Holdings Inc 400 W Ontario St Ste 1003 ... Chicago IL 60610 *Web:* www.oakridgeholdingsinc.com	312-505-9267		22
Oaks Amusement Park 7805 SE Oaks Pkwy ... Portland OR 97202 *Web:* www.oakspark.com	503-233-5777	236-9143	32
Oaks at Denville, The 19 Pocono Rd ... Denville NJ 07834 *TF:* 877-693-7650 ■ *Web:* oaksatdenville.org	973-586-6000	586-6030	672
Oaks at Ojai 122 E Ojai Ave ... Ojai CA 93023 *TF:* 800-753-6257 ■ *Web:* www.oaksspa.com	805-646-5573		706
Oaks Correctional Facility 1500 Caberfae Hwy ... Manistee MI 49660 *Web:* www.michigan.gov	231-723-8272		213
Oaks, The 350 W Hillcrest Dr ... Thousand Oaks CA 91360 *Web:* www.shoptheoaksmall.com	805-495-2032		460
Oakton Community College 1600 E Golf Rd ... Des Plaines IL 60016 *Web:* www.oakton.edu	847-635-1600	635-1890	162
Oakton Pavilion Healthcare Facility Inc 1660-1665 OAKTON Pl ... Des Plaines IL 60018 *Web:* generationsoakton.com	847-299-5588	493-6525	450
Oakview Manor 929 Mixon School Rd ... Ozark AL 36360 *Web:* www.oakviewmanor.com	334-774-2631	774-4252	371
Oakville Chamber of Commerce 700 Kerr St Ste 200 ... Oakville ON L6K3W5 *Web:* oakvillechamber.com	905-845-6613	845-6475	137
Oakville-Trafalgar Memorial Hospital 3001 Hospital Gate ... Oakville ON L6M0L8 *Web:* www.haltonhealthcare.on.ca	905-845-2571	338-4636	374-2
Oakwood Bank 36328 Main St PO Box 37 ... Whitehall WI 54773 *Web:* oakwoodbankwi.com	715-538-1500		70
Oakwood Capital Management LLC 12121 Wilshire Blvd Ste 1250 ... Los Angeles CA 90025 *TF:* 800-586-0600 ■ *Web:* www.oakwoodcap.com	310-772-2600		194
Oakwood Crystal City 400 15th St S ... Arlington VA 22202 *TF:* 877-902-0832 ■ *Web:* www.oakwood.com	866-730-8916		210
Oakwood Ctr 197 Westbank Expy ... Gretna LA 70053 *Web:* www.oakwoodcenter.com	504-361-1550		460
Oakwood Friends School 22 Spackenkill Rd ... Poughkeepsie NY 12603 *Web:* www.oakwoodfriends.org	845-462-4200		622
Oakwood Laboratories LLC 27070 Miles Rd Ste A ... Oakwood OH 44146 *Web:* oakwoodlabs.com	440-359-0000	359-0001	85
Oakwood Lakes State Park 46109 202nd St ... Bruce SD 57220 *Web:* sd.gov	605-627-5441		565
Oakwood Lanes Inc 234 SR- 31 N ... Washington NJ 07882 *Web:* www.oakwoodlanes.com	908-689-0310		99
Oakwood Metal Fabricating Co 1100 Oakwood Blvd ... Dearborn MI 48124 *Web:* www.theoakwoodgroup.com	313-561-7740	561-7784	328
Oakwood Products Inc 1741 Old Dunbar Rd ... West Columbia SC 29172 *TF:* 800-467-3386 ■ *Web:* www.oakwoodchemical.com	803-739-8800	739-6957	144
Oakwood University 7000 Adventist Blvd ... Huntsville AL 35896 *Web:* www2.oakwood.edu	256-726-7000	726-7154	166
Oakwood Village Prairie Ridge 5565 Tancho Dr ... Madison WI 53718 *Web:* www.oakwoodvillage.net	608-230-4000		672
Oakworks Inc 923 E Wellspring Rd ... New Freedom PA 17349 *TF:* 800-558-8850 ■ *Web:* www.oakworks.com	717-235-6807	235-6798	475
Oanda Corp 1441 Broadway 6 FL Ste 6027 ... New York NY 10005 *TF:* 800-826-8164 ■ *Web:* www1.oanda.com	212-858-7690		69
OAP Inc PO Box 3309 ... Suwanee GA 30024 *TF:* 888-732-2478 ■ *Web:* peachstateaudio.com	888-732-2478		35
Oar Net 1224 Kinnear Rd ... Columbus OH 43212 *TF:* 800-627-6420 ■ *Web:* www.oar.net	614-292-9191		180
Oasis Air Conditioning Heating & Sheet Metal Inc 1931 Grimes St ... Fallon NV 89406 *Web:* www.oasishvacnv.com	775-423-5258		189-10
Oasis Alignment Services Inc 255 Pickering Rd ... Rochester NH 03867 *TF:* 888-488-0236 ■ *Web:* www.oasisalignment.com	603-332-9641		261
Oasis Audio LLC 289 S Main Pl ... Carol Stream IL 60188 *Web:* www.oasisaudio.com	630-668-5367	668-0158	637-10
Oasis Cafe 151 South 500 East ... Salt Lake City UT 84102 *Web:* www.oasiscafeslc.com	801-322-0404		671
Oasis Carwash LLC 3425 E Flamingo Rd ... Las Vegas NV 89121 *Web:* www.oasishandcarwash.com	702-433-3680		62-1
Oasis Community Services 81557 Dr Carreon Blvd Ste C-10 ... Indio CA 92201 *Web:* www.starsinc.com	760-391-4972		374-5
Oasis Computing Inc 1595 16th Ave ... Richmond Hill ON L4B3N9 *Web:* www.oasiscomputing.com	905-709-7456		177
Oasis Deck & Restaurant 4000 A1A ... Saint Augustine FL 32080 *Web:* www.worldfamousoasis.com	904-471-3424		671
Oasis Foods Inc 2222 Kirkman St ... Lake Charles LA 70601 *Web:* www.oasisfoodservice.com	337-439-5262		345
Oasis Mediterranean Cuisine 1520 W Laskey Rd ... Toledo OH 43612 *Web:* www.omcfood.com	419-269-1459	324-7777	296-37
Oasis Outsourcing Inc 2054 Vista Pkwy Ste 300 ... West Palm Beach FL 33411 *TF:* 888-627-4735 ■ *Web:* www.oasisadvantage.com	888-627-4735		631
Oasis Ranch Management 86235 Ave 52 ... Coachella CA 92236 *Web:* seaviewsales.com	760-398-8850		196
Oasis Restaurant 2355 Schoenersville Rd ... Allentown PA 18109 *Web:* www.georgesoasis.com	610-264-1955		671
Oasis Stage Werks Inc 249 S Rio Grande St ... Salt Lake City UT 84101 *Web:* www.oasisstage.com	801-363-0364	575-7121	264-3
Oasis Systems Inc 24 Hartwell Ave ... Lexington MA 02421 *Web:* www.oasissystems.com	781-676-7333		225
Oasis Technology Inc 601 E Daily Dr Ste 226 ... Camarillo CA 93010 *Web:* www.oasistechnology.com	805-445-4833	445-4839	180
Oasis, The 6550 Comanche Trl ... Austin TX 78732 *Web:* www.oasis-austin.com	512-266-2442		671
Oates Energy Inc 14286 Beach Blvd Ste 12 ... Jacksonville FL 32250 *TF:* 800-717-9811 ■ *Web:* www.oatesenergy.com	800-717-9811		78
Oates Veterinary Clinic 715 E Columbus St ... Kenton OH 43326 *Web:* oatesvet.com	419-673-0473		794
Oatey Co 4700 W 160th St ... Cleveland OH 44135 **Fax Area Code: 800* ■ *TF:* 800-321-9532 ■ *Web:* www.oatey.com	216-267-7100	321-9535*	609
O-AT-KA Milk Products Co-opeartive Inc 700 Ellicott St ... Batavia NY 14020 *TF:* 800-828-8152 ■ *Web:* www.oatkamilk.com	585-343-0536	343-4473	296-3
Oatmeal Studios Inc Po Box 191 ... Rochester VT 05767 *Web:* www.oatmealstudios.com	802-767-3181		627
Oats & Marino 100 E Vermilion Ste 400 ... LaFayette LA 70501 *Web:* oatsmarino.com	337-233-1100		41
OATS Inc 2501 Maguire Blvd Ste 101 ... Columbia MO 65201 *TF:* 800-831-9219 ■ *Web:* www.oatstransit.org	573-443-4516		314
OB Macaroni Co 108 South Fwy ... Fort Worth TX 76140 *TF:* 800-553-4336 ■ *Web:* www.obmacaroni.com	817-335-4629		296-31
OB Sports Golf Management LLC 7025 E Greenway Pkwy Ste 550 ... Scottsdale AZ 85254 *Web:* www.obsports.com	480-948-1300		463
Obagi Medical Products Inc 3760 Kilroy Airport Way Ste 500 ... Long Beach CA 90806 *TF:* 800-636-7546 ■ *Web:* www.obagi.com	562-628-1007	628-1008	214
OBC (Ohio Brake and Clutch) 1460 Wolf Creek Trl ... Sharon Center OH 44274 *TF:* 800-622-1990 ■ *Web:* www.ohiobrake.com	330-239-2345	239-4995	385
OBC Northwest Inc 1076 SW Berg Pkwy ... Canby OR 97013 *TF:* 800-477-4744 ■ *Web:* obcnw.com	503-266-2021	266-6837	67
OBCI (Ocean Bio-Chem Inc) 4041 SW 47th Ave ... Fort Lauderdale FL 33314 *NASDAQ: OBCI* ■ *TF:* 800-327-8583 ■ *Web:* www.oceanbiochem.com	954-587-6280	587-2813	151
ObdEdge LLC 2370 Towne Center Blvd ... Baton Rouge LA 70806 *TF:* 888-896-9753 ■ *Web:* www.cellcontrol.com	888-896-9753		809
Obed Wild & Scenic River 208 N Maiden St ... Wartburg TN 37887 *Web:* www.nps.gov	423-346-6294		564
Obelisk 2029 P St NW ... Washington DC 20036 *Web:* www.obeliskdc.com	202-872-1180		671
Ober Gatlinburg Inc 1001 Pkwy Ste 2 ... Gatlinburg TN 37738 *TF:* 800-251-9202 ■ *Web:* obergatlinburg.com	865-436-5423		31
Oberbeck Grain Co 700 Walnut St ... Highland IL 62249 *TF:* 800-632-2012 ■ *Web:* www.oberbeckgrainco.com	618-654-2387	654-5862	447

	Phone	Fax	Class
Oberfields LLC 1165 Alum Creek Dr . . . . Columbus OH 43209 *TF:* 800-845-7644 ■ *Web:* oberfields.com	614-252-0955		191-4
Oberg Industries Inc 2301 Silverville Rd PO Box 368 . . . . .Freeport PA 16229 *Web:* www.oberg.com	724-295-2121	295-2588	757
Oberlin College & Conservatory 38 E College St. . . . . .Oberlin OH 44074 *TF:* 800-622-6243 ■ *Web:* www.oberlin.edu	440-775-8411		166
Oberlin Inn 7 N Main St. . . . . .Oberlin OH 44074 *Web:* thehotelatoberlin.com	440-775-7001		379
Obermeyer Wood Investment Counsel LLLP 200 Columbine St Ste 600 . . . . Aspen CO 81611 *Web:* www.obermeyerwood.com	970-925-8747		401
Oberon Asset Management LLC 51 Wooster St 4th Fl. . . . . .New York NY 10013 **Fax Area Code:* 212 ■ *Web:* www.oberonasset.com	917-237-0147	226-4698*	401
Oberto Sausage Co 7060 S 238th St . . . . .Kent WA 98032 *TF:* 877-453-7591 ■ *Web:* www.oberto.com	877-453-7591		296-26
Oberweis Securities Inc 3333 Warrenville Rd Ste 500 . . . . .Lisle IL 60532 **Fax Area Code:* 630 ■ *TF:* 800-323-6166 ■ *Web:* oberweis.net	800-323-6166	245-0467*	690
OB-GYN Physicians Inc 118 Fairview Dr Ste 100. . . . . .Franklin VA 23851 *Web:* www.ob-gyndocs.com	757-562-4156		415
OBI (Ocean Breeze Intl) 3910 Via Real . . . . .Carpinteria CA 93013 *Web:* www.oceanbreezeintl.com	805-684-1747	684-0235	369
OBI (Oklahoma Blood Institute) 1001 N Lincoln Blvd. . . . . .Oklahoma City OK 73104 **Fax Area Code:* 918 ■ *TF:* 866-708-4995 ■ *Web:* obi.org	405-278-3100	477-0446*	89
OBI Creative 2920 Farnam St. . . . . .Omaha NE 68131 *Web:* www.obicreative.com	402-493-7999		195
Obion County Nursing Home 1084 E County Home Rd . . . . .Union City TN 38261 *Web:* obioncountynursinghome.com	731-885-9065		371
Obion County Public Library 1221 E Reelfoot Ave . . . . .Union City TN 38261 *Web:* www.oclibrary.org	731-885-7000		434-3
Obion River Regional Library Ctr 542 N Lindell . . . . Martin TN 38237 *Web:* www.tn.gov	731-587-2347		434-3
Object CTalk Inc 1013 W Ninth Ave. . . . . King of Prussia PA 19406 *Web:* www.octalk.com	610-265-1278	992-0780	41
Object Edge Inc 488 N Wiget Ln. . . . . .Walnut Creek CA 94598 *Web:* www.objectedge.com	925-943-5558	943-5597	196
Object Management Group (OMG) 140 Kendrick St Ste 300. .Needham MA 02494 *Web:* www.omg.org	781-444-0404	444-0320	48-9
Object Research Systems Inc 760 St-Paul W Ste 101. . . . . Montreal QC H3C1M4 *Web:* www.theobjects.com	514-843-3861		809
Object Systems Group Inc 1505 LBJ Fwy Ste 240 . . . . .Farmers Branch TX 75234 *Web:* www.osgcorp.com	972-650-2026	650-9020	196
ObjectBuilders Inc 20134 W Vly Forge Cir. . . . . King of Prussia PA 19406 *Web:* www.objectbuilders.com	610-783-7748		177
ObjectDC 8212 Old Courthouse Rd . . . . .Vienna VA 22182 *Web:* www.objectdc.com	703-917-0023		344
Objectiva Software Solutions Inc 12770 El Camino Real Ste 300. . . . . San Diego CA 92130 *TF:* 800-878-6975 ■ *Web:* www.objectivasoftware.com	408-809-5950		196
Objective Arts Inc 20 N Wacker Ave. . . . . .Chicago IL 60606 *Web:* www.objectivearts.com	312-977-1150		177
Objective Interface Systems Inc 220 Spring St Ste 530 . . . . .Herndon VA 20170 *Web:* www.ois.com	703-295-6500		177
Objective Systems Inc 55 Dowlin Forge Rd . . . . .Exton PA 19341 *Web:* obj-sys.com	484-875-9841		180
Objective Technologies Inc 90-07 68th Ave. . . . . Forest Hills NY 11375 *Web:* www.object.com	718-997-9741		178-1
Objectivity Inc 3099 N First St Ste 200 . . . . San Jose CA 95134 *TF:* 800-767-6259 ■ *Web:* www.objectivity.com	408-992-7100	992-7171	178-1
ObjectRiver Inc 21 Pemberton Rd. . . . . .Wayland MA 01778 *Web:* www.objectriver.net	508-651-0767		177
Objectstream Inc 7725 W Reno Ave Ste 307 . . . . .Oklahoma City OK 73127 **Fax Area Code:* 866 ■ *Web:* objectstream.com	405-942-4477	814-0174*	178
ObjectVideo Labs 8281 Greensboro Dr Ste 100 . . . . .Tysons VA 22102 **Fax Area Code:* 703 ■ *Web:* www.objectvideolabs.com	571-327-3673	654-9399*	178-7
Objectwin Technology Inc 19219 Katy Fwy Ste 275. . . . . .Houston TX 77079 *Web:* objectwin.com	713-782-8200	782-8283	177
Oblate School of Theology 285 Oblate Dr. . . . . .San Antonio TX 78216 *Web:* ost.edu	210-341-1366		167-3
Oblong Industries Inc 923 E Third St Ste 111 .Los Angeles CA 90013 *Web:* www.oblong.com	213-683-8863		256
Oboxmedia Inc 4200 St Laurent Blvd Ste 900. . . . . Montreal QC H2W2R2 *Web:* oboxmedia.com	514-282-5020		5
Obrien et Al Advertising Inc 3113 Pacific Ave. . . . . .Virginia Beach VA 23451 *Web:* www.obrienetal.com	757-422-3231		7
OBS (Ohio Biological Survey) PO Box 21370 . . . . Columbus OH 43221 *Web:* www.ohiobiologicalsurvey.org	614-457-8787	457-6005	49-19
OBS Inc 1324 W Tuscarawas St PO Box 6210 . . . . .Canton OH 44706 *TF:* 800-362-9592 ■ *Web:* www.obsinc.net	330-453-3725	580-2429	516
Observer 1 Whitehall St 7th Fl . . . . New York NY 10004 *TF:* 800-571-7363 ■ *Web:* observer.com	212-755-2400		532-4
Observer Dispatch Inc 221 Oriskany Plz . . . . Utica NY 13501 *TF:* 800-765-5216 ■ *Web:* www.uticaod.com	315-797-9150	792-5033	637-8
Observer Newspaper 201 N Federal Hwy Ste 103 . . . . .Deerfield Beach FL 33441 *Web:* observernewspaperonline.com	954-428-9045	428-9096	532-4
Observer, The 140 S Front St . . . . Sarnia ON N7T7M8 *Web:* www.theobserver.ca	519-344-3641	332-2951	532-1
Observer/Enterprise PO Box 1329. . . . . .Robert Lee TX 76945 *Web:* observerenterprise.com	325-453-2433	453-4643	532-2
Observera Inc 3856 Dulles S Ct Ste I . . . . Chantilly VA 20151 *Web:* observera.com	703-378-3153		225
Observer-Reporter 122 S Main St . . . . .Washington PA 15301 *TF:* 800-222-6397 ■ *Web:* observer-reporter.com	724-222-2200		532-2
Obsidian Energy Ltd Penn W Plz 207 - Ninth Ave SW Ste 200 . . . . Calgary AB T2P1K3 *TF:* 866-693-2707 ■ *Web:* www.obsidianenergy.com	403-777-2500		675
Obsidian Mortgage Corp 35 Grand Marshall Dr 2nd Fl . . . . Toronto ON M1B5W9 *Web:* obsidianmortgages.com	416-283-2377		509
Obstetrics & Gynecology of Indiana 11595 N Meridian St Ste 375. . . . . .Carmel IN 46032 *Web:* www.obgynindiana.com	317-575-7300	575-7333	374-3
Obzerv Technologies Inc 400 Jean-Lesage Ste 201 . . . . .Quebec City QC G1K8W1 *Web:* www.obzerv.com	418-524-3522	524-6745	544
OC Jones & Sons Inc 1520 Fourth St. . . . . .Berkeley CA 94710 *Web:* www.ocjones.com	510-526-3424		77
OC Seacrets Inc 117 49th St. . . . . .Ocean City MD 21842 *Web:* seacrets.com	410-524-4900		54
OC Systems Inc 9990 Fairfax Blvd Ste 270. . . . . Fairfax VA 22030 *Web:* www.ocsystems.com	703-359-8160		177
OC Tanner Co 1930 S State St . . . . .Salt Lake City UT 84115 *TF:* 800-453-7490 ■ *Web:* www.octanner.com	800-453-7490		409
OC Weekly 2975 Red Hill Ave Ste 150 . . . . Costa Mesa CA 92626 *TF:* 800-300-4345 ■ *Web:* www.ocweekly.com	714-550-5900	550-5908	532-5
OC Wholesale Flowers 603 W Dyer Rd . . . . Santa Ana CA 92707 *Web:* www.ocwholesaleflowers.com	714-542-6181	542-5947	293
OCA (Organization of Chinese Americans) 1322 18th St NW . . . . .Washington DC 20036 *Web:* www.ocanational.org	202-223-5500	296-0540	48-14
OCA (Orthodox Church in America) 6850 N Hempstead Tpke. . . . . Syosset NY 11791 *Web:* www.oca.org	516-922-0550	922-0954	637-10
OCA Ventures 351 W Hubbard St Ste 600. . . . . .Chicago IL 60654 *Web:* www.ocaventures.com	312-327-8400	542-8952	792
Ocala Equine Hospital PA 10855 NW Hwy 27 . . . . Ocala FL 34482 *Web:* ocalaequinehospital.com	352-368-1616		794
Ocala-Marion County Chamber of Commerce 310 SE Third St . . . . Ocala FL 34471 *TF:* 800-466-5055 ■ *Web:* ocalacep.com	352-629-8051	629-7651	139
Ocasio-Cortez Alexandria (Rep D - NY) 229 Cannon House Office Bldg. . . . . .Washington DC 20515 *Web:* www.ocasio-cortez.house.gov	202-225-3965		342-2
OCB (Opera Company of Brooklyn) 33 Indian Rd 600 W 218th St Ste 1G . . . . .New York NY 10034 *Web:* operabrooklyn.org	212-567-3283		573-2
OCB (Old Country Buffet Restaurants) 120 Chula Vista . . . . .Hollywood Park TX 78232 *Web:* www.oldcountrybuffet.com	210-403-3725	403-3580	670
OCBJ (Orange County Business Journal) 18500 Von Karman Ave Ste 150. . . . . Irvine CA 92612 *Web:* www.ocbj.com	949-833-8373	833-8751	457-5
OCC (Optical Cable Corp) 5290 Concourse Dr . . . . .Roanoke VA 24019 *NASDAQ: OCC* ■ *TF:* 800-622-7711 ■ *Web:* www.occfiber.com	540-265-0690	265-0724	814
OCC (Ohio Chamber of Commerce) 34 S 3rd St Ste 100 . . . . Columbus OH 43215 *Web:* ohiochamber.com	614-228-4201		139
OCC Systems 1330 Hilton Rd. . . . . .Ferndale MI 48220 *Web:* www.occsystems.com	248-547-3800	547-8344	207
Occasions Group, The 1750 Tower Blvd. . . . . .North Mankato MN 56003 *TF:* 800-296-9029 ■ *Web:* www.theoccasionsgroup.com	800-296-9029		687
OCCC (Orange County Convention Ctr) 9800 International Dr . . . . Orlando FL 32819 *TF:* 800-345-9845 ■ *Web:* www.occc.net	407-685-9800	685-9876	205
Occidental College 1600 Campus Rd . . . . .Los Angeles CA 90041 *TF:* 800-825-5262 ■ *Web:* www.oxy.edu	323-259-2700	341-4875	166
Occidental Entertainment Group Holdings Inc 1149 N Mccadden Pl . . . . .Los Angeles CA 90038 *Web:* occidentalentertainment.com	323-464-7441	464-3681	653
Occidental Petroleum Corp 5 Greenway Plz Ste 110 . . . . .Houston TX 77046 *Web:* www.oxy.com	713-215-7000		579
OCCK Inc 1710 W Schilling Rd. . . . . Salina KS 67401 *TF:* 800-526-9731 ■ *Web:* occk.com	785-827-9383	823-2015	476
Occoneechee State Park 1192 Occoneechee Park Rd . . . . Clarksville VA 23927 *Web:* www.dcr.virginia.gov	434-374-2210		565
Occupational Health Dynamics 197 Cahaba Vly Pkwy. . . . . Pelham AL 35124 *Web:* www.ohdusa.com	205-980-0180	980-5764	194
Occupational Safety & Health Administration (OSHA) 200 Constitution Ave NW . . . . .Washington DC 20210 *TF:* 800-321-6742 ■ *Web:* www.osha.gov	202-693-2121		340-15
Occupational Safety & Health Administration Regional Offices			
Region 1 JFK Federal Bldg Rm E-340 . . . . .Boston MA 02203 *Web:* www.osha.gov	617-565-9860	565-9827	340-15
Region 2 201 Varick St Rm 670. . . . . .New York NY 10014 *Web:* www.osha.gov	212-337-2378	337-2371	340-15
Region 3 Curtis Ctr 170 S Independence Mall W Ste 740W. . . . . .Philadelphia PA 19106 *Web:* www.osha.gov	215-861-4900	861-4904	340-15
Region 4 61 Forsyth St SW Rm 6T50 . . . . Atlanta GA 30303 *Web:* www.osha.gov	678-237-0400		340-15

Phone | Fax | Class

Region 5 230 S Dearborn St Rm 3244 Chicago IL 60604 312-353-2220 353-7774 340-15
Web: www.osha.gov
Region 6 525 Griffin St Ste 602 Dallas TX 75202 972-850-4145 850-4149 340-15
Web: www.osha.gov
Region 7
2 Pershing Square Bldg 2300 Main St
Ste 1010 Kansas City MO 64108 816-283-8745 283-0547 340-15
Web: www.osha.gov
Region 8 1244 Speer Blvd Ste 551 Denver CO 80204 720-264-6550 264-6585 340-15
Web: www.osha.gov
Region 9 90 Seventh St Ste 2650 San Francisco CA 94103 415-625-2547 625-2534 340-15
Web: www.osha.gov
Region 10 300 Fifth Ave Ste 1280 Seattle WA 98104 206-757-6700 757-6705 340-15
Web: www.osha.gov

Occupational Safety & Health Review Commission
1120 20th St NW 9th Fl Washington DC 20036 202-606-5400 606-5050 340-20
Web: www.oshrc.gov

Occupational Safety & Health Review Commission Regional Offices
Atlanta Region
100 Alabama St SW Rm 2R90 Atlanta GA 30303 404-562-1640 562-1650 340-20
Web: www.oshrc.gov

Ocean 1218 20th St S Birmingham AL 35205 205-933-0999 671
Web: www.oceanbirmingham.com

Ocean Aire PO Box 1245 Toms River NJ 08754 732-797-1077 797-1076 63
Web: www.oceanaire.net

Ocean Bank 780 NW 42nd Ave Miami FL 33126 305-442-2660 70
TF: 877-688-2265 ■ *Web:* www.oceanbank.com

Ocean Bio-Chem Inc (OBCI)
4041 SW 47th Ave Fort Lauderdale FL 33314 954-587-6280 587-2813 151
NASDAQ: OBCI ■ *TF:* 800-327-8583 ■ *Web:* www.oceanbiochem.com

Ocean Breeze Intl (OBI)
3910 Via Real Carpinteria CA 93013 805-684-1747 684-0235 369
Web: www.oceanbreezeintl.com

Ocean Breeze Waterpark
849 General Booth Blvd Virginia Beach VA 23451 757-422-4444 31
Web: www.oceanbreezewaterpark.com

Ocean Bridge Group
2032 Armacost Ave Los Angeles CA 90025 310-392-3200 4
Web: www.oceanbridgemedia.com

Ocean City - City Hall
301 Baltimore Ave Ocean City MD 21842 410-289-8931 289-7385 337
TF: 800-626-2326 ■ *Web:* www.oceancitymd.gov

Ocean City Animal Hospital
11843 Ocean Gtwy Ocean City MD 21842 410-213-1170 213-2128 794
Web: oceancityvet.com

Ocean City Convention & Visitors Bureau
4001 Coastal Hwy Ocean City MD 21842 410-723-8600 206
Web: www.ococean.com

Ocean City Hotel-Motel-Restaurant Assn
PO Box 340 Ocean City MD 21843 410-289-6733 376
Web: ocvisitor.com

Ocean City Life-Saving Station Museum
813 S Atlantic Ave Ocean City MD 21842 410-289-4991 520
Web: www.ocmuseum.org

Ocean City Public Library
1735 Simpson Ave Ste 4 Ocean City NJ 08226 609-399-2434 434-3
Web: www.oceancitylibrary.org

Ocean City State Park 148 SR-115 Hoquiam WA 98550 360-289-3553 565
Web: www.parks.wa.gov

Ocean Club Night Club
10100 Coastal Hwy Ocean City MD 21842 410-703-1970 671
Web: www.oceancity.com

Ocean Conservancy
1300 19th St NW 8th Fl Washington DC 20036 202-429-5609 872-0619 48-13
TF: 800-519-1541 ■ *Web:* oceanconservancy.org

Ocean County 118 Washington St Toms River NJ 08753 732-929-2018 349-4336 338
TF: 800-722-0291 ■ *Web:* www.co.ocean.nj.us

Ocean County College
College Dr PO Box 2001 Toms River NJ 08754 732-255-0400 255-0444 162
Web: www.ocean.edu

Ocean County Library
101 Washington St Toms River NJ 08753 732-349-6200 473-1356 434-3
Web: theoceancountylibrary.org

Ocean Ctr 101 N Atlantic Ave Daytona Beach FL 32118 386-254-4500 254-4512 205
TF: 800-858-6444 ■ *Web:* www.oceancenter.com

Ocean Deck 127 S Ocean Ave Daytona Beach FL 32118 386-253-5224 671
Web: oceandeck.com

Ocean Divers 522 Caribbean Dr Key Largo FL 33037 305-451-1113 451-5765 167-3
TF: 800-451-1113 ■ *Web:* www.oceandivers.com

Ocean Downs 10218 Racetrack Rd Berlin MD 21811 410-641-0600 642
TF: 888-622-9743 ■ *Web:* www.oceandowns.com

Ocean Drive Clevelander Inc
1020 Ocean Dr Miami Beach FL 33139 877-532-4006 707
TF: 877-532-4006 ■ *Web:* www.clevelander.com

Ocean Edge Resort & Golf Club
2907 Main St Brewster MA 02631 508-896-9000 669
TF: 800-343-6074 ■ *Web:* www.oceanedge.com

Ocean Embassy Panama Inc
6426 Milner Blvd Ste 101 Orlando FL 32809 407-852-9129 787
Web: www.oceanembassy.com

Ocean Eyes Optical Inc
2907 Ocean Ave Brooklyn NY 11235 718-332-1017 237
Web: www.coolframes.com

Ocean Five Hotel 436 Ocean Dr Miami Beach FL 33139 305-532-7093 379
Web: oceanfive.com

Ocean Flow International LLC
2100 W Loop S Ste 500 Houston TX 77027 713-328-6700 328-6798 313
Web: www.ocean-flow.com

Ocean Futures Society
325 Chapala St Santa Barbara CA 93101 805-899-8899 899-8898 48-13
Web: www.oceanfutures.org

Ocean House Hotel Partners LLC
1 Bluff Ave Watch Hill RI 02891 401-584-7000 707
Web: www.oceanhouseri.com

Ocean Kayak
125 Gilman Falls Ave Bldg B Old Town ME 04468 800-852-9257 827-3647* 710
**Fax Area Code: 207* ■ *TF:* 800-852-9257 ■ *Web:* www.oceankayak.com

Ocean Key Resort
424 Atlantic Ave Virginia Beach VA 23451 757-425-2200 379
TF: 800-955-9700 ■ *Web:* vsaresorts.com

Ocean Key Resort & Spa 0 Duval St Key West FL 33040 305-296-7701 669
TF: 800-328-9815 ■ *Web:* www.oceankey.com

Ocean Management Systems Inc
2021 Goshen Tpke Wallkill NY 12589 619-236-1203 710
TF: 800-325-8439 ■ *Web:* omsdive.com

Ocean Manor Resort
4040 Galt Ocean Dr Fort Lauderdale FL 33308 954-566-7500 564-3075 669
TF: 800-955-0444 ■ *Web:* www.oceanmanor.com

Ocean Medical Ctr (OMC)
425 Jack Martin Blvd Brick NJ 08724 732-840-2200 374-3
TF: 800-560-9990 ■ *Web:* www.oceanmedicalcenter.com

Ocean Mist Beach Hotel & Suites
97 S Shore Dr South Yarmouth MA 02664 508-398-2633 398-2122 669
TF: 800-655-1972 ■ *Web:* www.oceanmistcapecod.com

Ocean Mist Farms
10855 Ocean Mist Pkwy Castroville CA 95012 831-633-2144 10-11
Web: www.oceanmist.com

Ocean One Cruise Outlet
3264 Marilynn St Lancaster CA 93536 661-949-2873 771
Web: www.oceanone.com

Ocean Optics Inc 830 Douglas Ave Dunedin FL 34698 727-733-2447 733-3962 544
Web: www.oceaninsight.com

Ocean Place Resort & Spa
1Ocean Blvd Long Branch NJ 07740 800-411-6493 669
TF: 800-411-6493 ■ *Web:* www.oceanplace.com

Ocean Pointe Suites at Key Largo
500 Burton Dr Tavernier FL 33070 305-853-3000 853-3007 379
TF: 800-882-9464 ■ *Web:* www.providentresorts.com

Ocean Products Research Inc 19 Butts Ln Diggs VA 23045 804-725-3406 208
Web: www.opr-rope.com

Ocean Properties Hotels Resorts & Affiliates
1001 E Atlantic Ave Ste 202 Delray Beach FL 33483 561-279-9900 377
Web: www.ophotels.com

Ocean Quest Pools Inc 10208 N Fm 620 Austin TX 78726 512-258-7379 186
Web: www.oceanquest.com

Ocean Reef Club
35 Ocean Reef Dr Ste 200 Key Largo FL 33037 305-367-2611 367-2224 379
TF: 800-741-7333 ■ *Web:* www.oceanreef.com

Ocean Reef Resort
7100 N Ocean Blvd Myrtle Beach SC 29572 843-315-3000 497-3041 669
TF: 888-322-6411 ■ *Web:* www.oceanreefmyrtlebeach.com

Ocean Seafood 750 N Hill St Los Angeles CA 90012 213-687-3088 671
Web: www.oceanseafoodchinatown.com

Ocean Shipholdings Inc
16211 Pk Ten Pl Houston TX 77084 281-579-3700 579-0671 698
Web: www.oceanshipholdings.com

Ocean Shores Convention Ctr
120 W Chance a La Mer Ave Ocean Shores WA 98569 360-289-4411 205
Web: www.oceanshoresconventioncenter.com

Ocean Sky Hotel & Resort
4060 Galt Ocean Dr Fort Lauderdale FL 33308 954-565-6611 564-7730 379
TF: 800-678-9022 ■ *Web:* www.oceanskyresort.com

Ocean Spray Cranberries Inc
1 Ocean Spray Dr Middleboro MA 02349 508-946-1000 946-4594 296-20
TF: 800-662-3263 ■ *Web:* www.oceanspray.com

Ocean Springs Seafood Market Inc
555 Bayview Ave Ste B Biloxi MS 39530 228-436-0052 296-14
Web: usagulfshrimp.com

Ocean State Creations
1044 Mineral Spring Ave North Providence RI 02904 401-728-0490 728-8577 157-4
Web: oscjewelry.com

Ocean State Jobbers Inc
375 Commerce Park Rd North Kingstown RI 02852 401-295-2672 791
Web: www.oceanstatejoblot.com

Ocean State Technical Services
55 Chapman St Providence RI 02905 401-467-8661 794
Web: www.ostservices.com

Ocean State Tire Company Inc
51 Worthington Rd Cranston RI 02920 401-946-0880 944-6783 755
TF: 888-834-8518 ■ *Web:* www.oceanstatetire.com

Ocean State Veterinary Specialists Ltd
1480 S County Trl East Greenwich RI 02818 401-886-6787 794
Web: www.osvs.net

Ocean Steel & Construction Ltd
400 Chesley Dr Saint John NB E2K5L6 506-632-2600 480
Web: www.oceansteel.com

Ocean Tug & Barge Engineering Corp
257 Main St Milford MA 01757 508-473-0545 261
Web: www.oceantugbarge.com

Ocean Walk Resort
300 N Atlantic Daytona Beach FL 32118 386-323-4800 379
Web: www.wyndhamoceanwalk.com

Ocean Walk Shoppes at the Village
250 N Atlantic Ave Ste 201 Daytona Beach FL 32118 386-258-9544 238-3864 50-6
Web: www.oceanwalkshoppes.com

Ocean Waters Spa
600 N Atlantic Ave Daytona Beach FL 32118 386-267-1660 706
TF: 844-284-2685 ■ *Web:* www.plazaresortandspa.com

Ocean's Eleven Casino 121 Brooks St Oceanside CA 92054 760-439-6988 452
Web: oceans11.com

Oceana 120 W 49th St New York NY 10020 212-759-5941 759-6076 671
Web: www.oceanarestaurant.com

Oceana County 100 S State St Ste 1 Hart MI 49420 231-873-4328 873-1391 338
Web: oceana.mi.us

Oceana Natural Foods Coop
159 SE Second St Newport OR 97365 541-265-8285 345
Web: www.oceanafoods.org

Oceana's Herald 123 S State St Hart MI 49420 231-873-5602 873-4775 532-2

OCEANAIR Inc 186A Lee Burbank Hwy Revere MA 02151 781-286-2700 311
TF: 800-456-4176 ■ *Web:* oceanair.net

Oceanaire Seafood Room, The
40 Court St Boston MA 02108 617-742-2277 671
Web: www.theoceanaire.com

Oceancliff Hotel & Resort 65 Ridge Rd Newport RI 02840 401-849-6683 379
Web: www.newportexperience.com

				Phone	Fax	Class

Oceane Marine Shipping Inc
407 E Maple St . . . Cumming GA 30040 770-888-5941 311
Web: oceanems.com

Oceaneering International Inc
11911 FM 529 . . . Houston TX 77041 713-329-4500 329-4951 539
NYSE: OII ■ *TF:* 844-381-9324 ■ *Web:* www.oceaneering.com

Oceanex
630 Boul Rene-Levesque W Ste 2550 . . . Montreal QC H3B1S6 514-875-9595 392-0200 311
TF: 888-875-9595 ■ *Web:* www.oceanex.com

Oceanex Services International Inc
10607 Haddington Ste 190 . . . Houston TX 77043 713-722-7300 722-7301 385
Web: www.oceanexservices.com

OceanFirst Bank 975 Hooper Ave . . . Toms River NJ 08753 732-240-4500 349-5070 70
TF: 888-623-2633 ■ *Web:* www.oceanfirstonline.com

Oceanfootage.com 810 Cannery Row . . . Monterey CA 93940 831-375-2313 621-9559 344
TF: 866-375-2313 ■ *Web:* www.naturefootage.com

Oceanfront Lodging Inc
305 N First St . . . Jacksonville Beach FL 32250 904-249-4949 378
Web: www.bestwesternjacksonvillebeach.com

OceanGate Inc
1205 Craftsman Way Ste 112 . . . Everett WA 98201 425-595-5017 393
Web: www.oceangate.com

Oceania Cruises Inc
8300 NW 33rd St Ste 308 . . . Miami FL 33122 305-514-2300 514-2222 220
TF: 800-531-5619 ■ *Web:* www.oceaniacruises.com

Oceanic Companies Inc
91-462 Komohana St . . . Kapolei HI 96707 808-682-0113 186
Web: www.oceaniccompanies.com

Oceanic Institute
41-202 Kalanianaole Hwy . . . Waimanalo HI 96795 808-259-7951 259-5971 668
Web: www.oceanicinstitute.org

Oceanic Medical Products Inc
8005 Shannon Industrial Park Ln . . . Atchison KS 66002 913-874-2000 874-2005 476
Web: www.oceanicmedical.com

Oceanic USA 2002 Davis St . . . San Leandro CA 94577 888-270-8595 569-5404* 710
**Fax Area Code:* 510 ■ *TF:* 800-435-3483 ■ *Web:* www.oceanicworldwide.com

Oceano Hotel & Spa Half Moon Bay Harbor
280 Capistrano Rd . . . Half Moon Bay CA 94019 650-726-5400 378
TF: 888-623-2001 ■ *Web:* www.oceanohalfmoonbay.com

Oceanos Inc 892 Plain St . . . Marshfield MA 02050 781-804-1010 5
Web: www.oceanosinc.com

Oceanpro Industries Ltd
1900 Fenwick St NE . . . Washington DC 20002 202-529-3003 297-5
TF: 800-967-9726 ■ *Web:* www.profish.com

Oceanside Chamber of Commerce
928 N Coast Hwy . . . Oceanside CA 92054 760-722-1534 722-8336 139
Web: www.oceansidechamber.com

Oceanside Chamber of Commerce
2721 Harrison Ave . . . Oceanside NY 11572 516-763-9177 139
Web: oceansidechamber.org

Oceanside Community Service Television Corp
3038 Industry St . . . Oceanside CA 92054 760-722-4433 116
Web: www.koct.org

Oceanside Museum of Art
704 Pier View Way . . . Oceanside CA 92054 760-435-3720 522
Web: oma-online.org

Oceanside Photo & Telescope (OPT)
918 Mission Ave . . . Oceanside CA 92054 760-400-0164 179
TF: 800-483-6287 ■ *Web:* optcorp.com

Oceanside Public Library
330 N Coast Hwy . . . Oceanside CA 92054 760-435-5600 434-3
Web: www.ci.oceanside.ca.us

Oceanside Unified School District (OUSD)
2111 Mission Ave . . . Oceanside CA 92058 760-966-4000 186
Web: www.oside.k12.ca.us

Oceanside Union Free School District 11
145 Merle Ave . . . Oceanside NY 11572 516-678-1200 685
Web: oceansideschools.org

Oceanus Partners
16540 Pointe Village Dr Ste 208 . . . Lutz FL 33558 888-496-1117 196
TF: 888-496-1117 ■ *Web:* www.oceanuspartners.com

OceanWorks International Inc
11611 Tanner Rd Ste A . . . Houston TX 77041 281-598-3940 350
Web: www.oceanworks.com

Ocenco Inc 10225 82nd Ave . . . Pleasant Prairie WI 53158 262-947-9000 947-9020 678
Web: www.ocenco.com

Oceus Networks Inc
1895 Preston White Dr Ste 300 . . . Reston VA 20191 703-234-9200 387
Web: www.oceusnetworks.com

OCF (International OCD Foundation)
PO Box 961029 . . . Boston MA 02196 617-973-5801 973-5803 48-17
TF: 800-331-3131 ■ *Web:* iocdf.org

OCF (Omaha Community Foundation)
302 S 36th St Ste 100 . . . Omaha NE 68131 402-342-3458 342-3582 303
TF: 800-794-3458 ■ *Web:* omahafoundation.org

OCGS (Orange County Genealogical Society)
101 Main St . . . Goshen NY 10924 845-294-5871 49-19
Web: www.ocgsny.org

OCH Regional Medical Ctr
400 Hospital Rd . . . Starkville MS 39759 662-323-4320 374-3
Web: www.och.org

Ochiltree County 511 S Main St . . . Perryton TX 79070 806-435-8039 435-2081 338
Web: www.co.ochiltree.tx.us

Ochlockonee River State Park
429 State Park Rd . . . Sopchoppy FL 32358 850-962-2771 565
Web: www.floridastateparks.org

Ochsner 1514 Jefferson Hwy . . . New Orleans LA 70121 504-842-3000 394-0840 374-3
TF: 800-343-0269 ■ *Web:* www.ochsner.org

Ochsner Journal, The
1319 Jefferson Hwy . . . New Orleans LA 70121 504-842-7398 637-9
Web: www.ochsnerjournal.org

OCI Sitwell
14815 Radburn Ave . . . Santa Fe Springs CA 90670 562-802-0464 319-1
TF: 866-624-4968 ■ *Web:* ocisitwell.com

Ocker & Associates PC
4148 Lincoln Way E . . . Fayetteville PA 17222 717-352-3737 2
Web: ockeraccounting.com

Ockers Co 830 W Chestnut St . . . Brockton MA 02301 508-586-4642 584-9180 175
TF: 800-346-0122 ■ *Web:* ockers.com

OCLC Inc 6565 Kilgour Pl . . . Dublin OH 43017 614-764-6000 764-6096 647
TF: 800-848-5878 ■ *Web:* www.oclc.org

OCLS Press PO Box 1137 . . . Huntsville AR 72740 501-559-2273 637-2
Web: www.adrr.com

OCM (One Call Medical Inc) PO Box 614 . . . Parsippany NJ 07054 973-257-1000 382
TF: 800-872-2875 ■ *Web:* onecallcm.com

Ocmulgee Electric Membership Corp
5722 Eastman St . . . Eastman GA 31023 478-374-7001 245
TF: 800-342-5509 ■ *Web:* www.ocmulgeeemc.com

Ocmulgee National Monument
1207 Emery Hwy . . . Macon GA 31217 478-752-8257 752-8259 564
Web: www.nps.gov

Oconee County 415 S Pine St . . . Walhalla SC 29691 864-638-4280 338
Web: oconeesc.com

Oconee County Library
501 W S Broad St . . . Walhalla SC 29691 864-638-4133 434-3
Web: oconeelibrary.org

Oconee County School District
34 School St PO Box 146 . . . Watkinsville GA 30677 706-769-5130 769-3500 685
Web: www.oconeeschools.org

Oconee Electric Membership Corp
3445 US Hwy 80 W PO Box 37 . . . Dudley GA 31022 478-676-3191 245
TF: 800-522-2930 ■ *Web:* www.oconeeemc.com

Oconee Fall Line Technical College - South Campus
560 Pinehill Rd . . . Dublin GA 31021 478-275-6589 167-3
TF: 800-200-4484 ■ *Web:* www.oftc.edu

Oconee State Park
624 State Park Rd . . . Mountain Rest SC 29664 864-638-5353 565
Web: southcarolinaparks.com

Oconee Station State Historic Site
500 Oconee Stn Rd . . . Walhalla SC 29691 864-638-0079 565
Web: southcarolinaparks.com

OConnor Engineering 2701 N Ontario St . . . Burbank CA 91504 818-847-8666 847-1205 591
Web: www.ocon.com

Oconomowoc Area Chamber of Commerce
175 E Wisconsin Ave . . . Oconomowoc WI 53066 262-567-2666 567-3477 139
Web: www.oconomowoc.org

Oconomowoc Convention & Visitors Bureau
174 E Wisconsin Ave . . . Oconomowoc WI 53066 262-569-2186 569-2164 206
Web: www.oconomowoc-wi.gov

Oconomowoc Memorial Hospital
791 Summit Ave . . . Oconomowoc WI 53066 262-569-9400 569-0336 374-3
TF: 800-242-0313 ■ *Web:* www.prohealthcare.org

Oconto County 301 Washington St . . . Oconto WI 54153 920-834-6800 834-6867 338
TF: 855-492-2372 ■ *Web:* www.co.oconto.wi.us

Oconto County Reporter 648 Brazeau Ave . . . Oconto WI 54153 920-834-4242 834-4878 532-2
Web: www.greatnorthernconn.com

Oconto Electric Co-op PO Box 168 . . . Oconto Falls WI 54154 920-846-2816 245
TF: 800-472-8410 ■ *Web:* ocontoelectric.com

Ocotillo Lumber Sales Inc
3121 N 28th Ave . . . Phoenix AZ 85017 602-258-6951 258-6172 191-3
Web: ocotillolumber.com

Ocotillo Wells State Vehicular Recreation Area
5172 Hwy 78 Ste 10 . . . Borrego Springs CA 92004 760-767-1302 565
Web: www.parks.ca.gov

OCP (Oregon Catholic Press)
5536 NE Hassalo St . . . Portland OR 97213 503-281-1191 462-7329* 637-3
**Fax Area Code:* 800 ■ *TF:* 877-596-1653 ■ *Web:* www.ocp.org

Ocsea-Afscme Local
390 Worthington Rd Ste A . . . Westerville OH 43082 614-865-4700 414
TF: 800-969-4702 ■ *Web:* www.ocsea.org

Octa Inc PO Box 217 . . . Buckner KY 40010 502-222-8985 454
Web: octainc.com

Octal Corp Unit B & C 125 Galway Pl . . . Teaneck NJ 07666 201-862-1010 360-3
Web: www.octalcorporation.com

Octane Interlounge 124 N Main St . . . Rockford IL 61101 815-965-4013 671
Web: www.octane.net

Octapharma Plasma Inc
10644 Westlake Dr . . . Charlotte NC 28273 704-654-4600 743
TF: 866-326-8689 ■ *Web:* octapharmaplasma.com

Octasic Inc 30-2901 rue Rachel . . . Montreal QC H2W2B1 514-282-8858 201
Web: www.octasic.com

Octex Corp 901 Sarasota Center Blvd . . . Sarasota FL 34240 941-371-6767 608
Web: www.octexgroup.com

OCTG LLP 9200 Sheldon Rd . . . Houston TX 77049 281-456-9057 41
Web: www.octg.org

October Company Inc 51 Ferry St . . . Easthampton MA 01027 413-527-9380 527-0091 295
TF: 800-628-9346 ■ *Web:* www.octobercompany.com

October Mountain State Forest
317 Woodland Rd . . . Lee MA 01238 413-243-1778 565
Web: www.mass.gov

OctoClean Franchising Systems
3357 Chicago Ave . . . Riverside CA 92507 951-683-5859 310
TF: 888-540-0828 ■ *Web:* octoclean.com

Ocu-ease Optical Products Inc
920 San Pablo Ave . . . Pinole CA 94564 510-724-0384 483-0292 237
TF: 800-521-8984 ■ *Web:* ocuease.weebly.com

Oculus VisionTech Inc
507 837 W Hastings St . . . Vancouver BC V6C3N6 604-685-1017 180
Web: www.ovtz.com

Ocwen Federal Bank FSB
1661 Worthington Rd Ste 100 . . . West Palm Beach FL 33409 561-681-8000 70
TF: 800-746-2936 ■ *Web:* www.ocwen.com

OCZ Storage Solutions Inc
6373 San Ignacio Ave . . . San Jose CA 95119 408-733-8400 624
Web: ssd.toshiba-memory.com

Odan Laboratories
325 Stillview Ave . . . Pointe-Claire QC H9R2Y6 514-428-1628 428-9783 231
TF: 888-252-6467 ■ *Web:* www.odanlab.com

ODaniel Chrysler Dodge Jeep Ram
5611 Illinois Rd . . . Fort Wayne IN 46804 855-631-1400 516
TF: 855-631-1400 ■ *Web:* odanielauto.com

Odawa Casino Resort, The
1760 Lears Rd . . . Petoskey MI 49770 877-442-6464 452
TF: 877-442-6464 ■ *Web:* www.odawacasino.com

Odawara Automation Inc
4805 S County Rd 25a . . . Tipp City OH 45371 937-667-8433 667-8435 454
Web: www.odawara.com

	Phone	Fax	Class
ODC 3153 17th St. San Francisco CA 94110 Web: odc.dance	415-863-6606		573-1
ODC Tooling & Molds 119 Roger St. Waterloo ON N2J3Z6 Web: www.odctooling.com	519-576-8950		757
Odea, Nordeen & Burink PC 122 W Spring St. Marquette MI 49855 Web: marquettelawpc.com	906-225-1770		41
Odebrecht Construction Inc 201 Alhambra Cir Ste 1000 Coral Gables FL 33134 Web: www.odebrecht.com	305-341-8800	569-1500	186
ODEC (Old Dominion Electric Co-op) 4201 Dominion Blvd. Glen Allen VA 23060 Web: www.odec.com	804-747-0592		245
Odee Co, The 10630 Control Pl. Dallas TX 75238 TF: 800-486-6333 ■ Web: www.odeecompany.com	214-340-0415	340-8526	534
ODEF (Old Dominion Eye Bank) 9200 Arboretum Pkwy Ste 104 Richmond VA 23236 TF: 800-832-0728 ■ Web: odef.org	804-560-7540	560-4752	269
Odell Associates Inc 212 S Tryon St Ste 980 Charlotte NC 28281 Web: www.odell.com	704-414-1000		261
Odell Brewing Co 800 E Lincoln Ave. Fort Collins CO 80524 Web: www.odellbrewing.com	970-498-9070		102
Odell Electronics Cleaning Stations 1061 Bradley Rd. Westlake OH 44145 TF: 888-779-0011 ■ Web: www.odellstations.com	440-617-9294	617-9296	45
Odell Simms & Lynch Inc 7704 Leesburg Pk. Falls Church VA 22043 Web: www.odellsimms.com	703-903-9797	903-8850	5
Oden & Associates Inc 158 Vance Ave Memphis TN 38103 TF: 800-371-6233 ■ Web: www.oden.com	901-578-8055		344
Oden Industries Inc 301 E Vanderbilt Way Ste 425 San Bernardino CA 92408 TF: 800-845-4637 ■ Web: odenindustries.com	909-386-0310	386-0476	177
Odeon Capital Group LLC 750 Lexington Ave 27th Fl New York NY 10022 Web: www.odeoncap.com	212-257-6970		690
Odesia Decision inc 1 Pl Ville-Marie Ste 560 Montreal QC H3B0E9 Web: www.odesia.com	514-876-1155		317
Odessa American PO Box 2952 Odessa TX 79760 TF: 800-592-4433 ■ Web: www.oaoa.com	432-333-7770	333-7742	532-2
Odessa Chamber of Commerce 700 N Grant Ave Ste 200 Odessa TX 79761 TF: 800-780-4678 ■ Web: odessachamber.com	432-332-9111	333-7858	139
Odessa College 201 W University Blvd. Odessa TX 79764 Web: www.odessa.edu	432-335-6400	335-6824	162
Odessa Pumps 7950 I-20 E Odessa TX 79764 Web: www.distributionnow.com	432-333-2817		641
Odessa Record, The 1 W 1st Ave. Odessa WA 99159 Web: www.odessarecord.com	509-982-2632		532-2
Odessa Regional Medical Ctr 520 E Sixth St. Odessa TX 79761 Web: www.odessaregionalmedicalcenter.org	432-582-8000		374-7
ODG (Ontario Drive & Gear Ltd) 220 Bergey Ct. New Hamburg ON N3A2J5 TF: 877-274-6288 ■ Web: www.odg.com	519-662-2840		29
ODIN Technologies Inc 21631 Red Rum Dr Ste 165 Ashburn VA 20147 Web: www.odinrfid.com	703-968-0000	456-0148	180
Odiorne Point State Park 570 Ocean Blvd Rye NH 03870 Web: www.nhstateparks.org	603-436-7406		565
Odjfs Federal Credit Union 4020 E Fifth Ave Columbus OH 43219 Web: www.odjfscu.com	614-237-3200	237-3210	219
ODL Inc 215 E Roosevelt Ave. Zeeland MI 49464 TF: 800-253-3900 ■ Web: www.odl.com	616-772-9111		329
Odlum Brown Ltd 250 Howe St Ste 1100 Vancouver BC V6C3S9 TF: 866-636-8222 ■ Web: www.odlumbrown.com	604-669-1600	844-5342	401
ODM Tool & Manufacturing Co 9550 Joliet Rd McCook IL 60525 Web: www.odmtool.com	708-485-6130	485-6540	489
Odom Corp, The 11400 SE 8th St Ste 300 Bellevue WA 98004 TF: 800-767-6366 ■ Web: www.odomcorp.com	800-767-6366		81-3
Odom Correctional Institution PO Box 36 Jackson NC 27845 Web: www.ncdps.gov	252-534-5611	574-2011	213
Odom Industries Inc 800 Odom Industrial Rd Waynesboro MS 39367 Web: www.odomind.com	601-735-0088	735-0089	143
Odon Wagner Gallery 196 Davenport Rd Toronto ON M5R1J2 TF: 800-551-2465 ■ Web: www.odonwagnergallery.com	416-962-0438	962-1581	42
Odonnell, Weiss & Mattei PC 41 E High St Pottstown PA 19464 Web: owmlaw.com	610-323-2800		41
Odopod 350 Bush St San Francisco CA 94102 Web: www.odopod.com	415-436-9980		344
ODW Logistics Inc 1580 Williams Rd Columbus OH 43207 Web: www.odwlogistics.com	614-497-1660		449
Odyssey Fun World 3440 Odyssey Ct. Naperville IL 60563 Web: ofwtinleypark.com	630-416-2222		31
Odyssey Industries Inc 3020 Indianwood Rd. Lake Orion MI 48362 Web: ascentaerospace.com	248-814-8800	814-8895	20
Odyssey Landscaping Company Inc 5400 W Hwy 12 Lodi CA 95242 Web: odysseylandscape.com	209-369-6197	369-6965	776
Odyssey Marine Exploration Inc 5215 W Laurel St Tampa FL 33607 NASDAQ: OMEX ■ Web: www.shipwreck.net	813-876-1776		465
Odyssey Medical Technologies LLC 2975 Brother Blvd. Bartlett TN 38133 Web: www.odysseymedicaltech.com	901-383-7777	786-6791	475
Odyssey Press (SCP) 1842 Santa Margarita Dr. Fallbrook CA 92028 Web: www.roadtripcurope.com	760-826-3182		637-2
Odyssey Re Holdings Corp 300 First Stamford Pl Stamford CT 06902 TF: 866-745-4440 ■ Web: www.odysseyre.com	203-977-8000		391-4
Odyssey Systems Consulting Group Ltd 201 Edgewater Dr Ste 270 Wakefield MA 01880 Web: www.odysseyconsult.com	781-245-0111		180
OEA (Ohio Education Assn) 225 E Broad St Columbus OH 43215 TF: 800-282-1500 ■ Web: www.ohea.org	614-228-4526	228-8771	457-8
OEA (Oregon Education Magazine) 6900 SW Atlanta St Bldg 1 Portland OR 97223 TF: 800-858-5505 ■ Web: www.oregoned.org	503-684-3300	684-8063	457-8
OEC (Otsego Electric Co-opeartive Inc) PO Box 128 Hartwick NY 13348 TF: 844-843-6842 ■ Web: www.otsegoec.coop	607-293-6622	293-6624	245
OEC 104 E I65 Service Rd N. Mobile AL 36607 TF: 800-759-3368 ■ Web: www.oecbi.com	251-471-3368	479-0641	393
OEC (Offshore Energy Ctr) 5555 San Felipe St Ste 2119 Houston TX 77056 *Fax Area Code: 281 ■ Web: www.oceanstaroec.com	713-840-1753	783-1200*	520
OEC Business Interiors 1601 NW 80th Blvd Gainesville FL 32606 Web: www.oec-fl.com	352-332-1192	333-8002	320
Oeco LLC 4607 SE International Way Milwaukie OR 97222 Web: www.oeco.com	503-659-5999		253
Oeconnection LLC 4205 Highlander Pkwy Richfield OH 44286 *Fax Area Code: 330 ■ TF: 888-776-5792 ■ Web: oeconnection.com	888-776-5792	523-1700*	177
Oehm Automation LLC 11 Fifth St Ste 104 Petaluma CA 94952 Web: oehmautomation.com	415-659-8900		177
Oehrlein School of Cosmetology 100 Meadow Ave East Peoria IL 61611 Web: www.oehrleinschool.com	309-699-1561		685
OEM Controls Inc 10 Controls Dr. Shelton CT 06484 Web: www.oemcontrols.com	203-929-8431	929-3867	203
Oem Fabricators Inc 300 Mcmillan Rd Woodville WI 54028 Web: www.oemfab.com	715-698-2111		567
OEM Group Inc 2120 W Guadalupe Rd Gilbert AZ 85233 Web: www.oemgroupinc.com	480-558-9200		696
OEM Inc 8500 S Tryon St Charlotte NC 28273 Web: www.oemdisc.com	704-504-1877	504-9877	658
OEM Industries Inc 1015 N Justin Ave. Dallas TX 75211 Web: www.oemindustries.net	214-330-7271	330-6978	483
OEM Systems LLC 210 W Oklahoma Ave Okarche OK 73762 TF: 800-810-7252 ■ Web: oemtruckequipment.com	405-263-7488	263-4765	61
Oemmcco Inc 9606 58th Pl Kenosha WI 53144 Web: www.oemmcco.com	262-605-1170		454
OEP (Ohio Energy Project) 200 E Wilson Bridge Rd Ste 320 Worthington OH 43085 Web: www.ohioenergy.org	614-785-1717		196
OERM (Orange Empire Railway Museum) 2201 S A St Perris CA 92570 Web: www.oerm.org	951-943-3020	943-2676	520
Oesterlen-services for Youth Inc 1918 Mechanicsburg Rd. Springfield OH 45503 Web: www.oesterlen.org	937-399-6101		726
OF Mossberg & Sons Inc 7 Grasso Ave. North Haven CT 06473 TF: 800-363-3555 ■ Web: www.mossberg.com	203-230-5300	230-5420	284
OFA (Orphan Foundation of America) 23811 Chagrin Blvd Ste 210 Cleveland OH 44122 *Fax Area Code: 855 ■ TF: 800-950-4673 ■ Web: www.fc2success.org	571-203-0270	773-8299*	48-6
OFB (Oklahoma Farm Bureau Mutual Insurance Co) 2501 N Stiles Ave Oklahoma City OK 73105 Web: www.okfarmbureau.org	405-523-2300	523-2362	391-4
OFD Foods 525 25th Ave SW Albany OR 97322 Web: www.ofd.com	541-926-6001		296-18
Off Broadway Theatre 272 S Main St. Salt Lake City UT 84101 Web: www.theobt.org	801-355-4628		572
Off Madison Ave Inc 5555 E Van Buren St Ste 215 Phoenix AZ 85008 Web: www.offmadisonave.com	480-505-4500		4
Off Road Unlimited (ORU) 2636 N Ontario St. Burbank CA 91504 TF: 888-365-0244 ■ Web: www.offroadunlimited.com	818-563-1208	729-1919	54
Off the Beaten Path 7 E Beall St Bozeman MT 59715 TF: 800-445-2995 ■ Web: www.offthebeatenpath.com	406-586-1311	587-4147	760
Off The Wall Company Inc 4814 Bethlehem Pk. Telford PA 18969 Web: www.otwcompany.com	215-453-9400		344
Off Wall Street Consulting Group Inc PO Box 382107 Cambridge MA 02238 Web: www.offwallstreet.com	617-868-7880	868-4933	401
OffBeat Publications 421 Frenchman St Ste 200 New Orleans LA 70116 TF: 877-944-4300 ■ Web: www.offbeat.com	504-944-4300	944-4306	637-9
Offen Petroleum Inc 5100 E 78th Ave Commerce City CO 80022 TF: 866-657-3835 ■ Web: offenpetro.com	303-297-3835		579
Offender Preparation & Education Network Inc (OPEN) PO Box 472223 Garland TX 75047 *Fax Area Code: 972 ■ TF: 800-966-1966 ■ Web: www.openinc.org	800-966-1966	278-5884*	637-2
Offenhauser Co 2201 Telephone Rd Houston TX 77023 Web: www.offenhauser.com	713-928-2981	928-2465	91
Offerpad 2150 E Germann Rd Ste 1 Chandler AZ 85286 TF: 844-388-4539 ■ Web: www.offerpad.com	844-388-4539		652
Office & Professional Employees International Union Local 277 641 N Cherry Ln. Fort Worth TX 76108 Web: opeiu277.org	817-246-4981		414
Office & Professional Employers 6136 Mission Gorge Rd Ste 214 San Diego CA 92120 Web: opeiulocal30.org	619-640-4840		414
Office Automation Technologies 11919 W 1-70 Frontage Rd N Ste 123 Wheat Ridge CO 80033 Web: www.oati1.com	303-202-5152		180

	Phone	Fax	Class
Office Depot Inc 2200 Old Germantown Rd. Delray Beach FL 33445 *NASDAQ:* ODP ■ *TF:* 800-937-3600 ■ *Web:* www.officedepot.com	561-438-4800		535
Office Designs 722 landwehr Rd. Northbrook IL 60062 **Fax Area Code:* 847 ■ *TF:* 877-978-0062 ■ *Web:* officedesigns.com	877-978-0062	504-1700*	320
Office Environments Inc 11407 Granite St. Charlotte NC 28273 *TF:* 888-861-2525 ■ *Web:* www.office-environments.com	704-714-7200	714-7400	320
Office Express Supply Inc 8005 W 20th Ave Hialeah FL 33014 *Web:* xpressbuy.com	305-557-1667	824-9211	321
Office Furniture Installers Inc 3167 Spaulding St Omaha NE 68111 *Web:* www.ofi-usa.com	402-451-8009		321
Office Furniture Team 4204 Lindbergh Dr Addison TX 75001 *Web:* www.oftoffice.com	972-503-8326		320
Office Liquidators Inc 11111 W Sixth Ave Denver CO 80215 *TF:* 800-279-3375 ■ *Web:* www.officeliquidators.com	303-759-3375		317
Office of Congressional Workplace Rights 110 2nd St SE Rm LA 200 Washington DC 20540 *Web:* www.ocwr.gov	202-724-9250	426-1913	340-20
Office of Crime Victim Services PO Box 7951 Madison WI 53707 *TF:* 800-446-6564 ■ *Web:* www.doj.state.wi.us	608-266-1221	264-6368	339-50
Office of Disability Employment Policy 200 Constitution Ave NW Washington DC 20210 *TF:* 866-633-7365 ■ *Web:* www.dol.gov	202-693-7880	693-7888	340-15
Office of General Services Corning Tower Empire State Plz 41st Fl Empire State Plz Albany NY 12242 *TF:* 877-426-6006 ■ *Web:* ogs.ny.gov	518-474-3899	457-3081	205
Office of Intergovernmental & External Affairs *Region II* 26 Federal Plz Ste 3835 New York NY 10278 *Web:* www.hhs.gov	212-616-2229		340-10
Office of Justice Programs (OJP) 810 Seventh St NW Washington DC 20531 *Web:* ojp.gov	202-307-0703		340-14
Office of Justice Programs			
Bureau of Justice Assistance 810 7th St NW Washington DC 20531 *TF:* 888-744-6513 ■ *Web:* bja.ojp.gov	202-616-6500	305-1367	340-14
National Institute of Justice 810 7th St NW Washington DC 20531 *Web:* nij.ojp.gov	202-307-2942		340-14
Office of Juvenile Justice & Delinquency Prevention 810 7th St NW Washington DC 20531 *Web:* ojjdp.ojp.gov	202-307-5911	307-2093	340-14
Office of Management & Budget (OMB) 725 17th St NW Washington DC 20503 *Web:* www.whitehouse.gov	202-395-3080	395-3888	340
Office of Personnel Management (OPM) 1900 E St NW Washington DC 20415 *Web:* www.opm.gov	202-606-1800		340-20
Office of Public Health & Science 200 Independence Ave SW Rm 716G Washington DC 20201 *Web:* www.hhs.gov	202-690-7694		340-10
Region I John F Kennedy Federal Bldg Rm 2100 Boston MA 02203 *Web:* www.hhs.gov	617-565-1491		340-10
Region IX 90 Seventh St Ste 5-100 San Francisco CA 94103 *Web:* www.hhs.gov	415-437-8500	437-8004	340-10
Office of Public Health & Science Regional Offices			
Region 3 150 S Independence Mall W Ste 436 Philadelphia PA 19106 *Web:* www.hhs.gov	215-861-4639	861-4617	340-10
Region 4 61 Forsyth St SW Ste 5B95 Atlanta GA 30303 *Web:* www.hhs.gov	404-562-7888	562-7899	340-10
Office of Special Counsel			
OSC Headquarters 1730 M St NW Ste 218 Washington DC 20036 *TF:* 800-872-9855 ■ *Web:* osc.gov	202-254-3600	254-3711	340-20
Office of Surface Mining Reclamation & Enforcement 1849 C St NW Washington DC 20240 *Web:* www.osmre.gov	202-208-2565		340-13
Office of the Assistant Secretary for Health *Region VIII* 1961 Stout St Rm 08-148 Denver CO 80294 *Web:* www.hhs.gov	303-844-3100	844-2019	340-10
Office of the Governor - American Samoa A P Lutali Executive Office Bldg Utulei Third Fl Pago Pago AS 96799 *Web:* www.americansamoa.gov	684-633-4116	633-2269	343
Office of the Governor - Arizona 1700 West Washington St. Phoenix AZ 85007 *Web:* www.azgovernor.gov	602-542-4331		343
Office of the Governor - Connecticut 210 Capitol Ave Hartford CT 06106 *TF:* 800-406-1527 ■ *Web:* www.portal.ct.gov	860-566-4840		343
Office of the Governor - Delaware 150 Martin Luther King Jr Blvd. Wilmington DE 19801 *Web:* www.governor.delaware.gov	302-577-3210		343
Office of the Governor - District of Columbia John A Wilson Bldg 1350 Pennsylvania Ave NW Washington DC 20004 *Web:* www.mayor.dc.gov	202-727-2643		343
Office of the Governor - Idaho State Capitol PO Box 83720 Boise ID 83720 *Web:* www.gov.idaho.gov	208-334-2100	854-3036	343
Office of the Governor - Indiana 302 W Washington St Rm E018 Indianapolis IN 46204 *Web:* www.in.gov	317-519-4563		343
Office of the Governor - Kansas Capitol 300 SW 10th Ave Ste 241S Topeka KS 66612 *TF:* 877-579-6757 ■ *Web:* www.governor.kansas.gov	785-296-3232		343
Office of the Governor - Maryland 100 State Cir. Annapolis MD 21401 *TF:* 800-811-8336 ■ *Web:* www.governor.maryland.gov	410-974-3901		343
Office of the Governor - Massachusetts Massachusetts State House 24 Beacon St Office of the Governor Rm 280 Boston MA 02133 *Web:* www.mass.gov	617-725-4005	727-3666	343
Office of the Governor - Mississippi PO Box 139 Jackson MS 39205 *Web:* www.usa.gov	601-359-3150	359-3741	343
Office of the Governor - Missouri PO Box 720 Jefferson City MO 65102 *Web:* www.governor.mo.gov	573-751-3222	751-1495	343
Office of the Governor - Montana PO Box 200801 Helena MT 59620 *TF:* 855-318-1330 ■ *Web:* www.governor.mt.gov	406-444-3111	444-5529	343
Office of the Governor - Nevada State Capitol Bldg 101 N Carson St Carson City NV 89701 *Web:* www.gov.nv.gov	775-684-5670	684-5683	343
Office of the Governor - New Hampshire State House 107 North Main St Concord NH 03301 *Web:* www.governor.nh.gov	603-271-2121	271-7680	343
Office of the Governor - New Jersey Office of Governor PO Box 001 Trenton NJ 08625 *Web:* www.state.nj.us	609-292-6000		343
Office of the Governor - New Mexico 490 Old Santa Fe Trl Rm 400 Santa Fe NM 87501 *Web:* www.governor.state.nm.us	505-476-2200		343
Office of the Governor - North Carolina 20301 Mail Service Ctr. Raleigh NC 27699 *Web:* www.governor.nc.gov	919-814-2000		343
Office of the Governor - Oklahoma State Capitol 2300 N Lincoln Blvd Oklahoma City OK 73105 *Web:* www.ok.gov	405-521-2342		343
Office of the Governor - Pennsylvania Office of the Governor 508 Main Capitol Bldg Harrisburg PA 17120 *Web:* www.governor.pa.gov	717-787-2500	772-8284	343
Office of the Governor - Rhode Island 82 Smith St. Providence RI 02903 *Web:* www.governor.ri.gov	401-222-2080	222-8096	343
Office of the Governor - South Dakota Office of the Governor 500 East Capitol Ave Pierre SD 57501 *Web:* www.sd.gov	605-773-3148		343
Office of the Governor - Tennessee State Capitol 1st Fl Nashville TN 37243 *Web:* www.tn.gov	615-741-2001		343
Office of the Governor - Utah 350 North State St Ste 200 PO Box 142220 Salt Lake City UT 84114 *TF:* 800-705-2464 ■ *Web:* www.utah.gov	801-538-1000		343
Office of the Governor - Vermont 109 State Street Pavilion Montpelier VT 05609 *Web:* www.governor.vermont.gov	802-828-3333	828-3339	343
Office of the Governor - Virginia PO Box 1475 Richmond VA 23218 *Web:* www.governor.virginia.gov	804-786-2211		343
Office of the Governor - Washington Office of the Governor PO Box 40002 Olympia WA 98504 *Web:* www.governor.wa.gov	360-902-4111	753-4110	343
Office of the Governor - West Virginia State Capitol 1900 Kanawha Blvd E Charleston WV 25305 *Web:* www.governor.wv.gov	304-558-2000		343
Office of the Governor - Wisconsin PO Box 7863 Madison WI 53707 *Web:* evers.wi.gov	608-266-1212		343
Office of the Pardon Attorney 145 N St NE Rm 5E Washington DC 20530 *TF:* 800-514-0301 ■ *Web:* www.justice.gov	202-616-6070		340-14
Office of the US Trade Representative 600 17th St NW Washington DC 20508 *Web:* ustr.gov	202-395-7360		340
Office of the Vice President 1650 Pennsylvania Ave NW Eisenhower Executive Office Bldg Washington DC 20504 *Web:* www.whitehouse.gov	202-456-4444		340
Office of Tribal Justice 950 Pennsylvania Ave NW Washington DC 20530 *Web:* www.justice.gov	202-514-2203		340-14
Office on Violence Against Women 145 N St Ste 10W 121 Washington DC 20530 *Web:* www.justice.gov	202-307-6026	307-2277	340-14
Office Pavilion 10030 Bent Oak Dr Houston TX 77040 *Web:* ophouston.com	713-803-0000	803-0001	320
Office Plus of Lake County 1428 Glen Flora Ave Waukegan IL 60085 *Web:* www.getofficeplus.com	847-662-5393	662-8761	320
Office Products Inc (Opi) 121 Freeport Cir Fallon NV 89406 *Web:* officeproinc.net	775-423-5403		535
Office Products Recycling Associates Inc 100 W 18th Ave North Kansas City MO 64116 *Web:* www.oprausa.com	816-584-1000		690
Office Resources Inc 263 Summer St Boston MA 02210 *Web:* www.ori.com	617-423-9100		535
Office Solutions Inc 217 Mt Horeb Rd Warren NJ 07059 *TF:* 800-677-1778 ■ *Web:* www.osi-technology.com	800-677-1778		179
Office Star Products 1901 S Archibald PO Box 3520 Ontario CA 91761 *TF:* 800-950-7262 ■ *Web:* www.officestar.net	909-930-2000		320
Office Systems of Texas 104 Lockhaven Dr. Houston TX 77073 *Web:* www.osot.com	281-443-2996	443-1494	174
Officepro Inc 8 Granite Pl Ste 26 Gaithersburg MD 20878 *Web:* officeproinc.com	301-468-3312		177
OfficeSuperSavers.com 4865 19th St NW Ste 110 Rochester MN 55901 **Fax Area Code:* 507 ■ *TF:* 877-591-4881 ■ *Web:* officesupersavers.com	877-591-4881	529-9756*	534
Official Payments Corp 3550 Engineering Dr. Norcross GA 30092 *TF:* 877-754-4413 ■ *Web:* www.officialpayments.com	770-325-3100		180

Name / Address	City	State	ZIP	Phone	Fax	Class
Official Reporters Inc						
421 W Church St Ste 701	Jacksonville	FL	32202	904-358-2090	358-0062	478
Web: www.officialreportersinc.com						
Offit Capital						
485 Lexington Ave 24th Fl	New York	NY	10017	212-588-3276		401
Web: www.offitcapital.com						
Offshore Energy Ctr (OEC)						
5555 San Felipe St Ste 2119	Houston	TX	77056	713-840-1753	783-1200*	520
**Fax Area Code:* 281 ■ *Web:* www.oceanstaroec.com						
Offshore Energy Services Inc						
5900 US Hwy 90 E	Broussard	LA	70518	337-837-1024		539
TF: 800-489-6202 ■ *Web:* www.offshoreenergyservices.com						
Offshore International Inc						
8350 E Old Vail Rd	Tucson	AZ	85747	800-897-3158		803-1
TF: 800-897-3158 ■ *Web:* tetakawi.com						
Offshore Process Services Inc						
1206 Park Dr	Mandeville	LA	70471	985-727-2900	727-2950	261
Web: www.opsincusa.com						
Offutt Air Force Base						
906 Sac Blvd Ste 1	Offutt AFB	NE	68113	402-294-1110		497-1
Web: www.offutt.af.mil						
Offwhite 521 Ft St	Marietta	OH	45750	740-373-9010		344
TF: 800-606-1610 ■ *Web:* www.offwhite.com						
OFS 1204 E 6th St	Huntingburg	IN	47542	800-983-4415	683-7155*	319-1
**Fax Area Code:* 812 ■ *TF:* 800-983-4415 ■ *Web:* ofs.com						
OFS (OFS Capital Corp)						
10 S Wacker Dr Ste 2500	Chicago	IL	60606	847-734-2000		69
Web: www.ofscapital.com						
OFS Capital Corp (OFS)						
10 S Wacker Dr Ste 2500	Chicago	IL	60606	847-734-2000		69
Web: www.ofscapital.com						
OG & E Electric Services						
PO Box 24990	Oklahoma City	OK	73124	405-272-9741		787
TF: 800-272-9741 ■ *Web:* www.oge.com						
Ogar & Miller 108 W Monroe St	Bloomington	IL	61701	309-827-8551	827-0881	41
Web: ogarmiller.com						
OGB Architectural Millwork						
3711 Paseo Del Norte NE	Albuquerque	NM	87113	505-998-0000		499
Web: www.ogb-am.com						
Ogden City Hall 2549 Washington Blvd	Ogden	UT	84401	801-629-8150	629-8154	337
Web: www.ogdencity.com						
Ogden Companies Inc						
606 Green Meadow St N	Colleyville	TX	76034	817-656-8570		734
Ogden Eccles Conference Ctr						
2415 Washington Blvd	Ogden	UT	84401	801-689-8600	689-8651	205
TF: 866-472-4627 ■ *Web:* oeccutah.com						
Ogden Eccles Dinosaur Park						
1544 E Pk Blvd	Ogden	UT	84401	801-393-3466		520
Web: www.dinosaurpark.org						
Ogden Museum of Southern Art						
925 Camp St	New Orleans	LA	70130	504-539-9650		520
Web: ogdenmuseum.org						
Ogden Nature Ctr 966 W 12th St	Ogden	UT	84404	801-621-7595	621-1867	50-5
Web: ogdennaturecenter.org						
Ogden Publications Inc 1503 SW 42nd St	Topeka	KS	66609	800-678-5779		4
TF: 800-678-5779 ■ *Web:* www.ogdenpubs.com						
Ogden Reporter 222 W Walnut St	Ogden	IA	50212	515-275-2101	275-2678	532-2
Web: www.ogdenreporter.com						
Ogden Telephone Co						
4726 E Weston Rd	Blissfield	MI	49228	517-443-5595		393
Web: www.ogdentel.com						
Ogden Telephone Co 202 W Walnut St	Ogden	IA	50212	515-275-4990		224
Web: www.ogdentelephone.com						
Ogden Welding Systems Inc						
372 Div St	Schererville	IN	46375	219-322-5252	865-1825	811
Web: ogdenwelding.com						
Ogden, Gibson, Broocks, Longoria & Hall LLP						
1900 Pennzoil S Twr 711 Louisiana St	Houston	TX	77002	713-844-3000		428
Web: www.keanmiller.com						
Ogden/Weber Convention & Visitors Bureau						
2438 Washington Blvd	Ogden	UT	84401	801-778-6250		206
TF: 800-255-8824 ■ *Web:* www.visitogden.com						
Ogdensburg Bridge & Port Authority						
1 Bridge Plz	Ogdensburg	NY	13669	315-393-4080	393-7068	618
Web: www.ogdensport.com						
Ogden-Weber Applied Technology College Foundation						
200 N Washington Blvd	Ogden	UT	84404	801-627-8300		305
Web: www.owatc.edu						
Ogdir Research Inc PO Box 7352	Princeton	NJ	08543	609-275-0208		178-1
Web: www.ogdir.com						
O-Gee Paint Co 6995 Bird Rd	Miami	FL	33155	305-666-3300	666-5169	802
TF: 866-666-1935 ■ *Web:* www.go.o-geepaint.com						
Ogeechee Technical College						
1 Joseph E Kennedy Blvd	Statesboro	GA	30458	912-681-5500	486-7413	167-3
TF: 800-646-1316 ■ *Web:* www.ogeecheetech.edu						
Ogemaw County 806 W Houghton Ave	West Branch	MI	48661	989-345-5040	345-1071	338
Web: www.ocmi.us						
Ogemaw County Herald						
215 W Houghton Ave	West Branch	MI	48661	989-345-0044	345-5609	532-2
Web: www.ogemawherald.com						
Ogg, Murphy & Perkosky PC						
245 Ft Pitt Blvd 4th Fl	Pittsburgh	PA	15222	412-471-8500		41
TF: 866-269-5149 ■ *Web:* yourpghlawyer.com						
Ogilvy Public Relations Worldwide						
636 11th Ave	New York	NY	10036	212-237-4000	370-4636	636
Web: www.ogilvypr.com						
Oglala Lakota College PO Box 629	Martin	SD	57551	605-455-6000	455-2787	166
Web: www.olc.edu						
Ogle County 2501 Broadway	Oregon	IL	61061	815-732-3201	732-6273	338
TF: 800-242-7642 ■ *Web:* www.oglecounty.org						
Ogle County Life 311 W Washington	Oregon	IL	61061	815-732-2156	732-6154	532-2
Web: www.oglecountylife.com						
Ogle Design 12512 N Gray Rd	Carmel	IN	46033	317-843-1102		344
Web: ogle-design.com						
Oglebay 465 Lodge Dr	Wheeling	WV	26003	304-243-4030	243-4110	823
TF: 877-436-1797 ■ *Web:* oglebay.com						
Oglethorpe County 341 W Main St	Lexington	GA	30648	706-743-5270	743-8371	338
Web: www.onlineoglethorpe.com						
Oglethorpe Inc						
201 N Franklin St Ste 1910	Tampa	FL	33647	813-978-1933		195
Web: www.oglethorpeinc.com						
Oglethorpe Mall 7804 Abercorn Ext	Savannah	GA	31406	912-354-7038		460
Web: www.oglethorpemall.com						
Oglethorpe Speedway Park						
200 Jesup Rd PO Box 687	Pooler	GA	31322	912-964-8200	964-9501	515
Web: www.ospracing.net						
Oglethorpe University						
4484 Peachtree Rd NE	Atlanta	GA	30319	404-364-8307	364-8491	166
TF: 800-428-4484 ■ *Web:* oglethorpe.edu						
Oglevee Ltd 152 Oglevee Ln	Connellsville	PA	15425	724-628-8360		369
Ogne Alberts & Stuart Pc 1869 E Maple Rd	Troy	MI	48083	248-362-3707	362-0422	428
Web: oaspc.com						
Ogontz Corp 2835 Terwood Rd	Willow Grove	PA	19090	215-657-4770	657-0460	789
TF: 800-523-2478 ■ *Web:* www.ogontz.com						
OGR (International Order of the Golden Rule)						
3520 Executive Center Dr Ste 300	Austin	TX	78731	512-334-5504	334-5514	49-4
TF: 800-637-8030 ■ *Web:* www.ogr.org						
Ogren Insurance 6929 Hohman Ave	Hammond	IN	46324	800-936-4736	933-0080*	390
**Fax Area Code:* 219 ■ *TF:* 800-936-4736 ■ *Web:* www.ogreninsurance.com						
OGS (Oklahoma Genealogical Society)						
1125 NW 50th St	Oklahoma City	OK	73118	405-637-1907		637-2
Web: www.okgensoc.org						
OGS Industries 976 Evans Ave	Akron	OH	44305	800-321-2438		454
TF: 800-321-2438 ■ *Web:* lehnerscrewmachine.com						
OH (Oroville Hospital) 2767 Olive Hwy	Oroville	CA	95966	530-533-8500		374-3
Web: www.orovillehospital.com						
O-H Community Partners						
125 S Clark St Ste 1700	Chicago	IL	60603	312-767-9228		463
Web: ohcommunitypartners.com						
Ohana Companies LLC, The						
1405 Foulk Rd Foulkstone Plz Ste 200	Wilmington	DE	19803	302-225-5505		195
Web: ohanacompanies.com						
Ohana Health Plan Inc PO Box 31372	Tampa	FL	33631	877-247-6272		391-3
TF: 877-247-6272 ■ *Web:* www.ohanahealthplan.com						
Ohanesian / Lecours Inc						
433 S Main St	West Hartford	CT	06110	860-521-4751	521-4755	690
TF: 800-525-9295 ■ *Web:* ol-advisors.com						
Ohaus Corp 7 Campus Dr Ste 310	Parsippany	NJ	07054	973-377-9000		684
TF: 800-672-7722 ■ *Web:* asiapacific.ohaus.com						
Ohel Children's Home & Family Services Inc						
156 Beach 9th St 2nd Fl Ste D	Far Rockaway	NY	11691	718-851-6300		363
TF: 800-603-6435 ■ *Web:* www.ohelfamily.org						
OHI Co 820 S Pershing Ave	Stockton	CA	95206	209-466-8921	466-8933	298
Web: www.ohicompany.com						
OHIGRO Inc 6720 Gillette Rd	Waldo	OH	43356	740-726-2574		276
Web: www.ohigro.com						
Ohio						
Adjutant's General Dept						
2825 W Dublin Granville Rd	Columbus	OH	43235	614-336-7000		339-36
Web: www.ong.ohio.gov						
Aging Dept 246 N High St 1st Fl	Columbus	OH	43215	614-466-5500	466-5741	339-36
TF: 800-266-4346 ■ *Web:* aging.ohio.gov						
Agriculture Dept 8995 E Main St	Reynoldsburg	OH	43068	614-728-6201	728-6310	339-36
TF: 800-282-1955 ■ *Web:* www.agri.ohio.gov						
Arts Council 30 E Broad St 33rd Fl	Columbus	OH	43215	614-466-2613	466-4494	339-36
Web: www.oac.ohio.gov						
Commerce Dept 77 S High St 23rd Fl	Columbus	OH	43215	614-466-3636		339-36
Web: www.com.ohio.gov						
Consumer Protection Section						
30 E Broad St 14th Fl	Columbus	OH	43215	614-466-4986		339-36
Web: www.ohioattorneygeneral.gov						
Department of Veterans Services						
77 S High St 7th Fl	Columbus	OH	43215	614-466-9287	387-7317	339-36
TF: 888-387-6446 ■ *Web:* www.dvs.ohio.gov						
Dept of Rehabilitation & Correction						
770 W Broad St	Columbus	OH	43222	614-752-0800		339-36
Web: www.drc.ohio.gov						
Education Dept 25 S Front St	Columbus	OH	43215	877-644-6338		339-36
TF: 877-644-6338 ■ *Web:* education.ohio.gov						
Emergency Management Agency						
2855 W Dublin-Granville Rd	Columbus	OH	43235	614-889-7150	889-7183	339-36
Web: www.ema.ohio.gov						
Environmental Protection Agency						
PO Box 1049	Columbus	OH	43216	614-644-3020		339-36
Web: www.epa.state.oh.us						
Ethics Commission 30 W Spring St L3	Columbus	OH	43215	614-466-7090	466-8368	265
Web: www.ethics.ohio.gov						
Financial Institutions Div						
77 S High St 21st Fl	Columbus	OH	43266	614-728-8400	728-0380	339-36
TF: 866-278-0003 ■ *Web:* www.com.ohio.gov						
Governor						
77 S High St Riffe Ctr 30th Fl	Columbus	OH	43215	614-466-3555	466-9354	339-36
Web: www.governor.ohio.gov						
Health Dept 246 N High St	Columbus	OH	43215	614-466-3543		339-36
Web: www.odh.ohio.gov						
Highway Patrol (OSHP)						
1970 W Broad St PO Box 182074	Columbus	OH	43223	614-466-2660	752-8410	339-36
Web: statepatrol.ohio.gov						
Housing Finance Agency 57 E Main St	Columbus	OH	43215	614-466-7970		339-36
TF: 888-362-6432 ■ *Web:* www.ohiohome.org						
Information Technology						
30 E Broad St 39th Fl	Columbus	OH	43215	614-466-6930		339-36
TF: 800-409-1205 ■ *Web:* www.das.ohio.gov						
Insurance Dept						
50 W Town St Ste 300 Third Fl	Columbus	OH	43215	614-644-2658		339-36
TF: 800-686-1526 ■ *Web:* www.insurance.ohio.gov						
Job & Family Services Dept						
30 E Broad St 38th Fl	Columbus	OH	43215	614-466-6894	728-7740	339-36
Web: www.jfs.ohio.gov						
Legislative Information Office						
77 S High St	Columbus	OH	43215	614-728-0711		433
Web: www.lis.state.oh.us						
Mental Health Dept						
30 E Broad St 8th Fl	Columbus	OH	43215	614-466-2596		339-36
TF: 877-275-6364 ■ *Web:* mha.ohio.gov						

Name / Address	City	State	Zip	Phone	Fax	Class
Motor Vehicles Bureau 1970 W Broad St *TF:* 844-644-6268 ■ *Web:* www.bmv.ohio.gov	Columbus	OH	43223	614-752-7500	752-7220	339-36
Office of Governor 77 S High St 30th Fl *Web:* governor.ohio.gov	Columbus	OH	43215	614-466-3396		339-36
Parole Board 770 W Broad St *TF:* 888-344-1441 ■ *Web:* www.drc.state.oh.us	Columbus	OH	43222	614-752-1164	752-1251	339-36
Public Utilities Commission 180 E Broad St *TF:* 800-686-7826 ■ *Web:* www.puco.ohio.gov	Columbus	OH	43215	614-466-3016	752-8351	339-36
Racing Commission 77 S High St 18th Fl *Web:* www.racingohio.net	Columbus	OH	43215	614-466-2757	466-1900	712
Regents Board 25 S Front St *Web:* www.ohiohighered.org	Columbus	OH	43215	614-466-6000	466-5866	339-36
Secretary of State 22 N 4th St 16th Fl *TF:* 877-767-6446 ■ *Web:* www.sos.state.oh.us	Columbus	OH	43215	614-466-2655		339-36
Securities Div 77 S High St 22nd Fl *Web:* www.com.ohio.gov	Columbus	OH	43215	614-644-7381		339-36
Supreme Court 65 S Front St *Web:* www.sconet.state.oh.us	Columbus	OH	43215	614-387-9000	387-9349	339-36
Taxation Dept PO Box 530 *TF:* 888-405-4089 ■ *Web:* www.tax.ohio.gov	Columbus	OH	43216	614-466-2166	466-7979	339-36
Transportation Dept 1980 W Broad St *Web:* dot.state.oh.us	Columbus	OH	43223	614-466-7170		339-36
Travel & Tourism Div PO Box 1001 *TF:* 800-282-5393 ■ *Web:* www.ohio.org	Columbus	OH	43216	614-466-8844		339-36
Treasurer 30 E Broad St 9th Fl *TF:* 800-228-1102 ■ *Web:* www.tos.ohio.gov	Columbus	OH	43215	614-466-2160		339-36
Tuition Trust Authority 35 E Chestnut St 8th Fl *TF:* 800-233-6734 ■ *Web:* www.ohio.gov	Columbus	OH	43215	614-752-9400	644-5009	725
Vital Statistics Unit 246 N High St *Web:* www.odh.ohio.gov	Columbus	OH	43215	614-466-2531		339-36
Wildlife Div 2045 Morse Rd Bldg G *TF:* 800-945-3543 ■ *Web:* wildlife.ohiodnr.gov	Columbus	OH	43229	614-265-6300		339-36
Workers' Compensation Bureau 30 W Spring St *TF:* 800-644-6292 ■ *Web:* info.bwc.ohio.gov	Columbus	OH	43215	614-728-7605		339-36
Workforce Development Office 4020 E Fifth Ave PO Box 1618 **Fax Area Code:* 614 ■ *TF:* 888-296-7541 ■ *Web:* www.jfs.ohio.gov	Columbus	OH	43219	888-296-7541	728-8366*	339-36
Youth Services Dept 30 W Spring St *TF:* 855-577-7714 ■ *Web:* ohio.gov	Columbus	OH	43215	614-466-4314	752-9859	339-36
Ohio ACEP 3510 Snouffer Rd Ste 100 *Web:* www.ohacep.org	Columbus	OH	43235	614-792-6506		533
Ohio Art Co, The 1 Toy St *OTC:* OART ■ *TF:* 800-800-3141 ■ *Web:* ohioart.com	Bryan	OH	43506	419-636-3141		762
Ohio Associated Enterprises LLC 97 Corwin Dr *TF:* 888-637-4832 ■ *Web:* meritec.com	Painesville	OH	44077	440-354-2100	354-5692	815
Ohio Association of Realtors 200 E Town St *Web:* www.ohiorealtors.org	Columbus	OH	43215	614-228-6675	228-2601	656
Ohio Biological Survey (OBS) PO Box 21370 *Web:* www.ohiobiologicalsurvey.org	Columbus	OH	43221	614-457-8787	457-6005	49-19
Ohio Brake and Clutch (OBC) 1460 Wolf Creek Trl *TF:* 800-622-1990 ■ *Web:* www.ohiobrake.com	Sharon Center	OH	44274	330-239-2345	239-4995	385
Ohio Broach & Machine Co 35264 Topps Industrial Pkwy *Web:* www.ohiobroach.com	Willoughby	OH	44094	440-946-1040	946-0725	455
Ohio Business College 5202 Timber Commons Dr *TF:* 888-514-3126 ■ *Web:* ohiobusinesscollege.edu	Sandusky	OH	44870	419-627-8345		166
Ohio Casualty 9450 Seward Rd *TF:* 800-843-6446 ■ *Web:* www.ohiocasualty-ins.com	Fairfield	OH	45014	800-843-6446		391-4
Ohio Catholic Federal Credit Union 13623 Rockside Rd *TF:* 888-696-4462 ■ *Web:* ohiocatholicfcu.com	Garfield Heights	OH	44125	216-663-6800	663-8610	219
Ohio Chamber of Commerce (OCC) 34 S 3rd St Ste 100 *Web:* ohiochamber.com	Columbus	OH	43215	614-228-4201		139
Ohio Contractors Assn 1313 Dublin Rd *TF:* 800-229-1388 ■ *Web:* ohiocontractors.org	Columbus	OH	43215	614-488-0724		138
Ohio Council of Community Schools 3131 Executive Pkwy Ste 306 *Web:* ohioschools.org	Toledo	OH	43606	419-720-5200		685
Ohio County 130 E Washington St Ste 209 *Web:* ohiocounty.ky.gov	Hartford	KY	42347	270-298-4400	298-4408	338
Ohio County 1500 Chapline St *Web:* www.ohiocountyhealth.com	Wheeling	WV	26003	304-234-3628	234-3829	338
Ohio County Board of Education 315 E Union St *Web:* www.ohio.k12.ky.us	Hartford	KY	42347	270-298-3249		685
Ohio County Convention Tourism & Visitors Commission 100 S Walnut St *Web:* www.enjoyrisingsun.com	Rising Sun	IN	47040	812-438-4933		206
Ohio County Public Library 52 16th St *Web:* www.ohiocountylibrary.org	Wheeling	WV	26003	304-232-0244	232-6848	434-3
Ohio Craft Museum 1665 W Fifth Ave *Web:* www.ohiocraft.org	Columbus	OH	43212	614-486-4402	486-7110	520
Ohio Democratic Party 340 E Fulton St *TF:* 833-648-6776 ■ *Web:* ohiodems.org	Columbus	OH	43215	614-221-6563	221-0721	616-1
Ohio Dental Assn 1370 Dublin Rd *Web:* www.oda.org	Columbus	OH	43215	614-486-2700	486-0381	227
Ohio Desk Co 1122 Prospect Ave E *Web:* www.ohiodesk.com	Cleveland	OH	44115	216-623-0600	623-0611	320
Ohio Dominican University 1216 Sunbury Rd *TF:* 800-955-6446 ■ *Web:* www.ohiodominican.edu	Columbus	OH	43219	614-251-4500	251-0156	166
Ohio Drilling Co, The 2405 Bostic Blvd SW *TF:* 800-272-1711 ■ *Web:* ohiodrilling.company	Massillon	OH	44647	330-832-1521		189-15
Ohio Edison Co 76 S Main St *TF:* 800-736-3402 ■ *Web:* www.firstenergycorp.com	Akron	OH	44308	330-436-4122		787
Ohio Education Assn (OEA) 225 E Broad St *TF:* 800-282-1500 ■ *Web:* www.ohea.org	Columbus	OH	43215	614-228-4526	228-8771	457-8
Ohio Electric Motors Inc 30 Paint Fork Rd PO Box 168 *Web:* www.ohioelectricmotors.com	Barnardsville	NC	28709	828-626-2901	626-2155	518
Ohio Energy Project (OEP) 200 E Wilson Bridge Rd Ste 320 *Web:* www.ohioenergy.org	Worthington	OH	43085	614-785-1717		196
Ohio Exterminating Company Inc 1347 N High St *Web:* www.ohioexterminating.com	Columbus	OH	43201	614-294-6311		577
Ohio Fabricators Co 111 N 14th St PO Box 207 *Web:* www.ohfab.com	Coshocton	OH	43812	740-622-5922	622-3307	454
Ohio Federation of Teachers 1251 E Broad St Frnt *Web:* oh.aft.org	Columbus	OH	43205	614-258-3240		414
Ohio Gas Co PO Box 528 *TF:* 800-331-7396 ■ *Web:* www.ohiogas.com	Bryan	OH	43506	419-636-1117		536
Ohio Grantmakers Forum 401 N High St *Web:* www.philanthropyohio.org	Columbus	OH	43215	614-224-1344		533
Ohio Gratings Inc 5299 Southway St SW *Web:* www.ohiogratings.com	Canton	OH	44706	330-477-6707		480
Ohio Health Care Assn, The 55 Green Meadows Dr S PO Box 447 *Web:* www.ohca.org	Lewis Center	OH	43035	614-436-4154		138
Ohio Hi-Point Career Ctr 2280 State Rte 540 *Web:* www.ohiohipoint.com	Bellefontaine	OH	43311	937-599-3010	599-2318	167-3
Ohio Hispanic Coalition 100 E Campus View Blvd Ste 130 *Web:* ohiohispaniccoalition.org	Columbus	OH	43235	614-840-9934	840-9935	226
Ohio Historical Society 1982 Velma Ave *TF:* 800-686-6124 ■ *Web:* www.ohiohistory.org	Columbus	OH	43211	614-297-2571		520
Ohio House Motel 600 N La Salle Dr *TF:* 866-601-6446 ■ *Web:* www.ohiohousemotel.com	Chicago	IL	60654	312-943-6000		707
Ohio Indemnity Co 250 E Broad St *TF:* 800-628-8581 ■ *Web:* www.ohioindemnity.com	Columbus	OH	43215	800-628-8581		391-4
Ohio Light Opera, The 1189 Beall Ave *Web:* ohiolightopera.org	Wooster	OH	44691	330-263-2345	263-2272	573-2
Ohio Loan Company Inc 1171 W Third St *Web:* ohioloanco.com	Dayton	OH	45402	937-228-5991		217
Ohio Lottery Commission 615 W Superior Ave *TF:* 800-686-4208 ■ *Web:* www.ohiolottery.com	Cleveland	OH	44113	216-787-3200	787-3313	452
Ohio Machinery Co 3993 E Royalton Rd *TF:* 800-837-6200 ■ *Web:* www.ohiocat.com	Broadview Heights	OH	44147	440-526-6200		358
Ohio Magnetics Inc 5400 Dunham Rd *TF:* 800-486-6446 ■ *Web:* www.ohiomagnetics.com	Maple Heights	OH	44137	216-662-8484	662-2911	470
Ohio Manufacturers' Assn 33 N High St *TF:* 800-662-4463 ■ *Web:* www.ohiomfg.com	Columbus	OH	43215	614-224-5111		138
Ohio Medical Transportation Inc 2827 W Dblin Granville Rd *TF:* 877-633-3598 ■ *Web:* www.medflight.com	Columbus	OH	43235	614-734-8001		13
Ohio Metal Technologies Inc 470 John Alford Pky *Web:* www.ohiometal.net	Hebron	OH	43025	740-928-8288	928-8286	483
Ohio Motorcycle Dealers Assn 655 Metro Pl S Ste 270 *TF:* 800-686-9100 ■ *Web:* www.oada.com	Dublin	OH	43017	614-766-9100		138
Ohio Municipal Advisory Council 9321 Ravenna Rd Ste K *Web:* www.ohiomac.com	Twinsburg	OH	44087	330-963-7444		401
Ohio Northern University 525 S Main St *TF:* 888-408-4668 ■ *Web:* www.onu.edu	Ada	OH	45810	419-772-2000	772-2313	166
Ohio Nurses Assn (ONA) 4000 E Main St *TF:* 800-735-0056 ■ *Web:* www.ohnurses.org	Columbus	OH	43213	614-237-5414	237-6074	533
Ohio Nut & Bolt Co 5250 W 164th St **Fax Area Code:* 216 ■ *TF:* 800-437-1689 ■ *Web:* www.buckeyefasteners.com	Brook Park	OH	44142	800-437-1689	267-3228*	278
Ohio Oil & Gas Energy Education Program (OOGEEP) 1718 Columbus Rd SW *Web:* oogeep.org	Granville	OH	43023	740-587-0410	587-0408	423
Ohio Paper Tube Co 3422 Navarre Rd SW *Web:* www.ohiopapertube.com	Canton	OH	44706	330-478-5171		125
Ohio Poultry Assn 5930 Sharon Woods Blvd *Web:* www.ohiopoultry.org	Columbus	OH	43229	614-882-6111		533
Ohio Precision Molding Inc 122 E Tuscarawas Ave *Web:* www.ohioprecisionmolding.com	Barberton	OH	44203	330-745-9393	745-0825	604
Ohio Quarter Horse 101 Tawa Rd *Web:* www.oqha.com	Richwood	OH	43344	740-943-2346		533
Ohio Reformatory for Women 1479 Collins Ave *Web:* drc.ohio.gov	Marysville	OH	43040	937-642-1065	642-7678	213
Ohio Republican Party 211 S Fifth St *TF:* 800-282-0515 ■ *Web:* www.ohiogop.org	Columbus	OH	43215	614-228-2481		616-2
Ohio Restaurant Assn 1525 Bethel Rd Ste 201 *TF:* 800-282-9049 ■ *Web:* www.ohiorestaurant.org	Columbus	OH	43220	614-442-3535		242
Ohio River Collieries Co 70245 Bannock Uniontown Rd *Web:* www.orcproperties.com	Saint Clairsville	OH	43950	740-391-5925		653
Ohio Roll Grinding Inc 5156 Louisville St *Web:* www.ohioroll.com	Louisville	OH	44641	330-453-1884		454
Ohio Screw Products Inc 818 Lowell St *Web:* www.ohioscrew.com	Elyria	OH	44035	440-322-6341	322-0750	621

Name	Address	City	State	ZIP	Phone	Fax	Class
Ohio Space Grant Consortium	22800 Cedar Point Rd *TF:* 800-828-6742 ■ *Web:* www.osgc.org	Cleveland	OH	44142	440-962-3032	962-3057	167-3
Ohio Stadium	2450 Fred Taylor Dr *Web:* www.ohiostatebuckeyes.com	Columbus	OH	43210	614-292-7572	292-0506	720
Ohio Star Forge Co (OSF)	4000 Mahoning Ave NW *Web:* www.ohiostar.com	Warren	OH	44483	330-847-6360		483
Ohio State Bar Assn (OSBA)	1700 Lake Shore Dr *TF:* 800-282-6556 ■ *Web:* www.ohiobar.org	Columbus	OH	43204	614-487-2050	487-1008	72
Ohio State Medical Assn	3401 Mill Run Dr *TF:* 800-766-6762 ■ *Web:* osma.org	Hilliard	OH	43026	614-527-6753	527-6763	474
Ohio State Penitentiary	878 Coitsville Hubbard Rd *Web:* drc.ohio.gov	Youngstown	OH	44505	330-743-0700	743-0841	213
Ohio State University	154 W 12th Ave *TF:* 800-426-5046 ■ *Web:* www.osu.edu	Columbus	OH	43210	614-292-3980	292-4818	166
Ohio State University							
Lima	4240 Campus Dr *Web:* lima.osu.edu	Lima	OH	45804	419-995-8391	995-8483	166
Mansfield	1660 University Dr *Web:* mansfield.osu.edu	Mansfield	OH	44906	419-755-4011		166
Newark	1179 University Dr *TF:* 800-963-9275 ■ *Web:* newark.osu.edu	Newark	OH	43055	740-366-3321	364-9645	166
Ohio State University College of Medicine & Public Health	370 W Ninth Ave *Web:* medicine.osu.edu	Columbus	OH	43210	614-292-2220		167-2
Ohio State University Health Plan Inc	700 Ackerman Rd Ste 580 *TF:* 800-678-6269 ■ *Web:* www.osuhealthplan.com	Columbus	OH	43202	614-292-4700		391-3
Ohio State University Moritz College of Law	55 W 12th Ave *Web:* www.moritzlaw.osu.edu	Columbus	OH	43210	614-292-2631	292-1492	167-1
Ohio State University Press	1070 Carmack Rd *Web:* ohiostatepress.org	Columbus	OH	43210	614-292-7818	292-2065	637-4
Ohio State University Wexner Medical Ctr, The	410 W Tenth Ave *TF:* 800-240-4477 ■ *Web:* wexnermedical.osu.edu	Columbus	OH	43210	614-293-8000		374-3
Ohio State University, The							
Secrest Arboretum	1680 Madison Ave *Web:* secrest.osu.edu	Wooster	OH	44691	330-263-3761	263-3667	97
University Libraries	1858 Neil Ave Mall *Web:* www.library.osu.edu	Columbus	OH	43210	614-292-6785	292-7859	434-6
Ohio Steel Industries Inc	2575 Ferris Rd *TF:* 800-652-2321 ■ *Web:* www.ohiosteel.com	Columbus	OH	43224	800-652-2321		429
Ohio Steel Sheet & Plate Inc	7845 Chestnut Ridge Rd *TF:* 800-827-2401 ■ *Web:* www.ohiosteelplate.com	Hubbard	OH	44425	800-827-2401		492
Ohio Technical College	1374 E 51st St **Fax Area Code:* 216 ■ *TF:* 800-322-7000 ■ *Web:* www.ohiotech.edu	Cleveland	OH	44103	800-322-7000	881-9145*	167-3
Ohio Telecom Inc	115 W 2nd St *Web:* www.ohiotelecom.us	Port Clinton	OH	43452	419-734-2369		224
Ohio Telecom LLC	2324 Stanley Ave *Web:* www.ohiotele.com	Dayton	OH	45404	937-222-2269		681
Ohio Tool Systems Inc	3863 Congress Pkwy *Web:* www.ohiotool.com	Richfield	OH	44286	330-659-4181		358
Ohio Travel Assn	1801 Watermark Dr Ste 375 *TF:* 800-896-4682 ■ *Web:* www.ohiotravel.org	Columbus	OH	43215	614-572-1931		772
Ohio Travel Bag Manufacturing Co	6481 Davis Industrial Pkwy *Web:* ohiotravelbag.com	Solon	OH	44139	440-498-1955		772
Ohio University	120 Chubb Hall *TF:* 800-858-6843 ■ *Web:* www.ohio.edu	Athens	OH	45701	740-593-0560		166
Ohio University Press	The Ridges 19 Cir Dr *Web:* www.ohioswallow.com	Athens	OH	45701	740-593-1154	593-4536	637-4
Ohio Valley Aluminum Company LLC	1100 Brooks Industrial Rd *TF:* 800-692-4145 ■ *Web:* www.ovaco.com	Shelbyville	KY	40065	502-633-2783		492
Ohio Valley Banc Corp	420 Third Ave *NASDAQ: OVBC* ■ *TF:* 800-468-6682 ■ *Web:* www.ovbc.com	Gallipolis	OH	45631	740-446-2631		360-2
Ohio Valley Coal Co	56854 Pleasant Ridge Rd *Web:* www.dysartwoods.org	Alledonia	OH	43902	740-926-1351		501
Ohio Valley Federal Credit Union	2091 James E Sauls Sr Dr *Web:* ovfcu.org	Batavia	OH	45103	513-724-6098	724-6093	219
Ohio Valley Flooring Inc	5555 Murray Ave *Web:* www.ovf.com	Cincinnati	OH	45227	513-561-3399		361
Ohio Valley Mall	67800 Mall Rd *Web:* www.ohiovalleymall.net	Saint Clairsville	OH	43950	740-695-4526	695-4451	460
Ohio Valley Medical Ctr	2000 Eoff St *Web:* www.ovmc-eorh.com	Wheeling	WV	26003	304-234-0123		374-3
Ohio Valley Supply Co	3512 Spring Grove Ave *TF:* 800-696-5608 ■ *Web:* ovsco.com	Cincinnati	OH	45223	513-681-8300	853-3307	191-3
Ohio Valley University	1 Campus View Dr *TF:* 877-446-8668 ■ *Web:* www.ovu.edu	Vienna	WV	26105	304-865-6000		166
Ohio Valley Veneer Inc	165 No Name Rd *Web:* www.ohiovalleyveneer.com	Piketon	OH	45661	740-493-2901	289-4750	683
Ohio Veterans Home	3416 Columbus Ave *TF:* 800-572-7934 ■ *Web:* www.dvs.ohio.gov	Sandusky	OH	44870	419-625-2454		793
Ohio Veterinary Medical Assn (OVMA)	3168 Riverside Dr *TF:* 800-662-6862 ■ *Web:* www.ohiovma.org	Columbus	OH	43221	614-486-7253	486-1325	795
Ohio Wesleyan University	Slocum Hall 61 S Sandusky St *TF:* 800-922-8953 ■ *Web:* www.owu.edu	Delaware	OH	43015	740-368-2000	368-3314	166
OhioHealth	3430 OhioHealth Pkwy Ste 2100 *Web:* www.ohiohealth.com	Columbus	OH	43202	614-788-8860	544-4301	353
Ohios First Class Credit Union	1800 Carnegie Ave *Web:* ofcu.com	Cleveland	OH	44115	216-241-1088		219
Ohiya Casino	53142 Hwy 12 *Web:* ohiyacasino.com	Niobrara	NE	68760	402-857-3860		452
Ohlinger Industries Inc	1211 W Melinda Ln *Web:* www.ohlingerind.com	Phoenix	AZ	85027	602-285-0911		757
Ohly Americas	1115 Tiffany St *TF:* 800-321-2689 ■ *Web:* www.ohly.com	Boyceville	WI	54725	320-587-2481	587-8617	296-42
Ohly Law Office Ltd	1850 N Broadway *Web:* ohlylaw.com	Rochester	MN	55906	507-289-4529		41
OHM (Orchard Hiltz & McCliment Inc)	34000 Plymouth Rd *TF:* 888-522-6711 ■ *Web:* www.ohm-advisors.com	Livonia	MI	48150	734-522-6711	522-6427	261
Ohm Systems Inc	10250 Chester Rd *TF:* 800-878-0646 ■ *Web:* www.ohmworld.com	Cincinnati	OH	45215	513-771-0008	771-0101	463
Ohmart/VEGA Corp	4241 Allendorf Dr *TF:* 800-367-5383 ■ *Web:* www.vega.com	Cincinnati	OH	45209	513-272-0131	272-0133	472
Ohmite Manufacturing Co	1600 Golf Rd Ste 850 *TF:* 866-964-6483 ■ *Web:* www.ohmite.com	Rolling Meadows	IL	60008	866-964-6483		253
Ohmstede	895 N Main St *TF:* 800-568-2328 ■ *Web:* www.ohmstede.com	Beaumont	TX	77704	409-833-6375	839-4948	91
Ohmx Corp	1801 Maple Ave Ste 6143 *Web:* www.ohmxbio.com	Evanston	IL	60201	847-491-8500		231
OHOP Mutual Light Co	34014 Mountain Hwy E *Web:* ohop.coop	Eatonville	WA	98328	253-847-4363	847-2877	245
Ohr-O'Keefe Museum of Art	386 Beach Blvd *Web:* www.georgeohr.org	Biloxi	MS	39530	228-374-5547	436-3641	520
OI Corp	151 Graham Rd PO Box 9010 *TF:* 800-653-1711 ■ *Web:* www.oico.com	College Station	TX	77842	979-690-1711	690-0440	419
OIA (Outdoor Industry Assn)	4909 Pearl E Cir Ste 200 *Web:* outdoorindustry.org	Boulder	CO	80301	303-444-3353	444-3284	49-4
OIA (Outpatient Imaging Affiliates)	840 Crescent Centre Dr Ste 200 *TF:* 866-591-5559 ■ *Web:* www.oiarad.com	Franklin	TN	37067	615-550-6000		415
OIA Global Logistics Inc	2100 SW River Pkwy *TF:* 800-938-3109 ■ *Web:* www.oiaglobal.com	Portland	OR	97201	503-736-5900		311
OIC (Ophthalmic Instrument Company Inc)	50 Strafello Dr *TF:* 800-272-2070 ■ *Web:* www.oic2020.com	Avon	MA	02322	781-341-2070	341-5060	542
Oic Group Inc	112 State St Ste Llb *Web:* www.oicgroup.net	Peoria	IL	61602	309-680-5600		180
OIC Intl	1875 Connecticut Ave NW 10th Fl **Fax Area Code:* 215 ■ *Web:* oici.org	Washington	DC	20009	202-846-6798	842-2276*	48-5
OIC of Washington	815 Fruitvale Blvd *Web:* www.yvoic.org	Yakima	WA	98902	509-248-6751	575-0482	167-3
OII (Ophthalmic Instrument Inc)	3322 Arden Rd *TF:* 800-728-6895 ■ *Web:* www.oiica.com	Hayward	CA	94545	510-265-1389		542
Oil & Gas Asset Clearinghouse LLC	1235 N Loop W Ste 510 *Web:* www.ogclearinghouse.com	Houston	TX	77008	281-873-4600		653
Oil & Gas Equipment Corp	8 Rd 350 *TF:* 800-868-9624 ■ *Web:* www.ogequip.com	Flora Vista	NM	87415	505-333-2300	333-2301	386
Oil & Gas Journal	1455 W Loop S *TF:* 800-633-1656 ■ *Web:* www.ogj.com	Houston	TX	77027	918-831-9423	831-9482	457-21
Oil Can Henry's	19150 SW 90th Ave *TF:* 800-765-6244 ■ *Web:* oilcanhenrys.com	Tualatin	OR	97062	503-783-3888		195
Oil Center Research LLC	106 Montrose Ave *TF:* 800-256-8977 ■ *Web:* www.oilcenter.com	LaFayette	LA	70503	337-993-3559	993-3149	541
Oil Chem Inc	711 W 12th St *Web:* www.oilcheminc.com	Flint	MI	48503	810-235-3040	238-5260	541
Oil Creek District Library Ctr	2 Central Ave *Web:* www.oilcreek.org	Oil City	PA	16301	814-678-3054	676-0359	434-3
Oil Creek Plastics Inc	45619 State Hwy 27 PO Box 385 *TF:* 800-537-3661 ■ *Web:* oilcreekplastics.com	Titusville	PA	16354	800-537-3661		596
Oil Creek State Park	305 State Park Rd *Web:* www.dcnr.pa.gov	Oil City	PA	16301	814-676-5915		565
Oil Field Development Engineering LLC	12121 Wickchester Ln *Web:* www.ofdeng.com	Houston	TX	77079	281-679-9060		261
Oil Mop LLC	131 Keating Dr *Web:* www.omies.com	Belle Chasse	LA	70037	504-394-6110		192
Oil Palace, The	10408 Tx Hwy 64 E *Web:* www.oilpalace.com	Tyler	TX	75707	903-566-2122		205
Oil Price Information Service	3349 Hwy 138 Bldg D Ste D *TF:* 888-301-2645 ■ *Web:* www.opisnet.com	Wall	NJ	07719	732-901-8800		531-5
Oil Producers Incorporated of Kansas	3209 N Ridge Port Cir *Web:* www.oilprod.com	Wichita	KS	67206	316-681-0231	682-3136	536
Oil States International Inc	333 Clay St Three Allen Ctr Ste 4620 *NYSE: OIS* ■ *Web:* www.oilstatesintl.com	Houston	TX	77002	713-652-0582	652-0499	539
Oil States Skagit SMATCO LLC	1180 Mulberry Rd *Web:* oilstates.com	Houma	LA	70363	985-868-0630		539
Oil-Dri Corporation of America	PO Box 11279 Cat's Pride Consumer Relations Ste 400 *NYSE: ODC* ■ *TF:* 800-645-3747 ■ *Web:* www.oildri.com	Chicago	IL	60611	312-321-1515	321-1271	500

Name / Address	Phone	Fax	Class
Oiles America Corp 4510 Enterprise Dr NW.......................Concord NC 28027 *TF:* 888-645-3726 ■ *Web:* www.oilesglobal.com	704-784-4500	784-4501	75
Oilfield Pipe and Supply Inc (OPS) 7227 Devonshire ....Shrewsbury MO 63119 **Fax Area Code:* 314 ■ *TF:* 800-783-7477 ■ *Web:* www.oilfieldpipe.com	800-783-7477	771-3177*	612
Oilgear Co 2430 S 179th St..................New Berlin WI 53146 *Web:* oilgear.com	414-327-1700	327-0532	640
Oil-Law Records Corp 8 N W 65th St.........................Oklahoma City OK 73116 *TF:* 888-464-5529 ■ *Web:* oil-law.com	405-840-1631		224
Oilmen's Equipment Corp 140 Cedar Springs Rd ....Spartanburg SC 29302 *Web:* oilmens.com	864-573-9311		579
Oil-Rite Corp 4325 Clipper Dr................Manitowoc WI 54221 *Web:* www.oilrite.com	920-682-6173	682-7699	386
Oilseeds International Ltd 8 Jackson St.......................... San Francisco CA 94111 *TF:* 888-967-8312 ■ *Web:* www.oilseedssf.com	415-956-7251	394-9023	803-1
Oiltanking Houston LP 15602 Jacinto Port Blvd......................Houston TX 77015 *Web:* www.oiltanking.com	281-457-7900		581
Oishii Boston 1166 Washington St ....Boston MA 02118 *Web:* www.oishiiboston.com	617-482-8868	482-8869	671
Oishii Sushi 277 Bernard Ouest .... Montreal QC H2V1T5 *Web:* www.oishii.ca	514-271-8863		671
OIT (Operator Interface Technology) 650 Weaver Park Rd....................... Longmont CO 80501 *Web:* www.oitkeypad.com	303-684-0094	684-0062	173-2
Ojai Culinary School c/o Lavender Inn 210 E Matilija St .... Ojai CA 93023 *Web:* www.lavenderinn.com	805-646-6635		685
Ojai Valley Chamber of Commerce 201 S Signal St................................ Ojai CA 93023 *Web:* www.ojaichamber.org	805-646-8126	646-9762	139
Ojai Valley Inn & Spa 905 Country Club Rd .... Ojai CA 93023 **Fax Area Code:* 805 ■ *TF:* 800-422-6524 ■ *Web:* www.ojaivalleyinn.com	855-697-8780	646-0904*	669
Ojai Valley News Inc 408 Bryant Cir Ste A........... Ojai CA 93023 *Web:* www.ojaivalleynews.com	805-646-1476	646-4281	637-8
Ojai Valley School 723 El Paseo Rd................ Ojai CA 93023 *Web:* www.ovs.org	805-646-1423	646-0362	622
Ojeda's 2001 Coit Rd Ste 102.....................Plano TX 75075 *Web:* www.ojedasrestaurant.com	972-599-1300		671
Oji Intertech Inc 906 W Hanley Rd .... North Manchester IN 46962 *Web:* www.ojiintertech.com	260-982-1544	982-4856	561
Ojo Caliente Mineral Springs Resort 50 Los Banos Dr PO Box 68...............Ojo Caliente NM 87549 *TF:* 800-222-9162 ■ *Web:* www.ojospa.com	505-583-2233	583-2045	706
OJP (Office of Justice Programs) 810 Seventh St NW.......................Washington DC 20531 *Web:* ojp.gov	202-307-0703		340-14
OK Co-Operative Grain & Mercantile Co 130 Main St ....Kiowa KS 67070 *Web:* www.okcoop.com	620-825-4212		276
OK Corral 326 E Allen St....................Tombstone AZ 85638 *Web:* www.ok-corral.com	520-457-3456		50-3
OK Foods Inc PO Box 1787 ....Fort Smith AR 72902 *TF:* 800-635-9441 ■ *Web:* www.okfoods.com	800-635-9441		619
OK International Corp 73 Bartlett St...........................Marlborough MA 01752 *Web:* www.okcorp.com	508-303-8286	303-8207	476
OK Intl 12151 Monarch St..................Garden Grove CA 92841 *Web:* www.okinternational.com	714-799-9910	799-9533	253
Ok Kosher Certification 391 Troy Ave.......... Brooklyn NY 11213 *Web:* www.ok.org	718-756-7500		743
OK Local Technical Assistance Program, The 5202 N Richmond Hill Dr.................... Stillwater OK 74078 *Web:* www.clgtokstate.com	405-744-9907		800
OK Tire Stores Inc 19082 21st Ave............... Surrey BC V3S3M3 *TF:* 800-663-1749 ■ *Web:* www.oktire.com	604-542-7999		755
OK3 Air 1980 Airport Rd Hngr A............ Heber City UT 84032 *TF:* 800-388-4445 ■ *Web:* www.ok3.aero	435-654-3962		23
Okaloosa - Walton Security & Surveillance 593 Hubbard St ....Defuniak Springs FL 32433 *Web:* www.larrythesecurityguyfl.com	850-259-9776		693
Okaloosa Correctional 3189 Little Silver Rd........................Crestview FL 32539 *Web:* dc.state.fl.us	850-682-0931	689-7803	213
Okaloosa County 101 E James Lee Blvd........................Crestview FL 32536 *Web:* www.co.okaloosa.fl.us	850-689-5000	689-5818	338
Okaloosa Technical College 1976 Lewis Turner Blvd ....Fort Walton Beach FL 32547 *Web:* www.otcollege.net	850-833-3500	833-3466	167-3
Okanagan College 1000 KLO Rd ....Kelowna BC V1Y4X8 *TF:* 800-621-3038 ■ *Web:* www.okanagan.bc.ca	250-762-5445		162
Okanjo Partners Inc 220 E Buffalo St Ste 303...................Milwaukee WI 53202 *Web:* www.okanjo.com	414-810-1760		224
Okanogan County 149 N Third Ave PO Box 980 .... Okanogan WA 98840 *Web:* www.okanogancounty.org	509-422-7170	422-7174	338
Okanogan County Energy Inc 93 W Chewuch Rd ....Winthrop WA 98862 *Web:* ocec.coop	509-996-2228		245
Okaw Truss Inc 368 E St Rt 133 .... Arthur IL 61911 *Web:* www.okawtruss.com	217-543-3371		817
Okawville Times 109 E Walnut................Okawville IL 62271 *Web:* www.okawvilletimes.com	618-243-5563		532-2
Okay Industries Inc 200 Ellis St............. New Britain CT 06051 *Web:* www.okayind.com	860-225-8707	225-7047	488
Okee Industries Inc 91 Shield St ....West Hartford CT 06110 *Web:* www.okee.net	860-953-1234	953-7462	351
Okeechobee Chamber of Commerce 55 S Parrott Ave ....Okeechobee FL 34972 *Web:* www.okeechobeebusiness.com	863-467-6246		139
Okeechobee Correctional Institution 3420 NE 168th St.........................Okeechobee FL 34972 *TF:* 800-574-5729 ■ *Web:* dc.state.fl.us	863-462-5400	462-5402	213
Okeechobee County 304 NW Second St ......Okeechobee FL 34972 *Web:* www.co.okeechobee.fl.us	863-763-6441	763-9529	338
Okeechobee Steakhouse 2854 Okeechobee Blvd................West Palm Beach FL 33409 *Web:* www.okeesteakhouse.com	561-683-5151		671
Okeeffe & Company Marketing Inc 921 King St.............................. Alexandria VA 22314 *Web:* www.okco.com	703-883-9000		7
Okeene Record, The PO Box 664 ....Okeene OK 73763 *Web:* www.okeenerecord.com	580-822-4401	822-3051	532-2
Okefenoke Rural Electric Membership Corp (REMC) 14384 Cleveland St PO Box 602................Nahunta GA 31553 *TF:* 800-262-5131 ■ *Web:* oremc.com	912-462-5131	462-6100	245
Oki Data Americas Inc 2000 Bishops Gate Blvd.................Mount Laurel NJ 08054 *TF:* 800-654-3282 ■ *Web:* www.oki.com	856-235-2600	222-5320	173-6
OKI Developments Inc 1416 112th Ave NE..........................Bellevue WA 98004 *TF:* 877-465-3654 ■ *Web:* www.okigolf.com	425-454-2800	646-6999	360-3
Okiok Data Ltd 655 Promenade du Centropolis Ste 230............ Laval QC H7T0A3 *TF:* 877-561-1681 ■ *Web:* www.okiok.com	450-681-1681		180
OKK Trading Inc 5705 Union Pacific Ave....................Los Angeles CA 90022 *Web:* www.okktoys.com	323-585-6800		241
OKL Can Line Inc 11235 Sebring Dr........... Cincinnati OH 45240 *Web:* www.oklcan.com	513-825-1655		757
Oklahoma			
Aging Services Div 2401 NW 23rd St Ste 40 ....Oklahoma City OK 73107 *Web:* www.okdhs.org	405-521-2281	521-2086	339-37
Agriculture Food & Forestry Dept 2800 N Lincoln Blvd ....Oklahoma City OK 73105 *Web:* www.oda.state.ok.us	405-521-3864	522-4912	339-37
Arts Council 2101 N Lincoln Blvd Ste 640...........Oklahoma City OK 73105 *Web:* arts.ok.gov	405-521-2931	521-6418	339-37
Attorney General 313 NE 21st St..........Oklahoma City OK 73105 *Web:* ok.gov	405-521-3921		339-37
Banking Dept 4545 N Lincoln Blvd Ste 164...........Oklahoma City OK 73105 *Web:* ok.gov	405-521-2782	522-2993	339-37
Chief Medical Examiner 921 NE 23rd St ....Oklahoma City OK 73105 *Web:* www.ok.gov	405-239-7141	239-2430	339-37
Commerce Dept 900 N Stiles Ave ....Oklahoma City OK 73104 *TF:* 800-879-6552 ■ *Web:* okcommerce.gov	405-815-6552		339-37
Conservation Commission 9101 S W Ave Ste 117................Oklahoma City OK 73105 *Web:* www.okcc.state.ok.us	405-522-4728		339-37
Consumer Protection Div 3613 NW 56th Ste 240 ....Oklahoma City OK 73112 *Web:* ok.gov	405-521-4274		339-37
Corporation Commission (OCC) Jim Thorpe Bldg 2101 N Lincoln PO Box 52000......................Oklahoma City OK 73152 *Web:* www.occeweb.com	405-521-2211	522-1623	339-37
Corrections Dept 3400 N Martin Luther King Ave ....Oklahoma City OK 73111 *Web:* ok.gov	405-425-2607	425-2578	339-37
Development Finance Authority 9220 N Kelley Ave ....Oklahoma City OK 73131 *Web:* ok.gov	405-848-9761	848-3314	339-37
Dewey County PO Box 368 .... Taloga OK 73667 *Web:* www.ok.gov	580-328-5361		338
Education Dept Hodge Bldg..............Oklahoma City OK 73105 *Web:* ok.gov	405-521-3301	521-6205	339-37
Emergency Management Dept 2401 Lincoln Blvd Ste C51 ....Oklahoma City OK 73105 *Web:* ok.gov	405-521-2481	521-4053	339-37
Employment Security Commission 2401 N Lincoln Blvd Will Rogers Memorial Bldg ....Oklahoma City OK 73152 *Web:* www.ok.gov	405-557-7200		259
Ethics Commission 2300 N Lincoln Blvd G 27 ....Oklahoma City OK 73105 *Web:* ok.gov	405-521-3451	521-4905	265
Health Dept 1000 NE 10th St.............Oklahoma City OK 73117 *Web:* www.ok.gov	405-271-6868	271-7360	339-37
Housing Finance Agency 100 NW 63rd St Ste 200 ....Oklahoma City OK 73116 *TF:* 800-256-1489 ■ *Web:* www.ok.gov	405-848-1144	879-8822	339-37
Human Services Dept 2400 N Lincoln Blvd Sequoyah Memorial Office Bldg.........Oklahoma City OK 73105 *Web:* www.okdhs.org	405-521-3646	521-6458	339-37
Insurance Dept (OID) 5 Corporate Plz 3625 NW 56th St Ste 100 ....Oklahoma City OK 73112 *TF:* 800-522-0071 ■ *Web:* ok.gov	405-521-6636	521-6635	339-37
John Lilley Correctional Ctr 407971 Hwy 62 E...........................Boley OK 74829 *Web:* www.ok.gov	918-667-3381	667-3959	213
Labor Dept 3017 N Stiles Ste 100.........Oklahoma City OK 73105 *Web:* ok.gov	405-521-6100	528-6018	339-37
Lieutenant Governor 2300 N Lincoln Blvd Rm 117...........Oklahoma City OK 73105 *Web:* ok.gov	405-521-2161	522-8694	339-37
Mental Health & Substance Abuse Services Dept 1200 NE 13th St PO Box 53277.........Oklahoma City OK 73152 *Web:* www.ok.gov	405-522-3908	522-3650	339-37
Motor Vehicle Commission 4334 NW Expy Ste 183 ....Oklahoma City OK 73116 *Web:* ok.gov	405-607-8227	607-8909	339-37

Name / Address	City	State	ZIP	Phone	Fax	Class
Pardon & Parole Board 2915 N Classen Blvd Ste 405 *Web:* www.ok.gov	Oklahoma City	OK	73106	405-521-6600	602-6437	339-37
Real Estate Commission Denver N. Davison Bldg 1915 N Stiles Ave Ste 200 *TF:* 866-521-3389 ■ *Web:* ok.gov	Oklahoma City	OK	73105	405-521-3387	521-2189	339-37
Rehabilitative Services Dept 3535 NW 58th St Ste 500 *TF:* 800-845-8476 ■ *Web:* www.okrehab.org	Oklahoma City	OK	73112	405-951-3400	951-3529	339-37
Secretary of State 421 NW 13 Ste 210 *Web:* www.sos.ok.gov	Oklahoma City	OK	73103	405-521-3912	521-3771	339-37
Securities Dept 204 N Robinson Ave Ste 400 *Web:* www.securities.ok.gov	Oklahoma City	OK	73102	405-280-7700	280-7742	339-37
State Regents for Higher Education 655 Research Pkwy Ste 200 *Web:* www.okhighered.org	Oklahoma City	OK	73104	405-225-9100	225-9235	725
Supreme Court 2100 N Lincoln Blvd Ste 3 *Web:* ok.gov	Oklahoma City	OK	73105	405-556-9300		339-37
Tax Commission 2501 N Lincoln Blvd *Web:* ok.gov	Oklahoma City	OK	73194	405-521-3160		339-37
Travel Promotion Div 900 N Stiles Ave *TF:* 800-652-6552 ■ *Web:* www.travelok.com	Oklahoma City	OK	73104	800-652-6552		339-37
Treasurer 2300 N Lincoln Rd Rm 217 *Web:* ok.gov	Oklahoma City	OK	73105	405-522-4215	521-4994	339-37
Veterans Affairs Dept 2311 N Central *TF:* 888-655-2838 ■ *Web:* ok.gov	Oklahoma City	OK	73105	405-521-3684	521-6533	339-37
Vital Records Div 1000 NE 10th St *TF:* 800-522-0203 ■ *Web:* ok.gov	Oklahoma City	OK	73117	405-271-5600		339-37
Wildlife Conservation Dept (ODWC) PO Box 53465 *Web:* wildlifedepartment.com	Oklahoma City	OK	73111	405-521-3851		339-37
Oklahoma Alliance for Manufacturing Excellence Inc 525 S Main St Ste 210 *Web:* www.okalliance.com	Tulsa	OK	74103	918-592-0722		138
Oklahoma Aquarium 300 S Aquarium Dr *Web:* www.okaquarium.org	Jenks	OK	74037	918-296-3474		40
Oklahoma Association of Realtors 9807 N Broadway *TF:* 800-375-9944 ■ *Web:* okrealtors.com	Oklahoma City	OK	73114	405-848-9944	848-9947	656
Oklahoma Baptist University 500 W University St *TF:* 800-654-3285 ■ *Web:* www.okbu.edu	Shawnee	OK	74804	405-275-2850		166
Oklahoma Bar Assn 1901 N Lincoln Blvd PO Box 53036 *TF:* 800-522-8065 ■ *Web:* www.okbar.org	Oklahoma City	OK	73105	405-416-7000	416-7001	72
Oklahoma Blood Institute (OBI) 1001 N Lincoln Blvd **Fax Area Code:* 918 ■ *TF:* 866-708-4995 ■ *Web:* obi.org	Oklahoma City	OK	73104	405-278-3100	477-0446*	89
Oklahoma Botanical Garden & Arboretum 358 Agricultural Hall *Web:* botanicgarden.okstate.edu	Stillwater	OK	74078	405-744-4531		97
Oklahoma Christian University PO Box 11000 **Fax Area Code:* 405 ■ *TF:* 800-877-5010 ■ *Web:* www.oc.edu	Oklahoma City	OK	73136	800-877-5010	425-5069*	166
Oklahoma City - City Hall 200 N Walker Ave *Web:* okc.gov	Oklahoma City	OK	73102	405-297-2578	297-3124	337
Oklahoma City Ballet 7421 N Classen Blvd *Web:* www.okcballet.org	Oklahoma City	OK	73116	405-843-9898	843-9894	573-1
Oklahoma City Community College 7777 S May Ave *Web:* www.occc.edu	Oklahoma City	OK	73159	405-682-1611	682-7521	162
Oklahoma City Convention & Visitors Bureau 123 Park Ave *Web:* www.visitokc.com	Oklahoma City	OK	73102	405-297-8912	297-8888	206
Oklahoma City Museum of Art 415 Couch Dr *TF:* 800-579-9278 ■ *Web:* www.okcmoa.com	Oklahoma City	OK	73102	405-236-3100	236-3122	520
Oklahoma City National Memorial & Museum 620 N Harvey Ave *Web:* memorialmuseum.com	Oklahoma City	OK	73102	405-235-3313		520
Oklahoma City Philharmonic 424 Colcord Dr Ste B *Web:* www.okcphil.org	Oklahoma City	OK	73102	405-232-7575	232-4353	573-3
Oklahoma City Public Schools 2500 NE 30th St *Web:* www.okcps.org	Oklahoma City	OK	73111	405-587-0000		685
Oklahoma City University 2501 N Blackwelder Ave *TF:* 800-633-7242 ■ *Web:* www.okcu.edu	Oklahoma City	OK	73106	405-208-5050		166
Oklahoma City Zoological Park & Botanical Gardens 2101 NE 50th St *Web:* www.okczoo.org	Oklahoma City	OK	73111	405-424-3344	425-0243	823
Oklahoma Correctional Industries 3402 N Martin Luther King Ave *TF:* 800-522-3565 ■ *Web:* www.ocisales.com	Oklahoma City	OK	73111	405-425-7500		630
Oklahoma Democratic Party 4100 N Lincoln Blvd *TF:* 800-547-5600 ■ *Web:* www.okdemocrats.org	Oklahoma City	OK	73105	405-427-3366		616-1
Oklahoma Dental Assn 317 NE 13th St *TF:* 800-876-8890 ■ *Web:* www.okda.org	Oklahoma City	OK	73104	405-848-8873	848-8875	227
Oklahoma Department of Career & Technology Education 1500 W 7th Ave *TF:* 800-522-5810 ■ *Web:* www.okcareertech.org	Stillwater	OK	74074	405-377-2000		242
Oklahoma Department of Libraries 200 NE 18th St *TF:* 800-522-8116 ■ *Web:* libraries.ok.gov	Oklahoma City	OK	73105	405-521-2502	525-7804	434-5
Oklahoma Education Assn 323 E Madison PO Box 18485 *TF:* 800-522-8091 ■ *Web:* www.okea.org	Oklahoma City	OK	73154	405-528-7785	524-0350	457-8
Oklahoma Electric Co-op 242 24th Ave NW *TF:* 800-522-6543 ■ *Web:* www.okcoop.org	Norman	OK	73069	405-321-2024	217-6900	245
Oklahoma Farm Bureau Mutual Insurance Co (OFB) 2501 N Stiles Ave *Web:* www.okfarmbureau.org	Oklahoma City	OK	73105	405-523-2300	523-2362	391-4
Oklahoma Federal Credit Union 517 NE 36th St *TF:* 800-522-8510 ■ *Web:* oklahomafederalcreditunion.org	Oklahoma City	OK	73105	405-524-6467	524-1067	219
Oklahoma Flower Market Inc, The 36 N Broadway Cir *Web:* www.okflowermarket.com	Oklahoma City	OK	73103	405-232-3143		293
Oklahoma Forensic Ctr 24800 S 4420 Rd *TF:* 800-752-9475 ■ *Web:* ok.gov	Vinita	OK	74301	918-256-7841		374-5
Oklahoma Gazette 3701 N Shartel Ave *Web:* www.okgazette.com	Oklahoma City	OK	73118	405-528-6000	528-4600	532-5
Oklahoma Genealogical Society (OGS) 1125 NW 50th St *Web:* www.okgensoc.org	Oklahoma City	OK	73118	405-637-1907		637-2
Oklahoma Historical Society 800 Nazih Zuhdi Dr *Web:* www.okhistory.org	Oklahoma City	OK	73105	405-521-2491		637-9
Oklahoma Horseshoeing School 26446 Horseshoe Cir *TF:* 800-538-1383 ■ *Web:* www.horseshoes.net	Purcell	OK	73080	405-288-6085	288-1004	685
Oklahoma Interactive LLC 6501 Broadway Ext Ste 250 *TF:* 866-521-2444 ■ *Web:* oklahomainteractive.com	Oklahoma City	OK	73116	405-524-3468	524-3469	339-37
Oklahoma Jazz Hall of Fame Upper Level 111 E First St *Web:* www.okjazz.org	Tulsa	OK	74103	918-281-8600	948-7737	520
Oklahoma Leather Products Inc 500 26th St NW *Web:* www.oklahomaleatherproducts.com	Miami	OK	74354	918-542-6651	542-4340	432
Oklahoma Lions Eye Bank 3840 N Lincoln Blvd *Web:* www.oklahomalionseyebank.org	Oklahoma City	OK	73105	405-557-1393	557-0086	269
Oklahoma Medical Research Foundation (OMRF) 825 NE 13th St *TF:* 800-522-0211 ■ *Web:* omrf.org	Oklahoma City	OK	73104	405-271-6673		668
Oklahoma Methodist Manor Inc 4134 E 31st St *Web:* www.ommtulsa.org	Tulsa	OK	74135	918-743-2565		48-20
Oklahoma Museum of Natural History 2401 Chautaugua Ave *Web:* samnoblemuseum.ou.edu	Norman	OK	73072	405-325-4712		520
Oklahoma Natural Gas Co 401 N Harvey PO Box 401 *TF:* 800-664-5463 ■ *Web:* www.oklahomanaturalgas.com	Oklahoma City	OK	73101	800-664-5463		787
Oklahoma Nurses Assn (ONA) 6608 NW Ste 627 *Web:* ona.nursingnetwork.com	Oklahoma City	OK	73103	405-840-3476	840-3013	533
Oklahoma Panhandle State University 323 Eagle Blvd *TF:* 800-664-6778 ■ *Web:* www.opsu.edu	Goodwell	OK	73939	580-349-2611	349-2302	166
Oklahoma Pharmacists Assn 3000 E Memorial Rd *Web:* www.opha.com	Edmond	OK	73013	405-528-3338	528-1417	585
Oklahoma Press Service Inc 3601 N Lincoln Blvd *TF:* 888-815-2672 ■ *Web:* www.okpress.com	Oklahoma City	OK	73105	405-499-0020		624
Oklahoma Primary Care Assn 6501 N Broadway Ext Ste 200 *Web:* okpca.org	Oklahoma City	OK	73116	405-424-2282	424-1111	138
Oklahoma Republican Party 4031 N Lincoln Blvd *Web:* www.okgop.com	Oklahoma City	OK	73105	405-528-3501	521-9531	616-2
Oklahoma Sports Hall of Fame & Jim Thorpe Museum 4040 N Lincoln Blvd *Web:* www.oklahomasportshalloffame.org	Oklahoma City	OK	73105	405-427-1400		522
Oklahoma State Penitentiary 1301 N West St PO Box 97 *Web:* doc.ok.gov	McAlester	OK	74502	918-423-4700	423-3862	213
Oklahoma State University 219 Student Union Bldg *TF:* 800-852-1255 ■ *Web:* go.okstate.edu	Stillwater	OK	74078	405-744-5000	744-7092	166
Oklahoma Telephone & Telegraph Inc 26 N Otis Ave *TF:* 800-869-1989 ■ *Web:* oklatel.net	Dustin	OK	74839	800-869-1989		387
Oklahoma Territorial Museum 406 E Oklahoma Ave *Web:* www.okterritorialmuseum.org	Guthrie	OK	73044	405-282-1889	282-7286	520
Oklahoma Veterans Center Ardmore 1015 S Commerce *TF:* 800-941-2160 ■ *Web:* ok.gov	Ardmore	OK	73401	580-223-2266	221-5606	793
Oklahoma Veterans Center Claremore 3001 W Blue Starr Dr PO Box 988 *Web:* odva.ok.gov	Claremore	OK	74018	918-342-5432	342-0835	793
Oklahoma Veterans Center Clinton Hwy 183 S *Web:* ok.gov	Clinton	OK	73601	580-331-2200	323-4834	793
Oklahoma Veterans Center Norman 1776 E Robinson St *TF:* 800-782-5218 ■ *Web:* ok.gov	Norman	OK	73070	405-360-5600		450
Oklahoma Veterans Center Sulphur 304 E Fairlane *Web:* ok.gov	Sulphur	OK	73086	580-622-2144		793
Oklahoma Veterans Center Talihina 10014 SE 1138th Ave PO Box 1168 *Web:* ok.gov	Talihina	OK	74571	918-567-2251	567-2950	793
Oklahoma Veterinary Medical Assn PO Box 14521 *Web:* okvma.org	Oklahoma City	OK	73113	405-478-1002	478-7193	795

Listing	City	State	ZIP	Phone	Fax	Class
Oklahoman, The 100 W Main St Ste 100 *TF:* 877-987-2737 ■ *Web:* oklahoman.com	Oklahoma City	OK	73102	405-475-3311		532-2
Okland Oil Co 110 N Robinson Ave *Web:* www.oklandoil.com	Oklahoma City	OK	73102	405-236-3046	232-4818	536
Oklee Herald, The PO Box 9 Corner 2nd Ave & Main *Web:* www.tricocanary.com	Oklee	MN	56742	218-796-5181		532-2
Okolona Carnegie Library 321 Main St *Web:* dixie.lib.ms.us	Okolona	MS	38860	662-447-2401		434-3
Okonite Co 102 Hilltop Rd *TF:* 800-631-7188 ■ *Web:* www.okonite.com	Ramsey	NJ	07446	201-825-0300	825-3524	813
Okuma America Corp 11900 W Hall Dr *Web:* www.okuma.com	Charlotte	NC	28278	704-588-7000	588-6503	455
Okuma Fishing Tackle Corp 2310 E Locust Ct *Web:* www.okumafishing.com	Ontario	CA	91761	909-923-2828		711
Olam Peanut Shelling Company Inc 205 E River Park Cir Ste 310 *Web:* www.mccleskeymills.com	Fresno	CA	93720	229-846-2003		275
Olan Mills Inc PO Box 23456 *Web:* www.olanmills.com	Chattanooga	TN	37406	423-622-5141		590
Olan Plastics Inc 6550 Olan Dr *TF:* 888-803-4645 ■ *Web:* www.olanplastics.com	Canal Winchester	OH	43110	614-834-6526	834-5536	604
Olana State Historic Site 5720 SR-9G *Web:* www.olana.org	Hudson	NY	12534	518-828-0135	828-6742	565
Olathe Chamber of Commerce 18001 W 106th St Ste 160 *TF:* 855-565-2843 ■ *Web:* olathe.org	Olathe	KS	66061	913-764-1050	782-4636	139
Olathe Medical Ctr 20333 W 151st St *Web:* www.olathehealth.org	Olathe	KS	66061	913-791-4200		374-3
Olathe Toyota 685 N Rawhide Dr *Web:* www.olathetoyota.com	Olathe	KS	66061	913-440-0053		516
Olbrich Botanical Gardens 3330 Atwood Ave *Web:* www.olbrich.org	Madison	WI	53704	608-246-4550	246-4719	97
Olcott Plastics Inc 95 N 17th St *Web:* www.olcottplastics.com	Saint Charles	IL	60174	630-584-0555		604
Old Alabama Town 301 Columbus St *TF:* 888-240-1850 ■ *Web:* www.oldalabamatown.com	Montgomery	AL	36104	334-240-4500		50-3
Old Army Press PO Box 1650 *TF:* 800-627-0079 ■ *Web:* www.oldarmypress.com	Johnstown	CO	80534	800-627-0079		637-2
Old Arsenal Museum 900 State Capitol Dr *Web:* www.sos.la.gov	Baton Rouge	LA	70802	225-342-0401		520
Old Barracks Museum 101 Barrack St *Web:* www.barracks.org	Trenton	NJ	08608	609-396-1776	777-4000	520
Old Bridge Chemicals Inc 554 Waterworks Rd *TF:* 800-275-3924 ■ *Web:* oldbridgechem.com	Old Bridge	NJ	08857	732-727-2225	727-2653	143
Old Bridge Public Library 1 Old Bridge Plz *Web:* www.oldbridgelibrary.org	Old Bridge	NJ	08857	732-721-5600	607-4816	434-3
Old Capitol Museum 100 S State St *Web:* www.mdah.state.ms.us	Jackson	MS	39201	601-576-6920	576-6981	520
Old Cathedral Library and Museum 205 Church St *TF:* 800-886-6443 ■ *Web:* www.vincennescvb.org	Vincennes	IN	47591	812-882-5638		434-3
Old Chicago 327 Lake Ave S *Web:* www.oldchicago.com	Duluth	MN	55802	218-720-2966		671
Old Chickahominy House 1211 Jamestown Rd *Web:* oldchickahominy.com	Williamsburg	VA	23185	757-229-4689		671
Old City Cemetery Museums & Arboretum 401 Taylor St *Web:* www.gravegarden.org	Lynchburg	VA	24501	434-847-1465	856-2004	97
Old City House Inn 115 Cordova St *Web:* www.oldcityhouse.com	Saint Augustine	FL	32084	904-826-0113		379
Old Colony Correctional Ctr 1 Admin Rd *Web:* www.mass.gov	Bridgewater	MA	02324	508-279-6000	279-6754	213
Old Colony Hospice 1 Credit Union Way *TF:* 800-370-1322 ■ *Web:* www.oldcolonyhospice.org	Randolph	MA	02368	781-341-4145	297-7345	371
Old Country Buffet Restaurants (OCB) 120 Chula Vista *Web:* www.oldcountrybuffet.com	Hollywood Park	TX	78232	210-403-3725	403-3580	670
Old Country Inn 9906 72nd Ave *Web:* oldcountryinnedmonton.com	Edmonton	AB	T6E0Z3	780-433-3242		671
Old Courthouse Museum 200 W Sixth St *Web:* siouxlandmuseums.com	Sioux Falls	SD	57104	605-367-4210	367-6004	520
Old Cowtown Museum 1865 W Museum Blvd *Web:* www.oldcowtown.org	Wichita	KS	67203	316-219-1871		520
Old Croton Aqueduct State Historic Park 15 Walnut St *Web:* parks.ny.gov	Dobbs Ferry	NY	10522	914-693-5259		565
Old Davidsonville State Park 7953 Hwy 166 S *Web:* www.arkansasstateparks.com	Pocahontas	AR	72455	870-892-4708		565
Old Dominion Brush Co 5118 Glen Alden Dr *TF:* 800-446-9823 ■ *Web:* www.odbco.com	Henrico	VA	23231	800-446-9823		586
Old Dominion Capital Management Inc 815 E Jefferson St *TF:* 800-446-2029 ■ *Web:* www.odcm.com	Charlottesville	VA	22902	434-977-1550		528
Old Dominion Electric Co-op (ODEC) 4201 Dominion Blvd *Web:* www.odec.com	Glen Allen	VA	23060	804-747-0592		245
Old Dominion Eye Bank (ODEF) 9200 Arboretum Pkwy Ste 104 *TF:* 800-832-0728 ■ *Web:* odef.org	Richmond	VA	23236	804-560-7540	560-4752	269
Old Dominion Freight Line Inc 500 Old Dominion Way *NASDAQ: ODFL* ■ *TF:* 800-432-6335 ■ *Web:* www.odfl.com	Thomasville	NC	27360	336-889-5000		780
Old Dominion University Rollins Hall *TF:* 800-348-7926 ■ *Web:* www.odu.edu	Norfolk	VA	23529	757-683-3685	683-3255	166
Old Dominion University Credit Union 2701 Hampton Blvd *Web:* oducreditunion.org	Norfolk	VA	23517	757-533-9308		219
Old Dutch Foods Inc 2375 Terminal Rd *Web:* www.olddutchfoods.com	Roseville	MN	55113	651-633-8810		297-3
Old Dutch Mustard Co 98 Cutter Mill Rd *Web:* pilgrimfoods.net	Great Neck	NY	11021	516-466-0522	466-0762	296-19
Old Ebbitt Grill 675 15th St NW *Web:* www.ebbitt.com	Washington	DC	20005	202-347-4800		671
Old Economy Village 270 16th St *Web:* www.oldeconomyvillage.org	Ambridge	PA	15003	724-266-4500	266-7506	520
Old Edwards Inn & Spa 445 Main St *TF:* 866-526-8008 ■ *Web:* www.oldedwardshospitality.com	Highlands	NC	28741	866-526-8008		378
Old Exchange & Provost Dungeon 122 E Bay St *TF:* 888-763-0448 ■ *Web:* www.oldexchange.org	Charleston	SC	29401	843-727-2165		50-3
Old First Reformed Church of Christ 151 N Fourth St *Web:* oldfirstucc.org	Philadelphia	PA	19106	215-922-4566		50-1
Old Fishermans Grotto 39 Fishermans Wharf *Web:* www.oldfishermansgrotto.com	Monterey	CA	93940	831-375-4604	375-0391	671
Old Florida Museum 259 San Marco Ave *TF:* 800-813-3208 ■ *Web:* www.oldfloridamuseum.com	Saint Augustine	FL	32084	904-824-8874		520
Old Fort Harrod State Park 100 S College St *Web:* parks.ky.gov	Harrodsburg	KY	40330	859-734-3314		565
Old Fort Niagara State Historic Site PO Box 169 *Web:* www.oldfortniagara.org	Youngstown	NY	14174	716-745-7611	745-9141	565
Old Fort Pub 65 Skull Creek Dr *Web:* www.oldfortpub.com	Hilton Head Island	SC	29926	843-681-2386		671
Old Fort Western 16 Cony St *Web:* www.augustamaine.gov	Augusta	ME	04330	207-626-2385	626-2304	520
Old Fourth Street Filling Station, The 871 W Fourth St *Web:* theoldfourthstreetfillingstation.com	Winston-Salem	NC	27101	336-724-7600		671
Old Globe, The 1363 Old Globe Way *Web:* www.theoldglobe.org	San Diego	CA	92101	619-231-1941	231-5879	573-4
Old Guard Museum 201 Lee Ave Ft Myer *Web:* www.army.mil	Fort Myer	VA	22211	703-696-6670		520
Old Harbor Outfit 480 Barnum Ave *Web:* www.oldharboroutfitters.com	Bridgeport	CT	06608	203-540-5150		711
Old Hill Partners 1120 Boston Post Rd 2nd Fl *Web:* oldhill.com	Darien	CT	06820	203-656-3004		401
Old Homestead Steakhouse 56 Ninth Ave *Web:* www.theoldhomesteadsteakhouse.com	New York	NY	10011	212-242-9040	727-1637	671
Old Idaho Penitentiary State Historic Site 2445 Old Penitentiary Rd *Web:* history.idaho.gov	Boise	ID	83712	208-334-2844	334-3225	50-3
Old Las Vegas Mormon Fort State Historic Park 500 E Washington Ave *Web:* www.parks.nv.gov	Las Vegas	NV	89101	702-486-3511		565
Old Louisville Historic Preservation District 1340 S Fourth St *Web:* www.oldlouisville.com	Louisville	KY	40208	502-635-5244	635-5245	50-3
Old Mansion Foods 3811 Corporate Rd PO Box 1838 *TF:* 800-476-1877 ■ *Web:* www.oldmansion.com	Petersburg	VA	23805	804-862-9889	861-8816	296-7
Old Maps PO Box 54 *Web:* www.old-maps.com	West Chesterfield	NH	03466	413-772-2801		637-10
Old Master Products Inc 7751 Hayvenhurst Ave *TF:* 800-300-5158 ■ *Web:* www.oldmasterproducts.com	Van Nuys	CA	91406	800-300-5158		550
Old Meeting House (OMH) 4004 S Macdill Ave *Web:* www.omhicecream.com	Tampa	FL	33611	813-254-0977	258-5747	297-6
Old Mill Antique Mall 310 State St *Web:* oldmillantiquemall.com	West Columbia	SC	29169	803-796-4229		460
Old Mill State Park 33489 240th Ave NW *Web:* www.dnr.state.mn.us	Argyle	MN	56713	218-437-8174		565
Old Mill Toronto 21 Old Mill Rd *TF:* 866-653-6455 ■ *Web:* www.oldmilltoronto.com	Toronto	ON	M8X1G5	416-236-2641		379
Old Mill Winery 403 S Broadway **Fax Area Code: 440* ■ *TF:* 800-227-6972 ■ *Web:* www.ohiowines.org	Geneva	OH	44041	800-227-6972	466-4417*	80-3
Old Mission Investment Company LLC 880 Munson Ave Ste B *Web:* omico.net	Traverse City	MI	49686	231-929-4100		690
Old Mission San Jose 43148 Mission Blvd *Web:* www.saintjosephmsj.org	Fremont	CA	94539	510-657-1797	656-2438	50-1
Old Mission San Luis Rey de Francia 4050 Mission Ave *Web:* www.sanluisrey.org	Oceanside	CA	92057	760-757-3651		50-1
Old Mission State Park 31732 S Mission Rd *Web:* parksandrecreation.idaho.gov	Cataldo	ID	83810	208-682-3814		565
Old Mulkey Meetinghouse State Historic Site 38 Old Mulkey Park Rd *Web:* parks.ky.gov	Tompkinsville	KY	42167	270-487-8481		565
Old National Bancorp 1 Main St *TF:* 800-731-2265 ■ *Web:* www.oldnational.com	Evansville	IN	47708	812-464-1294		70
Old Newbury Crafters PO Box 196 *TF:* 800-343-1388 ■ *Web:* oldnewburycrafterssilver.com	Amesbury	MA	01913	978-388-4026	388-8430	702
Old Original Bookbinder's 2306 E Cary St *Web:* bookbindersrichmond.com	Richmond	VA	23223	804-643-6900		671
Old Oyster Factory 101 Marshland Rd *Web:* www.oldoysterfactory.com	Hilton Head Island	SC	29926	843-681-6040	681-6418	671

	Phone	Fax	Class
Old Pine Street Presbyterian Church 412 Pine St ... Philadelphia PA 19106 *Web:* oldpine.org	215-925-8051		50-1
Old Point Financial Corp 1 W Mellen St PO Box 3392 ... Hampton VA 23663 *NASDAQ: OPOF* ■ *TF:* 800-952-0051 ■ *Web:* oldpoint.com	757-728-1200		360-2
Old Pueblo Archaeology Ctr 2201 W 44th St ... Tucson AZ 85713 *Web:* www.oldpueblo.org	520-798-1201	798-1966	520
Old Republic Insurance Co 133 Oakland Ave ... Greensburg PA 15601 *Web:* www.oldrepublicinsurancegroup.com	724-834-5000	834-4025	391-4
Old Republic Insured Automotive Services Inc 8282 S Memorial Dr ... Tulsa OK 74133 *TF:* 800-331-3780 ■ *Web:* www.orias.com	800-331-3780		391-5
Old Republic International Corp 307 N Michigan Ave ... Chicago IL 60601 *Web:* www.oldrepublic.com	312-346-8100		391-4
Old Republic National Title Insurance Co (ORTIG) 400 2nd Ave S ... Minneapolis MN 55401 **Fax Area Code:* 612 ■ *TF:* 800-328-4441 ■ *Web:* www.oldrepublictitle.com	800-328-4441	371-1191*	391-6
Old Republic Surety 445 S Moorlands Rd Ste 200 ... Brookfield WI 53005 *TF:* 800-217-1792 ■ *Web:* www.orsurety.com	262-797-2640		391-5
Old Sacramento 1014 Second St Ste 200 ... Sacramento CA 95814 *Web:* oldsacramento.com	916-970-5226	442-2053	50-3
Old Sacramento Schoolhouse, The 1200 Front St ... Sacramento CA 95814 *Web:* www.oldsacschoolhouse.org	916-483-8818		50-3
Old Saint Ferdinand's Shrine 1 Rue St Francois ... Florissant MO 63031 *Web:* www.oldstferdinandshrine.com	314-837-2110		50-1
Old Saint Joseph's Church 321 Willings Alley ... Philadelphia PA 19106 *Web:* oldstjoseph.org	215-923-1733	574-8529	50-1
Old Saint Mary's Church 123 E 13th St ... Cincinnati OH 45202 *Web:* www.oldstmarys.org	513-721-2988		50-1
Old Saint Patrick's Church 700 W Adams St ... Chicago IL 60661 *Web:* www.oldstpats.org	312-648-1021	648-9025	50-1
Old Salem 600 S Main St ... Winston-Salem NC 27101 *TF:* 800-441-5305 ■ *Web:* www.oldsalem.org	336-721-7300	721-7335	520
Old Salty Dog 1601 Ken Thompson Pkwy ... Sarasota FL 34236 *Web:* theoldsaltydog.com	941-388-4311		671
Old San Francisco Steak House 10223 Sahara Dr ... San Antonio TX 78216 *Web:* www.theoldsanfrancisco.com	210-342-2321	340-3135	671
Old Saybrook Chamber of Commerce 1 Main St PO Box 625 ... Old Saybrook CT 06475 *Web:* www.oldsaybrookchamber.com	860-388-3266	388-9433	139
Old School Square Cultural Arts Ctr 51 N Swinton Ave ... Delray Beach FL 33444 *Web:* oldschoolsquare.org	561-243-7922	243-7018	572
Old Second Bancorp Inc 37 S River St ... Aurora IL 60506 *NASDAQ: OSBC* ■ *TF:* 877-866-0202 ■ *Web:* www.oldsecond.com	630-892-0202	892-9630	360-2
Old State House 800 Main St ... Hartford CT 06103 *Web:* www.cga.ct.gov	860-522-6766		50-3
Old State House Museum 300 W Markham St ... Little Rock AR 72201 *Web:* www.oldstatehouse.com	501-324-9685		520
Old Stone Fort State Archaeological Park 732 Stone Ft Dr ... Manchester TN 37355 *Web:* www.state.tn.us	931-684-3426		565
Old Stone House 3051 M St NW ... Washington DC 20007 *Web:* www.nps.gov	202-426-6851		50-3
Old Sturbridge Village 1 Old Sturbridge Village Rd ... Sturbridge MA 01566 *Web:* www.osv.org	508-347-3362		520
Old Swedes Church & Hendrickson House Museum 606 Church St ... Wilmington DE 19801 *Web:* www.oldswedes.org	302-652-5629	652-8615	520
Old Time Pottery Inc 480 River Rock Blvd ... Murfreesboro TN 37128 *Web:* oldtimepottery.com	615-890-6060		362
Old Town 522 W Lincoln Ave ... Milwaukee WI 53207 *Web:* www.oldtownserbian.com	414-672-0206		671
Old Town Canoe Co 125 Gilman Falls Ave Bldg B ... Old Town ME 04468 **Fax Area Code:* 207 ■ *TF:* 800-343-1555 ■ *Web:* www.oldtowncanoe.com	800-343-1555	827-3647*	710
Old Town Endoscopy Center LLC 5500 Greenville Ave Ste 1100 ... Dallas TX 75206 *Web:* www.dhat.com	214-739-9544		415
Old Town Museum 265 Main St ... Old Town ME 04468 *Web:* www.old-town.org	207-827-3965	827-3979	520
Old Town San Diego State Historic Park 4002 Wallace St ... San Diego CA 92110 *Web:* www.parks.ca.gov	619-220-5422	688-3229	565
Old Toy Soldier PO Box 13324 ... Pittsburgh PA 15243 *Web:* www.oldtoysoldier.com	412-343-8733	344-5273	637-9
Old Trail Printing Company Inc, The 100 Fornoff Rd ... Columbus OH 43207 *Web:* www.oldtrailprinting.com	614-443-4852		627
Old Warsaw, The 2512 Maple Ave ... Dallas TX 75201 *Web:* www.oldwarsaw.com	214-528-0032		671
Old Wisconsin Sausage Co 4036 Weeden Creek Rd ... Sheboygan WI 53083 **Fax Area Code:* 708 ■ *TF:* 877-451-7988 ■ *Web:* www.oldwisconsin.com	920-458-4304	798-1284*	296-26
Old World Industries Inc 4065 Commercial Ave ... Northbrook IL 60062 *TF:* 800-323-5440 ■ *Web:* www.oldworldind.com	847-559-2000		145
Old World Wisconsin W372 S9727 Hwy 67 ... Eagle WI 53119 *Web:* oldworldwisconsin.wisconsinhistory.org	262-594-6301	594-6342	520
Oldcastle APG Inc Three Glenlake Pkwy FL 12 ... Atlanta GA 30328 *TF:* 800-899-8455 ■ *Web:* www.oldcastleapg.com	800-899-8455		191-1
Oldcastle BuildingEnvelope 5005 Lyndon B Johnson Fwy Ste 1050 ... Dallas TX 75244 *TF:* 866-653-2278 ■ *Web:* obe.com	866-653-2278		329
Oldcastle Infractructure Inc 7000 Central Pkwy Ste 800 ... Atlanta GA 30328 *Web:* www.oldcastleinfrastructure.com	770-270-5000		261
Oldcastle Precast Building Systems Div 1401 Trimble Rd ... Edgewood MD 21040 *TF:* 800-523-9144 ■ *Web:* oldcastleinfrastructure.com	410-612-1213		189-3
Oldcastle Precast Inc 7921 Southpark Plz Ste 200 ... Littleton CO 80120 *TF:* 800-642-3755 ■ *Web:* oldcastleinfrastructure.com	303-209-8000	794-4297	183
Oldcastle Publishing PO Box 1193 ... Escondido CA 92025 *Web:* www.abcurtiss.com	760-747-0633		637-2
Olde Mill Inn 5835 Dixie Hwy ... Clarkston MI 48346 *Web:* www.oldemillinnofclarkston.com	248-623-0300		379
Olde Ship, The 1120 W 17th St ... Santa Ana CA 92706 *Web:* www.theoldeship.com	714-550-6700		671
Olde Tyme Pastries 2225 Geer Rd ... Turlock CA 95382 *Web:* www.otpastries.com	209-668-0928		68
Oldenburg Group Inc 1717 W Civic Dr ... Milwaukee WI 53209 *Web:* www.oldenburggroup.com	414-354-6600	977-1700	358
Oldfields School 1500 Glencoe Rd ... Glencoe MD 21152 *Web:* www.oldfieldsschool.org	410-472-4800	472-6839	622
Oldham County PO Box 360 ... Vega TX 79092 *Web:* www.co.oldham.tx.us	806-267-2667		338
Oldham County Chamber of Commerce 412 E Main St ... LaGrange KY 40031 *TF:* 800-264-0521 ■ *Web:* www.oldhamcountychamber.com	502-222-1635	222-3159	139
Oldham County Fiscal Court 100 W Jefferson St ... LaGrange KY 40031 *Web:* www.oldhamcountyky.gov	502-222-1476	222-3210	338
Oldham Resource Group Inc 70 New Canaan Ave ... Norwalk CT 06850 *Web:* oldhamresourcegroup.com	203-847-5300		690
Olds College 4500-50 St ... Olds AB T4H1R6 *TF:* 800-661-6537 ■ *Web:* www.oldscollege.ca	403-556-8281		162
Olds Products Co 10700 88th Ave ... Pleasant Prairie WI 53158 *TF:* 800-233-8064 ■ *Web:* www.oldsproducts.com	262-947-3500		296-19
Olds-olympic Inc PO Box 180 ... Lynnwood WA 98046 *Web:* www.olds-olympic.com	425-778-1000	771-4346	324
Ole Bull State Park 31 Valhella VW ... Cross Fork PA 17729 *Web:* www.dcnr.pa.gov	814-435-5000		565
Ole Mexican Foods Inc 6585 Crescent Dr ... Norcross GA 30071 *Web:* olemex.com	770-582-9200		296-36
Ole Mole 1030 High Ridge Rd ... Stamford CT 06905 *Web:* www.olemolestamford.com	203-461-9962		671
Ole South Properties Inc 262 Robert Rose Dr Ste 300 ... Murfreesboro TN 37129 *Web:* www.olesouth.com	615-896-0019	896-9380	187
Olean General Hospital 515 Main St ... Olean NY 14760 *Web:* www.ogh.org	716-373-2600		374-3
Olean Times-Herald 639 Norton Dr ... Olean NY 14760 *TF:* 800-722-8812 ■ *Web:* www.oleantimesherald.com	716-372-3121		532-2
Olean Wholesale Grocery Co-opeartive Inc 1587 Haskell Rd PO Box 1070 ... Olean NY 14760 *TF:* 888-835-3026 ■ *Web:* www.oleanwholesale.com	716-372-2020		297-8
Oleana Restaurant 134 Hampshire St ... Cambridge MA 02139 *Web:* www.oleanarestaurant.com	617-661-0505		671
Oleary Law Associates LLC 4060 Post Rd ... Warwick RI 02886 *Web:* olearymurphy.com	401-615-8584		41
Oleco Inc 18683 Trimble Ct ... Spring Lake MI 49456 *TF:* 800-575-3282 ■ *Web:* globaltec.com	616-842-6790		814
Olentangy Indian Caverns 1779 Home Rd ... Delaware OH 43015 *Web:* www.olentangyindiancaverns.com	740-548-7917		50-5
Olesky Associates Inc 865 Washington St Ste 3 ... Newton MA 02460 *TF:* 800-486-4330 ■ *Web:* www.olesky.com	781-235-4330		260
Oleson's Foods Inc 3850 N Long Lake Rd Ste A ... Traverse City MI 49684 *Web:* www.olesonsfoods.com	231-947-6510	947-2907	345
Oleta River State Park 3400 NE 163rd St ... North Miami Beach FL 33160 *Web:* www.floridastateparks.org	305-919-1846	919-1845	565
Oley Foundation Albany Medical Ctr 214 Hun Memorial MC-28 ... Albany NY 12208 *TF:* 800-776-6539 ■ *Web:* www.oley.org	518-262-5079	262-5528	48-17
Olga Korper Gallery 17 Morrow Ave ... Toronto ON M6R2H9 *Web:* www.olgakorpergallery.com	416-538-8220		42
Olga's Kitchen Inc 1940 Northwood Dr ... Troy MI 48084 *Web:* www.olgas.com	248-362-0001		670
Olgoonik Development LLC 3201 C St Ste 700 ... Anchorage AK 99503 *Web:* www.olgoonik.com	907-562-8728	562-8751	187
Oliff & Berridge PLC 277 S Washington St Ste 500 ... Alexandria VA 22314 *Web:* www.oliff.com	703-836-6400		428
Olin Chlor Alkali Products Vinyls 490 Stuart Rd NE ... Cleveland TN 37312 *Web:* olinchloralkali.com	423-336-4850		143
Olin Corp 190 Carondelet Plz Ste 1530 ... Clayton MO 63105 *NYSE: OLN* ■ *Web:* www.olin.com	314-355-8285		185
Olin Corp *Winchester Div* 600 Powder Mill Rd ... East Alton IL 62024 *Web:* winchester.com	618-258-2000		284
Olis Inc 130 Conway Dr Ste A B & C ... Bogart GA 30622 *TF:* 800-852-3504 ■ *Web:* www.olisweb.com	706-353-6547	353-1972	419
Oliva Tobacco Co 3104 N Armenia Ave ... Tampa FL 33607 *Web:* olivatobacco.com	813-248-4921		756
Olive Branch Chamber of Commerce 9123 Pigeon Roost PO Box 608 ... Olive Branch MS 38654 *TF:* 800-948-3090 ■ *Web:* www.olivebranchms.com	662-895-2600		139
Olive Garden 1000 Darden Center Dr PO Box 695017 ... Orlando FL 32869 *Web:* www.olivegarden.com	407-245-4336		670

	Phone	Fax	Class
Olive Grove Consulting 540 Ralston Ave Ste 2c........Belmont CA 94002 *Web:* theolivegrove.com	650-591-4155		463
Olive Hill Greenhouses Inc 3508 Olive Hill Rd........Fallbrook CA 92028 *Web:* olivehill.net	760-728-4596		192
Olive Real Estate Group 102 N Cascade Ave Ste 250........Colorado Springs CO 80903 *TF:* 866-708-2014 ■ *Web:* www.olivereg.com	719-598-3000	578-0089	652
Olive Software Inc 3033 S Parker Rd Ste 502........Aurora CO 80014 *TF:* 866-654-8387 ■ *Web:* www.olivesoftware.com	720-747-1220	747-1217	178-1
Olive View Medical Ctr (OVMC) 14445 Olive View Dr........Sylmar CA 91342 *Web:* www.uclaoliveview.org	747-210-3000		374-3
Oliver & Company Inc 1300 S 51st St........Richmond CA 94804 *Web:* www.oliverandco.net	510-412-9090		186
Oliver Capital Partners Inc 102 3016 Fifth Ave NE........Calgary AB T2A6K4 *Web:* olcapa.com	403-313-4645		691
Oliver Construction Co 1770 Executive Dr........Oconomowoc WI 53066 *Web:* oliverconstruction.com	262-567-6677		780
Oliver Equipment Co 4620 Brittmoore Rd........Houston TX 77041 *Web:* www.oliverequip.com	713-856-9206	856-9299	385
Oliver Finley Academy of Cosmetology 6843 N Strawberry Glenn Rd Ste 140........Boise ID 83714 *Web:* www.oliverfinley.com	208-658-1115		167-3
Oliver Fire Protection & Security 501 Feheley Dr........King of Prussia PA 19406 *Web:* www.oliverfps.com	610-277-1331		189-13
Oliver M Dean Inc 125 Brooks St........Worcester MA 01606 *TF:* 800-648-3326 ■ *Web:* www.omdean.com	508-856-9100		429
Oliver Machinery Co 6902 S 194th St........Kent WA 98032 *TF:* 800-559-5065 ■ *Web:* www.olivermachinery.net	253-867-0334	867-0387	821
Oliver of Adrian Inc 1111 E Beecher St PO Box 189........Adrian MI 49221 *TF:* 877-668-0885 ■ *Web:* www.oliverinstrument.com	517-263-2132	265-8698	455
Oliver Printing Company Inc 1760 Enterprise Pkwy........Twinsburg OH 44087 *Web:* www.oliverprinting.com	330-425-7890	425-8138	627
Oliver Products Co 445 Sixth St NW........Grand Rapids MI 49504 *TF:* 800-253-3893 ■ *Web:* www.oliverproducts.com	616-456-7711	456-5820	298
Oliver Russell & Associates Inc 217 S 11th St........Boise ID 83702 *Web:* www.oliverrussell.com	208-344-1734		636
Oliver Staffing Inc 350 Lexington Ave Ste 401........New York NY 10016 *Web:* www.oliverstaffing.com	212-634-1234		260
Oliver Technologies Inc 467 Swan Ave........Hohenwald TN 38462 *Web:* www.olivertechnologies.com	931-796-4555	796-8811	610
Oliver Winery 8024 N SR-37........Bloomington IN 47404 *TF:* 800-258-2783 ■ *Web:* www.oliverwinery.com	812-876-5800		50-7
Oliver Wolcott Library (OWL) 160 S St........Litchfield CT 06759 *Web:* www.owlibrary.org	860-567-8030	567-4784	434-3
Oliver Wolcott Technical High School 75 Oliver St........Torrington CT 06790 *Web:* wolcott.cttech.org	860-496-5300	496-9022	685
Oliver's 2095 Delaware Ave........Buffalo NY 14216 *Web:* www.oliverscuisine.com	716-877-9662		671
Oliver's 130 S Fifth Ave........Pocatello ID 83201 *Web:* oliversdining.com	208-234-0672		671
Oliver, Price & Rhodes 1212 S Abington Rd........Clarks Summit PA 18411 *Web:* www.oprlaw.com	570-585-1200		428
Oliverio's Ristorante on the Wharf 52 Clay St........Morgantown WV 26505 *Web:* oliveriosrestaurant.com	304-296-2565		671
Olives 3131 Olive St........Las Vegas NV 89109 *Web:* cheftoddenglish.com	702-693-8181		671
Olivet College 320 S Main St........Olivet MI 49076 *TF:* 800-456-7189 ■ *Web:* www.olivetcollege.edu	269-749-7000	749-6617	166
Olivet Nazarene University 1 University Ave........Bourbonnais IL 60914 *TF:* 800-648-1463 ■ *Web:* www.olivet.edu	815-939-5011	935-4998	166
Oliveto Cafe & Restaurant 5655 College Ave........Oakland CA 94618 *Web:* oliveto.com	510-547-5356		671
Olivia 434 Brannan St........San Francisco CA 94107 *TF:* 800-631-6277 ■ *Web:* www.olivia.com	415-962-5700	962-5710	760
Ollie's Bargain Outlet Inc 6295 Allentown Blvd Ste 1........Harrisburg PA 17112 *TF:* 800-219-7052 ■ *Web:* www.ollies.us	717-657-2300		791
OLM LLC 4 Trefoil Dr........Trumbull CT 06611 *Web:* olm.net	203-445-7700		808
Olmec Systems Inc 85 Bloomfield Ave........Denville NJ 07834 *Web:* www.olmec.com	973-586-6590		180
Olmstead Place State Park 921 N Ferguson Rd........Ellensburg WA 98926 *Web:* www.parks.wa.gov	509-925-1943		565
Olmstead Properties Inc 575 Eighth Ave Ste 2400........New York NY 10018 *Web:* olmsteadinc.com	212-564-6662	564-6667	652
Olmsted Medical Ctr 210 Ninth St SE........Rochester MN 55904 *Web:* www.olmmed.org	507-288-3443		363
Olney Chamber of Commerce 3460 Olney-Laytonsville Rd Ste 211........Olney MD 20832 *Web:* www.olneymd.org	301-774-7117	774-4944	139
Olney Friends School 61830 Sandy Ridge Rd........Barnesville OH 43713 *Web:* olneyfriends.org	740-425-3655	425-3202	622
OLogic 544 E Weddell Dr Ste 7........Sunnyvale CA 94089 *Web:* www.ologicinc.com	650-996-1490		387
Ologie LLC 447 E Main St........Columbus OH 43215 *TF:* 800-962-1107 ■ *Web:* ologie.com	614-221-1107		463

	Phone	Fax	Class
Olompali State Historic Park PO Box 1016........Novato CA 94948 *Web:* www.parks.ca.gov	415-892-3383		565
Olon Industries Inc 42 Armstrong Ave........Georgetown ON L7G4R9 *Web:* www.olon.ca	905-877-7300	877-7383	599
Olon Ricerca Bioscience 7528 Auburn Rd........Painesville OH 44077 *TF:* 888-742-3722 ■ *Web:* olonricerca.com	440-357-3300	354-6276	668
Olsen & Thompson PA 970 Mt Kemble Ave........Morristown NJ 07960 *Web:* www.otcpa.com	973-425-3212		2
Olshan Lumber Co 2600 Commerce St........Houston TX 77003 *Web:* www.olshanlumber.com	713-225-5551	220-9400	364
Olson & Breckner PA 150 S Fifth St Ste 2825........Minneapolis MN 55402 *Web:* www.olsonandbreckner.com	612-315-1905		41
Olson & Company Steel Inc 1941 Davis St........San Leandro CA 94577 *Web:* www.olsonsteel.com	510-567-2200		480
Olson Bros Co 829 Chambers St........South Haven MI 49090	269-637-4494		803-3
Olson Communications Inc 445 W Erie St Ste 109........Chicago IL 60654 *Web:* www.olsoncom.com	312-280-4573	280-9203	4
Olson Engineering Inc 365 W Round Bunch Rd........Bridge City TX 77611 *Web:* www.o-engr.com	409-697-3333		261
Olson Pete (Rep R - TX) 2133 Rayburn House Office Bldg........Washington DC 20515 *Web:* www.olson.house.gov	202-225-5951		342-2
Olson Research Associates Inc 10290 Old Columbia Rd........Columbia MD 21046 *TF:* 888-657-6680 ■ *Web:* www.olsonresearch.com	410-290-6999	290-6726	178-10
Olsson Assoc 601 P St Ste 200........Lincoln NE 68508 *Web:* www.olsson.com	402-474-6311	474-5160	261
Olsson Roofing Company Inc 740 S Lake St........Aurora IL 60506 *Web:* www.olssonroofing.com	630-892-0449		189-12
Olsun Electrics Corp 10901 Commercial St........Richmond IL 60071 **Fax Area Code:* 815 ■ *TF:* 800-336-5786 ■ *Web:* www.olsun.com	800-336-5786	678-4909*	767
Oltmans Construction Co 10005 Mission Mill Rd........Whittier CA 90601 *Web:* www.oltmans.com	562-948-4242	695-5299	186
Olum's of Binghamton Inc 3701 Vestal Pkwy E........Vestal NY 13850 *TF:* 855-264-8674 ■ *Web:* www.olums.com	607-729-5775	729-6166	321
Oly Penn Inc 245 E Washington St........Sequim WA 98382 *TF:* 800-303-8696 ■ *Web:* startpage.olypen.com	360-683-1456	683-3159	225
Olymel LP 2200 Pratte Ave Pratte........Saint-Hyacinthe QC J2S4B6 *TF:* 800-361-7990 ■ *Web:* www.olymel.ca	450-771-0400	773-6436	619
Olympia City Hall PO Box 1967........Olympia WA 98507 *TF:* 800-451-7985 ■ *Web:* olympiawa.gov	360-753-8447	709-2791	337
Olympia Cos 11411 Southern Highlands Pkwy........Las Vegas NV 89141 *Web:* www.olympiacompanies.com	702-220-6565	220-6566	653
Olympia Financial Group Inc 125 Ninth Ave SE Ste 2300........Calgary AB T2G0P6 *TF:* 888-668-8384 ■ *Web:* www.olympiatrust.com	403-261-0900	261-7512	787
Olympia Lacey Tumwater Visitor & Convention Bureau 103 Sid Snyder Ave SW........Olympia WA 98501 *TF:* 877-704-7500 ■ *Web:* www.experienceolympia.com	360-704-7544		206
Olympia Medical Ctr 5900 W Olympic Blvd........Los Angeles CA 90036 *Web:* www.olympiamc.com	310-657-5900		374-3
Olympia Promotions & Distribution 226 E Jericho Tpke........Mineola NY 11501 *TF:* 800-846-7874 ■ *Web:* olympiapromo.com	516-775-4500		327
Olympia Resort & Spa 1350 Royale Mile Rd........Oconomowoc WI 53066 *TF:* 800-558-9573 ■ *Web:* www.olympiaresort.com	262-369-4999	369-4998	669
Olympia School District 1113 Legion Way SE........Olympia WA 98501 *Web:* www.osd.wednet.edu	360-596-6100	596-6111	685
Olympia Sports 5 Bradley Dr........Westbrook ME 04092 *TF:* 844-511-1721 ■ *Web:* www.olympiasports.net	207-854-2794		711
Olympia Theater 174 E Flagler St........Miami FL 33131 *Web:* www.olympiatheater.org	305-374-2444		572
Olympia Tile International Inc 1000 Lawrence Ave W........Toronto ON M6A1C6 *TF:* 800-268-1613 ■ *Web:* www.olympiatile.com	416-785-6666		191-4
Olympia/Thurston County Chamber of Commerce 809 Legion Way........Olympia WA 98501 *Web:* www.thurstonchamber.com	360-357-3362	357-3376	139
Olympian Academy of Cosmetology 1011 E 10th St Ste B........Alamogordo NM 88310 *TF:* 877-275-4442 ■ *Web:* www.olympusbeauty.com	575-437-2221	437-1375	167-3
Olympic Airways 7000 Austin St........Forest Hills NY 11375 *Web:* www.patch.com	718-269-2200		25
Olympic College 1600 Chester Ave........Bremerton WA 98337 *TF:* 800-259-6718 ■ *Web:* www.olympic.edu	360-792-6050	475-7202	162
Olympic Corrections Ctr 11235 Hoh Mainline........Forks WA 98331 *Web:* doc.wa.gov	360-374-6181		213
Olympic Flight Museum 7637A Old Hwy 99 SE........Olympia WA 98501 *Web:* www.olympicflightmuseum.com	360-705-3925	236-9839	520
Olympic Foundry Inc 5200 Airport Way S........Seattle WA 98108 *Web:* www.olympicfoundry.com	206-764-6200		492
Olympic Lanes 12751 New Halls Ferry Rd........Florissant MO 63033 *Web:* www.olympiclanesbowling.com	314-830-2695		99
Olympic Medical Ctr 939 Caroline St........Port Angeles WA 98362 *TF:* 888-362-6260 ■ *Web:* www.olympicmedical.org	360-417-7000		374-3

Phone | Fax | Class

Olympic Mountain School Press (OMSP)
PO Box 1114 .... Gig Harbor WA 98335 253-858-4448 637-2
TF: 800-819-1179 ■ *Web:* www.mountainschoolpress.com

Olympic Resource Management
19950 Seventh Ave NE Ste 200 .... Poulsbo WA 98370 360-697-6626 697-1156 752
NASDAQ: POPE ■ *TF:* 800-522-6645 ■ *Web:* www.orminc.com

Olympic Security Services Inc
631 Strander Blvd Ste A .... Tukwila WA 98188 206-575-8531 575-8640 693
Web: www.olympiksecurity.com

Olympic Staffing Services
588 S Grand Ave .... Covina CA 91724 626-447-3558 260
Web: www.olystaffing.com

Olympic Steel Inc
5096 Richmond Rd .... Bedford Heights OH 44146 216-292-3800 292-3974 492
NASDAQ: ZEUS ■ *Web:* olysteel.com

Olympic Tavern 2327 N Main St .... Rockford IL 61103 815-962-8758 671
Web: theolympictavern.com

Olympic Tool & Machine Company Inc
2100 Bridgewater Rd .... Aston PA 19014 610-494-1600 494-8320 454
Web: www.olymtool.com

Olympique Expert Building Care
26232 Enterprise Ct .... Lake Forest CA 92630 949-455-0796 463
TF: 866-659-6747 ■ *Web:* www.olympique.net

Olympus Flag & Banner
9000 W Heather Ave .... Milwaukee WI 53224 414-355-2010 355-1931 287
TF: 800-558-9620 ■ *Web:* www.olympusgrp.com

Olympus Homes Inc PO Box 2999 .... Westerville OH 43086 614-523-2000 187
Web: www.olympushomes.com

Olympus Partners 1 Stn Pl 4th Fl .... Stamford CT 06902 203-353-5900 792
Web: www.olympuspartners.com

Olympus Press Inc 3400 S 150th St .... Seattle WA 98188 206-242-2700 627
Web: www.olympuspress.com

OlympusNet PO Box 1824 .... Port Townsend WA 98368 360-385-0464 681
TF: 800-896-1751 ■ *Web:* www.olympus.net

OM Records
1890 Bryant St Ste 305 .... San Francisco CA 94110 415-904-1800 317
Web: www.om-records.com

OM Seafood Restaurant
3514 SE 76th Ave .... Portland OR 97206 503-788-1984 671
Web: www.omseafood.com

OMA (Oregon Medical Assn)
11740 SW 68th Pkwy Ste 100 .... Portland OR 97223 503-619-8000 619-0609 474
Web: www.theoma.org

Omadi 3451 Triumph Blvd Ste 650 .... Lehi UT 84043 801-800-8250 177
Web: omadi.com

Omaha Bedding Co 4011 S 60th St .... Omaha NE 68117 402-733-8600 471

Omaha Children's Museum 500 S 20th St .... Omaha NE 68102 402-342-6164 342-6165 521
Web: www.ocm.org

Omaha Community Foundation (OCF)
302 S 36th St Ste 100 .... Omaha NE 68131 402-342-3458 342-3582 303
TF: 800-794-3458 ■ *Web:* omahafoundation.org

Omaha Community Playhouse 6915 Cass St .... Omaha NE 68132 402-553-0800 553-6288 573-4
TF: 888-782-4338 ■ *Web:* www.omahaplayhouse.com

Omaha Correctional Ctr
2323 Ave J PO Box 11099 .... Omaha NE 68110 402-595-3963 213
Web: corrections.nebraska.gov

Omaha Douglas Federal Credit Union
8251 W Center Rd .... Omaha NE 68124 402-444-5999 444-5484 219
Web: omahadouglasfcu.org

Omaha Firefighters Credit Union
4630 S 143rd St .... Omaha NE 68137 402-894-5005 219
Web: omahafirefighterscu.org

Omaha Paper Co 6936 L St .... Omaha NE 68117 402-331-3243 638
TF: 800-288-7026 ■ *Web:* omahapaper.com

Omaha Performing Arts Society (OPAS)
1200 Douglas St .... Omaha NE 68102 402-345-0202 345-0222 572
TF: 866-434-8587 ■ *Web:* o-pa.org

Omaha Printing Co 4700 F St .... Omaha NE 68117 402-734-4400 626
Web: www.omahaprint.com

Omaha Public Library 215 S 15th St .... Omaha NE 68102 402-444-4800 434-3
Web: omahalibrary.org

Omaha Public Power District (OPPD)
444 S 16th St Mall .... Omaha NE 68102 402-536-4131 192
Web: www.oppd.com

Omaha Public Schools 3215 Cuming St .... Omaha NE 68131 402-557-2222 685
Web: www.district.ops.org

Omaha Steel Castings Co 921 E 12th St .... Wahoo NE 68066 402-277-7400 277-7410 307
Web: www.omahasteel.com

Omaha Symphony 1905 Harney St Ste 400 .... Omaha NE 68102 402-342-3836 342-3819 573-3
Web: www.omahasymphony.org

Omak Chronicle Inc 618 Okoma Dr .... Omak WA 98841 509-826-1110 826-5819 532-2
TF: 800-572-3446 ■ *Web:* www.omakchronicle.com

Oman Systems Inc 3334 Powell Ave .... Nashville TN 37204 615-385-2500 188
TF: 800-541-0803 ■ *Web:* omanco.com

Omar Ilhan (Rep D - MN)
1517 Longworth House Office Bldg .... Washington DC 20515 202-225-4755 342-2
Web: www.omar.house.gov

Omar Inc
4601 S Cottage Groove Ste 53452 .... Chicago IL 60653 708-679-0347 679-0384 475
Web: www.omarinc.com

Omar's Carriage House 313 W Bute St .... Norfolk VA 23510 757-622-4990 671
Web: omarscarriagehouse.com

OMAX Corp 21409 72nd Ave S .... Kent WA 98032 253-872-2300 697
TF: 800-838-0343 ■ *Web:* www.omax.com

OMB (Office of Management & Budget)
725 17th St NW .... Washington DC 20503 202-395-3080 395-3888 340
Web: www.whitehouse.gov

OMB Watch 1742 Connecticut Ave NW .... Washington DC 20009 202-234-8494 234-8584 48-7
TF: 866-544-7573 ■ *Web:* www.foreffectivegov.org

OMC (Ocean Medical Ctr)
425 Jack Martin Blvd .... Brick NJ 08724 732-840-2200 374-3
TF: 800-560-9990 ■ *Web:* www.oceanmedicalcenter.com

OMD Corp 3705 Missouri Blvd .... Jefferson City MO 65109 573-893-8930 893-3487 178-1
TF: 866-440-8664 ■ *Web:* www.omdcorp.com

Omeda Communications 555 Huehl Rd .... Northbrook IL 60062 847-564-8900 225
Web: main.omeda.com

Phone | Fax | Class

Omedix Inc
7114 E Stetson Dr Ste 360 .... Scottsdale AZ 85251 877-866-3349 396
TF: 877-866-3349 ■ *Web:* omedix.com

Omega Airline Software
116 N Eighth St .... Midlothian TX 76065 972-775-3693 177
Web: www.omegaair.com

Omega Alpha Pharmaceuticals Inc
795 Pharmacy Ave .... Scarborough ON M1L3K2 416-297-6900 297-8
Web: www.omegaalpha.us

Omega Biologicals Inc
910 Technology Blvd .... Bozeman MT 59718 406-586-3790 586-3792 231
Web: omegabiologicals.com

Omega Cabinetry Ltd 1205 Peters Dr .... Waterloo IA 50703 319-235-5700 235-5860 115
Web: www.omegacabinetry.com

Omega Communications Inc
41 E Washington Ste 110 .... Indianapolis IN 46204 317-264-4000 264-4020 116
Web: www.omegac.com

Omega Communications Inc
256 N Main St 2nd Fl .... Southington CT 06489 860-276-8504 276-0192 225
TF: 800-290-0461 ■ *Web:* www.omegamcomminc.com

Omega Construction Inc
1100 S Stratford Rd Bldg C Ste 110 .... Winston-Salem NC 27103 336-701-1100 368-2277 186
Web: omegaconstruction.com

Omega Design Corp 211 Philips Rd .... Exton PA 19341 610-363-6555 458-8829 547
Web: www.omegadesign.com

Omega Engineering Inc
1 Omega Dr PO Box 4047 .... Stamford CT 06907 203-359-1660 359-7700 201
TF: 800-826-6342 ■ *Web:* www.omega.com

Omega Engineers Inc
16360 Park Ten Pl Ste 325 .... Houston TX 77084 281-647-9182 261
Web: omegaengineers.com

Omega Flex Inc 451 Creamery Way .... Exton PA 19341 610-524-7272 524-7282 790
NASDAQ: OFLX ■ *TF:* 800-355-1039 ■ *Web:* www.omegaflex.com

Omega Healthcare Investors Inc
300 International Cir Ste 200 .... Hunt Valley MD 21030 410-427-1700 655
NYSE: OHI ■ *TF:* 877-511-2891 ■ *Web:* www.omegahealthcare.com

Omega Institute for Holistic Studies
150 Lake Dr .... Rhinebeck NY 12572 845-266-4444 266-3769 673
TF: 800-944-1001 ■ *Web:* www.eomega.org

Omega International Inc
1937 NE Loop 410 Ste 200 .... San Antonio TX 78217 210-805-8808 805-0828 360-3
Web: omegaco.com

Omega Laboratories Inc
400 N Cleveland Ave .... Mogadore OH 44260 330-628-5748 628-5803 415
TF: 800-665-5569 ■ *Web:* www.omegalabs.net

Omega Leads Inc
1509 Colorado Ave .... Santa Monica CA 90404 310-394-6785 253
TF: 800-338-2536 ■ *Web:* www.omegaleads.com

Omega Medical Health Systems Inc
1200 E High St Ste 106 .... Pottstown PA 19464 866-716-6342 475
TF: 866-716-6342 ■ *Web:* www.omegamedicalsystems.com

Omega Moulding Company Ltd
1 Saw Grass Dr .... Bellport NY 11713 800-289-6634 361
TF: 800-289-6634 ■ *Web:* www.omegamoulding.com

Omega Plastics Inc
24401 Capital Blvd .... Clinton Township MI 48036 586-954-2100 596
Web: www.opinc.com

Omega Plastics LLC 2636 Byington Rd .... Knoxville TN 37931 865-690-2211 691-6273 600
Web: www.omegaplastics.com

Omega Precision
13040 Telegraph Rd .... Santa Fe Springs CA 90670 562-946-2491 946-5240 454
Web: www.omegaprecision.us

Omega Printing Inc
201 Williams St .... Bensenville IL 60106 630-595-6344 595-0291 627
Web: omegaprinting.com

Omega Products Intl
1681 California Ave .... Corona CA 92881 951-737-7447 520-2594 191-3
TF: 800-600-6634 ■ *Web:* omega-products.com

Omega Protein Corp
2105 City W Blvd Ste 500 .... Houston TX 77042 713-623-0060 940-6122 296-12
TF: 866-421-0831 ■ *Web:* omegaprotein.com

Omega Psi Phi Fraternity Inc
3951 Snapfinger Pkwy .... Decatur GA 30035 404-284-5533 284-0333 48-16
TF: 800-829-4933 ■ *Web:* www.oppf.org

Omega Rail Management
4721 Trousdale Dr Ste 206 .... Nashville TN 37220 800-990-1961 649
TF: 800-990-1961 ■ *Web:* omegarail.com

Omega Securities Inc
300 Throckmorton Ste 1450 .... Fort Worth TX 76102 817-335-5739 336-4326 690
Web: www.omegawp.com

Omega Shielding Products Inc
1384 Pompton Ave .... Cedar Grove NJ 07009 973-366-0080 326
TF: 800-828-5784 ■ *Web:* www.omegashielding.com

Omega Sports Inc
2431 Battleground Ave .... Greensboro NC 27408 336-288-9741 711
Web: www.omegasports.net

Omega Steel Co 3460 Hollenberg Dr .... Bridgeton MO 63044 314-209-0992 595-5021 492
TF: 800-325-9000 ■ *Web:* www.omegasteel.com

Omega Studios School of Applied Recording Arts & Sciences
12712 Rock Creek Mill Rd .... Rockville MD 20852 301-230-9100 230-9203 685
Web: www.omegastudios.com

Omega Surgical Instruments Inc
8305 S Saginaw St Ste 6G .... Grand Blanc MI 48439 810-695-9800 475
TF: 800-656-6342 ■ *Web:* www.omegasurgical.com

Omega Waste Management Inc
957 Colusa St .... Corning CA 96021 530-824-1890 463
Web: www.omegawaste.com

Omega World Travel Inc
3102 Omega Office Pk Dr .... Fairfax VA 22031 703-359-0200 771
TF: 800-756-6342 ■ *Web:* www.omegatravel.com

Omegachem 480 Rue Perreault .... Saint-Romuald QC G6W7V6 418-837-4444 837-5196 238
TF: 800-661-6342 ■ *Web:* omegachem.com

OmegaNet Inc
2056 W Pk Place Blvd Ste H .... Stone Mountain GA 30087 770-482-3012 482-2741 344
TF: 800-726-1423 ■ *Web:* www.omeganetinc.net

Omega-R 31 W 34th St Ste 8101 .... New York NY 10001 646-586-2025 180
Web: omega-r.com

Omelet 3540 Hayden Ave .... Culver City CA 90232 213-427-6400 195
Web: www.omeletla.com

Company	City	State	Zip	Phone	Fax	Class
OMG (Object Management Group) 140 Kendrick St Ste 300 *Web:* www.omg.org	Needham	MA	02494	781-444-0404	444-0320	48-9
OMG Inc 153 Bowles Rd *Web:* www.omgroofing.com	Agawam	MA	01001	413-789-0252		350
OMH (Old Meeting House) 4004 S Macdill Ave *Web:* www.omhicecream.com	Tampa	FL	33611	813-254-0977	258-5747	297-6
OMI (OMI Industries) 1 Corporate Dr Ste 100 **Fax Area Code:* 847 ■ *TF:* 800-662-6367 ■ *Web:* ecosorbindustrial.com	Long Grove	IL	60047	800-662-6367	304-0989*	582
OMI (Opportunity Management Inc) 15455 NW Greenbrier Pky Ste 210 *TF:* 888-664-4408 ■ *Web:* www.sales-tools.com	Beaverton	OR	97075	503-626-5312	614-0565	194
Omi Gems Inc 100 N Barranca St Ste 970 **Fax Area Code:* 626 ■ *TF:* 877-664-4367 ■ *Web:* omigems.com	West Covina	CA	91791	877-664-4367	331-4532*	411
OMI Industries (OMI) 1 Corporate Dr Ste 100 **Fax Area Code:* 847 ■ *TF:* 800-662-6367 ■ *Web:* ecosorbindustrial.com	Long Grove	IL	60047	800-662-6367	304-0989*	582
Omicron Architecture Engineering Construction Ltd 595 Burrard St Three Bentall Centre Fifth Fl PO Box 49369 *TF:* 877-632-3350 ■ *Web:* omicronaec.com	Vancouver	BC	V7X1L4	604-632-3350		256
Omicron Biochemicals Inc 115 S Hill St *Web:* www.omicronbio.com	South Bend	IN	46617	574-287-6910	287-7165	143
Omimex Resources Inc 7950 John T White Rd *Web:* www.omimex.com	Fort Worth	TX	76120	817-460-7777	460-1381	536
Omitron Inc 7051 Muirkirk Meadows Dr Ste A *Web:* www.omitron.com	Beltsville	MD	20705	301-474-1700		387
Omix-Ada Inc 460 Horizon Dr Ste 400 *Web:* www.omix-ada.com	Suwanee	GA	30024	770-614-6101		54
Omnetics Connector Corp 7260 Commerce Cir E *TF:* 800-343-0025 ■ *Web:* www.omnetics.com	Minneapolis	MN	55432	763-572-0656	572-3925	815
Omnex Engineering & Management Inc 315 E Eisenhower Pkwy Ste 214 **Fax Area Code:* 315 ■ *Web:* www.omnex.com	Ann Arbor	MI	48108	734-761-4940	214-4810*	463
Omni Agent Solutions 5955 De Soto Ave Ste 100 *Web:* omniagentsolutions.com	Woodland Hills	CA	91367	818-906-8300	783-2737	463
Omni Baking Co 2621 Freddy Ln *Web:* www.omnibaking.com	Vineland	NJ	08360	856-691-5642		296-1
Omni Behavioral Health 5115 F St *Web:* www.omnibehavioralhealth.com	Omaha	NE	68117	402-397-9866	397-1404	726
Omni Cable Corp 2 Hagerty Blvd *TF:* 888-292-6664 ■ *Web:* www.omnicable.com	West Chester	PA	19382	610-701-0100	701-9870	246
Omni Cubed Inc 6125 Enterprise Dr Ste B155 *TF:* 877-311-1976 ■ *Web:* omnicubed.com	Diamond Springs	CA	95619	877-311-1976		226
Omni Custom Meats Inc 151 Vanderbilt Ct *Web:* www.omnimeats.com	Bowling Green	KY	42103	270-796-6147		296-26
Omni Data LLC 4 Industry Dr Ext Bldg 2 *Web:* www.myomnidata.com	West Haven	CT	06516	203-387-6664	387-8745	180
Omni Die Casting Inc 1100 Nova Dr SE *Web:* www.omnidiecasting.com	Massillon	OH	44646	330-830-5500		308
Omni Engineering Services Inc 370 W Second St Ste 100 *Web:* omnimn.com	Winona	MN	55987	507-454-5293		256
Omni Gear 7502 Mesa Rd *Web:* www.omnigear.com	Houston	TX	77028	713-635-6331	635-6360	60
Omni Hotels 4001 Maple Ave *TF:* 800-843-6664 ■ *Web:* www.omnihotels.com	Dallas	TX	75219	402-952-6664		379
Omni Information Systems Inc PO Box 1429 *TF:* 888-653-6664 ■ *Web:* www.omni-info.com	Dacula	GA	30019	678-377-5560		180
Omni Jet Trading Ctr 9415 Jet Ln Ste 3 *Web:* www.omnijet.com	Easton	MD	21601	410-820-7300	820-5082	770
Omni Life Assocates Inc 375 N Broadway Ste 203 **Fax Area Code:* 800 ■ *TF:* 800-966-6583 ■ *Web:* www.omniquote.net	Jericho	NY	11753	516-938-2465	966-6641*	390
Omni Link Corp 1750 Valley View Ln Ste 320 *Web:* www.omnilinkcorp.com	Dallas	TX	75234	972-620-9000		194
Omni Manufacturing Inc 901 Mckinley Rd *Web:* www.omnimfg.com	Saint Marys	OH	45885	419-394-7424		483
Omni Marketing Interactive 847 S Randall Rd Ste 312 *Web:* www.search-usability.com	Elgin	IL	60123	847-426-4256	426-4257	631
Omni Optical Lab 3255 Executive Blvd *Web:* www.omnioptical.com	Beaumont	TX	77705	409-842-4113		543
OMNI Products Inc 3911 Dayton St *TF:* 800-275-9848 ■ *Web:* www.omnirail.com	Mchenry	IL	60050	815-344-3100		677
Omni Tucson National Golf Resort & Spa 2727 W Club Dr *Web:* www.tucsonnational.com	Tucson	AZ	85742	520-297-2271	297-7544	669
Omni Valve Company LLC 4520 Chandler Rd *Web:* www.omnivalve.com	Muskogee	OK	74403	918-687-6100		536
Omni Vision Inc 504 Congress Cir N Unit B *Web:* www.omnivisionusa.com	Roselle	IL	60172	630-893-1720	893-9991	647
Omni W.C. Inc 166 National Rd *Web:* www.omniwcinc.com	Edison	NJ	08817	732-248-0999		550
Omnia Group Inc, The 1501 W Cleveland St Ste 300 *TF:* 800-525-7117 ■ *Web:* omniagroup.com	Tampa	FL	33606	813-254-9449	254-8558	196
Omnia Industries Incorporated Cedar Grove Plant 5 Cliffside Dr *Web:* www.omniaindustries.com	Cedar Grove	NJ	07009	973-239-7272		350
Omnibus Press 257 Park Ave S *Web:* www.omnibuspress.com	New York	NY	10010	212-254-2100	254-2013	637-2
Omnicare Inc 201 E Fourth St *NYSE:* OCR ■ **Fax Area Code:* 859 ■ *TF:* 800-342-5627 ■ *Web:* www.omnicare.com	Cincinnati	OH	45202	800-990-6664	392-3333*	587
Omnicell Inc 1201 Charleston Rd *NASDAQ:* OMCL ■ *TF:* 800-850-6664 ■ *Web:* www.omnicell.com	Mountain View	CA	94043	650-251-6100	251-6266	420
Omnicom Group Inc 437 Madison Ave *NYSE:* OMC ■ *Web:* www.omnicomgroup.com	New York	NY	10022	212-415-3600	415-3530	360-3
Omnience Inc 1350 Center Dr Ste 100 *Web:* omnienceevents.com	Atlanta	GA	30338	770-399-3199		184
Omnifics Inc 5845 Richmond Hwy Ste 300 *Web:* www.omnifics.com	Alexandria	VA	22303	703-548-4040		393
Omnifilm Entertainment Ltd 111 Water St *Web:* www.omnifilm.com	Vancouver	BC	V6B1A7	604-681-6543		514
Omnigraphics Inc PO Box 31-1640 *TF:* 800-234-1340 ■ *Web:* www.omnigraphics.com	Detroit	MI	48231	800-234-1340	875-1340	637-2
Omnikron Systems 20920 Warner Center Ln Ste A *Web:* www.omnikron.com	Woodland Hills	CA	91367	818-591-7890		196
Omnilife Health Care Systems Inc PO Box 8309 *Web:* www.omnilife.org	Columbus	OH	43201	614-299-3100	299-3813	450
Omnilift Inc Warwick Commons Industrial Pk 1938 Stout Dr *Web:* www.omnilift.com	Warminster	PA	18974	215-443-9090		358
Omnilingua Worldwide LLC 306 Sixth Ave SE *TF:* 800-395-6664 ■ *Web:* www.omnilingua.com	Cedar Rapids	IA	52401	800-395-6664		317
Omni-Lite Industries Canada Inc 17210 Edwards Rd *TF:* 800-577-6664 ■ *Web:* www.omni-lite.com	Cerritos	CA	90703	562-404-8510		621
Omnilogic Systems Inc 1420 Broad St *Web:* www.omnilogic.net	Regina	SK	S4R1Y9	306-586-6116		180
Omni-Medcom 160 Pope St **Fax Area Code:* 819 ■ *TF:* 888-780-6081 ■ *Web:* www.omnimed.com	Cookshire-Eaton	QC	J0B1M0	888-780-6081	875-3929*	179
OmniMetrix LLC 5225 Belle Wood Ct *TF:* 800-854-7342 ■ *Web:* www.omnimetrix.net	Buford	GA	30519	770-209-0012		407
OMNIPLEX World Services Corp 14151 Pk Meadow Dr *Web:* www.omniplex.com	Chantilly	VA	20151	703-652-3100	652-3101	271
Omnipress 2600 Anderson St *TF:* 800-828-0305 ■ *Web:* www.omnipress.com	Madison	WI	53704	608-246-2600		196
Omnipure Filter Company Inc 1904 Industrial Way *TF:* 800-398-0833 ■ *Web:* www.omnipure.com	Caldwell	ID	83605	208-454-2597		45
Omnis Network LLC 3655 Torrance Blvd Ste 180 *TF:* 877-393-4678 ■ *Web:* www.omnis.com	Torrance	CA	90503	310-316-9600	347-4075	224
OmniSource Corp 7575 W Jefferson Blvd *TF:* 800-666-4789 ■ *Web:* www.omnisource.com	Fort Wayne	IN	46804	260-422-5541	423-8500	686
OmniSYS-LLC 15950 Dallas Pkwy Ste 350 *TF:* 800-666-4797 ■ *Web:* www.omnisys.com	Dallas	TX	75248	214-459-2574		809
Omnitech Inc 5841 S Corporate Pl *Web:* www.omnitech-inc.com	Sioux Falls	SD	57108	605-336-0888		177
Omnitech Labs 215 Seminaire Blvd S Ste 1305 *TF:* 800-971-6860 ■ *Web:* www.omnitechlabs.net	Saint-Jean-sur-Richelieu	QC	J3B8W1	450-359-0891		180
Omnithruster Inc 2201 Pinnacle Pky *Web:* www.omnithruster.com	Twinsburg	OH	44087	330-963-6310	963-6325	815
OmniTI Computer Consulting Inc 11830 W Market Pl Ste B *Web:* omniti.com	Fulton	MD	20759	240-646-0770		631
Omnitracs 717 N Harwood St Ste 1300 *TF:* 800-348-7227 ■ *Web:* www.omnitracs.com	Dallas	TX	75201	800-348-7227		736
Omnitrans Inc 500 Merrick Rd *TF:* 877-806-2541 ■ *Web:* www.omnitrans.com	Lynbrook	NY	11563	516-561-9300	561-9326	449
OmniTRAX Inc 252 Clayton St 4th Fl *TF:* 800-533-9416 ■ *Web:* omnitrax.com	Denver	CO	80206	303-398-4500	398-4540	651
Omnitrend Software Inc 211 Millers Way *Web:* www.omnitrend.com	Simsbury	CT	06070	860-673-8910	673-3023	178-1
Omnitronics LLC 6573 Cochran Rd *TF:* 800-762-9266 ■ *Web:* www.cadaudio.com	Solon	OH	44139	440-349-4900		52
Omnivex Corp 3300 Hwy 7 Ste 501 *TF:* 800-745-8223 ■ *Web:* www.omnivex.com	Concord	ON	L4K4M3	905-761-6640		179
OmniVision Technologies Inc (OVT) 4275 Burton Dr *NASDAQ:* OVTI ■ *Web:* www.ovt.com	Santa Clara	CA	95054	408-542-3000		696
OmniVue Business Solutions LLC 1355 Windward Concourse Ste 200 *TF:* 866-900-6348 ■ *Web:* omnivue.net	Alpharetta	GA	30005	770-587-0095		196
Omni-X USA Inc 2751 W Mansfield Ave *TF:* 800-275-6664 ■ *Web:* www.omnibend.com	Englewood	CO	80110	303-789-3575	789-4755	456
Omnni Associates Inc 1 Systems Dr *TF:* 800-571-6677 ■ *Web:* omnni.com	Appleton	WI	54914	920-735-6900		261
OMNOVA Solutions Inc 25435 Harvard Rd *Web:* www.omnova.com	Beachwood	OH	44122	216-682-7000		385
OMP (Overmountain Press) PO Box 1261 *TF:* 800-992-2691 ■ *Web:* www.overmtn.com	Johnson City	TN	37605	800-992-2691		637-2
OMRF (Oklahoma Medical Research Foundation) 825 NE 13th St *TF:* 800-522-0211 ■ *Web:* omrf.org	Oklahoma City	OK	73104	405-271-6673		668
Omron Healthcare Inc 1925 W Field Ct *TF:* 877-216-1333 ■ *Web:* omronhealthcare.com	Lake Forest	IL	60045	847-680-6200	680-6269	475
Omron Microscan Systems Inc 700 SW 39th St Ste 100 *TF:* 800-762-1149 ■ *Web:* www.microscan.com	Renton	WA	98057	425-226-5700	226-8250	647
OMRON Scientific Technologies Inc 6550 Dumbarton Cir *TF:* 800-556-6766 ■ *Web:* www.omron.com	Fremont	CA	94555	510-608-3400	744-1442	203
OMSP (Olympic Mountain School Press) PO Box 1114 *TF:* 800-819-1179 ■ *Web:* www.mountainschoolpress.com	Gig Harbor	WA	98335	253-858-4448		637-2

Name / Address	City	State	ZIP	Phone	Fax	Class
OMW Corp 354 Bel Marin Keys Blvd. Web: www.omwcorp.com	Novato	CA	94949	415-382-1669	382-9069	454
OMYA Inc 62 Main St TF: 800-451-4468 ■ Web: www.omya.com	Proctor	VT	05765	802-499-8131		143
On 3 Promotional Partners 1543 Sheridan Rd TF: 877-247-7157 ■ Web: www.on3promopartners.com	Kenosha	WI	53140	262-551-8715		317
On Assignment Inc 26745 Malibu Hills Rd NYSE: ASGN ■ Web: asgn.com	Calabasas	CA	91301	919-334-0375		721
On Broadway 106 Broadway Web: onbroadwayinhelena.com	Helena	MT	59601	406-443-1929		671
On Campus Marketing LLC 305 W Commerce St Ste 650 Web: www.ocm.com	Bethesda	MD	20817	301-652-1580	941-0514	387
On Center Software Inc 8708 Technology Forest Pl Ste 175 TF: 866-627-6246 ■ Web: www.oncenter.com	The Woodlands	TX	77381	281-297-9000	297-9001	177
On Demand Books 584 Broadway Rm 1100 Web: www.ondemandbooks.com	New York	NY	10012	212-966-2222		95
On Demand Technologies Inc 9291 Cody St Web: www.odtinc.com	Overland Park	KS	66214	913-438-1800	438-3077	178-1
On Line Controls Inc 9 Kane Industrial Dr A Web: onlinecontrols.com	Hudson	MA	01749	978-562-5353	562-8986	476
On My Own Independent Living Services 6939 Sunrise Blvd Ste 215 Web: onmyown-web.com	Citrus Heights	CA	95610	916-726-0792	728-1005	363
ON Search Partners LLC 6240 SOM Center Rd Ste 230 Web: www.onpartners.com	Solon	OH	44139	440-318-1006		260
ON Semiconductor Corp 5005 E McDowell Rd NASDAQ: ON ■ TF: 800-282-9855 ■ Web: www.onsemi.com	Phoenix	AZ	85008	602-244-6600		696
ON Services 6779 Crescent Dr TF: 800-967-2419 ■ Web: onservices.com	Norcross	GA	30071	770-457-0966		738
On Site Gas Systems Inc 35 Budney Rd Budney Industrial Pk Web: www.onsitegas.com	Newington	CT	06111	860-667-8888		579
On Site Marketing 1901 Strasburg Rd TF: 866-314-3104 ■ Web: onsitemarketing.com	Coatesville	PA	19320	610-486-6900		463
On Tap Credit Union 816 Washington Ave Web: www.ontapcu.org	Golden	CO	80401	303-279-6414	279-6336	219
On Target Staffing LLC 1040 Orchard St Web: www.ontargetstaffingllc.com	New Brunswick	NJ	08901	732-249-8344	249-7341	260
On the Border Cafe 1350 NW Hwy Web: www.ontheborder.com	Garland	TX	75041	972-865-7988		671
On The Go Transportation Service 12383 Lewis St Ste 200 TF: 800-845-1190 ■ Web: onthegotrans.com	Garden Grove	CA	92840	714-621-3200	748-0226	225
On the Scene 500 N Dearborn St Ste 550 Web: www.onthescene.com	Chicago	IL	60654	312-661-1440		184
On Time Delivery Inc 1800 Preble Ave *Fax Area Code: 412 ■ TF: 800-248-6695 ■ Web: www.otdinc.net	Pittsburgh	PA	15233	800-248-6695	231-4987*	780
On Time Staffing 535 Rte 38 E Ste 412 *Fax Area Code: 856 ■ TF: 855-866-2910 ■ Web: www.ontimestaffing.com	Cherry Hill	NJ	08002	866-333-3007	668-4634*	260
On Time Transport Inc 135 E Highland Pkwy TF: 800-858-8463 ■ Web: www.ontimetransport.com	Roselle	NJ	07203	908-298-9500	298-9509	30
On Track Marketing Inc 1910 W N Ave Web: www.otmarketing.com	Chicago	IL	60622	773-235-0017		195
ON24 Inc 50 Beale St 8th Fl TF: 877-202-9599 ■ Web: www.on24.com	San Francisco	CA	94105	415-369-8000	369-8388	395
ONA (Ohio Nurses Assn) 4000 E Main St TF: 800-735-0056 ■ Web: www.ohnurses.org	Columbus	OH	43213	614-237-5414	237-6074	533
ONA (Oklahoma Nurses Assn) 6608 NW Ste 627 Web: ona.nursingnetwork.com	Oklahoma City	OK	73103	405-840-3476	840-3013	533
ONA (Oregon Nurses Assn) 18765 SW Boones Ferry Rd TF: 800-634-3552 ■ Web: www.oregonrn.org	Tualatin	OR	97062	503-293-0011	293-0013	533
Ona Beach State Park 5580 S Coast Hwy Web: stateparks.oregon.gov	Newport	OR	97366	541-867-4715		565
Onamac Industries Inc 6300 Merrill Creek Pkwy Web: www.onamac.com	Everett	WA	98204	425-743-6676	742-2718	454
Onboard Systems Intl 13915 NW Third Ct TF: 800-275-0883 ■ Web: www.onboardsystems.com	Vancouver	WA	98685	360-546-3072	546-3073	529
On-Call Nursing Agency & Associates of New Orleans 7900 Earhart Blvd Web: ldh.la.gov	New Orleans	LA	70125	504-866-0442		793
ONCAP 161 Bay St 49th Fl Web: www.oncap.com	Toronto	ON	M5J2S1	416-214-4300		792
OnCard Marketing Inc 132 W 31st St Ste 702 TF: 866-996-8729 ■ Web: www.revtrax.com	New York	NY	10001	866-996-8729		466
OnCell 1160D Pittsford-Victor Rd Web: oncell.com	Pittsford	NY	14534	585-419-9844	419-9843	178
Oncenter Complex 800 S State St TF: 800-776-7548 ■ Web: www.oncenter.org	Syracuse	NY	13202	315-435-8000	435-8099	205
Oncology Nursing Society (ONS) 125 Enterprise Dr *Fax Area Code: 877 ■ TF: 866-257-4667 ■ Web: www.ons.org	Pittsburgh	PA	15275	412-859-6100	369-5497*	49-8
Oncolytics Biotech Inc 1167 Kensington Crescent NW Ste 210 NASDAQ: ONCY ■ Web: www.oncolyticsbiotech.com	Calgary	AB	T2N1X7	403-670-7377	283-0858	85
Oncor 1616 Woodall Rodgers Fwy Ste 2M-012 TF: 888-313-6862 ■ Web: www.oncor.com	Dallas	TX	75202	888-313-4747		787
Oncore Manufacturing Services LLC 225 Carando Dr	Springfield	MA	01104	413-736-2121		625
OnCorp Direct Inc 1033 Bay St Ste 313 TF: 800-461-7772 ■ Web: www.oncorp.com	Toronto	ON	M5S3A5	416-964-2677		317
Oncoscope Inc 324 Blackwell St Ste 1120	Durham	NC	27701	919-251-8030		743
OnCure Medical Corp 188 Inverness Dr W Ste 650 Web: www.oncure.com	Englewood	CO	80112	303-643-6500	643-6560	374-3
Ondal USA 540 Eastpark Ct Ste A Web: www.ondal.com	Richmond	VA	23150	804-532-1440	532-1494	475
OndaVia Inc 26102 Eden Landing Rd Ste 1 Web: www.ondavia.com	Hayward	CA	94545	510-887-3180		407
OnDemand Resources LLC 265 Turkeysag Trl Ste 102 *Fax Area Code: 434 ■ TF: 800-403-8578 ■ Web: www.ondemandresources.com	Palmyra	VA	22963	800-403-8578	208-1388*	631
On-Demand Services Group 2604 Lyndale Ave S Web: ondemandgroup.com	Minneapolis	MN	55408	612-367-8101		180
Onder Shelton O'Leary & Peterson LLC 110 E Lockwood Ave Web: www.onderlaw.com	Saint Louis	MO	63119	314-963-9000		445
Ondine Biomedical Inc 1100 Melville St TF: 866-669-0555 ■ Web: www.ondinebio.com	Vancouver	BC	V6E4A6	604-669-0555	669-0533	231
Onduline North America Inc 4900 Ondura Dr TF: 800-777-7663 ■ Web: us.onduline.com	Fredericksburg	VA	22407	540-898-7000	898-4991	191-4
One & All 2 N Lake Ave Ste 600 TF: 800-241-9351 ■ Web: oneandall.com	Pasadena	CA	91101	626-449-6100		5
One 2 One Bodyscapes 1197 Walnut St Web: www.one2onebodyscapes.com	Newton	MA	02461	617-796-8808		354
One 8 Inc PO Box 2075 TF: 800-504-1818 ■ Web: www.mountainmanleatherworks.com	Forks	WA	98331	360-374-7500		430
One Acadiana 804 E St Mary Blvd Web: www.oneacadiana.org	LaFayette	LA	70503	337-233-2705	234-8671	139
One Call Concepts Inc 7223 Pkwy Dr Ste 210 TF: 800-257-7777 ■ Web: www.occinc.com	Hanover	MD	21076	410-712-0082	712-0838	171
One Call Medical Inc (OCM) PO Box 614 TF: 800-872-2875 ■ Web: onecallcm.com	Parsippany	NJ	07054	973-257-1000		382
One Consulting Group 448 Ralph David Abernathy Blvd Bldg 7 Web: onecginc.com	Atlanta	GA	30312	404-815-8005	815-8002	196
One DOT Systems Inc 6566 NW 13th Ct Web: www.onedotsystems.net	Plantation	FL	33313	954-327-1490		180
One Eighty Consulting Inc 413 N Meridian St Web: 180consultinginc.com	Tallahassee	FL	32301	850-412-0300		196
One if by Land Two if by Sea 17 Barrow St Web: www.oneifbyland.com	New York	NY	10014	212-255-8649		671
One Inc 620 Coolidge Dr Ste 200 TF: 866-343-6940 ■ Web: oneincsystems.com	Folsom	CA	95630	866-343-6940		177
One Incorporated Systems 400 Imperial Blvd PO Box 9002 *Fax Area Code: 321 ■ TF: 800-749-3160 ■ Web: www.calloneonline.com	Cape Canaveral	FL	32920	800-749-3160	799-9222*	735
One Lambda 21001 Kittridge St *Fax Area Code: 800 ■ TF: 800-822-8824 ■ Web: www.onelambda.com	Canoga Park	CA	91303	818-449-3230	992-2111*	479
One Market 1 Market St Web: onemarket.com	San Francisco	CA	94105	415-777-5577	777-3366	671
One More Pallet 9891 Montgomery Rd Ste 122 TF: 855-438-1667 ■ Web: www.onemorepallet.com	Cincinnati	OH	45242	855-438-1667		387
One Napili Way 5355 Lower Honoapiilani Hwy Web: www.onenapiliway.com	Lahaina	HI	96761	808-669-2007		753
One Nation Energy Solutions 4404 Blossom St Web: www.onenationenergy.com	Houston	TX	77007	713-861-0600	861-0608	538
One Planet Corp 850 Ridge Ave TF: 888-677-1010 ■ Web: www.one-planet.net	Pittsburgh	PA	15212	412-323-1050		768
One Point Solutions Inc 43422 W Oaks Dr Ste 294 Web: www.one-point.com	Novi	MI	48377	248-887-8470		177
One Reverse Mortgage LLC 4445 Eastgate Mall Ste 320 TF: 800-401-8114 ■ Web: www.onereversemortgage.com	San Diego	CA	92121	858-652-5990		509
One Smooth Stone 5222 Main St Web: www.onesmoothstone.com	Downers Grove	IL	60515	630-427-4226		463
One Source Industries LLC 185 Technology Dr TF: 800-899-4990 ■ Web: www.osicreative.com	Irvine	CA	92618	800-899-4990		546
One Source Safety & Health Inc 140 S Village Ave Ste 130 Web: www.1ssh.com	Exton	PA	19341	610-524-5525		196
One Source Toxicology Laboratory Inc 1213 Genoa Red Bluff Rd *Fax Area Code: 281 ■ TF: 888-747-3774 ■ Web: www.onesourcetox.com	Pasadena	TX	77504	713-920-2559	998-8587*	415
One Southern Indiana 4100 Charlestown Rd TF: 800-521-2232 ■ Web: www.1si.org	New Albany	IN	47150	812-945-0266	948-4664	139
One Step Logic 17615 Mayall St Web: www.onesteplogic.com	Northridge	CA	91325	818-700-7837		77
One Stop Environmental LLC (OSE) 4800 Division Ave Web: www.onestopenv.com	Birmingham	AL	35222	205-595-8188	595-8901	660
One Technologies LLC 8144 Walnut Hill Ln Ste 600 TF: 888-550-8471 ■ Web: onetechnologies.net	Dallas	TX	75231	469-916-1700		225
One Touch Global Technologies Inc 901 Dove St Ste 210 TF: 800-233-3619 ■ Web: www.otgt.com	Newport Beach	CA	92660	800-233-3619		174
One Touch Systems Inc 2528 Qume Dr Unit 14 Web: www.onetouchsys.com	San Jose	CA	95131	408-436-4600		178-7
One Trick Pony 136 E Fulton St Web: onetrick.biz	Grand Rapids	MI	49503	616-235-7669		671
One Washington Cir Hotel 1 Washington Cir NW Web: www.thecirclehotel.com	Washington	DC	20037	202-872-1680		379

				Phone	Fax	Class
One Way Wireless Construction 6811 Washington Ave S *Web:* www.owwc.com	Minneapolis	MN	55439	952-942-0412		186
One Workplace 475 Brannan St Ste 210 *Web:* www.oneworkplace.com	San Francisco	CA	94107	415-357-2200		320
One World Direct 10 First Ave E *Web:* www.owd.com	Mobridge	SD	57601	605-845-7172		459
One World Theatre 7701 Bee Caves Rd *TF:* 888-616-0522 ■ *Web:* www.oneworldtheatre.org	Austin	TX	78746	512-330-9500	330-9600	572
One Yellow Rabbit Performance Theatre 225 8 Ave SE *Web:* www.oyr.org	Calgary	AB	T2G0K8	403-264-3224		749
OneAero 175 N Applewood Dr *TF:* 888-820-8551 ■ *Web:* www.one.aero	Alpine	UT	84004	801-492-4070		770
OneBeacon Insurance Group 605 Hwy 169 N Ste 800 *TF:* 800-662-0156 ■ *Web:* www.onebeacon.com	Plymouth	MN	55441	781 332 7000	332-7904	391-4
OneCoast Network LLC 230 Spring St Ste 1800 *TF:* 866-592-5514 ■ *Web:* www.onecoast.com	Atlanta	GA	30303	866-592-5514	469-9517	361
Oneida City School District Inc 565 Sayles St *Web:* www.oneidacsd.org	Oneida	NY	13421	315-363-2550	363-6728	685
Oneida County 1 S Oneida Ave *Web:* www.co.oneida.wi.us	Rhinelander	WI	54501	715-369-6144	369-6230	338
Oneida County 310 Main St *Web:* ican.family	Utica	NY	13501	315-792-9039		338
Oneida County Convention & Visitors Bureau PO Box 551 *TF:* 800-426-3132 ■ *Web:* www.oneidacountytourism.com	Utica	NY	13503	315-724-7221	724-7335	206
Oneida Healthcare 321 Genesee St *Web:* www.oneidahealth.org	Oneida	NY	13421	315-363-6000	361-2043	374-3
Oneida-Madison Electric Co-opeartive Inc 6630 SR-20 *Web:* www.oneida-madison.coop	Bouckville	NY	13310	315-893-1851	893-1857	245
ONeill & Borges LLC 250 Munoz Rivera Ave Ste 800 *Web:* www.oneillborges.com	San Juan	PR	00918	787-764-8181	753-8944	428
OneIQ Corp 51 Breithaupt St Ste 100 Kitchener *Web:* www.oneiq.com	Toronto	ON	N2H5G5	416-342-1960	342-1961	179
OneLegacy Transplant Donor Network 221 S Figueroa St Ste 500 *TF:* 800-786-4077 ■ *Web:* www.onelegacy.org	Los Angeles	CA	90012	213-229-5600	229-5601	545
OneMedPlace 219 E 83rd St 4 Fl *Web:* www.onemedplace.com	New York	NY	10028	212-734-1008		466
OneName Corp 18 W Mercer Ste 300 *Web:* onename.com	Seattle	WA	98119	206-812-6000	812-6001	525
Oneonta City School District 31 Center St *Web:* www.oneontacsd.org	Oneonta	NY	13820	607-433-8200	433-8290	186
OneRoof Inc 495 E Brokaw Rd Ste 1100 *Web:* www.oneroof.com	San Francisco	CA	94111	415-391-0556	391-0559	196
OneSCM 6805 Capital of Texas Hwy Ste 370 *TF:* 800-324-5143 ■ *Web:* www.takesupplychain.com	Austin	TX	78731	512-231-8191		178-1
Oneshield Inc 62 Forest St *Web:* oneshield.com	Marlborough	MA	01752	774-348-1000		177
Onesmartworld Inc 79 Simcoe St *TF:* 800-387-6278 ■ *Web:* www.onesmartworld.com	Collingwood	ON	L9Y1H7	705-444-1234		193
OneSource Communication 4800 Keller Hicks Rd *TF:* 800-810-9848 ■ *Web:* www.1scom.com	Fort Worth	TX	76244	817-745-3000	745-2020	681
OneSource Distributors 3951 Oceanic Dr *Web:* 1sourcedist.com	Oceanside	CA	92056	760-966-4500	966-4599	246
OneSource Inc 1124 Hwy 315 *Web:* www.onesourcehrsolutions.com	Wilkes-Barre	PA	18702	570-825-3411		260
OneSource Virtual 5601 N MacArthur Blvd Ste 100 *Web:* www.onesourcevirtual.com	Irving	TX	75038	972-916-9847		631
OneSpan 121 W Wacker Dr Ste 2050 *NASDAQ: VDSI* ■ *Web:* www.onespan.com	Chicago	IL	60601	630-932-8844	932-8852	692
OneSpring LLC 980 Birmingham Rd Ste 501-165 *TF:* 888-472-1840 ■ *Web:* onespring.net	Alpharetta	GA	30004	888-472-1840		180
OneSubsea Processing Inc 4646 W Sam Houston Pkwy N *Web:* connect.slb.com	Houston	TX	77041	713-939-2211		539
Oneta Co 1401 S Padre Island Dr *Web:* www.onetacc.com	Corpus Christi	TX	78416	361-853-0123	853-5327	80-2
OneTech LLC 233 SE 2nd Ave *TF:* 800-968-8867 ■ *Web:* www.onetechllc.com	Hillsboro	OR	97123	503-648-8523	640-8639	177
OneTouch Direct LLC 4902 W Sligh Ave *TF:* 866-948-4005 ■ *Web:* www.onetouchdirect.com	Tampa	FL	33634	813-549-7500		41
Onetravel Inc 1050 E Flamingo Rd Ste S-302 *TF:* 888-204-1671 ■ *Web:* www.onetravel.com	Las Vegas	NV	89119	888-204-1671		771
OneUnited Bank 3683 Crenshaw Blvd *TF:* 877-663-8648 ■ *Web:* www.oneunited.com	Los Angeles	CA	90016	323-290-4848	389-0548	70
One-Write Co 3750 Lancaster New Lexington Rd SE *TF:* 800-268-6070 ■ *Web:* www.onewriteco.com	Lancaster	OH	43130	800-268-6070		627
Onex Corp 161 Bay St PO Box 700 *Web:* www.onex.com	Toronto	ON	M5J2S1	416-362-7711		185
OnForce Inc 10 Maguire Rd Bldg 2 Ste 232 *TF:* 888-515-0100 ■ *Web:* onforce.com	Lexington	MA	02421	888-515-0100		631
Ongig Inc 708 Montgomery St *Web:* www.ongig.com	San Francisco	CA	94111	415-857-2304		260
ONICON Inc 11451 Belcher Rd S *Web:* www.onicon.com	Largo	FL	33773	727-447-6140		201
Onion River Outdoors 20 Langdon St *Web:* www.onionriver.com	Montpelier	VT	05602	802-225-6736		711
Onit 1360 Post Oak Blvd Unit 2200 *TF:* 800-281-1330 ■ *Web:* www.onit.com	Houston	TX	77056	800-281-1330		178-1

				Phone	Fax	Class
OnIt Digital Inc PO Box 922 *Web:* www.onitdigital.com	New City	NY	10956	212-655-9632		195
Onity 2232 Northmont Pky Ste 100 *TF:* 800-248-6189 ■ *Web:* www.onity.com	Duluth	GA	30096	800-248-6189		425
Onity Inc 4001 Fairview Industrial Dr SE *TF:* 800-424-1433 ■ *Web:* en.onity.com	Salem	OR	97302	800-424-1433		351
Onix Networking Corp 18519 Detroit Ave *TF:* 800-664-9638 ■ *Web:* www.onixnet.com	Lakewood	OH	44107	800-664-9638		174
ONLC (Oregon Nikkei Legacy Ctr) 121 NW 2nd Ave *Web:* www.oregonnikkei.org	Portland	OR	97209	503-224-1458		192
Online Accounting 462 E Shore Dr Ste 140 **Fax Area Code:* 888 ■ *TF:* 888-254-9252 ■ *Web:* www.onlineaccounting.com	Eagle	ID	83616	208-939-9842	308-8413*	180
Online Commerce Group LLC 946 Plantation Way *Web:* www.onlinecommercegroup.com	Montgomery	AL	36117	334-558-0863		393
Online Computers & Communications LLC 110 S Jefferson Rd Ste 200 *TF:* 800-985-9368 ■ *Web:* onlinecomputers.com	Whippany	NJ	07981	800-985-9368		180
Online Copy Corp 48815 Kato Rd *TF:* 800-833-4460 ■ *Web:* onlinecopycorp.com	Fremont	CA	94539	800-833-4460		240
Online Development Inc 7209 Chapman Hwy *Web:* oldi.com	Knoxville	TN	37920	865-251-5252		180
Online Electronics Inc 1261 Jarvis Ave *Web:* www.pcb4less.com	Elk Grove Village	IL	60007	847-871-1700	871-1710	625
Online Engineering Inc 400 N Cedar St *Web:* online-engineering.com	Manistique	MI	49854	906-341-0090	341-0099	475
Online Paper Airplane Museum, The 6020 Green Pond Rd *Web:* www.theonlinepaperairplanemuseum.com	Polk City	FL	33868	813-766-4564		520
On-Line Strategies Inc 7920 Belt Line Rd Ste 1150 *Web:* olspayments.com	Dallas	TX	75254	214-466-1000		253
On-line Taxes Inc 724 Jules St **Fax Area Code:* 816 ■ *TF:* 800-829-1040 ■ *Web:* www.olt.com	Saint Joseph	MO	64501	800-829-1040	232-1591*	463
Online Transport System Inc 6311 W Stoner Dr *TF:* 866-543-1235 ■ *Web:* www.onlinetransport.com	Greenfield	IN	46140	317-894-2159		780
On-line Video Design Inc 710 Acacia Ave *Web:* www.onlinevid.com	Melbourne	FL	32904	321-676-5677		514
OnlineMetals.com 1848 Westlake Ave N Ste A **Fax Area Code:* 206 ■ *TF:* 800-704-2157 ■ *Web:* www.onlinemetals.com	Seattle	WA	98109	800-704-2157	285-7836*	492
Only in San Francisco Pier 39 Ste A01 *Web:* www.pier39.com	San Francisco	CA	94133	415-397-0143		327
Ono Pharma USA Inc 2000 Lenox Dr *Web:* www.ono.co.jp	Trenton	NJ	08648	609-219-1010	219-9229	582
Onondaga Cave State Park 7556 Hwy H *Web:* mostateparks.com	Leasburg	MO	65535	573-245-6576		565
Onondaga Coach Corp PO Box 277 *TF:* 800-451-1570 ■ *Web:* www.onondagacoach.com	Auburn	NY	13021	315-255-2216	255-0925	107
Onondaga Community College 4941 Onondaga Rd *Web:* www.sunyocc.edu	Syracuse	NY	13215	315-498-2622	498-2107	162
Onondaga County 401 Montgomery St *Web:* www.ongov.net	Syracuse	NY	13202	315-435-2226	435-3455	338
Onondaga County Public Library 447 S Salina St *Web:* www.onlib.org	Syracuse	NY	13202	315-435-1900		434-3
Onondaga Flooring Inc 1510 N Salina St *Web:* onondagaflooring.com	Syracuse	NY	13208	315-471-2243		290
OnPath Business Solutions Inc 1165 Kenaston St *TF:* 855-420-3244 ■ *Web:* www.onpath.com	Ottawa	ON	K1B3N9	855-420-3244		180
Onprocess Technology Inc 200 Homer Ave *Web:* www.onprocess.com	Ashland	MA	01721	508-520-2711		463
On-Q-ity Inc 610 Lincoln St N Bldg 3rd Fl *Web:* on-q-ity.com	Waltham	MA	02451	781-895-8100	890-4636	743
ONRAD Inc 1770 Iowa Ave Ste 280 *TF:* 800-848-5876 ■ *Web:* www.onradinc.com	Riverside	CA	92507	800-848-5876		177
Onramp Access LLC 2916 Montopolis Dr Ste 300 *Web:* www.onr.com	Austin	TX	78741	512-322-9200		177
ONS (Oncology Nursing Society) 125 Enterprise Dr **Fax Area Code:* 877 ■ *TF:* 866-257-4667 ■ *Web:* www.ons.org	Pittsburgh	PA	15275	412-859-6100	369-5497*	49-8
Onset Computer Corp PO Box 3450 **Fax Area Code:* 508 ■ *TF:* 800-564-4377 ■ *Web:* www.onsetcomp.com	Pocasset	MA	02559	800-564-4377	759-9100*	201
Onset Marketing LLC 28525 Beck Rd Ste 125 *Web:* www.onsetmarketing.com	Wixom	MI	48393	248-596-9788		463
Onset Ventures 2400 Sand Hill Rd Ste 150 *Web:* onset.com	Menlo Park	CA	94025	650-529-0700	529-0777	792
Onset Worldwide LLC 843 SR-12 Ste B15 *Web:* onsetworldwide.com	Frenchtown	NJ	08825	908-777-5151		366
onShore Networks LLC 1407 W Chicago Ave *Web:* www.onshore.com	Chicago	IL	60642	312-850-5200		225
Onsite Energy Corp 2701 Loker Ave W Ste 107 *Web:* www.onsitenergy.com	Carlsbad	CA	92010	760-931-2400		192
Onsite Health Diagnostics 1199 S Beltline Rd Ste 120 *TF:* 877-366-7483 ■ *Web:* www.onsitehealthdiagnostics.com	Coppell	TX	75019	877-366-7483		416
Onsite Occupational Health & Safety Inc 101 N Hart St *TF:* 855-220-2441 ■ *Web:* www.onsiteohs.com	Princeton	IN	47670	812-770-4480		194

Phone | Fax | Class

Onslow County 4024 Richland Hwy........... Jacksonville NC 28540 910-347-4717 455-7878 338
Web: onslowcountync.gov

Onslow County Public Library
58 Doris Ave E.......................... Jacksonville NC 28540 910-455-7350 434-3
Web: www.onslowcountync.gov

Onslow County Tourism
1099 Gum Branch Rd.................... Jacksonville NC 28540 800-932-2144 347-4705* 206
**Fax Area Code:* 910 ■ *TF:* 800-932-2144 ■ *Web:* www.onlyinonslow.com

Onslow Memorial Hospital
317 Western Blvd........................ Jacksonville NC 28546 910-577-2345 374-3
Web: www.onslow.org

Ontario Area Chamber of Commerce
251 SW Ninth St............................. Ontario OR 97914 541-889-8012 889-8331 206
TF: 866-989-8012 ■ *Web:* www.ontariochamber.com

Ontario Association of Archietects
111 Moatfield Dr.......................... North York ON M3B3L6 416-449-6898 449-5756 138
TF: 800-565-2724 ■ *Web:* www.oaa.on.ca

Ontario Centres of Excellence Inc
156 Front St W Ste 200 .... Toronto ON M5J2L6 416-861-1092 217
TF: 866-759-6014 ■ *Web:* www.oce-ontario.org

Ontario Chamber of Commerce
3200 Inland Empire Blvd Ste 130................ Ontario CA 91764 909-984-2458 139
Web: ontario.org

Ontario Chamber of Commerce
180 Dundas St W Ste 505..................... Toronto ON M5G1Z8 416-482-5222 137
Web: www.occ.ca

Ontario Christian High School
931 W Philadelphia St .... Ontario CA 91762 909-984-1756 685
Web: www.ocschools.org

Ontario City Library 303 E B St .... Ontario CA 91764 909-395-2206 434-3
Web: www.ontarioca.gov

Ontario Clean Water Agency
1 Yonge St Ste 1700.......................... Toronto ON M5E1E5 416-775-0500 314-8300 192
TF: 800-667-6292 ■ *Web:* www.ocwa.com

Ontario College of Art & Design
100 McCaul St.............................. Toronto ON M5T1W1 416-977-6000 977-6006 785
TF: 800-382-6516 ■ *Web:* www.ocadu.ca

Ontario Convention & Visitors Bureau
2000 E Convention Center Way .... Ontario CA 91764 909-937-3000 937-3080 206
TF: 800-455-5755 ■ *Web:* www.ontariocc.org

Ontario County 20 Ontario St .... Canandaigua NY 14424 585-396-4200 338
TF: 800-247-7273 ■ *Web:* www.co.ontario.ny.us

Ontario Dental Nurses & Assistants Assn
869 Dundas St .... London ON N5W2Z8 519-679-2566 138
TF: 800-461-4348 ■ *Web:* odaa.org

Ontario Die Company of America
1755 Busha Hwy........................... Marysville MI 48040 810-987-5060 987-3688 757
Web: www.ontariodie.com

Ontario Drive & Gear Ltd (ODG)
220 Bergey Ct......................... New Hamburg ON N3A2J5 519-662-2840 29
TF: 877-274-6288 ■ *Web:* www.odg.com

Ontario Equestrian
1 W Pearce St Ste 201 .... Richmond Hill ON L4B3K3 905-709-6545 138
TF: 877-441-7112 ■ *Web:* ontarioequestrian.ca

Ontario Hockey Federation
400 Sheldon Dr Unit 9..................... Cambridge ON N1T2H9 226-533-9070 620-7476* 78
**Fax Area Code:* 519 ■ *Web:* www.ohf.on.ca

Ontario International Airport
1923 E Avion St .... Ontario CA 91761 909-544-5300 27
Web: lawa.org

Ontario Knife Co 26 Empire St .... Franklinville NY 14737 716-676-5527 299-2618* 222
**Fax Area Code:* 800 ■ *Web:* www.ontarioknife.com

Ontario Lottery & Gaming Corp
70 Foster Dr Ste 800................ Sault Sainte Marie ON P6A6V2 305-712-8052 642
TF: 800-563-5357 ■ *Web:* home.olg.ca

Ontario Medical Assn
150 Bloor St W Ste 900 .... Toronto ON M5S3C1 416-599-2580 78
Web: www.oma.org

Ontario Medical Supply Ltd
1100 Algoma Rd............................ Ottawa ON K1B0A3 613-244-8620 363
TF: 800-267-1069 ■ *Web:* www.oms.ca

Ontario Minor Hockey Assn
25 Brodie Dr Unit 3.................... Richmond Hill ON L4B3K7 905-780-6642 717
Web: www.omha.net

Ontario Northland Transportation Commission
555 Oak St E.............................. North Bay ON P1B8L3 705-472-4500 311
TF: 800-363-7512 ■ *Web:* ontarionorthland.ca

Ontario Nurses Assn
85 Grenville St Ste 400...................... Toronto ON M5S3A2 416-964-8833 414
TF: 800-387-5580 ■ *Web:* www.ona.org

Ontario Pc Party
59 Adelaide St E Ste 400 .... Toronto ON M5C1K6 416-861-0020 615
TF: 800-903-6453 ■ *Web:* www.ontariopc.ca

Ontario Real Estate Assn
99 Duncan Mill Rd .... Don Mills ON M3B1Z2 416-445-9910 652
TF: 866-444-5557 ■ *Web:* www.orea.com

Ontario Refrigeration Service
635 S Mountain Ave.......................... Ontario CA 91762 909-984-2771 610
Web: www.ontariorefrigeration.com

Ontario Research & Innovation Optical Network
211 Yonge St Second Fl .... Toronto ON M5B1M4 416-507-9860 507-9862 224
Web: www.orion.on.ca

Ontario Science Ctr 770 Don Mills Rd........... Toronto ON M3C1T3 416-696-1000 696-3166 520
TF: 888-696-1110 ■ *Web:* www.ontariosciencecentre.ca

Ontario Society of Professional Engineers
4950 Yonge St Ste 502.................... North York ON M2N6K1 416-223-9961 223-9963 261
TF: 866-763-1654 ■ *Web:* www.ospe.on.ca

Ontario Systems Corp
1150 W Kilgore Ave .... Muncie IN 47305 765-751-7000 751-7099 177
TF: 800-488-4420 ■ *Web:* www.ontariosystems.com

Ontario Tourism Marketing Partnership Corp
10 Dundas St E Ste 900 .... Toronto ON M7A2A1 905-282-1721 774
Web: www.ontariotravel.net

Ontario Universities Application Ctr (OUAC)
170 Research Ln............................. Guelph ON N1G5E2 519-823-1063 165
Web: www.ouac.on.ca

Ontash & Ermac Inc
876 Kndrkamak Rd Ste 201 .... River Edge NJ 07661 201-265-2189 224
Web: www.ontash.com

Ontellus 1010 Lamar 18th Fl .... Houston TX 77002 800-467-9181 467-0822 41
TF: 800-467-9181 ■ *Web:* www.ontellus.com

Ontility LLC
3403 N Sam Houston Pkwy Ste 300............. Houston TX 77086 281-854-1400 194
Web: www.ontility.com

Ontonagon County 725 Greenland Rd.......... Ontonagon MI 49953 906-884-4699 338
Web: www.ontonagoncounty.org

Ontonagon County Rural Assn
500 James K Paul St...................... Ontonagon MI 49953 906-884-4151 245
Web: www.countrylines.com

Ontor Ltd 12 Leswyn Rd .... Toronto ON M6A1K3 416-781-5286 664
TF: 800-567-1631 ■ *Web:* www.ontor.com

On-Track Computer Training Corp
609 Granville St Ste 450 PO Box 10381........ Vancouver BC V7Y1G6 604-683-0020 764
Web: www.on-track.com

OnTrack Inc 1968 Williams St Ste A .... Medford OR 97501 541-772-1777 734-2410 726
Web: www.ontrackrecovery.org

Onug Communications Inc
3315 Atlantic Ave .... Raleigh NC 27604 919-876-5455 876-5353 260
Web: onugsolutions.com

Ony Inc 1576 Sweet Home Rd.................. Amherst NY 14228 877-274-4669 582
TF: 877-274-4669 ■ *Web:* www.onyinc.com

Onyx Computing 10 Avon St .... Cambridge MA 02138 617-876-3876 178-8
Web: www.onyxtree.com

Onyx Hotel 155 Portland St .... Boston MA 02114 617-557-9955 557-0005 379
TF: 866-660-6699 ■ *Web:* www.onyxhotel.com

Onyx Meetings & Events Inc
7200 W 75th St........................ Overland Park KS 66204 913-831-7200 463
Web: www.onyxmeetingsandevents.com

Onyx Specialty Papers Inc
40 Willow St.............................. South Lee MA 01260 413-243-1231 243-4602 552-1
Web: onyxpapers.com

OO (Overseas Operations Inc)
222 Avenida del Norte Ste 201........... Redondo Beach CA 90277 310-540-4600 540-8382 44
Web: www.overseas-operations.com

OOGEEP (Ohio Oil & Gas Energy Education Program)
1718 Columbus Rd SW .... Granville OH 43023 740-587-0410 587-0408 423
Web: oogeep.org

Oohology 908 S Eighth St..................... Louisville KY 40203 502-416-0143 5
TF: 855-664-6564 ■ *Web:* www.oohology.com

Ooo La La! 2413 SE Dixie Hwy.................... Stuart FL 34996 772-233-0456 670
Web: ooolalacaters.com

Oostburg State Bank 905 Center Ave........... Oostburg WI 53070 920-564-2336 564-3889 70
Web: www.oostburgbank.com

OP Center, The 49 Eight Rod Rd................ Augusta ME 04330 207-632-3807 459
Web: www.theopcenter.com

OP Schuman & Sons Inc
2001 County Line Rd .... Warrington PA 18976 215-343-1530 343-1633 454
Web: www.opschuman.com

OPA Restaurant 230 Atwells Ave.............. Providence RI 02903 401-351-8282 671
Web: www.opaprovidence.com

Opac Consulting Engineers Inc
315 Bay St .... San Francisco CA 94133 415-989-4551 989-4135 261
Web: opacengineers.com

Opal Financial Group Inc
10 E 38th St 4th Fl .... New York NY 10016 212-532-9898 196
Web: opalgroup.net

Opal Soft 1288 Kifer Rd Ste 201............... Sunnyvale CA 94086 408-267-2211 225
TF: 800-632-2022 ■ *Web:* opalsoft.com

Opamp Labs Inc
1033 N Sycamore Ave..................... Los Angeles CA 90038 323-934-3566 462-6490 52
Web: www.opamplabs.com

OPB (Oregon Public Broadcasting Inc)
7140 SW Macadam Ave .... Portland OR 97219 503-244-9900 632
TF: 800-241-8123 ■ *Web:* www.opb.org

OPC (Overseas Press Club of America)
40 W 45th St.............................. New York NY 10036 212-626-9220 626-9210 49-14
Web: opcofamerica.org

OPCMIA (Operative Plasterers' & Cement Masons' International Assn)
9700 Patuxent Woods Dr Ste 200............. Columbia MD 21046 301-623-1000 623-1032 49-3
TF: 888-379-1558 ■ *Web:* www.opcmia.org

Opechee Construction Corp
11 Corporate Dr .... Belmont NH 03220 603-527-9090 186
Web: www.opechee.com

OPEI (Outdoor Power Equipment Institute)
341 S Patrick St .... Alexandria VA 22314 703-549-7600 49-4
Web: opei.org

Opelika-Auburn News
2901 Society Hill Rd......................... Opelika AL 36803 334-749-6271 749-1228 532-2
Web: www.oanow.com

Opelousas Public Libraries
212 E Grolee St........................... Opelousas LA 70570 337-948-3693 434-3
Web: opelousaspubliclibrary.org

OPEN (Offender Preparation & Education Network Inc)
PO Box 472223 .... Garland TX 75047 800-966-1966 278-5884* 637-2
**Fax Area Code:* 972 ■ *TF:* 800-966-1966 ■ *Web:* www.openinc.org

Open Air Cinema
1349 S 500 E Ste 203.................. American Fork UT 84042 866-442-4644 796-6806* 748
**Fax Area Code:* 801 ■ *TF:* 866-319-3280 ■ *Web:* www.openaircinema.us

Open Applications Group Inc (OAGI)
PO Box 4897 .... Marietta GA 30061 404-402-1962 740-0100* 49-13
**Fax Area Code:* 801 ■ *Web:* oagi.org

Open Arms Hospice
1836 W Georgia Rd .... Simpsonville SC 29680 864-688-1700 688-1705 371
TF: 866-473-6276 ■ *Web:* www.openarmshospice.org

Open Automation Software
5077 Bear Mtn Dr........................ Evergreen CO 80439 303-679-0898 179
TF: 800-533-4994 ■ *Web:* openautomationsoftware.com

Open City Inc
270 Lafayette St Ste 1412.................... New York NY 10012 212-625-9048 637-10
Web: www.opencity.org

Open Court Publishing Co
70 E Lake St Ste 800......................... Chicago IL 60601 800-815-2280 701-1728* 637-2
**Fax Area Code:* 312 ■ *TF:* 800-815-2280 ■ *Web:* www.opencourtbooks.com

Open Dental Software
3995 Fairview Industrial Dr SE Ste 110 .... Salem OR 97302 503-363-5432 177
TF: 866-239-0469 ■ *Web:* www.opendental.com

Name / Address	City	State	Zip	Phone	Fax	Class
Open Door Family Medical Center Inc 165 Main St *Web:* www.opendoormedical.org	Ossining	NY	10562	914-632-2737		352
Open Door Inc PO Box 855 *Web:* www.chestermichael.org	Charlottesville	VA	22902	434-242-2686		48-20
Open Door Mission 5803 Harrisburg Blvd *Web:* www.opendoorhouston.org	Houston	TX	77011	713-921-7520	921-4602	48-20
Open Geospatial Consortium Inc 35 Main St Ste 5 *Web:* www.ogc.org	Wayland	MA	01778	508-655-5858		138
Open Group 44 Montgomery St Ste 960 *TF:* 800-433-6611 ■ *Web:* www.opengroup.org	San Francisco	CA	94104	415-374-8280	374-8293	48-9
Open Hand Publishing LLC PO Box 20207 *TF:* 866-888-9229 ■ *Web:* www.openhand.com	Greensboro	NC	27420	336-292-8585	292-8588	637-2
Open Kitchens 1161 W 21st St *Web:* www.openkitchens.com	Chicago	IL	60608	312-666-5335		299
Open Logic Corp 28345 Beck Rd Ste 308 *Web:* www.open-logix.com	Wixom	MI	48393	248-869-0080		225
Open Mind Technologies USA Inc 1492 Highland Ave Unit 3 **Fax Area Code:* 270 ■ *TF:* 888-516-1232 ■ *Web:* www.openmind-tech.com	Needham	MA	02492	888-516-1232	912-5822*	178-1
Open Minds 163 York St *TF:* 877-350-6463 ■ *Web:* www.openminds.com	Gettysburg	PA	17325	717-334-1329		466
Open Options Corp 1203-20 Erb St W *Web:* www.openoptions.com	Waterloo	ON	N2L1T2	519-884-5898		463
Open Pantry Food Marts of Wisconsin 10505 Corporate Dr Ste 101 *Web:* www.openpantry.com	Pleasant Prairie	WI	53158	262-857-1156	857-9667	204
Open Plan Systems Inc 4700 Deepwater Terminal Rd *Web:* www.openplan.com	Richmond	VA	23234	804-275-2468	275-2329	319-1
Open Society Institute 400 W 59th St Ste 4 *Web:* www.opensocietyfoundations.org	New York	NY	10019	212-548-0600	548-4679	305
Open Space Institute (OSI) 1350 Broadway Ste 201 *Web:* www.openspaceinstitute.org	New York	NY	10018	212-290-8200	244-3441	48-13
Open Spatial Inc 5701 Lonetree Blvd Ste 211 *TF:* 800-696-1238 ■ *Web:* www.openspatial.com	Rocklin	CA	95765	800-696-1238		196
Open Storage Solutions Inc 2 Castleview Dr *TF:* 800-387-3419 ■ *Web:* www.openstore.com	Toronto	ON	L6T5S9	905-790-0660		174
Open Systems Inc 4301 Dean Lakes Blvd **Fax Area Code:* 952 ■ *TF:* 800-328-2276 ■ *Web:* www.osas.com	Shakopee	MN	55379	800-328-2276	403-5870*	178-1
Open Systems International Inc (OSI) 4101 Arrowhead Dri *Web:* www.osii.com	Medina	MN	55340	763-551-0559		809
Open Systems of Cleveland Inc 22999 Forbes Rd Ste A *TF:* 888-881-6660 ■ *Web:* www.osinc.com	Cleveland	OH	44146	440-439-2332	439-3794	174
Open Technology Solutions LLC 8085 S Chester St Ste 100 *Web:* www.open-techs.com	Centennial	CO	80112	303-708-7140		180
Open Text Corp 275 Frank Tompa Dr *NASDAQ:* OTEX ■ *TF:* 800-499-6544 ■ *Web:* www.opentext.com	Waterloo	ON	N2L0A1	519-888-7111	888-0677	178-7
Open Works 1400 Greenmount Ave *Web:* www.openworksbmore.com	Baltimore	MD	21202	410-862-0424		393
OpenBase International Ltd 4905 34th St S Ste 5500 *Web:* www.openbase.com	Saint Petersburg	FL	33711	863-450-3310		178-1
Openbay Inc 222 Third St Ste 4000 *TF:* 888-601-0399 ■ *Web:* www.openbay.com	Cambridge	MA	02142	888-601-0399		387
OpenCon Systems Inc 377 Hoes Ln *Web:* www.opencon.com	Piscataway	NJ	08854	732-463-3131	463-3557	178-7
Openet Telecom Inc 1886 Metro Center Dr Ste 310 *Web:* www.openet.com	Reston	VA	20190	703-480-1820		177
OpenEye Inc 23221 E Knox Ave *TF:* 888-542-1103 ■ *Web:* www.openeye.net	Liberty Lake	WA	99019	509-232-5261		692
OpenEye Scientific Software Inc 9 Bisbee Ct Ste D *Web:* www.eyesopen.com	Santa Fe	NM	87508	505-473-7385		174
OpenGate Capital 10250 Constellation Blvd 17th Fl *Web:* www.opengatecapital.com	Los Angeles	CA	90067	310-432-7000		792
Openjar Concepts Inc 27710 Jefferson Ave Ste 302 *Web:* www.openjar.com	Temecula	CA	92590	951-296-9222		7
OpenLink Software Inc 10 Burlington Mall Rd Ste 265 *Web:* www.openlinksw.com	Burlington	MA	01803	781-273-0900	229-8030	178-1
OPENonline 1650 Lake Shore Dr Ste 350 *TF:* 888-381-5656 ■ *Web:* www.openonline.com	Columbus	OH	43204	614-481-6999	481-6980	635
OpenRules Inc 53 Riveria Dr *Web:* openrules.com	Monroe Township	NJ	08831	732-993-3131		809
OpenSesame Inc 1629 SW Salmon St *Web:* www.opensesame.com	Portland	OR	97205	503-808-1268		387
OpenTable Inc 1 Montgomery St Ste 700 *Web:* www.opentable.com	San Francisco	CA	94104	415-344-4200		39
OpenTV Corp 275 Sacramento St *Web:* www.nagra.com	San Francisco	CA	94111	415-962-5000	962-5300	178-7
Openwave Systems Inc 400 Seaport Ct Ste 104 *Web:* owmobility.com	Redwood City	CA	94063	650-480-7200		178-7
OpenWorks 4742 N 24th St Ste 450 *TF:* 800-777-6736 ■ *Web:* www.openworksweb.com	Phoenix	AZ	85016	602-224-0440	468-3788	310
Opera Atelier 157 King St E *Web:* operaatelier.com	Toronto	ON	M5C1G9	416-703-3767		749
Opera Birmingham 3601 Sixth Ave S *Web:* www.operabirmingham.org	Birmingham	AL	35222	205-322-6737	322-6206	573-2
Opera Carolina 345 N College St Ste 409 *Web:* operacarolina.org	Charlotte	NC	28202	704-332-7177	332-6448	573-2
Opera Colorado 695 S Colorado Blvd Ste 20 *TF:* 800-414-2251 ■ *Web:* www.operacolorado.org	Denver	CO	80246	303-778-1500	778-0479	573-2
Opera Company of Brooklyn (OCB) 33 Indian Rd 600 W 218th St Ste 1G *Web:* operabrooklyn.org	New York	NY	10034	212-567-3283		573-2
Opera Company of North Carolina 612 Wade Ave Ste 100 *Web:* www.ncopera.org	Raleigh	NC	27605	919-792-3850		573-2
Opera Company of Philadelphia 1420 Locust St Ste 210 *Web:* www.operaphila.org	Philadelphia	PA	19102	215-893-3600	893-7801	573-2
Opera Memphis 6745 Wolf River Pkwy *Web:* www.operamemphis.org	Memphis	TN	38120	901-257-3100		573-2
Opera News Magazine 70 Lincoln Center Plz 6th Fl *Web:* www.operanews.com	New York	NY	10023	212-769-7080	769-8500	457-9
Opera Omaha 1850 Farnam St *Web:* www.operaomaha.org	Omaha	NE	68102	402-346-7372	346-7323	573-2
Opera Roanoke 541 Luck Ave *Web:* www.operaroanoke.org	Roanoke	VA	24016	540-982-2742		573-2
Opera San Jose 2149 Paragon Dr *TF:* 877-707-7827 ■ *Web:* www.operasj.org	San Jose	CA	95131	408-437-4450	437-4455	573-2
Opera Santa Barbara 1330 State St *Web:* www.operasb.org	Santa Barbara	CA	93101	805-898-3890	898-3892	573-2
Opera Theatre at Wildwood 20919 Denny Rd *Web:* connect2india.com	Little Rock	AR	72223	501-821-7275		573-2
OperaDelaware 4 S Poplar St *Web:* www.operade.org	Wilmington	DE	19801	302-658-8063		573-2
Operation Technology Inc 17 Goodyear Ste 100 *Web:* etap.com	Irvine	CA	92618	949-900-1000		177
Operation USA 7421 Beverly Blvd PH *TF:* 800-678-7255 ■ *Web:* www.opusa.org	Los Angeles	CA	90036	323-413-2353		48-5
Operational Innovations Inc 2060 Fairport 9 Mile Point Rd *Web:* www.op-in.com	Penfield	NY	14526	585-265-9000	377-1080	194
Operational Technologies Corp 4100 NW Loop 410 Ste 100 *Web:* www.otcorp.com	San Antonio	TX	78229	210-926-8888	731-0008	261
OperationsInc 535 Connecticut Ave 2nd Fl *TF:* 800-307-5513 ■ *Web:* www.operationsinc.com	Norwalk	CT	06854	203-322-0538		260
Operative Plasterers' & Cement Masons' International Assn (OPCMIA) 9700 Patuxent Woods Dr Ste 200 *TF:* 888-379-1558 ■ *Web:* www.opcmia.org	Columbia	MD	21046	301-623-1000	623-1032	49-3
Operator Interface Technology (OIT) 650 Weaver Park Rd *Web:* www.oitkeypad.com	Longmont	CO	80501	303-684-0094	684-0062	173-2
Opex Corp 305 Commerce Dr *TF:* 800-673-9288 ■ *Web:* www.opex.com	Moorestown	NJ	08057	856-727-1100	727-1955	178-10
OPGI (Original Parts Group Inc) 1770 Saturn Way *TF:* 800-243-8355 ■ *Web:* www.opgi.com	Seal Beach	CA	90740	562-594-1000	594-1050	54
Ophelia's on the Bay 9105 Midnight Pass Rd *Web:* opheliasonthebay.net	Siesta Key	FL	34242	941-349-2212		671
Region I John F Kennedy Federal Bldg Rm 2100 *Web:* www.hhs.gov	Boston	MA	02203	617-565-1491		340-10
Ophthalmic Consultants of Boston Inc 50 Staniford St Ste 600 *TF:* 800-635-0489 ■ *Web:* www.eyeboston.com	Boston	MA	02114	617-367-4800		543
Ophthalmic Instrument Company Inc (OIC) 50 Strafello Dr *TF:* 800-272-2070 ■ *Web:* www.oic2020.com	Avon	MA	02322	781-341-2070	341-5060	542
Ophthalmic Instrument Inc (OII) 3322 Arden Rd *TF:* 800-728-6895 ■ *Web:* www.oiica.com	Hayward	CA	94545	510-265-1389		542
Ophthalmic Intl 16857 E Saguaro Blvd *Web:* www.oi-pnt.com	Fountain Hills	AZ	85268	480-837-6165	837-6870	502
Ophthalmic Plastic & Reconstructive Surgery 1615 Ellis St *Web:* www.oprsbilling.com	Kewaunee	WI	54216	920-388-2788		2
OPIC (Overseas Private Investment Corp) 1100 New York Ave NW *TF:* 800-225-5722 ■ *Web:* www.opic.gov	Washington	DC	20527	202-336-8400	408-9859	340-20
Opici Import Co 25 Deboer Dr *Web:* www.opici.com	Glen Rock	NJ	07452	201-689-1200		80-3
Opies Transport Inc 21 Hwy FF PO Box 89 *TF:* 800-341-9963 ■ *Web:* opiestransport.com	Eldon	MO	65026	573-392-6525		768
Opinion Access Corp 47-10 32nd Pl *Web:* www.opinionaccess.com	Long Island City	NY	11101	718-729-2622		225
Opinion Centers America Inc 896 Corporate Way *TF:* 800-779-3003 ■ *Web:* www.opinioncenters.com	Westlake	OH	44145	440-779-3000		466
Opis Management Resources 10150 Highlands Manor Dr Ste 300 *Web:* www.opismr.com	Tampa	FL	33610	813-558-6600		371
OPL (Oxnard Public Library) 4300 Saviers Rd *Web:* www.oxnard.org	Oxnard	CA	93033	805-247-8937	488-1336	434-3
OPM (Office of Personnel Management) 1900 E St NW *Web:* www.opm.gov	Washington	DC	20415	202-606-1800		340-20
Opmedic Group Inc 1361 Beaumont Ave Ste 300 *TF:* 888-776-2732 ■ *Web:* www.opmedic.com	Mount Royal	QC	H3P2W3	514-345-8535		418
Opotek Inc 2233 Faraday Ave Ste E *Web:* www.opotek.com	Carlsbad	CA	92008	760-929-0770	929-8782	544
Opp & Seibold General Construction Inc 1220 W Poplar St *Web:* www.oppseibold.com	Walla Walla	WA	99362	509-525-1373		186

Name / Address	City	State	ZIP	Phone	Fax	Class
OPPD (Omaha Public Power District) 444 S 16th St Mall *Web:* www.oppd.com	Omaha	NE	68102	402-536-4131		192
Oppenheim & Nickerson LLP 156 Locust St *Web:* onllplaw.com	Falmouth	MA	02540	508-548-8255		41
Oppenheimer & Company Inc 300 Madison Ave *Web:* www.oppenheimer.com	New York	NY	10017	212-885-4646		401
Oppenheimer Companies Inc 877 W Main Ste 700 *TF:* 800-727-9939 ■ *Web:* www.oppcos.com	Boise	ID	83702	208-343-4883		297-8
Oppenheimer Precision Products 173 Gibraltar Rd *Web:* www.oppiprecision.com	Horsham	PA	19044	215-674-9100	674-0423	253
Opportune 711 Louisiana Ste 3100 *Web:* opportune.com	Houston	TX	77002	713-490-5050		539
Opportunities for a Better Tomorrow 783 4th Ave *TF:* 800-662-1220 ■ *Web:* www.obtjobs.org	Brooklyn	NY	11232	718-369-0303	369-1518	167-3
Opportunity Finance Network 620 Chestnut St Ste 572 *Web:* ofn.org	Philadelphia	PA	19106	215-923-4754	923-4755	49-7
Opportunity Management Inc (OMI) 15455 NW Greenbrier Pky Ste 210 *TF:* 888-664-4408 ■ *Web:* www.sales-tools.com	Beaverton	OR	97075	503-626-5312	614-0565	194
Opposing Views Inc 371 Dalkeith Ave *Web:* www.opposingviews.com	Los Angeles	CA	90049	310-433-3833		5
Oproma Inc 116 Avenue Gatineau *Web:* oproma.com	Gatineau	QC	J8T4J6	819-568-4069		180
OPS (Oilfield Pipe and Supply Inc) 7227 Devonshire **Fax Area Code:* 314 ■ *TF:* 800-783-7477 ■ *Web:* www.oilfieldpipe.com	Shrewsbury	MO	63119	800-783-7477	771-3177*	612
Opsahl Dawson & Company PS 959 11th Ave Ste A *Web:* opsahlco.com	Longview	WA	98632	360-425-2000		2
OPSD (Oak Park School District) 13900 Granzon *Web:* www.oakparkschools.org	Oak Park	MI	48237	248-336-7700	336-7738	360-2
OpSec Security Inc 1857 Colonial Village Ln *Web:* www.opsecsecurity.com	Lancaster	PA	17601	717-293-4110		693
Opsol Integrators Inc 1566 La Pradera Dr *Web:* www.opsol.com	Campbell	CA	95008	408-364-9915		180
OPSWAT Inc 398 Kansas St *Web:* www.opswat.com	San Francisco	CA	94103	415-590-7300		177
OPT (Oceanside Photo & Telescope) 918 Mission Ave *TF:* 800-483-6287 ■ *Web:* optcorp.com	Oceanside	CA	92054	760-400-0164		179
Optek Systems Inc 12 Pilgrim Rd *Web:* www.opteksystems.com	Greenville	SC	29607	864-272-2640	272-2630	544
Optel Vision Inc 2680 Boul du Parc Technologique *TF:* 800-100-5995 ■ *Web:* www.optelpharmaceutical.com	Quebec City	QC	G1P4S6	418-688-0334	688-9397	407
Optelian Inc 1700 Enterprise Way SE Ste 101 *Web:* www.optelian.com	Marietta	GA	30067	770-690-9575		735
Optessa Inc 5555 Calgary Trl NW Ste 1045 *Web:* www.optessa.com	Edmonton	AB	T6H5P9	780-431-8426		179
Optex Inc 13661 Benson Ave Bldg C *TF:* 800-966-7839 ■ *Web:* www.optexamerica.com	Chino	CA	91710	909-993-5770	628-5560	692
Optex Systems Holdings Inc 1420 Presidential Dr *OTC:* OPXS ■ *Web:* www.optexsys.com	Richardson	TX	75081	972-644-0722	234-3544	502
Opti Staffing Group 3601 C St Ste 1220 *Web:* www.optistaffing.com	Anchorage	AK	99503	907-677-9675		260
Optical Cable Corp (OCC) 5290 Concourse Dr *NASDAQ:* OCC ■ *TF:* 800-622-7711 ■ *Web:* www.occfiber.com	Roanoke	VA	24019	540-265-0690	265-0724	814
Optical Data Associates LLC 5237 E 7th St *Web:* www.opdata.com	Tucson	AZ	85711	520-748-7333		743
Optical Discount Corp 12020 Mora Dr *Web:* www.icoatcompany.com	Santa Fe Springs	CA	90670	562-946-3050		31
Optical Dynamics Corp 1950 Production Ct **Fax Area Code:* 888 ■ *TF:* 800-587-2743 ■ *Web:* www.opticaldynamics.com	Louisville	KY	40299	502-671-2020	900-5504*	544
Optical Fashions 3617 Dayton Xenia Rd *Web:* www.optical-fashions.com	Dayton	OH	45432	937-429-2270		543
Optical Filters 13447 S Mosiertown Rd Ste A *Web:* www.opticalfiltersusa.com	Meadville	PA	16335	814-333-2222	333-4338	599
Optical Gaging Products Inc 850 Hudson Ave *TF:* 800-647-4243 ■ *Web:* www.ogpnet.com	Rochester	NY	14621	585-544-0450	544-4998	544
Optical Image Technology Inc 328 Innovation Blvd Ste 200 *TF:* 800-678-3241 ■ *Web:* www.docfinity.com	State College	PA	16803	814-238-0038		177
Optical Physics Co 4133 Guardian St **Fax Area Code:* 805 ■ *Web:* www.opci.com	Simi Valley	CA	93063	818-880-2907	578-3428*	237
Optical Society of America (OSA) 2010 Massachusetts Ave NW *TF:* 800-766-4672 ■ *Web:* www.osa.org	Washington	DC	20036	202-223-8130	223-1096	49-8
Optical Supply Inc 1526 Plainfield Ave NE *Web:* www.essilorlabs.com	Grand Rapids	MI	49505	616-361-7177		544
Optical Telecom 16837 Addison Rd Ste 400 *Web:* optelsol.com	Addison	TX	75001	972-931-0360		224
OptiCare PC 87 Grandview Ave *TF:* 800-225-5393 ■ *Web:* opticarepc.com	Waterbury	CT	06708	203-574-2020	596-2230	543
OptiCat LLC 1204 W S Jordan Pkwy Ste C2 *Web:* www.opticat.net	South Jordan	UT	84095	801-542-0560		393
Opticians Association of America (OAA) 3740 Canada Rd *Web:* oaa.org	Lakeland	TN	38002	901-388-2423	388-2348	49-8
Opti-Com Manufacturing Network LLC 259 Plauche St *Web:* opti-com.info	Harahan	LA	70123	504-736-0331	733-9046	246
Opticote Inc 10455 Seymour *TF:* 800-248-6784 ■ *Web:* www.opticote.com	Franklin Park	IL	60131	847-678-8900		484
Opti-Craft 12130 NE Ainsworth Cir Ste 260 **Fax Area Code:* 800 ■ *TF:* 800-288-8048 ■ *Web:* essilorlabs.com	Portland	OR	97230	503-256-5330	873-3291*	544
Optim LLC 64 Technology Park Rd *Web:* www.optim-llc.com	Sturbridge	MA	01566	508-347-5100		544
Optima Alliance LLC 4501 Forbes Blvd Ste 200 *Web:* optimaalliance.com	Lanham	MD	20706	301-577-3900		366
Optima Chemical Group LLC 200 Willacoochee Hwy *Web:* optimachem.com	Douglas	GA	31535	912-384-5101		146
Optima Global Solutions Inc 3131 Princeton Pk Ste 207 *Web:* www.optimags.com	Lawrenceville	NJ	08648	609-586-8811		177
Optima Graphics Inc 1540 Fencorp Ct *Web:* www.optimagfx.com	Fenton	MO	63026	636-349-3396		344
Optima Group Inc 2150 Post Rd *Web:* www.optimagroupinc.com	Fairfield	CT	06824	203-255-1066		194
Optima Health 4417 Corporation Ln *Web:* www.optimahealth.com	Virginia Beach	VA	23462	757-552-7174		391-3
Optima Neuroscience Inc 13400 Progress Blvd *Web:* www.optimaneuro.com	Alachua	FL	32615	352-371-8281		476
Optima Telecom Inc 4-20 Cachet Woods Ct *Web:* www.optimatele.com	Markham	ON	L6C3G1	905-477-0987		180
Optimae LifeServices Inc 301 W Burlington Ave *TF:* 800-735-2942 ■ *Web:* www.optimaelifeservices.com	Fairfield	IA	52556	641-472-1684		363
Optimal Control Systems Inc 2324 Three Lakes Rd SE *Web:* www.optimalcontrol.net	Albany	OR	97322	541-967-9323	967-9485	729
Optimal Data Group Inc 251 Laurier Ave W Ste 900 *Web:* www.optimal.ca	Ottawa	ON	K1P5J6	613-566-7080		180
Optimal Electronics Corp 13915 Burnet Rd Ste 312 *Web:* www.optelco.com	Austin	TX	78728	512-372-3415	372-3416	177
Optimal Engineering Systems 6901 Woodley Ave *TF:* 888-777-1826 ■ *Web:* oesincorp.com	Van Nuys	CA	91406	818-222-9200		358
Optimal Hospice Care 1675 Chester Ave Ste 401 *Web:* www.optimalcares.com	Bakersfield	CA	93301	661-716-4000	716-4004	363
Optimal Networks Inc 15201 Diamondback Dr Ste 220 *Web:* www.optimalnetworks.com	Rockville	MD	20850	240-499-7900		809
Optimal Outsource 7 Rancho Cir *Web:* optimaloutsource.com	Lake Forest	CA	92630	949-916-3700		41
Optimal Satcom Inc 600 Herndon Pkwy Ste 100 *TF:* 888-430-4050 ■ *Web:* www.optimalsatcom.com	Herndon	VA	20170	703-657-8800	547-0145	196
Optimal Strategix Group Inc 140 Terry Dr Ste 118 *Web:* www.osganalytics.com	Newtown	PA	18940	215-867-1880		196
Optimation Inc 18600 E 37th Terr S *TF:* 877-827-2100 ■ *Web:* www.optinest.com	Independence	MO	64057	816-228-2100		178-1
Optimetra Inc 1710 Chapel Hills Dr *TF:* 800-758-9710 ■ *Web:* www.optimetra.com	Colorado Springs	CO	80920	800-758-9710		225
Optimist Intl 4494 Lindell Blvd *TF:* 800-500-8130 ■ *Web:* www.optimist.org	Saint Louis	MO	63108	314-371-6000	371-6006	48-15
Optimization Group Inc 320 S Main St Ste D *Web:* www.optimizationgroup.com	Ann Arbor	MI	48104	734-212-2044		7
Optimized Process Designs LLC 25610 Clay Rd *Web:* www.opdepc.com	Katy	TX	77493	281-371-7500		261
Optimum Asset Management Inc 425 De Maisonneuve Blvd W Ste 1620 *Web:* www.optimumgestion.com	Montreal	QC	H3A3G5	514-288-7545		528
Optimum Card Solution LLC 855 S Fiene Dr *Web:* www.optimumcard.com	Addison	IL	60101	630-458-0077	458-0022	317
Optimum Computer Solutions Inc 780 Westridge Rd *Web:* ocscorp.com	The Woodlands	TX	77380	281-364-0539		224
Optimum Engineering Solutions Inc 1 Country Club View Dr *Web:* www.openso.com	Edwardsville	IL	62025	618-656-8600	656-1700	256
Optimum Financial & Tax Services 500 Rahway Ave *Web:* optimumfinancialtax.com	Elizabeth	NJ	07202	908-289-0082		734
Optimum Health Institute 6970 Central Ave *TF:* 800-993-4325 ■ *Web:* www.optimumhealth.org	Lemon Grove	CA	91945	619-464-3346		706
Optimum Logistic Solutions 3540 Seven Bridges Dr Ste 300 *TF:* 800-356-0595 ■ *Web:* www.optimumlogistic.com	Woodridge	IL	60517	630-350-0595	766-3479	631
Optimum Outsourcing LLC 2530 Red Hill Ave Ste 200 *Web:* optimumhr.net	Santa Ana	CA	92705	949-650-7800		631
Optimum Solutions Corp 170 Earle Ave *TF:* 800-227-0672 ■ *Web:* www.oscworld.com	Lynbrook	NY	11563	516-247-5300		177
Optimum Talent Inc 25 York St Ste 1802 *TF:* 888-237-2060 ■ *Web:* optimumtalent.com	Toronto	ON	M5J2V5	416-364-2605		764

Phone Fax Class

Optimum Technologies Inc
570 Joe Frank Harris Pkwy PO Box 1537 Cartersville GA 30120 770-386-3470 382-9047 234
Web: www.otitech.com

Optimum Technologies Inc
114 Pleasant St Southbridge MA 01550 508-765-8100 261
Web: optimum-tech.com

Optimum Technology Inc
100 E Campus View Blvd Ste 380 Columbus OH 43235 614-785-1110 177
Web: otech.com

Optimum Window Manufacturing
28 Canal St Ellenville NY 12428 845-647-1900 234
Web: optimumwindow.com

OPTIMUS | SBR 30 Adelaide St E Ste 600 Toronto ON M5C3G8 416-649-6000 463
Web: optimussbr.com

Optimus Corp 5727 S Lewis Ave Ste 600 Tulsa OK 74105 918-491-9191 480
Web: www.optimus-tulsa.com

Optimus Health Care Inc
982 E Main St Bridgeport CT 06608 203-696-3260 353
Web: www.optimushealthcare.org

Optimus Inc 161 E Grand Ave Chicago IL 60611 312-276-2661 512
Web: www.optimus.com

Optimus Information Inc
510-900 Howe St Vancouver BC V6Z2M4 604-736-4600 631
Web: www.optimusinfo.com

Optimus Solutions LLC
22 Technology Pk S Norcross GA 30092 770-447-1951 196
Web: www.softchoice.com

OptiNose US Inc
1010 Stony Hill Rd Ste 375 Yardley PA 19067 267-364-3500 475
Web: www.optinose.com

Options Credit Union
5935 S Zang St Unit 4 Littleton CO 80127 303-860-1117 219
Web: optionscreditunion.com

Options For Senior America Corp
555 Quince Orchard Rd Gaithersburg MD 20878 301-562-1100 363
Web: optionscorp.com

Options Group Inc 121 E 18th St New York NY 10003 212-982-0900 982-5577 193
Web: www.optionsgroup.com

Options University LLC
925 S Federal Hwy Ste 510 Boca Raton FL 33432 866-561-8227 166
TF: 866-561-8227 ■ *Web:* www.optionsuniversity.com

OptionsXpress Inc
311 W Monroe Ste 1000 Chicago IL 60606 888-280-8020 629-5256* 169
**Fax Area Code:* 312 ■ *TF:* 888-280-8020 ■ *Web:* www.optionsxpress.com

Optistreams Inc
381 W Warwick Ave Ste 68 Clovis CA 93611 559-440-6366 354-8487* 396
**Fax Area Code:* 415 ■ *Web:* www.optistreams.com

Optiva Inc
2233 Argentia Rd East Tower Ste 302 Mississauga ON L5N2X7 905-625-2622 736
Web: optiva.com

Optiwave Systems Inc 7 Capella Ct Ottawa ON K2E7X1 613-224-4700 179
TF: 866-576-6784 ■ *Web:* optiwave.com

Opto 22 Inc 43044 Business Park Dr Temecula CA 92590 951-695-3000 201
TF: 800-321-6786 ■ *Web:* www.opto22.com

OptoAtmospherics Inc
1777 Highland Dr Ste B Ann Arbor MI 48108 734-975-8777 407
Web: www.optoatmospherics.com

Optometrics Corp
8 Nemco Way Stony Brook Industrial Pk Ayer MA 01432 978-772-1700 544
Web: www.dynasil.com

Optoplex Corp 3374-3390 Gateway Blvd Fremont CA 94538 510-490-9930 735
Web: www.optoplex.com

Optoro Inc 1001 G St NW Ste 1200 Washington DC 20001 301-760-7003 393
Web: www.optoro.com

Optovue Inc 2800 Bayview Dr Fremont CA 94538 866-344-8948 543
TF: 866-344-8948 ■ *Web:* www.optovue.com

OPT-Sciences Corp 1912 Bannard St Cinnaminson NJ 08077 856-829-2800 829-0482 544
TF: 800-733-1121 ■ *Web:* www.optsciences.com

Opttech.com 2875 Idlewild Dr Unit 10 Reno NV 89509 775-348-8008 348-8009 178-1
Web: www.opttech.com

OptumHealth Allies PO Box 1459 Minneapolis MN 55414 800-860-8773 405-2193* 352
**Fax Area Code:* 855 ■ *TF:* 800-860-8773 ■ *Web:* www.optumhealthallies.com

Opus 21 Management Solutions
680 Commerce Dr Ste 160 Saint Paul MN 55125 651-905-0400 2
Web: www.opus21ms.com

Opus Agency 9000 SW Nimbus Ave Beaverton OR 97008 971-223-0777 195
TF: 888-887-8908 ■ *Web:* www.opusagency.com

Opus Bank 19900 MacArthur Blvd 12th Fl Irvine CA 92612 949-250-9800 360-2
TF: 855-678-7226 ■ *Web:* www.opusbank.com

Opus Capital Management LLC
221 E Fourth St Ste 2700 Cincinnati OH 45202 513-621-6787 401
Web: www.opusinc.com

Opus Framing Ltd 3445 Cornett Rd Vancouver BC V5M2H3 604-435-9991 435-9941 535
TF: 800-663-6953 ■ *Web:* www.opusartsupplies.com

Opus Group of Cos 10350 Bren Rd W Minnetonka MN 55343 952-656-4444 186
Web: www.opus-group.com

Opus Hotel 322 Davie St Vancouver BC V6B5Z6 866-642-6787 379
TF: 866-642-6787 ■ *Web:* vancouver.opushotel.com

Opus Interactive
1225 W Burnside St Ste 310 Portland OR 97209 503-972-6677 225
TF: 866-678-7955 ■ *Web:* opusinteractive.com

Opus One 565 E Larned St Detroit MI 48226 313-961-7766 671
Web: www.opus-one.com

Opus Restaurant 37 Prince Arthur Ave Toronto ON M5R1B2 416-921-3105 671
Web: www.opusrestaurant.com

Opvantek Inc 28 S State St Newtown PA 18940 215-968-7790 463
Web: www.opvantek.com

OPW, A Dover Co
9393 Princeton-Glendale Rd Hamilton OH 45011 800-422-2525 421-3297 145
TF: 800-422-2525 ■ *Web:* www.opwglobal.com

Oquaga Creek State Park
5995 County Rt 20 Bainbridge NY 13733 607-467-4160 565
Web: parks.ny.gov

OR Co, The 1625 S Tacoma Way Tacoma WA 98409 253-441-6509 333-9524* 475
**Fax Area Code:* 866 ■ *Web:* theorcompany.com

Oracle Applications & Technology Users Group
3525 Piedmont Rd NE Bldg 5 Ste 300 Atlanta GA 30305 404-240-0897 177
Web: www.oatug.org

Oracle Capital LLC
1985 E River Rd Ste 111 Tucson AZ 85718 520-319-9958 668
Web: www.oraclecapital.com

Oracle Corp 500 Oracle Pkwy Redwood City CA 94065 800-633-0738 506-7200* 178-1
NYSE: ORCL ■ **Fax Area Code:* 650 ■ *TF:* 800-392-2999 ■ *Web:* www.oracle.com

Oracle Packaging 220 Polo Rd Winston-Salem NC 27105 888-260-3947 777-5440* 548
**Fax Area Code:* 336 ■ *TF:* 800-634-3645 ■ *Web:* www.tekni-plex.com

Oracle State Park 3820 Wildlife Dr Oracle AZ 85623 520-896-2425 565
Web: azstateparks.com

Oradell Animal Hospital Inc
580 Winters Ave Paramus NJ 07652 201-262-0010 794
TF: 800-624-1883 ■ *Web:* www.oradell.com

ORAFOL Americas Inc 1100 Oracal Pkwy Ellabell GA 31308 888-672-2251 496
TF: 888-672-2251 ■ *Web:* www.orafol.com

Oral Arts Dental Laboratory Inc
2700 S Memorial Pkwy Huntsville AL 35801 256-533-6670 415
Web: www.oralartsdental.com

Oral Health America
180 N Michigan Ave Ste 1150 Chicago IL 60601 312-836-9900 836-9986 48-17
TF: 800-523-3438 ■ *Web:* oralhealthamerica.org

OralDNA Labs Inc
7400 Flying Cloud Dr Ste 150 Eden Prairie MN 55344 952-400-7772 415
Web: www.oraldna.com

Oran Safety Glass Inc
48 Industrial Pkwy Emporia VA 23847 434-336-1620 329
Web: www.osg.co.il

Orange & Rockland Utilities Inc
390 W Rte 59 Spring Valley NY 10977 877-434-4100 787
TF: 877-434-4100 ■ *Web:* www.oru.com

Orange Bakery Inc 17751 Cowan Ave Irvine CA 92614 949-863-1377 863-1932 68
Web: orangebakery.com

Orange Belt Stages PO Box 949 Visalia CA 93279 559-733-4408 733-0538 760
TF: 800-266-7433 ■ *Web:* www.orangebelt.com

Orange Chamber of Commerce
1940 N Tustin St Orange CA 92865 714-538-3581 532-1675 139
TF: 888-676-1040 ■ *Web:* www.orangechamber.com

Orange City Area Health System
1000 Lincoln Cir SE Orange City IA 51041 712-737-4984 374-3
TF: 800-808-6264 ■ *Web:* www.ochealthsystem.org

Orange Coast Chrysler Jeep Dodge
2929 Harbor Blvd Costa Mesa CA 92626 714-549-8023 57
TF: 877-291-5568 ■ *Web:* www.ocauto.com

Orange Coast College
2701 Fairview Rd PO Box 5005 Costa Mesa CA 92628 714-432-0202 162
Web: orangecoastcollege.edu

Orange Coast Magazine
3701 Birch St Ste 100 Newport Beach CA 92660 949-862-1133 862-0133 457-22
TF: 800-397-8179 ■ *Web:* www.orangecoast.com

Orange Coast Title Company Inc
640 N Tustin Ave Ste 106 Santa Ana CA 92705 714-558-2836 391-6
Web: www.octitle.com

Orange Correctional Ctr
2110 Clarence Walters Rd Hillsborough NC 27278 919-732-9301 644-1395 213
Web: www.ncdps.gov

Orange County 1055 N Main St Santa Ana CA 92701 714-347-8118 338
TF: 855-886-5400 ■ *Web:* www.css.ocgov.com

Orange County 255 Main St Goshen NY 10924 845-291-2700 291-2724 338
Web: www.orangecountygov.com

Orange County
200 S Cameron St PO Box 8181 Hillsborough NC 27278 919-732-8181 338
Web: www.co.orange.nc.us

Orange County 9227 Cajun Way Orange TX 77630 409-882-7055 882-7012 338
Web: www.co.orange.tx.us

Orange County 200 Dailey Dr Orange VA 22960 540-661-4550 661-4599 338
TF: 866-803-8641 ■ *Web:* www.ocss-va.org

Orange County
201 S Rosalind Ave 5th Fl Orlando FL 32802 407-836-7350 836-5879 338
TF: 888-949-3303 ■ *Web:* www.orangecountyfl.net

Orange County 3568 N County Rd 100 W Paoli IN 47454 812-723-2411 723-0239 338
Web: www.co.orange.in.us

Orange County 12 Civic Center Plz Santa Ana CA 92702 714-834-2500 834-2675 338
Web: www.ocgov.com

Orange County Bartending School
1819 E Chapman Ave Orange CA 92867 714-289-8600 266-8440 685
Web: www.orangebartendingschool.com

Orange County Business Council
2 Park Plz Ste 100 Irvine CA 92614 949-476-2242 476-9240 139
Web: www.ocbc.org

Orange County Business Journal (OCBJ)
18500 Von Karman Ave Ste 150 Irvine CA 92612 949-833-8373 833-8751 457-5
Web: www.ocbj.com

Orange County Chamber of Commerce
30 Scott's Corners Dr Montgomery NY 12549 845-457-9700 457-8799 139
Web: orangeny.com

Orange County Community College
115 S St Middletown NY 10940 845-344-6222 342-8662 162
TF: 866-694-4700 ■ *Web:* www.sunyorange.edu

Orange County Convention Ctr (OCCC)
9800 International Dr Orlando FL 32819 407-685-9800 685-9876 205
TF: 800-345-9845 ■ *Web:* www.occc.net

Orange County Genealogical Society (OCGS)
101 Main St Goshen NY 10924 845-294-5871 49-19
Web: www.ocgsny.org

Orange County Industrial Plastics Inc
4811 E La Palma Ave Anaheim CA 92807 800-974-6247 630-6489* 603
**Fax Area Code:* 714 ■ *TF:* 800-974-6247 ■ *Web:* www.ocip.com

Orange County Library System
101 E Central Blvd Orlando FL 32801 407-835-7611 434-3
Web: oclsfriends.info

Orange County Public Library
1501 E St Andrew Pl Santa Ana CA 92705 714-566-3000 434-3
Web: www.ocpl.org

Orange County Public Schools
445 W Amelia St Orlando FL 32801 407-317-3200 317-3392 685
TF: 800-378-9264 ■ *Web:* www.ocps.net

Orange County Regional History Ctr
65 E Central Blvd Orlando FL 32801 407-836-8500 520
Web: www.thehistorycenter.org

Phone | Fax | Class

Orange County Register, The
2190 S Towne Center Pl ..... Anaheim CA 92806 714-796-7000 532-2
Web: www.ocregister.com

Orange County Rural Electric Membership Corp
7133 N State Rd 337 PO Box 208 ..... Orleans IN 47452 812-865-2229 865-2061 245
TF: 888-337-5900 ■ *Web:* www.myremc.coop

Orange County Transportation Authority
550 S Main St PO Box 14184 ..... Orange CA 92863 714-560-6282 468
TF: 800-600-9191 ■ *Web:* www.octa.net

Orange County Zoo 1 Irvine Park Rd ..... Orange CA 92869 714-973-6847 823
Web: www.ocparks.com

Orange County's Credit Union
PO Box 11777 ..... Santa Ana CA 92711 714-755-5900 219
TF: 888-354-6228 ■ *Web:* www.orangecountyscu.org

Orange Door Inc
370 San Bruno Ave W Ste E ..... San Bruno CA 94066 650-952-1773 396

Orange Empire Railway Museum (OERM)
2201 S A St ..... Perris CA 92570 951-943-3020 943-2676 520
Web: www.oerm.org

Orange Enterprises Inc
2377 W Shaw Ste 205 ..... Fresno CA 93711 559-229-2195 229-9348 178-1
TF: 800-656-7264 ■ *Web:* www.orangesoftware.com

Orange Fence & Supply
205 Boston Post Rd ..... Orange CT 06477 203-904-2272 200
TF: 844-703-4267 ■ *Web:* www.orangefence.com

Orange Frazer Press Inc
37 1/2 W Main St ..... Wilmington OH 45177 937-382-3196 383-3159 637-2
Web: www.orangefrazer.com

Orange Label Art & Advrtg
4000 MacArthur Blvd Ste 520 ..... Newport Beach CA 92660 949-631-9900 4
Web: orangelabeladvertising.com

Orange Line Oil Company Inc
404 E Commercial St ..... Pomona CA 91767 909-623-0533 579
TF: 800-492-6864 ■ *Web:* www.orangelineoil.com

Orange Park Medical Ctr
2001 Kingsley Ave ..... Orange Park FL 32073 904-639-8500 374-3
TF: 855-432-7285 ■ *Web:* orangeparkmedical.com

Orange Products Inc 1929 Vultee St ..... Allentown PA 18103 610-791-9711 791-9531 604
Web: orangeproducts.com

Orange Public Library 348 Main St ..... Orange NJ 07050 973-673-0153 673-1847 434-3
Web: www.orangepl.org

Orange Public Library
407 E Chapmen Ave ..... Orange CA 92866 714-288-2400 771-6126 434-3
Web: www.cityoforange.org

Orange Regional Medical Ctr
707 E Main St ..... Middletown NY 10940 845-343-2424 333-1560 374-3
TF: 888-321-6762 ■ *Web:* www.ormc.org

Orange Research Inc 140 Cascade Blvd ..... Milford CT 06460 203-877-5657 201
TF: 800-989-5657 ■ *Web:* www.orangeresearch.com

Orange Street Food Farm
701 S Orange St ..... Missoula MT 59801 406-543-3188 345
Web: orangestreetfoodfarm.com

Orange Tree Employment Screening
7275 Ohms Ln ..... Minneapolis MN 55439 800-886-4777 941-9041* 635
**Fax Area Code:* 952 ■ *TF:* 800-886-4777 ■ *Web:* www.orangetreescreening.com

Orange Water & Sewer Authority (Inc)
400 Jones Ferry Rd ..... Carrboro NC 27510 919-968-4421 968-4464 787
Web: www.owasa.org

Orangeburg County 1406 Amelia St ..... Orangeburg SC 29118 803-533-6160 531-7256 338
Web: orangeburgcounty.org

Orangeburg County Chamber of Commerce
155 Riverside Dr SW PO Box 328 ..... Orangeburg SC 29116 803-534-6821 531-9435 139
TF: 800-545-6153 ■ *Web:* orangeburgchamber.com

Orangeburg County School District
102 Founders Ct ..... Orangeburg SC 29115 803-534-5454 533-7953 685
Web: www.ocsdsc.org

Orangeburg Pecan Company Inc
761 Russell St ..... Orangeburg SC 29115 800-845-6970 276
TF: 800-845-6970 ■ *Web:* uspecans.com

Orangeburg Public Library
20 S Greenbush Rd ..... Orangeburg NY 10962 845-359-2244 435
Web: www.orangeburg-library.org

Orangeburg-Calhoun Technical College
3250 St Matthews Rd ..... Orangeburg SC 29118 803-536-0311 162
Web: www.octech.edu

Orangeseed Design Inc
901 N Third St Ste 305 ..... Minneapolis MN 55401 612-252-9757 4
Web: www.orangeseed.com

OrangeSoda Inc
732 E Utah Vly Dr ..... American Fork UT 84003 801-610-2500 195
Web: www.orangesoda.com

Orangetheory Fitness
8960 University Center Ln ..... San Diego CA 92122 858-450-3355 671
Web: www.orangetheory.com

Orange-Ulster BOCES 53 Gibson Rd ..... Goshen NY 10924 845-291-0100 167-3
Web: www.ouboces.org

Orangevale Chamber of Commerce
9267 Greenback Ln Ste B-91 ..... Orangevale CA 95662 916-988-0175 988-1049 139
TF: 800-962-1106 ■ *Web:* www.orangevalechamber.com

Orano USA 4747 Bethesda Ave 10th Fl ..... Bethesda MD 20814 301-841-1600 787
Web: us.areva.com

Orasi Software Inc
114 Townpark Dr Ste 400 ..... Kennesaw GA 30144 678-819-5300 177
TF: 855-466-7274 ■ *Web:* www.orasi.com

OraSure Technologies Inc
220 E First St ..... Bethlehem PA 18015 610-882-1820 882-1830 231
NASDAQ: OSUR ■ *TF:* 800-869-3538 ■ *Web:* www.orasure.com

ORAU 100 Orau Way PO Box 117 ..... Oak Ridge TN 37831 865-576-3146 241-2923 49-5
Web: orau.org

Orban Inc 8350 E Evans Rd Ste C-4 ..... Scottsdale AZ 85260 480-403-8300 246
Web: www.orban.com

ORBCOMM 22970 Indian Creek Dr Ste 300 ..... Sterling VA 20166 703-433-6300 433-6380 681
TF: 800-672-2666 ■ *Web:* www.orbcomm.com

Orbis Books 79 Ryder Rd ..... Ossining NY 10562 800-258-5838 637-2
TF: 800-258-5838 ■ *Web:* www.orbisbooks.com

ORBIS Corp
1055 Corporate Center Dr ..... Oconomowoc WI 53066 800-890-7292 560-5841* 199
**Fax Area Code:* 262 ■ *TF:* 800 999 8683 ■ *Web:* www.orbiscorporation.com

Orbis Education Services Inc
11595 N Meridian Ste 400 ..... Carmel IN 46032 317-663-0260 242
Web: orbiseducation.com

ORBIS International Inc
520 Eigth Ave 12th Fl ..... New York NY 10018 800-672-4787 674-5599* 48-5
**Fax Area Code:* 646 ■ *TF:* 800-672-4787 ■ *Web:* www.orbis.org

Orbit Design 2560 Sheridan Blvd Ste 4 ..... Denver CO 80214 303-433-1616 195
Web: orbit-design.com

Orbit International Corp
80 Cabot Ct ..... Hauppauge NY 11788 631-435-8300 435-8458 529
NASDAQ: ORBT ■ *Web:* www.orbitintl.com

Orbit/FR Inc 506 Prudential Rd ..... Horsham PA 19044 215-674-5100 674-5108 647
OTC: ORFR ■ *Web:* www.mvg-world.com

Orbital Energy Group
20050 SW 112th Ave ..... Tualatin OR 97062 503-612-2300 360-3
NASDAQ: CUI ■ *TF:* 800-275-4899 ■ *Web:* www.orbitalenergygroup.com

Orbital Engineering Inc
1344 Fifth Ave ..... Pittsburgh PA 15219 412-261-9100 261-2308 261
Web: www.orbitalengr.com

Orbitel Communications LLC
21116 N John Wayne Pkwy Ste B-9 ..... Maricopa AZ 85239 520-568-8890 387
TF: 800-998-8084 ■ *Web:* www.orbitelcom.com

Orca Bay Seafoods Inc
900 Powell Ave SW ..... Renton WA 98057 425-204-9100 204-9200 296-14
TF: 800-932-6722 ■ *Web:* orcabayseafoods.com

Orca Systems Inc
3990 Old Town Ave Ste C307 ..... San Diego CA 92110 858-679-9175 668
Web: www.orcasystems.com

Orcas International Inc 9 Lenel Rd ..... Landing NJ 07850 973-448-2801 448-2806 345
Web: orcasnaturals.com

Orcas Island Library District
500 Rose St ..... Eastsound WA 98245 360-376-4985 435
Web: orcaslibrary.org

Orcas Power & Light Co-op
183 Mt Baker Rd ..... Eastsound WA 98245 360-376-3500 245
Web: www.opalco.com

Orchard Beach State Park
2064 N Lakeshore Rd ..... Manistee MI 49660 231-723-7422 565
Web: www.michigan.org

Orchard Garden Hotel
466 Bush St ..... San Francisco CA 94108 415-399-9807 393-9917 379
TF: 877-525-7749 ■ *Web:* www.theorchardgardenhotel.com

Orchard Hiltz & McCliment Inc (OHM)
34000 Plymouth Rd ..... Livonia MI 48150 734-522-6711 522-6427 261
TF: 888-522-6711 ■ *Web:* www.ohm-advisors.com

Orchard Homes 31 W 27th St 4th Fl ..... New York NY 10001 844-819-1373 652
TF: 844-819-1373 ■ *Web:* orchard.com

Orchard Hotel 665 Bush St ..... San Francisco CA 94108 415-362-8878 362-8088 379
Web: www.theorchardhotel.com

Orchard Machinery Corp
2700 Colusa Hwy ..... Yuba City CA 95993 530-673-2822 673-0296 273
Web: shakermaker.com

Orchard Manor Inc 500 Ohio St ..... Medina NY 14103 716-798-4100 371

Orchard Park Chamber of Commerce
4211 N Buffalo St Ste 14 ..... Orchard Park NY 14127 716-662-3366 662-5946 139
Web: www.orchardparkchamber.org

Orchard School 615 W 64th St ..... Indianapolis IN 46260 317-251-9253 623
Web: www.orchard.org

Orchard Software Corp
701 Congressional Blvd Ste 360 ..... Carmel IN 46032 317-573-2633 177
TF: 800-856-1948 ■ *Web:* www.orchardsoft.com

Orchard View Inc 4055 Skyline Rd ..... The Dalles OR 97058 541-298-4496 298-1808 315-3
Web: orchardview.com

Orchard, The 23 E Fourth St ..... New York NY 10003 916-239-6010 523
Web: www.theorchard.com

Orchards Hotel, The 222 Adams Rd ..... Williamstown MA 01267 413-458-9611 458-3273 379
Web: www.orchardshotel.com

Orchards Inn of Sedona 254 Hwy N 89 A ..... Sedona AZ 86336 855-474-7719 282-5710* 379
**Fax Area Code:* 928 ■ *TF:* 855-474-7719 ■ *Web:* www.orchardsinn.com

Orchestra Iowa 119 Third Ave SE ..... Cedar Rapids IA 52401 319-366-8206 573-3
Web: www.artsiowa.com

Orchestra New England PO Box 200123 ..... New Haven CT 06520 203-777-4690 573-3
Web: orchestranewengland.org

Orchestre Metropolitain du Grand Montreal
486 St Catherine St W Ste 401 ..... Montreal QC H3B1A6 514-598-0870 573-3
Web: www.orchestremetropolitain.com

Orchestre Symphonique de Montreal
1600 Saint-Urbain St ..... Montreal QC H2X0S1 514-842-9951 842-0728 573-3
TF: 888-842-9951 ■ *Web:* www.osm.ca

Orchid 350 21st St ..... Monroe WI 53566 608-325-9161 483
Web: www.orchidinternational.com

Orchid Orthopedic Solutions
1365 N Cedar St ..... Mason MI 48842 517-694-2300 247
Web: www.orchid-ortho.com

Orchids Paper Products Co 4826 Hunt St ..... Pryor OK 74361 918-825-0616 558
NYSE: TIS ■ *Web:* orchidspaper.com

Orco Block Company Inc
11100 Beach Blvd ..... Stanton CA 90680 714-527-2239 183
Web: www.orco.com

Orcon Corp 1570 Atlantic St ..... Union City CA 94587 800-227-0605 600
TF: 800-227-0505 ■ *Web:* www.orcon.com

Orcutt Union School District
500 Dyer St ..... Orcutt CA 93455 805-938-8900 938-8919 780
Web: www.orcuttschools.net

Orcutt/Winslow 3003 N Central Ave ..... Phoenix AZ 85012 602-257-1764 257-9029 186
Web: www.owp.com

Order Sons of Italy in America (OSIA)
219 E St NE ..... Washington DC 20002 202-547-2900 546-8168 48-14
TF: 800-552-6742 ■ *Web:* www.osia.org

Ordre Des Ingenieurs Du Quebec
Gare Windsor Bereau 350 ..... Montreal QC H3B2S2 514-845-6141 78
TF: 800-461-6141 ■ *Web:* www.oiq.qc.ca

Ordway Center for the Performing Arts
345 Washington St ..... Saint Paul MN 55102 651-282-3000 572
Web: ordway.org

Oreck Corp 1400 Salem Rd ..... Cookeville TN 38506 800-289-5888 788
TF: 800-289-5888 ■ *Web:* www.oreck.com

	City	State	ZIP	Phone	Fax	Class
Oregon						
Arts Commission 775 Summer St NE Ste 200 — *Web:* www.oregonartscommission.org	Salem	OR	97301	503-986-0082	986-0260	339-38
Attorney General 1162 Ct St NE Justice Bldg — *Web:* www.doj.state.or.us	Salem	OR	97301	503-378-4400	378-4017	339-38
Children Adults & Families Div (CAF) 500 Summer St NE E-15 — *Web:* www.oregon.gov	Salem	OR	97301	503-945-5600	581-6198	339-38
Community Colleges & Workforce Development Dept 605 Cottage St NE — *Web:* www.worksourceoregon.org	Salem	OR	97301	503-378-8648	378-8434	339-38
Corrections Dept (DOC) 2575 Center St NE — *Web:* www.oregon.gov	Salem	OR	97301	503-945-9090	373-1173	339-38
Department of Education 255 Capitol St NE — *Web:* www.oregon.gov	Salem	OR	97310	503-947-5600	378-5156	339-38
Dept of Consumer & Business Services 350 Winter St NE PO Box 14480 — *Web:* www.oregon.gov	Salem	OR	97309	503-378-4100	378-6444	339-38
Dept of Human Services 500 Summer St NE — *Web:* www.oregon.gov	Salem	OR	97301	503-947-5448	378-2897	339-38
Dept of Transportation 355 Capitol St NE MS 11 — *TF:* 888-275-6368 ■ *Web:* www.oregon.gov	Salem	OR	97301	503-986-3700		339-38
Driver & Motor Vehicle Services Div 1905 Lana Ave NE — *Web:* www.oregon.gov	Salem	OR	97314	503-945-5052		339-38
Emergency Management 3225 State St Rm 115 — *Web:* www.oregon.gov	Salem	OR	97301	503-584-3985		339-38
Energy Dept 550 Capitol St NE — *TF:* 800-221-8035 ■ *Web:* www.oregon.gov	Salem	OR	97301	503-378-4040	373-7806	339-38
Environmental Quality Dept 700 NE Multnomah St — *TF:* 800-452-4011 ■ *Web:* www.oregon.gov	Portland	OR	97204	503-229-5696	229-6124	339-38
Fish & Wildlife Dept (ODFW) 4034 Fairview Industrial Dr SE — *TF:* 800-720-6339 ■ *Web:* www.dfw.state.or.us	Salem	OR	97302	503-947-6000	947-6042	339-38
Forestry Dept 2600 State St — *Web:* www.oregon.gov	Salem	OR	97310	503-945-7200	945-7212	339-38
Government Standards & Practices Commission 3218 Pringle Rd SE Ste 220 — *Web:* www.oregon.gov	Salem	OR	97302	503-378-5105	373-1456	265
Governor 900 Ct St Ste 254 — *Web:* www.oregon.gov	Salem	OR	97301	503-378-4582	378-6827	339-38
Housing & Community Services Dept N Mall Office Bldg 725 Summer St NE Ste B — *Web:* www.oregon.gov	Salem	OR	97301	503-986-2000	986-2020	339-38
Labor & Industries Bureau 800 NE Oregon St Ste 1045 — *Web:* www.oregon.gov	Portland	OR	97232	971-673-0761	673-0762	339-38
Land Conservation & Development Dept 635 Capitol St NE Ste 150 — *Web:* www.oregon.gov	Salem	OR	97301	503-373-0050	378-5518	339-38
Legislative Assembly 900 Ct St NE — *TF:* 800-332-2313 ■ *Web:* www.oregonlegislature.gov	Salem	OR	97301	800-332-2313		339-38
Lottery 500 Airport Rd SE — *TF:* 888-311-0029 ■ *Web:* oregonlottery.org	Salem	OR	97301	503-540-1000	540-1001	452
Measurement Standards Div 635 Capitol St NE — *Web:* www.oregon.gov	Salem	OR	97301	503-986-4670		339-38
Military Dept 1776 Militia Way SE PO Box 14350 — *TF:* 800-452-7500 ■ *Web:* www.oregon.gov	Salem	OR	97309	503-584-3980	584-3987	339-38
Oregon Business Development Dept (OBDD) 775 Summer St NE Ste 200 — *Web:* www.oregon4biz.com	Salem	OR	97301	503-986-0123	581-5115	339-38
Parole & Post-Prison Supervision Board 2575 Center St NE Ste 100 — *Web:* www.oregon.gov	Salem	OR	97301	503-378-7558	373-7558	339-38
Publication & Distribution Services 550 Airport Rd SE Ste A — *Web:* www.oregon.gov	Salem	OR	97301	503-986-1243		433
Revenue Dept 955 Center St NE — *TF:* 800-356-4222 ■ *Web:* www.oregon.gov	Salem	OR	97301	503-378-4988	945-8738	339-38
Secretary of State 136 State Capitol — *Web:* www.sos.oregon.gov	Salem	OR	97310	503-986-1523	986-1616	339-38
State Court Administrator Office 1163 State St — *Web:* www.courts.oregon.gov	Salem	OR	97301	503-986-5500	986-5503	339-38
State Hospital 2600 Center St NE — *TF:* 800-544-7078 ■ *Web:* www.oregon.gov	Salem	OR	97301	503-945-2800	945-2807	374-5
State Library 250 Winter St NE — *Web:* www.oregon.gov	Salem	OR	97301	503-378-4243	585-8059	434-5
State Police Dept 3565 Trelstad Ave SE — *Web:* www.oregon.gov	Salem	OR	97317	503-378-3720	378-8282	339-38
Student Assistance Commission 1500 Valley River Dr Ste 100 — *TF:* 800-452-8807 ■ *Web:* oregonstudentaid.gov	Eugene	OR	97401	541-687-7400	687-7414	725
Supreme Court 1163 State St — *Web:* www.courts.oregon.gov	Salem	OR	97301	503-986-5555	986-5730	339-38
Treasurer 350 Winter St NE Ste 100 — *Web:* www.oregon.gov	Salem	OR	97301	503-378-4000		339-38
Veterans' Affairs Dept 700 Summer St NE — **Fax Area Code:* 503 ■ *TF:* 800-828-8801 ■ *Web:* www.oregon.gov	Salem	OR	97301	800-692-9666	373-2362*	339-38
Vocational Rehabilitation Services Office (OVRS) 700 Summer St NE Ste 150 — *TF:* 800-692-9666 ■ *Web:* www.oregon.gov	Salem	OR	97310	503-373-2085		339-38
Worker's Compensation Board 2601 SE 25th St Ste 150 — *Web:* www.cbs.state.or.us	Salem	OR	97302	503-378-3308	373-1600	339-38
Oregon Advanced Imaging LLC 881 Ohare Pkwy — *TF:* 800-462-1098 ■ *Web:* www.oaimaging.com	Medford	OR	97504	541-608-0350	773-7009	418
Oregon Aero Inc 34020 Skyway Dr — *TF:* 800-888-6910 ■ *Web:* www.oregonaero.com	Scappoose	OR	97056	503-543-7399		529
Oregon Air & Space Museum 90377 Boeing Dr — *Web:* www.oasmuseum.com	Eugene	OR	97402	541-461-1101		520
Oregon Association of Realtors 2110 Mission St SE — *TF:* 800-252-9115 ■ *Web:* oregonrealtors.org	Salem	OR	97308	503-362-3645	362-9615	656
Oregon Ballet Theatre 0720 SW Bancroft St — *Web:* www.obt.org	Portland	OR	97239	503-227-0977	227-4186	573-1
Oregon Bankers Assn 777 13th St SE Ste 130 — *Web:* www.oregonbankers.com	Salem	OR	97301	503-581-3522		138
Oregon Business Council 1100 SW Sixth Ave Ste 1608 — *Web:* orbusinesscouncil.org	Portland	OR	97204	503-220-0691		78
Oregon Canadian Forest Products Inc 31950 Comml St NW — *Web:* www.ocfp.com	North Plains	OR	97133	503-647-5011		683
Oregon Catholic Press (OCP) 5536 NE Hassalo St — **Fax Area Code:* 800 ■ *TF:* 877-596-1653 ■ *Web:* www.ocp.org	Portland	OR	97213	503-281-1191	462-7329*	637-3
Oregon Caves National Monument 19000 Caves Hwy — *TF:* 877-245-9022 ■ *Web:* www.nps.gov	Cave Junction	OR	97523	541-592-2100	592-3981	564
Oregon Cherry Growers Inc 1520 Woodrow NE — *TF:* 800-367-2536 ■ *Web:* oregoncherry.com	Salem	OR	97301	503-585-7710		315-3
Oregon City Chamber of Commerce 1201 Washington St — *Web:* www.oregoncity.org	Oregon City	OR	97045	503-656-1619	656-2274	139
Oregon City Public Library 606 John Adams — *Web:* www.orcity.org	Oregon City	OR	97045	503-657-8269		434-3
Oregon City School District 62 Department of HR PO Box 2110 — *Web:* ocsd62.org	Oregon City	OR	97045	503-785-8000		685
Oregon Coast Aquarium 2820 SE Ferry Slip Rd — *TF:* 800-452-7888 ■ *Web:* www.aquarium.org	Newport	OR	97365	541-867-3474	867-6846	40
Oregon Coast Magazine 88906 Hwy 101 N Ste 2 — *TF:* 800-348-8401 ■ *Web:* www.oregoncoastmagazine.com	Florence	OR	97439	541-997-8401	997-1124	457-22
Oregon College of Art & Craft 8245 SW Barnes Rd — *TF:* 800-390-0632 ■ *Web:* ocac.edu	Portland	OR	97225	503-297-5544		166
Oregon Community Foundation, The 1221 SW Yamhill St Ste 100 — *Web:* www.oregoncf.org	Portland	OR	97205	503-227-6846	274-7771	303
Oregon Convention Ctr 777 NE Martin Luther King Jr Blvd — *TF:* 800-791-2250 ■ *Web:* www.oregoncc.org	Portland	OR	97232	503-235-7575	235-7417	205
Oregon Culinary Institute 1717 SW Jefferson St — *TF:* 888-624-2433 ■ *Web:* www.oregonculinaryinstitute.com	Portland	OR	97201	503-961-6200		167-3
Oregon Democratic Party 232 NE Ninth Ave — *Web:* www.dpo.org	Portland	OR	97232	503-224-8200	224-5335	616-1
Oregon Dental Assn PO Box 3710 — *TF:* 800-452-5628 ■ *Web:* www.oregondental.org	Wilsonville	OR	97070	503-218-2010	218-2009	227
Oregon Education Magazine (OEA) 6900 SW Atlanta St Bldg 1 — *TF:* 800-858-5505 ■ *Web:* www.oregoned.org	Portland	OR	97223	503-684-3300	684-8063	457-8
Oregon Electric Station 27 E Fifth Ave — *Web:* www.oesrestaurant.com	Eugene	OR	97401	541-485-4444		671
Oregon Employment Dept 875 Union St NE — *TF:* 877-345-3484 ■ *Web:* www.oregon.gov	Salem	OR	97311	503-451-2400	947-1472	259
Oregon Environmental Council 222 NW Davis St Ste 309 — *Web:* oeconline.org	Portland	OR	97209	503-222-1963		804
Oregon Episcopal School 6300 SW Nicol Rd — *Web:* www.oes.edu	Portland	OR	97223	503-246-7771		622
Oregon Equipment Service Corp 180 NE Irving Ave — *Web:* orequipmentservices.com	Bend	OR	97701	541-388-2235		189-10
Oregon Food Bank 7900 NE 33rd Dr — *TF:* 800-777-7427 ■ *Web:* www.oregonfoodbank.org	Portland	OR	97211	503-282-0555	282-0922	48-5
Oregon Fruit Products LLC 150 Patterson St NW — *Web:* www.oregonfruit.com	Salem	OR	97304	503-581-6211	588-9519	296-21
Oregon Garden, The 879 W Main St PO Box 155 — *TF:* 877-674-2733 ■ *Web:* www.oregongarden.org	Silverton	OR	97381	503-874-8100	339-2996	97
Oregon Historical Society 1200 SW Park Ave — *Web:* www.ohs.org	Portland	OR	97205	503-222-1741	221-2035	520
Oregon Industrial Repair Inc 1885 16th St SE — *Web:* www.oirinc.com	Salem	OR	97302	503-399-1926	588-3499	454
Oregon Institute of Technology 3201 Campus Dr — *TF:* 800-422-2017 ■ *Web:* www.oit.edu	Klamath Falls	OR	97601	541-885-1000	885-1024	166
Oregon International Port of Coos Bay 125 W Central Ave Ste 300 — *Web:* www.portofcoosbay.com	Coos Bay	OR	97420	541-267-7678	269-1475	618
Oregon Labor Press Publishing Company Inc 4275 NE Halsey St — *Web:* www.nwlaborpress.org	Portland	OR	97213	503-288-3311		532-2
Oregon Lions Sight & Hearing Foundation 1010 NW 22nd Ave Ste 144 — *TF:* 800-635-4667 ■ *Web:* www.olshf.org	Portland	OR	97210	503-413-7399		269
Oregon Lox Co 4828 W 11th Ave — *TF:* 800-233-1850 ■ *Web:* www.oregonlox.com	Eugene	OR	97402	541-726-7824	747-7713	296-14
Oregon Maritime Center & Museum 115 SW Ash St Ste 400-C — *Web:* www.oregonmaritimemuseum.org	Portland	OR	97204	503-224-7724		520
Oregon Medical Assn (OMA) 11740 SW 68th Pkwy Ste 100 — *Web:* www.theoma.org	Portland	OR	97223	503-619-8000	619-0609	474

Name / Address	City	State	ZIP	Phone	Fax	Class
Oregon Museum of Science & Industry						
1945 SE Water Ave	Portland	OR	97214	503-797-4000	797-4500	520
TF: 800-955-6674 ■ *Web:* omsi.edu						
Oregon Mutual Insurance Co						
PO Box 808	McMinnville	OR	97128	503-472-2141		391-4
TF: 800-888-2141 ■ *Web:* www.ormutual.com						
Oregon Nikkei Legacy Ctr (ONLC)						
121 NW 2nd Ave	Portland	OR	97209	503-224-1458		192
Web: www.oregonnikkei.org						
Oregon Nurses Assn (ONA)						
18765 SW Boones Ferry Rd	Tualatin	OR	97062	503-293-0011	293-0013	533
TF: 800-634-3552 ■ *Web:* www.oregonrn.org						
Depoe Bay Whale Watching Ctr						
119 SW Hwy 101	Depoe Bay	OR	97341	541-765-3304	765-3402	565
Web: stateparks.oregon.gov						
Oregon Parks and Recreation Dept						
Devil's Lake State Recreation Area						
1452 NE 6th Dr	Lincoln City	OR	97367	541-994-2002		565
Web: stateparks.oregon.gov						
Parks & Recreation Dept (OPRD)						
725 Summer St NE Ste C	Salem	OR	97301	503-986-0707	986-0794	339-38
Web: stateparks.oregon.gov						
Oregon Potato Co PO Box 3110	Pasco	WA	99302	509-545-4545		296-18
TF: 800-336-6311 ■ *Web:* www.oregonpotato.com						
Oregon Primary Care Assn						
310 SW Fourth Ave Ste 200	Portland	OR	97204	503-228-8852		138
Web: www.orpca.org						
Oregon Public Broadcasting Inc (OPB)						
7140 SW Macadam Ave	Portland	OR	97219	503-244-9900		632
TF: 800-241-8123 ■ *Web:* www.opb.org						
Oregon Recreation Dept 5330 Seaman Rd	Oregon	OH	43616	419-693-9999		706
Web: www.oregonohio.org						
Oregon School of Massage						
9500 SW Barbur Blvd Ste 100	Portland	OR	97219	800-844-3420	244-1815*	685
**Fax Area Code:* 503 ■ *TF:* 800-844-3420 ■ *Web:* www.oregonschoolofmassage.com						
Oregon Scientific Inc						
10778 SW Manhasset Dr	Tualatin	OR	97062	503-783-5100	691-6208	38
Web: global.oregonscientific.com						
Oregon Screw Machine Products Inc						
9291 SE 64th Ave	Portland	OR	97206	503-774-2750		488
Web: www.osmpi.com						
Oregon Shakespeare Festival						
15 S Pioneer St	Ashland	OR	97520	541-482-2111		749
TF: 800-219-8161 ■ *Web:* www.osfashland.org						
Oregon Society of CPAS						
10206 SW Laurel St	Beaverton	OR	97005	503-641-7200		533
TF: 800-255-1470 ■ *Web:* www.orcpa.org						
Oregon State Archives (OSA)						
800 Summer St NE	Salem	OR	97310	503-373-0701	378-4118	387
Web: www.arcweb.sos.state.or.us						
Oregon State Bar Ctr						
16037 SW Upper Boones Ferry Rd	Tigard	OR	97224	503-620-0222	684-1366	72
Web: www.osbar.org						
Oregon State Correctional Institution						
3405 Deer Pk Dr SE	Salem	OR	97310	503-378-8919		213
Web: www.oregon.gov						
Oregon State Fair & Expo Ctr						
2330 17th St NE	Salem	OR	97301	971-701-6573		205
Web: oregonstatefair.org						
Oregon State Penitentiary 2605 State St	Salem	OR	97301	503-378-2453	378-3897	213
Web: www.oregon.gov						
Oregon State Pharmacy Assn (OSPA)						
147 SE 102nd Ave	Portland	OR	97216	503-582-9055	253-9172	585
Web: www.oregonpharmacy.org						
Oregon State Public Interest Research Group (OSPIRG)						
1536 SE 11th Ave	Portland	OR	97214	503-231-4181		633
Web: ospirg.org						
Oregon State University						
1500 Jefferson St	Corvallis	OR	97331	541-737-3166		167-3
Web: www.oregonstate.edu						
Oregon Symphony Orchestra						
921 SW Washington St Ste 200	Portland	OR	97205	503-228-4294	228-4150	573-3
TF: 800-228-7343 ■ *Web:* www.orsymphony.org						
Oregon Trail Electric Co-op (OTEC)						
4005 23rd St PO Box 226	Baker City	OR	97814	541-523-3616		245
Web: otec.coop						
Oregon Veterans' Home						
700 Veterans Dr	The Dalles	OR	97058	541-296-7190	296-7862	793
TF: 800-846-8460 ■ *Web:* www.oregon.gov						
Oregon Veterinary Clinic Sc						
1145 Park St	Oregon	WI	53575	608-835-7323		794
Web: oregonvetclinic.com						
Oregon Veterinary Medical Assn						
1880 Lancaster Dr NE Ste 118	Salem	OR	97305	503-399-0311	363-4218	795
TF: 800-235-3502 ■ *Web:* www.oregonvma.org						
Oregon Wine Services and Storage						
2803 Orchard Ave	McMinnville	OR	97128	503-474-9800		803-1
Web: www.oregonwineservices.com						
Oregon Winegrowers Assn (OWA)						
4640 SW Macadam Ave Ste 240	Portland	OR	97239	503-228-8336		139
Web: www.oregonwinegrowers.org						
Oregon Youth Authority Riverbend (OYA)						
58231 Oregon Hwy 244	La Grande	OR	97850	541-663-8801	663-9181	412
Web: www.oregon.gov						
Oregon Zoo 4001 SW Canyon Rd	Portland	OR	97221	503-226-1561		823
Web: www.oregonzoo.org						
Oregon-California Trails Assn						
524 S Osage St PO Box 1019	Independence	MO	64051	816-252-2276	836-0989	48-23
TF: 888-811-6282 ■ *Web:* www.octa-trails.org						
Orelube Corp, The 20 Sawgrass Dr	Bellport	NY	11713	631-205-9700	205-9797	541
TF: 800-645-9124 ■ *Web:* www.orelube.com						
Orem Public Library 58 N State St	Orem	UT	84057	801-229-7050		434-3
Web: www.oremlibrary.org						
Orem Rehabilitation & Nursing Ctr						
575 E 1400 S	Orem	UT	84097	801-225-4741		371
Web: oremrehab.com						
Oren Dunn City Museum						
689 Rutherford Rd Ballard Pk	Tupelo	MS	38801	662-841-6438		520
Web: www.tupeloms.gov						
Oren Elliott Products Inc						
128 W Vine St	Edgerton	OH	43517	419-298-2306	298-3545	253
Web: www.orenelliottproducts.com						
Orenco Systems Inc 814 Airway Ave	Sutherlin	OR	97479	541-459-4449	459-2884	427
TF: 800-348-9843 ■ *Web:* www.orenco.com						
Orfalea Family Foundation						
1283 Coast Village Cir Ste 2	Santa Barbara	CA	93108	805-565-7550	565-7554	305
Web: www.orfaleafoundation.org						
Orfila Vineyards & Winery						
13455 San Pasqual Rd	Escondido	CA	92025	760-738-6500		50-7
Web: www.orfila.com						
Orgain Bell & Tucker LLP						
470 Orleans St	Beaumont	TX	77704	409-838-6412		428
Web: obt.com						
Orgain Building Supply Co						
65 Commerce St	Clarksville	TN	37040	931-647-1567		191-3
Web: www.orgainbuilding.com						
Organ Recovery Systems Inc						
1 Pierce Pl Ste 475W	Itasca	IL	60143	847-824-2600		475
TF: 866-682-4800 ■ *Web:* www.organ-recovery.com						
Organ Supply Industries Inc						
2320 W 50th St	Erie	PA	16506	814-835-2244	838-0349	527
TF: 800-458-0289 ■ *Web:* www.organsupply.com						
Organ Transport Systems Inc						
2611 Internet Blvd Ste 109	Frisco	TX	75034	972-987-1312		476
Web: www.organtransportsystems.com						
Organic Avenue LLC 149 5th Ave Fl 5	New York	NY	10002	212-358-0500	202-7623	345
Web: www.organicavenue.com						
Organic By Nature inc						
2610 Homestead Pl	Rancho Dominguez	CA	90220	562-285-9863		583
Web: www.organicbynatureinc.com						
Organic Inc						
600 California St 7th Fl	San Francisco	CA	94108	415-581-5300		7
Web: www.organic.com						
Organic Milling Co 505 W Allen Ave	San Dimas	CA	91773	909-599-0961		296-4
Web: www.organicmilling.com						
Organic Products Trading Compa						
2908 NW 93rd St	Vancouver	WA	98665	360-573-4433		805
Web: www.optco.com						
Organic Valley 1 Organic Way	La Farge	WI	54639	888-444-6455	625-2600*	10-4
**Fax Area Code:* 608 ■ *TF:* 888-444-6455 ■ *Web:* www.organicvalley.coop						
Organifi 7535 Metropolitan Dr	San Diego	CA	92108	760-487-8587		296-21
Web: organifi.com						
Organization for Tropical Studies (OTS)						
410 Swift Ave	Durham	NC	27705	919-684-5774	684-5661	49-5
Web: tropicalstudies.org						
Organization Management Group						
638 Independence Pkwy Ste 100	Chesapeake	VA	23320	757-473-8701	473-9897	47
Web: www.managegroup.com						
Organization of American Historians (OAH)						
112 N Bryan Ave	Bloomington	IN	47408	812-855-7311	855-0696	49-5
Web: www.oah.org						
Organization of Chinese Americans (OCA)						
1322 18th St NW	Washington	DC	20036	202-223-5500	296-0540	48-14
Web: www.ocanational.org						
Organizational Dynamics Inc						
790 Boston Rd Ste 201	Billerica	MA	01821	978-671-5454	671-5005	194
TF: 800-634-4636 ■ *Web:* www.orgdynamics.com						
Organo Gold International Inc						
5505 Hovander Rd	Ferndale	WA	98248	877-674-2661		463
TF: 877-674-2661 ■ *Web:* www.organogold.com						
Organogenesis Inc 150 Dan Rd	Canton	MA	02021	781-575-0775		85
TF: 888-432-5232 ■ *Web:* organogenesis.com						
Orgill Inc 3742 Tyndale Dr	Memphis	TN	38125	901-754-8850	752-8989	351
TF: 800-347-2860 ■ *Web:* www.orgill.com						
Orgill Singer						
8360 W Sahara Ave Ste 110	Las Vegas	NV	89117	702-796-9100		48-20
TF: 800-745-3065 ■ *Web:* www.orgillsinger.com						
Oriana House Inc						
885 E Buchtel Ave PO Box 1501	Akron	OH	44305	330-535-8116		726
Web: www.orianahouse.org						
Orica USA Inc 33101 E Quincy Ave	Watkins	CO	80137	303-268-5000	268-5250	268
TF: 800-800-3855 ■ *Web:* www.oricaminingservices.com						
Oricom Internet Inc						
400 Rue Nolin Bureau	Vanier	QC	G1M1E7	418-683-4557		387
TF: 866-967-4266 ■ *Web:* www.oricom.ca						
Oriel Stat A Matrix						
1095 Morris Ave Ste 103B	Union	NJ	07083	732-548-0600	548-4085	463
TF: 800-472-6477 ■ *Web:* www.orielstat.com						
Oriental Institute Museum						
University of Chicago 1155 E 58th St	Chicago	IL	60637	773-702-9514	702-9853	520
TF: 800-791-9354 ■ *Web:* oi.uchicago.edu						
Oriental Jade Bangor Mall Blvd	Bangor	ME	04401	207-947-6969		671
Web: www.orientaljade.com						
Oriental Trading Company Inc						
5455 S 90th St	Omaha	NE	68127	402-596-1200		459
TF: 800-875-8480 ■ *Web:* www.orientaltrading.com						
Oriental Weavers of America						
3295 Lower Dug Gap Rd	Dalton	GA	30720	706-277-9666		131
Web: www.orientalweavers.com						
Origami Owl LLC 450 N 54th St	Chandler	AZ	85226	888-491-0331		408
TF: 888-491-0331 ■ *Web:* www.origamiowl.com						
Origen Financial Inc						
27777 Franklin Rd Ste 1700	Southfield	MI	48034	248-746-7000		509
OTC: ORGN ■ *Web:* www.origenfinancial.com						
Origin Materials						
930 Riverside Pkwy Ste 10	West Sacramento	CA	95605	916-231-9329		192
Web: www.originmaterials.com						
Origin Title & Escrow Inc						
160 Clairemont Ave Ste 490	Decatur	GA	30030	404-377-6783		653
Web: origintitle.com						
Original Appalachian Artworks Inc						
1721 Hwy 75 S PO Box 714	Cleveland	GA	30528	706-865-2171		762
Web: www.cabbagepatchkids.com						
Original Artists						
9465 Wilshire Blvd Ste 870	Beverly Hills	CA	90212	310-275-6765		731
Web: www.original-artists.com						

				Phone	Fax	Class
Original Benjamin's, The 9593 N Kings Hwy *Web:* www.originalbenjamins.com	Myrtle Beach	SC	29572	843-449-0821		671
Original Cake Candle Co, The 102 Sundale Rd *TF:* 888-444-2253 ■ *Web:* www.cakecandle.com	Norwich	OH	43767	740-872-3248		122
Original Engineered Products Inc 160 Abbott Dr *TF:* 888-566-2637 ■ *Web:* www.oep.com	Wheeling	IL	60090	847-459-9528	459-4076	551
Original Impressions LLC 12900 SW 89th Ct *TF:* 888-853-8644 ■ *Web:* www.originalimpressions.com	Miami	FL	33176	305-233-1322		627
Original Lincoln Logs Ltd 5 Riverside Dr PO Box 135 *TF:* 800-833-2461 ■ *Web:* www.lincolnlogs.com	Chestertown	NY	12817	800-833-2461		106
Original Mattress Factory Inc, The 4930 State Rd *TF:* 866-841-1421 ■ *Web:* www.originalmattress.com	Cleveland	OH	44134	216-661-8388	661-2337	471
Original Pancake House Franchising Inc 8601 SW 24th Ave *Web:* www.originalpancakehouse.com	Portland	OR	97219	503-246-9007		670
Original Parts Group Inc (OPGI) 1770 Saturn Way *TF:* 800-243-8355 ■ *Web:* www.opgi.com	Seal Beach	CA	90740	562-594-1000	594-1050	54
Original Q Shack, The 2510 University Dr *Web:* theqshackoriginal.com	Durham	NC	27707	919-402-4227		671
Original Tandoori Kitchen 7215 Main St *Web:* originaltandoorikitchen.com	Vancouver	BC	V5X3J3	604-327-8900		671
OriginClear Inc 5645 W Adams Blvd *TF:* 877-999-6645 ■ *Web:* www.originclear.com	Los Angeles	CA	90016	323-939-6645		536
OriginLab Corp 1 Roundhouse Plz Ste 303 *TF:* 800-969-7720 ■ *Web:* www.originlab.com	Northampton	MA	01060	413-586-2013		177
Origins Natural Resources Inc 767 Fifth Ave *TF:* 800-674-4467 ■ *Web:* www.origins.com	New York	NY	10153	800-674-4467		214
Origo Direct Marketing Communications 20-4480 Chesswood Dr *Web:* www.origo.ca	Toronto	ON	M3J2B9	416-398-7678		41
Orillia Soldiers' Memorial Hospital (OSMH) 170 Colborne St W *TF:* 866-797-0000 ■ *Web:* www.osmh.on.ca	Orillia	ON	L3V2Z3	705-325-2201	325-7953	374-2
Orinda Asset Management LLC 4 Orinda Way Ste 150-A *Web:* orindamanagement.com	Orinda	CA	94563	925-253-1300		528
O-Rings Inc 3311 Pepper Ave *Web:* www.oringsusa.com	Los Angeles	CA	90065	323-343-9500	343-9505	326
Orion Advisor Solutions 17605 Wright St *Web:* orion.com	Omaha	NE	68130	402-895-1600	431-4442	690
Orion Area Chamber of Commerce 1335 Joslyn Rd Ste 1 *Web:* www.orionareachamber.com	Lake Orion	MI	48360	248-693-6300		139
Orion Building Corp 9025 Overlook Blvd Ste 100 *Web:* www.orionbldg.com	Brentwood	TN	37027	615-321-4499		186
Orion Communications Inc 7650 Standish Pl Ste 102 *Web:* www.oricomm.com	Rockville	MD	20855	301-921-9056		175
Orion Development Group 177 Beach 116th St Ste 4 *TF:* 800-510-2117 ■ *Web:* www.odgroup.com	Rockaway Park	NY	11694	718-474-4600		194
Orion Drilling Company LLC 674 Flato Rd *Web:* oriondrilling.com	Corpus Christi	TX	78405	361-299-9800		540
Orion Fittings Inc PO Box 17-1580 *Web:* www.watts.com	Kansas City	KS	66115	913-342-1653		605-2
Orion Food Systems LLC 2930 W Maple *TF:* 800-648-6227 ■ *Web:* orionfoods.com	Sioux Falls	SD	57107	800-336-1320		393
Orion Genomics 20 S Sarah St *Web:* www.oriongenomics.com	Saint Louis	MO	63108	314-615-6977	615-6975	231
Orion HealthCorp Inc 1805 Old Alabama Rd Ste 350 *OTC:* ORNHQ ■ *Web:* www.orionhealthcorp.com	Roswell	GA	30076	678-832-1800	832-1888	352
Orion Industries Inc 1 Orion Park Dr *Web:* www.orionindustries.com	Ayer	MA	01432	978-772-6000		179
Orion Instruments LLC 2105 Oak Villa Blvd *TF:* 866-556-7466 ■ *Web:* www.orioninstruments.com	Baton Rouge	LA	70815	225-906-2343	906-2344	201
Orion Magazine 187 Main St *TF:* 888-909-6568 ■ *Web:* orionmagazine.org	Great Barrington	MA	01230	413-528-4422		457-19
Orion Mobility LLC 4 Mountainview Terr Ste 101 *Web:* www.orionmobility.com	Danbury	CT	06810	203-762-0365		194
Orion Press Inc 1224 W Melinda Ln *TF:* 800-528-0592 ■ *Web:* www.orionpress.com	Phoenix	AZ	85027	623-582-1010	582-0309	627
Orion Registrar Inc 7850 Vance Dr *TF:* 800-446-0674 ■ *Web:* www.orion4value.com	Arvada	CO	80003	303-456-6010		463
Orion Systems Inc 1800 Byberry Rd Ste 1300 *TF:* 800-301-0724 ■ *Web:* www.orionsystemsinc.net	Huntingdon Valley	PA	19006	215-659-1207		735
Orion Systems Integrators LLC 333 Thornall St 7th Fl **Fax Area Code:* 732 ■ *TF:* 877-456-9922 ■ *Web:* www.orioninc.com	Edison	NJ	08837	877-456-9922	422-6445*	809
Orion Township Public Library 825 Joslyn Rd *Web:* orionlibrary.org	Lake Orion	MI	48362	248-693-3000	693-3009	434-3
Orionnet Systems LLC 510 E Memorial Rd Ste C2 *Web:* www.iorion.com	Oklahoma City	OK	73114	405-286-1674	286-1007	809
Oriska Insurance Co 1310 Utica St *Web:* oriskainsurance.com	Oriskany	NY	13424	315-768-2726		390
Oristech Inc PO Box 310069 *TF:* 800-929-9078 ■ *Web:* www.oristech.com	New Braunfels	TX	78131	830-620-7422		225
Orkal Industries LLC 333 Westbury Ave *Web:* www.orkal.com	Carle Place	NY	11514	516-333-2121		770
ORKIN LLC 2170 Piedmont Rd NE **Fax Area Code:* 510 ■ *TF:* 877-250-1652 ■ *Web:* www.orkin.com	Atlanta	GA	30324	877-250-1652	265-0238*	577
Orland Park Area Chamber of Commerce 8799 W 151 St *Web:* www.orlandparkchamber.org	Orland Park	IL	60462	708-349-2972	349-7454	139
Orland Park Public Library 14921 Ravinia Ave *Web:* www.orlandparklibrary.org	Orland Park	IL	60462	708-428-5100	349-8196	434-3
Orlandi Inc 131 Executive Blvd *Web:* orlandi-usa.com	Farmingdale	NY	11735	631-756-0110		629
Orlando Baking Company Inc 7777 Grand Ave *TF:* 800-362-5504 ■ *Web:* www.orlandobaking.com	Cleveland	OH	44104	216-361-1872	391-3469	296-1
Orlando Bartending School 8250 Jamaican Ct *TF:* 800-262-5824 ■ *Web:* www.pbsa.com	Orlando	FL	32819	800-262-5824		685
Orlando Diefenderfer Co 116 S Second St *Web:* www.diefenderfer.com	Allentown	PA	18105	610-434-9595		246
Orlando Dodge Chrysler Jeep Ram 4101 W Colonial Dr *Web:* www.orlandododge.com	Orlando	FL	32808	407-299-1120		57
Orlando Economic Partnership 301 E Pine St Ste 900 *Web:* orlando.org	Orlando	FL	32801	407-422-7159	425-6428	139
Orlando Endodontic Specialists 670 N Mills Ave Ste 203 *Web:* www.midfloridarootcanals.com	Orlando	FL	32751	407-755-4700	755-4699	360-3
Orlando Fashion Square 3201 E Colonial Dr *Web:* www.orlandofashionsquare.com	Orlando	FL	32803	407-896-1132		460
Orlando Institute of Electrolysis Inc 6900 Turkey Lake Rd Ste 1-8 *Web:* www.orlandoinstitute.com	Orlando	FL	32819	407-295-2081	295-3170	167-3
Orlando International Airport 1 Jeff Fuqua Blvd *Web:* www.orlandoairports.net	Orlando	FL	32827	407-825-2001		27
Orlando Magazine 801 N Magnolia Ave Ste 201 *Web:* www.orlandomagazine.com	Orlando	FL	32803	407-423-0618	237-6258	457-22
Orlando Museum of Art 2416 N Mills Ave *Web:* www.omart.org	Orlando	FL	32803	407-896-4231	896-9920	520
Orlando North, Seminole County Tourism 1515 International Pkwy Ste 1013 *TF:* 800-800-7832 ■ *Web:* doorlandonorth.com	Lake Mary	FL	32746	407-665-2900	665-2920	206
Orlando Philharmonic Orchestra 425 N Bumby Ave *Web:* www.orlandophil.org	Orlando	FL	32803	407-896-6700		573-3
Orlando Regional Medical Ctr (ORMC) 1414 Kuhl Ave *TF:* 800-424-6998 ■ *Web:* www.orlandohealth.com	Orlando	FL	32806	321-841-5111		374-3
Orlando Repertory Theatre 1001 E Princeton St *Web:* www.orlandorep.com	Orlando	FL	32803	407-896-7365	897-3284	572
Orlando Science Ctr 777 E Princeton St *Web:* www.osc.org	Orlando	FL	32803	407-514-2000		520
Orlando Sentinel 633 N Orange Ave *TF:* 800-974-7488 ■ *Web:* www.orlandosentinel.com	Orlando	FL	32801	407-420-5000		532-2
Orlando Spring Corp 11131 Winners Cir *Web:* orlandospring.com	Los Alamitos	CA	90720	562-594-8411		492
Orlando Times, The 4403 Vineland Rd Ste B-5 *Web:* www.orlando-times.com	Orlando	FL	32811	407-841-3710	849-0434	532-2
Orlando Union Rescue Mission 1525 W Washington St *Web:* www.ourm.org	Orlando	FL	32805	407-423-2131		48-20
Orlando Weekly 16 W Pine St *Web:* www.orlandoweekly.com	Orlando	FL	32801	407-377-0400	377-0420	532-5
Orlando's 2402 Ave Q *Web:* www.orlandos.com	Lubbock	TX	79411	806-747-5998		671
Orlando, The 8384 W Third St *Web:* www.theorlando.com	Los Angeles	CA	90048	323-658-6600	653-3464	379
Orlando/Orange County Convention & Visitors Bureau Inc 6277 Sea Harbor Dr Ste 400 *Web:* www.visitorlando.com	Orlando	FL	32821	407-363-5872		206
Orlans 1650 W Big Beaver Rd *Web:* orlans.com	Troy	MI	48084	248-502-1400		428
Orlantech Inc 230 Lookout Pl *Web:* www.orlantech.com	Maitland	FL	32751	407-228-7290		180
Orleans Correctional Facility 3531 Gaines Basin Rd *Web:* www.doccs.ny.gov	Albion	NY	14411	585-589-6820		213
Orleans County 247 Main St *Web:* bgs.vermont.gov	Newport	NY	13416	802-895-2535		338
Orleans County Chamber of Commerce PO Box 501 *Web:* www.orleanschamber.com	Medina	NY	14103	585-301-8464		139
Orleans Grapevine Wine Bar & Bistro 718 - 720 Orleans Ave *Web:* www.orleansgrapevine.com	New Orleans	LA	70116	504-523-1930		671
Orleans Las Vegas Hotel & Casino 4500 W Tropicana Ave *TF:* 800-675-3267 ■ *Web:* www.orleanscasino.com	Las Vegas	NV	89103	702-365-7111		133
Orleans Parish School Board 3520 General DeGaulle Dr *Web:* nolapublicschools.com	New Orleans	LA	70114	504-304-4123		685
Orleans Technical Institute 2770 Red Lion Rd *Web:* www.orleanstech.edu	Philadelphia	PA	19114	215-728-4700		167-3
Orleans/Niagara BOCES Inc 4232 Shelby Basin Rd *TF:* 800-836-7510 ■ *Web:* www.onboces.org	Medina	NY	14132	716-731-6800		167-3
Orlo School of Hair Design & Cosmetology 232 N Allen St *Web:* www.theorloschool.com	Albany	NY	12206	518-459-7832		685

				Phone	Fax	Class
Orly International Inc 7710 Haskell Ave *Web:* www.orlybeauty.com	Van Nuys	CA	91406	818-994-1001		214
Orman House 177 Fifth St *Web:* www.floridastateparks.org	Apalachicola	FL	32320	850-653-1209		565
Ormat Technologies Inc 6225 Neil Rd Ste 300 *NYSE:* ORA ■ *Web:* www.ormat.com	Reno	NV	89511	775-356-9029	356-9039	620
ORMC (Orlando Regional Medical Ctr) 1414 Kuhl Ave *TF:* 800-424-6998 ■ *Web:* www.orlandohealth.com	Orlando	FL	32806	321-841-5111		374-3
ORMCO Corp 1717 W Collins Ave **Fax Area Code:* 800 ■ *TF:* 800-854-1741 ■ *Web:* ormco.com	Orange	CA	92867	714-516-7400	317-6012*	228
Orme School HC 63 PO Box 3040 *Web:* www.ormeschool.org	Mayer	AZ	86333	928-632-7601		622
Ormec Systems Corp 19 Linden Pk *TF:* 800-656-7632 ■ *Web:* www.ormec.com	Rochester	NY	14625	585-385-3520		203
Ormond Beach Chamber of Commerce 165 W Granada Blvd *Web:* www.ormondchamber.com	Ormond Beach	FL	32174	386-677-3454	677-4363	139
Ormond Memorial Art Museum & Gardens 78 E Granada Blvd *Web:* ormondartmuseum.org	Ormond Beach	FL	32176	386-676-3347	676-3244	520
Ormsby Insurance Agency Inc 698 Westfield St *Web:* ormsbyins.com	West Springfield	MA	01089	413-737-0300		390
Ormsby Trucking Inc 888 W Railroad St PO Box 67 *TF:* 800-348-2089 ■ *Web:* ormtrk.com	Uniondale	IN	46791	260-543-2233	543-2842	780
Ornamental Moulding 3804 Comanche Rd **Fax Area Code:* 888 ■ *TF:* 800-779-1135 ■ *Web:* www.ornamental.com	Archdale	NC	27263	800-779-1135	220-6290*	499
Orndorff & Spaid Inc 11722 Old Baltimore Pk *Web:* www.osroofing.com	Beltsville	MD	20705	301-937-5911		189-12
ORNL (Oak Ridge National Laboratory) PO Box 2008 *Web:* www.ornl.gov	Oak Ridge	TN	37831	865-576-9219	574-0595	668
Orocal Gold Nugget Co 1720 Bird St *TF:* 800-367-6225 ■ *Web:* www.orocal.com	Oroville	CA	95965	530-533-5065		409
Oronoque Eye Care 7365 Main St *Web:* www.oronoqueeyecare.com	Stratford	CT	06614	203-378-1111		237
Oroville Adult Education Career & Technical Ctr 2750 Mitchell Ave *Web:* www.orovilleadulted.com	Oroville	CA	95966	530-538-5350	538-5396	230
Oroville Area Chamber of Commerce 1789 Montgomery St *TF:* 800-655-4653 ■ *Web:* www.orovillechamber.com	Oroville	CA	95965	530-538-2542	538-2546	139
Oroville Hospital (OH) 2767 Olive Hwy *Web:* www.orovillehospital.com	Oroville	CA	95966	530-533-8500		374-3
Oroville Union High School District 2211 Washington Ave *Web:* www.ouhsd.org	Oroville	CA	95966	530-538-2300	538-2308	685
Orphan Foundation of America (OFA) 23811 Chagrin Blvd Ste 210 **Fax Area Code:* 855 ■ *TF:* 800-950-4673 ■ *Web:* www.fc2success.org	Cleveland	OH	44122	571-203-0270	773-8299*	48-6
Orpheum Children's Science Museum 346 N Neil St *Web:* www.orpheumkids.com	Champaign	IL	61820	217-352-5895	352-8160	521
Orpheum Performing Arts Ctr 200 N Broadway *Web:* wichitaorpheum.com	Wichita	KS	67202	316-263-0884		572
Orpheum Theatre 203 S Main St *Web:* orpheum-memphis.com	Memphis	TN	38103	901-525-3000	526-0829	572
Orpheus Chamber Orchestra 490 Riverside Dr 11th Fl *Web:* orpheusnyc.org	New York	NY	10027	212-896-1700	896-1717	573-3
Orr & Boss Inc 10 Shawfield Cr *Web:* www.orrandboss.com	Toronto	ON	M3A1S1	734-453-3033		463
ORR Associates Inc 2801 M St NW *Web:* orrgroup.com	Washington	DC	20007	202-338-6100		196
ORR Associates LLC 191 Peachtree St NE Ste 3720 *Web:* www.orrcpa.com	Atlanta	GA	30303	404-525-3007		2
ORR FELT Co, The 750 S Main St *Web:* www.orrfelt.com	Piqua	OH	45356	937-773-0551		745-6
ORR Group, The 110 S Stratford Rd Ste 402 *Web:* www.theorrgroup.com	Winston-Salem	NC	27104	336-722-7881	722-7517	194
ORR Safety Corp 11601 Interchange Dr *TF:* 800-726-6789 ■ *Web:* www.orrsafety.com	Louisville	KY	40229	502-774-5791	776-8030	679
Orrell's Food Service 9827 S NC Hwy 150 *Web:* www.orrellsfoodservice.com	Linwood	NC	27299	336-752-2114	752-2060	297-9
Orrick 666 Fifth Ave *TF:* 866-342-5259 ■ *Web:* www.orrick.com	New York	NY	10103	212-506-5000	506-5151	428
Orrstown Bank 77 E King St *TF:* 888-677-7869 ■ *Web:* www.orrstown.com	Shippensburg	PA	17257	888-677-7869		70
Orscheln Farm & Home LLC 1800 Overcenter Dr PO Box 698 **Fax Area Code:* 660 ■ *TF:* 800-498-5090 ■ *Web:* www.orscheln.com	Moberly	MO	65270	800-577-2580	269-3500*	276
Orscheln Products LLC 1177 N Morley St *Web:* orschelnproducts.com	Moberly	MO	65270	660-263-4377		247
ORT American Inc 75 Maiden Ln 10th Fl *TF:* 800-519-2678 ■ *Web:* www.ortamerica.org	New York	NY	10038	212-505-7700	674-3057	48-5
ORT Tool & Die Corp 6555 S Dixie Hwy **Fax Area Code:* 734 ■ *Web:* www.orttool.com	Erie	MI	48133	419-242-9553	848-4308*	757
Ortanique Restaurant 278 Miracle Mile *Web:* ortaniquerestaurants.com	Coral Gables	FL	33134	305-446-7710	446-9895	671
Ortco Inc 1317 SE 25th St *TF:* 800-654-4891 ■ *Web:* www.ortcoinc.com	Oklahoma City	OK	73129	405-670-2803	672-5681	537
Ortec Inc 505 Gentry Memorial Hwy PO Box 1469 *Web:* ortecinc.com	Easley	SC	29641	864-859-1471		145
Orthman Manufacturing Inc 75765 Rd 435 PO Box B *TF:* 800-658-3270 ■ *Web:* www.orthman.com	Lexington	NE	68850	308-324-4654	324-5001	273

				Phone	Fax	Class
Ortho Computer Systems Inc 1107 Buckeye Ave *TF:* 800-678-4644 ■ *Web:* www.ortho2.com	Ames	IA	50010	515-233-1026		177
Ortho Development Corp 12187 S Business Pk Dr *TF:* 800-429-8339 ■ *Web:* www.odev.com	Draper	UT	84020	801-553-9991		477
Ortho Kinematics Inc 110 Wild Basin Rd Ste 250 *Web:* www.orthokinematics.com	Austin	TX	78746	512-334-5490		475
Ortho Technology Inc 17401 Commerce Park Blvd *Web:* www.orthotechnology.com	Tampa	FL	33647	813-991-5896		476
OrthoAccel Technologies Inc 8275 El Rio St Ste 100 *Web:* acceledent.com	Houston	TX	77054	832-631-1660		228
Ortho-Clinical Diagnostics Inc 1001 US Rt 202 N **Fax Area Code:* 585 ■ *TF:* 800-828-6316 ■ *Web:* www.orthoclinicaldiagnostics.com	Raritan	NJ	08869	800-828-6316	453-3660*	476
OrthoCor Medical Inc 1251 Red Fox Rd *Web:* www.orthocormedical.com	Arden Hills	MN	55112	952-217-6366		477
Orthodent Ltd 311 Viola Ave *TF:* 800-267-8463 ■ *Web:* www.orthodentus.com	Oshawa	ON	L1H3A7	905-436-3133		415
Orthodox Church in America (OCA) 6850 N Hempstead Tpke *Web:* www.oca.org	Syosset	NY	11791	516-922-0550	922-0954	637-10
Orthodox Union (OU) 11 Broadway *TF:* 855-505-7500 ■ *Web:* www.ou.org	New York	NY	10004	212-563-4000	564-9058	48-20
Orthofeet Inc 152A Veterans Dr *Web:* www.orthofeet.com	Northvale	NJ	07647	201-767-6224		477
Orthofix Inc 1720 Bray Central Dr *TF:* 800-527-0404 ■ *Web:* www.orthofix.com	McKinney	TX	75069	469-742-2500	742-2556	477
Orthogonal 222 W Merchandise Mart Plz Ste 1230 *Web:* www.pathfindersoftware.com	Chicago	IL	60654	312-372-1058		180
Orthopaedic Hospital 403 W Adams Blvd *Web:* ortho-institute.org	Los Angeles	CA	90007	213-742-1000	741-8338	374-7
OrthoPediatrics Corp 2850 Frontier Dr *TF:* 877-268-6339 ■ *Web:* www.orthopediatrics.com	Warsaw	IN	46582	574-268-6379	269-3692	477
Orthopedic and Sports Physical Therapy Associates Inc (OSPTA) 625 Lincoln Plz Ste 208 **Fax Area Code:* 724 ■ *TF:* 800-337-6452 ■ *Web:* www.osptainc.com	Charleroi	PA	15022	800-337-6452	483-4793*	371
Orthopedic Designs North America Inc 5912 Breckenridge Pkwy Ste F *TF:* 888-635-8535 ■ *Web:* odi-na.com	Tampa	FL	33610	888-635-8535		475
OrthoSensor Inc 1855 Griffin Rd Ste A-310 *Web:* www.orthosensor.com	Dania Beach	FL	33004	954-577-7770		477
Orthotic & Prosthetic Lab Inc 748 Marshall Ave *Web:* www.oandplabinc.com	Saint Louis	MO	63119	314-968-8555	968-0037	477
Orthotic Prosthetic Center Inc 8330 Professional Hill Dr *Web:* www.opc1.com	Fairfax	VA	22031	703-698-5007		45
ORTIG (Old Republic National Title Insurance Co) 400 2nd Ave S **Fax Area Code:* 612 ■ *TF:* 800-328-4441 ■ *Web:* www.oldrepublictitle.com	Minneapolis	MN	55401	800-328-4441	371-1191*	391-6
Ortiz Enterprises Inc 6 Cushing Way Ste 200 *Web:* www.ortizent.com	Irvine	CA	92618	949-753-1414		189-5
Ortman Fluid power 1400 N 30th St Ste 20 *TF:* 844-759-4922 ■ *Web:* www.ortmanfluidpower.com	Quincy	IL	62301	217-277-0321	222-1773	223
Ortonville Recreation Area 5779 Hadley Rd *Web:* www.michigan.org	Ortonville	MI	48462	810-797-4439		565
ORU (Off Road Unlimited) 2636 N Ontario St *TF:* 888-365-0244 ■ *Web:* www.offroadunlimited.com	Burbank	CA	91504	818-563-1208	729-1919	54
Orvis International Travel 178 Conservation Way **Fax Area Code:* 802 ■ *TF:* 800-547-4322 ■ *Web:* www.orvis.com	Sunderland	VT	05250	888-235-9763	362-8795*	710
Orycon Control Technology Inc 3407 Rose Ave *Web:* www.oryconeu.cz	Ocean	NJ	07712	732-922-2400	922-2403	757
Oryx Insurance Brokerage Inc 2 Court St Ste 401 *TF:* 888-462-6799 ■ *Web:* www.oryxinsurance.com	Binghamton	NY	13901	607-724-0173		390
Oryx Midstream Services LLC 4000 N Big Spring Ste 400 *TF:* 844-394-0841 ■ *Web:* www.oryxmidstream.com	Midland	TX	79705	432-684-4272		536
OSA (Optical Society of America) 2010 Massachusetts Ave NW *TF:* 800-766-4672 ■ *Web:* www.osa.org	Washington	DC	20036	202-223-8130	223-1096	49-8
OSA (Oregon State Archives) 800 Summer St NE *Web:* www.arcweb.sos.state.or.us	Salem	OR	97310	503-373-0701	378-4118	387
Osage County 205 E Main St *Web:* www.osagecountyhd.org	Linn	MO	65051	573-897-2139	897-4915	338
Osage County 900 S St Paul Ave *TF:* 888-287-3150 ■ *Web:* ocso.net	Pawhuska	OK	74056	918-287-3535	287-6011	338
Osage Hills State Park 2131 Osage Hills State Park Rd *Web:* www.travelok.com	Pawhuska	OK	74056	918-336-4141	337-2176	565
Osage Valley Electric Cooperative Assn 1321 N Orange St *Web:* osagevalley.com	Butler	MO	64730	660-679-3131		245
Osaka Japanese Bistro 4205 W Sahara Ave *Web:* www.lasvegas-sushi.com	Las Vegas	NV	89102	702-876-4988		671
Osaka Japanese Restaurant 515 Westheimer Rd *Web:* www.osakahoustontx.com	Houston	TX	77006	713-533-9098		671
Osaka Restaurant 244 Adams Ave *Web:* osakarestaurant.business.site	Scranton	PA	18503	570-341-9600		671
OSBA (Ohio State Bar Assn) 1700 Lake Shore Dr *TF:* 800-282-6556 ■ *Web:* www.ohiobar.org	Columbus	OH	43204	614-487-2050	487-1008	72

Name / Address	City	State	ZIP	Phone	Fax	Class
Osbee Industries Inc 99 Calvert St 100 — *Web:* osbee.com	Harrison	NY	10528	914-777-6611		180
Osborn Barr Paramore OBP 914 Spruce St — *Web:* obpagency.com	Saint Louis	MO	63102	314-726-5511		4
Osborn Health & Rehabilitation 3333 N Civic Center Plz — *Web:* osbornhealth.com	Scottsdale	AZ	85251	480-994-1333		450
Osborn Intl 5401 Hamilton Ave — *TF:* 800-720-3358 ■ *Web:* www.osborn.com	Cleveland	OH	44114	216-361-1900	361-1913	103
Osborn Medical Corp 100 W Main St — *Web:* www.osbornmedical.com	Utica	MN	55979	507-932-5028		477
Osborne Assn 809 Westchester Ave — *Web:* www.osborncny.org	Bronx	NY	10455	718-707-2600		48-8
Osborne Bros 201 Eddings Ln — *Web:* osbornefoods.com	Nashville	TN	37214	615-885-7338	872-7295	345
Osborne Coinage Co, The 2851 Massachusetts Ave — *TF:* 877-480-0456 ■ *Web:* www.osbornecoin.com	Cincinnati	OH	45225	513-681-5424	681-5604	488
Osborne Construction Company Inc 10602 NE 38th Pl Ste 100 — *Web:* www.osborne.cc	Kirkland	WA	98033	425-827-4221	828-4314	186
Osborne County 114 County Rd — *Web:* www.osbornecounty.org	Osborne	KS	67473	785-346-2431	346-5252	338
Osborne Industries Inc 120 N Industrial Ave — *TF:* 800-255-0316 ■ *Web:* www.osborneindustries.com	Osborne	KS	67473	785-346-2192		273
Osborne Partners Capital Management LLC 580 California St Ste 1900 — *TF:* 800-362-7734 ■ *Web:* osbornepartners.com	San Francisco	CA	94104	415-362-5637		401
Osborne Wood Products Inc 4618 Hwy 123 — *TF:* 800-849-8876 ■ *Web:* www.osbornewood.com	Toccoa	GA	30577	800-849-8876		321
Osbornedale State Park 555 Roosevelt Dr — *TF:* 800-208-2018 ■ *Web:* portal.ct.gov	Derby	CT	06418	800-208-2018		565
Osbrink Talent Agency Inc 4343 Lankershim Blvd Ste 100 — *Web:* www.osbrinkagency.com	North Hollywood	CA	91602	818-760-2488		506
Oscar De La Renta Ltd 11 W 42nd St — *TF:* 888-782-6357 ■ *Web:* www.oscardelarenta.com	New York	NY	10036	888-782-6357		277
Oscar Gruss & Son Inc 430 Park Ave 6th Fl — *Web:* www.oscargruss.com	New York	NY	10022	212-419-4000	317-5907	690
Oscar Printing Co 57 Columbia Sq — *Web:* opportunitymart.com	San Francisco	CA	94103	415-626-8818		687
Oscar Scherer State Park 1843 S Tamiami Trl — *Web:* www.floridastateparks.org	Osprey	FL	34229	941-483-5956	480-3007	565
Oscar W. Larson Co 10100 Dixie Hwy — *TF:* 800-482-1200 ■ *Web:* www.larsonco.com	Clarkston	MI	48348	248-620-0070		579
Oscar Wilson Engines & Parts Inc 826 Lone Star Dr — **Fax Area Code:* 800 ■ *TF:* 800-873-6722 ■ *Web:* oscar-wilson.com	O'Fallon	MO	63366	636-978-1313	873-6720*	386
Oscar Winski Company Inc 2407 N Ninth St — *Web:* www.oscarwinski.com	LaFayette	IN	47904	765-742-1102		492
Osceola County 1 Courthouse Sq — *Web:* www.osceola.org	Kissimmee	FL	34741	407-742-2000		338
Osceola County 301 W Upton Ave — *Web:* www.osceola-county.org	Reed City	MI	49677	231-832-3261	832-6149	338
Osceola County 300 7th St — *Web:* osceolacountyia.org	Sibley	IA	51249	712-754-2241		338
Osceola Electric Co-opeartive Inc 1102 Egret Dr PO Box 127 — *TF:* 888-754-2519 ■ *Web:* www.osceolaelectric.com	Sibley	IA	51249	712-754-2519		245
Osceola Mills Public Library 600 Lingle St POBox 212 — *Web:* aruathite.tripod.com	Osceola Mills	PA	16666	814-339-7229		434-3
Osceola News-Gazette 108 Church St — *Web:* www.aroundosceola.com	Kissimmee	FL	34741	407-846-7600		532-4
Osco Industries Inc PO Box 1388 — *Web:* oscoind.com	Portsmouth	OH	45662	740-354-3183		307
Oscoda County 311 S Morenci Ave — *Web:* www.oscodacountymi.com	Mio	MI	48647	989-826-1109		338
Oscor Inc 3816 DeSoto Blvd — *TF:* 800-726-7267 ■ *Web:* www.oscor.com	Palm Harbor	FL	34683	727-937-2511		250
Osda Contract Services Inc 291 Pepes Farm Rd — *Web:* www.osda.com	Milford	CT	06460	203-878-2155		253
OSE (One Stop Environmental LLC) 4800 Division Ave — *Web:* www.onestopenv.com	Birmingham	AL	35222	205-595-8188	595-8901	660
Oseberg LLC 914 N Broadway Ave Ste 230 — *Web:* oseberg.io	Oklahoma City	OK	73102	405-415-7754		396
Oseman Insurance Agency 6750 Poplar Ave Ste 410 — *Web:* osemaninsurance.com	Memphis	TN	38138	901-762-8211		390
OSF (Ohio Star Forge Co) 4000 Mahoning Ave NW — *Web:* www.ohiostar.com	Warren	OH	44483	330-847-6360		483
OSF Digital 5600 Blvd des Galeries Bur 530 — *TF:* 888-548-4344 ■ *Web:* osf.digital	Quebec City	QC	G2K1M1	888-548-4344		631
OSF Healthcare System 800 NE Glen Oak Ave — *TF:* 877-574-5678 ■ *Web:* www.osfhealthcare.org	Peoria	IL	61603	877-574-5678		353
OSF International Inc 0715 SW Bancroft St — *Web:* www.osf.com	Portland	OR	97239	503-225-0433	226-6214	670
OSG Tap & Die Inc 676 E Fullerton Ave — *TF:* 800-837-2223 ■ *Web:* www.osgtool.com	Glendale Heights	IL	60139	630-790-1400	790-1477	493
Osgood Industries Inc 601 Burbank Rd — *Web:* www.osgoodinc.com	Oldsmar	FL	34677	813-448-9041	855-3068	641
Osgood Textile Company Inc 333 Park St — *TF:* 888-674-6638 ■ *Web:* www.osgoodtextile.com	West Springfield	MA	01089	413-737-6488		258
OSHA (Occupational Safety & Health Administration) 200 Constitution Ave NW — *TF:* 800-321-6742 ■ *Web:* www.osha.gov	Washington	DC	20210	202-693-2121		340-15
OSHEAN Inc 6946 Post Rd Ste 402 — *Web:* www.oshean.org	North Kingstown	RI	02852	401-398-7500		180
Oshkosh Chamber of Commerce 120 Jackson St — *Web:* www.oshkoshchamber.com	Oshkosh	WI	54901	920-303-2266	303-2263	139
Oshkosh Coil Spring Inc 3575 N Main St — *TF:* 800-638-8360 ■ *Web:* www.oshkoshcoilspring.com	Oshkosh	WI	54901	920-235-7620		492
Oshkosh Convention & Visitors Bureau 2401 W Waukau Ave — *Web:* visitoshkosh.com	Oshkosh	WI	54904	920-303-9200		48-20
Oshkosh Correctional Institution 1730 W Snell Rd — *Web:* doc.wi.gov	Oshkosh	WI	54901	920-231-4010	236-2615	213
Oshkosh Door Co 2501 Universal St — *Web:* oshkoshdoor.com	Oshkosh	WI	54904	920-233-6161		499
Oshkosh Northwestern Co 224 State St — *TF:* 800-924-6168 ■ *Web:* www.thenorthwestern.com	Oshkosh	WI	54901	920-235-7700		637-8
Oshkosh Public Library 106 Washington Ave — *Web:* www.oshkoshpubliclibrary.org	Oshkosh	WI	54901	920-236-5205		434-3
Oshkosh Public Museum 1331 Algoma Blvd — *Web:* www.oshkoshmuseum.org	Oshkosh	WI	54901	920-236-5799		520
Oshkosh Specialty Vehicles LLC 12770 44th St N — *Web:* www.oshkoshsv.com	Clearwater	FL	33762	727-573-0400		489
Oshkosh Truck Corp 2307 Oregon St — *TF:* 800-392-9921 ■ *Web:* oshkoshdefense.com	Oshkosh	WI	54903	920-235-9150		516
Oshkosh Truck Credit Union 2772 Oregon St — *Web:* oshkoshtruckcu.org	Oshkosh	WI	54902	920-233-2611	426-4428	219
OSI (Open Space Institute) 1350 Broadway Ste 201 — *Web:* www.openspaceinstitute.org	New York	NY	10018	212-290-8200	244-3441	48-13
OSI (Open Systems International Inc) 4101 Arrowhead Dri — *Web:* www.osii.com	Medina	MN	55340	763-551-0559		809
OSI Digital Inc 5950 Canoga Ave Ste 300 — *Web:* osidigital.com	Woodland Hills	CA	91367	818-992-2700	992-8700	194
OSI North America 1225 Corporate Blvd — *Web:* www.osigroup.com	Aurora	IL	60505	630-851-6600		473
OSI Software Inc 777 Davis St Ste 250 — *Web:* www.osisoft.com	San Leandro	CA	94577	510-297-5800	357-8136	178-10
OSI Systems Inc 12525 Chadron Ave — *NASDAQ: OSIS* ■ *TF:* 800-579-1639 ■ *Web:* www.osi-systems.com	Hawthorne	CA	90250	310-978-0516		696
OSIA (Order Sons of Italy in America) 219 E St NE — *TF:* 800-552-6742 ■ *Web:* www.osia.org	Washington	DC	20002	202-547-2900	546-8168	48-14
Osiris Therapeutics Inc 7015 Albert Einstein Dr — *OTC: OSIR* ■ *TF:* 888-674-9551 ■ *Web:* www.osiris.com	Columbia	MD	21046	443-545-1800	283-4419	85
OSKI Technology Inc 2513 E Charleston Rd Ste 203 — *Web:* www.oskitechnology.com	Mountain View	CA	94043	408-216-7728		225
OSKO Inc 8085 NW 90th St — *Web:* www.oskomedical.com	Miami	FL	33166	305-599-7161	599-7144	475
Osler Hoskin & Harcourt LLP 100 King St W 1 First Canadian Pl Ste 6100 — *Web:* www.osler.com	Toronto	ON	M5X1B8	416-362-2111		41
OSMH (Orillia Soldiers' Memorial Hospital) 170 Colborne St W — *TF:* 866-797-0000 ■ *Web:* www.osmh.on.ca	Orillia	ON	L3V2Z3	705-325-2201	325-7953	374-2
Osmose Inc 2475 George Urban Blvd Ste 160 — *TF:* 800-877-7653 ■ *Web:* www.osmose.com	Depew	NY	14043	770-632-6700		818
OSO (Ottawa Symphony Orchestra) 2 Daly Ave Ste 250 — *Web:* ottawasymphony.com	Ottawa	ON	K1N6E2	613-231-7802		573-3
Osoyoos Lake State Park 2207 Juniper St — *Web:* oroville-wa.com	Oroville	WA	98844	509-476-3321		565
OSP Sling Inc 803 S 3rd Ave — *Web:* www.ospsling.com	Sequim	WA	98382	360-683-4109	683-6092	287
OSPA (Oregon State Pharmacy Assn) 147 SE 102nd Ave — *Web:* www.oregonpharmacy.org	Portland	OR	97216	503-582-9055	253-9172	585
OSPIRG (Oregon State Public Interest Research Group) 1536 SE 11th Ave — *Web:* ospirg.org	Portland	OR	97214	503-231-4181		633
Osprey Central School 408053 Grey Rd 4 — *TF:* 800-661-7509 ■ *Web:* www.bwdsb.on.ca	Maxwell	ON	N0C1J0	519-922-2341		685
Osprey Medical Inc 7600 Executive Dr — *Web:* ospreymed.com	Eden Prairie	MN	55344	952-955-8230		250
Osprey Software & Systems Inc 13 Osprey Dr	Berkley	MA	02779	508-821-4486		180
Osprey Valley 18821 Main St — *TF:* 800-833-1561 ■ *Web:* www.ospreyvalley.com	Caledon	ON	L7K1R1	519-927-9034		707
OSPTA (Orthopedic and Sports Physical Therapy Associates Inc) 625 Lincoln Plz Ste 208 — **Fax Area Code:* 724 ■ *TF:* 800-337-6452 ■ *Web:* www.osptainc.com	Charleroi	PA	15022	800-337-6452	483-4793*	371
OSRAM Sylvania Inc 100 Endicott St — *Web:* www.sylvania.com	Danvers	MA	01923	978-750-2513	750-2152	437
OSS Inc 1 Dell Way Ste 114 — *Web:* www.ossjobs.com	Round Rock	TX	78664	512-255-2424		809
Ossian State Bank 102 N Jefferson St — *Web:* ossianstatebank.com	Ossian	IN	46777	260-622-4141		70
Ossid Corp 4000 College Rd — *TF:* 800-334-8369 ■ *Web:* www.ossid.com	Battleboro	NC	27809	252-446-6177	442-7694	547

	Phone	Fax	Class
Ossining Union Free School District 190 Croton Ave. Ossining NY 10562 *TF:* 877-769-7447 ■ *Web:* ossiningufsd.org	914-941-7700	941-7291	685
OSSNet Inc PO Box 369 Oakton VA 22124 *Web:* www.oss.net	703-242-1701	281-0888	194
Ossur 27412 Aliso Viejo Pkwy Aliso Viejo CA 92656 *TF:* 800-233-6263 ■ *Web:* www.ossur.com	800-233-6263		111
OST Inc 2001 M St NW Ste 3000 Washington DC 20036 *Web:* www.ostglobal.com	202-466-8099		463
Ostbye & Anderson Inc 10055 51st Ave N. Minneapolis MN 55442 **Fax Area Code:* 877 ■ *TF:* 866-553-1515 ■ *Web:* www.ostbye.com	866-553-1515	553-1515*	409
Osteogenics Biomedical Inc 4620 71st St. Lubbock TX 79424 *TF:* 888-796-1923 ■ *Web:* www.osteogenics.com	806-796-1923	796-0059	476
Osteomed Corp 3885 Arapaho Rd Addison TX 75001 *TF:* 800-456-7779 ■ *Web:* www.osteomed.com	972-677-4600		476
Osteoporosis Canada Resource Ctr 1090 Don Mills Rd Ste 301 Toronto ON M3C3R6 *TF:* 800-463-6842 ■ *Web:* www.osteoporosis.ca	416-696-2663	696-2673	434-3
Osterhout Free Library 71 S Franklin St Wilkes-Barre PA 18701 *Web:* osterhout.info	570-823-0156		434-3
Osteria 177 177 Main St Annapolis MD 21401 *Web:* www.osteria177.com	410-267-7700		671
Osteria Il Centro 5101 Main St. Kansas City MO 64112 *Web:* osteriailcentro.com	816-561-2369		671
Osteria Panevino 722 Fifth Ave San Diego CA 92101 *Web:* www.osteriapanevino.com	619-595-7959		671
Osterkamp Transportation Group 1350 E Philadelphia St Pomona CA 91766 *Web:* www.osterkampgrp.com	909-590-8200	590-8239	780
Osterman & Company Inc 726 S Main St Cheshire CT 06410 *Web:* www.osterman-co.com	203-272-2233		605-2
Ostermancron Inc 10830 Millington Ct Cincinnati OH 45242 *Web:* ostermancron.com	513-771-3377		321
Osterville Free Library 43 Wianno Ave Osterville MA 02655 *Web:* ostervillevillagelibrary.org	508-428-5757	428-5557	434-3
Osthoff Resort, The 101 Osthoff Ave PO Box 151 Elkhart Lake WI 53020 *TF:* 800-876-3399 ■ *Web:* www.osthoff.com	855-671-6870		669
Ostler Group Inc, The 7430 S Creek Rd Ste 204 Sandy UT 84093 *Web:* www.ostlergroup.com	801-566-6081		7
Ostrem Tool Company Inc 205 Inman Rd Lyman SC 29365 *Web:* www.ostremtool.com	864-879-7451	877-1633	493
Ostrom Mushroom Farms 8323 Steilacoom Rd SE Olympia WA 98513 *Web:* www.ostrommushrooms.com	360-491-1410		10-7
Ostrow Reisin Berk & Abrams Ltd 455 N Cityfront Plaza Dr Chicago IL 60611 *Web:* www.orba.com	312-670-7444	670-8301	2
OSU Medical Ctr 744 W Ninth St Tulsa OK 74127 *Web:* www.osumc.com	918-599-1000		374-3
Oswald Company Inc 308 E Eigth St Ste 500 Cincinnati OH 45202 *Web:* oswaldco.com	513-793-8080		610
Oswald Cos 1100 Superior Ave Ste 1500 Cleveland OH 44114 *TF:* 855-467-9253 ■ *Web:* www.oswaldcompanies.com	216-367-8787		390
Oswego County 46 E Bridge St Oswego NY 13126 *Web:* www.oswegocounty.com	315-349-8621	349-8237	338
Oswego County Opportunities Inc 239 Oneida St Fulton NY 13069 *TF:* 877-342-7618 ■ *Web:* www.oco.org	315-598-4717	592-7533	48-15
Oswego Hospital 110 W 6th St Oswego NY 13126 *Web:* www.oswegohealth.org	315-349-5511		374-3
Otani 1625 Golden Gate Plz Mayfield Heights OH 44124 *Web:* www.otanicleveland.com	440-442-7098		671
OTB Solutions Group LLC 12345 Lake City Way NE Ste 2055 Seattle WA 98125 *Web:* www.otbsolutions.com	206-445-7400		196
OTC Global Holdings 5151 San Felipe Ste 2200 Houston TX 77056 *TF:* 877-737-8511 ■ *Web:* www.otcgh.com	713-358-5450		360-3
OTC Markets Group Inc 300 Vesey St 12th Fl New York NY 10282 *Web:* www.otcmarkets.com	212-896-4400		822
OTEC (Oregon Trail Electric Co-op) 4005 23rd St PO Box 226 Baker City OR 97814 *Web:* otec.coop	541-523-3616		245
Oteco Inc PO Box 1849 Houston TX 77251 *Web:* oteco.com	713-695-3693	695-3520	641
Otelco Inc 505 Third Ave E Oneonta AL 35121 *NASDAQ:* OTT ■ *Web:* www.otelco.com	205-625-3574		736
Otero County 1000 New York Ave Ste 109 Alamogordo NM 88310 *Web:* www.co.otero.nm.us	575-434-8849	443-2941	338
Otero County 13 W Third St Rm 210 La Junta CO 81050 *TF:* 800-438-3752 ■ *Web:* www.oterogov.com	719-383-3020	383-3026	338
Otero County Electric Cooperative Inc 404 Burro Ave PO Box 227 Cloudcroft NM 88317 *TF:* 800-548-4660 ■ *Web:* www.ocec-inc.com	575-682-2521	682-3109	245
Otero Junior College 1802 Colorado Ave La Junta CO 81050 *Web:* www.ojc.edu	719-384-6831	384-6933	162
Otesaga, The 60 Lake St Cooperstown NY 13326 *TF:* 800-348-6222 ■ *Web:* www.otesaga.com	607-547-9931	547-9675	669
Other Firm LLC, The 618 NW Glisan St Ste 201 Portland OR 97209 *Web:* www.theotherfirm.com	503-336-5359		177
Otherwise Inc 840 S Canal St Fl 7 Chicago IL 60607 *Web:* www.otherwiseinc.com	312-226-1144		344
OtherWorld Enterprises Inc PO Box 1721 Simi Valley CA 93062 **Fax Area Code:* 203 ■ *TF:* 800-493-2237 ■ *Web:* www.other-world.com	805-768-4638	779-4638*	225
Otics USA Inc 5555 Interstate View Dr. Morristown TN 37813 *Web:* oticsusa.com	423-581-9933		60
OTIS 10 Farm Springs Rd. Farmington CT 06032 *Web:* expressevanslift.com	860-676-6000		256
OTIS College of Art & Design 9045 Lincoln Blvd Los Angeles CA 90045 *TF:* 800-527-6847 ■ *Web:* www.otis.edu	310-665-6820	665-6821	164
Otis Graphics Inc 290 Grant Ave. Lyndhurst NJ 07071 *Web:* www.otisgraphics.com	201-438-7120	438-5546	687
OTIS McAllister Inc 300 Frank H Ogawa Plz Ste 400 Oakland CA 94612 *Web:* www.otismcallister.com	415-421-6010	421-6016	297-11
Otis Technology 6987 Laura St PO Box 582 Lyons Falls NY 13368 *Web:* otistec.com	315-348-4300		711
OTO Development LLC 100 Dunbar St Ste 402 Spartanburg SC 29306 *Web:* www.otodevelopment.com	864-596-8930		378
Otoe County Otoe County Country Nebraska City NE 68410 *Web:* www.newschannelnebraska.com	402-873-9505	873-9506	338
Otomix Inc 7585 Commercial Way Ste E Henderson NV 89011 *TF:* 800-701-7867 ■ *Web:* www.otomix.com	310-215-6100		301
OTP Industrial Solutions 3601 N Fruitridge Ave Terre Haute IN 47804 *Web:* www.otpnet.com	812-466-2734		385
OTR Wheel Engineering Inc 6 Riverside Industrial Pk NE Rome GA 30161 *TF:* 800-833-6309 ■ *Web:* otrwheel.com	706-235-9781	234-8137	754
OTS (Organization for Tropical Studies) 410 Swift Ave Durham NC 27705 *Web:* tropicalstudies.org	919-684-5774	684-5661	49-5
OTS 3924 Clock Pointe Trl Stow OH 44224 *TF:* 877-445-2058 ■ *Web:* www.ots.net	877-445-2058		41
OTS Astracon 3115 Beam Rd. Charlotte NC 28219 **Fax Area Code:* 704 ■ *Web:* www.otsusa.com	877-769-8879	424-5622*	311
OTS International Inc 2615 Industrial Ln Conroe TX 77301 *Web:* www.otsintl.com	936-539-0099		537
Otsego Club 696 M-32 E Main St PO Box 556 Gaylord MI 49734 *TF:* 800-752-5510 ■ *Web:* www.otsegoclub.com	989-732-5181	732-0497	669
Otsego County 197 Main St. Cooperstown NY 13326 *Web:* www.otsegocounty.com	607-547-4202	547-4260	338
Otsego County 225 W Main St Gaylord MI 49735 *Web:* www.otsegocountymi.gov	989-732-6484		338
Otsego County Chamber 189 Main St Ste 201 Oneonta NY 13820 *Web:* otsegocc.com	607-267-4010	432-4506	139
Otsego Electric Co-opeartive Inc (OEC) PO Box 128 Hartwick NY 13348 *TF:* 844-843-6842 ■ *Web:* www.otsegoec.coop	607-293-6622	293-6624	245
Otsego Mutual Fire Insurance Co 143 Arnold Rd PO Box 40 Burlington Flats NY 13315 *Web:* www.otsegomutual.com	607-965-8211		390
Otsuka America Inc 1 Embarcadero Ctr Ste 2020 San Francisco CA 94111 *Web:* otsuka-america.com	415-986-5300		360-3
Otsuka America Pharmaceutical Inc 2440 Research Blvd Rockville MD 20850 *TF:* 800-562-3974 ■ *Web:* www.otsuka-us.com	301-424-9055		582
OTT Inc 2675 Long Lake Rd Saint Paul MN 55113 *Web:* www.ott-inc.com	651-262-2600	262-2601	178-1
Ottawa Board of Trade 328 Somerset St W Ottawa ON K2P0J9 *Web:* www.ottawabot.ca	613-236-3631	236-7498	137
Ottawa Citizen 1101 Baxter Rd PO Box 5020 Ottawa ON K2C3M4 *TF:* 800-267-6100 ■ *Web:* www.ottawacitizen.com	613-829-9100	726-1198	532-1
Ottawa City Hall 110 Laurier Ave W Ottawa ON K1P1J1 *TF:* 866-261-9799 ■ *Web:* www.ottawa.ca	613-580-2400		337
Ottawa County 414 Washington St Grand Haven MI 49417 *Web:* www.miottawa.org	616-846-8320	846-8179	338
Ottawa County 102 E Central Ave Ste 103 Miami OK 74354 *Web:* ottawa.okcounties.org	918-542-3332	542-8260	338
Ottawa County 307 N Concord St Minneapolis KS 67467 *Web:* www.ottawacounty.org	785-392-2279	392-2011	338
Ottawa County 315 Madison St. Port Clinton OH 43452 *TF:* 800-697-9807 ■ *Web:* www.co.ottawa.oh.us	419-734-6710	734-6898	338
Ottawa Fringe Festival 100-2 Daly Ave Ottawa ON K1N6E2 *Web:* ottawafringe.com	613-232-6162		747
Ottawa Herald, The 214 S Hickory St Ottawa KS 66067 *Web:* www.ottawaherald.com	785-242-4700		532-3
Ottawa Macdonald-Cartier International Airport 1000 Airport Pkwy Private Ste 2500 Ottawa ON K1V9B4 *Web:* yow.ca	613-248-2000	248-2003	27
Ottawa Regional Cancer Foundation, The 1500 Alta Vista Dr. Ottawa ON K1G3Y9 *TF:* 855-247-3527 ■ *Web:* www.ottawacancer.ca	613-247-3527		305
Ottawa Symphony Orchestra (OSO) 2 Daly Ave Ste 250 Ottawa ON K1N6E2 *Web:* ottawasymphony.com	613-231-7802		573-3
Ottawa Tourism & Convention Authority 150 Elgin St Ste 1405 Ottawa ON K2P1L4 **Fax Area Code:* 613 ■ *TF:* 800-363-4465 ■ *Web:* www.ottawatourism.ca	800-363-4465	237-7339*	206
Ottawa University 1001 S Cedar St Ottawa KS 66067 *TF:* 800-755-5200 ■ *Web:* www.ottawa.edu	785-242-5200		166
Ottawa Visitors Ctr 106 W Lafayette St Ottawa IL 61350 *Web:* pickusottawail.com	815-434-2737	434-4530	206
Otten Johnson Robinson Neff & Ragonetti PC 950 17th St Ste 1600 Denver CO 80202 *Web:* www.ottenjohnson.com	303-825-8400		428
Ottenweller Company Inc 3011 Congressional Pkwy Fort Wayne IN 46808 *Web:* www.ottenweller.com	260-484-3166	484-9798	91
Otter Computer Inc 3350 Scott Blvd Bldg 4 Santa Clara CA 95054 *Web:* www.otterusa.com	408-982-9358	982-9335	174

Name / Address	City	State	ZIP	Phone	Fax	Class
Otter Creek Management Inc 222 Lakeview Ave Ste 1100 *Web:* ottercreekfunds.com	West Palm Beach	FL	33401	561-832-4110		401
Otter Creek State Park PO Box 43 *Web:* stateparks.utah.gov	Antimony	UT	84712	435-624-3268	624-3203	565
Otter Tail Corp 4334 18th Ave SW PO Box 9156 *NASDAQ:* OTTR ■ *TF:* 866-410-8780 ■ *Web:* www.ottertail.com	Fargo	ND	58106	701-232-4108		360-3
Otter Tail County, Minnesota 520 Fir Ave W *TF:* 800-232-9077 ■ *Web:* ottertailcountymn.us	Fergus Falls	MN	56537	218-998-8000	998-8438	338
Otter Tail Power Co 215 S Cascade St *TF:* 800-257-4044 ■ *Web:* www.otpco.com	Fergus Falls	MN	56537	218-739-8200		787
Otter Tail Telcom 230 W Lincoln Ave *TF:* 800-247-2706 ■ *Web:* www.parkregion.com	Fergus Falls	MN	56537	218-998-2000		116
Otterbein College 1 S Grove St *TF:* 800-488-8144 ■ *Web:* www.otterbein.edu	Westerville	OH	43081	614-823-1500	823-1200	166
Otterbein senior lifestyle choices 580 N SR 741 *TF:* 888-513-9131 ■ *Web:* www.otterbein.org	Lebanon	OH	45036	513-933-5400	932-1054	672
Otterbine Barebo Inc 3840 Main Rd E *TF:* 800-237-8837 ■ *Web:* www.otterbine.com	Emmaus	PA	18049	610-965-6018		321
Otto Baum Company Inc 866 N Main St *Web:* www.ottobaum.com	Morton	IL	61550	309-266-7114	263-1050	189-7
Otto Brehm Inc PO Box 249 *TF:* 800-272-6886 ■ *Web:* www.ottobrehm.com	Yonkers	NY	10710	914-968-6100	968-8926	297-11
Otto Bremer Foundation 445 Minnesota St Ste 2250 *Web:* ottobremer.org	Saint Paul	MN	55101	651-227-8036		305
Otto Candies LLC 17271 US 90 *Web:* ottocandies.com	Des Allemands	LA	70030	504-469-7700	469-7740	465
Otto Design & Marketing 1611 Colley Ave *Web:* www.thinkotto.com	Norfolk	VA	23517	757-622-4050		636
Otto Engineering Inc 2 E Main St *TF:* 888-234-6886 ■ *Web:* www.ottoexcellence.com	Carpentersville	IL	60110	847-428-7171	428-1956	729
Otto Frei and Jules Borel 126 2nd St **Fax Area Code:* 800 ■ *Web:* www.ofrei.com	Oakland	CA	94604	510-832-0355	900-3734*	411
Otto Instrument Service Inc 1441 Valencia Pl *Web:* www.ottoinstrument.com	Ontario	CA	91761	909-930-5800		22
Otto Naumann Ltd 22 E 80th St *Web:* www.ottonaumannltd.com	New York	NY	10075	212-734-4443	535-0617	42
Otto Trucking Inc 4220 E McDowell Ste 108 *Web:* www.ottotrucking.com	Mesa	AZ	85215	480-641-3500	641-3550	780
Otto's Restaurant & Bar 6405 Mineral Pt Rd *Web:* www.ottosrestaurant.com	Madison	WI	53705	608-274-4044	274-1358	671
Ottobock North America 11501 Alterra Pky Ste 600 *TF:* 800-328-4058 ■ *Web:* www.ottobockus.com	Austin	TX	78758	800-328-4058		475
Ottosen Propeller & Accessories Inc 105 S 28th St *TF:* 800-528-7551 ■ *Web:* hartzellprop.com	Phoenix	AZ	85034	602-275-8514	275-8594	770
Ottoville Mutual Telephone Co 245 3rd St *Web:* ottovillemutual.com	Fort Jennings	OH	45844	419-453-3324	453-2468	224
Ottr Inc 10202 F St *Web:* ottr.com	Omaha	NE	68127	402-836-0000		180
Ottumwa Area Chamber of Commerce 217 E Main St *Web:* www.gopip.org	Ottumwa	IA	52501	641-682-3465	682-3466	139
Ottumwa Courier 213 E Second St *TF:* 800-532-1504 ■ *Web:* www.ottumwacourier.com	Ottumwa	IA	52501	641-684-4611	684-7326	532-2
Ottumwa Public Library 102 W Fourth St *Web:* blog.ottumwapubliclibrary.org	Ottumwa	IA	52501	641-682-7563	682-4970	434-3
Ottumwa Regional Health Ctr 1001 Pennsylvania Ave *TF:* 800-933-6742 ■ *Web:* www.ottumwaregionalhealth.com	Ottumwa	IA	52501	641-684-2300		374-3
O-Two Medical Technologies Inc 7575 Kimbel St *TF:* 800-387-3405 ■ *Web:* otwo.com	Mississauga	ON	L5S1C8	905-677-9410		250
OTZ Telephone Co-opeartive Inc PO Box 324 *TF:* 800-478-3111 ■ *Web:* otz.net	Kotzebue	AK	99752	907-442-3114		736
OU (Orthodox Union) 11 Broadway *TF:* 855-505-7500 ■ *Web:* www.ou.org	New York	NY	10004	212-563-4000	564-9058	48-20
Ouabache State Park 4930 E State Rd 201 *Web:* www.in.gov	Bluffton	IN	46714	260-824-0926		565
OUAC (Ontario Universities Application Ctr) 170 Research Ln *Web:* www.ouac.on.ca	Guelph	ON	N1G5E2	519-823-1063		165
Ouachita Baptist University 410 Ouachita St *TF:* 800-342-5628 ■ *Web:* obu.edu	Arkadelphia	AR	71998	870-245-5000	245-5500	166
Ouachita Citizen 4423 Cypress St *Web:* www.hannapub.com	West Monroe	LA	71291	318-396-0602		532-4
Ouachita County Medical Ctr 638 California Ave SW *Web:* www.ouachitamedcenter.com	Camden	AR	71701	870-836-1000	231-4329	338
Ouachita Electric Co-opeartive Corp 700 Bradley Ferry Rd PO Box 877 *TF:* 877-252-4538 ■ *Web:* www.oecc.com	Camden	AR	71711	870-836-5791		245
Ouachita Machine Works Inc 120 N Hilton St *Web:* www.omwinc.com	West Monroe	LA	71291	318-396-1468	396-1668	189-9
Ouachita Parish 301 S Grand St Ste 104 *Web:* www.opclerkofcourt.com	Monroe	LA	71201	318-327-1444	327-1462	338
Ouachita Parish Public Library 1800 Stubbs Ave *Web:* www.oplib.org	Monroe	LA	71201	318-327-1490	327-1373	434-3
Ouellette Machinery Systems Inc 1761 Chase Dr *TF:* 800-545-7619 ■ *Web:* www.omsinc.net	Fenton	MO	63026	636-343-7200		547
Ouellette Plumbing & Heating 36 Dorset Ln *Web:* www.ouelletteplumbing.com	Williston	VT	05495	802-878-6004		189-10
Ouimette Goldstein & Andrews LLP 88 Markte St PO Box 192 *Web:* ogandalaw.com	Poughkeepsie	NY	12602	845-454-9700		41
Ouisi Bistro 3014 Granville St *Web:* www.ouisibistro.com	Vancouver	BC	V6H3J8	604-732-7550		671
Ounce of Prevention Fund of Florida Inc, The 111 N Gadsden St Ste 200 *Web:* www.ounce.org	Tallahassee	FL	32301	850-921-4494		317
Our Coop 525 Old Bellefonte Rd *Web:* www.oursc.k12.ar.us	Harrison	AR	72601	870-743-9100	302-3099	148
Our Credit Union 3070 Normandy Rd *Web:* ourcuonline.org	Royal Oak	MI	48073	248-549-3838		219
Our Family Veterinary Services 649 Lowell St *Web:* ourfamilyvetservices.com	Peabody	MA	01960	978-535-8200		794
Our Lady of Fatima Retreat House 5353 E 56th St *TF:* 800-382-9836 ■ *Web:* www.archindy.org	Indianapolis	IN	46226	317-545-7681	545-0095	673
Our Lady of Lourdes Memorial Hospital 169 Riverside Dr *Web:* www.lourdes.com	Binghamton	NY	13905	607-798-5111	729-7667	374-3
Our Lady of Lourdes Regional Medical Ctr 4801 Ambassador Caffery Pkwy *Web:* www.lourdesrmc.com	LaFayette	LA	70508	337-470-2000		374-3
Our Lady of the Lake Regional Medical Ctr 5000 Hennessy Blvd *Web:* ololrmc.com	Baton Rouge	LA	70808	225-765-6565		374-3
Our Lady of the Lake University 411 SW 24th St *TF:* 800-436-6558 ■ *Web:* www.ollusa.edu	San Antonio	TX	78207	210-434-6711	431-4036	166
Our Lady Queen of Peace Catholic School 1600 Hwy 2004 *Web:* www.olqpschool.org	Richwood	TX	77531	979-265-3909	265-9780	685
Our Lady Queen of the Most Holy Rosary Cathedral 2535 Collingwood Blvd *Web:* rosarycathedral.org	Toledo	OH	43610	419-244-9575		50-1
Our Sunday Visitor Inc 200 Noll Plz *TF:* 800-348-2440 ■ *Web:* www.osv.com	Huntington	IN	46750	260-356-8400	356-8472	637-8
Our Town 30 Browns Crossing Rd *Web:* ourtownnews.com	Pearl River	NY	10965	845-735-1342	620-9533	532-4
Ouray County PO Box C *Web:* www.ouraycountyco.gov	Ouray	CO	81427	970-325-4961	325-0452	338
OUSD (Oceanside Unified School District) 2111 Mission Ave *Web:* www.oside.k12.ca.us	Oceanside	CA	92058	760-966-4000		186
Out of Africa Wildlife Park 4020 N Cherry Rd *Web:* outofafricapark.com	Camp Verde	AZ	86322	928-567-2840	567-2839	823
Out There Advertising Inc 22 E Second St *Web:* outthereadvertising.com	Duluth	MN	55802	218-720-6002		7
Outback Steakhouse Inc 2202 NW Shore Blvd 5th Fl *Web:* www.outback.com	Tampa	FL	33607	813-282-1225		670
OutboundEngine 98 San Jacinto Blvd Ste 1300 *TF:* 800-562-7315 ■ *Web:* www.outboundengine.com	Austin	TX	78701	800-562-7315		195
Outbrain Inc 39 W 13th St 3rd Fl *Web:* www.outbrain.com	New York	NY	10011	212-867-0149		194
OutCast Agency, The 100 Montgomery St Ste 1201 *Web:* theoutcastagency.com	San Francisco	CA	94104	415-392-8282		636
Outdoor Adv Association of America Inc (OAAA) 1850 M St NW Ste 1040 *Web:* oaaa.org	Washington	DC	20036	202-833-5566	833-1522	615
Outdoor Adventure River Specialists Inc PO Box 67 *TF:* 800-346-6277 ■ *Web:* www.oars.com	Angels Camp	CA	95222	209-736-4677		760
Outdoor Amusement Business Association Inc (OABA) 1035 S Semoran Blvd Ste 1045A **Fax Area Code:* 952 ■ *TF:* 800-517-6222 ■ *Web:* oaba.org	Winter Park	FL	32792	407-848-4958	300-2419*	615
Outdoor Connection Inc 424 Neosho *Web:* outdoor-connection.com	Burlington	KS	66839	620-364-5500	364-5563	771
Outdoor Decor Store Inc 3375 Tamiami Trail N *Web:* outdoordecorstoreinc.com	Naples	FL	34103	239-659-6595		321
Outdoor Industry Assn (OIA) 4909 Pearl E Cir Ste 200 *Web:* outdoorindustry.org	Boulder	CO	80301	303-444-3353	444-3284	49-4
Outdoor Photographer Magazine 25 Braintree Hill Office Pk Ste 404 *TF:* 800-283-4410 ■ *Web:* www.outdoorphotographer.com	Braintree	MA	02184	617-706-9110	536-0102	457-14
Outdoor Power Equipment Institute (OPEI) 341 S Patrick St *Web:* opei.org	Alexandria	VA	22314	703-549-7600		49-4
Outdoor Sports Ctr 80 Danbury Rd *Web:* www.outdoorsports.com	Wilton	CT	06897	203-762-8797		711
Outdoor Ventures 10579 S Main St *Web:* outdoorventureshayward.com	Hayward	WI	54843	715-634-4447		711
Outdoorsy 1475 Folsom St 2nd Fl *Web:* www.outdoorsy.com	San Francisco	CA	94103	415-930-4841		449
Outer Banks Chamber of Commerce 101 Town Hall Dr PO Box 1757 *Web:* www.outerbankschamber.com	Kill Devil Hills	NC	27948	252-441-8144	441-0338	139
Outer Banks Press 75 E Dogwood Trail **Fax Area Code:* 800 ■ *Web:* www.outerbankspress.com	Kitty Hawk	NC	27949	252-261-0612	215-9698*	637-2
Outer Banks Visitors Bureau 1 Visitor Center Cir *TF:* 877-629-4386 ■ *Web:* www.outerbanks.org	Manteo	NC	27954	252-473-2138	473-5777	206
OuterBox Inc 325 S Main St 3rd Fl **Fax Area Code:* 877 ■ *TF:* 866-647-9218 ■ *Web:* www.outerboxdesign.com	Akron	OH	44308	866-647-9218	217-1347*	809
Outerlink Corp 187 Ballardvale St Ste A260 *TF:* 877-688-3770 ■ *Web:* www.outerlink.com	Wilmington	MA	01887	978-284-6070	268-5444	681

	Phone	Fax	Class
Outermost Inn 81 Lighthouse Rd. Aquinnah MA 02535 *Web:* www.outermostinn.com	508-645-3511		671
Outfest-Los Angeles Gay & Lesbian Film Festival 3470 Wilshire Blvd Ste 935 Los Angeles CA 90010 *TF:* 800-726-7147 ■ *Web:* www.outfest.org	213-480-7088	480-7099	282
Out-Fit 25 W Easy St Ste 304 Simi Valley CA 93065 *Web:* www.out-fit.net	310-410-1200		711
OUTFRONT Media Inc 405 Lexington Ave New York NY 10174 *Web:* www.outfrontmedia.com	212-297-6400		8
Outlet Collection Seattle, The 1101 Supermall Way Auburn WA 98001 *Web:* outletcollectionseattle.com	253-833-9500		460
Outlet Coworking 2110 K St. Sacramento CA 95816 *Web:* www.outletcoworking.com	916-476-9606		393
Outlets at Loveland 5661 McWhinney Blvd Loveland CO 80538 *Web:* www.outletsatloveland.com	970-663-1916		460
Outlook Computing Inc PO Box 375 Deerfield IL 60015 *Web:* www.outlookcomputing.com	847-236-1850	236-1851	180
Outlook Group Corp 1180 American Dr Neenah WI 54956 *Web:* www.outlookgroup.com	920-722-2333		627
Outlook Newspaper 800 Foothill Blvd La Canada Flintridge CA 91011 *Web:* outlooknewspapers.com	818-790-7500		532-3
Outokumpu 1 Steel Dr Calvert AL 36513 *Web:* www.outokumpu.com	251-829-3655		490
Outotec (Canada) Ltd 1551 Corporate Dr Burlington ON L7L6M3 *Web:* www.outotec.com	905-335-0002		111
Outpatient Imaging Affiliates (OIA) 840 Crescent Centre Dr Ste 200 Franklin TN 37067 *TF:* 866-591-5559 ■ *Web:* www.oiarad.com	615-550-6000		415
Outpost Lodge 28229 Cow Creek Rd. Pierre SD 57501 *Web:* www.theoutpostlodge.com	605-264-5450		671
Output Services Inc 6410 O'Dell Pl Boulder CO 80301 *Web:* www4.outputservices.com	303-530-3403		627
Outreach Communications 2801 Glenda St. Haltom City TX 76117 *TF:* 800-982-3760 ■ *Web:* www.thriftbenefits.com	817-288-7200		224
Outreach Healthcare Inc 269 W Renner Pkwy Richardson TX 75080 *TF:* 800-793-0081 ■ *Web:* www.outreachhealth.com	800-793-0081		363
Outreach Intl 129 W Lexington PO Box 210 Independence MO 64050 *TF:* 888-833-1235 ■ *Web:* outreach-international.org	816-833-0883	833-0103	48-5
Outrigger Energy LLC 1200 Seventeenth St Ste 900 Denver CO 80202 *Web:* www.outriggerenergy.com	720-638-7312		580
Outrigger Hotels & Resorts 2375 Kuhio Ave Honolulu HI 96815 **Fax Area Code:* 800 ■ *TF:* 800-688-7444 ■ *Web:* www.outrigger.com	866-956-4262	622-4852*	379
Outset Media Corp 106-4226 Commerce Cir Victoria BC V8Z6N6 *Web:* www.outsetmedia.com	250-592-7374	592-7522	761
Outside Magazine 400 Market St Santa Fe NM 87501 *TF:* 888-909-2382 ■ *Web:* www.outsideonline.com	505-989-7100		457-14
Outside Source Inc 7202 E 71st St Indianapolis IN 46256 *Web:* www.outsidesource.com	317-842-4853		344
Outside the Lines Inc 529 W Blueridge Ave Orange CA 92865 *Web:* www.otl-inc.com	714-637-4747		186
Outsource Staffing Inc 2611 Laurel St Beaumont TX 77702 *Web:* outsourcestaffinginc.com	409-813-2900		260
Outsource Testing Inc 1278 Center Court Dr Covina CA 91724 *Web:* www.outsourcetesting.com	909-592-8898		809
OUTSOURCEIT Inc 6810 Crain Hwy La Plata MD 20646 *TF:* 800-497-4078 ■ *Web:* www.outsourceitcorp.com	301-539-0200		180
Outspoken Media Inc 5 State St 3rd Fl Troy NY 12180 *Web:* outspokenmedia.com	518-326-5500	874-5130	631
OutStar One Inc 147 W 24 St New York NY 10011 *Web:* www.outstar1.com	212-242-6416		637-10
Outstart Inc 745 Atlantic Ave 4th Fl Boston MA 02111 *TF:* 877-971-9171 ■ *Web:* www.outstart.com	617-897-6800	897-6801	39
Outten & Whitby PC 102 N Main St Lawrenceville VA 23868 *Web:* outtenwhitby.com	434-848-3184		41
Outten Chevrolet Inc 1701 W Tilghman St. Allentown PA 18104 *Web:* www.outtenchevyallentown.com	610-628-3600	820-5774	57
OUTtv 53 E 6th Ave Vancouver BC V5T1J3 *Web:* www.outtv.ca	604-874-4300	874-4305	647
Outward Bound 910 Jackson St Ste 140 Golden CO 80401 **Fax Area Code:* 207 ■ *TF:* 866-467-7651 ■ *Web:* www.outwardbound.org	866-467-7651	510-7535*	766
Ovadia Diamonds 589 5th Ave Ste 905 New York NY 10017 *Web:* ovadiadiamonds.com	212-319-8840		411
Ovarian Cancer Research Fund Alliance 1101 14th St NW Ste 850 Washington DC 20005 *TF:* 866-399-6262 ■ *Web:* ocrfa.org	202-331-1332	331-2292	474
Ovation Data Services Inc 14199 Westfair E Dr Houston TX 77041 *TF:* 800-802-1635 ■ *Web:* www.ovationdata.com	713-464-1300		224
Ovation Development Corp 6021 S Ft Apache Rd Ste 100 Las Vegas NV 89148 *Web:* ovationdev.com	702-990-2390		653
Ovation Hair Design 18 Davenport St Somerville NJ 08876 *Web:* ovationhairdesign.com	908-526-5110		77
Ovation Instore 57-13 49th Pl. Maspeth NY 11378 *TF:* 800-553-2202 ■ *Web:* www.ovationinstore.com	718-628-2600		233
Ovation Networks Inc 222 Third Ave SE Ste 276 Cedar Rapids IA 52401 *TF:* 877-275-9444 ■ *Web:* www.ovationnetworks.com	319-365-6200		225
Ovation The Arts Network 2850 Ocean Pk Blvd Ste 225 Santa Monica CA 90405 *Web:* www.ovationtv.com	310-430-7575		740
Ovation Travel 71 Fifth Ave New York NY 10003 *TF:* 800-431-1112 ■ *Web:* www.ovationtravel.com	800-431-1112		771
Ovation Wireless Management Inc 19315 W Catawba Ave Ste 220 Cornelius NC 28031 *TF:* 866-207-2111 ■ *Web:* ovationwireless.com	704-714-2111	714-2113	736
Oven, The 201 N Eigth St Lincoln NE 68508 *Web:* theoven-lincoln.com	402-475-6118		671
Over The Mountain Journal 2016 Columbiana Rd Vestavia Hills AL 35216 *Web:* otmj.com	205-823-9646	824-1246	532-4
Over The Rainbow 8300 Tampa Ave Ste C Northridge CA 91324 *Web:* otrsalon.org	818-886-9325		77
Overbrook Entertainment Inc 10202 W Washington Blvd Culver City CA 90232	310-432-2400	432-2401	514
Overcomers in Christ PO Box 34460 Omaha NE 68134 *TF:* 866-573-0966 ■ *Web:* overcomersinchrist.org	866-573-0966		48-21
Overcomers Outreach PO Box 922950 Sylmar CA 91392 *TF:* 800-310-3001 ■ *Web:* www.overcomersoutreach.org	800-310-3001		48-21
OverDrive Inc 1 Overdrive Way Cleveland OH 44125 *Web:* www.overdrive.com	216-573-6886	573-6888	178-10
Overeaters Anonymous Inc (OA) PO Box 44020 Rio Rancho NM 87174 *TF:* 866-505-4966 ■ *Web:* oa.org	505-891-2664	891-4320	48-21
Overfelt Gardens 368 Educational Pk Dr San Jose CA 95133 *Web:* www.sanjoseca.gov	408-535-4905		97
Overhead Door Company of Sacramento Inc 6756 Franklin Blvd Sacramento CA 95823 *TF:* 800-929-3667 ■ *Web:* www.overheaddoor.com	916-421-3747		189-2
Overhead Door Company of Tulsa 5740 E Admiral Pl. Tulsa OK 74115 *Web:* www.overheaddoortulsa.com	918-836-2546	838-9731	191-3
Overhill Farms Inc 2727 E Vernon Ave Vernon CA 90058 *NYSE: OFI* ■ *TF:* 800-859-6406 ■ *Web:* www.overhillfarms.com	323-582-9977	582-6122	296-36
Overit 435 New Scotland Ave Albany NY 12208 *TF:* 888-978-8147 ■ *Web:* overit.com	518-465-8829		7
Overlake Hospital Medical Ctr 1035 116th Ave NE Bellevue WA 98004 *Web:* www.overlakehospital.org	425-688-5000		374-3
Overland Contracting Inc 600 N Greenfield Pky Garner NC 27529 *TF:* 800-790-2149 ■ *Web:* www.overlandcontracting.com	919-329-8400	329-8401	188-10
Overland Express Co 5539 Harvey Wilson Dr. Houston TX 77020 *Web:* overlandexp.com	713-672-6161		780
Overland Park Chamber of Commerce 9001 W 110th St Ste 150 Overland Park KS 66210 *Web:* opchamber.org	913-491-3600	491-0393	139
Overland Park Convention & Visitors Bureau 9001 W 110th St Ste 100 Overland Park KS 66210 *TF:* 800-262-7275 ■ *Web:* www.visitoverlandpark.com	913-491-0123	491-0015	206
Overland Park Convention Center Hotel 6100 College Blvd Overland Park KS 66211 *Web:* opconventioncenter.com	913-234-2100		378
Overland Park Regional Medical Ctr 10500 Quivira Rd Overland Park KS 66215 *TF:* 800-849-0829 ■ *Web:* oprmc.com	913-541-5000		374-3
Overland Rentals Inc 1901 N State Hwy 360 Ste 340 Grand Prairie TX 75050 *TF:* 844-943-7368 ■ *Web:* www.point-of-rental.com	800-944-7368		177
Overland Sheepskin Co 2096 Nutmeg Ave Fairfield IA 52556 *TF:* 800-683-7526 ■ *Web:* www.overland.com	641-472-8434		157-5
Overland Solutions Inc 10975 Grandview Dr Ste 400 Overland Park KS 66210 **Fax Area Code:* 913 ■ *TF:* 888-827-2118 ■ *Web:* www.overlandsolutionsinc.com	888-827-2118	451-3285*	2
Overland Stockyard Inc 10565 Ninth Ave. Hanford CA 93230 *Web:* www.overlandstockyard.com	559-582-0404	582-6261	446
Overland Supply Inc 42 Samuel Ave PO Box 498 Pawtucket RI 02862 *TF:* 800-899-4669 ■ *Web:* overlandsupply.com	800-899-4669		104
Overland, Pacific & Cutler Inc 3750 Schaufele Ave Ste 150 Long Beach CA 90808 *TF:* 800-400-7356 ■ *Web:* opcservices.com	562-304-2000	304-2020	652
Overlay TV Inc 80 Aberdeen St Ste 401 Ottawa ON K1S5R5 *Web:* www.overlay.tv	613-761-6152		4
Overlook Lodge PO Box 351 Bear Mountain NY 10911 *TF:* 855-548-1184 ■ *Web:* www.visitbearmountain.com	845-786-2731	786-2543	379
Overlook Systems Technologies Inc 1950 Old Gallows Rd Ste 400 Vienna VA 22182 *Web:* www.overlooksys.com	703-893-1411	356-9029	261
Overly Manufacturing Co 574 W Otterman St Greensburg PA 15601 *TF:* 800-979-7300 ■ *Web:* www.overly.com	724-834-7300	830-2871	491
Overmountain Press (OMP) PO Box 1261 Johnson City TN 37605 *TF:* 800-992-2691 ■ *Web:* www.overmtn.com	800-992-2691		637-2
Overnight Prints 7582 S Las Vegas Blvd Ste 487 Las Vegas NV 89123 *TF:* 888-677-2000 ■ *Web:* www.overnightprints.com	888-677-2000		627
Oversea-Chinese Banking Corporation Ltd 1700 Broadway 18th Fl. New York NY 10019 *Web:* www.ocbc.com	212-586-6222	586-0636	70
Overseas Adventure Travel 347 Congress St. Boston MA 02210 *TF:* 800-221-0814 ■ *Web:* www.oattravel.com	800-221-0814		760
Overseas Development Corp 953 Washington Blvd Stamford CT 06901 *Web:* www.overseasdevelopment.com	203-964-0111		492
Overseas Express Consolidators (Canada) Inc 725 Montee De Liesse Saint-Laurent QC H4T1P5 *Web:* www.oecgroup.ca	514-905-1246		314
Overseas Freight Inc 1525 Seabright Ave. Long Beach CA 90813 *Web:* www.overseasfreight.net	562-980-1811	980-1808	780

Name	Address	City	State	ZIP	Details	Phone	Fax	Class
Overseas Operations Inc (OO)	222 Avenida del Norte Ste 201	Redondo Beach	CA	90277	*Web:* www.overseas-operations.com	310-540-4600	540-8382	44
Overseas Press Club of America (OPC)	40 W 45th St	New York	NY	10036	*Web:* opcofamerica.org	212-626-9220	626-9210	49-14
Overseas Private Investment Corp (OPIC)	1100 New York Ave NW	Washington	DC	20527	*TF:* 800-225-5722 ■ *Web:* www.opic.gov	202-336-8400	408-9859	340-20
Overseas Shipholding Group Inc	302 Knights Run Ave Ste 1200	Tampa	FL	33602	*TF:* 800-851-9677 ■ *Web:* www.osg.com	813-209-0600	221-2769	313
Oversee.net	312 Arizona Ave 2nd Fl	Santa Monica	CA	90071	*Web:* oversee.wpengine.com	213-408-0080		530
Oversight Systems Inc	1165 Northchase Pky SE Ste 400	Atlanta	GA	30301	*TF:* 866-876-5578 ■ *Web:* www.oversightsystems.com	770-984-4650		178-1
Overstockcom Inc	6350 South 3000 East	Salt Lake City	UT	84121	*NASDAQ: OSTK* ■ *TF:* 800-843-2446 ■ *Web:* www.overstock.com	801-947-3100	944-4629	791
Over-the-Rhine Chamber of Commerce	1805 Elm St 3rd Fl	Cincinnati	OH	45202	*Web:* www.otrchamber.com	513-512-5668		140
Overton Brooks Veterans Affairs Medical Ctr	510 E Stoner Ave	Shreveport	LA	71101	*TF:* 800-863-7441 ■ *Web:* www.shreveport.va.gov	318-221-8411		374-8
Overton Chicago Gear Inc	530 Westgate Dr	Addison	IL	60101	*Web:* www.ocgear.com	630-543-9570		709
Overton County	317 E University St Rm 22	Livingston	TN	38570	*Web:* www.overtoncountytn.com	931-823-2631	823-2696	338
Overton County News	415 W Main St	Livingston	TN	38570	*Web:* www.overtoncountynews.com	931-823-6485		532-3
Overton Hotel & Conference Ctr	2320 Mac Davis Ln	Lubbock	TX	79401	*Web:* www.overtonhotel.com	806-776-7000		132
Overture Center for the Arts	201 State St	Madison	WI	53703	*TF:* 800-373-6376 ■ *Web:* www.overture.org	608-258-4141	258-4966	572
Overture Partners LLC	57 Wells Ave Ste 22	Newton	MA	02459	*Web:* overturepartners.com	617-614-9600		196
Overwaitea Food Group	19855 92A Ave	Langley	BC	V1M3B6	*Web:* www.owfg.com	604-888-1213		345
Overwraps Packaging LP	3950 La Reunion Pkwy	Dallas	TX	75212	*Web:* www.overwraps.com	214-634-0427		548
Ovid Technologies Inc	333 Seventh Ave 20th Fl	New York	NY	10001	*TF:* 800-950-2035 ■ *Web:* www.ovid.com	646-674-6300	674-6301	387
Ovintiv	500 Center St SE PO Box 2850	Calgary	AB	T2G1A6	*TSE: ECA* ■ *TF:* 888-568-6322 ■ *Web:* www.ovintiv.com	403-645-2000	645-3400	536
OvisLink Technologies Corp	203 Lemon Creek Dr Ste C	Walnut	CA	91789	*Web:* www.ovislink.com	909-869-8666		176
OVMA (Ohio Veterinary Medical Assn)	3168 Riverside Dr	Columbus	OH	43221	*TF:* 800-662-6862 ■ *Web:* www.ohiovma.org	614-486-7253	486-1325	795
OVMC (Olive View Medical Ctr)	14445 Olive View Dr	Sylmar	CA	91342	*Web:* www.uclaoliveview.org	747-210-3000		374-3
OVT (OmniVision Technologies Inc)	4275 Burton Dr	Santa Clara	CA	95054	*NASDAQ: OVTI* ■ *Web:* www.ovt.com	408-542-3000		696
OW Lee Company Inc	1822 E Francis St	Ontario	CA	91761	**Fax Area Code:* 909 ■ *TF:* 800-776-9533 ■ *Web:* www.owlee.com	800-776-9533	947-6614*	319-4
OWA (Oregon Winegrowers Assn)	4640 SW Macadam Ave Ste 240	Portland	OR	97239	*Web:* www.oregonwinegrowers.org	503-228-8336		139
Owasso Chamber of Commerce	315 S Cedar St	Owasso	OK	74055	*Web:* owassochamber.com	918-272-2141	272-8564	139
Owatonna Area Business Development Ctr	1065 24th Ave SW	Owatonna	MN	55060	*Web:* www.owatonna.biz	507-451-0517		393
Owatonna Area Chamber of Commerce & Tourism	320 Hoffman Dr	Owatonna	MN	55060	*TF:* 800-423-6466 ■ *Web:* owatonna.org	507-451-7970	451-7972	139
Owatonna Peoples Press	135 W Pearl St	Owatonna	MN	55060	*Web:* www.southernminn.com	507-451-2840	444-2382	637-8
Owatonna Public Library	105 N Elm St	Owatonna	MN	55060	*TF:* 800-657-3864 ■ *Web:* ci.owatonna.mn.us	507-444-2460	444-2465	434-3
Owatonna Senior High School	333 E School St	Owatonna	MN	55060	*Web:* www.isd761.org	507-444-8800		685
Owen Brennan's Restaurant	6150 Poplar Ave	Memphis	TN	38119	*Web:* www.brennansmemphis.com	901-761-0990	761-9177	671
Owen Community Bank	279 E Morgan St	Spencer	IN	47460	*TF:* 800-690-2095 ■ *Web:* www.ocbconnect.com	812-829-2095	829-3069	360-2
Owen County	100 N Thomas St	Owenton	KY	40359	*Web:* www.owencountyky.us	502-484-3405	484-1004	338
Owen County	60 S Main St	Spencer	IN	47460	*Web:* www.owencounty.in.gov	812-829-5030		338
Owen Electric Co-opeartive Inc	8205 Hwy 127 N PO Box 400	Owenton	KY	40359	*TF:* 800-372-7612 ■ *Web:* www.owenelectric.com	502-484-3471		245
Owen Equipment Co	13101 NE Whitaker Way	Portland	OR	97230	*TF:* 800-992-3656 ■ *Web:* www.owenequipment.com	503-255-9055		358
Owen G Dunn Company Inc	3731 Trent Rd	New Bern	NC	28562	*TF:* 800-682-4500 ■ *Web:* www.printelect.com	252-633-3197	637-9320	627
Owen Group Inc	220 Technology Dr Ste 100	Irvine	CA	92618	*TF:* 800-600-6936 ■ *Web:* www.owengroup.com	949-860-4800	860-4810	261
Owen Industries Inc	501 Ave H	Carter Lake	IA	51510	*TF:* 800-831-9252 ■ *Web:* www.owenind.com	712-347-5500		492
Owen Media Inc	3130 E Madison St Ste 206	Seattle	WA	98112	*Web:* owenmedia.com	206-322-1167		7
Owen Oil Tools Inc	12001 County Rd 1000	Godley	TX	76044	*TF:* 800-333-6936 ■ *Web:* www.owentools.com	817-551-0540	551-1674	537
Owen Sound Minor Hockey Group	PO Box 13	Owen Sound	ON	N4K5P1	*Web:* owensoundminorhockey.com	519-371-2467		706
Owen Sound Sun Times	290 Ninth St E	Owen Sound	ON	N4K5P2	*Web:* www.owensoundsuntimes.com	519-376-2250	376-7190	532-1
Owen Steel Company Inc	727 Mauney Dr	Columbia	SC	29201	*Web:* www.owensteel.com	803-251-7680	251-7613	480
Owen-Ames-Kimball Co	300 Ionia Ave NW	Grand Rapids	MI	49503	*Web:* www.owen-ames-kimball.com	616-456-1521	458-0770	186
Owenhouse Hardware Co	36 E Main St	Bozeman	MT	59715	*Web:* owenhouse.com	406-587-5401	587-5406	351
Owens & Associates Investigations	8765 Aero Dr Ste 306	San Diego	CA	92123	**Fax Area Code:* 619 ■ *TF:* 800-297-1343 ■ *Web:* owenspi.com	800-297-1343	297-1343*	400
Owens & Minor Inc	9120 Lockwood Blvd	Mechanicsville	VA	23116	*NYSE: OMI* ■ *TF:* 800-488-8850 ■ *Web:* www.owens-minor.com	804-723-7000	723-7100	475
Owens Community College	*Toledo* 30335 Oregon Rd	Perrysburg	OH	43551	*TF:* 800-466-9367 ■ *Web:* www.owens.edu	567-661-7357		162
Owens Corning	1 Owens Corning Pkwy	Toledo	OH	43659	*NYSE: OC* ■ *TF:* 888-317-6003 ■ *Web:* www.owenscorning.com	419-248-8000		389
Owens Design Inc	47427 Fremont Blvd	Fremont	CA	94538	*Web:* www.owensdesign.com	510-659-1800		454
Owens Healthcare	2247 Court St	Redding	CA	96001	**Fax Area Code:* 800 ■ *Web:* www.myowens.com	530-246-1075	696-9367*	237
Owens Industries Inc	7815 S 6th St	Oak Creek	WI	53154	*Web:* www.owensind.com	414-764-1212	764-6030	454
Owens Liquors Inc	8000 N Kings Hwy	Myrtle Beach	SC	29572	*Web:* owensliquors.com	843-449-6833		443
Owens Precision Inc	5966 Morgan Mill Rd	Carson City	NV	89701	*Web:* owensprecision.com	775-883-4690		757
Owensboro Community & Technical College	4800 New Hartford Rd	Owensboro	KY	42303	*TF:* 866-755-6282 ■ *Web:* owensboro.kctcs.edu	270-686-4400	686-4496	800
Owensboro Daviess County Convention & Visitors Bureau	215 E Second St	Owensboro	KY	42303	*TF:* 800-489-1131 ■ *Web:* visitowensboro.com	270-926-1100		206
Owensboro Federal Credit Union	717 Harvard Dr PO Box 1189	Owensboro	KY	42302	*TF:* 800-264-1054 ■ *Web:* www.ofcuonline.com	270-683-1054	685-3987	219
Owensboro Grain Co	822 E Second St	Owensboro	KY	42303	*TF:* 800-874-0305 ■ *Web:* www.owensborograin.com	270-926-2032	686-6509	296-29
Owensboro Health	811 E Parish Ave PO Box 20007	Owensboro	KY	42303	*TF:* 877-888-6647 ■ *Web:* www.owensborohealth.org	270-691-8040	691-8049	374-3
Owensboro Symphony Orchestra	211 E Second St	Owensboro	KY	42303	*Web:* theoso.com	270-684-0661		573-3
Owens-Illinois Inc	1 Michael Owens Way	Perrysburg	OH	43551	*NYSE: OI* ■ *Web:* www.o-i.com	567-336-5000		331
OWL (Oliver Wolcott Library)	160 S St	Litchfield	CT	06759	*Web:* www.owlibrary.org	860-567-8030	567-4784	434-3
Owl Cos	2465 Campus Dr	Irvine	CA	92612	*Web:* www.owlcompanies.com	949-797-2000	660-4936	360-3
Owl Magazine	10 Lower Spadina Ave Ste 400	Toronto	ON	M5V2Z2	*TF:* 800-551-6957 ■ *Web:* www.owlkids.com	416-340-2700	340-9769	457-6
Owl Wire & Cable Inc	3127 Seneca Tpke	Canastota	NY	13032	*TF:* 800-765-9473 ■ *Web:* www.owlwire.com	315-697-2011		813
Owlett & Lewis PC	1 Charles St PO Box 878	Wellsboro	PA	16901	*Web:* owlettlewis.com	570-723-1000		41
Owlstone Nanotech Inc	19 Ludlow Rd	Westport	CT	06880	*Web:* www.owlstoneinc.com	203-908-4848	908-4849	692
Ownby Insurance Service Inc	400 Court Ave	Sevierville	TN	37862	*Web:* ownbyinsurance.com	865-453-1414		390
Ownersite Technologies LLC	1425 Market Blvd Ste 330-179	Roswell	GA	30076	*Web:* www.ownersite.com	404-402-7117		226
Owosso Automation Inc	1650 E South St	Owosso	MI	48867	*Web:* www.owossofeeders.com	989-725-8804	720-7271	493
Owosso Public Library	502 W Main St	Owosso	MI	48867	*Web:* sdl.lib.mi.us	989-725-5134		434-3
Owosso Public Schools	645 Alger St	Owosso	MI	48867	*Web:* www.owosso.k12.mi.us	989-723-8131	723-7777	685
Owsley County	PO Box 500	Booneville	KY	41314	*Web:* www.elect.ky.gov	606-593-5735	593-5737	338
Owyhee County	20381 State Hwy 78 PO Box 128	Murphy	ID	83650	*Web:* www.owyheecounty.net	208-495-2421	495-1173	338
Owyhee, The	1109 Main St	Boise	ID	83702	*Web:* www.theowyhee.com	208-343-4611		379
OX Bow Press	PO Box 4045	Woodbridge	CT	06525	*Web:* www.oxbowpress.net	203-387-5900		637-2
OX Industries	600 W Elm Ave	Hanover	PA	17331	*TF:* 800-414-2476 ■ *Web:* oxindustries.com	800-414-2476		125
OX International Inc	13111 NW Fwy 5th Fl	Houston	TX	77040	*Web:* www.oxinternational.com	713-895-6610	895-6691	177
Oxarc Inc	4003 E Broadway	Spokane	WA	99202	*TF:* 800-765-9055 ■ *Web:* www.oxarc.com	509-535-7794		385

Name / Address	City	State	ZIP	Phone	Fax	Class
Oxbo International Corp 7275 Batavia Byron Rd *Web:* www.oxbocorp.com	Byron	NY	14422	585-548-2665		273
Oxbow Carbon LLC 1601 Forum Pl Ste 1400 *Web:* www.oxbow.com	West Palm Beach	FL	33401	561-907-5422	640-8747	536
OxBow Data Management Systems LLC 3802 Raynor Pky Ste 200 *Web:* www.oxbowdms.com	Bellevue	NE	68123	402-991-8600	991-9331	225
Oxbow Machine Products Inc 12743 Merriman Rd *Web:* www.oxbow-machine.com	Livonia	MI	48150	734-422-7730	422-7750	757
Oxbow Meadows Environmental Learning Ctr 3535 S Lumpkin Rd *Web:* oxbow.columbusstate.edu	Columbus	GA	31903	706-507-8550	507-8549	50-5
Oxbow Park 5731 County Rd 105 NW *Web:* www.co.olmsted.mn.us	Byron	MN	55920	507-328-7340		823
OXD 210-12 Water St *Web:* oxd.com	Vancouver	BC	V6B1A5	604-694-0554		809
Oxendine Publishing Inc 412 NW 16th Ave *TF:* 888-547-6310 ■ *Web:* studentleader.com	Gainesville	FL	32601	352-373-6907	373-8120	637-9
Oxfam America 226 Cswy St 5th Fl *TF:* 800-776-9326 ■ *Web:* www.oxfamamerica.org	Boston	MA	02114	617-482-1211	728-2594	48-5
Oxford Academy 1393 Boston Post Rd *Web:* www.oxfordacademy.net	Westbrook	CT	06498	860-399-6247		622
Oxford Academy & Central School 50 S Washington Ave PO Box 192 *Web:* www.oxac.org	Oxford	NY	13830	607-843-2025	843-3241	685
Oxford Alloys Inc 2632 Tee Dr *TF:* 800-562-3355 ■ *Web:* www.oxfordalloys.com	Baton Rouge	LA	70814	225-273-4800		358
Oxford Bank PO Box 129 *Web:* www.oxford.bank	Addison	IL	60101	630-629-5000	628-1575	70
Oxford Bank Corp 60 S Washington St *Web:* www.oxfordbank.com	Oxford	MI	48371	248-628-2533	969-7230	70
Oxford Biomedical Research Inc 2165 Avon Industrial Dr *TF:* 800-692-4633 ■ *Web:* www.oxfordbiomed.com	Rochester Hills	MI	48309	248-852-8815	852-4466	231
Oxford College of Emory University 110 Few Cir *Web:* www.oxford.emory.edu	Oxford	GA	30054	770-784-8888		786
Oxford Communications LLC 321 S Washington St Ste 6 *Web:* www.oxfordcomm.net	Alexandria	VA	22314	703-535-6712		393
Oxford Convention & Visitors Bureau 102 Ed Perry Blvd *TF:* 800-758-9177 ■ *Web:* visitoxfordms.com	Oxford	MS	38655	662-232-2367		206
Oxford County 26 Western Ave PO Box 179 *Web:* www.oxfordcounty.org	South Paris	ME	04281	207-743-6359	743-1545	338
Oxford Development Co 2545 Railroad St Ste 300 *Web:* oxforddevelopment.com	Pittsburgh	PA	15219	412-261-1500	642-7543	655
Oxford Financial Group Ltd 11711 N Meridian St Ste 600 *TF:* 800-722-2289 ■ *Web:* ofgltd.com	Carmel	IN	46032	317-843-5678		401
Oxford General Industries Inc 3 Gramar Ave *Web:* www.ogict.com	Prospect	CT	06712	203-758-4467	758-6259	482
Oxford Global Resources Inc 100 Cummings Ctr Ste 206L *TF:* 800-536-3562 ■ *Web:* www.oxfordcorp.com	Beverly	MA	01915	978-236-1182		721
Oxford Graduate School Inc 500 Oxford Dr *TF:* 800-933-6188 ■ *Web:* ogs.edu	Dayton	TN	37321	423-775-6596		166
Oxford Health Plans LLC 48 Monroe Tpke *TF:* 800-444-6222 ■ *Web:* www.oxhp.com	Trumbull	CT	06611	203-459-9100	459-6464	391-3
Oxford Hills Chamber of Commerce 4 Western Ave *Web:* www.oxfordhillsmaine.com	South Paris	ME	04281	207-743-2281	743-0687	139
Oxford Hotel 1600 17th St *TF:* 800-228-5838 ■ *Web:* www.theoxfordhotel.com	Denver	CO	80202	303-628-5400		379
Oxford Industries Inc 999 Peachtree St NE Ste 688 *NYSE:* OXM ■ *Web:* www.oxfordinc.com	Atlanta	GA	30309	404-659-2424	653-1545	155-12
Oxford Instruments 300 Bake Ave Ste 150 *Web:* www.oxinst.com	Concord	MA	01742	978-369-9933		472
Oxford Insurance Agency Inc 300 Main St *Web:* oxfordinsurance.com	Oxford	MA	01540	508-987-0333	987-5517	390
Oxford Life Insurance Co 2721 N Central Ave *Web:* oxfordlife.com	Phoenix	AZ	85004	602-263-6666	277-5901	391-2
Oxford Palace 745 S Oxford Ave *Web:* oxfordhotel.com	Los Angeles	CA	90005	213-389-8000		379
Oxford Parks & Recreation 6025 Fairfield Rd *Web:* oprd.recdesk.com	Oxford	OH	45056	513-523-6314		564
Oxford Plains Speedway 877 Main St *Web:* www.oxfordplains.com	Oxford	ME	04270	207-539-8865	539-8860	515
Oxford Properties Group 100 Adelaide St W Ste 900 *Web:* www.oxfordproperties.com	Toronto	ON	M5H0E2	416-865-8300	369-9704	655
Oxford Public Library 129 S Franklin Ave *Web:* oxfordlibrary.org	Oxford	WI	53952	608-586-4458		434-3
Oxford Recycling Inc 2400 W Oxford Ave *Web:* www.oxfordrecycling.com	Englewood	CO	80110	303-762-1160	762-1746	191-1
Oxford Suites Boise 1426 S Entertainment Ave *TF:* 888-322-8001 ■ *Web:* www.oxfordsuitesboise.com	Boise	ID	83709	208-322-8000	322-8002	379
Oxford Suites Spokane Valley 15015 E Indiana Ave *TF:* 866-668-7848 ■ *Web:* www.oxfordsuitesspokanevalley.com	Spokane Valley	WA	99216	509-847-1000	847-1001	379
Oxford Suites Spokane-Downtown 115 W N River Dr *Web:* www.oxfordsuitesspokane.com	Spokane	WA	99201	509-353-9000	353-9164	379
Oxford University Press 198 Madison Ave **Fax Area Code:* 919 ■ *Web:* global.oup.com	New York	NY	10016	212-726-6000	677-1303*	637-2
Oxford-Lafayette County Chamber of Commerce 299 W Jackson Ave *Web:* oxfordms.com	Oxford	MS	38655	662-234-4651		139
Oxley Enterprises Inc 685 Garrisonville Rd Ste 101 *Web:* www.oxleyenterprises.com	Stafford	VA	22554	540-752-8822		627
Oxman College 318 Westlake Ctr **Fax Area Code:* 415 ■ *TF:* 800-249-5661 ■ *Web:* www.oxmancollege.com	Daly City	CA	94015	800-249-5661	668-3025*	167-3
Oxnard Airport 2889 W 5th St *Web:* iflyoxnard.com	Oxnard	CA	93030	805-382-3022		27
Oxnard Chamber of Commerce 400 E Esplanade Dr Ste 302 *Web:* www.oxnardchamber.org	Oxnard	CA	93036	805-983-6118	604-7331	139
Oxnard City Hall 251 S "C" St *Web:* www.oxnard.org	Oxnard	CA	93030	805-385-7803		337
Oxnard College 4000 S Rose Ave *Web:* www.oxnardcollege.edu	Oxnard	CA	93033	805-986-5800	986-5943	162
Oxnard Convention & Visitors Bureau 2775 N Ventura Rd Ste 204 *TF:* 800-269-6273 ■ *Web:* www.visitoxnard.com	Oxnard	CA	93036	805-385-7545	385-7571	206
Oxnard Public Library (OPL) 4300 Saviers Rd *Web:* www.oxnard.org	Oxnard	CA	93033	805-247-8937	488-1336	434-3
Oxus America Inc 2676 Paldan Dr *TF:* 888-475-1568 ■ *Web:* www.oxusamerica.com	Auburn Hills	MI	48326	248-475-0925	475-0938	476
Oxxford Clothes Inc 1220 W Van Buren St *Web:* www.oxxfordclothes.com	Chicago	IL	60607	312-829-3600		155-12
Oxygen Ventures 2000 Technology Pkwy *Web:* oxygenventures.com	Mechanicsburg	PA	17050	717-540-9730		809
OxygenPac 1776 N Water St *TF:* 800-700-0202 ■ *Web:* www.lifecorporation.com	Milwaukee	WI	53202	414-272-4000	272-0000	476
OYA (Oregon Youth Authority Riverbend) 58231 Oregon Hwy 244 *Web:* www.oregon.gov	La Grande	OR	97850	541-663-8801	663-9181	412
OYO Hotel & Casino Las Vegas 115 E Tropicana Ave *TF:* 866-584-6687 ■ *Web:* www.oyolasvegas.com	Las Vegas	NV	89109	866-584-6687		133
Oyster Consulting LLC 4128 Innslake Dr *TF:* 888-965-5401 ■ *Web:* www.oysterllc.com	Glen Allen	VA	23060	804-965-5400		463
Oyster House 1516 Sansom St *Web:* www.oysterhousephilly.com	Philadelphia	PA	19102	215-567-7683		671
Oyster House 320 Fourth Ave W *Web:* www.oysterhouse.com	Olympia	WA	98501	360-753-7000		671
Oyster Point Hotel, The 146 Bodman Pl *TF:* 800-345-3484 ■ *Web:* www.theoysterpointhotel.com	Red Bank	NJ	07701	732-530-8200	747-1875	379
Oyster Pub 555 Seabreeze Blvd *Web:* www.oysterpub.com	Daytona Beach	FL	32118	386-255-6348		671
OZ Systems Inc 2201 E Lamar Blvd Ste 260 *TF:* 888-727-3366 ■ *Web:* www.ozsystems.com	Arlington	TX	76006	888-727-3366		194
Ozanne Construction Company Inc 1635 E 25th St *Web:* www.ozanne.com	Cleveland	OH	44114	216-696-2876	696-8613	186
Oz-Arc/Gas Equipment & Supply Inc 1021 Southern Expy *TF:* 800-800-2848 ■ *Web:* ozarc.com	Cape Girardeau	MO	63703	800-800-2848		316
Ozark Area Chamber of Commerce 294 Painter Ave *TF:* 800-582-8497 ■ *Web:* www.ozarkalchamber.com	Ozark	AL	36360	334-774-9321	774-8736	139
Ozark Bible Institute & College 906 Summit St PO Box 398 *Web:* obicollege.com	Neosho	MO	64850	417-451-2057	451-2059	166
Ozark Border Electric Co-op 3281 S Westwood *TF:* 800-392-0567 ■ *Web:* www.ozarkborder.org	Poplar Bluff	MO	63901	573-785-4631		245
Ozark Christian College 1111 N Main St *Web:* www.occ.edu	Joplin	MO	64801	417-624-2518		161
Ozark County 361 Main St PO Box 605 *Web:* www.ozarkcounty.net	Gainesville	MO	65655	417-679-4913		338
Ozark Empire Distributors Inc 2301 S 1st St *Web:* www.harrisbaking.com	Rogers	AR	72758	479-636-3313	631-3895	296-1
Ozark Folk Center State Park 1032 Park Ave *TF:* 800-264-3655 ■ *Web:* www.arkansasstateparks.com	Mountain View	AR	72560	870-269-3851		565
Ozark Foothills Region 3019 Fair St *Web:* www.ofrpc.org	Poplar Bluff	MO	63901	573-785-6402	686-5467	338
Ozark Guidance Center Inc 2400 S 48th St *TF:* 800-234-7052 ■ *Web:* www.ozarkguidance.org	Springdale	AR	72762	479-750-2020		726
Ozark Motor Lines Inc 3934 Homewood Rd *TF:* 800-264-4100 ■ *Web:* www.ozark.com	Memphis	TN	38118	901-251-9711	375-8661	780
Ozark Mountain Poultry 1000 N 2nd St *Web:* www.ozarkmountainpoultry.com	Rogers	AR	72756	479-633-8700		619
Ozark Mountain Publishing Inc PO Box 754 *TF:* 800-935-0045 ■ *Web:* www.ozarkmt.com	Huntsville	AR	72740	479-738-2348	738-2448	637-2
Ozark National Life Insurance Co 500 E Ninth St *Web:* www.ozark-national.com	Kansas City	MO	64106	816-842-6300	471-6981	391-2
Ozark National Scenic Riverways 404 Watercress Dr PO Box 490 *Web:* www.nps.gov	Van Buren	MO	63965	573-323-4236	323-4140	564
Ozark Natural Foods 1554 N College Ave *Web:* onf.coop	Fayetteville	AR	72703	479-521-7558	521-5230	297-2

Name / Address	City	State	Zip	Phone	Fax	Class
Ozark Ready Mix Company Inc 1115 Bluff Dr *TF:* 866-920-2417 ■ *Web:* ozarkreadymix.com	Osage Beach	MO	65065	573-348-5946		182
Ozark Regional Transit 2423 E Robinson Ave *TF:* 800-865-5901 ■ *Web:* www.ozark.org	Springdale	AR	72764	479-756-5901		108
Ozark Riverview Manor Inc 1200 W Hall St *Web:* ormanor.com	Ozark	MO	65721	417-581-6025		371
Ozark Steel Fabricators Inc 1 Ozark Steel Dr *Web:* www.ozarksteel.com	Farmington	MO	63640	573-756-5741		480
Ozark Trucking Inc 4916 Dudley Blvd *Web:* www.ozarktruckinginc.com	Mcclellan	CA	95652	916-561-5400		314
Ozarka College 218 College Dr *TF:* 800-821-4335 ■ *Web:* www.ozarka.edu	Melbourne	AR	72556	870-368-7371	368-2091	162
Ozarka Water Co 729 SW Third St *TF:* 800-310-8474 ■ *Web:* www.ozarkah2o.com	Oklahoma City	OK	73109	405-235-8474		366
Ozarks Coca-Cola Dr Pepper Bottling Co 1777 N Packer Rd *TF:* 866-223-4498 ■ *Web:* www.cocacolaozarks.com	Springfield	MO	65803	417-865-9900	865-7967	98
Ozarks Electric Co-opeartive Corp 3641 W Wedington Dr *TF:* 800-521-6144 ■ *Web:* www.ozarksecc.com	Fayetteville	AR	72704	479-521-2900		245
Ozarks Medical Ctr 1100 N Kentucky Ave *TF:* 800-356-5395 ■ *Web:* www.ozarksmedicalcenter.com	West Plains	MO	65775	417-256-9111	257-6770	374-3
Ozarks Technical Community College 1001 E Chestnut Expy *Web:* www.otc.edu	Springfield	MO	65802	417-447-7500	447-2605	162
Ozaukee County 121 W Main St PO Box 994 *Web:* www.co.ozaukee.wi.us	Port Washington	WI	53074	262-284-9411	284-8100	338
Ozeki Sake (USA) Inc 249 Hillcrest Rd *Web:* www.ozekisake.com	Hollister	CA	95023	831-637-9217		80-3
Ozel Fine Jewelers Inc 12200 Amargosa Rd *Web:* www.ozeljewelry.com	Victorville	CA	90066	310-301-9797		410
Ozone Ranch PO Box 1068 *Web:* www.ozoneranch.com	Sandpoint	ID	83864	208-266-1668		344
Ozotech Inc 2401 Oberlin Rd *Web:* www.ozotech.com	Yreka	CA	96097	530-842-4189		806
Ozumo Concepts International LLC 161 Steuart St *Web:* www.ozumo.com	San Francisco	CA	94105	415-882-1333		671
OZZ Electric Inc 20 Floral Pkwy **Fax Area Code:* 905 ■ *TF:* 844-699-6100 ■ *Web:* www.ozzelectric.com	Concord	ON	L4K4R1	416-637-7237	326-1733*	610

P

Name / Address	City	State	Zip	Phone	Fax	Class
P & C Construction Co 2133 NW York St *Web:* builtbypandc.com	Portland	OR	97210	503-665-0165	667-2565	186
P & D Hobby Shop Oak Ridge Shopping Ctr 31280 Groesbeck *TF:* 800-874-7443 ■ *Web:* www.pdhobbyshop.com	Fraser	MI	48026	586-296-6116	296-5642	44
P & D Mechanical Inc 627 Old Hartford Rd	Colchester	CT	06415	860-537-0617		189-10
P & E Distributors Inc 709 Rivergate Pkwy *TF:* 800-251-2034 ■ *Web:* www.pedistributors.com	Goodlettsville	TN	37072	615-851-8060	851-4053	54
P & E Engineering Co 245 S 5th St *Web:* peengr.weebly.com	Carlisle	IA	50047	515-989-3083		101
P & E Microcomputer Systems Inc 98 Galen St 2nd Fl *Web:* www.pemicro.com	Watertown	MA	02472	617-923-0053	923-0808	173-1
P & F Industries Inc 445 Broadhollow Rd Ste 100 *NASDAQ: PFIN* ■ *TF:* 800-327-9403 ■ *Web:* www.pfina.com	Melville	NY	11747	631-694-9800	694-9804	759
P & G Steel Products Company Inc 54 Gruner Rd *Web:* www.pgsteel.com	Buffalo	NY	14227	716-896-7900	896-4129	488
P & H Manufacturing Co 604 S Lodge St *Web:* www.phmfg.com	Shelbyville	IL	62565	217-774-2123	774-5341	273
P & J Machining Inc 2601 Inter Ave *Web:* www.pnjmachining.com	Puyallup	WA	98372	253-841-0500	840-1695	454
P & K Research 6323 N Avondale Ave *TF:* 800-747-5522 ■ *Web:* www.pk-research.com	Chicago	IL	60631	773-774-3100		668
P & P Industries Inc 2100 Enterprise Dr *Web:* www.ppind.com	Sterling	IL	61081	815-632-3297		604
P & P Press Inc 6513 N Galena Rd *Web:* pppress.com	Peoria	IL	61614	309-691-8511	691-1972	627
P & R Communications Service Inc 700 E First St *Web:* www.pandrcommunications.com	Dayton	OH	45402	937-512-8100		736
P & R Enterprises Inc 5681 Columbia Pk Ste 101 *Web:* www.p-and-r.com	Falls Church	VA	22041	703-931-1000		256
P & R Fasteners Inc 325 Pierce St *Web:* www.prfasteners.com	Somerset	NJ	08873	732-302-3600	302-3636	621
P & R Industries Inc 1524 N Clinton Ave *Web:* www.pandrindustries.com	Rochester	NY	14621	585-266-6725		455
P & R Specialty Inc 1835 W High St *Web:* www.prspecialty.com	Piqua	OH	45356	937-773-0263	773-4243	820
P & S Machining and Fabrication Inc 2900 Tucker St *Web:* www.psmachine.com	Burlington	NC	27215	336-227-0151	222-1066	695
P & S Products Inc 781 Enterprise Dr *Web:* www.molders.com	Lexington	KY	40510	859-231-0031		604
P & S Ravioli Co 2001 S 26th St *Web:* www.psravioli.com	Philadelphia	PA	19145	215-465-8888	465-3559	159
P & W Industries LLC 68668 Hwy 59 *Web:* www.pandwindustries.com	Mandeville	LA	70471	985-892-2461	892-2618	492
P & W Quality Machines Inc 707 S Hwy 67 *Web:* www.pwmachine.com	Cedar Hill	TX	75104	972-299-0500	299-0505	454
P & W Sales Inc 405 N Hwy 135 *Web:* www.p-wsales.com	Kilgore	TX	75662	903-984-2102		358
P A Landers Inc 351 Winter St *TF:* 800-660-6404 ■ *Web:* www.palanders.com	Hanover	MA	02339	781-826-8818		186
P B Cosmetology Education Ctr 110 Monmouth St *TF:* 800-336-4247 ■ *Web:* www.pbbeautyschool.com	Gloucester City	NJ	08030	856-456-4927		167-3
P C Whip 4451 Henderson Rd *Web:* www.pcwhip.com	Hickory	PA	15340	724-356-4070		177
P E La Moreaux & Associates Inc 2703 39th St *Web:* www.pela.com	Tuscaloosa	AL	35401	205-752-5543	752-4043	192
P Flanigan & Sons Inc 2444 Loch Raven Rd *Web:* www.pflanigan.com	Baltimore	MD	21218	410-467-5900	467-3127	188-4
P Gagnon & Son Inc 215 Main St *Web:* pgagnon.com	South Berwick	ME	03908	888-815-8384		316
P Gioioso & Sons Inc 50 Sprague St *Web:* pgioioso.com	Hyde Park	MA	02136	617-364-5800	364-9462	188-10
P I Incentive 220 Duncan Mill Rd Ste 315 *Web:* www.piincentives.com	Toronto	ON	M3B3J5	416-383-0766		196
P J Hoerr Inc 107 Commerce Pl *Web:* www.pjhoerr.com	Peoria	IL	61604	309-688-9567	688-9556	780
P J Morgan Real Estate Auctioneers 7801 Wakeley Plz *Web:* pjmorgan.com	Omaha	NE	68114	402-397-7775	397-6065	652
P J Wine 4898 Broadway *Web:* www.pjwine.com	New York	NY	10034	212-567-5501		443
P K Electrical 681 Sierra Rose Dr Ste B *Web:* pkelectrical.com	Reno	NV	89511	775-826-9010		261
P K W Associates Inc 705 E Ordnance Rd Ste 108 *TF:* 888-358-3900 ■ *Web:* www.pkwassoc.com	Baltimore	MD	21226	443-773-1000		225
P L Consulting LLC 119 Old Court Rd *Web:* plcfo.com	Pikesville	MD	21208	410-764-3731		570
P M C Property Group 3600 W Broad St *Web:* www.pmcpropertygroup.com	Richmond	VA	23230	215-241-0200		186
P M Engineered Solutions Inc 140 Commercial St *Web:* www.psmindustries.com	Watertown	CT	06795	860-274-8877		596
P M F Industries Inc 2601 Reach Rd *Web:* www.pmfind.com	Williamsport	PA	17701	570-323-9944		222
P M Industrial Supply Co 9613 Canoga Ave *TF:* 800-382-3684 ■ *Web:* www.pmindustrial.com	Chatsworth	CA	91311	818-341-9180		350
P Marshall & Associates LLC 1000 Holcomb Woods Pkwy Ste 210 *Web:* www.pmass.com	Roswell	GA	30076	678-280-2325		387
P Murphy & Associates Inc 2301 W Olive Ave *Web:* www.pmurphy.com	Burbank	CA	91506	818-841-2002		225
P V Rentals Ltd 5810 S Rice Ave *TF:* 800-275-7878 ■ *Web:* www.pvrentals.com	Houston	TX	77081	713-667-0665		126
P. D. Q. Tooling, Inc 940 Grnock Buena Vista Rd *Web:* www.pdqtooling.com	McKeesport	PA	15135	412-751-2214	751-2666	757
P. H. Hagopian Contractor Inc 778 W Town & Country Rd *Web:* www.phhagopian.com	Orange	CA	92868	714-543-4185		186
P. T. M. Corp 6560 Bethuy Rd *TF:* 800-486-2212 ■ *Web:* www.ptmcorporation.com	Fair Haven	MI	48023	586-725-2211	725-6753	60
P. W. Gillibrand Company Inc 4537 Ish Dr *Web:* www.pwgillibrand.com	Simi Valley	CA	93063	805-526-2195		41
P.A.T. Products Inc 21 White Pine Rd *Web:* www.patproducts.com	Hermon	ME	04401	207-942-6348	942-9662	146
P.C. Drilling Inc 101 S Southgate Dr *Web:* www.pcdrilling.com	Chandler	AZ	85224	480-785-9127	785-9128	625
P.C. Transport Inc 2063 Skyview Dr *Web:* www.pctiwy.com	Casper	WY	82604	307-235-3367	265-8200	780
P.D.Q. Manufacturing Inc 201 Victory Cir *TF:* 800-248-2401 ■ *Web:* www.pdqonline.com	Ellijay	GA	30540	706-636-1848		151
P.J. Wallbank Springs Inc 2121 Beard St *Web:* www.pjws.com	Port Huron	MI	48060	810-987-2992	987-2997	718
P.K. Data Inc 11340 Lakefield Dr Ste 200 *Web:* www.pkdata.net	Johns Creek	GA	30097	770-931-9677	931-9564	466
P.M. Testing Laboratory Inc 3921 Pacific Hwy E Fife *Web:* www.pm-testing.com	Tacoma	WA	98424	253-922-1321	922-1329	743
P.R.I.D.E. Foundation Inc 391 Long Hill Rd *TF:* 800-332-9122 ■ *Web:* www.sewtiqueonline.com	Groton	CT	06340	800-332-9122		48-13
P1 Group Inc 2151 Haskell Ave Bldg 1 *TF:* 800-376-2911 ■ *Web:* www.p1group.com	Lawrence	KS	66046	785-843-2910		189-10
P2i Inc 1236 Main St *Web:* www.p2ionline.com	Hellertown	PA	18055	610-814-0550		225
P2S Engineering Inc 5000 E Spring St 8th Fl *Web:* www.p2sinc.com	Long Beach	CA	90815	562-497-2999		261
P3 Inc 213 Hwy 35 *TF:* 866-222-5169 ■ *Web:* power.pereless.com	Red Bank	NJ	07701	866-222-5169		180
P3I Inc 77 Main St *Web:* www.p3i-inc.com	Hopkinton	MA	01748	508-435-7882		463
PA Capital LLC 901 E Byrd St Ste 1400 *Web:* pacapital.com	Richmond	VA	23219	804-289-6000		401

				Phone	Fax	Class
PA Department of Human Services *Clarks Summit State Hospital* 1451 Hillside Dr. *Web:* www.dhs.pa.gov	Clarks Summit	PA	18411	570-586-2011		374-5
PA Inc 6626 Gulf Fwy *Web:* www.painc.com	Houston	TX	77087	713-570-4900	570-4950	492
Paarlo Plastics Inc 7720 Tim Ave Nw *TF:* 800-476-1645 ■ *Web:* www.paarloplastics.com	North Canton	OH	44720	330-494-3798	494-2493	604
Paasche Airbrush Co 4311 N Normandy Ave **Fax Area Code:* 773 ■ *TF:* 800-621-1907 ■ *Web:* www.paascheairbrush.com	Chicago	IL	60634	800-621-1907	867-9198*	43
PABCO Building Products LLC 10600 White Rock Rd Ste 100 *TF:* 800-829-1577 ■ *Web:* www.pabcobuildingproducts.com	Rancho Cordova	CA	95670	916-631-6044		347
PABCO Gypsum 37851 Cherry St. *TF:* 877-449-7786 ■ *Web:* www.pabcogypsum.com	Newark	CA	94560	510-792-9555		347
Pabla Indian Cuisine 1516 Second Ave *Web:* pablaindiacuisine.com	Seattle	WA	98101	206-623-2868	667-0385	671
Pablo Historical Park 381 Beach Blvd. *Web:* www.beachesmuseum.org	Jacksonville Beach	FL	32250	904-241-5657		50-3
Pabrai Investment Funds 1220 Roosevelt Ste 200 *Web:* www.pabraifunds.com	Irvine	CA	92620	949-453-0609		796
PABST 10635 Santa Monica Blvd Ste 350 *TF:* 800-947-2278 ■ *Web:* pabst.com	Los Angeles	CA	90025	800-947-2278		102
Pabst Mansion 2000 W Wisconsin Ave. *Web:* www.pabstmansion.com	Milwaukee	WI	53233	414-931-0808		50-3
Pabst Theater 144 E Wells St *Web:* pabsttheater.org	Milwaukee	WI	53202	414-286-3205		572
PAC (Pocatello Art Ctr) 444 N Main St *Web:* www.pocatelloartcenter.org	Pocatello	ID	83204	208-232-0970		50-2
PAC (Public Affairs Council) 2121 K St NW Ste 9 *Web:* pac.org	Washington	DC	20037	202-787-5950	787-5942	48-7
Pac Global Insurance Brokerage Inc 898 N Sepulveda Blvd Ste 700 *Web:* pacglobalins.com	El Segundo	CA	90245	310-227-8500		390
PAC Industries Inc 5341 Jaycee Ave *Web:* www.pacindustries.com	Harrisburg	PA	17112	717-657-0407		426
Pac Tec 12365 Haynes St. *TF:* 877-554-2544 ■ *Web:* www.pactecinc.com	Clinton	LA	70722	877-554-2544		608
PAC Tech USA - Packaging Technologies Inc 328 Martin Ave *Web:* www.pactech.com	Santa Clara	CA	95050	408-588-1925		557
PACC (Peabody Area) *Chamber of Commerce* 49 Lowell St 1st Fl *TF:* 888-287-9400 ■ *Web:* www.peabodychamber.com	Peabody	MA	01960	978-531-0384		139
PACCAR Financial Corp 777 106th Ave NE *TF:* 800-333-4998 ■ *Web:* www.paccarfinancial.com	Bellevue	WA	98004	800-333-4998		216
PACCAR Inc *International Div* 777 106th Ave NE *Web:* www.paccar.com	Bellevue	WA	98004	425-468-7400	468-8216	516
Pace Communications Inc 1301 Carolina St. *Web:* www.paceco.com	Greensboro	NC	27401	336-378-6065		637-9
Pace Computer Solutions Inc 10500 Little Patuxent Pkwy Ste 310 *TF:* 888-225-7223 ■ *Web:* www.pace-solutionsinc.com	Columbia	MD	21044	443-539-0290	539-0292	177
Pace Dairy Foods Co 2700 Vly High Dr NW *Web:* kroger.com	Rochester	MN	55901	507-288-6315		296-5
Pace Engineering Inc 4800 Beidler Rd *Web:* www.paceparts.net	Willoughby	OH	44094	440-942-1234		190
PACE Engineering Inc 1730 S St *Web:* www.paceengineering.us	Redding	CA	96001	530-244-0202		727
Pace Gallery, The 32 E 57th St 2th Fl *Web:* www.pacegallery.com	New York	NY	10022	212-421-3292	421-0835	42
PACE Inc 255 Air Tool Dr *TF:* 877-882-7223 ■ *Web:* www.paceworldwide.com	Southern Pines	NC	28387	910-695-7223		253
Pace Learning Systems Inc 10852 Mallard Lake Ln. **Fax Area Code:* 205 ■ *TF:* 800-826-7223 ■ *Web:* www.pacelearning.com	Cottondale	AL	35453	800-826-7223	758-3222*	637-2
Pace Machine & Tool Inc 7986 SW Jack James Dr. *Web:* www.pacemachine.com	Stuart	FL	34997	561-747-5444		757
Pace Packaging LLC 3 Sperry Rd *Web:* www.pacepackaging.com	Fairfield	NJ	07004	973-227-1040		547
Pace Prints 32 E 57th St 3rd Fl *Web:* www.paceprints.com	New York	NY	10022	212-421-3237	832-5162	42
Pace Products Inc 4510 W 89th St Ste 110 **Fax Area Code:* 913 ■ *TF:* 888-389-8203 ■ *Web:* www.paceproducts.com	Prairie Village	KS	66207	888-389-8203	469-4067*	46
Pace Resources Federal Credit Union 445 W Philadelphia St PO Box 15040 *Web:* paceresourcesfcu.virtualcu.net	York	PA	17401	717-852-1390	852-1391	360-3
Pace Scientific Inc PO Box 4418 *Web:* www.pace-sci.com	Mooresville	NC	28117	704-799-0688	799-0177	52
Pace Staffing Network Inc 14450 NE 29th Pl Ste 113 *Web:* www.pacestaffing.com	Bellevue	WA	98007	425-637-3312		260
Pace Suburban Bus 550 W Algonquin Rd *Web:* www.pacebus.com	Arlington Heights	IL	60005	847-364-8130		468
Pace University *Pleasantville/Briarcliff* 861 Bedford Rd *TF:* 866-722-3338 ■ *Web:* www.pace.edu	Pleasantville	NY	10570	914-773-3200	773-3851	166
Pace's Lodging Corp 4265 45th St S Ste 200. *Web:* www.propertyresourcesgroup.com	Fargo	ND	58104	701-356-8888	281-9501	379
Paceco Corp 25503 Whitesell St *Web:* www.pacecocorp.com	Hayward	CA	94545	510-264-9288	264-9280	470
Pace-Edwards 2400 Commercial Rd. *TF:* 800-338-3697 ■ *Web:* www.pace-edwards.com	Centralia	WA	98531	360-736-9991	736-9992	120
Pacer Financial Inc 16 Industrial Blvd. *Web:* www.pacerfinancial.com	Paoli	PA	19301	610-644-8100		401
Pacesetter Claims Service Inc 2871 N Hwy 167 *TF:* 888-218-4880 ■ *Web:* www.pacesetterclaims.com	Catoosa	OK	74015	918-665-8887		390
Pacesetter Steel Service Inc 1045 Big Shanty Rd **Fax Area Code:* 678 ■ *TF:* 800-749-6505 ■ *Web:* www.teampacesetter.com	Kennesaw	GA	30144	770-919-8000	581-8800*	492
Pachaug State Forest Rt 49 PO Box 5. *Web:* portal.ct.gov	Voluntown	CT	06384	860-376-4075		565
Pacheco State Park 38787 Dinosaur Point Rd *Web:* www.parks.ca.gov	Hollister	CA	95023	209-826-6283		565
Pachulski Stang Ziehl Young & Jones Professional Corp 10100 Santa Monica Blvd. *Web:* www.pszjlaw.com	Los Angeles	CA	90067	310-277-6910		428
Pachyderm Consulting LLC 66 W 38th St Apt 11k Ste 33c. *Web:* www.pachyderm.net	New York	NY	10018	212-629-7600		180
Paciello Group LLP, The 5 Pine St Ext Ste 6 *Web:* www.paciellogroup.com	Nashua	NH	03060	603-882-4122		196
Pacific Adhesives Company Inc 8670 23rd Ave *Web:* pacificadhesives.com	Sacramento	CA	95826	916-383-1509		3
Pacific Aerospace & Electronics Inc 434 Olds Stn Rd *TF:* 855-285-5200 ■ *Web:* www.pacaero.com	Wenatchee	WA	98801	509-667-5346		621
Pacific Agenda Inc PO Box 10142. *Web:* www.pacificagendainc.com	Portland	OR	97210	503-957-8661		184
Pacific Agri Lands Inc 5206 Hammett Rd.	Modesto	CA	95358	209-545-1623		315-5
Pacific Air Cargo 6041 W Imperial Hwy *Web:* pacificaircargo.com	Los Angeles	CA	90045	310-645-2178	645-5290	25
Pacific Alliance Medical Ctr (PAMC) 531 W College St *Web:* pamc.net	Los Angeles	CA	90012	213-624-8411		374-3
Pacific Alloy Castings Company Inc 5900 E Firestone Blvd. *Web:* pacificalloy.com	South Gate	CA	90280	562-928-1387		492
Pacific American Group LLC 104 Caledonia St *Web:* pacamgroup.com	Sausalito	CA	94965	415-331-3838		653
Pacific Asia Museum 46 N Los Robles Ave. *Web:* pacificasiamuseum.usc.edu	Pasadena	CA	91101	626-449-2742	449-2754	520
Pacific Bay International Inc 72 Banana Way. *TF:* 800-272-2229 ■ *Web:* www.fishpacbay.com	Sequim	WA	98382	360-683-2080	683-2234	710
Pacific Bearing Co 6402 Rockton Rd. *TF:* 888-389-6266 ■ *Web:* www.pbclinear.com	Roscoe	IL	61073	815-389-5600	389-5790	75
Pacific Beverage Co 5305 Ekwill St. *Web:* www.pacificbeveragecompany.com	Santa Barbara	CA	93111	805-964-3574		81-1
Pacific Biosciences Inc 1305 O'Brien Dr *TF:* 877-920-7222 ■ *Web:* www.pacb.com	Menlo Park	CA	94025	650-521-8000		250
Pacific Building Group 9752 Aspen Creek Ct Ste 150. *Web:* www.pacificbuildinggroup.com	San Diego	CA	92126	858-552-0600	552-0604	685
Pacific Building Maintenance Inc 2646 Palma Dr Ste 320. *TF:* 800-300-4094 ■ *Web:* www.pacificbuildingmaintenance.com	Ventura	CA	93003	805-642-0214		104
Pacific Building Systems (PBS) 2100 N Pacific Hwy *TF:* 800-727-7844 ■ *Web:* www.pbsbuildings.com	Woodburn	OR	97071	503-981-9581	981-9584	105
Pacific Cataract & Laser Institute 2517 NE Kresky Ave *TF:* 800-888-9903 ■ *Web:* www.pcli.com	Chehalis	WA	98532	360-748-8632	748-3869	798
Pacific Center for Awareness & Bodywork PO Box 1049 *TF:* 844-687-7222 ■ *Web:* www.awarenessandbodywork.com	Kilauea	HI	96754	844-687-7222		800
Pacific Choice 4652 E Date Ave *Web:* www.pacificchoice.com	Fresno	CA	93725	559-237-5583		296-19
Pacific Choice Seafoods Co 16797 SE 130th Ave *TF:* 800-882-0212 ■ *Web:* www.pacificseafood.com	Clackamas	OR	97015	707-442-2981		296-13
Pacific City Financial Corp 3701 Wilshire Blvd Ste 402 *OTC: PFCF* ■ *TF:* 888-227-3096 ■ *Web:* www.paccity.net	Los Angeles	CA	90010	213-210-2000	210-2032	70
Pacific Clay Products Inc 14741 Lake St. *Web:* www.pacificclay.com	Lake Elsinore	CA	92530	951-674-2131		150
Pacific Clinics 800 S Santa Anita Ave. *Web:* www.pacificclinics.org	Arcadia	CA	91006	626-254-5000		374-3
Pacific Coast Building Products Inc 10600 White Rock Rd Bldg B Ste 100. *Web:* paccoast.com	Rancho Cordova	CA	95670	916-631-6500		191-4
Pacific Coast Container Inc 432 Estudillo Ave *TF:* 800-458-4788 ■ *Web:* pcclogistics.com	San Leandro	CA	94577	510-346-6100		650
Pacific Coast Feather Co 1736 4th Ave S Ste B *TF:* 888-297-1778 ■ *Web:* www.pacificcoast.com	Seattle	WA	98134	888-297-1778		746
Pacific Coast Fruit Co 201 NE Second Ave *TF:* 800-423-4945 ■ *Web:* www.pcfruit.com	Portland	OR	97232	503-234-6411		297-7
Pacific Coast Jet Charter Inc 10600 White Rock Rd. *TF:* 800-655-3599 ■ *Web:* www.pacificjet.com	Rancho Cordova	CA	95670	916-631-6507	631-6687	13
Pacific Coast Lighting 20238 Plummer St *TF:* 800-709-9004 ■ *Web:* www.pacificcoastlighting.com	Chatsworth	CA	91311	818-886-9751	886-5751	439
Pacific Coast Producers 631 N Cluff Ave *TF:* 877-618-4776 ■ *Web:* pacificcoastproducers.com	Lodi	CA	95240	209-367-8800	367-1084	296-20

Name / Address	City	State	ZIP	Phone	Fax	Class
Pacific Coast Valuations 740 Corporate Center Dr. *TF:* 888-623-4001 ■ *Web:* www.pcvmurcor.com	Pomona	CA	91768	888-623-4001		652
Pacific College 3160 Red Hill Ave *TF:* 800-867-2243 ■ *Web:* www.pacific-college.edu	Costa Mesa	CA	92626	714-662-4402		167-3
Pacific College Oriental Med Inc 7445 Mission Valley Rd Ste 105 *TF:* 800-729-0941 ■ *Web:* www.pacificcollege.edu	San Diego	CA	92108	619-574-6909		166
Pacific Color Graphics 440 Boulder Ct 100d *TF:* 888-551-1482 ■ *Web:* www.pacificcolor.com	Pleasanton	CA	94566	925-600-3006		627
Pacific Combustion Engineering Co 2107 Border Ave *TF:* 800-342-4442 ■ *Web:* www.pacificcombustion.com	Torrance	CA	90501	310-212-6300	212-5333	420
Pacific Communications 18581 Teller Ave *Web:* www.pacificcommunications.com	Irvine	CA	92612	714-427-1900		4
Pacific Compensation Insurance Co 1 Baxter Way Ste 170 *TF:* 866-378-8500 ■ *Web:* www.pacificcomp.com	Thousand Oaks	CA	91362	818-575-8500	474-7076	390
Pacific Consolidated Industries LLC 12201 Magnolia Ave *TF:* 800-309-8935 ■ *Web:* www.pcigases.com	Riverside	CA	92503	951-479-0860		386
Pacific Consulting Group 643 Bair Island Rd Ste 212 *Web:* www.pcgfirm.com	Redwood City	CA	94063	650-327-8108		463
Pacific Continental Corp 111 W 7th Ave PO Box 10727 *NASDAQ: PCBK* ■ *TF:* 877-231-2265 ■ *Web:* www.therightbank.com	Eugene	OR	97440	541-686-8685		70
Pacific Cookie Co 303 Potrero St Bldg 40 A/B *TF:* 800-969-9709 ■ *Web:* www.pacificcookie.com	Santa Cruz	CA	95060	800-969-9709		296-9
Pacific Crest Trail Assn (PCTA) 1331 Garden Hwy *Web:* www.pcta.org	Sacramento	CA	95833	916-285-1846	285-1865	48-23
Pacific Crystal Guild PO Box 1371 *Web:* www.crystalfair.com	Sausalito	CA	94966	415-383-7837		393
Pacific Design Ctr 8687 Melrose Ave *Web:* www.pacificdesigncenter.com	West Hollywood	CA	90069	310-657-0800	652-8576	320
Pacific Design Engineering (1996) Ltd 8505 Eastlake Dr *Web:* www.pde.com	Burnaby	BC	V5A4T7	604-421-1311		393
Pacific Dialogue 33 Ferry Ct *Web:* www.pacificdialogue.com	Stratford	CT	06615	203-378-2803		317
Pacific Die Casting Corp 6155 S Eastern Ave *Web:* www.pacdiecast.com	Commerce	CA	90040	323-725-1332	728-1115	308
Pacific Digital Image 333 Broadway *Web:* www.pacdigital.com	San Francisco	CA	94133	415-274-7234		781
Pacific Disaster Ctr 1305 N Holopono St Ste 2 *TF:* 888-808-6688 ■ *Web:* www.pdc.org	Kihei	HI	96753	808-891-0525	891-0526	668
Pacific Diversified Insurance Services Inc 15005 Concord Cir Ste 110 **Fax Area Code:* 925 ■ *Web:* pdins.com	Morgan Hill	CA	95037	408-842-2131	686-6118*	390
Pacific Division of the American Association for the Advancement of Science (AAASPD) Dept. of Biology Southern Oregon University 1250 Siskiyou Blvd *Web:* associations.sou.edu	Ashland	OR	97520	541-552-6869	552-8457	49-19
Pacific Dualies Inc 13637 Cimarron Ave *TF:* 800-426-0584 ■ *Web:* www.pacific-dualies.com	Gardena	CA	90249	310-516-9898	516-8797	60
Pacific Echo Inc 23540 Telo Ave *Web:* pacificecho.com	Torrance	CA	90505	310-539-1822		360-3
Pacific Edge Hotel 647 S Coast Hwy *Web:* www.pacificedgehotel.com	Laguna Beach	CA	92651	949-494-8566		379
Pacific Egg and Poultry Assn (PEPA) 1521 I St *Web:* www.pacificegg.org	Sacramento	CA	95814	916-441-0801	446-1063	139
Pacific Empire Radio Corp 403 Capital St	Lewiston	ID	83501	208-743-6564		645-124
Pacific Ethanol Inc 400 Capitol Mall Ste 2060 *NASDAQ: PEIX* ■ *TF:* 866-508-4969 ■ *Web:* www.pacificethanol.com	Sacramento	CA	95814	916-403-2123	446-3937	145
Pacific Event Productions Inc 6989 Corte Santa Fe *Web:* www.pacificevents.com	San Diego	CA	92121	858-458-9908	458-1173	113
Pacific Eyecare 20669 Bond Rd NE Ste 200 *Web:* pacificsurgerycenter.com	Poulsbo	WA	98370	360-779-9300		543
Pacific Fence & Wire Co 13770 SE Ambler Rd *Web:* www.pacificfence.com	Clackamas	OR	97015	503-233-6248		350
Pacific Fibre & Rope Company Inc 903 Flint St *TF:* 800-825-7673 ■ *Web:* pacificfibre.com	Wilmington	CA	90744	310-834-4567		208
Pacific Fibre Products Inc 20 Fibre Way *Web:* www.pacfibre.com	Longview	WA	98632	360-577-7112	577-1362	683
Pacific Firm, The 2407 Fourth St *Web:* www.pacfirm.com	Berkeley	CA	94710	510-647-1000		193
Pacific Fisherman 5351 24th Ave NW *Web:* www.pacificfishermen.com	Seattle	WA	98107	206-784-2562	784-1986	698
Pacific Flooring Supply Co 4220 Hubbard St *Web:* pacificflooringsupply.com	Emeryville	CA	94608	510-654-0485	654-2813	361
Pacific Floral Exchange Inc 16-685 Milo St *TF:* 800-752-7779 ■ *Web:* www.pacflor.com	Keaau	HI	96749	808-966-7427	966-7684	293
Pacific Food Importers Inc 18620 80th Ct S Bldg F *TF:* 800-225-4029 ■ *Web:* www.pacificfoodimporters.com	Kent	WA	98032	206-682-2740	622-6259	360-3
Pacific Forge Inc 10641 Etiwanda Ave *Web:* www.pacificforge.com	Fontana	CA	92337	909-390-0701		483
Pacific Gas & Electric Co 77 Beale St *TF:* 800-743-5000 ■ *Web:* www.pge.com	San Francisco	CA	94105	415-973-7000		787
Pacific Giant Inc 4625 District Blvd *Web:* www.pacificgiant.com	Vernon	CA	90058	323-587-5000		297-5
Pacific Grain Products International Inc 351 Hanson Way PO Box 2060 *TF:* 800-333-0110 ■ *Web:* www.pgpint.com	Woodland	CA	95776	530-631-5786	662-6074	296-23
Pacific Grip and Lighting Inc 6550 NE Portland Hwy *Web:* www.pacificgrip.com	Portland	OR	97218	503-233-4747	233-5830	512
Pacific Group, The 5755 Dupree Dr Ste 130 *Web:* pacificgroupinc.com	Atlanta	GA	30327	678-385-2889		652
Pacific Grove Museum of Natural History 165 Forest Ave *Web:* www.pgmuseum.org	Pacific Grove	CA	93950	831-648-5716		520
Pacific Guardian Life Insurance Company Ltd 1440 Kapiolani Blvd Ste 1700 *TF:* 800-367-5354 ■ *Web:* www.pacificguardian.com	Honolulu	HI	96814	808-955-2236		391-2
Pacific Handy Cutter Inc 17819 Gillette Ave *TF:* 800-229-2233 ■ *Web:* www.phcsafety.com	Irvine	CA	92614	714-662-1033	662-7595	222
Pacific Health Laboratories Inc 800 Lanidex Plz Ste 220 *TF:* 877-363-8769 ■ *Web:* www.pacifichealthlabs.com	Parsippany	NJ	07054	732-739-2900		799
Pacific Horizon Ventures 800 Fifth Ave Ste 4120 *Web:* www.pacifichorizon.com	Seattle	WA	98104	206-682-1181	682-8077	792
Pacific Hospitality Group LLC 2532 Dupont Dr *Web:* pacifichospitality.com	Irvine	CA	92612	949-861-4700		707
Pacific Income Advisers Inc 1299 Ocean Ave Ste 210 Second Fl *Web:* www.pacificincome.com	Santa Monica	CA	90401	310-393-1424		401
Pacific Industrial Development Corp 4788 Runway Blvd *Web:* www.pidc.com	Ann Arbor	MI	48108	734-930-9292		492
Pacific Inn 600 Marina Dr *TF:* 866-466-0300 ■ *Web:* www.thepacificinn.com	Seal Beach	CA	90740	562-493-7501		379
Pacific Institute 12101 Tukwila Int'l Blvd Ste 330 *TF:* 800-426-3660 ■ *Web:* www.thepacificinstituteretail.com	Seattle	WA	98168	206-628-4800	587-6007	765
Pacific Institute for Research & Evaluation 11720 Beltsville Dr Ste 900 *Web:* www.pire.org	Calverton	MD	20705	301-755-2700	755-2799	668
Pacific Integrated Handling Inc 10215 Portland Ave *Web:* www.pacificintegrated.com	Tacoma	WA	98445	253-535-5888		358
Pacific International Center for High Technology Research (PICHTR) 1440 Kapiolani Blvd Ste 1225 *Web:* www.pichtr.org	Honolulu	HI	96814	808-943-9581	943-9582	668
Pacific International Rice Mills Inc 845 Kentucky Ave *TF:* 800-747-4764 ■ *Web:* www.pirmirice.com	Woodland	CA	95695	530-661-6028		296-23
Pacific Internet 105 W Clay St *Web:* www.pacific.net	Ukiah	CA	95482	707-468-1005	468-5822	808
Pacific Investment Management Company LLC 840 Newport Center Dr *TF:* 800-387-4626 ■ *Web:* www.pimco.com	Newport Beach	CA	92660	949-720-6000	720-1376	401
Pacific Island Books 2802 E 132nd Cir **Fax Area Code:* 603 ■ *TF:* 866-491-2799 ■ *Web:* www.pacificislandbooks.com	Thornton	CO	80241	303-920-8338	372-5979*	637-2
Pacific Islands Club Saipan San Antonio 502370 Beach Rd *Web:* www.picresorts.com	Saipan	MP	96950	670-234-7976		378
Pacific Language Institute 755 Burrard St Ste 300 *Web:* www.kaplaninternational.com	Vancouver	BC	V6Z1X6	604-688-8330	688-0638	423
Pacific Legal Foundation 930 G St *Web:* pacificlegal.org	Sacramento	CA	95814	916-419-7111		305
Pacific Life Insurance Co 700 Newport Center Dr *TF:* 800-800-7646 ■ *Web:* www.pacificlife.com	Newport Beach	CA	92660	949-219-3011		391-2
Pacific Lighting & Standards Co 2815 Los Flores Blvd *Web:* www.pacificlighting.com	Lynwood	CA	90262	310-603-9344	603-9421	439
Pacific Lutheran Theological Seminary 2770 Marin Ave **Fax Area Code:* 510 ■ *TF:* 800-235-7587 ■ *Web:* www.plts.edu	Berkeley	CA	94708	800-235-7587	524-2408*	167-3
Pacific Lutheran University 12180 Park Ave S *Web:* www.plu.edu	Tacoma	WA	98447	253-535-7411		167-3
Pacific Manufacturing Ohioinc 8955 Seward Rd *Web:* www.pacific-ind.co.jp	Fairfield	OH	45011	513-642-0055		247
Pacific Marine Environmental Laboratory (PMEL) 7600 Sand Pt Way NE *Web:* pmel.noaa.gov	Seattle	WA	98115	206-526-6239	526-6815	668
Pacific Material Handling Solutions Inc 30361 Whipple Rd *Web:* www.pmhsi.com	Hayward	CA	94545	510-878-3065	372-0444	194
Pacific Mdf Products Inc 4312 Anthony Ct *TF:* 800-472-2874 ■ *Web:* pactrim.com	Rocklin	CA	95677	916-660-1882		499
Pacific Mechanical Corp 2501 Annalisa Dr *Web:* www.pmcorporation.com	Concord	CA	94520	925-827-4940	827-0519	189-10
Pacific Medical Inc 1700 N Chrisman Rd *TF:* 800-726-9180 ■ *Web:* www.pacmedical.com	Tracy	CA	95304	800-726-9180	861-5950	477
Pacific Mercantile Bancorp 949 S Coast Dr Ste 105 *NASDAQ: PMBC* ■ *Web:* www.pmbank.com	Costa Mesa	CA	92626	714-438-2600	438-1088	360-2
Pacific Meridian Group 222 Juana Ave *Web:* pacificfarms.com	San Leandro	CA	94577	510-618-1600		770
Pacific Metallurgical Inc 925 Fifth Ave S *TF:* 800-428-9436 ■ *Web:* www.pacmet.com	Kent	WA	98032	800-428-9436		484

Company	Phone	Fax	Class
Pacific Mobile Structures Inc 1554 Bishop Rd .... Chehalis WA 98532 *TF:* 800-225-6539 ■ *Web:* www.pacificmobile.com	360-748-0121		505
Pacific Modern Homes Inc (PMHI) 9723 Railroad St........ Elk Grove CA 95624 *TF:* 800-395-1011 ■ *Web:* pmhi.com	800-395-1011		106
Pacific Northwest Ballet (PNB) 301 Mercer St........ Seattle WA 98109 *Web:* www.pnb.org	206-441-2424	441-2420	573-1
Pacific Northwest College of Art 511 NW Broadway .... Portland OR 97209 *TF:* 888-390-7499 ■ *Web:* www.pnca.edu	503-226-4391	821-8978	166
Pacific Northwest Inlander 1227 W Summit Pkwy .... Spokane WA 99201 *TF:* 866-444-3066 ■ *Web:* www.inlander.com	509-325-0634	626-5875	532-5
Pacific Northwest National Laboratory (PNNL) 902 Battelle Blvd PO Box 999........ Richland WA 99352 *TF:* 888-375-7665 ■ *Web:* www.pnnl.gov	509-375-2121	375-2507	668
Pacific NW Federal Credit Union (PNWFCU) 12106 NE Marx St .... Portland OR 97220 *TF:* 866-692-8669 ■ *Web:* www.pnwfcu.org	503-256-5858	253-5858	219
Pacific Oaks College 55 W Eureka St .... Pasadena CA 91103 *TF:* 877-314-2380 ■ *Web:* www.pacificoaks.edu	877-314-2380		166
Pacific Oasis Inc 1045 Benson Way........ Ashland OR 97520 *Web:* pacificoasisinc.com	541-488-4287		302
Pacific Office Interiors 5304 Derry Ave Ste U........ Agoura Hills CA 91301 *Web:* pacificofficeinteriors.com	818-735-0333		393
Pacific Packaging Products Inc 24 Industrial Way .... Wilmington MA 01887 *TF:* 800-777-0300 ■ *Web:* www.pacificpkg.com	978-657-9100	658-4933	559
Pacific Palisades Post Co 839 Via de la Paz .... Pacific Palisades CA 90272 *Web:* www.palipost.com	310-454-1321	454-1078	637-8
Pacific Palms Conference Resort 1 Industry Hills Pkwy .... City of Industry CA 91744 *TF:* 800-524-4557 ■ *Web:* www.pacificpalmsresort.com	626-810-4455	964-9535	669
Pacific Paper Tube Inc 1025 98th Ave .... Oakland CA 94603 *TF:* 888-377-8823 ■ *Web:* pacificpapertube.com	510-562-8823	562-9002	125
Pacific Pathology Associates Inc 665 Winter St SE .... Salem OR 97301 *Web:* www.auroradx.com	503-814-3350		418
Pacific Piston Ring Company Inc 3620 Eastham Dr PO Box 987 .... Culver City CA 90232 *Web:* www.pacificpistonring.com	310-836-3322	836-3327	128
Pacific Place 600 Pine St........ Seattle WA 98101 *Web:* www.pacificplaceseattle.com	206-405-2655		460
Pacific Plaza Hotels Inc 1000 Marina Village Pkwy Ste 100........ Alameda CA 94501 *Web:* www.pacificplazahotels.com	510-832-6868		378
Pacific Polymers Inc 12271 Monarch St .... Garden Grove CA 92841 *TF:* 800-888-8340 ■ *Web:* pacpoly.com	714-898-0025		3
Pacific Power Group 805 Broadway St Ste 700........ Vancouver WA 98660 *TF:* 877-769-7436 ■ *Web:* www.pacificpowergroup.com	360-887-7400		385
Pacific Power Source Inc 17692 Fitch........ Irvine CA 92614 *TF:* 800-854-2433 ■ *Web:* www.pacificpower.com	949-251-1800	756-0756	253
Pacific Premier Bancorp Inc 17901 Von Karman Ave Ste 1200........ Irvine CA 92614 *NASDAQ: PPBI* ■ *Web:* www.ppbi.com	714-431-4000		360-2
Pacific Press 1350 N Kings Rd........ Nampa ID 83687 *TF:* 800-765-6955 ■ *Web:* www.pacificpress.com	208-465-2500	465-2531	637-9
Pacific Press PO Box 1452........ Melville NY 11747 **Fax Area Code: 631* ■ *TF:* 877-390-7730 ■ *Web:* www.pacificpressnewyork.com	877-390-7730	390-0053*	637-2
Pacific Press Technologies 714 Walnut St........ Mount Carmel IL 62863 *TF:* 800-851-3586 ■ *Web:* www.pacific-press.com	618-262-8666	262-7000	456
Pacific Propeller Inc 5802 S 228th St........ Kent WA 98032 *TF:* 800-722-7767 ■ *Web:* www.pacprop.com	253-872-7767		22
Pacific Radomes Inc 2543 Precision Dr .... Minden NV 89423 *Web:* www.pacificradomes.com	775-267-5480		647
Pacific Records 523 N Hunter St .... Stockton CA 95202 *TF:* 888-823-5467 ■ *Web:* www.pacific-records.com	209-320-7771	465-9533	803-1
Pacific Repertory Theater PO Box 222035 .... Carmel By The Sea CA 93922 *TF:* 866-622-0709 ■ *Web:* www.pacrep.org	831-622-0700	622-0703	573-4
Pacific Research Institute (PRI) 101 Montgomery St Ste 1300........ San Francisco CA 94104 *Web:* www.pacificresearch.org	415-989-0833	989-2411	634
Pacific Resources for Education & Learning 1136 Union Mall 9th Fl........ Honolulu HI 96813 *TF:* 800-377-4773 ■ *Web:* www.prel.org	808-441-1300		242
Pacific Ridge School 6269 El Fuerte St .... Carlsbad CA 92009 *Web:* www.pacificridge.org	760-448-9820		685
Pacific Rim 114 W Liberty St........ Ann Arbor MI 48104 *Web:* www.pacificrimbykana.com	734-662-9303		671
Pacific Rim 2061 Paramount Blvd........ Amarillo TX 79109 *Web:* www.pacificrimam.com	806-353-9179		671
Pacific Rim Bistro 303 Peachtree Center Ave........ Atlanta GA 30303 *Web:* www.pacificrimbistro.com	404-893-0018		671
Pacific Rim Capital Inc 15231 Laguna Canyon Rd Ste 250........ Irvine CA 92618 *Web:* pacificrimcapital.com	949-389-0800	389-0900	216
Pacific Rim Manufacturing Inc 5456 SE International Way .... Milwaukie OR 97222 *Web:* www.pacificrimmfg.com	503-654-9543	654-8050	621
Pacific Rim Mechanical 7655 Convoy Ct........ San Diego CA 92111 *TF:* 800-891-4822 ■ *Web:* www.prmech.com	858-974-6500	974-6501	14
Pacific Rivers 317 SW Alder St Ste 900 .... Portland OR 97204 *Web:* pacificrivers.org	503-228-3555	228-3556	48-13
Pacific Roller Die Co 1321 W Winton Ave .... Hayward CA 94545 *Web:* www.prdcompany.com	510-782-7242	887-5639	456

Company	Phone	Fax	Class
Pacific Salmon Foundation 1682 Seventh Ave W Ste 300 .... Vancouver BC V6J4S6 *Web:* www.psf.ca	604-664-7664		303
Pacific School of Religion 1798 Scenic Ave........ Berkeley CA 94709 *TF:* 800-999-0528 ■ *Web:* www.psr.edu	510-848-0528		167-3
Pacific Science Ctr 200 Second Ave N .... Seattle WA 98109 *Web:* www.pacificsciencecenter.org	206-443-2001	443-3631	520
Pacific Scientific Energetic Materials Company Inc 7073 W Willis Rd .... Chandler AZ 85226 *Web:* psemc.com	480-763-3000		21
Pacific Seacraft PO Box 189 .... Washington NC 27889 *TF:* 800-561-3357 ■ *Web:* www.pacificseacraft.com	252-948-1421	948-1422	90
Pacific Security Integrations Inc *LTS Holdings Inc* 99-930 Iwaena St Unit B-102........ Aiea HI 96701	808-484-4000		693
Pacific Service Federal Credit Union PO Box 8191 .... Walnut Creek CA 94596 *TF:* 888-858-6878 ■ *Web:* www.pacificservice.org	925-296-6200		219
Pacific Ship Repair 1625 Rigel St .... San Diego CA 92113 *Web:* www.pacship.com	619-232-3200		698
Pacific Shipyards International LLC Pier 41 Honolulu Harbor PO Box 31328........ Honolulu HI 96820 *Web:* www.pacificshipyards.com	808-848-6211	848-6279	698
Pacific Shores Inn 4802 Mission Blvd........ San Diego CA 92109 *Web:* www.pacificshoresinn.com	858-483-6300	483-9276	379
Pacific Software Publishing Inc 1404 140th Pl NE........ Bellevue WA 98007 *TF:* 800-232-3989 ■ *Web:* www.pspinc.com	800-232-3989		180
Pacific Source Inc PO Box 2323 .... Woodinville WA 98072 *TF:* 888-343-1515 ■ *Web:* www.pacsource.com	888-343-1515		191-3
Pacific Southwest Railway Museum 4695 Nebo Dr........ La Mesa CA 91941 *Web:* www.psrm.org	619-465-7776		520
Pacific Southwest Research Station 800 Buchanan St .... Albany CA 94710 *Web:* www.fs.usda.gov	510-883-8830	559-6440	668
Pacific Specialty Insurance Co 3601 Haven Ave .... Menlo Park CA 94025 **Fax Area Code: 650* ■ *TF:* 800-962-1172 ■ *Web:* www.pacificspecialty.com	800-962-1172	780-4820*	391-4
Pacific Stainless Products Inc 58500 Mcnulty Way .... Saint Helens OR 97051 *TF:* 888-618-2122 ■ *Web:* www.pacificstainless.com	503-397-1277		697
Pacific State Pipe 4118 Wilmarth Rd........ Stockton CA 95215 *Web:* pacificstatepipe.com	209-931-7862		366
Pacific States Cast Iron Pipe Co 1401 E 2000 S .... Provo UT 84603 *Web:* www.mcwaneductile.com	801-373-6910	377-0338	307
Pacific States Felt & Manufacturing Company Inc 23850 Clawiter Rd .... Hayward CA 94545 *TF:* 800-566-8866 ■ *Web:* www.pacificstatesfelt.net	510-783-0277	783-4725	326
Pacific States Marine Fisheries Commission 205 SE Spokane St Ste 100 .... Portland OR 97202 *Web:* www.psmfc.org	503-595-3100		743
Pacific States University 3424 Wilshire Blvd 12th Fl........ Los Angeles CA 90010 *TF:* 888-200-0383 ■ *Web:* www.psuca.edu	323-731-2383	731-7276	166
Pacific Steel & Recycling 1401 Third St NW........ Great Falls MT 59404 *TF:* 800-889-6264 ■ *Web:* www.pacific-steel.com	406-727-6222		492
Pacific Sun 1200 Fifth Ave Ste 200 .... San Rafael CA 94901 *Web:* pacificsun.com	415-485-6700	485-6226	532-5
Pacific Sunwear of California Inc 3450 E Miraloma Ave........ Anaheim CA 92806 *NASDAQ: PSUN* ■ *Web:* www.pacsun.com	714-414-4000		157-4
Pacific Supermarket Inc 1420 Southgate Ave .... Daly City CA 94015 *Web:* www.pacificsupermarket.com	650-994-1688		345
Pacific Surveying & Engineering Services Inc 909 Squalicum Way Ste 111........ Bellingham WA 98225 *Web:* www.psesurvey.com	360-671-7387	671-4685	261
Pacific Systems Group 501 4th St........ Lake Oswego OR 97034 *TF:* 800-572-5517 ■ *Web:* www.pacsys.com	503-675-5982		178-1
Pacific Tech Solutions LLC 15530 Rckfeld Blvd Ste B4........ Irvine CA 92618 *Web:* www.pts1.com	949-830-1623		177
Pacific Telecommunications Council (PTC) 914 Coolidge St .... Honolulu HI 96826 *Web:* www.ptc.org	808-941-3789	944-4874	139
Pacific Terminals Ltd 3480 W Marginal Way SW .... Seattle WA 98106 *Web:* www.pacificterminals.com	206-923-2155	923-2165	311
Pacific Terrace Hotel 610 Diamond St........ San Diego CA 92109 *TF:* 800-344-3370 ■ *Web:* www.pacificterrace.com	858-581-3500	274-2534	379
Pacific Theatres Corp 189 The Grove Dr........ Los Angeles CA 90036 *Web:* www.pacifictheatres.com	323-615-2202		748
Pacific Tile Imports 2995 Aukele St .... Lihue HI 96766 *Web:* www.pacific-tile.com	808-245-1765	246-9395	191-1
Pacific Timesheet 5348 Vegas Dr .... Las Vegas NV 89108 *TF:* 866-416-2061 ■ *Web:* www.pacifictimesheet.com	650-641-2760	331-3509	178-1
Pacific Title Archives 10717 Vanowen St .... North Hollywood CA 91605 *TF:* 800-968-9111 ■ *Web:* www.pacifictitlearchives.com	818-760-4223		514
Pacific Tool Inc 15235 NE 92nd St........ Redmond WA 98052 *Web:* www.pacifictool.com	425-882-1970	869-7724	757
Pacific Tower Properties 425 G St Ste 711 .... Anchorage AK 99501 *Web:* www.pacifictower.com	907-561-4010	562-6387	104
Pacific Trading 1200 S Fretz Ave .... Edmond OK 73003 *TF:* 800-464-1136 ■ *Web:* www.pacifictradingonline.com	405-216-9258	216-9273	44
Pacific Transit System 216 N Second St........ Raymond WA 98577 *Web:* www.pacifictransit.org	360-875-9418	942-3193	108
Pacific Union College 1 Angwin Ave........ Angwin CA 94508 *TF:* 800-862-7080 ■ *Web:* www.puc.edu	707-965-6336	965-6432	166

Name / Address	City	State	Zip	Phone	Fax	Class
Pacific University 2043 College Way *TF:* 800-677-6712 ■ *Web:* www.pacificu.edu	Forest Grove	OR	97116	503-352-2007	352-2975	166
Pacific Veterinary Hospital 9715 SW Barbur Blvd *Web:* pacificveterinaryhospital.com	Portland	OR	97219	503-246-3373		794
Pacific Vista Capital LLC 2211 Encinitas Blvd *Web:* www.pacvista.com	Encinitas	CA	92024	760-479-0601		401
Pacific Warriors Inc PO Box 1410 *Web:* pacificwarriors.com	Boulder Creek	CA	95006	831-338-7857		637-10
Pacific Wave 2001 6th Ave Westin Bldg *TF:* 888-722-9283 ■ *Web:* www.pacificwave.net	Seattle	WA	98105	206-722-9283		681
Pacific Western Bank 5404 Wisconsin Ave *NYSE: CSE* ■ *Web:* www.pacwest.com	Chevy Chase	MD	20815	301-272-3710		509
Pacific Western Transportation Ltd 6999 Ordan Dr *Web:* www.pacificwesterntoronto.com	Mississauga	ON	L5T1K6	905-564-6333		107
Pacific Wood Laminates Inc 885 Railroad Ave PO Box 820 *Web:* www.pacificwoodlaminates.com	Brookings	OR	97415	541-469-2136		191-3
Pacifica Chamber of Commerce 225 Rockaway Beach Ave Ste 1 *Web:* pacificachamber.com	Pacifica	CA	94044	650-355-4122	355-6949	139
Pacifica Graduate Institute 249 Lambert Rd *Web:* www.pacifica.edu	Carpinteria	CA	93013	805-969-3626		166
Pacifica Nursing & Rehabilitation Ctr 385 Esplanade Ave *Web:* www.pacificarehab.com	Pacifica	CA	94044	650-993-5576	359-9388	450
Pacifica Radio Archives (PRA) 3729 Cahuenga Blvd W *TF:* 800-735-0230 ■ *Web:* www.pacificaradioarchives.org	Studio City	CA	91604	818-506-1077	506-1084	226
Pacifica Radio Foundation 1925 ML King Jr Way *Web:* www.pacifica.org	Berkeley	CA	94704	510-849-2590	849-2617	644
Pacifica Services Inc 106 S Mentor Ave Ste 200 *Web:* www.pacificaservices.com	Pasadena	CA	91106	626-405-0131		261
Pacifica State Beach 1416 Ninth St *Web:* www.parks.ca.gov	Sacramento	CA	95814	650-738-7381		565
Pacifico Inc 1953 OToole Way *Web:* pacifico.com	San Jose	CA	95131	408-327-8888		7
PacifiCord 185 Technology Dr Ste 150 **Fax Area Code: 949* ■ *TF:* 888-379-2670 ■ *Web:* www.pacificord.com	Irvine	CA	92618	888-379-2670	789-0337*	352
PacifiCorp 825 NE Multnomah St *Web:* www.pacificorp.com	Portland	OR	97232	503-813-5000		787
PacificSource Community Solutions 2965 NE Conners Ave *TF:* 888-863-3637 ■ *Web:* medicare.pacificsource.com	Bend	OR	97708	541-385-5315	322-6423	352
Pacificsource Health Plans 110 International Way *Web:* www.pacificsource.com	Springfield	OR	97477	541-686-1242		391-3
Pacira Inc 5 Sylvan Way *Web:* www.pacira.com	Parsippany	NJ	07054	973-254-3560		85
Package Concepts & Materials Inc 1023 Thousand Oaks Blvd *TF:* 800-424-7264 ■ *Web:* packageconcepts.com	Greenville	SC	29607	864-458-7291		600
Package Development Company Inc 100 Roundhill Dr *Web:* www.packagedevelopmentcompany.com	Rockaway	NJ	07866	973-983-8500		596
Package Machinery Co 380 Union St Ste 58 *Web:* www.packagemachinery.com	West Springfield	MA	01089	413-732-4000	732-1163	547
Package Pavement Company Inc PO Box 400 *TF:* 800-724-8193 ■ *Web:* www.packagepavement.com	Stormville	NY	12582	845-221-2224	221-0433	46
Package Printing Company Inc 33 Myron St *Web:* www.pkgprinting.com	West Springfield	MA	01089	413-736-2748	739-7618	548
Package Right Corp 811 Development Dr *TF:* 800-964-3794 ■ *Web:* www.packageright.com	Tipton	IN	46072	800-964-3794		88
Package Steel Systems Inc 15 Harback Rd *TF:* 800-225-7242 ■ *Web:* packagesteelsystem.com	Sutton	MA	01590	508-865-5871	865-9130	105
PackageX Inc 17100 Ventura Blvd Ste 223 *Web:* www.packagex.com	Encino	CA	91316	818-789-6910		88
Packaging Concepts Inc 9832 Evergreen Indus Dr *Web:* www.packagingconceptsinc.com	Saint Louis	MO	63123	314-329-9700	487-2666	548
Packaging Distribution Services Inc (PDS) 2308 Sunset Rd *TF:* 800-747-2699 ■ *Web:* www.pdspack.com	Des Moines	IA	50321	515-243-3156	243-1741	559
Packaging Inc 7200 93rd Ave N Ste 190 *TF:* 800-328-6650 ■ *Web:* www.packinc.com	Brooklyn Park	MN	55445	952-935-3421	935-0978	492
Packaging Innovators Corp 6650 National Dr *Web:* www.packaginginnovators.com	Livermore	CA	94550	925-371-2000	371-2001	596
Packaging Machinery Manufacturers Institute (PMMI) 4350 N Fairfax Dr Ste 600 *TF:* 888-275-7664 ■ *Web:* www.pmmi.org	Arlington	VA	22203	703-243-8555	243-8556	49-13
Packaging Material Direct Inc 30405 Solon Rd Ste 9 *TF:* 800-456-2467 ■ *Web:* www.packagingsuppliesbymail.com	Solon	OH	44139	800-456-2467		690
Packaging Materials Inc 62805 Bennett Ave *Web:* www.packagingmaterialsinc.com	Cambridge	OH	43725	740-432-6337	439-4718	600
Packaging Personified Inc 246 Kehoe Blvd *Web:* packagingpersonified.com	Carol Stream	IL	60188	630-653-1655		629
Packaging Progressions Inc 102 G P Clement Dr *Web:* www.pacproinc.com	Collegeville	PA	19426	610-489-8601		96
Packaging Services of Maryland Inc 16461 Elliott Pkwy *TF:* 800-223-6255 ■ *Web:* www.psimd.com	Williamsport	MD	21795	301-223-6200	223-8247	549
Packaging Solutions Co Bo Guaraguao Carr 174 Km 51 *Web:* www.flepak.com	Bayamon	PR	00959	787-622-7225		601
Packaging Specialties Inc 300 Lake Rd *TF:* 800-344-9271 ■ *Web:* www.packspec.com	Medina	OH	44256	330-723-6000	725-8180	198
Packaging Strategies Inc 6711-B Moravia Park Dr *Web:* psicases.com	Baltimore	MD	21237	410-547-7877	547-1616	601
Packaging Systems International Inc 4990 Acoma St *TF:* 800-525-6110 ■ *Web:* www.pkgsys.com	Denver	CO	80216	303-296-4445	298-1016	547
Packaging Technology Inc 118 Pickering Way Ste 103 *Web:* www.packtec.net	Exton	PA	19341	610-363-8830	363-1368	601
Packard & Appleby PC 2158 N Gilbert Rd Ste 117 *Web:* packard-appleby.com	Mesa	AZ	85203	480-834-3550	834-3650	2
Packard Cos, The 9555 Chesapeake Dr Ste 202 *Web:* www.packard-1.com	San Diego	CA	92123	858-277-4305	277-4308	652
Packard Humanities Institute, The (PHI) 300 Second St *Web:* www.packhum.org	Los Altos	CA	94022	650-948-0150		305
Packard Industries Inc 1515 N US Hwy 31	Niles	MI	49120	269-684-2550		286
Packard Transport Inc 24021 S Municipal Dr PO Box 380 *TF:* 800-467-9260 ■ *Web:* www.packardtransport.com	Channahon	IL	60410	815-467-9260	467-6939	468
Packer Engineering Inc 420 N Main St *TF:* 866-264-4126 ■ *Web:* solutionengineering.com	Montgomery	IL	60538	630-701-7703	701-7732	261
Packer Thomas 6601 Westford Pl Ste 101 *TF:* 800-943-4278 ■ *Web:* www.packerthomas.com	Canfield	OH	44406	330-533-9777		2
Packerland Rent-a-mat Inc 12580 W Rohr Ave *TF:* 800-472-9339 ■ *Web:* www.packerland.net	Butler	WI	53007	262-781-5321		131
Packers Distributing Co 1301 E Commercial St *Web:* www.packersdist.com	Springfield	MO	65803	417-866-7230	863-9511	297-9
Packers Manufacturing Inc 30467 Rd 158 *Web:* www.thepacker.com	Visalia	CA	93292	559-732-4886		547
Packers of Indian River Ltd 5700 W Midway Rd *Web:* packersindianriver.com	Fort Pierce	FL	34981	772-464-6575		11-1
Packet Design Inc 2455 Augustine Dr *Web:* www.packetdesign.com	Santa Clara	CA	95054	408-490-1000	562-0080	178-10
PackLatecom Inc 100 Four Falls Corporate Ctr Ste 104 **Fax Area Code: 815* ■ *TF:* 877-472-2552 ■ *Web:* www.packlate.com	West Conshohocken	PA	19428	877-472-2552	550-2502*	387
Packless Metal Hose Inc PO Box 20668 *TF:* 800-347-4859 ■ *Web:* packless.com	Waco	TX	76702	254-666-7700	666-7893	14
Packnet Ltd 2950 Lexington Ave S Ste 500 *Web:* www.packnetltd.com	Eagan	MN	55121	952-944-9124		683
Packworld USA 539 S Main St *Web:* www.packworldusa.com	Nazareth	PA	18064	610-746-2765	746-2754	641
PacLand 10135 SE Sunnyside Rd Ste 200 *Web:* www.pacland.com	Clackamas	OR	97015	503-659-9500	659-2227	463
Pacmoore Products Inc 1844 Summer St *TF:* 866-610-2666 ■ *Web:* www.pacmoore.com	Hammond	IN	46320	219-932-2666		393
Paco Steel & Engineering Corp 19818 S Alameda St *TF:* 800-421-1473 ■ *Web:* www.pacosteel.com	Compton	CA	90221	310-537-6375		492
Pacon Corp 2525 N Casaloma Dr *TF:* 800-333-2545 ■ *Web:* pacon.com	Appleton	WI	54912	800-333-2545		554
Pacon Inc 15604 Cypress Ave *Web:* paconinc.com	Baldwin Park	CA	91706	626-814-4654		601
Pacon Mfg 400 Pierce St *Web:* www.paconmfg.com	Somerset	NJ	08873	732-764-9070		558
Pacotech Inc 1739 Nina Lee Ln *Web:* pacotech.com	Houston	TX	77018	713-688-0404	682-6768	196
PacPizza LLC 220 Porter Dr Ste 100 *Web:* www.pacpizza.com	San Ramon	CA	94583	925-838-8567	838-5801	670
Pacrim Engineering 233 W Cerritos Ave *Web:* pacrimengineering.com	Anaheim	CA	92805	714-683-0470	683-0460	186
Pacrim Hospitality Services Inc 30 Damascus Rd *TF:* 800-561-7666 ■ *Web:* www.pacrimhospitality.com	Bedford	NS	B4A0C1	800-561-7666		194
Pacs Industries Inc 1211 Stewart Ave *Web:* www.pacsswitchgearllc.com	Bethpage	NY	11714	516-465-7100	465-7057	729
Pactiv Corp 1900 W Field Ct *TF:* 888-828-2850 ■ *Web:* www.pactiv.com	Lake Forest	IL	60045	847-482-2000		561
Pact-One Solutions Inc 8215 S Eastern Ave Ste 101 *TF:* 866-722-8663 ■ *Web:* www.pact-one.com	Las Vegas	NV	89123	702-492-6105		174
Pacur LLC 3555 Moser St *Web:* www.pacur.com	Oshkosh	WI	54901	920-236-2888		600
Pad Print Machinery of Vermont Inc 201 Tennis Way *TF:* 800-272-7764 ■ *Web:* www.epsvt.com	East Dorset	VT	05253	802-362-0844		628
Pad Thai Restaurant 1681 Grand Ave *Web:* www.padthaisp.com	Saint Paul	MN	55105	651-690-1393		671
Padberg, Corrigan & Appelbaum PC 1926 Chouteau Ave *Web:* padbergcorrigan.com	Saint Louis	MO	63103	314-621-2900		41
Padco Inc 2220 Elm St SE *TF:* 800-328-5513 ■ *Web:* www.padco.com	Minneapolis	MN	55414	612-378-7270	378-9388	103
Paddle Tramps Manufacturing Co 1317 University Ave *Web:* www.paddletramps.com	Lubbock	TX	79401	806-765-9901		279
Paddock Chevrolet Inc 3232 Delaware Ave *Web:* www.paddockchevrolet.com	Kenmore	NY	14217	716-941-4093		57

Name / Address	Phone	Fax	Class
Paddock Laboratories Inc *Perrigo Company Plc* 3940 Quebec Ave N .... Minneapolis MN 55427 *Web:* www.perrigodocs.com	763-546-4676	546-4842	479
Paddock Pool Equipment Company Inc 555 Paddock Pky .... Rock Hill SC 29730 *TF:* 800-849-2729 ■ *Web:* www.paddockindustries.com	803-324-1111	324-1116	806
PADF (Pan American Development Foundation) 1889 F St NW 2nd Fl .... Washington DC 20006 *TF:* 877-572-4484 ■ *Web:* www.padf.org	202-458-3969	458-6316	48-5
Padgett Business Services 160 Hawthorne Pk .... Athens GA 30606 **Fax Area Code:* 706 ■ *TF:* 800-723-4388 ■ *Web:* www.padgettbusinessservices.com	800-723-4388	543-8537*	2
Padgett Inc 901 E Fourth St................. New Albany IN 47150 *Web:* padgett-inc.com	812-945-2391		480
Padgett Services 140 Mountain Brook Dr .... Canton GA 30115 *TF:* 888-323-0777 ■ *Web:* padgettservices.com	678-880-1600		610
PADI Americas 30151 Tomas St .... Rancho Santa Margarita CA 92688 **Fax Area Code:* 800 ■ *TF:* 800-527-8378 ■ *Web:* www.padi.com	949-858-7234	878-4364*	513
PADIC Inc 1609 E Broadway.................. Gainesville TX 76240 *Web:* www.padic.com	940-665-6130	665-7486	400
Padilla Speer Beardsley Inc 1101 W River Pkwy Ste 400 .... Minneapolis MN 55415 *Web:* padillaco.com	612-455-1700		636
Padma Publishing PO Box 279............ Junction City CA 96048 *TF:* 877-479-6129 ■ *Web:* www.tibetantreasures.com	530-623-2714	623-4039	637-2
Padre Associates Inc 1861 Knoll Dr .... Ventura CA 93003 *Web:* www.padreinc.com	805-644-2220		261
Padre Island National Seashore PO Box 181300 .... Corpus Christi TX 78480 *TF:* 800-343-2368 ■ *Web:* www.nps.gov	361-949-8068	949-8023	564
Padre Janitorial Supplies 3380 Market St............................ San Diego CA 92102 *TF:* 800-400-3060 ■ *Web:* padrejanitorial.com	619-237-4360	237-4371	104
Padre Pio Foundation of America Inc 463 Main St .... Cromwell CT 06416 *Web:* www.padrepio.com	860-635-4996		305
Paducah & Louisville Railway Inc 200 Clark St .... Paducah KY 42003 *Web:* www.palrr.com	270-444-4300		648
Paducah Area Chamber of Commerce 300 S Third St .... Paducah KY 42003 *Web:* www.paducahchamber.org	270-443-1746	442-9152	139
Paducah Beauty School 124 S 4th St........... Paducah KY 42001 *Web:* www.paducahbeauty.com	270-442-0990		685
Paducah Power System 1500 Broadway......... Paducah KY 42001 *Web:* paducahpower.com	270-575-4000		787
Paducah Sun 408 Kentucky Ave................ Paducah KY 42003 *TF:* 800-599-1771 ■ *Web:* www.paducahsun.com	270-575-8600		532-2
Paducah Symphony Orchestra 222 Kentucky Ave Ste 10 .... Paducah KY 42003 *Web:* paducahsymphony.org	270-444-0065	444-0456	573-3
Paesano's 555 E Basse .... San Antonio TX 78209 *Web:* www.paesanos.com	210-828-5191	828-6329	671
Paesano's 3411 Washtenaw Ave .... Ann Arbor MI 48104 *Web:* www.paesanoannarbor.com	734-971-0484	971-0419	671
PAFCO LLC 201 S Orange Ave Ste 1575........... Orlando FL 32801 *TF:* 800-313-3835 ■ *Web:* www.pafcollc.com	407-206-5300		316
Page & Jones Inc 52 N Jackson St PO Box 2167 .... Mobile AL 36652 *Web:* pagejones.com	251-287-8700		311
Page County 112 E Main St.................... Clarinda IA 51632 *TF:* 877-899-0007 ■ *Web:* www.co.page.ia.us	712-542-2516	542-6005	338
Page County 103 S Court St .... Luray VA 22835 *Web:* www.pagecounty.virginia.gov	540-743-4142	743-4533	338
Page International Hose 4700 Lone Star Blvd .... Fort Worth TX 76106 *TF:* 800-847-7280 ■ *Web:* www.pageintl.com	800-847-7280		370
Page One Bookstore 5850 Eubank Blvd Ste B-41 .... Albuquerque NM 87111 *Web:* www.page1book.com	505-294-2026	294-5576	95
Page Public Library 479 Lake Powell Blvd.......... Page AZ 86040 *Web:* www.pagepubliclibrary.org	928-645-4270		434-3
Page Southerland Page Inc 1100 Louisiana St Ste 1 .... Houston TX 77002 *Web:* www.pagethink.com	713-871-8484	871-8440	261
Pageantry, Talent and Entertainment Services Inc PO Box 160307 .... Altamonte Springs FL 32716 *Web:* www.pageantrymagazine.com	407-260-2262	260-5131	637-9
Pageau Morel et Associes Inc 210 Cremazie Blvd W Ste 110 .... Montreal QC H2P1C6 *Web:* www.pageaumorel.com	514-382-5150	384-9872	261
Pageplus Cellular 9700 NW 112th Ave .... Miami FL 33178 *TF:* 800-550-2436 ■ *Web:* www.pagepluscellular.com	800-550-2436		387
Page-Walker Arts & History Ctr 119 Ambassador Loop PO Box 8005 .... Cary NC 27512 *Web:* www.townofcary.org	919-460-4963		50-2
Pagnotti Enterprises Inc 46 Public Sq Ste 600 .... Wilkes-Barre PA 18701 *Web:* www.jeddocoal.com	570-825-0138	820-8369	360-2
Pagoda Federal Credit Union 833 Washington St.......................... Reading PA 19601 *Web:* pagodafcu.org	610-373-3840	373-4479	219
Pagoda Hotel Inc 1525 Rycroft St.............. Honolulu HI 96814 *TF:* 866-536-7977 ■ *Web:* www.pagodahotel.com	808-941-6611		378
PAH (Punxsutawney Area Hospital Inc) 81 Hillcrest Dr .... Punxsutawney PA 15767 *Web:* www.pah.org	814-938-1800		374-3
PAH (Passavant Area Hospital) 1600 W Walnut St........................ Jacksonville IL 62650 *Web:* www.passavanthospital.com	217-245-9541		374-3
Pahio Resorts Inc 3970 Wyllie Rd .... Princeville HI 96722 *TF:* 800-428-1932 ■ *Web:* www.pahio.com	808-826-6549		378
Pahrump Nugget Hotel & Gambling Hall 681 S Hwy 160............................ Pahrump NV 89048 *Web:* www.pahrumpnugget.com	775-751-6500		452
Pahrump Valley Times 1570 E Hwy 372 .... Pahrump NV 89048 *TF:* 800-417-4791 ■ *Web:* pvtimes.com	775-727-5102	727-5309	532-2
PAI (Population Action Intl) 1300 19th St NW Ste 200.................. Washington DC 20036 *Web:* pai.org	202-557-3400	728-4177	48-5
PAI Management Corp 5272 River Rd Ste 630 .... Bethesda MD 20816 *Web:* www.paimgmt.com	301-656-4224		47
Paiboon Publishing Inc 1442A Walnut St Ste 256 .... Berkeley CA 94709 *TF:* 800-837-2979 ■ *Web:* www.paiboonpublishing.com	510-848-7086		637-10
Paideia School Inc, The 1509 Ponce De Leon Ave NE .... Atlanta GA 30307 *Web:* www.paideiaschool.org	404-377-3491	377-0032	685
Paielli's Bakery Inc 6020 39th Ave .... Kenosha WI 53142 *Web:* www.paiellisbakery.com	262-654-0785	654-0848	296-1
Paier College of Art Inc 20 Gorham Ave......... Hamden CT 06514 **Fax Area Code:* 203 ■ *Web:* www.paier.edu	475-256-0845	287-3021*	166
Paige Electric Company LP 200 Sheffield St Ste 302.................. Mountainside NJ 07083 *TF:* 800-327-2443 ■ *Web:* paigeconnected.com	908-687-7810		246
Paige Hendricks Public Relations Inc (PHPR) 1617 Park Place Ave Ste 110-4 .... Fort Worth TX 76110 *Web:* www.phprinc.com	817-798-4004		317
Pain Therapeutics Inc 7801 N Capital of Texas Hwy Ste 260............. Austin TX 78731 *NASDAQ: PTIE* ■ *Web:* www.paintrials.com	512-501-2444	614-0414	582
Paine College 1235 15th St.................... Augusta GA 30901 *TF:* 800-476-7703 ■ *Web:* www.paine.edu	706-821-8200		166
Paine, Hamblen, Coffin, Brooke & Miller LLP 717 W Sprague Ave Washington Trust Financial Ctr Ste 1200.................................. Spokane WA 99201 *Web:* painehamblen.com	509-455-6000		428
Painful Pleasures Inc 7410 Coca Cola Dr Unit 108.................. Hanover MD 21076 *Web:* www.painfulpleasures.com	410-712-0145		410
Paint & Decorating Retailers Assn (PDRA) 1401 Triad Center Dr...................... Saint Peters MO 63376 *TF:* 800-737-0107 ■ *Web:* www.pdra.org	636-326-2636		49-18
Paint and Coatings Industry 2401 W Big Beaver Rd Ste 700.................... Troy MI 48084 *Web:* www.pcimag.com	248-244-3915		637-9
Paint Applicator Corporation of America 7 Harbor Park Dr..................... Port Washington NY 11050 *Web:* www.pacoa.com	516-284-3000		690
Paint Sundries Solutions Inc 930 Seventh Ave............................ Kirkland WA 98033 *Web:* www.paintsundries.com	425-827-9200		297-8
Painted Bride Art Ctr 230 Vine St............................. Philadelphia PA 19106 *Web:* paintedbride.org	215-925-9914	925-7402	50-2
Painted Pony Petroleum Ltd 736 Sixth Ave SW Ste 1800 .... Calgary AB T2P3T7 *TF:* 866-975-0440 ■ *Web:* www.paintedpony.ca	403-475-0440		539
Painters Supply & Equipment Co 25195 Brest Rd.............................. Taylor MI 48180 *TF:* 800-589-8100 ■ *Web:* www.painters-supply.com	734-946-8119		550
Painting Contractors Assn 2316 Millpark Dr .... Maryland Heights MO 63043 *TF:* 800-332-7322 ■ *Web:* pcapainted.org	314-514-7322	514-9417	49-3
Painweek 6 Erie St.......................... Montclair NJ 07042 *Web:* www.painweek.org	973-415-5100		195
Paisan's 4826 Longley Ln .... Reno NV 89502 *Web:* www.paisanscatering.com	775-826-9444		671
Paisano Publications LLC 28210 Dorothy Dr....................... Agoura Hills CA 91301 *TF:* 800-323-3484 ■ *Web:* www.paisanopub.com	818-889-8740		637-9
Paisano's 4043 SW Tenth St..................... Topeka KS 66604 *Web:* www.paisanoskansas.com	785-273-0100		671
Paiute Pipeline Co 5241 W Spring Mtn Rd..................... Las Vegas NV 89146 *Web:* paiutepipeline.com	702-876-7178	873-3820	325
Pajarito Scientific Security Corp 2532 Camino Entrada........................ Santa Fe NM 87507 *Web:* www.pajaritoscientific.com	505-424-6660		639
Pajaro Valley Chamber of Commerce 44 Brennan St PO Box 1748................ Watsonville CA 95076 *Web:* www.pajarovalleychamber.com	831-724-3900		139
Pajcic & Pajcic PA 1 Independent Dr Ste 1900................. Jacksonville FL 32202 *Web:* pajcic.com	904-358-8881	354-1180	41
PAK Mail Centers of America Inc 8601 W Cross Dr Ste F5...................... Littleton CO 80123 *TF:* 800-778-6665 ■ *Web:* www.pakmail.com	303-971-0088		113
PAK Technologies Inc 7025 W Marcia Rd .... Milwaukee WI 53223 *Web:* www.paktech.com	414-371-3100	371-3110	463
PAK West Paper & Packaging 4042 W Garry Ave.......................... Santa Ana CA 92704 *TF:* 800-927-7299 ■ *Web:* pakwest.com	714-557-7420		548
Pakarang 303 S Main St .... Providence RI 02903 *Web:* www.pakarangrestaurant.com	401-453-3660		671
Pakistan 8 E 65th St......................... New York NY 10065 *Web:* www.pakun.org	212-879-8600	744-7348	784
Pakistan			
Consulate General 10850 Wilshire Blvd Ste 1250............ Los Angeles CA 90024 *Web:* www.pakconsulatela.org	310-441-5114	441-9256	257
Consulate General 12 E 65th St............... New York NY 10065 *Web:* www.pakistanconsulateny.org	212-879-3117		257
Embassy 3517 International Ct NW.......... Washington DC 20008 *Web:* www.embassyofpakistanusa.org	202-243-6500	686-1534	257
Pakistan International Airlines Corp (PIA) 1200 New Jersey Ave SE.................. Washington DC 20590 *TF:* 800-578-6786 ■ *Web:* www.piac.com.pk	800-578-6786		25
PAK-it Products 120 Roop Rd............... Rising Sun MD 21911 **Fax Area Code:* 410 ■ *TF:* 800-447-2548 ■ *Web:* www.pakitproducts.com	800-447-2548	658-1383*	548
Pak-Lite Inc 550 Old Peachtree Rd .... Suwanee GA 30024 *Web:* www.pliusa.com	770-447-5123		601
Pak-Rite Ltd 2395 S Burrell St................ Milwaukee WI 53207 *Web:* www.pak-rite.com	414-489-0450		88

	Phone	Fax	Class
Paksys Software LLC 10 Schalks Crossing Rd Ste 501A-335. . . . . Plainsboro NJ 08536 *Web:* www.paksys.com	732-297-8908		177
Paktech 1680 Irving Rd . . . . Eugene OR 97402 *Web:* paktech-opi.com	541-461-5000		608
PAL General Engineering Inc 10675 Treena St Ste 103. San Diego CA 92131 *Web:* www.palsd.com	858-860-5300	860-5556	261
PALA (Pennsylvania Library Assn) 220 Cumberland Pkwy Ste 10. . . . . Mechanicsburg PA 17055 *TF:* 800-622-3308 ■ *Web:* www.palibraries.org	717-766-7663	766-5440	435
Pala Casino Resort & Spa 11154 Hwy 76. . . . . Pala CA 92059 *TF:* 877-946-7252 ■ *Web:* www.palacasino.com	760-510-5100	510-5191	669
Pala Group 16347 Old Hammond Hwy. . . . . Baton Rouge LA 70816 *Web:* www.palagroup.com	225-272-5194		188
Pala International Inc 912 S Live Oak Park Rd . . . . Fallbrook CA 92028 *TF:* 800-854-1598 ■ *Web:* www.palagems.com	760-728-9121	728-5827	410
Pala Mesa Resort 2001 Old Hwy 395. . . . . Fallbrook CA 92028 *TF:* 800-722-4700 ■ *Web:* www.palamesa.com	760-728-5881		669
Palace Cafe 605 Canal St . . . . New Orleans LA 70130 *Web:* www.palacecafe.com	504-523-1661		671
Palace Casino 158 Howard Ave . . . . Biloxi MS 39530 *TF:* 800-725-2239 ■ *Web:* www.palacecasinoresort.com	228-386-2315		132
Palace Construction Company Inc 7 S Galapago St . . . . Denver CO 80223 *Web:* www.palaceconst.com	303-777-7999		186
Palace of Fine Arts Theatre 3301 Lyon St . . . . San Francisco CA 94123 *Web:* palaceoffinearts.org	415-563-6504		572
Palace Production Ctr 29 N Main St . . . . South Norwalk CT 06854 *Web:* www.palaceproductioncenter.com	203-853-1740	855-9608	658
Palace Renaissance & Royale 11355 SW 84th St . . . . Miami FL 33173 *Web:* www.thepalace.org	305-270-7000		672
Palace Rug Gallery Inc 10644 NE Eighth St . . . . Bellevue WA 98004 *Web:* palacerug.com	425-454-7879		290
Palace Station Hotel & Casino 2411 W Sahara Ave. . . . . Las Vegas NV 89102 *Web:* palacestation.sclv.com	702-367-2411		133
Palace Theatre 80 Hanover St . . . . Manchester NH 03101 *Web:* www.palacetheatre.org	603-668-5588	668-5804	572
Palace Theatre 19 Clinton Ave. . . . . Albany NY 12207 *Web:* www.palacealbany.org	518-465-3335		572
Palace Theatre 1564 Broadway . . . . New York NY 10036 *Web:* broadwaydirect.com	212-730-8200		747
Paladin Associates Inc 4709 Layfield Dr Ste 100B . . . . Dunwoody GA 30338 *Web:* www.paladinassociatesinc.com	770-395-9156		463
Paladin Law Group LLP 1176 Blvd Way . . . . Walnut Creek CA 94595 *Web:* paladinlaw.com	925-947-5700		428
Paladin Partners 838 Kirkland Ave. . . . . Kirkland WA 98033 *Web:* www.paladinpartners.com	425-260-5354		260
Paladin Registry LLC 69 Lincoln Blvd Ste A 275 . . . . Lincoln CA 95648 *Web:* www.paladinregistry.com	916-253-3334		260
Paladin Technologies Inc 703 Palomar Airport Rd Ste 150. . . . . Carlsbad CA 92011 *Web:* paladingroup.com	858-947-0101		631
Palais de Jade 960 W Moana Ln . . . . Reno NV 89509 *Web:* palaisdejadereno.net	775-827-5233		671
Palani Drive 401 Libbie Ave. . . . . Richmond VA 23226 *Web:* www.palanidrive.com	804-285-3200		671
Palatin Technologies Inc 4 B Cedar Brook Dr Cedar Brook Corporate Ctr . . . . Cranbury NJ 08512 *NYSE:* PTN ■ *Web:* www.palatin.com	609-495-2200		85
Palatine Area Chamber of Commerce 579 First Bank Dr Ste 205. Palatine IL 60067 *Web:* www.palatinechamber.com	847-359-7200	359-7246	139
Palau *Embassy* 1701 Pennsylvania Ave NW Ste 200 . . . . Washington DC 20006 *Web:* www.palauembassy.org	202-349-8598		257
Palay Display Industries Inc 10901 Louisiana Ave S Ste 106 . . . . Bloomington MN 55438 *TF:* 800-437-5377 ■ *Web:* www.palaydisplay.com	952-983-2026		791
Palazzo Creative PO Box 2022. . . . . Vashon Island WA 98070 *Web:* palazzocreative.com	206-328-5555	826-6212	4
Palazzo Steven (Rep R - MS) 2349 Rayburn House Office Bldg . . . . Washington DC 20515 *Web:* www.palazzo.house.gov	202-225-5772	225-7074	342-2
Palcam Technologies Ltd 1300 Ringwell Dr . . . . Newmarket ON L3Y9C7 *Web:* www.palcam.com	905-853-1675	853-1584	454
Paleotechnics PO Box 876 . . . . Boonville CA 95415 *Web:* www.paleotechnics.com	707-391-8683		344
Palermo's Pizza 3301 W Canal St. . . . . Milwaukee WI 53208 *TF:* 888-571-7181 ■ *Web:* www.palermospizza.com	414-455-0347		297-6
Palestine Regional Medical Ctr 2900 S Loop 256 . . . . Palestine TX 75801 *Web:* www.palestineregional.com	903-731-1000	731-2236	374-3
Paley Center in Los Angeles, The 1901 Avenue of the Stars Ste 1775. . . . . Los Angeles CA 90210 *Web:* www.paleycenter.org	310-786-1000		520
Paley's Place 1204 NW 21st Ave . . . . Portland OR 97209 *Web:* www.paleysplace.net	503-243-2403		671
PALHACC (President Abraham Lincoln Hotel & Conference Ctr) 701 E Adams St . . . . Springfield IL 62701 *Web:* www.doubletree3.hilton.com	217-544-8800	544-9607	379
Pali Adventures Summer Camp 30778 Hwy 18 . . . . Running Springs CA 92382 *TF:* 800-858-3334 ■ *Web:* paliadventures.com	909-867-5743		239
Palisade 2601 W Marina Pl . . . . Seattle WA 98199 *Web:* palisaderestaurant.com	206-285-1000		671
Palisade Corp 130 E Seneca St Ste 505 . . . . Ithaca NY 14850 *TF:* 800-432-7475 ■ *Web:* www.palisade.com	607-277-8000	277-8001	178-1
Palisade State Park 2200 E Palisade Rd PO Box 650070. . . . . Sterling UT 84665 *Web:* stateparks.utah.gov	435-835-7275		565
Palisades Charter High School 15777 Bowdoin St . . . . Pacific Palisades CA 90272 *Web:* www.palihigh.org	310-230-6623	454-6076	685
Palisades Convention Management Inc 411 Lafayette St Ste 201 . . . . New York NY 10003 *Web:* www.pcm411.com	212-460-9700	460-5460	393
Palisades Hudson Financial Group LLC 200 SW First Ave Ste 1250. . . . . Fort Lauderdale FL 33301 *Web:* www.palisadeshudson.com	954-524-5552		401
Palisades Medical Ctr 7600 River Rd. . . . . North Bergen NJ 07047 *Web:* www.palisadesmedical.org	201-854-5000		374-3
Palisades Safety and Insurance Assn PO Box 902 . . . . Lincroft NJ 07738 *TF:* 800-437-3535 ■ *Web:* www.plymouthrock.com	800-437-3535		391-4
Palisades Tennis Club 1171 Jamboree Rd . . . . Newport Beach CA 92660 *Web:* www.palisadestennis.com	949-644-6900		354
Palisades-Kepler State Park 700 Kepler Dr . . . . Mount Vernon IA 52314 *Web:* www.iowadnr.gov	319-895-6039		565
Palitto Consulting Services Inc 150 Main St . . . . Wadsworth OH 44281 *Web:* www.palittoconsulting.com	330-335-7271		196
Pall Corp 2200 Northern Blvd. . . . . East Hills NY 11548 *NYSE:* PLL ■ *TF:* 800-645-6532 ■ *Web:* www.pall.com	516-484-5400	801-9754	386
PALLAB (WestPac Labs) 9830 Brimhall Rd . . . . Bakersfield CA 93312 *TF:* 800-675-2271 ■ *Web:* www.pallab.org	661-829-2260	829-1317	418
Palladian Partners Inc 8484 Georgia Ave Ste 400 . . . . Silver Spring MD 20910 *Web:* palladianpartners.com	301-650-8660		463
Palladin Precision Products Inc 57 Bristol St . . . . Waterbury CT 06708 *Web:* www.palladin.com	203-574-0246	756-9478	621
Palladium Equity Partners LLC 1270 Avenue of the Americas 31st Fl . . . . New York NY 10020 *Web:* www.palladiumequity.com	212-218-5150		690
Palladium Group Inc 1331 Pennsylvania Ave NW Ste 600. . . . . Washington DC 20004 *Web:* www.thepalladiumgroup.com	202-775-9680		194
Palladium Impact Capital 1200 18th St NW Ste 700. . . . . Washington DC 20036 *Web:* capital.thepalladiumgroup.com	202-822-9100		466
Palladium Technical Academy 10229 Lower Azusa Rd. . . . . Temple City CA 91780 **Fax Area Code:* 626 ■ *TF:* 888-893-0160 ■ *Web:* www.palladiumta.com	888-893-0160	444-4441*	167-3
Palladium-Item 1175 N a St . . . . Richmond IN 47374 *Web:* www.pal-item.com	765-962-1575	973-4570	532-2
Pallet Consultants Corp 810 NW 13th Ave . . . . Pompano Beach FL 33069 *TF:* 888-782-2909 ■ *Web:* www.palletconsultants.com	954-946-2212		551
Pallet Factory Inc, The 3740 Arnold Rd . . . . Memphis TN 38118 *TF:* 800-329-8055 ■ *Web:* www.thepalletfactory.com	901-795-8300		200
Pallet Logistics of America LLC 4100 Platinum Way. . . . . Dallas TX 75237 *Web:* www.plofa.com	972-850-5000		820
Pallet Masters Inc 655 E Florence Ave. . . . . Los Angeles CA 90001 *TF:* 800-675-2579 ■ *Web:* palletmasters.com	323-758-6559	758-9600	551
Pallet Repair Systems Inc 2 Eastgate Dr . . . . Jacksonville IL 62650 *TF:* 866-546-8864 ■ *Web:* www.pallet-repair.com	217-291-0009	291-0008	470
Pallet Services Inc 201 E Fairhaven Ave. . . . . Burlington WA 98233 *TF:* 800-769-2245 ■ *Web:* www.palletservices.com	360-776-1130		200
PalletOne Inc 1470 US Hwy 17 S . . . . Bartow FL 33830 *TF:* 800-771-1148 ■ *Web:* www.palletone.com	863-533-1147	533-3065	551
Pallett Valo LLP 77 City Center Dr Ste 300. . . . . Mississauga ON L5B1M5 *TF:* 800-323-3781 ■ *Web:* www.pallettvalo.com	905-273-3300		428
Palliser Furniture Upholstery Ltd 70 Lexington Pk . . . . Winnipeg MB R2G4H2 **Fax Area Code:* 204 ■ *TF:* 866-444-0777 ■ *Web:* www.palliser.com	866-444-0777	988-5604*	471
Palliser Regional Library 366 Coteau St W. . . . . Moose Jaw SK S6H5C9 *Web:* palliserlibrary.ca	306-693-3669	692-5657	436
Pallone Frank Jr (Rep D - NJ) 2107 Rayburn House Office Bldg . . . . Washington DC 20515 *Web:* www.pallone.house.gov	202-225-4671	225-9665	342-2
Palm Beach Atlantic University PO Box 24708 . . . . West Palm Beach FL 33416 *TF:* 888-468-6722 ■ *Web:* www.pba.edu	561-803-2000	803-2115	166
Palm Beach Chamber of Commerce 400 Royal Palm Way. . . . . Palm Beach Gardens FL 33480 *Web:* www.palmbeachchamber.com	561-655-3282		138
Palm Beach Community College *Palm Beach Gardens* 3160 PGA Blvd . . . . Palm Beach Gardens FL 33410 *TF:* 866-576-7222 ■ *Web:* www.palmbeachstate.edu	561-207-5340		162
Palm Beach County Public Library System 3650 Summit Blvd . . . . West Palm Beach FL 33406 *TF:* 888-780-4962 ■ *Web:* www.pbclibrary.org	561-233-2600		434-3
Palm Beach County School District, The 3300 Forest Hill Blvd . . . . West Palm Beach FL 33406 *TF:* 866-930-8402 ■ *Web:* www.palmbeachschools.org	561-434-8000		685
Palm Beach Daily Business Review 324 Datura St Ste 140. . . . . West Palm Beach FL 33401 *TF:* 800-777-7300 ■ *Web:* www.law.com	561-820-2060	820-2077	457-5
Palm Beach Gardens Medical Ctr 3360 Burns Rd . . . . Palm Beach Gardens FL 33410 *Web:* www.pbgmc.com	561-622-1411	694-7160	374-3

Name / Address	City	State	ZIP	Phone	Fax	Class
Palm Beach Illustrated Magazine 1000 N Dixie Hwy Ste C *TF:* 800-308-7346 ■ *Web:* www.palmbeachillustrated.com	West Palm Beach	FL	33401	561-659-6160		457-22
Palm Beach International Airport 846 Palm Beach International Airport *Web:* www.pbia.org	West Palm Beach	FL	33406	561-471-7420		27
Palm Beach Motor Cars Limited Inc 915 S Dixie Hwy *Web:* www.jaguarpalmbeach.com	West Palm Beach	FL	33401	561-659-6206		57
Palm Beach Motoring Accessories Inc 7744 SW Jack James Dr *TF:* 800-869-3011 ■ *Web:* www.autogeek.net	Stuart	FL	34997	772-286-2701		54
Palm Beach National Golf and Country Club 7500 Saint Andrews Rd *Web:* www.palmbeachnational.com	Lake Worth	FL	33467	561-965-3381		48-22
Palm Beach Newspapers Inc 2751 S Dixie Hwy *TF:* 800-432-7595 ■ *Web:* www.palmbeachpost.com	West Palm Beach	FL	33416	561-820-4100		637-8
Palm Beach North Chamber of Commerce 5520 PGA Blvd Ste 200 *Web:* www.pbnchamber.com	Palm Beach Gardens	FL	33418	561-746-7111	745-7519	139
Palm Beach Opera 1800 S Australian Ste 301 *Web:* pbopera.org	West Palm Beach	FL	33409	561-833-7888		573-2
Palm Beach Photographic Ctr 415 Clematis St *Web:* www.workshop.org	West Palm Beach	FL	33401	561-253-2600		520
Palm Beach Tan Inc 633 E State Hwy 121 Ste 500 *Web:* palmbeachtan.com	Coppell	TX	75019	972-966-5300		310
Palm Beach Zoo at Dreher Park 1301 Summit Blvd *Web:* www.palmbeachzoo.org	West Palm Beach	FL	33405	561-547-9453	585-6085	823
Palm Canyon Theatre 538 N Palm Canyon Dr *Web:* www.palmcanyontheatre.org	Palm Springs	CA	92262	760-323-5123		572
Palm Desert Chamber of Commerce (PDCC) 72559 Hwy 111 *Web:* pdacc.org	Palm Desert	CA	92260	760-346-6111	346-3263	139
Palm Desert Tobacco 73580 El Paseo *Web:* www.palmdeserttobacco.com	Palm Desert	CA	92260	760-340-1954		756
Palm Garden Hotel 495 N Ventu Park Rd *Web:* www.palmgardenhotel.com	Thousand Oaks	CA	91320	805-716-4200	716-4300	707
Palm Gardens Center for Nursing & Rehabilitation 615 Ave C *Web:* www.palmgardenscenter.com	Brooklyn	NY	11218	718-633-3300		450
Palm Mountain Resort & Spa 155 S Belardo Rd *TF:* 800-622-9451 ■ *Web:* www.palmmountainresort.com	Palm Springs	CA	92262	760-325-1301		669
Palm Peterbilt Truck Centers Inc 2441 S State Rd 7 *TF:* 800-432-1257 ■ *Web:* www.palmtruck.com	Davie	FL	33317	954-584-3200	584-3228	385
Palm Press Inc 1442A Walnut St Ste 120 *Web:* www.palmpressinc.com	Berkeley	CA	94709	510-486-0502		130
Palm Printing 6001 Business Blvd *Web:* palmprinting.com	Sarasota	FL	34240	941-907-0090	907-0091	627
Palm Restaurant 250 W 50th St *TF:* 866-333-7256 ■ *Web:* www.thepalm.com	New York	NY	10019	212-333-7256		671
Palm Springs Air Museum 745 N Gene Autry Trl *Web:* palmspringsairmuseum.org	Palm Springs	CA	92262	760-778-6262		520
Palm Springs Chamber of Commerce 190 W Amado Rd *Web:* pschamber.org	Palm Springs	CA	92262	760-325-1577		139
Palm Springs Convention Ctr 277 N Avenida Caballeros *Web:* www.palmspringscc.com	Palm Springs	CA	92262	760-325-6611	778-4102	205
Palm Springs Desert Resorts Convention & Visitors Authority 70-100 Hwy 111 *TF:* 800-967-3767 ■ *Web:* www.visitgreaterpalmsprings.com	Rancho Mirage	CA	92270	760-770-9000		206
Palm Springs Disposal Services 4690 E Mesquite Ave *Web:* www.palmspringsdisposal.com	Palm Springs	CA	92264	760-327-1351	323-5132	804
Palm Springs International Airport 3200 E Tahquitz Canyon Way *TF:* 800-847-4389 ■ *Web:* www.palmspringsca.gov	Palm Springs	CA	92262	760-318-3800	318-3815	27
Palm Springs Life Magazine 303 N Indian Canyon *TF:* 800-775-7256 ■ *Web:* www.palmspringslife.com	Palm Springs	CA	92262	760-325-2333	325-7008	457-22
Palma Ceia United Methodist Church 3723 W Bay To Bay Blvd *Web:* palmaceiaumc.org	Tampa	FL	33629	813-837-1541	837-3600	48-20
Palma Insurance Agency Inc 547 Hwy 67 PO Box 317 *Web:* chuckpalma.com	Fontana	WI	53125	262-275-5786		390
Palm-Aire Country Club in Pompano Beach 3701 Oaks Clubhouse Dr *Web:* palmaire.clublink.com	Pompano Beach	FL	33069	954-975-6225		671
Palmas Printing Inc 200 East Dr *Web:* palmasprinting.com	Melbourne	FL	32904	321-984-4451		627
Palmdale Chamber of Commerce 817 E Ave Q-9 *Web:* www.palmdalechamber.org	Palmdale	CA	93550	661-273-3232	273-8508	139
Palmdale City Library 700 E Palmdale Blvd *Web:* cityofpalmdale.org	Palmdale	CA	93550	661-267-5600		434-3
Palmdale Oil Company Inc 911 N Second St *Web:* www.palmdaleoil.com	Fort Pierce	FL	34950	772-461-2300		579
Palmer & Barr PC 607 Easton Rd Ste E-3 *Web:* palmerbarr.net	Willow Grove	PA	19090	215-659-2200		41
Palmer & Sicard Inc 140 Epping Rd *Web:* palmerandsicard.com	Exeter	NH	03833	603-778-1841	778-3168	189-10
Palmer Advertising 466 Geary St Ste 301 *Web:* palmeradagency.com	San Francisco	CA	94102	415-771-2327		7
Palmer Asphalt Co 196 W Fifth St PO Box 58 *TF:* 800-352-9898 ■ *Web:* www.palmerasphalt.com	Bayonne	NJ	07002	201-339-0855	339-8320	46
Palmer Candy Co 2600 Hwy 75 N PO Box 326 *Web:* palmercandy.com	Sioux City	IA	51105	712-258-5543	258-3224	296-8
Palmer College-chiropractic 4705 S Clyde Morris Blvd *Web:* www.palmer.edu	Port Orange	FL	32129	386-763-2709		165
Palmer Distributors Inc 33525 Groesbeck Hwy *Web:* www.palmerretailsolutions.com	Fraser	MI	48026	586-772-4225	772-4627	604
Palmer Electric & Showcase Lighting 875 Jackson Ave *Web:* www.palmer-electric.com	Winter Park	FL	32789	407-646-8700	647-8951	189-4
Palmer Family Insurance Agency 8 Cortland St *TF:* 800-741-7919 ■ *Web:* palmerfamilyins.com	Marathon	NY	13803	607-849-4322	849-4323	390
Palmer Food Services (PFS) 900 Jefferson Rd Ste 1000 *TF:* 800-888-3474 ■ *Web:* www.palmerfoods.com	Rochester	NY	14623	585-424-3210	424-1035	297-9
Palmer Gary (Rep R - AL) 207 Cannon House Office Bldg *Web:* palmer.house.gov	Washington	DC	20515	202-225-4921	225-2082	342-2
Palmer Gas Company Inc 13 Hall Farm Rd *TF:* 800-420-9045 ■ *Web:* palmergas.com	Atkinson	NH	03811	603-898-7986		316
Palmer Holland Inc 25000 Country Club Blvd Ste 444 *TF:* 800-635-4822 ■ *Web:* www.palmerholland.com	North Olmsted	OH	44070	800-635-4822		146
Palmer International Inc PO Box 315 *Web:* www.palmerint.com	Skippack	PA	19474	610-584-4241		487
Palmer Investigative Services 624 W Gurley St Ste A *TF:* 800-280-2951 ■ *Web:* www.palmerinvestigative.com	Prescott	AZ	86304	928-778-2951	445-7204	400
Palmer Manufacturing 18 N Bechtle Ave *TF:* 800-457-5456 ■ *Web:* www.palmermfg.com	Springfield	OH	45504	937-323-6339		492
Palmer Moving & Storage 24660 Dequindre Rd *TF:* 800-521-3954 ■ *Web:* www.palmermoving.com	Warren	MI	48091	586-834-3400	834-3414	519
Palmer Paving Corp 25 Blanchard St *TF:* 800-244-8354 ■ *Web:* palmerpaving.com	Palmer	MA	01069	413-283-8354	289-1939	188-4
Palmer Printing Company Inc 2902 Third St S *TF:* 800-336-3504 ■ *Web:* www.palmerprinting.com	Waite Park	MN	56387	320-252-0033		627
Palmer Products Inc 920 Moe Dr *TF:* 800-692-2179 ■ *Web:* www.shaftsaver.com	Akron	OH	44310	330-630-9397	630-9759	454
Palmer School of Floral Design 3710 Mitchell Dr *Web:* www.palmerschoolofloraldesign.com	Fort Collins	CO	80525	970-207-9476		685
Palmer Square 40 Nassau St *Web:* www.palmersquare.com	Princeton	NJ	08542	609-921-2333	921-3797	460
Palmer Steel Supplies Inc 4300 Acapulco Ave *Web:* www.palmersteel.com	Mcallen	TX	78503	956-686-6575	686-7022	190
Palmer Theological Seminary 588 N Gulph Rd *TF:* 800-220-3287 ■ *Web:* www.palmerseminary.edu	King of Prussia	PA	19406	610-896-5000	649-3834	167-3
Palmer Wahl Instrumentation Group 234 Old Weaverville Rd *TF:* 800-421-2853 ■ *Web:* www.palmerwahl.com	Asheville	NC	28804	828-658-3131	658-0728	201
Palmer-christiansen Company Inc 2510 S West Temple *Web:* palmerchris.com	Salt Lake City	UT	84115	801-466-1679		610
Palmer-Donavin Manufacturing Co 1200 Steelwood Rd *TF:* 800-589-4412 ■ *Web:* www.palmerdonavin.com	Columbus	OH	43212	800-652-1234	883-2811	191-3
Palmerton Area School District 680 Fourth St *Web:* www.palmerton.org	Palmerton	PA	18071	610-826-7101	826-4958	685
Palmetto Brick Co 3501 Brickyard Rd **Fax Area Code:* 843 ■ *TF:* 800-922-4423 ■ *Web:* palmettobrick.com	Wallace	SC	29596	800-922-4423	537-4802*	150
Palmetto Chevrolet Company Inc 1122 Fourth Ave *Web:* www.palmettochevy.com	Conway	SC	29526	843-248-4283		57
Palmetto Dunes Resort 4 Queens Folly Rd *TF:* 866-380-1778 ■ *Web:* www.palmettodunes.com	Hilton Head Island	SC	29928	866-380-1778		669
Palmetto GBA LLC 17 Technology Cir AG-905 *TF:* 800-833-4455 ■ *Web:* www.palmettogba.com	Columbia	SC	29203	803-735-1034		177
Palmetto Industries International Inc 6001 Horizon W Pkwy *Web:* www.palmetto-industries.com	Grovetown	GA	30813	706-737-7999	737-7995	601
Palmetto Infusion Services LLC 172 Mcswain Dr Ste A *Web:* www.palmettoinfusion.com	West Columbia	SC	29169	803-771-7740		557
Palmetto Island State Park Inc 19501 Pleasant Rd *Web:* www.lastateparks.com	Abbeville	LA	70510	337-893-3930		565
Palmetto Pig 530 Devine St *Web:* www.palmettopig.com	Columbia	SC	29201	803-733-2556		671
Palmetto State Bank 601 First St W *TF:* 800-943-2644 ■ *Web:* www.palmettostatebank.com	Hampton	SC	29924	803-943-2671		70
Palmetto State Park 78 Park Rd 11 S *Web:* tpwd.texas.gov	Gonzales	TX	78629	830-672-3266		565
Palmetto State Transportation Company Inc 1050 Pk W Blvd *TF:* 800-269-0175 ■ *Web:* www.palmettostatetrans.com	Greenville	SC	29611	864-672-3800		780
Palms of Pasadena Hospital 1501 Pasadena Ave S *Web:* palmspasadena.com	Saint Petersburg	FL	33707	727-381-1000		374-3
Palms Resort 2500 N Ocean Blvd *TF:* 800-300-1198 ■ *Web:* www.palmsresort.com	Myrtle Beach	SC	29577	843-626-8334		669

Name / Address	City	State	ZIP	Phone	Fax	Class
Palms Thai 5900 Hollywood Blvd — *Web:* palmsthai.com	Los Angeles	CA	90028	323-462-5073		671
Palms West Hospital (PWH) 13001 S Blvd — *Web:* palmswesthospital.com	Loxahatchee	FL	33470	561-798-3300		374-3
Palms, The 3025 Collins Ave — *TF:* 800-550-0505 ■ *Web:* www.thepalmshotel.com	Miami Beach	FL	33140	305-534-0505	534-0515	669
Palmyra Area School District 1125 Pk Dr — *Web:* www.palmyraportal.org	Palmyra	PA	17078	717-838-3144		685
Palmyra Bologna Company Inc 230 N College St — *TF:* 800-282-6336 ■ *Web:* www.seltzerslebanon.com	Palmyra	PA	17078	717-838-6336		296-26
Palo Alto Airport 1925 Embarcadero Rd — *TF:* 866-638-2344 ■ *Web:* www.cityofpaloalto.org	Palo Alto	CA	94303	408-918-7700		27
Palo Alto Chamber of Commerce 355 Alma St — *Web:* www.paloaltochamber.com	Palo Alto	CA	94301	650-324-3121	324-1215	139
Palo Alto City Library 1213 Newell Rd — *Web:* www.cityofpaloalto.org	Palo Alto	CA	94303	650-329-2436		434-3
Palo Alto Networks Inc 4401 Great America Pkwy — *TF:* 866-898-9087 ■ *Web:* www.paloaltonetworks.com	Santa Clara	CA	95054	408-753-4000		196
Palo Alto Research Center Inc (PARC) 3333 Coyote Hill Rd — *Web:* www.parc.com	Palo Alto	CA	94304	650-812-4000		668
Palo Alto Staffing 2479 E Bayshore Rd Ste 165 — *Web:* www.paloaltostaffing.com	Palo Alto	CA	94303	650-493-0223		260
Palo Alto Weekly 450 Cambridge Ave — *Web:* www.paloaltoonline.com	Palo Alto	CA	94306	650-326-8210	326-3928	532-5
Palo Duro Canyon State Park 11450 Park Rd 5 — *Web:* tpwd.texas.gov	Canyon	TX	79015	806-488-2227		565
Palo Petroleum Inc 5944 Luther Ln Ste 900 — *Web:* www.palopetro.com	Dallas	TX	75225	214-601-3676	601-8785	630
Palo Pinto County PO Box 219 — *TF:* 844-769-4976 ■ *Web:* www.co.palo-pinto.tx.us	Palo Pinto	TX	76484	940-659-1277		338
Palo Verde College Foundation 1 College Dr — *Web:* www.paloverde.edu	Blythe	CA	92225	760-921-5500	921-3608	162
Paloma Energy Consultants, Lp 14405 Brown Rd — *Web:* palomaec.com	Tomball	TX	77377	281-890-8800		261
Paloma Systems Inc 11250 Waples Mill Rd — *Web:* www.palomasys.com	Fairfax	VA	22030	703-626-5024		809
Palomar Community College District 1140 W Mission Rd — *Web:* www2.palomar.edu	San Marcos	CA	92069	760-744-1150		162
Palomar Health 2185 Citracado Pkwy — *Web:* www.palomarhealth.org	Escondido	CA	92029	442-281-5000		462
Palomar Institute of Cosmetology 355 Via Vera Cruz — *Web:* www.pic.edu	San Marcos	CA	92078	760-744-7900		167-3
Palomar Insurance Corp 4525 Executive Park Dr Ste 202 — *Web:* palomarins.com	Montgomery	AL	36116	334-270-0105		390
Palomar Mountain State Park 200 Palm Canyon Dr — *Web:* www.parks.ca.gov	Borrego Springs	CA	92004	760-742-3462		565
Palomar Technologies 2728 Loker Ave W — *Web:* www.palomartechnologies.com	Carlsbad	CA	92010	760-931-3600	931-5191	811
Palomar Ventures 233 Wilshire Blvd Ste 900 — *Web:* www.palomarventures.com	Santa Monica	CA	90401	310-260-6050		792
Palomino 49 W Maryland St — *Web:* www.palomino.com	Indianapolis	IN	46204	317-974-0400		671
Palomino 1420 Fifth Ave — *Web:* palomino.com	Seattle	WA	98101	206-623-1300		671
Palomino Inc 404-533 College St — *TF:* 866-360-0360 ■ *Web:* www.palominosys.com	Toronto	ON	M5V1M1	416-964-7333		179
Palomino RV 1200 New Jersey Ave SE — *Web:* www.palominorv.com	Washington	DC	20590	269-432-3271	432-2516	120
Paloras Corp 228 Hamilton Ave 3rd Fl — *Web:* paloras.com	Palo Alto	CA	94301	650-440-7663		177
Palos Sports Inc 11711 S Austin Ave — *TF:* 800-233-5484 ■ *Web:* www.palossports.com	Alsip	IL	60803	708-396-2555		711
Palos Verdes Inn 1700 S Pacific Coast Hwy — *Web:* www.palosverdesinn.com	Redondo Beach	CA	90277	310-316-4211		379
Palos Verdes Library District 701 Silver Spur Rd — *Web:* www.pvld.org	Rolling Hills Estates	CA	90274	310-377-9584		434-3
Palos Verdes Peninsula Chamber of Commerce 707 Silver Spur Rd Ste 100 — *Web:* www.palosverdeschamber.com	Rolling Hills Estates	CA	90274	310-377-8111	377-0614	139
Palos Verdes Peninsula News 609 Deep Valley Dr Ste 200 — *Web:* www.pvnews.com	Rolling Hills Estates	CA	90274	310-377-6877	372-6113	532-4
Pals Intl 900 Wilshire Dr Ste 105 — *Web:* www.palsintl.com	Troy	MI	48084	248-362-2060		768
Palstar Inc 9676 Looney Rd — *TF:* 800-773-7931 ■ *Web:* palstar.com	Piqua	OH	45356	937-773-6255	773-8003	248
Paltech Enterprises Inc 2560 Bing Miller Ln — *TF:* 800-949-1006 ■ *Web:* www.paltech-entrps.com	Urbana	IA	52345	319-443-2700		499
PAM and Dean Blehert 11919 Moss Point Ln — *Web:* www.blehert.com	Reston	VA	20194	703-471-7907		637-10
Pam Lychner State Jail 2350 Atascocita Rd — *Web:* www.tdcj.texas.gov	Humble	TX	77396	281-454-5036		213
PAM Transportation Services Inc 297 W Henri De Tonti Blvd — *NASDAQ: PTSI* ■ *TF:* 800-879-7261 ■ *Web:* www.pamtransport.com	Tontitown	AR	72770	479-361-9111	361-5338	780
Pamal Broadcasting Ltd 6 Johnson Rd — *Web:* www.pamal.com	Latham	NY	12110	518-786-6600		643
Pamarco 171 E Marquardt Dr — *TF:* 800-323-7735 ■ *Web:* www.pamarco.com	Wheeling	IL	60090	847-459-6000		677
Pambiche 2811 NE Glisan St — *Web:* www.pambiche.com	Portland	OR	97232	503-233-0511		671
PAMC (Pacific Alliance Medical Ctr) 531 W College St — *Web:* pamc.net	Los Angeles	CA	90012	213-624-8411		374-3
Pamco Inc 1301 S 7th St — *Web:* www.pamco.biz	Oskaloosa	IA	52577	641-672-2576	672-2354	273
Pamlico Capital 150 N College St Ste 2400 — *Web:* www.pamlicocapital.com	Charlotte	NC	28202	704-414-7150		41
Pamlico Community College PO Box 185 — *Web:* www.pamlicocc.edu	Grantsboro	NC	28529	252-249-1851	249-2377	162
Pamlico County PO Box 776 — *Web:* www.pamlicocounty.org	Bayboro	NC	28515	252-745-3133	745-5514	338
Pampa Regional Medical Ctr 1 Medical Plz — *Web:* www.prmctx.com	Pampa	TX	79065	806-665-3721		374-3
Pampas Bar & Grill 6333 W 3rd St Ste 618 — *Web:* www.pampas-grill.com	Los Angeles	CA	92123	858-278-5971		671
Pampered Chef Ltd 1 Pampered Chef Ln — *TF:* 888-687-2433 ■ *Web:* www.pamperedchef.com	Addison	IL	60101	888-687-2433		366
Pampered Pet School of Dog Grooming 109 Dewalt Ave DeWalt Professional Bldg — *Web:* www.pamperedpetschool.com	Pittsburgh	PA	15227	412-881-4744	885-0211	685
Pamplemousse Le Restaurant 400 E Sahara Ave — *Web:* www.pamplemousselerestaurant.com	Las Vegas	NV	89104	702-733-2066		671
Pams Inc 3361 Pomona Blvd — *Web:* pamsinc.com	Pomona	CA	91768	909-869-7267		196
Pan Abode Cedar Homes Inc 1100 Maple Ave SW — *TF:* 800-782-2633 ■ *Web:* www.panabodehomes.com	Renton	WA	98057	425-255-8260	255-8630	106
Pan Am Railways 1700 Iron Horse Pk — *TF:* 800-955-9212 ■ *Web:* panamrailways.com	North Billerica	MA	01862	800-955-9212		648
Pan American Development Foundation (PADF) 1889 F St NW 2nd Fl — *TF:* 877-572-4484 ■ *Web:* www.padf.org	Washington	DC	20006	202-458-3969	458-6316	48-5
Pan American Express Inc 4848 Riverside Dr — *TF:* 866-472-6263 ■ *Web:* www.panamex-zero.com	Laredo	TX	78041	956-723-4848	723-9979	519
Pan American Finance LLC 601 Brickell Key Dr Ste 604 — *Web:* panamfinance.com	Miami	FL	33131	305-577-9799		401
Pan American Screw Inc 630 Reese Dr SW — *TF:* 800-951-2222 ■ *Web:* www.panamericanscrew.com	Conover	NC	28613	828-466-0060	466-0070	278
Pan American Silver Corp 625 Howe St Ste 1500 — *TF:* 800-564-6253 ■ *Web:* www.panamericansilver.com	Vancouver	BC	V6C2T6	604-684-1175	684-0147	502
Pan American Travel Services 320 East 900 South — *TF:* 800-364-4359 ■ *Web:* www.panam-tours.com	Salt Lake City	UT	84111	801-364-4300		772
Pan Asian Publications Inc 29564 Union City Blvd — *TF:* 800-909-8088 ■ *Web:* panap.com	Union City	CA	94587	510-475-1185	475-1489	95
Pan Glo 1550 Custer Ave — *TF:* 800-652-2151 ■ *Web:* www.bundybakingsolutions.com	San Francisco	CA	94124	415-648-3325		393
Pan Pacific Express Corp 19481 Harborgate Way — *Web:* www.panpacificusa.com	Torrance	CA	90501	310-638-3888		311
Pan Pacific Hotels Group Wells Fargo Center 999 3rd Ave — *TF:* 877-324-4856 ■ *Web:* www.panpacific.com	Seattle	WA	98104	877-324-4856		379
Pan Star Express Corp 1134 Tower Ln — *Web:* www.panstarexpress.com	Bensenville	IL	60106	630-787-1672		311
Panacea Inc 14905 Paramount Blvd Ste H — *Web:* panenv.com	Paramount	CA	90723	562-860-2869	633-3180	261
Panacea Technologies Inc 160 Commerce Dr Ste 500 — *Web:* www.panaceatech.com	Montgomeryville	PA	18936	267-421-5300		463
Panache Partners LLC 1424 Gables Ct — *Web:* www.panache.com	Plano	TX	75075	469-246-6060	246-6062	637-2
Panacore Corp 2015 E Eighth St Ste 242 — *TF:* 877-726-2267 ■ *Web:* www.panacore.com	Odessa	TX	79761	877-726-2267		809
PANalytical Inc 117 Flanders Rd — *Web:* www.malvernpanalytical.com	Westborough	MA	01581	508-647-1100		419
Panama						
Consulate General 1100 Poydras St Ste 2615 — *Web:* www.consulateofpanama.com	New Orleans	LA	70163	504-525-3458	524-8960	257
Embassy 2862 McGill Terr NW — *Web:* embassyofpanama.org	Washington	DC	20008	202-483-1407	483-8413	257
Panama City Beach Convention & Visitors Bureau 17001 Panama City Beach Pkwy — *Web:* www.visitpanamacitybeach.com	Panama City Beach	FL	32413	850-233-5070		206
Panama City Beaches Chamber of Commerce 309 Richard Jackson Blvd Ste 101 — *TF:* 800-224-4853 ■ *Web:* www.pcbeach.org	Panama City Beach	FL	32407	850-235-1159	235-2301	139
Panama Jack Inc 230 Ernestine St — *TF:* 800-840-5225 ■ *Web:* www.panamajack.com	Orlando	FL	32801	800-840-5225		361
Pan-American Life Insurance Co 601 Poydras St — *TF:* 877-939-4550 ■ *Web:* www.palig.com	New Orleans	LA	70130	877-939-4550		391-2
Panaram Intl 126 Greylock Ave — *TF:* 800-872-8695 ■ *Web:* usatowl.com	Belleville	NJ	07109	973-751-1100		362
Panasas Inc 969 W Maude Ave — *TF:* 888-726-2727 ■ *Web:* www.panasas.com	Sunnyvale	CA	94085	408-215-6800	215-6801	177

Name / Address	City	State	ZIP	Phone	Fax	Class
Panasonic 2 Riverfront Plz *Web:* www.na.panasonic.com	Newark	NJ	07102	201-348-7000		52
Panasonic Avionics Corp 26200 Enterprise Way *TF:* 877-627-2300 ■ *Web:* www.panasonic.aero	Lake Forest	CA	92630	949-672-2000	462-7100	52
Panavise Products Inc 7540 Colbert Dr *TF:* 800-759-7535 ■ *Web:* www.panavise.com	Reno	NV	89511	775-850-2900		697
Panavision Inc 6219 DeSoto Ave *TF:* 800-260-1846 ■ *Web:* www.panavision.com	Woodland Hills	CA	91367	818-316-1000	316-1111	591
Panchero's Mexican Grill 2475 Coral Ct Ste B *Web:* www.pancheros.com	Coralville	IA	52241	319-545-6565		670
Pancho Villa Restaurant Ottawa 361 Elgin St *Web:* www.panchovilla.ca	Ottawa	ON	K2P1M7	613-234-8872		671
Pancho's Mexican Buffet Inc 4001 Wheatland Rd *Web:* www.panchosmexicanbuffetdfw.com	Dallas	TX	75237	972-709-4685		186
Pancio Law Group LLC 2028 N Broad St *Web:* walshpancio.com	Lansdale	PA	19446	215-368-8660		41
Panda Express 1717 Walnut Grove Ave *TF:* 800-877-8988 ■ *Web:* www.pandaexpress.com	Rosemead	CA	91770	626-312-5401		670
Panda Inn PO Box 1159 *TF:* 800-877-8988 ■ *Web:* www.pandainn.com	Rosemead	CA	91206	800-877-8988		671
Panda Kitchen 1986 Hwy 50 E *Web:* www.pandakitchencarsoncity.com	Carson City	NV	89701	775-882-8128		671
Panda Restaurant Group 1683 Walnut Grove Ave *TF:* 888-532-7126 ■ *Web:* pandarg.com	Rosemead	CA	91770	626-799-9898		670
Panda Travel 1017 Kapahulu Ave *TF:* 800-303-6702 ■ *Web:* www.pandaonline.com	Honolulu	HI	96816	808-738-3898		772
PandaDoc Inc 101 California St Ste 3975 *Web:* www.pandadoc.com	San Francisco	CA	94111	415-779-0222		788
Pandel Inc 21 River Dr *TF:* 800-537-3868 ■ *Web:* www.pandel.com	Cartersville	GA	30120	770-382-1034		364
Pandell Technology Corp 4954 Richard Rd SW Ste 400 *Web:* www.pandell.com	Calgary	AB	T3E6L1	403-271-0701	217-0730	180
Pandjiris Inc 5151 Northrup Ave *Web:* www.pandjiris.com	Saint Louis	MO	63110	314-776-6893	776-8763	811
Pandol Bros Inc 33150 Pond Rd *Web:* www.pandol.com	Delano	CA	93215	661-725-3755		297-7
Pandora Bancshares Inc 102 E Main St *Web:* e-fnb.com	Pandora	OH	45877	419-384-3221		70
Pandora Quaker Bridge Mall 1299 Rt 38 Ste 3 *Web:* stores.pandora.net	Lawrenceville	NJ	08648	609-799-8177		460
Panduit Corp 17301 Ridgeland Ave *TF:* 888-506-5400 ■ *Web:* www.panduit.com	Tinley Park	IL	60477	708-532-1800		815
Pane e Vino 365 Atwells Ave *Web:* panevino.net	Providence	RI	02903	401-223-2230	223-4322	671
Pane e Vino 1715 Union St *Web:* www.paneevinotrattoria.com	San Francisco	CA	94123	415-346-2111		671
Panef Inc 5700 W Douglas Ave *TF:* 800-448-1247 ■ *Web:* www.panef.com	Milwaukee	WI	53218	414-464-7200		579
Panel Processing Inc 120 N Industrial Hwy **Fax Area Code:* 989 ■ *TF:* 800-433-7142 ■ *Web:* www.panel.com	Alpena	MI	49707	800-433-7142	356-9000*	819
Panelfold Inc 10700 NW 36th Ave *TF:* 800-433-3222 ■ *Web:* www.panelfold.com	Miami	FL	33167	305-688-3501	688-0185	286
Panella Trucking LLC 5000 E Fremont *TF:* 800-696-4007 ■ *Web:* panellatrucking.com	Stockton	CA	95215	209-943-5000		311
Paneloc Corp 142 Brickyard Rd PO Box 547 *Web:* www.paneloc.com	Farmington	CT	06034	860-677-6711	677-8606	350
Panera Bread Co 3630 S Geyer Rd *NASDAQ:* PNRA ■ *TF:* 800-301-5566 ■ *Web:* www.panerabread.com	Saint Louis	MO	63127	314-984-1000	909-3300	68
Panetta Institute for Public Policy, The California State University Monterey Bay 100 Campus Ctr Bldg 86E *Web:* www.panettainstitute.org	Seaside	CA	93955	831-582-4200	582-4082	634
Panetta Jimmy (Rep D - CA) 212 Cannon House Office Bldg *Web:* panetta.house.gov	Washington	DC	20515	202-225-2861	225-6791	342-2
Pangaea Information Technologies Ltd 219 W Chicago Ave *Web:* www.pangaeatech.com	Chicago	IL	60654	312-337-5404		177
Pangaea Partners Ltd 1210 N Wfield Rd *Web:* www.pangaeapartners.com	Madison	WI	53717	608-347-0192	836-5060	690
Pangaea Publishing 226 Wheeler St S *Web:* www.pangaea.org	Saint Paul	MN	55105	651-690-3320		637-2
Pangere Corp 4050 W Fourth Ave *Web:* www.pangere.com	Gary	IN	46406	219-949-1368	944-3028	186
Pango Technology Inc 502 E Fireweed Ln *Web:* www.pangotechnology.com	Anchorage	AK	99503	907-868-8092	563-2264	177
Pangolin Laser Systems Inc 9501 Satellite Blvd Ste 109 *Web:* pangolin.com	Orlando	FL	32837	407-299-2088	299-6066	177
Panhandle Cooperative Assn 401 S Beltline Hwy W *TF:* 800-732-4546 ■ *Web:* www.panhandlecoop.com	Scottsbluff	NE	69361	308-632-5301	632-5375	276
Panhandle Food Sales Inc 1980 Smith Township State Rd *Web:* panhandlefoodsales.com	Burgettstown	PA	15021	724-947-2216		296-36
Panhandle Northern Railroad LLC 100 E Grand *Web:* www.omnitrax.com	Borger	TX	79007	806-273-3513		649
Panhandle PBS PO Box 447 *Web:* www.panhandlepbs.org	Amarillo	TX	79178	806-371-5222	371-5258	741-4
Panhandle Royalty Co 5400 N Grand Blvd Grand Ctr Bldg Ste 300 *TF:* 800-884-4225 ■ *Web:* www.panhandleoilandgas.com	Oklahoma City	OK	73112	405-948-1560	948-2038	538
Panhandle Telecommunication Systems Inc (PTSI) 2222 NW Hwy 64 *TF:* 800-562-2556 ■ *Web:* www.ptci.net	Guymon	OK	73942	580-338-2556		736
Panhandle-Plains Higher Education Authority Inc (PPHEA) 1303 23rd St *Web:* www.pphea.org	Canyon	TX	79015	806-324-4100		48-11
Panhandle-Plains Historical Museum 2503 Fourth Ave *Web:* www.panhandleplains.org	Canyon	TX	79015	806-651-2244		520
Pankl Aerospace Systems Inc 16615 Edwards Rd *Web:* www.pankl.com	Cerritos	CA	90703	562-926-0432		21
Pannell Kerr Forster of Texas Pc 5847 San Felipe St *Web:* www.pkftexas.com	Houston	TX	77057	713-860-1400	355-3909	2
Pannier Corp 207 Sandusky St *TF:* 877-726-6437 ■ *Web:* www.pannier.com	Pittsburgh	PA	15212	412-323-4900	323-4962	494
Pannier Graphics 345 Oak Rd *TF:* 800-544-8428 ■ *Web:* www.panniergraphics.com	Gibsonia	PA	15044	724-265-4900		701
Pan-O-Gold Baking Co 444 E St Germain *TF:* 800-444-7005 ■ *Web:* www.panogold.com	Saint Cloud	MN	56304	320-251-9361		296-1
Panola College 1109 W Panola St *TF:* 800-252-9152 ■ *Web:* www.panola.edu	Carthage	TX	75633	903-693-2000	693-2031	162
Panola County 110 Sycamore St *Web:* www.co.panola.tx.us	Carthage	TX	75633	903-693-0300	693-4125	338
Panola County Chamber of Commerce 300 W Panola St *Web:* www.carthagetexas.us	Carthage	TX	75633	903-693-6634	693-8578	139
Panola Mountain State Park 2600 Georgia 155 *Web:* gastateparks.org	Stockbridge	GA	30281	770-389-7801		565
Panola Partnership Inc 150-A Public Sq *TF:* 888-872-6652 ■ *Web:* www.panolacounty.com	Batesville	MS	38606	662-563-3126	563-0704	139
Panola Watchman 109 W Panola St *Web:* www.panolawatchman.com	Carthage	TX	75633	903-693-7888		637-9
Panola-Harrison Electric Co-op 410 E Houston St *TF:* 800-972-1093 ■ *Web:* www.phec.us	Marshall	TX	75670	903-935-7936		245
Panolam Decorative Surfaces 1 Pionite Rd *Web:* panolam.com	Auburn	ME	04210	207-689-9433		291
Panolam Industries International Inc 1 Corporate Dr Ste 725 *TF:* 877-726-6526 ■ *Web:* www.panolam.com	Shelton	CT	06484	877-726-6526		49-9
Panoptic Development Inc 131 Wayland Ave **Fax Area Code:* 717 ■ *Web:* www.panopticdev.com	Providence	RI	02906	401-239-2192	924-9606*	809
PanOptica Inc 150 Morristown Rd Ste 205 *Web:* www.panopticapharma.com	Bernardsville	NJ	07924	908-766-2202		238
Panora Cooperative Telephone Association Inc 114 E Main St *Web:* panoratelco.com	Panora	IA	50216	641-755-2424		116
Panorama Balloon Tours 2683 Via De La Valle 625G *TF:* 800-455-3592 ■ *Web:* www.gohotair.com	Del Mar	CA	92014	760-271-3467		760
Panorama City 1751 Cir Ln SE *TF:* 800-999-9807 ■ *Web:* www.panorama.org	Lacey	WA	98503	360-456-0111	438-5901	672
Panorama Consulting Solutions 5975 S Quebec St Ste 207 *Web:* www.panorama-consulting.com	Greenwood Village	CO	80111	720-515-1377		196
Panorama Helicopters Ltd 360 Airport Rd *Web:* www.helicopterespanorama.com	Alma	QC	G8B5V2	418-668-3046		13
Panoramic Corp 4321 Goshen Rd *TF:* 800-654-2027 ■ *Web:* www.pancorp.com	Fort Wayne	IN	46818	800-654-2027		757
Panoramic Inc 1500 N Parker Dr *TF:* 800-333-1394 ■ *Web:* www.panoramicinc.com	Janesville	WI	53545	608-754-8850	754-5703	101
Panoramic Press Inc 2920 N 35th St *Web:* panoramicpress.com	Phoenix	AZ	85018	602-955-2001		627
Panos Greek Taverna 654 SE Marine Dr *Web:* www.panosgreekvancouver.ca	Vancouver	BC	V5X2T4	604-322-8824		671
Panos Restaurant 1504 W 38 St *Web:* www.panosrestaurant.com	Erie	PA	16508	814-866-0517		671
Pan-Osten Co 6944 Louisville Rd *TF:* 800-472-6678 ■ *Web:* www.panoston.com	Bowling Green	KY	42101	270-783-3900	783-3911	286
Pan-Pacific Plumbing Co 18250 Euclid St *Web:* www.ppmechanical.com	Fountain Valley	CA	92708	949-474-9170		609
Pantages Hotel 200 Victoria St *TF:* 855-852-1777 ■ *Web:* www.pantageshotel.com	Toronto	ON	M5B1V8	416-362-1777		379
Pantages Theatre 6233 Hollywood Blvd *TF:* 800-430-8903 ■ *Web:* www.pantages-theater.com	Los Angeles	CA	90028	800-430-8903		572
Pantagraph PO Box 2907 *TF:* 800-747-7323 ■ *Web:* www.pantagraph.com	Bloomington	IL	61702	309-829-9000		532-2
Pantagraph Printing and Stationery Co PO Box 1406 *Web:* pantagraphprinting.com	Bloomington	IL	61702	309-829-1071		627
Pantera Energy Co 817 S Polk St Ste 201 *Web:* www.panteraenergy.com	Amarillo	TX	79101	806-376-6625	376-5833	536
Pantera Global Technology 10411 Corporate Dr Ste 208 *TF:* 877-219-9777 ■ *Web:* panteratools.com	Pleasant Prairie	WI	53158	877-219-9777		177
Pantheon 717 California St 2nd Fl *TF:* 855-927-9387 ■ *Web:* pantheon.io	San Francisco	CA	94108	855-927-9387		177
Panther Creek State Park 2010 Panther Creek Park Rd *Web:* www.state.tn.us	Morristown	TN	37814	423-587-7046		565
Panther Graphics Inc 465 Central Ave *Web:* www.panthergraphics.net	Rochester	NY	14605	585-546-7163		627
Panther Racing LLC 5101 Decatur Blvd *Web:* pantherracing.com	Indianapolis	IN	46241	317-856-9500		642
Panthera Interactive LLC 2831 St Rose Pkwy Ste 232 *Web:* www.pantherainteractive.com	Henderson	NV	89052	702-202-4740		7

Name / Address	City	State	ZIP	Phone	Fax	Class
Pants Store, The 8029 Pkwy Dr *Web:* pantsstore.com	Leeds	AL	35094	205-699-6166		229
Panurgy Inc 3 Wing Dr Ste 225 *Web:* www.panurgy.com	Cedar Knolls	NJ	07927	973-625-9686		175
Panzano 909 17th St *Web:* www.panzano-denver.com	Denver	CO	80202	303-296-3525		671
Panzer Dermatology Cosmetic Surgery 537 Stanton Christiana Rd *Web:* premierdermde.com	Newark	DE	19713	302-633-7550		77
Panzer Nursery Inc 17980 W Baseline Rd *TF:* 888-212-5327 ■ *Web:* www.panzernursery.com	Beaverton	OR	97006	503-645-1185	629-9023	369
PAOC (Pentecostal Assemblies of Canada, The) 2450 Milltower Ct *TF:* 800-779-7262 ■ *Web:* www.paoc.org	Mississauga	ON	L5N5Z6	905-542-7400	542-7313	48-20
Paolo's Restaurant 333 W San Carlos St Ste 150 *Web:* www.paolosrestaurant.com	San Jose	CA	95110	408-294-2558		671
Papa Advertising Inc 1673 W Eighth St *Web:* papaadvertising.com	Erie	PA	16505	814-454-6236		7
Papa Cantella's Inc 3341 E 50th St *Web:* www.papacantella.com	Vernon	CA	90058	323-584-7272		296-26
Papa Cristos 2771 W Pico Blvd *Web:* papacristos.com	Los Angeles	CA	90006	323-737-2970		671
Papa Dio's 10712 N May Ave *Web:* papadiosokc.com	Oklahoma City	OK	73120	405-755-2255		671
Papa Gino's Inc 600 Providence Hwy *Web:* www.papaginos.com	Dedham	MA	02026	781-467-1600	326-7552	670
Papa Joe's 1561 Akron Peninsula Rd *Web:* www.papajoes.com	Akron	OH	44313	330-923-7999	923-8009	671
Papa John's International Inc 2002 Papa John's Blvd *NASDAQ: PZZA* ■ *TF:* 877-547-7272 ■ *Web:* www.papajohns.com	Louisville	KY	40299	502-261-7272		670
Papa Murphy's International Inc 8000 NE Pkwy Dr Ste 350 **Fax Area Code:* 360 ■ *TF:* 877-777-5062 ■ *Web:* www.papamurphys.com	Vancouver	WA	98662	800-257-7272	260-0500*	670
Papachino's 1212 J St *Web:* www.mypapachinos.com	Modesto	CA	95354	209-578-5225		671
Papalote Press PO Box 32058 *TF:* 888-229-7109 ■ *Web:* www.papalotepress.com	Santa Fe	NM	87594	888-229-7109	229-8862	637-2
Papapavlo's Bistro & Bar 501 N Lincoln Ctr *Web:* www.papapavlos.com	Stockton	CA	95207	209-477-6133		671
Paparone Corp 702 N White Horse Pk *Web:* www.paparonenewhomes.com	Stratford	NJ	08084	856-784-0550		653
Papas Bakery Inc 6055 S Howell Ave *Web:* www.papasbakery.com	Milwaukee	WI	53207	414-483-9003	483-9087	68
Papas Jeep Ram 585 E Main St *Web:* www.papasjeepram.com	New Britain	CT	06051	860-225-8751		516
Papco Inc 4920 S Blvd *TF:* 800-899-0747 ■ *Web:* www.wfscorp.com	Virginia Beach	VA	23462	757-499-5977		579
Pape-Dawson Engineers Inc 2000 NW Loop 410 *Web:* www.pape-dawson.com	San Antonio	TX	78213	210-375-9000	375-9010	261
Paper Chase Farms Publishing Group 23532 Chase Hollow Ln *Web:* www.paperchasefarms.com	Middleburg	VA	20117	540-687-3364		637-2
Paper Converting Machine Co (PCMC) 2300 S Ashland Ave *Web:* www.pcmc.com	Green Bay	WI	54307	920-494-5601	494-8865	556
Paper Crafts Magazine 14512 S Center Point Way Ste 600 *TF:* 800-815-3538 ■ *Web:* www.papercraftsmag.com	Bluffdale	UT	84065	801-816-8302		457-14
Paper Cut Inc, The 234 W Northland Ave *Web:* thepapercut.com	Appleton	WI	54911	920-954-6210		561
Paper Epiphanies 687 N Tillamook St Ste C *Web:* www.paperepiphanies.com	Portland	OR	97227	424-272-5817		637-10
Paper Machinery Corp 8900 W Bradley Rd PO Box 240100 *Web:* www.papermc.com	Milwaukee	WI	53224	414-354-8050	354-8614	556
Paper Pak Industries (PPI) 1941 N White Ave *TF:* 888-293-6529 ■ *Web:* www.paperpakindustries.com	La Verne	CA	91750	909-392-1750	392-1760	297-9
Paper Pigeon 14701 SW 94 Ave *Web:* paperpigeonmiami.com	Miami	FL	33157	305-235-7887		535
Paper Place 4130 N Marshall Way *Web:* thepaperplaceaz.com	Scottsdale	AZ	85251	480-941-2858		535
Paper Pop Cards 54 W 40th St **Fax Area Code:* 646 ■ *TF:* 866-906-2044 ■ *Web:* www.paperpopcards.com	New York	NY	10018	866-906-2044	219-3365*	637-10
Paper Products Company Inc 760 Commonwealth Dr *TF:* 800-837-2702 ■ *Web:* www.paperproducts-pgh.com	Warrendale	PA	15086	724-741-9700	741-9901	559
Paper Shack & Party Store Inc, The 2430 E Texas St *Web:* www.papershackandpartystore.com	Bossier City	LA	71111	318-746-4108		566
Paper Source Converting 4800 S Santa Fe Ave *Web:* www.papersourcemfg.com	Vernon	CA	90058	323-583-3800		557
Paper Store Inc 20 Main St *TF:* 844-480-7100 ■ *Web:* www.thepaperstore.com	Acton	MA	01720	844-480-7100		566
Paper Systems Inc 185 S Pioneer Blvd *TF:* 888-564-6774 ■ *Web:* www.papersystems.com	Springboro	OH	45066	937-746-6841	746-1089	554
Paper Tiger 1248 San Felipe Ave *Web:* www.ptig.com	Santa Fe	NM	87505	505-983-3101		627
Paper Tigers, The 2201 Waukegan Rd Ste 180 *TF:* 800-621-1774 ■ *Web:* www.papertigers.com	Bannockburn	IL	60015	847-919-6500	919-6501	660
Paper Transport Inc 1250 Mid Valley Dr *TF:* 800-317-3650 ■ *Web:* www.papertransport.com	De Pere	WI	54115	800-317-3650		780
Paper Wise PO Box 2196 *Web:* www.paperwise.net	Glenwood Springs	CO	81602	970-945-2885		559
PaperChase PO Box 54 **Fax Area Code:* 540 ■ *TF:* 800-722-2075 ■ *Web:* www.paperchase.com	Hood	VA	22723	781-325-6086	948-4841*	225
Paperclip Software Inc 1 University Plz *TF:* 800-929-3503 ■ *Web:* www.paperclip.com	Hackensack	NJ	07601	201-525-1221	525-1511	178-1
Papercone Corp 3200 Fern Valley Rd *TF:* 800-626-5308 ■ *Web:* papercone.com	Louisville	KY	40213	502-961-9493	961-9346	263
Papercutz 160 Broadway Ste 700E **Fax Area Code:* 212 ■ *Web:* www.papercutz.com	New York	NY	10038	646-559-4681	643-1545*	637-2
PaperDirect Inc 1005 E Woodmen Rd *TF:* 800-272-7377 ■ *Web:* www.paperdirect.com	Colorado Springs	CO	80920	800-338-3346		553
Papers Inc 206 S Main St *TF:* 800-733-4111 ■ *Web:* www.the-papers.com	Milford	IN	46542	574-658-4111	658-4701	637-8
PaperThin Inc 300 Congress St Ste 303 *Web:* www.paperthin.com	Quincy	MA	02169	617-471-4440		177
PaperWise Inc 3171 E Sunshine *TF:* 888-828-7505 ■ *Web:* www.paperwise.com	Springfield	MO	65804	417-886-7505		177
PaperWorks Industries Inc 5000 Flat Rock Rd *Web:* www.paperworksindustries.com	Philadelphia	PA	19127	215-984-7000		561
Papillon Restaurant 37296 Mission Blvd *Web:* www.papillonrestaurant.com	Fremont	CA	94536	510-793-6331	793-2789	671
Pappadeaux Seafood Kitchen 1304 E Copeland Rd *Web:* www.pappadeaux.com	Arlington	TX	76011	817-543-0545		671
Pappajohn Capital Resources 666 Walnut St *Web:* www.pappajohn.com	Des Moines	IA	50309	515-244-5746		792
Pappas Capital LLC 2520 Meridian Pkwy *Web:* www.pappasventures.com	Durham	NC	27713	919-998-3300	998-3301	792
Pappas Chris (Rep D - NH) 323 Cannon House Office Bldg *Web:* www.pappas.house.gov	Washington	DC	20515	202-225-5456		342-2
Pappas Macdonnell Inc 135 Rennell Dr *Web:* www.pappasmacdonnell.com	Southport	CT	06890	203-254-1944		7
Pappas Rehabilitation Hospital for Children 3 Randolph St *Web:* www.mass.gov	Canton	MA	02021	781-828-2440	821-4086	371-1
Pappas Restaurants Inc 13939 NW Fwy *Web:* www.pappas.com	Houston	TX	77040	713-869-0151		670
Pappasito's Cantina 13070 Hwy 290 *Web:* www.pappasitos.com	Houston	TX	77040	713-462-0246		670
Pappy's Place 943 N Main Ave *Web:* www.pappysplace.business.site	Springfield	MO	65802	417-866-8744		671
Par 4 Plastics Inc 351 Industrial Dr *Web:* www.par4plastics.com	Marion	KY	42064	270-965-9141		596
PAR Capital Management Inc 200 Clarendon St 48th Fl *Web:* www.parcapital.com	Boston	MA	02116	617-526-8990		690
PAR Excellence Systems Inc 11500 Northlake Dr *TF:* 800-888-7279 ■ *Web:* www.parexcellencesystems.com	Cincinnati	OH	45249	800-888-7279		177
Par Kut International Inc 40961 Production Dr *Web:* www.parkut.com	Harrison Township	MI	48045	586-468-2947		480
Par Mar Stores 114 A Westview Ave *Web:* www.parmarstores.com	Marietta	OH	45750	304-572-3500		297-8
Par Pharmaceutical Companies Inc 1 State Street Plz 24th Fl *NASDAQ: ENDP* ■ *TF:* 800-828-9393 ■ *Web:* www.parpharm.com	Chestnut Ridge	NY	10977	800-462-3636		583
Par Plumbing Company Inc 60 N Prospect Ave *Web:* pargroup.com	Lynbrook	NY	11563	516-887-4000		189-10
Par Springer-Miller Systems Inc 782 Mountain Rd *Web:* www.springermiller.com	Stowe	VT	05672	802-253-7377		764
Par Systems Inc 707 County Rd E *TF:* 800-464-1320 ■ *Web:* www.par.com	Shoreview	MN	55126	651-484-7261		207
PAR Technology Corp 8383 Seneca Tpke *NYSE: PAR* ■ *TF:* 800-448-6505 ■ *Web:* www.partech.com	New Hartford	NY	13413	315-738-0600		614
Para Systems Inc *Minuteman UPS* 1455 LeMay Dr *TF:* 800-238-7272 ■ *Web:* www.minutemanups.com	Carrollton	TX	75007	972-446-7363	446-9011	253
Paraben Corp 21690 Red Rum Dr Ste 137 *Web:* www.paraben.com	Ashburn	VA	20147	801-796-0944		177
Parable Christian Stores 3563 Empleo St *Web:* www.parable.com	San Luis Obispo	CA	93401	805-248-7395	201-9026	95
Parade Publications Inc 711 Third Ave *Web:* parade.com	New York	NY	10017	212-450-7000		637-9
Par-A-Dice Hotel 21 Blackjack Blvd *TF:* 800-727-2342 ■ *Web:* www.paradicecasino.com	East Peoria	IL	61611	309-699-7711		379
Paradies Shops 2849 Paces Ferry Rd *Web:* paradieslagardere.com	Atlanta	GA	30339	404-344-7905		327
Paradigm 1672 Merriman Rd Ste A *Web:* www.paradigmequity.com	Akron	OH	44313	330-475-1690	475-1695	390
Paradigm Capital Inc 95 Wellington St W Ste 2101 *Web:* www.paradigmcap.com	Toronto	ON	M5J2N7	416-361-9892		401
Paradigm Design Associates Inc 4 Center Rd Unit 5 *TF:* 800-495-3295 ■ *Web:* www.pda4.com	Old Saybrook	CT	06475	800-495-3295		525
Paradigm Financial Advisors LLC 12231 Manchester Rd *Web:* www.pfaclient.com	Des Peres	MO	63131	314-966-3400	966-0422	401
Paradigm Imaging Group Inc 3010 Red Hill Ave *TF:* 888-221-7226 ■ *Web:* www.paradigmimaging.com	Costa Mesa	CA	92626	714-432-7226	432-7222	627
Paradigm Learning Inc 100 Second Ave S Ste 1201 *Web:* paradigmlearning.com	Saint Petersburg	FL	33701	727-471-3170		194
Paradigm Medical Industries Inc 2355 S 1070 W *OTC: PDMI* ■ *Web:* www.paradigm-medical.com	Salt Lake City	UT	84119	801-977-8970	977-8973	250

				Phone	Fax	Class
Paradigm Metals Inc 15811 Vision Dr *Web:* www.paradigmmetals.com	Pflugerville	TX	78660	512-255-2622		697
Paradigm Precision Holdings 404 W Guadalupe Rd *Web:* paradigmprecision.com	Tempe	AZ	85283	480-839-0501		454
Paradigm Precision Holdings LLC 3651 SE Commerce Ave *Web:* www.paradigmprecision.com	Stuart	FL	34997	772-287-7770		21
Paradigm Printing Inc 429 Virgil Dr *Web:* www.paradigmprinting.com	Dalton	GA	30721	706-226-7474	278-7474	627
Paradigm Talent & Literary Agency 360 N Crescent Dr N Bldg *Web:* paradigmagency.com	Beverly Hills	CA	90210	310-288-8000	288-2000	731
Paradigm Transportation Solutions Ltd 22 King St S Ste 300 *Web:* www.ptsl.com	Waterloo	ON	N2J1N8	519-896-3163		463
Paradigms Consulting Group 1200-1881 Scarth St *Web:* www.paradigmconsulting.com	Regina	SK	S4P4K9	306-522-8588		463
Paradise Adv & Marketing Inc 150 Second Ave N Ste 800 *Web:* www.paradiseadv.com	Saint Petersburg	FL	33701	727-821-5155		4
Paradise Bank 2420 N Federal Hwy *Web:* paradisebank.com	Boca Raton	FL	33431	561-392-5444		70
Paradise Beverages Inc 94-1450 Moaniani St *Web:* www.paradisebeverages.com	Waipahu	HI	96797	808-678-4000	677-8280	81-1
Paradise Cay Publications Inc PO Box 29 *TF:* 800-736-4509 ■ *Web:* www.paracay.com	Arcata	CA	95521	707-822-9063	822-9163	637-2
Paradise Chamber of Commerce 5550 Sky Way Ste 1 *TF:* 800-247-9889 ■ *Web:* www.paradisechamber.com	Paradise	CA	95969	530-877-9356	877-1865	139
Paradise Chevrolet 6350 Leland St *TF:* 800-942-1694 ■ *Web:* www.paradisechevrolet.com	Ventura	CA	93003	805-642-0111		57
Paradise Cove Luau 1860 Ala Moana Blvd Ste 401 *TF:* 800-775-2683 ■ *Web:* www.paradisecove.com	Honolulu	HI	96815	808-842-5911		572
Paradise Guest Ranch PO Box 790 **Fax Area Code: 720* ■ *Web:* www.paradiseranch.com	Buffalo	WY	82834	307-684-7876	862-2126*	239
Paradise Inc 1200 W MLK Jr Blvd *OTC:* PARF ■ *TF:* 800-330-8952 ■ *Web:* www.paradisefruitco.com	Plant City	FL	33563	800-330-8952		296-8
Paradise Inc 1200 Dr Martin Luther King Jr Blvd *Web:* www.paradisefruitco.com	Plant City	FL	33563	813-752-1155	754-3168	602
Paradise Point State Park 33914 NW Paradise Park Rd *Web:* www.parks.wa.gov	Ridgefield	WA	98642	360-263-2350		565
Paradise Post 5399 Clark Rd *Web:* www.paradisepost.com	Paradise	CA	95969	530-877-4413		532-4
Paradise Valley Community College 18401 N 32nd St *Web:* www.paradisevalley.edu	Phoenix	AZ	85032	602-787-6500	787-7025	162
Paradise Valley Mall 13440 N 44th St *Web:* www.theparadisevalleymall.com	Phoenix	AZ	85032	602-996-8840		460
Paradise Valley Unified School District 15002 N 32nd St *Web:* www.pvschools.net	Phoenix	AZ	85032	602-449-2000		685
Paradise Ventures Inc 2901 Rigsby Ln *Web:* www.paradiseventuresinc.com	Safety Harbor	FL	34695	727-726-1115	726-2337	360-2
Paradise Video Inc 10148 Springtree Dr NW 47th St *Web:* www.paradisevideo.com	Fort Lauderdale	FL	33351	954-747-1118		514
Paradocs Worldwide Inc 550 Vanderbilt Ave *TF:* 855-727-2362 ■ *Web:* www.paradocsworldwide.com	Brooklyn	NY	11238	855-727-2362		113
Paradowski Creative 349 Marshall Ave Ste 200 *Web:* paradowski.com	Saint Louis	MO	63119	314-241-2150		195
Paradox 6330 E Thomas Rd Ste 200 *TF:* 888-283-4817 ■ *Web:* www.paradox.ai	Scottsdale	AZ	85251	888-283-4817		178-1
Parady Financial Group Inc 340 Heald Way Ste 226 *Web:* www.paradyfinancial.com	The Villages	FL	32163	352-751-3016	751-3017	401
Paraflex *Fast flexible focused lighting* 3 Luger Rd Ste 1 *Web:* www.paraflex.com	Denville	NJ	07834	973-340-6040		439
Paragon Advising Group LP 3200 SW Fwy Ste 2350	Houston	TX	77027	713-599-0111		70
Paragon Advisors LLC PO Box 332 *Web:* www.paragonenergyadvisors.com	Madison	CT	06443	203-245-9131		463
Paragon Agency, The PO Box 1281 *Web:* www.theparagonagency.com	Orange	CA	92856	714-771-0652		637-2
Paragon Application Systems Inc 326 Raleigh St *Web:* www.paragonedge.com	Holly Springs	NC	27540	919-567-9890		177
Paragon Casino Resort 711 Paragon Pl *TF:* 800-946-1946 ■ *Web:* www.paragoncasinoresort.com	Marksville	LA	71351	800-946-1946		133
Paragon Communications Inc 41 Main St *TF:* 877-483-5366 ■ *Web:* www.paragonnt.com	Bolton	MA	01740	508-881-0500	881-8887	38
Paragon Controls Inc 2371 Circadian Way *Web:* www.paragoncontrols.com	Santa Rosa	CA	95407	707-579-1424	579-8480	202
Paragon Culinary School 505 Popes Bluff Trl PO Box 7820 *Web:* www.paragonculinaryschool.org	Colorado Springs	CO	80907	719-578-5740	578-5742	685
Paragon D & E 5225 33rd St SE *Web:* paragonde.com	Grand Rapids	MI	49512	616-949-2220	949-2536	757
Paragon Data Systems Inc 2218 Superior Ave *TF:* 800-211-0768 ■ *Web:* paragondsi.com	Cleveland	OH	44114	216-621-7571		180
Paragon Development Systems Inc (PDS) 13400 Bishops Ln Ste 190 *TF:* 800-966-6090 ■ *Web:* pdsit.net	Brookfield	WI	53005	262-569-5300		174
Paragon Engineering Services Inc 2201 S Queen St *Web:* www.peservices.org	York	PA	17402	717-854-7374	854-5533	261
Paragon Environmental Construction Inc 5664 Mud Mill Rd *Web:* paragonec.net	Brewerton	NY	13029	315-699-0840	699-0845	667
Paragon Events 352 NE Third Ave *Web:* www.paragon-events.com	Delray Beach	FL	33444	561-243-3073		463
Paragon Films Inc 3500 W Tacoma *TF:* 800-274-9727 ■ *Web:* www.paragonfilms.com	Broken Arrow	OK	74012	918-250-3456		600
Paragon Furniture Management Inc 2224 E Randol Mill Rd *TF:* 800-451-8546 ■ *Web:* www.paragoninc.com	Arlington	TX	76011	817-633-3242		320
Paragon Gaming Corp 6650 Via Austi Pkwy Ste 150 *Web:* paragongaming.com	Las Vegas	NV	89119	702-631-5161	631-9820	360-3
Paragon Geophysical Services Inc 3500 N Rock Rd Bldg 800 *Web:* paragongeo.com	Wichita	KS	67226	316-636-5552	636-5572	538
Paragon Health Pc 2318 Gull Rd Ste B *Web:* www.paragonhealthpc.com	Kalamazoo	MI	49048	269-341-4554		374-8
Paragon Hotel Corp PO Box 14065 *Web:* www.paragonhotels.com	Phoenix	AZ	85063	602-248-0811		379
Paragon Industries Inc 2011 S Town E Blvd *TF:* 800-876-4328 ■ *Web:* www.paragonweb.com	Mesquite	TX	75149	972-288-7557	222-0646	318
Paragon International Inc 2885 N Berkeley Lake Rd Ste 17 *TF:* 800-526-1095 ■ *Web:* www.paragonint.net	Duluth	GA	30096	800-526-1095		393
Paragon IT Professionals 108 Third St Ste 200 *Web:* www.paragonitpros.com	Des Moines	IA	50309	515-288-2128	243-4009	809
Paragon Laboratories 20433 Earl St *TF:* 800-231-3670 ■ *Web:* www.paragonlabsusa.com	Torrance	CA	90503	310-370-1563		799
Paragon Management Company LLC 4370 La Jolla Village Dr Ste 640 *Web:* www.paragoncompany.com	San Diego	CA	92122	858-535-9000		652
Paragon Manufacturing Company Inc 2001 N 15th Ave *Web:* www.paragonmanufacturing.com	Melrose Park	IL	60160	708-345-1717	345-1721	199
Paragon Manufacturing Inc 61 Union St *Web:* www.paragonmfg.com	Westfield	MA	01085	413-562-7202	562-7178	454
Paragon Medical Inc 8 Matchett Industrial Park Dr *TF:* 800-225-6975 ■ *Web:* www.paragonmedical.com	Pierceton	IN	46562	574-594-2140		475
Paragon National Bank 5400 Poplar Ave Ste 350 *Web:* bankparagon.com	Memphis	TN	38119	901-273-2900		70
Paragon Offshore PLC 3151 Briarpark Dr Ste 700 *Web:* www.paragonoffshore.com	Houston	TX	77042	832-783-4000		539
Paragon Packaging Inc 7700 Centerville Rd *Web:* www.paragonpackaging.com	Ferndale	CA	95536	707-786-4004		101
Paragon Packaging Products Inc 625 Beaver Rd *TF:* 800-458-0425 ■ *Web:* www.parapack.com	Girard	PA	16417	814-774-9621	774-3689	100
Paragon Press Inc 2532 South 3270 West *Web:* www.paragonpress.com	Salt Lake City	UT	84119	801-978-3500		627
Paragon Products LLC 4475 Golden Foothill Pkwy *Web:* www.paragonproducts.net	El Dorado Hills	CA	95762	916-941-9717		641
Paragon Salons Inc 6775 Harrison Ave *Web:* paragonsalon.com	Cincinnati	OH	45247	513-574-7610		77
Paragon School of Pet Grooming, The 110 Chicago Dr *Web:* www.paragonpetschool.com	Jenison	MI	49428	616-667-7297	667-9851	685
Paragon Space Development Corp 3481 E Michigan St *TF:* 800-866-7248 ■ *Web:* www.paragonsdc.com	Tucson	AZ	85714	520-903-1000	903-2000	504
Paragon Sporting Goods Corp 867 Broadway 18th St *TF:* 800-961-3030 ■ *Web:* www.paragonsports.com	New York	NY	10003	212-255-8889		711
Paragon Steel 4211 County Rd 61 *TF:* 800-411-5677 ■ *Web:* paragon-steel.com	Butler	IN	46721	260-868-1100	868-1101	492
Paragon Supply Co 160 Reaser Ct *TF:* 800-726-8041 ■ *Web:* www.paragon-supply.com	Elyria	OH	44035	440-365-8040		186
Paragon Systems Inc 13655 Dulles Technology Dr Ste 100 *Web:* parasys.com	Herndon	VA	20171	703-263-7176	263-9527	692
Paragon Technologies Inc 101 Larry Holmes Dr Ste 500 *OTC:* PGNT ■ *Web:* pgntgroup.com	Easton	PA	18042	610-252-3205	252-3102	470
Paragon Water Systems Inc 13805 Monroes Pk *TF:* 800-288-9708 ■ *Web:* www.paragonwater.com	Tampa	FL	33635	727-538-4704		806
Paragould Light Water & Cable (PLWC) 1901 Jones Rd *Web:* www.paragould.com	Paragould	AR	72450	870-239-7700		116
Paragould Regional Chamber of Commerce 300 W Ct St PO Box 124 *Web:* www.paragould.org	Paragould	AR	72451	870-236-7684	236-7142	139
Paraguay *Consulate General* 25 SE Second Ave Ste 720 *Web:* www.consulparmiami.org	Miami	FL	33131	305-374-9090	374-5522	257
Embassy 2209 Massachusetts Ave NW *Web:* www.mre.gov.py	Washington	DC	20008	202-483-6960	234-4508	257
Paragus Strategic I T 112 Russell St *Web:* www.paragusit.com	Hadley	MA	01035	413-587-2666		180
Parallax 2179 W 11th St *Web:* parallaxtremont.com	Cleveland	OH	44113	216-583-9999		671
Parallax Capital Partners LLC 23332 Mill Creek Dr Ste 155 *Web:* www.parallaxcap.com	Laguna Hills	CA	92653	949-296-4800		690

	Phone	Fax	Class
Parallax Consulting LLC 325 Wood Rd Ste 107 ... Braintree MA 02184 *Web:* parallax-consulting.com	781-535-6004		196
Parallax Inc 599 Menlo Dr Ste 100 ... Rocklin CA 95765 *TF:* 888-512-1024 ■ *Web:* www.parallax.com	916-624-8333	624-8003	625
Parallax Press PO Box 7355 ... Berkeley CA 94710 *TF:* 800-863-5290 ■ *Web:* www.parallax.org	510-540-6411		196
Parallel Edge Inc 718 Benson St ... Philadelphia PA 19111 *Web:* www.paralleledge.com	610-293-0101	293-0102	180
Parallel Infrastructure LLC 7411 Fullerton St Ste 110 ... Jacksonville FL 32256 *Web:* pitowers.com	904-274-4686		188-10
Parallel Partners Inc 1212 S Naper Blvd Ste 119-307 ... Naperville IL 60540 *Web:* www.parallelpartners.com	630-428-0600		260
Parallels Holding 500 SW 39th St Ste 200 ... Renton WA 98057 *Web:* www.parallels.com	425-282-6400	282-6444	178-11
Parallon Business Solutions LLC 6640 Carothers Pkwy ... Franklin TN 37067 *Web:* parallon.com	615-807-8000		317
Parametric Solutions Inc 831 Jupiter Park Dr ... Jupiter FL 33458 *Web:* www.psnet.com	561-747-6107		256
Parametric Technology Corp (PTC) 140 Kendrick St ... Needham MA 02494 *NASDAQ: PTC* ■ *TF:* 800-613-7535 ■ *Web:* www.ptc.com	781-370-5000	370-6000	178-5
Parametrix Inc 1002 15th St SW ... Auburn WA 98001 *TF:* 888-863-5128 ■ *Web:* www.parametrix.com	888-863-5128		261
Paramit Corp 18735 Madrone Pkwy ... Morgan Hill CA 95037 *Web:* www.paramit.com	408-782-5600	782-9991	476
Paramont EO Inc 1000 Davey Rd Ste 100 ... Woodridge IL 60517 *Web:* paramont-eo.com	708-345-0000	345-0816	249
Paramount Apparel International Inc 1 Paramount Dr ... Bourbon MO 65441 *TF:* 866-274-4287 ■ *Web:* www.paramountapparel.com	573-732-4411		155-9
Paramount Bakeries Inc 61 Davenport Ave ... Newark NJ 07107 *Web:* www.paramountbakeries.com	973-482-6638		296-1
Paramount Beauty Distributing Associates Inc 41 Mercedes Way Unit 34 ... Edgewood NY 11717 *TF:* 800-755-7475 ■ *Web:* www.paramountbeauty.com	631-242-3737		231
Paramount Builders Inc 501 Central Dr ... Virginia Beach VA 23454 *TF:* 888-340-9002 ■ *Web:* www.paramountbuilders.com	757-340-9000		364
Paramount Building Solutions Inc 3003 N Central Ave Ste 920 ... Phoenix AZ 85283 *Web:* www.paramountbuildingsolutions.com	877-633-5100		256
Paramount Chamber of Commerce 15357 Paramount Blvd ... Paramount CA 90723 *Web:* paramountchamber.com	562-634-3980	634-0891	139
Paramount Chemical Specialties Inc 14750 NE 95th St ... Redmond WA 98052 *TF:* 877-846-7826 ■ *Web:* www.kidsnpetsbrand.com	425-882-2673		151
Paramount Coffee Co 5133 W Grand River Ave ... Lansing MI 48906 *TF:* 800-968-1222 ■ *Web:* paramountcoffee.com	800-968-1222		296-7
Paramount Components Ltd 2130 Paramount Cres ... Abbotsford BC V2T6A5 *Web:* www.paramount.bc.ca	604-852-2564		480
Paramount Convention Services Inc 5015 Fyler Ave ... Saint Louis MO 63139 *TF:* 800-883-6578 ■ *Web:* www.paramountcs.com	314-621-6677		184
Paramount Cosmetics Inc 93 Entin Rd Ste 4 ... Clifton NJ 07014 *TF:* 800-522-9880 ■ *Web:* www.paramountcosmetics.net	973-472-2323	472-5005	214
Paramount Defenses Inc 620 Newport Center Dr Ste 1100 ... Newport Beach CA 92660 *Web:* www.paramountdefenses.com	949-468-5770		387
Paramount Export Co 175 Filbert St Ste 201 ... Oakland CA 94607 *Web:* www.paramountexport.net	510-839-0150		297-7
Paramount Graphics Inc 6075 Pkwy N Dr Ste D ... Cumming GA 30040 **Fax Area Code: 770* ■ *TF:* 800-714-8071 ■ *Web:* www.thinkparamount.com	800-714-8071	628-0471*	627
Paramount Group Inc 1633 Broadway Ste 1801 ... New York NY 10019 *Web:* www.paramount-group.com	212-237-3100		653
Paramount Health Care 1901 Indian Wood Cir ... Maumee OH 43537 *Web:* www.paramounthealthcare.com	419-887-2525		391-3
Paramount Home Entertainment 5555 Melrose Ave ... Los Angeles CA 90038 *Web:* www.paramount.com	323-956-5000		511
Paramount Hospitality Management LLC 12562 International Dr S ... Orlando FL 32821 *Web:* www.paramounthospitality.com	407-238-7700		378
Paramount Hotel 724 Pine St ... Seattle WA 98101 *Web:* www.paramounthotelseattle.com	206-292-9500	292-8610	379
Paramount Hotel 235 W 46th St ... New York NY 10036 *Web:* www.nycparamount.com	212-764-5500	354-5237	379
Paramount Hotel 808 SW Taylor St ... Portland OR 97205 *TF:* 855-215-0160 ■ *Web:* www.portlandparamount.com	503-223-9900	223-7900	379
Paramount Hotel Group 710 Rt 46 E Ste 206 ... Fairfield NJ 07004 *Web:* paramounthotelgroup.com	973-882-0505		379
Paramount Industrial Companies Inc 1112 Kingwood Ave ... Norfolk VA 23502 *Web:* www.paramountsleep.com	757-855-3321	855-2029	471
Paramount Industries Inc 304 N Howard St ... Croswell MI 48422 *TF:* 800-521-5405 ■ *Web:* www.paramountlighting.com	810-679-2551	679-4045	439
Paramount Landscape & Maintenance Inc 402 W Orion St ... Tempe AZ 85283 *Web:* paramountlandscape.com	480-668-6109		776
Paramount Pallet Inc 1330 Martin Grove Rd ... Toronto ON M9W4X3 *Web:* www.paramountpallet.com	416-742-6006		820
Paramount Panels Inc 1531 E Cedar St ... Ontario CA 91761 *Web:* www.paramountpanels.com	909-947-8008	947-8012	22
Paramount Property Management Inc 142 Broad St 2nd Fl ... Elizabeth NJ 07201 *Web:* www.paramountassets.com	201-858-8500	858-4445	652
Paramount Resources Ltd 421 7 Ave SW Ste 2800 ... Calgary AB T2P4K9 *Web:* www.paramountres.com	403-290-3600		539
Paramount Supply Company Inc 816 SE Ash St ... Portland OR 97214 *Web:* www.paramountsupply.com	503-232-4137		612
Paramount Theatre 23 E Galena Blvd ... Aurora IL 60506 *Web:* paramountaurora.com	630-896-7676	892-1084	572
Paramount Theatre 352 Cypress St ... Abilene TX 79601 *Web:* www.paramountabilene.com	325-676-9620	676-0642	572
Paramount Theatre 2025 Broadway ... Oakland CA 94612 *Web:* www.paramounttheatre.com	510-465-6400	893-5098	572
Paramount Theatre 123 Third Ave SE ... Cedar Rapids IA 52401 *Web:* www.paramounttheatrecr.com	319-398-5226		572
Paramount Theatre, The 713 Congress Ave ... Austin TX 78701 *TF:* 888-325-3589 ■ *Web:* www.austintheatre.org	512-472-5470	472-5824	572
Paramount Tool LLC 473 Pleasant St ... Fall River MA 02721 *Web:* www.paramount-tool.com	508-672-0844		488
Paramount WorkPlace 1374 E West Maple Rd ... Walled Lake MI 48390 *TF:* 800-725-4408 ■ *Web:* paramountworkplace.com	248-960-0909	960-1919	39
Parapsychology Press c/o Rhine Research Ctr 2741 Campus Walk Ave Bldg 500 ... Durham NC 27705 *Web:* www.rhine.org	919-309-4600		637-9
Parasec Inc 2804 Gateway Oaks Dr Ste 200 PO Box 160568 ... Sacramento CA 95833 *TF:* 800-533-7272 ■ *Web:* www.parasec.com	800-533-7272	603-5868	635
Paratech Ambulance Service 9401 W Brown Deer Rd ... Milwaukee WI 53224 *TF:* 866-525-8888 ■ *Web:* www.paratechambulance.com	414-365-8900		30
Paratech Incorp 1025 Lambrecht Rd ... Frankfort IL 60423 *TF:* 800-435-9358 ■ *Web:* paratech.com	800-435-9358		59
Paratek Pharmaceuticals Inc 75 Park Plz 4th Fl ... Boston MA 02116 *TF:* 833-727-2835 ■ *Web:* paratekpharma.com	617-275-0040		85
Paratransit Services 4810 Auto Ctr Way ... Bremerton WA 98312 *TF:* 800-933-3468 ■ *Web:* www.paratransit.net	800-933-3468		772
Paravista Inc 1055 Centennial Ave ... Piscataway NJ 08854 *Web:* www.paravistainc.com	732-752-1222		627
PARC (Palo Alto Research Center Inc) 3333 Coyote Hill Rd ... Palo Alto CA 94304 *Web:* www.parc.com	650-812-4000		668
Parc Environmental 2706 S Railroad Ave ... Fresno CA 93725 *TF:* 800-955-7761 ■ *Web:* parcenvironmental.com	559-233-7156	233-4284	365
Parc Safari 280 Rang Roxham ... Saint-Bernard-de-Lacolle QC J0L1H0 *Web:* www.parcsafari.com	450-247-2727	247-3563	823
Parc Specialty Contractors 1400 Vinci Ave ... Sacramento CA 95838 *Web:* www.parcspecialty.com	916-992-5405	992-6177	667
Parcel Plus Inc 13121 Louetta Rd ... Cypress TX 77429 *Web:* www.parcelpluscypress.com	281-376-0054	376-0056	113
Parcel Pro Inc 1867 Western Way ... Torrance CA 90501 *TF:* 888-683-2300 ■ *Web:* www.parcelpro.com	310-328-8484	328-1221	113
Parchem Trading Ltd 415 Huguenot St ... New Rochelle NY 10801 *TF:* 800-282-3982 ■ *Web:* www.parchem.com	914-654-6800		231
Parchman Vaughan & Company LLC Symphony Ctr 1040 Park Ave Ste 120 ... Baltimore MD 21201 *Web:* www.parchmanvaughan.com	410-244-8971		690
Parco Inc 1801 S Archibald Ave ... Ontario CA 91761 *Web:* www.parcoinc.com	909-947-2200	923-0288	326
Pardee Home Museum 672 11th St ... Oakland CA 94607 *Web:* www.pardeehome.org	510-444-2187		520
Pardee-Morris House 325 Lighthouse Rd ... New Haven CT 06512 *Web:* www.newhavenmuseum.org	203-562-4183	562-2002	50-3
Pare Corp 8 Blackstone Valley Pl ... Lincoln RI 02865 *Web:* parecorp.com	401-334-4100		261
Parent Co, The 241 Wilson Pk Cir PO Box 5036 ... Brentwood TN 37027 *Web:* www.theparentco.com	615-221-7000	221-7013	186
Parent Petroleum inc 3340 W Main St ... Saint Charles IL 60175 *TF:* 877-584-2509 ■ *Web:* www.parentpetroleum.com	630-584-2505	584-2576	579
Parental Drug Assn (PDA) 4350 East-West Hwy ... Bethesda MD 20814 *Web:* www.pda.org	301-656-5900	986-1093	49-8
Parenti & Raffaelli Ltd 215 Prospect Ave E ... Mount Prospect IL 60056 *Web:* www.parentiwoodwork.com	847-253-5550	253-6055	499
Parents Families & Friends of Lesbians & Gays 1828 L St NW Ste 660 ... Washington DC 20036 *Web:* www.pflag.org	202-467-8180	467-8194	48-8
Parents Helping Parents (PHP) 1400 Parkmoor Ave Ste 100 ... San Jose CA 95126 *TF:* 855-727-5775 ■ *Web:* www.php.com	408-727-5775	286-1116	48-6
Parents of Murdered Children (POMC) 4960 Ridge Ave Ste 2 ... Cincinnati OH 45209 *TF:* 888-818-7662 ■ *Web:* www.pomc.com	513-721-5683	345-4489	48-6
Parents Television Council (PTC) 707 Wilshire Blvd Ste 2075 ... Los Angeles CA 90017 *Web:* www.w2.parentstv.org	213-629-9255	629-9254	49-14
Parenty Reitmeier Inc 605 Des Meurons St ... Winnipeg MB R2H2R1 *TF:* 877-445-3737 ■ *Web:* www.parentyreitmeier.com	204-237-3737		317
Pareto Building Improvement 1220 Bristol ... Westchester IL 60154 *Web:* www.paretobi.com	708-344-4355	547-5131	637-2

Name / Address	City	State	Zip	Phone	Fax	Class
ParetoLogic Inc 1827 Ft St *Web:* www.paretologic.com	Victoria	BC	V8R1J6	250-370-9229		179
Parfums Givenchy LLC 598 Madison Ave *Web:* www.givenchybeauty.com	New York	NY	10022	212-931-2682		574
Parham Santana Inc 41 E 11 St 1st Fl *Web:* www.parhamsantana.com	New York	NY	10003	212-645-7501		506
PARI Respiratory Equipment Inc 2412 Pari Way *TF:* 800-327-8632 ■ *Web:* www.pari.com	Midlothian	VA	23112	800-327-8632		476
Paric Corp 77 Westport Plz Ste 250 *TF:* 800-500-4320 ■ *Web:* www.paric.com	Saint Louis	MO	63146	636-561-9500		194
Parijat Controlware Inc 9603 Neuens St *Web:* www.parijat.com	Houston	TX	77080	713-935-0900	935-9565	177
Paris 1624 Knowlton St *Web:* www.paristiaras.com	Cincinnati	OH	45223	513-542-8345		409
Paris Beauty College 1655 Willow Pass Rd *Web:* www.parisbeautycollege.com	Concord	CA	94520	925-685-7600		167-3
Paris Business Products 800 Highland Dr *TF:* 800-523-6454 ■ *Web:* www.pariscorp.com	Westampton	NJ	08060	609-265-9200	261-4853	110
Paris Farmers' Union PO Box D *TF:* 800-639-3603 ■ *Web:* www.parisfarmersunion.com	South Paris	ME	04281	207-743-8976	743-8564	276
Paris Foods Corp 3965 Ocean Gateway PO Box 121 *Web:* www.parisfoods.com	Trappe	MD	21673	410-200-9595		297-6
Paris Gibson Square Museum of Art 1400 First Ave N *Web:* www.the-square.org	Great Falls	MT	59401	406-727-8255	727-8256	520
Paris Gourmet of New York Inc 145 Grand St **Fax Area Code:* 201 ■ *TF:* 800-727-8791 ■ *Web:* www.parisgourmet.com	Carlstadt	NJ	07072	800-727-8791	939-5613*	297-8
Paris Junior College 2400 Clarksville St *TF:* 800-232-5804 ■ *Web:* www.parisjc.edu	Paris	TX	75460	903-785-7661	782-0427	162
Paris Kitchens 245 W Beaver Creek Rd *Web:* pariskitchens.com	Richmond Hill	ON	L4B1L1	905-886-5751		321
Paris Landing State Park 400 Lodge Rd *Web:* www.state.tn.us	Buchanan	TN	38222	731-641-4465		565
Paris Machining Company Inc 1020 Wes-Lee Dr *Web:* www.parismachining.com	Paris	KY	40361	859-987-6320	987-2583	350
Paris Miki Usa Inc 600th Ave S Ste 109 *Web:* parismikiusa.com	Seattle	WA	98104	206-652-8436	652-8475	543
Paris Mountain State Park 2401 State Park Rd *Web:* southcarolinaparks.com	Greenville	SC	29609	864-244-5565		565
Paris National Bank 118 N Main St *TF:* 888-639-0852 ■ *Web:* www.tpnbbank.com	Paris	MO	65275	660-327-4181		70
Paris Regional Medical Ctr 820 Clarksville St *Web:* www.parisregionalmedical.com	Paris	TX	75460	903-785-4521		374-3
Paris Technologies Inc 200 Hyde Pk *Web:* paristech.com	Doylestown	PA	18902	215-340-2890	340-2894	192
Paris Transport Inc 500 W Monroe St *TF:* 800-359-3341 ■ *Web:* www.paristransportinc.com	Paris	IL	61944	217-463-7030	466-5285	780
Paris Veterinary Clinic Inc 25010 Business Hwy 24 *Web:* parisvetclinic.net	Paris	MO	65275	660-327-5121		794
Parish International Inc PO Box 468 **Fax Area Code:* 979 ■ *Web:* www.parishforge.com	Hempstead	TX	77445	281-463-9233	826-8224*	483
Parish of Caddo 505 Travis St Ste 800 *Web:* www.caddo.org	Shreveport	LA	71101	318-226-6900		338
Paris-Henry County Chamber of Commerce 2508 Eastwood St *TF:* 800-345-1103 ■ *Web:* paristnchamber.com	Paris	TN	38242	731-642-3431	642-3454	139
Parisi 4401 Tennyson St *Web:* www.parisidenver.com	Denver	CO	80212	303-561-0234	480-5514	671
Parisi Associates Inc 16 Esquire Rd Unit 1 *Web:* www.parisiassociatesinc.com	Billerica	MA	01821	978-667-8700	667-8703	253
Parisi Royal Inc 120 Pheasant Run *Web:* www.parisischool.com	Newtown	PA	18940	215-968-6677		319-3
Parisi's Italian Ristorante 1412 S Bend Ave *Web:* www.parisisrestaurant.com	South Bend	IN	46617	574-232-4244		671
Parisian Beauty Academy 362 State St *Web:* www.paulmitchell.edu	Hackensack	NJ	07601	201-257-5956		167-3
Parity Computing Inc 6160 Lusk Blvd Ste C205 *Web:* www.paritycomputing.com	San Diego	CA	92121	858-535-0516		177
Pariyatti Publishing 867 Larmon Rd *TF:* 800-829-2748 ■ *Web:* www.pariyatti.org	Onalaska	WA	98570	541-357-8185		637-2
Parizade 2200 W Main St *Web:* parizadedurham.com	Durham	NC	27705	919-286-9712		671
Park 'N Fly 2060 Mt Paran Rd Ste 207 *TF:* 800-325-4863 ■ *Web:* www.pnf.com	Atlanta	GA	30327	800-325-4863		562
Park 100 Foods Inc 326 E Adams St *TF:* 800-854-6504 ■ *Web:* www.park100foods.com	Tipton	IN	46072	765-675-3480		296-26
Park Avenue Auto Group 216 Rte 17 *TF:* 866-719-4466 ■ *Web:* www.parkavebmw.com	Rochelle Park	NJ	07662	201-843-7900	843-4941	289
Park Avenue Building & Roofing Supplies LLC 2120 Atlantic Ave *Web:* www.parkavebenmoore.com	Brooklyn	NY	11233	718-403-0100	596-5085	191-3
Park Bank 7540 W Capitol Dr *Web:* www.parkbankonline.com	Milwaukee	WI	53216	414-466-8000		360-2
Park Cafe 4403 Murphy Rd *Web:* parkcafenashville.com	Nashville	TN	37209	615-383-4409		671
Park Center Inc 909 E State Blvd *Web:* www.parkcenter.org	Fort Wayne	IN	46805	260-481-2700		726
Park Central New York 870 Seventh Ave *Web:* www.parkcentralny.com	New York	NY	10019	212-247-8000		379
Park City Ctr 142 Pk City Ctr *Web:* www.parkcitycenter.com	Lancaster	PA	17601	717-650-0185		460
Park City Group Inc 299 S Main St Ste 2225 *Web:* parkcitygroup.com	Salt Lake City	UT	84111	435-645-2000		225
Park City Mountain Resort 1345 Lowell Ave *Web:* www.parkcitymountain.com	Park City	UT	84060	435-649-8111		669
Park Community Federal Credit Union PO Box 18630 *TF:* 800-626-2870 ■ *Web:* www.parkcommunity.com	Louisville	KY	40261	502-968-3681	964-6704	216
Park Compounding Pharmacy Inc 4333 Park Terrace Dr Ste 160 *Web:* parkcompounding.com	Westlake Village	CA	91361	805-497-8258	496-7099	238
Park Construction Company Inc 1481 81st Ave NE *TF:* 800-328-2556 ■ *Web:* parkconstructionco.com	Minneapolis	MN	55432	763-786-9800	786-2952	189-5
Park County 1002 Sheridan Ave *TF:* 800-786-2844 ■ *Web:* www.parkcounty.us	Cody	WY	82414	307-527-8510	527-8515	338
Park County 501 Main St PO Box 1373 *Web:* www.parkco.us	Fairplay	CO	80440	719-836-2771	836-3273	338
Park County 414 E Callender St *Web:* www.parkcounty.org	Livingston	MT	59047	406-222-4110	222-4160	338
Park County District No 6 919 Cody Ave *Web:* www.park6.org	Cody	WY	82414	307-587-4283		685
Park County Travel Council (PCTC) 836 Sheridan Ave PO Box 2454 *TF:* 800-393-2639 ■ *Web:* www.codyyellowstone.org	Cody	WY	82414	307-587-2297	527-6228	206
Park Dietz & Associates Inc 2906 Lafayette Rd *Web:* www.parkdietzassociates.com	Newport Beach	CA	92663	949-723-2211	723-2212	463
Park Distributors Inc 347 Railroad Ave *Web:* www.parkdistributors.com	Bridgeport	CT	06604	203-366-7200		350
Park Electric Co-opeartive Inc 5706 US Hwy 89 S PO Box 1119 *TF:* 888-298-0657 ■ *Web:* www.parkelectric.coop	Livingston	MT	59047	406-222-3100	222-3418	245
Park Electrochemical Corp 48 S Service Rd Ste 300 *NYSE: PKE* ■ *Web:* parkelectro.com	Melville	NY	11747	631-465-3600	465-3100	625
Park Energy Services LLC 1015 N Broadway Ave Ste 301 *Web:* www.parkenergyservices.com	Oklahoma City	OK	73102	405-896-3169		536
Park Enterprises Inc 226 Jay St *Web:* www.parkent.com	Rochester	NY	14608	585-546-4200	546-7088	203
Park Expo & Conference Ctr, The 800 Briar Creek Rd *Web:* theparkexponc.com	Charlotte	NC	28205	704-333-7709		205
Park Forest Coop Area B 206 Birch St *Web:* parkforest.coop	Park Forest	IL	60466	708-748-3602		390
Park Forest Public Library 400 Lakewood Blvd *Web:* www.pfpl.org	Park Forest	IL	60466	708-748-3731	748-8829	434-3
Park Hill Veterinary Medical Center PC 2255 Oneida St *Web:* parkhillvet.com	Denver	CO	80207	303-388-2255		794
Park Hills Leadington Chamber of Commerce (PHLCOC) 12 Municipal Dr *Web:* www.phlcoc.net	Park Hills	MO	63601	573-431-1051	431-2327	139
Park House Eatery 4574 Pk Blvd *Web:* parkhousesd.com	San Diego	CA	92116	619-295-7275		671
Park House Hotel Corp 1206 48th St *Web:* parkhousehotelbrooklyn.com	Brooklyn	NY	11219	718-871-8100		132
Park Hyatt Beaver Creek 100 E Thomas Pl *Web:* www.allegriaspa.com	Beaver Creek	CO	81620	970-748-7500	748-7501	707
Park Lane Jewelry 100 E Commerce Dr **Fax Area Code:* 847 ■ *TF:* 800-621-0088 ■ *Web:* parklanejewelry.com	Schaumburg	IL	60173	800-621-0088	884-7064*	410
Park Lane, The 200 Glenwood Cir *Web:* www.srgseniorliving.com	Monterey	CA	93940	831-298-0100		672
Park Li Group 1776 Broadway Ste 705 *Web:* www.parkli.com	New York	NY	10019	212-505-5324		194
Park Maintenance 20500 Madrona Ave *Web:* www.torranceca.gov	Torrance	CA	90503	310-781-6901		564
Park Manor of Quail Valley 2350 Fm 1092 Rd *Web:* www.parkmanor-quailvalley.com	Missouri City	TX	77459	281-499-9333		371
Park Meadows 8401 Pk Meadows Center Dr *Web:* www.parkmeadows.com	Lone Tree	CO	80124	303-792-2533		460
Park National Bank 50 N Third St PO Box 3500 *NYSE: PRK* ■ *TF:* 888-791-8633 ■ *Web:* investor.parknationalcorp.com	Newark	OH	43058	740-349-8451		360-2
Park Place 5870 E Broadway Blvd *Web:* www.parkplacemall.com	Tucson	AZ	85711	520-747-7575		460
Park Place Assisted Living 2305 Ives Ct *Web:* www.parkplaceassistedliving.com	Reno	NV	89503	775-746-1188		793
Park Place Behavioral Health Care 206 Park Pl Blvd *Web:* www.ppbh.org	Kissimmee	FL	34741	407-846-0023		726
Park Place Technologies Inc 5910 Landerbrook Dr *TF:* 877-778-8707 ■ *Web:* www.parkplacetechnologies.com	Cleveland	OH	44124	877-778-8707		177
Park Place Volvo 3515 Inwood Rd *TF:* 888-437-0906 ■ *Web:* parkplace.com	Dallas	TX	75209	855-272-5915		57
Park Plaza Hotel Oakland 150 Hegenberger Rd *Web:* apps.usfa.fema.gov	Oakland	CA	94621	510-635-5300	635-9661	379
Park Plaza Mall 6000 W Markham St *Web:* www.parkplazamall.com	Little Rock	AR	72205	501-664-4956		460
Park Printing Inc 2801 California St NE *TF:* 800-789-3877 ■ *Web:* www.parkprint.com	Minneapolis	MN	55418	612-789-4333		627
Park Record PO Box 3688 *Web:* www.parkrecord.com	Park City	UT	84060	435-649-9014	649-4942	532-3

Name / Address	City	State	ZIP	Phone	Fax	Class
Park Regency Care Ctr 1770 W La Habra Blvd *Fax Area Code: 562 ■ *Web:* www.parkregencycare.com	La Habra	CA	90631	714-773-0750	697-8478*	450
Park Regency Real Estate 10146 Balboa Blvd *Web:* www.parkregency.com	Granada Hills	CA	91344	818-363-6116		652
Park Ridge Child Care Ctr 1555 Long Pond Rd *Web:* www.rochesterregional.org	Rochester	NY	14626	585-723-7543		374-3
Park Ridge Public Library 20 S Prospect Ave *Web:* www.parkridgelibrary.org	Park Ridge	IL	60068	847-825-3123	825-0001	434-3
Park Ridge Recreation & Park District 2701 Sibley Ave *Web:* www.prparks.org	Park Ridge	IL	60068	847-692-5127		31
Park Seed Co 1 Parkton Ave *TF:* 800-845-3369 ■ *Web:* parkseed.com	Greenwood	SC	29647	800-845-3369		694
Park Shore 1630 43rd Ave E *Web:* www.parkshore.org	Seattle	WA	98112	206-329-0770		672
Park Shore Resort 600 Neapolitan Way *TF:* 855-923-8197 ■ *Web:* www.parkshorefl.com	Naples	FL	34103	855-923-8197		669
Park Shore Waikiki Hotel 2586 Kalakaua Ave *TF:* 866-536-7975 ■ *Web:* www.parkshorewaikiki.com	Honolulu	HI	96815	808-954-7426	923-0311	379
Park Slope Veterinary Ctr 639 Fourth Ave *Web:* parkslopevetcenter.com	Brooklyn	NY	11215	718-369-7387		794
Park To Fly 1900 Jetport Dr Exit 8 off S R 528 (Beachline) *TF:* 888-851-8875 ■ *Web:* www.parktofly.com	Orlando	FL	32809	407-851-8875	851-8011	562
Park Tudor School 7200 N College Ave *Web:* www.parktudor.org	Indianapolis	IN	46240	317-415-2700		685
Park University 8700 NW River Pk Dr *TF:* 800-745-7275 ■ *Web:* www.park.edu	Parkville	MO	64152	816-741-2000	741-9668	166
Park Vista Resort Hotel 705 Cherokee Orchard Rd PO Box 30 *TF:* 800-227-5622 ■ *Web:* www.parkvista.com	Gatlinburg	TN	37738	865-436-9211	430-7533	379
Park West Asset Management LLC 900 Larkspur Landing Cir Ste 165 *Web:* www.parkwestllc.com	Larkspur	CA	94939	415-524-2900		401
Park West Companies Inc 22421 Gilberto Ste A *Web:* www.parkwestinc.com	Rancho Santa Margarita	CA	92688	949-546-8300	546-8301	422
Parkade Health Shoppe Inc 378 Middle Tpke W *Web:* cthealthshop.com	Manchester	CT	06040	860-646-8178		237
Par-Kan Co 2915 W 900 S *TF:* 800-291-5487 ■ *Web:* www.par-kan.net	Silver Lake	IN	46982	260-352-2141		470
Parkdale Mills Inc 531 Cotton Blossom Cir *TF:* 800-331-1843 ■ *Web:* www.parkdalemills.com	Gastonia	NC	28054	704-874-5000	874-5175	745-9
Parke County 116 W High St *Web:* www.parkecounty-in.gov	Rockville	IN	47872	765-569-5132		338
Parke County Rural Electric Membership Corp 119 W High St *TF:* 800-537-3913 ■ *Web:* safer.fmcsa.dot.gov	Rockville	IN	47872	765-569-3133	569-3360	245
Parke Regency Hotel & Conference Ctr, The 1413 Leslie Dr *Web:* www.parkehotel.com	Bloomington	IL	61704	309-662-4300		378
Parke-Bell Limited Inc 709 W 12th St *TF:* 800-457-7456 ■ *Web:* www.touchofclass.com	Huntingburg	IN	47542	812-683-3707		114
Parker 3025 W Croft Cir *Web:* www.parker.com	Spartanburg	SC	29302	864-573-7332	583-4299	326
Parker & Irwin, A Professional Corp 348 W Hospitality Ln Ste 202 *Web:* parkerirwinlaw.com	San Bernardino	CA	92408	909-890-1800		41
Parker & Parker 411 Hamilton Blvd Ste 1900 *Web:* parkerandparkerattorneys.com	Peoria	IL	61602	309-673-0069		41
Parker & Zubkoff LLP 110 W A St Ste 615 *Web:* pzfirm.com	San Diego	CA	92101	619-233-8292	233-8636	41
Parker Boats 2570 NC Hwy 101 *Web:* www.parkerboats.com	Beaufort	NC	28516	252-728-5621		90
Parker Boiler Co 5930 Bandini Blvd *Web:* www.parkerboiler.com	Los Angeles	CA	90040	323-727-9800	722-2848	357
Parker Bows 3022 Lee Jackson Hwy *Web:* www.parkerbows.com	Staunton	VA	24401	540-337-5426	337-0887	710
Parker Chamber of Commerce 19590 E Main St Ste 100 *Web:* www.parkerchamber.com	Parker	CO	80138	303-841-4268	841-8061	139
Parker County 1112 Santa Fe Dr *Web:* parkercountytx.com	Weatherford	TX	76086	817-598-6163	594-9540	338
Parker Dam State Park 28 Fairview Rd *Web:* www.dcnr.pa.gov	Penfield	PA	15849	814-765-0630		565
Parker Development Company Inc 4525 Serrano Pkwy *Web:* www.parkerdevco.com	El Dorado Hills	CA	95762	916-939-4060		261
Parker Drilling Co 1401 Enclave Pkwy Ste 600 *NYSE:* PKD ■ *Web:* www.parkerdrilling.com	Houston	TX	77077	281-406-2000	406-2001	540
Parker Furniture 10375 SW Beaverton-Hillsdale Hwy *Fax Area Code: 971 ■ *TF:* 866-515-9673 ■ *Web:* www.parker-furniture.com	Beaverton	OR	97005	503-644-0155	275-1087*	321
Parker Gallini LLP 460 Totten Pond Rd Ste 350 *Web:* parkergallini.com	Waltham	MA	02451	781-810-8990	290-4985	41
Parker Goodman Gordon & Hammock LLC 129 N Washington St PO Box 1209 *Web:* parkercountslaw.com	Easton	MD	21601	410-822-1122		41
Parker Hannifin Corp *Electromechanical Automation Div* 5500 Business Pk Dr *TF:* 800-358-9068 ■ *Web:* www.parkermotion.com	Rohnert Park	CA	94928	707-584-7558	584-8015	203
Parker Industries Inc 1650 Sycamore Ave *Web:* www.parkerind.com	Bohemia	NY	11716	631-567-1000	567-1355	386
Parker Industries Inc 4867 Rhoney Rd *Web:* www.parkerindustriesinc.com	Connelly Springs	NC	28612	828-437-7779	437-6686	488
Parker Laboratories Inc 286 Eldridge Rd *TF:* 800-631-8888 ■ *Web:* www.parkerlabs.com	Fairfield	NJ	07004	973-276-9500		476
Parker Lumber Company Inc 2192 Eastex Fwy *Web:* www.parkersbuildingsupply.com	Beaumont	TX	77703	409-898-7000		191-3
Parker Majestic Inc 300 N Pike Rd *TF:* 866-572-7537 ■ *Web:* www.pennunited.com	Sarver	PA	16055	724-352-1551	353-1196	455
Parker Marketing Research LLC 5405 Dupont Cir *Web:* www.parkerinsights.com	Milford	OH	45150	513-248-8100		668
Parker McCay PA 9000 Midlantic Dr Ste 300 *Web:* www.parkermccay.com	Mount Laurel	NJ	08054	856-596-8900		428
Parker McCrory Manufacturing Co 2000 Forest Ave *TF:* 800-662-1038 ■ *Web:* parmakusa.com	Kansas City	MO	64108	816-221-2000	221-9879	203
Parker Oil Company Inc PO Box 120 *Web:* parkeroilcompany.com	South Hill	VA	23970	434-447-3146	447-2646	579
Parker Oil Products Inc 508 California Ave *Web:* www.parkeroilproducts.com	Parker	AZ	85344	928-669-2617		579
Parker Palm Springs 4200 E Palm Canyon Dr *Web:* www.parkerpalmsprings.com	Palm Springs	CA	92264	760-770-5000		565
Parker Playhouse 707 NE Eigth St *Web:* www.parkerplayhouse.com	Fort Lauderdale	FL	33304	954-462-0222	524-9952	572
Parker Poe Adams & Bernstein LLP 3 Wachovia Ctr 401 S Tryon St Ste 3000 *Web:* www.parkerpoe.com	Charlotte	NC	28202	704-372-9000		428
Parker Powis Inc 775 Heinz Ave *TF:* 800-321-2463 ■ *Web:* mypowis.com	Berkeley	CA	94710	510-848-2463		92
Parker Remick Inc 1106 Harris Ave Ste 201 *Web:* www.parkerremick.com	Bellingham	WA	98225	360-527-2555		193
Parker Rose Design Inc 10075 Mesa Rim Rd Ste A *TF:* 800-403-2711 ■ *Web:* parkerrosedesign.com	San Diego	CA	92121	800-403-2711		41
Parker Smith & Feek Inc 2233 112th Ave NE *Fax Area Code: 425 ■ *TF:* 800-457-0220 ■ *Web:* www.psfinc.com	Bellevue	WA	98004	800-457-0220	709-7460*	390
Parker Stanbury LLP 444 S Flower St 19th Fl *Web:* www.parkstan.com	Los Angeles	CA	90071	213-622-5124	622-4858	428
Parker Steel Co 1625 Indian Wood Cir *TF:* 800-333-4140 ■ *Web:* www.metricmetal.com	Maumee	OH	43537	419-473-2481	471-2655	492
Parker Stevenson Brokerage Co 4030 Truxel Rd Ste D *Web:* www.parkerstevenson.com	Sacramento	CA	95834	916-928-3800	928-3808	690
Parker Surplus Sales 2859 Hwy 43 S *Web:* www.parkersurplus.com	Loretto	TN	38469	931-852-2356	852-2358	328
Parker Swearngin LLP 215 SE Douglas St *Web:* www.parkerswearngin.com	Lee's Summit	MO	64063	816-434-6770	434-6771	2
Parker Towing Company Inc PO Box 20908 *Web:* www.parkertowing.com	Tuscaloosa	AL	35402	205-349-1677	758-0061	465
Parker Trutec Inc 4700 Gateway Blvd *Web:* www.parkertrutec.com	Springfield	OH	45502	937-323-8833	323-9192	482
Parker University 2540 Walnut Hill Ln *TF:* 800-637-8337 ■ *Web:* www.parker.edu	Dallas	TX	75229	972-438-6932		764
Parker's Lighthouse 435 Shoreline Village Dr *Web:* www.parkerslighthouse.com	Long Beach	CA	90802	562-432-6500	436-3551	671
Parker, Kern, Nard & Wenzel 1111 E Herndon Ave Ste 202 *Web:* pknwlaw.com	Fresno	CA	93720	559-449-2558		428
Parker-Helac 225 Battersby Ave *TF:* 800-327-2589 ■ *Web:* www.helac.com	Enumclaw	WA	98022	360-825-1601	825-1603	223
Parkersburg & Wood County Public Library 3100 Emerson Ave *Web:* parkwoodlib.com	Parkersburg	WV	26104	304-420-4587		434-3
Parkersburg News 519 Juliana St *TF:* 800-642-1997 ■ *Web:* www.newsandsentinel.com	Parkersburg	WV	26101	304-485-1891	485-5122	532-2
Parkersville Landing Historical Park 24 South A St *Web:* portcw.com	Washougal	WA	98671	360-835-2196	835-2197	50-5
ParkerVision Inc 7915 Baymeadows Way *NASDAQ:* PRKR ■ *TF:* 800-532-8034 ■ *Web:* www.parkervision.com	Jacksonville	FL	32256	904-732-6100	731-0958	647
Parkerwhite Inc 230 Birmingham Dr *Web:* www.parkerwhite.com	Cardiff-By-The-Sea	CA	92007	760-783-2020		4
Parkett Publishers Inc 145 Avenue of the Americas Spring St *Web:* www.parkettart.com	New York	NY	10013	212-673-2660		637-2
Parkhill Smith & Cooper Inc 4222 85th St *TF:* 800-400-6646 ■ *Web:* www.team-psc.com	Lubbock	TX	79423	806-473-2200		261
Parkhouse Tire Service Inc 5960 Shull St *Web:* www.parkhousetire.com	Bell Gardens	CA	90201	562-927-8333		54
Parkhurst Manufacturing Co 18999 Hwy Y *TF:* 800-821-7380 ■ *Web:* parkhurstmfg.com	Sedalia	MO	65301	660-826-8685		516
Parkin Archeological State Park PO Box 1110 *Web:* www.arkansasstateparks.com	Parkin	AR	72373	870-755-2500		565
Parking Company of America (PCA) 11101 Lakewood Blvd *TF:* 888-220-1282 ■ *Web:* www.parkpca.com	Downey	CA	90241	562-862-2118		562

				Phone	Fax	Class
Parking Company of America 250 W Court St Ste 100E *Web:* www.parkplaceparking.com	Cincinnati	OH	45202	513-381-2179		562
Parking Concepts Inc 12 Mauchly Bldg I *TF:* 800-540-7275 ■ *Web:* parkingconcepts.com	Irvine	CA	92618	949-753-7525		562
Parking Management Inc 1725 Desales St NW Ste 300 *Web:* www.pmi-parking.com	Washington	DC	20036	202-785-9191		562
Parking Panda Corp 3422 Fait Ave *TF:* 800-232-6415 ■ *Web:* www.parkingpanda.com	Baltimore	MD	21224	800-232-6415		562
Parking Solutions Inc 353 W Nationwide Blvd *TF:* 888-469-7690 ■ *Web:* www.parkingsolutionsinc.com	Columbus	OH	43215	614-469-7000		562
Parkinson Construction Company Inc 3905 Perry St *Web:* www.parkinsonconstruction.com	Brentwood	MD	20722	301-985-6080	985-6083	186
Parkinson's Disease Foundation (PDF) 1359 Broadway *TF:* 800-457-6676 ■ *Web:* parkinson.org	New York	NY	10018	212-923-4700	923-4778	48-17
Parkit Enterprise Inc 666 Burrard Ste 500 *Web:* www.parkitenterprise.com	Vancouver	BC	V6C2X8	604-424-8700		653
Parkland College 2400 W Bradley Ave *TF:* 888-467-6065 ■ *Web:* parkland.edu	Champaign	IL	61821	217-351-2200	353-2640	162
Parkland Community Library 4422 Walbert Ave *Web:* www.parklandlibrary.org	Allentown	PA	18104	610-398-1361		435
Parkland Health & Hospital System 5201 Harry Hines Blvd *Web:* www.parklandhospital.com	Dallas	TX	75235	214-590-8000	266-8704	374-3
Parkland Health Ctr 1101 W Liberty St *TF:* 800-734-3944 ■ *Web:* www.parklandhealthcenter.org	Farmington	MO	63640	573-756-6451		374-3
Parkland Light & Water Co 12918 Park Ave *Web:* www.plw.coop	Tacoma	WA	98444	253-531-5666	531-2684	245
Parkland Medical Ctr 1 Parkland Dr *Web:* parklandmedicalcenter.com	Derry	NH	03038	603-432-1500		374-3
Parkland Plastics Inc 104 Yoder Dr PO Box 339 *TF:* 800-835-4110 ■ *Web:* www.parklandplastics.com	Middlebury	IN	46540	574-825-4336		661
Parkland School District 1210 Springhouse Rd *Web:* www.parklandsd.org	Allentown	PA	18104	610-351-5503	351-5509	685
Parkline Inc PO Box 65 *TF:* 800-786-4855 ■ *Web:* www.parkline.com	Winfield	WV	25213	304-586-2113	586-3842	105
Park-Ohio Holdings Corp (PKOH) 6065 Parkland Blvd *NASDAQ: PKOH* ■ *Web:* pkoh.com	Cleveland	OH	44124	440-947-2000	947-2099	449
Parks & Ratliff Pc 620 Main St *Web:* parksandratliff.com	Klamath Falls	OR	97601	541-882-6331		41
Parks Associates Inc 15950 N Dallas Pkwy Ste 575 *Web:* www.parksassociates.com	Dallas	TX	75248	972-490-1113		668
Parks at Arlington 3811 S Cooper St *Web:* www.theparksmallarlington.com	Arlington	TX	76015	817-467-0200		460
Parks at Chehaw 105 Chehaw Park Rd *Web:* chehaw.org	Albany	GA	31701	229-430-5275		823
Parks Auto Parts Professionals 2320 Savannah Hwy *Web:* parksautoparts.com	Charleston	SC	29414	843-556-4703		54
Parks Bros Farm Inc 6733 Parks Rd *TF:* 800-334-5770 ■ *Web:* www.parksbrothers.com	Van Buren	AR	72956	479-410-2217		369
Parks Canada 30 Victoria St *Web:* www.pc.gc.ca	Gatineau	QC	J8X0B3	819-420-9486		563
Carleton Martello Tower National Historic Site 454 Whipple St *Web:* www.pc.gc.ca	Saint John	NB	E2M2R3	506-636-4011	887-6011	563
Parks Chamber of Commerce 100 Heart Blvd *Web:* www.parkschamber.com	Loves Park	IL	61111	815-633-3999	633-4057	139
Parks Huffman Mcvay Shepard & Wells PC 503 E Border St *Web:* phmsw.com	Arlington	TX	76010	817-261-2000		41
Parks Medical Electronics Sales Inc 6000 SE Ave Ste 10-B *TF:* 800-547-6427 ■ *Web:* www.parksmed.com	Las Vegas	NV	89119	702-736-6317	739-9305	119
Parks Moving and Storage Inc 740 Commonwealth Dr *TF:* 866-790-1560 ■ *Web:* www.parksmoving.com	Warrendale	PA	15086	866-790-1560		780
Parks Productions Ltd 2250 Pontiac Rd *Web:* www.parkspro.com	Auburn Hills	MI	48326	248-370-9200	370-9207	195
Parkside Animal Hospital 12962 Publishers Dr *Web:* www.parksidepets.com	Fishers	IN	46038	317-849-1440	849-1490	794
Parkside Management Services LLC 5215 Old Orchard Rd Ste 860 *Web:* parksidesenior.com	Skokie	IL	60077	847-779-8500		653
Parkside Publications Inc 601 Union St Ste 2600 *Web:* www.parksidepublications.com	Seattle	WA	98101	206-839-1191		637-2
Parkside Rotisserie & Bar 76 S Main St *Web:* www.parksideprovidence.com	Providence	RI	02903	401-524-5252		671
Parksite Inc 1563 Hubbard Ave **Fax Area Code:* 630 ■ *TF:* 800-338-3355 ■ *Web:* www.parksite.com	Batavia	IL	60510	800-338-3355	761-6820*	191-3
Parkson Corp 1401 W Cyperess Creek Rd **Fax Area Code:* 954 ■ *TF:* 888-727-5766 ■ *Web:* www.parkson.com	Fort Lauderdale	FL	33309	888-727-5766	974-6182*	386
Parksville Chamber of Commerce PO Box 99 *Web:* www.parksvillechamber.com	Parksville	BC	V9P2G3	250-248-3613	248-5210	137
Parkview Community Hospital Medical Ctr (PCHMC) 3865 Jackson St *Web:* www.pchmc.org	Riverside	CA	92503	951-688-2211		374-3
Parkview Hospital 2200 Randallia Dr *TF:* 888-737-9311 ■ *Web:* www.parkview.com	Fort Wayne	IN	46805	260-373-4000		374-3
Parkview Medical Ctr 400 W 16th St *TF:* 800-543-4046 ■ *Web:* www.parkviewmc.com	Pueblo	CO	81003	719-584-4000	584-7376	374-3
Parkville Insurances Services Inc 15242 E Whittier Blvd PO Box 1275 *TF:* 800-350-2702 ■ *Web:* www.parkvilleinsurance.com	Whittier	CA	90603	562-945-2702	945-4297	390
Parkway Bancorp Inc 4800 N Harlem Ave *Web:* www.parkwaybank.com	Harwood Heights	IL	60706	708-867-6600		70
Parkway Chevrolet Inc 25500 Tomball Pkwy *TF:* 888-929-4556 ■ *Web:* www.parkwaychevrolet.com	Tomball	TX	77375	888-929-4556		516
Parkway Clinical Laboratories Inc 3494 Progress Dr *TF:* 800-327-2764 ■ *Web:* parkwayclinical.com	Bensalem	PA	19020	215-245-5112		418
Parkway Construction & Associates LP 1000 Civic Cir *Web:* parkwayconstruction.com	Lewisville	TX	75067	972-221-1979	219-0061	186
Parkway Corp 150 N Broad St *Web:* www.parkwaycorp.com	Philadelphia	PA	19102	215-575-4000	636-9596	562
Parkway Electric & Communications LLC 11952 James St **Fax Area Code:* 616 ■ *TF:* 800-574-9553 ■ *Web:* www.parkway.us	Holland	MI	49424	800-574-9553	392-6880*	787
Parkway Grill 510 S Arroyo Pkwy *Web:* www.theparkwaygrill.com	Pasadena	CA	91105	626-795-1001	796-6221	671
Parkway Inn 125 N Jackson St PO Box 494 *TF:* 800-247-8390 ■ *Web:* www.parkwayinn.com	Jackson	WY	83001	800-247-8390		379
Parkway Metal Products Inc 130 Rawls Rd *Web:* www.parkwaymetal.com	Des Plaines	IL	60018	847-789-4000	789-4001	480
Parkway Place Mall 2801 Memorial Pkwy SW *Web:* www.parkwayplacemall.com	Huntsville	AL	35801	256-533-0700		460
Parkway Plastics Inc 561 Stelton Rd *Web:* parkwayjars.com	Piscataway	NJ	08854	732-752-3636		596
Parkway Products Inc 1400 Jamike Ave *Web:* www.parkwayproducts.com	Erlanger	KY	41018	859-525-8040		21
Parkway Properties Inc 188 E Capitol St Ste 1000 *NYSE: PKY* ■ *TF:* 800-748-1667 ■ *Web:* www.pky.com	Jackson	MS	39201	601-948-4091		655
Parkwest Medical Ctr 9352 Park West Blvd *Web:* www.treatedwell.com	Knoxville	TN	37923	865-373-1000		374-3
Parlay Intl 712 Bancroft Rd Ste 505 **Fax Area Code:* 925 ■ *TF:* 800-457-2752 ■ *Web:* www.parlay.com	Walnut Creek	CA	94598	800-457-2752	939-1414*	387
Parlec Inc 101 Perinton Pkwy *TF:* 800-866-5872 ■ *Web:* www.parlec.com	Fairport	NY	14450	585-425-4400		358
Parlee McLaws LLP 3300 TD Canada Trust Tower 421 Seventh Ave SW *Web:* www.parlee.com	Calgary	AB	T2P4K9	403-294-7000	265-8263	428
Parlor Press LLC 816 Robinson St *Web:* www.parlorpress.com	West Lafayette	IN	47906	765-409-2649		637-2
Parma Area Chamber of Commerce 7908 Day Dr *Web:* parmaareachamber.org	Parma	OH	44129	440-886-1700	886-1770	139
Parma Tile Mosaic & Marble Inc 29-10 14th St *Web:* www.parmatile.com	Astoria	NY	11102	718-278-3060		191-1
Parmalat Canada Ltd 405 the W Mall 10th Fl *TF:* 800-563-1515 ■ *Web:* parmalat.ca	Toronto	ON	M9C5J1	800-563-1515		296-27
Parman Energy Corp 7101 Cockrill Bend Blvd *TF:* 800-727-7920 ■ *Web:* www.parmanenergy.com	Nashville	TN	37209	615-350-7920		316
Parmed Pharmaceuticals Inc 4220 Hyde Pk Blvd **Fax Area Code:* 800 ■ *TF:* 800-727-6331 ■ *Web:* www.parmed.com	Niagara Falls	NY	14305	716-284-5666	727-6330*	238
Parmenter Realty Partners 701 Brickell Ave Ste 2020 *Web:* www.parmco.com	Miami	FL	33131	305-379-7500	379-0009	653
Parmer County 401 3rd St *Web:* www.parmercounty.org	Farwell	TX	79325	806-481-3691		338
Parnassus Investments 1 Market St Steuart Tower Ste 1600 *TF:* 800-999-3505 ■ *Web:* www.parnassus.com	San Francisco	CA	94105	415-778-0200		690
Parnell & Crum PA 641 S Lawrence St PO Box 2189 *Web:* www.crumellis.com	Montgomery	AL	36104	334-832-4200		41
Paroscientific Inc 4500 148th Ave NE *Web:* www.paroscientific.com	Redmond	WA	98052	425-883-8700	867-5407	407
Parr Brown Gee & Loveless 101 South 200 East Ste 700 *Web:* www.parrbrown.com	Salt Lake City	UT	84111	801-532-7840	532-7750	428
Parr Instrument Co 211 53rd St *TF:* 800-872-7720 ■ *Web:* www.parrinst.com	Moline	IL	61265	309-762-7716	762-9453	420
Parr Lumber Co 14023 Ramona Ave *Web:* www.parrlumberchino.com	Chino	CA	91710	909-627-0953	591-9132	364
Parr Moto 13120 Westlinks Ter Blvd Unit 4 *TF:* 866-772-1381 ■ *Web:* www.parrmoto.com	Fort Myers	FL	33913	866-772-1381		6
Parr Richey Frandsen Patterson Kruse LLP Capital Ctr N 251 N Illinois St Ste 1800 *TF:* 888-337-7766 ■ *Web:* www.parrlaw.com	Indianapolis	IN	46204	317-269-2500	269-2514	428
Parrett Insurance Agency Inc 100 N Glenn Ave *Web:* parrettinsurance.com	Washington Court House	OH	43160	740-335-6081		390
Parrett, Porto, Parese & Colwell PC 1 Hamden Ctr 2319 Whitney Ave Ste 1-D *Web:* www.pppclaw.com	Hamden	CT	06518	203-281-2700	281-0700	428
Parris & Associates Construction Management 333 Richmond St *Web:* www.parrisinc.com	Raynham	MA	02767	508-230-0255	230-2543	610
PARRIS Law 43364 10th St W *TF:* 877-773-9669 ■ *Web:* www.parris.com	Lancaster	CA	93534	661-429-3399	949-7524	445

	City	State	Zip	Phone	Fax	Class
Parris Printing 211 Whitsett Rd *Web:* www.parrisprinting.com	Nashville	TN	37210	615-832-7170	832-1169	627
Parrish & Heimbecker Ltd (P&H) 201 Portage Ave Ste 1400 *TF:* 800-665-8937 ■ *Web:* parrishandheimbecker.com	Winnipeg	MB	R3B3K6	204-956-2030	943-8233	275
Parrish Law Offices 788 Washington Rd *Web:* dparrishlaw.com	Pittsburgh	PA	15228	412-561-6250	561-6253	41
Parrish Medical Ctr 951 N Washington Ave *TF:* 800-227-9954 ■ *Web:* www.parrishhealthcare.com	Titusville	FL	32796	321-268-6111	268-6231	374-3
Parrish Tire Company Inc 5130 Indiana Ave *TF:* 800-849-8473 ■ *Web:* www.parrishtire.com	Winston-Salem	NC	27106	336-767-0202	744-2716	62-5
Parrish-Hare Electrical Supply LP 1211 Regal Row *Web:* www.parrish-hare.com	Dallas	TX	75247	214-905-1001	951-8101	246
Parry Law Office LLC 115 E Fulton St *Web:* maroneyandparry.com	Waupaca	WI	54981	715-258-5990		41
PARS (Pittsburgh Antique Radio Society) Brentwood Presbyterian Church 3725 Brownsville Rd *Web:* pittantiqueradios.org	Pittsburgh	PA	15227	724-942-1113		637-2
Pars International Corp 253 W 35th St 7th Fl *Web:* www.parsintl.com	New York	NY	10001	212-221-9595	221-9195	532-3
Parsec Financial Management Inc 6 Wall St *TF:* 888-877-1012 ■ *Web:* www.parsecfinancial.com	Asheville	NC	28801	828-255-0271		194
Parsec Inc 1100 Gest St *Web:* parsecinc.com	Cincinnati	OH	45203	513-621-6111		317
Parsippany Area Chamber of Commerce 14 N Beverwyck Rd *Web:* www.parsippanychamber.org	Lake Hiawatha	NJ	07034	973-402-6400		139
Parsippany-Troy Hills Public Library 449 Halsey Rd *Web:* www.parsippanylibrary.org	Parsippany	NJ	07054	973-887-5150		434-3
Parsley Energy Inc 303 Colorado St Ste 3000 *TF:* 855-214-5200 ■ *Web:* www.parsleyenergy.com	Austin	TX	78701	737-704-2300		536
Parsons & Associates Inc 440 S Warren St Ste 704 *Web:* parsonsinsurance.com	Syracuse	NY	13202	315-472-5420		390
Parsons Capital Management Inc 10 Weybosset St Ste 1000 *TF:* 888-521-2440 ■ *Web:* parsonscapital.com	Providence	RI	02903	401-521-2440		401
Parsons Child & Family Ctr 60 Academy Rd *Web:* www.parsonscenter.org	Albany	NY	12208	518-426-2600	447-5234	48-6
Parsons Company Inc 1386 SR- 117 *Web:* www.parsonscompany.com	Roanoke	IL	61561	309-467-9100		454
Parsons Corp 100 W Walnut St *Web:* www.parsons.com	Pasadena	CA	91124	626-440-2000	440-2630	261
Parsons Dance Co 229 W 42nd St 8th Fl *Web:* www.parsonsdance.org	New York	NY	10036	212-869-9275		573-1
Parsons Electric LLC 5960 Main St NE **Fax Area Code:* 763 ■ *Web:* www.pecsolutions.com	Minneapolis	MN	55432	651-735-2195	571-7210*	189-4
Parsons Elem School 899 Hollywood St *Web:* nbtschools.org	North Brunswick	NJ	08902	732-289-3400		685
Parsons State Hospital & Training Ctr 2601 Gabriel St *Web:* kdads.ks.gov	Parsons	KS	67357	620-421-6550	421-3623	230
Partec Inc 9301 Belmont Ave *Web:* partec-inc.com	Franklin Park	IL	60131	847-678-9520		543
Par-Tech Inc 139 Premier Dr *Web:* www.partechgss.com	Lake Orion	MI	48359	248-276-0213	364-0370	344
Partek Inc 624 Trade Center Blvd *Web:* www.partek.com	Chesterfield	MO	63005	314-878-2329	275-8453	178-1
Parter Medical Products Inc 17015 Kingsview Ave *TF:* 800-666-8282 ■ *Web:* www.partermedical.com	Carson	CA	90746	310-327-4417	327-8601	420
Partex Marking Systems Inc 1155 N Main St *Web:* www.partexmarker.com	Lombard	IL	60148	630-516-0400	833-7631	640
Parthenon 5500 S 56th St Ste 8 *Web:* www.theparthenon.net	Lincoln	NE	68516	402-423-2222		671
Parthenon Prints Inc PO Box 2505 *Web:* www.parthenonprints.com	Panama City	FL	32402	850-769-8321	769-5374	745-7
Parthenon, The 511 Oman St *Web:* www.nashville.gov	Nashville	TN	37203	615-862-8431	880-2265	520
Participant Inc 253 E Houston St Ste 1 *Web:* www.participantinc.org	New York	NY	10002	212-254-4334		637-2
Participant Media LLC 331 Foothill Rd 3rd Fl *Web:* participant.com	Beverly Hills	CA	90210	310-550-5100		514
Particle 126 Post St *Web:* particle.io	San Francisco	CA	94108	415-316-1024		178-1
Particle Measuring Systems Inc 5475 Airport Blvd *TF:* 800-238-1801 ■ *Web:* www.pmeasuring.com	Boulder	CO	80301	303-443-7100	449-6870	419
PartiLife Publications 65 Sussex St *Web:* www.balloonsandparties.com	Hackensack	NJ	07601	201-441-4224	342-8118	637-9
Partner Assessment Corp 2154 Torrance Blvd Ste 200 *TF:* 800-419-4923 ■ *Web:* www.partneresi.com	Torrance	CA	90501	800-419-4923		192
Partner in Publishing 50 Nye Rd *Web:* www.partnerinpublishing.com	Glastonbury	CT	06033	860-430-9440		637-2
Partner Reinsurance Company of the US 200 First Stamford Pl Ste 400 *Web:* partnerre.com	Stamford	CT	06902	203-485-4200	485-4300	391-2
Partner Software Inc PO Box 748 *TF:* 844-778-4717 ■ *Web:* www.partnersoftware.com	Athens	GA	30603	800-964-1833		809
Partnercomm Inc 2304 I-20 W *Web:* www.partnercomm.net	Arlington	TX	76017	817-465-9277		463
Partners 1st Federal Credit Union 1330 Directors Row *TF:* 800-728-8943 ■ *Web:* www.partners1stcu.org	Fort Wayne	IN	46808	260-471-8336		219
Partners A Tasteful Choice Co 20232 72nd Ave *TF:* 800-632-7477 ■ *Web:* www.partnerscrackers.com	Kent	WA	98032	253-867-1580		68
Partners Bank of California 27201 Puerta Real Ste 160 *Web:* www.partnersbankca.com	Mission Viejo	CA	92691	949-732-4000	348-0180	70
Partners Capital Investment Group LLC 50 Rowes Wharf 4th Fl *Web:* www.partners-cap.com	Boston	MA	02110	617-292-2570		401
Partners Data Systems Inc 3663 Via Mercado *TF:* 800-550-3005 ■ *Web:* www.partnersdata.com	La Mesa	CA	91941	619-415-2000	415-2001	174
Partners HealthCare Accountable Care Organization LLC 800 Boylston St Ste 1150 *Web:* www.massgeneralbrigham.org	Boston	MA	02199	857-282-2149		353
Partners In Computing Services 1608 20th St NW Ste B *Web:* pintl.net	Washington	DC	20009	202-223-8401		180
Partners in Human Resources International Inc 9 E 37th St *Web:* www.partners-international.com	New York	NY	10016	212-685-0400	685-0545	194
Partners Napier Inc 192 Mill St Ste 600 *Web:* www.partnersandnapier.com	Rochester	NY	14614	585-454-1010		7
Partners of the Americas 1424 K St NW Ste 700 *Web:* www.partners.net	Washington	DC	20005	202-628-3300		48-5
Partners Press Inc 98 Highland Ave *Web:* www.partners-press.com	Oaks	PA	19456	610-666-7960	666-7963	637-2
Partners Riley 1375 Euclid Ave Ste 410 *Web:* www.partnersriley.com	Cleveland	OH	44115	216-241-2141		4
Partners Trust Real Estate Brokerage & Acquisitions 9378 Wilshire Blvd Ste 200 *Web:* pacificunionla.com	Beverly Hills	CA	90212	424-249-7162		652
Partnership Capital Growth LLC PO Box 7 *Web:* www.pcg-investors.com	Los Gatos	CA	95031	415-705-8008	705-5279	691
Partnership for a Drug-Free America 405 Lexington Ave Ste 1601 *TF:* 855-378-4373 ■ *Web:* drugfree.org	New York	NY	10174	212-922-1560	922-1570	48-17
Partnership for Philanthropic Planning PO Box 293106 *Web:* pppgd.org	Kettering	OH	45429	317-269-6274		48-5
Partnerships In Community Living Inc 480 Main St E PO Box 129 *Web:* www.pclpartnership.org	Monmouth	OR	97361	503-838-2403	838-5815	48-15
Partnersolve LLC 30 Southville Rd *TF:* 855-445-2837 ■ *Web:* www.partnersolve.com	Southborough	MA	01772	855-445-2837		260
Parton Lumber Company Inc 251 Parton Rd *TF:* 800-624-1501 ■ *Web:* partonlumber.com	Rutherfordton	NC	28139	800-624-1501		683
Partridge Snow & Hahn LLP 40 Westminster St Ste 1100 *Web:* www.psh.com	Providence	RI	02903	401-861-8200		428
Parts Authority Inc 495 Merrick Rd *Web:* partsauthority.com	Rockville Centre	NY	11570	516-678-3900		61
Parts Central Inc 3243 Whitfield St *TF:* 800-226-9396 ■ *Web:* www.partscentral.net	Macon	GA	31204	478-745-0878	746-1177	61
Parts Inc 210 Andrew Dr *Web:* partsinc.net	Stockbridge	GA	30281	678-325-6950	325-6957	686
Parts Specialists Inc 14639 Short St *Web:* www.partsspecialistsinc.com	Posen	IL	60469	708-371-2444	371-2477	385
PartsBase Inc 905 Clint Moore Rd *TF:* 888-322-6896 ■ *Web:* www.partsbase.com	Boca Raton	FL	33487	561-953-0700	953-0793	770
Party Cat Inc 2727 Exposition Blvd Ste 119 *Web:* partycat.com	Austin	TX	78703	512-472-8250		627
Party City Corp 25 Green Pond Rd Ste 1 *TF:* 800-727-8924 ■ *Web:* www.partycity.com	Rockaway	NJ	07866	973-453-8690		566
Party Fair Inc 4345 US Hwy 9 *Web:* www.partyfair.com	Freehold	NJ	07728	732-780-1110		566
Party Rental Ltd 275 N St *Web:* www.partyrentalltd.com	Teterboro	NJ	07608	201-727-4700	727-4701	264-2
Party Time Manufacturing Co 421 Parsonage St **Fax Area Code:* 570 ■ *TF:* 800-346-3847 ■ *Web:* www.partytimemfg.com	Hughestown	PA	18640	800-346-3847	655-8535*	554
Party.com Inc 14856 Knollview Dr *Web:* www.partyandpaperwarehouse.com	Dallas	TX	75248	214-310-6599		241
Partylite Gifts Inc 59 Armstrong Rd *TF:* 888-999-5706 ■ *Web:* www.partylite.com	Plymouth	MA	02360	508-830-3100	732-5818	366
PartySecret.com 29995 Technology Dr Ste 205 *Web:* www.partysecret.com	Murrieta	CA	92563	951-461-8222	445-4363	459
Parvin State Park 701 Almond Rd *Web:* www.njparksandforests.org	Pittsgrove	NJ	08318	856-358-8616		565
Par-Way Tryson Co 107 Bolte Ln *TF:* 800-844-4554 ■ *Web:* parwaytryson.com	Saint Clair	MO	63077	636-629-4545	629-1330	296-30
PAS (Percussive Arts Society) 110 W Washington St *Web:* www.pas.org	Indianapolis	IN	46204	317-974-4488	974-4499	48-4
Pas Technologies Inc 10301 N Commerce Pkwy *Web:* www.pas-technologies.com	Miramar	FL	33025	305-624-3173		21
PAS USA Inc 2010 W 15th St *Web:* www.pas-net.biz	Washington	NC	27889	252-974-5500	974-5515	596
Pasadena Capital Partners LLC PO Box 60786 *Web:* pasadenacapital.com	Pasadena	CA	91116	626-432-7070	432-7470	528
Pasadena Chamber of Commerce 4334 Fairmont Pkwy *Web:* www.pasadenachamber.org	Pasadena	TX	77504	281-487-7871	487-5530	139

Name / Address	City	State	ZIP	Phone	Fax	Class
Pasadena Chamber of Commerce & Civic Assn						
844 E Green St Ste 208	Pasadena	CA	91101	626-795-3355	795-5603	139
Web: www.pasadena-chamber.org						
Pasadena City College						
1570 E Colorado Blvd	Pasadena	CA	91106	626-585-7123	585-7915	162
Web: pasadena.edu						
Pasadena Convention & Visitors Bureau						
300 E Green St	Pasadena	CA	91101	626-795-9311	795-9656	206
Web: www.visitpasadena.com						
Pasadena Heritage 651 S St John Ave	Pasadena	CA	91105	626-441-6333		533
Web: pasadenaheritage.org						
Pasadena Playhouse, The						
39 S El Molino Ave	Pasadena	CA	91101	626-356-7529		749
Web: www.pasadenaplayhouse.org						
Pasadena Public Library						
207 N Garfield Ave	Pasadena	CA	91101	626-794-8585	585-8396	434-3
Web: www.cityofpasadena.net						
Pasadena Public Library						
1149 Ellsworth Dr	Pasadena	TX	77506	713-477-1511	473-9640	434-3
Web: www.pasadenatx.gov						
Pasadena Service Federal Credit Union						
670 N Rosemead Blvd	Pasadena	CA	91107	877-297-4707		219
TF: 877-297-4707 ■ *Web:* mypsfcu.org						
Pasadena Star-News						
2 N Lake Ave Ste 150	Pasadena	CA	91101	626-445-1585		532-2
Web: www.pasadenastarnews.com						
Pasadena Weekly						
50 S Delacey Ave Ste 200	Pasadena	CA	91105	626-584-1500	795-0149	532-5
Web: www.pasadenaweekly.com						
Pasadera Capital LLC						
115 W El Prado Ste 1	San Antonio	TX	78212	210-804-4240		70
Web: www.pasaderacapital.com						
Pasand Indian Cuisine						
2600 N Belt Line Rd	Irving	TX	75062	972-594-0693	594-8935	671
Web: www.pasandrestaurant.com						
Pascal Engineering Inc						
64 W Seegers Rd	Arlington Heights	IL	60005	847-427-1234	427-1222	493
Web: www.pascalenginc.com						
Pascal International Inc						
2929 NE Northup Way	Bellevue	WA	98004	425-827-4694	827-6893	475
TF: 800-426-8051 ■ *Web:* www.pascaldental.com						
Pascal Pour Elle 368 Park Ave	Glencoe	IL	60022	847-501-3100		77
Web: pascalpourelle.com						
Pascal's on Ponce						
2611 Ponce de Leon Blvd	Coral Gables	FL	33134	305-444-2024	444-9798	671
Web: www.pascalmiami.com						
Pascap Company Inc 4250 Boston Rd	Bronx	NY	10475	718-325-7200	325-7595	686
Web: pascapco.com						
Pasco 2600 S Hanley Rd Ste 450	Saint Louis	MO	63144	314-781-2212		551
TF: 800-489-3300 ■ *Web:* pascosystems.com						
Pasco County 7530 Little Rd	New Port Richey	FL	34654	727-847-2411	847-8969	338
TF: 800-368-2411 ■ *Web:* www.pascocountyfl.net						
Pasco County Library System						
8012 Library Rd	Hudson	FL	34667	727-861-3020	861-3025	434-3
Web: www.pascolibraries.org						
Pasco Inc 1140 Terex Rd	Hudson	OH	44236	330-655-7000		225
Web: www.pasco-group.com						
Pasco Specialty & Manufacturing Inc						
11156 Wright Rd	Lynwood	CA	90262	310-537-7782		612
TF: 800-737-2726 ■ *Web:* www.pascospecialty.com						
Pasco-Hernado State College						
10230 Ridge Rd	New Port Richey	FL	34654	727-847-2727	816-3389	162
TF: 855-669-7472 ■ *Web:* phsc.edu						
Pascrell Bill Jr (Rep D - NJ)						
2409 Rayburn House Office Bldg	Washington	DC	20515	202-225-5751	225-5782	342-2
Web: www.pascrell.house.gov						
Pasek Corp 9 W Third St	South Boston	MA	02127	617-269-7110		693
TF: 800-628-2822 ■ *Web:* www.pasek.com						
Paseo 4225 Fremont Ave N	Seattle	WA	98103	206-545-7440		671
Web: www.paseorestaurants.com						
Pasha Group Inc						
4040 Civic Center Dr Ste 350	San Rafael	CA	94903	415-927-6400	924-5672	313
Web: www.pashagroup.com						
Pasha Middle East Cafe						
919 W International Speedway Blvd	Daytona Beach	FL	32114	386-257-7753		671
Web: pashamideastcafe.com						
Paslin Co 25303 Ryan Rd	Warren	MI	48091	586-758-0200		757
Web: www.paslin.com						
Paslode 888 Forest Edge Dr	Vernon Hills	IL	60061	847-634-1900	634-6602	759
Web: www.paslode.com						
PASNAP (Pennsylvania Association of Staff Nurses & Allied Professionals)						
1 Fayette St Ste 475	Conshohocken	PA	19428	610-567-2907	567-2915	533
TF: 800-500-7850 ■ *Web:* www.pasnap.com						
Paso Fino Horse Assn						
4047 Iron Works Pkwy Ste 1	Lexington	KY	40511	859-825-6000	258-2125	48-3
TF: 800-844-1409 ■ *Web:* www.pfha.org						
Paso Robles Inn 1103 Spring St	Paso Robles	CA	93446	805-238-2660	238-4707	379
TF: 800-676-1713 ■ *Web:* www.pasoroblesinn.com						
Paso Robles Press						
935 Riverside Ave Ste 8A	Paso Robles	CA	93446	805-237-6060	237-6066	532-4
Web: www.pasoroblespress.com						
Pason Systems Inc 6130 Third St SE	Calgary	AB	T2H1K4	403-301-3400	301-3499	178-10
TSX: PSI ■ *TF:* 877-255-3158 ■ *Web:* www.pason.com						
Pasquier Panel Products Inc						
1510 Puyallup St PO Box 1170	Sumner	WA	98390	253-863-6323	891-7993	819
Web: www.pasquierpanel.com						
Pasquotank Correctional Institution						
527 Commerce Dr	Elizabeth City	NC	27906	252-331-4881	331-4866	213
Web: www.ncdps.gov						
Pasquotank County PO Box 39	Elizabeth City	NC	27907	252-335-0865	335-0866	338
Web: www.pasquotankcountync.org						
Pass Security LLC						
15 Executive Dr Ste 6	Fairview Heights	IL	62208	618-394-1144		693
Web: www.passsecurity.com						
Passage to India 520 Race St	Harrisburg	PA	17104	717-233-1202		671
Web: www.passagetoindiaharrisburgpa.com						
PassageMaker Magazine						
105 Eastern Ave Ste 203	Annapolis	MD	21403	410-990-9086		457-4
Web: www.passagemaker.com						
Passaic County 401 Grand St	Paterson	NJ	07505	973-225-3632	754-1920	338
Web: www.passaiccountynj.org						
Passaic County Community College						
1 College Blvd	Paterson	NJ	07505	973-684-6800	684-6778	162
Web: www.pccc.cc.nj.us						
Passaic Metal Products Co						
5 Central Ave	Clifton	NJ	07015	973-546-9000		697
Web: www.pampco.com						
Passaic River Coalition (PRC)						
330 Speedwell Ave	Morristown	NJ	07960	973-532-9830	889-9172	48-13
Web: passaicriver.org						
Passaic Rubber Co 45 Demarest Dr	Wayne	NJ	07474	973-696-9500		677
Web: www.passaic.com						
Passaic Valley Water Commission						
1525 Main Ave	Clifton	NJ	07011	973-340-4300	340-5598	787
TF: 877-772-7077 ■ *Web:* www.pvwc.com						
Passavant Area Hospital (PAH)						
1600 W Walnut St	Jacksonville	IL	62650	217-245-9541		374-3
Web: www.passavanthospital.com						
Passenger Vessel Assn (PVA)						
103 Oronoco St Ste 200	Alexandria	VA	22314	703-518-5005	518-5151	49-21
TF: 800-807-8360 ■ *Web:* www.passengervessel.com						
Passero Assoc 242 W Main St Ste 100	Rochester	NY	14614	585-325-1000		261
TF: 800-836-0365 ■ *Web:* www.passero.com						
Passionfish 701 Lighthouse Ave	Pacific Grove	CA	93950	831-655-3311		671
Web: www.passionfish.net						
Passionist Academic Institute Library						
660 Busse Hwy	Park Ridge	IL	60068	847-518-8844	518-0461	434-3
TF: 800-295-9048 ■ *Web:* www.passionist.org						
Passkeys Foundation Jefferson Center for Character Education						
PO Box 4137	Mission Viejo	CA	92690	949-770-7602	450-1100	194
Web: passkeys.org						
Passman & Jones						
2500 Renaissance Tower 1201 Elm St	Dallas	TX	75270	214-742-2121		428
Web: www.passmanjones.com						
Passport Corp 16 West St	Warwick	NY	10990	800-926-6736		178-1
TF: 800-926-6736 ■ *Web:* www.passportcorp.com						
Passport Health Communications Inc						
720 Cool Springs Blvd Ste 200	Franklin	TN	37067	615-661-5657	376-3552	180
TF: 888-661-5657 ■ *Web:* www.passporthealth.com						
Passport Online Inc						
9786 SW Nimbus Ave	Beaverton	OR	97008	503-626-7766	626-8676	225
Web: www.passportonlineinc.com						
Passport Services Regional Offices						
Boston Agency						
10 Cswy St Tip O'Neill Federal Bldg Rm 247	Boston	MA	02222	877-487-2778		340-16
TF: 877-487-2778 ■ *Web:* www.travel.state.gov						
Passport Systems Inc						
70 Treble Cove Rd 1st Fl	Billerica	MA	01862	978-263-9900	263-9971	743
Web: www.passportsystems.com						
Passport Telecom Inc						
1404 San Ignacio	Solana Beach	CA	92075	858-764-4200		681
Web: www.passporttele.com						
PASSUR Aerospace Inc						
1 Landmark Sq Ste 1900	Stamford	CT	06901	203-622-4086		177
Web: www.passur.com						
Passy-Muir Inc 4521 Campus Dr Pmb 273	Irvine	CA	92612	949-833-8255		477
TF: 800-634-5397 ■ *Web:* www.passy-muir.com						
Pasta House Co 700 New Ballas Rd	Saint Louis	MO	63141	314-535-6644	531-2499	670
Web: pastahouse.com						
Pasta Jays 1001 Pearl St	Boulder	CO	80302	303-444-5800		671
Web: pastajays.com						
Paster & Harpootian Ltd						
1000 Chapel View Blvd	Cranston	RI	02920	401-455-9800		41
Web: ph-estplan.com						
Pastian's Bakery 3320 2nd St NW	Albuquerque	NM	87107	505-345-7773	345-2088	296-1
Web: www.pastiansbakery.com						
Pastiche Modern Eatery						
3025 N Campbell Ave	Tucson	AZ	85719	520-325-3333		671
Web: www.pasticheme.com						
Pastore's of Rosedale						
8442 Philadelphia Rd	Baltimore	MD	21237	410-686-1884	686-1798	345
Web: pastores.net						
Pastorelli Food Products Inc						
162 N Sangamon St	Chicago	IL	60607	312-666-2041	666-2415	296-36
TF: 800-767-2829 ■ *Web:* www.pastorelli.com						
Pastries By Randolph Inc						
4500 Lee Hwy	Arlington	VA	22207	703-243-0070		68
Web: www.pastriesbyrandolph.com						
Pastry Star 9445 Washington Blvd N	Laurel	MD	20723	301-498-0912		361
TF: 800-886-0912 ■ *Web:* www.pastrystar.com						
Pat Campbell Insurance LLC						
141 Roadrunner Pkwy Ste 109	Las Cruces	NM	88011	575-524-8642		390
Web: campbell-ins.com						
Pat Hoey Productions 167 Auburn St	Auburn	MA	01501	508-832-3300		184
Web: www.thebostonhomeshow.com						
Pat Milliken Ford 9600 Telegraph Rd	Redford	MI	48239	855-803-3131		57
TF: 855-803-3131 ■ *Web:* www.patmillikenford.com						
Pat O'Brien's International Inc						
718 St Peter St	New Orleans	LA	70116	504-525-4823		670
TF: 800-597-4823 ■ *Web:* www.patobriens.com						
Pat's Steak House						
2437 Brownsboro Rd	Louisville	KY	40206	502-893-2062		671
Web: www.patssteakhouselouisville.com						
Patagonia 259 W Santa Clara St	Ventura	CA	93001	805-643-8616		157-4
TF: 800-638-6464 ■ *Web:* www.patagonia.com						
Patagonia Lake State Park						
400 Patagonia Lake Rd	Patagonia	AZ	85624	520-287-6965		565
Web: azstateparks.com						
Patch Rubber Co PO Box H	Roanoke Rapids	NC	27870	252-536-2574		676
Web: www.patchrubber.com						
Patchogue-Medford Library						
54-60 E Main St	Patchogue	NY	11772	631-654-4700	289-3999	434-3
Web: www.pmlib.org						
Pa-Ted Spring Company LLC						
137 Vincent P Kelly Rd	Bristol	CT	06010	860-582-6368	583-1044	719
Web: pa-ted.com						
Patel & Assoc 266 17th St Ste 200	Oakland	CA	94612	510-452-5051		2
Web: patelcpa.com						

Name / Address	City	State	ZIP	Phone	Fax	Class
Patel & Dalrymple LLC 5200 Fort Ave *Web:* pdlaw.us	Lynchburg	VA	24502	434-832-7030		41
Patel Burica & Associates Inc 9283 Research Dr **Fax Area Code:* 714 ■ *Web:* pbastructural.com	Irvine	CA	92618	949-943-8080	352-2209*	261
Patel Consultants Corp 1525 Morris Ave *Web:* www.patelcorp.com	Union	NJ	07083	908-964-7575		177
Patel Law Pc 108 W University Ave *Web:* patellawteam.com	Urbana	IL	61801	217-384-1111		41
Patene Building Supplies Ltd 641 Speedvale Ave W *TF:* 800-265-8319 ■ *Web:* www.patene.com	Guelph	ON	N1K1E6	519-824-4030		191-1
Patent & Trademark Office Federal Credit Union 501 Dulany St 1st Fl *Web:* ptofcu.org	Alexandria	VA	22314	571-272-0350	273-0190	219
Patent Calls Inc (PCI) 214 W Fannin St *Web:* www.patentcalls.com	Marshall	TX	75670	512-371-4120		387
Patented Acquisition Corp 2490 CrossPointe Dr *Web:* thinkpatented.com	Miamisburg	OH	45342	937-353-2299	254-9638	317
Paternity Testing Corp (PTC) 300 Portland St *TF:* 888-837-8323 ■ *Web:* www.ptclabs.com	Columbia	MO	65201	573-442-9948	442-9870	417
Paterson Free Public Library 250 Broadway *Web:* www.patersonpl.org	Paterson	NJ	07501	973-321-1223	321-1205	434-3
Paterson Museum 2 Market St *Web:* www.thepatersonmuseum.com	Paterson	NJ	07501	973-321-1260		520
Paterson Pacific Parchment Co 625 Greg St **Fax Area Code:* 800 ■ *TF:* 800-678-8104 ■ *Web:* www.patersonpaper.com	Sparks	NV	89431	775-353-3000	456-8104*	559
Paterson Papers PO Box 2286 *Web:* www.patersonpapers.com	Paterson	NJ	07501	973-278-2410	278-0677	553
PATH 1455 NW Leary Way *Web:* www.path.org	Seattle	WA	98107	206-285-3500	285-6619	48-17
Path Master Inc 1960 Midway Dr *Web:* www.pathmasterinc.com	Twinsburg	OH	44087	330-425-4994	425-9338	246
Path-2 Ventures LLC 3729 Monique Ln *TF:* 888-692-1057 ■ *Web:* www.path-2.com	Charlotte	NC	28203	888-692-1057		463
Patheon 4815 Emperor Blvd *Web:* www.patheon.com	Durham	NC	27703	919-226-3200		583
Pathfinder Bancorp Inc 214 W 1st St *NASDAQ:* PBHC ■ *TF:* 800-811-5620 ■ *Web:* www.pathfinderbank.com	Oswego	NY	13126	315-343-0057	342-9403	360-2
Pathfinder Consulting 70 E Lake St Ste 1120 *Web:* pathfinderconsulting.org	Chicago	IL	60601	312-498-7166		194
Pathfinder Group Park Lane Terr 502 - 5657 Spring Garden Rd PO Box 142 *TF:* 800-200-7284 ■ *Web:* pathfinder-group.ca	Halifax	NS	B3J3R4	902-425-2445	425-2441	47
Pathfinder Intl 9 Galen St Ste 217 *Web:* www.pathfinder.org	Watertown	MA	02472	617-924-7200	924-3833	48-5
Pathfinder Regional Vocational Technical High School 240 Sykes St *Web:* www.pathfindertech.org	Palmer	MA	01069	413-283-9701		800
Pathfinder/LI & D Insurance Group LLC 12141 Wickchester Ln Ste 500 *Web:* pathfinderlld.com	Houston	TX	77079	281-556-9999		390
PathGroup 5301 Virginia Way *TF:* 800-366-5847 ■ *Web:* www.pathgroup.com	Brentwood	TN	37027	615-221-4511		194
PathLogic 1166 National Dr Ste 80 *TF:* 844-603-3071 ■ *Web:* www.pathlogic.com	Sacramento	CA	95834	866-863-1496		418
Pathlore Software Corp 7965 N High St Ste 300 *Web:* www.sumtotalsystems.com	Columbus	OH	43235	614-781-0036	781-7200	463
Pathmaker Group LP 635 Fritz Dr Ste 110 *Web:* www.pathmaker-group.com	Coppell	TX	75019	817-704-3644		174
Pathologists' Regional Laboratory 1225 Highland Ave *Web:* pathregional.com	Clarkston	WA	99403	509-758-5576		416
Pathology & Cytology Laboratories Inc 290 Big Run Rd *TF:* 800-264-0514 ■ *Web:* www.pandclab.com	Lexington	KY	40503	859-278-9513		415
Pathology Ctr, The 8303 Dodge St *Web:* thepathologycenter.org	Omaha	NE	68114	402-354-4540		418
Pathology Group of The Mid South 7550 Wolf River Blvd Ste 200 *TF:* 877-608-2756 ■ *Web:* www.trumbulllabs.com	Germantown	TN	38138	901-542-6800	542-6873	415
Pathology Laboratories Inc 1946 N 13th St Ste 301 *TF:* 800-281-8804 ■ *Web:* www.pathlabs.org	Toledo	OH	43604	419-255-4600		415
Path-Tec LLC 5700 Old Brim Rd *Web:* path-tec.com	Midland	GA	31820	706-569-6368	569-6369	476
Pathway Bank 306 S High St *Web:* pathwaybank.com	Cairo	NE	68824	308-485-4232		70
Pathway Book Service 4 White Brook Rd *TF:* 800-345-6665 ■ *Web:* www.pathwaybook.com	Gilsum	NH	03448	603-357-0236		96
Pathway Health 11240 Stillwater Blvd N *TF:* 877-777-5463 ■ *Web:* www.pathwayhealth.com	Lake Elmo	MN	55042	877-777-5463		196
Pathway Press 1080 Montgomery Ave NE *Web:* www.pathwaybookstore.com	Cleveland	TN	37311	423-476-4512		637-2
Pathways 200 W Spring St *Web:* pathwaysup.org	Marquette	MI	49855	906-225-1181		371
Pathways Consulting LLC 240 Mechanic St Ste 100 *Web:* pathwaysconsult.com	Lebanon	NH	03766	603-448-2200		261
Pathways Home Health Hospice 585 N Mary Ave *TF:* 888-755-7855 ■ *Web:* www.pathwayshealth.org	Sunnyvale	CA	94085	888-755-7855		363
Pathways to Independence 289 Pinnacle St *TF:* 866-775-1608 ■ *Web:* www.pathwaysind.com	Belleville	ON	K8N3B3	613-962-2541	962-6357	138
Pathwayz Communications Inc 4176 Canyon Dr *TF:* 888-778-4241 ■ *Web:* www.pathwayz.com	Amarillo	TX	79109	806-350-9000		506
Patience Press LLC PO Box 2757 *Web:* www.patiencepress.com	High Springs	FL	32655	352-215-9251		637-2
Patient Advocate Foundation Inc 700 Thimble Shoals Blvd Ste 200 *TF:* 800-532-5274 ■ *Web:* www.patientadvocate.org	Newport News	VA	23606	800-532-5274		305
Patient Aids 100 Crossing Dr *Web:* www.patientaids4u.com	Wilder	KY	41076	859-441-8876	441-5850	475
Patient Recruiting Agency LLC, The 6207 Bee Cave Rd Ste 288 *Web:* tpra.com	Austin	TX	78746	512-345-7788		4
PatientKeeper Inc 880 Winter St Ste 300 *TF:* 888-994-2443 ■ *Web:* www.patientkeeper.com	Waltham	MA	02451	781-373-6100		476
PatientPing Inc 225 Franklin St *Web:* patientping.com	Boston	MA	02110	617-701-7816		89
Patients Best Choice Home Health Inc 3427 W Fm 120 Ste 105 *Web:* patientsbestchoice.com	Denison	TX	75020	903-462-0604	462-0603	363
Patients Rights Council (PRC) PO Box 760 *TF:* 800-958-5678 ■ *Web:* www.patientsrightscouncil.org	Steubenville	OH	43952	740-282-3810		48-8
PatientSafe Solutions Inc 5375 Mira Sorrento Pl Ste 500 *Web:* www.patientsafesolutions.com	San Diego	CA	92121	858-746-3100		475
Patina Restaurant Group 141 S Grand Ave *TF:* 866-972-8462 ■ *Web:* www.patinagroup.com	Los Angeles	CA	90012	866-972-8462		670
Patio Drugs 5208 Veterans Blvd *Web:* www.patiodrugs.com	Metairie	LA	70006	504-889-7070		582
Patioshoppers Inc 41188 Sandalwood Cir *TF:* 800-940-6123 ■ *Web:* www.patioshoppers.com	Murrieta	CA	92562	951-696-1700		321
Patoka Lake 3084 N Dillard Rd	Birdseye	IN	47513	812-685-2464		565
Patpatia & Associates Inc 1803 Sixth St Ste A *Web:* patpatia.com	Berkeley	CA	94710	510-559-7140		195
Patpro Inc 2111 Eisenhower Ave Ste 404 *Web:* www.epatpro.com	Alexandria	VA	22314	703-299-8500	299-9925	41
Patreon 600 Townsend St *Web:* www.patreon.com	San Francisco	CA	94103	415-967-2735		178-1
Patricia Egen Consulting LLC 803 Creek Overlook *Web:* www.egenconsulting.com	Chattanooga	TN	37415	423-875-2652		196
Patricia Lynch Associates Inc 677 Broadway Ste 305 *Web:* www.plynchassociates.com	Albany	NY	12207	518-432-9220		463
Patricia Seybold Group 210 Commercial St *Web:* www.customers.com	Boston	MA	02109	617-742-5200		463
Patricio Enterprises Inc 525 Corporate Dr Ste 201 *Web:* www.patricioenterprises.com	Stafford	VA	22554	703-441-4760	441-4798	463
Patrick & Co 560 Market St *Web:* www.patrickandco.com	San Francisco	CA	94104	415-392-2640	591-0773	535
Patrick Air Force Base 1225 Jupiter St *Web:* www.patrick.af.mil	Patrick Afb	FL	32925	321-494-5933	494-2133	497-1
Patrick Buzarellos Kendrick 1900 Point W Way Ste 102 *Web:* www.pbkcpas.com	Sacramento	CA	95815	916-920-1604		2
Patrick County 106 Rucker St PO Box 466 *Web:* www.co.patrick.va.us	Stuart	VA	24171	276-694-6094	694-2160	338
Patrick Engineering Inc 4970 Varsity Dr *Web:* www.patrickengineering.com	Lisle	IL	60532	630-795-7200		261
Patrick Henry Community College 645 Patriot Ave *TF:* 855-874-6692 ■ *Web:* www.ph.vccs.edu	Martinsville	VA	24112	276-638-8777		162
Patrick Henry Creative Promotions Inc 1177 WS Loop Ste 800 *Web:* www.phcp.com	Houston	TX	77027	281-983-5500		393
Patrick Henry Mall 12300 Jefferson Ave *TF:* 855-466-7467 ■ *Web:* shoppatrickhenrymall.com	Newport News	VA	23602	757-249-4305		460
Patrick Industries Inc 107 W Franklin St PO Box 638 *NASDAQ:* PATK ■ *TF:* 800-331-2151 ■ *Web:* patrickind.com	Elkhart	IN	46515	574-294-7511	522-5213	115
Patrick Industries Inc *Patrick Metals Div* 5020 Lincolnway E *Web:* www.patrickmetals.com	Mishawaka	IN	46544	574-255-9692	256-6577	485
Patrick J. Flynn & Associates PC 7979 Old Georgetown Rd Ste 550 *Web:* flynncpas.com	Bethesda	MD	20814	301-951-1019		2
Patrick J. Kozlowski Accountancy 1127 11th St 225	Sacramento	CA	95814	916-448-5191		2
Patrick James Inc 780 W Shaw Ave *TF:* 888-427-6003 ■ *Web:* www.patrickjames.com	Fresno	CA	93704	559-224-5500	448-0601	157-3
Patrick Mechanical LLC 3307 International St *Web:* www.patrickmechanical.com	Fairbanks	AK	99701	907-452-3334	452-3369	189-10
Patrick S. Gray Insurance Agency Inc 2743 Maguire Rd *Web:* patrickgrayinsurance.com	Ocoee	FL	34761	407-877-0081		390
Patrick Solutions Inc 955 W 3rd Ave *Web:* www.patricksolutions.com	Columbus	OH	43212	614-255-0300		525
Patrick T. Hsu CPA 7927 Garden Grove Blvd *Web:* www.hsuaccounting.com	Garden Grove	CA	92841	714-895-6516		2
Patrick's Hawaiian Cafe 316 SE 123rd Ave Ste D1 *Web:* hawaiiancafe.com	Vancouver	WA	98683	360-885-0881		671
Patrick's Point State Park 4150 Patrick's Pt Dr *Web:* www.parks.ca.gov	Trinidad	CA	95570	707-677-3570		565
Patriot Advertising Inc 1801 E Ave *Web:* www.patriotadvertising.com	Katy	TX	77493	832-437-1477		7

	Phone	Fax	Class
Patriot Benefit Solutions Insu 17 Cobblestone Cir. .... North Andover MA 01845 *Web:* patriotbenefit.com	978-683-1799		390
Patriot Buick GMC 4600 E Central Texas Expy .... Killeen TX 76543 *Web:* www.patriotcars.com	254-781-0452		516
Patriot Chevrolet of Warminister 829 W St Rd .... Warminster PA 18974 *Web:* www.chevyofwarminster.com	215-259-5827		57
Patriot Engineering & Environmental Inc 6150 E 75th St .... Indianapolis IN 46250 *Web:* patrioteng.com	317-576-8058	576-1965	261
Patriot Equity Credit Union 1450 Union University Dr .... Jackson TN 38305 *Web:* pecujax.org	731-668-1155		219
Patriot Fire Protection Inc 2707 70th Ave E .... Fife WA 98424 *Web:* www.patriotfire.com	253-926-2290		610
Patriot Gaming & Electronics Inc 217 N Lindberg St .... Griffith IN 46319 *Web:* patriotgaming.com	219-922-6400		452
Patriot Industries Inc PO Box 909 .... Monticello KY 42633 *Web:* www.patriotindustries.com	606-340-8080	340-8100	287
Patriot League 3897 Adler Pl .... Bethlehem PA 18017 *Web:* www.patriotleague.org	610-691-2414		713
Patriot Ledger 400 Crown Colony Dr PO Box 699159 .... Quincy MA 02269 *Web:* www.patriotledger.com	617-786-7000	786-7025	532-2
Patriot Machining & Maintenance Services Inc 512 Linden St .... Carlisle OH 45005 *Web:* www.patriot-mg.com	937-746-2117		454
Patriot National Bancorp Inc 900 Bedford St .... Stamford CT 06901 *NASDAQ: PNBK* ■ **Fax Area Code:* 203 ■ *TF:* 888-728-7468 ■ *Web:* bankpatriot.com	888-728-7468	324-8804*	360-2
Patriot Properties Inc 123 Pleasant St .... Marblehead MA 01945 *TF:* 800-527-9991 ■ *Web:* www.patriotproperties.com	781-586-9670		655
Patriot Rail Co 10752 Deerwood Park Blvd Ste 300 .... Jacksonville FL 32246 *TF:* 855-258-4514 ■ *Web:* patriotrailandports.com	904-423-2540		649
Patriot Software Inc 2925 E 96th St Ste 100 .... Indianapolis IN 46240 *Web:* patriotsoftware.net	317-573-5431		179
Patriot Staffing & Services LLC 47 Eggert Ave .... Metuchen NJ 08840 *TF:* 888-412-6999 ■ *Web:* www.patstaffing.com	888-412-6999		570
Patriot Technologies Inc 5108 Pegasus Ct Ste F .... Frederick MD 21704 *TF:* 888-417-9899 ■ *Web:* patriot-tech.com	301-695-7500	695-4711	177
Patriot Transportation Holding Inc 200 W Forsyth St 7th Fl .... Jacksonville FL 32202 *NASDAQ: PATI* ■ *TF:* 877-704-1776 ■ *Web:* www.patriottrans.com	877-704-1776		780
Patriot-News 2020 Technology Pkwy Ste 300 .... Mechanicsburg PA 17050 *TF:* 800-692-7207 ■ *Web:* www.pennlive.com	717-255-8100		532-2
Patriots Theater Memorial Dr. .... Trenton NJ 08608 *TF:* 866-847-7682 ■ *Web:* www.state.nj.us	609-984-8484		572
Patrol One 1820 E First St .... Santa Ana CA 92705 *Web:* www.patrol-one.com	714-541-0999		693
Patrona Corp 1919 S Eads St Ste 202 .... Arlington VA 22202 *Web:* www.patronacorp.com	571-255-4707		195
Pattee Hotel LLC 1112 Willis Ave. .... Perry IA 50220 *Web:* hotelpattee.com	515-465-3511		378
Patten & Patten Inc 520 Lookout St .... Chattanooga TN 37403 *TF:* 800-757-3480 ■ *Web:* www.patteninc.com	423-756-3480		194
Patten Monument Co 3980 W River Dr NE .... Comstock Park MI 49321 *TF:* 800-627-5371 ■ *Web:* pattenmonument.com	800-627-5371		45
Patten University 2100 Franklin St Ste 350 .... Oakland CA 94612 *TF:* 866-841-1986 ■ *Web:* patten.edu	866-841-1986		166
Patten, Wornom, Hatten & Diamonstein 12350 Jefferson Ave Ste 300 .... Newport News VA 23602 *TF:* 800-459-1881 ■ *Web:* www.pwhd.com	757-223-4500		428
Pattern Insight Inc 465 Fairchild Dr Ste 209 .... Mountain View CA 94043 *TF:* 866-582-2655 ■ *Web:* patterninsight.com	866-582-2655		177
Pattern Press PO Box 2737 .... Fallbrook CA 92088 *Web:* www.patternpress.com	760-728-3731		637-2
Patterson and Murphy Public Relations 2018 Sul Ross St .... Houston TX 77098 *Web:* www.pattersonandmurphy.com	713-520-7111	520-6346	317
Patterson Dental Supply Inc 1031 Mendota Heights Rd .... Saint Paul MN 55120 *NASDAQ: PDCO* ■ **Fax Area Code:* 651 ■ *TF:* 800-328-5536 ■ *Web:* www.pattersondental.com	800-328-5536	686-9331*	475
Patterson Harkavy LLP 100 Europa Dr Ste 420 .... Chapel Hill NC 27517 *TF:* 800-458-2541 ■ *Web:* pathlaw.com	919-755-1812		41
Patterson Law Firm LLP 505 Fifth Ave Ste 729 .... Des Moines IA 50309 *Web:* pattersonfirm.com	515-283-2147		41
Patterson Office Supplies 3310 N Duncan Rd .... Champaign IL 61822 *TF:* 800-637-1140 ■ *Web:* pattersonofficesupplies.com	217-351-5400		110
Patterson Power Engineers LLC 329 Wauhatchie Pk .... Chattanooga TN 37419 *TF:* 888-679-1306 ■ *Web:* pattersonpowerengineers.com	423-702-9981		261
Patterson Pump Co 2129 Ayersville Rd .... Toccoa GA 30577 *Web:* www.pattersonpumps.com	706-886-2101		641
Patterson Services Inc 2828 Technology Forest Blvd .... The Woodlands TX 77381 *Web:* www.pattersonservices.com	281-875-4006		23
Patterson-Schwartz & Associates Inc 7234 Lancaster Pk Ste 100A .... Hockessin DE 19707 *TF:* 877-456-4663 ■ *Web:* www.pattersonschwartz.com	302-234-5270		652
Patterson-UTI Energy Inc 10713 W Sam Houston Pkwy N Ste 800 .... Houston TX 77064 *NASDAQ: PTEN* ■ *Web:* www.patenergy.com	281-765-7100	765-7175	540
Pattersonville Telephone Co (PTC) 1309 Main St .... Rotterdam Junction NY 12150 *Web:* www.ptcconnect.net	518-887-2121		224
Patti & Sons Inc 8 Berry St .... Brooklyn NY 11249	718-963-3700		189-13
Pattison Sign Group 555 Ellesmere Rd .... Scarborough ON M1R4E8 *Web:* pattisonsign.com	416-759-1111		701
Pattison State Park 6294 S State Rd 35 .... Superior WI 54880 *Web:* dnr.wi.gov	715-399-3111		565
Patton Electronics Co 7622 Rickenbacker Dr .... Gaithersburg MD 20879 *Web:* patton.com	301-975-1000	869-9293	176
Patton Sales Corp 1095 E California St .... Ontario CA 91761 *Web:* www.pattonscorp.com	909-988-0661		320
Patton State Hospital 3102 E Highland Ave .... Patton CA 92369 *Web:* dsh.ca.gov	909-425-7000		374-5
Patton's Inc 3201 S Blvd .... Charlotte NC 28209 *Web:* pattonsinc.com	704-523-4122	525-5148	385
Patton-Kiehl Group Inc 17026 Bull Church Rd .... Woodford VA 22580 *Web:* www.pattonkiehl.com	804-448-8900		5
Patty Palace Ltd 595 Middlefield Rd .... Scarborough ON M1V3S2 *Web:* pattypalace.net	416-297-0510		297-8
Patuxent Cos 2124 Priest Bridge Dr Ste 18 .... Crofton MD 21114 *TF:* 800-628-4942 ■ *Web:* www.paxcos.com	410-793-0181		189-16
Patuxent Wildlife Research Ctr 12100 Beech Forest Rd .... Laurel MD 20708 *Web:* www.usgs.gov	301-497-5500		668
Patz & Hall Wine Co 851 Napa Vly Corporate Way Ste A .... Napa CA 94558 *TF:* 877-265-6700 ■ *Web:* www.patzhall.com	707-931-2440		443
Paul & Dixon Insurance Agency Inc 388 County St .... New Bedford MA 02740 *Web:* pd-ins.com	508-996-8593		390
Paul A. Hundt Financial Services Inc 375 Bishops Way Ste 235 .... Brookfield WI 53005 *Web:* hundtfs.com	262-784-1337		690
Paul B. Brickfield PC 70 Grand Ave .... River Edge NJ 07661 *Web:* brickdonlaw.com	201-488-7707		41
Paul B. Sullivan Insurance Agency 1467 So Main St .... Fall River MA 02724 *Web:* paulsullivanins.com	508-678-9611		390
Paul Baker Printing Inc 220 Riverside Ave .... Roseville CA 95678 *Web:* www.pbaker.com	916-969-8317	783-8950	627
Paul Bunyan Broadcasting Co 502 Beltrami Ave NW .... Bemidji MN 56601 *Web:* www.paulbunyanbroadcasting.com	216-444-1500		647
Paul C. Buff Inc 2725 Bransford Ave .... Nashville TN 37204 *TF:* 800-443-5542 ■ *Web:* www.paulcbuff.com	615-383-3982	383-0676	439
Paul C. Rizzo Associates Inc 500 Penn Center Blvd .... Pittsburgh PA 15235 *Web:* www.rizzoassoc.com	412-856-9700		261
Paul Cribbs Insurance Agency Inc 3565 N Crossing Cir .... Valdosta GA 31602 *Web:* paulcribbs.net	229-247-7127		390
Paul D. Camp Community College 100 N College Dr PO Box 737 .... Franklin VA 23851 *TF:* 855-877-3918 ■ *Web:* www.pdc.edu	757-569-6700	569-6795	162
Paul Davis Systems Canada Ltd 38 Crockford Blvd .... Toronto ON M1R3C2 *TF:* 800-661-5975 ■ *Web:* pauldavis.ca	416-299-8890		192
Paul deLima Company Inc 7546 Morgan Rd .... Liverpool NY 13090 *TF:* 800-962-8864 ■ *Web:* www.delimacoffee.com	315-457-3725	457-3730	296-7
Paul Dry Books Inc (PDB) 1700 Sansom St Ste 700 .... Philadelphia PA 19103 *Web:* pauldrybooks.com	215-231-9939	231-9942	637-2
Paul F. Shanahan 101 Sullys Trail Bldg 20 .... Pittsford NY 14534 *Web:* paulshanahan.com	585-381-9500		41
Paul Frank Collins PC 1 Church St PO Box 1307 .... Burlington VT 05401 *Web:* pfclaw.com	802-658-2311		41
Paul Fredrick Menstyle 223 W Poplar St .... Fleetwood PA 19522 *TF:* 800-247-1417 ■ *Web:* www.paulfredrick.com	610-944-0909	944-6452	157-3
Paul Gauguin Cruises Inc 11100 Main St Ste 300 .... Bellevue WA 98004 *Web:* www.pgcruises.com	425-440-6171		31
Paul Giordano and Sons 6700 Essington Ave .... Philadelphia PA 19153 *Web:* www.pwpm.net	215-755-7900	755-7160	297-7
Paul H. Gesswein & Co 255 Hancock Ave .... Bridgeport CT 06605 *TF:* 800-544-2043 ■ *Web:* www.gesswein.com	203-366-5400	366-3953	407
Paul Hastings Janofsky & Walker LLP 515 S Flower St 25th Fl .... Los Angeles CA 90071 *Web:* www.paulhastings.com	213-683-6000	627-0705	428
Paul Hemmer Construction Co 226 Grandview Dr .... Fort Mitchell KY 41017 *Web:* www.paulhemmer.com	859-341-8300		186
Paul Heuring Motors Inc 720 N Hobart Rd .... Hobart IN 46342 *Web:* www.heuringford.com	219-942-3673		57
Paul J. Krez Co 7831 N Nagle Ave .... Morton Grove IL 60053 *Web:* www.krezgroup.com	847-581-0017		189-9
Paul K. Guillow Inc 40 New Salem St PO Box 229 .... Wakefield MA 01880 *Web:* www.guillow.com	781-245-5255	245-4738	762
Paul King Co 1030 N Owasso Ave .... Tulsa OK 74106 *Web:* www.paulkingco.com	918-592-5464	584-4120	385
Paul Kuhn Gallery 724 11th Ave SW .... Calgary AB T2R0E4 *Web:* www.paulkuhngallery.com	403-263-1162		42

Name / Address	City	State	ZIP	Phone	Fax	Class
Paul L. Jernigan CPA 3103 Airport Blvd Ste 667 *Web:* pljcpa.com	Mobile	AL	36606	251-471-6770	471-6780	2
Paul M. Grist State Park 1546 Grist Rd *Web:* www.alapark.com	Selma	AL	36701	334-872-5846		565
Paul May & Associates Inc 17220 Browning Dr *Web:* paulmayassociates.com	Orland Park	IL	60467	708-479-1111		463
Paul Mitchell the School - Birmingham 1694 Montgomery Hwy *Web:* www.birmingham.paulmitchell.edu	Hoover	AL	35216	205-824-4442		685
Paul Mitchell The School - Boise 50 S 6TH ST STE 1500 *Web:* www.boise.paulmitchell.edu	Boise	ID	83709	208-287-4032		685
Paul Mitchell the School - Dallas Campus 2389 Midway Rd Ste A *Web:* www.dallas.paulmitchell.edu	Carrollton	TX	75006	972-669-0494		685
Paul Mitchell The School - North Haven 97 Washington Ave *TF:* 866-942-5627 ■ *Web:* www.north-haven.paulmitchell.edu	North Haven	CT	06473	203-985-0222		685
Paul Mitchell the School Miami 8905 Dadeland Blvd *Web:* www.miami.paulmitchell.edu	Miami	FL	33156	305-487-9997		685
Paul Moak Automotive Inc 740 Larson St *Web:* www.paulmoak.com	Jackson	MS	39202	601-352-2700		57
Paul Mueller Co 1600 W Phelps St *OTC:* MUEL ■ *TF:* 800-683-5537 ■ *Web:* www.paulmueller.com	Springfield	MO	65802	417-575-9000		386
Paul Quinn College 3837 Simpson Stuart Rd *Web:* pqc-edu.squarespace.com	Dallas	TX	75241	214-379-5449	379-5448	166
Paul Rand (Sen R - KY) 167 Russell Senate Office Bldg *Web:* www.paul.senate.gov	Washington	DC	20510	202-224-4343		342-2
Paul Reed Smith Guitars 380 Log Canoe Cir *Web:* www.prsguitars.com	Stevensville	MD	21666	410-643-9970	643-9980	527
Paul Revere House, The 19 North Sq *Web:* www.paulreverehouse.org	Boston	MA	02113	617-523-2338	523-1775	520
Paul Revere's Pizza International Ltd 47 Kirkwood Court Southwest *Web:* paulreverespizza.com	Cedar Rapids	IA	52404	319-399-1500		670
Paul Risk Associates Inc 11 W State St *Web:* www.paulrisk.com	Quarryville	PA	17566	717-786-7308	786-2848	685
Paul Sawyier Public Library 319 Wapping St *Web:* www.pspl.org	Frankfort	KY	40601	502-352-2665	227-2250	434-3
Paul Schurman Machine Inc 23201 NE 10th Ave *Web:* www.schurmanmfg.com	Ridgefield	WA	98642	360-887-3193	887-4914	454
Paul Smith's College 7833 New York 30 *TF:* 800-421-2605 ■ *Web:* www.paulsmiths.edu	Paul Smiths	NY	12970	518-327-6227		166
Paul Stuart Inc Madison Ave & 45th St *TF:* 800-678-8278 ■ *Web:* www.paulstuart.com	New York	NY	10017	212-682-0320		157-4
Paul Taylor Dance Co 551 Grand St *Web:* www.ptamd.org	New York	NY	10002	212-431-5562		573-1
Paul W. Bryant Museum 300 Paul W Bryant Dr **Fax Area Code:* 205 ■ *TF:* 866-772-2327 ■ *Web:* bryantmuseum.ua.edu	Tuscaloosa	AL	35487	866-772-2327	348-8883*	522
Paul Webb PC 221 N Houston *Web:* paulwebbpc.com	Wharton	TX	77488	979-532-5331		41
Paul Weiss Rifkind Wharton & Garrison LLP 1285 Avenue of the Americas *Web:* www.paulweiss.com	New York	NY	10019	212-373-3000	757-3990	428
Paul Werth Associates 10 N High St Ste 300 *Web:* werthpr.com	Columbus	OH	43215	614-224-8114		636
Paul Wilmot Communications LLC 581 Sixth Ave *Web:* www.paulwilmot.com	New York	NY	10011	212-206-7447		636
Paul Wissmach Glass Company Inc 420 Stephen St PO Box 228 *Web:* www.wissmachglass.com	Paden City	WV	26159	304-337-2253	337-8800	329
Paul's Hauling Ltd 250 Oak Point Hwy *Web:* www.paulshauling.com	Winnipeg	MB	R2R1V1	204-633-4330		314
Paul's Homewood Cafe 919 W St *Web:* www.paulshomewoodcafe.com	Annapolis	MD	21401	410-267-7891		671
Paul's Pharmacy Inc 2345 W Franklin St *TF:* 844-358-1775 ■ *Web:* paulsrx.com	Evansville	IN	47712	812-425-4364	425-5399	237
Paul, Elkind, Branz & Kelton PA 142 E New York Ave *TF:* 800-309-4386 ■ *Web:* paulandelkind.com	Deland	FL	32724	386-734-3020	574-5665	41
Paula Black and Associates 3006 Aviation Ave Ste 3B *Web:* www.paulablack.com	Coconut Grove	FL	33133	305-859-9554	860-0016	344
Paula Cooper Gallery 534 W 21st St *Web:* www.paulacoopergallery.com	New York	NY	10011	212-255-1105	255-5156	42
Paulaur Corp 105 Melrich Rd *Web:* www.paulaur.com	Cranbury	NJ	08512	609-395-8844	395-8850	123
Paulding County 240 Constitution Blvd *Web:* www.paulding.gov	Dallas	GA	30132	770-443-7550	443-7537	338
Paulding County 115 N Williams St Ste 101 *Web:* www.pauldingcountyauditor.com	Paulding	OH	45879	419-399-8205	399-5713	338
Paulding County Carnegie Library 205 S Main St *Web:* www.pauldingcountylibrary.org	Paulding	OH	45879	419-399-2032		434-3
Paulding County Chamber of Commerce 455 Jimmy Campbell Pkwy *Web:* www.pauldingchamber.org	Dallas	GA	30132	770-445-6016		139
Paulding-Putman Electric Co-op 910 N Williams St *TF:* 800-686-2357 ■ *Web:* ppec.coop	Paulding	OH	45879	419-399-5015	399-3026	245
Pauler Communications Inc 7271 Engle Rd Ste 309 *Web:* www.townplanner.com	Cleveland	OH	44130	234-400-0068		627
Paulette Wolf Events & Entertainment Inc 1165 N Clark St Ste 613 *Web:* pwe-e.com	Chicago	IL	60610	312-981-2600		184
Pauli Systems Inc 1820 Walters Ct *TF:* 800-370-1115 ■ *Web:* www.paulisystems.com	Fairfield	CA	94533	707-429-2434		295
Pauline & Thomas Healthcare Inc 610 W College St Ste 170 *Web:* paulineandthomashealthcare.com	Murfreesboro	TN	37130	615-896-8231	896-8232	363
Pauline Books & Media 50 St Paul's Ave *TF:* 800-876-4463 ■ *Web:* www.pauline.org	Boston	MA	02130	617-522-8911	524-8035	637-3
Pauline's 1834 Shelburne Rd *Web:* paulinescafe.com	Burlington	VT	05403	802-862-1081		671
Paull Associates Inc 1311 Chapline St *Web:* paullassociates.com	Wheeling	WV	26003	304-233-3303		390
Paulo Products Company Inc 5711 W Park Ave *Web:* www.paulo.com	Saint Louis	MO	63110	314-647-7500		484
Paulsen Inc 1116 E Hwy 30 *Web:* www.paulseninc.com	Cozad	NE	69130	308-784-3333	784-3310	188-4
Paulsen Marketing Inc 3510 S First Ave Cir *Web:* www.paulsen.ag	Sioux Falls	SD	57105	605-336-1745		195
Paulson Investment Company Inc 2141 W North Ave 2nd Fl *TF:* 855-653-3444 ■ *Web:* www.paulsoninvestment.com	Chicago	IL	60647	503-243-6000		690
Paulson Manufacturing Corp 46752 Rainbow Canyon Rd *TF:* 800-542-2451 ■ *Web:* www.paulsonmfg.com	Temecula	CA	92592	951-676-2451		596
Paulson Press Inc 904 Cambridge Dr *Web:* paulsonpressinc.com	Elk Grove Village	IL	60007	847-290-0080	290-0140	627
Paulus Engineering Inc 2871 Coronado St *Web:* www.paulusengineering.com	Anaheim	CA	92806	714-632-3975		261
Paulus Sokolowski & Sartor LLC 67B Mountain Blvd *Web:* www.psands.com	Warren	NJ	07059	732-560-9700		261
Pav & Broome Watchmakers & Jewelers Inc 2413 14th St *Web:* pavandbroome.com	Gulfport	MS	39501	228-863-3699		410
Pavco Inc 1935 John Crosland Jr Dr *TF:* 800-321-7735 ■ *Web:* www.pavco.com	Charlotte	NC	28208	704-496-6800	496-6810	145
Pavco Industries Inc PO Box 612 *Web:* www.pavcoind.com	Pascagoula	MS	39568	228-762-3172	762-3170	613
Pavek Museum of Broadcasting 3517 Raleigh Ave *Web:* www.pavekmuseum.org	Saint Louis Park	MN	55416	952-926-8198	929-6105	520
Pavement Saw Press (PSP) 321 Empire St *Web:* www.pavementsaw.org	Montpelier	OH	43543	419-485-0524		637-2
Pavex Inc 4400 Gettysburg Rd *Web:* pavexinc.com	Camp Hill	PA	17011	717-761-1502	761-0329	189-5
Pavillion Agency Inc 15 E 40 St Ste 400 *Web:* pavillionagency.com	New York	NY	10016	212-889-6609		260
Pavliks Com 80 Bell Farm Rd *TF:* 877-728-5457 ■ *Web:* www.pavliks.com	Barrie	ON	L4M5K5	705-726-2966		180
Pavone Inc 1006 Market St *Web:* www.pavone.net	Harrisburg	PA	17101	717-234-8886		4
Pavsner Press Inc 9008 Yellow Brick Rd *Web:* pavsnerpress.com	Baltimore	MD	21237	410-687-7550		627
Paw Prints Animal Hospital PC 1229 Powdersville Rd *Web:* pawprintseasley.com	Easley	SC	29642	864-442-9000		794
Pawleys Plantation 70 Tanglewood Dr *TF:* 877-283-2122 ■ *Web:* www.pawleysplantation.com	Pawleys Island	SC	29585	877-283-2122		669
Pawlik/Dorman Partners 2639 N Southport *Web:* www.pawlikdorman.com	Chicago	IL	60614	773-296-0950		194
Pawling Central School District 515 Rt 22 *Web:* www.pawlingschools.org	Pawling	NY	12564	845-855-4600		685
Pawling Corp 32 Nelson Hill Rd PO Box 200 **Fax Area Code:* 845 ■ *TF:* 800-431-3456 ■ *Web:* www.pawling.com	Wassaic	NY	12592	800-431-3456	373-9300*	676
Pawnee County 715 Broadway *TF:* 800-211-4401 ■ *Web:* www.pawneecountykansas.com	Larned	KS	67550	620-285-3721	285-2559	338
Pawnee County 513 Sixth St *TF:* 800-299-1267 ■ *Web:* www.cityofpawnee.com	Pawnee	OK	74058	918-762-3741	392-4408	338
Pawnee State Recreation Area 3900 NW 105th *Web:* outdoornebraska.gov	Lincoln	NE	68524	402-796-2362		565
PAWS (Performing Animal Welfare Society) 11435 Simmerhorn Rd *TF:* 800-513-6560 ■ *Web:* www.pawsweb.org	Galt	CA	95632	209-745-2606	745-1809	48-3
Paws Up Outfitters 40060 Paws Up Rd *Web:* www.pawsup.com	Greenough	MT	59823	406-244-5200		393
Pawsitively Heaven Pet Resort 10051 Kitty Ave *Web:* pawsitivelyheavenpetresort.com	Chicago Ridge	IL	60415	708-636-3647		794
Pawtuckaway State Park 128 Mountain Rd *Web:* www.nhstateparks.org	Nottingham	NH	03290	603-895-3031		565
Pawtucket Credit Union 1200 Central Ave *TF:* 800-298-2212 ■ *Web:* www.pcu.org	Pawtucket	RI	02861	401-722-2212		219
Pawtucket Public Library 13 Summer St *TF:* 800-359-3090 ■ *Web:* www.pawtucketlibrary.org	Pawtucket	RI	02860	401-725-3714		434-3
Pax Machine Works Inc PO Box 338 *Web:* paxmachine.com	Celina	OH	45822	419-586-2337	586-7123	488
Paxcell Group Inc 360 S Abbott Ave *Web:* www.paxcell.com	Milpitas	CA	95035	510-612-5649		393

Name / Address	City	State	ZIP	Phone	Fax	Class
Paxful 3422 Old Capitol Trl Ste 989 *Web:* paxful.com	Wilmington	DE	19808	865-272-9385		39
Paxton Co 1111 Ingleside Rd *TF:* 800-234-7290 ■ *Web:* www.paxtonco.com	Norfolk	VA	23502	757-853-6781		770
Paxton Van Lines Inc 5300 Port Royal Rd *TF:* 800-336-4536 ■ *Web:* www.paxton.com	Springfield	VA	22151	703-321-7600		519
Paxton-Mitchell Co 108 S 12th St *Web:* www.paxton-mitchell.com	Blair	NE	68008	402-426-3131		307
Pay Connect 17701 Cowan Ste 250 *TF:* 800-576-6412 ■ *Web:* www.payconnect.net	Irvine	CA	92614	800-576-6412	866-0006	569
Pay Forward LLC 27200 Tourney Rd Ste 450 *TF:* 844-944-9273 ■ *Web:* payforward.com	Valencia	CA	91355	844-944-9273		49-2
Pay It Forward House 719 Somonauk St *Web:* www.payitforwardhouse.org	Sycamore	IL	60178	815-762-4882		372
Pay Plus Benefits Inc 1110 N Center Pkwy Ste B *TF:* 888-531-5781 ■ *Web:* www.payplusbenefits.com	Kennewick	WA	99336	509-735-1143	735-7668	631
Pay USA Inc 680 American Ave Ste 103 *Web:* payusa.com	King of Prussia	PA	19406	610-337-3000		570
Payability 61 Broadway *Web:* www.payability.com	New York	NY	10006	646-494-8675		49-2
Payan & Payan CPA 7936 W Sahara Ave *Web:* p2cpa.com	Las Vegas	NV	89117	702-233-9526		2
Paychex Inc 911 Panorama Trl S *NASDAQ: PAYX* ■ *TF:* 833-729-8200 ■ *Web:* www.paychex.com	Rochester	NY	14625	585-385-6666		570
Paycom 7501 W Memorial Rd *TF:* 800-580-4505 ■ *Web:* www.paycomonline.com	Oklahoma City	OK	73142	800-580-4505		734
Paycor Inc 4811 Montgomery Rd *TF:* 855-551-2013 ■ *Web:* www.paycor.com	Cincinnati	OH	45212	855-551-2013		2
PayData Payroll Services Inc PO Box 706 *TF:* 800-639-9058 ■ *Web:* www.paydata.com	Essex Junction	VT	05453	802-655-6160	655-7263	570
Payday Payroll Services 6465 College Park Sq Ste 200 *Web:* www.paydaypayroll.com	Virginia Beach	VA	23464	757-523-0605		570
Payden & Rygel 333 S Grand Ave *TF:* 800-572-9336 ■ *Web:* www.payden.com	Los Angeles	CA	90071	213-625-1900		401
PayEase Inc 2332-A Walsh Ave *Web:* www.payeasenet.com	Santa Clara	CA	95051	408-567-9300	567-9370	387
Payette Associates Inc 290 Congress St 5th Fl *Web:* www.payette.com	Boston	MA	02210	617-895-1000		261
Payfactors 2 Adams Pl 2nd Fl *TF:* 800-251-9267 ■ *Web:* payfactors.com	Quincy	MA	02169	800-251-9267		178-8
Payless 3231 SE 6th Ave *TF:* 877-474-6379 ■ *Web:* www.payless.com	Topeka	KS	66607	785-233-5171		301
Payless Drugs Inc 4901 Gary Ave *Web:* mypaylessdrugs.com	Fairfield	AL	35064	205-785-4343		237
Payliance 3 Easton Oval Ste 210 **Fax Area Code:* 614 ■ *TF:* 866-627-2927 ■ *Web:* www.payliance.com	Columbus	OH	43219	866-627-2927	465-1700*	225
Paylogic 2843 Brownsboro Rd Ste 111 *Web:* www.epaylogic.com	Louisville	KY	40206	502-894-0088		2
Paylogix 1025 Old Country Rd Ste 310 *Web:* www.paylogix.com	Westbury	NY	11590	516-408-7800		2
Payment America Systems Inc 450 Tenth Cir N *Web:* www.paymentamerica.com	Nashville	TN	37203	615-255-9200		160
Paymetric Inc 300 Colonial Center Pkwy Ste 130 *TF:* 855-476-0134 ■ *Web:* www.paymetric.com	Roswell	GA	30076	678-242-5281		251
Payne & Garlow Insurance Agency Inc 3744 Teays Valley Rd Ste 101 *Web:* payneandgarlow.com	Hurricane	WV	25526	304-757-6880		390
Payne & Henderson CPAS PC 1240 Southridge Ct Ste 103 *Web:* paynehenderson.com	Hurst	TX	76053	915-592-9696	592-9924	2
Payne and Dolan Inc N3W23650 Badinger Rd *Web:* www.payneanddolan.com	Waukesha	WI	53187	262-524-1700	524-1845	188-4
Payne County 315 W Sixth *Web:* www.paynecounty.org	Stillwater	OK	74074	405-747-8310	747-8304	338
Payne Engineering Co PO Box 70 *TF:* 800-331-1345 ■ *Web:* www.payneng.com	Scott Depot	WV	25560	304-757-7353	757-7305	203
Payne Jr Donald (Rep D - NJ) 103 Cannon House Office Bldg *Web:* www.payne.house.gov	Washington	DC	20515	202-225-3436	225-4160	342-2
Payne Oil Company Inc 962 E Elm St *Web:* payneoil.com	Graham	NC	27253	336-578-0404		316
Payne Printery Inc 3235 Memorial Hwy *TF:* 800-724-3188 ■ *Web:* www.payneinc.net	Dallas	PA	18612	570-675-1147	675-3159	627
Payne Publishers Inc 8707 Quarry Rd Ste B *TF:* 800-854-8669 ■ *Web:* www.paynepub.com	Manassas	VA	20110	703-369-5454	369-0492	637-10
Payne Theological Seminary 1230 Wilberforce Clifton Rd *TF:* 888-816-8933 ■ *Web:* payne.edu	Wilberforce	OH	45384	937-376-2946	376-3330	167-3
Payne Trucking Co 10411 Hall Industrial Dr *Web:* paynetrucking.com	Fredericksburg	VA	22408	540-898-1346		62-5
PayneCrest Electric Inc 10411 Baur Blvd *Web:* www.paynecrest.com	Saint Louis	MO	63132	314-996-0400		189-4
PayneGroup Inc 1218 3rd Ave 19th Fl *TF:* 800-467-2963 ■ *Web:* new.thepaynegroup.com	Seattle	WA	98101	206-344-8966	344-8268	196
Paynes Creek Historic State Park 888 Lake Branch Rd *Web:* www.floridastateparks.org	Bowling Green	FL	33834	863-375-4717	375-4510	565
Paynes Prairie Preserve State Park 100 Savannah Blvd *Web:* www.floridastateparks.org	Micanopy	FL	32667	352-466-3397		565
PayNet Inc 5750 Old Orchard Rd Ste 250 **Fax Area Code:* 847 ■ *TF:* 866-825-3400 ■ *Web:* paynet.com	Skokie	IL	60077	866-825-3400	965-9828*	466
Pay-O-Matic Corp 160 Oak Dr *TF:* 888-545-6311 ■ *Web:* www.payomatic.com	Syosset	NY	11791	888-545-6311		141
PayPal PO Box 45950 *Web:* www.paypal.com	Omaha	NE	68145	402-935-7733		251
Payphone Solutions LLC 123 S 22nd St *TF:* 888-341-4678 ■ *Web:* www.pay-telephones.com	Philadelphia	PA	19103	570-947-9456		393
Paypro Corp 450 Wireless Blvd *Web:* www.payprocorp.com	Hauppauge	NY	11788	631-777-1100		570
PayReel 211 Violet St Ste 100 *Web:* payreel.com	Golden	CO	80401	303-526-4900		514
Payright Payroll Service Inc 468 Great Rd (2A) *Web:* www.payrightpayroll.com	Acton	MA	01720	978-263-5004		2
Payroll 1 PO Box 1568 Ste 250 *TF:* 888-999-7291 ■ *Web:* www.payroll1.com	Birmingham	MI	48009	888-999-7291		2
Payroll Factory, The 18 E Lancaster Ave *Web:* thepayrollfactory.com	Malvern	PA	19355	610-644-4569	647-1364	570
Payroll Masters 855 Bordeaux Way *TF:* 800-963-1428 ■ *Web:* www.payrollmasters.com	Napa	CA	94558	707-226-1428		2
Payroll Network Inc 2092 Gaither Rd *Web:* payrollnetwork.com	Rockville	MD	20850	301-339-6000		570
PAYS (Public Auction Yards) 1802 Minnesota Ave *Web:* www.publicauctionyards.com	Billings	MT	59101	406-245-6447	256-6270	446
Payscape Advisors 1438 W Peachtree St NW Ste 220 *TF:* 888-351-6565 ■ *Web:* www.payscape.com	Atlanta	GA	30324	888-351-6565		509
PaySimple 1515 Wynkoop St Ste 250 *TF:* 800-466-0992 ■ *Web:* www.paysimple.com	Denver	CO	80202	800-466-0992		2
Payson Roundup Newspaper 708 N Beeline Hwy *Web:* www.paysonroundup.com	Payson	AZ	85541	928-474-5251		532-3
Payspan Inc 7751 Belfort Pkwy Ste 200 *TF:* 877-331-7154 ■ *Web:* payspan.com	Jacksonville	FL	32256	877-331-7154		178-1
PayStream Advisors Inc 5334 Lila Wood Cir *Web:* www.paystreamadvisors.com	Charlotte	NC	28209	704-523-7357		195
Payworks Inc 1565 Willson Pl **Fax Area Code:* 204 ■ *TF:* 866-788-3500 ■ *Web:* www.payworks.ca	Winnipeg	MB	R3T4H1	866-788-3500	779-0538*	734
Pazazz Printing Inc 5584 Cote-de-Liesse *Web:* www.pazazz.com	Montreal	QC	H4P1A9	514-856-3330		627
Pazzaluna 360 St Peter St *Web:* www.pazzaluna.com	Saint Paul	MN	55102	651-223-7000		671
Pazzo Pazzo Italian Cuisine 10016-103 Ave NW *Web:* www.pazzopazzo.ca	Edmonton	AB	T5J0G7	780-425-7711		671
Pazzo! 853 Fifth Ave S *Web:* www.gr8food.net	Naples	FL	34102	239-434-8494		671
PB Express Inc 20800 Ctr Ridge Rd Ste 301 *Web:* www.pbexpress.com	Rocky River	OH	44116	440-356-8988		780
PB Hoidale Company Inc 3801 W Harry *TF:* 800-362-0784 ■ *Web:* www.hoidale.com	Wichita	KS	67213	316-942-1361		791
PBA (Professional Bowlers Assn) 719 Second Ave Ste 701 *Web:* www.pba.com	Seattle	WA	98104	206-332-9688	654-6030	48-22
PBA (Professional Beauty Assn) 15825 N 71st St Ste 100 *TF:* 800-468-2274 ■ *Web:* probeauty.org	Scottsdale	AZ	85254	480-281-0424	905-0708	49-18
PBA Engineering PC 12 Kulick Rd *Web:* www.pbanj.com	Fairfield	NJ	07004	973-276-1700		261
PBA Health 6300 Enterprise Rd *TF:* 800-333-8097 ■ *Web:* www.pbahealth.com	Kansas City	MO	64120	816-245-5700		231
PBBS Equipment Corp N59W16500 Greenway Cir *TF:* 800-236-9620 ■ *Web:* pbbs.com	Menomonee Falls	WI	53051	262-252-7575		612
PBCVB (Pine Bluff Convention & Visitors Bureau) 1 Convention Center Plz *TF:* 800-536-7660 ■ *Web:* www.pinebluffconvention.center	Pine Bluff	AR	71601	870-536-7600	850-2105	206
PBE Group, The 1459 Wittens Mill Rd *Web:* pbegrp.com	North Tazewell	VA	24630	276-988-5505		735
PBE Warehouse Inc 12171 Pangborn Ave *Web:* aapcq.nationaloak.com	Downey	CA	90241	562-803-4691		61
PBEC (Polk-Burnett Electric Co-op) 1001 State Rd 35 *TF:* 800-421-0283 ■ *Web:* www.polkburnett.com	Centuria	WI	54824	715-646-2191	646-2404	245
PBG Builders Inc 1000 NorthChase Dr Ste 307 *Web:* www.pbgbuilders.com	Goodlettsville	TN	37072	615-256-2200		186
PBI (Pulse Biomedical Inc) 112 Ivy Ln *Web:* www.qrscard.com	King of Prussia	PA	19406	610-666-5510		475
PBI Market Equipment Inc 2667 Gundry Ave *TF:* 800-421-3753 ■ *Web:* www.pbimarketing.com	Signal Hill	CA	90755	562-595-4785	426-2262	300
PBI/Gordon Corp 1217 W 12th St *TF:* 800-821-7925 ■ *Web:* www.pbigordon.com	Kansas City	MO	64101	816-421-4070	474-0462	280
PBK Bank Inc 120 Frontier Blvd *TF:* 877-230-3711 ■ *Web:* pbkbank.com	Stanford	KY	40484	606-365-7098		70
PBM Corp 20600 Chagrin Blvd Ste 450 *TF:* 800-341-5809 ■ *Web:* www.pbmcorp.com	Cleveland	OH	44122	216-283-7999	283-7931	39
PBM Graphics Inc PO Box 13603 *TF:* 800-849-8100 ■ *Web:* www.pbmgraphics.com	Durham	NC	27703	919-544-6222	544-6695	627
PBM Inc 1070 Sandy Hill Rd *TF:* 800-967-4726 ■ *Web:* www.pbmvalve.com	Irwin	PA	15642	724-863-0550	864-9255	790
PBP (Powered by Professionals) 1460 Broadway *Web:* poweredbyprofessionals.com	New York	NY	10036	646-278-6735		194
PBR (Professional Bull Riders Inc) 101 W Riverwalk *TF:* 800-732-1727 ■ *Web:* www.pbr.com	Pueblo	CO	81003	719-242-2800		48-15
PBS 7013 S 216th St *TF:* 877-727-7515 ■ *Web:* pbsbuilds.com	Kent	WA	98032	253-395-5550	395-5575	534
PBS (Public Broadcasting Service) 2100 Crystal Dr *TF:* 866-864-0828 ■ *Web:* www.pbs.org	Arlington	VA	22202	703-739-5051		739

Name / Address	City	State	ZIP	Phone	Fax	Class
PBS (Pacific Building Systems) 2100 N Pacific Hwy TF: 800-727-7844 ■ Web: www.pbsbuildings.com	Woodburn	OR	97071	503-981-9581	981-9584	105
PBS (Precision Blasting Services) 6990 Summers Rd Web: www.idc-pbs.com	Montville	OH	44064	440-474-6700	968-3967	261
PBS Engineering & Environmental Inc 1500 D St Web: www.pbsenv.com	Vancouver	WA	98663	360-690-4331		261
PBS39 2501 E Coliseum Blvd Web: wfwa.org	Fort Wayne	IN	46805	260-484-8839		741-51
PBSP (Pelican Bay State Prison) 5905 Lake Earl Dr PO Box 7000 Web: cdcr.ca.gov	Crescent City	CA	95531	707-465-1000		213
PC Age Career Institute 2815 Kennedy Blvd 3rd Fl TF: 888-269-5760 ■ Web: www.pcage.edu	Jersey City	NJ	07306	201-761-0144	761-0199	167-3
PC Campana Inc 1374 E 28th St Web: www.pccampana.com	Lorain	OH	44055	440-246-6500		492
PC Connection Inc 730 Milford Rd Rt 101A NASDAQ: PCCC ■ TF: 888-213-0607 ■ Web: www.connection.com	Merrimack	NH	03054	603-683-2000	683-5766	179
PC Connection Inc MacConnection Div 730 Milford Rd TF: 888-213-0260 ■ Web: www.macconnection.com	Merrimack	NH	03054	888-213-0260		179
PC Doctors LLC 2001 S Central Ave Web: pcdrs.com	Medford	WI	54451	715-748-1911		175
PC Focus Computer Co 7500 Mountain Ave Web: pcfocus.net	Orangevale	CA	95662	916-988-0404		177
PC Godfrey Inc 1816 Rozzelles Ferry Rd Web: www.pcgodfreyservice.com	Charlotte	NC	28208	704-334-9715	376-5186	189-10
PC Innovations 3699 W Henrietta Rd Ste 15 Web: www.pcinnovations.com	Rochester	NY	14623	585-340-1555		175
PC Krause & Associates Inc 3000 Kent Ave Web: pcka.com	West Lafayette	IN	47906	765-464-8997		261
PC Professional Inc 1615 Webster St Web: www.pcprofessional.com	Oakland	CA	94612	510-874-5871		175
PC Professor Computer Training & Repair 7146 Beracasa Way Web: www.pcprofessor.com	Boca Raton	FL	33433	561-750-7879		507
PC Richard & Son Inc 150 Price Pkwy TF: 800-696-2000 ■ Web: www.pcrichard.com	Farmingdale	NY	11735	631-773-4900		35
PC Synergy Inc 804 N Twin Oaks Valley Rd Ste 122 Web: pcsynergy.com	San Marcos	CA	92069	760-410-1677		177
PC Treasures Inc 3720 Lapeer Rd Web: www.pctreasures.com	Auburn Hills	MI	48326	248-969-7800		174
PC Works Plus Inc 109 Stadium Dr PO Box 190 TF: 800-626-4293 ■ Web: www.pcworksplus.com	Bellwood	PA	16617	814-742-9750		180
PC/Nametag 124 Horizon Dr *Fax Area Code: 800 ■ TF: 877-626-3824 ■ Web: www.pcnametag.com	Verona	WI	53593	888-354-7868	233-9787*	178-8
PCA (Pittsburgh Center for the Arts) 1047 Shady Ave Web: pghartsmedia.org	Pittsburgh	PA	15232	412-361-0455	361-8338	50-2
PCA (Parking Company of America) 11101 Lakewood Blvd TF: 888-220-1282 ■ Web: www.parkpca.com	Downey	CA	90241	562-862-2118		562
PCA (Portland Cement Assn) 5420 Old Orchard Rd Web: www.cement.org	Skokie	IL	60077	847-966-6200	966-9781	49-3
PCA (Presbyterian Church in America) 1700 N Brown Rd Ste 105 Web: pcanet.org	Lawrenceville	GA	30043	678-825-1000		48-20
PCA (PCA Technology Solutions) 12824 Cantrell Rd Ste 200 Web: www.pcatechsolutions.com	Little Rock	AR	72223	501-907-4722		180
PCA Engineering Inc 57 Cannonball Rd PO Box 196 TF: 800-666-7221 ■ Web: www.pcaengineering.com	Pompton Lakes	NJ	07442	973-616-4501	616-4451	261
PCA Technology Group 303 Cayuga Rd Ste 100 Web: pcatg.com	Buffalo	NY	14225	716-632-5881		177
PCA Technology Solutions (PCA) 12824 Cantrell Rd Ste 200 Web: www.pcatechsolutions.com	Little Rock	AR	72223	501-907-4722		180
PCB Group Inc 3425 Walden Ave TF: 800-828-8840 ■ Web: www.pcb.com	Depew	NY	14043	716-684-0001	684-0987	253
PCC (Pensacola Cultural Ctr) 400 S Jefferson St Web: www.pensacolalittletheatre.com	Pensacola	FL	32502	850-432-2042		572
PCC Structurals Inc 4600 SE Harney Dr Web: www.pccstructurals.com	Portland	OR	97206	503-777-3881		306
PCCC (Pennsylvania Commission for Community Colleges) 800 N 3rd St Ste 405 Web: pacommunitycolleges.org	Harrisburg	PA	17102	717-232-7584		49-19
PCCI 300 N Lee St Web: www.pccii.com	Alexandria	VA	22314	703-684-2060		256
Pcd Carbide Tool Co Precorp Inc 2024 N Chappel Dr Web: www.precorp.net	Spanish Fork	UT	84660	801-798-5425		697
PCE Pacific Inc 22011 26th Ave SE TF: 800-321-4723 ■ Web: www.pcepacific.com	Bothell	WA	98021	425-487-9600	487-1114	358
PCE Systems 28530 Orchard Lake Rd Web: www.pcesystems.com	Farmington Hills	MI	48334	248-932-4888		138
PCES (Power & Control Engineering Solutions LLC) 12611 E 60th St Web: www.pcescorp.com	Tulsa	OK	74146	918-627-7237		261
PCG (Piedmont Construction Group LLC) 107 Gateway Dr Ste B Web: www.piedmontconstructiongroup.com	Macon	GA	31210	478-405-8907	405-8908	186
PCH Litho Inc 1497 Poinsettia Ave 159 Web: www.pchlitho.com	Vista	CA	92081	760-798-1190	798-1186	627
PCHMC (Parkview Community Hospital Medical Ctr) 3865 Jackson St Web: www.pchmc.org	Riverside	CA	92503	951-688-2211		374-3
PCI (Pioneer Circuits Inc) 3000 S Shannon St Web: www.pioneercircuits.com	Santa Ana	CA	92704	714-641-3132		625
PCI (Peninsula Copper Industries Inc) 220 Calumet St Web: www.pencopper.com	Lake Linden	MI	49945	906-296-9918		145
PCI (Protect Controls Inc) 3212 Old Hwy 105 E Web: www.protectcontrols.com	Conroe	TX	77301	713-691-5183	691-0159	105
PCI (Phoenix Cable Inc) 10801 N 24th Ave Ste 115-116 TF: 833-807-3855 ■ Web: www.phoenixcable.com	Phoenix	AZ	85029	602-870-8870	870-8464	116
PCI (Precast/Prestressed Concrete Institute) 200 W Adams St Ste 2100 Web: www.pci.org	Chicago	IL	60606	312-786-0300	786-0353	49-3
PCI (Patent Calls Inc) 214 W Fannin St Web: www.patentcalls.com	Marshall	TX	75670	512-371-4120		387
PCI (Pierson Construction Inc) 2103 Burlington Ste 201 Web: www.piersonconstruction.net	Columbia	MO	65202	573-445-8493	445-5015	186
PCI (Project Concern Intl) 5151 Murphy Canyon Rd Ste 320 Web: www.pciglobal.org	San Diego	CA	92123	858-279-9690	694-0294	48-5
PCI (Professional Communications Inc) 1223 W Main St Ste 1427 TF: 800-337-9838 ■ Web: pcibooks.com	Durant	OK	74702	580-745-9838	745-9837	637-2
PCI Academy Iowa (Ames) 309 Kitty Hawk Dr TF: 800-956-3781 ■ Web: www.pci-academy.com	Ames	IA	50010	515-232-7250	956-3783	167-3
PCI Dealer's School 4575 W Flamingo Rd Web: www.pcidealerschool.com	Las Vegas	NV	89103	702-877-4724		685
PCI Geomatics Inc 90 Allstate Pkwy Ste 501 Web: www.pcigeomatics.com	Markham	ON	L3R6H3	905-764-0614		174
PCI Group Inc 11632 Harrisburg Rd Web: www.pcigroup.com	Fort Mill	SC	29707	803-578-7700		627
PCI Health Training Ctr 8101 John W Carpenter Fwy Web: www.pcihealth.edu	Dallas	TX	75247	214-380-4322		167-3
PCI LLC 6811 Benjamin Franklin Dr Ste 200 Web: gopci.com	Columbia	MD	21046	410-312-0885	312-0888	463
PCI Paper Conversions Inc 6761 Thompson Rd N Web: www.stikwithit.com	Syracuse	NY	13211	315-437-1641		548
PCIO 172 Via Serena Web: pcioit.com	Alamo	CA	94507	925-552-7953		175
PCiRoads LLC 14123 42nd St NE Web: www.pciroads.com	Saint Michael	MN	55376	763-497-6100	497-6101	188-4
PCL (Planning and Conservation League) 1107 9th St Ste 901 Web: www.pcl.org	Sacramento	CA	95814	916-822-5631	822-5650	48-13
PCL Construction Enterprises Inc 2000 S Colorado Blvd Ste 2 500 Web: www.pcl.com	Denver	CO	80222	303-365-6500		186
PCLD (Pinal County Library District) 92 W Butte Ave Web: www.pinalcountyaz.gov	Florence	AZ	85132	520-866-6457	866-6533	431-3
Pcm Networking 2121 W First St TF: 866-726-6381 ■ Web: www.pcmnetworking.com	Fort Myers	FL	33901	239-334-1615	334-3275	180
Pcm Products Inc 1225 White Dr Web: www.pcmproducts.com	Titusville	FL	32780	321-267-7500	267-9138	481
PCMA (Pharmaceutical Care Management Assn) 325 Seventh St NW Web: www.pcmanet.org	Washington	DC	20004	202-756-5700		49-8
PCMA (Professional Convention Management Assn) 35 E Wacker Dr Ste 500 TF: 877-827-7262 ■ Web: www.pcma.org	Chicago	IL	60601	312-423-7262	423-7222	49-12
PCMC (Paper Converting Machine Co) 2300 S Ashland Ave Web: www.pcmc.com	Green Bay	WI	54307	920-494-5601	494-8865	556
PCO Services Corp 5840 Falbourne St TF: 800-800-6754 ■ Web: www.orkincanada.ca	Mississauga	ON	L5R4B5	905-502-9700		577
PCOM (Philadelphia College of Osteopathic Medicine) 4170 City Ave TF: 800-999-6998 ■ Web: www.pcom.edu	Philadelphia	PA	19131	215-871-6100		800
PCPS (Pulaski County School District) 202 N Washington Ave Web: www.pcva.us	Pulaski	VA	24301	540-994-2550		685
PCRM (Physicians Committee for Responsible Medicine) 5100 Wisconsin Ave NW Ste 400 TF: 866-416-7276 ■ Web: www.pcrm.org	Washington	DC	20016	202-686-2210	686-2216	49-8
PCS (Portland Center Stage) 128 NW Eleventh Ave Web: www.pcs.org	Portland	OR	97209	503-445-3700	445-3701	573-4
PCS (Petaluma City Schools) 200 Douglas St Web: www.petalumacityschools.org	Petaluma	CA	94952	707-778-4813		685
PCS (Precision Computer Services Inc) 175 Constitution Blvd S Web: precisiongroup.com	Shelton	CT	06484	203-929-0000	929-8800	175
PCS (People Creating Success Inc) 1000 Hill St Ste 320 Web: www.pcs-services.org	Ventura	CA	93003	805-644-9480	644-9473	672
PCS Co 34488 Doreka Dr TF: 800-521-0546 ■ Web: www.pcs-company.com	Fraser	MI	48026	586-294-7780		757
PCSB (Putnam County Savings Bank) 2477 Rt 6 PO Box 417 Web: www.pcsb.com	Brewster	NY	10509	845-279-7101	279-9175	71
PCSC Corp 3541 Challenger St TF: 800-899-7272 ■ Web: www.pcscsecurity.com	Torrance	CA	90503	310-303-3600	303-3609	692

	Phone	Fax	Class
PCSD (Pickens County School District) 1348 Griffin Mill Rd .... Easley SC 29640 *Web:* www.pickens.k12.sc.us	864-397-1000	855-8159	685
PCstar Communications PO Box 26141 .... Salt Lake City UT 84126 *Web:* www.pcstarnet.com	801-232-8713		175
PCT (Power & Composite Technologies LLC) 200 Wallins Corners Rd .... Amsterdam NY 12010 *Web:* www.pactinc.com	518-843-6825	843-6723	249
PCT Enterprises Inc 145 Middlefield Ct .... Brentwood CA 94513 *Web:* www.precisioncabinets.com	925-634-5552		115
PCTA (Pacific Crest Trail Assn) 1331 Garden Hwy .... Sacramento CA 95833 *Web:* www.pcta.org	916-285-1846	285-1865	48-23
PCTC (Park County Travel Council) 836 Sheridan Ave PO Box 2454 .... Cody WY 82414 *TF:* 800-393-2639 ■ *Web:* www.codyyellowstone.org	307-587-2297	527-6228	206
PCTEL Inc 471 Brighton Dr .... Bloomingdale IL 60108 *NASDAQ: PCTI* ■ *TF:* 800-323-9122 ■ *Web:* www.pctel.com	630-372-6800	372-8077	178-7
PCTV Inc PO Box 286 .... Keene NH 03431 *Web:* www.pctv.com	603-863-9322		514
PCX Aerosystems 300 Fenn Rd .... Newington CT 06111 *Web:* pcxaero.com	860-666-2471		22
PD Holdings LLC 2629 S Hanley Rd .... Saint Louis MO 63144 *TF:* 800-452-4682 ■ *Web:* particledynamics.com	314-968-2376	781-3354	582
PDA (Presbyterian Disaster Assistance) 100 Witherspoon St .... Louisville KY 40202 **Fax Area Code:* 502 ■ *TF:* 800-728-7228 ■ *Web:* www.presbyterianmission.org	800-728-7228	569-8039*	48-5
PDA (Property Damage Appraisers Inc) 6100 SW Blvd Ste 200 .... Fort Worth TX 76109 *TF:* 800-749-7324 ■ *Web:* www.pdacorporation.com	800-749-7324	866-4732	310
PDA (Parental Drug Assn) 4350 East-West Hwy .... Bethesda MD 20814 *Web:* www.pda.org	301-656-5900	986-1093	49-8
PDA-Pro 915 LeMay Dr .... Evansville IN 47712 **Fax Area Code:* 815 ■ *Web:* mochau.com	812-449-4216	327-0997*	177
PDB (Paul Dry Books Inc) 1700 Sansom St Ste 700 .... Philadelphia PA 19103 *Web:* pauldrybooks.com	215-231-9939	231-9942	637-2
PDC (Porterville Developmental Ctr) 26501 Ave 140 PO Box 2000 .... Porterville CA 93258 *Web:* www.dds.ca.gov	559-782-2222	784-5630	230
PDC (PDC Energy Inc) 1775 Sherman St Ste 3000 .... Denver CO 80203 *NASDAQ: PDCE* ■ *TF:* 800-624-3821 ■ *Web:* www.pdce.com	303-860-5800		536
PDC Energy Inc (PDC) 1775 Sherman St Ste 3000 .... Denver CO 80203 *NASDAQ: PDCE* ■ *TF:* 800-624-3821 ■ *Web:* www.pdce.com	303-860-5800		536
PDC Facilities Inc 700 Walnut Ridge Dr .... Hartland WI 53029 *TF:* 800-545-5998 ■ *Web:* www.pdcbiz.com	262-367-7700		186
PDC Machines Inc 1875 Stout Dr .... Warminster PA 18974 *Web:* www.pdcmachines.com	215-443-9442	443-8530	454
PDCC (Palm Desert Chamber of Commerce) 72559 Hwy 111 .... Palm Desert CA 92260 *Web:* pdacc.org	760-346-6111	346-3263	139
PDE & Excelle College 3251 Adams Ave Ste A .... San Diego CA 92116 *Web:* www.sandiegodentaltraining.com	619-584-6262		167-3
PDEMC (Pee Dee Electric Membership Corp) 575 US Hwy 52 S .... Wadesboro NC 28170 *TF:* 800-992-1626 ■ *Web:* www.pdemc.com	704-694-2114	694-9636	245
PDF (Parkinson's Disease Foundation) 1359 Broadway .... New York NY 10018 *TF:* 800-457-6676 ■ *Web:* parkinson.org	212-923-4700	923-4778	48-17
PDF Solutions Inc 333 W San Carlos St Ste 700 .... San Jose CA 95110 *NASDAQ: PDFS* ■ *Web:* www.pdf.com	408-280-7900	280-7915	178-10
PDG (Publishers Design Group Inc) 1655 Booth Rd .... Roseville CA 95747 *TF:* 800-587-6666 ■ *Web:* www.publishersdesign.com	916-784-0500		637-2
PDI 100 American Metro Blvd Ste 201 ..... Hamilton Township NJ 08619 *TF:* 800-242-7494 ■ *Web:* www.ph-pdi.com	215-525-5207		195
PDI (Preservation Delaware Inc) 211 Delaware St .... New Castle DE 19720 *Web:* preservationde.org	302-322-7100		50-3
PDI 3407 S 31st St .... Temple TX 76502 *Web:* www.pdisoftware.com	254-771-7100	771-7117	178-1
PDI 4200 Oakleys Ct .... Richmond VA 23223 *TF:* 800-225-4838 ■ *Web:* www.pdicorp.com	804-737-9880		729
PDI (Priority Distribution Inc) 330 Milltown Rd Ste C31 .... East Brunswick NJ 08816 **Fax Area Code:* 877 ■ *Web:* www.prioritydistribution.com	732-234-1950	734-3751*	311
PDI Communications Inc 6353 W Rogers Cir .... Boca Raton FL 33487 *TF:* 800-242-1606 ■ *Web:* pdiconnected.com	561-998-0600		246
PDI Financial Group 601 N Lynndale Dr .... Appleton WI 54914 *TF:* 800-234-7341 ■ *Web:* pdifinancial.com	920-739-2303	739-2205	690
PDK (Phi Delta Kappa Intl) 408 N Union St .... Bloomington IN 47407 *TF:* 800-766-1156 ■ *Web:* pdkintl.org	812-339-1156	339-0018	48-16
PDM Healthcare 24700 Ctr Ridge Rd Ste 110 .... Cleveland OH 44145 *Web:* www.pdmhealthcare.com	440-871-1721	871-1722	194
PDMA (Product Development & Management Assn) 330 N Wabash Ave Ste 2000 .... Chicago IL 60611 *TF:* 800-232-5241 ■ *Web:* www.pdma.org	312-321-5145		49-12
PDMA Corp 5909-C Hampton Oaks Pkwy .... Tampa FL 33610 *TF:* 800-476-6463 ■ *Web:* www.pdma.com	813-621-6463		201
PDQ Manufacturing 2754 Creek Hill Rd .... Leola PA 17540 *TF:* 800-441-9692 ■ *Web:* www.pdqlocks.com	717-656-4281		350
PDQ Print Center Inc 301 Mulberry St .... Taylor PA 18517 *Web:* www.pdqprint.com	570-343-0414		627
PDQ Printing Inc 3820 S Vly View Blvd .... Las Vegas NV 89103 *TF:* 800-437-2920 ■ *Web:* www.pdqvegas.com	702-876-3235		627

	Phone	Fax	Class
PDQ Tool & Stamping Co 14901 Greenwood Rd .... Dolton IL 60419 *Web:* www.pdqtoolandstamping.com	708-841-3000	841-7936	757
PDR (Professional Desk References Inc) 5543 Edmondson Pike Ste 183 .... Nashville TN 37211 *TF:* 888-335-7664 ■ *Web:* www.greenbookofsongs.com	615-832-1942		637-2
PDR CPA Inc 29750 US Hwy 19 N .... Clearwater FL 33761 *Web:* www.pdr-cpa.com	727-785-4447		2
PDRA (Paint & Decorating Retailers Assn) 1401 Triad Center Dr .... Saint Peters MO 63376 *TF:* 800-737-0107 ■ *Web:* www.pdra.org	636-326-2636		49-18
PDS (Personnel Data Systems Inc) 470 Norritown Rd .... Blue Bell PA 19422 *TF:* 800-243-8737 ■ *Web:* www.pdssoftware.com	610-238-4600	238-4550	178-1
PDS (Packaging Distribution Services Inc) 2308 Sunset Rd .... Des Moines IA 50321 *TF:* 800-747-2699 ■ *Web:* www.pdspack.com	515-243-3156	243-1741	559
PDS (Paragon Development Systems Inc) 13400 Bishops Ln Ste 190 .... Brookfield WI 53005 *TF:* 800-966-6090 ■ *Web:* pdsit.net	262-569-5300		174
PDS Agent Inc 2333 Bergdolt Rd .... Evansville IN 47711 *TF:* 800-735-0087 ■ *Web:* www.pdsagent.com	812-422-8700		780
PDS Gaming Corp 6280 Annie Oakley Dr .... Las Vegas NV 89120 *TF:* 800-479-3612 ■ *Web:* www.pdsgaming.com	702-736-0700		216
PDT (Product Development Technologies Inc) 1 Corporate Dr Ste 110 .... Lake Zurich IL 60047 *Web:* pdt.com	847-821-3033	821-3020	261
PDX Inc 101 Jim Wright Fwy S Ste 200 .... Fort Worth TX 76108 *TF:* 800-433-5719 ■ *Web:* www.pdxinc.com	800-433-5719		180
PE (Pump Engineering Co) 9807 Jordan Cir .... Santa Fe Springs CA 90670 **Fax Area Code:* 562 ■ *TF:* 800-560-7867 ■ *Web:* www.pumpengineering.net	800-560-7867	944-4768*	385
PE Guerin Inc 23 Jane St .... New York NY 10014 *Web:* peguerin.com	212-243-5270	727-2290	350
PE Kramme Inc 404 Monroeville Rd .... Monroeville NJ 08343 *Web:* www.pekramme.com	856-358-8151		780
Pea Ridge National Military Park 15930 Hwy 62 E .... Garfield AR 72732 *Web:* www.nps.gov	479-451-8122	451-0219	564
Pea River Electric Co-op 1311 W Roy Parker Rd PO Box 969 .... Ozark AL 36361 *TF:* 800-264-7732 ■ *Web:* www.peariver.com	334-774-2545		245
Peabody & Arnold LLP 600 Atlantic Ave .... Boston MA 02210 *Web:* www.peabodyarnold.com	617-951-2100	951-2125	428
Peabody Area (PACC) *Chamber of Commerce* 49 Lowell St 1st Fl .... Peabody MA 01960 *TF:* 888-287-9400 ■ *Web:* www.peabodychamber.com	978-531-0384		139
Peabody Auditorium 600 Auditorium Blvd .... Daytona Beach FL 32118 *Web:* www.peabodyauditorium.org	386-671-3460	239-6435	572
Peabody Energy Corp Peabody Plz 701 Market St .... Saint Louis MO 63101 *Web:* www.peabodyenergy.com	314-342-3400		501
Peabody Essex Museum E India Sq 161 Essex St .... Salem MA 01970 *TF:* 866-745-1876 ■ *Web:* www.pem.org	978-745-9500		520
Peabody Institute Library 82 Main St .... Peabody MA 01960 *Web:* www.peabodylibrary.org	978-531-0100		434-3
Peabody Institute of the Johns Hopkins University *Peabody Conservatory of Music* 1 E Mt Vernon Pl .... Baltimore MD 21202 **Fax Area Code:* 410 ■ *TF:* 800-368-2521 ■ *Web:* www.peabody.jhu.edu	667-208-6500	659-8102*	166
Peabody Landscape Construction Inc 2253 Dublin Rd .... Columbus OH 43228 *Web:* www.peabodylandscape.com	614-488-2877		776
Peabody Memphis, The 149 Union Ave .... Memphis TN 38103 *Web:* www.peabodymemphis.com	901-529-4000		379
Peabody Museum of Archaeology & Ethnology 11 Divinity Ave .... Cambridge MA 02138 *Web:* www.peabody.harvard.edu	617-496-1027	495-7535	520
Peabody Office Furniture Corp 234 Congress St .... Boston MA 02110 *Web:* www.peabodyoffice.com	617-542-1902		320
Peabody Properties Inc 536 Granite St .... Braintree MA 02184 *Web:* www.ayerlofts.com	781-794-1000		652
Peabody River King State Fish & Wildlife Area 10981 Conservation Rd .... Baldwin IL 62217 *Web:* www.dnr.illinois.gov	618-785-2555		565
Peace Action 8630 Fenton St .... Silver Spring MD 20910 *TF:* 800-228-1228 ■ *Web:* www.peaceaction.org	301-565-4050	565-0850	48-5
Peace Arch Historical State Park 19 A St .... Blaine WA 98231 *Web:* www.parks.state.wa.us	360-332-8221		565
Peace Arch Hospital 15521 Russell Ave .... White Rock BC V4B2R4 *Web:* www.pahfoundation.ca	604-535-4520	541-5820	374-2
Peace Bridge Duty Free Inc 1 Peace Bridge Plz .... Fort Erie ON L2A5N1 *TF:* 800-361-1302 ■ *Web:* www.dutyfree.ca	800-361-1302		241
Peace Corps 1111 20th St NW .... Washington DC 20526 *TF:* 800-424-8580 ■ *Web:* www.peacecorps.gov	855-855-1961		340-20
Peace Corps Regional Offices *Chicago Regional Office* 230 S Dearborn St Ste 2020 .... Chicago IL 60604 *Web:* www.peacecorps.gov	312-353-4990	353-4192	340-20
Los Angeles Regional Office 800 N State College Blvd .... Fullerton CA 92831 *Web:* www.peacecorps.gov	310-356-1100	356-1125	340-20
Mid-Atlantic Regional Office 1525 Wilson Blvd Ste 100 .... Arlington VA 22209 *Web:* www.peacecorps.gov	202-692-1040		340-20
New York Regional Office 201 Varick St Ste 1025 .... New York NY 10014 *Web:* www.peacecorps.gov	212-352-5440	352-5441	340-20

Name / Address	City	State	ZIP	Phone	Fax	Class
Northwest Regional Office 1275 First Street NE	Washington	DC	20002	206-553-5490	553-2343	340-20
Web: www.peacecorps.gov						
San Francisco Regional Office 1301 Clay St Ste 620-N	Oakland	CA	94612	510-452-8444	452-8441	340-20
Web: www.peacecorps.gov						
Peace Health Medical Group 1162 Willamette St	Eugene	OR	97401	541-687-6234		374-3
Web: www.peacehealth.org						
Peace Operations Training Institute Inc 1309 Jamestown Rd Ste 202	Williamsburg	VA	23185	757-253-6933		166
Web: www.peaceopstraining.org						
Peace River Chamber of Commerce 10006 96 Ave PO Box 6599	Peace River	AB	T8S1S4	780-624-4166	525-4423*	137
**Fax Area Code:* 888 ■ *Web:* peaceriverchamber.com						
Peace River Electric Cooperative Inc 210 Metheny Rd PO Box 1310	Wauchula	FL	33873	800-282-3824	201-1814*	245
**Fax Area Code:* 866 ■ *TF:* 800-282-3824 ■ *Web:* www.preco.coop						
Peace River Regional Medical Ctr 2500 Harbor Blvd	Port Charlotte	FL	33952	941-766-4122		374-3
Web: www.bayfrontcharlotte.com						
Peace Wapiti Public School Division No 76 8611 108 St	Grande Prairie	AB	T8V4C5	780-532-8133		685
Web: www.pwsd76.ab.ca						
PeaceHealth Laboratories 123 International Way	Springfield	OR	97477	541-341-8010		415
TF: 800-826-3616 ■ *Web:* www.peacehealthlabs.org						
Peach County 205 W Church St	Fort Valley	GA	31030	478-825-2535	825-2678	338
Web: www.peachcounty.net						
Peach County School District Inc 523 Vineville St	Fort Valley	GA	31030	478-825-5933	825-9970	685
Web: www.peachschools.org						
Peach Farm 4 Tyler St	Boston	MA	02111	617-482-3332		671
Web: peachfarmboston.com						
Peach State Ambulance Inc 105 Peach State Ct	Tyrone	GA	30290	440-497-4021		30
Web: www.b-global.biz						
Peach Trader Inc 6286 Dawson Blvd	Norcross	GA	30093	404-752-6715		791
TF: 888-949-9613 ■ *Web:* www.acitydiscount.com						
Peach Tree 6800 Eastwood Tfwy	Kansas City	MO	64129	816-923-0099		671
Web: www.peachtreerestaurants.com						
Peachin Schwartz & Weingardt Pc 9775 Crosspoint Blvd Ste 100	Indianapolis	IN	46256	317-574-4280	574-4286	2
Web: psw-cpa.com						
Peachtree Hotel Group LLC 1 Alliance Ctr 3500 Lenox Rd Ste 625	Atlanta	GA	30326	404-497-4111		379
Web: peachtreehotelgroup.com						
Peachtree Lighting Inc 7230 Industrial Blvd NE	Covington	GA	30014	770-787-8490	787-8521	439
Web: www.peachtreelighting.com						
Peachtree Packaging Inc 770 Marathon Pkwy	Lawrenceville	GA	30046	770-822-1304		8
Web: www.peachtreepackaging.com						
Peachtree Planning Corp 5040 Roswell Rd NE	Atlanta	GA	30342	404-260-1600	260-1700	113
TF: 800-366-0839 ■ *Web:* www.peachtreeplanning.com						
Peachtree Publishers Ltd 1700 Chattahoochee Ave NW	Atlanta	GA	30318	404-876-8761	875-2578	637-2
TF: 800-241-0113 ■ *Web:* www.peachtree-online.com						
Peachtree Residential Properties 7380 McGinnis Ferry Rd	Suwanee	GA	30024	770-622-2522		187
Web: www.peachtreeresidential.com						
Peacock Alley 422 E Main St	Bismarck	ND	58501	701-221-2333		671
Web: www.peacock-alley.com						
Peacock Cafe 3251 Prospect St NW	Washington	DC	20007	202-625-2740	625-1402	671
Web: www.peacockcafe.com						
Peacock Construction Inc 3421 Golden Gate Way	LaFayette	CA	94549	925-283-4550		186
Web: www.peacockconstruction.com						
Peacock, Keller, & Ecker LLP 70 E Beau St	Washington	PA	15301	724-222-4520		41
Web: peacockkeller.com						
Peak Completion Technologies Inc 7710 W Hwy 80	Midland	TX	79706	432-684-4155		539
TF: 866-684-7325 ■ *Web:* peakcompletions.com						
Peak Energy Inc PO Box 1110	Waynesville	NC	28786	828-456-9035	456-9031	324
Web: peakenergyonline.com						
Peak Environmental LLC 26 Kennedy Blvd Ste A	East Brunswick	NJ	08816	732-326-1010	326-1012	196
Web: www.peak-environmental.com						
Peak Financial Management Inc The Wellesley Office Pk 20 William St Ste 135	Wellesley	MA	02481	781-487-9500	487-9501	401
TF: 877-567-9500 ■ *Web:* www.peak-financial.com						
Peak International Inc 3432 Greystone Dr Ste 202	Austin	TX	78731	512-339-4684		124
Web: www.peakf.com						
Peak of the Market 1200 King Edward St	Winnipeg	MB	R3H0R5	204-632-7325		297-7
Web: www.peakmarket.com						
Peak Oilfield Service Company LLC 5015 Business Park Blvd Ste 4000	Anchorage	AK	99503	907-263-7000	263-7070	539
Web: www.peakalaska.com						
Peak Organization Inc, The 25 W 31st St 1st Fl	New York	NY	10001	212-947-6600	947-6780	463
Web: www.peakorg.com						
Peak Physique Inc 67 Holly Hill Ln	Greenwich	CT	06830	203-625-9595		354
Web: www.peak360greenwich.com						
Peak Publications PO Box 34850	Los Angeles	CA	90034	310-475-8236		637-2
Web: www.georgegamez.com						
PEAK Resources Inc 2750 W Fifth Ave	Denver	CO	80204	303-934-1200		180
TF: 800-925-7325 ■ *Web:* www.peakresources.com						
Peak Sales & Marketing Inc 6330 Flank Dr	Harrisburg	PA	17112	717-986-0301	986-0354	195
Web: www.peaksalesmkt.com						
Peak Sales Recruiting Inc 64 Beaver St Ste 119	New York	NY	10005	646-291-8960		41
Web: www.peaksalesrecruiting.com						
Peak Technical Services Inc 583 Epsilon Dr	Pittsburgh	PA	15238	833-850-7325		721
TF: 888-888-7325 ■ *Web:* www.peaktechnical.com						
Peak Technologies Inc 10330 Old Columbia Rd	Columbia	MD	21046	800-926-9212		174
TF: 800-926-9212 ■ *Web:* www.peak-ryzex.com						
Peak Tool Works 1180 Wernsing Rd	Jasper	IN	47546	812-482-2000	457-7458*	455
**Fax Area Code:* 800 ■ *TF:* 800-457-7468 ■ *Web:* www.peaktoolworks.com						
Peak Wellness Ctr 1263 N 15th St	Laramie	WY	82072	307-745-8915		726
Web: www.peakwellnesscenter.org						
Peaklogix Inc 14409 Justice Rd	Midlothian	VA	23113	800-849-6332		186
TF: 800-849-6332 ■ *Web:* www.peaklogix.com						
Peaks Resort & Golden Door Spa 136 Country Club Dr	Telluride	CO	81435	866-282-4557		669
TF: 800-789-2220 ■ *Web:* www.thepeaksresort.com						
Peaksware LLC 7007 Winchester Cir Ste 200	Boulder	CO	80301	720-406-1839		180
Web: www.peaksware.com						
Peapack-Gladstone Bank 500 Hills Dr Ste 300 PO Box 700	Bedminster	NJ	07921	908-234-0700		360-2
NASDAQ: PGC ■ *TF:* 800-742-7595 ■ *Web:* www.pgbank.com						
Peapod LLC 580 Capital Dr	Chicago	IL	60606	800-573-2763		345
TF: 800-573-2763 ■ *Web:* www.peapod.com						
Pear Therapeutics Inc 200 State St	Boston	MA	02109	617-925-7848		668
Web: peartherapeutics.com						
Pear Workplace Solutions 1515 Arapahoe St Ste 100	Denver	CO	80202	303-824-2000	824-2001	320
Web: www.pearwork.com						
Pearce & Durick 314 E Thayer Ave	Bismarck	ND	58502	701-223-2890		428
Web: www.pearce-durick.com						
Pearce Bevill Leesburg & Moore Pc 110 Office Pk Dr	Birmingham	AL	35223	205-323-5440	328-8523	2
Web: www.pearcebevill.com						
Pearl City High School 100 S Summit St	Pearl City	IL	61062	815-443-2715	443-2237	685
Web: www.pcwolves.net						
Pearl City Nursing Home 919 Lehua Ave	Pearl City	HI	96782	808-453-1919		793
TF: 800-596-0026 ■ *Web:* pearlcitynursinghome.com						
Pearl Dragon 15229 W Sunset Blvd	Pacific Palisades	CA	90272	310-459-9790		671
Web: www.thepearldragon.com						
Pearl Engineering Corp 110 E Grand Ave PO Box 425	Wisconsin Rapids	WI	54494	715-424-4008		261
Web: pearlengineering.com						
Pearl Harbor Aviation 319 Lexington Blvd	Honolulu	HI	96818	808-441-1000		520
Web: www.pearlharboraviationmuseum.org						
Pearl Harbor Federal Credit Union (PHFCU) 94-449 Ukee St	Waipahu	HI	96797	800-987-5583	218-6299*	219
**Fax Area Code:* 808 ■ *TF:* 800-987-5583 ■ *Web:* pearlhawaii.com						
Pearl Hotel Waikiki 415 Nahua St	Honolulu	HI	96815	808-922-1616		378
TF: 855-518-3455 ■ *Web:* www.pearlhotelwaikiki.com						
Pearl Hotel, The 1410 Rosecrans St	San Diego	CA	92106	619-226-6100		379
Web: thepearlsd.com						
Pearl Laguna LLC, The 21095 Raquel Rd	Laguna Beach	CA	92651	949-715-1674		378
Web: thepearllaguna.com						
Pearl Lake State Park PO Box 750	Clark	CO	80428	970-879-3922		565
Web: cpw.state.co.us						
Pearl Law Firm PA, The 7400 Tamiami Trail N Ste 101	Naples	FL	34108	239-653-9330		41
Web: investorattorneys.com						
Pearl Law Group 567 Sutter St 3rd Fl	San Francisco	CA	94102	415-771-7500		41
Web: www.immigrationlaw.com						
Pearl Meat Packing Company Inc 27 York Ave	Randolph	MA	02368	781-228-5100	228-5123	473
TF: 800-462-3022 ■ *Web:* www.pearlmeat.com						
Pearl Oyster Bar 18 Cornelia St	New York	NY	10014	212-691-8211		671
Web: www.pearloysterbar.com						
Pearl River Community College 101 Hwy 11 N	Poplarville	MS	39470	601-403-1000		162
TF: 877-772-2338 ■ *Web:* www.prcc.edu						
Pearl River County 200 S Main St PO Box 530	Poplarville	MS	39470	601-403-2300		338
Web: www.pearlrivercounty.net						
Pearl River County Library System 900 Goodyear Blvd	Picayune	MS	39466	601-798-5081	798-5082	434-3
Web: pearlriver.lib.ms.us						
Pearl River Restaurant 4728 99th St NW	Edmonton	AB	T6E5H5	780-435-2015	431-2758	671
Web: www.pearlriverrestaurant.com						
Pearl River Valley Electric Power Assn 1422 Hwy 13 N PO Box 1217	Columbia	MS	39429	601-736-2666		245
TF: 855-277-8372 ■ *Web:* www.prvepa.com						
Pearl S. Buck Birthplace 8129 Seneca Trl PO Box 126	Hillsboro	WV	24946	304-653-4430		50-3
Web: www.pearlsbuckbirthplace.com						
Pearl Street Grill & Brewery 76 Pearl St	Buffalo	NY	14202	716-856-2337		671
Web: pearlstreetgrill.com						
Pearl's Restaurant Group 5641 N Classen Blvd	Oklahoma City	OK	73118	405-842-2102	840-0382	670
Web: www.pearlsokc.com						
Pearland Area Chamber of Commerce 6117 Broadway St	Pearland	TX	77581	281-485-3634	485-2420	139
Web: www.pearlandtexaschamber.us						
Pearlman Industries Inc 4900 Zambrano St	Commerce	CA	90040	562-927-5561		295
Web: www.pearlabrasive.com						
Pearlridge Ctr 98-1005 Moana Lua Rd	Aiea	HI	96701	808-488-0981		460
Web: pearlridgeonline.com						
Pearlsong Press PO Box 58065	Nashville	TN	37205	615-356-5188	352-4222	637-2
TF: 866-427-3275 ■ *Web:* www.pearlsong.com						
Pearman Motor Company Ltd 240 N Marcus	Alto	TX	75925	936-858-4188		57
Web: www.pearmanmotor.com						

	Phone	Fax	Class
Pearne & Gordon LLP 1801 E Ninth St Ste 1200 Cleveland OH 44114 *Web:* pearne.com	216-579-1700	579-6073	428
Pearpoint Inc 39-740 Garand Ln Unit B Palm Desert CA 92211 *TF:* 800-688-8094 ■ *Web:* www.pearpoint.com	760-343-7350	343-7351	647
Pearrygin Lake State Park 561 Bear Creek Rd Winthrop WA 98862 *Web:* www.parks.state.wa.us	509-996-2370		565
Pearson Animal Hospital Inc 1903 W San Marcos Blvd Ste 140 San Marcos CA 92078 *Web:* pearsonvet.com	760-598-2512		794
Pearson Co 1420 Progress Ave High Point NC 27260 *Web:* www.pearsonco.com	336-882-8135		319-2
Pearson College 650 Pearson College Dr Victoria BC V9C4H7 *Web:* www.pearsoncollege.ca	250-391-2411		166
Pearson Dental Supplies Inc 13161 Telfair Ave Sylmar CA 91342 **Fax Area Code:* 800 ■ *TF:* 800-535-4535 ■ *Web:* www.pearsondental.com	818-362-2600	835-3100*	475
Pearson Engineering Associates Inc 8825 N 23rd Ave Ste 11 Phoenix AZ 85021 *TF:* 866-747-9754 ■ *Web:* peaeng.com	602-264-0807		261
Pearson Foods Corp 1024 Ken O Sha Ind Park Dr SE Grand Rapids MI 49508 *Web:* www.pearsonfoods.com	616-245-5053		297-8
Pearson Group 904 Princess Anne St Fredericksburg VA 22401 *Web:* pearsonplanners.com	540-373-4493		184
Pearson Inc 1330 Avenue of the Americas 7th Fl New York NY 10019 **Fax Area Code:* 212 ■ *TF:* 877-311-0948 ■ *Web:* www.pearson.com	877-311-0948	641-2500*	360-3
Pearson Packaging Systems 8120 W Sunset Hwy Spokane WA 99224 *TF:* 800-732-7766 ■ *Web:* www.pearsonpkg.com	800-732-7766		547
Pearson Vue 5601 Green Vly Dr Bloomington MN 55437 *Web:* home.pearsonvue.com	952-681-3000		244
Pearson's Candy Co 2140 W Seventh St Saint Paul MN 55116 *TF:* 800-328-6507 ■ *Web:* pearsonscandy.com	651-698-0356	696-2222	296-8
Peasant 194 Elizabeth St New York NY 10012 *Web:* www.peasantnyc.com	212-965-9511		671
Pease & Sons Inc 10601 Waller Rd E Tacoma WA 98448 *Web:* www.peaseandsons.com	253-531-7700		188
Peavey Electronics Corp 5022 Hartley Peavey Dr Meridian MS 39305 *TF:* 877-732-8391 ■ *Web:* peavey.com	601-483-5365	486-1278	52
Peavey Performance Systems 10749 W 84th Terr Lenexa KS 66214 *Web:* www.safetyjackpot.com	913-888-0600		279
Peavy & Son Construction Company Inc 39 Schwall Rd Havana FL 32333 *Web:* www.peavyandson.com	850-539-5019	539-6669	188-4
Pebble Beach Co 17-Mile Dr Pebble Beach CA 93953 *TF:* 800-877-0597 ■ *Web:* www.pebblebeach.com	800-877-0597		669
PEC (Preferred Excellent Care) 10521 Garden Grove Blvd Garden Grove CA 92843 *TF:* 877-590-3620 ■ *Web:* www.preferredexcellentcare.com	714-590-3620	590-3628	363
PEC (Pennsylvania Equine Council) PO Box 303 Windsor PA 17366 *TF:* 888-304-0281 ■ *Web:* www.pennsylvaniaequinecouncil.org	888-304-0281		48-13
Pecan Grove Press (PGP) 1 Camino Santa Maria San Antonio TX 78228 *Web:* www.library.stmarytx.edu	210-436-3442	436-3782	637-2
Pecan Row Press 603 Duling Ave Ste 202 Jackson MS 39216 *TF:* 877-362-3201 ■ *Web:* www.pecanrowpress.com	601-842-1700	829-0063	637-2
Pecci Educational Publishers 440 Davis Ct No 405 San Francisco CA 94111 **Fax Area Code:* 970 ■ *Web:* www.onlinereadingteacher.com	415-391-8579	493-8781*	637-2
Pechanga Resort & Casino 45000 Pechanga Pkwy Temecula CA 92592 *TF:* 877-711-2946 ■ *Web:* www.pechanga.com	951-693-1819	695-7410	669
Pechters Baking 840 Jersey St Harrison NJ 07029 *Web:* www.xn--pechters-ip3d.com	973-483-3374		296-1
Peck & Associates Pc 401 W Main Ste 400 Norman OK 73069 *Web:* peckandassociates.com	405-364-3040		2
Peck & Hale LLC 180 Div Ave West Sayville NY 11796 *Web:* www.peckhale.com	631-589-2510	589-2925	678
Peck & Peck CPAs PC 312 S Pacific Dillon MT 59725 *Web:* peckandpeckcpas.com	406-683-4254		2
Peck B. G. Company Inc 50 Shepard St Lawrence MA 01843 *Web:* bgpeck.com	978-686-4181		326
Peckham Industries Inc 20 Haarlem Ave White Plains NY 10603 *Web:* www.peckham.com	914-949-2000	949-2075	46
Peco Fasteners Inc 1218 Six Flags Rd Austell GA 30168 *Web:* www.pecofasteners.com	770-745-1300		350
Peco Foods Inc 1101 Greensboro Ave Tuscaloosa AL 35401 *Web:* pecofoods.com	205-345-3955	343-2401	619
Peco Products 3812 US Hwy 641 N Murray KY 42071 *TF:* 866-477-0600 ■ *Web:* www.pecoproducts.com	270-767-0085		344
Peconic Bay Medical Ctr 1300 Roanoke Ave Riverhead NY 11901 *Web:* www.pbmchealth.org	631-548-6000	548-6048	374-3
Peconic Bay Originals Inc 6800 Alvah's Ln Cutchogue NY 11935 *Web:* www.peconicbayoriginals.com	631-734-6798		637-10
Pecora Corp 165 Wambold Rd Harleysville PA 19438 *TF:* 800-523-6688 ■ *Web:* www.pecora.com	215-723-6051	799-2518	3
Pecos Benedictine Monastery *Our Lady of Guadalupe Abbey* PO Box 1080 Pecos NM 87552 *Web:* www.pecosmonastery.org	505-757-6415		673
Pecos County 103 W Callaghan St Fort Stockton TX 79735 *Web:* www.co.pecos.tx.us	432-336-7555		338
Pecos Enterprise PO Box 2057 Pecos TX 79772 *Web:* www.pecos.net	432-445-5475	445-4321	532-2
Pecos National Historical Park PO Box 418 Pecos NM 87552 *Web:* www.nps.gov	505-757-7207		564
Pecos Valley Broadcasting 105 W 3rd St-No 242 Roswell NM 88202 *Web:* www.ksvpradio.com	575-578-1198	748-3748	647
Pedal Valves Inc 13625 River Rd Luling LA 70070 *TF:* 800-431-3668 ■ *Web:* pedalvalve.com	985-785-9997		610
PEDCo E & A Services Inc 11499 Chester Rd Ste 301 Cincinnati OH 45246 *Web:* pedcoea.com	513-782-4920		261
Peddie School 201 S Main St Hightstown NJ 08520 *Web:* www.peddie.org	609-944-7500	944-7901	622
Peddinghaus Corp 300 N Washington Ave Bradley IL 60915 *TF:* 800-786-2448 ■ *Web:* www.peddinghaus.com	815-937-3800	937-4003	455
Pedernales Electric Co-opeartive Inc PO Box 1 Johnson City TX 78636 *TF:* 888-554-4732 ■ *Web:* www.pec.coop	830-868-7155	868-4767	245
Pedernales Falls State Park 2585 Park Rd 6026 Johnson City TX 78636 *Web:* tpwd.texas.gov	830-868-7304		565
Pederson Law Offices, A Professional Law Corp 280 E Thousand Oaks Blvd Ste A Thousand Oaks CA 91360 *Web:* pedersonlawoffices.com	805-495-3444		41
Pederson Tool & Design Inc 700 Lund Blvd Anoka MN 55303 *Web:* www.pedersontoolanddesign.com	763-421-0355		757
Pediatric Home Respiratory Services Inc 2800 Cleveland Ave N Roseville MN 55113 *TF:* 800-225-7477 ■ *Web:* www.pediatrichomeservice.com	651-642-1825		363
Pediatrix Medical Group Inc 1301 Concord Terr Sunrise FL 33323 *TF:* 800-243-3839 ■ *Web:* www.pediatrix.com	954-384-0175		463
PediaVascular Inc 7181 Chagrin Rd SU 250 Chagrin Falls OH 44023 **Fax Area Code:* 888 ■ *Web:* www.pediavascular.com	216-236-5533	691-6161*	476
Pedigo Products Inc 4000 SE Columbia Way Vancouver WA 98661 *Web:* pedigo-usa.com	360-695-3500		567
Pedigree Ski Shop Inc 355 Mamaroneck Ave White Plains NY 10605 *Web:* pedigreeskishop.com	914-948-2995		711
Pedigree Technologies 4776 28th Ave S Ste 101 Fargo ND 58104 *TF:* 844-407-9307 ■ *Web:* www.pedigreetechnologies.com	800-470-6581		809
Pedipress Inc 125 Red Gate Ln Amherst MA 01002 *TF:* 800-611-6081 ■ *Web:* www.pedipress.com	413-549-7798	549-4095	637-2
Pedone 49 W 27th St New York NY 10001 *Web:* www.pedonepartners.com	212-627-3300	627-3966	4
Pedorthic Footwear Assn (PFA) 2025 M St NW Ste 800 Washington DC 20036 *TF:* 800-673-8447 ■ *Web:* www.pedorthics.org	202-367-1145	367-2145	48-17
Pedowitz Group, The 810 Mayfield Rd Milton GA 30009 *TF:* 855-738-6584 ■ *Web:* www.pedowitzgroup.com	855-738-6584		195
Pedro's 4938 W Glendale Ave Glendale AZ 85301 *Web:* pedrosmexicanfood.com	623-937-0807		671
Pedro's Mexican Restaurante 3555 E Washington Ave Madison WI 53704 *Web:* www.pedrosmadison.com	608-241-8110		671
Peduzzi Associates Ltd 221 S Alfred St Alexandria VA 22314 *Web:* peduzziassociates.com	703-836-7990		196
Pee Dee Electric Co-opeartive Inc PO Box 491 Darlington SC 29540 *TF:* 866-747-0060 ■ *Web:* pdec.com	843-665-4070		245
Pee Dee Electric Membership Corp (PDEMC) 575 US Hwy 52 S Wadesboro NC 28170 *TF:* 800-992-1626 ■ *Web:* www.pdemc.com	704-694-2114	694-9636	245
Peebles Corp, The 2020 Pone de Leon Blvd Ste 907 Coral Gables FL 33134 *Web:* peeblescorp.com	305-993-5050		653
Peebles Island State Park 1 Delaware Ave N Cohoes NY 12047 *Web:* sites.google.com	518-268-2188		565
Peeco 7050 W Ridge Rd Fairview PA 16415 *TF:* 800-235-9382 ■ *Web:* www.autodev.com	814-474-5561		454
Peek 'n Peak Resort 1405 Olde Rd Clymer NY 14724 *TF:* 800-772-6906 ■ *Web:* www.pknpk.com	716-355-4141	355-4542	669
Peel Plastic Products Ltd 49 Rutherford Rd S Brampton ON L6W3J3 *Web:* www.peelplastics.com	905-456-3660		601
Peelle Co 34 E Main St Ste 372 Smithtown NY 11787 *TF:* 800-787-5020 ■ *Web:* www.peelledoor.com	905-846-4545	846-2161	234
PeelMaster Packaging Corp 6153 W Mulford St Unit C Niles IL 60714 *TF:* 855-966-6200 ■ *Web:* www.peelmaster.com	855-966-6200		477
Peer Bearing Co 2200 Norman Dr S Waukegan IL 60085 *TF:* 800-433-7337 ■ *Web:* www.peerbearing.com	847-578-1000	578-1200	75
PEER Consultants PC 409 12th St SW Ste 603 Washington DC 20024 *Web:* peercpc.com	202-478-2060	478-2050	192
Peer Foods Group Inc 1200 W 35th St Chicago IL 60609 *TF:* 800-365-5644 ■ *Web:* www.peerfoods.com	773-475-2375		296-26
Peerfit 1060 Woodcock Rd Ste 128 Orlando FL 32803 *Web:* peerfit.com	813-392-3333		354
Peerless Chain Co 1416 E Sanborn St Winona MN 55987 *TF:* 800-533-8056 ■ *Web:* www.peerlesschain.com	800-873-1916	356-1149	678
Peerless Cleaners Inc 519 N Monroe St Decatur IL 62522 *Web:* www.peerlessrestoration.com	217-423-7703		83
Peerless Concrete Products Co 246 Main St Butler NJ 07405 *Web:* www.peerlessconcrete.com	973-838-3060		183
Peerless Electric 1401 W Market St Warren OH 44485 **Fax Area Code:* 330 ■ *TF:* 800-676-3651 ■ *Web:* www.peerlesselectric.com	800-676-3651	393-6041*	518
Peerless Electronics Inc 700 Hicksville Rd Bethpage NY 11714 *TF:* 800-285-2121 ■ *Web:* www.peerlesselectronics.com	516-594-3500	593-2179	246
Peerless Food Equipment 500 S Vandenmark Rd Sidney OH 45365 *TF:* 877-795-7377 ■ *Web:* www.peerlessfood.com	937-492-4158	492-3688	298
Peerless Inc 79 Perry St Buffalo NY 14203 *TF:* 800-234-3033 ■ *Web:* www.peerless-inc.com	716-852-4784		111

Company	City	State	ZIP	Phone	Fax	Class
Peerless Insurance Co 62 Maple Ave *Web:* www.peerless-ins.com	Keene	NH	03431	603-352-3221		391-4
Peerless Maintenance Service Inc PO Box 2772 *Web:* peerlesssvc.com	La Habra	CA	90632	714-871-3380	871-2232	104
Peerless Manufacturing Co US Hwy 82 E *TF:* 800-225-4617 ■ *Web:* www.peerlessmfg.cc	Shellman	GA	39886	229-679-5353	679-5542	273
Peerless Network Inc 222 S Riverside Plz Ste 2730 *TF:* 888-380-2721 ■ *Web:* www.peerlessnetwork.com	Chicago	IL	60606	312-506-0920		387
Peerless of America Inc 1201 Wabash Ave *Web:* www.peerlessofamerica.com	Effingham	IL	62401	217-342-0400		14
Peerless Pattern Works Inc 3325 NW Yeon Ave *Web:* www.peerlesspatternworks.com	Portland	OR	97210	503-227-6561		547
Peerless Plastics 510 Willow St *Web:* www.peerlessplastics.com	Farmington	MN	55024	651-463-7147		596
Peerless Pottery Inc 2827 W State Rd 66 Ste E *TF:* 866-457-5785 ■ *Web:* www.peerlesspottery.com	Rockport	IN	47635	812-649-9920	649-6429	611
Peerless Premier Appliance Co 119 S 14th St *Fax Area Code: 618 ■ *TF:* 800-858-5844 ■ *Web:* www.premierrange.com	Belleville	IL	62222	800-858-5844	235-1771*	36
Peerless Products Inc 2403 S Main St *TF:* 866-420-4000 ■ *Web:* www.peerlessproducts.com	Fort Scott	KS	66701	620-223-4610	224-3107	234
Peerless Pump Co 2005 Dr Martin Luther King Jr St *TF:* 800-879-0182 ■ *Web:* www.peerlesspump.com	Indianapolis	IN	46202	317-925-9661	924-7388	641
Peerless Saw Co, The 4353 Directors Blvd *Web:* www.peerlesssaw.com	Groveport	OH	43125	614-836-5790		273
Peerless Steak House 2531 N Roan St *Web:* www.peerlesssteakhousegrill.com	Johnson City	TN	37601	423-282-2351		671
Peerless Steel Corp 2450 Austin *TF:* 800-482-3947 ■ *Web:* www.peerlesssteel.com	Troy	MI	48083	248-528-3200	528-9144	492
Peerless Systems Corp 1055 Washington Blvd 8th Fl *NASDAQ: PVOFU* ■ *Web:* www.peerless.com	Stamford	CT	06901	203-350-0040		178-8
Peerless Tire Co 5000 Kingston St *TF:* 800-999-7810 ■ *Web:* peerlesstyreco.com	Denver	CO	80239	800-999-7810		54
Peerless-Winsmith Inc 172 Eaton St *Web:* www.winsmith.com	Springville	NY	14141	716-592-9310	592-9546	709
PeerStreet 2121 Park Pl Ste 250 *TF:* 844-733-7787 ■ *Web:* peerstreet.com	El Segundo	CA	90245	844-733-7787		49-17
Peery Hotel 110 West 300 South *TF:* 800-331-0073 ■ *Web:* www.peeryhotel.com	Salt Lake City	UT	84101	801-521-4300		379
Peet Frate Line Inc 650 S Eastwood Dr PO Box 1129 *TF:* 800-435-6909 ■ *Web:* www.peetfrateline.com	Woodstock	IL	60098	815-338-5500	338-1052	780
Peg Poulin-Horton Ins. Agency Inc 224 Main St *Web:* pegpoulin.com	Saco	ME	04072	207-283-9166		390
Pegalis Law Group LLC 1 Hollow Ln Ste 107 *Web:* pegalislawgroup.com	Lake Success	NY	11042	516-684-2900		41
Pegasi Energy Resources Corp 1999 Bryan St Ste 900 *Web:* www.pegasienergy.com	Dallas	TX	75701	903-595-4139	595-0344	536
Pegasus 4711 Poplar Level Rd *TF:* 800-582-5576 ■ *Web:* www.takepegasus.com	Louisville	KY	40218	502-458-1862	458-3608	441
Pegasus Engineering Inc 301 W State Rd 434 Ste 309 *Web:* www.pegasusengineering.net	Winter Springs	FL	32708	407-992-9160	358-5155	261
Pegasus Home Health Care 132 N Maryland Ave *Web:* pegasushomecare.com	Glendale	CA	91206	818-551-1932		363
Pegasus International Hotel 501 Southard St *TF:* 800-397-8148 ■ *Web:* www.pegasuskeywest.com	Key West	FL	33040	305-294-9323	294-4741	379
Pegasus Laboratories Inc 8809 Ely Rd *Web:* www.pegasuslabs.com	Pensacola	FL	32514	850-478-2770		582
Pegasus Logistics Group Inc 306 Airline Dr Ste 100 *TF:* 800-997-7226 ■ *Web:* www.pegasuslogisticsgroup.com	Coppell	TX	75019	469-671-0300	671-0317	449
Pegasus Manufacturing Inc 422 Timber Ridge Rd *Web:* www.pegasusmfg.com	Middletown	CT	06457	860-635-8811		697
Pegasus Originals Inc 129 Minnie Fallaw Rd *Web:* www.pegasusoriginals.com	Lexington	SC	29073	803-755-1141		637-2
Pegasus Productions PO Box 1869 *Web:* www.pegasusproductions.com	Jupiter	FL	33468	561-745-0525	379-3490	344
Pegasus Residential LLC 1750 Founders Pkwy Ste 180 *Web:* www.pegasusresidential.com	Alpharetta	GA	30009	678-347-2802	347-2902	652
Pegasus Taverna 558 Monroe St *Web:* pegasustavernas.com	Detroit	MI	48226	313-964-6800	964-0869	671
PegasusTSI Inc 5310 Cypress Center Dr Ste 200 *Web:* www.pegasustsi.com	Tampa	FL	33609	813-876-2424		261
Pegasystems Inc 101 Main St *NASDAQ: PEGA* ■ *Web:* www.pega.com	Cambridge	MA	02142	617-374-9600	374-9620	178-1
PegEx Inc 2693 Research Park Dr Ste 201 *TF:* 888-681-9616 ■ *Web:* pegex.com	Fitchburg	WI	53711	888-681-9616		192
Peggy Lauritsen Design Grp Inc (PLDG) 125 Main St SE Ste 340 *Web:* pldg.com	Minneapolis	MN	55414	612-623-4200		344
Peggy Notebaert Nature Museum 2430 N Cannon Dr *Web:* www.naturemuseum.org	Chicago	IL	60614	773-755-5100		520
Peg-Perego USA Inc 3625 Independence Dr *TF:* 800-671-1701 ■ *Web:* www.en.pegperego.com	Fort Wayne	IN	46808	260-482-8191	484-2940	64
PEI (Photofabrication Engineering Inc) 500 Fortune Blvd *TF:* 800-253-8518 ■ *Web:* www.photofabrication.com	Milford	MA	01757	508-478-2025	478-3582	454
Pei Cobb Freed & Partners Architects LLP 88 Pine St *Web:* www.pcf-p.com	New York	NY	10005	212-751-3122	872-5443	261
PEI-Genesis 2180 Hornig Rd *TF:* 800-675-1214 ■ *Web:* www.peigenesis.com	Philadelphia	PA	19116	215-673-0400	552-8022	246
Peirce College 1420 Pine St *TF:* 888-467-3472 ■ *Web:* www.peirce.edu	Philadelphia	PA	19102	215-545-6400	670-9366	166
Peirce-Phelps Inc 516 E Township Line Rd Blue Bell *TF:* 800-222-2096 ■ *Web:* www.peirce.com	Philadelphia	PA	19131	215-879-7217		38
Peirson Patterson LLP 2310 W I-20 Ste 100 *TF:* 800-800-9975 ■ *Web:* www.peirsonpatterson.com	Arlington	TX	76017	817-461-5500		428
Pekin Area Chamber of Commerce 402 Court St *Web:* www.pekinchamber.com	Pekin	IL	61554	309-346-2106	346-2104	139
Pekin Daily Times 306 Court St *Web:* www.pekintimes.com	Pekin	IL	61554	309-346-1111		532-2
Pekin Insurance 2505 Court St *TF:* 800-322-0160 ■ *Web:* www.pekininsurance.com	Pekin	IL	61558	888-735-4611		391-4
Pekin Public Library 301 S Fourth St *Web:* www.pekinpubliclibrary.org	Pekin	IL	61554	309-347-7111	347-6587	434-3
Peking 120 Waller Mill Rd *Web:* www.peking-va.com	Williamsburg	VA	23185	757-229-2288		671
Peking Garden 1831 Zaragosa *Web:* www.pekinggarden.club	El Paso	TX	79930	915-565-9090		671
Peking Garden 1488 University Ave *Web:* www.pekinggardenmn.com	Saint Paul	MN	55104	651-644-0888	644-1738	671
Peking Handicraft Inc 1388 San Mateo Ave *Web:* www.pkhc.com	South San Francisco	CA	94080	650-871-3788		361
Peking House 1125 Van Voorhis Rd *Web:* www.pekinghousewv.com	Morgantown	WV	26505	304-598-3333		671
Peking Noodle Company Inc 1514 N San Fernando Rd *TF:* 877-735-4648 ■ *Web:* www.pekingnoodle.com	Los Angeles	CA	90065	323-223-2023		296-31
Peko Precision Products Inc 1400 Emerson St *Web:* www.pekoprecision.com	Rochester	NY	14606	585-647-3010	647-1366	454
PEL (Pennsylvania Economy League Inc) 88 N Franklin St *Web:* pelcentral.org	Wilkes-Barre	PA	18701	570-824-3559	829-8099	637-2
Pel Hughes Printing Inc 3801 Toulouse St *Web:* pelhughes.com	New Orleans	LA	70119	504-486-8646		627
Pelanchos Mexican Grill 1516 Downtown W Blvd *Web:* pelanchos.com	Knoxville	TN	37919	865-694-9060		671
Pelco Products Inc 320 W 18th St *Web:* www.pelcoinc.com	Edmond	OK	73013	405-340-3434	340-3435	350
Pelco Structural LLC 1501 Industrial Blvd *Web:* www.pelcostructural.com	Claremore	OK	74017	918-283-4004		492
Pelerei Inc 2379 Broad Run Ct *Web:* www.madelynblair.com	Jefferson	MD	21755	301-371-7100		195
Pelesys Learning Systems Inc 13500 Maycrest Way Ste 125 *Web:* website.pelesys.com	Richmond	BC	V6V2N8	604-233-6268		380
Pelfrey & Company CPAS Inc 10855 Indeco Dr *Web:* pelfreycpa.com	Cincinnati	OH	45241	513-793-1200		2
Pelham Hotel 444 Common St *Web:* www.thepelhamhotel.com	New Orleans	LA	70130	504-522-4444		379
Pelham Plastics Inc 42 Dick Tracy Dr *Web:* www.pelhamplastics.com	Pelham	NH	03076	603-886-7226	886-3311	608
Pelican Aviation 1314 Hangar Dr *Web:* pelican-aviation-corp.ueniweb.com	New Iberia	LA	70560	337-367-1401		63
Pelican Bay State Prison (PBSP) 5905 Lake Earl Dr PO Box 7000 *Web:* cdcr.ca.gov	Crescent City	CA	95531	707-465-1000		213
Pelican Cafe 826 Ocean Dr *Web:* pelicanhotel.com	Miami Beach	FL	33139	305-673-3373		671
Pelican Club 312 Exchange Alley *Web:* www.pelicanclub.com	New Orleans	LA	70130	504-523-1504	522-2331	671
Pelican Grand Beach Resort 2000 N Ocean Blvd *TF:* 800-525-6232 ■ *Web:* www.pelicanbeach.com	Fort Lauderdale	FL	33305	954-568-9431		379
Pelican Ice & Cold Storage Inc 711 Oxley St *Web:* pelicanice.com	Kenner	LA	70062	504-602-0013		380
Pelican Press 5011 Ocean Blvd Ste 206 *Web:* www.pelicanpressonline.com	Sarasota	FL	34242	941-349-4949		532-4
Pelican Products Inc 147 N Main St *TF:* 800-542-7344 ■ *Web:* www.pelican.com	South Deerfield	MA	01373	413-665-2163	665-4801	199
Pelican Rope Works Inc 4001 W Carriage Dr *TF:* 800-464-7673 ■ *Web:* www.pelicanrope.com	Santa Ana	CA	92704	714-545-0116	545-7673	208
Pelican's Restaurant 9800 Montgomery Blvd NE *Web:* www.pelicans-restaurant.com	Albuquerque	NM	87111	505-298-7678		671
Pelicans 291 N Air Depot Blvd *Web:* pelicansok.com	Midwest City	OK	73110	405-732-4392		671
Pelicans Perch Marina & Boatyard 40 Audusson Ave Bayou Chico *Web:* www.pelicansperchmarina.com	Pensacola	FL	32507	850-453-3471	457-1662	465
Pelion Investment Advisors 369 Lexington Ave Ste 311 *Fax Area Code: 646 ■ *Web:* www.peliongroup.com	New York	NY	10017	917-639-5476	224-8240*	691
PELITAS 2745 Dallas Pkwy Ste 605 *Web:* pelitas.com	Plano	TX	75093	972-781-2030		177

Phone | Fax | Class

Pelivan Transit
333 S Oak St PO Box B .... Big Cabin OK 74332 918-783-5793 783-5051 108
TF: 800-482-4594 ■ *Web:* www.pelivantransit.org
Pella Cooperative Electric Assn
2615 Washington St .... Pella IA 50219 641-628-1040 245
TF: 800-619-1040 ■ *Web:* pella-cea.org
Pella Corp 102 Main St .... Pella IA 50219 641-621-1000 236
TF: 877-473-5527 ■ *Web:* www.pella.com
Pella Historical Village
507 Franklin St .... Pella IA 50219 641-628-4311 520
Web: www.pellahistorical.org
Pella Products Inc
345 Enterprise Way .... Pittston PA 18640 570-346-7722 366
Web: pella.com
Pellegrino Honick Mcfarland & Miller PA
1800 Second St
The Bb T Bank Bldg East Tower Ste 810 .... Sarasota FL 34236 941-365-1172 957-0423 2
Web: phmmcpa.com
Pellerin Milnor Corp 700 Jackson St .... Kenner LA 70062 504-467-9591 469-1849 427
TF: 800-469-8780 ■ *Web:* www.milnor.com
Pelletizer Knives Inc 9703 Telge Rd .... Houston TX 77095 281-859-4492 859-4493 758
Web: www.pelletizerknivesinc.com
Pellettieri Rabstein & Altman
100 Nassau Pk Blvd .... Princeton NJ 08540 609-520-0900 428
TF: 800-432-5297 ■ *Web:* www.pralaw.com
Pellissippi State Technical Community College
10915 Hardin Valley Rd .... Knoxville TN 37933 865-694-6400 539-7217 162
Web: www.pstcc.edu
Pelorus Management Consultants (PMC)
19 Crossfield Ct .... Bedminster NJ 07921 862-368-0038 194
Web: www.pmcinfo.com
Pelosi Nancy (Rep D - CA)
1236 Longworth House Office Bldg .... Washington DC 20515 202-225-4965 342-2
Web: pelosi.house.gov
Peloton Therapeutics Inc
2330 Inwood Rd Ste 226 .... Dallas TX 75235 972-629-4100 231
Web: www.pelotontherapeutics.com
Pelvalon Inc 923 Thompson Pl .... Sunnyvale CA 94085 650-276-0130 646-2213 475
Web: eclipsesystem.com
PEM (Power Engineering and Manufacturing Ltd)
2635 WCF&N Dr .... Waterloo IA 50703 319-232-2311 232-6100 709
TF: 877-898-4327 ■ *Web:* www.pemltd.com
Pemberton & Englund Law Offices LLC
214 First St .... Baraboo WI 53913 608-356-5700 355-0725 41
Web: baraboodellslaw.com
Pemberton Truck Lines Inc
2530 Mitchell St .... Knoxville TN 37917 865-524-5592 523-9449 780
TF: 800-621-5530 ■ *Web:* ptlapp.com
Pembina County 301 Dakota St W Ste 1 .... Cavalier ND 58220 701-265-4231 265-4876 338
Web: www.pembinacountynd.gov
Pembina Pipeline Corp
2000 700 - 9 Ave SW .... Calgary AB T2P1G1 403-231-7500 237-0254 405
TSE: PPL ■ *TF:* 888-428-3222 ■ *Web:* www.pembina.com
Pembroke
1002 Sherbrooke St W Ste 1700 .... Montreal QC H3A3S4 514-848-0716 796
TF: 800-667-0716 ■ *Web:* private.pml.ca
Pembroke Commercial Realty Corp
4460 Corporation Ln Ste 300 .... Virginia Beach VA 23462 757-490-3141 652
Web: www.pembrokerealty.com
Pembroke Consulting Inc
1515 Market St Ste 960 .... Philadelphia PA 19102 215-523-5700 463
Web: www.pembrokeconsulting.com
Pembroke Hill School
400 W 51st St .... Kansas City MO 64112 816-936-1200 685
Web: www.pembrokehill.org
Pembroke Hospital 199 Oak St .... Pembroke MA 02359 781-829-7000 374-5
TF: 800-222-2237 ■ *Web:* arbourhealth.com
Pembroke Lakes Mall
11401 Pines Blvd .... Pembroke Pines FL 33026 954-436-3311 460
Web: www.pembrokelakesmall.com
Pembroke Regional Hospital
705 MacKay St .... Pembroke ON K8A1G8 613-732-2811 732-9986 374-2
TF: 866-996-0991 ■ *Web:* www.pemreghos.org
Pembroke Telephone Co 185 E Bacon St ...... Pembroke GA 31321 912-653-4389 653-2929 224
TF: 888-382-1222 ■ *Web:* www.pemtelco.com
PEMCO (Hunt Engine Inc) 14805 S Main St ...... Houston TX 77035 713-721-9400 721-7346 386
Web: www.huntengine.com
Pemco Ltd 1632 S King St Ste 100 .... Honolulu HI 96826 808-949-0414 955-0414 463
TF: 888-909-5007 ■ *Web:* pemco-limited.com
Pemco World Air Services
4102 N Westshore Blvd .... Tampa FL 33614 813-322-9600 24
Web: www.pemcoair.com
Pemex Procurement International Inc
10344 Sam Houston Park Dr .... Houston TX 77064 713-430-3100 536
TF: 888-254-1487 ■ *Web:* pemexprocurement.com
Pemi-Baker Community Health
101 Boulder Point Dr Ste 3 .... Plymouth NH 03264 603-536-2232 363
Web: www.pemibakercommunityhealth.org
Pemiscot County
610 Ward Ave Ste 1A .... Caruthersville MO 63830 573-333-4203 333-0440 338
Web: www.pemiscotcounty.org
Pemiscot-Dunklin Electric Co-op
Hwy 412 W PO Box 509 .... Hayti MO 63851 573-757-6641 757-6656 245
TF: 800-558-6641 ■ *Web:* www.pemdunk.com
Pemko Manufacturing Company Inc
4226 Transport St .... Ventura CA 93003 805-642-2600 283-4050* 234
**Fax Area Code:* 800 ■ *TF:* 800-283-9988 ■ *Web:* www.assaabloy.com
PEN American Ctr 588 Broadway .... New York NY 10012 212-334-1660 48-8
Web: pen.org
PEN Products 2010 E New York St .... Indianapolis IN 46201 317-955-6800 630
TF: 800-736-2550 ■ *Web:* www.in.gov
Pen Publishing Interactive Inc
239 S Pattie St .... Wichita KS 67211 316-651-0551 396
Web: www.collegefans.com
Penacook Place 150 Water St .... Haverhill MA 01830 978-374-0707 371
Web: www.penacookplace.org
Penasco Valley Telephone Cooperative Inc (PVT)
4011 W Main St .... Artesia NM 88210 575-748-1241 746-4142 736
TF: 800-505-4844 ■ *Web:* www.pvt.com

Pencco Inc
831 Bartlett Rd PO Box 600 .... San Felipe TX 77473 979-885-0005 144
TF: 800-864-1742 ■ *Web:* www.pencco.com
Pence Greg (Rep R - IN)
222 Cannon House Office Bldg .... Washington DC 20515 202-225-3021 342-2
Web: www.pence.house.gov
Pence Kelly Construction LLC
2747 Pence Loop SE .... Salem OR 97302 503-399-7223 186
Web: pencekelly.com
Penchant Publishing PO Box 109 .... Jackson NH 03846 603-383-4000 383-8108 637-2
TF: 800-235-7221 ■ *Web:* www.penchantpublishing.com
Penco Products Inc
1820 Stonehenge Dr .... Greenville NC 27858 800-562-1000 248-1555 319-1
TF: 800-562-1000 ■ *Web:* www.pencoproducts.com
Pencom Systems Inc 152 Remsen St .... Brooklyn NY 11201 718-923-1111 923-6065 631
Web: www.pencom.com
Pencor Services Inc 613 Third St .... Palmerton PA 18071 610-826-2552 637-2
Web: www.pencor.com
Pend Oreille County 229 S Garden Ave .... Newport WA 99156 509-447-2435 338
Web: pendoreilleco.org
Penda 2344 W Wisconsin St .... Portage WI 53901 800-933-4200 60
TF: 800-356-7704 ■ *Web:* penda.com
Penda Aiken Inc 330 Livingston St .... Brooklyn NY 11217 718-643-4880 260
Web: pendaaiken.com
Pender Correctional Institution
906 Penderlea Hwy .... Burgaw NC 28425 910-259-8735 213
Web: www.ncdps.gov
Pender County PO Box 5 .... Burgaw NC 28425 910-259-1200 259-1402 338
Web: www.pendercountync.gov
Pender County Public Library
805 S Walker St .... Burgaw NC 28425 910-259-1234 434-3
Web: www.pendercountync.gov
Pendle Hill 338 Plush Mill Rd .... Wallingford PA 19086 610-566-4507 566-3679 673
TF: 800-742-3150 ■ *Web:* pendlehill.org
Pendleton County 233 Main St .... Falmouth KY 41040 859-654-4321 654-5047 338
Web: www.pendletoncounty.ky.gov
Pendleton County
3882 Agler Rd PO Box 187 .... Franklin WV 26807 304-358-7573 358-2473 338
Web: www.pendletoncounty.wv.gov
Pendleton Manor 414 Summit Dr .... Greenville SC 29609 864-271-7562 652
Web: pendletonmanor.com
Pendleton Woolen Mills Inc
220 NW Broadway .... Portland OR 97209 503-226-4801 535-5502 155-5
TF: 800-760-4844 ■ *Web:* www.pendleton-usa.com
PendoPharm Inc 6111 Royalmount Ave .... Montreal QC H4P2T4 514-340-5045 733-9684 479
TF: 866-926-7653 ■ *Web:* pendopharm.com
Pendu Manufacturing Inc
718 N Shirk Rd .... New Holland PA 17557 717-354-4348 355-2148 821
TF: 800-233-0471 ■ *Web:* pendu.com
Penfield Fire Company Inc
1838 Penfield Rd .... Penfield NY 14526 585-586-2413 186
Web: www.penfieldfire.org
Penfund
Bay Adelaide Centre 333 Bay St Ste 610 .... Toronto ON M5H2R2 416-865-0707 528
Web: penfund.com
Pengate Handling Systems Inc
3 Interchange Pl .... York PA 17406 717-764-3050 386
Web: www.pengate.com
Pengo Corp 500 E Hwy 10 .... Laurens IA 50554 712-845-2540 845-2497 190
TF: 800-599-0211 ■ *Web:* www.pengoattachments.com
Penguin Air Conditioning Corp
5 Penn Plz 16th Fl .... New York NY 10001 718-706-6500 189-10
TF: 866-533-2098 ■ *Web:* penguinac.com
Penguin Audiobooks 375 Hudson St .... New York NY 10014 212-366-2372 366-2933 637-2
Web: www.us.penguingroup.com
Penguin Computing Inc
45800 Northport Loop W .... Fremont CA 94538 415-954-2800 180
TF: 888-736-4846 ■ *Web:* www.penguincomputing.com
Penguin Group (USA) Inc
375 Hudson St .... New York NY 10014 212-366-2000 366-2933 637-2
TF: 800-847-5515 ■ *Web:* www.penguin.com
Penguin Hotel 1418 Ocean Dr .... Miami Beach FL 33139 305-534-9334 379
Web: www.penguinhotel.com
Penguin Point Franchise Systems Inc
2691 E US 30 .... Warsaw IN 46580 574-267-3107 267-3154 670
TF: 800-557-5755 ■ *Web:* www.penguinpoint.com
Penguin Random House 1745 Broadway .... New York NY 10019 212-782-9000 782-5157 637-2
Web: www.penguinrandomhouse.com
Peniel Solutions LLC
3885 Crestwood Pkwy Ste 275 .... Duluth GA 30096 866-878-2490 113
TF: 866-878-2490 ■ *Web:* www.penielsolutions.com
Peninsula Asset Management Inc
1111 Third Ave W Ste 340 .... Bradenton FL 34205 800-269-6417 748-2654* 401
**Fax Area Code:* 941 ■ *TF:* 800-269-6417 ■ *Web:* www.peninsulaasset.com
Peninsula Ballet Theatre
1880 S Grant St .... San Mateo CA 94402 650-342-3262 573-1
Web: www.peninsulaballet.org
Peninsula Behavioral Health
2347 Jones Bend Rd .... Louisville TN 37777 865-970-9800 374-5
Web: www.peninsulabehavioralhealth.org
Peninsula Beverly Hills
9882 S Santa Monica Blvd .... Beverly Hills CA 90212 310-551-2888 788-2319 379
TF: 800-462-7899 ■ *Web:* www.peninsula.com
Peninsula Chamber of Commerce
PO Box 6015 .... San Diego CA 92166 619-223-1629 139
Web: www.peninsulachamber.com
Peninsula Cleaning Service Inc
12610 Patrick Henry Dr Ste A .... Newport News VA 23602 757-833-1603 104
Web: www.peninsulacleaning.com
Peninsula College
1502 E Lauridsen Blvd .... Port Angeles WA 98362 360-452-9277 162
Web: pencol.edu
Peninsula Community Health Services
PO Box 960 .... Bremerton WA 98337 360-377-3776 373-2096 374-3
TF: 866-418-1002 ■ *Web:* www.pchsweb.org
Peninsula Community Theatre
10251 Warwick Blvd PO Box 11056 .... Newport News VA 23601 757-595-5728 572
Web: www.pctlive.org

Company	Address	City	State	ZIP	Phone	Fax	Class	Notes
Peninsula Copper Industries Inc (PCI)	220 Calumet St	Lake Linden	MI	49945	906-296-9918		145	Web: www.pencopper.com
Peninsula Daily News	305 W First St PO Box 1330	Port Angeles	WA	98362	360-452-2345	417-3521	532-2	TF: 800-826-7714 ■ Web: www.peninsuladailynews.com
Peninsula Fine Arts Ctr	101 Museum Dr	Newport News	VA	23606	757-596-8175		50-2	Web: pfac-va.org
Peninsula Gaming Corp	301 Bell St	Dubuque	IA	52001	563-690-4975		133	Web: www.diamondjo.com
Peninsula Grill	112 N Market St	Charleston	SC	29401	843-723-0700		671	Web: www.peninsulagrill.com
Peninsula High School	14105 Purdy Dr NW	Gig Harbor	WA	98332	253-530-4400	530-4420	685	Web: www.psd401.net
Peninsula Light Co	13315 Goodnough Dr NW	Gig Harbor	WA	98332	253-857-5950		245	TF: 888-809-8021 ■ Web: www.penlight.org
Peninsula Plastics Co	2800 Auburn Ct	Auburn Hills	MI	48326	248-852-3731	852-5482	596	Web: www.peninsulaplastics.com
Peninsula Regent, The	1 Baldwin Ave	San Mateo	CA	94401	650-579-5500		672	Web: www.peninsularegent.com
Peninsula Regional Medical Ctr	100 E Carroll St	Salisbury	MD	21801	410-546-6400	543-7102	374-3	TF: 800-543-7780 ■ Web: www.peninsula.org
Peninsula State Park	9462 Shore Rd	Fish Creek	WI	54212	920-868-3258		565	Web: dnr.wi.gov
Peninsula Town Ctr	1620 Merchant Ln	Hampton	VA	23666	757-838-1505		460	Web: peninsulatowncenter.com
Peninsular Cylinder Co	27650 Groesbeck	Roseville	MI	48066	586-775-7211		223	Web: www.peninsularcylinders.com
Penland School of Crafts	310 1/2 W Franklin St PO Box 37	Penland	NC	28765	828-765-2359	765-7389	766	Web: penland.org
Pen-Link Ltd	5944 VanDervoort Dr	Lincoln	NE	68516	402-421-8857		177	Web: www.penlink.com
Penlyric Press	PO Box 10332	Seattle	WA	98110	206-795-6682		637-2	Web: www.luckystarsandgoldbars.com
Penmac Staffing Services Inc	447 South Ave	Springfield	MO	65806	417-831-9100	865-1692	260	TF: 877-473-6622 ■ Web: www.penmac.com
Penmar Industries Inc	35 Ontario St	Stratford	CT	06615	203-853-4868	855-8136	559	Web: www.penmar-industries.com
Penmor Lithographers Inc	8 Lexington St PO Box 2003	Lewiston	ME	04241	800-339-1341		627	TF: 800-339-1341 ■ Web: penmor.com
Penn Air & Hydraulics Corp	580 Davies Dr	York	PA	17402	888-631-7638		641	TF: 888-631-7638 ■ Web: pennair.com
Penn Aluminum International Inc	1117 N Second St	Murphysboro	IL	62966	618-684-2146		485	TF: 800-445-7366 ■ Web: www.pennaluminum.com
Penn Brewery, The	800 Vinial St	Pittsburgh	PA	15212	412-237-9400		671	Web: www.pennbrew.com
Penn Cigar Machines Inc	1 Line St	Nanticoke	PA	18634	570-740-1112		454	Web: www.penncigar.com
Penn Color Inc	400 Old Dublin Pk	Doylestown	PA	18901	215-345-6550	345-0270	550	TF: 866-617-7366 ■ Web: www.penncolor.com
Penn Commercial Inc	242 Oak Spring Rd	Washington	PA	15301	724-222-5330	222-4722	800	TF: 888-309-7484 ■ Web: penncommercial.edu
Penn Dutch Foods	3201 N State Rd 7	Margate	FL	33063	954-974-3900		345	Web: www.penn-dutch.com
Penn Emblem Co	10909 Dutton Rd	Philadelphia	PA	19154	800-793-7366	632-6166*	258	*Fax Area Code: 215 ■ TF: 800-793-7366 ■ Web: pennemblem.com
Penn Engineering Components	29045 Ave Penn	Valencia	CA	91355	661-295-2080	295-2084	295	Web: www.pennengineering.com
Penn Fibre Plastics	2434 Bristol Rd	Bensalem	PA	19020	800-662-7366	702-9552*	600	*Fax Area Code: 215 ■ TF: 800-662-7366 ■ Web: www.pennfibre.com
Penn Fishing Tackle Manufacturing Co	7 Science Ct	Columbia	SC	29203	800-892-5444		710	TF: 800-892-5444 ■ Web: www.pennfishing.com
Penn Foster Career School	925 Oak St	Scranton	PA	18515	570-342-7701		800	TF: 800-275-4410 ■ Web: www.pennfoster.edu
Penn Hills Chamber of Commerce	12013 Frankstown Rd	Pittsburgh	PA	15235	412-795-8741	795-7993	139	Web: www.pennhillschamber.org
Penn Hills School District	260 Aster St	Pittsburgh	PA	15235	412-793-7000		685	Web: www.phsd.k12.pa.us
Penn Inc	306 S 45th Ave	Phoenix	AZ	85043	800-289-7366	329-7366*	710	*Fax Area Code: 888 ■ TF: 800-289-7366 ■ Web: www.pennracquet.com
Penn Lighting Associates	417 N 8th St Ste 302	Philadelphia	PA	19123	215-735-5000	735-5459	361	Web: www.pennlighting.com
Penn Line Service Inc	300 Scottdale Ave	Scottdale	PA	15683	724-887-9110	887-0545	188-10	TF: 800-448-9110 ■ Web: www.pennline.com
Penn Machine Co	106 Stn St	Johnstown	PA	15905	814-288-1547	497-3325*	595	*Fax Area Code: 610 ■ TF: 800-736-6872 ■ Web: www.pennusa.com
Penn Maid Foods Inc	10975 Dutton Rd	Philadelphia	PA	19154	800-242-2423		296-27	Web: pennmaid.com
Penn Manor Senior High School	100 E Cottage Ave	Millersville	PA	17551	717-872-9520		685	Web: www.pennmanor.net
Penn Manufacturing Industries Inc (PMI)	506 Stump Rd	Montgomeryville	PA	18936	215-362-1217	362-3918	757	Web: www.pennmfg.com
Penn Mar Castings Inc	500 Broadway	Hanover	PA	17331	717-632-4165	632-6912	492	Web: www.pennmarcastings.com
Penn Metal Fabricators Inc	2103 New Germany Rd	Ebensburg	PA	15931	814-472-6000		198	Web: pennmetalfab.com
Penn Mutual Life Insurance Co	600 Dresher Rd	Horsham	PA	19044	215-956-8000		391-2	TF: 800-523-0650 ■ Web: www.pennmutual.com
Penn National Gaming	825 Berkshire Blvd	Wyomissing	PA	19610	610-373-2400	373-4966	322	Web: www.pngaming.com
Penn National Insurance Co	2 N Second St PO Box 2361	Harrisburg	PA	17101	717-234-4941		391-4	TF: 800-388-4764 ■ Web: www.pennnationalinsurance.com
Penn Parking Inc	7257 Pkwy Dr Ste 100	Hanover	MD	21076	410-782-9110		562	Web: www.pennparking.com
Penn Pro Inc	4000 State Rd 60 E PO Box 89	Mulberry	FL	33860	863-648-9990		261	Web: www.pennpro.net
Penn Shore Vineyards & Winery	10225 Lake Rd	North East	PA	16428	814-725-8688	725-8689	50-7	Web: www.pennshore.com
Penn State Behrend	4701 College Dr	Erie	PA	16563	814-898-6160	898-6461	97	TF: 800-231-2222 ■ Web: behrend.psu.edu
Penn State College of Medicine	500 University Dr Rm C1805	Hershey	PA	17033	717-531-6955		167-2	TF: 800-243-1455 ■ Web: www.hmc.pennstatehealth.org
Penn State Scranton *Worthington Scranton*	120 Ridge View Dr	Dunmore	PA	18512	570-963-2500	963-2524	162	Web: scranton.psu.edu
Penn State Tool & Die Corp	260 Westec Dr	Mount Pleasant	PA	15666	724-613-5500	696-4014	757	Web: www.pennstatetool.com
Penn State York	1031 Edgecomb Ave	York	PA	17403	717-771-4000	771-4005	162	Web: york.psu.edu
Penn Systems Group Inc	5068 W Chester Pk	Edgemont	PA	19028	610-353-3800	353-3801	196	Web: pennsys.com
Penn Treaty Network America Insurance Co	3440 Lehigh St	Allentown	PA	18103	800-362-0700	967-4616*	391-2	*Fax Area Code: 610 ■ TF: 800-362-0700 ■ Web: www.penntreaty.com
Penn Veterinary Supply Inc	53 Industrial Cir	Lancaster	PA	17601	717-656-4121		794	TF: 800-233-0210 ■ Web: www.pennvet.com
Penn Virginia Corp	100 Matsonford Rd Ste 200	Radnor	PA	19087	610-687-8900	687-3688	536	NASDAQ: PVAC ■ TF: 877-316-5288 ■ Web: www.pennvirginia.com
Penn's Landing	301 S Columbus Blvd	Philadelphia	PA	19106	215-922-2386	923-2801	50-6	Web: www.delawareriverwaterfront.com
Penn's View Hotel	14 N Front St	Philadelphia	PA	19106	215-922-7600	922-7642	379	TF: 800-331-7634 ■ Web: www.pennsviewhotel.com
Penna State Education Association Harrisburg (PSEA)	400 N Third St PO Box 1724	Harrisburg	PA	17105	717-255-7000		474	TF: 800-944-7732 ■ Web: www.psea.org
Pennag Industries Assn	2215 Forest Hills Dr Ste 39	Harrisburg	PA	17112	717-651-5920		138	Web: pennag.com
Penn-America Group	3 Bala Plaza E Ste 300	Bala Cynwyd	PA	19004	215-443-3600	660-8886*	391-4	*Fax Area Code: 610 ■ Web: www.penn-america.com
Pennco Tech	3815 Otter St	Bristol	PA	19007	215-785-0111		800	Web: www.penncotech.edu
Penncomp	2050 N Loop W Ste 200	Houston	TX	77018	713-669-0965		196	Web: www.penncomp.com
Penncorp Servicegroup Inc	600 N Second St Ste 401	Harrisburg	PA	17101	717-234-2300		635	TF: 800-544-9050 ■ Web: www.penncorp.net
Pennebaker Hegedus Films Inc	262 W 91st St	New York	NY	10024	212-496-9195	496-8195	514	Web: www.phfilms.com
PennEngineering & Manufacturing Corp	5190 Old Easton Rd	Danboro	PA	18916	215-766-8853	766-3680	278	TF: 800-237-4736 ■ Web: www.pemnet.com
Pennex Aluminum Company LLC	50 Community St	Wellsville	PA	17365	717-432-9647		492	Web: www.pennexaluminum.com
Penney Group Inc	1309 Topsail Rd PO Box 8274 Stn A	Saint John	NL	A1B3N4	709-782-3404	782-0129	360-3	Web: www.penneygroup.ca
Pennfab Inc	20 Steel Rd S	Morrisville	PA	19067	215-245-1577	245-1868	492	Web: www.pennfab.com
Penn-Florida Cos	1515 N Federal Hwy Ste 306	Boca Raton	FL	33432	561-750-1030		652	Web: www.pennflorida.com
Pennian Bank	2 N Main St PO Box 96	Mifflintown	PA	17059	717-436-2144		70	Web: pennianbank.com
Pennichuck Corp	25 Manchester St	Merrimack	NH	03054	603-882-5191	913-2362	787	NASDAQ: PNNW ■ TF: 800-553-5191 ■ Web: pennichuck.com
Pennington County	315 St Joseph St	Rapid City	SD	57701	605-394-2171		338	Web: www.pennco.org
Pennington County	101 Main Ave N PO Box 616	Thief River Falls	MN	56701	218-683-7000	683-7026	338	Web: co.pennington.mn.us
Pennington Law Firm LLC	1501 Main St Ste 700	Columbia	SC	29201	803-929-1070		41	Web: pennlawfirm.com
Pennington School	112 W Delaware Ave	Pennington	NJ	08534	609-737-1838		622	Web: www.pennington.org
Pennington Seed Inc	1280 AtlantaHwy	Madison	GA	30650	706-342-1234	342-8071	694	Web: www.pennington.com
Pennock Acheson Nielsen Devaney Chartered Accountants	701-10088 102 Ave NW TD Tower Ste 10088	Edmonton	AB	T5J2Z1	780-496-7774		2	Web: www.pand.ca
Pennock Co	7135 Colonial Ln	Pennsauken Township	NJ	08109	215-492-7900		293	TF: 800-248-1557 ■ Web: www.preferred.pennock.com
PENNPIRG (Pennsylvania Public Interest Research Group)	1429 Walnut St Ste 1100	Philadelphia	PA	19102	215-732-3747		633	Web: pennpirg.org
Penn-Plax	35 Marcus Blvd	Hauppauge	NY	11788	866-625-2385		578	Web: www.penn-plax.com

Listing	City	State	ZIP	Phone	Fax	Class
Pennridge Chamber of Commerce 538 W Market St *Web:* www.pennridge.com	Perkasie	PA	18944	215-257-5390	257-6840	139
Pennridge School District 1200 N 5th St *Web:* sites.google.com	Perkasie	PA	18944	215-257-5011		685
Penns Grove-Carneys Point Regional Board of Education 100 Iona Ave *Web:* pgcpschools.org	Penns Grove	NJ	08069	856-299-4250		685
Penns Valley Publishers (PVP) 154 E Main St *TF:* 800-422-4412 ■ *Web:* www.pennsvalleypublishers.com	Lansdale	PA	19446	215-855-4948	855-7238	637-10
Pennsauken Free Public Library 5605 N Crescent Blvd *Web:* www.pennsaukenlibrary.org	Pennsauken Township	NJ	08110	856-665-5959	486-0142	434-3
Pennstar Federal Credit Union 4139 E State St *Web:* pennstarfederal.com	Hermitage	PA	16148	724-981-2973		219
PennStuart 208 E Main St *Web:* www.pennstuart.com	Abingdon	VA	24210	276-628-5151		428
PennSuburban Chamber of Commerce 217 Church Rd Ste C **Fax Area Code:* 267 ■ *Web:* www.chambergmc.org	North Wales	PA	19454	215-362-9200	613-8865*	139
Pennswood Village 1382 Newtown-Langhorne Rd *TF:* 888-454-1122 ■ *Web:* pennswood.org	Newtown	PA	18940	215-968-9110		672
Pennsy Supply Inc 1001 Paxton St *TF:* 800-300-6426 ■ *Web:* www.pennsysupply.com	Harrisburg	PA	17104	717-233-4511		182
Pennsylvania						
Aging Dept 555 Walnut St 5th Fl *Web:* www.aging.pa.gov	Harrisburg	PA	17101	717-783-1550	783-6842	339-39
Agriculture Dept 2301 N Cameron St *Web:* www.agriculture.pa.gov	Harrisburg	PA	17110	717-787-4737	346-3229	339-39
Attorney General Strawberry Sq 16th Fl *TF:* 800-385-1044 ■ *Web:* www.attorneygeneral.gov	Harrisburg	PA	17120	717-787-3391	787-8242	339-39
Community & Economic Development Dept 400 N St 4th Fl *TF:* 866-466-3972 ■ *Web:* dced.pa.gov	Harrisburg	PA	17120	866-466-3972		339-39
Conservation & Natural Resources Dept 400 Market St 6th Fl *Web:* www.dcnr.pa.gov	Harrisburg	PA	17101	717-787-2703		339-39
Consumer Advocate 555 Walnut St 5th Fl Forum Pl *TF:* 800-684-6560 ■ *Web:* www.oca.state.pa.us	Harrisburg	PA	17101	717-783-5048	783-7152	339-39
Corrections Dept PO Box 598 *Web:* www.cor.pa.gov	Camp Hill	PA	17001	717-728-2573	346-5622	339-39
Driver & Vehicle Services Bureau 1101 S Front St *TF:* 800-932-4600 ■ *Web:* www.dmv.pa.gov	Harrisburg	PA	17104	800-265-0921		339-39
Education Dept 333 Market St *Web:* www.education.pa.gov	Harrisburg	PA	17126	717-783-6788		339-39
Emergency Management Agency 1310 Elmerton Ave *Web:* pema.pa.gov	Harrisburg	PA	17110	717-651-2001	651-2021	339-39
Environmental Protection Dept 400 Market St *Web:* www.dep.pa.gov	Harrisburg	PA	17101	717-783-8727		339-39
Fish & Boat Commission 1601 Elmerton Ave *Web:* pfbc.pa.gov	Harrisburg	PA	17110	717-705-7800		339-39
Game Commission 2001 Elmerton Ave *Web:* www.pgc.pa.gov	Harrisburg	PA	17110	717-787-4250	772-2411	339-39
General Assembly Capitol Bldg *TF:* 800-868-7672 ■ *Web:* www.legis.state.pa.us	Harrisburg	PA	17120	717-787-5920		339-39
Higher Education Assistance Agency 1200 N Seventh St **Fax Area Code:* 717 ■ *TF:* 800-213-9827 ■ *Web:* www.pheaa.org	Harrisburg	PA	17102	800-213-9827	720-3901*	725
Historical & Museum Commission 300 N St *Web:* www.phmc.pa.gov	Harrisburg	PA	17120	717-787-3362		339-39
Housing Finance Agency 211 N Front St *Web:* www.phfa.org	Harrisburg	PA	17101	717-780-3800		339-39
Information Technology Office 209 Finance Bldg *Web:* www.oa.pa.gov	Harrisburg	PA	17120	717-787-5440	787-4523	339-39
Insurance Dept 1326 Strawberry Sq *TF:* 877-881-6388 ■ *Web:* www.insurance.pa.gov	Harrisburg	PA	17120	717-787-2317	787-8585	339-39
Military & Veterans Affairs Dept Fort Indiantown Gap Bldg 0-47 *Web:* www.dmva.pa.gov	Annville	PA	17003	717-861-8910		339-39
Public Utility Commission 400 N St Keystone Bldg PO Box 3265 *TF:* 800-692-7380 ■ *Web:* www.puc.state.pa.us	Harrisburg	PA	17120	717-783-1740	787-6641	339-39
Public Welfare Dept PO Box 2675 *Web:* www.dhs.pa.gov	Harrisburg	PA	17105	717-787-6443	772-2062	339-39
Revenue Dept Strawberry Sq *Web:* www.revenue.pa.gov	Harrisburg	PA	17128	717-783-1405		339-39
Secretary of the Commonwealth 210 N Office Bldg *Web:* www.dos.pa.gov	Harrisburg	PA	17120	717-787-5280	787-1734	339-39
State Ethics Commission Rm 309 Finance Bldg PO Box 11470 *TF:* 800-932-0936 ■ *Web:* www.ethics.pa.gov	Harrisburg	PA	17108	717-783-1610	787-0806	265
State Parks Rachel Carson State Office Bldg 400 Market St PO Box 8551 *TF:* 888-727-2757 ■ *Web:* www.dcnr.pa.gov	Harrisburg	PA	17105	717-787-6640	787-8817	339-39
State Police 1800 Elmerton Ave *Web:* www.psp.pa.gov	Harrisburg	PA	17110	717-783-5599	705-2185	339-39
State System of Higher Education 2986 N Second St *Web:* www.passhe.edu	Harrisburg	PA	17110	717-720-4000	720-4011	339-39
Transportation Dept 400 N St *Web:* www.penndot.gov	Harrisburg	PA	17120	717-787-2838		339-39
Treasury Dept 129 Finance Bldg *TF:* 800-222-2040 ■ *Web:* www.patreasury.gov	Harrisburg	PA	17120	717-787-2465		339-39
Victims Compensation Assistance Program PO Box 1167 *TF:* 800-233-2339 ■ *Web:* www.pcv.pccd.pa.gov	Harrisburg	PA	17108	717-783-5153	787-4306	339-39
Vital Records Div PO Box 1528 *TF:* 844-228-3516 ■ *Web:* www.health.pa.gov	New Castle	PA	16103	800-254-5164		339-39
Vocational Rehabilitation Office (OVR) 417 Walnut St *TF:* 800-442-6351 ■ *Web:* www.portal.state.pa.us	Harrisburg	PA	17102	717-787-5244		339-39
Workers Compensation Bureau 1171 S Cameron St Rm 324 *TF:* 800-482-2383 ■ *Web:* www.dli.pa.gov	Harrisburg	PA	17104	717-783-5421		339-39
Pennsylvania AAA Federation 600 N Third St *Web:* www.aaapa.org	Harrisburg	PA	17101	717-238-7192	238-6574	53
Pennsylvania Academy of the Fine Arts *School of Fine Arts* 118 128 N Broad St *Web:* www.pafa.org	Philadelphia	PA	19102	215-972-7600	569-0153	164
Pennsylvania Anthracite Heritage Museum 22 Bald Mountain Rd McDade Pk Bald Mountain Rd *Web:* www.anthracitemuseum.org	Scranton	PA	18504	570-963-4804	963-4194	520
Pennsylvania Association of Realtors 500 N 12th St Ste 100 **Fax Area Code:* 717 ■ *TF:* 800-555-3390 ■ *Web:* www.parealtors.org	Lemoyne	PA	17043	800-555-3390	561-8796*	656
Pennsylvania Association of Staff Nurses & Allied Professionals (PASNAP) 1 Fayette St Ste 475 *TF:* 800-500-7850 ■ *Web:* www.pasnap.com	Conshohocken	PA	19428	610-567-2907	567-2915	533
Pennsylvania Ballet Shop 100 S Broad St Ste 2226 *Web:* shop.paballet.org	Philadelphia	PA	19110	215-551-7000	551-7224	573-1
Pennsylvania Bar Assn 100 South St *TF:* 800-932-0311 ■ *Web:* www.pabar.org	Harrisburg	PA	17101	717-238-6715	238-1204	72
Pennsylvania Chamber of Business & Industry 417 Walnut St *TF:* 800-225-7224 ■ *Web:* www.pachamber.org	Harrisburg	PA	17101	717-255-3252	255-3298	140
Pennsylvania College of Art & Design 204 N Prince St *TF:* 800-689-0379 ■ *Web:* pcad.edu	Lancaster	PA	17603	717-396-7833	396-1339	164
Pennsylvania College of Technology 1 College Ave *Web:* www.pct.edu	Williamsport	PA	17701	570-326-3761	321-5551	800
Pennsylvania Commission for Community Colleges (PCCC) 800 N 3rd St Ste 405 *Web:* pacommunitycolleges.org	Harrisburg	PA	17102	717-232-7584		49-19
Pennsylvania Convention Ctr 1101 Arch St *TF:* 800-428-9000 ■ *Web:* www.paconvention.com	Philadelphia	PA	19107	215-418-4700		205
Pennsylvania Correctional Industries PO Box 47 *TF:* 877-673-3724 ■ *Web:* www.cor.pa.gov	Camp Hill	PA	17011	717-425-7292	425-7291	630
Pennsylvania Crusher Corp 600 Abbott Dr *Web:* terrasource.com	Broomall	PA	19008	610-544-7200		190
Pennsylvania Democratic Party 229 State St *Web:* www.padems.com	Harrisburg	PA	17101	717-920-8470	901-7829	616-1
Pennsylvania Dental Assn 3501 N Front St *Web:* www.padental.org	Harrisburg	PA	17110	717-234-5941	232-7169	227
Pennsylvania Dutch Candies 1250 Slate Hill Rd *TF:* 800-233-7082 ■ *Web:* www.padutchcandies.com	Camp Hill	PA	17011	800-233-7082		296-8
Pennsylvania Economy League Inc (PEL) 88 N Franklin St *Web:* pelcentral.org	Wilkes-Barre	PA	18701	570-824-3559	829-8099	637-2
Pennsylvania Employees Benefit Trust Fund 150 S 43rd St *TF:* 800-522-7279 ■ *Web:* www.pebtf.org	Harrisburg	PA	17111	717-561-4750		41
Pennsylvania Equine Council (PEC) PO Box 303 *TF:* 888-304-0281 ■ *Web:* www.pennsylvaniaequinecouncil.org	Windsor	PA	17366	888-304-0281		48-13
Pennsylvania Gunsmith School 812 Ohio River Blvd *Web:* www.pagunsmith.edu	Pittsburgh	PA	15202	412-766-1812		685
Pennsylvania Highlands Community College 101 Community College Way *Web:* www.pennhighlands.edu	Johnstown	PA	15904	814-471-0010	262-6420	162
Pennsylvania Homeschoolers 105 Richman Ln *Web:* www.pahomeschoolers.com	Kittanning	PA	16201	724-783-6512		423
Pennsylvania Institute of Technology (PIT) 800 Manchester Ave *TF:* 800-422-0025 ■ *Web:* www.pit.edu	Media	PA	19063	610-892-1500	892-1533	800
Pennsylvania Library Assn (PALA) 220 Cumberland Pkwy Ste 10 *TF:* 800-622-3308 ■ *Web:* www.palibraries.org	Mechanicsburg	PA	17055	717-766-7663	766-5440	435
Pennsylvania Macaroni Co 2010-2012 Penn Ave *Web:* www.pennmac.com	Pittsburgh	PA	15222	412-227-1982		360-3
Pennsylvania Manufacturers Association Co 380 Sentry Pkwy *TF:* 800-222-2749 ■ *Web:* www.pmacompanies.com	Blue Bell	PA	19422	800-222-2749		391-4
Pennsylvania Medical Society 777 E Park Dr PO Box 8820 *TF:* 800-228-7823 ■ *Web:* www.pamedsoc.org	Harrisburg	PA	17105	717-558-7750	558-7818	391-5
Pennsylvania Municipal League 414 N 2nd St *Web:* www.pml.org	Harrisburg	PA	17101	717-236-9469	236-6716	49-19
Pennsylvania Pharmacists Assn 508 N Third St *Web:* www.papharmacists.com	Harrisburg	PA	17101	717-234-6151		585
Pennsylvania Precision Cast Parts Inc 521 N Third Ave PO Box 1429 *Web:* www.ppcpinc.com	Lebanon	PA	17042	717-273-3338	273-2662	306
Pennsylvania Public Interest Research Group (PENNPIRG) 1429 Walnut St Ste 1100 *Web:* pennpirg.org	Philadelphia	PA	19102	215-732-3747		633

	Phone	Fax	Class
Pennsylvania Real Estate Investment Trust 200 S Broad St 3rd Fl . . . . Philadelphia PA 19102 *NYSE:* PEI ■ *TF:* 866-875-0700 ■ *Web:* www.preit.com	215-875-0700	546-7311	655
Pennsylvania Renaissance Faire 2775 Lebanon Rd . . . . Manheim PA 17545 *Web:* www.parenfaire.com	717-665-7021	664-3466	31
Pennsylvania Republican State Committee 112 State St . . . . Harrisburg PA 17101 *Web:* www.pagop.org	717-234-4901	231-3828	616-2
Pennsylvania Restaurant and Lodging Assn (PRLA) 100 State St . . . . Harrisburg PA 17101 *TF:* 800-345-5353 ■ *Web:* www.prla.org	717-232-4433	236-1202	49-19
Pennsylvania State Athletic Commission 2601 N Third St . . . . Harrisburg PA 17110 **Fax Area Code:* 717 ■ *TF:* 877-868-3772 ■ *Web:* www.dos.pa.gov	877-868-3772	783-0824*	712
Pennsylvania State Employees Credit Union 1 Innovation Way . . . . Harrisburg PA 17110 *TF:* 800-237-7328 ■ *Web:* www.psecu.com	717-255-1760	772-2272	219
Pennsylvania State University			
Abington College 1600 Woodland Rd . . . . Abington PA 19001 *Web:* abington.psu.edu	215-881-7300	881-7412	166
Altoona 3000 Ivyside Pk . . . . Altoona PA 16601 *TF:* 800-848-9843 ■ *Web:* altoona.psu.edu	814-949-5466		166
Beaver 100 University Dr . . . . Monaca PA 15061 *TF:* 877-564-6778 ■ *Web:* beaver.psu.edu	724-773-3500	773-3578	162
Berks Tulpehocken Rd PO Box 7009 . . . . Reading PA 19610 *Web:* berks.psu.edu	610-396-6000	396-6077	162
DuBois 1 College Park Dr . . . . DuBois PA 15801 *TF:* 800-346-7627 ■ *Web:* dubois.psu.edu	814-375-4700	375-4784	162
Fayette 2201 University Dr . . . . Lemont Furnace PA 15456 *TF:* 877-568-4130 ■ *Web:* fayette.psu.edu	724-430-4100	430-4175	162
Harrisburg 777 W Harrisburg Pk . . . . Middletown PA 17057 *TF:* 800-222-2056 ■ *Web:* harrisburg.psu.edu	717-948-6000	948-6325	166
Hazleton 76 University Dr . . . . Hazleton PA 18202 *TF:* 800-279-8495 ■ *Web:* hazleton.psu.edu	570-450-3000		162
Libraries 510 Paterno Library . . . . University Park PA 16802 *Web:* libraries.psu.edu	814-865-6368	865-3665	434-6
Mont Alto 1 Campus Dr . . . . Mont Alto PA 17237 *TF:* 800-392-6173 ■ *Web:* montalto.psu.edu	717-749-6000	749-6132	162
New Kensington 3550 Seventh St Rd Rt 780 . . . . New Kensington PA 15068 *Web:* newkensington.psu.edu	724-334-5466	334-6111	162
Schuylkill 200 University Dr . . . . Schuylkill Haven PA 17972 *Web:* schuylkill.psu.edu	570-385-6000	385-6113	162
Shenango 147 Shenango Ave . . . . Sharon PA 16146 *TF:* 888-275-7009 ■ *Web:* shenango.psu.edu	724-983-2803	983-2820	162
Pennsylvania State University Dickinson Law 150 S College St . . . . Carlisle PA 17013 *Web:* dickinsonlaw.psu.edu	717-240-5000	241-3503	167-1
Pennsylvania State University Press 820 N University Dr USB1 Ste C . . . . University Park PA 16802 *TF:* 800-326-9180 ■ *Web:* www.psupress.org	814-865-1327	863-1408	637-4
Pennsylvania State University, The			
Brandywine 25 Yearsley Mill Rd . . . . Media PA 19063 *Web:* brandywine.psu.edu	610-892-1200	892-1357	166
Penn State Lehigh Valley 2809 Saucon Valley Rd . . . . Center Valley PA 18034 *Web:* lehighvalley.psu.edu	610-285-5000	285-5220	162
Pennstate Wilkes-Barre Old Rt 115 PO Box PSU . . . . Lehman PA 18627 *Web:* wilkesbarre.psu.edu	570-675-2171	675-9113	162
Pennsylvania Steel Company Inc 1717 Woodhaven Dr . . . . Bensalem PA 19020 *TF:* 800-999-2997 ■ *Web:* www.pasteel.com	215-633-9600	633-9601	492
Pennsylvania Tool & Gages Inc PO Box 534 . . . . Meadville PA 16335 *TF:* 877-827-8285 ■ *Web:* www.patool.com	814-336-3136	333-9131	757
Pennsylvania Transformer Technology Inc 30 Curry Ave . . . . Canonsburg PA 15317 *Web:* www.patransformer.com	724-873-2100		767
Pennsylvania Trust Co 5 Radnor Corp Ctr Ste 450 . . . . Radnor PA 19087 *TF:* 800-975-4316 ■ *Web:* www.penntrust.com	610-975-4300	975-4324	690
Pennsylvania Youth Ballet (PYB) 556 Main St . . . . Bethlehem PA 18018 *Web:* www.bglv.org	610-865-0353		573-1
Penn-Tech International Inc 3 S Bacton Hill Rd Unit 2 . . . . Frazer PA 19355 *Web:* www.ptii.net	484-395-0145		189-11
Penntecq Inc 106 Kuder Dr . . . . Greenville PA 16125 *Web:* www.penntecq.com	724-646-4250	646-4261	60
Pennterra Engineering Inc 3075 Enterprise Dr Ste 100 . . . . State College PA 16801 *Web:* pennterra.com	814-231-8285	237-2308	261
Penn-Union Corp 229 Waterford St . . . . Edinboro PA 16412 *Web:* www.penn-union.com	814-734-1631	734-4946	815
Pennville Custom Cabinetry 600 E Votaw St . . . . Portland IN 47371 *Web:* www.pennvillecabinetry.com	260-726-9357	726-7044	115
Penny Group Inc, The 1328 Harding Pl . . . . Charlotte NC 28204 *Web:* www.thepennygroup.com	704-372-1400		195
Penny Hill Publishing PO Box 257 . . . . Franklin TN 37065 *Web:* www.pennyhillpublishing.com	615-830-4181		637-2
Penny Ohlmann Neiman Inc 1605 N Main St . . . . Dayton OH 45405 *Web:* ohlmanngroup.com	937-278-0681		4
Penny-Farthing Productions Inc 2000 W Sam Houston Pky S . . . . Houston TX 77042 *TF:* 800-926-2669 ■ *Web:* www.pfpress.com	713-780-0300	780-4004	637-2
Penn-York Medical Supplies Inc 69 Main St . . . . Binghamton NY 13905 *Web:* www.penn-yorkmedical.com	607-773-3622	773-0063	475
Pennypack Supply Co 8030 Frankford Ave . . . . Philadelphia PA 19136 *TF:* 877-439-0272 ■ *Web:* www.pennypacksupply.com	877-439-0272		364
Pennyrile Forest State Resort Park 20781 Pennyrile Lodge Rd . . . . Dawson Springs KY 42408 *TF:* 800-325-1711 ■ *Web:* parks.ky.gov	270-797-3421		565
Pennyrile Rural Electric Co-opeartive Corp 2000 Harrison St PO Box 2900 . . . . Hopkinsville KY 42241 *TF:* 800-297-4710 ■ *Web:* www.precc.com	270-886-2555		245
Pennyroyal Hospice Inc 220 Burley Ave . . . . Hopkinsville KY 42240 *TF:* 888-611-0121 ■ *Web:* pennyroyalhospice.com	270-885-6428		363
Pennysaveronline.com 18-20 Mechanic St . . . . Norwich NY 13815 *Web:* pennysaveronline.com	607-334-4714	336-7318	532-2
Pennysmith's 4022 Rio Grande Blvd NW . . . . Albuquerque NM 87107 *Web:* www.pennysmiths.com	505-345-2353		534
Pennzoil 1321 W Tyler Ave Ste 125 . . . . Houston TX 77002 *Web:* www.pennzoil.com	713-546-4000	546-6639	541
Penobscot Community Health Center Inc 103 Maine Ave . . . . Bangor ME 04401 *Web:* pchc.com	207-992-9200		237
Penobscot County 97 Hammond St . . . . Bangor ME 04401 *Web:* www.penobscot-county.net	207-942-8535		338
Penobscot Investment Management Company Inc 50 Congress St Ste 410 . . . . Boston MA 02109 *Web:* www.pimboston.com	617-227-3111		401
Penobscot Marine Museum 5 Church St PO Box 498 . . . . Searsport ME 04974 *TF:* 800-268-8030 ■ *Web:* penobscotmarinemuseum.org	207-548-2529	548-2520	520
Penobscot McCrum LLC 28 Pierce St . . . . Belfast ME 04915 *TF:* 800-435-4456 ■ *Web:* www.penobscotmccrum.com	207-338-4360	338-5742	296-21
Penobscot Theatre Co 131 Main St . . . . Bangor ME 04401 *Web:* www.penobscottheatre.org	207-942-3333		573-4
PenRad Technologies Inc 114 Commerce Cir . . . . Buffalo MN 55313 *Web:* www.penrad.com	763-475-3388		475
Penray Companies Inc 440 Denniston Ct . . . . Wheeling IL 60090 **Fax Area Code:* 847 ■ *TF:* 800-373-6729 ■ *Web:* penray.com	800-323-6329	459-5043*	145
Penrod & George 421 Independence Dr . . . . Napoleon OH 43545 *Web:* penrodcpa.com	419-599-8045		2
Penrod Co 272 Bendix Rd Ste 550 . . . . Virginia Beach VA 23452 *TF:* 800-537-3497 ■ *Web:* www.thepenrodcompany.com	757-498-0188	498-1075	191-2
Penrose Academy 13402 N Scottsdale Rd Ste B160 . . . . Scottsdale AZ 85254 *Web:* www.penrose.edu	480-222-9540	222-9541	167-3
Penrose Chun & Gorman LLP 1200 Pacific Ave Ste 260 . . . . Santa Cruz CA 95060 *Web:* pcg-llp.com	831-515-3344		41
Penrose Point State Park 321 158th KPS . . . . Lakebay WA 98349 *Web:* www.parks.state.wa.us	253-884-2514		565
Pensacola Area Chamber of Commerce 117 W Garden St . . . . Pensacola FL 32502 *Web:* www.pensacolachamber.com	850-438-4081	438-6369	139
Pensacola Christian College 250 Brent Ln . . . . Pensacola FL 32503 **Fax Area Code:* 800 ■ *TF:* 800-722-4636 ■ *Web:* www.pcci.edu	850-478-8496	722-3355*	166
Pensacola City Hall 222 W Main St . . . . Pensacola FL 32502 *Web:* www.cityofpensacola.com	850-435-1626		337
Pensacola Civic Ctr 201 E Gregory St . . . . Pensacola FL 32502 *Web:* www.pensacolabaycenter.com	850-432-0800	432-1707	572
Pensacola Convention & Visitors Bureau 1401 E Gregory St . . . . Pensacola FL 32502 *TF:* 800-874-1234 ■ *Web:* www.visitpensacola.com	850-434-1234		206
Pensacola Cultural Ctr (PCC) 400 S Jefferson St . . . . Pensacola FL 32502 *Web:* www.pensacolalittletheatre.com	850-432-2042		572
Pensacola Greyhound Track 951 Dog Track Rd . . . . Pensacola FL 32506 *TF:* 800-345-3997 ■ *Web:* www.pensacolagreyhoundtrack.com	850-455-8595		642
Pensacola Gulf Coast Regional Airport 2430 Airport Blvd Ste 225 . . . . Pensacola FL 32504 *TF:* 800-874-6580 ■ *Web:* www.flypensacola.com	850-436-5000	436-5006	27
Pensacola Junior College 1000 College Blvd . . . . Pensacola FL 32504 *TF:* 888-897-3605 ■ *Web:* www.pensacolastate.edu	850-484-1000	484-1829	162
Pensacola Museum of Art 407 S Jefferson St . . . . Pensacola FL 32502 *Web:* www.pensacolamuseum.org	850-432-6247	469-1532	520
Pensacola Opera 75 S Tarragona St . . . . Pensacola FL 32502 *Web:* pensacolaopera.com	850-433-6737		573-2
Pensacola School of Massage Therapy & Health Careers 2409 Creighton Rd . . . . Pensacola FL 32504 *Web:* www.psmthc.com	850-474-1330	475-4294	685
Pensacola Symphony Orchestra 205 E Zaragossa St PO Box 1752 . . . . Pensacola FL 32502 *Web:* www.pensacolasymphony.com	850-435-2533		573-3
Pensar Development Inc 1011 W Ave Ste 1000 . . . . Seattle WA 98122 *Web:* pensar.com	206-284-3134		256
Pension Administrators & Consultants Inc 1544 Woodlake Dr . . . . Chesterfield MO 63017 *Web:* pension-administrators.com	314-878-1544		390
Pension Benefit Guaranty Corp 1200 K St NW . . . . Washington DC 20005 *TF:* 800-400-7242 ■ *Web:* www.pbgc.gov	202-326-4000		340-20
Pension Corp Stn Prov Govt Po Box 9460 . . . . Victoria BC V8W9V8 *Web:* www.pensionsbc.ca	250-387-1002		528
Pension Real Estate Assn (PREA) 100 Pearl St 13th Fl . . . . Hartford CT 06103 *Web:* www.prea.org	860-692-6341	692-6351	49-2
Pension Rights Ctr 1350 Connecticut Ave NW Ste 206 . . . . Washington DC 20036 *TF:* 866-735-7737 ■ *Web:* www.pensionrights.org	202-296-3776	833-2472	48-6
Pensionmark Retirement Group 24 E Cota St . . . . Santa Barbara CA 93101 *Web:* pensionmark.com	805-456-6260		401
Penske Vehicle Services Inc 1225 E Maple Rd . . . . Troy MI 48083 *TF:* 877-210-5290 ■ *Web:* penskevehicleservices.com	248-729-5400		194

Listing	Phone	Fax	Class
Penso Capital Markets LLC 68 Carman Ave . . . . Cedarhurst NY 11516 *Web:* www.penso.com	516-791-3800		690
Penstan Supply 501 Broad St . . . . Johnstown PA 15906 *TF:* 800-634-0684 ■ *Web:* www.penstanjohnstown.com	814-536-0754	539-2808	612
Penta Communications Inc 208 Turnpike Rd Ste 200 . . . . Westborough MA 01581 *Web:* www.pentamarketing.com	508-616-9900	366-0781	463
Penta Engineering Corp 10123 Corporate Square Dr . . . . Saint Louis MO 63132 *Web:* penta.net	314-878-0123		261
Penta Laboratories (PL) 7868 Deering Ave . . . . Canoga Park CA 91304 *TF:* 800-421-4219 ■ *Web:* pentalabs.com	818-882-3872	882-3968	418
Penta Technologies Inc 250 S Executive Dr Ste 201 . . . . Brookfield WI 53005 *Web:* www.penta.com	262-782-7700	780-2444	178-1
Pentacle Theater 324 52nd Ave NW . . . . Salem OR 97304 *TF:* 800-333-0774 ■ *Web:* pentacletheatre.org	503-364-7200		572
Pentaflex Inc 4981 Gateway Blvd . . . . Springfield OH 45502 *Web:* pentaflex.com	937-325-5551		488
Pentagon 2000 Software Inc 15 W 34 St 5th Fl . . . . New York NY 10001 *TF:* 800-643-1806 ■ *Web:* www.pentagon2000.com	212-629-7521	629-7513	178-1
Pentagon Federal Credit Union 2930 Eisenhower Ave . . . . Alexandria VA 22314 *TF:* 800-247-5626 ■ *Web:* www.penfed.org	800-247-5626	253-6589	219
Pentair 5500 Wayzata Blvd Ste 600 . . . . Minneapolis MN 55416 *Web:* www.pentair.com	763-545-1730		641
Pentair 1101 Myers Pkwy . . . . Ashland OH 44805 **Fax Area Code:* 800 ■ *TF:* 855-274-8948 ■ *Web:* www.pentaircom.com	855-274-8948	426-9446*	641
Pentair 1620 Hawkins Ave . . . . Sanford NC 27330 *TF:* 800-831-7133 ■ *Web:* www.pentair.com	800-831-7133	284-4151	641
Pentair Residential Filtration LLC 13845 Bishops Dr Ste 200 . . . . Brookfield WI 53008 *TF:* 888-784-9065 ■ *Web:* www.waterpurification.pentair.com	262-784-4490	785-6535	91
Pentalpha Capital Group LLC 1 Greenwich Office Pk North Bldg. . . . . Greenwich CT 06831 *Web:* www.pentalphaglobal.com	203-660-6100		401
Pentastar Aviation 7310 Highland Rd . . . . Waterford MI 48327 *TF:* 800-662-9612 ■ *Web:* www.pentastaraviation.com	248-666-3630		13
Pentax Imaging Co 633 17th St Ste 2600. . . . . Denver CO 80202 *TF:* 800-877-0155 ■ *Web:* us.ricoh-imaging.com	303-799-8000		173-6
Pentec Health 50 Applied Card Way. . . . . Glen Mills PA 19342 **Fax Area Code:* 866 ■ *TF:* 844-742-6150 ■ *Web:* www.pentechealth.com	610-494-8700	495-7659*	363
Pentecostal Assemblies of Canada, The (PAOC) 2450 Milltower Ct. . . . . Mississauga ON L5N5Z6 *TF:* 800-779-7262 ■ *Web:* www.paoc.org	905-542-7400	542-7313	48-20
Pentecostal Publishing House (PPH) 5584 Mt View Rd . . . . Antioch TN 37013 *TF:* 866-819-7667 ■ *Web:* www.pentecostalpublishing.com	866-819-7667		637-2
Pentecostal Theological Seminary 900 Walker St NE . . . . Cleveland TN 37311 *TF:* 800-228-9126 ■ *Web:* www.ptseminary.edu	423-478-1131		167-3
Pentek Inc 1 Pk Way . . . . Upper Saddle River NJ 07458 *Web:* www.pentek.com	201-818-5900	818-5692	625
Pentel of America Ltd 2715 Columbia St. . . . . Torrance CA 90503 *TF:* 855-528-4101 ■ *Web:* www.pentel.com	760-200-0547	200-0586	571
PenTeleData 540 Delaware Ave PO Box 197 . . . . Palmerton PA 18071 *TF:* 800-281-3564 ■ *Web:* www.penteledata.net	800-281-3564		225
Pentera Inc 8650 Commerce Park Pl Ste G . . . . Indianapolis IN 46268 *Web:* pentera.com	317-875-0910		195
Penterra Services 1700 Kaliste Saloom Rd Bldg 5 . . . . LaFayette LA 70508 *Web:* penterraservices.com	337-706-8650	706-8655	653
Penticton & Wine Country Chamber of Commerce 101 - 553 Vees Dr. . . . . Penticton BC V2A8S3 *Web:* www.penticton.org	250-490-2006		137
Pentron Clinical Technologies LLC 1717 W Collins Ave . . . . Orange CA 92867 **Fax Area Code:* 877 ■ *TF:* 800-551-0283 ■ *Web:* www.pentron.com	714-516-7557	677-8844*	228
Pentucket Bank 1 Merrimack St. . . . . Haverhill MA 01830 *Web:* www.pentucketbank.com	978-372-7731	372-4499	70
Pentwater Wire Products Inc (PWP) 474 Carroll St PO Box 947 . . . . Pentwater MI 49449 *TF:* 877-869-6911 ■ *Web:* www.pentwaterwire.com	231-869-6911	869-4020	286
Pentz Design Pattern & Foundry 14823 Main St NE . . . . Duvall WA 98019 *TF:* 800-411-6555 ■ *Web:* www.pentzcastsolutions.com	425-788-6490		492
Penumbra Theatre 270 Kent St . . . . Saint Paul MN 55102 *Web:* penumbratheatre.org	651-224-3180	288-6789	572
Penwood State Park 560 Simsburry Rd. . . . . Bloomfield CT 06002 *Web:* portal.ct.gov	860-560-9036		565
Penworthy Co, The 219 N Milwaukee St . . . . Milwaukee WI 53202 *TF:* 800-262-2665 ■ *Web:* www.penworthy.com	414-287-4600	287-4602	96
Penzeys Spices Inc 12001 W Capitol Dr . . . . Wauwatosa WI 53222 *Web:* www.penzeys.com	414-760-7307		459
PENZONE Salons + Spas! 1480 Manning Pkwy. . . . . Powell OH 43065 *Web:* www.penzonesalons.com	614-898-1200		77
People Bank 201 N Bardstown Rd. . . . . Mount Washington KY 40047 *Web:* www.peoplesbankmtw.com	502-538-7301	538-6606	70
People Care Inc 116 W 32nd St 15th Fl . . . . New York NY 10001 *Web:* www.peoplecare.com	212-631-7300		363
People Creating Success Inc (PCS) 1000 Hill St Ste 320 . . . . Ventura CA 93003 *Web:* www.pcs-services.org	805-644-9480	644-9473	672
People First Federal Credit Union 2141 Downyflake Ln . . . . Allentown PA 18103 *TF:* 800-446-5598 ■ *Web:* www.peoplefirstcu.org	610-797-7440		219
People For Animals Inc 401 Hillside Ave . . . . Hillside NJ 07205 *Web:* pfaonline.org	973-282-0890		794
People for the American Way (PFAW) 2000 M St NW Ste 400. . . . . Washington DC 20036 *TF:* 800-326-7329 ■ *Web:* www.pfaw.org	202-467-4999	293-2672	48-7
People for the Ethical Treatment of Animals (PETA) 501 Front St . . . . Norfolk VA 23510 *TF:* 800-566-9768 ■ *Web:* www.peta.org	757-622-7382	622-0457	48-3
People Inc 1219 N Forest Rd . . . . Williamsville NY 14231 *Web:* www.people-inc.org	716-634-8132		672
People Lease Inc 689 Towne Center Blvd. . . . . Ridgeland MS 39157 *TF:* 800-723-3025 ■ *Web:* www.peoplelease.com	601-987-3025	987-3029	631
People Magazine Time & Life Bldg 1271 Avenue of the Americas 28th Fl . . . . New York NY 10020 *TF:* 800-541-9000	212-522-3347	522-0883	457-11
People Newspapers 750 N St Paul St Ste 2100 . . . . Dallas TX 75201 *Web:* www.peoplenewspapers.com	214-739-2244		532-4
People Plus Industrial Inc 1095 Nebo Rd. . . . . Madisonville KY 42431 *TF:* 888-825-1500 ■ *Web:* www.peopleplusinc.com	270-825-8939		260
People Productions Video Services Inc 1737 15th St Ste 200 . . . . Boulder CO 80302 *Web:* peopleproductions.com	303-449-6086		514
People Services Center Inc 10868 W Dodge Rd . . . . Omaha NE 68154 *Web:* catchintelligence.com	402-715-5800		180
People's Electric Co-op 1600 N Country Club Rd . . . . Ada OK 74820 *TF:* 877-456-3031 ■ *Web:* www.peopleselectric.coop	580-332-3031	272-1558	245
People's Energy Co-op 1775 Lake Shady Ave S . . . . Oronoco MN 55960 *TF:* 800-214-2694 ■ *Web:* www.peoplesrec.com	507-367-7000	367-7001	245
People's Food Co-op 315 Fifth Ave S. . . . . La Crosse WI 54601 *Web:* www.pfc.coop	608-784-5798		345
People's Light & Theatre Co 39 Conestoga Rd . . . . Malvern PA 19355 *Web:* www.peopleslight.org	610-647-1900	640-9521	749
People's Securities Inc 850 Main St . . . . Bridgeport CT 06604 *TF:* 800-894-0300 ■ *Web:* psi.peoples.com	800-894-0300		690
People's United Bank Bridgeport Ctr 850 Main St. . . . . Bridgeport CT 06604 *TF:* 800-772-1090 ■ *Web:* www.peoples.com	203-338-7171		70
People's Weekly World 235 W 23rd St . . . . New York NY 10011 *Web:* www.peoplesworld.org	212-924-2523	229-1713	532-4
Peoplefit Health & Fitness Ctr 237 Lexington St . . . . Woburn MA 01801 *TF:* 855-784-4663 ■ *Web:* peoplefit.net	781-932-9332	491-0477	354
Peoplelink Staffing Solutions LLC 431 E Colfax Ave Ste 200 . . . . South Bend IN 46617 *Web:* www.peoplelinkstaffing.com	574-232-5400	245-5822	260
PeopleNet 4400 Baker Rd . . . . Minnetonka MN 55343 **Fax Area Code:* 425 ■ *TF:* 888-346-3486 ■ *Web:* www.peoplenetonline.com	905-332-2329	675-8218*	681
PeopleReady Inc 1015 A St . . . . Tacoma WA 98401 **Fax Area Code:* 877 ■ *TF:* 877-733-0430 ■ *Web:* www.peopleready.com	253-383-9101	733-0399*	631
Peoples 9738 Up River Rd . . . . Corpus Christi TX 78410 *Web:* www.peoplesrestaurant.com	361-241-8087		671
Peoples Bancorp Inc 138 Putnam St. . . . . Marietta OH 45750 *NASDAQ:* PEBO ■ *TF:* 800-374-6123 ■ *Web:* www.peoplesbancorp.com	740-373-3155		360-2
Peoples Bancorp of North Carolina Inc 518 W 'C' St . . . . Newton NC 28658 *NASDAQ:* PEBK ■ *TF:* 800-948-7195 ■ *Web:* peoplesbanknc.com	828-464-5620		360-2
Peoples Bank 5820 82nd St . . . . Lubbock TX 79424 *Web:* peoplesbanktexas.com	806-794-0044	794-9262	70
Peoples Bank & Trust 805 Hospital Rd PO Box 747 . . . . New Roads LA 70760 *Web:* www.thefriendlybank.com	225-638-3713	638-6772	780
Peoples Bank of Kankakee County 315 Main NW . . . . Bourbonnais IL 60914 *Web:* peoplesbankdirect.com	815-936-7600		70
Peoples Cartage Inc 2207 Kimball Rd SE . . . . Canton OH 44707 *Web:* www.peoplesservices.com	330-453-3709	453-5170	780
Peoples Community Bank, The 222 W Commercial St PO Box 8. . . . . Mazomanie WI 53560 *Web:* thepeoplescommunitybank.com	608-795-2120		70
Peoples Electric Company Inc 277 E Fillmore Ave . . . . Saint Paul MN 55107 *Web:* www.peoplesco.com	651-227-7711		189-4
Peoples Financial Services Corp 82 Franklin Ave. . . . . Hallstead PA 18822 *NASDAQ:* PFIS ■ *TF:* 888-868-3858 ■ *Web:* www.psbt.com	570-879-2175		70
Peoples Health 3838 N Causeway Blvd Ste 2600 . . . . Metairie LA 70002 *TF:* 800-222-8600 ■ *Web:* www.peopleshealth.com	504-849-4500		391-3
Peoples Insurance Agency Ltd 1700 Eighth St SW . . . . Waverly IA 50677 *TF:* 800-932-4801 ■ *Web:* peoples-insurance.com	319-352-6327		390
Peoples Jewellers 1100 Pembroke St E. . . . . Pembroke ON K8A6Y7 *TF:* 800-211-2272 ■ *Web:* www.peoplesjewellers.com	613-735-1536		410
Peoples Savings Bank (PSB) 414 N Adams PO Box 248 . . . . Wellsburg IA 50680 *TF:* 877-508-2265 ■ *Web:* www.bankpsb.com	641-869-3721	869-3855	70
Peoples Savings Bank 101 Bluff St. . . . . Rhineland MO 65069 *Web:* www.ourpsb.com	573-236-4414	236-4368	70
Peoples State Bank 445 S Lewis Ave . . . . Tulsa OK 74104 *Web:* peoplesbanktulsa.com	918-583-9800	587-9307	70
Peoples Telecommunications LLC 208 N Broadway . . . . La Cygne KS 66040 *TF:* 877-876-4434 ■ *Web:* www.peoplestelecom.net	913-757-2500		224
Peopleschoice Credit Union 23 Industrial Park Rd . . . . Saco ME 04072 *TF:* 877-785-6328 ■ *Web:* peopleschoicecreditunion.com	207-282-4156		219
PeopleShare 1601 Market St 17th Fl. . . . . Philadelphia PA 19103 *Web:* www.peopleshareworks.com	215-988-0700		631

Name / Address	City	State	ZIP	Phone	Fax	Class
PeopleSpace 17800 Mitchell N *Web:* www.interiorofficesolutions.com	Irvine	CA	92614	949-724-9444		321
PeopleStrategy Inc 5883 Glenridge Dr Ste 200 *TF:* 855-488-4100 ■ *Web:* www.peoplestrategy.com	Atlanta	GA	30328	855-488-4100		178-1
PeopleTec Inc 4901-I Corporate Dr NW *Web:* www.peopletec.com	Huntsville	AL	35805	256-319-3800		261
People-to-People Health Foundation 255 Carter Hall Ln *TF:* 800-544-4673 ■ *Web:* www.projecthope.org	Millwood	VA	22646	540-837-2100	837-1813	48-5
PeopleWorks Inc 224 Main St *Web:* www.peopleworksinc.com	Alta	IA	51002	712-284-2881		463
Peoria Area Chamber of Commerce 100 SW Water St *Web:* www.peoriachamber.org	Peoria	IL	61602	309-676-0755	676-7534	139
Peoria Area Convention & Visitors Bureau 456 Fulton St Ste 300 *TF:* 800-747-0302 ■ *Web:* www.peoria.org	Peoria	IL	61602	309-676-0303	676-8470	206
Peoria Ballet 809 W Detweiller Dr *Web:* peoriaballet.com	Peoria	IL	61615	309-690-7990	690-7991	573-1
Peoria City Hall 419 Fulton St *Web:* www.peoriagov.org	Peoria	IL	61602	309-494-2273		337
Peoria Civic Ctr 201 SW Jefferson Ave *Web:* www.peoriaciviccenter.com	Peoria	IL	61602	309-673-8900	673-9223	572
Peoria County Courthouse 324 Main St Rm 101 *TF:* 800-843-6154 ■ *Web:* www.peoriacounty.org	Peoria	IL	61602	309-672-6047	672-6054	338
Peoria Disposal Co 4700 N Sterling Ave *Web:* www.pdcarea.com	Peoria	IL	61615	309-688-0760	688-0881	660
Peoria Journal Star 1 News Plz *Web:* www.pjstar.com	Peoria	IL	61643	309-686-3000	686-3296	532-2
Peoria Packing Ltd 1307-9 W Lake St *Web:* www.peoriapacking.com	Chicago	IL	60607	312-226-2600	226-8752	473
Peoria Park District 1125 W Lake Ave *Web:* peoriaparks.org	Peoria	IL	61614	309-682-1200	686-3352	97
Peoria Public Library 8463 W Monroe St *Web:* www.peoriaaz.gov	Peoria	AZ	85345	623-773-7555		434-3
Peoria Public Library 107 NE Monroe St *Web:* www.peoriapubliclibrary.org	Peoria	IL	61602	309-497-2135		434-3
Peoria Riverfront Museum 222 SW Washington St *Web:* www.peoriariverfrontmuseum.org	Peoria	IL	61602	309-686-7000		520
Peoria Speedway 3520 W Farmington Rd *Web:* www.peoriaspeedway.com	Peoria	IL	61604	309-357-3339		515
Peoria Symphony Orchestra 101 State St *Web:* peoriasymphony.org	Peoria	IL	61602	309-671-1096		573-3
PEP (Performance Engineered Products Inc) 3270 Pomona Blvd *Web:* pepincplastics.com	Pomona	CA	91768	909-594-7487		604
PEP Filters Inc 322 Rolling Hill Rd *TF:* 800-243-4583 ■ *Web:* www.pepfilters.com	Mooresville	NC	28117	704-662-3133	662-3155	806
PEPA (Pacific Egg and Poultry Assn) 1521 I St *Web:* www.pacificegg.org	Sacramento	CA	95814	916-441-0801	446-1063	139
PEPCO (Professional Electric Products Co) 33210 Lakeland Blvd **Fax Area Code:* 440 ■ *TF:* 800-872-7000 ■ *Web:* www.pepconet.com	Eastlake	OH	44095	800-872-7000	942-5883*	246
Pepco Sales of Dallas Inc 11310 Gemini Ln *TF:* 877-737-2699 ■ *Web:* pepcosales.com	Dallas	TX	75229	972-823-8700		612
Pepe's 2429 W Ball Rd *Web:* pepesmexicanfood.com	Anaheim	CA	92804	714-257-7373		671
Pepe's Inc 1325 W 15th St *Web:* pepes.com	Chicago	IL	60608	312-733-2500		670
Pepg LLC 9270 S Sandy Pkwy *Web:* pepg.net	Sandy	UT	84070	801-562-2521	562-2661	261
Pepin County Wisconsin 740 7th Ave W PO Box 39 *Web:* www.co.pepin.wi.us	Durand	WI	54736	715-672-8857	672-8677	338
Pepin Distributing Co 4121 N 50th St *TF:* 800-331-2829 ■ *Web:* www.pepindistributing.com	Tampa	FL	33610	813-626-6176	626-5800	81-1
Pepin Farm Implements PO Box 158 *TF:* 800-637-3746 ■ *Web:* www.pepinharrows.com	Pepin	WI	54759	715-442-4111		273
Pepin Manufacturing Inc 1875 Hwy 61 S *TF:* 800-291-6505 ■ *Web:* www.pepinmfg.com	Lake City	MN	55041	651-345-5655		476
Pepose Vision Institute PC 1815 Clarkson Rd *TF:* 877-862-2020 ■ *Web:* www.peposevision.com	Chesterfield	MO	63017	636-728-0111		476
Pepper Construction 643 N Orleans St *Web:* www.pepperconstruction.com	Chicago	IL	60654	312-266-4700		186
Pepper Group, The 220 N Smith St *Web:* www.peppergroup.com	Palatine	IL	60067	847-963-0333		4
Pepper Hamilton LLP 3000 Two Logan Sq 18th & Arch St *Web:* www.pepperlaw.com	Philadelphia	PA	19103	215-981-4000	981-4750	428
Pepper Sprout 378 Main St *Web:* peppersprout.com	Dubuque	IA	52001	563-556-2167		671
Pepper Tree, The 888 W Moreno *Web:* www.peppertreecs.com	Colorado Springs	CO	80905	719-471-4888	471-0997	671
Pepperball Technologies Inc 6540 Lusk Blvd Ste C137 *TF:* 877-887-3773 ■ *Web:* www.pepperball.com	San Diego	CA	92121	858-638-0236		762
PepperCom Inc 470 Park Ave S *Web:* www.peppercomm.com	New York	NY	10016	212-931-6100		636
Peppercorn's Grill 357 Main St *Web:* www.peppercornsgrill.com	Hartford	CT	06106	860-547-1714	724-7612	671
Pepperdine University 24255 Pacific Coast Hwy *TF:* 800-413-0848 ■ *Web:* www.pepperdine.edu	Malibu	CA	90263	310-506-4000	506-4861	166
Pepperell Braiding Company Inc 22 Lowell St *TF:* 800-343-8114 ■ *Web:* pepperell.com	Pepperell	MA	01463	800-343-8114		596
Pepperidge Farm Inc 595 Westport Ave *TF:* 888-737-7374 ■ *Web:* www.pepperidgefarm.com	Norwalk	CT	06851	888-737-7374		296-1
Pepperl Fuchs Inc 1600 Enterprise Pkwy *Web:* www.pepperl-fuchs.com	Twinsburg	OH	44087	330-425-3555	425-4607	203
Peppermill Hotel & Casino 2707 S Virginia St *TF:* 800-648-6992 ■ *Web:* www.peppermillreno.com	Reno	NV	89502	866-821-9996		133
Peppermill Restaurant 3524 Severn Ave *Web:* www.riccobonos.com	Metairie	LA	70002	504-455-2266		671
Peppermint Ridge Inc 825 Magnolia Ave *Web:* www.peppermintridge.org	Corona	CA	92879	951-273-7320		672
Peppers Unlimited of Louisiana Inc 602 W Bridge St *Web:* peppersunlimitedofla.com	Saint Martinville	LA	70582	337-394-8035		297-8
Peppler & Associates Inc 22 E Dundee Rd *Web:* www.peppler.com	Barrington	IL	60010	847-382-6866		177
Peppler Agency Inc, The 20658 Harper Ave *Web:* peppleragy.com	Harper Woods	MI	48225	313-881-4623		390
Pepsi Bottling Ventures LLC 4141 Parklake Ave Ste 600 *TF:* 800-662-8792 ■ *Web:* www.pepsibottlingventures.com	Raleigh	NC	27612	919-865-2300		296-37
PepsiCo Inc 700 Anderson Hill Rd *NYSE:* PEP ■ *TF:* 800-433-2652 ■ *Web:* www.pepsico.com	Purchase	NY	10577	914-253-2000		185
Pepsi-Cola Bottling Company of La Crosse PO Box 998 *TF:* 877-606-4313 ■ *Web:* www.gillettepepsicola.com	La Crosse	WI	54602	608-785-0450	782-0722	805
Pepsi-Cola Bottling Company of New Haven 101 Hickory St *Web:* www.pepsi.com	New Haven	MO	63068	573-237-3076		805
Peptides International Inc 11621 Electron Dr *TF:* 800-777-4779 ■ *Web:* www.pepnet.com	Louisville	KY	40299	502-266-8787	267-1329	231
Pequannock Animal Hospital 591 Newark Pompton Tpke *Web:* pequannockveterinarian.com	Pompton Plains	NJ	07444	973-616-0400		794
Pequot Library 720 Pequot Ave *Web:* www.pequotlibrary.org	Southport	CT	06890	203-259-0346	259-5602	434-3
Per Mar Security 1910 E Kimberly Rd *TF:* 800-473-7627 ■ *Web:* www.permarsecurity.com	Davenport	IA	52807	563-359-3200		692
Perani's Hockey World 1600 Cochran Rd *TF:* 800-888-4625 ■ *Web:* www.hockeyworld.com	Pittsburgh	PA	15220	412-343-5857		711
Perantinides & Nolan Company LPA 80 S Summit St Ste 300 *TF:* 800-253-5452 ■ *Web:* www.perantinides.com	Akron	OH	44308	330-253-5454	253-6524	428
Peraso Technologies Inc 144 Front St W Ste 685 *Web:* perasotech.com	Toronto	ON	M5J2L7	416-637-1048		225
PERC (Propane Education and Research Council) 1140 Connecticut Ave NW Ste 1075 *Web:* www.propanecouncil.org	Washington	DC	20036	202-452-8975	452-9054	48-6
PERC Water Corp 959 S Coast Dr Ste 315 *Web:* www.percwater.com	Costa Mesa	CA	92626	714-352-7750	352-7765	192
Percepta LLC 1320 S Babcock St Ste 610 *Web:* www.percepta.com	Dearborn	MI	48126	313-390-0157		636
Perceptics Corp 9737 Cogdill Rd Ste 200 **Fax Area Code:* 865 ■ *TF:* 800-448-8544 ■ *Web:* www.perceptics.com	Knoxville	TN	37932	800-448-8544	966-9330*	178-12
PerceptiMed Inc 365 San Antonio Rd *Web:* perceptimed.com	Mountain View	CA	94040	650-941-7000		475
Perception Programs Inc 54 North St *Web:* www.perceptionprograms.org	Willimantic	CT	06226	860-450-7122		726
Perceptions Inc 1030 Hinsburg Rd *Web:* www.perceptionsvermont.com	Charlotte	VT	05445	802-425-2783	425-3628	514
Perceptron Inc 47827 Halyard Dr *NASDAQ:* PRCP ■ *Web:* perceptron.com	Plymouth	MI	48170	734-414-6100	414-4700	472
Percival Scientific Inc 505 Research Dr *TF:* 800-695-2743 ■ *Web:* www.percival-scientific.com	Perry	IA	50220	800-695-2743		420
Percussion Software Inc 600 Unicorn Pk Dr *TF:* 800-283-0800 ■ *Web:* www.percussion.com	Woburn	MA	01801	781-438-9900	438-9955	178-1
Percussive Arts Society (PAS) 110 W Washington St *Web:* www.pas.org	Indianapolis	IN	46204	317-974-4488	974-4499	48-4
PercuVision LLC 2030 Dividend Dr *Web:* percuvision.com	Columbus	OH	43228	614-891-4800	891-3500	345
Percy Quin State Park 2036 Percy Quin Dr *Web:* mdwfp.com	McComb	MS	39648	601-684-3938		565
Perdido Beach Resort 27200 Perdido Beach Blvd *TF:* 800-634-8001 ■ *Web:* www.perdidobeachresort.com	Orange Beach	AL	36561	251-981-9811		669
Perdoceo Education Corp 231 N Martingale Rd *NASDAQ:* CECO ■ *Web:* www.perdoceoed.com	Schaumburg	IL	60173	847-781-3600	781-3610	242
Perdue David (Sen R - GA) 455 Russell Senate Office Bldg *Web:* www.perdue.senate.gov	Washington	DC	20510	202-224-3521	228-1031	342-2
Perdue Farms Inc PO Box 1537 *TF:* 800-473-7383 ■ *Web:* www.perdue.com	Salisbury	MD	21804	410-543-3000		619
Perdue Inc 5 W Forsyth St Ste 100 *TF:* 800-732-5857 ■ *Web:* www.perdueoffice.com	Jacksonville	FL	32202	904-737-5858		362
Perdue Woodworks Inc 2415 Creek Dr *Web:* www.perduesinc.com	Rapid City	SD	57703	605-341-2101		319-2
Pere Bruin Press PO Box 781 *Web:* www.perebruin.com	Alamo	CA	94507	925-944-7017	945-8360	637-2
Pere Marquette State Park 13112 Visitor Center Ln *Web:* www2.illinois.gov	Grafton	IL	62037	618-786-3323		565
Peregrine Capital Partners LLC 732 Pittsford-Victor Rd *Web:* www.peregrinecapitalpartners.com	Pittsford	NY	14534	585-218-5220	218-9005	401

Phone | Fax | Class

Peregrine Pharmaceuticals Inc
14282 Franklin Ave Ste 100 .... Tustin CA 92780 714-508-6000 838-5817 85
NASDAQ: CDMO ■ *TF:* 800-987-8256 ■ *Web:* www.avidbio.com

Peregrine Semiconductor Corp
9380 Carroll Pk Dr .... San Diego CA 92121 858-731-9400 731-9499 696
Web: www.psemi.com

Peregrine Surgical Ltd
51 Britain Dr .... New Britain PA 18901 215-348-0456 476
TF: 877-348-0456 ■ *Web:* www.peregrinesurgical.com

Pereira & Azevedo CPA LLC
52-54 Rome St .... Newark NJ 07105 973-466-1663 2
Web: www.njcpas.com

Perelson Weiner LLP
1 Dag Hammarskjold Plz 42nd Fl .... New York NY 10017 212-605-3100 2
Web: www.pwcpa.com

Perennial Mgmt Ltd 40 Aberdeen Ave .... Saint John NL A1A5T3 709-754-2057 652
Web: perennialmanagement.ca

Perennial Properties Inc
1924 Piedmont Cir NE Ste 100 .... Atlanta GA 30324 404-881-0759 653
Web: perennialproperties.net

Perennial Public Power District
2122 S Lincoln Ave .... York NE 68467 402-362-3355 362-3623 245
TF: 800-289-0288 ■ *Web:* perennialpower.com

Perey Turnstiles Inc
308 Bishop Ave .... Bridgeport CT 06610 203-333-9400 693
Web: www.turnstile.com

Perez Art Museum Miami
1103 Biscayne Blvd .... Miami FL 33132 305-375-3000 375-1725 520
Web: www.pamm.org

Perez Trading Company Inc
3490 NW 125th St .... Miami FL 33167 305-769-0761 559
Web: www.pereztrading.com

PERF (Police Executive Research Forum)
1120 Connecticut Ave NW Ste 930 .... Washington DC 20036 202-466-7820 466-7826 49-7
Web: www.policeforum.org

Perfect 85 Degrees C Inc
2700 Alton Pkwy .... Irvine CA 92606 949-553-8585 345
Web: www.85cbakerycafe.com

Perfect Commerce Inc
1 Compass Way Ste 120 .... Newport News VA 23606 757-766-8211 39
TF: 877-871-3788 ■ *Web:* www.perfect.com

Perfect Fit Placement Inc
1253 Berlin Tpke .... Berlin CT 06037 860-828-3127 828-0301 260
TF: 800-290-2168 ■ *Web:* www.pfpjobs.com

Perfect Game Softball LLC
850 Twixt Town Rd NE .... Cedar Rapids IA 52402 319-298-2923 761
Web: www.perfectgame.org

Perfect Home Care Inc
4210 Middlebrook Dr .... Fort Worth TX 76103 817-534-9600 363
Web: perfecthomecare.net

Perfect North Slopes Inc
19074 Perfect Pl Ln .... Lawrenceburg IN 47025 812-537-3754 537-3352 379
Web: www.perfectnorth.com

Perfect Parties Usa
147 Summit St Unit 6 .... Peabody MA 01960 978-977-0500 366
Web: www.perfectpartiesusa.com

Perfect Patterns Inc 2221 Pensar Dr .... Appleton WI 54911 920-734-6643 567
Web: www.perfectpatterns.com

Perfect Plastic Printing Corp
311 Kautz Rd .... Saint Charles IL 60174 630-584-1600 584-0648 704
Web: www.perfectplastic.com

Perfect Shutters Inc 12213 Rte 173 .... Hebron IL 60034 815-648-2401 648-4510 699
TF: 800-548-3336 ■ *Web:* www.perfectshutters.com

Perfect Sweep Inc 1202 S Expressway Dr .... Toledo OH 43608 419-726-1801 63
Web: www.perfectsweep.com

Perfect Turf Inc 622 Sandpebble Dr .... Schaumburg IL 60193 888-796-8873 601
TF: 888-796-8873 ■ *Web:* perfectturf.com

Perfect World Entertainment Inc
101 Redwood Shores Pkwy 4th Fl .... Redwood City CA 94065 650-590-7700 591-1211 395
Web: www.perfectworld.com

PerfectData Corp
1323 Conshohocken Rd .... Plymouth Meeting PA 19462 800-973-7332 534
TF: 800-973-7332 ■ *Web:* www.perfectdata.com

PerfectForms Inc
2035 Corte Del Nogal Ste 165 .... Carlsbad CA 92011 866-900-8588 174
TF: 866-900-8588 ■ *Web:* www.perfectforms.com

Perfection Group Inc
2649 Commerce Blvd .... Cincinnati OH 45241 513-772-7545 326-2380 610
Web: perfectiongroup.com

Perfection Learning Corp 1000 N 2nd Ave .... Logan IA 51546 712-644-2831 543-2745* 637-2
**Fax Area Code:* 800 ■ *TF:* 800-831-4190 ■ *Web:* www.perfectionlearning.com

Perfection Spring & Stamping Corp
1449 E Algonquin Rd .... Mount Prospect IL 60056 847-437-3900 718
Web: www.pss-corp.com

Perfection Type Inc (PT)
1050 33rd Ave SE Ste 1000 .... Minneapolis MN 55414 651-917-8444 917-8440 385
TF: 800-829-4815 ■ *Web:* www.perfectiontype.com

PerfectMind Inc
4333 Still Creek Dr 2nd Fl .... Burnaby BC V5C6S6 877-774-5425 809
TF: 877-774-5425 ■ *Web:* www.perfectmind.com

Perfecto's Caffe 79 N Main St .... Andover MA 01810 978-749-7022 68
Web: perfectoscaffe.com

Perfekta Inc 480 E 21st St N .... Wichita KS 67214 316-263-2056 263-0106 454
Web: www.perfekta-inc.com

Per-Fil Industries Inc 407 Adams St .... Riverside NJ 08075 856-461-5700 547
Web: www.per-fil.com

Perforated Tubes Inc 4850 Fulton St E .... Ada MI 49301 616-942-4550 942-2121 492
TF: 888-869-5736 ■ *Web:* www.perftubes.com

Perforce Software Inc
2320 Blanding Ave .... Alameda CA 94501 510-864-7400 864-5340 177
TF: 888-081-7363 ■ *Web:* www.perforce.com

Perform Better Inc PO Box 8090 .... Cranston RI 02920 401-942-9363 942-7645 711
TF: 888-556-7464 ■ *Web:* www.everythingtrackandfield.com

Performance Assessment Network Inc
11590 N Meridian St Ste 200 .... Carmel IN 46032 317-814-8800 814-8888 631
Web: www.panpowered.com

Performance Co, The
1263 US Hwy 59 N .... Cleveland TX 77328 281-593-8888 779
Web: www.performancetruck.com

Performance Coating Intl 600 Murray St .... Bangor PA 18013 610-588-7900 588-7901 600
Web: www.pcoatingsintl.com

Performance Contracting Group Inc
11145 Thompson Ave .... Lenexa KS 66219 913-888-8600 492-8723 189-10
TF: 800-255-6886 ■ *Web:* www.performancecontracting.com

Performance Contractors Inc
9901 Pecu Ln .... Baton Rouge LA 70810 225-751-4156 188-7
Web: www.performance-contractors.com

Performance Designs Inc
1300 E International Speedway Blvd .... DeLand FL 32724 386-738-2224 734-8297 576
Web: www.performancedesigns.com

Performance Engineered Products Inc (PEP)
3270 Pomona Blvd .... Pomona CA 91768 909-594-7487 604
Web: pepincplastics.com

Performance Engineering Group Inc
32995 Industrial Rd .... Livonia MI 48150 734-266-5300 612
Web: www.performanceengineering.com

Performance Engineering Inc
10027 Park Cedar Dr Ste 200 .... Charlotte NC 28210 704-542-6789 542-5851 261
Web: performancenc.com

Performance Feeders Inc 251 Dunbar .... Oldsmar FL 34677 813-855-2685 855-4296 273
Web: performancefeeders.com

Performance Food Group Co
12500 W Creek Pkwy .... Richmond VA 23238 804-484-7700 297-8
Web: www.pfgc.com

Performance Inc 1 Performance Way .... Chapel Hill NC 27514 800-727-2453 942-5431* 711
**Fax Area Code:* 919 ■ *TF:* 800-727-2453 ■ *Web:* www.performancebike.com

Performance Machining Inc
79 Pennsylvania Ave .... Irwin PA 15642 724-864-2499 454
Web: www.performancemachine.com

Performance Management Group, The (PMG)
3125 Geddes Ave .... Ann Arbor MI 48104 734-216-4849 555-5555 194
Web: www.pmga2.com

Performance Medical Group Inc
103 Deer Tree Dr .... Lafayette LA 70507 337-237-1924 232-9143 475
TF: 800-960-2010 ■ *Web:* www.performancemedicalgroup.com

Performance Office Papers
21565 Hamburg Ave .... Lakeville MN 55044 800-458-7189 488-5058 110
TF: 800-458-7189 ■ *Web:* www.perfpapers.com

Performance Plants Inc
700 Gardiners Rd .... Kingston ON K7M3X9 613-545-0390 292
Web: www.performanceplants.com

Performance Plus Tire and Auto
3910 Cherry Ave .... Long Beach CA 90807 562-988-0211 981-2688 755
Web: www.performanceplustire.com

Performance Polymer Technologies Co
8801 Washington Blvd Ste 109 .... Roseville CA 95678 916-677-1414 677-1474 370
Web: www.pptech.com

Performance POP 2929 Stemmons Fwy .... Dallas TX 75247 214-665-1000 393
TF: 800-727-7335 ■ *Web:* www.performancepop.com

Performance Pulsation Control Inc
3309 Essex Dr Ste 200 .... Richardson TX 75082 972-699-8600 699-8602 610
Web: www.pulsationcontrol.com

Performance Safety Group Inc
781A Rudder Rd .... Fenton MO 63026 636-326-4568 774-1329* 523
**Fax Area Code:* 877 ■ *TF:* 877-774-4568 ■ *Web:* www.PSGgear.com

Performance Software
2095 W Pinnacle Peak Rd Ste 120 .... Phoenix AZ 85027 623-780-1517 177
Web: www.psware.com

Performance Stamping Company Inc
20 Lake Marian Rd .... Carpentersville IL 60110 847-426-2233 483
TF: 800-935-0393 ■ *Web:* www.performancestamping.com

Performance Strategies Inc
9350 Castlegate Dr .... Indianapolis IN 46256 317-842-0393 578-4711 384
Web: www.performancestrategies.com

Performance Trends Inc
31531 W 8 Mile Rd .... Livonia MI 48152 248-473-9230 442-7750 178-1
Web: www.performancetrends.com

Performance Water Products Inc
6902 Aragon Cir .... Buena Park CA 90620 714-736-0137 736-0153 610
Web: pwqa.com

Performing Animal Welfare Society (PAWS)
11435 Simmerhorn Rd .... Galt CA 95632 209-745-2606 745-1809 48-3
TF: 800-513-6560 ■ *Web:* www.pawsweb.org

Performing Arts Ctr
735 Anderson Hill Rd .... Purchase NY 10577 914-251-6200 251-6171 572
Web: www.artscenter.org

PerformLine Inc 58 South St .... Morristown NJ 07960 973-590-2305 393
Web: performline.com

Perfumania.com 251 International Pky .... Sunrise FL 33325 866-557-2368 45
TF: 866-557-2368 ■ *Web:* www.perfumania.com

Pergo Inc 3128 Highwoods Blvd Ste 100 .... Raleigh NC 27604 800-337-3746 773-6004* 291
**Fax Area Code:* 919 ■ *TF:* 800-337-3746 ■ *Web:* na.pergo.com

Pergolis-Swartz Associates Inc
12 W 37th St 8th Fl .... New York NY 10018 212-643-5663 695-8656 509
Web: www.pergolis.com

Perham Stockyards 45240 County Hwy 80 .... Perham MN 56573 218-346-3415 346-9004 446
Web: www.perhamstockyards.com

Peri & Sons Farms Inc PO Box 35 .... Yerington NV 89447 775-463-4444 463-4028 10-11
Web: www.periandsons.com

Peri Formwork Systems Inc
7135 Dorsey Run Rd .... Elkridge MD 21075 410-712-7225 796-8682 190
Web: www.peri-usa.com

Peri Software Solutions Inc
570 Broad St .... Newark NJ 07102 973-735-9500 177
Web: www.perisoftware.com

Periculum Capital Company LLC
4 Ctr Green Ste 200 .... Carmel IN 46032 317-636-1800 70
Web: www.periculumcapital.com

Peridot Corp 1072 Serpentine Ln .... Pleasanton CA 94566 925-461-8830 461-8833 492
Web: www.peridotcorp.com

Perillo Tours
Perillo Plaza 577 Chestnut Ridge Rd .... Woodcliff Lake NJ 07677 201-307-1234 307-1808 760
TF: 800-431-1515 ■ *Web:* www.perillotours.com

Perimeter Church
9500 Medlock Bridge Rd .... Johns Creek GA 30097 678-405-2000 405-2009 48-20
Web: www.perimeter.org

Name / Address	City	State	ZIP	Phone	Fax	Class
Perimeter Financial Corp 2 Queen St E Ste 1800 *Web:* www.pfin.ca	Toronto	ON	M5C3G7	416-703-7800		690
Perimeter Mall 4400 Ashford-Dunwoody Rd *Web:* www.perimetermall.com	Atlanta	GA	30346	770-394-4270		460
Perimeter Security Solutions Inc 1900 Fannin St Ste 301	Vernon	TX	76384	940-552-2942		693
Perini Management Services Inc 73 Mt Wayte Ave *Web:* tutorperini.com	Framingham	MA	01701	508-628-2000	628-2357	655
Perio Sciences LLC 11700 Preston Rd Ste 660 *TF:* 800-915-8110 ■ *Web:* www.periosciences.com	Dallas	TX	75230	800-915-8110		475
Periodical Publishers' Service Bureau 653 W Fallbrook Ave Ste 101 *TF:* 888-206-0350 ■ *Web:* www.ppsb.com	Fresno	CA	93711	888-206-0350		317
Periop Anesthesia Billing 111 Continental Dr Ste 412 *TF:* 800-250-7063 ■ *Web:* periop.com	Newark	DE	19713	800-250-7063		2
Peripheral Dynamics Inc 5150 Campus Dr *TF:* 800-523-0253 ■ *Web:* www.pdiscan.com	Plymouth Meeting	PA	19462	610-825-7090	834-7708	173-7
Peripheral Visions Inc 500 26th St NE *TF:* 800-728-4146 ■ *Web:* www.peripheralvisions.com	Auburn	WA	98002	253-735-3910	735-3920	476
Peris Companies Inc 282 N Washington St *Web:* www.peris.com	Falls Church	VA	22046	703-533-4700	533-4710	186
Periscope Inc 921 Washington Ave S *Web:* www.periscope.com	Minneapolis	MN	55415	612-399-0500		4
Periscope Post & Audio 6860 Lexington Ave *Web:* www.periscopepa.com	Los Angeles	CA	90038	323-460-4649		514
Perishable Distributors of Iowa Ltd 2741 SE PDI Pl *Web:* contactpdi.com	Ankeny	IA	50021	515-965-6300		297-8
Peritech Home Health Associates Inc PO Box 525 *TF:* 000-034-5670 ■ *Web:* peritech.com	Dubois	PA	15801	814-375-1040	375-1100	303
Peritus Partners Inc 703 Briar Ranch Ln *Web:* www.peritusp.com	San Jose	CA	95120	408-228-3724		195
Peritus Public Relations 2829 Second Ave S Ste 335 *Web:* www.perituspr.com	Birmingham	AL	35233	205-267-6673		636
Periyali 35 W 20th St *Web:* www.periyali.com	New York	NY	10011	212-463-7890		671
PerkinElmer Genomics 90 Emerson Ln *Web:* www.perkinelmergenomics.com	Bridgeville	PA	15017	412-220-2300		418
Perkins & Will 410 N Michigan Ave Ste 1600 *Web:* perkinswill.com	Chicago	IL	60611	312-755-0770	755-0775	261
Perkins Capital Management Inc 730 E Lake St *Web:* www.perkinscapital.comdefault.htm	Wayzata	MN	55391	952-473-8367		401
Perkins Coie LLP 1201 Third Ave Ste 4900 *TF:* 888-720-8382 ■ *Web:* www.perkinscoie.com	Seattle	WA	98101	206-359-8000	359-9000	428
Perkins County PO Box 156 *Web:* www.co.perkins.ne.us	Grant	NE	69140	308-352-7560	352-7562	338
Perkins County Clerk of Courts 101 Main St *Web:* www.perkinscounty.org	Bison	SD	57620	605-244-5626	244-7110	338
Perkins Group PO Box 472285 Ste D *Web:* www.perkinsgroup.com	Charlotte	NC	28226	704-543-1111		260
Perkins Investment Management LLC 311 S Wacker Dr Ste 6000 *TF:* 866-922-0355 ■ *Web:* cdn.janushenderson.com	Chicago	IL	60606	866-922-0355		401
Perkins Law Firm LLC 200 N Main St Ste 301 *Web:* johnperkinslaw.com	Greenville	SC	29601	864-908-3900		41
Perkins Medical Supply 4005 20th St *TF:* 888-837-5467 ■ *Web:* www.perkinsmedicalsupply.net	Vero Beach	FL	32960	772-569-3797	567-1567	476
Perkins Oil Company Inc 4707 Pflaum Rd *TF:* 800-634-9937 ■ *Web:* perkinsoil.com	Madison	WI	53718	608-221-4736		541
Perkins Restaurant & Bakery 6075 Poplar Ave Ste 800 *TF:* 800-225-5939 ■ *Web:* www.perkinsrestaurants.com	Memphis	TN	38119	901-766-6400		670
Perkins Stone Mansion 550 Copley Rd *Web:* www.summithistory.org	Akron	OH	44320	330-535-1120	535-0250	50-3
Perkins Thompson, Attorneys & Counselors at Law 1 Canal Plz *Web:* www.perkinsthompson.com	Portland	ME	04101	207-774-2635		428
Perkinson Reprographics Inc 735 E Brill St *TF:* 888-330-8782 ■ *Web:* www.prigraphics.com	Phoenix	AZ	85006	602-393-3131		627
Perkiomen Animal Hospital PLLC 919 Gravel Pk *Web:* perkiomenanimalhospital.com	Palm	PA	18070	215-679-7019	541-0231	794
Perkiomen School 200 Seminary St *TF:* 866-966-9998 ■ *Web:* www.perkiomen.org	Pennsburg	PA	18073	215-679-9511	679-1146	622
Perkiomen Valley Chamber of Commerce 351 E Main St *Web:* perkiomenvalleychamber.org	Collegeville	PA	19426	610-489-6660	454-1270	139
Perko Inc 16490 NW 13th Ave *Web:* www.perko.com	Miami	FL	33169	305-621-7525	620-9978	350
Perlectric 2711 Prosperity Ave *Web:* perlectric.com	Fairfax	VA	22031	703-352-5151	352-5155	189-4
Perley & Rideau Veterans' Health Ctr 1750 Russell Rd *Web:* www.perleyrideau.ca	Ottawa	ON	K1G5Z6	613-526-7173		371
Perley-Halladay Association Inc 1037 Andrew Dr *TF:* 800-248-5800 ■ *Web:* www.perleyhalladay.com	West Chester	PA	19380	610-296-5800	647-1711	803-2
Perlick Corp 8300 W Good Hope Rd *TF:* 800-558-5592 ■ *Web:* www.perlick.com	Milwaukee	WI	53223	414-353-7060	353-7069	664
Perlmutter Ed (Rep D - CO) 1226 Longworth House Office Bldg *Web:* perlmutter.house.gov	Washington	DC	20515	202-225-2645	225-5278	342-2
Perlson LLP 977 N Broadway *Web:* perlsonllp.com	North Massapequa	NY	11758	516-541-0022		2
Perma Graphics Inc 2470 Schuetz Rd *Web:* permagraphics.net	Maryland Heights	MO	63043	314-567-4606		130
Perma Pom LLC 9611 TX-60 *Web:* www.pepcopoms.com	Lane City	TX	77453	979-532-3106		535
Perma Pools Corp 5245 Elmwood Ave *Web:* permapools.com	Indianapolis	IN	46203	317-782-9956	782-9935	422
Perma Treat Corp 74 Airline Dr	Durham	CT	06422	860-349-1133		818
Perma-Bound 617 E Vandalia Rd **Fax Area Code:* 800 ■ *TF:* 800-637-6581 ■ *Web:* www.perma-bound.com	Jacksonville	IL	62650	217-243-5451	551-1169*	92
Permac Industries Inc 14401 Ewing Ave S *Web:* permacindustries.com	Burnsville	MN	55306	952-894-7231	894-7198	757
Permacharts Inc 60 Industrial Pky Ste 616 **Fax Area Code:* 905 ■ *TF:* 800-387-3626 ■ *Web:* www.permacharts.com	Cheektowaga	NY	14227	800-387-3626	660-1604*	637-2
Permadur Industries Inc 186 Rt 206 S *TF:* 800-392-0146 ■ *Web:* www.permadur.com	Hillsborough	NJ	08844	908-359-9767	359-9773	386
Perma-Fix Environmental Services Inc 8302 Dunwoody Pl Ste 250 *NASDAQ: PESI* ■ *TF:* 800-365-6066 ■ *Web:* www.perma-fix.com	Atlanta	GA	30350	770-587-9898	587-9937	667
Perma-Glaze Inc 1638 Research Loop Rd Ste 160 **Fax Area Code:* 520 ■ *TF:* 800-332-7397 ■ *Web:* www.permaglaze.com	Tucson	AZ	85710	800-332-7397	296-4393*	189-11
Permanent Mission of Afghanistan to the United Nations in New York 633 3rd Ave 27th Fl *Web:* www.afghanistan-un.org	New York	NY	10017	212-972-1212	972-1216	784
Permanent Mission of Albania 320 E 79th St *Web:* www.punetejashtme.gov.al	New York	NY	10075	212-249-2059	535-2917	784
Permanent Mission of Australia to the United Nations 150 E 42nd St 33rd Fl *Web:* unny.mission.gov.au	New York	NY	10017	212-351-6600	351-6610	784
Permanent Mission of Belize to the United Nations 675 Third Ave Ste 1911 *Web:* www.belizemission.com	New York	NY	10017	212-986-1240	593-0932	784
Permanent Mission of Cambodia 327 E 58th St *Web:* www.unohrlls.org	New York	NY	10022	212-336-0777		784
Permanent Mission of Cyprus To The United Nations 15 W 38th St 11th Fl **Fax Area Code:* 212 ■ *Web:* www.cyprusun.org	New York	NY	10018	646-905-1140	685-7316*	784
Permanent Mission of Germany to the United Nations 871 UN Plz *Web:* new-york-un.diplo.de	New York	NY	10017	212-940-0400	940-0402	784
Permanent Mission of Iraq 14 E 79th St *Web:* www.iraqmission.us	New York	NY	10075	212-737-4433	772-1794	784
Permanent Mission of Mali 111 E 69th St *Web:* www.un.int	New York	NY	10021	212-737-4150	472-3778	784
Permanent Mission of Sweden to the United Nations 885 2nd Ave 1 Dag Hammarskjold Plz 46th Fl *Web:* www.swedenabroad.com	New York	NY	10017	212-583-2500		784
Permanent Mission of The Angola To The United Nations 820 Second Ave 12th Fl *Web:* www.un.int	New York	NY	10017	212-861-5656	861-9295	784
Permanent Mission of The Armenia To The United Nations 119 E 36th St *Web:* un.mfa.am	New York	NY	10016	212-686-9079	686-3934	784
Permanent Mission of The Belarus To The United Nations 136 E 67th St 4th Fl *Web:* un.mfa.gov.by	New York	NY	10065	212-535-3420	734-4810	784
Permanent Mission of The Benin To The United Nations 125 E 38th St *Web:* www.un.int	New York	NY	10016	212-684-1339	684-2058	784
Permanent Mission of The Chad Mission 129 E 36th St *Web:* www.un.int	New York	NY	10016	212-986-0980		784
Permanent Mission of The Comoros To The United Nations 866 UN Plz Ste 417 *Web:* www.un.int	New York	NY	10017	212-750-1637	750-1657	784
Permanent Mission of The Costa Rica To The United Nations 211 E 43rd St Rm 1002 *Web:* www.un.int	New York	NY	10017	212-986-6373	986-6842	784
Permanent Mission of the Czech Republic to the UN, The 1109-1111 Madison Ave *Web:* www.mzv.cz	New York	NY	10028	646-981-4001	981-4099	784
Permanent Mission of The Dominican Republic To The United Nations 144 E 44th St 4th Fl *Web:* www.un.int	New York	NY	10017	212-867-0833	297-2509	784
Permanent Mission of The Ecuador To The United Nations 866 UN Plz RM 516 *Web:* www.un.int	New York	NY	10017	212-935-1680	935-1835	784
Permanent Mission of The France To The United Nations 245 E 47th St 44 th Fl *Web:* onu.delegfrance.org	New York	NY	10017	212-702-4900		784
Permanent Mission of The Grenada To The United Nations 800 Second Ave Ste 400K *Web:* www.un.int	New York	NY	10017	212-599-0301	599-1540	784
Permanent Mission of The Guatemala To The United Nations 57 Park Ave *Web:* www.un.int	New York	NY	10016	212-679-4760	685-8741	784
Permanent Mission of The Honduras To The United Nations 866 UN Plz Ste 302 *Web:* www.un.int	New York	NY	10017	212-421-4741	486-1985	784
Permanent Mission of The Hungary To The United Nations 227 E 52nd St *Web:* ensz-newyork.mfa.gov.hu	New York	NY	10022	212-752-0209	755-5395	784

Name / Address	City	State	ZIP	Phone	Fax	Class
Permanent Mission of The India To The United Nations 235 E 43rd St *Web:* www.un.int	New York	NY	10017	212-490-9660	490-9656	784
Permanent Mission of The Ireland To The United Nations 1 Dag Hammarskjold Plz Ste 885 *Web:* www.un.int	New York	NY	10017	212-421-6934	752-4726	784
Permanent Mission of The Islamic Republic of Iran to the United Nations 622 Third Ave *Web:* www.un.int	New York	NY	10017	212-687-2020	867-7086	784
Permanent Mission of The Jamaica To The United Nations 767 Third Ave 9th Fl *Web:* www.un.int	New York	NY	10017	212-935-7509	935-7607	784
Permanent Mission of The Kingdom of Bahrain to The United Nations 866 Second Ave 14th & 15th Fl *Web:* www.un.int	New York	NY	10017	212-223-6200	223-6206	784
Permanent Mission of The Lao People's Democratic Republic 317 E 51st St *Web:* www.un.int	New York	NY	10022	212-832-2734	750-0039	784
Permanent Mission of The Lesotho To The United Nations 204 E 39th St *Web:* www.un.int	New York	NY	10016	212-661-1690	682-4388	784
Permanent Mission of The Malawi To The United Nations 866 UN Plz Ste 486 *Web:* www.un.int	New York	NY	10017	212-317-8738	317-8729	784
Permanent Mission of The Malaysia To The United Nations 313 E 43rd St *Web:* www.un.int	New York	NY	10017	212-986-6310	490-8576	784
Permanent Mission of The Mauritania To The United Nations 116 E 38th St *Web:* www.un.int	New York	NY	10016	212-252-0113	252-0175	784
Permanent Mission of The Mongolia To The United Nations 6 E 77th St *Web:* www.un.int	New York	NY	10075	212-861-9460	861-9464	784
Permanent Mission of The Mozambique To The United Nations 420 E 50th St *Web:* www.un.int	New York	NY	10022	212-644-6800	644-5972	784
Permanent Mission of The Nepal To The United Nations 820 Second Ave Ste 17B *Web:* www.un.int	New York	NY	10017	212-370-3988	953-2038	784
Permanent Mission of the Netherlands 666 3rd Ave 19th Fl *Web:* www.permanentrepresentations.nl	New York	NY	10017	212-519-9500	370-1954	784
Permanent Mission of The Niger To The United Nations 417 E 50th St *Web:* www.un.int	New York	NY	10022	212-421-3260	753-6931	784
Permanent Mission of The Oman To The United Nations 305 E 47th St 11th &12th Fl *Web:* www.un.int	New York	NY	10017	212-355-3505	644-0070	784
Permanent Mission of The Peru To The United Nations 820 Second Ave Ste 1600 *Web:* www.un.int	New York	NY	10017	212-687-3336	972-6975	784
Permanent Mission of The Philippines To The United Nations 556 Fifth Ave 5th Fl *Web:* www.un.int	New York	NY	10036	212-764-1300	840-8602	784
Permanent Mission of The Republic of Cape Verde to the United Nations 27 E 69th St *Web:* www.un.int	New York	NY	10021	212-472-0333	794-1398	784
Permanent Mission of the Republic of Fiji to the United Nations 801 Second Ave 4th Fl Ste 402 *Web:* unohrlls.org	New York	NY	10017	212-682-8132	937-0079	784
Permanent Mission of The Republic of Madagascar To The United Nations 820 Second Ave Ste 800 *Web:* www.un.int	New York	NY	10017	212-986-9491	986-6271	784
Permanent Mission of the Republic of Poland to the United Nations in New York 750 3rd Ave 30th Fl **Fax Area Code:* 212 ■ *Web:* www.gov.pl	New York	NY	10017	646-559-7552	517-6771*	784
Permanent Mission of The Republic of Serbia to the United Nations - New York 854 Fifth Ave. *Web:* www.un.int	New York	NY	10065	212-879-8700	879-8705	784
Permanent Mission of the Republic of the Union of Myanmar 10 E 77th St *Web:* mmnewyork.org	New York	NY	10075	212-744-1271		784
Permanent Mission of The Romania To The United Nations 573-577 3rd Ave. *Web:* mpnewyork.mae.ro	New York	NY	10016	212-682-3273	682-9746	784
Permanent Mission of The Senegal To The United Nations 747 Third Ave 21st Fl *Web:* www.un.int	New York	NY	10017	212-517-9030	517-3032	784
Permanent Mission of The Sierra Leone To The United Nations 245 E 49th St *Web:* www.un.int	New York	NY	10017	212-688-1656	688-4924	784
Permanent Mission of The Somalia To The United Nations 425 E 61st St Ste 702 *Web:* www.un.int	New York	NY	10065	212-688-9410		784
Permanent Mission of The Sudan To The United Nations 305 E 47th St 4th Fl *Web:* www.un.int	New York	NY	10017	212-573-6033	573-6160	784
Permanent Mission of The Suriname To The United Nations 866 UN Plz Ste 320 *Web:* www.un.int	New York	NY	10017	212-826-0660	980-7029	784
Permanent Mission of The Syria To The United Nations 820 Second Ave 15th Fl *Web:* www.un.int	New York	NY	10017	212-661-1313	983-4439	784
Permanent Mission of The Tanzania To The United Nations 307 E 53rd St *Web:* www.tzmissionun.org	New York	NY	10022	212-697-3612	697-3618	784
Permanent Mission of The United Nations 79 Madison Ave *Web:* visit.un.org	New York	NY	10017	212-963-1234	963-4260	783
Permanent Mission of The United States of America To The United Nations 799 United Nations Plz *Web:* www.un.int	New York	NY	10017	212-415-4000	415-4443	784
Permanent Mission of The Uruguay To The United Nations 866 UN Plz Ste 322 *Web:* www.un.int	New York	NY	10017	212-752-8240	593-0935	784
Permanent Mission of The Zambia To The United Nations 237 E 52nd St *Web:* www.zambiamissionun.com	New York	NY	10022	212-888-5770	888-5213	784

Name / Address	City	State	ZIP	Phone	Fax	Class
Permanent Mission of Uganda to the United Nations, The 336 E 45th St *Web:* newyork.mofa.go.ug	New York	NY	10017	212-949-0110	687-4517	784
Permanent Mission of Ukraine 220 E 51st St *Web:* www.ukraineun.org	New York	NY	10022	212-759-7003	355-9455	784
Permatech Inc 911 E Elm St *Web:* www.permatech.net	Graham	NC	27253	336-578-0701	578-7758	663
Permatile Concrete Products Co 100 Beacon Rd *TF:* 800-662-5332 ■ *Web:* permatile.com	Bristol	VA	24203	276-669-5332		135
PermaTreat Pest & Termite Control 501 Lafayette Blvd *TF:* 866-737-6287 ■ *Web:* permatreat.com	Fredericksburg	VA	22401	540-373-6655		192
Permatron Group 2020 Touhy Ave *TF:* 800-882-8012 ■ *Web:* www.permatron.com	Elk Grove Village	IL	60007	847-434-1421		17
Perma-Type Company Inc 83 NW Dr *TF:* 800-243-4234 ■ *Web:* www.perma-type.com	Plainville	CT	06062	860-747-9999	747-1986	477
Permco Inc 1500 Frost Rd *TF:* 800-626-2801 ■ *Web:* www.permco.com	Streetsboro	OH	44241	330-626-2801	626-2805	640
Permenent Mission of Turkey 821 UN Plz 10th Fl *Web:* www.mfa.gov.tr	New York	NY	10017	212-949-0150	949-0086	784
Permian Plastics LLC 1477 Hoff Industrial Dr *Web:* permianplastics.com	O Fallon	MO	63366	636-978-4655	978-0557	604
Permobil Inc 300 Duke Dr *TF:* 800-736-0925 ■ *Web:* www.permobil.com	Lebanon	TN	37090	800-736-0925	400-1354	475
Pernod Ricard USA 250 Park Ave *Web:* www.pernod-ricard-usa.com	New York	NY	10177	212-372-5400		81-3
Perot Theatre 219 Main St *Web:* www.trahc.org	Texarkana	TX	75501	903-792-4992	793-8511	572
Perpetual Energy Inc 605 5 Ave SW Ste 3200 *TF:* 800-811-5522 ■ *Web:* www.perpetualenergyinc.com	Calgary	AB	T2P3H5	403-269-4400		536
Perpetual Financial Group Inc, The 1838 Old Norcross Rd Ste 400 *Web:* theperpetual.com	Lawrenceville	GA	30044	770-972-4955		653
Perq LLC 7225 Georgetown Rd *TF:* 800-873-3117 ■ *Web:* perq.com	Indianapolis	IN	46268	800-873-3117		4
Perquimans County 128 N Church St PO Box 45 *Web:* www.co.perquimans.nc.us	Hertford	NC	27944	252-312-5314	426-4034	338
Perreca Electric Co 520 Broadway *Web:* perreca.com	Newburgh	NY	12550	845-562-4080		189-4
Perricone's Marketplace & Cafe 15 SE Tenth St *Web:* www.perricones.com	Miami	FL	33131	305-374-9449	371-6647	671
Perrier & Lacoste L L C 365 Canal St Ste 2550 *TF:* 877-212-7280 ■ *Web:* www.perrierlacoste.com	New Orleans	LA	70130	504-212-8820		445
Perrigo Co 515 Eastern Ave *NYSE:* PRGO ■ *TF:* 800-719-9260 ■ *Web:* www.perrigo.com	Allegan	MI	49010	269-673-8451	673-9128	583
Perris Union High School District 155 E Fourth St *Web:* www.puhsd.org	Perris	CA	92570	951-943-6369		685
Perrot State Park W26247 Sullivan Rd *Web:* dnr.wi.gov	Trempealeau	WI	54661	608-534-6409		565
Perrotta, Fraser & Forrester LLC 16 Valley Rd *Web:* pffp-law.com	Clark	NJ	07066	732-680-1400		41
Perry & Assoc 948 11th St Ste 16 *Web:* perrylawyers.com	Modesto	CA	95354	209-544-5727		41
Perry & Associates LLC 221 N LaSalle St Ste 3100 *Web:* www.perryllc.com	Chicago	IL	60601	312-364-9112	364-9163	261
Perry Anthony Design Group 5331 Limestone Rd *Web:* perryanthony.com	Wilmington	DE	19808	302-239-6161		77
Perry Baromedical Corp 3750 Prospect Ave *TF:* 800-741-4376 ■ *Web:* perrybaromedical.com	Riviera Beach	FL	33404	561-840-0395		476
Perry Color Card 685 W Ter Dr *Web:* www.perrycolorcard.com	San Dimas	CA	91773	909-599-7954		393
Perry Communications Group Inc 980 Ninth St Ste 410 *Web:* perrycom.com	Sacramento	CA	95814	916-658-0144		636
Perry Construction Group Inc 1440 W 21st St *Web:* www.perryconst.com	Erie	PA	16502	814-459-8551	453-5653	186
Perry County 333 Seventh St PO Box 721 *TF:* 888-343-6262 ■ *Web:* www.pickperry.com	Tell City	IN	47586	812-547-7933	547-8378	338
Perry County 601 Main St PO Box 210 *Web:* www.perrycounty.ky.gov	Hazard	KY	41701	606-439-1816	439-1686	338
Perry County 215 E Main St PO Box 177 *Web:* www.perrycountytennessee.com	Linden	TN	37096	931-589-2453	589-2585	338
Perry County 105 N Main St PO Box 207 *Web:* www.perrycountycourt.com	New Lexington	OH	43764	740-342-3156	342-2188	338
Perry County 310 W Main St Ste 101 *Web:* www.perrycoarkansas.org	Perryville	AR	72126	501-889-5128	889-2574	338
Perry County 3764 SR-13 127 Rm 110 PO Box 438 *Web:* www.perryil.com	Pinckneyville	IL	62274	618-357-5116	357-3365	338
Perry County District Library 117 S Jackson St *Web:* www.pcdl.org	New Lexington	OH	43764	740-342-4194	342-4204	434-3
Perry County Public Library 289 Black Gold Blvd *Web:* www.perrycountylibrary.org	Hazard	KY	41701	606-436-4747		435
Perry County Tax Assessment 25 W Main St *TF:* 800-852-2102 ■ *Web:* www.perryco.org	New Bloomfield	PA	17068	717-582-2131	582-5189	338
Perry Engineering Company Inc 1945 Millwood Pk *Web:* perryeng.com	Winchester	VA	22602	540-667-4310	667-7618	189-5

Name / Address	City	State	Zip	Phone	Fax	Class
Perry Foam Products 2335 S 30th St *TF:* 800-592-6614 ■ *Web:* www.perrychemical.com	LaFayette	IN	47909	765-474-3404	474-3423	596
Perry GA Convention & Visitors Bureau 101 Gen Courtney Hodges Blvd *Web:* www.visitperry.com	Perry	GA	31069	478-988-8000		206
Perry Green Valley Nursing Home Inc 1103 Birch St *Web:* greenvalleyhealthcare.net	Perry	OK	73077	580-336-2285		371
Perry Group Intl 1 Market Plz Ste 3600 *TF:* 800-580-3950 ■ *Web:* www.perrygroup.com	San Francisco	CA	94105	800-580-3950		378
Perry Heights Press LLC PO Box 102 *Web:* www.cttrips.com	Georgetown	CT	06829	203-767-6509		637-10
Perry Insurance 522 Chickering Rd *Web:* perryins.com	North Andover	MA	01845	978-685-7690	687-0149	390
Perry Johnson Registrars Inc 755 W Big Beaver Rd Ste 1340 *TF:* 800-800-7910 ■ *Web:* www.pjr.com	Troy	MI	48084	248-358-3388		194
Perry Memorial Library 205 Breckenridge St *Web:* www.library.perrylibrary.org	Henderson	NC	27536	252-438-3316		434-3
Perry Null Trading Co 1710 S 2nd St *Web:* www.perrynulltrading.com	Gallup	NM	87301	505-863-5249		459
Perry Olson State Farm 9850 S Maryland Pkwy Ste 7 *Web:* perryolson.com	Las Vegas	NV	89183	702-309-6655		390
Perry Products Corp 25 Mt Laurel Rd *Web:* www.perryproducts.com	Hainesport	NJ	08036	609-267-1600		14
Perry Scott (Rep R - PA) 1207 Longworth House Office Bldg *Web:* perry.house.gov	Washington	DC	20515	202-225-5836	226-1000	342-2
Perry State Park 5441 Westlake Rd *Web:* www.ksoutdoors.com	Ozawkie	KS	66070	785-246-3449		565
Perry Supply Company Inc 2625 Vassar NE *Web:* www.perrysupply.net	Albuquerque	NM	87107	505-884-6972		612
Perry Technical Institute 2011 W Washington Ave *TF:* 888-528-8586 ■ *Web:* www.perrytech.edu	Yakima	WA	98903	509-453-0374		162
Perry Technology Corp 120 Industrial Park Rd *Web:* www.perrygear.com	New Hartford	CT	06057	860-738-2525		22
Perry's Ice Cream Company Inc 1 Ice Cream Plz *TF:* 800-873-7797 ■ *Web:* www.perrysicecream.com	Akron	NY	14001	716-542-5492	542-2544	296-25
Perry's Victory & International Peace Memorial 93 Delaware Ave PO Box 549 *Web:* www.nps.gov	Put-in-Bay	OH	43456	419-285-2184		564
Perryman Financial Advisory Inc 12221 Merit Dr Ste 1660 *Web:* billperryman.com	Dallas	TX	75251	972-770-4800		401
Perrysburg Area Chamber of Commerce 105 W Indiana Ave *Web:* www.perrysburgchamber.com	Perrysburg	OH	43551	419-874-9147	872-9347	139
Perry-Spencer Rural Telephone Coop 11877 E State Rd 62 *TF:* 800-511-4899 ■ *Web:* www.psci.net	Saint Meinrad	IN	47577	812-357-2123	357-2211	224
Perryville Area Career & Technology Ctr 326 College St *Web:* www.perryville.k12.mo.us	Perryville	MO	63775	573-547-7500	517-0396	230
Perryville Pet Hospital Inc 1917 Daimler Rd *TF:* 888-426-4435 ■ *Web:* perryvillepet.com	Rockford	IL	61112	815 229 1234	229-7990	794
Persante Health Care Inc 200 E Park Dr Ste 600 *TF:* 800-753-3779 ■ *Web:* www.persante.com	Mount Laurel	NJ	08054	800 753-3779		418
Perseverance Theatre 914 Third St *Web:* www.ptalaska.org	Douglas	AK	99824	907-364-2421	364-2603	573-4
Pershing & Company Inc 20 Central Sq *Web:* pershingcpas.com	Greencastle	IN	46135	765-653-4120		2
Pershing County 398 Main St PO Box 89 *TF:* 877-368-7828 ■ *Web:* www.pershingcounty.net	Lovelock	NV	89419	775-273-2401	273-5037	338
Pershing State Park 29277 Hwy 130 *Web:* mostateparks.com	Laclede	MO	64651	660-963-2299		565
Persimmon Group, The 11 E Fifth St Ste 300 *Web:* www.thepersimmongroup.com	Tulsa	OK	74103	918-592-4121		194
Persimmon Press Inc PO Box 297 **Fax Area Code:* 800 ■ *TF:* 800-910-5080 ■ *Web:* www.persimmoncards.com	Belmont	CA	94002	650-802-8325	910-5095*	130
Persimmon Technologies Corp 200 Harvard Mill Sq Ste 110 *Web:* www.persimmontech.com	Wakefield	MA	01880	781-587-0677	587-0675	196
Persis Corp 900 Ft St Mall Ste 1720 *Web:* persis.com	Honolulu	HI	96813	808-599-8000	526-4114	655
Person & Covey Inc 616 Allen Ave *TF:* 800-423-2341 ■ *Web:* www.personandcovey.com	Glendale	CA	91201	800-423-2341		214
Person Centered Services 240 N Union St *Web:* pcs4dd.com	Stockton	CA	95207	209-466-2448		685
Person County Schools 304 S Morgan St *TF:* 866-724-6650 ■ *Web:* www.pcsnc.org	Roxboro	NC	27573	336-599-2191		685
Persona Inc 700 21st St SW *Web:* www.personasigns.com	Watertown	SD	57201	605-882-2244	882-3521	9
Personal Capital Corp 1 Circle Star Way 1st Fl *TF:* 855-855-8005 ■ *Web:* www.personalcapital.com	San Carlos	CA	94070	855-855-8005		401
Personal Care Inc 321 Sycamore St *Web:* personalcare.net	Decatur	GA	30030	404-373-2727		363
Personal Data Systems Inc 638 Sobrato Ln *Web:* www.personaldatasystems.com	Campbell	CA	95008	408-866-1126		177
Personal Genome Diagnostics Inc 2809 Boston St Ste 503 *Web:* www.personalgenome.com	Baltimore	MD	21224	443-602-8833		418
Personal Touch Home Healthcare Inc 15700 W 10 Mile Rd Ste 219 **Fax Area Code:* 866 ■ *Web:* www.pthhc.com	Southfield	MI	48075	248-416-1695	655-1320*	363
Personal Touch Systems Inc 125 E Main St Ste 245 *TF:* 800-950-6767 ■ *Web:* www.personaltouchsystems.net	American Fork	UT	84003	801-649-6691		177
Personal-Touch Home Care Inc 186-18 Hillside Ave **Fax Area Code:* 412 ■ *TF:* 888-275-4147 ■ *Web:* www.pthomecare.com	Jamaica	NY	11432	718-468-2500	681-2550*	363
Personnel Data Systems Inc (PDS) 470 Norriftown Rd *TF:* 800-243-8737 ■ *Web:* www.pdssoftware.com	Blue Bell	PA	19422	610-238-4600	238-4550	178-1
Personnel Management Inc PO Box 6657 *TF:* 800-259-4126 ■ *Web:* www.pmiresource.com	Shreveport	LA	71136	318-869-4555	841-4350	631
Personnel Systems Associates Inc 7551 E Moonridge Ln *Web:* personnelsystems.com	Anaheim	CA	92808	714-281-8337	281-2949	196
Persons Majestic Manufacturing Co PO Box 370 *TF:* 800-772-2453 ■ *Web:* www.permaco.com	Huron	OH	44839	419-433-9057	433-0182	517
Perspectives Inc 352 Longview Plz *Web:* www.perspectives-usa.com	Lexington	KY	40503	859-277-0525	278-4441	350
Perspectives Ltd 20 N Clark St Ste 2650 **Fax Area Code:* 312 ■ *TF:* 800-866-7556 ■ *Web:* www.perspectivesltd.com	Chicago	IL	60602	800-866-7556	558-1570*	462
Perstorp Polyols Inc 600 Matzinger Rd *TF:* 800-537-0280 ■ *Web:* www.perstorp.com	Toledo	OH	43612	419-729-5448	729-3291	144
PerSys Medical 5310 Elm St *TF:* 888-737-7978 ■ *Web:* persysmedical.com	Houston	TX	77081	888-737-7978		475
Persyst Consulting LLC 17815 80th Avw NE Ste C-1 *Web:* www.persystconsulting.com	Kenmore	WA	98028	206-396-5825		463
Perteet Inc 2707 Colby Ave Ste 900 *Web:* www.perteet.com	Everett	WA	98201	425-252-7700		261
Perth & District Chamber of Commerce 34 Herriott St *TF:* 888-319-3204 ■ *Web:* perthchamber.com	Perth	ON	K7H1T2	613-267-3200	267-6797	137
Perth Amboy Public Library 196 Jefferson St *Web:* www.perthamboynj.org	Perth Amboy	NJ	08861	732-826-2600		434-3
Perth Amboy Spring Works 185 Sheridan St *Web:* www.leafspring.com	Perth Amboy	NJ	08861	732-442-4420		57
Perthera Inc 8200 Greensboro Dr Ste 350 *TF:* 877-827-7893 ■ *Web:* perthera.com	McLean	VA	22102	877-827-7893		225
Perth-Smiths Falls District Hospital 60 Cornelia St W *Web:* www.psfdh.on.ca	Smiths Falls	ON	K7A2H9	613-283-2330	283-8990	374-2
Pertronix LLC 440 E Arrow Hwy *TF:* 800-827-3758 ■ *Web:* pertronixbrands.com	San Dimas	CA	91773	909-599-5955		57
Peru State College 600 Hoyt St PO Box 10 *TF:* 800-742-4412 ■ *Web:* www.peru.edu	Peru	NE	68421	402-872-3815	872-2296	166
PES (PES Environmental Inc) 7665 Redwood Blvd Ste 200 *Web:* www.pesenv.com	Novato	CA	94945	415-899-1600	899-1601	261
PES Environmental Inc (PES) 7665 Redwood Blvd Ste 200 *Web:* www.pesenv.com	Novato	CA	94945	415-899-1600	899-1601	261
PES Structural engineers 1852 Century Pl NE *Web:* pesengineers.com	Atlanta	GA	30345	770-457-5923		261
Peschio's Classic Beauty College 4601 E Bell Rd Ste A-15 *Web:* www.classicbeautycollege.com	Phoenix	AZ	85032	602-992-2282		167-3
Pesco Inc 3333 N American St *TF:* 800 035-0007 ■ *Web:* www.pitchblock.com	North Charleston	SC	29418	843-697-2117		00
Peshtigo River State Forest N10008 Paust Ln *Web:* dnr.wi.gov	Crivitz	WI	54114	715-757-3965		565
Pest Routes 4500 W Eldorado Pkwy Ste 3200 *TF:* 888-496-8293 ■ *Web:* www.pestroutes.com	McKinney	TX	75070	888-496-8293		177
Pestmaster Services Inc 137 E S St *Web:* www.pestmaster.com	Bishop	CA	93514	760-873-8100		577
Pet Adoption Network, The 4261 Culver Rd *Web:* www.petadoptionnetwork.org	Rochester	NY	14622	585-338-9175		794
Pet Care Center PLLC 2950 SW Avalon Way *Web:* petcarecenteratlunapark.com	Seattle	WA	98126	206-935-3600		794
Pet Factory Inc 845 E High St *Web:* www.petfactory.com	Mundelein	IL	60060	847-837-8900		578
Pet Food Experts Inc 1 John C Dean Memorial Blvd *TF:* 800-637-7338 ■ *Web:* www.pfxne.com	Cumberland	RI	02864	800-637-7338	935-2150	45
Pet Food Express 500 85th Ave *Web:* www.petfood.express	Oakland	CA	94621	510-609-3600		578
Pet Food Institute (PFI) 2025 M St NW Ste 800 *Web:* www.petfoodinstitute.org	Washington	DC	20036	202-367-1120	367-2120	49-4
Pet Health Pharmacy 12012 N 111th Ave *TF:* 800-742-0516 ■ *Web:* www.pethealthpharmacy.com	Youngtown	AZ	85363	800-742-0516		237
Pet Industry Distributors Assn (PIDA) 2105 Laurel Bush Rd Ste 200 *Web:* www.pida.org	Bel Air	MD	21015	443-640-1060		49-18
Pet Industry Joint Advisory Council (PIJAC) 1220 19th St NW Ste 400 *TF:* 800-553-7387 ■ *Web:* www.pijac.org	Washington	DC	20036	202-452-1525	293-4377	49-4
Pet Network 105 Gordon Baker Rd *Web:* www.thepetnetwork.tv	Toronto	ON	M2H3P8	416-756-2404	756-5526	740
Pet Qwerks Inc 9 Studebaker Dr *Web:* www.petqwerks.com	Irvine	CA	92618	949-916-3733	916-3734	45
Pet Safe Intl 10427 Electric Ave *TF:* 800-732-2677 ■ *Web:* www.petsafe.net	Knoxville	TN	37932	865-777-5404		578
Pet Shotz Inc 210 Tuleta Bldg 3 *Web:* petshotzinc.com	San Antonio	TX	78212	210-735-1004		794

Name / Address	City	State	Zip	Phone	Fax	Class
Pet Sitters Intl (PSI) 213 East Dalton Rd *Web:* www.petsit.com	King	NC	27021	336-983-9222		48-3
Pet Supermarket Inc 1100 International Pkwy *TF:* 866-434-1990 ■ *Web:* www.petsupermarket.com	Sunrise	FL	33323	954-351-0834	351-0897	578
Pet Supplies "Plus" Inc 17197 N Laurel Prk Dre Ste 402 *Web:* www.petsuppliesplus.com	Livonia	MI	48152	248-615-0039		578
Pet Terra Systems Inc 110 Evans Mill Dr *Web:* www.petsystems.com	Dallas	GA	30157	770-445-2233	445-2290	463
Pet Valu Canada Inc 121 McPherson St *TF:* 800-845-4759 ■ *Web:* petvalu.com	Markham	ON	L3R3L3	905-946-1200		578
Pet Vet Animal Health Care Inc 19748 Sherman Way *Web:* petvetanimalhospital.com	Canoga Park	CA	91306	818-346-2455		794
Pet Vet Animal Hospitals 4520 Katy Fwy *Web:* www.petvethospitals.com	Houston	TX	77007	281-879-7387		794
Pet's Playground Grooming School 1296 N Federal Hwy *Web:* www.petsplayground.com	Pompano Beach	FL	33062	954-782-4994		685
PETA (People for the Ethical Treatment of Animals) 501 Front St *TF:* 800-566-9768 ■ *Web:* www.peta.org	Norfolk	VA	23510	757-622-7382	622-0457	48-3
Petal Card Inc 483 Broadway *Web:* www.petalcard.com	New York	NY	10013	914-874-3352		113
Petal Designs School of Flowers 21090 St Andrews Blvd *Web:* www.petal-designs.com	Boca Raton	FL	33433	561-391-5394		685
Petaluma Adobe State Historic Park 3325 Old Adobe Rd *Web:* www.parks.ca.gov	Petaluma	CA	94954	707-762-4871		565
Petaluma Area Chamber of Commerce 6 Petaluma Blvd N Ste A-2 *Web:* www.petalumachamber.com	Petaluma	CA	94952	707-762-2785	762-4721	139
Petaluma City Schools (PCS) 200 Douglas St *Web:* www.petalumacityschools.org	Petaluma	CA	94952	707-778-4813		685
Petaluma Fairgrounds Speedway 100 Fairgrounds Dr *Web:* www.petaluma-speedway.com	Petaluma	CA	94952	707-763-7223		642
Petaluma Poultry PO Box 7368 *Web:* www.petalumapoultry.com	Petaluma	CA	94954	707-763-1904		619
PETCO Animal Supplies Inc 9125 Rehco Rd *TF:* 877-738-6742 ■ *Web:* www.petco.com	San Diego	CA	92121	858-453-7845	784-3489	578
Pete Fowler Construction Services 931 Calle Negocio Ste J *Web:* www.petefowler.com	San Clemente	CA	92673	949-240-9971		196
Pete Lien & Sons Inc 3401 Universal Dr Ste 9360 *Web:* www.petelien.com	Rapid City	SD	57702	605-342-7224		503-4
Pete Moore Imports 106 N New Warrington Rd **Fax Area Code:* 850 ■ *TF:* 866-307-7995 ■ *Web:* www.petemoorevolkswagen.com	Pensacola	FL	32506	866-307-7995	453-3690*	57
Pete Soro Machine Works Inc 5542 Universal Dr *TF:* 800-688-4267 ■ *Web:* www.petesoro.com	Memphis	TN	38118	901-360-8957		454
Pete's Road Service Inc 2230 E Orangethorpe Ave *TF:* 800-352-8349 ■ *Web:* www.petesrs.com	Fullerton	CA	92831	800-352-8349		754
Pete's Tire Barns Inc 114 New Athol Rd *TF:* 800-239-1833 ■ *Web:* www.petestire.com	Orange	MA	01364	978-544-8811		755
Peter A. Mayer Advertising Inc 324 Camp St *Web:* www.peteramayer.com	New Orleans	LA	70130	504-581-7191		7
Peter Andjelkovich & Assoc 135 S La Salle St Ste 3950 *Web:* paalaw.net	Chicago	IL	60603	312-782-8345	782-6517	41
Peter Baker & Son Co 1349 Rockland Rd *Web:* www.peterbaker.com	Lake Bluff	IL	60044	847-362-3663	362-0707	188-4
Peter Basso Associates Inc 5145 Livernois Ste 100 *TF:* 866-950-9760 ■ *Web:* www.peterbassoassociates.com	Troy	MI	48098	248-879-5666		261
Peter Becker Community 800 Maple Ave *Web:* peterbeckercommunity.com	Harleysville	PA	19438	215-256-9501		672
Peter Bell CPA 1735 Dilworth Rd E *Web:* peterbellpllc.com	Charlotte	NC	28203	704-525-9999		2
Peter Bowers PC 441 N Fifth St *Web:* peterbowerspc.com	Philadelphia	PA	19123	215-440-0300	440-8390	41
Peter C. Merani PC 1001 Avenue of the Americas Ste 1800 *Web:* meranilaw.com	New York	NY	10018	212-629-9690		41
Peter C. Wachowski PC 15 N Northwest Hwy *Web:* bellas-wachowski.com	Park Ridge	IL	60068	847-823-9030		41
Peter Dag Portfolio Strategy & Management, The 65 Lake Front Dr *TF:* 800-833-2782 ■ *Web:* www.peterdag.com	Akron	OH	44319	330-644-2782		531-9
Peter E. Randall Publisher LLC 5 Greenleaf Woods Dr Ste 102 *Web:* www.perpublisher.com	Portsmouth	NH	03801	603-431-5667	431-3566	637-2
Peter G. Carchedi, Clu Inc 2017 Genesee St *Web:* romechamber.com	Utica	NY	13501	315-732-3921		690
Peter Glenn Ski & Sports 2901 W Oakland Pk Blvd *TF:* 800-818-0946 ■ *Web:* www.peterglenn.com	Fort Lauderdale	FL	33311	954-484-3606		711
Peter Grandich & Co PO Box 763 *Web:* www.petergrandich.com	Spring Lake	NJ	07762	732-642-3992		637-10
Peter H. Burgher 5699 Head Cliff Dr *Web:* www.peterburgher.com	Gaylord	MI	49735	989-732-1864		192
Peter J. Bertuglia CPA PC 775 Park Ave *Web:* bertugliacpa.com	Huntington	NY	11743	631-385-7003		2
Peter J. Jaensch Immigration 2198 Main St *TF:* 800-870-3676 ■ *Web:* visaamerica.com	Sarasota	FL	34237	941-366-9841		428
Peter King Corp 11040 N 19th Ave *Web:* petekingaz.com	Phoenix	AZ	85029	602-944-4441	943-4876	189-8
Peter L. Cedeno & Associates Pc 111 Broadway Ste 707 *Web:* nyc-divorces.com	New York	NY	10006	212-235-1382		41
Peter Lang Publishing Inc 29 Broadway *TF:* 800-770-5264 ■ *Web:* www.peterlang.com	New York	NY	10006	212-647-7706	647-7707	637-2
Peter Luger Steak House 178 Broadway *Web:* peterluger.com	Brooklyn	NY	11211	718-387-7400	387-3523	671
Peter P. Briggs Insurance Agency Inc 19 County Rd PO Box 96 *Web:* peterbriggsins.com	Mattapoisett	MA	02739	508-758-6929		390
Peter Pan Bus Lines PO Box 1776 *TF:* 800-343-9999 ■ *Web:* peterpanbus.com	Springfield	MA	01102	800-343-9999		107
Peter Parts Electronics 34 Foley Dr *Web:* www.paceelectronics.com	Sodus	NY	14551	800-228-7223		246
Peter Paul Electronics Company Inc 480 John Downey Dr *TF:* 800-825-8377 ■ *Web:* peterpaul.com	New Britain	CT	06051	860-229-4884	223-1734	789
Peter Pauper Press Inc 202 Mamaroneck Ave Ste 400 *Web:* www.peterpauper.com	White Plains	NY	10601	914-681-0144	681-0389	637-2
Peter Pepper Products Inc (PPP) 17929 S Susana Rd PO Box 5769 **Fax Area Code:* 310 ■ *TF:* 800-496-0204 ■ *Web:* www.peterpepper.com	Compton	CA	90224	800-496-0204	639-6013*	591
Peter Piper Pizza Inc 6049 E Grant Rd Ste 350 *Web:* www.peterpiperpizza.com	Phoenix	AZ	85014	480-609-6400		670
Peter Scherrer Group Inc, The 448 Falcon Ridge Dr Ste B *Web:* psgwisconsin.com	Burlington	WI	53105	262-758-6064		360-3
Peter Shannon & Co 6412 Joliet Rd Ste 1 *Web:* petershannonco.com	Countryside	IL	60525	708-482-3000		2
Peter Smith Associates 75 Arlington St Ste 500 *Web:* www.petersmithassociates.biz	Boston	MA	02116	857-241-3655		194
Peter Thomas Roth Labs LLC 460 Park Ave 16th Fl *TF:* 800-787-7546 ■ *Web:* peterthomasroth.com	New York	NY	10022	212-581-5800	581-5810	214
Peter Yegen Jr Yellowstone County Museum 1950 Terminal Cir *Web:* www.pyjrycm.org	Billings	MT	59105	406-256-6811	254-6031	520
Peter's Choice Nutrition Ctr 4879 Fountain Ave *TF:* 888-324-9904 ■ *Web:* www.vites.com	Los Angeles	CA	90029	888-324-9904		297-8
Peter's Inn 504 S Ann St *Web:* www.petersinn.com	Baltimore	MD	21231	410-675-7313		671
Peterbilt Motors Co 1700 Woodbrook St *Web:* www.peterbilt.com	Denton	TX	76205	940-591-4000	591-4260	516
Peterborough Regional Health Ctr 1 Hospital Dr *Web:* prhc.on.ca	Peterborough	ON	K9J7C6	705-743-2121		374-2
Peterman Associates Inc 3840 N Main St *Web:* petermanaes.com	Findlay	OH	45840	419-422-6672		261
Peters & Company PC 610 S W Alder St 910 *Web:* peterscopc.com	Portland	OR	97205	503-241-8080		2
Peters Gary C (Sen D - MI) 724 Hart Senate Office Bldg *Web:* www.peters.senate.gov	Washington	DC	20510	202-224-6221		342-2
Peters Main Street Photography 314 N Main St *Web:* www.petersphotography.com	London	OH	43140	740-852-2731		590
Peters Murdaugh Parker Eltzroth & Detrick PA (PMPED) 123 S Walter St PO Box 1164 *Web:* www.pmped.com	Walterboro	SC	29488	843-549-9544	549-9546	428
Peters of Nashua 300 Amherst St *Web:* www.petersauto.com	Nashua	NH	03063	603-889-1166		57
Peters Scott (Rep D - CA) 2338 Rayburn House Office Bldg *Web:* scottpeters.house.gov	Washington	DC	20515	202-225-0508		342-2
Petersburg Chamber of Commerce 325 E Washington St *Web:* www.petersburgchamber.com	Petersburg	VA	23804	804-733-8131		139
Petersburg Fisheries PO Box 1147 *TF:* 877-772-4294 ■ *Web:* www.hookedonfish.com	Petersburg	AK	99833	907-772-4294	772-4472	296-13
Petersburg (Independent City) 135 N Union St *Web:* www.petersburg-va.org	Petersburg	VA	23803	804-733-2300		338
Petersburg National Battlefield 1539 Hickory Hill Rd *Web:* www.nps.gov	Petersburg	VA	23803	804-732-3531	732-0835	564
Petersburg Public Library 201 W Washington St *Web:* www.ppls.org	Petersburg	VA	23803	804-733-2387		434-3
Petersburg Public Library 14 S 2nd St *Web:* www.psglib.org	Petersburg	AK	99833	907-772-3349		434-3
Petersen Aluminum Corp 1005 Tonne Rd *TF:* 800-323-1960 ■ *Web:* www.pac-clad.com	Elk Grove Village	IL	60007	800-722-2523	722-7150	697
Petersen Automotive Museum 6060 Wilshire Blvd *Web:* www.petersen.org	Los Angeles	CA	90036	323-930-2277		520
Petersen Engineering Inc 8902 Vincennes Cir Ste F *Web:* pei-engineering.com	Indianapolis	IN	46268	317-217-1701		261
Petersen Health Care Inc 830 W Trailcreek Dr *Web:* www.petersenhealthcare.net	Peoria	IL	61614	309-691-8113		371
Petersen Inc 1527 North 2000 West *TF:* 800-410-6789 ■ *Web:* www.peterseninc.com	Ogden	UT	84404	801-732-2000		358

Name / Address	City	State	ZIP	Phone	Fax	Class
Petersen Industries Inc 4000 SR 60 West *Web:* www.petersenind.com	Lake Wales	FL	33859	863-676-1493		45
Petersen-Arne 4310 W Fifth Ave *TF:* 800-547-2509 ■ *Web:* www.petersen-arne.com	Eugene	OR	97402	541-485-1406	485-3459	44
PetersenDean Roofing & Solar 39300 Civic Center Dr Ste 300 *TF:* 877-552-4418 ■ *Web:* petersendean.com	Fremont	CA	94538	877-552-4418		46
Peterson & Peterson Pc 8555 Westland West Blvd *Web:* petersonandpeterson.com	Houston	TX	77041	832-237-1040	237-1042	2
Peterson & Smith Equine Hospital LLC 4747 SW 60th Ave *Web:* www.petersonsmith.com	Ocala	FL	34474	352-237-6151		794
Peterson Associates Consulting Engineers Inc 7201 N Dreamy Draw Dr Ste 200 *Web:* www.mpeconsult.com	Phoenix	AZ	85020	602-943-4116	943-2507	261
Peterson Collin C (Rep D - MN) 2204 Rayburn House Office Bldg *Web:* collinpeterson.house.gov	Washington	DC	20515	202-225-2165	225-1593	342-2
Peterson Construction Co 18817 State Rte 501 *Web:* www.petersonconstructionco.com	Wapakoneta	OH	45895	419-941-2233		186
Peterson Cos, The 12500 Fair Lakes Cir Ste 400 *Web:* www.petersoncos.com	Fairfax	VA	22033	703-227-2000	631-6481	655
Peterson Farms Inc 3104 W Baseline Rd PO Box 115 *Web:* www.petersonfarmsinc.com	Shelby	MI	49455	231-861-7101		296-21
Peterson Health 551 Hill Country Dr *Web:* www.petersonhealth.com	Kerrville	TX	78028	830-896-4200		374-3
Peterson Industries Inc Rr 2 PO Box 95 *Web:* www.petersonind.com	Smith Center	KS	66967	785-282-6825		120
Peterson Institute for International Economics 1750 Massachusetts Ave NW *Web:* piie.com	Washington	DC	20036	202-328-9000	328-5432	634
Peterson Johnson Murray 788 N Jefferson St Ste 500 *Web:* pjmlaw.com	Milwaukee	WI	53202	414-278-8800	278-0920	41
Peterson Manufacturing Co 4200 E 135th St *TF:* 800-821-3490 ■ *Web:* www.pmlights.com	Grandview	MO	64030	816-765-2000	761-6693	438
Peterson Milla Hooks 1315 Harmon Pl *Web:* pmhadv.com	Minneapolis	MN	55403	612-349-9116		4
Peterson Pacific Corp 29408 Airport Rd *TF:* 800-269-6520 ■ *Web:* www.petersoncorp.com	Eugene	OR	97402	541-689-6520	689-0804	190
Peterson Picture Co 2720 W Belmont Ave *Web:* peterson-picture.com	Chicago	IL	60618	773-463-8888	463-4603	309
Peterson Power Systems Inc 2828 Teagarden St *Web:* www.petersonpower.com	San Leandro	CA	94577	510-895-8400		23
Peterson Products Inc 10 Airpark Vista Blvd *Web:* www.petersonproducts.com	Dayton	NV	89403	650-591-7311		606
Peterson School 25 Montvale Ave *Web:* www.petersonschool.com	Woburn	MA	01801	781-938-5656	932-6864	685
Peterson Spring 21200 Telegraph Rd *Web:* www.pspring.com	Southfield	MI	48033	248-799-5400	357-3176	719
Peterson Steel Corp 61 W Mountain St *TF:* 800-325-3245 ■ *Web:* www.petersonsteel.com	Worcester	MA	01606	508-853-3630		492
Peterson Structural Engineers Inc (PSE) 9400 SW Barnes Rd Ste 100 *Web:* psengineers.com	Portland	OR	97225	503-292-1635	292-9846	261
Peterson Tool Company Inc 739 Fesslers Ln PO Box 100830 *Web:* petersontool.com	Nashville	TN	37224	615-242-7341	242-7362	454
Peterson Tractor Co 955 Marina Blvd *TF:* 800-590-5945 ■ *Web:* www.petersoncat.com	San Leandro	CA	94577	510-357-6200	352-4570	274
Peterson Transportation Inc 1950 Tabor Ave *Web:* petersontrans.com	Manson	IA	50563	712-469-2303		311
Peterson's LLC 8740 Lucent Blvd Ste 400 *TF:* 800-338-3282 ■ *Web:* www.petersons.com	Highlands Ranch	CO	80129	800-338-3282		637-2
Peterson's North Branch Mill Inc 39015 Branch Ave *Web:* www.petersonscountrymill.com	North Branch	MN	55056	651-674-4425		276
Petillo Masterpiece Guitars 1206 Herbert Ave *Web:* www.petilloguitars.com	Ocean	NJ	07712	732-531-6338	531-3045	527
Petit Jean Electric Co-op 270 Quality Dr PO Box 37 *TF:* 800-786-7618 ■ *Web:* www.pjecc.com	Clinton	AR	72031	501-745-2493		245
Petit Jean State Park 1285 Petit Jean Mtn Rd *Web:* www.arkansasstateparks.com	Morrilton	AR	72110	501-727-5441		565
Petit Louis Bistro 4800 Roland Ave *Web:* www.petitlouis.com	Baltimore	MD	21210	410-366-9393		671
Petite Petal Inc 381 E Campbell Ave *Web:* petitepetalco.com	Campbell	CA	95008	408-540-7429		292
Petitt Barraza LLC 1651 N Glenville Dr Ste 212 *Web:* www.petittbarraza.com	Richardson	TX	75081	214-221-9955	340-3550	261
Petitti Garden Centers 24964 Broadway Ave *Web:* www.petittigardencenter.com	Oakwood	OH	44146	440-439-6511	439-7736	369
Petland Inc 250 Riverside St *TF:* 800-221-5935 ■ *Web:* petland.com	Chillicothe	OH	45601	740-775-2464	775-2575	578
Petlovers Animal Hospital 6425 E Livingston Ave *Web:* petloversah.com	Reynoldsburg	OH	43068	614-866-1912		794
PetManufacturers.com PO Box 2202 **Fax Area Code:* 646 ■ *TF:* 888-248-4301 ■ *Web:* www.petmanufacturers.com	Secaucus	NJ	07096	888-248-4301	607-4025*	328
Petmate 2300 E Randol Mill Rd *TF:* 877-738-6283 ■ *Web:* www.petmate.com	Arlington	TX	76011	877-738-6283		578
PetMed Express Inc 1441 SW 29th Ave *NASDAQ: PETS* ■ *TF:* 800-738-6337 ■ *Web:* www.1800petmeds.com	Pompano Beach	FL	33069	954-979-5995	971-0544	578
Peto MacCallum Ltd 165 Cartwright Ave *Web:* www.petomaccallum.com	Toronto	ON	M6A1V5	416-785-5110		261
Petol Gearench 4450 S Hwy 6 PO Box 192 *Web:* petol.com	Clifton	TX	76634	254-675-8651	675-6100	537
Petoskey Area Visitors Bureau 401 E Mitchell St *TF:* 800-845-2828 ■ *Web:* www.petoskeyarea.com	Petoskey	MI	49770	231-348-2755		206
Petoskey Plastics Inc 1 Petoskey St *Web:* www.petoskeyplastics.com	Petoskey	MI	49770	231-347-2602		600
Petoskey Regional Chamber of Commerce 401 E Mitchell St *Web:* www.petoskeychamber.com	Petoskey	MI	49770	231-347-4150	348-1810	139
Petra Allied Health Inc PO Box 6611 *TF:* 800-785-9876 ■ *Web:* www.petraalliedhealth.com	Springdale	AR	72766	479-750-9876	750-4655	167-3
Petra Financial Advisors Inc 2 N Cascade Ave Ste 720 *Web:* www.petrafinancial.com	Colorado Springs	CO	80903	719-636-9000		401
Petra Industries Inc 2101 S Kelly Ave *Web:* www.petra.com	Edmond	OK	73013	405-216-2146		360-3
Petra Manufacturing Co 6600 W Armitage Ave *TF:* 800-888-7387 ■ *Web:* www.petraandholum.com	Chicago	IL	60707	773-622-1475		687
Petracca Design & Engineering PC 199 E Main St Ste 3 *Web:* tompetracca.com	Smithtown	NY	11787	631-361-9825		261
Petrella's Italian Cafe 2174 W Nine Mile Rd *Web:* www.petrellasitaliancafe.com	Pensacola	FL	32534	850-471-9444		671
Petrey W. L. Wholesale Company Inc 10345 Petrey Hwy *Web:* www.petrey.com	Luverne	AL	36049	334-230-5674	335-2422	345
Petrie Raymond, Professional Chartered Accountants LLP 255 Cromazie Blvd E Ste 1000 *Web:* www.petrieraymond.qc.ca	Montreal	QC	H2M1M2	514-342-4740		463
Petrified Forest National Park PO Box 2217 *Web:* www.nps.gov	Petrified For	AZ	86028	928-524-6228	524-3567	564
Petrini & Associates PC 372 Union Ave *Web:* petrinilaw.com	Framingham	MA	01702	508-665-4310		41
Petrini Corp 187 Rosemary St *Web:* www.petrinicorp.com	Needham	MA	02494	781-444-1963		186
Petro 49 Inc 234 4th Ave *TF:* 800-478-7586 ■ *Web:* www.petromarineservices.com	Seward	AK	99664	907-224-3190	224-3937	579
Petro Amigos Supply Inc 777 N Eldridge Pkwy Ste 400 *Web:* www.petro-amigos.com	Houston	TX	77079	281-497-0858	497-1575	755
Petro Cohen PC 2111 New Rd Ste 202 *TF:* 888-675-7607 ■ *Web:* petrocohen.com	Northfield	NJ	08225	609-677-1700		41
Petro Lock Inc 45315 N Trevor Ave *Web:* petrolock.com	Lancaster	CA	93534	661-948-6044	948-9524	579
Petro Lucrum Inc 3525 Sage Rd Ste 1416 *Web:* www.petrolucrum.com	Houston	TX	77056	832-993-5426		536
Petro Packaging Company Inc 16 Quine St *Web:* www.petropackaging.com	Cranford	NJ	07016	908-272-4054	272-2836	605-2
Petro Plastics Company Inc 450 S Ave *TF:* 800-486-4738 ■ *Web:* www.petroplastics.com	Garwood	NJ	07027	908-789-1200	789-1381	599
Petrobras 10350 Richmond Ave Ste 1400 *Web:* www.petrobras.com.br	Houston	TX	77042	713-808-8000		536
PetroCard Systems Inc 730 Central Ave S *TF:* 800-950-3835 ■ *Web:* www.petrocard.com	Kent	WA	98032	253-852-7777		579
Petrocco Farms 14110 Brighton Rd *TF:* 888-876-2207 ■ *Web:* www.petroccofarms.com	Brighton	CO	80601	303-659-6498	659-7645	10-11
Petrochem Field Services Inc 2429 Wilson Rd *TF:* 800-255-4737 ■ *Web:* www.pfs-us.com	Humble	TX	77396	281-441-2550	441-2022	539
Petrol Adv Inc 443 N Varney St *Web:* petrolad.com	Burbank	CA	91502	323-644-3720		4
Petroleum Accounting Consultants PLLC 2123 SW 119th St Ste A *Web:* pacpllc.com	Oklahoma City	OK	73170	405-759-2708	759-2714	2
Petroleum Analyzer Company LP 8824 Fallbrook Dr *TF:* 800-444-8378 ■ *Web:* www.paclp.com	Houston	TX	77064	281-940-1803		419
Petroleum County 302 E Main PO Box 226 *Web:* petroleumcountymt.org	Winnett	MT	59087	406-429-6551	429-6328	338
Petroleum Geo-Services Inc W Memorial Pl I 15375 Memorial Dr Ste 100 *Web:* www.pgs.com	Houston	TX	77079	281-509-8000	509-8500	538
Petroleum Heat & Power Company Inc 1000 Woodbury Rd 3rd Fl Ste 110 *TF:* 800-645-4328 ■ *Web:* www.petro.com	Stamford	CT	06902	800-645-4328		316
Petroleum Marketers Association of America (PMAA) 1901 N Ft Myer Dr Ste 500 *Web:* www.pmaa.org	Arlington	VA	22209	703-351-8000	351-9160	49-18
Petroleum Rx LLC 424 E Southern Ave Ste 101 *Web:* petroleumrx.com	Tempe	AZ	85282	480-464-6053	219-6759	177
Petroleum Strategies Inc 303 W Wall St *Web:* www.petroleumstrategies.com	Midland	TX	79701	432-682-0292		539
Petroleum Traders Corp 7120 Pointe Inverness Way *TF:* 800-348-3705 ■ *Web:* www.petroleumtraders.com	Fort Wayne	IN	46804	800-348-3705		579
Petroleum Wholesale LP 2204 Timberlock Palace Ste 270 *Web:* petroleumwholesale.com	The Woodlands	TX	77381	281-681-1000		579
PetroLiance LLC 739 N State St *TF:* 800-628-7231 ■ *Web:* www.petroliance.com	Elgin	IL	60123	877-738-7699		579
Petron Automation Inc 65 Mountain View Rd *Web:* www.petronautomation.com	Watertown	CT	06795	860-274-9091	274-7451	621

Company	Phone	Fax	Class
PetroQuest Energy Inc 400 E Kaliste Saloom Rd Ste 6000 . . . LaFayette LA 70508 *NYSE: PQ* ■ *Web:* www.petroquest.com	337-232-7028	232-0044	538
Petros Energy Products Inc 3035 Walnut Ave. . . . Long Beach CA 90807 *Web:* petrosenergy.com	562-424-7030		612
PetroSkills LLC 2930 S Yale Ave. . . . Tulsa OK 74114 *Web:* www.petroskills.com	918-828-2500	828-2580	539
Petrosouth Inc 234 N Hill St. . . . Griffin GA 30224 *Web:* www.petrosouth.com	770-227-8804	412-8851	579
Petrotech Inc 151 Brookhollow Esplanade . . . New Orleans LA 70123 *Web:* petrotechinc.com	504-620-6600		518
Petro-Techna Intl 31 Scarsdale Rd. . . . Toronto ON M3B2R2 *Web:* www.petro-techna.com	416-444-0071	444-0072	539
Petrow Kane Leemhuis PC 8440 Woodfield Crossing Blvd Ste 345 . . . Indianapolis IN 46240 *Web:* www.petrowkane.com	317-452-4700		2
Petroway Inc 926 Bautista Ct . . . Palo Alto CA 94303 *Web:* www.petroway.com	650-427-9049		192
Petruccelli & Osher Attorneys at Law 5100 N Federal Hwy Ste 300 B. . . . Fort Lauderdale FL 33308 *Web:* www.equaljustice.law	954-771-4118		428
Petsky Prunier LLC 60 Broad St 38th Fl. . . . New York NY 10004 *Web:* petskyprunier.com	212-842-6020		70
PETsMART Inc 19601 N 27th Ave . . . Phoenix AZ 85027 *NASDAQ: PETM* ■ *TF:* 800-738-1385 ■ *Web:* www.petsmart.com	623-580-6100		578
Petterino's 150 N Dearborn St. . . . Chicago IL 60601 *Web:* www.petterinos.com	312-422-0150		671
Pettey Machine Works Inc 16 N Seneca Dr. . . . Trinity AL 35673 *Web:* www.petteymachineworks.com	256-355-0085	355-0243	454
Pettibone Michigan 1100 Superior Ave. . . . Baraga MI 49908 *TF:* 800-467-3884 ■ *Web:* www.gopettibone.com	906-353-4800	353-6325	470
Pettigrew & Associates PA 100 E Navajo . . . Hobbs NM 88240 *Web:* pettigrew.us	575-393-9827		261
Pettigrew & Sons Casket Co 6151 Power Inn Rd. . . . Sacramento CA 95824 *TF:* 800-852-1701 ■ *Web:* www.pettigrewcaskets.com	916-383-0777	383-2445	134
Pettigrew State Park 2252 Lake Shore Rd . . . Creswell NC 27928 *Web:* www.ncparks.gov	252-797-4475		565
Pettus Mechanical Services 12647 Hwy 72 . . . Rogersville AL 35652 *Web:* www.pettushvac.com	256-389-8181		186
Petty & Associates Inc 1375 Greg St Ste 106. . . . Sparks NV 89431 *Web:* pettyengineering.com	775-359-5777	359-1119	261
Petty Machine Company Inc 2403 Forbes Rd . . . Gastonia NC 28056	704-864-3254	861-1937	744
PETZL America Inc 2929 Decker Lake Dr . . . West Valley City UT 84119 *Web:* www.petzl.com	801-926-1500		711
Peugeot Motors of America Inc 150 Clove Rd . . . Little Falls NJ 07424 *Web:* frenchcarsinamerica.over-blog.com	973-812-4444		59
Pevarnik Bros Inc 1302 Memorial Dr. . . . Latrobe PA 15650 *Web:* www.pevarnik.com	724-539-3516		189-3
Pevco Sys International Inc 1401 Tangier Dr . . . Baltimore MD 21220 *TF:* 800-296-7382 ■ *Web:* www.pevco.com	410-931-8800		595
Pew Charitable Trusts 2005 Market St 1 Commerce Sq Ste 2800 . . . Philadelphia PA 19103 *Web:* www.pewtrusts.org	215-575-9050		305
Pewag Inc 600 W Crossroad Pky. . . . Bolingbrook IL 60440 **Fax Area Code:* 630 ■ *TF:* 800-526-3924 ■ *Web:* pewagchain.com	800-526-3924	759-0788*	483
Pexagon Technology Inc 14 Business Park Dr. . . . Branford CT 06405 *Web:* www.pexagontech.com	203-458-3364		173-8
Pexco LLC 2500 Northwinds Pkwy Ste 472 . . . Alpharetta GA 30009 *Web:* pexco.com	404-564-8560	564-8579	600
Pexx Inc PO Box 210 . . . Plantersville TX 77363 *Web:* www.pexx.net	832-237-5888	487-8050	180
Peyton's Place 5344 Atlanta Hwy . . . Montgomery AL 36109 *Web:* peytonsplacelunch.tripod.com	334-396-3630		671
PEZ Candy Inc 35 Prindle Hill Rd . . . Orange CT 06477 *Web:* us.pez.com	203-795-0531		296-8
PF Chang's China Bistro Inc 7676 E Pinnacle Peak Rd . . . Scottsdale AZ 85255 *TF:* 844-737-7333 ■ *Web:* www.pfchangs.com	480-888-3000	888-3002	671
PFA (Pedorthic Footwear Assn) 2025 M St NW Ste 800. . . . Washington DC 20036 *TF:* 800-673-8447 ■ *Web:* www.pedorthics.org	202-367-1145	367-2145	48-17
Pfaltzgraff Co PO Box 21769 . . . York PA 17402 *TF:* 800-999-2811 ■ *Web:* www.pfaltzgraff.com	800-999-2811	757-6872	730
PFAU Industrial Animal Oils PO Box 7 . . . Jeffersonville IN 47130 *Web:* www.pfauoil.com	812-283-6697		579
Pfaudler Inc 1000 W Ave. . . . Rochester NY 14611 *Web:* www.pfaudler.com	585-235-1000		386
PFAW (People for the American Way) 2000 M St NW Ste 400. . . . Washington DC 20036 *TF:* 800-326-7329 ■ *Web:* www.pfaw.org	202-467-4999	293-2672	48-7
PFB Corp 100-2886 Sunridge Way NE . . . Calgary AB T1Y7H9 *Web:* www.pfbcorp.com	403-569-4300		787
PFE Group, The Cordaville Office Bldg 153 Cordaville Rd Ste 230. . . . Southborough MA 01772 *Web:* www.unitedcp.com	508-683-1400	683-1401	463
Pfeffer Hanniford & Palka CPAS PC 225 E Grand River Ave Ste 104. . . . Brighton MI 48116 *Web:* phpcpa.com	810-229-5550	229-5578	2
Pfeiffer Big Sur State Park Pfeiffer Big Sur Rd & Cabrillo Hwy. . . . Big Sur CA 93920 *Web:* www.parks.ca.gov	831-667-1112	647-6239	565
Pfeiffer University 48380 Hwy 52 N. . . . Misenheimer NC 28109 *TF:* 800-338-2060 ■ *Web:* www.pfeiffer.edu	704-463-1360	463-1363	166
Pfeiffer Vacuum Inc 24 Trafalgar Sq . . . Nashua NH 03063 *TF:* 800-248-8254 ■ *Web:* www.pfeiffer-vacuum.com	603-578-6500		358
Pfeiler & Associates Engineers Inc 22609 La Palma Ave Ste 202 . . . Yorba Linda CA 92887 *Web:* pfeilerassociates.com	909-993-5800		261
Pfenex Inc 10790 Roselle St . . . San Diego CA 92121 *Web:* www.pfenex.com	858-352-4400	352-4602	668
PFERD Milwaukee Brush Co 30 Jytek Dr . . . Leominster MA 01453 *TF:* 800-342-9015 ■ *Web:* www.pferd.com	978-840-6420	840-6421	103
PFF (Progress & Freedom Foundation) 1444 Eye St NW Ste 500. . . . Washington DC 20005 *Web:* www.pff.org	202-289-8928	289-6079	634
PFI (Pet Food Institute) 2025 M St NW Ste 800. . . . Washington DC 20036 *Web:* www.petfoodinstitute.org	202-367-1120	367-2120	49-4
PFI Precision Inc 2011 N Dayton Lakeview Rd . . . New Carlisle OH 45344 *TF:* 800-248-4734 ■ *Web:* www.pfiprecision.com	937-845-3081	845-0475	454
PFI Tech 5761 Rickenbacker Rd . . . Commerce CA 90040 *Web:* www.pfitech.com	310-824-1800		196
Pfingsten Partners LLC 300 N LaSalle St Ste 5400 . . . Chicago IL 60654 *Web:* www.pfingsten.com	312-222-8707	222-8708	792
Pfister Hotel 424 E Wisconsin Ave . . . Milwaukee WI 53202 *TF:* 800-558-8222 ■ *Web:* www.thepfisterhotel.com	414-273-8222	273-5025	379
Pfister Roofing Inc 80 E Fifth St. . . . Paterson NJ 07524 *Web:* pfisterroofing.com	973-569-9330	569-9333	191-4
Pfizer Animal Health 5 Giralda Farms . . . Madison NJ 07940 *TF:* 888-963-8471 ■ *Web:* www.zoetisus.com	888-963-8471		582
Pfizer Canada Inc 17300 TransCanada Hwy . . . Kirkland QC H9J2M5 *TF:* 800-463-6001 ■ *Web:* www.pfizer.ca	514-695-0500		582
Pfizer Inc 235 E 42nd St. . . . New York NY 10017 *NYSE: PFE* ■ *TF:* 800-879-3477 ■ *Web:* www.pfizer.com	212-733-2323		582
PFLOW Industries 6720 N Teutonia Ave. . . . Milwaukee WI 53209 *Web:* www.pflow.com	414-352-9000		207
PFM Capital Inc 1925 Victoria Ave 2nd Fl . . . Regina SK S4P0R3 *Web:* www.pfm.ca	306-791-4855		528
PFMS (Professional Furniture Management Services) 5101 LeTourneau Cir . . . Tampa FL 33610 *Web:* www.pfms.org	813-621-6700	973-9888	189-1
PFS (Palmer Food Services) 900 Jefferson Rd Ste 1000 . . . Rochester NY 14623 *TF:* 800-888-3474 ■ *Web:* www.palmerfoods.com	585-424-3210	424-1035	297-9
PFSB (Piedmont Federal Savings Bank) 201 S Stratford Rd . . . Winston-Salem NC 27103 *Web:* www.piedmontfederal.bank	336-770-1000		70
PFSweb Inc 505 Millennium Dr Ste 500 . . . Allen TX 75013 *NASDAQ: PFSW* ■ *TF:* 888-330-5504 ■ *Web:* www.pfsweb.com	972-881-2900		463
PFT Alexander Inc 3250 E Grant St . . . Signal Hill CA 90755 *TF:* 800-696-1331 ■ *Web:* www.pft-alexander.com	562-595-1741		246
PFund Mcdonnell PC 139 Prospect St 2nd Fl. . . . Ridgewood NJ 07450 *Web:* pfundmcdonnell.com	201-857-5040		41
PFW Systems Corp 850 Medway Park Ct . . . London ON N6G5C6 *Web:* www.pfw.com	519-474-3300		177
PG & E Corp 77 Beale St 24th Fl . . . San Francisco CA 94105 *NYSE: PCG* ■ *Web:* www.pgecorp.com	415-973-8200	973-8719	360-5
PG Exhibits 3510 Himalaya Rd. . . . Aurora CO 80011 *Web:* www.pgexhibits.com	303-722-6565		8
PG Life Link Inc 167 Gap Way. . . . Erlanger KY 41018 *TF:* 800-287-4123 ■ *Web:* www.pglifelink.com	859-283-5900	372-6272	253
PGA of America 100 Avenue of the Champions . . . Palm Beach Gardens FL 33418 *TF:* 800-477-6465 ■ *Web:* www.pga.com	561-624-8400		48-22
PGA Tour Inc 112 PGA Tour Blvd. . . . Ponte Vedra Beach FL 32082 *Web:* www.pgatour.com	904-285-3700		48-22
PGA Worldwide Golf Exhibitions 383 Main Ave . . . Norwalk CT 06851 *TF:* 800-840-5628 ■ *Web:* www.pgalasvegas.com	203-840-5628	840-9628	637-10
PGC (Precision Gasket Co) 5732 Lincoln Dr. . . . Edina MN 55436 *Web:* pgc-solutions.com	952-942-6711		326
PGF (PGF Technology Group Inc) 2993 Technology Dr. . . . Rochester Hills MI 48309 *TF:* 800-342-0422 ■ *Web:* www.pgftech.com	248-852-2800	852-2992	253
PGF Technology Group Inc (PGF) 2993 Technology Dr. . . . Rochester Hills MI 48309 *TF:* 800-342-0422 ■ *Web:* www.pgftech.com	248-852-2800	852-2992	253
PGM Inc PO Box 1933 . . . Orem UT 84058 *Web:* www.pgminc.com	801-426-0889		466
PGP (Professional Group Plans Inc) 225 Wireless Blvd Ste 200 . . . Hauppauge NY 11788 *Web:* www.pgpbenefits.com	631-951-9200	951-9623	631
PGP (Pecan Grove Press) 1 Camino Santa Maria . . . San Antonio TX 78228 *Web:* www.library.stmarytx.edu	210-436-3442	436-3782	637-2
PGR Media 34 Farnsworth St 2nd Fl . . . Boston MA 02210 *Web:* www.pgrmedia.com	617-502-8400		6
PGT 1070 Technology Dr. . . . Nokomis FL 34275 *TF:* 800-282-6019 ■ *Web:* pgtwindows.com	941-480-1600	486-8369	234
PGW (Publishers Group West) 1700 Fourth St . . . Berkeley CA 94710 *TF:* 866-400-5351 ■ *Web:* www.pgw.com	510-809-3700	809-3777	96
PGW (Philadelphia Gas Works) 800 W Montgomery Ave. . . . Philadelphia PA 19122 *TF:* 800-242-1776 ■ *Web:* www.pgworks.com	215-235-1000		787
P&H (Parrish & Heimbecker Ltd) 201 Portage Ave Ste 1400 . . . Winnipeg MB R3B3K6 *TF:* 800-665-8937 ■ *Web:* parrishandheimbecker.com	204-956-2030	943-8233	275
PH Hoeft State Park 5001 US Hwy 23 N. . . . Rogers City MI 49779 *Web:* www.michigan.org	989-734-2543		565

	Phone	Fax	Class
Phacil Inc 601 California St . . . San Francisco CA 94108 *Web:* www.phacil.com	703-526-1800		180
Phadia US Inc 4169 Commercial Ave . . . Portage MI 49002 *TF:* 800-346-4364 ■ *Web:* www.phadia.com	269-492-1940		231
Phagans' Beauty College 1565 SW 53rd St . . . Corvallis OR 97333 *Web:* www.phagans-schools.com	541-753-6466	752-2647	167-3
Phagans' School of Hair Design 1542 NE Weidler St. . . . Portland OR 97232 *Web:* www.phagans.com	503-239-0838		685
Phalcon Ltd 505 Main St . . . Farmington CT 06032 *Web:* phalconusa.com	860-677-9797		787
Phantom Canyon Brewing Co 2 E Pikes Peak Ave . . . Colorado Springs CO 80903 *Web:* www.phantomcanyon.com	719-635-2800	635-9930	671
Phantom Laboratory Inc, The 2727 SR- 29 . . . Greenwich NY 12834 *TF:* 800-525-1190 ■ *Web:* www.phantomlab.com	518-692-1190		668
Phaostron Instrument & Electronic Co 717 N Coney Ave . . . Azusa CA 91702 *Web:* www.phaostron.com	626-969-6801	334-8057	729
Pharma eMarket LLC 15 E Ridge Pk Ste 225 . . . Conshohocken PA 19428 *Web:* www.monitorforhire.com	610-862-0909		237
Pharma Tech Industries Inc 1310 Stylemaster Dr . . . Union MO 63084 *Web:* www.pharma-tech.net	636-583-8664	583-5373	479
PharmaCentra LLC 105 Industrial Dr . . . Americus GA 31719 **Fax Area Code:* 770 ■ *TF:* 866-395-0088 ■ *Web:* www.pharmacentra.com	866-395-0088	395-0989*	195
Pharmaceutical Advisors LLC 330 Wall St. . . . Princeton NJ 08540 *Web:* www.pharmadvisors.com	609-688-1330	228-5889	237
Pharmaceutical Associates Inc 1700 Perimeter Rd . . . Greenville SC 29605 *Web:* www.paipharma.com	864-277-7282		231
Pharmaceutical Calibrations & Instrumentation LLC 8100 Brownleigh Dr Ste 100-A. . . . Raleigh NC 27617 *TF:* 877-724-2257 ■ *Web:* www.pci-llc.com	877-724-2257		583
Pharmaceutical Care Management Assn (PCMA) 325 Seventh St NW. . . . Washington DC 20004 *Web:* www.pcmanet.org	202-756-5700		49-8
Pharmaceutical Innovations Inc 897 Frelinghuysen Ave . . . Newark NJ 07114 *Web:* www.pharminnovations.com	973-242-2900	242-0578	231
Pharmaceutical Media Inc 30 E 33rd St 4th Fl . . . New York NY 10016 *Web:* www.pminy.com	212-685-5010	685-6126	4
Pharmaceutical Representative Magazine 641 Lexington Ave 8th Fl . . . New York NY 10022 *Web:* www.pharmexec.com	212-951-6600	951-6604	457-5
Pharmaceutical Research & Manufacturers of America (PHRMA) 950 F St NW Ste 300 . . . Washington DC 20004 *Web:* www.phrma.org	202-835-3400	835-3414	49-8
Pharmaceutics International Inc 10819 Gilroy Rd . . . Hunt Valley MD 21031 *Web:* www.pharm-int.com	410-584-0001		231
Pharmacists Mutual Insurance Co 808 US Hwy 18 W PO Box 370. . . . Algona IA 50511 **Fax Area Code:* 515 ■ *TF:* 800-247-5930 ■ *Web:* www.phmic.com	800-247-5930	295-9306*	391-4
Pharmacists Society of the State of New York Inc 210 Washington Ave Ext . . . Albany NY 12203 **Fax Area Code:* 518 ■ *TF:* 800-632-8822 ■ *Web:* pssny.site-ym.com	800-632-8822	464-0618*	585
Pharmacommunications Group Inc 5 - 501 Apple Creek Blvd . . . Markham ON L3R9R6 *TF:* 800-267-5409 ■ *Web:* www.pharmacommunications.com	905-477-3100		238
Pharmacy Consultants & Investigtors 830 W Rte 22 Ste 118. . . . Lake Zurich IL 60047 *Web:* www.piconsulting.org	847-540-9590		237
Pharmacy Providers of OK (PPOK) 3000 E Memorial Rd . . . Edmond OK 73013 **Fax Area Code:* 405 ■ *TF:* 877-557-5707 ■ *Web:* www.ppok.com	877-557-5707	525-2196*	237
Pharmacy Society of Wisconsin 701 Heartland Trl . . . Madison WI 53717 *Web:* www.pswi.org	608-827-9200	827-9292	585
Pharmacy Systems Inc 5050 Bradenton Ave PO Box 130 . . . Dublin OH 43017 *Web:* www.pharmacysystems.com	614-766-0101	766-4448	587
Pharmacyclics Inc 995 E Arques Ave. . . . Sunnyvale CA 94085 *NASDAQ:* PCYC ■ *Web:* www.pharmacyclics.com	408-774-0330		85
PharmaLogic Holdings Corp 1 S Ocean Blvd Ste 206 . . . Boca Raton FL 33432 *Web:* radiopharmacy.com	561-416-0085		238
Pharmalucence Inc 29 Dunham Rd . . . Billerica MA 01821 *TF:* 800-221-7554 ■ *Web:* www.pharmalucence.com	781-275-7120		231
Pharmapoint LLC 2 Perimeter Pk S Ste 300E . . . Birmingham AL 35243 *Web:* pharmapointrx.com	205-795-8800		237
Pharmaports LLC 1 E Uwchlan Ave Ste 116 . . . Exton PA 19341 *Web:* www.pharmaports.com	610-524-7888	524-7288	582
Pharmasave Drugs (National) Ltd 8411 - 200th St Ste 201 . . . Langley BC V2Y0E7 *TF:* 800-661-6106 ■ *Web:* pharmasave.com	604-455-2400	455-2493	231
Pharmascience Inc 6111 Royalmount Ave Ste 100 . . . Montreal QC H4P2T4 *TF:* 866-853-1178 ■ *Web:* www.pharmascience.com	514-340-9800		231
PharmaSeq Inc 11 Deer Park Dr Ste 104. . . . Monmouth Junction NJ 08852 *Web:* www.pharmaseq.com	732-355-0100	355-0102	194
Pharmaspectra Group Ltd 1359 Broadway Ste 600 . . . New York NY 10018 *Web:* medmeme.com	212-725-5990		237
PharmaSys Inc 216 Towne Village Dr . . . Cary NC 27513 *Web:* www.pharma-sys.com	919-468-2547		177
Pharmavite LLC 8510 Balboa Blvd Ste 100 . . . Northridge CA 91325 *TF:* 800-423-2405 ■ *Web:* www.pharmavite.com	818-221-6200	221-6618	583
PharmEcology Associates LLC 1001 Fannin . . . Houston TX 77002 **Fax Area Code:* 262 ■ *TF:* 877-247-7430 ■ *Web:* pharmecology.com	877-247-7430	250-8314*	192
PharMethod Inc 1170 Wheeler Way . . . Langhorne PA 19047 *TF:* 877-200-0736 ■ *Web:* www.pharmethod.com	877-200-0736		195
Pharmgate LLC 161 N Franklin Tpke. . . . Ramsey NJ 07446 *Web:* www.pharmgate.com	201-327-3800		238
Pharmore Ingredients 12569 S 2700 W Ste 201 . . . Riverton UT 84065 *Web:* pharmore.com	801-446-8188		297-8
Pharmout Laboratories Inc 1151 Sonora Ct . . . Sunnyvale CA 94086 *Web:* www.pharmoutlabs.net	408-481-3090		743
Pharos Hospitality LLC 320 S Tryon St Ste 202. . . . Charlotte NC 28202 *Web:* www.pharoshospitality.com	704-333-1818		378
Pharr Memorial Library 118 S Cage Blvd . . . Pharr TX 78577 *Web:* pharr-tx.gov	956-787-3966	787-3345	434-3
Pharr Yarns LLC 100 Main St PO Box 1939 . . . McAdenville NC 28101 *Web:* www.pharryarns.com	704-824-3551	824-0072	745-9
Phase 3 Marketing & Communications 3560 Atlanta Industrial Dr. . . . Atlanta GA 30331 *Web:* www.phase3mc.com	404-367-9898		344
Phase Matrix Inc 109 Bonaventura Dr . . . San Jose CA 95134 *Web:* www.phasematrix.net	408-428-1000	428-1500	248
Phase One Inc 200 Broadhollow Rd Ste 312 . . . Melville NY 11747 *TF:* 888-742-7366 ■ *Web:* www.phaseone.com	631-757-0400	547-9898	591
Phase Technology 6400 Youngerman Cir. . . . Jacksonville FL 32244 *TF:* 888-742-7385 ■ *Web:* phasetech.mseaudio.com	904-777-0700		52
PhaseBio Pharmaceuticals Inc 1 Great Vly Pkwy Ste 30 . . . Malvern PA 19355 *Web:* phasebio.com	610-981-6500		231
Phasetek Inc 550 California Rd Unit 11 . . . Quakertown PA 18951 *Web:* www.phasetekinc.com	215-536-6648		647
Phasetronics Inc 1600 Sunshine Dr. . . . Clearwater FL 33765 *Web:* www.phasetronics.com	727-573-1819	573-1803	203
PhaseWare Inc 1700 N Redbud Blvd Ste 190 . . . McKinney TX 75069 **Fax Area Code:* 214 ■ *TF:* 866-838-4789 ■ *Web:* www.phaseware.com	866-838-4789	975-1280*	178-1
Phasor Engineering Services LLC 14 Industrial Park Pl . . . Middletown CT 06457 *Web:* phasor.net	860-635-9777		261
PHB Inc 7900 W Ridge Rd. . . . Fairview PA 16415 *Web:* www.phbcorp.com	814-474-5511		308
PHCC (Plumbing-Heating-Cooling Contractors NA) 180 S Washington St Ste 100. . . . Falls Church VA 22046 *TF:* 800-533-7694 ■ *Web:* www.phccweb.org	703-237-8100	237-7442	49-3
PHD Inc 9009 Clubridge Dr. . . . Fort Wayne IN 46809 *TF:* 800-624-8511 ■ *Web:* www.phdinc.com	260-747-6151	747-6754	223
PHD Manufacturing Inc 44018 Columbiana-Waterford Rd . . . Columbiana OH 44408 *Web:* phd-mfg.com	330-482-9256		612
PhDx Systems Inc 5901 Indian School Rd NE . . . Albuquerque NM 87110	505-764-0174	764-0074	39
Pheasant Run Resort & Spa 4051 E Main St. . . . Saint Charles IL 60174 *TF:* 800-474-3272 ■ *Web:* www.pheasantrun.com	630-584-6300		669
Pheasant, The 905 Main St. . . . Dennis MA 02638 *Web:* www.pheasantcapecod.com	508-385-2133		671
Phelan & Taylor Produce Co 1860 Front St . . . Oceano CA 93445	805-489-2413		11-1
Phelan Hallinan & Schmieg LLP 400 Fellowship Rd Ste 100. . . . Mount Laurel NJ 08054 *TF:* 800-382-8746 ■ *Web:* www.phelanhallinan.com	800-382-8746		428
Phelps County 200 N Main St. . . . Rolla MO 65401 *Web:* www.phelpscounty.org	573-458-6000	458-6119	338
Phelps Courthouse 715 5th Ave. . . . Holdrege NE 68949 *Web:* phelpsgov.org	308-995-4469	995-4368	338
Phelps Dunbar LLP Canal Pl 365 Canal St Ste 2000 . . . New Orleans LA 70130 *Web:* www.phelps.com	504-566-1311		428
Phelps Fan LLC 10701 I-30 PO Box 190718 . . . Little Rock AR 72209 *Web:* www.phelpsfan.com	501-568-5550	568-3363	14
Phelps Industries Inc 1700 E 9th St . . . Little Rock AR 72202 *Web:* www.phelpsindustries.com	501-375-1141	375-6568	470
Phelps School 583 Sugartown Rd. . . . Malvern PA 19355 *Web:* thephelpsschool.org	610-644-1754	644-6679	622
Phelps Sungas Inc 224 Cross Rd. . . . Geneva NY 14456 *TF:* 800-458-1085 ■ *Web:* sungas.com	315-789-3285		316
Phenix & Crump PLLC 118 S Main. . . . Henderson TX 75654 *TF:* 800-940-1047 ■ *Web:* phenixlawfirm.com	903-657-3595		41
Phenix Technologies Inc 75 Speicher Dr . . . Accident MD 21520 *Web:* www.phenixtech.com	301-746-8118	895-5570	248
Phenomenex Inc 411 Madrid Ave. . . . Torrance CA 90501 *TF:* 800-543-3681 ■ *Web:* www.phenomenex.com	310-212-0555	328-7768	419
Phenopath Laboratories PLLC 551 N 34th St Ste 100 . . . Seattle WA 98103 *TF:* 888-927-4366 ■ *Web:* phenopath.com	206-374-9000		415
Phenova Inc 6390 Joyce Dr Ste 100 . . . Golden CO 80403 *Web:* www.phenova.com	303-940-0033	940-0043	743
Pherin Pharmaceuticals Inc PO Box 4081 . . . Los Altos CA 94024 *Web:* www.pherin.com	650-636-7064		231
PHF (Phoenix House Foundation Inc) 164 W 74th St. . . . New York NY 10023 *TF:* 888-671-9392 ■ *Web:* www.phoenixhouse.org	646-505-2018		726
PHFCU (Pearl Harbor Federal Credit Union) 94-449 Ukee St. . . . Waipahu HI 96797 **Fax Area Code:* 808 ■ *TF:* 800-987-5583 ■ *Web:* pearlhawaii.com	800-987-5583	218-6299*	219
PHH Mortgage Corp 3000 Leadenhall Rd . . . Mount Laurel NJ 08054 *TF:* 800-210-8849 ■ *Web:* www.phhmortgage.com	800-210-8849		509
PHI (Packard Humanities Institute, The) 300 Second St . . . Los Altos CA 94022 *Web:* www.packhum.org	650-948-0150		305

				Phone	Fax	Class
Phi Alpha Theta *National History Honor Society* 4202 E Fowler Ave SOC 107 *Fax Area Code: 813 ■ TF: 800-394-8195 ■ Web: www.phialphatheta.org	Tampa	FL	33620	800-394-8195	974-8215*	48-16
Phi Beta Sigma Fraternity Inc 145 Kennedy St NW Web: phibetasigma1914.org	Washington	DC	20011	202-726-5434	882-1681	48-16
Phi Chi Theta 1508 E Beltline Rd Ste 104 Web: www.phichitheta.org	Carrollton	TX	75006	972-245-7202		48-16
Phi Delta Kappa Intl (PDK) 408 N Union St TF: 800-766-1156 ■ Web: pdkintl.org	Bloomington	IN	47407	812-339-1156	339-0018	48-16
Phi Delta Phi International Legal Fraternity 1426 21st St NW Web: www.phideltaphi.org	Washington	DC	20036	202-223-6801	223-6808	48-16
Phi Delta Theta 2 S Campus Ave TF: 888-373-9855 ■ Web: www.phideltatheta.org	Oxford	OH	45056	513-523-6345	523-9200	48-16
PHI Environmental Consulting 4844 Jackson Rd Web: www.phiconsulting.com	Ann Arbor	MI	48103	734-332-0800		463
Phi Eta Sigma 1906 College H8s Blvd Ste 11062 Web: www.phietasigma.org	Bowling Green	KY	42101	270-745-6540	745-3893	48-16
PHI Inc 2001 SE Evangeline Thwy PO Box 90808 NASDAQ: PHII ■ TF: 866-815-7101 ■ Web: www.phihelico.com	LaFayette	LA	70508	337-235-2452	235-1357	359
PHI Inc 14955 E Salt Lake Ave Web: phihydraulics.com	City of Industry	CA	91746	626-968-9680	333-3610	456
Phi Kappa Phi Foundation 7576 Goodwood Blvd TF: 800-804-9880 ■ Web: www.phikappaphi.org	Baton Rouge	LA	70806	225-388-4917		305
Phi Kappa Psi 5395 Emerson Way TF: 800-486-1852 ■ Web: www.phikappapsi.com	Indianapolis	IN	46226	317-632-1852		48-16
Phi Kappa Sigma International Fraternity Inc 2 Timber Dr TF: 800-344-7335 ■ Web: www.pks.org	Chester Springs	PA	19425	610-469-3282	469-3286	48-16
Phi Kappa Tau 5221 Morning Sun Rd Web: www.phikappatau.org	Oxford	OH	45056	513-523-4193	523-9325	48-16
Phi Kappa Theta National Fraternity 3901 W 86th St Ste 360 Web: www.phikaps.org	Indianapolis	IN	46268	317-872-9934		48-16
Phi Mu Alpha Sinfonia Fraternity of America Inc 10600 Old State Rd TF: 800-473-2649 ■ Web: www.sinfonia.org	Evansville	IN	47711	812-867-2433	867-0633	48-16
Phi Mu Fraternity 400 Westpark Dr TF: 888-744-6824 ■ Web: www.phimu.org	Peachtree City	GA	30269	770-632-2090	632-2136	48-16
Phi Sigma Kappa Intl 2925 E 96th St TF: 888-846-6851 ■ Web: phisigmakappa.org	Indianapolis	IN	46240	317-573-5420	573-5430	48-16
Phi Sigma Pi National Honor Fraternity Inc 2119 Ambassador Cir TF: 800-366-1916 ■ Web: phisigmapi.org	Lancaster	PA	17603	717-299-4710	390-3054	48-16
Phi Sigma Sigma Inc 8178 Lark Brown Rd Ste 202 Web: www.onephisigmasigma.org	Elkridge	MD	21075	410-799-1224	799-9186	48-16
Phi Theta Kappa International Honor Society 1625 Eastover Dr *Fax Area Code: 601 ■ TF: 800-946-9995 ■ Web: www.ptk.org	Jackson	MS	39211	800-946-9995	984-3550*	48-16
Phibro Animal Health Corp 300 Frank W Burr Blvd Ste 21 TF: 800-223-0434 ■ Web: www.pahc.com	Teaneck	NJ	07666	201-329-7300	329-7399	143
Phifer Inc 4400 Kauloosa Ave PO Box 1700 TF: 800-633-5955 ■ Web: www.phifer.com	Tuscaloosa	AL	35401	205-345-2120	759-4450	413
Phil Long Dealerships 1020 Motor City Dr TF: 866-644-1378 ■ Web: www.phillong.com	Colorado Springs	CO	80905	866-644-1378		57
Phil Rulloda School of Floral Design 843 S State College Blvd Ste D TF: 800-981-7445 ■ Web: www.philrulloda.com	Anaheim	CA	92806	714-776-7445	776-7485	685
Phil Smith Automotive Group 4250 N Federal Hwy TF: 800-785-9608 ■ Web: www.philsmithauto.com	Lighthouse Point	FL	33064	954-867-1234		57
Phil Trani's 3490 Long Beach Blvd Web: philtrani.com	Long Beach	CA	90807	562-426-3668		671
Phil's BBQ 3750 Sports Arena Blvd Web: philsbbq.net	San Diego	CA	92110	619-226-6333		671
Philadelphia City Hall 1234 Market St 17th Fl Web: www.phila.gov	Philadelphia	PA	19107	215-686-9749	686-9853	337
Philadelphia City Paper 123 Chestnut St 3rd Fl Web: mycitypaper.com	Philadelphia	PA	19106	215-735-8444		532-5
Philadelphia College of Osteopathic Medicine (PCOM) 4170 City Ave TF: 800-999-6998 ■ Web: www.pcom.edu	Philadelphia	PA	19131	215-871-6100		800
Philadelphia Consolidated Holding Corp 231 St Asaph's Rd Ste 100 TF: 888-647-8639 ■ Web: www.phly.com	Bala Cynwyd	PA	19004	610-617-7900	617-7940	391-4
Philadelphia Contributionship Insurance Co 212 S Fourth St *Fax Area Code: 267 ■ TF: 888-627-1752 ■ Web: 1752.com	Philadelphia	PA	19106	215-627-1752	765-4611*	391-4
Philadelphia Convention & Visitors Bureau 1601 Market St Ste 200 Web: www.discoverphl.com	Philadelphia	PA	19103	215-636-3300	636-3327	206
Philadelphia County City Hall Broad & Market St Web: www.phila.gov	Philadelphia	PA	19107	215-686-1776	567-7380	338
Philadelphia Dance Co Philadanco Way 9 N Preston St Web: www.philadanco.org	Philadelphia	PA	19104	215-387-8200	387-8203	573-1
Philadelphia Eagles NovaCare Complex 1 NovaCare Way Web: www.philadelphiaeagles.com	Philadelphia	PA	19145	215-463-2500		715-3
Philadelphia Gas Works (PGW) 800 W Montgomery Ave TF: 800-242-1776 ■ Web: www.pgworks.com	Philadelphia	PA	19122	215-235-1000		787
Philadelphia Gay News 505 S Fourth St Web: www.epgn.com	Philadelphia	PA	19147	215-625-8501		532-3
Philadelphia Inquirer, Pbc, The PO Box 8263 Web: www.inquirer.com	Philadelphia	PA	19101	215-854-2000		532-2
Philadelphia Instruments & Controls Inc 4401 N 6th St TF: 800-863-9351 ■ Web: www.philadelphiainstrument.com	Philadelphia	PA	19140	215-329-8828	329-0729	201
Philadelphia International Airport 8000 Essington Ave Web: www.phl.org	Philadelphia	PA	19153	215-937-6937	937-6497	27
Philadelphia Macaroni Co 760 S 11th St Web: www.philamacaroni.com	Philadelphia	PA	19147	215-923-3141	925-4298	296-31
Philadelphia Magazine 1818 Market St 36th Fl Web: www.phillymag.com	Philadelphia	PA	19103	215-564-7700	656-3500	457-22
Philadelphia Mixing Solutions Ltd 1221 E Main St Web: www.philamixers.com	Palmyra	PA	17078	717-832-2800		298
Philadelphia Museum of Art 2600 Benjamin Franklin Pkwy Web: www.philamuseum.org	Philadelphia	PA	19130	215-763-8100	236-4465	520
Philadelphia Opportunities Industrialization Center Inc 1231 N Broad St Web: www.philaoic.org	Philadelphia	PA	19122	215-236-7700		167-3
Philadelphia Orchestra 1 S Broad St 14th Fl Web: www.philorch.org	Philadelphia	PA	19107	215-893-1955		573-3
Philadelphia Protestant Home 6500 Tabor Rd Web: pphfamily.org	Philadelphia	PA	19111	215-697-8000	697-8137	672
Philadelphia Regional Port Authority 3460 N Delaware Ave 2nd Fl Web: www.philaport.com	Philadelphia	PA	19134	215-426-2600	426-6800	618
Philadelphia Reserve Supply Co 200 Mack Dr TF: 800-347-7726 ■ Web: www.prsco.org	Croydon	PA	19021	215-785-3141		191-4
Philadelphia Sign Co 707 W Spring Garden St Web: www.philadelphiasign.com	Palmyra	NJ	08065	856-829-1460		701
Philadelphia Soft Pretzels Inc 4315 N 3rd St Web: www.philasoftpretzels.com	Philadelphia	PA	19140	215-324-4315		68
Philadelphia Sports Hall of Fame Foundation 2701 Grant Ave Web: www.phillyhall.org	Philadelphia	PA	19114	215-254-5049		522
Philadelphia Sunday Sun, The 6661-63 Germantown Ave Web: www.philasun.com	Philadelphia	PA	19119	215-848-7864	848-7893	532-2
Philadelphia Theatre Co 215 S Broad St 10th Fl Web: philadelphiatheatrecompany.org	Philadelphia	PA	19107	215-985-1400	985-5800	749
Philadelphia Toboggan Coaster Inc 3195 Penn St Web: www.philadelphiatoboggancoastersinc.com	Hatfield	PA	19440	215-799-2155	799-2158	454
Philadelphia Tribune Co 520 S 16th St Web: www.phillytrib.com	Philadelphia	PA	19146	215-893-4050	735-3612	637-8
Philadelphia Trust Co, The 1760 Market St 2nd Fl Web: philadelphiatrust.com	Philadelphia	PA	19103	215-979-3434	751-9283	69
Philadelphia University 4201 Henry Ave TF: 800-951-7287 ■ Web: www.philau.edu	Philadelphia	PA	19144	215-951-2800	951-2907	166
Philadelphia Vietnam Veterans Memorial 4715-25 Mercer St Web: pvvms646.org	Philadelphia	PA	19137	215-535-0643		50-4
Philadelphia Weekly 1520 Locust St Fifth Fl Web: www.philadelphiaweekly.com	Philadelphia	PA	19102	215-336-2500	563-0620	532-5
Philadelphia Zoo 3400 W Girard Ave Web: www.philadelphiazoo.org	Philadelphia	PA	19104	215-243-1100	243-5385	823
Philander Smith College 900 Daisy Bates Dr TF: 800-446-6772 ■ Web: www.philander.edu	Little Rock	AR	72202	501-370-5221	370-5225	166
Philatelic Foundation 22 E 35th St 4th Fl Web: www.philatelicfoundation.org	New York	NY	10016	212-221-6555	221-6208	48-18
Philbrook Museum of Art & Gardens 2727 S Rockford Rd Web: www.philbrook.org	Tulsa	OK	74114	918-749-7941		520
Phil-Good Products Inc 3500 W Reno Web: www.philgood.com	Oklahoma City	OK	73107	405-942-5527	942-8002	604
Philharmonia Baroque Orchestra 180 Redwood St Ste 200 Web: philharmonia.org	San Francisco	CA	94102	415-252-1288	252-1488	573-3
Philharmonic Center for the Arts 5833 Pelican Bay Blvd TF: 800-597-1900 ■ Web: artisnaples.org	Naples	FL	34108	239-597-1111		572
Philip Crosby Assn 120 Saint James Ave TF: 877-276-7295 ■ Web: discovercrosby.com	Boston	MA	02116	877-276-7295		194
Philip Lief Group Inc (PLG) 130 Wall St Web: www.philipliefgroup.com	Princeton	NJ	08540	609-430-1000		94
Philip R. Lee Institute for Health Policy Studies 3333 California St Web: www.healthpolicy.ucsf.edu	San Francisco	CA	94118	415-476-4921	476-0705	634
Philipp Lithographing Co 1960 Wisconsin Ave PO Box 4 TF: 800-657-0871 ■ Web: philipplitho.com	Grafton	WI	53024	262-377-1100	377-6660	627
Philippi-Hagenbuch Inc 7424 W Plank Rd TF: 800-447-6464 ■ Web: www.philsystems.com	Peoria	IL	61604	309-697-9200	697-2400	489

Name / Address	City	State	ZIP	Phone	Fax	Class
Philippine Department of Tourism 556 Fifth Ave *Web:* www.tourism.gov.ph	New York	NY	10036	212-575-7915	302-6759	775
Philippines *Consulate General* 30 N Michigan Ave Ste 2100 *TF:* 888-259-7838 ■ *Web:* www.chicagopcg.com	Chicago	IL	60602	312-332-6458	332-3657	257
Consulate General 447 Sutter St 6th Fl Philippine Ctr Bldg *Web:* www.philippinessanfrancisco.org	San Francisco	CA	94108	415-433-6666	421-2641	257
Consulate General 3435 Wilshire Blvd Ste 550 *Web:* www.philippineconsulatela.org	Los Angeles	CA	90010	213-639-0980	639-0990	257
Consulate General 556 Fifth Ave *TF:* 866-589-1878 ■ *Web:* www.newyorkpcg.org	New York	NY	10036	212-764-1330	764-6010	257
Embassy 1600 Massachusetts Ave NW *Web:* www.philippineembassy-usa.org	Washington	DC	20036	202-467-9300	467-9417	257
Philips & Cohen LLP 2000 Massachusetts Ave NW Ste 100 *Web:* www.phillipsandcohen.com	Washington	DC	20036	202-833-4567		428
Philips Arena 1 Philips Dr *Web:* www.philipsarena.com	Atlanta	GA	30303	404-878-3000		720
Philips Healthcare 22100 Bothell Everett Hwy *TF:* 888-744-5477 ■ *Web:* www.dunlee.com	Bothell	WA	98021	888-744-5477		475
Philips Healthcare Informatics Inc 4100 E 3rd Ave Ste 101 *Web:* www.usa.philips.com	Foster City	CA	94404	650-293-2300	293-2301	382
Philips Lighting Co 200 Franklin Sq Dr *TF:* 800-555-0050 ■ *Web:* www.usa.lighting.philips.com	Somerset	NJ	08873	800-555-0050		437
Philipse Manor Hall State Historic Site 29 Warburton Ave *Web:* philipsemanorhall.blogspot.com	Yonkers	NY	10701	914-965-4027		565
Phillip Roy Inc 13064 Indian Rocks Rd *TF:* 800-255-9085 ■ *Web:* www.philliproy.com	Largo	FL	33774	727-593-2700	595-2685	637-2
Phillip's Flower Shops Inc 524 N Cass Ave *TF:* 800-356-7257 ■ *Web:* www.800florals.com	Westmont	IL	60559	630-719-5200	719-2202	292
Phillippi Creek Village Restaurant & Oyster Bar 5353 S Tamiami Trl *Web:* www.creekseafood.com	Sarasota	FL	34231	941-925-4444		671
Phillippi Engineering Inc 425 Merchant St Ste200 *Web:* phillippieng.com	Vacaville	CA	95688	707-451-6556		261
Phillips & Assoc PO Box 241040 *Web:* www.phillipsontheweb.com	Los Angeles	CA	90024	310-247-0963	247-0966	317
Phillips & Company Securities Inc 1300 SW Fifth Ave Ste 2100 *TF:* 800-572-4765 ■ *Web:* phillipsandco.com	Portland	OR	97201	503-224-0858		690
Phillips & Johnston Inc 21w179 Hill Ave *TF:* 877-411-8823 ■ *Web:* www.pjtube.com	Glen Ellyn	IL	60137	630-469-8150	469-8048	492
Phillips & Jordan Inc 10201 Parkside Dr Ste 300 *TF:* 800-955-0876 ■ *Web:* www.pandj.com	Knoxville	TN	37922	865-688-8342	688-8369	189-5
Phillips & Temro Industries 9700 W 74th St *TF:* 800-328-6108 ■ *Web:* phillipsandtemro.com	Eden Prairie	MN	55344	952-941-9700	941-2285	60
Phillips & Webster Pllc Attys 17410 133rd Ave NE Ste 301 *TF:* 800-708-6000 ■ *Web:* www.justiceforyou.com	Woodinville	WA	98072	425-482-1111		428
Phillips 66 3010 Briarpark Dr *Web:* www.phillips66.com	Houston	TX	77042	281-293-6600		787
Phillips Academy 180 Main St *TF:* 877-445-5477 ■ *Web:* www.andover.edu	Andover	MA	01810	978-749-4000		622
Phillips Air Compressor Inc 5946 SW Ave *TF:* 800-966-4931 ■ *Web:* www.pac1913.com	Chicago	IL	60636	773-434-3000		172
Phillips Beach Plaza Hotel 1301 Atlantic Ave *Web:* www.beachplazaoc.com	Ocean City	MD	21842	410-289-9121		379
Phillips Brooks School 2245 Avy Ave *Web:* www.phillipsbrooks.org	Menlo Park	CA	94025	650-854-4545	854-6532	305
Phillips Bros Electrical Contractors Inc 235 Sweet Spring Rd **Fax Area Code:* 610 ■ *TF:* 800-220-5051 ■ *Web:* philipsbrothers.com	Glenmoore	PA	19343	800-220-5051	458-8438*	189-4
Phillips Buick GMC 2160 US Hwy 441 *TF:* 888-664-7454 ■ *Web:* www.phillipsbuickgmctruck.com	Fruitland Park	FL	34731	352-728-1212		57
Phillips Collection 1600 21st St NW *Web:* www.phillipscollection.org	Washington	DC	20009	202-387-2151	387-2436	520
Phillips Community College 1000 Campus Dr PO Box 785 *TF:* 800-582-6953 ■ *Web:* www.pccua.edu	Helena	AR	72342	870-338-6474	338-7542	162
Phillips Contracting Co PO Box 2069 *Web:* www.phillipscontracting.com	Columbus	MS	39704	662-328-6250	329-3291	188-4
Phillips Corp 7390 Coca Cola Dr *TF:* 800-878-4242 ■ *Web:* www.phillipscorp.com	Hanover	MD	21076	410-564-2929	564-2949	493
Phillips County 620 Cherry St *Web:* phillipscounty.arkansas.gov	Helena	AR	72342	870-338-5500	338-5509	338
Phillips County PO Box 484 *Web:* www.phillipscofair.com	Holyoke	CO	80734	970-854-3616		338
Phillips County Chamber of Commerce 111 Hickory Hills Dr PO Box 447 *Web:* www.phillipscountychamber.org	Helena	AR	72342	870-338-8327		139
Phillips County Kansas 301 State St *Web:* www.phillipscountyks.org	Phillipsburg	KS	67661	785-543-6895		338
Phillips Crab House 2004 N Philadelphia Ave *Web:* www.phillipsseafood.com	Ocean City	MD	21842	410-289-6821		671
Phillips Dean (Rep D - MN) 1305 Longworth House Office Bldg *Web:* www.phillips.house.gov	Washington	DC	20515	202-225-2871		342-2
Phillips Distributing Corp 3010 Nob Hill Rd *TF:* 800-236-7269 ■ *Web:* www.phillipsdistributing.com	Madison	WI	53713	608-222-9177	222-0558	81-3
Phillips Diversified Manufacturing Inc 120 Industrial Park Rd *Web:* www.phillipsdminc.com	Manchester	KY	40962	606-596-0313		425
Phillips European Restaurant 26 Corporate Woods *Web:* www.phillipseuropean.com	Rochester	NY	14623	585-272-9910		671
Phillips Exeter Academy 20 Main St *TF:* 800-245-2525 ■ *Web:* www.exeter.edu	Exeter	NH	03833	603-772-4311		622
Phillips Financial Management LLC 6920 Pointe Inverness Way Ste 230 *Web:* www.1phillips.com	Fort Wayne	IN	46804	260-420-7732		194
Phillips Food Service 3000 E Houston St *TF:* 800-580-2397 ■ *Web:* phillipsfoodservice.net	San Antonio	TX	78219	210-227-2397		559
Phillips Garcia Law 13 Ventura Dr *Web:* phillipsgarcialaw.com	North Dartmouth	MA	02747	508-998-0800		41
Phillips Gold & Company LLP 1430 Broadway Rm 1200 *Web:* www.phillipsgold.com	New York	NY	10018	212-730-1112	719-1737	2
Phillips Graduate University 19900 Plummer St *Web:* www.pgu.edu	Chatsworth	CA	91311	818-861-6627	386-5699	166
Phillips Lifestyles 5161 N US 31 S *Web:* www.phillipslifestyles.com	Grawn	MI	49637	231-929-1396		362
Phillips Machine Service Inc 367 George St *TF:* 800-733-1521 ■ *Web:* phillipsmachine.com	Beckley	WV	25801	304-255-0537		386
Phillips Manufacturing Co 4949 S 30th St *TF:* 800-822-5055 ■ *Web:* www.phillipsmfg.com	Omaha	NE	68107	402-339-3800		234
Phillips Murrah 101 N Robinson Ave Corporate Tower 13th Fl *Web:* phillipsmurrah.com	Oklahoma City	OK	73102	405-235-4100	235-4133	428
Phillips Mushroom Farms Inc 1011 Kaolin Rd *TF:* 800-722-8818 ■ *Web:* www.phillipsmushroomfarms.com	Kennett Square	PA	19348	800-722-8818		10-7
Phillips Pharmacy 123 E State St *Web:* www.milebluffrx.com	Mauston	WI	53948	608-847-5949		238
Phillips Plywood Company Inc 13599 Desmond St *TF:* 800-649-6410 ■ *Web:* www.phillipsplywood.com	Pacoima	CA	91331	818-897-7736	897-6571	613
Phillips Precision Inc 7 Paul Kohner Pl *Web:* www.phillipsmedicraft.com	Elmwood Park	NJ	07407	201-797-8820		757
Phillips Property Management 6106 Macarthur Blvd Ste 102 *Web:* www.phillipspm.com	Bethesda	MD	20816	301-320-0422	229-0937	652
Phillips Service Industries Inc 11878 Hubbard *Web:* www.psi-online.com	Livonia	MI	48150	734-853-5000		360-3
Phillips Sheet Metal Company Inc 700 Elk St *Web:* psmbuffalo.com	Buffalo	NY	14210	716-824-3374		697
Phillips State Prison 2989 W Rock Quarry Rd *Web:* dcor.state.ga.us	Buford	GA	30519	770-932-4500	932-4544	213
Phillips Syrup Corp 28025 Ranney Pkwy *TF:* 800-350-8443 ■ *Web:* www.phillipssyrup.com	Westlake	OH	44145	440-835-8001	835-1148	296-15
Phillips Tax & Accounting Inc 1508 Oregon St *Web:* phillips-tax.com	Oshkosh	WI	54902	920-231-1227	231-1228	734
Phillips Theological Seminary 901 N Mingo Rd *TF:* 800-843-4675 ■ *Web:* www.ptstulsa.edu	Tulsa	OK	74116	918-610-8303	610-8404	167-3
Phillips, Gerstein & Channen LLP 25 Kenoza Ave *Web:* pgclawoffice.com	Haverhill	MA	01830	978-374-1131	372-3086	41
Phillips, Hager & North Investment Management Ltd 200 Burrard St 20th Fl *TF:* 800-661-6141 ■ *Web:* www.phn.com	Vancouver	BC	V6C3N5	800-661-6141		528
Phillipsburg Board of Education 50 Sargent Ave *Web:* www.pburgsd.net	Phillipsburg	NJ	08865	908-454-3400		685
Philly POPS, The 1518 Walnut St Ste 1706 *Web:* www.phillypops.org	Philadelphia	PA	19102	215-875-8004		573-3
PhillyLaw 2021 Locust St *Web:* phillylaw.com	Philadelphia	PA	19103	215-515-2050		41
Phillystran Inc 151 Commerce Dr *Web:* www.phillystran.com	Montgomeryville	PA	18936	215-368-6611		208
Philosophy Inc 3809 E Watkins *TF:* 800-568-3151 ■ *Web:* www.philosophy.com	Phoenix	AZ	85034	800-568-3151		214
Philotechnics Ltd 201 Renovare Blvd *TF:* 888-723-9278 ■ *Web:* www.philotechnics.com	Oak Ridge	TN	37830	865-483-1551		271
Philpot Law Firm Pa 115 Broadus Ave *Web:* philpotlawfirm.com	Greenville	SC	29601	864-242-1366	242-1566	41
Philpott Solutions Group 1010 Industrial Pkwy *Web:* philpottsolutions.com	Brunswick	OH	44212	330-225-3344	225-1999	676
Philpotts 40 S School St Ste 200 *Web:* www.philpotts.net	Honolulu	HI	96813	808-523-6771	521-9569	393
Philz Coffee Inc 1258 Minnesota St *Web:* www.philzcoffee.com	San Francisco	CA	94107	415-834-5933	834-5493	670
Phin Solutions Inc 14245 St Francis Blvd Ste 105 *Web:* phinsolutions.com	Ramsey	MN	55303	763-633-7007		180
Phinney Bischoff Design House Inc 614 Boylston Ave E *Web:* phinneybischoff.com	Seattle	WA	98102	206-322-3484		344

	Phone	Fax	Class
Phinney Tool & Die Co 11023 W Center St Ext PO Box 270 ... Medina NY 14103 *Web:* www.phinneytool.com	585-798-3000	798-5612	757
Phipps Conservatory & Botanical Gardens 1 Schenley Pk ... Pittsburgh PA 15213 *Web:* www.phipps.conservatory.org	412-622-6914	622-7363	97
Phipps Houses 902 Broadway 13th Fl ... New York NY 10010 *Web:* www.phippsny.org	212-243-9090		186
Phipps Pharmacy Inc 205 B Hospital Dr ... Mckenzie TN 38201 *Web:* www.phippspharmacy.com	731-352-0820		237
PHLCOC (Park Hills Leadington Chamber of Commerce) 12 Municipal Dr ... Park Hills MO 63601 *Web:* www.phlcoc.net	573-431-1051	431-2327	139
PHM International Inc 509 Acacia Ave ... Sebastian FL 32958 *Web:* www.phmintl.com	772-388-6496		463
PHM Management 3300 Oak Lawn Ave Ste 408 ... Dallas TX 75219 *Web:* phmmanagement.com	214-521-0002		463
PHMSA (Pipeline & Hazardous Materials Safety Administration) 1200 New Jersey Ave SE E Bldg Second Fl ... Washington DC 20590 *Web:* www.phmsa.dot.gov	202-366-4433	366-3666	340-17
PHMSA (Pipeline & Hazardous Materials Safety Administration Regional Offices)			
Central Region (Pipeline) 901 Locust St Rm 462 ... Kansas City MO 64106 *Web:* www.phmsa.dot.gov	816-329-3800	329-3831	340-17
Southern Region 233 Peachtree St NE Ste 602 ... Atlanta GA 30303 *Web:* www.phmsa.dot.gov	404-832-1140	832-1168	340-17
Phnom Penh 27080 Lorain Ave ... North Olmsted OH 44070 *Web:* ohiorestaurant.com	216-201-9141		671
Pho 777 Vietnamese Restaurant 102 E 2nd St ... Reno NV 89501 *Web:* www.pho777reno.com	775-323-7777		671
Pho 79 9941 W Hazard Ave ... Garden Grove CA 92844 *Web:* pho79.com	714-531-2490		671
Pho Bang New York 1001 St-Laurent Blvd ... Montreal QC H2Z1J4 *Web:* www.phobangnewyork.com	514-954-2032		671
Pho Grand 3195 S Grand Blvd ... Saint Louis MO 63118 *Web:* www.phogrand.com	314-664-7435		671
Pho Saigon 400 Dickinson St ... Springfield MA 01108 *Web:* phosaigonspringfield.com	413-781-4488		671
Pho Tre Bien 6946 Gateway E ... El Paso TX 79915 *Web:* orderphotrebien.com	915-598-0166		671
PHO VIET 2 1589 W El Camino Ave Ste 105 ... Sacramento CA 95833 *Web:* www.phoviet2.com	916-925-2138		671
Pho84 354 17th St ... Oakland CA 94612 *Web:* www.pho84.com	510-832-1338		671
Phoebe Micro Inc 47606 Kato Rd ... Fremont CA 94538 *Web:* www.phoebemicro.com	510-360-0800		173-3
Phoebe Putney Health System 427 W Third Ave ... Albany GA 31701 *Web:* www.phoebehealth.com	229-312-7141		374-3
Phoebe's 900 E Genesee St ... Syracuse NY 13210 *Web:* www.phoebessyracuse.com	315-475-5154		671
Phoenecia Restaurant 4717 42nd Ave SW ... West Seattle WA 98116 *Web:* phoeneciawestseattle.com	206-492-5694		671
Phoenix Aerospace Inc 220 W 80th Terr ... Kansas City MO 64114 *TF:* 800-437-6556 ■ *Web:* www.phoenixaerospace.com	816-333-3400		21
Phoenix Air Group Inc 100 Phoenix Air Dr SW ... Cartersville GA 30120 *Web:* phoenixair.com	770-387-2000		25
Phoenix AMD International Inc 41 Butler Ct ... Bowmanville ON L1C4P8 **Fax Area Code:* 905 ■ *TF:* 800-661-7313 ■ *Web:* www.phoenixamd.com	800-661-7313	427-2166*	361
Phoenix American Inc 2401 Kerner Blvd ... San Rafael CA 94901 *TF:* 866-895-5050 ■ *Web:* www.phxa.com	866-895-5050		216
Phoenix Analysis & Design Inc 7755 S Research Dr Ste 110 ... Tempe AZ 85284 *TF:* 800-293-7238 ■ *Web:* www.padtinc.com	480-813-4884		261
Phoenix Art Museum 1625 N Central Ave ... Phoenix AZ 85004 *Web:* www.phxart.org	602-257-1222	253-8662	520
Phoenix Audio Technologies 2934 N Naomi St ... Burbank CA 91504 *Web:* www.phnxaudio.com	818-937-4774	230-9116	392
Phoenix Cable Inc (PCI) 10801 N 24th Ave Ste 115-116 ... Phoenix AZ 85029 *TF:* 833-807-3855 ■ *Web:* www.phoenixcable.com	602-870-8870	870-8464	116
Phoenix Center for Advanced Legal & Economic Public Policy Studies 5335 Wisconsin Ave NW Ste 440 ... Washington DC 20015 *Web:* www.phoenix-center.org	202-274-0235	244-8257	634
Phoenix Children's Hospital 1919 E Thomas Rd ... Phoenix AZ 85016 *TF:* 888-908-5437 ■ *Web:* www.phoenixchildrens.org	602-933-1000	933-0628	374-1
Phoenix City Hall 200 W Washington St 11th Fl ... Phoenix AZ 85003 *Web:* www.phoenix.gov	602-262-7111	495-5583	337
Phoenix College 1202 W Thomas Rd ... Phoenix AZ 85013 *Web:* www.phoenixcollege.edu	602-285-7777	285-7813	162
Phoenix Color 18249 Phoenix Dr ... Hagerstown MD 21742 *Web:* www.phoenixcolor.com	301-733-0018		626
Phoenix Company of Chicago Inc, The 22 Great Hill Rd ... Naugatuck CT 06770 *TF:* 800-323-9562 ■ *Web:* www.phoenixofchicago.com	203-729-9090	723-1794	815
Phoenix Controls 75 Discovery Way ... Acton MA 01720 *TF:* 800-340-0007 ■ *Web:* www.phoenixcontrols.com	978-795-1285	795-1111	202
Phoenix Convention Ctr 100 N Third St ... Phoenix AZ 85004 *Web:* www.phoenixconventioncenter.com	602-262-6225		205
Phoenix Converting Co 211 W Booneslick ... Jonesburg MO 63351 *Web:* www.phoenixconvertingco.com	636-488-3200		548

	Phone	Fax	Class
Phoenix Creative Co 555 Washington Ave Ste 510 ... Saint Louis MO 63101 *Web:* www.phoenixcreative.com	314-421-5646		344
Phoenix Data Inc 8813 State Rte 405 ... Montgomery PA 17752 *Web:* www.phoenixdatainc.com	570-547-1665	547-6349	110
Phoenix Dogs 24/7 3618 W Bell Rd Ste 1 ... Glendale AZ 85308 *Web:* phxdogs.com	602-588-7833		794
Phoenix Down Corp 85 US 46 ... Totowa NJ 07512 *Web:* www.phoenixdown.com	973-812-8100	812-9077	746
Phoenix East Aviation Inc 561 Pearl Harbor Dr ... Daytona Beach FL 32114 *TF:* 800-868-4359 ■ *Web:* www.pea.com	386-258-0703	254-6842	167-3
Phoenix Electric Manufacturing Co 3625 N Halsted St ... Chicago IL 60613 *Web:* phoenixelectric.com	773-477-8855		518
Phoenix Electronic Enterprises Inc 131 Tillson Ave EXT ... Highland Falls NY 12528 *Web:* www.phoenixmfg.com	845-691-7700	691-7759	492
Phoenix Elementary School District 1817 N Seventh St ... Phoenix AZ 85006 *Web:* phxschools.org	602-257-3755		685
Phoenix Engineering & Consulting Inc 110 Londonderry Ct Ste 136-C ... Woodstock GA 30188 *Web:* phoenixengineering.com	404-330-9513		393
Phoenix Environmental Laboratories Inc 587 Middle Tpke E ... Manchester CT 06040 *TF:* 800-827-5426 ■ *Web:* www.phoenixlabs.com	860-645-3513		743
Phoenix Fabricators & Erectors Inc 182 S Country Rd 900 E ... Avon IN 46123 *Web:* phoenixtank.com	317-271-7002		480
Phoenix Film Festival 7000 E Mayo Blvd Ste 1059 ... Phoenix AZ 85054 *Web:* www.phoenixfilmfestival.com	602-955-6444		282
Phoenix Films Inc PO Box 3816 ... Clearwater FL 33767 *Web:* www.phoenixfilms.com	727-446-0300		600
Phoenix Flower Shops 5733 E Thomas Rd Ste 4 ... Scottsdale AZ 85251 *TF:* 888-311-0404 ■ *Web:* www.phoenixflowershops.com	480-289-4000		292
Phoenix Foods Inc 723 Cowan St ... Nashville TN 37207 *Web:* www.phoenixfoods.com	615-742-4989	742-3864	619
Phoenix Footwear Group Inc 5937 Darwin Ct Ste 109 ... Carlsbad CA 92008 *OTC:* PXFG ■ *Web:* www.phoenixfootwear.com	760-602-9688		301
Phoenix Forging Company Inc 800 Front St ... Catasauqua PA 18032 *TF:* 800-444-3674 ■ *Web:* www.phoenixforge.com	610-264-2861	266-0530	483
Phoenix Grand Hotel Salem 201 Liberty St SE ... Salem OR 97301 *TF:* 877-540-7800 ■ *Web:* grandhotelsalem.com	503-540-7800		379
Phoenix Graphics Inc 1525 Emerson St ... Rochester NY 14606 *TF:* 800-262-3202 ■ *Web:* www.phoenix-graphics.com	585-232-4040	232-5642	627
Phoenix Group of Virginia Inc 630C Woodlake Dr ... Chesapeake VA 23320 *Web:* phoenix-group.com	757-228-1730		463
Phoenix Home Care Inc 3033 S Kansas Expy ... Springfield MO 65807 *TF:* 855-881-7442 ■ *Web:* phoenixhomehc.com	417-881-7442		363
Phoenix Hotel 601 Eddy St ... San Francisco CA 94109 *Web:* www.phoenixsf.com	415-776-1380		379
Phoenix House Foundation Inc (PHF) 164 W 74th St ... New York NY 10023 *TF:* 888-671-9392 ■ *Web:* www.phoenixhouse.org	646-505-2018		726
Phoenix Inc 1899 High Grove Ln ... Naperville IL 60540 *Web:* phxpkg.com	630-420-4750		154
Phoenix Innovate Inc 1775 Bellingham ... Troy MI 48083 *TF:* 888-831-1184 ■ *Web:* www.phoenixinnovate.com	248-457-9000		627
Phoenix Integration Inc 1715 Pratt Dr Ste 2000 ... Blacksburg VA 24060 *TF:* 800-500-1936 ■ *Web:* www.phoenix-int.com	540-961-7215		180
Phoenix Intl 812 W Southern Ave ... Orange CA 92865 *Web:* www.phenxint.com	714-283-4800	283-1169	173-8
Phoenix Learning Resources (PLR) 812 Court St ... Honesdale PA 18431 *TF:* 800-228-9345 ■ *Web:* www.phoenixlearningresources.com	570-251-6871	253-3227	637-2
Phoenix Lithographing Corp 11631 Caroline Rd ... Philadelphia PA 19154 *Web:* www.phoenixlitho.com	215-698-9000		627
Phoenix Magazine 15169 N Scottsdale Rd Ste 310 ... Scottsdale AZ 85254 *TF:* 866-481-6970 ■ *Web:* www.phoenixmag.com	480-664-3960		457-22
Phoenix Manufacturing Inc 3655 E Roeser Rd ... Phoenix AZ 85040 *TF:* 800-325-6952 ■ *Web:* phoenixmanufacturing.com	602-437-4833		14
Phoenix Manufacturing of Georgia Inc 34 Industrial Ct E ... Villa Rica GA 30180	770-459-5255		499
Phoenix Medical Management Inc 1401 S Ocean Blvd Ste 402 ... Pompano Beach FL 33062 *TF:* 877-941-6505 ■ *Web:* www.phoenixmed.net	877-941-6505		194
Phoenix Metals Co 4685 Buford Hwy ... Norcross GA 30071 *TF:* 800-241-2290 ■ *Web:* phoenixmetals.com	770-447-4211		492
Phoenix Modular Inc 5301 W Madison St ... Phoenix AZ 85043 *Web:* www.phoenixmodular.com	602-447-6460		186
Phoenix New Times 1201 E Jefferson ... Phoenix AZ 85034 *Web:* www.phoenixnewtimes.com	602-271-0040	340-8806	532-5
Phoenix Noise & Vibration LLC 5216 Chairmans Ct Ste 107 ... Frederick MD 21703 *Web:* phoenixnv.com	301-846-4227		261
Phoenix Park 'n Swap 3801 E Washington St ... Phoenix AZ 85034 *TF:* 800-772-0852 ■ *Web:* www.americanparknswap.com	602-273-1250		271
Phoenix Park Hotel 520 N Capitol St ... Washington DC 20001 *TF:* 800-824-5419 ■ *Web:* www.phoenixparkhotel.com	202-638-6900	393-3236	379
Phoenix Pharmaceuticals Inc 330 Beach Rd ... Burlingame CA 94010 *TF:* 800-988-1205 ■ *Web:* www.phoenixpeptide.com	650-558-8898		231

Company	Address	City	State	ZIP	Phone	Fax	Class
Phoenix Pictures Inc	10203 W Washington Blvd Ste 400 *Web:* www.phoenixpictures.com	Los Angeles	CA	90067	424-298-2788	298-2588	514
Phoenix Police Museum	17 S Second Ave Historic City Hall First Fl. *TF:* 888-223-7275 ■ *Web:* phxpdmuseum.org	Phoenix	AZ	85003	602-534-7278		520
Phoenix Precast Products Inc	1856 E Deer Valley Rd *Web:* www.phoenixprecastproducts.com	Phoenix	AZ	85024	602-569-6090	569-2483	183
Phoenix Press Inc	15 James St *Web:* www.phoenixpressinc.com	New Haven	CT	06513	203-865-5555		627
Phoenix Process Equipment Co	2402 Watterson Trial *Web:* www.dewater.com	Louisville	KY	40299	502-499-6198	499-1079	386
Phoenix Public Library	1221 N Central Ave *Web:* www.phoenixpubliclibrary.org	Phoenix	AZ	85004	602-261-8847	261-8836	434-3
Phoenix Realty & Trust Co	One E Washington St Ste 1900 PO Box 87420	Phoenix	AZ	85080	602-494-0202		652
Phoenix Renovation & Restoration Inc	16250 Foster *Web:* www.kcphoenix.com	Overland Park	KS	66085	913-599-0055		186
Phoenix Seminary	4222 E Thomas Rd Ste 400 *TF:* 888-443-1020 ■ *Web:* www.ps.edu	Phoenix	AZ	85018	602-850-8000	850-8080	167-3
Phoenix Sky Harbor International Airport	3400 E Sky Harbor Blvd Ste 3300 *TF:* 800-781-1010 ■ *Web:* www.skyharbor.com	Phoenix	AZ	85034	602-273-3300		27
Phoenix Society for Burn Survivors Inc	1835 RW Berends Dr SW *TF:* 800-888-2876 ■ *Web:* www.phoenix-society.org	Grand Rapids	MI	49519	616-458-2773	458-2831	48-17
Phoenix Solutions Co	5480 Nathan Ln N Ste 110 *Web:* www.phoenixsolutionsco.com	Plymouth	MN	55442	763-544-2721	546-5617	318
Phoenix Stamping Group LLC	6100 Emmanuel Dr *Web:* phoenixstamping.com	Atlanta	GA	30336	404-699-2882		488
Phoenix Symphony	1 N First St Ste 200 *TF:* 800-776-9080 ■ *Web:* www.phoenixsymphony.org	Phoenix	AZ	85004	602-495-1117	253-1772	573-3
Phoenix Technologies Ltd	915 Murphy Ranch Rd *TF:* 800-677-7305 ■ *Web:* www.phoenix.com	Milpitas	CA	95035	408-570-1000	570-1001	178-12
Phoenix Transportation Services LLC	335 E Yusen Dr *TF:* 800-860-0889 ■ *Web:* www.phoenix-transportation.net	Georgetown	KY	40324	502-863-0108	863-0029	780
Phoenix Tube Company Inc	1185 Win Dr *TF:* 800-526-2124 ■ *Web:* www.phoenixtube.com	Bethlehem	PA	18017	610-865-5337		492
Phoenix Union High School District (PUHSD)	4502 N Central Ave *Web:* www.phxhs.k12.az.us	Phoenix	AZ	85012	602-764-1100		685
Phoenix USA Inc	51 E Borden St *TF:* 800-786-8785 ■ *Web:* www.phoenixusa.com	Cookeville	TN	38501	800-786-8785		54
Phoenix Veterinary Internal Medicine Services Inc	10645 N Tatum Blvd Ste 200-527 *Web:* phoenixvetinternalmedicine.com	Phoenix	AZ	85028	602-953-9541		794
Phoenix Zoo	455 N Galvin Pkwy *Web:* www.phoenixzoo.org	Phoenix	AZ	85008	602-273-1341		823
PhoeniXongs	PO Box 8101 *TF:* 888-560-5755 ■ *Web:* phoenixsongsbio.com	White Plains	NY	10602	914-997-1433		637-2
Phoenixville Hospital	140 Nutt Rd *Web:* phoenixville.towerhealth.org	Phoenixville	PA	19460	610-983-1000		374-3
Phoenixville Regional Chamber of Commerce	171 Bridge St *Web:* phoenixvillechamber.org	Phoenixville	PA	19460	610-933-3070	917-0503	139
Phoinix Group Inc, The	10300 California Ste 100 - 105 *Web:* www.phoinixgroup.com	Tampa	FL	33624	813-962-4000		180
Phone Card Hotline	7324 Valleyview Dr *TF:* 800-524-9299 ■ *Web:* www.phonecardhotline.com	Independence	OH	44131	440-457-7209	201-6340	45
Phone Ware Inc	8902 Activity Rd *TF:* 800-243-8329 ■ *Web:* www.phonewareinc.com	San Diego	CA	92126	858-459-3000		317
Phonecom Inc	211 Warren St *Web:* www.phone.com	Newark	NJ	07103	973-577-6380		387
PhoneTree	301 N Main St Ste 1800 *TF:* 800-951-8733 ■ *Web:* www.phonetree.com	Winston-Salem	NC	27101	336-722-5008		224
Phonic Ear Inc	2080 Lakeville Hwy *TF:* 800-227-0735 ■ *Web:* www.phonicear.com	Petaluma	CA	94954	707-769-1110		477
Phonoscope Ltd	6105 Wline Dr *Web:* www.phonoscope.com	Houston	TX	77036	713-272-4600		116
Photo Antiquities-Museum of Photographic History	531 E Ohio St *Web:* www.photoantiquities.org	Pittsburgh	PA	15212	412-231-7881		520
Photo Den	315 SE Seventh St *Web:* photoden.com	Grants Pass	OR	97526	541-479-1833	479-8855	119
Photo Diagnostic Systems Inc	85 Swanson Rd *Web:* www.photodiagnostic.com	Boxborough	MA	01719	978-266-0420	266-0425	476
Photo Protective Technologies Inc (PPT)	6610 Topper Ridge *Web:* www.melaninproducts.com	San Antonio	TX	78233	210-493-6353	493-7043	543
Photo Researchers Inc	307 Fifth Ave 3rd Fl *TF:* 800-833-9033 ■ *Web:* www.sciencesource.com	New York	NY	10016	212-758-3420		593
Photo Resource Hawaii	PO Box 1082 *Web:* www.photoresourcehawaii.com	Honokaa	HI	96727	808-754-5698		593
Photo USA	2140 Colonial Ave *Web:* www.photousa.com	Roanoke	VA	24015	540-344-0961		588
Photocrazy Inc	509 Raindance St *Web:* www.photocrazy.com	Thousand Oaks	CA	91360	805-492-0562		592
Photodex Corp	11100 Metric Blvd Ste 400 *Web:* www.photodex.com	Austin	TX	78758	512-419-7000		225
Photofabrication Engineering Inc (PEI)	500 Fortune Blvd *TF:* 800-253-8518 ■ *Web:* www.photofabrication.com	Milford	MA	01757	508-478-2025	478-3582	454
Photograph America	PO Box 86 *Web:* www.photographamerica.com	Novato	CA	94948	415-898-9677		592
Photographic Center Northwest	900 12th Ave *Web:* www.pcnw.org	Seattle	WA	98122	206-720-7222	720-0306	167-3
Photography	1919 Madison Ave 522 *Web:* www.photographmag.com	New York	NY	10035	212-787-0401		637-2
PhotoMachining Inc	4 Industrial Dr Unit 40 *Web:* www.photomachining.com	Pelham	NH	03076	603-882-9944	886-8844	757
Photon Kinetics Inc (PK)	9305 SW Gemini Dr *Web:* www.pkinetics.com	Beaverton	OR	97008	503-644-1960	526-4700	385
PhotonicsComm Solutions Inc	65 Rachel Rd *Web:* www.photonicscomm.com	Newton Center	MA	02459	617-916-1676	332-4851	196
Photo-Scan of Los Angeles Inc (PSLA)	743 Cochran St Ste C *TF:* 800-820-7752 ■ *Web:* www.pslasecurity.com	Simi Valley	CA	93065	805-581-4448	526-4406	693
Photo-Sonics Inc	9131 Independence Ave *Web:* photosonics.com	Chatsworth	CA	91311	818-842-2141		52
PhotoSource	5106 Louetta Rd *Web:* www.photosource.com	Spring	TX	77379	281-370-2220		531-13
Photronics Inc	15 Secor Rd *NASDAQ: PLAB* ■ *TF:* 800-292-9396 ■ *Web:* www.photronics.com	Brookfield	CT	06804	203-775-9000		696
PHP (Parents Helping Parents)	1400 Parkmoor Ave Ste 100 *TF:* 855-727-5775 ■ *Web:* www.php.com	San Jose	CA	95126	408-727-5775	286-1116	48-6
PHPC (Pictorial Histories Publishing Company Inc)	713 S 3rd St W *Web:* www.pictorialhistoriespublishing.com	Missoula	MT	59801	406-549-8488	728-9280	96
PHPR (Paige Hendricks Public Relations Inc)	1617 Park Place Ave Ste 110-4 *Web:* www.phprinc.com	Fort Worth	TX	76110	817-798-4004		317
PHR (Physicians for Human Rights)	256 W 38th St 9th Fl *Web:* secure.phr.org	New York	NY	10018	646-564-3720	564-3750	48-5
PHRI (Public Health Research Institute)	225 Warren St Rm E240M *Web:* www.phri.org	Newark	NJ	07103	973-854-3100	854-3101	668
PHRMA (Pharmaceutical Research & Manufacturers of America)	950 F St NW Ste 300 *Web:* www.phrma.org	Washington	DC	20004	202-835-3400	835-3414	49-8
Phronesis Publishing LLC	10151 SW Barbur Blvd Ste 10149b *Web:* www.downsyndromenutrition.com	Portland	OR	97219	971-258-1837	202-1577	637-2
Phunware Inc	7800 Shoal Creek Blvd *TF:* 855-521-8485 ■ *Web:* www.phunware.com	Austin	TX	78757	855-521-8485		177
PHX Energy Services Corp	1400-250 2 St SW *TF:* 800-909-9819 ■ *Web:* www.phxtech.com	Calgary	AB	T2P0C1	403-543-4466		536
Phyle Inventory Control Specialists Inc	4150 Grange Hall Rd *TF:* 888-303-8482 ■ *Web:* www.picsinv.com	Holly	MI	48442	888-303-8482		393
PhyleTec	4150 Grange Hall Rd *Web:* www.phyletec.com	Holly	MI	48442	248-634-4000		253
Phyllis Browning Co	4372 N Loop 1604 W Ste 102 *Web:* www.phyllisbrowning.com	San Antonio	TX	78249	210-408-2500		463
Phyllis Kind Gallery	236 W 26th St Ste 503 *Web:* www.phylliskindgallery.com	New York	NY	10001	212-925-1200	941-7841	42
Phylway Construction LLC	1074a Hwy 1 *Web:* phylway.com	Thibodaux	LA	70301	985-446-9644		188-10
Phyphar Inc	29 Walter Hammond Pl *Web:* phyphar.com	Waldwick	NJ	07463	201-444-4648		734
Physcient Inc	112 S Duke St Ste 4A *Web:* physcient.com	Durham	NC	27701	919-686-0300		475
Physical Acoustics Corp	195 Clarksville Rd *Web:* www.physicalacoustics.com	Princeton Junction	NJ	08550	609-716-4000	716-4145	639
Physical Electronics Inc	18725 Lake Dr E *Web:* www.phi.com	Chanhassen	MN	55317	952-828-6100	828-6451	419
Physical Optics Corp	1845 W 205th St *Web:* www.poc.com	Torrance	CA	90501	310-320-3088	320-4667	402
Physical Therapy Association of Washington Inc	208 Rogers St NW *TF:* 800-554-5569 ■ *Web:* ptwa.org	Olympia	WA	98502	360-352-7290	352-7298	414
Physician Insurers Association of America (PIAA)	2275 Research Blvd Ste 250 *TF:* 800-688-2421 ■ *Web:* www.mplassociation.org	Rockville	MD	20850	301-947-9000	947-9090	49-9
Physicians Committee for Responsible Medicine (PCRM)	5100 Wisconsin Ave NW Ste 400 *TF:* 866-416-7276 ■ *Web:* www.pcrm.org	Washington	DC	20016	202-686-2210	686-2216	49-8
Physicians for Human Rights (PHR)	256 W 38th St 9th Fl *Web:* secure.phr.org	New York	NY	10018	646-564-3720	564-3750	48-5
Physicians for Social Responsibility (PSR)	1875 Connecticut Ave NW Ste 1012 *Web:* www.psr.org	Washington	DC	20009	202-667-4260	667-4201	49-8
Physicians Laboratory Services Inc	4840 "F" St *TF:* 800-642-1117 ■ *Web:* www.physlab.com	Omaha	NE	68117	402-731-4145		415
Physicians Mutual Insurance Co	2600 Dodge St *TF:* 800-228-9100 ■ *Web:* www.physiciansmutual.com	Omaha	NE	68131	402-633-1000		391-2
Physicians Record Company Inc	3000 Ridgeland Ave **Fax Area Code:* 708 ■ *Web:* www.physiciansrecord.com	Berwyn	IL	60402	800-323-9268	749-0171*	627
Physicians Regional Medical Ctr	6101 Pine Ridge Rd *Web:* www.physiciansregional.com	Naples	FL	34119	239-348-4000		374-3
Physicians Weight Loss Centers of America Inc	395 Springside Dr **Fax Area Code:* 330 ■ *TF:* 800-205-7887 ■ *Web:* www.pwlc.com	Akron	OH	44333	800-205-7887	666-2197*	810
Physicians World	125 Chubb Ave *Web:* www.physiciansworld.com	Lyndhurst	NJ	07071	201-549-5777		352

Name / Address	City	State	ZIP	Phone	Fax	Class
Physick House 321 S Fourth St. *Web:* www.philalandmarks.org	Philadelphia	PA	19106	215-925-2251		50-3
Physics Today One Physics Ellipse *Web:* physicstoday.scitation.org	College Park	MD	20740	301-209-3040		457-19
Phytron Inc 600 Blair Park Rd Ste 220 *Web:* www.phytron.com	Williston	VT	05495	802-872-1600	872-0311	518
Pi Beta Phi Fraternity for Women 1154 Town & Country Commons Dr. *Web:* www.pibetaphi.org	Town and Country	MO	63017	636-256-0680	256-8095	48-16
PI Inc 213 Dennis St *Web:* www.pi-inc.com	Athens	TN	37303	423-368-1890		608
Pi Kappa Alpha Fraternity 8347 W Range Cove *Web:* www.pikes.org	Memphis	TN	38125	901-748-1868	748-3100	48-16
Pi Kappa Phi Fraternity 2015 Ayrsley Town Blvd Ste 200 *Web:* www.pikapp.org	Charlotte	NC	28273	704-504-0888	504-0880	48-16
Pi Lambda Phi Fraternity Inc 60 Newtown Rd Ste 118 *Web:* www.pilambdaphi.org	Danbury	CT	06810	203-740-1044	740-1644	48-16
PI Marketing 8505 Crown Crescent Ct *Web:* www.perfectimagemktg.com	Charlotte	NC	28227	704-841-2464		627
PI Services LLC 4550 SW Betts Ste 157 *Web:* pi-info.com	Beaverton	OR	97005	503-643-4274	643-5474	400
Pi Sigma Alpha 1527 New Hampshire Ave NW *Web:* www.pisigmaalpha.org	Washington	DC	20036	202-349-9285		48-16
Pi Sigma Epsilon (PSE) 3747 S Howell Ave *Web:* www.pse.org	Milwaukee	WI	53207	414-328-1952	328-1953	48-16
PIA (Pakistan International Airlines Corp) 1200 New Jersey Ave SE *TF:* 800-578-6786 ■ *Web:* www.piac.com.pk	Washington	DC	20590	800-578-6786		25
PIA (Pittsburgh Institute of Aeronautics) 5 Allegheny County Airport *TF:* 800-444-1440 ■ *Web:* pia.edu	West Mifflin	PA	15122	412-346-2100		800
PIA Management Services Inc 25 Chamberlain St **Fax Area Code:* 888 ■ *Web:* www.pia.org	Glenmont	NY	12077	800-424-4244	225-6935*	637-9
PIA/GATF (Printing Industries of America/Graphic Arts Technical Foundation) 200 Deer Run Rd *TF:* 800-910-4283 ■ *Web:* www.printing.org	Sewickley	PA	15143	412-741-6860	741-2311	49-16
PIAA (Physician Insurers Association of America) 2275 Research Blvd Ste 250 *TF:* 800-688-2421 ■ *Web:* www.mplassociation.org	Rockville	MD	20850	301-947-9000	947-9090	49-9
Piad Precision Casting Corp 112 Industrial Park Rd *TF:* 800-441-9858 ■ *Web:* piad.com	Greensburg	PA	15601	724-838-5500	838-5520	308
Piaggio Group Americas Inc 257 Park Ave S 4th Fl *Web:* www.piaggiogroup.com	New York	NY	10010	212-380-4400	380-4459	82
Piano Press PO Box 85 **Fax Area Code:* 858 ■ *Web:* www.pianopress.com	Del Mar	CA	92014	619-884-1401	755-1104*	637-2
Piano Software Inc One World Trade Ctr Ste 46 D *Web:* piano.io	New York	NY	10007	646-350-1999		178-8
Piano Technicians Guild 4444 Forest Ave *Web:* www.ptg.org	Kansas City	KS	66106	913-432-9975	432-9986	49-4
PianoDisc 4111 N Fwy Blvd *TF:* 866-566-3472 ■ *Web:* www.pianodisc.com	Sacramento	CA	95834	916-567-9999	567-1941	527
Piantedosi Baking Company Inc 240 Commercial St *TF:* 800-339-0080 ■ *Web:* www.piantedosi.com	Malden	MA	02148	781-321-3400	324-5647	296-1
Piasecki Aircraft Corp 519 W Second St *Web:* www.piasecki.com	Essington	PA	19029	610-521-5700		256
Piatt County 101 W Washington St *Web:* www.piattcounty.org	Monticello	IL	61856	217-762-9487	762-7563	338
Piatti 2182 Avenida de la Playa *Web:* piatti.com	La Jolla	CA	92037	858-454-1589		671
Piatti Mill Valley Italian Restaurant & Bar 625 Redwood Hwy *Web:* millvalley.piatti.com	Mill Valley	CA	94941	415-380-2525	380-2530	670
Piatti Sacramento 571 Pavilions Ln *Web:* www.piatti.com	Sacramento	CA	95825	916-649-8885	649-8907	671
Piatto Ristorante 4925 W Alabama St *Web:* piattoristorante.com	Houston	TX	77056	713-871-9722	871-9190	671
Piazza Italia 1129 NW Johnson St *Web:* www.piazzaportland.com	Portland	OR	97209	503-478-0619	227-5199	671
Piazza Italia 904 E Las Olas Blvd *Web:* thepiazzaitalia.com	Fort Lauderdale	FL	33301	954-533-7130		671
Piazzano's Restaurant 1825 N Grand River Ave *Web:* www.piazzanos.com	Lansing	MI	48906	517-484-9922		671
Pibbs Industries 133-15 32nd Ave *TF:* 800-551-5020 ■ *Web:* www.pibbs.com	Flushing	NY	11354	718-445-8046	461-3910	76
PIC Business Systems Inc 5119 Beckwith Blvd Ste 106 *TF:* 800-742-7378 ■ *Web:* picbusiness.com	San Antonio	TX	78249	800-742-7378		177
Pic Design Corp 86 Benson Rd PO Box 1004 *TF:* 800-243-6125 ■ *Web:* www.pic-design.com	Middlebury	CT	06762	203-758-8272	758-8271	620
PIC North America 100 Bluegrass Commons Blvd Ste 2200 *TF:* 800-325-3398 ■ *Web:* www.pic.com	Hendersonville	TN	37075	800-325-3398		10-6
PIC Skate 22 Village Dr *TF:* 800-882-3448 ■ *Web:* www.picskate.com	Riverside	RI	02915	401-490-9334	438-5419	710
Picaboo Corp 1160 Chestnut St *Web:* www.picaboo.com	Menlo Park	CA	94025	650-326-3200		177
Picacho Peak State Park PO Box 907 *Web:* azstateparks.com	Eloy	AZ	85131	520-466-3183		565
Picante Mexican Restaurant 3235 NW Evangeline Thwy *Web:* www.picantesrestaurant.com	LaFayette	LA	70508	337-896-1200		671
Picarro Inc 480 Oakmead Pkwy *Web:* www.picarro.com	Sunnyvale	CA	94085	408-962-3900		419
Picasso Travel 300 N Continental Blvd Ste 310 *Web:* picassotravel.com	El Segundo	CA	90245	310-645-4400		16
Picasso's 62 W Santa Clara St *Web:* www.picassostapas.com	San Jose	CA	95113	408-298-4400		671
Picayune Drug Company Inc 110 Hwy 11 N PO Box 10 *TF:* 800-798-4846 ■ *Web:* picayunedrug.com	Picayune	MS	39466	601-798-4846		237
Piccadilly Books Ltd PO Box 25203 *Web:* www.piccadillybooks.com	Colorado Springs	CO	80936	719-550-9887		637-2
Piccadilly Cafeterias Inc 3332 S Sherwood Forest Blvd **Fax Area Code:* 318 ■ *Web:* www.piccadilly.com	Baton Rouge	LA	70816	225-293-4853	445-4740*	670
Piccadilly Circus Pizza 1007 Okoboji Ave PO Box 188 *TF:* 800-338-4340 ■ *Web:* www.pcpizza.com	Milford	IA	51351	800-338-4340		670
Piccadilly Printing Co 1000 Valley Ave *Web:* www.picprinting.com	Winchester	VA	22601	540-662-3804		627
Picco Engineering 8611 Jane St Ste 200 *TF:* 888-772-0773 ■ *Web:* picco-engineering.com	Concord	ON	L4K2M6	905-760-9688	760-9699	261
Piccola Italia 815 Elm St *Web:* www.piccolaitalianh.com	Manchester	NH	03101	603-606-5100		671
Piccolina Toscana 1412 N DuPont St *Web:* www.piccolinatoscana.com	Wilmington	DE	19806	302-654-8001		671
Piccolo Mondo 829 E Lamar Blvd *Web:* www.piccolomondo.com	Arlington	TX	76011	817-265-9174		671
Picerne Real Estate Group 75 Lambert Lind Hwy *Web:* www.picerne.com	Warwick	RI	02886	401-732-3700	738-6452	653
PICHTR (Pacific International Center for High Technology Research) 1440 Kapiolani Blvd Ste 1225 *Web:* www.pichtr.org	Honolulu	HI	96814	808-943-9581	943-9582	668
Picis Inc 100 Quannapowitt Pkwy Ste 405 *Web:* www.picis.com	Wakefield	MA	01880	781-557-3000		178-10
Pick Instrument Products Company Inc 102 Eastway St *Web:* www.pickinstrument.com	Galena Park	TX	77547	713-672-1686		454
Pick N Save 6950 W State St *Web:* www.picknsave.com	Wauwatosa	WI	53213	414-475-7181		345
Pick Your Part Auto Wrecking Inc 1235 S Beach Blvd *TF:* 800-962-2277 ■ *Web:* www.lkqpickyourpart.com	Anaheim	CA	92804	800-962-2277		54
Pickaway Correctional Institution 11781 St Rte 762 PO Box 209 *Web:* www.drc.ohio.gov	Orient	OH	43146	614-877-4362	877-4514	213
Pickaway County 139 W Franklin St *Web:* www.pickaway.org	Circleville	OH	43113	740-474-6093	474-8988	338
Pickaway County Chamber of Commerce 114 E Main St *Web:* www.pickawaychamber.com	Circleville	OH	43113	740-474-4923		139
Pickaway County District Public Library 1160 N Court St *Web:* pickawaylib.org	Circleville	OH	43113	740-477-1644	474-2855	434-3
Pickaway County Visitors Bureau 325 W Main St *Web:* pickaway.com	Circleville	OH	43113	740-474-3636	420-9181	206
Pickaway-Ross County Joint Vocational School District 895 Crouse Chapel Rd *Web:* www.pickawayross.com	Chillicothe	OH	45601	740-642-1200		685
Pickens County Herald Inc PO Box 390 *Web:* www.pcherald.com	Carrollton	AL	35447	205-367-2217		532-2
Pickens County Library System 304 Biltmore Rd *Web:* pickenscountylibrarysystem.com	Easley	SC	29640	864-850-7077		434-3
Pickens County School District (PCSD) 1348 Griffin Mill Rd *Web:* www.pickens.k12.sc.us	Easley	SC	29640	864-397-1000	855-8159	685
Pickens Snodgrass Koch & Company PC 3001 Medlin Dr Ste 100 *TF:* 800-424-5790 ■ *Web:* www.pskcpa.com	Arlington	TX	76015	817-664-3000		2
Pickens Technical College 500 Airport Blvd *Web:* www.pickenstech.org	Aurora	CO	80011	720-502-8544		167-3
Pickens-Kane Moving Co 410 N Milwaukee Ave *TF:* 888-871-9998 ■ *Web:* www.pickenskane.com	Chicago	IL	60610	312-942-0330		519
Pickerel Lake Recreation Area 12980 446th Ave *Web:* gfp.sd.gov	Grenville	SD	57239	605-486-4753		565
Pickering College 16945 Bayview Ave *Web:* www.pickeringcollege.on.ca	Newmarket	ON	L3Y4X2	905-895-1700	895-9076	622
Pickerington Local School District 90 N East St *Web:* www.pickerington.k12.oh.us	Pickerington	OH	43147	614-833-2110		685
Picket Fences Realty School 531 Fairmont Ave *Web:* www.pfrealty.net	Fairmont	WV	26554	304-367-0543	363-0589	685
Pickett County 1 Courthouse Sq Ste 200 *TF:* 888-406-4704 ■ *Web:* www.dalehollow.com	Byrdstown	TN	38549	931-864-3798	864-6615	338
Pickett Group Inc 14500 N Outer Forty Ste 210 *TF:* 800-333-1999 ■ *Web:* pickettgroup.com	Chesterfield	MO	63017	636-519-0977	519-5233	390
Pickett State Park 4605 Pickett Pk Hwy *TF:* 877-260-0010 ■ *Web:* tnstateparks.com	Jamestown	TN	38556	931-879-5821		565
Pickett's Mill Battlefield State Historic Site 4432 Mt Tabor Church Rd *Web:* gastateparks.org	Dallas	GA	30157	770-443-7850		565
PickPoint 3149 Skyway Ct Ste 101 *TF:* 800-636-1288 ■ *Web:* www.pickpoint.com	Fremont	CA	94539	925-924-1700	924-1900	475

Name / Address	City	State	Zip	Phone	Fax	Class
Pickrel Schaeffer & Ebeling 40 N Main St - Kettering Tower *Web:* www.pselaw.com	Dayton	OH	45423	937-223-1130		428
Pickwick Electric Co-op 672 Hwy 142 *TF:* 800-372-8258 ■ *Web:* www.pickwickec.com	Selmer	TN	38375	731-645-3411	645-7167	245
Pickwick Landing State Resort Park PO Box 15 *Web:* tnstateparks.com	Pickwick Dam	TN	38365	731-689-3129		565
Picnic Time Inc 5131 Maureen Ln *TF:* 888-742-6429 ■ *Web:* www.picnictime.com	Moorpark	CA	93021	805-529-7400	529-7474	200
Pico Envirotec Inc 222 Snidercroft Rd *Web:* www.picoenvirotec.com	Concord	ON	L4K2K1	905-760-9512		180
Pico Holdings Inc 7979 Ivanhoe Ave Ste 300 *NASDAQ: PICO* ■ *TF:* 888-389-3222 ■ *Web:* www.picoholdings.com	La Jolla	CA	92037	858-456-6022	456-6480	360-4
Pico Quantitative Trading LLC 32 Old Slip 16th Fl *Web:* www.pico.net	New York	NY	10005	646-362-4420		690
Pico Rivera Chamber of Commerce 5016 Passons Blvd *Web:* www.picoriverachamber.org	Pico Rivera	CA	90660	562-949-2477		139
Pico Systems 543 Lindeman Rd *Web:* www.pico-systems.com	Kirkwood	MO	63122	314-965-5523		246
PicoSearch LLC 10 Fawcett St	Cambridge	MA	02138	617-547-4020		39
PICS (Professional Implementation Consulting Services Inc) 46 High St *Web:* www.pics.com	Mount Holly	NJ	08060	609-702-3920		194
Pics Telecom International Corp 1920 Lyell Ave *TF:* 800-521-7427 ■ *Web:* www.picstelecom.com	Rochester	NY	14606	585-295-2000		735
Pictorial Histories Publishing Company Inc (PHPC) 713 S 3rd St W *Web:* www.pictorialhistoriespublishing.com	Missoula	MT	59801	406-549-8488	728-9280	96
Pictou County Chamber of Commerce 115 MacLean St *Web:* pictouchamber.com	New Glasgow	NS	B2H4M5	902-755-3463		137
Pictron Inc 1250 Oakmead Pky Ste 210 *Web:* www.pictron.com	Sunnyvale	CA	94085	408-725-8888		178-1
Pictsweet Co, The 10 Pictsweet Dr **Fax Area Code:* 888 ■ *Web:* pictsweetfarms.com	Bells	TN	38006	731-663-6525	662-7651*	206-21
Picture Marketing Inc 1202 Grant Ave Ste D **Fax Area Code:* 888 ■ *Web:* picturemarketing.com	Novato	CA	94945	949-623-9889	337-8288*	636
Pictured Rocks National Lakeshore N8391 Sandpoint Rd PO Box 40 *Web:* www.nps.gov	Munising	MI	49862	906-387-2607		564
PIDA (Pet Industry Distributors Assn) 2105 Laurel Bush Rd Ste 200 *Web:* www.pida.org	Bel Air	MD	21015	443-640-1060		49-18
Pie Consulting & Engineering Inc 6275 Joyce Dr Ste 200 *TF:* 866-552-5246 ■ *Web:* www.pieglobal.com	Arvada	CO	80403	303-552-0177	552-0178	261
Pied Piper Mills Inc 423 E Lake Dr	Hamlin	TX	79520	325-576-3684		447
Piedmont Airlines Inc 5443 Airport Terminal Rd *Web:* piedmont-airlines.com	Salisbury	MD	21804	410-572-5100		25
Piedmont Baptist College 420 S Broad St *TF:* 800-937-5097 ■ *Web:* www.piedmontu.edu	Winston-Salem	NC	27101	336-725-8344	725-5522	166
Piedmont Chemical Industries Inc 331 Burton Ave *Web:* www.piedmontchemical.com	High Point	NC	27262	336-885-5131	887-5563	144
Piedmont College 165 Central Ave *TF:* 800-277-7020 ■ *Web:* www.piedmont.edu	Demorest	GA	30535	706-776-0103	776-6635	166
Piedmont Community College 1715 College Dr PO Box 1197 *Web:* www.piedmont.cc.nc.us	Roxboro	NC	27573	336-599-1181	597-3817	162
Piedmont Community Health Plan Inc 2512 Langhorne Rd *Web:* www.pchp.net	Lynchburg	VA	24501	434-947-4463		390
Piedmont Concrete Inc 197 Quarry Rd *Web:* www.piedmontconcrete.net	Union	SC	29379	864-427-1756		183
Piedmont Construction Group LLC (PCG) 107 Gateway Dr Ste B *Web:* www.piedmontconstructiongroup.com	Macon	GA	31210	478-405-8907	405-8908	186
Piedmont Electric Membership Corp 2500 Nc 86 PO Box 1179 *TF:* 800-222-3107 ■ *Web:* pemc.coop	Hillsborough	NC	27278	919-732-2123	732-9978	245
Piedmont Federal Savings Bank (PFSB) 201 S Stratford Rd *Web:* www.piedmontfederal.bank	Winston-Salem	NC	27103	336-770-1000		70
Piedmont Geotechnical Consultants 3000 Northfield Pl *Web:* pgci.com	Roswell	GA	30076	770-752-9205	752-0890	256
Piedmont Geriatric Hospital PO Box 427 *Web:* www.pgh.dbhds.virginia.gov	Burkeville	VA	23922	434-767-4401		374-7
Piedmont Graphics Inc 6903 International Dr *Web:* www.piedmontgraphics.com	Greensboro	NC	27409	336-230-0040		627
Piedmont Graphics Inc 1007 Industrial Park Dr Ste 100 *Web:* www.piedmontgraphicsinc.com	Marietta	GA	30062	770-425-1222		627
Piedmont Healthcare 1133 Eagle's Landing Pkwy *Web:* www.piedmont.org	Stockbridge	GA	30281	678-604-1000		374-3
Piedmont Mechanical Inc 116 John Dodd Rd PO Box 4925 *Web:* www.piedmontmechanical.com	Spartanburg	SC	29305	864-578-9114	578-5314	189-10
Piedmont Medical Ctr 222 S Herlong Ave *TF:* 800-222-4218 ■ *Web:* www.piedmontmedicalcenter.com	Rock Hill	SC	29732	803-329-1234		374-3
Piedmont Natural Gas 4720 Piedmont Row Dr PO Box 33068 *NYSE: PNY* ■ *TF:* 800-752-7504 ■ *Web:* www.piedmontng.com	Charlotte	NC	28233	704-364-3120		787
Piedmont Precision Machine Company Inc 150 Airside Dr *Web:* www.ppmmach.com	Danville	VA	24540	434-793-0677		757
Piedmont Recreation Dept 358 Hillside Ave *Web:* www.ci.piedmont.ca.us	Piedmont	CA	94611	510-420-3070		564
Piedmont Systems Inc PO Box 2088 *Web:* www.piedmontsystems.com	Advance	NC	27006	336-998-2800		178-1
Piedmont Technical College 620 N Emerald Rd *TF:* 800-868-5528 ■ *Web:* www.ptc.edu	Greenwood	SC	29646	800-868-5528		800
Piedmont Triad International Airport 1000 A Ted Johnson Pkwy *Web:* flyfrompti.com	Greensboro	NC	27409	336-665-5600		27
Piedmont Triad Regional Council (PTRC) 1398 Carrolton Crossing Dr *Web:* www.ptrc.org	Kernersville	NC	27284	336-904-0300	904-0301	48-6
Piedmont Truck Tires Inc PO Box 18228 *TF:* 800-274-8473 ■ *Web:* www.piedmonttrucktires.com	Greensboro	NC	27419	336-668-0091		755
Piedmont Virginia Community College 501 College Dr *Web:* www.pvcc.edu	Charlottesville	VA	22902	434-977-3900	961-5425	162
Piehl, Hanson, Beckman PA 700 S Grade Rd SW *Web:* www.phbcpa.com	Hutchinson	MN	55350	320-234-4430	234-4426	2
Piemonte & Liebhauser LLC 325 Columbia Tpke Ste 108 *Web:* piemonteandliebhauser.com	Florham Park	NJ	07932	973-937-6201		734
Pieper Electric Inc 5477 S Westridge Ct *Web:* pieperpower.com	New Berlin	WI	53151	414-462-7700		189-4
Pieper O'Brien Herr Architects Ltd 3000 Royal Blvd S *Web:* poharchitects.com	Alpharetta	GA	30022	770-569-1706		261
Pier 1 Imports Inc 100 Pier 1 Pl *NYSE: PIR* ■ *TF:* 800-245-4595 ■ *Web:* pier1.com	Fort Worth	TX	76102	817-252-8000	252-8174	362
Pier 99 2822 N Shoreline Blvd *Web:* www.pier99restaurant.com	Corpus Christi	TX	78402	361-887-0764		671
Pier Foundry & Pattern Shop Inc 51 State St *Web:* www.pierfoundry.com	Saint Paul	MN	55107	651-222-4461	222-4185	492
Pier House Resort Caribbean Spa 1 Duval St *TF:* 800-723-2791 ■ *Web:* www.pierhouse.com	Key West	FL	33040	305-296-4600	296-7569	669
Pieratt's 110 Mt Tabor Rd *TF:* 855-743-7288 ■ *Web:* www.pieratts.com	Lexington	KY	40517	859-268-6000		35
Pierce & Shearer LLP 730 Polhemus Rd Ste 101 *Web:* www.pierceshearer.com	San Mateo	CA	94402	650-573-9300		428
Pierce Aluminum 34 Forge Pkwy *TF:* 800-336-1358 ■ *Web:* www.piercealuminum.com	Franklin	MA	02038	508-541-7007	541-6077	492
Pierce College 6201 Winnetka Ave *Web:* www.piercecollege.edu	Woodland Hills	CA	91371	818-719-6401		162
Pierce College 9401 Farwest Dr SW *Web:* www.pierce.ctc.edu	Lakewood	WA	98498	253-964-6500	964-6427	162
Pierce County 414 W Main St PO Box 119 *Web:* www.co.pierce.wi.us	Ellsworth	WI	54011	715-273-6744	273-6861	338
Pierce County 240 SE Second St *Web:* www.piercecountynd.gov	Rugby	ND	58368	701-776-6161	776-5707	338
Pierce County 930 Tacoma Ave S Rm 110 *Web:* www.co.pierce.wa.us	Tacoma	WA	98402	253-798-7455	798-3428	338
Pierce County Library System 3005 112th St E *TF:* 800-346-0995 ■ *Web:* www.piercecountylibrary.org	Tacoma	WA	98446	253-548-3300	537-4600	434-3
Pierce County Security Inc 2002 99th St E *TF:* 800-773-4432 ■ *Web:* pcswa.com	Tacoma	WA	98445	253-535-4433		693
Pierce County Tax Commissioner 312 Nichols St, Ste 4 PO Box 192 *Web:* www.piercegatax.com	Blackshear	GA	31516	912-449-2026	449-2024	338
Pierce Courthouse 111 W Ct St *Web:* co.pierce.ne.us	Pierce	NE	68767	402-329-4225	329-6439	338
Pierce Distribution Services Co PO Box 15600 **Fax Area Code:* 815 ■ *TF:* 800-466-7397 ■ *Web:* www.piercedistribution.com	Loves Park	IL	61132	800-466-7397	636-5660*	449
Pierce Group Benefits LLC 4928 Linksland Dr Ste 201 *TF:* 888-662-7500 ■ *Web:* piercegroupbenefits.com	Holly Springs	NC	27540	919-577-0700	577-0710	390
Pierce Manufacturing Inc 2600 American Dr PO Box 2017 *TF:* 888-974-3723 ■ *Web:* www.piercemfg.com	Appleton	WI	54912	920-832-3000		516
Pierce Pacific Manufacturing Inc 4424 NE 158th PO Box 30509 *TF:* 800-760-3270 ■ *Web:* piercepacific.com	Portland	OR	97294	503-808-9110	808-9111	190
Pierce Pepin Co-opeartive Services W7725 US Hwy 10 PO Box 420 *TF:* 800-924-2133 ■ *Web:* www.piercepepin.coop	Ellsworth	WI	54011	715-273-4355		245
Pierce Promotions and Event Management LLC 178 Middle St 2nd Fl *Web:* www.pierceglobal.com	Portland	ME	04101	207-523-1700		7
Pierce Pump Company LP 9010 John W Carpenter Fwy *Web:* piercepump.com	Dallas	TX	75247	214-320-3604		358
Pierce Telephone Company Inc (PTC) 112 S 5th St *TF:* 888-329-6225 ■ *Web:* www.piercetelephone.com	Pierce	NE	68767	402-329-6225	329-4006	224
Pierce Transit 3701 96th St SW PO Box 99070 *TF:* 800-562-8109 ■ *Web:* www.piercetransit.org	Lakewood	WA	98499	253-581-8000	581-8075	468
Pierce-Cote Advertising 683 Main St *Web:* pierce-cote.com	Osterville	MA	02655	508-420-5566		7
Pierce-Eislen Inc 9200 E Pima Center Pkwy Ste 150 *Web:* www.yardimatrix.com	Scottsdale	AZ	85258	480-663-1149		652
Piercey Automotive Group 16901 Millikan Ave *Web:* www.pierceyautogroup.com	Irvine	CA	92606	949-396-6000		57

				Phone	Fax	Class
Piercon Solutions LLC 63 Beaverbrook Rd Ste 201 *Web:* www.piercon.net	Lincoln Park	NJ	07035	973-628-9330	628-9321	261
Piergrossi & Peterman LLP 2344 Eastchester Rd *Web:* bronxlawoffice.com	Bronx	NY	10469	718-515-6000		41
Pierpont Inn 550 Sanjon Rd *Web:* www.pierpontinn.com	Ventura	CA	93001	805-643-0245		379
Pierpont's at Union Station 30 W Pershing Rd Union Stn *Web:* www.herefordhouse.com	Kansas City	MO	64108	816-842-8718	221-4478	671
Pierre Area Chamber of Commerce 800 W Dakota Ave *TF:* 800-962-2034 ■ *Web:* www.pierre.org	Pierre	SD	57501	605-224-7361	224-6485	139
Pierre Fabre Dermo Cosmetique 8 Campus Dr *Web:* www.pierre-fabre.com	Parsippany	NJ	07054	973-898-1042		231
Pierre Part Store LLC 3421 Hwy 70 S *Web:* www.pierrepartstore.com	Pierre Part	LA	70339	985-252-6261	252-6607	812
Pierre Regional Airport 222 E Dakota Ave *Web:* www.cityofpierre.org	Pierre	SD	57501	605-773-7447		27
Pierson & Fendley LLC 1705 Lamar *TF:* 855-784-0836 ■ *Web:* pierson-fendley.com	Paris	TX	75460	903-784-0836	785-8434	390
Pierson Co 1200 W Harris St *Web:* piersoncompany.com	Eureka	CA	95503	707-268-1800	268-1801	186
Pierson Construction Inc (PCI) 2103 Burlington Ste 201 *Web:* www.piersonconstruction.net	Columbia	MO	65202	573-445-8493	445-5015	186
Pierson Industries Inc 7 Astro Pl *Web:* www.piersonindustriesinc.com	Rockaway	NJ	07866	973-627-7945	627-1638	596
Pierson Products Inc 419 S Arch St *Web:* www.piersonproductsinc.com	Janesville	WI	53548	608-754-7733	754-1480	454
Pietragallo Gordon Alfano Bosick & Raspanti LLP 1 Oxford Centre 301 Grant St 3rd Fl *Web:* www.pietragallo.com	Pittsburgh	PA	15219	412-263-2000	263-2001	428
Pietrantoni Mendez & Alvarez LLP Popular Ctr Bldg 208 Ponce de Leon Ave 19th Fl *Web:* www.pmalaw.com	San Juan	PR	00918	787-274-1212		428
Piezo-Metrics Inc 4509 Runway St *Web:* www.microninstruments.com	Simi Valley	CA	93063	805-522-4676	522-4982	696
Piezotech LLC 8431 Georgetown Rd Ste 300 *Web:* piezotechnologies.com	Indianapolis	IN	46268	317-876-4670		407
Pig Pen Studios Inc 30 Manorhaven Blvd *Web:* www.pigpenstudiosinc.com	Port Washington	NY	11050	516-883-2500		344
Pigeon Brands Inc 179 John St 2nd Fl *Web:* www.pigeonbrands.com	Toronto	ON	M5T1X4	416-532-9950		344
Pigeon Forge Department of Tourism PO Box 1390 *TF:* 800-251-9100 ■ *Web:* www.mypigeonforge.com	Pigeon Forge	TN	37868	865-453-8574		206
Pigeon Point Light Station State Historic Park 210 Pigeon Pt Rd *Web:* www.parks.ca.gov	Pescadero	CA	94060	650-879-0633		565
Pigeon Telephone Co 20 S Main St *TF:* 800-292-0614 ■ *Web:* www.pigeontelephone.com	Pigeon	MI	48755	989-453-4321		224
Piggly Wiggly 2400 J Terrell Wooten Dr *Web:* www.pwadc.com	Bessemer	AL	35020	205-481-2300	481-2336	297-8
Piggly Wiggly Carolina Company Inc 176 Croghan Spur Rd Ste 301 *TF:* 800-243-9880 ■ *Web:* www.thepig.net	Charleston	SC	29407	843-554-9880	202-8200	345
Piggly Wiggly Midwest LL 2215 Union Ave *Web:* pigglywiggly.com	Sheboygan	WI	53081	920-457-4433		345
Pignataro Volkswagon 10633 Evergreen Way *Web:* www.pignatarovw.com	Everett	WA	98204	425-348-3141		57
Pigott Inc 3815 Ingersoll Ave *Web:* pigottnet.com	Des Moines	IA	50312	515-279-8879	279-7338	320
Pigs Unlimited Inc 23802 FM 2978 Ste C1 *TF:* 800-578-7436 ■ *Web:* www.pigsunlimited.com	Tomball	TX	77375	281-351-2749	351-4658	454
PIIRS (Princeton Institute for International & Regional Studies) Princeton University Louis A Simpson International Bldg *Web:* piirs.princeton.edu	Princeton	NJ	08544	609-258-7497	258-3988	634
PIJAC (Pet Industry Joint Advisory Council) 1220 19th St NW Ste 400 *TF:* 800-553-7387 ■ *Web:* www.pijac.org	Washington	DC	20036	202-452-1525	293-4377	49-4
PIKA Technologies Inc 535 Legget Dr Ste 400 *Web:* www.pikatech.com	Ottawa	ON	K2K3B8	613-591-1555		256
Pike County 115 W Main St *Web:* www.pikecountymo.net	Bowling Green	MO	63334	573-324-2412		338
Pike County PO Box 309 *TF:* 866-545-7876 ■ *Web:* www.co.pike.ms.us	Magnolia	MS	39652	601-783-3362	783-4104	338
Pike County 506 Broad St *TF:* 866-681-4947 ■ *Web:* www.pikepa.org	Milford	PA	18337	570-296-7613	296-6055	338
Pike County 146 Main St *Web:* www.revenue.ky.gov	Pikeville	KY	41501	606-432-6201		338
Pike County 120 W Church St *Web:* sos.alabama.gov	Troy	AL	36081	334-566-1757		338
Pike County 126 W Second St PO Box 134 *Web:* www.piketravel.com	Waverly	OH	45690	740-947-9650	941-0255	338
Pike County Chamber of Commerce 178 College St *Web:* www.sekchamber.com	Pikeville	KY	41501	606-432-5504	432-7295	139
Pike County Chamber of Commerce 201 Broad St Ste 2 *TF:* 877-345-0691 ■ *Web:* www.pikechamber.com	Milford	PA	18337	570-296-8700	296-3921	139
Pike County Coop 105 Nehi Rd *Web:* www.pikecountycoop.biz	McComb	MS	39649	601-684-1651	684-0057	276
Pike County Courthouse 100 E Washington St *Web:* www.pikeil.org	Pittsfield	IL	62363	217-285-6812		338
Pike Distributors Inc 353 US 41 E *Web:* pikedistributors.com	Newberry	MI	49868	906-475-9936	475-9937	81-1
Pike Electric LLC 100 Pike Way PO Box 868 *NYSE: PIKE* ■ **Fax Area Code: 336* ■ *Web:* pike.com	Mount Airy	NC	27030	919-231-6134	719-7453*	189-4
Pike Industries Inc 3 Eastgate Park Rd *TF:* 800-283-0803 ■ *Web:* pikeindustries.com	Belmont	NH	03220	603-527-5100	527-5101	188-4
Pike Lumber Company Inc PO Box 247 *TF:* 800-356-4554 ■ *Web:* www.pikelumber.com	Akron	IN	46910	574-893-4511	893-7400	683
Pike National Forest 601 S Weber St *Web:* www.fs.usda.gov	Colorado Springs	CO	80903	719-636-1602	477-4233	50-5
Pike Nurseries Holding LLC 3555 Koger Blvd Ste 360 *Web:* www.pikenursery.com	Duluth	GA	30096	770-921-1022		323
Pike Outlets, The 95 S Pine Ave *TF:* 877-225-5337 ■ *Web:* thepikeoutlets.com	Long Beach	CA	90802	562-432-8325		50-6
Pike Place Market (PPM) 85 Pike St Rm 500 *Web:* www.pikeplacemarket.org	Seattle	WA	98101	206-682-7453	625-0646	50-6
Pike-Lincoln Technical Ctr 342 VoTech Rd *Web:* www.pltc.edu	Eolia	MO	63344	573-485-2900	485-2388	167-3
Pikes Peak Community College *Centennial* 5675 S Academy Blvd *TF:* 800-456-6847 ■ *Web:* www.ppcc.edu	Colorado Springs	CO	80906	719-502-2000		162
Pikes Peak Ctr 190 S Cascade Ave *Web:* www.pikespeakcenter.com	Colorado Springs	CO	80903	719-477-2100	477-2199	572
Pikes Peak Library District PO Box 1579 *Web:* ppld.org	Colorado Springs	CO	80901	719-531-6333		434-3
Pikes Peak of Texas Inc 4340 Directors Row *Web:* pikespeakfloral.com	Houston	TX	77092	713-686-4500		293
Pikes Peak State Park 15316 Great River Rd *Web:* www.iowadnr.gov	McGregor	IA	52157	563-873-2341		565
Pikes Peak Test Labs Inc 4750 Edison Ave *Web:* troybennettpptli.wixsite.com	Colorado Springs	CO	80915	719-596-0802		743
Pikesville-Owings Mills Regional Chamber of Commerce *Chamber of Commerce* 7 Church Ln Ste 6 *Web:* www.pomchamber.org	Pikesville	MD	21208	410-484-2337	484-4151	139
Pikeville College 147 Sycamore St *TF:* 866-232-7700 ■ *Web:* upike.edu	Pikeville	KY	41501	606-218-5250	218-5255	166
Pikeville Medical Ctr 911 Bypass Rd *Web:* www.pikevillehospital.org	Pikeville	KY	41501	606-218-3500		374-3
Pilarski Sinkel & Hankes Ltd 5100 Eden Ave S Ste 304	Edina	MN	55436	952-929-2580		2
Pilat 75 SR-17 Ste 408 *TF:* 800-338-9701 ■ *Web:* www.pilat.com	Whitehouse Station	NJ	08889	800-338-9701		196
Pilcher Hamilton Corp 6845 Kingery Hwy *Web:* www.pilcherhamilton.com	Willowbrook	IL	60527	630-655-8100		603
Pilgrim Bank 2401 S Jefferson Ave *TF:* 877-303-3111 ■ *Web:* pilgrimbank.com	Mount Pleasant	TX	75455	903-575-2150	575-0383	70
Pilgrim Hall Museum 75 Ct St *Web:* pilgrimhall.org	Plymouth	MA	02360	508-746-1620		520
Pilgrim Home & Hearth Alliance LLC 5600 Imhoff Dr Ste G *TF:* 800-227-1044 ■ *Web:* www.pilgrimhearth.com	Concord	CA	94520	800-227-1044		364
Pilgrim Instrument & Controls Inc 38 Union St *TF:* 800-536-7990 ■ *Web:* www.pilgrim-instrument.com	East Walpole	MA	02032	800-536-7990		385
Pilgrim Monument & Provincetown Museum 1 High Pole Hill Rd *Web:* www.pilgrim-monument.org	Provincetown	MA	02657	508-487-1310		50-4
Pilgrim Psychiatric Ctr 998 Crooked Hill Rd *Web:* omh.ny.gov	West Brentwood	NY	11717	631-761-3500	761-2600	374-5
Pilgrim Quality Solutions 2807 W Busch Blvd *Web:* www.pilgrimquality.com	Tampa	FL	33618	813-915-1663	915-1948	178-1
Pilgrim Title Insurance Co 450 Veterans Memorial Pkwy Ste 7A *Web:* pilgrimtitle.com	East Providence	RI	02914	401-274-9100		390
Pilgrim Tours & Travel Inc PO Box 268 *TF:* 800-322-0788 ■ *Web:* www.pilgrimtours.com	Morgantown	PA	19543	610-286-0788	286-6262	760
Pilgrims Tales Inc PO Box 791613 *TF:* 866-829-0820 ■ *Web:* www.pilgrimstales.com	Paia	HI	96779	866-829-0820		637-2
Pilieromazza PLLC 888 17th St NW Ste 1100 *Web:* pilieromazza.com	Washington	DC	20006	202-857-1000		41
Pilkey-Hopping & Ekberg Inc 2102 N Pearl St Ste 102 *Web:* pheinsurance.com	Tacoma	WA	98406	253-756-2000	756-5336	390
Pilkington Holdings Inc 811 Madison Ave *Web:* www.pilkington.com	Toledo	OH	43697	419-247-3731	247-3821	329
Pill Club 133 Arch St *Web:* www.thepillclub.com	Redwood City	CA	94062	772-217-4557		374-7
Pillar Financial Advisors LLC 3046 Breckenridge Ln Ste 104 *Web:* pillar.net	Louisville	KY	40220	502-384-3890		401
Pillar Hotels & Resorts LP 6031 Connection Dr Ste 500 *Web:* pillarhotels.com	Irving	TX	75039	972-830-3100		379
Pillar Induction Co 21905 Gateway Rd *TF:* 800-558-7733 ■ *Web:* www.pillar.com	Brookfield	WI	53045	262-317-5300	317-5353	318
Pillar Innovations LLC 92 Corporate Dr *Web:* pillarinnovations.com	Grantsville	MD	21536	301-245-4007		407

Name / Address	City	State	ZIP	Phone	Fax	Class
Pillar Ministries 1302 Sherman St *Web:* pillarministries.org	Denver	CO	80203	303-839-1500		506
Pillar Technologies 475 Industrial Dr PO Box 110 *Web:* www.pillartech.com	Hartland	WI	53029	262-367-3060	912-7272	201
Pillar Technology Group LLC 301 E Liberty St Ste 700 *TF:* 888-374-5527 ■ *Web:* pillartechnology.com	Ann Arbor	MI	48104	888-374-5527		809
Pillars Hotel at New River Sound 111 N Birch Rd *Web:* pillarshotel.com	Fort Lauderdale	FL	33304	954-467-9639		379
Piller Inc 45 Turner Rd **Fax Area Code:* 845 ■ *TF:* 800-597-6937 ■ *Web:* www.piller.com	Middletown	NY	10941	800-597-6937	692-0295*	518
Pillsbury State Park 100 Pillsbury State Park Rd *Web:* www.nhstateparks.org	Washington	NH	03280	603-863-2860		565
Pillsbury Winthrop Shaw Pittman LLP 50 Fremont St *Web:* www.pillsburylaw.com	San Francisco	CA	94105	415-983-1000	983-1200	428
Pilot 302 Locust St *Web:* dixonpilot.com	Dixon	MO	65459	573-759-2127	759-6226	532-2
Pilot Contracting Corp 1452 Donaldson Hwy *Web:* www.pilotbuilds.com	Erlanger	KY	41018	859-525-8585		610
Pilot Digital Marketing 4619 N Ravenswood Ave Ste 104 *Web:* pilotdigital.com	Chicago	IL	60640	773-809-5002		5
Pilot Freight Services Inc 314 N Middletown Rd *TF:* 800-447-4568 ■ *Web:* www.pilotair.com	Lima	PA	19037	610-891-8100		311
Pilot Knob State Park 2148 340th St *Web:* www.iowadnr.gov	Forest City	IA	50436	641-581-4835		565
Pilot LLC, The 145 W Pennsylvania Ave PO Box 58 *Web:* www.thepilot.com	Southern Pines	NC	28388	910-692-7271	692-9382	532-4
Pilot Mountain State Park 1792 Pilot Knob Park Rd *Web:* www.ncparks.gov	Pinnacle	NC	27043	336-325-2355		565
Pilot Travel Centers LLC 5508 Lonas Dr *TF:* 800-562-6210 ■ *Web:* pilotflyingj.com	Knoxville	TN	37939	865-938-1439		324
Pilot Tribune 527 Cayuga St *TF:* 800-447-1985 ■ *Web:* www.stormlakepilottribune.com	Storm Lake	IA	50588	712-732-3130	732-3152	532-2
Piltz Williams Larosa & Co 1077 Tommy Munro Dr *Web:* pwlcpa.com	Biloxi	MS	39532	228-374-4141		2
Pilz Automation Safety LP 7150 Commerce Blvd *Web:* www.pilz.com	Canton	MI	48187	734-354-0272	354-3355	455
PIM (Printing Industry Midwest) 1300 Godward St NE Ste 2650 *Web:* www.pimw.org	Minneapolis	MN	55413	612-400-6200		139
PIMA (Professional Insurance Marketing Assn) 35 E Wacker Dr Ste 850 *Web:* www.pimainsights.org	Chicago	IL	60601	817-569-7462		49-9
Pima Air & Space Museum 6000 E Valencia Rd *Web:* www.pimaair.org	Tucson	AZ	85730	520-574-0462	574-9238	520
Pima Community College 401 N Bonita Ave *TF:* 800-860-7462 ■ *Web:* pima.edu	Tucson	AZ	85709	520-206-2733	206-4790	162
Pima County 130 W Congress St *Web:* webcms.pima.gov	Tucson	AZ	85701	520-724-9999		338
Pima County *Dept of Transportation Transportation Systems Div* 201 N Stone Ave 4th Fl *Web:* www.webcms.pima.gov	Tucson	AZ	85701	520-740-6410		108
Pima County Public Library 101 N Stone Ave *TF:* 877-705-5437 ■ *Web:* www.library.pima.gov	Tucson	AZ	85701	520-791-4010	594-5621	434-3
Pima County School Superintendent 200 N Stone Ave *Web:* www.schools.pima.gov	Tucson	AZ	85701	520-724-8451	770-4210	685
Pima Medical Institute 3350 E Grant Rd Ste 200 *TF:* 888-556-7334 ■ *Web:* pmi.edu	Tucson	AZ	85716	520-326-1600		507
Pimlico Race Course 5201 Park Heights Ave *TF:* 800-638-1859 ■ *Web:* www.pimlico.com	Baltimore	MD	21215	410-542-9400		133
Pin Oak Investment Advisors Inc 510 Bering Dr Ste 100 *Web:* www.pinoak.com	Houston	TX	77057	713-871-8300	871-8307	401
Pin Oak Stud 830 Grassy Spring Rd PO Box 68 *Web:* pinoakstud.com	Versailles	KY	40383	859-873-1420	873-2391	368
Pinal County 31 N Pinal St *Web:* www.pinalcountyaz.gov	Florence	AZ	85232	520-509-3555	866-6512	338
Pinal County Library District (PCLD) 92 W Butte Ave *Web:* www.pinalcountyaz.gov	Florence	AZ	85132	520-866-6457	866-6533	434-3
Pinchin Group, The 2470 Milltower Ct *TF:* 855-746-2446 ■ *Web:* www.pinchin.com	Mississauga	ON	L5N7W5	905-363-0678	363-0681	192
Pinck & Company Inc 98 Magazine St *Web:* pinck-co.com	Boston	MA	02119	617-445-3555		188
Pinckney Community Schools 2130 E MI 36 *Web:* www.pinckneypirates.org	Pinckney	MI	48169	810-225-3900		685
Pinckney Hugo Group 760 W Genesee St *Web:* www.pinckneyhugo.com	Syracuse	NY	13204	315-478-6700		7
Pinckneyville Correctional Ctr 5835 SR-154 *Web:* www2.illinois.gov	Pinckneyville	IL	62274	618-357-9722	357-2083	213
Pincock Allen & Holt Inc 165 S Union Blvd Ste 950	Lakewood	CO	80228	303-986-6950	987-8907	261
Pindler & Pindler Inc 11910 Poindexter Ave *TF:* 800-669-6002 ■ *Web:* www.pindler.com	Moorpark	CA	93021	805-531-9090		194
Pine Bluff Commercial 300 S Beech St *Web:* www.pbcommercial.com	Pine Bluff	AR	71601	870-534-3400	534-0113	532-2
Pine Bluff Convention & Visitors Bureau (PBCVB) 1 Convention Center Plz *TF:* 800-536-7660 ■ *Web:* www.pinebluffconvention.center	Pine Bluff	AR	71601	870-536-7600	850-2105	206
Pine Bluff Cotton Belt Federal Credit Union 1703 River Pines Blvd *TF:* 888-249-1904 ■ *Web:* www.pbcbcu.org	Pine Bluff	AR	71601	870-535-6365	535-0765	219
Pine Bluff Sand & Gravel Co 1501 Heart Wood *Web:* pbsgc.applicantharbor.com	White Hall	AR	71602	870-534-7120		182
Pine Bluffs Post 201 E 2nd *Web:* www.pinebluffspost.com	Pine Bluffs	WY	82082	307-245-3763		532-2
Pine Cliff Energy Ltd 1015 Fourth St SW Ste 850 *TF:* 877-486-0470 ■ *Web:* www.pinecliffenergy.com	Calgary	AB	T2R1J4	403-269-2289		539
Pine Club, The 1926 Brown St *Web:* www.thepineclub.com	Dayton	OH	45409	937-228-7463		671
Pine Country Bank 412 N Hwy 10 PO Box 25 *Web:* www.pinecountrybank.com	Royalton	MN	56373	320-584-5522	584-8385	70
Pine County 635 Northridge Dr NW *TF:* 800-450-7463 ■ *Web:* www.co.pine.mn.us	Pine City	MN	55063	320-591-1400		338
Pine Crest Inn 85 Pine Crest Ln *TF:* 800-633-3001 ■ *Web:* www.pinecrestinn.com	Tryon	NC	28782	828-859-9135		379
Pine Drive Telephone Co 8611 Central Ave *Web:* www.pinedrivetel.com	Beulah	CO	81023	719-485-3400		224
Pine Grove Area School Dist 103 School St *Web:* www.pgasd.com	Pine Grove	PA	17963	570-345-2731		685
Pine Grove Furnace State Park 1100 Pine Grove Rd *Web:* www.dcnr.pa.gov	Gardners	PA	17324	717-486-7174		565
Pine Grove Manufactured Homes Inc 2 Pleasant Valley Rd *Web:* www.pinegrovehomes.com	Pine Grove	PA	17963	570-345-6500	345-4440	505
Pine Hall Brick Co 2701 Shorefair Dr **Fax Area Code:* 336 ■ *TF:* 800-334-8689 ■ *Web:* www.pinehallbrick.com	Winston-Salem	NC	27105	800-334-8689	725-3940*	150
Pine Hills Youth Correctional Facility 4 N Haynes Ave *Web:* www.cor.mt.gov	Miles City	MT	59301	406-232-1377	232-7432	412
Pine Instrument Co 101 Industrial Dr *Web:* www.pineinstrument.com	Grove City	PA	16127	724-458-6391	458-4648	203
Pine Island Sportswear Ltd 1609b N Rocky River Rd *TF:* 800-545-7548 ■ *Web:* pineislandsportswear.com	Monroe	NC	28110	704-289-5600		155-12
Pine Jog Environmental Education Ctr 6301 Summit Blvd *Web:* www.pinejog.fau.edu	West Palm Beach	FL	33415	561-686-6600	687-4968	50-5
Pine Lake State Park 22620 County Hwy S56 *Web:* www.iowadnr.gov	Eldora	IA	50627	641-858-5832	858-5641	565
Pine Lakes Animal Hospital 2 Pine Lakes Pkwy N Ste 4-5 *Web:* pinelakesanimal.com	Palm Coast	FL	32137	386-447-7381		794
Pine Manor College 400 Heath St *TF:* 800-762-1357 ■ *Web:* www.pmc.edu	Chestnut Hill	MA	02467	617-731-7104	731-7102	166
Pine Mountain Lake Assn 19228 Pine Mtn Dr *Web:* www.pinemountainlake.com	Groveland	CA	95321	209-962-8600	962-6796	671
Pine Mountain State Resort Park 1050 State Park Rd *TF:* 800-325-1712 ■ *Web:* parks.ky.gov	Pineville	KY	40977	800-325-1712		565
Pine Pointe Hospice & Palliative Care 6261 Peak Rd *TF:* 800-211-1084 ■ *Web:* pinepointehospice.org	Macon	GA	31210	478-633-5660	633-6247	371
Pine Rest Christian Mental Health Services 300 68th St SE PO Box 165 *TF:* 800-678-5500 ■ *Web:* www.pinerest.org	Grand Rapids	MI	49501	616-455-5000	831-2608	374-5
Pine Ridge Farms 1800 SE Maury St *Web:* www.pineridgefarmspork.com	Des Moines	IA	50317	515-266-4100		296-26
Pine Ridge Winery LLC 5901 Silverado Trl *TF:* 800-575-9777 ■ *Web:* www.pineridgevineyards.com	Napa	CA	94558	800-575-9777		80-3
Pine River Capital Management LP 601 Carlson Pkwy 7th Fl *Web:* pinerivercapital.com	Minnetonka	MN	55305	612-238-3300		463
Pine Road Elementary School 2551 Murray Ave *Web:* www.lmtsd.org	Huntingdon Valley	PA	19006	215-938-0290		685
Pine Run Community 777 Ferry Rd *TF:* 800-992-8992 ■ *Web:* www.pinerun.org	Doylestown	PA	18901	215-345-9000		672
Pine State Trading Co 100 Enterprise Ave *TF:* 800-452-4633 ■ *Web:* www.pinestatetrading.com	Gardiner	ME	04345	800-452-4633		81-1
Pine Street Animal Hospital LLC 980 S Pine St *Web:* pinestreetanimalhospital.com	Spartanburg	SC	29302	864-585-0231		794
Pine Technical & Community College 900 4th St SE *TF:* 800-521-7463 ■ *Web:* www.pine.edu	Pine City	MN	55063	320-629-5100	629-5101	162
Pine Telephone System Inc 104 Center St PO Box 706 *Web:* www.pinetel.com	Halfway	OR	97834	541-742-2201		116
Pine to Prairie Broadcasting 2524 S Washington St Ste 1 *Web:* www.yourqfm.com	Grand Forks	ND	58201	701-757-4120		645-141
Pine Tree Equity Management LP 777 Brickell Ave Ste 1070 *Web:* www.pinetreeequity.com	Miami	FL	33131	305-808-9820		41
Pine Tree Furniture & Lighting Inc 1405 S Lapeer Rd *Web:* pinetreelighting.com	Lake Orion	MI	48360	248-693-6248		362
Pine Tree Lumber Co 707 N Andreasen Dr *Web:* pinetreelumber.com	Escondido	CA	92029	760-745-0411		364

Name / Address	City	State	ZIP	Phone	Fax	Class
Pineapple Hospitality Co 155 108th Ave NE *TF:* 866-866-7977 ■ *Web:* www.staypineapple.com	Bellevue	WA	98004	866-866-7977		707
Pinecrest Gardens 11000 Red Rd *Web:* www.pinecrest-fl.gov	Pinecrest	FL	33156	305-669-6990	669-6944	97
Pinehurst LLC 80 Carolina Vista *TF:* 855-235-8507 ■ *Web:* www.pinehurst.com	Pinehurst	NC	28374	855-235-8507		669
Pinehurst Southern Pines Aberdeen Area 165 NE Broad St *TF:* 800-346-5362 ■ *Web:* homeofgolf.com	Southern Pines	NC	28387	910-692-6926	692-2493	206
Pineland Telephone Cooperative Inc 30 S Rountree St *TF:* 800-247-1266 ■ *Web:* pineland.net	Metter	GA	30439	912-685-2121		387
Pinelands National Reserve 15 Springfield Rd *Web:* www.nps.gov	New Lisbon	NJ	08064	609-894-7300		564
Pinelands Regional School District 520 Nugentown Rd *Web:* www.pinelandsregional.org	Little Egg Harbor Township	NJ	08087	609-296-3106		685
Pinellas County Heritage Village 11909 125th St N *Web:* www.pinellascounty.org	Largo	FL	33774	727-582-2123		520
Pinellas Park Mid-County Chamber of Commerce 5851 Pk Blvd *Web:* www.pinellasparkchamber.com	Pinellas Park	FL	33781	727-544-4777	209-0837	139
Pinellas Technical Education Centers 6100 154th Ave N *Web:* www.pcsb.org	Clearwater	FL	33760	727-538-7167	538-7203	167-3
Pineloch Management Corp 102 W Pineloch Ave Ste 10 *Web:* www.pineloch.com	Orlando	FL	32806	407-859-3550	650-0303	653
Pinemoor, The 1101 N Highland St *Web:* www.thepinemoor.com	Arlington	VA	22201	571-970-2592		671
Pineries Bank, The 3601 Main St *Web:* www.pineries.com	Stevens Point	WI	54481	715-341-5600		70
Pines at Davidson 400 Avinger Ln *TF:* 877-574-8203 ■ *Web:* www.thepinesatdavidson.org	Davidson	NC	28036	704-896-1100		672
Pines Bach 122 W Washington Ave Ste 900 *TF:* 866-443-8661 ■ *Web:* www.pinesbach.com	Madison	WI	53703	608-807-0752		428
Pines Lodge 141 Scott Hill Rd *TF:* 855-395-7625 ■ *Web:* pineslodge.rockresorts.com	Beaver Creek	CO	81620	970-429-5043	754-7295	379
Pines of Sarasota Inc 1501 N Orange Ave *Web:* www.pinesofsarasota.org	Sarasota	FL	34236	941-365-0250		371
Pines One Publications 3870 Crenshaw Blvd Ste 3911 *Web:* aalbc.com	Los Angeles	CA	90008	213-290-1182	295-3880	637-10
Pines Resort, The 103 Shore Rd *TF:* 800-667-4637 ■ *Web:* www.digbypines.ca	Digby	NS	B0V1A0	800-667-4637		669
Pinestar Technology Inc 1000 E Jamestown Rd *TF:* 800-682-2226 ■ *Web:* www.pinestar.com	Jamestown	PA	16134	724-932-2121	932-3176	809
Pinestone Resort 4252 County Rd Ste 21 *TF:* 800-461-0357 ■ *Web:* www.pinestone-resort.com	Haliburton	ON	K0M1S0	705-457-1800	457-1783	669
Pinetree Group Inc 548 W 28th St Ste 645 *Web:* www.pinetreegroup.com	New York	NY	10001	212-279-5600		655
Pineville Beauty School 1008 Main St *Web:* www.pinevillebeauty.com	Pineville	LA	71360	318-445-1040	448-6090	685
Pineville Community Hospital 850 Riverview Ave	Pineville	KY	40977	606-337-3051	337-4284	374-3
Pinewood Preparatory School 1114 Orangeburg Rd *Web:* www.pinewoodprep.com	Summerville	SC	29483	843-873-1643	821-4257	685
Piney Creek Ravine 2280 Piney Creek Rd *Web:* www2.illinois.gov	Chester	IL	62233	618-826-2706		565
Piney Mountain Press Inc PO Box 986 *TF:* 800-255-3127 ■ *Web:* www.pineymountain.com	Dahlonega	GA	30533	800-255-3127	905-3127	637-10
Piney Woods School, The 5096 Hwy 49 S *Web:* www.pineywoods.org	Piney Woods	MS	39148	601-845-2214	845-2604	622
Ping Inc 2201 W Desert Cove Ave PO Box 82000 *TF:* 800-474-6434 ■ *Web:* ping.com	Phoenix	AZ	85071	602-687-5000		710
Ping's Cafe *J n J's Asian Restaurant* 34 Baltimore St *Web:* www.gettysburgpings.com	Gettysburg	PA	17325	717-334-2234		671
Pinger Inc 97 S Second St Ste 210 *Web:* www.pinger.com	San Jose	CA	95113	408-271-5700		224
Pingree Chellie (Rep D - ME) 2162 Rayburn House Office Bldg *TF:* 888-862-6500 ■ *Web:* pingree.house.gov	Washington	DC	20515	202-225-6116	225-5590	342-2
Pingree School 537 Highland St *Web:* www.pingree.org	South Hamilton	MA	01982	978-468-4415		148
Pink Door, The 1919 Post Alley *Web:* www.thepinkdoor.net	Seattle	WA	98101	206-443-3241		671
Pink Gorilla Pizzeria 7018-109th St NW *TF:* 855-822-6854 ■ *Web:* www.pinkgorillapizzeria.com	Edmonton	AB	T6H3C1	780-660-0060		671
Pink Palace Museum 3050 Central Ave *Web:* www.memphismuseums.org	Memphis	TN	38111	901-636-2362		520
Pink Pearl Chinese Seafood 1132 E Hastings St *Web:* www.pinkpearl.com	Vancouver	BC	V6A1S2	604-253-4316		671
Pinkard Construction Co 9195 W Sixth Ave *Web:* www.pinkardcc.com	Lakewood	CO	80215	303-986-4555	985-5050	186
Pinkerton & Laws Inc 1165 N Chase Pkwy Ste 100 *Web:* pinkerton-laws.com	Marietta	GA	30067	770-956-9000	618-8688	186
Pinkie's Inc 1426 E Eigth St *Web:* www.pinkiestexas.com	Odessa	TX	79761	432-580-0439	580-0918	443
Pinkpalacefilm 1160 King George Hwy *TF:* 800-667-2248 ■ *Web:* www.pinkpalacefilm.com	Surrey	BC	V4A4Z2	604-535-1432	531-6979	379
Pinnacle Actuarial Resources Inc 3109 Cornelius Dr *Web:* www.pinnacleactuaries.com	Bloomington	IL	61704	309-807-2300	807-2301	194
Pinnacle Advertising & Marketing 1435 N Plum Grove Rd Ste C *Web:* pinnacleadvertising.com	Schaumburg	IL	60173	847-255-0000		7
Pinnacle Bancshares Inc 1811 2nd Ave *OTC:* PCLB ■ *Web:* www.pinnaclebanc.com	Jasper	AL	35501	205-221-4111	221-8860	360-2
Pinnacle Bank 18181 Butterfield Blvd Ste 135 *Web:* pinnaclebankonline.com	Morgan Hill	CA	95037	408-762-7171	762-2462	70
Pinnacle Brokers Insurance Solutions Inc 1330 N Broadway Ste 204 *Web:* pinnbrokers.com	Walnut Creek	CA	94596	925-952-8680		390
Pinnacle Business Finance Inc 5407 12th St E Ste A **Fax Area Code:* 800 ■ *TF:* 800-566-1993 ■ *Web:* www.pinnaclecap.com	Tacoma	WA	98402	253-284-5600	821-5903*	216
Pinnacle Business Systems Inc 3824 S Blvd St Ste 200 *TF:* 800-311-0757 ■ *Web:* www.pbsnow.com	Edmond	OK	73013	800-311-0757	444-3439	225
Pinnacle Career Institute 10301 Hickman Mills Dr *TF:* 877-241-3097 ■ *Web:* www.pcitraining.edu	Kansas City	MO	64137	816-331-5700		167-3
Pinnacle Communications PO Box 230 *Web:* www.pinncom.com	Lavaca	AR	72941	479-674-2211		224
Pinnacle Communications Corp 19821 Executive Park Cir *TF:* 800-644-9101 ■ *Web:* www.pinnaclecommunications.com	Germantown	MD	20874	301-601-0777		387
Pinnacle Converting Equipment 1720 Toal St *Web:* pinnacleconverting.com	Charlotte	NC	28206	704-376-3855		455
Pinnacle Corp, The 201A E Abram St *Web:* www.pinncorp.com	Arlington	TX	76010	817-795-5555		179
Pinnacle Engineering Inc 7660 Woodway Dr Ste 350 *Web:* www.pinnacleengr.com	Houston	TX	77063	713-784-1005		261
Pinnacle Exhibits Inc 22400 NW Westmark Dr *Web:* www.pinnacle-exhibits.com	Hillsboro	OR	97124	503-844-4848		7
Pinnacle Foods Corp 399 Jefferson Rd *Web:* www.pinnaclefoodscorp.com	Parsippany	NJ	07054	973-541-6620		296-39
Pinnacle Frames & Accents Inc 12303 Technology Blvd Ste 950 **Fax Area Code:* 512 ■ *TF:* 888-846-6847 ■ *Web:* www.nielsenbainbridgegroup.com	Austin	TX	78727	888-846-6847	506-3933*	361
Pinnacle Group Intl c/o CT Corporation System 111 Eighth Ave *Web:* www.pinnaclegroup.com	New York	NY	10011	480-994-6173		260
Pinnacle Hotels USA Inc 8369 Vickers St Ste 101 *Web:* pinnaclehotelsusa.com	San Diego	CA	92111	858-974-8201	974-8203	463
Pinnacle Management Systems Inc 2140 East Southlake Blvd Ste L-803 **Fax Area Code:* 888 ■ *TF:* 888-975-1119 ■ *Web:* www.pinnaclemanagement.com	Southlake	TX	76092	703-382-9161	975-9991*	194
Pinnacle Motor Club 800 Point Vista Rd *Web:* viewpinnacle.com	Hickory Creek	TX	75065	940-321-8105		53
Pinnacle Mountain State Park 11901 Pinnacle Valley Rd *Web:* www.arkansasstateparks.com	Little Rock	AR	72223	501-868-5806	868-5018	565
Pinnacle Peak Lending 8655 E Via De Ventura Ste G151 *Web:* pinnaclepeaklending.com	Scottsdale	AZ	85258	480-538-5333		70
Pinnacle Performance Improvement Worldwide (PPIW) 101 Main St *Web:* ppiw.com	Pepperell	MA	01463	978-433-2040	925-9798	194
Pinnacle Plastic Products 513 Napoleon Rd *Web:* pinnacleplasticproducts.com	Bowling Green	OH	43402	419-352-8688	354-4164	608
Pinnacle Precision Sheet Metal Corp 5410 E La Palma Ave *Web:* www.pinnacleprecisionsheetmetal.com	Anaheim	CA	92807	714-777-3129		483
Pinnacle Precision Technologies LLC 2607 Eaton Ln *Web:* pinnacleprecisiontech.com	Racine	WI	53404	262-632-2232		483
Pinnacle Rock State Park 6407 Coal Heritage Rd *Web:* wvstateparks.com	Bluefield	WV	24701	304-248-8565		565
Pinnacle Sports LLC 313 Medina Rd *Web:* pinnaclesports.org	Medina	OH	44256	330-239-0616		713
Pinnacle Staffing Inc PO Box 17589 **Fax Area Code:* 864 ■ *TF:* 888-297-4212 ■ *Web:* www.pinnaclestaffing.com	Greenville	SC	29606	888-297-4212	987-7351*	721
Pinnacle State Park 1904 Pinnacle Rd *Web:* parks.ny.gov	Addison	NY	14801	607-359-2767		565
Pinnacle Technical Resources Inc 5501 Lyndon B Johnson Fwy *Web:* www.pinnacle1.com	Dallas	TX	75240	214-740-2424		180
Pinnacle Trust Partners LLC 540 Hopmeadow St *Web:* www.pinnacletrustpartners.com	Simsbury	CT	06070	860-264-1595		70
Pinnacle Wealth & Benefits Strategies Inc 51 Haddonfield Rd **Fax Area Code:* 856 ■ *TF:* 888-528-2987 ■ *Web:* pinnaclewealthinc.com	Cherry Hill	NJ	08002	888-528-2987	348-0258*	390
Pinnacle West Capital Corp 400 N Fifth St *NYSE:* PNW ■ *TF:* 800-457-2983 ■ *Web:* www.pinnaclewest.com	Phoenix	AZ	85004	602-250-1000		360-5
PinnacleART 1 Pinnacle Way *Web:* pinnacleart.com	Pasadena	TX	77504	281-598-1330		256
PinnacleCart Inc 3320 W Cheryl Dr Ste B200 *TF:* 800-506-0398 ■ *Web:* www.pinnaclecart.com	Phoenix	AZ	85051	800-506-0398		225
Pinnacles National Monument 5000 Hwy 146 *Web:* www.nps.gov	Paicines	CA	95043	831-389-4485		564
Pinnacol Assurance 7501 E Lowry Blvd *TF:* 800-873-7242 ■ *Web:* www.pinnacol.com	Denver	CO	80230	303-361-4000	361-5000	391-4
Pinner Construction Company Inc 1255 S Lewis St *Web:* www.pinnerconstruction.com	Anaheim	CA	92805	714-490-4000		186

Name / Address	City	State	ZIP	Phone	Fax	Class
Pinnergy Ltd 111 Congress Ave Ste 2020 *Web:* www.pinnergy.com	Austin	TX	78701	512-343-8880	343-8885	539
Pinney Associates Inc 4800 Montgomery Ln Ste 400 *Web:* www.pinneyassociates.com	Bethesda	MD	20814	301-718-8440		194
PinnPack 1151 Pacific Ave. *Web:* www.pinnpack.com	Oxnard	CA	93033	805-385-4100	385-4880	596
Pino's Salon & Spa 70 Victoria St N *Web:* www.pinosalon.com	Kitchener	ON	N2H5C2	519-578-8898		77
Pinole Valley Trucking Inc 202 S Rochester *TF:* 800-878-9993 ■ *Web:* www.pvtservices.com	Ontario	CA	91761	909-390-6161	390-5161	780
Pinon Family Practice 2300 E 30th St Bldg C2 *Web:* www.pinonfp.com	Farmington	NM	87401	505-324-1000		416
Pinons 105 S Mill St *Web:* www.pinons.net	Aspen	CO	81611	970-920-2021		671
Pinpoint Data 339 Somerset St *Web:* www.couponchek.com	North Plainfield	NJ	07060	908-756-9400		225
Pinpoint Technologies 17802 Irvine Blvd Ste 215 *TF:* 866-603-7770 ■ *Web:* www.pinpoint-tech.com	Tustin	CA	92780	714-505-7600		463
Pinsly Railroad Company Inc 94 N Elm St Ste 404 *Web:* www.pinsly.com	Westfield	MA	01085	413-568-6426		649
Pinson Mounds State Archaeological Park 460 Ozier Rd *Web:* www.state.tn.us	Pinson	TN	38366	731-988-5614		565
Pinto Horse Association of America 7330 NW 23rd St *Web:* www.pinto.org	Bethany	OK	73008	405-491-0111		48-3
Pinto Mucenski Hooper VanHouse & Company CPA PC 42 Market St *Web:* www.pmhvcpa.com	Potsdam	NY	13676	315-265-6080	393-9231	2
Pintoresco Advisors LLC 466 Foothill Blvd Ste 333 *TF:* 866-217-1140 ■ *Web:* www.pintorescoadvisors.com	La Canada Flintridge	CA	91011	213-223-2070		70
Pinyon Environmental Inc 3222 S Vance St Unit 200 *TF:* 888-641-7337 ■ *Web:* pinyon-env.net	Lakewood	CO	80227	303-980-5200	980-0089	463
Piolax Corp 139 Etowah Industrial Ct. *Web:* www.piolaxusa.com	Canton	GA	30114	770-479-2227	479-2399	608
Pioneer Air Systems Inc 210 Flatfork Rd *Web:* www.pioneerair.com	Wartburg	TN	37887	423-346-6693		14
Pioneer Arizona Living History Museum 3901 W Pioneer Rd *Web:* pioneeraz.org	Phoenix	AZ	85086	623-465-1052		520
Pioneer Automotive Industries 5184 Pioneer Rd *Web:* www.pioneerautoinc.com	Meridian	MS	39301	601-483-5211		61
Pioneer Bank 21 Second St *TF:* 866-873-9573 ■ *Web:* www.pioneerbanking.com	Troy	NY	12180	518-274-4800		71
Pioneer Broach Co 6434 Telegraph Rd *TF:* 800-621-1945 ■ *Web:* www.pioneerbroach.com	Los Angeles	CA	90040	323-728-1263	722-1699	455
Pioneer Circuits Inc (PCI) 3000 S Shannon St. *Web:* www.pioneercircuits.com	Santa Ana	CA	92704	714-641-3132		625
Pioneer Clubs 123 E Elk *TF:* 800-694-2582 ■ *Web:* www.pioneerclubs.org	Carol Stream	IL	60188	800-694-2582		148
Pioneer Construction Company Inc 550 Kirtland St SW *TF:* 800-861-0874 ■ *Web:* www.pioneerinc.com	Grand Rapids	MI	49507	616-247-6966	247-0186	186
Pioneer Contract Services Inc 8090 Kempwood Dr *Web:* pioneercontract.com	Houston	TX	77055	713-464-8200	464-7100	186
Pioneer Credit Co 1870 Executive Pk NW *Web:* www.pioneercredit.net	Cleveland	TN	37311	423-479-9615		216
Pioneer Credit Recovery Inc 26 Edward St *TF:* 800-836-2442 ■ *Web:* www.pioneercreditrecovery.com	Arcade	NY	14009	585-492-1234		160
Pioneer Electric Co-op 300 Herbert St *TF:* 800-239-3092 ■ *Web:* www.pioneerelectric.com	Greenville	AL	36037	334-382-6636		245
Pioneer Electric Co-op 344 W US Rt 36 *TF:* 800-762-0997 ■ *Web:* www.pioneerec.com	Piqua	OH	45356	937-773-2523		245
Pioneer Electronics (USA) Inc 1925 E Dominguez St *TF:* 800-421-1404 ■ *Web:* www.pioneerelectronics.com	Long Beach	CA	90810	800-421-1404		52
Pioneer Equipment Co 2545 S Sarah St *Web:* www.pioneerequipmentca.com	Fresno	CA	93706	559-486-7580	486-7587	274
Pioneer Equipment Inc 3738 E Miami Ave. *TF:* 800-523-9998 ■ *Web:* pioneerequip.com	Phoenix	AZ	85040	602-437-4312	437-0174	385
Pioneer Exploration LLC 15603 Kuykendahl Ste 200 **Fax Area Code:* 832 ■ *Web:* www.pecogas.com	Houston	TX	77090	281-893-9400	249-1270*	536
Pioneer Frozen Foods Inc 627 Big Stone Gap *Web:* www.chguenther.com	Duncanville	TX	75137	972-298-4281		68
Pioneer Golf Inc 609 Castle Ridge Rd Ste 335 *TF:* 800-262-5725 ■ *Web:* www.pioneergolf.com	Austin	TX	78746	512-327-2680	327-8120	760
Pioneer Hi-Bred International Inc PO Box 1000 *TF:* 800-247-6803 ■ *Web:* www.pioneer.com	Johnston	IA	50131	515-535-3200		10-5
Pioneer Industries Inc 111 Kero Rd *Web:* www.pioneerindustries.com	Carlstadt	NJ	07072	201-933-1900	933-9580	234
Pioneer Library System 300 Norman Center Ct *Web:* pioneerlibrarysystem.org	Norman	OK	73072	405-801-4500	701-2608	434-3
Pioneer Long Distance Inc PO Box 539 *TF:* 888-782-2667 ■ *Web:* gopioneer.com	Kingfisher	OK	73750	888-782-2667		736
Pioneer Manufacturing Inc 740 Beechcroft Rd *Web:* www.pioneerleveler.com	Spring Hill	TN	37174	931-486-2296		757
Pioneer Metal Finishing LLC 486 Globe Ave **Fax Area Code:* 920 ■ *TF:* 877-721-1100 ■ *Web:* www.pioneermetal.com	Green Bay	WI	54304	877-721-1100	884-1790*	481
Pioneer Millworks 1180 Commercial Dr *Web:* pioneermillworks.com	Farmington	NY	14425	585-924-9970		752
Pioneer National Bank of Duluth 331 NoCentral Ave *Web:* parkstatebank.com	Duluth	MN	55807	218-624-3676		70
Pioneer Natural Resources Co 5205 N O'Connor Blvd Ste 200. *NYSE:* PXD ■ *TF:* 888-234-6372 ■ *Web:* www.pxd.com	Irving	TX	75039	972-444-9001		536
Pioneer Oil & Gas 1206 W S Jordan Pkwy Unit B *Web:* www.piol.com	South Jordan	UT	84095	801-566-3000		536
Pioneer Oil LLC 1728 Lampman Dr Ste A *Web:* www.pioneeroil-co.com	Billings	MT	59102	406-254-7071	254-2560	579
Pioneer Pacific College 27375 SW Pkwy Ave. *TF:* 866-772-4636 ■ *Web:* www.pioneerpacific.edu	Wilsonville	OR	97070	503-682-3903		166
Pioneer Paper Stock 155 Irving Ave N *TF:* 800-821-8512 ■ *Web:* www.pioneerintl.com	Minneapolis	MN	55405	612-374-2280	374-5982	660
Pioneer Petrotech Services Inc 1431-40 Ave NE Ste 1 *TF:* 888-774-2843 ■ *Web:* www.pioneerps.com	Calgary	AB	T2E8N6	403-282-7669		536
Pioneer Photo Albums Inc 9801 Deering Ave *Web:* www.pioneerphotoalbums.com	Chatsworth	CA	91311	818-882-2161	882-6239	86
Pioneer Pipe Inc 2021 Hanna Rd *Web:* www.pioneerpipeinc.com	Marietta	OH	45750	740-376-2400	373-8964	595
Pioneer Production Services Inc 10628 Hwy 1 *Web:* pioneerprod.net	Lockport	LA	70374	985-532-2577	532-2580	192
Pioneer Products Inc 1917 S Memorial Dr *Web:* pioneerproducts.com	Racine	WI	53403	262-633-6304		454
Pioneer Railcorp 1318 S Johanson Rd. *OTC:* PRRR ■ *Web:* www.pioneer-railcorp.com	Peoria	IL	61607	309-697-1400	697-5387	648
Pioneer Security Life Insurance Co 425 Austin Ave **Fax Area Code:* 254 ■ *TF:* 800-736-7311 ■ *Web:* www.pioneersecuritylife.com	Waco	TX	76701	800-736-7311	297-2105*	796
Pioneer Square 1221 2nd Ave 320 *Web:* www.pioneersquare.org	Seattle	WA	98104	206-667-0687		50-6
Pioneer Steel Corp 7447 Intervale St *TF:* 800-999-9440 ■ *Web:* www.pioneersteel.us	Detroit	MI	48238	313-933-9400		492
Pioneer Super Market 289 Columbus Ave *Web:* www.pioneersupermarkets.com	New York	NY	10023	212-874-9506		345
Pioneer Technology Ctr 2101 N Ash. *TF:* 866-612-4782 ■ *Web:* www.pioneertech.edu	Ponca City	OK	74601	580-762-8336		167-3
Pioneer Telephone Association Inc PO Box 707 *TF:* 800-308-7536 ■ *Web:* www.pioncomm.net	Ulysses	KS	67880	620-356-3211	356-3242	736
Pioneer Tool & Forge Inc 101 Sixth St *TF:* 800-359-6408 ■ *Web:* www.breakersteel.com	New Kensington	PA	15068	724-337-4700	337-4707	759
Pioneer Transfer LLC 2034 S St Aubin St PO Box 2567 *TF:* 800-325-4650 ■ *Web:* www.pioneertransfer.com	Sioux City	IA	51106	712-274-2946		311
Pioneer Transportation Corp 2890 Arthur Kill Rd. *Web:* pioneerbus.com	Staten Island	NY	10309	718-984-8077	984-6588	109
Pioneer Wholesale Co 500 W Bagley Rd. *TF:* 800-234-5400 ■ *Web:* www.pioneerwholesaleco.com	Berea	OH	44017	440-234-5400	234-5403	44
Pioneer/Eclipse Corp 1 Eclipse Rd *TF:* 800-367-3550 ■ *Web:* www.pioneereclipse.com	Sparta	NC	28675	336-372-8080	372-2895	386
Pioneerland Library System 410 SW Fifth St *Web:* www.pioneerland.lib.mn.us	Willmar	MN	56201	320-235-6106	214-0187	434-3
Pioneers 10123 William Carey Dr *TF:* 800-755-7284 ■ *Web:* www.pioneers.org	Orlando	FL	32832	407-382-6000		48-20
Pioneers Medical Ctr 100 Pioneers Medical Center Dr. *TF:* 800-332-1168 ■ *Web:* pioneershospital.org	Meeker	CO	81641	970-878-5047		363
Pioneers Memorial Healthcare District (PMHD) 207 W Legion Rd *Web:* www.pmhd.org	Brawley	CA	92227	760-351-3333		374-3
Pioneers Volunteer 1801 California St Ste 225 *TF:* 800-872-5995 ■ *Web:* www.pioneersvolunteer.org	Denver	CO	80202	303-571-1200	572-0520	48-15
Piotte Enterprises Inc 179 Great Rd Ste 210 *Web:* cfwms.com	Acton	MA	01720	978-266-1930		734
PIP Printing & Document Services Inc 26722 Plaza Dr. *Web:* www.pip.com	Mission Viejo	CA	92691	949-348-5000	348-5066	310
Pipco Companies Ltd, The 1409 W Altorfer Dr *Web:* www.pipco-co.com	Peoria	IL	61615	309-692-4060		189-10
Pipco Transportation Inc PO Box 515 *TF:* 800-524-2702 ■ *Web:* www.pipcotrans.com	Rosenhayn	NJ	08352	856-378-7000	451-9146	780
Pipe & Tube Supply Inc 1407 N Cypress *TF:* 800-770-8823 ■ *Web:* www.pipeandtubesupply.com	North Little Rock	AR	72114	501-372-6556	372-7694	386
Pipe Fabricating & Supply Co 1235 N Kraemer Blvd *Web:* www.pipefab.com	Anaheim	CA	92806	714-630-5200		490
Pipe Spring National Monument 406 N Pipe Spring Rd HC 65 PO Box 5 *Web:* www.nps.gov	Fredonia	AZ	86022	928-643-7105	643-7583	564
Pipe Valves Inc 1200 E Fifth Ave *Web:* www.pipevalves.com	Columbus	OH	43219	614-294-4971		358
Pipe Welders Inc 2965 W State Rd 84 *Web:* www.pipewelders.com	Fort Lauderdale	FL	33312	954-587-8400	587-3007	480

				Phone	Fax	Class
Pipefy 10 Jackson St.	San Francisco	CA	94111	617-832-3057		657
Web: www.pipefy.com						
Pipelife Jet Stream Inc						
1700 S Lincoln St.	Siloam Springs	AR	72761	479-524-5151	524-3516	596
Web: www.pipelife.com						
Pipeline & Hazardous Materials Safety Administration (PHMSA)						
1200 New Jersey Ave SE E Bldg Second Fl	Washington	DC	20590	202-366-4433	366-3666	340-17
Web: www.phmsa.dot.gov						
Southern Region						
233 Peachtree St NE Ste 602	Atlanta	GA	30303	404-832-1140	832-1168	340-17
Web: www.phmsa.dot.gov						
Pipeline & Hazardous Materials Safety Administration Regional Offices (PHMSA)						
Central Region (Pipeline)						
901 Locust St Rm 462	Kansas City	MO	64106	816-329-3800	329-3831	340-17
Web: www.phmsa.dot.gov						
Eastern Region (Pipeline)						
840 Bear Tavern Rd Ste 300	West Trenton	NJ	08628	609-989-2256	882-1209	340-17
Web: www.phmsa.dot.gov						
Southwest Region Office						
8701 S Gessner Rd Ste 900	Houston	TX	77074	713-272-2820	272-2821	340-17
Web: www.phmsa.dot.gov						
Pipeline Development Co, The						
870 Canterbury Rd	Westlake	OH	44145	440-871-5700	871-9577	595
Web: plidco.com						
Pipeline Industry Benefit Fund						
4845 S 83rd E Ave	Tulsa	OK	74145	918-280-4800		414
Web: www.pibf.org						
Piper Products Inc 300 S 84th Ave	Wausau	WI	54401	715-842-2724	842-3125	298
TF: 800-544-3057 ■ *Web:* www.piperonline.net						
Piper Sandler						
800 Nicollet Mall Ste 1000	Minneapolis	MN	55402	800-333-6000		690
NYSE: PJC ■ *TF:* 800-333-6000 ■ *Web:* www.pipersandler.com						
Piper Weatherford Co 10755 Rockwall Rd	Dallas	TX	75238	214-343-9000		351
Web: www.piperweatherford.com						
Piperade 1015 Battery St	San Francisco	CA	94111	415-391-2555	391-1159	671
Web: www.piperade.com						
Pipestem Resort State Park						
PO Box 150	Pipestem	WV	25979	304-466-1800		565
Web: wvstateparks.com						
Pipestone County Historical Society						
113 S Hiawatha Ave	Pipestone	MN	56164	507-825-2563		49-19
TF: 866-747-3687 ■ *Web:* www.pipestoneminnesota.com						
Pipestone Livestock Auction Market						
1500 Seventh St SE	Pipestone	MN	56164	507-825-3306		446
Web: pipestonelivestock.com						
Pipestone Publishing Co PO Box 277	Pipestone	MN	56164	507-825-3333	825-2168	637-8
TF: 800-325-6440 ■ *Web:* www.pipestonestar.com						
Pipestone Veterinary Clinic LLC						
1300 Hwy 75 S PO Box 188	Pipestone	MN	56164	507-825-4211		794
TF: 800-658-2523 ■ *Web:* pipevet.com						
Piping Resources Inc 4502 F St	Omaha	NE	68117	402-738-8100		358
Web: www.pipingresources.com						
Piping Systems Engineering (PSE)						
1905 S Lindsay Rd	Mesa	AZ	85201	480-345-0052		261
Web: piping-systems.com						
Piping Technology & Products Inc						
3701 Holmes Rd PO Box 34506	Houston	TX	77051	713-731-0030	731-8640	595
TF: 866-746-9172 ■ *Web:* pipingtech.com						
Pipitone Group						
3933 Perrysville Ave	Pittsburgh	PA	15214	412-321-0879	321-2217	194
Web: www.pipitonegroup.com						
Pipka's of Door County						
2340 Mill Rd	Sister Bay	WI	54234	920-854-4392		327
Web: pipkas.com						
Pipkins Inc						
14515 N Outer 40 Rd Ste 130	Chesterfield	MO	63017	314-469-6106	222-2459	177
TF: 800-469-6106 ■ *Web:* www.pipkins.com						
Pippin Law Firm PC 111 E Broadway	Williston	ND	58801	701-572-5544		41
Web: pippinlawfirm.com						
Piqua Manor 1840 W High St	Piqua	OH	45356	937-773-0040	773-4836	371
Web: piquamanor.com						
Piqua State Bank 1356 Xylan Rd	Piqua	KS	66761	620-468-2555		70
Web: www.piquastatebank.com						
Piqua Transfer and Storage Co						
9782 Looney Rd	Piqua	OH	45356	937-773-3743		519
TF: 800-278-0617 ■ *Web:* www.piquatransfer.com						
Piranha Killer Sushi						
7100 Blvd 26 Ste 208	Richland Hills	TX	76180	682-626-5953	626-5954	671
Web: www.piranhakillersushi.com						
Piranha Marketing Inc						
4440 S Rural Rd Bldg F	Tempe	AZ	85282	480-858-0008		195
TF: 800-275-2643 ■ *Web:* joepolish.com						
Pirate's Cove 109 Gainsborough Sq	Chesapeake	VA	23320	757-549-7272		671
Web: www.piratescoveva.com						
Pirates' House 20 E Broad St	Savannah	GA	31401	912-233-5757		671
Web: www.thepirateshouse.com						
PIREL Inc 1315 Rue Gay-Lussac	Boucherville	QC	J4B7K1	450-449-5199	449-7196	180
TF: 800-449-5199 ■ *Web:* www.pirel.com						
PIRG (Georgia Public Interest Research Group)						
108 E Ponce de Leon Ave Ste 210	Decatur	GA	30030	404-370-1762		633
Web: www.georgiapirg.org						
Piscataquis County						
Economic Development Council						
214 Foxcroft Center Rd	Dover-Foxcroft	ME	04426	207-564-3638		338
Web: www.pcedc.org						
Piscataway Park						
National Park Service						
13551 Ft Washington Rd	Fort Washington	MD	20744	301-763-4600		564
Web: www.nps.gov						
Pisces 1007 Simonton St	Key West	FL	33040	305-294-7100		671
Web: www.pisceskeywest.com						
Pisces Fish Machinery Inc PO Box 189	Wells	MI	49894	906-789-1636	789-1211	298
Web: pisces-ind.com						
Pisgah Inn PO Box 749	Waynesville	NC	28786	828-235-8228		379
Web: www.pisgahinn.com						
Pismo Coast Village RV Resort						
165 S Dolliver St	Pismo Beach	CA	93449	805-755-5406	773-1507	669
TF: 888-782-3224 ■ *Web:* pismocoastvillage.com						
PIT (Pennsylvania Institute of Technology)						
800 Manchester Ave	Media	PA	19063	610-892-1500	892-1533	800
TF: 800-422-0025 ■ *Web:* www.pit.edu						
Pita Jungle 4 E University Dr	Tempe	AZ	85281	480-804-0234		671
Web: www.pitajungle.com						
Pitango Venture Capital						
540 Cowper St Ste 200	Palo Alto	CA	94301	650-322-2201	473-1347	792
Web: www.pitango.com						
Pitcairn Properties Inc						
165 Township Line Rd	Jenkintown	PA	19046	215-690-3000		653
Web: www.pitcairnproperties.com						
Pitch 8825 National Blvd	Culver City	CA	90232	424-603-6000		5
Web: www.thepitchagency.com						
Pitch, The 1701 Main St	Kansas City	MO	64108	816-561-6061	756-0502	532-5
Web: www.pitch.com						
Pitcher Inn 275 Main St	Warren	VT	05674	802-496-6350		379
Web: www.pitcherinn.com						
Pitco Frialator Inc PO Box 501	Concord	NH	03302	603-225-6684		298
Web: pitco.com						
Pitkin County 530 E Main St Ste 101	Aspen	CO	81611	970-920-5200	920-5230	338
Web: www.pitkincounty.com						
Pitman Animal Hospital 654 N Delsea Dr	Pitman	NJ	08071	856-582-7500		794
Web: pitmananimalhospital.com						
Pitmar Tours 7549 140th St Ste 9	Surrey	BC	V3W5J9	604-596-9670	596-3444	760
TF: 877-596-9670 ■ *Web:* www.pitmartours.com						
Pitney Bowes Group 1 Software						
4200 Parliament Pl Ste 600	Lanham	MD	20706	800-368-5806		178-1
TF: 800-367-6950 ■ *Web:* www.pbinsight.com						
Pitney Bowes inc 3001 Summer St	Stamford	CT	06926	203-356-5000		463
TF: 844-256-6444 ■ *Web:* www.pitneybowes.com						
Pitot House Museum 1440 Moss St	New Orleans	LA	70119	504-482-0312		520
Web: www.pitothouse.org						
Pitt Community College						
1986 Pitt Tech Rd PO Box 7007	Winterville	NC	28590	252-493-7200	321-4401	162
Web: pittcc.edu						
Pitt County 1717 W 5th St	Greenville	NC	27834	252-902-1000		338
Web: www.pittcountync.gov						
Pitt Grill Inc						
3048 Gertsner Memorial Dr	Lake Charles	LA	70601	337-478-2925		670
Web: pittgrill.com						
Pitt Ohio Express 15 27th St	Pittsburgh	PA	15222	412-232-3015	232-0944	780
TF: 800-366-7488 ■ *Web:* www.works.pittohio.com						
Pitt Plastics Inc 1400 Atkinson Ave	Pittsburg	KS	66762	800-835-0366	314-8449	66
TF: 800-835-0366 ■ *Web:* www.pittplastics.com						
Pittcon						
300 Penn Center Blvd Ste 332	Pittsburgh	PA	15235	412-825-3220		184
TF: 800-825-3221 ■ *Web:* pittcon.org						
Pittenger & Anderson Inc						
5533 S 27th St Ste 201	Lincoln	NE	68512	402-328-8800		401
TF: 800-897-1588 ■ *Web:* pittand.com						
Pittleman & Assoc 336 E 43rd St	New York	NY	10017	212-370-9600	370-9608	266
Web: www.pittlemanassociates.com						
Pittman Dental Laboratory						
2355 Centennial Cir	Gainesville	GA	30504	770-534-4457		415
TF: 800-235-4720 ■ *Web:* www.pittmandental.com						
Pittman McLenagan Group LC, The (PMGLC)						
6626 Wilson Ln	Bethesda	MD	20817	855-512-9430		194
TF: 855-512-9430 ■ *Web:* www.pmglc.com						
Pitts Enterprises Inc 5734 Hwy 431	Pittsview	AL	36871	334-855-4754		779
Web: pittstrailers.com						
Pitts Toyota 210 N Jeffreson St	Dublin	GA	31021	478-272-3244		57
Web: www.pittstoyota.com						
Pittsburg Area Chamber of Commerce						
117 W Fourth St	Pittsburg	KS	66762	620-231-1000	231-3178	139
Web: pittsburgareachamber.com						
Pittsburg Chamber of Commerce						
985 Railroad Ave	Pittsburg	CA	94565	925-432-7301		139
Web: pittsburgchamber.org						
Pittsburg County						
115 E Carl Albert Pkwy	McAlester	OK	74501	918-423-6895	423-7379	338
Web: okcountytreasurers.com						
Pittsburg State University						
1701 S Broadway St	Pittsburg	KS	66762	620-235-4251	235-6003	166
TF: 800-854-7488 ■ *Web:* www.pittstate.edu						
Pittsburg Tank & Tower Group						
1 Watertank Pl	Henderson	KY	42420	270-826-9000	827-4417	189-14
Web: www.pttg.com						
Pittsburg Wholesale Groceries Inc						
727 Kennedy St	Oakland	CA	94606	800-200-4244		345
TF: 800-200-4244 ■ *Web:* www.pitcofoods.com						
Pittsburgh Airport Area Chamber of Commerce						
850 Beaver Grade Rd	Moon Township	PA	15108	412-264-6270	264-1575	139
Web: www.paacc.com						
Pittsburgh Antique Radio Society (PARS)						
Brentwood Presbyterian Church						
3725 Brownsville Rd	Pittsburgh	PA	15227	724-942-1113		637-2
Web: pittantiqueradios.org						
Pittsburgh Ballet Theatre						
2900 Liberty Ave	Pittsburgh	PA	15201	412-281-0360	281-9901	573-1
Web: www.pbt.org						
Pittsburgh Catholic Publishing Associates Inc						
111 Blvd of the Allies Ste 200	Pittsburgh	PA	15222	412-471-1252	471-4228	637-9
TF: 800-392-4670 ■ *Web:* www.pittsburghcatholic.org						
Pittsburgh Center for the Arts (PCA)						
1047 Shady Ave	Pittsburgh	PA	15232	412-361-0455	361-8338	50-2
Web: pghartsmedia.org						
Pittsburgh City Hall						
414 Grant St City-County Bldg	Pittsburgh	PA	15219	412-255-2883	255-2821	337
TF: 800-932-0313 ■ *Web:* pittsburghpa.gov						
Pittsburgh City Paper						
650 Smithfield St Ste 2200	Pittsburgh	PA	15222	412-316-3342	316-3388	532-5
Web: www.pghcitypaper.com						
Pittsburgh Civic Light Opera						
719 Liberty Ave	Pittsburgh	PA	15222	412-281-3973	281-5339	573-2
Web: www.pittsburghclo.org						
Pittsburgh Design Services Inc						
PO Box 469	Carnegie	PA	15106	412-276-3000	276-6843	261
Web: www.pittsdesign.com						

Name / Address	City	State	ZIP	Phone	Fax	Class
Pittsburgh Foundation, The						
5 PPG Pl Ste 250	Pittsburgh	PA	15222	412-391-5122	391-7259	303
TF: 800-392-6900 ■ *Web:* pittsburghfoundation.org						
Pittsburgh History & Landmarks Foundation						
100 W Station Square Dr Ste 450	Pittsburgh	PA	15219	412-471-5808	471-1633	637-2
Web: www.phlf.org						
Pittsburgh Institute of Aeronautics (PIA)						
5 Allegheny County Airport	West Mifflin	PA	15122	412-346-2100		800
TF: 800-444-1440 ■ *Web:* pia.edu						
Pittsburgh Institute of Mortuary Science Inc						
5808 Baum Blvd	Pittsburgh	PA	15206	412-362-8500	362-1684	800
Web: pims.edu						
Pittsburgh International Airport						
Landside Terminal 4th Fl Mezz						
PO Box 12370	Pittsburgh	PA	15231	412-472-3500	472-3636	27
TF: 888-429-5377 ■ *Web:* www.flypittsburgh.com						
Pittsburgh Opera 2425 Liberty Ave	Pittsburgh	PA	15222	412-281-0912	281-4324	573-2
Web: www.pittsburghopera.org						
Pittsburgh Public Schools (PPS)						
341 S Bellefield Ave	Pittsburgh	PA	15213	412-622-7920		685
Web: www.pghschools.org						
Pittsburgh Public Theater						
621 Penn Ave	Pittsburgh	PA	15222	412-316-1600	316-8219	573-4
Web: ppt.org						
Pittsburgh School of Massage Therapy						
3600 Laketon Rd	Pittsburgh	PA	15235	800-860-1114	241-4933*	685
**Fax Area Code:* 412 ■ *TF:* 800-860-1114 ■ *Web:* www.massageschoolpittsburgh.com						
Pittsburgh Steelers						
3400 S Water St	Pittsburgh	PA	15203	412-432-7800		715-3
Web: www.steelers.com						
Pittsburgh Supercomputing Ctr						
300 S Craig St	Pittsburgh	PA	15213	412-268-4960	268-5832	668
TF: 800-221-1641 ■ *Web:* www.psc.edu						
Pittsburgh Symphony Orchestra						
600 Penn Ave	Pittsburgh	PA	15222	412-392-4900	392-3311	573-3
TF: 800-743-8560 ■ *Web:* www.pittsburghsymphony.org						
Pittsburgh Technical College (PTI)						
1111 McKee Rd	Oakdale	PA	15071	412-809-5100	809-5121	800
TF: 800-784-9675 ■ *Web:* www.pti.edu						
Pittsburgh Theological Seminary						
616 N Highland Ave	Pittsburgh	PA	15206	412-362-5610	363-3260	167-3
TF: 800-451-4194 ■ *Web:* www.pts.edu						
Pittsburgh Toy Lending Library Inc						
5401 Centre Ave	Pittsburgh	PA	15232	412-682-4430		434-3
Web: www.pghtoys.org						
Pittsburgh Zoo & PPG Aquarium						
7370 Baker St	Pittsburgh	PA	15206	412-665-3640	665-3661	823
Web: www.pittsburghzoo.org						
Pittsfield Plastics Engineering Inc						
1510 W Housatonic St	Pittsfield	MA	01201	413-442-0067		596
Web: www.pittsplas.com						
Pittsfield State Forest						
1041 Cascade St	Pittsfield	MA	01201	413-442-8992		565
Web: www.mass.gov						
Pittsford Federal Cu						
1321 Pittsford Mendon Rd PO Box 726	Mendon	NY	14506	585-624-7474	624-7939	219
TF: 800-836-8010 ■ *Web:* www.pittsfordfcu.org						
Pittsville Pdq Inc						
549 NW State Rte 131	Holden	MO	64040	816-850-6915		297-8
Pittsylvania County						
1 Center St PO Box 426	Chatham	VA	24531	434-432-7700		338
Web: www.pittsylvaniacountyva.gov						
Pittsylvania County Public Library						
24 Military Dr	Chatham	VA	24531	434-432-3271	432-1405	434-3
Web: pcplib.org						
Pittsylvania County Schools						
39 Bank St SE PO Box 232	Chatham	VA	24531	434-432-2761	432-0660	605
TF: 888-440-6520 ■ *Web:* www.pcs.k12.va.us						
Pitzer College 1050 N Mills Ave	Claremont	CA	91711	909-621-8129	621-8770	166
TF: 800-748-9371 ■ *Web:* www.pitzer.edu						
Piute County 550 N Main	Junction	UT	84740	435-577-2840	577-2433	338
Web: www.piute.org						
Pivot Interiors						
3355 Scott Blvd Ste 110	Santa Clara	CA	95054	408-432-5600	432-5601	320
Web: www.pivotinteriors.com						
Pivot Point International Inc						
8725 Higgins Rd Ste 700	Chicago	IL	60631	847-866-0500		514
Web: www.pivot-point.com						
Pivot Point Security						
1245 Whitehorse Mercerville Rd Ste 423	Trenton	NJ	08619	609-581-4600	581-4660	693
Web: www.pivotpointsecurity.com						
Pivot Systems Inc						
2480 N First St Ste 150	San Jose	CA	95131	408-435-1000		177
Web: www.pivotsys.com						
Pivotal Fitness						
1401 Sam Rittenberg Blvd	Charleston	SC	29407	843-571-5858		354
Web: www.pivotalfitness.com						
Pivotal Law Firm Inc 25 Mauchly Ste 319	Irvine	CA	92618	949-287-8015		41
Web: pivotallawfirm.com						
PIX 11 220 E 42nd St	New York	NY	10017	212-949-1100		741-91
Web: pix11.com						
Pixar Animation Studios						
1200 Park Ave	Emeryville	CA	94608	510-922-3000		33
Web: www.pixar.com						
Pixel Systems Inc 47 Greylynne Dr	Princeton	NJ	08540	609-945-3190		177
Web: www.pixelsystemsinc.com						
Pixel Velocity Inc PO Box 2566	Ann Arbor	MI	48106	734-213-3715	369-5031	529
Web: www.pixel-velocity.com						
Pixeled Business Systems Inc						
PO Box 3386	Vista	CA	92085	858-566-6060		225
Web: www.pixeled.com						
Pixelgate						
733 Lakefield Rd Ste A	Westlake Village	CA	91361	805-446-6254		387
Web: www.pixelgate.net						
Pixels & Dots LLC						
3181 Linwood Ave Ste 25	Cincinnati	OH	45208	513-405-3687	651-0051	344
Web: www.pixelsanddots.com						
Pixelworks Inc						
224 Airport Pkwy Ste 400	San Jose	CA	95110	408-200-9200	200-9201	696
NASDAQ: PXLW ■ *Web:* www.pixelworks.com						
Pixia Corp 45615 Willow Pond Plz	Sterling	VA	20164	571-203-9665		809
Web: www.pixia.com						
Pizza Boli's 3 Greenwood Pl Ste 208	Pikesville	MD	21208	800-234-2654	544-1505*	670
**Fax Area Code:* 443 ■ *TF:* 800-234-2654 ■ *Web:* www.pizzabolis.com						
Pizza Factory Inc 49430 Rd 426	Oakhurst	CA	93644	559-683-3377	683-6879	670
TF: 800-654-4840 ■ *Web:* www.pizzafactory.com						
Pizza Fusion						
1013 N Federal Hwy	Fort Lauderdale	FL	33304	954-358-5353	358-5354	670
Web: pizzafusion.com						
Pizza Inn Inc 3551 Plano Pkwy	The Colony	TX	75056	877-574-9924		670
NASDAQ: RAVE ■ *TF:* 877-574-9924 ■ *Web:* www.pizzainn.com						
Pizza King Inc 221 Farabee Dr	LaFayette	IN	47905	765-447-2172		670
Web: theoriginalpizzaking.com						
Pizza Plus Inc 299 Franklin Dr	Blountville	TN	37617	423-323-5555		670
Web: www.pizzaplusinc.com						
Pizza Pro Inc						
2107 N Second St PO Box 1285	Cabot	AR	72023	501-605-1175		670
TF: 800-777-7554 ■ *Web:* www.pizzapro.com						
Pizza Ranch Inc 204 19th St SE	Orange City	IA	51041	800-321-3401		670
TF: 800-321-3401 ■ *Web:* pizzaranch.com						
Pizza Today 908 S 8th St Ste 200	Louisville	KY	40203	502-736-9500	736-9511	670
Web: www.pizzatoday.com						
Pizzagalli Construction Co						
193 Tilley Dr	South Burlington	VT	05403	802-658-4100		186
Web: www.pcconstruction.com						
Pizzazz Hair Design & Spa						
771 Village Blvd	West Palm Beach	FL	33409	561-689-1177		77
Web: www.pizzazzhair.com						
Pizzeria Bianco 623 E Adams St	Phoenix	AZ	85004	602-258-8300		671
Web: www.pizzeriabianco.com						
Pizzuti Inc 629 N High St Ste 500	Columbus	OH	43215	614-280-4000	280-5000	653
Web: www.pizzuti.com						
PJ Cook Web Designs Inc						
2034 Rainbow Farms Dr	Safety Harbor	FL	34695	727-712-9493		180
Web: pjcook.com						
PJ Hoffmaster State Park						
6585 Lake Harbor Rd	Muskegon	MI	49441	231-798-3711		565
Web: www.michigan.org						
PJ Keating Co 998 Reservoir Rd	Lunenburg	MA	01462	978-582-5200	582-7130	188-4
TF: 800-441-4119 ■ *Web:* www.pjkeating.com						
PJ Noah PetSalon						
27762 Antonio Pkwy Ste L1-622	Ladera Ranch	CA	92694	855-577-7669	329-5779	794
TF: 855-577-7669 ■ *Web:* pjnoahpetsalon.com						
PJ Sohnciders & Company LLP						
152 Himmelein Rd Village Greene E Ste 400	Medford	NJ	08055	609-654-8300	654-7026	2
Web: corrugatedcpa.com						
PJ's Auto Parts Inc 2708 W Main Rd	Caledonia	NY	14423	716-538-2391	538-6192	54
TF: 800-946-5787 ■ *Web:* www.pjs4lkq.com						
PJ's College of Cosmetology						
1901 Russellville Rd	Bowling Green	KY	42101	270-842-8149		166
TF: 800-627-2566 ■ *Web:* www.gotopjs.com						
PJA Advertising + Marketing						
12 Arrow St	Cambridge	MA	02138	617-492-5899		4
Web: www.agencypja.com						
PJT Partners Inc 280 Park Ave	New York	NY	10017	212-364-7800		690
Web: pjtpartners.com						
PK (Promise Keepers) PO Box 11798	Denver	CO	80211	866-776-6473	433-1036*	48-20
**Fax Area Code:* 303 ■ *TF:* 866-776-6473 ■ *Web:* promisekeepers.org						
PK (Photon Kinetics Inc)						
9305 SW Gemini Dr	Beaverton	OR	97008	503-644-1960	526-4700	385
Web: www.pkinetics.com						
PK Network Communications Inc						
11 E 47th St	New York	NY	10017	212-888-4700		463
Web: pknetwork.com						
PK Partners LLC						
3610 River Crossing Pkwy	Indianapolis	IN	46240	317-817-8888		652
Web: www.pkpartners.com						
PK Safety Supply						
1829 Clement Ave Ste 200	Alameda	CA	94501	510-337-8880	337-8890	679
TF: 800-829-9580 ■ *Web:* www.pksafety.com						
PK USA Inc 600 W Northridge Dr	Shelbyville	IN	46176	317-395-5500	395-5501	489
Web: www.pkusa.com						
PK4 Media 2250 E Maple Ave	El Segundo	CA	90245	888-320-6281		387
TF: 888-320-6281 ■ *Web:* www.pk4media.com						
PKA Marketing						
1009 W Glen Oaks Ln Ste 107	Mequon	WI	53092	262-241-9414		4
Web: pkamarcom.com						
PKC Construction 7802 Barton St	Lenexa	KS	66214	913-782-4646		186
Web: www.pkcc.com						
PKC Corp 1 Mill St C13 Ste 355	Burlington	VT	05401	802-658-5351	658-3078	178-10
PKF PC 99 Summer St Ste 1660	Boston	MA	02110	617-753-9985	753-9986	2
Web: pkfboston.com						
PKF-Mark III Inc						
17 BlackSmith Rd Ste 101	Newtown	PA	18940	215-968-5031	968-3829	188-4
Web: www.pkfmarkiii.com						
PKM Electric Co-opeartive Inc						
406 N Minnesota St	Warren	MN	56762	218-745-4711		245
TF: 800-552-7366 ■ *Web:* www.pkmcoop.com						
PKM Steel Service Inc 228 E Ave A	Salina	KS	67401	785-827-3638		697
Web: www.pkmsteel.com						
PKMM Inc 265 E Main St Ste B	Oceanport	NJ	07757	732-935-1927		177
Web: pkmminc.com						
PKOH (Park-Ohio Holdings Corp)						
6065 Parkland Blvd	Cleveland	OH	44124	440-947-2000	947-2099	449
NASDAQ: PKOH ■ *Web:* pkoh.com						
PKWare Inc						
201 E Pittsburgh Ave Ste 400	Milwaukee	WI	53204	414-289-9788	289-9789	178-12
TF: 866-583-1795 ■ *Web:* pkware.com						
PL (Penta Laboratories)						
7868 Deering Ave	Canoga Park	CA	91304	818-882-3872	882-3968	418
TF: 800-421-4219 ■ *Web:* pentalabs.com						
PL Communications 417 Victor St	Scotch Plains	NJ	07076	908-889-8888		7
Web: www.plcommunications.com						

Phone | Fax | Class

PL Custom Body & Equipment Company Inc
2201 Atlantic Ave ... Manasquan NJ 08736 732-223-1411 30
TF: 800-752-8786 ■ *Web:* www.plcustom.com

PLA (Pro Lingua Associates Inc)
PO Box 1348 ... Brattleboro VT 05302 802-257-7779 257-5117 637-2
TF: 800-366-4775 ■ *Web:* www.proliguaassociates.com

Place D'Armes Hotel 625 St Ann St ... New Orleans LA 70116 504-524-4531 379
TF: 888-626-5917 ■ *Web:* www.placedarmes.com

Place de la Cite
2600 Laurier Blvd ... Quebec City QC G1V4T3 418-657-6920 657-6924 460
Web: www.placedelacite.com

Place Pigalle 81 Pike St ... Seattle WA 98101 206-624-1756 671
Web: www.placepigalle-seattle.com

PlaceFull Inc 122 S Jackson St Ste 310 ... Seattle WA 98104 206-624-0295 387
Web: placefull.com

Placemaking Group LLC
505 14th St 5th Fl ... Oakland CA 94612 510-835-7900 393
Web: www.placemakinggroup.com

Placemark Investments Inc
16633 Dallas Pkwy ... Addison TX 75001 972-404-8100 401
Web: www.placemark.com

Placement Strategies Inc
UPS Store Inc, The
6965 El Camino Real Ste 105-200 ... Carlsbad CA 92009 760-438-7704 438-4329 260
TF: 866-445-0710 ■ *Web:* www.placementstrategies.com

Placentia Chamber of Commerce
117 N Main St ... Placentia CA 92870 714-528-1873 528-1879 139
TF: 844-730-0418 ■ *Web:* www.placentiachamber.com

Placentia-Linda Hospital
1301 N Rose Dr ... Placentia CA 92870 714-993-2000 961-5980 374-3
Web: www.placentialinda.com

Placentia-Yorba Linda Unified School District (PYLUSD)
1301 E Orangethorpe Ave ... Placentia CA 92870 714-996-2550 685
Web: www.pylusd.org

Placer County 2954 Richardson Dr ... Auburn CA 95603 530-886-5600 886-5687 338
Web: www.placer.ca.gov

Placer County Library 350 Nevada St ... Auburn CA 95603 530-886-4500 886-4555 434-3
TF: 800-488-4308 ■ *Web:* www.placer.ca.gov

Placer County Water Agency
144 Ferguson Rd PO Box 6570 ... Auburn CA 95604 530-823-4850 787
Web: pcwa.net

Placer Title Co 189 Fulweiler Ave ... Auburn CA 95603 530-887-2410 885-0207 391-6
TF: 800-317-8407 ■ *Web:* www.placertitle.com

Placer Union High School District
13000 New Airport ... Auburn CA 95603 530-886-4400 685
Web: www.puhsd.k12.ca.us

Placeteco inc 3763 Burrill St ... Shawinigan QC G9N6T6 819-539-8808 539-9224 360-2
Web: www.placeteco.com

Placid Refining Company LLC
1940 Louisiana Hwy 1 N ... Port Allen LA 70767 225-387-0278 580
Web: www.placidrefining.com

Placitas Realty
03 Homesteads Rd Ste A ... Placitas NM 87043 505-867-8000 867-4113 652
Web: www.placitasrealty.com

Plaid Enterprises Inc
3225 Westech Dr ... Norcross GA 30092 800-842-4197 291-8368* 43
**Fax Area Code:* 678 ■ *TF:* 800-842-4197 ■ *Web:* plaidonline.com

Plaid Pantries Inc
10025 SW Allen Blvd ... Beaverton OR 97005 503-646-4246 646-3071 204
Web: www.plaidpantry.com

Plain Dealer 1801 Superior Ave ... Cleveland OH 44114 216-999-5000 532-2
Web: www.cleveland.com

Plain Local School District
901 44th St NW ... Canton OH 44709 330-492-3500 493-5542 685
Web: www.plainlocal.org

Plainfield Asset Management LLC
60 Arch St 2nd Fl ... Greenwich CT 06830 203-302-1700 463
Web: www.pfam.com

Plainfield Central School District
75 Canterbury Rd ... Plainfield CT 06374 860-564-6437 564-1147 685
Web: pcs.plainfieldschools.org

Plainfield Community Consolidated School District 202
15732 S Howard St ... Plainfield IL 60544 815-577-4000 436-7824 685
Web: www.psd202.org

Plainfield Correctional Facility
727 Moon Rd ... Plainfield IN 46168 317-839-2513 837-1875 213
Web: www.in.gov

Plainfield Public Library
800 Park Ave ... Plainfield NJ 07060 908-757-1111 754-0063 434-3
Web: www.plainfieldlibrary.info

Plains All American Pipeline LP
333 Clay St Ste 1600 ... Houston TX 77002 713-646-4100 597
NYSE: PAA ■ *TF:* 800-708-5071 ■ *Web:* www.plainsallamerican.com

Plains Conservation Ctr
21901 E Hampden Ave ... Aurora CO 80013 303-693-3621 693-3379 50-5
Web: www.plainsconservationcenter.org

Plains Cotton Cooperative Assn
3301 E 50th St PO Box 2827 ... Lubbock TX 79408 806-763-8011 275
TF: 800-333-8011 ■ *Web:* www.pcca.com

Plains Dairy Products
300 N Taylor St ... Amarillo TX 79107 806-374-0385 297-4
TF: 800-365-5608 ■ *Web:* www.plainsdairy.com

Plains Grain & Agronomy LLC
109 Third Ave ... Enderlin ND 58027 701-437-2400 10-4
TF: 800-950-2219 ■ *Web:* plainsgrain.com

Plains Midstream Canada
607 Eighth Ave SW Ste 1400 ... Calgary AB T2P0A7 403-298-2100 233-0399 538
TF: 866-343-5182 ■ *Web:* www.plainsmidstream.com

Plains Regional Medical Ctr
2100 N ML King Blvd ... Clovis NM 88101 505-769-2141 374-3
TF: 800-923-6980 ■ *Web:* www.phs.org

Plains Reporter PO Box 1447 ... Williston ND 58802 701-572-2165 572-9563 532-4
TF: 800-950-2165 ■ *Web:* www.willistonherald.com

Plains State Bank, The
411 Grand Ave PO Box 38 ... Plains KS 67869 620-563-7242 70
Web: plainsstatebank.com

PlainsCapital Bank
325 N St Paul St Ste 800 ... Dallas TX 75201 866-762-8392 360-2
TF: 866-762-8392 ■ *Web:* www.plainscapital.com

Plaintree Systems Inc 110 Decosta St ... Arnprior ON K7S0B5 613-623-3434 623-4647 176
Web: www.plaintree.com

Plainview Chamber of Commerce
1906 W Fifth St ... Plainview TX 79072 806-296-7431 296-0819 139
Web: www.plainviewtexaschamber.com

Plainview Milk Products Co-Op
130 Second St SW ... Plainview MN 55964 507-534-3872 534-3992 296-3
TF: 800-356-5606 ■ *Web:* www.plainviewmilk.com

Plainview News, The PO Box 9 ... Plainview NE 68769 402-582-4921 582-4922 532-4
Web: www.theplainviewnews.com

Plainville Farms Inc
304 S Water St PO Box 38 ... New Oxford PA 17350 717-624-2191 10-8
Web: www.plainvillefarms.com

Plainwell Community School District
600 School Dr ... Plainwell MI 49080 269-685-5823 685-1108 685
Web: www.plainwellschools.org

Plaisted Companies Inc
11555 205th Ave Nw ... Elk River MN 55330 763-441-1100 441-7782 780
Web: www.plaistedcompanies.com

Plaj Scandinavian Restaurant
333 Fulton St ... San Francisco CA 94102 415-294-8925 379
Web: www.plajrestaurant.com

Plan Administrators Inc
1300 Enterprise Dr ... De Pere WI 54115 800-236-7400 194
TF: 800-236-7400 ■ *Web:* www.pai.com

Plan B Advertising
116 W Illinois St Ste 2W ... Chicago IL 60654 312-222-0303 4
Web: www.thisisplanb.com

Plan B Technologies Inc
185 Admiral Cochrane Dr Ste 150 ... Annapolis MD 21401 301-860-1006 860-1005 177
TF: 888-925-1602 ■ *Web:* www.planbtech.net

Plan First Technologies Inc
120 Groton Ave ... Cortland NY 13045 607-756-9347 196
Web: p1tech.net

Plan Publishing Co 146-23 61st Rd ... Queens NY 11367 718-939-5800 637-10
TF: 800-843-7526 ■ *Web:* www.theplan.com

Plan Tech Inc 7031 Shaker Rd ... Loudon NH 03307 603-783-4767 783-4827 604
TF: 877-349-0620 ■ *Web:* www.plantech.com

Plan USA 155 Plan Way ... Warwick RI 02886 401-738-5600 738-5608 48-6
TF: 800-556-7918 ■ *Web:* www.planusa.org

Planar Systems Inc
1195 NW Compton Dr ... Beaverton OR 97006 503-748-1100 748-1244 173-4
NASDAQ: PLNR ■ *TF:* 866-475-2627 ■ *Web:* www.planar.com

Planaxis 60 St-Jacques St 7th Fl ... Montreal QC H2Y1L5 514-878-2295 476-0324* 196
**Fax Area Code:* 844 ■ *Web:* www.planaxis.com

Planemasters Ltd
DuPage Airport 32 W 611 Tower Rd ... West Chicago IL 60185 630-513-2100 377-3283 13
TF: 800-994-6400 ■ *Web:* planemasters.com

Planes of Fame Air Museum
7000 Merrill Ave Ste 17 ... Chino CA 91710 909-597-3722 597-4755 520
Web: www.planesoffame.org

Planesmart! Aviation LLC
Addison Airport 15841 Addison Rd ... Addison TX 75001 972-380-8004 20
Web: www.planesmart.com

PLANET (Professional Landcare Network)
950 Herndon Pkwy Ste 450 ... Herndon VA 20170 703-736-9666 736-9668 48-2
TF: 800-395-2522 ■ *Web:* www.landscapeprofessionals.org

Planet 21 8040 Providence Rd Ste 300 ... Charlotte NC 28277 704-543-1083 77
Web: www.planet21salon.com

Planet Bike 2402 Vondron Rd ... Madison WI 53718 866-256-8510 711
TF: 866-256-8510 ■ *Web:* www.planetbike.com

Planet Biotechnology Inc
20980 Corsair Blvd ... Hayward CA 94545 510-887-1461 668
Web: www.planetbiotechnology.com

Planet Forward LLC
800 Hillgrove Ave Ste 201 ... Western Springs IL 60558 888-845-2539 505-4039* 260
**Fax Area Code:* 708 ■ *TF:* 888-845-2539 ■ *Web:* www.theplanetforward.com

Planet Granite 815 Stewart Dr ... Sunnyvale CA 94085 408-991-9090 148
Web: planetgranite.com

Planet Hollywood International Inc
4700 Millenia Blvd Ste 400 ... Orlando FL 32839 407-903-5500 670
Web: www.planethollywoodintl.com

Planet Honda 2421 Iorio St ... Union NJ 07083 877-411-8066 57
TF: 855-439-7120 ■ *Web:* www.planethondanj.com

Planet One Networks LLC
4555 Knightsbridge Blvd ... Columbus OH 43214 614-602-4222 225
TF: 888-306-0319 ■ *Web:* planet1networks.com

Planet Paper Box Inc
2841 Langstaff Rd ... Concord ON L4K4W7 416-798-7641 100
Web: www.planetpaper.com

Planet Products Corp
4200 Malsbary Rd ... Cincinnati OH 45242 513-984-5544 984-5580 298
Web: www.planet-products.com

Planet Propaganda 605 Williamson St ... Madison WI 53703 608-256-0000 256-1975 7
Web: planetpropaganda.com

Planet Smoothie 3393 Peachtree Rd NW ... Atlanta GA 30326 404-816-1438 670
Web: planetsmoothie.com

Planet Studio LLC 7820 Roswell Rd ... Atlanta GA 30350 770-392-1000 4
Web: www.planetstudio.com

Planet Technologies Inc
20400 Observation Dr Ste 107 ... Germantown MD 20876 301-721-0100 179
Web: go-planet.com

Planet4it 55 Yonge St ... Toronto ON M5E1J4 416-363-9888 193
Web: www.planet4it.com

Planetbids Inc
5850 Canoga Ave Ste 301 ... Woodland Hills CA 91367 888-614-2437 175
Web: solutions.planetbids.com

Planetfone Inc
101 Convention Center Dr ... Las Vegas NV 89109 626-792-9978 463
Web: planetfone.com

PlanetMagpie 2762 Bayview Dr ... Fremont CA 94538 510-344-1200 463
Web: planetmagpie.com

PlanetMind Internetworks Inc
PO Box 1244 ... Nederland CO 80466 303-258-1103 407-8478* 225
**Fax Area Code:* 720 ■ *Web:* www.planetmind.net

Planetree Inc 130 Division St ... Derby CT 06418 203-732-1365 533
TF: 800-222-2818 ■ *Web:* planetree.org

Name / Address	Phone	Fax	Class
Plan-it Interactive 150 W Industrial Way .... Benicia CA 94510 *Web:* www.interactivegame.com	707-752-6010		232
Planit Measuring Co, The 94 Lkshore Rd E Unit C .... Mississauga ON L5G1E3 *TF:* 800-933-5136 ■ *Web:* planitmeasuring.com	905-271-7010		317
Plank Enterprises Inc 4404 Anderson Dr .... Eau Claire WI 54703 *TF:* 800-657-6956 ■ *Web:* www.plankenterprises.com	715-839-1225	839-8158	194
PlanMember Financial Corp 6187 Carpinteria Ave .... Carpinteria CA 93013 *TF:* 800-964-5632 ■ *Web:* www.planmember.com	805-684-1199		401
Planned Administrators Inc PO Box 6927 .... Columbia SC 29260 *TF:* 800-768-4375 ■ *Web:* www.paisc.com	803-462-0151		390
Planned Furniture Promotions Inc 9 Moody Rd Ste 18 Bldg D .... Enfield CT 06082 *Web:* www.pfpnow.com	860-749-1472		320
Planned Parenthood Action Fund Inc 1110 Vermont Ave NW .... Washington DC 20005 *TF:* 800-430-4907 ■ *Web:* www.plannedparenthoodaction.org	202-973-4800	296-3242	615
Planned Systems International Inc 10632 Lttle Patuxent Pkwy Ste 200............ Columbia MD 21044 *TF:* 800-275-7749 ■ *Web:* www.plan-sys.com	410-964-8000	964-8001	180
Planners Network Inc, The 43418 Business Park Dr..................... Temecula CA 92590 **Fax Area Code: 951* ■ *TF:* 866-676-6288 ■ *Web:* theplannersnetwork.com	866-676-6288	695-0511*	463
Planning and Conservation League (PCL) 1107 9th St Ste 901 .... Sacramento CA 95814 *Web:* www.pcl.org	916-822-5631	822-5650	48-13
planning NEXT 75 W 3rd Ave................. Columbus OH 43201 *Web:* www.planning-next.com	614-586-1500	586-1515	196
Plano Chamber of Commerce 1200 E 15th St .... Plano TX 75074 *TF:* 800-594-5420 ■ *Web:* www.planochamber.org	972-424-7547	422-5182	139
Plano Convention & Visitors Bureau 2000 E Spring Creek Pkwy .... Plano TX 75074 *TF:* 800-817-5266 ■ *Web:* www.visitplano.com	972-941-5840	424-0002	206
Plano Molding Co 431 E South St .... Plano IL 60545 *Web:* www.planomolding.com	630-552-3111		199
Plano Municipal Ctr 1520 K Ave .... Plano TX 75074 *Web:* www.plano.gov	972-941-7000		339-44
Plano Public Library System 5024 Custer Rd................................ Plano TX 75023 *TF:* 800-473-5707 ■ *Web:* www.plano.gov	972-769-4200		434-3
Plano Super Bowl Inc 2521 K Ave................ Plano TX 75074 *Web:* planosuperbowl.com	972-881-0242		99
Plano Symphony Orchestra 5236 Tennyson Pkwy Ste 200.................... Plano TX 75024 *Web:* www.planosymphony.org	972-473-7262		573-3
Planogramming Solutions Inc 9080 Golfside Dr .... Jacksonville FL 32256	904-448-0834		195
Plansee USA LLC 115 Constitution Blvd........................ Franklin MA 02038 *Web:* www.plansee-usa.com	508-553-3800		482
Plant Affair, The 1931 Blake Ave .... Los Angeles CA 90039 *Web:* plantaffair.com	323-661-4571		393
Plant Delights Nursery Inc 9241 Sauls Rd .... Raleigh NC 27603 *Web:* www.plantdelights.com	919-772-4794	662-0370	323
Plant Engineering Magazine 2000 Clearwater Dr......................... Oak Brook IL 60523 *Web:* www.plantengineering.com	630-288-8780	288-8781	457-21
Plant Machine Works Inc 4633 Blount Rd......................... Baton Rouge LA 70807 *Web:* www.plantmachineworks.com	225-775-7163	775-2743	454
Plant Maintenance Service Corp 3000 Fite Rd............................ Millington TN 38053 *Web:* www.pmscmphs.com	901-353-9880	353-0882	91
Plant Process Equipment Inc 280 Reynolds Ave........................ League City TX 77573 *Web:* plant-process.com	281-333-7850	332-6280	537
Plant Reclamation 941 Marina Way S Ste C.................... Richmond CA 94804 *Web:* www.plantreclamation.com	510-233-6552	237-6739	189-16
Plant Sciences Inc 342 Green Valley Rd...................... Watsonville CA 95076 *Web:* www.plantsciences.com	831-728-7771		238
Plantation Agriculture Museum PO Box 87 .... Scott AR 72142 *Web:* www.arkansasstateparks.com	501-961-1409		565
Plantation At Ponte Vedra Inc, The 101 Plantation Dr.................. Ponte Vedra Beach FL 32082 *Web:* theplantationpvb.com	904-543-2999		653
Plantation Inn & Golf Resort 9301 W Fort Island Trl .... Crystal River FL 34429 *TF:* 800-632-6262 ■ *Web:* www.plantationoncrystalriver.com	352-795-4211	795-1156	669
Plantation Pharmacy LLC 776 Daniel Ellis Dr Ste 2C .... Charleston SC 29412 *Web:* plantationpharmacy.com	843-795-9554		237
Plante & Moran PLLC 27400 Northwestern Hwy .... Southfield MI 48034 *Web:* www.plantemoran.com	248-352-2500		2
Planters Cotton Oil Mill Inc 2901 Planters Dr.......................... Pine Bluff AR 71601 *TF:* 800-264-7070 ■ *Web:* www.plantersoil.com	870-534-3631	534-1421	296-29
Planters Electric Membership Corp 1740 Hwy 25 N PO Box 979..................... Millen GA 30442 *Web:* www.plantersemc.com	478-982-4722	982-4798	245
Planters Inn 112 N Market St................ Charleston SC 29401 *TF:* 800-845-7082 ■ *Web:* www.plantersinn.com	843-722-2345		379
Planters Oil Inc 217 S Main St................ Fitzgerald GA 31750	229-423-2231		316
Planters Telephone Cooperative Inc 100 Ogeechee St........................... Newington GA 30446 *Web:* www.planters.net	912-857-4411	857-9800	224
PlantForm Corp 1920 Yonge St Ste 200.......... Toronto ON M4S3E2 *Web:* www.plantformcorp.com	416-452-7242		231
Plantique Inc 6344 Schantz Rd............... Allentown PA 18104 *Web:* plantique.com	610-395-6940		422
PlantIt Wise Inc 215 Industrial Dr .... New Glarus WI 53574 *Web:* www.planetwiseinc.com	608-225-6625		192
Plantronics Inc 345 Encinal St............... Santa Cruz CA 95060 *NYSE: PLT* ■ *TF:* 800-544-4660 ■ *Web:* www.poly.com	831-426-5858	426-6098	735
Plants of the Southwest 3095 Agua Fria Rd .... Santa Fe NM 87507 *TF:* 800-788-7333 ■ *Web:* plantsofthesouthwest.com	505-438-8888	438-8800	323
Plantscape Inc 3101 Liberty Ave .... Pittsburgh PA 15201 *TF:* 800-303-1380 ■ *Web:* www.plantscape.com	412-281-6352		393
Plantscape Inc 9901 W 74th St Ste 150 .... Eden Prairie MN 55344 *Web:* plantscapeinc.com	952-934-7666		422
Planview Inc 12301 Research Blvd Research Park Plz Ste 101 .... Austin TX 78759 *TF:* 800-856-8600 ■ *Web:* www.planview.com	512-346-8600	346-9180	178-1
Plaquemine Bancshares Corp 24025 Eden St .... Plaquemine LA 70764 *Web:* plaqbank.com	225-687-6388		70
Plaquemine Lock State Historic Site 57730 Main St .... Plaquemine LA 70764 *TF:* 877-987-7158 ■ *Web:* crt.state.la.us	225-687-7158		520
Plaquemines Parish Government 8056 Hwy 23 Ste 200.................... Belle Chasse LA 70037 *Web:* plaqueminesparish.com	504-297-2462		338
Plaquemines Parish School Board 557 F Edward Hebert Blvd .... Belle Chasse LA 70037 *Web:* www.ppsb.org	504-595-6400	392-4973	685
PLASA North America 630 Ninth Ave Ste 609 .... New York NY 10036 *Web:* www.plasa.org	212-244-1505	244-1502	48-4
Plasco Conversion Technologies Inc 515 Legget D Ste 100.......................... Kanata ON K2K3G4 *Web:* plascotechnologies.com	613-287-3127		196
Plascore Inc 615 N Fairview .... Zeeland MI 49464 *TF:* 800-630-9257 ■ *Web:* www.plascore.com	616-772-1220	772-1289	696
Plasencia Group Inc, The 1 N Dale Mabry Hwy Ste 100 .... Tampa FL 33609 *Web:* tpghotels.com	813-932-1234		463
Plasidyne Engineering & Manufacturing Inc 3230 E 59th St .... Long Beach CA 90805 *Web:* plasidyne.com	562-531-0510	531-1377	757
Plaskett Stacey (Rep D - VI) 2404 Rayburn House Office Bldg .... Washington DC 20515 *Web:* plaskett.house.gov	202-225-1790	225-5517	342-2
Plaskolite Inc 1770 Joyce Ave .... Columbus OH 43219 *TF:* 800-848-9124 ■ *Web:* www.plaskolite.com	614-294-3281	297-7287	600
Plas-Labs Inc 401 E North St................... Lansing MI 48906 *TF:* 800-866-7527 ■ *Web:* www.plas-labs.com	517-372-7177	372-2857	420
Plasma Protein Therapeutics Assn (PPTA) 147 Old Solomon's Island Rd Ste 100 .... Annapolis MD 21401 *Web:* www.pptaglobal.org	202-789-3100		49-8
Plasma Ruggedized Solutions Inc 2284 Ringwood Ave Ste A .... San Jose CA 95131 *TF:* 800-994-7527 ■ *Web:* www.plasmarugged.com	408-954-8405		481
Plasma Services Group Inc 1840 County Line Rd Unit 100......... Huntingdon Valley PA 19006 *Web:* www.plasmaservicesgroup.com	215-355-1288		238
Plasma Technology Inc 1754 Crenshaw Blvd......................... Torrance CA 90501 *Web:* www.ptise.com	310-320-3373	533-1677	481
PlasmaNet Inc 420 Lexington Ave Ste 1648.................. New York NY 10170 *Web:* freelotto.com	212-931-6760	931-6761	225
Plaspack USA Inc 753 Amron Ave .... Antigo WI 54409	715-623-4449		596
Plaspros Inc 1143 Ridgeview Dr .... McHenry IL 60050 *Web:* www.plaspros.com	815-430-2300	430-2600	604
Plasser American Corp 2001 Myers Rd PO Box 5464............... Chesapeake VA 23324 *TF:* 800-388-4825 ■ *Web:* www.plasseramerican.com	757-543-3526	494-7186	650
Plast O Foam LLC 24601 Capital Blvd................... Clinton Township MI 48036 *Web:* www.plastofoam.com	586-307-3790		247
Plas-Tanks Industries Inc 39 Standen Dr........................... Hamilton OH 45015 *TF:* 800-247-6709 ■ *Web:* www.plastanks.com	513-942-3800	942-3993	199
Plastatech Engineering Ltd 725 Morley Dr .... Saginaw MI 48601 *TF:* 800-892-9358 ■ *Web:* plastatech.com	989-754-6500		191-4
Plasteak Inc 3489 Sawmill Rd................... Copley OH 44321 *TF:* 800-320-1841 ■ *Web:* www.plasteak.com	330-668-2587	666-0844	186
Plastech Corp 920 S Field Ave .... Rush City MN 55069 *Web:* www.plastechcorporation.com	651-407-5700	407-5495	604
Plastek Group 2425 W 23rd St .... Erie PA 16506 *Web:* www.plastekgroup.com	814-878-4400	878-4529	604
Plaster Fun Time Ltd 72 Joy St............. Somerville MA 02143 *Web:* plasterfuntime.com	617-262-1230		761
Plasterer Equipment Company Inc 2550 E Cumberland St .... Lebanon PA 17042 *Web:* www.plasterer.com	717-273-2616		358
Plasti Dip Intl 3920 Pheasant Ridge Dr............ Blaine MN 55449 *TF:* 800-969-5432 ■ *Web:* plastidip.com	800-969-5432		596
Plastic & Steel Supply Company Inc 50 Tannery Rd Bldg 3 .... Branchburg NJ 08876 *Web:* www.pep-plastic.com	908-534-5556	534-5287	601
Plastic Card Systems Inc 31 Pierce St .... Northborough MA 01532 *TF:* 800-742-2273 ■ *Web:* www.plasticard-systems.com	508-351-6210		173-6
Plastic Components Inc N 116 W 18271 Morse Dr.................. Germantown WI 53022 *TF:* 877-253-1496 ■ *Web:* www.plasticcomponents.com	262-253-0353		604
Plastic Composites Co 8301 Clinton Park Dr .... Fort Wayne IN 46825 *Web:* www.buckettruckparts.com	260-484-3139		463
Plastic Concepts Inc 2 Sterling Rd Unit 2 .... North Billerica MA 01862 *Web:* www.plastic-concepts.com	978-663-7996	663-7880	604
Plastic Container Corp 2508 N Oak St .... Urbana IL 61802 *Web:* www.netpcc.com	217-352-2722		601

	Phone	Fax	Class
Plastic Design International Inc 111 Industrial Park Rd ... Middletown CT 06457 *Web:* www.plasticdesign.com	860-632-2001	632-1776	604
Plastic Designs Inc 1330 S Vermillion St ... Paxton IL 60957 *TF:* 866-734-1988 ■ *Web:* www.agsolutionsonline.com	866-734-1988		604
Plastic Development Company Inc 75 Palmer Industrial Rd PO Box 4007 ... Williamsport PA 17701 **Fax Area Code:* 570 ■ *TF:* 800-451-1420 ■ *Web:* www.pdcspas.com	800-451-1420	323-8485*	375
Plastic Engineering & Technical Services Inc 4141 Luella Ln ... Auburn Hills MI 48326 *Web:* petsgroupintl.com	248-373-0800		261
Plastic Film Corporation of America Inc 1287 Naperville Dr ... Romeoville IL 60446 *TF:* 800-654-6589 ■ *Web:* www.plasticfilmcorporation.com	630-887-0800		603
Plastic Forming Company Inc 20 S Bradley Rd ... Woodbridge CT 06525 *TF:* 800-732-2060 ■ *Web:* www.pfccases.com	203-397-1338	389-0420	199
Plastic Ingenuity Inc 1017 Park St ... Cross Plains WI 53528 *Web:* www.plasticingenuity.com	608-798-3071	798-4452	596
Plastic Lumberyard LLC 220 E Washington St ... Norristown PA 19401 *Web:* plasticlumberyard.com	610-277-3900	277-3970	661
Plastic Mart Inc 43535 Gadsden Ave Ste F ... Lancaster CA 93534 *TF:* 800-200-4228 ■ *Web:* theplasticmart.com	800-200-4228		605-2
Plastic Molded Concepts Inc PO Box 490 ... Eagle WI 53119 *Web:* www.pmcplastics.com	262-594-5050	594-5075	604
Plastic Monofil Company Ltd 28 Industrial Dr ... Milton VT 05468 *Web:* www.plasticmonofil.com	802-893-1543		596
Plastic Omnium Auto Inergy USA LLC 2710 Bellingham Dr Ste 400 ... Troy MI 48083 *Web:* www.plasticomnium.com	248-743-5700		247
Plastic Products Company Inc 30355 Akerson St ... Lindstrom MN 55045 *Web:* www.plasticproductsco.com	651-257-5980	257-9774	604
Plastic Products Inc 1051 York Rd ... Kings Mountain NC 28086 *TF:* 800-752-7770 ■ *Web:* www.plastic-products.com	704-739-7463	739-5566	603
Plastic Recycling of Iowa Falls Inc 10252 Hwy 65 ... Iowa Falls IA 50126 *TF:* 800-338-1438 ■ *Web:* plasticrecycling.us	641-648-5073	648-5074	661
Plastic Safety Systems Inc 2444 Baldwin Rd ... Cleveland OH 44104 **Fax Area Code:* 216 ■ *TF:* 800-662-6338 ■ *Web:* pss-innovations.com	800-662-6338	231-2702*	678
Plastic Source LLC 3219 E Camelback Rd Blvd 481 ... Phoenix AZ 85018 *Web:* www.plasticsourceus.com	602-277-9380	233-9725	604
Plastic Suppliers Inc 2450 Marilyn Ln ... Columbus OH 43219 **Fax Area Code:* 614 ■ *TF:* 800-722-5577 ■ *Web:* www.plasticsuppliers.com	800-722-5577	475-0264*	600
Plastic Technologies Inc 1440 Timberwolf Dr ... Holland OH 43528 *Web:* www.plastictechnologies.com	419-867-5400		194
Plastic Technology Inc 1115 Farrington St ... Conover NC 28613 *Web:* ptifoam.com	828-328-2201		601
Plasticap 177 Crosby Ave ... Richmond Hill ON L4C2R3 *Web:* plasticap.com	905-883-4343		553
Plasticoid Co 249 W High St ... Elkton MD 21921 *Web:* www.plasticoid.com	410-398-2800	398-2803	676
Plasticolors Inc 2600 Michigan Ave PO Box 816 ... Ashtabula OH 44005 *TF:* 888-661-7675 ■ *Web:* www.chromaflo.com	440-997-5137	992-3613	143
Plasticrest Products Inc 4519 W Harrison St ... Chicago IL 60624 *TF:* 800-828-2163 ■ *Web:* www.signaturejewelrypackaging.com	773-826-2163	826-4227	286
Plastics Advanced Research Technology Inc 1427 Old N Main St ... Clover SC 29710 *Web:* www.partinc.com	803-222-7771		191-3
Plastics Color & Compounding Inc 14201 Paxton Ave ... Calumet City IL 60409 *TF:* 800-922-9936 ■ *Web:* www.plasticscolor.com	800-922-9936		605-2
Plastics Design & Mfg 6284 S Nome Ct ... Centennial CO 80111 *Web:* plasticsdesign-mfg.com	303-768-8380		596
Plastics Engineering Company Inc 3518 Lake Shore Rd ... Sheboygan WI 53083 *Web:* plenco.com	920-458-2121	458-1923	605-2
Plastics Extrusion Machinery Inc 900 Kit Blvd ... McPherson KS 67460 *Web:* www.pemusa.com	620-241-3873	241-7707	695
Plastics International Inc 7600 Anagram Dr ... Eden Prairie MN 55344 *TF:* 800-776-7769 ■ *Web:* www.plasticsintl.com	952-934-2303		603
Plastics Molding Company Inc 4211 N Broadway ... Saint Louis MO 63147 *Web:* www.plasticsmoldingco.com	314-241-2479	241-3757	604
Plastics One Inc 6591 Merriman Rd ... Roanoke VA 24018 *Web:* www.p1tec.com	540-772-7950		596
Plastics Plus Technology Inc 1495 Research Dr ... Redlands CA 92374 *Web:* www.plasticsplus.com	909-747-0555		608
Plastics Research Corp 1400 S Campus Ave ... Ontario CA 91761 *Web:* www.prccal.com	909-391-2006		199
Plastics Resources Inc 495 N 1000 W ... Logan UT 84321 *Web:* www.pri-plastics.com	435-753-7458		596
Plastics Unlimited Inc 12012 W Fairview Ave ... Wauwatosa WI 53226 *TF:* 800-657-0724 ■ *Web:* www.plastics-unlimited.com	414-771-3834	771-5246	604
Plasti-Fab Inc 2305 Hilton Rd ... Ferndale MI 48220 *Web:* www.plasti-fabinc.com	248-206-0672	543-3959	604
PlastiFab/Leed Plastics 1425 Palomares Ave ... La Verne CA 91750 **Fax Area Code:* 909 ■ *TF:* 800-842-4593 ■ *Web:* www.plastifabonline.com	800-842-4593	596-3020*	599

	Phone	Fax	Class
Plastiform Packaging Inc 114 Beach St Bldg 6 ... Rockaway NJ 07866 *Web:* plastiformpkg.com	973-983-8900	983-8989	557
Plastikon Industries Inc 688 Sandoval Way ... Hayward CA 94544 *TF:* 800-370-0858 ■ *Web:* www.plastikon.com	510-400-1010	400-1133	608
Plastikos Inc 8165 Hawthorne Dr ... Erie PA 16509 *Web:* www.plastikoserie.com	814-868-1656		596
Plastipak Industries Inc 150 Industriel Blvd ... Boucherville QC J4B2X3 *TF:* 800-387-7452 ■ *Web:* www.plastipak.ca	450-650-2200	650-2201	601
Plastipak Packaging Inc 41605 Ann Arbor Rd ... Plymouth MI 48170 *Web:* www.plastipak.com	734-455-3600	354-7391	98
Plastiq 360 9th St ... San Francisco CA 94103 *TF:* 866-313-9823 ■ *Web:* www.plastiq.com	866-313-9823		251
Plastiques Milsi Incorporated Les 2310 Rue de la Province ... Longueuil QC J4G1G1 *Web:* www.plastiquesmilsi.com	450-463-4568		608
Plast-O-Matic Valves Inc 1384 Pompton Ave ... Cedar Grove NJ 07009 *Web:* plastomatic.com	973-256-3000	256-4745	789
Plastomer Corp 37819 Schoolcraft Rd ... Livonia MI 48150 *Web:* www.plastomer.com	734-464-0700	464-4792	601
Plastpro Inc 5200 W Century Blvd Ste 09 ... Los Angeles CA 90045 *TF:* 800-779-0561 ■ *Web:* www.plastproinc.com	310-693-8600	693-8620	608
Plastronics Socket Company Inc 2601 Texas Dr ... Irving TX 75062 *TF:* 800-582-5822 ■ *Web:* plastronics.com	972-258-2580	258-6771	253
Plastruct Inc 1020 Wallace Ave ... City of Industry CA 91748 *TF:* 800-666-7015 ■ *Web:* www.plastruct.com	626-912-7016	965-2036	761
Plastube Inc 590 Simonds S ... Granby QC J2J1E1 *Web:* www.plastube.com	450-378-2633		601
Plateau Electric Cooperative 16200 Scott Hwy ... Oneida TN 37841 *Web:* plateauelectric.com.temp.omnis.com	423-569-8591		245
Plateau Excavation Inc 375 Lee Industrial Blvd ... Austell GA 30168 *Web:* plateauexcavation.com	770-948-2600		261
Plath & Company Inc 1575 Francisco Blvd E ... San Rafael CA 94901 *Web:* plathco.com	415-460-1575		186
Platinum Advisors LLC 1215 K St Ste 1150 ... Sacramento CA 95814 *Web:* www.platinumadvisors.com	916-443-8891		401
Platinum Business Corp 14662 Cambridge Cir ... Laurel MD 20707 **Fax Area Code:* 800 ■ *Web:* www.platinumcorporation.com	301-498-4149	853-7990*	809
Platinum Control Technologies Corp 2822 W 5th St ... Fort Worth TX 76107 *TF:* 877-374-1115 ■ *Web:* www.platinumcontrol.com	817-529-6485	977-4896	539
Platinum Dragon 814 W Market St ... Akron OH 44303 *Web:* www.platinumdragonakron.com	330-434-8108		671
Platinum Equity Holdings *Platinum Equity LLC* 360 N Crescent Dr ... Beverly Hills CA 90210 *Web:* www.platinumequity.com	310-712-1850		405
Platinum Federal Credit Union 2035 Sugarloaf Cir ... Duluth GA 30097 *Web:* platinumfcu.org	404-297-9797		219
Platinum Home Health Care Inc 16634 107th Ct ... Orland Park IL 60467 *Web:* platinumhomehealthcare.com	708-995-7758		363
Platinum Homes LLC 155 County Rd 351 ... Lynn AL 35575 *Web:* www.platinumhomes-llc.com	205-893-5182		505
Platinum Hotel 211 E Flamingo Rd ... Las Vegas NV 89169 *TF:* 877-211-9211 ■ *Web:* www.theplatinumhotel.com	702-365-5000		379
Platinum HR Management LLC 4512 Farragut Rd ... Brooklyn NY 11203 *Web:* www.platinumhrm.com	718-859-1600		260
Platinum Maintenance Services Corp 120 Broadway 36th Fl ... New York NY 10271 *Web:* platinuminc.com	212-535-9700	480-2699	152
Platinum Partners Real Estate Team Inc 2080 E 20th St Ste 170 ... Chico CA 95928 *Web:* platinumpartnersteam.com	530-771-6940		652
Platinum Personnel 1475 Ellis St Ste 202 ... Kelowna BC V1Y2A3 *TF:* 800-652-1511 ■ *Web:* www.platinumrecruiting.ca	250-979-7200		260
Platinum Systems 4600 Green Bay Rd ... Kenosha WI 53144 *TF:* 888-910-4407 ■ *Web:* platinumsystems.net	262-652-6671		225
Platinum Systems Specialists Inc 4715 Yender Ave ... Lisle IL 60532 *Web:* www.platinum-universe.com	630-375-6800	375-9069	194
Platinum Vault Inc 10554 Norwalk Blvd ... Santa Fe Springs CA 90670 *TF:* 888-671-2888 ■ *Web:* www.hartleymedical.com	562-903-1494		196
Plato Woodwork Inc 200 Third St SW ... Plato MN 55370 *TF:* 800-328-5924 ■ *Web:* www.platowoodwork.com	800-328-5924		115
Plato's Closet 23021 Outer Dr ... Allen Park MI 48101 *Web:* www.platoscloset.com	313-278-2300		310
Platon Craft & Floral Inc 1415 Rollins Rd Ste 110 ... Burlingame CA 94010	650-373-7888		292
Platon Digital Graphics 136 Oregon St ... El Segundo CA 90245 **Fax Area Code:* 310 ■ *TF:* 800-499-0292 ■ *Web:* platongraphics.com	800-499-0292	227-8026*	627
Platsky Company Inc 298 Montrose Rd ... Westbury NY 11590 *Web:* www.platsky.com	516-333-9292		612
Platt & Labonia Co 70 Stoddard Ave ... North Haven CT 06473 *TF:* 800-505-9099 ■ *Web:* www.plattlabonia.com	203-239-5681	234-7978	697
Platt College 6250 El Cajon Blvd ... San Diego CA 92115 *TF:* 866-752-8826 ■ *Web:* www.platt.edu	866-752-8826		167-3
Platt Electric Supply 10605 SW Allen Blvd ... Beaverton OR 97005 *TF:* 800-257-5288 ■ *Web:* www.platt.com	503-641-6121	277-7497	246

Name / Address	City	State	ZIP	Phone	Fax	Class
Platt Irwin Law Firm PS 403 S Peabody *Web:* plattirwin.com	Port Angeles	WA	98362	360-457-3327		41
Platt Luggage Inc 4051 W 51st St *TF:* 800-222-1555 ■ *Web:* www.plattcases.com	Chicago	IL	60632	773-838-2000	838-2010	453
Platt Technical High School 600 Orange Ave *Web:* platt.cttech.org	Milford	CT	06461	203-783-5300	783-3970	685
Plattco Corp 7 White St *TF:* 800-352-1731 ■ *Web:* www.plattco.com	Plattsburgh	NY	12901	518-563-4640	563-4892	789
Platte County 415 Third St *TF:* 888-875-2883 ■ *Web:* www.co.platte.mo.us	Platte City	MO	64079	816-858-2232	858-3363	338
Platte County PO Box 728 *Web:* www.plattecountywyoming.com	Wheatland	WY	82201	307-322-2315	322-2245	338
Platte County Citizen 1110 Branch St *Web:* www.plattecountycitizen.com	Platte City	MO	64079	816-858-5154		532-2
Platte County Community Center North 3101 Running Horse Rd *Web:* kansascityymca.org	Platte City	MO	64079	816-858-0114		354
Platte River State Park 14421 346th St *Web:* outdoornebraska.gov	Louisville	NE	68037	402-234-2217		565
Platte Valley Bank 606 Main St PO Box 500 *Web:* pvbonline.com	North Bend	NE	68649	402-652-3221		70
Platte Valley Youth Services Ctr 2200 'O' St *Web:* www.colorado.gov	Greeley	CO	80631	970-304-6220		412
Platte-Clay Electric Co-opeartive Inc 1000 W Hwy 92 PO Box 100 *Web:* www.pcec.coop	Kearney	MO	64060	816-628-3121	628-3141	245
Plattsburgh North Country Chamber of Commerce 7061 Rt 9 *Web:* www.northcountrychamber.com	Plattsburgh	NY	12901	518-563-1000	563-1028	139
Platzi Inc 535 St 14th Fl *Web:* platzi.com	San Francisco	CA	94105	415-894-0755		48-11
Plauche & Carr LLP 811 First Ave Ste 630 *Web:* plauchecarr.com	Seattle	WA	98104	206-588-4188		41
Plaudit Design 2470 University Ave W *Web:* www.plaudit.com	Saint Paul	MN	55114	651-646-0696		180
Plave Koch Plc 12005 Sunrise Valley Dr Ste 200 *Web:* plavekoch.com	Reston	VA	20191	703-774-1200		41
Play 107 5241 Calgary Trl Centre 104 Ste 700 *Web:* www.play107.com	Edmonton	AB	T6H5G8	780-435-3023	988-2387	647
Play It Again Sports 5600 W 95th St *Web:* www.playitagainsportsoaklawn.com	Oak Lawn	IL	60453	708-636-6311		711
Play Safe Playground Systems of NY 3 Laurel Ln *Web:* www.playsafeny.com	Syosset	NY	11791	516-677-9240	677-9241	711
Playa Azul Mexican Restaurant 415 E William St	Carson City	NV	89701	775-883-2244		671
Playback Now Inc 3139 Campus Dr Ste 700 *TF:* 800-241-7785 ■ *Web:* www.playbacknow.com	Norcross	GA	30071	770-447-0616		463
Playbill Inc 525 Seventh Ave Ste 1801 *Web:* www.playbill.com	New York	NY	10018	212-557-5757		457-9
Playbooks Inc 111 Corporate Dr Ste 240 **Fax Area Code:* 949 ■ *TF:* 800-375-2926 ■ *Web:* www.readerstheater.com	Ladera Ranch	CA	92694	800-375-2926	595-4741*	637-2
PlayCore Inc 544 Chestnut St **Fax Area Code:* 423 ■ *TF:* 877-762-7563 ■ *Web:* www.playcore.com	Chattanooga	TN	37402	877-762-7563	425-3124*	346
Player's Club Resort 35 Deallyon Ave *TF:* 800-497-7529 ■ *Web:* www.spinnakerresorts.com	Hilton Head Island	SC	29928	843-785-3355		669
Playground King Inc 3744 W Lambright St *Web:* www.playgroundking.com	Tampa	FL	33614	813-875-5500		44
Playhouse on the Square 66 S Cooper St *Web:* www.playhouseonthesquare.org	Memphis	TN	38104	901-725-0776	726-5521	572
Playhouse Square 1501 Euclid Ave Ste 200 *TF:* 866-546-1353 ■ *Web:* www.playhousesquare.org	Cleveland	OH	44115	216-771-4444	771-0217	572
PlayMakers Repertory Co 120 Country Club Rd *Web:* playmakersrep.org	Chapel Hill	NC	27599	919-962-7529		749
Playmobil USA Inc 26 Commerce Dr *TF:* 800-351-8697 ■ *Web:* www.playmobil.us	Cranbury	NJ	08512	609-395-5566	395-3015	762
PlayMyAd Inc 7545 Irvine Center Dr Ste 200 *TF:* 888-411-6923 ■ *Web:* www.playmyad.com	Irvine	CA	92618	949-988-2500		5
Playnation of Wnc 542 Hendersonville Rd *Web:* playnationofwnc.com	Asheville	NC	28803	828-776-2731		711
PlayNetwork Inc 8727 148th Ave NE *TF:* 888-567-7529 ■ *Web:* www.playnetwork.com	Redmond	WA	98052	425-497-8100		524
Playscripts Inc 7 Penn Plz Ste 904 *TF:* 866-639-7529 ■ *Web:* www.playscripts.com	New York	NY	10001	866-639-7529		791
Playspace Design LLC 5698 Shady Farm Ln *Web:* www.playspacedesign.com	Murray	UT	84107	801-274-0212		711
Playwell Group, The 4743 Iberia Ave Ste C *TF:* 800-726-1816 ■ *Web:* www.playwellgroup.com	Dallas	TX	75207	800-726-1816		711
Playworks Inc 340 Blalock Rd *Web:* www.playworksinc.com	Boiling Springs	SC	29316	864-814-2230	814-2232	711
Playworld Systems Inc 1000 Buffalo Rd *TF:* 800-233-8404 ■ *Web:* playworld.com	Lewisburg	PA	17837	570-522-9800	522-3030	346
Plaza Art 633 Middleton St *TF:* 866-668-6714 ■ *Web:* www.plazaart.com	Nashville	TN	37203	615-254-3368		45
Plaza Azteca 4292 Holland Rd *Web:* www.plazaazteca.com	Virginia Beach	VA	23452	757-431-8135		671

Name / Address	City	State	ZIP	Phone	Fax	Class
Plaza Fleet Parts Inc 1520 S Broadway *TF:* 800-325-7618 ■ *Web:* www.plazafleetparts.com	Saint Louis	MO	63104	314-231-5047	231-5109	61
Plaza Group Inc 10375 Richmond Ave Ste 1620 *TF:* 800-876-3738 ■ *Web:* www.theplazagrp.com	Houston	TX	77042	713-266-0707	266-8660	146
Plaza Home Mortgage Inc 4820 Eastgate Mall Ste 100 *TF:* 866-260-2529 ■ *Web:* plazahomemortgage.com	San Diego	CA	92121	858-346-1208	677-6741	509
Plaza Hotel & Casino 1 Main St *TF:* 800-634-6575 ■ *Web:* www.plazahotelcasino.com	Las Vegas	NV	89101	702-386-2110		379
Plaza Inn 900 Medical Arts NE	Albuquerque	NM	87102	505-243-5693		379
Plaza Library 2100 Clarendon Blvd 1st Fl Lobby *Web:* library.arlingtonva.us	Arlington	VA	22201	703-228-3352		434-3
Plaza Live, The 425 N Bumby Ave *Web:* www.eventbritesites.com	Orlando	FL	32803	407-228-1220		572
Plaza Resort Club 121 W St *TF:* 800-628-5974 ■ *Web:* plazaresortclub.com	Reno	NV	89501	775-786-2200		379
Plaza Square Motel Lodge 2255 Central Blvd	Brownsville	TX	78520	956-546-5104		379
Plaza Suite Resort 620 S Peters St *Web:* www.plazaresort.com	New Orleans	LA	70130	504-524-9500	524-2135	379
Plaza Suites Silicon Valley 3100 Lakeside Dr *TF:* 800-345-1554 ■ *Web:* www.theplazasuites.com	Santa Clara	CA	95054	408-748-9800		379
Plaza Tire Service PO Box 2048 **Fax Area Code:* 573 ■ *TF:* 800-334-5036 ■ *Web:* www.plazatireservice.com	Cape Girardeau	MO	63702	800-334-5036	334-0322*	62-5
Plaza Travel 16530 Ventura Blvd Ste 106 *TF:* 800-347-4447 ■ *Web:* www.plazatravel.com	Encino	CA	91436	818-990-4053		775
Plaza View 245 N Wildwood Dr *Web:* bransongrandplaza.com	Branson	MO	65616	417-336-6646		671
PLB Sports and Entertainment 2 Penn Center W Ste 314 Bldg 2 *Web:* plbse.com	Pittsburgh	PA	15276	412-787-8800		296-8
PLDA Group 2570 N 1st St 2nd Fl *Web:* www.pldagroup.com	San Jose	CA	95131	408-273-4528		253
PLDG (Peggy Lauritsen Design Grp Inc) 125 Main St SE Ste 340 *Web:* pldg.com	Minneapolis	MN	55414	612-623-4200		344
Pleasant Care 508 Westline Dr *Web:* www.pleasantcare.com	Alameda	CA	94501	510-521-5765		793
Pleasant Creek State Recreation Area 4530 McClintock Rd *Web:* www.iowadnr.gov	Palo	IA	52324	319-436-7716		565
Pleasant Gardens Machine Inc 2708 US 70 W *Web:* www.pgmachine.com	Marion	NC	28752	828-724-4173		454
Pleasant Hill Chamber of Commerce 91 Gregory Ln Ste 11 *Web:* www.pleasanthillchamber.com	Pleasant Hill	CA	94523	925-687-0700	676-7422	139
Pleasant Holidays LLC 2404 Townsgate Rd *TF:* 800-742-9244 ■ *Web:* www.pleasantholidays.com	Westlake Village	CA	91361	818-991-3390		771
Pleasant Nursery Inc 4234 W Wabash *Web:* www.pleasant-nursery.com	Springfield	IL	62711	217-522-2222		292
Pleasant River Lumber Co 432 Milo Rd *Web:* www.pleasantriverlumber.com	Dover-Foxcroft	ME	04426	207-564-8520		683
Pleasant Trucking 2250 Industrial Dr **Fax Area Code:* 724 ■ *TF:* 800-245-2402 ■ *Web:* pleasanttrucking.com	Connellsville	PA	15425	800-245-2402	628-5868*	780
Pleasant Valley Hospital 2520 Valley Dr *Web:* www.pvalley.org	Point Pleasant	WV	25550	304-675-4340		374-3
Pleasant Valley Nursing Ctr 8 Peabody Rd	Derry	NH	03038	603-434-1566		450
Pleasant Valley Potato Inc 275 E Elmore Ave *Web:* www.pleasantvalleypotato.com	Aberdeen	ID	83210	208-397-4194		11-1
Pleasant Valley Sch District 600 Temple Ave *Web:* www.pvsd.k12.ca.us	Camarillo	CA	93010	805-482-2763	987-5511	685
Pleasant Valley State Prison 24863 W Jayne Ave PO Box 8500 *Web:* cdcr.ca.gov	Coalinga	CA	93210	559-935-4900	386-7461	213
Pleasant Valley Vet Clinic Inc 1710 Otsego Ave *Web:* pvvetclinic.com	Coshocton	OH	43812	740-622-3376		794
Pleasant View Gardens Inc 7316 Pleasant St *TF:* 866-862-2974 ■ *Web:* pwpvg.com	Loudon	NH	03307	603-435-8361	435-6849	323
Pleasanton Chamber of Commerce 777 Peters Ave *Web:* www.pleasanton.org	Pleasanton	CA	94566	925-846-5858	846-9697	139
Pleasanton Garbage Service Inc 3110 Busch Rd *Web:* www.pleasantongarbageservice.com	Pleasanton	CA	94566	925-846-2042	846-9323	660
Pleasanton Weekly 5506 Sunol Blvd Ste 100 *Web:* www.pleasantonweekly.com	Pleasanton	CA	94566	925-600-0840		532-3
Pleasants County 40 Vaughn Rd	Saint Marys	WV	26170	304-684-9942		338
Pleasantville Union Free School District 60 Romer Ave *Web:* pleasantvilleschools.org	Pleasantville	NY	10570	914-741-1400	741-1499	685
Please Touch Museum Memorial Hall Fairmount Pk 4231 Ave of the Republic *Web:* www.pleasetouchmuseum.org	Philadelphia	PA	19131	215-581-3181	581-3183	521
Pleasure Bar & Restaurant 4729 Liberty Ave *Web:* pleasurebarpittsburgh.com	Pittsburgh	PA	15224	412-682-9603		671
Pleiger Plastics Co PO Box 1271 *TF:* 800-753-4437 ■ *Web:* pleiger.com	Washington	PA	15301	724-228-2244	228-2253	608
Pleora Technologies Inc 340 Terry Fox Dr Ste 300 *TF:* 888-687-6877 ■ *Web:* www.pleora.com	Kanata	ON	K2K3A2	613-270-0625	270-1425	668

Company / Address	City	State	ZIP	Phone	Fax	Class
Pletronics Inc 19013 36th Ave W Ste H *Web:* www.pletronics.com	Lynnwood	WA	98036	425-776-1880	776-2760	253
Pleune Service Co 750 Himes SE *Web:* www.pleuneservice.com	Grand Rapids	MI	49548	616-243-6374		189-10
Plews Shadley Racher & Braun LLP 1346 N Delaware St *Web:* www.psrb.com	Indianapolis	IN	46202	317-637-0700		428
Plex Systems Inc 1731 Harmon Rd *Web:* www.plex.com	Auburn Hills	MI	48326	248-391-8001		178-12
Plexsys Interface Products Inc 4900 NW Camas Meadows Dr *Web:* www.plexsys.com	Camas	WA	98607	360-838-2500		180
Plexus Corp 1 Plexus Way PO Box 156 *NASDAQ: PLXS* ■ *TF:* 877-733-7260 ■ *Web:* www.plexus.com	Neenah	WI	54957	920-722-3451	751-5395	625
Plexus Ventures LLC 1701 Waterford Way **Fax Area Code:* 267 ■ *Web:* www.plexusventures.com	Maple Glen	PA	19002	215-715-0539	937-2081*	463
Plexxikon Inc 91 Bolivar Dr *Web:* www.plexxikon.com	Berkeley	CA	94710	510-647-4000	548-8014	668
PLF (Public Lands Foundation) PO Box 7226 *TF:* 866-985-9636 ■ *Web:* publicland.org	Arlington	VA	22207	703-935-0916		48-13
PLG (Philip Lief Group Inc) 130 Wall St *Web:* www.philipliefgroup.com	Princeton	NJ	08540	609-430-1000		94
PLH Products Inc 6655 Knott Ave *TF:* 800-946-6001 ■ *Web:* healthmatesauna.com	Buena Park	CA	90620	714-739-6600		791
PLI (Practising Law Institute) 1177 Avenue of the Americas 2nd Fl **Fax Area Code:* 800 ■ *TF:* 800-260-4754 ■ *Web:* www.pli.edu	New York	NY	10036	212-824-5700	321-0093*	49-10
Plibrico Co 1010 N Hooker St *TF:* 800-255-8793 ■ *Web:* plibrico.com	Chicago	IL	60622	312-337-9000	337-9003	663
Plimoth Plantation 137 Warren Ave *Web:* www.plimoth.org	Plymouth	MA	02360	508-746-1622		520
Plitek LLC 69 Rawls Rd *TF:* 800-966-1250 ■ *Web:* www.plitek.com	Des Plaines	IL	60018	800-966-1250		608
Pliteq Inc 1370 Don Mills Rd Unit 300 *Web:* pliteq.com	Toronto	ON	M3B3N7	416-449-0049		261
PLK Consulting Group LLC 3 Stone Dr *Web:* www.plkconsulting.com	Westport	CT	06880	203-221-8221		194
PLMA (Private Label Manufacturers Assn) 630 Third Ave *Web:* plma.com	New York	NY	10017	212-972-3131	983-1382	49-18
PLN & Associates Inc 15400 Jennings Ln Ste 300 *TF:* 800-699-0299 ■ *Web:* www.pln-inc.com	Bowie	MD	20721	301-390-4635		463
Plochman Inc 1333 N Boudreau Rd *Web:* www.plochman.com	Manteno	IL	60950	815-468-3434		296-19
Plote Inc 1100 Brandt Dr *Web:* www.plote.com	Hoffman Estates	IL	60192	847-695-9300		188-4
Plough Publishing House 151 Bowne Dr *TF:* 800-521-8011 ■ *Web:* www.plough.com	Walden	NY	12586	845-572-3455		637-2
Ploughshares (PS) Emerson College 120 Boylston St *Web:* www.pshares.org	Boston	MA	02116	617-824-3757		637-9
Plouse Precision Manufacturing 401 Aviation Way *Web:* www.plousemanufacturing.com	Highspire	PA	17034	717-558-8530	564-1919	454
Plowshare Group Inc 1 Dock St *Web:* www.plowsharegroup.com	Stamford	CT	06902	203-425-3949		4
PLP (Pro Lingua Press) PO Box 24368 *Web:* www.prolinguapress.com	Los Angeles	CA	90024	310-472-8396	472-0770	637-2
PLR (Phoenix Learning Resources) 812 Court St *TF:* 800-228-9345 ■ *Web:* www.phoenixlearningresources.com	Honesdale	PA	18431	570-251-6871	253-3227	637-2
PLRB (Property Loss Research Bureau) 3025 Highland Pkwy Ste 800 *TF:* 888-711-7572 ■ *Web:* www.plrb.org	Downers Grove	IL	60515	630-724-2200	724-2260	49-9
PLS Custom House Broker Inc 5200 W Loomis Rd *Web:* plschb.com	Greendale	WI	53129	414-858-1051		653
PLSN (Pro Lights & Staging News) 6000 S Eastern Ste 14-J *Web:* www.plsn.com	Las Vegas	NV	89119	702-932-5585	932-5584	457-21
Plug Power Inc 968 Albany-Shaker Rd *TF:* 800-283-1922 ■ *Web:* www.plugpower.com	Latham	NY	12110	518-782-7700		253
Plum Creek Specialty Hospital 5601 Plum Creek Dr	Amarillo	TX	79124	806-351-1000		450
Plum Grove Inc 2160 Stoningtone Ave *TF:* 866-738-3702 ■ *Web:* plumgroveinc.com	Hoffman Estates	IL	60169	847-882-4020		627
Plum Island Animal Disease Ctr 1400 Independence Ave SW *Web:* www.ars.usda.gov	Washington	DC	20250	631-323-3200	323-3006	668
Plum Market Corp 30777 Northwestern Hwy Ste 301 *Web:* www.plummarket.com	Farmington Hills	MI	48334	248-706-1600		345
Plumas County 520 Main St Rm 309 *Web:* www.countyofplumas.com	Quincy	CA	95971	530-283-6155	283-6415	338
Plumas County Visitors Bureau 550 Crescent St *TF:* 800-326-2247 ■ *Web:* www.plumascounty.org	Quincy	CA	95971	530-283-6345		206
Plumas-Eureka State Park 310 Johnsville Rd *Web:* www.parks.ca.gov	Blairsden	CA	96103	530-836-2380		565
Plumas-Sierra Rural Electric Co-op 73233 SR-70 *TF:* 800-555-2207 ■ *Web:* www.psrec.coop	Portola	CA	96122	530-832-4261	832-5761	245
Plumb Memorial Library 65 Wooster St *Web:* sheltonlibrarysystem.org	Shelton	CT	06484	203-924-1580	924-8422	434-3
Plumb Supply Co 1622 NE 51st Ave *TF:* 800-483-9511 ■ *Web:* www.plumbsupply.com	Des Moines	IA	50313	515-262-9511	262-9790	612
Plumbers & Steamfitters Local 166 2930 W Ludwig Rd *Web:* www.ualocal166.org	Fort Wayne	IN	46818	260-490-5696	490-5697	167-3
Plumbers Local Union No 68 502 Link Rd *TF:* 800-798-1074 ■ *Web:* www.plu68.com	Houston	TX	77009	713-869-3592	869-3671	414
Plumbers Supply Co 1000 E Main St *TF:* 800-626-5133 ■ *Web:* www.plumbers-supply-co.com	Louisville	KY	40206	502-582-2261	585-5521	612
Plumbing Concepts Inc 2445 Railroad St *Web:* www.plumbingconcepts.com	Corona	CA	92880	951-520-8590		610
Plumbing Distributors Inc 1025 Old Norcross Rd *TF:* 800-262-9231 ■ *Web:* relyonpdi.com	Lawrenceville	GA	30046	770-963-9231		612
Plumbing Industry Board Trade Education Committee 3711 47th Ave *TF:* 800-638-7442 ■ *Web:* www.ualocal1.org	Long Island City	NY	11101	718-752-9630		414
Plumbing Manufacturers Intl (PMI) 1921 Rohlwing Rd Unit G *Web:* www.safeplumbing.org	Rolling Meadows	IL	60008	847-481-5500	481-5501	49-3
Plumbing Wholesale Outlet 520 N Fair Oaks Ave *Web:* www.pwooutlet.com	Pasadena	CA	91103	626-744-3170	744-3175	612
Plumbing-Heating-Cooling Contractors NA (PHCC) 180 S Washington St Ste 100 *TF:* 800-533-7694 ■ *Web:* www.phccweb.org	Falls Church	VA	22046	703-237-8100	237-7442	49-3
Plumley Engineering PC 8232 Loop Rd *Web:* plumleyeng.com	Baldwinsville	NY	13027	315-638-8587	638-9740	261
Plummer Forest Products Inc 401 N Poltatch Rd *Web:* plummerforestproducts.com	Post Falls	ID	83854	208-773-7521		683
Plummer House 1091 SW Plummer Ln *Web:* www.rochestermn.gov	Rochester	MN	55902	507-328-2900	328-2901	50-3
Plummer Slade Inc 428 Forbes Ave Ste 2450 *Web:* plummerslade.com	Pittsburgh	PA	15219	412-261-5600	261-1528	180
Plump Engineering Inc 914 E Katella Ave *Web:* peica.com	Anaheim	CA	92805	714-385-1835		539
Plump Jack's Squaw Valley Inn 1920 Squaw Valley Rd PO Box 2407 *TF:* 800-323-7666 ■ *Web:* plumpjacksquawvalleyinn.com	Olympic Valley	CA	96146	530-583-1576	583-1734	379
Plump's Last Shot 6416 Cornell Ave *Web:* www.plumpslastshot.com	Indianapolis	IN	46220	317-257-5867		671
PlumpJack Group 3138 Fillmore St *Web:* www.plumpjack.com	San Francisco	CA	94123	415-346-5712	474-8792	671
Plumrose USA Inc 1901 Butterfield Rd Ste 305 *TF:* 800-526-4909 ■ *Web:* www.plumroseusa.com	Downers Grove	IL	60515	732-624-4040		473
Plums Bank 35 S Lindan Ave *NASDAQ: PLBC* ■ *Web:* plumasbank.com	Quincy	CA	95971	530-283-7305		70
Plunge LLC 225 Ocean Dr W *TF:* 844-758-6434 ■ *Web:* www.plungedigital.com	Stamford	CT	06902	844-758-6434		196
Plunkett Research Ltd PO Box 541737 *Web:* www.plunkettresearch.com	Houston	TX	77254	713-932-0000		626
Plunkett's Pest Control 40 NE 52nd Way *TF:* 866-906-1780 ■ *Web:* www.plunketts.net	Fridley	MN	55421	866-906-1780		577
Plus Group 135 Merchant St Ste 300 *Web:* www.plusgroups.com	Cincinnati	OH	45246	513-742-7590		256
Plus Group Inc, The (TPG) 7425 Janes Ave Ste 201 *Web:* theplusgroup.com	Woodridge	IL	60517	630-515-0500	515-0510	721
PlusOne Solutions Inc 3501 Quadrangle Blvd Ste 120 *TF:* 877-943-0100 ■ *Web:* plusonesolutions.net	Orlando	FL	32817	407-359-5929		196
Plustech Inc 735 E Remington Rd *Web:* www.plustech-inc.com	Schaumburg	IL	60173	847-490-8130	490-3192	757
Pluto Corp PO Box 391 *Web:* www.plutocorp.com	French Lick	IN	47432	812-936-9988	936-2828	98
Pluymert, Macdonald, Hargrove & Lee Ltd 2300 Barrington Rd Ste 220 *Web:* lawpmh.com	Hoffman Estates	IL	60169	847-310-0025	310-0054	41
PLWC (Paragould Light Water & Cable) 1901 Jones Rd *Web:* www.paragould.com	Paragould	AR	72450	870-239-7700		116
PLX Pharma Inc 8285 El Rio Ste 130 *Web:* plxpharma.com	Houston	TX	77054	713-842-1249		231
Ply Gem 5020 Weston Pkwy Ste 400 *TF:* 800-786-2726 ■ *Web:* www.plygem.com	Cary	NC	27513	888-975-9436	842-3991	697
Plyler Construction 3505 Texoma Pkwy PO Box 912406 *Web:* www.plylerbuilds.com	Sherman	TX	75091	903-893-6393	892-3523	189-10
PlymKraft Inc 479 Export Cir *TF:* 800-992-0854 ■ *Web:* www.plymkraft.com	Newport News	VA	23601	757-595-0364	595-3993	208
Plymold 615 Centennial Dr *TF:* 800-759-6653 ■ *Web:* www.plymold.com	Kenyon	MN	55946	800-759-6653		319-1
Plymouth Area Chamber of Commerce 134 Court St *Web:* plymouthchamber.com	Plymouth	MA	02360	508-830-1620	830-1621	139
Plymouth Community Chamber of Commerce 850 W Ann Arbor Trl *Web:* www.plymouthchamber.org	Plymouth	MI	48170	734-453-1540		139
Plymouth County 215 4th Ave SE *Web:* www.co.plymouth.ia.us	Le Mars	IA	51031	712-546-6100	546-5784	338
Plymouth Foam Inc 1800 Sunset Dr *TF:* 800-669-1176 ■ *Web:* www.plymouthfoam.com	Plymouth	WI	53073	920-893-0535		601
Plymouth Foundry Inc 523 W Harrison St *Web:* www.plymouthfoundry.com	Plymouth	IN	46563	574-936-2106		492
Plymouth Harbor 700 John Ringling Blvd *Web:* plymouthharbor.org	Sarasota	FL	34236	941-365-2600		672
Plymouth Place Inc 315 N LaGrange Rd *Web:* www.plymouthplace.org	LaGrange	IL	60526	708-354-0340		450
Plymouth Public Library 132 S St *Web:* www.plymouthpubliclibrary.org	Plymouth	MA	02360	508-830-4250		434-3
Plymouth Rubber Company Inc 960 Turnpike St **Fax Area Code:* 844 ■ *TF:* 800-458-0336 ■ *Web:* www.plymouthrubber.com	Canton	MA	02021	800-458-0336	849-7219*	732
Plymouth Spring Company Inc 281 Lake Ave *Web:* www.plymouthspring.com	Bristol	CT	06010	860-584-0594	584-0943	719

Name / Address	City	State	ZIP	Phone	Fax	Class
Plymouth State University 17 High St *TF:* 800-842-6900 ■ *Web:* www.plymouth.edu	Plymouth	NH	03264	603-535-2237	535-2714	166
Plymouth Technology Inc 2925 Waterview Dr *TF:* 800-535-5053 ■ *Web:* www.plymouthtechnology.com	Rochester Hills	MI	48309	248-537-0081		612
Plymouth Tube Co 29W150 Warrenville Rd *TF:* 800-323-9506 ■ *Web:* www.plymouth.com	Warrenville	IL	60555	630-393-3550	393-3551	490
Plywood Hawaii Inc 1062 Kikowaena Pl *TF:* 800-263-7049 ■ *Web:* www.plywoodhawaii.com	Honolulu	HI	96819	808-834-1144	834-1232	364
Plywood Supply Inc 7036 NE 175th St *TF:* 888-774-9663 ■ *Web:* www.plywoodsupply.com	Kenmore	WA	98028	425-485-8585	485-6195	613
PM Construction Company Inc PO Box 728 *TF:* 800-646-0068 ■ *Web:* www.pmconstruction.com	Saco	ME	04072	207-282-7697		186
PM Environmental Inc 3340 Ranger Rd *TF:* 800-313-2966 ■ *Web:* www.pmenv.com	Lansing	MI	48906	517-321-3331		194
PM Group, The 7550 I-10 W Ste 510 *Web:* thepmgrp.com	San Antonio	TX	78229	210-490-2554		4
PM Machining Inc 8630 Argent St Ste C *Web:* www.pmmachining.com	Santee	CA	92071	619-449-8989	258-7958	454
PM Parties Inc 701 Matthews Mint Hill Rd Ste C	Matthews	NC	28105	704-841-1370		327
PM Press PO Box 23912 *Web:* www.pmpress.org	Oakland	CA	94623	510-658-3906		637-2
PM Realty Group (PMRG) 1000 Main St Ste 2400 *Web:* www.pmrg.com	Houston	TX	77002	713-209-5800	209-5702	655
PM Recovery Inc 106 Calvert St *Web:* www.pmrecovery.com	Harrison	NY	10528	914-835-1900		411
PM Resource Group LLC 10 Sams Point Way Ste B-1 Ste 165 *Web:* www.pmresourcegroup.com	Beaufort	SC	29907	404-247-6968		765
PMA (Polish Museum of America) 984 N Milwaukee Ave *Web:* www.polishmuseumofamerica.org	Chicago	IL	60642	773-384-3352	384-3799	520
PMA (Polyurethane Manufacturers Assn) 6737 W Washington St Ste 1420 *Web:* www.pmahome.org	Milwaukee	WI	53214	414-431-3094		49-13
PMA (Precision Metalforming Assn) 6363 Oak Tree Blvd *Web:* www.pma.org	Independence	OH	44131	216-901-8800	901-9190	49-3
PMA (Produce Marketing Assn) 1500 Casho Mill Rd *Web:* www.pma.com	Newark	DE	19711	302-738-7100	731-2409	49-6
PMA Canada Ltd 231 Oak Park Blvd Ste 400 *TF:* 800-667-9463 ■ *Web:* www.pmacanada.com	Oakville	ON	L6H7S8	905-257-2116	257-2286	41
PMA Consultants LLC 1 Woodward Ave Ste 1400 *Web:* pmaconsultants.com	Detroit	MI	48226	313-963-8863		194
PMA Engineering 6717 Shawnee Mission Pkwy Ste 100 *Web:* pmaengineering.com	Overland Park	KS	66202	913-831-1262	831-0148	261
PMA Inc 17128 Edwards Rd *Web:* www.printmgt.com	Cerritos	CA	90703	562-407-9977		627
PMA Sleep Wellness Ctr 826 Main St Ste 100 *Web:* pmadoctor.com	Phoenixville	PA	19460	610-933-0200	917-0320	352
PMAA (Petroleum Marketers Association of America) 1901 N Ft Myer Dr Ste 500 *Web:* www.pmaa.org	Arlington	VA	22209	703-351-8000	351-9160	49-18
Pmalliance Inc 2075 Spencers Way Ste 201 *Web:* pm-alliance.com	Stone Mountain	GA	30087	770-938-4947		463
PMB Broadcasting LLC 1820 Wynnton Rd *Web:* pmbsites.com	Columbus	GA	31904	706-327-1217		645-39
PMB Helin Donovan LLP 12301 Research Blvd Bldg V Ste 160 *TF:* 877-762-4360 ■ *Web:* pmbhd.com	Austin	TX	78759	512-258-9670	233-0530	2
PMC (Power Management Concepts LLC) 510 Grumman Rd W Ste 211 *Web:* powermanage.com	Bethpage	NY	11714	516-605-9451		463
PMC (Pelorus Management Consultants) 19 Crossfield Ct *Web:* www.pmcinfo.com	Bedminster	NJ	07921	862-368-0038		194
PMC Biogenix Inc 1231 Pope St *Fax Area Code: 800 ■ *TF:* 800-641-2152 ■ *Web:* pmcbiogenix.com	Memphis	TN	38108	901-325-4930	641-2153*	601
PMC Commercial Trust 17950 Preston Rd Ste 600 *NASDAQ: CMCT* ■ *TF:* 800-486-3223 ■ *Web:* www.cimgroup.com	Dallas	TX	75252	972-349-3200	349-3265	216
PMC Engineering LLC 11 Old Sugar Hollow Rd *TF:* 800-869-5747 ■ *Web:* www.pmc1.com	Danbury	CT	06810	203-792-8686	743-2051	201
PMC Global Inc 12243 Branford St *Web:* www.pmcglobalinc.com	Sun Valley	CA	91352	818-896-1101	897-0180	145
PMC Group Inc 1288 Rt 73 S Pmc Group Bldg Ste 401 *Web:* pmc-group.com	Mount Laurel	NJ	08054	856-533-1866		608
PMC Industries 275 Hudson St *Web:* www.pmc-industries.com	Hackensack	NJ	07601	201-342-3684	342-3568	547
PMC Industries Inc 12155 Commissioner Dr *Web:* www.pmc-colinet.com	Wickliffe	OH	44092	440-943-3300	944-1974	455
PMC Insurance Agency Inc 209 Burlington Rd Ste 109 *Web:* pmcinsurance.com	Bedford	MA	01730	781-449-7744		390
PMC Lenco 10240 Deer Park Rd *TF:* 877-789-5844 ■ *Web:* www.pmc-group.com	Waverly	NE	68462	402-786-2000	786-5050	604
PMC Mechanical Contractors Inc 15 S Ridge Ave *Web:* www.mcaepa.org	Ambler	PA	19002	215-628-3806		610
PMC SMART Solutions LLC 9825 Kenwood Rd Ste 302 *Web:* pmcsmartsolutions.com	Cincinnati	OH	45242	513-921-5040		604
PMC Specialties Group Inc 501 Murray Rd *TF:* 800-543-2466 ■ *Web:* www.pmcsg.com	Cincinnati	OH	45217	800-543-2466		144
PMC Systems Ltd 12155 Commissioner Dr *Web:* www.pmcsystems.com	North Jackson	OH	44451	330-538-2268	538-2270	203
PMD Healthcare 1555 Bustard Rd Ste 200 *Web:* remetrichealth.com	Lansdale	PA	19446	484-664-7600		363
PME Equip Inc 304 Garden Oaks Blvd	Houston	TX	77018	713-691-3081		358
PMEL (Pacific Marine Environmental Laboratory) 7600 Sand Pt Way NE *Web:* pmel.noaa.gov	Seattle	WA	98115	206-526-6239	526-6815	668
PMG (Performance Management Group, The) 3125 Geddes Ave *Web:* www.pmga2.com	Ann Arbor	MI	48104	734-216-4849	555-5555	194
PMG Indiana LLC 1751 Arcadia Dr *Web:* www.pmgsinter.com	Columbus	IN	47201	812-379-4606	379-1216	60
PMG Project Management Group LLC 2723 Houston Ave *Web:* www.pmgunited.com	Houston	TX	77009	713-880-2626		186
PMGLC (Pittman McLenagan Group LC, The) 6626 Wilson Ln *TF:* 855-512-9430 ■ *Web:* www.pmglc.com	Bethesda	MD	20817	855-512-9430		194
PMHD (Pioneers Memorial Healthcare District) 207 W Legion Rd *Web:* www.pmhd.org	Brawley	CA	92227	760-351-3333		374-3
PMHI (Pacific Modern Homes Inc) 9723 Railroad St *TF:* 800-395-1011 ■ *Web:* pmhi.com	Elk Grove	CA	95624	800-395-1011		106
PMI (Plumbing Manufacturers Intl) 1921 Rohlwing Rd Unit G *Web:* www.safeplumbing.org	Rolling Meadows	IL	60008	847-481-5500	481-5501	49-3
PMI (Penn Manufacturing Industries Inc) 506 Stump Rd *Web:* www.pennmfg.com	Montgomeryville	PA	18936	215-362-1217	362-3918	757
PMI (Project Management Institute) 14 Campus Blvd *TF:* 866-276-4764 ■ *Web:* www.pmi.org	Newtown Square	PA	19073	610-356-4600	356-4647	49-12
PMI (Professional Machining Inc) 3840 SW 113th St *Web:* www.hepman.com	Oklahoma City	OK	73173	405-691-1215		60
PMI KYOTO Packaging Systems 850 Pratt Blvd *Web:* www.pmikyoto.com	Elk Grove Village	IL	60007	847-437-1427		547
PMI Mortgage Insurance Co 3003 Oak Rd *OTC: PMI* ■ *TF:* 800-288-1970 ■ *Web:* www.pmi-us.com	Walnut Creek	CA	94597	800-288-1970		360-4
PML Inc 201 W Beach Ave *TF:* 800-335-4345 ■ *Web:* www.yourcovers.com	Inglewood	CA	90302	310-671-4345	671-0858	54
PMMC (Pottstown Memorial Medical Ctr) 1600 E High St *Web:* pottstown.towerhealth.org	Pottstown	PA	19464	610-327-7000		374-3
PMMI (Packaging Machinery Manufacturers Institute) 4350 N Fairfax Dr Ste 600 *TF:* 888-275-7664 ■ *Web:* www.pmmi.org	Arlington	VA	22203	703-243-8555	243-8556	49-13
PMOLink LLC 2001 Lakeshore Dr *TF:* 800-401-5701 ■ *Web:* www.pmolink.com	Mandeville	LA	70448	985-674-5968		196
PMP Corp 25 Security Dr *TF:* 800-243-6628 ■ *Web:* www.pmp-corp.com	Avon	CT	06001	860-677-9656	674-0196	495
PMP Network PO Box 639 *Web:* www.pmpnetwork.com	Randolph	MA	02368	781-341-8332	344-7207	647
PMPA (Precision Machined Products Assn) 6700 W Snowville Rd *Web:* www.pmpa.org	Brecksville	OH	44141	440-526-0300	526-5803	49-13
PMPED (Peters Murdaugh Parker Eltzroth & Detrick PA) 123 S Walter St PO Box 1164 *Web:* www.pmped.com	Walterboro	SC	29488	843-549-9544	549-9546	428
PMRG (PM Realty Group) 1000 Main St Ste 2400 *Web:* www.pmrg.com	Houston	TX	77002	713-209-5800	209-5702	655
PMRS Inc 202 Precision Rd *Web:* www.pmrsinc.com	Horsham	PA	19044	267-960-3300		743
PMS (Portsmouth Marine Society) PO Box 728 *Web:* portsmouthhistory.org	Portsmouth	NH	03802	603-436-8433		637-2
PMS Systems Corp 26707 Agoura Rd Ste 201 *TF:* 800-755-3968 ■ *Web:* www.assetsmart.com	Calabasas	CA	91302	310-450-2566	450-1311	178-5
PMT Corp 1500 Park Rd *Web:* www.pmtcorp.com	Chanhassen	MN	55317	952-470-0866	470-0865	475
PMX Industries Inc 5300 Willow Creek Dr SW *TF:* 800-531-5268 ■ *Web:* www.ipmx.com	Cedar Rapids	IA	52404	319-368-7700	368-7721	492
PNB (Pacific Northwest Ballet) 301 Mercer St *Web:* www.pnb.org	Seattle	WA	98109	206-441-2424	441-2420	573-1
PNBC (Progressive National Baptist Convention Inc) 601 50th St NE *TF:* 800-876-7622 ■ *Web:* www.pnbc.org	Washington	DC	20019	202-396-0558	398-4998	48-20
PNC Arena 1400 EdWards Mill Rd *Web:* www.pncarena.com	Raleigh	NC	27607	919-861-2300	861-2310	720
PNC Bank 1 PNC Plz 300 Fifth Ave 29th Fl *TF:* 888-762-2265 ■ *Web:* www.pnc.com	Pittsburgh	PA	15222	412-762-2000	762-7829	70
PNC Inc 115 E Centre St *Web:* www.pnconline.com	Nutley	NJ	07110	973-284-1600	284-1925	625
Pneudraulics Inc 8575 Helms Ave *Web:* www.pneudraulics.com	Rancho Cucamonga	CA	91730	909-980-5366	945-2821	790
Pneumadyne Inc 14425 23rd Ave N *Web:* www.pneumadyne.com	Plymouth	MN	55447	763-559-0177		789
Pneumatic & Hydraulic Systems Company Inc 1338 Petroleum Pkwy *TF:* 877-836-1999 ■ *Web:* pneumaticandhydraulic.com	Broussard	LA	70518	337-839-1999		358
Pneumatic Scale Angelus 4485 Allen Rd *Web:* psangelus.com	Stow	OH	44224	330-923-0491		547
Pneumatrek Inc 2037 S 4130 W Ste B *Web:* www.pneumatrek.com	Salt Lake City	UT	84104	801-486-2178	466-0737	385

Name / Address	City	State	Zip	Phone	Fax	Class
Pneumech Systems Manufacturing LLC 201 Pneu Mech Dr	Statesville	NC	28625	704-873-2475		18
TF: 800-274-5724 ■ *Web:* www.pneu-mech.com						
Pneumercator Inc 120 Finn Ct	Farmingdale	NY	11735	631-293-8450		61
Web: www.pneumercator.com						
Pneumex Inc 2605 N Boyer Ave	Sandpoint	ID	83864	208-265-4105		196
TF: 800-447-5792 ■ *Web:* www.pneumex.com						
Pneutek 17 Friars Dr	Hudson	NH	03051	603-883-1660	882-9165	759
TF: 800-431-8665 ■ *Web:* www.pneutek.com						
PNGTS (Portland Natural Gas Transmission System) 1 Harbour Pl	Portsmouth	NH	03801	603-559-5500	427-2807	325
TF: 855-895-8754 ■ *Web:* www.pngts.com						
PNK (River City) LLC 777 River City Casino Blvd	Saint Louis	MO	63125	888-578-7289		377
TF: 888-578-7289 ■ *Web:* www.rivercity.com						
PNM Resources Inc Alvarado Sq	Albuquerque	NM	87158	505-241-2700		360-5
NYSE: PNM ■ *TF:* 888-342-5766 ■ *Web:* www.pnmresources.com						
PNNL (Pacific Northwest National Laboratory) 902 Battelle Blvd PO Box 999	Richland	WA	99352	509-375-2121	375-2507	668
TF: 888-375-7665 ■ *Web:* www.pnnl.gov						
PNR RailWorks Inc 2595 Deacon St PO Box 2280	Abbotsford	BC	V2T4X2	604-850-9166		188
Web: www.pnrail.com						
PNT Marketing Services Inc 2420 Jackson Ave Ste 203	Long Island City	NY	11101	718-433-4053		195
Pnucor Inc 10525 Granite St PO Box 7209	Charlotte	NC	28273	704-588-3333	588-6002	640
TF: 800-849-8097 ■ *Web:* www.pnucor.com						
PNWFCU (Pacific NW Federal Credit Union) 12106 NE Marx St	Portland	OR	97220	503-256-5858	253-5858	219
TF: 866-692-8669 ■ *Web:* www.pnwfcu.org						
PNY Technologies Inc 100 Jefferson Rd	Parsippany	NJ	07054	973-560-5382	560-5590	288
TF: 800-769-0143 ■ *Web:* www.pny.com						
Poarch Thompson Law Immigration & Adoption 203 S College Ave	Salem	VA	24153	540-387-1005		41
Web: poarchthompsonlaw.com						
Poblocki Sign Company LLC 922 S 70th St	Milwaukee	WI	53214	414-453-4010	453-3070	701
TF: 800-776-7064 ■ *Web:* www.poblocki.com						
Pocahontas Aluminum Coinc 2001 Industrial Dr	Pocahontas	AR	72455	870-892-3689		234
Web: www.pocahontasaluminum.com						
Pocahontas County PO Box 275	Marlinton	WV	24954	800-336-7009		338
TF: 800-336-7009 ■ *Web:* pocahontascountywv.com						
Pocahontas State Park 10301 State Park Rd	Chesterfield	VA	23832	804-796-4255	796-4004	565
Web: www.dcr.virginia.gov						
Pocan Mark (Rep D - WI) 1421 Longworth House Office Bldg	Washington	DC	20515	202-225-2906	225-6942	342-2
Web: www.pocan.house.gov						
Pocatello Art Ctr (PAC) 444 N Main St	Pocatello	ID	83204	208-232-0970		50-2
Web: www.pocatelloartcenter.org						
Pocatello Downs 10588 Fairgrounds Rd	Pocatello	ID	83202	208-238-1721	238-5877	642
Web: www.theracingjournal.com						
Pocatello Women's Correctional Ctr 1451 Fore Rd	Pocatello	ID	83204	208-236-6360	236-6362	213
Web: www.idoc.idaho.gov						
Pocatello Zoo 2900 S Second Ave	Pocatello	ID	83204	208-234-6264		823
Web: www.zooidaho.org						
Pocino Foods Co 14250 Lomitas Ave	City of Industry	CA	91746	626-968-8000	968-0196	296-26
TF: 800-345-0150 ■ *Web:* www.pocinofoods.com						
Pocket Opera 469 Bryant St	San Francisco	CA	94107	415-972-8930		573-2
Web: pocketopera.org						
Pocket Press Inc PO Box 25124	Portland	OR	97298	888-237-2110	643-3732*	637-2
**Fax Area Code:* 877 ■ *TF:* 888-237-2110 ■ *Web:* www.pocketpressinc.com						
PocketiNet Communications Inc 45 Terminal Loop Rd Ste 210	Walla Walla	WA	99362	509-526-5026		224
Web: www.pocketinet.com						
Pocketwatch Inc 8500 Steller Dr Bldg 7	Culver City	CA	90232	424-298-8234		242
Web: pocket.watch						
Poclain Hydraulics Inc PO Box 801	Sturtevant	WI	53177	262-321-0676	321-0703	385
Web: www.poclain-hydraulics.com						
Pocock Racing Shells 615 80th St SW	Everett	WA	98203	425-438-9048		698
TF: 888-762-6251 ■ *Web:* www.pocock.com						
Pocomoke River State Park 3461 Worcester Hwy	Snow Hill	MD	21863	410-632-2566	632-2914	565
Web: www.dnr.maryland.gov						
Pocono Manor Golf Resort & Spa 1 Manor Dr Rt 314	Pocono Manor	PA	18349	800-944-8392	839-3407*	669
**Fax Area Code:* 570 ■ *TF:* 800-233-8150 ■ *Web:* www.poconomanor.com						
Pocono Mountain Villas By Exploria Resorts 5785 Milford Rd	East Stroudsburg	PA	18302	888-337-6966	588-7112*	669
**Fax Area Code:* 570 ■ *TF:* 888-337-6966 ■ *Web:* www.exploriaresorts.com						
Pocono Mountains Vacation Bureau 1004 W Main St	Stroudsburg	PA	18360	570-421-5791	421-6927	206
TF: 800-722-9199 ■ *Web:* www.poconomountains.com						
Pocono Produce Company Inc (PPC) Chipperfield Dr Rte 191	Stroudsburg	PA	18360	570-421-4990	476-5149	297-2
TF: 800-366-4550 ■ *Web:* poconoprofoods.com						
Pocono Raceway Long Pond Rd PO Box 500	Long Pond	PA	18334	570-646-2300	646-2010	515
TF: 800-722-3929 ■ *Web:* www.poconoraceway.com						
Pocono Record 511 Lenox St	Stroudsburg	PA	18360	570-421-3000	421-6284	532-2
TF: 800-530-6310 ■ *Web:* www.poconorecord.com						
Pocumtuck Valley Memorial Assn (PVMA) 10 Memorial St	Deerfield	MA	01342	413-774-7476		49-19
Web: deerfield-ma.org						
POD 3636 Sansom St	Philadelphia	PA	19104	215-387-1803		671
Web: podrestaurant.com						
Podiatry Insurance Company of America 3000 Meridian Blvd Ste 400	Franklin	TN	37067	615-984-2005	370-9021	391-5
TF: 800-251-5727 ■ *Web:* www.picagroup.com						
Podium 1650 W Digital Dr	Lehi	UT	84043	801-758-0580		39
Web: www.podium.com						
Podoll & Podoll PC 5619 Dtc Pkwy Ste 1100	Greenwood Village	CO	80111	303-861-4000		41
Web: podoll.net						
Poepping Stone Bach & Associates Incorporated Engr 100 S 54th St PO Box 709	Quincy	IL	62305	217-223-4605		727
Web: www.psba.com						
Poersch Metal Manufacturing Co 4027 W Kinzie St	Chicago	IL	60624	773-722-0890	722-4122	482
Web: www.poerschmetal.com						
Poet LLC 4615 N Lewis Ave	Sioux Falls	SD	57104	605-965-2200		580
Web: poet.com						
Poetry Pals Inc 295 SW Brushy Mound Rd	Burleson	TX	76028	817-295-6680	295-4657	95
Web: www.poetrypals.com						
Poets & Writers Magazine 90 Broad St Ste 2100	New York	NY	10004	212-226-3586	226-3963	457-10
Web: www.pw.org						
Poets on the Line PO Box 020292	Brooklyn	NY	11202	971-655-9491		637-9
Web: www.echonyc.com						
Poggemeyer Design Group Inc 1168 N Main St	Bowling Green	OH	43402	419-352-7537	353-0187	261
Web: www.poggemeyer.com						
Pogonias Press Inc 1411 Shannock Rd	Charlestown	RI	02813	800-296-6310		637-2
TF: 800-296-6310 ■ *Web:* www.awpdb.com						
Pohanka of Salisbury 2007 N Salisbury Blvd	Salisbury	MD	21801	410-202-3450		516
Web: www.pohankaofsalisbury.com						
Pohl Transportation Inc 9297 McGreevey Rd	Versailles	OH	45380	800-837-2122	526-4810*	780
**Fax Area Code:* 937 ■ *TF:* 800-837-2122 ■ *Web:* www.pohltransportation.com						
Pohler & Associates LLC 766 Northwest Blvd	Grandview Heights	OH	43212	614-459-2700		41
Web: pohlerlaw.com						
Pohlman LLC 2316 Schuetz Rd	Saint Louis	MO	63146	636-537-1909		621
Web: www.pohlman.com						
Pohly Co 867 Boylston St 5th Fl	Boston	MA	02116	617-451-1700	338-7767	637-9
TF: 800-383-0888 ■ *Web:* www.pohlyco.com						
Poinsett County 1500 Justice Dr	Harrisburg	AR	72432	870-578-5411	578-4417	338
Web: www.poinsettcountysheriff.org						
Poinsett State Park 6660 Poinsett Park Rd	Wedgefield	SC	29168	803-494-8177		565
Web: southcarolinaparks.com						
Point Alliance Inc 20 Adelaide St E Ste 500	Toronto	ON	M5C2T6	855-947-6468		180
TF: 855-947-6468 ■ *Web:* www.pointalliance.com						
Point Au Roche State Park 19 Camp Red Cloud Rd	Plattsburgh	NY	12901	518-563-0369		565
Web: parks.ny.gov						
Point B Communications 600 W Fulton Ste 710	Chicago	IL	60661	312-867-7750		193
Web: www.pointbcommunications.com						
Point Beach State Forest 9400 County Hwy O	Two Rivers	WI	54241	920-794-7480		565
Web: dnr.wi.gov						
Point Defiance Zoo & Aquarium 5400 N Pearl St	Tacoma	WA	98407	253-591-5337	591-5448	823
Web: www.pdza.org						
Point Dume State Beach 1925 Las Virgenes Rd	Calabasas	CA	91302	818-880-0363		565
Web: www.parks.ca.gov						
Point Eight Power Inc 1510 Engineers Rd	Belle Chasse	LA	70037	504-394-6100		729
TF: 800-284-1522 ■ *Web:* www.pointeightpower.com						
Point Group, The 5949 Sherry Ln Ste 1800	Dallas	TX	75225	214-378-7970		466
Web: www.thepointgroup.com						
Point Lighting Corp 61 W Dudley Town Rd	Bloomfield	CT	06002	860-243-0600		362
Web: www.pointlighting.com						
Point Loma Nazarene University 3900 Lomaland Dr	San Diego	CA	92106	619-849-2200	849-2601	166
TF: 800-733-7770 ■ *Web:* www.pointloma.edu						
Point Lookout State Park 11175 Pt Lookout Rd	Scotland	MD	20687	301-872-5688	872-5084	565
Web: www.dnr.maryland.gov						
Point Medical Corp 891 E Summit St	Crown Point	IN	46307	219-663-1775	663-2877	476
Web: pointmedical.com						
Point of View Productions 2477 Folsom St	San Francisco	CA	94110	415-821-0435	821-0434	514
Web: www.karildaniels.com						
Point Park University 201 Wood St	Pittsburgh	PA	15222	412-391-4100	392-3902	166
TF: 800-321-0129 ■ *Web:* pointpark.edu						
Point Pelee National Park of Canada 407 Monarch Ln RR 1	Leamington	ON	N8H3V4	519-322-2365	322-1277	563
Web: www.pc.gc.ca						
Point Pleasant Beach Chamber of Commerce 517-A Arnold Ave	Point Pleasant Beach	NJ	08742	732-899-2424		139
Web: www.pointpleasantbeachchamber.com						
Point Reyes National Seashore 1 Bear Valley Rd	Point Reyes Station	CA	94956	415-464-5100	663-8132	564
Web: www.nps.gov						
Point Riders Press 520 W Eufaula St	Norman	OK	73069	405-321-7961		637-2
Web: www.pointriderspress.com						
Point Source Power Inc 132 Tharp Dr	Moraga	CA	94556	925-708-7845		696
Web: www.pointsourcepower.com						
Point State Park 601 Commonwealth Pl	Pittsburgh	PA	15222	412-565-2850		565
Web: dcnr.state.pa.us						
Point Studios, The 169 River St	Montpelier	VT	05602	802-223-2396		645
Web: pointfm.com						
Point to Point Inc 23240 Chagrin Blvd Ste 200	Cleveland	OH	44122	216-831-4421		4
Web: www.pointtopoint.com						
Point, The 222 Beaverwood Rd	Saranac Lake	NY	12983	518-891-5674	891-1152	669
TF: 800-255-3530 ■ *Web:* thepointresort.com						
Point360 2701 Media Center Dr	Los Angeles	CA	90065	818-565-1400	847-2503	512
NASDAQ: PTSX ■ *Web:* www.point360.com						

Name / Address	City	State	Zip	Phone	Fax	Class
PointCare Technologies Inc 19 Brigham St Office 9-A *Web:* www.pointcare.net	Marlborough	MA	01752	508-537-9769		476
Pointclear LLC 6470 E Johns Crossing Ste 160 *TF:* 877-582-9909 ■ *Web:* www.pointclear.com	Johns Creek	GA	30097	678-533-2700	533-2703	7
PointCross Life Sciences 1291 E Hillsdale Blvd Ste 304 *TF:* 866-468-1900 ■ *Web:* www.pointcrosslifesciences.com	Foster City	CA	94404	650-350-1900		463
Pointe Coupee Electric Membership Corp 2506 False River Dr PO Box 160 *TF:* 800-738-7232 ■ *Web:* www.pcemc.org	New Roads	LA	70760	225-638-3751	638-8124	245
Pointe General Contractors LLC 1209 Pointe Centre Dr Ste 101 *Web:* www.pointecentre.com	Chattanooga	TN	37421	423-755-0844		186
Pointe Scientific Inc 5449 Research Dr PO Box 87188 *TF:* 800-445-9853 ■ *Web:* www.pointescientific.com	Canton	MI	48188	734-487-8300	483-1592	231
Pointe-a-Calliere - The Montreal Museum of Archaeology & History 350 Royale Pl *Web:* www.pacmusee.qc.ca	Old Montreal	QC	H2Y3Y5	514-872-9150	872-9151	520
Pointivity 10201 Wateridge Cir Ste 260 *Web:* www.pointivity.com	San Diego	CA	92121	858-777-6900		39
Pointmail Inc 101 W Renner Rd Ste 300 *Fax Area Code:* 512 ■ *Web:* www.vcsy.com	Richardson	TX	75082	972-437-5200	692-1836*	178-1
Pointon Communications 202 South Blvd *Web:* pointon.com	Baraboo	WI	53913	608-355-0257	355-0261	179
Points International Ltd 171 John St 5th Fl *Web:* www.points.com	Toronto	ON	M5T1X3	416-595-0000		195
Points North Inc 371 Canal Park Dr Ste 210 *Web:* www.points-north.com	Duluth	MN	55802	218-726-1195		179
Points of Light Foundation & Volunteer Center National Network 1875 K St Ste 800 *TF:* 866-545-5307 ■ *Web:* www.pointsoflight.org	Washington	DC	20005	202-729-8000	729-8100	48-5
Pointwise Inc 213 S Jennings Ave *Web:* www.pointwise.com	Fort Worth	TX	76104	817-377-2807	377-2799	177
Poisoned Pen Bookstore 4014 N Goldwater Blvd *TF:* 888-560-9919 ■ *Web:* poisonedpen.com	Scottsdale	AZ	85251	480-947-2974	945-1023	95
Poka Lambro Telephone Cooperative Inc 560 US Hwy 87 *TF:* 877-867-0203 ■ *Web:* poka.com	Wilson	TX	79381	806-924-7234	924-5001	225
Pokagon State Park 450 Ln 100 Lake James *Web:* www.in.gov	Angola	IN	46703	260-833-2012		565
Poke Restaurant 343 E 85th St *Web:* pokesushinyc.com	New York	NY	10028	212-249-0569		671
Polack Corp, The 1400 Keystone Ave *TF:* 800-392-8759 ■ *Web:* www.polackcorp.com	Lansing	MI	48911	517-272-1400		535
Polar Asset Management Partners 401 Bay St Ste 1900 PO Box 19 *Web:* polaramp.com	Toronto	ON	M5H2Y4	416-367-4364	367-0564	528
Polar Beverages 1001 Southbridge St *TF:* 800-734-9800 ■ *Web:* polarbeverages.com	Worcester	MA	01610	800-734-9800		80-2
Polar Communications 110 Fourth St E PO Box 270 *TF:* 800-284-7222 ■ *Web:* www.polarcomm.com	Park River	ND	58270	701-284-7221	284-7205	116
Polar Hardware Manufacturing Co 1813 W Montrose Ave *Web:* www.polarmfg.com	Chicago	IL	60613	773-935-8600	935-8749	350
Polar Instruments Inc 18640 SW Farmington Rd *Web:* www.polarinstruments.com	Beaverton	OR	97007	503-356-5270		177
Polar King International Inc 4424 New Haven Ave *TF:* 800-752-7178 ■ *Web:* www.polarking.com	Fort Wayne	IN	46803	260-428-2530		14
Polar Plastics Inc 6959 N 55th St *TF:* 800-328-3155 ■ *Web:* www.polar-plastics.com	Oakdale	MN	55128	651-770-2925	770-7578	600
Polar Service Centers 7600 E Sam Houston Pkwy N *TF:* 800-955-8558 ■ *Web:* www.polartank.com	Houston	TX	77049	281-459-6400		779
Polar Systems Inc 21890 Willamette Dr *Web:* polarsystems.com	West Linn	OR	97068	503-775-4410		180
Polar Tech Industries Inc 415 E Railroad Ave *Web:* www.polar-tech.com	Genoa	IL	60135	815-784-9000		124
Polar ware 502 Hgwy 67 *TF:* 800-237-3655 ■ *Web:* polarware.com	Kiel	WI	53042	800-237-3655		489
Polaris Capital Management LLC 121 High St *Web:* www.polariscapital.com	Boston	MA	02110	617-951-1365		41
Polaris Career Ctr 7285 Old Oak Blvd *Web:* www.polaris.edu	Middleburg Heights	OH	44130	440-891-7600	243-3952	165
Polaris Consulting Engineers 214 W Main St 208 *Web:* www.polarisce.com	Moorestown	NJ	08057	856-778-5400	778-1788	261
Polaris Engineering Inc 212 Pine St *Web:* www.polarisengr.com	Lake Charles	LA	70601	337-497-0652		186
Polaris Fashion Place 1500 Polaris Pkwy *Web:* polarisfashionplace.com	Columbus	OH	43240	614-846-1500		460
Polaris Industries Inc 2100 Minnesota 55 *NYSE:* PII ■ *Web:* www.polaris.com	Medina	MN	55340	763-542-0500	542-0599	705
Polaris Pharmaceuticals Inc 9373 Towne Centre Dr Ste 150 *Web:* polarispharma.com	San Diego	CA	92121	858-452-6688		231
Polaris Project PO Box 77892 *Web:* polarisproject.org	Washington	DC	20013	202-745-1001		533
Polarity Inc 11294 Sunrise Park Dr *Web:* www.polarity.net	Rancho Cordova	CA	95742	916-635-3050		261
PolarSat Inc 549 Meloche Ave *Web:* www.polarsat.com	Dorval	QC	H9P2W2	514-635-0040		647
Polestar Capital Inc 180 N Michigan Ave Ste 1905 *Web:* www.polestarvc.com	Chicago	IL	60601	312-984-9090	984-9877	403
Polhemus Savery DaSilva Architects Builders 157 Brewster-Chatham Rd (Rt 137) *Web:* www.psdab.com	East Harwich	MA	02645	508-945-4500	945-9803	186
Poliac Research Corp 12233 Wood Lake Dr *Web:* www.poliac.com	Burnsville	MN	55337	952-882-1772		809
Police & Fire Federal Credit Union 901 Arch St *TF:* 800-228-8801 ■ *Web:* www.pffcu.org	Philadelphia	PA	19107	215-931-0300		219
Police Bookshelf PO Box 122 *TF:* 800-624-9049 ■ *Web:* www.ayoob.com	Concord	NH	03302	603-224-6814		637-2
Police Equipment Worldwide Inc 11155 Lu Wista Ln *Fax Area Code:* 800 ■ *TF:* 888-668-6860 ■ *Web:* www.police-equipment-worldwide.com	Brooksville	FL	34601	888-668-6860	834-9850*	459
Police Executive Research Forum (PERF) 1120 Connecticut Ave NW Ste 930 *Web:* www.policeforum.org	Washington	DC	20036	202-466-7820	466-7826	49-7
Police Jury Association of Louisiana 707 North 7th St *TF:* 888-551-2832 ■ *Web:* www.lpgov.org	Baton Rouge	LA	70802	225-343-2835	336-1344	48-5
Police Science Institute 5133 N Gates Ave Ste 102 *Web:* www.policescience.com	Fresno	CA	93722	559-276-9800	276-9898	167-3
Policemen's Annuity & Benefit Fund of Chicago 221 N LaSalle St Ste 1626 *TF:* 800-656-6606 ■ *Web:* www.chipabf.org	Chicago	IL	60601	312-744-3891	726-3216	390
Policy Research Associates Inc 345 Delaware Ave *TF:* 800-311-4246 ■ *Web:* www.prainc.com	Delmar	NY	12054	518-439-7415		141
Policygenius 50 W 23rd St 9th Fl *TF:* 855-695-2255 ■ *Web:* www.policygenius.com	New York	NY	10010	855-695-2255		390
Polimaster Inc 44873 Falcon Pl Ste 128 *Web:* polimaster.us	Arlington	VA	20166	703-525-5075	525-5079	407
Poling Law 300 E Broad St Ste 350 *Web:* poling-law.com	Columbus	OH	43215	614-737-2900	737-2929	445
Poliquin & Degrave LLP 22972 Mill Creek Dr *Web:* pdattorneys.com	Laguna Hills	CA	92653	949-716-8230		41
Polish American Cultural Center Museum 308 Walnut St *TF:* 800-422-1275 ■ *Web:* www.polishamericancenter.org	Philadelphia	PA	19106	215-922-1700	922-1518	520
Polish Library in Washington 1503 21st St NW *Web:* www.polishlibrary.org	Washington	DC	20036	202-466-2665		48-13
Polish Museum of America (PMA) 984 N Milwaukee Ave *Web:* www.polishmuseumofamerica.org	Chicago	IL	60642	773-384-3352	384-3799	520
Polish National Alliance of the US of North America 6100 N Cicero Ave *Web:* www.pna-znp.org	Chicago	IL	60646	773-286-0500		391-2
Polish National Tourist Office 5 Marina View Plz Ste 303b *Web:* www.poland.travel	Hoboken	NJ	07030	201-420-9910	584-9153	775
Polisher Research Institute Abramson Center for Jewish Life 1425 Horsham Rd *TF:* 888-340-0080 ■ *Web:* www.abramsoncenter.org	North Wales	PA	19454	215-371-1895	371-3015	668
Political Branding Associates 6600 College Blvd Ste 310 *Web:* politicalbrandingassociates.com	Overland Park	KS	66211	816-753-0200		194
Politics & Prose Bookstore 5015 Connecticut Ave NW *TF:* 800-722-0790 ■ *Web:* www.politics-prose.com	Washington	DC	20008	202-364-1919	966-7532	95
Polk Audio Inc 5601 Metro Dr *TF:* 800-377-7655 ■ *Web:* www.polkaudio.com	Baltimore	MD	21215	410-358-3600	764-5266	52
Polk County 100 Polk County Plz *Web:* www.co.polk.wi.us	Balsam Lake	WI	54810	715-485-9226	485-9104	338
Polk County 330 W Church St PO Box 9005 *TF:* 800-780-5346 ■ *Web:* polk-county.net	Bartow	FL	33831	863-534-6000		338
Polk County 6239 Hwy 411 PO Box 128 *Web:* www.polkgovernment.com	Benton	TN	37307	423-338-4527	338-4558	338
Polk County 102 E Broadway Ste 6 *Web:* www.polkcountycollector.com	Bolivar	MO	65613	417-326-4032	777-8693	338
Polk County 40 Courthouse St PO Box 308 *Web:* www.polknc.org	Columbus	NC	28722	828-894-3301	894-2263	338
Polk County 612 N Broadway Rm 211 *Web:* www.co.polk.mn.us	Crookston	MN	56716	218-281-5408	281-3808	338
Polk County 850 Main St *Web:* www.co.polk.or.us	Dallas	OR	97338	503-623-8391	831-3015	338
Polk County 111 Court Ave Administration Bldg *TF:* 800-848-0869 ■ *Web:* www.polkcountyiowa.gov	Des Moines	IA	50309	515-286-3000	323-5225	338
Polk County 101 W Church St *Web:* www.co.polk.tx.us	Livingston	TX	77351	936-327-6804	327-6891	338
Polk County 211 DeQueen St *Web:* www.uaex.edu	Mena	AR	71953	479-394-6018	394-8137	338
Polk County Chamber of Commerce/Development Authority 133 S Marble St *Web:* polkgeorgia.com	Rockmart	GA	30153	770-684-8760		139
Polk County Convention Complex 730 Third St *Web:* www.iowaeventscenter.com	Des Moines	IA	50309	515-564-8001		205
Polk County Rural Public Power District 115 W Third St PO Box 465 *TF:* 888-242-5265 ■ *Web:* www.pcrppd.com	Stromsburg	NE	68666	402-764-4381	764-4382	245
Polk County Schools Employee Credit Union 423 E Court Ave *Web:* servecu.org	Des Moines	IA	50309	515-243-2677		219
Polk State College 999 Ave H NE *Web:* www.polk.edu	Winter Haven	FL	33881	863-297-1000	297-1060	162

Name / Address	City	State	Zip	Phone	Fax	Class
Polk Tractor Co 3450 Havendale Blvd NW *TF:* 866-417-4303 ■ *Web:* www.polktractorco.com	Winter Haven	FL	33881	863-967-0651	967-0705	274
Polka Dot Publishing 9034 W Skies Dr *Web:* www.stanleyschmidt.com	Reno	NV	89521	775-852-2690		637-2
Polk-Burnett Electric Co-op (PBEC) 1001 State Rd 35 *TF:* 800-421-0283 ■ *Web:* www.polkburnett.com	Centuria	WI	54824	715-646-2191	646-2404	245
Pollan, Mauner & Wess LLP 888 Veterans Memorial Hwy *Web:* pollanmaunerwess.com	Hauppauge	NY	11788	631-232-1777	232-4411	2
Pollard Friendly Ford Co 3301 S Loop 289 *TF:* 866-239-3735 ■ *Web:* www.pollardfriendlyford.com	Lubbock	TX	79423	888-473-0791		57
Pollard Memorial Library 401 Merrimack St *Web:* lowelllibrary.org	Lowell	MA	01852	978-674-4120		434-3
Pollard, The 2 Broadway Ave N *Web:* www.thepollardhotel.com	Red Lodge	MT	59068	406-446-0001		379
Pollock & Maguire 4 W Red Oak Ln Ste 302 *Web:* pollock-maguire.com	White Plains	NY	10604	914-251-1525		41
Pollock Orora 1 Pollock Pl *TF:* 800-843-7320 ■ *Web:* www.pollock.com	Grand Prairie	TX	75050	972-263-2126	262-4737	559
Pollock Printing Company Inc 928 Sixth Ave S *TF:* 800-349-1205 ■ *Web:* www.pollockprinting.com	Nashville	TN	37203	615-255-0526		627
Pollstar 4697 W Jacquelyn Ave *Web:* www.pollstarpro.com	Fresno	CA	93722	559-271-7900	271-7979	637-9
Pollution Control Corp 500 W Country Club Rd *Fax Area Code: 405* ■ *TF:* 800-966-1265 ■ *Web:* www.pollutioncontrolcorp.com	Chickasha	OK	73018	800-966-1265	224-7424*	196
Pollution Probe 150 Ferrand Dr Ste 208 *TF:* 877-926-1907 ■ *Web:* www.pollutionprobe.org	Toronto	ON	M3C3E5	416-926-1907	926-1601	48-13
Polly Hill Arboretum 809 State Rd PO Box 561 *Web:* www.pollyhillarboretum.org	West Tisbury	MA	02575	508-693-9426		97
Polly's Pies Restaurant 17198 Norwalk Blvd *Web:* www.pollyspies.com	Cerritos	CA	90703	562-402-2758		671
Polman Transfer Inc 63425 Hwy 10 W *TF:* 800-777-1753 ■ *Web:* www.polmantransfer.com	Wadena	MN	56482	218-631-1753	631-3969	780
Polo Grill 2038 Utica Sq *Web:* www.pologrill.com	Tulsa	OK	74114	918-744-4280	749-7082	671
Polpo Restaurant & Saloon 554 Old Post Rd Ste 3 *Web:* www.polporestaurantgreenwich.com	Greenwich	CT	06830	203-629-1999		671
Polsinelli Shalton Flanigan Suelthaus PC 700 W 47th St Ste 1000 *Web:* www.polsinelli.com	Kansas City	MO	64112	816-753-1000	753-1536	428
Polsinello Fuels Inc 241 Riverside Ave Drawer 211 *TF:* 800-334-5823 ■ *Web:* www.polsinello.com	Rensselaer	NY	12144	518-463-0084		316
POLY (Poly Languages Institute Inc) 5757 Wilshire Blvd Ste 510 *TF:* 877-738-5787 ■ *Web:* www.polylanguages.edu	Los Angeles	CA	90036	323-933-9399	686-5384	423
Poly Cast Inc 14140 SW 72nd Ave *Web:* www.poly-cast.com	Tigard	OR	97224	503-620-9850		596
Poly Expert Inc 850 Ave Munck *TF:* 877-384-5060 ■ *Web:* www.polyexpert.com	Laval	QC	H7S1B1	877-384-5060		366
Poly Languages Institute Inc (POLY) 5757 Wilshire Blvd Ste 510 *TF:* 877-738-5787 ■ *Web:* www.polylanguages.edu	Los Angeles	CA	90036	323-933-9399	686-5384	423
Poly Molding LLC 96 Fourth Ave *TF:* 800-229-7161 ■ *Web:* polymoldingllc.com	Haskell	NJ	07420	973-835-7161		601
Poly Plant Project Inc 3099 N Lima St *Web:* www.polyplantproject.com	Burbank	CA	91504	818-848-2111		261
Poly Plastics Inc 3280 Park Dr *Web:* www.recycleyourplastic.com	Owatonna	MN	55060	507-451-8659	451-8054	604
Poly Processing 2201 Old Sterlington Rd PO Box 4150 *TF:* 800-523-9871 ■ *Web:* www.polyprocessing.com	Monroe	LA	71211	866-765-9957		280
Poly Sat Inc 7240 State Rd *TF:* 888-839-2661 ■ *Web:* www.vexcon.com	Philadelphia	PA	19135	215-332-7709	332-9997	145
Poly Systems Inc 3 Industrial Dr *Web:* www.polysystems.com	Steelville	MO	65565	573-775-3300		596
Poly Tech Diamond Co 4 E St PO Box 6 *TF:* 800-365-7659 ■ *Web:* polytechdiamond.com	North Attleboro	MA	02761	508-695-3561	695-3564	697
Poly Tech Industries Inc 238 Industrial Park Dr *Web:* www.polyskid.com	Monticello	GA	31064	706-468-2801	468-2881	604
Poly Tek Inc 1900 Marina Blvd *Web:* www.poly-tek.com	San Leandro	CA	94577	510-895-6001		677
Poly Vinyl Company Inc 320 Range Line Rd *Web:* www.polyvinyl.com	Kohler	WI	53044	920-467-4685		596
Poly-America 2000 W Marshall Dr *TF:* 800-527-3322 ■ *Web:* www.poly-america.com	Grand Prairie	TX	75051	972-337-7100	337-7600	66
Polycast Industries Inc 130 S 2nd St *TF:* 800-486-3512 ■ *Web:* www.polycastindustries.com	Bay Shore	NY	11706	631-595-2530	595-2537	253
Polychem Corp 6277 Heisley Rd *TF:* 800-548-9557 ■ *Web:* www.polychem.com	Mentor	OH	44060	440-357-1500	352-9553	596
Poly-Clip System Corp 1000 Tower Rd *Web:* www.polyclip.com	Mundelein	IL	60060	847-949-2800		429
Polycom Inc 4750 Willow Rd *TF:* 800-765-9266 ■ *Web:* www.poly.com	Pleasanton	CA	94588	800-765-9266		735
Polycon Industries Inc 8919 Colorado St *TF:* 800-621-4620 ■ *Web:* www.crownpolycon.com	Merrillville	IN	46410	219-738-1024		604
PolyConversions Inc 505 Condit Dr *TF:* 888-893-3330 ■ *Web:* www.polycousa.com	Rantoul	IL	61866	217-893-3330	893-3003	576
Polycor Inc 139 St-Pierre St *Web:* www.polycor.com	Quebec City	QC	G1K8B9	418-692-4695		724
Polycycle Industrial Products Inc 5501 Campbells Run Rd	Pittsburgh	PA	15205	412-747-1101	747-0749	454
Polydeck Screen Corp 1790 Dewberry Rd *Web:* www.polydeck.com	Spartanburg	SC	29307	864-579-4594	579-4173	596
Polyengineering Inc 1885 Headland Ave PO Box 837 *Web:* www.poly-inc.com	Dothan	AL	36303	334-793-4700	793-9015	261
Polyethics Industries Inc 301 Forest Ave N *Web:* www.polyethics.com	Orillia	ON	L3V6H9	705-329-2266		600
Polyfab Display Co 14892 Persistence Dr *Web:* www.polyfab-display.com	Woodbridge	VA	22191	703-497-4577	490-6401	604
Polyfet Rf Devices Inc 1110 Avenida Acaso *Web:* www.polyfet.com	Camarillo	CA	93012	805-484-4210	484-3393	696
Poly-Flex Inc Hwy B & Ridge Rd *Fax Area Code: 414* ■ *Web:* www.polyflexinc.com	Walworth	WI	53184	262-275-2156	275-2284*	604
Polyflon Co 1 Willard Rd *Web:* www.polyflon.com	Norwalk	CT	06851	203-840-7555	840-7565	253
Polyform Inc 3125 22nd St SE *Web:* www.polyforminc.net	Salem	OR	97302	503-585-0163		599
Polyform Products Co 1901 Estes Ave *Web:* www.sculpey.com	Elk Grove Village	IL	60007	847-427-0020		791
Polyform U.S. Ltd 7030 S 224th St *TF:* 800-423-0664 ■ *Web:* www.polyformus.com	Kent	WA	98032	253-872-0300	395-4650	604
Polygenesis Corp 4260 US Hwy 1 Ste 5 *Web:* www.polygenesis.com	Monmouth Junction	NJ	08852	732-355-1001		195
Polygon Network PO Box 4806 *TF:* 800-221-4435 ■ *Web:* www.polygon.net	Dillon	CO	80435	800-221-4435		393
Polyguard Products Inc PO Box 755 *TF:* 800-541-4994 ■ *Web:* www.polyguardproducts.com	Ennis	TX	75120	972-875-8421	875-9425	745-2
PolyJohn Enterprises Corp 2500 Gaspar Ave *TF:* 800-292-1305 ■ *Web:* www.polyjohn.com	Whiting	IN	46394	800-292-1305		610
Polymedco Inc 510 Furnace Dock Rd *TF:* 800-431-2123 ■ *Web:* www.polymedco.com	Cortlandt Manor	NY	10567	914-739-5400	739-5890	231
Polymer Conversions Inc 5732 Big Tree Rd *Web:* polymerconversions.com	Orchard Park	NY	14127	716-662-8550	662-8555	608
Polymer Corp 180 Pleasant St *Web:* polymercorporation.com	Rockland	MA	02370	781-871-4606	871-5460	604
Polymer Industries LLC 10526 Alabama Hwy 40 PO Box 32 *TF:* 877-489-0039 ■ *Web:* www.polymerindustries.com	Henagar	AL	35978	256-657-5197		601
Polymer Machinery Company Inc 154 Potomac Ave Ste B *Web:* www.polymermachineryco.com	Tallmadge	OH	44278	330-633-5734	633-6367	385
Polymer Resources Ltd 656 New Britain Ave *TF:* 800-243-5176 ■ *Web:* prlresins.com	Farmington	CT	06032	800-243-5176		596
Polymer Solutions Inc 2903-C Commerce St *TF:* 877-961-4341 ■ *Web:* www.polymersolutions.com	Blacksburg	VA	24060	877-961-4341		317
Polymerics Inc 2828 2nd St *Web:* www.polymericsinc.com	Cuyahoga Falls	OH	44221	330-928-2210	929-8819	676
Polymers Center of Excellence University Research Pk 8900 Research Dr *Web:* polymers-center.org	Charlotte	NC	28262	704-602-4100	602-4114	637-2
Polymet Alloys Inc 1701 Providence Pk Ste 100 *Web:* www.polymetalloys.com	Birmingham	AL	35242	205-981-2200	981-1583	492
Polymos Inc 150 Fifth Blvd *TF:* 855-765-9667 ■ *Web:* www.polymos.com	Terrasse-Vaudreuil	QC	J7V5M3	514-453-1920	453-0295	608
Polyneer Inc 259-D Samuel Barnet Blvd *Web:* www.ar-tex.it	New Bedford	MA	02745	508-998-5225		677
Polynesian Adventure Tours Inc 2880 Kilihau St *TF:* 800-622-3011 ■ *Web:* www.polyad.com	Honolulu	HI	96819	808-833-3000	833-3473	760
Polynesian Cultural Ctr 55-370 Kamehameha Hwy *TF:* 800-367-7060 ■ *Web:* www.polynesia.com	Laie	HI	96762	808-293-3005		520
Polynesian Resort, The 615 Ocean Shores Blvd NW *TF:* 800-562-4836 ■ *Web:* www.thepolynesian.com	Ocean Shores	WA	98569	360-289-3361		669
PolyOne Corp 33587 Walker Rd *NYSE: POL* ■ *TF:* 866-765-9663 ■ *Web:* www.polyone.com	Avon Lake	OH	44012	440-930-1000	930-3064	605-2
Poly-Pak Industries Inc 125 Spagnoli Rd *Fax Area Code: 631* ■ *TF:* 800-969-1993 ■ *Web:* www.poly-pak.com	Melville	NY	11747	800-969-1993	454-6366*	66
PolyPeptide Laboratories Inc 365 Maple Ave *TF:* 800-338-4965 ■ *Web:* www.polypeptide.com	Torrance	CA	90503	310-782-3569		231
PolyQuest Inc 6770 Parker Farm Dr Ste 100 *Web:* www.polyquest.com	Wilmington	NC	28405	910-342-9554	342-9558	5
Polysciences Inc 400 Valley Rd *TF:* 800-523-2575 ■ *Web:* www.polysciences.com	Warrington	PA	18976	215-343-6484	343-0214	231
Poly-Seal Corp 11 E CHASE St	Baltimore	MD	21202	410-633-1990		596
PolySource LLC 3730 S Elizabeth St Ste B *Web:* polysource.net	Independence	MO	64057	816-540-5300		225
Polyspede Electronics Company Inc 6770 Twin Hills Ave *TF:* 888-476-5944 ■ *Web:* www.polyspede.com	Dallas	TX	75231	214-363-7245		518
Poly-Tainer Inc 450 W Los Angeles Ave *Web:* www.polytainer.com	Simi Valley	CA	93065	805-526-3424	526-3430	98
Polytec Products Corp 1190 Obrien Dr *Web:* polytecproducts.com	Menlo Park	CA	94025	650-322-7555		608
Poly-Tech Dental Studio 868 N Garfield Ave *Web:* dentallabspoly-tech.com	Montebello	CA	90640	323-890-9004		415
Polytex 820 E 140th St *Web:* www.polytcxink.com	Bronx	NY	10454	718-402-2000		388

Name / Address	City	State	Zip	Phone	Fax	Class
Polytop LLC 110 Graham Dr	Slatersville	RI	02896	401-767-2400		154
Polytron Corp 4400 Wyland Dr *TF:* 888-228-0246 ■ *Web:* www.polytron-corp.com	Elkhart	IN	46516	574-522-0246	522-0457	203
Polytype America Corp 10 Industrial Ave *Web:* www.wifag-polytype.com	Mahwah	NJ	07430	201-995-1000	995-1080	627
Polyurethane Engineering Techniques Company Inc 28041 N Bradley Rd *TF:* 800-551-5665 ■ *Web:* www.petcorolls.com	Lake Forest	IL	60045	847-362-1820	362-1833	385
Polyurethane Machinery Corp 1 Komo Dr *Web:* polymac-usa.com	Lakewood	NJ	08701	732-415-4400	364-4025	172
Polyurethane Manufacturers Assn (PMA) 6737 W Washington St Ste 1420 *Web:* www.pmahome.org	Milwaukee	WI	53214	414-431-3094		49-13
Polyurethane Molding Industries Inc 100 Founders Dr *Web:* pmirim.com	Woonsocket	RI	02895	401-765-6700	765-7271	757
Polyvel Inc 100 Ninth St *Web:* www.polyvel.com	Hammonton	NJ	08037	609-567-0080		608
Polyvinyl Films Inc PO Box 753 *TF:* 800-343-6134 ■ *Web:* www.stretchtite.com	Sutton	MA	01590	508-865-3558	865-1562	600
PolyVision Corp 10700 Abbotts Bridge Rd Ste 100 *TF:* 888-325-6351 ■ *Web:* polyvision.com	Johns Creek	GA	30097	678-542-3100	542-3200	173-1
Polywest Ltd 110-3240 Idylwyld Dr N *TF:* 866-750-0725 ■ *Web:* www.polywest.ca	Saskatoon	SK	S7L5Y7	306-956-7788		770
Polyzen Inc 1041 Classic Rd *Web:* www.polyzen.com	Apex	NC	27539	919-319-9599	319-8458	476
POM Inc 200 S Elmira Ave *TF:* 800-331-7275 ■ *Web:* www.pom.com	Russellville	AR	72802	479-968-2880		495
POMC (Parents of Murdered Children) 4960 Ridge Ave Ste 2 *TF:* 888-818-7662 ■ *Web:* www.pomc.com	Cincinnati	OH	45209	513-721-5683	345-4489	48-6
Pomegranate Communications Inc 19018 NE Portal Way *Web:* pomegranate.com	Portland	OR	97230	503-328-6500		42
Pomeranian Pictures 20236 Leadwell St *Web:* www.pompixweb.com	Winnetka	CA	91306	818-998-1983		514
Pomerantz Marketing 175 Admiral Cochrane Dr Ste 104 *Web:* pomagency.com	Annapolis	MD	21401	410-216-9447	216-9320	7
Pomeroy IT Solutions Inc 1020 Petersburg Rd *TF:* 800-846-8727 ■ *Web:* www.pomeroy.com	Hebron	KY	41048	859-586-0600	586-4414	180
Pomfret School 398 Pomfret St PO Box 128 *Web:* www.pomfret.org	Pomfret	CT	06258	860-963-6100	963-2042	622
Pomme de Terre State Park 23451 Park Entrance Rd *Web:* mostateparks.com	Pittsburg	MO	65724	417-852-4291		565
Pomona Box Co 301 W Imperial Hwy PO Box 536 *Web:* www.pomonabox.com	La Habra	CA	90631	714-871-0932	871-3483	200
Pomona Capital 780 Third Ave 46th Fl *TF:* 800-992-0180 ■ *Web:* www.pomonacapital.com	New York	NY	10017	800-992-0180		792
Pomona Chamber of Commerce 101 W Mission Blvd Ste 222 *Web:* www.pomonachamber.org	Pomona	CA	91766	909-622-1256	620-5986	139
Pomona College 333 N College Way *Web:* www.pomona.edu	Claremont	CA	91711	909-621-8134	621-8952	166
Pomona Public Library 625 S Garey Ave *Web:* www1.youseemore.com	Pomona	CA	91766	909-620-2043	620-3713	434-3
Pomona State Park 22900 S Hwy 368 *Web:* www.ksoutdoors.com	Vassar	KS	66543	785-828-4933		565
Pomona Valley Hospital Medical Ctr 1798 N Garey Ave *Web:* www.pvhmc.org	Pomona	CA	91767	909-865-9500		374-3
Pompaction Inc 119 Blvd Hymus *Web:* www.pompaction.com	Pointe-Claire	QC	H9R1E5	514-697-8600		358
Pompano Beach Amphitheater 1806 NE 6th St *Web:* www.pompanobeacharts.org	Pompano Beach	FL	33060	954-786-4111		572
Pompanoosuc Mills 3184 Rte 5 S *TF:* 800-841-6671 ■ *Web:* www.pompy.com	East Thetford	VT	05043	800-841-6671		361
Pomperaug Woods 80 Heritage Rd *Web:* www.pomperaugwoods.com	Southbury	CT	06488	203-262-6555		672
Pomps Tire Service Inc 1123 Cedar St *TF:* 800-236-8911 ■ *Web:* www.pompstire.com	Green Bay	WI	54301	920-435-8301		755
Ponca City Area Chamber of Commerce 420 E Grand Ave *TF:* 866-763-8092 ■ *Web:* www.poncacitychamber.com	Ponca City	OK	74601	580-765-4400	765-2798	139
Ponca City Library 515 E Grand Ave *Web:* www.poncacityok.gov	Ponca City	OK	74601	580-767-0345	767-0374	434-3
Ponca City Publishing Company Inc 300 N Third St *Web:* www.poncacity.com	Ponca City	OK	74601	580-765-3311		637-8
Ponca State Park 88090 Spur 26 E *Web:* outdoornebraska.gov	Ponca	NE	68770	402-755-2284		565
Ponca Tribe 2602 J St *Web:* www.poncatribe-ne.org	Omaha	NE	68107	402-734-5275		418
Ponce Bank 2244 Westchester Ave *Web:* www.poncebank.com	Bronx	NY	10462	718-931-9000	542-9733	71
Ponce de Leon Springs State Park 2860 Ponce de Leon Springs Rd *Web:* www.floridastateparks.org	Ponce de Leon	FL	32455	850-836-4281		565
Ponce de Leon's Fountain of Youth 11 Magnolia Ave *Web:* www.fountainofyouthflorida.com	Saint Augustine	FL	32084	904-829-3168		50-3
Pond & Co 3500 Pkwy Ln Ste 600 *Web:* www.pondco.com	Norcross	GA	30092	678-336-7740		261
Pond House Cafe 1555 Asylum Ave *Web:* www.pondhousecafe.com	West Hartford	CT	06117	860-231-8823	231-8731	671
Ponder Pro Serve PO Box 674257 *Web:* www.ponderproserve.com	Griffin	GA	30223	770-490-2767		809
Pondera County Montana *Treasurer / Assessor and Superintendent of Schools* 20 4th Ave SW Ste 211 *Web:* ponderacountymontana.org	Conrad	MT	59425	406-271-4000	271-4070	338
Ponderosa Motor Inn 1206 Trans Canada Hwy *Web:* www.ponderosamotorinn.bc.ca	Golden	BC	V0A1H0	250-344-2205		378
Ponderosa State Park 1920 N Davis Ave *Web:* parksandrecreation.idaho.gov	McCall	ID	83638	208-634-2164		565
Pong Studios 201 Creditview Rd *Web:* www.pongstudios.com	Woodbridge	ON	L4L9T1	905-264-3555		387
Poniard Pharmaceuticals Inc 7000 Shoreline Court S *OTC: PARD*	San Francisco	CA	94080	650-583-3774		85
Pontarelli Limousine Service 5584 N Northwest Hwy *TF:* 800-322-5466 ■ *Web:* www.pontarelliischicago.com	Chicago	IL	60630	312-226-1300		441
Pontchartrain 2031 St Charles Ave *TF:* 800-708-6652 ■ *Web:* thepontchartrainhotel.com	New Orleans	LA	70130	800-708-6652		379
Pontchartrain Ctr 4545 Williams Blvd *Web:* www.pontchartraincenter.com	Kenner	LA	70065	504-465-9985	468-6692	205
Pontchartrain Materials Corp 3819 France Rd *Web:* www.pontchartrain.com	New Orleans	LA	70126	504-949-7571		183
Pontiac Coil Inc 5800 Moody Dr *Web:* www.pontiaccoil.com	Clarkston	MI	48348	248-922-1100		567
Pontiac Correctional Ctr 700 W Lincoln St *TF:* 800-275-7877 ■ *Web:* www2.illinois.gov	Pontiac	IL	61764	815-842-2816	842-3420	213
Pontiac Lake Recreation Area 7800 Gale Rd *Web:* www.michigan.org	Waterford	MI	48327	248-666-1020		565
Pontiac Public Library 60 E Pike St *Web:* www.pontiac.lib.mi.us	Pontiac	MI	48342	248-758-3942	758-3990	434-3
Pontiac Regional Chamber of Commerce 402 N Telegraph Rd *TF:* 800-477-3172 ■ *Web:* www.pontiacrc.com	Pontiac	MI	48341	248-335-9600		139
Pontifical College Josephinum 7625 N High St *TF:* 888-252-5812 ■ *Web:* www.pcj.edu	Columbus	OH	43235	614-885-5585	885-2307	167-3
Pontis Research Inc (PRI) 4195 Thousand Oaks Blvd Ste 105 *Web:* www.pontisresearch.com	Westlake Village	CA	91362	805-777-7424		693
Pontotoc County County Courthouse PO Box 1425 *Web:* ltap.okstate.edu	Ada	OK	74820	580-327-2126	436-5613	338
Pontotoc Electric Power Assn 12 S Main St *Web:* www.pepa.com	Pontotoc	MS	38863	662-489-3211	489-5156	245
Pontotoc Technology Ctr 601 W 33rd St *Web:* www.pontotoctech.edu	Ada	OK	74820	580-310-2200		167-3
Ponvia Technology Inc 804 E Park Ave Ste 112 *Web:* www.ponvia.com	Libertyville	IL	60048	847-362-8484		449
PONY Baseball/Softball Inc 1951 Pony Pl PO Box 225 *TF:* 800-853-2414 ■ *Web:* www.pony.org	Washington	PA	15301	724-225-1060	225-9852	48-22
Pony Express National Museum 914 Penn St *TF:* 800-530-5930 ■ *Web:* www.ponyexpress.org	Saint Joseph	MO	64503	816-279-5059	233-9370	520
Poogan's Porch 72 Queen St *Web:* www.pooganssporch.com	Charleston	SC	29401	843-577-2337		671
Pool Doctor, The 4038 San Pablo Dam Rd *Web:* thepooldoctors.com	El Sobrante	CA	94803	510-223-7537		186
Pool Management Group Inc 1210 Warsaw Rd Ste 900 *Web:* www.poolmanagementgroup.com	Roswell	GA	30076	770-993-4665		463
Pool Works Inc 765 Lawrence Dr *TF:* 800-638-8822 ■ *Web:* www.poolworksinc.com	De Pere	WI	54115	920-339-9801	339-9765	189-11
Poole & Kent Corp 4530 Hollins Ferry Rd *TF:* 800-468-0851 ■ *Web:* poole-kent.com	Baltimore	MD	21227	410-247-2200	247-2331	189-10
Poolmaster Inc 770 Del Paso Rd *TF:* 800-854-1492 ■ *Web:* www.poolmaster.com	Sacramento	CA	95834	916-567-9800	567-9880	710
Poolpak Technologies Corp 3491 Industrial Dr *Web:* www.poolpak.com	York	PA	17402	717-757-2648		14
Poor Boy's Gourmet 300 Main St *Web:* www.poorboysgourmet.com	Bar Harbor	ME	04609	207-288-4148		671
POP Displays USA LLC 1 International Dr Ste 100 *Web:* www.popdisplaysusa.com	Rye Brook	NY	10573	914-771-4200		5
Pop Warner Little Scholars Inc 586 Middletown Blvd Ste C-100 *Web:* www.popwarner.com	Langhorne	PA	19047	215-752-2691	752-2879	48-22
Popcorn Board 330 N Wabash Ave Ste 2000 *Web:* www.popcorn.org	Chicago	IL	60611	312-321-5166		49-6
Popcorn Press and Media PO Box 3375 **Fax Area Code:* 206 ■ *Web:* www.popcornpressandmedia.com	Rancho Santa Fe	CA	92067	858-759-2779	984-3977*	4
Pope Aylward Sweeney & Stephenson LLP 6701 Carmel Rd Ste 105 *Web:* passlawyers.com	Charlotte	NC	28226	704-374-1600		445
Pope County 100 W Main *Web:* www.popecountyar.com	Russellville	AR	72801	479-968-6064	967-2291	338
Pope County Community Unit School District #1 125 State Hwy 146 W *Web:* es.popek12.org	Golconda	IL	62938	618-683-2301	683-5181	338
Pope County Library System 116 E Third St *Web:* popelibrary.org	Russellville	AR	72801	479-968-4368	968-3222	434-3
Pope John Paul Ii High School Office 1901 Jaguar Dr *Web:* www.pjp.org	Slidell	LA	70461	985-649-0914		685
Pope Scientific Inc 351 N Dekora Woods Blvd *TF:* 844-400-7673 ■ *Web:* www.popeinc.com	Saukville	WI	53080	844-400-7673		292

Name / Address	City	State	Zip	Phone	Fax	Class
Pope, Houser & Barnes PLLC 1605 Cooper Point Rd NW *Web:* wbpopelawfirm.com	Olympia	WA	98502	360-866-4000	866-3832	41
Popejoy Hall UNM Public Events Popejoy Hall UNM Ctr for the Arts MSC 04 2580 *TF:* 877-664-8661 ■ *Web:* www.popejoypresents.com	Albuquerque	NM	87131	505-277-3824	277-7353	572
Popeyes Louisiana Kitchen 5555 Glenridge Connector NE Ste 300 *Web:* popeyes.com	Atlanta	GA	30342	404-459-4450		670
Poplar Bluff Regional Medical Center - Westwood 2620 N Westwood Blvd. *Web:* www.pbrmc.com	Poplar Bluff	MO	63901	573-785-7721		374-3
Poplar Bluff Regional Medical Ctr 3100 Oak Grove Rd. *TF:* 855-444-7276 ■ *Web:* www.pbrmc.com	Poplar Bluff	MO	63901	855-444-7276		374-3
Poplar Forest Capital LLC 70 S Lake Ave Ste 930 *Web:* poplarforestllc.com	Pasadena	CA	91101	626-304-6000		528
Poplar Springs Hospital 350 Poplar Dr. *TF:* 888-490-3601 ■ *Web:* poplarsprings.com	Petersburg	VA	23805	804-733-6874	862-6322	374-5
Popp Communications 620 Mendelssohn Ave N. *Web:* popp.com	Golden Valley	MN	55427	763-797-7900		387
Poppee's Popcorn Inc 38727 Taylor Pky **Fax Area Code:* 440 ■ *TF:* 800-452-3235 ■ *Web:* www.jennyspopcorn.com	North Ridgeville	OH	44039	800-452-3235	327-9349*	297-3
Popular Kinetics Press 6005 Yale Ave. *Web:* www.popularkinetics.com	Glen Echo	MD	20812	301-229-2213		637-2
Popular Mechanics Magazine 300 W 57th St. *TF:* 800-333-4948 ■ *Web:* www.popularmechanics.com	New York	NY	10019	800-333-4948		457-14
Population Action Intl (PAI) 1300 19th St NW Ste 200. *Web:* pai.org	Washington	DC	20036	202-557-3400	728-4177	48-5
Population Communication 1250 E Walnut St Ste 220. *Web:* populationcommunication.com	Pasadena	CA	91106	626-793-4750	793-4791	48-5
Population Connection 2120 L St NW Ste 500 *TF:* 800-767-1956 ■ *Web:* www.populationconnection.org	Washington	DC	20037	202-332-2200	332-2302	48-5
Population Council 1 Dag Hammarskjold Plz 3rd Fl *TF:* 877-339-0500 ■ *Web:* www.popcouncil.org	New York	NY	10017	212-339-0500	755-6052	668
Population Reference Bureau (PRB) 1875 Connecticut Ave NW Ste 520. *TF:* 800-877-9881 ■ *Web:* www.prb.org	Washington	DC	20009	202-483-1100	328-3937	48-7
Population Research Ctr 1155 60th St. *Web:* edirc.repec.org	Chicago	IL	60637	773-256-6315	256-6313	668
Population Research Institute Pennsylvania State University 601 Oswald Tower *Web:* www.pop.psu.edu	University Park	PA	16802	814-865-7760	863-8342	668
Population Services Intl (PSI) 1120 19th St NW Ste 600. *Web:* www.psi.org	Washington	DC	20036	202-785-0072	785-0120	48-17
Population-Environment Balance Inc 2000 P St NW Ste 600 *TF:* 800-866-6269 ■ *Web:* www.balance.org	Washington	DC	20036	202-955-5700	955-6161	48-7
Populus Group LLC 3001 W Big Beaver Rd Ste 400. *Web:* www.populusgroup.com	Troy	MI	48084	248-712-7900	928-0530	195
Poquoson 500 City Hall Ave. *Web:* www.ci.poquoson.va.us	Poquoson	VA	23662	757-868-3000	868-3101	338
Por La Mar Nursery 905 S Patterson Ave *TF:* 800-733-5286 ■ *Web:* www.porlamarnursery.com	Santa Barbara	CA	93111	805-699-4500	967-3266	323
Por Mor Construction 2901 S Sante Fe Dr. *Web:* www.pormor.com	Englewood	CO	80110	303-789-1551		697
Porchlight Real Estate Group 838 Broadway *Web:* porchlightgroup.com	Denver	CO	80203	303-733-5335		652
Porcia Publishing Corp 13155 SW 123 Ave Ste 11 **Fax Area Code:* 786 ■ *TF:* 866-828-8972 ■ *Web:* edicionesporcia.com	Miami	FL	33186	305-364-0035	573-0000*	637-2
Porcupine Mountains Wilderness State Park 33303 Headquarters Rd *Web:* www.michigan.org	Ontonagon	MI	49953	906-885-5275		565
Poretta & Orr Inc 450 East St. *Web:* www.porettaorr.com	Doylestown	PA	18901	215-345-1515		7
Porex Technologies Corp 500 Bohannon Rd. *TF:* 800-241-0195 ■ *Web:* www.porex.com	Fairburn	GA	30213	770-964-1421	969-0954	608
Pork and Beans 440 Hahn Rd. *TF:* 800-227-7675 ■ *Web:* www.porkandbeansstore.com	Westminster	MD	21157	410-848-4200	848-1247	473
Pork checkoff 1776 NW 114th St. *TF:* 800-456-7675 ■ *Web:* www.pork.org	Des Moines	IA	50325	515-223-2600	223-2646	457-1
Pork King Packing Inc 8808 S Rte 23 *Web:* www.porkkingpacking.com	Marengo	IL	60152	815-568-8024	568-9054	473
Porker's BBQ 1251 Market St.	Chattanooga	TN	37402	423-267-2726		671
Porky Products Corp 400 Port Carteret Dr *Web:* www.porky.com	Carteret	NJ	07008	732-541-0200	969-6110	297-9
Porsche Cars North America Inc 980 Hammond Dr Ste 1000 *TF:* 800-505-1041 ■ *Web:* www.porsche.com	Atlanta	GA	30328	770-290-3500	290-3708	59
Porsche St Paul 2490 Maplewood Dr. *Web:* stpaul.porschedealer.com	Maplewood	MN	55109	612-439-5943		57
Port & Company CPAS 5730 Commons Park Dr. *Web:* www.portcompanycpas.com	East Syracuse	NY	13057	315-449-1200	449-2650	2
Port Alberni Port Authority 2750 Harbour Rd *Web:* www.portalberniportauthority.ca	Port Alberni	BC	V9Y7X2	250-723-5312	723-1114	618
Port Angeles Coast Guard Air Station Ediz Hook Rd *Web:* www.uscg.mil	Port Angeles	WA	98362	360-417-5840		158
Port Arthur 11137 Warwick Blvd *Web:* www.portarthurva.com	Newport News	VA	23601	757-599-6474		671
Port Arthur News 3501 Turtle Creek Dr Ste 105 *Web:* www.panews.com	Port Arthur	TX	77642	409-729-6397	724-6840	532-2
Port Authority of Allegheny County 345 Sixth Ave 3rd Fl. *Web:* www.portauthority.org	Pittsburgh	PA	15222	412-566-5500		468
Port Authority of New York/New Jersey 225 Park Ave S 15th Fl. *Web:* www.panynj.gov	New York	NY	10003	212-435-7777		618
Port Canaveral 445 Challanger Rd *TF:* 888-767-8226 ■ *Web:* www.portcanaveral.com	Cape Canaveral	FL	32920	321-783-7831	784-6223	618
Port City Java Inc 101 Portwatch Way. *Web:* www.portcityjava.com	Wilmington	NC	28412	910-796-6646		296-7
Port Colborne-Wainfleet Chamber of Commerce 296 Fielden Ave *Web:* southniagaracc.com	Port Colborne	ON	L3K3K1	905-834-9765	834-1542	137
Port Columbus International Airport 4600 International Gateway. *Web:* columbusairports.com	Columbus	OH	43219	614-239-4000		27
Port Consolidated Inc 3141 SE 14th Ave. *Web:* www.portconsolidated.com	Fort Lauderdale	FL	33316	954-522-1182		579
Port Coquitlam Senior Citizens' Housing Society 2111 Hawthorne Ave. *Web:* hawthornecare.com	Port Coquitlam	BC	V3C1W3	604-941-4051		371
Port Crescent State Park 1775 Port Austin Rd *Web:* www.michigan.org	Port Austin	MI	48467	989-738-8663		565
Port Discovery Children's Museum in Baltimore 35 Market Pl. *Web:* www.portdiscovery.org	Baltimore	MD	21202	410-727-8120	727-3042	521
Port Erie Plastics Inc 909 Troupe Rd *Web:* www.porterie.com	Harborcreek	PA	16421	814-899-7602	899-7854	604
Port Everglades 1850 Eller Dr. *TF:* 800-421-0188 ■ *Web:* porteverglades.org	Fort Lauderdale	FL	33316	954-523-3404	525-1910	618
Port Freeport 1001 N Gulf Blvd. *TF:* 800-362-5743 ■ *Web:* www.portfreeport.com	Freeport	TX	77541	979-233-2667	233-5625	618
Port Harbor Marine 1 Spring Point Dr *Web:* www.portharbormarine.com	South Portland	ME	04106	207-767-3254	767-5940	90
Port Health Care 113 Low St *Web:* www.whittierhealth.com	Newburyport	MA	01950	978-462-7373	462-6510	450
Port Houston 111 E Loop N. *Web:* porthouston.com	Houston	TX	77029	713-670-2400	671-0359	618
Port Hudson National Cemetery 20978 Port Hickey Rd. *Web:* www.cem.va.gov	Zachary	LA	70791	225-654-1988	654-1989	136
Port Huron Music Ctr 2700 Pine Grove Ave *Web:* porthuronmusic.com	Port Huron	MI	48060	810-984-5081		526
Port Isabel Lighthouse State Historic Site 421 E Queen Isabella Blvd *Web:* portisabelmuseums.com	Port Isabel	TX	78578	956-943-2262		565
Port Jervis City School District 9 Thompson St. *Web:* www.pjschools.org	Port Jervis	NY	12771	845-858-3100	858-8693	186
Port Kashdin & Mcsherry CPAs 3535 W Rd *Web:* www.pkmcpa.com	Cortland	NY	13045	607-756-5681	756-8320	2
Port Lavaca Wave 107 E Austin St. *Web:* www.portlavacawave.com	Port Lavaca	TX	77979	361-552-9788		532-3
Port Ludlow Associates LLC 70 Breaker Ln *TF:* 877-805-0868 ■ *Web:* portludlowresort.com	Port Ludlow	WA	98365	360-437-2101	437-7410	379
Port of Albany *Albany Port District Commission* 106 Smith Blvd *Web:* www.portofalbany.us	Albany	NY	12202	518-463-8763		618
Port of Anacortes 100 Commercial Ave. *Web:* www.portofanacortes.com	Anacortes	WA	98221	360-293-3134	293-9608	618
Port of Astoria 10 Pier 1 Bldg Ste 308 *TF:* 800-860-4093 ■ *Web:* portofastoria.com	Astoria	OR	97103	503-741-3300	741-3345	618
Port of Baltimore *Maryland Port Administration* 401 E Pratt St. *TF:* 800-638-7519 ■ *Web:* www.mpa.maryland.gov	Baltimore	MD	21202	800-638-7519		618
Port of Beaumont 1225 Main St. *Web:* www.portofbeaumont.com	Beaumont	TX	77701	409-835-5367	832-9592	618
Port of Belledune 112 Shannon Dr *Web:* www.portofbelledune.ca	Belledune	NB	E8G2W2	506-522-1200		342
Port of Bellingham 1801 Roeder Ave. *Web:* www.portofbellingham.com	Bellingham	WA	98225	360-676-2500	671-6411	618
Port of Brownsville 1000 Foust Rd *TF:* 800-378-5395 ■ *Web:* www.portofbrownsville.com	Brownsville	TX	78521	956-831-4592	831-5006	618
Port of Call 838 Esplanade Ave *Web:* portofcallnola.com	New Orleans	LA	70116	504-523-0120		671
Port of Columbia County 100 E St PO Box 190 *Web:* www.portofcolumbiacounty.org	Columbia City	OR	97018	503-397-2888	397-6924	618
Port of Corpus Christi 222 Power St *TF:* 800-580-7110 ■ *Web:* www.portofcc.com	Corpus Christi	TX	78401	361-882-5633	882-7110	618
Port of Duluth *Duluth Seaway Port Authority* 1200 Port Terminal Dr *TF:* 800-232-0703 ■ *Web:* www.duluthport.com	Duluth	MN	55802	218-727-8525	727-6888	618
Port of Everett 2911 Bond St Ste 202. *TF:* 800-729-7678 ■ *Web:* www.portofeverett.com	Everett	WA	98201	425-259-3164	252-7366	618
Port of Galveston 123 25th St *Web:* www.portofgalveston.com	Galveston	TX	77550	409-765-9321	766-6107	618

Name / Address	City	State	ZIP	Phone	Fax	Class
Port of Grays Harbor 111 S Wooding St *Web:* www.portofgraysharbor.com	Aberdeen	WA	98520	360-533-9528	533-9505	618
Port of Greater Baton Rouge *Greater Baton Rouge Port Commission* 2425 Ernest Wilson Dr PO Box 380 *Web:* www.portgbr.com	Port Allen	LA	70767	225-342-1660	342-1666	618
Port of Homer 4350 Homer Spit Rd *Web:* www.cityofhomer-ak.gov	Homer	AK	99603	907-235-3160	235-3152	618
Port of Iberia 4611 S Lewis St PO Box 9986 *Web:* www.portofiberia.com	New Iberia	LA	70560	337-364-1065	364-3136	618
Port of Jacksonville *Jacksonville Port Authority* 2831 Talleyrand Ave PO Box 3005 *TF:* 800-874-8050 ■ *Web:* www.jaxport.com	Jacksonville	FL	32206	904-357-3000	357-3060	618
Port of Lake Charles 150 Marine St *TF:* 800-228-3848 ■ *Web:* www.portlc.com	Lake Charles	LA	70601	337-439-3661	493-3523	618
Port of Long Beach 925 Harbor Plz *Web:* www.polb.com	Long Beach	CA	90801	562-437-0041	901-1725	618
Port of Longview 10 Port Way *Web:* www.portoflongview.com	Longview	WA	98632	360-425-3305	425-8650	618
Port of Los Angeles 330 Centre St *Web:* www.portoflosangeles.org	San Pedro	CA	90731	310-732-3508		618
Port of Miami Dante B Fascell 1015 N America Way *Web:* www.miamidade.gov	Miami	FL	33132	305-347-4800		618
Port of Miami Terminal Operating Company LC 635 Australia Way *Web:* www.pomtoc.com	Miami	FL	33132	305-416-7600	374-6724	465
Port of Milwaukee 2323 S Lincoln Memorial Dr *Web:* www.city.milwaukee.gov	Milwaukee	WI	53207	414-286-3511	286-8506	618
Port of Monroe *Monroe Port Commission* 10 Port Ave PO Box 585 **Fax Area Code:* 721 ■ *Web:* www.portofmonroe.com	Monroe	MI	48161	734-241-6480	241-2964*	618
Port of New Orleans 1350 Port of New Orleans Pl *TF:* 800-776-6652 ■ *Web:* www.portnola.com	New Orleans	LA	70130	504-522-2551	524-4156	618
Port of Newport 600 SE Bay Blvd *Web:* www.portofnewport.com	Newport	OR	97365	541-265-7758	265-4235	618
Port of Nome 307 Belmont St *Web:* www.nomealaska.org	Nome	AK	99762	907-443-6619	443-5473	618
Port of Oakland 530 Water St *Web:* www.portofoakland.com	Oakland	CA	94607	510-627-1100		618
Port of Olympia 915 Washington St NE *Web:* www.portolympia.com	Olympia	WA	98501	360-528-8000	528-8090	618
Port of Orange *Orange County Navigation Port District* 1201 Childers Rd *Web:* www.portoforange.com	Orange	TX	77630	409-883-4363	883-5607	618
Port of Oswego Authority 1 E Second St *Web:* www.portoswego.com	Oswego	NY	13126	315-343-4503	343-5498	618
Port of Palm Beach 1 E 11th St Ste 600 *Web:* www.portofpalmbeach.com	Riviera Beach	FL	33404	561-842-4201	842-4240	618
Port of Pascagoula *Jackson County Port Authority* 3033 Pascagoula St *Web:* www.portofpascagoula.com	Pascagoula	MS	39567	228-762-4041	762-7476	618
Port of Pittsburgh 4955 Steubenville Pk Ste 245A *Web:* www.portpitt.com	Pittsburgh	PA	15205	412-201-7330	722-1190	618
Port of Port Angeles 338 W First St PO Box 1350 *Web:* portofpa.com	Port Angeles	WA	98362	360-457-8527	452-3959	618
Port of Port Arthur 221 Houston Ave *Web:* portpa.com	Port Arthur	TX	77640	409-983-2011	983-7572	618
Port of Port Lavaca-Point Comfort *Calhoun Port Authority* PO Box 397 *Web:* www.calhounport.com	Point Comfort	TX	77978	361-987-2813	987-2189	618
Port of Portland 7200 NE Airport Way *TF:* 800-547-8411 ■ *Web:* www.portofportland.com	Portland	OR	97218	503-415-6000		618
Port of Portland 389 Congress St *Web:* portlandmaine.gov	Portland	ME	04101	207-874-8892	874-8473	618
Port of Redwood City 675 Seaport Blvd *Web:* www.redwoodcityport.com	Redwood City	CA	94063	650-306-4150	369-7636	618
Port of Sacramento 1110 W Capitol Ave *Web:* www.cityofwestsacramento.org	West Sacramento	CA	95691	916-617-4500		618
Port of San Diego 3165 Pacific Hwy *TF:* 800-854-2757 ■ *Web:* www.portofsandiego.org	San Diego	CA	92101	619-686-6200		618
Port of San Francisco Pier 1 The Embarcadero *TF:* 800-479-5314 ■ *Web:* sfport.com	San Francisco	CA	94111	415-274-0400	732-0400	618
Port of Seattle 2711 Alaskan Way *TF:* 800-426-7817 ■ *Web:* www.portseattle.org	Seattle	WA	98111	206-787-3000		618
Port of Sept-Iles 1 Mgr-Blanche Dock *Web:* www.portsi.com	Sept-Iles	QC	G4R5P3	418-968-1231	962-4445	618
Port of South Louisiana 171 Belle Terre Blvd PO Box 909 *Web:* www.portsl.com	LaPlace	LA	70068	985-652-9278		618
Port of Stockton 2201 W Washington St *TF:* 800-344-3213 ■ *Web:* www.portofstockton.com	Stockton	CA	95203	209-946-0246	465-7244	618
Port of Tacoma 1 Sitcum Way *Web:* www.portoftacoma.com	Tacoma	WA	98421	253-383-5841	593-4570	618
Port of Vancouver 3103 NW Lower River Rd *TF:* 800-475-8012 ■ *Web:* www.portvanusa.com	Vancouver	WA	98660	360-693-3611	735-1565	618
Port of Vancouver 100 The Pointe 999 Canada Pl **Fax Area Code:* 866 ■ *TF:* 888-767-8826 ■ *Web:* www.portvancouver.com	Vancouver	BC	V6C3T4	604-665-9000	284-4271*	618
Port of Wilmington 1 Hausel Rd *Web:* www.portofwilmington.com	Wilmington	DE	19801	302-472-7740		618
Port Orange-South Daytona Chamber of Commerce 3431 S Ridgewood Ave *TF:* 800-848-3984 ■ *Web:* www.pschamber.com	Port Orange	FL	32129	386-761-1601	788-9165	139
Port Orchard Chamber of Commerce 1014 Bay St Ste 8 *TF:* 800-475-7526 ■ *Web:* www.portorchard.com	Port Orchard	WA	98366	360-876-3505	895-1920	139
Port Panama City 1 Seaport Dr *TF:* 855-347-8371 ■ *Web:* www.panamacityportauthority.com	Panama City	FL	32401	855-347-8371		618
Port Plastics Inc 15325 Fairfield Ranch Rd Ste 150 **Fax Area Code:* 909 ■ *TF:* 800-800-0039 ■ *Web:* www.portplastics.com	Chino Hills	CA	91709	480-813-6118	597-0116*	603
Port Richmond Glass & Storefronts Inc 1288 Forest Ave *Web:* portrichmondglass.com	Staten Island	NY	10302	718-720-1616		362
Port Salerno Animal Hospital I 4515 SE Dixie Hwy *Web:* mypsah.com	Stuart	FL	34997	772-286-3833		794
Port Townsend Marine Science Ctr 532 Battery Way *TF:* 800-566-3932 ■ *Web:* ptmsc.org	Port Townsend	WA	98368	360-385-5582	385-7248	520
Port Townsend Paper Corp 100 Mill Rd *Web:* www.ptpc.com	Port Townsend	WA	98368	360-385-3170		554
Port Washington Chamber of Commerce 329 Main St *Web:* www.pwguide.com	Port Washington	NY	11050	516-883-6566		139
Port Washington Teachers Federal Credit Union 101 Sands Point Rd *Web:* pwtfcu.org	Port Washington	NY	11050	516-883-1227	883-3088	219
Porta Bella 425 N Frances St *Web:* www.portabellarest.com	Madison	WI	53703	608-256-3186	256-1210	671
Portabellos.net 2109 N Pollard St *Web:* www.portabellos.net	Arlington	VA	22207	703-528-1557		671
Portable Buildings Inc 3235 Bay Rd *TF:* 800-205-5030 ■ *Web:* www.portablebuildingsinc.com	Milford	DE	19963	302-335-1300		186
Portable Church Industries Inc 1923 Ring Dr *TF:* 800-939-7722 ■ *Web:* www.portablechurch.com	Troy	MI	48083	800-939-7722		190
Portable Rechargeable Battery Assn (PRBA) 1776 K St 4th Fl *Web:* www.prba.org	Washington	DC	20006	202-719-4978		49-13
Portable Technology Solutions LLC 221 David Ct *TF:* 877-640-4152 ■ *Web:* www.ptsmobile.com	Calverton	NY	11933	631-727-8084		177
Porta-Bote Intl 1074 Independence Ave *TF:* 800-227-8882 ■ *Web:* www.porta-bote.com	Mountain View	CA	94043	650-961-5334	961-3800	90
Portaco Inc 1805 Second Ave N *Web:* www.portaco.com	Moorhead	MN	56560	218-236-0223		640
Porta-Fab Corp 18080 Chesterfield Airport Rd *TF:* 800-325-3781 ■ *Web:* www.portafab.com	Chesterfield	MO	63005	636-537-5555	537-2955	105
Portage & District Chamber of Commerce 56 Royal Rd N *Web:* www.portagechamber.com	Portage la Prairie	MB	R1N1V1	204-857-7778	856-5001	137
Portage Community School District 904 De Witt St *Web:* www.portage.k12.wi.us	Portage	WI	53901	608-742-4867		685
Portage County 449 S Meridian St 1st Fl *TF:* 800-772-3799 ■ *Web:* www.co.portage.oh.us	Ravenna	OH	44266	330-297-9422	297-3696	338
Portage County 1516 Church St *Web:* www.co.portage.wi.us	Stevens Point	WI	54481	715-346-1327	346-1486	338
Portage County Business Council 5501 Vern Holmes Dr *TF:* 800-333-6668 ■ *Web:* portagecountybiz.com	Stevens Point	WI	54481	715-344-1940	344-4473	139
Portage County District Library 10482 S St *TF:* 800-500-5179 ■ *Web:* www.portagelibrary.org	Garrettsville	OH	44231	330-527-4378	527-4370	434-3
Portage District Library 300 Library Ln *Web:* www.portagelibrary.info	Portage	MI	49002	269-329-4544	324-9222	434-3
Portage Electric Products Inc 7700 Freedom Ave NW *TF:* 888-464-7374 ■ *Web:* www.pepiusa.com	North Canton	OH	44720	330-499-2727	499-1853	202
Portage Lakes Career Ctr 4401 Shriver Rd *Web:* plcc.edu	Uniontown	OH	44685	330-896-8200		507
Portage Lakes State Park 5031 Manchester Rd *Web:* www.stateparks.com	Akron	OH	44319	330-644-2220		565
Portage Park Chamber of Commerce 5829 W Irving Park Rd *Web:* www.portageparkchamber.org	Chicago	IL	60634	773-777-2020	777-0202	139
Portage Tire & Auto Service 3520 Scottsdale St *Web:* www.portagetire.com	Portage	IN	46368	219-762-0405	762-5585	755
Porta-King Building Systems 4133 Shoreline Dr *TF:* 800-284-5346 ■ *Web:* www.portaking.com	Earth City	MO	63045	888-481-1671		186
Portal Inc 10 Tracy Dr *Web:* www.portalincorporated.com	Avon	MA	02322	508-588-3030		234
Portal Instruments Inc 190 Fifth St *Web:* www.portalinstruments.com	Cambridge	MA	02141	617-500-4348		475
Portal Planet PO Box 18251 *Web:* www.portalplanet.net	Erlanger	KY	41018	859-795-4566		180
PortalFront Hosting 1260 N Hancock St Ste 102 *TF:* 888-890-1935 ■ *Web:* www.portalfronthosting.com	Anaheim	CA	92807	888-890-1935		180
Porta-Lung Inc 1790 Glen Ayre Dr *Web:* www.portalung.com	Lakewood	CO	80215	303-288-7575	288-7577	475
Porteous, Hainkel & Johnson LLP 704 Carondelet St *Web:* www.phjlaw.com	New Orleans	LA	70130	504-581-3838		428
Porter & Chester Institute Inc 670 Lordship Blvd *TF:* 800-870-6789 ■ *Web:* porterchester.edu	Stratford	CT	06615	203-375-4463		148

Name / Address	City	State	ZIP	Phone	Fax	Class
Porter & Company PC CPAS 241 Summit Ave Ste 100 *Web:* www.porterandco.com	Greensboro	NC	27401	336-370-1000		2
Porter Capital Corp 2112 First Ave N *TF:* 800-737-7344 ■ *Web:* www.portercap.net	Birmingham	AL	35203	205-322-5442		272
Porter Consulting Engineers PC 552 State St *TF:* 800-541-5941 ■ *Web:* www.pceengineers.com	Meadville	PA	16335	814-337-4447		261
Porter County 155 Indiana Ave *Web:* porterco.org	Valparaiso	IN	46383	219-465-3445		338
Porter Henry & Company Inc 455 E 86th St *Web:* porterhenry.com	New York	NY	10028	212-953-5544		194
Porter Hills 3600 E Fulton St *Web:* www.porterhills.org	Grand Rapids	MI	49546	616-949-4971		672
Porter Inc 2200 W Monroe St *TF:* 800-736-7685 ■ *Web:* www.formulaboats.com	Decatur	IN	46733	260-724-9111		90
Porter Instrument Company Inc 245 Township Line Rd PO Box 907 *TF:* 888-723-4001 ■ *Web:* www.porterinstrument.com	Hatfield	PA	19440	215-723-4000	723-2199	201
Porter Katie (Rep D - CA) 1117 Longworth House Office Bldg *Web:* www.porter.house.gov	Washington	DC	20515	202-225-5611		342-2
Porter Khouw Consulting Inc PO Box 4028 *Web:* www.porterkhouwconsulting.com	Crofton	MD	21114	410-451-3617		463
Porter Lee Corp 1901 Wright Blvd *Web:* www.porterlee.com	Schaumburg	IL	60193	847-985-2060		177
Porter Medical Center Inc 115 Porter Dr *Web:* www.portermedical.org	Middlebury	VT	05753	802-388-4701	382-3440	463
Porter Novelli Intl 75 Varick St 6th Fl *Web:* www.porternovelli.com	New York	NY	10013	212-601-8000		636
Porter Pipe & Supply Co 303 S Rohlwing Rd *Web:* www.porterpipe.com	Addison	IL	60101	630-543-8145	543-6830	612
Porter Rogers Dahlman & Gordon P C 1 Shoreline Plz 800 N Shoreline Ste 800 S *Web:* www.prdg.com	Corpus Christi	TX	78401	361-880-5808	880-5844	445
Porter Truck Sales LP 135 McCarty St *TF:* 800-956-2408 ■ *Web:* www.portertrk.com	Houston	TX	77029	713-672-2400	672-7343	516
Porter's 200 W First St *Web:* hiduluth.com	Duluth	MN	55802	218-727-6746	722-0233	671
PorterCorp 4240 136th Ave *TF:* 800-354-7721 ■ *Web:* www.portercorp.com	Holland	MI	49424	616-399-1963	399-9123	105
Porters Building Center Inc 700 E 92 Hwy *Web:* www.portersbuilding.com	Kearney	MO	64060	816-628-6111		191-3
Porter-Simon Professional Corp 40200 Truckee Airport Rd *Web:* portersimon.com	Truckee	CA	96161	530-587-2002		41
Porterville Chamber of Commerce 93 N Main St Ste A *Web:* www.portervillechamber.org	Porterville	CA	93257	559-784-7502		139
Porterville College 100 E College Ave *Web:* portervillecollege.edu	Porterville	CA	93257	559-791-2200		162
Porterville Developmental Ctr (PDC) 26501 Ave 140 PO Box 2000 *Web:* www.dds.ca.gov	Porterville	CA	93258	559-782-2222	784-5630	230
Porterville Public Library 41 W Thurman Ave *Web:* www.ci.porterville.ca.us	Porterville	CA	93257	559-784-0177	781-4396	434-3
Portfolio Defense 7 Mt Lassen Dr Ste D150 *Web:* portfoliodefense.com	San Rafael	CA	94903	415-492-8262		261
Portfolio Gallery & Educational Ctr 3514 Delmar Blvd *Web:* www.portfoliogallerystl.org	Saint Louis	MO	63103	314-533-3323		50-2
Portfolio Strategy Group Inc, The 81 Main St *Web:* www.portfoliostrategygroup.com	White Plains	NY	10601	914-328-6660		401
Portico Healthnet 1600 University Ave W Ste 211 *TF:* 866-489-4899 ■ *Web:* www.porticohealthnet.org	Saint Paul	MN	55104	651-489-2273	603-5101	463
Portland Art Museum 1219 SW Park Ave *Web:* portlandartmuseum.org	Portland	OR	97205	503-226-2811	226-4842	520
Portland Baroque Orchestra 1020 SW Taylor St Ste 200 *Web:* pbo.org	Portland	OR	97205	503-222-6000	226-6635	573-3
Portland Bible College 9150 NE Fremont St *Web:* www.portlandbiblecollege.org	Portland	OR	97220	503-255-3540	257-2209	167-3
Portland Bolt & Manufacturing Company Inc 3441 NW Guam St *TF:* 800-547-6758 ■ *Web:* www.portlandbolt.com	Portland	OR	97210	503-227-5488		351
Portland Bottling Co 1321 NE Couch St *Web:* www.portlandbottling.com	Portland	OR	97232	503-231-5035	231-8994	805
Portland Business Alliance 200 SW Market St Ste 150 *Web:* portlandalliance.com	Portland	OR	97201	503-224-8684	323-9186	139
Portland Cement Assn (PCA) 5420 Old Orchard Rd *Web:* www.cement.org	Skokie	IL	60077	847-966-6200	966-9781	49-3
Portland Center for the Performing Arts 1111 SW Broadway *Web:* www.portland5.com	Portland	OR	97205	503-248-4335		572
Portland Center Stage (PCS) 128 NW Eleventh Ave *Web:* www.pcs.org	Portland	OR	97209	503-445-3700	445-3701	573-4
Portland Children's Museum 4015 SW Canyon Rd *Web:* www.portlandcm.org	Portland	OR	97221	503-223-6500	223-6600	521
Portland City Grill 111 SW Fifth Ave 30th Fl *Web:* portlandcitygrill.com	Portland	OR	97204	503-450-0030		671
Portland Clinic, The 800 SW 13th Ave *Web:* www.theportlandclinic.com	Portland	OR	97205	503-221-0161		353
Portland Community College *Sylvania* 12000 SW 49th Ave *TF:* 866-922-1010 ■ *Web:* www.pcc.edu	Portland	OR	97219	503-244-6111	977-4740	162
Portland Federal Credit Union 9077 Charlotte Hwy *TF:* 844-517-3611 ■ *Web:* pfcu4me.com	Portland	MI	48875	517-647-7571	647-4145	219
Portland General Electric 121 SW Salmon St *NYSE: POR* ■ *TF:* 800-542-8818 ■ *Web:* www.portlandgeneral.com	Portland	OR	97204	503-464-8000		787
Portland Global Advisors LLC 217 Commercial St *Web:* www.portlandglobal.com	Portland	ME	04101	207-773-2773		401
Portland Harbor Hotel 468 Fore St *TF:* 888-798-9090 ■ *Web:* www.portlandharborhotel.com	Portland	ME	04101	207-775-9090	775-9990	379
Portland Housing Center Inc 3233 NE Sandy Blvd *Web:* portlandhousingcenter.org	Portland	OR	97232	503-282-7744		509
Portland Institute for Contemporary Art 15 NE Hancock *Web:* pica.org	Portland	OR	97212	503-242-1419	243-1167	50-2
Portland International Jetport 1001 Westbrook St *Web:* www.portlandjetport.org	Portland	ME	04102	207-874-8877	774-7740	27
Portland International Raceway 1940 N Victory Blvd *Web:* www.portlandraceway.com	Portland	OR	97217	503-823-7223	823-5896	642
Portland Investment Counsel Inc 1375 Kerns Rd *TF:* 888-710-4242 ■ *Web:* www.portlandic.com	Burlington	ON	L7P4V7	905-331-4242	319-4939	403
Portland Lobster Co 180 Commercial St *Web:* www.portlandlobstercompany.com	Portland	ME	04112	207-775-2112		671
Portland (ME) City Hall 389 Congress St *Web:* www.portlandmaine.gov	Portland	ME	04101	207-874-8610	874-8612	337
Portland Meadows Horse Track 8102 NE Killingsworth **Fax Area Code:* 503 ■ *Web:* www.portlandmeadows.com	Portland	OR	97218	971-254-4450	286-9763*	642
Portland Metropolitan Exposition Ctr 2060 N Marine Dr *Web:* www.expocenter.org	Portland	OR	97217	503-736-5200	736-5201	205
Portland Museum of Art 7 Congress Sq *Web:* www.portlandmuseum.org	Portland	ME	04101	207-775-6148	773-7324	520
Portland Natural Gas Transmission System (PNGTS) 1 Harbour Pl *TF:* 855-895-8754 ■ *Web:* www.pngts.com	Portsmouth	NH	03801	603-559-5500	427-2807	325
Portland Observatory 138 Congress St *Web:* www.portlandlandmarks.org	Portland	ME	04101	207-774-5561		598
Portland Opera 211 SE Caruthers St *TF:* 866-739-6737 ■ *Web:* www.portlandopera.org	Portland	OR	97214	503-241-1407	241-4212	573-2
Portland Products Inc 271 Morse Dr *Web:* www.portlandproducts.com	Portland	MI	48875	517-647-4191		492
Portland Public Library 5 Monument Sq *TF:* 800-848-5800 ■ *Web:* www.portlandlibrary.com	Portland	ME	04101	207-871-1700	871-1703	434-3
Portland Public Schools 501 N Dixon St *Web:* www.pps.net	Portland	OR	97227	503-916-2000	916-3110	685
Portland Regency Hotel 20 Milk St *TF:* 800-727-3436 ■ *Web:* www.theregency.com	Portland	ME	04101	207-774-4200	775-2150	379
Portland Regional Chamber 443 Congress St *Web:* www.portlandregion.com	Portland	ME	04101	207-772-2811	772-1179	139
Portland Stage Co PO Box 1458 *Web:* www.portlandstage.org	Portland	ME	04104	207-774-1043	774-0576	749
Portland State University Millar Library 1875 SW Park Ave *Web:* library.pdx.edu	Portland	OR	97201	503-725-5874		434-6
Portland Symphony Orchestra 50 Monument Sq 2nd Fl *Web:* www.portlandsymphony.org	Portland	ME	04101	207-773-6128	773-6089	573-3
Portland Teachers Credit Union PO Box 3750 *TF:* 800-527-3932 ■ *Web:* onpointcu.com	Portland	OR	97208	503-228-7077	273-2698	219
Portland Terminal Railroad Co 3500 NW Yeon Ave *Web:* www.up.com	Portland	OR	97210	503-241-9898	241-4494	651
Portland Water District 225 Douglass St PO Box 3553 *Web:* www.pwd.org	Portland	ME	04104	207-761-8310		787
Portland Webworks Inc 5 Milk St *Web:* www.portlandwebworks.com	Portland	ME	04101	207-773-6600		180
Portlogic Systems Inc 2 Toronto St Ste 209 *Web:* new.portlogicsystems.com	Toronto	ON	M5C2B5	786-924-4200		809
Portman Architects 303 Peachtree Center Ave NE Ste 575 *Web:* portmanarchitects.com	Atlanta	GA	30303	404-614-5555		321
Portman Holdings LLC 303 Peachtree St NE Ste 575 *Web:* www.portmanholdings.com	Atlanta	GA	30303	404-614-5252		655
Portman Rob (Sen R - OH) 448 Russell Senate Office Bldg *TF:* 800-205-6446 ■ *Web:* www.portman.senate.gov	Washington	DC	20510	202-224-3353		342-2
Portneuf Health Partners 777 Hospital Way *Web:* www.portneuf.org	Pocatello	ID	83201	208-239-1000		374-3
Portnoff Law Associates Ltd 2700 Horizon Dr Ste 100 **Fax Area Code:* 484 ■ *TF:* 866-211-9466 ■ *Web:* www.portnoffonline.com	King of Prussia	PA	19406	866-211-9466	690-9301*	428
Portnoy CPA 9283 San Jose Blvd *Web:* www.portnoycpa.com	Jacksonville	FL	32257	904-731-8005	732-5004	2
Port-O-Call Hotel 1510 Boardwalk *TF:* 800-334-4546 ■ *Web:* www.portocallhotel.com	Ocean City	NJ	08226	609-399-8812		379

				Phone	Fax	Class
Portofino 249 E Main St *Web:* portofinolexington.com	Lexington	KY	40507	859-253-9300	258-2488	671
Portofino 3124 Eastway Dr *Web:* portofinos-us.com	Charlotte	NC	28205	704-568-7933		671
Portofino Hotel & Yacht Club 260 Portofino Way *TF:* 800-468-4292 ■ *Web:* www.hotelportofino.com	Redondo Beach	CA	90277	310-379-8481		379
Portofino Inn & Suites Anaheim 1831 S Harbor Blvd *TF:* 800-398-3963 ■ *Web:* www.portofinoinnanaheim.com	Anaheim	CA	92802	714-782-7600		379
Porto-Fino Restaurant 3124 S Atlantic Ave *Web:* portofinodaytona.com	Daytona Beach	FL	32118	386-767-9484		671
Portofino Spa at Portofino Island Resort 10 Portofino Dr *TF:* 877-523-2016 ■ *Web:* portofinoisland.com	Pensacola	FL	32561	877-523-2016		707
Portola Elementary School 300 Amador Ave *Web:* sbpsd.k12.ca.us	San Bruno	CA	94066	650-624-3175	624-3199	685
Portola Plaza Hotel 2 Portola Plz *TF:* 888-222-5851 ■ *Web:* www.portolahotel.com	Monterey	CA	93940	831-649-2684	649-4511	379
Portola Redwoods State Park 9000 Portola State Park Rd *Web:* www.parks.ca.gov	La Honda	CA	94020	650-948-9098		565
Portola Systems Inc 7064 Corline Ct Ste B5 *Web:* www.portolasystems.net	Sebastopol	CA	95472	707-824-8800	824-8866	180
Portrait Displays Inc 6663 Owens Dr *Web:* www.portrait.com	Pleasanton	CA	94588	925-227-2700		177
Portrait Express 441 N Water St *TF:* 800-228-3759 ■ *Web:* portraitexpress.com	Silverton	OR	97381	503-873-6365		590
Portrait Innovations Inc 2016 Ayrsley Town Blvd Ste 200 *Web:* www.portraitinnovations.com	Charlotte	NC	28273	704-499-9359		590
Portraits Intl 10835 Rockley Rd *TF:* 888-838-1495 ■ *Web:* www.portraitsinternational.com	Houston	TX	77099	281-879-8444		590
Ports America Inc 525 Washington Blvd Ste 1660 **Fax Area Code:* 201 ■ *Web:* www.portsamerica.com	Jersey City	NJ	07310	732-635-3899	216-9366*	465
Ports O'Call Village Berth 77 *Web:* www.sanpedro.com	San Pedro	CA	90731	310-832-4251		50-6
Ports Petroleum Company Inc 1337 Blachleyville Rd PO Box 1046 *TF:* 800-562-0373 ■ *Web:* www.portspetroleum.com	Wooster	OH	44691	330-264-1885		324
Portsmouth Abbey School 285 Cory's Ln *Web:* www.portsmouthabbey.org	Portsmouth	RI	02871	401-683-2000		622
Portsmouth Area Chamber of Commerce 342 Second St PO Box 509 *Web:* www.portsmouth.org	Portsmouth	OH	45662	740-353-7647	353-5824	139
Portsmouth Athenaeum 9 Market Sq *Web:* portsmouthathenaeum.org	Portsmouth	NH	03801	603-431-2538		434-4
Portsmouth Daily Times 637 Sixth St *TF:* 800-582-7277 ■ *Web:* www.portsmouth-dailytimes.com	Portsmouth	OH	45662	740-353-3101		532-2
Portsmouth Marine Society (PMS) PO Box 728 *Web:* portsmouthhistory.org	Portsmouth	NH	03802	603-436-8433		637-2
Portsmouth Public Library 1220 Gallia St *Web:* www.yourppl.org	Portsmouth	OH	45662	740-354-5688		434-3
Portsmouth Public Library 601 Ct St *Web:* www.portsmouthpubliclibrary.org	Portsmouth	VA	23704	757-393-8501		434-3
Portsmouth Regional Hospital 333 Borthwick Ave *TF:* 800-685-8282 ■ *Web:* portsmouthhospital.com	Portsmouth	NH	03801	603-436-5110		374-3
Portugal-US Chamber of Commerce 35 W 44th St *Web:* portugal-us.com	New York	NY	10036	212-354-4627		138
Porzak Browning & Bushong LLP 2120 13th St *Web:* pbblaw.com	Boulder	CO	80302	303-443-6800	443-6864	41
Porzio Bromberg & Newman PC 100 Southgate Pkwy *Web:* pbnlaw.com	Morristown	NJ	07962	973-538-4006		428
Porzio Life Sciences LLC 100 Southgate Pky *Web:* www.porziolifesciences.com	Morristown	NJ	07962	973-538-1690	538-5146	476
Posados Cafe 3421 N Central Expy *Web:* posados.com	Plano	TX	75023	972-509-4999		671
Posca Bros Dental Laboratory Inc 641 W Willow St *TF:* 800-537-6722 ■ *Web:* poscabrothers.com	Long Beach	CA	90806	562-427-1811		415
POSDATA Inc 5775 Soundview Dr Bldg E **Fax Area Code:* 253 ■ *TF:* 800-852-3282 ■ *Web:* www.posdata.com	Gig Harbor	WA	98335	800-852-3282	858-6059*	174
Poses & Poses PA 169 E Flagler St Ste 1600 *Web:* posesandposes.com	Miami	FL	33131	305-577-0200		41
Posey Bill (Rep R - FL) 2150 Rayburn House Office Bldg *TF:* 888-681-1776 ■ *Web:* posey.house.gov	Washington	DC	20515	202-225-3671	225-3516	342-2
Posey Co 5635 Peck Rd **Fax Area Code:* 800 ■ *TF:* 800-447-6739 ■ *Web:* www.posey.com	Arcadia	CA	91006	626-443-3143	767-3933*	477
Posey County 126 E Third St *Web:* www.poseycountyin.gov	Mount Vernon	IN	47620	812-838-1300	838-1344	338
Poshmark 203 Redwood Shores Pkwy 8th Fl *Web:* poshmark.com	Redwood City	CA	94065	650-262-4771		459
Positech Corp 191 N Rush Lake Rd *TF:* 800-831-6026 ■ *Web:* positech.com	Laurens	IA	50554	712-841-4548	841-4765	470
Positek.net LLC 1934 Old Gallows Rd Ste 350 *TF:* 855-767-4835 ■ *Web:* www.positek.net	Vienna	VA	22182	855-767-4835		180
Position 2 Process Ltd 707 Canopy Dr *Web:* www.position2process.com	Naperville	IL	60540	630-983-8762		194

				Phone	Fax	Class
Positive Education Program Inc 3100 Euclid Ave *Web:* www.pepcleve.org	Cleveland	OH	44115	216-361-4400	361-8600	685
Positive Potentials LLC 12756 W Maya Way *TF:* 877-547-3713 ■ *Web:* www.positivepotentials.com	Peoria	AZ	85383	480-510-7166		637-2
Positive Promotions Inc 15 Gilpin Ave **Fax Area Code:* 800 ■ *TF:* 800-635-2666 ■ *Web:* www.positivepromotions.com	Hauppauge	NY	11788	631-648-1200	635-2329*	317
Positive Software Co 723 The Pkwy *TF:* 800-735-6860 ■ *Web:* www.positiveforbusiness.com	Richland	WA	99352	509-392-6636		175
Positron Corp 530 Oakmont Ln *Web:* www.positron.com	Westmont	IL	60559	317-576-0183		250
Positron Corp 4614 Wyland Dr *TF:* 800-882-6404 ■ *Web:* positroncorp.com	Elkhart	IN	46516	574-295-8777	293-1872	247
Positron Inc 5101 Buchan St Ste 220 *Web:* www.positronpower.com	Montreal	QC	H4P2R9	514-345-2220	345-2271	668
Positronic Industries Inc 423 N Campbell Ave PO Box 8247 *TF:* 800-641-4054 ■ *Web:* www.connectpositronic.com	Springfield	MO	65801	417-866-2322	866-4115	253
Posner Industries Inc 8641 Edgeworth Dr *TF:* 888-767-6377 ■ *Web:* posners.com	Capitol Heights	MD	20743	301-350-1000	350-1050	492
Possum Kingdom State Park 362 N FM 2353 *Web:* tpwd.texas.gov	Graford	TX	76449	940-549-1803		565
Post & Courier 134 Columbus St *Web:* www.postandcourier.com	Charleston	SC	29403	843-577-7111		532-2
Post & Nickel 144 N 14th St *TF:* 877-667-6107 ■ *Web:* www.postandnickel.com	Lincoln	NE	68508	402-476-3432	476-3454	157-5
Post & Schell PC 4 Penn Ctr 1600 John F Kennedy Blvd *Web:* www.postschell.com	Philadelphia	PA	19103	215-587-1000		428
Post Acute Medical LLC 1828 Good Hope Rd Ste 102 **Fax Area Code:* 412 ■ *TF:* 888-590-3888 ■ *Web:* postacutemedical.com	Enola	PA	17025	717-731-9660	247-2333*	374-7
Post Alarm Systems Inc 47 E St Joseph St *TF:* 877-432-9629 ■ *Web:* www.postalarm.com	Arcadia	CA	91006	626-446-7159	446-6811	603
Post Asylum Inc 5642 Dyer St *Web:* postasylum.com	Dallas	TX	75206	214-363-0162		637-10
Post Gardens Inc 3055 Michigan Ave W *Web:* www.postgardens.com	Rockwood	MI	48173	734-379-9688		369
Post Glover Resistors Inc 1369 Cox Rd *TF:* 800-537-6144 ■ *Web:* www.postglover.com	Erlanger	KY	41018	859-283-0778	283-2978	253
Post Hotel, The 200 Pipestone Rd PO Box 69 *TF:* 800-661-1586 ■ *Web:* posthotel.com	Lake Louise	AB	T0L1E0	403-522-3989	522-3966	379
Post Masters 2101 Fillmore St *Web:* www.postmastersmailing.com	Fort Wayne	IN	46802	260-744-7400		5
Post Modern Co 2734 Walnut St *Web:* postmodernco.com	Denver	CO	80205	303-539-7001		512
Post Modern Inc 100 Ross St Ste 310 *Web:* www.postmodern-pgh.com	Pittsburgh	PA	15219	412-391-6635		514
Post No Bills 1316 Rutledge Ave *Web:* www.postnobills.com	Charleston	SC	29403	843-577-1071		4
Post Office Employees Cu of New Orleans Louisiana 4624 W Napoleon Ave *Web:* poecu.org	Metairie	LA	70001	504-885-6871		219
Post Precision Castings Inc 21 Walnut St *Web:* www.postprecision.com	Strausstown	PA	19559	610-488-1011	488-6928	306
Post Ranch Inn Hwy 1 PO Box 219 *TF:* 800-527-2200 ■ *Web:* www.postranchinn.com	Big Sur	CA	93920	831-667-2200		707
Post University 800 Country Club Rd *TF:* 800-345-2562 ■ *Web:* www.post.edu	Waterbury	CT	06723	203-596-4500	756-5810	166
Postal Connections of America 6136 Frisco Sq Blvd Ste 400 *TF:* 800-767-8257 ■ *Web:* www.postalconnections.com	Frisco	TX	75034	800-767-8257		310
Postal Family Credit Union Inc 1243 W 8th St *TF:* 800-265-4527 ■ *Web:* www.urmycu.org	Cincinnati	OH	45203	513-381-8600		219
Postal Presort Inc 820 W Second St N *TF:* 800-235-3033 ■ *Web:* www.postalpresort.com	Wichita	KS	67203	316-262-3333		5
Postal Regulatory Commission 901 New York Ave NW Ste 200 *Web:* www.prc.gov	Washington	DC	20268	202-789-6800	789-6891	340-20
PostalAnnex+ Inc 7580 Metropolitan Dr Ste 200 **Fax Area Code:* 619 ■ *TF:* 800-456-1525 ■ *Web:* www.postalannex.com	San Diego	CA	92108	866-964-3142	563-9850*	113
PostcardMania 2145 Sunnydale Blvd Bldg 101 *TF:* 800-628-1804 ■ *Web:* www.postcardmania.com	Clearwater	FL	33765	800-628-1804		366
Post-Gazette PO Box 130135 *Web:* www.bostonpostgazette.com	Boston	MA	02113	617-227-8929	227-5307	532-2
Postgraduate Center for Mental Health Residence 516 W 50th St *Web:* www.pgcmh.org	New York	NY	10019	212-889-5500		726
Postive Feed Ltd 15077 N Yates Rd *Web:* www.pf4feed.com	Franklinton	LA	70438	979-885-2903		447
Post-Journal 15 W Second St *TF:* 866-756-9600 ■ *Web:* www.post-journal.com	Jamestown	NY	14701	716-487-1111		532-2
Postler & Jaeckle Corp 615 S Ave *TF:* 800-724-4252 ■ *Web:* www.postlerandjaeckle.com	Rochester	NY	14620	585-546-7450	546-4316	189-10
Postman Inc 595 Market St *Web:* www.getpostman.com	San Francisco	CA	94105	415-796-6470		788
Postmark Ink Inc 755 Middle St *Web:* www.postmarkink.com	Fairhope	AL	36532	251-928-1095		5
PostMark Press Inc 16 Spruce St *Web:* www.postmarkpress.com	Watertown	MA	02472	617-926-1165		130
Postmasters Inc 701 Brazos St Ste 1616	Austin	TX	78701	512-693-4040		387
Postmedia Network Inc 365 Bloor St E *Web:* www.postmedia.com	Toronto	ON	M4W3L4	416-383-2300		530
PostNet International Franchise Corp 1819 Wazee St *TF:* 800-841-7171 ■ *Web:* www.postnet.com	Denver	CO	80202	303-771-7100	771-7133	113

	Phone	Fax	Class
ostpartum Support Intl 6706 SW 54th Ave ..... Portland OR 97219 *TF:* 800-944-4773 ■ *Web:* www.postpartum.net	503-894-9453	894-9452	48-17
Post-Register PO Box 1800 ..... Idaho Falls ID 83403 *TF:* 800-574-6397 ■ *Web:* www.postregister.com	208-522-1800		532-2
Post-Standard 220 S Warren St ..... Syracuse NY 13202 *TF:* 866-447-3787 ■ *Web:* www.syracuse.com	315-470-0011		532-2
Post-Star 76 Lawrence St ..... Glens Falls NY 12801 *TF:* 800-724-2543 ■ *Web:* poststar.com	518-792-3131	761-1255	532-2
Postworks New York 110 Leroy St ..... New York NY 10014 *Web:* www.postworks.com	212-609-9400		512
Posty Cards 1600 Olive St ..... Kansas City MO 64127 **Fax Area Code:* 888 ■ *TF:* 800-821-7968 ■ *Web:* www.postycards.com	816-231-2323	577-3800*	130
Pot Au Feu 44 Custom House St ..... Providence RI 02903 *Web:* potaufeuri.com	401-273-8953	273-8963	671
Pot O' Gold Cinema Advertising 11555 Central Pkwy ..... Jacksonville FL 32224 *TF:* 800-446-5330 ■ *Web:* pogusa.com	904-744-7478		514
Potager 1109 Ogden St ..... Denver CO 80218 *Web:* www.potagerrestaurant.com	303-832-5788		671
Potamkin Automotive 6200 NW 167th ..... Miami Lakes FL 33014 *TF:* 855-799-9965 ■ *Web:* www.potamkin.com	855-799-9965		57
Potato Creek State Park 25601 State Rd 4 PO Box 908 ..... North Liberty IN 46554 *Web:* www.in.gov	574-656-8186		565
Potatoes USA 4949 S Syracuse St Ste 400 ..... Denver CO 80237 *Web:* www.potatogoodness.com	303-369-7783	369-7718	48-2
Potawatomi Business Development Corp 3215 W State St Ste 300 ..... Milwaukee WI 53208 *Web:* www.potawatomibdc.com	414-290-9490		393
Potawatomi Hotel & Casino 1721 W Canal St ..... Milwaukee WI 53233 *Web:* www.paysbig.com	414-847-7910		133
Potawatomi Inn Pokagan State Pk 6 Ln 100A Lk James ..... Angola IN 46703 *TF:* 877-768-2928 ■ *Web:* www.in.gov	260-833-1077		669
Potawatomi State Park 3740 County Rd PD ..... Sturgeon Bay WI 54235 *Web:* dnr.wi.gov	920-746-2890	746-2896	565
Potbelly Sandwich Works 222 Merchandise Mart Plz Ste 2300 ..... Chicago IL 60654 *Web:* www.potbelly.com	312-951-0600		670
Potdevin Machine Co 26 Fairfield Pl ..... West Caldwell NJ 07006 *Web:* www.potdevin.com	201-288-1941	288-3770	594
Poteau Chamber of Commerce 201 Hillview Pkwy ..... Poteau OK 74953 *Web:* poteauchamber.com	918-647-9178	647-4099	139
Poteet Strawberry Festival Assn 9199 N State Hwy 16 ..... Poteet TX 78065 *Web:* www.strawberryfestival.com	830-742-8144		138
Potelco Inc 14103 Stewart Rd ..... Sumner WA 98390 *TF:* 800-662-8670 ■ *Web:* www.potelco.net	253-863-0484	863-1813	256
Potemkin Industries Inc 8043 Columbus Rd ..... Mount Vernon OH 43050 **Fax Area Code:* 740 ■ *TF:* 800-445-8434 ■ *Web:* www.potemkinindustries.com	800-445-8434	397-8529*	172
Poten & Partners Inc 805 Third Ave ..... New York NY 10022 *Web:* www.poten.com	212-230-2000	355-0295	311
Potential Industries Inc 922 E E St ..... Wilmington CA 90744 *Web:* www.potentialindustries.com	310-807-4466		660
Potesta & Associates Inc 7012 MacCorkle Ave SE ..... Charleston WV 25304 *Web:* www.potesta.com	304-342-1400		192
Potestio Brothers Equipment 19020 Longs Way ..... Parker CO 80134 *TF:* 800-866-2298 ■ *Web:* www.pbequip.com	303-841-2299	841-7039	274
Potestivo & Associates PC 251 Diversion St ..... Rochester MI 48307 *Web:* www.potestivolaw.com	248-853-4400	853-0404	428
Potholes State Park 6762 Hwy 262 SE ..... Othello WA 99344 *Web:* parks.state.wa.us	509-346-2759		565
Potlatch Corp *Wood Products Div* 805 Mill Rd PO Box 1388 ..... Lewiston ID 83501 *Web:* potlatchdeltic.com	509-835-1500		613
Potlatch State Park 21020 N US Hwy 101 ..... Shelton WA 98584 *Web:* www.parks.wa.gov	360-877-5361		565
Potluck Press 920 S Bayview St ..... Seattle WA 98134 *TF:* 877-818-5500 ■ *Web:* www.potluckpress.com	206-328-1300	328-4633	130
Potomac Appalachian Trail Club Inc, The 118 Park St SE ..... Vienna VA 22180 *TF:* 800-732-0911 ■ *Web:* www.patc.net	703-242-0965		148
Potomac Assn, The Jack London Sq 540 Water St ..... Oakland CA 94607 *Web:* www.usspotomac.org	510-627-1215	839-4729	50-4
Potomac Basin Group Associates LLC 4740 Corridor Pl ..... Beltsville MD 20705 *TF:* 800-311-1031 ■ *Web:* www.potomacbasin.com	301-937-0422	937-7892	390
Potomac College 4000 Chesapeake St NW ..... Washington DC 20016 *Web:* potomac.edu	202-686-0876		166
Potomac Communications Group Inc 1133 20th St NW Ste 400 ..... Washington DC 20036 *Web:* pcgpr.com	202-466-7391		196
Potomac Conference Corporation of Seventh Day Adventists 606 Greenville Ave ..... Staunton VA 24401 *TF:* 800-732-1844 ■ *Web:* www.pcsda.org	540-886-0771		48-20
Potomac Electric Corp 1 Westinghouse Plz ..... Boston MA 02136 *TF:* 877-737-2662 ■ *Web:* www.pepco.com	617-364-0400		454
Potomac Floral Wholesale Inc 2403 Linden Ln ..... Silver Spring MD 20910 *TF:* 800-770-8353 ■ *Web:* www.flowerwholesale.com	301-589-4747	589-4992	293
Potomac Healthcare Solutions LLC 1549 Old Bridge Rd Ste 201 ..... Woodbridge VA 22192 *Web:* www.potomachealthcare.com	703-436-9009		196
Potomac Heritage National Scenic Trail PO Box B ..... Harpers Ferry WV 25425 *Web:* www.nps.gov	304-535-4014		564
Potomac Massage Training Institute 8380 Colesville Rd Ste 600 ..... Silver Spring MD 20910 *Web:* www.pmti.org	202-686-7046		167-3
Potomac State College 101 Ft Ave ..... Keyser WV 26726 *TF:* 800-262-7332 ■ *Web:* www.potomacstatecollege.edu	304-788-6800	788-6939	162
Potomac Supply Corp 1398 Kinsale Rd ..... Kinsale VA 22488 *TF:* 800-365-3900 ■ *Web:* www.potomacsupply.com	804-472-2527	472-5058	551
Potomac Valley Brick & Supply Co 15810 Indianola Dr Ste 100 ..... Rockville MD 20855 *Web:* www.pvbrick.com	301-309-9600	309-0929	150
PotomacWave Consulting 44 Canal Center Plz Ste 410 ..... Alexandria VA 22314 *Web:* www.potomacwave.com	703-997-6066	842-6169	196
Potosi Correctional Ctr 11593 State Hwy O ..... Mineral Point MO 63660 *Web:* www.mo.gov	573-438-6000	438-6006	213
PotPie 904 Westport Rd ..... Kansas City MO 64111 *Web:* www.kcpotpie.com	816-561-2702		671
Potsdam Specialty Paper Inc 547A Sissonville Rd ..... Potsdam NY 13676 *Web:* www.pspi.us.com	315-265-4000		557
Pottawatomie County 325 N Broadway ..... Shawnee OK 74801 *Web:* www.pottcoso.com	405-273-1727		338
Pottawatomie County PO Box 187 ..... Westmoreland KS 66549 *Web:* www.pottcounty.org	785-457-3314	457-3507	338
Potter Anderson & Corroon LLP Hercules Plz 1313 N Market St ..... Wilmington DE 19801 *Web:* www.potteranderson.com	302-984-6000		428
Potter County Santa Fe Bldg 900 S Polk St Ste 705 ..... Amarillo TX 79101 *Web:* www.co.potter.tx.us	806-349-4835	379-2296	338
Potter County 1 N Main St ..... Coudersport PA 16915 *Web:* www.pottercountypa.net	814-274-8290	274-8284	338
Potter Distributing Inc 4037 Roger B Chaffee Blvd ..... Grand Rapids MI 49548 *TF:* 800-748-0568 ■ *Web:* potterdistributing.com	616-531-6860	531-9578	38
Potter Electric Signal Company Inc 5757 Phantom Dr Ste 125 ..... Hazelwood MO 63042 *TF:* 800-325-3936 ■ *Web:* pottersignal.com	314-878-4321	595-6999	283
Potter Lawson Inc 749 University Row Ste 300 ..... Madison WI 53705 *Web:* potterlawson.com	608-274-2741		261
Potter Park Zoo 1301 S Pennsylvania Ave ..... Lansing MI 48912 *Web:* potterparkzoo.org	517-483-4222	316-3894	823
Potter State Bank of Potter, The 301 Chestnut St ..... Potter NE 69156 *Web:* www.potterstatebank.com	308-879-4451		70
Potter, Cohen & Samulon 3852 E Colorado Blvd ..... Pasadena CA 91107 *Web:* pottercohenlaw.com	626-795-0681		41
Potter-Randall Appraisal District 5701 Hollywood Rd (Loop 335) Po Box 7190 ..... Amarillo TX 79118 *Web:* www.prad.org	806-355-8426		393
Potter-Roemer 17451 Hurley St ..... City of Industry CA 91744 *TF:* 800-366-3473 ■ *Web:* www.potterroemer.com	626-336-4561	937-4777	678
Potter-Webster Co 41 NE Walker St ..... Portland OR 97211 *TF:* 877-731-4792 ■ *Web:* www.potterwebster.com	503-283-4792	735-3305	57
Pottle's Transportation Inc 15 Page Rd W ..... Bangor ME 04401 **Fax Area Code:* 207 ■ *TF:* 800-370-5623 ■ *Web:* www.pottlestrans.com	800-370-5623	947-5613*	780
Pottorff 5101 Blue Mound Rd ..... Fort Worth TX 76106 **Fax Area Code:* 206 ■ *Web:* www.pottorffcorporate.com	817-509-2300	339-9455*	198
Pottstown Memorial Medical Ctr (PMMC) 1600 E High St ..... Pottstown PA 19464 *Web:* pottstown.towerhealth.org	610-327-7000		374-3
Pottsville Free Public Library 215 W Market St ..... Pottsville PA 17901 *Web:* www.pottsvillelibrary.org	570-622-8880	622-2157	434-3
Pottsville Republican 111 Mahantongo St ..... Pottsville PA 17901 *Web:* www.republicanherald.com	717-628-6092		532-2
Poudre River Public Library 301 E Olive St ..... Fort Collins CO 80524 *Web:* www.poudrelibraries.org	970-221-6740		434-3
Poudre School District 2407 LaPorte Ave ..... Fort Collins CO 80521 *Web:* www.psdschools.org	970-482-7420		685
Poudre Valley Hospital 1024 S Lemay Ave ..... Fort Collins CO 80524 *Web:* www.uchealth.org	970-495-7000		374-3
Poudre Valley Rural Electric Association Inc 7649 Rea Pkwy ..... Fort Collins CO 80528 *TF:* 800-432-1012 ■ *Web:* pvrea.coop	970-226-1234		245
Poughkeepsie Journal 85 Civic Center Plz ..... Poughkeepsie NY 12601 *TF:* 800-765-1120 ■ *Web:* www.poughkeepsiejournal.com	845-437-4800	437-4921	532-2
Poultry Products Northeast Inc 11 Bemis Rd ..... Hooksett NH 03106 *TF:* 800-334-2449 ■ *Web:* www.morethanchicken.net	800-334-2449		297-10
Pound Ridge Veterinary Ctr 35 Westchester Ave ..... Pound Ridge NY 10576 *Web:* poundridgevet.com	914-764-4644		794
Pounding Mill Quarry Corp 171 St Clair S Crossing ..... Bluefield VA 24605 *TF:* 888-661-7625 ■ *Web:* www.pmqc.com	276-326-1145	322-6805	503-5
Poverty Point Reservoir State Park 1500 Poverty Pt Pkwy ..... Delhi LA 71232 *TF:* 800-474-0392 ■ *Web:* crt.state.la.us	318-878-7536		565
Poverty Point State Historic Site 6859 Hwy 577 ..... Pioneer LA 71266 *TF:* 888-926-5492 ■ *Web:* crt.state.la.us	318-926-5492		565
POW! Kids Books 37 Main St ..... Brooklyn NY 11201 *Web:* www.powkidsbooks.com	212-604-9074		637-2

Name / Address	City	State	ZIP	Phone	Fax	Class
Poway Chamber of Commerce 13325 Civic Center Dr *Web:* www.poway.com	Poway	CA	92064	858-748-0016	748-1710	139
Poway Pilates 14053 Midland Rd *Web:* www.powaypilates.net	Poway	CA	92064	858-748-7864		354
Powder River Correctional Facility 3600 13th St *Web:* www.oregon.gov	Baker City	OR	97814	541-523-6680	523-6678	213
Powder River County PO Box 200 *Web:* prco.mt.gov	Broadus	MT	59317	406-436-2361		338
Powder River Energy Corp (PRE) 221 Main St PO Box 930 **Fax Area Code:* 307 ■ *TF:* 800-442-3630 ■ *Web:* www.precorp.coop	Sundance	WY	82729	800-442-3630	283-3527*	245
Powder Valley Conservation Nature Ctr 11715 Cragwold Rd *Web:* mdc.mo.gov	Saint Louis	MO	63122	314-301-1500	301-1501	50-5
Powdermet Inc 24112 Rockwell Dr *Web:* www.powdermetinc.com	Euclid	OH	44117	216-404-0053		487
POWDR Corp 1794 Olympic Pkwy Ste 210 *Web:* www.powdr.com	Park City	UT	84098	435-608-6564		787
Powell Broadcasting 5667 Bankers Ave *Web:* www.powellgroup.com	Baton Rouge	LA	70808	850-249-8802		647
Powell County 409 Missouri Ave *Web:* www.powellcountymontana.com	Deer Lodge	MT	59722	406-846-3680		338
Powell County PO Box 506 *Web:* www.powellcounty.ky.gov	Stanton	KY	40380	606-663-2834	663-2905	338
Powell Electro Systems LLC 5 Briar Dr *Web:* www.powellelectrosystems.com	West Grove	PA	19390	610-869-8393	869-0591	370
Powell Electronics Inc 200 Commodore Dr *TF:* 800-235-7880 ■ *Web:* www.powell.com	Swedesboro	NJ	08085	856-241-8000	241-8630	246
Powell Fabrication & Manufacturing Inc 740 E Monroe Rd *TF:* 888-800-2310 ■ *Web:* www.powellfab.com	Saint Louis	MI	48880	989-681-2158	681-5013	695
Powell Gardens 1609 NW US Hwy 50 *Web:* powellgardens.org	Kingsville	MO	64061	816-697-2600	697-2619	97
Powell Industries Inc 8550 Mosely Dr *NASDAQ:* POWL ■ *TF:* 800-400-7273 ■ *Web:* www.powellind.com	Houston	TX	77075	713-944-6900	947-4453	729
Powell Radomsky PLLC 11350 Random Hills Rd Ste 420 *Web:* www.powellradomsky.com	Fairfax	VA	22030	866-368-2617		41
Powell River Public Library 100-6975 Alberni St **Fax Area Code:* 866 ■ *Web:* prpl.ca	Powell River	BC	V8A2S3	604-485-4796	489-5778*	435
Powell Systems Inc 162 Churchill-Hubbard Rd *Web:* www.powellsystems.com	Youngstown	OH	44505	330-759-9220	759-9434	470
Powell Technologies 3003 Industrial Dr *Web:* powell-tech.com	Johnson City	TN	37601	423-282-0111	282-6230	188-7
Powell Trachtman PC *Powell, Trachtman, Logan, Carrle & Lombardo PC* 475 Allendale Rd Ste 200 *Web:* www.powelltrachtman.com	King of Prussia	PA	19406	610-354-9700		428
Powell's Books Inc 7 NW Ninth Ave *TF:* 800-878-7323 ■ *Web:* www.powells.com	Portland	OR	97209	503-228-0540		95
Power & Composite Technologies LLC (PCT) 200 Wallins Corners Rd *Web:* www.pactinc.com	Amsterdam	NY	12010	518-843-6825	843-6723	249
Power & Control Engineering Solutions LLC (PCES) 12611 E 60th St *Web:* www.pcescorp.com	Tulsa	OK	74146	918-627-7237		261
Power & Industrial Air Systems 5281 Hamilton Blvd *Web:* pias-usa.com	Allentown	PA	18106	610-395-3242		358
Power & Motoryacht Magazine 10 Bokum Rd *TF:* 800-284-8036 ■ *Web:* www.powerandmotoryacht.com	Essex	CT	06426	860-767-3200		457-4
Power & Telephone Supply Company Inc 2673 Yale Ave *TF:* 800-238-7514 ■ *Web:* www.ptsupply.com	Memphis	TN	38112	901-866-3300		246
Power Beck & Matzureff Law Offices 308 W Burke St *Web:* lawpbm.com	Martinsburg	WV	25401	304-264-8870		41
Power Brake Dies Inc 263 W 154th St *Web:* www.powerbrakedies.com	South Holland	IL	60473	708-339-5951	339-7737	757
Power City Electric Inc 3327 E Olive Ave *Web:* www.powercityelectric.com	Spokane	WA	99202	509-535-8500	535-4665	189-4
Power Construction Company LLC 8750 W Bryn Mawr Ave Ste 500 *Web:* www.powerconstruction.net	Chicago	IL	60631	312-596-6960		186
Power County 543 Bannock Ave *Web:* www.co.power.id.us	American Falls	ID	83211	208-226-7610		338
Power Creative 11701 Commonwealth Dr *Web:* www.poweragency.com	Louisville	KY	40299	502-267-0772		4
Power Depot Inc 3553 NW 78th Ave *Web:* powerdepot.com	Miami	FL	33122	305-592-7100		196
Power Engineering and Manufacturing Ltd (PEM) 2635 WCF&N Dr *TF:* 877-898-4327 ■ *Web:* www.pemltd.com	Waterloo	IA	50703	319-232-2311	232-6100	709
Power Engineering Corp PO Box 766 *TF:* 800-626-0903 ■ *Web:* www.powerengineeringcorp.com	Wilkes-Barre	PA	18703	570-823-8822	823-8143	261
Power Equipment Co 3300 Alcoa Hwy *Web:* www.powerequipco.com	Knoxville	TN	37920	865-577-5563	579-7355	358
Power Equipment Systems 1331 Tandem Ave NE *TF:* 800-782-2700 ■ *Web:* www.pesnet.com	Salem	OR	97301	800-782-2700	637-9243	274
Power Flame Inc 2001 S 21st St PO Box 974 *TF:* 877-421-0480 ■ *Web:* www.powerflame.com	Parsons	KS	67357	620-421-0480	421-0948	357
Power Grid Engineering LLC 100 Colonial Center Pkwy Ste 400 *TF:* 877-819-1171 ■ *Web:* www.powergridengineering.com	Lake Mary	FL	32746	321-244-0170	578-3720	188
Power Gripps Usa Inc 41 Pomola Ave *Web:* www.versagripps.com	Sorrento	ME	04677	207-422-2051		711
Power Integrations 5245 Hellyer Ave *NASDAQ:* POWI ■ *Web:* www.power.com	San Jose	CA	95138	408-414-9200	414-9201	696
Power Law Firm LLP 433 Hackensack Ave 1St Fl *TF:* 800-281-1515 ■ *Web:* powerlawfirm.com	Hackensack	NJ	07601	800-281-1515		41
Power Machinery Ctr 3450 Camino Ave *Web:* www.powermachinery.com	Oxnard	CA	93030	805-485-0577	983-2773	385
Power Management Co 1600 Moseley Rd Ste 100 *Web:* powermgt.com	Victor	NY	14564	585-249-1360		261
Power Management Concepts LLC (PMC) 510 Grumman Rd W Ste 211 *Web:* powermanage.com	Bethpage	NY	11714	516-605-9451		463
Power Marketing Administrations *Southeastern Power Administration* 1166 Athens Tech Rd *Web:* www.energy.gov	Elberton	GA	30635	706-213-3800	213-3884	340-9
Power Motive Corp 5000 Vasquez Blvd *TF:* 800-627-0087 ■ *Web:* www.powermotivecorp.com	Denver	CO	80216	303-355-5900	388-9328	358
Power Organics 301 S Old Stage Rd PO Box 1626 *TF:* 877-769-3795 ■ *Web:* powerorganics.com	Mount Shasta	CA	96067	530-926-6684	926-6685	799
Power Partners Inc 200 Newton Bridge Rd *Web:* www.powerpartners-usa.com	Athens	GA	30607	706-548-3121	548-1929	767
Power Plant Live! 34 Market St *Web:* www.powerplantlive.com	Baltimore	MD	21202	410-727-5483		50-6
Power Plus Sound & Lighting Inc 2445 Grand Ave *Web:* www.powerpluscorp.com	Vista	CA	92081	760-727-1717		38
Power PR 20521 Earl St *Web:* powerpr.com	Torrance	CA	90503	310-787-1940		636
Power Process Piping Inc 45780 Port St *Web:* www.ppphq.com	Plymouth	MI	48170	734-451-0130	451-0763	189-10
Power Quality Engineering Inc 3001 Woodall Dr *Web:* www.pqeinc.com	Cedar Park	TX	78613	512-267-6656		256
Power Repair Service Inc 314 Mcbride Ln *TF:* 888-289-1599 ■ *Web:* powerrepair.net	Corpus Christi	TX	78408	361-289-1471		454
Power Service Products Inc PO Box 1089 *TF:* 800-643-9089 ■ *Web:* powerservice.com	Weatherford	TX	76086	817-599-9486		538
Power Station Inc 7360 Reseda Blvd Ste D	Reseda	CA	91335	818-344-8148		54
Power System Engineering Inc 1532 W Broadway Ste 100 *TF:* 866-825-8895 ■ *Web:* powersystem.org	Madison	WI	53713	608-222-8400	222-9378	261
Power Systems & Controls Inc 3206 Lanvale Ave *Web:* www.pscpower.com	Richmond	VA	23230	804-355-2803		112
Power Technical Services LLC 1195 Yuma Dr *Web:* ptswyo.com	Douglas	WY	82633	307-351-1305		261
Power Tool & Supply Co 3699 Leharps Rd *TF:* 800-228-3699 ■ *Web:* powertoolandsupply.com	Youngstown	OH	44515	330-792-1487		351
Power Transmission Distributors Assn (PTDA) 230 W Monroe St Ste 1410 *Web:* www.ptda.org	Chicago	IL	60606	312-516-2100		49-18
Power Vac Services 50 Goebel Ave *Web:* powervac.ca	Cambridge	ON	N3C1Z1	519-658-4140		104
Power Wellness 851 Oak Creek Dr *TF:* 877-888-2988 ■ *Web:* www.powerwellness.com	Lombard	IL	60148	630-570-2600		403
Power Worker's Union, The 244 Eglinton Ave E *TF:* 800-958-8798 ■ *Web:* www.pwu.ca	Toronto	ON	M4P1K2	416-481-4491		414
Powerboss Inc 175 Anderson St *Web:* powerboss.com	Aberdeen	NC	28315	910-944-2105		386
Powercast Corp 620 Alpha Dr *Web:* www.powercastco.com	Pittsburgh	PA	15238	724-238-3700		261
PowerChord Inc 360 Central Ave 5th Fl *TF:* 800-350-0981 ■ *Web:* www.powerchord.com	Saint Petersburg	FL	33701	727-823-1530		5
Powercon Corp PO Box 477 *TF:* 800-638-5055 ■ *Web:* www.powerconcorp.com	Severn	MD	21144	410-551-6500	551-8451	729
PowerData Corp 11431 Willows Rd NE Ste 130 *Web:* www.powerdata.com	Redmond	WA	98052	425-732-0149		178-1
Powered by Professionals (PBP) 1460 Broadway *Web:* poweredbyprofessionals.com	New York	NY	10036	646-278-6735		194
Powered By Search Inc 505 Consumers Rd Ste 507 *TF:* 866-611-5535 ■ *Web:* www.poweredbysearch.com	Toronto	ON	M2J4V8	416-840-9044		224
Powerex Inc 173 Pavilion Ln *TF:* 800-451-1415 ■ *Web:* www.pwrx.com	Youngwood	PA	15697	724-925-7272	925-4393	696
Powerfilm Inc 2337 230th St *TF:* 888-354-7773 ■ *Web:* www.powerfilmsolar.com	Ames	IA	50014	515-292-7606		696
PowerFleet 123 Tice Blvd Ste 101 *NASDAQ:* IDSY ■ *TF:* 866-410-0152 ■ *Web:* www.powerfleet.com	Woodcliff Lake	NJ	07677	201-996-9000	996-9144	647
Powerhouse Gym Intl 355 S Old Woodward Ste 150 *Web:* powerhousegym.com	Birmingham	MI	48009	248-476-2888		354
Powerlink Facilities Management Services 3031 W Grand Blvd Ste 640 *Web:* www.powerlinkonline.com	Detroit	MI	48202	313-309-2020		104
Powermag Inc 2639 Lavery Ct Ste 4 *Web:* www.powermaginc.com	Newbury Park	CA	91320	805-499-7471	499-3001	253
PowerMed Corp 48 Free St *Web:* www.powermed.com	Portland	ME	04101	207-772-3920		179
Powernail Co 1300 Rose Rd *TF:* 800-323-1653 ■ *Web:* www.powernail.com	Lake Zurich	IL	60047	847-847-3000	634-4943	759
PowerPhone Inc 1321 Boston Post Rd *Web:* powerphone.com	Madison	CT	06443	203-245-8911		180

	Phone	Fax	Class
PowerPhysics 877 Production Pl Newport Beach CA 92663 *Web:* powerphysics.com	949-371-6202		52
PowerPlan Corp 2130 Main St Ste 245 Huntington Beach CA 92648 *Web:* www.questica.com	714-969-5353		809
Powerplant Consultants Inc (PPC) 1106 E Emporia St Ontario CA 91761 *Web:* www.gesco.org	909-986-1141	986-1147	194
Powers & Miller A Professional Corp 3500 Douglas Blvd Ste 100 Roseville CA 95661 *Web:* powersmiller.com	916-924-7900		41
Powers & Santola LLP 39 N Pearl St Albany NY 12207 *Web:* powers-santola.com	518-465-5995		41
Powers & Sons Construction Company Inc 2636 W 15th Ave Gary IN 46404 *Web:* www.powersandsons.com	219-949-3100	949-5906	186
Powers & Sons LLC 1613 Magda Dr Montpelier OH 43543 *Web:* www.powersandsonsllc.com	419-485-3151	485-5490	60
Powers Agency Inc 1 W Fourth St 5th Fl Cincinnati OH 45202 *Web:* www.powersagency.com	513-721-5353		7
Powers David J & Associates Inc 1871 The Alameda Ste 200 San Jose CA 95126 *Web:* davidjpowers.com	408-248-3500	248-9641	463
Powers Distributing Company Inc 3700 Giddings Rd Orion MI 48359 *Web:* powersdistributing.com	248-393-3700		81-1
Powers Fasteners Inc 2 Powers Ln Brewster NY 10509 **Fax Area Code:* 914 ■ *TF:* 800-524-3244 ■ *Web:* www.powers.com	800-524-3244	576-6483*	493
Powers Law 411 S 13th St Ste 300 Lincoln NE 68508 *Web:* www.vincepowerslaw.com	402-474-8000		428
Powers Manufacturing Co 1340 Sycamore St PO Box 2157 Waterloo IA 50704 *Web:* www.powersathletic.com	319-233-6118	234-8048	155-1
Powers Products Co 2695 W Third Ave Denver CO 80219 *Web:* powersproducts.com	303-791-1010		191-2
Powers Pyles Sutter & Verville PC 1501 M St NW 7th Fl Washington DC 20005 *Web:* www.powerslaw.com	202-466-6550	785-1756	428
PowerScore Inc 57 Hasell St Charleston SC 29401 *TF:* 800-545-1750 ■ *Web:* www.powerscore.com	800-545-1750		764
PowerSecure International Inc 1609 Heritage Commerce Ct Wake Forest NC 27587 *NYSE: POWR* ■ *Web:* powersecure.com	919-556-3056	556-3596	787
PowerServe International Inc 961 Broad St Augusta GA 30901 *Web:* www.powerserve.net	706-826-1506		177
Powerserve Technologies Inc 15074 Park of Commerce Blvd Ste 4 Jupiter FL 33478 *Web:* powerservetech.com	561-840-1441		261
Powersmiths International Corp 10 Devon Rd Brampton ON L6T5B5 *TF:* 800-747-9627 ■ *Web:* www.powersmiths.com	905-791-1493		767
Powersports Business 10405 Sixth Ave N Ste 210 Minneapolis MN 55441 *Web:* www.powersportsbusiness.com	763-383-4400	383-4499	637-9
Powers-Swain Chevrolet Inc 4709 Bragg Blvd Fayetteville NC 28303 *TF:* 800-476-5135 ■ *Web:* www.pschevy.com	910-864-9500		516
Powersteering Software Inc 401 Congress Ave Ste 1850 Austin TX 78701 *TF:* 866-390-9088 ■ *Web:* uplandsoftware.com	617-492-0707	492-9444	178-7
Powerstream LLC PO Box 1333 Royal Oak MI 48068 *TF:* 800-842-1015 ■ *Web:* www.powerstream.net	248-862-7271		225
Powertex Inc 1 Lincoln Ave Rouses Point NY 12979 *Web:* www.powertex.com	518-297-4000		596
Powertronix Inc 1120 Chess Dr Foster City CA 94404 *Web:* www.powertronix.com	650-345-6800	345-7240	767
Powerzone Volleyball Inc 3 Luger Rd Denville NJ 07834 *TF:* 800-772-2222 ■ *Web:* www.powerzonevb.com	973-983-8208		708
Poweshiek County PO Box 218 Montezuma IA 50171 *Web:* www.poweshiekcounty.org	641-623-5644		338
Powhatan County 3880 Old Buckingham Rd Powhatan VA 23139 *Web:* www.powhatanva.com	804-598-5612	598-5608	338
Powhatan County School District 2320 Skaggs Rd Powhatan VA 23139 *Web:* www.powhatan.k12.va.us	804-598-5700		685
Powill Manufacturing & Engineering Inc 21039 N 27th Ave Phoenix AZ 85027 *Web:* www.powill.com	623-780-4100		21
Powin Corp 20550 SW 115th Ave Tualatin OR 97062 *Web:* powinenergy.com	503-598-6659		621
Powmet Inc 2625 Sewell St Rockford IL 61125 *Web:* www.powmet.com	815-398-6900		350
Powrtek Engineering Inc 20711 Watertown Rd Ste C Waukesha WI 53186 *Web:* powrtek.com	262-827-9575		261
Powr-Ups Corp 1 Roned Rd Brookhaven R&D Plz Shirley NY 11967 *Web:* www.powrupscorp.com	631-345-5700	345-0060	203
Poyner & Spruill LLP 301 Fayetteville St Ste 1900 Raleigh NC 27601 **Fax Area Code:* 704 ■ *Web:* www.poynerspruill.com	919-783-6400	342-5264*	428
Poynter Institute for Media Studies Inc, The 801 Third St S Saint Petersburg FL 33701 *Web:* www.poynter.org	727-821-9494		507
Pozas Bros Trucking Company Inc 8130 Enterprise Dr Newark CA 94560 *TF:* 800-874-8383 ■ *Web:* pozasbros.com	510-742-9939	742-9979	780
Pozzetta Products Inc 3219 S Platte River Dr Englewood CO 80110 *Web:* www.pozzetta.com	303-783-3172		88
PP Systems International Inc 110 Haverhill Rd Ste 301 Amesbury MA 01913 *TF:* 866-211-9346 ■ *Web:* ppsystems.com	978-834-0505		250
PPA (Professional Photographers of America Inc) 229 Peachtree St NE Ste 2200 Atlanta GA 30303 *TF:* 800-786-6277 ■ *Web:* www.ppa.com	404-522-8600	614-6400	48-4
PPA (Premium Press America) 2606 Eugenia Ave Ste C Nashville TN 37211 *TF:* 800-891-7323 ■ *Web:* www.premiumpressamerica.com	615-353-7902	353-7905	637-2
PPAI (Promotional Products Association Intl) 3125 Skyway Cir N Irving TX 75038 *TF:* 888-426-7724 ■ *Web:* www.ppai.org	972-252-0404		49-18
PPC (Powerplant Consultants Inc) 1106 E Emporia St Ontario CA 91761 *Web:* www.gesco.org	909-986-1141	986-1147	194
PPC (Pocono Produce Company Inc) Chipperfield Dr Rte 191 Stroudsburg PA 18360 *TF:* 800-366-4550 ■ *Web:* poconoprofoods.com	570-421-4990	476-5149	297-2
PPC (PPC Lubricants Inc) 305 Micro Dr Jonestown PA 17038 **Fax Area Code:* 866 ■ *TF:* 800-772-5823 ■ *Web:* www.ppclubricants.com	800-772-5823	772-5823*	541
PPC Industries 3000 E Marshall Ave Longview TX 75601 *Web:* www.ppcair.com	903-758-3395	758-6487	386
Ppc Industries Inc 10101 78th Ave Pleasant Prairie WI 53158 *TF:* 800-769-1172 ■ *Web:* www.ppcind.com	262-947-0900	947-0933	596
PPC Lubricants Inc (PPC) 305 Micro Dr Jonestown PA 17038 **Fax Area Code:* 866 ■ *TF:* 800-772-5823 ■ *Web:* www.ppclubricants.com	800-772-5823	772-5823*	541
PPC Mechanical Seals 2769 Mission Dr Baton Rouge LA 70805 *TF:* 800-731-7325 ■ *Web:* www.ppcmechanicalseals.com	225-356-4333	355-2126	326
PPD Inc 929 N Front St Wilmington NC 28401 *Web:* www.ppd.com	910-251-0081		743
PPF (Public Policy Forum) 633 W Wisconsin Ave Ste 406 Milwaukee WI 53203 *Web:* www.publicpolicyforum.org	414-276-8240	276-9962	48-13
PPG & Associates Federal Credit Union 101 Bailies Run Rd Creighton PA 15030 *TF:* 800-449-7728 ■ *Web:* ppgfcu.org	724-224-1777	224-3226	219
PPG Aerospace 12780 San Fernando Rd Sylmar CA 91342 *Web:* www.ppg.com	818-362-6711	362-0603	20
PPG Industries Inc 17451 Von Karman Ave Irvine CA 92614 *TF:* 800-544-3338 ■ *Web:* www.ppgaerospace.com	949-474-0400	474-7269	550
PPG Industries Inc 1 PPG Pl Pittsburgh PA 15272 *NYSE: PPG* ■ **Fax Area Code:* 724 ■ *Web:* www.corporate.ppg.com	412-434-3131	325-5105*	550
PPH (Pentecostal Publishing House) 5584 Mt View Rd Antioch TN 37013 *TF:* 866-819-7667 ■ *Web:* www.pentecostalpublishing.com	866-819-7667		637-2
PPHEA (Panhandle-Plains Higher Education Authority Inc) 1303 23rd St Canyon TX 79015 *Web:* www.pphea.org	806-324-4100		48-11
PPI (Paper Pak Industries) 1941 N White Ave La Verne CA 91750 *TF:* 888-293-6529 ■ *Web:* www.paperpakindustries.com	909-392-1750	392-1760	297-9
PPI (Progressive Policy Institute) 1101 14th St NW Ste 1250 Washington DC 20005 *Web:* www.progressivepolicy.org	202-525-3926	525-3941	634
PPI Construction Management Inc 8200 NW 15th Pl Ste B Gainesville FL 32606	352-331-1141	331-9084	194
PPIW (Pinnacle Performance Improvement Worldwide) 101 Main St Pepperell MA 01463 *Web:* ppiw.com	978-433-2040	925-9798	194
PPL Corp 2 N Ninth St Allentown PA 18101 *NYSE: PPL* ■ *Web:* www.pplweb.com	610-774-5151		360-5
PPL Electric Utilities Corp 827 Hausman Rd Allentown PA 18104 *TF:* 800-342-5775 ■ *Web:* www.pplelectric.com	800-358-6623		787
PPM (Pike Place Market) 85 Pike St Rm 500 Seattle WA 98101 *Web:* www.pikeplacemarket.org	206-682-7453	625-0646	50-6
PPM America Inc 225 W Wacker Dr Ste 1200 Chicago IL 60606 *Web:* www.ppmamerica.com	312-634-2500		401
PPM Consultants Inc 1600 Lamy Ln Monroe LA 71201 *Web:* ppmco.com	318-323-7270	323-6593	261
PPO USA Inc 310 NE Mulberry Lee's Summit MO 64086 *TF:* 800-505-8880 ■ *Web:* www.ppousa.com	800-505-8880		391-3
PPOK (Pharmacy Providers of OK) 3000 E Memorial Rd Edmond OK 73013 **Fax Area Code:* 405 ■ *TF:* 877-557-5707 ■ *Web:* www.ppok.com	877-557-5707	525-2196*	237
ppoONE Inc 1311 W President George Bush Hwy 1st Fl Richardson TX 75080 *Web:* www.ppoone.com	214-273-8923		178-1
PPOplus LLC 400 Poydras St Ste 2040 New Orleans LA 70130 *TF:* 888-965-1180 ■ *Web:* www.ppoplus.com	504-680-4498		390
PPP (Peter Pepper Products Inc) 17929 S Susana Rd PO Box 5769 Compton CA 90224 **Fax Area Code:* 310 ■ *TF:* 800-496-0204 ■ *Web:* www.peterpepper.com	800-496-0204	639-6013*	591
PPPL (Princeton Plasma Physics Laboratory) PO Box 451 Princeton NJ 08543 *Web:* www.pppl.gov	609-243-2000	243-2751	668
PPS (Pittsburgh Public Schools) 341 S Bellefield Ave Pittsburgh PA 15213 *Web:* www.pghschools.org	412-622-7920		685
PPS Parking & Transportation Inc 1800 E Garry Ave Ste 107 Santa Ana CA 92705 *TF:* 800-701-3763 ■ *Web:* ppsparkingandtrans.com	949-223-8707	588-5979	562
PPT (Photo Protective Technologies Inc) 6610 Topper Ridge San Antonio TX 78233 *Web:* www.melaninproducts.com	210-493-6353	493-7043	543
PPTA (Plasma Protein Therapeutics Assn) 147 Old Solomon's Island Rd Ste 100 Annapolis MD 21401 *Web:* www.pptaglobal.org	202-789-3100		49-8
PPV Inc 4927 NW Front Ave Portland OR 97210 *Web:* www.ppvnw.com	503-261-9800		539
P-Q Controls Inc 95 Dolphin Rd Bristol CT 06010 *Web:* www.pqcontrols.com	860-583-6994		179
PQ Media LLC 370 Hope St Ste 2815 Stamford CT 06906 *Web:* www.pqmedia.com	203-921-5249		466
PQC 4211 Hobson Ct Ste A Fort Wayne IN 46815 *Web:* www.pqcworks.com	260-420-7374		463
P-R Farms Inc 2917 E Shepherd Ave Clovis CA 93619 *Web:* www.prfarms.com	559-299-0201	299-7292	315-3

Phone | Fax | Class

PR Hoffman Machine Products
1517 Commerce Ave. Carlisle PA 17015 717-243-9900 494
Web: www.prhoffman.com

PRA (PRA Health Sciences)
4130 Parklake Ave Ste 400 Raleigh NC 27612 919-786-8200 786-8201 85
Web: prahs.com

PRA (Pacifica Radio Archives)
3729 Cahuenga Blvd W Studio City CA 91604 818-506-1077 506-1084 226
TF: 800-735-0230 ■ *Web:* www.pacificaradioarchives.org

PRA Health Sciences (PRA)
4130 Parklake Ave Ste 400 Raleigh NC 27612 919-786-8200 786-8201 85
Web: prahs.com

PRA Inc 1501 Broadway New York NY 10036 212-354-9440 184
Web: pra.com

Prab Inc 5944 E Kilgore Rd. Kalamazoo MI 49048 269-382-8200 349-2477 207
TF: 800-968-7722 ■ *Web:* www.prab.com

Prabhav Services Inc
181 New Rd Ste 304 Parsippany NJ 07054 862-251-3528 177
Web: prabhavonline.com

Practical Automation Inc
45 Woodmont Rd Milford CT 06460 203-882-5640 882-5648 173-6
Web: www.practicalautomation.com

Practical Business Systems
3598 W Blue Ridge Dr Greenville SC 29611 864-242-6896 837-2748* 177
**Fax Area Code:* 888 ■ *Web:* www.pbsit.com

Practical Computer Inc
1510 Mohawk Blvd. Springfield OR 97477 541-726-7775 726-7852 173-8
Web: www.practicalcomputersinc.com

Practical Horseman Magazine
656 Quince Orchard Rd Ste 600 Gaithersburg MD 20878 800-365-5548 457-14
TF: 800-365-5548 ■ *Web:* practicalhorsemanmag.com

Practical Imagination Enterprising
18 Losey Rd Ringoes NJ 08551 908-237-2246 195
Web: www.practical-imagination.com

Practical Nurse Program of Canton City Schools
305 McKinley Ave NW Canton OH 44702 330-453-2500 685
Web: www.ccsdistrict.org

Practical Political Consulting Inc
920 N Washington Ave Lansing MI 48906 517-351-5105 192
Web: www.practicalpoliticalconsulting.com

Practice CFO
13400 Sabre Springs Pkwy Ste. San Diego CA 92128 800-675-2712 251-0015* 2
**Fax Area Code:* 858 ■ *TF:* 800-675-2712 ■ *Web:* practicecfo.com

Practice Concepts 2706 Harbor Blvd. Costa Mesa CA 92626 714-545-5110 317
TF: 877-778-2020 ■ *Web:* www.practiceconcepts.com

Practice Technology Inc
2311 Mount Vernon St Orlando FL 32803 407-228-4400 177
TF: 866-974-3946 ■ *Web:* www.prevail.net

Practicon Inc 1112 Sugg Pkwy Greenville NC 27834 252-752-5183 228
TF: 800-959-9505 ■ *Web:* www.practicon.com

Practising Law Institute (PLI)
1177 Avenue of the Americas 2nd Fl New York NY 10036 212-824-5700 321-0093* 49-10
**Fax Area Code:* 800 ■ *TF:* 800-260-4754 ■ *Web:* www.pli.edu

Prada 609 W 51st St New York NY 10019 212-307-9300 277
Web: www.prada.com

Prader-Willi Syndrome Association (USA)
8588 Potter Park Dr Ste 500 Sarasota FL 34238 800-926-4797 312-0142* 48-17
**Fax Area Code:* 941 ■ *TF:* 800-926-4797 ■ *Web:* www.pwsausa.org

Pradip Patel & Co
1701 E Woodfield Rd Ste 817 Schaumburg IL 60173 847-413-0414 2
Web: patelcpas.com

Prado Group Inc, The
150 Post St Ste 320 San Francisco CA 94108 415-395-0880 528
Web: www.pradogroup.com

Prado Vision & Lasik Ctr
7522 N Himes Ave Tampa FL 33614 813-931-0500 798
Web: www.pradovision.com

Praemittias Group Inc
8871 Ridgeline Blvd Highlands Ranch CO 80129 720-344-0611 196
Web: praemittias.com

Praet Tool & Engineering Inc
51214 Industrial Dr. Macomb MI 48042 586-677-3800 677-3900 757
Web: www.praettool.com

Pragma Corp, The 116 E Broad St Falls Church VA 22046 703-237-9303 195
Web: www.pragmacorp.com

Pragma Systems Inc
13809 Research Blvd Ste 675 Austin TX 78750 512-219-7270 219-7110 178-12
TF: 800-224-1675 ■ *Web:* www.pragmasys.com

Pragmatek
5775 Wayzata Blvd Ste 700 Saint Louis Park MN 55416 952-525-2217 194
Web: www.pragmatek.com

Pragmatic Institute
8960 E Raintree Dr Scottsdale AZ 85260 480-515-1411 195
Web: www.pragmaticinstitute.com

Pragmatic Works
1845 Town Center Blvd Ste 505 Fleming Island FL 32003 904-413-1911 180
Web: pragmaticworks.com

Pragmatics Inc 1761 Business Center Dr Reston VA 20190 703-761-4033 438-1779 178-10
Web: www.pragmatics.com

Prairie Band Casino & Resort
12305 150th Rd Mayetta KS 66509 785-966-7777 133
TF: 888-727-4946 ■ *Web:* www.prairieband.com

Prairie Capital Management LLC
4900 Main St Ste 700 Kansas City MO 64112 816-531-1101 401
Web: www.prairiecapital.com

Prairie City State Vehicular Recreation Area
13300 White Rock Rd Rancho Cordova CA 95742 916-985-7378 565
Web: www.parks.ca.gov

Prairie College
350 Fifth Ave NE PO Box 4000 Three Hills AB T0M2N0 403-443-5511 443-5540 785
TF: 800-661-2425 ■ *Web:* prairie.edu

Prairie County 1 Commerce Dr Ste 101 Des Arc AR 72040 870-256-4137 338
Web: prairiecountysheriff.org

Prairie County, Justice of the Peace
217 West Park St PO Box 124 Terry MT 59349 406-635-4466 635-5576 338
Web: www.prairiecounty.org

Prairie Dog LLC 6155 Oak St. Kansas City MO 64113 816-822-3636 7
Web: pdog.com

Prairie du Chien Correctional Institution
500 E Parrish St Prairie du Chien WI 53821 608-326-7828 213
Web: www.doc.wi.gov

Prairie Engineers PC 404 N Main St Columbia IL 62236 618-719-2580 261
Web: prairieengineers.com

Prairie Farms Dairy Inc
1100 N Broadway St. Carlinville IL 62626 217-854-2547 854-6426 296-27
TF: 800-654-2547 ■ *Web:* www.prairiefarms.com

Prairie Group Inc
PO Box 65820 West Des Moines IA 50265 515-225-3720 225-2422 178-1
TF: 800-346-5392 ■ *Web:* www.prgrsoft.com

Prairie Grove Battlefield State Park
506 E Douglas St Prairie Grove AR 72753 479-846-2990 565
Web: www.arkansasstateparks.com

Prairie Heart Institute
619 E Mason St Springfield IL 62701 217-788-0706 194
Web: www.st-johns.org

Prairie Holdings Group LLC
1525 Bio Science Dr. Worthington MN 56187 507-372-4722 794
Web: prairieholdings.com

Prairie Hotel 700 Prairie Pk Ln Yelm WA 98597 360-458-8300 379
Web: www.prairiehotel.com

Prairie Inc 300 E Fifth Ave Ste 300 Naperville IL 60563 630-983-6400 983-6466 180
Web: www.prairieinc.com

Prairie Industries Inc
800 N State Prairie Du Chien WI 53821 608-326-2500 1
Web: www.pind.com

Prairie Knights Casino & Resort
7932 Hwy 24 Fort Yates ND 58538 701-854-7777 854-7786 133
TF: 800-425-8277 ■ *Web:* prairieknights.com

Prairie Lakes Area Education Agency
1235 Fifth Ave S Fort Dodge IA 50501 515-574-5500 685
TF: 800-669-2325 ■ *Web:* www.plaea.org

Prairie Lakes Hospital & Care Ctr
401 Ninth Ave NW Watertown SD 57201 605-882-7000 374-3
TF: 877-917-7547 ■ *Web:* www.prairielakes.com

Prairie Land Electric Co-opeartive Inc
14035 US Hwy 36 Norton KS 67654 785-877-3323 245
TF: 800-577-3323 ■ *Web:* www.prairielandelectric.com

Prairie Lights Bookstore
15 S Dubuque St Iowa City IA 52240 319-337-2681 95
TF: 800-295-2665 ■ *Web:* www.prairielights.com

Prairie Management & Development Inc
333 N Michigan Ave Ste 1700 Chicago IL 60601 312-644-1055 644-0686 653

Prairie Material 7601 W 79th St. Bridgeview IL 60455 708-458-0400 182
Web: www.prairie.com

Prairie Meadows 1 Prairie Meadows Dr Altoona IA 50009 515-967-1000 967-1344 133
TF: 800-325-9015 ■ *Web:* www.prairiemeadows.com

Prairie Mission Retirement Village Inc
242 Carroll St Saint Paul KS 66771 620-449-2400 672
Web: www.pmrv.com

Prairie Plastics Inc
522 Progress Way Sun Prairie WI 53590 608-834-9122 604
Web: www.prairieplastics.com

Prairie Public Broadcasting Inc
207 N Fifth St Fargo ND 58102 701-241-6900 239-7650 741-48
TF: 800-359-6900 ■ *Web:* www.prairiepublic.org

Prairie River Home Care Inc
4432 State Hwy 25 SE Ste 200 Buffalo MN 55313 507-252-9844 363
Web: prairieriver.com

Prairie Rose State Park 680 Rd M47 Harlan IA 51537 712-773-2701 773-2702 565
Web: www.iowadnr.gov

Prairie Schooner Restaurant 445 Pk Blvd Ogden UT 84401 801-392-2712 671
Web: www.prairieschoonerrestaurant.com

Prairie Spirit Trail 419 S Oak St. Garnett KS 66032 785-448-6767 565
Web: bikeprairiespirit.com

Prairie State Bank & Trust
1361 Toronto Rd Springfield IL 62712 217-786-2509 70
Web: www.psbank.net

Prairie State College
202 S Halsted St Chicago Heights IL 60411 708-709-3500 709-3951 162
Web: prairiestate.edu

Prairie State Park
128 NW 150th Ln Mindenmines MO 64769 417-843-6711 565
Web: mostateparks.com

Prairie Valley School Division No 208
3080 Albert St N PO Box 1937 Regina SK S4P3E1 306-949-3366 543-1771 623
TF: 877-266-1666 ■ *Web:* www.pvsd.ca

Prairie View A & M University
700 University Dr PO Box 519 Prairie View TX 77446 936-261-3311 166
TF: 877-241-1752 ■ *Web:* www.pvamu.edu

Prairie View Sr High School
13731 Ks Hwy 152 Lacygne KS 66040 913-757-4447 685
Web: www.pv362.org

Prairie Wetlands Learning Ctr
602 State Hwy 210 E. Fergus Falls MN 56537 218-998-4480 50-5
Web: www.fws.gov

Prairie Winds Veterinary Center Inc
5370 51st Ave S Ste A Fargo ND 58104 701-356-5600 356-5601 794
Web: prairiewindsvet.com

Prairie's Edge Casino Resort
5616 Prairies Edge Ln Granite Falls MN 56241 320-564-2121 452
Web: www.prairiesedgecasino.com

PrairieCoast Equipment
15102 101 St Grande Prairie AB T8V0P7 780-532-8402 612
Web: www.prairiecoastequipment.com

Praise 93.3 142 Skyland Blvd Tuscaloosa AL 35405 205-752-4800 645-168
Web: praise933.com

Praise Broadcasting Network Inc
PO Box 2468 Asheboro NC 27204 336-626-7729 645-141
Web: pbnradio.com

Praj Americas Inc
14511 Old Katy Rd Ste 370 Houston TX 77079 281-372-6082 372-6391 668
Web: www.praj.net

Prakat Solutions Inc
6016 Annandale Dr Fort Worth TX 76132 817-846-7541 177
Web: www.prakat.com

	Phone	Fax	Class
Pran Systems 399 Jacquard St Ste 100 .... Quebec City QC G1N4J6 *TF:* 866-688-7726 ■ *Web:* www.pransystems.com	418-688-7726	688-7738	253
Prangley Marks LLP 333 Bridge St NW 11th Fl .... Grand Rapids MI 49504 *Web:* www.pmcpa.com	616-774-9004	774-9081	2
Prasco LLC 6125 Commerce Ct .... Mason OH 45040 *TF:* 866-525-0688 ■ *Web:* www.prasco.com	513-618-3333		231
Prasek's Hillje Smokehouse 29714 US 59 Hwy .... El Campo TX 77437 *TF:* 800-207-6653 ■ *Web:* www.praseks.com	979-543-8312		297-9
Prassel Lumber Company Inc 275 Hwy 51 .... Ridgeland MS 39157 *TF:* 800-852-6873 ■ *Web:* www.prassellumber.com	601-856-4191		364
Prater Way College of Beauty 1627 Prater Way .... Sparks NV 89431 *Web:* www.praterway.net	775-355-6677	355-6679	167-3
Prather Engineering Inc 199 S Business Rte 5 .... Camdenton MO 65020 *Web:* www.pratherengineering.com	562-634-5566		454
Pratt & Radford PL 380 Columbia Dr Ste 108 .... West Palm Beach FL 33409 *Web:* prattradford.com	561-640-0330	471-4240	41
Pratt & Whitney 400 Main St .... East Hartford CT 06108 *Web:* prattwhitney.com	860-565-4321		21
Pratt & Whitney AutoAir Inc 5640 Enterprise Dr .... Lansing MI 48911 *Web:* www.autoair.com	517-394-9448		529
Pratt & Whitney Canada Inc 1000 Marie-Victorin Blvd .... Longueuil QC J4G1A1 *TF:* 800-268-8000 ■ *Web:* www.pwc.ca	450-677-9411	647-3620	21
Pratt Communications 2913 Tech Ctr .... Santa Ana CA 92705 *Web:* www.prattcommunications.com	714-540-6840		787
Pratt Community College 348 NE SR-61 .... Pratt KS 67124 *TF:* 800-794-3091 ■ *Web:* www.prattcc.edu	620-672-5641		162
Pratt Computing Technologies Inc 10420 Jackson Oaks Way Ste 202 .... Knoxville TN 37922 *Web:* www.prattonline.com	865-693-0900		177
Pratt County *Pratt County Court House* 300 S Ninnescah .... Pratt KS 67124 *Web:* www.prattcounty.org	620-672-4112	672-9541	338
Pratt Feeders LLC PO Box 945 .... Pratt KS 67124 *Web:* www.prattfeeders.com	620-672-6448		10-1
Pratt Fine Arts Ctr 1902 S Main St .... Seattle WA 98144 *Web:* www.pratt.org	206-328-2200		720
Pratt Industries Inc 1800C Sarasota Pkwy .... Conyers GA 30013 *TF:* 800-835-2088 ■ *Web:* www.prattindustries.com	770-918-5678	918-5679	548
Pratt Industries Inc 11365 Red Arrow Hwy .... Bridgman MI 49106 *TF:* 800-546-7728 ■ *Web:* prattinc.com	269-465-7676	465-7677	779
Pratt Institute 200 Willoughby Ave .... Brooklyn NY 11205 *TF:* 800-755-8920 ■ *Web:* www.pratt.edu	718-636-3669	636-3670	166
Pratt Regional Medical Center Corp 200 Commodore St .... Pratt KS 67124 *Web:* www.prmc.org	620-672-7451		374-3
Pratt, Vreeland, Kennelly, Martin & White Ltd 64 N Main St PO Box 280 .... Rutland VT 05702 *Web:* vermontcounsel.com	802-775-7141		41
Prattville Machine & Tool Company Inc 240 Jubilee Dr .... Peabody MA 01960 *Web:* 02f7839.netsolhost.com	978-538-5229		454
Prava Construction Services Inc 2032 Corte Del Nogal Ste 100 .... Carlsbad CA 92011 *Web:* www.pravacsi.com	760-929-9787		186
Praxair Inc 39 Old Ridgebury Rd .... Danbury CT 06810 *NYSE:* PX ■ *TF:* 800-772-9247 ■ *Web:* www.praxair.com	203-837-2000		143
Praxis Companies LLC, The 435 Industrial Rd .... Savannah TN 38372	731-925-7656		610
Praxis Consulting Group Inc 9 A/B W Highland Av .... Philadelphia PA 19118 *Web:* praxiscg.com	215-753-0303		463
Praxis Engineering Technologies Inc 135 National Business Pkwy .... Annapolis Junction MD 20701 *Web:* www.praxiseng.com	301-490-4299	490-1290	177
Praxis Institute, The 1850 SW 8th St 4th Fl .... Miami FL 33135 *Web:* www.praxis.edu	305-642-4104	642-6063	167-3
Pray, Walker, Jackman, Williamson, & Marlar 900 Oneok Plz 100 W Fifth St .... Tulsa OK 74103 *Web:* www.praywalker.com	918-581-5500		428
PRB (Population Reference Bureau) 1875 Connecticut Ave NW Ste 520 .... Washington DC 20009 *TF:* 800-877-9881 ■ *Web:* www.prb.org	202-483-1100	328-3937	48-7
PRB Productions 963 Peralta Ave .... Albany CA 94706 *Web:* www.prbmusic.com	510-526-0722	527-4763	637-10
PRBA (Portable Rechargeable Battery Assn) 1776 K St 4th Fl .... Washington DC 20006 *Web:* www.prba.org	202-719-4978		49-13
PRC (Patients Rights Council) PO Box 760 .... Steubenville OH 43952 *TF:* 800-958-5678 ■ *Web:* www.patientsrightscouncil.org	740-282-3810		48-8
PRC (Passaic River Coalition) 330 Speedwell Ave .... Morristown NJ 07960 *Web:* passaicriver.org	973-532-9830	889-9172	48-13
PRC Group of Companies, The 40 Monmouth Pk Hwy PO Box 70 .... West Long Branch NJ 07764 *Web:* www.prcgroup.com	732-222-2000	222-6410	655
PRCA (Professional Rodeo Cowboys Assn) 101 Pro Rodeo Dr .... Colorado Springs CO 80919 *TF:* 800-234-7722 ■ *Web:* www.prorodeo.com	719-593-8840		48-22
PRE (Powder River Energy Corp) 221 Main St PO Box 930 .... Sundance WY 82729 **Fax Area Code:* 307 ■ *TF:* 800-442-3630 ■ *Web:* www.precorp.coop	800-442-3630	283-3527*	245
PREA (Pension Real Estate Assn) 100 Pearl St 13th Fl .... Hartford CT 06103 *Web:* www.prea.org	860-692-6341	692-6351	49-2
Preach Inc 1601 W Hatcher Rd .... Phoenix AZ 85021 *Web:* www.preachbuildingsupply.com	602-944-4594	943-2554	191-1
Preble County 101 E Main St .... Eaton OH 45320 *Web:* www.prebco.org	937-456-8143	456-8114	338
Preble County Chamber of Commerce 122 W Decatur St PO Box 303 .... Eaton OH 45320 *Web:* www.preblecountyohio.com	937-456-4949		139
Preble Feed & Grain Inc 6035 N 400 W PO Box 52 .... Preble IN 46782 *Web:* kentfeeds.com	260-547-4452		447
Preble-Shawnee School District 124 Bloomfield St .... Camden OH 45311 *Web:* www.preble-shawnee.k12.oh.us	937-452-1283		685
Precast Specialties Corp 999 Adams St .... Abington MA 02351 *Web:* www.precastspecialtiescorp.com	781-878-7220		183
Pre-Cast Specialties LLC 3898 Selvitz Rd .... Fort Pierce FL 34981 **Fax Area Code:* 954 ■ *Web:* www.precastspecialties.com	772-266-5701	781-3539*	183
Precast/Prestressed Concrete Institute (PCI) 200 W Adams St Ste 2100 .... Chicago IL 60606 *Web:* www.pci.org	312-786-0300	786-0353	49-3
Precept Medical Communications Inc 3 Mtn View Rd .... Warren NJ 07059 *Web:* www.preceptmedical.com	908-605-4801	605-4777	242
Precept Medical Products Inc 370 Airport Rd .... Arden NC 28704 *TF:* 800-438-5827 ■ *Web:* preceptmed.com	828-681-0209	687-3605	576
Precept Ministries of Reach Out Inc 7324 Noah Reid Rd .... Chattanooga TN 37421 *TF:* 800-763-8280 ■ *Web:* www.precept.org	800-763-8280		637-2
PreCheck Inc 2500 E T C Jester Blvd .... Houston TX 77008 *TF:* 800-999-9861 ■ *Web:* www.precheck.com	800-999-9861		363
Precipio 4 Science Pk 3rd Fl .... New Haven CT 06511 *Web:* precipiodx.com	203-787-7888		415
Precise Aerospace Manufacturing Inc 224 Glider Cir .... Corona CA 92880 *Web:* www.precisemfg.com	951-898-0500	898-0600	604
Precise Cables Inc 1801 Iron Horse Dr Ste A .... Longmont CO 80501 *Web:* www.precisecables.com	303-678-1166		253
Precise Flight Inc 63354 Powell Butte Hwy .... Bend OR 97701 *TF:* 800-547-2558 ■ *Web:* www.preciseflight.com	541-382-8684		22
Precise Industries Inc 610 Neptune Ave .... Brea CA 92821 *Web:* www.preciseind.com	714-482-2333	482-2332	697
Precise Light Surgical Inc 310 W Hamilton Ave Ste 210 .... Campbell CA 95008 *Web:* preciselightsurgical.com	831-539-3323		475
Precise Mailing Inc 168 Beacon St .... South San Francisco CA 94080 *Web:* www.precisemailing.com	650-589-4000	588-3144	627
Precise Packaging 300 Riggenbach Rd .... Fall River MA 02720 *Web:* www.precisepackaging.com	508-677-2600	677-2606	596
Precise Plastics Inc 7700 Middle Rd .... Fairview PA 16415 *Web:* www.ppi-erie.com	814-474-5504		604
Precise Resource Group Inc 3016 Skyway Cir S .... Irving TX 75038 *Web:* preciseresourcegroup.com	972-570-0121	570-0149	627
Precise Tool & Gage Company Inc 30540 SE 84th St Unit 2 .... Preston WA 98050 *Web:* www.precisetoolco.com	425-222-9567		246
Precision Abrasives 3176 Abbott Rd .... Orchard Park NY 14127 *TF:* 800-722-3967 ■ *Web:* www.wesand.com	800-722-3967		1
Precision Aerospace Corp 5300 Corporate Grove Dr SE Ste 350 .... Grand Rapids MI 49512 *Web:* www.precision-aerospace.com	616-243-8112		22
Precision Aircraft Components Inc 2787 Armstrong Ln .... Dayton OH 45414 *Web:* www.precisionaircraftinc.com	937-278-0264	278-4466	529
Precision Airmotive LLC 17716 48th Dr NE .... Arlington WA 98223 *Web:* www.precisionairmotive.com	360-651-8282	651-8080	24
Precision Associates Inc 3800 N Washington Ave .... Minneapolis MN 55412 *TF:* 800-394-6590 ■ *Web:* www.precisionassoc.com	612-333-7464	342-2417	677
Precision Auto Care Inc 748 Miller Dr SE .... Leesburg VA 20175 *OTC:* PACI ■ **Fax Area Code:* 703 ■ *TF:* 866-944-8863 ■ *Web:* www.precisiontune.com	866-944-8863	771-7108*	62-5
Precision Automation Company Inc 1841 Old Cuthbert Rd .... Cherry Hill NJ 08034 *Web:* precisionautomationinc.com	856-428-7400		194
Precision BioLogic Inc 140 Eileen Stubbs Ave .... Dartmouth NS B3B0A9 *TF:* 800-267-2796 ■ *Web:* www.precisionbiologic.com	902-468-6422		475
Precision Blasting Services (PBS) 6990 Summers Rd .... Montville OH 44064 *Web:* www.idc-pbs.com	440-474-6700	968-3967	261
Precision Boring Co 24400 Maplehurst Dr .... Clinton Township MI 48036 *Web:* www.precisionboring.com	586-463-3900	463-3905	757
Precision Cable Assemblies LLC 16830 Pheasant Dr .... Brookfield WI 53005 *Web:* www.pca-llc.com	262-784-7887	784-0681	253
Precision Cable Inc 3255 NW 29th Ave .... Portland OR 97210 *Web:* www.precision-cable.com	503-222-4323	223-0656	253
Precision Castparts Corp 28 Sword St .... Auburn MA 01501 *TF:* 800-343-6068 ■ *Web:* www.ptgtools.com	508-753-6530	753-0127	456
Precision Castparts Corp 915 118th Ave SE Ste 320 .... Bellevue WA 98005 *Web:* www.pccaero.com	425-688-0444		350
Precision Coating Company Inc 51 Parmenter Rd .... Hudson MA 01749 **Fax Area Code:* 978 ■ *Web:* www.precisioncoating.com	781-329-1420	562-9622*	481
Precision Coatings Inc 8120 Goldie St .... Commerce Charter Township MI 48390 *TF:* 800-521-8380 ■ *Web:* www.pcicoatings.com	248-363-8361		596

Phone | Fax | Class

Precision Coil Spring Co
10107 Rose Ave .... El Monte CA 91731 626-444-0561 444-3712 719
Web: www.pcspring.com

Precision Component Industries
5325 Southway St SW .... Canton OH 44706 330-477-6287 477-1052 757
Web: www.precision-component.com

Precision Computer Services Inc (PCS)
175 Constitution Blvd S .... Shelton CT 06484 203-929-0000 929-8800 175
Web: precisiongroup.com

Precision Concepts Group LLC
2701 Boulder Park Ct .... Winston-Salem NC 27101 336-761-8572 488
Web: www.precisionconcepts.com

Precision Countertops Inc
26200 SW 95th Ave Ste 303 .... Wilsonville OR 97070 503-660-3023 115
TF: 800-548-4445 ■ *Web:* precisioncountertops.com

Precision Custom Components
500 Lincoln St .... York PA 17401 717-848-1126 843-5733 91
Web: www.pcc-york.com

Precision Die & Stamping Inc
1704 W Tenth St .... Tempe AZ 85281 480-967-2038 483
Web: precisiondie.com

Precision Die- Cutting Inc
27595 SW 95th Ave Bldg C-7 Ste 760 .... Wilsonville OR 97070 503-685-9130 682-6249 454
Web: www.diecutinc.com

Precision Drawn Metals Inc
1345 Plainfield Ave .... Janesville WI 53545 608-755-1495 483
Web: www.drawnmetals.com

Precision Dynamics Corp
27770 N Entertainment Dr Ste 200 .... Valencia CA 91355 661-257-0233 477
TF: 800-847-0670 ■ *Web:* www.pdcorp.com

Precision Econowind Inc
8940 N Fork Dr .... North Fort Myers FL 33903 239-997-3860 997-3243 52
TF: 866-856-4783 ■ *Web:* www.precisioneconowind.com

Precision Edge Surgical Products Co
415 W 12th Ave .... Sault Sainte Marie MI 49783 906-632-4800 632-5619 476
Web: www.precisionedge.com

Precision Electronic Glass Inc
1013 Hendee Rd .... Vineland NJ 08360 856-691-2234 691-3090 332
TF: 800-982-4734 ■ *Web:* www.pegglass.com

Precision Engineered Products LLC
262 Broad St .... North Attleboro MA 02760 508-695-7700 695-7512 485
Web: www.polymet.com

Precision Engineered Products LLC
821 W Algonquin Rd .... Algonquin IL 60102 847-658-4588 658-0788 488
Web: wauconda.wpengine.com

Precision Extrusion Inc
12 Glens Falls Technical Pk .... Glens Falls NY 12801 518-792-1199 596
Web: www.spectrumplastics.com

Precision Fabricating & Cleaning Company Inc
3975 E Railroad Ave .... Cocoa FL 32926 321-635-2000 201
TF: 800-508-9736 ■ *Web:* www.precgroup.com

Precision Fabrics Group Inc
301 N Elm St Ste 600 .... Greensboro NC 27401 800-284-8001 510-8004* 745-1
**Fax Area Code:* 336 ■ *TF:* 800-284-8001 ■ *Web:* www.precisionfabrics.com

Precision Fasteners Tooling Inc
11530 Western Ave .... Stanton CA 90680 714-898-8558 891-4988 757
Web: www.precisionfastenertooling.com

Precision Filters Inc 240 Cherry St .... Ithaca NY 14850 607-277-3550 668
Web: www.pfinc.com

Precision Foods Inc
11457 Olde Cabin Rd Ste 100 .... Saint Louis MO 63141 314-567-7400 296-37
TF: 800-442-5242 ■ *Web:* www.precisionfoods.com

Precision Gasket Co (PGC) 5732 Lincoln Dr .... Edina MN 55436 952-942-6711 326
Web: pgc-solutions.com

Precision Gears Inc
N 13 W 24705 Bluemound Rd .... Pewaukee WI 53072 262-542-4261 542-1592 454
Web: www.precisiongears.com

Precision Governors Inc 2322 7th Ave .... Rockford IL 61104 815-229-5300 203
Web: www.pgcontrols.com

Precision Graphics Inc
21 County Line Rd .... Somerville NJ 08876 908-707-8880 481
Web: www.precisiongraphics.us

Precision Grinding & Manufacturing Corp
1305 Emerson St .... Rochester NY 14606 585-458-4300 458-7281 493
Web: www.pgmcorp.com

Precision H2O Inc 6328 E Utah Ave .... Spokane WA 99212 509-536-9214 536-9205 1
TF: 800-425-2098 ■ *Web:* www.precisionh2o.com

Precision Heat Treating Corp
2711 Adams Center Rd .... Fort Wayne IN 46803 260-749-5125 484
Web: www.phtc.net

Precision Hose
2200 Centre Park Ct .... Stone Mountain GA 30087 770-413-5680 295
TF: 877-850-2662 ■ *Web:* www.precisionhose.com

Precision Husky Corp
850 Markeeta Spur Rd .... Moody AL 35004 205-640-5181 640-1147 190
Web: precisionhusky.com

Precision Hydraulic Cylinders Inc
196 N Hwy 41 .... Beulaville NC 28518 910-298-0100 358
Web: www.phc-global.com

Precision IBC Inc 8054 Mcgowin Dr .... Fairhope AL 36532 251-990-6789 690
TF: 800-544-7069 ■ *Web:* www.precisionibc.com

Precision Instruments
20780 Hugo .... Farmington Hills MI 48336 248-987-4743 987-4851 542
TF: 800-262-6008 ■ *Web:* www.precision-instruments.net

Precision Intl 25 W Miller Rd .... Iola KS 66749 620-365-7255 365-7746 537
Web: prec-int.com

Precision Kidd Steel Company Inc
1 Quality Way .... Aliquippa PA 15001 724-378-7670 697
TF: 800-945-5003 ■ *Web:* www.precisionkidd.com

Precision Laboratories Inc
1429 S Shields Dr .... Waukegan IL 60085 847-596-3001 596-3017 145
TF: 800-323-6280 ■ *Web:* www.precisionlab.com

Precision Machine & Manufacturing Inc
1290 S Bertelsen Rd .... Eugene OR 97402 541-484-9841 454
Web: www.premach.com

Precision Machined Products Assn (PMPA)
6700 W Snowville Rd .... Brecksville OH 44141 440-526-0300 526-5803 49-13
Web: www.pmpa.org

Precision Machining Sheet Metal Inc
2250 N Forbes Blvd .... Tucson AZ 85745 520-622-0050 624-9643 454
Web: www.bestinquality.com

Precision Manufacturing Group LLC
501 Little Falls Rd .... Cedar Grove NJ 07009 973-785-4630 295
Web: servometer.com

Precision Masking Inc 721 Lavoy Rd .... Erie MI 48133 734-848-4200 480
Web: www.precisionmasking.com

Precision Medical Products Inc
44 Denver Rd .... Denver PA 17517 717-335-3700 335-0007 476
Web: www.pmp.net

Precision Metal Industries Inc
1408 SW Eighth St .... Pompano Beach FL 33069 954-942-6303 942-6715 567
Web: www.pmiquality.com

Precision Metal Products Co
353 Garden Ave PO Box 1047 .... Holland MI 49422 616-886-1085 298-3524 621
Web: www.pmpc1.com

Precision Metal Products Inc
850 W Bradley Ave .... El Cajon CA 92020 619-448-2711 483
Web: www.pmp-elcajon.com

Precision Metal Products Inc
307 Pepe's Farm Rd .... Milford CT 06460 203-877-4258 878-8353 454
Web: www.pmpinc.biz

Precision Metal Services Inc
418 Stump Rd .... Montgomeryville PA 18936 215-661-0225 492
Web: www.precisionmetalservices.com

Precision Metal Works
6901 Preston Hwy .... Louisville KY 40219 877-511-9695 757
TF: 877-511-9695 ■ *Web:* www.nth-works.com

Precision Metal Works Inc
1080 Kershaw St .... Montgomery AL 36108 334-265-1678 269-5783 454
Web: www.precisionmetalinc.com

Precision Metalforming Assn (PMA)
6363 Oak Tree Blvd .... Independence OH 44131 216-901-8800 901-9190 49-3
Web: www.pma.org

Precision Mold & Machining Services Inc
13143 E 9th Mile Rd .... Warren MI 48089 586-774-2330 774-2441 196
Web: www.precisionmold.com

Precision Molded Plastics Inc
880 W 9th St .... Upland CA 91786 909-981-9662 981-9251 604
Web: www.precisionmoldedplastics.com

Precision Molding Inc
5500 Roberts Matthews Hwy .... Sparta TN 38583 931-738-8376 738-8429 602
Web: www.precision-molding.com

Precision Multiple Controls Inc
33 Greenwood Ave .... Midland Park NJ 07432 201-444-0600 445-8575 203
TF: 800-775-5862 ■ *Web:* www.pmcontrols.com

Precision Opinion Inc
101 Convention Center Dr Plaza 125 .... Las Vegas NV 89109 702-483-4000 483-4100 748
TF: 800-780-2790 ■ *Web:* precisionopinion.com

Precision Optical Group Inc
701 S Oak St .... Creston IA 50801 641-782-6685 782-8410 415
Web: www.precisionopticalgroup.com

Precision Optics Corporation Inc
22 E Broadway .... Gardner MA 01440 978-630-1800 630-1487 382
OTC: PEYE ■ *TF:* 800-447-2812 ■ *Web:* www.poci.com

Precision Paper Converters LLC
2600 Northridge Dr .... Kaukauna WI 54130 920-436-9890 558
Web: www.cornerstone-business.com

Precision Paper Tube Company Inc
1033 S Noel Ave .... Wheeling IL 60090 847-537-4250 537-5777 125
Web: www.pptube.com

Precision Parts & Remanufacturing Co
4411 SW 19th St .... Oklahoma City OK 73108 405-681-2592 681-2596 247
TF: 800-654-3846 ■ *Web:* www.pprok.com

Precision Pipeline Solutions LLC
617 Little Britain Rd Ste 200 .... New Windsor NY 12553 845-566-8332 597
Web: www.precisionpipelinesolutions.com

Precision Plastics Inc
900 W Connexion Way .... Columbia City IN 46725 260-244-6114 604
Web: www.pplastic.com

Precision Plus Inc 840 Koopman Ln .... Elkhorn WI 53121 262-743-1700 743-1701 621
Web: www.preplus.com

Precision Printer Services Inc
9185 Portage Industrial Dr .... Portage MI 49024 269-384-5725 589
Web: www.precisionprinterservices.com

Precision Products Group Inc
10201 N Illinois St Ste 390 .... Indianapolis IN 46290 888-808-4341 601
TF: 888-808-4341 ■ *Web:* www.ppgintl.com

Precision Products Inc 316 Limit St .... Lincoln IL 62656 217-735-1590 735-2435 429
TF: 800-225-5891 ■ *Web:* www.precisionprodinc.com

Precision Products Machine & Fab. Inc
58 Latimer St .... Hazlehurst GA 31539 912-375-9159 375-9161 697
Web: www.precisionpro.com

Precision Products of Asheville Inc
118 Glenn Bridge Rd .... Arden NC 28704 828-684-4207 454
Web: www.ppofa.com

Precision pulley and idler PO Box 69 .... Humboldt IA 50548 515-332-4040 332-4923 207
Web: www.ppi-global.com

Precision Pump & Valve Service Inc
517 Old Goff Mtn Rd .... Cross Lanes WV 25313 304-776-1710 14
Web: www.ppvs.com

Precision Resource 25 Forest Pkwy .... Shelton CT 06484 203-925-0012 488
TF: 844-154-1000 ■ *Web:* www.precisionresource.com

Precision Roll Grinders Inc
6356 Chapmans Rd .... Allentown PA 18106 610-395-6966 481-9130 454
Web: www.precisionrollgrinders.com

Precision Samplers Inc
147 11th Ave .... South Charleston WV 25303 304-744-5534 744-3113 472
Web: www.precisionsamplers.com

Precision Scheduling Consultants LLC
10715 Gulfdale Dr Ste 260 .... San Antonio TX 78216 210-380-5691 495-0120 194
Web: www.precisionschedulingconsultants.com

Precision Screw Machine Products Inc
20 Gooch St .... Biddeford ME 04005 207-283-0121 283-4824 621
Web: www.psmp.com

Precision Screw Thread Corp
S82w19275 Apollo Dr .... Muskego WI 53150 262-679-9000 454
Web: thepstgroup.com

Listing	Phone	Fax	Class
Precision Sensors Inc 50 Seemans Ln . . . . Milford CT 06460 *Web:* www.precisionsensors.com	203-877-2795		790
Precision Small Engine Co 2510 NW 16th Ln . . . . Pompano Beach FL 33064 *TF:* 800-345-1960 ■ *Web:* www.precisionusa.com	954-974-1960	973-8032	429
Precision Solutions Inc 2525 Tollgate Rd. . . . . Quakertown PA 18951 *Web:* www.precisionsolutionsinc.com	215-536-4400		362
Precision Southeast Inc 4900 Hwy 501 . . . . Myrtle Beach SC 29579 *Web:* www.precisionsoutheast.com	843-347-4218		604
Precision Specialties Co 1201 E Pecan St. . . . . Sherman TX 75090 **Fax Area Code:* 903 ■ *TF:* 800-527-3295 ■ *Web:* www.presco.com	800-527-3295	893-2328*	407
Precision Speed Instruments Inc 2022 W Clarendon Ave. . . . . Phoenix AZ 85015 *TF:* 800-873-1055 ■ *Web:* www.precisionspeed.com	602-973-1055	242-8577	472
Precision Steel Manufacturing Corp 1723 Seibel Dr NE . . . . Roanoke VA 24012 *Web:* precisionsteelmfg.com	540-985-8963		492
Precision Steel Warehouse Inc 3500 Wolf Rd . . . . Franklin Park IL 60131 *TF:* 800-323-0740 ■ *Web:* www.precisionsteel.com	847-455-7000	455-1341	492
Precision Strip Inc 86 S Ohio St PO Box 104 . . . . Minster OH 45865 *Web:* www.precision-strip.com	419-628-2343		494
Precision Tank & Equipment Company Inc 3503 Conover Rd . . . . Virginia IL 62691 *TF:* 800-258-4197 ■ *Web:* www.precisiontank.com	217-452-7228		273
Precision Technologies Inc 65 W Century Pkwy PO Box 65446. . . . . Salt Lake City UT 84115 *Web:* www.circuitboards-pti.com	801-487-6266	486-4243	454
Precision Technology Inc 3601 E Plano Pky Ste 200 . . . . Plano TX 75074 **Fax Area Code:* 214 ■ *Web:* www.ptiassembly.com	469-326-5900	343-8216*	425
Precision Thermoplastic Components Inc PO Box 1296 . . . . Lima OH 45802 *TF:* 800-860-4505 ■ *Web:* ptclima.com	419-227-4500		608
Precision Time Systems Inc 5433 Main St . . . . Shallotte NC 28470 *TF:* 877-416-6660 ■ *Web:* www.precisiontime.com	910-253-9850	253-8720	407
Precision Tool Technologies Inc 309 13th Ave NW . . . . Little Falls MN 56345 *Web:* precisiontooltech.com	320-632-5320		543
Precision Trading Corp 15800 NW 48th Ave . . . . Miami Gardens FL 33014 *Web:* precisiontrading.com	305-592-4500	593-6169	38
Precision Trailer Hitches and Welding 10919 Randall St Ste 3 & Ste 4 . . . . Sun Valley CA 91352 *Web:* www.precisionhitchandwelding.com	818-256-1118	771-9272	45
Precision Tube Company Inc 287 Wissahickon Ave . . . . North Wales PA 19454 *Web:* www.precisiontube.com	215-699-5801		492
Precision Tube Inc 1025 Fortune Dr . . . . Richmond KY 40475 *Web:* www.ptube.net	859-623-5595	623-6116	454
Precision Valve Corp 5711 Old Buncombe Rd . . . . Greenville SC 29609 *Web:* www.precisionglobal.com	864-246-2200		487
Precision Wall Systems Inc 102 Vander Horck St. . . . . Britton SD 57430	605-448-2929		499
Precision Walls Inc 1230 NE Maynard Rd. . . . . Cary NC 27513 *TF:* 800-849-9255 ■ *Web:* www.precisionwalls.com	919-832-0380	839-1402	189-9
Precision Waveguide Components Inc 561 E Overdrive Cir . . . . Hernando FL 34442 *Web:* www.precisionwaveguide.com	352-489-9893	489-2251	253
Precision X-Ray Inc 15 Commerce Dr . . . . North Branford CT 06471 *Web:* www.pxinc.com	203-484-2011		475
Precisionform Inc 148 W Airport Rd . . . . Lititz PA 17543 *TF:* 800-233-3821 ■ *Web:* www.precisionform.com	717-560-7610		621
Precitech 44 Blackbrook Rd. . . . . Keene NH 03431 *Web:* www.precitech.com	603-357-2511	358-6174	493
Precix Inc 744 Bellville Ave . . . . New Bedford MA 02745 *TF:* 800-225-8505 ■ *Web:* www.precixinc.com	508-998-4000	998-4100	677
Preco Electronics Inc 10335 W Emerald St. . . . . Boise ID 83704 *TF:* 866-977-7326 ■ *Web:* preco.com	208-323-1000		472
Precoat Metals 1310 Papin St 3rd Fl. . . . . Saint Louis MO 63103 *Web:* precoat.com	317-462-7761		481
Precor Inc 20031 142nd Ave NE . . . . Woodinville WA 98072 *TF:* 800-786-8404 ■ *Web:* www.precor.com	425-486-9292	486-3856	267
Predator Trucking Co 3181 Trumbull Ave . . . . McDonald OH 44437 *TF:* 800-235-5624 ■ *Web:* web.predatortrucking.com	330-530-0712		780
Predicate Logic Inc 6155 Cornerstone Ct E . . . . San Diego CA 92121 *Web:* www.predicate.com	858-715-0100		177
Prediction Sciences LLC 3252 Holiday Ct Ste 209. . . . . La Jolla CA 92037 *Web:* www.predict.net	858-404-0404	777-3614	463
Prediction Systems Inc 309 Morris Ave Ste J . . . . Spring Lake NJ 07762 *Web:* www.predictsys.com	732-449-6800	449-0897	178-8
PredictWallStreet LLC 1840 41st Ave Ste 102-171 . . . . Capitola CA 95010 *Web:* www.predictwallstreet.com	831-464-0308	401-2391	466
Preece Inc 26845 Vista Terr. . . . . Lake Forest CA 92630 *Web:* www.preeceinc.com	949-770-9411		21
Preemo 9655 S Dixie Hwy Ste 202 . . . . Miami FL 33156 *Web:* preemo.com	305-306-8518		180
PreEmptive 767 Beta Dr Ste A . . . . Mayfield Village OH 44143 *Web:* www.preemptive.com	440-443-7200	460-0680	178-1
Preference Employment Solutions 2605 42nd St S. . . . . Fargo ND 58104 *Web:* www.preferenceemploymentsolutions.com	701-293-6905		260
Preferred Bank Los Angeles 601 S Figueroa St 29th Fl. . . . . Los Angeles CA 90017 *NASDAQ:* PFBC ■ *TF:* 888-673-1808 ■ *Web:* www.preferredbank.com	213-891-1188	622-0369	70
Preferred CommunityChoice PPO 218 W Sixth St . . . . Tulsa OK 74119 *TF:* 800-884-4776 ■ *Web:* www.ccok.com	918-594-5200		391-3
Preferred Dental Laboratory Inc 37 Woodland Rd. . . . . Roseland NJ 07068 *TF:* 800-548-2613 ■ *Web:* www.pdldentallab.com	800-548-2613		415
Preferred Employers Group Inc 10800 Biscayne Blvd . . . . Miami FL 33161	305-899-0404		391-4
Preferred Employers Insurance Co PO Box 85478 . . . . San Diego CA 92186 **Fax Area Code:* 619 ■ *TF:* 888-472-9001 ■ *Web:* www.peiwc.com	866-472-9602	688-3913*	391-4
Preferred Excellent Care (PEC) 10521 Garden Grove Blvd. . . . . Garden Grove CA 92843 *TF:* 877-590-3620 ■ *Web:* www.preferredexcellentcare.com	714-590-3620	590-3628	363
Preferred Health Professionals LLC 10740 Nall Ste 100. . . . . Overland Park KS 66211 **Fax Area Code:* 855 ■ *TF:* 800-544-3014 ■ *Web:* www.phpkc.com	913-945-4770	804-9546*	352
Preferred Healthcare Systems Inc PO Box 1015 . . . . Duncansville PA 16635 *TF:* 800-238-9900 ■ *Web:* www.phsppo.com	814-317-5063	317-5139	391-3
Preferred Home Health Agency Inc 13831 SW 59 Ave Ste 105 . . . . Miami FL 33183 *Web:* www.phhagency.com	305-388-4851	388-4852	363
Preferred Homecare Infusion LLC 4601 E Hilton Ave Ste 100 . . . . Phoenix AZ 85034 *TF:* 800-636-2123 ■ *Web:* preferredhomecare.com	480-446-9010		363
Preferred Hospice of Missouri Central 1900 N Providence Rd Ste 311. . . . . Columbia MO 65202 *Web:* www.preferredhospice.com	573-499-4540		450
Preferred Hotel Group 311 S Wacker Dr Ste 1900 . . . . Chicago IL 60606 *Web:* preferredhotels.com	312-913-0400	913-5124	379
Preferred Meal Systems Inc 5240 St Charles Rd. . . . . Berkeley IL 60163 **Fax Area Code:* 708 ■ *TF:* 800-886-6325 ■ *Web:* www.preferredmeals.com	800-886-6325	493-2690*	296-36
Preferred Medical Marketing Corp 15720 Brixham Hill Ave Ste 460. . . . . Charlotte NC 28277 *TF:* 800-543-8176 ■ *Web:* www.pmmconline.com	704-543-8103		177
Preferred Mental Health Management Inc 7309 E 21st St N Ste 110 . . . . Wichita KS 67206 *TF:* 800-819-9571 ■ *Web:* www.pmhm.com	316-262-0444		462
Preferred Mutual Insurance Co 1 Preferred Way . . . . New Berlin NY 13411 *TF:* 800-333-7642 ■ *Web:* www.preferredmutual.com	607-847-6161	847-8046	391-4
Preferred Plastics Inc 800 E Bridge St. . . . . Plainwell MI 49080 *Web:* www.preferredplastics.com	269-685-5873		608
Preferred Popcorn LLC 1132 Ninth Rd . . . . Chapman NE 68827 *Web:* www.preferredpopcorn.com	308-986-2526	986-2626	123
Preferred Professional Insurance Company Inc 11605 Miracle Hills Dr Ste 200 . . . . Omaha NE 68154 *Web:* coverage.ppicins.com	402-392-1566		390
Preferred Properties of Venice Inc 325 W Venice Ave. . . . . Venice FL 34285 *Web:* www.veniceflproperties.com	941-485-9602		652
Preferred Sands LLC 100 Matsonford Rd One Radnor Corporate Ctr Ste 101 . . . . Radnor PA 19087 *TF:* 855-372-2435 ■ *Web:* preferredsands.com	610-834-1969		191-1
Preferred Strategies LLC 2425 Porter St Ste 20 . . . . Soquel CA 95073 *TF:* 888-232-7337 ■ *Web:* preferredstrategies.com	888-232-7337		177
Preferred Systems Solutions Inc 1945 Old Gallows Rd Ste 450. Vienna VA 22182 *Web:* www.pssfed.com	703-663-2777	663-2780	180
Preferred Technology Systems LLC (PTI) 9160 E Bahia Dr Ste 100. Scottsdale AZ 85260 *TF:* 800-331-6224 ■ *Web:* www.ptisecurity.com	480-257-2600	257-2599	392
PreferredOne Administrative Services Inc 6105 Golden Hills Dr . . . . Golden Valley MN 55416 *TF:* 800-451-9597 ■ *Web:* www.preferredone.com	763-847-4000		463
Prefin Inc 12 N 4th St. . . . . Clear Lake IA 50428 *Web:* www.clreporter.com	641-357-2131	357-2133	532-2
Prefix Corp 1300 W Hamlin Rd . . . . Rochester Hills MI 48309 *Web:* www.prefix.com	248-650-1330	650-1334	261
Preformed Line Products 660 Beta Dr . . . . Cleveland OH 44143 *NASDAQ:* PLPC ■ *Web:* www.preformed.com	440-461-5200	442-8816	815
Prego 2520 Amherst St . . . . Houston TX 77005 *Web:* www.prego-houston.com	713-529-2420		671
Prein & Newhof Inc 3355 Evergreen Dr NE . . . . Grand Rapids MI 49525 *Web:* www.preinnewhof.com	616-364-8491	364-6955	261
Preis PLC Versailles Ctr 102 Versailles Blvd Ste 400 . . . . LaFayette LA 70501 *Web:* www.preisplc.com	337-237-6062	237-9129	428
Prejean's Restaurant 3480 NE Evangeline Trwy . . . . Lafayette LA 70507 *Web:* prejeans.com	337-896-3247	896-3278	671
Prelco Inc 94 Blvd Cartier . . . . Riviere-du-Loup QC G5R2M9 *TF:* 800-463-1325 ■ *Web:* www.prelco.ca	418-862-2274	862-8181	329
Preload Inc 125 Kennedy Dr Ste 500. . . . . Hauppauge NY 11788 *TF:* 888-773-5623 ■ *Web:* preload.com	631-231-8100	231-8881	183
Prelude Systems Inc 5095 Ritter Rd Ste 112 . . . . Mechanicsburg PA 17055 **Fax Area Code:* 717 ■ *TF:* 800-579-1047 ■ *Web:* www.preludeservices.com	800-579-1047	441-2410*	177
Premac Inc 167 Wescott Dr . . . . Rahway NJ 07065 *Web:* www.premac.us	732-381-7550		529
Premco Inc Shore Industrial Pk 55 Research Rd S . . . . Hingham MA 02043 *Web:* www.premco.net	781-749-0333	740-2043	454
Premcom Corp 85 Northpointe Pkwy Ste 100 . . . . Amherst NY 14228 *Web:* www.premcom.com	716-691-0791	691-0795	180
Premedia Group LLC 7605 Business Park Dr Ste F . . . . Greensboro NC 27409 *Web:* www.premediagroup.com	336-274-2421	274-2763	344
Premera Blue Cross Blue 7001 220th St SW Bldg 1. . . . . Mountlake Terrace WA 98043 *TF:* 855-629-0987 ■ *Web:* www.premera.com	800-817-3049		391-3

Name / Address	City	State	ZIP	Phone	Fax	Class
Premier Access Insurance Co PO Box 659010 *TF:* 888-634-6074 ■ *Web:* www.premierlife.com	Sacramento	CA	95865	916-920-2500	646-9000	390
Premier Alaska Tours Inc 1900 Premier Ct *TF:* 888-486-8725 ■ *Web:* premieralaskatours.com	Anchorage	AK	99502	907-279-0001		760
Premier Aluminum LLC 3633 S Memorial Dr *TF:* 800-254-9261 ■ *Web:* premieraluminum.com	Racine	WI	53403	262-554-2100		492
Premier America Credit Union 19867 Prairie St PO Box 2178 *TF:* 800-772-4000 ■ *Web:* www.premieramerica.com	Chatsworth	CA	91313	818-772-4000		219
Premier Bank 275 W Federal St *TF:* 888-822-4751 ■ *Web:* www.yourpremierbank.com	Youngstown	OH	44503	330-742-0500		70
Premier Bank 2866 White Bear Ave N *TF:* 800-772-6497 ■ *Web:* www.premierbanks.com	Maplewood	MN	55109	651-777-7700	777-3761	70
Premier Bank Inc 2883 5th Ave *NASDAQ: PFBI* ■ *TF:* 800-657-7682	Huntington	WV	25702	800-657-7682		360-2
Premier Benefit Plans Inc 35 Pinelawn Rd Ste 208E *Web:* premier-benefits.com	Melville	NY	11747	631-719-8205		390
Premier BPO Inc 102 Country Ln Ste B *Web:* www.premierbpo.com	Clarksville	TN	37043	931-551-8888		393
Premier Civil Engineering LLC 1302 Calle Del Norte Ste 2 *Web:* premier-ce.com	Laredo	TX	78041	956-717-1199		261
Premier Coach Company Inc 946 Rte 7 S *TF:* 800-532-1811 ■ *Web:* premiercoach.com	Milton	VT	05468	802-655-4456	655-4213	107
Premier Communications 339 First Ave NE *Web:* www.mtcnet.net	Sioux Center	IA	51250	712-722-3451		116
Premier Concrete Products 5102 Galveston Rd *TF:* 800-575-7293 ■ *Web:* www.premier-concrete.com	Houston	TX	77017	713-641-2727	641-1112	183
Premier Co-opeartive Inc 2104 W Pk Ct *Web:* www.premiercooperative.net	Champaign	IL	61821	217-355-1983	355-3478	275
Premier Courier Service Inc 410 Eighth Ave *Web:* www.premier-nyc.com	New York	NY	10001	212-684-0901		317
Premier Credit Union 800 Ninth St *Web:* premiercu.org	Des Moines	IA	50309	515-282-1611		219
Premier Dental Products Co 1710 Romano Dr *TF:* 888-670-6100 ■ *Web:* www.premusa.com	Plymouth Meeting	PA	19462	610-239-6000	239-6171	228
Premier Die Casting Co 1177 Rahway Ave *TF:* 800-394-3006 ■ *Web:* diecasting.com	Avenel	NJ	07001	732-634-3000	634-0590	308
Premier Direct Marketing Inc 5051 Commerce Crossings Dr *TF:* 800-737-0205 ■ *Web:* premierdm.net	Louisville	KY	40229	502-367-6441		195
Premier Electrical Corp 4401 85th Ave N *Web:* www.premiercorp.net	Brooklyn Park	MN	55443	763-424-6551	424-5225	189-4
Premier Elevator Company Inc 230 Andrew Dr *Web:* www.premier-elevator.com	Stockbridge	GA	30281	770-389-4951		791
Premier Engineering Group Inc 439 Rt 46 E *Web:* www.pegmcp.com	Rockaway	NJ	07866	973-586-3004		261
Premier Equipment Inc 990 Sunshine Ln *Web:* www.premierequipment.com	Altamonte Springs	FL	32714	407-786-2000		385
Premier Equipment LLC 2025 US Hwy 14 W *TF:* 800-627-5469 ■ *Web:* www.premiereqhuron.com	Huron	SD	57350	605-352-7100	352-7071	274
Premier Eyecare Group Inc 1524 Cedar Cliff Dr *Web:* www.premiereyes.com	Camp Hill	PA	17011	717-761-3077		543
Premier Gear & Machine Works 387 S Sequoia Pkwy *Web:* www.premier-gear.com	Canby	OR	97013	503-227-3514	266-4328	821
Premier Golf 4355 River Green Pkwy *TF:* 866-260-4409 ■ *Web:* www.premiergolf.com	Duluth	GA	30096	770-291-4202	291-5157	771
Premier Homecare Inc 6123 Montrose Rd *Web:* www.jssa.org	Rockville	MD	20852	301-984-1742		363
Premier Inc 12255 El Camino Real *TF:* 877-777-1552 ■ *Web:* www.premierinc.com	San Diego	CA	92130	858-481-2727		353
Premier Incentives 6 Admiral Ln *Web:* www.premierincentives.com	Salem	MA	01970	978-607-0135		384
Premier Insurance Agency Ltd 2409 Dovercourt Dr *TF:* 877-794-8001 ■ *Web:* yourpremierins.com	Midlothian	VA	23113	804-794-8000	794-9077	390
Premier Insurance Corporation Inc 1326 Cape Coral Pkwy E *Web:* www.premierinsurancecorp.com	Cape Coral	FL	33904	239-542-7101		390
Premier Integrity Solutions Inc 7 Jamestown St *Web:* www.premierintegrity.com	Russell Springs	KY	42642	270-866-3144		743
Premier Jets 2140 NE 25th Ave *TF:* 800-635-8583 ■ *Web:* www.premierjets.com	Hillsboro	OR	97124	503-640-2927		13
Premier Kitchens Inc 3373 Mt Diablo Blvd *Web:* premierkitchens.net	LaFayette	CA	94549	925-283-6500		362
Premier Malt Products Inc 88 Market St *TF:* 800-521-1057 ■ *Web:* www.premiermalt.com	Saddle Brook	NJ	07663	586-443-3355		461
Premier Management Corp 8894 Stanford Blvd Ste 405 *Web:* www.premgtcorp.com	Columbia	MD	21045	443-656-3550		225
Premier Medical Group Pc 1850 Business Pk Dr PO Box 3799 *Web:* premiermed.com	Clarksville	TN	37043	931-245-7000		374-3
Premier Members Credit Union 5505 Arapahoe Ave *TF:* 800-468-0634 ■ *Web:* pmfcu.org	Boulder	CO	80303	303-657-7000	657-7353	219
Premier Network Solutions Inc 5070 Oaklawn Dr *Web:* prenet.com	Cincinnati	OH	45227	513-631-6381	631-6121	180
Premier Nursing Services Inc 444 W Ocean Blvd Ste 1050 *Web:* www.premiernursing.com	Long Beach	CA	90802	562-437-4313		260
Premier One Insurance Services I 100 Pacifica Ste 480 *Web:* premierone.com	Irvine	CA	92618	949-727-2025		390
Premier Pacific Seafoods Inc 111 W Harrison St *Web:* prempac.com	Seattle	WA	98119	206-286-8584	286-8810	297-5
Premier Paint Roller LLC 131-11 Atlantic Ave *Web:* www.premierpaintroller.com	Richmond Hill	NY	11418	718-441-7700		586
Premier Pan Company Inc 33 Mcgovern Blvd *Web:* www.prestigehomes.com	Crescent	PA	15046	724-457-4220	457-4222	483
Premier Payroll Services Inc 290 Main St *Web:* premiernow.com	Royersford	PA	19468	610-917-2281		570
Premier Performance LLC 278 E Dividend Dr *TF:* 888-497-3666 ■ *Web:* premierwd.com	Rexburg	ID	83440	208-356-0106	359-1414	146
Premier Pump & Supply Inc 19 Fruite St *Web:* www.premierpumponline.com	Belmont	NH	03220	603-528-3100		358
Premier Pyrotechnics Inc 25255 Hwy K **Fax Area Code: 573* ■ *TF:* 888-647-6863 ■ *Web:* premierpyro.com	Richland	MO	65556	417-322-6595	213-2210*	45
Premier Realty Group 2 N Sewalls Point Rd *TF:* 800-915-8517 ■ *Web:* www.premierrealtygroup.com	Stuart	FL	34996	772-287-1777		652
Premier Safety & Service Inc 2 Industrial Pk Dr *TF:* 800-828-1080 ■ *Web:* www.premiersafety.com	Oakdale	PA	15071	724-693-8699	693-8698	386
Premier Steel 1330 N Knollwood Cir *TF:* 800-220-9940 ■ *Web:* www.premiersteel.com	Anaheim	CA	92801	714-220-9940	220-1095	492
Premier Subaru LLC 150 N Main St *TF:* 888-690-6710 ■ *Web:* www.premiersubaru.com	Branford	CT	06405	203-481-0687	481-1861	57
Premier System Integrators Inc 140 Weakley Ln *Web:* www.premier-system.com	Smyrna	TN	37167	615-355-7200		203
Premier Tax & Financial Services 121 W 27th St Ste 1003A *Web:* www.premiertaxandfinancial.com	New York	NY	10001	212-807-8201		734
Premier Tech Chronos 1 Premier Ave *TF:* 866-571-7354 ■ *Web:* www.ptchronos.com	Riviere-du-Loup	QC	G5R6C1	418-868-8324	862-6642	684
Premier Technology Inc 1858 W Bridge Rd *Web:* www.premiertechnology.cc	Blackfoot	ID	83221	208-785-2274		480
Premier Tours 1120 South St *TF:* 800-545-1910 ■ *Web:* premiertours.com	Philadelphia	PA	19147	800-545-1910		760
Premier Truck Parts Inc 5800 W Canal Rd *Web:* www.premiertruckparts.com	Cleveland	OH	44125	216-642-5000		60
Premier Valley Bank 255 E River Pk Cir Ste 180 *TF:* 877-438-2002 ■ *Web:* www.premiervalleybank.com	Fresno	CA	93720	559-438-2002		70
Premiere Career College 12901 Ramona Blvd *TF:* 888-988-8198 ■ *Web:* www.premierecollege.edu	Irwindale	CA	91706	888-988-8198		167-3
Premiere Concrete Inc 11332 Red Lion Rd *Web:* premierconcrete.biz	White Marsh	MD	21162	410-344-1604		186
Premiere Credit of North America LLC PO Box 19309 *TF:* 866-808-7118 ■ *Web:* www.premierecredit.com	Indianapolis	IN	46219	866-808-7118		160
Premiere Hotel 625 N Fort Lauderdale Beach Blvd *Web:* www.premierehotel.com	Fort Lauderdale	FL	33304	954-566-7676		379
PremierGarage 335 Victory Dr *TF:* 866-590-9411 ■ *Web:* www.premiergarage.com	Herndon	VA	20170	703-707-0009		310
Premins Company Inc, The 1407 Ave M *Web:* www.preminsco.com	Brooklyn	NY	11230	718-375-8300		390
Premio Foods Inc 50 Utter Ave *TF:* 800-864-7622 ■ *Web:* www.premiofoods.com	Hawthorne	NJ	07506	800-864-7622		296-26
Premium Color Group LLC 95-B Industrial *Web:* premiumcolor.com	Clifton	NJ	07012	973-472-7007		627
Premium Connection Inc, The 6165 S Pecos Rd *TF:* 800-683-0933 ■ *Web:* www.thepremiumconnection.com	Las Vegas	NV	89120	702-434-6900	434-9715	328
Premium Feeders Inc 705 US Hwy 36 PO Box 230	Scandia	KS	66966	785-335-2221		10-1
Premium Press America (PPA) 2606 Eugenia Ave Ste C *TF:* 800-891-7323 ■ *Web:* www.premiumpressamerica.com	Nashville	TN	37211	615-353-7902	353-7905	637-2
Premium Retail Services Inc 618 Spirit Dr *Web:* premiumretail.com	Chesterfield	MO	63005	636-728-0592		193
Premium Rx National LLC 15809 Crabbs Branch Way **Fax Area Code: 571* ■ *TF:* 877-862-7796 ■ *Web:* www.prnpharma.com	Rockville	MD	20855	301-230-0908	934-6999*	237
Premium Transit Services 1415 Riding Mall E *Web:* www.premiumtransit.com	South Bend	IN	46614	574-291-8020		61
Premium Transportation Staffing Inc 190 Highland Dr *Web:* www.premiumdrivers.com	Medina	OH	44256	330-722-7974		734
Premix Inc 3365 E Center St *Web:* www.premix.com	Conneaut	OH	44030	440-224-2181	224-2766	604
Premix Marbletite 1259 NW 21st St *TF:* 800-432-5097 ■ *Web:* www.pmmproducts.com	Pompano Beach	FL	33069	800-432-5097		1
Prenia Corp 16625 Redmond Way Ste M-418 *Web:* www.prenia.com	Redmond	WA	98052	425-999-4330		177
Prent Corp 2225 Kennedy Rd *Web:* www.prent.com	Janesville	WI	53545	608-754-0276		602

Company / Address	City	State	Zip	Phone	Fax	Class
Prentex Alloy Fabricators Inc 3108 Sylvan Ave *Web:* www.prentex.com	Dallas	TX	75212	214-748-7837	748-7850	295
Prentice Products 4236 W Ferguson Rd *Web:* www.prenticeproducts.com	Fort Wayne	IN	46809	260-747-3195		627
Prentiss County 1901-B E Chambers *Web:* www.prentisscounty.org	Booneville	MS	38829	662-728-6232		338
Prentiss County Electric Power Assn 302 W Church St *Web:* www.pcepa.com	Booneville	MS	38829	662-728-4433	728-4059	245
Prentke Romich Co 1022 Heyl Rd *TF:* 800-262-1984 ■ *Web:* prentrom.com	Wooster	OH	44691	330-262-1984	263-4829	800
PREP 3300 Marjan Dr *Web:* prepatl.com	Atlanta	GA	30340	404-920-4150		196
Pre-Paid Legal Casualty Inc 1 Pre-Paid Way *TF:* 800-654-7757 ■ *Web:* www.legalshield.com	Ada	OK	74820	580-436-1234		41
Preparis Inc 3340 Peachtree Rd NE Ste 2050 *TF:* 855-447-3750 ■ *Web:* www.preparis.com	Atlanta	GA	30326	855-447-3750		178-1
Prepress Supply Inc 17336 Mount Wynne Cr *Web:* www.prepresssupply.com	Fountain Valley	CA	92708	714-557-4560		174
Preproduction Plastics Inc 210 Teller St *Web:* www.ppiplastics.com	Corona	CA	92879	951-340-9680		608
Presbyterian Childrens Services Inc 1220 N Lindbergh Blvd *TF:* 800-383-8147 ■ *Web:* www.pchas.org	Saint Louis	MO	63132	314-989-9727	427-2682	48-20
Presbyterian Church in America (PCA) 1700 N Brown Rd Ste 105 *Web:* pcanet.org	Lawrenceville	GA	30043	678-825-1000		48-20
Presbyterian Church (USA) 100 Witherspoon St *TF:* 888-728-7228 ■ *Web:* www.pcusa.org	Louisville	KY	40202	502-569-5288		48-20
Presbyterian College 503 S Broad St *TF:* 800-476-7272 ■ *Web:* www.presby.edu	Clinton	SC	29325	800-476-7272		166
Presbyterian Communities of South Carolina Equal Opportunity Housing 2817 Ashland Rd *Web:* www.prescommunities.org	Columbia	SC	29210	803-772-5885	772-5872	672
Presbyterian Disaster Assistance (PDA) 100 Witherspoon St **Fax Area Code:* 502 ■ *TF:* 800-728-7228 ■ *Web:* www.presbyterianmission.org	Louisville	KY	40202	800-728-7228	569-8039*	48-5
Presbyterian Espanola Hospital 1010 Spruce St *Web:* espanola-hospital.phs.org	Espanola	NM	87532	505-753-7111		374-3
Presbyterian Homes Inc, The 2109 Sandy Ridge Rd *TF:* 800-225-9573 ■ *Web:* www.presbyhomesinc.org	Colfax	NC	27235	336-886-6553		48-15
Presbyterian SeniorCare-Southminster Place 835 S Main St *Web:* www.srcare.org	Washington	PA	15301	724-222-4300		450
Presbyterian Villages of Michigan 25300 W Six Mile Rd *Web:* www.pvm.org	Redford	MI	48240	313-541-6000	541-6004	672
Presbyterian/St Luke's Medical Ctr 1719 E 19th Ave *Web:* pslmc.com	Denver	CO	80218	303-839-6000		769
Prescient Digital Media Ltd 80 Sherbourne St Unit 101 *Web:* www.prescientdigital.com	Toronto	ON	M5A2R1	416-926-8800		396
Prescient Infotech Inc 3930 Pender Dr Ste 160 *Web:* www.prescientinfotech.com	Fairfax	VA	22030	703-218-6233	991-7630	180
Prescott Chamber of Commerce 117 W Goodwin St *TF:* 800-266-7534 ■ *Web:* www.prescott.org	Prescott	AZ	86303	928-445-2000	445-0068	139
Prescott College 220 Grove Ave **Fax Area Code:* 928 ■ *TF:* 877-350-2100 ■ *Web:* www.prescott.edu	Prescott	AZ	86301	877-350-2100	776-5242*	166
Prescott National Cemetery 500 Hwy 89 N *Web:* www.cem.va.gov	Prescott	AZ	86301	928-717-7569	717-7570	136
Prescott Pines Camp 855 E Schoolhouse Gulch Rd *Web:* prescottpines.org	Prescott	AZ	86303	928-445-5225		239
Prescott Precision Die Inc 3231 Tower Dr *Web:* www.prescottprecision.com	Prescott	AZ	86305	928-778-3774	771-1038	454
Prescott Valley Chamber of Commerce 3001 N Main St Ste 2A *TF:* 800-355-0843 ■ *Web:* www.pvchamber.org	Prescott Valley	AZ	86314	928-772-8857	772-4267	139
Prescott's Inc 18940 Microscope Way *TF:* 800-438-3937 ■ *Web:* www.surgicalmicroscopes.com	Monument	CO	80132	719-481-3353	488-2268	475
Prescreen America Inc 505 W Abram St 2ND FL	Arlington	TX	76010	817-861-6666		260
Prescription Pad LLC, The 1118 NW 16th St Ste 150B *Web:* rxpadonline.com	Fruitland	ID	83619	208-452-7075	452-7446	237
Prescription Solutions 3515 Harbor Blvd *TF:* 800-788-4863 ■ *Web:* www.optumrx.com	Costa Mesa	CA	92626	800-788-4863		586
Prescription Supply Inc 2233 Tracy Rd *Web:* www.prescriptionsupply.com	Northwood	OH	43619	419-661-6600		231
Prescriptives Inc 767 Fifth Ave *TF:* 866-290-6471 ■ *Web:* www.prescriptives.com	New York	NY	10153	866-290-6471		214
Presentation College 1500 N Main St *TF:* 800-437-6060 ■ *Web:* www.presentation.edu	Aberdeen	SD	57401	605-225-1634		166
Presentation Concepts Corp 6517 Basile Rowe *TF:* 888-262-7596 ■ *Web:* www.pccav.com	East Syracuse	NY	13057	315-437-1314	437-0110	45
Presentek Inc 987 University Ave Ste 11 *Web:* www.presentek.com	Los Gatos	CA	95032	408-354-1264	354-6261	225
Preservation Action 1307 New Hampshire Ave NW 3rd Fl *Web:* preservationaction.org	Washington	DC	20036	202-463-0970		48-7
Preservation Delaware Inc (PDI) 211 Delaware St *Web:* preservationde.org	New Castle	DE	19720	302-322-7100		50-3
Preservation Education Institute 54 Main St PO Box 21 *Web:* www.preservationworks.org	Windsor	VT	05089	802-674-6752	674-6179	167-3
Preservation Hall 726 St Peter St *Web:* www.preservationhall.com	New Orleans	LA	70116	504-522-2841		572
Preservation Technologies LP 111 Thomson Park Dr *TF:* 800-416-2665 ■ *Web:* www.ptlp.com	Cranberry Township	PA	16066	724-779-2111		321
President Abraham Lincoln Hotel & Conference Ctr (PALHACC) 701 E Adams St *Web:* www.doubletree3.hilton.com	Springfield	IL	62701	217-544-8800	544-9607	379
President Asset Group LLC 260 Newport Center Dr 3rd Fl *Web:* president-llc.com	Newport Beach	CA	92660	949-999-3368	999-3367	653
President Container Inc 200 W Commercial Ave *Web:* www.presidentcontainergroup.com	Moonachie	NJ	07074	201-933-7500		100
President Global Corp 6965 Aragon Cir *Web:* www.tung-i.com	Buena Park	CA	90620	714-994-2990		296-20
President William Jefferson Clinton Birthplace Home National Historic Site 117 S Hervey St *Web:* www.nps.gov	Hope	AR	71801	870-777-4455		564
President's Council on Fitness Sports & Nutrition 1101 Wootton Pkwy Ste 560 *Web:* www.hhs.gov	Rockville	MD	20852	240-276-9567	276-9860	340-10
Presidential Aviation 1725 NW 51st Pl Ft Lauderdale Executive Airport *TF:* 888-772-8622 ■ *Web:* www.presidential-aviation.com	Fort Lauderdale	FL	33309	954-772-8622		13
Presidential Online Bank 4520 East-West Hwy *TF:* 800-383-6266 ■ *Web:* www.presidential.com	Bethesda	MD	20814	301-652-0700	951-3582	70
Presidents Federal Credit Union 4135 SR-128 *TF:* 800-416-8703 ■ *Web:* presidentsfcu.org	Cleves	OH	45002	513-941-6675	941-8240	219
Presidio Engineering Inc 190 S Stratford Dr Ste 105 *Web:* presidioengineering.com	Tucson	AZ	85716	520-795-7255		261
Presidio Networked Solutions Inc 7601 Ora Glen Dr Ste 100 *TF:* 800-452-6926 ■ *Web:* www.presidio.com	Greenbelt	MD	20770	301-313-2000	313-2400	180
Presidio Trust 103 Montgomery St *Web:* www.presidio.gov	San Francisco	CA	94129	415-561-5300		340-20
Presima Inc 1000 Jean-Paul-Riopelle Pl Herald Bldg Fourth Fl *Web:* www.presima.com	Montreal	QC	H2Z2B6	514-673-1375		528
PresiNET Systems Corp 645 Fort St Ste L109 *Web:* www.presinet.com	Victoria	BC	V8W1G2	250-405-5380		387
Presley Tours Inc 16 Presley Pk Dr PO Box 58 *TF:* 800-621-6100 ■ *Web:* www.presleytours.com	Makanda	IL	62958	618-549-0704		760
Presnell Gage PLLC 1216 Idaho St *Web:* www.presnellgage.com	Lewiston	ID	83501	208-746-8281	746-5174	2
Presnell's Bayside Marina and R.V. Resort 2115 State Rd 30A *Web:* presnells.com	Port Saint Joe	FL	32456	850-229-9229		379
Presqu'ile Provincial Park 328 Presqu Pkwy *Web:* www.ontarioparks.com	Brighton	ON	K0K1H0	613-475-4324		520
Presque Isle County PO Box 110 *Web:* www.presqueislecounty.org	Rogers City	MI	49779	989-734-3810	734-7635	338
Presque Isle Electric & Gas Co-op PO Box 308 *TF:* 800-423-6634 ■ *Web:* www.pieg.com	Onaway	MI	49765	989-733-8515	733-2247	245
Presque Isle State Park 301 Peninsula Dr Ste 1 *Web:* www.dcnr.pa.gov	Erie	PA	16505	814-833-7424		565
Presray Corp 32 Nelson Hill Rd PO Box 200 *Web:* www.presray.com	Wassaic	NY	12592	845-855-1220	855-8034	326
Presrite Corp 3665 E 78th St *Web:* www.presrite.com	Cleveland	OH	44105	216-441-5990	441-2644	483
Press Democrat 427 Mendocino Ave *TF:* 800-675-5056 ■ *Web:* www.pressdemocrat.com	Santa Rosa	CA	95401	707-546-2020	521-5330	532-2
Press Ganey Associates Inc 404 Columbia Pl *TF:* 800-232-8032 ■ *Web:* www.pressganey.com	South Bend	IN	46601	800-232-8032		194
Press of Atlantic City 1000 W Washington Ave *Web:* www.pressofatlanticcity.com	Pleasantville	NJ	08232	609-272-7000	272-7224	532-2
Press on Scroll Road 3387 Ormond Rd *Web:* www.thepressonscrollroad.com	Cleveland Heights	OH	44118	216-704-6203		637-2
Press One Publishing PO Box 563 *TF:* 888-775-4410 ■ *Web:* www.debtsmart.com	Barnegat	NJ	08005	609-660-0682	660-1412	637-2
Press Toward the Mark Publications PO Box 02099 *Web:* www.elretadodds.com	Detroit	MI	48202	313-527-0068		637-2
Press-A-Print International LLC 1463 Commerce Way *TF:* 888-880-0004 ■ *Web:* www.pressaprint.com	Idaho Falls	ID	83401	888-880-0004		393
Pressco Technology Inc 29200 Aurora Rd *Web:* www.pressco.com	Cleveland	OH	44139	440-498-2600	498-2615	639
Presscut Industries Inc 1730 Briercroft Ct *TF:* 800-442-4924 ■ *Web:* www.presscut.com	Carrollton	TX	75006	972-389-0615	245-2488	326
Pressed Juicery LLC 1550 17th St **Fax Area Code:* 310 ■ *TF:* 855-755-8423 ■ *Web:* www.pressedjuicery.com	Santa Monica	CA	90404	855-755-8423	477-7474*	345
Pressed4Time Inc 50 Mendon St *TF:* 800-423-8711 ■ *Web:* www.pressed4time.com	Upton	MA	01568	508-879-5966		426

	Phone	Fax	Class
Press-Enterprise Inc 3185 Lackawanna Ave. . . . . Bloomsburg PA 17815 *TF:* 888-484-6345 ■ *Web:* www.pressenterprise.net	570-784-3057		637-8
Pressler & Pressler LLP 7 Entin Rd. . . . . Parsippany NJ 07054 *Web:* www.pressler-pressler.com	973-753-5100		428
Pressley Ayanna (Rep D - MA) 1108 Longworth House Office Bldg . . . . . Washington DC 20515 *Web:* www.pressley.house.gov	202-225-5111		342-2
Pressley Ridge 5500 Corporate Dr Ste 400. . . . . Pittsburgh PA 15237 *TF:* 888-777-0820 ■ *Web:* www.pressleyridge.org	412-872-9400	872-9478	48-6
Pressman Toy Corp 3701 W Plano Pkwy Ste 100. . . . . Plano TX 75075 *TF:* 800-800-0298 ■ *Web:* www.pressmantoy.com	855-258-8214		762
Pressnet Express Inc 7283 Engineer Rd Ste A/B . . . . . San Diego CA 92111 *Web:* www.pressnetexpress.com	858-694-0070	633-1186	627
Press-Republican 170 Margaret St PO Box 459 . . . . . Plattsburgh NY 12901 *TF:* 800-288-7323 ■ *Web:* www.pressrepublican.com	518-561-2300	561-3362	532-2
Pressroom Restaurant 26-28 W King St. . . . . Lancaster PA 17603 *Web:* pressroomrestaurant.com	717-399-5400		671
Press-Seal Gasket Corp 2424 W State Blvd . . . . . Fort Wayne IN 46808 *TF:* 800-348-7325 ■ *Web:* www.press-seal.com	260-436-0521	436-1908	326
Presstek Inc 55 Executive Dr. . . . . Hudson NH 03051 *NASDAQ: PRST* ■ *TF:* 800-422-3616 ■ *Web:* www.presstek.com	603-595-7000		781
Press-Telegram 727 Pine Ave. . . . . Long Beach CA 90813 *Web:* www.presstelegram.com	562-435-1161		532-2
Pressure BioSciences Inc 14 Norfolk Ave . . . . . South Easton MA 02375 *OTC: PBIO* ■ *Web:* pressurebiosciences.com	508-230-1828	230-1829	85
Pressure Profile Systems Inc 5757 Century Blvd Ste 600. . . . . Los Angeles CA 90045 *Web:* pressureprofile.com	310-641-8100		201
Pressure Service Inc (PSI) 2361 S Plaza Dr . . . . . Rapid City SD 57702 *TF:* 800-666-3664 ■ *Web:* www.pressureservices.com	605-341-5154	341-4843	76
Prestage Farms 4651 Taylors Bridge Hwy . . . . . Clinton NC 28329 *TF:* 800-558-9585 ■ *Web:* www.prestagefarms.com	910-596-5700		10-6
Presteligence Inc 8328 Cleveland Ave NW. . . . . Canton OH 44720 *TF:* 888-438-6050 ■ *Web:* presteligence.com	888-438-6050		180
Prestera Center for Mental Health Services Inc 3375 Us Rt 60. . . . . Huntington WV 25705 *TF:* 877-399-7776 ■ *Web:* www.prestera.org	304-525-7851		726
Prestera Trucking 19129 US Rt 52. . . . . South Point OH 45680 *TF:* 855-761-7943 ■ *Web:* www.prestera.com	740-894-4770		780
Prestige Accommodations Intl 1231 E Dyer Rd Ste 240 . . . . . Santa Ana CA 92705 *TF:* 800-321-6338 ■ *Web:* www.meetingplanners.com	714-957-9100		184
Prestige Alarm & Specialty Products Inc 7640 Commerce Ln . . . . . Trussville AL 35173 *Web:* www.prestigealarm.com	205-661-4822	661-4823	693
Prestige Bar Academy PBA 200 S Citrus Ave. . . . . Covina CA 91723 *TF:* 800-996-6499 ■ *Web:* www.prestigebaracademy.com	626-343-9641		685
Prestige Brands Inc 660 White Plains Rd Ste 250 . . . . . Tarrytown NY 10591 *Web:* www.prestigebrands.com	914-524-6819		214
Prestige Capital Corp 400 Kelby St 14th Fl. . . . . Fort Lee NJ 07024 *Web:* www.prestigecapital.com	201-944-4455	944-9477	272
Prestige Care Inc 7700 NE Pkwy Dr Ste 300. . . . . Vancouver WA 98662 *Web:* www.prestigecare.com	360-735-7155		371
Prestige Chrysler Dodge Inc 200 Alpine St . . . . . Longmont CO 80501 *Web:* www.prestigechryslerdodge.com	303-651-3000		57
Prestige Cleaners Inc 7536 Taggart Ln . . . . . Knoxville TN 37938 *Web:* prestigecleanersinc.net	865-938-7701		426
Prestige Cosmetics Corp 5001 NW 13th Ave Ste L. . . . . Pompano Beach FL 33064 *Web:* www.prestigecosmetics.com	954-480-9202	480-9220	214
Prestige Fabricators Inc 2206 Dumont St. . . . . Asheboro NC 27204 *Web:* www.prestigefab.com	336-672-2751		601
Prestige Financial Services Inc 351 W Opportunity Way . . . . . Draper UT 84020 *TF:* 888-822-7422 ■ *Web:* www.myprestige.com	888-822-7422		217
Prestige Graphics Inc 9630 Ridgehaven Ct Ste B . . . . . San Diego CA 92123 *TF:* 800-383-9361 ■ *Web:* pgisd.com	858-560-8213	560-1473	535
Prestige Group 26155 Groesbeck Hwy . . . . . Warren MI 48089 *Web:* prestige-grp.com	989-635-8037		393
Prestige Harbourfront Resort & Convention Ctr 251 Harbourfront Dr NE . . . . . Salmon Arm BC V1E2W7 *TF:* 877-737-8443 ■ *Web:* www.prestigehotelsandresorts.com	250-833-5800		379
Prestige Maintenance USA Ltd 1808 Tenth St Ste 300 . . . . . Plano TX 75074 *TF:* 800-321-4773 ■ *Web:* www.prestigeusa.net	972-578-9801		192
Prestige Medical Corporation Intl 8600 Wilbur Ave. . . . . Northridge CA 91324 *TF:* 800-762-3333 ■ *Web:* www.prestigemedical.com	818-993-3030		475
Prestige Properties & Development Company Inc 546 5th Ave Ste 15B. . . . . New York NY 10036	212-944-0444		653
Prestige Security 5721 W Slauson Ave Ste 120 . . . . . Culver City CA 90230 *Web:* www.prestigesecurity.com	310-670-5999		693
Prestige Stamping Inc 23513 Groesbeck Hwy . . . . . Warren MI 48089 *Web:* www.prestigestamping.com	586-773-2700		488
Prestige Technicall Services 7908 Cincinnati Dayton Rd Ste T . . . . . West Chester OH 45069 *Web:* www.prestigetechnical.com	513-779-6800		261
Prestige Travel & Cruises Inc 6175 Spring Mountain Rd . . . . . Las Vegas NV 89146 *TF:* 800-758-5693 ■ *Web:* www.prestigecruises.com	702-251-5552		771
Prestige Wealth Management Group LLC 31 SR-12 . . . . . Flemington NJ 08822 *TF:* 800-743-4768 ■ *Web:* prestigewmg.com	908-782-0001	450-1495	690
Prestini Corp 351 E Patagonia Hwy Ste 4. . . . . Nogales AZ 85621 *TF:* 800-528-6569 ■ *Web:* www.prestiniusa.com	520-287-4931		527
Presto Food Stores Inc 1513 James L Redman Pkwy . . . . . Plant City FL 33563	813-754-3511		204
Presto Lifts Inc 50 Commerce Way . . . . . Norton MA 02766 **Fax Area Code:* 888 ■ *TF:* 800-343-9322 ■ *Web:* www.prestolifts.com	800-343-9322	788-6496*	470
Presto Products Co 670 N Perkins St PO Box 2399. . . . . Appleton WI 54912 **Fax Area Code:* 920 ■ *TF:* 800-558-3525 ■ *Web:* prestoproducts.com	800-558-3525	738-1432*	66
Presto Tape Inc 1626 Bridgewater Rd. . . . . Bensalem PA 19020 *TF:* 800-331-1373 ■ *Web:* prestotape.com	215-245-8555	245-8554	732
Prestolite Wire Corp 200 Galleria Office Ctr Ste 212. . . . . Southfield MI 48034 *TF:* 800-498-3132 ■ *Web:* www.prestolitewire.com	248-355-4422	386-4462	814
Preston Citizen 1250 Industrial Park Rd . . . . . Preston ID 83263 *Web:* prestoncitizen.com	208-852-0155	852-0158	532-2
Preston Feather Building Ctr PO Box 637 . . . . . Petoskey MI 49770 *Web:* prestonfeather.com	231-347-2501		364
Preston Industries Inc 6600 W Touhy Ave . . . . . Niles IL 60714 *TF:* 800-229-7569 ■ *Web:* www.polyscience.com	847-647-0611	647-1155	420
Preston Mobility Inc 13071 Vanier Pl Ste 128. . . . . Richmond BC V6V2J1 *Web:* www.prestonmobility.com	604-629-8526		736
Preston Partnership 115 Perimeter Center Pl Ste 950. . . . . Atlanta GA 30346 *Web:* www.theprestonpartnership.com	770-396-7248	396-2945	261
Preston Phipps Inc 6400 Vanden Abeele. . . . . Montreal QC H4S1R9 *Web:* prestonphipps.com	514-333-5340		111
Preston Refrigeration Company Inc 3200 Fiberglass Rd. . . . . Kansas City KS 66115 *Web:* www.prestonrefrigeration.com	913-225-5500	621-6962	665
Preston Wynne Spa Inc 14567 Big Basin Way . . . . . Saratoga CA 95070 *Web:* www.prestonwynne.com	408-741-5525		77
Preston, Wilson & Crandley PLC 2404 Potters Rd Ste 500. . . . . Virginia Beach VA 23454 *Web:* pwcattorneys.com	757-486-2700	486-7227	41
Prestone Press LLC 47-50 30th St. . . . . Long Island City NY 11101 *Web:* www.prestoneprinting.com	347-468-7900		627
Preston-Eastin Inc 9490 N Ridgeway St. . . . . Tulsa OK 74131 *TF:* 800-615-5432 ■ *Web:* www.prestoneastin.com	918-834-5591	834-5595	811
PrestoTech Solutions 4595 Broadmoor Ave SE Ste 200 . . . . . Grand Rapids MI 49512 *Web:* www.prestotech.net	616-891-4100		387
Presto-X Co 10421 Portal Rd Ste 101 . . . . . La Vista NE 68128 *TF:* 800-759-1942 ■ *Web:* www.prestox.com	800-759-1942		577
Prestress Engineering Corp 2220 Rt 176 . . . . . Prairie Grove IL 60012 *Web:* www.pre-stress.com	815-459-4545	459-6855	183
Prestress Services Inc 7855 NW Winchester Rd. . . . . Decatur IN 46733 *Web:* www.prestressservices.com	260-724-7117	724-3349	183
Prestressed Casting Co PO Box 3499 . . . . . Springfield MO 65807 *Web:* prestressedcasting.com	417-869-7350		183
Prestressed Systems Inc 4955 Walker Rd Hwy 401 . . . . . Windsor ON N9A6J3 *Web:* www.theprecaster.com	519-737-1216		135
Prestwood Elementary School 343 E Macarthur St. . . . . Sonoma CA 95476 *Web:* www.sonomaschools.org	707-935-6030		685
Pretend City, The Childrens Museum of Orange County 17752 Sky Park Cir Ste 280 . . . . . Irvine CA 92614 *Web:* www.pretendcity.org	949-428-3900		522
PreTesting Group 38 Franklin St. . . . . Tenafly NJ 07670 *Web:* pretesting.com	201-569-4800		466
Preti, Flaherty, Beliveau, Pachios & Haley LLC 45 Memorial Cir . . . . . Augusta ME 04330 *Web:* www.preti.com	207-623-5300		428
Pretium Packaging LLC 8112 Maryland Ste 250 . . . . . Clayton MO 63105 *Web:* pretiumpkg.com	314-727-8200		601
Pretium Partners 3240 Henderson Rd . . . . . Columbus OH 43220 *Web:* pretiumpartners.com	614-457-1726		196
Prettl Electric Corp 1721 White Horse Rd . . . . . Greenville SC 29605 *Web:* www.prettl.com	864-220-1010		247
Pretzelmaker 5555 Glenridge Connector Ste 850. . . . . Atlanta GA 30342 *TF:* 877-639-2361 ■ *Web:* pretzelmaker.com	877-639-2361		670
Pretzels Inc 123 Harvest Rd PO Box 503 . . . . . Bluffton IN 46714 *TF:* 800-456-4838 ■ *Web:* pretzels-inc.com	260-824-5782	824-0895	296-9
Pretzelworks Inc 5331-37 Oxford Ave . . . . . Philadelphia PA 19124 *Web:* www.pretzelworks.com	215-288-4002		297-3
Preusser Jewelers 125 Ottawa NW . . . . . Grand Rapids MI 49503 *Web:* preusserjewelers.com	616-458-1425		410
Prevail Health Inc 1105 W Chicago Ave Ste 203 . . . . . Chicago IL 60642 *Web:* prevailhealth.com	312-441-9137		363
Prevea Health Services Inc PO Box 13008 . . . . . Green Bay WI 54304 *Web:* www.prevea.com	920-496-4700		363
Prevent Blindness America 211 W Wacker Dr Ste 1700. . . . . Chicago IL 60606 *TF:* 800-331-2020 ■ *Web:* www.preventblindness.org	800-331-2020		48-17

Name / Address	City	State	ZIP	Phone	Fax	Class
Prevention Magazine 733 Third Ave *TF:* 800-813-8070 ■ *Web:* www.prevention.com	New York	NY	10017	212-697-2040		457-13
PreventionGenetics LLC 3700 Downwind Dr *Web:* www.preventiongenetics.com	Marshfield	WI	54449	715-387-0484		743
Preventure Inc 2000 Nooseneck Hill Rd *TF:* 888-321-4326 ■ *Web:* preventure.com	Coventry	RI	02816	888-321-4326		706
Preverco Inc 285 Rue De Rotterdam *TF:* 877-667-2725 ■ *Web:* www.preverco.com	Saint-Augustin-de-Desmaures	QC	G3A2E5	418-878-8930		364
Providence Corp 5685 S 1475 E Ste 2b *Web:* www.previdence.com	Ogden	UT	84403	801-409-0904		463
PreViser Corp 20849 Cascade Ridge Dr *Web:* www.previser.com	Mount Vernon	WA	98274	360-941-4715		177
Prevost Car Inc 35 Boul Gagnon *TF:* 877-773-8678 ■ *Web:* www.prevostcar.com	Sainte-Claire	QC	G0R2V0	418-883-3391	883-4157	516
Prevue Pet Products Inc 224 N Maplewood Ave *TF:* 800-243-3624 ■ *Web:* prevuepet.com	Chicago	IL	60612	312-243-3624		578
Prewitt and Company LLC 756 10th Ave SE *Web:* www.prewittandco.com	Sidney	MT	59270	406-482-5251	482-6644	446
Prezacor Inc 170 Cold Soil Rd *TF:* 855-792-3335 ■ *Web:* prezacor.com	Princeton	NJ	08540	855-792-3335		743
Prezza 24 Fleet St *Web:* www.prezza.com	Boston	MA	02113	617-227-1577		671
PRG Nocturne Productions Inc 300 Harvestore Dr *Web:* www.trichromes.com	Dekalb	IL	60115	815-756-9600		514
PRG-Schultz International Inc 600 Galleria Pkwy Ste 100 *Web:* www.prgx.com	Atlanta	GA	30339	770-779-3900	779-3133	2
PRI (Public Radio Intl) 401 Second Ave N Ste 500 *Web:* www.pri.org	Minneapolis	MN	55401	612-330-9251	330-9222	644
PRI (Pacific Research Institute) 101 Montgomery St Ste 1300 *Web:* www.pacificresearch.org	San Francisco	CA	94104	415-989-0833	989-2411	634
PRI (Pontis Research Inc) 4195 Thousand Oaks Blvd Ste 105 *Web:* www.pontisresearch.com	Westlake Village	CA	91362	805-777-7424		693
PRI Group LLC 600 Thomas Dr **Fax Area Code:* 630 ■ *Web:* theprigroup.com	Bensenville	IL	60106	708-492-1777	477-4044*	463
Pri Mar Petroleum Inc 1207 Broad St *Web:* www.primarpetro.com	Saint Joseph	MI	49085	269-983-7314		580
Pribila, Aquino & Fields PC 628 N Weber St *Web:* pribila.com	Colorado Springs	CO	80903	719-473-1238	473-2542	41
Pribuss Engineering Inc 523 Mayfair Ave *Web:* www.pribuss.com	South San Francisco	CA	94080	650-588-0447		261
Price Bros Equipment Co 619 S Washington St **Fax Area Code:* 316 ■ *TF:* 877-957-9577 ■ *Web:* www.pricebroseq.com	Wichita	KS	67211	877-957-9577	265-1062*	274
Price Companies Inc, The 218 Midway Rt *Web:* www.thepricecompanies.com	Monticello	AR	71655	870-367-9751	367-3309	820
Price County 126 Cherry St *Web:* www.co.price.wi.us	Phillips	WI	54555	715-339-3325	339-3089	338
Price David (Rep D - NC) 2108 Rayburn House Office Bldg *Web:* www.price.house.gov	Washington	DC	20515	202-225-1784	225-2014	342-2
Price Edwards & Co 210 Park Ave Ste 1000 *Web:* www.priceedwards.com	Oklahoma City	OK	73102	405-843-7474	236-1849	655
Price Electric Co-op 508 N Lake Ave PO Box 110 *TF:* 800-884-0881 ■ *Web:* price-electric.com	Phillips	WI	54555	715-339-2155	339-2921	245
Price Ford of Turlock 5200 N Golden State Blvd *Web:* www.pricefordofturlock.com	Turlock	CA	95382	209-669-5200		57
PRICE Futures Group Inc, The 141 W Jackson Blvd Ste 1340A *TF:* 800-769-7021 ■ *Web:* www.pricegroup.com	Chicago	IL	60604	312-264-4300		690
Price Industries Inc 2975 Shawnee Ridge Ct *Web:* www.priceindustries.com	Suwanee	GA	30024	770-623-8050		14
Price Pfister Inc 19701 Da Vinci St *TF:* 800-732-8238 ■ *Web:* www.pfisterfaucets.com	Lake Forest	CA	92610	949-672-4000		609
Price Postel & Parma LLP 200 E Carrillo St Ste 400 *Web:* ppplaw.com	Santa Barbara	CA	93101	805-962-0011		428
Price Products Inc 106 State Pl *Web:* www.priceproducts.com	Escondido	CA	92029	760-745-5602	745-9419	454
Price Pump Co 21775 Eighth St E *Web:* www.pricepump.com	Sonoma	CA	95476	707-938-8441		641
Price Rubber Corp 2733 Gunter Park Dr W *TF:* 800-633-1470 ■ *Web:* www.pricerubber.com	Montgomery	AL	36109	334-277-5470	271-3194	207
Price Stagner & Company PLLC 501 Darby Creek Rd No 6 *Web:* www.pricestagner.com	Lexington	KY	40509	859-263-1944		2
Price Steel Ltd 13500 156 St *TF:* 800-661-6789 ■ *Web:* www.pricesteel.com	Edmonton	AB	T5V1L3	780-447-9999		480
Price Systems LLC 17000 Commerce Pky Ste A *TF:* 800-437-7423 ■ *Web:* www.pricesystems.com	Mount Laurel	NJ	08054	856-608-7200	608-7247	23
Price, Heneveld, Cooper, De Witt & Litton 695 Kenmoor Ave SE *Web:* priceheneveld.com	Grand Rapids	MI	49546	616-949-9610		428
Priced Rite Suites 2327 University Ave *Web:* www.pricedritesuites.com	Green Bay	WI	54302	920-469-2130		379
Pricekubecka PLLC 16775 Addison Rd Ste 500 *Web:* pricekubecka.com	Addison	TX	75001	972-888-0950		2
Priceline LLC 800 Connecticut Ave *TF:* 800-774-2354 ■ *Web:* www.trvl.priceline.com	Norwalk	CT	06854	800-774-2354		51
PriceSmart Inc 9740 Scranton Rd *NASDAQ: PSMT* ■ *Web:* www.pricesmart.com	San Diego	CA	92121	858-404-8800		812
PriceWaiter LLC 426 Market St *TF:* 855-671-9889 ■ *Web:* www.pricewaiter.com	Chattanooga	TN	37421	855-671-9889		387
PricewaterhouseCoopers LLP 300 Madison Ave **Fax Area Code:* 813 ■ *TF:* 800-993-9971 ■ *Web:* www.pwc.com	New York	NY	10017	646-471-4000	286-6000*	2
PriceWeber Marketing Communications Inc 10701 Shelbyville Rd *Web:* www.priceweber.com	Louisville	KY	40243	502-499-9220		7
Prichard Communications 620 SW 5th Ave Ste 702 *Web:* www.prichardcommunications.com	Portland	OR	97204	503-517-2773		317
Pricing Advisor Inc 3535 Roswell Rd Ste 59 *Web:* pricingsociety.com	Marietta	GA	30062	770-509-9933	509-1963	195
Prickett, Jones & Elliott PA 1310 King St PO Box 1328 *TF:* 800-669-5460 ■ *Web:* www.prickett.com	Wilmington	DE	19899	302-888-6500	658-8111	428
Picketts Fort State Park 106 Overfort Ln *Web:* wvstateparks.com	Fairmont	WV	26554	304-363-3030		565
Prickly Pear Southwest Cafe 328 S Main St *Web:* pricklypearcafe.com	Ann Arbor	MI	48104	734-930-0047		671
Pricon Inc 1831 W Lincoln Ave *TF:* 800-660-1831 ■ *Web:* www.pricon.com	Anaheim	CA	92801	714-758-8832		225
PRIDE (Prison Rehabilitative Industries & Diversified Enterprises Inc) 223 Morrison Rd *Web:* www.pride-enterprises.org	Brandon	FL	33511	813-324-8700	890-2132	630
Pride Cleaners 13613 S US 71 Hwy *Web:* www.pridecleaners.com	Grandview	MO	64030	816-442-8555		426
Pride Computer Systems 4006 3rd St South Ste 101 *Web:* www.pridecomputersystems.com	Jacksonville Beach	FL	32250	904-242-9522		175
Pride Engineering LLC 10301 Xylon Ave N Ste 100 *Web:* www.pridecan.com	Minneapolis	MN	55445	763-427-6250	427-6226	454
Pride Hospitality LLC 2129 S Germantown Rd Ste 1 *Web:* www.pridehospitality.com	Germantown	TN	38138	901-751-2212	751-2940	463
Pride Institute 14400 Martin Dr *TF:* 800-547-7433 ■ *Web:* www.pride-institute.com	Eden Prairie	MN	55344	952-934-7554		352
Pride International Inc 5847 San Felipe St Ste 3300 *TF:* 877-736-3772 ■ *Web:* www.rigzone.com	Houston	TX	77057	713-789-1400		539
Pride Mobility Products Corp 182 Susquehanna Ave *TF:* 800-800-8586 ■ *Web:* www.pridemobility.com	Exeter	PA	18643	800-800-8586		477
Pride of Main Street Dairy 214 Main St S	Sauk Centre	MN	56378	320-351-8300		296-27
Pride Products Corp 4333 Veterans Memorial Hwy *TF:* 800-898-5550 ■ *Web:* www.prideproducts.com	Ronkonkoma	NY	11779	631-737-4444		791
Pride Signs Ltd 255 Pinebush Rd *TF:* 877-551-5529 ■ *Web:* www.pridesigns.com	Cambridge	ON	N1T1B9	519-622-4040		261
Pride Solvents & Chemical Company of New York Inc 6 Long Island Ave *Web:* www.pridesol.com	Holtsville	NY	11742	631-758-0200	758-0290	146
Pride South Florida 4233 NE 6th Ave *Web:* pridesouthflorida.org	Oakland Park	FL	33334	954-561-2020		474
Pride Transport Inc 5499 W 2455 S *TF:* 800-877-1320 ■ *Web:* www.pridetransport.com	Salt Lake City	UT	84120	800-827-7743		780
Pridestaff Inc 7535 N Palm Ave Ste 101 *Web:* www.pridestaff.com	Fresno	CA	93711	559-432-7780		193
Pridgeon & Clay Inc 50 Cottage Grove St SW *Web:* www.pridgeonandclay.com	Grand Rapids	MI	49507	616-241-5675	241-1799	489
Priefert Manufacturing 2630 S Jefferson Ave PO Box 1540 *TF:* 800-527-8616 ■ *Web:* www.priefert.com	Mount Pleasant	TX	75455	903-572-1741	572-2798	311
Prier Products Inc 4515 E 139th St *TF:* 800-362-1463 ■ *Web:* www.prier.com	Grandview	MO	64030	800-362-9055		610
Priest Lake State Park 314 Indian Creek Park Rd *Web:* parksandrecreation.idaho.gov	Coolin	ID	83821	208-443-2200		565
Priester Aviation 1061 S Wolf Rd *TF:* 888-323-7887 ■ *Web:* www.priesterav.com	Wheeling	IL	60090	847-537-1133	459-0778	24
Priester Pecan Company Inc 208 Old Fort Rod E *TF:* 800-277-3226 ■ *Web:* www.priesters.com	Fort Deposit	AL	36032	334-227-4301	227-4294	296-28
Prikos & Becker Tool Co 8109 N Lawndale Ave	Skokie	IL	60076	847-675-3910		757
Prima 5325 Lyndale Ave S *Web:* primampls.com	Minneapolis	MN	55419	612-827-7376	827-7534	671
PRIMA (Public Risk Management Assn) 700 S Washington St Ste 218 *Web:* www.primacentral.org	Alexandria	VA	22314	703-528-7701	739-0200	49-7
Prima Supply Inc 4603 Poplar Level Rd Ste 1 *Web:* primasupply.com	Louisville	KY	40213	502-966-4578		612
Primacy 1577 New Britain Ave *Web:* www.theprimacy.com	Farmington	CT	06032	860-679-9332		7
Primal AI 605-305 King St W *Web:* primal.ai	Kitchener	ON	N2G1B9	519-741-1243		177
Primal Essence Inc 1351 Maulhardt Ave *TF:* 877-774-6253 ■ *Web:* primalessence.com	Oxnard	CA	93030	877-774-6253		80-2
Primal Technologies Inc 3615 Laird Rd Ste 13 *TF:* 800-603-6035 ■ *Web:* www.primaltech.com	Mississauga	ON	L5L5Z8	416-548-3376		179
Primanti Bros 46 18th St *Web:* www.primantibros.com	Pittsburgh	PA	15222	412-263-2142		671

Company	City	State	ZIP	Phone	Fax	Class
Primary Automation Systems Inc 13361 Aberdeen St NE *TF:* 888-313-4502 ■ *Web:* www.primaryautomation.com	Ham Lake	MN	55304	763-755-3500	755-3744	596
Primary Color Inc 9239 Premier Row *TF:* 800-581-9555 ■ *Web:* www.primarycolorinc.com	Dallas	TX	75247	800-581-9555		687
Primary Design Inc 90 Washington St 3rd Fl *Web:* primary360.com	Haverhill	MA	01832	978-373-1565		344
Primary Flow Signal Inc 800 Wellington Ave *TF:* 877-737-3569 ■ *Web:* www.primaryflowsignal.com	Cranston	RI	02910	401-461-6366	461-4450	358
Primary Freight Services Inc 6545 Caballero Blvd *TF:* 800-635-0013 ■ *Web:* www.primaryfreight.com	Buena Park	CA	90620	310-635-3000		311
Primary Instruments Inc 9553 Vassar Ave *Web:* www.primaryinstruments.com	Chatsworth	CA	91311	818-993-4971	701-5516	743
Primary Land Services LLC 3033 Express Dr N *Web:* primaryland.com	Islandia	NY	11749	631-864-4460		653
Primary Media Outdoor Advertising 2511 Boll St *Web:* www.primarymedia.com	Dallas	TX	75204	214-880-0440		7
Primary Packaging Inc 10810 Industrial Pkwy NW *Web:* www.primarypackaging.com	Bolivar	OH	44612	330-874-3131		88
Primary Staffing Inc 4247 S Kedzie Ave *Web:* www.primary-staffing.net	Chicago	IL	60632	773-376-0486		631
Primatech Inc 50 Northwoods Blvd *Web:* www.primatech.com	Columbus	OH	43235	614-841-9800	841-9805	463
Prima-Temp Inc 2820 Wilderness Pl Ste C *TF:* 866-398-1032 ■ *Web:* www.prima-temp.com	Boulder	CO	80301	866-398-1032		261
Primavista 810 Matson Pl *Web:* www.pvista.com	Cincinnati	OH	45204	513-251-6467		671
Primax Compozit Home Systems LLC 5611 Fern Valley Rd *Web:* www.chswindows.com	Louisville	KY	40228	502-653-3705		499
Primco Dene Ltd PO Box 2070 *TF:* 855-355-2223 ■ *Web:* primcodene.com	Cold Lake	AB	T9M1P5	780-594-4034	594-4759	314
Prime Alliance Bank 1868 South 500 West *Web:* primealliancebank.com	Woods Cross	UT	84087	801-296-2200	296-0300	70
Prime Buchholz & Associates Inc 273 Corporate Dr Ste 250 *Web:* www.primebuchholz.com	Portsmouth	NH	03801	603-433-1143	433-8661	401
Prime Capital Services Inc 11 Raymond Ave *Web:* www.primefs.com	Poughkeepsie	NY	12603	845-485-3338		690
Prime Care Technologies Inc 6650 Sugarloaf Pkwy Ste 400 *Web:* www.primecaretech.com	Duluth	GA	30097	770-870-2888		225
Prime Coatings and Supply 875 W 2600 S *TF:* 800-851-9693 ■ *Web:* www.primecoatings.com	Salt Lake City	UT	84119	800-851-9693		802
Prime Concepts Group Inc 1807 S Eisenhower St *TF:* 800-946-7804 ■ *Web:* www.primeconcepts.com	Wichita	KS	67209	316-942-1111		195
Prime Contractors Inc 17355 Village Green Dr *Web:* www.primecontractorsinc.com	Houston	TX	77040	281-999-0875	999-0885	186
Prime Controls LP 1725 Lakepointe D *Web:* www.prime-controls.com	Lewisville	TX	75057	972-221-4849	420-4842	177
Prime Engineered Components 1012 Buckingham St PO Box 359 *Web:* www.primeeci.com	Watertown	CT	06795	860-274-6773	274-7939	621
Prime Equipment Group Inc 2000 E Fulton St *Web:* www.primeequipmentgroup.com	Columbus	OH	43205	614-253-8590		296
Prime Financial Credit Union 5656 S Packard Ave *TF:* 800-835-9680 ■ *Web:* primefinancialcu.org	Cudahy	WI	53110	414-486-4500		219
Prime Financial Inc 753 W River Rd *Web:* primefinancial.biz	Waterville	ME	04901	207-877-9450		690
Prime Holdings Insurance Services Inc 8722 S Harrison St *TF:* 800-257-5590 ■ *Web:* primeis.com	Sandy	UT	84070	800-257-5590		360-3
Prime Inc 2740 N Mayfair PO Box 4208 *TF:* 800-321-4552 ■ *Web:* www.primeinc.com	Springfield	MO	65803	417-521-3950	521-6878	780
Prime Industries Inc 406 Dividend Dr *Web:* primeindustriesusa.com	Peachtree City	GA	30269	770-632-1851		21
Prime Line *Prime Resources Corp* 1100 Boston Ave *Web:* www.primeline.com	Bridgeport	CT	06610	203-331-9100	330-0123	9
Prime Management Services 3416 Primm Ln *TF:* 866-609-1599 ■ *Web:* www.primemanagement.net	Birmingham	AL	35216	205-823-6106	823-2760	47
Prime Marine Services Inc 312 S Bernard Rd *Web:* primemarineinc.com	Broussard	LA	70518	337-837-6500		539
Prime Meridian Bank 1897 Capital Cir NE PO Box 13629 *Web:* primemeridianbank.com	Tallahassee	FL	32317	850-907-2301		70
Prime NDT Services Inc 4345 Independence Dr *Web:* primendt.com	Schnecksville	PA	18078	610-262-4954		41
Prime Osborn Convention Ctr 1000 Water St *Web:* www.jaxevents.com	Jacksonville	FL	32204	904-630-4000		205
Prime Payroll Relief Inc 16 Church St *Web:* primepayrollrelief.com	Cortland	NY	13045	607-428-0225		570
Prime Products Inc 2755 Remico St SW *Web:* www.primeproductsinc.com	Wyoming	MI	49519	616-531-8970		22
Prime Publishing LLC 3400 Dundee Rd Ste 220 *Web:* www.primecp.com	Northbrook	IL	60062	847-205-9375	513-6099	637-10
Prime Rate Premium Finance Corp 2141 Enterprise Dr PO Box 100507 *TF:* 800-777-7458 ■ *Web:* www.primeratepfc.com	Florence	SC	29501	843-669-0937	292-1080	217
Prime Rib, The 2020 K St NW *Web:* www.theprimerib.com	Washington	DC	20006	202-466-8811	466-2010	671
Prime Solutions Inc 4261 Business Ctr Dr *Web:* www.primesol.com	Fremont	CA	94538	510-490-2255	490-2177	696
Prime Staffing Inc 3806 N Cicero Ave	Chicago	IL	60641	773-685-9399		721
Prime Systems Inc 416 Mission St *Web:* www.primeuv.com	Carol Stream	IL	60188	630-681-2100		190
Prime Technology LLC 344-352 Twin Lakes Rd PO Box 185 *Web:* www.primetechnology.com	North Branford	CT	06471	203-481-5721	481-8937	248
Prime Therapeutics Inc 1305 Corporate Center Dr *TF:* 800-858-0723 ■ *Web:* www.primetherapeutics.com	Eagan	MN	55121	612-777-4000		586
Prime Time Intl 86-705 Ave 54 Ste A *Web:* www.primetimeproduce.com	Coachella	CA	92236	760-399-4278	399-4281	10-11
Prime Wheel Corp 17705 S Main St *Web:* www.primewheel.com	Gardena	CA	90248	310-516-9126	516-9676	60
Prime360 1450 American Ln Ste 700 *Web:* prime360.com	Schaumburg	IL	60173	815-544-6001		200
PrimeArray Systems Inc 127 Riverneck Rd *TF:* 800-433-5133 ■ *Web:* www.primearray.com	Chelmsford	MA	01824	978-654-6250	654-6249	176
Primebank 37 First Ave NW *Web:* www.primebank.com	Le Mars	IA	51031	712-546-4175		70
PrimeGenesis LLC 200 W Hill Rd *Web:* www.primegenesis.com	Stamford	CT	06902	203-323-8501		463
Prime-Line Products Inc 26950 San Bernardino Ave *Web:* www.primeline.net	Redlands	CA	92374	909-887-8118		350
PrimeLink 99 Kansas Ave *TF:* 800-300-0145 ■ *Web:* www.primelink1.net	Plattsburgh	NY	12903	518-324-5465		224
Primelite Manufacturing Corp 407 S Main St *Web:* www.primelite-mfg.com	Freeport	NY	11520	516-868-4411		361
PrimeNet Direct Marketing Solutions LLC 7320 Bryan Dairy Rd *TF:* 800-826-2869 ■ *Web:* www.primenet.com	Largo	FL	33777	727-447-6245		5
Primepak 133 Cedar Ln *TF:* 800-786-5613 ■ *Web:* www.primepak.com	Teaneck	NJ	07666	201-836-5060		603
Prime-Pak FoodsInc 2076 Memorial Park Rd	Gainesville	GA	30504	770-536-8708		619
PrimeQ Solutions Inc 26035 Acero Ste 100	Mission Viejo	CA	92691	949-268-3680	707-8600	195
Primera Engineers Ltd 100 S Wacker Dr Ste 700 *Web:* primeraeng.com	Chicago	IL	60606	312-606-0910	606-0415	196
Primera Partners Real Estate Services 8500 Vlg Ste 300 *Web:* primerapartners.com	San Antonio	TX	78217	210-444-1400	444-1401	652
Primera Plastics Inc 3424 Production Ct *Web:* www.primera-inc.com	Zeeland	MI	49464	616-748-6248		596
Primera Technology Inc 2 Carlson Pkwy N *TF:* 800-797-2772 ■ *Web:* www.primera.com	Plymouth	MN	55447	763-475-6676	475-6677	173-6
PrimeRevenue Inc 1100 Peachtree St NE 11th Fl *TF:* 877-217-3838 ■ *Web:* www.primerevenue.com	Atlanta	GA	30309	678-904-7100		569
Primerica Financial Services 3120 Breckinridge Blvd *Web:* www.primerica.com	Duluth	GA	30099	770-381-1000		401
Primeritus Financial Services Inc 440 Metroplex Dr *TF:* 888-833-4238 ■ *Web:* www.primeritus.com	Nashville	TN	37211	888-833-4238		393
PrimeSource Building Products Inc 1321 Greenway Dr *TF:* 800-676-7777 ■ *Web:* www.primesourcebp.com	Irving	TX	75038	972-999-8500		191-3
Primesource Staffing LLC 5250 Leetsdale Dr Ste 101 *Web:* primesourcestaffing.com	Denver	CO	80246	303-869-2990	869-2997	194
Primestream Corp 15590 NW 15th Ave *Web:* www.primestream.com	Miami	FL	33169	305-625-4415		809
Primevest Capital Corp 400 Burrard St Ste 1730 *Web:* www.primevestcapital.ca	Vancouver	BC	V6C3A6	604-630-7011		528
Primeway Federal Credit Union 12811 Northwest Fwy *TF:* 800-554-5690 ■ *Web:* www.primewayfcu.com	Houston	TX	77040	713-799-6200		219
Primewood Inc 2217 N 9th St	Wahpeton	ND	58075	701-642-2727		200
Primex Clinical Laboratories Inc 16742 Stagg St Ste 120 *Web:* primexlab.com	Van Nuys	CA	91406	818-779-0496		415
Primex Plastics Corp 1235 N 'F' St *TF:* 800-222-5116 ■ *Web:* www.primexplastics.com	Richmond	IN	47374	765-966-7774	935-1083	600
Primitives by Kathy Inc 1817 William Penn Way *TF:* 866-295-2849 ■ *Web:* www.primitivesbykathy.com	Lancaster	PA	17601	866-295-2849		292
Primmer & Piper P C 100 E State St PO Box 1309 *Web:* www.primmer.com	Montpelier	VT	05601	802-223-2102	223-2628	445
Primo Medical Group 75 Mill St *Web:* www.primomedicalgroup.com	Stoughton	MA	02072	781-828-4400	344-5895	476
Primo Microphones Inc 1805 Couch Dr *Web:* www.primomic.com	McKinney	TX	75069	972-548-9807	548-1351	52
Primo Water Corp 6525 Viscount Rd *TSX: BCB* ■ *Web:* primowatercorp.com	Mississauga	ON	L4V1H6	813-313-1798		80-2
Primo's 3309 McKinney Ave *Web:* www.primosdallas.com	Dallas	TX	75204	214-220-0510		671
Primorigen Biosciences Inc 510 Charmany Dr *TF:* 866-372-7442 ■ *Web:* www.primorigen.com	Madison	WI	53719	608-441-8332		85

Name / Address	City	State	ZIP	Phone	Fax	Class
Primrose Candy Co 4111 W Parker Ave *Web:* www.primrosecandy.com	Chicago	IL	60639	773-276-9522		296-8
Primrose Oil Company Inc 11444 Denton Dr *TF:* 800-275-2772 ■ *Web:* www.primrose.com	Dallas	TX	75229	800-275-2772		541
Primrose School Franchising Co 3660 Cedarcrest Rd *TF:* 800-745-0677 ■ *Web:* www.primroseschools.com	Acworth	GA	30101	770-529-4100	529-1551	148
Primus Builders Inc 8294 Hwy 92 Ste 210 *Web:* www.primusbuilders.com	Woodstock	GA	30189	770-928-7120	928-6548	186
Primus Electronics 4180 E Sand Ridge Rd *Web:* primuselectronics.com	Morris	IL	60450	800-435-1636	767-7605	246
PRIMUS Global Services Inc 1431 Greenway Dr Ste 750 *Web:* primusglobal.com	Irving	TX	75038	972-753-6500	753-6501	260
Primus Power Corp 3967 Trust Way *Web:* www.primuspower.com	Hayward	CA	94545	510-342-7600		74
Primus Software Corp 3061 Peachtree Industrial Blvd Ste 110 *Web:* www.primussoft.com	Duluth	GA	30097	770-300-0004		178-2
Primus Venture Partners 28601 Chagrin Blvd Ste 525 *Web:* www.primuscapital.com	Cleveland	OH	44122	440-684-7300		792
Prince & Izant Co 12999 Plaza Dr *TF:* 800-634-0437 ■ *Web:* princeizant.com	Cleveland	OH	44130	216-362-7000	362-7456	492
Prince Albert & District Chamber of Commerce 3700 Second Ave W *Web:* www.princealbertchamber.com	Prince Albert	SK	S6W1A2	306-764-6222		137
Prince Albert Historical Museum 10 River St E *Web:* www.historypa.com	Prince Albert	SK	S6V8A9	306-764-2992		520
Prince Albert National Park of Canada Northern Prairies Field Unit PO Box 100 *Web:* www.pc.gc.ca	Waskesiu Lake	SK	S0J2Y0	306-663-4522		563
Prince Associates Inc 270 Duffy Ave Ste D *Web:* princeins.com	Hicksville	NY	11801	516-822-6550	822-6564	390
Prince Castle Inc 355 E Kehoe Blvd *TF:* 800-722-7853 ■ *Web:* www.princecastle.com	Carol Stream	IL	60188	630-462-8800	462-1460	298
Prince Conti Hotel 830 Conti St *Web:* www.princecontihotel.com	New Orleans	LA	70112	504-529-4172		379
Prince Contracting LLC 10210 Highland Manor Dr Ste 110 *Web:* www.princecontracting.com	Tampa	FL	33610	813-699-5900	699-5901	188-4
Prince Corp 8351 County Rd H *TF:* 800-777-2486 ■ *Web:* www.prince-corp.com	Marshfield	WI	54449	800-777-2486		578
Prince County Hospital 65 Roy Boapes Ave PO Box 3000 *Web:* pchcare.com	Summerside	PE	C1N2A9	902-438-4200	432-2551	374-2
Prince Edward County 111 S St 2nd Fl PO Box 304 *Web:* www.co.prince-edward.va.us	Farmville	VA	23901	434-392-5145	392-3913	338
Prince Edward County public School 35 Eagle Dr *Web:* www.pecps.k12.va.us	Farmville	VA	23901	434-315-2100	392-1911	685
Prince Edward Island Museum & Heritage Foundation 2 Kent St *Web:* www.peimuseum.ca	Charlottetown	PE	C1A1M6	902-368-6600	368-6608	520
Prince Edward Island National Park of Canada 2 Palmers Ln *TF:* 800-663-7192 ■ *Web:* www.pc.gc.ca	Charlottetown	PE	C1A5V8	902-672-6350	672-6370	563
Prince Edward Island Tourism PO Box 2000 *TF:* 800-463-4734 ■ *Web:* www.gov.pe.ca	Charlottetown	PE	C1A7N8	902-368-4000	368-4438	774
Prince Gallitzin State Park 966 Marina Rd *Web:* www.dcnr.pa.gov	Patton	PA	16668	814-674-1000		565
Prince George Chamber of Commerce 890 Vancouver St *Web:* www.pgchamber.bc.ca	Prince George	BC	V2L2P5	250-562-2454	562-6510	137
Prince George Citizen 150 Brunswick St *Web:* www.princegeorgecitizen.com	Prince George	BC	V2L2B3	250-562-2441		532-1
Prince George County 6602 Courts Dr PO Box 68 *Web:* www.princegeorgecountyva.gov	Prince George	VA	23875	804-722-8600	732-1967	338
Prince George County Public Schools 6410 Courts Dr *Web:* www.pgs.k12.va.us	Prince George	VA	23875	804-733-2700	733-2737	186
Prince George Electric Co-op 7103 General Mahone Hwy PO Box 168 *Web:* www.pgec.coop	Waverly	VA	23890	804-834-2424		245
Prince George Hotel, The 1725 Market St *TF:* 800-565-1567 ■ *Web:* www.princegeorgehotel.com	Halifax	NS	B3J3N9	902-425-1986		379
Prince George's Chamber of Commerce 4640 Forbes Blvd Ste 130 *Web:* www.pgcoc.org	Lanham	MD	20706	301-731-5000	731-8015	139
Prince George's Community College 301 Largo Rd *Web:* www.pgcc.edu	Largo	MD	20774	301-336-6000	322-0119	162
Prince George's Community Federal Credit Union 15201 Hall Rd *TF:* 800-952-7428 ■ *Web:* princegeorgescfcu.org	Bowie	MD	20721	301-627-2666		219
Prince George's Community Television 9475 Lottsford Rd Ste 125 *Web:* pgctv.org	Largo	MD	20774	301-773-0900		514
Prince George's County 14741 Governor Oden Bowie Dr *Web:* www.princegeorgescountymd.gov	Upper Marlboro	MD	20772	301-952-3600		338
Prince George's County Memorial Library System 9601 Capital Ln *Web:* pgcmls.info	Largo	MD	20774	301-699-3500		434-3
Prince George's County, MD Conference & Visitors Bureau 9200 Basil Ct Ste 101 *Web:* www.experienceprincegeorges.com	Largo	MD	20774	301-925-8300	925-2053	206
Prince Industries Inc 745 N Gary Ave *Web:* www.princeind.com	Carol Stream	IL	60188	630-588-0088	588-0099	493
Prince Law Firm, The 800 W Long Lake Rd Ste 200 *TF:* 866-383-1125 ■ *Web:* probateprince.com	Bloomfield Hills	MI	48302	248-865-8810	865-0640	41
Prince Lionheart Inc 2421 Westgate Rd *TF:* 800-544-1132 ■ *Web:* www.princelionheart.com	Santa Maria	CA	93455	805-922-2250	922-9442	64
Prince Minerals 15311 Vantage Pkwy W Ste 350 *Web:* www.princecorp.com	Houston	TX	77032	646-747-4200		447
Prince of Peace United Methodist Church of Elk Group 1400 S Arlington Heights Rd *Web:* www.princeofpeaceumc.org	Elk Grove Village	IL	60007	847-439-0668		48-20
Prince Preferred Guest Program 100 Holomoana St **Fax Area Code:* 808 ■ *TF:* 800-774-6234 ■ *Web:* www.princepreferred.com	Honolulu	HI	96815	800-774-6234	943-4158*	378
Prince Publishing 149 So Barrington Ave 514 *TF:* 888-837-2665 ■ *Web:* www.princepublishing.com	Los Angeles	CA	90049	310-472-0548	471-4677	637-2
Prince Resorts Hawaii 100 Holomoana St *TF:* 888-977-4623 ■ *Web:* www.princewaikiki.com	Honolulu	HI	96815	808-956-1111	944-4491	669
Prince Rubber & Plastics Company Inc 137 Arthur St *Web:* www.princerp.com	Buffalo	NY	14207	716-877-7400	877-0743	677
Prince Rupert Port Authority 200-215 Cow Bay Rd *Web:* www.rupertport.com	Prince Rupert	BC	V8J1A2	250-627-8899	627-8980	618
Prince Service & Manufacturing Inc 7539 Hawkinsville Rd *Web:* www.princeservice.com	Macon	GA	31216	478-788-8162	788-0381	697
Prince Telecom Inc 551 Mews Dr Ste A *Web:* www.princetelecom.com	New Castle	DE	19720	302-324-1800		187
Prince Theater 1412 Chestnut St *Web:* www.princetheater.org	Philadelphia	PA	19102	267-239-2941		749
Prince William County 1 County Complex Ct *Web:* www.pwcgov.org	Woodbridge	VA	22192	703-792-6800		338
Prince William County-Greater Manassas Chamber of Commerce 9720 Capital Ct Ste 203 *TF:* 877-867-3853 ■ *Web:* pwchamber.org	Manassas	VA	20110	703-368-6600	368-4733	139
Prince William Forest Park 18100 Pk Headquarters Rd *Web:* www.nps.gov	Triangle	VA	22172	703-221-7181	221-3258	564
Princess Bayside Beach Hotel & Golf Ctr 4801 Coastal Hwy *Web:* princessbayside.com	Ocean City	MD	21842	410-723-2900		379
Princess Cruises 24844 Rockefeller Ave *TF:* 800-774-6237 ■ *Web:* www.princess.com	Santa Clarita	CA	91355	661-753-0000	284-4771	220
Princess House Inc 470 Miles Standish Blvd *TF:* 800-622-0039 ■ *Web:* www.princesshouse.com	Taunton	MA	02780	508-884-8541		366
Princess Margaret Hospital 610 University Ave *Web:* www.uhn.ca	Toronto	ON	M5G2M9	416-946-2000		374-7
Princess Pub & Grille 1665 India St *Web:* www.princesspub.com	San Diego	CA	92101	619-702-3021		671
Princess Royale Oceanfront Hotel & Conference Ctr 9100 Coastal Hwy *Web:* www.princessroyale.com	Ocean City	MD	21842	410-524-7777	524-7787	379
Princeton Battlefield State Park 500 Mercer Rd *Web:* www.njparksandforests.org	Princeton	NJ	08540	609-921-0074		565
Princeton Capital Management LLC 17 Hulfish St Ste 220 *Web:* www.princap.com	Princeton	NJ	08542	609-924-6867		194
Princeton Community Hospital 122 12th St *Web:* www.pchonline.org	Princeton	WV	24740	304-487-7000	487-2161	374-3
Princeton Flying School Princeton Airport 41 Airpark Rd *Web:* www.princetonairport.com	Princeton	NJ	08540	609-921-3100	921-1291	685
Princeton Forrestal Village 206 Rockingham Row *Web:* pfvillage.com	Princeton	NJ	08540	609-799-7400		460
Princeton Gamma Tech Instruments 1026 Rte 518	Rocky Hill	NJ	08553	609-924-7310		472
Princeton HealthCare System 905 Herrontown Rd *TF:* 866-460-4776 ■ *Web:* www.princetonhcs.org	Princeton	NJ	08540	609-497-3300		363
Princeton Industrial Products Inc 2119 Stonington Ave *Web:* www.princetonind.com	Hoffman Estates	IL	60169	847-839-8500	839-8526	621
Princeton Institute for International & Regional Studies (PIIRS) Princeton University Louis A Simpson International Bldg *Web:* piirs.princeton.edu	Princeton	NJ	08544	609-258-7497	258-3988	634
Princeton Instruments Inc 3660 Quakerbridge Rd *TF:* 877-474-2286 ■ *Web:* www.princetoninstruments.com	Trenton	NJ	08619	609-587-9797		544
Princeton Insurance Co 746 Alexander Rd PO Box 5322 *TF:* 800-334-0588 ■ *Web:* www.princetoninsurance.com	Princeton	NJ	08540	609-452-9404	734-8461	391-4
Princeton Mercer Regional Chamber 600 Alexander Rd Ste 3-2 *Web:* princetonmercerchamber.org	Princeton	NJ	08540	609-924-1776	924-5776	139
Princeton Packet, The 300 Witherspoon St PO Box 350 *TF:* 888-747-1122 ■ *Web:* www.centraljersey.com	Princeton	NJ	08542	609-924-3244	921-2714	637-8
Princeton Partners Inc 205 Rockingham Row *Web:* princetonpartners.com	Princeton	NJ	08540	609-452-8500		4

Phone | Fax | Class

Princeton Plasma Physics Laboratory (PPPL)
PO Box 451 Princeton NJ 08543 609-243-2000 243-2751 668
Web: www.pppl.gov

Princeton Public Library
65 Witherspoon St Princeton NJ 08542 609-924-9529 305
Web: www.princetonlibrary.org

Princeton Public Schools
25 Valley Rd Princeton NJ 08540 609-806-4200 685
TF: 800-322-8174 ■ *Web:* www.princetonk12.org

Princeton Radiology 3674 Rt 27 Kendall Park NJ 08824 732-821-4800 418
Web: www.princetonradiology.com

Princeton Review Inc, The
Cochituate Pl 24 Prime Pkwy Ste 201 Natick MA 01760 508-663-5050 242
TF: 800-273-8439 ■ *Web:* www.princetonreview.com

Princeton Scapes Inc 47 Chocksett Rd Sterling MA 01564 978-422-0420 422
Web: princetonscapes.com

Princeton Survey Research Assoc
600 Alexander Rd Princeton NJ 08540 609-924-9204 466
Web: psrai.com

Princeton Theological Seminary
64 Mercer St Princeton NJ 08540 609-921-8300 924-2973 167-3
Web: www.ptsem.edu

Princeton University
33 Washington Rd Princeton NJ 08544 609-258-3000 258-6743 166
TF: 877-609-2273 ■ *Web:* www.princeton.edu

Princeton University
Fine Hall Washington Rd Princeton NJ 08544 609-258-4200 258-1367 637-9
Web: www.math.princeton.edu

Princeton University Library
1 Washington Rd Princeton NJ 08544 609-258-4820 258-0441 434-6
Web: library.princeton.edu

Princeton University Press
41 William St Princeton NJ 08540 609-258-4900 258-6305 637-4
TF: 800-777-4726 ■ *Web:* press.princeton.edu

Princeton University Store
36 University Pl Princeton NJ 08540 609-921-8500 526
TF: 800-624-4236 ■ *Web:* www.pustore.com

Principal Financial Services Inc
711 High St Des Moines IA 50392 800-986-3343 304
TF: 800-986-3343 ■ *Web:* www.principal.com

Principal Properties Inc 3295 W 4 Ave Hialeah FL 33012 305-883-7555 883-5046 652
Web: principalproperties.com

Principal Technical Services (PTS)
2860 Michelle Dr Ste 150 Irvine CA 92606 949-268-4000 721
TF: 888-787-3711 ■ *Web:* www.ptsadvance.com

Principia College
13201 Clayton Rd Saint Louis MO 63131 618-374-2131 166
TF: 800-277-4648 ■ *Web:* www.principia.edu

Principia Partners
101 Lindenwood Dr Ste 225 Malvern PA 19355 610-363-7815 193
Web: www.principiaconsulting.com

Principle Business Enterprises Inc
PO Box 129 Dunbridge OH 43414 419-352-1551 558
TF: 800-467-3224 ■ *Web:* tranquilityproducts.com

Princo Instruments Inc
1020 Industrial Hwy Southampton PA 18966 215-355-1500 201
Web: www.princoinstruments.com

Pringle & Pringle, A Professional Corp
9251 N Pennsylvania Pl Oklahoma City OK 73120 405-848-4810 41
Web: www.pringleandpringle.com

Prinsco Inc 1717 16th St NE Willmar MN 56201 320-222-6800 978-8602 600
TF: 800-992-1725 ■ *Web:* www.prinsco.com

Print Basics Inc
1061 SW 30th Ave Deerfield Beach FL 33442 866-324-3270 627
Web: www.printbasics.com

Print Communications Inc
PO Box 11578 Indianapolis IN 46201 317-266-8208 626

Print Direction Inc
1600 Indian Brook Way Norcross GA 30093 770-446-6446 627
TF: 877-435-1672 ■ *Web:* www.printdirection.com

Print House, The 200 Maplewood St Malden MA 02148 781-324-4455 627
Web: www.printhouse.com

Print Magazine
10151 Carver Rd Ste 200 Blue Ash OH 45242 715-445-4612 457-5
TF: 877-860-9145 ■ *Web:* www.printmag.com

Print NW 9914 32nd Ave S Lakewood WA 98499 253-284-2300 627
TF: 800-826-8260 ■ *Web:* printnw.rocks

Print PAC 1001 G St NW Ste 800 Washington DC 20001 202-627-6924 730-7987 615
Web: www.printpaconline.org

Print Papa 1920 Lafayette St Ste L Santa Clara CA 95050 408-567-9553 567-9554 627
TF: 800-657-7181 ■ *Web:* printpapa.com

Print Resources Inc
1500 E Riverside Dr Indianapolis IN 46202 317-833-7000 41
Web: printindy.com

Print Services & Distribution Assn (PSDA)
330 N Wabash Ave Ste 2000 Chicago IL 60611 800-230-0175 48-9
TF: 800-230-0175 ■ *Web:* www.psda.org

Print Source Inc, The 404 S Tracy St Wichita KS 67209 316-945-7052 687
TF: 800-535-9498 ■ *Web:* www.theprintsourceinc.com

Print Tech LLC 49 Fadem Rd Springfield NJ 07081 908-232-2287 627
Web: print-tech.com

Print Time 1105 W 24th Kansas City MO 64108 816-756-3900 756-2982 627
Web: www.printtime.com

Print Turnaround Inc
3025 Malmo Dr Arlington Heights IL 60005 847-228-1762 627
Web: www.printturnaround.com

Printco Graphics Inc
14112 Industrial Rd Omaha NE 68144 402-593-1080 225
TF: 888-593-1080 ■ *Web:* www.printcographics.com

Printco Inc 1434 Progress Ln Omro WI 54963 920-685-5662 541-5967* 627
**Fax Area Code:* 800 ■ *Web:* www.printco.com

Printed Circuits Assembly Corp
13221 SE 26th St Ste E Bellevue WA 98005 425-644-7754 644-6430 625
Web: www.pcacorporation.com

Printed Image, The 41 S Grant Ave Columbus OH 43215 614-221-1412 627
Web: printedimage.com

Printed Matter Inc 231 11th Ave New York NY 10001 212-925-0325 95
Web: www.printedmatter.org

Phone | Fax | Class

Printed Systems 1265 Gillingham Rd Neenah WI 54956 800-352-2332 321-8247* 413
**Fax Area Code:* 888 ■ *TF:* 800-352-2332 ■ *Web:* www.psdtag.com

PrintEdd Products Ltd
2641 Forum Dr Grand Prairie TX 75052 972-660-3800 641-2564 110
TF: 800-367-6728 ■ *Web:* www.printedd.com

Printek Inc 1517 Townline Rd Benton Harbor MI 49022 269-925-3200 925-8539 173-6
TF: 800-368-4636 ■ *Web:* www.printek.com

Printer Inc, The
1220 Thomas Beck Rd Des Moines IA 50315 515-288-7241 288-9234 627
Web: www.the-printer.com

Printers & Stationers Inc
113 N Court St Florence AL 35630 256-764-8061 764-5024 535
TF: 800-624-5334 ■ *Web:* printersandstationers.com

Printfection LLC
3700 Quebec St Unit 100-136 Denver CO 80207 866-459-7990 195
TF: 866-459-7990 ■ *Web:* www.printfection.com

Printify 814 Mission St San Francisco CA 94103 415-992-7720 39
Web: printify.com

Printing Arts Press
8028 Newark Rd Mount Vernon OH 43050 740-397-6106 627
TF: 866-998-9575 ■ *Web:* www.printingartspress.com

Printing Co, The
112 S Broadview St Cape Girardeau MO 63703 573-651-3377 627
Web: capeprinting.com

Printing House Ltd, The
1403 Bathurst St Toronto ON M5R3H8 416-536-6113 344
TF: 800-874-0870 ■ *Web:* www.tph.ca

Printing Industries of America/Graphic Arts Technical Foundation (PIA/GATF)
200 Deer Run Rd Sewickley PA 15143 412-741-6860 741-2311 49-16
TF: 800-910-4283 ■ *Web:* www.printing.org

Printing Industry Midwest (PIM)
1300 Godward St NE Ste 2650 Minneapolis MN 55413 612-400-6200 139
Web: www.pimw.org

Printing Partners Inc
929 W 16th St Indianapolis IN 46202 317-635-2282 627
Web: www.printingpartners.net

Printing Port Inc
150 April Gray Ln Myrtle Beach SC 29579 843-236-1225 236-8612 627
Web: www.theprintingport.com

PrintingForLesscom Inc 100 PFL Way Livingston MT 59047 800-930-6040 627
TF: 800-930-6040 ■ *Web:* www.printingforless.com

Printmail Systems Inc 23 Friends Ln Newtown PA 18940 215-860-4250 225
TF: 800-910-4844 ■ *Web:* www.printmailsolutions.com

Print-O-Stat Inc 1011 W Market St York PA 17404 717-854-7821 846-4084 727
TF: 800-711-8014 ■ *Web:* www.printostat.com

Print-O-Tape Inc 755 Tower Rd Mundelein IL 60060 847-362-1476 949-7449 413
TF: 800-346-6311 ■ *Web:* www.printotape.com

Printpack Inc 2800 Overlook Pkwy NE Atlanta GA 30339 404-460-7000 548
Web: www.printpack.com

PrintPlace.com LLC 1130 Ave H E Arlington TX 76011 817-701-3555 627
Web: www.printplace.com

Printpoint Printing Inc
150 S Patterson Blvd Dayton OH 45402 937-223-9041 627
Web: www.printpointprinting.com

Printronix Inc 6440 Oak Canyon Ste 200 Irvine CA 92618 714-368-2300 368-2600 173-6
TF: 800-665-6210 ■ *Web:* www.printronix.com

Printscape Inc
700 Vista Park Dr Ste 7 Pittsburgh PA 15205 412-788-0640 627
Web: myprintscape.com

Printsouth Printing Inc
1114 Silstar Rd West Columbia SC 29170 803-796-2619 796-2744 627
Web: www.myprintsouth.com

Printswell Inc 135 Cahaba Valley Pkwy Pelham AL 35124 800-476-4723 627
TF: 800-476-4723 ■ *Web:* www.printswell.com

Printware LLC 2935 Waters Rd Ste 160 Eagan MN 55121 651-456-1400 629
TF: 800-456-1400 ■ *Web:* www.printwareinc.com

Prinzo Group, The
12600 Deerfield Pkwy Ste 100 Alpharetta GA 30004 678-883-5340 466
Web: www.prinzogroup.com

Prior Aviation Service Inc
50 N Airport Dr Buffalo NY 14225 716-633-1000 633-1432 63
Web: www.prioraviation.com

Prior Lake-Savage Area Public School District 719
4540 Tower St SE Prior Lake MN 55372 952-226-0000 226-0049 685
TF: 855-346-1650 ■ *Web:* www.priorlake-savage.k12.mn.us

Priority 1 Consulting 42 Fairview Ln Plymouth MA 02360 508-224-5128 445

Priority Business Services Inc
19712 MacArthur Blvd Ste 110 Irvine CA 92612 949-222-1122 222-2827 260
TF: 800-710-8775 ■ *Web:* prioritystaffing.biz

Priority Capital Inc 174 Green St Melrose MA 02176 800-761-2118 321-4108* 216
**Fax Area Code:* 781 ■ *TF:* 800-761-2118 ■ *Web:* prioritycapital.com

Priority Chevrolet
1495 S Military Hwy Chesapeake VA 23320 757-424-1811 57
Web: www.priorityauto.com

Priority Designs Inc
100 S Hamilton Rd Columbus OH 43213 614-337-9979 337-9499 261
Web: www.prioritydesigns.com

Priority Distribution Inc (PDI)
330 Milltown Rd Ste C31 East Brunswick NJ 08816 732-234-1950 734-3751* 311
**Fax Area Code:* 877 ■ *Web:* www.prioritydistribution.com

Priority Envelope Inc
2920 NW Blvd Ste 160 Plymouth MN 55441 763-519-9190 519-9199 263
TF: 800-822-0523 ■ *Web:* www.priorityenv.com

Priority Express Courier
5 Chelsea Pkwy Boothwyn PA 19061 610-364-3300 546
TF: 800-526-4646 ■ *Web:* www.priorityexpress.com

Priority Health
1231 E Beltline NE Grand Rapids MI 49525 616-942-0954 942-0145 391-3
TF: 800-942-0954 ■ *Web:* www.priorityhealth.com

Priority Management Systems Inc
1595 Cliveden Ave Unit 7 Delta BC V3M6M2 604-214-7772 765
TF: 800-437-1032 ■ *Web:* www.prioritymanagement.com

Priority Plus Federal Credit Union
6 Lynam St Wilmington DE 19804 302-633-6480 219
Web: priorityplusfcu.org

Priority Staffing Solutions Inc
15 W 39th St Rm 500 New York NY 10018 212-213-2244 213-2255 260

	City	State	ZIP	Phone	Fax	Class
Priority Wire & Cable Inc PO Box 398 *TF:* 800-945-5542 ■ *Web:* www.prioritywire.com	North Little Rock	AR	72115	501-372-5444	372-3988	246
Priory Spirituality Ctr 500 College St NE *Web:* www.stplacid.org	Lacey	WA	98516	360-438-2595	438-9236	673
Priory, The 614 Pressley St *Web:* www.thepriory.com	Pittsburgh	PA	15212	412-231-3338		379
Pri-Pak Inc 2000 Schenley Pl *TF:* 800-274-7632 ■ *Web:* pripak.com	Greendale	IN	47025	800-274-7632		88
Prism Associates Inc 9747 Business Park Ave Ste 217 *Web:* callprism.com	San Diego	CA	92131	858-695-7099		366
Prism Career Institute 3 Executive Campus *TF:* 888-966-8146 ■ *Web:* www.prismcareerinstitute.edu	Cherry Hill	NJ	08002	888-966-8146		167-3
Prism Contractors & Engineers Inc 1568 Manufacture Dr *Web:* prismce.com	Williamsburg	VA	23185	757-874-5670		261
Prism Energy Services *Prism Consulting Inc* 1150 Hancock St Ste 400 *Web:* www.prismconsultinginc.com	Quincy	MA	02169	617-328-9896	328-0496	196
Prism Hotels & Resorts 14800 Landmark Blvd Ste 800 *TF:* 877-299-0519 ■ *Web:* prismhotels.com	Dallas	TX	75254	214-987-9300		379
Prism International Inc 1st Sanford Twr 312 W 1st St Ste 500 *TF:* 888-997-7476 ■ *Web:* www.prismdiversity.com	Sanford	FL	32771	407-324-5290	324-0148	194
Prism Maritime LLC 1416 Kelland Dr Ste B *Web:* prismmaritime.com	Chesapeake	VA	23320	757-460-8800		261
Prism Plastics Products Inc Hwy 65 PO Box 446 *TF:* 877-246-7535 ■ *Web:* www.prismplasticsinc.com	New Richmond	WI	54017	715-246-7535	246-5661	608
Prism Pointe Technologies LLC 1950 Sullivan Rd **Fax Area Code:* 678 ■ *TF:* 866-323-4146	College Park	GA	30337	866-323-4146	610-4950*	175
Prism Systems Inc 200 Virginia St *Web:* prismsystems.com	Mobile	AL	36603	251-341-1140		177
Prism Visual Software Inc 1 Sagamore Hl Dr Ste 2B *TF:* 800-260-2793 ■ *Web:* www.prismvs.com	Port Washington	NY	11050	516-944-5920		225
Prisma Graphic Corp 2937 E Broadway Rd *TF:* 800-379-5777 ■ *Web:* www.prismagraphic.com	Phoenix	AZ	85040	602-243-5777	268-4804	627
Prismaflex Inc 1645 Queens Way E *Web:* www.prismaflex.com	Mississauga	ON	L4X3A3	905-279-9793	279-1330	701
Prismatic Development Inc 60 Rt 46 *Web:* www.prisdev.com	Fairfield	NJ	07004	973-882-1133		186
PrismOne Group Inc 37 N Boyd St Ste 100 *Web:* www.prismone.com	Winter Garden	FL	34787	321-293-1000	293-1001	2
Prison Enterprises 504 Mayflower St PO Box 94304 *Web:* doc.louisiana.gov	Baton Rouge	LA	70802	225-342-6633	342-5556	630
Prison Rehabilitative Industries & Diversified Enterprises Inc (PRIDE) 223 Morrison Rd *Web:* www.pride-enterprises.org	Brandon	FL	33511	813-324-8700	890-2132	630
Pristech Products Inc 6952 Fairgrounds Pkwy Ste 107 *TF:* 800-432-8722 ■ *Web:* www.pristech.com	San Antonio	TX	78238	210-520-8051	509-7463	172
Pristine Engineers Inc 534 New State Hwy Ste 5 *Web:* pristineengineers.com	Raynham	MA	02767	508-977-9353		261
Pritchard & Jerden Inc 950 E Paces Ferry NE Ste 2000 *Web:* pjins.com	Atlanta	GA	30305	404-238-9090	261-5440	390
Pritchard Bieler Gruver & Willison PC 590 Bethlehem Pk Ste A *Web:* www.pbgw.com	Colmar	PA	18915	215-997-6700	997-7208	2
Pritchard Electric Company Inc 2425 Eigth Ave *Web:* www.pritchardelectric.com	Huntington	WV	25703	304-529-2566	529-2567	189-4
Pritchard Management Associates Inc 517 Wilson Pl Ste 1000 *Web:* carlpritchard.com	Frederick	MD	21702	301-662-7877		463
Pritchett and Hull Associates Inc 3440 Oakcliff Rd Ste 110 *TF:* 800-241-4925 ■ *Web:* www.p-h.com	Atlanta	GA	30340	770-451-0602	454-7130	637-2
Pritchett Ball & Wise Inc 2295 Parklake Dr Ste 425 *Web:* pbwatlanta.com	Atlanta	GA	30345	404-874-4499		41
Pritchett Controls Inc 6980 Muirkirk Meadows Dr *TF:* 877-743-2363 ■ *Web:* www.pritchettcontrols.com	Beltsville	MD	20705	301-470-7300		189-10
Pritchett LLC 8150 N Central Expy Ste 1350 *TF:* 800-992-5922 ■ *Web:* www.pritchettnet.com	Dallas	TX	75206	214-239-9600	239-9650	194
Pritchett Technology Inc 929 Dalton St *Web:* www.pritchetttechnology.com	Ellijay	GA	30540	706-635-7745	635-7716	529
Pritchett Trucking Inc 1050 SE 6th St PO Box 311 *TF:* 800-486-7504	Lake Butler	FL	32054	386-496-2630	496-2883	780
Pritikin Longevity Center & Spa 8755 NW 36th St *TF:* 800-327-4914 ■ *Web:* www.pritikin.com	Doral	FL	33178	888-254-1462		706
Pritzker Hageman PA 45 S Seventh St Plaza VII Ste 2950 *Web:* pritzkerlaw.com	Minneapolis	MN	55402	612-338-0202		41
Pritzlaff Wholesale Meats Inc 17025 W Glendale Dr *TF:* 866-290-0507 ■ *Web:* www.pritzlaffmeats.com	New Berlin	WI	53151	262-786-1151		297-9
Privacy Journal PO Box 28577 *Web:* www.privacyjournal.net	Providence	RI	02908	401-274-7861	274-4747	637-9
Privacy Rights Clearinghouse 3100 Fifth Ave Ste B *TF:* 800-269-0271 ■ *Web:* www.privacyrights.org	San Diego	CA	92103	619-298-3396	298-5681	48-10
Privacy Times Inc PO Box 302 *Web:* www.privacytimes.com	Cabin John	MD	20818	301-229-7002	229-8011	637-10
Private Capital Management 8889 Pelican Bay Blvd Ste 500 *TF:* 800-763-0337 ■ *Web:* www.private-cap.com	Naples	FL	34108	239-254-2500		792
Private Citizen Inc PO Box 233 *Web:* www.private-citizen.com	Naperville	IL	60566	630-393-2370		48-10
Private Client Resources LLC 187 Danbury Rd *Web:* www.pcrinsights.com	Wilton	CT	06897	203-885-3114		463
Private Club Assoc 2750 Holcomb Bridge Rd Ste 220 **Fax Area Code:* 478 ■ *Web:* www.privateclubassociates.com	Alpharetta	GA	30022	678-585-9120	741-6743*	463
Private Export Funding Corp 280 Park Ave 4th Fl *Web:* pefco.com	New York	NY	10017	212-916-0300	286-0304	216
Private Eyes Inc 2700 Ygnacio Valley Rd Ste 100 *TF:* 877-292-3331 ■ *Web:* www.privateeyesinc.com	Walnut Creek	CA	94598	925-927-3333	927-3330	400
Private Label Manufacturers Assn (PLMA) 630 Third Ave *Web:* plma.com	New York	NY	10017	212-972-3131	983-1382	49-18
Private Lodging Service 1978 Coltman Rd *Web:* privatelodgings.com	Cleveland	OH	44106	216-291-1209		376
Private Party Consignments 11344 I-10 E	Baytown	TX	77520	281-303-3000		366
Privateer Publications PO Box 29427 *TF:* 888-700-4333 ■ *Web:* www.privateerpublications.com	San Antonio	TX	78229	210-308-8191		637-2
Prive Jets LLC 1250 E Hallandale Beach Blvd Ste 505 *Web:* privejets.com	Hallandale Beach	FL	33009	305-917-1600		23
Privilege International Inc 2419 Firestone Blvd *Web:* www.privilegeinc.com	South Gate	CA	90280	323-585-0777		321
Priviti Capital Corp 850 444 5th Ave S W *TF:* 855-333-9943 ■ *Web:* www.priviticapital.com	Calgary	AB	T2P2T8	403-263-9943	265-1134	528
Privy 201 S St 2nd Fl *Web:* www.privy.com	Boston	MA	02111	617-852-5292		737
Prizm LLC 10 E Stow Rd Ste 100 *Web:* www.prizmllc.com	Marlton	NJ	08053	856-596-5600		463
Prizm Medical Inc 3400 Corporate Way Ste I *Web:* www.prizm-medical.com	Duluth	GA	30096	770-622-0933		476
PRL Aluminum 14760 Don Julian Rd *TF:* 877-775-2586 ■ *Web:* www.prlglass.com	City of Industry	CA	91746	877-775-2586		492
PRLA (Pennsylvania Restaurant and Lodging Assn) 100 State St *TF:* 800-345-5353 ■ *Web:* www.prla.org	Harrisburg	PA	17101	717-232-4433	236-1202	49-19
PRN Computer Systems Inc 16435 SW Second Dr *Web:* prncomp.com	Pembroke Pines	FL	33027	954-431-5071		809
PRN Health Services Inc 4321 W College Ave Ste 200 *TF:* 888-830-8811 ■ *Web:* www.prnhealthservices.com	Appleton	WI	54914	888-830-8811		260
PRN Medical Services LLC 2311 W Utopia Rd *Web:* www.symbiusmedical.com	Phoenix	AZ	85027	623-780-8686		475
Pro Athlete Inc 10800 N Pomona Ave *Web:* www.proathleteinc.com	Kansas City	MO	64153	816-587-6050		791
Pro Bono Partnership 237 Mamaroneck Ave Ste 300 *Web:* www.probonopartner.org	White Plains	NY	10605	914-328-0674		428
PRO Building Systems Inc 3678 N Peachtree Rd *Web:* probldgsystems.com	Atlanta	GA	30341	770-455-1791		186
Pro Care Horticultural Services 9801 Commerce Dr *Web:* procarelandscapers.com	Carmel	IN	46032	317-872-4800		422
Pro Careers Inc 5051 Washington St W *TF:* 800-992-0566 ■ *Web:* procareersinc.com	Cross Lanes	WV	25313	800-992-0566		363
Pro Cat Testing LLC 30844 Century Dr *Web:* www.procat-testing.com	Wixom	MI	48393	248-926-8200	926-8300	247
Pro Clear Aquatic Systems Inc 2959 Mercury Rd *Web:* www.pro-clear.com	Jacksonville	FL	32207	904-448-6800		520
Pro Comm Inc 6403 W Pierson Rd *Web:* www.procomminc.net	Flushing	MI	48433	810-659-5000		736
Pro Comp 2360 Boswell Rd *Web:* www.procompusa.com	Chula Vista	CA	91914	619-216-1444		454
Pro Computer Service 304 Harper Dr Ste 130 *TF:* 877-596-4446 ■ *Web:* www.helpmepcs.com	Moorestown	NJ	08057	856-596-4446		624
Pro Controls Inc 1312 Gordon Rd Ste1 *TF:* 800-488-3386 ■ *Web:* www.proctrl.com	Yakima	WA	98901	509-457-3386	457-3491	203
Pro Copy 5219 E Fowler Ave *Web:* www.pro-copy.com	Tampa	FL	33617	813-988-5900		627
PRO EM - Party Concepts 4691 S Butterfield Dr *Web:* proem.org	Tucson	AZ	85714	520-750-0550	750-0060	129
Pro Equipment Company Inc PO Box 441 *TF:* 800-544-7767 ■ *Web:* www.procarwashequipment.com	Benton	KY	42025	270-527-1366		806
Pro Fabrication Inc 201 First St *Web:* www.pro-fabrication.com	Madison Lake	MN	56063	507-243-3441		697
Pro Football Hall of Fame 2121 George Halas Dr NW *Web:* www.profootballhof.com	Canton	OH	44708	330-456-8207	456-8175	522
Pro Hockey Life Sporting Goods Inc 4440 Autoroute 440 *Web:* prohockeylife.com	Laval	QC	H7T2P7	450-681-8440	681-1144	711

Company	Phone	Fax	Class
Pro HR Plus 724 Garland - State and Cantrell PO Box 1300 ... Little Rock AR 72203 *Fax Area Code:* 501 ■ *TF:* 877-621-3247 ■ *Web:* www.prohrplus.com	877-621-3247	537-0542*	2
Pro Image Sports 233 N 1250 W Ste 200 ... Centerville UT 84014 *Web:* proimagesports.com	801-296-9999		157-5
Pro Lights & Staging News (PLSN) 6000 S Eastern Ste 14-J ... Las Vegas NV 89119 *Web:* www.plsn.com	702-932-5585	932-5584	457-21
Pro Lingua Associates Inc (PLA) PO Box 1348 ... Brattleboro VT 05302 *TF:* 800-366-4775 ■ *Web:* www.prolinguaassociates.com	802-257-7779	257-5117	637-2
Pro Lingua Press (PLP) PO Box 24368 ... Los Angeles CA 90024 *Web:* www.prolinguapress.com	310-472-8396	472-0770	637-2
Pro Mark Graphics 861 Winnebago Ave ... Olmsted IL 62970 *Web:* www.pro-mark.com	618-742-6430		344
Pro Motion Inc 18405 Edison Ave ... Chesterfield MO 63005 *Web:* promotion1.com	636-449-3162		636
Pro Mujer Inc 253 W 35th St 11th Fl ... New York NY 10001 *Web:* promujer.org	646-626-7000		403
Pro Net Communications Inc 1152 Mainland St Ste 230 ... Vancouver BC V6B5L1 *Web:* www.pro.net	604-606-0660	606-0661	225
Pro Orthopedic Devices Inc 2884 E Ganley Rd ... Tucson AZ 85706 *TF:* 800-523-5611 ■ *Web:* www.proorthopedic.com	520-294-4401		477
Pro Pac Labs Inc 3804 Airport Rd ... Ogden UT 84405 *Web:* www.globalhealthindustries.com	801-621-0900	621-0930	582
Pro Park America Inc 1 Union Pl ... Hartford CT 06103 *Web:* www.propark.com	860-527-2378		192
Pro Pay LLC 7450 W 130th St Ste 220 ... Overland Park KS 66213	913-826-6300	492-9171	2
Pro Petroleum Inc 4985 N Sloan Ln ... Las Vegas NV 89115 *TF:* 877-791-4900 ■ *Web:* www.propetroleum.com	877-791-4900		579
Pro Printing & Graphics Inc 2719 Halligan Dr ... North Platte NE 69101 *Web:* www.proprintingandgraphics.com	308-532-1111		627
Pro Products LLC 7201 Engle Rd ... Fort Wayne IN 46804 *TF:* 800-357-5063 ■ *Web:* proproducts.com	260-483-2519		806
Pro Sales Inc 917 Valley Ave NW Ste C ... Puyallup WA 98371 *Web:* www.prosalesinc.com	253-852-6046	852-6067	523
Pro Security Group 541 N Valley Mills Dr ... Waco TX 76710 *TF:* 855-753-7766 ■ *Web:* prosecuritygroup.com	254-753-7766		693
Pro Staff Personnel Services 2999 W County Rd 42 Ste 220 ... Burnsville MN 55306 *Web:* www.prostaff.com	952-892-3240		721
Pro Staff Sales Inc 1840 Old Norcross Rd Ste 100 ... Lawrenceville GA 30044 *Web:* prostaffsales.com	678-407-0382	407-0386	260
Pro Star Aviation LLC 5 Industrial Dr ... Londonderry NH 03053 *Web:* prostaraviation.com	603-627-7827		261
Pro Tapes & Specialties Inc 621 Rte One S ... North Brunswick NJ 08902 *TF:* 800-345-0234 ■ *Web:* www.protapes.com	732-346-0900	729-7373	732
Pro Tec Equipment Inc 4837 W Grand River Ave ... Charlotte MI 48813 *Fax Area Code:* 517 ■ *TF:* 800-292-1225 ■ *Web:* www.pro-tecequipment.com	800-292-1225	827-3263*	190
Pro Tech Products Inc 3003 N 73rd St ... Scottsdale AZ 85251 *Web:* www.pro-techproducts.com	480-945-7303	945-8873	188-3
Pro Unlimited Inc 301 Yamato Rd Ste 3199 ... Boca Raton FL 33431 *TF:* 800-291-1099 ■ *Web:* prounlimited.com	800-291-1099		734
Pro Way Hair School 5684 Memorial Dr ... Stone Mountain GA 30083 *Web:* www.prowayhairschool.com	404-299-5156	299-5159	685
Proa Medical Inc 2512 Artesia Blvd Ste 305-C ... Redondo Beach CA 90278 *Fax Area Code:* 888 ■ *TF:* 800-899-3385 ■ *Web:* www.proamedical.com	800-899-3385	395-9288*	475
Proactive Business Solutions Inc 428 13th St 5th Fl ... Oakland CA 94612 *Web:* www.proactiveok.com	510-302-0120		463
Proactive Communications Inc 100 E Whitestone Blvd Ste 148-303 ... Cedar Park TX 76542	254-699-0067		194
Proactive Diagnostics 2235 Faraday Ave Ste O ... Carlsbad CA 92008 *Web:* www.pro-dx.com	805-405-4620		111
Proactive Management Consulting LLC 2700 Cumberland Pkwy SE ... Atlanta GA 30339 *TF:* 877-319-2198 ■ *Web:* proactive-management.com	770-319-7468		196
Proactive Networking 9240 NW 63rd St Ste 6 ... Platte City MO 64152	816-587-7878		180
Proactive Performance Solution 560 Peoples Plz 139 ... Newark DE 19702 *Web:* www.proactiveusa.com	302-375-0451	375-0452	809
Proactive Sports Inc 1200 SE 2nd Ave ... Canby OR 97013 *TF:* 800-369-8642 ■ *Web:* www.proactivesports.com	503-263-8583		711
Proair LLC 28731 County Rd 6 ... Elkhart IN 46514 *TF:* 800-338-8544 ■ *Web:* www.proairllc.com	574-264-5494	264-2194	14
Pro-Am Safety Inc 551 Keystone Dr ... Warrendale PA 15086 *TF:* 800-351-2477 ■ *Web:* www.proamsafety.com	800-351-2477		178-1
ProAssurance Mid-Continent Underwriters Inc 2 Riverway Ste 750 ... Houston TX 77056 *Fax Area Code:* 877 ■ *Web:* www.proassurancemidcontinent.com	713-965-6900	405-5211*	796
Probing Solutions Inc 78 Rattler Way Ste B ... Carson City NV 89706 *Web:* www.probingsolutions.com	775-246-0999	246-0480	248
Prob-Test Inc 364 W Tullock St ... Rialto CA 92376 *Web:* www.probtest.com	909-421-4444	421-4440	425
Procacci Bros Sales Corp 3333 S Front St ... Philadelphia PA 19148 *Web:* www.procaccibrothers.com	215-463-8000		297-7
Procaccianti Group, The 1140 Reservoir Ave ... Cranston RI 02920 *Web:* www.procaccianti.com	401-946-4600		379
Pro-cad Software Ltd 12 Elbow River Rd ... Calgary AB T3Z2V2 *TF:* 888-477-6223 ■ *Web:* www.procad.com	403-216-3375		177
Procal Innovations LLC PO Box 115 ... Alpena MI 49707 *TF:* 800-323-0966 ■ *Web:* www.pcimfg.com	989-358-7070	358-7075	173-2
ProCamps Inc 4600 McAuley Pl 4th Fl ... Cincinnati OH 45242 *Web:* www.procamps.com	513-793-2267		239
ProCare Medical Associates LLC 776 Northfield Ave ... West Orange NJ 07052 *Web:* www.drkelly.us	973-736-1939		352
ProCare Rx 1267 Professional Pkwy ... Gainesville GA 30507 *TF:* 800-377-1037 ■ *Web:* www.procarerx.com	800-377-1037		809
ProCare Vision Center Inc 1955 Newark-Granville Rd ... Granville OH 43023 *Web:* www.procarevisioncenters.com	740-587-3937	587-3589	543
Procase Consulting 180 Caster Ave Unit 55 ... Woodbridge ON L4L5Y7 *Web:* www.procaseconsulting.com	905-856-7479		180
Procedyne Corp 11 Industrial Dr ... New Brunswick NJ 08901 *Web:* www.procedyne.com	732-249-8347	249-7220	318
Procel Temporary Services 2447 Pacific Coast Hwy Ste 207 ... Hermosa Beach CA 90254 *TF:* 800-338-9905 ■ *Web:* www.procelnurses.com	310-372-0560		260
Process Combustion Corp 300 Weyman Rd Ste 400 ... Pittsburgh PA 15236 *Web:* www.pcc-group.com	412-655-0955	650-5569	318
Process Construction Inc 1421 Queen City Ave ... Cincinnati OH 45214 *Web:* www.processconstruction.com	513-251-2211		189-10
Process Control Corp 6875 Mimms Dr ... Atlanta GA 30340 *Web:* www.process-control.com	770-449-8810		111
Process Data Control Corp 1803-A W Park Row Dr ... Arlington TX 76013 *Web:* www.pdccorp.com	817-459-4488		180
Process Development & Control Inc 1075 Montour W Industrial Pk ... Coraopolis PA 15108 *Web:* www.pdcvalve.com	724-695-3440		350
Process Displays 7108 31st Ave N ... Minneapolis MN 55427 *TF:* 800-233-5012 ■ *Web:* pdinstore.com	763-541-1245		627
Process Engineering Corp PO Box 279 ... Crystal Lake IL 60039 *Web:* www.pecfrictionfighters.com	815-459-1734	459-3676	127
Process Equipment & Service Company Inc 5680 Hwy 64 ... Farmington NM 87401 *Web:* www.pescoinc.biz	505-327-2222	327-7550	91
Process Equipment Co 6555 S SR-202 ... Tipp City OH 45371 *Web:* www.peco-us.com	937-667-4451	667-9322	454
Process Equipment Inc 2770 Welborn St PO Box 1607 ... Pelham AL 35124 *TF:* 888-663-2028 ■ *Web:* processbarron.com	205-663-5330	663-6037	18
Process Innovations Inc 4219 King Graves Rd ... Vienna OH 44473 *Web:* www.processinnovations-ohio.com	330-856-5192		386
Process Iv Inc 7209 Chagrin Falls Rd Ste D ... Chagrin Falls OH 44023 *Web:* process4.com	440-247-4452		261
Process Materials Inc 5625 Brisa St Ste B ... Livermore CA 94550 *Web:* processmaterials.com	925-245-9626	245-9629	567
Process Screw Products Inc 10 N Shannon Rte ... Shannon IL 61078 *Web:* www.processscrewproducts.com	815-864-2220	864-2254	621
Process Sensors Corp 113 Cedar St ... Milford MA 01757 *Web:* www.processsensors.com	508-473-9901		492
Process Software Corp 959 Concord St ... Framingham MA 01701 *TF:* 800-722-7770 ■ *Web:* www.process.com	508-879-6994	879-0042	178-12
Process Technology 7010 Lindsay Dr ... Mentor OH 44060 *Web:* www.process-technology.com	440-974-1300		14
Processed Metals Innovators LLC 600 21st Ave ... Bloomer WI 54724 *TF:* 888-877-7277 ■ *Web:* www.pmillc.com	715-568-1700		480
Processed World 1310 Mission St ... San Francisco CA 94103 *Web:* www.processedworld.com	415-626-2060		637-9
ProcessMAP 13450 W Sunrise Blvd Ste 160 ... Sunrise FL 33323 *Web:* www.processmap.com	954-515-5040	846-1233	177
Processmodel Inc 10602 S Cvered Bridge Cyn ... Spanish Fork UT 84660 *Web:* www.processmodel.com	801-356-7165		809
Prochem Inc 5100 Enterprise Dr ... Elliston VA 24087 *TF:* 800-290-2295 ■ *Web:* www.prochemwater.com	540-268-9884	268-9874	806
Proco Machinery 1111 Brevik Pl ... Mississauga ON L4W3R7 *Web:* procomachinery.com	905-602-6066		111
Proco Products Inc PO Box 590 ... Stockton CA 95201 *TF:* 800-344-3246 ■ *Web:* www.procoproducts.com	209-943-6088	943-0242	676
ProCo Sound Inc 5278 Lovers Ln ... Portage MI 49002 *Fax Area Code:* 269 ■ *TF:* 800-253-7360 ■ *Web:* www.procosound.com	800-253-7360	388-9681*	492
ProCom Inc 28838 US Hwy 69 E PO Box 27 ... Lamoni IA 50140 *Web:* www.procom-inc.com	641-784-8841		737
ProComp Software Consultants Inc 4629 Aicholtz Rd ... Cincinnati OH 45244 *TF:* 800-783-1668 ■ *Web:* www.procompsoftware.com	513-685-5245	685-5293	179
Procon Consulting LLC 1005 N Glebe Rd Ste 325 ... Arlington VA 22201 *Web:* www.proconconsulting.com	703-527-7059		196
Procon Engineering Inc 7240 SW 39 Ter ... Miami FL 33155 *Web:* proconengineers.net	305-262-7630	266-7798	261
Procon Products 869 7 Oaks Blvd Ste 120 ... Smyrna TN 37167 *Web:* www.proconpumps.com	615-355-8000	355-8001	641
Proconex Management Group Inc 103 Enterprise Dr ... Royersford PA 19468 *Web:* www.proconexdirect.com	610-495-1835		358
Procopio Cory Hargreaves & Savitch LLP 525 B St Ste 2200 ... San Diego CA 92101 *Web:* www.procopio.com	619-238-1900	235-0398	428
Procor Ltd 2001 Speers Rd ... Oakville ON L6L2X9 *Web:* www.procor.com	905-827-4111		264-5

Company	Phone	Fax	Class
Procter & Gamble Co, The 1 Procter & Gamble Plz .... Cincinnati OH 45202 *NYSE:* PG ■ *Web:* us.pg.com	513-983-1100		214
Proctor Academy 204 Main St PO Box 500 .... Andover NH 03216 *Web:* www.proctoracademy.org	603-735-6000		622
Proctor Engineering Group Ltd 418 Mission Ave. .... San Rafael CA 94901 *TF:* 888-455-5742 ■ *Web:* www.proctoreng.com	415-451-2480		261
Proctor Gas Inc 2 Market St .... Proctor VT 05765 *Web:* proctorgas.com	802-459-3340		316
Proctor Journal 215 E Fifth St. .... Proctor MN 55810 *Web:* www.proctorjournal.com	218-624-3344		532-4
Proctor Sales Inc 20715 50th Ave W .... Lynnwood WA 98036 *Web:* www.proctorsales.com	425-774-1441		612
Proctor Speedway 800 N Boundary Ave. .... Proctor MN 55810 *Web:* www.halvorlinesspeedway.com	218-624-0606		515
Proctor's Theatre 432 State St .... Schenectady NY 12305 *Web:* www.proctors.org	518-382-3884	346-2468	572
Proctorio 6840 E Indian School Rd .... Scottsdale AZ 85251 *Web:* proctorio.com	480-428-4076		39
Procurity Inc 160 Eagle Dr .... Winnipeg MB R2R1V5	204-632-5506		238
Procurri LLC 5825 Peachtree Corners E Ste A .... Norcross GA 30092 *TF:* 866-687-1760 ■ *Web:* www.procurri.com	770-817-9092		196
Pro-data Computer Services Inc 2809 S 160th St Ste 401 .... Omaha NE 68130 *TF:* 800-228-6318 ■ *Web:* dodbu.com	402-697-7575		175
Prodata Systems Inc 11007 Slater Ave NE .... Kirkland WA 98033 *TF:* 866-582-7485 ■ *Web:* www.prodata.com	425-296-4168	822-3443	39
Prodco International Inc 9408 Boul du Golf .... Montreal QC H1J3A1 *TF:* 888-577-6326 ■ *Web:* www.prodcotech.com	514-324-9796		693
Prodeva Inc 100 Jerry Dr. .... Jackson Center OH 45334 *Web:* www.prodeva.com	937-596-6713	596-5145	207
Pro-Dex Inc 2361 McGaw Ave .... Irvine CA 92614 *NASDAQ:* PDEX ■ *TF:* 800-562-6204 ■ *Web:* www.pro-dex.com	800-562-6204		360-3
Prodigy Diabetes Care LLC 2701-A Hutchison McDonald Rd PO Box 481928 . Charlotte NC 28269 *TF:* 800-366-5901 ■ *Web:* www.prodigymeter.com	800-366-5901		476
Prodo Laboratories 27402 Aliso Viejo Pkwy .... Aliso Viejo CA 92656 *Web:* prodolabs.com	949-727-1972		41
Prodo-Pak Corp 77 Commerce St .... Garfield NJ 07026 *Web:* www.prodo-pak.com	973-772-4500	772-0471	547
Produce Junction Inc 2241 Bryn Mawr Ave .... Philadelphia PA 19131 *Web:* producejunction.com	215-477-5007	477-5032	297-7
Produce Marketing Assn (PMA) 1500 Casho Mill Rd .... Newark DE 19711 *Web:* www.pma.com	302-738-7100	731-2409	49-6
Produce Source Partners 13167 Telcourt Rd. .... Ashland VA 23005 *TF:* 800-344-4728 ■ *Web:* producesourcepartners.com	804-262-8300		297-7
Producers Co-opeartive Assoc 300 E Buffalo St .... Girard KS 66743 *TF:* 800-442-2809 ■ *Web:* www.girardcoop.com	620-724-8241		447
Producers Dairy Foods Inc 250 E Belmont Ave .... Fresno CA 93701 *Web:* www.producersdairy.com	559-264-6583		296-27
Producers Financial 5350 Tomah Dr Ste 3800 .... Colorado Springs CO 80918 *TF:* 800-985-5549 ■ *Web:* www.pfnco.com	719-535-0739		401
Producers Library Service 10832 Chandler Blvd .... North Hollywood CA 91601 *TF:* 800-944-2135 ■ *Web:* www.producerslibrary.com	818-752-9097	752-9196	434-3
Producers Livestock Auction Co 1131 N Bell St .... San Angelo TX 76903 *Web:* www.producersandcargile.com	325-653-3371	653-3370	446
Producers Livestock Marketing Assn 4809 S 114th St .... Omaha NE 68137 *TF:* 800-257-4046 ■ *Web:* producerslivestock.net	402-597-9189	597-9505	446
Producers Management Television Pmtv 681 Moore Rd Ste 100 .... King of Prussia PA 19406 *Web:* www.pmtv.com	610-768-1770		514
Producers Peanut Company Inc PO Box 250 .... Suffolk VA 23434 *TF:* 800-847-5491 ■ *Web:* www.producerspeanut.com	757-539-7496	934-7730	296-32
Producers Rice Mill Inc PO Box 1248 .... Stuttgart AR 72160 *TF:* 800-369-7675 ■ *Web:* www.producersrice.com	870-673-4444		296-23
Producers Service Corp 109 Graham St .... Zanesville OH 43701 *Web:* www.producersservicecorp.com	740-454-6253	454-0775	539
Product Development & Management Assn (PDMA) 330 N Wabash Ave Ste 2000. .... Chicago IL 60611 *TF:* 800-232-5241 ■ *Web:* www.pdma.org	312-321-5145		49-12
Product Development Consulting Inc 343 Commercial St Ste 309 .... Boston MA 02109 *Web:* pdcinc.com	617-723-1150		177
Product Development Corp 20 Ragsdale Dr Ste 100 .... Monterey CA 93940 **Fax Area Code:* 831 ■ *Web:* deliverphonebooks.com	209-383-6655	333-0110*	96
Product Development Technologies Inc (PDT) 1 Corporate Dr Ste 110. .... Lake Zurich IL 60047 *Web:* pdt.com	847-821-3033	821-3020	261
Product Distributors Inc 4200 Beach Dr Ste 2. .... Rapid City SD 57702 *Web:* www.forpd.com	605-341-6500		191-3
Product Evaluation Systems Inc 637 Donohoe Rd. .... Latrobe PA 15650 *Web:* www.productevaluationsystems.com	724-834-8848	834-9151	743
Product Liability Speciality LLC 16801 Addison Rd Ste 300. .... Addison TX 75001 *Web:* jordanjordaninsurance.com	972-398-6222		390
Product Manufacturing Inc 555 SW 2nd Ave. .... Canby OR 97013 *Web:* www.productmfg.com	503-266-6196	266-2340	454
Product Marketing Group Inc 978 Douglas Ave. .... Altamonte Springs FL 32714 *Web:* www.productmarketingfl.com	407-774-6363	774-6548	4
Product Miniature Co 627 Capitol Dr .... Pewaukee WI 53072 *Web:* www.pmplastic.com	262-691-1700		604
Product Packaging West Inc 11921 Vose St .... North Hollywood CA 91605 *Web:* www.productpackagingwest.com	818-765-8037	765-6387	393
Product Safety Consulting Inc (PSC) 605 Country Club Dr Ste I & J .... Bensenville IL 60106 *TF:* 877-804-3066 ■ *Web:* www.productsafetyinc.com	630-238-0188	238-0269	196
Product Safety Labs 2394 Hwy 130. .... Dayton NJ 08810 *Web:* www.productsafetylabs.com	732-438-5100	230-4209	743
Product Slingshot Inc 2221 Rutherford Rd .... Carlsbad CA 92008 *TF:* 800-549-5414 ■ *Web:* www.forecast3d.com	760-929-9380	929-9357	757
Productboard Inc 612 Howard St. .... San Francisco CA 94105 *TF:* 844-472-5273 ■ *Web:* www.productboard.com	844-472-5273		39
Production Automation Co 6200 Bury Dr .... Eden Prairie MN 55346 *TF:* 888-903-0333 ■ *Web:* www.gotopac.com	952-903-0333		57
Production Design Services Inc 401 Fame Rd .... Dayton OH 45449 *Web:* www.pdsicorp.com	937-866-3377	866-3437	386
Production Equipment Co 401 Liberty St. .... Meriden CT 06450 *TF:* 800-758-5697 ■ *Web:* productionequipmentcompany.com	800-758-5697	563-4150	470
Production Haus LLC, The 112 Renford Rd. .... Ball Ground GA 30107 *Web:* www.theproductionhaus.com	770-704-9248		4
Production Machining of Alma Inc 6595 N Jerome Rd .... Alma MI 48801 *Web:* www.productionmachining.net	989-463-1495	463-5924	454
Production Management Industries LLC 9761 Hwy 90 E .... Morgan City LA 70380 *TF:* 888-229-3837 ■ *Web:* www.pmi.net	985-631-3837	631-0729	539
Production Masters Inc 204 Fifth Ave. .... Pittsburgh PA 15222 *Web:* pmi.tv	412-281-8500		514
Production Pattern Co 560 Solon Rd .... Cleveland OH 44146	440-439-3243		567
Production Press Inc 307 E Morgan St. .... Jacksonville IL 62650 *TF:* 800-231-3880 ■ *Web:* www.productionpress.com	217-243-3353	245-0400	627
Production Products Co 6176 E Molloy Rd. .... East Syracuse NY 13057 *TF:* 800-800-6652 ■ *Web:* www.ppc-online.com	315-431-7200	431-7201	621
Production Ready Programming Inc 4200 E La Palma Ave .... Anaheim CA 92807 *Web:* www.prpca.com	714-528-5001	528-4421	177
Production Resource Group LLC 539 Temple Hill Rd .... New Windsor NY 12553 *TF:* 877-774-7088 ■ *Web:* www.prg.com	845-567-5700	567-5800	722
Production Systems Solutions Inc PO Box 700 .... Hurt VA 24563 *Web:* www.pss-inc.biz	434-324-7843	324-7099	203
Production Technologies Inc 7651 Washington Ave S .... Edina MN 55439 *Web:* www.ptimn.com	952-944-1076		253
Production Tool Supply 8655 E Eight Mile Rd .... Warren MI 48089 **Fax Area Code:* 586 ■ *TF:* 800-366-3600 ■ *Web:* www.pts-tools.com	800-366-3600	755-4921*	385
ProductionHUB Inc 1806 Hammerlin Ave .... Winter Park FL 32789 *Web:* www.productionhub.com	407-629-4122		530
Productions USA Inc 1960 N Lincoln Pk W .... Chicago IL 60614 *Web:* www.productionsusa.com	773-296-6200	296-6333	184
Productive Alternatives Inc 1205 N Tower Rd .... Fergus Falls MN 56537 *Web:* www.productivemn.org	218-998-5630	736-2541	230
Productive Plastics Inc 103 W Pk Dr. .... Mount Laurel NJ 08054 *Web:* www.productiveplastics.com	856-778-4300	234-3310	602
Productivity Apex Inc 11301 Corporate Blvd Ste 303 .... Orlando FL 32817 *Web:* www.productivityapex.com	407-384-0800		177
Productivity Inc 375 Bridgeport Ave 3rd Fl. .... Shelton CT 06484 *TF:* 800-966-5423 ■ *Web:* www.productivityinc.com	203-225-0451	225-0771	765
Productivity Point International Inc 2950 Gateway Center Blvd .... Morrisville NC 27560	919-379-5611		764
Products Engineering Corp 2645 Maricopa St. .... Torrance CA 90503 *TF:* 800-923-6255 ■ *Web:* pec.tools	310-787-4500	787-4501	493
Produits Alimentaires Berthelet Inc 1805 Berlier St .... Laval QC H7L3S4 *Web:* www.berthelet.com	514-334-5503	334-3584	296-37
ProEd Communications Inc 25101 Chagrin Blvd Ste 230. .... Beachwood OH 44122 *Web:* www.proedcom.com	216-595-7919		4
Pro-Ed Inc 8700 Shoal Creek Blvd. .... Austin TX 78757 **Fax Area Code:* 800 ■ *TF:* 800-897-3202 ■ *Web:* www.proedinc.com	512-451-3246	397-7633*	637-2
Pro-Ed Professional Education 3101 W 41st St Ste 212 .... Sioux Falls SD 57105 *TF:* 800-658-3959 ■ *Web:* www.southdakotarealestateeducation.com	605-331-4900	331-0111	167-3
Proenergy Services LLC 2001 ProEnergy Blvd .... Sedalia MO 65301 **Fax Area Code:* 660 ■ *TF:* 844-367-4948 ■ *Web:* www.proenergyservices.com	844-367-4948	829-1160*	463
Profab Electronics Inc 2855 W Mcnab Rd .... Pompano Beach FL 33069 *Web:* www.profabelectronics.com	954-917-1998		253
Pro-Fab Manufacturing Inc 45300 Industrial Pl Ste 5 .... Fremont CA 94538 *Web:* www.pfmfg.com	510-651-5570		454
Professional Aircraft Accessories Inc 7035 Center Ln. .... Titusville FL 32780 *Web:* www.gopaa.com	321-267-1040		529

Name / Address	City	State	ZIP	Phone	Fax	Class
Professional Bank Services Inc 6200 Dutchmans Ln Ste 305 *TF:* 800-523-4778 ■ *Web:* www.probank.com	Louisville	KY	40205	502-451-6633	451-6755	194
Professional Bartending School 2961 W Liberty Ave Ste 217 *Web:* www.pittsburghbartendingschool.com	Pittsburgh	PA	15216	412-344-9100		685
Professional Bartending School 2440 Wilson Blvd *Web:* www.bartending-school.com	Arlington	VA	22201	703-841-9700		685
Professional Beauty Assn (PBA) 15825 N 71st St Ste 100 *TF:* 800-468-2274 ■ *Web:* probeauty.org	Scottsdale	AZ	85254	480-281-0424	905-0708	49-18
Professional Books Inc 50 Conrad Dr Ste 105 **Fax Area Code:* 731 ■ *TF:* 800-241-8645 ■ *Web:* www.yeastconnection.com	Jackson	TN	38305	800-241-8645	660-5029*	637-2
Professional Bowlers Assn (PBA) 719 Second Ave Ste 701 *Web:* www.pba.com	Seattle	WA	98104	206-332-9688	654-6030	48-22
Professional Building Systems Inc 72 E Market St *TF:* 800-837-4552 ■ *Web:* www.pbsmodular.com	Middleburg	PA	17842	800-837-4552		106
Professional Bull Riders Inc (PBR) 101 W Riverwalk *TF:* 800-732-1727 ■ *Web:* www.pbr.com	Pueblo	CO	81003	719-242-2800		48-15
Professional Career Institute 9200 Arboretum Pky Ste 110 *Web:* www.procareerinstitute.org	Richmond	VA	23236	804-327-9740	327-9745	167-3
Professional Coaters Inc 100 Commerce Park Dr **Fax Area Code:* 501 ■ *TF:* 800-962-0344 ■ *Web:* www.procoatinc.com	Cabot	AR	72023	800-962-0344	843-9261*	818
Professional Communications Inc (PCI) 1223 W Main St Ste 1427 *TF:* 800-337-9838 ■ *Web:* pcibooks.com	Durant	OK	74702	580-745-9838	745-9837	637-2
Professional Computer Systems Co 3710 Timberline Dr *TF:* 888-843-3106 ■ *Web:* www.pcsco.com	Denison	IA	51442	712-263-3106	263-8145	177
Professional Contract Services Inc 718 W FM 1626 *Web:* www.pcsi.org	Austin	TX	78748	512-358-8887	358-8890	152
Professional Convention Management Assn (PCMA) 35 E Wacker Dr Ste 500 *TF:* 877-827-7262 ■ *Web:* www.pcma.org	Chicago	IL	60601	312-423-7262	423-7222	49-12
Professional Desk References Inc (PDR) 5543 Edmondson Pike Ste 183 *TF:* 888-335-7664 ■ *Web:* www.greenbookofsongs.com	Nashville	TN	37211	615-832-1942		637-2
Professional Drivers Academy 2300 Housels Run Rd PO Box 475 *TF:* 800-875-2511 ■ *Web:* www.pdacdl.com	Milton	PA	17847	570-523-3100	523-3114	167-3
Professional Electric Products Co (PEPCO) 33210 Lakeland Blvd **Fax Area Code:* 440 ■ *TF:* 800-872-7000 ■ *Web:* www.pepconet.com	Eastlake	OH	44095	800-872-7000	942-5883*	246
Professional Engineering Consultants PA 303 S Topeka St *Web:* www.pec1.com	Wichita	KS	67202	316-262-2691	262-3003	261
Professional Evaluation Group PC 380 S Broadway *Web:* www.pegexams.com	Hicksville	NY	11801	516-935-1730	931-3117	194
Professional Furniture Management Services (PFMS) 5101 LeTourneau Cir *Web:* www.pfms.org	Tampa	FL	33610	813-621-6700	973-9888	189-1
Professional Graphic Communications Inc 2260 Big Swckly Crk Rd *Web:* www.pgcinc.com	Sewickley	PA	15143	724-318-1222	318-1212	534
Professional Graphics Inc 25 Perry Ave *Web:* www.progi.net	Norwalk	CT	06850	203-846-4291	847-6396	174
Professional Group Plans Inc (PGP) 225 Wireless Blvd Ste 200 *Web:* www.pgpbenefits.com	Hauppauge	NY	11788	631-951-9200	951-9623	631
Professional Hair Design Academy 3408 Mall Dr *Web:* www.thesalonprofessionalacademy.com	Eau Claire	WI	54701	715-835-2345		167-3
Professional Healthcare Inc 3005 Village Park Dr Ste 101 *Web:* phicare.com	Knightdale	NC	27545	919-872-7999		363
Professional Healthcare Resources Inc 7619 Little River Tpke Ste 600 **Fax Area Code:* 866 ■ *TF:* 866-243-1234 ■ *Web:* www.phri.com	Annandale	VA	22003	703-379-9012	845-0762*	363
Professional Help Computer Services Inc 432 N Duncan Bypass Ste A *Web:* www.professionalhelp.com	Union	SC	29379	864-427-7334		179
Professional Imaging LLC 523 N Sam Houston Pky E Ste 125 **Fax Area Code:* 877 ■ *TF:* 866-676-6277 ■ *Web:* www.mbssonline.com	Houston	TX	77060	866-676-6277	675-6277*	352
Professional Implementation Consulting Services Inc (PICS) 46 High St *Web:* www.pics.com	Mount Holly	NJ	08060	609-702-3920		194
Professional Institute of Beauty 10801 Valley Mall *Web:* www.pib.edu	El Monte	CA	91731	626-443-9401	443-0401	167-3
Professional Instruments Co 7800 Powell Rd *Web:* www.airbearings.com	Hopkins	MN	55343	952-933-1222		75
Professional Insurance Marketing Assn (PIMA) 35 E Wacker Dr Ste 850 *Web:* www.pimainsights.org	Chicago	IL	60601	817-569-7462		49-9
Professional Janitorial Service of Houston Inc 2303 Nance St *Web:* www.pjs.com	Houston	TX	77020	713-850-0287	963-9420	152
Professional Landcare Network (PLANET) 950 Herndon Pkwy Ste 450 *TF:* 800-395-2522 ■ *Web:* www.landscapeprofessionals.org	Herndon	VA	20170	703-736-9666	736-9668	48-2
Professional Liability Underwriting Society 5353 Wayzata Blvd Ste 600 *TF:* 800-845-0778 ■ *Web:* www.plusweb.org	Minneapolis	MN	55416	952-746-2580	746-2599	49-9
Professional Machining Inc (PMI) 3840 SW 113th St *Web:* www.hepman.com	Oklahoma City	OK	73173	405-691-1215		60
Professional Maintenance Care 4912 Naples St *Web:* pmsjanitorial.com	San Diego	CA	92110	619-276-1150		104
Professional Marketing Insurance 115 W California Blvd Ste 434 *TF:* 866-558-6365 ■ *Web:* letterprinting.net	Pasadena	CA	91105	866-558-6365		390
Professional Medical 12545 Lake City Way *Web:* www.professionalmedicalcorp.com	Seattle	WA	98125	206-366-9544		475
Professional Mental Health Associates Burke Center Plz 9554 Old Keene Mill Rd Ste F *Web:* www.psychologicalevaluations.org	Burke	VA	22015	703-786-3703	425-7435	374-5
Professional Pharmacy & Convalescent Products Ltd 920 N Charlotte St *Web:* professionalpharmacy.com	Pottstown	PA	19464	610-323-2115		237
Professional Pharmacy of Oxford LLC 140 Roxboro Rd *Web:* professionalpharmacyoxford.com	Oxford	NC	27565	919-693-8555		237
Professional Photographers of America Inc (PPA) 229 Peachtree St NE Ste 2200 *TF:* 800-786-6277 ■ *Web:* www.ppa.com	Atlanta	GA	30303	404-522-8600	614-6400	48-4
Professional Placement Inc 3923 S McClintock Dr Ste 408 *Web:* www.proplacement.com	Tempe	AZ	85282	602-955-0870	955-0604	721
Professional Planning Services Inc 4809 Vue Du Lac Pl Ste 205 *Web:* 4ppsinc.com	Manhattan	KS	66503	785-776-9118		390
Professional Plastics Inc 1810 E Valencia Dr *TF:* 800-878-0755 ■ *Web:* www.professionalplastics.com	Fullerton	CA	92831	714-446-6500	447-9231	601
Professional Power Products Inc 448 W Madison St *Web:* www.professionalpowerproducts.com	Darien	WI	53114	262-882-9000		729
Professional Press PO Box 4371 *TF:* 800-277-8960 ■ *Web:* www.profpress.com	Chapel Hill	NC	27515	919-942-8020	942-3094	637-2
Professional Pride Training Company Inc PO Box 1090 *TF:* 800-830-8228 ■ *Web:* www.911trainer.com	Sumner	WA	98390	253-435-0911	435-6031	423
Professional Refrigeration PO Box 518 *Web:* www.professionalrefrigerationac.com	Millersport	OH	43046	740-467-2206		665
Professional Research Consultants Inc 11326 P St *TF:* 800-428-7455 ■ *Web:* www.prccustomresearch.com	Omaha	NE	68137	800-428-7455		194
Professional Risk Associates Inc 2909 Polo Pkwy Ste 100 *TF:* 800-318-9930 ■ *Web:* profrisk.com	Midlothian	VA	23113	804-794-0574	794-3468	390
Professional Risk Solutions LLC 37 Mountain Blvd Ste 3 *Web:* prsbrokers.com	Warren	NJ	07059	908-834-8401	834-8411	390
Professional Rodeo Cowboys Assn (PRCA) 101 Pro Rodeo Dr *TF:* 800-234-7722 ■ *Web:* www.prorodeo.com	Colorado Springs	CO	80919	719-593-8840		48-22
Professional Sales & Service LC 1720 W Indiana Ave *Web:* pro-sales.com	Salt Lake City	UT	84104	801-977-3961		690
Professional School of Bartending 660 N Main St *Web:* www.professionalschoolofbartending.com	Brockton	MA	02301	508-588-8204		685
Professional School of Bartending 108 Spruce St *Web:* www.probarschool.com	Providence	RI	02903	401-831-6446		685
Professional Service Industries Inc (PSI) 1901 S Meyers Rd Ste 400 *TF:* 800-548-7901 ■ *Web:* www.psiusa.com	Oakbrook Terrace	IL	60181	630-691-1490	691-1587	261
Professional Services Council (PSC) 4401 Wilson Blvd Ste 1110 *Web:* www.pscouncil.org	Arlington	VA	22203	703-875-8059	875-8922	49-12
Professional Shorthand Reporters Inc (PSR) 601 Poydras St Ste 1615 *TF:* 800-536-5255 ■ *Web:* www.psrdepo.com	New Orleans	LA	70130	504-529-5255	529-5257	445
Professional Software Engineering Inc 780 Lynnhaven Pkwy Ste 350 *Web:* prosoft-eng.com	Virginia Beach	VA	23452	757-431-2400	463-1071	180
Professional Sports Publications 519 Eigth Ave 25th Fl *Web:* www.pspsports.com	New York	NY	10018	212-697-1460		637-9
Professional Staffing Group 155 Federal St *Web:* psgstaffing.com	Boston	MA	02110	617-250-1000	250-1099	721
Professional Systems Associates Inc 1308 Florida Ave *TF:* 800-373-3453 ■ *Web:* psasys.com	Panama City	FL	32401	800-373-3453		177
Professional Tennis Registry PO Box 4739 *TF:* 800-421-6289 ■ *Web:* www.ptrtennis.org	Hilton Head Island	SC	29938	843-785-7244	686-2033	48-22
Professional Translating Services Inc Douglas Rd *TF:* 888-532-7887 ■ *Web:* www.protranslating.com	Coral Gables	FL	33134	305-371-7887	371-8366	768
Professional Travel Inc 25000 Great Northern Corporate Ctr Ste 170 *TF:* 800-247-0060 ■ *Web:* www.protrav.com	North Olmsted	OH	44070	440-734-8800	734-4528	771
Professional Village Pharmacy 1701 Professional Dr *Web:* professionalvillagerx.com	Sacramento	CA	95825	916-483-3455		237
Professional's Choice Hair Design Academy Stadium Plz 2719 W Jefferson St *Web:* www.bgi-online.com	Joliet	IL	60433	815-741-8224	744-4243	167-3
Professors World Peace Academy (PWPA) 3600 Labore Rd Ste 1 *Web:* www.paragonhouse.com	Saint Paul	MN	55110	651-644-3087	644-0997	637-2
Profex Medical Products Inc 2224 E Person Ave PO Box 140188 **Fax Area Code:* 901 ■ *Web:* www.profexmed.com	Memphis	TN	38114	800-325-0196	454-9850*	476
Proffitt & Goodson Inc 6283 Clinton Hwy Ste 200 *TF:* 866-776-3355 ■ *Web:* www.proffittgoodson.com	Knoxville	TN	37919	865-584-1850		229

Name / Address	City	State	ZIP	Phone	Fax	Class
Proficient Learning LLC 1508 Military Cutoff Rd Ste 304 *Web:* proficientlearning.com	Wilmington	NC	28403	910-509-0104		195
Proficio 1555 Faraday Ave *TF:* 800-779-5042 ■ *Web:* www.proficio.com	Carlsbad	CA	92008	800-779-5042		631
Profile Bank 45 Wakefield St PO Box 1808 *Web:* profilebank.com	Rochester	NH	03866	603-332-2610	332-2519	70
Profile Food Ingredients LLC 1151 Timber Dr *TF:* 877-632-1700 ■ *Web:* profilefoodingredients.com	Elgin	IL	60123	847-622-1700		358
Profile Plastics Inc 65 Waukegan Rd *Web:* www.thermoform.com	Lake Bluff	IL	60044	847-604-5100	604-8030	604
Profiles International LLC 510 N Valley Mills Dr Ste 600 *Web:* www.profilesinternational.com	Waco	TX	76710	254-751-1644		721
Profiles Placement 217 N Charles St Fl 5 *Web:* www.careerprofiles.com	Baltimore	MD	21201	410-244-6400		260
Profisee Group Inc 3655 Brookside Pkwy **Fax Area Code:* 770 ■ *Web:* www.profisee.com	Alpharetta	GA	30022	678-202-8990	619-5186*	387
Profit Point Inc 24 Ayers St *Web:* profitpt.com	North Brookfield	MA	01535	610-645-5557		463
Profit Programming Inc 120 Cockysville Rd *Web:* www.profitprogramming.com	Hunt Valley	MD	21030	410-316-1000		177
Profit Recovery Partners 2995 Red Hill Ave *TF:* 877-484-7776 ■ *Web:* www.prpllc.com	Costa Mesa	CA	92626	877-484-7776		196
Profit Sharing/401(k) Council of America (PSCA) 20 N Wacker Dr Ste 3700 *TF:* 866-614-8407 ■ *Web:* www.psca.org	Chicago	IL	60606	312-419-1863	419-1864	49-12
Profitable Investing 9201 Corporate Blvd *TF:* 800-211-8566 ■ *Web:* www.profitableinvesting.investorplace.com	Rockville	MD	20850	800-211-8566		531-9
Profitkey International LLC 2 Keewaydin Dr *Web:* profitkey.com	Salem	NH	03079	603-898-9800		360-3
Profi-Vision Inc 1150 Glenlivet Dr Ste C-40 *Web:* profi-vision.com	Allentown	PA	18106	610-530-2025		261
Proflowers 4840 Eastgate Mall *TF:* 800-580-2913 ■ *Web:* www.proflowers.com	San Diego	CA	92121	800-565-6609		292
Profold Inc 10300 99th Way *Web:* www.profold.com	Sebastian	FL	32958	772-589-0063	589-0213	556
ProForma 8800 E Pleasant Valley Rd *TF:* 800-825-1525 ■ *Web:* www.proforma.com	Independence	OH	44131	216-520-8400		627
Profound Logic Software Inc 396 Congress Park Dr *TF:* 877-224-7768 ■ *Web:* www.profoundlogic.com	Dayton	OH	45459	937-439-7925		525
ProFutures Inc 11719 Bee Cave Rd Ste 200 *Web:* www.profutures.com	Austin	TX	78738	512-263-3800		691
Progenics Pharmaceuticals Inc 1 World Trade Ctr 47th Fl Ste J *NASDAQ: PGNX* ■ *TF:* 866-644-7188 ■ *Web:* www.progenics.com	New York	NY	10007	646-975-2500	707-3626	85
Progeny Linux Systems Inc 9100 Keystone Crossing Ste 440	Indianapolis	IN	46240	317-833-0313	833-0315	177
Progeny Software LLC 190 Congress Park Dr Ste 140 *TF:* 800-776-4369 ■ *Web:* www.progenygenetics.com	Delray Beach	FL	33445	574-968-0822		177
Progeny Systems Corp 9500 Innovation Dr *Web:* www.progeny.net	Manassas	VA	20110	703-368-6107		180
Progesys Inc 1980 Post Oak Blvd Ste 1500 *TF:* 877-764-3797 ■ *Web:* progesys.ca	Houston	TX	77056	713-360-4814		463
Programmable Orienting Systems Inc 1547 Sartwell Creek Rd *Web:* posifeeders.com	Port Allegany	PA	16743	814-544-4000		385
Progress & Freedom Foundation (PFF) 1444 Eye St NW Ste 500 *Web:* www.pff.org	Washington	DC	20005	202-289-8928	289-6079	634
Progress Container Corp 635 Patrick Mill Rd SW *Web:* www.progresscontainer.com	Winder	GA	30680	678-425-2000	425-2001	100
Progress Group Inc, The 918 Kennedy Ave *Web:* theprogressgroupinc.com	Schererville	IN	46375	219-322-3700		757
Progress Investment Management Co 33 New Montgomery St 19th Fl *Web:* www.progressinvestment.com	San Francisco	CA	94105	415-512-3480	512-3475	401
Progress Printing Co 2677 Waterlick Rd **Fax Area Code:* 434 ■ *TF:* 800-572-7804 ■ *Web:* www.progressprintplus.com	Lynchburg	VA	24502	800-572-7804	237-1618*	627
Progress Rail Services 1600 Progress Dr PO Box 1037 *TF:* 800-476-8769 ■ *Web:* www.progressrail.com	Albertville	AL	35950	256-505-6600	593-1249	686
Progress Software Corp 14 Oak Pk *NASDAQ: PRGS* ■ *TF:* 800-477-6473 ■ *Web:* www.progress.com	Bedford	MA	01730	781-280-4000	280-4095	178-1
Progress Tool and Stamping Inc 207 Southgate Dr *Web:* www.progresstoolandstamping.com	Minster	OH	45865	419-628-2384		757
Progress Unlimited Inc 11431 Cronhill Dr Ste C *Web:* www.progressunlimited.org	Owings Mills	MD	21117	410-363-8550		726
Progress Wire Products Inc 532 Co Rd 1600 *Web:* www.progresswire.com	Ashland	OH	44805	419-496-0964	496-0967	73
Progress-Index 15 Franklin St *Web:* www.progress-index.com	Petersburg	VA	23803	804-732-3456		532-2
Progressions Cu 2919 E Mission Ave *Web:* progressionscu.org	Spokane	WA	99202	509-535-0191		219
Progressive Animal Wellness 70 E Main St *Web:* progressiveanimalwellness.com	Avon	CT	06001	860-325-2124		794
Progressive Chevrolet 8000 Hills & Dales Rd NW *Web:* progressivechevrolet.com	Massillon	OH	44646	330-833-8564		516
Progressive Communications Corp 18 E Vine St *TF:* 800-772-5333 ■ *Web:* mountvernonnews.com	Mount Vernon	OH	43050	740-397-5333	397-1321	637-8
Progressive Companies Inc 1301 18th St *TF:* 800-831-5174 ■ *Web:* www.sfishinc.com	Spirit Lake	IA	51360	712-336-1750	336-4681	297-5
Progressive Contracting Company Inc 115 Chatham St Ste 301 *Web:* www.progressivecci.com	Sanford	NC	27330	919-718-5454	718-5455	186
Progressive Converting Inc 2430 E Glendale Ave *Web:* www.pro-con.net	Appleton	WI	54911	920-832-8844	832-1115	554
Progressive Die & Stamping Inc 169 E Main St *Web:* www.pdsinctn.com	Cookeville	TN	38506	931-537-6528	537-6045	488
Progressive Dynamics Inc 507 Industrial Rd *TF:* 800-848-0558 ■ *Web:* www.progressivedyn.com	Marshall	MI	49068	269-781-4241	781-7802	253
Progressive Employer Services 6407 Parkland Dr *TF:* 888-925-2990 ■ *Web:* www.progressiveemployer.com	Sarasota	FL	34243	941-925-2990		631
Progressive Furniture Inc PO Box 308 *Web:* www.progressivefurniture.com	Archbold	OH	43502	828-459-2151	459-9702	319-2
Progressive Home Health Care Inc 312 S Old Dixie Hwy Ste 101 *Web:* www.progressivehomehealthcare.com	Jupiter	FL	33458	561-748-8700	748-8702	363
Progressive Hydraulics Inc 350 N Midland Ave *Web:* www.phionline.com	Saddle Brook	NJ	07663	201-791-3400		641
Progressive Marketing Products Inc 2620 Palisades Dr *TF:* 800-368-9700 ■ *Web:* www.premiermounts.com	Corona	CA	92882	714-632-7100		194
Progressive Metal Manufacturing Co 1300 Channing St *Web:* www.pmmco.com	Ferndale	MI	48220	248-546-2827		489
Progressive Microtechnology Inc 5717 Kugler Mill Rd Unit A *TF:* 800-325-7636 ■ *Web:* scanpmi.com	Cincinnati	OH	45236	513-782-5050		178-1
Progressive National Baptist Convention Inc (PNBC) 601 50th St NE *TF:* 800-876-7622 ■ *Web:* www.pnbc.org	Washington	DC	20019	202-396-0558	398-4998	48-20
Progressive Plastics Inc 14801 Emery Ave *TF:* 800-252-0053 ■ *Web:* www.progressive-plastics.com	Cleveland	OH	44135	216-252-5595	252-6327	98
Progressive Plumbing Inc 1064 W Hwy 50 *Web:* progressiveplumbing.com	Clermont	FL	34711	352-394-7171		610
Progressive Policy Institute (PPI) 1101 14th St NW Ste 1250 *Web:* www.progressivepolicy.org	Washington	DC	20005	202-525-3926	525-3941	634
Progressive Produce Co 5790 Peachtree St *TF:* 800-900-0757 ■ *Web:* www.progressiveproduce.com	Los Angeles	CA	90040	323-890-8100		297-7
Progressive Promotions Inc 145 Cedar Ln *Web:* www.progressivepromotions.com	Englewood	NJ	07631	201-945-0500		701
Progressive Recovery Inc 700 Industrial Dr *TF:* 800-732-3793 ■ *Web:* www.progressive-recovery.com	Dupo	IL	62239	618-286-5000		386
Progressive Tool & Manufacturing Co 290 Fifth St NE *Web:* www.ptmmn.com	Pine Island	MN	55963	507-356-8345	356-4557	482
Progressive, The PO Box 952 *Web:* www.theprogressnews.com	Clearfield	PA	16830	814-765-5581	765-5165	637-8
Progrexion Marketing Inc 257 East 200 South Ste 1200 *Web:* www.progrexion.com	Salt Lake City	UT	84111	801-384-4100		393
ProgyMedia 1040 Boul Michele-bohec *Web:* www.progymedia.com	Blainville	QC	J7C5E2	514-272-0599		180
Project Access Inc 2100 W Orangewood Ave Ste 230 **Fax Area Code:* 714 ■ *Web:* www.project-access.org	Orange	CA	92868	949-253-6200	940-9803*	41
Project Adventure Inc 719 Cabot St *TF:* 800-468-8898 ■ *Web:* www.pa.org	Beverly	MA	01915	978-524-4500	524-4501	242
Project Concern Intl (PCI) 5151 Murphy Canyon Rd Ste 320 *Web:* www.pciglobal.org	San Diego	CA	92123	858-279-9690	694-0294	48-5
Project Consulting Services Inc 3300 W Esplanade Ave S Ste 500 *TF:* 855-468-7473 ■ *Web:* www.projectconsulting.com	Metairie	LA	70002	504-833-5321		196
Project Corps 1325 Fourth Ave Ste 1925 *Web:* projectcorps.com	Seattle	WA	98101	206-932-7077		463
Project for Public Spaces 419 Lafayette St 7th Fl *Web:* www.pps.org	New York	NY	10003	212-620-5660	620-3821	48-13
Project Inform 273 Ninth St *TF:* 877-435-7443 ■ *Web:* www.projectinform.org	San Francisco	CA	94103	415-558-8669	558-0684	48-17
Project Lifesaver International Headquarters 815 Battlefield Blvd S *TF:* 877-580-5433 ■ *Web:* projectlifesaver.org	Chesapeake	VA	23322	757-546-5502		138
Project Management Institute (PMI) 14 Campus Blvd *TF:* 866-276-4764 ■ *Web:* www.pmi.org	Newtown Square	PA	19073	610-356-4600	356-4647	49-12
Project Partners Inc 23195 La Cadena Dr Ste 101 *Web:* projectpartners.com	Laguna Hills	CA	92653	949-852-9300	852-9322	261
Project Resources Inc 3760 Convoy St Ste 230 *Web:* www.priworld.com	San Diego	CA	92111	858-505-1000	505-1010	261
Project Vote 1350 I St NW Ste 1250 *Web:* www.projectvote.org	Washington	DC	20005	202-546-4173		48-7
Project X Ltd 200 Yorkland Blvd Ste 720 *TF:* 888-501-5424 ■ *Web:* www.pxltd.ca	North York	ON	M2J5C6	416-422-8900	422-8901	196

Company	City	State	ZIP	Phone	Fax	Class
Projectbits Consulting Inc 236 Lead King Dr *Web:* www.projectbits.com	Castle Rock	CO	80108	720-319-8160		809
ProjectDesign Consultants 701 B St Ste 800 *Web:* www.projectdesign.com	San Diego	CA	92101	619-235-6471		261
Projection Presentation Technology 5803 Rolling Rd *TF:* 800-377-7650 ■ *Web:* projection.com	Springfield	VA	22152	703-912-1334	912-1350	264-2
Projections Unlimited Inc 15311 Varrenca Pkwy **Fax Area Code:* 949 ■ *TF:* 800-551-4405 ■ *Web:* www.shoppui.com	Irvine	CA	92618	714-544-2700	789-0318*	246
Projectline Services Inc 506 Second Ave Ste 400 *Web:* www.projectlineservices.com	Seattle	WA	98104	206-382-2025		195
Projectools Company Inc 4099 Hwy 36 N *Web:* projectools.com	Bellville	TX	77418	713-371-9840		225
Projects in Knowledge Inc 290 W Mount Pleasant Ave Ste 2350 *TF:* 800-772-8277 ■ *Web:* www.projectsinknowledge.com	Livingston	NJ	07039	973-890-8988		423
Projects Plus Inc 254 W 29th St 5th Fl *Web:* www.projectsplusinc.com	New York	NY	10001	212-997-0100		194
Projects Unlimited Inc 6300 Sand Lake Rd *Web:* www.pui.com	Dayton	OH	45414	937-918-2200		625
PROJECTXYZ Inc 1500 Perimeter Pkwy Ste 426 *Web:* www.projectxyz.com	Huntsville	AL	35806	256-721-9001		261
ProKarma Inc 8705 SW Nimbus Ave Ste 118 **Fax Area Code:* 503 ■ *Web:* pkglobal.com	Beaverton	OR	97008	877-527-6226	521-8454*	317
Prolab Nutrition 21411 Prairie St *Web:* prolab.com	Chatsworth	CA	91311	818-739-6000		799
ProLender Solutions Inc 6050 Santo Rd Ste 160 *Web:* www.prolender.com	San Diego	CA	92124	858-974-4888		175
Proliance Surgeons Inc 805 Madison Ste 901 *Web:* www.proliancesurgeons.com	Seattle	WA	98104	206-264-8100		374-3
Pro-Life Action League 6160 N Cicero Ave Ste 600 *Web:* prolifeaction.org	Chicago	IL	60646	773-777-2900	777-3061	48-8
Prolifics 24025 Park Sorrento Ste 405 **Fax Area Code:* 818 ■ *TF:* 800-458-3313 ■ *Web:* www.prolifics.com	Calabasas	CA	91302	800-458-3313	224-5269*	178-2
Prolifiq Software Inc 8585 SW Cascade Ave Ste 200 *TF:* 800-840-7183 ■ *Web:* www.prolifiq.com	Beaverton	OR	97008	503-684-1415		179
Proline Concrete Tools Inc 2560 Jason Ct *Web:* www.prolinestamps.com	Oceanside	CA	92056	760-758-7240		111
Proline Distributors Inc 1191 S Rogers Cir *Web:* www.prolinedist.com	Boca Raton	FL	33487	561-241-7000		711
Proline Supply Co 6711 Bingle Rd *Web:* www.prolinesupplyco.com	Houston	TX	77092	713-939-9730	939-9729	45
Pro-line Water Screen Services Inc 4525 S Main St *Web:* www.intakescreens.com	Pearland	TX	77581	281-992-6730		454
Prolink Computer Inc 15336 E Valley Blvd *Web:* www.prolink-usa.com	City of Industry	CA	91746	626-369-3833	369-4883	173-1
Pro-Link Inc 510 Chapman St *Web:* www.prolinkhq.com	Canton	MA	02021	781-828-9550		77
Prolitec Inc 1235 W Canal St *TF:* 844-247-7599 ■ *Web:* prolitec.com	Milwaukee	WI	53233	844-247-7599		261
ProLiteracy Worldwide 1320 Jamesville Ave *Web:* proliteracy.org	Syracuse	NY	13210	315-422-9121	422-6369	48-5
Prolog Ventures 7733 Forsyth Blvd Ste 1100 *Web:* www.prologventures.com	Clayton	MO	63105	314-743-2400	743-2403	792
ProLogis Pier 1 Bay 1 *NYSE:* PLD ■ *TF:* 800-566-2706 ■ *Web:* www.prologis.com	San Francisco	CA	94111	415-394-9000		655
Promac Inc 1153 Timber Dr *Web:* www.promac.com	Elgin	IL	60123	847-695-8181		186
Promag Ltd 11552 Merchant Dr *Web:* www.promagltd.com	Baton Rouge	LA	70809	225-751-7755	751-7750	201
ProManage LLC 130 E Randolph St Ste 2825 *Web:* promanageplan.com	Chicago	IL	60603	312-456-0665		194
ProMark Direct Inc 300 N Midland Ave Ste 2 *Web:* www.promarkdirect.com	Saddle Brook	NJ	07663	201-398-9000	398-9212	7
Promark Technology Inc 10900 Pump House Rd Ste B **Fax Area Code:* 301 ■ *TF:* 800-634-0255 ■ *Web:* promarktech.com	Annapolis Junction	MD	20701	240-280-8030	725-7869*	174
PRO-MART Industries Inc 17421 Von Karman Ave *Web:* www.deltanovaltd.com	Irvine	CA	92614	949-428-7700		361
Promation Engineering Inc 16138 Flight Path Dr *Web:* promationei.com	Brooksville	FL	34604	352-544-8436		261
Promax Tools LP 11312 Sunrise Gold Cir *Web:* www.promaxtools.com	Rancho Cordova	CA	95742	916-638-0501		456
PromaxBDA 5700 Wilshire Blv Ste 275 *Web:* www.promax.org	Los Angeles	CA	90404	310-788-7600		138
ProMed Molded Products Inc 15600 Medina Rd *TF:* 855-331-3800 ■ *Web:* promedmolding.com	Plymouth	MN	55447	763-331-3800	331-3888	475
ProMedical Inc 1 Militia Dr *TF:* 800-722-1555 ■ *Web:* promedllc.com	Lexington	MA	02421	781-325-7239		463
Promega Corp 2800 Woods Hollow Rd *TF:* 800-356-9526 ■ *Web:* www.promega.in	Madison	WI	53711	608-274-4330	277-2516	231
Promenade Rehabilitation & Health Care Ctr 140 Beach 114th St *Web:* www.promenadenh.com	Rockaway Park	NY	11694	718-945-4600	634-8274	450
Promera Health 61 Accord Park Dr *TF:* 888-878-9058 ■ *Web:* promerasports.com	Norwell	MA	02061	888-878-9058		363
Promerus LLC 9921 Brecksville Rd *Web:* www.promerus.com	Brecksville	OH	44141	440-922-0300		548
Promess Inc PO Box 748 *Web:* www.promessinc.com	Brighton	MI	48116	810-229-9334	229-8125	472
Prometheus Biosciences 9410 Carroll Pk Dr **Fax Area Code:* 877 ■ *TF:* 888-892-8391 ■ *Web:* www.prometheusbiosciences.com	San Diego	CA	92121	858-824-0895	816-4019*	582
Prometric 1501 S Clinton St *TF:* 866-776-6387 ■ *Web:* www.prometric.com	Baltimore	MD	21224	443-455-8000		244
Promex Industries Inc 3075 Oakmead Village Dr *Web:* www.promex-ind.com	Santa Clara	CA	95051	408-496-0222		696
Promex Technologies LLC 3049 Hudson St	Franklin	IN	46131	317-736-0128	736-0793	475
Promiles Software Development 1900 Texas Ave *TF:* 800-324-8588 ■ *Web:* www.promiles.com	Bridge City	TX	77611	800-324-8588		177
Prominence Health Plan 1510 Meadow Wood Ln *Web:* www.prominencehealthplan.com	Reno	NV	89502	775-770-6230	770-6253	391-3
Prominent Fluid Controls Inc 136 Industry Dr *Web:* www.prominent.us	Pittsburgh	PA	15275	412-787-2484	787-0704	248
Promise Hotels Inc 2201 N 77th E Ave *Web:* www.promisehotels.com	Tulsa	OK	74115	918-858-2779		707
Promise Jobs Culinary School 211 Livingston Ave *Web:* www.elijahspromise.org	New Brunswick	NJ	08901	732-545-9002	246-1138	685
Promise Keepers (PK) PO Box 11798 **Fax Area Code:* 303 ■ *TF:* 866-776-6473 ■ *Web:* promisekeepers.org	Denver	CO	80211	866-776-6473	433-1036*	48-20
Promise Technology Inc 580 Cottonwood Dr *TF:* 800 000 0245 ■ *Web:* promise.com	Milpitas	CA	95035	400 220-1400		625
Promised Land State Park PO Box 96 *Web:* www.dcnr.pa.gov	Greentown	PA	18426	570-676-3428		565
Promium LLC 3350 Monte Villa Pkwy Ste 220 *Web:* www.promium.com	Bothell	WA	98021	425-286-9200		177
PromoCentric 5 Forbes Rd *TF:* 877-776-6641 ■ *Web:* www.promocentric.com	Newmarket	NH	03857	603-758-6377	758-6388	226
Promodel Corp 3400 Bath Pk Ste 200 *TF:* 888-900-3090 ■ *Web:* promodel.com	Bethlehem	PA	18017	001-223-4600	226-6046	178-10
Pro-Mold Inc 55 Chancellor Dr **Fax Area Code:* 847 ■ *Web:* www.promolddie.com	Roselle	IL	60172	630-893-3594	893-4773*	757
Promontory Financial Group LLC 801 17th St NW Ste 1100 *Web:* www.promontory.com	Washington	DC	20006	202-384-1200	783-2924	194
Promontory Point Capital 322 E Michigan St Ste 500 *Web:* www.promontorypointcapital.com	Milwaukee	WI	53202	414-225-0484	225-0485	194
Promoshop Inc 5420 McConnell Ave *TF:* 877-776-6699 ■ *Web:* promoshopinc.com	Los Angeles	CA	90066	310-821-1780		791
ProMost Inc 1616 16th St Ste 350 *Web:* www.promost.com	San Francisco	CA	94103	415-575-1358		809
Promotion Fulfillment Ctr 311 21st St **Fax Area Code:* 563 ■ *TF:* 800-493-7063 ■ *Web:* pfcfulfills.com	Camanche	IA	52730	800-493-7063	259-0110*	41
Promotional Products Association Intl (PPAI) 3125 Skyway Cir N *TF:* 888-426-7724 ■ *Web:* www.ppai.org	Irving	TX	75038	972-252-0404		49-18
Prompt Mailers Inc 66 Willow Ave *Web:* www.promptmailers.com	Staten Island	NY	10305	718-447-6206	981-7333	5
Promptime Home Healthcare 5409 S Collins St Ste 131 *Web:* www.promptime.com	Arlington	TX	76018	817-300-8314	466-2685	363
Prompton Tool Inc 120 Sunrise Ave *Web:* www.promptontool.com	Honesdale	PA	18431	570-253-4141	253-0548	454
ProMusica Chamber Orchestra 620 E Broad St Ste 300 *Web:* promusicacolumbus.org	Columbus	OH	43215	614-464-0066	464-4141	573-3
Pronghorn Controls Ltd 101 4919 72 Ave SE *Web:* www.pronghorn.ca	Calgary	AB	T2C3H3	403-720-2526		358
Pronk Technologies Inc 8933 Lankershim Blvd *TF:* 800-609-9802 ■ *Web:* www.pronktech.com	Sun Valley	CA	91352	818-768-5600		476
Pronto Networks 1966 Tice Valley Blvd **Fax Area Code:* 267 ■ *Web:* www.prontonetworks.com	Walnut Creek	CA	94595	925-860-6200	873-8803*	178-1
Proof Advertising LLC 114 W Seventh St Ste 500 *Web:* www.proof-advertising.com	Austin	TX	78701	512-345-6658	345-6227	7
ProOrbis 112 Moores Rd Ste 400 *Web:* proorbis.com	Malvern	PA	19355	610-240-0200	240-0508	195
ProPacific Fresh 70 Pepsi Way *TF:* 888-232-0908 ■ *Web:* www.propacificfresh.com	Durham	CA	95938	530-893-0596	893-3249	297-7
Propaganda Inc 3115 S Grand Blvd Ste 500 *Web:* www.propaganda-india.com	Saint Louis	MO	63118	314-664-8516	664-8596	7
Pro-Pak Industries Inc 1125 Ford St *Web:* www.pro-pakindustries.com	Maumee	OH	43537	419-729-0751		100
Propak Systems Ltd 440 E Lake Rd NE *TF:* 800-408-4434 ■ *Web:* www.propaksystems.com	Airdrie	AB	T4A2J8	403-912-7000		261
Propane Education and Research Council (PERC) 1140 Connecticut Ave NW Ste 1075 *Web:* www.propanecouncil.org	Washington	DC	20036	202-452-8975	452-9054	48-6
Propane Resources LLC 6950 Squibb Rd Ste 306 *Web:* www.propaneresources.com	Mission	KS	66201	913-262-8345		466
Propane Services LLC 27481 Beverly Rd *Web:* propaneservices.net	Romulus	MI	48174	313-292-9100		316

Company	Address	City	State	ZIP	Phone	Fax	Class	Details
ProPath Laboratory Inc	1355 River Bend Dr	Dallas	TX	75247	214-638-2000		418	*TF:* 800-258-1253 ■ *Web:* www.propathlab.com
ProPay Inc	3400 N Ashton Blvd Ste 200	Lehi	UT	84043	801-341-5300		569	*TF:* 888-227-9856 ■ *Web:* www.propay.com
Propel Software Corp	2216 O'Toole Ave	San Jose	CA	95131	408-571-6300	577-1070	178-7	*Web:* www.propel.com
Propel Tax	PO Box 100350	San Antonio	TX	78201	877-324-8445		194	*TF:* 877-324-8445 ■ *Web:* www.propeltax.com
Propeller Consulting	220 NW 8th Ave	Portland	OR	97209	503-278-7055		194	*Web:* propellerconsulting.com
ProPeople Staffing Services Inc	10369 W Emerald St	Boise	ID	83704	208-345-5747		260	*Web:* www.propeoplestaffing.com
Proper Tooling	13870 E 11-Mile Rd	Warren	MI	48089	586-779-8787	779-4530	604	*Web:* propergroupintl.com
Property Advisers Realty Inc	6012 W Campus Circle Dr Ste 210	Irving	TX	75063	972-465-9900		653	*Web:* propertyadvisers.com
Property Casualty Insurers Association of America	8700 W Bryn Mawr Ave Ste 1200S	Chicago	IL	60631	847-297-7800	297-5064	49-9	*Web:* www.pciaa.net
Property Damage Appraisers Inc (PDA)	6100 SW Blvd Ste 200	Fort Worth	TX	76109	800-749-7324	866-4732	310	*TF:* 800-749-7324 ■ *Web:* www.pdacorporation.com
Property Loss Research Bureau (PLRB)	3025 Highland Pkwy Ste 800	Downers Grove	IL	60515	630-724-2200	724-2260	49-9	*TF:* 888-711-7572 ■ *Web:* www.plrb.org
Property Management Consulting Services Inc	829 W Genesee St	Syracuse	NY	13204	315-451-2423		652	*Web:* www.pmcsinc.com
Property One Inc	4141 Veterans Memorial Blvd Ste 300	Metairie	LA	70002	504-681-3400		113	*Web:* propertyone.com
Property Owners Exchange Inc	6630 Baltimore National Pk Ste 208	Catonsville	MD	21228	410-719-0100		635	*TF:* 800-869-3200 ■ *Web:* poeknows.com
Property Panorama Inc	9475 Pinecone Dr	Mentor	OH	44060	440-290-2200		177	*TF:* 877-299-6306 ■ *Web:* propertypanorama.com
Property Tax Advisors LLC	620 Manhattan Beach Blvd	Manhattan Beach	CA	90266	310-374-1216	374-2023	463	*Web:* propertytaxadvisors.com
Property Tax Advocates Inc	1303 W Walnut Hill Ln Ste 260	Irving	TX	75038	972-550-8877		653	*Web:* proptaxadv.com
Property Tax Consultants Inc	9810 Winter Gardens Blvd	Lakeside	CA	92040	619-390-7000	390-7005	734	*Web:* www.propertytaxconsultantsinc.com
Propet USA Inc	2415 W Valley Hwy N	Auburn	WA	98001	253-854-7600	854-7607	301	*TF:* 800-877-6738 ■ *Web:* www.propetusa.com
ProPetro Services Inc	1706 S Midkiff Rd Bldg B PO Box 873	Midland	TX	79701	432-688-0012		540	*TF:* 800-221-1037 ■ *Web:* www.propetroservices.com
ProPhase Labs Inc	621 Shady Retreat Rd	Doylestown	PA	18901	215-345-0919		582	*NASDAQ: PRPH* ■ *TF:* 800-505-2653 ■ *Web:* www.prophaselabs.com
Prophet Equity LLC	1460 Main St Ste 200	Southlake	TX	76092	817-898-1500		194	*Web:* prophetequity.com
Propheta Communications	70 E Tenth St Ste 6P	New York	NY	10003	212-901-6914		636	*Web:* propheta.com
Prophetline Inc	2120 S Waldron Rd	Fort Smith	AR	72903	800-875-6592		809	*TF:* 800-875-6592 ■ *Web:* prophetline.com
Prophetstown State Park	Riverside Dr PO Box 181	Prophetstown	IL	61277	815-537-2926		565	*Web:* www2.illinois.gov
ProPhotonix Inc	13 Red Roof Ln Ste 200	Salem	NH	03079	603-893-8778		544	*OTC: STKR* ■ *Web:* www.prophotonix.com
Propipe Technologies Inc	1800 Clayton Ave	Middletown	OH	45042	513-424-5311		595	
Proplanner	2321 N Loop Dr Ste 104	Ames	IA	50010	515-296-0738	296-3229	809	*Web:* www.proplanner.com
Proportion-Air Inc	8250 N 600 W PO Box 218	Mccordsville	IN	46055	317-335-2602		201	*Web:* proportionair.com
Propper Manufacturing Company Inc	36-04 Skillman Ave	Long Island City	NY	11101	718-392-6650	482-8909	476	*TF:* 800-832-4300 ■ *Web:* www.proppermfg.com
Propylon Inc	3429 Derry St	Harrisburg	PA	17111	717-265-0400		809	*Web:* www.propylon.com
Prores Group Inc	16526 W 78th St Ste 310	Eden Prairie	MN	55346	952-449-1000		138	*Web:* www.proresgroup.com
ProRodeo Hall of Fame & Museum of the American Cowboy	101 ProRodeo Dr	Colorado Springs	CO	80919	719-528-4764		522	*Web:* www.prorodeo.org
Pros Holdings Inc	3100 Main St Ste 900	Houston	TX	77002	713-335-5151	335-8144	178-10	*NYSE: PRO* ■ *Web:* www.pros.com
Prosatcomm	1470 NW 107th Ave Ste N	Doral	FL	33172	305-677-3812		692	*Web:* www.prosatcomm.com
ProScan Imaging LLC	5400 Kennedy Ave	Cincinnati	OH	45213	513-618-1063	351-3100	418	*TF:* 877-776-7226 ■ *Web:* proscan.com
ProSchools	20225 Water Tower Blvd 4th Fl	Brookfield	WI	53045	800-299-2207		685	*TF:* 800-299-2207 ■ *Web:* www.proschools.com
Prosci Inc	5042 Technology Pkwy Ste 500	Fort Collins	CO	80528	970-825-5232		463	*Web:* www.prosci.com
ProSep (USA) Inc	5353 W Sam Houston Pkwy N Ste 150	Houston	TX	77041	281-504-2040		539	*Web:* www.prosep.com
Proserv Anchor Crane Group	455 Aldine Bender Rd	Houston	TX	77060	281-405-9048	448-7508	470	*TF:* 800-835-2223 ■ *Web:* www.proservanchor.com
Proshot Concrete Inc	4158 Musgrove Dr	Florence	AL	35630	256-263-0445	764-5946	189-3	*TF:* 800-633-3141 ■ *Web:* www.proshotconcrete.com
Prosite Business Solutions	732 Third St	New Martinsville	WV	26155	304-455-5900		180	*Web:* www.probusinesstools.com
ProSites Inc	27919 Jefferson Ave Ste 103	Temecula	CA	92590	951-693-9101		177	*TF:* 888-932-3644 ■ *Web:* www.prosites.com
Proskauer Rose LLP	11 Times Sq	New York	NY	10036	212-969-3000	969-2900	428	*TF:* 866-444-3272 ■ *Web:* www.proskauer.com
Proske Plastic Products Inc	6701 Supply Row	Houston	TX	77011	713-926-9941	926-9943	599	*Web:* www.proskeplastics.com
Prosoco Inc	3741 Greenway Cir	Lawrence	KS	66046	800-255-4255	830-9797*	151	**Fax Area Code: 785* ■ *TF:* 800-255-4255 ■ *Web:* prosoco.com
Prosource Fitness Equipment	6503 Hilburn Dr	Raleigh	NC	27613	919-781-8077		627	*TF:* 877-781-8077 ■ *Web:* www.prosourcefitness.com
Prosource Industries Inc	1700 111th St	Grand Prairie	TX	75050	972-660-1400	660-8437	815	*Web:* www.prosourceind.com
ProSource Solutions LLC	4199 Kinross Lakes Pkwy Ste 150	Richfield	OH	44286	866-549-0279		196	*TF:* 866-549-0279 ■ *Web:* prosource-corp.com
Prospec Technologies Inc	3235 Wharton Way	Mississauga	ON	L4X2B6	905-629-3100		358	*TF:* 888-797-7867 ■ *Web:* prospectech.com
Prospect Airport Services Inc	2130 S Wolf Rd	Des Plaines	IL	60018	847-299-3636	789-8489	27	*Web:* www.prospectair.com
Prospect College	1720 I St NW Ste 200	Washington	DC	20006	202-844-4216	223-7200	167-3	*Web:* prospectcollege.edu
Prospect Fastener Corp	1295 Kyle Ct	Wauconda	IL	60084	847-526-2950		350	*Web:* www.prospectfastener.com
Prospect Foundry LLC	1225 Winter St NE	Minneapolis	MN	55413	612-331-9282		307	*Web:* prospectfdry.com
Prospect Medical Holdings Inc	3415 S Sepulveda Blvd 9th Fl	Los Angeles	CA	90034	310-943-4500		463	*TF:* 800-708-3230 ■ *Web:* pmh.com
Prospect Mold Inc	1100 Main St	Cuyahoga Falls	OH	44221	330-929-3311		757	*Web:* www.prospectmold.com
Prospect Steel	8900 Fourche Dam Pke	Little Rock	AR	72206	501-490-2300		480	*Web:* www.prospectsteel.com
Prospect Venture Partners	435 Tasso St Ste 200	Palo Alto	CA	94301	650-327-8800		792	*Web:* www.prospectventures.com
Prospection Inc	1750 Av De Vitre	Quebec City	QC	G1J1Z6	418-521-2248		225	*Web:* prospection.qc.ca
Prospectiv Direct Inc	40 Harvard Mill Sq Ste 1	Wakefield	MA	01880	781-305-2100	938-6634	195	*Web:* www.prospectiv.com
Prospector Hotel	375 Whittier St	Juneau	AK	99801	907-586-3737	586-1204	379	*Web:* prospectorhotel.com
Prospectr Marketing	575 SE Ninth St Ste 205	Minneapolis	MN	55414	612-200-0874		5	*Web:* prospectrmarketing.com
Prospects Influential Inc	1313 E Maple St Ste 548	Bellingham	WA	98225	800-352-2282		7	*TF:* 800-352-2282 ■ *Web:* www.prospectsinfluential.com
Prospera Financial Services Inc	5429 LBJ Fwy Ste 400	Dallas	TX	75240	972-581-3000		390	*Web:* www.prosperafinancial.com
Prosperity Advisors	10955 Lowell Ave Ste 900	Overland Park	KS	66210	913-451-4501		690	*TF:* 800-344-7285 ■ *Web:* www.prosperityadvisors.com
Prosperity Bank	1301 N Mechanic	El Campo	TX	77437	800-531-1401	543-1906*	360-2	*NYSE: PB* ■ **Fax Area Code: 979* ■ *TF:* 800-531-1401 ■ *Web:* www.prosperitybankusa.com
Prosser Career Education Ctr	4202 Charlestown Rd	New Albany	IN	47150	812-542-8508	542-4799	167-3	*Web:* www.prosser.nafcs.k12.in.us
Prosser Wilbert Construction Inc	13730 W 108th St	Lenexa	KS	66215	913-906-0104		186	*Web:* www.prosserwilbert.com
Prostar Computer Inc	837 Lawson St	City of Industry	CA	91748	626-839-6472		174	*TF:* 888-576-4742 ■ *Web:* www.pro-star.com
Prostate Cancer Foundation	1250 Fourth St	Santa Monica	CA	90401	310-570-4700	570-4701	303	*TF:* 800-757-2873 ■ *Web:* www.pcf.org
ProSteel Security Products Inc	1400 S State St	Provo	UT	84603	801-373-2385		295	*Web:* www.prosteel.us
Prosthetic Design Inc	700 Harco Dr	Clayton	OH	45315	800-459-0177		477	*TF:* 800-459-0177 ■ *Web:* prostheticdesign.com
Prostrollo Motor Sales Inc	500 Fourth St NE	Huron	SD	57350	866-466-4515	352-9286*	57	**Fax Area Code: 605* ■ *TF:* 866-466-4515 ■ *Web:* www.prostrollo.com
Prosum Inc	2201 Park Pl Ste 102	El Segundo	CA	90245	310-426-0600		192	*TF:* 888-477-6786 ■ *Web:* www.prosum.com
Prosurance Group Inc	2685 Marine Way Ste 1408	Mountain View	CA	94043	650-428-0818		390	*Web:* prosurancegroup.com
Prosurg Inc	2195 Trade Zone Blvd	San Jose	CA	95131	408-945-4044	945-1390	476	*Web:* prosurg.com
Prosync Technology Group LLC	6021 University Blvd Ste 300	Ellicott City	MD	21043	410-772-7969		177	*Web:* www.prosync.com
Prosys Industries Inc	47576 Halyard Dr	Plymouth	MI	48170	734-207-3710		358	*Web:* www.prosys-group.com
Pro-System Inc	121 Oakpark Dr	Mooresville	NC	28115	704-799-8100		22	*Web:* www.prosystems.com
Protagon Display Inc	719 Tapscott Rd	Toronto	ON	M1X1A2	416-293-9500		7	*Web:* protagon.com

Phone | Fax | Class

Protameen Chemicals Inc
375 Minnisink Rd — Totowa NJ 07512 — 973-256-4374 — 256-6764 — 143
Web: www.protameen.com

ProtaTek International Inc
2635 University Ave W Ste 140 — Saint Paul MN 55114 — 651-644-5391 — 644-6831 — 584
Web: www.protatek.com

Protean Design Group
100 E Pine St Ste 600 — Orlando FL 32801 — 407-246-0044 — 246-0040 — 261
Web: proteandg.com

Protec Arisawa America Inc 2455 Ash St — Vista CA 92081 — 760-599-4800 — 597-4830 — 91
Web: www.protec-arisawa.com

Pro-Tec Fire Services Ltd
2129 S Oneida St — Green Bay WI 54304 — 800-242-6352 — 63
TF: 800-242-6352 ■ *Web:* www.protecfire.com

Pro-Tec Refrigeration Inc
3640 N 39th Ave — Phoenix AZ 85019 — 602-222-9881 — 189-10
Web: protecref.com

ProTech Associates Inc
5457 Twin Knolls Rd Ste 400 — Columbia MD 21045 — 310-206-0070 — 539-9599* — 178-1
**Fax Area Code:* 443 ■ *TF:* 800-310-8813 ■ *Web:* www.protechassociates.com

Protech Coatings Inc
1213 Harrison Ave — Arlington TX 76011 — 817-274-7336 — 274-7378 — 145
Web: www.protechcoatingsinc.com

Pro-Tech Design & Manufacturing Inc
14561 Marquardt Ave — Santa Fe Springs CA 90670 — 562-207-1680 — 207-1699 — 88
Web: www.protechdesign.com

Pro-Tech Energy Solutions LLC
215 Executive Dr — Moorestown NJ 08057 — 856-437-6220 — 466
Web: www.pro-techenergy.com

Pro-tech Security Sales
1313 W Bagley Rd — Berea OH 44017 — 440-239-0100 — 237
TF: 800-888-4002 ■ *Web:* www.protechsales.com

Protech Systems Group
3350 Players Club Pkwy — Memphis TN 38125 — 901-767-7550 — 177
TF: 800-459-5100 ■ *Web:* www.psgi.net

Protect Computer Products Inc
2216 N 640 W — West Bountiful UT 84087 — 801-295-7739 — 295-7786 — 174
TF: 800-669-7739 ■ *Web:* www.protectcovers.com

Protect Controls Inc (PCI)
3212 Old Hwy 105 E — Conroe TX 77301 — 713-691-5183 — 691-0159 — 105
Web: www.protectcontrols.com

Protect-All Inc 109 Badger Pkwy — Darien WI 53114 — 888-432-8526 — 554
TF: 888-432-8526 ■ *Web:* www.protect-all.com

Protected Investors of America Inc
235 Montgomery St Ste 1050 — San Francisco CA 94104 — 800-786-2559 — 398-6789* — 194
**Fax Area Code:* 415 ■ *TF:* 800-786-2559 ■ *Web:* www.protectedinvestors.com

Protection Controls Inc
7317 Lawndale Ave — Skokie IL 60076 — 847-674-7676 — 674-7009 — 729
Web: www.protectioncontrolsinc.com

Protection Engineering Consultants LLC
14144 Trautwein Rd — Austin TX 78737 — 512-380-1988 — 261
Web: www.protection-consultants.com

Protection One Alarm Monitoring
1035 N Third St Ste 101 — Lawrence KS 66044 — 877-776-1911 — 692
TF: 800-438-4357 ■ *Web:* www.protection1.com

Protection Technologies Inc
529 Vista Blvd — Sparks NV 89434 — 775-856-7333 — 856-7658 — 253
TF: 800-428-9662 ■ *Web:* www.protechusa.com

Protective Armored Systems Inc
100 Valley St — Lee MA 01238 — 413-637-1060 — 329
Web: pasarmor.com

Protective Group Inc, The
14100 NW 58th Ct — Miami Lakes FL 33014 — 305-820-4240 — 791
Web: www.protectivegroup.com

Protective Insurance Co
111 Congressional Blvd Ste 500 — Carmel IN 46032 — 800-644-5501 — 391-5
TF: 800-644-5501 ■ *Web:* www.protectiveinsurance.com

Protective Life Corp
2801 Hwy 280 S — Birmingham AL 35223 — 844-733-5433 — 360-4
NYSE: PL ■ *TF:* 800-866-9933 ■ *Web:* www.protective.com

Protective Lining Corp 601 39th St — Brooklyn NY 11232 — 800-221-9712 — 854-4658* — 273
**Fax Area Code:* 718 ■ *TF:* 800-221-9712 ■ *Web:* www.prolining.com

Protectolite Inc 84 Railside Rd — Toronto ON M3A1A3 — 416-444-4484 — 393
Web: www.protectolite.com

Protectoseal Co 225 W Foster Ave — Bensenville IL 60106 — 630-595-0800 — 595-8059 — 124
TF: 800-323-2268 ■ *Web:* www.protectoseal.com

Protegrity Properties
260 Wekiva Springs Rd Ste 1040 — Longwood FL 32779 — 407-960-7703 — 682-7719 — 390
Web: www.protegrityproperties.com

Protegrity USA Inc
333 Ludlow St 8th Fl — Stamford CT 06902 — 203-326-7200 — 348-1251 — 255
Web: www.protegrity.com

Protein Sciences Corp
1000 Research Pkwy — Meriden CT 06450 — 203-686-0800 — 686-0268 — 85
TF: 800-488-7099 ■ *Web:* www.proteinsciences.com

Protek Cargo 1568 Airport Blvd — Napa CA 94558 — 707-254-9627 — 283
TF: 800-439-1426 ■ *Web:* www.protekcargo.com

Pro-Tek Manufacturing Inc
4849 Southfront Rd — Livermore CA 94551 — 925-454-8100 — 697
Web: www.protekmfg.com

Protel Inc 4150 Kidron Rd — Lakeland FL 33811 — 863-644-5558 — 646-5855 — 735
TF: 800-925-8882 ■ *Web:* www.protelinc.com

Protelo Inc 340 Palladio Pkwy Ste 520 — Folsom CA 95630 — 916-235-8601 — 177
Web: proteloinc.com

Protelus 11000 NE 33rd Pl Ste 320 — Bellevue WA 98004 — 800-585-0207 — 466
TF: 800-585-0207 ■ *Web:* protelus.com

Protenergy Natural Foods Inc
904 Woods Rd — Cambridge MD 21613 — 410-901-8625 — 228-1646 — 296-37
Web: www.protenergyfoods.com

Protential 3722 Illinois Ave — Saint Charles IL 60174 — 630-663-0567 — 663-0578 — 195
Web: www.protential.com

Protenus Inc 1629 Thames St — Baltimore MD 21231 — 410-995-8811 — 788
Web: www.protenus.com

Proteon Therapeutics Inc 200 W St — Waltham MA 02451 — 781-890-0102 — 231
Web: www.proteontherapeutics.com

Proteos Inc 4717 Campus Dr — Kalamazoo MI 49008 — 269-372-3480 — 231
Web: proteos.business.site

Protestant Episcopal Theological Seminary in Virginia
3737 Seminary Rd — Alexandria VA 22304 — 703-370-6600 — 167-3
TF: 800-941-0083 ■ *Web:* www.vts.edu

Proteus Applied Technologies Inc
100 PRODUCE Ave Ste K — South San Francisco CA 94080 — 650-588-7774 — 476

Proteus Inc 1830 N Dinuba Blvd — Visalia CA 93291 — 559-733-5423 — 685
TF: 888-776-9998 ■ *Web:* www.proteusinc.org

Proteus Industries
340 Pioneer Way — Mountain View CA 94041 — 650-964-4163 — 201
Web: proteusind.com

Proteus On-Demand Facilities LLC
6727 Oak Ridge Commerce Way SW — Austell GA 30168 — 770-333-1886 — 184
TF: 877-533-2637 ■ *Web:* www.proteusondemand.com

Prothro, Wilhelmi & Company PLLC
6855 Oak Hill Blvd — Tyler TX 75703 — 903-534-8811 — 534-8891 — 2
Web: pw-tx.com

Protide Pharmaceuticals Inc
505 Oakwood Rd Ste 200 — Lake Zurich IL 60047 — 847-726-3100 — 726-3110 — 582
TF: 800-552-3569 ■ *Web:* protidepharma.com

Protiscom 7212 Mcneil Dr Ste 202 — Austin TX 78729 — 512-258-1282 — 258-1664 — 179
Web: protis.com

Proto Corp 10500 47th St N — Clearwater FL 33762 — 727-573-4665 — 596
TF: 800-875-7768 ■ *Web:* www.protocorporation.com

Proto-1 Manufacturing LLC
10 Tower Rd — Winneconne WI 54986 — 920-582-4491 — 757
Web: proto1mfg.com

Protocall Group, The
1 Mall Dr Ste 105 — Cherry Hill NJ 08002 — 856-249-0487 — 260
Web: protocallgroup.com

Protocase Inc
Harbourside Industrial Pk 46 Wabana Ct — Sydney NS B1P0B9 — 902-567-3335 — 697
TF: 866-849-3911 ■ *Web:* www.protocase.com

Protochips Inc
3800 Gateway Centre Blvd Ste 306 — Morrisville NC 27560 — 919-377-0800 — 256
Web: www.protochips.com

Protoco Enterprises LLC
28757 NW W Union Rd — North Plains OR 97133 — 503-647-0082 — 604
Web: www.protoco.com

Protocol Driven Healthcare Inc
40 Morristown Rd Ste 1-A — Bernardsville NJ 07924 — 973-785-8686 — 785-8680 — 463
TF: 888-816-4006 ■ *Web:* www.pdhi.com

Protocol Link Inc
175 E Hawthorn Pkwy Ste 210 — Vernon Hills IL 60061 — 847-549-0390 — 463
Web: www.protocollink.com

Protocol LLC
2110 Cheshire Way Ste A — Greensboro NC 27405 — 336-553-0755 — 553-0756 — 76
TF: 800-227-5336 ■ *Web:* www.protocolvending.com

Protocol Networks Inc 15 Shore Dr — Johnston RI 02919 — 877-676-0146 — 180
TF: 877-676-0146 ■ *Web:* www.protocolnetworks.com

Protocol Telecommunications Inc
16844 Saticoy St — Van Nuys CA 91406 — 818-782-5705 — 23
TF: 800-400-5705 ■ *Web:* www.walkietalkie.com

Protogate Inc 12225 World Trade Dr — San Diego CA 92128 — 858-451-0865 — 225
TF: 877-473-0190 ■ *Web:* www.protogate.com

Protoline Inc 10650 Stancliff Rd — Houston TX 77099 — 281-561-0802 — 561-0021 — 625
Web: www.protoline.com

Protolink Inc
1755 N Collins Blvd Ste 550 — Richardson TX 75080 — 972-644-9763 — 809
Web: www.protolink.com

Protomatic Inc 2125 Bishop Cir W — Dexter MI 48130 — 734-426-3655 — 426-2725 — 476
Web: www.protomaticaerospace.com

Proton Onsite 10 Technology Dr — Wallingford CT 06492 — 203-949-8697 — 253
Web: www.protononsite.com

Proton PRC Ltd 4805 S Colony Blvd — The Colony TX 75056 — 972-931-8200 — 580
Web: www.protonprc.com

ProtonMedia Inc 1690 Sumneytown Pk — Lansdale PA 19446 — 215-631-1401 — 703
Web: www.protonmedia.com

Protostatix Engineering Consultants Inc
10410 - 102 Ave NW Ste 500 — Edmonton AB T5J0E9 — 780-423-5855 — 261
Web: protostatix.com

Prototype & Plastic Mold Co
35 Industrial Pk Pl — Middletown CT 06457 — 860-632-2800 — 632-2249 — 454
Web: www.proppm.com

Prototypes
1000 N Alameda St Ste 390 — Los Angeles CA 90012 — 213-542-3838 — 726
Web: www.prototypes.org

Proto-Vest Inc
7400 N Glen Harbor Blvd — Glendale AZ 85307 — 623-872-8300 — 872-6150 — 806
TF: 800-521-8218 ■ *Web:* www.protovest.com

ProTrak International Inc
237 W 35th St — New York NY 10001 — 212-265-9833 — 180
Web: protrak.com

Protran Technology LLC 52 Paterson Ave — Newton NJ 07860 — 973-250-4176 — 779-7436* — 693
**Fax Area Code:* 856 ■ *Web:* www.protrantechnology.com

ProTrans International Inc
8311 N Perimeter Rd — Indianapolis IN 46241 — 317-240-4100 — 240-4101 — 311
TF: 888-744-7669 ■ *Web:* www.protrans.com

Protravel International Inc
515 Madison Ave 10th Fl — New York NY 10022 — 212-755-4550 — 593-4907 — 771
TF: 800-227-1059 ■ *Web:* www.protravelinc.com

Protronics Inc 861 Old Knight Rd — Knightdale NC 27545 — 919-217-0007 — 625
Web: www.protronics-inc.com

Proturn Inc 14192 Fir St Ste 100 — Oregon City OR 97045 — 503-657-3858 — 657-3969 — 454
Web: www.proturnmfg.com

Proudfoot Associates Inc
2005 Michael Owens Way — Perrysburg OH 43551 — 419-865-7195 — 261
Web: proudfootassociates.com

Proulx Mfg 11433 Sixth St — Rancho Cucamonga CA 91730 — 909-980-0662 — 596
TF: 888-612-0662 ■ *Web:* www.proulxmfg.com

Prousys Inc 4700 New Horizon Blvd — Bakersfield CA 93313 — 661-837-4001 — 837-4004 — 261
Web: www.prousys.com

Prouty Place State Park 1201 Prouty Rd — Austin PA 16720 — 814-435-5010 — 565
Web: www.dcnr.pa.gov

Provantage Corp
7249 Whipple Ave NW — North Canton OH 44720 — 330-494-8715 — 494-5260 — 174
TF: 800-336-1166 ■ *Web:* www.provantage.com

Provation Medical Inc
800 Washington Ave N Ste 400 — Minneapolis MN 55401 — 612-313-1500 — 341-4355 — 177
TF: 888-952-6673 ■ *Web:* www.provationmedical.com

Phone | Fax | Class

Provco Group
795 E Lancaster Ave Two Villanova Ctr — Villanova PA 19085 — 610-520-2010 — 520-1905 — 792
Web: www.provcogroup.com

Provenance Consulting
301 W 6th St Ste 200 — Borger TX 79007 — 806-273-5100 — 194
Web: provpsm.com

Provenance Hotels
808 SW Park Alder Ste 300 — Portland OR 97205 — 503-295-2122 — 241-9399 — 379
Web: provenancehotels.com

Provence
1475 Western Ave Stuyvesant Plz — Albany NY 12203 — 518-689-7777 — 671
Web: provence-restaurant.net

Provia Door Inc 2150 SR- 39 — Sugarcreek OH 44681 — 403-555-5555 — 852-2107* — 235
**Fax Area Code:* 330 ■ *TF:* 800-669-4711 ■ *Web:* www.provia.com

Proviatek Inc 80 Broad St Ste 507 — New York NY 10004 — 212-500-6037 — 525
Web: www.proviatek.com

Provide-A-Care LLC
500 E Higgins Rd — Elk Grove Village IL 60007 — 773-326-6860 — 690-1539* — 363
**Fax Area Code:* 847 ■ *Web:* www.provideacare.com

Providence Athenaeum
251 Benefit St — Providence RI 02903 — 401-421-6970 — 520
Web: providenceathenaeum.org

Providence Business News
400 Wminster St Ste 600 — Providence RI 02903 — 401-273-2201 — 274-6580 — 457-5
TF: 855-813-5805 ■ *Web:* www.pbn.com

Providence Casket Co 1 Industrial Cir — Lincoln RI 02865 — 401-726-1700 — 134

Providence Children's Museum
100 S St — Providence RI 02903 — 401-273-5437 — 273-1004 — 521
Web: providencechildrensmuseum.org

Providence City Hall
25 Dorrance St — Providence RI 02903 — 401-421-7740 — 337
Web: www.providenceri.gov

Providence College 1 Cunningham Sq — Providence RI 02918 — 401-865-1000 — 865-2826 — 166
TF: 800-721-6444 ■ *Web:* www.providence.edu

Providence College & Seminary
10 College Crescent — Otterburne MB R0A1G0 — 204-433-7488 — 167-3
TF: 800-668-7768 ■ *Web:* www.prov.ca

Providence County 1 Dorrance Plz — Providence RI 02903 — 401-458-5400 — 338
Web: www.courts.ri.gov

Providence Equity Partners LLC
50 Kennedy Plz 18th Fl — Providence RI 02903 — 401-751-1700 — 751-1790 — 792
Web: www.provequity.com

Providence Health 2435 Forest Dr — Columbia SC 29204 — 803-256-5300 — 256-5935 — 374-3
Web: www.yourprovidencehealth.com

Providence Health & Services
9205 SW Barnes Rd — Portland OR 97225 — 503-216-1234 — 216-4041 — 374-3
TF: 800-562-8964 ■ *Web:* oregon.providence.org

Providence Health & Services
2201 Lind Ave SW Ste 130 — Renton WA 98057 — 800-832-0319 — 374-3
TF: 800-832-0319 ■ *Web:* www.providence.org

Providence Homes Inc
4901 Belfort Rd Ste 140 — Jacksonville FL 32256 — 904-262-9898 — 187
Web: www.providencehomesinc.com

Providence Hospital 6801 Airport Blvd — Mobile AL 36608 — 251-633-1000 — 633-1679 — 374-3
Web: www.providencehospital.org

Providence Hospital
1150 Varnum St NE — Washington DC 20017 — 202-854-7000 — 374-3
Web: www.provhosp.org

Providence Hospitality Partners
709 Clarkson St — Denver CO 80218 — 303-831-1114 — 379
Web: providencehospitality.com

Providence Jewelry Museum
1 Spectacle St — Cranston RI 02910 — 401-274-0999 — 520
Web: providencemuseum.org

Providence Journal 75 Fountain St — Providence RI 02902 — 401-277-7303 — 532-2
TF: 888-697-7656 ■ *Web:* www.providencejournal.com

Providence Lacquer & Supply Centre Inc
1155 Park Ave — Cranston RI 02910 — 401-943-1700 — 802
TF: 888-943-1700 ■ *Web:* www.providencelacquer.net

Providence Medical Ctr
8929 Parallel Pkwy — Kansas City KS 66112 — 913-596-4000 — 596-4801 — 374-3
TF: 800-281-7777 ■ *Web:* www.providencekc.com

Providence Metallizing Company Inc
51 Fairlawn Ave — Pawtucket RI 02860 — 401-722-5300 — 724-3410 — 481
Web: www.providencemetallizing.com

Providence Mutual Fire Insurance Co
340 E Ave — Warwick RI 02886 — 401-827-1800 — 822-1872 — 391-4
TF: 877-763-1800 ■ *Web:* www.providencemutual.com

Providence Oyster Bar
283 Atwells Ave — Providence RI 02903 — 401-272-8866 — 671
Web: www.provoysterbar.com

Providence Performing Arts Ctr
220 Weybosset St — Providence RI 02903 — 401-421-2997 — 351-7827 — 572
Web: www.ppacri.org

Providence Playhouse
1256 Providence Rd — Scranton PA 18508 — 570-342-9707 — 572

Providence Public Library
150 Empire St — Providence RI 02903 — 401-455-8000 — 434-3
Web: www.provlib.org

Providence Rest 3304 Waterbury Ave — Bronx NY 10465 — 718-931-3000 — 450
Web: www.providencerest.org

Providence Service Corp 700 Canal St — Stamford CT 06902 — 203-307-2800 — 307-2799 — 462
NASDAQ: PRSC ■ *Web:* www.prscholdings.com

Providence Software Solutions Inc
2054 Kildaire Farm Rd Ste 331 — Cary NC 27518 — 919-854-1800 — 178-1
Web: www.xvt.com

Providence Warwick Convention & Visitors Bureau
10 Memorial Blvd — Providence RI 02903 — 401-456-0200 — 351-2090 — 206
TF: 800-233-1636 ■ *Web:* www.goprovidence.com

Provident Bank 3756 Central Ave — Riverside CA 92506 — 951-686-6060 — 360-2
NASDAQ: PROV ■ *TF:* 800-442-5201 ■ *Web:* www.myprovident.com

Provident Bank 239 Washington Ave — Jersey City NJ 07302 — 732-590-9200 — 70
Web: www.provident.bank

Provident Central Credit Union
303 Twin Dolphin Dr — Redwood City CA 94065 — 650-508-0300 — 508-7202 — 219
TF: 800-632-4600 ■ *Web:* www.providentcu.org

Provident Construction Inc
12424 E Weaver Pl — Centennial CO 80111 — 720-482-0200 — 186
Web: www.providentconstruction.com

Provident Federal Credit Union
401 S New St — Dover DE 19904 — 302-734-1133 — 734-2683 — 219
TF: 888-328-7120 ■ *Web:* providentfcu.com

Provident Home Health Inc
725 E Broadway Ste 201 — Glendale CA 91205 — 818-241-9500 — 241-9509 — 363
Web: www.providenthomehealth.com

Provident Hotels & Resorts
107 Hampton Rd Ste 100 — Clearwater FL 33759 — 727-726-4770 — 379
Web: www.providentresorts.com

Provident Investment Management
39555 Orchard Hill Pl Ste 139 — Novi MI 48375 — 248-380-1700 — 380-1701 — 196
TF: 800-449-6970 ■ *Web:* www.investprovident.com

Provident Real Estate Ventures LLC
2800 Niagara Ln N — Plymouth MN 55447 — 952-345-5200 — 401
Web: www.providentrev.com

Provident Travel
11309 Montgomery Rd — Cincinnati OH 45249 — 513-247-1100 — 384
TF: 800-354-8108 ■ *Web:* www.providenttravel.com

Provider Trust
406 11th Ave N Ste 250 — Nashville TN 37203 — 615-938-7878 — 353
Web: www.providertrust.com

Providge Consulting
2207 Concord Pk Ste 537 — Wilmington DE 19803 — 888-927-6583 — 177
TF: 888-927-6583 ■ *Web:* providge.com

ProviDRs Care 1102 S Hillside — Wichita KS 67211 — 316-683-4111 — 683-6255 — 391-3
TF: 800-801-9772 ■ *Web:* www.providrscare.net

Provimi Foods Inc W2103 County Rd W — Seymour WI 54165 — 920-833-6861 — 10-3
Web: www.provimifoods.com

Provimi North America Inc
10 Nutrition Way PO Box 69 — Brookville OH 45309 — 800-257-3788 — 458-2539 — 447
TF: 800-257-3788 ■ *Web:* www.provimius.com

Provincetown Arts Inc
650 Commercial St — Provincetown MA 02657 — 508-487-3167 — 637-9
Web: www.provincetownarts.org

Provincetown Public Library
356 Commercial St — Provincetown MA 02657 — 508-487-7094 — 434-3
Web: provincetownlibrary.org

Provincial Archives of Alberta
8555 Roper Rd — Edmonton AB T6E5W1 — 780-427-1750 — 434-3
Web: provincialarchives.alberta.ca

Provincial Information & Library Resources Board
West Newfoundland-Labrador Div
4 West St — Corner Brook NL A2H0C1 — 709-634-7333 — 634-7313 — 436
Web: nlpl.ca

Provincial Wildlife Park
149 Creighton Rd — Shubenacadie NS B0N2H0 — 902-758-2040 — 823
Web: wildlifepark.novascotia.ca

Provine Helicopter Service Inc
308 Airport Rd — Greenwood MS 38930 — 662-453-9406 — 455-1160 — 302
TF: 800-559-6580 ■ *Web:* provinehelicopters.com

Provisio Group Ltd, The
10910 W Sam Houston Pkwy N Ste 500 — Houston TX 77064 — 281-894-7700 — 571-8080 — 45
Web: www.provisiogroup.com

ProVision Partners Coop PO Box 14 — Stratford WI 54484 — 715-687-4443 — 276
Web: provisionpartners.coop

ProVision solar Inc
69 Railroad Ave Ste A-7 — Hilo HI 96720 — 808-969-3281 — 934-7462 — 357
Web: provisionsolar.com

Provista 250 E John Carpenter Fwy — Irving TX 75062 — 888-538-4662 — 317
TF: 888-538-4662 ■ *Web:* www.provista.com

Provista Diagnostics Inc
17301 N Perimeter Dr — Scottsdale AZ 85255 — 855-552-7439 — 743
TF: 855-552-7439 ■ *Web:* www.provistadx.com

Provisur Technologies Inc
9150 191st St — Mokena IL 60448 — 708-479-3500 — 479-3598 — 298
Web: www.provisur.com

Provo City Hall 351 W Center St — Provo UT 84601 — 801-852-6100 — 852-6107 — 337
Web: www.provo.org

Provo City Library 550 N University Ave — Provo UT 84601 — 801-852-6650 — 852-6688 — 434-3
TF: 800-914-8931 ■ *Web:* www.provolibrary.com

Provo College 1450 West 820 North — Provo UT 84601 — 801-333-7133 — 167-3
TF: 877-777-5886 ■ *Web:* www.provocollege.edu

Provo School District 280 W 940 N — Provo UT 84604 — 801-374-4800 — 374-4808 — 685
Web: www.provo.edu

Provo Towne Ctr 1200 Towne Centre Blvd — Provo UT 84601 — 801-852-2400 — 460
Web: www.provotownecentre.com

Provo/Orem Chamber of Commerce
111 S University Ave — Provo UT 84601 — 801-851-2555 — 139
Web: www.thechamber.org

Provoast Automation Controls
12635 Danielson Ct Ste 205 — Poway CA 92064 — 858-748-2237 — 385
Web: www.proautocon.com

Provost-Umphrey Law Firm LLP
490 Park St — Beaumont TX 77704 — 409-835-6000 — 428
TF: 888-588-1695 ■ *Web:* www.provostumphrey.com

Proware 7621 E Kemper Rd — Cincinnati OH 45249 — 513-489-5477 — 177
Web: www.proware.com

Prowess Inc 1844 Clayton Rd — Concord CA 94520 — 925-356-0360 — 177
Web: www.prowess.com

Pro-west & Associates Inc
8239 State 371 NW — Walker MN 56484 — 320-207-6868 — 302
Web: www.prowestgis.com

Proworks Corp
777 NE Second St Ste 300 — Corvallis OR 97330 — 541-752-9885 — 177
Web: proworks.com

Proxibid Inc 4411 S 96 St — Omaha NE 68127 — 402-505-7770 — 177
TF: 877-505-7770 ■ *Web:* www.proxibid.com

Proxim Wireless Corp 1561 Buckeye Dr — Milpitas CA 95035 — 408-383-7600 — 383-7680 — 735
OTC: PRXM ■ *TF:* 800-229-1630 ■ *Web:* www.proxim.com

Proximex Corp 300 Santana Row Ste 200 — San Jose CA 95128 — 408-215-9000 — 338-0806 — 177
Web: www.proximex.com

Proximity Hotel
704 Green Valley Rd — Greensboro NC 27408 — 336-379-8200 — 132
TF: 800-379-8200 ■ *Web:* www.proximityhotel.com

Proximo Consulting Services Inc
2500 Plaza Five — Jersey City NJ 07311 — 800-236-9250 — 177
TF: 800-236-9250 ■ *Web:* www.proximo.com

Proz.com 235 Harrison St — Syracuse NY 13202 — 315-463-7323 — 261
Web: www.proz.com

Name / Address	City	State	ZIP	Phone	Fax	Class
PRP 5620 Elmwood Ave *Web:* www.prpgraphics.com	Indianapolis	IN	46203	317-783-3226		629
PRR Inc 1501 Fourth Ave Ste 550 *Web:* www.prrbiz.com	Seattle	WA	98101	206-623-0735		636
PRS Group Inc, The 5800 Heritage Landing Dr Ste E *Web:* www.prsgroup.com	East Syracuse	NY	13057	315-431-0511		637-10
PRS Inc 1761 Old Meadow Rd Ste 100 *Web:* prsinc.org	McLean	VA	22102	703-536-9000	448-3723	363
PRSA (Public Relations Society of America) 33 Maiden Ln 11th Fl *Web:* www.prsa.org	New York	NY	10038	212-460-1400	995-0757	49-18
PRTC (PRTC Inc) 201 Anderson Dr *Web:* www.prtcnet.com	Laurens	SC	29360	864-682-3131		736
PRTC Inc (PRTC) 201 Anderson Dr *Web:* www.prtcnet.com	Laurens	SC	29360	864-682-3131		736
Prudent Software Services Inc 8919 Donaker St *Web:* prudentglobal.com	San Diego	CA	92129	858-225-0406		177
Prudential Bank 1834 W Oregon Ave *Web:* www.psbanker.com	Philadelphia	PA	19145	215-755-1500		70
Prudential Builders Ctr 3902 E Ferry Ave	Spokane	WA	99202	509-535-2401		38
Prudential Financial Inc 751 Broad St *NYSE: PRU* ■ *TF:* 800-843-7625 ■ *Web:* www.prudential.com	Newark	NJ	07102	973-802-6000		401
Prudential Ltd 1737 E 22nd St *Web:* www.prulite.com	Los Angeles	CA	90058	213-746-0360	741-8590	439
Prudential Overall Supply PO Box 11210 *TF:* 800-767-5536 ■ *Web:* www.prudentialuniforms.com	Santa Ana	CA	92711	949-250-4855	261-1947	442
PruittHealth 1626 Jeurgens Ct *TF:* 800-222-0321 ■ *Web:* www.pruitthealth.com	Norcross	GA	30093	770-279-6200		450
Pruntytown Correctional Center and Jail 2006 Trap Springs Rd *Web:* dcr.wv.gov	Grafton	WV	26354	304-265-6111	265-6120	213
PRWT Services Inc 1835 Market St 8th Fl *Web:* www.prwt.com	Philadelphia	PA	19103	215-569-8810	569-9893	721
PRX Inc 991 W Hedding St Ste 201 *Web:* www.prxdigital.com	San Jose	CA	95126	408-287-1700		636
Prym-Dritz USA Inc PO Box 5028 *Web:* www.dritz.com	Spartanburg	SC	29304	864-576-5050		594
Pryor Products 1819 Peacock Blvd *TF:* 800-854-2280 ■ *Web:* www.pryorproducts.com	Oceanside	CA	92056	760-724-8244		476
PS (Ploughshares) Emerson College 120 Boylston St *Web:* www.pshares.org	Boston	MA	02116	617-824-3757		637-9
PS & Associates Underwriting Agency Inc 1776 Legacy Cir Ste 104 *Web:* www.psassociate.com	Naperville	IL	60563	630-416-0004	416-2246	390
PS & M Communication Arts 2101 E El Segundo Blvd Ste 202 *Web:* www.psmcommarts.com	El Segundo	CA	90245	310-791-2755		4
PS Business Parks Inc 701 Western Ave *NYSE: PSB* ■ *TF:* 888-782-6110 ■ *Web:* www.psbusinessparks.com	Glendale	CA	91201	818-244-8080	242-0566	655
PS Energy Group Inc 4480 N Shallowford Rd Ste 100 **Fax Area Code:* 404 ■ *TF:* 800-334-7548 ■ *Web:* www.psenergy.com	Dunwoody	GA	30338	770-350-3000	321-3938*	787
PS Engineering Inc 9800 Martel Rd *Web:* ps-engineering.com	Lenoir City	TN	37772	865-988-9800		261
PS Marcato Elevator Co 4411 11th St *Web:* www.psmarcato.com	Long Island City	NY	11101	718-392-6400		189-1
PS Marston Associates 38B S Rd *TF:* 800-643-9537 ■ *Web:* www.abenaquicarriers.com	North Hampton	NH	03862	603-379-8819	964-9343	780
PS Websolutions Inc 906 Carriage Path SE Ste 100 *TF:* 877-571-7829 ■ *Web:* pswebsolution.com	Smyrna	GA	30082	877-571-7829		177
PSA Airlines Inc 3400 Terminal Dr **Fax Area Code:* 937 ■ *TF:* 800-235-0986 ■ *Web:* www.psaairlines.com	Vandalia	OH	45377	800-235-0986	665-2510*	25
PSA Management Inc 1516 E Hillcrest St Ste 310 *Web:* www.psaonline.com	Orlando	FL	32803	407-898-9119	898-9077	196
PSARA Technologies Inc 10925 Reed Hartman Hwy Ste 220 *Web:* psara.com	Cincinnati	OH	45242	513-791-4418		261
PSB (Peoples Savings Bank) 414 N Adams PO Box 248 *TF:* 877-508-2265 ■ *Web:* www.bankpsb.com	Wellsburg	IA	50680	641-869-3721	869-3855	70
PSB Industries Inc PO Box 1318 *TF:* 800-829-1119 ■ *Web:* www.psbindustries.com	Erie	PA	16512	814-453-3651		386
Psbank 76 Church St PO Box 217 *Web:* psbanking.com	Wyalusing	PA	18853	570-746-1011		70
PSC (Professional Services Council) 4401 Wilson Blvd Ste 1110 *Web:* www.pscouncil.org	Arlington	VA	22203	703-875-8059	875-8922	49-12
PSC (Product Safety Consulting Inc) 605 Country Club Dr Ste I & J *TF:* 877-804-3066 ■ *Web:* www.productsafetyinc.com	Bensenville	IL	60106	630-238-0188	238-0269	196
PSC Distribution 72 Commercial Dr *Web:* www.pscia.com	Iowa City	IA	52246	319-338-3601	337-7937	612
PSC Electronics 2307 Calle Del Mundo *Web:* pscelex.com	Santa Clara	CA	95054	408-737-1333		602
PSC Industries 1100 W Market St *Web:* pscindustries.com	Louisville	KY	40203	502-625-7700	625-7837	605-2
PSCA (Profit Sharing/401(k) Council of America) 20 N Wacker Dr Ste 3700 *TF:* 866-614-8407 ■ *Web:* www.psca.org	Chicago	IL	60606	312-419-1863	419-1864	49-12
PSD Global LLC 505 N Mansfield St *Web:* www.psdglobal.com	Alexandria	VA	22304	703-531-8773		195
PSDA (Print Services & Distribution Assn) 330 N Wabash Ave Ste 2000 *TF:* 800-230-0175 ■ *Web:* www.psda.org	Chicago	IL	60611	800-230-0175		48-9
PSE (Pi Sigma Epsilon) 3747 S Howell Ave *Web:* www.pse.org	Milwaukee	WI	53207	414-328-1952	328-1953	48-16
PSE (Piping Systems Engineering) 1905 S Lindsay Rd *Web:* piping-systems.com	Mesa	AZ	85201	480-345-0052		261
PSE (Peterson Structural Engineers Inc) 9400 SW Barnes Rd Ste 100 *Web:* psengineers.com	Portland	OR	97225	503-292-1635	292-9846	261
PSEA (Penna State Education Association Harrisburg) 400 N Third St PO Box 1724 *TF:* 800-944-7732 ■ *Web:* www.psea.org	Harrisburg	PA	17105	717-255-7000		474
PSF Industries Inc 65 S Horton St *TF:* 800-426-1204 ■ *Web:* www.psfindustries.com	Seattle	WA	98134	206-622-1252		189-10
PSF Mechanical Inc 9322 14th Ave S *Web:* www.psfmechanical.com	Seattle	WA	98108	206-764-9663		610
PSFEG Inc 5700 Ralston St Ste 300 *Web:* psfeg.com	Ventura	CA	93003	805-644-1370		261
PSI (Pet Sitters Intl) 213 East Dalton Rd *Web:* www.petsit.com	King	NC	27021	336-983-9222		48-3
PSI (Population Services Intl) 1120 19th St NW Ste 600 *Web:* www.psi.org	Washington	DC	20036	202-785-0072	785-0120	48-17
PSI (Professional Service Industries Inc) 1901 S Meyers Rd Ste 400 *TF:* 800-548-7901 ■ *Web:* www.psiusa.com	Oakbrook Terrace	IL	60181	630-691-1490	691-1587	261
PSI (Pressure Service Inc) 2361 S Plaza Dr *TF:* 800-666-3664 ■ *Web:* www.pressureservices.com	Rapid City	SD	57702	605-341-5154	341-4843	76
PSI (Pump Systems Inc) 530 25th Ave E *TF:* 800-437-8076 ■ *Web:* www.pumpsystems.com	Dickinson	ND	58601	701-225-4494	225-0320	385
PSI Chi National Honor Society in Psychology 651 E Fourth St Ste 600 *Web:* www.psichi.org	Chattanooga	TN	37403	423-756-2044	265-1529	48-16
PSI Contact Ctr 3160 Haggerty Rd Ste D *Web:* www.psicontactcenter.com	West Bloomfield	MI	48323	313-879-4895		737
PSI Control Solutions Inc 9900 Twin Lakes Pkwy *Web:* www.psicontrolsolutions.com	Charlotte	NC	28269	704-596-5617		729
PSI Health Solutions Inc 1013 Morse Dr *Web:* www.psibands.com	Pacific Grove	CA	93950	831-373-7712		476
PSI Industries Inc PO Box 70127 *TF:* 800-238-6430 ■ *Web:* www.psiindustries.com	Memphis	TN	38107	901-525-0422	526-4901	625
PSI International Inc 11200 Waples Mill Rd Ste 200 **Fax Area Code:* 888 ■ *Web:* www.psiint.com	Fairfax	VA	22030	703-352-8700	767-6418*	178-10
PSI Personnel LLC 252 W Swamp Rd Ste 29 *Web:* www.psipersonnel.com	Doylestown	PA	18901	215-345-6778		260
PSI Services LLC 611 N Brand Blvd 1st Fl *TF:* 800-367-1565 ■ *Web:* www.psionline.com	Glendale	CA	91203	800-367-1565		180
PSI Software Inc 7326 Remcon Cir *Web:* www.psisoftware.com	El Paso	TX	79912	915-584-4100		179
PSI Upsilon Fraternity 3003 E 96th St *TF:* 800-394-1833 ■ *Web:* psiu.org	Indianapolis	IN	46240	317-571-1833	844-5170	48-16
Psilos Group Managers LLC 140 Broadway 51st Fl *Web:* psilos.com	New York	NY	10005	212-242-8844		792
PsiNapse Technology 1063 Serpentine Ln Ste A *Web:* www.psinapse.com	Pleasanton	CA	94566	925-225-0400		260
PSLA (Photo-Scan of Los Angeles Inc) 743 Cochran St Ste C *TF:* 800-820-7752 ■ *Web:* www.pslasecurity.com	Simi Valley	CA	93065	805-581-4448	526-4406	693
PSM Partners 209 W Jackson Blvd *Web:* www.psmpartners.com	Chicago	IL	60606	312-940-7830		177
PSMJ Resources Inc 10 Midland Ave *TF:* 800-537-7765 ■ *Web:* www.psmj.com	Newton	MA	02458	617-965-0055	965-5152	194
PSNC Energy Corp PO Box 1398 *TF:* 877-776-2427 ■ *Web:* www.psncenergy.com	Gastonia	NC	28053	877-776-2427		579
Psomas 555 S Flower St Ste 4300 *Web:* psomas.com	Los Angeles	CA	90071	213-223-1400		261
PSP (Pavement Saw Press) 321 Empire St *Web:* www.pavementsaw.org	Montpelier	OH	43543	419-485-0524		637-2
PSP Industries Inc 9885 Doerr Ln *Web:* www.pspindustries.com	Schertz	TX	78154	210-651-9595	646-5999	537
PSPrint LLC 2861 Mandela Pkwy *TF:* 800-511-2009 ■ *Web:* www.psprint.com	Oakland	CA	94608	800-511-2009		627
PSR (Physicians for Social Responsibility) 1875 Connecticut Ave NW Ste 1012 *Web:* www.psr.org	Washington	DC	20009	202-667-4260	667-4201	49-8
PSR (Professional Shorthand Reporters Inc) 601 Poydras St Ste 1615 *TF:* 800-536-5255 ■ *Web:* www.psrdepo.com	New Orleans	LA	70130	504-529-5255	529-5257	445
PSR Associates Inc 6629 Thornton Palms Dr *TF:* 855-717-4777 ■ *Web:* psrassociates.com	Tampa	FL	33647	813-412-5246	978-8670	260
Pssc Labs 20432 N Sea Cir *Web:* www.pssclabs.com	Lake Forest	CA	92630	949-380-7288	380-9788	173-8
PSTG Consulting 72 Scollard St	Toronto	ON	M5R1G2	416-593-0000		193
Psychemedics Corp 289 Great Rd Ste 200 *NASDAQ: PMD* ■ **Fax Area Code:* 978 ■ *TF:* 800-628-8073 ■ *Web:* www.psychemedics.com	Acton	MA	01720	877-517-2033	264-9236*	85
Psychiatric Institute of Washington 4228 Wisconsin Ave NW *TF:* 800-369-2273 ■ *Web:* psychinstitute.com	Washington	DC	20016	202-885-5600	885-5614	374-5
Psychic Readings by Sylvia 546 Rogers St *Web:* www.sylviaspsychicreadings.com	Lowell	MA	01852	978-937-0998		226
Psycho-Cybernetics Foundation Inc 10339 Birdwatch Dr *Web:* www.psycho-cybernetics.com	Tampa	FL	33647	813-994-8267	994-4947	96
Psychological Software Solutions Inc 4119 Montrose Blvd STE 500	Houston	TX	77006	713-965-6941		177
Psychology Software Tools Inc Sharpsburg Business Pk 311 23rd Street Ext Ste 200 *TF:* 888-540-9664 ■ *Web:* pstnet.com	Sharpsburg	PA	15215	412-449-0078	449-0079	177

				Phone	Fax	Class
Psychology Today 115 E 23rd St 9th Fl *Web:* www.psychologytoday.com	New York	NY	10010	212-260-7210	260-7445	457-11
Psychopathic Record 32575 Folsom Rd *Web:* www.psychopathicrecords.com	Farmington Hills	MI	48336	248-426-0800		657
Psychotherapy Networker 5135 MacArthur Blvd NW *TF:* 888-851-9498 ■ *Web:* www.psychotherapynetworker.org	Washington	DC	20016	888-851-9498		457-16
Psychsoft PO Box 232 *Web:* www.psych-soft.com	Quincy	MA	02171	617-471-8733		180
PsyComNet 1556 3rd Ave *TF:* 800-332-1088 ■ *Web:* www.psycom.net	New York	NY	10128	212-876-7800		387
PsyMax Solutions LLC 25550 Chagrin Blvd Ste 100 *TF:* 866-774-2273 ■ *Web:* www.psymaxsolutions.com	Cleveland	OH	44122	216-896-9991		194
Psyop Inc 45 Howard St 5th Fl *Web:* www.psyop.com	New York	NY	10013	212-533-9055		344
Psytech Solutions 1138 Stone Creek Dr *TF:* 866-377-9832 ■ *Web:* www.psytechsolutions.net	Hummelstown	PA	17036	866-377-9832		177
PT (Perfection Type Inc) 1050 33rd Ave SE Ste 1000 *TF:* 800-829-4815 ■ *Web:* www.perfectiontype.com	Minneapolis	MN	55414	651-917-8444	917-8440	385
PT Ferro Construction Co 700 Rowell Ave *Web:* www.ptferro.com	Joliet	IL	60433	815-726-6284	726-5614	189-5
PTA Corp 148 Christian St *Web:* www.ptaplastics.com	Oxford	CT	06478	203-888-0585		604
PTC (Paternity Testing Corp) 300 Portland St *TF:* 888-837-8323 ■ *Web:* www.ptclabs.com	Columbia	MO	65201	573-442-9948	442-9870	417
PTC (Parents Television Council) 707 Wilshire Blvd Ste 2075 *Web:* www.w2.parentstv.org	Los Angeles	CA	90017	213-629-9255	629-9254	49-14
PTC (Parametric Technology Corp) 140 Kendrick St *NASDAQ: PTC* ■ *TF:* 800-613-7535 ■ *Web:* www.ptc.com	Needham	MA	02494	781-370-5000	370-6000	178-5
PTC (Pierce Telephone Company Inc) 112 S 5th St *TF:* 888-329-6225 ■ *Web:* www.piercetelephone.com	Pierce	NE	68767	402-329-6225	329-4006	224
PTC (Pattersonville Telephone Co) 1309 Main St *Web:* www.ptcconnect.net	Rotterdam Junction	NY	12150	518-887-2121		224
PTC (Pacific Telecommunications Council) 914 Coolidge St *Web:* www.ptc.org	Honolulu	HI	96826	808-941-3789	944-4874	139
PTC Alliance Copperleaf Corporate Ctr 6051 Wallace Road Ext Ste 200 *TF:* 800-274-8823 ■ *Web:* www.ptcalliance.com	Wexford	PA	15090	412-299-7900	299-2619	490
PTC Enterprises Inc 3047 County Rd K *Web:* www.ptc-enterprises.com	Edon	OH	43518	419-272-2524		604
PTC International Inc 345 N Charles St *Web:* www.ptcintl.com	Baltimore	MD	21201	443-682-9127		809
PTC Organics Inc 900 Briggs Rd Ste 145 *TF:* 800-782-7118 ■ *Web:* www.ptcorganics.com	Mount Laurel	NJ	08054	856-222-1146	222-1124	192
PTC Select LLC 2450 N Knoxville Ave *TF:* 800-225-2320 ■ *Web:* www.ptcselect.com	Peoria	IL	61604	309-685-8400		175
PTC Therapeutics Inc 100 Corporate Ct *Web:* www.ptcbio.com	South Plainfield	NJ	07080	908-222-7000		231
PTCFO Inc 48 Walkley Rd *Web:* www.ptcfo.com	West Hartford	CT	06119	860-232-9858	232-9438	194
PTDA (Power Transmission Distributors Assn) 230 W Monroe St Ste 1410 *Web:* www.ptda.org	Chicago	IL	60606	312-516-2100		49-18
PTI (Pittsburgh Technical College) 1111 McKee Rd *TF:* 800-784-9675 ■ *Web:* www.pti.edu	Oakdale	PA	15071	412-809-5100	809-5121	800
PTI (Preferred Technology Systems LLC) 9160 E Bahia Dr Ste 100 *TF:* 800-331-6224 ■ *Web:* www.ptisecurity.com	Scottsdale	AZ	85260	480-257-2600	257-2599	392
PTI Engineered Plastics Inc 50900 Corporate Dr *Web:* www.teampti.com	Macomb	MI	48044	586-263-5100	263-6680	261
PTI Technologies Inc 501 Del Norte Blvd *TF:* 800-331-2701 ■ *Web:* www.ptitechnologies.com	Oxnard	CA	93030	805-604-3700	604-3701	386
Ptm & W Industries Inc 10640 S Painter Ave *TF:* 800-421-1518 ■ *Web:* www.ptm-w.com	Santa Fe Springs	CA	90670	562-946-4511	941-4773	605-2
PTMW Inc 5040 NW US Hwy 24 *Web:* www.ptmw.com	Topeka	KS	66618	785-232-7792		697
PTR Baler & Compactor Co 2207 E Ontario St *TF:* 800-523-3654 ■ *Web:* ptrco.com	Philadelphia	PA	19134	800-523-3654		470
PTRC (Piedmont Triad Regional Council) 1398 Carrollton Crossing Dr *Web:* www.ptrc.org	Kernersville	NC	27284	336-904-0300	904-0301	48-6
PTR-Precision Technologies Inc 120 Post Rd *Web:* www.ptreb.com	Enfield	CT	06082	860-741-2281	745-7932	425
PTS Data Center Solutions Inc 16 Thornton Rd *Web:* www.ptsdcs.com	Oakland	NJ	07436	201-337-3833		180
PTS Laboratories 8100 Secura Way *Web:* www.ptslabs.com	Santa Fe Springs	CA	90670	562-347-2500		743
PTSD (Department of Veterans Affairs) *National Center for Post-Traumatic Stress Disorder* 215 N Main St *Web:* www.ptsd.va.gov	White River Junction	VT	05009	802-296-5132	296-5135	668
PTSI (Panhandle Telecommunication Systems Inc) 2222 NW Hwy 64 *TF:* 800-562-2556 ■ *Web:* www.ptci.net	Guymon	OK	73942	580-338-2556		736
Pub Cite 191 Rue Theberge *Web:* pubcite.com	Delson	QC	J5B2J9	450-635-0635		627
Pub Italia 434 1/2 Preston St *Web:* www.pubitalia.ca	Ottawa	ON	K1S4N4	613-232-2326		671
Pub Saint-Alexandre 1087 St Jean St *Web:* pubstalexandre.com	Quebec City	QC	G1R1S3	418-694-0015	694-0178	671
Pub St Patrick 1200 St-Jean St *Web:* www.pubsaintpatrick.com	Quebec City	QC	G1R1S8	418-694-0618		671
Pub St-Paul 124 St Paul St E *Web:* pubstpaul.com	Montreal	QC	H2Y1G6	514-874-0485		671
Pubco Corp 3830 Kelley Ave *TF:* 800-878-3399 ■ *Web:* www.fundinguniverse.com	Cleveland	OH	44114	216-881-5300	881-8380	111
Public Affairs 1290 Avenue of the Americas 5th Fl *Web:* www.publicaffairsbooks.com	New York	NY	10104	212-364-1100		637-2
Public Affairs Associates Inc 1 Michigan Avenue 120 N Washington Sq Ste 1050 *Web:* www.paa-online.com	Lansing	MI	48933	517-371-3800		317
Public Affairs Council (PAC) 2121 K St NW Ste 9 *Web:* pac.org	Washington	DC	20037	202-787-5950	787-5942	48-7
Public Agenda 6 E 39th St *Web:* www.publicagenda.org	New York	NY	10016	212-686-6610	889-3461	634
Public Auction Yards (PAYS) 1802 Minnesota Ave *Web:* www.publicauctionyards.com	Billings	MT	59101	406-245-6447	256-6270	446
Public Belt Railroad Commission 4822 Tchoupitulas St *TF:* 800-524-3421 ■ *Web:* www.nopb.com	New Orleans	LA	70115	504-896-7410	896-7452	651
Public Broadcasting Service (PBS) 2100 Crystal Dr *TF:* 866-864-0828 ■ *Web:* www.pbs.org	Arlington	VA	22202	703-739-5051		739
Public Chicago 1301 N State Pkwy *Web:* www.publichotels.com	Chicago	IL	60610	312-787-3700	573-5817	671
Public Company Accounting Oversight Board (PCAOB) 125 E Lake St Ste 303 *Web:* pcaobus.org	Washington	DC	20006	202-207-9100		533
Public Consulting Group Inc 148 State St **Fax Area Code:* 617 ■ *TF:* 800-210-6113 ■ *Web:* www.publicconsultinggroup.com	Boston	MA	02109	800-210-6113	426-4632*	194
Public Forum Institute 2300 M St NW *Web:* www.ncdd.org	Washington	DC	20037	202-467-2774		48-7
Public Health Institute 555 12th St 10th Fl *Web:* www.phi.org	Oakland	CA	94607	510-285-5500	285-5501	48-17
Public Health Research Institute (PHRI) 225 Warren St Rm E240M *Web:* www.phri.org	Newark	NJ	07103	973-854-3100	854-3101	668
Public Health Solutions 40 Worth St 5th Fl *Web:* www.healthsolutions.org	New York	NY	10013	646-619-6400		231
Public Impact 504 Dogwood Dr *Web:* publicimpact.com	Chapel Hill	NC	27516	919-240-7955	903-8649	195
Public Interest Network 1543 Wazee St Ste 400 *TF:* 800-401-6511 ■ *Web:* publicinterestnetwork.org	Denver	CO	80202	303-573-5995		305
Public Lands Foundation (PLF) PO Box 7226 *TF:* 866-985-9636 ■ *Web:* publicland.org	Arlington	VA	22207	703-935-0916		48-13
Public Law Ctr 601 W Civic Center Dr *Web:* publiclawcenter.org	Santa Ana	CA	92701	714-541-1010	541-5157	41
Public Libraries of Saginaw 505 Janes St *Web:* www.saginawlibrary.org	Saginaw	MI	48607	989-755-0904	755-9829	434-3
Public Library of Cincinnati & Hamilton County 800 Vine St *Web:* www.cincinnatilibrary.org	Cincinnati	OH	45202	513-369-6900		434-3
Public Library of Steubenville & Jefferson County 407 S 4th St *Web:* www.steubenvillelibrary.org	Steubenville	OH	43952	740-282-9782	282-2919	434-3
Public Library of Youngstown & Mahoning County 305 Wick Ave *Web:* www.libraryvisit.org	Youngstown	OH	44503	330-744-8636	744-2258	434-3
Public Market of Newington LLC 437 New Britain Ave *Web:* publicmarketnewington.com	Newington	CT	06111	860-667-1454		345
Public Media Nj Inc PO Box 5776 *Web:* www.njtvonline.org	Englewood	NJ	07631	609-777-0031		647
Public Opinion 77 N Third St *TF:* 800-782-0661 ■ *Web:* www.publicopiniononline.com	Chambersburg	PA	17201	717-264-6161	264-0377	532-2
Public Opinion Strategies LLC 214 N Fayette St *Web:* pos.org	Alexandria	VA	22314	703-836-7655		636
Public Partnerships LLC 40 Broad St 4th Fl *TF:* 866-709-3319 ■ *Web:* www.publicpartnerships.com	Boston	MA	02109	617-426-2026		466
Public Policy Forum (PPF) 633 W Wisconsin Ave Ste 406 *Web:* www.publicpolicyforum.org	Milwaukee	WI	53203	414-276-8240	276-9962	48-13
Public Protection Cabinet *Economic Development Cabinet* 500 Mero St 218NC *Web:* ppc.ky.gov	Frankfort	KY	40601	502-782-2736		339-18
Public Radio 89.5 800 Tucker Dr *TF:* 888-594-5947 ■ *Web:* publicradiotulsa.org	Tulsa	OK	74104	918-631-2577	631-3695	645-166
Public Radio Intl (PRI) 401 Second Ave N Ste 500 *Web:* www.pri.org	Minneapolis	MN	55401	612-330-9251	330-9222	644
Public Relations Society of America (PRSA) 33 Maiden Ln 11th Fl *Web:* www.prsa.org	New York	NY	10038	212-460-1400	995-0757	49-18
Public Resources Advisory Group Inc 39 Broadway Ste 1210 *Web:* pragadvisors.com	New York	NY	10006	212-566-7800		194
Public Risk Management Assn (PRIMA) 700 S Washington St Ste 218 *Web:* www.primacentral.org	Alexandria	VA	22314	703-528-7701	739-0200	49-7

Phone | Fax | Class

Public Salt Co 2927 Harrisburg Rd NE ....Canton OH 44705 330-454-7913 454-7978 297-2
TF: 800-686-7439 ■ *Web:* www.publicsalt.com

Public Sector Consultants Inc
230 N Washington Sq Ste 300 ....Lansing MI 48933 517-484-4954 484-6549 196
Web: www.publicsectorconsultants.com

Public Service Commission of West Virginia
201 Brooke St PO Box 812..................Charleston WV 25301 304-340-0300 340-0325 339-49
TF: 800-344-5113 ■ *Web:* www.psc.state.wv.us

Public Service Enterprise Group Inc
80 Park Plz ....Newark NJ 07102 973-430-7000 360-5
NYSE: PEG ■ *TF:* 800-436-7734 ■ *Web:* www.pseg.com

Public Service Research Foundation
320-D Maple Ave E...........................Vienna VA 22180 703-242-3575 48-7
Web: psrf.org

Public Technology Inc
1420 Prince St Ste 200.....................Alexandria VA 22314 202-626-2400 49-7
TF: 866-664-6368 ■ *Web:* www.pti.org

Public Theater San Antonio, The
800 W Ashby Pl ....San Antonio TX 78212 210-733-7258 734-2651 572
Web: www.thepublicsa.org

Public Theater, The 425 Lafayette St...........New York NY 10003 212-539-8500 573-4
Web: publictheater.org

Public Utilities Reports Inc (PUR)
11410 Isaac Newton Sq Ste 220.................Reston VA 20190 703-847-7720 847-0683 637-10
TF: 800-368-5001 ■ *Web:* www.fortnightly.com

Public Utility District #1 of Ferry County
686 S Clark Ave PO Box 1039 .... Republic WA 99166 509-775-3325 775-3326 245
Web: fcpud.com

Public Welfare Foundation
1200 U St NW...........................Washington DC 20009 202-965-1800 305
TF: 800-275-7934 ■ *Web:* www.publicwelfare.org

Public Works Commission of The City of Fayetteville North Carolina
955 Old Wilmington Rd PO Box 1089 ....Fayetteville NC 28301 910-483-1382 787
TF: 877-687-7921 ■ *Web:* www.faypwc.com

Publication Printers Corp
2001 S Platte River Dr ....Denver CO 80223 303-936-0303 934-6712 627
TF: 888-824-0303 ■ *Web:* www.publicationprinters.com

Publications & Communications Inc
13552 Hwy 183 N Ste A .... Austin TX 78750 512-250-9023 637-9
TF: 800-678-9724 ■ *Web:* pcinews.com

Publications International Ltd
7373 N Cicero Ave .... Lincolnwood IL 60712 847-676-3470 676-3671 637-2
TF: 800-777-5582 ■ *Web:* pilbooks.com

PublicData
7750 N MacArthur Blvd Ste 120-320 ....Irving TX 75063 877-762-6266 393
TF: 877-762-6266 ■ *Web:* www.publicdata.com

Publicis USA 1675 Broadway..................New York NY 10019 212-474-5000 4
Web: publicisna.com

Publick House Historic Resort
277 Main St Rt 131........................Sturbridge MA 01566 508-347-3313 347-1460 379
TF: 800-782-5425 ■ *Web:* www.publickhouse.com

Publicom Inc
333 Albert Ave Ste 400.................. East Lansing MI 48823 517-487-3700 317
Web: www.publicom.com

Publipage Inc 2055 Rue Peel .... Montreal QC H3A1V4 514-286-1550 7
TF: 800-544-8614 ■ *Web:* www.publitech.com

Publish or Perish Inc
1302 Waugh Dr Ste 377......................Houston TX 77019 713-893-6100 637-2
Web: www.mathpop.com

PublishAmerica LLP PO Box 151..............Frederick MD 21705 301-695-1707 637-2
Web: www.publishamerica.com

Publishers Design Group Inc (PDG)
1655 Booth Rd ....Roseville CA 95747 916-784-0500 637-2
TF: 800-587-6666 ■ *Web:* www.publishersdesign.com

Publishers Group West (PGW)
1700 Fourth St ....Berkeley CA 94710 510-809-3700 809-3777 96
TF: 866-400-5351 ■ *Web:* www.pgw.com

Publishers' Warehouse
150 Industrial Rd .... Alabaster AL 35007 205-980-2820 96
Web: www.publisherswarehouse.com

Publishing Group of America Media
131 3rd Ave N Ste 200 ....Franklin TN 37064 615-468-6000 637-9

Publix Super Markets Inc
3300 Publix Corporate Pkwy .... Lakeland FL 33811 863-688-1188 345
TF: 800-242-1227 ■ *Web:* www.publix.com

PUC Inc
500 Second Line E PO Box 9000 ....Sault Sainte Marie ON P6B4K1 705-759-6500 759-6510 224
TF: 800-400-2255 ■ *Web:* www.ssmpuc.com

Pucci Foods 25447 Industrial Blvd ....Hayward CA 94545 510-300-6800 887-0151 297-9
Web: puccifoods.com

Pucel Enterprises Inc
1440 E 36th St ....Cleveland OH 44114 216-881-4604 881-6731 470
TF: 800-336-4986 ■ *Web:* www.pucelenterprises.com

Puckett Publishing 629 Jackson St SE .... Decatur AL 35601 256-682-0783 637-10
Web: www.puckettpublishing.com

PuddleDancer Press
2240 Encinitas Blvd Ste D-911................ Encinitas CA 92024 866-693-5293 759-6967* 637-2
**Fax Area Code:* 858 ■ *TF:* 866-693-5293 ■ *Web:* www.nonviolentcommunication.com

Pudik Graphics Inc 111 Oakwood Rd..........East Peoria IL 61611 309-694-2900 344
Web: www.pudik.com

Pudney & Company PC 1689 Rte 22 Ste 6........Brewster NY 10509 845-279-6300 279-4705 2
Web: www.pudneycpa.com

Pueblo Bank & Trust Co 301 W 5th St ....Pueblo CO 81003 719-545-1834 70
Web: pbandt.bank

Pueblo Bonito Golf & Spa Resorts
4350 La Jolla Village Dr................. San Diego CA 92122 858-642-2050 378
TF: 800-990-8250 ■ *Web:* www.pueblobonito.com

Pueblo Chieftain 825 W Sixth St ....Pueblo CO 81003 719-544-3520 532-2
TF: 800-279-6397 ■ *Web:* www.chieftain.com

Pueblo Community College
900 W Orman Ave.............................Pueblo CO 81004 719-549-3200 162
TF: 888-642-6017 ■ *Web:* www.pueblocc.edu

Pueblo County Courthouse 215 W 10th St........Pueblo CO 81003 719-583-6000 583-4894 338
Web: county.pueblo.org

Pueblo Fruits Inc
3333 Los Arboles Ave NE .... Albuquerque NM 87107 505-344-2554 297-7
Web: www.pueblofruits.com

Pueblo Government Agencies Federal Credit Union
720 N Greenwood St..........................Pueblo CO 81003 719-542-3379 219
Web: pgafcu.org

Pueblo Grande Museum & Archaeological Park
4619 E Washington St ....Phoenix AZ 85034 602-495-0901 520
Web: www.phoenix.gov

Pueblo Youth Services Ctr
1406 W 17th St..............................Pueblo CO 81003 719-544-1406 412
Web: www.colorado.gov

Pueblo Zoo 3455 Nuckolls Ave...................Pueblo CO 81005 719-561-1452 823
Web: www.pueblozoo.org

Puente Hills Mall
1600 Azusa Ave .... City of Industry CA 91748 626-912-8777 913-2719 460
TF: 800-743-3463 ■ *Web:* www.puentehills-mall.com

Puerto Rican Chamber of Commerce of South Florida
3550 Biscayne Blvd Ste 306.................... Miami FL 33137 305-571-8006 571-8007 138
Web: www.puertoricanchamber.com

Puerto Rico
Secretary of State PO Box 9020082............San Juan PR 00902 787-721-7000 340-16
Web: www.fortaleza.pr.gov

Puerto Rico Chamber of Commerce
PO Box 9024033 ....San Juan PR 00902 787-721-6060 723-1891 140
Web: www.camarapr.org

Puerto Rico Convention Ctr
500 Tanca Ste 402 ....San Juan PR 00901 800-875-4765 725-2133* 206
**Fax Area Code:* 787 ■ *TF:* 800-875-4765 ■ *Web:* www.prconvention.com

Puerto Rico Farm Credit Aca
PO Box 363649 ....San Juan PR 00936 787-753-0579 216
TF: 800-981-3323 ■ *Web:* prfarmcredit.com

Puffin Inn 4400 Spenard Rd.................Anchorage AK 99517 907-243-4044 248-6853 379
TF: 800-478-3346 ■ *Web:* www.puffininn.net

Puget Bindery Inc 7820 S 228th St ....Kent WA 98032 253-872-5707 872-5221 92
Web: www.pugetbindery.com

Puget Consumers Coop
3131 Elliott Ave Ste 500.......................Seattle WA 98121 206-547-1222 390
Web: www.pccmarkets.com

Puget Energy 10885 NE Fourth St...............Bellevue WA 98004 888-225-5773 456-2707* 360-5
**Fax Area Code:* 425 ■ *TF:* 888-225-5773 ■ *Web:* www.pugetenergy.com

Puget Sound Educational Service District
800 Oakesdale Ave SW........................Renton WA 98057 425-917-7600 685
TF: 800-664-4549 ■ *Web:* www.psesd.org

Puget Sound Rope Corp
1012 Second St ....Anacortes WA 98221 360-293-8488 293-8480 208
TF: 888-525-8488 ■ *Web:* www.cortlandcompany.com

Puget Western Inc
19515 N Creek Pkwy Ste 310..................Bothell WA 98011 425-487-6550 487-6565 653
Web: pugetwestern.com

Pugh Capital Management Inc
520 Park St Ste 2900 .... Seattle WA 98101 206-322-4985 401
Web: www.pughcapital.com

Pugh Lubricants
701 McDowell Rd PO Box 4006...............Asheboro NC 27205 336-629-2061 579
Web: www.pughoil.com

Puglisi Egg Farms Inc
75 Easy St.........................Howell Township NJ 07731 732-938-2373 10-8

Pugster Inc 2835 Sierra Grande St.............Pasadena CA 91107 626-356-1881 411
Web: pugster.com

PugTale Publishing
1601 W Main St Ste 90 No 403 .... Willimantic CT 06226 860-456-9173 637-2
TF: 877-456-7847 ■ *Web:* www.pugtalepublishing.com

PUHSD (Phoenix Union High School District)
4502 N Central Ave.........................Phoenix AZ 85012 602-764-1100 685
Web: www.phxhs.k12.az.us

Pukaskwa National Park of Canada
PO Box 212 ....Heron Bay ON P0T1R0 807-229-0801 229-2097 563
Web: www.pc.gc.ca

Puklich Chevrolet Inc 3701 State St ...... Bismarck ND 58502 701-223-5800 57
Web: www.puklichchevrolet.com

Pulaski County 143 Third St NW Ste 1............Pulaski VA 24301 540-980-7705 980-7717 338
TF: 800-211-5540 ■ *Web:* www.pulaskicounty.org

Pulaski County
137 St Robert Bldg Ste A ....Saint Robert MO 65584 573-336-6355 338
TF: 877-858-8687 ■ *Web:* www.visitpulaskicounty.org

Pulaski County 28 Pkwy Dr PO Box 720.........Somerset KY 42502 606-679-6361 338
Web: pulaski.ca.uky.edu

Pulaski County Chamber of Commerce
4440 Cleburne Blvd ....Dublin VA 24084 540-674-1991 674-4163 139
TF: 866-256-8864 ■ *Web:* www.pulaskichamber.info

Pulaski County Library 60 W Third St............Pulaski VA 24301 540-980-7770 980-7775 434-3
Web: www.pclibs.org

Pulaski County Public Library
304 S Main St.............................Somerset KY 42501 606-679-8401 434-3
Web: pulaskipubliclibrary.org

Pulaski County School District (PCPS)
202 N Washington Ave........................Pulaski VA 24301 540-994-2550 685
Web: www.pcva.us

Pulaski Meat Products Co
123 N Wood Ave.............................Linden NJ 07036 908-925-5380 296-26
Web: www.pulaskimeats.com

Pulaski State Prison
373 Upper River Rd .... Hawkinsville GA 31036 478-783-6000 783-6008 213
Web: www.dcor.state.ga.us

Pulaski Technical College
3000 W Scenic Dr.................... North Little Rock AR 72118 501-812-2200 771-2844 162
Web: www.uaptc.edu

Pulaski White Rural Telephone Coop (PWRTC)
5549 S US Hwy 35 ....Star City IN 46985 574-946-1377 278-8448 224
TF: 800-760-0848 ■ *Web:* www.lightstreamin.com

Pulau Electronics Corp
12633 Challenger Pkwy ....Orlando FL 32826 407-380-9191 311
Web: www.pulau.com

Pulice Construction Inc
2033 W Mountain View Rd....................Phoenix AZ 85021 602-944-2241 188-4
Web: www.pulice.com

Pullan Consulting
9360 W Flamingo Rd Ste 110-554 .... Las Vegas NV 89147 805-558-0361 463
Web: www.pullanconsulting.com

Pulley-Kellam Company Inc
245 Erie St ....Huntington IN 46750 260-356-6326 356-1928 482

Company / Address	City	State	Zip	Phone	Fax	Class
Pulliam Enterprises Inc 13790 E Jefferson Blvd *TF:* 800-443-2307 ■ *Web:* www.pullrite.com	Mishawaka	IN	46545	574-259-1520	258-0289	60
Pullman Chamber of Commerce 415 N Grand Ave *Web:* pullmanchamber.com	Pullman	WA	99163	509-334-3565	332-3232	139
Pullman Public Schools 240 SE Dexter St *Web:* www.pullmanschools.org	Pullman	WA	99163	509-332-3581		685
Pullstring Inc 133 Kearny St Ste 400 *Web:* pullstring.com	San Francisco	CA	94108	415-758-3339		761
Pulmonary and Sleep Specialists 2665 N Decatur Rd Ste 230 *Web:* www.pssatl.com	Decatur	GA	30033	404-499-0533		352
Puls Technologies 444 Spear St *Web:* puls.com	San Francisco	CA	94105	415-993-5176		113
Pulsafeeder Inc 2883 Brighton-Henrietta Town Line Rd *Web:* www.pulsa.com	Rochester	NY	14623	585-292-8000	424-5619	641
Pulsar It Consulting Inc 9200 Worthington Rd Ste 101	Westerville	OH	43082	614-781-3787		196
Pulsar Vascular Inc 4030 Moorpark Ave Ste 110 *Web:* www.pulsarvascular.com	San Jose	CA	95117	408-260-9264		475
PULSE 1301 McKinney St Ste 2500 *TF:* 800-420-2122 ■ *Web:* www.pulsenetwork.com	Houston	TX	77010	800-420-2122		69
Pulse Biomedical Inc (PBI) 112 Ivy Ln *Web:* www.qrscard.com	King of Prussia	PA	19406	610-666-5510		475
Pulse Communications Inc 2900 Towerview Rd *TF:* 800-381-1997 ■ *Web:* www.pulse.com	Herndon	VA	20171	703-471-2900	471-2951	735
Pulse Engineering Inc 12220 World Trade Dr *Web:* www.pulseelectronics.com	San Diego	CA	92128	858-674-8100	674-8262	253
Pulse Home Health Care Inc 2325 Severn Ave Ste 5 *Web:* pulsehomehealthcare.com	Metairie	LA	70001	504-831-7778	831-7760	363
Pulse Needlefree Systems Inc 8210 Marshall Dr *Web:* www.pulse-nfs.com	Lenexa	KS	66214	913-599-1590		476
Pulse Seismic Inc 421 Seventh Ave SW Ste 2700 *TF:* 877-460-5559 ■ *Web:* www.pulseseismic.com	Calgary	AB	T2P4K9	403-237-5559		624
Pulse Technologies Inc 2000 Am Dr *Web:* www.pulsetechinc.com	Quakertown	PA	18951	267-733-0200		454
Pulse Technology 312 Roberts Rd **Fax Area Code:* 219 ■ *TF:* 800-922-5226 ■ *Web:* www.pulsetechnology.com	Chesterton	IN	46304	800-837-1400	929-4686*	535
PulseTech Products Corp 1100 S Kimball Ave *TF:* 800-580-7554 ■ *Web:* www.pulsetech.net	Southlake	TX	76092	817-329-6099		74
Puma Industries Inc 1992 Airways Blvd *TF:* 888-848-1668 ■ *Web:* www.pumaairusa.com	Memphis	TN	38114	901-744-7979		172
Puma NA 10 Lyberty Way *TF:* 888-565-7862 ■ *Web:* us.puma.com	Westford	MA	01886	978-698-1000		301
Pummills Sporting Goods Inc 2400 W 16th St *Web:* pummillsports.com	Sedalia	MO	65301	660-826-0150		711
Pump Engineering Co (PE) 9807 Jordan Cir **Fax Area Code:* 562 ■ *TF:* 800-560-7867 ■ *Web:* www.pumpengineering.net	Santa Fe Springs	CA	90670	800-560-7867	944-4768*	385
Pump House, The 796 Chena Pump Rd *Web:* www.pumphouse.com	Fairbanks	AK	99709	907-479-8452	479-8432	671
Pump It Up Party 11411 W 183rd St *Web:* www.pumpitupparty.com	Orland Park	IL	60467	480-371-1200		138
Pump Systems Inc (PSI) 530 25th Ave E *TF:* 800-437-8076 ■ *Web:* www.pumpsystems.com	Dickinson	ND	58601	701-225-4494	225-0320	385
Pumper's Premium Stores Inc 4931 Earle Morris Hwy *Web:* www.pumperspremium.com	Easley	SC	29642	864-306-2999		345
Pumpernickel Press PO Box 603 *TF:* 888-760-9012 ■ *Web:* www.pumpernickelpress.com	Berryville	VA	22611	540-955-5770		637-10
Pumping Solutions Inc 1906 S Quaker Ridge Pl **Fax Area Code:* 909 ■ *TF:* 800-603-0399 ■ *Web:* www.apumpstore.com	Ontario	CA	91761	800-603-0399	930-6603*	610
Pumpkin Hollow Farm 1184 Rt 11 *Web:* www.pumpkinhollow.org	Craryville	NY	12521	518-325-3583	325-5633	673
Pumpkin Seed Press 43668 355th Ave *Web:* www.pumpkinseedpress.net	Humphrey	NE	68642	402-276-0370		637-10
Pun's Toy Shop 839 1/2 Lancaster Ave *Web:* www.punstoys.com	Bryn Mawr	PA	19010	610-525-9789	527-5514	761
Punahou School 1601 Punahou St *Web:* www.punahou.edu	Honolulu	HI	96822	808-944-5711		623
Punch & Associates Inc 7701 France Ave S Ste 300 *TF:* 800-241-5552 ■ *Web:* punchinvest.com	Edina	MN	55435	952-224-4350		528
Punch Media 10 N Third St *Web:* punchmedia.biz	Philadelphia	PA	19106	215-592-0120		195
Punch Press Products Inc 2035 E 51st St *Web:* www.punch-press.com	Los Angeles	CA	90058	323-581-7151		567
Punchbowl Inc 50 Speen St Ste 202 *TF:* 877-570-4340 ■ *Web:* www.punchbowl.com	Framingham	MA	01701	508-589-4486		107
Punchcut LLC 150 California St 9th Fl *Web:* www.punchcut.com	San Francisco	CA	94111	415-445-8855		180
Punchkick Interactive Inc 150 N Michigan Ave Ste 3900 *TF:* 800-549-4104 ■ *Web:* www.punchkick.com	Chicago	IL	60601	800-549-4104		195
Punderson State Park 11755 Kinsman Rd P O BOX 292	Newbury	OH	44065	440-564-9144		565
Punxsutawney Area Hospital Inc (PAH) 81 Hillcrest Dr *Web:* www.pah.org	Punxsutawney	PA	15767	814-938-1800		374-3
Puppet Labs 308 SW Second Ave 5th Fl *Web:* puppet.com	Portland	OR	97204	503-575-9775		225
Puppy Paws Press 7814 Edmunds Way *Web:* www.dayonedogtraining.com	Elkridge	MD	21075	410-796-5349		637-2
PUR (Public Utilities Reports Inc) 11410 Isaac Newton Sq Ste 220 *TF:* 800-368-5001 ■ *Web:* www.fortnightly.com	Reston	VA	20190	703-847-7720	847-0683	637-10
Purafil Inc 2654 Weaver Way *TF:* 800-222-6367 ■ *Web:* www.purafil.com	Doraville	GA	30340	770-662-8545	263-6922	18
Purakal Cylinders Inc 1017 S Danebo Ave *Web:* www.purakal.com	Eugene	OR	97402	541-345-4199	345-6522	223
Puratos Corp 1941 Old Cuthbert Rd *Web:* www.puratos.com	Cherry Hill	NJ	08034	856-428-4300	428-2939	296-16
Purcell Construction Inc 277 Dennis St *Web:* www.purcellc.com	Humble	TX	77338	281-548-1000	548-2998	187
Purcell International Group 1640 S Sepulveda Blvd Ste 208 *Web:* www.purcellintl.com	Brea	CA	92821	714-524-0640		193
Purcell Tire & Rubber Co 301 N Hall St *Web:* www.purcelltire.com	Potosi	MO	63664	623-848-4200		754
Purchase College 735 Anderson Hill Rd *TF:* 800-553-8118 ■ *Web:* www.purchase.edu	Purchase	NY	10577	914-251-6360	251-6314	166
Purchasing Magazine 225 Wyman St *TF:* 888-393-5000 ■ *Web:* www.buyerzone.com	Waltham	MA	02451	888-393-5000		457-5
Purdie Rogers Inc 2288 W Commodore Way Ste 200 *Web:* www.purdierogers.com	Seattle	WA	98199	206-628-7700		4
Purdue Pharma 575 Granite Ct *TF:* 800-387-5349 ■ *Web:* www.purdue.ca	Pickering	ON	L1W3W8	905-420-6400		231
Purdue Student Publishing Foundation 460 NW Ave *Web:* www.purdueexponent.org	West Lafayette	IN	47906	765-743-1111	743-6087	532-2
Purdue University Schleman Hall 475 Stadium Mall Dr *TF:* 800-743-3333 ■ *Web:* www.purdue.edu	West Lafayette	IN	47907	765-494-1776	494-0544	166
Purdue University 2200 169th St *TF:* 800-447-8738 ■ *Web:* www.pnw.edu	Hammond	IN	46323	219-989-2400	989-2775	166
Libraries 1880 Ellison Dr *Web:* www.lib.purdue.edu	West Lafayette	IN	47907	765-494-2900	494-0156	434-6
Purdue University Global Inc 18618 Crestwood Dr *TF:* 800-987-7734 ■ *Web:* www.purdueglobal.edu	Hagerstown	MD	21742	301-766-3600		786
Purdue University Press 504 W State St Stewart Ctr 370 *Web:* www.thepress.purdue.edu	West Lafayette	IN	47907	765-496-2442		637-4
Purdy Corp 101 Prospect Ave *TF:* 800-547-0780 ■ *Web:* www.purdy.com	Cleveland	OH	44115	800-547-0780		350
Purdy Insurance Agency Inc 136 Market St *Web:* purdyinsurance.com	Sunbury	PA	17801	570-286-5855		390
Purdyco Ltd 2836 Ualena St *Web:* www.islandprincesshawaii.com	Honolulu	HI	96819	808-839-5222	836-2019	296-8
Purdy-McGuire Inc 17300 Dallas Pkwy Ste 3000 *Web:* www.purdy-mcguire.com	Dallas	TX	75248	972-239-5357		261
Pure & Secure LLC 4511 NW 42nd St *TF:* 800-875-5915 ■ *Web:* mypurewater.com	Lincoln	NE	68524	402-467-9300		806
Pure Aesthetics 2850 E Speedway Blvd *Web:* www.pureaesthetics.edu	Tucson	AZ	85716	520-514-7873		167-3
Pure Auto LLC 164 Market St Ste 250 *TF:* 877-860-7873 ■ *Web:* purecars.com	Charleston	SC	29401	877-860-7873		387
Pure Brand 621 Kalamath St Ste 150 *Web:* pure-brand.com	Denver	CO	80204	303-297-0170	845-9588	194
Pure Canadian Gaming Corp 7055 Argyll Rd *Web:* purecanadiangaming.com	Edmonton	AB	T6C4A5	780-465-5377		133
Pure Energy Corp 61 S Paramus Rd *Web:* www.pure-energy.com	Paramus	NJ	07652	201-843-8100		579
Pure Essence Laboratories Inc 6155 S Sandhill Rd Ste 200 *Web:* www.pureessencelabs.com	Las Vegas	NV	89120	702-990-7400		345
Pure Express Mart 4002 Knight Arnold Rd	Memphis	TN	38118	901-794-3100		297-8
Pure Financial Advisors Inc 3131 Camino del Rio N Ste 1550 *TF:* 877-222-6044 ■ *Web:* purefinancial.com	San Diego	CA	92108	619-814-4100		401
Pure Hair Studio Inc 5515 Utica Ridge Rd Ste 350 *Web:* purehairstudioinc.com	Davenport	IA	52807	563-424-2327		77
Pure Humidifier Co 141 Jonathan Blvd N *Web:* www.purehumidifier.com	Chaska	MN	55318	952-368-9335	368-9338	14
PURE Storage Inc 650 Castro St Ste 400 *TF:* 800-379-7873 ■ *Web:* www.purestorage.com	Mountain View	CA	94041	650-290-6088		173-8
Pure Strategies Inc 47R Englewood Rd *Web:* purestrategies.com	Gloucester	MA	01930	978-525-0480		192
Pure Sweet Honey Farm Inc 514 Commerce Pkwy *TF:* 800-355-9601 ■ *Web:* www.puresweethoney.com	Verona	WI	53593	800-355-9601		296-24
Pureflex Inc 4855 Broadmoor Ave *Web:* www.pureflex.com	Kentwood	MI	49512	616-554-1100	554-3633	326
pureHOPE 5742 Hamilton Ave *Web:* www.purehope.net	Cincinnati	OH	45224	513-521-6227		48-6
Pure-logic Industries Inc 1730 W Sunrise Blvd Ste A102 *Web:* www.purelogicind.com	Gilbert	AZ	85233	480-892-9395	892-9323	608
Purematter 350 W Julian St Bldg 3 *Web:* www.purematter.com	San Jose	CA	95110	408-297-7800		4
PurEnergy LLC 4488 Onondaga Blvd *Web:* www.purenergyllc.com	Syracuse	NY	13219	315-448-2266	448-0264	463
Pure-Seed Testing Inc 29975 S Barlow Rd *Web:* pureseed.com	Canby	OR	97013	503-651-2130	651-2351	668
Purestream Services 2401 Foothill Dr *TF:* 855-778-7342 ■ *Web:* www.purestream.com	Salt Lake City	UT	84109	801-869-4455		538

Name / Address	City	State	ZIP	Phone	Fax	Class
PureTech Health 501 Boylston St Ste 6102 *Web:* puretechhealth.com	Boston	MA	02116	617-482-2333	482-3337	792
Purgatory Chasm State Reservation Purgatory Rd. *Web:* www.mass.gov	Sutton	MA	01590	508-234-3733		565
Puritan Backroom Restaurant 245 Hooksett Rd *Web:* puritanbackroom.com	Manchester	NH	03104	603-669-6890		671
Puritan Bakery Inc 1624 E Carson St. *Web:* www.puritanbakery.com	Carson	CA	90745	310-830-5451		68
Puritan Manufacturing Inc 1302 Grace St *TF:* 800-331-0487 ■ *Web:* www.purmfg.com	Omaha	NE	68110	402-341-3753		697
Puritan of Cape Cod 408 Main St *TF:* 800-924-0606 ■ *Web:* www.puritancapecod.com	Hyannis	MA	02601	508-775-2400		157-2
PuriTec 4705 S Durango Dr Ste 100-102 **Fax Area Code:* 888 ■ *TF:* 888-491-4100 ■ *Web:* www.puriteam.com	Las Vegas	NV	89147	610-268-5420	759-8905*	17
Purity Cylinder Gases Inc PO Box 9390 *Web:* www.puritygas.com	Grand Rapids	MI	49509	616-532-2375	532-5626	146
Purity Dairies Inc 360 Murfreesboro Rd	Nashville	TN	37210	615-244-1900		296-27
Purity Ice Cream Company Inc 700 Cascadilla St *Web:* www.purityicecream.com	Ithaca	NY	14850	607-272-1545	272-1546	296-25
Purity Wholesale Grocers Inc 5300 Broken Sound Blvd NW *TF:* 800-323-6838 ■ *Web:* www.pwg-inc.com	Boca Raton	FL	33487	800-323-6838		297-8
Purk & Associates Pc 1034 S Brentwood Blvd Ste 2000 *Web:* purkpc.com	Saint Louis	MO	63117	314-884-4000		2
Purmort Co, The 101 W Crawford St. *Web:* purmortbros.com	Van Wert	OH	45891	419-238-6214		390
Purnell School 51 Pottersville Rd PO Box 500 *Web:* www.purnell.org	Pottersville	NJ	07979	908-439-2154	439-4088	622
PuroClean 6001 Hiatus Rd Ste 13 *TF:* 800-775-7876 ■ *Web:* www.puroclean.com	Tamarac	FL	33321	800-775-7876		463
Purolator Inc 5995 Avebury Rd *TF:* 888-744-7123 ■ *Web:* www.purolator.com	Mississauga	ON	L5R3T8	905-712-0101		546
Pur-O-Zone Inc 345 N Iowa St *Web:* www.purozone.com	Lawrence	KS	66044	785-843-0771	843-0798	76
Purple Communications Inc 595 Menlo Dr *TF:* 800-900-9478 ■ *Web:* www.purplevrs.com	Rocklin	CA	95765	800-900-9478		387
Purple Diamond Packaging LLC 183 Mikron Rd *Web:* purple-diamond.com	Bethlehem	PA	18020	610-264-5080		261
Purple Heart Service Foundation 7008 Little River Tpke PO Box 49 *TF:* 888-414-4483 ■ *Web:* purpleheartfoundation.org	Annandale	VA	22003	703-256-6139	256-6142	303
Purple Parrot Cafe 3810 Hardy St Ste 30 *Web:* purpleparrotcafe.net	Hattiesburg	MS	39402	601-264-0657		671
Purple Pomegranate Productions 60 Haight St *TF:* 877-463-7742 ■ *Web:* www.store.jewsforjesus.org	San Francisco	CA	94102	877-463-7742		637-2
Purple Room Publishing 1314 S Grand Blvd Ste 2-321 **Fax Area Code:* 815 ■ *Web:* www.purpleroom.com	Spokane	WA	99202	509-879-4121	642-8206*	637-2
Purple Sage Motel 1501 E Coliseum Dr. *Web:* www.thepurplesagemotel.com	Snyder	TX	79549	325-573-5491		378
Purple Strategies LLC 815 Slaters Ln *Web:* www.purplestrategies.com	Alexandria	VA	22314	703-548-7877		5
Purple Toes Inc 102 Thistle Meadow **Fax Area Code:* 413 ■ *TF:* 877-863-9463 ■ *Web:* www.purpletoes.com	Laurel Springs	NC	28644	336-803-2452	403-9821*	81-3
Pursuant 12770 Coit Rd Ste 1000 *Web:* www.pursuant.com	Dallas	TX	75254	214-866-7700		317
Pursuit (NYBDC) 50 Beaver St Ste 500 *TF:* 800-923-2504 ■ *Web:* www.nybdc.com	Albany	NY	12207	518-463-2268	463-0240	216
Pursuit Boats 3901 St Lucie Blvd *TF:* 800-947-8778 ■ *Web:* www.pursuitboats.com	Fort Pierce	FL	34946	772-465-6006	465-6177	90
Pursuit of Excellence Inc 10440 N Central Expy Ste 1250 *Web:* poehr.com	Dallas	TX	75231	214-452-7881	265-9587	734
Purtis Creek State Park 14225 FM 316 *Web:* tpwd.texas.gov	Eustace	TX	75124	903-425-2332		565
Purves & Associates Insurance 500 Fourth St *TF:* 800-681-2025 ■ *Web:* purvesinsurance.com	Davis	CA	95616	530-756-5561		390
Purvis Ford Inc 3660 Jefferson Davis Hwy Ste 1 *Web:* www.purvisford.net	Fredericksburg	VA	22408	540-898-3000		57
Purvis Systems 88 Silva Ln. *Web:* www.purvis.com	Middletown	RI	02842	401-849-4750	849-0121	177
Puryear Law Group PLLC 104 Woodmont Blvd Ste 201 *Web:* puryearlawgroup.com	Nashville	TN	37205	615-630-6601		41
PUSH 22 30300 Telegraph Rd *Web:* push22.com	Bingham Farms	MI	48025	248-335-9500		5
Push Inc 101 Ernestine St. *Web:* www.push.inc	Orlando	FL	32801	407-841-2299		7
Push Product Design 813 Shades Creek Pkwy Ste 104 *Web:* www.pushpd.com	Birmingham	AL	35209	205-453-4423		463
Pushcart Press PO Box 380 *Web:* pushcartprize.com	Wainscott	NY	11975	631-324-9300		637-2
Pushmataha County 302 SW B St *Web:* www.usgennet.org	Antlers	OK	74523	580-298-2512	298-3641	338
Putman Group 9911 Irvine Center Dr Ste 100 *Web:* putmancpa.com	Irvine	CA	92618	949-502-6700	502-6701	2
Putnam & Lieb Incorporated PS 907 Legion Way SE. *Web:* putnamlieb.com	Olympia	WA	98507	360-754-7707		41
Putnam Bank 40 Main St PO Box 151. *Web:* www.putnambank.com	Putnam	CT	06260	860-928-6501		70
Putnam Career & Technical Ctr 300 Roosevelt Blvd. *Web:* www.pctc.edu	Eleanor	WV	25070	304-586-3494		250
Putnam County 40 Gleneida Ave *Web:* www.putnamcountyny.com	Carmel	NY	10512	845-225-3641		338
Putnam County 121 S Dixie Ave *Web:* putnamcountytn.gov	Cookeville	TN	38501	931-526-7106	372-8201	338
Putnam County 117 Putnam Dr Ste A *TF:* 800-253-1077 ■ *Web:* www.putnamcountyga.us	Eatonton	GA	31024	706-485-5826	923-2345	338
Putnam County 1 Courthouse Sq St *Web:* www.co.putnam.in.us	Greencastle	IN	46135	765-653-2648		338
Putnam County 120 N Fourth St *Web:* www.co.putnam.il.us	Hennepin	IL	61327	815-925-7129	925-7549	338
Putnam County 12093 Winfield Rd *Web:* www.putnamcounty.org	Winfield	WV	25213	304-586-0202	586-0200	338
Putnam County Chamber of Commerce 1100 Reid St *Web:* www.putnamcountychamber.com	Palatka	FL	32177	386-328-1503	328-7076	139
Putnam County Chamber of Commerce 971 WV-34 *TF:* 800-216-9805 ■ *Web:* putnamchamber.org	Hurricane	WV	25526	304-757-6510	757-6562	139
Putnam County Commissioners 115 S Fair Ave Ste 101 *Web:* www.putnamcountyohio.com	Ottawa	OH	45875	419-523-3656		338
Putnam County Convention & Visitors Bureau 971 WV Rt 34 Ste 1 *Web:* www.visitputnamwv.com	Hurricane	WV	25526	304-757-7282		206
Putnam County District Library 136 Putnam Pkwy *Web:* mypcdl.org	Ottawa	OH	45875	419-523-3747	523-6477	434-3
Putnam County Library 50 E Broad St *Web:* www.pclibrary.org	Cookeville	TN	38501	931-526-2416	372-8517	434-3
Putnam County Public Library 103 E Poplar St. *Web:* pcpl21.org	Greencastle	IN	46135	765-653-2755		434-3
Putnam County Savings Bank (PCSB) 2477 Rt 6 PO Box 417 *Web:* www.pcsb.com	Brewster	NY	10509	845-279-7101	279-9175	71
Putnam County Sentinel 224 E Main St *Web:* putnamsentinel.com	Ottawa	OH	45875	419-523-5709	523-3512	532-2
Putnam County Sheriff's Office 130 Orie Griffin Blvd. *TF:* 800-426-9975 ■ *Web:* www.putnamsherifffl.com	Palatka	FL	32177	386-329-0800		338
Putnam Family of Funds PO Box 41203 *TF:* 800-225-1581 ■ *Web:* www.putnam.com	Providence	RI	02940	800-225-1581		528
Putnam Lexus 390 Convention Way *TF:* 888-231-8005 ■ *Web:* www.putnamlexus.com	Redwood City	CA	94063	650-363-8500		57
Putnam Memorial State Park 499 Black Rock Tpke *Web:* portal.ct.gov	Redding	CT	06896	203-938-2285		565
Putnam Museum of History & Natural Science 1717 W 12th St. *Web:* putnam.org	Davenport	IA	52804	563-324-1933		522
Putnam Rolling Ladder Inc 32 Howard St *Web:* www.putnamrollingladder.com	New York	NY	10013	212-226-5147	941-1836	421
Putnam Valley School District Inc 146 Peekskill Hollow Rd. *TF:* 800-666-5327 ■ *Web:* www.pvcsd.org	Putnam Valley	NY	10579	845-528-8143		685
Putnam White Lewis Insurance Agency Inc 4161 N High St. *TF:* 800-267-6724 ■ *Web:* pwlinsurance.com	Columbus	OH	43214	614-267-1269	267-6380	390
Putnamville Correctional Facility 1946 W Hwy 40 *Web:* www.in.gov	Greencastle	IN	46135	765-653-8441	653-7461	213
Putney School 418 Houghton Brook Rd *Web:* www.putneyschool.org	Putney	VT	05346	802-387-5566	387-6278	622
Putters & Associates Apc 22 Battery St Ste 512 *Web:* putterslaw.com	San Francisco	CA	94111	415-788-8377		41
Puttin' on the Tips School 2620 SW 17th Rd Ste 700 *Web:* www.puttinonthetips.com	Ocala	FL	34471	352-351-2373		685
Putzmeister America 1733 90th St *TF:* 800-553-3414 ■ *Web:* www.putzmeister.com	Sturtevant	WI	53177	800-553-3414		190
Puukohola Heiau National Historic Site 62-3601 Kawaihae Rd. *Web:* www.nps.gov	Kawaihae	HI	96743	808-882-7218		564
Puyallup Public Library 333 S Meridian. *TF:* 844-821-8911 ■ *Web:* www.cityofpuyallup.org	Puyallup	WA	98371	253-841-4321	841-5483	434-3
PV Fluid Products 11245 - Vly Ridge Dr NW Suit 322. *Web:* www.pvfluid.com	Calgary	AB	T3B5V4	403-640-0331		358
PV Labs Inc 1074 Cooke Blvd *TF:* 888-667-7202 ■ *Web:* www.pv-labs.com	Burlington	ON	L7T4A8	905-667-7202		692
PVA (Passenger Vessel Assn) 103 Oronoco St Ste 200. *TF:* 800-807-8360 ■ *Web:* www.passengervessel.com	Alexandria	VA	22314	703-518-5005	518-5151	49-21
PVA Consulting Group Inc 20865 Ch de la Cote Nord Ste 200. *TF:* 877-970-1970 ■ *Web:* www.pva.ca	Boisbriand	QC	J7E4H5	450-970-1970	970-1969	463
PVA Inc 2814 Eric Ln *Web:* www.pvaglobal.com	Burlington	NC	27215	336-217-4600		463
PVA Tepla America Inc 251 Corporate Terr *TF:* 800-527-5667 ■ *Web:* www.pvateplaamerica.com	Corona	CA	92879	951-371-2500		203
PVC Industries Inc 107 Pierce Rd *TF:* 800-727-3488 ■ *Web:* www.pvcindustries.com	Clifton Park	NY	12065	800-727-3488		604
PVEC 420 Straight Creek Rd PO Box 1528. 	New Tazewell	TN	37825	423-626-5204	626-0711	245
PVG Asset Management Corp 24918 Genesee Trl Rd. *TF:* 800-777-0818 ■ *Web:* pvgassetmanagement.com	Golden	CO	80401	800-777-0818		401

Phone | Fax | Class

PVH 200 Madison Ave, New York NY 10016 — 212-381-3500 — 155-12
NYSE: PVH ■ *TF:* 888-203-1112 ■ *Web:* www.pvh.com

PVI Industries LLC 3209 Galvez Ave, Fort Worth TX 76111 — 817-335-9531 — 332-6742 — 91
TF: 800-784-8326 ■ *Web:* www.pvi.com

PVMA (Pocumtuck Valley Memorial Assn)
10 Memorial St, Deerfield MA 01342 — 413-774-7476 — 49-19
Web: deerfield-ma.org

PVP (Penns Valley Publishers)
154 E Main St, Lansdale PA 19446 — 215-855-4948 — 855-7238 — 637-10
TF: 800-422-4412 ■ *Web:* www.pennsvalleypublishers.com

PVS Chemicals Inc 10900 Harper Ave, Detroit MI 48213 — 313-921-1200 — 921-1378 — 145
TF: 800-932-8860 ■ *Web:* www.pvschemicals.com

PVT (Penasco Valley Telephone Cooperative Inc)
4011 W Main St, Artesia NM 88210 — 575-748-1241 — 746-4142 — 736
TF: 800-505-4844 ■ *Web:* www.pvt.com

PV-Tron Inc 8810 Blvd Langelier, Saint-Leonard QC H1P3H2 — 514-723-2131 — 196
Web: www.pvtron.com

PW Stephens Inc
15201 Pipeline Ln Unit B, Huntington Beach CA 92649 — 714-892-2028 — 891-9807 — 667
TF: 800-750-7733 ■ *Web:* www.pwsei.com

PWC Employees Credit Union
12715 Ridgefield Village Dr Ste 101, Woodbridge VA 22193 — 703-680-1143 — 680-5998 — 219
Web: pwcecu.org

PWC Industries Inc
6650 Leopard St, Corpus Christi TX 78409 — 361-289-0557 — 289-2408 — 537
Web: www.pwcindustries.com

PWH (Palms West Hospital)
13001 S Blvd, Loxahatchee FL 33470 — 561-798-3300 — 374-3
Web: palmswesthospital.com

PWP (Pentwater Wire Products Inc)
474 Carroll St PO Box 947, Pentwater MI 49449 — 231-869-6911 — 869-4020 — 286
TF: 877-869-6911 ■ *Web:* www.pentwaterwire.com

PWPA (Professors World Peace Academy)
3600 Labore Rd Ste 1, Saint Paul MN 55110 — 651-644-3087 — 644-0997 — 637-2
Web: www.paragonhouse.com

PWR LLC 6402 Deere Rd, Syracuse NY 13206 — 315-701-0210 — 701-0217 — 767
TF: 800-342-0878 ■ *Web:* www.pwrllc.com

PWRTC (Pulaski White Rural Telephone Coop)
5549 S US Hwy 35, Star City IN 46985 — 574-946-1377 — 278-8448 — 224
TF: 800-760-0848 ■ *Web:* www.lightstreamin.com

PXP Solutions 2485 Merritt Dr, Garland TX 75041 — 214-221-7669 — 627
Web: www.pxpsolutions.com

PYB (Pennsylvania Youth Ballet)
556 Main St, Bethlehem PA 18018 — 610-865-0353 — 573-1
Web: www.bglv.org

Pybus Point Lodge PO Box 33497, Juneau AK 99803 — 907-789-9150 — 790-4866 — 669
TF: 800-947-9287 ■ *Web:* www.pybus.com

Pyco Industries PO Box 841, Lubbock TX 79404 — 806-747-3434 — 296-29
Web: www.pycoindustriesinc.com

Pyle Machine Company Inc
4201 Clay Ave, Fort Worth TX 76117 — 817-485-6011 — 581-7660 — 454
Web: www.pylemachine.com

PYLUSD (Placentia-Yorba Linda Unified School District)
1301 E Orangethorpe Ave, Placentia CA 92870 — 714-996-2550 — 685
Web: www.pylusd.org

Pymatuning State Park
2660 Williamsfield Rd, Jamestown PA 16134 — 724-932-3142 — 565
Web: www.dcnr.pa.gov

Pymatuning Telephone Co
7 Edgewood Dr, Greenville PA 16125 — 724-646-5321 — 646-5441 — 224
Web: www.pymtele.net

Pymetrics 102 Madison Ave 5th Fl, New York NY 10016 — 646-397-7998 — 39
Web: www.pymetrics.com

Pyne-Davidson Co 237 Weston St, Hartford CT 06120 — 860-522-9106 — 627
Web: www.pynedavidson.com

PYR 221 River St 9th FL, Hoboken NJ 07030 — 800-223-2336 — 943-9831 — 637-2
TF: 800-223-2336 ■ *Web:* www.pyrsf.com

Pyramax Bank FSB
7001 W Edgerton Ave, Greenfield WI 53220 — 414-421-8200 — 421-6802 — 70

Pyramid America, Lp 1 Haven Ave, Mount Vernon NY 10553 — 914-668-6666 — 664-3415 — 42
Web: pyramidamerica.com

Pyramid Brewing Co
91 S Royal Brougham Way, Seattle WA 98134 — 206-682-8322 — 682-8420 — 102
Web: www.pyramidbrew.com

Pyramid Brokerage Co
5786 Widewaters Pkwy PO Box 3, Syracuse NY 13214 — 315-445-1030 — 652
Web: www.pyramidbrokerage.com

Pyramid Checks & Printing Inc
208 Riverside Indus Pkwy, Portland ME 04103 — 207-878-9832 — 627
Web: www.pyramidchecks-printing.com

Pyramid Communications Inc
1932 First Ave Ste 507, Seattle WA 98101 — 206-374-7788 — 636
Web: pyramidcommunications.com

Pyramid Construction Inc
275 N Franklin Tpke, Ramsey NJ 07446 — 201-327-1919 — 327-0054 — 187
Web: www.pyramidgroup.biz

Pyramid Consulting Inc
11100 Atlantis Pl, Alpharetta GA 30022 — 678-514-3500 — 225
TF: 877-248-0024 ■ *Web:* www.pyramidci.com

Pyramid Cos 4 Clinton Sq, Syracuse NY 13202 — 315-422-7000 — 655
Web: www.pyramidmg.com

Pyramid Educational Consultants
350 Churchmans Rd Ste B, New Castle DE 19720 — 302-368-2515 — 368-2516 — 196
TF: 888-732-7462 ■ *Web:* www.pecs-usa.com

Pyramid Enterprises Inc
320 Industrial Rd, Summerville SC 29483 — 843-873-4500 — 873-4565 — 454
Web: www.pyramidenterprisesinc.com

Pyramid Floor Covering Inc
38 Harbor Park Dr, Port Washington NY 11050 — 516-932-7200 — 290
Web: www.pyramidfloors.com

Pyramid Healthcare Solutions Inc
14141 46th St N Ste 1212, Clearwater FL 33762 — 727-431-3000 — 196
Web: www.pyramidhs.com

Pyramid Hotel Group LLC
1 Post Office Sq Ste 1950, Boston MA 02109 — 617-412-2800 — 946-2040 — 378
Web: pyramidhotelgroup.com

Pyramid Interiors Distributors Inc
PO Box 181058, Memphis TN 38181 — 901-375-4197 — 191-3
TF: 800-456-0592 ■ *Web:* pyramidinteriors.com

Pyramid Masonry Contractors Inc
2330 Mellon Ct, Decatur GA 30035 — 770-987-4750 — 981-7142 — 189-7
Web: www.pyramidmasonry.net

Pyramid Mountain Lumber Inc
379 Boy Scout Rd PO Box 549, Seeley Lake MT 59868 — 406-677-2201 — 677-2509 — 683
Web: www.pyramidlumber.com

Pyramid Peak Group
2950 N Academy, Colorado Springs CO 80917 — 719-598-1186 — 809
Web: www.pyramidpeak.com

Pyramid Precision Machine Inc
6721 Cobra Way, San Diego CA 92121 — 858-642-0713 — 454
Web: www.pyramidprecision.com

Pyramid Printing 58 Mathewson Dr, Weymouth MA 02189 — 781-337-7609 — 627
Web: www.pyramidprinting.net

Pyramid Restaurant & Bar
1717 N Akard St, Dallas TX 75201 — 214-720-5249 — 671
Web: www.pyramidrestaurant.com

Pyramid Software Development Inc
4008 Louetta Rd Ste 404, Spring TX 77388 — 281-350-2535 — 177
Web: pyramidsdi.com

Pyramid State Recreation Area
1562 Pyramid Park Rd, Pinckneyville IL 62274 — 618-357-2574 — 565
Web: www2.illinois.gov

Pyramid Studios Inc 10 State St, Ellsworth ME 04605 — 207-667-3321 — 624-9301* — 410
**Fax Area Code:* 888 ■ *Web:* www.pyramid.gold

Pyramid Tubular Products LP
2 Northpoint Dr Ste 610, Houston TX 77060 — 281-405-8090 — 481-9495* — 539
**Fax Area Code:* 817 ■ *Web:* www.pyramidtubular.com

Pyro Shows Inc 115 N 1ST St, Lafollette TN 37766 — 423-566-5729 — 562-9171 — 145
TF: 800-662-1331 ■ *Web:* www.pyroshows.com

Pyro-Comm Systems Inc
15531 Container Ln, Huntington Beach CA 92649 — 714-902-8000 — 693
Web: www.pyrocomm.com

Pyromation Inc 5211 Industrial Rd, Fort Wayne IN 46825 — 260-484-2580 — 482-6805 — 201
TF: 800-837-6805 ■ *Web:* pyromation.com

Pyronics Inc 17700 Miles Rd, Cleveland OH 44128 — 216-662-8800 — 663-8954 — 318
TF: 800-883-9218 ■ *Web:* www.selas.com

Pyrotechnic Specialties Inc
1661 Juniper Creek Rd, Byron GA 31008 — 478-956-5400 — 956-5108 — 268
Web: pyrotechnicspecialties.com

Pyrotek Inc
9503 E Montgomery Ave, Spokane Valley WA 99206 — 509-926-6212 — 927-2408 — 127
Web: www.pyrotek.com

Pyrotek Special Effects Inc
201 Whitehall Dr Ste 6, Markham ON L3R9Y3 — 905-479-9991 — 479-3515 — 149
Web: www.pyrotekfx.com

Pyrros & Serres LLP
31-19 Newtown Ave Ste 501, Astoria NY 11102 — 718-804-5430 — 41
Web: nylaw.net

Pythia Press PO Box 2010, Reston VA 20195 — 703-709-0919 — 709-1333* — 637-2
**Fax Area Code:* 707 ■ *Web:* www.pythiapress.com

Pyure Brands LLC 5405 Taylor Rd Unit 10, Naples FL 34109 — 305-509-5096 — 296-37
Web: pyuresweet.com

Pzena Investment Management Inc
320 Park Ave 8th Fl, New York NY 10022 — 212-355-1600 — 308-0010 — 401
NYSE: PZN ■ *Web:* www.pzena.com

Q

Phone | Fax | Class

Q & A Reporting Inc
7115 Virginia Rd Ste 105, Crystal Lake IL 60014 — 815-477-2230 — 768
Web: qareportinginc.com

Q & D Construction Inc 1050 S 21st St, Sparks NV 89431 — 775-786-2677 — 186
Web: qdconstruction.com

Q Analysts LLC
4320 Stevens Creek Blvd Ste 130, San Jose CA 95129 — 408-907-8500 — 907-8515 — 194
Web: www.qanalysts.com

Q Carriers Inc 1415 Maras St, Shakopee MN 55379 — 952-445-8718 — 445-8794 — 780
Web: www.qcarriers.com

Q Ctr 1405 N Fifth Ave, Saint Charles IL 60174 — 630-377-3100 — 31
TF: 877-774-4627 ■ *Web:* www.qcenter.com

Q Grady Minor & Associates PA
3800 Via Del Rey, Bonita Springs FL 34134 — 239-947-1144 — 261
Web: gradyminor.com

Q Haute Cuisine 100 LaCaille Pl SW, Calgary AB T2P5E2 — 403-262-5554 — 671
Web: www.qhautecuisine.com

Q Perfumes 1965 Tubeway Ave, Commerce CA 90040 — 323-728-3434 — 728-4221 — 238
Web: www.qperfumesinc.com

Q Prime Inc 729 Seventh Ave, New York NY 10019 — 212-302-9790 — 344
Web: qprime.com

Q Up Arts.com LLC PO Box 794, Dana Point CA 92629 — 310-714-9547 — 511
Web: www.quparts.com

Q. B. Johnson Manufacturing Inc
9000 S Sunnylane Rd, Oklahoma City OK 73165 — 405-677-6676 — 670-3270 — 537
Web: www.qbjohnson.com

Q.A. Technologies Inc
222 South 15th St Ste 1001 N, Omaha NE 68102 — 402-391-9200 — 180
Web: www.qat.com

Q.E.D. Environmental Systems Inc
2355 Bishop Cir W, Dexter MI 48130 — 734-995-2547 — 995-1170 — 641
Web: www.qedenv.com

Q104.5
950 Houston Northcutt Blvd Ste 201, Mount Pleasant SC 29464 — 843-721-1045 — 645
Web: q1045.iheart.com

Q105.1 Rocks 2720 Seventh Ave S, Fargo ND 58103 — 701-237-4500 — 645-56
Web: www.q1051rocks.com

Q93 929 Howard Ave, New Orleans LA 70113 — 504-679-7300 — 645-107
Web: q93.iheart.com

QA Systems Inc 5811 Blue Bluff Rd, Austin TX 78724 — 512-637-6100 — 180
Web: qasystems.com

Qa1 Precision Products Inc
21730 Hanover Ave, Lakeville MN 55044 — 952-985-5675 — 985-5679 — 620
TF: 800-721-7761 ■ *Web:* www.qa1.net

Name / Address	City	State	ZIP	Phone	Fax	Class
QACVB (Quincy Area Convention & Visitors Bureau) 532 Gardner Expy	Quincy	IL	62301	217-214-3700		206
TF: 800-978-4748 ■ *Web:* seequincy.com						
QAD Inc 100 Innovation Pl	Santa Barbara	CA	93108	805-566-6100	565-4202	178-1
NASDAQ: QADB ■ *Web:* www.qad.com						
QAI Inc 9191 Towne Centre Dr Ste 200	San Diego	CA	92122	858-792-3531		194
Web: www.qai-inc.com						
Qal-Tek Associates LLC 3998 Commerce Cir	Idaho Falls	ID	83401	208-523-5557		582
Web: www.qaltek.com						
Qantas Airways Cargo 6555 W Imperial Hwy	Los Angeles	CA	90045	310-665-2280	665-2201	12
TF: 800-227-0290 ■ *Web:* www.qantas.com						
Qantel Technologies Inc 3506 Breakwater Ct	Hayward	CA	94545	510-731-2080	731-2121	173-2
TF: 800-666-3686 ■ *Web:* www.qantel.com						
Qatar						
Consulate General 1990 Post Oak Blvd Ste 900	Houston	TX	77056	713-355-8221	355-8184	257
Web: houston.consulate.qa						
Embassy 2555 M St NW	Washington	DC	20037	202-274-1600	237-0682	257
Web: washington.embassy.qa						
QB Corp 1420 Hwy 28	Salmon	ID	83467	208-756-4248		817
Web: qbcorp.com						
QBE Farmers Union Insurance 5619 DTC Pkwy Ste 300	Greenwood Village	CO	80111	303-337-5500	338-2211	391-4
TF: 800-347-1961 ■ *Web:* www.farmersunioninsurance.com						
QBE LLC 14604 Washington St	Haymarket	VA	20169	571-766-1022		174
Web: www.qbe.net						
QC Data International Inc 8000 E Maplewood Ave Ste 300	Greenwood Village	CO	80111	303-783-8888		225
Web: www.qcdata.com						
QC Electronics Inc 1635 La Dawn Dr	Portage	WI	53901	608-742-1661		547
Web: www.qcelectronics.com						
QC Laboratories Inc 10810 NW Fwy	Houston	TX	77092	713-695-1133		743
QCA Systems Ltd 101-6951 72nd St	Delta	BC	V4G0A2	604-940-0868	940-0869	261
TF: 877-940-0868 ■ *Web:* www.qcasystems.com						
QCC (Quality Control Corp) 7315 W Wilson Ave	Chicago	IL	60706	708-887-5400	887-5009	621
Web: www.qccorp.com						
Qcera Inc 11041 Santa Monica Blvd Ste 818	Los Angeles	CA	90025	310-473-7988		180
Web: qcera.com						
QCHC Inc 200 Narrows Pkwy	Birmingham	AL	35242	205-437-1512		363
Web: www.qchcweb.com						
QCHI 8208 Melrose Dr	Lenexa	KS	66214	913-234-5000		141
OTC: QCCO ■ *TF:* 866-660-2243 ■ *Web:* www.qchi.com						
QCI Asset Management 40A Grove St	Pittsford	NY	14534	585-218-2060	218-2013	401
TF: 800-836-3960 ■ *Web:* e-qci.com						
QCM Inc 5040 Brooklake Rd NE	Brooks	OR	97305	503-371-9335	371-9745	253
Web: www.qcm-inc.com						
QCP (Quaker City Plating) 11729 Washington Blvd	Whittier	CA	90606	800-922-4799		482
Web: www.qcpent.com						
QCSI (Quality Control Solutions Inc) 43339 Business Park Dr Ste 101 & 102	Temecula	CA	92590	951-676-1616	676-8970	472
TF: 888-355-7274 ■ *Web:* www.qc-solutions.com						
QCSS Inc 21925 Field Pkwy Ste 210	Deer Park	IL	60010	847-229-7046		317
TF: 888-229-7046 ■ *Web:* www.qcssinc.com						
Qdigital Corp 6037 S Ft Apache Rd Ste 100	Las Vegas	NV	89148	702-360-9371	360-9198	180
Web: www.qdigital.com						
Qdoba Restaurant Corp 4865 Ward Rd Ste 500	Wheat Ridge	CO	80033	720-898-2300	629-2396*	670
**Fax Area Code: 303* ■ *Web:* www.qdoba.com						
QED Group LLC, The 1820 N Ft Myer Dr Ste 700	Arlington	VA	22209	703-678-4700		463
Web: www.qedgroupllc.com						
QED Inc 1001 W Third Ave	Denver	CO	80223	303-825-5011	893-5019	246
TF: 800-700-5011 ■ *Web:* www.qedelectric.com						
QED Inc 2920 S Halladay St	Santa Ana	CA	92705	714-546-6010		21
Web: qedaero.com						
QED Inc 218 Terrace Ave	Riverside	RI	02915	401-433-4045		45
Web: www.qedusa.com						
QED Systems Inc 4646 N Witchduck Rd	Virginia Beach	VA	23455	757-490-5000	490-5027	547
Web: www.qedsysinc.com						
QeH2 401 S Wilcox St Ste 100	Castle Rock	CO	80104	303-688-7531		179
Web: qeh2.com						
QEP Company Inc 1001 Broken Sound Pkwy NW Ste A	Boca Raton	FL	33487	561-994-5550	241-2830	758
OTC: QEPC ■ *TF:* 800-777-8665 ■ *Web:* www.qep.com						
QFD Institute 1140 Morehead Ct	Ann Arbor	MI	48103	734-995-0847	203-3575*	637-2
**Fax Area Code: 206* ■ *Web:* www.qfdi.org						
Q-Flex Inc 1301 E Hunter Ave	Santa Ana	CA	92705	714-664-0101		625
Web: www.qflexinc.com						
QFlow Systems 9317 Manchester Rd	Saint Louis	MO	63119	314-968-9906	968-0670	177
TF: 877-652-1439 ■ *Web:* www.qflow.com						
QHR Technologies Inc 1620 Dickson Ave Ste 300	Kelowna	BC	V1Y9Y2	855-550-5004		177
TF: 855-550-5004 ■ *Web:* www.qhrtechnologies.com						
QIAGEN Sciences LLC 19300 Germantown Rd	Germantown	MD	20874	800-426-8157	718-2056	85
TF: 800-426-8157 ■ *Web:* www.qiagen.com						
QIS (Quantum Internet Services Inc) 2975B Manchester Rd	Manchester	MD	21102	410-239-6920		681
TF: 888-889-4638 ■ *Web:* www.qis.net						
Qivana 5255 Edgewood Dr Ste 225	Provo	UT	84604	801-610-4600		366
Q-Lab Corp 800 Canterbury Rd	Westlake	OH	44145	440-835-8700		201
Web: www.q-lab.com						
QLE (Quantum Leap Engineering) 11 Toner Blvd Ste 5-353	North Attleboro	MA	02763	508-954-0185		194
Web: www.quantumleapengineering.com						
QlikTech International AB 150 N Radnor Chester Rd Ste E220	Radnor	PA	19087	888-828-9768		178-10
NASDAQ: QLIK ■ *TF:* 888-828-9768 ■ *Web:* www.qlik.com						
QME Inc 9070 First St	Baroda	MI	49101	269-422-2137	422-1846	757
Web: www.quality-molds.com						
Qmf Metal & Electronic Solutions Inc 324 Berry Garden Rd	Kernersville	NC	27284	336-996-5570		697
Web: www.qmf-usa.com						
QMI (Quebecor Media Inc) 612 Saint-Jacques St	Montreal	QC	H3C4M8	514-380-1999		637-2
Web: www.quebecor.com						
QMI (Quality Manufacturing Company Inc) PO Box 616	Winchester	KY	40392	859-744-0420		454
TF: 866-460-6459 ■ *Web:* www.qmiky.com						
QMS (Quality Management Solutions LLC) 146 Lowell St Ste 300B	Wakefield	MA	01880	800-645-6430		196
TF: 800-645-6430 ■ *Web:* www.qmsinc.com						
QMSI (Quintessential Mailing Software Inc) 5800 Ager Beswick Rd	Montague	CA	96064	866-284-1001	459-3191*	178-1
**Fax Area Code: 530* ■ *TF:* 866-284-1001 ■ *Web:* www.qmsi.software						
QNB Corp 15 N Third St PO Box 9005	Quakertown	PA	18951	215-538-5600	538-5765	70
OTC: QNBC ■ *TF:* 800-491-9070 ■ *Web:* www.qnbbank.com						
Qosina Corp 2002-Q Orville Dr N	Ronkonkoma	NY	11779	631-242-3000		476
Web: www.qosina.com						
Qosmedix 2002 Orville Dr N	Ronkonkoma	NY	11779	631-242-3270	242-3291	214
Web: www.qosmedix.com						
QPE Technical Institute 1557 N Gemini Pl	Anaheim	CA	92801	714-778-5518	778-0292	167-3
Web: www.qpetech.com						
Q-Peak Inc 135 S Rd	Bedford	MA	01730	781-275-9535	275-9726	393
Web: www.qpeak.com						
QPI (Quality Perforating Inc) 166 Dundaff St	Carbondale	PA	18407	570-282-4344	282-4627	488
TF: 800-872-7373 ■ *Web:* www.qualityperf.com						
QPI Multipress Inc 2222 S Third St	Columbus	OH	43207	614-228-0185	228-2358	456
Web: www.multipress.com						
QRP Inc 2307 Mercantile Dr NE	Leland	NC	28451	910-371-0700	371-9055	350
Web: www.camaerospace.com						
QRS Music Technologies 2011 Seward Ave	Naples	FL	34109	239-597-5888		527
Web: www.qrsmusic.com						
QS Quarterhouse Software Inc 3445 Executive Center Dr Ste 151	Austin	TX	78731	512-351-8783	351-9522	178-1
Web: www.quarterhouse.net						
QS/Togo Inc 355 Jay St	Coldwater	MI	49036	517-278-2391	279-4680	719
Web: www.qsti.com						
QSA ToolWorks LLC 3100 47th Ave	Long Island City	NY	11101	516-935-9151		178-7
TF: 800-784-7018 ■ *Web:* www.qsatoolworks.com						
QSC Audio Products LLC 1675 MacArthur Blvd	Costa Mesa	CA	92626	714-754-6175	754-6174	52
TF: 800-854-4079 ■ *Web:* www.qsc.com						
QSL Print Communications Inc 3000 Pierce Pkwy	Springfield	OR	97477	541-687-1184		194
TF: 800-382-1184 ■ *Web:* qslprinting.com						
QSR Automations Inc 2301 Stanley Gault Pkwy	Louisville	KY	40223	502-297-0221		177
TF: 855-980-7328 ■ *Web:* www.qsrautomations.com						
Qst Consultations Ltd 11275 Edgewater Dr	Allendale	MI	49401	616-895-5461		231
TF: 866-757-4751 ■ *Web:* mail.qstconsultations.com						
QST Industries Inc 550 W Adams St Ste 200	Chicago	IL	60661	312-930-9400	648-0312	34
Web: www.qst.com						
QStar Technologies Inc 8738 Ortega Park Dr	Navarre	FL	32566	850-243-0900		177
Web: www.qstar.com						
QTEC Solutions Inc 355 E Rincon St Ste 219	Corona	CA	92879	951-270-5357	270-5369	463
Web: www.qtec.us						
Q-Tech Corp 10150 Jefferson Blvd	Culver City	CA	90232	310-836-7900	836-2157	253
Web: q-tech.com						
QTF (Quality Texas Foundation) 201 Woodland Pk	Georgetown	TX	78633	512-656-8946		303
Web: quality-texas.org						
QTI (Qual-Tron Inc) 9409 E 55th Pl	Tulsa	OK	74145	918-622-7052		253
Web: www.qual-tron.com						
QTI Group, The 1010 E Washington Ave Ste 314	Madison	WI	53703	608-257-1057	258-5523	194
Web: qtigroup.com						
QTM Inc 300 Stevens Ave	Oldsmar	FL	34677	813-891-1300		454
Web: www.qtminc.com						
Q-tran Inc 155 Hill St	Milford	CT	06460	203-367-8777		253
Web: www.q-tran.com						
QTS Payroll Services Inc 8170 W Sahara Ave Ste 100	Las Vegas	NV	89117	702-796-3855		570
TF: 866-787-7297 ■ *Web:* qtspayroll.com						
Quabbin Capital Inc 160 Federal St	Boston	MA	02110	617-330-9041		401
Web: www.quabbincapital.com						
Quaboag Hills Chamber of Commerce 3 Converse St	Palmer	MA	01069	413-283-2418		139
Web: qhma.com						
Quad Cities Chamber 1601 River Dr Ste 310	Moline	IL	61265	309-757-5416		139
Web: quadcitieschamber.com						
Quad Cities Convention & Visitors Bureau 1601 River Dr Ste 110	Moline	IL	61265	309-277-0937	764-9443	206
TF: 800-747-7800 ■ *Web:* www.visitquadcities.com						
Quad Cities Realty 1053 Ripon Ave	Lewiston	ID	83501	208-798-7798		652
TF: 877-798-7798 ■ *Web:* www.qcrhomes.com						
Quad City Bank & Trust 3551 Seventh St	Moline	IL	61265	309-736-3580		360-2
NASDAQ: QCRH ■ *TF:* 866-676-0551 ■ *Web:* www.qcbt.bank						
Quad City Botanical Ctr 2525 Fourth Ave	Rock Island	IL	61201	309-794-0991		97
Web: www.qcgardens.com						
Quad City Conservation Alliance Expo Ctr 2621 Fourth Ave	Rock Island	IL	61201	309-788-5912	788-9619	205
Web: www.qccaexpocenter.com						
Quad City Engineering Company Inc 3650 Morton Dr	East Moline	IL	61244	309-755-9762	755-9765	757
Web: www.quadcityeng.com						
Quad Group Inc 1815 S Lewis St	Spokane	WA	99224	509-458-4558	458-4555	495
TF: 800-342-2430 ■ *Web:* www.quadgroupinc.com						

Company / Address	City	State	Zip	Phone	Fax	Class
Quad Three Group Inc 72 Glenmaura National Blvd *Web:* www.quad3.com	Wilkes-Barre	PA	18701	570-829-4200		261
Quad/Graphics Inc N61 W23044 Harry's Way *NYSE: QUAD* ■ *Web:* www.quad.com	Sussex	WI	53089	888-782-3226		627
Quad656 LLC 656 E Swedesford Rd *Web:* quad656.com	Wayne	PA	19087	610-687-6441	687-6442	260
Quadbase Systems Inc 275 Saratoga Ave Ste 105 *Web:* www.quadbase.com	Santa Clara	CA	95050	408-982-0835	982-0838	178-7
Quad-City Times 500 E Third St *TF:* 800-437-4641 ■ *Web:* www.qctimes.com	Davenport	IA	52801	563-383-2200		532-2
Quadel Consulting 1200 G St NW Ste 700 *TF:* 866-640-1019 ■ *Web:* quadel.com	Washington	DC	20005	202-789-2500	898-0632	194
Quadel Industries Inc 93759 Troy Ln *TF:* 800-289-7659 ■ *Web:* www.quadel.net	Coos Bay	OR	97420	541-269-7351		596
Quadlogic Controls Corp 33-00 Northern Blvd *Web:* www.quadlogic.com	Long Island City	NY	11101	212-930-9300		196
QuadMed *Sussex Health Ctr* W227 N6103 Sussex Rd *Web:* myquadmedical.com	Sussex	WI	53089	414-566-8100	566-8038	793
Quadra Chemicals Ltd 3901 Fixtessier *TF:* 800-665-6553 ■ *Web:* www.quadra.ca	Vaudreuil-Dorion	QC	J7V5V5	800-665-6553		146
Quadra Tech Inc 864 E Jenkins Ave *TF:* 800-443-2766 ■ *Web:* www.quadra-techinc.com	Columbus	OH	43207	800-443-2766		198
Quadramed Inc 12110 Sunset Hills Rd Ste 600 *TF:* 800-393-0278 ■ *Web:* www.quadramed.com	Reston	VA	20190	703-709-2300		177
Quadrant Chemical LLC 1002 Abby Ln *Web:* www.quadrantchemical.com	Lucas	TX	75002	972-542-0072		3
Quadrant Homes 15900 SE Eastgate Way Ste 300 *Web:* www.quadranthomes.com	Bellevue	WA	98008	425-452-6589		653
Quadrants Inc 49140 Wixom Tech Dr	Wixom	MI	48393	248-960-3900	960-9867	186
Quadrants Scientific Inc 10840 Thornmint Rd Ste 113 *Web:* www.quadscience.com	San Diego	CA	92127	858-618-4708		743
Quadratec Inc 1028 Saunders Ln *TF:* 800-745-6037 ■ *Web:* www.quadratec.com	West Chester	PA	19380	800-745-6037		791
Quadravest Capital Management Inc 200 Front St W Ste 2510 PO Box 51 *Web:* www.quadravest.com	Toronto	ON	M5V3K2	416-304-4443		401
Quadrel Labeling Systems 7670 Jenther Dr *Web:* www.quadrel.com	Mentor	OH	44060	440-602-4700		547
Quadrex Corp PO Box 3881 *TF:* 800-275-7033 ■ *Web:* quadrexcorp.com	Woodbridge	CT	06525	203-393-3112	393-0391	333
Quadriscan Inc 6600 Saint-Urbain St Ste 102 *Web:* quadriscan.com	Montreal	QC	H2S3G8	514-277-6022		627
QuadriSpace Corp 705 N Greenville Ave Ste 800 *Web:* www.quadrispace.com	Allen	TX	75002	972-359-6700		809
Quadros Systems Inc 13850 Gulf Fwy Ste 122 *Web:* quadros.com	Houston	TX	77034	832-351-2830		809
QuadW Technologies 600 Enterprise Dr Ste 225 *Web:* www.quadwtech.com	Oak Brook	IL	60523	630-694-4444		5
Quail Creek State Park 472 N 5300 W *Web:* stateparks.utah.gov	Hurricane	UT	84737	435-879-2378		565
Quail Hollow Resort 11080 Concord-Hambden Rd	Painesville	OH	44077	440-710-0876		669
Quail Lodge Resort & Golf Club 8205 Valley Greens Dr *TF:* 866-675-1101 ■ *Web:* www.quaillodge.com	Carmel By The Sea	CA	93923	866-675-1101		669
Quail Pointe Veterinary Hospital 868 North 2000 West *Web:* qpvh.com	Clinton	UT	84015	801-825-9191		794
Quail Ridge Press Inc PO Box 123 **Fax Area Code:* 800 ■ *TF:* 800-343-1583 ■ *Web:* www.quailridge.com	Brandon	MS	39043	601-825-2063	864-1082*	637-2
Quail Springs Mall 2501 W Memorial Rd *Web:* www.quailspringsmall.com	Oklahoma City	OK	73134	405-755-6530		460
Quail Tools LP 3713 Hwy 14 *Web:* www.quailtools.com	New Iberia	LA	70560	337-364-0407	365-9997	540
Quaintance-Weaver Inc 324 W Wendover Ave *Web:* www.qwrh.com	Greensboro	NC	27408	336-370-0966	370-0965	379
Quaker Chemical Corp 901 E Hector St *NYSE: KWR* ■ *TF:* 800-523-7010 ■ *Web:* www.quakerchem.com	Conshohocken	PA	19428	610-832-4000	832-8682	145
Quaker City Castings 310 E Euclid Ave *Web:* quakercitycastings.com	Salem	OH	44460	330-332-1566	332-1159	307
Quaker City Paper Co 300 N Sherman St *TF:* 800-533-2553 ■ *Web:* quakercitypaper.com	York	PA	17403	717-843-9061	843-7850	559
Quaker City Plating (QCP) 11729 Washington Blvd *Web:* www.qcpent.com	Whittier	CA	90606	800-922-4799		482
Quaker Gardens 12151 Dale St *Web:* rowntreegardens.org	Stanton	CA	90680	714-530-9100		672
Quaker Hill Conference Ctr 10 Quaker Hill Dr *Web:* www.qhcc.org	Richmond	IN	47374	765-962-5741		673
Quaker Oats Co 555 W Monroe St *TF:* 800-367-6287 ■ *Web:* www.quakeroats.com	Chicago	IL	60661	312-821-1000		296-36
Quaker Oats Credit Union 3535 Center Point Rd NE *Web:* quakeroatscu.com	Cedar Rapids	IA	52402	319-395-7060		219
Quaker Partners 2929 Arch St Cira Ctr *Web:* www.quakerbio.com	Philadelphia	PA	19104	215-988-6800	988-6801	792
Quaker Valley School District 203 Graham St *Web:* www.qvsd.org	Sewickley	PA	15143	412-749-3600		685
Quaker Window Products Inc 504 S Hwy 63 S *TF:* 800-347-0438 ■ *Web:* www.quakerwindows.com	Freeburg	MO	65035	800-347-0438		234
Quala-Die Inc 1250 Brusselles St *Web:* quala-die.com	Saint Marys	PA	15857	814-781-6280	781-3673	757
Qualaroo Inc 122 E Houston St *TF:* 888-449-3364 ■ *Web:* qualaroo.com	San Antonio	TX	78205	888-449-3364		387
Qualastat Electronics Inc 1270 Fairfield Rd Ste 50 *Web:* www.qualastat.org	Gettysburg	PA	17325	717-253-9301	334-9110	815
Qualchoice of Arkansas Inc 12615 Chenal Pkwy Ste 300 *TF:* 800-235-7111 ■ *Web:* www.qualchoice.com	Little Rock	AR	72211	800-235-7111		363
Qualcomm Inc 5775 Morehouse Dr *NASDAQ: QCOM* ■ *Web:* www.qualcomm.com	San Diego	CA	92121	858-587-1121		735
Qualcomm Stadium 9449 Friars Rd **Fax Area Code:* 619 ■ *TF:* 800-400-7115 ■ *Web:* www.sandiego.gov	San Diego	CA	92108	858-694-3900	283-0460*	720
QualCorp Inc 27240 Turnberry Ln Ste 200 *TF:* 888-367-6775 ■ *Web:* qualcorp.com	Valencia	CA	91355	661-799-0033	799-0020	809
Qual-Craft Industries PO Box 559 *TF:* 800-231-5647 ■ *Web:* www.qualcraft.com	Stoughton	MA	02072	800-231-5647		350
Quale Press 2 Hillcrest Rd *Web:* www.quale.com	Niantic	CT	06357	860-739-9153		179
Qualex Consulting Services Inc 1111 Kane Concourse Ste 320 *TF:* 877-887-4727 ■ *Web:* www.qlx.com	Bay Harbor Islands	FL	33154	877-887-4727		180
Qual-Fab Inc 34250 Mills Rd *Web:* www.qual-fab.net	Avon	OH	44011	440-327-5000		697
Quali Tech Inc 318 Lake Hazeltine Dr *TF:* 800-328-5870 ■ *Web:* www.qualitechco.com	Chaska	MN	55318	952-448-5151	448-3603	447
Qualia 201 Mission St Ste 1800 *TF:* 855-441-5498 ■ *Web:* www.qualia.com	San Francisco	CA	94105	855-441-5498		39
Qualicaps Inc 6505 Franz Warner Pkwy *TF:* 800-227-7853 ■ *Web:* qualicaps.com	Whitsett	NC	27377	336-449-3900	449-3333	582
Qualico Steel Company Inc 7797 E State Hwy 52 *TF:* 866-234-5382 ■ *Web:* www.qualicosteel.com	Webb	AL	36376	334-793-1290	794-0996	480
Qualified Printers Inc 2803 N Big Spring St *Web:* www.qualifiedprinters.net	Midland	TX	79705	432-683-4676		627
Qualified Resources International LLC 78 Kenwood St *Web:* www.qristaffing.com	Cranston	RI	02907	401-946-1002		631
Qualigen Inc 2042 Corte Del Nogal *Web:* www.qualigeninc.com	Carlsbad	CA	92011	760-918-9165		419
Qualigence Inc 35200 Schoolcraft Rd *Web:* qualigence.com	Livonia	MI	48150	734-432-6300		193
Qualis Corp 689 Discovery Dr NW Ste 400 *Web:* www.qualis-corp.com	Huntsville	AL	35806	256-971-1707		261
Qualis Health PO Box 33400 *TF:* 800-949-7536 ■ *Web:* www.qualishealth.org	Seattle	WA	98133	206-364-9700		374-3
QualiTau Inc 830 Maude Ave **Fax Area Code:* 650 ■ *Web:* qualitau.com	Mountain View	CA	94043	408-522-9200	230-9192*	253
Qualitek International Inc 315 Fairbank St *Web:* qualitek.com	Addison	IL	60101	630-628-8083	628-6543	145
Qualitek Services Inc 700 N Wickham Rd Ste 101 *Web:* www.qualitek.biz	Melbourne	FL	32935	321-259-2400		260
Qualitel Corp 11831 Beverly Park Rd *Web:* qualitel.com	Everett	WA	98204	425-423-8388	423-8398	253
QualiTest Ltd 1 Post Rd 3rd Fl *TF:* 877-882-9540 ■ *Web:* www.qualitestgroup.com	Fairfield	CT	06824	877-882-9540		393
Qualitex Co 4248 N Elston Ave *Web:* www.qualitexco.com	Chicago	IL	60618	773-463-6777	463-5731	151
Qualitrol Company LLC 1385 Fairport Rd *Web:* www.qualitrolcorp.com	Fairport	NY	14450	585-586-1515	377-0220	201
Quality & Regulatory Consulting LLC 5105 Fairoaks Rd *Web:* www.qandrconsulting.com	Durham	NC	27712	919-247-0479		194
Quality Administration LLC 610 Indian Trail Ct *TF:* 866-902-2090 ■ *Web:* www.qualityadmin.com	Smithville	MO	64089	816-532-2090	532-2099	463
Quality Air Heating & Cooling Inc 3395 Kraft Ave SE *Web:* www.qualityairinc.com	Grand Rapids	MI	49512	616-956-0200		697
Quality Aluminum Products Inc 14544 Telegraph Rd *Web:* www.qualityaluminum.com	Flat Rock	MI	48134	734-783-0990		697
Quality America Inc PO Box 30591 **Fax Area Code:* 520 ■ *TF:* 800-722-6154 ■ *Web:* www.qualityamerica.com	Tucson	AZ	85751	800-722-6154	722-6154*	178-1
Quality Asset Recovery 7 Foster Ave Ste 101 *TF:* 800-796-1476 ■ *Web:* www.qarcollect.com	Gibbsboro	NJ	08026	856-925-1010		160
Quality Bakery Products Inc 14330 Interdrive W *TF:* 866-449-4977 ■ *Web:* www.qualitybakeryproducts.net	Houston	TX	77032	281-449-4977	449-7820	296-1
Quality Beef Producers LP PO Box 145	Wildorado	TX	79098	806-426-3325		10-1
Quality Bending & Fabrication Inc 10005 SW Herman Rd *Web:* www.qpacmfg.com	Tualatin	OR	97062	503-692-0430		454
Quality Beverage Inc 525 Miles Standish Blvd *Web:* www.qblp.com	Taunton	MA	02780	508-822-6200		81-1
Quality Bicycle Products 6400 W 105th St *TF:* 800-346-0004 ■ *Web:* qbp.com	Bloomington	MN	55438	952-941-9391		82
Quality Biological Inc 7581 Lindbergh Dr *TF:* 800-443-9331 ■ *Web:* www.qualitybiological.com	Gaithersburg	MD	20879	301-840-9331		231
Quality Bioresources Inc 1015 N Austin St *TF:* 888-674-7224 ■ *Web:* qualbio.com	Seguin	TX	78155	830-372-4797		415

Company	Phone	Fax	Class
Quality Borate Company LLC 3690 Orange Pl Ste 495 Cleveland OH 44122 *TF:* 866-267-2837 ■ *Web:* www.qualityborate.com	216-896-1949		280
Quality Building Stone Inc 993 W 14730 S Riverton UT 84065 *Web:* www.qualitybuildingstone.com	801-255-2911		191-1
Quality Built LLC 401 SE 12th St Ste 200 Fort Lauderdale FL 33316 *TF:* 800-547-5125 ■ *Web:* www.qualitybuilt.com	954-358-3500		194
Quality Business Solutions Inc 280 Hindman Rd Travelers Rest SC 29690 *TF:* 877-834-3985 ■ *Web:* qualitybsolutions.net	864-834-3985	834-5642	194
Quality Castings Co 1200 N Main St Orrville OH 44667 *Web:* www.qcfoundry.com	330-682-6010	683-3153	307
Quality Chain Corp 3365 NW 215th Ave Hillsboro OR 97124 *Web:* qualitychaincorp.com	503-614-9664		350
Quality Circuit Assembly 1709 Junction Ct Ste 380 San Jose CA 95112 *Web:* qcamfg.com	408-441-1001		625
Quality Circuits Inc 1102 Progress Dr Fergus Falls MN 56537 *Web:* www.qciusa.com	218-739-9707	739-9705	625
Quality Contract Assemblies Inc 100 Boxart St Ste 251 Rochester NY 14612 *Web:* www.qcacorp.com	585-663-9030	663-1432	253
Quality Control Corp (QCC) 7315 W Wilson Ave Chicago IL 60706 *Web:* www.qccorp.com	708-887-5400	887-5009	621
Quality Control Inspection Inc 40 Tarbell Ave Cleveland OH 44146 *Web:* www.qcigroup.com	440-359-1900	359-1935	365
Quality Control Solutions Inc (QCSI) 43339 Business Park Dr Ste 101 & 102 Temecula CA 92590 *TF:* 888-355-7274 ■ *Web:* www.qc-solutions.com	951-676-1616	676-8970	472
Quality Craft Ltd 17750-65A Ave Ste 301 Surrey BC V3S5N4 *TF:* 800-663-2252 ■ *Web:* www.qualitycraft.com	604-575-5550	575-1121	290
Quality Custom Cabinetry Inc 125 Peters Rd New Holland PA 17557 *Web:* www.qcc.com	717-661-6900		115
Quality Customs Broker Inc 4464 S Whitnall Ave Saint Francis WI 53235 *TF:* 888-813-4647 ■ *Web:* www.qualitybrokers.com	414-482-9447	482-9448	311
Quality Dining Inc 4220 Edison Lakes Pkwy Mishawaka IN 46545 *TF:* 800-589-3820 ■ *Web:* www.qdi.com	574-271-4600	271-4612	670
Quality Distribution Inc 4041 Pk Oaks Blvd Ste 200 Tampa FL 33610 *NASDAQ: QLTY* ■ *TF:* 800-282-2031 ■ *Web:* www.qualitydistribution.com	800-282-2031		780
Quality Edge Inc 2712 Walkent Dr NW Walker MI 49544 *TF:* 888-784-0878 ■ *Web:* www.qualityedge.com	888-784-0878		490
Quality Electrodynamics LLC 700 Beta Dr Mayfield Village OH 44143 *Web:* qedinnovations.com	440-638-5106		383
Quality Elevator Products Inc 7760 Merrimac Ave Niles IL 60714 *TF:* 800-222-3688 ■ *Web:* qualityelev.com	847-581-0085	581-0095	256
Quality Enclosures Inc 2025 Porter Lake Dr Sarasota FL 34240 *TF:* 800-881-0051 ■ *Web:* www.qualityenclosures.com	941-378-0051		320
Quality Engineering Services 122 N Plains Industrial Rd Wallingford CT 06492 *TF:* 800-637-6809 ■ *Web:* qes1.com	203-269-5054	269-9277	454
Quality Extrusion Inc 1904 Willow St Mankato MN 56001 *Web:* www.qualityextrusion.net	507-387-4131	387-4597	600
Quality Fabrication Inc 9631 Irondale Ave Chatsworth CA 91311 *Web:* www.quality-fab.com	818-709-8505	709-4530	697
Quality Filters Inc 7215 Jackson Rd Ann Arbor MI 48103 *Web:* www.qualityfiltersinc.com	734-668-0211		483
Quality Flow Systems Inc 800 Sixth St NW New Prague MN 56071 *Web:* qfsi.net	952-758-9445	758-9661	358
Quality Food Centers QFC 10116 NE 8th Bellevue WA 98004 *Web:* www.qfc.com	425-455-0870		345
Quality Forms 4317 W US Rt 36 Piqua OH 45356 **Fax Area Code: 888* ■ *TF:* 866-773-4595 ■ *Web:* www.qualforms.com	937-773-4595	550-3937*	110
Quality Frozen Foods Inc 1663 62nd St Brooklyn NY 11204 *Web:* www.qualityfrozenfoods.com	718-256-9100		297-6
Quality Fuel Networks Inc 15227 Herriman Blvd Noblesville IN 46060 *Web:* www.qualityfuel.com	317-774-1076		463
Quality Gold Inc 500 Quality Blvd Fairfield OH 45014 *TF:* 800-354-9833 ■ *Web:* www.qgold.com	800-354-9833		411
Quality Grinding Company Inc 6800 Caballero Blvd Buena Park CA 90620 *Web:* www.qualitygrinding.net	714-228-2100		493
Quality Group Inc, The 5825 Glenridge Dr NE Bldg 3 Ste 101 Atlanta GA 30328 *TF:* 800-772-3071 ■ *Web:* opusworks.com	404-843-9525	252-4475	194
Quality Healthcare Services 235 High St Burlington NJ 08016 *Web:* www.qualityhealthcareservices.com	609-499-8844	228-6645	363
Quality Hill Playhouse 303 W Tenth St Kansas City MO 64105 *Web:* www.qualityhillplayhouse.com	816-421-1700		572
Quality Home Health Care 18100 Meyers Rd Detroit MI 48235 *TF:* 866-270-2558 ■ *Web:* www.qualityhomehealthcare.net	313-340-1240		363
Quality Honeycomb LP 624 107th St Arlington TX 76011 *Web:* www.qualityhoneycomb.com	817-640-1190		21
Quality Hotel-airport 7228 Wminster Hwy Richmond BC V6X1A1 *TF:* 877-244-3051 ■ *Web:* www.qualityhotelvancouverairport.com	604-244-3051		379
Quality Hydraulics & Pneumatics Inc 1415 Wilhelm Rd Mundelein IL 60060 *Web:* www.qualityhydraulics.com	847-680-8400	680-5325	358
Quality Incentive Co 3962 Willow Lake Blvd Memphis TN 38118 *TF:* 800-621-9745 ■ *Web:* qualityincentivecompany.com	901-367-8200	367-8265	463
Quality Industrial Products Inc 21835 N 23rd Ave Phoenix AZ 85027 *Web:* www.quality-industrial.com	602-861-2930	581-0208	326
Quality Industries Inc 130 Jones Blvd La Vergne TN 37086 *TF:* 800-745-8613 ■ *Web:* www.qualityindustries.com	615-793-3000		697
Quality Inn & Suites Naples Golf Resort 4100 Golden Gate Pkwy Naples FL 34116 *TF:* 800-277-0017 ■ *Web:* www.naplesgolfresort.com	239-455-1010	455-4038	669
Quality Inn Flamingo 1300 N Stone Ave Tucson AZ 85705 *Web:* www.flamingohoteltucson.com	520-770-1910	770-0750	379
Quality Inn Halifax Airport 60 Sky Blvd Goffs NS B2T1K3 *TF:* 800-667-3333 ■ *Web:* www.airporthotelhalifax.com	902-873-3000		379
Quality Insurance Services Inc 241 E Pomona Blvd Monterey Park CA 91755 *Web:* qualityins.com	323-727-7755		390
Quality IP LLC 145 S River St Kent OH 44240 *TF:* 833-566-9748 ■ *Web:* qualityip.com	330-931-4141		562
Quality King Distributors Inc 35 Sawgrass Dr Ste 3 Bellport NY 11713 *Web:* www.qkd.com	631-737-5555		238
Quality Life Health Care LLC 46 Prince St Prince Professional Bldg Ste 201 New Haven CT 06519 *Web:* qualitylifehealthcare.com	203-562-0656	562-0657	352
Quality Liquid Feeds Inc PO Box 240 Dodgeville WI 53533 *TF:* 800-236-2345 ■ *Web:* www.qlf.com	608-935-2345		276
Quality Logistics Systems Inc PO Box 5637 Meridian MS 39302 *TF:* 877-223-4570 ■ *Web:* www.qualitylogistics.com	601-483-0265	483-7928	803-1
Quality Machine & Tool Works Inc 1201 Michigan Ave Columbus IN 47201 *Web:* www.qmtw.net	812-379-2660	379-2669	454
Quality Machine & Welding Company Inc PO Box 27345 Knoxville TN 37927 *Web:* www.qmwkx.com	865-524-2162	524-1830	480
Quality Machine Engineering Inc 5600 Skylane Blvd Santa Rosa CA 95403 *Web:* www.qmeinc.com	707-528-1900	528-1999	454
Quality Machine Works Inc 32838 La 642 N Paulina LA 70763 *Web:* www.qualitymachine.net	225-869-9809	869-8860	454
Quality Management Solutions LLC (QMS) 146 Lowell St Ste 300B Wakefield MA 01880 *TF:* 800-645-6430 ■ *Web:* www.qmsinc.com	800-645-6430		196
Quality Manufacturing Company Inc (QMI) PO Box 616 Winchester KY 40392 *TF:* 866-460-6459 ■ *Web:* www.qmiky.com	859-744-0420		454
Quality Manufacturing Corp 4300 NW Urbandale Dr Urbandale IA 50322 *Web:* qualitymfgcorp.com	515-331-4300	331-4400	492
Quality Manufacturing Inc 969 Labore Industrial Ct Saint Paul MN 55110 *TF:* 800-243-5473 ■ *Web:* www.qualitymanufacturing.com	651-483-5473	483-1101	701
Quality Mat Co 6550 Tram Rd Beaumont TX 77713 *TF:* 800-227-8159 ■ *Web:* www.qmat.com	409-722-4594		131
Quality Meats & Seafoods 700 Center St West Fargo ND 58078 *TF:* 800-342-4250 ■ *Web:* www.qualitymeats.com	701-282-0202		473
Quality Media Resources Inc 10929 SE 23rd St Bellevue WA 98004 *TF:* 800-800-5129 ■ *Web:* qmr.com	800-800-5129		463
Quality Metal Fabricators Inc 2610 E Fifth Ave Tampa FL 33605 *Web:* www.qmf.com	813-831-7320		697
Quality Metal Finishing Company Inc 421 N Walnut St Byron IL 61010 *Web:* www.qmfco.com	815-234-2711		609
Quality Metal Products Inc 720 Orange Rd Dallas PA 18612 *TF:* 888-251-2805 ■ *Web:* www.qualmet.com	570-333-4248	333-4967	697
Quality Metals Inc 2575 Doswell Ave Saint Paul MN 55108 *TF:* 800-328-4893 ■ *Web:* www.qualitymetalsinc.com	651-645-5875		492
Quality Name Plate Inc 22 Fisher Hill Rd East Glastonbury CT 06025 *Web:* www.qnp.com	860-633-9495	633-4391	729
Quality of Life Health Services Inc 1411 Piedmont Cutoff Gadsden AL 35903 *TF:* 888-490-0131 ■ *Web:* www.qolhs.org	256-492-0131		374-3
Quality Oil Company LLC 1540 Silas Creek Pkwy Winston-Salem NC 27127 *Web:* www.qualityoilnc.com	336-722-3441	721-9520	324
Quality Oil Inc 55 N 400 Valparaiso IN 46383	219-462-2951		690
Quality Packaging Industries 5830 State Hwy V Jackson MO 63755 *Web:* qpimo.com	573-334-6700	334-8032	549
Quality Perforating Inc (QPI) 166 Dundaff St Carbondale PA 18407 *TF:* 800-872-7373 ■ *Web:* www.qualityperf.com	570-282-4344	282-4627	488
Quality Petroleum Inc 11610 Maybelline Dr North Little Rock AR 72117 *Web:* www.qualitypetroleuminc.com	501-955-2166		579
Quality Plastic Products Inc 830 Maple Ln Bensenville IL 60106 *Web:* www.qualityplastics.org	630-766-7593	599-8620	604
Quality Pork Processors Inc 711 Hormel Century Pkwy Austin MN 55912 *Web:* www.qppinc.net	507-434-6300		473
Quality Porks International Inc 10404 F Plz Omaha NE 68127 *Web:* www.qpii.com	402-339-1911	339-8383	473
Quality Press Inc 222 S Orcas St Seattle WA 98108 *Web:* www.qualitypress.com	206-768-2655	768-0970	627

	Phone	Fax	Class
Quality Quartz Engineering Inc 8484 Central Ave .... Newark CA 94560 *Web:* www.qqe.com	510-745-9200	745-7948	330
Quality Sausage Company Ltd 1925 Lone Star Dr .... Dallas TX 75212 *Web:* www.qualitysausage.com	214-634-3400		296-26
Quality Solutions Inc 128 N First St .... Colwich KS 67030 *TF:* 888-328-2454 ■ *Web:* www.qsifacilities.com	316-721-3656		271
Quality Sprinkler Company Inc 10301 Old Concord Rd .... Charlotte NC 28213 *Web:* www.qualitysprinkler.com	704-549-8220		610
Quality State Oil Company Inc 2201 Calumet Dr .... Sheboygan WI 53083 *TF:* 800-236-5640 ■ *Web:* www.qualitystateoil.biz	920-459-5640		579
Quality Surface Mount Inc 965 Dillon Dr .... Wood Dale IL 60191 *Web:* www.qsmt.com	630-350-8556	350-9868	625
Quality Switch Inc 715 Arlington Blvd .... Newton Falls OH 44444 *Web:* www.qualityswitch.com	330-872-5707		425
Quality Synthetic Rubber Inc 1700 Highland Rd .... Twinsburg OH 44087 *Web:* qsr-inc.com	330-425-8472		677
Quality Systems Integrated Corp 6720 Cobra Way .... San Diego CA 92121 *Web:* www.qsic.com	858-587-9797		625
Quality Systems Solutins Inc 6905 Zachary Dr .... Carpentersville IL 60110 *Web:* www.qualitysystemssolutions.com	847-426-9548		809
Quality Tech Services Inc 10525 Hampshire Ave S .... Bloomington MN 55438 *Web:* qtspackage.com	952-942-8321	942-8361	476
Quality Technical Training Ctr 3139 Westwood Dr .... Las Vegas NV 89109 *TF:* 800-858-2653 ■ *Web:* www.qualitytrainingcenters.com	702-597-0861	597-2731	167-3
Quality Texas Foundation (QTF) 201 Woodland Pk .... Georgetown TX 78633 *Web:* quality-texas.org	512-656-8946		303
Quality Tool & Stamping Company Inc 541 E Sherman Blvd .... Muskegon MI 49444 *Web:* www.qtstamping.com	231-733-2538	733-0983	488
Quality Tool Inc 1220 Energy Park Dr .... Saint Paul MN 55108 *TF:* 866-997-4647 ■ *Web:* www.qualitytool.com	651-646-7433		697
Quality Transformer & Electronics 963 Ames Ave .... Milpitas CA 95035 *Web:* www.qte.com	408-263-8444		767
Quality Transportation 36-40 37th St Ste 201 .... Long Island City NY 11101 *TF:* 800-677-2838 ■ *Web:* www.qualitytca.com	212-308-6333		311
Quality Transportation Inc 511 W Montana Ave .... Baker MT 59313 **Fax Area Code:* 406 ■ *TF:* 800-423-0141 ■ *Web:* www.quality-transportation.com	800-423-0141	778-3196*	780
Quality Truck Bodies & Repair Inc 5316 Rock Quarry Rd .... Elm City NC 27822 *TF:* 800-334-5182 ■ *Web:* www.qualitytruckbodies.com	252-245-5100	245-5153	61
Quality Wholesale Building Inc 11701 Kinard Rd .... North Little Rock AR 72117	501-945-3442		191-3
Quality Window & Door Inc 27888 County Rd 32 W .... Elkhart IN 46517 *TF:* 888-674-0867 ■ *Web:* www.qwd-online.com	574-862-1613	862-4090	234
Qualnetics Corp 6197 Everson Goshen Rd .... Everson WA 98247	360-733-4151		177
Qualortran Inc 236 Carpenter Rd NE .... Calhoun GA 30701 *Web:* qualortran.com	706-295-4510		261
Qual-Pro Corp 18510 S Figueroa St .... Gardena CA 90248 *Web:* www.qual-pro.com	310-329-7535		625
QualPro Inc 3117 Pellissippi Pkwy .... Knoxville TN 37931 *Web:* qualproinc.com	865-927-0491		196
Qualstar Corp 3990-B Heritage Oak Ct .... Simi Valley CA 93063 *NASDAQ: QBAK* ■ *TF:* 800-468-0680 ■ *Web:* www.qualstar.com	805-583-7744	583-7749	173-8
Qualtech Inc 1880 Leon-Harmel St .... Quebec City QC G1N4K3 *TF:* 888-339-3801 ■ *Web:* www.qualtech.ca	418-686-3802		296
Qualtech Laboratories Inc 104 Green Grove Rd .... Ocean City NJ 07712 *Web:* qualtechlabsinc.com	732-918-0207		743
Qualtech Systems 100 Corporate Pl Ste 220 .... Rocky Hill CT 06067 *Web:* teamqsi.com	860-257-8014		177
Qualtrics 2250 N University Pkwy Ste 48 C .... Provo UT 84604 *Web:* www.qualtrics.com	385-203-4999		466
Qual-Tron Inc (QTI) 9409 E 55th Pl .... Tulsa OK 74145 *Web:* www.qual-tron.com	918-622-7052		253
Qualys Inc 1600 Bridge Pkwy .... Redwood City CA 94065 *TF:* 800-745-4355 ■ *Web:* www.qualys.com	650-801-6100	801-6101	692
Quam-Nichols Company Inc 234 E Marquette Rd .... Chicago IL 60637 *TF:* 800-633-3669 ■ *Web:* www.quamspeakers.com	773-488-5800	488-6944	52
Quanah Tribune-Chief 310 Mercer St .... Quanah TX 79252 *TF:* 866-600-5333 ■ *Web:* www.quanahtribunechief.com	940-663-5333	663-5073	532-2
Quandel Group Inc 3003 N Front St Ste 203 .... Harrisburg PA 17110 *Web:* quandel.com	717-657-0909	652-6282	186
Quanex Building Products 2270 Woodale Dr .... Mounds View MN 55112 *TF:* 800-233-4383 ■ *Web:* www.quanex.com	763-231-4000		499
Quang 2719 Nicollet Ave .... Minneapolis MN 55408 *Web:* www.quang-restaurant.com	612-870-4739		671
Quanta Laboratories 3199 De La Cruz Blvd .... Santa Clara CA 95054 *Web:* www.quantalabs.com	408-988-0770		743
Quanta Services Inc 1360 Post Oak Blvd Ste 2100 .... Houston TX 77056 *NYSE: PWR* ■ *Web:* www.quantaservices.com	713-629-7600	629-7676	188-1
Quantcast Corp 201 3rd St 2nd Fl .... San Francisco CA 94103 *TF:* 800-293-5706 ■ *Web:* www.quantcast.com	800-293-5706		387
Quantec Geoscience Ltd 146 Sparks Ave .... Toronto ON M2H2S4 *TF:* 877-782-6832 ■ *Web:* quantecgeo.com	416-306-1941		727
Quantech Corp 369 Lexington Ave .... New York NY 10016 *TF:* 833-256-8367 ■ *Web:* www.quantech.net	212-323-2660	323-2661	809
Quantenna Communications Inc 3450 W Warren Ave .... Fremont CA 94538 *Web:* www.quantenna.com	510-743-2260		201
Quantiam Technologies Inc 1651 - 94 St NW .... Edmonton AB T6N1E6 *TF:* 877-461-0707 ■ *Web:* www.quantiam.com	780-462-0707	465-6603	668
Quantico National Cemetery 18424 Joplin Rd .... Triangle VA 22172 *Web:* www.cem.va.gov	703-221-2183	221-2185	136
Quantifi Inc 17 Union Pl 2nd Fl .... Summit NJ 07901 **Fax Area Code:* 646 ■ *Web:* www.quantifisolutions.com	908-273-9455	304-3440*	178-1
Quantimetrix Corp 2005 Manhattan Beach Blvd .... Redondo Beach CA 90278 *TF:* 800-624-8380 ■ *Web:* quantimetrix.com	310-536-0006	536-9977	231
QuantiTech Inc 360A Quality Cir Ste 100 .... Huntsville AL 35806 *Web:* www.quantitech.com	256-650-6263	650-5569	463
Quantlab Financial LLC 3 Greenway Plz Ste 200 .... Houston TX 77046 *Web:* www.quantlab.com	713-333-5440		401
Quantopian Inc 100 Franklin St 5th Fl .... Boston MA 02110 *Web:* www.quantopian.com	617-752-1454		387
Quantronix Inc 380 S 200 W .... Farmington UT 84025 **Fax Area Code:* 801 ■ *TF:* 800-488-2823 ■ *Web:* www.cubiscan.com	800-488-2823	451-0502*	173-1
Quantros Inc 691 S Milpitas Blvd Ste 100 .... Milpitas CA 95035 *TF:* 877-782-6876 ■ *Web:* www.quantros.com	877-782-6876		177
Quantrum LLC 2371 Lkview Dr .... Beavercreek OH 45431 *Web:* quantrum-llc.com	937-458-3913		525
Quantum Analytical Services Inc 1210 E 223rd St Ste 314 .... Carson CA 90745 *Web:* quantumairlab.com	310-830-2226		261
Quantum Analytics 3400 E Third Ave .... Foster City CA 94404 *TF:* 800-992-4199 ■ *Web:* www.lqa.com	650-312-0900	312-0303	264-3
Quantum Audio Designs Inc PO Box 130 .... Benton MO 63736 *TF:* 888-545-4404 ■ *Web:* www.quantumaudiodesigns.com	573-545-4404	545-4411	526
Quantum Automation Inc 4400 E La Palma Ave .... Anaheim CA 92807 *Web:* www.quantumautomation.com	714-854-0800	854-0803	463
Quantum Aviation Solutions 1720 Epps Bridge Pkwy Ste 108 Number 304 .... Athens GA 30606 *Web:* quantum.aero	404-348-4839		177
Quantum Capital Management LLC 105 E Mill Rd .... Northfield NJ 08225 *Web:* www.quantumadv.com	609-677-4949	677-8825	401
Quantum Communications Ltd 123 State St .... Harrisburg PA 17101 *Web:* www.quantumcomms.com	717-213-4955		681
Quantum Controls Inc 1691 Lake Dr W .... Chanhassen MN 55317 *TF:* 888-276-9131 ■ *Web:* www.quantum-controls.com	952-361-3694	361-3794	203
Quantum Corp 224 Airport Pkwy Ste 300 .... San Jose CA 95110 *NYSE: QTM* ■ *TF:* 800-677-6268 ■ *Web:* www.quantum.com	408-944-4000		173-8
Quantum Corporate Funding Ltd 1140 Avenue of the Americas 16th Fl .... New York NY 10036 *TF:* 800-352-2535 ■ *Web:* www.quantumfunding.com	212-768-1200	944-8216	272
Quantum Credit Union 6300 W 21st Ste N .... Wichita KS 67205 *TF:* 877-287-3783 ■ *Web:* theq.org	316-263-5756		219
Quantum Crossings LLC 111 E Wacker Dr Ste 990 .... Chicago IL 60601 *Web:* www.quantumcrossings.com	312-467-0065		186
Quantum Dental Technologies Inc 748 Briar Hill Ave .... Toronto ON M6B1L3 *TF:* 866-993-9910 ■ *Web:* www.thecanarysystem.com	866-993-9910		228
Quantum Design Inc 6325 Lusk Blvd .... San Diego CA 92121 *Web:* www.qdusa.com	858-481-4400		419
Quantum Devices Inc 112 Orbison St .... Barneveld WI 53507 *Web:* www.quantumdev.com	608-924-3000		696
Quantum Dimension Inc 18672 Florida St Ste 302-D .... Huntington Beach CA 92648 *Web:* quantumdimension.com	714-893-6004		681
Quantum House 987 45th St .... West Palm Beach FL 33407 *Web:* www.quantumhouse.org	561-494-0515	494-0522	372
Quantum Inc PO Box 2791 .... Eugene OR 97402 *TF:* 800-448-1448 ■ *Web:* www.quantumhealth.com	541-345-5556		297
Quantum Information Systems Solutions Inc 2805 Pontiac Lake Rd Ste 2C .... Waterford MI 48328 *Web:* www.qinfosys.com	248-393-3621		196
Quantum Internet Services Inc (QIS) 2975B Manchester Rd .... Manchester MD 21102 *TF:* 888-889-4638 ■ *Web:* www.qis.net	410-239-6920		681
Quantum Laboratories Inc 28221 Beck Rd Ste A-11 .... Wixom MI 48393 *Web:* www.quantumlaboratories.com	248-348-8378		743
Quantum Labs Inc 452 Northco Dr Ste 180 .... Minneapolis MN 55432 **Fax Area Code:* 800 ■ *TF:* 888-328-8213 ■ *Web:* www.quantumlabs.com	888-328-8213	485-9565*	475
Quantum Leap Engineering (QLE) 11 Toner Blvd Ste 5-353 .... North Attleboro MA 02763 *Web:* www.quantumleapengineering.com	508-954-0185		194
Quantum Legal LLC 513 Central Ave Ste 300 .... Highland Park IL 60035 *Web:* qulegal.com	847-433-4500		41
Quantum Management Services Ltd 2000 McGill College Ave Ste 1800 .... Montreal QC H3A3H3 *TF:* 800-978-2688 ■ *Web:* www.quantum.ca	514-842-5555		734
Quantum Marine Stabilizers 3790 SW 30th Ave .... Fort Lauderdale FL 33312 *Web:* quantumstabilizers.com	954-587-4205		261
Quantum Plastics 1000 Davis Rd .... Elgin IL 60123 *Web:* www.quantumplastics.com	847-695-9700		596
Quantum Signal AI LLC 200 N Ann Arbor St .... Saline MI 48176 *Web:* quantumsignalai.com	734-429-9100	429-9113	261

	City	State	Zip	Phone	Fax	Class
Quantum Technology Sciences Inc 1980 N Atlantic Ave Ste 201 *Web:* www.qtsi.com	Cocoa Beach	FL	32931	321-868-0288		692
Quantum Utility Generation 1401 McKinney St Ste 1800 *Web:* www.quantumug.com	Houston	TX	77010	713-485-8600	485-8601	787
Quantum3D Inc 1759 McCarthy Blvd *TF:* 888-747-1020 ■ *Web:* quantum3d.com	Milpitas	CA	95035	408-600-2500	600-2608	173-2
QuantumDigital Inc 8702 Cross Park Dr *TF:* 800-637-7373 ■ *Web:* quantumdigital.com	Austin	TX	78754	800-637-7373		5
Quantus Creative 8211 E Regal Blvd Ste 103 *Web:* www.quantuscreative.com	Tulsa	OK	74133	918-794-2758		194
Quantus Software 62 Scurfield Blvd	Winnipeg	MB	R3Y1M5	204-478-1308		193
Quapaw Quarter Assn 615 E Capitol Ave PO Box 165023 *Web:* www.quapaw.com	Little Rock	AR	72216	501-371-0075		50-3
Quark Inc 1800 Grant St *TF:* 800-676-4575 ■ *Web:* www.quark.com	Denver	CO	80203	800-676-4575		178-8
Quark Pharmaceuticals Inc 6501 Dumbarton Cir *Web:* quarkpharma.com	Fremont	CA	94555	510-402-4020	402-4021	231
Quarles & Brady LLP 411 E Wisconsin Ave Ste 2400 *Web:* www.quarles.com	Milwaukee	WI	53202	414-277-5000	271-3552	428
Quarles Petroleum Inc 1701 Fall Hill Ave *Web:* www.quarlesinc.com	Fredericksburg	VA	22401	540-371-2400		581
Quarry Hill Nature Ctr 701 Silver Creek Rd NE *Web:* qhnc.org	Rochester	MN	55906	507-328-3950	287-1345	50-5
Quarryhill Botanical Garden 12841 Sonoma Hwy PO Box 232 *Web:* www.quarryhillbg.org	Glen Ellen	CA	95442	707-996-3166	996-3198	97
Quarryville Presbyterian Retirement Community 625 Robert Fulton Hwy *Web:* www.quarryville.com	Quarryville	PA	17566	717-786-7321		672
Quartech Systems Ltd 650 - 2889 East 12th Ave *Web:* www.quartech.com	Vancouver	BC	V5M4T5	604-291-9686		196
Quarter Master Industries Inc 510 Telser Rd *Web:* www.quartermasterusa.com	Lake Zurich	IL	60047	847-540-8999		247
Quartino Ristorante & Wine Bar 626 N State St *Web:* www.quartinoristorante.com	Chicago	IL	60654	312-698-5000		671
Quarto Publishing Group USA 400 1st Ave N Ste 400 *Web:* qbookshop.com	Minneapolis	MN	55401	612-344-8100	344-8691	454
Quarton Partners LLC 300 Park St Ste 480 *Web:* www.quartoninternational.com	Birmingham	MI	48009	248-594-0400	594-0401	70
Quartz 2650 Novation Pkwy Ste 400 *TF:* 800-545-5015 ■ *Web:* quartzbenefits.com	Madison	WI	53713	608-282-8900		391-3
Quartz Lake State Recreation Area 3700 Airport Way *Web:* www.dnr.alaska.gov	Fairbanks	AK	99709	907-451-2695		565
Quartz Mountain Resort & Conference Ctr 22469 Lodge Rd *TF:* 877-999-5567 ■ *Web:* www.quartzmountainresort.com	Lone Wolf	OK	73655	580-563-2424	563-2422	669
Quartzdyne Inc 4334 W Links Dr *TF:* 800-222-3611 ■ *Web:* www.quartzdyne.com	Salt Lake City	UT	84120	801-839-1000	266-7985	253
Quasius Investment Corp 4200 W Cypress St Ste 375 *TF:* 888-422-9786 ■ *Web:* www.gca.net	Tampa	FL	33607	813-249-2514		196
Quast Janke & Co 1010 N Johnson St *Web:* www.qjc.com	Bay City	MI	48708	989-892-4549	892-4030	2
Quatela Chimeri PLLC 888 Veterans Memorial Hwy Ste 530 *Web:* www.qclaw.com	Hauppauge	NY	11788	631-482-9700		41
Quatred LLC 532 Fourth Range Rd *TF:* 888-395-8534 ■ *Web:* www.quatred.com	Pembroke	NH	03275	888-395-8534		41
Quattlebaum, Grooms & Tull PLLC 111 Center St Ste 1900 *Web:* qgtlaw.com	Little Rock	AR	72201	501-379-1700		41
Quay County PO Box 1246 **Fax Area Code:* 505 ■ *Web:* www.quaycounty-nm.gov	Tucumcari	NM	88401	575-461-2112	461-6208*	338
Quazar Capital Corp 3535 Plymouth Blvd Ste 210 *Web:* quazarcapital.com	Minneapolis	MN	55447	763-550-9000		401
Quebe Holdings Inc 1985 Founders Dr *Web:* www.quebe.com	Dayton	OH	45420	937-222-2290		246
Quebec Inn 7175 Blvd Hamel Ouest *Web:* www.hotelsjaro.com	Quebec City	QC	G2G1B6	418-872-9831	872-1336	379
Quebec Port Authority 150 Dalhousie St PO Box 80 Stn Haute-Ville *TF:* 800-465-1213 ■ *Web:* www.portquebec.ca	Quebec City	QC	G1R4M8	418-648-3640	648-4160	618
Quebecor Media Inc (QMI) 612 Saint-Jacques St *Web:* www.quebecor.com	Montreal	QC	H3C4M8	514-380-1999		637-2
Quechee State Park 1 National Life Dr Davis 2 *Web:* www.vtstateparks.com	Montpelier	VT	05620	802-295-2990		565
Queen Anne Hotel 1590 Sutter St *TF:* 800-227-3970 ■ *Web:* www.queenanne.com	San Francisco	CA	94109	415-441-2828	775-5212	379
Queen Anne's County 107 N Liberty St *Web:* www.qac.org	Centreville	MD	21617	410-758-4098	758-1170	338
Queen Anne's County Chamber of Commerce 1561 Postal Rd *Web:* www.qacchamber.com	Chester	MD	21619	410-643-8530	643-8477	139
Queen Anne's County Library 121 S Commerce St *Web:* www.quan.lib.md.us	Centreville	MD	21617	410-758-0980	758-0614	434-3
Queen B 51 Means Dr	Platteville	WI	53818	608-349-2000		645
Queen Beach Printers Inc 937 Pine Ave *Web:* www.qbprinters.com	Long Beach	CA	90813	562-436-8201	435-2209	174

	City	State	Zip	Phone	Fax	Class
Queen City Grill 2209 1st Ave Ste 252	Seattle	WA	98121	206-443-0975		671
Queen City Polymers Inc 6101 Schumacher Park Dr *TF:* 888-298-5529 ■ *Web:* www.qcpinc.net	West Chester	OH	45069	888-298-5529		604
Queen City Printers Inc 701 Pine St *TF:* 800-639-8099	Burlington	VT	05401	802-864-4566		627
Queen City TV & Appliance Company Inc 2430 Queen City Dr *Web:* www.queencityonline.com	Charlotte	NC	28208	704-391-6000	391-6038	35
Queen Communications LLC 1215 Anthony Ave *Web:* www.queencommunicationsllc.com	Columbia	SC	29201	803-779-0340		47
Queen Emma Summer Palace 2913 Pali Hwy *Web:* daughtersofhawaii.org	Honolulu	HI	96817	808-595-3167	595-4395	50-3
Queen Kapiolani Hotel 150 Kapahulu Ave *Web:* www.queenkapiolani.com	Honolulu	HI	96815	808-922-1941		379
Queen of Angels Monastery 840 S Main St *Web:* www.benedictine-srs.org	Mount Angel	OR	97362	503-845-6141		50-1
Queen of the Valley Medical Ctr 1000 Trancas St *Web:* www.thequeen.org	Napa	CA	94558	707-252-4411		374-3
Queen Wilhelmina State Park 3877 Arkansas 88 *Web:* www.arkansasstateparks.com	Mena	AR	71953	479-394-2863		565
Queen's College Faculty of Theology 210 Prince Philip Dr *TF:* 877-753-0116 ■ *Web:* queenscollegenl.ca	Saint John	NL	A1B3R6	709-753-0116		167-3
Queen's Medical Ctr, The 1301 Punchbowl St *Web:* www.queens.org	Honolulu	HI	96813	808-691-7171	691-8865	374-3
Queen's School of Business Goodes Hall 143 Union St Rm 130 *Web:* www.smith.queensu.ca	Kingston	ON	K7L3N6	613-533-2301	533-2316	162
Queen's University 99 University Ave *TF:* 800 267-7037 ■ *Web:* www.queensu.ca	Kingston	ON	K7L3N6	613 583-7402	533-2068	785
Queen's University Faculty of Health Sciences 18 Barrie St *Web:* healthsci.queensu.ca	Kingston	ON	K7L3N6	613-533-2544		167-2
Queens Borough Public Library 89-11 Merrick Blvd *Web:* www.queenslibrary.org	Jamaica	NY	11432	718-990-0700		434-3
Queens Botanical Garden 43-50 Main St *Web:* www.queensbotanical.org	Flushing	NY	11355	718-886-3800	463-0263	97
Queens Boulevard Extended Care Facility Corp 61-11 Queens Blvd *Web:* www.qbecf.com	Woodside	NY	11377	718-205-0287	205-0297	793
Queens Chamber of Commerce 75-20 Astoria Blvd Ste 140 *Web:* www.queenschamber.org	East Elmhurst	NY	11370	718-898-8500	898-8599	139
Queens College 65-30 Kissena Blvd *TF:* 888-888-0606 ■ *Web:* www.qc.cuny.edu	Flushing	NY	11367	718-997-5000	997-5617	166
Queens County 120-55 Queens Blvd *Web:* www.queensda.org	Kew Gardens Hills	NY	11415	718-286-6000		338
Queens County Farm Museum 73-50 Little Neck Pkwy *Web:* www.queensfarm.org	Floral Park	NY	11004	718-347-3276		520
Queens Courier 38-15 Bell Blvd *Web:* qns.com	Bayside	NY	11361	718-224-5863	224-5441	532-4
Queens Museum of Art New York City Bldg *Web:* www.queensmuseum.org	Queens	NY	11368	718-592-9700	592-5778	520
Queens University of Charlotte 1900 Selwyn Ave *TF:* 800-849-0202 ■ *Web:* www.queens.edu	Charlotte	NC	28274	704-337-2212	337-2403	166
Queensboro Farm Products Inc 105-03 150th St Ste 2	Jamaica	NY	11435	718-658-5000		297-4
Queensborough Community College 222-05 56th Ave *Web:* www.qcc.cuny.edu	Bayside	NY	11364	718-631-6262	281-5189	162
Queensborough National Bank & Trust 113 E Broad St *Web:* www.qnbtrust.bank	Louisville	GA	30434	478-625-2001	625-2008	780
Queensbury Union Free School 429 Aviation Rd *Web:* www.queensburyschool.org	Queensbury	NY	12804	518-824-5699		685
Queenston Heights National Historic Site 14184 Niagara River Pky *Web:* www.pc.gc.ca	Niagara-on-the-Lake	ON	L0S1J0	905-468-6614	468-6621	563
Queenstown Bank of Maryland 7101 Main St PO Box 120 *TF:* 888-827-4300 ■ *Web:* www.queenstownbank.com	Queenstown	MD	21658	410-827-8881		70
Queensway-Carleton Hospital 3045 Baseline Rd *Web:* www.qch.on.ca	Ottawa	ON	K2H8P4	613-721-4700	721-2000	374-2
Quehanna Boot Camp 4395 Quehanna Hwy Staff *Web:* www.cor.pa.gov	Karthaus	PA	16845	814-263-4125		213
Quenzel Associates Inc 12801 University Dr *Web:* quenzel.com	Fort Myers	FL	33907	239-226-0040		7
Quest Capital Management Inc 8117 Preston Rd Ste 700 *TF:* 800-668-1283 ■ *Web:* www.questadvisor.com	Dallas	TX	75225	214-691-6090	691-7240	401
Quest College 5430 Fredericksburg Rd Ste 310 *Web:* www.questcollege.edu	San Antonio	TX	78229	210-366-2701		167-3
Quest Companies Inc 8011 N Point Blvd Ste 201 **Fax Area Code:* 336 ■ *TF:* 800-467-9409 ■ *Web:* www.questcompaniesinc.com	Winston-Salem	NC	27106	800-467-9409	723-0026*	7
Quest Continuing Education Solutions 10850 W Park Pl Ste 1000 *TF:* 877-593-3366 ■ *Web:* www.questce.com	Milwaukee	WI	53224	414-375-3400	375-3449	423

Company	Phone	Fax	Class
Quest Controls Inc 208 Ninth St Dr W.......... Palmetto FL 34221 *TF:* 800-373-6331 ■ *Web:* www.questcontrols.com	800-373-6331		625
Quest Corporation of America 17220 Camelot Ct...................... Land O' Lakes FL 34638 *TF:* 866-662-6273 ■ *Web:* qcausa.com	866-662-6273		636
Quest Diagnostics 1300 Avenida Vista Hermosa Ste 160....... San Clemente CA 92673	949-940-7200		382
Quest Diagnostics 500 Plaza Dr............... Secaucus NJ 07094 *TF:* 800-222-0446 ■ *Web:* www.questforhealthsystems.com	800-222-0446		418
Quest Diagnostics at Nichols Institute 33608 Ortega Hwy .... San Juan Capistrano CA 92675 *TF:* 800-642-4657 ■ *Web:* www.questdiagnostics.com	949-728-4000		418
Quest Engineering Inc 2300 Edgewood Ave S .... Minneapolis MN 55426 *TF:* 800-328-4853 ■ *Web:* www.questenginc.com	952-546-4441		358
Quest Graphics LLC 2423 Northline Indus Dr.............. Maryland Heights MO 63043 *TF:* 800-997-6260 ■ *Web:* questgraphics.com	314-432-4565		627
Quest Integrated Inc 19823 58th Pl S.............. Kent WA 98032 *Web:* www.qi2.com	253-872-9500		419
Quest Investment Management LLC 5335 Meadows Rd Ste 400................ Lake Oswego OR 97035 *Web:* www.questinvestment.com	503-221-0158		401
Quest Marketing Inc N152 Rogers Ln.......... Appleton WI 54915 *Web:* www.questahead.com	920-996-0563		4
Quest Partners LLC 126 E 56th St 25th Fl .... New York NY 10022 *Web:* www.questpartnersllc.com	212-838-7222	838-4440	401
Quest Personnel Resources Inc 50 Briar Hollow Ste 510 E..................... Houston TX 77027 *Web:* www.questpersonnel.com	713-961-0605	961-1857	260
Quest Plastics Inc 89 Commercial Blvd....................... Torrington CT 06790 *Web:* www.questplastics.com	860-489-1404	489-1091	604
Quest Service Group LLC 439 Oak St .... Garden City NY 11530 *Web:* questservicegroup.com	516-594-7079		393
Quest Software Inc 5 Polairis Way............ Aliso Viejo CA 92656 *TF:* 800-306-9329 ■ *Web:* www.quest.com	949-754-8000	754-8999	178-1
Quest Turnaround Advisors LLC 800 Westchester Ave Ste S-520 .... Rye Brook NY 10573 *Web:* www.qtadvisors.com	914-253-8100		194
Questa Engineering Corp 1220 Brickyard Cove Rd Ste 206 .... Point Richmond CA 94801 *Web:* www.questaec.com	510-236-6114		535
Questar Assessment Inc 5550 Upper 147th St W .... Apple Valley MN 55124 *OTC: QUSA* ■ *TF:* 800-800-2598 ■ *Web:* www.questarai.com	952-997-2700		243
Questar Capital Corp 5701 Golden Hills Dr .... Minneapolis MN 55416 *TF:* 888-446-5872 ■ *Web:* www.questarcapital.com	888-446-5872		690
Questar Pipeline Co PO Box 45360 .... Salt Lake City UT 84145 *Web:* www.questarpipeline.com	801-324-5604	324-5245	325
Questco 100 Commercial Cir.................... Conroe TX 77304 *TF:* 800-256-7823 ■ *Web:* questco.net	936-756-1980		734
Questec Inc 1390 Boone Industrial Dr Ste 260............. Columbia MO 65202 *Web:* www.questec.us	573-875-0260		189-10
Questech Corp 92 Park St..................... Rutland VT 05701 *Web:* www.questech.com	802-773-1228		608
Questek Innovations LLC 1820 Ridge Ave............................ Evanston IL 60201 *Web:* www.questek.com	847-328-5800		177
Questel Orbit 1725 Duke St Ste 625 .... Alexandria VA 22314 **Fax Area Code: 703* ■ *TF:* 800-456-7248 ■ *Web:* www.questel.com	800-456-7248	519-1821*	635
Questerre Energy Corp 1650 AMEC Pl 801 Sixth Ave SW............... Calgary AB T2P3W2 *Web:* www.questerre.com	403-777-1185		536
Questex LLC 275 Grove St Ste 2-130............. Newton MA 02466 *TF:* 888-552-4346 ■ *Web:* www.questex.com	617-219-8300	219-8310	531-13
Questionmark Corp 5 Hillandale Ave .... Stamford CT 06902 *TF:* 800-863-3950 ■ *Web:* www.questionmark.com	203-358-3950		177
Questionpro Inc 548 Market St Ste 62790 .... San Francisco CA 94104 *TF:* 800-531-0228 ■ *Web:* questionpro.com	800-531-0228		180
Questmark Information Management Inc 9440 Kirby Dr............................. Houston TX 77054 *Web:* questmark.net	713-662-9022		627
Questor 700 E Maple Rd.................... Birmingham MI 48009 *Web:* www.questor.com	248-593-1930		194
Questor Technology Inc 1121 940 - Sixth Ave SW..................... Calgary AB T2P3T1 *TF:* 844-477-8669 ■ *Web:* www.questortech.com	403-571-1530		539
QuestSoft Corp 23441 S Pointe Dr Ste 220................ Laguna Hills CA 92653 *TF:* 800-575-4632 ■ *Web:* www.questsoft.com	800-575-4632		35
Questus Inc 675 Davis St................. San Francisco CA 94111 *Web:* www.questus.com	415-677-5700		7
Quetico LLC 5521 Schaefer Ave................... Chino CA 91710 *Web:* www.queticollc.com	909-628-6200		88
Queue Inc 3552 Whitney Ave.................... Fairfield CT 06824 *TF:* 800-232-2224 ■ *Web:* www.queueinc.com	800-232-2224	775-2729	178-3
Quez Media Marketing 1138 Prospect Ave E........................ Cleveland OH 44115 *Web:* www.quezmedia.com	216-910-0202		737
Quick Cable Corp 3700 Quick Dr .... Franksville WI 53126 *TF:* 800-558-8667 ■ *Web:* www.quickcable.com	262-824-3100		116
Quick Color Solutions Inc 829 Knox Rd............................. McLeansville NC 27301 *TF:* 877-698-0951 ■ *Web:* www.quickcolorsolutions.com	336-698-0951		627
Quick Crete Products 731 Parkridge Ave .... Norco CA 92860 *TF:* 866-703-3434 ■ *Web:* www.quickcrete.com	866-703-3434		191-1
Quick Electronics Inc 10800 76th Ct .... Largo FL 33777 *Web:* www.quickelectronics.com	727-546-9299		175
Quick Fuel Fleet Services Inc 11815 W Bradley Rd....................... Milwaukee WI 53224 **Fax Area Code: 414* ■ *TF:* 800-522-6287 ■ *Web:* www.quickfuel.com	800-522-6287	359-1469*	316
Quick Point Inc 1717 Fenpark Dr .... Fenton MO 63026 *Web:* www.quickpoint.com	636-343-9400		9
Quick Rx Drugs Inc 5204 Augusta Rd .... Garden City GA 31408 *Web:* quickrxdrugs.com	912-966-5665	966-1985	237
Quick Search 4155 Buena Vista.................. Dallas TX 75204 *Web:* quicksi.com	214-358-2880		635
Quick Tab II Inc 241 Heritage Dr.................. Tiffin OH 44883 *TF:* 800-332-5081 ■ *Web:* www.qt2.com	419-448-6622		627
Quick Tanks Inc PO Box 338 .... Kendallville IN 46755 *TF:* 800-348-2514 ■ *Web:* quicktanks.com	260-347-3850	347-3853	481
Quick Technologies Inc 16301 Quorum Dr Ste 200A.................. Addison TX 75001 *Web:* www.qti.com	214-631-6000	631-2323	177
Quick Test Inc 1061 E Indiantown Rd Ste 300 .... Jupiter FL 33477 *TF:* 800-523-1288 ■ *Web:* www.quicktest.com	561-748-0931		466
Quick USA Inc 551 5th Ave Ste 620............. New York NY 10176 *Web:* www.919usa.com	212-692-0850		192
Quick Way Manufacturing Inc 915 Stanley Dr .... Euless TX 76040 *Web:* www.quick-way.com	817-267-1515		483
QuickCompliance Inc 8 Canal Ct................. Avon CT 06001	860-676-9400		177
Quickdraft Inc 1525 Perry Dr SW .... Canton OH 44710 *Web:* www.quickdraft.com	330-477-4574		358
Quicken Loans LLC 1050 Woodward Ave .... Detroit MI 48226 *Web:* www.quickenloans.com	800-769-6133		387
Quickie Manufacturing Corp PO Box 156 .... Riverton NJ 08077 *TF:* 800-257-5751 ■ *Web:* www.quickie.com	800-257-5751		103
QuickLogic Corp 1277 Orleans Dr............. Sunnyvale CA 94089 *NASDAQ: QUIK* ■ *Web:* www.quicklogic.com	408-990-4000	990-4040	696
Quickmill Inc 760 Rye St.................. Peterborough ON K9J6W9 *TF:* 800-295-0509 ■ *Web:* www.quickmill.com	705-745-2961	745-8130	491
Quicksilver Manufacturing Inc 42214 Sarah Way .... Temecula CA 92590 *TF:* 800-840-4806 ■ *Web:* www.quicksilveraircraft.com	951-506-0061		20
QuickStart 5910 Courtyard Dr Ste 170............. Austin TX 78731 *TF:* 866-991-3924 ■ *Web:* www.quickstart.com	866-991-3924		177
Quidel Corp 10165 McKellar Ct............... San Diego CA 92121 *NASDAQ: QDEL* ■ *TF:* 800-874-1517 ■ *Web:* www.quidel.com	858-552-1100	453-4338	231
Quiel Bros Sign Co 272 S 'I' St .... San Bernardino CA 92410 *TF:* 800-874-7446 ■ *Web:* www.quielsigns.com	909-885-4476	888-2239	701
Quiet Light Communications Inc 220 E State St............................. Rockford IL 61104 *Web:* www.quietlightcom.com	815-398-6860		7
Quiet Light Publishing 2331 Hartzell St .... Evanston IL 60201 *Web:* www.quietlightpublishing.com	847-864-4911		637-2
Quiet Waters Publications PO Box 34........... Bolivar MO 65613 *Web:* www.quietwaterspub.com	417-429-0834		637-2
Quigley Mike (Rep D - IL) 2458 Rayburn House Office Bldg .... Washington DC 20515 *Web:* quigley.house.gov	202-225-4061	225-5603	342-2
Quigley Tax Service 5822 W Fond Du Lac Ave................... Milwaukee WI 53218 *Web:* quigleytaxserv.com	414-461-1800		734
Quik Mart Inc 8351 E Broadway Blvd .... Tucson AZ 85710 *Web:* www.quikmartstores.com	520-298-8929	298-6881	345
Quik Stop Markets Inc 4567 Enterprise St .... Fremont CA 94538 *Web:* quikstop.com	510-657-8500	657-1544	204
Quik Travel Staffing Inc 175 E Olive Ave Ste 101...................... Burbank CA 91502 *TF:* 800-554-7501 ■ *Web:* www.qtstaffing.com	800-554-2230		260
Quikbook 381 Park Ave S..................... New York NY 10016 *TF:* 800-789-9887 ■ *Web:* www.quikbook.com	212-779-7666		376
Quikey Manufacturing Co 1500 Industrial Pkwy .... Akron OH 44310 *Web:* www.quikey.com	330-633-8106		9
Quikey Manufacturing Company Inc 100 Thorpe Rd .... Orlando FL 32824 *Web:* m.quikey.com	407-859-7517		232
QUIKRETE Cos 3490 Piedmont Rd Ste 1300 .... Atlanta GA 30305 *TF:* 800-282-5828 ■ *Web:* www.quikrete.com	404-634-9100	842-1424	183
Quiksilver Inc 15202 Graham St .... Huntington Beach CA 92649 *NYSE: ZQK* ■ **Fax Area Code: 714* ■ *TF:* 800-435-9917 ■ *Web:* www.quiksilver.com	800-435-9917	889-2325*	155-3
Quikstik Labels 220 Broadway .... Everett MA 02149 *TF:* 800-225-3496 ■ *Web:* www.qsxlabels.com	617-389-7570	381-9280	413
Quikteks LLC 373 US 46 .... Fairfield NJ 07004 *Web:* www.quikteks.com	973-882-4644		180
Quiktrak Inc 9700 SW Nimbus Ave............. Beaverton OR 97008 *TF:* 800-927-8725 ■ *Web:* www.quiktrak.com	800-927-8725		41
QuikTrip Corp 4705 S 129th E Ave................. Tulsa OK 74134 *TF:* 800-441-0253 ■ *Web:* www.quiktrip.com	918-615-7700		204
Quilling Card 47 Mellen St Ste C-1 .... Framingham MA 01702 *Web:* www.quillingcard.com	508-405-2888	302-1289	637-10
Quiltcraft Industries Inc 1230 E Ledbetter Dr .... Dallas TX 75216 *Web:* www.quiltcraft.com	214-376-1841	376-1852	361
Quilting Daily 741 Corporate Cir Ste A .... Golden CO 80401 *TF:* 800-388-7023 ■ *Web:* www.quiltingdaily.com	800-881-6634		457-14
Quimby House Inn 109 Cottage St .... Bar Harbor ME 04609 *TF:* 800-344-5811 ■ *Web:* www.quimbyhouse.com	207-288-5811		379
Quince 470 Pacific Ave.................. San Francisco CA 94133 *Web:* www.quincerestaurant.com	415-775-8500		671
Quincy & Company Inc 57 Dedham Ave .... Needham MA 02494 *Web:* www.quincycompany.com	781-431-9600		390
Quincy Area Chamber of Commerce 300 Civic Center Plz Ste 245 .... Quincy IL 62301 *Web:* www.quincychamber.org	217-222-7980	222-3033	139
Quincy Area Convention & Visitors Bureau (QACVB) 532 Gardner Expy.............................. Quincy IL 62301 *TF:* 800-978-4748 ■ *Web:* seequincy.com	217-214-3700		206
Quincy College 1250 Hancock St .... Quincy MA 02169 *TF:* 800-698-1700 ■ *Web:* quincycollege.edu	617-984-1700	984-1794	162

				Phone	Fax	Class
Quincy Compressor 3501 Wismann Ln *Web:* www.quincycompressor.com	Quincy	IL	62301	217-277-0343		172
Quincy Correctional Institution 2225 Pat Thomas Pkwy *Web:* dc.state.fl.us	Quincy	FL	32351	850-627-5400	875-3572	213
Quincy Herald-Whig 130 S Fifth St *TF:* 800-373-9444 ■ *Web:* www.whig.com	Quincy	IL	62301	217-223-5100	221-3395	532-2
Quincy Mutual Fire Insurance Co 57 Washington St *TF:* 800-899-1116 ■ *Web:* www.quincymutual.com	Quincy	MA	02169	800-899-1116	899-7790	391-4
Quincy Public Library 526 Jersey St *Web:* quincylibrary.org	Quincy	IL	62301	217-223-1309		434-3
Quincy Raceways 8000 Broadway St *Web:* www.qcyraceways.com	Quincy	IL	62305	217-224-4100		515
Quincy Street Inc 13350 Quincy St *TF:* 800-784-6290 ■ *Web:* www.quincystreetinc.com	Holland	MI	49424	616-399-3330	399-0952	473
Quincy University 1800 College Ave *Web:* www.quincy.edu	Quincy	IL	62301	217-222-8020		166
Quine IP Law Group 2033 Clement Ave Ste 200 *Web:* www.quinelaw.com	Alameda	CA	94501	510-337-7871	337-7877	428
Quinebaug Valley Community College 742 Upper Maple St *Web:* qvcc.edu	Danielson	CT	06239	860-932-4000		162
Quinlan & Co 726 Exchange St Ste 612 *Web:* www.quinlanco.com	Buffalo	NY	14210	716-691-6200		7
Quinlan & Fabish Music Co 166 Shore Dr *Web:* www.qandf.com	Burr Ridge	IL	60527	630-654-4111		526
Quinn Fable Advertising Inc 131 W 35h St *Web:* www.quinnfable.com	New York	NY	10001	212-974-8700	974-0554	4
Quinn Medical Day Spa 6920 W 121st St Ste 10 *Web:* www.quinnplasticsurgery.com	Overland Park	KS	66209	913-492-3443	492-1881	77
Quinn's Lighthouse 1951 Embarcadero Cove *Web:* www.quinnslighthouse.com	Oakland	CA	94606	510-536-2050	535-1285	671
Quinn, Johnston, Henderson, Pretorius & Cerulo 227 N E Jefferson St *Web:* www.quinnjohnston.com	Peoria	IL	61602	309-674-1133		428
Quinnipiac Chamber of Commerce 50 N Main St *Web:* www.quinncham.com	Wallingford	CT	06492	203-269-9891	269-1358	139
Quinnipiac University 275 Mt Carmel Ave *TF:* 800-462-1944 ■ *Web:* www.qu.edu	Hamden	CT	06518	203-582-8600	582-8906	166
Quinnipiac Valley Community Federal Credit Union 285 Broad St *Web:* membersfirstctfcu.com	Meriden	CT	06450	203-237-6424		219
Quinsigamond Community College 670 W Boylston St *Web:* www.qcc.edu	Worcester	MA	01606	508-853-2300	854-4357	162
Quinsigamond State Park 10 N Lake Ave *Web:* www.mass.gov	Worcester	MA	01612	508-755-6880		565
QuinStreet Inc 950 Tower Ln 6th Fl *Web:* www.quinstreet.com	Foster City	CA	94404	650-578-7700		171
Quint Measuring Systems Inc 1541 3rd Ave *TF:* 800-745-5045 ■ *Web:* quintmeasuring.com	Walnut Creek	CA	94597	800-745-5045	745-5043	472
Quintel Management Consulting 5910 S University Blvd Ste C18-193 *Web:* quintel-mc.com	Greenwood Village	CO	80121	303-434-0215		463
Quintel Technology Ltd 1200 Ridgeway Ave Ste 132 *Web:* www.quintelsolutions.com	Rochester	NY	14615	585-420-8720		253
Quintess Collection LLC 11101 W 120th Ave Ste 200 *TF:* 800-895-4301 ■ *Web:* quintess.com	Broomfield	CO	80021	800-895-4301		377
Quintessence Publishing Co 4350 Chandler Dr *TF:* 800-621-0387 ■ *Web:* www.quintpub.com	Hanover Park	IL	60133	630-736-3600		781
Quintessential Mailing Software Inc (QMSI) 5800 Ager Beswick Rd *Fax Area Code: 530 ■ *TF:* 866-284-1001 ■ *Web:* www.qmsi.software	Montague	CA	96064	866-284-1001	459-3191*	178-1
Quintevents LLC 9300 Harris Corners Pkwy Ste 120 *TF:* 866-834-8663 ■ *Web:* quintevents.com	Charlotte	NC	28269	866-834-8663		195
Quintron Systems Inc 2105 S Blosser Rd *Web:* www.quintron.com	Santa Maria	CA	93458	805-928-4343		735
QuiqMeds 40 General Warren Blvd Ste 160 *Web:* www.quiqmeds.com	Malvern	PA	19355	484-328-3048		582
Quirch Foods Co 7600 NW 82nd Pl *TF:* 800-458-5252 ■ *Web:* www.quirchfoods.com	Miami	FL	33166	305-691-3535		297-9
QuirkRoberts Publishing PO Box 71 *Web:* www.quirkroberts.com	Troy	MI	48099	248-879-2598	879-2599	637-2
Quirks Enterprises Inc 4662 Slater Rd *TF:* 800-827-0676 ■ *Web:* quirks.com	Eagan	MN	55122	651-379-6200		7
Quitman County 220 Chestnut St Ste 2 *Web:* www.quitmancountyms.org	Marks	MS	38646	662-326-2661		338
Quixote Group Research Marketing 3107 Brassfield Rd Ste 106 *Web:* www.quixotegroup.com	Greensboro	NC	27401	336-402-5314		195
Quiznos Corp 7595 Technology Way Ste 200 *TF:* 866-486-2783 ■ *Web:* www.quiznos.com	Denver	CO	80237	720-359-3300		670
Quoddy Head State Park 973 S Lubec Rd *Web:* www.maine.gov	Lubec	ME	04652	207-733-0911		565
Quoizel Inc 6 Corporate Pkwy *Web:* www.quoizel.com	Goose Creek	SC	29445	843-553-6700		439
Quore 5000 Meridian Blvd Ste 400 *TF:* 877-974-9774 ■ *Web:* www.quore.com	Franklin	TN	37067	877-974-9774		178-8
Quorex Construction Ltd 142 Cardinal Crescent *Web:* www.quorex.ca	Saskatoon	SK	S7L6H6	306-244-3717		186
Quorum Associates LLC 1005 Chapman St *Web:* www.quorumassociates.com	Yorktown Heights	NY	10598	914-320-6251		260
Quorum Business Solutions Inc 811 Main St Ste 2000 *Web:* www.quorumsoftware.com	Houston	TX	77002	713-430-8601		177
Quorum Health Resources LLC 1573 Mallory Ln Ste 200 *Web:* www.qhr.com	Brentwood	TN	37027	615-371-7979		194
Quorum Hotels & Resorts 5429 Lyndon B Johnson Fwy Ste 625 *Web:* www.quorumhotels.com	Dallas	TX	75240	972-458-7265	991-5647	379
Quota International Inc 1420 21st St NW *Web:* www.quota.org	Washington	DC	20036	202-331-9694		48-15
Quotable Cards Inc 611 Broadway Rm 810 *Web:* www.quotablecards.com	New York	NY	10012	212-420-7552	420-7558	130
Quttinirpaaq National Park PO Box 278 *Web:* www.pc.gc.ca	Iqaluit	NU	X0A0H0	867-975-4673	975-4674	563
QV Investors Inc Livingston Pl, South Tower 222 - 3rd Ave SW Ste 1008 *Web:* www.qvinvestors.com	Calgary	AB	T2P0B4	403-265-7007	266-6524	528
QVC Inc 1200 Wilson Dr *TF:* 800-367-9444 ■ *Web:* www.qvc.com	West Chester	PA	19380	484-701-1000		740
Qvinci Software LLC 1601 S Mopac Expy Ste 475 *TF:* 844-422-5037 ■ *Web:* qvinci.com	Austin	TX	78746	512-637-7337		180
QVS Software Inc 5950 Six Forks Rd *Web:* qvssoftware.com	Raleigh	NC	27609	919-676-1991		180
Qwest Investment Management Corp 750 W Pender St Ste 802 *TF:* 866-602-1142 ■ *Web:* qwestfunds.com	Vancouver	BC	V6C2T8	604-601-5804		528

R

				Phone	Fax	Class
R & A Tool & Engineering Co 39127 Ford Rd *Web:* www.randatool.com	Westland	MI	48185	734-981-2000		261
R & B Car Company Inc 3811 S Michigan St *TF:* 800-260-1833 ■ *Web:* www.rbcarcompany.com	South Bend	IN	46614	800-260-1833		516
R & B Commercial Service Inc 3110 Los Arboles Ave NE *TF:* 800-376-1821 ■ *Web:* www.rbcommserv.com	Albuquerque	NM	87107	505-889-4090	889-3845	665
R & B Electronics Inc 1520 Industrial Park Dr Sault *Web:* www.randbelectronics.com	Sault Sainte Marie	MI	49783	906-632-1542		22
R & B Grinding Company Inc 1900 Clark St *Web:* www.rbgrinding.com	Racine	WI	53403	262-634-5538		454
R & B Marine Power Engineers Inc 913 NW 31st Ave *Web:* rb-marine.com	Pompano Beach	FL	33069	954-979-4038		261
R & B Wagner Inc 10600 W Brown Deer Rd *TF:* 888-243-6914 ■ *Web:* www.wagnercompanies.com	Butler	WI	53007	414-214-0444	214-0450	595
R & B Wholesale Distributors Inc 2350 S Milliken Ave *TF:* 800-627-7539 ■ *Web:* www.rbdist.com	Ontario	CA	91761	909-230-5400	230-5405	38
R & D Associates Inc 100 10th St *Web:* www.rdassociates.com	Catlettsburg	KY	41129	606-739-4166		698
R & D Batteries Inc 3300 Corporate Center Dr PO Box 5007 *TF:* 800-950-1945 ■ *Web:* www.rdbatteries.com	Burnsville	MN	55306	952-890-0629	890-7912	74
R & D Computers Inc 3190 Reps Miller Rd Ste 390 *TF:* 800-350-3071 ■ *Web:* www.randdcomp.com	Norcross	GA	30071	770-416-0103	416-0155	589
R & D Industries Inc 812 10th St *TF:* 800-659-3529 ■ *Web:* www.rdi.com	Milford	IA	51351	712-338-2999		180
R & D Logic Inc 1611 Borel Pl Ste 2 *Web:* www.rdlogic.com	San Mateo	CA	94402	650-356-9207	571-1276	177
R & D Machine & Engineering Inc 130 Scarlet Blvd *Web:* www.rdmachine.com	Oldsmar	FL	34677	813-891-9109		454
R & D Professional Services LLC 3000 Keller Springs Rd Ste 200	Carrollton	TX	75006	214-483-5342		693
R & D Systems Inc 614 McKinley Pl NE *Web:* www.rndsystems.com	Minneapolis	MN	55413	612-379-2956	656-4400	231
R & D Transportation Services Inc 4036 Adolfo Rd *TF:* 800-966-7114 ■ *Web:* rdtsi.com	Camarillo	CA	93012	805-529-7511		311
R & h Construction Co 1530 SW Taylor St *Web:* www.rhconst.com	Portland	OR	97205	503-228-7177		186
R & H Wholesale Supply Inc 81 Dorman Ave Ste A *TF:* 800-367-5625 ■ *Web:* www.plsgroup.com	San Francisco	CA	94124	415-970-5000	641-0455	351
R & J Public Relations LLC 1140 Rt 22 E Ste 200 *Web:* www.randjsc.com	Bridgewater	NJ	08807	908-722-5757		636
R & K Building Supplies Inc 25 W Baseline Rd *Web:* www.randk.com	Gilbert	AZ	85233	480-892-0025		499
R & K Industrial Products Co 1945 Seventh St *TF:* 800-842-7655 ■ *Web:* www.rkwheels.com	Richmond	CA	94801	510-234-7212	234-1923	676
R & L Spring Co 1097 Geneva Pkwy *Web:* www.rlspring.com	Lake Geneva	WI	53147	262-249-7854	249-7866	719
R & M Consultants Inc 9101 Vanguard Dr *Web:* www.rmconsult.com	Anchorage	AK	99507	907-522-1707		727

Company / Address	City	State	Zip	Phone	Fax	Class
R & M Manufacturing Company LLC 200 Centennial Dr.	Buffalo	MN	55313	763-574-9225	574-9344	198
TF: 866-929-0468 ■ Web: www.rmmco.com						
R & M Materials Handling Inc 4501 Gateway Blvd	Springfield	OH	45502	937-328-5100		358
TF: 800-955-9967 ■ Web: rmhoist.com						
R & M Office Furniture 9615 Oates Dr.	Sacramento	CA	95827	916-362-1756	362-1086	320
TF: 800-660-1756 ■ Web: www.randmoffice.com						
R & O Construction Co 933 Wall Ave.	Ogden	UT	84404	801-627-1403		186
Web: www.randoco.com						
R & R Bindery Service Inc 499 Rachel Rd	Girard	IL	62640	217-627-2143		92
Web: www.rrbindery.com						
R & R Contracting Inc 5201 N Washington St	Grand Forks	ND	58203	701-772-7667		188
TF: 800-872-5975 ■ Web: www.rrcontracting.net						
R & R Corrugated Packaging Group 360 Minor Rd	Bristol	CT	06107	860-584-1194		100
Web: randrbox.com						
R & R General Contractors Inc 505 N State Hwy 121	Mount Zion	IL	62549	217-864-4407	864-2877	186
Web: www.randrgc.com						
R & R Partners Inc 900 S Pavillion Center Dr	Las Vegas	NV	89144	702-228-0222		636
Web: www.rrpartners.com						
R & R Products Inc 3334 E Milber St.	Tucson	AZ	85714	520-889-3593		386
TF: 800-528-3446 ■ Web: www.rrproducts.com						
R & R Rubber Molding Inc 2444 Loma Ave.	South El Monte	CA	91733	626-575-8105	575-3756	677
Web: www.rrrubber.com						
R & R Technologies LLC 7560 E County Line Rd.	Edinburgh	IN	46124	812-526-2655	526-9294	604
Web: www.rrtech.com						
R & R Trucking Inc 302 Thunder Rd PO Box 545	Duenweg	MO	64841	417-623-6885		780
TF: 800-625-6885 ■ Web: www.randrtruck.com						
R & S Processing Company Inc 15712 Illinois Ave PO Box 2037	Paramount	CA	90723	562-531-1403	531-4318	605-3
Web: rsprocessing.com						
R & S Steel Co 3811 Joliet St	Denver	CO	80239	303-321-9660	321-9677	492
TF: 800-231-1034 ■ Web: www.rssteel.com						
R & S/Godwin Truck Body Company LLC 5168 US Hyw 23 S PO Box 420	Ivel	KY	41642	606-874-2151	874-9136	516
TF: 800-826-7413 ■ Web: rstruckbody.com						
R A Burch Construction Company Inc 405 Maple St Bldg B PO Box 1590	Ramona	CA	92065	760-788-0800	789-3549	186
Web: www.raburch.com						
R A Zweig Inc 2500 Ravine Way	Glenview	IL	60025	847-832-9001	832-9019	454
Web: www.zweig-cnc.com						
R and R Publishing Inc 1836 N 900 Rd	Baldwin City	KS	66006	785-691-6806		637-10
Web: www.mountaindirectory.com						
R B M Co 2700 Texas Ave	Knoxville	TN	37921	865-524-8621		385
Web: rbmcompany.com						
R C Mc Lean & Associates Inc 210 N Tustin Ave.	Santa Ana	CA	92705	714-347-1000		445
TF: 800-883-7243 ■ Web: www.rcmclean.com						
R C Romine & Associates Advertising & Marketing 1250 Executive Pl Ste 601	Geneva	IL	60134	630-208-1020		7
Web: www.rcromine.com						
R C Willey Home Furnishings 2301 South 300 West	Salt Lake City	UT	84115	801-461-3800		321
Web: www.rcwilley.com						
R D A Container Corp 70 Cherry Rd.	Gates	NY	14624	585-247-2323		100
Web: www.rdacontainer.com						
R D D Associates LLC 930 Riverview Dr Ste 400	Totowa	NJ	07512	973-812-8070		317
Web: www.rddassociates.com						
R D Jones & Assoc 400 E Pratt St Ste 902.	Baltimore	MD	21202	410-332-4700		393
Web: www.rdjones.com						
R D S Delivery Service Company Inc 436 E 11th St Frnt A	New York	NY	10009	212-260-5800		314
Web: www.rdsdelivery.com						
R David Thomas Executive Conference Ctr (RDTC) 100 Fuqua Dr PO Box 90120	Durham	NC	27708	919-660-6400	660-3607	377
Web: www.fuqua.duke.edu						
R E Chaix & Associates Insurance Brokers Inc 3200 El Camino Real Ste 290	Irvine	CA	92602	949-722-4177		390
Web: rechaixinsurance.com						
R E Dimond & Associates Inc 732 N Capitol Ave.	Indianapolis	IN	46204	317-634-4672		261
Web: redimond.com						
R E Warner & Associates Inc 25777 Detroit Rd Ste 200	Westlake	OH	44145	440-835-9400		727
Web: www.rewarner.com						
R F R Metal Fabrication Inc 3204 Knotts Grove Rd.	Oxford	NC	27565	919-693-1354		480
Web: www.rfr-metalfab.com						
R F Stearns Inc 4000 Kruse Way Pl Bldg 3 Ste 100	Lake Oswego	OR	97035	503-601-8700		186
R G Canning Cos 4515 E 59th Pl.	Maywood	CA	90270	323-560-7469		232
Web: www.rgcshows.com						
R G S Financial Corp 1700 Jay Ell Dr	Richardson	TX	75081	469-791-4700		317
Web: www.rgsfinancial.com						
R H K Hydraulic Cylinder Services Inc 13111 159th St.	Edmonton	AB	T5V1H6	780-452-2876		393
TF: 800-406-3111 ■ Web: www.rhkhydraulics.com						
R I Merrell Institute of Bootmaking 3400 North 3500 West	Vernal	UT	84078	801-789-3079		167-3
Web: www.merrellfootlab.com						
R J Behar & Company Inc 6861 SW 196th Ave Ste 302	Fort Lauderdale	FL	33332	954-680-7771		261
Web: www.rjbehar.com						
R J Julia Booksellers LLC 768 Boston Post Rd	Madison	CT	06443	203-245-3959		95
Web: booksasgifts.com						
R J Lanthier Company Inc 485 Corporate Dr	Escondido	CA	92029	760-738-9798		610
R J Schinner Company Inc 16950 W Lincoln Ave	New Berlin	WI	53151	262-797-7180	797-7190	791
TF: 800-234-1460 ■ Web: www.rjschinner.com						
R J Williams 585 Rugh St	Greensburg	PA	15601	724-834-3403		2
R J Wood & Co 652 Arlington Pl	Macon	GA	31201	478-741-7044		261
R K Allen Oil Inc 36002 AL Hwy 21.	Talladega	AL	35161	256-362-4261		579
TF: 800-445-5823 ■ Web: www.rkallenoil.com						
R K Electric Inc 49211 Milmont Dr.	Fremont	CA	94538	510-770-5660		189-4
Web: rkelectric.com						
R K Sport Inc 26900 Jefferson Ave.	Murrieta	CA	92562	951-894-7883		21
Web: www.stretchformingcorp.com						
R l Bryan Co, The 301 Greystone Blvd	Columbia	SC	29210	803-779-3560		627
Web: www.rlbryan.com						
R L f Communications LLC 532 S Elm St.	Greensboro	NC	27406	336-553-1800		636
Web: rlfcommunications.com						
R L Hulett & Company Inc 8000 Maryland Ave Ste 245	Saint Louis	MO	63105	314-721-0607	721-2783	194
Web: rlhulett.com						
R L Turner Corp 1000 W Oak St.	Zionsville	IN	46077	317-873-2712	873-1262	187
Web: rlturner.com						
R L Vallee Inc 282 S Main St.	Saint Albans	VT	05478	802-524-8710	524-8714	579
R Lazy S Ranch PO Box 308	Teton Village	WY	83025	307-733-2655		239
Web: rlazys.com						
R M Kaul & Associates Inc 10 Bennett Ave	New York	NY	10033	646-706-1807		195
Web: www.rmkaul.com						
R M Roach & Sons Inc 301 E Stephen St	Martinsburg	WV	25401	304-263-3329	263-3275	538
Web: www.roachenergy.com						
R Mcclure Electric 706 Portal St Ste D	Cotati	CA	94931	707-792-2101		390
R N Croft Financial Group Inc 218 Steeles Ave E	Thornhill	ON	L3T1A6	905-695-7777		401
TF: 877-249-2884 ■ Web: www.croftgroup.com						
R O I Media Solutions LLC 11500 W Olympic Blvd Ste 400	Los Angeles	CA	90064	866-211-2580		5
TF: 866-211-2580 ■ Web: www.roims.com						
R O Whitesell & Associates Inc 11711 N Pennsylvania St Ste 240.	Carmel	IN	46032	317-564-8008	564-8766	246
Web: www.whitesell.com						
R R Floody Co 5065 27th Ave	Rockford	IL	61109	815-399-1931		358
TF: 800-678-6639 ■ Web: www.rrfloody.com						
R Seelaus & Company Inc 25 Deforest Ave Ste 304	Summit	NJ	07901	800-922-0584		690
TF: 800-922-0584 ■ Web: www.rseelaus.com						
R Studio T 14 Horatio St 8K	New York	NY	10014	212-929-8851		92
Web: www.rstudiot.com						
R T Group Inc 70 Romano Vineyard Way Ste 134	North Kingstown	RI	02852	401-438-3100		261
Web: rtg-eng.com						
R T Patterson Company Inc 230 Third Ave.	Pittsburgh	PA	15222	412-227-6600		261
Web: www.rtpatterson.com						
R Value Inc 2267 N Interstate Ave	Portland	OR	97227	503-284-2260		499
Web: indowwindows.com						
R W Armstrong 300 S Meridian St.	Indianapolis	IN	46225	317-786-0461		47
Web: www.rwa.com						
R W Collins Co 7225 W 66th St.	Chicago	IL	60638	708-458-6868		667
Web: www.rwcollins.com						
R W Mercer Co 2322 Brooklyn Rd PO Box 180	Jackson	MI	49204	517-787-2960	787-8111	186
TF: 877-763-7237 ■ Web: www.rwmercer.com						
R W Rog & Company Inc 630 Johnson Ave Ste 103.	Bohemia	NY	11716	631-218-0077		194
TF: 877-218-0085 ■ Web: www.rwroge.com						
R W Wentworth & Company Inc 311 W 24th St Ste 18C	New York	NY	10011	212-627-0467		466
Web: www.rwwentworth.com						
R Y Timber Inc 85 Mill Rd.	Townsend	MT	59644	406-266-3111		683
Web: rytimber.com						
R Zoppo Corp 160 Old Maple St.	Stoughton	MA	02072	781-344-8822		186
Web: www.zoppo.com						
R. & S. Mexican Food Products Inc 5818 W Maryland Ave	Glendale	AZ	85301	602-272-2727	435-1377	296-37
Web: www.rsmexfoods.com						
R. A. Industries LLC 3207 W Pendleton Ave.	Santa Ana	CA	92704	714-557-2322	557-3138	454
Web: www.ra-industries.com						
R. A. Smith National Inc 16745 W Bluemound Rd Ste 200	Brookfield	WI	53005	262-781-1000	781-8466	189-12
Web: www.rasmith.com						
R. C. Brayshaw & Company Inc 45 Waterloo St	Warner	NH	03278	603-456-3101		627
Web: www.rcbrayshaw.com						
R. G. Niederhoffer Capital Management Inc 1700 Broadway 39th Fl.	New York	NY	10019	212-245-0400		528
Web: www.niederhoffer.com						
R. H. Bluestein & Co 260 E Brown St Ste 100	Birmingham	MI	48009	248-646-4000		401
Web: www.rhbco.com						
R. H. Smith Distributing Co 315 E Wine Country Rd PO Box 6.	Grandview	WA	98930	509-882-3377	882-5755	581
Web: www.rhsmith.com						
R. J. Graphics Inc 206 Crown Point Rd	Thorofare	NJ	08086	856-848-1986	848-5040	344
Web: www.rjgraphicsprinting.com						
R. M. Davis Inc 24 City Ctr	Portland	ME	04101	207-774-0022		401
Web: www.rmdavis.com						
R. M. Stark & Company Inc 701 SE Sixth Ave Ste 203	Delray Beach	FL	33483	561-243-3815		690
Web: rmstark.com						
R. Mastrangelo Landscaping 71 Pine Aire Dr	Bay Shore	NY	11706	631-242-1683		422
Web: rmastrangelolandscaping.com						

				Phone	Fax	Class
R. P. C. Contracting Inc 934 W Kitty Hawk Rd *Web:* rpccontracting.com	Kitty Hawk	NC	27949	252-261-3336	261-8471	393
R. P. N. Inc 908 Cherokee Dr *Web:* www.rpnmachineshop.com	Morristown	TN	37814	423-586-8663		454
R. Shane Chance CPA PC 1000 W Aztec Blvd *Web:* www.chancecpa.com	Aztec	NM	87410	505-334-4375		194
R. W. Fernstrum & Co 1716 11th Ave PO Box 97 *Web:* www.fernstrum.com	Menominee	MI	49858	906-863-5553	863-5634	91
R. W. Lynch Company Inc 2333 San Ramon Vly Blvd *TF:* 800-594-8940 ■ *Web:* www.rwlynch.com	San Ramon	CA	94583	925-837-3877		428
R. Weinstein Pharmaceuticals & Medical Products 846 Pohukaina St *Web:* www.rweinstein.com	Honolulu	HI	96813	808-591-8331	591-8339	238
R.A Jones & Co 2701 Crescent Springs Rd *Web:* www.rajones.com	Covington	KY	41017	859-341-0400	341-0519	547
R.B. Zack and Associates Inc 23844 Hawthorne Blvd Ste 101 *Web:* www.rbza.com	Torrance	CA	90505	310-709-2011		177
R.C. Musson Rubber Co, The 1320 E Archwood Ave PO Box 7038 *TF:* 800-321-2381 ■ *Web:* mussonrubber.com	Akron	OH	44306	330-773-7651	773-3254	676
R.C. Sports Inc 17501 W 98th St Ste 18-51 *Web:* rcsports.com	Lenexa	KS	66219	913-894-5177	894-5179	711
R.C.A. Rubber Co 1833 E Market St *TF:* 800-321-2340 ■ *Web:* www.rcarubber.com	Akron	OH	44305	330-784-1291	794-6446	676
R.D. Bitzer Company Inc 776 American Dr W Port Industrial Pk *TF:* 800-523-3862 ■ *Web:* www.rdbitzer.com	Bensalem	PA	19020	215-604-6600	604-6601	609
R.E. Barry Pumps Inc 415 Atwood Ave *Web:* barrypumps.com	Cranston	RI	02920	401-942-5300	942-0618	612
R.E. Crawford Construction LLC 6650 Professional Pkwy W Ste 100 *Web:* www.recrawford.com	Sarasota	FL	34240	941-907-0010		685
R.E. West Inc 14 Bluegrass Dr *TF:* 800-792-9552 ■ *Web:* www.rewest.com	Ashland City	TN	37015	615-792-1528		780
R.F. Fager Company Inc 2058 State Rd *Web:* www.rffager.com	Camp Hill	PA	17011	717-761-0660	761-6428	612
R.F. Lafferty & Company Inc 40 Wall St 19th Fl *Web:* rflafferty.com	New York	NY	10005	212-293-9090		690
R.H. Boyd Publishing Corp 6717 Centennial Blvd *TF:* 877-474-2693 ■ *Web:* www.rhboydpublishing.com	Nashville	TN	37209	615-350-8000	350-9018	637-2
R.H. Johnson Co, The 4520 Madison Ave Ste 300 *Web:* rhjohnson.com	Kansas City	MO	64111	816-561-5111		652
R.I. Carbide Tool Co 339C Farnum Pke *Web:* www.ricarbide.com	Smithfield	RI	02917	401-231-1020	231-1676	493
R.J. Caruso 364 E Ave *Web:* rjcarusotax.com	Oswego	NY	13126	315-342-4900		2
R.J. Fregenti Associates Inc 350 Jericho Tpke *Web:* rjfassoc.com	Jericho	NY	11753	516-681-0101		390
R.J. Gagnon Publishing 701 Palmetto St *Web:* www.053803.com	West Palm Beach	FL	33405	561-533-9103		637-2
R.L. Shep Publications PO Box 2706 *Web:* www.rlshep.com	Fort Bragg	CA	95437	707-964-8662		637-10
R.M.Flagg Co 1212 State St *TF:* 800-432-7814 ■ *Web:* www.rmflagg.com	Veazie	ME	04401	207-945-9463		300
R.O. Anderson Engineering Inc 1603 Esmeralda *Web:* www.roanderson.com	Minden	NV	89423	775-782-2322		261
R.P.S. Engineering Inc 1300 Crispin Dr *Web:* www.rpsengineering.com	Elgin	IL	60123	847-931-1950	931-4274	697
R.R. Donnelley & Sons Co (RRD) 35 W Wacker Dr *TF:* 800-742-4455 ■ *Web:* www.rrd.com	Chicago	IL	60601	800-742-4455		5
R.S. Semler & Associates Insurance 870 W Sumner St *TF:* 800-414-5875 ■ *Web:* rssemler.com	Hartford	WI	53027	262-673-3160	673-9466	390
R.S.V.P. 887 Forest Ave *Web:* rsvpdiscountbeverage.com	Portland	ME	04103	207-773-8808		443
R.V. Nuccio & Associates Insurance Brokers Inc 10148 Riverside Dr *Web:* rvnuccio.com	Toluca Lake	CA	91602	818-980-1413		390
R.W. Beckett Corp 38251 Center Ridge Rd *TF:* 800-645-2876 ■ *Web:* www.beckettcorp.com	North Ridgeville	OH	44039	440-327-1060	327-1064	641
R.W. Raddatz Inc 280 SW 12th Ave *Web:* www.rwraddatz.com	Deerfield Beach	FL	33442	954-480-9327	480-9399	454
R.W. Smith & Co 8555 Miralani Dr *TF:* 800-942-1101 ■ *Web:* www.rwsmithco.com	San Diego	CA	92196	800-942-1101		45
R/GA 350 W 39th St *Web:* www.rga.com	New York	NY	10018	212-946-4000		7
R/J Florig Industrial Company Inc 910 Brook Rd *Web:* www.rjflorig.com	Conshohocken	PA	19428	610-825-6655	825-7424	480
R2 Unified Technologies 980 N Federal Hwy Ste 410 *TF:* 866-464-7381 ■ *Web:* www.r2ut.com	Boca Raton	FL	33432	561-515-6800		196
R2t Inc 580 W Crssvlle Rd *Web:* r2tinc.com	Roswell	GA	30075	770-569-7038		261
R2W Inc 5957 McLeod Dr	Las Vegas	NV	89120	702-434-6500		189-4
r4 Technologies LLC 38C Grove St *Web:* www.r4.ai	Ridgefield	CT	06877	203-461-7100		113
RA (Ruotolo Associates Inc) 580 Sylvan Ave Ste M-B *Web:* www.ruotoloassociates.com	Englewood Cliffs	NJ	07632	201-568-3898	568-8783	317
RA (Romney Associates Inc) 64 Carriage Ln *Web:* www.romneyassociates.com	Amherst	MA	01002	413-253-5630		192
RA Miller Industries Inc 14500 168th Ave PO Box 858 *TF:* 888-845-9450 ■ *Web:* www.rami.com	Grand Haven	MI	49417	616-842-9450		647
RA Serafini Inc 111 Lagrande St *Web:* www.raserafini.com	Gastonia	NC	28056	704-864-6763		757
RAA (Regional Airline Assn) 2025 M St NW Ste 800 *Web:* www.raa.org	Washington	DC	20036	202-367-1170	367-2170	49-21
RAB (Radio Adv Bureau) 125 W 55th St 5th Fl *TF:* 800-232-3131 ■ *Web:* www.rab.com	New York	NY	10019	800-232-3131		49-18
RAB Lighting Inc 170 Ludlow Ave *TF:* 888-722-1000 ■ *Web:* www.rablighting.com	Northvale	NJ	07647	201-784-8600		439
Raba-Kistner Consultants Inc 12821 W Golden Ln *TF:* 866-722-2547 ■ *Web:* www.rkci.com	San Antonio	TX	78249	210-699-9090	699-6426	189-15
Rabbinical Assembly 3080 Broadway *TF:* 866-907-2761 ■ *Web:* www.rabbinicalassembly.org	New York	NY	10027	866-907-2761		48-20
Rabbit Air 125 N Raymond Ave Ste 308 *TF:* 888-866-8862 ■ *Web:* www.rabbitair.com	Pasadena	CA	91103	562-861-4688		45
Rabbit Creek Journal PO Box 309 *Web:* www.rcj.net	Clipper Mills	CA	95930	530-675-2270		637-9
Rabbit Hill Inn 48 Lower Waterford Rd PO Box 55 *TF:* 800-626-3215 ■ *Web:* www.rabbithillinn.com	Lower Waterford	VT	05848	802-748-5168	748-8342	379
Rabe Environmental Systems Inc 2300 W 23 St *Web:* www.rabehvac.com	Erie	PA	16506	814-456-5374	456-5654	610
Rabe Hardware Inc 317 Locust St NW *Web:* rabehardware.com	Blairstown	IA	52209	319-454-6514		351
Rabe's Quality Meat Inc 13075 Renfro Cir *Web:* www.rabes.com	Omaha	NE	68137	402-895-5399	895-7048	473
Raben Tire Company Inc 2100 N New York Ave *Web:* www.rabentire.com	Evansville	IN	47711	812-465-5505		62-5
Rabenhorst Funeral Home Inc 825 Government St *Web:* rabenhorst.com	Baton Rouge	LA	70802	225-383-6831		510
Raber Packing Co 1413 N Raber Rd *Web:* raberpacking.com	Peoria	IL	61604	309-673-0721		473
Rabinovici & Associates Inc 800 Silks Run Ste 2320 *Web:* www.rabinovicionline.com	Hallandale Beach	FL	33009	305-655-0021		4
Rabinowitz, Lubetkin & Tully LLC 293 Eisenhower Pkwy Ste 100 *Web:* rltlawfirm.com	Livingston	NJ	07039	973-597-9100		41
Rable Machine Inc 30 Paragon Pkwy *Web:* www.rablemachineinc.com	Mansfield	OH	44901	419-525-2255		621
Rabobank Intl 245 Park Ave *Web:* www.rabobank.com	New York	NY	10167	212-916-7800		360-2
Rabun County 25 Courthouse Sq Ste 201 *Web:* rabuncounty.ga.gov	Clayton	GA	30525	706-782-5271	782-7588	338
Rabun County School District 963 Tiger Connector *Web:* www.rabuncountyschools.org	Tiger	GA	30576	706-212-4350	782-6224	685
Rabun Gap-Nacoochee School 339 Nacoochee Dr *TF:* 800-543-7467 ■ *Web:* www.rabungap.org	Rabun Gap	GA	30568	706-746-7467	746-2594	622
Raccoon Creek State Park 3000 SR-18 *Web:* www.dcnr.pa.gov	Hookstown	PA	15050	724-899-3611		565
Raccoon Mountain Caverns 319 W Hills Dr *TF:* 800-823-2267 ■ *Web:* www.raccoonmountain.com	Chattanooga	TN	37419	423-821-9403		50-5
Raccoon Valley Electric Co-op 28725 Hwy 30 PO Box 486 *TF:* 800-253-6211 ■ *Web:* www.rvec.coop	Glidden	IA	51443	712-659-3649	659-3716	245
Racer Parts Wholesale 1725 Wales Ave Ste A *Web:* www.racerpartswholesale.com	Indianapolis	IN	46202	317-639-0725		61
RaceTrac Petroleum Inc 3225 Cumberland Blvd Ste 100 *TF:* 888-636-5589 ■ *Web:* racetrac.com	Atlanta	GA	30339	770-431-7600		324
Raceway Park 230 Pension Rd *Web:* etownracewaypark.com	Englishtown	NJ	07726	732-446-7800	446-1373	515
Rachlin & Wolfson LLP 390 Bay St Ste 1500 *Web:* www.rachlinlaw.com	Toronto	ON	M5H2Y2	416-367-0202		428
Rachman Group, The 33 Walt Whitman Rd Ste 232 *Web:* www.mrhuntington.com	Huntington Station	NY	11746	631-547-5464	547-5465	41
Racine Area Manufacturing & Commerce 300 Fifth St *Web:* www.racinechamber.com	Racine	WI	53403	262-634-1931	634-7422	139
Racine Correctional Institution 2019 Wisconsin St *Web:* www.doc.wi.gov	Sturtevant	WI	53177	262-886-3214	886-3514	213
Racine County 730 Wisconsin Ave 1st Fl North end *TF:* 800-242-4202 ■ *Web:* racinecounty.com	Racine	WI	53403	262-636-3121	636-3491	338
Racine County Convention & Visitors Bureau 14015 Washington Ave *TF:* 800-272-2463 ■ *Web:* www.realracine.com	Sturtevant	WI	53177	262-884-6400		206
Racine Metal-Fab Ltd 1520 Grandview Pky *Web:* www.rm-f.com	Sturtevant	WI	53177	262-554-1140	554-1266	454
Racine Public Library 75 Seventh St *Web:* www.racinelibrary.info	Racine	WI	53403	262-636-9241	636-9260	434-3
Racine Railroad Products Inc 1955 Norwood Ct *Web:* www.racinerailroad.com	Mount Pleasant	WI	53403	262-637-9681	637-9069	650
Racine Zoo 200 Goold St *Web:* www.racinezoo.org	Racine	WI	53402	262-636-9189	636-9307	823
Rack Attack-car Rack & Hitch Ctr 745 Worcester Rd *Web:* www.rackattack.com	Framingham	MA	01701	508-879-1444		791

Name / Address	City	State	Zip	Phone	Fax	Class
Rack Room Shoes 8310 Technology Dr *Web:* www.rackroomshoes.com	Charlotte	NC	28262	704-501-4674		301
Racket Group 713 Walnut St *Web:* www.racketgroup.com	Kansas City	MO	64106	816-842-2380	842-8998	361
Racking Horse Breeders Association of America (RHBAA) 67 Horse Center Rd *Web:* www.rackinghorse.com	Decatur	AL	35603	256-353-7225		48-3
Racks Inc PO Box 530840 *Web:* www.racksinc.com	San Diego	CA	92153	619-661-0987		286
Raco General Contractors 1401 Dalon Rd NE *Web:* www.racogc.com	Atlanta	GA	30306	404-873-3567	876-1394	186
Raco Interior Products Inc 7354 Denny Rd Ste 100 *TF:* 800-272-7226 ■ *Web:* www.racointeriors.com	Houston	TX	77040	713-682-6100	682-2079	234
RACO Manufacturing & Engineering Company Inc 1400-62nd St *TF:* 800-722-6999 ■ *Web:* www.racoman.com	Emeryville	CA	94608	800-722-6999		201
RAD Data Communications Ltd 900 Corporate Dr *TF:* 800-444-7234 ■ *Web:* www.rad.com	Mahwah	NJ	07430	201-529-1100		735
Rad Law Firm 2001 Beach St Ste 225 *Web:* www.radlawfirm.com	Fort Worth	TX	76103	817-543-1999		428
Radar Inc 22214 20th Ave SE Ste 101 *TF:* 800-282-2524 ■ *Web:* www.radarinc.com	Bothell	WA	98021	800-282-2524		246
Radar Marine Electronics Inc 909 Squalicum Way *Web:* www.radarmarine.com	Bellingham	WA	98225	360-733-2012		246
Radar Media Group Inc 12 Blossom Hill Rd Ste 101a *Web:* www.radarmedia.com	Winchester	MA	01890	781-721-1910		463
Radcliff (HCCC) *Hardin County Chamber of Commerce* 306 N Wilson Rd *Web:* www.hardinchamber.com	Radcliff	KY	40160	270-351-4450	352-4449	139
Radcliff Wire Inc 97 Ronzo Rd *Web:* radcliffwire.com	Bristol	CT	06010	860-583-1305	583-6553	492
Radcliffe Telephone Company Inc 202 Isabella St *Web:* www.radcliffetelephone.com	Radcliffe	IA	50230	515-899-2341	899-2499	224
Rad-Comm Systems Corp 2931 Portland Dr *TF:* 800-588-5229 ■ *Web:* www.radcommsystems.com	Oakville	ON	L6H5S4	905-829-8290		407
Rader Solutions Ltd 537 Cajundome Blvd Ste 209 *Web:* www.radersolutions.com	LaFayette	LA	70506	337-205-4652		196
Radewagen Amata (Rep R - AS) 1339 Longworth House Office Bldg *Web:* radewagen.house.gov	Washington	DC	20515	202-225-8577	225-8757	342-2
Radey Thomas Yon & Clark 301 S Bronough St Ste 200 *Web:* www.radeylaw.com	Tallahassee	FL	32301	850-425-6654	425-6694	428
Radford (Independent City) 619 Second St *Web:* www.courts.state.va.us	Radford	VA	24141	540-731-3610	731-3692	338
Radford University 801 E Main St *TF:* 800-890-4265 ■ *Web:* www.radford.edu	Radford	VA	24142	540-831-5371	831-5038	166
Radgov Inc 6750 N Andrews Ave Ste 200 *Web:* www.radgov.com	Fort Lauderdale	FL	33309	954-938-2800		196
Radiac Abrasives Inc 1015 S College Ave *TF:* 800-851-1095 ■ *Web:* radiac.com	Salem	IL	62881	618-548-4200	548-4207	1
Radial Drilling Services Inc 4921 Spring Cypress Rd *Web:* www.radialdrilling.com	Spring	TX	77379	281-374-7507	374-7509	540
Radian Group Inc 1500 Market St *TF:* 800-523-1988 ■ *Web:* radian.com	Philadelphia	PA	19102	800-523-1988		391-5
Radian Memory Systems Inc 5010 N Parkway Calabasas Unit 205 *Web:* radianmemory.com	Calabasas	CA	91302	818-222-4080		180
Radian Research Inc 3852 Fortune Dr *Web:* www.radianresearch.com	LaFayette	IN	47905	765-449-5500	448-4614	201
Radiance 4788 Heyer Ave Ste B *Web:* www.radiancemagazine.com	Castro Valley	CA	94546	510-885-1505		637-9
Radiance Home Health Care Inc 10 Center St Ste 302 *Web:* radiancehhc.com	Chicopee	MA	01013	413-592-0101		363
Radiance Technologies Inc 350 Wynn Dr *Web:* www.radiancetech.com	Huntsville	AL	35805	256-704-3400		692
Radiant Clipper 9014 Heritage Pkwy Ste 300 *TF:* 800-678-2547 ■ *Web:* www.radiantclipper.com	Woodridge	IL	60517	630-739-0700	739-1817	449
Radiant Communication Inc 5512 Merrick Rd	Massapequa	NY	11758	516-798-0465		194
Radiant Communications Corp 1600-1050 W Pender St *TSX: RCN* ■ *TF:* 888-219-2111 ■ *Web:* www.radiant.net	Vancouver	BC	V6E4T3	888-219-2111		808
Radiant Electric Co-opeartive Inc PO Box 390 *TF:* 800-821-0956 ■ *Web:* radiantec.coop	Fredonia	KS	66736	620-378-2161		245
Radiant Energy Systems Inc 175 N Ethel Ave *TF:* 800-486-7786 ■ *Web:* www.radiantenergy.com	Hawthorne	NJ	07506	973-423-5220	423-5228	318
Radiant Global Logistics 405 114th Ave SE 3rd Fl *TF:* 800-843-4784 ■ *Web:* www.radiantdelivers.com	Bellevue	WA	98004	425-462-1094	462-0768	449
Radiant Logic Inc 75 Rowland Way Ste 300 *TF:* 877-727-6442 ■ *Web:* www.radiantlogic.com	Novato	CA	94945	415-209-6800	798-5697	177
Radiant Networks 13000 Middletown Industrial Blvd Ste D **Fax Area Code: 866* ■ *TF:* 866-411-9526 ■ *Web:* www.radiant-networks.com	Louisville	KY	40223	502-379-4800	455-4001*	180
Radiant Pools 440 N Pearl St *TF:* 866-697-5870 ■ *Web:* radiantpools.com	Albany	NY	12207	518-434-4161	432-6554	728
Radiant Power Corp 7135 16th St E Ste 101 *Web:* www.radiantpowercorp.com	Sarasota	FL	34243	941-739-3200	739-3201	22
Radiant Systems Inc 107 B Corporate Blvd *Web:* www.radiants.com	South Plainfield	NJ	07080	908-668-1080	668-1081	178-1
Radiant Technologies Inc 2835 Pan American Fwy NE *TF:* 800-289-7176 ■ *Web:* www.ferrodevices.com	Albuquerque	NM	87107	505-842-8007		256
Radiant Vision Systems 22908 NE Alder Crest Dr Ste 100 *Web:* www.radiantvisionsystems.com	Redmond	WA	98053	425-844-0152	844-0153	407
Radianta Inc 9012 Research Dr Ste 200 *TF:* 866-467-9695 ■ *Web:* www.radianta.com	Irvine	CA	92618	866-467-9695		809
Radiation Monitoring Devices Inc (RMD) 44 Hunt St Ste 2 *Web:* www.dynasil.com	Watertown	MA	02472	617-668-6975		472
Radiation Safety Associates Inc 19 Pendleton Dr *Web:* www.radpro.com	Hebron	CT	06248	860-228-0487	228-4402	637-10
Radiator Specialty Co 1900 Wilkinson Blvd *Web:* www.gunk.com	Charlotte	NC	28208	704-688-2405		145
Radiator Specialty Co 600 Radiator Rd *Web:* www.rscbrands.com	Indian Trail	NC	28079	704-821-7643		541
RadicalMedia 435 Hudson St 6th Fl *Web:* www.radicalmedia.com	New York	NY	10014	212-462-1500		514
Radicchio 402 Wood St	Philadelphia	PA	19106	215-627-6850		671
Radice Law Firm Pc 34 Sunset Blvd *Web:* radicelawfirm.com	Long Beach	NJ	08008	646-245-8502		41
RadiciSpandex Corp 3145 NW Blvd *Web:* www.radicigroup.com	Gastonia	NC	28052	704-864-5495		605-1
Radio Abilene 402 Cypress St Ste 510 *Web:* www.radioabilene.com	Abilene	TX	79601	325-672-5442	672-6128	645-1
Radio Adv Bureau (RAB) 125 W 55th St 5th Fl *TF:* 800-232-3131 ■ *Web:* www.rab.com	New York	NY	10019	800-232-3131		49-18
Radio America 1100 N Glebe Rd Ste 900 *TF:* 800-807-4703 ■ *Web:* www.radioamerica.com	Arlington	VA	22201	703-302-1000		644
Radio Bilingue Inc 5005 E Belmont Ave *TF:* 800-509-4772 ■ *Web:* www.radiobilingue.org	Fresno	CA	93727	559-455-5746		647
Radio City Entertainment LLC 1260 Sixth Ave *Web:* www.msg.com	New York	NY	10020	212-485-7200		181
Radio Communications Co 8035 Chapel Hill Rd *TF:* 800-508-7580 ■ *Web:* rccws.com	Cary	NC	27513	919-467-2421		194
Radio Connection Broadcasting School 1201 W 5th St Ste M130 *TF:* 800-990-9445 ■ *Web:* www.radioconnection.com	Los Angeles	CA	90017	310-456-8341	461-6016	685
Radio Distributing Company Inc 27015 Trolley Industrial Dr *Web:* www.radiodistributing.com	Taylor	MI	48180	313-295-4500		38
Radio Express Inc 2501 W Burbank Blvd Ste 205 *Web:* www.radioexpress.com	Burbank	CA	91505	818-295-5800	295-5801	646
Radio Fiesta Network L L C 4887 Melrose Ave *Web:* www.radiofiestanetwork.com	Los Angeles	CA	90029	323-462-0903		644
Radio Flyer Inc 6515 W Grand Ave *TF:* 800-621-7613 ■ *Web:* www.radioflyer.com	Chicago	IL	60707	773-637-7100	637-8874	762
Radio Free Asia 2025 M St NW Ste 300 *Web:* www.rfa.org	Washington	DC	20036	202-530-4900		644
Radio Free Europe/Radio Liberty (RFE/RL) 1201 Connecticut Ave NW 4th Fl *Web:* www.rferl.org	Washington	DC	20036	202-457-6900		644
Radio Frequency Company Inc (RFC) 150 Dover Rd *Web:* www.radiofrequency.com	Millis	MA	02054	508-376-9555	376-9944	318
Radio Frequency Systems 200 Pondview Dr *TF:* 877-737-9675 ■ *Web:* www.rfsworld.com	Meriden	CT	06450	203-630-3311	634-2273	647
Radio Guys 2061 Fwy Dr Ste E *Web:* www.theradioguys.com	Woodland	CA	95776	530-406-0700		179
Radio Holland USA Inc 8943 Gulf Fwy *Web:* www.radioholland.com	Houston	TX	77017	713-378-2100	378-2101	647
Radio Iowa 2700 Grand Ave Ste 103 *Web:* www.radioiowa.com	Des Moines	IA	50312	515-282-1984	282-1879	647
Radio Kansas 815 N Walnut Ste 300 *TF:* 800-723-4657 ■ *Web:* www.radiokansas.org	Hutchinson	KS	67501	800-723-4657		645
Radio Latina 104.5FM 1690 W Frontage Rd *Web:* 1045radiolatina.com	Chula Vista	CA	91911	619-336-7800		645
Radio LOBO 102.9 5100 Commerce Dr *Web:* www.radiolobo.com	Bakersfield	CA	93309	661-327-0797		645-14
Radio Maria 119 N Walnut St *Web:* radiomariarestaurant.com	Champaign	IL	61820	217-398-7729		671
Radio Medford 1438 Rossanley Dr *Web:* www.radiomedford.com	Medford	OR	97501	541-779-1550	776-2360	647
Radio North 2682 Garfield Rd N Ste 22 *TF:* 800-274-8255 ■ *Web:* radionorth.com	Traverse City	MI	49686	800-274-8255		647
Radio People, The 265 Highpoint Dr *Web:* www.radiopeople.com	Ridgeland	MS	39157	601-956-0102	978-3980	643
Radio Research Consortium Inc (RRC) PO Box 1309 *Web:* www.rrconline.org	Olney	MD	20830	301-774-6686	774-0976	632
Radio Systems Inc 601 Heron Dr *Web:* www.radiosystems.com	Logan Township	NJ	08085	856-467-8000	467-3044	647
Radio Training Network Inc 5015 S Florida Ave	Lakeland	FL	33813	863-644-3464		643
Radio VM Montreal 5000 Rue d'Iberville Ste 303 *TF:* 855-212-2020 ■ *Web:* www.radiovm.com	Montreal	QC	H2H2S6	514-382-3913	858-0965	647
Radiocat 32-A Mellor Ave *TF:* 800-323-9729 ■ *Web:* radiocat.com	Baltimore	MD	21228	800-323-9729		794
Radio-Classique montrEal Parc Jean-Drapeau 1260 rue Mill bureau 100 *Web:* www.cjpx.ca	Montreal	QC	H3K2B4	514-871-0995	871-0990	647

Company	City	ST	ZIP	Phone	Fax	Class
Radiofrequency Safety Intl (RSI) 543 Main St *TF:* 888-830-5648 ■ *Web:* www.rsicorp.com	Kiowa	KS	67070	888-830-5648		196
Radiological Imaging Technology Inc 5065 List Dr *TF:* 888-992-1077 ■ *Web:* radimage.com	Colorado Springs	CO	80919	719-590-1077	590-1071	174
Radiological Society of North America (RSNA) 820 Jorie Blvd *TF:* 800-381-6660 ■ *Web:* www.rsna.org	Oak Brook	IL	60523	630-571-2670	571-7837	49-8
Radiology Business Management Assn (RBMA) 9990 Fairfax Blvd Ste 430 *TF:* 888-224-7262 ■ *Web:* www.rbma.org	Fairfax	VA	22030	703-621-3355	621-3356	49-8
Radiology Support Devices Inc 1904 E Dominguez St *Web:* www.rsdphantoms.com	Long Beach	CA	90810	310-518-0527		476
Radiometrics Midwest Corp 12 E Devonwood *Web:* www.radiomet.com	Romeoville	IL	60446	815-293-0772	293-0820	743
Radiophone Engineering Inc 534 W Walnut St *TF:* 800-369-2929 ■ *Web:* www.radiophonewireless.com	Springfield	MO	65806	417-862-6653		246
Radio-Television News Directors Assn (RTNDA) 1600 K St NW Ste 700 *Web:* www.rtdna.org	Washington	DC	20006	202-659-6510	223-4007	49-14
RadioU PO Box 1887 *TF:* 877-272-3468 ■ *Web:* www.radiou.com	Westerville	OH	43086	877-272-3468		645
Radiowirenet Inc 314 Lafayette St *Web:* radiowire.net	Jefferson City	MO	65101	573-659-7950		396
RadioWorks Inc 3207 Dogwood Dr *Web:* www.radioworks.com	Portsmouth	VA	23703	757-484-0140		647
Radish Tools 12 Mckendree Ave *Web:* radishtools.com	Annapolis	MD	21401	443-321-2732		317
Radisson Hotel & Suites Fort Mc Murray 435 Gregoire Dr *Web:* www.radissonfortmcmurray.com	Fort McMurray	AB	T9H4K7	780-743-2400		379
RadiSys Corp 5445 NE Dawson Creek Dr *NASDAQ: RSYS* ■ *TF:* 800-950-0044 ■ *Web:* www.radisys.com	Hillsboro	OR	97124	503-615-1100		625
RADIUS 7700 Wisconsin Ave Ste 400 *Web:* www.radiustravel.com	Bethesda	MD	20814	301-718-9500		772
Radius Advertising 10883 Pearl Rd Ste 100 *Web:* www.radiuscleveland.com	Strongsville	OH	44136	440-638-3800		5
Radius Engineering Inc 1042 West 2780 South *Web:* www.radiuseng.com	Salt Lake City	UT	84119	801-886-2624		256
Radius Global Solutions LLC 50 W Skippack Pk *Web:* www.radiusgs.com	Ambler	PA	19002	267-419-1111		160
Radius Partners LLC 2 Burlington Woods Dr Ste 100 *Web:* www.radius-partners.com	Burlington	MA	01803	978-824-2777		690
Radius Professional HDD Tools 2525 Ranger Hwy PO Box 3106 **Fax Area Code:* 817 ■ *TF:* 800-892-9114 ■ *Web:* www.radiushdd.com	Weatherford	TX	76088	800-892-9114	599-3024*	538
Radius Technology Group 4835 Cordell Ave Ste 1309 *Web:* www.radius360.net	Bethesda	MD	20814	301-565-3400		225
Radius Ventures LLC 250 Park Ave Ste 1102 *Web:* radiusventures.com	New York	NY	10017	212-897-7778	397-2656	792
Radix Health 887 W Marietta St NW Ste E *TF:* 833-723-4999 ■ *Web:* www.radixhealth.com	Atlanta	GA	30318	833-723-4999		657
Radix Law PLC 15205 N Kierland Blvd Ste 200 *Web:* radixlaw.com	Scottsdale	AZ	85254	602-606-9300		41
Radixx Solutions International Inc 6310 Hazeltine National Dr *Web:* www.radixx.com	Orlando	FL	32822	407-856-9009		224
Radley Corp 23077 Greenfield Rd Ste 440 *Web:* www.radley.com	Southfield	MI	48075	248-559-6858		177
Radnor Financial Advisors Inc 485 Devon Park Dr Ste 119 *TF:* 888-271-9922 ■ *Web:* www.radnorfinancial.com	Wayne	PA	19087	610-975-0280		401
Radnor Lake State Park 1160 Otter Creek Rd *Web:* tnstateparks.com	Nashville	TN	37220	615-373-3467		565
Radnor Township School Authority 135 S Wayne Ave *Web:* www.rtsd.org	Wayne	PA	19087	610-688-8100	971-0742	685
Rado Enterprises 20 Industrial Dr *Web:* www.morocorp.com	Bloomsburg	PA	17815	570-759-0303		595
Radon Control Systems Inc 160 US Rt 1 *TF:* 800-698-9655 ■ *Web:* www.awqinc.com	Freeport	ME	04032	207-865-9200		35
Radoslovich Shapiro PC 701 University Ave Ste 100 *Web:* radshap.com	Sacramento	CA	95825	916-565-8161		41
RadView Software Inc 991 Hwy 22 W Ste 200 *TF:* 888-723-8439 ■ *Web:* www.radview.com	Bridgewater	NJ	08807	908-526-7756		178-12
Radware Inc 575 Corporate Dr Lobby 2 *TF:* 888-234-5763 ■ *Web:* www.radware.com	Mahwah	NJ	07430	201-512-9771	512-9774	178-11
Radwell International Ltd 1 Millennium Dr *TF:* 800-884-5500 ■ *Web:* www.radwell.co.uk	Willingboro	NJ	08046	609-288-9393	288-9417	190
Rady Children's Hospital (RCH) 3020 Children's Way 3rd Fl *TF:* 800-788-9029 ■ *Web:* www.rchsd.org	San Diego	CA	92123	858-576-1700	966-5859	374-1
Radyne Corp 211 W Boden St *TF:* 800-236-8360 ■ *Web:* www.radyne.com	Milwaukee	WI	53207	414-481-8360	481-8303	318
RAE Corp 4492 Hunt St PO Box 1206 *Web:* raecorp.com	Pryor	OK	74361	918-825-7222	825-0723	14
RAE DC Products Group 4615 Prime Pkwy *TF:* 800-323-7049 ■ *Web:* www.raemotors.com	McHenry	IL	60050	815-385-3500		518
Rae Engineering & Inspection Ltd 4810 93 St NW *Web:* www.raeengineering.ca	Edmonton	AB	T6E5M4	780-469-2401		261
Raeford-Hoke Chamber of Commerce 101 N Main St	Raeford	NC	28376	910-875-5929		139
RAF Industries Inc 1 Pitcairn Pl 165 Township Line Rd Ste 2100 *Web:* www.rafind.com	Jenkintown	PA	19046	215-572-0738	576-1640	194
RAF Technology Inc 15400 NE 90th St Ste 300 *Web:* www.raf.com	Redmond	WA	98052	425-867-0700		177
Raff Printing Inc PO Box 42365 *TF:* 800-994-4044 ■ *Web:* raffprinting.com	Pittsburgh	PA	15203	412-431-4044		627
Raffa Consulting Economists Inc 17 S Osceola Ave Ste 200 *Web:* raffaconsulting.com	Orlando	FL	32801	407-648-5141		196
Raffaello 201 E Delaware Pl **Fax Area Code:* 312 ■ *TF:* 844-874-4253 ■ *Web:* www.chicagoraffaello.com	Chicago	IL	60611	844-874-4253	924-9158*	379
Rafferty's Inc 1750 Scottsville Rd Ste 2 *Web:* www.raffertys.com	Bowling Green	KY	42104	270-842-0123		670
Raffield Fisheries Inc PO Box 309 *Web:* www.raffieldfisheries.com	Port Saint Joe	FL	32457	850-229-8229	229-8782	285
Raffles Capital Group Inc 1 Burning Tree Rd *Web:* www.rafflescapital.com	Greenwich	CT	06830	203-629-5604		401
Rafi Systems Inc 23453 Golden Spring Dr *Web:* www.rafisystems.com	Diamond Bar	CA	91765	909-861-6574	396-7933	542
RAFN Co 1721 132nd Ave NE *Web:* www.rafn.com	Bellevue	WA	98005	425-702-6600		186
Raft River Rural Electric Co-opeartive Inc PO Box 617 *TF:* 800-342-7732 ■ *Web:* www.rrelectric.com	Malta	ID	83342	208-645-2211		245
Rag Co, The 5430 W State St *Web:* theragcompany.com	Boise	ID	83703	208-888-6821		459
Rag Man Inc 14076 SE 82nd Dr *TF:* 877-572-4626 ■ *Web:* ragmanonline.com	Clackamas	OR	97015	503-657-5694		686
Ragan & Massey Inc 100 Ponchatoula Pkwy *TF:* 800-264-5281 ■ *Web:* raganandmassey.com	Ponchatoula	LA	70454	985-386-6042		237
Ragan & Ragan p C (R&R) 3100 Rt 138 W Brinley Plz 1st Bldg *Web:* www.raganlaw.com	Wall Township	NJ	07719	732-280-4100	280-4112	428
Rage Administrative and Marketing Services Inc PO BOX 789749 *Web:* www.rage-inc.com	Wichita	KS	67278	316-634-1888		196
Rage Corp 3949 Lyman Dr *Web:* pcgrp.squarespace.com	Hilliard	OH	43026	614-771-4771		596
Rage Unlimited Inc 1715 Pearl St *Web:* www.rageunlimited.com	Boulder	CO	80302	303-444-6506	440-7243	344
Raging Waters 2333 S White Rd *Web:* www.rwsplash.com	San Jose	CA	95148	408-238-9900	270-2022	32
Raging Waters Sacramento 1600 Exposition Blvd *Web:* www.rwsac.com	Sacramento	CA	95815	916-924-3747	924-1314	32
RagingWire Data Centers Inc 5470 Kietzke Ln Ste 230 *Web:* www.ragingwire.com	Reno	NV	89511	916-286-3000		387
Ragland Clay Products LLC 61 Industrial Dr *Web:* www.raglandclay.com	Ragland	AL	35131	205-472-2136	472-2119	191-1
Ragland Mills Inc 14079 Hammer Rd *TF:* 888-549-8014 ■ *Web:* www.raglandmills.com	Neosho	MO	64850	417-451-2510		447
Ragnar Benson Construction LLC 223 W Jackson Blvd Ste 350 *Web:* www.rbic.com	Park Ridge	IL	60068	847-698-4900	692-9320	186
Rago & Son Inc 1029 51st Ave *Web:* www.rago-son.com	Oakland	CA	94601	510-536-5700		483
Rago and Associates 525 S Washington St *Web:* www.ragotherapy.com	Naperville	IL	60540	630-637-9300		374-5
RAH Federal Credit Union 45 Diauto Dr *Web:* rahfcu.org	Randolph	MA	02368	781-961-2417		219
Rahal Letterman Lanigan 4601 Lyman Dr *Web:* rahal.com	Hilliard	OH	43026	614-529-7000		642
Rahmberg Stover & Associates LLC 789 Vinewood Ave *Web:* rahmbergstover.com	Birmingham	MI	48009	248-203-7712	498-6593	261
Rahr Malting Co 800 W 1st Ave *Web:* www.rahr.com	Shakopee	MN	55379	952-445-1431		461
Rahway Public Library 2 City Hall Plz *Web:* www.rahwaylibrary.org	Rahway	NJ	07065	732-340-1551	340-0393	434-3
Raia & Associates Inc 930 Bunty Station Rd	Delaware	OH	43015	740-369-6882		193
Rail Car Service Co 584 Fairground Rd *TF:* 800-521-2151 ■ *Web:* parailcar.com	Mercer	PA	16137	724-662-3660		650
Rail City Casino 2121 Victorian Ave *Web:* www.railcity.com	Sparks	NV	89431	775-359-9440		452
Rail Delivery Services Inc (RDS) 8600 Bannana Ave *Web:* www.raildelivery.com	Fontana	CA	92335	909-355-4105	822-3135	780
Rail Europe Inc 44 S Broadway 11th Fl *TF:* 800-361-7245 ■ *Web:* www.raileurope.com	White Plains	NY	10601	914-682-2999		775
Rail Exchange Inc 1150 State St *Web:* railexchangeinc.com	Chicago Heights	IL	60411	708-757-3317		770
Rail Transit Consultants Inc 901 S Railroad St *Web:* www.railtransit.com	Penn Run	PA	15675	724-527-2386		108
Railex Corp 89-02 Atlantic Ave *Web:* www.railexcorp.com	Ozone Park	NY	11416	718-845-5454	738-1020	207
Railhead Corp 224 Shore Ct *TF:* 800-235-1782 ■ *Web:* www.railheadcorp.com	Burr Ridge	IL	60527	708-844-5500	844-5559	770

Name / Address	City	State	ZIP	Phone	Fax	Class
Railhead Smokehouse 2900 Montgomery St *Web:* www.railheadsmokehouse.com	Fort Worth	TX	76107	817-738-9808	732-4059	671
Railinc Corp 7001 Weston Pkwy Ste 200 *TF:* 877-724-5462 ■ *Web:* www.railinc.com	Cary	NC	27513	919-651-5000		577
Railmark Holdings Inc PO Box 1185 *Fax Area Code: 888 ■ *Web:* www.railmark.com	Madisonville	KY	42431	248-860-7219	998-7245*	648
Railplan International Inc 1200 Bernard Dr *Web:* www.railplan.com	Baltimore	MD	21223	410-947-5900		261
Railroad Bazaar LLC 1207 Eidson St *Web:* railroadbazaar.com	Athens	AL	35611	256-232-5800		526
Railroad Construction Co 75-77 Grove St *Web:* www.railroadconstruction.com	Paterson	NJ	07503	973-684-0362	684-1355	186
Railroad Pass Hotel & Casino 2800 S Boulder Hwy *TF:* 800-654-0877 ■ *Web:* www.railroadpass.com	Henderson	NV	89002	702-294-5000	294-0092	133
RAILS (Reaching Across Illinois Library System) 125 Tower Dr *TF:* 866-940-4081 ■ *Web:* www.railslibraries.info	Burr Ridge	IL	60527	630-734-5000	734-5050	434-3
Rails Co 101 Newark Way *TF:* 800-217-2457 ■ *Web:* www.railsco.com	Maplewood	NJ	07040	973-763-4320	763-2585	770
Railserve Inc 1691 Phoenix Blvd Ste 250 *TF:* 800-345-7245 ■ *Web:* www.railserve.biz	Atlanta	GA	30349	770-996-6838		651
Rails-to-Trails Conservancy (RTC) 2121 Ward Ct NW 5th Fl *TF:* 800-944-6847 ■ *Web:* www.railstotrails.org	Washington	DC	20037	202-331-9696	223-9257	48-13
Railtown 1897 State Historic Park PO Box 1250 *Web:* railtown1897.org	Jamestown	CA	95327	209-984-3953		565
Railway & Industrial Services Inc 2201 N Ctr St *Web:* www.risxinc.com	Joliet	IL	60403	815-726-4224	726-4265	605-2
Railway Credit Union 1006 E Main St *TF:* 800-601-9580 ■ *Web:* railwaycu.com	Mandan	ND	58554	701-667-9500	667-9600	219
Railway Specialties Corp 2979 State Rd *Web:* www.railwayspecialties.com	Croydon	PA	19021	215-788-9242		350
Railway Supply Institute Inc (RSI) 425 Third St Ste 920 *Web:* www.rsiweb.org	Washington	DC	20024	202-347-4664	347-0047	49-21
RailWorks Corp 5 Penn Plz *Web:* www.railworks.com	New York	NY	10001	212-502-7900		188-8
Raimondo Pettit & Glassman 21515 Hawthorne Blvd Ste 1250 *Web:* www.rpgcpa.com	Torrance	CA	90503	310-540-5990		2
Rain & Hail LLC 9200 Northpark Dr Ste 100 *TF:* 800-776-4045 ■ *Web:* www.rainhail.com	Johnston	IA	50131	515-559-1000	559-1001	390
Rain City Publishing PO Box 15378 *Web:* www.raincitypublishing.com	Seattle	WA	98115	206-527-8778		637-2
Rain Technologies LP, The 11522 W Washington Blvd *TF:* 888-652-7529 ■ *Web:* www.thebrain.com	Los Angeles	CA	90066	310-751-5000		174
Rain the Growth Agency 207 NW Park Ave *TF:* 866-402-1124 ■ *Web:* www.rainforgrowth.com	Portland	OR	97209	866-402-1124		4
Rain Trade Corp 19 Skokie Valley Rd *TF:* 888-909-7246 ■ *Web:* www.guttersupply.com	Lake Bluff	IL	60044	847-283-0006		697
Rainbo Record Manufacturing Corp 8960 Eton Ave *Web:* www.rainborecords.com	Canoga Park	CA	91304	818-280-1100		797
Rainbow Advertising Lp 3904 W Vickery Blvd *TF:* 800-645-7377 ■ *Web:* www.rainbowadvertising.com	Fort Worth	TX	76107	817-738-3838		7
Rainbow Art Glass Inc 1761 Rt 34 S *Web:* www.orderrag.com	Farmingdale	NJ	07727	732-681-6003	681-4984	329
Rainbow Balloons Inc 65 Holton St *Fax Area Code: 781 ■ *TF:* 800-200-8181 ■ *Web:* rainbowballoons.com	Woburn	MA	01801	800-200-8181	935-5959*	366
Rainbow Books Inc PO Box 430 *Web:* www.rainbowbooksinc.com	Highland City	FL	33846	863-648-4420	647-5951	637-2
Rainbow Chinese 2739 Nicollet Ave S *Web:* rainbowrestaurant.com	Minneapolis	MN	55408	612-870-7084		671
Rainbow Computers Corp 6000 NW 97th Ave Ste 21 *Web:* www.rainbowcc.com	Doral	FL	33178	305-592-2611		179
Rainbow Courts Motel & Apartments 915 E Cameron Ave *Web:* www.rainbowcourts.com	Rockdale	TX	76567	512-446-2361		707
Rainbow Falls State Park 633 Leudinghaus Rd *Web:* parks.state.wa.us	Chehalis	WA	98532	360-291-3767		565
Rainbow Graphics Inc 933 Tower Rd *Web:* www.rainbowgraphics.com	Mundelein	IL	60060	847-824-9600	824-9656	627
Rainbow Grocery Co-opeartive Inc 1745 Folsom St *TF:* 877-720-2667 ■ *Web:* www.rainbow.coop	San Francisco	CA	94103	415-863-0620		345
Rainbow Hospice 1550 Bishop Ct *Web:* rainbowhospice.org	Mount Prospect	IL	60056	847-685-9900	294-9613	371
Rainbow Inc 1051 Industrial Park Rd *Web:* www.rainbowsvc.com	Clarksville	TN	37040	931-552-7783	552-7784	454
Rainbow Inc 888 N Nimitz Hwy 3rd Fl *Web:* www.rsmhawaii.com	Honolulu	HI	96817	808-487-6455	487-0888	297-6
Rainbow Intl 204 N Lacy Dr *TF:* 855-724-6269 ■ *Web:* rainbowintl.com	Waco	TX	76707	254-756-5463		152
Rainbow Light 100 Avenue Tea *TF:* 800-475-1890 ■ *Web:* www.rainbowlight.com	Santa Cruz	CA	95060	831-429-9089	429-0189	479
Rainbow Lodge 2011 Ella Blvd *TF:* 866-861-8666 ■ *Web:* www.rainbow-lodge.com	Houston	TX	77008	713-861-8666		671
Rainbow Manufacturing Co 1 Rainbow Dr PO Box 70 *Web:* www.rainbowirrigation.com	Fitzgerald	GA	31750	229-423-4341	423-4645	273
Rainbow Palace 2787 E Oakland Pk Blvd *Web:* www.rainbowpalace.com	Fort Lauderdale	FL	33306	954-565-5652		671
Rainbow Research Inc 621 W Lake St Ste 300 *Web:* www.rainbowresearch.org	Minneapolis	MN	55408	612-824-0724		194
Rainbow Restaurant 212 W Laurel St *Web:* rainbowfoco.com	Fort Collins	CO	80521	970-221-2664		671
Rainbow Sandals Inc 900 Calle Negocio *Web:* rainbowsandals.com	San Clemente	CA	92673	949-276-4431		301
Rainbow Scientific Inc 83 Maple Ave *Web:* rainbowscientific.com	Windsor	CT	06095	860-298-8382	298-8586	475
Rainbow Springs State Park 19158 SW 81st Pl Rd *Web:* www.floridastateparks.org	Dunnellon	FL	34432	352-465-8555		565
Rainbow Travel 5831 NE 1st Ave *TF:* 800-889-9747 ■ *Web:* www.rainbowtravel.com	Fort Lauderdale	FL	33334	954-491-9747		771
Rainbow Treecare Inc 11571 K-Tel Dr *Web:* www.rainbowtreecare.com	Minnetonka	MN	55343	952-922-3810		776
Rainbow Trout Ranch (RTR) 1484 FDR 250 PO Box 458 *TF:* 800-633-3397 ■ *Web:* www.rainbowtroutranch.com	Antonito	CO	81120	719-376-2440		239
Rainbow Veterinary Clinic Inc 2636 Noble Rd *Web:* rainbowvet.com	Cleveland	OH	44121	216-291-3931		414
Rainbow/PUSH Coalition Inc 930 E 50th St *Web:* rainbowpush.org	Chicago	IL	60615	773-373-3366	373-3571	48-5
Rainbows 614 Dempster St Ste C *Web:* rainbows.org	Evanston	IL	60202	847-952-1770	952-1774	48-6
Raindancer Steak House 2300 Palm Beach Lakes Blvd *Web:* www.raindancersteakhouse.com	West Palm Beach	FL	33409	561-684-2810		671
Raines and Fischer 555 5th Ave 4th Fl *Web:* www.rainesfischer.com	New York	NY	10017	212-953-9200	953-9366	2
Rainey, Austin, P.C. 401K Plan 3737 Government Blvd Ste 517 *Web:* raineyaustin.com	Mobile	AL	36693	251-433-8088		41
Rainforest Action Network (RAN) 425 Bush St Ste 300 *TF:* 800-368-1819 ■ *Web:* www.ran.org	San Francisco	CA	94108	415-398-4404	398-2732	48-13
Rainforest Cafe 12801 W Sunrise Blvd *Web:* www.rainforestcafe.com	Sunrise	FL	33323	954-851-1015		671
Rainhart Co PO Box 4533 *TF:* 800-628-0021 ■ *Web:* rainhart.com	Austin	TX	78765	512-452-8848	452-9883	318
Rainier Group Investment Advisory LLC 500 108th Ave N E Ste 2000 *Web:* www.rainiergroup.com	Bellevue	WA	98004	425-463-3000		656
Rainier Industries Ltd 18375 Olympic Ave S *TF:* 800-869-7162 ■ *Web:* www.rainier.com	Tukwila	WA	98188	425-251-1800	251-5065	733
Rainier Plastics Inc 1101 Ledwich Ave *Web:* www.rainierplastics.com	Yakima	WA	98902	509-248-1473	453-7385	660
Rainier Surgical Inc 4150 B Pl Northwest S *Web:* www.rainiersurgical.com	Auburn	WA	98001	253-486-0500	486-0501	475
RainMaker Securities LLC 11390 W Olympic Blvd Ste 380 *TF:* 888-333-1091 ■ *Web:* www.rainmakersecurities.com	Los Angeles	CA	90064	888-333-1091		691
Rainmaker Studios 1901 E Franklin St Ste 101 *Web:* www.rainmakerstudios.com	Richmond	VA	23223	804-771-1300		657
RAINN (Rape Abuse & Incest National Network) 2000 L St NW Ste 406 *TF:* 800-656-4673 ■ *Web:* www.rainn.org	Washington	DC	20036	202-544-1034	544-3556	48-6
Raintree Graphics Inc 5921 Richard St *Web:* www.raintreegraphics.com	Jacksonville	FL	32216	904-396-1653		627
Raintree Resorts Management Company LLC 3340 W Cody Ln PO Box 350 *Web:* www.tetonclub.com	Teton Village	WY	83025	307-734-9777		378
Raintree Restaurant 102 San Marco Ave *Web:* www.raintreerestaurant.com	Saint Augustine	FL	32084	904-824-7211		671
Raintree Systems Inc 27307 Via Industria *TF:* 800-333-1033 ■ *Web:* www.raintreeinc.com	Temecula	CA	92590	951-252-9400		177
Rainwater, Holt & Sexton PA 801 Technology Dr *TF:* 800-434-4800 ■ *Web:* www.callrainwater.com	Little Rock	AR	72223	501-868-2500		428
Rainwise Inc 18 River Field Rd *TF:* 800-762-5723 ■ *Web:* www.rainwise.com	Trenton	ME	04605	207-288-5169	288-3477	407
Rainy River Community College 1501 Hwy 71 *TF:* 800-456-3996 ■ *Web:* www.rainyriver.edu	International Falls	MN	56649	218-285-7722	285-2239	162
Raisbeck Engineering Inc 4411 S Ryan Way *Web:* www.raisbeck.com	Seattle	WA	98178	206-723-2000		256
Raising Arizona Kids 5229 N 7th Ave Ste 102 *Web:* www.raisingarizonakids.com	Phoenix	AZ	85013	480-991-5437	991-5460	637-9
Raj, The 1734 Jasmine Ave *TF:* 800-248-9050 ■ *Web:* www.theraj.com	Fairfield	IA	52556	641-472-9580	472-2496	706
Raja Rani Fine Indian Cuisine 400 S Division St	Ann Arbor	MI	48104	734-995-1545		671
Rajason Tools Inc 11664 County Rd 42 *Web:* www.rajasontools.com	Tecumseh	ON	N8N2M1	519-979-1263		358
Rajdoot 2424 Fourth St SW *Web:* www.rajdoot.ca	Calgary	AB	T2S2T4	403-245-0181		671
Rajkowski Hansmeier Ltd 11 Seventh Ave N *TF:* 800-445-9617 ■ *Web:* www.rajhan.com	Saint Cloud	MN	56303	320-251-1055		428
Rajput Indian Cuisine 742 W 21st St *Web:* www.rajputonline.com	Norfolk	VA	23517	757-625-4634		671

Name / Address	City	State	ZIP	Phone	Fax	Class
Rak Medical Inc 340 Duquesne Way *Web:* rakmedical.com	Sewickley	PA	15143	412-741-2880		366
Rakar Inc 1700 Emerson Ave *Web:* www.rakarinc.com	Oxnard	CA	93033	805-487-2721	483-2778	604
Raken 5600 Avenida Encinas Ste 140e *TF:* 866-438-0646 ■ *Web:* www.rakenapp.com	Carlsbad	CA	92008	866-438-0646		177
Rakuten Marketing 215 Park Ave S 2nd Fl *TF:* 888-880-8430 ■ *Web:* rakutenmarketing.com	New York	NY	10003	646-943-8200	943-8204	7
Ralco Industries Inc 2720 Auburn Ct *Web:* www.ralcoind.com	Auburn Hills	MI	48326	248-853-3200		483
Ralco Nutrition Inc 1600 Hahn Rd *TF:* 800-533-5306 ■ *Web:* www.ralconutrition.com	Marshall	MN	56258	800-533-5306		447
Raleigh City Museum 220 Fayetteville St *Web:* www.cityofraleighmuseum.org	Raleigh	NC	27601	919-996-2220		520
Raleigh Convention Ctr 500 S Salisbury St *Web:* www.raleighconvention.com	Raleigh	NC	27601	919-996-8500	996-8550	205
Raleigh Correctional Center for Women 1201 S State St	Raleigh	NC	27610	919-733-4248		213
Raleigh County 215 Main St *TF:* 800-509-6568 ■ *Web:* raleighcountyassessor.com	Beckley	WV	25801	304-255-9178		338
Raleigh County Public Library 221 N Kanawha St *Web:* www.rcplwv.org	Beckley	WV	25801	304-255-0511	255-9161	434-3
Raleigh Enterprises 5300 Melrose Ave 4th Fl *Web:* www.raleighenterprises.com	Hollywood	CA	90038	310-899-8900	899-8910	185
Raleigh General Hospital 1710 Harper Rd *Web:* www.raleighgeneral.com	Beckley	WV	25801	304-256-4100	256-4009	374-3
Raleigh Licensee Inc 3012 Highwoods Blvd Ste 101 *Web:* www.raleighcw.com	Raleigh	NC	27604	919-872-9535	878-6588	647
Raleigh Studios 5300 Melrose Ave *TF:* 888-960-3456 ■ *Web:* raleighstudios.com	Hollywood	CA	90038	888-960-3456		514
Raleigh Symphony Orchestra PO Box 26878 *Web:* www.raleighsymphony.org	Raleigh	NC	27611	919-546-9755		573-3
Raleigh, The 1775 Collins Ave *Web:* www.raleighhotel.com	Miami Beach	FL	33139	305-534-6300		707
Raleigh-Durham International Airport PO Box 80001 *Web:* www.rdu.com	Raleigh	NC	27623	919-840-2123	840-0175	27
Raley's 500 W Capitol Ave *TF:* 800-925-9989 ■ *Web:* www.raleys.com	West Sacramento	CA	95605	916-373-3333	373-0881	345
RA-LIN & Associates Inc 101 Parkwood Cir *Web:* www.ra-lin.com	Carrollton	GA	30117	770-834-4884	828-0670	186
Ralls County Courthouse 311 S Main St PO Box 466 *Web:* www.rallscountymo.net	New London	MO	63459	573-985-7111	985-3446	338
Ralls County Electric Co-op 17594 Hwy 19 PO Box 157 *TF:* 877-985-8711 ■ *Web:* www.rallscountyelectric.com	New London	MO	63459	573-985-8711		245
Rally Education 22 Railroad Ave *TF:* 888-997-2559 ■ *Web:* rallyeducation.com	Glen Head	NY	11545	516-671-9300	671-7900	196
Rally House & Kansas Sampler 9750 Quivira Rd *TF:* 800-645-5409 ■ *Web:* www.rallyhouse.com	Lenexa	KS	66215	800-645-5409		791
Rally Point Management LLC 630C Anchors St NW *Web:* www.rallypointmanagement.com	Fort Walton Beach	FL	32548	850-226-7589		396
Rally.org 995 Market St 2nd Fl *TF:* 888-648-2220 ■ *Web:* rally.org	San Francisco	CA	94105	888-648-2220		387
Ralm Inc 4620 Moroaoon Rd	Fayetteville	NC	28311	910-486-4491		463
Ralph & Kacoo's 1700 Old Minden Rd Ste 141 *Web:* www.ralphandkacoos.com	Bossier City	LA	71111	318-747-6660		671
Ralph 'N Rich's 815 Main St *Web:* www.ralphnrichs.com	Bridgeport	CT	06604	203-366-3597		671
Ralph Andersen & Assoc 5800 Stanford Ranch Rd Ste 410 *Web:* www.ralphandersen.com	Rocklin	CA	95765	916-630-4900		463
Ralph Brennan's Jazz Kitchen Downtown Disney 1590 S Disneyland Dr *Web:* www.rbjazzkitchen.com	Anaheim	CA	92802	714-776-5200	999-2123	671
Ralph C. Mehler Agency Inc 62 E Shenango St *Web:* mehlerinsurance.com	Sharpsville	PA	16150	724-962-5757		390
Ralph Dowd Agency Inc 13 River St *Web:* dowdinsurancect.com	Canton	CT	06019	860-693-8876		390
Ralph E. Ames Machine Works 2301 Dominguez Way *Web:* www.amesmachine.com	Torrance	CA	90501	310-320-2637	320-6511	454
Ralph Friedland & Bros 17 Industrial Dr *TF:* 800-631-2162 ■ *Web:* www.friedlandshades.com	Keyport	NJ	07735	732-290-9800		87
Ralph H. Johnson VA Medical Ctr 109 Bee St *TF:* 888-878-6884 ■ *Web:* www.charleston.va.gov	Charleston	SC	29401	843-577-5011		374-8
Ralph J Steinhauer Elementary School 25 N Fellowship Rd *Web:* rjse.mapleshade.org	Maple Shade	NJ	08052	856-779-7323	779-2921	685
Ralph L. Wadsworth Construction Company Inc 166 E 14000 S Ste 200 *Web:* www.wadsco.com	Draper	UT	84020	801-553-1661	553-1696	188-4
Ralph Moyle Inc (RMI) 23599 Freedom Ln *TF:* 800-845-6062 ■ *Web:* www.ralphmoyle.com	Mattawan	MI	49071	269-668-4531		780
Ralph Pill Electrical Supply Co 50 Von Hillern St *TF:* 800-897-1769 ■ *Web:* www.needco.com	Boston	MA	02125	617-265-8800	288-1776	246
Ralph Rosenberg Court Reporters Inc 1001 Bishop St Ste 2460 *TF:* 888-524-5888 ■ *Web:* www.hawaiicourtreporters.com	Honolulu	HI	96813	888-524-5888		445
Ralph S. Inouye Company Ltd 500 Alakawa St Rm 220E *Web:* www.rsinouye.com	Honolulu	HI	96817	808-839-9002	833-5971	256
Ralph Stover State Park 6011 State Park Rd *Web:* www.dcnr.pa.gov	Pipersville	PA	18947	610-982-5560		565
Ralph W. Earl Company Inc 5930 E Molloy Rd *Web:* www.rwearl.com	Syracuse	NY	13211	315-454-4431	454-0977	358
Ralph Warner & Sons Incorporated Plumbing & Heating 161 Berlin St	Southington	CT	06489	860-628-6826		189-10
Ralph'S Foods Inc 630 N Carol Malone Blvd *Web:* foodfairmarkets.com	Grayson	KY	41143	606-474-5522		345
Ralph's Packing Co 500 W Freeman Ave *Web:* www.ralphspacking.com	Perkins	OK	74059	405-547-2464	547-2364	473
Ralphs Grocery Co 1014 Vine St *TF:* 800-576-4377 ■ *Web:* www.ralphs.com	Cincinnati	OH	45202	800-576-4377		345
Ralphs-pugh Company Inc 3931 Oregon St **Fax Area Code:* 800 ■ *TF:* 800-486-0021 ■ *Web:* www.ralphs-pugh.com	Benicia	CA	94510	707-745-6222	995-3942*	207
Ralston Discount Liquor 3147 Southmore Blvd *Web:* www.ralstonliquor.com	Houston	TX	77004	713-524-3045	524-5981	237
Ralston Metal Products Ltd 50 Watson Rd S *TF:* 800-265-7611 ■ *Web:* www.ralstonmetal.com	Guelph	ON	N1L1E2	800-265-7611		480
Ralston Public School 8545 Park Dr *TF:* 844-964-7103 ■ *Web:* www.ralstonschools.org	Ralston	NE	68127	402-331-4700	331-4843	685
RAM Co 3172 E Deseret Dr S *Web:* ramcompany.com	Saint George	UT	84790	435-673-4603	673-8239	790
RAM Computer Supply Inc 14901 E Hampden Ave Ste 315 *Web:* ramcomputersupply.com	Aurora	CO	80014	303-690-1300		175
RAM Electronic Industries Inc 1704 Taylors Ln *Web:* www.ramelectronics.net	Cinnaminson	NJ	08077	856-864-0999		253
RAM Enterprise Inc 1225 W Main St *TF:* 800-738-0308 ■ *Web:* ram-enterprise.com	Elko	NV	89801	775-738-3997		631
RAM Freezers and Coolers 783 W 18th St *Web:* www.ramrefri.com	Hialeah	FL	33010	305-887-1000	433-7096	189-10
RAM Inc 808 E 6th St *Web:* www.raminc-cisco.com	Cisco	TX	76437	254-442-1008	442-1009	604
RAM Industrial Services Inc 5460B Pottsville Pk *Web:* rammotors.com	Leesport	PA	19533	610-916-8000		203
RAM Industries Inc 13119 Mula Ct *Web:* www.ramwindows.com	Stafford	TX	77477	281-495-9056		236
RAM Mechanical Inc 3506 Moore Rd *Web:* ram-mechanical.com	Ceres	CA	95307	209-531-9155		261
RAM Offset Lithographers LLC 2651 Ave G *TF:* 800-352-6888 ■ *Web:* www.ramoffset.com	White City	OR	97503	541-826-3155	826-5467	627
RAM Precision Industries Inc 11125 Yankee Rd *Web:* www.ramprecision.com	Dayton	OH	45458	937-885-7700	885-7727	454
RAM Printing Inc 5 Commerce Park Dr *TF:* 800-860-7045 ■ *Web:* www.ramprinting.com	East Hampstead	NH	03826	603-382-7045	382-7629	627
RAM Publications & Distributions Inc 2525 Michigan Ave Bldg A2 *Web:* www.rampub.com	Santa Monica	CA	90404	310-453-0043	264-4888	637-10
RAM Restaurant & Brewery 10013 59th Ave SW *Web:* www.theram.com	Lakewood	WA	98499	253-588-1788	588-9617	670
RAM Sensors Inc 876 Canterbury Rd *TF:* 800-888-8987 ■ *Web:* www.ramsensors.com	Cleveland	OH	44145	440-835-3540	835-8603	201
RAM Software Systems Inc 892 New Castle Rd *Web:* aim-system.com	Slippery Rock	PA	16057	724-794-1222		177
RAM Steelco Inc 2249 Madrona Ave SE *TF:* 800-452-7880 ■ *Web:* ramsteelco.net	Salem	OR	97302	503-588-1311	581-2521	492
RAM Technologies LLC 29 Soundview Rd *Web:* www.ramtechno.com	Guilford	CT	06437	203-453-3916	453-3913	250
RAM Threading Inc 2640 Crockett St *Web:* www.ramthreading.com	Beaumont	TX	77701	409-833-2658	832-4014	351
RAM Tool & Supply Co 3620 Eigth Ave S *Web:* ramtool.com	Birmingham	AL	35222	205-714-3300		351
RAM Tool Inc 1420 Cheyenne Ave *Web:* www.ramtoolinc.com	Grafton	WI	53024	262-375-3036	375-3025	757
RAM Trucking Inc 27037 Weber Rd *TF:* 800-345-1416 ■ *Web:* www.ramtrucking.com	Brownsville	OR	97327	800-345-1416		780
RAM Welding Company Inc 93 Rado Dr *TF:* 800-927-6485 ■ *Web:* www.ramwelding.com	Naugatuck	CT	06770	203-729-2289		480
RAM Winch & Hoist 14603 Chrisman Rd *Web:* ramwinch.com	Houston	TX	77039	281-999-8665	999-8666	351
Ram's Horn Restaurant 26200 W 12 Mile Rd *Web:* www.ramshornrestaurants.com	Southfield	MI	48034	248-353-3232		670
Rama Corp 600 W Esplanade Ave *TF:* 800-472-5670 ■ *Web:* ramacorporation.com	San Jacinto	CA	92583	951-654-7351	654-3748	14
Rama Restaurant 327 4th Ave	San Diego	CA	92101	619-501-8424		671
Ramah Navajo School Board Inc PO Box 10 *Web:* rnsb.k12.nm.us	Pinehill	NM	87357	505-775-3256	775-3799	423
Ramaker & Associates Inc 1120 Dallas St *TF:* 800-332-7532 ■ *Web:* www.ramaker.com	Sauk City	WI	53583	608-643-4100	643-7999	261
Ramakrishna-Vivekananda Center of New York Inc 17 E 94th St *Web:* www.ramakrishna.org	New York	NY	10128	212-534-9445	828-1618	637-2
Ramallo Bros Printing Inc PO Box 70225	San Juan	PR	00936	787-287-0303		627
Ramapo Catskill Library System 619 Rt 17-M *Web:* www.rcls.org	Middletown	NY	10940	845-343-1131		434-3

	Phone	Fax	Class
Ramapo College of New Jersey 505 Ramapo Valley Rd . . . . Mahwah NJ 07430 *Web:* www.ramapo.edu	201-684-7500	684-7964	166
Ramapo Sales & Marketing Inc 4760 Goer Dr Ste F . . . . North Charleston SC 29406 *TF:* 800-866-9173 ■ *Web:* www.ramapoglass.com	800-866-9173		195
Ramar-Hall Inc 26 Old Indian Trl . . . . Middlefield CT 06455 *Web:* www.ramarhall.com	860-349-1081	349-1949	22
Ramberg & Associates PA 1080 SW Wanamaker Rd . . . . Topeka KS 66604 *Web:* rambergandassociates.com	785-273-7276	273-4579	2
Ramblin Express Transportation 3465 Astrozon Pl . . . . Colorado Springs CO 80910 *TF:* 800-772-6254 ■ *Web:* www.ramblinexpress.com	719-590-8687		108
Ramblin Jack's 520 E Fourth Ave . . . . Olympia WA 98501 *Web:* www.ramblinjacks.com	360-754-8909		671
Ramboll Environ 4350 N Fairfax Dr Ste 300 . . . . Arlington VA 22203 *Web:* www.ramboll.com	703-516-2300	516-2345	192
Rambus Inc 1050 Enterprise Way Ste 700 . . . . Sunnyvale CA 94089 *NASDAQ: RMBS* ■ *Web:* www.rambus.com	408-462-8000	462-8001	696
Rambusch Decorating Co 160 Cornelison Ave . . . . Jersey City NJ 07304 *Web:* rambusch.com	201-333-2525	433-3355	329
Ramcar Batteries Inc 2700 Carrier Ave . . . . Commerce CA 90040 *Web:* www.ramcarbattery.com	323-726-1212		74
Ramcel Engineering Co 2926 MacArthur Blvd . . . . Northbrook IL 60062 *Web:* www.ramcel.com	847-272-6980	272-7196	488
RAMCO (Reliable Architectural Metals Co) 9751 Erwin . . . . Detroit MI 48213 *TF:* 800-445-0263 ■ *Web:* www.ramcometals.com	313-924-9750	924-8877	191-2
Ramco Laboratories Inc 4100 Greenbriar Dr Ste 200 . . . . Stafford TX 77477 *TF:* 800-231-6238 ■ *Web:* ramcolab.com	281-313-1200	313-1251	476
Ramco Systems Corp 3150 Brunswick Pk Ste 130 . . . . Lawrenceville NJ 08648 *TF:* 800-472-6261 ■ *Web:* www.ramco.com	609-620-4800		225
Ramco-Gershenson Properties Trust 31500 NW Hwy Ste 300 . . . . Farmington Hills MI 48334 *NYSE: RPT* ■ *Web:* ramcoproperties.com	248-350-9900	350-9925	655
Ramec Engineering 1736 W 130th St . . . . Gardena CA 90249 *Web:* www.ramec.net	310-532-2573	532-2576	20
Ramen-Ya 181 W Fourth St . . . . New York NY 10014 *Web:* www.ramenya.nyc	212-989-5440		671
Ramey Chandler Quinn & Zito 750 Bering Dr Ste 600 . . . . Houston TX 77057 *Web:* www.ramey-chandler.com	713-266-0074		445
Ramey Kemp & Associates Inc 5808 Faringdon Pl Ste 100 . . . . Raleigh NC 27609 *Web:* www.rameykemp.com	919-872-5115		261
Ramius Corp 283 Blvd Alexandre Tache Ste F2014 . . . . Gatineau QC J9A1L8 *TF:* 888-932-2299 ■ *Web:* recollective.com	613-230-3808	230-8718	225
Ramon Worthington PLLC 900 Kerria Ave . . . . Mcallen TX 78501 *Web:* ramonworthington.com	956-294-4800		41
Ramona Chamber of Commerce 960 Main St . . . . Ramona CA 92065 *TF:* 877-985-5267 ■ *Web:* ramonachamber.com	760-789-1311	789-1317	139
Ramona's Mexican Food Products Inc 13633 SW Ave . . . . Gardena CA 90249 *Web:* www.ramonas.com	310-323-1950		296-37
Ramos Oil Company Inc 1515 S River Rd . . . . West Sacramento CA 95691 *TF:* 800-477-7266 ■ *Web:* www.ramosoil.com	916-371-2570	371-0635	579
Rampart Brokerage Corp 1983 Marcus Ave Ste C130 . . . . New Hyde Park NY 11042 *TF:* 800-772-6727 ■ *Web:* rampartinsurance.com	516-538-7000	390-3555	390
Rampart Investment Management 1540 Broadway 16th Fl . . . . New York NY 10036 *Web:* rampart-im.com	212-395-9470		401
Rampart Supply Inc 1801 N Union Blvd . . . . Colorado Springs CO 80909 *TF:* 800-748-1837 ■ *Web:* www.rampartsupply.com	719-482-7333		612
RamQuest Software Inc 5801 Tennyson Pkwy Ste 500 . . . . Plano TX 75024 *Web:* www.ramquest.com	214-291-1600		177
Ramrod Industries LLC 800 S Monroe St . . . . Spencer WI 54479 *TF:* 888-233-0876 ■ *Web:* www.ramrodindustries.com	715-659-4996	659-4696	641
Rams Head Inn 9 W White Horse Pk . . . . Galloway NJ 08205 *Web:* www.ramsheadinn.com	609-652-1910		671
Ramsay Law Firm PA 10610 Metromont Pkwy Ste 205 . . . . Charlotte NC 28269 *TF:* 800-388-1612 ■ *Web:* deweyramsayhunt.com	704-376-1616		41
Ramsbottom Printing Inc 135 Waldron Rd . . . . Fall River MA 02720 *Web:* www.rpiprinting.net	508-730-2220		627
Ramsell Corp 200 Webster St Ste 200 . . . . Oakland CA 94607 *TF:* 888-900-6635 ■ *Web:* ramsellcorp.com	510-587-2600	587-2799	225
Ramsey Board of Education 266 E Main St . . . . Ramsey NJ 07446 *Web:* www.ramsey.k12.nj.us	201-785-2300	934-6623	685
Ramsey County 524 Fourth Ave NE . . . . Devils Lake ND 58301 *Web:* www.co.ramsey.nd.us	701-662-7001		338
Ramsey County 15 W Kellogg Blvd . . . . Saint Paul MN 55102 *TF:* 866-520-7225 ■ *Web:* www.ramseycounty.us	651-266-8000	266-8039	338
Ramsey County Public Library 4570 N Victoria St . . . . Shoreview MN 55126 *Web:* www.rclreads.org	651-486-2200	486-2220	434-3
Ramsey House 2614 Thorngrove Pk . . . . Knoxville TN 37914 *Web:* www.ramseyhouse.org	865-546-0745	546-1851	50-3
Ramsey Lake State Recreation Area Ramsey Lake Rd PO Box 97 . . . . Ramsey IL 62080 *Web:* www.dnr.illinois.gov	618-423-2215		565
Ramsey Land Surveying LLC 8718 SW Pkwy . . . . Austin TX 78735 *Web:* www.rlsurveying.com	512-301-9398		727
Ramsey Law Group Apc 3736 Mt Diablo Blvd Ste 300 . . . . LaFayette CA 94549 *Web:* ramseylawgroup.com	925-284-2800		41
Ramsey Popcorn Company Inc 5645 Clover Valley Rd NW . . . . Ramsey IN 47166 *Web:* www.cousinwillies.com	812-347-2441		123
Ramsey Products Corp 3701 Performance Rd PO Box 668827 . . . . Charlotte NC 28266 *Web:* www.ramseychain.com	704-394-0322	394-9134	620
Ramsey Winch Company Inc 1600 N Garnett Rd . . . . Tulsa OK 74116 *TF:* 800-777-2760 ■ *Web:* www.ramsey.com	918-438-2760	438-6688	190
Ramsey, Skiles, & Streva Ltd 1915 Hwy 182 E . . . . Morgan City LA 70380 *Web:* rsslawoffice.com	985-395-9247		41
Ramsgate Veterinary 843 Sundown Dr . . . . Waco TX 76712 *Web:* ramsgatevet.com	254-848-4083		794
Ramsoft Systems Inc 29777 Telegraph Rd Ste 2250 . . . . Southfield MI 48034 *Web:* ramsoft.net	248-354-0100		177
Ramson's Imports Inc (RI) 5159 Sinclair Rd . . . . Columbus OH 43229 *TF:* 800-669-0874 ■ *Web:* www.ramsonsimports.com	614-846-4447	846-4809	328
Ramtech Building Systems Inc 1400 Hwy 287 S . . . . Mansfield TX 76063 *TF:* 800-568-9376 ■ *Web:* www.ramtechmodular.com	817-473-9376	473-3485	186
RAN (Rainforest Action Network) 425 Bush St Ste 300 . . . . San Francisco CA 94108 *TF:* 800-368-1819 ■ *Web:* www.ran.org	415-398-4404	398-2732	48-13
Ran One Inc 7567 Amador Valley Blvd Ste 304 . . . . Dublin CA 94568 **Fax Area Code:* 925 ■ *Web:* global.ranone.com	510-535-9730	833-9658*	463
Ranac 11650 Lantern Rd Ste 111 . . . . Fishers IN 46038 *TF:* 888-335-0427 ■ *Web:* ranac.com	888-335-0427		180
Ranalli & Zaniel - Reno LLC 50 W Liberty St Ste 1050 . . . . Reno NV 89501 *Web:* ranallilawyers.com	775-786-4441		41
Ranalli Zaniel Fowler & Moran LLC 2400 W Horizon Ridge Pkwy . . . . Henderson NV 89052 *Web:* www.ranallilawyers.com	702-477-7774	477-7778	341
Ra-Nav Laboratories Inc 3100 W I 44 Service Rd . . . . Oklahoma City OK 73112 *Web:* www.rnlinc.com	405-947-3361	947-8343	261
Rance Industries Inc 1361 Heck Rd . . . . Columbiana OH 44408 *Web:* www.ranceindustries.com	330-482-1745	482-1727	480
Ranch at Steamboat 1800 Ranch Rd . . . . Steamboat Springs CO 80487 *TF:* 888-686-8075 ■ *Web:* www.ranch-steamboat.com	970-879-3000		379
Ranch at Ucross, The 1701 Sheridan Ave . . . . Cody WY 82414 *Web:* www.blairhotels.com	307-737-2281		206
Ranch Inn 45 E Pearl St . . . . Jackson WY 83001 *TF:* 800-348-5599 ■ *Web:* www.ranchinn.com	307-733-6363	733-0623	379
Rancher Labs 19409 Stevens Creek Blvd Ste 260 . . . . Cupertino CA 95014 *Web:* rancher.com	408-775-7190		788
Ranchers Club of New Mexico 1901 University Blvd NE . . . . Albuquerque NM 87102 *Web:* www.theranchersclubofnm.com	505-889-8071		671
Rancho Alegre Lodge 3600 S Pk Loop Rd PO Box 998 . . . . Jackson WY 83001 *Web:* www.ranchoalegre.com	307-733-7988		379
Rancho Bernardo Inn 17550 Bernardo Oaks Dr . . . . San Diego CA 92128 *TF:* 877-517-9340 ■ *Web:* www.ranchobernardoinn.com	858-675-8500	675-8501	671
Rancho Building Materials Inc 4701 Wible Rd . . . . Bakersfield CA 93313	661-831-0831		183
Rancho Chico Family Restaurant 9205 N Division St . . . . Spokane WA 99218 *Web:* www.mexicanrestaurantspokane.com	509-467-0022		671
Rancho Cordova Chamber of Commerce 2729 Prospect Park Dr Ste 117 . . . . Rancho Cordova CA 95670 *Web:* ranchocordova.org	916-273-5700	384-2046	139
Rancho Cucamonga Chamber of Commerce 9047 Arrow Rt Ste 180 . . . . Rancho Cucamonga CA 91730 *Web:* www.ranchochamber.org	909-987-1012	987-5917	139
Rancho de la Osa Guest Ranch 1 La Osa Ranch Rd . . . . Sasabe AZ 85633 *Web:* ranchodelaosa.com	520-339-1086		239
Rancho de los Caballeros 1551 S Vulture Mine Rd . . . . Wickenburg AZ 85390 *TF:* 800-684-5030 ■ *Web:* www.ranchodeloscaballeros.com	928-684-5484		669
Rancho Grande 1789 Central Park Ave . . . . Yonkers NY 10710 *Web:* www.ranchograndemex.com	914-337-3056		671
Rancho Los Alamitos Historic Ranch & Gardens 6400 E Bixby Hill Rd . . . . Long Beach CA 90815 *Web:* rancholosalamitos.com	562-431-3541	430-9694	520
Rancho Los Amigos National Rehabilitation Ctr 7601 E Imperial Hwy . . . . Downey CA 90242 *TF:* 877-726-2461 ■ *Web:* www.dhs.lacounty.gov	562-385-7111		374-6
Rancho Los Cerritos Historic Ranch 4600 Virginia Rd . . . . Long Beach CA 90807 *Web:* www.rancholoscerritos.org	562-206-2040	206-2049	520
Rancho Mission Viejo 28811 Ortega Hwy . . . . San Juan Capistrano CA 92675 *Web:* www.ranchomissionviejo.com	949-240-3363		653
Rancho Pinot Grill 6208 N Scottsdale Rd . . . . Scottsdale AZ 85253 *Web:* ranchopinot.com	480-367-8030		671
Rancho San Carlos Pet Clinic Inc 7850 Golfcrest Dr . . . . San Diego CA 92119 *Web:* ranchosancarlospet.com	619-462-6820		794
Rancho Santa Ana Botanic Garden 1500 N College Ave . . . . Claremont CA 91711 *Web:* www.rsabg.org	909-625-8767	626-7670	97
Rancho Santa Fe Protective Services Inc 1991 Vlg Pk Way Ste 100 . . . . Encinitas CA 92024 **Fax Area Code:* 760 ■ *TF:* 800-303-8877 ■ *Web:* www.rsfsecurity.com	800-303-8877	942-9387*	693

Phone | Fax | Class

Rancho Simi Insurance Agency
1611 E Los Angeles Ave . . . Simi Valley CA 93065 805-581-2128 390
Web: ranchosimiinsurance.com
Rancho Valencia Resort
5921 Valencia Cir PO Box 9126 . . . Rancho Santa Fe CA 92067 858-756-1123 756-0165 669
TF: 800-548-3664 ■ *Web:* www.ranchovalencia.com
Rancho Viejo Resort & Country Club
1 Rancho Viejo Dr . . . Rancho Viejo TX 78575 956-350-4000 365-2961 669
TF: 800-531-7400 ■ *Web:* www.rvrcc.com
Ranch-Way Inc 416 Linden St . . . Fort Collins CO 80524 970-482-1662 482-6963 447
Web: www.ranch-way.com
Ranco Fertiservice Inc
701 Hwy 71 . . . Sioux Rapids IA 50585 712-283-2525 283-2303 273
Web: www.rancofertiservice.com
Rancocas Nature Ctr
794 Rancocas Rd . . . Westampton NJ 08060 609-261-2495 544
Web: njaudubon.org
Rand & Jones Enterprises 18 Tracy St . . . Buffalo NY 14201 716-626-1080 626-1214 187
Web: www.randjones.com
Rand Capital Corp 2200 Rand Bldg . . . Buffalo NY 14203 716-853-0802 854-8480 405
NASDAQ: RAND ■ *Web:* www.randcapital.com
Rand Construction Co
1428 W Ninth St . . . Kansas City MO 64101 816-421-4143 421-4144 186
Web: www.randsc.com
Rand Corp 1776 Main St . . . Santa Monica CA 90401 310-393-0411 393-4818 634
TF: 877-584-8642 ■ *Web:* www.rand.org
Rand Financial Services Inc
111 W Jackson Blvd Ste 1250 . . . Chicago IL 60604 312-559-8800 169
TF: 800-842-7263 ■ *Web:* www.randfinancial.com
Rand Graphics Inc 500 S Florence St . . . Wichita KS 67209 316-942-1218 627
TF: 800-435-7263 ■ *Web:* www.randgraphics.com
Rand Insurance Inc
1100 E Putnam Ave . . . Riverside CT 06878 203-637-1006 390
Web: www.randinsurance.com
Rand Logistics Inc
333 Washington St Ste 201 . . . Jersey City NJ 07302 212-863-9403 313
Web: www.randlogisticsinc.com
Rand Machine Products Inc
2072 Allen St Ext . . . Falconer NY 14733 716-665-5217 665-3374 757
Web: www.randmachine.com
Rand McNally 9855 Woods Dr PO Box 7600 . . . Skokie IL 60077 800-333-0136 637-1
TF: 800-333-0136 ■ *Web:* www.randmcnally.com
Rand Mintzer Attorney at Law
1523 Yale St . . . Houston TX 77008 713-862-8880 869-1517 41
Web: www.mintzerlaw.com
Randall & Danskin P S
601 W Riverside Ave Ste 1500 . . . Spokane WA 99201 509-747-2052 445
Web: www.randalldanskin.com
Randall & Stein PA 70 S Orange Ave . . . Livingston NJ 07039 973-994-4710 41
Web: randallandstein.com
Randall Bearings Inc
1046 Greenlawn Ave PO Box 1258 . . . Lima OH 45802 419-223-1075 228-0200 483
Web: www.randallbearings.com
Randall Bros Inc 665 Marietta St NW . . . Atlanta GA 30313 404-892-6666 875-6102 499
TF: 800-476-4539 ■ *Web:* www.randallbrothers.com
Randall County 501 16th St Ste 305 . . . Canyon TX 79015 806-468-5505 338
Web: randallcounty.com
Randall Foods Inc PO Box 2669 . . . Huntington Park CA 90255 323-261-6565 619
TF: 800-427-2632 ■ *Web:* www.randallfoods.com
Randall Manufacturing LLC
722 Church Rd . . . Elmhurst IL 60126 630-782-0001 608
TF: 800-323-7424 ■ *Web:* www.randallmfg.com
Randall Metals Corp
2483 Greenleaf Ave . . . Elk Grove Village IL 60007 847-952-9690 492
Web: www.randallmetals.com
Randall Museum 199 Museum Way . . . San Francisco CA 94114 415-554-9600 554-9609 520
TF: 866-807-7148 ■ *Web:* www.randallmuseum.org
Randall S. Miller & Associates PC
43252 Woodward Ave Ste 180 . . . Bloomfield Hills MI 48302 248-335-9200 41
TF: 844-322-6558 ■ *Web:* www.millerlaw.biz
Randall-Reilly Publishing Co
3200 Rice Mine Rd NE . . . Tuscaloosa AL 35406 205-349-2990 637-9
TF: 800-633-5953 ■ *Web:* www.randallreilly.com
Randcastle Extrusion Systems Inc
220 Little Falls Rd Ste 6 . . . Cedar Grove NJ 07009 973-239-1150 239-0830 604
Web: www.randcastle.com
Randles Sand & Gravel Inc
5802 192nd St E . . . Puyallup WA 98375 253-531-6800 503-4
Web: www.randlessandandgravel.net
Rando Machine Corp
1071 Rt 31 PO Box 614 . . . Macedon NY 14502 315-986-2761 986-7943 744
Web: www.randomachine.com
Randol International Ltd
21578 Mountsfield Dr . . . Golden CO 80401 303-526-1626 401
Web: www.randol.com
Randolph Area Chamber of Commerce
PO Box 391 . . . Mount Freedom NJ 07970 973-361-3462 139
TF: 800-366-3922 ■ *Web:* randolphchamber.org
Randolph Austin Company Inc
2119 FM 1626 PO Box 988 . . . Manchaca TX 78652 512-282-1590 641
TF: 800-531-5263 ■ *Web:* www.randolphaustin.com
Randolph Broadcasting Inc
1119 Eastview Dr . . . Asheboro NC 27203 336-625-2187 626-9292 645-141
Web: www.wkxr.com
Randolph Builders PO Box 410283 . . . Charlotte NC 28241 704-588-7116 588-8280 186
Web: www.randolphbuilders.com
Randolph College 2500 Rivermont Ave . . . Lynchburg VA 24503 434-947-8000 947-8996 166
TF: 800-745-7692 ■ *Web:* www.randolphcollege.edu
Randolph Community College
629 Industrial Park Ave PO Box 1009 . . . Asheboro NC 28203 336-633-0200 629-4695 162
Web: www.randolph.edu
Randolph Correctional Ctr
2760 US Hwy 220 PO Box 4128 . . . Asheboro NC 27203 336-625-2578 625-5717 213
Web: www.ncdps.gov
Randolph County 725 McDowell Rd . . . Asheboro NC 27205 336-318-6200 338
Web: www.co.randolph.nc.us
Randolph County 1 Taylor St . . . Chester IL 62233 618-826-5000 338
Web: randolphcountyclerk.com
Randolph County 1302 N Randolph Ave . . . Elkins WV 26241 304-636-2780 338
TF: 800-422-3304 ■ *Web:* www.randolphcountywv.com
Randolph County 372 Hwy JJ . . . Huntsville MO 65259 844-277-6555 338
TF: 844-277-6555 ■ *Web:* www.randolphcounty-mo.com
Randolph County
100 S Main St PO Box 230 . . . Winchester IN 47394 765-584-7207 338
Web: www.randolphcounty.us
Randolph County Chamber of Commerce
3355 US Hwy 431 Ste 11 PO Box 431 . . . Roanoke AL 36274 334-863-6612 863-7280 338
Web: randolphcountyal.com
Randolph Electric Membership Corp
879 McDowell Rd PO Box 40 . . . Asheboro NC 27204 336-625-5177 626-1551 245
TF: 800-672-8212 ■ *Web:* www.randolphemc.com
Randolph Health
364 White Oak St PO Box 1048 . . . Asheboro NC 27204 336-625-5151 625-4393 374-3
Web: www.randolphhealth.org
Randolph Packing Co
275 Roma Jean Pkwy . . . Streamwood IL 60107 630-830-3100 296-26
TF: 800-451-1607 ■ *Web:* www.randolphpacking.com
Randolph Public Library 201 Worth St . . . Asheboro NC 27203 336-318-6800 318-6823 434-3
Web: www.randolphlibrary.org
Randolph Savings Bank 129 N Main St . . . Randolph MA 02368 781-963-2100 70
TF: 877-963-2100 ■ *Web:* www.envisionbank.com
Randolph-Brooks Federal Credit Union
PO Box 2097 . . . Universal City TX 78148 210-945-3300 219
TF: 800-580-3300 ■ *Web:* www.rbfcu.org
Randolph-Macon Academy
200 Academy Dr . . . Front Royal VA 22630 540-636-5200 636-5419 622
TF: 800-272-1172 ■ *Web:* www.rma.edu
Randolph-Macon College PO Box 5005 . . . Ashland VA 23005 804-752-7200 752-4707 166
TF: 800-888-1762 ■ *Web:* www.rmc.edu
Random Lengths News
1300 S Pacific Ave . . . San Pedro CA 90731 310-519-1442 832-1000 532-5
Web: www.randomlengthsnews.com
Randr Inc 3764 Ninth St . . . Riverside CA 92501 951-369-3427 275
Web: www.randrinc.com
Randsman Artist Management
400 W 43rd St Ste 18E . . . New York NY 10036 212-244-5874 731
Web: www.randsman.com
Randstad Canada
810 Boul De Maisonneuve Ste 1 . . . Montreal QC H3A3E6 514-350-0033 631
Web: www.randstad.ca
Randstad Engineering
6200 the Corners Pkwy Ste 100 . . . Norcross GA 30092 770-390-9888 193
Web: www.randstadusa.com
Rand-Whitney Container LLC
1 Agrand St . . . Worcester MA 01607 508-890-7000 792-1578 100
Web: www.randwhitney.com
Randy Potter School of Piano Technology
61592 SE Orion Dr . . . Bend OR 97702 541-382-5411 382-5400 685
Web: www.pianotuning.com
Randy Wilcox Insurance Agency Inc
11115 S Eastern Ave Ste 130 . . . Henderson NV 89052 702-617-9111 390
Web: randywilcox.net
Randy's Jewelry Inc 309 S Main St . . . O'Fallon MO 63366 636-978-1953 410
Web: www.randys-jewelry.com
Randys Environmental Services
4351 US Hwy 12 SE PO Box 169 . . . Delano MN 55328 763-972-3335 192
Web: www.randysenvironmentalservices.com
Rane Corp 10802 47th Ave W . . . Mukilteo WA 98275 425-355-6000 347-7757 52
TF: 877-764-0093 ■ *Web:* www.rane.com
Rane Precision Die Casting Inc
232 Hopkinsville Rd . . . Russellville KY 42276 270-726-2441 726-6468 60
Web: www.pdc-na.com
R-Anell Custom Homes Inc
235 Anthony Grave Rd . . . Crouse NC 28033 800-951-5511 505
TF: 800-951-5511 ■ *Web:* www.r-anell.com
Ranfac Corp PO Box 635 . . . Avon MA 02322 508-588-4400 584-8588 476
Web: www.ranfac.com
Rangam Consultants Inc
270 Davidson Ave Ste 103 . . . Somerset NJ 08873 908-704-8843 253-6550 225
TF: 877-388-1858 ■ *Web:* rangam.com
Rangaswamy & Associates Inc
304 W Liberty St . . . Louisville KY 40202 502-589-2212 589-2240 261
Web: rangaswamy.com
Range Commanders Council (RCC)
Bldg. 1510 . . . White Sands Missile Range NM 88002 505-678-1107 678-7519 637-2
Web: www.wsmr.army.mil
Range LP Gas 1613 E Camp St . . . Ely MN 55731 218-365-8888 316
Web: rangelp.com
Range Ponds State Park PO Box 475 . . . Poland ME 04274 207-998-4104 565
Web: www.maine.gov
Range Printing 1022 Madison St . . . Brainerd MN 56401 218-829-5982 627
Web: www.rangeprinting.com
Range Resources Corp
100 Throckmorton St Ste 1200 . . . Fort Worth TX 76102 817-870-2601 869-9100 536
NYSE: RRC ■ *Web:* www.rangeresources.com
Range-Ledger, The
41 S 1st E St . . . Cheyenne Wells CO 80810 719-767-5615 767-5113 433
Web: townofcheyennewells.com
Rangeley Lake State Park
HC 32 PO Box 5000 . . . Rangeley ME 04970 207-864-3858 565
Web: www.maine.gov
Rangely Times 713 E Main . . . Rangely CO 81648 970-675-5033 675-8709 532-2
Web: www.theheraldtimes.com
Rangen Inc 115 13th Ave S . . . Buhl ID 83316 208-543-6421 543-6090 447
TF: 800-657-6446 ■ *Web:* www.rangen.com
Ranger American
Calle Marginal Lodi 605 Ave 65 Infanteria Villa Capri
PO Box 29105 . . . San Juan PR 00924 787-999-6060 999-6050 693
Web: www.rangeramerican.com
Ranger Automation Systems Inc
9 Railroad Ave . . . Millbury MA 01527 508-865-0151 386
Web: rangerautomation.com
Ranger College 1100 College Cir . . . Ranger TX 76470 254-647-3234 647-3739 162
Web: www.rangercollege.edu
Ranger Construction Industries Inc
101 Sansbury's Way . . . West Palm Beach FL 33411 561-793-9400 790-4332 188-4
TF: 800-969-9402 ■ *Web:* www.rangerconstruction.com

Name / Address	City	State	ZIP	Phone	Fax	Class
Ranger Creek Ranch PO Box 47	Shell	WY	82441	307-765-4636		239
Web: www.rangercreekranch.net						
Ranger Industries Inc 15 Park Rd	Tinton Falls	NJ	07724	732-389-3535	389-1102	388
TF: 800-244-2211 ■ *Web:* rangerink.com						
Ranger Steel Supply Corp						
1225 N Loop W Ste 650	Houston	TX	77008	713-633-1306		492
Web: www.rangersteel.com						
Ranger Tool & Die Co						
317 S Westervelt Rd	Saginaw	MI	48604	989-754-1403	754-4803	757
Web: www.ranger-tool.com						
Rangers Die Casting Co						
10828 S Alameda St	Lynwood	CA	90262	310-764-1800		492
TF: 877-386-9969 ■ *Web:* www.rangersdiecasting.com						
Rangeview Library District						
5877 E 120th Ave	Thornton	CO	80602	303-288-2001	451-0190	434-3
Web: www.anythinklibraries.org						
Ranken Energy Corp 457 W 18th St	Edmond	OK	73013	405-340-2363		536
Web: www.ranken-energy.com						
Ranken Technical College						
4431 Finney Ave	Saint Louis	MO	63113	314-371-0236	286-3309	167-3
TF: 866-472-6536 ■ *Web:* www.ranken.edu						
Rankin Automation Company LLC						
888 Sussex Blvd	Broomall	PA	19008	610-544-6800	328-6594	385
Web: www.rankinautomation.com						
Rankin County						
211 E Government St Ste A	Brandon	MS	39042	601-825-1475	825-9600	338
Web: www.rankinchamber.com						
Rankin, Hill, Porter & Clark LLP						
23755 Lorain Rd Ste 200	North Olmsted	OH	44070	216-566-9700		428
Web: rankinhill.com						
Ranor Inc 1 Bella Dr	Westminster	MA	01473	978-874-0591	874-2748	480
Web: www.ranor.com						
Ran-Pro Farms Inc PO Box 300	Tyler	TX	75710	903-593-7381	592-8108	192
TF: 800-749-6266 ■ *Web:* www.ranprofarms.com						
Ransdell, Roach & Royse PLLC						
176 Pasadena Dr Bldg One	Lexington	KY	40503	859-276-6262		41
Web: rrrfirm.com						
Ransom & Randolph Co						
3535 Briarfield Blvd	Maumee	OH	43537	419-865-9497	865-9997	663
TF: 800-800-7496 ■ *Web:* www.ransom-randolph.com						
Ransom County Gazette PO Box 473	Lisbon	ND	58054	701-683-4128		532-2
Web: www.rcgazette.com						
Rantec Microwave Systems Inc						
24003 Ventura Blvd	Calabasas	CA	91302	818-223-5000	223-5199	647
Web: www.rantecantennas.com						
Rantec Power Systems Inc						
1173 Los Olivos Ave	Los Osos	CA	93402	805-596-6000		767
Web: www.rantec.com						
Rao Design International Inc						
9451 Ainslie	Schiller Park	IL	60176	847-671-6182	671-9276	695
Web: www.newraodesign.com						
Rapafusyn Research & Development						
855 N Wolfe St	Baltimore	MD	21205	410-995-8234		237
Web: rapafusyn.com						
Rapaport Diamond Corp (RDC)						
1212 Avenue of the Americas Ste 801	New York	NY	10036	702-893-9400	840-0243*	637-9
**Fax Area Code:* 212 ■ *Web:* www.diamonds.net						
Rapat Corp 919 Odonnel St	Hawley	MN	56549	218-483-3344	483-3535	207
TF: 800-325-6377 ■ *Web:* www.rapat.com						
RAPCO Inc 445 Cardinal Ln	Hartland	WI	53029	262-367-2292	367-7158	22
TF: 800-527-2726 ■ *Web:* rapcoinc.com						
Rape Abuse & Incest National Network (RAINN)						
2000 L St NW Ste 406	Washington	DC	20036	202-544-1034	544-3556	48-6
TF: 800-656-4673 ■ *Web:* www.rainn.org						
Raphael Kansas City 325 Ward Pkwy	Kansas City	MO	64112	816-756-3800	802-2131	379
TF: 800-821-5343 ■ *Web:* www.raphaelkc.com						
Raphael's School of Beauty Culture						
2445 W State St	Alliance	OH	44601	330-823-3884	240-7277	685
TF: 800-511-6405 ■ *Web:* www.raphaelsbeautyschool.edu						
Rapid Bind Inc 2728 SE 14th Ave	Portland	OR	97202	503-231-8898	232-6452	92
Web: www.rapidbind.com						
Rapid Chevrolet Company Inc						
2323 E Mall Dr	Rapid City	SD	57701	605-343-1282		516
Web: www.dennymenholtrapidchevrolet.com						
Rapid City Journal 507 Main St	Rapid City	SD	57701	605-394-8300		532-2
TF: 800-843-2300 ■ *Web:* www.rapidcityjournal.com						
Rapid City Regional Health						
353 Fairmont Blvd	Rapid City	SD	57701	605-755-8829		374-3
Web: www.regionalhealth.com						
Rapid Controls Inc						
2693 Commerce Rd Ste G	Rapid City	SD	57702	605-348-7688	341-5496	253
TF: 888-510-7688 ■ *Web:* www.rapidcontrols.com						
Rapid Displays 4300 W 47th St	Chicago	IL	60632	773-927-1091		233
TF: 800-356-5775 ■ *Web:* www.rapiddisplays.com						
Rapid Engineering Inc						
1100 7-Mile Rd NW	Comstock Park	MI	49321	616-784-0500		318
TF: 800-536-3461 ■ *Web:* www.rapidengineering.com						
Rapid Fire Marketing Inc						
311 W Third St Ste 1234	Carson City	NV	89703	404-261-1196		477
Web: rapid-fire-marketing.com						
Rapid Global Business Solutions Inc						
1200 Stephenson Hwy	Troy	MI	48083	248-589-1135		261
Web: www.rgbsi.com						
Rapid Industries 4003 Oaklawn Dr	Louisville	KY	40219	502-968-3645	968-6331	207
TF: 800-727-4381 ■ *Web:* www.rapidindustries.com						
Rapid Insight Inc						
53 Technology Ln Ste 112	Conway	NH	03818	888-585-6511		177
TF: 888-585-6511 ■ *Web:* www.rapidinsightinc.com						
Rapid Line Industries Inc						
455 N Ottawa St	Joliet	IL	60432	815-727-4362		111
TF: 877-444-9955 ■ *Web:* rapidline.com						
Rapid Pathogen Screening Inc						
7227 Delainey Ct	Sarasota	FL	34240	941-556-1850		476
Web: www.rpsdetectors.com						
Rapid Press Printing & Copy Center Inc						
608 Lake St S	Forest Lake	MN	55025	651-464-6200	464-2645	627
Web: www.rapidpressprinting.com						
Rapid Printers of Monterey						
201 Foam St	Monterey	CA	93940	831-373-1822		627
Web: rapidprinters.com						
Rapid Pump & Meter Service Company Inc						
285 Straight St PO Box AY	Paterson	NJ	07509	973-345-5600	345-0301	627
Web: www.rapidservice.com						
Rapid Rater Co PO Box 13055	Tallahassee	FL	32317	850-893-7346		627
Web: www.rapidpress.com						
Rapid Ratings Pty Ltd						
86 Chambers St Ste 701	New York	NY	10007	646-233-4600		194
Web: www.rapidratings.com						
Rapid Response Marketing LLC						
Xy7Elite						
7500 W Lake Mead Blvd Ste 9463	Las Vegas	NV	89128	702-848-3954		193
Web: www.xy7elite.com						
Rapid Response Monitoring Services Inc						
400 W Division St	Syracuse	NY	13204	800-558-7767		693
TF: 800-558-7767 ■ *Web:* www.rrms.com						
Rapid Software Corp 3079 Parr Ln	Grapevine	TX	76051	817-251-0615		177
Web: www.rapidsw.com						
Rapid Transcript Inc						
4311 Wilshire Blvd	Los Angeles	CA	90010	323-964-0400		478
Web: www.rapidtranscript.com						
rapid! PayCard 5300 W Cypress St Ste 150	Tampa	FL	33607	888-727-4314		2
TF: 888-727-4314 ■ *Web:* www.rapidpaycard.com						
RAPIDES FOUNDATION, The						
2001 Macarthur Dr	Alexandria	LA	71301	318-769-3000		374-3
TF: 877-801-8441 ■ *Web:* rapidesregional.com						
Rapides Parish PO Box 952	Alexandria	LA	71309	318-473-8153	473-4667	338
Web: rapidesclerk.org						
Rapides Parish Library						
411 Washington St	Alexandria	LA	71301	318-445-2411		434-3
Web: www.rpl.org						
Rapids Christian Press Inc						
3031 Plover Rd	Wisconsin Rapids	WI	54494	715-421-3250	423-5404	627
Web: www.the-printshop.com						
RAPIDS Wholesale Equipment Co						
6201 S Gateway Dr	Marion	IA	52302	319-447-1670	447-1680	300
TF: 800-472-7431 ■ *Web:* rapidswholesale.com						
Rapidsoft Systems Inc						
7 Diamond Ct	Princeton Junction	NJ	08550	609-439-4775		631
Web: www.rapidsoftsystems.com						
RapidValue						
7901 Stoneridge Dr Ste 225	Pleasanton	CA	94588	925-398-3344		180
Web: www.rapidvaluesolutions.com						
Rapier Solutions Inc 3095 Senna Dr	Matthews	NC	28105	704-321-2271		180
Web: rapiersolutions.com						
Rapit Printing Inc						
1415 First Ave NW	New Brighton	MN	55112	651-633-4600	633-9512	627
Web: rapit.com						
Rapoport Law Offices PC						
20 N Clark St Ste 3500	Chicago	IL	60602	312-327-9880	327-9881	41
TF: 877-216-4213 ■ *Web:* rapoportlaw.com						
Rapp Advertising Inc						
150 Morris Ave Ste 200	Springfield	NJ	07081	973-467-5570		7
Web: www.rappadvertising.com						
Rappahannock Community College						
Glenns 12745 College Dr	Glenns	VA	23149	804-758-6700	758-6830	162
TF: 800-836-9381 ■ *Web:* www.rappahannock.edu						
Rappahannock County						
290 Gay St PO Box 519	Washington	VA	22747	540-675-5330	675-5331	338
Web: www.rappahannockcountyva.gov						
Rappahannock Electric Coop						
247 Industrial Ct	Fredericksburg	VA	22404	540-898-8500	891-5878	245
TF: 800-552-3904 ■ *Web:* www.myrec.coop						
RAPS (Regulatory Affairs Professionals Society)						
5635 Fishers Ln Ste 550	Rockville	MD	20852	301-770-2920	770-2924	49-8
Web: www.raps.org						
Raptim Humanitarian Travel						
6420 Inducon Dr W Ste A	Sanborn	NY	14132	716-754-9232	754-2881	772
TF: 800-272-7846 ■ *Web:* www.raptim.org						
Raque Food Systems LLC						
PO Box 99594	Louisville	KY	40269	502-267-9641	267-2352	547
Web: www.raque.com						
Rare Bird Inc						
8555 Cedar Pl Dr Ste 114	Indianapolis	IN	46240	317-251-6744		7
Web: www.rarebirdinc.com						
Rare Earth Hardwoods Inc						
6778 E Traverse Hwy	Traverse City	MI	49684	231-946-0043	968-0094*	683
**Fax Area Code:* 800 ■ *TF:* 800-968-0074 ■ *Web:* www.rare-earth-hardwoods.com						
Raritan Bay Medical Ctr						
530 New Brunswick Ave	Perth Amboy	NJ	08861	732-442-3700		374-3
TF: 800-701-0710 ■ *Web:* www.rbmc.org						
Raritan Center Travel II						
110 Fieldcrest Ave	Edison	NJ	08837	732-225-2900		772
Web: www.sairealestate.com						
Raritan Computer Inc						
400 Cottontail Ln	Somerset	NJ	08873	732-764-8886	764-8887	253
TF: 800-724-8090 ■ *Web:* www.raritan.com						
Raritan Pharmaceuticals Inc						
8 Joanna Ct	East Brunswick	NJ	08816	732-432-8200	432-8255	231
Web: www.raritanpharm.com						
Raritan Valley Community College						
PO Box 3300	Somerville	NJ	08876	908-526-1200	704-3442	162
TF: 888-326-4058 ■ *Web:* www.raritanval.edu						
Ras Kassa's Ethiopian Restaurant						
802 S Public Rd	LaFayette	CO	80026	303-604-6885		671
Web: www.raskassas.com						
Rasansky Law Firm						
2525 McKinnon Ave Ste 550	Dallas	TX	75201	214-651-6100	651-6150	637-6
OTC: ATTY ■ *TF:* 877-405-4313 ■ *Web:* www.jrlawfirm.com						
Rasar State Park 38730 Cape Horn Rd	Concrete	WA	98237	360-826-3942		565
Web: parks.state.wa.us						
Rash, Chapman, Schreiber, Leaverton & Morrison LLP						
2112 Rio Grande St	Austin	TX	78705	512-477-7543		428
Web: www.rashchapman.com						
Rasi Laboratories Inc						
20 Roosevelt Ave	Somerset	NJ	08873	732-873-8500		231
Web: www.rasilabs.com						

	Phone	Fax	Class
RASIRC Inc 7815 Silverton Ave ... San Diego CA 92126 *Web:* www.rasirc.com	858-259-1220		610
Raskin Jamie (Rep D - MD) 412 Cannon House Office Bldg ... Washington DC 20515 *Web:* raskin.house.gov	202-225-5341		342-2
Raskob Kambourian Financial Advisors Ltd 4100 N First Ave ... Tucson AZ 85719 *Web:* www.rkfin.com	520-690-1999		401
Rasmussen College 130 Saint Andrews Dr ... Mankato MN 56001 *TF:* 800-657-6767 ■ *Web:* www.rasmussen.edu	507-625-6556	625-6557	166
Rasmussen Equipment Co 3333 West 2100 South ... Salt Lake City UT 84119 *TF:* 800-453-8032 ■ *Web:* www.raseq.com	801-972-5588	972-2215	358
Rasmussen Equipment Co 2220 Engineers Rd ... Belle Chasse LA 70037 *TF:* 800-227-7920 ■ *Web:* www.rasmussenco.com	504-392-0442	392-0107	358
Rasmussen Iron Works Inc 12028 E Philadelphia St ... Whittier CA 90601 *Web:* www.rasmussen.biz	562-696-8718	698-3510	357
Rasmussen Software Inc 10240 SW Nimbus Ave Ste L9 ... Portland OR 97223 *Web:* anzio.com	503-624-0360	624-0760	177
Rasmussen Teller O Neil & Christman Pc 555 Michigan St ... Petoskey MI 49770 *Web:* rtoccpa.com	231-347-5555		2
Rast Iron Works PO Box 792002 ... San Antonio TX 78279 *Web:* www.rastironworks.com	210-659-6704		480
Rata Associates LLC 1916 Boothe Cir ... Longwood FL 32750 *Web:* www.rataassociates.com	407-831-7282		177
Ratcliffe Hicks School of Agriculture University of Connecticut Office of Academic Programs ... Storrs CT 06269 *Web:* www.rhsa.uconn.edu	860-486-2919	486-4643	685
RateHubca 411 Richmond St E Ste 208 ... Toronto ON M5A3S5 *TF:* 800-679-9622 ■ *Web:* www.ratehub.ca	800-679-9622		466
RateMyProfessorscom LLC 1515 Broadway ... New York NY 10036 *Web:* www.ratemyprofessors.com	212-654-7763		387
Ratespecial LLC 35 N Arroyo Pkwy Ste 250 ... Pasadena CA 91103 *Web:* www.ratespecial.com	626-376-4702		5
Rathbun's Restaurant 112 Krog St ... Atlanta GA 30307 *Web:* www.kevinrathbun.com	404-524-8280		671
Rathgeber Goss Associates PC 15871 Crabbs Branch Way ... Rockville MD 20855 *Web:* rath-goss.com	301-590-0071		261
Rathgeber Hospitality House 1615 12th St ... Wichita Falls TX 76301 *Web:* rathgeberhospitalityhouse.org	940-764-2400	764-2456	372
Rathskeller Restaurant 401 E Michigan St ... Indianapolis IN 46204 *Web:* www.rathskeller.com	317-636-0396		671
Rational Energies LLC 14920 27th Ave N ... Plymouth MN 55447 *Web:* www.rationalenergies.com	952-807-0080		196
Ratliff CPA Inc 2020 E 15th St Ste A ... Edmond OK 73013 *Web:* ratliffcpa.com	405-478-1800		2
Ratner Steel Supply Company Inc 2500 W County Rd B ... Roseville MN 55113 *Web:* www.ratnersteel.com	651-631-8515		492
Rattikin Title Co 201 Main St Ste 800 ... Fort Worth TX 76102 *Web:* www.rattikintitle.com	817-332-1171	882-9886	391-6
Rauch Industries Inc 3800A Little Mountain Rd ... Gastonia NC 28056	704-867-5333		334
Raulerson GYN LLC 1713 Hwy 441 N Ste F ... Okeechobee FL 34972 *Web:* raulersongyn.com	863-763-8000	763-8212	352
Raulerson Hospital 1796 Hwy 441 N ... Okeechobee FL 34972 *TF:* 877-549-9337 ■ *Web:* raulersonhospital.com	863-763-2151		374-3
Raulli & Sons Inc 213 Teall Ave ... Syracuse NY 13210 *Web:* www.raulliandsons.com	315-479-6693		480
Raute Wood Inc 4836 Hickory Hill Rd Ste 128 ... Memphis TN 38141 *TF:* 800-448-8592 ■ *Web:* www.raute.com	800-448-8592	615-1379	821
Rauxa Direct LLC 275 McCormick Ave A ... Costa Mesa CA 92626 *Web:* www.rauxa.com	714-427-1271		5
Ravalli County 215 S Fourth St Ste C ... Hamilton MT 59840 *Web:* ravalli.us	406-375-6555	375-6595	338
Ravalli County Electric Co-opeartive Inc 1051 Eastside Hwy ... Corvallis MT 59828 *Web:* www.ravallielectric.com	406-961-3001	961-3230	245
Ravalli Republic 232 W Main St ... Hamilton MT 59840 *Web:* www.ravallirepublic.com	406-363-3300	363-1767	532-2
Rave Computer Association Inc 7171 Sterling Ponds Ct ... Sterling Heights MI 48312 *TF:* 800-966-7283 ■ *Web:* www.rave.com	800-966-7283		174
Rave Mobile Safety 492 Old Connecticut Path 2nd Fl ... Framingham MA 01701 *TF:* 888-605-7164 ■ *Web:* www.ravemobilesafety.com	508-848-2484	532-0564	177
Rave/Eagles Club, The 2401 W Wisconsin Ave ... Milwaukee WI 53233 *Web:* www.therave.com	414-342-7283		572
Raven Capital Management LLC 110 Greene St Ste 9G ... New York NY 10012 *Web:* www.ravencm.com	212-966-7926		528
Raven Computers 5956 Odana Rd ... Madison WI 53719 *Web:* ravencomputers.com	608-661-1372		175
Raven Industries Inc 205 E Sixth St ... Sioux Falls SD 57104 *NASDAQ:* RAVN ■ *TF:* 800-243-5435 ■ *Web:* ravenind.com	605-336-2750	335-0268	600
Raven One to One Marketing 1020 Airport Rd ... Allentown PA 18109 *Web:* raven121.com	484-240-6500	240-6505	195
Raven Printing 325 S Union ... Lakewood CO 80228 *Web:* www.ravenprinting.com	303-989-9888		627
Raven Rock State Park 3009 Raven Rock Rd ... Lillington NC 27546 *Web:* www.ncparks.gov	910-893-4888		565
Raven Rocks Press 53650 Belmont Ridge Rd ... Beallsville OH 43716 *Web:* www.raven-rocks.org	740-926-1481		637-2
Raven Software Corp 8496 Greenway Blvd ... Middleton WI 53562 *Web:* www.ravensoftware.com	608-833-5791		225
Raven Transport Company Inc 6800 Broadway Ave ... Jacksonville FL 32254 *Web:* raventransport.com	904-880-1515		780
Ravenna Pattern & Manufacturing Inc 13101 E Apple Ave ... Ravenna MI 49451 *Web:* www.ravennapattern.com	231-853-2264		757
Ravens Grin inn 411 N Carroll St ... Mount Carroll IL 61053 *Web:* www.hauntedravensgrin.com	815-244-4746		760
Ravensberg Inc 1338 Strassner Dr ... Saint Louis MO 63144 *Web:* www.ravensberg.com	314-968-4020		321
Ravenswood Special Events 1100 W Cermak Rd Unit C411 ... Chicago IL 60608 *Web:* www.ravenswoodevents.com	312-633-2600		366
Ravenswood Studio Inc 6900 N Central Park Ave ... Lincolnwood IL 60712 *Web:* www.ravenswoodstudio.com	847-679-2800	679-2805	393
Ravenswood Winery Inc 18701 Gehricke Rd ... Sonoma CA 95476 *TF:* 888-669-4679 ■ *Web:* www.ravenswoodwinery.com	888-669-4679		80-3
Ravi Engineering & Land Surveying PC 2110 S Clinton Ave Ste 1 ... Rochester NY 14618 *Web:* www.ravieng.com	585-223-3660		261
Ravid & Associates P C 23855 Northwestern Hwy ... Southfield MI 48075 *Web:* ravidandassociates.com	248-948-9696		41
Ravine Gardens State Park 1600 Twigg St ... Palatka FL 32177 *Web:* www.floridastateparks.org	386-329-3721	329-3718	565
Raving Consulting Co 475 Hill St Ste G ... Reno NV 89501 *Web:* www.ravingconsulting.com	775-329-7864		463
Ravinia Festival Assn 418 Sheridan Rd ... Highland Park IL 60035 *Web:* www.ravinia.org	847-266-5000		720
Raw Art Works 37 Central Sq ... Lynn MA 01901 *Web:* www.rawartworks.org	781-593-5515		149
Rawah Ranch 11447 N County Rd 103 ... Jelm WY 82063 *TF:* 800-510-7071 ■ *Web:* rawahranch.com	800-510-7071		239
Rawhide Chemoil Inc 2650 N Rawhide Dr ... Fremont NE 68025 *TF:* 800-700-7601 ■ *Web:* www.rawhidechemoil.com	402-721-7601		316
Rawlco Radio Ltd 715 Saskatchewan Cres W ... Saskatoon SK S7M5V7 *Web:* www.rawlco.com	306-934-2222	477-0002	647
Rawle & Henderson 1339 Chestnut St One S Penn Sq The Widener Bldg 16th Fl ... Philadelphia PA 19107 *Web:* www.rawle.com	215-575-4200	563-2583	428
Rawlings Manufacturing Inc 1780 Idaho St ... Missoula MT 59801 *TF:* 866-762-9327 ■ *Web:* www.rawlingsmanufacturing.com	406-728-6182	728-7957	821
Rawlins County 205 N Fourth St Ste 1 ... Atwood KS 67730 *Web:* www.usd105.org	785-626-3236	626-3083	338
Rawlins Municipal Library 1000 E Church St ... Pierre SD 57501 *Web:* www.rawlinslibrary.org	605-773-7421		434-3
Rawls, Scheer, Clary & Mingo PLLC 1011 E Morehead St Ste 300 ... Charlotte NC 28204 *TF:* 866-388-0627 ■ *Web:* rdslaw.com	704-376-3200	332-3716	41
Rawson Inc 2010 McAllister ... Houston TX 77092 *TF:* 800-779-1414 ■ *Web:* www.rawsonlp.com	800-779-1414		246
Raxco Software Inc 6 Montgomery Village Ave Ste 500 ... Gaithersburg MD 20879 *TF:* 800-546-9728 ■ *Web:* www.raxco.com	301-527-0803	519-7711	178-12
Ray Allen Inc 400 W Erie Ste 400 ... Chicago IL 60654 *Web:* www.rayalleninc.com	312-895-0222		225
Ray Cammack Shows Inc PO Box 10 ... Laveen AZ 85339 *Web:* rcsfun.com	602-237-3333	237-2753	239
Ray Carlson & Associates Inc 411 Russell Ave ... Santa Rosa CA 95403 *Web:* rcmaps.com	707-528-7649	571-5541	261
Ray Catena Motor Car Corp 910 US Hwy 1 N ... Edison NJ 08817 *TF:* 800-639-2886 ■ *Web:* www.raycatena.com	732-549-6600		57
Ray County County Courthouse 100 W Main St ... Richmond MO 64085 *Web:* raycountymo.com	816-776-3377		338
Ray Gruver Insurance Financial Services 2802 S Laurel St ... Port Angeles WA 98362 *Web:* raygruver.com	360-457-4567		390
Ray H. Morris Co (RHM) 30 Precision Ct ... New Britain CT 06051 *TF:* 800-243-0662 ■ *Web:* www.rhmorris.com	860-224-2678	224-4134	385
Ray L. Hellwig Plumbing & Heating Inc 1301 Laurelwood Rd ... Santa Clara CA 95054 *TF:* 800-631-7013 ■ *Web:* www.rlhellwig.com	408-727-5612		189-10
Ray Machine Inc 12 Lynbrook Rd ... Baltimore MD 21220 *TF:* 800-801-6955 ■ *Web:* www.crumber.com	410-686-6955	686-5860	454
Ray Norbut State Fish & Wildlife Area 46816 290th Ave ... Griggsville IL 62340 *Web:* www.dnr.illinois.gov	217-833-2811		565
Ray Products Company Inc 1700 Chablis Ave ... Ontario CA 91761 *TF:* 800-423-7859 ■ *Web:* www.rayplastics.com	800-423-7859		602
Ray Quinney & Nebeker 36 S State St Ste 1400 ... Salt Lake City UT 84111 *Web:* rqn.com	801-532-1500		445
Ray Roberts Lake State Park 100 PW 4137 ... Pilot Point TX 76258 *Web:* tpwd.texas.gov	940-686-2148		565

Company	City	State	ZIP	Phone	Fax	Class
Ray Seraphin Ford Inc 100 Windsor Ave *TF:* 866-981-4724 ■ *Web:* www.rayseraphinfordinc.com	Vernon Rockville	CT	06066	866-981-4724		57
Ray Stone Inc (RSI) 550 Howe Ave Ste 100 *Web:* www.raystoneinc.com	Sacramento	CA	95825	916-649-7500		652
Ray's Boathouse 6049 Seaview Ave NW *Web:* www.rays.com	Seattle	WA	98107	206-789-3770	781-1960	671
Ray's in the City 240 Peachtree St NW *Web:* www.raysrestaurants.com	Atlanta	GA	30303	404-524-9224		671
Ray's the Steaks 2300 Wilson Blvd *Web:* www.raysthesteaks.com	Arlington	VA	22201	703-841-7297		671
Ray's Wholesale Meats Inc 2113 S 3rd Ave *Web:* raysmeats.com	Yakima	WA	98903	509-575-0729		297-9
Raybestos Powertrain LLC 711 Tech Dr *TF:* 800-729-7763 ■ *Web:* www.raybestospowertrain.com	Crawfordsville	IN	47933	800-729-7763		60
Raybourn Group Intl 9100 PuRdue Rd Ste 200 *TF:* 800-362-2546 ■ *Web:* raybourn.com	Indianapolis	IN	46268	317-328-4636	280-8527	47
Raycap Inc 806 S Clearwater Loop **Fax Area Code:* 800 ■ *Web:* www.raycap.com	Post Falls	ID	83854	208-777-1166	890-2569*	815
Rayco Industries Inc 1502 Valley Rd *TF:* 800-505-7111 ■ *Web:* www.raycoindustries.com	Richmond	VA	23222	804-321-7111		492
Raycom Electronics Inc 1 Raycom Rd *Web:* www.raycomelectronics.com	Dover	PA	17315	717-292-3641	292-2919	425
Raycom Media Inc 201 Monroe St RSA Tower 20th Fl *Web:* www.raycommedia.com	Montgomery	AL	36104	334-206-1400		738
Raycom Sports Inc 1900 W Morehead St *Web:* raycomsports.com	Charlotte	NC	28208	704-378-4400		739
Rayle Electric Membership Corp 616 Lexington Ave *Web:* www.rayleemc.com	Washington	GA	30673	706-678-2116	678-5381	245
Raymar Information Technology Inc 7325 Roseville Rd *TF:* 800-695-1951 ■ *Web:* raymar-telenetics.com	Sacramento	CA	95842	916-783-1951	783-1952	177
Raymarine Inc 9 Townsend W *TF:* 800-539-5539 ■ *Web:* www.raymarine.com	Nashua	NH	03063	603-324-7900	324-7995	529
Raymath Company Inc 2323 W SR-55 *Web:* www.raymath.com	Troy	OH	45373	937-335-1860	335-2500	757
Rayment & Collins Ltd 119 Ferrier St *Web:* www.raymentcollins.com	Markham	ON	L3R3K6	905-940-4030		627
Raymond Building Supply Corp 7751 Bayshore Rd *TF:* 877-731-7272 ■ *Web:* www.rbsc.net	North Fort Myers	FL	33917	239-731-8300	731-3299	191-3
Raymond Case Elementary School 8565 Shasta Lily Dr *Web:* www.blogs.egusd.net	Elk Grove	CA	95624	916-681-8820	681-8807	685
Raymond Communications Inc PO Box 4311 *Web:* www.raymond.com	Silver Spring	MD	20914	301-879-0628		196
Raymond Corp 22 S Canal St *TF:* 800-235-7200 ■ *Web:* www.raymondcorp.com	Greene	NY	13778	607-656-2311	656-9005	470
Raymond Excavating Company Inc 800 Gratiot Blvd *TF:* 800-837-6770 ■ *Web:* www.raymondexcavating.com	Marysville	MI	48040	810-364-6881		189-5
Raymond Express Intl (REI) 573 Forbes Blvd *Web:* www.reiexpress.com	South San Francisco	CA	94080	650-871-8560		311
Raymond F. Kravis Center for the Performing Arts 701 Okeechobee Blvd *TF:* 800-572-8471 ■ *Web:* www.kravis.org	West Palm Beach	FL	33401	561-832-7469	833-0691	572
Raymond Gary State Park HC 63 PO Box 1450 *Web:* www.travelok.com	Fort Towson	OK	74735	580-873-2307	326-2305	565
Raymond Group Inc, The 8333 Greenway Blvd Ste 200 *Web:* www.raymondteam.com	Middleton	WI	53562	608-833-4100		652
Raymond Handling Concepts Corp 41400 Boyce Rd *TF:* 800-675-2500 ■ *Web:* raymondhandling.com	Fremont	CA	94538	510-745-7500	745-7686	264-3
Raymond Intl PO Box 591 *Web:* www.globalrecruiter.com	Santa Cruz	CA	95060	831-429-1234	429-1272	721
Raymond James Ltd 2200-925 W Georgia St Cathedral Pl *TF:* 888-545-6624 ■ *Web:* www.raymondjames.ca	Vancouver	BC	V6C3L2	604-659-8000		401
Raymond James Stadium 4201 N Dale Mabry Hwy *Web:* www.tampasportsauthority.com	Tampa	FL	33607	813-350-6500	673-4308	720
Raymond James (USA) Ltd 925 W Georgia St Ste 2100 *TF:* 844-654-7357 ■ *Web:* www.rjlu.com	Vancouver	BC	V6C3L2	844-654-7357		691
Raymond L. Goodson Jr Inc 12001 N Central Expy Ste 300 *Web:* www.rlginc.com	Dallas	TX	75243	214-739-8100	739-6354	261
Raymond Martin Co 4709 Bluebonnet Blvd Ste A *Web:* www.raymondmartin.com	Baton Rouge	LA	70809	225-291-9300	291-5300	528
Raymond of New Jersey LLC 1000 Brighton St *Web:* www.raymond-nj.com	Union	NJ	07083	908-624-9570		358
Raymond R. Andy Guest Jr Shenandoah River State Park 350 Daughter of Stars Dr *Web:* www.dcr.virginia.gov	Bentonville	VA	22610	540-622-6840		565
Raymond Vineyard 849 Zinfandel Ln *TF:* 800-525-2659 ■ *Web:* raymondvineyards.com	Saint Helena	CA	94574	707-963-3141		80-3
Raymore Veterinary Center Inc 411 Remington Plaza Ct *Web:* raymorevetcenter.vetstreet.com	Raymore	MO	64083	816-331-2626		794
Raymour & Flanigan Furniture PO Box 220 *TF:* 866-383-4484 ■ *Web:* www.raymourflanigan.com	Liverpool	NY	13088	315-453-2500		321
Rayne Plane Inc 9107 Grand Prairie Hwy **Fax Area Code:* 713 ■ *Web:* www.rayneplane.com	Church Point	LA	70525	337-334-2101	634-2813*	273
Rayner Covering Systems Inc 665 Schneider Dr *TF:* 800-648-0757 ■ *Web:* www.raynercovering.com	South Elgin	IL	60177	847-695-2264	695-2363	608
Rayner's Seafood House 7343 Hwy 49 *Web:* www.raynersseafood.com	Hattiesburg	MS	39401	601-268-2639		671
Raynor Garage Doors 1101 E River Rd *TF:* 800-472-9667 ■ *Web:* www.raynor.com	Dixon	IL	61021	815-288-1431		234
Raynor Garage Doors of Lexingt 1033 Rushwood Ct *Web:* lexingtondoorauthority.com	Lexington	KY	40511	859-233-0802		378
Rayonier Inc Wildlight 1 Rayonier Way *TF:* 844-877-5263 ■ *Web:* www.rayonier.com	Yulee	FL	32097	904-357-9100		403
Rayotek Scientific Inc 11499 Sorrento Valley Rd *Web:* rayotek.com	San Diego	CA	92121	858-558-3671		696
Raypak Inc 2151 Eastman Ave *TF:* 800-438-4328 ■ *Web:* www.raypak.com	Oxnard	CA	93030	805-278-5300	278-5468	357
Raytech Industries 475 Smith St **Fax Area Code:* 860 ■ *TF:* 800-243-7163 ■ *Web:* www.raytech-ind.com	Middletown	CT	06457	800-243-7163	632-1699*	1
Raytex Fabrics Inc 130 Crossways Pk Dr *Web:* www.raytexindustries.com	Woodbury	NY	11797	516-584-1111		594
Raytheon Co 870 Winter St *NYSE: RTN* ■ *Web:* www.raytheon.com	Waltham	MA	02451	781-522-3000		529
Raytown Area Chamber of Commerce 5909 Raytown Trafficway *Web:* raytownchamber.com	Raytown	MO	64133	816-353-8500	353-8525	139
Raytrans Management Inc 56 W Maiden St *Web:* www.raytrans.com	Washington	PA	15301	412-321-0100	321-4343	194
Rayven Inc 431 Griggs St N *TF:* 800-878-3776 ■ *Web:* www.rayven.com	Saint Paul	MN	55104	651-642-1112	642-9497	628
Razberi Technologies Inc 13755 Hutton Dr Ste 500 *Web:* www.razberi.net	Farmers Branch	TX	75234	469-828-3380		693
Razoom Inc 420 Maple Way *Web:* www.razoom.com	Woodside	CA	94062	650-561-3037	561-3279	246
Razorgator 4216 3/4 Glencoe Ave *Web:* www.razorgator.com	Marina	CA	90292	310-481-3400		366
Razorleaf Corp 3766 Fishcreek Rd Ste 291 *Web:* www.razorleaf.com	Stow	OH	44224	330-676-0022		177
RAZR Marketing Inc 10590 Wayzata Blvd *Web:* razrmarketinginc.com	Minnetonka	MN	55305	763-404-6100		195
RB (Rosenthal Bros Inc) 740 Waukegan Rd PO Box 700 *Web:* www.rosenthalbros.com	Deerfield	IL	60015	847-940-4300	940-4315	390
RB Financial-mortgages Inc 44028 Mound Rd Ste 3 *Web:* www.rbfinancial.com	Sterling Heights	MI	48314	586-254-8435	254-8438	509
RB Humphreys Inc 5549 State Rte 233 *Web:* www.rbhumphreys.com	Westmoreland	NY	13490	315-838-2650	838-2651	780
RB Manufacturing Inc 140 W North St *Web:* www.rbmfg.com	Kirkland	IL	60146	815-522-3100	522-3131	625
RB Milestone Group 125 Park Ave 25th Fl *Web:* www.rbmilestone.com	New York	NY	10168	212-661-0075		401
RB Royal Industries Inc 1350 S Hickory St *TF:* 800-892-1550 ■ *Web:* www.rbroyal.com	Fond du Lac	WI	54937	920-921-1550	921-4713	621
RBC Bearings Inc 102 Willenbrock Rd **Fax Area Code:* 203 ■ *TF:* 800-390-3300 ■ *Web:* www.rbcbearings.com	Oxford	CT	06478	800-390-3300	267-5000*	620
RBC Capital Markets 200 Bay St S Tower 10th Fl *TF:* 800-769-2511 ■ *Web:* www.rbc.com	Toronto	ON	M5J2T6	800-769-2511		690
RBC Dain Rauscher Inc 60 S Sixth St *TF:* 800-933-9946 ■ *Web:* www.rbcwealthmanagement.com	Minneapolis	MN	55402	800-933-9946		690
RBC Global Asset Management 225 Franklin St Ste 2700 *Web:* bostonsri.org	Boston	MA	02110	617-722-4700		401
RBC Inc 100 N Pitt St Ste 300 *Web:* www.rbcinc.com	Alexandria	VA	22314	703-549-6921	549-6926	261
RBC Insurance Services PO Box 789 *TF:* 800-551-8354 ■ *Web:* www.rbcinsurance.com	Greenville	SC	29602	864-609-8111		391-2
RBC Royal Bank 1127 Decarie Blvd **Fax Area Code:* 514 ■ *TF:* 800-769-2599 ■ *Web:* www.rbcroyalbank.com	Saint-Laurent	QC	H4L3M8	800-769-2599	874-3055*	70
RBC Trust Company (Delaware) Ltd 4550 New Linden Hill Rd Ste 200 *TF:* 800-441-7698 ■ *Web:* www.rbctrust.com	Wilmington	DE	19808	302-892-6976		70
RBCM (Royal British Columbia Museum) 675 Belleville St *TF:* 888-447-7977 ■ *Web:* www.royalbcmuseum.bc.ca	Victoria	BC	V8W9W2	250-356-7226		520
RBF (Ross Buehler Falk & Company LLP) 1500 Lititz Pk *Web:* www.rbfco.com	Lancaster	PA	17601	717-393-2700	393-1743	2
RBG (Royal Botanical Gardens) 680 Plains Rd W *TF:* 800-694-4769 ■ *Web:* www.rbg.ca	Burlington	ON	L7T4H4	905-527-1158	577-0375	97
RBI (Riddleberger Bros Inc) 6127 S Valley Pk *Web:* www.rbiva.com	Mount Crawford	VA	22841	540-434-1731	432-1691	186
RBI Corp 10201 Cedar Ridge Dr *TF:* 800-444-7370 ■ *Web:* www.rbicorp.com	Ashland	VA	23005	804-550-2210		358
RBL Group, The 3507 N University Ave Ste 100 *Web:* rbl.net	Provo	UT	84604	801-373-4238		765
Rbm Conveyor Systems Inc 1570 W Mission Blvd *TF:* 800-367-7260 ■ *Web:* www.rbmcsi.com	Pomona	CA	91766	909-620-1333	620-6119	298
RBMA (Radiology Business Management Assn) 9990 Fairfax Blvd Ste 430 *TF:* 888-224-7262 ■ *Web:* www.rbma.org	Fairfax	VA	22030	703-621-3355	621-3356	49-8
RBMA (Reed Brennan Media Assoc) 628 Virginia Dr *TF:* 800-708-7311 ■ *Web:* www.rbma.com	Orlando	FL	32803	407-894-7300	894-7900	317

Phone | Fax | Class

RBN Energy LLC
2323 S Shepherd Dr Ste 1010 ... Houston TX 77019 888-400-9838 463
TF: 888-400-9838 ■ *Web:* rbnenergy.com

RBP (Regular Baptist Press)
3715 N Ventura Dr ... Arlington Heights IL 60004 847-843-1600 843-3757 637-2
TF: 800-727-4440 ■ *Web:* www.rbpstore.org

RBS (Rutgers Business School)
1 Washington Pk 3rd Fl ... Newark NJ 07102 973-353-1821 668
Web: www.business.rutgers.edu

RBS (Remote Backup Systems Inc)
324 Poplar View Pky ... Collierville TN 38017 901-405-1234 178-1
TF: 800-519-7643 ■ *Web:* www.remote-backup.com

RBS Bulk Systems Inc 9910 -48 St SE ... Calgary AB T2C2R2 403-248-1530 248-9122 314
TF: 800-882-5930 ■ *Web:* www.rbsbulk.com

RBS Fab Inc 230 N Hoernerstown Rd ... Hummelstown PA 17036 717-566-9513 566-9268 454
Web: www.rbsfab.com

RBT Services Inc
218 Corporate Dr ... Elizabethtown KY 42701 270-763-6649 763-6653 207
Web: www.rbtsi.com

RBTEL (Rice Belt Telephone Company Inc)
228 Kings Hwy ... Weiner AR 72479 870-684-2288 684-2226 224
Web: www.ricebelt.net

RBX Inc PO Box 2118 ... Springfield MO 65802 800-245-5507 780
TF: 877-450-2200 ■ *Web:* rbxinc.com

RC Aluminum Industries 2805 NW 75th Ave ... Miami FL 33122 305-592-1515 234
Web: www.miamidade.gov

RC Components Inc
373 Mitch Mcconnell Way ... Bowling Green KY 42101 270-842-6000 82
Web: www.rccomponents.com

RC Fine Foods PO Box 236 ... Belle Mead NJ 08502 908-359-5500 359-6957 296-11
TF: 800-526-3953 ■ *Web:* www.rcfinefoods.com

RC Moore Inc 8 Ginn Rd ... Scarborough ME 04074 800-831-6362 311
TF: 800-831-6362 ■ *Web:* rcmoore.com

RC Productions Inc 1756 Lakeshore Dr ... Muskegon MI 49441 231-759-3160 7
Web: rcproductions.com

RC Smith Co 14200 Southcross Dr W ... Burnsville MN 55306 952-854-0711 854-8160 286
TF: 800-747-7648 ■ *Web:* www.rcsmith.com

RC Telecom 6250 W Tenth St ... Greeley CO 80634 970-356-4572 387
Web: www.rctelecom.com

RC Tronics Inc 2573 E Kercher Rd ... Goshen IN 46528 574-642-3857 642-3858 45
TF: 866-457-7790 ■ *Web:* www.rctronics.com

RCA Records 550 Madison Ave ... New York NY 10022 212-930-4000 930-4512 657
Web: www.rcarecords.com

RCC (Riverside Chemical Company Inc)
871 River Rd ... North Tonawanda NY 14120 716-692-1350 692-1485 146
TF: 800-748-2436 ■ *Web:* www.rivchem.com

RCC (Range Commanders Council)
Bldg. 1510 ... White Sands Missile Range NM 88002 505-678-1107 678-7519 637-2
Web: www.wsmr.army.mil

RCC (Rogue Community College)
Riverside 114 S Bartlett St ... Medford OR 97501 541-245-7500 162
Web: web.roguecc.edu

RCCI (Royal Crown Cola Intl)
1001 10th Ave ... Columbus GA 31901 706-494-7552 494-7502 297-2
Web: www.rccolainternational.com

RCEC (Roosevelt County Electric Co-opeartive Inc)
121 N Main Ave PO Box 389 ... Portales NM 88130 575-356-4491 245
Web: www.rcec.org

RCF Information Systems Inc
4200 Colonel Glenn Hwy Ste 100 ... Beavercreek OH 45431 937-427-5680 225
Web: rcfinfo.com

RCG (Rosenthal Collins Group LLC)
216 W Jackson Blvd Ste 400 ... Chicago IL 60606 312-460-9200 795-7730 169
Web: www.rcgdirect.com

RCG (Risk Consulting Group)
23120 Alicia Pky Ste 200 ... Mission Viejo CA 92692 949-583-1161 583-0245 194
Web: www.rcgcorp.com

RCGS (Riley County Genealogical Society)
2005 Claflin Rd ... Manhattan KS 66502 785-565-6495 48-13
Web: www.rileycgs.com

RCGT Inc 7950 Asheville Hwy ... Spartanburg SC 29303 864-503-0879 401

RCH (Rady Children's Hospital)
3020 Children's Way 3rd Fl ... San Diego CA 92123 858-576-1700 966-5859 374-1
TF: 800-788-9029 ■ *Web:* www.rchsd.org

RCI (Resort Condominiums Intl)
9998 N Michigan Rd ... Carmel IN 46032 317-805-8000 753
TF: 800-338-7777 ■ *Web:* www.rci.com

RCI (Records Consultants Inc)
12829 Wetmore Rd ... San Antonio TX 78247 210-366-4127 366-0776 393
TF: 877-363-4127

RCI (Retail Confectioners Intl)
3029 E Sunshine St Ste A ... Springfield MO 65804 417-883-2775 883-1108 49-6
TF: 800-545-5381 ■ *Web:* www.retailconfectioners.org

RCI Capital Group Inc
1055 Dunsmuir St Ste 2184 ... Vancouver BC V7X1L3 604-689-0881 690
Web: www.rcicapitalgroup.com

RCI Consultants Inc
17314 State Hwy 249 Ste 350 ... Houston TX 77064 281-970-4221 970-4241 194
Web: www.rcigroup.us

RCI Custom Products
801 N East St Ste 2A ... Frederick MD 21701 301-620-9130 620-9103 203
TF: 800-546-4724 ■ *Web:* www.rcicustom.com

RCI Sound Systems 10721 Hanna St ... Beltsville MD 20705 301-931-9001 931-9002 246
Web: www.rcisystems.com

RCI Technologies Inc 1133 Green St ... Iselin NJ 08830 732-382-3000 177
Web: www.rci-technologies.com

Rcl Structural Engineers Inc
570 E El Camino Real Ste D ... Sunnyvale CA 94087 408-463-6832 261
Web: rclse.com

RCM Technologies Inc
2500 McClellan Ave Ste 350 ... Pennsauken Township NJ 08109 856-356-4500 356-4600 721
NASDAQ: RCMT ■ *Web:* www.rcmt.com

RCMA (Religious Conference Management Association Inc)
7702 Woodland Dr Ste 120 ... Indianapolis IN 46278 317-632-1888 632-7909 49-12
Web: www.rcmaweb.org

RCMC (Rush-Copley Medical Ctr)
2000 Ogden Ave ... Aurora IL 60504 630-978-6200 374-3
TF: 866-426-7539 ■ *Web:* www.rushcopley.com

RCMP (Royal Canadian Mounted Police)
73 Leikin Dr ... Ottawa ON K1A0R2 613-993-7267 993-0260 303
Web: www.rcmp-grc.gc.ca

RCMP Heritage Ctr 5907 Dewdney Ave ... Regina SK S4T0P4 306-522-7333 520
TF: 866-567-7267 ■ *Web:* rcmphc.com

RCO Engineering Inc
29200 Calahan Rd ... Roseville MI 48066 586-771-8400 247
Web: www.rcoeng.com

RCO Systems Inc 251 James Jackson Ave ... Cary NC 27513 919-319-3612 180
Web: www.rconet.com

RCP (Rubbermaid Commercial Products)
3124 Valley Ave ... Winchester VA 22601 540-667-8700 542-8770 608
TF: 800-347-9800 ■ *Web:* www.rubbermaidcommercial.com

RCP Block & Brick Inc
8240 Broadway ... Lemon Grove CA 91945 619-460-7250 460-3926 183
TF: 800-794-4727 ■ *Web:* www.rcpblock.com

RCPL (Richland County Public Library)
1431 Assembly St ... Columbia SC 29201 803-799-9084 434-3
Web: www.richlandlibrary.com

RCR (Red Cedar Review)
600 Auditorium Rd ... East Lansing MI 48824 517-355-7610 166
Web: www.art.msu.edu

RCR Technology Corp
251 N Illinois St ... Indianapolis IN 46204 317-624-9500 194
Web: www.rcrtechnology.com

RCS (Retail Construction Services Inc)
11343 39th St N ... Lake Elmo MN 55042 651-704-9000 704-9100 685
Web: retail-construction.com

RCS Innovations 7075 W Parkland Ct ... Milwaukee WI 53223 414-354-6900 8
TF: 800-373-6873 ■ *Web:* rcsinnovations.com

RCS Technology 12860 Danielson Crt Ste A ... Poway CA 92064 916-635-6784 202
Web: www.rcstechnology.com

RCS Wireless Technology
800 Megahertz Dr ... Winston-Salem NC 27107 336-788-9191 650-1124 246
TF: 800-441-9191 ■ *Web:* rcscom.com

RCSD (Redwood City School District)
750 Bradford St ... Redwood City CA 94063 650-423-2200 423-2294 685
Web: www.rcsdk8.net

RCT (Rural Community Transportation Inc)
1677 Industrial Pkwy ... Lyndonville VT 05851 802-748-8170 748-5275 108
Web: www.riderct.org

RCTV Intl 888 Brickell Ave 6th Fl ... Miami FL 33131 305-688-7475 742
Web: www.rctvintl.com

R-Cubed Service & Sales Inc
11126 Shady Trl Ste 101 ... Dallas TX 75229 972-243-3830 175

RCW Energy Services
6270 Morningstar Dr Ste 100 ... The Colony TX 75056 972-394-1000 536
Web: www.rcwenergyservices.com

RD Data Solutions LLC (RDDS)
2340 E Trinity Mills Ste 300 ... Carrollton TX 75006 972-417-2835 594-9080* 525
**Fax Area Code:* 214 ■ *Web:* www.rddatasolutions.com

RD Herbert & Sons Company Inc
7336 Cockrill Bend Blvd ... Nashville TN 37208 615-242-3501 256-4056 189-12
Web: www.rdherbert.com

RD Legal Funding LLC 45 Legion Dr ... Cresskill NJ 07626 800-565-5177 403
TF: 800-565-5177 ■ *Web:* www.legalfunding.com

RD Management LLC
810 Seventh Ave 10th Fl ... New York NY 10019 212-265-6600 459-9133 655
Web: www.rdmanagement.com

RD Olson Construction
2955 Main St 3rd Fl ... Irvine CA 92614 949-474-2001 474-1534 186
Web: www.rdolson.com

RD Rubber Products Inc 1600 S Rd ... Garrett IN 46738 260-357-3571 357-6739 677
Web: rdrubberinc.com

RD Walker Engineering
750 Westbrook Rd ... West Milford NJ 07480 973-728-0344 728-1353 104
Web: www.rdwalker.com

RDA (Retail Design Associates)
9984 Niblick Dr Ste 2 ... Roseville CA 95678 800-722-4922 393
TF: 800-722-4922 ■ *Web:* www.retaildesignassociates.com

RDA (J.S. Fleming Associates Inc)
28 Lord Rd ... Marlborough MA 01752 508-460-0904 460-0909 179
TF: 800-498-0904 ■ *Web:* jsfleming.com

RDA (Richard Dean Associates Inc)
1 Harris St ... Newburyport MA 01950 978-462-1150 462-4431 761
Web: www.richarddean.com

RDA Corp
303 International Cir Ste 340 ... Hunt Valley MD 21030 410-308-9300 308-9600 177
TF: 888-441-1278 ■ *Web:* www.rdacorp.com

RDC (Roche Diagnostics Corp)
9115 Hague Rd PO Box 50457 ... Indianapolis IN 46256 800-428-5076 231
TF: 800-428-5076 ■ *Web:* www.usdiagnostics.roche.com

RDC (Rapaport Diamond Corp)
1212 Avenue of the Americas Ste 801 ... New York NY 10036 702-893-9400 840-0243* 637-9
**Fax Area Code:* 212 ■ *Web:* www.diamonds.net

RDC (Redding Distributing Co)
6450 Lockheed Dr ... Redding CA 96003 530-226-5700 226-1173 81-1
Web: www.reddingdistributing.com

RDD Enterprises Inc
3200 S Grand Ave ... Los Angeles CA 90007 213-742-0666 742-9366 523
Web: www.rddusa.com

RDDS (RD Data Solutions LLC)
2340 E Trinity Mills Ste 300 ... Carrollton TX 75006 972-417-2835 594-9080* 525
**Fax Area Code:* 214 ■ *Web:* www.rddatasolutions.com

Rdk Truck Sales Inc 3214 Adamo Dr ... Tampa FL 33605 813-241-0711 516
TF: 877-735-4636 ■ *Web:* www.rdk.com

Rdm Industrial Electronics Inc
850 Harmony Grove Rd ... Nebo NC 28761 800-282-5183 652-2697* 425
**Fax Area Code:* 828 ■ *TF:* 800-282-5183 ■ *Web:* www.rdm.net

RDO Equipment Co 700 Seventh St S ... Fargo ND 58103 877-444-7363 274
TF: 800-247-4650 ■ *Web:* www.rdoequipment.com

RDR Group Inc
5250 Grand Ave No 206 Ste 14 ... Gurnee IL 60031 727-444-0647 317
Web: rdrgroup.com

RDS (Rail Delivery Services Inc)
8600 Bannana Ave ... Fontana CA 92335 909-355-4105 822-3135 780
Web: www.raildelivery.com

RDS Associates Inc 41 Brainerd Rd ... Niantic CT 06357 860-691-0081 194
TF: 800-363-8867 ■ *Web:* www.businessbookpress.com

	Phone	Fax	Class
RDS Global Ltd 2707 Congress St Ste 1-E . . . . San Diego CA 92110 *TF:* 888-510-0801 ■ *Web:* www.rdsglobal.com	619-542-0801	542-0946	194
RDS Media LLC PO Box 828 . . . . Southington CT 06489 *Web:* www.rdsmediallc.com	860-681-4943		637-9
RDS Solutions LLC 99 Grayrock Rd. . . . . Clinton NJ 08809 *TF:* 888-473-7435 ■ *Web:* rdssolutions.com	888-473-7435		196
RDSI (RDSI Banking Systems Inc) c/o SB Financial Group 401 Clinton St. . . . . Defiance OH 43512 *Web:* www.yoursbfinancial.com	419-783-8950	782-6393	225
RDSI Banking Systems Inc (RDSI) c/o SB Financial Group 401 Clinton St. . . . . Defiance OH 43512 *Web:* www.yoursbfinancial.com	419-783-8950	782-6393	225
RDT Inc 9022 Vincik Ehlert PO Box 73 . . . . Beasley TX 77417 *Web:* www.rdt-usa.co	979-387-3223	387-3232	190
RDTC (R David Thomas Executive Conference Ctr) 100 Fuqua Dr PO Box 90120 . . . . Durham NC 27708 *Web:* www.fuqua.duke.edu	919-660-6400	660-3607	377
RDW Group Inc 125 Holden St. . . . . Providence RI 02908 *Web:* rdwgroup.com	401-521-2700		4
RE Carroll Inc 1570 N Olden Ave. . . . . Trenton NJ 08638 *Web:* www.recarroll.com	609-695-6211		579
RE Darling Company Inc 3749 N Romero Rd . . . . Tucson AZ 85705 *Web:* www.redarling.com	520-887-2400	887-4551	370
RE Garrison Trucking 1103 County Rd 1194. . . . . Vinemont AL 35179 *Web:* www.regarrison.com	256-255-5500		780
RE Group Inc 213 W Liberty St Ste 100 . . . . Ann Arbor MI 48104 *Web:* regroup.us	734-213-0200		4
RE Lewis Refrigeration Inc 803 S Lincoln St PO Box 92. . . . . Creston IA 50801 *TF:* 800-264-0767 ■ *Web:* www.relewisinc.com	641-782-8183	782-8156	665
RE Olds Transportation Museum 240 Museum Dr . . . . Lansing MI 48933 *Web:* www.reoldsmuseum.org	517-372-0529	372-2901	520
RE Phelon Company Inc 2063 University Pkwy . . . . Aiken SC 29801 *Web:* fenix-mfg.com	803-649-1381		247
RE Uptegraff Manufacturing Co PO Box 182 . . . . Scottdale PA 15683 *Web:* www.uptegraff.com	724-887-7700	887-4748	767
RE/MAX International Inc 5075 S Syracuse St . . . . Denver CO 80237 *TF:* 800-525-7452 ■ *Web:* www.remax.com	303-770-5531	796-3599	652
REA 50 Grafton Ave . . . . Basking Ridge NJ 07920 *Web:* www.r-e-a.com	908-484-7200		193
REA & Associates Inc 419 W High Ave PO Box 1020 . . . . New Philadelphia OH 44663 *Web:* www.reacpa.com	330-339-6651	308-9506	2
REA Energy Co-opeartive Inc 75 Airport Rd . . . . Indiana PA 15701 *TF:* 800-211-5667 ■ *Web:* www.reaenergy.com	724-349-4800		245
REA Magnet Wire Company Inc 3400 E Coliseum Blvd Ste 200. . . . . Fort Wayne IN 46805 *TF:* 800-732-9473 ■ *Web:* www.reawire.com	800-732-9473		813
Reach Air Medical Services 451 Aviation Blvd . . . . Santa Rosa CA 95403 *Web:* reachair.com	707-324-2400	324-2478	26
Reach Christian Schools 1390 Red Lion Rd. . . . . Bear DE 19701 *Web:* www.reachschools.online	302-834-2526	836-6346	685
Reach Media Inc 13760 Noel Rd Ste 750. . . . . Dallas TX 75240 *Web:* www.reachmediainc.com	972-789-1058		645-141
Reach Out & Read 29 Mystic Ave. . . . . Somerville MA 02145 *Web:* www.reachoutandread.org	617-629-8042		242
Reach Resort 1435 Simonton St. . . . . Key West FL 33040 *TF:* 888-318-4317 ■ *Web:* www.reachresort.com	305-296-5000	296-2830	669
Reaching Across Illinois Library System (RAILS) 125 Tower Dr . . . . Burr Ridge IL 60527 *TF:* 866-940-4081 ■ *Web:* www.railslibraries.info	630-734-5000	734-5050	434-3
ReachLocal Inc 21700 Oxnard St Ste 1600 . . . . Woodland Hills CA 91367 *TF:* 877-525-6084 ■ *Web:* www.reachlocal.com	818-274-0260		4
Reachsolutions LLC 7540 Potomac Fall Rd . . . . McLean VA 22102 *Web:* www.reachsolutions.com	703-893-4114		463
Reaction Audio Visual LLC 30400 Esperanza . . . . Rancho Santa Margarita CA 92688 **Fax Area Code:* 949 ■ *TF:* 877-273-6887 ■ *Web:* www.reactionav.com	877-273-6887	600-8238*	514
Reaction Design Inc 5930 Cornerstone Ct W Ste 230. . . . . San Diego CA 92121 *Web:* www.reactiondesign.com	858-550-1920	550-1925	178-1
Reaction Engineering International Inc 746 E Winchester Ste 120. . . . . Murray UT 84107 *Web:* www.reaction-eng.com	801-364-6925		261
Reaction Technology Inc 3400 Bassett St. . . . . Santa Clara CA 95054 *Web:* www.reactiontechnology.com	408-970-9601	970-9695	696
Reactrix Systems Inc 233 Franklin Tpke . . . . Ramsey NJ 07446 *TF:* 888-444-2323 ■ *Web:* www.reactrix.com	888-444-2323		637-10
Read Between The Lines 2412 Victory Park Ln . . . . Dallas TX 75219 *Web:* www.readbetweenthelines.com	469-904-8034		637-10
Read Jones Christoffersen Ltd 1285 W Broadway Ste 300 . . . . Vancouver BC V6H3X8 *Web:* www.rjc.ca	604-738-0048		256
Read's Uniforms Inc 123 Sweeten Creek Rd Ste D . . . . Asheville NC 28803 *Web:* readsuniforms.net	828-277-6380		157-5
Readco Kurimoto LLC 460 Grim Ln . . . . York PA 17406 *TF:* 800-395-4959 ■ *Web:* www.readco.com	800-395-4959		494
Reader's Catalog, The 435 Hudson St Ste 300. . . . . New York NY 10014 **Fax Area Code:* 212 ■ *Web:* www.readerscatalog.com	646-215-2500	333-5374*	459
Reader, The 2314 M St PO Box 7360 . . . . Omaha NE 68107 *Web:* thereader.com	402-341-7323	341-6967	532-5
Readerlink Distribution Services LLC 1420 Kensington Rd Ste 300 . . . . Oak Brook IL 60523 *TF:* 800-549-5389 ■ *Web:* www.readerlink.net	708-547-4400		96
Reading Anthracite Co 200 Mahantongo St PO Box 1200 . . . . Pottsville PA 17901 *TF:* 800-654-7792 ■ *Web:* readinganthracite.com	570-622-5150		501
Reading Area Community College 10 S Second St. . . . . Reading PA 19603 *TF:* 800-626-1665 ■ *Web:* www.racc.edu	610-372-4721	607-6290	162
Reading Hospital & Medical Ctr PO Box 16052 . . . . Reading PA 19612 *Web:* reading.towerhealth.org	610-988-8000		374-3
Reading International Inc 5995 Sepulveda Blvd Ste 300. . . . . Culver City CA 90230 *NASDAQ: RDI* ■ *Web:* www.readingrdi.com	213-235-2240	235-2229	748
Reading Is Fundamental Inc (RIF) 1825 Connecticut Ave NW Ste 400. . . . . Washington DC 20009 *TF:* 877-743-7323 ■ *Web:* www.rif.org	202-536-3400		48-11
Reading Precast Inc 5494 Pottsville Pk. . . . . Leesport PA 19533 *TF:* 800-724-4881 ■ *Web:* www.readingprecast.com	800-724-4881		183
Reading Public Library 64 Middlesex Ave. . . . . Reading MA 01867 *Web:* www.readingpl.org	781-944-0840		434-3
Reading Public Library 100 S Fifth St. . . . . Reading PA 19602 *Web:* readingpubliclibrary.org	610-655-6355	655-6609	434-3
Reading Public Museum & Art Gallery 500 Museum Rd. . . . . Reading PA 19611 *Web:* www.readingpublicmuseum.org	610-371-5850	371-5632	520
Reading Rock Inc 4600 Devitt Dr. . . . . Cincinnati OH 45246 *TF:* 800-482-6466 ■ *Web:* www.readingrock.com	513-874-2345	874-2520	183
Reading Royals Hockey Club 645 Penn St 3rd Fl . . . . Reading PA 19601 *Web:* royalshockey.com	610-898-7825		717
Reading Truck Body Inc 201 Hancock Blvd. . . . . Reading PA 19611 *TF:* 800-458-2226 ■ *Web:* www.readingbody.com	800-458-2226		516
Reading-muhlenberg Area Vocational-technical School 2615 Warren Rd . . . . Reading PA 19604 *Web:* www.rmctc.org	610-921-7300		764
Reading-North Reading Chamber of Commerce PO Box 771 . . . . Reading MA 01867 *Web:* www.readingnreadingchamber.org	978-664-5060		139
Readington Farms Inc 12 Mill Rd. . . . . Whitehouse Station NJ 08888	908-534-2121	534-5235	296-27
Ready At Dawn 15201 Laguna Canyon Rd Ste 200. . . . . Irvine CA 92618 *Web:* www.readyatdawn.com	949-724-1234		809
Ready Electric Company Inc 3300 Gilmore Industrial Blvd . . . . Louisville KY 40213 *Web:* www.readyelec.com	502-893-2511	893-2519	189-4
Ready Logistics 1030 N Colorado St Ste 109. . . . . Gilbert AZ 85233 *Web:* readylogistics.com	480-558-3200		311
Ready Pac Produce Inc 4401 Foxdale Ave. . . . . Irwindale CA 91706 *TF:* 800-800-7822 ■ *Web:* www.readypac.com	800-800-7822		296-33
Ready Reading 3703 Watts Dr. . . . . Columbia MO 65203 *Web:* www.readyreading.com	573-356-3900	447-2716	637-2
Ready Reading Glasses Inc 1003 Dragon St . . . . Dallas TX 75207 *TF:* 800-238-0904 ■ *Web:* readingglasses.com	800-238-0904		543
Ready Set Work LLC (RSW) 1487 Dunwoody Dr Ste 200 . . . . West Chester PA 19380 **Fax Area Code:* 215 ■ *TF:* 877-507-3706 ■ *Web:* www.readysetwork.com	877-507-3706	689-4323*	387
Ready Technologies Inc 101 Capitol Way N Ste 301. . . . . Olympia WA 98501 *TF:* 877-892-9104 ■ *Web:* www.readyengineering.com	360-413-9800		261
Ready Telecom Inc (RTI) 220 Sunset Ave . . . . Asheboro NC 27203 *Web:* www.readytelecom.com	336-610-3001	629-5961	224
Ready, Kiernan & Mcnally LLP 267 Main St . . . . Wareham MA 02571 *Web:* rkm-law.com	508-295-0286		41
Readyforce Inc 1010 Doyle St Ste 200 . . . . Menlo Park CA 94025	650-543-1400		260
ReadyGo Inc 1761 Pilgrim Ave . . . . Mountain View CA 94040 *Web:* www.readygo.com	650-559-8990		177
Ready-to-run Software Inc 212 Cedar Cv . . . . Lansing NY 14882 *Web:* www.rtr.com	607-533-4002		177
Reagan County PO Box 100 . . . . Big Lake TX 76932	325-884-2090	884-4160	338
Reagan Middle School 620 Division St. . . . . Dixon IL 61021 *Web:* www.dps170.org	815-284-7725	284-8576	685
Reagan Outdoor Advertising 1775 N Warm Springs Rd. . . . . Salt Lake City UT 84116 *Web:* reaganoutdoor.com	801-521-1775		8
Reagan Wireless Corp 720 S Powerline Rd Ste D. . . . . Deerfield Beach FL 33442 *TF:* 877-724-3266 ■ *Web:* www.reaganwireless.com	954-596-2355	596-0070	246
Reagent Chemical & Research Inc 2915 Toccoa St. . . . . Ringoes NJ 08551 *TF:* 800-231-1807 ■ *Web:* www.reagentchemical.com	908-284-2800	284-6090	146
Real & Hernandez 400 N Tustin Ave Ste 220 . . . . Santa Ana CA 92705 *Web:* workerscompcounsels.com	714-542-4100		41
Real Asset Management 309 Court Ave Ste 244 . . . . Des Moines IA 50309 *Web:* www.realassetmgt.com	515-699-8574	699-8575	174
Real Barber's College 451 W Lincoln Ave Ste B100 . . . . Anaheim CA 92805 *Web:* www.therealbarbercollege.com	714-991-1222	991-1441	167-3
Real Beer Media Inc 1459 18th St Ste 287 . . . . San Francisco CA 94107 *Web:* www.realbeer.com	650-260-5178		387
Real Capital Analytics Inc 110 Fifth Ave. . . . . New York NY 10011 *Web:* www.rcanalytics.com	212-387-7103		395

Company / Address	City	State	ZIP	Phone	Fax	Class
Real Capital Solutions 371 Centennial Pky Ste 200 *Web:* www.realcapitalsolutions.com	Louisville	CO	80027	303-466-2500		652
Real County PO Box 750 *Web:* www.co.real.tx.us	Leakey	TX	78873	830-232-5202	232-6888	338
Real Estate Advisory Services Inc 2050 Catawba Valley Blvd SE 2nd Fl *Web:* www.reasinc.com	Hickory	NC	28602	828-466-5037	466-5039	652
Real Estate Board of New York Inc 570 Lexington Ave 2nd Fl *Web:* rebny.com	New York	NY	10022	212-532-3100		653
Real Estate Business Institute 430 N Michigan Ave **Fax Area Code:* 312 ■ *TF:* 800-621-8738 ■ *Web:* www.rebinstitute.com	Chicago	IL	60611	800-621-8738	329-8882*	49-17
Real Estate Buyer's Agent Council (REBAC) 430 N Michigan Ave **Fax Area Code:* 312 ■ *TF:* 800-648-6224 ■ *Web:* www.rebac.net	Chicago	IL	60611	800-648-6224	329-8632*	49-17
Real Estate Errors & Omissions Insurance Corp 1604 700 W Pender St *Web:* www.reeoic.com	Vancouver	BC	V6C1G8	604-669-0019		390
Real Estate Express 12977 N 40 Dr Ste 108 *TF:* 866-739-7277 ■ *Web:* www.realestateexpress.com	Saint Louis	MO	63141	866-739-7277		652
Real Estate III Inc 2271 Seminole Trl *Web:* timcarson.com	Charlottesville	VA	22901	434-817-9200		652
Real Estate Institute of Bc 1750 - 355 Burrard St *TF:* 800-667-2166 ■ *Web:* www.reibc.org	Vancouver	BC	V6C2G8	604-685-3702		652
Real Estate Institute of Canada 5407 Eglinton Ave W Unit 208 *TF:* 800-542-7342 ■ *Web:* www.reic.ca	Toronto	ON	M9C5K6	416-695-9000	695-7230	656
Real Estate Management Services Group LLC 1100 Fifth Ave S Ste 305 *Web:* www.remsgroup.com	Naples	FL	34102	239-262-3017		401
Real Estate One Inc 25800 NW Hwy *TF:* 800-521-0508 ■ *Web:* www.realestateone.com	Southfield	MI	48075	248-208-2900	263-0092	652
Real Estate Roundtable 801 Pennsylvania Ave NW Ste 720 *Web:* www.rer.org	Washington	DC	20004	202-639-8400	639-8442	49-17
Real Floors Inc 1791 Williams Dr *Web:* realfloors.com	Marietta	GA	30066	770-590-7334		362
Real Foundation Inc 13737 Noel Rd Ste 900 *Web:* www.realfoundations.net	Dallas	TX	75240	214-292-7000		655
Real Fundraising 6C Lyle Ct **Fax Area Code:* 866 ■ *Web:* www.real-fundraising.com	Farmington	CT	06032	860-674-9528	615-1185*	393
Real Good Foods 111 Artsakh Ave Ste 201 *Web:* realgoodfoods.com	Glendale	CA	91205	818-299-4179		296-11
Real Goods Solar 833 W S Boulder Rd Bldg B *NASDAQ: RSGE* ■ *TF:* 888-391-9944 ■ *Web:* rgsenergy.com	Louisville	CO	80027	888-391-9944		620
Real Goods Trading Corp 13771 S Hwy 101 *TF:* 800-919-2400 ■ *Web:* www.realgoods.com	Hopland	CA	95449	717-472-2403	472-2430	812
Real Hip-Hop Network 1717 Pennsylvania Ave NW Ste 1020 *TF:* 888-742-9993 ■ *Web:* www.rhn.tv	Washington	DC	20006	888-742-9993		116
Real Info Inc 701 Seneca St Ste 641 *TF:* 877-630-7028 ■ *Web:* real-info.com	Buffalo	NY	14210	716-608-4370		653
Real Integrated 40900 Woodward Ave *Web:* www.realintegrated.com	Bloomfield Hills	MI	48304	248-540-0660		7
Real Intent Inc 990 Almanor Ave Ste 220 *Web:* www.realintent.com	Sunnyvale	CA	94085	408-830-0700		225
Real Living First Service Realty 10155 SW 42nd St Ste 200 *TF:* 800-899-8477 ■ *Web:* www.realliving.com	Miami	FL	33175	305-226-0061		652
Real People Press Inc 1221 Left Hand Canyon Dr *Web:* www.realpeoplepress.com	Boulder	CO	80302	303-442-2902		637-2
Real Property Research Group Inc 10400 Little Patuxent Pkwy Ste 450 *Web:* rprg.net	Columbia	MD	21044	410-772-1004		653
Real Salt Lake 9256 S State St *Web:* www.realsaltlake.com	Sandy	UT	84070	801-727-2700	727-1469	714-1
Real Seafood Co 22 Main St *Web:* realseafoodcotoledo.com	Toledo	OH	43605	419-697-5427		671
Real Soft Inc 2540 Rt 130 N Ste 118 *Web:* www.realsoftinc.com	Cranbury	NJ	08512	609-409-3636	409-3637	178-11
Real Software Systems LLC 21255 Burbank Blvd Ste 220 *Web:* www.realsoftwaresystems.com	Woodland Hills	CA	91367	818-313-8038		178-1
Real Story Group, The 3470 Olney-Laytonsville Rd Ste 131 *TF:* 800-325-6190 ■ *Web:* www.realstorygroup.com	Olney	MD	20832	617-340-6464		463
Real Time Consultants Inc 777 Corporate Dr Ste 1 *Web:* rtcnt.com	Mahwah	NJ	07430	201-512-1777	512-1900	174
Real Time Information Services Inc 191 W Shaw Ave Ste 106 *Web:* www.realtimeca.com	Fresno	CA	93704	559-222-6456		177
Real Time Measurements Inc 4615 - 112th Ave SE Ste 125 *TF:* 866-720-3444 ■ *Web:* www.rty.ca	Calgary	AB	T2C5J3	403-720-3444		539
Real Time Risk Systems LLC 80 Wall St Ste 500 *Web:* realtimerisksystems.com	New York	NY	10005	212-425-0721		226
Real Trends Inc 7501 Village Sq Dr Ste 200 *Web:* www.realtrends.com	Castle Rock	CO	80108	303-741-1000	741-1070	637-10
Real View Books (RVB) PO Box 10 *Web:* www.realviewbooks.com	New Hope	KY	40052	270-325-3061	325-3091	637-2
Real Vision Software Inc 3700 Jackson St Ste 203 *Web:* www.realvisionsoftware.com	Alexandria	LA	71303	318-449-4579	448-3033	177
Real Watersports Inc 25706 Hwy 12 PO Box 476 *Web:* realwatersports.com	Waves	NC	27982	252-987-6000		711
Real World Inc 8098 N Via De Negocio *Web:* realworldinc.com	Scottsdale	AZ	85258	480-296-0160		7
Real X Software Inc 800 W El Camino Real Ste 180 *TF:* 888-411-2221 ■ *Web:* www.realx.com	Mountain View	CA	94040	888-411-2221		177
RealCapitalMarketscom LLC 5780 Fleet St Ste 130 *TF:* 888-546-5281 ■ *Web:* www.rcm1.com	Carlsbad	CA	92008	888-546-5281		652
Realdecoy Inc 205 Catherine St *Web:* www.realdecoy.com	Ottawa	ON	K2P1C3	613-234-9330		177
RealEnergy LLC 1500 Soscol Ferry Rd *Web:* realenergy.com	Napa	CA	94558	707-944-2400		188
Realistic Computing Inc 10461 Mill Run Cir *TF:* 877-667-9503 ■ *Web:* www.realistic-computing.com	Owings Mills	MD	21117	410-744-8144	744-8145	175
Reality Interactive LLC 213 Court St on Fl 2 & 10 *Web:* realityi.com	Middletown	CT	06457	860-346-2700	852-5046	652
Reality Technology Inc 2444 Washington St Ste 215 *Web:* www.reality-technology.com	Denver	CO	80205	303-757-1107		225
RealityCheck Inc 2033 N Geyer Rd *TF:* 866-751-2094 ■ *Web:* www.realitycheckinc.com	Saint Louis	MO	63131	314-909-9095		466
Realized Financial Solutions Inc 413 E St *Web:* www.realizedfinancialsolutions.com	Plainville	CT	06062	860-747-0002		180
Realizing Global Health 4710 Olley Ln *Web:* www.realizingglobalhealth.com	Fairfax	VA	22032	571-331-4158		196
Realizing Your Potential 11181 Yonge St No 210 *Web:* www.realizingyourpotential.ca	Richmond Hill	ON	L4S1L2	905-751-1076		167-3
RealNetworks Inc 2601 Elliott Ave Ste 1000 *NASDAQ: RNWK* ■ *Web:* www.realnetworks.com	Seattle	WA	98121	206-674-2700	674-2696	178-8
Realogy Corp 175 Park Ave *Web:* www.realogy.com	Madison	NJ	07940	973-407-2000		652
RealReal, The 253 Post St *Web:* www.therealreal.com	San Francisco	CA	94108	415-554-3700		366
RealSTEEL 1684 Medina Rd *TF:* 866-965-2688 ■ *Web:* www.realsteelsoftware.com	Medina	OH	44256	866-965-2688		180
Realstreet Staffing 2500 Wallington Way Ste 208 *TF:* 877-480-8002 ■ *Web:* www.realstreet.com	Marriottsville	MD	21104	410-480-8002		463
RealTime Group Inc, The 5217 Tennyson Pkwy Ste 200 *Web:* therealtimegroup.com	Plano	TX	75024	972-985-9100		463
Real-Time Innovations Inc 232 E Java Dr *Web:* rti.com	Sunnyvale	CA	94089	408-990-7400	990-7402	180
Real-Time Laboratories LLC 990 S Rogers Cir Ste 5 *Web:* www.real-timelabs.com	Boca Raton	FL	33487	561-988-8826		419
Realtime Software Corp 24 Deane Rd *TF:* 800-323-1143 ■ *Web:* www.realtimesw.com	Bernardston	MA	01337	847-803-1100	954-4764	178-1
Realtors Association of Metropolitan Pittsburgh 1427 W Liberty Ave *Web:* realtorspgh.com	Pittsburgh	PA	15226	412-563-5200		653
Realtors Association of New Mexico 2201 Bros Rd *TF:* 800-224-2282 ■ *Web:* www.nmrealtor.com	Santa Fe	NM	87505	505-982-2442	983-8809	656
Realty Bancorp Equities LLC 21800 Oxnard St Ste 500 *Web:* rbellc.com	Woodland Hills	CA	91367	818-251-9911		653
Realty Capital Partners LLC 8333 Douglas Ave Ste 300 *Web:* rcpinvestments.com	Dallas	TX	75225	469-533-4000		41
Realty Executives International Inc 645 E Missouri Ave Ste 210 *TF:* 800-252-3366 ■ *Web:* www.realtyexecutives.com	Phoenix	AZ	85020	480-239-2038		652
Realty Income Corp 11995 El Camino Real *NYSE: O* ■ *TF:* 877-924-6266 ■ *Web:* www.realtyincome.com	San Diego	CA	92130	877-924-6266		655
Realty Landscaping Corp 2585 Second St Pk *Web:* www.realtylandscaping.com	Newtown	PA	18940	215-598-7334		776
Realty Plus Chicago Inc 453 E 111th St Ste 16	Chicago	IL	60628	773-785-1400		652
Realty School of Kansas 3241 E Douglas Ave *Web:* www.rsk.net	Wichita	KS	67218	316-685-3652	382-4152	685
Realty World 1101 Dove St Ste 228 *Web:* www.realtyworld.com	Newport Beach	CA	92660	714-436-9009	436-9010	652
RealtyBid International Inc 3225 Rainbow Dr Ste 248 *TF:* 877-518-5600 ■ *Web:* www.realtybid.com	Rainbow City	AL	35906	877-518-5600		393
RealtyShares Inc 525 Market St Ste 2800 *Web:* www.realtyshares.com	San Francisco	CA	94105	415-450-6234		387
Ream's Food Stores 160 E Claybourne Ave *Web:* www.reamsfoods.com	Salt Lake City	UT	84115	801-485-8451		355
Reams Asset Management Company LLC 227 Washington St *Web:* www.reamsasset.com	Columbus	IN	47202	812-372-6606		690
Reardon & Associates LLC 985 Old Eagle School Rd Ste 516 *Web:* dreardonlaw.com	Wayne	PA	19087	610-687-3942	687-5817	41
Reardon Associates Inc 27 Cambridge St Ste 103 *Web:* www.reardonassociates.com	Dedham	MA	02026	781-329-2660		260
Reardon Law Firm PC, The 160 Hempstead St Drawer 1430 *Web:* reardonlaw.com	New London	CT	06320	860-442-0444	444-6445	41

Company	Phone	Fax	Class
Reardon Machine Company Inc 5015 Se Hwy 169 ... Saint Joseph MO 64507 *Web:* www.reardonmachine.com	816-279-0906		454
Reata 310 Houston St ... Fort Worth TX 76102 *Web:* www.reata.net	817-336-1009		671
Reaveley Engineers & Associates Inc 675 East 500 South ... Salt Lake City UT 84102 *Web:* www.reaveley.com	801-486-3883		539
Reaxis Inc 941 Robinson Hwy ... Mcdonald PA 15057 *TF:* 800-426-7273 ■ *Web:* www.reaxis.com	800-426-7273		388
REBAC (Real Estate Buyer's Agent Council) 430 N Michigan Ave ... Chicago IL 60611 **Fax Area Code:* 312 ■ *TF:* 800-648-6224 ■ *Web:* www.rebac.net	800-648-6224	329-8632*	49-17
Rebar Engineering Inc 10706 Painter Ave ... Santa Fe Springs CA 90670	562-946-2461		189-14
Re-Bath LLC 16879 N 75th Ave Ste 101 ... Peoria AZ 85382 *TF:* 800-426-4573 ■ *Web:* www.rebath.com	800-426-4573		189-11
Rebco Inc 1171-1225 Madison Ave ... Paterson NJ 07509 *TF:* 800-777-0787 ■ *Web:* www.rebcoinc.com	973-684-0200	684-0118	234
Rebecca Taylor Inc 307 W 36th St ... New York NY 10018 *TF:* 888-485-6738 ■ *Web:* www.rebeccataylor.com	888-485-6738		594
Rebecca's Cafe 99 S Bedford St Ste 7 ... Burlington MA 01803 *Web:* www.rebeccascafe.com	781-272-0539		670
Rebel Interactive Inc 1217 S 13th St ... Omaha NE 68108 *Web:* www.rebelinteractive.com	402-561-0520		809
Rebel State Historic Site 1260 Hwy 1221 ... Marthaville LA 71450 *TF:* 888-677-3600 ■ *Web:* crt.state.la.us	318-472-6255		565
Rebellion Photonics Inc 2327 Commerce St Ste 200 ... Houston TX 77002 *Web:* rebellionphotonics.com	713-218-0101		693
Reber Machine & Tool Company Inc 1112 S Liberty ... Muncie IN 47302 *Web:* rebermachine.com	765-288-0297		757
Reboot Computer Services Inc 70-11 Austin St Ste 3L ... Forest Hills NY 11375 **Fax Area Code:* 718 ■ *TF:* 866-228-6286 ■ *Web:* www.rebootcs.com	866-228-6286	897-9665*	175
Reborn Cabinets 2981 E La Palma Ave ... Anaheim CA 92806 *TF:* 888-273-2676 ■ *Web:* www.reborncabinets.com	714-630-2220		321
Rebsco Inc 4362 Us Rte 36 ... Greenville OH 45331 *Web:* www.rebsco.com	937-548-2246	548-8506	186
Rebuilders Automotive Supply Company Inc 1650 Flat River Rd ... Coventry RI 02816 *TF:* 800-633-0162 ■ *Web:* www.coresupply.com	401-822-3030		61
Rebuilding Together Inc 1899 L St NW Ste 1000 ... Washington DC 20036 *TF:* 800-473-4229 ■ *Web:* rebuildingtogether.org	800-473-4229		48-5
REC (Rural Electric Coop) 13942 Hwy 76 ... Lindsay OK 73052 *TF:* 800-259-3504 ■ *Web:* www.rural-electric.com	405-756-3104	756-8957	245
REC Consulting Inc 2442 Second Ave ... San Diego CA 92101 *Web:* rec-consultants.com	619-232-9200		261
REC Room, The 512 York Rd ... Towson MD 21204 *Web:* www.recroomtowson.com	410-337-7178		572
RECARO Aircraft Seating Americas LLC 2275 Eagle Pkwy ... Fort Worth TX 76177 *Web:* www.recaro-as.com	817-490-9160	490-9175	22
Receivable Management Inc 107 W Randol Mill Rd ... Arlington TX 76011 *TF:* 866-433-7534 ■ *Web:* receivablemanagement.net	817-261-7534		160
ReceptoPharm Inc 1537 NW 65th Ave ... Plantation FL 33313 *Web:* www.receptopharm.com	954-356-1460		238
Recipe Unlimited Corp 199 Four Valley Dr ... Vaughan ON L4K0B8 *TF:* 800-860-4082 ■ *Web:* www.recipeunlimited.com	905-760-2244		299
Reciprocal of America 4200 Innslake Dr Ste 102 ... Glen Allen VA 23060 *Web:* www.reciprocalgroup.com	804-747-8600		391-5
Reciprocal Results 193 A Rice Ave ... Staten Island NY 10314 *Web:* reciprocalresults.com	718-370-3977	761-7103	194
Recker & Boerger Inc 10115 Transportation Way ... Cincinnati OH 45246 *TF:* 800-299-5039 ■ *Web:* thecomfortzone.com	513-942-9663		35
Reckitt Benckiser Inc 399 Interpace Pkwy PO Box 225 ... Parsippany NJ 07054 *Web:* www.rb.com	973-404-2600		151
Reco Constructors Inc 710 Hospital St ... Richmond VA 23219 *Web:* www.recoconstructors.com	804-644-2611	643-3561	91
Reco Equipment Inc 41245 Reco Rd ... Belmont OH 43718 *TF:* 800-686-7326 ■ *Web:* www.recoequip.com	740-782-1314	782-1020	190
Recognition Co, The 7960 Goodwood Blvd ... Baton Rouge LA 70806 *TF:* 866-924-2778 ■ *Web:* www.therecognitionco.com	225-924-2778	924-2664	637-2
Recognition Specialties Inc 1710 Harbeck Rd ... Grants Pass OR 97527 *Web:* nicebadge.com	541-476-3166		701
Recology Sunset Scavenger 250 Executive Pk Ste 2100 ... San Francisco CA 94134 *Web:* www.recology.com	415-330-1300		804
RECON (Remedial Construction Services LP) 9977 W Sam Houston Pky N Ste 304 ... Houston TX 77064 *Web:* www.reconservices.com	281-955-2442	890-5172	194
RECON Dynamics LLC 18323 Bothell Everett Hwy Ste 330 ... Bothell WA 98012 *TF:* 877-480-3551 ■ *Web:* www.recondynamics.com	877-480-3551		693
RECON Environmental Inc 1927 Fifth Ave ... San Diego CA 92101 *Web:* www.recon-us.com	619-308-9333		192
Recon Logistics LLC 384 Inverness Pkwy Ste 270 ... Englewood CO 80112 *TF:* 866-424-7153 ■ *Web:* reconlogistics.com	866-424-7153		311
Recon Management Services Inc 1907 Ruth St ... Sulphur LA 70663 *TF:* 888-301-4662 ■ *Web:* www.recon-group.com	337-583-4662	583-7565	631
Reconditioned Systems Inc (RSI) 235 S 56th St ... Chandler AZ 85226 **Fax Area Code:* 480 ■ *TF:* 800-280-5000 ■ *Web:* www.rsisystemsfurniture.com	800-280-5000	894-1907*	319-1
Reconnect Mental Health Services 1281 St Clair Ave W ... Toronto ON M6E1B8 *Web:* www.reconnect.on.ca	416-248-2050		726
Reconstructionist Rabbinical Assn (RRA) 1299 Church Rd ... Wyncote PA 19095 *Web:* www.therra.org	215-576-5210	576-8051	48-20
Record 4324 Phil Hargett Ct PO Box 3099 ... Monroe NC 28111 *TF:* 800-438-1937 ■ *Web:* www.record-usa.com	704-289-9212	289-2024	253
Record Center Innovations Inc 3919 W Washington St ... Phoenix AZ 85009	602-258-4000		463
Record Exchange, The 1105 W Idaho St ... Boise ID 83702 *Web:* www.therecordexchange.com	208-344-8010		525
Record Herald Publishing 30 Walnut St ... Waynesboro PA 17268 *Web:* www.therecordherald.com	717-762-2151		532-3
Record Plant Inc 1032 N Sycamore Ave ... Hollywood CA 90038 *Web:* www.recordplant.com	323-993-9300	466-8835	657
Record Play Tek Inc 110 E Vistula St ... Bristol IN 46507 *TF:* 800-809-5233 ■ *Web:* www.recordplaytek.com	574-848-5233	848-5333	52
Record Research Inc PO Box 200 ... Menomonee Falls WI 53051 *TF:* 800-827-9810 ■ *Web:* www.recordresearch.com	262-251-5408		637-2
Record Search America Inc 1201 N Liberty St ... Boise ID 83704	208-375-1906		635
Record Searchlight 1101 Twin View Blvd ... Redding CA 96003 *Web:* www.redding.com	530-243-2424		532-2
Record Technology Inc (RTI) 486 Dawson Dr ... Camarillo CA 93012 *Web:* www.recordtech.com	805-484-2747	987-0508	657
Record Town Inc 38 Corporate Cir ... Albany NY 12203 *Web:* www.twec.com	518-452-1242		525
Record, The 501 Broadway ... Troy NY 12180 *Web:* www.troyrecord.com	518-270-1200		532-2
Record, The 160 King St E ... Kitchener ON N2G4E5 *TF:* 800-265-8261 ■ *Web:* www.therecord.com	519-894-2231	894-3829	532-1
Record, The 1195 Galt St E ... Sherbrooke QC J1G1Y7 *Web:* www.sherbrookerecord.com	819-569-9525	821-3179	532-1
Record-Courier 1050 W Main St ... Kent OH 44240 *TF:* 800-560-9657 ■ *Web:* www.record-courier.com	330-541-9400	296-2698	532-2
Record-Courier 126 N Chestnut St ... Ravenna OH 44266 *Web:* www.recordpub.com	330-296-9657	296-2698	532-2
Recordflow 1751 E Garry Ave ... Santa Ana CA 92705 *TF:* 877-896-7350 ■ *Web:* www.advantmed.com	877-896-7350		463
Record-Gazette 218 N Murray St ... Banning CA 92220 *Web:* www.recordgazette.net	951-849-4586	849-2437	532-2
Recording Engineers Institute 100-5 Patco Ct ... Islandia NY 11749 *Web:* www.audiotraining.com	631-582-8999	582-8213	167-3
Recording for the Blind & Dyslexic (RFB&D) 20 Roszel Rd ... Princeton NJ 08540 **Fax Area Code:* 609 ■ *TF:* 800-221-4792 ■ *Web:* www.rfbd.org	800-221-4792	987-8116*	48-17
Recording Industry Association of America Inc (RIAA) 1025 F St NW 10th Fl ... Washington DC 20004 *Web:* www.riaa.com	202-775-0101		48-4
Record-Journal 500 S Broad St 2nd Fl ... Meriden CT 06450 *TF:* 800-228-6915 ■ *Web:* www.myrecordjournal.com	203-235-1661	639-0210	532-2
Recordnet.com 530 E Market St ... Stockton CA 95202 *TF:* 800-606-9741 ■ *Web:* www.recordnet.com	209-943-6568	547-8186	532-2
Records Consultants Inc (RCI) 12829 Wetmore Rd ... San Antonio TX 78247 *TF:* 877-363-4127	210-366-4127	366-0776	393
RecordSetter LLC 228 Park Ave S Ste 29280 ... New York NY 10003 *Web:* recordsetter.com	646-912-6611		387
Recordtrak Inc 651 Allendale Rd PO Box 61591 ... King of Prussia PA 19406 **Fax Area Code:* 610 ■ *TF:* 800-355-7400 ■ *Web:* www.recordtrak.com	800-355-7400	354-8946*	224
Recourse Communications Inc 112 Intracoastal Pointe Dr ... Jupiter FL 33477 *Web:* www.rciars.com	561-686-6800		184
Recovered Energy Inc 11455 N Rio Vista Rd ... Pocatello ID 83202 *Web:* recoveredenergy.com	208-637-0645		697
Recovery Partners LLC 4151 N Marshall Way Ste 12 ... Scottsdale AZ 85251 **Fax Area Code:* 480 ■ *TF:* 866-661-5203 ■ *Web:* www.recoverypartners.com	866-661-5203	747-9889*	160
Recreation Supply Company Inc 515 Airport Rd ... Bismarck ND 58504 *TF:* 800-437-8072 ■ *Web:* www.recsupply.com	701-222-4860	255-7895	459
Recreation Unlimited 15150 Herriman Blvd ... Noblesville IN 46060 *Web:* www.recunlimited.com	317-773-3545	773-2675	711
Recreation Vehicle Dealers Assn (RVDA) 3930 University Dr ... Fairfax VA 22030 *Web:* www.rvda.org	703-591-7130	591-0734	49-18
Recreation Vehicle Industry Assn (RVIA) 1896 Preston White Dr ... Reston VA 20191 *TF:* 800-336-0154 ■ *Web:* www.rvia.org	703-620-6003	620-5071	49-21
Recreation.gov 1849 C St NW ... Washington DC 20240 *Web:* www.recreation.gov	202-208-4743		197
National Recreation Reservation Service PO Box 140 ... Ballston NY 12020 *Web:* www.recreation.gov	518-885-3639		773
Recreational Equipment Inc (REI) 6750 S 228th St ... Kent WA 98032 *TF:* 800-426-4840 ■ *Web:* www.rei.com	253-395-3780	891-2523	711
Recreational Sports and Imports Inc 2436 N Woodruff Ave ... Idaho Falls ID 83401 *TF:* 800-825-7999 ■ *Web:* www.rsiinc.com	800-825-7999		38
Recreatives Industries Inc 60 Depot St ... Buffalo NY 14206 *TF:* 800-255-2511 ■ *Web:* www.maxatvs.com	716-855-2226		29
Recruit Wise PO Box 5231 ... Oak Ridge TN 37831 *Web:* www.recruitwise.jobs	865-425-0405	425-9925	260
Recruitech Internationa 500 Office Center Dr Ste 400 ... Fort Washington PA 19034 *Web:* recruitech.com	215-293-1300		193

Name / Address	City	State	ZIP	Phone	Fax	Class
Recruiters of Minnesota 6110 Blue Circle Dr Ste 280 *Web:* www.recruitersofmn.com	Minnetonka	MN	55343	952-767-0089		260
Recruiters Online Inc 3599 E Normandy Park Dr Q7 *TF:* 888-364-4667 ■ *Web:* www.recruitersonline.com	Medina	OH	44256	888-364-4667		631
Recruitics 437 5th Ave 5th Fl *Web:* recruitics.com	New York	NY	10016	646-612-7181		49-18
Recruiting Network Inc, The PO Box 487 *TF:* 888-844-4939 ■ *Web:* www.recruitingpipeline.com	Winnetka	IL	60093	888-844-4939		631
Recruiting Toolbox PO Box 2573 *Web:* recruitingtoolbox.com	Redmond	WA	98073	425-557-2100		393
Recruitmilitary LLC 422 W Loveland Ave *TF:* 800-226-0841 ■ *Web:* recruitmilitary.com	Loveland	OH	45140	513-683-5020		260
Recto Molded Products Inc (RMP) 4425 Appleton St *Web:* www.rectomolded.com	Cincinnati	OH	45209	513-871-5544		604
Rector Communications Inc 12 W Willow Grove Ave *Web:* rector.com	Philadelphia	PA	19118	215-963-9661		7
Rector Phillips Morse Inc 1501 N University Ste 800 *TF:* 888-664-7761 ■ *Web:* www.rpmrealty.com	Little Rock	AR	72207	501-664-7807	664-0104	652
Rectory School 528 Pomfret St PO Box 68 *Web:* www.rectoryschool.org	Pomfret	CT	06258	860-928-7759	928-4961	622
Recupero & Associates Inc 31877 Del Obispo St Ste 204 *Web:* recupero.net	San Juan Capistrano	CA	92675	949-429-6300		653
Recursion Pharmaceuticals 41 400 W *Web:* www.recursionpharma.com	Salt Lake City	UT	84101	385-269-0203		582
Recursion Software Inc 2591 Dallas Pkwy Ste 200 *TF:* 800-727-8674 ■ *Web:* www.recursionsw.com	Frisco	TX	75034	972-731-8800	731-8881	179
Recycle Ann Arbor Inc 2420 S Industrial Hwy *Web:* recycleannarbor.org	Ann Arbor	MI	48104	734-662-6288		660
Recycled Paperboard Technical Assn PO Box 5774 *Web:* www.rpta.org	Elgin	IL	60121	847-622-2544		49-13
Recycling Center Inc 630 S M St *TF:* 800-826-9222 ■ *Web:* www.recyclingcenterinc.com	Richmond	IN	47374	765-966-8295		686
Recycling Center of Live Oak Inc, The 700 Houston Ave NW *Web:* www.biggreenball.org	Live Oak	FL	32064	386-364-5865		660
Red 5 Studios Inc 24022 Calle De La Plata Ste 200 *Web:* www.red5studios.com	Laguna Hills	CA	92653	949-754-0919		178-1
Red Angus Association of America 4201 N IH-35 *Fax Area Code: 888 ■ *TF:* 800-422-2117 ■ *Web:* redangus.org	Denton	TX	76207	940-387-3502	829-6069*	48-2
Red Arrow Delivery Service 1120 Visco Dr *Web:* redarrowdelivery.com	Nashville	TN	37210	615-883-1702	871-9816	311
Red Ball Oxygen Company Inc 609 N Market *TF:* 800-551-8150 ■ *Web:* www.redballoxygen.com	Shreveport	LA	71107	318-425-3211	425-6323	385
Red Barn 455 Riverside Dr *Web:* theredbarnmaine.org	Augusta	ME	04330	207-623-9485		671
Red Barn Investments 5215 Old Orchard Rd Ste 675 *Web:* www.redbarnllc.com	Skokie	IL	60077	847-920-7100		796
Red Barn Theatre 319 Duval St Rear *Web:* www.redbarntheatre.com	Key West	FL	33040	305-296-9911		572
Red Bell Real Estate LLC 7730 S Union Park Ave Ste 400 *Web:* www.redbellre.com	Salt Lake City	UT	84115	801-483-4300		656
Red Blazer, The 72 Manchester St *Web:* www.theredblazer.com	Concord	NH	03301	603-224-4101		671
Red Brick Design Inc 150 Westford Rd	Tyngsboro	MA	01879	978-649-4411		395
Red Bud Industries 200 B & E Industrial Dr *TF:* 800-851-4612 ■ *Web:* www.redbudindustries.com	Red Bud	IL	62278	618-282-3801	282-6718	494
Red Butte Garden & Arboretum University of Utah 300 Wakara Way *Web:* www.redbuttegarden.org	Salt Lake City	UT	84108	801-585-0556		97
Red Canoe Credit Union 1418 15th Ave *TF:* 800-562-5611 ■ *Web:* www.redcanoecu.com	Longview	WA	98632	360-425-2130		219
Red Cap Cards PO Box 412019 *Fax Area Code: 815 ■ *Web:* redcapcards.com	Los Angeles	CA	90041	310-926-3773	927-0129*	637-10
Red Capital Group LLC 10 W Broad St 8th Fl *TF:* 800-837-5100 ■ *Web:* www.redcapitalgroup.com	Columbus	OH	43215	800-837-5100		360-3
Red Card Media 100 State St Ste 301 *Web:* www.isthmus.com	Madison	WI	53703	608-256-2273		637-9
Red Carpet Charters 4820 SW 20th *TF:* 888-878-5100	Oklahoma City	OK	73128	405-672-5100		107
Red Cedar Review (RCR) 600 Auditorium Rd *Web:* www.art.msu.edu	East Lansing	MI	48824	517-355-7610		166
Red Cedar Technology Inc 4572 S Hagadorn Rd Ste 3-A *Web:* www.redcedartech.com	East Lansing	MI	48823	517-664-1137		256
Red Chamber Co 1912 E Vernon Ave *Web:* redchamber.com	Vernon	CA	90058	323-234-9000	231-8888	297-5
Red Clay Consolidated School District 1502 Spruce Ave *Web:* www.redclayschools.com	Wilmington	DE	19805	302-552-3700		685
Red Clay Interactive 22 Buford Village Way Ste 221 *TF:* 866-251-2800 ■ *Web:* www.redclayinteractive.com	Buford	GA	30519	770-297-2430		225
Red Clay State Historic Park 1140 Red Clay Park Rd *Web:* www.state.tn.us	Cleveland	TN	37311	423-478-0339		565
Red Cloud Promotions 1600 Sawtelle Blvd Ste 108 *Web:* www.redcloudagency.com	Los Angeles	CA	90025	310-444-5583		195
Red Cross Pharmacy 420 Main St *Web:* www.rcrx.com	Forest City	PA	18421	570-785-5400		237
Red Deer Advocate 2950 Bremner Ave *TF:* 877-223-3311 ■ *Web:* www.reddeeradvocate.com	Red Deer	AB	T4R1M9	403-343-2400	341-6560	532-1
Red Deer Chamber of Commerce 3017 Gaetz Ave *Web:* www.reddeerchamber.com	Red Deer	AB	T4N5Y6	403-347-4491	343-6188	137
Red Deer Public Library 4818 49 St *Web:* www.rdpl.org	Red Deer	AB	T4N1T9	403-346-4576		435
Red Devil Inc 1437 S Boulder *Fax Area Code: 918 ■ *TF:* 800-423-3845 ■ *Web:* www.reddevil.com	Tulsa	OK	74119	800-423-3845	585-8120*	3
Red Diamond Inc 400 Park Ave *TF:* 800-292-4651 ■ *Web:* reddiamond.com	Moody	AL	35004	205-577-4000		296-7
Red Dolly Casino 530 Gregory St *Web:* www.thereddollycasino.com	Black Hawk	CO	80422	303-582-1100	582-1435	133
Red Door By Elizabeth Arden, The 400 E Fairway Ln *Web:* www.thereddoor.com	Galloway	NJ	08205	609-404-4100		707
Red Door Interactive Inc 350 Tenth Ave Ste 100 *Web:* www.reddoor.biz	San Diego	CA	92101	619-398-2670		7
Red Dot Corp 1209 W Corsicana St *TF:* 800-657-2234 ■ *Web:* www.reddotbuildings.com	Athens	TX	75751	800-657-2234		105
Red Dot Corp 495 Andover Pk E *Web:* www.rdac.com	Tukwila	WA	98188	206-575-3840		172
Red Dragonfly Press PO Box 98 *Web:* www.reddragonflypress.org	Northfield	MN	55057	507-321-1551		637-2
Red Earth Publishing Inc 301 SW 62nd St *Web:* www.redearthpublish.com	Oklahoma City	OK	73139	405-395-8686		637-2
Red Ewald Inc 2669 US 181 *TF:* 800-242-3524 ■ *Web:* www.redewald.com	Karnes City	TX	78118	830-780-3304		606
Red Feather Marketing Group Inc 332 Main St *Web:* red-feather.com	Madison	NJ	07940	973-966-1399		195
Red Fedeles Brookhouse 920 Elmridge Center Dr *Web:* fedelesbrookhouse.com	Rochester	NY	14626	585-723-9988		671
Red Fish 8 Archer Rd *Web:* www.redfishofhiltonhead.com	Hilton Head Island	SC	29928	843-686-3388	686-4628	671
Red Fish Grill 115 Bourbon St *Web:* www.redfishgrill.com	New Orleans	LA	70130	504-598-1200		671
Red Fleet State Park 8750 N Hwy 191 *Web:* stateparks.utah.gov	Vernal	UT	84078	435-789-4432	789-4475	565
Red Gold Inc 120 E Oak St *TF:* 800-772-5726 ■ *Web:* www.redgoldfoods.com	Orestes	IN	46063	765-754-7527		296-20
Red Hat Society Store 431 S Acacia Ave *TF:* 866-386-2850 ■ *Web:* www.redhatsociety.com	Fullerton	CA	92831	714-738-0001		533
Red Haw State Park 24550 US Hwy 34 *Web:* www.iowadnr.gov	Chariton	IA	50049	641-774-5632	774-8821	565
Red Hawk Casino 1 Red Hawk Pkwy *TF:* 888-573-3495 ■ *Web:* www.redhawkcasino.com	Placerville	CA	95667	530-677-7000		452
Red Hill Grinding Wheel 335 Dotts St *Web:* www.rhgrindingwheel.com	Pennsburg	PA	18073	215-679-7964		1
Red Hill Patrick Henry National Memorial 1250 Red Hill Rd *TF:* 800-514-7463 ■ *Web:* www.redhill.org	Brookneal	VA	24528	434-376-2044		564
Red Hill Studios 1017 E St Ste C *Web:* www.redhillstudios.com	San Rafael	CA	94901	415-457-0440	457-0450	344
Red Hills State Park 3571 Ranger Ln *Web:* www.dnr.illinois.gov	Sumner	IL	62466	618-936-2469		565
Red Hot & Blue Restaurants Inc 1600 Wilson Blvd *TF:* 888-509-7100 ■ *Web:* www.redhotandblue.com	Arlington	VA	22209	703-276-7427		670
Red Hour Films 9200 Sunset Blvd Penthouse 22 *Web:* www.redhourfilms.com	Los Angeles	CA	90069	323-602-5000		514
Red Iguana 736 W N Temple St *Web:* www.rediguana.com	Salt Lake City	UT	84116	801-322-1489		671
Red Incorporated Communications 510 Energy Pl *Web:* www.redinc.com	Idaho Falls	ID	83401	208-528-0051		393
Red Inn 15 Commercial St *TF:* 866-473-3466 ■ *Web:* theredinn.com	Provincetown	MA	02657	508-487-7334	487-5115	671
Red Jacket Beach Resort 39 Todd Rd *Web:* redjacketresorts.com	South Yarmouth	MA	02664	508-398-6941		379
Red Label Vacations Inc 5450 Explorer Dr Ste 100 *TF:* 866-573-3824 ■ *Web:* www.redtag.ca	Mississauga	ON	L4W5N1	905-283-6020		772
Red Lake County 124 Langevin Ave 2nd Fl *Web:* www.co.red-lake.mn.us	Red Lake Falls	MN	56750	218-253-2590		338
Red Lake County Cooperative Inc 106 Hwy 59 *TF:* 800-253-6269 ■ *Web:* www.redlakecocoop.com	Brooks	MN	56715	800-253-6269		579
Red Lake Electric Co-opeartive Inc 412 International Dr PO Box 430 *TF:* 800-245-6068 ■ *Web:* www.redlakeelectric.com	Red Lake Falls	MN	56750	218-253-2168	253-2630	245
Red Lake Gaming Enterprises Inc PO Box 543 *TF:* 888-679-2501 ■ *Web:* www.sevenclanscasino.com	Redlake	MN	56671	218-679-2111	679-2191	132
Red Lambda Inc 400 Colonial Center Pkwy Ste 270 *Web:* www.redlambda.com	Lake Mary	FL	32746	407-732-7507		387
Red Letter Press (RLP) 4710 University Way NE Ste 100 *Web:* www.redletterpress.org	Seattle	WA	98105	206-985-8965		637-2
Red Letter Publishing PO Box 272682 *Fax Area Code: 970 ■ *TF:* 800-445-5614 ■ *Web:* www.christianbusinessdirectoryonline.com	Fort Collins	CO	80527	800-445-5614	267-9669*	637-2
Red Level Networks LLC 40200 Grand River Ste 200 *Web:* redlevelnetworks.com	Novi	MI	48375	248-412-8200		180

	Phone	Fax	Class
Red Lion Controls Inc 20 Willow Springs Cir ... York PA 17406 *TF:* 877-432-9908 ■ *Web:* www.redlion.net	717-767-6511		201
Red Lion Hotels Corp 201 W N River Dr Ste 100 ... Spokane WA 99201 *NYSE: RLH* ■ **Fax Area Code:* 509 ■ *TF:* 800-733-5466 ■ *Web:* www.redlion.com	800-733-5466	325-7324*	379
Red Lion Inn 30 Main St ... Stockbridge MA 01262 *Web:* www.redlioninn.com	413-298-5545		379
Red Lodge Beverages and Refreshments Inc 7 Pepsi Dr ... Red Lodge MT 59068 *Web:* www.redlodgechamber.org	406-446-2040		297-8
Red Lodge Mountain 305 Ski Run Rd ... Red Lodge MT 59068 *TF:* 800-444-8977 ■ *Web:* www.redlodgemountain.com	406-446-2610		226
Red Mesa Restaurant 4912 Fourth St N ... Saint Petersburg FL 33703 *Web:* www.redmesarestaurant.com	727-527-8728		671
Red Oak Greenhouses Inc 401 W Coolbaugh St ... Red Oak IA 51566 *Web:* redoakgreenhouse.com	712-623-5191		192
Red Onion State Prison 10800 H Jack Rose Hwy PO Box 970 ... Pound VA 24279 *Web:* vadoc.virginia.gov	276-796-7510		213
Red Ox Inn 9420 91st St ... Edmonton AB T6C1Z5 *Web:* www.theredoxinn.com	780-465-5727		671
Red Parrot, The 348 Thames St ... Newport RI 02840 *Web:* www.redparrotrestaurant.com	401-847-3800		671
Red Path Consulting Group 1011 Washington Ave S Ste 350 ... Minneapolis MN 55415 *Web:* redpathcg.com	612-843-3360		196
Red Peacock International Inc 12070 Delante Way ... Granada Hills CA 91344 *Web:* www.redpeacock.com	818-265-7722		246
Red Pepper 1011 University Ave ... Grand Forks ND 58203 *Web:* www.redpepper.com	701-775-9671		671
Red Pig Bar-B-Q 2201 Ferguson Rd ... Johnson City TN 37604 *Web:* redpigbarbq.com	423-282-6585		671
Red Privet LLC 415 Market St ... Harrisburg PA 17101 *Web:* redprivet.com	717-260-5239		466
Red River Broadcasting Company LLC 2001 London Rd ... Duluth MN 55812 *Web:* www.fox21online.com	218-728-1622		738
Red River Commodities Inc 501 42nd St N ... Fargo ND 58102 *TF:* 800-437-5539 ■ *Web:* redriv.com	701-282-2600		694
Red River Computer Company Inc 21 Water St Ste 500 ... Claremont NH 03743 *TF:* 800-769-3060 ■ *Web:* www.redriver.com	603-448-8880		121
Red River County 200 N Walnut St ... Clarksville TX 75426 *Web:* www.co.red-river.tx.us	903-427-2401	427-5510	338
Red River Parish Clerk of Court's Office 615 E Carroll St PO Box 485 ... Coushatta LA 71019 *Web:* www.redriverclerk.com	318-932-6741	932-3126	338
Red River Sanitors Inc 1522 Corporate Dr ... Shreveport LA 71107 *TF:* 800-832-7654 ■ *Web:* www.sanitors.com	318-222-6070	227-0101	192
Red River Specialties Inc 1324 N Hearne Ave Ste 120 ... Shreveport LA 71107 *TF:* 800-256-3344 ■ *Web:* www.rrsi.com	318-425-5944		276
Red River Valley Cooperative Power Assn 109 Second Ave E ... Halstad MN 56548 *TF:* 800-788-7784 ■ *Web:* www.rrvcoop.com	218-456-2139		245
Red River Valley School Division 233 Main St N ... Morris MB R0G1K0 *Web:* rrvsd.ca	204-746-2317	746-2785	685
Red River Zoo 4255 23rd Ave S ... Fargo ND 58104 *Web:* redriverzoo.org	701-277-9240	277-9238	823
Red Robin Gourmet Burgers Inc 6312 S Fiddlers Green Cir Ste 200-N ... Greenwood Village CO 80111 *NASDAQ: RRGB* ■ *Web:* www.redrobin.com	303-846-6000	846-6013	670
Red Rock Brewing Co 254 South 200 West ... Salt Lake City UT 84101 *Web:* redrockbrewing.com	801-521-7446		671
Red Rock Canyon National Conservation Area 1000 Scenic Loop Dr ... Las Vegas NV 89161 *Web:* www.redrockcanyonlv.org	702-515-5350	363-6779	50-5
Red Rock Canyon State Park 116 Red Rock Canyon Rd ... Hinton OK 73047 *Web:* www.travelok.com	405-542-6344		565
Red Rock Distributing Co 1 NW 50th St ... Oklahoma City OK 73118 *TF:* 800-323-7109 ■ *Web:* www.redrockdist.com	405-677-3373		449
Red Rock Ranch, The PO Box 38 ... Kelly WY 83011 *Web:* theredrockranch.com	307-733-6288	733-6287	239
Red Rock Research Ctr 5701 W Charleston Blvd Ste 100 ... Las Vegas NV 89146 *Web:* www.redrockmedical.com	702-602-6839		743
Red Rock Resort Spa & Casino 11011 W Charleston Blvd ... Las Vegas NV 89135 *TF:* 866-767-7773 ■ *Web:* redrock.sclv.com	702-797-7777		379
Red Rock State Park 4050 Red Rock Loop Rd ... Sedona AZ 86336 *Web:* azstateparks.com	928-282-6907		565
Red Rocket Media Group LLC 2720 Council Tree Ave Ste 218 ... Fort Collins CO 80525 **Fax Area Code:* 800 ■ *Web:* www.redrocketmg.com	970-674-0079	783-8047*	463
Red Rocks Amphitheater 18300 W Alameda Pkwy ... Morrison CO 80465 *Web:* www.redrocksonline.com	720-865-2494		572
Red Rocks Community College 13300 W Sixth Ave ... Lakewood CO 80228 *Web:* www.rrcc.edu	303-914-6308	914-6318	162
Red Roof Inn 4271 Sidco Dr ... Nashville TN 37204 *Web:* www.redroof.com	615-832-0093		379
Red Roof Inn Monterey 2227 N Fremont St ... Monterey CA 93940 *Web:* www.redroofinnmonterey.com	831-372-7586		379
Red Rooster Group 22 E 49th St 7th Fl ... New York NY 10017 *Web:* www.redroostergroup.com	212-673-9353		194
Red Rose Studio 358 Flintlock Dr ... Willow Street PA 17584 *TF:* 888-839-5673 ■ *Web:* www.redrosestudio.com	717-464-3873	464-3250	637-2
Red Sage Publishing Inc PO Box 4844 ... Seminole FL 33775 *Web:* www.eredsage.com	727-391-3847		637-2
Red Sea Press Inc (RSP) 541 W Ingham Ave Ste B ... Trenton NJ 08638 *Web:* www.africaworldpressbooks.com	609-695-3200	695-6466	637-2
Red Seal Electric Co 3835 W 150th St ... Cleveland OH 44111 *Web:* www.redseal.com	216-941-3900	941-5305	816
Red Sky Solutions LLC 11925 S 700 E ... Draper UT 84020 *TF:* 844-369-4593 ■ *Web:* www.redskysolutions.com	949-273-2639		226
Red Snapper 144 E 9th St ... Durango CO 81301 *Web:* www.durangoredsnapper.com	970-259-3417		671
Red Snapper 8430 Ward Pkwy ... Kansas City MO 64114 *Web:* www.kcredsnapper.com	816-333-8899		671
Red Spot Interactive 1001 Jupiter Park Dr ... Jupiter FL 33458 *TF:* 800-401-7931 ■ *Web:* www.redspotinteractive.com	800-401-7931		463
Red Spot Paint & Varnish Company Inc 1107 E Louisiana St ... Evansville IN 47711 *Web:* www.redspot.com	812-428-9100	435-1706	550
Red Square Agency Inc 54 St Emanuel St ... Mobile AL 36602 *Web:* www.redsquareagency.com	251-476-1283		7
Red Star Oil 802 Purser Dr ... Raleigh NC 27603 *TF:* 800-774-6033 ■ *Web:* www.redstaroil.com	919-772-1944	779-8871	449
Red Star Tavern & Roast House 503 SW Alder St ... Portland OR 97204 *Web:* www.redstartavern.com	503-222-0005	417-3334	671
Red Stone Education Consulting Group PO Box 1685 ... Rapid City SD 57709 *Web:* www.redstoneeducation.org	605-341-3585	341-4001	244
Red Streak Corp 1627 Main St ... Kansas City MO 64108 *Web:* www.redstreakcorp.com	816-471-6979		111
Red Tettemer Inc 1 S Broad St 24th Fl ... Philadelphia PA 19107 *Web:* rtop.com	267-402-1410		4
Red Thread 300 E River Dr ... East Hartford CT 06108 *TF:* 800-635-4874 ■ *Web:* www.red-thread.com	860-528-9981	528-1843	320
Red Tree inc 1374 W 130 S ... Orem UT 84097 *Web:* www.redtreeleadership.com	801-655-0200		463
Red Triangle Oil Co 2809 S Chestnut Ave ... Fresno CA 93725 *Web:* redtriangleoil.com	559-485-4320		579
Red Valve Company Inc 600 N Bell Ave ... Carnegie PA 15106 *Web:* www.redvalve.com	412-279-0044		789
Red Wind Casino 12819 Yelm Hwy ... Olympia WA 98513 *TF:* 866-946-2444 ■ *Web:* redwindcasino.com	866-946-2444		133
Red Wing Shoe Company Inc 314 Main St ... Red Wing MN 55066 *TF:* 800-733-9464 ■ *Web:* www.redwingheritage.com	844-314-6246		301
Red Wing Software Inc 491 Hwy 19 ... Red Wing MN 55066 *TF:* 800-732-9464 ■ *Web:* www.redwingsoftware.com	651-388-1106	388-7950	178-1
Red's Old 395 Grill 1055 S Carson St ... Carson City NV 89701 *Web:* www.reds395.com	775-887-0395		671
Red7e Inc 637 W Main St ... Louisville KY 40202 *Web:* red7e.com	502-585-3403		7
Redapt Inc 12226 134th Ct NE Bldg D ... Redmond WA 98052 *TF:* 888-800-5633 ■ *Web:* www.redapt.com	425-882-0400		196
RedBrick Health Corp 510 Marquette Ave Ste 500 ... Minneapolis MN 55402 **Fax Area Code:* 612 ■ *TF:* 866-322-1255 ■ *Web:* www.redbrickhealth.com	866-322-1255	659-3001*	393
Redbud E & P Inc 16000 Stuebner Airline Ste 320 ... Spring TX 77379 *Web:* www.redbudinc.com	832-698-4901		536
RedBuilt LLC 200 E Mallard Dr ... Boise ID 83706 *TF:* 866-859-6757 ■ *Web:* www.redbuilt.com	866-859-6757		817
Redbury Hotel, The 1717 Vine St ... Los Angeles CA 90028 *Web:* theredbury.com	323-962-1717		378
REDCAT (Roy & Edna Disney/CALARTS Theater (REDCAT)) 631 W Second St ... Los Angeles CA 90012 *Web:* www.redcat.org	213-237-2800	237-2811	50-2
Redcliffe Plantation State Historic Site 181 Redcliffe Rd ... Beech Island SC 29842 *Web:* southcarolinaparks.com	803-827-1473		565
Redco Foods Inc One Hansen Island ... Little Falls NY 13365 *TF:* 800-556-6674 ■ *Web:* redrosetea.com	315-823-1300		296-40
Redco Machine Inc 3032 Forest Rd ... Bedford VA 24523 *Web:* www.redcomachine.com	540-586-3545	586-3566	454
Redcom Laboratories Inc 1 Redcom Ctr ... Victor NY 14564 *Web:* www.redcom.com	585-924-7550	924-6572	735
Redd Brown & Williams Real Estate services 201 Bridge St ... Paintsville KY 41240 *Web:* www.rbandw.com	606-789-8119	789-5414	653
Redd Paper Co 3851 Ctr Loop ... Orlando FL 32808 *TF:* 800-961-6656 ■ *Web:* www.reddpaper.com	407-299-6656	299-8142	553
Red-D-Arc Inc 667 S Service Rd PO Box 40 ... Grimsby ON L3M4G1 *Web:* www.red-d-arc.com	905-643-4212		23
Reddick, Riggs & Hunter PC 23 Siebald St PO Box 725 ... Statesboro GA 30458 *Web:* rrhcpa.com	912-764-9843	489-3036	2
Redding Civic Auditorium 700 Auditorium Dr ... Redding CA 96001 *Web:* www.reddingcivic.com	530-229-0036		572
Redding Distributing Co (RDC) 6450 Lockheed Dr ... Redding CA 96003 *Web:* www.reddingdistributing.com	530-226-5700	226-1173	81-1
Redding Oil Co 4990 Mountain Lake Rd ... Redding CA 96003 *TF:* 800-223-1217 ■ *Web:* www.reddingoilcompany.com	530-243-1217	243-3432	579
Redding Printing Company Inc 1130 Continental St ... Redding CA 96001 *TF:* 800-633-7991 ■ *Web:* www.reddingprinting.com	530-243-0525	243-0427	627
Redding Resources Inc 8140 Mayfield Rd ... Chesterland OH 44026 *Web:* www.surgicalbilling.com	440-729-1001	729-6001	2

Name / Address	City	State	ZIP	Phone	Fax	Class
Reddog Industries Inc 2012 E 33rd St *Web:* reddog-erie.com	Erie	PA	16510	814-898-4321	899-5671	757
Reddy Ice Holdings Inc 8750 N Central Expy Ste 1800 *OTC:* RDDYQ ■ *TF:* 800-683-4423 ■ *Web:* www.reddyice.com	Dallas	TX	75231	214-526-6740		380
Redeemer Catholic Schools 1 McRae St PO Box 1318 *Web:* www.redeemer.ab.ca	Okotoks	AB	T1S1B3	403-938-2659		623
Redeemer Lutheran Church of Waverly Bremer County Iowa 2001 W Bremer Ave *Web:* redeemerwaverly.org	Waverly	IA	50677	319-352-1325		48-20
Redeemer Radio 4618 E State Blvd Ste 200 *TF:* 888-436-1450 ■ *Web:* www.redeemerradio.com	Fort Wayne	IN	46815	260-436-9598	432-6179	645-141
Redeemer University College 777 Garner Rd E *TF:* 877-779-0913 ■ *Web:* www.redeemer.ca	Ancaster	ON	L9K1J4	905-648-2131	648-2134	166
Redemption Church 105 Nortech Pkwy *Web:* www.myredemption.cc	San Jose	CA	95134	408-262-0900		685
Redemption Press 1730 Railroad St *Web:* redemption-press.com	Enumclaw	WA	98022	360-226-3488		637-2
Redemptorist Retreat Ctr 1800 N Timber Trail Ln *Web:* www.redemptoristretreat.org	Oconomowoc	WI	53066	262-567-6900		673
Redemptorist, The 1 Liguori Dr *TF:* 800-325-9521 ■ *Web:* www.liguori.org	Liguori	MO	63057	636-464-2500		48-20
Redex Industries Inc 1176 Salem Pkwy *TF:* 800-345-7339 ■ *Web:* udderlysmooth.com	Salem	OH	44460	330-332-9800		77
Redeye Distribution Inc 449a Trollingwood Rd *TF:* 877-733-3931 ■ *Web:* www.redeyeworldwide.com	Haw River	NC	27258	877-733-3931		317
Redfield Financial Group LLC 4120 E Beltline Ave Ste 100 *Web:* redfieldfinancialgroup.com	Grand Rapids	MI	49525	616-447-1600		390
Redfin 9890 S Maryland Pkwy *TF:* 844-759-7732 ■ *Web:* www.redfin.com	Las Vegas	NV	89183	877-973-3346		5
Redflex Traffic Systems Inc 5651 W Talavi Blvd Ste 200 *TF:* 866-703-8097 ■ *Web:* www.redflex.com	Glendale	AZ	85306	866-703-8097		196
Redford Township Chamber of Commerce 26050 5-Mile Rd *Web:* redfordchamber.com	Redford	MI	48239	313-535-0960	535-6356	139
Redgrave & Rosenthal LLP 120 E Palmetto Park Rd Ste 400 *Web:* redgraveandrosenthal.com	Boca Raton	FL	33432	561-347-1700		41
Redgwick Construction 21 Hegenberger Ct *Web:* www.redgwick.com	Oakland	CA	94621	510-792-1727	792-1728	188-4
RedHawk Energy Corp PO Box 53929 *Web:* www.redhawkenergycorp.com	LaFayette	LA	70505	337-269-5933	269-5935	538
Redhawk Network Security LLC 62958 Layton Ave Ste One *TF:* 866-605-6328 ■ *Web:* redhawksecurity.com	Bend	OR	97701	541-382-4360		196
Redhead Publishing PO Box 178 *Web:* www.tonybender.net	Ashley	ND	58413	701-288-3531		532-2
Redhills Ventures LLC PO Box 370369 *Web:* redhillsventures.com	Las Vegas	NV	89137	702-233-2160		401
RedHouse Associates LLC 802 Lovett Blvd *Web:* www.redhouseassociates.com	Houston	TX	77006	713-338-2151		463
Redi Bag USA 135 Fulton Ave *TF:* 800-517-2247 ■ *Web:* www.redibagusa.com	New Hyde Park	NY	11040	516-746-0600		98
Redi-Carpet Inc 10101 Fountaingate Dr *Web:* www.redicarpet.com	Stafford	TX	77477	832-310-2000	310-2001	290
Redico Inc 1850 S Lee Ct **Fax Area Code:* 770 ■ *TF:* 800-242-3920 ■ *Web:* www.redicoinc.com	Buford	GA	30519	800-242-3920	614-1403*	665
Redi-Data Inc 107 Little Falls Rd *TF:* 800-635-5833 ■ *Web:* www.redidata.com	Fairfield	NJ	07004	973-227-4380		387
Rediker Software Inc 2 Wilbraham Rd *TF:* 800-213-9860 ■ *Web:* www.rediker.com	Hampden	MA	01036	413-566-3463		177
Redi-Mail Direct Marketing Inc 107 Little Falls Rd *Web:* www.redimail.com	Fairfield	NJ	07004	973-808-4500	808-5511	5
Redington Inc 49 Richmondville Ave *Web:* www.redingtoninc.com	Westport	CT	06880	203-222-7399	222-1819	401
Redlands Bowl 25 Grant St *Web:* redlandsbowl.org	Redlands	CA	92373	909-793-7316	793-5086	572
Redlands Chamber of Commerce 47 N First St *TF:* 800-966-6428 ■ *Web:* www.redlandschamber.org	Redlands	CA	92373	909-793-2546	335-6388	139
Redlands Community College 1300 S Country Club Rd *TF:* 866-415-6367 ■ *Web:* www.redlandscc.edu	El Reno	OK	73036	405-262-2552	422-1200	162
Redlands Symphony 1200 E Colton Ave *Web:* www.redlandssymphony.com	Redlands	CA	92373	909-748-8018		573-3
Redleaf Press 10 Yorkton Ct *TF:* 800-423-8309 ■ *Web:* www.redleafpress.org	Saint Paul	MN	55117	651-641-0508	641-0115	637-10
RedLegg 319 1/2 State St Ste A *TF:* 877-811-5040 ■ *Web:* redlegg.com	Geneva	IL	60134	877-811-5040		196
Redline Communications Inc 302 Town Centre Blvd 4th Fl *TF:* 866-633-6669 ■ *Web:* rdlcom.com	Markham	ON	L3R0E8	905-479-8344		224
Redline Trading Solutions Inc 18 Commerce Way Ste 6800 *Web:* www.redlinetrading.com	Woburn	MA	01801	781-995-3403		174
Redman Equipment & Manufacturing Co 19800 Normandie Ave *TF:* 888-733-2602 ■ *Web:* www.redmaneq.com	Torrance	CA	90502	310-329-1134	324-5656	91
Redman Technologies Inc 10172-108 St *TF:* 866-425-0022 ■ *Web:* www.redmantech.com	Edmonton	AB	T5J1L3	866-425-0022		180
RedMane Technology LLC 8614 W Catalpa Ave Ste 1001 *TF:* 833-276-2003 ■ *Web:* www.redmane.com	Chicago	IL	60656	773-331-0000	693-3627	177
Redmon, Peyton & Braswell LLP 510 King St Ste 301 *Web:* www.rpb-law.com	Alexandria	VA	22314	703-684-2000		428
Redmond Chamber of Commerce 8383 158th Ave NE Ste 225 *Web:* www.oneredmond.org	Redmond	WA	98052	425-885-4014		139
Redmond Co, The W228 N745 Westmound Dr *Web:* theredmondco.com	Waukesha	WI	53186	262-549-9600	549-1314	194
Redmond Regional Medical Ctr 501 Redmond Rd *TF:* 800-242-5662 ■ *Web:* redmondregional.com	Rome	GA	30165	706-291-0291		374-3
Redmond School District 145 SE Salmon Ave *Web:* www.redmond.k12.or.us	Redmond	OR	97756	541-923-5437	923-5142	685
Redmonk 95 High St Ste 206 *TF:* 866-733-6665 ■ *Web:* www.redmonk.com	Portland	ME	04101	866-733-6665		463
Redneck Trailer Supplies 2100 NW By-Pass *TF:* 877-973-3632 ■ *Web:* www.redneck-trailer.com	Springfield	MO	65803	417-864-5856		779
Redner's Markets Inc 3 Quarry Rd *Web:* www.rednersmarkets.com	Reading	PA	19605	610-926-3700		345
Redniss & Mead Inc 22 First St *TF:* 800-404-2060 ■ *Web:* rednissmead.com	Stamford	CT	06905	203-327-0500	357-1118	261
Redondo Beach Chamber of Commerce & Visitors Bureau 200 N Pacific Coast Hwy *Web:* www.redondochamber.org	Redondo Beach	CA	90277	310-376-6911	374-7373	139
Redondo Beach Public Library 303 N Pacific Coast Hwy *Web:* www.redondo.org	Redondo Beach	CA	90277	310-318-0675	318-3809	434-3
Redondo Systems Inc 4025 Spencer St Ste 104 *Web:* www.redondosystems.com	Torrance	CA	90503	310-542-6730	542-6771	180
RedPeg Marketing 727 N Washington St *Web:* redpegmarketing.com	Alexandria	VA	22314	703-519-9000		7
RedRick Technologies Inc 21624 Adelaide Rd *TF:* 800-340-9511 ■ *Web:* www.redricktechnologies.com	Mount Brydges	ON	N0L1W0	800-340-9511		475
Redrock Canyon Grill 9221 Lake Hefner Pkwy *Web:* www.redrockcanyongrill.com	Oklahoma City	OK	73120	405-749-1995		671
RedRock Consultants 1450 Sutter St No 527 *Web:* www.redrockconsultants.com	San Francisco	CA	94109	415-246-7625	928-7259	195
Redrock Security & Cabling Inc 6 Morgan Ste 150 *Web:* www.itredrock.com	Irvine	CA	92618	949-900-3460		693
Reds Wine Tavern 77 Adelaide St W *Web:* redsrestaurants.com	Toronto	ON	M5H1P9	416-862-7337		671
Redshift Business Networks Inc 900 Reichert Ave Ste 535 *Web:* www.redshift-networks.com	Novato	CA	94945	415-462-6262	704-3277	631
RedSky Technologies Inc 333 N Michigan Ave Ste 1600 *TF:* 866-778-2435 ■ *Web:* www.redskye911.com	Chicago	IL	60601	312-432-4300	432-4320	179
Redspin, a Division of CynergisTek 11410 Jollyville Rd Ste 2201 *TF:* 800-721-9177 ■ *Web:* www.redspin.com	Austin	TX	78759	800-721-9177		177
Redsson Ltd 104 N Summit St **Fax Area Code:* 866 ■ *Web:* www.redsson.com	Toledo	OH	43604	419-244-1111	644-8510*	809
Redstone Communications Group Inc 10031 Maple St *Web:* www.redstoneweb.com	Omaha	NE	68134	402-393-5435		4
Redstone Federal Credit Union 220 Wynn Dr NW *TF:* 800-234-1234 ■ *Web:* www.redfcu.org	Huntsville	AL	35893	256-837-6110	722-3655	219
Redstone Highlands Health Care Ctr 6 Garden Center Dr *Web:* www.redstonehighlands.org	Greensburg	PA	15601	724-832-8400	836-3710	450
Redstone Inn 82 Redstone Blvd *Web:* redstoneinn.thegilmorecollection.com	Redstone	CO	81623	970-963-2526		379
Redstone Inn & Suites 504 Bluff St *Web:* www.theredstoneinn.com	Dubuque	IA	52001	563-582-1894	582-1893	379
Redstone Properties 1120 W SR- 89A Ste D5 *Web:* redstonesedona.com	Sedona	AZ	86336	928-204-2500	203-0109	652
RedWind Group Inc 1220 Southmore *Web:* www.redwindgroup.com	Houston	TX	77004	713-522-2472		194
Redwing Book Company Inc 202 Bendix Dr *TF:* 800-873-3946 ■ *Web:* www.redwingbooks.com	Taos	NM	87571	575-758-7758	758-7768	96
Redwire LLC 1136 Thomasville Rd *TF:* 877-371-9473 ■ *Web:* redwire.com	Tallahassee	FL	32303	850-219-9473		693
Redwood Adventure LLC 1512 Colonial Ter N *TF:* 855-222-5885 ■ *Web:* www.c21redwood.com	Arlington	VA	22209	703-858-5676		652
Redwood Capital Group LLC 1 E Wacker Dr Ste 1600 *Web:* www.redwoodcapgroup.com	Chicago	IL	60601	312-995-7300		690
Redwood City Public Library 1044 Middlefield Rd *Web:* www.redwoodcity.org	Redwood City	CA	94063	650-780-7018		434-3
Redwood City School District (RCSD) 750 Bradford St *Web:* www.rcsdk8.net	Redwood City	CA	94063	650-423-2200	423-2294	685
Redwood City Seed Co PO Box 361 *Web:* www.ecoseeds.com	Redwood City	CA	94064	650-325-7333		323
Redwood City-San Mateo County Chamber of Commerce 1450 Veterans Blvd Ste 125 *Web:* redwoodcitychamber.com	Redwood City	CA	94063	650-364-1722	364-1729	139
Redwood Coast Trucking 2210 Peninsula Dr	Arcata	CA	95521	707-443-0857		780
Redwood County 403 S Mill St PO Box 130 *Web:* www.co.redwood.mn.us	Redwood Falls	MN	56283	507-637-4016	637-4017	338
Redwood Credit Union PO Box 6104 *TF:* 800-479-7928 ■ *Web:* www.redwoodcu.org	Santa Rosa	CA	95406	707-545-4000		217
Redwood Day School Parents & Guardians Assn 3245 Sheffield Ave *Web:* www.rdschool.org	Oakland	CA	94602	510-534-0800		685

Phone | Fax | Class

Redwood Library & Athenaeum
50 Bellevue Ave Newport RI 02840 401-847-0292 841-5680 434-4
Web: redwoodlibrary.org

Redwood National & State Parks
1111 Second St Crescent City CA 95531 707-465-7335 564
Web: www.nps.gov

Redwood Products of Chino Inc
9301 Remington Ave Site E Chino CA 91710 909-923-5656 499
Web: www.redwoodchino.com

Redwood Steakhouse
5304 Gateway Center Dr Flint MI 48507 810-233-8000 233-8833 671
Web: theredwoodlodge.com

Redwood Toxicology Laboratory Inc
3650 W Wind Blvd Santa Rosa CA 95403 707-577-7959 743
Web: www.redwoodtoxicology.com

Redwood Trust Inc
1 Belvedere Pl Ste 300 Mill Valley CA 94941 415-389-7373 509
NYSE: RWT ■ *TF:* 866-269-4976 ■ *Web:* www.redwoodtrust.com

Redwood Veterinary Clinic Inc
1946 Santa Rosa Ave Santa Rosa CA 95407 707-542-4012 794
Web: redwoodvetclinic.com

RedXDefense LLC 7642 Standish Pl Rockville MD 20855 301-279-7970 279-7973 21
Web: www.redxdefense.com

Reeb Millwork Corp
7475 Henry Clay Blvd Liverpool NY 13088 315-451-6699 499
TF: 800-862-8622 ■ *Web:* reeb.com

Reece & Nichols Realtors
11601 Granada Leawood KS 66211 913-945-3704 491-0930 652
Web: www.reecenichols.com

Reece, Noland, & Mcelrath Inc
94 Main St Canton NC 28716 828-492-0677 261
Web: rnm-engineers.com

Reed & Brinkman Accounting 413 3rd St Jackson MN 56143 507-847-4222 2

Reed - Dallas Inc 3118 Ridge Pk Pottstown PA 19464 610-970-2002 390
Web: reeddallas.com

Reed & Davidson LLP
515 S Figueroa St Ste 1110 Los Angeles CA 90071 213-624-6200 623-1692 41
Web: www.politicallaw.com

Reed Bingham State Park
542 Reed Bingham Rd Adel GA 31620 229-896-3551 565
Web: gastateparks.org

Reed Brennan Media Assoc (RBMA)
628 Virginia Dr Orlando FL 32803 407-894-7300 894-7900 317
TF: 800-708-7311 ■ *Web:* www.rbma.com

Reed Candle Co 1531 W Poplar St San Antonio TX 78207 210-734-2342 122
Web: www.reedcandlecompany.com

Reed City Tool & Die Inc
603 E Church St Reed City MI 49677 231-832-7500 757
Web: www.reedcitytool.com

Reed College 3203 SE Woodstock Blvd Portland OR 97202 503-777-7511 777-7553 166
TF: 800-547-4750 ■ *Web:* www.reed.edu

Reed College of Media, The
1511 University Ave Morgantown WV 26506 304-293-3505 293-3072 637-9
Web: reedcollegeofmedia.wvu.edu

Reed Credit Union
10200 East Fwy Ste 125 Houston TX 77029 713-673-3333 673-2420 219
Web: reedcreditunion.com

Reed Gold Mine State Historic Site
9621 Reed Mine Rd Midland NC 28107 704-721-4653 721-4657 50-3
Web: www.nchistoricsites.org

Reed Group
10355 Westmoor Dr Ste 210 Westminster CO 80021 800-347-7443 194
TF: 800-347-7443 ■ *Web:* reedgroup.com

Reed Jack (Sen D - RI)
728 Hart Senate Office Bldg Washington DC 20510 202-224-4642 224-4680 342-2
TF: 800-745-5555 ■ *Web:* www.reed.senate.gov

Reed Lallier Chevrolet Inc
4500 Raeford Rd Fayetteville NC 28304 910-426-2000 516
Web: www.reedlallier.com

Reed Law Firm PA
220 Stoneridge Dr Ste 301 Columbia SC 29210 803-726-4888 41
Web: reedlawsc.com

Reed LLC 13822 Oaks Ave Chino CA 91710 909-287-2100 287-2140 190
TF: 888-779-7333 ■ *Web:* www.reedmfg.com

Reed Machinery Inc 10A New Bond St Worcester MA 01606 508-595-9090 111
Web: www.reed-machinery.com

Reed Manufacturing Co 1425 W Eigth St Erie PA 16502 814-452-3691 455-1697 758
TF: 800-456-1697 ■ *Web:* www.reedmfgco.com

Reed Manufacturing Company Inc
1321 S Veterans Blvd Tupelo MS 38804 662-842-4472 237-5898* 155-11
**Fax Area Code:* 800 ■ *TF:* 800-466-1154 ■ *Web:* www.reedmanufacturing.com

Reed Motors Inc 3776 W Colonial Dr Orlando FL 32808 407-297-7333 57
Web: www.reednissan.com

Reed Oil Company Inc
106 Washington St Doniphan MO 63935 573-996-2321 581

Reed Oven Co 1720 Nicholson Ave Kansas City MO 64120 816-842-7446 421-0422 298
Web: www.reedovenco.com

Reed Presentations Inc 17 Water St Lebanon NJ 08833 908-753-8800 753-8823 86
Web: www.reedpresentations.com

Reed Smith LLP 20 Stanwix St Pittsburgh PA 15222 412-288-3330 288-3063 428
Web: www.reedsmith.com

Reed Technology & Information Services Inc
7 Walnut Grove Dr Horsham PA 19044 215-441-6400 781
Web: www.reedtech.com

Reed Tom (Rep R - NY)
2263 Rayburn House Office Bldg Washington DC 20515 202-225-3161 226-6599 342-2
Web: www.reed.house.gov

Reeder & Associates Ltd
1905 Woodstock Rd Ste 7200 Roswell GA 30075 770-649-7523 260
Web: reederassoc.com

Reeder Distributors Inc
5450 Wilbarger St Fort Worth TX 76119 817-429-5957 429-9052 579
TF: 800-722-3103 ■ *Web:* www.reederdistributors.com

Reed-Lane Inc 359 Newark-Pompton Tpke Wayne NJ 07470 973-709-1090 476
Web: www.reedlane.com

Reedley College 995 N Reed Ave Reedley CA 93654 559-638-3641 638-5040 162
TF: 877-253-7122 ■ *Web:* www.rcedleycollege.edu

Phone | Fax | Class

Reed-Ramsey Inc
1315 W 22nd St Ste 205 Oak Brook IL 60523 630-571-4585 571-4630 192
Web: www.reed-ramsey.com

Reeds Family Outdoor Outfitters
522 Minnesota Ave NW Walker MN 56484 800-346-0019 711
TF: 800-346-0019 ■ *Web:* www.reedssports.com

Reeds Gap State Park
1405 New Lancaster Valley Rd Milroy PA 17063 717-667-3622 565
Web: www.dcnr.pa.gov

Reeds Jewelers Inc PO Box 2229 Wilmington NC 28402 877-406-3266 410
TF: 877-406-3266 ■ *Web:* www.reeds.com

Reedsville Cooperative Association Inc
PO Box 460 Reedsville WI 54230 920-754-4321 276
TF: 800-236-4047 ■ *Web:* www.countryvisionscoop.com

Reedy Industries Inc
2440 Ravine Way Ste 200 Glenview IL 60025 847-729-9450 189-10
Web: www.reedyindustries.com

Reedy Press PO Box 5131 Saint Louis MO 63139 314-644-3400 637-2
Web: www.reedypress.com

Reef Caribbean Restaurants, The
4172 Main St Vancouver BC V5V3P6 604-874-5375 671
Web: www.thereefrestaurant.com

Reef Industries Inc
9209 Almeda Genoa Rd Houston TX 77075 713-507-4200 507-4295 599
TF: 800-231-6074 ■ *Web:* www.reefindustries.com

Reef Restaurant, The
4100 Coastal Hwy Saint Augustine FL 32084 904-824-8008 671
Web: www.thereefstaugustine.com

Reef Restaurant, The
880 S Harbor Scenic Dr Long Beach CA 90802 562-435-8013 671
Web: www.reefrestaurant.com

Reef, The 105 S Sixth St Boise ID 83702 208-287-9200 671
Web: www.reefboise.com

Reel FX Inc 301 N Crowdus St Dallas TX 75226 214-979-0961 514
Web: www.reelfx.com

Reel Games Inc
1501 NE 13th Ave Fort Lauderdale FL 33304 954-563-8253 761
Web: www.reelgamesinc.com

Reel-Core Inc 904 3rd Ave SW Waukon IA 52172 563-568-6307 568-3688 604
Web: www.reelcore.com

Reell Precision Manufacturing Corp
1259 Willow Lake Blvd Saint Paul MN 55110 651-484-2447 484-3867 620
Web: reell.com

Reema Consulting Services Inc
8106 Hallmark Pl Gaithersburg MD 20879 443-303-3630 463
Web: reemacsi.com

Reemployability Inc
3212 Parkside Center Cir Tampa FL 33619 866-663-9880 78
TF: 866-663-9880 ■ *Web:* www.reemployability.com

Reenders Blueberries Farms
14079 168th Ave Grand Haven MI 49417 616-842-5238 315-1
Web: www.reendersblueberryfarms.com

Rees Broome PC 1900 Gallows Rd Tysons VA 22182 703-790-1911 848-2530 428
Web: www.reesbroome.com

Rees Inc 405 S Reed Rd Fremont IN 46737 260-495-9811 203
Web: www.reesinc.com

Rees Scientific Corp
1007 Whitehead Rd Ext Trenton NJ 08638 609-530-1055 530-1854 407
Web: www.reesscientific.com

Reese Engineering Inc
2021 Pine Hall Rd State College PA 16801 814-234-2548 261
Web: www.reeseinc.com

Reese Enterprises Inc
16350 Asher Ave Rosemount MN 55068 651-423-1126 423-2662 234
TF: 800-328-0953 ■ *Web:* www.reeseusa.com

Reese Law Group, Aplc
3168 Lionshead Ave Carlsbad CA 92010 760-842-5850 41
TF: 800-609-6050 ■ *Web:* reeselawgroup.com

Reese Military Sales Inc
2820 Bransford Ave Nashville TN 37204 615-298-5774 195
Web: reesemilitarysales.com

Reese Pharmaceutical Co
10617 Frank Ave Cleveland OH 44106 800-321-7178 231-6444* 238
**Fax Area Code:* 216 ■ *TF:* 800-321-7178 ■ *Web:* www.reesepharmaceutical.com

Reeve Shima PC
500 Union St Logan Bldg Ste 800 Seattle WA 98101 206-624-4004 41
Web: reeveshima.com

Reeve Store Equipment Co
9131 Bermudez St Pico Rivera CA 90660 562-949-2535 949-3862 286
TF: 800-927-3383 ■ *Web:* www.reeveco.com

Reeve Trucking Co 5050 Carpenter Rd Stockton CA 95215 209-948-4061 948-1791 780
TF: 800-842-6677 ■ *Web:* www.reevetrucking.com

Reeves Brothers Trucking Inc
16105 Hwy 412 E Lexington TN 38351 731-968-6839 967-1813 780
TF: 800-892-7067 ■ *Web:* www.reevesbrostrucking.com

Reeves Construction Company Inc
101 Sheraton Ct Macon GA 31210 478-474-9092 474-9192 188-4
TF: 800-743-0593 ■ *Web:* www.reevescc.com

Reeves County 2340 Balmorhea Pecos TX 79772 432-445-5467 445-3997 338
Web: reevescountytexas.net

Reeves Law Group, The
200 W Santa Ana Blvd Ste 600 Santa Ana CA 92701 714-550-6000 41
Web: robertreeveslaw.com

Reeves Plastics LLC
507 Omalley Dr Coopersville MI 49404 616-997-0777 604
Web: www.reevesplastics.com

Reeves-Reed Arboretum 165 Hobart Ave Summit NJ 07901 908-273-8787 97
Web: www.reeves-reedarboretum.org

Reeves-Wiedeman Company Inc
14861 W 100th St Lenexa KS 66215 913-492-7100 492-6962 612
TF: 800-365-0024 ■ *Web:* rwco.com

Ref-Chem LP
1128 S Grandview PO Box 2588 Odessa TX 79761 432-332-8531 188-9
TF: 888-685-8531 ■ *Web:* www.ref-chem.com

Refectory Restaurant & Bistro
1092 Bethel Rd Columbus OH 43220 614-451-9774 671
Web: www.therefectoryrestaurant.com

Company / Address	Phone	Fax	Class
Reference Desk Press Inc 305 Briarwood Ave Haddonfield NJ 08033 *Web:* www.referencedeskpress.com	856-858-1010		637-2
ReferencePointPress PO Box 27779 San Diego CA 92198 *TF:* 888-479-6436 ■ *Web:* www.referencepointpress.com	858-618-1314	618-1730	637-2
Referentia Systems Inc 550 Paiea St Ste 236 Honolulu HI 96819 *TF:* 800-569-6255 ■ *Web:* www.referentia.com	808-840-8500		177
Reflection Riding Arboretum & Botanical Garden 400 Garden Rd Chattanooga TN 37419 *Web:* www.reflectionriding.org	423-821-1160		97
Reflectix Inc 1 School St PO Box 108 Markleville IN 46056 *Web:* www.reflectixinc.com	765-533-4332		548
Reflector, The PO Box 2020 Battle Ground WA 98604 *Web:* www.thereflector.com	360-687-5151	687-5162	532-4
Reflexite Corp 120 Darling Dr Avon CT 06001 *TF:* 800-654-7570 ■ *Web:* www.orafol.com	860-676-7100	676-7199	745-2
Reformed Church in America 4500 60th St SE Grand Rapids MI 49512 **Fax Area Code: 212* ■ *TF:* 800-722-9977 ■ *Web:* www.rca.org	616-698-7071	870-2499*	48-20
Reformed Episcopal Seminary 826 Second Ave Blue Bell PA 19422 *Web:* www.reseminary.edu	610-292-9852	292-9853	167-3
Reformed Presbyterian Theological Seminary 7418 Penn Ave Pittsburgh PA 15208 *Web:* www.rpts.edu	412-731-6000	731-4834	167-3
Reformed Theological Seminary 5422 Clinton Blvd Jackson MS 39209 *TF:* 800-543-2703 ■ *Web:* www.rts.edu	601-923-1600	923-1654	167-3
Refplus Inc 2777 Grande Allee Saint-Hubert QC J4T2R4 *TF:* 888-816-2665 ■ *Web:* www.refplus.com	450-641-2665		664
Refricenter of Miami Inc 7101 NW 43rd St Miami FL 33166 *Web:* www.refricenter.net	305-477-8880	599-9323	665
Refrigerated Food Express Inc 57 Littlefield St Avon MA 02322 *TF:* 800-342-8822 ■ *Web:* www.rfxinc.com	508-587-4600	588-9655	780
Refrigeration Contractors Inc 17246 NE San Rafael St Portland OR 97230 *Web:* www.refconinc.com	503-257-8668		665
Refrigeration Research Inc 525 N Fifth St PO Box 869 Brighton MI 48116 *Web:* www.refresearch.com	810-227-1151	227-3700	14
Refrigeration Sales Corp 9450 Allen Dr Valley View OH 44125 *TF:* 866-894-8200 ■ *Web:* www.refrigerationsales.net	216-525-8200		612
Refrigeration Sales Inc 1810 E High St Jackson MI 49203 *TF:* 800-482-0781 ■ *Web:* www.refsales.com	517-784-8579	784-7373	665
Refrigeration School Inc 4210 E Washington St Phoenix AZ 85034 *TF:* 888-943-4822 ■ *Web:* www.refrigerationschool.com	602-344-9600	267-4805	685
Refrigeration Service Engineers Society (RSES) 1666 Rand Rd Des Plaines IL 60016 *TF:* 800-297-5660 ■ *Web:* www.rses.org	847-297-6464	297-5038	49-3
Refrigeration Supplies Distributor (RSD) 26021 Atlantic Ocean Dr Lake Forest CA 92630 *TF:* 800-773-5359 ■ *Web:* www.rsd.net	949-380-7878	380-0755	665
Refrigerator Manufacturers Inc 17018 Edwards Rd Cerritos CA 90703 *TF:* 800-776-7178 ■ *Web:* www.rmi-econocold.com	562-926-2006	926-2007	14
RefrigiWear Inc 54 Breakstone Dr Dahlonega GA 30533 *TF:* 800-645-3744 ■ *Web:* www.refrigiwear.com	706-864-5757	864-5898	155-5
Refuge Media Group 806 E 4th St Duluth MN 55805 *Web:* www.refugeradio.com	218-722-2727		645-141
Refugees Intl (RI) 2001 S St NW Ste 700 Washington DC 20009 *TF:* 800-733-8433 ■ *Web:* www.refugeesinternational.org	202-828-0110	828-0819	48-5
Refugio County 808 Commerce St Refugio TX 78377 *Web:* www.co.refugio.tx.us	361-526-2233	526-1325	338
RefurbUPS com Inc 379 Spook Rock Rd Bldg J Suffern NY 10901 *Web:* www.refurbups.com	845-357-6911		180
RefWorks LLC 7200 Wisconsin Ave Ste 601 Bethesda MD 20814 *TF:* 800-843-7751 ■ *Web:* www.refworks.com	301-961-6700		387
Rega Engineering Group Inc 601 Old Cheney Rd Ste A Lincoln NE 68512 *Web:* regaengineering.com	402-484-7342	484-7344	261
Regal Air Flight School 10100 30th Ave W Hangar C51 Everett WA 98204 *TF:* 800-337-0345 ■ *Web:* www.regalair.com	425-353-9123	347-4507	685
Regal Art Press Inc 134 Fairfax Rd Saint Albans VT 05478 *Web:* www.regalartpress.com	802-524-4855	524-9795	627
Regal Beloit Corp 200 State St Beloit WI 53511 *Web:* www.regalbeloit.com	608-364-8800	364-8816	640
Regal Discount Securities Inc 950 Milwaukee Ave Ste 102 Glenview IL 60025 *TF:* 877-488-6534 ■ *Web:* www.eregal.com	800-927-3425		690
Regal Electronics Inc 2029 Otoole Ave San Jose CA 95131 *Web:* www.regalusa.net	408-988-2288		253
Regal Entertainment Group 7132 Regal Ln Knoxville TN 37918 *NASDAQ: RGC* ■ *TF:* 877-835-5734 ■ *Web:* www.regmovies.com	865-922-1123	922-3188	748
Regal Food Inc 3040 Ualena St Honolulu HI 96819 *Web:* www.regalfoodsusa.org	808-838-1229	834-4910	297-2
Regal Machine & Engineering Inc 5200 E 60th St Maywood CA 90270 *Web:* www.regalmachine.com	323-773-7462	784-8500	454
Regal Manufacturing Company Inc 990 3rd Ave SE Hickory NC 28602	828-328-5381		745-9
Regal Marine Industries Inc 2300 Jetport Dr Orlando FL 32809 *TF:* 800-877-3425 ■ *Web:* www.regalboats.com	407-851-4360	857-1256	90
Regal Metal Products Co 3615 Union Ave SE Minerva OH 44657 *Web:* www.regalmetalproducts.com	330-868-6343		295
Regal Mold & Die 25208 Leer Dr Elkhart IN 46514 *Web:* www.regalmold.com	574-262-4110		791
Regal Plastic Supply Co 111 E Tenth Ave North Kansas City MO 64116 *TF:* 800-627-2102 ■ *Web:* www.regalplastic.com	816-421-6290	421-8206	603
Regal Press 79 Astor Ave Norwood MA 02062 *TF:* 800-447-3425 ■ *Web:* www.regalpress.com	781-769-3900	352-3930	627
Regal Recycling Inc 645 Lucy Rd Howell MI 48843 *Web:* www.regalrecycling.net	517-546-3820		686
Regal Research & Manufacturing Company Inc 1200 E Plano Pkwy Plano TX 75074 *TF:* 888-589-9925 ■ *Web:* www.regalresearch.com	972-494-0359	272-0220	253
Regal Travel 615 Piikoi St Ste 104 Honolulu HI 96814 *TF:* 800-799-0865 ■ *Web:* www.regaltravel.com	808-566-7620		771
Regal Ware Inc 1675 Reigle Dr Kewaskum WI 53040 *Web:* www.regalware.com	262-626-2121	626-8565	486
Regali Inc 518 N Interurban St Richardson TX 75081 *Web:* regaliinc.com	972-726-8830		45
Regalia Manufacturing Co 2018 Fourth Ave Rock Island IL 61201 *TF:* 800-798-7471 ■ *Web:* www.regaliamfg.com	309-788-7471	788-0788	777
Regalix Inc 1121 San Antonio Rd Ste B200 Palo Alto CA 94303 *TF:* 888-683-4875 ■ *Web:* www.regalix.com	631-230-2629		195
Regan Communications Group Inc 106 Union Wharf Boston MA 02109 *Web:* regancomm.com	617-488-2800		636
Regan Group Inc, The 444 Regency Parkway Dr Ste 101 Omaha NE 68114 *Web:* theregangroup.wfadv.com	402-391-8000		690
Regan Group, The 360 W 132nd St Los Angeles CA 90061 *Web:* www.theregangroup.com	310-935-0413	327-7336	4
Regan Insurance Agency Inc 90144 Overseas Hwy Tavernier FL 33070 *Web:* reganinsuranceinc.com	305-852-3234		390
Regence Blue Cross Blue Shield of Oregon PO Box 1071 Portland OR 97207 *TF:* 888-734-3623 ■ *Web:* www.regence.com	888-675-6570		391-3
Regency Centers 1 Independent Dr Ste 114 Jacksonville FL 32202 *NYSE: REG* ■ *TF:* 800-950-6333 ■ *Web:* www.regencycenters.com	904-598-7000	634-3428	655
Regency Enterprises 10201 W Pico Blvd Bldg 12 Los Angeles CA 90035 *Web:* www.newregency.com	310-369-8300		514
Regency Fairbanks Hotel 95 10th Ave Fairbanks AK 99701 *TF:* 800-478-1320 ■ *Web:* www.regencyfairbankshotel.com	907-459-2700		379
Regency Fire Protection Inc 7651 Densmore Ave Van Nuys CA 91406 *Web:* regencyfire.com	818-982-0126		610
Regency Furniture Inc 7900 Cedarville Rd Brandywine MD 20613 *Web:* www.regencyfurniture.com	301-782-3800		321
Regency Hotel Management LLC 3211 W Sencore Dr Sioux Falls SD 57107 *Web:* regency-mgmt.com	605-334-2371		194
Regency House Hotel 140 Rt 23 N Pompton Plains NJ 07444 *Web:* www.regencyhousehotel.com	973-696-0900	696-0201	379
Regency Lighting Co 9261 Jordan Ave Chatsworth CA 91311 *TF:* 800-284-2024 ■ *Web:* www.regencylighting.com	800-284-2024		246
Regency Mall 5538 Durand Ave Racine WI 53406 *Web:* www.shopregency-mall.com	262-554-7903		460
Regency Outdoor Adv Inc 8820 Sunset Blvd West Hollywood CA 90069 *Web:* www.regencyoutdoor.com	310-657-8883	657-8073	4
Regency Plastics Company Ltd 50 Brisbane Rd North York ON M3J2K2 *Web:* www.regencyplastics.com	416-661-3000		608
Regency Seating Inc 2375 Romig Rd Akron OH 44320 *TF:* 866-816-9822 ■ *Web:* www.regencyof.com	330-848-3700		321
Regency Square Mall 9501 Arlington Expy Ste 100 Jacksonville FL 32225 *Web:* www.regencysquaremall.com	904-725-3830		460
Regency Suites Calgary 610 Fourth Ave SW Calgary AB T2P0K1 *TF:* 800-468-4044 ■ *Web:* www.regencycalgary.com	403-231-1000		379
Regency Theatres Inc 1440 Eastman Ave Ventura CA 93003 *Web:* regencymovies.com	805-658-6544		748
Regeneron Pharmaceuticals Inc 777 Old Saw Mill River Rd Tarrytown NY 10591 *NASDAQ: REGN* ■ *Web:* www.regeneron.com	914-345-7400		85
RegeneRx Biopharmaceuticals Inc 15245 Shady Grove Rd Ste 470 Rockville MD 20850 *OTC: RGRX* ■ *Web:* www.regenerx.com	301-208-9191		582
Regenesis Biomedical Inc 5301 N Pima Rd Scottsdale AZ 85250 *TF:* 877-970-4970 ■ *Web:* www.regenesisbio.com	480-970-4970		582
Regenexx Network 403 Summit Blvd Ste 201 Broomfield CO 80021 *TF:* 888-525-3005 ■ *Web:* www.regenexx.com	888-525-3005		668
Regent Association Services 2740 N Grand Ave Ste 200 Santa Ana CA 92705 *Web:* regentcmc.com	714-634-0611		652
Regent College 5800 University Blvd Vancouver BC V6T2E4 *TF:* 800-663-8664 ■ *Web:* www.regent-college.edu	604-224-3245	224-3097	167-3
Regent Education Inc 340 E Patrick St Ste 201 Frederick MD 21701 *TF:* 800-639-0927 ■ *Web:* www.regenteducation.com	301-662-5592	662-5866	178-1
Regent Entertainment Partnership LP 8411 Preston Rd Ste 650 Dallas TX 75225 *Web:* www.regententertainment.com	214-373-3434		514
Regent Group Inc 4501 Forbes Blvd Ste 100 Lanham MD 20706 *TF:* 888-354-6309 ■ *Web:* preferredtraveller.com	301-459-8020	459-3247	531-6

	Phone	Fax	Class
Regent Pacific Insurance Services Inc 265 S Randolph Ave Ste 240 ..... Brea CA 92821 *Web:* regentpacificins.com	714-671-1200		390
Regent Products Corp 8999 Palmer St ..... River Grove IL 60171 *TF:* 800-583-1002 ■ *Web:* www.regentproducts.com	708-583-1000		361
Regent University *Library* 1000 Regent University Dr ..... Virginia Beach VA 23464 *TF:* 888-249-1822 ■ *Web:* www.regent.edu	757-352-4916	226-4167	434-6
Regents of the University of California 1111 Franklin St 12th Fl ..... Oakland CA 94607 *Web:* www.regents.universityofcalifornia.edu	510-987-9691	987-9685	167-3
Regiment Capital Advisors LLC 222 Berkeley St 12th Fl ..... Boston MA 02116	617-488-1600		401
Regina Chamber of Commerce 2145 Albert St ..... Regina SK S4P2V1 *Web:* www.reginachamber.com	306-757-4658	757-4668	137
Regina Leader Post 1964 Park St PO Box 2020 ..... Regina SK S4P3G4 *TF:* 800-667-9999 ■ *Web:* leaderpost.com	306-781-5211	565-2588	532-1
Regina USA Inc 824 Chesapeake Dr ..... Cambridge MD 21613 *Web:* www.reginachain.net	410-221-2800		350
Regina Villa Associates Inc 51 Franklin St Ste 400 ..... Boston MA 02110 *Web:* www.reginavilla.com	617-357-5772		194
Reginald F. Lewis Museum of Maryland African American History & Culture 830 E Pratt St ..... Baltimore MD 21202 **Fax Area Code:* 410 ■ *Web:* www.lewismuseum.org	443-263-1800	333-1138*	520
Reginella's 4000 Virginia Beach Blvd ..... Virginia Beach VA 23452 *Web:* www.reginellas.com	757-498-9770		671
Region 4 Education Service Ctr 7145 W Tidwell Rd ..... Houston TX 77092 *Web:* www.esc4.net	713-462-7708	744-6514	764
Regional Acceptance Corp 1424 E Fire Tower Rd ..... Greenville NC 27858 *TF:* 877-722-7299 ■ *Web:* www.regionalacceptance.com	252-321-7700		217
Regional Airline Assn (RAA) 2025 M St NW Ste 800 ..... Washington DC 20036 *Web:* www.raa.org	202-367-1170	367-2170	49-21
Regional Care Inc 905 W 27th St ..... Scottsbluff NE 69361 *TF:* 800-795-7772 ■ *Web:* www.regionalcare.com	308-635-2260		390
Regional Chamber of Commerce San Gabriel Valley 19720 E Walnut Dr Ste 100A ..... Walnut CA 91789 **Fax Area Code:* 626 ■ *Web:* www.regionalchambersgv.com	714-245-5540	810-8475*	139
Regional Economic Models Inc 433 W St ..... Amherst MA 01002 *Web:* www.remi.com	413-549-1169	549-1038	177
Regional Educational Laboratory Midwest Resource Ctr 1120 E Diehl Rd Ste 200 ..... Naperville IL 60563 *TF:* 866-730-6735 ■ *Web:* ies.ed.gov	866-730-6735		434-3
Regional Group of Companies Inc, The 1737 Woodward Dr 2nd Fl ..... Ottawa ON K2C0P9 *Web:* regionalgroup.com	613-230-2100		652
Regional Heating & Air Conditioning Inc 2525 Won Rd ..... Colorado Springs CO 80910	719-392-6171		189-10
Regional Hospice of Western Connecticut 30 Milestone Rd ..... Danbury CT 06810 *Web:* regionalhospicect.org	203-702-7400		371
Regional International Corp 1007 Lehigh Stn Rd ..... Henrietta NY 14467 *Web:* www.regionalinternational.com	585-359-2011		61
Regional Jet Ctr 12344 Tower Dr ..... Bentonville AR 72712 *Web:* regionaljetcenter.com	479-205-1100		63
Regional Medical Center at Memphis 877 Jefferson Ave ..... Memphis TN 38103 *Web:* www.regionalonehealth.org	901-545-7100	545-6991	374-3
Regional Medical Center Bayonet Point 14000 Fivay Rd ..... Hudson FL 34667 *TF:* 800-861-0141 ■ *Web:* bayonetpointhospital.com	727-819-2929		374-3
Regional Medical Center of San Jose (RMCSJ) 225 N Jackson Ave ..... San Jose CA 95116 *TF:* 800-307-7135 ■ *Web:* regionalmedicalsanjose.com	408-259-5000	729-2884	374-3
Regional Medical Ctr, The 3000 St Matthews Rd ..... Orangeburg SC 29118 *TF:* 800-476-3377 ■ *Web:* www.trmchealth.org	803-395-2200		374-3
Regional Occupational Programs 300 Dana St ..... Fort Bragg CA 95437 *Web:* mcoe.us	707-964-9000		507
Regional Personnel Services Inc 502 US Hwy 22 Ste 1 ..... Lebanon NJ 08833 *Web:* regionalpersonnel.com	908-534-8113		260
Regional Plan Association Inc 4 Irving Pl 7th Fl ..... New York NY 10003 *Web:* www.rpa.org	212-253-2727		138
Regional Radio Group L L C 238 Bay Rd ..... Queensbury NY 12804 *Web:* www.regionalradiogroup.com	518-761-9890	761-9893	643
Regional Supply Inc 3571 S 300 W ..... Salt Lake City UT 84115 *TF:* 800-365-8920 ■ *Web:* www.regionalsupply.com	800-365-8920		603
Regional Transit Authority (RTA) 2817 Canal St ..... New Orleans LA 70119 *Web:* www.norta.com	504-827-8300		468
Regional Transit Service Inc 1372 E Main St ..... Rochester NY 14609 *Web:* www.myrts.com	585-654-0200		468
Regional Transit System (RTS) Stn 5 PO Box 490 ..... Gainesville FL 32627 *Web:* go-rts.com	352-334-2600	334-2607	468
Regional Transportation Authority 175 W Jackson Blvd Ste 1550 ..... Chicago IL 60604 *Web:* rtachicago.org	312-913-3200		468
Regional Transportation Commission of Southern Nevada (RTC) 600 S Grand Central Pkwy Ste 350 ..... Las Vegas NV 89106 *TF:* 800-228-3911 ■ *Web:* www.rtcsnv.com	702-676-1500	676-1518	468
Regional Transportation District (RTD) 1600 Blake St ..... Denver CO 80202 *TF:* 800-366-7433 ■ *Web:* www.rtd-denver.com	303-628-9000		468
Regional West Medical Ctr 4021 Ave B ..... Scottsbluff NE 69361 *Web:* www.rwhs.org	308-635-3711		374-3
Regions Bank 1900 Fifth Ave N ..... Birmingham AL 35203 *TF:* 800-734-4667 ■ *Web:* www.regions.com	800-734-4667		70
Regions Hospital 640 Jackson St ..... Saint Paul MN 55101 *Web:* www.regionshospital.com	651-254-3456	254-9426	374-3
Regis College 15 St Mary St ..... Toronto ON M4Y2R5 *Web:* regiscollege.ca	416-922-5474	922-2898	167-3
Regis College 235 Wellesley St ..... Weston MA 02493 *TF:* 866-438-7344 ■ *Web:* www.regiscollege.edu	781-768-7000	768-7071	166
Regis Group Inc, The PO Box 3323 ..... Leesburg VA 20177 *Web:* www.regisgroup.com	703-777-2233		77
Regis School 7330 Westview Dr ..... Houston TX 77055 *Web:* www.theregisschool.org	713-682-8383		685
Regis Technologies Inc 8210 Austin Ave ..... Morton Grove IL 60053 *TF:* 800-323-8144 ■ *Web:* www.registech.com	847-967-6000	967-5876	582
Regis University 3333 Regis Blvd ..... Denver CO 80221 *TF:* 800-388-2366 ■ *Web:* www.regis.edu	303-458-4100	964-5473	166
Register Graphics Inc 220 Main St ..... Randolph NY 14772 *Web:* www.registergraphics.com	716-358-2921	358-5695	627
Register Publications 126 W High St ..... Lawrenceburg IN 47025 *Web:* thedcregister.com	812-537-0063	537-5576	532-2
Register Tapes Unlimited Inc 1445 Langham Creek ..... Houston TX 77084 *TF:* 800-247-4793 ■ *Web:* www.indoormedia.com	800-247-4793		4
Registercom Inc 575 Eigth Ave 8th Fl ..... New York NY 10018 *TF:* 888-734-4783 ■ *Web:* www.register.com	888-734-4783		396
Register-Herald 801 N Kanawha St ..... Beckley WV 25801 *TF:* 800-950-0250 ■ *Web:* www.register-herald.com	304-255-4400	255-4427	532-2
Register-Star 364 Warren St ..... Hudson NY 12534 *TF:* 800-836-4069 ■ *Web:* www.hudsonvalley360.com	518-828-1616		532-2
Registrar Corp 144 Research Dr ..... Hampton VA 23666 *Web:* www.registrarcorp.com	757-224-0177	224-0179	463
Registry of Interpreters for the Deaf Inc (RID) 333 Commerce St ..... Alexandria VA 22314 *Web:* www.rid.org	703-838-0030	838-0454	49-5
Regitar USA Inc 2575 Container Dr ..... Montgomery AL 36109 *Web:* regitar.com	334-244-1885	244-1901	351
Regnery Publishing Inc 300 New Jersey Ave NW Ste 500 ..... Washington DC 20001 *Web:* www.regnery.com	202-216-0600	393-1781	637-2
Rego Manufacturing Company Inc 1870 E Mansfield St ..... Bucyrus OH 44820 *Web:* www.regoonline.com	419-562-0466		411
Rego-fix Tool Corp 4420 Anson Blvd ..... Whitestown IN 46075 *TF:* 800-999-7346 ■ *Web:* www.in.rego-fix.com	317-870-5959		358
Regular Baptist Press (RBP) 3715 N Ventura Dr ..... Arlington Heights IL 60004 *TF:* 800-727-4440 ■ *Web:* www.rbpstore.org	847-843-1600	843-3757	637-2
Regulator Bookshop 720 Ninth St ..... Durham NC 27705 *Web:* www.regulatorbookshop.com	919-286-2700		95
Regulatory Affairs Professionals Society (RAPS) 5635 Fishers Ln Ste 550 ..... Rockville MD 20852 *Web:* www.raps.org	301-770-2920	770-2924	49-8
Regulus 238 N Main St ..... Woodstock VA 22664 *Web:* www.regulus-group.com	540-459-2142		261
Regupol America 11 Ritter Way ..... Lebanon PA 17042 **Fax Area Code:* 717 ■ *TF:* 800-537-8737 ■ *Web:* www.regupol.com	800-537-8737	675-2199*	291
Regus 4449 Easton Way 2nd Fl ..... Columbus OH 43219 *Web:* www.regus.com	226-786-9165		809
Reh Holdings Inc 150 S Sumner St ..... York PA 17404 *Web:* www.rehholdings.com	717-843-0021		697
Rehab at Home 1 Father DeValles Blvd Ste 401 ..... Fall River MA 02723 *TF:* 888-687-5778 ■ *Web:* www.trmrehab.com	508-673-5500	300-0273	363
Rehab Plus Therapeutic Products 726 Donald Preston Dr ..... Wolfforth TX 79382	806-791-2288		477
Rehabilities, The PO Box 1565 ..... Rancho Cucamonga CA 91730 *Web:* rehababilities.com	909-989-5699		260
Rehabilitation Engineering & Assistive Technology Society of North America (RESNA) 1560 Wilson Blvd Ste 850 ..... Arlington VA 22209 *Web:* www.resna.org	703-524-6686	524-6630	48-17
Rehabilitation Hospital of Colorado Springs Inc 325 Parkside Dr ..... Colorado Springs CO 80910 *Web:* www.healthsouthcoloradosprings.com	719-630-8000		374-3
Rehabilitation Hospital of Dayton 1 Elizabeth Pl ..... Dayton OH 45417 *Web:* healthsouthdayton.com	937-424-8200		726
Rehabilitation Hospital of Indiana 4141 Shore Dr ..... Indianapolis IN 46254 *TF:* 866-510-2273 ■ *Web:* www.rhin.com	317-329-2000	566-9111	374-6
Rehabilitation Hospital of the Pacific 226 N Kuakini St ..... Honolulu HI 96817 *Web:* www.rehabhospital.org	808-531-3511		374-6
Rehabilitation Institute of Michigan 261 Mack Blvd ..... Detroit MI 48201 *Web:* www.rimrehab.org	313-745-1203		374-6
Rehau Inc 1501 Edwards Ferry Rd NE ..... Leesburg VA 20176 *TF:* 800-247-9445 ■ *Web:* www.rehau.com	703-777-5255	777-3053	235
Rehman Technology Services Inc 34646 Rust Rd ..... Eustis FL 32736 *Web:* www.electronicdiscovery.com	352-357-0500		180
Rehmann Group 5800 Gratiot St Ste 201 ..... Saginaw MI 48638 *TF:* 866-799-9580 ■ *Web:* www.rehmann.com	989-799-9580	799-0227	2
Rehoboth Beach City Hall 229 Rehoboth Ave ..... Rehoboth Beach DE 19971 *Web:* www.cityofrehoboth.com	302-227-6181	227-4643	337
Rehoboth Beach Public Library 226 Rehoboth Ave ..... Rehoboth Beach DE 19971 *Web:* www.rehobothlibrary.org	302-227-8044	227-0597	434-3
Rehoboth Beach-Dewey Beach Chamber of Commerce 501 Rehoboth Ave ..... Rehoboth Beach DE 19971 *TF:* 800-441-1329 ■ *Web:* www.beach-fun.com	302-227-2233	227-8351	139

Name	Address	City	State	ZIP	Phone	Fax	Class
Rehoboth McKinley Christian Hospital	1900 Redrock Dr	Gallup	NM	87301	505-863-7000		374-3
	Web: www.rmch.org						
Rehrig Pacific Co	4010 E 26th St	Los Angeles	CA	90058	323-262-5145	269-8506	199
	TF: 800-421-6244 ■ *Web:* www.rehrigpacific.com						
REI (Raymond Express Intl)	573 Forbes Blvd	South San Francisco	CA	94080	650-871-8560		311
	Web: www.reiexpress.com						
REI (Recreational Equipment Inc)	6750 S 228th St	Kent	WA	98032	253-395-3780	891-2523	711
	TF: 800-426-4840 ■ *Web:* www.rei.com						
REI (Rollinger Engineering Inc)	20333 State Hwy 249 1 Chasewood	Houston	TX	77077	281-558-5000	558-4999	261
	Web: www.reifirepro.com						
REI do Gado	939 Fourth Ave	San Diego	CA	92101	619-702-8464		671
	Web: www.reidogado.net						
REI Service Corp	763 Chestnut St	Manchester	NH	03104	603-645-6450		653
	Web: reiservice.com						
REI Systems Inc	45335 Vintage Park Plz	Sterling	VA	20166	703-480-9100	689-4680	177
	Web: www.reisystems.com						
Reich Tool & Design Inc	W175 N 5750 Technology Dr	Menomonee Falls	WI	53051	262-252-3440		757
	Web: www.reichtool.com						
Reichard Buick GMC	161 Salem Ave	Dayton	OH	45406	937-401-2034		57
	Web: www.reichardbuick.com						
Reichdrill Inc	99 Troy Hawk Run Hwy	Philipsburg	PA	16866	814-342-5500	342-1135	537
	Web: reichdrill.com						
Reichel Foods Inc	3706 Enterprise Dr SW	Rochester	MN	55902	507-289-7264		123
	Web: www.reichelfoods.com						
Reichert Inc	3362 Walden Ave	Depew	NY	14043	716-686-4500		544
	Web: www.reichert.com						
Reichhold Inc	2400 Ellis Rd	Durham	NC	27703	919-990-7500	990-7711	605-2
	TF: 800-448-3482 ■ *Web:* www.reichhold.com						
Reicker, Pfau, Pyle & McRoy LLP	1421 State St Ste B	Santa Barbara	CA	93101	805-966-2440		428
	Web: www.reickorpfau.com						
Reid Hospital & Health Care Services	1401 Chester Blvd	Richmond	IN	47374	765-983-3000		374-3
	Web: www.reidhosp.com						
Reid Hurst Nagy	105-13900 Maycrest Way	Richmond	BC	V6V3E2	604-273-9338		2
	TF: 888-764-3188 ■ *Web:* www.rhncpa.com						
Reid Insurance Group Inc	423 S Main Ave	Lovington	NM	88260	575-396-3645		390
	Web: reidinsurance.biz						
Reid Middleton Inc	728 134th St SW Ste 200	Everett	WA	98204	425-741-3800		261
	Web: www.reidmiddleton.com						
Reid Park Zoo	1100 S Randolph Way	Tucson	AZ	85716	520-791-3204		823
	Web: reidparkzoo.org						
Reid State Park	375 Seguinland Rd	Georgetown	ME	04548	207-371-2303		565
	Web: www.maine.gov						
Reid Temple African Methodist Episcopal Church	11400 Glenn Dale Blvd	Glenn Dale	MD	20769	301-352-0320		48-20
	Web: reidtemple.org						
Reid-Ashman Manufacturing Inc	582 N 3050 E	Saint George	UT	84790	435-986-6000	986-6100	425
	Web: www.reidashman.com						
Reidler Decal Corp	264 Industrial Park Rd PO Box 8	Saint Clair	PA	17970	800-628-7770	429-1528*	413
	**Fax Area Code:* 570 ■ *TF:* 800-628-7770 ■ *Web:* www.reidlerdecal.com						
Reidsville Recreation Dept	200 N Franklin St	Reidsville	NC	27320	336-349-1090		564
	Web: ci.reidsville.nc.us						
Reif Carbide Tool Company Inc	11055 E 9 Mile Rd	Warren	MI	48090	586-754-1890	754-0378	493
	Web: www.reifcarbidetool.com						
Reif Performing Arts Ctr	720 NW Conifer Dr	Grand Rapids	MN	55744	218-327-5780		572
	Web: reifcenter.org						
Reiff & Nestor Co	50 Reiff St	Lykens	PA	17048	717-453-7113	453-7555	493
	TF: 800-521-3422 ■ *Web:* www.rntap.com						
Reigel Plumbing & Heating Inc	1701 S Galvin Ave	Marshfield	WI	54449	715-387-3411		189-10
	TF: 888-734-4351 ■ *Web:* www.reigelplumbing.com						
Reigstad & Associates Inc	192 W Ninth St	Saint Paul	MN	55102	651-292-1123		261
	TF: 800-355-8414 ■ *Web:* reigstad.com						
Reiko Wireless Inc	55 Mall Dr	Commack	NY	11725	631-913-6700	821-5749*	736
	**Fax Area Code:* 718 ■ *TF:* 888-797-3456 ■ *Web:* reikowireless.com						
Reilly Construction Company Inc	PO Box 99	Ossian	IA	52161	563-532-9211	532-9759	188-4
	Web: www.reilly-construction.com						
Reilly Financial Advisors	7777 Alvarado Rd Ste 116	La Mesa	CA	91942	800-682-3237		796
	TF: 800-682-3237 ■ *Web:* www.rfadvisors.com						
Reilly Green Mountain	300 Boston Post Rd	Orange	CT	06477	203-795-5696	795-9120	710
	TF: 800-950-5049 ■ *Web:* www.platformtennis.com						
Reilly Like & Tenety	179 Little E Neck Rd N	West Babylon	NY	11704	631-669-3000		428
	Web: www.reillylikeandtenety.com						
Reilly Penner & Benton LLP	1233 N Mayfair Rd	Milwaukee	WI	53226	414-271-7800		2
	Web: rpb.biz						
Reilly Windows & Doors	901 Burman Blvd Bldg 701	Calverton	NY	11933	631-208-0710	208-0711	499
	Web: www.reillywd.com						
Reily Foods Co	400 Poydras St 10th Fl	New Orleans	LA	70130	800-535-1961	539-5427*	296-7
	**Fax Area Code:* 504 ■ *TF:* 800-535-1961 ■ *Web:* www.frenchmarketcoffee.com						
Reimagine Office Furnishings	1212 N 39th St Ste 200	Tampa	FL	33605	877-763-4400		321
	TF: 877-763-4400 ■ *Web:* www.rofinc.net						
Reiman Gardens	*Iowa State University* 1407 University Blvd	Ames	IA	50011	515-294-2710		97
	Web: www.reimangardens.com						
Reimers & Jolivette Inc	2344 NW 24th Ave	Portland	OR	97210	503-228-7691	228-2721	187
	Web: www.reimersandjolivette.com						
Reimers Electra Steam Inc	4407 Martinsburg Pk	Clear Brook	VA	22624	540-662-3811	726-4215*	357
	**Fax Area Code:* 800 ■ *TF:* 800-872-7562 ■ *Web:* www.reimersinc.com						
Reimers-kaufman Concrete Prods	6200 Cornhusker Hwy	Lincoln	NE	68507	402-434-1855	434-1877	191-1
	Web: reimerskaufman.com						
Reinauer Transportation Companies Inc	1983 Richmond Terr	Staten Island	NY	10302	718-816-8167	876-5183	314
	Web: www.reinauer.com						
Reinberger Printwerks	20275 Paseo Del Prado	Walnut	CA	91789	909-594-9377	594-9828	627
	TF: 800-585-9377 ■ *Web:* www.reinbergerprintwerks.com						
Reindl Bindery Company Inc	W194 N11381 McCormick Dr	Germantown	WI	53022	262-293-1444	293-1445	92
	TF: 800-878-1121 ■ *Web:* www.reindlbindery.com						
Reindl Printing Inc	1300 Johnson St	Merrill	WI	54452	715-536-9537		627
	TF: 800-236-9637 ■ *Web:* www.reindlprinting.com						
Reinforcement Unlimited	335 Pky 575 Ste 220	Woodstock	GA	30188	770-591-9552	218-8249*	196
	**Fax Area Code:* 800 ■ *Web:* www.behavior-consultant.com						
Reingold Inc	433 E Monroe Ave	Alexandria	VA	22301	202-333-0400		463
	Web: www.reingold.com						
Reinhardt College	5692 Reinhardt College Pkwy	Waleska	GA	30183	770-720-5526	720-5899	166
	TF: 877-346-4273 ■ *Web:* www.reinhardt.edu						
Reinhardt Corp	3919 State Hwy 23	West Oneonta	NY	13861	607-432-6633		316
	TF: 800-421-2867 ■ *Web:* www.reinhardthomeheating.com						
Reinhart Boerner Van Deuren SC	1000 N Water St Ste 1700	Milwaukee	WI	53202	414-298-1000	298-8097	41
	TF: 800-553-6215 ■ *Web:* www.reinhartlaw.com						
Reinhart Food Service	7735 Westside Industrial Dr	Jacksonville	FL	32219	904-781-9888		300
	Web: rfsdelivers.com						
Reinhart Grounds Maintenance Inc	10051 Mccue Dr	Bloomington	IL	61705	309-821-1711		422
	Web: www.reinhartservices.com						
Reinhart Partners Inc	1500 W Market St	Mequon	WI	53092	262-241-2020	241-2025	796
	TF: 800-969-1159 ■ *Web:* reinhart-partnersinc.com						
Reinhold Industries Inc	12827 E Imperial Hwy	Santa Fe Springs	CA	90670	562-944-3281	944-7238	504
	Web: reinhold-ind.com						
Reinke Manufacturing Company Inc	5325 Reinke Rd	Deshler	NE	68340	402-365-7251	365-4370	273
	TF: 866-365-7381 ■ *Web:* www.reinke.com						
Reinsel Kuntz Lesher	1330 Broadcasting Rd	Wyomissing	PA	19610	610-376-1595		463
	Web: www.rklcpa.com						
Reinsurance Group of America Inc	16600 Swingley Ridge Rd	Chesterfield	MO	63017	636-736-7000		360-4
	NYSE: RGA ■ *TF:* 800-985-4326 ■ *Web:* www.rgare.com						
Reis Inc	530 Fifth Ave 5th Fl	New York	NY	10036	800-366-7347	921-2533*	466
	NASDAQ: REIS ■ **Fax Area Code:* 212 ■ *TF:* 800-366-7347 ■ *Web:* www.reis.com						
Reis Nichols Jewelers	3535 E 86th St	Greenwood	IN	46142	317-883-4467		410
	Web: www.reisnichols.com						
Reischling Press Inc	3325 S 116th St Ste 161	Seattle	WA	98168	206-905-5999		627
	Web: www.rpiprint.com						
Reisterstown Lumber Co, The	PO Box 337	Reisterstown	MD	21136	410-833-1300	833-6803	364
	Web: www.reisterstownlumber.com						
Reiter Affiliated Cos	1767 San Juan Rd	Aromas	CA	95004	805-483-1000		315-1
	Web: www.berry.net						
Reiter Giuliani Group LLC	1 Penn Plz 36th Fl	New York	NY	10119	212-786-7626		463
	Web: www.rggllc.com						
Reitmans (Canada) Ltd	250 Sauve St W	Montreal	QC	H3L1Z2	514-384-1140		229
	TSE: RET.A ■ *Web:* www.reitmans.com						
Reitz Home Museum	224 SE First St	Evansville	IN	47706	812-426-1871	426-2179	520
	Web: www.reitzhome.com						
Rejoice Church	13413 E 106th St N	Owasso	OK	74055	918-272-5291		148
	Web: www.rejoicechurch.com						
Rejoice Radio	PO Box 18000	Pensacola	FL	32523	850-479-6570		645-118
	TF: 800-726-1191 ■ *Web:* www.rejoice.org						
Rejuvenation Inc	2550 NW Nicolai St	Portland	OR	97210	503-238-1900	526-7329*	439
	**Fax Area Code:* 800 ■ *TF:* 888-401-1900 ■ *Web:* www.rejuvenation.com						
Rekon Technologies Inc	150 S Los Robles Ave Ste 660	Pasadena	CA	91101	626-577-4350		809
	Web: www.rekon.com						
Relais Intl	1690 Woodward Dr Ste 215	Ottawa	ON	K2C3R8	613-226-5571	226-0998	178-12
	TF: 888-294-5244 ■ *Web:* www.relais-intl.com						
Relate Corp	5141 Verdugo Way Ste C	Camarillo	CA	93012	800-428-3708		180
	TF: 800-428-3708 ■ *Web:* www.relate.com						
Related Group of Florida	315 S Biscayne Blvd	Miami	FL	33131	305-460-9900		653
	Web: www.relatedgroup.com						
Related Midwest	350 W Hubbard St Ste 300	Chicago	IL	60654	312-595-7400		653
	Web: www.relatedmidwest.com						
Relational Architects International Inc	33 Newark St	Hoboken	NJ	07030	201-420-0400	420-4080	178-1
	TF: 800-776-0771 ■ *Web:* www.relarc.com						
Relationship One LLC	8009 34th Ave S Ste 300	Minneapolis	MN	55425	763-355-1025		463
	Web: www.relationshipone.com						
Relay Specialties Inc	17 Raritan Rd	Oakland	NJ	07436	800-526-5376		203
	TF: 800-526-5376 ■ *Web:* www.relayspec.com						
Relay Therapeutics	399 Binney St	Cambridge	MA	02139	617-370-8837		85
	Web: relaytx.com						
Relay2 Inc	1525 Mccarthy Blvd Ste 209	Milpitas	CA	95035	408-380-0031		180
	Web: relay2.com						

	Phone	Fax	Class
Relco LLC 2331 Third Ave ..... Willmar MN 56201 *Web:* relco.net	320-231-2210		360-3
Relco Systems Inc 7310 Chestnut Ridge Rd ..... Lockport NY 14094 *TF:* 800-262-1020 ■ *Web:* www.relcosystems.com	716-434-8100	434-7229	780
ReleaseTEAM Inc 1400 W 122nd Ave Ste 202 ..... Denver CO 80234 *TF:* 866-887-0489 ■ *Web:* www.releaseteam.com	720-887-0489		177
Relevancy Group, The 505 Congress St Ste 602 ..... Boston MA 02210 *TF:* 877-972-6886 ■ *Web:* relevancygroup.com	877-972-6886		466
Relevant Radio 3256 Penryn Rd Ste 100 ..... Loomis CA 95650 **Fax Area Code:* 916 ■ *TF:* 888-887-7120 ■ *Web:* relevantradio.com	888-914-9149	535-0504*	647
Relevante Inc 1000 Westlakes Dr Ste 130 ..... Berwyn PA 19312 **Fax Area Code:* 610 ■ *Web:* www.relevante.com	484-403-4100	644-3234*	734
Reliability Ctr 501 Westover Ave ..... Hopewell VA 23860 *TF:* 800-457-0645 ■ *Web:* www.reliability.com	804-458-0645		194
Reliable Architectural Metals Co (RAMCO) 9751 Erwin ..... Detroit MI 48213 *TF:* 800-445-0263 ■ *Web:* www.ramcometals.com	313-924-9750	924-8877	191-2
Reliable Carriers Inc 41555 Koppernick Rd ..... Canton MI 48187 *TF:* 800-521-6393 ■ *Web:* reliable-carriers.com	734-453-6677	453-8609	468
Reliable Castings Corp 3530 Spring Grove Ave ..... Cincinnati OH 45223 *Web:* www.reliablecastings.com	513-541-2627	541-5696	308
Reliable Chevrolet Inc 800 N Central Expy ..... Richardson TX 75080 *Web:* www.reliablechevytexas.com	972-330-4326		57
Reliable Container Corp 9206 Santa Fe Springs Rd ..... Santa Fe Springs CA 90670 *Web:* www.reliablecontainer.com	562-861-6226		100
Reliable Contracting Company Inc 2410 Evergreen Rd Ste 200 ..... Gambrills MD 21054 *Web:* www.reliablecontracting.com	410-987-0313	721-7700	188-4
Reliable Factory Supply Co PO Box 340 ..... Thomaston CT 06787 *TF:* 800-288-8464 ■ *Web:* rfsupply.com	800-288-8464		361
Reliable Fire Equipment Co 12845 S Cicero Ave ..... Alsip IL 60803 *Web:* reliablefire.com	708-597-4600	389-1150	679
Reliable Hardware Co 11319 Vanowen St ..... North Hollywood CA 91605 *Web:* www.reliablehardware.com	818-753-8558	753-4778	350
Reliable Health Systems Inc (RHS) 2610 Nostrand Ave ..... Brooklyn NY 11210 *Web:* www.reliablehealth.com	718-338-2400	338-2741	178-1
Reliable Life Insurance Co 100 King St W PO Box 557 ..... Hamilton ON L8N3K9 **Fax Area Code:* 866 ■ *TF:* 800-465-0661 ■ *Web:* www.reliablelifeinsurance.com	905-523-5587	551-1704*	391-2
Reliable Machine Co 1327 Tenth Ave ..... Rockford IL 61104 *Web:* reliablemachine.com	815-968-8803		488
Reliable Manufacturing Inc 1900 N A W Grimes Blvd ..... Round Rock TX 78665 *Web:* www.reliable-mfg.com	512-255-6572	255-9123	454
Reliable Market 36 Circuit Av ..... Oak Bluffs MA 02557 *Web:* thereliablemarket.com	508-693-1102		345
Reliable Medical Supply Inc 9401 Winnetka Ave N ..... Brooklyn Park MN 55445 *Web:* www.reliamed.com	763-255-3800		475
Reliable of Milwaukee Inc 6737 W Washington St ..... Milwaukee WI 53214 *Web:* reliableofmilwaukee.com	414-272-5084		155-18
Reliable Production Service Inc 9095 US Hwy 190 ..... Livonia LA 70755 *Web:* www.reliableproduction.com	225-637-4835	637-4842	539
Reliable Propane Corp 10140 County Rd ..... Clarence NY 14032 *Web:* reliablepropane.com	716-741-3000		316
Reliable Software Resources Inc 22260 Haggerty Rd Ste 285 ..... Northville MI 48167 *Web:* www.rsrit.com	248-477-3555		177
Reliable Source Inc 11109 Jasmine St ..... Fontana CA 92337 *Web:* www.reliablesourcemetals.com	909-357-1211	357-1311	492
Reliable Tire Co 805 N Blackhorse Pk ..... Blackwood NJ 08012 *TF:* 800-342-3426 ■ *Web:* www.reliabletire.com	800-342-3426		755
Reliable Title & Escrow LLC 508 Princeton Rd Ste 302 ..... Johnson City TN 37601 *Web:* rte-llc.com	423-282-1300		653
Reliable Transportation Specialists Inc 139 Venturi Dr ..... Chesterton IN 46304 *Web:* www.reliabletrans.com	219-926-8850		468
Reliable Wholesale Lumber Inc 7600 Redondo Cir ..... Huntington Beach CA 92648 *TF:* 877-795-4638 ■ *Web:* www.rwli.net	714-848-8222	847-1605	191-3
Reliance Bancshares Inc 10401 Clayton Rd ..... Saint Louis MO 63131 *OTC: RLBS* ■ *Web:* reliancebankstl.com	314-569-7200		70
Reliance Connects 61 W Mesquite Blvd ..... Mesquite NV 89027 *TF:* 866-894-4657 ■ *Web:* relianceconnects.com	702-346-5211		387
Reliance Consulting LLC 13940 N Dale Mabry Hwy ..... Tampa FL 33618 *Web:* reliancecpa.com	813-931-7258		2
Reliance Controls Corp 2001 Young Ct ..... Racine WI 53404 *TF:* 800-634-6155 ■ *Web:* www.reliancecontrols.com	262-634-6155		729
Reliance Data 3543 88th Ave NE Ste 200 ..... Circle Pines MN 55014 *Web:* www.reliancedata.net	763-231-7684		175
Reliance Heating & Air Conditioning Inc 1694 Hwy 138 NE ..... Conyers GA 30013 *Web:* www.reliance-hvac.com	770-483-3850		610
Reliance One Inc 1700 Harmon Rd Ste 1 ..... Auburn Hills MI 48326 *Web:* www.reliance-one.com	248-922-4500	922-5660	260
Reliance Paper Co 1404 W 12th St ..... Kansas City MO 64101 *Web:* www.reliancepaper.com	816-471-2008		559
Reliance Pathology Partners LLC 5747 Hoover Blvd ..... Tampa FL 33634 *TF:* 866-944-0404 ■ *Web:* www.pims-inc.com	866-944-0404		415
Reliance Standard Life Insurance 2001 Market St Ste 1500 ..... Philadelphia PA 19103 *TF:* 800-351-7500 ■ *Web:* www.reliancestandard.com	267-256-3500		391-2
Reliance Steel & Aluminum Co 350 S Grand Ave Ste 5100 ..... Los Angeles CA 90071 *NYSE: RS* ■ *Web:* www.rsac.com	213-687-7700	687-8792	492
Reliance Tool & Manufacturing Co 900 N State St Ste 101 ..... Elgin IL 60123 *Web:* www.reliancetool.com	847-695-1234	695-0931	757
Reliance Trading Corporation of America 55 Watermill Ln ..... Great Neck NY 11021 *Web:* www.beautysilk.com	516-466-6240		192
Reliant Energy Retail Services LLC 1201 Fannin St ..... Houston TX 77002 **Fax Area Code:* 713 ■ *TF:* 866-660-4900 ■ *Web:* www.reliant.com	866-222-7100	488-4422*	787
Reliant Federal Credit Union 4015 Plaza Dr ..... Casper WY 82604 *TF:* 800-329-1551 ■ *Web:* reliantfcu.com	307-234-1429		219
Reliant Molding Inc 10525 Crosby Cir ..... Cranesville PA 16410 *Web:* www.reliantmolding.com	814-756-5522	756-5710	604
Reliant Realty LLC 401(K) Plan 1517 Hunt Club Blvd Ste 200 ..... Gallatin TN 37066 *Web:* reliantrealty.com	615-724-5222		652
Reliant Sales Inc 18956 Freeport Dr Ste B ..... Montgomery TX 77356 *Web:* reliant-sales.com	936-582-1160	582-1187	261
Reliant Transportation Inc 4411 S 86th St Ste 101 PO Box 67009 ..... Lincoln NE 68526 *Web:* reliant-transportation.com	402-464-7771	464-8124	449
Relias 111 Corning Rd Ste 250 ..... Atlanta GA 30326 *Web:* www.relias.com	404-262-5476		637-9
Religence Inc 2090 Green St ..... San Francisco CA 94123 *Web:* www.religence.com	415-771-7473		393
Religion News Service (RNS) 529 14th St NW 13th Fl ..... Washington DC 20045 *Web:* religionnews.com	202-463-8777		530
Religious and Theological Abstracts Inc (R&TA) PO Box 215 ..... Myerstown PA 17067 *Web:* www.rtabst.org	717-866-6734	866-9280	637-9
Religious Conference Management Association Inc (RCMA) 7702 Woodland Dr Ste 120 ..... Indianapolis IN 46278 *Web:* www.rcmaweb.org	317-632-1888	632-7909	49-12
Relin, Goldstein & Crane LLP 28 E Main St Ste 1800 ..... Rochester NY 14614 **Fax Area Code:* 585 ■ *TF:* 888-984-2351 ■ *Web:* www.rgcattys.net	888-984-2351	325-6201*	428
Relios Inc 6815 Academy Pkwy W NE ..... Albuquerque NM 87109 *TF:* 800-827-6543 ■ *Web:* carolynpollackjewelry.com	505-345-5304		409
Reliv International Inc 136 Chesterfield Industrial Blvd ..... Chesterfield MO 63005 *NASDAQ: RELV* ■ *TF:* 800-735-4887 ■ *Web:* reliv.com	636-537-9715	537-9753	366
Reller Risk Management LLC 6315 Fly Rd ..... East Syracuse NY 13057	315-432-8210		390
Relli Technology Inc 1200 S Rogers Cir ..... Boca Raton FL 33487 *Web:* www.relli.com	561-886-0200	886-0201	770
RELO Direct Inc 161 N Clark St Ste 1200 ..... Chicago IL 60601 *TF:* 800-621-7356 ■ *Web:* www.relodirect.com	312-384-5900		666
Relocation America Intl 25800 Northwestern Hwy Ste 210 ..... Southfield MI 48075 *TF:* 877-500-4466 ■ *Web:* relocationamericainternational.com	877-500-4466		666
Relode 7000 Executive Center Dr Ste 190 ..... Brentwood TN 37027 *TF:* 844-773-5633 ■ *Web:* relode.com	844-773-5633		788
Relton Corp 317 Rolyn Pl ..... Arcadia CA 91007 **Fax Area Code:* 626 ■ *TF:* 800-423-1505 ■ *Web:* www.relton.com	323-681-2551	446-9671*	758
Rely Services Inc 957 N Plum Grove Rd Ste B ..... Schaumburg IL 60173 *TF:* 866-735-9328 ■ *Web:* relyservices.com	847-310-8750	842-2200	195
Relypsa Inc 700 Saginaw Dr ..... Redwood City CA 94063 *Web:* www.relypsa.com	650-421-9500		582
Rem Sales Inc 910 Gay Hill Rd ..... Windsor CT 06095 *Web:* www.remsales.com	860-687-3400	687-3401	385
Rema Dri-Vac Corp 45 Ruby St ..... Norwalk CT 06850 *Web:* www.remadrivac.com	203-847-2464	847-3609	427
Rema Foods Inc 140 Sylvan Ave ..... Englewood Cliffs NJ 07632 *Web:* www.foodimportgroup.com	201-947-1000		360-3
Remanco Hydraulics Inc 7917 Beech St NE ..... Minneapolis MN 55432 *Web:* www.superswivels.com	763-784-5531	784-7423	488
Remax Villa Realtors 7515 Bergenline Ave ..... North Bergen NJ 07047 *Web:* www.remaxvilla.com	201-868-3100	537-8380	652
Rembolt Ludtke LLP 3 Landmark Ctr 1128 Lincoln Mall Ste 300 ..... Lincoln NE 68508 *Web:* remboltlawfirm.com	402-475-5100	475-5087	445
Rembrandt Commercial Cleaning 20900 Swenson Dr Ste 250 ..... Waukesha WI 53186 *Web:* rembrandtcleaning.com	262-798-1038		104
Rembrandt Group LLC 2 N Rd Ste 3 ..... Warren NJ 07059 *Web:* www.rembrandtgroup.com	732-356-1600		180
Rembrandt Venture Partners 600 Montgomery St 44th Fl ..... San Francisco CA 94111 **Fax Area Code:* 415 ■ *Web:* rembrandtvc.com	650-326-7070	528-2901*	792
REMC (Okefenoke Rural Electric Membership Corp) 14384 Cleveland St PO Box 602 ..... Nahunta GA 31553 *TF:* 800-262-5131 ■ *Web:* oremc.com	912-462-5131	462-6100	245
REMC (International Division Inc) PO Box 1275 ..... Springfield MO 65801 *Web:* www.indiv.com	417-862-2673	862-5434	297-10
Remco Inc 195 Hempt Rd ..... Mechanicsburg PA 17050 *TF:* 877-297-0389 ■ *Web:* remcopa.com	717-697-0389		189-10

Name / Address	City	State	Zip	Phone	Fax	Class
Remco Products Corp 4735 W 106th St *TF:* 800-585-8619 ■ *Web:* remcoproducts.com	Zionsville	IN	46077	317-876-9856		296
Remcom Inc 315 S Allen St Ste 222 *TF:* 888-773-6266 ■ *Web:* www.remcom.com	State College	PA	16801	814-861-1299		174
Remcon Plastics Inc 208 Chestnut St *TF:* 800-360-3636 ■ *Web:* www.remcon.com	Reading	PA	19602	800-360-3636		599
Remcor Technical Industries Inc 7025 Alamitos Ave *Web:* www.remcortech.com	San Diego	CA	92154	619-424-8878	424-9218	529
REMEDI Electronic Commerce Group 96 Northwoods Blvd *Web:* www.remedi.com	Columbus	OH	43235	614-436-4040		196
Remedial Construction Services LP (RECON) 9977 W Sam Houston Pky N Ste 304 *Web:* www.reconservices.com	Houston	TX	77064	281-955-2442	890-5172	194
Remediation Services Inc 2735 S Tenth St PO Box 587 *TF:* 800-335-1201 ■ *Web:* www.rsi-ks.com	Independence	KS	67301	800-335-1201		667
Remedy Engineering Inc 2510 Old Eurka Way *Web:* remedyengineering.com	Redding	CA	96001	530-241-7658		261
Remedy Temp Inc 3820 State St *Web:* www.remedystaffing.com	Santa Barbara	CA	93105	513-541-5696		721
Remelt Sources Inc 27151 Tungsten Rd *TF:* 800-227-8638 ■ *Web:* www.remeltsources.com	Cleveland	OH	44132	216-289-4555		492
Remer Inc 205 Marion St *Web:* www.remerinc.com	Seattle	WA	98104	206-624-1010		7
Remet Corp 210 Commons Rd *Web:* www.remet.com	Utica	NY	13502	315-797-8700		306
Reminder Media Inc 130 Old Town Rd PO Box 27	Vernon	CT	06066	860-875-3368	875-2089	637-8
Reminder Newspaper 2 W Vine St PO Box 1600 *Web:* www.reminderusa.net	Millville	NJ	08332	856-825-8811	825-0011	532-4
Reminderband Inc 917 W 600 N Ste 107 **Fax Area Code:* 435 ■ *TF:* 800-922-5401 ■ *Web:* www.reminderband.com	Logan	UT	84321	800-922-5401	753-2558*	594
Reminger 101 W Prospect Ave Ste 1400 *TF:* 800-486-1311 ■ *Web:* www.reminger.com	Cleveland	OH	44115	216-687-1311	687-1841	428
Remington & Vernick Engineers Inc 232 Kings Hwy E *Web:* www.rve.com	Haddonfield	NJ	08033	856-795-9595		261
Remington Arms Company Inc 870 Remington Dr PO Box 700 *TF:* 800-243-9700 ■ *Web:* www.remington.com	Madison	NC	27025	336-548-8700	548-7801	284
Remington College 303 Rue Louis XIV *Web:* lafayette.remingtoncollege.edu	LaFayette	LA	70508	337-981-4010		800
Remington College *Little Rock* 10600 Colonel Glenn Rd Ste 100 *Web:* www.remingtoncollege.edu	Little Rock	AR	72204	501-312-0007		800
Remington Hotel Corp 14185 Dallas Pkwy Ste 1150 *Web:* www.remingtonhotels.com	Dallas	TX	75254	972-980-2700	991-6365	379
Remington Park Race Track 1 Remington Pl *TF:* 866-456-9880 ■ *Web:* www.remingtonpark.com	Oklahoma City	OK	73111	405-424-1000		642
Remington Seeds 4746 W US Hwy 24 PO Box 9 *Web:* www.remingtonseeds.com	Remington	IN	47977	219-261-3444	261-2220	10-5
Remington's Restaurant 425 Merchants Rd	Rochester	NY	14609	585-482-4434		671
Remke Markets Inc 1299 Cox Ave *Web:* www.remkes.com	Erlanger	KY	41018	859-594-3400		345
Remland Insurance Services Inc 636 E Chapman Ave *Web:* remlandinsurance.com	Orange	CA	92866	714-532-3341	532-1344	390
Remo Inc 28101 Industry Dr *TF:* 800-525-5134 ■ *Web:* www.remo.com	Valencia	CA	91355	661-294-5600		527
Remodelers Advantage Inc 14440 Cherry Ln Ct Ste 201 *Web:* www.remodelersadvantage.com	Laurel	MD	20707	301-490-5620		463
Remote Access Technology Inc 61 Atlantic St *TF:* 877-356-2728	Dartmouth	NS	B2Y4P4	902-434-4405		365
Remote Backup Systems Inc (RBS) 324 Poplar View Pky *TF:* 800-519-7643 ■ *Web:* www.remote-backup.com	Collierville	TN	38017	901-405-1234		178-1
Remote Logistics International LLC 6430 Richmond Ave Ste 320	Houston	TX	77057	713-780-9933		393
Remote Technologies Inc 5775 12th Ave E Ste 180 *Web:* www.rticorp.com	Shakopee	MN	55379	952-253-3100	253-3131	52
Rempco Acquisition Inc 251 Bell Ave *Web:* www.rempco.com	Cadillac	MI	49601	231-775-0108	775-9936	621
REMPREX LLC 7501 S Quincy St Ste 100 *TF:* 877-473-6773 ■ *Web:* www.remprex.com	Willowbrook	IL	60527	630-910-0600	910-0634	631
Remstar International Inc 41 Eisenhower Dr **Fax Area Code:* 207 ■ *TF:* 800-639-5805 ■ *Web:* www.kardexremstar.com	Westbrook	ME	04092	800-639-5805	854-1610*	385
Remtec Intl 1100 Haskins Rd *TF:* 888-873-6832 ■ *Web:* www.remtec.net	Bowling Green	OH	43402	419-867-8990	867-3279	192
Rem-Tronics Inc 659 Brigham Rd *Web:* www.rem-tronics.com	Dunkirk	NY	14048	716-203-7344		253
Remy Cointreau USA Inc 1290 Avenue of the Americas *Web:* www.remy-cointreau.com	New York	NY	10104	212-399-4200		81-3
Ren Potterfield Trucking Inc 404 US Hwy 24-36 E *Web:* www.renpotterfield.com	Monroe City	MO	63456	573-735-4528		780
Rena Ware International Inc 15885 NE 28th St *TF:* 800-721-5156 ■ *Web:* renaware.com	Bellevue	WA	98008	425-881-6171	882-7500	486
Renaissance Capital LLC 165 Mason St *Web:* www.renaissancecapital.com	Greenwich	CT	06830	203-622-2978		401
Renaissance College 566 West 1350 South *Web:* www.renaissancecollege.edu	Bountiful	UT	84010	801-292-8515		167-3
Renaissance Computing Institute (RENCI) 100 Europa Dr Ste 540 *Web:* renci.org	Chapel Hill	NC	27517	919-445-9640	445-9669	668
Renaissance Cos, The 8925 E Pima Center Pkwy Ste 205 *Web:* renaissancecos.com	Scottsdale	AZ	85258	480-967-0880	967-0879	186
Renaissance Group 981 Worcester St *TF:* 800-514-2667 ■ *Web:* www.renaissanceins.com	Wellesley	MA	02482	800-514-2667		390
Renaissance Learning Inc 2911 Peach St *Web:* www.renaissance.com	Wisconsin Rapids	WI	54494	715-424-3636		178-3
Renaissance Macro Research LLC 116 E 16th St 12th Fl *Web:* www.renmac.com	New York	NY	10003	212-537-8811		401
Renaissance Technologies Corp 800 Third Ave Ste 34 *Web:* www.rentec.com	New York	NY	10022	212-829-4460		690
Renaissance Westchester Hotel 80 W Red Oak Ln	West Harrison	NY	10604	914-694-5400		378
Renal Physicians Assn (RPA) 1700 Rockville Pk Ste 220 *Web:* www.renalmd.org	Rockville	MD	20852	301-468-3515	468-3511	49-8
RenalGuard Solutions Inc 459 Fortune Blvd *Web:* www.renalguard.com	Milford	MA	01757	508-541-8800		250
Renasant Corp 209 Troy St *NASDAQ: RNST* ■ *TF:* 800-680-1601 ■ *Web:* www.renasantbank.com	Tupelo	MS	38804	800-680-1601		360-2
Renaud Cook Drury Mesaros PA 1 N Central Ste 900 *TF:* 888-307-2499 ■ *Web:* rcdmlaw.com	Phoenix	AZ	85004	602-307-9900		428
Renault Winery Resort 72 N Bremen Ave *Web:* www.renaultwinery.com	Egg Harbor City	NJ	08215	609-965-2111		80-3
Renbor Sales Solutions Inc 256 Thornway Ave *TF:* 855-257-2537 ■ *Web:* www.tiborshanto.com	Thornhill	ON	L4J7X8	416-671-3555		393
RENCI (Renaissance Computing Institute) 100 Europa Dr Ste 540 *Web:* renci.org	Chapel Hill	NC	27517	919-445-9640	445-9669	668
Renco Corp 116 Third Ave N *TF:* 800-359-8181 ■ *Web:* www.rencocorp.com	Minneapolis	MN	55401	612-338-6124	333-9026	584
Renco Electronics Inc 595 International Pl *TF:* 800-645-5828 ■ *Web:* www.rencousa.com	Rockledge	FL	32955	321-637-1000	637-1600	246
Renco Group 1 Rockefeller Plz Ste 29 *Web:* www.rencogroup.net	New York	NY	10020	212-541-6000		185
Renco Machine Co 1730 Radisson St *Web:* www.rencomachine.com	Green Bay	WI	54302	920-448-8000		454
Rencor Controls Inc 21 Sullivan Pkwy *TF:* 866-472-7030 ■ *Web:* rencor.com	Fort Edward	NY	12828	518-747-4171		358
Rend Lake College 468 N Ken Gray Pkwy *TF:* 800-369-5321 ■ *Web:* rlc.edu	Ina	IL	62846	618-437-5321	437-5677	162
Rend Lake State Fish Wildlife Area 10885 E Jefferson Rd *Web:* www.stateparks.com	Bonnie	IL	62816	618-279-3110		565
Renda Broadcasting Corp 900 Parish St 4th Fl *Web:* www.rendabroadcasting.com	Pittsburgh	PA	15220	412-875-1800	875-1801	643
Rendersoft Inc 5801 Christie Ave Ste 275 *Web:* www.rendersoftinc.com	Emeryville	CA	94608	510-652-3936	652-3079	180
Rendigs, Fry, Kiely & Dennis LLP 600 Vine St Ste 2650 *TF:* 800-274-2330 ■ *Web:* www.rendigs.com	Cincinnati	OH	45202	513-381-9200		428
Rendon Group Inc 1875 Connecticut Ave NW Ste 716 *Web:* www.rendon.com	Washington	DC	20009	202-745-4900		636
Rene Bates Auctioneers Inc 4660 County Rd 1006 *Web:* www.renebates.com	McKinney	TX	75071	972-548-9636	542-5495	51
Rene Cazares 1111 S Jellick Ave *Web:* renecazares.com	City of Industry	CA	91748	626-964-4100		321
Rene of Paris 9135 Independence Ave *TF:* 800-353-7363 ■ *Web:* www.reneofparis.com	Chatsworth	CA	91311	800-353-7363		348
Rene S. Randel CPA PC 1601 Carmen Dr Ste 213 *Web:* rsrcpa.com	Camarillo	CA	93010	805-389-3330		2
Rene Swiss Corp 14 Townline Rd *Web:* www.reneswiss.com	Wolcott	CT	06716	203-879-4822	879-0732	385
Renee Manley, Agent State Farm Insurance 3768 Humbert Rd *Web:* reneemanley.net	Alton	IL	62002	618-462-0417		390
Renee's Garden 6060 Graham Hill Rd *TF:* 888-880-7228 ■ *Web:* www.reneesgarden.com	Felton	CA	95018	831-335-8257	335-7227	694
Renegade LLC 151 W 25th St 11th Fl *Web:* renegade.com	New York	NY	10001	646-486-7702		7
Renegade Productions Inc 10950 Gilroy Rd Ste J *Web:* renegadecommunications.com	Hunt Valley	MD	21031	410-667-1400		514
Renegade Theatre Co 222 E Superior St *Web:* www.zeitgeistarts.com	Duluth	MN	55802	218-722-6775		572
ReNew Life Formulas Inc 2076 Sunnydale Blvd *TF:* 800-830-1800 ■ *Web:* www.renewlife.com	Clearwater	FL	33765	800-830-1800		297-11
Renew Plastics PO Box 480 *TF:* 800-666-5207 ■ *Web:* www.renewplastics.com	Luxemburg	WI	54217	920-845-2326	845-2335	661
Renewable Choice Energy Inc 4775 Walnut St Ste 230 *Web:* www.renewablechoice.com	Boulder	CO	80301	303-468-0405		194
Renewable Fuels Assn (RFA) 425 Third St SW *Web:* www.ethanolrfa.org	Washington	DC	20024	202-289-3835	289-7519	48-12

Phone | Fax | Class

Renewable Natural Resources Foundation (RNRF)
5430 Grosvenor Ln. Bethesda MD 20814 301-770-9101 493-6148 48-13
Web: rnrf.org
Renewable NRG Systems 110 Riggs Rd Hinesburg VT 05461 802-482-2255 177
Web: www.nrgsystems.com
Renewal By Andersen Corp
9900 Jamaica Ave S Cottage Grove MN 55016 651-769-2210 499
Web: www.renewalbyandersen.com
Renfro Corp
661 Linville Rd PO Box 908 Mount Airy NC 27030 800-334-9091 719-8215* 155-10
**Fax Area Code:* 336 ■ *TF:* 800-334-9091 ■ *Web:* www.renfro.com
Renfrow & Company Inc
1123 Agnes St Corpus Christi TX 78401 361-884-5541 110
Web: www.renfrowprint.com
Renfrow Bros Inc 855 Gossett Rd. Spartanburg SC 29307 864-579-0558 186
Web: www.renfrowbros.com
Renhill Staffing Services of Texas Inc
102 Rilla Vista Dr San Antonio TX 78216 210-828-0508 828-0589 260
Web: renhillmgmt.com
Renier Construction Corp
2164 Citygate Dr. Columbus OH 43219 614-866-4580 866-0115 186
Web: www.renier.com
Renishaw Inc
5277 Trillium Blvd Hoffman Estates IL 60192 847-286-9953 286-9974 385
Web: www.renishaw.com
Renkert Oil 3817 Main St PO Box 246. Morgantown PA 19543 610-286-8012 579
TF: 800-423-6457 ■ *Web:* www.renkertoil.com
Renkim Corp 13333 Allen Rd. Southgate MI 48195 734-374-8300 5
Web: www.renkim.com
Renkus-heinz Inc 19201 Cook St. Foothill Ranch CA 92610 949-588-9997 588-9514 52
TF: 855-411-2364 ■ *Web:* www.renkus-heinz.com
Rennco LLC 300 Elm St Homer MI 49245 800-409-5225 791
TF: 800-409-5225 ■ *Web:* www.rennco.com
Renner Sports Surfaces 775 Canosa Ct Denver CO 80204 800-738-8106 188-3
TF: 800-738-8106 ■ *Web:* www.rennersports.com
Rennert Bilingual 216 E 45th St. New York NY 10017 212-867-8700 867-7666 423
Web: www.rennert.com
Rennert Vogel Mandler & Rodriguez PA
100 Se Second St Ste 2900 Miami FL 33131 305-577-4177 41
Web: rvmrlaw.com
Rennhack Marketing Services Inc
752 Port America Pl Grapevine TX 76051 817-481-6516 195
Web: www.gorms.com
Rennies Advertising Ideas Inc
711 Twinridge Ln Richmond VA 23235 804-272-4442 7
Web: www.renniesadv.com
Rennoc Corp 645 Pine St. Greenville OH 45331 800-372-7100 675-1727 155-5
TF: 800-372-7100 ■ *Web:* www.rennoc.com
Renntech Inc 1369 N Killian Dr. Lake Park FL 33403 561-845-7888 57
Web: www.renntechmercedes.com
Reno Chamber Orchestra
925 Riverside Dr Ste 5 Reno NV 89503 775-348-9413 348-0643 573-3
Web: www.renochamberorchestra.org
Reno City Hall PO Box 1900 Reno NV 89505 775-334-2030 334-2432 337
Web: www.reno.gov
Reno Computer Repair 8710 Dixon Ln Reno NV 89511 775-722-6969 175
Web: www.renocomputerrepair.com
Reno County 206 W First St. Hutchinson KS 67501 620-694-2934 694-2534 338
Web: www.renogov.org
Reno Gazette-Journal PO Box 22000 Reno NV 89520 775-788-6397 532-2
TF: 800-970-7366 ■ *Web:* www.rgj.com
Reno Machine Company Inc
170 Pane Rd Newington CT 06111 860-666-5641 455
Web: www.reno-machine.com
Reno Media Group 961 Matley Ln Ste 120. RENO NV 89502 775-829-1964 645-131
Web: www.renomediagroup.com
Reno Philharmonic Orchestra
925 Riverside Dr Ste 3 Reno NV 89503 775-323-6393 323-6711 573-3
Web: www.renophil.com
RENO Refractories Inc
Reftech Div 601 Reno Dr Morris AL 35116 800-741-7366 663
TF: 800-741-7366 ■ *Web:* renorefractories.com
Reno Rodeo Assn 1350 N Wells Ave. Reno NV 89512 775-329-3877 720
Web: www.renorodeo.com
Renodis Inc 476 Robert St N Saint Paul MN 55101 651-556-1200 449
TF: 866-200-8986 ■ *Web:* www.renodis.com
Renoir Staffing Services Inc
1301 Marina Vlg Pkwy Ste 350. Alameda CA 94501 866-672-3709 260
TF: 866-672-3709 ■ *Web:* www.renoirstaffing.com
Renold Ajax Inc 100 Bourne St. Westfield NY 14787 716-326-3121 326-6121 620
Web: www.renold.com
Renold Jeffrey 2307 Maden Dr. Morristown TN 37813 800-251-9012 581-2399* 207
**Fax Area Code:* 423 ■ *TF:* 800-251-9012 ■ *Web:* www.renoldjeffrey.com
Reno-Sparks Convention Ctr
4590 S Virginia St Reno NV 89502 775-827-7620 827-7701 205
TF: 800-367-7366 ■ *Web:* www.visitrenotahoe.com
Reno-Tahoe International Airport
2001 E Plumb Ln Reno NV 89502 775-328-6400 328-6510 27
Web: www.renoairport.com
Renova Lighting Systems Inc
36 Bellair Ave Warwick RI 02886 401-737-6700 737-6750 439
TF: 800-635-6682 ■ *Web:* www.renova.com
Renovator's Supply Inc
1 River St Millers Falls MA 01349 413-423-3300 350
TF: 800-659-2211 ■ *Web:* www.rensup.com
Renown Regional Medical Ctr 1155 Mill St Reno NV 89502 775-982-4100 374-3
Web: www.renown.org
RenoWorks Software Inc 2816 21 St NE Calgary AB T2E6Z2 403 296-3880 177
TF: 877-980-3880 ■ *Web:* www.renoworks.com
Rensselaer County 1600 Seventh Ave Troy NY 12180 518-270-2900 270-2961 338
Web: www.rensco.com
Rensselaer County Regional Chamber of Commerce
90 Fourth St Ste 200. Troy NY 12180 518-274-7020 139
Web: www.renscochamber.com
Rensselaer Polytechnic Institute
110 Eigth St Troy NY 12180 518-276-6000 276-4072 166
TF: 800-433-4723 ■ *Web:* www.rpi.edu

Phone | Fax | Class

Rent 'N Drive 4103 S 48 St Lincoln NE 68506 402-441-4835 53
Web: www.rentndrive.com
Rent Com Inc
131 Garlisch Dr Elk Grove Village IL 60007 847-678-7000 678-9378 23
Web: www.rentcom.com
Rent-A-Bit Inc
3880 Pendleton Way Ste 100 Indianapolis IN 46250 317-568-0393 568-4839 264-1
TF: 800-673-7350 ■ *Web:* www.rentabit.com
Rent-A-Center Inc 5501 Headquarters Dr. Plano TX 75024 800-422-8186 943-0113* 264-2
NASDAQ: RCII ■ **Fax Area Code:* 972 ■ *TF:* 800-422-8186 ■ *Web:* www.rentacenter.com
Rental Research Services Inc
7525 Mitchell Rd Ste 301. Eden Prairie MN 55344 952-935-5700 935-9212 635
TF: 800-328-0333 ■ *Web:* www.rentalresearch.com
Rentals Inc
3230 Peachtree Corners Cir Ste D Norcross GA 30092 888-501-7368 387
TF: 888-501-7368 ■ *Web:* www.rentals.com
Rent-A-PC Inc 265 Oser Ave Hauppauge NY 11788 631-273-8888 264-1
TF: 800-888-8686 ■ *Web:* www.smartsourcerentals.com
Rent-A-Wheel
2500 Firestone Blvd Ste G South Gate CA 90280 323-249-5668 54
Web: www.rentawheel.com
Rentbits 383 Corona St Ste 301. Denver CO 80218 303-640-3160 387
Web: rentbits.com
Rentec Direct LLC 231 SW I St. Grants Pass OR 97526 800-881-5139 177
TF: 800-881-5139 ■ *Web:* rentecdirect.com
Rentech Inc 10877 Wilshire Blvd Los Angeles CA 90024 310-571-9800 571-9799 579
NASDAQ: RTK ■ *Web:* www.rentechinc.com
Renton Technical College
3000 NE Fourth St Renton WA 98056 425-235-2352 235-7832 162
Web: www.rtc.edu
RentPath LLC
950 E Paces Ferry Rd NE Ste 2600. Atlanta GA 30326 678-421-3000 637-9
TF: 800-216-1423 ■ *Web:* www.rentpath.com
Rentping LLC 1001 S 70th St Ste 201 Lincoln NE 68510 402-204-0465 653
Web: rentping.com
Rentschler Field 615 Silver Ln. East Hartford CT 06118 860-610-4700 31
Web: www.rentschlerfield.com
Renville County PO Box 68. Mohall ND 58761 701-756-6398 756-6494 338
Web: www.ndcourts.gov
Renville County 500 E DePue Ave. Olivia MN 56277 320-523-3663 523-3692 338
Web: www.renvillecountymn.com
Renville-Sibley Cooperative Power Assn
103 Oak St PO Box 68 Danube MN 56230 320-826-2593 245
TF: 800-826-2593 ■ *Web:* www.renville-sibley.coop
RenWeb School Management Software
820 SW Wilshire Blvd. Burleson TX 76028 866-800-6593 623
TF: 866-800-6593 ■ *Web:* www.renweb.com
Renwick Gallery of the Smithsonian American Art Museum
1661 Pennsylvania Ave NW Washington DC 20006 202-633-7970 520
Web: americanart.si.edu
Renze Display Inc 6847 N 16th St Omaha NE 68112 402-342-1111 342-2864 393
TF: 800-627-9131 ■ *Web:* www.renze.com
Renzios Greek Food
1400 Dell Range Blvd Cheyenne WY 82007 307-637-5411 671
Web: renziosgreekfood.com
REO Plastics Inc 11850 93rd Ave N Maple Grove MN 55369 763-425-4171 425-0735 604
Web: www.reoplastics.com
Reonomy 767 3rd Ave. New York NY 10017 646-882-6260 39
Web: www.reonomy.com
REOTEMP Instrument Corp
10656 Roselle St San Diego CA 92121 858-784-0710 784-0720 201
Web: reotemp.com
Rep Works Marketing LLC
1745 S Alma School Rd Ste 260. Mesa AZ 85210 602-279-1987 279-1988 61
Web: www.repworksmktg.com
Repaircliniccom Inc 48600 Michigan Ave. Canton MI 48188 734-495-3079 351
TF: 800-269-2609 ■ *Web:* www.repairclinic.com
Repairtech International Inc
16134 Saticoy St Van Nuys CA 91406 818-989-2681 989-4358 359
Web: www.repairtechinternational.com
Repco Replacement Parts Inc
1021 W Enon Ave Everman TX 76140 817-293-3639 293-7213 202
TF: 800-433-7146 ■ *Web:* www.erepco.com
Repeat Business Systems Inc
4 Fritz Blvd Albany NY 12205 518-869-8116 45
Web: www.repeatbusinesssystems.com
Repeated Signal Solutions Inc
5383 Hollister Ave Ste 150. Santa Barbara CA 93111 805-685-6700 179
Web: www.repeatedsignal.com
Repertory Theatre of Saint Louis
130 Edgar Rd Saint Louis MO 63119 314-968-7340 573-4
Web: www.repstl.org
Repforce Inc 210 Turner Industrial Way Aston PA 19014 610-485-7800 364-0530 366
Web: repforce.com
Replex Mirror Co
11 Mt Vernon Ave. Mount Vernon OH 43050 740-397-5535 596
Web: www.replex.com
Repligen Corp 41 Seyon St Waltham MA 02453 781-250-0111 250-0115 85
NASDAQ: RGEN ■ *TF:* 800-622-2259 ■ *Web:* www.repligen.com
Reply Inc 111 Deerwood Rd Ste 200 San Ramon CA 94583 925-983-3400 4
Web: www.reply.eu
Reporter
333 W Irving Park Rd Ste 331. Palos Heights IL 60463 708-448-6161 448-4012 532-2
Web: thereporteronline.net
Reporter, The 916 Cotting Ln Vacaville CA 95688 707-448-6401 532-2
Web: www.thereporter.com
Reporter, The 307 Derstine Ave. Lansdale PA 19446 215-855-8440 532-2
TF: 888-955-0355 ■ *Web:* www.thereporteronline.com
Reporting Systems Inc
2200 Rimland Dr Ste 305 Bellingham WA 98226 844-752-6066 177
TF: 844-752-6066 ■ *Web:* www.emergencyreporting.com
Repository 500 Market Ave S. Canton OH 44702 330-580-8300 454-5745 532-2
Web: www.cantonrep.com
Representative of German Industry & Trade
1776 I St NW Ste 1000. Washington DC 20006 202-659-4777 659-4779 138
Web: www.rgit-usa.com
Reprint Company Publishers
PO Box 5401 Spartanburg SC 29304 864-579-4433 637-2
Web: www.reprintcompany.com

Name / Address	Phone	Fax	Class
Reproduction Enterprises Inc 908 N Prairie Rd . . . . . Stillwater OK 74075 *Web:* reproductionenterprises.com	405-377-8037	377-4541	11-2
Reproductive Genetics Institute Inc 2910 MacArthur Blvd . . . . . Northbrook IL 60062 *Web:* www.rgipgd.com	773-472-4900		415
Repros Therapeutics Inc 1999 Bryan St Ste 900 . . . . . Dallas TX 77380 *NASDAQ: RPRX* ■ *TF:* 800-895-6554 ■ *Web:* www.reprosrx.com	281-719-3400	719-3446	85
Republic Airways Holdings Inc 8909 Purdue Rd Ste 300 . . . . . Indianapolis IN 46268 *NASDAQ: RJET* ■ *Web:* rjet.com	317-484-6000		360-1
Republic Bancorp Inc 601 W Market St . . . . . Louisville KY 40202 *NASDAQ: RBCAA* ■ *TF:* 888-540-5363 ■ *Web:* www.republicbank.com	502-584-3600		360-2
Republic County 702 K St . . . . . Belleville KS 66935 *Web:* www.republiccounty.org	785-527-2114	527-2668	338
Republic Elite Holdings 15167 Business Ave . . . . . Addison TX 75001 **Fax Area Code:* 903 ■ *Web:* www.republicind.com	972-606-9667	935-3680*	115
Republic Finance 7031 Commerce Cir . . . . . Baton Rouge LA 70809 *TF:* 800-317-7662 ■ *Web:* www.republicfinance.com	225-927-0005		217
Republic Financial Corp 5251 DTC Pkwy Ste 300 . . . . . Greenwood Village CO 80111 *TF:* 800-596-3608 ■ *Web:* republic-financial.com	303-751-3501		216
Republic First Bancorp Inc 50 S 16th St Ste 2400 . . . . . Philadelphia PA 19102 *NASDAQ: FRBK* ■ *TF:* 888-875-2265 ■ *Web:* www.myrepublicbank.com	888-875-2265		360-2
Republic Jewelry & Collectibles 212 Center St . . . . . Auburn ME 04210 *TF:* 877-422-7979 ■ *Web:* www.republicjewelry.com	207-784-4444	782-7351	410
Republic Metals Corp 12900 NW 38th Ave . . . . . Opa Locka FL 33054 *TF:* 888-685-8505 ■ *Web:* www.republicmetalscorp.com	888-685-8505		410
Republic Mills Inc 888 School St . . . . . Okolona OH 43545 *Web:* www.republicmills.com	419-758-3511		447
Republic Mortgage Insurance Co 101 N Cherry St Ste 101 . . . . . Winston-Salem NC 27101 *TF:* 800-999-7642 ■ *Web:* www.rmic.com	800-999-7642		391-5
Republic National Distributing Co (RNDC) 6511 Tri County Pkwy . . . . . Schertz TX 78154 *Web:* www.rndc-usa.com	210-224-7531		81-3
Republic of Croatia *Embassy of the Republic of Croatia in the United States* 2343 Massachusetts Ave NW . . . . . Washington DC 20008 *Web:* us.mvep.hr	202-588-5899	588-8937	257
Republic Packaging Corp 9160 S Green St . . . . . Chicago IL 60620 *Web:* www.repco.com	773-233-6530	233-6005	601
Republic Parking System 633 Chestnut St Ste 2000 . . . . . Chattanooga TN 37450 *Web:* www.republicparking.com	423-756-2771	265-5728	562
Republic Plastics 355 Schumann Rd . . . . . McQueeney TX 78123 *Web:* www.republicplastics.com	830-557-5574		600
Republic Plumbing Supply Company Inc 890 Providence Hwy . . . . . Norwood MA 02062 **Fax Area Code:* 781 ■ *TF:* 800-696-3900 ■ *Web:* www.republicsupplyco.com	800-696-3900	769-7842*	612
Republic Powdered Metals Inc 2628 Pearl Rd . . . . . Medina OH 44256 *TF:* 800-382-1218 ■ *Web:* www.tremcoroofing.com	800-382-1218		550
Republic Properties Corp 1201 MD Ave SW Ste 850 . . . . . Washington DC 20024 *Web:* www.republicfamilyofcompanies.com	202-552-5300		653
Republic Storage Systems LLC 1038 Belden Ave NE . . . . . Canton OH 44705 *TF:* 800-477-1255 ■ *Web:* republicstorage.com	330-438-5800	454-7772	286
Republic, The 2900 N National Rd Ste A . . . . . Columbus IN 47201 *Web:* www.therepublic.com	812-372-7811	379-5711	532-2
Republican Co, The 1860 Main St . . . . . Springfield MA 01103	413-788-1000	788-1301	637-8
Republican Governors Assn (RGA) 1747 Pennsylvania Ave NW Ste 250 . . . . . Washington DC 20006 *Web:* www.rga.org	202-662-4140		48-7
Republican National Committee (RNC) 310 First St SE . . . . . Washington DC 20003 *TF:* 800-445-5768 ■ *Web:* www.gop.com	202-863-8500		616
Republican Party of New Mexico (RPNM) 5150-A San Francisco Rd NE PO Box 94083 . . Albuquerque NM 87109 *Web:* newmexico.gop	505-298-3662		616-2
Republican-American Inc 389 Meadow St . . . . . Waterbury CT 06702 *TF:* 800-992-3232 ■ *Web:* www.rep-am.com	203-574-3636	596-9277	637-8
Republican-Rustler PO Box 640 . . . . . Basin WY 82410 *Web:* www.basinrepublican-rustler.com	307-568-2458		532-2
Reputation Institute Inc 222 3rd St . . . . . Cambridge MA 02142 *Web:* www.reputationinstitute.com	617-758-0955		466
Reputation Rhino LLC 300 Park Ave 12th Fl . . . . . New York NY 10022 *TF:* 888-975-3331 ■ *Web:* www.reputationrhino.com	888-975-3331		387
Repwest Insurance Co 2721 N Central Ave . . . . . Phoenix AZ 85004 *TF:* 800-528-7134 ■ *Web:* www.repwest.com	800-528-7134		391-4
Request Foods Inc PO Box 2577 . . . . . Holland MI 49422 *Web:* www.requestfoods.com	616-786-0900	786-9180	296-36
ReQuest Inc 100 Saratoga Village Blvd Ste 45 . . . . . Ballston NY 12020 *TF:* 800-236-2812 ■ *Web:* www.request.com	518-899-1254	899-1251	52
Requitest Inc 8614 N Bali Ct . . . . . Ellicott City MD 21043 *Web:* www.requitest.com	410-465-8637		809
Res Engineers Inc 1250 Missouri St Ste 207 . . . . . San Francisco CA 94107 *Web:* resengineers.com	415-822-4625		261
RES Exhibit Services LLC 435 Smith St . . . . . Rochester NY 14608 *TF:* 800-482-4049 ■ *Web:* www.res-exhibits.com	585-546-2040		7
RES Manufacturing Co 7801 N 73rd St . . . . . Milwaukee WI 53223 *Web:* www.resmfg.com	414-354-4530	354-9434	488

Name / Address	Phone	Fax	Class
Res Title Inc 175 Metro Center Blvd Ste 4 . . . . . Warwick RI 02886 *TF:* 866-737-8485 ■ *Web:* res-title.com	866-737-8485		41
Rescar Inc 1101 31st St Ste 250 . . . . . Downers Grove IL 60515 *TF:* 800-851-5196 ■ *Web:* www.rescar.com	630-963-1114	963-6342	651
Reschenthaler Guy (Rep R - PA) 531 Cannon House Office Bldg . . . . . Washington DC 20515 *Web:* www.reschenthaler.house.gov	202-225-2065		342-2
Resco Plastics Inc 93783 Newport Ln . . . . . Coos Bay OR 97420 *TF:* 800-266-5097 ■ *Web:* rescoplastics.com	541-269-5485		661
Resco Products Inc 2 Penn Ctr W Ste 430 . . . . . Pittsburgh PA 15276 **Fax Area Code:* 412 ■ *TF:* 888-283-5505 ■ *Web:* www.rescoproducts.com	888-283-5505	494-4571*	662
Rescraft Plastic Products Inc 9 Woodslee Ave . . . . . Paris ON N3L3V1 *Web:* www.rescraft.com	519-442-4339		393
Rescuecom Corp 2560 Burnet Ave . . . . . Syracuse NY 13206 **Fax Area Code:* 315 ■ *TF:* 800-737-2837 ■ *Web:* www.rescuecom.com	800-737-2837	433-5228*	310
Rescuetime Inc 811 First Ave Ste 480 . . . . . Seattle WA 98104 *TF:* 888-215-8635 ■ *Web:* rescuetime.com	888-215-8635		225
Research & Development Solutions Inc 7921 Jones Branch Dr . . . . . McLean VA 22102 *Web:* rdsi.com	703-893-9533		261
Research & Diagnostic Antibodies 2645 W Cheyenne Ave . . . . . North Las Vegas NV 89032 *TF:* 800-858-7322 ■ *Web:* www.rdabs.com	702-638-7800	638-7801	231
Research & Innovative Technology Administration *Office of Research, Development & Technology Programs & Activities* 1200 New Jersey Ave SE . . . . . Washington DC 20590 **Fax Area Code:* 202 ■ *TF:* 800-853-1351 ■ *Web:* www.transportation.gov	800-853-1351	366-3759*	340-17
Research 1166 Federal Credit Union 600 Billingsport Rd . . . . . Paulsboro NJ 08066 *Web:* 1166fcu.org	856-224-3136		219
Research Associates Inc 27999 Clemens Rd . . . . . Cleveland OH 44145 *TF:* 800-255-9693 ■ *Web:* www.raiglobal.com	440-892-9439		400
Research Corp 4703 E Camp Lowell Dr Ste 201 . . . . . Tucson AZ 85712 *Web:* www.rescorp.org	520-571-1111	571-1119	305
Research Corporation Technologies 101 N Wilmot Rd Ste 600 . . . . . Tucson AZ 85711 *Web:* rctech.com	520-748-4400	748-0025	792
Research Data Inc 3900-A Carolina Ave . . . . . Richmond VA 23222 *Web:* www.researchdata.com	804-591-3328		180
Research Director Inc 914 Bay Ridge Rd Ste 215 . . . . . Annapolis MD 21403 *Web:* www.researchdirectorinc.com	410-295 6619	268-1915	466
Research Electro-optics Inc 5505 Airport Blvd . . . . . Boulder CO 80301 *Web:* www.reoinc.com	303-938-1960	245-4396	544
Research Financial Strategies Inc 5929 S Fashion Point Dr Ste 203 . . . . . Ogden UT 84403 *Web:* rfsadvisors.com	385-715-0120		690
Research First Consulting Inc 8 Mockingbird Ln . . . . . Gulfport MS 39507 *Web:* www.researchfirst.com	205-995-8866		737
Research for Good Inc 1037 NE 65th St Ste 80212 . . . . . Seattle WA 98115 *Web:* www.researchforgood.com	425-610-7294		466
Research Foundation of City University of New York, The 230 W 41st St 7th Fl . . . . . New York NY 10036 *Web:* www.rfcuny.org	212-417-8300		668
Research Frontiers Inc 240 Crossways Park Dr . . . . . Woodbury NY 11797 *Web:* www.smartglass.com	516-364-1902		544
Research Horizons LLC 6423 Montgomery St Ste 12 . . . . . Rhinebeck NY 12572 *TF:* 888-876-7641 ■ *Web:* www.phoenixmi.com	845-876-8228		4
Research Inc 7128 Shady Oak Rd . . . . . Eden Prairie MN 55344 *Web:* pcscontrols.com	952-941-3300	941-3628	201
Research into Action Inc 3934 NE Mlking Jr Blvd Ste 300 . . . . . Portland OR 97212 *TF:* 888-492-9100 ■ *Web:* www.researchintoaction.com	503-287-9136		196
Research Laboratory of Electronics Massachusetts Institute of Technology 77 Massachusetts Ave . . . . . Cambridge MA 02139 *Web:* www.rle.mit.edu	617-253-2519	253-1301	668
Research Management Consultants Inc 816 Camarillo Springs Rd Ste J . . . . . Camarillo CA 93012 *Web:* www.rmci.com	805-987-5538	987-2868	261
Research Medical Ctr 2316 E Meyer Blvd . . . . . Kansas City MO 64132 *TF:* 855-422-6625 ■ *Web:* researchmedicalcenter.com	816-276-4000		374-3
Research Products Corp 1015 E Washington Ave . . . . . Madison WI 53703 *TF:* 800-334-6011 ■ *Web:* www.aprilaire.com	608-257-8801	257-4357	17
Research Psychiatric Ctr 2323 E 63rd St . . . . . Kansas City MO 64130 *TF:* 844-207-4511 ■ *Web:* researchpsychiatriccenter.com	816-444-8161		374-5
Research Solutions Inc 5435 Balboa Blvd Ste 202 . . . . . Encino CA 91316 *Web:* researchsolutions.investorroom.com	310-477-0354		466
Research to Prevent Blindness Inc (RPB) 360 Lexington Ave 22nd Fl . . . . . New York NY 10017 *TF:* 800-621-0026 ■ *Web:* www.rpbusa.org	212-752-4333	688-6231	48-17
Research Triangle Institute 3040 Cornwallis Rd PO Box 12194 . . . . . Research Triangle Park NC 27709 *TF:* 800-334-8571 ■ *Web:* www.rti.org	919-541-6000	541-5985	668
Research Triangle Park Laboratories 7201 Acc Blvd Ste 104 . . . . . Raleigh NC 27617 *Web:* www.rtp-labs.com	919-510-0228	510-0141	85
Research Wizard of Tulsa City-County Library 400 Civic Ctr . . . . . Tulsa OK 74103 *Web:* www.researchwizard.org	918-549-7431	549-7433	434-5
Research!America 241 18th St S Ste 501 . . . . . Arlington VA 22202 *Web:* www.researchamerica.org	703-739-2577	739-2372	48-5

Phone | Fax | Class

Reseau BIBLIO de la Monteregie
275 Rue Conrad-Pelletier . . . La Prairie QC J5R4V1 450-444-5433 659-3364 436
Web: www.reseaubibliomonteregie.qc.ca

Reseau BIBLIO des Laurentides
29 Rue Brissette . . . Sainte-Agathe-des-Monts QC J8C3L1 819-326-6440 326-0885 436
Web: www.mabibliotheque.ca

Reser's Fine Foods Inc
15570 SW Jenkins Rd . . . Beaverton OR 97006 503-643-6431 296-33
TF: 800-333-6431 ■ *Web:* www.resers.com

Reserve National Insurance Co
601 E Britton Rd . . . Oklahoma City OK 73114 405-848-7931 391-2
Web: www.reservenational.com

Reserve Officers Association of the US (ROA)
1 Constitution Ave NE . . . Washington DC 20002 202-479-2200 547-1641 48-19
TF: 800-809-9448 ■ *Web:* www.roa.org

Reserve Petroleum Co
6801 Broadway Ext Ste 300 . . . Oklahoma City OK 73116 405-848-7551 536
Web: www.reserve-petro.com

Reserve Telephone Company Inc
3750 Nicole St . . . Paulina LA 70763 985-536-1111 536-4815 736
TF: 888-611-6111 ■ *Web:* rtconline.com

Reservoir Capital Group
767 5th Ave 16th Fl . . . New York NY 10153 212-610-9000 690
Web: www.reservoircap.com

Reservoir State Park
c/o Niagara Frontier Reg PO Box 1132 . . . Niagara Falls NY 14303 716-284-4691 565
Web: parks.ny.gov

Residence & Conference Centre - Toronto
1760 Finch Ave E . . . Toronto ON M2J5G3 416-491-8811 491-0486 379
TF: 877-225-8664 ■ *Web:* www.stayrcc.com

Residence Inn Mystic 40 Whitehall Ave . . . Mystic CT 06355 603-286-8008 707
Web: www.lakesregion.org

Residences on Georgia
101-1288 W Georgia St . . . Vancouver BC V6E4R3 604-891-6101 891-6103 379
Web: www.respal.com

Residential Mortgage LLC
100 Calais Dr . . . Anchorage AK 99503 907-222-8800 222-8801 509
TF: 888-357-2707 ■ *Web:* www.residentialmtg.com

Residential Properties Management Inc
1105 Brookstown Ave . . . Winston-Salem NC 27101 336-724-1110 724-6765 652
Web: www.residentialpropertiesmanagement.com

Resideo Technologies Inc
3400 Intertech Dr Ste 200 . . . Brookfield WI 53045 262-783-5440 250
Web: lifecaresolutions.resideo.com

Resilite Sports Products PO Box 764 . . . Sunbury PA 17801 800-843-6287 473-8988* 710
**Fax Area Code:* 570 ■ *TF:* 800-843-6287 ■ *Web:* www.resilite.com

Resilux America LLC
265 John Brooks Rd . . . Pendergrass GA 30567 706-693-7110 601
Web: www.uniqueplastics.com

Resin Systems Corp 62 Rt 101A . . . Amherst NH 03031 603-673-1234 673-4512 610
Web: resinsystems.com

Resin Systems Inc 1586 Swisco Rd . . . Sulphur LA 70665 337-625-4541 625-4557 596
Web: www.rsiswla.com

Resina West Inc 27455 Bostik Ct . . . Temecula CA 92590 951-296-6585 296-5018 298
TF: 800-207-4804 ■ *Web:* resina.com

Resinall Corp PO Box 195 . . . Severn NC 27877 800-421-0561 605-2
TF: 800-421-0561 ■ *Web:* www.resinall.com

Resinart East Inc 201 Old Airport Rd . . . Fletcher NC 28732 828-687-0215 687-0182 596
TF: 877-655-6506 ■ *Web:* east.resinart.com

Resinoid Engineering Corp
251 O'Neill Dr . . . Hebron OH 43025 740-928-6115 596
Web: www.resinoid.com

ResMed Inc
9001 Spectrum Center Blvd . . . San Diego CA 92123 858-836-5000 836-5501 476
NYSE: RMD ■ *TF:* 800-424-0737 ■ *Web:* www.resmed.com

RESNA (Rehabilitation Engineering & Assistive Technology Society of North America)
1560 Wilson Blvd Ste 850 . . . Arlington VA 22209 703-524-6686 524-6630 48-17
Web: www.resna.org

Resolute Energy Corp
1700 N Lincoln St Ste 2800 . . . Denver CO 80203 303-534-4600 536
Web: www.resoluteenergy.com

Resolute Forest Products
111 Robert-Bourassa Blvd Ste 5000 . . . Montreal QC H3C2M1 514-875-2160 557
TF: 800-361-2888 ■ *Web:* www.resolutefp.com

RESOLUTE Partners LLC
37 W Center St Ste 301 . . . Southington CT 06489 860-628-6800 225
Web: www.resolutepartners.com

Resolute Systems Inc
1550 N Prospect Ave . . . Milwaukee WI 53202 414-276-4774 270-0932 41
TF: 800-776-6060 ■ *Web:* resolutesystems.com

Resolute Technology Solutions Inc
600-433 Main St . . . Winnipeg MB R3B1B3 204-927-3520 927-3521 177
Web: resolutets.com

Resolute Tissue 3301 NW 107th St . . . Miami FL 33167 800-562-2860 558
Web: resolutetissue.com

Resolution Digital Studios
2226 W Walnut St . . . Chicago IL 60612 312-846-4226 514
Web: www.rdschicago.com

Resolve Inc 1255 23rd St NW Ste 275 . . . Washington DC 20037 202-944-2300 196
Web: www.resolv.org

RESOLVE Partners LLC
2733 Horse Pen Creek Rd Ste 101 . . . Greensboro NC 27410 336-217-1005 346-3228 41
TF: 866-921-5388 ■ *Web:* www.resolve-partners.com

Resolve Tech Solutions Inc
15851 N Dallas Pkwy Ste 1103 . . . Addison TX 75001 214-310-1020 310-1021 463
Web: resolvetech.com

RESOLVE: National Infertility Assn
1760 Old Meadow Rd Ste 500 . . . McLean VA 22102 703-556-7172 506-3266 48-17
Web: resolve.org

Resonetics 2941 College Dr . . . Kettering OH 45420 937-865-4070 425
Web: resonetics.com

Resort Condominiums Intl (RCI)
9998 N Michigan Rd . . . Carmel IN 46032 317-805-8000 753
TF: 800-338-7777 ■ *Web:* www.rci.com

Resort Data Processing Inc 211 Eagle Rd . . . Avon CO 81620 970-845-1140 177
TF: 877-779-3717 ■ *Web:* www.resortdata.com

Resort Internet
719 Ten Mile Dr Ste A PO Box 2718 . . . Frisco CO 80443 970-262-3515 455-3069 387
Web: www.resortinternet.com

Resort Parks Intl 2901 Cherry Ave . . . Signal Hill CA 90755 562-595-8818 490-0669 564
TF: 800-456-7774 ■ *Web:* www.resortparks.com

Resort Semiahmoo 9565 Semiahmoo Pkwy . . . Blaine WA 98230 360-318-2000 318-2087 669
TF: 855-917-3767 ■ *Web:* www.semiahmoo.com

Resorts Casino Hotel
1133 Boardwalk . . . Atlantic City NJ 08401 800-334-6378 669
TF: 800-334-6378 ■ *Web:* resortsac.com

Resorts of the Canadian Rockies Inc
1505 17th Ave SW . . . Calgary AB T2T0E2 403-254-7669 378
TF: 800-258-7669 ■ *Web:* skircr.com

Resource & Financial Management Systems Inc
3073 Palisades Ct . . . Tuscaloosa AL 35405 800-701-7367 177
TF: 800-701-7367 ■ *Web:* www.rfms.com

Resource Alliance LLC
1725 Windward Concourse Ste 100 . . . Alpharetta GA 30005 678-691-6600 570
Web: real-hr.com

Resource America Inc
712 Fifth Ave 12th Fl . . . New York NY 10019 212-506-3899 401
Web: www.resourceamerica.com

Resource Building Materials
10961 Dale Ave . . . Stanton CA 90680 800-274-2549 952-2710* 191-1
**Fax Area Code:* 714 ■ *TF:* 800-274-2549 ■ *Web:* www.resourcebuildingmaterials.com

Resource Center for Associations
10200 W 44th Ave Ste 304 . . . Wheat Ridge CO 80033 303-422-2615 47

Resource Connection Inc
161 S Main St . . . Middleton MA 01949 978-777-9333 777-3360 184
TF: 800-649-5228 ■ *Web:* www.resource-connection.com

Resource Data Inc
560 E 34th Ave Ste 100 . . . Anchorage AK 99503 907-563-8100 177
Web: www.resourcedata.com

Resource Development Company Inc
716 Dekalb Pke Ste 212 . . . Blue Bell PA 19422 215-628-2293 628-2780 194
Web: rdcinc.com

Resource Development Corp
280 Daines St Ste 200 . . . Birmingham MI 48009 248-646-2300 646-0789 39
TF: 800-360-7222 ■ *Web:* www.resourcedev.com

Resource Federal Credit Union
525 Old Hickory Blvd . . . Jackson TN 38305 731-668-3464 668-5573 219
TF: 800-643-9212 ■ *Web:* resourcefcu.com

Resource Foundation, The
237 W 35th St Ste 1203 . . . New York NY 10001 212-675-6170 268-5325 48-5
Web: www.resourcefnd.org

Resource Label Group LLC
147 Seaboard Ln . . . Franklin TN 37067 615-661-5900 661-5950 552-1
Web: resourcelabel.com

Resource Land Holdings LLC
1400 16th St Ste 320 . . . Denver CO 80202 720-723-2850 723-2851 360-3
Web: www.rlholdings.com

Resource Management Inc
281 Main St Ste 5 . . . Fitchburg MA 01420 800-508-0048 631
TF: 800-508-0048 ■ *Web:* rmi-solutions.com

Resource Management Service LLC
31 Inverness Center Pkwy Ste 360 . . . Birmingham AL 35242 800-995-9516 991-2807* 302
**Fax Area Code:* 205 ■ *TF:* 800-995-9516 ■ *Web:* www.resourcemgt.com

Resource Mfg
7033 Commonwealth Ave Ste 4 . . . Jacksonville FL 32220 904-693-3686 260
Web: www.resourcemfg.com

Resource Network, The
1119 Brentfield Dr . . . McLean VA 22101 703-506-0203 506-0205 180
Web: www.resnet.org

Resource One 40 School St . . . Framingham MA 01701 508-906-6075 104
Web: r1ne.com

Resource One International LLC
2225 Bohm Dr . . . Little Chute WI 54140 920-788-1550 788-5757 393
Web: www.resoneint.com

Resource Options Inc 200 Highland Ave . . . Needham MA 02494 781-455-0224 455-7132 192
TF: 800-505-4764 ■ *Web:* www.resourceoptions.com

Resource Plus 9636 Heckscher Dr . . . Jacksonville FL 32226 888-678-8966 345
TF: 888-678-8966 ■ *Web:* www.resourcep.com

Resource Publications 2205 Benton . . . Searcy AR 72143 501-305-1472 637-2
Web: www.resourcepublications.net

Resource Technology Management Inc
251 Maitland Av Ste 215 . . . Maitland FL 32751 407-998-8000 225
Web: www.rtm-inc.com

Resources Applications Designs & Controls Inc
3220 E 59th St . . . Long Beach CA 90805 562-272-7231 261

Resources For Living Ltd
4407 Monterey Oaks Blvd . . . Austin TX 78749 512-358-8400 194
Web: www.resourcesforliving.com

Resources for Rehabilitation (RFR)
22 Bonad Rd . . . Winchester MA 01890 781-368-9080 368-9096 637-2
Web: www.rfr.org

Resources for the Future
1616 P St NW . . . Washington DC 20036 202-328-5000 939-3460 634
Web: www.rff.org

Resources Global Professionals
17101 Armstrong Ave . . . Irvine CA 92614 714-430-6400 721
NASDAQ: RECN ■ *Web:* www.rgp.com

Resources Unlimited Co
2680 Berkshire Pkwy Ste 110 . . . Des Moines IA 50325 515-270-0694 193
TF: 800-278-1292 ■ *Web:* resourcesunlimited.com

Resourcing Edge Inc
1309 Ridge Rd Ste 200 . . . Rockwall TX 75087 214-771-4411 771-4420 734
TF: 877-703-8010 ■ *Web:* resourcingedge.com

Respec Inc 3824 Jet Dr . . . Rapid City SD 57703 605-394-6400 394-6456 261
Web: www.respec.com

Respiratory Home Care Specialists Inc
PO Box 29099 . . . Honolulu HI 96820 808-832-1600 832-1607 264-4
Web: rhcs.net

Respondus Inc
8201 164th Ave NE Ste 200 PO Box 3247 . . . Redmond WA 98052 425-881-3329 225
Web: www.respondus.com

Response Design Corp
5541 Simpson Ave . . . Ocean City NJ 08226 800-366-4732 196
TF: 800-366-4732 ■ *Web:* www.responsedesign.com

Response Envelope Inc
1340 S Baker Ave . . . Ontario CA 91761 909-923-5855 923-3639 263
TF: 800-750-0046 ■ *Web:* response-envelope.com

	Phone	Fax	Class
Response Staffing Solutions Inc			
56 W 45th St 16th Fl........New York NY 10036	212-983-8870	532-0660	260
Web: www.responseco.com			
Response Technology Inc P O Box 1569........Renton WA 98057	425-254-8687		177
TF: 800-523-5201 ■ *Web:* www.responsetech.com			
Ressler Motor Co 8474 Huffine Ln........Bozeman MT 59718	406-587-5501		516
TF: 866-623-5532 ■ *Web:* www.resslermotors.com			
Rest Haven-York 1050 S George St........York PA 17403	717-843-9866	846-5894	450
Web: www.resthavenyork.com			
Rest Ministries Inc PO Box 502928........San Diego CA 92150	858-486-4685		48-21
Web: restministries.com			
Restaurant & Stores Equipment Co			
230 West 700 South........Salt Lake City UT 84101	801-364-1981		300
TF: 800-877-0087 ■ *Web:* rescoslc.com			
Restaurant Associates Inc			
132 W 31st St Ste 601........New York NY 10001	212-613-5500		670
Web: www.restaurantassociates.com			
Restaurant at the Phoenix			
812 Race St........Cincinnati OH 45202	513-721-8901		671
Web: www.thephx.com			
Restaurant Avo 5908 Magazine St........New Orleans LA 70115	504-509-6550		671
Web: restaurantavo.com			
Restaurant Beffroi Steak House			
775 Honore-Mercier Ave........Quebec City QC G1R6A5	418-380-2638		671
Web: www.beffroisteakhouse.com			
Restaurant Bouchard 505 Thames St........Newport RI 02840	401-846-0123		671
Web: bouchardnewport.com			
Restaurant Bricco 78 LaSalle Rd........West Hartford CT 06107	860-233-0220		671
Web: www.billygrant.com			
Restaurant Developers Corp			
7002 Engle Rd Ste 100........Middleburg Heights OH 44130	440-625-3080		670
TF: 888-860-5082 ■ *Web:* www.mrhero.com			
Restaurant Europea			
1227 de la Montagne........Montreal QC H3G1Z2	514-398-9229	398-9718	671
Web: www.europea.ca			
Restaurant Gandhi			
230 Rue St Paul Oeust........Montreal QC H2Y1Z9	514-845-5866		671
Web: www.restaurantgandhi.com			
Restaurant Gary Danko			
800 N Pt St........San Francisco CA 94109	415-749-2060	775-1805	671
Web: garydanko.com			
Restaurant Initial			
54 St-Pierre St........Quebec City QC G1K4A1	418-694-1818	694-2387	671
Web: restaurantinitiale.com			
Restaurant Jano Grillades			
3883 St-Laurent Blvd........Montreal QC H2W1X9	514-849-0646		671
Web: www.janogrillades.ca			
Restaurant Partners Inc			
1030 N Orange Ave Ste 200........Orlando FL 32801	407-839-5070	839-3388	463
Web: www.restaurantpartnersinc.com			
Restaurant School at Walnut Hill College			
4207 Walnut St........Philadelphia PA 19104	215-222-4200		163
Web: www.walnuthillcollege.edu			
Restaurant Solutions Inc			
1423 Austell Rd........Marietta GA 30008	770-421-1999	421-1090	45
Web: www.restaurantsolutionsinc.com			
Restaurant Technologies Inc			
2250 Pilot Knob Rd Ste 100........Mendota Heights MN 55120	651-796-1600	379-4082	300
TF: 888-796-4997 ■ *Web:* www.rti-inc.com			
Restaurant365 500 Technology Dr Ste 200........Irvine CA 92618	949-652-7800		39
Web: www.restaurant365.com			
Restaurants Unlimited Inc			
411 First Ave S Ste 200........Seattle WA 98104	206-634-0550		670
TF: 877-855-6106 ■ *Web:* www.r-u-i.com			
Restek Corp 110 Benner Cir........Bellefonte PA 16823	814-353-1300		201
Web: www.restek.com			
Restless Legs Syndrome Foundation Inc			
3006 Bee Caves Rd Ste D206........Austin TX 70740	507-287-6465	287-6312	48-17
Web: www.rls.org			
Resto Gare 630 Des Meurons St........Winnipeg MB R2H2P9	204-237-7072		671
Web: www.restogare.com			
Reston Hospital Ctr			
1850 Town Center Pkwy........Reston VA 20190	703-689-9000		374-3
TF: 888-327-8882 ■ *Web:* restonhospital.com			
Restoration Hardware Inc			
2900 N MacArthur Dr Ste 100........Tracy CA 95376	800-910-9836		362
TF: 800-910-9836 ■ *Web:* www.restorationhardware.com			
Result Data Consulting Ltd			
110 Polaris Pkwy........Westerville OH 43082	614-505-0770	505-0779	809
Web: www.resultdata.com			
Resultly LLC 116 W Hubbard St 4th Fl........Chicago IL 60654	312-273-9400		387
Results 1101 15th St NW Ste 1200........Washington DC 20005	202-783-7100	452-9346	48-5
Web: www.results.org			
Results Driven Marketing			
8534 NE Alderwood Rd Ste 300........Wichita KS 67208	877-689-8555		194
Web: www.resultsdm.com			
Results Radio LLC			
1355 N Dutton Ave Ste 225........Santa Rosa CA 95401	707-546-9185		643
Web: resultsradio.com			
Results Telemarketing Inc			
100 NE 3rd Ave Ste 200........Fort Lauderdale FL 33301	954-921-2400	923-8070	737
Web: www.theresultscompanies.com			
RESUMate Inc 2500 Packard St Ste 200........Ann Arbor MI 48104	734-477-9402		178-10
TF: 800-530-9310 ■ *Web:* resumate.com			
Resurrection Medical Ctr			
7435 W Talcott Ave........Chicago IL 60631	773-774-8000		374-3
Web: www.presencehealth.org			
Resuscitation International LLC			
17797 N Perimeter Dr Ste 105........Scottsdale AZ 85255	480-240-9495		743
Web: resusintl.com			
Retail Alliance 838 Granby St........Norfolk VA 23510	757-466-1600		78
Web: retailalliance.com			
Retail Computer Group LLC, The			
8194 Traphagen St NW........Massillon OH 44646	800-944-0917		525
TF: 800-944-0917 ■ *Web:* www.trcgllc.com			
Retail Concepts Inc			
10225 Mula Rd Ste 120........Stafford TX 77477	281-340-5000		711
Web: www.retailconcepts.cc			
Retail Confectioners Intl (RCI)			
3029 E Sunshine St Ste A........Springfield MO 65804	417-883-2775	883-1108	49-6
TF: 800-545-5381 ■ *Web:* www.retailconfectioners.org			
Retail Construction Services Inc (RCS)			
11343 39th St N........Lake Elmo MN 55042	651-704-9000	704-9100	685
Web: retail-construction.com			
Retail Design Associates (RDA)			
9984 Niblick Dr Ste 2........Roseville CA 95678	800-722-4922		393
TF: 800-722-4922 ■ *Web:* www.retaildesignassociates.com			
Retail Industry Leaders Assn (RILA)			
1700 N Moore St Ste 2250........Arlington VA 22209	703-841-2300	841-1184	49-18
Web: www.rila.org			
Retail Planning Corp			
35 Johnson Ferry Rd........Marietta GA 30068	770-956-8383		652
Web: retailplanningcorp.com			
Retail Pro International LLC			
400 Plaza Dr Ste 200........Folsom CA 95630	916-605-7200		178-10
OTC: RTPRQ ■ *TF:* 800-738-2457 ■ *Web:* www.retailpro.com			
Retail Resource Group International LLC			
226 New Gate Loop........Lake Mary FL 32746	407-878-6650	732-4565	601
Web: www.mybevi.com			
Retail Service Co (RSC)			
2108 W Broadway........South Portland ME 04106	207-772-8888		112
TF: 800-548-4028 ■ *Web:* www.retailserviceco.com			
Retail Solutions Providers Assn (RSPA)			
9920 Couloak Dr Unit 120........Charlotte NC 28216	800-782-2693	357-3127*	49-18
**Fax Area Code:* 704 ■ *TF:* 800-782-2693 ■ *Web:* www.gorspa.org			
RetailMLS LLC 12 W 23rd St 4th Fl........New York NY 10010	212-729-1041		387
Retama Park 1 Retama Pkwy........Selma TX 78154	210-651-7000		642
Web: www.retamapark.com			
Retco Tool Company Inc			
9030 Viscount Row........Dallas TX 75247	214-358-5039	350-2810	493
TF: 800-562-0552 ■ *Web:* retcotool.com			
Retcomp Inc 2nd NH Tpke S........New Boston NH 03070	603-487-5010	487-5181	625
Web: www.retcomp.com			
Retech Systems LLC 100 Henry Stn Rd........Ukiah CA 95482	707-462-6522		386
Web: www.retechsystemsllc.com			
Rethink Autism Inc			
19 W 21st St Ste 403........New York NY 10010	646-257-2919		177
Web: www.rethinkfirst.com			
Rethink Innovations 77 Elbo Ln........Mount Laurel NJ 08054	609-784-8427		317
Web: myrethink.com			
Retif Oil & Fuel Inc 527 Destrehan Ave........Harvey LA 70058	800-349-9000		579
TF: 800-349-9000 ■ *Web:* www.retif.com			
Retina Consultants of Oklahoma			
9821 S May Ave Ste C........Oklahoma City OK 73159	405-691-0505		543
Web: retinaconsultantsoklahoma.com			
Retired Enlisted Assn			
15821 E Centre Tech Cir........Aurora CO 80011	303-340-3939		48-19
Web: trea.org			
Retirement Advantage Inc, The			
47 Park Pl Ste 850........Appleton WI 54914	888-872-2364		463
TF: 888-872-2364 ■ *Web:* tra401k.com			
Retirement Investment Advisors Inc			
3001 United Founders Blvd Ste A........Oklahoma City OK 73112	405-842-3443	842-3471	401
Web: www.theretirementpath.com			
Retirement Plan Advisors LLC			
105 W Adams St Ste 2175........Chicago IL 60603	312-701-1100		401
Web: retirementplanadvisors.com			
Retirement Research Foundation			
8765 W Higgins Rd Ste 430........Chicago IL 60631	773-714-8080	714-8089	305
Web: www.rrf.org			
Retirement System Group Inc			
41 E 42nd St........New York NY 10017	212-503-0100		401
Retlif Incorporated Testing Laboratories			
795 Marconi Ave........Ronkonkoma NY 11779	631-737-1500	737-1497	743
Web: www.retlif.com			
Retractable Technologies Inc			
511 Lobo Ln........Little Elm TX 75068	972-294-1010	292-3600	477
NYSE: RVP ■ *TF:* 888-806-2626 ■ *Web:* www.retractable.com			
Retreat Spa & Salon LLC			
4246 Washington Rd........Evans GA 30809	706-364-8292		77
Web: retreatspaandsalon.com			
Retro-Fit Technologies Inc			
455 Fortune Blvd........Milford MA 01757	508-478-2222	478-2040	174
TF: 800-966-2222 ■ *Web:* www.retrofit.com			
Retrospect, The 732 Haddon Ave........Collingswood NJ 08108	609-854-1400		532-2
Web: www.theretrospect.com			
Rettew Associates Inc			
3020 Columbia Ave........Lancaster PA 17603	717-394-3721		261
TF: 800-738-8395 ■ *Web:* www.rettew.com			
Return Management Services Inc			
800 Berkshire Ln N........Plymouth MN 55441	952-475-0242		463
Web: www.rmsincorporated.com			
Reuben & Junius LLP			
1 Bush St Ste 600........San Francisco CA 94104	415-567-9000	399-9480	428
Web: www.reubenlaw.com			
Reuben H. Fleet Science Ctr			
1875 El Prado........San Diego CA 92101	619-238-1233	685-5771	520
Web: www.rhfleet.org			
Reuland Electric Co			
17969 E Railroad St........City of Industry CA 91748	888-964-6411		518
TF: 888-964-6411 ■ *Web:* reuland.com			
Reunion Tower 300 Reunion Blvd E........Dallas TX 75207	214-712-7040		671
Web: reuniontower.com			
Reuter Associates LLC			
Ten Vaughan Mall Ste 201A........Portsmouth NH 03801	603-430-2081		192
Web: www.reuterassociates.com			
Reuter Organ Co 1220 Timberedge Rd........Lawrence KS 66049	785-843-2622	843-3302	527
Web: www.reuterorgan.com			
Reuther Engineering 126 S 14th St........Newark NJ 07107	973-485-5800	482-6005	454
Web: www.reutherengineering.com			
Reuther Mold & Manufacturing Inc			
1225 Munroe Falls Ave........Cuyahoga Falls OH 44221	330-923-5266	923-9930	757
Web: www.reuthermold.com			
REV GROUP Inc 52216 State Rd 15........Bristol IN 46507	574-848-1126	848-1127	120
TF: 888-522-1126 ■ *Web:* renegaderv.com			

Phone | Fax | Class

REV Rocket LLC
9000 Executive Pk Dr Bldg D Ste 300 ... Knoxville TN 37923 865-693-4343 691-6904 741-69
Web: www.wtnzfox43.revrocket.us

REVA Air Ambulance Inc
1745 NW 51 Pl Hngr 73 ... Fort Lauderdale FL 33309 954-730-9300 30
Web: www.flyreva.com

Reva Capital Markets LLC
45 Broadway 8th Fl ... New York NY 10025 212-464-7363 964-6629* 690
**Fax Area Code:* 646 ■ *Web:* www.revacap.com

REVA Medical Inc 5751 Copley Dr ... San Diego CA 92111 858-966-3000 477
Web: www.revamedical.com

Revcom Inc 251 Kearny St 8th Fl ... San Francisco CA 94108 888-369-0701 393
TF: 888-369-0701 ■ *Web:* www.rev.com

Revcor Inc 251 E Edwards Ave ... Carpentersville IL 60110 800-323-8261 426-4630* 18
**Fax Area Code:* 847 ■ *TF:* 800-323-8261 ■ *Web:* www.revcor.com

Reveal Global Intelligence
10800 Sikes Pl ... Charlotte NC 28277 704-844-6000 815-0399 260
Web: revealglobal.com

Revel Consulting
2226 Third Ave Ste 300 ... Seattle WA 98121 206-407-3173 463
Web: revelconsulting.com

Revelation Software
99 Kinderkamack Rd ... Westwood NJ 07675 201-594-1422 722-9815 178-2
TF: 800-262-4747 ■ *Web:* www.revelation.com

Revelations Entertainment
1990 S Bundy Dr Ste 850 ... Los Angeles CA 90025 310-394-3131 514
Web: revelationsent.com

Revelex Corp
6405 Congress Ave Ste 120 ... Boca Raton FL 33487 561-988-5588 180
Web: www.revelex.com

Revels Tractor Company Inc
2217 N Main St ... Fuquay-Varina NC 27526 919-552-5697 274
TF: 800-849-5469 ■ *Web:* www.revelstractor.com

Revenew International LLC
9 Greenway PlZ Ste 1950 ... Houston TX 77046 281-276-4500 734
Web: www.revenew.net

Revens Revens & St Pierre
946 Centerville Rd ... Warwick RI 02886 401-822-2900 428
Web: www.rrsplaw.com

Revens-Gates Insurance Inc
1130 Ten Rod Rd Ste E-201 ... North Kingstown RI 02852 401-294-9537 390
TF: 800-284-9537 ■ *Web:* revensgatesins.com

Revent Inc 100 Ethel Rd W ... Piscataway NJ 08854 732-777-9433 296
TF: 800-822-9642 ■ *Web:* www.revent.com

Revention Inc
1315 W Sam Houston Pkwy N Ste 100 ... Houston TX 77043 877-738-7444 196
TF: 877-738-7444 ■ *Web:* www.revention.com

Revenue Well
2275 Half Day Rd Ste 337 ... Bannockburn IL 60015 855-415-9355 39
TF: 855-415-9355 ■ *Web:* www.revenuewell.com

RevenueAds Affiliate Network
322 NE Second St 2nd Fl ... Oklahoma City OK 73104 405-455-9053 5
TF: 800-441-1136 ■ *Web:* www.revenueads.com

RevenueWire Inc
3962 Borden St Ste 102 ... Victoria BC V8P3H8 250-590-2273 393
Web: www.revenuewire.com

Revera Long Term Care Inc
55 Standish Ct ... Mississauga ON L5R4B2 519-376-3212 371
Web: www.reveraliving.com

Reverb Music LLC 3316 N Lincoln Ave ... Chicago IL 60657 773-525-7773 525-2775 526
TF: 888-686-7872 ■ *Web:* www.chicagomusicexchange.com

Revere Academy of Jewelry Arts
785 Market St Ste 900 ... San Francisco CA 94103 415-391-4179 795-1407 409
Web: www.revereacademy.com

Revere Control Systems Inc
2240 Rocky Ridge Rd ... Birmingham AL 35216 205-824-0004 824-0439 729
TF: 800-536-2525 ■ *Web:* www.reverecontrol.com

Revere Copper Products Inc 1 Revere Pk ... Rome NY 13440 800-448-1776 338-2224* 485
**Fax Area Code:* 315 ■ *TF:* 800-448-1776 ■ *Web:* www.reverecopper.com

Revere Electric Supply Co
2501 W Washington Blvd ... Chicago IL 60612 312-738-3636 249
Web: www.revereelectric.com

Revere Healthcare Ltd 112 Carry St ... Cary IL 60013 847-516-4900 476
Web: www.reverehc.com

Revere Hotel Boston Common
200 Stuart St ... Boston MA 02116 617-482-1800 707
TF: 855-673-8373 ■ *Web:* www.reverehotel.com

Revere Mills Inc
2860 S River Rd Ste 250 ... Des Plaines IL 60018 847-759-6800 361
Web: www.reveremills.com

Revere Public Library 179 Beach St ... Revere MA 02151 781-286-8380 434-3
Web: www.reverepubliclibrary.org

Reverse Logistics Trends Inc
2300 Lakeview Pkwy Ste 700 ... Alpharetta GA 30009 801-331-8949 216-8672* 184
**Fax Area Code:* 866 ■ *TF:* 866-801-6332 ■ *Web:* www.reverselogisticstrends.com

Revestor
505 Montgomery St 11th Fl ... San Francisco CA 94111 800-569-2674 387
TF: 800-569-2674 ■ *Web:* revestor.com

ReviewPush 701 Brazos St Ste 670 ... Austin TX 78701 512-669-5000 387
Web: www.reviewpush.com

Revionics Inc
2998 Douglas Blvd Ste 350 ... Roseville CA 95661 866-580-7277 253
TF: 866-580-7277 ■ *Web:* www.revionics.com

Revision Military Ltd
7 Corporate Dr ... Essex Junction VT 05452 802-879-7002 543
TF: 800-383-6049 ■ *Web:* www.revisionmilitary.com

Revision Technologies Inc
30 Richard Rd ... Edison NJ 08820 781-910-3273 180
Web: www.revisiontek.com

Revision3 Corp
2415 3rd St Ste 232 ... San Francisco CA 94107 415-734-3500 514
Web: www.revision3.com

Reviva Inc 5130 Main St NE ... Fridley MN 55421 763-535-8900 390-3727 247
TF: 877-357-7634 ■ *Web:* reviva.com

Reviva Pharmaceuticals Inc
1250 Oakmead Pkwy Ste 210 ... Sunnyvale CA 94085 408-816-1470 904-6270 231
Web: www.revivapharma.com

Revival Christian Ctr
5601 Hemlock St ... Sacramento CA 95841 916-572-6121 48-20
Web: revivalscc.com

Revivicor Inc
1700 Kraft Dr Ste 2400 ... Blacksburg VA 24060 540-961-5559 961-7958 85
Web: www.revivicor.com

REVL Communications & Systems
650 W 58th Ave Ste J ... Anchorage AK 99518 907-563-8302 647
Web: www.revlinc.net

Revlon Consumer Products Corp
1501 Williamsboro St ... Oxford NC 27565 212-527-4000 214
TF: 800-473-8566 ■ *Web:* www.revlon.com

Revman International Inc
350 Fifth Ave 70th Fl ... New York NY 10118 800-237-0658 361
TF: 800-237-0658 ■ *Web:* www.revman.com

Revo America Inc
850 Freeport Pkwy Ste 100 ... Coppell TX 75019 866-625-7386 692
TF: 866-625-7386 ■ *Web:* www.revoamerica.com

Revolution Eyewear Inc
2853 Eisenhower St Ste 100 ... Carrollton TX 75007 800-986-0010 908-2900* 237
**Fax Area Code:* 866 ■ *TF:* 800-986-0010 ■ *Web:* www.revolutioneyewear.com

Revolution Studios
225 Santa Monica Blvd 9th Fl ... Santa Monica CA 90401 310-255-7000 514
Web: www.revolutionstudios.com

Revolve Clothing Exchange
1620 E Seventh Ave ... Tampa FL 33605 813-242-5970 157-6
Web: revolve.cx

REVShare Corp 32836 Wolf Store Rd ... Temecula CA 92592 800-819-9945 195
TF: 800-819-9945 ■ *Web:* www.revshare.com

Revzero Inc 2431 Galpin Ct Ste 150 ... Chanhassen MN 55317 952-380-9966 454
Web: www.revzeroinc.com

Rewards Network Establishment Services Inc
300 S Park Rd Ste 300 ... Hollywood FL 33021 877-491-3463 393
TF: 877-491-3463 ■ *Web:* www.idine.com

Rewind 1009 420 Western Ave ... South Portland ME 04106 207-774-4561 774-3788 645
Web: rewind1009.com

Rewind 103.5/104.3
4401 Carriage Hill Ln ... Columbus OH 43220 614-451-2191 451-1831 645-40
Web: rewindcolumbus.com

Rewind 92.5 2603 W Bradley Ave ... Champaign IL 61821 217-352-4141 352-1256 645-29
Web: rewind925.com

Rex American Resources Corp
7720 Paragon Rd ... Dayton OH 45459 937-276-3931 35
Web: rexstores.com

Rex Art Co 3160 SW 22 St ... Miami FL 33145 305-445-1413 445-1412 45
TF: 800-739-2782 ■ *Web:* www.rexart.com

Rex Black Consulting Services Inc
31520 Beck Rd ... Bulverde TX 78163 830-438-4830 180
TF: 866-438-4830 ■ *Web:* rbcs-us.com

Rex Energy Corp 366 Walker Dr ... State College PA 16801 814-278-7267 536
Web: www.rexenergycorp.com

Rex Engineering Corp
1200 Chaffee Dr ... Titusville FL 32780 321-268-5500 518
Web: rex-engineering.com

Rex Fine Foods Inc
1536 River Oaks Rd W ... Harahan LA 70123 504-602-9487 296-37
TF: 800-341-4694 ■ *Web:* www.rexfoods.com

Rex Healthcare 4420 Lake Boone Trl ... Raleigh NC 27607 919-784-3100 374-3
Web: www.rexhealth.com

Rex Heat Treat
951 W Eigth St PO Box 270 ... Lansdale PA 19446 215-855-1131 855-2028 484
TF: 800-220-4739 ■ *Web:* www.rexht.com

Rex Lumber Co 840 Main St ... Acton MA 01720 978-263-0055 263-9806 819
TF: 800-343-0567 ■ *Web:* www.rexlumber.com

Rex Lumber LLC 5299 Alabama St ... Graceville FL 32440 850-263-2056 683
Web: www.rex-lumber.com

Rex Medical LP
1100 E Hector St Ste 245 ... Conshohocken PA 19428 610-940-0665 476
Web: rexmedical.com

Rex Oil Company Inc
1000 Lexington Ave ... Thomasville NC 27360 336-472-3000 472-3368 579
Web: www.rexoil.com

Rex Pak Ltd 85 Thornmount Dr ... Toronto ON M1B5V3 416-755-3324 393
Web: www.rexpak.com

Rex Pipe & Supply Co
1245 Middle Rowsburg Rd ... Ashland OH 44805 419-281-4577 281-2089 610
Web: rexpipe.com

Rex Wine Vinegar Co 828 Raymond Blvd ... Newark NJ 07105 973-589-6911 296-41
Web: www.rexwinevinegar.com

Rexair Inc 50 W Big Beaver Rd Ste 350 ... Troy MI 48084 248-643-7222 643-7676 788
Web: www.rainbowsystem.com

Rexarc Inc 35 E Third St ... West Alexandria OH 45381 937-839-4604 839-5897 790
TF: 877-739-2721 ■ *Web:* www.rexarc.com

RexburgStandardJournal.com PO Box 10 ... Rexburg ID 83440 208-356-5441 532-2
Web: www.rexburgstandardjournal.com

Rexel Canada Inc
5600 Keaton Crescent ... Mississauga ON L5R3G3 905-712-4004 246
Web: www.rexel.ca

Rexel Inc 14951 Dallas Pkwy PO Box 9085 ... Dallas TX 75254 972-387-3600 246
TF: 888-739-3577 ■ *Web:* www.rexelusa.com

Rexford Industrial Realty Inc
11620 Wilshire Blvd ... Los Angeles CA 90025 310-966-1680 653
Web: rexfordindustrial.com

Rexius Forest By-Products Inc
1275 Bailey Hill Rd ... Eugene OR 97402 541-342-1835 343-4802 293
Web: rexius.com

Rexon Components Inc
24500 Highpoint Rd ... Beachwood OH 44122 216-292-7373 639
Web: www.rexon.com

Rexton Inc
10800 Normandale Blvd Ste 103M ... Minneapolis MN 55446 763-553-0787 553-9129 250
Web: www.rexton.com

Rey's 1130 Buck Jones Rd ... Raleigh NC 27606 919-380-0122 671
Web: reysrestaurant.com

Reyers 40 S Water Ave ... Sharon PA 16146 724-981-2200 301
TF: 800-245-1550 ■ *Web:* www.reyers.com

Reyes Holdings LLC
6250 N River Rd Ste 9000 ... Rosemont IL 60018 847-227-6500 227-6550 360-3
Web: www.reyesholdings.com

				Phone	Fax	Class
Reymond Products International Inc 2066 Brightwood Rd SE *Web:* www.reymondproducts.com	New Philadelphia	OH	44663	330-339-3583		454
Reynard Corp 1020 Calle Sombra *Web:* www.reynardcorp.com	San Clemente	CA	92673	949-366-8866	498-9528	544
Reynold R. Bonaldi Agency 38 Kiinderkamack Rd *Web:* bonaldiinsurance.com	Oradell	NJ	07649	201-262-8100		390
Reynolda Gardens of Wake Forest University 100 Reynolda Vlg *Web:* reynoldagardens.org	Winston-Salem	NC	27106	336-758-5593		97
Reynolda House Museum of American Art 2250 Reynolda Rd *TF:* 888-663-1149 ■ *Web:* www.reynoldahouse.org	Winston-Salem	NC	27106	336-758-5150	758-5704	520
Reynolda Village 2201 Reynolda Rd *Web:* www.reynoldavillage.com	Winston-Salem	NC	27106	336-758-5584		460
Reynoldo V. Lopez State Jail 1203 El Cibolo Rd *Web:* www.tdcj.texas.gov	Edinburg	TX	78542	956-316-3810	316-7447	213
Reynolds & Assoc 823 Las Vegas Blvd S Ste 280 *Web:* reynoldslawyers.com	Las Vegas	NV	89101	702-445-7000		445
Reynolds & Reynolds Co 1 Reynolds Way *TF:* 800-767-0080 ■ *Web:* www.reyrey.com	Dayton	OH	45430	937-485-2000		178-10
Reynolds Co, The 10 Gates St *Web:* reynoldsglue.com	Greenville	SC	29611	864-232-6791		3
Reynolds Hix & Company PA 6729 Academy Rd NE *Web:* rhcocpa.com	Albuquerque	NM	87109	505-828-2900	828-2913	2
Reynolds Manufacturing Co 501 38th St *Web:* www.reynoldsmfg.com	Rock Island	IL	61201	309-788-7443		757
Reynolds Plantation One Lake Ochonee Trail *TF:* 800-800-5250 ■ *Web:* www.reynoldslakeoconee.com	Greensboro	GA	30642	706-467-0600		669
Reynolds Polymer Technology Inc 607 Hollingsworth St *Web:* www.reynoldspolymer.com	Grand Junction	CO	81505	970-241-4700	241-4747	604
Reynolds School District 7 Inc 1204 NE 201st Ave *Web:* www.reynolds.k12.or.us	Fairview	OR	97024	503-661-7200	667-6932	685
Reynolds Service Inc 860 Brentwood Dr *Web:* www.rsi.biz	Greenville	PA	16125	724-646-2600		492
Reynolds Smith & Hills Inc 10748 Deerwood Pk Blvd *TF:* 800-741-2014 ■ *Web:* www.rsandh.com	Jacksonville	FL	32256	904-256-2500	256-2501	261
Reynolds Tavern 7 Church Cir *Web:* www.reynoldstavern.org	Annapolis	MD	21401	410-295-9555		671
Reynolds Telephone Co 221 W Main St *Web:* www.reytel.net	Reynolds	IL	61279	309-372-4214	372-8888	224
Reynolds, Caronia, Gianelli & Lapinta PC 35 Arkay Dr *Web:* rcgllaw.com	Hauppauge	NY	11788	631-231-1199	300-4380	41
Reynolds, Jensen, Swan & Pershing LLP 3233 Arlington Ave Ste 203 *Web:* rjslaw.com	Riverside	CA	92506	951-787-9400		41
Reynolds, Mirth, Richards & Farmer LLP Manulife Pl 10180-101 St Ste 3200 *TF:* 800-661-7673 ■ *Web:* www.rmrf.com	Edmonton	AB	T5J3W8	780-425-9510		428
Reynolds, Rappaport, Kaplan & Hackney LLC 106 Cooke St PO Box 2540 *Web:* rrklaw.net	Edgartown	MA	02539	508-627-3711		41
Reynolds-Alberta Museum 6426 40 Ave PO Box 6360 *TF:* 800-661-4726 ■ *Web:* reynoldsmuseum.ca	Wetaskiwin	AB	T9A2G1	780-312-2065	361-1239	520
Reynoldsburg Animal Hospital LLC 7295 E Main St *Web:* rah4pets.com	Reynoldsburg	OH	43068	614-861-5755		794
Reynoldsburg Area Chamber of Commerce 1580 Brice Rd *Web:* www.reynoldsburgchamber.com	Reynoldsburg	OH	43068	614-866-4753	866-7313	139
REZ-1 Inc 100 William St Ste 100 *Web:* www.rez1.com	Wellesley	MA	02481	617-928-5000		750
Rezac Livestock Commission Co 27425 Drew Rd *Web:* www.rezaclivestock.com	Saint Marys	KS	66536	785-286-1107		446
Reznick Group PC 7501 Wisconsin Ave Ste 400 E *Web:* www.cohnreznick.com	Bethesda	MD	20814	301-652-9100		2
Rezometry 120 S University Dr Ste D *TF:* 888-387-4266 ■ *Web:* rezometry.com	Plantation	FL	33324	954-370-6050		178-1
RF Connect LLC 37735 Enterprise Ct Ste 200 *Web:* www.rfconnect.com	Farmington Hills	MI	48331	248-489-5800		624
RF Cook Manufacturing Co 4585 Allen Rd *TF:* 800-430-7536 ■ *Web:* www.rfcook.com	Stow	OH	44224	330-923-9797	923-8641	455
RF Industries 7610 Miramar Rd *NASDAQ: RFIL* ■ *TF:* 800-233-1728 ■ *Web:* www.rfindustries.com	San Diego	CA	92126	858-549-6340	549-6345	253
RF Knox Company Inc 4865 Martin Ct SE *Web:* www.rfknox.com	Smyrna	GA	30082	770-434-7401		697
RF Macdonald Co 25920 Eden Landing Rd *Web:* www.rfmacdonald.com	Hayward	CA	94545	510-784-0110		610
RF Murray & Company CPAS PC 3741 Wilder Rd *Web:* rfmurraycpa.com	Bay City	MI	48706	989-686-7740	686-7742	2
RF Ougheltree & Associates LLC 300 Executive Dr Ste 350 *TF:* 800-388-0215 ■ *Web:* www.rfoins.com	West Orange	NJ	07052	800-388-0215		390
RF Owens Company Inc 1062 Broadway *Web:* www.trucchis.com	Raynham	MA	02767	508-824-7514		345
RF Products Inc 1500 Davis St *Web:* www.rfproducts.com	Camden	NJ	08103	856-365-5500	342-9757	647
RF|Binder Partners Inc 950 Third Ave 7th Fl *Web:* www.rfbinder.com	New York	NY	10022	212-994-7600		636
RFA (Renewable Fuels Assn) 425 Third St SW *Web:* www.ethanolrfa.org	Washington	DC	20024	202-289-3835	289-7519	48-12
RFB&D (Recording for the Blind & Dyslexic) 20 Roszel Rd **Fax Area Code:* 609 ■ *TF:* 800-221-4792 ■ *Web:* www.rfbd.org	Princeton	NJ	08540	800-221-4792	987-8116*	48-17
RFC (Radio Frequency Company Inc) 150 Dover Rd *Web:* www.radiofrequency.com	Millis	MA	02054	508-376-9555	376-9944	318
RFD & Associates Inc 401 Camp Craft Rd *Web:* www.rfdinc.com	Austin	TX	78746	512-347-9411		177
RFE Investment Partners 36 Grove St *Web:* www.rfeip.com	New Canaan	CT	06840	203-966-2800		402
RFE/RL (Radio Free Europe/Radio Liberty) 1201 Connecticut Ave NW 4th Fl *Web:* www.rferl.org	Washington	DC	20036	202-457-6900		644
RFH (Robert Family Holdings Inc) 12430 Tesson Ferry Rd Ste 313 **Fax Area Code:* 314 ■ *Web:* www.rf-holdings.com	Saint Louis	MO	63128	636-305-2830	965-0309*	548
RFI Communications & Security Systems 360 Turtle Creek Ct *Web:* www.rfi.com	San Jose	CA	95125	408-298-5400	882-4401	189-4
RFIP Inc 7720 N Robinson Ave Ste B3 *Web:* www.rfip.com	Oklahoma City	OK	73116	405-286-0928		736
RFK (Robert F. Kennedy Stadium) 2400 E Capitol St SE *Web:* www.eventsdc.com	Washington	DC	20003	202-608-1100		720
RFL Electronics Inc 353 Powerville Rd *Web:* rflelect.com	Boonton	NJ	07005	973-334-3100	334-3863	735
Rfmx Corp 500 E 76th Ave Bldg 2 *Web:* rfmx.net	Denver	CO	80229	303-853-0169		311
RFR (Resources for Rehabilitation) 22 Bonad Rd *Web:* www.rfr.org	Winchester	MA	01890	781-368-9080	368-9096	637-2
RFWP (Royal Fireworks Publishing Co) PO Box 399 *Web:* www.rfwp.com	Unionville	NY	10900	845-726-4444	726-3824	637-2
RG & Associates LLC 4885 Ward Rd Ste 100 *Web:* rgengineers.com	Wheat Ridge	CO	80033	303-293-8107		261
RG Associates Inc 201 N Charles St Ste 806 *Web:* www.rgassociates-assetmanagement.com	Baltimore	MD	21201	443-977-4370		401
RG Egan Equipment Inc 1049 Gravel Rd *Web:* www.rgegan.com	Webster	NY	14580	585-671-0465		385
RG Johnson Company Inc 25 S College St *Web:* www.rgjohnsoninc.com	Washington	PA	15301	724-222-6810	222-6815	501
RG Smith Co 1249 Dueber Ave SW *Web:* www.rgscontractors.com	Canton	OH	44706	330-456-3415	456-9638	697
RGA (Republican Governors Assn) 1747 Pennsylvania Ave NW Ste 250 *Web:* www.rga.org	Washington	DC	20006	202-662-4140		48-7
RGA Tire & Auto Repair Inc 9 Ledge Rd *Web:* www.rgatire.com	Pelham	NH	03076	603-505-7671		54
RGB Group Inc 4141 N Miami Ave Ste 300 *Web:* www.rgbgroupinc.com	Miami	FL	33127	305-573-1672	573-4447	514
RGBS Enterprises 2842 Richmond Terr *TF:* 888-467-7427 ■ *Web:* www.rgbse.com	Staten Island	NY	10303	718-981-0734	981-0736	194
RGC Resources Inc 519 Kimball Ave PO Box 13007 *NASDAQ: RGCO* ■ *Web:* www.rgcresources.com	Roanoke	VA	24016	540-777-4427		360-5
RGE USA Inc 365 Oliver Cromwell Dr *Web:* www.rgegroup.com	Newport	TN	37821	423-625-1000		008
Rgen Solutions 4062 148th Ave NE *Web:* www.rgensolutions.com	Redmond	WA	98052	425-867-1350		180
RGF Environmental Group 1101 W 13th St *TF:* 800-842-7771 ■ *Web:* www.rgf.com	Riviera Beach	FL	33404	561-848-1826	848-9454	201
RGFCC Corp 9900 Traverse Way **Fax Area Code:* 301 ■ *Web:* www.rgfcc.com	Fort Washington	MD	20744	202-251-6391	839-3780*	463
RGH (Riverside General Hospital) *Houston Recovery Ctr* 3204 Ennis St *Web:* riversidegeneralhospital.org	Houston	TX	77004	713-526-2441		726
RGH Enterprises Inc 1810 Summit Commerce Pk **Fax Area Code:* 330 ■ *TF:* 800-307-5930	Twinsburg	OH	44087	800-860-8027	963-6839*	475
Rgi Inc 2245 Gilbert Ave *Web:* rgidesign.com	Cincinnati	OH	45206	513-221-2121		344
RGIS LLC 2000 E Taylor Rd *TF:* 800-551-9130 ■ *Web:* www.rgis.com	Auburn Hills	MI	48326	248-651-2511		317
RGL Consultants 13724 Venetian Ct *Web:* www.rglconsultants.com	Orland Park	IL	60467	708-301-6425		194
RGL Reservoir Management Inc 610 700-2nd St SW Ste 610 *Web:* www.rglrm.com	Calgary	AB	T2P2W1	403-269-8088	269-9099	539
Rgm Commercial Real Estate Services LLC 10423 Main St Ste 5 *Web:* rgmcommercial.com	Bellevue	WA	98004	425-452-3052		652
RGR Pharma Ltd 103 Crystal Harbour Dr *Web:* www.rgrpharma.com	LaSalle	ON	N9J3R6	519-734-6600		231
RGS (Ruffed Grouse Society) 451 McCormick Rd *TF:* 888-564-6747 ■ *Web:* www.ruffedgrousesociety.org	Coraopolis	PA	15108	412-262-4044	262-9207	48-3
R-G-T Plastics Co 600 Penn St *Web:* rgt-plastics.com	Linesville	PA	16424	814-683-2161		604
RGV Partnership 322 S Missouri Ave *Web:* rgvpartnership.com	Weslaco	TX	78596	956-968-3141	968-0210	139
RH (Russell Hall Co, The) 19 N George St *Web:* www.russellhall.com	Meriden	CT	06451	203-235-6391	237-4336	559
RH Murphy Company Inc 3 Howe Dr *Web:* www.rhmurphy.com	Amherst	NH	03031	603-889-2255	889-3129	604
RH Nicholson & Company Inc 3998 Fair Ridge Dr Ste 200 *Web:* rhnicholson.com	Fairfax	VA	22033	703-261-6100		390

Name / Address	City	State	ZIP	Phone	Fax	Class
RH Reny Inc 731 Rt 1 *Web:* www.renys.com	Newcastle	ME	04553	207-563-3177	563-5681	229
RH Wealth Advisors Inc 5700 Ralston St Ste 102 *Web:* rhwealth.com	Ventura	CA	93003	805-658-1500	658-1515	690
RH White Construction Company Inc 41 Central St PO Box 404 *Web:* www.rhwhite.com	Auburn	MA	01501	508-832-3295	832-7084	188-10
RHA (Richard Heath & Associates Inc) 590 W Locust Ave Ste 103 *Web:* www.rhainc.com	Fresno	CA	93650	559-447-7000	447-7099	463
RHA Health Services Inc 17 Church St *TF:* 866-742-2428 ■ *Web:* rhahealthservices.org	Asheville	NC	28801	828-232-6844		463
RHBAA (Racking Horse Breeders Association of America) 67 Horse Center Rd *Web:* www.rackinghorse.com	Decatur	AL	35603	256-353-7225		48-3
RHCOC (Richmond Hill Chamber of Commerce) 376 Church St S *Web:* www.rhcoc.com	Richmond Hill	ON	L4C9V8	905-884-1961	884-1962	137
Rhea & Kaiser 400 E Diehl Rd *Web:* www.rkconnect.com	Naperville	IL	60563	630-505-1100		4
Rhea County 9460 Rhea County Hwy *Web:* www.rheacountytn.gov	Dayton	TN	37321	423-775-7832		338
Rhee Bros Inc 7461 Coca Cola Dr *Web:* www.rheebros.com	Hanover	MD	21076	410-381-9000	381-4989	296
Rheem Manufacturing Co *Air Conditioning Div* 5600 Old Greenwood Rd *TF:* 800-268-6966 ■ *Web:* www.rheem.com	Fort Smith	AR	72903	479-646-4311		14
Rhein Consulting Laboratories 4475 SW Scholls Ferry Rd Ste 101 *Web:* www.rheinlabs.com	Portland	OR	97225	503-292-1988		196
Rheinland Restaurant 208 N Main St *Web:* www.rheinlandrestaurant.com	Independence	MO	64050	816-461-5383		671
Rheinmetall Canada Information Ctr 225 du Seminaire Sud *Web:* www.rheinmetall.ca	Saint Jean sur Richelieu	QC	J3B8E9	450-358-2000	358-1744	434-3
Rhema 1751 Brigantine Dr *Web:* www.rhemamade.com	Coquitlam	BC	V3K7B4	604-516-0199		345
RheTech Inc 1500 E N Territorial Rd *TF:* 800-869-1230 ■ *Web:* rhetech.com	Whitmore Lake	MI	48189	734-769-0585	769-3565	605-2
Rhett House Inn 1009 Craven St *TF:* 888-480-9530 ■ *Web:* www.rhetthouseinn.com	Beaufort	SC	29902	843-524-9030		379
Rhinehart Oil Company Inc 585 E State Rd *Web:* www.rhinehartoil.com	American Fork	UT	84003	801-756-9681		579
Rhinehart's Oyster Bar 3051 Washington Rd *Web:* www.rhineharts.com	Augusta	GA	30907	706-860-2337		671
Rhinelander Flying Service Inc Oneida County Airport PO Box 501 *TF:* 800-236-3131 ■ *Web:* www.rhinelanderflyingservice.com	Rhinelander	WI	54501	715-365-3456	365-3461	167-3
Rhinestahl Corp 7687 Innovation Way *Web:* www.rhinestahl.com	Mason	OH	45040	513-229-5300		256
Rhino Fire Protection Engineering PLLC 12359 Sunrise Valley Dr Ste 350 *Web:* rhinofpe.com	Reston	VA	20191	703-476-5034		261
Rhino Foods Inc 79 Industrial Pkwy *TF:* 800-639-3350 ■ *Web:* www.rhinofoods.com	Burlington	VT	05401	802-862-0252		296-2
Rhino Inc 411 Congress St W *Web:* www.rhinoroto.com	Maple Lake	MN	55358	320-963-5995	963-6192	604
Rhino Linings Corp 9151 Rehco Rd *Web:* www.rhinolatino.com	San Diego	CA	92121	858-450-0441		550
Rhino Medical Staffing 2000 E Lamar Blvd Ste 250 *TF:* 866-267-4466 ■ *Web:* www.rhinomedical.com	Arlington	TX	76006	817-795-2295		507
Rhino Metals Inc 607 Garber St *Web:* www.rhinosafe.com	Caldwell	ID	83605	208-454-5545		386
Rhino Mfg 16705 Tye St SE *Web:* www.rhinomfginc.com	Monroe	WA	98272	360-568-0572		697
Rhino Resource Partners LP 424 Lewis Hargett Cir Ste 250 *Web:* www.rhinolp.com	Lexington	KY	40503	859-389-6500		501
RhinoCorps Limited Co 1128 Pennsylvania St NE Ste 100 *Web:* www.rhinocorps.com	Albuquerque	NM	87110	505-323-9836		180
RhinoDox 20 N Upper Wacker Dr Ste 1229 *Web:* www.rhinodox.com	Chicago	IL	60606	630-372-8861		196
Rhintek Inc 8835c Columbia 100 Pkwy *Web:* www.rhintek.com	Columbia	MD	21045	410-730-2575		178-12
Rhiza Inc 5850 Ellsworth Ave Ste 200 *Web:* rhiza.com	Pittsburgh	PA	15232	412-488-0600		224
RHM (Ray H. Morris Co) 30 Precision Ct *TF:* 800-243-0662 ■ *Web:* www.rhmorris.com	New Britain	CT	06051	860-224-2678	224-4134	385
RHM (Strybuc Industries) 500 W 84 St *TF:* 800-780-5051 ■ *Web:* www.strybuc.com	Hialeah	FL	33014	305-558-5051	557-5239	234
RHM Fluid Power Inc 375 Manufacturers Dr *Web:* www.rhmfluidpower.com	Westland	MI	48186	734-326-5400	326-0339	385
RHO Capital Partners Inc 152 W 57th St 23rd Fl *Web:* www.rhoventures.com	New York	NY	10019	212-751-6677	751-3613	792
Rhoades Levy Law Group PC 3400 Dundee Rd Ste 340 *Web:* rhoadeslevylaw.com	Northbrook	IL	60062	847-870-7600	380-2036	41
Rhoades McKee PC 55 Campau Ave NW Ste 300 *Web:* www.rhoadesmckee.com	Grand Rapids	MI	49503	616-235-3500	233-5269	428
Rhoads & Sinon LLP 1 S Market Sq 12th Fl *Web:* www.rhoadssinon.com	Harrisburg	PA	17101	717-233-5731		445
Rhode Island *Arts Council* 1 Capitol Hill 3rd Fl *Web:* arts.ri.gov	Providence	RI	02908	401-222-3880	222-3018	339-40
Attorney General 150 S Main St *Web:* www.riag.ri.gov	Providence	RI	02903	401-274-4400		339-40
Board of Governors for Higher Education (RIBGHE) 80 Washington St Shepard Bldg Ste 524 *Web:* www.ribghe.org	Providence	RI	02903	401-456-6000	456-6028	339-40
Child Support Services 77 Dorrance St *Web:* www.cse.ri.gov	Providence	RI	02903	401-458-4400	458-4465	339-40
Children Youth & Families Dept 101 Friendship St *TF:* 800-742-4453 ■ *Web:* www.dcyf.state.ri.us	Providence	RI	02903	401-528-3502	528-3590	339-40
Commerce Corp 315 Iron Horse Way Ste 101 *Web:* commerceri.com	Providence	RI	02908	401-278-9100	273-8270	339-40
Corrections Dept 40 Howard Ave	Cranston	RI	02920	401-462-2611		339-40
Court Administrators Office 250 Benefit St *Web:* www.courts.ri.gov	Providence	RI	02903	401-222-3215		339-40
Crime Victim Compensation Program 50 Service Ave *Web:* www.treasury.ri.gov	Warwick	RI	02886	401-462-7650	222-6140	339-40
Elderly Affairs Dept 74 W Rd Hazard Bldg *Web:* www.dea.ri.gov	Cranston	RI	02920	401-462-3000		339-40
Elementary & Secondary Education Dept 255 Westminster St *Web:* www.ride.ri.gov	Providence	RI	02903	401-222-4600		339-40
Emergency Management Agency 645 New London Ave *Web:* www.riema.ri.gov	Cranston	RI	02920	401-946-9996	944-1891	339-40
Environmental Management Dept 235 Promenade St *Web:* www.dem.ri.gov	Providence	RI	02908	401-222-6800		339-40
Ethics Commission 40 Fountain St *Web:* www.ethics.ri.gov	Providence	RI	02903	401-222-3790	222-3382	265
General Assembly 82 Smith St *Web:* www.rilin.state.ri.us	Providence	RI	02903	401-222-2466		339-40
Health Dept 3 Capitol Hill *Web:* www.health.ri.gov	Providence	RI	02908	401-222-5960	222-6548	339-40
Historical Preservation & Heritage Commission 401 Broadway *Web:* www.riparks.com	Providence	RI	02903	401-222-2678	222-2968	339-40
Housing & Mortgage Finance Corp 44 Washington St *TF:* 800-427-5560 ■ *Web:* www.rihousing.com	Providence	RI	02903	401-457-1234		339-40
Human Services Dept 10 Ross Simons Dr	Cranston	RI	02920	401-462-5300		339-40
Labor & Training Dept Center General Complex 1511 Pontiac Ave *Web:* www.dlt.state.ri.us	Cranston	RI	02920	401-462-8000	462-8872	259
Library & Information Services Office 1 Capitol Hil 2nd Fl *Web:* www.olis.ri.gov	Providence	RI	02908	401-574-9300	574-9320	339-40
Lieutenant Governor 82 Smith St Rm 116 *Web:* www.ltgov.ri.gov	Providence	RI	02903	401-222-2371		339-40
Lottery 1425 Pontiac Ave *TF:* 833-486-7170 ■ *Web:* www.rilot.com	Cranston	RI	02920	401-463-6500	463-5669	452
Medical Examiner 401 Broadway *Web:* www.health.ri.gov	Providence	RI	02908	401-222-5500		339-40
Parks & Recreation Div 1100 Tower Hill Rd *Web:* www.riparks.com	North Kingstown	RI	02852	401-667-6200	667-3970	339-40
Public Utilities Commission 89 Jefferson Blvd *Web:* www.ripuc.org	Warwick	RI	02888	401-941-4500		339-40
RI Office of the Postsecondary Commissioner 560 Jefferson Blvd Ste 100 *Web:* www.riopc.edu	Warwick	RI	02886	401-736-1100	732-3541	725
State Government Information 40 Fountain St *Web:* www.ri.gov	Providence	RI	02903	401-421-7005		339-40
State Police 311 Danielson Pk *Web:* risp.ri.gov	North Scituate	RI	02857	401-444-1000	555-5555	339-40
Supreme Court 250 Benefit St *Web:* www.courts.ri.gov	Providence	RI	02903	401-222-3272		339-40
Transportation Dept 2 Capitol Hill *Web:* rhodeislandbids.com	Providence	RI	02903	401-222-2495	222-2086	339-40
Treasurer 82 Smith St Rm 102 *Web:* www.treasury.ri.gov	Providence	RI	02903	401-222-2397	222-6140	339-40
Veterans Affairs Div 480 Metacom Ave *Web:* www.vets.ri.gov	Bristol	RI	02809	401-253-8000		339-40
Weights & Measures Office 1511 Pontiac Ave *Web:* www.dlt.ri.gov	Cranston	RI	02920	401-462-8570	462-8576	339-40
Rhode Island Airport Corp 2000 Post Rd *TF:* 888-268-7222 ■ *Web:* www.pvdairport.com	Warwick	RI	02886	401-691-2000		27
Rhode Island Association of Realtors 100 Bignall St *Web:* www.rirealtors.org	Warwick	RI	02888	401-785-9898	941-5360	656
Rhode Island Bar Assn 115 Cedar St *TF:* 877-659-0801 ■ *Web:* www.ribar.com	Providence	RI	02903	401-421-5740	421-2703	72
Rhode Island Beverage Journal Inc 2508 Whitney Ave *Web:* www.thebeveragejournal.com	Hamden	CT	06518	203-288-3375	288-2693	637-9
Rhode Island Blood Ctr 405 Promenade St *TF:* 800-283-8385 ■ *Web:* www.ribc.org	Providence	RI	02908	401-453-8360	453-8557	89
Rhode Island College 600 Mt Pleasant Ave *TF:* 800-669-5760 ■ *Web:* www.ric.edu	Providence	RI	02908	401-456-8000	456-8817	166
Rhode Island Convention Ctr 1 Sabin St *Web:* www.riconvention.com	Providence	RI	02903	401-458-6000	458-6500	205
Rhode Island Correctional Industries 40 Howard Ave *Web:* www.doc.ri.gov	Cranston	RI	02920	401-462-3900		630

Name / Address	City	State	ZIP	Phone	Fax	Class
Rhode Island Democratic Party 151 Broadway Ste 310 *Web:* www.ridemocrats.org	Providence	RI	02903	401-272-3367	272-3368	616-1
Rhode Island Foundation 1 Union Stn *Web:* www.rifoundation.org	Providence	RI	02903	401-274-4564	331-8085	303
Rhode Island Hospital 593 Eddy St *Web:* www.rhodeislandhospital.org	Providence	RI	02903	401-444-4000		374-3
Rhode Island Medical Society 405 Promenade St Ste A *Web:* www.rimed.org	Providence	RI	02908	401-331-3207	751-8050	457-16
Rhode Island PBS 50 Pk Ln *Web:* www.ripbs.org	Providence	RI	02907	401-222-3636	222-3407	632
Rhode Island Philharmonic Orchestra 667 Waterman Ave *Web:* www.ri-philharmonic.org	East Providence	RI	02914	401-248-7070	248-7071	573-3
Rhode Island Public Interest Research Group (RIPIRG) 11 S Angell St Ste 150 *Web:* ripirg.org	Providence	RI	02906	401-608-1201		633
Rhode Island Public Transit Authority 265 Melrose St *Web:* www.ripta.com	Providence	RI	02907	401-781-9400		468
Rhode Island Publications Society (RIPS) 1445 Wampanoag Trail Ste 201 *Web:* www.ripublications.org	Riverside	RI	02915	401-272-1776	273-1791	48-6
Rhode Island School of Design 2 College St *TF:* 800-364-7473 ■ *Web:* www.risd.edu	Providence	RI	02903	401-454-6100	454-6309	164
Rhode Island School of Design - Museum of Art 224 Benefit St *Web:* risdmuseum.org	Providence	RI	02903	401-454-6502	454-6556	520
Rhode Island State Employees Credit Union 160 Francis St *TF:* 855-322-7428 ■ *Web:* www.ricreditunion.org	Providence	RI	02903	401-751-7440	331-5907	219
Rhode Island State Nurses Assn (RISNA) 100 Wsetminster St Ste 1500 *Web:* www.risna.org	Providence	RI	02903	401-331-5644	331-5646	533
Rhode Island Veterinary Medical Assn 302 Pearl St Ste 108 *Web:* rivma.org	Providence	RI	02907	401-751-0944	780-0940	705
Rhodes College 2000 N Pkwy *TF:* 800-844-5969 ■ *Web:* www.rhodes.edu	Memphis	TN	38112	901-843-3700	843-3631	166
Rhodes Computer Services Inc 4324 Washington Rd Ste 103 *Web:* rhodesmurphy.com	Evans	GA	30809	706-868-1298	868-7935	401
Rhodes International Inc PO Box 25487 *TF:* 800-876-7333 ■ *Web:* rhodesbakenserv.com	Salt Lake City	UT	84125	801-972-0122		296-16
Rhodes Manufacturing Inc 7045 Buckeye Valley Rd NE *Web:* www.rhodesmfg.com	Somerset	OH	43783	740-743-2614		537
Rhodes State College 4240 Campus Dr *Web:* www.rhodesstate.edu	Lima	OH	45804	419-995-8320	995-8098	800
Rhodeside Grill 1836 Wilson Blvd *Web:* www.rhodesidegrill.com	Arlington	VA	22201	703-243-0145		671
Rhodes-Joseph & Tobiason Advisors LLC 1177 High Ridge Rd *Web:* www.rjtadvisors.com	Stamford	CT	06905	203-883-8144		463
Rhododendron Species Botanical Garden 2525 S 336th St PO Box 3798 *TF:* 877-242-2528 ■ *Web:* www.rhodygarden.org	Federal Way	WA	98063	253-838-4646	838-4686	97
Rhodunda & Williams LLC 1220 N Market St Ste 700 *Web:* rawlaw.com	Wilmington	DE	19801	302-576-2000		41
Rhody Transportation 600 Callahan Rd *Web:* rhodytrans.com	North Kingstown	RI	02852	401-294-0037		311
Rhoe B. Henderson Agency Inc 552 W 3rd St PO Box 1238 *Web:* rhoebhenderson.com	Jamestown	NY	14702	716-483-1886		390
Rhombus Publishing Co PO Box 806 *Web:* www.rhombusbooks.com	Corrales	NM	87048	505-897-3700	898-4706	637-2
Rhorer Law Firm 10566 Airline Hwy *Web:* rhorerlaw.com	Baton Rouge	LA	70816	225-292-2767		41
RHP Mechanical Systems Inc 1008 E Fourth St *Web:* www.rhpinc.net	Reno	NV	89512	775-322-9434		189-10
RHR International LLP 233 S Wacker Dr No9500 95th Fl *Web:* www.rhrinternational.com	Chicago	IL	60606	312-924-0800		194
RHS (Reliable Health Systems Inc) 2610 Nostrand Ave *Web:* www.reliablehealth.com	Brooklyn	NY	11210	718-338-2400	338-2741	178-1
Rhumbline Advisers Corp 265 Franklin St 21st Fl *Web:* www.rhumblineadvisers.com	Boston	MA	02110	617-345-0434		401
Rhythm & Hues Inc 5890 W Jefferson Blvd Ste Q *Web:* www.rhythm.com	Los Angeles	CA	90016	310-448-7500	448-7600	512
Rhythm Band Instruments LLC 2051 Franklin Dr *Web:* www.rhythmband.com	Fort Worth	TX	76106	817-335-2561		390
Rhythm Cafe 3800 S Dixie Hwy *Web:* www.rhythmcafe.cc	West Palm Beach	FL	33405	561-833-3406		671
Rhythm Organism LLC, The 400 N State St Ste 410 *Web:* www.fanfueled.com	Chicago	IL	60654	312-321-0111		387
Rhythm Tech 29 Beechwood Ave *TF:* 800-726-2279 ■ *Web:* www.rhythmtech.com	New Rochelle	NY	10801	800-726-2279		527
RI (Ramson's Imports Inc) 5159 Sinclair Rd *TF:* 800-669-0874 ■ *Web:* www.ramsonsimports.com	Columbus	OH	43229	614-846-4447	846-4809	328
RI (Refugees Intl) 2001 S St NW Ste 700 *TF:* 800-733-8433 ■ *Web:* www.refugeesinternational.org	Washington	DC	20009	202-828-0110	828-0819	48-5
RI Lampus Co 816 RI Lampus Ave PO Box 167 **Fax Area Code:* 724 ■ *Web:* www.lampus.com	Springdale	PA	15144	412-362-3800	274-2181*	183
Ri Ra 123 Church St *Web:* rira.com	Burlington	VT	05401	802-860-9401		671
RIA (Robotic Industries Assn) 900 Victors Way Ste 140 *Web:* www.robotics.org	Ann Arbor	MI	48108	734-994-6088	994-3338	49-19
Ria Compliance Consultants Inc 11640 Arbor St Ste 100 *TF:* 877-345-4034 ■ *Web:* www.ria-compliance-consultants.com	Omaha	NE	68144	877-345-4034		196
Ria Federal Credit Union 4343 Utica Ridge Rd *TF:* 800-742-2848 ■ *Web:* riafcu.com	Bettendorf	IA	52722	563-355-3800		219
RIAA (Recording Industry Association of America Inc) 1025 F St NW 10th Fl *Web:* www.riaa.com	Washington	DC	20004	202-775-0101		48-4
Rialto Center for the Arts 80 Forsyth St NW *Web:* rialto.gsu.edu	Atlanta	GA	30303	404-413-9800	413-9850	572
Rialto Chamber of Commerce 120 N Riverside Ave *TF:* 800-597-4955 ■ *Web:* www.rialtochamber.org	Rialto	CA	92376	909-875-5364	875-6790	139
Rialto Record PO Box 110 *Web:* iecn.com	Colton	CA	92324	909-381-9898		532-4
Rialto Theater 310 S 9th St *Web:* www.broadwaycenter.org	Tacoma	WA	98402	253-591-5890	591-2013	572
Rialto, The 318 E Congress St *Web:* www.rialtotheatre.com	Tucson	AZ	85701	520-740-1000		572
Riata Financial Services Inc 245 Landa St *Web:* riatafinancial.com	New Braunfels	TX	78130	830-606-5100		251
Rib Crib Corp 4535 S Harvard Ave *Web:* www.ribcrib.com	Tulsa	OK	74135	918-712-7427		670
Riba Foods Inc 3735 Arc St *TF:* 800-327-7422 ■ *Web:* www.ribafoods.com	Houston	TX	77063	713-975-7001	975-7036	297-8
Ribbeck Engineering Inc 14335 SW 120th St Ste 205 *Web:* www.ribbeck.co	Miami	FL	33186	305-383-5909		261
Ribbon Technology Corp 825 Taylor Stn Rd *TF:* 800-848-0477 ■ *Web:* www.ribtec.com	Gahanna	OH	43230	614-864-5444	864-5305	013
Ribbond Inc 1402 3rd Ave Ste 1030 *TF:* 800-624-4554 ■ *Web:* www.ribbond.com	Seattle	WA	98101	206-340-8870	382-9354	228
Ribbons Unlimited Inc 6 Park Center Ct Ste 100 **Fax Area Code:* 410 ■ *TF:* 800-250-7426 ■ *Web:* www.ribbonsunlimited.com	Owings Mills	MD	21117	800-250-7426	902-1620*	459
Ribelin Sales Inc 3857 Miller Pk Dr **Fax Area Code:* 877 ■ *TF:* 800-374-1594 ■ *Web:* www.ribelin.com	Garland	TX	75042	972-272-1594	474-2354*	146
Ribollita 41 Middle St *Web:* ribollitamaine.com	Portland	ME	04101	207-774-2972		671
Ricardo's 5629 E 41st St *Web:* ricardostulsa.com	Tulsa	OK	74135	918-622-2668		671
Ricardo's Restaurant 2112 E Lake Rd *Web:* ricardosrestauranterie.com	Erie	PA	16511	814-455-4947		671
Ricart Automotive Group 4255 S Hamilton Rd *TF:* 800-438-2733 ■ *Web:* www.ricart.com	Groveport	OH	43125	614-836-5321		57
Ricci & Company LLC 6200 Uptown Blvd NE Ste 400 *Web:* riccicpa.com	Albuquerque	NM	87110	505-338-0800		2
Ricci Fava LLC 16 Furler St 2nd Fl *Web:* riccifavalaw.com	Totowa	NJ	07512	973-837-1900		41
Ricci's Toni & Guy Hairdressing Academy 99 S Main St Ste 3 *Web:* www.newtown.toniguy.edu	Newtown	CT	06470	203-426-8770		167-3
Rice Associates Inc 10625 Gaskins Way *Web:* www.ricesurveys.com	Manassas	VA	20109	703-968-3200		727
Rice Belt Telephone Company Inc (RBTEL) 228 Kings Hwy *Web:* www.ricebelt.net	Weiner	AR	72479	870-684-2288	684-2226	224
Rice Cohen Intl 301 Oxford Valley Rd Ste 1506A *Web:* www.ricecoheninternational.com	Yardley	PA	19067	215-321-4100		266
Rice County 320 NW Third St *Web:* www.co.rice.mn.us	Faribault	MN	55021	507-332-6101	332-5999	338
Rice County 101 W Commercial St *Web:* www.ricecounty.us	Lyons	KS	67554	620-257-2232	257-3039	338
Rice Epicurean Markets Inc 5333 Gulfton St *Web:* www.riceepicurean.com	Houston	TX	77081	713-662-7700		345
Rice Financial Products Co 55 Broad St 27th Fl *Web:* www.ricefinancialproducts.com	New York	NY	10004	212-908-9200	908-9299	690
Rice Fruit Co 2760 Carlisle Rd *TF:* 800-627-3359 ■ *Web:* www.ricefruit.com	Gardners	PA	17324	717-677-8131		315-3
Rice Hall James & Associates LLC 600 W Broadway Ste 1000 *Web:* www.ricehalljames.com	San Diego	CA	92101	619-239-9005		401
Rice Kathleen (Rep D - NY) 2435 Rayburn House Office Bldg *Web:* www.kathleenrice.house.gov	Washington	DC	20515	202-225-5516	225-5758	342-2
Rice Lake Weighing Systems Inc 230 W Coleman St *TF:* 800-472-6703 ■ *Web:* www.ricelake.com	Rice Lake	WI	54868	800-472-6703		639
Rice Packaging Inc 356 Somers Rd *TF:* 800-367-6725 ■ *Web:* www.ricepackaging.com	Ellington	CT	06029	860-872-8341		101
Rice Restaurant 1608 14th St NW *Web:* www.ricerestaurant.com	Washington	DC	20009	202-234-2400		671
Rice Tom (Rep R - SC) 512 Cannon House Office Bldg *Web:* rice.house.gov	Washington	DC	20515	202-225-9895	225-9690	342-2
Rice Toyota 2630 Battleground Ave *Web:* www.ricetoyota.com	Greensboro	NC	27408	336-288-1190		198
Rice University 6100 Main St *TF:* 866-294-4633 ■ *Web:* www.rice.edu	Houston	TX	77005	713-348-0000	348-5323	166
Rice, Davis, Daley & Krenz Inc 50 Washington St *Web:* rddk.com	Middletown	CT	06457	860-346-6611		390
Riceland Foods Inc PO Box 927 *Web:* www.riceland.com	Stuttgart	AR	72160	870-673-5500		296-23

Name	Address	City	State	Zip	Phone	Fax	Class	Additional
RiceTec Inc	1925 FM 2917 PO Box 1305	Alvin	TX	77511	281-393-3532		296-23	*TF:* 877-580-7423 ■ *Web:* www.ricetec.com
Rich & Campbell Pc	30665 NW Hwy Ste 201	Farmington Hills	MI	48334	248-406-8000		41	*Web:* richandcampbell.com
Rich & Gillis Law Group LLC	6400 Riverside Dr Ste D	Dublin	OH	43017	614-228-5822		41	*Web:* richgillislawgroup.com
Rich County	20 S Main St	Randolph	UT	84064	435-793-2415		338	*Web:* www.richcountyut.org
Rich Gelwarg & Lampf LLP	4 Ethel Rd	Edison	NJ	08817	732-287-5565	287-5152	2	*Web:* www.rglcpas.com
Rich Greenberg Rosenthal & Costle LLP	201 N Union St Ste 230	Alexandria	VA	22314	703-299-3440		41	*Web:* rrbmdk.com
Rich Ltd	3809 Ocean Ranch Blvd Ste 110	Oceanside	CA	92056	760-722-2300		119	*Web:* www.richltd.com
Rich Metals Co (RMC)	510 Schmidt Rd	Davenport	IA	52802	563-322-0975	322-8774	686	*Web:* richmetalsco.com
Rich Mountain Electric Co-opeartive Inc	515 Janssen Ave	Mena	AR	71953	479-394-4140		245	*TF:* 877-828-4074 ■ *Web:* www.rmec.com
Rich N Ton Calls Inc	2315 Hwy 63 N	Stuttgart	AR	72160	870-673-4274		711	*Web:* rntcalls.com
Rich Products Corp	1 Robert Rich Way	Buffalo	NY	14213	716-878-8000		578	*Web:* www.richs.com
Rich Ranch	939 Cottonwood Lakes Rd	Seeley Lake	MT	59868	406-677-2317		239	*TF:* 800-532-4350 ■ *Web:* richranch.com
Rich Worldwide Travel Inc	500 Mamaroneck Ave	Harrison	NY	10528	914-835-7600	835-1666	771	
Richard & Karen Carpenter Performing Arts Ctr	6200 Atherton St	Long Beach	CA	90815	562-985-7000	985-7023	572	*Web:* www.carpenterarts.org
Richard & Richard Construction Company Inc	234 Venture St Ste 100	San Marcos	CA	92078	760-759-2260		186	*Web:* www.rrconstruction.com
Richard A. Feare & Associates Ltd	840 S Northwest Hwy Ste 207	Barrington	IL	60010	847-381-5300		390	*Web:* richardafeare.com
Richard A. Foreman Associates Inc	330 Emery Dr E	Stamford	CT	06902	203-327-2800	967-9393	116	*Web:* www.rafamedia.com
Richard A. Granowitz, Aplc	650 E Hospitality Ln Ste 570	San Bernardino	CA	92408	909-890-1717	890-4610	41	*Web:* gwwlaw.com
Richard A. Handlon Correctional Facility	1728 Bluewater Hwy	Ionia	MI	48846	616-527-3100		213	*Web:* www.michigan.gov
Richard A. Kennedy Law Office	3773 Tibbetts St Ste D	Riverside	CA	92506	951-715-5000		428	*Web:* www.richardakennedy.com
Richard A. Schurr PA	100 Almeria Ave Ste 340	Coral Gables	FL	33134	305-204-4924	483-7828*	41	*Fax Area Code: 786 ■ *Web:* richardschurr.com
Richard A. Urbanek Jr DDS Ms PA	5 Eureka Cir Ste B	Wichita Falls	TX	76308	940-696-2002		363	*Web:* www.oralsurgeonwichitafalls.com
Richard B. Russell State Park	2650 Russell State Park Rd	Elberton	GA	30635	706-213-2045		565	*Web:* gastateparks.org
Richard Bland College	11301 Johnson Rd	Petersburg	VA	23805	804-862-6100	862-6490	162	*Web:* www.rbc.edu
Richard Bong State Recreation Area	26313 Burlington Rd	Kansasville	WI	53139	262-878-5600		565	*Web:* dnr.wi.gov
Richard Bowers and Co	260 Peachtree St Ste 2400	Atlanta	GA	30303	404-816-1600	880-0077	652	*Web:* www.richardbowers.com
Richard Brady & Assoc	3710 Ruffin Rd	San Diego	CA	92123	858-496-0500	496-0505	261	*Web:* richardbrady.com
Richard Carlton Consulting Inc	1941 Rollingwood Dr	Fairfield	CA	94534	707-422-4053		196	*TF:* 800-325-2747 ■ *Web:* www.rcconsulting.com
Richard Childress Racing Enterprises Inc	425 Industrial Dr	Welcome	NC	27374	336-731-3334		713	*Web:* www.rcrracing.com
Richard Curtis Associates Inc	171 E 74th St Ste 2	New York	NY	10021	212-772-7363		444	*Web:* www.curtisagency.com
Richard D. Burbidge, A Professional Corp	215 S State St Ste 920	Salt Lake City	UT	84111	801-355-6677		41	*Web:* burbidgemitchell.com
Richard Dean Associates Inc (RDA)	1 Harris St	Newburyport	MA	01950	978-462-1150	462-4431	761	*Web:* www.richarddean.com
Richard E. Jacobs Group Inc	25425 Ctr Ridge Rd	Cleveland	OH	44145	440-871-4800	808-6902	655	*Web:* www.rejacobsgroup.com
Richard Franco Agency Inc, The	60 Morris Tpke 3rd Fl	Summit	NJ	07901	973-376-4111	376-8196	169	*Web:* richardfranco.com
Richard Goettle Inc	12071 Hamilton Ave	Cincinnati	OH	45231	513-825-8100		189-3	*Web:* www.goettle.com
Richard Gray Gallery	875 N Michigan Ave 38th Fl	Chicago	IL	60611	312-642-8877	642-8488	42	*Web:* www.richardgraygallery.com
Richard Gumz Farms	8905 S Gumz Rd	North Judson	IN	46366	574-896-5441		10-5	
Richard H. Hutchings Psychiatric Ctr	620 Madison St	Syracuse	NY	13210	315-426-3600		374-5	*Web:* omh.ny.gov
Richard H. Thornton Public Library	210 Main St	Oxford	NC	27565	919-693-1121	693-2244	434-3	*Web:* www.granville.lib.nc.us
Richard Harrison Bailey Inc	121 S Niles Ave	South Bend	IN	46617	317-634-2120		4	*Web:* www.rhb.com
Richard Heath & Associates Inc (RHA)	590 W Locust Ave Ste 103	Fresno	CA	93650	559-447-7000	447-7099	463	*Web:* www.rhainc.com
Richard Henry Group LLC	PO Box 45422	Westlake	OH	44145	440-724-2658		41	*Web:* www.rhgsolutions.com
Richard I Green Inc	959 Sampsonville Rd	Enosburg Falls	VT	05450	802-933-6693	933-4744	780	*TF:* 800-639-3199 ■ *Web:* www.rigreen.com
Richard J. Donovan Correctional Facility at Rock Mountain (RJD)	480 Alta Rd	San Diego	CA	92179	619-661-6500	661-6253	213	*Web:* www.cdcr.ca.gov
Richard L. Feigen & Co	16 E 77th St	New York	NY	10075	212-628-0700		42	*Web:* www.rlfeigen.com
Richard L. Roudebush VA Medical Ctr	1481 W Tenth St	Indianapolis	IN	46202	317-554-0000		374-8	*TF:* 888-878-6889 ■ *Web:* www.va.gov
Richard Lubin PA	1217 S Flagler Dr 2nd Fl	West Palm Beach	FL	33401	561-655-2040		41	*Web:* lubinlaw.com
Richard M. Campbell Veterans Home	4605 Belton Hwy	Anderson	SC	29621	864-261-6734		793	
Richard N. Best Associates Inc	300 N Oxford Valley Rd	Fairless Hills	PA	19030	215-945-9240	945-9277	261	*Web:* rnbest.com
Richard Nixon Foundation, The	18001 Yorba Linda Blvd	Yorba Linda	CA	92886	714-993-5075	528-0544	434-2	*Web:* www.nixonfoundation.org
Richard Oil & Fuel LLC	2330 Hwy 70 PO Box 686	Donaldsonville	LA	70346	225-473-8389		581	*Web:* popingos.com
Richard P. Johnson PC	2400 Lakeside Blvd Ste 120	Richardson	TX	75082	972-497-1010		41	*Web:* johnsonfirmpc.com
Richard Petty Museum	309 Branson Mill Rd	Randleman	NC	27317	336-495-1143		520	*Web:* www.richardpettymotorsports.com
Richard Rodgers Theatre	226 W 46th St	New York	NY	10036	212-221-1211		747	*TF:* 866-755-3075 ■ *Web:* broadwaydirect.com
Richard Sandoval Hospitality	3377 Blake St	Denver	CO	80205	303-586-3099		671	*Web:* www.richardsandoval.com
Richard Shapiro, Attorney	1327 Chicago Ave	Evanston	IL	60201	847-869-8686		41	*Web:* richardshapiro.com
Richard Stockton College of New Jersey	Jimmie Leeds Rd	Pomona	NJ	08240	609-652-4593	626-6050	166	*Web:* intraweb.stockton.edu
Richard V. Ellis PA	3202 N Tamiami Trl	Sarasota	FL	34234	941-351-9111		41	*Web:* sarasotabankruptcy.com
Richard Winger	PO Box 470296	San Francisco	CA	94147	415-922-9779		637-10	*Web:* richardwinger.com
Richard Wolf Medical Instruments Corp	353 Corporate Woods Pkwy	Vernon Hills	IL	60061	800-323-9653	913-1488*	250	*Fax Area Code: 847 ■ *TF:* 800-323-9653 ■ *Web:* www.richardwolfusa.com
Richards & Richards	1741 Elm Hill Pk	Nashville	TN	37210	615-242-9600	242-2100	608	*Web:* www.richardsandrichards.com
Richards & Southern Inc	PO Box 37	Goodlettsville	TN	37070	615-851-9655		194	*Web:* www.richardsandsouthern.com
Richards Brick Co	234 Springer Ave	Edwardsville	IL	62025	618-656-0230	656-0944	150	*Web:* www.richardsbrick.com
Richards Electric Supply Company Inc	4620 Reading Rd	Cincinnati	OH	45229	513-242-8800		246	*TF:* 800-234-4614 ■ *Web:* www.richardselectric.com
Richards Energy Group	781 S Chiques Rd	Manheim	PA	17545	717-898-6330		463	*Web:* richardsenergy.com
Richards Graphic Communications Inc	2700 Van Buren St	Bellwood	IL	60104	708-547-6000	547-6044	781	*TF:* 866-827-3686 ■ *Web:* www.rgcnet.com
Richards Group	2801 N Central Expy Ste 100	Dallas	TX	75204	214-891-5700	891-5230	4	*Web:* richards.com
Richards Industries Inc	3170 Wasson Rd	Cincinnati	OH	45209	513-533-5600	871-0105	595	*TF:* 800-543-7311 ■ *Web:* www.richardsind.com
Richards Layton & Finger	PO Box 551	Wilmington	DE	19899	302-651-7700	651-7701	428	*Web:* www.rlf.com
Richards Maple Products Inc	545 Water St	Chardon	OH	44024	800-352-4052		296-39	*TF:* 800-352-4052 ■ *Web:* www.richardsmapleproducts.com
Richards Memorial Library	118 N Washington St	North Attleboro	MA	02760	508-699-0122		434-3	*Web:* rmlonline.org
Richards Packaging Inc	2321 NE Argyle St Ste D	Portland	OR	97211	503-290-0000		601	*Web:* www.richardspackaging.com
Richards Sheet Metal Works Inc	2680 Industrial Dr	Ogden	UT	84401	801-621-3341	392-9567	480	*Web:* www.richards-fab.com
Richards/Carlberg	1900 W Loop S Ste 1100	Houston	TX	77027	713-965-0764		4	*Web:* www.richardscarlberg.com
Richards-Apex Inc	4202-24 Main St	Philadelphia	PA	19127	215-487-1100	487-3090	541	*Web:* www.richardsapex.com
Richards-DAR House Museum	256 N Joachim St	Mobile	AL	36603	251-208-7320		520	*Web:* www.richardsdarhouse.com

Name / Address	City	State	ZIP	Phone	Fax	Class
Richardson Bike Mart Inc 1451 W Campbell Rd; *Web:* bikemart.com	Richardson	TX	75080	972-231-3993		711
Richardson Chamber of Commerce 411 Belle Grove Dr; *Web:* www.richardsonchamber.com	Richardson	TX	75080	972-792-2800	792-2825	139
Richardson Convention & Visitors Bureau 411 W Arapaho Rd Ste 105; *TF:* 888-690-7287 ■ *Web:* www.richardsontexas.org	Richardson	TX	75080	972-744-4034	744-5834	206
Richardson County 1700 Stone St; *Web:* co.richardson.ne.us	Falls City	NE	68355	402-245-2911	245-2946	338
Richardson Electrical Company Inc 17 Batchelder Rd; *Web:* www.richardsonelectrical.us	Seabrook	NH	03874	603-474-3900	474-7755	189-4
Richardson Electronics Ltd 40 W 267 Keslinger Rd PO Box 393; *NASDAQ:* RELL ■ *TF:* 800-348-5580 ■ *Web:* www.rell.com	La Fox	IL	60147	630-208-2200	208-2550	246
Richardson Grove State Park 1600 US Hwy 101 Ste 8; *Web:* www.parks.ca.gov	Garberville	CA	95542	707-247-3318		565
Richardson Manufacturing Co 2209 Old Jacksonville Rd; *Web:* www.rmc-bigcnc.com	Springfield	IL	62704	217-546-2249	546-9433	757
Richardson Molding Inc 2405 Norcross Dr; *Web:* richardsonmolding.com	Columbus	IN	47201	812-342-0139		596
Richardson Public Library 900 Civic Center Dr; *Web:* www.cor.net	Richardson	TX	75080	972-744-4350	744-5806	434-3
Richardson Seeds Inc PO Box 60; *Web:* www.richardsonseeds.com	Vega	TX	79092	806-267-2379	267-2820	276
Richardson Smith Gardner & Assoc 14 N Boylan Ave; *Web:* www.smithgardnerinc.com	Raleigh	NC	27603	919-828-0577		261
Richards-Wilcox Inc 600 S Lake St; **Fax Area Code:* 630 ■ *TF:* 800-253-5668 ■ *Web:* www.richardswilcox.com	Aurora	IL	60506	800-253-5668	897-6994*	207
Richelieu Foods Inc 222 Forbes Rd Ste 4400; *Web:* www.richelieufoods.com	Braintree	MA	02184	781-786-6800	843-1784	296-37
Richey Equipment Inc 3213 Honeysuckle Rd; *TF:* 800-207-2086 ■ *Web:* www.richeyequipment.com	White Pine	TN	37890	865-674-6042	674-7510	274
Richey May & Company PC 9605 S Kingston Ct Ste 200; *Web:* www.richeymay.com	Englewood	CO	80112	303-721-6131		2
Richey Restoration Inc 9574 Lebanon Rd; *Web:* www.richeyrestoration.com	Mount Juliet	TN	37122	615-758-8760		83
Richfield Chamber of Commerce 6601 Lyndale Ave S Ste 106; *Web:* richfieldmnchamber.org	Minneapolis	MN	55423	612-866-5100		139
Richfield Hospitality Services 1900 W Loop S Ste 700; *Web:* www.richfield.com	Houston	TX	77027	303-220-2000		379
Richie, Guettinger & Manydeeds, SC 3410 Oakwood Mall Dr; *Web:* rgmlawec.com	Eau Claire	WI	54701	715-832-5777		41
Richland Area Chamber of Commerce 55 N Mulberry St; *Web:* www.richlandareachamber.com	Mansfield	OH	44902	419-522-3211	526-6853	139
Richland Communities 3161 Michelson Dr Ste 425; *Web:* richlandcommunities.com	Irvine	CA	92612	949-261-7010	261-7016	401
Richland Community College 1 College Pk; *TF:* 800-899-4722 ■ *Web:* www.richland.edu	Decatur	IL	62521	217-875-7200	875-6965	162
Richland Correctional Institution 1001 Olivesburg Rd; *Web:* ohio.gov	Mansfield	OH	44905	419-526-2100	521-2810	213
Richland County 2020 Hampton St; *Web:* www.richlandcountysc.gov	Columbia	SC	29204	803-576-2050	576-2137	338
Richland County 50 Park Ave E; *Web:* www.richlandcountyoh.us	Mansfield	OH	44902	419-774-5550	774-5862	338
Richland County 103 W Main St Ste 21; *Web:* richlandcountycourt.org	Olney	IL	62450	618-392-2151	392-5041	338
Richland County 181 W Seminary St PO Box 310; *Web:* co.richland.wi.us	Richland Center	WI	53581	608-647-2197	647-6134	338
Richland County 201 W Main St; *Web:* www.richland.org	Sidney	MT	59270	406-433-1708	433-3731	338
Richland County 418 Second Ave N; *Web:* www.co.richland.nd.us	Wahpeton	ND	58075	701-642-7700	642-7701	338
Richland County Public Library (RCPL) 1431 Assembly St; *Web:* www.richlandlibrary.com	Columbia	SC	29201	803-799-9084		434-3
Richland Electric Co-op 1027 N Jefferson St; *TF:* 844-843-6845 ■ *Web:* rec.coop	Richland Center	WI	53581	608-647-3173		245
Richland Federal Credit Union 201 W Holly St; *Web:* richlandfcu.com	Sidney	MT	59270	406-482-2704		219
Richland Glass Company Inc 1640 SW Blvd; *Web:* www.richlandglass.com	Vineland	NJ	08360	856-691-1697		332
Richland Hospital Inc, The 333 E Second St; *TF:* 888-467-7485 ■ *Web:* www.richlandhospital.com	Richland Center	WI	53581	608-647-6321		374-3
Richland LLC 1905 Mines Rd; *Web:* www.richlandllc.com	Pulaski	TN	38478	931-424-3900		190
Richland Parish 708 Julia St; *Web:* www.lpgov.org	Rayville	LA	71269	318-728-2061		338
Richland Public Library 955 Northgate Dr; *Web:* www.richland.lib.wa.us	Richland	WA	99352	509-942-7454		434-3
Richland Ventures 1201 16th Ave S	Nashville	TN	37212	615-383-8030		792
Richline Group Inc 6701 Nob Hill Rd; *TF:* 800-327-1808 ■ *Web:* www.richlinegroup.com	Tamarac	FL	33321	954-718-3200	718-3206	360-2
Richloom Fabrics Group 261 Fifth Ave; *Web:* www.richloom.com	New York	NY	10016	212-685-5400		594

Name / Address	City	State	ZIP	Phone	Fax	Class
Richman Chemical Inc 768 N Bethlehem Pk Ste 204; *Web:* www.richmanchemical.com	Lower Gwynedd	PA	19002	215-628-2946		194
Richman Group of Cos 340 Pemberwick Rd; *TF:* 800-425-9503 ■ *Web:* www.therichmangroup.com	Greenwich	CT	06831	203-869-0900		653
Richmar Associates Inc 283 Brokaw Rd; *TF:* 866-282-7424 ■ *Web:* www.richmarstaffing.com	Santa Clara	CA	95050	408-727-6070	727-4465	260
Richmond Agency Inc, The 833 Laurence Ave PO Box 907; *Web:* richmondagency.com	Jackson	MI	49204	517-788-9130		390
Richmond Animal Hospital 233 E Main St; *Web:* richmondanimalhospitalvt.com	Richmond	VT	05477	802-434-4935		794
Richmond Auto Parts Technology Inc 5000 Corporate Way; *Web:* www.raptech.com	Richmond	KY	40475	859-625-1101		247
Richmond Baking Co 520 N Sixth St; *Web:* www.richmondbaking.com	Richmond	IN	47374	765-962-8535	962-2253	296-9
Richmond Ballet 407 E Canal St; *Web:* richmondballet.com	Richmond	VA	23219	804-344-0906	344-0901	573-1
Richmond Capital Management Inc 10800 Midlothain Tpke Ste 217; *Web:* www.richmondcap.com	Richmond	VA	23235	804-379-8280		401
Richmond Cedric (Rep D - LA) 506 Cannon House Office Bldg; *Web:* richmond.house.gov	Washington	DC	20515	202-225-6636	225-1988	342-2
Richmond Chamber of Commerce 3925 Macdonald Ave; *Web:* www.rcoc.com	Richmond	CA	94805	510-234-3512	234-3540	139
Richmond Chamber of Commerce 5811 Cooney Rd Ste 101; *Web:* www.richmondchamber.ca	Richmond	BC	V6X3M1	604-278-2822	278-2972	137
Richmond City Hall 450 Civic Center Plz; *TF:* 800-833-2900 ■ *Web:* www.ci.richmond.ca.us	Richmond	CA	94804	510-620-6555		434-3
Richmond Coliseum 601 E Leigh St; *Web:* richmondcoliseum.net	Richmond	VA	23219	804-780-4970	780-4606	720
Richmond Communications Group Inc 2750 Northaven Rd Ste 202; *TF:* 866-627-0853 ■ *Web:* www.richmondcomm.com	Dallas	TX	75229	972-241-1982	241-1976	189-4
Richmond Community College PO Box 1189; *Web:* www.richmondcc.edu	Hamlet	NC	28345	910-410-1700	582-7102	162
Richmond County 1401 Fayetteville Rd; *Web:* richmondnc.com	Rockingham	NC	28379	910-997-8200	997-8208	338
Richmond County 101 Court Cir PO Box 1000; *Web:* co.richmond.va.us	Warsaw	VA	22572	804-333-3781	333-5396	338
Richmond County Hospice 1119 N US Hwy 1; *Web:* www.richmondcountyhospice.com	Rockingham	NC	28379	910-997-4464	997-4484	371
Richmond County School System 864 Broad St; *Web:* www.rcboe.org	Augusta	GA	30901	706-826-1000		685
Richmond Ford 4600 W Broad St; *TF:* 877-709-7947 ■ *Web:* www.richmondford.com	Richmond	VA	23230	804-358-5521		57
Richmond Ford West 10751 W Broad St; *Web:* www.richmondfordwest.com	Glen Allen	VA	23060	804-474-0571		516
Richmond Gear PO Box 238; *Web:* www.richmondgear.com	Liberty	SC	29657	864-843-9231	843-1276	709
Richmond Hill Chamber of Commerce (RHCOC) 376 Church St S; *Web:* www.rhcoc.com	Richmond Hill	ON	L4C9V8	905-884-1961	884-1962	137
Richmond International Airport 1 Richard E Byrd Terminal D Ste C; *Web:* www.flyrichmond.com	Richmond	VA	23250	804-226-3000		27
Richmond International Forest Products Inc 4050 Innslake Dr Ste 100; *TF:* 800-767-0111 ■ *Web:* www.rifp.com	Glen Allen	VA	23060	804-747-0111	270-4547	191-3
Richmond Kickers Soccer Club Inc 2001 Maywill St Ste 203; *Web:* www.richmondkickers.com	Richmond	VA	23230	804-644-5425		717
Richmond Metropolitan Convention & Visitors Bureau 401 N Third St; *TF:* 800-370-9004 ■ *Web:* www.visitrichmondva.com	Richmond	VA	23219	804-782-2777		206
Richmond National Battlefield Park 3215 E Broad St; *TF:* 866-733-7768 ■ *Web:* www.nps.gov	Richmond	VA	23223	804-226-1981		520
Richmond North Associates Inc 4232 Ridge Lea Rd; *Web:* www.rnacollects.com	Amherst	NY	14226	716-832-5668	832-4236	160
Richmond Printing LLC 5825 Schumacher; *Web:* www.richmondprinting.com	Houston	TX	77057	713-952-0800	952-0932	627
Richmond Public Library 101 E Franklin St; *Web:* rvalibrary.org	Richmond	VA	23219	804-646-7223		434-3
Richmond Public Relations 1601 5th Ave Ste 1100; *Web:* www.richmondpr.com	Seattle	WA	98101	206-682-6979		636
Richmond Public Schools 301 N Ninth St; *Web:* www.rvaschools.net	Richmond	VA	23219	804-780-7700	780-4122	685
Richmond State Hospital (RSH) 3771 S A St; *Web:* www.in.gov	Richmond	IN	47374	765-966-0511		374-5
Richmond Symphony Orchestra 380 Hubelchison Pkwy PO Box 982; *Web:* richmondsymphony.org	Richmond	IN	47375	765-966-5181	962-8447	573-3
Richmond Tours 1828 Hylan Blvd; *Web:* richmond-tours.org	Staten Island	NY	10305	718-979-3111	979-7143	760
Richmond University Medical Ctr 355 Bard Ave; *TF:* 800-422-8798 ■ *Web:* www.rumcsi.org	Staten Island	NY	10310	718-818-1234		374-3
Richmond, The 1757 Collins Ave; *Web:* www.richmondhotel.com	Miami Beach	FL	33139	305-538-2331	531-9021	379

Name / Address	City	State	ZIP	Phone	Fax	Class
Richmond/Wayne County Convention & Tourism Bureau 5701 National Rd E. TF: 800-828-8414 ■ Web: visitrichmond.org	Richmond	IN	47374	765-935-8687	935-0440	206
Richmor Aviation Inc 1142 Rte 9H PO Box 423 TF: 800-331-6101 ■ Web: www.richmor.com	Hudson	NY	12534	518-828-9461	828-1303	63
Richner Communications Inc 2 Endo Blvd Web: www.liherald.com	Garden City	NY	11530	516-569-4000	569-4942	532-3
Richter & Ratner Builders 45 W 36th St 12th Fl. Web: www.richterratner.com	New York	NY	10018	212-936-4500	710-5858	610
Richter LLP 1981 McGill College 11th Fl. TF: 888-805-1793 ■ Web: www.richter.ca	Montreal	QC	H3A0G6	514-934-3400		734
Richter Publishing LLC 3001 N Rocky Point Dr E Ste 200 Web: richterpublishing.com	Tampa	FL	33607	727-940-7647		637-2
Richter Studios 1143 W Rundell Pl. Web: www.richterstudios.com	Chicago	IL	60607	312-861-9999		514
Richter102 Media Group LLC 600 Cleveland St Bank of America Tower Ste 920 Web: www.richter10point2.com	Clearwater	FL	33755	727-447-3600		395
Richter7 280 South 400 West Ste 200 Web: www.richter7.com	Salt Lake City	UT	84101	801-521-2903		636
Richway Industries Ltd 504 N Maple St. TF: 800-553-2404 ■ Web: richway.com	Janesville	IA	50647	319-987-2976	987-2251	273
Richweb Inc 9680 Atlee Commons Dr. Web: richweb.com	Ashland	VA	23005	804-368-0421		225
Richwood Meat Company Inc 2751 N Santa Fe Ave. Web: richwoodmeat.com	Merced	CA	95348	209-722-8171		296-26
Rick Engineering Co 5620 Friars Rd Web: www.rickengineering.com	San Diego	CA	92110	619-291-0707		77
Rick Husband Amarillo International Airport 10801 Airport Blvd Web: fly-ama.com	Amarillo	TX	79111	806-335-1671	335-1672	27
Rick Johnson & Associates of Colorado 1649 Downing St TF: 800-530-2300 ■ Web: www.denverpi.com	Denver	CO	80218	303-296-2200	296-3038	400
Rick Linn LLC 933 N Charlotte St. Web: ricklinn.com	Pottstown	PA	19464	610-850-9036		41
Rick Steves' Europe Through The Back Door 130 Fourth Ave N Web: www.ricksteves.com	Edmonds	WA	98020	425-771-8303		772
Rick's Cafe Boatyard 4050 Dandy Trl Web: ricksboatyard.com	Indianapolis	IN	46254	317-290-9300		671
Rickard Circular Folding Co 325 N Ashland Ave TF: 800-747-1389 ■ Web: www.rickardbindery.com	Chicago	IL	60607	312-243-6300	243-6323	92
Rickard Metals Inc (RM) 2043 Elm Ct Web: www.rickardmetals.com	Ontario	CA	91761	909-947-4922		492
Rickenbacker International Corp 3895 S Main St. Web: www.rickenbacker.com	Santa Ana	CA	92707	714-545-5574		527
Rickenbaugh Cadillac Co 777 Broadway Web: www.rickenbaughcadillac.com	Denver	CO	80203	303-573-7773		57
Ricker Pond State Park 18 Ricker Pond Camp Ground Rd. Web: www.vtstateparks.com	Groton	VT	05046	802-584-3821		565
Ricker, Atkinson, Mcbee & Associates Inc 2105 S Hardy Dr Ste 13 Web: www.rammeng.com	Tempe	AZ	85282	480-921-8100		261
Rickert & Wessel Law Office PC 115 Broad St PO Box 193 Web: rickertlawoffice.com	Reinbeck	IA	50669	319-345-6438	345-2911	41
Ricketts Company LPA 50 Hill Rd S Web: ricketts-law.com	Pickerington	OH	43147	614-834-8246		41
Ricketts Glen State Park 695 SR-487 Web: www.dcnr.pa.gov	Benton	PA	17814	570-477-5675		565
Ricks Barbecue 2367 Hwy 43 South TF: 800-544-5864 ■ Web: ricksbbq.com	Leoma	TN	38468	931-852-2324		186
Rickwood Caverns State Park 370 Rickwood Park Rd Web: www.alapark.com	Warrior	AL	35180	205-647-9692		565
Rico Auto Complex 220 S 5th St TF: 877-389-9544 ■ Web: www.ricoautocomplex.com	Gallup	NM	87301	877-389-9544		57
Rico Auto Industries Inc 6338 Sashabaw Rd Web: www.ricoauto.com	Clarkston	MI	48346	248-409-0960	409-0965	60
Rico Foods Inc 578 E 19th St Web: www.ricofood.com	Paterson	NJ	07514	973-278-0589	278-0378	345
Rico Intl 8484 San Fernando Rd. Web: www.woodwinds.daddario.com	Sun Valley	CA	91352	818-394-2700		527
Ricochet Fuel Distributors Inc 1201 Royal Pkwy TF: 800-284-2540 ■ Web: www.ricochetfuel.com	Euless	TX	76040	800-284-2540		316
Ricoh Electronics Inc 1100 Valencia Ave Web: www.rei.ricoh.com	Tustin	CA	92780	770-338-7200		173-7
Ricoh Printing Systems America Inc 2390-A Ward Ave TF: 888-372-6659 ■ Web: www.rpsa.ricoh.com	Simi Valley	CA	93065	805-578-4000	578-4001	173-6
Ricoh USA Inc 5 Dedrick Pl Web: www.ricoh-usa.com	West Caldwell	NJ	07006	973-882-2000	808-7523	112
Ricon Corp 7900 Nelson Rd. TF: 800-322-2884 ■ Web: www.riconcorp.com	Panorama City	CA	91402	818-267-3000		256
Ricos Products Company Inc 830 S Presa St Web: www.ricos.com	San Antonio	TX	78210	210-222-1415	226-6453	300
RID (Registry of Interpreters for the Deaf Inc) 333 Commerce St. Web: www.rid.org	Alexandria	VA	22314	703-838-0030	838-0454	49-5
Ridco Casting Co 6 Beverage Hill Ave. Web: www.ridco.com	Pawtucket	RI	02860	401-724-0400	724-6320	308
Riddle Village 1048 W Baltimore Pk. Web: www.riddlevillage.com	Media	PA	19063	610-891-3700	891-3671	672
Riddleberger Bros Inc (RBI) 6127 S Valley Pk. Web: www.rbiva.com	Mount Crawford	VA	22841	540-434-1731	432-1691	186
Ride & Show Engineering Inc PO Box 3240 Web: www.rideshow.com	San Dimas	CA	91773	909-592-5575	599-9837	261
Ride Inc PO Box 6213. Web: www.rideinc.com	Drayton Valley	AB	T7A1R7	780-621-1570		711
Rideau Inc 473 Deslauriers TF: 800-363-6464 ■ Web: rideau.com	Montreal	QC	H4N1W2	800-363-6464		463
Ridenbaugh Press PO Box 834. Web: ridenbaughpress.com	Carlton	OR	97111	503-852-0010		637-10
Rider Levett Bucknall (RLB) 4343 E Camelback Rd Ste 350 Web: rlb.com	Phoenix	AZ	85018	602-443-4848		194
Rider University 2083 Lawrenceville Rd TF: 800-257-9026 ■ Web: www.rider.edu	Lawrenceville	NJ	08648	609-896-5000	895-6645	166
Ridewell Corp PO Box 4586 TF: 877-434-8088 ■ Web: www.ridewellcorp.com	Springfield	MO	65808	417-833-4565		60
Ridge Behavioral Health System 3050 Rio Dosa Dr TF: 800-753-4673 ■ Web: www.ridgebhs.com	Lexington	KY	40509	859-269-2325		374-5
Ridge Engineering Inc 3987 Hampstead Mexico Rd. Web: www.ridgeeng.com	Hampstead	MD	21074	410-239-7716	239-8710	454
Ridge Printing Corp 8900 Yellow Brick Rd Web: www.ridgeprinting.com	Baltimore	MD	21237	410-668-4780	668-0469	627
Ridge Tahoe 400 Ridge Club Dr PO Box 5790 TF: 800-334-1600 ■ Web: www.ridgetahoeresort.com	Stateline	NV	89449	775-588-3553	588-1551	669
Ridge Technical College 7700 State Rd 544 Web: www.polkedpathways.com	Winter Haven	FL	33881	863-419-3060	419-3062	167-3
Ridge Tool Co 400 Clark St Web: www.ridgid.com	Elyria	OH	44035	440-323-5581		758
Ridge Ventures 1 Letterman Dr Bldg D Ste P100. Web: ridge.vc	San Francisco	CA	94129	415-439-4420		792
Ridgedale Ctr 12401 Wayzata Blvd Web: www.ridgedalecenter.com	Minnetonka	MN	55305	952-541-4864		460
Ridgefield Symphony Orchestra 77 Danbury Rd Web: ridgefieldsymphony.org	Ridgefield	CT	06877	203-438-3889		573-3
Ridgeline Consulting Group Inc 1110 Winchester Trl	Downingtown	PA	19335	610-518-1430		196
Ridgestone Corp 10880 Wilshire Blvd Ste 910 Web: www.ridgestonecorp.com	Los Angeles	CA	90024	310-209-5300	209-0040	401
Ridgetop Group Inc 3580 W Ina Rd Web: www.ridgetopgroup.com	Tucson	AZ	85741	520-742-3300		261
Ridgeview Animal Hospital 816 N Ridgeview Rd Web: ridgeviewanimalhosp.com	Olathe	KS	66061	913-780-0078		794
Ridgeview Institute Inc 3995 S Cobb Dr TF: 844-350-8800 ■ Web: ridgeviewinstitute.com	Smyrna	GA	30080	844-350-8800		726
Ridgeview Medical Ctr (RMC) 500 S Maple St. TF: 800-967-4620 ■ Web: www.ridgeviewmedical.org	Waconia	MN	55387	952-442-2191	442-6524	374-3
Ridgeview Publishing Co (RPC) PO Box 686 Web: www.ridgeviewpublishing.com	Atascadero	CA	93423	805-466-7252		637-2
Ridgewater College *Hutchinson* 2 Century Ave SE TF: 800-722-1151 ■ Web: www.ridgewater.edu	Hutchinson	MN	55350	320-234-8500		800
Ridgeway Pharmacy Ltd 2824 Hwy 93 N TF: 800-630-3214 ■ Web: ridgewayrx.com	Victor	MT	59875	406-642-6040		237
Ridgewood High School 7500 W Montrose Ave Web: www.d234.org	Norridge	IL	60706	708-456-4242	456-0342	449
Ridgewood Racquet Club 249 Ackerman Ave Web: www.ridgewoodracquet.com	Ridgewood	NJ	07450	201-652-1991		354
Ridgewood Savings Bank 71-02 Forest Ave TF: 800-250-4832 ■ Web: www.ridgewoodbank.com	Ridgewood	NY	11385	718-240-4800		70
Ridgmar Mall 1888 Green Oaks Rd Web: www.ridgmar.com	Fort Worth	TX	76116	817-731-6591	763-5146	460
Ridg-U-Rak Inc 120 S Lake St. TF: 866-479-7225 ■ Web: www.ridgurak.com	North East	PA	16428	814-725-8751	725-5659	286
Ridgway State Park 28555 Hwy 550 Web: cpw.state.co.us	Ridgway	CO	81432	970-626-5822		565
Riding Mountain Park East Gate Registration Complex National Historic Site of Canada 135 Wasagaming Dr PO Box 299 Web: www.pc.gc.ca	Onanole	MB	R0J1N0	204-848-7275	848-2596	563
Ridley College 2 Ridley Rd PO Box 3013 Web: www.ridleycollege.com	Saint Catharines	ON	L2R7C3	905-684-1889	684-8875	622
Ridley Creek State Park 1023 Sycamore Mills Rd Web: www.dcnr.pa.gov	Media	PA	19063	610-892-3900		565
Ridley Feed Ingredients 1609 1st Ave & 17th St. TF: 866-376-3336 ■ Web: www.ridleyfeedingredients.com	Mendota	IL	61342	866-376-3336		447
Ridley-Lowell Business & Technical Institute 470 Bank St TF: 877-611-8603	New London	CT	06320	877-611-8603		668
Ridley-Lowell Business & Technical Institute 116 Front St TF: 877-606-5325	Binghamton	NY	13905	877-606-5325		167-3
Ridout Lumber Co 125 Henry Farrar Dr. Web: www.ridoutlumber.com	Searcy	AR	72143	501-268-3929		191-3

Name	Address	City	State	Zip	Phone	Fax	Class
Ridout Plastics Company Inc	5535 Ruffin Rd *Web:* www.eplastics.com	San Diego	CA	92123	858-560-1551	560-1941	600
Riechmann Transport Inc	3328 W Chain of Rocks Rd *TF:* 800-844-4225 ■ *Web:* www.riechmanntransport.com	Granite City	IL	62040	618-797-0523		780
Rieck & Crotty PC	55 W Monroe Ste 3625 *Web:* rieckcrotty.com	Chicago	IL	60603	312-726-4646		41
Ried & Agee PLLC	3633 26th St W *Web:* www.reidagee.com	Bradenton	FL	34205	941-756-8791		445
Riedel Marketing Group	5327 E Pinchot Ave *Web:* 4rmg.com	Phoenix	AZ	85018	602-840-4948		345
Riedell Shoes Inc	122 Cannon River Ave *TF:* 800-698-6893 ■ *Web:* www.riedellskates.com	Red Wing	MN	55066	651-388-8251	385-5500	710
Rieders, Travis, Humphrey, Waters & Dohrmann	161 W Third St *TF:* 800-326-9259 ■ *Web:* www.riederstravis.com	Williamsport	PA	17701	570-323-8711		428
Riege Software International USA	73 Redding Rd *Web:* www.riege.com	Georgetown	CT	06829	203-544-9475		311
Riegel Consumer Products	51 Riegel Rd *TF:* 800-845-3251 ■ *Web:* riegellinen.com	Johnston	SC	29832	803-275-2541	275-2219	746
Rieger & Fried LLP	100 Quentin Roosevelt Blvd Ste 208 *Web:* riegerllp.com	Garden City	NY	11530	516-280-8880		41
Riegle Press Inc, The	1282 N Gale Rd *Web:* www.rieglepress.com	Davison	MI	48423	810-653-9631	653-6878	627
Rieke Corp	500 W 7th St *Web:* www.riekepackaging.com	Auburn	IN	46706	260-925-3700		608
Rieke Office Interiors	2000 Fox Ln *Web:* rieke.com	Elgin	IL	60123	847-622-9711	622-9750	320
Riekes Equipment Co	6703 L St *TF:* 800-856-0931 ■ *Web:* www.riekesequipment.com	Omaha	NE	68117	402-593-1181	593-9295	385
Riel House National Historic Site of Canada	330 River Rd **Fax Area Code:* 866 ■ *Web:* www.pc.gc.ca	Winnipeg	MB	R2M3Z8	519-826-5391	787-6221*	563
Riemer & Braunstein LLP	1 Center Plz *Web:* www.riemerlaw.com	Boston	MA	02108	617-523-9000	880-3456	428
Riephoff Sawmill Inc	763 Rt 524 *Web:* www.riephoffsawmill.com	Allentown	NJ	08501	609-259-7265	259-7267	683
Ries Graphics Ltd	12727 W Custer Ave *Web:* www.riesgraphics.com	Butler	WI	53007	262-781-5720		627
Riesbeck Food Markets Inc	48661 National Rd *Web:* www.riesbeckfoods.com	Saint Clairsville	OH	43950	740-695-7050	695-7555	345
Riester	3344 E Camelback Rd *TF:* 844-602-3344 ■ *Web:* www.riester.com	Phoenix	AZ	85018	044-602-3344		7
Riesterer & Schnell Inc	N2909 Hwy 32 *Web:* www.rands.com	Pulaski	WI	54162	920-822-3077	822-3704	274
Rieter Automotive North America	38555 Hills Tech Dr **Fax Area Code:* 248 ■ *Web:* www.rieter.com	Farmington Hills	MI	48331	803-649-1371	848-0130*	60
Rieth-Riley Construction Company Inc	3626 Elkhart Rd *Web:* www.rieth-riley.com	Goshen	IN	46526	574-875-5183	875-8405	188-4
RIF (Reading Is Fundamental Inc)	1825 Connecticut Ave NW Ste 400 *TF:* 877-743-7323 ■ *Web:* www.rif.org	Washington	DC	20009	202-536-3400		48-11
Rife Resources Ltd	400 144 - Fourth Ave SW *TF:* 888-257-1873 ■ *Web:* www.rife.com	Calgary	AB	T2P3N4	403-221-0800		536
Rifenburg Construction Inc	159 Brick Church Rd *Web:* www.rifenburg.com	Troy	NY	12180	518-279-3265	279-4260	188-4
Rifle Correctional Ctr	200 County Rd 219	Rifle	CO	81650	970-625-1700		213
Rifle Falls State Park	5775 Hwy 325 *Web:* cpw.state.co.us	Rifle	CO	81650	970-625-1607		565
Rifle River Recreation Area	2550 Rose City Rd *Web:* www.michigan.org	Lupton	MI	48635	989-473-2258		565
Rigaku Americas Corp	9009 New Trails Dr *TF:* 855-785-1064 ■ *Web:* www.rigaku.com	The Woodlands	TX	77381	281-362-2300	364-3628	475
Rig-Chem Inc	132 Thompson Rd *TF:* 800-375-7208 ■ *Web:* www.rigchem.com	Houma	LA	70363	985-873-7208		539
Rigel Networks LLC	1500 Quail St Ste 280 *Web:* www.rigelnetworks.com	Newport Beach	CA	92660	949-891-2571		196
Rigel Pharmaceuticals Inc	1180 Veterans Blvd *NASDAQ: RIGL* ■ *Web:* www.rigel.com	South San Francisco	CA	94080	650-624-1100	624-1101	85
Rigel Shipping Canada Inc	3521 Rt 134 *Web:* rigelcanada.com	Shediac	NB	E4P3G6	506-533-9000		314
Rigg Darlington Group Inc, The	14 E Welsh Pool Rd *Web:* www.rdgins.com	Exton	PA	19341	484-876-2222		390
Riggers Inc	901 Holly Springs Ave *TF:* 800-343-2878 ■ *Web:* www.riggersinc.com	Richmond	VA	23224	804-232-1281		780
Riggins Company Lc	410 Rotary St *Web:* www.rigginscompany.com	Hampton	VA	23661	757-826-0525		480
Riggins Inc	3938 S Main Rd *TF:* 800-642-9148 ■ *Web:* rigginsoil.com	Vineland	NJ	08360	856-825-7600		316
Riggleman Denver (Rep R - VA)	1022 Longworth House Office Bldg *Web:* www.riggleman.house.gov	Washington	DC	20515	202-225-4711		342-2
Riggs Abney Neal Orbison & Lewis Inc	502 W Sixth St Frisco Bldg *Web:* www.riggsabney.com	Tulsa	OK	74119	918-587-3161		428
Riggs Machine & Fabricating Inc	3850 Belford St *Web:* www.riggsmachine.com	Ashland	KY	41101	606-324-0090		454
Right at Home Inc	6464 Center St Ste 150 *TF:* 877-697-7537 ■ *Web:* www.rightathome.net	Omaha	NE	68106	402-697-0289		310
Right at Home Properties	PO Box 631154 *Web:* www.rightathomeproperties.com	Irving	TX	75063	972-333-4164		652

Name	Address	City	State	Zip	Phone	Fax	Class
Right Mfg	7949 Stromesa Ct Ste G *Web:* www.rightmfg.com	San Diego	CA	92126	858-566-7002	566-7623	482
Right Systems Inc	2600 Willamette Dr NE Ste C *TF:* 800-571-1717 ■ *Web:* www.rightsys.com	Lacey	WA	98516	360-956-0414	956-0336	225
Right/Pointe Co	234 Harvestore Dr PO Box 467 *Web:* www.rightpointe.com	Dekalb	IL	60115	815-754-5700		3
RightAnswercom Inc	2900 Rodd St Ste 1911 *Web:* www.rightanswer.com	Midland	MI	48641	989-835-5000		387
Righteous Babe	341 Delaware Ave *TF:* 800-664-3769 ■ *Web:* www.righteousbabe.com	Buffalo	NY	14202	716-852-8020	852-2741	657
Right-Gard Corp	531 N 4th St	Denver	PA	17517	717-336-7594		576
RightHand Technologies Inc	6545 N Olmsted Ave *Web:* www.righthandtech.com	Chicago	IL	60631	773-774-7600		393
Rightline Equipment Inc	29120 Dike Rd *Web:* www.rightline.com	Rainier	OR	97048	503-556-1761	556-2421	470
RightScale Inc	402 E Gutierrez St *TF:* 888-989-1856 ■ *Web:* www.rightscale.com	Santa Barbara	CA	93101	805-500-4164		177
Rightsline	448 S Hill St *Web:* www.rightsline.com	Los Angeles	CA	90013	310-507-1270		657
RightStaff Inc	4919 McKinney Ave *Web:* www.rightstaffinc.com	Dallas	TX	75205	214-953-0900		260
RightsTrade LLC	12001 Ventura Pl Ste 500 *Web:* www.rightstrade.com	Studio City	CA	91604	818-762-5811	753-0322	224
Rightware Inc	850 Stephenson Hwy Ste 618 *TF:* 877-775-2694 ■ *Web:* www.rightware.com	Troy	MI	48083	877-775-2694		178-1
Rightway Gate Inc	2720 Loker Ave W Ste Q *TF:* 888-398-4703 ■ *Web:* www.rwgusa.com	Carlsbad	CA	92008	760-736-3700		224
Rigid Hitch Inc	3301 W Burnsville Pkwy *TF:* 800-624-7630 ■ *Web:* www.rigidhitch.com	Burnsville	MN	55337	800-624-7630		763
Rigidized Metals Corp	658 Ohio St *TF:* 800-836-2580 ■ *Web:* www.rigidized.com	Buffalo	NY	14203	716-849-4760		492
Rigidply Rafters Inc	701 E Linden St *Web:* www.rigidply.com	Richland	PA	17087	717-866-6581		191-3
RigNet Inc	15115 Park Row Ste 300 *TF:* 800-638-8844 ■ *Web:* www.rig.net	Houston	TX	77084	281-674-0100	674-0101	224
RI-Go Lift Truck Ltd	175 Courtland Ave *TF:* 855-211-9673 ■ *Web:* www.rigolift.com	Concord	ON	L4K4T2	647-846-8475		358
RigUp Inc	111 Congress Ave Ste 900 *Web:* www.rigup.com	Austin	TX	78701	512-501-5452		48-12
Rihm Kenworth (RK)	425 Concord St S *TF:* 800-988-8235 ■ *Web:* www.rihmkenworth.com	South Saint Paul	MN	55075	651-646-7833	646-0630	516
Riiser Energy	709 S 20th Ave *TF:* 800-570-8024 ■ *Web:* www.myrstore.com	Wausau	WI	54401	715-845-7272		324
Riken of America Inc	4709 Golf Rd Ste 550 *Web:* www.rikencorp.com	Skokie	IL	60076	847-673-1400	673-1457	61
Riker, Danzig, Scherer, Hyland & Perretti LLP	1 Speedwell Ave *Web:* riker.com	Morristown	NJ	07962	973-538-0800	538-1984	428
RILA (Retail Industry Leaders Assn)	1700 N Moore St Ste 2250 *Web:* www.rila.org	Arlington	VA	22209	703-841-2300	841-1184	49-18
Riley Bennett Egloff LLP	141 E Washington St 4th Fl *Web:* rbelaw.com	Indianapolis	IN	46204	317-636-8000	636-8027	428
Riley Construction Company Inc	5301 00th Ave **Fax Area Code:* 414 ■ *Web:* www.rileycon.com	Kenosha	WI	53144	262-658-4381	359-0105*	186
Riley County	110 Courthouse Plz *Web:* rileycountyks.gov	Manhattan	KS	66502	785-537-6300	537-6394	338
Riley County Genealogical Society (RCGS)	2005 Claflin Rd *Web:* www.rileycgs.com	Manhattan	KS	66502	785-565-6495		48-13
Riley Gear Corp	1 Precision Dr *TF:* 866-487-0779 ■ *Web:* www.rileygear.com	Saint Augustine	FL	32092	904-829-5652		483
Riley Hayes Adv	333 S 1st St *Web:* rileyhayes.com	Minneapolis	MN	55401	612-338-7161		4
Riley Industrial Services Inc	2615 San Juan Blvd PO Box 2014 *Web:* rileyindustrial.com	Farmington	NM	87401	505-327-4947	326-0305	172
Riley Warnock & Jacobson PLC	1906 W End Ave *Web:* rwjplc.com	Nashville	TN	37203	615-320-3700		41
Riley White Inc	153 Park Sq NW *Web:* rileywhitedrugs.com	Russellville	KY	42276	270-726-7626		237
Riley's	312 Park St *Web:* rileys.restaurantsnapshot.com	Syracuse	NY	13203	315-471-7111		671
Rileys Floors & More Inc	3230 Marnie Ave *Web:* rileysfloors.com	Waterloo	IA	50701	319-233-9911		290
Rim Country Mechanical Inc	261 N Eighth St *Web:* rimcountrymechanical.com	Show Low	AZ	85901	928-537-1803		610
Rim Country Museum Library	700 S Green Valley Pkwy *Web:* www.rimcountrymuseums.com	Payson	AZ	85547	928-474-3483		434-3
Rim Country Regional Chamber of Commerce	100 W Main St *Web:* www.rimcountrychamber.com	Payson	AZ	85541	928-474-4515		139
Rim Forest Lumber Company Inc	26491 Pine Ave *Web:* www.rimlumber.com	Rimforest	CA	92378	909-337-6262		683
Rim Logistics Ltd	200 N Gary Ave *TF:* 888-275-0937 ■ *Web:* www.rimlogistics.com	Roselle	IL	60172	630-595-0610	595-0614	449
Rima Enterprises Inc	5340 Argosy Ave *Web:* www.rima-system.com	Huntington Beach	CA	92649	714-893-4534		628

Company / Address	City	State	ZIP	Phone	Fax	Class
Rima Manufacturing Co 3850 Munson Hwy *Web:* www.rimamfg.com	Hudson	MI	49247	517-448-8921	448-7142	621
Rimage Corp 7725 Washington Ave S *Web:* www.qumu.com	Minneapolis	MN	55439	952-944-8144		173-8
Rimex Metals (USA) Inc 2850 Woodbridge Ave *Web:* www.rimexmetals.com	Edison	NJ	08837	732-549-3800	549-6435	481
Rimex Supply Ltd 9726 186th St *TF:* 800-663-9883 ■ *Web:* www.rimex.com	Surrey	BC	V4N3N7	604-888-0025		111
Rimkus Consulting Group Inc 8 Greenway Plz Ste 500 *TF:* 800-580-3228 ■ *Web:* rimkus.com	Houston	TX	77046	800-580-3228		196
Rimnetics Inc 3141 Swetzer Rd *Web:* www.rimnetics.com	Loomis	CA	95650	916-652-5555		604
Rimrock Corp 1700 Jetway Blvd *Web:* www.rimrockcorp.com	Columbus	OH	43219	614-471-5926	471-7388	456
Rimrock Credit Union 952 Central Ave *Web:* rimrockcu.org	Billings	MT	59102	406-248-3685	248-3686	219
Rimrock Dude Ranch 2728 Northfork Rt *Web:* www.rimrockranch.com	Cody	WY	82414	307-587-3970		239
Rimrock Foundation 1231 N 29th St *TF:* 800-227-3953 ■ *Web:* www.rimrock.org	Billings	MT	59101	406-248-3175	248-3821	726
Rimrock Resort Hotel, The 300 Mountain Ave PO Box 1110 *TF:* 888-746-7625 ■ *Web:* www.rimrockresort.com	Banff	AB	T1L1J2	403-762-3356		669
RIMS (Risk & Insurance Management Society Inc) 1065 Avenue of the Americas 13th Fl *Web:* www.rims.org	New York	NY	10018	212-286-9292	986-9716	49-9
Rimtec Corp 1702 Beverly Rd *Web:* www.rimtec.com	Burlington	NJ	08016	609-387-0011	387-1436	605-2
RINA Systems LLC 8180 Corporate Park Dr Ste 140 *Web:* www.rinasystems.com	Cincinnati	OH	45242	513-469-7462		177
Rinaldi Printing Co 4514 E Adamo Dr *Web:* www.rinaldiprinting.com	Tampa	FL	33605	813-247-3921		627
Rinchem Company Inc 6133 Edith Blvd NE *Web:* www.rinchem.com	Albuquerque	NM	87107	505-345-3655	998-4378	449
Rinck Advertising 113 Lisbon St *Web:* rinckadvertising.com	Lewiston	ME	04240	207-755-9470		636
Rincon Broadcasting LLC 414 E Cota St *TF:* 800-234-6217 ■ *Web:* www.ktyd.com	Santa Barbara	CA	93101	805-879-8300		645-141
Rincon Research Corp 101 N Wilmot Rd Ste 101 *Web:* www.rincon.com	Tucson	AZ	85711	520-519-4600	519-4747	466
Rindt-McDuff Associates Inc 334 Cherokee St NE *Web:* www.rindt-mcduff.com	Marietta	GA	30060	770-427-8123		261
Rinehart Oil Inc 2401 N State St *Web:* www.rinehartoil.com	Ukiah	CA	95482	707-462-8811		579
Rinell Wood Systems Inc 2706 Kilihau St Unit A *Web:* www.rinellwoodsystems.com	Honolulu	HI	96819	808-834-1344	834-1409	191-3
RINET Company LLC 101 Federal St 14th Fl *Web:* www.rinetco.com	Boston	MA	02110	617-488-2700	423-3206	194
Ring Container Technology 1 Industrial Park Rd *TF:* 800-280-6333 ■ *Web:* www.ringcontainer.com	Oakland	TN	38060	800-280-6333		124
Ring Energy Inc 901 W Wall St 3rd Fl *Web:* ringenergy.com	Midland	TX	79701	432-682-7464		536
Ring of Fire Studios LLC 1702 Olympic Blvd Studio A *Web:* www.ringoffire.com	Santa Monica	CA	90404	310-966-5055		514
Ring's End Inc 181 W Ave *Web:* www.ringsend.com	Darien	CT	06820	203-655-2525		752
Ringdale Inc 101 Halmar Cove *TF:* 888-288-9080 ■ *Web:* www.ringdale.com	Georgetown	TX	78628	512-288-9080	288-7210	176
Ringfeder Power Transmission USA Corp 165 Carver Ave *Web:* www.ringfeder.com	Westwood	NJ	07675	201-666-3320		770
Ringgold County 109 W Madison St *Web:* ringgoldcountyia.wixsite.com	Mount Ayr	IA	50854	641-464-3239		338
Ringgold Telephone Company Inc 200 Evitt Pkwy PO Box 869 *Web:* www.rtctel.com	Ringgold	GA	30736	706-965-2345		224
Ringland-Johnson Construction 1725 Huntwood Dr *Web:* www.ringland.com	Cherry Valley	IL	61016	815-332-8600	332-8411	186
Ringler Associates Inc 27422 Aliso Creek Rd Ste 200 *Web:* ringlerassociates.com	Aliso Viejo	CA	92656	949-296-9000		509
Ringling College of Art & Design 2700 N Tamiami Trl *TF:* 800-255-7695 ■ *Web:* www.ringling.edu	Sarasota	FL	34234	941-351-5100	359-7517	164
Ringmaster Jewelers Inc 1990 Healy Dr *Web:* ringmasterjewelers.com	Winston-Salem	NC	27103	336-722-2218		410
Ringo Drilling Company Inc PO Box 400	Tye	TX	79563	325-695-5600		540
Ringold Financial Management Services Inc 850 S Wabash Ave Ste 210 *Web:* www.ringoldfinancial.com	Chicago	IL	60605	312-566-9705		2
Ringside SteakHouse 2165 W Burnside St *TF:* 800-688-4142 ■ *Web:* www.ringsidesteakhouse.com	Portland	OR	97210	503-223-1513	223-6908	671
RingTel Communications 19 W Maple St *TF:* 888-771-7464 ■ *Web:* www.ringtelco.com	Ringsted	IA	50578	712-866-8000	866-0002	681
Ringwood State Park 1304 Sloatsburg Rd *Web:* www.njparksandforests.org	Ringwood	NJ	07456	973-962-7031		565
Ring-Zero Software Inc 3800 N Lamar Blvd Ste 730-126 **Fax Area Code: 800* ■ *TF:* 800-842-1312 ■ *Web:* www.ring-zero.com	Austin	TX	78756	512-686-3022	742-1312*	178-1
Rink Printing Company Inc 814 S Main St *TF:* 877-617-1589 ■ *Web:* www.rinkprinting.com	South Bend	IN	46601	574-232-7935	288-2115	627
Rink Systems Inc 1103 Hershey St *TF:* 800-944-7930 ■ *Web:* www.rinksystems.com	Albert Lea	MN	56007	507-373-9175	377-1060	14
Rinke Noonan US Bank Plz 1015 W St Germain St Ste 300 *TF:* 888-899-6700 ■ *Web:* www.rinkenoonan.com	Saint Cloud	MN	56302	320-251-6700	656-3500	428
Rinker Materials Corp *Concrete Pipe Div* 8311 W Carder Ct *TF:* 800-909-7763 ■ *Web:* www.rinkerpipe.com	Littleton	CO	80125	303-791-1600	791-1710	183
Rio Bank 1655 N 23rd *Web:* www.riobk.com	Mcallen	TX	78501	956-631-7890	972-1574	70
Rio Blanco County 555 Main St PO Box 1067 *Web:* www.co.rio-blanco.co.us	Meeker	CO	81641	970-878-9460	878-3587	338
Rio Blanco Schools Federal Credit Union 402 W Main St Ste 139 *Web:* rioblancoschoolsfcu.com	Rangely	CO	81648	970-675-2372	675-5535	219
Rio Bravo Oil Inc 5868 Westheimer RD Ste 553	Houston	TX	77057	713-787-9060		536
Rio Chama Steakhouse 414 Old Santa Fe Trl *Web:* riochamasteakhouse.com	Santa Fe	NM	87501	505-955-0765		671
Rio City Cafe 1110 Front St *Web:* www.riocitycafe.com	Sacramento	CA	95814	916-442-8226		671
Rio Delmar Enterprises 8338 Elliott Rd *Web:* pages.stihldealer.net	Easton	MD	21601	410-822-8866		429
Rio Grande Bible Institute & Language School 4300 S US Hwy 281 *Web:* www.riogrande.edu	Edinburg	TX	78539	956-380-8100		48-20
Rio Grande Cafe 270 S Rio Grande St Ste 400 *Web:* riograndecafeslc.com	Salt Lake City	UT	84101	801-364-3302		671
Rio Grande Co 201 Santa Fe Dr *TF:* 800-935-8420 ■ *Web:* www.riograndeco.com	Denver	CO	80223	303-825-2211	629-0417	191-1
Rio Grande County 965 Sixth St PO Box 160 *Web:* www.riograndecounty.org	Del Norte	CO	81132	719-657-3334	657-2621	338
Rio Grande Electric Cooperative Inc 778 E US Hwy 90 PO Box 1509 *TF:* 800-749-1509 ■ *Web:* www.riogrande.coop	Brackettville	TX	78832	830-563-2444	563-2450	245
Rio Grande Mexican Restaurant 160 Ct St Ste 7 *Web:* eatriogrande.com	Charleston	WV	25301	304-344-8616		671
Rio Grande Nature Center State Park 2901 Candelaria Rd NW *Web:* www.rgnc.org	Albuquerque	NM	87107	505-344-7240	344-4505	565
Rio Grande Service Ctr 3005 Broadway Blvd SE Ste E *TF:* 800-374-8939 ■ *Web:* www.riograndeservicecenter.com	Albuquerque	NM	87102	505-877-2349	877-0086	45
Rio Grande Valley Credit Union 1221 Morgan Blvd *Web:* rgvcu.coop	Harlingen	TX	78550	956-423-5792		219
Rio Grande Valley Sugar Growers PO Box 459 *Web:* www.rgvsugar.com	Santa Rosa	TX	78593	956-636-1411	636-1449	296-38
Rio Grill 101 the Crossroads *Web:* www.riogrill.com	Carmel By The Sea	CA	93923	831-625-5436		671
Rio Hondo Community College 3600 Workman Mill Rd *Web:* www.riohondo.edu	Whittier	CA	90601	562-692-0921		162
Rio Products Intl 5050 S Yellowstone Hwy *Web:* www.rioproducts.com	Idaho Falls	ID	83402	208-524-7760		208
Rio Ranch 9999 Westheimer Rd *Web:* www.rioranch.com	Houston	TX	77042	713-952-5000	952-2263	671
Rio Rancho Chamber of Commerce 4001 Southern Blvd SE *TF:* 888-282-9232 ■ *Web:* rrrcc.org	Rio Rancho	NM	87124	505-892-1533	892-6157	139
Rio Rancho Observer 409 NM 528 NE Ste 101 *Web:* www.abqjournal.com	Rio Rancho	NM	87124	505-892-8080	892-5719	532-2
Rio Rio Cantina 421 E Commerce St *Web:* www.rioriorivercwalk.com	San Antonio	TX	78205	210-226-8462		671
Rio Salado College 2323 W 14th St *Web:* www.riosalado.edu	Tempe	AZ	85281	480-517-8000		162
Rio Technical Services LLC 4200 S Hulen *Web:* www.riotechnical.com	Fort Worth	TX	76109	817-735-8264		261
RioCan Real Estate Investment Trust 2300 Yonge St Ste 500 PO Box 2386 *TSE:* REI.UN ■ *TF:* 800-465-2733 ■ *Web:* riocan.com	Toronto	ON	M4P1E4	416-866-3033	866-3020	654
Riordan & Scully Insurance Service LLC 815 Commerce Dr *Web:* riordan-scully.com	Oak Brook	IL	60523	630-468-5400		390
Riordan Lewis & Haden 10900 Wilshire Blvd Ste 850 *Web:* www.rlhinvestors.com	Los Angeles	CA	90024	310-405-7200	405-7222	792
Riordan Mansion State Historic Park 409 W Riordan Rd *Web:* www.azstateparks.com	Flagstaff	AZ	86001	928-779-4395		565
Rios Golden Cut Inc 121 N Pk Blvd *Web:* www.riosgoldencuts.com	San Antonio	TX	78204	210-227-4996		77
Riotel Group 250 Ave du Phare Est *TF:* 877-566-2651 ■ *Web:* www.riotel.com	Matane	QC	G4W3N4	418-566-2651	562-7365	707
Riovida Networks 2133 Clinton Ave *Web:* www.riovida.net	Alameda	CA	94501	510-693-0166		195
RIP Curl Inc 3030 Airway Ave *Web:* www.ripcurl.com	Costa Mesa	CA	92626	714-422-3642		77
RIP Griffin Truck Travel Center Inc 4710 Fourth St *TF:* 800-333-9330 ■ *Web:* www.ripgriffin.com	Lubbock	TX	79416	806-795-8785	795-6574	324
Ripa Engineering Corp 9555 Owensmouth Ave Nbr 8 *Web:* ripaeng.com	Chatsworth	CA	91311	818-773-8722		261
Ripcho Studio 7630 Lorain Ave *TF:* 800-686-7427 ■ *Web:* www.ripchostudio.com	Cleveland	OH	44102	216-631-0664		590
Ripcord Solutions PO Box 1566 Ste 201 *Web:* ripcordsolutions.com	Edmonds	WA	98020	425-670-8700		7
Ripe Tomato 5064 N Palm Ave *Web:* www.tripadvisor.com	Fresno	CA	93704	559-225-1850		671

Name / Address	City	State	ZIP	Phone	Fax	Class
RIPIRG (Rhode Island Public Interest Research Group) 11 S Angell St Ste 150 *Web:* ripirg.org	Providence	RI	02906	401-608-1201		633
Ripley Co 46 Nooks Hill Rd *TF:* 800-528-8665 ■ *Web:* www.ripley-tools.com	Cromwell	CT	06416	860-635-2200	635-3631	758
Ripley County Hwy 160 E *Web:* www.ripleycountymissouri.org	Doniphan	MO	63935	573-996-2212		338
Ripley County 1015 S Main St *Web:* www.ripleycounty.com	Versailles	IN	47042	812-689-6115	689-6000	338
Ripley Entertainment Inc 601 E Palace Pkwy *Web:* www.ripleys.com	Grand Prairie	TX	75050	972-263-2391		520
Ripley Entertainment Inc 7576 Kingspointe Pkwy Ste 188 *Web:* www.ripleys.com	Orlando	FL	32819	407-345-8010	345-0801	31
Ripley's Aquarium 1110 Celebrity Cir *Web:* www.ripleys.com	Myrtle Beach	SC	29577	843-916-0888		40
Ripley's Believe It or Not! Museum 1441 Boardwalk *Web:* www.ripleys.com	Atlantic City	NJ	08401	609-347-2001		520
Ripley's Believe It or Not! Museum 3326 W Hwy 76 *Web:* www.ripleys.com	Branson	MO	65616	417-337-5300		520
Ripley's Believe It or Not! Museum 901 N Ocean Blvd *TF:* 800-905-4228 ■ *Web:* www.ripleys.com	Myrtle Beach	SC	29577	843-448-2331		520
Ripley's Believe It or Not! Museum 4960 Clifton Hill *Web:* www.ripleys.com	Niagara Falls	ON	L2G3N4	905-356-2238		520
Ripley's Believe It or Not! Museum 19 San Marco Ave *TF:* 800-226-6545 ■ *Web:* www.ripleys.com	Saint Augustine	FL	32084	904-824-1606	829-1790	520
Ripley's Believe It or Not! Museum 6780 Hollywood Blvd *Web:* www.ripleys.com	Hollywood	CA	90028	323-466-6335		520
Ripley's Believe It or Not! Orlando Odditorium 8201 International Dr *Web:* www.ripleys.com	Orlando	FL	32819	407-345-0501		520
Ripon Chamber of Commerce 114 Scott St *Web:* www.ripon-wi.com	Ripon	WI	54971	920-748-6764		139
Ripon College 300 Seward St PO Box 248 *TF:* 800-947-4766 ■ *Web:* www.ripon.edu	Ripon	WI	54971	800-947-4766		166
Ripon Elementary School 304 N Acacia Ave *Web:* www.riponusd.net	Ripon	CA	95366	209-599-2131		685
Ripon Printers Inc 656 S Douglas St *TF:* 800-321-3136 ■ *Web:* www.riponprinters.com	Ripon	WI	54971	920-748-3136		256
Ripon Society 1155 15th St NW Ste 550 *Web:* www.riponsociety.org	Washington	DC	20005	202-216-1008		48-7
Riposta, Lawyers LLC 432 Ridge Rd *Web:* ripostalaw.com	North Arlington	NJ	07031	201-991-0067		41
Rippe Keane Marketing Inc 525 Junction Rd Ste 8200 *Web:* www.rippekeane.com	Madison	WI	53717	608-277-9097		194
Ripped Enterprises 528 Chama St NE *Web:* www.cbass.com	Albuquerque	NM	87108	505-266-5858		637-2
Rippey Corp 5000 Hillsdale Cir *Web:* www.rippey.com	El Dorado Hills	CA	95762	916-939-4332	939-4338	174
Ripple 315 Montgomery St *Web:* ripple.com	San Francisco	CA	94104	415-213-4838		113
Ripple6 Inc 520 8th Ave 17th Fl *Web:* www.ripple6.com	New York	NY	10018	646-254-6780		5
Rippling 55 2nd St *Web:* www.rippling.com	San Francisco	CA	94110	415-555-5555		657
Rippy Cadillac 4951 New Centre Dr *Web:* www.rippyautomotive.com	Wilmington	NC	28403	910-799-2421		57
RIPS (Rhode Island Publications Society) 1445 Wampanoag Trail Ste 201 *Web:* www.ripublications.org	Riverside	RI	02915	401-272-1776	273-1791	48-6
Riptide Communications Inc 2621 Palisade Ave Ste C *Web:* www.riptidecommunications.com	Bronx	NY	10463	212-260-5000	260-5191	636
Ririe-Woodbury Dance Co 138 West Broadway *Web:* ririewoodbury.com	Salt Lake City	UT	84101	801-297-4241	297-4235	573-1
RIS (Russian Information Services Inc) PO Box 567 *TF:* 800-639-4301 ■ *Web:* russianlife.com	Montpelier	VT	05601	802-223-4955		637-9
RIS Corp 5905 Weisbrook Ln Ste 101 *Web:* www.ris-corp.com	Knoxville	TN	37909	865-588-4456		196
RIS Inc 901 24th St *TF:* 800-526-6565 ■ *Web:* risnet.com	Anacortes	WA	98221	360-293-2135	293-2385	390
RIS Media Inc 69 E Ave *TF:* 800-724-6000 ■ *Web:* rismedia.com	Norwalk	CT	06851	203-855-1234		652
Risch James E (Sen R - ID) 483 Russell Senate Office Bldg *Web:* www.risch.senate.gov	Washington	DC	20510	202-224-2752	224-2573	342-2
Riscky's Barbecue 2314 Azle Ave *Web:* risckys.com	Fort Worth	TX	76164	817-624-8662	624-3777	670
RISD Store Art Supplies 30 N Main St *Web:* risdstore.com	Providence	RI	02903	401-454-6464	454-6453	45
Risdall Adv Agency 2685 Long Lake Rd Ste 100 *TF:* 888-747-3255 ■ *Web:* www.risdall.com	Roseville	MN	55113	651-286-6700	631-2561	4
Rise Brands 134 E Long St *Web:* www.risebrands.com	Columbus	OH	43215	614-754-7522		49-12
Rise Broadband 61 Inverness Dr E Ste 250 *TF:* 844-411-7473 ■ *Web:* www.risebroadband.com	Englewood	CO	80112	844-411-7473		387
Rise Community Development 1627 Washington Ave 1st Fl *Web:* risestl.org	Saint Louis	MO	63103	314-333-7008		653

Name / Address	City	State	ZIP	Phone	Fax	Class
Rise Sushi & Sake Lounge 756 W Webster Ave *Web:* www.shinerestaurant.com	Chicago	IL	60614	773-296-0101	525-3522	671
Risetime Inc 130 S Jefferson St Ste 100 *Web:* www.risetime.com	Chicago	IL	60661	312-362-9930		196
Rish Equipment Co PO Box 330 *Web:* www.rish.com	Bluefield	WV	24701	304-327-5124	327-8821	358
Rishi Tea LLC 185 S 33rd Ct *TF:* 866-747-4483 ■ *Web:* www.rishi-tea.com	Milwaukee	WI	53208	414-747-4001		297-8
Rising Media Inc 211 E Victoria St Ste E **Fax Area Code:* 916 ■ *Web:* risingmedia.com	Santa Barbara	CA	93101	805-965-3184	314-9080*	232
Rising Pharmaceuticals Inc 3 Pearl Ct *Web:* www.risingpharma.com	Allendale	NJ	07401	201-961-9000		231
Rising Results Inc 201 Edward Curry Ave Ste 202 *Web:* www.risingresults.com	Staten Island	NY	10314	718-370-8300		401
Rising Star Casino Resort 777 Rising Star Dr *TF:* 800-472-6311 ■ *Web:* www.risingstarcasino.com	Rising Sun	IN	47040	812-438-1234		133
Rising Sun Publishing PO Box 70906 *Web:* www.rspublishing.com	Marietta	GA	30007	770-518-0369	587-0862	637-2
Rising Tide Capital Inc 334 Martin Luther King Dr *Web:* www.risingtidecapital.org	Jersey City	NJ	07305	201-432-4316	432-3504	194
Risk & Insurance Management Society Inc (RIMS) 1065 Avenue of the Americas 13th Fl *Web:* www.rims.org	New York	NY	10018	212-286-9292	986-9716	49-9
Risk Consulting Group (RCG) 23120 Alicia Pky Ste 200 *Web:* www.rcgcorp.com	Mission Viejo	CA	92692	949-583-1161	583-0245	194
Risk Focus Inc 225 W 35th St 11th Fl *Web:* riskfocus.com	New York	NY	10001	917-725-6006		177
Risk Information Inc 33765 Magellan Isle *Web:* www.riskinformation.com	Dana Point	CA	92629	949-443-0330		637-10
Risk Integrated LLC 37 Main St *Web:* www.riskintegrated.com	Cold Spring	NY	10516	845-598-1620		655
Risk Management Agency 1400 Independence Ave SW Rm 6092-S *Web:* www.rma.usda.gov	Washington	DC	20250	202-690-2803	690-2818	340-1
Risk Management Assn (RMA) 1801 Market St Ste 300 *TF:* 800-677-7621 ■ *Web:* www.rmahq.org	Philadelphia	PA	19103	215-446-4000	446-4101	49-2
Risk Management Services Co (RMSC) 9100 Marksfield Rd **Fax Area Code:* 888 ■ *Web:* www.rmsc.com	Louisville	KY	40222	502-326-5900	326-5909*	194
Risk Management Solutions Inc 7575 Gateway Blvd *Web:* www.rms.com	Newark	CA	94560	510-505-2500	505-2501	178-10
Risk Sciences Group Inc PO Box 5047 *TF:* 800-241-2541 ■ *Web:* www.crawfordandcompany.com	Atlanta	GA	30302	800-241-2541		463
RiskSpan 281 Tresser Blvd Ste 1203 *Web:* riskspan.com	Stamford	CT	06901	203-355-1510		396
RiskWatch 1237 N Gulfstream Ave *TF:* 800-360-1898 ■ *Web:* www.riskwatch.com	Sarasota	FL	34236	800-360-1898		178-10
RISNA (Rhode Island State Nurses Assn) 100 Wsetminster St Ste 1500 *Web:* www.risna.org	Providence	RI	02903	401-331-5644	331-5646	533
RISO Inc 800 District Ave Ste 390 *TF:* 800-942-7476 ■ *Web:* www.riso.com	Burlington	MA	01803	978-777-7377	777-2517	173-6
RISQ Inc 625 Rene-Levesque Blvd W Bureau 300 *Web:* www.risq.quebec	Montreal	QC	H3B1R2	514-845-7181		387
Risse Racing Technology Inc 1240 Redwood Blvd *Web:* www.risseracing.com	Redding	CA	96003	530-246-8700		711
Rissers Poultry Inc 12 Wynfield Dr PO Box 52 *Web:* risserspoultry.com	Lititz	PA	17543	717-626-5466		311
Rist-Frost-Shumway Engineering PC 71 Water St *Web:* www.rfsengineering.com	Laconia	NH	03246	603-524-4647		261
Ristorante Bacco 737 Diamond St *Web:* baccosf.com	San Francisco	CA	94114	415-282-4969		671
Ristorante Ciao 835 Fourth Ave S *Web:* www.ristoranteciao.com	Naples	FL	34102	239-263-3889		671
Ristorante DaVinci 1180 Bishop St *Web:* davinci.ca	Montreal	QC	H3G2E3	514-874-2001		671
Ristorante SOTTO SOTTO 120 Ave Rd *Web:* www.sottosotto.ca	Toronto	ON	M5R2H4	416-962-0011		671
Rita A. Meiser PLC 7012 N 18th St *Web:* meiserlaw.com	Phoenix	AZ	85020	602-650-2473		41
Rita Hazan Salon 720 Fifth Ave 1st Fl *Web:* ritahazan.com	New York	NY	10019	212-586-4343		77
Rita's Italian ice 1401 Bridgetown Pk *Web:* www.ritasice.com	Feasterville-Trevose	PA	19053	215-322-8774		381
Ritatsu Manufacturing Inc 700 Old Liberty Church Rd *Web:* www.ritatsu.co.jp	Beaver Dam	KY	42320	270-730-7010	730-7011	483
Ritchey Mock & Associates PC 2038 Sandy Dr Ste 100A *Web:* ritcheymock.com	State College	PA	16803	814-826-2155		2
Ritchie Commercial 34 W Santa Clara St *Web:* ritchiecommercial.com	San Jose	CA	95113	408-971-2700	971-1600	652
Ritchie County 115 E Main St *Web:* www.ritchiecounty.wv.gov	Harrisville	WV	26362	304-643-2164	643-2906	338
Ritchie Engineering Company Inc 10950 Hampshire Ave S **Fax Area Code:* 800 ■ *TF:* 800-769-8370 ■ *Web:* yellowjacket.com	Bloomington	MN	55438	952-943-1300	322-8684*	14
Ritchie Tractor 1746 W Lmar Alxander Pkwy *TF:* 855-319-3484 ■ *Web:* www.ritchietractor.com	Maryville	TN	37801	865-981-3199		323

	Phone	Fax	Class
Ritchie, Dillard, Davies & Johnson PC 606 W Main St Ste 300 Knoxville TN 37902 *Web:* www.rddjlaw.com	865-637-0661	524-4623	428
Rite Aid Corp 30 Hunter Ln Camp Hill PA 17011 *NYSE:* RAD ■ *TF:* 800-748-3243 ■ *Web:* www.riteaid.com	717-761-2633		237
Rite Choice Home Health Care LLC 2200 N Canton Center Rd Ste 160 Canton MI 48187 *Web:* www.ritechoicehomehealthcare.com	734-981-1818	981-1888	363
Rite Engineering & Manufacturing Corp 5832 Garfield Commerce CA 90040 *Web:* www.riteboiler.com	562-862-2135	861-9821	357
Rite Rug Co 3949 Business Park Dr Columbus OH 43204 *Web:* www.riterug.com	614-261-6060		131
Rite Technology 1744 Independence Blvd Sarasota FL 34234 *TF:* 877-492-7725 ■ *Web:* ritefl.com	941-955-2737	351-0586	708
Rite Track Inc 8655 Rite Track Way West Chester OH 45069 *Web:* www.ritetrack.com	513-881-7820		454
Rite-Hite Corp 8900 N Arbon Dr Milwaukee WI 53224 *TF:* 800-456-0600 ■ *Web:* www.ritehite.com	414-355-2600	355-9248	678
Ritescreen Company Inc, The 4314 Rt 209 Elizabethville PA 17023 *Web:* www.ritescreen.com	717-362-7483		234
Rite-solutions Inc 1 Corporate Pl 2nd Fl Middletown RI 02842 *Web:* www.rite-solutions.com	860-599-1969		317
Riteway Bus Service Inc *Motorcoach Div* W201 N13900 Fond du Lac Ave Richfield WI 53076 *Web:* www.goriteway.com	262-677-3282	677-3121	107
Ritewood Inc 3643 S 4000 E Franklin ID 83237	208-646-2213	646-2217	10-8
Ritrama 800 Kasota Ave SE Minneapolis MN 55414 **Fax Area Code:* 612 ■ *TF:* 800-328-5071 ■ *Web:* www.ritrama.com	800-328-5071	378-9327*	3
Ritron Wireless Solutions 505 W Carmel Dr Carmel IN 46032 *TF:* 800-872-1872 ■ *Web:* www.ritron.com	317-846-1201		647
Ritta & Assoc 568 Grand Ave Englewood NJ 07631 *Web:* ritta.com	201-567-4400		4
RITTAL North America LLC Woodfield Corporate Ctr 425 N Martingale Rd Ste 400 Schaumburg IL 60173 **Fax Area Code:* 937 ■ *TF:* 800-477-4000 ■ *Web:* www.rittal.com	800-477-4000	390-5599*	816
Rittenhouse Book Distributors Inc 511 Feheley Dr King of Prussia PA 19406 *TF:* 800-345-6425 ■ *Web:* www.rittenhouse.com	800-345-6425	223-7488	96
Ritter Technology LLC 100 Williams Dr Zelienople PA 16063 *Web:* www.ritter1.com	724-452-6000		790
Ritter, Robinson, Mccready & James Ltd 405 Madison Ave Ste 1850 Toledo OH 43604 *Web:* rrmjlaw.com	419-241-3213	241-4925	41
Rittner Products Inc 150 Elizabeth Ln Rochester MI 48307 **Fax Area Code:* 248 ■ *TF:* 800-732-4773 ■ *Web:* www.rittnerfrench.com	800-732-4773	651-2650*	350
Rittners Floral School 345 Marlborough St Boston MA 02115 *Web:* www.floralschool.com	617-267-3824		685
Ritz Barbecue 302 17th St Allentown PA 18104	610-432-0952		671
Ritz Camera & Image 2 Bergen Tpke Ridgefield Park NJ 07660 *TF:* 855-622-7489 ■ *Web:* www.ritzcamera.com	855-622-7489		119
Ritz Tours Inc 208 S First St Alhambra CA 91801 **Fax Area Code:* 626 ■ *Web:* www.ritztours.com	650-259-9983	281-0117*	772
Ritz, Holman, Butala, Fine LLP 330 E Kilbourn Ave Two Plz E Ste 550 Milwaukee WI 53202 *Web:* www.ritzholman.com	414-271-1451	271-7464	2
Ritz-Carlton Hotel Company LLC, The 4445 Willard Ave Ste 800 Chevy Chase MD 20815 **Fax Area Code:* 801 ■ *TF:* 800-241-3333 ■ *Web:* www.ritzcarlton.com	301-547-4893	468-4069*	669
Ritz-Craft Corporation of Pennsylvania Inc 15 Industrial Park Rd Mifflinburg PA 17844 *TF:* 800-326-9836 ■ *Web:* www.ritz-craft.com	570-966-1053		505
Ritzman Pharmacies Inc 473 High St Wadsworth OH 44281 *Web:* www.ritzmanrx.com	330-335-2318	335-3222	237
Riu Hotel Florida Beach 3101 Collins Ave Miami FL 33140 *Web:* www.riu.com	305-673-5333		379
Rival Capital Management Inc 99 Scurfield Bvld Winnipeg MB R3Y1M6 *Web:* rivalcapital.ca	204-992-6210		317
RivalHealth LLC 6601 Hillsborough St Ste 109 Raleigh NC 27606 *TF:* 888-949-1001 ■ *Web:* www.rivalhealth.com	919-803-6709		387
Rivco Products Inc 440 S Pine St Burlington WI 53105 *TF:* 888-801-8222 ■ *Web:* rivcoproducts.com	262-763-8222	763-8949	517
Rivel Research Group Inc 830 Post Rd E Westport CT 06880 *Web:* rivel.com	203-226-0800		668
Rivendell Books PO Box 29348 Saint Louis MO 63126 *Web:* www.rivendellbooks.com	314-609-6534		637-2
River 95.7 208 N Thomas Dr Shreveport LA 71107 *Web:* www.klkl.fm	318-222-3122		645-148
River 97.3 WRVV, The 600 Corporate Cir Harrisburg PA 17110 *Web:* theriver973.iheart.com	717-540-8076		645-68
River Bank Laboratories Inc 18 S 8th St Geneva IL 60134 *Web:* www.riverbanklabs.com	630-232-2207		476
River Bend Business Products 304 Downtown Plz Fairmont MN 56031 *TF:* 800-783-3877 ■ *Web:* www.riverbendbusiness.com	507-235-3800		316
River Bend Industries 2421 16th Ave S Moorhead MN 56560 *TF:* 800-365-3070 ■ *Web:* www.riverbendind.com	800-365-3070		199
River Birch Homes Inc 400 River Birch Dr Hackleburg AL 35564 *Web:* www.riverbirchhomes.com	205-935-1997		505
River Bluff Nursing Home 4401 N Main Rockford IL 61103 *Web:* rbnh.org	815-921-9200	877-1069	371
River Cafe 1 Water St Brooklyn NY 11201 *Web:* rivercafe.com	718-522-5200	875-0037	671
River Cafe 25 Prince's Island Pk Calgary AB T2P0R1 *Web:* www.river-cafe.com	403-261-7670		671
River Cities Capital Funds 221 E 4th St Ste 2400 Cincinnati OH 45202 *Web:* rccf.com	513-621-9700		402
River Cities Engineering Inc 125 W 76th St Davenport IA 52806 *Web:* rivercities.us	563-386-4777		261
River City Ale Works 1400 Main St Wheeling WV 26003 *Web:* www.rivercitybanquets.com	304-233-4555		671
River City Bank PO Box 15247 Sacramento CA 95851 *OTC:* RCBC ■ *TF:* 800-564-7144 ■ *Web:* rivercitybank.com	916-567-2899		70
River City Brass Band Inc 500 Grant St Ste 2720 Pittsburgh PA 15219 *TF:* 800-292-7222 ■ *Web:* www.rivercitybrass.org	412-434-7222		573-3
River City Construction LLC 101 Hoffer Ln East Peoria IL 61611 *Web:* www.rccllc.com	309-694-3120	694-1332	186
River City Engineering 1795 Kuehler Ave New Braunfels TX 78130 *Web:* www.rcetx.com	830-626-3588	626-3601	77
River City Enterprises PO Box 9365 Peoria IL 61612 *Web:* www.pistontech.com	309-688-3223	688-3258	45
River City Metal Products Inc 655 Godfrey Ave SW Grand Rapids MI 49503 *Web:* www.rcmpinc.com	616-235-3746		295
River City Petroleum Inc 840 Delta Ln West Sacramento CA 95691 *Web:* rcpfuel.com	916-371-4960		780
River Community Credit Union 644 W Second St Ottumwa IA 52501 *Web:* rivercommunitycu.org	641-684-6302		219
River Country Co-op 9072 Cahill Ave Inver Grove Heights MN 55076 *TF:* 800-657-3285 ■ *Web:* www.rivercountry.coop	651-451-1151		48-2
River Country Tourism Council of Greater St Joseph County PO Box 214 Three Rivers MI 49093 *Web:* rivercountry.com	269-321-0640		338
River East Transcona School Division 589 Roch St Winnipeg MB R2K2P7 *Web:* www.retsd.mb.ca	204-667-7130		685
River Falls Journal 2815 Prairie Dr River Falls WI 54022 *TF:* 800-535-1660 ■ *Web:* www.rivertowns.net	715-426-1039		532-3
River Falls Public Library 140 Union St River Falls WI 54022 *Web:* www.riverfallspubliclibrary.org	715-425-0905	425-0914	434-3
River Forest Public Schools 90 7776 W Lake St River Forest IL 60305 *Web:* www.district90.org	708-771-8282	771-8291	780
River Garden Farms Co 41758 County Rd 112 Knights Landing CA 95645 *Web:* www.rivergardenfarms.com	530-735-6274		10-4
River Garden Hebrew Home for the Aged 11401 Old St Augustine Rd Jacksonville FL 32258 *Web:* www.rivergarden.org	904-260-1818	260-9733	450
River Heights Chamber of Commerce 5782 Blackshire Path Inver Grove Heights MN 55076 *Web:* riverheights.com	651-451-2266	451-0846	139
River House Seafood Restaurant 125 W River St Savannah GA 31401 *Web:* www.savannahriverhouse.com	912-234-1900		671
River Inn 924 25th St NW Washington DC 20037 *Web:* www.theriverinn.com	202-337-7600		379
River Legacy Park 701 NW Green Oaks Blvd Arlington TX 76006 *Web:* riverlegacy.org	817-860-6752	860-1595	520
River Metals Recycling 2045 River Rd Louisville KY 40206 *Web:* www.rmrecycling.com	502-585-5331		686
River Oaks Country Club Inc 1600 River Oaks Blvd Houston TX 77019 *Web:* www.riveroakscc.net	713-529-4321		354
River Oaks Hospital 1525 River Oaks Rd W New Orleans LA 70123 **Fax Area Code:* 504 ■ *TF:* 800-366-1740 ■ *Web:* riveroakshospital.com	800-366-1740	733-3229*	374-3
River Park Hospital 1230 Sixth Ave Huntington WV 25701 *TF:* 800-621-2673 ■ *Web:* www.riverparkhospital.net	304-526-9111		374-5
River Recycling Industries Inc 4195 Bradley Rd Cleveland OH 44109 *Web:* www.riverrecyclingind.com	216-459-2100	749-8107	686
River Region Credit Union 3124 W Edgewood Dr Jefferson City MO 65109 *Web:* rrcu.org	573-636-9198		219
River Road Partners LLC 462 S Fourth St Louisville KY 40202 *Web:* www.riverroadllc.com	502-371-4100		463
River Rock Casino Resort 8811 River Rd Richmond BC V6X3P8 *TF:* 866-748-3718 ■ *Web:* www.riverrock.com	604-247-8900	207-2641	669
River Rock Entertainment Authority 3250 Hwy 128 E Geyserville CA 95441 *TF:* 877-883-7777 ■ *Web:* www.riverrockcasino.com	707-857-2777		452
River Run Computers Inc 2320 W Camden Rd Milwaukee WI 53209 *Web:* www.river-run.com	414-228-7474		180
River School 4880 Macarthur Blvd NW Washington DC 20007 *Web:* riverschool.net	202-337-3554		685
River States Truck & Trailer 3959 N Kinney Coulee Rd La Crosse WI 54601 *Web:* www.riverstates.com	608-784-1149		57
River Street Inn 124 E Bay St Savannah GA 31401 *Web:* www.riverstreetinn.com	912-234-6400		379

				Phone	Fax	Class
River Technical Design Inc 2811 Sharon Copley Rd *Web:* www.rivertechnicaldesign.com	Medina	OH	44256	330-241-5397		695
River Terrace Inn 1600 Soscol Ave. *TF:* 866-627-2386 ■ *Web:* www.riverterraceinn.com	Napa	CA	94559	707-320-6910		379
River Trading Company LTD 10900 89th Ave N *Web:* www.rtcltd.com	Maple Grove	MN	55369	763-463-3400		791
River Valley Coop 254 E 90th St. *TF:* 800-247-0797 ■ *Web:* www.rivervalleycoop.com	Davenport	IA	52807	563-452-3805		276
River Valley Telecommunications Coop & Cable Tv 1607 Rolling St. *Web:* www.ruthventel.com	Ruthven	IA	51358	712-837-5522		116
River Valley Veterinary Service Inc 15900 Jordan Ave SE *Web:* rivervalleyveterinary.com	Prior Lake	MN	55372	952-447-4118		794
River View Local School District 26496 SR- 60 *Web:* www.river-view.k12.oh.us	Warsaw	OH	43844	740-824-3521		685
River Village PO Box 208 **Fax Area Code:* 336 ■ *TF:* 800-242-0115 ■ *Web:* www.river-village.com	Mayodan	NC	27027	800-242-0115	427-9759*	361
River Walk 110 Broadway Ste 500 *TF:* 800-417-4139 ■ *Web:* www.thesanantonioriverwalk.com	San Antonio	TX	78204	210-227-4262	212-7602	50-6
River West Meeting Associates Inc 3616 N Lincoln Ave *TF:* 888-534-5292 ■ *Web:* www.riverwestmeetings.com	Chicago	IL	60613	773-755-3000		463
River's Edge Hotel & Spa 0455 SW Hamilton Ct. *Web:* www.riversedgehotel.com	Portland	OR	97239	503-802-5800		379
River's Edge Resort Cottages 4200 Boat St. *TF:* 800-770-3343 ■ *Web:* www.riversedge.net	Fairbanks	AK	99709	907-474-0286	474-3665	379
Rivera Law Offices PLLC 1800 Cooper Point Rd SW Ste 14. *Web:* riveralawoffices.com	Olympia	WA	98502	360-705-8200		41
Riverbank State Park 679 Riverside Dr. *Web:* parks.ny.gov	New York	NY	10031	212-694-3600		565
Riverbank Veterinary Clinic 2814 Maybank Hwy *Web:* riverbankvet.com	Johns Island	SC	29455	843-277-2250		794
Riverbanks Zoo & Botanical Garden 500 Wildlife Pkwy. *Web:* www.riverbanks.org	Columbia	SC	29210	803-779-8717	253-6381	823
Riverbay Corp 2049 Bartow Ave *Web:* www.riverbaycorp.com	Bronx	NY	10475	718-320-3300	671-4733	652
Riverbend Maximum Security Institution 7475 Cockrill Bend Blvd. *Web:* www.tn.gov	Nashville	TN	37243	615-350-3100	350-3400	213
Riverbend Music Ctr 6295 Kellogg Ave *Web:* www.riverbend.org	Cincinnati	OH	45230	513-232-5882		572
Riverbend Technology 850 Elder Dr *Web:* www.riverbendtech.com	West Sacramento	CA	95605	916-372-1766		180
RiverCenter Adler Theatre 136 E Third St. *Web:* www.riverctr.com	Davenport	IA	52801	563-326-8500	326-8505	205
RiverCenter for the Performing Arts 900 Broadway Po Box 2425 *Web:* www.rivercenter.org	Columbus	GA	31902	706-256-3607		749
Riverchase Galleria 2000 Riverchase Galleria *Web:* www.riverchasegalleria.com	Hoover	AL	35244	205-985-3020		460
Rivercrest Realty Assoc 8816 Six Forks Rd Ste 201 *Web:* rivercrestrealty.com	Raleigh	NC	27615	919-846-4046		652
Rivercrest Technologies Inc 3811 Creekside Ln *Web:* www.rtihosted.us	Holmen	WI	54636	608-779-2000		180
Riverdale Country School 5250 Fieldston Rd *Web:* www.riverdale.edu	Bronx	NY	10471	718-549-8810	519-2795	685
Riverdale Global 1 Walnut St *Web:* riverdaleglobal.com	Perth Amboy	NJ	08861	732-376-9300		608
Riverdale Mills Corp 130 Riverdale St *TF:* 800-762-6374 ■ *Web:* riverdale.com	Northbridge	MA	01534	508-234-8715	234-9593	279
Riverdale Plating & Heat Treating Inc 680 W 134th St. *Web:* www.rpht.com	Riverdale	IL	60827	708-849-2050		484
Riveredge Nature Ctr 4458 W Hawthorne Dr PO Box 26. *TF:* 800-287-8098 ■ *Web:* www.riveredgenaturecenter.org	Newburg	WI	53060	262-375-2715		50-5
Riveredge Resort Hotel 17 Holland St *TF:* 800-365-6987 ■ *Web:* riveredge.com	Alexandria Bay	NY	13607	315-482-9917	482-5010	379
River-FM 107.5 (CHR), The 55 Music Sq W. *Web:* 1075theriver.iheart.com	Nashville	TN	37203	615-664-2400		645-106
Riverfork Federal Credit Union 711 N Washington St Ste 101. *TF:* 800-991-4965 ■ *Web:* riverforkfcu.com	Grand Forks	ND	58203	701-775-0593	780-9545	219
Riverfront Barbeque & Grill 300 Water St. *Web:* riverfrontbbq.com	Augusta	ME	04330	207-622-8899		671
Riverfront Investment Group LLC 1214 E Cary St *Web:* www.riverfrontig.com	Richmond	VA	23219	804-549-4800		401
Riverfront Times 6358 Delmar Blvd Ste 200 *Web:* www.riverfronttimes.com	Saint Louis	MO	63130	314-754-5966	754-5955	532-5
Rivergate Mall 1000 Rivergate Pkwy Ste 1 *Web:* www.rivergate-mall.com	Goodlettsville	TN	37072	615-859-3458		460
Riverhawk Company LP 215 Clinton Rd *Web:* riverhawk.com	New Hartford	NY	13413	315-768-4855		295
Riverhead Building Supply Corp 1093 Pulaski St *TF:* 800-378-3650 ■ *Web:* www.rbscorp.com	Riverhead	NY	11901	631-727-3650	727-7713	191-3
Riverhead Raceway PO Box 1743 *Web:* www.riverheadraceway.com	Riverhead	NY	11901	631-842-7223		515
Riverland Community College 1900 Eigth Ave NW. *TF:* 800-247-5039 ■ *Web:* www.riverland.edu	Austin	MN	55912	507-433-0600	433-0515	162
Riverland Energy Co-op N28988 State Rd 93 PO Box 277 *TF:* 800-411-9115 ■ *Web:* www.riverlandenergy.com	Arcadia	WI	54612	608-323-3381		245
Rivermaid Travelling Co PO Box 350 *Web:* www.rivermaid.com	Lodi	CA	95240	209-369-3586	369-5465	11-1
RiverMead Retirement Community 150 RiverMead Rd *TF:* 800-200-5433 ■ *Web:* www.rivermead.org	Peterborough	NH	03458	603-924-0062		672
Rivermoor Engineering LLC 146 Front St *Web:* rivermoorengineering.com	Scituate	MA	02066	781-545-2848		261
RIVEROAK Technical College 415 SW Pinewood Dr *Web:* riveroakcollege.com	Live Oak	FL	32064	386-647-4200	364-4698	167-3
RiverPoint Group LLC 2200 E Devon Ave Ste 385 *TF:* 800-297-5601 ■ *Web:* riverpoint.com	Des Plaines	IL	60018	847-233-9600	233-9602	180
Riverrun International Film Festival 305 W Fourth St Ste 1A *Web:* www.riverrunfilm.com	Winston-Salem	NC	27101	336-724-1502	724-1112	282
Rivers Bridge State Historic Site 325 State Park Rd *Web:* southcarolinaparks.com	Ehrhardt	SC	29081	803-267-3675		565
Rivers Metal Products Inc 3100 N 38th St. *Web:* www.riversmetal.com	Lincoln	NE	68504	402-466-2329		295
Rivers Oceans & Mountains Adventures Inc (ROAM) 24-622 Front St *TF:* 888-639-1114 ■ *Web:* iroamtheworld.com	Nelson	BC	V1L4B7	888-639-1114		760
Riverside Air Service 6741 Gemende Dr. *Web:* www.ralair.com	Riverside	CA	92504	951-321-0091	352-1855	167-3
Riverside Animal Clinic 905 W Central St *Web:* rivanclinic.com	Springfield	MN	56087	507-723-5211		794
Riverside Art Museum 3425 Mission Inn Ave. *Web:* www.riversideartmuseum.org	Riverside	CA	92501	951-684-7111		520
Riverside Art Shop 1600 Grand Army Hwy *Web:* www.riversideart.com	Somerset	MA	02726	508-672-6735		45
Riverside Arts Ctr 76 N Huron St *Web:* www.riversidearts.org	Ypsilanti	MI	48197	734-480-2787		572
Riverside Campus of Ottawa Hospital 1967 Riverside Dr. *Web:* www.ottawahospital.on.ca	Ottawa	ON	K1H7W9	613-738-7100	761-5292	374-2
Riverside Chemical Company Inc (RCC) 871 River Rd. *TF:* 800-748-2436 ■ *Web:* www.rivchem.com	North Tonawanda	NY	14120	716-692-1350	692-1485	146
Riverside City Hall 3900 Main St 5th Fl *Web:* riversideca.gov	Riverside	CA	92522	951-826-5557		337
Riverside City Public Library 3581 Mission Inn Ave. *Web:* riversideca.gov	Riverside	CA	92501	951-826-5201	826-5407	434-3
Riverside Clay Company Inc 201 Truss Ferry Rd *Web:* www.riversiderefractories.com	Pell City	AL	35128	205-338-3366		503-2
Riverside Clubhouse 2033 Riverside Blvd *Web:* www.riversideclubhouse.com	Sacramento	CA	95818	916-448-9988		671
Riverside Community College 4800 Magnolia Ave. *Web:* www.rcc.edu	Riverside	CA	92506	951-222-8000		162
Riverside Community Credit Union 185 N Fraser Ave *Web:* riversidecu.com	Kankakee	IL	60901	815-933-1101	933-1181	219
Riverside Convention & Visitors Bureau 3750 University Ave Ste 175. *TF:* 800-600-7080 ■ *Web:* www.riversidecvb.com	Riverside	CA	92501	951-222-4700		206
Riverside Correctional Facility 777 W Riverside Dr. *Web:* www.michigan.gov	Ionia	MI	48846	616-527-4174		213
Riverside County Record 4080 Lemon St. *Web:* www.countyofriverside.us	Riverside	CA	92501	951-955-1000		532-4
Riverside Dental Group 7251 Magnolia Ave. *Web:* www.riversidedentalgroup.com	Riverside	CA	92504	951-689-5031		227
Riverside Electronics Ltd 1 Riverside Dr. *Web:* www.riversideelectronics.com	Lewiston	MN	55952	507-523-3220	523-2831	625
Riverside Farnsley-Moremen Landing 7410 Moorman Rd *Web:* www.riverside-landing.org	Louisville	KY	40272	502-935-6809	935-6821	50-3
Riverside Foods Inc 2520 Wilson St *TF:* 800-678-4511 ■ *Web:* riversidefoods.com	Two Rivers	WI	54241	800-678-4511		296-14
Riverside Ford 2625 Ludington St. *TF:* 877-774-3171 ■ *Web:* www.riversidefordescanaba.com	Escanaba	MI	49829	877-774-3171		57
Riverside Ford Inc 2089 Riverside Dr. *TF:* 800-395-6210 ■ *Web:* www.riversideford.net	Macon	GA	31204	478-464-2900		57
Riverside Forest Products Inc 2912 Professional Pkwy PO Box 211663 *TF:* 888-855-8733 ■ *Web:* www.riversideforest.com	Augusta	GA	30907	706-855-5500	863-3362	191-3
Riverside Furniture Corp PO Box 1427 *Web:* www.riverside-furniture.com	Fort Smith	AR	72901	479-785-8100		319-2
Riverside General Hospital (RGH) *Houston Recovery Ctr* 3204 Ennis St. *Web:* riversidegeneralhospital.org	Houston	TX	77004	713-526-2441		726

Phone | Fax | Class

Riverside Health System
701 Town Center Dr Ste 1000 .... Newport News VA 23606 757-534-7000 534-7087 353
TF: 800-759-1001 ■ *Web:* riversideonline.com

Riverside Hotel
620 E Las Olas Blvd .... Fort Lauderdale FL 33301 954-467-0671 462-2148 379
Web: www.riversidehotel.com

Riverside Machine Company Inc
3306 N Hawthorne St .... Chattanooga TN 37406 423-698-4597 624-6943 454
TF: 800-754-9330 ■ *Web:* www.riversidemachineinc.com

Riverside Machine Works Inc
6301 Baldwin Ave .... Riverside CA 92509 951-685-7416 454
Web: www.riversidemachineworks.com

Riverside Manufacturing LLC
14510 Lima Rd .... Fort Wayne IN 46818 260-637-4470 203
Web: www.riversidemfg.com

Riverside Marine Inc 600 Riverside Dr .... Essex MD 21221 410-686-1500 686-3345 90
TF: 800-448-6872 ■ *Web:* www.riversideboats.com

Riverside Medical Clinic
6405 Day St .... Riverside CA 92507 951-683-6370 186
Web: riversidemedicalclinic.com

Riverside Medical Ctr (RMC)
350 N Wall St .... Kankakee IL 60901 815-933-1671 374-3
Web: www.riversidehealthcare.org

Riverside Metropolitan Museum
3580 Mission Inn Ave .... Riverside CA 92501 951-826-5273 369-4970 520
Web: riversideca.gov

Riverside Military Academy
2001 Riverside Dr .... Gainesville GA 30501 770-532-6251 622
TF: 800-462-2338 ■ *Web:* www.riversidemilitary.com

Riverside National Cemetery
22495 Van Buren Blvd .... Riverside CA 92518 951-653-8417 653-5233 136
Web: www.cem.va.gov

Riverside Paper Company Inc
3505 NW 112th St .... Miami FL 33167 305-722-0110 559
Web: www.rpconline.com

Riverside Plastics Inc
900 Washington St .... Bonaparte IA 52620 319-592-3166 592-3117 604
Web: www.rpimolding.com

Riverside Scrap Iron 2993 Sixth St .... Riverside CA 92507 951-686-2129 686
Web: www.riversidemetalrecycling.com

Riverside Spline & Gear Inc
1390 S Parker St .... Marine City MI 48039 810-765-8302 765-9595 483
Web: www.splineandgear.com

Riverside Staffing Services Inc
2322 E Kimberly Rd Paul Revere Sq Ste 20S .... Davenport IA 52807 563-355-5212 355-5437 260
Web: www.riversidestaffing.com

Riverside Transit Agency (RTA)
1825 Third St PO Box 59968 .... Riverside CA 92517 951-565-5000 468
TF: 800-800-7821 ■ *Web:* www.riversidetransit.com

Riverside Travel Group Inc
3100 525 First St .... Lake Oswego OR 97034 503-255-2950 772
Web: www.riversidetravel.com

Riverside Unified School District (RUSD)
3380 14th St PO Box 2800 .... Riverside CA 92501 951-788-7135 778-5669 685
TF: 800-782-7463 ■ *Web:* www.riversideunified.org

Riverside University Health System
26520 Cactus Ave .... Moreno Valley CA 92555 951-486-4000 374-3
Web: www.ruhealth.org

Riverside Veterinary Hospital
512 S Second Ave .... Elizabeth PA 15037 412-384-6884 794
Web: riversidevethospitalpc.com

Riverside Vocational Technical School
8000 Correction Cir PO Box 1179 .... Pine Bluff AR 71603 870-267-6900 267-6902 800
Web: www.riversidevtech.com

Riverside Youth Correctional Facility
2 Riverside Rd PO Box 88 .... Boulder MT 59632 406-225-4500 412
Web: mt.gov

Riverside Zoo
1600 S Beltline Hwy W .... Scottsbluff NE 69361 308-630-6236 823
Web: riversidediscoverycenter.org

Riverside-San Bernardino County Indian Health Inc (RSBCIH)
11555 1/2 Potrero Rd .... Banning CA 92220 951-849-4761 353
TF: 800-732-8805 ■ *Web:* www.rsbcihi.org

Riverso Associates Inc
1088 Central Park Ave .... Scarsdale NY 10583 914-723-3474 261
Web: riversoassociates.com

Riverstone Billings Inn
880 N 29th St .... Billings MT 59101 406-252-6800 379
TF: 800-231-7782 ■ *Web:* www.riversageinns.com

RiverStone Group Inc 1701 Fifth Ave .... Moline IL 61265 309-757-8250 182
TF: 800-906-2489 ■ *Web:* www.riverstonegroup.com

Riverstone Holdings LLC
712 Fifth Ave 36th Fl .... New York NY 10019 212-993-0076 360-3
Web: www.riverstonellc.com

Riverton Elementary School
209 N Seventh St .... Riverton IL 62561 217-629-6001 685
Web: rivertonschools.org

Riverton Memorial Hospital LLC
1320 Bishop Randall Dr .... Riverton WY 82501 307-856-4161 857-3571 374-3
Web: www.sagewesthealthcare.com

RiverTown Crossings
3700 Rivertown Pkwy .... Grandville MI 49418 616-257-5000 460
Web: www.rivertowncrossings.com

Rivertown School of Beauty
4747-E Hamilton Rd .... Columbus GA 31904 706-653-8032 653-7109 685
Web: www.rivertownschoolofbeauty.com

Rivervalley Behavioral Health Hospital
1100 Walnut St PO Box 1637 .... Owensboro KY 42302 270-689-6800 726
TF: 800-737-0696 ■ *Web:* www.rvbh.com

Riverview Animal Clinic PC
4640 Hwy 280 S .... Birmingham AL 35242 205-991-9580 794
Web: riverviewanimalclinic.net

Riverview Bancorp Inc
900 Washington St Ste 900 .... Vancouver WA 98660 360-693-6650 360-2
NASDAQ: RVSB ■ *Web:* www.riverviewbank.com

Riverview Estates 303 Bank Ave .... Riverton NJ 08077 856-829-2274 371
Web: www.riverviewestates.org

Riverview Hospital
395 Westfield Rd .... Noblesville IN 46060 317-773-0760 374-3
TF: 800-523-6001 ■ *Web:* riverview.org

Riverview Intermediate Unit Number 6 Administrative Services
270 Mayfield Rd .... Clarion PA 16214 814-226-7103 685
TF: 800-672-7123 ■ *Web:* www.riu6.org

Riverview Medical Ctr
1 Riverview Plz .... Red Bank NJ 07701 732-530-2305 374-3
Web: www.meridianhealth.com

Riverview Psychiatric Ctr
250 Arsenal St 11 State House Stn .... Augusta ME 04332 207-624-4600 374-5
TF: 888-261-6684 ■ *Web:* www.maine.gov

Riverview Regional Medical Ctr
600 S Third St .... Gadsden AL 35901 256-543-5200 543-5888 374-3
Web: www.riverviewregional.com

Riverwalk Casino Hotel
1046 Warrenton Rd .... Vicksburg MS 39180 601-634-0100 452
TF: 866-615-9125 ■ *Web:* www.riverwalkvicksburg.com

Riverwalk Marketplace
500 Port of New Orleans Pl .... New Orleans LA 70130 504-522-1555 460
Web: www.riverwalkneworleans.com

Riverwalk Plaza Hotel
100 Villita St .... San Antonio TX 78205 210-225-1234 707
Web: www.riverwalkplaza.com

Riverwalk Theatre 228 Museum Dr .... Lansing MI 48933 517-482-5700 482-9812 572
Web: www.riverwalktheatre.com

Riverway Lobster House
1338 Massachusetts 28 .... South Yarmouth MA 02664 508-398-2172 671
Web: riverwaylobsterhouserestaurant.com

Riverwise Inc 70 1/2 E 4th St .... Winona MN 55987 507-454-5949 344
TF: 800-303-8201 ■ *Web:* www.riverwise.com

Riverwood Ctr 1485 M139 .... Benton Harbor MI 49022 269-925-0585 726
TF: 800-336-0341 ■ *Web:* www.riverwoodcenter.org

Riverwood Solutions
3964 Rivermark Plz .... Santa Clara CA 95054 408-422-9554 463
Web: rwsops.com

Riveter, The 5021 Colorado Ave S .... Seattle WA 98134 206-492-5809 352
Web: theriveter.co

Riviana Foods Inc PO Box 2636 .... Houston TX 77252 713-529-3251 296-23
Web: www.riviana.com

Rivier College 420 S Main St .... Nashua NH 03060 603-888-1311 891-1799 166
TF: 800-447-4843 ■ *Web:* www.rivier.edu

Riviera Advisors Inc
2222 East St Ste 3 .... Long Beach CA 90853 800-635-9063 193
TF: 800-635-9063 ■ *Web:* rivieraadvisors.com

Riviera Beach Public Library
600 W Blue Heron Blvd .... Riviera Beach FL 33404 561-845-4195 434-3
Web: rivierabch.com

Riviera Finance 220 Ave I .... Redondo Beach CA 90277 310-540-3993 454-8122* 272
**Fax Area Code:* 651 ■ *TF:* 800-872-7484 ■ *Web:* www.rivierafinance.com

Riviera Fitness Centers
3908 Veterans Blvd .... Metairie LA 70002 504-454-5855 454-7717 354
Web: rivierafitnesscenters.com

Riviera Hotel 1431 Robson St .... Vancouver BC V6G1C1 604-685-1301 685-1335 379
TF: 888-699-5222 ■ *Web:* www.rivieravancouver.com

Riviera Telephone Co
103 S 8th PO Box 997 .... Riviera TX 78379 361-296-3232 296-3125 387
TF: 877-296-3232 ■ *Web:* www.rivnet.com

Riviere Insurance Agency Inc
412 Canal Blvd .... Thibodaux LA 70301 985-447-2625 390
Web: riviereinsurance.com

Rivkin Radler LLP 926 RXR Plz .... Uniondale NY 11556 516-357-3000 428
Web: www.rivkinradler.com

RIWI Corp, The 459 Bloor St W Ste 200 .... Toronto ON M5S1X9 416-205-9984 224
Web: riwi.com

RIX Industries Inc
4900 Industrial Way .... Benicia CA 94510 707-747-5900 172
Web: www.rixindustries.com

Rix North America LLC
2717 Topside Rd Ste B .... Louisville TN 37777 865-977-7475 806
Web: www.rix.co.jp

Rizzetta & Company Inc
3434 Colwell Ave Ste 200 .... Tampa FL 33614 813-933-5571 514-0401 463
Web: rizzetta.com

Rizzieri Aveda School for Beauty & Wellness
8200 Town Center Blvd .... Voorhees NJ 08043 856-985-5500 685
Web: www.rizzierischools.com

Rizzoli International Publications Inc
300 Park Ave S 3rd Fl .... New York NY 10010 212-387-3400 387-3535 637-2
Web: www.rizzoliusa.com

RJ & Makay LLC
100 S Ridge St Ste 101 .... Breckenridge CO 80424 970-306-0600 138

RJ Burnside & Associates Ltd
15 Townline .... Orangeville ON L9W3R4 519-941-5331 256
TF: 800-265-9662 ■ *Web:* www.rjburnside.com

RJ Computer Networks Inc
13215 E Penn St Ste 210 .... Whittier CA 90602 562-464-3644 464-3641 180
Web: rjcomputers.com

RJ Lee Group Inc 350 Hochberg Rd .... Monroeville PA 15146 724-325-1776 733-1799 417
TF: 800-860-1775 ■ *Web:* www.rjlg.com

RJ Marshall Co 26776 W 12-Mile Rd .... Southfield MI 48034 248-353-4100 338-7900* 724
**Fax Area Code:* 800 ■ *TF:* 888-514-8600 ■ *Web:* www.rjmarshall.com

RJ O'Brien & Assoc
222 S Riverside Plz Ste 900 .... Chicago IL 60606 312-373-5000 373-5238 169
Web: www.rjobrien.com

RJ Reynolds Tobacco Co
401 N Main St .... Winston-Salem NC 27102 336-741-5000 741-2998 756
Web: www.rjrt.com

RJ Rippey Od PA 1635A S Voss Rd .... Houston TX 77057 713-954-2020 954-2046 543

RJ Singer International Inc
4801 W Jefferson Blvd PO Box 78189 .... Los Angeles CA 90016 323-735-1717 453
Web: www.rjsinger.com

RJ Thomas Manufacturing Company Inc
PO Box 946 .... Cherokee IA 51012 712-225-5115 225-5796 319-4
TF: 800-762-5002 ■ *Web:* www.pilotrock.com

RJ Torching Inc 5061 Energy Dr .... Flint MI 48505 810-785-9759 492

RJC Designs Inc
1916 Crain Hwy S Ste 10 .... Glen Burnie MD 21061 410-760-7712 196
Web: rjcdesigns.com

	Phone	Fax	Class
RJD (Richard J. Donovan Correctional Facility at Rock Mountain) 480 Alta Rd. . . . . San Diego CA 92179 *Web:* www.cdcr.ca.gov	619-661-6500	661-6253	213
RJE Business Interiors Inc 623 Broadway St. . . . . Cincinnati OH 45202 *TF:* 800-236-8232 ■ *Web:* www.rjebusinessinteriors.com	513-641-3700		393
RJG Inc 3111 Park Dr . . . . . Traverse City MI 49686 *Web:* www.rjginc.com	231-947-3111		201
RJH Air Conditioning & Refrige 12232 Distribution Pl . . . . . Beltsville MD 20705 *Web:* rjhhvacr.com	301-776-7270		189-10
RJK Partners LLC 1756 Forest Oaks Dr. . . . . Hudson OH 44236 *Web:* www.rjkpartners.com	330-414-8705		196
RJM Sales Inc 454 Park Ave . . . . . Scotch Plains NJ 07076 *TF:* 800-752-9055 ■ *Web:* rjmsales.com	908-322-7880		358
RJM Systems Inc 712 Madelyn Dr . . . . . Des Plaines IL 60016 *Web:* www.rjmsys.com	847-228-1130	228-1233	178-1
RJM Wireless Consulting Services 12300 Perry Hwy Ste 206. . . . . Wexford PA 15090 *Web:* rjmwireless.com	724-934-1055		196
RJN Group Inc 200 W Front St. . . . . Wheaton IL 60187 *TF:* 800-227-7838 ■ *Web:* rjn.com	630-682-4700	682-4754	192
RJR Fashion Fabrics 2610 Columbia St Ste B. . . . . Torrance CA 90503 *TF:* 800-422-5426 ■ *Web:* www.rjrfabrics.com	310-222-8782	222-8792	270
RJR Innovations 1400 St Laurent Blvd . . . . . Ottawa ON K1K4H4 *Web:* rjrinnovations.com	613-233-1915		193
RJS & Associates Inc 1675 Sabre St. . . . . Hayward CA 94545 *Web:* www.rjsdesignbuild.com	510-670-9111		135
RK (Rihm Kenworth) 425 Concord St S. . . . . South Saint Paul MN 55075 *TF:* 800-988-8235 ■ *Web:* www.rihmkenworth.com	651-646-7833	646-0630	516
RK & K 81 Mosher St . . . . . Baltimore MD 21217 *Web:* www.rkk.com	410-728-2900		261
RK Black Inc 8343 E 32nd St N. . . . . Wichita KS 67226 *Web:* www.rkblack.com	316-636-5400		321
RK Consulting LLC 1313 Valley View Rd Ste 201 . . . . . Glendale CA 91202 *Web:* rkconsulting.com	818-406-9968		180
RK Controls 5901 Corvette St . . . . . Commerce CA 90040 *Web:* www.rkcontrols.com	323-887-7066		358
RK Electronics Inc 7405 Industrial Row. . . . . Mason OH 45040 *TF:* 800-543-4936 ■ *Web:* www.rke.com	800-543-4936		203
RK Engineering Group Inc 4000 Werly Pl Ste 280 . . . . . Newport Beach CA 92660 *Web:* rkengineer.com	949-474-0809	474-0902	261
RK Inc 6962 State Rte 17. . . . . West Plains MO 65775 *Web:* www.rkincorporated.com	417-256-9225		695
RK Mechanical Inc 3800 Xanthia St. . . . . Denver CO 80238 *TF:* 877-576-9696 ■ *Web:* www.rkmi.com	303-355-9696	355-8666	189-10
RK Taylor & Assoc 2890 N Main St Ste 305. . . . . Walnut Creek CA 94597 *Web:* www.rktaylor.com	925-944-7660	944-7665	2
RKA Petroleum Companies Inc 28340 Wick Rd. . . . . Romulus MI 48174 *TF:* 866-509-3288 ■ *Web:* www.rkapetroleum.com	800-875-3835		579
RKI Inc 2301 Central Pkwy . . . . . Houston TX 77092 *TF:* 800-346-8988 ■ *Web:* www.rki-us.com	713-688-4414	688-8982	470
RKL eSolutions LLC 1800 Fruitville Pk. . . . . Lancaster PA 17604 *TF:* 888-222-8827 ■ *Web:* www.rklesolutions.com	717-735-9109		631
RKO Pictures Inc 11301 W Olympic Blvd Ste 510 . . . . . Los Angeles CA 90064 *Web:* www.rko.com	310-277-0707	566-8940	514
RKR Hess Associates Inc 112 N Courtland St. . . . . East Stroudsburg PA 18301 *Web:* www.rkrhess.com	570-421-1550	421-6720	261
RL Adams Plastics Inc 5955 Crossroads Commerce . . . . . Wyoming MI 49519 *Web:* www.goadams.com	616-261-4400		601
RL Deppmann Co 20929 Bridge St . . . . . Southfield MI 48033 *TF:* 800-589-6120 ■ *Web:* www.deppmann.com	248-354-3710		641
RL Drake Co 710 Pleasant Valley Dr. . . . . Springboro OH 45066 *TF:* 800-276-4523 ■ *Web:* www.rldrake.com	937-746-4556	806-1510	647
RL Hudson & Co 2000 W Tacoma . . . . . Broken Arrow OK 74012 *Web:* rlhudson.com	918-259-6600		608
RL Winston Rod Co 500 S Main St. . . . . Twin Bridges MT 59754 *TF:* 866-946-7637 ■ *Web:* winstonrods.com	406-684-5674	684-5533	710
RLA Insurance Intermediaries LLC 75 Federal St Ste 1250. . . . . Boston MA 02114 *Web:* rlainsurance.com	617-419-2600		390
RLB (Rider Levett Bucknall) 4343 E Camelback Rd Ste 350 . . . . . Phoenix AZ 85018 *Web:* rlb.com	602-443-4848		194
RLB (RLB Food Distributors LP) 2 Dedrick Pl . . . . . West Caldwell NJ 07007 *Web:* www.rlbfood.com	973-575-9526	575-1019	297-7
RLB Food Distributors LP (RLB) 2 Dedrick Pl . . . . . West Caldwell NJ 07007 *Web:* www.rlbfood.com	973-575-9526	575-1019	297-7
RLC Electronics Inc 83 Radio Cir Dr. . . . . Mount Kisco NY 10549 *Web:* www.rlcelectronics.com	914-241-1334	241-1753	253
RLE Technologies Inc 104 Racquette Dr . . . . . Fort Collins CO 80524 *TF:* 800-518-1519 ■ *Web:* rletech.com	970-484-6510		693
RLI Press PO Box 1115. . . . . Wilsonville OR 97070 *TF:* 888-522-8747 ■ *Web:* www.roadtripdream.com	888-522-8747		637-2
RLJ Companies LLC, The 3 Bethesda Metro Ctr Ste 1000. . . . . Bethesda MD 20814 *TF:* 888-600-7655 ■ *Web:* www.rljcompanies.com	301-280-7700	280-7750	360-3
Rlj Financial Services Inc 1788 Mitchell Rd Ste 102. . . . . Ceres CA 95307 *TF:* 800-240-1050 ■ *Web:* www.rljfinancial.com	209-538-7758		138
RLM Communications Inc 1027 E Manchester Rd . . . . . Spring Lake NC 28390 *TF:* 877-223-1345 ■ *Web:* www.rlm-communications.com	910-223-1350		179
RLM Public Relations Inc 228 E 45 St 11th Fl. . . . . New York NY 10017 *Web:* rlmpr.com	212-741-5106		636
RLP (Red Letter Press) 4710 University Way NE Ste 100 . . . . . Seattle WA 98105 *Web:* www.redletterpress.org	206-985-8965		637-2
RLR Management Consulting Inc 77806 Flora Rd Ste D. . . . . Palm Desert CA 92211 *TF:* 888-757-7330 ■ *Web:* rlrmgmt.com	760-200-4800	200-4825	193
RLS Logistics 2260 Industrial Way . . . . . Vineland NJ 08360 *Web:* www.rlslogistics.com	856-691-2040		196
RLTV 5525 Research Park Dr 2nd Fl . . . . . Baltimore MD 21228 *TF:* 800-754-8464 ■ *Web:* www.rl.tv	800-754-8464		116
RM (Rickard Metals Inc) 2043 Elm Ct . . . . . Ontario CA 91761 *Web:* www.rickardmetals.com	909-947-4922		492
RM Bradley 1 Financial Plz . . . . . Hartford CT 06103 *Web:* www.rmbradley.com	860-278-2040		652
RM Burritt Motors Inc 340 Rt 104 E . . . . . Oswego NY 13126 *Web:* www.burrittchevy.com	315-343-8948		60
RM Design Studio Ltd 850 W Bartlett Rd Ste 1c. . . . . Bartlett IL 60103 *Web:* www.rmdesignstudio.com	630-540-1222	540-0212	396
RM Education 310 Barnstable Rd . . . . . Hyannis MA 02601 *Web:* shop.rm.com	508-862-0700		242
RM Kerner Co 2208 E 33rd St . . . . . Erie PA 16510 *Web:* www.rmkco.com	814-898-2000		454
RM King Co 315 N Marks Ave . . . . . Fresno CA 93706 *Web:* www.rmking.com	559-266-0258	266-1672	273
RM Mechanical Inc 5998 W Gowen Rd . . . . . Boise ID 83709 *Web:* www.rmmechanical.net	208-362-0131		256
RM Palmer Co 77 S Second Ave . . . . . West Reading PA 19611 *Web:* www.rmpalmer.com	610-372-8971		296-8
RM Strategic Marketing 800 W End Ave . . . . . New York NY 10025 *Web:* www.rmstrategicmarketing.com	212-961-1120		194
RM Towill Corp 2024 N King St Ste 200 . . . . . Honolulu HI 96819 *Web:* www.rmtowill.com	808-842-1133	842-1937	261
RMA (Risk Management Assn) 1801 Market St Ste 300 . . . . . Philadelphia PA 19103 *TF:* 800-677-7621 ■ *Web:* www.rmahq.org	215-446-4000	446-4101	49-2
RMA Electronics Inc 35 Pond Park Rd Unit No 12. . . . . Hingham MA 02043 *Web:* www.rmaelectronics.com	781-749-9700	749-9707	246
RMA Group Inc 12130 Santa Margarita Ct. . . . . Rancho Cucamonga CA 91730 *TF:* 800-480-4808 ■ *Web:* rmacompanies.com	909-989-1751		261
RMC (Riverside Medical Ctr) 350 N Wall St. . . . . Kankakee IL 60901 *Web:* www.riversidehealthcare.org	815-933-1671		374-3
RMC (Ridgeview Medical Ctr) 500 S Maple St. . . . . Waconia MN 55387 *TF:* 800-967-4620 ■ *Web:* www.ridgeviewmedical.org	952-442-2191	442-6524	374-3
RMC (Rich Metals Co) 510 Schmidt Rd. . . . . Davenport IA 52802 *Web:* richmetalsco.com	563-322-0975	322-8774	686
RMC Medical 7940 A State Rd. . . . . Philadelphia PA 19136 *Web:* rmcmedical.com	215-824-4100	824-1371	477
RMC Research Corp 1000 Market St Bldg 2 . . . . . Portsmouth NH 03801 *TF:* 800-258-0802 ■ *Web:* rmcresearchcorporation.com	603-422-8888		743
RMCF (Rocky Mountain Chocolate Factory Inc) 265 Turner Dr. . . . . Durango CO 81303 *NASDAQ: RMCF* ■ *TF:* 888-525-2462 ■ *Web:* www.rmcf.com	970-247-4943		123
RMCN Credit Services Inc 1611 Wilmeth Rd Ste B. . . . . McKinney TX 75069 *TF:* 888-469-7372 ■ *Web:* www.RepairMyCreditNow.com	972-529-0900	562-0225	160
RMCSJ (Regional Medical Center of San Jose) 225 N Jackson Ave. . . . . San Jose CA 95116 *TF:* 800-307-7135 ■ *Web:* regionalmedicalsanjose.com	408-259-5000	729-2884	374-3
RMD (Radiation Monitoring Devices Inc) 44 Hunt St Ste 2. . . . . Watertown MA 02472 *Web:* www.dynasil.com	617-668-6975		472
RMD Advertising 6116 Cleveland Ave. . . . . Columbus OH 43231 *Web:* www.rmdadvertising.com	614-794-2008		4
RMD Instruments LLC 44 Hunt St . . . . . Watertown MA 02472 *Web:* rmdinc.com	617-668-6801		492
RME360 4805 Independence Pkwy Ste 250 . . . . . Tampa FL 33634 *TF:* 888-383-8770 ■ *Web:* www.rme360.com	888-383-8770		5
RMF (Rocky Mountain Fabrication) 1125 West 2300 North PO Box 16409 . . . . . Salt Lake City UT 84116 *TF:* 888-763-5307 ■ *Web:* www.rmf-slc.com	801-596-2400	322-2702	91
RMF Engineering Inc 5520 Research Pk Dr Ste 300. . . . . Baltimore MD 21228 *TF:* 800-938-5760 ■ *Web:* www.rmf.com	410-576-0505		261
RMF Printing Technologies Inc 50 Pearl St . . . . . Lancaster NY 14086 *TF:* 800-828-7999 ■ *Web:* www.rmfprinting.com	716-683-7500		627
RMF Steel Products Co 4417 E 119th St . . . . . Grandview MO 64030 *Web:* rmfworks.com	816-765-4101	765-0067	298
RMG Financial Consulting Inc 813 E Ballard Ave . . . . . Colbert WA 99005 *Web:* rmgfinancial.com	509-468-2956		196
RMH (Ross Memorial Hospital) 10 Angeline St N. . . . . Lindsay ON K9V4M8 *TF:* 800-510-7365 ■ *Web:* rmh.org	705-324-6111		374-2
RMH (Ronald McDonald House) 2524 N State St. . . . . Jackson MS 39216 *Web:* www.rmhcms.org	601-981-5683	981-3613	373
RMH (Roxborough Memorial Hospital) 5800 Ridge Ave. . . . . Philadelphia PA 19128 *Web:* www.roxboroughmemorial.com	215-483-9900	483-8012	374-3
RMHC (Ronald McDonald House Charities of Kentuckiana) 550 S First St . . . . . Louisville KY 40202 *Web:* rmhc-kentuckiana.org	502-581-1416		373
Omaha 620 S 38th Ave . . . . . Omaha NE 68105 *Web:* www.rmhcomaha.org	402-346-9377		373
RMHCA (Ronald McDonald House Charities of Arkansas) *Little Rock* 1009 Wolfe St . . . . . Little Rock AR 72202 *Web:* www.rmhcarkansas.org	501-374-1956		373

Name / Address	City	State	ZIP	Phone	Fax	Class
RMI (Ralph Moyle Inc) 23599 Freedom Ln *TF:* 800-845-6062 ■ *Web:* www.ralphmoyle.com	Mattawan	MI	49071	269-668-4531		780
RMI (Rocky Mountain Instrument Co) 106 Laser Dr *TF:* 866-678-4270 ■ *Web:* www.rmico.com	Lafayette	CO	80026	303-664-5000	664-5002	544
RMI (Michigan Department of corrections) *Michigan Reformatory* 1342 W Main *Web:* www.michigan.gov	Ionia	MI	48846	616-527-2500		213
RMI Direct Marketing Inc 44 Old Ridgebury Rd *Web:* www.rmidirect.com	Danbury	CT	06810	203-798-0448		195
RMLEB (Rocky Mountain Lions Eye Bank) 1675 Aurora Crt Ste El2049 PO Box 6026 *TF:* 800-444-7479 ■ *Web:* www.corneas.org	Aurora	CO	80045	720-848-3937	848-3938	269
RMMS (Rocky Mountain Medical Search) 5340 S Quebec St Ste 320 S *TF:* 800-735-6721 ■ *Web:* www.rmmedicalsearch.com	Greenwood Village	CO	80111	800-735-6721		194
RMO (Rocky Mountain Orthodontics Inc) 650 W Colfax Ave *TF:* 800-525-6375 ■ *Web:* www.rmortho.com	Denver	CO	80204	303-592-8200		228
RMP (Recto Molded Products Inc) 4425 Appleton St *Web:* www.rectomolded.com	Cincinnati	OH	45209	513-871-5544		604
RMP (Robert Mann Packaging Inc) 340 El Camino Real S Bldg 36 *TF:* 800-345-6766 ■ *Web:* www.rmp.com	Salinas	CA	93901	831-789-8300	783-3147	100
RMPersonnel Inc 4707 Montana Ave *Web:* www.rmpersonnel.com	El Paso	TX	79903	915-565-7674	565-7687	631
RMR (Rocky Mountain Recorders) 1250 W Cedar Ave *Web:* www.coloradorecordingstudios.net	Denver	CO	80223	303-777-3648	777-3923	393
RMR Associates Inc 5870 Hubbard Dr *Web:* rmr.com	Rockville	MD	20852	301-230-0045	230-0046	636
RMRC Services Inc 5870 S Walden Ct *Web:* rockymountainmold.com	Centennial	CO	80015	303-667-0400		83
RMS 8227 Northwest Blvd Ste 230 *Web:* rms-safety.com	Indianapolis	IN	46278	317-872-8227		463
RMS Titanic Inc 3340 Peachtree Rd NE Ste 2250 *Web:* premierexhibitions.com	Atlanta	GA	30326	404-842-2600		465
RMSC (Risk Management Services Co) 9100 Marksfield Rd **Fax Area Code:* 888 ■ *Web:* www.rmsc.com	Louisville	KY	40222	502-326-5900	326-5909*	194
RMS-Ross Corp 44325 Yale Rd W *Web:* www.rmsross.com	Chilliwack	BC	V2R4H2	604-792-5911	792-7148	454
RMT Woodworth Inc 45755 Five Mile Rd *Web:* www.rmtwoodworth.com	Plymouth	MI	48170	734-254-0566	254-0069	484
RMW Architecture & Interiors 160 Pine St 4th Fl *Web:* rmw.com	San Francisco	CA	94111	415-781-9800		393
Rmx Global Logistics 141 Union Blvd Ste 450 **Fax Area Code:* 303 ■ *TF:* 888-824-7365 ■ *Web:* www.rmxglobal.com	Evergreen	CO	80439	888-824-7365	674-3803*	311
RN Fink Manufacturing Company Inc 1530 Noble Rd PO Box 245 *Web:* www.rnfink.com	Williamston	MI	48895	517-655-4351	655-5119	98
RNA Consulting Inc 27820 Saddle Ct *Web:* rnaconsultinginc.com	Los Altos Hills	CA	94022	650-949-1092		743
RNC (Republican National Committee) 310 First St SE *TF:* 800-445-5768 ■ *Web:* www.gop.com	Washington	DC	20003	202-863-8500		616
RNC Genter Capital Management 11601 Wilshire Blvd Ste 2500 *TF:* 800-877-7624 ■ *Web:* rncgenter.com	Los Angeles	CA	90025	310-477-6543	479-6406	401
RND Consulting Inc 6710 Ridgecliff Dr *Web:* rndcredits.com	Solon	OH	44139	440-519-1905		2
RNDC (Republic National Distributing Co) 6511 Tri County Pkwy *Web:* www.rndc-usa.com	Schertz	TX	78154	210-224-7531		81-3
RNDT Incorporated Nondestructive Testing & Research Services 228 Maple Ave *TF:* 800-505-7638 ■ *Web:* www.rndt.net	Johnstown	PA	15901	814-535-5448		743
RNJ Electronics Inc 202 New Hwy **Fax Area Code:* 800 ■ *TF:* 800-645-5833 ■ *Web:* rnjelectronics-estore.com	Amityville	NY	11701	631-226-2700	765-3291*	246
RNR RV Ctr 23203 E Knox Ave *TF:* 866-386-4875 ■ *Web:* www.rnrrv.com	Liberty Lake	WA	99019	866-386-4875		57
RNR Tire Express 8030 Florida Blvd *Web:* www.rnrtires.com	Baton Rouge	LA	70806	225-245-3725		57
RNRF (Renewable Natural Resources Foundation) 5430 Grosvenor Ln *Web:* rnrf.org	Bethesda	MD	20814	301-770-9101	493-6148	48-13
RNS (Religion News Service) 529 14th St NW 13th Fl *Web:* religionnews.com	Washington	DC	20045	202-463-8777		530
ROA (Reserve Officers Association of the US) 1 Constitution Ave NE *TF:* 800-809-9448 ■ *Web:* www.roa.org	Washington	DC	20002	202-479-2200	547-1641	48-19
ROACO Logistics Services 500 Country Club Dr	Bensenville	IL	60106	630-595-8631		449
Road & Track Magazine 1350 Eisenhower Pl *Web:* www.roadandtrack.com	Ann Arbor	MI	48108	734-352-8000		457-3
Road America N 7390 Hwy 67 *TF:* 800-365-7223 ■ *Web:* www.roadamerica.com	Elkhart Lake	WI	53020	920-892-4576	892-4550	515
Road America Inc 4580 Schaefer Ave *Web:* roadamericadecals.com	Chino	CA	91710	909-591-6304	627-9560	627
Road Atlanta Raceway 5300 Winder Hwy *TF:* 800-849-7223 ■ *Web:* www.roadatlanta.com	Braselton	GA	30517	770-967-6143		515
Road Builders Machinery & Supply Company Inc 1001 S Seventh St *Web:* www.roadbuildersmachinery.com	Kansas City	KS	66105	913-371-3822	371-3870	385
Road Machinery Co 926 S Seventh St **Fax Area Code:* 602 ■ *TF:* 800-989-7121 ■ *Web:* www.roadmachinery.com	Phoenix	AZ	85034	800-989-7121	253-9690*	358
Road Race Management Inc 4904 Glen Cove Pky *Web:* www.rrm.com	Bethesda	MD	20816	301-320-6865	320-9164	637-10
Road Ranger LLC 4930 E State St *Web:* www.roadrangerusa.com	Rockford	IL	61108	815-387-1700		345
Road Sprinkler Fitters Local Union 669 7050 Oakland Mills Rd *Web:* www.sprinklerfitters669.org	Columbia	MD	21046	410-381-4300		414
Roadmaster Drivers School 1409 Pickettville Rd *TF:* 800-831-1300 ■ *Web:* www.roadmaster.com	Jacksonville	FL	32220	904-783-3333		685
Roadrunner Transportation Systems Inc 4900 S Pennsylvania Ave *NYSE: RRTS* ■ *TF:* 800-831-4394 ■ *Web:* www.rrts.com	Cudahy	WI	53110	414-615-1500	615-1513	651
Roadster Factory, The 328 Killen Rd *TF:* 800-234-1104 ■ *Web:* www.the-roadster-factory.com	Armagh	PA	15920	814-446-4444		54
Roadtec Inc 800 Manufacturers Rd PO Box 180515 *TF:* 800-272-7100 ■ *Web:* www.roadtec.com	Chattanooga	TN	37405	423-265-0600	267-7104	190
Roadtex Transportation Corp 13 Jensen Dr *TF:* 800-762-3839 ■ *Web:* www.roadtex.com	Somerset	NJ	08873	800-762-3839		780
Roadtrip Productions Ltd 1626 Placentia Ave *Web:* roadtripnation.com	Costa Mesa	CA	92627	949-764-9121		738
Roake & Associates Inc 1684 Quincy Ave Ste 100A *Web:* www.roake.com	Naperville	IL	60540	630-355-3232	355-3267	261
ROAM (Rivers Oceans & Mountains Adventures Inc) 24-622 Front St *TF:* 888-639-1114 ■ *Web:* iroamtheworld.com	Nelson	BC	V1L4B7	888-639-1114		760
Roam Data Inc 280 Summer St *TF:* 888-589-5885 ■ *Web:* www.roamdata.com	Boston	MA	02210	888-589-5885		180
Roam Mobility Holdings Inc 60 James St 3rd Fl *Web:* roammobility.com	Saint Catharines	ON	L2R7E7	613-995-8210	947-6850	224
Roaman's 2300 SE Ave **Fax Area Code:* 317 ■ *TF:* 800-840-6214 ■ *Web:* www.roamans.com	Indianapolis	IN	46201	212-613-9500	266-3393*	459
Roan Mountain State Park 1015 Hwy 143 *Web:* tnstateparks.com	Roan Mountain	TN	37687	423-547-3900		565
Roane Alliance 1209 N Kentucky St *TF:* 800-386-4686 ■ *Web:* www.roanealliance.org	Kingston	TN	37763	865-376-2093	376-4978	338
Roane County 200 Main St *Web:* www.roanewv.com	Spencer	WV	25276	304-927-2860	927-2489	338
Roane County News 204 Franklin St *Web:* www.roanecounty.com	Kingston	TN	37763	865-376-3481		532-2
Roane Jackson Technical Ctr 9450 Spencer Rd *Web:* www.rjtcwv.com	Le Roy	WV	25252	304-372-7335	372-7336	167-3
Roane State Community College 276 Patton Ln *TF:* 800-343-9104 ■ *Web:* www.roanestate.edu	Harriman	TN	37748	865-354-3000	882-4562	162
Roanoke College 221 College Ln *TF:* 800-388-2276 ■ *Web:* www.roanoke.edu	Salem	VA	24153	540-375-2270	375-2267	166
Roanoke County 5204 Bernard Dr *Web:* www.roanokecountyva.gov	Roanoke	VA	24018	540-772-2004	561-2884	338
Roanoke County Public Library 6303 Merriman Rd *Web:* www.roanokecountyva.gov	Roanoke	VA	24018	540-772-7507	989-3129	434-3
Roanoke Electric Co-op 518 NC 561 W *TF:* 800-433-2236 ■ *Web:* www.roanokeelectric.com	Aulander	NC	27805	800-433-2236		245
Roanoke Regional Airport 5202 Aviation Dr NW *Web:* www.flyroa.com	Roanoke	VA	24012	540-362-1999	563-4838	27
Roanoke Regional Chamber of Commerce 210 S Jefferson St *Web:* roanokechamber.org	Roanoke	VA	24011	540-983-0700	983-0723	139
Roanoke Symphony Orchestra 541 Luck Ave Ste 200 *Web:* www.rso.com	Roanoke	VA	24016	540-343-6221	343-0065	573-3
Roanoke Times 201 W Campbell Ave SW *TF:* 800-346-1234 ■ *Web:* www.roanoke.com	Roanoke	VA	24011	540-981-3340		532-2
Roanoke Valley Chamber of Commerce 260 Premier Blvd *TF:* 800-280-3999 ■ *Web:* www.rvchamber.com	Roanoke Rapids	NC	27870	252-537-3513	535-5767	139
Roanoke Valley Convention & Visitors Bureau 101 Shenandoah Ave NE *TF:* 800-635-5535 ■ *Web:* www.visitroanokeva.com	Roanoke	VA	24016	540-342-6025	342-7119	206
Roanoke Valley Wine Co 1250 Intervale *Web:* rvwc.com	Salem	VA	24153	540-444-4440	375-8877	80-3
Roanoke-Chowan Community College 109 Community College Rd *Web:* www.roanokechowan.edu	Ahoskie	NC	27910	252-862-1200	862-1355	162
Roanwell Corp 2564 Park Ave *Web:* www.roanwell.com	Bronx	NY	10451	718-401-0288	401-0663	52
Roar Foundation 6867 Soledad Canyon Rd *Web:* www.shambala.org	Acton	CA	93510	661-268-0380	268-8809	564
Roaring Brook Ranch & Tennis Resort Rte 9N S *TF:* 800-882-7665 ■ *Web:* www.roaringbrookranch.com	Lake George	NY	12845	518-668-5767		669
Roaring River State Park 12716 Farm Rd 2239 *Web:* mostateparks.com	Cassville	MO	65625	417-847-2539		565
Roaring Run Resort Sales 194 Tannery Rd *Web:* www.roaringrunresort.com	Champion	PA	15622	724-593-7837		377
Roaring Spring Blank Book Co 740 Spang St *Web:* www.rspaperproducts.com	Roaring Spring	PA	16673	814-224-5141		86
RoArk Group Inc, The 1600 N 35th St *TF:* 800-569-2616 ■ *Web:* www.roarkgroup.com	Rogers	AR	72756	479-636-1686	631-8101	627
Roasterie Inc, The 1204 W 27th St *TF:* 800-376-0245 ■ *Web:* www.theroasterie.com	Kansas City	MO	64108	816-931-4000		345
Rob Bailey Communications 310 NJ-17	Upper Saddle River	NJ	07458	201-760-0200		636
Rob Roy Academy 251 Main St *Web:* www.rob-roy.com	Woonsocket	RI	02895	401-769-1777	651-9042	167-3
Robar Enterprises Inc 17671 Bear Valley Rd *Web:* robar.com	Hesperia	CA	92345	760-244-5456	244-1819	182

Name / Address	Phone	Fax	Class
Robart Manufacturing 625 N 12th St .... Saint Charles IL 60174 *Web:* robart.com	630-584-7616	584-3712	3
Robata Grill 3658 The Barnyard .... Carmel By The Sea CA 93923 *Web:* robata-barnyard.com	831-624-2643		671
Robb & Stucky Intl 13170 S Cleveland Ave .... Fort Myers FL 33907 *Web:* robbstuckyintl.com	239-415-2800		321
Robbers Cave State Park 4575 NW 1024th Ave .... Wilburton OK 74578 *Web:* www.travelok.com	918-465-2565	465-5763	565
Robberson Ford Lincoln Mazda 2100 NE 3rd St .... Bend OR 97701 *Web:* www.robberson.com	541-382-4521		57
Robbie A. Mckinney CPA 746 Crossover Ln .... Memphis TN 38117 *Web:* ram-cpa.com	901-685-0098		2
Robbinex Inc 41 Stuart St .... Hamilton ON L8L1B5 *TF:* 888-762-2463 ■ *Web:* www.robbinex.com	905-523-7510	523-4998	317
Robbins & Lloyd Career Training Institute 11801 W Silver Spring Dr Ste 200 .... Milwaukee WI 53225 *Web:* www.robbinsandlloyd.net	414-464-0800	464-0850	653
Robbins Arroyo LLP 600 B St Ste 1900 .... San Diego CA 92101 *TF:* 800-350-6003 ■ *Web:* www.robbinsarroyo.com	800-350-6003		428
Robbins Inc 4777 Eastern Ave .... Cincinnati OH 45226 **Fax Area Code:* 513 ■ *TF:* 800-543-1913 ■ *Web:* www.robbinsfloor.com	800-543-1913	871-7998*	683
Robbins Library 700 Massachusetts Ave .... Arlington MA 02476 *Web:* www.robbinslibrary.org	781-316-3200		434-3
Robbins Lightning Inc 124 E 2nd St .... Maryville MO 64468 *TF:* 800-426-3792 ■ *Web:* www.robbinslightning.com	660-582-3156		815
Robbins LLC 3415 Thompson St .... Muscle Shoals AL 35661 *TF:* 800-633-3312 ■ *Web:* www.robbinsllc.com	256-383-5441		754
Robbins Lumber Co 53 Ghent Rd .... Searsmont ME 04973 *Web:* www.rlco.com	207-342-5221		683
Robbins Manufacturing Co 1003 E 131st Ave .... Tampa FL 33612 *TF:* 888-558-8199 ■ *Web:* www.robbinslumber.com	813-971-3030		818
Robbins Parking Service Ltd 1102 Fort St .... Victoria BC V8V3K8 *Web:* robbinsparking.com	250-382-4411		562
Robbins Ross Alloy Belinfante Littlefield LLC 999 Peachtree St Ste 1120 .... Atlanta GA 30309 **Fax Area Code:* 404 ■ *Web:* robbinsfirm.com	678-701-9381	856-3250*	41
Robbinsdale Area Schools 4148 Winnetka Ave N .... New Hope MN 55427 *Web:* www.rdale.org	763-504-8000		685
Robern Inc 701 N Wilson Ave .... Bristol PA 19007 *TF:* 800-877-2376 ■ *Web:* www.robern.com	215-826-9800		319-2
Roberson CPA Firm PLLC 1904 Front St Ste 420 .... Durham NC 27705 *Web:* robersoncpas.com	919-383-0441	383-8288	2
Roberson Motors Inc 3100 Ryan Dr SE .... Salem OR 97301 *TF:* 888-281-6220 ■ *Web:* www.robersonmotorschryslerjeep.com	503-363-4117		57
Roberson Museum & Science Ctr 30 Front St .... Binghamton NY 13905 *TF:* 888-269-5325 ■ *Web:* www.roberson.org	607-772-0660	771-8905	520
Roberson Wireline Inc 314 SE Ninth Ave .... Perryton TX 79070 *Web:* robersonwireline.com	806-435-3087	435-9668	539
Robert & Judi Newman Center for the Performing Arts, The 2344 E Iliff Ave .... Denver CO 80208 *Web:* www.newmancenterpresents.com	303-871-7720		572
Robert A. Bob Bowers Civic Ctr 3401 Cultural Center Dr .... Port Arthur TX 77642	409-985-8801		205
Robert A. Karn & Associates Inc 707 Beck Ave .... Fairfield CA 94533 *Web:* rakengineers.com	707-435-9999	435-9988	261
Robert A. Main & Sons Inc 555 Goffle Rd .... Wyckoff NJ 07481 *Web:* www.ramsco-inc.com	201-447-3700	447-0302	621
Robert A. Welch Foundation 5555 San Felipe St Ste 1900 .... Houston TX 77056 *Web:* www.welch1.org	713-961-9884		305
Robert A. Woloshen CPA PC 29 W 15th St Ste 1 .... New York NY 10011 *Web:* rawcpa.com	212-843-3486		2
Robert Abbey Inc 3166 Main Ave SE .... Hickory NC 28602 *Web:* www.robertabbey.biz	828-322-3480		601
Robert Allan Ltd 1639 Second Ave W Ste 230 .... Vancouver BC V6J1H3 *Web:* ral.ca	604-736-9466		261
Robert Allen Law 1441 Brickell Ave Ste 1400 .... Miami FL 33131 *Web:* www.robertallenlaw.com	305-372-3300		445
Robert Allerton Park & Conference Ctr 515 Old Timber Rd .... Monticello IL 61856 *Web:* allerton.illinois.edu	217-333-3287	300-3078	97
Robert B. Jones Inc 825 Colorado Blvd Ste 219 .... Los Angeles CA 90041 *Web:* jm-cpa.com	323-550-8400		2
Robert Bearden Inc 2601 Industrial Pk Dr PO Box 870 .... Cairo GA 39828 *TF:* 888-298-6928 ■ *Web:* www.rbitrucking.com	229-377-6928		780
Robert Bell Insurance Brokers 605 E Alvarado Ste 200 .... Fallbrook CA 92028 *TF:* 800-426-2634 ■ *Web:* robertbellinsurance.com	760-451-8556		390
Robert Bosch LLC 38000 Hills Tech Dr .... Farmington Hills MI 48331 *Web:* www.bosch.us	248-876-1000		52
Robert Bosch Tool Corp 1800 W Central Rd .... Mount Prospect IL 60056 **Fax Area Code:* 224 ■ *TF:* 877-267-2499 ■ *Web:* www.boschtools.com	877-267-2499	232-3169*	759
Robert Brady Law Office 1 Grove Ave .... East Providence RI 02914 *Web:* rhodeislandpilawyer.com	401-434-2800		41

Name / Address	Phone	Fax	Class
Robert Busse & Company Inc 75 Arkay Dr .... Hauppauge NY 11788 *TF:* 800-645-6526 ■ *Web:* www.busseinc.com	631-435-4711		596
Robert C. Bickerman CPA PC 1117 Perimeter Ctr W Ste E-201 .... Atlanta GA 30338 *Web:* bobbickerman.com	404-201-2301	393-7560	2
Robert C. Gardella PLLC 134 N First St Ste 201 .... Brighton MI 48116 *Web:* gardellalawoffice.com	810-220-4200		41
Robert C. Weisheit Company Inc 999 Regency Dr .... Glendale Heights IL 60139 *Web:* www.weisheit.com	847-648-4991	648-4956	454
Robert Clofine, Esquire 340 Pine Grove Commons .... York PA 17403 *Web:* estateattorney.com	717-747-5995		41
Robert Curtis Law Office 215 Central Ave NW Ste 200 .... Albuquerque NM 87102 *Web:* rcurtislaw.com	505-389-2031		41
Robert D. Niehaus Inc 140 E Carrillo St .... Santa Barbara CA 93101 *Web:* www.rdniehaus.com	805-962-0611	962-0097	466
Robert Derector Assoc 19 W 44th St .... New York NY 10036 *Web:* www.derector.com	212-764-7272		256
Robert Dietrick Company Inc PO Box 605 .... Fishers IN 46038 *TF:* 866-767-1888 ■ *Web:* rd-co.com	317-842-1991	842-2698	385
Robert E. Lee & Associates Inc 1250 Centennial Centre Blvd .... Hobart WI 54155 *TF:* 800-986-6388 ■ *Web:* releeinc.com	920-662-9641		261
Robert E. Miller Insurance Agency Inc 6363 College Blvd Ste 400 .... Overland Park KS 66211 *Web:* millercares.com	816-333-3000		390
Robert E. Morris Co 910 Gay Hill Rd .... Windsor CT 06095 *Web:* www.robertemorris.com	860-687-3300	687-3301	385
Robert E. Nolan Company Inc 92 Hopmeadow St .... Weatogue CT 06089 **Fax Area Code:* 860 ■ *TF:* 800-653-1941 ■ *Web:* www.renolan.com	877-736-6526	651-3465*	194
Robert E. Porter Construction Company Inc 1720 W Lincoln Ct .... Phoenix AZ 85007 *Web:* robertporterconstruction.com	602-253-4911	340-9533	186
Robert E. Webber Institute for Worship Studies, The (IWS) 4001 Hendricks Ave .... Jacksonville FL 32207 *TF:* 800-282-2977 ■ *Web:* iws.edu	904-264-2172	379-5534	685
Robert F. Henry Tile Company Inc 1008 Lagoon Business Loop .... Montgomery AL 36117 *Web:* henrytile.com	334-269-2518		191-1
Robert F. Kennedy Stadium (RFK) 2400 E Capitol St SE .... Washington DC 20003 *Web:* www.eventsdc.com	202-608-1100		720
Robert Family Holdings Inc (RFH) 12430 Tesson Ferry Rd Ste 313 .... Saint Louis MO 63128 **Fax Area Code:* 314 ■ *Web:* www.rf-holdings.com	636-305-2830	965-0309*	548
Robert Fiance Beauty Schools 312 State St .... Perth Amboy NJ 08861 *Web:* www.robertfiance.edu	732-442-6007		685
Robert Fiance Beauty Schools 121 Watchung Ave .... North Plainfield NJ 07060 *TF:* 800-842-3451 ■ *Web:* www.robertfiance.com	908-754-4247		685
Robert Fisher Co 10 E 38th St 6th Fl .... New York NY 10016 *Web:* www.rsfisher.com	212-532-3253	481-3394	409
Robert Frances Group 46 Kent Hills Ln .... Wilton CT 06897 *Web:* www.rfgonline.com	203-429-8951		196
Robert Frost Farm Historic Site 122 Rockingham Rd .... Derry NH 03038 *Web:* www.nhstateparks.org	603-432-3091		565
Robert Frost Middle School 2206 W 167th St .... Markham IL 60428 *Web:* www.sd1525.org	708-210-9929		685
Robert Gibb & Sons Inc 2011 Great Northern Dr .... Fargo ND 58102 *Web:* www.robertgibb.com	701-282-5900	281-0819	189-10
Robert Gordon Industries Ltd 1500 Plaza Ave .... New Hyde Park NY 11040 *Web:* www.gordonsinclair.com	516-354-8888		361
Robert Gray Palmer Company LPA 1335 Dublin Rd Ste 221B .... Columbus OH 43215 *Web:* rgpalmerlaw.com	614-484-1200		41
Robert Group Inc, The 3108 Los Feliz Blvd .... Los Angeles CA 90039 *Web:* www.therobertgroup.com	323-669-9100	669-9800	194
Robert H. Arrick, Dvm 1207 Ninth Ave .... San Francisco CA 94122 *Web:* parkanimalvetsf.com	415-753-8485		794
Robert H. Peterson Co 14724 Proctor Ave .... City of Industry CA 91746 *Web:* www.rhpeterson.com	626-369-5085		350
Robert H. Treman State Park 105 Enfield Falls Rd .... Ithaca NY 14850 *Web:* parks.ny.gov	607-273-3440		565
Robert H. Wager Co 570 Montroyal Rd .... Rural Hall NC 27045 *TF:* 800-562-7024 ■ *Web:* www.wagerusa.com	336-969-6909	969-6375	789
Robert Haber & Associates Inc 16 W 23rd St .... New York NY 10010 *Web:* rhancientart.com	212-243-3656		42
Robert Hale & Assoc 5405 Morehouse Dr Ste 320 .... San Diego CA 92121 *Web:* productsstrategy.com	858-404-0200		466
Robert Half International Inc *OfficeTeam Div* 2884 Sand Hill Rd Ste 200 .... Menlo Park CA 94025 *Web:* www.roberthalf.com	650-234-6000		721
Robert Heath Trucking Inc 10880 Rockwall Road .... Dallas TX 79404 *Web:* www.robertheath.com	806-747-1651		780
Robert Huber Associates 9446 E Jenan Dr .... Scottsdale AZ 85260 *TF:* 888-277-3118 ■ *Web:* www.allcampuscard.com	480-551-0520	551-0521	194

Name / Address	City	State	ZIP	Phone	Fax	Class
Robert Hughes Associates Inc 508 Twilight Trl Ste 200 *Web:* www.roberthughes.com	Richardson	TX	75080	972-980-0088	233-1548	390
Robert I. Goldstein 6507 Wilkins Ave Ste 202	Pittsburgh	PA	15217	412-362-9040		2
Robert I. Slater, A Law Corp 16633 Ventura Blvd Ste 730 *Web:* bobslaterlaw.com	Encino	CA	91436	818-377-3722		41
Robert J. Dole Institute of Politics 2350 Petefish Dr *Web:* doleinstitute.org	Lawrence	KS	66045	785-864-4900	864-1414	634
Robert J. Dole VA Medical Ctr 5500 E Kellogg St *TF:* 888-878-6881 ■ *Web:* www.wichita.va.gov	Wichita	KS	67218	316-685-2221	651-3666	374-3
Robert J. Kleberg Public Library 220 N 4th St	Kingsville	TX	78363	361-592-6381		434-3
Robert J. Klein CPA 4021 214 Pl *Web:* robertjkleincpa.com	Bayside	NY	11361	718-423-8984		2
Robert J. Kratz & Co 145 W Lancaster Ave *Web:* robertjkratz.com	Paoli	PA	19301	610-296-2500		2
Robert Jeffrey Hair Studio 3153 N Broadway *Web:* robertjeffrey.com	Chicago	IL	60657	773-525-8800		77
Robert Johnson Law Corp 34197 Pacific Coast Hwy *Web:* robertjohnsonlaw.com	Dana Point	CA	92629	949-498-4999	498-4998	41
Robert Jones Plumbing Inc 6071 SR- 128 *Web:* www.robertjonesplumbing.com	Cleves	OH	45002	513-353-2230	353-2247	189-10
Robert Kaplan Financial Management & Insurance Services Inc 16030 Ventura Blvd Ste 600 *Web:* kaplanfinancial.net	Encino	CA	91436	818-783-6620		390
Robert Kaufman Company Inc PO Box 59266 *TF:* 800-877-2066 ■ *Web:* www.robertkaufman.com	Los Angeles	CA	90059	310-538-3482	538-9235	594
Robert L. Bayless, Producer LLC 621 17th St Ste 2300 *Web:* www.rlbayless.com	Denver	CO	80293	303-296-9900		539
Robert L. Lovett PC 619 Arizona Ave *Web:* lovettlawfirm.com	El Paso	TX	79902	915-757-9999		41
Robert Lloyd Coutts & Sons 46 Washington St *Web:* couttsinsurance.com	Morristown	NJ	07960	973-539-4900		390
Robert Lloyd Sheet Metal Inc 4485 Independence Hwy *Web:* www.rlsm.net	Independence	OR	97351	503-838-3863	838-3964	189-10
Robert M Hadley Company Inc 4054 Transport St *Web:* www.rmhco.com	Ventura	CA	93003	805-658-7286	658-1907	604
Robert M. Bird Health Sciences Library 1105 N Stonewall Ave *TF:* 800-522-0222 ■ *Web:* www.library.ouhsc.edu	Oklahoma City	OK	73117	405-271-2285	271-3297	434-1
Robert M. Coplen PA 10225 Ulmerton Rd Ste 5A *Web:* coplenlaw.com	Largo	FL	33771	727-588-4550		41
Robert M. Grum Jr CPA 4540 Kearny Villa Rd Ste 108 *Web:* www.grumcpas.com	San Diego	CA	92123	858-560-5449	560-7403	2
Robert M. Saunders CPA LLC 241 N Ave W *Web:* fintax.com	Westfield	NJ	07090	908-233-7900		2
Robert Mann Packaging Inc (RMP) 340 El Camino Real S Bldg 36 *TF:* 800-345-6766 ■ *Web:* www.rmp.com	Salinas	CA	93901	831-789-8300	783-3147	100
Robert McConnell Productions 4303 67th Ave NW *TF:* 800-532-4017 ■ *Web:* www.parli.com	Gig Harbor	WA	98335	253-265-1550		514
Robert Miller Gallery 524 W 26th St *Web:* www.robertmillergallery.com	New York	NY	10001	212-366-4774		42
Robert Mitchell Inc 350 Decarie Blvd Via St-Louis & Crevier St *Web:* www.robertmitchell.com	Saint-Laurent	QC	H4L3K5	514-747-2471		595
Robert Mondavi Co 7801 St Helena Hwy *TF:* 888-766-6328 ■ *Web:* www.robertmondaviwinery.com	Oakville	CA	94562	888-766-6328		80-3
Robert Moreno Insurance Services 22860 Savi Ranch Pkwy PO Box 87023 *TF:* 800-815-7647 ■ *Web:* www.rmismga.com	Yorba Linda	CA	92887	714-738-1383	921-1106	390
Robert Morgan Educational Ctr 18180 SW 122nd Ave *Web:* www.hs.robertmorganeducenter.org	Miami	FL	33177	305-253-9920	259-1495	167-3
Robert Morris College *Springfield* 3101 Montvale Dr *Web:* robertmorris.edu	Springfield	IL	62704	217-793-2500		166
Robert Morris University 6001 University Blvd **Fax Area Code:* 412 ■ *TF:* 800-762-0097 ■ *Web:* www.rmu.edu	Moon Township	PA	15108	800-762-0097	397-2425*	166
Robert Moses State Park - Long Island Robert Moses State Pkwy PO Box 247 *Web:* parks.ny.gov	Babylon	NY	11702	631-669-0470		565
Robert Moses State Park - Thousand Islands 32 Beach Marina Rd *Web:* parks.ny.gov	Massena	NY	13662	315-769-8663		565
Robert Paul Academy of Cosmetology Arts & Sciences 29 Green Meadow Dr *Web:* www.robertpaulacademy.com	Timonium	MD	21093	410-252-4481		167-3
Robert Quackenbush Studios 460 E 79th St *Web:* www.rquackenbush.com	New York	NY	10075	212-744-3822		637-2
Robert R. McCormick Foundation 205 N Michigan Ave Ste 4300 *Web:* www.mccormickfoundation.org	Chicago	IL	60601	312-445-5000	445-5001	305
Robert Rippe & Associates Inc 6117 Blue Cir Dr *Web:* www.rippeassociates.com	Minnetonka	MN	55343	952-933-0313		196
Robert Schalkenbach Foundation Inc (RSF) 211 E 43rd St Ste 400 *TF:* 800-269-9555 ■ *Web:* schalkenbach.org	New York	NY	10017	212-683-6424	683-6454	637-2
Robert Sharp & Associates Inc 3615 Canyon Lake Dr Ste 1 *Web:* www.robertsharpassociates.com	Rapid City	SD	57702	605-341-5226	341-7390	177
Robert Sterling Clark Foundation Inc 135 E 64th St *Web:* www.rsclark.org	New York	NY	10065	212-288-8900		303
Robert T. Kirkwood Inc 91 Washington Ave *Web:* kirkwoodinsurance.net	Pleasantville	NY	10570	914-769-9070		390
Robert Talbott Inc 2901 Monterey-Salinas Hwy *Web:* www.roberttalbott.com	Monterey	CA	93940	831-649-6000		155-13
Robert Toombs House State Historic Site 216 E Robert Toombs Ave *Web:* gastateparks.org	Washington	GA	30673	706-678-2226		565
Robert Treat Hotel 50 Pk Pl *TF:* 800-569-2300 ■ *Web:* www.rthotel.com	Newark	NJ	07102	973-622-1000	622-6410	379
Robert V. Jensen Inc 4029 S Maple Ave *TF:* 800-366-8210 ■ *Web:* www.rvjensen.com	Fresno	CA	93725	559-485-8210	485-8503	579
Robert W. Baird & Company Inc 777 E Wisconsin Ave PO Box 672 *TF:* 800-792-2473 ■ *Web:* www.rwbaird.com	Milwaukee	WI	53202	414-765-3500		690
Robert W. Hughes & Associates P 390 W Crogan St Ste 2 *Web:* hughespclaw.com	Lawrenceville	GA	30046	770-469-8887		41
Robert W. Woodruff Foundation Inc 191 Peachtree St NE Ste 3540 *Web:* www.woodruff.org	Atlanta	GA	30303	404-522-6755	522-7026	305
Robert Weed Plywood Corp 705 Maple St PO Box 487 *Web:* robertweedcorp.com	Bristol	IN	46507	574-848-4408	848-5679	613
Robert Wood Johnson Foundation PO Box 2316 *TF:* 877-843-7953 ■ *Web:* www.rwjf.org	Princeton	NJ	08543	877-843-7953		305
Robert Wood Johnson Medical School 675 Hoes Ln *Web:* rwjms.rutgers.edu	Piscataway	NJ	08854	732-235-4576	235-5078	167-2
Robert Wooler Co 1755 Susquehanna Rd *Web:* www.robertwooler.com	Dresher	PA	19025	215-542-7600	542-0250	484
Robert-James Sales Inc 2585 Walden Ave *TF:* 800-666-0088 ■ *Web:* www.rjsales.com	Buffalo	NY	14225	716-651-6000	651-0234	492
Roberto Clemente State Park 301 W Tremont Ave *Web:* parks.ny.gov	Bronx	NY	10453	718-299-8750		565
Roberto's 908 E Amador Ave *Web:* www.robertosmexicanfoods.com	Las Cruces	NM	88001	575-523-1851		671
Roberto's 603 Crescent Ave *Web:* www.usmenuguide.com	Bronx	NY	10458	718-733-9503		671
Roberto-Venn School of Luthiery 1012 NW Grand Ave *TF:* 800-507-3738 ■ *Web:* www.roberto-venn.com	Phoenix	AZ	85007	602-243-1179	304-1175	685
Roberts & Holland LLP 1675 Broadway 17th Fl *Web:* www.robertsandholland.com	New York	NY	10019	212-903-8700	974-3059	428
Roberts & Schaefer Co 222 S Riverside Plz Ste 1800	Chicago	IL	60606	312-236-7292		261
Roberts Air Conditioning 780 Commerce Dr *Web:* robertsac.com	Gulf Shores	AL	36547	251-968-7600	968-7300	612
Roberts Automatic Products Inc 880 Lake Dr *Web:* www.robertsautomatic.com	Chanhassen	MN	55317	952-949-1000	949-9240	621
Roberts Beauty 9131 Oakdale Ave Ste 110 *Web:* www.robertsbeauty.com	Chatsworth	CA	91311	818-727-1700		361
Roberts Brothers Tire Service 1415 E Harding Ave *Web:* www.robertsbrotherstire.com	Pine Bluff	AR	71601	870-534-2911	534-3439	755
Roberts Communications Inc 64 Commercial St *Web:* www.robertscomm.com	Rochester	NY	14614	585-325-6000		4
Roberts Communications Network LLC 4175 Cameron St *Web:* www.robertscomnet.com	Las Vegas	NV	89103	702-227-7500		681
Roberts Company Inc 180 Franklin St **Fax Area Code:* 508 ■ *TF:* 800-729-1482 ■ *Web:* www.firecatalog.com	Framingham	MA	01702	800-729-1482	879-3735*	627
Roberts County 122 E Water St PO Box 458 *Web:* www.uccsource.com	Miami	TX	79059	806-868-2341	868-3381	338
Roberts Gallery Ltd 641 Yonge St *Web:* www.robertsgallery.net	Toronto	ON	M4Y1Z9	416-924-8731		42
Roberts Hawaii Inc 680 Iwilei Rd Ste 700 *TF:* 800-831-5541 ■ *Web:* www.robertshawaii.com	Honolulu	HI	96817	808-523-7750		760
Roberts Home Medical Inc 20465 Seneca Meadows Pkwy *Web:* www.robertshomemedical.com	Germantown	MD	20876	301-353-0300		475
Roberts House Museum 1207 N Carson St *Web:* www.nps.gov	Carson City	NV	89701	775-887-2174		520
Roberts Insurance Group LLC 211 Nokomis Ave S *Web:* robertsinsurancegroup.com	Venice	FL	34285	941-485-5686	485-5626	390
Roberts Mitani LLC 145 W 57th St	New York	NY	10019	212-582-9800	582-9789	690
Roberts PolyPro Inc 5416 Wyoming Ave *TF:* 800-269-7409 ■ *Web:* www.robertspolypro.com	Charlotte	NC	28273	704-588-1794		601
Roberts Printing Co 2049 Calumet St *Web:* www.robpri.com	Clearwater	FL	33765	727-442-4011		627
Roberts Sinto Corp 3001 W Main St *Web:* robertssinto.com	Lansing	MI	48917	517-371-2460	371-4930	386
Roberts Technology Group Inc 120 New Britain Blvd *Web:* rtgpkg.com	Chalfont	PA	18914	215-822-0600	822-0662	358
Roberts Tool & Die Co 401 Industrial Rd *Web:* www.r-t-d.com	Chillicothe	MO	64601	660-646-5950	646-4520	488

Name / Address	City	State	Zip	Phone	Fax	Class
Roberts Wesleyan College 2301 Westside Dr *TF:* 800-777-4792 ■ *Web:* www.roberts.edu	Rochester	NY	14624	585-594-6000	594-6371	166
Roberts-Gordon Inc 1250 William St PO Box 44 *TF:* 800-828-7450 ■ *Web:* www.rg-inc.com	Buffalo	NY	14240	716-852-4400	852-0854	357
Roberts-Hamilton Co 6601 Pkwy Cir Ste A *Web:* robertshamilton.com	Brooklyn Center	MN	55430	763-315-0100	315-0199	612
Robertshaw Industrial Products 1602 Mustang Dr *TF:* 800-228-7429 ■ *Web:* www.robertshawindustrial.com	Maryville	TN	37801	865-981-3100	981-3168	201
Robertson & Associates CPA'S 1101 N Main St *Web:* www.robertsoncpa.com	Lakeport	CA	95453	707-263-9012		2
Robertson & Gable LLC 5875 Peachtree Industrial Blvd Ste 170 *TF:* 888-736-5182 ■ *Web:* rglegal.com	Norcross	GA	30092	770-736-5182	736-5183	41
Robertson College 3-265 Notre Dame Ave *Web:* www.robertsoncollege.com	Winnipeg	MB	R3B1N9	204-943-5661		165
Robertson County PO Box 1029 *Web:* www.co.robertson.tx.us	Franklin	TX	77856	979-828-4130	828-1260	338
Robertson County PO Box 76 *Web:* www.robertsoncounty.ky.gov	Mount Olivet	KY	41064	606-724-5212	724-5022	338
Robertson County 523 S Brown St *TF:* 866-355-6134 ■ *Web:* www.robertsoncountytn.org	Springfield	TN	37172	615-384-0202	384-2218	338
Robertson County Chamber ofCommerce 503 W Ct Sq *TF:* 800-264-9011 ■ *Web:* robertsonchamber.org	Springfield	TN	37172	615-384-3800	384-1260	139
Robertson Fuel Systems LLC 800 W Carver Rd Ste 101 *Web:* www.robertsonfuelsystems.com	Tempe	AZ	85284	480-337-7050	968-3019	21
Robertson Furniture Company Inc 890 Elberton St *TF:* 800-241-0713 ■ *Web:* www.robertson-furniture.com	Toccoa	GA	30577	706-886-1494	886-8998	319-1
Robertson GeoConsultants Inc 580 Hornby St Ste 900 *Web:* www.rgc.ca	Vancouver	BC	V6C3B6	604-684-8072		463
Robertson Heating Supply Co 2155 W Main St *TF:* 800-433-9532 ■ *Web:* www.robertsonheatingsupply.com	Alliance	OH	44601	330-821-9180		612
Robertson Inc 1455 Lakeshore Rd Ste 204-S *TF:* 800-268-5090 ■ *Web:* www.robertsonscrew.com	Burlington	ON	L7L5V5	905-332-7776	336-7019	278
Robertson Manufacturing Inc 112 Woodland Ave	West Grove	PA	19390	610-869-9600	869-6365	733
Robertson Precision Inc 325 Sharon Park Dr Ste 444 *Web:* www.robertsonprecision.com	Menlo Park	CA	94025	650-363-2212	363-0178	696
Robertson Ryan & Associates Inc 330 E Kilbourn Ave *TF:* 800-258-0277 ■ *Web:* www.robertsonryan.com	Milwaukee	WI	53202	414-271-3575		390
Robertson Tire Company Inc PO Box 472287 *Web:* robertson-tire.com	Tulsa	OK	74147	918-664-2211		54
Robertson's Ready Mix Concrete Inc 200 S Main St Ste 200 *Web:* www.rrmca.com	Corona	CA	92882	951-493-6462		182
Robertsville State Park 900 State Pk Dr *Web:* mostateparks.com	Robertsville	MO	63072	636-257-3788		565
Robeson Community College 5160 Fayetteville Rd PO Box 1420 *Web:* robeson.edu	Lumberton	NC	28360	910-272-3700	272-3328	162
Robeson Correctional Ctr 803 NC Hwy 711 *Web:* ncdps.gov	Lumberton	NC	28360	910-618-5535		213
Robeson County 701 N Elm St *Web:* www.co.robeson.nc.us	Lumberton	NC	28358	910-671-3000	671-3010	338
Robesonian, The 2175 N Roberts Ave *Web:* www.robesonian.com	Lumberton	NC	28358	910-739-4322		532-3
Robetex Inc 2504 Fayetteville Rd *Web:* www.robetexinc.com	Lumberton	NC	28359	910-671-0503		604
Robie & Matthai A Professional Corp Biltmore Tower 500 S Grand Ave 15th Fl *Web:* www.romalaw.com	Los Angeles	CA	90071	213-706-8000		428
Robie's Food Center Inc 604 S State St *Web:* robies.net	Abbeville	LA	70510	337-893-4354		345
Robin America Inc 905 Telser Rd *Web:* www.subarupower.com	Lake Zurich	IL	60047	847-540-7300		518
Robin Enterprises Co 111 N Otterbein Ave *Web:* www.robinenterprises.com	Westerville	OH	43081	614-891-0250	891-4398	627
Robin Healthcare 1845 Berkeley Way *TF:* 800-708-3617 ■ *Web:* www.robinhealthcare.com	Berkeley	CA	94703	800-708-3617		352
Robin Hood Foundation 826 Broadway 9th Fl *Web:* www.robinhood.org	New York	NY	10003	212-227-6601		743
Robin Rug Inc 125 Thames St *Web:* www.constitutionrugs.com	Bristol	RI	02809	401-253-8350		131
Robinette Demolition Inc S 560 Hwy 83 *Web:* www.rdidemolition.com	Oakbrook Terrace	IL	60181	630-833-7997	833-8047	189-16
Robins & Morton Group 5500 Maryland Way Ste 100 *Web:* www.robinsmorton.com	Birmingham	AL	35209	205-870-1000		186
Robinson & Geraldo Prof Corp 1316 Pennsylvania Ave *Web:* www.rglaw.net	Washington	DC	20003	202-544-2888		428
Robinson & Henry P C 900 Castleton Rd Ste 200 *Web:* robinsonandhenry.com	Castle Rock	CO	80109	303-688-0944		41
Robinson & Mcelwee PLLC 700 Virginia St E Ste 400 *Web:* ramlaw.com	Charleston	WV	25301	304-344-5800		428
Robinson Aviation 50 Thompson Ave *Web:* www.robinsonaviation.com	East Haven	CT	06512	203-467-9555	467-6346	63
Robinson Ballet 107 Union St *Web:* www.robinsonballet.org	Bangor	ME	04401	207-990-3140		573-1
Robinson Bradshaw & Hinson PA 101 N Tryon St Ste 1900 *Web:* www.robinsonbradshaw.com	Charlotte	NC	28246	704-377-2536	378-4000	428
Robinson Correctional Ctr 13423 E 1150th Ave *Web:* www.illinois.gov	Robinson	IL	62454	618-546-5659	544-2166	213
Robinson Farms Feed Co 7000 S Inland Dr *Web:* www.robinsonfarmsfeedco.com	Stockton	CA	95206	209-466-7915		447
Robinson Fin Machines Inc 13670 US Hwy 68 *Web:* www.robfin.com	Kenton	OH	43326	419-674-4152		295
Robinson Helicopter Co 2901 Airport Dr *Web:* robinsonheli.com	Torrance	CA	90505	310-539-0508		20
Robinson Hughes & Christopher Psc 459 W Martin Luther King Blvd *Web:* www.rhccpas.com	Danville	KY	40422	859-236-6628		2
Robinson Industries Inc 3051 W Curtis Rd *TF:* 877-465-4055 ■ *Web:* www.robinsonind.com	Coleman	MI	48618	989-465-6111	465-1217	548
Robinson Industries Inc 400 Robinson Dr *Web:* www.robinsonfans.com	Zelienople	PA	16063	724-452-6121	452-0388	18
Robinson Intellectual Property Law Office 3975 Fair Ridge Dr Ste 20 N *Web:* riplo.com	Fairfax	VA	22033	571-434-6789		41
Robinson Jeffers Tor House Foundation 26304 Ocean View Ave *Web:* www.torhouse.org	Carmel By The Sea	CA	93923	831-624-1813	624-3696	50-3
Robinson Law PA 1501 Venera Ave Ste 300 *Web:* www.rrobinsonlaw.com	Miami	FL	33146	305-662-7618		445
Robinson Lumber Company Inc 4000 Tchoupitoulas St *TF:* 800-874-1165 ■ *Web:* www.roblumco.com	New Orleans	LA	70115	800-874-1165		191-3
Robinson Metal Inc 1740 Eisenhower Dr *Web:* www.robinsonmetal.com	De Pere	WI	54115	920-494-7411		454
Robinson MFG 798 Market St PO Box 338 *Web:* www.robinsonmfg.com	Dayton	TN	37321	423-775-2212		155-18
Robinson Pharma Inc 3330 S Harbor Blvd *Web:* robinsonpharma.com	Santa Ana	CA	92704	714-241-0235	751-6066	799
Robinson Plumbing & Heating Supply Co 195 Broadway *TF:* 800-838-1119 ■ *Web:* www.robinsonsupply.com	Fall River	MA	02721	508-675-7433	677-1266	612
Robinson Seiler & Anderson 2500 N University Ave *Web:* rsalawyers.com	Provo	UT	84604	801-375-1920		41
Robinson State Park 428 North St PO Box 42 *Web:* www.mass.gov	Feeding Hills	MA	01030	413-786-2877		565
Robinson Terminal Warehouse Corp 1 Oronoco St *Web:* www.robinsonterminal.com	Alexandria	VA	22314	703-836-8300	836-8307	803-1
Robinson Terrace 28652 New York 23 *Web:* robinsonterrace.org	Stamford	NY	12167	607-652-7521	652-3362	450
Robinson, Reagan, & Young PLLC 446 James Robertson Pkwy Ste 200 *Web:* rrylaw.com	Nashville	TN	37219	615-726-0900		41
Robishaw Engineering Inc 10106 Mathewson Ln *TF:* 800-877-1706 ■ *Web:* www.flexifloat.com	Houston	TX	77043	713-468-1706	468-5822	698
Robison Oil Corp 500 Executive Blvd *Web:* www.robisonoil.com	Elmsford	NY	10523	914-345-5700		316
Robmar Precision Manufacturing Inc 30100 Abruzzi Dr *Web:* www.robmar.com	Westland	MI	48185	734-326-2664		454
Robotech Cad Solutions 2 Marine View Plz Ste 7 *Web:* www.robotechcad.com	Hoboken	NJ	07030	201-792-6300	792-3600	396
Robotic Industries Assn (RIA) 900 Victors Way Ste 140 *Web:* www.robotics.org	Ann Arbor	MI	48108	734-994-6088	994-3338	49-19
Robotic Research LLC 555 Quince Orchard Rd Ste 300 *Web:* roboticresearch.com	Gaithersburg	MD	20878	240-631-0008	631-0092	261
Robotics Institute 5000 Forbes Ave *Web:* www.ri.cmu.edu	Pittsburgh	PA	15213	412-268-3818	268-6436	668
RobotsAppscom Inc 50 California St 15th Fl Ste 1500 *Web:* www.robotappstore.com	San Francisco	CA	94111	415-439-5291		387
RobotWorx Inc 370 W Fairground St *Web:* www.robots.com	Marion	OH	43302	740-251-4312		23
RoboVent 37900 Mound Rd *TF:* 888-298-4214 ■ *Web:* www.robovent.com	Sterling Heights	MI	48310	586-698-1800	698-1801	610
Robrad Tool & Engineering Inc 564 E Juanita Ave *Web:* www.robrad.com	Mesa	AZ	85204	480-892-2529	892-6210	454
Robshaw & Associates Pc 5672 Main St *Web:* robshawlaw.com	Williamsville	NY	14221	716-633-4030		41
Robson Communities 9532 E Riggs Rd *TF:* 800-732-9949 ■ *Web:* www.robson.com	Sun Lakes	AZ	85248	800-732-9949		653
Robson Forensic Inc 354 N Prince St *TF:* 800-813-6736 ■ *Web:* www.robsonforensic.com	Lancaster	PA	17603	717-293-9050		194
Robson Technologies Inc 135 E Main Ave *Web:* www.testfixtures.com	Morgan Hill	CA	95037	408-779-8008	782-7132	743
Robstan Group Inc 400 Admiral Blvd *Web:* www.robstan.com	Kansas City	MO	64106	816-472-8870	472-7765	47
Robstown High School 609 W Hwy 44 *TF:* 800-446-3142 ■ *Web:* www.robstownisd.org	Robstown	TX	78380	361-387-5999		685
Robus Leather Corp 10 W Market St Ste 1950 *Web:* www.robus.com	Indianapolis	IN	46204	317-704-7000		432

Name / Address	City	State	ZIP	Phone	Fax	Class
Robustelli Corporate Services 1717 Newfield Ave *Web:* www.rcsltd.com	Stamford	CT	06903	203-322-2790	912-6487	184
Roby Martha (Rep R - AL) 504 Cannon House Office Bldg. *Web:* roby.house.gov	Washington	DC	20515	202-225-2901	225-8913	342-2
Robyn Inc 7717 W Britton Rd *TF:* 877-211-9711 ■ *Web:* robynpromo.com	Oklahoma City	OK	73132	877-211-9711		627
ROC Software Systems Inc 3305 Northland Dr Ste 105 *Web:* rocsoftware.com	Austin	TX	78731	512-336-4200		177
ROC USA LLC 6 Loudon Rd Ste 501 *Web:* rocusa.org	Concord	NH	03301	603-513-2791		138
Rocco Altobelli Inc 14301 Burnsville Pkwy W *Web:* roccoaltobellisalons.com	Burnsville	MN	55306	952-707-1900		77
Rocco Building Supplies LLC 560 Pleasant Valley Rd *TF:* 877-476-7640 ■ *Web:* www.roccobuilding.com	Harrisonburg	VA	22801	540-434-1371	434-4593	364
Rocco's 537 N St Louis Blvd *Web:* roccosoriginalpizza.com	South Bend	IN	46617	574-233-2464		671
Rochdale Village Inc 169-65 137th Ave *Web:* rochdalevillage.com	Jamaica	NY	11434	718-276-5700		655
Roche & Roche PC 38 Pond St Ste 308 *Web:* roche-murphy.com	Franklin	MA	02038	508-528-8300	528-8889	41
Roche Bobios 200 Madison St *Web:* www.roche-bobois.com	New York	NY	10016	212-889-0700		321
Roche Bros Supermarkets Inc 70 Hastings St *Web:* www.rochebros.com	Wellesley	MA	02481	781-235-9400		345
Roche Constructors Inc 361 71st Ave. *Web:* www.rocheconstructors.com	Greeley	CO	80634	970-356-3611	356-3619	186
Roche Diagnostics Corp (RDC) 9115 Hague Rd PO Box 50457 *TF:* 800-428-5076 ■ *Web:* www.usdiagnostics.roche.com	Indianapolis	IN	46256	800-428-5076		231
Roche Molecular Systems Inc 4300 Hacienda Dr *Web:* molecular.roche.com	Pleasanton	CA	94588	925-730-8200		582
Rocheleau Tool & Die Company Inc 117 Industrial Rd *Web:* www.rocheleautool.com	Fitchburg	MA	01420	978-345-1723	345-5972	757
Rochelle Foods LLC 1001 S Main St	Rochelle	IL	61068	815-562-4141	562-4149	473
Rochester & Monroe County Efcu 460 Goodman St N *Web:* rocmon.org	Rochester	NY	14609	585-546-4279		219
Rochester Aluminum Smelting Canada Ltd 31-35 Freshway Dr *Web:* www.rochesteraluminum.com	Concord	ON	L4K1R9	905-669-1222		492
Rochester Area Chamber of Commerce 220 S Broadway Ste 100 *Web:* www.rochestermnchamber.com	Rochester	MN	55904	507-288-1122	282-8960	139
Rochester Art Ctr 40 Civic Center Dr SE *Web:* www.rochesterartcenter.org	Rochester	MN	55904	507-282-8629		50-2
Rochester Business Journal 45 E Ave Ste 500 *Web:* rbj.net	Rochester	NY	14604	585-232-4424	546-3398	457-5
Rochester City Ballet 1326 University Ave *Web:* rochestercityballet.org	Rochester	NY	14607	585-461-5850	473-8847	573-1
Rochester City School District 131 W Broad St *Web:* www.rcsdk12.org	Rochester	NY	14614	585-262-8100		685
Rochester Civic Theatre 30 Civic Center Dr *Web:* www.rochestercivictheatre.org	Rochester	MN	55904	507-282-8481		572
Rochester College 800 W Avon Rd *TF:* 800-521-6010 ■ *Web:* www.rc.edu	Rochester Hills	MI	48307	248-218-2000	218-2025	166
Rochester Colonial Manufacturing Inc 1794 Lyell Ave *Web:* www.rochestercolonial.com	Rochester	NY	14606	585-254-8191		234
Rochester Community & Technical College 851 30th Ave SE *TF:* 800-247-1296 ■ *Web:* www.rctc.edu	Rochester	MN	55904	507-285-7210	280-3529	162
Rochester Contemporary Art Ctr 137 East Ave *Web:* www.rochestercontemporary.org	Rochester	NY	14604	585-461-2222		50-2
Rochester Convention & Visitors Bureau 30 Civic Center Dr SE Ste 200 *TF:* 800-634-8277 ■ *Web:* www.experiencerochestermn.com	Rochester	MN	55904	507-288-4331	288-9144	206
Rochester Correctional Facility 470 Ford St *Web:* www.doccs.ny.gov	Rochester	NY	14608	585-454-2280		213
Rochester Electronics Inc 16 Malcolm Hoyt Dr *Web:* www.rocelec.com	Newburyport	MA	01950	978-462-9332	462-9512	246
Rochester Gas & Electric Corp 89 E Ave *TF:* 800-743-2110 ■ *Web:* www.rge.com	Rochester	NY	14649	800-743-2110		787
Rochester Gauges Incorporated of Texas 11616 Harry Hines Blvd *Web:* www.rochestergauges.com	Dallas	TX	75229	972-241-2161	620-1403	201
Rochester Hills Public Library 500 Olde Towne Rd *Web:* rhpl.org	Rochester	MI	48307	248-656-2900		434-3
Rochester Homes Inc 1345 N Lucas St *TF:* 800-860-4554 ■ *Web:* www.rochesterhomesinc.com	Rochester	IN	46975	800-860-4554		106
Rochester Industrial Control Inc 6400 Furnace Rd *Web:* rochesterindustrial.com	Ontario	NY	14519	315-524-4555		246
Rochester Institute of Technology 1 Lomb Memorial Dr *Web:* www.rit.edu	Rochester	NY	14623	585-475-2411	475-7424	166
Rochester International Airport 7600 Helgerson Dr SW *TF:* 800-227-4672 ■ *Web:* flyrst.com	Rochester	MN	55902	507-282-2328		27
Rochester International Film Festival PO Box 17746 *Web:* rochesterfilmfest.org	Rochester	NY	14617	585-496-4443		282
Rochester Mayor's 201 Fourth St SE *Web:* www.rochestermn.gov	Rochester	MN	55904	507-328-2700		337
Rochester Metal Products Corp 616 Indiana Ave PO Box 488 *TF:* 888-215-2233 ■ *Web:* www.rochestermetals.com	Rochester	IN	46975	574-223-3164	223-2326	295
Rochester Midland Corp 333 Hollenbeck St *TF:* 800-836-1627 ■ *Web:* www.rochestermidland.com	Rochester	NY	14621	585-336-2200	467-4406	145
Rochester Museum & Science Ctr 657 E Ave *Web:* www.rmsc.org	Rochester	NY	14607	585-271-4320	271-0492	520
Rochester (NY) City Hall 30 Church St *Web:* cityofrochester.gov	Rochester	NY	14614	585-428-5990	428-6059	337
Rochester Philharmonic Orchestra 108 E Ave *Web:* www.rpo.org	Rochester	NY	14604	585-454-7311	325-4905	573-3
Rochester Psychiatric Ctr 1111 Elmwood Ave *TF:* 800-310-1160 ■ *Web:* www.rochesterhealth.com	Rochester	NY	14620	585-454-1490		374-5
Rochester Public Library 101 2nd St SE *Web:* www.rochesterpubliclibrary.org	Rochester	MN	55904	507-328-2300	328-2384	434-3
Rochester Public Library (RPL) 65 S Main St *Web:* www.rpl.lib.nh.us	Rochester	NH	03867	603-332-1428	335-7582	434-3
Rochester Regional Chamber of Commerce 71 Walnut Blvd Ste 110 *Web:* www.rrc-mi.com	Rochester	MI	48307	248-651-6700		139
Rochester Repertory Theatre Co 103 Seventh St NE *Web:* www.rochesterrep.org	Rochester	MN	55906	507-289-1737		573-4
Rochester Riverside Convention Ctr 123 E Main St *Web:* www.rrcc.com	Rochester	NY	14604	585-232-7200	232-1510	205
Rochester Rotational Molding Inc 1952 E Lucas St *TF:* 800-633-9173 ■ *Web:* www.rrmplastics.com	Rochester	IN	46975	574-223-8844		604
Rochester Shoe Tree Company Inc 1 Cedar Ln *TF:* 866-627-3800 ■ *Web:* www.shoekeeper.com	Ashland	NH	03217	603-968-3301	968-3197	200
Rochester Symphony 1530 Greenview Dr SW Ste 120 *Web:* www.rochestersymphony.org	Rochester	MN	55902	507-286-8742		573-3
Rochester Teachers Assn 30 N Union St *Web:* rochesterteachers.com	Rochester	NY	14607	585-546-2681		414
Rochester Telephone Company Inc (RTC) 117 W 8th St *Web:* www.rtc1.com	Rochester	IN	46975	574-223-2191		224
Rochester Yacht Club 5555 St Paul Blvd *Web:* www.rochesteryc.com	Rochester	NY	14617	585-342-5511	342-8116	713
Rochester-Syracuse Auto Auction 1826 SR-414 PO Box 129 *Web:* www.rsautoauction.com	Waterloo	NY	13165	315-539-5006	539-9508	516
Rochon Corp 28 Second St NW Ste 200 *Web:* rochoncorp.com	Osseo	MN	55369	763-559-9393	559-8101	186
Rock & Gem Magazine 4635 McEwen Rd *TF:* 866-377-4666 ■ *Web:* www.rockngem.com	Dallas	TX	75244	805-644-3824		457-14
Rock & Roll Hall of Fame & Museum 1100 Rock & Roll Blvd *Web:* www.rockhall.com	Cleveland	OH	44114	216-781-7625		520
Rock 'N Learn Inc 105 Commercial Cir *TF:* 800-348-8445 ■ *Web:* www.rocknlearn.com	Conroe	TX	77304	936-539-2731	539-2659	243
Rock 100.5 780 Johnson Ferry Rd NE 5th Fl *Web:* www.atlantasrockstation.com	Atlanta	GA	30342	404-497-4700		645-11
Rock 106.9 WCCC, The 1039 Asylum Ave. *Web:* www.wccc.com	Hartford	CT	06105	860-525-1069		645-69
Rock 108 301 S Polk St Ste 100 *Web:* www.amarillosrockstation.com	Amarillo	TX	79101	806-342-5200		645-5
Rock Bottom Brewery 825 Hennepin Ave Ste 125 *Web:* rockbottom.com	Minneapolis	MN	55402	612-332-2739		671
Rock Bottom Restaurant & Brewery 4508 University Ave *Web:* www.rockbottom.com	West Des Moines	IA	50266	301-652-1311		671
Rock Bridge Memorial State Park 5901 S Hwy 163 *Web:* mostateparks.com	Columbia	MO	65203	573-449-7402	442-2249	565
Rock Canyon Bank 1376 N State St *Web:* rockcanyonbank.com	Orem	UT	84057	801-222-9006		70
Rock Cave IGA Junction of Rt 4 & Rt 20 *Web:* www.rockcaveiga.com	Rock Cave	WV	26234	304-924-5296		345
Rock City Gardens 1400 Patten Rd *TF:* 800-854-0675 ■ *Web:* www.seerockcity.com	Lookout Mountain	GA	30750	706-820-2531		50-5
Rock City Mechanical Company LLC 2715 Grandview Ave *Web:* rcm-nashville.com	Nashville	TN	37211	615-251-3045		610
Rock County PO Box 367 *TF:* 800-634-8951 ■ *Web:* www.rockcountynebraska.org	Bassett	NE	68714	402-684-3933	684-2741	338
Rock County 51 S Main St *TF:* 800-924-3570 ■ *Web:* www.co.rock.wi.us	Janesville	WI	53545	608-757-5660	757-5662	338
Rock Creek Outfitters 1530 Riverside Dr *TF:* 888-707-6708 ■ *Web:* www.rockcreek.com	Chattanooga	TN	37406	423-266-8200		711
Rock Creek Park 5200 Glover Rd NW *Web:* www.nps.gov	Washington	DC	20015	202-895-6000		564
Rock Creek Resort 6380 US Hwy 212 *TF:* 800-667-1119 ■ *Web:* www.rockcreekresort.com	Red Lodge	MT	59068	406-446-1111		669
Rock Creek State Park 5627 Rock Creek E *Web:* www.iowadnr.gov	Kellogg	IA	50135	641-236-3722	236-5599	565

Name / Address	City	State	Zip	Phone	Fax	Class
Rock Creek Station State Historical Park 57426 710th Rd *Web:* www.outdoornebraska.gov	Fairbury	NE	68352	402-729-5777		565
Rock Cut State Park 7318 Harlem Rd *Web:* www.dnr.illinois.gov	Loves Park	IL	61111	815-885-3311		565
Rock Family Worship Ctr, The 2300 Memorial Pkwy SW *Web:* www.therockfamily.org	Huntsville	AL	35801	256-533-9292		48-20
Rock Garden 1951 Bond St *Web:* www.comfortsuitesgb.com	Green Bay	WI	54303	920-497-4701	499-5242	671
Rock Hill Mechanical Corp 524 Clark Ave *TF:* 877-966-7792 ■ *Web:* www.rhmcorp.com	Saint Louis	MO	63122	314-966-0600	966-3679	189-10
Rock House Publishing Inc 6304 Caleigh Dr *Web:* www.rockhousepub.com	Charlestown	IN	47111	812-697-0419	948-9998	637-2
Rock Intl PO Box 4766 *Web:* www.rockintl.org	Greenville	SC	29608	864-235-6487		393
Rock Island Capital LLC 1415 W 22nd St Ste 1250 *Web:* www.rockislandcapital.com	Oak Brook	IL	60523	630-413-9136		360-3
Rock Island Communications 208 Enchanted Forest Dr Ste D *Web:* rockisland.com	Eastsound	WA	98245	360-378-5884		681
Rock Island County 1504 Third Ave *Web:* www.rockislandcounty.org	Rock Island	IL	61201	309-786-4451		338
Rock Island National Cemetery Bldg 118 *Web:* www.cem.va.gov	Rock Island	IL	61299	309-782-2094	782-2097	136
Rock Island Public Library 401 19th St *Web:* www.rockislandlibrary.org	Rock Island	IL	61201	309-732-7323		434-3
Rock Island State Park 82 Beach Rd *TF:* 800-713-6065 ■ *Web:* tnstateparks.com	Rock Island	TN	38581	931-686-2471		565
Rock Island State Park 1924 Indian Pt Rd *Web:* dnr.wi.gov	Washington Island	WI	54246	920-847-2235		565
Rock Island Trail State Park 311 E Williams St PO Box 64 *Web:* www.dnr.illinois.gov	Wyoming	IL	61491	309-695-2228		565
Rock of Ages Corp 560 Graniteville Rd *TF:* 800-421-0166 ■ *Web:* rockofages.com	Graniteville	VT	05654	802-476-3115		724
Rock Point School 1 Rock Pt Rd *Web:* www.rockpointschool.org	Burlington	VT	05408	802-863-1104	863-6628	622
Rock River Arms Inc 1042 Cleveland Rd *Web:* www.rockriverarms.com	Colona	IL	61241	309-792-5780		807
Rock River Lumber & Grain Co 5502 Lyndon Rd PO Box 68 *TF:* 888-537-5615 ■ *Web:* www.rockriverag.com	Prophetstown	IL	61277	815-537-5131		296-23
Rock River Times, The 128 N Church St *Web:* www.rockrivertimes.com	Rockford	IL	61107	815-964-9767	964-9825	532-2
Rock River Tool Inc 2953 63rd Ave E *TF:* 800-345-8924 ■ *Web:* www.rockrivertool.com	Bradenton	FL	34203	800-345-8924	867-9312	493
Rock River Valley Blood Ctr 3065 N Perryville Rd Ste 105 *TF:* 877-778-2299 ■ *Web:* www.rrvbc.org	Rockford	IL	61114	815-965-8751	965-8756	89
Rock Sports Complex LLC, The 7900 W Crystal Ridge Dr *Web:* www.rockcomplex.com	Franklin	WI	53132	414-529-7676		354
Rock Springs Chamber of Commerce 382 Hwy 370 *Web:* rockspringschamber.com	Rock Springs	WY	82901	307-352-6880	362-3838	139
Rock Springs Guest Ranch 64201 Tyler Rd *Web:* www.rocksprings.com	Bend	OR	97701	541-382-1957		239
Rock Springs National Bank 200 Second St PO Box 880 *TF:* 800-400-0001 ■ *Web:* www.rsnb.com	Rock Springs	WY	82902	307-362-0001	362-9432	69
Rock the Vote (RTV) 1001 Connecticut Ave NW Ste 640 *Web:* www.rockthevote.org	Washington	DC	20036	202-719-9910		48-7
Rock Trade Law LLC 134 N La Salle St Ste 1800 *Web:* www.rocktradelaw.com	Chicago	IL	60602	312-824-6190		428
Rock Valley College 3301 N Mulford Rd *TF:* 800-973-7821 ■ *Web:* www.rockvalleycollege.edu	Rockford	IL	61114	815-921-7821	921-4269	162
Rock Valley Oil & Chemical Co (RV) 1911 Windsor Rd *Web:* www.rockvalleyoil.com	Rockford	IL	61101	815-654-2400	654-2428	146
Rock Valley Publishing LLC 11512 N Second St *Web:* www.rvpublishing.com	Machesney Park	IL	61115	815-877-4044		637-8
Rock Ventures LLC 1074 Woodward Ave *Web:* www.rockventures.com	Detroit	MI	48226	313-373-7700		133
Rock Veterinary Clinic PA 1295 101st St *Web:* rockvetclinic.org	Luverne	MN	56156	507-283-9524		794
Rock View Resort 1049 Parkview Dr *TF:* 800-375-9530 ■ *Web:* www.rockviewresort.com	Hollister	MO	65672	417-334-4678		379
Rock Wool Manufacturing Co 8610 Spruiell St PO Box 506 *TF:* 800-874-7625 ■ *Web:* www.deltainsulation.com	Leeds	AL	35094	205-699-6121	699-3132	389
Rockaway Press LLC 1000 Boxelder Cir *Web:* www.rockawaypress.com	Longmont	CO	80503	303-517-5825		637-2
Rockbestos-Surprenant Cable Corp 20 Bradley Park Rd *TF:* 800-327-7625 ■ *Web:* www.r-scc.com	East Granby	CT	06026	860-653-8300		814
Rockbridge County 150 S Main St *TF:* 800-420-1663 ■ *Web:* www.co.rockbridge.va.us	Lexington	VA	24450	540-463-4361	463-5981	338
Rockbridge Global Village Inc 30 Crossing Ln Ste 206 *Web:* www.rockbridge.net	Lexington	VA	24450	540-463-4451		681
Rockcastle County 1050 W Main St *Web:* rockcastle.ca.uky.edu	Mount Vernon	KY	40456	606-256-2403	256-8643	338
Rockdale Citizen 969 S Main St NE *Web:* www.rockdalenewtoncitizen.com	Conyers	GA	30012	770-483-7108	483-5797	532-2
Rockdale County 922 Ct St *Web:* rockdaleclerk.com	Conyers	GA	30012	770-278-7900	278-7921	338
Rockdale Grocery Inc 7110 US 441 *Web:* www.pigglywiggly-atl.com	Dillard	GA	30537	706-746-2624		345
Rockdale Pipeline Inc PO Box 1157 *Web:* www.rockdalepipeline.com	Conyers	GA	30012	770-922-4123		186
Rockefeller Brothers Fund 475 Riverside Dr Ste 900 *Web:* www.rbf.org	New York	NY	10115	212-812-4200	812-4299	305
Rockefeller Foundation 420 Fifth Ave *Web:* www.rockefellerfoundation.org	New York	NY	10018	212-869-8500	764-3468	305
Rockefeller State Park Preserve 125 Phelps Way *Web:* parks.ny.gov	Pleasantville	NY	10570	914-631-1470		565
Rockefeller University *Library* 1230 York Ave *Web:* www.rockefeller.edu	New York	NY	10065	212-327-8904		434-6
Rockenwagner *3 Square Cafe + Bakery* 12835 W Washington Blvd *Web:* rockenwagner.com	Los Angeles	CA	90066	310-578-8171		671
Rocker Solenoid Co 1500 W 240th St *Web:* www.rockerindustries.com	Harbor City	CA	90710	310-534-5660	534-4285	789
Rocket Communications Inc 81 Langton St Ste 12 *TF:* 844-897-6253 ■ *Web:* www.rocketcom.com	San Francisco	CA	94103	415-863-0101		344
Rocket Federal Credit Union 905 W Mcgregor Dr *Web:* rocketfcu.com	Mcgregor	TX	76657	254-840-2873		219
Rocket Imaging Inc 12365 Rhea Dr	Plainfield	IL	60585	815-577-6315		627
Rocket Jewelry Packaging & Displays 375 Executive Blvd Ste W-4 *TF:* 800-762-5521 ■ *Web:* www.rocketbox.com	Elmsford	NY	10523	718-292-5370		199
Rocket media Inc 532 Central Dr *Web:* www.rocketmediamail.com	Virginia Beach	VA	23454	757-463-9161	463-9020	5
Rocket Media Inc 3335 E Baseline Rd *TF:* 800-339-7305 ■ *Web:* www.rocketmedia.com	Gilbert	AZ	85234	800-339-7305		195
Rocket Mortgage FieldHouse 1 Center Ct *TF:* 888-894-9424 ■ *Web:* www.rocketmortgagefieldhouse.com	Cleveland	OH	44115	888-894-9424		720
Rocket Pharmaceuticals Inc 430 E 29th St Ste 1040	New York	NY	10016	781-676-2100		231
Rocket Supply 404 N Rt 115 *TF:* 800-252-6871 ■ *Web:* www.rocketsupply.com	Roberts	IL	60962	800-252-6871		516
Rocket Ventures 2200 Sand Hill Rd Ste 240 *Web:* www.rocketventures.com	Menlo Park	CA	94025	650-561-9100		792
RocketCityNow.com 1309 N Memorial Pkwy *Web:* www.rocketcitynow.com	Huntsville	AL	35801	256-755-3246	203-8320	741-61
Rocket-Hire LLC 4537 N Robertson St *TF:* 844-426-2246 ■ *Web:* rocket-hire.com	New Orleans	LA	70117	504-236-7259		463
Rockets of Awesome 419 Park Ave S *TF:* 877-762-5387 ■ *Web:* www.rocketsofawesome.com	New York	NY	10016	877-762-5387		42
Rocketship Inc 110 S 300 W *Web:* www.rocketshipdesign.com	Provo	UT	84601	801-373-1922		393
Rockett Inc 3640 4th St *Web:* www.rockettinc.com	Flowood	MS	39232	601-939-9347	932-2307	91
Rockfish Seafood Grill 275 W Campbell Rd Ste 115 *Web:* www.rockfish.com	Richardson	TX	75080	214-887-9400	821-0138	670
Rockford Acromatic Products Co 611 Beacon St *Web:* www.rockfordacromatic.com	Loves Park	IL	61111	815-877-7473		454
Rockford Area Chamber of Commerce 17 S Monroe *Web:* rockfordmichamber.com	Rockford	MI	49341	616-866-2000	866-2141	139
Rockford Area Convention & Visitors Bureau 102 N Main St *Web:* www.gorockford.com	Rockford	IL	61101	815-963-8111	963-4298	206
Rockford Art Museum 711 N Main St *TF:* 800-521-0849 ■ *Web:* www.rockfordartmuseum.org	Rockford	IL	61103	815-968-2787	316-2179	520
Rockford Career College 1130 S Alpine Rd *Web:* www.rockfordcareercollege.edu	Rockford	IL	61108	815-965-8616		764
Rockford Chamber of Commerce 308 W State St Ste 190 *Web:* www.rockfordchamber.com	Rockford	IL	61101	815-987-8100	987-8122	139
Rockford City Hall 425 E State St *Fax Area Code: 815 ■ *Web:* rockfordil.gov	Rockford	IL	61104	779-348-7300	967-6952*	337
Rockford College 5050 E State St *TF:* 800-892-2984 ■ *Web:* www.rockford.edu	Rockford	IL	61108	815-226-4000	226-2822	166
Rockford Constant Velocity 1500 11th Ave *Web:* www.rockfordcv.com	Rockford	IL	61104	815-962-1411		61
Rockford Corp 600 S Rockford Dr *OTC: ROFO* ■ *Web:* www.rockfordcorp.com	Tempe	AZ	85281	480-967-3565	966-3983	52
Rockford Homes Inc 999 Polaris Pkwy Ste 200 *Web:* www.rockfordhomes.net	Columbus	OH	43240	614-785-0015		187
Rockford Institute 928 N Main St *TF:* 800-383-0680 ■ *Web:* www.chroniclesmagazine.org	Rockford	IL	61103	815-964-5053		634
Rockford It 6090 Strathmoor Dr *Web:* rockfordit.com	Rockford	IL	61107	815-316-7575	316-7574	175
Rockford Manufacturing Co 3901 Little River Rd	Rockford	TN	37853	865-970-3131		208
Rockford Manufacturing Group Inc 14343 Industrial Pky *Web:* www.rmgfelm.com	South Beloit	IL	61080	815-624-2500	624-7254	494
Rockford Memorial Hospital 2400 N Rockton Ave *Web:* mercyhealthsystem.org	Rockford	IL	61103	815-971-5000		374-3
Rockford Mercantile Agency Inc 2502 S Alpine Rd *TF:* 800-369-6116 ■ *Web:* www.rockfordmercantile.com	Rockford	IL	61108	815-229-3328		393

Name / Address	City	State	ZIP	Phone	Fax	Class
Rockford Metro Ctr 300 Elm St *Web:* thebmoharrisbankcenter.com	Rockford	IL	61101	815-968-5600	968-5451	720
Rockford Process Control Inc 2020 Seventh St *TF:* 800-228-3779 ■ *Web:* rockfordprocess.com	Rockford	IL	61104	815-966-2000	966-2026	350
Rockford Register Star 99 E State St *Web:* www.rrstar.com	Rockford	IL	61104	815-987-1359	987-1365	532-2
Rockford Road Animal Hospital PA 3900 Vinewood Ln N Ste 16 *Web:* rrahospital.com	Plymouth	MN	55441	763-559-7554		794
Rockford Spring Co 3801 S Central Ave *Web:* www.rockfordspring.com	Rockford	IL	61102	815-968-3000	968-3100	718
Rockford Symphony Orchestra 711 N Main St *Web:* www.rockfordsymphony.com	Rockford	IL	61103	815-965-0049	965-0642	573-3
Rockford Systems Inc 4620 Hydraulic Rd *TF:* 800-922-7533 ■ *Web:* www.rockfordsystems.com	Rockford	IL	61109	815-874-7891	874-6144	203
Rockford Toolcraft Inc 766 Research Pkwy *Web:* www.rockfordtoolcraft.com	Rockford	IL	61109	815-398-5507		488
Rockhill-York County Convention & Visitors Bureau 452 S Anderson Rd *TF:* 888-702-1320 ■ *Web:* www.visityorkcounty.com	Rock Hill	SC	29730	803-329-5200	329-0145	206
Rockhurst University 1100 Rockhurst Rd *TF:* 800-842-6776 ■ *Web:* www.rockhurst.edu	Kansas City	MO	64110	816-501-4000	501-4241	166
Rocking Horse Ranch Resort 600 SR-44/55 *TF:* 800-647-2624 ■ *Web:* www.rockinghorseranch.com	Highland Falls	NY	12528	800-647-2624		669
Rockingham Community College 215 Wrenn Memorial Rd *Web:* www.rockinghamcc.edu	Wentworth	NC	27375	336-342-4261	342-1809	162
Rockingham Co-op 1040 S High St *Web:* rockinghamcoop.com	Harrisonburg	VA	22801	540-434-3856	434-6890	275
Rockingham County 20 E Gay St *Web:* www.rockinghamcountyva.gov	Harrisonburg	VA	22802	540-564-3000		338
Rockingham County 371 US Hwy 65 PO Box 101 *Web:* www.co.rockingham.nc.us	Wentworth	NC	27375	336-342-8101	342-8105	338
Rockingham County Public Library 598 S Pierce St *Web:* rcpl.libguides.com	Eden	NC	27288	336-623-3168	623-1171	434-3
Rockingham Dragway 2153 Hwy US 1 N PO Box 70 *Web:* www.rockinghamdragway.com	Rockingham	NC	28379	910-582-3400	582-8667	515
Rockingham New Holland Inc 600 W Market St *Web:* rockinghamnh.com	Harrisonburg	VA	22802	540-434-6791	434-6780	274
Rockingham State Historic Site 84 Laurel Ave *Web:* www.rockingham.net	Kingston	NJ	08528	609-683-7132		565
Rockingham Steel Inc 2565 John Wayland Hwy *TF:* 800-738-1742 ■ *Web:* www.rockinghamsteel.com	Harrisonburg	VA	22803	800-738-1742		492
Rock-It Cargo USA Inc 5343 W Imperial Hwy Ste 900 *TF:* 800-973-1727 ■ *Web:* www.rockitcargo.com	Los Angeles	CA	90045	310-410-0935	410-0628	311
Rockland Bakery Inc 94 Demarest Mill Rd W *Web:* www.rocklandbakery.com	Nanuet	NY	10954	845-623-5800	623-6921	296-1
Rockland Community College 145 College Rd *TF:* 800-722-7666 ■ *Web:* www.sunyrockland.edu	Suffern	NY	10901	845-574-4000	574-4433	162
Rockland County 11 New Hempstead Rd *Web:* rocklandgov.com	New City	NY	10956	845-638-5100	638-5675	338
Rockland Federal Credit Union 241 Union St *TF:* 800-562-7328 ■ *Web:* www.rfcu.com	Rockland	MA	02370	781-878-0232	792-3866	219
Rockland Immunochemicals Inc PO Box 326 *TF:* 800-656-7625 ■ *Web:* www.rockland-inc.com	Gilbertsville	PA	19525	610-369-1008	367-7825	231
Rockland Inc 152 Weber Ln *Web:* www.rocklandmfg.com	Bedford	PA	15522	814-623-1115	623-7214	190
Rockland Industries Inc 1601 Edison Hwy *Web:* rocklandflooring.com	Baltimore	MD	21213	410-522-2505		819
Rockland Lake State Park PO Box 217 *Web:* parks.ny.gov	Congers	NY	10920	845-268-3020		565
Rockland Psychiatric Ctr 140 Old Orangeburg Rd *Web:* omh.ny.gov	Orangeburg	NY	10962	845-359-1000	680-5580	374-5
Rockland Trust 435 Market St *NASDAQ: PEOP* ■ *Web:* www.rocklandtrust.com	Boston	MA	02135	617-254-0813		70
Rocklands Barbeque & Grilling Co 25 S Quaker Ln *Web:* rocklands.com	Alexandria	VA	22314	703-778-8000		671
Rockledge Hook & Ladder Social Hall Rentals 505 Huntingdon Pk *Web:* www.rockledgefireco.org	Rockledge	PA	19046	215-379-8373		181
Rockler Press PO Box 8572 *TF:* 800-279-4441 ■ *Web:* www.woodworkersjournal.com	Red Oak	IA	51591	800-279-4441		637-9
Rocklin Academy, The 6532 Turnstone Way *Web:* www.rocklinacademy.com	Rocklin	CA	95765	916-632-6580		685
Rocklin Area Chamber of Commerce 3700 Rocklin Rd *TF:* 800-228-3380 ■ *Web:* www.rocklinchamber.com	Rocklin	CA	95677	916-624-2548	624-5743	139
Rocklin Park Hotel 5450 China Garden Rd *TF:* 888-630-9400 ■ *Web:* www.rocklinpark.com	Rocklin	CA	95677	916-630-9400	630-9448	379
Rockmount Ranch Wear Manufacturing Co 1626 Wazee St *TF:* 800-776-2566 ■ *Web:* www.rockmount.com	Denver	CO	80202	303-629-7777	629-5836	155-20
Rocknel Fastener Inc 5309 11th St *Web:* www.rocknel.com	Rockford	IL	61109	815-873-4000	873-4011	351
Rockoff Harlan & Rasof Ltd 3818 Oakton St *Web:* www.rhrcpa.com	Skokie	IL	60076	847-675-7777		734
Rockpoint Logistics LLC 901 Bilter Rd *Web:* www.rockpointlogistics.com	Aurora	IL	60502	630-801-2900		314
Rockport Capital Partners 160 Federal St 18th Fl *Web:* www.rockportcap.com	Boston	MA	02110	617-912-1420	912-1449	792
Rockport Center for the Arts 902 Navigation Cir *Web:* www.rockportartcenter.com	Rockport	TX	78382	361-729-5519	729-3551	572
Rockport Company Inc 1220 Washington St *TF:* 800-828-0545 ■ *Web:* www.rockport.com	Newton	MA	02465	781-401-5000	401-5230	301
Rockport State Park 51905 WA-20 *Web:* parks.state.wa.us	Rockport	WA	98283	360-853-8461		565
Rockport Technology Group Inc 5 Industrial Way Ste 2C *TF:* 800-399-7053 ■ *Web:* www.rockporttech.com	Salem	NH	03079	603-681-0333		180
Rocks State Park 3318 Rocks Chrome Hill Rd *Web:* www.dnr.maryland.gov	Jarrettsville	MD	21084	410-557-7994		565
Rock-Tred Corp 405 N Oakwood Ave *Web:* www.rocktred.com	Waukegan	IL	60085	847-673-8200	679-6665	189-2
Rockview Dairies Inc 7011 Stewart & Gray Rd *TF:* 800-423-2479 ■ *Web:* www.rockviewfarms.com	Downey	CA	90241	562-927-5511		297-4
Rockville Chamber of Commerce 1 Research Ct Ste 450 *Web:* www.rockvillechamber.org	Rockville	MD	20850	301-424-9300	762-7599	139
Rockville Correctional Facility 811 W 50 N *Web:* www.in.gov	Rockville	IN	47872	765-569-3178		213
Rockville Fuel & Feed Company Inc 14901 S Lawn Ln PO Box 1707 *Web:* rockvilleconcrete.com	Rockville	MD	20850	301-762-3988	309-3894	182
Rockville General Hospital 31 Union St *Web:* www.echn.org	Vernon	CT	06066	860-872-0501		374-3
Rockville Road Veterinarians Inc 7351 Rockville Rd *Web:* rockvilleroadanimal.com	Indianapolis	IN	46214	317-271-2200		794
Rockwall County Chamber of Commerce 697 E I-30 *Web:* rockwallchamber.org	Rockwall	TX	75087	972-771-7700	772-3642	139
Rockwall County Library 1215 E Yellowjacket Ln *Web:* www.rockwallcountytexas.com	Rockwall	TX	75087	972-204-7700	204-7709	435
Rockwell 1714 N Vermont Ave *Web:* rockwell-la.com	Los Angeles	CA	90027	323-669-1550		671
Rockwell Automation Canada Inc 135 Dundas St *Web:* www.rockwellautomation.com	Cambridge	ON	N1R5N9	519-623-1810		690
Rockwell Collins Inc 400 Collins Rd NE *NYSE: COL* ■ *TF:* 888-721-3094 ■ *Web:* www.rockwellcollins.com	Cedar Rapids	IA	52498	319-295-9000	295-1542	529
Rockwell Debt-Free Properties Inc 8494 South 700 East Ste 200 *Web:* rockwelltic.com	Sandy	UT	84070	801-568-1031		653
Rockwell Farms 332 Rockwell Farms Rd *TF:* 800-635-6576 ■ *Web:* www.rockwellfarms.com	Rockwell	NC	28138	800-635-6576		369
Rockwell Financial Group LLC 9085 E Mineral Cir Ste 320 *Web:* www.rockwellfinance.com	Centennial	CO	80112	720-257-7977	257-7976	401
Rockwell Laser Industries Inc 7754 Camargo Rd *TF:* 800-945-2737 ■ *Web:* www.rli.com	Cincinnati	OH	45243	513-272-9900	272-9901	543
Rockwell Medical Inc 30142 Wixom Rd *NASDAQ: RMTI* ■ *TF:* 800-449-3353 ■ *Web:* www.rockwellmed.com	Wixom	MI	48393	248-960-9009	960-9119	250
Rockwell's 27 Broadway St *Web:* www.mbaybrew.com	Toledo	OH	43604	419-243-1302		671
Rockwell's Neighborhood Grill 4632 N Rockwell St *Web:* www.rockwellsgrill.com	Chicago	IL	60625	773-509-1871		671
Rockwood Capital LLC 50 California St 30th Fl *Web:* rockwoodcap.com	San Francisco	CA	94111	415-645-4300		653
Rockwood Dry Cleaners 171 Granville St *Web:* rockwoodcleaners.com	Gahanna	OH	43230	614-471-3700		426
Rockwood Retaining Walls Inc 7200 Hwy 63 N **Fax Area Code: 507* ■ *TF:* 800-535-2375 ■ *Web:* www.rockwoodwalls.com	Rochester	MN	55906	888-288-4045	529-2879*	183
Rockwood Retirement Community 2903 E 25th Ave *TF:* 800-727-6650 ■ *Web:* www.rockwoodretirement.org	Spokane	WA	99223	509-536-6650	536-6662	672
Rockwood Service Corp 43 Arch St *TF:* 888-539-1849 ■ *Web:* www.rockwoodservice.com	Greenwich	CT	06830	203-869-6734		466
Rocky Brands Inc 39 E Canal St *NASDAQ: RCKY* ■ *TF:* 877-795-2410 ■ *Web:* www.rockyboots.com	Nelsonville	OH	45764	740-753-3130		301
Rocky Gap State Park 12500 Pleasant Valley Rd *Web:* www.dnr.maryland.gov	Flintstone	MD	21530	301-722-1480		565
Rocky Mount Area Chamber of Commerce 100 Coastline St Ste 200 *Web:* www.rockymountchamber.org	Rocky Mount	NC	27804	252-446-0323	446-5103	139
Rocky Mount Children's Museum 270 Gay St *Web:* imperialcentre.org	Rocky Mount	NC	27804	252-972-1167		521
Rocky Mount Cord Co 381 N Grace St *TF:* 800-342-9130 ■ *Web:* www.rmcord.com	Rocky Mount	NC	27804	252-977-9130	977-9123	208
Rocky Mount Museum 200 Hyder Hill Rd PO Box 160 *TF:* 888-538-1791 ■ *Web:* www.rockymountmuseum.com	Piney Flats	TN	37686	423-538-7396	538-1086	520
Rocky Mountain Bank 2615 King Ave W *Web:* www.rmbank.com	Billings	MT	59108	406-656-3140	655-5133	690
Rocky Mountain Children's Health Foundation 5394 Marshall St Ste 400 *TF:* 833-234-0555 ■ *Web:* rmchildren.org	Arvada	CO	80002	303-839-6782	839-7336	363

	Phone	Fax	Class
Rocky Mountain Chocolate Factory Inc (RMCF) 265 Turner Dr ... Durango CO 81303 *NASDAQ:* RMCF ■ *TF:* 888-525-2462 ■ *Web:* www.rmcf.com	970-247-4943		123
Rocky Mountain College 1511 Poly Dr ... Billings MT 59102 *TF:* 800-877-6259 ■ *Web:* www.rocky.edu	406-657-1000	657-1189	166
Rocky Mountain Escape PO Box 5029 ... Hinton AB T7V1X3 *Web:* www.ecolodge.com	780-865-0124		771
Rocky Mountain Fabrication (RMF) 1125 West 2300 North PO Box 16409 ... Salt Lake City UT 84116 *TF:* 888-763-5307 ■ *Web:* www.rmf-slc.com	801-596-2400	322-2702	91
Rocky Mountain Food Factory Inc 2825 S Raritan St ... Englewood CO 80110 *Web:* www.rockymtnfoodfactory.com	303-761-3330		297-8
Rocky Mountain Hardware Inc 1020 Airport Way ... Hailey ID 83333 *TF:* 888-788-2013 ■ *Web:* www.rockymountainhardware.com	208-788-2013	788-2577	350
Rocky Mountain Health Plans 2775 Crossroads Blvd PO Box 10600 ... Grand Junction CO 81502 **Fax Area Code:* 970 ■ *TF:* 800-843-0719 ■ *Web:* www.rmhp.org	800-843-0719	244-7880*	391-3
Rocky Mountain Instrument Co (RMI) 106 Laser Dr ... Lafayette CO 80026 *TF:* 866-678-4270 ■ *Web:* www.rmico.com	303-664-5000	664-5002	544
Rocky Mountain Lions Eye Bank (RMLEB) 1675 Aurora Crt Ste El2049 PO Box 6026 ... Aurora CO 80045 *TF:* 800-444-7479 ■ *Web:* www.corneas.org	720-848-3937	848-3938	269
Rocky Mountain Log Homes 1883 Hwy 93 S ... Hamilton MT 59840 *Web:* www.rockymountainloghomes.com	406-363-5680	363-2109	106
Rocky Mountain Medical Search (RMMS) 5340 S Quebec St Ste 320 S ... Greenwood Village CO 80111 *TF:* 800-735-6721 ■ *Web:* www.rmmedicalsearch.com	800-735-6721		194
Rocky Mountain Motorcycle Museum & Hall of Fame 5867 N Nevada Ave ... Colorado Springs CO 80918 *Web:* www.themotorcyclemuseum.com	719-487-8005		520
Rocky Mountain National Park 1000 Hwy 36 ... Estes Park CO 80517 *Web:* www.nps.gov	970-586-1206		564
Rocky Mountain Natural Meats Inc 9757 Alton Way ... Henderson CO 80640 *Web:* greatrangebison.com	303-287-7100		473
Rocky Mountain Orthodontics Inc (RMO) 650 W Colfax Ave ... Denver CO 80204 *TF:* 800-525-6375 ■ *Web:* www.rmortho.com	303-592-8200		228
Rocky Mountain Prestress 5801 Pecos St ... Denver CO 80221 *Web:* www.rmpprestress.com	303-480-1111		364
Rocky Mountain Quilt Museum 200 Violet St Ste 140 ... Golden CO 80401 *Web:* www.rmqm.org	303-277-0377		520
Rocky Mountain Recorders (RMR) 1250 W Cedar Ave ... Denver CO 80223 *Web:* www.coloradorecordingstudios.net	303-777-3648	777-3923	393
Rocky Mountain Recycling Inc 6510 Brighton Blvd ... Commerce City CO 80022 *Web:* www.mountainrecycling.com	303-288-6868	288-0250	686
Rocky Mountain Research Station *US Forest Service* 240 W Prospec ... Fort Collins CO 80526 *Web:* www.fs.usda.gov	970-498-1100	498-1010	668
Rocky Mountain Tissue Bank 2993 S Peoria St Ste 390 ... Aurora CO 80014 *TF:* 800-424-5169 ■ *Web:* www.rmtb.org	303-337-3330	337-9383	545
Rocky Mountain Transportation Inc 1410 E Edgewood ... Whitefish MT 59937 *Web:* www.rockymountaintrans.com	406-863-1200	863-1213	109
Rocky Mountain Wine Co 133 Big Horn Dr ... Kalispell MT 59901 *Web:* www.rockymountainwine.com	406-752-9463		443
Rocky Neck State Park PO Box 676 ... Niantic CT 06357 *Web:* portal.ct.gov	860-676-3120		565
Rocky Point Gold & Silver Exchange 137 Main Ct ... Stony Brook NY 11790 *Web:* rockypointjewelers.com	631-751-3751		410
Rocky Ridge Trucks 259 Westclock Ext ... Franklin Springs GA 30639 *Web:* www.rockyridgetrucks.com	706-245-8693		770
Rocky River Brewing Co 21290 Ctr Ridge Rd ... Rocky River OH 44116 *Web:* www.rockyriverbrewco.com	440-895-2739		102
Rocky River Public Library 1600 Hampton Rd ... Rocky River OH 44116 *Web:* www.rrpl.org	440-333-7610		435
Rocky Rococo 105 E Wisconsin Ave ... Oconomowoc WI 53066 *TF:* 800-888-7625 ■ *Web:* rockyrococo.com	262-569-5580		670
Rocky Top Furniture Inc 8957 Lexington Rd ... Lancaster KY 40444 *TF:* 800-332-1143 ■ *Web:* rockytopfurniture.com	859-548-2828		321
Rocky's Italian Restaurant 120 N Sycamore St ... Branson MO 65616	417-335-4765		671
RockYou Inc 642 Harrison St Ste 300 ... San Francisco CA 94107 *Web:* www.rockyou.com	415-580-6400		178-1
Roco Rescue 7077 Exchequer Dr ... Baton Rouge LA 70809 *TF:* 800-647-7626 ■ *Web:* www.rocorescue.com	225-755-7626		463
Rocscience 31 Balsam Ave ... Toronto ON M4E3B5 *Web:* www.rocscience.com	416-698-8217		178-10
Rod L Electronics Inc 935 Sierra Vista Ave F ... Mountain View CA 94043 *TF:* 800-548-6305 ■ *Web:* rodl.com	650-322-0711	326-1993	248
Roda Group, The 918 Parker St ... Berkeley CA 94710 *Web:* www.rodagroup.com	510-649-1900		41
Rodale Electronics Inc 20 Oser Ave ... Hauppauge NY 11788 *Web:* www.rodaleelectronics.com	631-231-0044	231-1345	248
Rodale Institute 611 Siegfriedale Rd ... Kutztown PA 19530 *TF:* 800-432-1565 ■ *Web:* www.rodaleinstitute.org	610-683-1400	683-8548	668
Rodbat Security Services 8125 Somerset Blvd ... Paramount CA 90723 *TF:* 877-676-3228 ■ *Web:* www.rmiintl.com	562-806-9098		693
Rodd Hotels & Resorts PO Box 432 ... Charlottetown PE C1A7K7 *TF:* 800-565-7633 ■ *Web:* roddvacations.com	902-892-7448	368-3569	377
Rodda Paint Co 6107 N Marine Dr ... Portland OR 97203 *TF:* 800-452-2315 ■ *Web:* www.roddapaint.com	503-521-4300		550
Roddey Engineering Services Inc 10100 Woolworth Rd ... Keithville LA 71047 *Web:* www.themartincompanies.com	318-221-1996		261
Rodeberg & Berryman Inc 119 S First St ... Montevideo MN 56265 *Web:* www.granitefalls.com	320-269-7695		261
Rodefer Moss & Company PLLC 608 Mabry Hood Rd ... Knoxville TN 37932 *Web:* www.rodefermoss.com	865-583-0091		2
Rodeo Plastic Bag & Film Inc 3328 Executive Blvd ... Mesquite TX 75149 *Web:* www.rodeoplastic.com	972-216-3331		596
Rodey Dickason Sloan Akin & Robb PA 201 Third St NW Ste 2200 PO Box 1888 ... Albuquerque NM 87102 *Web:* www.rodey.com	505-765-5900	768-7395	428
Rodgers & Hammerstein Organization, The 229 W 28th St 11th Fl ... New York NY 10001 *TF:* 800-400-8160 ■ *Web:* rodgersandhammerstein.com	212-541-6600		514
Rodgers Cathy McMorris (Rep R - WA) 1035 Longworth House Office Bldg ... Washington DC 20515 *Web:* www.mcmorris.house.gov	202-225-2006		342-2
Rodgers Group Ltd, The 3739 N Tripp Ave ... Chicago IL 60641 *Web:* therodgersgroup.com	773-316-9754		463
Rodgers Instruments LLC 1300 NE 25th Ave ... Hillsboro OR 97124 *Web:* www.rodgersinstruments.com	503-648-4181	681-0444	527
Rodgers Townsend LLC 200 N Broadway 12th Fl ... Saint Louis MO 63102 *Web:* rodgerstownsend.com	314-259-8319		7
Rodgers Travel Inc 512 W Lancaster Ave SteC ... Wayne PA 19087 *TF:* 877-636-1775 ■ *Web:* www.rodgerstravel.com	610-964-1775	964-1776	775
Rodheim Marketing Group 125 E Baker St Unit 266 ... Costa Mesa CA 92626	714-557-5100		194
Rodine Communications Inc PO Box 792 ... Sterling CO 80751 *Web:* rodine.com	970-522-5097		396
Rodizio Grill 600 South 700 East ... Salt Lake City UT 84102 *Web:* www.rodiziogrill.com	801-220-0500		671
Rodman Media Corp 70 Hilltop Rd 3rd Fl ... Ramsey NJ 07446 *Web:* rodmanmedia.com	201-825-2552		5
Rodman Public Library 215 E Broadway St ... Alliance OH 44601 *Web:* www.rodmanlibrary.com	330-821-2665		434-3
Rodman's Discount Food & Drugs 4301 Randolph Rd ... Silver Spring MD 20906 *Web:* www.rodmans.com	301-946-3100		237
Rodney Babar Inc 4222 Pilot Dr ... Memphis TN 38118 *Web:* www.baberweb.com	901-332-6300		113
Rodney G. Hughes CPA 388 17th St Ste 100 ... Oakland CA 94612 *Web:* rodhughescpa.com	510-891-9662		2
Rodney Hunt Co 46 Mill St ... Orange MA 01364 *Web:* www.rodneyhunt.com	978-633-4362		480
Rodney L. Rich & Company Inc 300 N Tarragona St ... Pensacola FL 32501 *Web:* rodneyrichco.com	850-434-5321		390
Rodney P. Kinney Associates Inc 16515 Centerfield Dr Ste 101 ... Eagle River AK 99577 *Web:* rpka.net	907-694-2332	694-1807	261
Rodney Strong Vineyards 11455 Old Redwood Hwy ... Healdsburg CA 95448 *TF:* 800-678-4763 ■ *Web:* www.rodneystrong.com	707-431-1533		80-3
Rodney's Oyster House 469 King St W ... Toronto ON M5V1K4 *Web:* rodneysoysterhouse.com	416-363-8105	363-6638	671
Rodolf & Todd PLLC 401 S Boston Ave Ste 2000 ... Tulsa OK 74103 *Web:* rodolftodd.com	918-295-2100		41
Rodrigo's Online Store 1320 N Manzanita ... Orange CA 92867 *Web:* www.rodrigos-shop.com	714-633-7844		299
Rodriguez Transportation Group Inc 11211 Taylor Draper Ln Ste 100 ... Austin TX 78759 *Web:* rtg-texas.com	512-231-9544	231-9133	261
Roe Comm Inc 1400 Ramona Ave ... Portage MI 49002 *TF:* 800-421-2621 ■ *Web:* www.roecomm.com	269-327-1045	327-8784	392
Roe Dental Laboratory Inc 7165 E Pleasant Valley Rd ... Independence OH 44131 *TF:* 800-228-6663 ■ *Web:* www.roedentallab.com	216-663-2233	663-2237	415
Roe Machine Inc 12725 Union Rd ... West Frankfort IL 62896 *Web:* www.roemachineco.com	618-983-5524	983-8390	454
Roe Phil (Rep R - TN) 102 Cannon House Office Bldg ... Washington DC 20515 *Web:* roe.house.gov	202-225-6356	225-5714	342-2
Roebbelen Construction Inc 1241 Hawks Flight Ct ... El Dorado Hills CA 95762 *Web:* www.roebbelen.com	916-939-4000	939-4028	186
Roeberg, Moore & Friedman PA 910 Gilpin Ave ... Wilmington DE 19806 *Web:* roebergmooreandfriedman.com	302-658-8700		41
Roebic Laboratories Inc 25 Connair Rd PO Box 927 ... Orange CT 06477 *Web:* www.roebic.com	203-795-1283	795-5227	145
Roedel Companies LLC 1134 Gibbons Hwy ... Wilton NH 03086 *Web:* roedelcompanies.com	603-654-2040	654-6005	378
Roedel, Parsons, Koch, Blache, Balhoff & Mccollister, A Law Corp 8440 Jefferson Hwy Ste 301 ... Baton Rouge LA 70809 *Web:* roedelparsons.com	225-929-7033		41
Roeder Implement Inc 2550 Rockdale Rd ... Dubuque IA 52003 *TF:* 800-557-1184 ■ *Web:* www.roederimplement.com	563-557-1184	583-1821	274
Roeder Implement Inc 781 120th Rd ... Seneca KS 66538 *Web:* www.roederimp.com	785-336-6103	336-0115	274
Roeder Travel Ltd 9805 York Rd ... Cockeysville MD 21030 *Web:* www.roedertravel.com	410-667-6090		771

Name	Address	City	State	ZIP	Phone	Fax	Class
Roehl & Yi Investment Advisors LLC	450 Country Club Rd Ste 200	Eugene	OR	97401	541-683-2085		690
TF: 888-683-4343 ■ *Web:* roehl-yi.com							
Roehl Transport Inc	1916 E 29th St PO Box 750	Marshfield	WI	54449	715-591-3795		780
TF: 800-826-8367 ■ *Web:* www.roehl.jobs							
Roemer Wallens Gold & Mineaux LLP	13 Columbia Cir	Albany	NY	12203	518-464-1300		41
Web: rwgmlaw.com							
Roesch Inc	100 N 24th St	Belleville	IL	62222	800-423-6243	233-1186*	481
**Fax Area Code:* 618 ■ *TF:* 800-423-6243 ■ *Web:* www.roeschinc.com							
Roettele Industries Inc	15485 Dupont Ave	Chino	CA	91710	909-606-8252		326
Web: www.roetteleindustries.com							
Roffe Container Inc	1802 2nd Ave N	Moorhead	MN	56560	218-233-5145		98
Roffe Enterprises Inc	438 N Frederick Ave	Gaithersburg	MD	20877	301-963-0762	963-9431	194
Web: www.hhcgroup.com							
Roffman Miller Associates Inc	1835 Market St Ste 500	Philadelphia	PA	19103	215-981-1030	981-0146	401
TF: 800-995-1030 ■ *Web:* www.roffmanmiller.com							
Rofin-Sinar Inc	40984 Concept Dr	Plymouth	MI	48170	734-455-5400	455-2741	425
Web: www.rofin-inc.com							
Rogan Corp	3455 Woodhead Dr	Northbrook	IL	60062	847-498-2300	498-2334	608
TF: 800-584-5662 ■ *Web:* www.rogancorp.com							
Roger A. Soape Inc	19450 State Hwy 249 Ste 460	Houston	TX	77070	281-440-6347	440-0609	690
Web: www.rasoape.com							
Roger Bates Garage	21026 State Hwy 81	Kewanee	IL	61443	309-852-2285		274
Web: www.rogerbatesgarage.com							
Roger Black Studio Inc	107 Third Ave	Saint Pete Beach	FL	33706	212-481-9800		317
Web: www.rogerblack.com							
Roger D. Fields & Assoc	4588 Kenny Rd	Columbus	OH	43220	614-451-2248		261
Web: rdfa.com							
Roger D. Perry, CPA PC	3050 Business Park Cir Ste 401	Goodlettsville	TN	37072	615-851-6081		2
Roger Dean Chevrolet West Palm Beach	2235 Okeechobee Blvd	West Palm Beach	FL	33409	561-594-1478		57
TF: 877-827-4705 ■ *Web:* www.rogerdeanchevrolet.com							
Roger Dean Stadium	4751 Main St	Jupiter	FL	33458	561-775-1818	691-6886	720
Web: rogerdeanchevroletstadium.com							
Roger Grace Associates LLC	109 Greenfield Ct	Naples	FL	34110	239-596-8738		193
Web: www.rgrace.com							
Roger L. Handy PC	1064 Laskin Rd Ste 25C	Virginia Beach	VA	23451	757-965-7501	965-7503	2
Web: handycpas.com							
Roger Mills County	500 E Broadway PO Box 708	Cheyenne	OK	73628	580-497-3350		338
Web: www.rogermills.org							
Roger Sherman Inn	195 Oenoke Rdg	New Canaan	CT	06840	203-966-4541		379
Web: www.rogershermaninn.com							
Roger Sipe CPA Firm LLC	5742 Coventry Ln	Fort Wayne	IN	46804	260-432-9996		2
TF: 888-747-3272 ■ *Web:* sipecpa.com							
Roger Smith Hotel	501 Lexington Ave	New York	NY	10017	212-755-1400	758-4061	379
TF: 800-445-0277 ■ *Web:* www.rogersmith.com							
Roger W. Wheeler State Beach	100 Sand Hill Cove Rd	Narragansett	RI	02882	401-789-3563		565
Web: www.riparks.com							
Roger Ward Inc	17275 Green Mtn Rd	San Antonio	TX	78247	210-551-0287	653-0919	780
TF: 888-909-3147 ■ *Web:* www.wardnorthamerican.com							
Roger Williams Medical Ctr	825 Chalkstone Ave	Providence	RI	02908	401-456-2000		374-3
Web: www.rwmc.org							
Roger Williams National Memorial	282 N Main St	Providence	RI	02903	401-521-7266		564
Web: www.nps.gov							
Roger Williams Park Zoo	1000 Elmwood Ave	Providence	RI	02907	401-785-3510	941-3988	823
Web: rwpzoo.org							
Roger Williams University	1 Old Ferry Rd	Bristol	RI	02809	401-254-3500	254-3557	166
TF: 800-458-7144 ■ *Web:* www.rwu.edu							
Roger Williams University Ralph R Papitto School of Law	10 Metacom Ave	Bristol	RI	02809	401-254-4500	254-4516	167-1
TF: 800-633-2727 ■ *Web:* law.rwu.edu							
Roger's Academy of Hair Design	2903 Mt Vernon Ave	Evansville	IN	47712	812-429-0110		167-3
Web: www.rogershair.com							
Roger's Manufacturing Corp	801 Industrial Pkwy	West Monroe	LA	71291	318-396-5700		817
Web: www.rogersmfg.com							
Rogers & Brown	2 Cumberland St	Charleston	SC	29401	843-577-3630		311
Web: www.rogers-brown.com							
Rogers & Cowan	1840 Century Pk E 18th Fl	Los Angeles	CA	90067	310-854-8100		731
Web: www.rogersandcowan.com							
Rogers & Greenberg LLP	40 N Main St Ste 2160	Dayton	OH	45423	937-223-8171		41
Web: rogersgreenberg.com							
Rogers & Lapan PA	355 Windy Ridge Rd	Chapel Hill	NC	27517	919-545-9259		428
Web: rogerslapan.com							
Rogers Arena	800 Griffiths Way	Vancouver	BC	V6B6G1	604-899-7400		720
Web: rogersarena.com							
Rogers Bros Corp	100 Orchard St	Albion	PA	16401	814-756-4121	756-4830	779
TF: 800-441-9880 ■ *Web:* www.rogerstrailers.com							
Rogers Communications Inc	333 Bloor St E 9th Fl	Toronto	ON	M4W1G9	877-490-9481	935-6304*	736
TSX: RCI.B ■ **Fax Area Code:* 416 ■ *TF:* 888-221-1687 ■ *Web:* www.rogers.com							
Rogers Consulting Ltd	4900 FM 1264	Lubbock	TX	79415	806-993-6101	993-6102	194
Web: www.rogersconsulting.com							
Rogers Corp	1 Technology Dr	Rogers	CT	06263	860-774-9605	779-5509	605-2
TF: 800-237-2267 ■ *Web:* www.rogerscorp.com							
Rogers County	200 S Lynn Riggs Blvd	Claremore	OK	74017	918-923-4400		338
Web: www.rogerscounty.org							
Rogers Ctr	1 Blue Jays Way Ste 3000	Toronto	ON	M5V1J1	416-341-2622		720
Web: www.rogerscentre.com							
Rogers Electro-Matics Inc	405 W Chicago St	Syracuse	IN	46567	574-457-2305	457-3170	625
Web: www.rogerselectromatics.com							
Rogers Engineering & Manufacturing Inc	112 S Center St	Cambridge City	IN	47327	765-478-5444		261
Web: rogersengineering.net							
Rogers Foam Corp	20 Vernon St	Somerville	MA	02145	617-623-3010	629-2585	601
Web: www.rogersfoam.com							
Rogers Group Inc	421 Great Cir Rd	Nashville	TN	37228	615-242-0585		503-4
Web: www.rogersgroupincint.com							
Rogers Harold (Rep R - KY)	2406 Rayburn House Office Bldg	Washington	DC	20515	202-225-4601	225-0940	342-2
Web: halrogers.house.gov							
Rogers Huber & Assoc	973 Lycoming Mall Dr	Muncy	PA	17756	570-546-2238		2
Web: rogershuber.com							
Rogers Industrial Products Inc	532 S Main St	Akron	OH	44311	330-535-3331	535-4408	456
Web: www.rogersusa.com							
Rogers Jewelry Co	PO Box 3151	Modesto	CA	95353	800-877-4221		410
TF: 800-877-4221 ■ *Web:* www.thinkrogers.com							
Rogers Kitchens Inc	130 Chestnut St	Norwich	CT	06360	860-886-0505		191-3
Web: www.rogerskitchens.com							
Rogers Lumber Company Inc	937 Hwy 7 N	Camden	AR	71701	870-574-0231	574-1206	683
Web: www.rogerslumberco.com							
Rogers Machinery Company Inc	14650 SW 72nd Ave PO Box 230429	Portland	OR	97224	503-639-0808		172
TF: 800-394-6151 ■ *Web:* www.rogers-machinery.com							
Rogers Manufacturing Company Inc	110 Transit Ave	Nashville	TN	37210	615-244-9720		190
TF: 877-407-6437 ■ *Web:* www.rogersdumpbodies.com							
Rogers Manufacturing Inc	Martin Luther King Jr St	Mineral Wells	TX	76067	940-325-7806		455
Web: www.rogers-mfg-inc.com							
Rogers Media	33 Dundas St E	Toronto	ON	M5B1B8	416-764-3003		741-136
TF: 888-336-9978 ■ *Web:* www.citytv.com							
Rogers Memorial Hospital Inc	34700 Valley Rd	Oconomowoc	WI	53066	262-646-4411	646-3158	374-5
TF: 800-767-4411 ■ *Web:* rogersbh.org							
Rogers Mike (Rep R - AL)	2184 Rayburn House Office Bldg	Washington	DC	20515	202-225-3261	226-8485	342-2
Web: mikerogers.house.gov							
Rogers Printing Inc	PO Box 215	Ravenna	MI	49451	231-853-2244	853-6558	627
TF: 800-622-5591 ■ *Web:* www.rogersprinting.net							
Rogers State University	1701 W Will Rogers Blvd	Claremore	OK	74017	918-343-7546	343-7595	166
TF: 800-256-7511 ■ *Web:* www.rsu.edu							
Rogers Stereo Inc	525 Woodruff Rd	Greenville	SC	29607	864-288-9999		791
Web: www.rogersstereo.com							
Rogers Supply Company Inc	PO Box 740	Champaign	IL	61824	217-356-0166	356-1768	665
TF: 800-252-0406 ■ *Web:* www.rogerssupply.com							
Rogers, Hofrichter & Karrh LLC	225 S Glynn St Ste 1	Fayetteville	GA	30214	770-884-6705	460-1920	41
TF: 877-572-3949 ■ *Web:* roholaw.com							
RogersGray	64 Fairhaven Rd	Mattapoisett	MA	02739	508-758-3731		390
Web: www.rogersgray.com							
Rogers-Lowell Area Chamber of Commerce	317 W Walnut St	Rogers	AR	72756	479-636-1240	636-5485	139
TF: 800-364-1240 ■ *Web:* www.rogerslowell.com							
Rogers-O'Brien Construction USA	1901 Regal Row	Dallas	TX	75235	214-962-3000		186
Web: www.r-o.com							
Rogerson Aircraft Corp	16940 Von Karman Ave	Irvine	CA	92606	949-660-0666		21
Web: www.rogersonaircraft.com							
Rogersville/Hawkins County Chamber of Commerce	107 E Main St Ste 100	Rogersville	TN	37857	423-272-2186		139
Web: www.rogersvillechamber.us							
Rogge Capital Management LP	3801 N Capital Of Texas Hwy Ste E240 c/o 601	Austin	TX	78746	512-322-0909		401
Rogosheske Rogosheske & Atkins PLLC	105 Hardman Ct Ste 110	South Saint Paul	MN	55075	651-451-6411	451-9956	41
Web: rogo-law.com							
Rogue Ales Co	2320 OSU Dr	Newport	OR	97365	541-867-3660		102
Web: www.rogue.com							
Rogue Community College	3345 Redwood Hwy	Grants Pass	OR	97527	541-956-7500	471-3585	162
TF: 800-411-6508 ■ *Web:* www.roguecc.edu							
Rogue Community College (RCC)	*Riverside* 114 S Bartlett St	Medford	OR	97501	541-245-7500		162
Web: web.roguecc.edu							
Rogue Credit Union	1370 Center Dr	Medford	OR	97501	541-858-7328		219
TF: 800-856-7328 ■ *Web:* www.roguecu.org							
Rogue Valley Manor	1200 Mira Mar Ave	Medford	OR	97504	541-857-7214		672
TF: 800-848-7868 ■ *Web:* www.retirement.org							
Rogue Valley Youth Correctional Facility	2001 NE 'F' St	Grants Pass	OR	97526	541-471-2862	471-2861	412
Web: www.oregon.gov							
Rogue Wave Software Inc	5500 Flatiron Pkwy	Boulder	CO	80301	303-473-9118	473-9137	178-2
TF: 800-487-3217 ■ *Web:* www.roguewave.com							
Rohde & Schwarz Inc	6821 Benjamin Franklin Dr	Columbia	MD	21046	410-910-7800		246
Web: www.rohde-schwarz.com							
Rohde Bros Inc	W5745 Woodchuck Ln	Plymouth	WI	53073	920-893-5905		610
Web: www.rohdebros.com							
Rohde Construction Company Inc	4087 Brockton Dr	Kentwood	MI	49512	616-698-0880		187
Web: rohdeconstruction.com							
ROHL LLC	3 Parker	Irvine	CA	92618	714-557-1933		612
Web: www.rohlhome.com							
Rohn Industries Inc	862 Hersey St	Saint Paul	MN	55114	651-647-1300		553
Web: rohnind.com							
ROHN Products LLC	1 Fairholm Ave	Peoria	IL	61603	309-566-3000		723
TF: 800-727-7646 ■ *Web:* www.rohnnet.com							

Phone | Fax | Class

Rohnert Park Chamber of Commerce
101 Golf Course Dr Ste C-7 . . . Rohnert Park CA 94928 707-584-1415 584-2945 139
Web: www.rohnertparkchamber.org

Rohrback Cosasco Systems Inc
11841 Smith Ave . . . Santa Fe Springs CA 90670 562-949-0123 949-3065 350
TF: 800-635-6898 ■ *Web:* www.cosasco.com

Rohrer Corp
717 Seville Rd PO Box 1009 . . . Wadsworth OH 44282 330-335-1541 336-5147 608
TF: 800-243-6640 ■ *Web:* www.rohrer.com

Roi Advertising & Communication
5001 Brentwood Stair Rd . . . Fort Worth TX 76112 800-464-9564 371-4160* 7
**Fax Area Code:* 877 ■ *TF:* 800-464-9564 ■ *Web:* www.roiac.com

Roi Communications Inc
5274 Scotts Vly Dr . . . Scotts Valley CA 95066 831-430-0170 196
Web: www.roico.com

Roi Consulting LL LLC
176 Logan St Ste 22 . . . Noblesville IN 46060 866-465-6470 196
TF: 866-465-6470 ■ *Web:* roillc.net

ROI4Sales Inc 3355 Quaas Dr . . . West Bend WI 53095 262-338-1824 463
Web: www.roi4sales.com

Roig Lawyers
1255 S Military Trl Ste 100 . . . Deerfield Beach FL 33442 954-462-0330 462-7798 428
Web: www.roiglawyers.com

Rokeby Museum 4334 Rt 7 . . . Ferrisburgh VT 05456 802-877-3406 520
Web: www.rokeby.org

Rolac Contracting Inc 1800 Valley St . . . Minot ND 58701 701-839-6525 610
Web: www.rolac-nd.com

Roland Berger & Partners
177 Huntington Ave 18th Fl . . . Boston MA 02115 617-310-6600 310-6601 194
Web: www.rolandberger.com

Roland Cooper State Park
285 Deer Run Dr . . . Camden AL 36726 334-682-4838 682-4050 565
Web: www.alapark.com

Roland Corporation US
5100 S Eastern Ave . . . Los Angeles CA 90040 323-890-3700 890-3701 527
Web: www.roland.com

Roland D. Kelly Infiniti Inc
155 Andover St Rt 114 . . . Danvers MA 01923 978-774-1000 57
TF: 855-885-3559 ■ *Web:* www.kellyauto.com

Roland D. Waller Chartered
5332 Main St . . . New Port Richey FL 34652 727-847-2288 41
Web: rdwaller.com

Roland DGA Corp 15363 Barranca Pkwy . . . Irvine CA 92618 949-727-2100 727-2112 173-6
TF: 800-542-2307 ■ *Web:* www.rolanddga.com

Roland Machinery Co
816 N Dirksen Pkwy . . . Springfield IL 62702 217-789-7711 744-7314 358
TF: 800-252-2926 ■ *Web:* www.rolandmachinery.com

Roland Park Place 830 W 40th St . . . Baltimore MD 21211 410-243-5700 672
Web: rolandparkplace.org

Roland Stock LLC
627 N Fourth St PO Box 902 . . . Reading PA 19603 610-372-5588 41
Web: rolandstock.com

Roland's Electric Inc
307 Suburban Ave . . . Deer Park NY 11729 631-242-8080 242-6392 787
TF: 800-981-8010 ■ *Web:* www.rolandselectric.com

Roland|Criss
2011 E Lamar Blvd Ste 150 . . . Arlington TX 76006 817-861-7963 466
TF: 800-440-3457 ■ *Web:* rolandcriss.com

Rolands & Associates Corp
120 Del Rey Gardens Dr . . . Del Rey Oaks CA 93940 831-373-2025 371-2841 177
Web: www.rolands.com

Rolcon Inc 134 Carthage Ave . . . Cincinnati OH 45215 513-821-7259 207
TF: 800-486-2472 ■ *Web:* www.rolconrollers.com

Rolenn Mfg 2065 Roberta St . . . Riverside CA 92507 951-682-1185 608
Web: www.rolenn.com

Rolette County PO Box 276 . . . Rolla ND 58367 701-477-3816 338
Web: www.rolettecounty.com

Rolex Watch Usa Inc 665 Fifth Ave . . . New York NY 10022 212-758-7700 205
Web: www.rolex.com

Rolf C. Hagen Corp 305 Forbes Blvd . . . Mansfield MA 02048 508-339-9531 578
TF: 800-724-2436 ■ *Web:* www.hagen.com

Rolf Institute of Structural Integration
5055 Chaparral Ct Ste 103 . . . Boulder CO 80301 303-449-5903 449-5978 48-17
TF: 800-530-8875 ■ *Web:* www.rolf.org

Rolf Prima Wheel Systems 940 Wilson St . . . Eugene OR 97402 541-868-1715 851-3748* 517
**Fax Area Code:* 888 ■ *TF:* 888-308-7700 ■ *Web:* rolfprima.com

Rolfe Hinderaker PLLC
2500 N Tucson Blvd Ste . . . Tucson AZ 85716 520-209-2550 41
Web: rolfefamilylaw.com

Rol-Flo Engineering Inc
85a Tom Harvey Rd . . . Westerly RI 02891 401-596-0060 596-0216 757
Web: www.rolflo.com

Rolinc Staffing
333 W Hampden Ave Ste 545 . . . Englewood CO 80110 303-781-0055 260
Web: www.rolinc.com

Roll Bond Converting
12855 Vly Branch Ln . . . Dallas TX 75234 972-866-0880 557
Web: www.rbconverting.com

Roll Forming Corp
1070 Brooks Industrial Rd . . . Shelbyville KY 40065 502-633-4435 697
Web: www.rfcorp.com

Roll Shutter Systems Inc
21633 N 14th Ave . . . Phoenix AZ 85027 623-869-7057 699
TF: 800-551-7655 ■ *Web:* www.rollshuttersystemsusa.com

Roll'n Oilfield Industries Ltd
5208 - 53rd Ave Ste 350 . . . Red Deer AB T4N5K2 403-343-1710 540
TF: 800-662-7139 ■ *Web:* www.rolln.com

Rolla Area Chamber of Commerce
1311 Kingshighway . . . Rolla MO 65401 573-364-3577 364-5222 139
TF: 888-809-3817 ■ *Web:* rollachamber.org

Rolla Farmers Exchange 209 E 8th St . . . Rolla MO 65401 573-364-1874 276
Web: www.rollamfa.com

Rolla Technical Institute
1304 E 10th St . . . Rolla MO 65401 573-458-0150 458-0155 167-3
Web: www.rolla.k12.mo.us

Roll-A-Way Conveyor Inc
2335 Delaney Rd . . . Gurnee IL 60031 847-336-5033 782-0158 207
TF: 800-747-9024 ■ *Web:* www.roll-away.com

Roll-A-Way Inc 1661 Glenlake Ave . . . Itasca IL 60143 866-749-5424 980-6364* 699
**Fax Area Code:* 630 ■ *TF:* 866-749-5424 ■ *Web:* roll-a-way.com

Rollease Acmeda 750 E Main St 7th Fl . . . Stamford CT 06902 800-552-5100 964-0513* 620
**Fax Area Code:* 203 ■ *Web:* www.rolleaseacmeda.com

Rolled Alloys Inc 125 W Sterns Rd . . . Temperance MI 48182 734-847-0561 847-6917 492
TF: 800-521-0332 ■ *Web:* www.rolledalloys.com

Rolled Steel Products Corp
2187 Garfield Ave . . . Los Angeles CA 90040 323-723-8836 888-9866 492
TF: 800-400-7833 ■ *Web:* www.rolledsteel.com

Rolleigh Inc 104 Enterprise St . . . Reading MI 49274 517-283-3811 757
Web: www.rolleigh.com

Roller Derby Skate Corp PO Box 930 . . . Litchfield IL 62056 217-324-3961 324-2213 710
Web: www.rollerderby.com

Roller Die & Forming Company of Alabama Inc
107 Industrial Park Dr . . . Eufaula AL 36027 334-687-4844 455
Web: www.rollerdie.com

Roller Skating Association Intl (RSAI)
6905 Corporate Dr . . . Indianapolis IN 46278 317-347-2626 347-2636 48-22
Web: www.rollerskating.com

Rollercoat Industries Inc
10135 E Hwy 92 . . . Tampa FL 33610 813-621-4668 620-0915 103
TF: 800-248-4351 ■ *Web:* www.rollercoat.com

Rollex Corp 800 Chasa Ave . . . Elk Grove Village IL 60007 800-251-3300 437-7561* 697
**Fax Area Code:* 847 ■ *TF:* 800-251-3300 ■ *Web:* rollex.com

Rollin J. Lobaugh Inc
240 Ryan Way . . . South San Francisco CA 94080 650-583-9682 621
Web: www.rjlobaugh.com

Rolling F Credit Union
2101 Geer Rd Ste 401 . . . Turlock CA 95382 209-634-2911 219
Web: rollingf.org

Rolling Hills Electric Co-opeartive Inc
3075B US Hwy 24 PO Box 339 . . . Beloit KS 67420 785-534-1601 245
TF: 800-530-5572 ■ *Web:* www.rollinghills.coop

Rolling Hills Library
1912 N Belt Hwy . . . Saint Joseph MO 64506 816-232-5479 434-3
Web: rhcl.org

Rolling Meadows Animal Hospital
795 NE SR-18 . . . Adrian MO 64720 816-297-2006 794
Web: adrianvet.com

Rolling Meadows Chamber of Commerce
3601 W Algonquin Rd Ste 322 . . . Rolling Meadows IL 60008 847-398-3730 398-3745 139
Web: rmchamber.org

Rolling Meadows Library
3110 Martin Ln . . . Rolling Meadows IL 60008 847-259-6050 435
TF: 800-232-3798 ■ *Web:* www.rmlib.org

Rolling Mix Management Ltd
7209 Railway St SE . . . Calgary AB T2H2V6 403-253-6426 252-5442 183
Web: rollingmix.com

Rolling Oaks Mall
6909 N Loop 1604 E . . . San Antonio TX 78247 210-651-5513 460
TF: 877-746-6642 ■ *Web:* rollingoaksmall.com

Rolling Pin Productions
9322 3rd Ave Ste 462 . . . Brooklyn NY 11209 212-243-1158 296-9
Web: www.rollingpinproductions.com

Rolling Shield Inc
9875 NW 79th Ave . . . Hialeah Gardens FL 33016 305-436-6661 436-5523 699
TF: 800-474-9404 ■ *Web:* www.rollingshield.com

Rolling Tomes Inc PO Box 1943 . . . Grand Junction CO 81502 970-243-8025 637-9
Web: www.b-dylan.com

Rollinger Engineering Inc (REI)
20333 State Hwy 249 1 Chasewood . . . Houston TX 77077 281-558-5000 558-4999 261
Web: www.reifirepro.com

Rollins College 1000 Holt Ave . . . Winter Park FL 32789 407-646-2000 646-1502 166
TF: 800-799-2586 ■ *Web:* rollins.edu

Rollins Inc 2170 Piedmont Rd NE . . . Atlanta GA 30324 404-888-2000 577
NYSE: ROL ■ *Web:* www.rollins.com

Rollins Moving & Storage Inc
1900 E Leffel Ln . . . Springfield OH 45505 937-325-2484 549
TF: 800-826-8094 ■ *Web:* www.rollins3pl.com

Rollins State Park
1066 Kearsarge Mountain Rd . . . Warner NH 03278 603-456-3808 565
Web: www.nhstateparks.org

Rolls Anderson & Rolls
115 Yellowstone Dr . . . Chico CA 95973 530-895-1422 261
Web: rarcivil.com

Rolls-Royce Engine Services Inc
7200 Earhart Rd . . . Oakland CA 94621 510-613-1000 635-3221 24
TF: 888-255-4766 ■ *Web:* www.rolls-royce.com

Rollstock Inc 5720 Brighton Ave . . . Kansas City MO 64130 616-570-0430 547
TF: 800-295-2949 ■ *Web:* rollstock.com

Roll-Tech Molding Products LLC
243 Performance Dr SE . . . Hickory NC 28602 828-431-4515 431-4450 754
TF: 866-431-4515 ■ *Web:* www.roll-tech.net

Rollx Vans 6591 Hwy 13 W . . . Savage MN 55378 952-890-7851 890-1903 62-7
TF: 800-956-6668 ■ *Web:* www.rollxvans.com

Rolo's Cafe
719 Stevens Ave PO Box 18591 . . . Huntsville AL 35801 256-883-7656 671
Web: www.rolos-cafe.com

Roloff Evangelistic Enterprises Inc
PO Box 100 . . . Fort Thomas AZ 85536 361-289-9215 645-141
Web: roloff.org

Rolta Tusc Inc
333 E Butterfield Rd Ste 900 . . . Lombard IL 60148 630-960-2909 180
TF: 800-755-8872 ■ *Web:* www.rolta.com

Roma Italian Restaurant 3 President Dr . . . Dover DE 19901 302-678-1041 671
Web: www.romadover.com

Roma Pizzeria Flint G5227 N Saginaw St . . . Flint MI 48505 810-787-1061 671
Web: www.romaspizza.com

Romac Industries Inc
21919 20th Ave SE . . . Bothell WA 98021 425-951-6200 951-6201 595
TF: 800-426-9341 ■ *Web:* www.romac.com

Romac Supply Company Inc
7400 Bandini Blvd . . . Commerce CA 90040 800-777-6622 729
TF: 800-777-6622 ■ *Web:* www.romacsupply.com

Roman Catholic Diocese of Fort Worth
800 W Loop 820 S . . . Fort Worth TX 76108 817-560-3300 244-8839 48-20
Web: www.fwdioc.org

Phone | Fax | Class

Roman Catholic Diocese of Fresno
1550 N Fresno St Fresno CA 93703 559-488-7400 685
Web: dioceseoffresno.org

Roman Catholic Diocese of Marquette
1004 Harbor Hills Dr Marquette MI 49855 906-225-1141 225-0437 532-2
Web: dioceseofmarquette.org

Roman Catholic Diocese of Tulsa
12300 E 91st St S Broken Arrow OK 74012 918-294-1904 294-0920 48-20
Web: www.dioceseoftulsa.org

Roman Electric Company Inc
640 S 70th St Milwaukee WI 53214 414-771-5400 471-8693 189-4
Web: www.romanelectric.com

Roman J. Claprood Co 242 N Grant Ave Columbus OH 43215 614-221-5515 221-4398 293
Web: rjclaprood.com

Roman Manufacturing Inc
861 47th St SW Grand Rapids MI 49509 616-530-8641 530-8953 811
Web: www.romanmfg.com

Roman Meal Company Inc 4014 15th Ave N Fargo ND 58102 866-245-8921 297-8
TF: 866-245-8921 ■ *Web:* www.romanmeal.com

Romance Monographs
C-115 Bondurant Hall University MS 38677 662-915-7298 915-1086 637-2
Web: modernlanguages.olemiss.edu

Romania
Consulate General 200 E 38th St New York NY 10016 212-682-9123 257
Web: newyork.mae.ro

Romanian National Tourist Office
600 Third Ave Ste 224 New York NY 10016 212-545-8484 775
Web: www.romaniatourism.com

Romano Law Offices & Assoc
5 Irving St Worcester MA 01609 508-791-8255 445
Web: www.romanoandromano.com

Romano Stancroff PC
801 W Ann Arbor Trail Ste 232 Plymouth MI 48170 734-207-3377 41
Web: thelemonlawattorneys.com

Romano's Macaroni Grill
4535 Belt Line Rd Addison TX 75001 972-386-3831 670
Web: www.macaronigrill.com

Romanoff Electric Company LLC
5570 Enterprise Blvd Toledo OH 43612 419-726-2627 726-5406 189-4
Web: quebe.com

Romanoff Group, The 1288 Research Rd Gahanna OH 43230 614-755-4500 116
Web: www.romanoffgroup.cc

Romanoff International Supply Corp
9 Deforest St Amityville NY 11701 800-221-7448 842-0028* 407
**Fax Area Code:* 631 ■ *TF:* 800-221-7448 ■ *Web:* www.romanoff.com

Romanow Inc 346 University Ave Westwood MA 02090 781-320-9200 100
Web: www.romanowcontainer.com

Romar Cabinet & Top Company Inc
23949 S Northern Illinois Dr Channahon IL 60410 815-467-9900 467-9985 321
Web: www.romarcabinet.com

Romar Learning Solutions LLC
28420 Hardy Toll Rd Ste 150 Spring TX 77373 281-292-5508 194
Web: romarlearning.com

Romar Transportation Systems Inc
3500 S Kedzie Ave Chicago IL 60632 773-376-8800 311
TF: 800-621-5416 ■ *Web:* www.romartrans.com

Rome Area Chamber of Commerce
139 W Dominick St Rome NY 13440 315-337-1700 337-1715 139
Web: www.romechamber.com

Rome City School District
508 E Second St Rome GA 30161 706-236-5050 802-4311 685
Web: www.rcs.rome.ga.us

Rome Fastener Corp 257 Depot Rd Milford CT 06460 203-874-6719 877-0201 594
Web: romefast.com

Rome Group Inc, The 3120 Locust Saint Louis MO 63103 314-533-0930 195
Web: www.theromegroup.com

Rome Memorial Hospital 1500 N James St Rome NY 13440 315-338-7000 338-7695 374-3
Web: www.romehosp.org

Rome News-Tribune 305 E Sixth Ave Rome GA 30161 706-290-5255 532-2
Web: www.northwestgeorgianews.com

Rome Research Corp 421 Ridge St Rome NY 13440 315-339-0491 393
Web: www.romeresearchcorp.com

Rome Sentinel Co
333 W Dominick St PO Box 471 Rome NY 13442 315-337-4000 339-6281 637-8
Web: romesentinel.com

Rome Snowboards 1 Derby Ln Waterbury VT 05676 802-244-1758 711
Web: www.romesnowboards.com

Rome Specialty Company Inc
Rosco Div 501 W Embargo St Rome NY 13440 315-337-8200 339-2523 710
TF: 800-794-8357 ■ *Web:* www.roscoinc.com

Rome Technologies Inc
412 Headquarters Dr Ste 4 Millersville MD 21108 410-923-2000 809
Web: www.rometech.com

Rome Tool & Die Company Inc
113 Hemlock St Rome GA 30161 800-241-3369 234-1242* 757
**Fax Area Code:* 706 ■ *TF:* 800-241-3369 ■ *Web:* stemco.com

Rome-Floyd County Library Heritage Room
205 Riverside Pkwy Rome GA 30161 706-236-4607 434-3
Web: www.rome.shrls.org

Romeo Community School District
316 N Main St Romeo MI 48065 586-752-0200 752-0228 685
TF: 888-427-6818 ■ *Web:* romeok12.org

Romeo Computer Co
76005 Van Dyke Rd Bruce Township MI 48065 586-752-5158 396
Web: www.romeocomp.com

Romeo Entertainment Group Inc
5247 N 129th St Omaha NE 68164 402-359-1010 317
Web: romeoent.com

Romeo Rim Inc
74000 Van Dyke Rd Bruce Township MI 48065 586-336-5800 752-5021 596
Web: romeorim.com

Romeo's Euro Cafe 207 N Gilbert Rd Gilbert AZ 85234 480-962-4224 671
Web: www.eurocafe.com

Romeo-Washington Chamber of Commerce
228 N Main St PO Box 175 Romeo MI 48065 586-752-4436 752-2835 139
Web: www.rwchamber.com

Romero Mazda 1307 Kettering Dr Ontario CA 91761 909-390-8484 57
TF: 888-317-2233 ■ *Web:* www.ontariohyundai.com

Romeros Food Products Inc
15155 Valley View Ave Santa Fe Springs CA 90670 562-802-1858 123
Web: romerosfood.com

Romet Ltd 1080 Matheson Blvd E Mississauga ON L4W2V2 905-624-1591 624-5668 407
TF: 800-387-3201 ■ *Web:* www.rometlimited.com

Romig Engineers Inc
1390 El Camino Real 2nd Fl San Carlos CA 94070 650-591-5224 591-5251 261
Web: romigengineers.com

Romney Associates Inc (RA)
64 Carriage Ln Amherst MA 01002 413-253-5630 192
Web: www.romneyassociates.com

Romney Mitt (Sen R - UT)
124 Russell Senate Office Bldg Washington DC 20510 202-224-5251 342-2
Web: www.romney.senate.gov

Romo Incentives Group
1156 Suncast Ln Ste 3 El Dorado Hills CA 95762 916-941-0350 463
TF: 866-941-8383 ■ *Web:* www.romogroup.com

Romulus Public Library 11121 Wayne Rd Romulus MI 48174 734-942-7589 434-3
Web: www.romulus.lib.mi.us

Ron Carter Automotive Group 3205 FM 528 Alvin TX 77511 281-331-3111 57
Web: www.roncarter.com

Ron Foth Adv 8100 N High St Columbus OH 43235 614-888-7771 4
Web: ronfoth.com

Ron Jon Surf Shop
3850 S Banana River Blvd Cocoa Beach FL 32931 321-799-8888 799-8805 711
TF: 888-757-8737 ■ *Web:* www.ronjonsurfshop.com

Ron Kendall Masonry Inc
101 Benoist Farms Rd West Palm Beach FL 33411 561-793-5924 795-2621 189-7
TF: 866-844-1404 ■ *Web:* www.ronkendallmasonry.com

Ron Sachs Communications Inc
114 S Duval St Tallahassee FL 32301 850-222-1996 636
Web: sachsmedia.com

Ron Tonkin Dealerships
122 NE 122nd Ave Portland OR 97230 503-255-4100 57
Web: www.tonkinchevrolet.com

Ron Turley Associates Inc
17437 N 71St Dr Ste 110 Glendale AZ 85308 623-581-2447 582-1747 178-1
TF: 800-279-0549 ■ *Web:* www.rtafleet.com

Ron West Barber College
3303 N Dixie Dr Dayton OH 45414 937-277-4444 167-3
Web: ronwestbarbercollege.com

Ron's Cabinets Inc
380 Industrial Blvd Sauk Rapids MN 56379 320-252-7667 257-0158 499
Web: www.ronscabinets.com

Ronald A. Chatterton PC 25 82nd Dr Gladstone OR 97027 503-557-1040 2
Web: chattertoncpa.com

Ronald Blue & Company LLC
300 Colonial Center Pkwy Ste 300 Roswell GA 30076 770-280-6000 280-6001 401
TF: 800-841-0362 ■ *Web:* www.ronblue.com

Ronald C. Markoff 144 Medway St Providence RI 02906 401-272-9330 41
Web: ronmarkoff.com

Ronald C. Wornick Jewish Day School
800 Foster City Blvd Foster City CA 94404 650-378-2600 685
Web: www.wornickjds.org

Ronald Feldman Fine Arts Inc
31 Mercer St New York NY 10013 212-226-3232 941-1536 42
Web: feldmangallery.com

Ronald L. Bonin, Esq
1070 Reservoir Ave Cranston RI 02910 401-943-5500 41
Web: morettiperlowandbonin.com

Ronald M. Stein Professionals
4521 Quail Lakes Dr Stockton CA 95207 209-957-2910 41
Web: ronsteinlaw.com

Ronald Mark Associates Inc
1227 Central Ave Hillside NJ 07205 908-558-0011 558-9366 41
TF: 800-969-0108 ■ *Web:* www.ronaldmark.com

Ronald McDonald House (RMH)
2524 N State St Jackson MS 39216 601-981-5683 981-3613 373
Web: www.rmhcms.org

Ronald McDonald House
Albany 139 S Lake Ave Albany NY 12208 518-438-2655 373
TF: 866-244-8464 ■ *Web:* rmhcofalbany.org
Albuquerque 1011 Yale Ave NE Albuquerque NM 87106 505-842-8960 764-0412 373
TF: 877-842-8960 ■ *Web:* www.rmhc-nm.org
Ann Arbor 1600 Washington Hts Ann Arbor MI 48104 734-994-4442 994-4919 373
TF: 800-544-8684 ■ *Web:* rmhcannarbor.org
Atlanta 795 Gatewood Rd NE Atlanta GA 30329 404-315-1133 315-7873 373
Web: armhc.org
Austin 1315 Barbara Jordan Blvd Austin TX 78723 512-472-9844 373
Web: rmhc-ctx.org
Baltimore 635 W Lexington St Baltimore MD 21201 410-528-1010 727-6177 373
Web: rmhcbaltimore.org
Bangor 654 State St Bangor ME 04401 207-942-9003 990-2984 373
Web: rmhcmaine.org
Bend 1700 NE Purcell Blvd Bend OR 97701 541-318-4950 318-4994 373
Web: www.rmhcoregon.org
Billings 1144 N 30th St Billings MT 59101 406-256-8006 373
Web: www.rmhc.org
Birmingham 1700 Fourth Ave S Birmingham AL 35233 205-638-7255 373
Web: www.rmhca.org
Bismarck 609 N Seventh St Bismarck ND 58501 701-258-8551 258-5076 373
Web: rmhcbismarck.org
Boise 101 Warm Springs Ave Boise ID 83712 208-336-5478 336-0587 373
Web: www.rmhcidaho.org
Buffalo 780 W Ferry St Buffalo NY 14222 716-883-1177 373
Web: rmhcwny.org
Burlington 16 S Winooski Ave Burlington VT 05401 802-862-4943 862-2175 373
Web: www.rmhcvt.org
Camden 550 Mickle Blvd Camden NJ 08103 856-966-4663 373
Web: ronaldhouse-snj.org
Chapel Hill 101 Old Mason Farm Rd Chapel Hill NC 27517 919-913-2040 951-0123 373
Web: rmhch.org
Charities of Central Iowa
1441 Pleasant St Des Moines IA 50314 515-243-2111 280-3111 373
Web: rmhdesmoines.org
Charities of the Central Valley
9161 Randall Way Madera CA 93636 559-447-6770 447-6778 373
Web: www.rmhccv.org

				Phone	Fax	Class
Charleston 81 Gadsden St	Charleston	SC	29401	843-723-7957	722-2204	373
Web: www.rmhcharleston.org						
Charlottesville 300 Ninth St SW	Charlottesville	VA	22903	434-295-1885	295-7735	373
Web: rmhcharlottesville.org						
Chattanooga 200 Central Ave	Chattanooga	TN	37403	423-778-4300	778-4350	373
Web: www.rmhchattanooga.com						
Chicago 211 E Grand Ave	Chicago	IL	60611	312-888-2500		373
Web: rmhccni.org						
Cleveland 10415 Euclid Ave	Cleveland	OH	44106	216-229-5758	229-0556	373
Web: www.rmhcleveland.org						
Colorado Springs 311 N Logan Ave	Colorado Springs	CO	80909	719-471-1814		373
Web: rmhcsoutherncolorado.org						
Columbus 1959 Hamilton Rd	Columbus	GA	31904	706-321-0033	321-0034	373
Web: www.rmhcwga.org						
Corpus Christi 3402 Ft Worth St	Corpus Christi	TX	78411	361-854-4073	854-9174	373
Web: rmhcofcc.org						
Dallas 4707 Bengal St	Dallas	TX	75235	214-631-7354	631-1527	373
Web: rmhdallas.org						
Danville 100 N Academy Ave PO Box 300	Danville	PA	17821	570-271-6300	271-8182	373
Web: rmhdanville.org						
Detroit 4707 St Antoine St Ste 200	Detroit	MI	48201	313-745-5909		373
Web: rmhc-detroit.org						
Durham 506 Alexander Ave	Durham	NC	27705	919-286-9305	286-7307	373
Web: www.rmhdurhamwake.org						
Edmonton 7726 107 St NW	Edmonton	AB	T6E4K3	780-439-5437		373
Web: rmhcalberta.org						
Falls Church 3312 Gallows Rd	Falls Church	VA	22042	703-698-7080	698-7745	373
Web: rmhcdc.org						
Fargo 1234 Broadway	Fargo	ND	58102	701-232-3980		373
Web: rmhcfargo.org						
Fort Worth 1001 Eighth Ave	Fort Worth	TX	76104	817-870-4942	870-0254	373
Web: rmhfw.org						
Galveston 301 14th St	Galveston	TX	77550	409-762-8770		373
Web: www.rmhg.org						
Grand Rapids 1323 Cedar St NE	Grand Rapids	MI	49503	616-776-1300	776-0368	373
Web: www.rmhwesternmichigan.org						
Greater Cincinnati 350 Erkenbrecher Ave	Cincinnati	OH	45229	513-636-7642	636-4887	373
Web: www.rmhcincinnati.org						
Greenville 529 Moye Blvd	Greenville	NC	27834	252-847-5435		373
Web: rmhenc.org						
Hamilton 1510 Main St W	Hamilton	ON	L8S1E3	905-521-9983		373
Web: www.rmhcsco.ca						
Hershey 745 W Governor Rd	Hershey	PA	17033	717-533-4001	533-1299	373
Web: www.rmhc-centralpa.org						
Honolulu 1970 Judd Hillside Rd	Honolulu	HI	96822	808-973-5683	955-8794	373
Web: ronaldhousehawaii.org						
Huntington 1500 17th St	Huntington	WV	25701	304-529-1122		373
Web: rmhchuntington.org						
Iowa City 730 Hawkins Dr	Iowa City	IA	52246	319-356-3939	353-6873	373
Web: rmhc-eiwi.org						
Jacksonville 824 Children's Way	Jacksonville	FL	32207	904-807-4663		373
Web: rmhcjacksonville.org						
Johnson City 418 N State of Franklin Rd	Johnson City	TN	37604	423-975-5437	434-8989	373
Web: www.rmhsa.org						
Joplin 3402 S Jackson Ave PO Box 2688	Joplin	MO	64804	417-624-2273		373
Web: rmhjoplin.org						
Kansas City 2502 Cherry St	Kansas City	MO	64108	816-842-8321		373
Web: www.rmhckc.org						
Knoxville 1705 W Clinch Ave	Knoxville	TN	37916	865-637-7475	525-7942	373
Web: knoxrmhc.org						
Las Vegas 2323 Potosi St	Las Vegas	NV	89146	702-252-4663	252-7345	373
TF: 888-248-1561 ■ *Web:* rmhlv.org						
Long Branch 131 Bath Ave	Long Branch	NJ	07740	732-222-8755		373
Web: www.rmh-cnj.org						
Los Angeles (LARMH) 4560 Fountain Ave	Los Angeles	CA	90029	323-644-3000	669-0552	373
Web: rmhcsc.org						
Macon 1160 Forsyth St	Macon	GA	31201	478-746-4090	746-0580	373
Web: www.rmhccga.org						
Marshfield 803 W N St	Marshfield	WI	54449	715-387-5899	389-5991	373
Web: www.rmhc-marshfield.org						
Memphis 535 Alabama Ave	Memphis	TN	38105	901-529-4055	523-0315	373
Web: rmhc-memphis.org						
Midtown 1110 N Emporia St	Wichita	KS	67214	316-269-4420	269-0665	373
Web: rmhcwichita.org						
Minneapolis 818 Fulton St SE	Minneapolis	MN	55414	612-331-5752	331-1255	373
Web: rmhtwincities.org						
Missoula 3003 Fort Missoula Rd	Missoula	MT	59804	406-541-7646		373
Web: www.rmhcwesternmontana.org						
Montreal 5800 Hudson Rd	Montreal	QC	H3S2G5	514-731-2871	739-8823	373
Web: www.manoirmontreal.qc.ca						
Morgantown 841 Country Club Dr	Morgantown	WV	26505	304-598-0050	599-0780	373
Web: rmhcpgh-mgtn.org						
New Hyde Park 267-07 76th Ave	New Hyde Park	NY	11040	718-343-5683	343-5798	373
Web: www.rmhlongisland.org						
New Orleans 4403 Canal St	New Orleans	LA	70119	504-486-6668		373
Web: rmhc-sla.org						
New York 405 E 73rd St	New York	NY	10021	212-639-0100		373
Web: www.rmh-newyork.org						
Norfolk 404 Colley Ave	Norfolk	VA	23507	757-627-5386		373
Web: rmhcnorfolk.org						
Northwest Ohio 3883 Monroe St	Toledo	OH	43606	419-471-4663	479-6961	373
Web: rmhctoledo.org						
Oklahoma City 1301 NE 14th St	Oklahoma City	OK	73117	405-424-6873	424-0919	373
Web: rmhc-okc.org						
Orange 383 S Batavia St	Orange	CA	92868	714-639-3600	516-3697	373
Web: rmhcsc.org						
Orlando 2201 Alden Rd	Orlando	FL	32803	407-898-6127		373
Web: www.rmhccf.org						
Ottawa 407 Smyth Rd	Ottawa	ON	K1H8M8	613-737-5523	737-5524	373
Web: www.rmhottawa.com						
Pasadena 763 S Pasadena Ave	Pasadena	CA	91105	626-585-1588		373
Web: rmhcsc.org						
Pensacola 5200 Bayou Blvd	Pensacola	FL	32503	850-477-2273	477-7607	373
Web: rmhc-nwfl.org						
Philadelphia 3925 Chestnut St	Philadelphia	PA	19104	215-387-8406	386-4977	373
Web: www.philarmh.org						
Phoenix 501 E Roanoke Ave	Phoenix	AZ	85004	602-264-2654	264-5670	373
TF: 877-333-2978 ■ *Web:* rmhccnaz.org						
Pittsburgh 451 44th St	Pittsburgh	PA	15201	412-362-3400	362-8540	373
Web: www.rmhcpgh.org						
Portland 2620 N Commercial Ave	Portland	OR	97227	971-230-6700		373
Web: rmhcoregon.org						
Richmond 2330 Monument Ave	Richmond	VA	23220	804-355-6517	358-3153	373
Web: www.rmhc-richmond.org						
Rio Grande Valley, The 1720 Treasure Hills Blvd	Harlingen	TX	78550	956-412-7200	412-6300	373
Web: www.rmhcrgv.org						
Roanoke 2224 S Jefferson St	Roanoke	VA	24014	540-857-0770	857-9584	373
Web: rmhc-swva.org						
Rochester 333 Westmoreland Dr	Rochester	NY	14620	585-442-5437		373
Web: www.rmhcrochester.org						
Sacramento 2555 49th St	Sacramento	CA	95817	916-734-4230		373
Web: www.rmhcnc.org						
San Diego 2929 Children's Way	San Diego	CA	92123	858-467-4750	467-4757	373
Web: rmhcsd.org						
Saskatoon 1011 University Dr	Saskatoon	SK	S7N0K4	306-244-5700	244-3099	373
Web: www.rmh.sk.ca						
Scranton 332 Wheeler Ave	Scranton	PA	18510	570-969-8998		373
Web: rmhscranton.org						
Seattle 5130 40th Ave NE	Seattle	WA	98105	206-838-0600		373
TF: 866-987-9330 ■ *Web:* www.rmhcseattle.org						
Spokane 1015 W Fifth Ave	Spokane	WA	99204	509-624-0500	624-3267	373
Web: rmhcinlandnw.org						
Springfield 34 Chapin Terr	Springfield	MA	01107	413-794-5683		373
Web: rmhc-ctma.org						
Springfield 949 E Primrose St	Springfield	MO	65807	417-886-0225		373
Web: rmhcozarks.org						
Tallahassee 712 E Seventh Ave	Tallahassee	FL	32303	850-222-0056	222-0086	373
Web: rmhctallahassee.org						
Tampa 35 Columbia Dr	Tampa	FL	33606	813-254-2398	258-6517	373
Web: rmhctampabay.org						
Temple 2415 S 47th St	Temple	TX	76504	254-770-0910		373
Web: www.rmhc-temple.org						
Topeka 825 SW Buchanan St	Topeka	KS	66606	785-235-6852		373
Web: www.rmhcneks.org						
Toronto 240 McCaul St	Toronto	ON	M5T1W5	416-977-0458	977-8807	373
Web: www.rmhctoronto.ca						
Tucson 2155 E Allen Rd	Tucson	AZ	85719	520-326-0060		373
Web: rmhctucson.org						
Tulsa 6102 S Hudson Ave	Tulsa	OK	74136	918-496-2727	496-2762	373
Web: rmhctulsa.org						
Wilmington 1901 Rockland Rd	Wilmington	DE	19803	302-656-4847		373
TF: 888-656-4847 ■ *Web:* rmhde.org						
Winnipeg 566 Bannatyne Ave	Winnipeg	MB	R3A0G7	204-774-4777	774-2160	373
Web: www.rmhcmanitoba.org						
Winston-Salem 419 S Hawthorne Rd	Winston-Salem	NC	27103	336-723-0228	723-0302	373
TF: 855-227-7435 ■ *Web:* www.rmhws.org						
Ronald McDonald House At Stanford						
Palo Alto 510 Sand Hill Rd	Palo Alto	CA	94304	650-470-6000	470-6018	373
Web: rmhcbayarea.org						
Ronald McDonald House BC						
4567 Heather St	Vancouver	BC	V5Z0C9	604-736-2957	736-5974	373
TF: 855-451-6703 ■ *Web:* rmhbc.ca						
Ronald McDonald House Charites						
Maine 250 Brackett St	Portland	ME	04102	207-780-6282	780-0198	373
Web: www.rmhcmaine.org						
Ronald McDonald House Charities						
Eastern Wisconsin 8948 W Watertown Plank Rd	Milwaukee	WI	53226	414-475-5333	475-6342	373
Web: rmhcmilwaukee.org						
Fort Myers 16100 Roserush Ct	Fort Myers	FL	33908	239-437-0202	437-3521	373
Web: rmhcswfl.org						
Halifax 1133 Tower Rd	Halifax	NS	B3H2Y7	902-429-4044		373
Web: rmhatlantic.com						
Madison 2716 Marshall Ct	Madison	WI	53705	608-232-4660	232-4670	373
Web: www.rmhcmadison.org						
Omaha 620 S 38th Ave	Omaha	NE	68105	402-346-9377		373
Web: www.rmhcomaha.org						
Reno 323 Maine St	Reno	NV	89502	775-322-4663		373
Web: www.rmhc-reno.org						
Saint Louis 3450 Park Ave	Saint Louis	MO	63104	314-773-1100		373
Web: www.rmhcstl.com						
San Antonio 4803 Sid Katz	San Antonio	TX	78229	210-614-2554	614-2905	373
Web: www.rmhcsanantonio.org						
Sioux City 2500 Nebraska St	Sioux City	IA	51104	712-255-4084	255-4281	373
Web: rmhc-siouxland.org						
Springfield 610 N Seventh St	Springfield	IL	62702	217-528-3314	528-6084	373
Web: rmhc-centralillinois.org						
Ronald McDonald House Charities Columbia						
2901 Colonial Dr	Columbia	SC	29203	803-254-0118	254-8688	373
Web: www.rmhcofcolumbia.org						
Ronald McDonald House Charities of Arkansas (RMHCA)						
Little Rock 1009 Wolfe St	Little Rock	AR	72202	501-374-1956		373
Web: www.rmhcarkansas.org						
Ronald McDonald House Charities of Central Ohio						
711 E Livingston Ave	Columbus	OH	43205	614-227-3700		373
Web: rmhc-centralohio.org						
Ronald McDonald House Charities of Denver						
1300 E 21st Ave	Denver	CO	80205	303-832-2667	832-3802	373
Web: rmhc-denver.org						
Ronald McDonald House Charities of Kentuckiana (RMHC)						
550 S First St	Louisville	KY	40202	502-581-1416		373
Web: rmhc-kentuckiana.org						
Ronald McDonald House Charities of Nashville						
2144 Fairfax Ave	Nashville	TN	37212	615-343-4000	343-4004	373
Web: www.rmhcnashville.com						
Ronald McDonald House Charities of North Central Florida						
1600 SW 14th St	Gainesville	FL	32608	352-374-4404	335-5325	373
Web: www.rmhcncf.org						

Phone | Fax | Class

Ronald McDonald House Charities of the Southwest
3413 Tenth St . . . Lubbock TX 79415 806-744-8877 744-3652 373
Web: www.rmhcsouthwest.com

Ronald McDonald House Charities Southwestern Ontario
741 Base Line Rd E. . . . London ON N6C2R6 519-685-3232 373
Web: www.rmhc-swo.ca

Ronald McDonald House Charities's
Salt Lake City 935 E Temple . . . Salt Lake City UT 84102 801-363-4663 363-0092 373
Web: www.rmhcslc.org

Ronald McDonald House Houston
1907 Holcombe Blvd . . . Houston TX 77030 713-795-3500 373
Web: rmhhouston.org

Ronald McDonald House of Mid-Michigan
121 S Holmes St. . . . Lansing MI 48912 517-485-9303 373
Web: rmhmm.org

Ronald Reagan Building & International Trade Ctr
1300 Pennsylvania Ave NW . . . Washington DC 20004 202-312-1300 312-1310 822
Web: itcdc.com

Ronald Reagan Medical Ctr
757 Westwood Plz . . . Los Angeles CA 90095 310-825-9111 825-7271 374-3
Web: www.uclahealth.org

Ronald Reagan Presidential Library & Museum
40 Presidential Dr. . . . Simi Valley CA 93065 805-522-2977 520-9702 434-2
TF: 800-410-8354 ■ *Web:* www.reaganfoundation.org

Ronald T. Jepson & Associates Ps
222 Grand Ave . . . Bellingham WA 98225 360-733-5760 647-8939 261
Web: www.jepsonengineering.com

Ronald T. Karpowich CPA 725 Front St. . . . Freeland PA 18224 570-636-2358 2

Ronald Thorn Insurance Agency Inc
114 Fourth Ave SE . . . Red Bay AL 35582 256-356-2700 390
Web: ronaldthorninsurance.com

Ronan Engineering Co
21200 Oxnard St. . . . Woodland Hills CA 91367 800-327-6626 992-6435* 201
**Fax Area Code:* 818 ■ *TF:* 800-327-6626 ■ *Web:* www.ronan.com

Roncalli High Sch Sisters
2000 Mirro Dr. . . . Manitowoc WI 54220 920-682-8801 685
Web: roncallijets.net

Roncelli Inc 6471 Metro Pkwy. . . . Sterling Heights MI 48312 586-264-2060 979-3190 401
Web: www.roncelli-inc.com

Roncelli Plastics Inc
330 W Duarte Rd . . . Monrovia CA 91016 626-359-2551 608
TF: 800-250-6516 ■ *Web:* www.roncelli.com

Ronco Communications
595 Sheridan Dr. . . . Tonawanda NY 14150 716-873-0760 681
TF: 888-879-8011 ■ *Web:* www.ronco.net

Ronco Consulting Corp
6710 Oxon Hill Rd Ste 200. . . . Oxon Hill MD 20745 240-493-3910 493-1440 692
Web: www.roncoconsulting.com

Rondaxe Pharma LLC
6443 Ridings Rd Ste 125 . . . Syracuse NY 13206 315-469-2800 469-3694 196
Web: www.rondaxe.com

Rondout Electric Inc 225 Upper N Rd . . . Highland NY 12528 845-471-4810 246
Web: rondoutelectric.net

Roney Furniture Inc
14000 Washington Ave. . . . San Leandro CA 94578 510-352-1175 321
Web: roneysfurniture.com

Ronin Corp 2 Research Way Ste 203 . . . Princeton NJ 08540 609-452-0060 195
Web: www.ronin.com

Ronin Publishing Inc PO Box 22900 . . . Oakland CA 94609 510-420-3669 420-3672 637-2
TF: 800-858-2665 ■ *Web:* www.roninpub.com

Ronis Bros 39 Harriet Pl. . . . Lynbrook NY 11563 516-887-5266 887-5288 464
Web: www.ronis.com

Ronnie Matthews 5910 Fm 2920 Ste A . . . Spring TX 77388 281-440-7900 652
Web: ronnieandcathy.com

Ronningen Research & Development Co
6700 E 'YZ' Ave. . . . Vicksburg MI 49097 269-649-0520 649-0526 602
Web: www.ronningenresearch.com

Ronnybrook Farm Dairy Inc
310 Prospect Hill Rd. . . . Ancram NY 12503 646-559-2828 10-3
Web: www.ronnybrook.com

Ronpak Inc
4301 New Brunswick Ave . . . South Plainfield NJ 07080 732-968-8000 66
Web: www.ronpak.com

Ron-Son Foods Inc PO Box 38 . . . Swedesboro NJ 08085 856-241-7333 241-7338 297-11
Web: www.ronsonfoods.com

Rood Riddle Equine Hospital
2150 Georgetown Rd . . . Lexington KY 40511 859-233-0371 794
Web: www.roodandriddle.com

Roof Line Supply & Delivery
700 N Victory Blvd . . . Burbank CA 91502 818-840-8851 191-4
Web: rooflinesupply.com

Roof Structures Inc 3333 Yale Way . . . Fremont CA 94538 510-226-7171 226-8989 817
Web: www.roofstructures.com

Roof to deck Decoration Inc
365 Webster St. . . . Saint Paul MN 55102 651-699-3504 104
Web: rooftodeckdecoration.com

Roofing & Insulation Supply Inc
12221 Merit Dr Ste 1015 . . . Dallas TX 75251 972-239-8309 239-8310 191-4
Web: www.risris.com

Roofing Products & Building Supply Company Inc
4955 River Rd. . . . Jefferson LA 70121 504-733-0404 191-4
Web: www.rfgproducts.com

Roofing Wholesale Company Inc
1918 W Grant St. . . . Phoenix AZ 85009 602-258-3794 256-0932 191-4
Web: www.rwc.org

Rooftop Media Inc
530 Howard St Ste 400. . . . San Francisco CA 94105 612-492-1197 116
TF: 800-860-0293 ■ *Web:* www.rooftopcomedy.com

Rook Security
11350 N Meridian St Ste 600 . . . Carmel IN 46032 888-712-9531 196
TF: 888-712-9531 ■ *Web:* www.rooksecurity.com

Rooke Johnson & Renslow Insurance Agency Inc
5720 Smetana Dr Ste 370. . . . Minnetonka MN 55343 952-931-9999 390
Web: rjrinsurance.com

Rooks County 115 N Walnut . . . Stockton KS 67669 785-425-6391 425-6015 338
Web: www.rookscounty.net

Room & Board Inc
4600 Olson Memorial Hwy . . . Golden Valley MN 55422 763-521-4431 319-2
TF: 800-301-9720 ■ *Web:* www.roomandboard.com

Phone | Fax | Class

Room 214 Inc 3340 Mitchell Ln. . . . Boulder CO 80301 303-444-9214 7
Web: room214.com

Roomplace, The 1000-46 Rohlwing Rd . . . Lombard IL 60148 630-261-3900 321
Web: www.theroomplace.com

Rooney Francis (Rep R - FL)
120 Cannon House Office Bldg. . . . Washington DC 20515 202-225-2536 226-3547 342-2
Web: francisrooney.house.gov

Roosevelt & Cross Inc
1 Exchange Plz 55 Broadway 22nd Fl. . . . New York NY 10006 212-344-2500 690
TF: 800-348-3426 ■ *Web:* www.roosevelt-cross.com

Roosevelt County 109 W First St . . . Portales NM 88130 575-356-8562 356-3560 338
Web: www.rooseveltcounty.com

Roosevelt County 400 Second Ave S . . . Wolf Point MT 59201 406-653-6250 653-6289 338
Web: rooseveltcounty.org

Roosevelt County Electric Co-opeartive Inc (RCEC)
121 N Main Ave PO Box 389 . . . Portales NM 88130 575-356-4491 245
Web: www.rcec.org

Roosevelt Hotel 45 E 45th St . . . New York NY 10017 212-661-9600 885-6168 379
Web: www.therooseveltho tel.com

Roosevelt Paper Co
1 Roosevelt Dr . . . Mount Laurel NJ 08054 856-303-4100 642-1949 553
TF: 800-523-3470 ■ *Web:* www.rooseveltpaper.com

Roosevelt Park Zoo 1219 Burdick Expy . . . Minot ND 58701 701-857-4166 857-4169 823
Web: www.rpzoo.com

Roosevelt State Park 2149 Hwy 13 S . . . Morton MS 39117 601-732-6316 565
Web: www.mdwfp.com

Roosevelt University
430 S Michigan Ave . . . Chicago IL 60605 312-341-3500 166
TF: 877-277-5978 ■ *Web:* www.roosevelt.edu

Roosevelt Warm Springs
6135 Roosevelt Hwy . . . Warm Springs GA 31830 706-655-5304 374-6

Roost 200 Gate Five Rd Number 116. . . . Sausalito CA 94965 415-339-9500 339-9400 321
Web: www.roostco.com

Rooster Park
2100 Westlake Ave N Ste 107. . . . Seattle WA 98109 206-801-0189 177
Web: www.roosterpark.com

Rooster's 253 25th St. . . . Ogden UT 84401 801-627-6171 671
Web: www.roostersbrewingco.com

Root Candles Co 623 W Liberty St . . . Medina OH 44256 330-723-4359 725-5624 122
TF: 800-289-7668 ■ *Web:* www.rootcandles.com

Root Consulting Inc
2010 N Loop West Ste 260. . . . Houston TX 77008 713-523-8976 809
Web: rootcon.com

Root Group Inc, The
1790 30th St Ste 140 . . . Boulder CO 80301 303-447-8093 447-0197 180
Web: www.rootgroup.com

Root Inc 5470 Main St . . . Sylvania OH 43560 800-852-1315 196
TF: 800-852-1315 ■ *Web:* www.rootinc.com

Root Insurance Co
80 E Rich St Ste 500. . . . Columbus OH 43215 866-980-9431 390
TF: 866-980-9431 ■ *Web:* www.joinroot.com

Root-Lowell Manufacturing Co
1000 Foreman Rd. . . . Lowell MI 49331 800-748-0098 968-3555 273
TF: 800-748-0098 ■ *Web:* www.rlflomaster.com

RootsWeb 1300 W Traverse Pkwy. . . . Lehi UT 84043 801-705-7000 397
Web: www.rootsweb.ancestry.com

Roper Corp 1507 Broomtown Rd . . . LaFayette GA 30728 706-638-5100 36
Web: roperappliances.com

Roper Lake State Park
101 E Roper Lake Rd . . . Safford AZ 85546 928-428-6760 565
Web: azstateparks.com

Roper Mountain Science Ctr
402 Roper Mtn Rd . . . Greenville SC 29615 864-355-8900 520
Web: www.ropermountain.org

Roper Performing Arts Ctr
340 Granby St. . . . Norfolk VA 23510 757-822-1450 572
Web: www.tccropercenter.org

Roper Pump Co 3475 Old Maysville Rd. . . . Commerce GA 30529 706-335-5551 335-5490 641
TF: 800-944-6769 ■ *Web:* www.roperpumps.com

Roper Whitney 2833 Huffman Blvd. . . . Rockford IL 61103 815-962-3011 962-2227 456
Web: www.roperwhitney.com

Ropes & Gray LLP 1 International Pl. . . . Boston MA 02110 617-951-7000 951-7050 428
Web: www.ropesgray.com

Ropes Associates Inc
333 N New River Dr E Ste 2000 . . . Fort Lauderdale FL 33301 954-525-6600 196
Web: www.ropesassociates.com

ROPH (Rush Oak Park Hospital)
520 S Maple Ave. . . . Oak Park IL 60304 708-383-9300 660-2310 374-3
Web: www.roph.org

Rophi Technical Services East
814 S Rosedale Ct . . . Grosse Pointe MI 48236 313-417-2021 180

Roplast Industries Inc
3155 S Fifth Ave. . . . Oroville CA 95965 530-532-9500 532-9576 66
TF: 800-767-5278 ■ *Web:* www.roplast.com

Roppe Corp 1602 N Union St. . . . Fostoria OH 44830 419-435-8546 435-1056 291
TF: 800-537-9527 ■ *Web:* roppe.com

Roque Bluffs State Park
145 Schoppee Pt Rd. . . . Roque Bluffs ME 04654 207-255-3475 565
Web: www.maine.gov

Roquemore & Roquemore Inc
310 E I-30 Ste 200 . . . Garland TX 75043 972-226-9266 160
Web: www.roquemore.com

Roquette America
1417 Exchange St PO Box 6647. . . . Keokuk IA 52632 319-524-5757 526-2345 296-23
Web: www.roquette.com

Rory Dolan's 890 McLean Ave. . . . Yonkers NY 10704 914-776-2946 776-6538 671
Web: www.rorydolans.com

Ros Technology Services Inc
8500 NW River Park Dr. . . . Parkville MO 64152 866-746-4100 809
TF: 866-746-4100 ■ *Web:* www.rosnet.com

Rosa + Wesley Inc 400 S Knoll St Ste B. . . . Wheaton IL 60187 630-588-9801 588-9804 94
Web: www.rosawesley.com

Rosa's Mexican Grill 328 E University Dr . . . Mesa AZ 85201 480-964-5451 671
Web: rosasgrill.com

Rosalie's 46 Cottage St . . . Bar Harbor ME 04609 207-288-5666 671
Web: rosaliespizza.com

Phone | Fax | Class

Rosalind Franklin University of Medicine & Science Learning Resource Ctr
3333 Green Bay Rd ... North Chicago IL 60064 847-578-3000 434-1
TF: 800-244-1177 ■ *Web:* www.rosalindfranklin.edu

Rosamond Gifford Zoo at Burnet Park
1 Conservation Pl ... Syracuse NY 13204 315-435-8511 435-8517 823
TF: 800-724-5006 ■ *Web:* rosamondgiffordzoo.org

Rosanne M. Duane PA
250 S Central Blvd Ste 202 ... Jupiter FL 33458 561-747-1646 41
Web: rmd-law.com

Rosario Resort & Spa
1400 Rosario Rd ... Eastsound WA 98245 360-376-2222 376-2289 669
TF: 800-562-8820 ■ *Web:* rosarioresort.com

Rosaryville State Park
7805 W Marlton Ave ... Upper Marlboro MD 20772 301-856-9656 565
Web: dnr.maryland.gov

Rosati's Pizza
28381 Davis Pkwy Ste 701 ... Warrenville IL 60555 630-393-2280 670
Web: www.rosatispizza.com

Rosauers Super Markets Inc
1815 W Garland Ave ... Spokane WA 99205 509-326-8900 328-2483 345
Web: www.rosauers.com

Rosback Co 125 Hawthorne Ave ... Saint Joseph MI 49085 269-983-2582 983-2516 629
TF: 800-542-2420 ■ *Web:* www.rosbackcompany.com

Rosboro Lumber Co 2509 Main St ... Springfield OR 97477 541-746-8411 726-8919 683
Web: rosboro.com

Rosco Laboratories Inc
52 Harbor View Ave ... Stamford CT 06902 203-708-8900 708-8919 722
TF: 800-767-2669 ■ *Web:* www.us.rosco.com

Roscoe & Swanson Accountancy Corp
23717 Hawthorne Blvd Ste 206 ... Torrance CA 90505 310-540-5300 2
Web: rscpa.com

Roscoe Co 3535 W Harrison St ... Chicago IL 60624 773-722-5000 722-0827 442
TF: 888-476-7263 ■ *Web:* www.eroscoe.com

Roscoe Medical Inc
21973 Commerce Pkwy ... Strongsville OH 44149 440-572-1962 194
TF: 800-376-7263 ■ *Web:* www.roscoemedical.com

Roscoe Moss Co 4360 Worth St ... Los Angeles CA 90063 323-263-4111 263-4497 595
Web: roscoemoss.com

Roscoe Steel 1501 S 30th St W ... Billings MT 59102 406-656-2253 480
TF: 866-982-9511 ■ *Web:* truenorthsteel.com

Roscoe Village 600 N Whitewoman St ... Coshocton OH 43812 740-622-7644 520
TF: 800-877-1830 ■ *Web:* roscoevillage.com

Roscoe's House of Chicken & Waffles
730 E Broadway ... Long Beach CA 90802 562-437-8355 671
Web: www.roscoeschickenandwaffles.com

Roscoe's Root Beer & Ribs
603 Fourth St SE ... Rochester MN 55904 507-285-0501 671
Web: www.roscoesbbq.com

Roscommon County 500 Lake St ... Roscommon MI 48653 989-275-8021 275-3161 338
Web: www.roscommoncounty.net

Rose & Kiernan Inc 99 Troy Rd ... East Greenbush NY 12061 518-244-4245 244-4262 391-5
Web: www.rkinsurance.com

Rose & Walker Supply Lafayette Inc (RWS)
5294 S Leonard Springs Rd ... Bloomington IN 47403 765-471-7070 474-7507 191-2
Web: www.roseandwalkersupply.com

Rose Aircraft Interiors Inc
132 Flight Ln ... Mena AR 71953 479-394-2551 63
Web: www.roseaircraft.com

Rose Alley Press
4203 Brooklyn Ave NE Ste 103A ... Seattle WA 98105 206-633-2725 637-2
Web: www.rosealleypress.com

Rose Associates Inc
777 Third Avenue 6th Fl ... New York NY 10016 212-210-6666 652
Web: www.rosenyc.com

Rose Bowl 1001 Rose Bowl Dr ... Pasadena CA 91103 626-577-3100 405-0992 720
Web: www.rosebowlstadium.com

Rose Bowl Aquatics Ctr
360 N Arroyo Blvd ... Pasadena CA 91103 626-564-0330 31
Web: www.rosebowlaquatics.org

Rose Bowl Hall of Fame
391 S Orange Grove Blvd ... Pasadena CA 91184 626-449-4100 522
Web: www.tournamentofroses.com

Rose Bros Inc 302 Main St ... Lingle WY 82223 307-837-2261 274
Web: rosebrosinc.com

Rose City Veterinary Hospital
2695 E Foothill Blvd ... Pasadena CA 91107 626-796-8387 796-9251 794
Web: rosecityvets.com

Rose Displays Ltd
500 Narragansett Park Dr ... Pawtucket RI 02861 800-631-9707 194
TF: 888-452-9528 ■ *Web:* www.rosedisplays.com

Rose F. Kennedy Ctr
Albert Einstein College of Medicine
1410 Pelham Pkwy S ... Bronx NY 10461 718-430-8500 918-7505 668
Web: www.einstein.yu.edu

Rose Financial Services LLC
2 Research Pl Ste 300 ... Rockville MD 20850 301-527-1130 527-1140 734
Web: www.rosefinancial.com

Rose Hill Plantation State Historic Site
2677 Sardis Rd ... Union SC 29379 864-427-5966 565
Web: southcarolinaparks.com

Rose Hotel 807 Main St ... Pleasanton CA 94566 925-846-8802 846-2272 379
TF: 800-843-9540 ■ *Web:* www.rosehotel.net

Rose Intl
16401 Swingley Ridge Rd Ste 300 ... Chesterfield MO 63017 636-812-4000 812-0076 177
Web: www.roseit.com

Rose John W (Rep R - TN)
1232 Longworth House Office Bldg ... Washington DC 20515 202-225-4231 342-2
Web: www.johnrose.house.gov

Rose L. Brand & Associates PC
7430 Washington St NE ... Albuquerque NM 87109 505-833-3036 41
Web: roselbrand.com

Rose Law Firm A Professional Assn
120 E Fourth St ... Little Rock AR 72201 501-375-9131 375-1309 428
Web: www.roselawfirm.com

Rose Leonard & Sons Inc
212 Decatur St ... Doylestown PA 18901 215-345-9263 610

Rose Max (Rep D - NY)
1529 Longworth House Office Bldg ... Washington DC 20515 202-225-3371 342-2
Web: www.maxrose.house.gov

Rose Metal Processing 2902 Center St ... Houston TX 77007 713-880-7000 686
Web: www.rosemetal.net

Rose Metal Products Inc
1955 E Division St ... Springfield MO 65803 417-865-1676 865-7673 482
Web: www.rosemetalproducts.com

Rose Packing Company Inc
65 S Barrington Rd ... South Barrington IL 60010 847-381-5700 381-9436 473
TF: 800-323-7363 ■ *Web:* www.rosepacking.com

Rose Plastic USA LLLP
525 Technology Dr ... Coal Center PA 15423 724-938-8530 938-8532 600
Web: www.rose-plastic.us

Rose Printing Company Inc
2503 Jackson Bluff Rd ... Tallahassee FL 32304 850-576-4151 626
TF: 800-227-3725 ■ *Web:* www.roseprinting.com

Rose Radiology Boot Ranch
4133 Woodlands Pkwy ... Palm Harbor FL 34685 727-781-3888 415
Web: www.roseradiology.com

Rose State College
6420 SE 15th St ... Midwest City OK 73110 405-733-7372 736-0309 162
TF: 866-621-0987 ■ *Web:* www.rose.edu

Rose Tattoo Cafe
1847 Callowhill St ... Philadelphia PA 19130 215-569-8939 671
Web: www.rosetattoocafe.com

Rose Thai 5333 Monroe St ... Toledo OH 43623 419-841-8467 671

Rose Tree Media School District
308 N Olive St ... Media PA 19063 610-627-6000 685
Web: www.rtmsd.org

Rose's Oil Service Inc 375 Main St ... Gloucester MA 01930 877-283-3334 283-3308* 579
**Fax Area Code:* 978 ■ *TF:* 877-283-3334 ■ *Web:* www.rosesmarine.com

Rose, Snyder & Jacobs LLP
15821 Ventura Blvd Ste 490 ... Encino CA 91436 818-461-0600 160
Web: www.rsjcpa.com

Roseau Electric Co-opeartive Inc
1107 Third St NE ... Roseau MN 56751 218-463-1543 463-3713 245
TF: 888-847-8840 ■ *Web:* roseauelectric.coop

Roseborough Travel Agency Inc
140 E Indiana Ave ... Deland FL 32724 386-734-7245 738-1415 775
TF: 800-346-0997 ■ *Web:* roseboroughtravel.com

Rosebud N3310 Asje Rd ... Cambridge WI 53523 608-423-9780 637 0
Web: www.rsbd.net

Rosebud Agency PO Box 170429 ... San Francisco CA 94117 415-386-3456 386-0599 731
Web: www.rosebudus.com

Rosebud County 1200 Main St PO Box 47 ... Forsyth MT 59327 406-346-7322 346-7551 338
Web: rosebudcountymt.gov

Rosebud Electric Co-opeartive Inc
512 Rosebud Ave PO Box 439 ... Gregory SD 57533 605-835-9624 245
TF: 888-464-9304 ■ *Web:* www.rosebudelectric.com

Rosebud Restaurant
1419 W Diversey Pkwy ... Chicago IL 60614 773-325-9700 670
Web: www.rosebudrestaurants.com

Rosebud Wood Products 701 SE 12th St ... Madison SD 57042 605-256-4561 256-3842 115
TF: 800-256-4561 ■ *Web:* www.rosebudwood.com

Roseburg 3660 Gateway St ... Springfield OR 97477 541-679-3311 679-2543 302
TF: 800-245-1115 ■ *Web:* www.roseburg.com

Roseburg National Cemetery
913 NW Garden Valley Blvd ... Roseburg OR 97471 541-677-3152 677-3044 136
Web: www.cem.va.gov

Rosecroft Raceway
6336 Rosecroft Dr ... Fort Washington MD 20744 301-567-4500 567-1053 133
Web: www.rosecroft.com

Rosedale Barbeque 600 SW Blvd ... Kansas City KS 66103 913-262-0343 671
Web: www.rosedalebarbeque.com

Rosedale Bible College 2270 Rosedale Rd ... Irwin OH 43029 740-857-1311 857-1312* 161
**Fax Area Code:* 877 ■ *Web:* rosedale.edu

Rosedale Development Assn
1403 SW Blvd ... Kansas City KS 66103 913-677-5097 50-4
Web: www.rosedale.org

Rosedale on Robson Suite Hotel
838 Hamilton St ... Vancouver BC V6B6A2 604-689-8033 689-4426 379
TF: 800-661-8870 ■ *Web:* www.rosedaleonrobson.com

Rosedale Products Inc
3730 W Liberty Rd PO Box 1085 ... Ann Arbor MI 48106 734-665-8201 520
Web: www.rosedaleproducts.com

Rosedale Technical Institute
215 Beecham Dr Ste 2 ... Pittsburgh PA 15205 800-521-6262 148
TF: 800-521-6262 ■ *Web:* www.rosedaletech.org

Rosedale Veterinary Hospital Inc
10611 Rosedale Hwy ... Bakersfield CA 93312 661-588-9630 794
Web: rosedalevet.com

Rosedown Plantation State Historic Site
12501 Hwy 10 ... Saint Francisville LA 70775 225-635-3332 50-3
TF: 888-376-1867 ■ *Web:* crt.state.la.us

Rose-Hulman Institute of Technology
5500 Wabash Ave ... Terre Haute IN 47803 812-877-1511 877-8941 166
TF: 800-248-7448 ■ *Web:* www.rose-hulman.edu

Roseland Community Hospital
45 W 111th St ... Chicago IL 60628 773-995-3000 374-3
Web: www.roselandhospital.org

Roseline Financial Group LLC, The
140 Virginia St Ste 300 ... Richmond VA 23219 804-545-7440 2
Web: theroselinegroup.com

Rosellen Suites at Stanley Park
2030 Barclay St ... Vancouver BC V6G1L5 604-689-4807 379
TF: 888-317-6648 ■ *Web:* www.rosellensuites.com

Rosemarie Arnold Law Offices
1386 Palisade Ave ... Fort Lee NJ 07024 201-461-1111 428
Web: www.rosemariearnold.com

Rosemary Beach Realty Inc
PO Box 611040 ... Rosemary Beach FL 32461 866-348-8952 652
TF: 866-348-8952 ■ *Web:* www.rosemarybeach.com

Rosemary Square
700 S Rosemary Ave ... West Palm Beach FL 33401 561-366-1000 366-1001 50-6
Web: www.rosemarysquarewpb.com

Rosemead Chamber of Commerce
3953 Muscatel Ave ... Rosemead CA 91770 626-288-0811 288-2514 139
Web: www.rosemeadchamber.org

Rosemead College of English
8705 E Valley Blvd ... Rosemead CA 91770 626-285-9668 285-1351 423
Web: www.rosemeadcollege.edu

				Phone	Fax	Class
Rosemont College 1400 Montgomery Ave TF: 888-521-0983 ■ Web: www.rosemont.edu	Rosemont	PA	19010	610-527-0200	526-2971	166
Rosemont Convention Bureau 9301 Bryn Mawr Ave Web: www.rosemont.com	Rosemont	IL	60018	847-823-2100	696-9700	206
Rosemont Landscaping & Lawncare LLC 3308 Mt Vernon Ave Web: rosemontlc.com	Alexandria	VA	22305	571-215-1275		422
Rosemont Suites 181 W Town St Web: rosemontnorwich.com	Norwich	CT	06360	860-889-2671		378
Rosemore Inc 1 N Charles St 22nd Fl Web: www.rosemoreinc.com	Baltimore	MD	21201	410-347-7080	347-7081	538
Rosen Associates Management Corp 33 S Service Rd Web: www.rosenmgmt.com	Jericho	NY	11753	516-333-2000	333-7555	655
Rosen Aviation LLC 1020 Owen Loop S TF: 888-668-4955 ■ Web: www.rosenaviation.com	Eugene	OR	97402	541-342-3802		57
Rosen Centre Hotel 9840 International Dr TF: 800-204-7234 ■ Web: www.rosencentre.com	Orlando	FL	32819	407-996-9840	996-0865	379
Rosen Consulting Group 1995 University Ave Ste 550 Web: rosenconsulting.com	Berkeley	CA	94704	510-549-4510		653
Rosen Group LLC, The 44 Wall St Ste 705 Web: rosengrouppr.com	New York	NY	10005	212-255-8455		636
Rosen Jacky (Sen D - NV) 144 Russell Senate Office Bldg Web: www.rosen.senate.gov	Washington	DC	20510	202-224-6244		342-2
Rosen Law Firm LLC 18 Broad St Ste 201 Web: www.rosen-lawfirm.com	Charleston	SC	29401	843-377-1700	377-1709	428
Rosen Plaza Hotel 9700 International Dr TF: 800-366-9700 ■ Web: www.rosenplaza.com	Orlando	FL	32819	407-996-9700	354-5774	379
Rosen Sapperstein & Friedlander Cht 300 Red Brook Blvd Web: rsfchart.com	Owings Mills	MD	21117	410-581-0800		2
Rosen Shingle Creek 9939 Universal Blvd TF: 866-996-9939 ■ Web: www.rosenshinglecreek.com	Orlando	FL	32819	407-996-9939		379
Rosen's Diversified Inc 1120 Lake Ave PO Box 933 Web: www.rosensdiversifiedinc.com	Fairmont	MN	56031	507-238-6001		360-3
Rosen, Bien, Galvan & Grunfeld LLP 50 Fremont St 19th Fl Web: rbgg.com	San Francisco	CA	94105	415-433-6830		41
Rosenbach Museum & Library 2008-2010 Delancey St Web: rosenbach.org	Philadelphia	PA	19103	215-732-1600		520
Rosenbaum & Assoc 1818 Market St Ste 3200 TF: 800-753-4257 ■ Web: rosenbauminjuryfirm.com	Philadelphia	PA	19103	215-569-0200		41
Rosenbaum Family House 30 Family House Dr PO Box 8228 TF: 855-988-2273 ■ Web: www.rosenbaumfamilyhouse.com	Morgantown	WV	26506	304-598-6094	598-6412	372
RosenbaumRollins & Olah PC 30057 Orchard Lake Rd Ste 200 Web: www.rrocpas.com	Farmington Hills	MI	48334	248-855-6640	855-3121	2
Rosenberg Advertising 12613 Detroit Ave Web: www.rosenbergadv.com	Lakewood	OH	44107	216-529-7910		7
Rosenberg Library 2310 Sealy Ave Web: rosenberg-library.org	Galveston	TX	77550	409-763-8854	763-0275	434-3
Rosenblatt Securities Inc 40 Wall St 59th Fl Web: rblt.com	New York	NY	10005	212-607-3100		401
Rosenblum Law Firm PC, The 200 Broadacres Dr Ste 325 TF: 888-883-5529 ■ Web: rosenblumlawfirm.com	Bloomfield	NJ	07003	888-883-5529		41
Rosenblum-silverman-sutton Investment Counsel (RSSIC) 1388 Sutter St Ste 725 Web: www.rssic.com	San Francisco	CA	94109	415-771-4500		401
Rosenboom Machine & Tool Inc 1530 Western Ave Web: www.rosenboom.com	Sheldon	IA	51201	712-324-4854		358
Rosencrantz-Bemis Water Well Co 1105 Hwy 281 Bypass TF: 800-466-2467 ■ Web: www.kansaswaterwelldrilling.com	Great Bend	KS	67530	620-793-5512		189-15
Rosendin Electric Inc 880 N Mabury Rd Web: www.rosendin.com	San Jose	CA	95133	408-286-2800		189-4
Rosenfeld, Hafron, Shapiro & Farmer 221 N Lasalle St Ste 1763 Web: rhsflawfirm.com	Chicago	IL	60601	312-372-6058		41
Rosenfeld, Meyer and Susman LLP 232 N Canon Dr Web: www.rmslaw.com	Beverly Hills	CA	90210	310-858-7700	860-2430	41
Rosengard Moving Systems Inc 177 Ferry Rd Web: rosengardmovingsystems.com	Haverhill	MA	01835	978-373-6272		311
Rosenn, Jenkins & Greenwald LLP 15 S Franklin St TF: 800-888-4754 ■ Web: www.rjglaw.com	Wilkes-Barre	PA	18711	570-826-5600		428
Rosenquist LLC PO Box 1162 Web: www.rosenquistllc.com	Wilkesboro	NC	28697	336-262-5595		821
Rosenstiel School of Marine & Atmospheric Science University of Miami 4600 Rickenbacker Causeway Rosenstiel School Web: www.rsmas.miami.edu	Miami	FL	33149	305-421-4000	421-4771	166
Rosenthal & Marsh LLP 26500 W Agoura Rd Ste 211 Web: rosenthalmarshlaw.com	Calabasas	CA	91302	818-746-9222		41
Rosenthal & Rosenthal Inc 1370 Broadway Web: www.rosenthalinc.com	New York	NY	10018	212-356-1400		272
Rosenthal Appraisal Company Inc 6 W Railroad Ave Web: www.rosappraisal.com	Tenafly	NJ	07670	201-567-4300		41
Rosenthal Automotive Organization 11050 Fairfax Blvd *Fax Area Code: 703 ■ TF: 877-446-4543 ■ Web: www.rosenthalauto.com	Arlington	VA	22203	877-446-4543	553-8435*	57
Rosenthal Bros Inc (RB) 740 Waukegan Rd PO Box 700 Web: www.rosenthalbros.com	Deerfield	IL	60015	847-940-4300	940-4315	390
Rosenthal Collins Group LLC (RCG) 216 W Jackson Blvd Ste 400 Web: www.rcgdirect.com	Chicago	IL	60606	312-460-9200	795-7730	169
Rosenthal Retirement Planning LP 1412 Main St 6th Fl TF: 800-336-2553 ■ Web: rrp.com	Dallas	TX	75202	214-752-1000		401
Rosenthal, Murphey, Coblentz & Donahue 30 N Lasalle Ste 1624 Web: rmcj.com	Chicago	IL	60602	312-541-1070	541-9191	41
Rosenwasser Grossman Consulting Engineers PC 519 8h Ave 20th Fl Web: www.rgce.com	New York	NY	10018	212-564-2424		261
RoseRyan Inc 35473 Dumbarton Ct Web: roseryan.com	Newark	CA	94560	510-456-3056		194
Roses Medical and Surgical Supply 90 Washington St Web: www.rosesmed.com	East Orange	NJ	07017	973-675-0725		475
Roses Southwest Papers Inc 1701 Second St SW Web: www.rosessouthwestpapers.com	Albuquerque	NM	87102	505-842-0134	242-0342	65
Rosetta Stone Ltd 1919 N Lynn St 7th Fl NYSE: RST ■ *Fax Area Code: 540 ■ TF: 800-788-0822 ■ Web: www.rosettastone.com	Arlington	VA	22209	800-788-0822	432-0953*	685
Roseville Chamber of Commerce 650 Douglas Blvd Web: rosevillechamber.com	Roseville	CA	95678	916-783-8136		139
Roseville Joint Union High School District 1750 Cirby Way Web: www.rjuhsd.us	Roseville	CA	95661	916-786-2051	786-2681	685
Roseville Public Library 29777 Gratiot Ave Web: www.libcoop.net	Roseville	MI	48066	586-445-5407	445-5499	434-3
Rosewater Supper Club 19 Toronto St Web: www.libertygroup.com	Toronto	ON	M5C2R1	416-214-5888	214-2412	671
Rosewell Toyota 2211 W Second St Web: www.roswelltoyota.com	Roswell	NM	88201	575-622-5860		57
Rosewood Capital 367 Ave U *Fax Area Code: 415 ■ Web: www.rosewoodcapitalgroup.com	Brooklyn	NY	11223	516-253-6423	362-1192*	792
Rosewood Industries Inc 1203 E Central Terr Web: www.rosewood.net	Stigler	OK	74462	918-967-3306		321
Rosey Baby 4587 N University Dr Web: www.roseybaby.com	Lauderhill	FL	33351	954-749-5627		671
Roshanian & Associates Inc 6404 Wilshire Blvd Web: www.roshanian.com	Los Angeles	CA	90048	323-933-5252		261
Roshi Tech Inc 5 Castleton Ct *Fax Area Code: 270 ■ Web: www.roshitech.com	Merrimack	NH	03054	603-889-2211	568-6295*	177
Rosicrucian Egyptian Museum 1342 Naglee Ave Web: www.rosicrucian.org	San Jose	CA	95191	408-947-3600	947-3677	520
Rosie the Riveter/World War II Home Front National Historical Park 1401 Marina Way S Web: www.nps.gov	Richmond	CA	94804	510-232-5050		564
Rosin Eyecare Ctr 6233 W Cermak Rd Web: www.rosineyecare.com	Berwyn	IL	60402	708-749-2020		542
Rosina Food Products Inc 170 French Rd Web: www.rosina.com	Buffalo	NY	14227	716-668-0123		296-26
Rosine's 434 Alvarado St Web: www.rosinesmonterey.com	Monterey	CA	93940	831-375-1400		671
Rosine's 721 S Weir Canyon Rd Web: www.rosines.com	Anaheim	CA	92808	714-283-5141		671
Rosner Law Group LLC 824 N Market St Ste 810 Web: teamrosner.com	Wilmington	DE	19801	302-777-1111		41
Rosner's Inc 1480 S Military Trail Web: rosners.com	West Palm Beach	FL	33415	561-967-8600		35
Ross & Baruzzini 6 S Old Orchard TF: 888-334-5831 ■ Web: www.rossbar.com	Saint Louis	MO	63119	314-918-8383		261
Ross & Matthews PC 3650 Lovell Ave TF: 800-458-6982 ■ Web: rossandmatthews.com	Fort Worth	TX	76107	800-458-6982		428
Ross & Wallace Paper Products Inc 204 Old Covington Hwy *Fax Area Code: 985 ■ TF: 800-854-2300 ■ Web: www.rossandwallace.com	Hammond	LA	70403	800-854-2300	345-1370*	65
Ross Aluminum Castings LLC 815 N Oak Ave Web: www.rossal.com	Sidney	OH	45365	937-492-4134		492
Ross Buehler Falk & Company LLP (RBF) 1500 Lititz Pk Web: www.rbfco.com	Lancaster	PA	17601	717-393-2700	393-1743	2
Ross Casting & Innovation LLC 402 S Kuther Rd PO Box 89 Web: www.rciwheels.com	Sidney	OH	45365	937-497-4500		492
Ross Controls 1250 Stephenson Hwy TF: 800-438-7677 ■ Web: www.rosscontrols.com	Troy	MI	48083	248-764-1800	764-1850	790
Ross Correctional Institution 16149 Sr 104 Web: drc.ohio.gov	Chillicothe	OH	45601	740-774-7050	774-7055	213
Ross County 2 N Paint St Ste B Web: www.co.ross.oh.us	Chillicothe	OH	45601	740-702-3085	702-3018	338
Ross Express Inc 195 N Main St TF: 800-762-5966 ■ Web: www.rossexpress.com	Boscawen	NH	03303	603-753-4176	753-8614	780
Ross Grill Whalers Wharf 237-241 Commercial St Web: rossgrillptown.com	Provincetown	MA	02657	508-487-8878		671
Ross Group Inc 2730 Indian Ripple Rd TF: 800-734-9304 ■ Web: www.rossgroupinc.com	Dayton	OH	45440	800-734-9304		225
Ross Industries Inc 5321 Midland Rd TF: 800-336-6010 ■ Web: www.rossindinc.com	Midland	VA	22728	540-439-3271		298

Phone | Fax | Class

Ross Insurance Agency LLC
1496 Lititz Pk . . . . . Lancaster PA 17601 717-397-4729 397-6756 390
Web: rossinsuranceagency.com

Ross Laboratories Inc
3138 Fairview Ave E . . . . . Seattle WA 98102 206-324-3950 529
Web: www.rosslabsllc.com

Ross Lane and Co
7000 Peachtree Dunwoody Rd Bldg 1 . . . . . Atlanta GA 30328 770-804-8044 2
Web: www.ross-lane.com

Ross Marketing International LLC
2214 Main St Ste A . . . . . Cedar Falls IA 50613 319-266-5881 195
Web: rossmarketing.net

Ross Matthews Mills Inc
372 Kilburn St . . . . . Fall River MA 02724 508-677-0601 745-5

Ross Medical Education Ctr
11590 Century Blvd Ste 210 . . . . . Cincinnati OH 45246 513-851-8500 668
TF: 866-815-5578 ■ *Web:* www.rosseducation.edu

Ross Memorial Hospital (RMH)
10 Angeline St N . . . . . Lindsay ON K9V4M8 705-324-6111 374-2
TF: 800-510-7365 ■ *Web:* rmh.org

Ross Metals Corp 54 W 47th St . . . . . New York NY 10036 800-334-7191 768-3018* 485
**Fax Area Code:* 212 ■ *TF:* 800-334-7191 ■ *Web:* rossmetals.com

Ross Neely Systems Inc
1500 Second St . . . . . Birmingham AL 35214 205-798-1137 780
Web: www.rossneely.com

Ross Optical Industries Inc
1410 Gail Borden Pl . . . . . El Paso TX 79935 915-595-5417 595-5466 544
TF: 800-880-5417 ■ *Web:* www.rossoptical.com

Ross Park Zoo 60 Morgan Rd . . . . . Binghamton NY 13903 607-724-5461 823
Web: rossparkzoo.org

Ross Realty Investments Inc
3325 S University Dr Ste 210 . . . . . Davie FL 33328 954-452-5000 452-4700 652
TF: 800-370-4202 ■ *Web:* www.ross-realty.com

Ross Reels 11 Ponderosa Ct . . . . . Montrose CO 81401 970-249-0606 710
Web: www.rossreels.com

Ross Simons Jewelers Inc
9 Ross Simons Dr . . . . . Cranston RI 02920 401-463-3100 410
TF: 800-835-0919 ■ *Web:* www.ross-simons.com

Ross Sinclaire & Associates LLC
700 Walnut St Ste 600 . . . . . Cincinnati OH 45202 513-381-3939 690
TF: 800-543-1831 ■ *Web:* www.rsanet.com

Ross Technology Corp 104 N Maple Ave . . . . . Leola PA 17540 800-345-8170 91
TF: 800-345-8170 ■ *Web:* www.rosstechnology.com

Ross Thiele & Sons Ltd
7425 Girard Ave . . . . . La Jolla CA 92037 858-454-2133 362
Web: rossthiele.com

Ross Valley School District
110 Shaw Dr . . . . . San Anselmo CA 94960 415-454-2162 454-6840 685
Web: www.rossvalleyschools.org

Ross Video Ltd 8 John St . . . . . Iroquois ON K0E1K0 613-652-4886 797
Web: www.rossvideo.com

Ross, Amsel, Raben, Nascimento PLLC
2250 SW Third Ave 4th Fl . . . . . Miami FL 33129 305-858-9550 858-7491 41
Web: crimlawfirm.com

Ross, Banks, May, Cron & Cavin PC
7700 San Felipe Ste 550 . . . . . Houston TX 77063 713-626-1200 428
Web: www.rossbanks.com

Ross, Brittain & Schonberg Company LPA
6480 Rockside Woods Blvd S Ste 350 . . . . . Cleveland OH 44131 216-447-1551 447-1554 428
Web: www.rbslaw.com

Rossbacher Insurance Service Inc
19 N Center St PO Box 404 . . . . . Corry PA 16407 814-664-7744 390
Web: teamrossbacher.com

Rosseau Lake College 1967 Bright St . . . . . Rosseau ON P0C1J0 705-732-4351 732-6319 622
TF: 800-265-0569 ■ *Web:* www.rosseaulakecollege.com

Rossetti & Devoto PC
20 Brace Rd Ste 115 . . . . . Cherry Hill NJ 08034 856-354-0900 41
Web: rossettidevoto.com

Ross-France PC 9417 Innovation Dr . . . . . Manassas VA 20110 703-361-4188 261
Web: rossfranceva.com

Rossi Building Materials Inc
835 Stewart St . . . . . Fort Bragg CA 95437 707-964-4086 752
Web: www.rossi-ace.com

Rossi Kimms & Mcdowell LLC
20609 Gordon Park Sq Ste 150 . . . . . Ashburn VA 20147 703-726-6020 726-6024 428
Web: rkmllp.com

Rossi Kitchen & Bar, The
895 N High St . . . . . Columbus OH 43215 614-525-0624 671
Web: rossikitchenandbar.com

Rossi Law Offices Ltd
28 Thurber Blvd . . . . . Smithfield RI 02917 401-231-7700 406-2843 41
TF: 800-747-6774 ■ *Web:* rossilaw.com

Rossmann Macdonald & Benetti Inc
3838 Watt Ave Ste E500 . . . . . Sacramento CA 95821 916-488-8360 488-9478 2
Web: www.rmb-cpa.com

Rosson House Historic Museum
113 N Sixth St . . . . . Phoenix AZ 85004 602-262-5070 520
Web: heritagesquarephx.org

Rossum Realty Unlimited
3875 S Jones Blvd Ste 101 . . . . . Las Vegas NV 89103 702-368-1850 652
Web: www.rossumrealty.com

Roster Carlsen Inc 555 Main St Ste 220 . . . . . Chico CA 95928 530-895-3163 2
Web: rostercarlsen.com

Rostra Precision Controls Inc
2519 Dana Dr . . . . . Laurinburg NC 28352 800-782-3379 276-1354* 529
**Fax Area Code:* 910 ■ *TF:* 800-782-3379 ■ *Web:* www.rostra.com

Roswell Bookbinding Co
2614 N 29th Ave . . . . . Phoenix AZ 85009 602-272-9338 272-9786 92
TF: 888-803-8883 ■ *Web:* www.roswellbookbinding.com

Roswell Chamber of Commerce
131 W Second St . . . . . Roswell NM 88201 575-623-5695 624-6870 139
TF: 877-849-7679 ■ *Web:* www.roswellnm.org

Roswell Correctional Ctr
578 W Chickasaw Rd . . . . . Hagerman NM 88232 575-625-3100 213
Web: cd.nm.gov

Roswell Livestock Auction Sales Inc
900 N Garden PO Box 2041 . . . . . Roswell NM 88202 575-622-5580 446
TF: 800-748-1541 ■ *Web:* www.roswelllivestockauction.com

Roswell Museum & Art Ctr
100 W 11th St . . . . . Roswell NM 88201 575-624-6744 520
Web: www.roswell-nm.gov

Roswell Park Cancer Institute
Elm & Carlton St . . . . . Buffalo NY 14263 716-845-2300 374-7
TF: 877-275-7724 ■ *Web:* www.roswellpark.org

Rosy's Fish City 2882 Story Rd . . . . . San Jose CA 95127 408-272-2088 671
Web: www.rosyfishcity.com

RotaDyne 1101 Windham Pkwy . . . . . Romeoville IL 60446 630-769-9700 769-9255 677
Web: www.rotadyne.com

Rotair Industries Inc
964 Crescent Ave . . . . . Bridgeport CT 06607 203-576-6545 22
Web: www.rotair.com

Rotary Botanical Gardens
1455 Palmer Dr . . . . . Janesville WI 53545 608-752-3885 97
Web: www.rotarybotanicalgardens.org

Rotary Forms Press Inc
835 S High St . . . . . Hillsboro OH 45133 937-393-3426 393-8473 110
TF: 800-654-2876 ■ *Web:* www.rotaryfp.com

Rotary Foundation, The
1560 Sherman Ave . . . . . Evanston IL 60201 847-866-3100 48-5
TF: 866-976-8279 ■ *Web:* www.rotary.org

Rotary Intl
1 Rotary Ctr 1560 Sherman Ave . . . . . Evanston IL 60201 847-866-3000 328-8554 48-15
Web: my.rotary.org

Rotary Lift 2700 Lanier Dr . . . . . Madison IN 47250 812-273-1622 386
TF: 800-640-5438 ■ *Web:* www.rotarylift.com

Rotary Multiforms Inc
1340 E 11 Mile Rd . . . . . Madison Heights MI 48071 586-558-7960 627
TF: 800-762-5644 ■ *Web:* www.rmi-printing.com

Rotary Offset Press Inc 6600 S 231st St . . . . . Kent WA 98032 253-813-9900 627
Web: www.rotaryoffsetpress.com

Rotary Park
1030-B Cumberland Heights Rd . . . . . Clarksville TN 37040 931-648-5732 920-1832 564
Web: mcgtn.org

Rotating Machinery Services Inc
2760 Baglyos Cir . . . . . Bethlehem PA 18020 484-821-0702 386
Web: rotatingmachinery.com

Rotating Right Inc 6120 Davies Rd NW . . . . . Edmonton AB T6E4M9 780-485-2010 485-1938 518

Rotec Industries Inc
270 Industrial Dr . . . . . Hampshire IL 60140 630-279-3300 207
Web: www.rotec-usa.com

Rotech Clarks Summit
335 Bedford St . . . . . Clarks Summit PA 18411 570-586-8969 475
Web: www.rotech.com

Rotek Inc
1400 S Chillicothe Rd PO Box 312 . . . . . Aurora OH 44202 330-562-4000 562-4620 75
TF: 800-221-8043 ■ *Web:* www.rotek-inc.com

Rotella's Italian Bakery Inc
6949 S 108th St . . . . . La Vista NE 68128 402-592-6600 592-2989 68
Web: www.rotellasbakery.com

Rotenberg Meril Solomon
Park 80 W Plaza 1 250 Pehle Ave Ste 101 . . . . . Saddle Brook NJ 07663 201-487-8383 2
Web: www.rmsbg.com

Roth Fabricating Inc 9600 Skyline Dr . . . . . Morenci MI 49256 517-458-7541 480
Web: www.rothfabricatinginc.com

Roth Farms Inc
232 NW Ave L PO Box 1300 . . . . . Belle Glade FL 33430 561-996-2991 996-8501 10-11
Web: www.rothfarms.com

Roth Heating Company Inc
400 W Drexel Ave . . . . . Oak Creek WI 53154 414-764-4700 764-0157 189-10
Web: www.rothheating.com

Roth Living 11300 W 47th St . . . . . Minnetonka MN 55343 952-933-4428 38
TF: 800-363-3818 ■ *Web:* www.rothliving.com

Roth Pump Co PO Box 4330 . . . . . Rock Island IL 61204 309-787-1791 787-5142 641
TF: 888-444-7684 ■ *Web:* www.rothpump.com

Roth Ready Mix Concrete Co
900 Kieley Pl . . . . . Cincinnati OH 45217 513-242-8400 182
Web: www.cincinnatireadymix.com

Roth Staffing Companies LP
450 N State College Blvd . . . . . Orange CA 92868 714-939-8600 721
Web: www.rothstaffing.com

Rothberg Logan & Warsco LLP
505 E Washington Blvd . . . . . Fort Wayne IN 46802 260-422-9454 428
Web: rlwlawfirm.com

Rothbury Farms PO Box 202 . . . . . Grand Rapids MI 49501 877-684-2879 296-1
TF: 877-684-2879 ■ *Web:* rothburyfarms.com

Rothe Development Inc
4614 Sinclair Rd . . . . . San Antonio TX 78222 210-648-3131 743
TF: 800-229-5209 ■ *Web:* www.rothe.com

Rothenberg & Peters PLLC
1 Linden Pl Ste 211 . . . . . Great Neck NY 11021 516-773-3200 2
Web: rothenbergpeters.com

Rothenberger USA LLC
7130 Clinton Rd . . . . . Loves Park IL 61111 815-397-0260 455
TF: 800-545-7698 ■ *Web:* rothenberger.com

Rothenbuhler Engineering
524 Rhodes Rd PO Box 708 . . . . . Sedro-Woolley WA 98284 360-856-0836 856-2183 700
Web: www.rothenbuhlereng.com

Rothman Consulting Group Inc
34 Bradley Rd . . . . . Arlington MA 02474 781-641-4046 194
Web: www.jrothman.com

Rothman Furniture Stores Inc
2101 E Terra Ln . . . . . O'Fallon MO 63366 636-978-3500 321
TF: 877-704-0002 ■ *Web:* www.rothmanfurniture.com

Rothman Goodman Managmnt Corp
27236 Grand Central Pkwy . . . . . Queens NY 11005 718-224-2880 652

Rothman Gordon PC
310 Grant St 3rd Fl Grant Bldg . . . . . Pittsburgh PA 15219 412-338-1100 281-7304 428
Web: www.rothmangordon.com

Rothmann's Steakhouse & Grill
3 E 54th St . . . . . New York NY 10022 212-319-5500 671
Web: www.rothmanns54.com

Rothschild 1407 Broadway 10th Fl . . . . . New York NY 10018 212-354-8550 155-3
Web: www.srothschild.com

Rothstein, Mandell, Strohm & Halm
150 Airport Rd Ste 600 PO Box 3017 . . . . . Lakewood NJ 08701 732-719-4156 905-6555 41
TF: 888-657-9720 ■ *Web:* rmsmlaw.com

Name / Address	City	State	ZIP	Phone	Fax	Class
Rothwell Landscape Inc 1607 Fair Ln	Manhattan	KS	66502	785-539-1799		422
Web: rothwelllandscape.com						
Rotier's 2413 Elliston Pl	Nashville	TN	37203	615-327-9892		671
Web: www.rotiersrestaurant.com						
Rotisserie Coco Rico						
3907 St-Laurent Blvd	Montreal	QC	H2W1X9	514-849-5554		671
Web: cocoricomtl.com						
Rotmans Furniture & Carpet						
725 Southbridge St	Worcester	MA	01610	800-768-6267		321
TF: 800-768-6267 ■ *Web:* www.rotmans.com						
Roto Pumps North America Inc						
5889 S Garnett Rd	Tulsa	OK	74147	918-280-9144	806-6853	641
Web: www.rotopumps.com						
Roto Rooter Corp						
300 Ashworth Rd	West Des Moines	IA	50265	515-223-1343		427
Web: www.rotorooter.com						
Roto Salt Company Inc 118 Monell St	Penn Yan	NY	14527	315-536-6234		145
Web: www.rotosalt.com						
Rotochopper Inc						
217 West St PO Box 295	Saint Martin	MN	56376	320-548-3586	548-3372	190
TF: 800-663-7574 ■ *Web:* www.rotochopper.com						
RotoMetrics Group 800 Howerton Ln	Eureka	MO	63025	636-587-3600	587-3701	757
TF: 800-325-3851 ■ *Web:* www.rotometrics.com						
Roton Products Inc 660 E Elliott Ave	Kirkwood	MO	63122	314-821-4400	821-4818	492
TF: 800-467-6866 ■ *Web:* www.roton.com						
Rotor Clip Company Inc						
187 Davidson Ave	Somerset	NJ	08873	732-469-7333	469-7898	326
TF: 800-557-6867 ■ *Web:* www.rotorclip.com						
Rotorcraft Services Group/Rsg Products						
3900 Falcon Way W	Fort Worth	TX	76106	817-624-6600		22
Web: rotorcraftservices.com						
Rotork Process Controls Inc						
5607 W Douglas Ave	Milwaukee	WI	53218	414-461-9200	461-1024	203
Web: www.rotork.com						
Rottler Mfg 8029 S 200th St	Kent	WA	98032	253-872-7050	395-0230	455
TF: 800-452-0534 ■ *Web:* www.rottlermfg.com						
Rottler Pest & Lawn Solutions						
2690 Masterson Ave	Saint Louis	MO	63114	314-426-0130		577
TF: 888-966-8919 ■ *Web:* www.rottler.com						
Rotz Pharmacy Inc 1338 Amherst St	Winchester	VA	22601	540-662-8312		237
Web: rotzpharmacy.com						
Rouda Harley (Rep D - CA)						
2300 Rayburn House Office Bldg	Washington	DC	20515	202-225-2415		342-2
Web: www.rouda.house.gov						
Rouge 1240 Eigth Ave SE	Calgary	AB	T2G0M7	403-531-2767	531-2768	671
Web: www.rougecalgary.com						
Rough Brothers Inc 5513 Vine St	Cincinnati	OH	45217	513-242-0310		186
Web: www.roughbros.com						
Rough Creek Lodge						
5165 County Rd 2013	Glen Rose	TX	76043	254-965-3700		379
Web: roughcreek.com						
Rough Notes Company Inc, The						
11690 Technology Dr	Carmel	IN	46032	317-582-1600	321-1909*	457-5
**Fax Area Code:* 800 ■ *TF:* 800-428-4384 ■ *Web:* www.roughnotes.com						
Rough Rider Industries						
3303 E Main Ave PO Box 5521	Bismarck	ND	58506	800-732-0557	328-6164*	630
**Fax Area Code:* 701 ■ *TF:* 800-732-0557 ■ *Web:* www.roughriderindustries.com						
Rough River Dam State Resort Park						
450 Lodge Rd	Falls of Rough	KY	40119	270-257-2311		565
TF: 800-325-1713 ■ *Web:* parks.ky.gov						
Roughrider Electric Cooperative Inc						
2156 4th Ave E	Dickinson	ND	58602	701-483-5111	483-6057	245
TF: 800-748-5533 ■ *Web:* www.roughriderelectric.com						
Round Butte Seed Growers Inc 505 C St	Culver	OR	97734	541-385-7001		323
TF: 866-385-7001 ■ *Web:* helenaculver.com						
Round Lake Area Chamber of Commerce & Industry						
2007 Civic Ctr Way	Round Lake Beach	IL	60073	847-546-2002	546-2254	139
TF: 800-334-7661 ■ *Web:* www.rlchamber.org						
Round Lake Library 31 Wesley Ave	Round Lake	NY	12151	518-899-2285	899-0061	434-3
Web: roundlake.sals.edu						
Round Lake State Park PO Box 170	Sagle	ID	83860	208-263-3489		565
Web: idahostateparks.reserveamerica.com						
Round River Records 301 Jacob St	Seekonk	MA	02771	508-336-9703	336-2254*	514
**Fax Area Code:* 503 ■ *Web:* www.billharley.com						
Round Rock Chamber of Commerce						
212 E Main St	Round Rock	TX	78664	512-255-5805		139
Web: roundrockchamber.org						
Round Rock ISD 1311 Round Rock Ave	Round Rock	TX	78681	512-464-6000		685
Web: roundrockisd.org						
Round Rock Public Library						
221 E Main St	Round Rock	TX	78664	512-218-7001		434-3
Web: www.roundrocktexas.gov						
Round Sky Inc						
848 N Rainbow Blvd Ste 326	Las Vegas	NV	89107	855-826-6284		317
TF: 855-826-6284 ■ *Web:* www.roundsky.com						
Round Table Wealth Management						
319 Lenox Ave	Westfield	NJ	07090	908-789-7310		194
Web: roundtablewealth.com						
Round Top State Bank						
301 N Washington PO Box 36	Round Top	TX	78954	979-249-3151		70
Web: roundtopstatebank.com						
Round Valley Recreation Area						
1220 Lebanon-Stanton Rd	Lebanon	NJ	08833	908-236-6355		565
Web: www.njparksandforests.org						
Roundabout Theatre Co						
231 W 39th St Ste 1200	New York	NY	10018	212-719-9393	869-8817	747
Web: www.roundabouttheatre.org						
Roundhouse Marketing Services Inc						
560 E Verona Ave	Verona	WI	53593	608-497-2550		463
Web: roundhouse-marketing.com						
Rounds Mike (Sen R - SD)						
502 Hart Senate Office Bldg	Washington	DC	20510	202-224-5842	224-7482	342-2
TF: 844-875-5268 ■ *Web:* www.rounds.senate.gov						
Roundtable Investment Partners LLC						
280 Park Ave E 23rd Fl	New York	NY	10017	212-488-4700		401
Web: www.roundtableip.com						
Rountree Group Inc						
12670 Crabapple Rd Ste 210	Milton	GA	30004	770-645-4545		317
Web: www.rountreegroup.com						
Rountree Transport & Rigging Inc						
2640 N Ln Ave	Jacksonville	FL	32254	904-781-1033	786-6229	780
TF: 800-342-5036 ■ *Web:* rountreetransport.com						
Rourke & Blumenthal LLP						
495 S High St Ste 450	Columbus	OH	43215	614-321-3212		428
Web: www.randbllp.com						
Rouse Consulting Group Inc 422 16th St	Moline	IL	61265	309-762-3589		196
Web: go2rcg.com						
Rouse's Enterprises LLC						
1301 St Mary St	Thibodaux	LA	70301	985-447-5998		345
Web: www.rouses.com						
Rouse-sirine Associates Ltd						
333 Office Sq Ln	Virginia Beach	VA	23462	757-490-2300		727
Web: www.rouse-sirine.com						
Roush & Yates Racing Engines LLC						
297 Rolling Hill Rd	Mooresville	NC	28117	704-799-6216		54
Web: roushyates.com						
Roush Enterprise 12447 Levan	Livonia	MI	48150	734-779-7006		60
TF: 800-215-9658 ■ *Web:* roush.com						
Roush Fenway Racing LLC						
4600 Roush Pl NW	Concord	NC	28027	704-720-4600		713
Web: www.roushfenway.com						
Roush Media 84 E Santa Anita Ave	Burbank	CA	91502	818-559-8648		514
Web: roush-media.com						
Rousseau Metal Inc						
105 Ave De Gasp Ouest	Saint Jean-Port-Joli	QC	G0R3G0	418-598-3381		350
TF: 866-463-4270 ■ *Web:* www.rousseaumetal.com						
Route 3 Press 19948 Shooting Star Rd	Anamosa	IA	52205	319-462-4623		637-9
Web: www.wapsialmanac.com						
Route 66 21 Cottage St	Bar Harbor	ME	04609	207-288-3708		671
Web: www.barharborroute66.com						
Route 66 Casino Hotel						
14500 Central Ave	Albuquerque	NM	87121	505-352-7866		133
TF: 866-352-7866 ■ *Web:* www.rt66casino.com						
Route 66 State Park 97 N Outer Rd Ste 1	Eureka	MO	63025	636-938-7198		565
Web: mostateparks.com						
Route Brokers Inc 107 N Blvd	Great Neck	NY	11021	516-482-8250		194
TF: 800-476-8837 ■ *Web:* www.routebrokers.com						
Routeware Inc 16575 SW 72nd Ave	Portland	OR	97224	503-906-8500		350
TF: 877-906-8550 ■ *Web:* routeware.com						
Routt County						
136 Sixth St PO Box 775227	Steamboat Springs	CO	80477	970-870-5405	871-8140	338
Web: www.co.routt.co.us						
Roux Associates Inc 209 Shafter St	Islandia	NY	11749	631-232-2600		193
TF: 800-322-7689 ■ *Web:* www.rouxinc.com						
Roux Insurance Services						
185 Webster St	Lewiston	ME	04240	207-784-9358		390
Web: nfp.com						
Rouzer David (Rep R - NC)						
2439 Rayburn House Office Bldg	Washington	DC	20515	202-225-2731	225-5773	342-2
Web: www.rouzer.house.gov						
Rovanco Piping Systems Inc						
20535 SE Frontage Rd	Joliet	IL	60431	815-741-6700	741-4229	595
Web: www.rovanco.com						
Rover Armstrong APC						
75100 Mediterreanean	Palm Desert	CA	92211	760-346-4741		41
Web: roverarmstrong.com						
Rovibec Inc 475 Rte du Port	Nicolet	QC	J3T1W3	819-293-5005	289-2203	190
Web: rovibecagrisolutions.com						
Rovisys Co, The 1455 Danner Dr	Aurora	OH	44202	330-562-8600	562-8688	261
Web: www.rovisys.com						
ROW2 Technologies Inc						
14 Walsh Dr Ste 200	Parsippany	NJ	07054	973-795-1141		809
Web: www.row2technologies.com						
Rowan College at Burlington County						
601 Pemberton Brown Mills Rd	Pemberton	NJ	08068	609-894-9311		167-3
Web: www.rcbc.edu						
Rowan College at Gloucester County						
1400 Tanyard Rd	Sewell	NJ	08080	856-468-5000		167-3
Web: www.rcgc.edu						
Rowan College of South Jersey - Cumberland Campus						
Cumberland County College						
3322 College Dr	Vineland	NJ	08360	856-691-8600	794-3368	162
Web: www.rcsj.edu						
Rowan Correctional Ctr						
4750 S Main St	Salisbury	NC	28147	704-639-7540	733-8272*	213
**Fax Area Code:* 919 ■ *Web:* www.ncdps.gov						
Rowan Cos 2800 Postoak Blvd Ste 5450	Houston	TX	77056	713-621-7800		185
NYSE: RDC ■ *Web:* www.rowan.com						
Rowan County 130 W Innes St	Salisbury	NC	28144	704-216-8170	216-8110	338
Web: www.rowancountync.gov						
Rowan County Chamber of Commerce						
204 E Innes St Ste 110	Salisbury	NC	28144	704-633-4221	639-1200	139
Web: www.rowanchamber.com						
Rowan County Convention & Visitors Bureau						
204 E Innes St Ste 120	Salisbury	NC	28144	704-638-3100	642-2011	206
Web: www.visitsalisburync.com						
Rowan Public Library						
201 W Fisher St	Salisbury	NC	28144	704-216-8228	216-8237	434-3
Web: www.rowancountync.gov						
Rowan Regional Medical Center Inc (RRMC)						
612 Mocksville Ave	Salisbury	NC	28144	704-210-5000	210-5562	374-3
TF: 888-844-0080						
Rowan University						
201 Mullica Hill Rd	Glassboro	NJ	08028	856-256-4200	256-4430	166
TF: 877-787-6926 ■ *Web:* www.rowan.edu						
Rowan Williams Davies & Irwin Inc						
650 Woodlawn Rd W	Guelph	ON	N1K1B8	519-823-1311		261
Web: rwdi.com						
Rowan-Cabarrus Community College						
North						
1333 Jake Alexander Blvd S PO Box 1595	Salisbury	NC	28146	704-216-7222		162
Web: www.rccc.edu						
Rowayton Arts Ctr 145 Rowayton Ave	Rowayton	CT	06853	203-866-2744		50-2
Web: rowaytonarts.org						
Rowe Camp & Conference Ctr						
22 Kings Hwy Rd PO Box 273	Rowe	MA	01367	413-339-4954	339-5728	673
Web: rowecenter.org						

Name / Address	City	State	Zip	Phone	Fax	Class
Rowe Foundry Inc 147 W Cumberland St PO Box 130 *Web:* www.rowefoundry.com	Martinsville	IL	62442	217-382-4135		492
Rowe Machinery & Automation Inc 76 Hinckley Rd *TF:* 800-247-2645 ■ *Web:* www.runwithrowe.com	Clinton	ME	04927	207-426-2351		494
Rowe Machinery Inc 287 County Hwy 85 *TF:* 800-833-9237 ■ *Web:* www.rowemachinery.com	Haleyville	AL	35565	205-486-9237	486-8343	780
Rowell Auctions Inc 1303 Fourth St SW *TF:* 800-323-8388 ■ *Web:* www.rowellauctions.com	Moultrie	GA	31768	229-985-8388		652
Rowell Chemical Corp 15 Salt Creek Ln Ste 205 *TF:* 888-261-7963 ■ *Web:* www.rowellchemical.com	Hinsdale	IL	60521	630-920-8833	920-8994	146
Rowland & Moore LLP 200 W Superior St Ste 400 *Web:* telecomreg.com	Chicago	IL	60654	312-803-1000		41
Rowland Institute for Science Inc, The 100 Edwin H Land Blvd *Web:* www.rowland.harvard.edu	Cambridge	MA	02142	617-497-4600		522
Rowland Technologies Inc 320 Barnes Rd *Web:* www.rowlandtechnologies.com	Wallingford	CT	06492	203-269-9500		600
Rowland Transportation Inc 40824 Messick Rd *TF:* 800-338-1146 ■ *Web:* www.rowlandtransportation.com	Dade City	FL	33525	352-567-2002		314
Rowlands Sales Company Inc Butler Industrial Pk *TF:* 800-582-6388 ■ *Web:* www.rowlands.com	Hazleton	PA	18201	570-455-5813		358
Rowlett Bowl-A-Rama 5021 Lakeview Pkwy *Web:* www.rowlettbowlarama.com	Rowlett	TX	75088	972-475-7080		99
Rowlett Chamber of Commerce 3910 Main St *Web:* www.rowlettchamber.com	Rowlett	TX	75088	972-475-3200		139
Rowley Biochemical Institute Danvers Industrial Park 10 Electronics Ave *Web:* www.rowleybio.com	Danvers	MA	01923	978-739-4883	739-5640	85
Rowley Chapman & Barney Ltd 63 E Main St Ste 501 *TF:* 888-476-8411 ■ *Web:* www.azlegal.com	Mesa	AZ	85201	480-833-1113		428
Rowley Properties Inc 1595 NW Gilman Blvd Ste 1 *Web:* www.rowleyproperties.com	Issaquah	WA	98027	425-392-6407		652
Rowley Spring & Stamping Corp 210 Redstone Hill Rd *Web:* www.rowleyspring.com	Bristol	CT	06010	860-582-8175	589-8718	719
Rowleys Tires & Automotive Services 3596 Wilder Rd *Web:* www.rowleystires.com	Bay City	MI	48706	989-686-1144		57
Rowman & Littlefield Publishers Inc 4501 Forbes Blvd Ste 200 *TF:* 800-462-6420 ■ *Web:* rowman.com	Lanham	MD	20706	301-459-3366	429-5748	637-2
Rowmark Inc 2040 Industrial Dr *TF:* 800-243-3339 ■ *Web:* www.rowmark.com	Findlay	OH	45840	419-425-2407	425-2927	599
Rowpar Pharmaceuticals Inc 16100 N Greenway Hayden Loop Ste 400 *Web:* closys.com	Scottsdale	AZ	85260	480-948-6997		583
Roxboro Area Chamber of Commerce 211 N Main St *Web:* www.roxboronc.com	Roxboro	NC	27573	336-599-8333	599-8335	139
Roxborough Memorial Hospital (RMH) 5800 Ridge Ave *Web:* www.roxboroughmemorial.com	Philadelphia	PA	19128	215-483-9900	483-8012	374-3
Roxborough State Park 4751 Roxborough Dr *Web:* cpw.state.co.us	Littleton	CO	80125	303-973-3959		565
Roxburgh Agency Inc 4300 Campus Dr Ste 100 *Web:* www.roxburgh.com	Newport Beach	CA	92660	714-556-4365		4
Roxbury Community College 1234 Columbus Ave *Web:* www.rcc.mass.edu	Roxbury	MA	02120	617-541-5310	427-5316	162
Roxbury Latin School 101 St Theresa Ave *Web:* www.roxburylatin.org	West Roxbury	MA	02132	617-325-4920	325-3585	623
Roxy Trading Inc 389 Humane Way *Web:* www.roxytrading.com	Pomona	CA	91768	626-610-1388	610-1339	297-11
Roy & Associates 15550 N Creek Dr *Web:* www.roy-associates.com	Porter	TX	77365	713-822-6970		194
Roy & Associates PC 433 Frye Farm Rd Ste 7 *Web:* royandassociates.wordpress.com	Greensburg	PA	15601	724-834-3900	834-3390	2
Roy & Edna Disney/CALARTS Theater (REDCAT) (REDCAT) 631 W Second St *Web:* www.redcat.org	Los Angeles	CA	90012	213-237-2800	237-2811	50-2
Roy Anderson Corp 11400 Reichold Rd *TF:* 800-688-4003 ■ *Web:* www.rac.com	Gulfport	MS	39503	228-896-4000		186
Roy Bros Inc 764 Boston Rd *TF:* 800-225-0830 ■ *Web:* www.roybrosinc.com	Billerica	MA	01821	978-667-1921	667-5091	780
Roy Chip (Rep R - TX) 1319 Longworth House Office Bldg *Web:* www.roy.house.gov	Washington	DC	20515	202-225-4236		342-2
Roy E. Hanson Jr Mfg 1600 E Washington Blvd *TF:* 800-421-9395 ■ *Web:* hansontank.com	Los Angeles	CA	90021	213-747-7514	747-7724	91
Roy E. Whitehead Inc 2245 Via Cerro *Web:* www.royewhitehead.com	Riverside	CA	92509	951-682-1490		115
Roy H. Reeve Agency Inc 13400 Main Rd *Web:* www.royreeve.agency	Mattituck	NY	11952	631-298-4700		390
Roy J. Carver Biotechnology Ctr 1206 W Gregory *Web:* biotech.illinois.edu	Urbana	IL	61801	217-333-1695	244-0466	668
Roy J. Carver Charitable Trust 202 Iowa Ave *Web:* www.carvertrust.org	Muscatine	IA	52761	563-263-4010	263-1547	305
Roy Jorgensen Associates Inc 3735 Buckeystown Pk *Web:* www.royjorgensen.com	Buckeystown	MD	21717	301-831-1000		194
Roy Kirby & Sons Inc 1403 Rome Rd *Web:* www.roykirby.com	Baltimore	MD	21227	410-536-0808	536-0799	186
Roy Lake State Park 11545 Northside Dr *Web:* gfp.sd.gov	Lake City	SD	57247	605-448-5701		565
Roy Miller Freight Lines LLC 3165 E Coronado St *TF:* 800-336-5673 ■ *Web:* www.roymiller.com	Anaheim	CA	92806	714-632-5511		314
Roy Motors Inc 929 N Main St *TF:* 800-960-6537 ■ *Web:* www.roymotors.com	Opelousas	LA	70570	337-942-9701		57
Roy Nichols Motors Ltd 2728 Courtice Rd *TF:* 866-232-9356 ■ *Web:* www.roynicholsmotors.com	Courtice	ON	L1E2M7	905-436-2222		57
Roy O. Martin 2189 Memorial Dr PO Box 1110 *TF:* 800-299-5174 ■ *Web:* royomartin.com	Alexandria	LA	71301	318-448-0405	473-2624	752
Roy W. Litherland, A Professional Corp 3425 S Bascom Ave Ste 240 *Web:* attorneyoffice.com	Campbell	CA	95008	408-356-9200		41
Roy's 7151 W Ray Rd *Web:* www.roysrestaurant.com	Chandler	AZ	85226	480-705-7697		671
Roy's Wood Products Inc 329 Thrush Ln *TF:* 800-727-1590 ■ *Web:* www.royswoodproducts.com	Lugoff	SC	29078	803-438-1590		115
Royal & SunAlliance Insurance Company of Canada (RSA) 18 York St Ste 800 *TF:* 800-268-8406 ■ *Web:* www.rsagroup.ca	Toronto	ON	M5J2T8	416-366-7511	367-9869	391-4
Royal Alberta Museum 9810 103a Ave NW *Web:* www.royalalbertamuseum.ca	Edmonton	AB	T5J0G2	825-468-6000		520
Royal Alliance Associates Inc 1 World Financial Ctr 15th Fl *TF:* 800-821-5100 ■ *Web:* www.royalalliance.com	New York	NY	10281	800-821-5100		690
Royal Aloha Vacation Club 1505 Dillingham Blvd Ste 212 *TF:* 800-367-5212 ■ *Web:* www.ravc.com	Honolulu	HI	96817	808-847-8050	841-5467	753
Royal Aluminum Company Inc 620 Market St *Web:* www.royalaluminum.net	Newark	NJ	07105	973-589-8880	589-3954	234
Royal American Construction Company Inc 1002 W 23rd St Ste 400 *Web:* royalamericanconstruction.com	Panama City	FL	32405	850-769-8981		187
Royal Bancshares Inc 202 Main St *Web:* www.royalbank-usa.com	Elroy	WI	53929	608-462-8401	462-8963	360-2
Royal Bavaria Brewery 3401 S Sooner Rd *Web:* www.royal-bavaria.com	Oklahoma City	OK	73165	405-799-7666		671
Royal Bearing Inc 17719 NE Sandy Blvd *TF:* 800-279-0992 ■ *Web:* www.royalbearing.com	Portland	OR	97230	503-231-0992		385
Royal Botanical Gardens (RBG) 680 Plains Rd W *TF:* 800-694-4769 ■ *Web:* www.rbg.ca	Burlington	ON	L7T4H4	905-527-1158	577-0375	97
Royal Brass Inc 2856 Anton Rd *TF:* 800-669-9650 ■ *Web:* www.royalbrassandhose.com	Madisonville	KY	42431	270-821-8150	825-0822	790
Royal British Columbia Museum (RBCM) 675 Belleville St *TF:* 888-447-7977 ■ *Web:* www.royalbcmuseum.bc.ca	Victoria	BC	V8W9W2	250-356-7226		520
Royal Broadcasting Inc 1106 Elm St *Web:* theriver953.com	Front Royal	VA	22630	540-635-4121		645-141
Royal Business Forms Inc 3301 Ave E E **Fax Area Code:* 817 ■ *TF:* 800-255-9303 ■ *Web:* www.royalbf.com	Arlington	TX	76011	800-255-9303	633-2164*	110
Royal Cabinets 1299 E Phillips Blvd *Web:* www.royalcabinets.com	Pomona	CA	91766	909-629-8565	629-7762	115
Royal Camp Services Ltd 7111 - 67 St *TF:* 877-884-2267 ■ *Web:* www.royalcamp.com	Edmonton	AB	T6B3L7	780-463-8000		779
Royal Canadian Military Institute 426 University Ave *TF:* 800-585-1072 ■ *Web:* www.rcmi.org	Toronto	ON	M5G1S9	416-597-0286	597-6919	520
Royal Canadian Mounted Police (RCMP) 73 Leikin Dr *Web:* www.rcmp-grc.gc.ca	Ottawa	ON	K1A0R2	613-993-7267	993-0260	303
Royal Canadian Yacht Club, The 141 St George St *Web:* rcyc.ca	Toronto	ON	M5R2L8	416-967-7245		138
Royal Capital Management LLC 4400 N Federal Hwy Ste 300 *Web:* www.royalcapitalmanagement.com	Boca Raton	FL	33431	561-394-4174	394-4420	401
Royal Caribbean Intl 1050 Caribbean Way *TF:* 800-327-6700 ■ *Web:* www.royalcaribbean.com	Miami	FL	33132	305-982-2625		220
Royal Carolina Corp 7305 Old Friendly Rd *Web:* www.royalcarolina.com	Greensboro	NC	27410	336-292-8845	294-2396	745-7
Royal Case Company Inc 419 E Lamar St *TF:* 844-769-2538 ■ *Web:* www.royalcase.com	Sherman	TX	75090	903-868-0288	893-7984	453
Royal Chemical Co 1755 Enterprise Pkwy Ste 600 *TF:* 844-462-7692 ■ *Web:* www.royalchemical.com	Twinsburg	OH	44087	844-462-7692		145
Royal Coach Lines Inc 924 Broadway *Web:* www.royalcoachlines.com	Thornwood	NY	10594	914-747-9494	747-9497	109
Royal Coach Tours 630 Stockton Ave *Web:* www.royal-coach.com	San Jose	CA	95126	408-279-4801		760
Royal Coachman Worldwide 88 Ford Rd Ste 26 *TF:* 800-472-7433 ■ *Web:* www.royalcoachman.com	Denville	NJ	07834	973-400-3200	675-4365	441
Royal College of Dental Surgeons of Ontario 6 Crescent Rd *TF:* 800-565-4591 ■ *Web:* rcdso.org	Toronto	ON	M4W1T1	416-961-6555		165
Royal Conservatory of Music, The 273 Bloor St W *TF:* 800-462-3815 ■ *Web:* www.rcmusic.com	Toronto	ON	M5S1W2	416-408-2824		627
Royal Consumer Information Products Inc 1160 US 22 **Fax Area Code:* 800 ■ *TF:* 888-261-4555 ■ *Web:* www.royalsupplies.com	Bridgewater	NJ	08807	908-864-4851	232-9769*	111

Name / Address	City	State	ZIP	Phone	Fax	Class
Royal Contracting Company Ltd 677 Ahua St *Web:* www.royalcontracting.com	Honolulu	HI	96819	808-839-9006	839-7571	188-4
Royal Crest Dairy Inc 350 S Pearl St *TF:* 888-226-6455 ■ *Web:* www.royalcrestdairy.com	Denver	CO	80209	303-777-2227	744-9173	296-27
Royal Crown Cola Intl (RCCI) 1001 10th Ave. *Web:* www.rccolainternational.com	Columbus	GA	31901	706-494-7552	494-7502	297-2
Royal Cup PO Box 170971 *TF:* 800-366-5836 ■ *Web:* royalcupcoffee.com	Birmingham	AL	35217	800-366-5836		159
Royal Cyber Inc 55 Shuman Blvd Ste 275 *Web:* www.royalcyber.com	Naperville	IL	60563	630-355-6292		177
Royal Diversified Products Inc 287 Market St *Web:* www.royalpins.com	Warren	RI	02885	401-245-6900	247-2231	757
Royal Engineering Inc 34450 Commerce Rd *Web:* royalinc.com	Fraser	MI	48026	586-294-9400	294-9455	261
Royal Envelope Co 4114 S Peoria St *Web:* www.royalenv.com	Chicago	IL	60609	773-376-1212	376-0011	263
Royal Farms Arena 201 W Baltimore St *Web:* www.royalfarmsarena.com	Baltimore	MD	21201	410-347-2020	347-2042	720
Royal Filter Manufacturing Co 4327 S 4th St *Web:* www.royalfilter.com	Chickasha	OK	73018	405-224-0229	224-9174	386
Royal Fireworks Publishing Co (RFWP) PO Box 399 *Web:* www.rfwp.com	Unionville	NY	10988	845-726-4444	726-3824	637-2
Royal Food Products LLC 2322 E Minnesota St *Web:* www.royalfp.com	Indianapolis	IN	46203	317-782-2660		296-37
Royal Food Service Company Inc 3720 Zip Industrial Blvd *Web:* www.royalfoodservice.com	Atlanta	GA	30354	404-366-4299		805
Royal Fox Country Club 4405 Royal & Ancient Dr *Web:* www.royalfoxcc.com	Saint Charles	IL	60174	330-887-0391		354
ROYAL Furniture 122 S Main St *Web:* www.royalfurniture.com	Memphis	TN	38103	901-527-6407		321
Royal George Theatre Ctr 1641 N Halsted St *Web:* www.theroyalgeorgetheatre.com	Chicago	IL	60614	312-988-9105		572
Royal Glass Company Inc 3200 De La Cruz Blvd *Web:* www.royalglasscoinc.com	Santa Clara	CA	95054	408-969-0444		329
Royal Gold Inc 1660 Wynkoop St Ste 1000 *NASDAQ: RGLD* ■ *Web:* www.royalgold.com	Denver	CO	80202	303-573-1660	595-9385	502
Royal Group 1301 S 47th Ave *Web:* teamtrg.com	Cicero	IL	60804	708-656-2020		100
Royal Group, The 71 Royal Group Crescent *TF:* 800-263-2353 ■ *Web:* www.royalbuildingproducts.com	Woodbridge	ON	L4H1X9	905-264-0701	850-9184	235
Royal Harvest Foods 55 Avocado St *Web:* www.royalharv.com	Springfield	MA	01104	413-737-8392	731-9336	619
Royal Hawaiian 2259 Kalakaua Ave *TF:* 866-716-8110 ■ *Web:* www.royal-hawaiian.com	Honolulu	HI	96815	808-923-7311	931-7098	669
Royal Hawaiian Orchards LP 688 Kinoole St Ste 121 *NYSE: NNUTD* ■ **Fax Area Code:* 808 ■ *Web:* rholp.com	Hilo	HI	96720	303-339-0500	969-8123*	10-10
Royal Hilltop 18581 E Hampden Ave *Web:* www.royalhilltop.com	Aurora	CO	80013	303-690-7738		671
Royal Holiday Beach Resort 1988 Beach Blvd *TF:* 800-874-0402 ■ *Web:* www.holidaybeachresort.com	Biloxi	MS	39531	228-388-7553		379
Royal Home Care 6381 Little River Tpke Ste 6 *Web:* www.royalhomecarellc.com	Alexandria	VA	22312	703-992-9032	436-6962	363
Royal Hotel South Beach 763 Pennsylvania Ave *Web:* www.royalsouthbeach.com	Miami Beach	FL	33139	305-673-9009	673-9244	379
Royal Industries Inc 225 25th St *Web:* www.royalindustries.com	Brooklyn	NY	11232	718-369-3046		629
Royal Industries Inc 4100 W Victoria St **Fax Area Code:* 800 ■ *TF:* 800-782-1200 ■ *Web:* www.royalindustriesinc.com	Chicago	IL	60646	773-478-6300	321-3295*	286
Royal Inland Hospital 311 Columbia St *Web:* www.rihfoundation.ca	Kamloops	BC	V2C2T1	250-314-2325		374-2
Royal Khyber S Coast Plz Vlg 1621 W Sunflower Ave *Web:* royalkhyber.com	Santa Ana	CA	92704	714-436-1010		671
Royal Lahaina Resort 2780 Kekaa Dr *TF:* 800-222-5642 ■ *Web:* www.hawaiihotels.com	Lahaina	HI	96761	808-661-3611		669
Royal Machine & Tool Corp 4 Willowbrook Dr PO Box Y *Web:* www.royalworkholding.com	Berlin	CT	06037	860-828-6555		493
Royal Management Corp 665 W N Ave *Web:* www.lexingtonhealth.com	Lombard	IL	60148	630-458-4700	748-3701	451
Royal Manufacturing 14635 Chrisman Rd *TF:* 800-826-0074 ■ *Web:* www.royal-mfg.com	Houston	TX	77039	281-442-3400	442-1455	375
Royal Master Grinders Inc 143 Bauer Dr *Web:* www.royalmaster.com	Oakland	NJ	07436	201-337-8500	337-2324	455
Royal Metal Products Inc 100 Royal Way *TF:* 800-520-6593 ■ *Web:* www.royalmetalproducts.com	Temple	GA	30179	678-563-0003	563-0094	697
Royal Neighbors of America 230 16th St *TF:* 800-627-4762 ■ *Web:* www.theroyalneighbor.org	Rock Island	IL	61201	309-788-4561		457-10
Royal Oak Foundation, The 35 W 35th St Ste 1200 *TF:* 800-913-6565 ■ *Web:* www.royal-oak.org	New York	NY	10001	212-480-2889	785-7234	48-13
Royal Oak Public Library 222 E Eleven Mile Rd *Web:* www.romi.gov	Royal Oak	MI	48067	248-246-3700		434-3
Royal Oaks Country Club Club House 7915 Greenville Ave *Web:* roccdallas.com	Dallas	TX	75231	214-691-6091		120
Royal Ontario Museum 100 Queen's Pk *Web:* www.rom.on.ca	Toronto	ON	M5S2C6	416-586-8000	586-5504	520
Royal Pacific Tea Company Inc, The PO Box 6277 *Web:* www.royalpacificintl.com	Scottsdale	AZ	85261	480-951-8251	951-0092	297-11
Royal Palm Coast Realtor Assn 2840 Winkler Ave *Web:* rpcra.org	Fort Myers	FL	33916	239-936-3537		653
Royal Palms Resort & Spa 5200 E Camelback Rd *TF:* 800-672-6011 ■ *Web:* www.royalpalmshotel.com	Phoenix	AZ	85018	602-840-3610	840-6927	669
Royal Paper Box Company of California Inc PO Box 458 *Web:* www.royalpaperbox.com	Montebello	CA	90640	323-728-7041	722-2646	101
Royal Paper Corp 10232 Palm Dr *Web:* www.royal-paper.com	Santa Fe Springs	CA	90670	562-903-9030	944-6000	194
Royal Park Hotel-brookshire & The Commons 600 E University Dr *TF:* 800-339-2761 ■ *Web:* www.royalparkhotel.net	Rochester	MI	48307	248-652-2600		379
Royal Park Uniforms Co 14139 Hwy 56 S	Prospect Hill	NC	27314	336-562-3345		155-19
Royal Plastics Inc 9410 Pineneedle Dr *Web:* www.royalplastics.com	Mentor	OH	44060	440-352-1357	352-6681	604
Royal Processing Co 5710 Old Concord Rd	Charlotte	NC	28213	704-599-2804	599-2805	745-8
Royal ready mix 1 Ridder Cir *Web:* royalenterprises.net	Saint Paul	MN	55107	651-224-5963		183
Royal Regency Hotel 165 Tuckahoe Rd *Web:* www.royalregencyhotelny.com	Yonkers	NY	10710	914-476-6200		379
Royal River Casino & Entertainment Complex 607 S Veterans St *Web:* www.royalrivercasino.com	Flandreau	SD	57028	605-997-3746		452
Royal Roads University 2005 Sooke Rd *TF:* 800-788-8028 ■ *Web:* www.royalroads.ca	Victoria	BC	V9B5Y2	250-391-2511	391-2500	785
Royal Saskatchewan Museum 2445 Albert St *Web:* www.royalsaskmuseum.ca	Regina	SK	S4P4W7	306-787-2815	787-2820	520
Royal Savings Bank 9226 S Commercial Ave *Web:* www.royalbankweb.com	Chicago	IL	60617	773-768-4800		70
Royal Screw Machine Products Co 409 Lake Ave *Web:* www.royalscrew.com	Bristol	CT	06010	860-845-8567		621
Royal Sonesta Chicago Riverfront 71 E Wacker Dr *Web:* wyndhamgrandchicagoriverfront.com	Chicago	IL	60601	312-346-7100	346-1721	379
Royal Staffing Services 14011 Ventura Blvd Ste 214-W *Web:* www.royalstaffing.com	Sherman Oaks	CA	91423	818-981-1080	981-1338	260
Royal State National Insurance Company Ltd 500 Ala Moana Blvd Ste 6-400 *Web:* royalstate.com	Honolulu	HI	96813	808-539-1600		391-2
Royal Suite Lodge 3811 Minnesota Dr	Anchorage	AK	99503	907-563-3114		379
Royal T Management 7419 N Cedar Ave Ste 102 *Web:* www.royaltmanagement.com	Fresno	CA	93720	559-447-9887		652
Royal Technocrats Inc 7447 Harwin Dr Ste 270 *Web:* royaltechnocrats.com	Houston	TX	77036	713-776-8300		180
Royal Textile Mills Inc 929 Firetower Rd *TF:* 800-334-9361 ■ *Web:* www.dukeathletic-tactical.com	Yanceyville	NC	27379	800-334-9361	934-9360	155-1
Royal Thai 5500 Greenville Ave *Web:* www.royalthaidallas.com	Dallas	TX	75206	214-691-3555		671
Royal Tine Guide School & Packer Training - Hunting Fishing & Camp Cook School PO Box 809 *Web:* www.royaltine.com	Philipsburg	MT	59858	406-859-5138		685
Royal Tire Inc 3955 Roosevelt Rd *TF:* 877-454-7070 ■ *Web:* www.royaltire.com	Saint Cloud	MN	56301	320-763-9618		755
Royal Tours And Travel LLC PO Box 372 *Web:* www.royaltoursllc.net	Smithfield	VA	23431	757-569-7616		760
Royal Travel & Tours Inc 122 N 1st St Ste C *Web:* www.royal-travel.com	Dekalb	IL	60115	815-758-8172		772
Royal Trucking Co 1323 Eshman Ave N PO Box 387 **Fax Area Code:* 662 ■ *TF:* 800-321-1293 ■ *Web:* www.royaltruck.com	West Point	MS	39773	800-321-1293	495-1066*	780
Royal Tyrrell Museum PO Box 7500 *TF:* 888-440-4240 ■ *Web:* www.tyrrellmuseum.com	Drumheller	AB	T0J0Y0	403-823-7707	823-7131	520
Royal University Hospital 103 Hospital Dr *TF:* 800-458-1179 ■ *Web:* www.saskatoonhealthregion.ca	Saskatoon	SK	S7N0W8	306-655-1000		374-2
Royal Victoria Hospital 201 Georgian Dr *Web:* www.rvh.on.ca	Barrie	ON	L4M6M2	705-728-9802	728-0982	374-2
Royal Waste Services Inc 18740 Hollis Ave *Web:* royalwaste.com	Hollis	NY	11423	718-468-3988		660
Royal Wine Corp 63 Le Fante Ln *Web:* www.royalwine.com	Bayonne	NJ	07002	718-384-2400	388-8444	80-3
Royal's Furniture 225 W Canal St N *Web:* royalsfurnitureinc.com	Belle Glade	FL	33430	561-996-7646	996-4480	321
Royale College of Beauty 27485 Commerce Center Dr *Web:* www.royalecollegeofbeauty.net	Temecula	CA	92590	951-676-0833	676-0653	167-3
Royale Energy Inc 3777 Willow Glen Dr *TF:* 800-447-8505 ■ *Web:* www.royl.com	El Cajon	CA	92019	619-383-6600		536
Royale Management Services Inc 2319 N Andrews Ave *Web:* rmsaccounting.com	Fort Lauderdale	FL	33311	954-563-1269		463
Royals Food Town 135 S Main *Web:* royalsfoodtown.com	Loa	UT	84747	435-836-2841		345
Royalty Cleaning Services 1331 Granite Ln *Web:* royaltycleaning.com	Modesto	CA	95351	209-529-3110		426

Phone | Fax | Class

Royalty Pharma 110 E 59th St 33rd Fl New York NY 10022 212-883-0200 85
Web: www.royaltypharma.com
Roybal-Allard Lucille (Rep D - CA)
2083 Rayburn House Office Bldg Washington DC 20515 202-225-1766 226-0350 342-2
Web: roybal-allard.house.gov
Royce & Associates LLC
745 5th Ave Ste 2300 New York NY 10151 800-221-4268 401
TF: 800-221-4268 ■ Web: www.roycefunds.com
Royco Inc
8121 Georgia Ave Ste 500 Silver Spring MD 20910 301-608-2212 652
Royer Corp 805 East St. Madison IN 47250 812-265-3133 604
TF: 800-457-8997 ■ Web: www.royercorp.com
Royer's Flowers Inc
201 Rohrerstown Rd Lancaster PA 17603 717-397-0376 292
TF: 888-276-9377 ■ Web: www.royers.com
Roylco Inc
3251 Abbeville Hwy PO Box 13409 Anderson SC 29624 864-296-0043 296-6736 243
TF: 800-362-8656 ■ Web: www.roylco.com
Royle Printing Co 745 S Bird St Sun Prairie WI 53590 608-837-5161 627
Web: www.royle.com
Roymal Inc 3 Roymal Ln Newport NH 03773 603-863-2410 550
Web: www.roymalinc.com
Royse Law Firm PC
1717 Embarcadero Rd Palo Alto CA 94303 650-813-9700 428
Web: rroyselaw.com
Roysons Corp 40 Vanderhoof Ave Rockaway NJ 07866 973-625-5570 625-5917 290
TF: 888-769-7667 ■ Web: www.roysons.com
Royster's Machine Shop LLC
215 Hwy 2084 S Henderson KY 42420 270-826-3396 826-2479 454
Web: www.roystersmachine.com
Roytex Inc 16 E 34th St 17th Fl New York NY 10016 212-686-3500 686-4336 155-15
Web: www.roytex.com
Roytman Info Svc Inc 504 Old Harbor Ct. Dayton OH 45458 937-885-0821 624
Web: www.roytmanis.com
Rozelle Cosmetics 4260 Loop Rd Westfield VT 05874 800-451-4216 214
TF: 800-451-4216 ■ Web: www.rozelle.com
Rozendal Associates Inc
9530 Pathway St. Santee CA 92071 619-562-5596 562-2529 529
Web: www.rozendalassociates.com
Rozhome Care LLC
8891 Watson St Ste 103 Cypress CA 90630 714-226-0366 363
Web: rozhomecare.com
Rozovics & Wojocicki PC
1580 N Northwest Hwy Ste 120 Park Ridge IL 60068 847-699-7600 299-7526 2
Web: rozcpa.com
RP Design Web Services
17 Meriden Ave Ste 2A Southington CT 06489 203-271-7991 177
TF: 800-847-3475 ■ Web: www.rpdesign.com
RP Fedder Corp 740 Driving Park Ave. Rochester NY 14613 585-288-1600 288-2481 18
Web: www.rpfedder.com
RP Funding Ctr 701 W Lime St Lakeland FL 33815 863-834-8100 834-8101 205
TF: 888-397-0100 ■ Web: rpfundingcenter.com
RP Lumber Company Inc
514 E Vandalia St Edwardsville IL 62025 618-656-1514 656-6785 191-3
Web: www.rplumber.com
RP Machine Enterprises Inc
860 Cochran St. Statesville NC 28677 704-872-8888 872-5777 455
Web: www.rpmachine.com
RPA (Renal Physicians Assn)
1700 Rockville Pk Ste 220 Rockville MD 20852 301-468-3515 468-3511 49-8
Web: www.renalmd.org
RPA Inc 2895 S Reach Rd Williamsport PA 17701 570-321-6111 321-7160 194
TF: 800-992-9277 ■ Web: www.rpainc.org
RPAC LLC 21490 S Ortigalita Rd Los Banos CA 93635 209-826-0272 11-1
Web: www.rpacalmonds.com
RPB (Research to Prevent Blindness Inc)
360 Lexington Ave 22nd Fl. New York NY 10017 212-752-4333 688-6231 40-17
TF: 800-621-0026 ■ Web: www.rpbusa.org
RPC (Ridgeview Publishing Co)
PO Box 686 Atascadero CA 93423 805-466-7252 637-2
Web: www.ridgeviewpublishing.com
RPC Inc 2801 Buford Hwy NE Ste 300 Atlanta GA 30329 404-321-2140 321-5483 539
NYSE: RES ■ TF: 866-796-3419 ■ Web: www.rpc.net
RPC Photonics Inc 330 Clay Rd Rochester NY 14623 585-272-2840 272-2845 544
Web: www.rpcphotonics.com
RPC Video Inc 50 Allegheny River Blvd. Verona PA 15147 412-828-1414 828-1488 38
TF: 800-837-0096 ■ Web: www.rpcvideo.com
RPI Industries Inc
12 Christopher Way Ste 200. Medford NJ 08055 609-714-2330 499
Web: rpiindustries.com
RPI Media Inc 265 Racine Dr Ste 201 Wilmington NC 28403 910-763-2100 656
TF: 800-736-0321 ■ Web: www.rpimedia.com
RPI Publishing Inc PO Box 66398 Scotts Valley CA 95067 831-438-8384 438-8332 637-2
TF: 800-873-8384 ■ Web: www.rpipublishing.com
RPL (Rochester Public Library)
65 S Main St. Rochester NH 03867 603-332-1428 335-7582 434-3
Web: www.rpl.lib.nh.us
RPL Associates Inc
21650 W 11 Mile Rd. Southfield MI 48076 248-353-0011 311
Web: rplassociates.com
RPL Supplies Inc
141 Lanza Ave Bldg 3A Garfield NJ 07026 973-767-0880 772-6601 174
TF: 800-524-0914 ■ Web: www.rplsupplies.com
RPM Direct 24 Arnett Ave Ste 100 Lambertville NJ 08530 609-566-7150 566-7155 195
Web: www.rpmdirectllc.com
RPM Industries Inc 1444 Lowell St Elyria OH 44035 440-268-8077 199
Web: rpmindustries.blogspot.com
RPM International Inc 2628 Pearl Rd Medina OH 44256 330-273-5090 225-8743 550
NYSE: RPM ■ TF: 800-776-4488 ■ Web: www.rpminc.com
RPM Mortgage Inc 3240 Stone Valley Rd W Alamo CA 94507 925-295-9300 217
TF: 888-776-7575 ■ Web: www.rpm-mtg.com
RPM Pizza LLC 15384 5th St. Gulfport MS 39503 228-832-4000 670
Web: www.rpmpizza.com
RPM Revenue Drivers LLC 429 N 1340 E Provo UT 84606 801-850-6750 463
RPM Tech 12 E Jarrettsville Rd. Forest Hill MD 21050 410-877-6168 261
Web: rpm-tech.com

Phone | Fax | Class

RPM Transportation Inc
13225 Marquardt Ave Santa Fe Springs CA 90670 562-777-9510 519
TF: 800-423-5840 ■ Web: www.rpmcsi.com
RPMG Inc 1157 Vly Park Dr Ste 100. Shakopee MN 55379 952-465-3220 465-3221 580
Web: www.rpmgllc.com
RpmOne Inc 4495 Military Trl Ste 207 Jupiter FL 33458 561-741-4447 390
Web: www.rpmone.com
RPNM (Republican Party of New Mexico)
5150-A San Francisco Rd NE PO Box 94083 Albuquerque NM 87109 505-298-3662 616-2
Web: newmexico.gop
RPP Corp 12 Ballard Way Lawrence MA 01843 978-689-2800 677
TF: 800-232-2239 ■ Web: www.rppcorp.com
Rpr Graphics Inc 87 Main St. Peapack NJ 07977 908-654-8080 781
Web: rprgraphicsinc.com
RPR Industries Inc PO Box 220 Grantsville WV 26147 304-354-7844 354-7132 676
Web: rprind.com
RPS Products Inc 281 Keyes Ave Hampshire IL 60140 847-683-3400 18
Web: www.rpsproducts.com
RPTS Express Inc
1220 Industrial Pky N Brunswick OH 44212 330-273-7303 273-6330 780
Web: www.rptsexpress.com
R&R (Ragan & Ragan p C)
3100 Rt 138 W Brinley Plz 1st Bldg Wall Township NJ 07719 732-280-4100 280-4112 428
Web: www.raganlaw.com
RR Bowker LLC 630 Central Ave New Providence NJ 07974 908-795-3500 637-2
TF: 888-269-5372 ■ Web: www.bowker.com
RR Donnelley 111 S Wacker Dr Chicago IL 60606 312-326-8000 951-1355* 626
*Fax Area Code: 925 ■ Web: www.rrdonnelley.com
RRA (Reconstructionist Rabbinical Assn)
1299 Church Rd Wyncote PA 19095 215-576-5210 576-8051 48-20
Web: www.therra.org
RRC (Radio Research Consortium Inc)
PO Box 1309 Olney MD 20830 301-774-6686 774-0976 632
Web: www.rrconline.org
RRC Assoc 4770 Baseline Rd Ste 360 Boulder CO 80303 303-449-6558 449-6587 466
TF: 888-449-4772 ■ Web: www.rrcassociates.com
RRD (R.R. Donnelley & Sons Co)
35 W Wacker Dr Chicago IL 60601 800-742-4455 5
TF: 800-742-4455 ■ Web: www.rrd.com
RRE Ventures LLC
130 E 59th St 17th Fl New York NY 10022 212-418-5100 792
Web: www.rre.com
RRK Associates Ltd
900 Tri-State Pkwy Ste 800. Gurnee IL 60031 847-856-8420 856-8421 196
Web: www.rrkassociates.net
RRMC (Rowan Regional Medical Center Inc)
612 Mocksville Ave. Salisbury NC 28144 704-210-5000 210-5562 374-3
TF: 888-844-0080
RRR Development Co
8817 Pleasantwood Ave NW North Canton OH 44720 330-966-8855 454
Web: www.rrrdev.com
RS Audley Inc 609 Rt 3A Bow NH 03304 603-224-7724 225-7614 188-4
Web: www.audleyconstruction.com
RS Braswell Company Inc
485 S Cannon Blvd. Kannapolis NC 28083 704-933-2269 933-7000 770
TF: 888-628-3550 ■ Web: rsbraswell.com
RS Consulting USA 39 S LaSalle St Chicago IL 60603 312-368-0800 195
Web: www.rsconsulting-usa.com
RS Corcoran Co 500 N Vine St New Lenox IL 60451 815-485-2156 641
TF: 800-637-1067 ■ Web: www.corcoranpumps.com
RS Harritan & Company Inc
3280 Formex Rd Richmond VA 23224 804-275-7821 195
Web: www.rsharritan.com
RS Hughes Company Inc
1162 Sonora Ct Sunnyvale CA 94086 408-739-3211 385
TF: 877-774-8443 ■ Web: www.rshughes.com
RS Marketing Services LLC
35 Ft Boone Ct Clayton NC 27527 919-585-4556 463
Web: www.rsmsinsights.com
RS Mowery & Sons Inc
1000 Bent Creek Blvd Mechanicsburg PA 17050 717-506-1000 506-1010 187
Web: rsmowery.com
RS Owens & Co 5535 N Lynch Ave Chicago IL 60630 773-282-6000 777
TF: 800-282-6200 ■ Web: www.stregisgrp.com
RS2 Technologies LLC
400 Fisher St Ste G. Munster IN 46321 219-836-9002 692
TF: 877-682-3532 ■ Web: www.rs2tech.com
RSA (Royal & SunAlliance Insurance Company of Canada)
18 York St Ste 800 Toronto ON M5J2T8 416-366-7511 367-9869 391-4
TF: 800-268-8406 ■ Web: www.rsagroup.ca
RSA Engineering Inc
670 W Fireweed Ln Ste 200 Anchorage AK 99503 907-276-0521 276-1751 261
Web: rsa-ak.com
RSA Security Inc 174 Middlesex Tpke Bedford MA 01730 781-515-5000 178-12
TF: 800-995-5095 ■ Web: www.rsa.com
RSAI (Roller Skating Association Intl)
6905 Corporate Dr Indianapolis IN 46278 317-347-2626 347-2636 48-22
Web: www.rollerskating.com
RSB Transmissions NA Inc 24425 W M 60 Homer MI 49245 517-568-4171 568-4174 454
Web: rsbna.com
RSBCIH (Riverside-San Bernardino County Indian Health Inc)
11555 1/2 Potrero Rd Banning CA 92220 951-849-4761 353
TF: 800-732-8805 ■ Web: www.rsbcihi.org
RSC (Retail Service Co)
2108 W Broadway South Portland ME 04106 207-772-8888 112
TF: 800-548-4028 ■ Web: www.retailserviceco.com
RSD (Refrigeration Supplies Distributor)
26021 Atlantic Ocean Dr. Lake Forest CA 92630 949-380-7878 380-0755 665
TF: 800-773-5359 ■ Web: www.rsd.net
RSDC of Michigan LLC 1775 Holloway Dr Holt MI 48842 877-881-7732 480
TF: 877-881-7732 ■ Web: rsdcmi.com
RSES (Refrigeration Service Engineers Society)
1666 Rand Rd. Des Plaines IL 60016 847-297-6464 297-5038 49-3
TF: 800-297-5660 ■ Web: www.rses.org
RSF (Robert Schalkenbach Foundation Inc)
211 W 43rd St Ste 400. New York NY 10017 212-683-6424 683-6454 637-2
TF: 800-269-9555 ■ Web: schalkenbach.org

Phone | Fax | Class

RSF Social Finance
1002A O'Reilly Ave ..... San Francisco CA 94129 415-561-3900 401
Web: rsfsocialfinance.org

RSH (Richmond State Hospital)
3771 S A St ..... Richmond IN 47374 765-966-0511 374-5
Web: www.in.gov

RSH Architects
363 Vanadium Rd Ste 200 ..... Pittsburgh PA 15243 412-429-1555 279-7285 186
Web: www.rsharc.com

R-S-H Engineering Inc
909 N 18th St Ste 200 ..... Monroe LA 71201 318-361-3000 387-4828 261
TF: 888-340-4884 ■ *Web:* www.rsh.com

RSI (Reconditioned Systems Inc)
235 S 56th St ..... Chandler AZ 85226 800-280-5000 894-1907* 319-1
**Fax Area Code:* 480 ■ *TF:* 800-280-5000 ■ *Web:* www.rsisystemsfurniture.com

RSI (Railway Supply Institute Inc)
425 Third St Ste 920 ..... Washington DC 20024 202-347-4664 347-0047 49-21
Web: www.rsiweb.org

RSI (Ray Stone Inc)
550 Howe Ave Ste 100 ..... Sacramento CA 95825 916-649-7500 652
Web: www.raystoneinc.com

RSI (Radiofrequency Safety Intl)
543 Main St ..... Kiowa KS 67070 888-830-5648 196
TF: 888-830-5648 ■ *Web:* www.rsicorp.com

RSI Building Products LLC
6504 Union Ave ..... Shreveport LA 71106 318-861-7091 866-2626 191-4
TF: 800-259-4400 ■ *Web:* www.rsibp.com

RSI Insurance Brokers Inc
4000 Westerly Pl Ste 110 ..... Newport Beach CA 92660 714-546-6616 390
TF: 800-828-5273 ■ *Web:* www.rsiinsurancebrokers.com

RSI Kitchen & Bath
9700 Manchester Rd ..... Rock Hill MO 63119 314-961-2000 222-4416 191-3
Web: www.rsikb.com

RSI Logistics Inc 2419 Science Pkwy ..... Okemos MI 48864 517-349-7713 349-7154 194
Web: www.rsilogistics.com

RSJ Machining 606 Charcot Ave ..... San Jose CA 95131 408-441-7891 441-7895 454
Web: www.rsjmachining.com

RSK Tool Inc 410 W Carob St ..... Compton CA 90220 310-537-3302 757
Web: www.rsktool.com

RSM Co 811 Pressley Rd PO Box 31605 ..... Charlotte NC 28231 704-525-6851 525-8368 745-8
Web: www.rsmcompany.com

RSNA (Radiological Society of North America)
820 Jorie Blvd ..... Oak Brook IL 60523 630-571-2670 571-7837 49-8
TF: 800-381-6660 ■ *Web:* www.rsna.org

RSP (Red Sea Press Inc)
541 W Ingham Ave Ste B ..... Trenton NJ 08638 609-695-3200 695-6466 637-2
Web: www.africaworldpressbooks.com

RSP Architects
1220 Marshall St NE ..... Minneapolis MN 55413 612-677-7100 677-7499 261
Web: rsparch.com

RSP Permian Inc 3141 Hood St Ste 500 ..... Dallas TX 75219 214-252-2700 252-2750 536
Web: www.rsppermian.com

RSPA (Retail Solutions Providers Assn)
9920 Couloak Dr Unit 120 ..... Charlotte NC 28216 800-782-2693 357-3127* 49-18
**Fax Area Code:* 704 ■ *TF:* 800-782-2693 ■ *Web:* www.gorspa.org

R-Squared Puckett Inc 6422 Hwy 18 ..... Puckett MS 39151 601-825-1171 247

RSR Corp 2777 Stemmons Fwy Ste 1800 ..... Dallas TX 75207 214-631-6070 631-6146 485
Web: rsrcorp.com

RSR Group Inc 4405 Metric Dr ..... Winter Park FL 32792 407-677-1000 677-4489 710
TF: 800-541-4867 ■ *Web:* www.rsrgroup.com

RSSIC (Rosenblum-silverman-sutton Investment Counsel)
1388 Sutter St Ste 725 ..... San Francisco CA 94109 415-771-4500 401
Web: www.rssic.com

Rstn Consulting LLC
1035 Pearl St 4th Fl ..... Boulder CO 80301 303-447-6878 196
Web: www.rstn.com

RSVP Publications
6730 W Linebaugh Ave Ste 201 ..... Tampa FL 33625 813-960-7787 310
TF: 800-360-7787 ■ *Web:* rsvppublications.com

RSVP Vacations LLC
9200 Sunset Blvd Ste 500 ..... West Hollywood CA 90069 310-432-2300 859-8886 760
TF: 800-328-7787 ■ *Web:* rsvpvacations.com

RSVP: The Directory of Illustration and Design
PO Box 050314 ..... Brooklyn NY 11205 718-857-9267 637-10
Web: www.rsvpdirectory.com

RSW (Ready Set Work LLC)
1487 Dunwoody Dr Ste 200 ..... West Chester PA 19380 877-507-3706 689-4323* 387
**Fax Area Code:* 215 ■ *TF:* 877-507-3706 ■ *Web:* www.readysetwork.com

RT Tanaka Engineers Inc
871 Kolu St Ste 201 ..... Wailuku HI 96793 808-242-6861 261

RT's Restaurant 3804 Mt Vernon Ave ..... Alexandria VA 22305 703-684-6010 548-0417 671
Web: www.rtsrestaurant.net

RTA (Riverside Transit Agency)
1825 Third St PO Box 59968 ..... Riverside CA 92517 951-565-5000 468
TF: 800-800-7821 ■ *Web:* www.riversidetransit.com

RTA (Greater Cleveland Regional Transit Authority)
1240 W Sixth St ..... Cleveland OH 44113 216-621-9500 781-4484 468
Web: www.riderta.com

RTA (Regional Transit Authority)
2817 Canal St ..... New Orleans LA 70119 504-827-8300 468
Web: www.norta.com

R&TA (Religious and Theological Abstracts Inc)
PO Box 215 ..... Myerstown PA 17067 717-866-6734 866-9280 637-9
Web: www.rtabst.org

RTC (Regional Transportation Commission of Southern Nevada)
600 S Grand Central Pkwy Ste 350 ..... Las Vegas NV 89106 702-676-1500 676-1518 468
TF: 800-228-3911 ■ *Web:* www.rtcsnv.com

RTC (Rails-to-Trails Conservancy)
2121 Ward Ct NW 5th Fl ..... Washington DC 20037 202-331-9696 223-9257 48-13
TF: 800-944-6847 ■ *Web:* www.railstotrails.org

RTC 2800 Golf Rd ..... Rolling Meadows IL 60008 847-640-2400 640-5175 195
Web: www.rtc.com

RTC (Rochester Telephone Company Inc)
117 W 8th St ..... Rochester IN 46975 574-223-2191 224
Web: www.rtc1.com

RTC Direct Mailing Inc
56 Seip Ln ..... Shoemakersville PA 19555 610-562-5122 5
Web: www.rtcdirect.net

RTCA Inc 1150 18th St NW Ste 910 ..... Washington DC 20036 202-833-9339 833-9434 139
Web: www.rtca.org

RTD (Regional Transportation District)
1600 Blake St ..... Denver CO 80202 303-628-9000 468
TF: 800-366-7433 ■ *Web:* www.rtd-denver.com

RTD Financial Advisors Inc
30 S 17th St United Plz Ste 1620 ..... Philadelphia PA 19103 215-557-3800 194
Web: www.rtdfinancial.com

RTEC (Rural Transit Enterprises Coordinated Inc)
100 E Main St ..... Mount Vernon KY 40456 606-256-9835 108
TF: 800-321-7832 ■ *Web:* www.4rtec.com

R-Tech Feeders Inc
5292 American Rd R-Tech Feeders ..... Rockford IL 61109 815-874-2990 874-4661 273
Web: www.rtechfeeders.com

RTI (Ready Telecom Inc) 220 Sunset Ave ..... Asheboro NC 27203 336-610-3001 629-5961 224
Web: www.readytelecom.com

RTI (Record Technology Inc)
486 Dawson Dr ..... Camarillo CA 93012 805-484-2747 987-0508 657
Web: www.recordtech.com

RTI Biologics Inc 11621 Research Cir ..... Alachua FL 32615 386-418-8888 418-0342 85
NASDAQ: RTIX ■ *Web:* www.rtix.com

RTKL Associates Inc 901 S Bond St ..... Baltimore MD 21231 410-537-6000 276-2136 261
Web: www.callisonrtkl.com

RTL Construction
350 Old Airport Rd ..... Yellowknife NT X1A3T4 867-873-6271 920-2661 186
Web: www.westcanbulk.ca

RTL Networks Inc
1391 Speer Blvd Ste 850 ..... Denver CO 80204 303-757-3100 180
TF: 877-785-2259 ■ *Web:* www.rtl-networks.com

Rtm Communications Inc
360 Rt 101 9 Pine Tree Pl ..... Bedford NH 03110 603-420-1230 180
Web: solutionsbyrtm.com

RTM Consulting Inc (RTMC)
4335 Ferguson Dr Ste 210 ..... Cincinnati OH 45245 855-786-2555 786-2329 463
TF: 855-786-2555 ■ *Web:* www.rtmconsulting.net

RTM Studios 130 SE Pkwy Ct ..... Franklin TN 37064 615-224-3107 503-9704 116
Web: www.rtmtv.com

RTMC (RTM Consulting Inc)
4335 Ferguson Dr Ste 210 ..... Cincinnati OH 45245 855-786-2555 786-2329 463
TF: 855-786-2555 ■ *Web:* www.rtmconsulting.net

RTN Federal Credit Union 600 Main St ..... Waltham MA 02452 781-736-9900 736-9856 219
TF: 800-338-0221 ■ *Web:* www.rtn.org

RTNDA (Radio-Television News Directors Assn)
1600 K St NW Ste 700 ..... Washington DC 20006 202-659-6510 223-4007 49-14
Web: www.rtdna.org

RTP Co 580 E Front St ..... Winona MN 55987 507-454-6900 454-2041 605-2
TF: 800-433-4787 ■ *Web:* www.rtpcompany.com

RTP Corp 1834 SW Second St ..... Pompano Beach FL 33069 954-974-5500 975-9815 201
Web: www.rtpcorp.com

RTR (Rainbow Trout Ranch)
1484 FDR 250 PO Box 458 ..... Antonito CO 81120 719-376-2440 239
TF: 800-633-3397 ■ *Web:* www.rainbowtroutranch.com

RTR Financial Services Inc
2 Teleport Dr Ste 302 ..... Staten Island NY 10311 718-668-2881 668-1937 251
TF: 855-399-4787 ■ *Web:* www.rtrfs.com

RTS (Regional Transit System)
Stn 5 PO Box 490 ..... Gainesville FL 32627 352-334-2600 334-2607 468
Web: go-rts.com

RTS Financial Service
9300 Metcalf Ste 301 ..... Overland Park KS 66212 844-206-6123 272
TF: 877-242-4390 ■ *Web:* www.rtsfinancial.com

RTS Packaging LLC 504 Thrasher St ..... Norcross GA 30071 800-558-6984 101
TF: 800-558-6984 ■ *Web:* www.rtspackaging.com

RTV (Rock the Vote)
1001 Connecticut Ave NW Ste 640 ..... Washington DC 20036 202-719-9910 48-7
Web: www.rockthevote.org

Rtz Associates Inc
150 Grand Ave Ste 201 ..... Oakland CA 94612 510-986-6700 177
Web: rtzsystems.com

RUAN Transportation Management Systems
666 Grand Ave 3200 Ruan Ctr ..... Des Moines IA 50309 866-782-6669 289
TF: 866-782-6669 ■ *Web:* www.ruan.com

Rubatino Refuse Removal Inc
2812 Hoyt Ave ..... Everett WA 98201 425-259-0044 339-4196 804
Web: www.rubatino.com

RubbAir Door Div Eckel Industries Inc
100 Groton Shirley Rd ..... Ayer MA 01432 978-772-0480 772-7114 235
TF: 800-966-7822 ■ *Web:* www.rubbair.com

Rubber & Plastics Inc
7401 NE 47th Ave ..... Vancouver WA 98661 360-567-4280 370
Web: www.conveyorbelt.com

Rubber & Plastics News 1725 Merriman Rd ..... Akron OH 44313 330-836-9180 532-3
Web: www.rubbernews.com

Rubber Associates
1522 W Turkeyfoot Lake Rd ..... Barberton OH 44203 330-745-2186 676
Web: www.rubberassociates.com

Rubber City Radio Group
1795 West Market St ..... Akron OH 44313 330-869-9797 645-2
Web: www.wone.net

Rubber Development Inc
701 Technology Pl ..... Waverly IA 50677 319-352-5600 352-5601 676
Web: www.rubberdevelopment.com

Rubber Industries Inc
200 Cavanaugh Dr ..... Shakopee MN 55379 952-445-1320 445-7934 676
Web: www.rubberindustries.com

Rubbercraft Corporation of California
3701 Conant St ..... Long Beach CA 90808 562-354-2800 354-2900 326
Web: www.rubbercraft.com

Rubberlite Inc 2501 Guyan Ave ..... Huntington WV 25703 304-525-3116 523-4316 601
Web: www.rubberlite.com

Rubbermaid Commercial Products (RCP)
3124 Valley Ave ..... Winchester VA 22601 540-667-8700 542-8770 608
TF: 800-347-9800 ■ *Web:* www.rubbermaidcommercial.com

Ruben Cos 600 Madison Ave ..... New York NY 10022 212-293-9400 293-9401 652
Web: www.rubenco.com

Rubenstein & Ziff Inc
11516 K-Tel Dr ..... Minnetonka MN 55343 952-854-1460 854-7254 594
Web: www.rzindustrial.com

Name / Address	City	State	ZIP	Phone	Fax	Class
Rubenstein Bros Inc 102 St Charles Ave *TF:* 800-725-7823 ■ *Web:* rubensteinsneworleans.com	New Orleans	LA	70130	504-581-6666		157-3
Rubenstein Supply Co 2800 San Pablo Ave *Web:* www.rubensteinsupply.com	Oakland	CA	94608	510-444-6614	444-2518	612
Rubicon Group Ltd, The 2625 Butterfield Rd Ste 217N *Web:* www.rubgrp.com	Oak Brook	IL	60523	630-574-7766		177
Rubicon Marketing Inc 10925 Estate Ln Ste 208 *Web:* rubiconmarketing.com	Dallas	TX	75238	214-478-3929	432-1112	463
Rubicon Minerals Corp 121 King St W Ste 830 *OTC:* RBYCF ■ *TF:* 844-818-1776 ■ *Web:* rubiconminerals.com	Toronto	ON	M5H3T9	416-766-2804	792-4601	502
Rubicon Programs 2500 Bissell Ave *Web:* rubiconprograms.org	Richmond	CA	94804	510-235-1516		260
Rubin & Levin PC 500 Marott Ctr 342 Massachusetts Ave *Web:* www.rubin-levin.com	Indianapolis	IN	46204	317-634-0300		428
Rubin Abramson LLP 225 Broadway Ste 400 *Web:* rubinabramson.com	New York	NY	10007	212-964-3300		41
Rubin Communications Group Inc 4542 Bonney Rd Ste B *Web:* rubincommunications.com	Virginia Beach	VA	23462	757-456-5212		636
Rubin Guttman & Associates LPA 55 Public Sq Ste 1860 *Web:* guttlaw.com	Cleveland	OH	44113	216-696-4006		41
Rubin Licatesi PC 591 Stewart Ave 4th Fl *Web:* www.rubinlicatesi.com	Garden City	NY	11530	516-227-2662	227-2739	445
Rubin Museum, The 150 W 17th St *TF:* 844-289-0473 ■ *Web:* rubinmuseum.org	New York	NY	10011	212-620-5000	620-0628	522
Rubin Postaer & Assoc 2525 Colorado Ave *Web:* www.rpa.com	Santa Monica	CA	90404	310-394-4000		4
Rubin Steel Co 1430 Fruitville Pke *Web:* rubinsteel.com	Lancaster	PA	17601	717-397-3613		492
RubinBrown LLP 1 N Brentwood Blvd Ste 1100 *Web:* www.rubinbrown.com	Saint Louis	MO	63105	314-290-3300		2
Rubino & McGeehin Consulting Group Inc 6903 Rockledge Dr Ste 1200 *Web:* rubino.com	Bethesda	MD	20817	301-564-3636		734
Rubino Brothers Inc 560 Canal St *Web:* www.rubinobrothersinc.com	Stamford	CT	06902	203-323-3195		686
Rubio Marco (Sen R - FL) 284 Russell Senate Office Bldg *TF:* 866-630-7106 ■ *Web:* www.rubio.senate.gov	Washington	DC	20510	202-224-3041		342-2
Rubio's Restaurants Inc 1902 Wright Pl Ste 300 *TF:* 800-354-4199 ■ *Web:* www.rubios.com	Carlsbad	CA	92008	760-929-8226	929-8203	670
Rubius Therapeutics 399 Binney St Ste 300 *Web:* www.rubiustx.com	Cambridge	MA	02139	617-679-9600		418
Ruby Falls 1720 S Scenic Hwy *TF:* 800-755-7105 ■ *Web:* www.rubyfalls.com	Chattanooga	TN	37409	423-821-2544	821-6705	50-5
Ruby Hill Golf Shop 3400 W Ruby Hill Dr *Web:* www.rubyhill.com	Pleasanton	CA	94566	925-417-5850		711
Ruby River Steak House 4286 Riverdale Rd *Web:* www.rubyriver.com	Ogden	UT	84405	801-622-2320		671
Ruby Stein Wagner 300 Leo-Pariseau Ste 1900 *TF:* 866-842-3911 ■ *Web:* rsw.ca	Montreal	QC	H2X4B5	514-842-3911		2
Ruby Tequila's 2001 S Georgia *Web:* rubytequilas.com	Amarillo	TX	79109	806-358-7829		671
Ruby's Diner 1 Main St *Web:* www.rubys.com	Huntington Beach	CA	92648	714-969-7829		671
Ruchi 11168 Antioch Rd *Web:* www.ruchicuisine.com	Overland Park	KS	66210	913-661-9088		671
Rucka, O'Boyle, Lombardo & Mckenna 245 W Laurel Dr *Web:* rolmlawyers.com	Salinas	CA	93906	831-443-1051	443-6419	41
Rucker & Associates Inc 7009 N Ridge Dr Ste 300 *Web:* www.ruckerassociates.com	Raleigh	NC	27615	919-873-1268	873-1769	463
Center for Ocean Observing Leadership 71 Dudley Rd **Fax Area Code:* 732 ■ *Web:* rucool.marine.rutgers.edu	New Brunswick	NJ	08901	848-932-6555	932-8578*	668
Rudd Container Corp 4600 S Kolin *Web:* www.ruddcontainer.com	Chicago	IL	60632	773-847-7600	847-7930	100
Rudd Equipment Co 4344 Poplar Level Rd *TF:* 800-527-2282 ■ *Web:* www.ruddequipment.com	Louisville	KY	40213	502-456-4050	459-8695	358
Ruder Finn 425 E 53rd St *Web:* www.ruderfinn.com	New York	NY	10022	212-593-6400		636
Rudick Forensic Engineering Inc 855 Tod Ave *TF:* 800-966-5392 ■ *Web:* rudick-forensic.com	Youngstown	OH	44502	330-744-5392		261
Rudnick, Addonizio, Pappa & Casazza PC 25 Village Ct *Web:* rudnicklaw.com	Hazlet	NJ	07730	732-264-4400		41
Rudolf Bass Inc 289 Central Ave *Web:* www.rudolfbassinc.net	Jersey City	NJ	07307	201-433-3800	433-6853	385
Rudolf Steiner College 9200 Fair Oaks Blvd *Web:* steinercollege.edu	Fair Oaks	CA	95628	916-963-4000		166
Rudolph & Sletten Inc 1600 Seaport Blvd Ste 350 *Web:* www.rsconstruction.com	Redwood City	CA	94063	650-216-3600	599-9112	186
Rudolph Bros 6550 Oley Speaks Way *TF:* 800-600-9508 ■ *Web:* www.rudolphbros.com	Canal Winchester	OH	43110	800-375-0605		732
Rudolph Foods Company Inc 6575 Bellefontaine Rd *TF:* 800-241-7675 ■ *Web:* www.rudolphfoods.com	Lima	OH	45804	419-648-3611	648-4087	296-9
Rudolph Kaplan 20 N Clark St Ste 2500 *Web:* rudolphkaplan.com	Chicago	IL	60602	312-236-8808		41
Rudy's Texas Bar-B-Q LLC 2780 North Expy 77-83A *TF:* 877-609-3337 ■ *Web:* rudysbbq.com	Brownsville	TX	78526	956-542-2532		671
Rue & Associates Inc 7264 Hanover Green Dr *Web:* rueassociates.com	Mechanicsville	VA	23111	804-730-7455		196
Ruekert & Mielke Inc W233 N2080 Ridgeview Pkwy *TF:* 800-236-0890 ■ *Web:* www.ruekertmielke.com	Waukesha	WI	53188	262-542-5733	542-5631	261
Ruemelin Manufacturing Company Inc 3860 N Palmer St *Web:* www.ruemelin.com	Milwaukee	WI	53212	414-962-6500	962-5780	386
Rues Principales 870 De Salaberry Ave Ste 309 *TF:* 877-694-9944 ■ *Web:* www.ruesprincipales.org	Quebec City	QC	G1R2T9	418-694-9944		78
Ruffalo Noel Levitz LLC 1025 Kirkwood Pky SW *Web:* www.noellevitz.com	Cedar Rapids	IA	52404	319-362-7483		196
Ruffed Grouse Society (RGS) 451 McCormick Rd *TF:* 888-564-6747 ■ *Web:* www.ruffedgrousesociety.org	Coraopolis	PA	15108	412-262-4044	262-9207	48-3
Ruffin & Payne Inc 4000 Vawter Ave *Web:* www.ruffin-payne.com	Richmond	VA	23222	804-329-2691	321-4940	499
Ruffin Flag Co 314 Water St *Web:* www.ruffinflagcompany.net	Washington	GA	30673	706-678-7777		45
Rug Doctor LP 4701 Old Shepard Pl *TF:* 800-784-3628 ■ *Web:* www.rugdoctor.com	Plano	TX	75093	800-784-3628		264-2
Rugg Manufacturing Corp 554 Willard St **Fax Area Code:* 978 ■ *TF:* 800-633-8772 ■ *Web:* www.rugg.com	Leominster	MA	01453	800-633-8772	401-2188*	429
Rugged Systems Inc 13000 Danielson St Q *Web:* www.coresystemsusa.com	Poway	CA	92064	858-391-1006		225
Ruggeri-Jensen-Azar & Assoc 4690 Chabot Dr *Web:* www.rja-gps.com	Pleasanton	CA	94588	925-227-9100		463
Ruggie Wealth Management 2100 Lake Eustis Dr *TF:* 888-343-2711 ■ *Web:* www.ruggiewealth.com	Tavares	FL	32778	352-343-2700		463
Ruggles Service Corp 2209 Dickens Rd *Web:* www.societyhq.com	Richmond	VA	23230	804-282-0062		47
Ruhle Companies Inc 99 Wall St *Web:* www.ruhle.com	Valhalla	NY	10595	914-761-2600	761-0405	253
Ruhlin Company Inc PO Box 190 *Web:* www.ruhlin.com	Sharon Center	OH	44274	330-239-2800	239-1828	186
Ruhof Corp, The 393 Sagamore Ave *TF:* 800-537-8463 ■ *Web:* www.ruhof.com	Mineola	NY	11501	516-294-5888	248-6456	194
Ruhrpumpen Inc 4501 S 86th E Ave *Web:* www.ruhrpumpen.com	Tulsa	OK	74145	918-627-8400		537
Ruiz Foods Inc PO Box 37 **Fax Area Code:* 559 ■ *TF:* 800-477-6474 ■ *Web:* www.elmonterey.com	Dinuba	CA	93618	800-477-6474	591-1593*	296-36
Ruiz Mexican Foods Inc 1200 Marlborough Ave A *Web:* www.ruizflourtortillas.com	Riverside	CA	92507	909-947-7811	947-2338	296-37
Ruiz Raul (Rep D - CA) 2342 Rayburn House Office Bldg *Web:* ruiz.house.gov	Washington	DC	20515	202-225-5330	225-1238	342-2
Rukert Terminals Corp 2021 S Clinton St *Web:* www.rukert.com	Baltimore	MD	21224	410-276-1013		465
RuleSphere International Inc PO Box 152 *Web:* www.rulesphere.com	Still River	MA	01467	978-456-8253		396
Rulesware LLC 10 N Martingale Rd Ste 400 *Web:* rulesware.com	Schaumburg	IL	60173	312-224-8501		196
Rulmeca Corp 6508 Windmill Way Ste B *Web:* www.rulmecacorp.com	Wilmington	NC	28405	910-794-9294	794-9296	636
Rulon Co 2000 Ring Way Rd *Web:* rulonco.com	Saint Augustine	FL	32092	904-584-1400		200
RuMar Manufacturing Corp 925 S St *Web:* www.rumar.com	Mayville	WI	53050	920-387-2104	387-2367	697
Rumbi Island Grill 358 South 700 East *Web:* www.rumbi.com	Salt Lake City	UT	84102	801-530-1000		671
Rumble Tuff Inc 865 N 1430 W *TF:* 855-228-8388 ■ *Web:* www.rumbletuff.com	Orem	UT	84057	801-609-8168		319-2
Rummel Industries Inc 697 Rahway Ave Rear *TF:* 800-526-4549 ■ *Web:* www.rummelindustries.com	Union	NJ	07083	908-688-6600	686-4612	605-2
Rumpke 10795 Hughes Rd *TF:* 800-582-3107 ■ *Web:* www.rumpke.com	Cincinnati	OH	45251	800-582-3107		804
Rumsey Electric Co 15 Colwell Ln *TF:* 800-462-2402 ■ *Web:* www.rumsey.com	Conshohocken	PA	19428	610-832-9000	941-8181	246
Rumsey Hall School 201 Romford Rd *Web:* www.rumseyhall.org	Washington Depot	CT	06794	860-868-0535	868-7907	622
Run Consultants LLC 925 N Point Pkwy Ste 160 *TF:* 866-457-2193 ■ *Web:* www.runconsultants.com	Alpharetta	GA	30005	866-457-2193		260
Run Energy LP 5009 S Danville Dr *Web:* www.runenergy.com	Abilene	TX	79602	325-795-1550		393
Rundle-Spence Manufacturing Co 2075 S Moorland Rd *TF:* 800-783-6060 ■ *Web:* www.rundle-spence.com	New Berlin	WI	53151	262-782-3000	782-5078	612
Runnells Specialized Hospital of Union County 40 Watchung Way *Web:* ucnj.org	Berkeley Heights	NJ	07922	908-771-5700		374-7
Runnels County 613 Hutchings Ave Rm 303 *Web:* www.co.runnels.tx.us	Ballinger	TX	76821	325-365-2137	365-4823	338
Runner Technologies Inc 6530 W Rogers Cir Ste 31 *Web:* www.runneredq.com	Boca Raton	FL	33487	561-395-9322		177
Runner's Edge Inc, The 3195 N Federal Hwy *TF:* 888-361-1950 ■ *Web:* runnersedgeboca.com	Boca Raton	FL	33431	561-361-1950		711

	Phone	Fax	Class
Runners Forum of Carmel Inc 620 Station Dr . . . . . Carmel IN 46032 *Web:* www.runnersforum.com	317-844-1558		711
Running Foxes Petroleum 14550 E Easter Ave Ste 200 . . . . . Centennial CO 80015 *Web:* www.runningfoxes.com	720-377-0923		579
Runtime Design Automation 2560 Mission College Blvd Ste 130 . . . . . Santa Clara CA 95054 *Web:* runtimeinc.com	408-492-0940		261
Runway Tire Service Inc 10 Park Cir E . . . . . New Hyde Park NY 11040 *Web:* www.runwaytireservice.com	718-545-5200		54
Runyon Saltzman Inc 2020 L St Ste 100 . . . . . Sacramento CA 95811 *Web:* www.rs-e.com	916-446-9900		4
Runyon's 9810 W Sample Rd . . . . . Coral Springs FL 33065 *Web:* www.runyonsofcoralsprings.com	954-752-2333		671
Runza National Inc PO Box 6042 . . . . . Lincoln NE 68506 *TF:* 800-929-2394 ■ *Web:* www.runza.com	402-423-2394	423-5726	670
Runzheimer Intl 1 Runzheimer Pk . . . . . Waterford WI 53185 *TF:* 800-558-1702 ■ *Web:* www.runzheimer.com	262-971-2200		193
Ruotolo Associates Inc (RA) 580 Sylvan Ave Ste M-B . . . . . Englewood Cliffs NJ 07632 *Web:* www.ruotoloassociates.com	201-568-3898	568-8783	317
Ruotolo, Speak & Co 101 Chestnut Ave . . . . . Mount Laurel NJ 08054 *Web:* nowfinancialnetwork.com	856-273-1282		2
Rupe's Hydraulics Sales & Service 725 N Twin Oaks Valley Rd . . . . . San Marcos CA 92069 *TF:* 800-354-7873 ■ *Web:* rupeshydraulics.com	760-744-9350		790
Ruppersberger C. A. Dutch (Rep D - MD) 2206 Rayburn House Office Bldg . . . . . Washington DC 20515 *Web:* ruppersberger.house.gov	202-225-3061	225-3094	342-2
Ruprecht Co 1301 Allanson Rd . . . . . Mundelein IL 60060 *TF:* 888-829-4100 ■ *Web:* ruprechtcompany.com	312-829-4100		296-26
Rural Coalition 1029 Vermont Ave NW Ste 601 . . . . . Washington DC 20005 *Web:* www.ruralco.org	202-628-7160	393-1816	48-2
Rural Community Transportation Inc (RCT) 1677 Industrial Pkwy . . . . . Lyndonville VT 05851 *Web:* www.riderct.org	802-748-8170	748-5275	108
Rural Electric Convenience Co-operative Co 3973 W SR-104 PO Box 19 . . . . . Auburn IL 62615 *TF:* 800-245-7322 ■ *Web:* www.recc.coop	217-438-6197	438-3212	245
Rural Electric Coop (REC) 13942 Hwy 76 . . . . . Lindsay OK 73052 *TF:* 800-259-3504 ■ *Web:* www.rural-electric.com	405-756-3104	756-8957	245
Rural Health Resource Ctr 525 S Lake Ave Ste 320 . . . . . Duluth MN 55802 *TF:* 800-997-6685 ■ *Web:* www.ruralcenter.org	218-727-9390		449
Rural Media Group Inc 9500 W Dodge Rd Ste 101 . . . . . Omaha NE 68114 *Web:* www.rfdtv.com	402-289-0192		116
Rural Mutual Insurance Co 1241 John Q Hammons Dr . . . . . Madison WI 53717 *TF:* 877-219-9550 ■ *Web:* www.ruralins.com	877-219-9550		391-4
Rural Resources Community Action 956 S Main St . . . . . Colville WA 99114 *TF:* 800-538-7659 ■ *Web:* www.ruralresources.org	509-684-8421	684-4740	148
Rural Telephone Service Company Inc 145 N Main PO Box 158 . . . . . Lenora KS 67645 *TF:* 877-625-7872 ■ *Web:* www.nex-tech.com	785-567-4281	567-4401	736
Rural Transit Enterprises Coordinated Inc (RTEC) 100 E Main St . . . . . Mount Vernon KY 40456 *TF:* 800-321-7832 ■ *Web:* www.4rtec.com	606-256-9835		108
Rural/Metro Corp 9221 E Via de Ventura . . . . . Scottsdale AZ 85258 *TF:* 800-352-2309 ■ *Web:* www.ruralmetro.com	480-606-3886		30
Rural-Urban Record 24487 Squire Rd . . . . . Columbia Station OH 44028 *Web:* rural-urbanrecord.com	440-236-8982	236-9198	532-4
Ruritan National 5451 Lyons Rd PO Box 487 . . . . . Dublin VA 24084 *TF:* 877-787-8727 ■ *Web:* www.ruritan.org	540-674-5431	674-2304	48-15
Ruro Inc 321 Ballenger Center Dr Ste 102 . . . . . Frederick MD 21703 *TF:* 888-881-7876 ■ *Web:* ruro.com	888-881-7876		177
Rusach International Inc 100 Raymond St . . . . . Hope IN 47246 *Web:* www.rusach.com	317-638-0298		493
Ruscilli Construction Company Inc 5000 Arlington Center Blvd Ste 300 . . . . . Columbus OH 43220 *Web:* www.ruscilli.com	614-876-9484	876-0253	186
Rusco Inc 203 Red Barn Rd Ste 220 . . . . . Willow Grove PA 19090	610-313-9955		809
RUSD (Riverside Unified School District) 3380 14th St PO Box 2800 . . . . . Riverside CA 92501 *TF:* 800-782-7463 ■ *Web:* www.riversideunified.org	951-788-7135	778-5669	685
Ruseto College 1750 30th St Ste 83 . . . . . Boulder CO 80301 *Web:* www.ruseto.com	303-449-1686		167-3
Rush Bobby L (Rep D - IL) 2188 Rayburn House Office Bldg . . . . . Washington DC 20515 *Web:* rush.house.gov	202-225-4372	226-0333	342-2
Rush County 101 E Second St Rm 212 . . . . . Rushville IN 46173 *Web:* www.rushcounty.in.gov	765-932-5974	938-1163	338
Rush Enterprises Inc 555 IH 35 S Ste 500 . . . . . New Braunfels TX 78130 *NASDAQ: RUSHA* ■ *TF:* 800-973-7874 ■ *Web:* www.rushenterprises.com	830-626-5200	626-5310	264-3
Rush Foundation Hospital 1314 19th Ave . . . . . Meridian MS 39301 *Web:* www.rushhealthsystems.org	601-483-0011	703-4427	374-3
Rush Gears Inc 550 Virginia Dr . . . . . Fort Washington PA 19034 *TF:* 800-523-2576 ■ *Web:* www.rushgears.com	800-523-2576	635-6273	709
Rush Industries Inc 118 N Wrenn St . . . . . High Point NC 27260 *Web:* www.rushfurniture.com	336-886-7700	886-2227	319-2
Rush Moore LLP 737 Bishop St Ste 2400 . . . . . Honolulu HI 96813 *Web:* rmhawaii.com	808-521-0400	521-0497	428
Rush Oak Park Hospital (ROPH) 520 S Maple Ave . . . . . Oak Park IL 60304 *Web:* www.roph.org	708-383-9300	660-2310	374-3
Rush Shelby Energy Inc 2777 S 840 W PO Box 55 . . . . . Manilla IN 46150 *TF:* 800-706-7362 ■ *Web:* www.rse.coop	765-544-2600		245
Rush Transportation and Logistics 2388 Arbor Blvd . . . . . Dayton OH 45439 *TF:* 800-989-7874 ■ *Web:* www.rush-delivery.com	937-297-6182		546
Rush Truck Center - Lubbock 4515 Ave A . . . . . Lubbock TX 79404 *TF:* 888-987-2458 ■ *Web:* www.rushtruckcenters.com	806-686-3600	747-4171	516
Rush University 600 S Paulina St . . . . . Chicago IL 60612 *Web:* www.rushu.rush.edu	312-942-7100		166
Rush-Copley Medical Ctr (RCMC) 2000 Ogden Ave . . . . . Aurora IL 60504 *TF:* 866-426-7539 ■ *Web:* www.rushcopley.com	630-978-6200		374-3
Rusher Loscavio & LoPresto 369 Pine St Ste 221 . . . . . San Francisco CA 94104 *Web:* www.rll.com	415-765-6583		266
Rush-Henrietta Central School District 2034 Lehigh Stn Rd . . . . . Henrietta NY 14467 *Web:* www.rhnet.org	585-359-5000	359-5045	685
Rushmore Cave 13622 Hwy 40 . . . . . Keystone SD 57751 *TF:* 800-344-8826 ■ *Web:* www.rushmtn.com	605-255-4384		50-5
Rushmore Forest Products 23848 Hwy 385 PO Box 619 . . . . . Hill City SD 57745 *TF:* 866-466-5254 ■ *Web:* neimanenterprises.com	605-574-2512		683
Rushmore Plaza Civic Ctr 444 Mt Rushmore Rd . . . . . Rapid City SD 57701 *Web:* www.gotmine.com	605-394-4115	394-4119	205
Rushmore View Inn 522 Hwy 16A . . . . . Keystone SD 57751 *TF:* 800-888-2603 ■ *Web:* www.rushmoreviewinn.com	800-888-2603		379
Rushworks 800 Parker Sq Ste 200 . . . . . Flower Mound TX 75028 *TF:* 888-894-7874 ■ *Web:* www.rushworks.tv	888-894-7874		179
Rusk County 115 N Main St Ste 206 PO Box 758 . . . . . Henderson TX 75653 *Web:* www.co.rusk.tx.us	903-657-0330	657-2387	338
Rusk County 311 Miner Ave E . . . . . Ladysmith WI 54848 *TF:* 800-535-7875 ■ *Web:* www.ruskcounty.org	715-532-2100	532-2237	338
Rusk County Electric Co-opeartive Inc 3162 State Hwy 43 E . . . . . Henderson TX 75652 *Web:* www.rcelectric.org	903-657-4571	657-5377	245
Rusk High School 203 E Seventh St . . . . . Rusk TX 75785 *Web:* www.ruskisd.net	903-683-5592		685
Rusk State Hospital 805 N Dickinson Dr . . . . . Rusk TX 75785 *Web:* www.dshs.texas.gov	903-683-3421	683-7400	374-5
Rusken Packaging Inc 64 Walnut St NW . . . . . Cullman AL 35055 *TF:* 800-232-8108 ■ *Web:* www.rusken.com	256-734-0092	734-3008	101
Ruskin Manufacturing Co 3900 Doctor Greaves Rd . . . . . Grandview MO 64030 *Web:* www.ruskin.com	816-761-7476	765-8955	697
Ruskin Moscou Faltischek PC East Tower 1425 RXR Plz 15th Fl . . . . . Uniondale NY 11556 *Web:* www.rmfpc.com	516-663-6600		428
Ruskin Rooftop Systems 1625 Diplomat Dr . . . . . Carrollton TX 75006 *TF:* 800-552-4822 ■ *Web:* www.ruskinrooftopsystems.com	972-247-7447		14
Russ Bassett Co 8189 Byron Rd . . . . . Whittier CA 90606 *TF:* 800-350-2445 ■ *Web:* www.russbassett.com	562-945-2445	698-8972	286
Russ Blakely & Assoc 246 E 11th St Ste 302 . . . . . Chattanooga TN 37402 *Web:* www.rbabenefits.com	423-266-8306		41
Russ Darrow Group Inc W133 N8569 Executive Pkwy . . . . . Menomonee Falls WI 53051 *Web:* www.russdarrow.com	262-250-9600		57
Russ Doughten Films Inc 5907 Meredith Dr . . . . . Des Moines IA 50322 *TF:* 800-247-3456 ■ *Web:* www.rdfilms.com	515-278-4737	278-4738	514
Russ Lyon Sotheby's International Realty 7669 E Pinnacle Peak Rd Ste 110 . . . . . Scottsdale AZ 85255 *Web:* russlyon.com	480-502-3500		652
Russ Swanay Real Estate 112 S Armed Forces Dr . . . . . Elizabethton TN 37643 *Web:* swanayproperties.com	423-543-5741		652
Russ' Restaurants Inc 390 E 8th St . . . . . Holland MI 49423 *TF:* 800-521-1778 ■ *Web:* www.russrestaurants.com	616-396-6571	396-6755	670
Russelectric Inc 99 Industrial Park Rd . . . . . Hingham MA 02043 *TF:* 800-225-5250 ■ *Web:* www.russelectric.com	781-749-6000		729
Russell C. Davis Planetarium 201 E Pascagoula St . . . . . Jackson MS 39201 *Web:* www.jacksonms.gov	601-960-1552		598
Russell Cave National Monument 3729 County Rd 98 . . . . . Bridgeport AL 35740 *Web:* www.nps.gov	256-495-2672	495-9220	564
Russell Cellular Inc 5624 S Hwy FF . . . . . Battlefield MO 65619 *Web:* www.russellcellular.com	417-886-7542		736
Russell Construction Company Inc 4600 E 53rd St . . . . . Davenport IA 52807 *Web:* www.russellco.com	563-459-4600		187
Russell County 137 Highland Dr . . . . . Lebanon VA 24266 *Web:* www.russellcountyva.us	276-971-0690	889-8011	338
Russell County 1000 Broad St . . . . . Phenix City AL 36867 *Web:* www.rcala.com	334-298-7979	297-7594	338
Russell County 401 N Main St PO Box 113 . . . . . Russell KS 67665 *Web:* ks-russellco.manatron.com	785-483-4641	483-5725	338
Russell County Clerk 410 Monument Sq Ste 103 . . . . . Jamestown KY 42629 *Web:* russell.clerkinfo.net	270-343-2125		338
Russell County News 958 Wichita Ave . . . . . Russell KS 67665	785-483-2116		532-2
Russell County Public Library 248 W Main St . . . . . Lebanon VA 24266 *Web:* russell.lib.va.us	276-889-8044	889-8045	434-3
Russell Development Company Inc 200 SW Market St Ste 1720 . . . . . Portland OR 97201 *Web:* www.russelldevelopment.net	503-228-2500		653
Russell Florist Inc 5001 Gravois Ave . . . . . Saint Louis MO 63116 *Web:* russellfloriststlouis.net	314-351-4676		292

	City	State	ZIP	Phone	Fax	Class
Russell Food Equipment Ltd 1255 Venables St *TF:* 800-663-0707 ■ *Web:* www.russellfood.ca	Vancouver	BC	V6A3X6	604-253-6611		14
Russell Forest Products Inc 719 Railroad St SW *Web:* www.russellforest.com	Hartselle	AL	35640	256-773-1607		111
Russell Hall Co, The (RH) 19 N George St. *Web:* www.russellhall.com	Meriden	CT	06451	203-235-6391	237-4336	559
Russell Hall Seafood Inc 2501 Old House Point Rd *TF:* 866-952-7227 ■ *Web:* www.tarbayseafood.com	Fishing Creek	MD	21634	866-952-7227		296-14
Russell Herder 275 Market St Ste 319 *Web:* russellherder.com	Minneapolis	MN	55405	612-455-2360		7
Russell Investments 1301 Second Ave 18th Fl *TF:* 800-426-7969 ■ *Web:* www.russellinvestments.com	Seattle	WA	98101	206-505-7877		401
Russell Johns Associates LLC 5020 W Linebaugh Ave Ste 210 *TF:* 800-237-9851 ■ *Web:* www.russelljohns.com	Tampa	FL	33624	727-443-7667		5
Russell Meerdink Company Ltd, The 1555 S Park Ave *TF:* 800-635-6499 ■ *Web:* www.horseinfo.com	Neenah	WI	54956	920-725-0955	725-0709	637-2
Russell Phillips & Associates LLC 500 Cross Keys Office Pk *Web:* www.phillipsllc.com	Fairport	NY	14450	585-223-1130	223-1189	463
Russell Reynolds Associates Inc 277 Park Ave Ste 3800 *TF:* 800-259-0470 ■ *Web:* www.russellreynolds.com	New York	NY	10166	212-351-2000		266
Russell Sage Foundation 112 E 64th St *Web:* www.russellsage.org	New York	NY	10065	212-750-6000	371-4761	668
Russell Standard Corp 285 Kappa Dr Ste 300 *TF:* 800-323-3053 ■ *Web:* www.russellstandard.com	Pittsburgh	PA	15238	800-323-3053		46
Russell Stover Candies Inc 4900 Oak St *TF:* 800-477-8683 ■ *Web:* www.russellstover.com	Kansas City	MO	64112	800-777-4004		296-8
Russell's 1918 Ash St	Scranton	PA	18510	570-961-8949		671
Russellville Area Chamber of Commerce 708 W Main St *Web:* www.russellvillechamber.org	Russellville	AR	72801	479-968-2530	968-5894	139
Russellville Steel Company Inc PO Box 1538 *Web:* www.rsvlsteel.com	Russellville	AR	72811	479-968-2211	968-3486	492
Russia 136 E 67th St *Web:* russiaun.ru	New York	NY	10065	212-861-4900	628-0252	784
Russia *Consulate General* 600 University St Ste 2510 *Web:* www.seattle.mid.ru	Seattle	WA	98121	206-728-0232	728-1871	257
Consulate General 2790 Green St *Web:* sanfrancisco.mid.ru	San Francisco	CA	94123	415-928-6878	929-0306	257
Consulate General 9 E 91st St *Web:* newyork.mid.ru	New York	NY	10128	212-534-3782	831-9162	257
Russian federation Washington DC *Embassy* 2650 Wisconsin Ave NW *Web:* www.russianembassy.org	Washington	DC	20007	202-298-5700	298-5735	257
Russian Information Services Inc (RIS) PO Box 567 *TF:* 800-639-4301 ■ *Web:* russianlife.com	Montpelier	VT	05601	802-223-4955		637-9
Russian National Tourist Office 224 W 30th St Ste 701 *TF:* 877-221-7120 ■ *Web:* www.russia-travel.com	New York	NY	10001	646-473-2233	473-2205	775
Russin Lumber Corp 21 Leonards Dr *TF:* 800-724-0010 ■ *Web:* www.russinlumber.com	Montgomery	NY	12549	845-457-4000	457-4010	191-3
Russ-Knits Inc 520 E Main St *Web:* www.russknits.com	Candor	NC	27229	910-974-4114	974-4023	745-4
Russo & Steele LLC 7722 E Gray Rd Ste C *Web:* russoandsteele.com	Scottsdale	AZ	85260	602-252-2697	252-6260	57
Russo Corp 1421 Mims Ave SW *Web:* www.russocorp.com	Birmingham	AL	35211	205-923-4434	925-0665	186
Russo Development LLC 570 Commerce Blvd *Web:* russodevelopment.com	Carlstadt	NJ	07072	201-487-5657		653
Russo Farms Inc 1962 SE Ave *Web:* russofarms.com	Vineland	NJ	08360	856-692-5942		10-11
Russo Music Ctr 1989 Arena Dr *Web:* russomusic.com	Hamilton Township	NJ	08610	609-888-0620		526
Russo Partners LLC 12 W 27th St 4th Fl *Web:* russopartnersllc.com	New York	NY	10001	212-845-4200	845-4260	636
Russo Rosalina Company LPA 691 Richmond Rd *Web:* rrlpa.com	Richmond Heights	OH	44143	440-565-5994		41
Russtech Inc 1338 Vickers Rd *Web:* www.russtechinc.com	Tallahassee	FL	32303	850-562-9811		768
Rust College 150 Rust Ave *TF:* 888-886-8492 ■ *Web:* www.rustcollege.edu	Holly Springs	MS	38635	662-252-8000	252-2258	166
Rust Constructors Inc 2 Perimeter Pk S Ste 300 W *Web:* rustconstructors.azurewebsites.net	Birmingham	AL	35243	205-995-7171		187
Rust Orling Architecture Inc 1215 Cameron St *Web:* www.rustorling.com	Alexandria	VA	22314	703-836-3205		186
Rusted Moon Outfitters Inc 6410 Cornell Ave *Web:* rustedmoonindy.com	Indianapolis	IN	46220	317-253-4453		711
Rustic Canyon 201 Santa Monica Blvd Ste 500 *Web:* www.rusticcanyon.com	Santa Monica	CA	90401	310-998-8000	998-8001	792
Rustler Lodge 10380 East Hwy 210 PO Box 8030 *TF:* 888-532-2582 ■ *Web:* www.rustlerlodge.com	Alta	UT	84092	801-742-2200	742-3832	669
Rust-Oleum Corp 11 E Hawthorn Pkwy *TF:* 800-323-3584 ■ *Web:* www.rustoleum.com	Vernon Hills	IL	60061	847-367-7700		550
Ruston/Lincoln Chamber of Commerce 2111 N Trenton St *TF:* 800-392-9032 ■ *Web:* www.rustonlincoln.org	Ruston	LA	71270	318-255-2031	255-3481	139
Rusty Hardin & Associates LLP 5 Houston Ctr 1401 McKinney Ste 2250 *Web:* www.rustyhardin.com	Houston	TX	77010	713-652-9000		428
Rusty Parrot Lodge & Spa PO Box 1657 *TF:* 800-458-2004 ■ *Web:* www.rustyparrot.com	Jackson	WY	83001	307-733-2000	733-5566	669
Rusty Pelican 2425 N Rocky Pt Dr *Web:* www.therustypelican.com	Tampa	FL	33607	813-281-1943		671
Rusty Rudder Restaurant 113 Dickinson St *Web:* www.rustyrudderdewey.com	Dewey Beach	DE	19971	302-227-3888		671
Rusty's Pizza Parlors Inc 232 W Carrillo St Ste F *Web:* www.rustyspizza.com	Santa Barbara	CA	93101	805-963-9127	962-5054	670
RustyBrick Inc 250 W Nyack Rd Ste 200 *TF:* 877-467-8789 ■ *Web:* www.rustybrick.com	West Nyack	NY	10994	845-369-6869	228-8177	194
Rutan Poly Industries Inc 39 Siding Pl. *TF:* 800-872-1474 ■ *Web:* rutanpoly.com	Mahwah	NJ	07430	201-529-1474		297-8
Rutgers Business School (RBS) 1 Washington Pk 3rd Fl *Web:* www.business.rutgers.edu	Newark	NJ	07102	973-353-1821		668
Rutgers Gardens Cook College/Rutgers University 112 Ryders Ln *Web:* rutgersgardens.rutgers.edu	New Brunswick	NJ	08901	732-932-8451	932-7060	97
Rutgers Magazine Department of University Communications and Marketing Rutgers The State University of New Jersey 96 Davidson Rd *Web:* magazine.rutgers.edu	Piscataway	NJ	08854	732-445-5925		637-9
Rutgers School of Social Work The State University of New Jersey 536 George St *Web:* socialwork.rutgers.edu	New Brunswick	NJ	08901	848-932-7520		166
Rutgers The State University of New Jersey *Camden* 406 Penn St *Web:* www.camden.rutgers.edu	Camden	NJ	08102	856-225-6104	225-6498	166
Center for Ocean Observing Leadership 71 Dudley Rd **Fax Area Code:* 732 ■ *Web:* rucool.marine.rutgers.edu	New Brunswick	NJ	08901	848-932-6555	932-8578*	668
Libraries 169 College Ave *Web:* www.libraries.rutgers.edu	New Brunswick	NJ	08901	732-932-7505	932-1101	434-6
Newark 249 University Ave Rm 100 *Web:* www.newark.rutgers.edu	Newark	NJ	07102	973-353-5205	353-1440	166
School of Law Camden 217 N Fifth St *TF:* 800-466-7561 ■ *Web:* law.rutgers.edu	Camden	NJ	08102	856-225-6375		167-1
Rutgers University Foundation 7 College Ave Winants Hall *Web:* www.rutgers.edu	New Brunswick	NJ	08901	732-932-7777		166
Rutgers University Press 106 Somerset St 3rd Fl **Fax Area Code:* 732 ■ *Web:* www.rutgersuniversitypress.org	New Brunswick	NJ	08901	848-445-7762	745-4935*	637-4
Ruth Bancroft Garden Inc 1552 Bancroft Rd *Web:* www.ruthbancroftgarden.org	Walnut Creek	CA	94598	925-944-9352	256-1889	97
Ruth C. Schwartz & Co 6 W 18th St *Web:* www.rcspr.com	New York	NY	10011	212-463-0684	463-0941	636
Ruth Eckerd Hall 1111 McMullen Booth Rd *TF:* 800-875-8682 ■ *Web:* www.rutheckerdhall.com	Clearwater	FL	33759	727-791-7060		572
Ruth Enlow Library 6 N Second St *Web:* www.relib.net	Oakland	MD	21550	301-334-3996	334-4152	434-3
Ruth Lilly Medical Library 975 W Walnut St Ib 100 *TF:* 877-952-1988 ■ *Web:* library.mednet.iu.edu	Indianapolis	IN	46202	317-274-7182		434-1
Ruth's Chris Steak House 267 Marietta St *Web:* ruthschris.net	Atlanta	GA	30313	404-223-6500		671
Ruth's Hospitality Group Inc 1030 W Canton Ave Ste 100' *NASDAQ: RUTH* ■ *Web:* www.ruthschris.com	Winter Park	FL	32789	407-333-7440	833-9625	670
Rutheford & Chekene 375 Beale St Ste 310 *Web:* www.ruthchek.com	San Francisco	CA	94105	415-568-4400		256
Rutherford B. Hayes Presidential Ctr Spiegel Grove *TF:* 800-998-7737 ■ *Web:* www.rbhayes.org	Fremont	OH	43420	419-332-2081	332-4952	434-2
Rutherford Correctional Ctr 549 Ledbetter Rd PO Box 127 *Web:* www.ncdps.gov	Spindale	NC	28160	828-286-4121	286-9285	213
Rutherford County 319 N Maple St Ste 121 *Web:* rutherfordcountytn.gov	Murfreesboro	TN	37130	615-898-7800	898-7830	338
Rutherford County 289 N Main St *Web:* rutherfordcountync.gov	Rutherfordton	NC	28139	828-287-6060	287-6210	338
Rutherford County Chamber of Commerce 501 Memorial Blvd *TF:* 800-716-7560 ■ *Web:* www.rutherfordchamber.org	Murfreesboro	TN	37129	615-278-2326	890-7600	139
Rutherford County Chamber of Commerce 162 N Main St *TF:* 866-478-4646 ■ *Web:* www.rutherfordcoc.org	Rutherfordton	NC	28139	828-287-3090	287-0799	139
Rutherford Electric Membership Corp 186 Hudlow Rd PO Box 1569 *TF:* 800-521-0920 ■ *Web:* www.remc.com	Forest City	NC	28043	828-245-1621	248-2319	245
Rutherford Farmers Coop 985 Middle Tennessee Blvd *Web:* www.rutherfordfarmerscoop.com	Murfreesboro	TN	37130	615-898-8801	898-8805	276
Rutherford Institute PO Box 7482 *TF:* 800-225-1791 ■ *Web:* rutherford.org	Charlottesville	VA	22906	434-978-3888	978-1789	48-8
Rutherford John (Rep R - FL) 1711 Longworth House Office Bldg *Web:* rutherford.house.gov	Washington	DC	20515	202-225-2501		342-2
Rutherford Regional Health System 288 S Ridgecrest Ave *TF:* 800-542-4225 ■ *Web:* www.myrutherfordregional.com	Rutherfordton	NC	28139	828-286-5000		374-3

Phone | Fax | Class

Rutkin, Oldham & Griffin LLC
5 Imperial Ave PO Box 295 .... Westport CT 06880 203-227-7301 41
Web: rutkinoldham.com
Rutland Herald PO Box 668 .... Rutland VT 05702 800-498-4296 532-2
TF: 800-498-4296 ■ *Web:* www.rutlandherald.com
Rutland Mental Health Services Inc
78 S Main St .... Rutland VT 05701 802-775-2381 726
Web: www.rmhsccn.org
Rutland Plastic Technologies
10021 Rodney St .... Pineville NC 28134 704-553-0046 552-6589 605-2
TF: 800-438-5134 ■ *Web:* www.rutlandinc.com
Rutland Plywood Corp 1 Ripley Rd .... Rutland VT 05701 802-747-4000 683
Web: www.rutply.com
Rutland Region Chamber of Commerce
50 Merchants Row .... Rutland VT 05701 802-773-2747 338
TF: 800-756-8880 ■ *Web:* rutlandvermont.com
Rutland Regional Medical Ctr
160 Allen St .... Rutland VT 05701 802-775-7111 374-3
Web: www.rrmc.org
Rutland State Park 2 Crawford Rd .... Rutland MA 01543 508-886-6333 565
Web: www.mass.gov
Rutledge State Prison 7175 Manor Rd .... Columbus GA 31907 706-568-2340 568-2126 213
Web: www.prisonhandbook.com
Rutt HandCrafted Cabinetry
215 Diller Ave .... New Holland PA 17557 717-351-1700 115
Web: ruttcabinetry.com
Ruttger's Bay Lake Lodge
25039 Tame Fish Lake Rd PO Box 400 .... Deerwood MN 56444 218-678-2885 678-2864 669
TF: 800-450-4545 ■ *Web:* ruttgers.com
Ruttura & Sons Construction Company Inc
200 Cabot St .... West Babylon NY 11704 631-454-0291 454-8804 189-5
Web: www.ruttura.com
Ruxer Ford Lincoln Inc 123 Place Rd .... Jasper IN 47546 812-482-1200 57
TF: 800-397-8937 ■ *Web:* www.ruxerford.com
RV (Rock Valley Oil & Chemical Co)
1911 Windsor Rd .... Rockford IL 61101 815-654-2400 654-2428 146
Web: www.rockvalleyoil.com
R-V Industries Inc 584 Poplar Rd .... Honey Brook PA 19344 610-273-2457 273-3361 386
Web: www.rvii.com
RVB (Real View Books) PO Box 10 .... New Hope KY 40052 270-325-3061 325-3091 637-2
Web: www.realviewbooks.com
RVDA (Recreation Vehicle Dealers Assn)
3930 University Dr .... Fairfax VA 22030 703-591-7130 591-0734 49-18
Web: www.rvda.org
RVIA (Recreation Vehicle Industry Assn)
1896 Preston White Dr .... Reston VA 20191 703-620-6003 620-5071 49-21
TF: 800-336-0154 ■ *Web:* www.rvia.org
RVing Women (RVW)
1075 S Idaho Rd Ste 213 .... Apache Junction AZ 85120 480-671-6226 671-6230 48-23
TF: 888-557-8464 ■ *Web:* www.rvingwomen.org
RVision Inc 2445 Fifth Ave Ste 450 .... San Diego CA 92101 619-233-1403 628
Web: www.rvisionusa.com
RVM Enterprises Inc
40 Rector St 17th Fl .... New York NY 10006 800-525-7915 41
TF: 800-525-7915 ■ *Web:* rvminc.com
RVW (RVing Women)
1075 S Idaho Rd Ste 213 .... Apache Junction AZ 85120 480-671-6226 671-6230 48-23
TF: 888-557-8464 ■ *Web:* www.rvingwomen.org
RW Advertising Inc 310 Canal St .... Lemont IL 60439 630-257-1179 7
RW Allen LLC 1015 Broad St .... Augusta GA 30901 706-733-2800 733-3879 186
Web: rwallen.com
RW Engineering & Surveying Inc
6225 N 89th Cir .... Omaha NE 68134 402-573-2205 261
Web: rwmidwest.com
RW Hartnett Co 2055 Bennett Rd .... Philadelphia PA 19116 215-969-9190 969-9030 629
Web: www.rwhartnett.com
RW Machine Inc 1414 E Richey Rd .... Houston TX 77073 281-784-1600 784-1604 454
Web: www.rwmachineinc.com
RW Norton Art Gallery
4747 Creswell Ave .... Shreveport LA 71106 318-865-4201 869-0435 520
Web: www.rwnaf.org
RW Pressprich & Company Inc
Research Div 452 Fifth Ave 12th Fl .... New York NY 10018 212-832-6297 401
Web: www.pressprich.com
RW Sauder Inc 570 Furnace Hills Pk .... Lititz PA 17543 717-626-2074 297-10
TF: 800-233-0413 ■ *Web:* www.saudereggs.com
RW Screw Products Inc
999 Oberlin Rd SW .... Massillon OH 44647 330-837-9211 837-9223 621
TF: 866-797-2739 ■ *Web:* rwscrew.com
RW Setterlin Building Co
560 Harmon Ave .... Columbus OH 43223 614-459-7077 754-9702 186
Web: www.setterlin.com
RW Summers Railroad Contractor Inc
3693 E Gandy Rd .... Bartow FL 33830 863-533-8107 533-8100 188-8
Web: www.rwsummers.net
RW Warner Inc 217 Monroe Ave .... Frederick MD 21701 301-662-5387 698-0451 189-10
Web: www.rwwarner.com
Rwanda 124 E 39th St .... New York NY 10016 212-679-9010 784
Web: rwandaun.org
Rwanda Embassy
1875 Connecticut Ave NW .... Washington DC 20009 202-232-2882 257
Web: rwandaembassy.org
RWC Inc 2105 S Euclid Ave PO Box 920 .... Bay City MI 48707 989-684-4030 684-3960 811
Web: www.rwcinc.com
RWDSU 30 E 29th St .... New York NY 10016 212-684-5300 414
TF: 866-781-4430 ■ *Web:* www.rwdsu.info
RWH Trucking Inc 2970 Old Oakwood Rd .... Oakwood GA 30566 800-256-8119 780
TF: 800-256-8119 ■ *Web:* www.rwhtrucking.com
RWI Ventures
545 Middlefield Rd Ste 220 .... Menlo Park CA 94025 650-543-3300 543-3339 401
Web: www.rwiventures.com
RWJBarnabas Health
95 Old Short Hills Rd .... West Orange NJ 07052 973-322-4800 322-4795 371
Web: www.rwjbh.org
RWM Casters Co PO Box 668 .... Gastonia NC 28053 800-634-7704 350
TF: 800-634-7704 ■ *Web:* www.rwmcasters.com
RWS (Rose & Walker Supply Lafayette Inc)
5294 S Leonard Springs Rd .... Bloomington IN 47403 765-471-7070 474-7507 191-2
Web: www.roseandwalkersupply.com

RWS 555 Montgomery St Ste 720 .... San Francisco CA 94111 415-981-5890 393
Web: www.rws.com
RX Inc 612 E 69th St .... Savannah GA 31405 912-352-0375 237
Web: locostpharmacy.com
RX Monitoring Services Inc
22A Eastman Ave .... Bedford NH 03110 603-666-6606 261
Web: rxms.com
RX Optical 1700 S Park St .... Kalamazoo MI 49001 269-342-0003 543
TF: 800-792-2737 ■ *Web:* www.rxoptical.com
RX Scan 2478 Lackey Old State Rd .... Delaware OH 43015 740-548-1725 548-1745 238
TF: 800-572-2648 ■ *Web:* rxscan.com
RX Systems Inc
121 Point West Blvd .... Saint Charles MO 63301 800-922-9142 548
TF: 800-922-9142 ■ *Web:* www.rxsystems.com
RX Worldwide Meetings Inc
3060 Communications Pkwy Ste 200 .... Plano TX 75093 214-291-2920 291-2930 184
TF: 800-562-1713 ■ *Web:* infinixglobal.com
Rxcom 1404 Vontress Dr Ste 2127 .... Fort Worth TX 76108 817-246-6760 237
Web: www.rx.com
Rxpert Inc 2177 Kingsley Ave Ste 1 .... Orange Park FL 32073 904-272-1690 237
Web: rxpertinc.com
RXR Realty 625 Rex Plz .... Uniondale NY 11556 516-506-6000 506-6800 655
Web: www.rxrrealty.com
RxResults LLC
320 Executive Ct Ste 301 .... Little Rock AR 72205 501-367-8402 463
Web: rxresults.com
Ryan & Coscia PC 256 Essex St .... Salem MA 01970 978-744-1760 2
Web: ryancoscia.com
Ryan Alexander Chtd
3017 W Charleston Ste 58 .... Las Vegas NV 89102 702-868-3311 41
Web: ryanalexander.us
Ryan Alternative Staffing Inc
6936 Market St .... Boardman OH 44512 330-781-1172 260
TF: 800-665-5627 ■ *Web:* www.ryanstaffing.com
Ryan Automotive LLC 200 Carter Dr Ste D .... Edison NJ 08817 732-650-1550 57
Ryan Chevrolet Inc 1800 S Broadway .... Minot ND 58701 701-852-3571 57
TF: 877-296-6860 ■ *Web:* www.ryanchevrolet.com
Ryan Companies US Inc
50 S Tenth St Ste 300 .... Minneapolis MN 55403 612-492-4000 186
Web: www.ryancompanies.com
Ryan FireProtection Inc
9740 E 148th St .... Noblesville IN 46060 800-409-7606 610
TF: 800-409-7606 ■ *Web:* indianasubcontractors.org
Ryan Group Inc, The 14110 Dallas Pkwy .... Dallas TX 75254 972-385-7781 194
Web: www.ryangroupinc.com
Ryan Herco Products Corp
3010 N San Fernando Blvd .... Burbank CA 91504 818-841-1141 973-2600 603
TF: 800-848-1141 ■ *Web:* www.rhfs.com
Ryan Incorporated Central
2700 E Racine St .... Janesville WI 53545 608-754-2291 754-3290 189-5
Web: www.ryancentral.com
Ryan Insurance Agency Inc 44 Front St .... Ashland MA 01721 508-875-5850 390
Web: atryaninsurance.com
Ryan International Airlines Inc
4949 Harrison Ave .... Rockford IL 61108 815-316-5420 12
Ryan Iron Works Inc 1830 Broadway .... Raynham MA 02767 508-822-8001 189-14
Web: www.ryanironworks.net
Ryan Labs Inc 500 5th Ave Ste 2520 .... New York NY 10110 212-635-2300 635-2309 401
TF: 800-321-2301 ■ *Web:* www.ryanlabs.com
Ryan Lawn & Tree Inc
9120 Barton St .... Overland Park KS 66214 913-381-1505 381-2378 274
TF: 855-216-2293 ■ *Web:* ryanlawn.com
Ryan Manufacturing Inc
6606 Machmueller St .... Schofield WI 54476 715-359-2565 359-4839 757
Web: ryanmfg.com
Ryan Miller & Assoc
9700 Reseda Blvd Ste 200 .... Northridge CA 91324 818-638-5080 260
Web: rmasearch.com
Ryan Public Safety Solutions Inc
12119 US Hwy 431 .... Guntersville AL 35976 256-279-0082 196
Web: www.rpss911.com
Ryan Smith & Carbine Ltd
Mead Bldg 98 Merchants Row .... Rutland VT 05702 802-786-1000 786-1100 428
TF: 800-660-4930 ■ *Web:* www.rsclaw.com
Ryan Tim (Rep D - OH)
1126 Longworth House Office Bldg .... Washington DC 20515 202-225-5261 225-3719 342-2
Web: www.timryan.house.gov
Ryan Trading Corp
2500 Westchester Ave Ste 102 .... Purchase NY 10577 914-253-6767 296-20
Web: ryantrading.com
Ryan's 719 Coliseum Dr .... Winston-Salem NC 27106 336-724-6132 724-5761 671
Web: www.ryansrestaurant.com
Ryan-Biggs Associates PC
257 Ushers Rd .... Clifton Park NY 12065 518-406-5506 261
Web: ryanbiggs.com
Ryansharkey LLP 12700 Sunrise Vly Dr .... Reston VA 20191 703-652-1124 2
Web: www.ryansharkey.com
Ryantech Cloud Services
60 E Rio Salado Pkwy 9th Fl .... Tempe AZ 85281 866-804-9040 225
TF: 866-804-9040 ■ *Web:* www.ryantechinc.com
Rybar Group Inc, The 3150 Owen Rd .... Fenton MI 48430 810-750-6822 750-6733 196
Web: therybargroup.com
Rybovich Spencer Group
4200 N Flagler Dr .... West Palm Beach FL 33407 561-840-8190 90
Web: www.rybovich.com
Rycon Construction Inc
2501 Smallman St Ste 100 .... Pittsburgh PA 15222 412-392-2525 392-2526 186
TF: 800-883-1901 ■ *Web:* www.ryconinc.com
Rydalch Electric Inc
250 Plymouth Ave .... Salt Lake City UT 84115 801-265-1813 189-4
Web: www.rydalchelectric.com
Rydell Chevrolet Buick GMC
2700 S Washington St .... Grand Forks ND 58201 701-772-7211 57
TF: 877-591-8318 ■ *Web:* www.rydellchev.com
Rydell Chevrolet Inc
18600 Devonshire St .... Northridge CA 91324 866-697-5167 516
TF: 866-697-5167 ■ *Web:* www.chevynorthridge.com

Company	City	State	ZIP	Phone	Fax	Class
Ryder Material Handling 210 Annagem Blvd *Fax Area Code: 905 ■ TF: 800-268-2125 ■ Web: www.rydermaterialhandling.com	Mississauga	ON	L5T2V5	800-268-2125	795-9311*	358
Ryder System Inc 11690 NW 105th St NYSE: R ■ TF: 800-297-9337 ■ Web: ryder.com	Miami	FL	33178	305-500-3726		778
Rydex Funds 805 King Farm Blvd Ste 600 TF: 800-820-0888 ■ Web: www.guggenheiminvestments.com	Rockville	MD	20850	301-296-5100		528
Rye Ford Inc 1151 Boston Post Rd TF: 877-332-9036 ■ Web: www.ryeford.com	Rye	NY	10580	877-332-9036		57
Rye Patch State Recreation Area 2505 Rye Patch Reservoir Rd Web: www.parks.nv.gov	Lovelock	NV	89419	775-538-7321		565
Rye Telephone Co 60 Beckwith Dr Web: www.ryetelephone.com	Colorado City	CO	81019	719-676-3131	676-3135	224
Ryeco Inc 2549 Park Ave Web: www.ryecoinc.com	Beloit	WI	53511	608-362-7007	362-8155	454
Ryerson Inc 227 W Monroe St 27th Fl Web: www.ryerson.com	Chicago	IL	60606	312-292-5000		492
Ryerson Station State Park 361 Bristoria Rd Web: www.dcnr.pa.gov	Wind Ridge	PA	15380	724-428-4254		565
Ryerson University 350 Victoria St TF: 866-592-8882 ■ Web: www.ryerson.ca	Toronto	ON	M5B2K3	416-979-5000	979-5170	785
Ryko Solutions Inc 1500 SE 37th St TF: 800-289-7956 ■ Web: www.ryko.com	Grimes	IA	50111	515-986-3700		427
Ryle Manufacturing Co 3116 Holliday Rd Web: www.rylesprocket.com	Wichita Falls	TX	76302	940-767-4354	767-4849	620
Ryley Carlock & Applewhite Pa 1 N Central Ave Ste 1200 Web: www.rcalaw.com	Phoenix	AZ	85004	602-258-7701	257-9582	428
Ryman Auditorium 116 Fifth Ave N Web: www.ryman.com	Nashville	TN	37219	615-458-8700	458-8701	572
Rymax Marketing Services Inc 19 Chapin Rd Bldg B PO Box 2024 *Fax Area Code: 973 ■ TF: 866-796-2911 ■ Web: rymaxinc.com	Pine Brook	NJ	07058	866-796-2911	808-4513*	195
Rynel Inc 11 Twin Rivers Dr Web: www.rynel.com	Wiscasset	ME	04578	207-882-0200		601
Ryness Company Inc, The 801 San Ramon Valley Blvd Web: www.ryness.com	Danville	CA	94526	925-820-3432		656
Rynone Manufacturing Corp 297 Dominic Pace Industrial Pwy TF: 800-839-1654 ■ Web: www.rynone.com	Sayre	PA	18840	570-888-5272	888-1175	115
Ryobi Die Casting Inc 800 W Mausoleum Rd Web: www.ryobidiecasting.com	Shelbyville	IN	46176	317-398-3398		60
Ryobi Technologies Inc 1428 Pearman Dairy Rd TF: 800-525-2579 ■ Web: www.ryobitools.com	Anderson	SC	29625	800-525-2579		351
Ryokan College 11965 Venice Blvd Ste 304 TF: 866-796-5261 ■ Web: www.ryokan.edu	Los Angeles	CA	90066	310-390-7560	391-9756	166
Ryosan Technologies USA Inc 41650 Gardenbrook Rd Ste 185 Web: www.ryosan.co.jp	Novi	MI	48375	248-380-4010		246
Ryosho USA Inc 2580 N 1st St Ste 230 Web: www.ryoden.co.jp	San Jose	CA	95131	408-474-7777	474-7722	246
Ryson International Inc 300 Newsome Dr Web: www.ryson.com	Yorktown	VA	23692	757-898-1530	898-1580	207
Ryte Byte Inc S4125A Rocky Point Rd TF: 866-356-6822 ■ Web: rytebyteinc.com	Baraboo	WI	53913	608-356-6822	356-0312	225
Rytec Corp 1 Cedar Pkwy TF: 800-628-1909 ■ Web: www.rytecdoors.com	Jackson	WI	53037	262-677-9046		234
Rythmos Inc 80 Yesler Way Ste 310 Web: rythmos.com	Seattle	WA	98104	206-257-2111		177
Rywant Alvarez Jones Russo & Guyton PA 407 Courthouse Sq TF: 888-378-4401 ■ Web: rywantalvarez.com	Inverness	FL	34450	352-341-4441		428
RZ & Company Inc 6602 Odana Rd Web: www.rzco.com	Madison	WI	53719	608-827-7979		77

S

Company	City	State	ZIP	Phone	Fax	Class
S & A Consulting Group LLP 2573 Butterwing Rd Web: www.sa-consultinggroup.com	Cleveland	OH	44124	216-593-0050	593-0053	2
S & A Homes 2121 Old Gatesburg Rd Ste 200 Web: www.sahomebuilder.com	State College	PA	16803	814-231-4780		653
S & A Supply Inc 20 Maple Ave TF: 800-348-6693 ■ Web: www.sasupplyinc.com	Great Barrington	MA	01230	413-528-3470	528-5062	364
S & B Engineers & Constructors Ltd 7825 Pk Pl Blvd Web: www.sbec.com	Houston	TX	77087	713-645-4141		261
S & B Industrial Minerals North America Inc 920 Cassatt Rd Ste 205 Web: www.industrialspecialtiesnews.com	Berwyn	PA	19312	610-647-1123		501
S & C Electric Co 6601 N Ridge Blvd TF: 800-621-5546 ■ Web: www.sandc.com	Chicago	IL	60626	773-338-1000		729
S & D Coffee Inc 300 Concord Pkwy S TF: 800-933-2210 ■ Web: sdcoffeetea.com	Concord	NC	28027	800-933-2210	950-4378	296-7
S & D Oyster Co 2701 McKinney Ave Web: sdoyster.com	Dallas	TX	75204	214-880-0111		671
S & G Manufacturing Group LLC 4830 Northwest Pkwy Web: www.sgmgroup.com	Hilliard	OH	43026	614-334-3600		427
S & H Consulting LLC 6056 K C Pl Web: www.stewartconsulting.net	Port Orchard	WA	98367	360-447-0141		194
S & H Engineering Inc 248 Mill Rd Web: www.s-and-h.com	Chelmsford	MA	01824	978-256-7231	250-8488	494
S & H Express Inc 400 Mulberry St TF: 800-637-9782 ■ Web: www.sandhexpress.com	York	PA	17403	717-848-5015	852-8722	449
S & J Transportation Services 251 Calef Hwy Web: sjtrans.com	Lee	NH	03861	603-659-3542		311
S & K Electronics Inc 56301 US Hwy 93 Web: www.skecorp.com	Ronan	MT	59864	406-883-6241	883-6228	253
S & L Intl 150 E Colorado Blvd Ste 203 Web: www.slinternational.com	Pasadena	CA	91105	626-405-0999		196
S & L Travel Partners Inc 210 Aspen Airport Business Ctr Ste AA Web: www.ski.com	Aspen	CO	81611	970-925-9500		772
S & M Machine Service Inc 109 E Highland Dr TF: 800-323-1579 ■ Web: www.snmmachine.com	Oconto Falls	WI	54154	920-846-8130	846-4803	455
S & M Moving Systems Inc 12128 Burke St TF: 800-528-4561 ■ Web: www.smmoving.com	Santa Fe Springs	CA	90670	562-567-2100		519
S & ME Inc 3201 Spring Forest Rd TF: 800-849-2517 ■ Web: www.smeinc.com	Raleigh	NC	27616	919-872-2660	876-3958	192
S & P Communications 6712 Randolph Blvd	Live Oak	TX	78233	210-656-5073		736
S & P Global Platts 2 Penn Plz 25th Fl TF: 800-752-8878 ■ Web: www.spglobal.com	New York	NY	10121	212-904-3070		637-9
S & P Tax Solutions Ltd 95 Revere Dr Ste A Web: www.sandptax.com	Northbrook	IL	60062	847-480-4400		2
S & P Whistlestop Inc 3216 Spangle St TF: 800-392-0160 ■ Web: www.spwhistlestop.com	Canandaigua	NY	14424	585-396-0160	396-9930	44
S & R Law Firm PLLC 4010 University Dr Ste 102 Web: novadefenders.com	Fairfax	VA	22030	703-273-6431	273-6487	41
S & R Truck Tire Center Inc 1402 Truckers Blvd TF: 800-488-2670 ■ Web: www.srtrucktire.com	Jeffersonville	IN	47130	812-282-4799		54
S & S Concrete & Materials LLC 3000 Pass Canyon Rd Web: www.snsconcrete.com	Bullhead City	AZ	86442	928-754-1999		190
S & S Cycle Inc 14025 County Hwy G Web: www.sscycle.com	Viola	WI	54664	608-627-1497		82
S & S Hvac Equipment LLC 18085 W Little York Web: sandshvacequipment.com	Katy	TX	77449	281-463-9999		290
S & S Industrial Equipment & Supply Company Inc 7 Chelten Way TF: 800-282-3506 ■ Web: www.sandsindustrial.com	Trenton	NJ	08638	609-695-3800		358
S & S Industries Inc 115 Clemmons Rd	Mount Juliet	TN	37122	615-754-8000	754-8011	389
S & S Industries of Mexico Inc 5 Odell Plz Web: www.sandsindustries.com	Yonkers	NY	10701	914-885-1500		813
S & S Management Services Inc 1 Regency Dr Web: www.ssmgt.com	Bloomfield	CT	06002	860-243-3977	286-0787	47
S & S Technology 10625 Telge Rd TF: 800-231-1747 ■ Web: www.ssxray.com	Houston	TX	77095	281-815-1300	815-1444	382
S & S Tire 1475 Jingle Bell Ln TF: 800-685-6794 ■ Web: www.sstire.com	Lexington	KY	40509	859-252-0151		54
S & S Transport Inc PO Box 12579 TF: 800-726-8022 ■ Web: www.sstransport.com	Grand Forks	ND	58208	800-726-8022		780
S & S Welding Inc 22131 68th Ave S Web: www.ssweld.com	Kent	WA	98032	253-872-3833		491
S & S Worldwide Inc 75 Mill St TF: 800-243-9232 ■ Web: www.ssww.com	Colchester	CT	06415	860-537-3451	537-2563	459
S & T Bancorp Inc 800 Philadelphia St NASDAQ: STBA ■ TF: 800-325-2265 ■ Web: www.stbank.com	Indiana	PA	15701	724-349-1800	465-6874	360-2
S & W Contracting Company Inc 952 New Salem Rd Web: www.sandwcontracting.com	Murfreesboro	TN	37129	615-893-2511		787
S & W Ready Mix Concrete Co 1300 Hwy 17 N Web: www.snwreadymix.com	New Bern	NC	28560	252-633-2115		190
S Abraham & Sons Inc (SAS) 4001 3 Mile Rd NW PO Box 1768 TF: 800-477-5455 ■ Web: www.sasinc.com	Grand Rapids	MI	49534	616-453-6358	453-9259	297-8
S and Y Industries Inc 606 Industrial Rd TF: 800-794-7671 ■ Web: www.sandyindustries.com	Winfield	KS	67156	800-794-7671		253
S B Foot Tanning Co 805 Bench St Web: www.sbfoot.com	Red Wing	MN	55066	651-388-4731		432
S Brewer Enterprises Inc 2151 Jamieson Ave Ste 1607	Alexandria	VA	22314	703-567-1284		667
S C & A Construction Inc 3411 Silverside Rd Shipley Bldg Ste 200 Web: scaconstructs.com	Wilmington	DE	19810	302-478-6030	478-3775	186
S D Associates PO Box 4565 TF: 800-786-8377 ■ Web: www.sdassociates.com	Hartford	CT	06147	860-278-3434		194
S Freedman & Sons Inc 3322 Pennsy Dr TF: 800-545-7277 ■ Web: www.sfreedman.com	Landover Hills	MD	20785	301-322-5000	772-7563	559
S Gordon Corp 87 Terrace Hall Ave Ste 2 Web: sgordoncorp.com	Burlington	MA	01803	781-222-0955		2
S Himmelstein & Co 2490 Pembroke Ave TF: 800-632-7873 ■ Web: www.himmelstein.com	Hoffman Estates	IL	60169	847-843-3300	843-8488	407
S Howes LLC 25 Howard St Web: www.showes.com	Silver Creek	NY	14136	716-934-2611		298
S I Metals N5820 Johnson Rd Web: www.simetals.com	Portage	WI	53901	608-742-9039		492
S I Systems Ltd 335 Eighth Ave SW Ste 1210 Web: www.sisystems.com	Calgary	AB	T2P1C9	403-450-5174		260
S Jet 1251 W Blee Rd Web: www.spectrajetinc.com	Springfield	OH	45502	937-323-5804	323-8168	13

	Phone	Fax	Class
S K C Communication Products Inc 8320 Hedge Ln Terr .... Shawnee Mission KS 66227 **Fax Area Code:* 800 ■ *TF:* 800-882-7779 ■ *Web:* www.skccom.com	913-422-4222	454-4752*	246
S L Nusbaum Insurance Agency Inc 500 W 21st St Ste 300 ....Norfolk VA 23517 *Web:* www.nusbauminsurance.com	757-622-4653	624-1573	390
S Lichtenberg & Company Inc 295 Fifth Ave............................... New York NY 10016 *Web:* www.lichtenberg.com	212-689-4510	689-4517	746
S Parker Hardware Manufacturing Corp PO Box 9882 ....Englewood NJ 07631 *TF:* 800-772-7537 ■ *Web:* www.sparker.com	201-569-1600	569-1082	350
S R C Corp PO Box 30676.................Salt Lake City UT 84130 *TF:* 800-888-4545 ■ *Web:* www.steveregan.com	801-268-4500		276
S R C Refrigeration 6620 19 Mile Rd......................Sterling Heights MI 48314 *TF:* 877-794-1870 ■ *Web:* www.srcrefrigeration.com	586-254-0610		610
S R Snodgrass AC 2009 Mackenzie Way Ste 340.........Cranberry Township PA 16066 *TF:* 800-580-7738 ■ *Web:* www.srsnodgrass.com	724-934-0344		2
S Rose Inc 1213 Prospect Ave E................Cleveland OH 44115	216-781-8200		321
S Systems Corp 5777 W Century Blvd Ste 520..............Los Angeles CA 90045 *Web:* www.s-sc.com	310-215-0248	642-3738	261
S T & P Communications Inc 320 Springside Dr Ste 150...................Fairlawn OH 44333 *Web:* stpinc.com	330-668-1932		224
S T Bunn Construction 1904 University Blvd ....Tuscaloosa AL 35401	205-752-8195	349-4288	780
S T Specialty Foods Inc 8700 Xylon Ave N...................... Brooklyn Park MN 55445 *Web:* www.stspecialtyfoods.com	763-493-9600		123
S V Microwave Inc 2400 Centre Pk W Dr ....West Palm Beach FL 33409 *Web:* www.svmicrowave.com	561-840-1800	842-6277	253
S W Cole Engineering Inc 37 Liberty Dr..........Bangor ME 04401 *Web:* www.swcole.com	207-848-5714	848-2403	256
S'more Entertainment 4335 Van Nuys Blvd Ste 313 ....Sherman Oaks CA 91403 *Web:* www.smoreent.com	818-905-7267		657
S. A. White Oil Company Inc 590 Atlanta St SE ....Marietta GA 30060 *Web:* sawhite.com	770-427-1387		579
S. D. Myers Inc 180 S Ave .... Tallmadge OH 44278 *Web:* www.sdmyers.com	330-630-7000	633-8081	743
S. H. Coleman Library *FAMU Libraries* 1500 S Martin Luther King Blvd........... Tallahassee FL 32307 *TF:* 800-540-6754 ■ *Web:* www.library.famu.edu	850-599-3370	561-2293	434-6
S. Harman & Associates Inc PO Box 1129 .... Sykesville MD 21784 *Web:* www.sharmansite.com	410-795-9296	549-1261	196
S. J. Smith Company Inc 3707 W River Dr.......................... Davenport IA 52802 *Web:* www.sjsmith.com	563-263-1829		385
S. M. Haw Associates Inc 2285 E Enterprise Pkwy .... Twinsburg OH 44087 *Web:* smhaw.com	330-405-4480	405-4484	261
S. R. Smith LLC 1017 Sw Berg Pky .... Canby OR 97013 *Web:* www.srsmith.com	800-824-4387		189-11
S. S. Papadopulos & Associates Inc 7944 Wisconsin Ave........................ Bethesda MD 20814 *Web:* www.sspa.com	301-718-8900		539
S.A.F.E. Management LLC Arizona 1 Cardinals Dr .... Glendale AZ 85305 *Web:* www.safemanagement.net	623-433-7300		184
S.C.I. Tronics Inc 4630 Churchill St Ste 2 .... Saint Paul MN 55126 *TF:* 800-698-1368 ■ *Web:* www.scitronics.com	651-415-9690	415-9691	392
S.D. Malkin Properties 35 Mason St .... Greenwich CT 06830 *Web:* sdmproperties.com	203-622-1800	622-3001	653
S.D.P. Manufacturing Inc 400 Industrial Dr........................... Dunkirk IN 47336 *Web:* www.sdpmfg.com	765-768-5000	768-5015	806
S.E. International Inc 436 Farm Rd.........Summertown TN 38483 *TF:* 800-293-5759 ■ *Web:* www.seintl.com	931-964-3561	964-3564	472
S.F. Advance Transportation Services Inc 100 Bridgepoint Way Ste 180........... South Saint Paul MN 55075 *TF:* 800-288-3339 ■ *Web:* sfadvance.com	651-451-2977	451-1810	311
S.H. Hirth & Associates Inc 36 W 44th St Ste 610....................... New York NY 10036 *Web:* hirthny.com	212-997-1187		195
S.J. Controls Inc 2248 Obispo Ave Ste 203................. Long Beach CA 90755 *Web:* www.sjcontrols.com	562-494-1400		201
S.J. Fuel Company Inc 601 Union St........... Brooklyn NY 11215 *Web:* sjfuelco.com	718-855-6060		316
S.K. Lavery Appliance Co 1003 Farmington Ave....................West Hartford CT 06107 *Web:* www.sklaveryappliance.com	860-523-5271	232-8950	38
S.M. Lawrence Co 245 Preston St ....Jackson TN 38301 *TF:* 800-627-0775 ■ *Web:* www.smlawrence.com	731-423-0112	423-0572	189-10
S.P. Richards Co 24 Wes Warren Dr.......... Middletown NY 10941 *TF:* 800-833-8658 ■ *Web:* www.sprichards.com	845-692-5534	692-2517	112
S.S. Mechanical Corp 17631 Metzler Ln .... Huntington Beach CA 92647 *Web:* www.ssmechanical.biz	714-847-1317		261
S.S. White Technologies Inc 151 Old New Brunswick Rd ....Piscataway NJ 08854 *Web:* www.sswhiteaerospace.com	732-474-1700	752-8315	620
S.USA Life Insurance Co PO Box 1050..........Newark NJ 07101 *TF:* 866-787-2123 ■ *Web:* www.prosperitylife.com	866-787-2123		796
S.X. Callahan Inc 824 S Laredo St...........San Antonio TX 78204 *Web:* www.sxcallahaninc.com	210-224-1641		61
S/L/A/M Collaborative 80 Glastonbury Blvd......................Glastonbury CT 06033 *Web:* www.slamcoll.com	860-657-8077	657-3141	261
S2L Inc 531 Versailles Dr Ste 202............... Maitland FL 32751 *Web:* www.s2li.com	407-475-9163	475-9169	804
S2Tech 720 Spirit 40 Park Dr ....Chesterfield MO 63005 *Web:* www.s2tech.com	636-530-9286		177
S2Verify LLC PO Box 2597.................... Roswell GA 30077 *Web:* www.s2verify.com	770-649-8282		260
S3 Ventures 6300 Bridgepoint Pkwy Bldg One Ste 405 .... Austin TX 78730 *Web:* www.s3vc.com	512-258-1759		792
S4 Inc 209 Burlington Rd Ste 105................ Bedford MA 01730 *Web:* www.s4inc.com	781-273-1600	276-3600	180
S4 NetQuest 580 N Fourth St Ste 600 .... Columbus OH 43215 *Web:* www.s4netquest.com	614-220-5700		463
S4i Systems Inc 616 S El Camino Real Ste M.............. San Clemente CA 92672 *TF:* 800-231-5280 ■ *Web:* www.s4isystems.com	949-366-5234	366-5338	178-1
S4Software Inc PO Box 3953 .... San Diego CA 92163 *Web:* www.s4software.com	619-574-5375		178-1
SA (Sexaholics Anonymous) PO Box 3565..... Brentwood TN 37024 *TF:* 866-424-8777 ■ *Web:* www.sa.org	615-370-6062	370-0882	48-21
SA (Salem Academy) 942 Lancaster Dr NE......... Salem OR 97301 *Web:* salemacademy.org	503-378-1219		622
Sa Bai Thong 6802 Odana Rd .... Madison WI 53719 *Web:* www.sabaithong.com	608-828-9565		671
SA Comunale Company Inc 2900 Newpark Dr ....Barberton OH 44203 **Fax Area Code:* 330 ■ *TF:* 800-776-7181 ■ *Web:* sacomunale.com	800-776-7181	861-0860*	189-13
SA Day Manufacturing Company Inc 1489 Niagara St ....Buffalo NY 14213 *TF:* 800-747-0030 ■ *Web:* www.saday.com	716-881-3030	881-4353	145
SA Intl 5296 S Commerce Dr Ste 102 ....Salt Lake City UT 84107 *TF:* 800-229-9066 ■ *Web:* thinksai.com	801-478-1900	401-7234	177
SA Recycling LLC 2411 N Glassell St.............Orange CA 92865 *Web:* www.sarecycling.com	714-637-4913	630-5836	686
SA Scientific Ltd 4919 Golden Quail ....San Antonio TX 78240 *TF:* 800-272-2710 ■ *Web:* www.sascientific.com	210-699-8800		231
SAA (Society of American Archivists) 17 N State St Ste 1425.......................Chicago IL 60602 *TF:* 866-722-7858 ■ *Web:* www2.archivists.org	312-606-0722	606-0728	48-4
SAA (Sex Addicts Anonymous) PO Box 70949....Houston TX 77270 *TF:* 800-477-8191 ■ *Web:* saa-recovery.org	713-869-4902	692-0105	48-21
SAA (Society for American Archaeology) 900 Second St NE Ste 12..................Washington DC 20002 *Web:* www.saa.org	202-789-8200	789-0284	49-5
Saab Barracuda LLC 608 E Mcneill St...........................Lillington NC 27546 *Web:* saabgroup.com	910-893-2094		21
Saad Enterprises Inc 1515 S University Blvd........................Mobile AL 36609 *Web:* www.saadhealthcare.com	251-343-9600		475
Saalfeld Griggs PC 250 Church St SE .... Salem OR 97301 *Web:* www.sglaw.com	503-399-1070		428
Saanich Peninsula Chamber of Commerce 10382 Pat Bay Hwy.................... North Saanich BC V8L5S8 *Web:* www.peninsulachamber.ca	250-656-3616	656-7111	137
Saar's Inc 32199 SR-20.................... Oak Harbor WA 98277 *Web:* www.saarsmarketplacefoods.com	360-675-3000		237
Saatchi & Saatchi 375 Hudson St.............New York NY 10014 *Web:* saatchiny.com	212-463-2000	463-2367	4
Saba Software Inc 2400 Bridge Pkwy...................... Redwood City CA 94065 *TSX:* SABA ■ *TF:* 877-722-2101 ■ *Web:* www.saba.com	650-581-2500	696-1773	178-3
Sababa 3311 Connecticut Ave NW ....Washington DC 20008 *Web:* www.sababauptown.com	202-244-6750		671
Sabak, Wilson & Lingo Inc 608 S Third St ....Louisville KY 40202 *Web:* swlinc.com	502-584-6271		261
Sabates Eye Centers *UMKC Department of Ophthalmology/Eye Foundation of Kansas City* 2101 Charlotte St...................... Kansas City MO 64108 *TF:* 800-742-0020 ■ *Web:* sabateseye.com	816-404-1780		303
Sabatini & Associates Ltd 5255 Longley Ln Ste 101 .... Reno NV 89511 *Web:* sabatiniltd.com	775-324-2066		734
Sabatino's 901 Fawn St......................Baltimore MD 21202 *Web:* www.sabatinos.com	410-727-9414	837-6540	671
Sabel Steel Industries Inc 749 N Ct St............................ Montgomery AL 36104 *Web:* www.sabelsteel.com	334-265-6771	264-3692	492
Saber Power Services LLC 3309 Texas St..............................Houston TX 77003 *TF:* 877-912-9102 ■ *Web:* www.saberpower.com	713-222-9102	236-8386	189-4
Sabert Corp 2288 Main St Ext ....Sayreville NJ 08872 **Fax Area Code:* 732 ■ *TF:* 800-722-3781 ■ *Web:* www.sabert.com	800-722-3781	721-0622*	548
Sabertooth Technology Group LLC 5944 Coral Ridge Dr Ste 389 .... Coral Springs FL 33076 *Web:* sabertoothweb.com	954-635-5545		196
Sabey Corp 12201 Tukwila International Blvd 4th Fl .... Seattle WA 98168 *Web:* www.sabey.com	206-281-8700	282-9951	655
SABIA Inc 10911 Technology Pl............... San Diego CA 92127 *Web:* sabiainc.com	858-217-2200		501
Sabian Ltd 219 Main St .... Meductic NB E6H2L5 *TF:* 800-817-2242 ■ *Web:* www.sabian.com	506-272-2019	272-2040	527
Sabina Motors & Controls Inc 1440 N Burton Pl .... Anaheim CA 92806 *Web:* www.sabinadrives.com	714-956-0480	956-0486	201
Sabinas Food Products Inc 1509 W 18th St.............................Chicago IL 60608 *Web:* sabinasfoods.com	312-738-2412	738-0042	296-37
Sabine County *Chamber of Commerce* 1555 Worth St PO Box 717 .... Hemphill TX 75948 *TF:* 800-986-5336 ■ *Web:* www.co.sabine.tx.us	409-787-2732	787-2158	338
Sabine County Reporter 610 Worth St .... Hemphill TX 75948 *Web:* www.sabinecountyreporter.com	409-787-2172		532-2
Sabine Parish 400 S Capital Rm 102 .... Many LA 71449 *Web:* www.sabineparishclerk.com	318-256-6223		338

				Phone	Fax	Class
Sabine River Authority of Texas 1922 Owens Illinois Rd	Orange	TX	77632	409-746-2192		202
Sabine Universal Products Inc PO Box 295 *Web:* supus.com	Port Arthur	TX	77640	409-982-9446		770
Sabinsa Corp 20 Lake Dr *Web:* www.sabinsa.com	East Windsor	NJ	08520	732-777-1111	777-1443	479
Sabio Information Technologies Inc 7715 NW 48th St Ste 350 *Web:* www.sabioit.com	Doral	FL	33166	305-676-7884		196
Sablan Gregorio (Rep D - MP) 2411 Rayburn House Office Bldg *TF:* 877-446-3465 ■ *Web:* www.sablan.house.gov	Washington	DC	20515	202-225-2646	226-4249	342-2
Sable Networks Inc 3171 Jay St	Santa Clara	CA	95054	408-727-5514		225
Sable Systems Intl 3840 N Commerce St **Fax Area Code:* 702 ■ *TF:* 866-217-6760 ■ *Web:* sablesys.com	North Las Vegas	NV	89032	800-330-0465	269-4445*	201
Sabol and Rice Inc 1834 S 900 W *Web:* www.sabolandrice.com	Salt Lake City	UT	84104	801-973-2300	972-5033	189-10
Sabor Latino Restaurant 112 Green Springs Hwy *Web:* www.misaborlatino.webs.com	Homewood	AL	35209	205-942-9480	942-9428	671
Sabra Dipping Company LLC 2420 49th St *TF:* 888-957-2272 ■ *Web:* sabra.com	Astoria	NY	11103	888-957-2272		296-37
Sabre Companies LLC, The 1891 New Scotland Rd *TF:* 800-349-2799 ■ *Web:* www.thesabrecompanies.com	Slingerlands	NY	12159	518-514-1572		192
Sabre Corp PO Box 134 *Web:* www.sabreyachts.com	South Casco	ME	04077	207-655-3831	655-5050	90
Sabre Holdings Corp 3150 Sabre Dr *Web:* www.sabre.com	Southlake	TX	76092	682-605-1000		360-3
Sabre Industries Inc 8653 E Hwy 67 *TF:* 866-254-3707 ■ *Web:* www.sabreindustriesinc.com	Alvarado	TX	76009	817-852-1700	852-1703	261
Sabre Solution, The 200 E 31st St *TF:* 888-494-7200 ■ *Web:* thesabresolution.com	Savannah	GA	31401	912-355-7200		180
Sabre Strategic Partners 5025 Orbitor Dr Bldg 3 Ste 300 *TF:* 800-314-3346 ■ *Web:* sabrelife.com	Mississauga	ON	L4W4Y5	905-206-0900	206-1600	301-2
Sabre Towers and Poles 7101 Southbridge Dr *TF:* 800-369-6690 ■ *Web:* www.sabreindustries.com	Sioux City	IA	51111	712-258-6690	279-0814	245
Sabreliner Corp 1390 Hwy H *Web:* www.sabrelineraviation.com	Perryville	MO	63775	573-543-2212		20
Sabretech Consulting LLC 154 Lewis St *Web:* sabretechllc.com	Hillsdale	MI	49242	517-437-7150		196
Sabrient Systems LLC 115 S La Cumbre Ln Ste 100 *Web:* www.sabrient.com	Santa Barbara	CA	93105	805-730-7777		668
SAC (Smith Affiliated Capital) 800 Third Ave 12th Fl *TF:* 888-387-3298 ■ *Web:* www.smithcapital.com	New York	NY	10022	212-644-9440	644-1979	403
SAC & Fox Casino Inc 1322 US Hwy 75 *TF:* 800-990-2946 ■ *Web:* www.sacandfoxcasino.com	Powhattan	KS	66527	800-990-2946		133
SAC County 100 NW State St *Web:* www.saccounty.org	Sac City	IA	50583	712-662-4492	662-7358	338
SAC Osage Electric Co-opeartive Inc 4815 E Hwy 54 PO Box 111 *TF:* 800-876-2701 ■ *Web:* www.sacosage.com	El Dorado Springs	MO	64744	417-876-2721	876-5368	245
SACA Technologies LLC 5101 E La Palma Ave Ste 200 *TF:* 888-603-9033 ■ *Web:* www.sacatech.com	Anaheim Hills	CA	92807	714-777-3222		78
Sacajawea Hotel 5 N Main *Web:* www.sacajaweahotel.com	Three Forks	MT	59752	406-285-6515	285-4210	379
Sacajawea State Park 2503 Sacajawea Park Rd *Web:* www.parks.state.wa.us	Pasco	WA	99301	509-545-2361		565
SACAM (Sousa Archives & Center for American Music) 1103 S Sixth St Harding Band Bldg *Web:* archives.library.illinois.edu	Champaign	IL	61820	217-333-2290	244-8695	520
SACAMA (Shemer Arts Center & Museum Association Inc) 5005 E Camelback Rd *Web:* shemerartcenter.org	Phoenix	AZ	85018	602-262-4727		520
SACC (Swedish-American Chamber of Commerce Georgia) 715 Peachtree St N E Ste 100 & 200 *Web:* www.sacc-georgia.org	Atlanta	GA	30308	470-378-1180		138
Saccani Distributing Co 2600 5th St PO Box 1764 *Web:* www.saccanidist.com	Sacramento	CA	95818	916-441-0213	441-0806	81-1
Saccucci Honda 1350 W Main Rd *TF:* 866-730-7656 ■ *Web:* www.saccuccihonda.com	Middletown	RI	02842	866-730-7656		57
Sachem Central School District 51 School Str *Web:* www.sachem.edu	Lake Ronkonkoma	NY	11779	631-471-1300	471-8976	685
Sachem Inc 821 E Woodward St *Web:* www.sacheminc.com	Austin	TX	78704	512-421-4900	445-5066	144
Sachse Real Estate Company Inc 315 S Beverly Dr Ste 415 *Web:* www.sachsere.com	Beverly Hills	CA	90212	310-284-7100		652
Sackett & Assoc 1055 Lincoln Ave *TF:* 800-913-3000 ■ *Web:* www.sackettlaw.com	San Jose	CA	95125	408-295-7755		428
Sackett Ranch Inc 2939 Neff Rd NE	Stanton	MI	48888	989-762-5049		10-11
Sackrider & Company Inc 1925 Wabash Ave *Web:* www.sackrider.com	Terre Haute	IN	47807	812-232-9492		2
Sacks Tierney PA 4250 N Drinkwater Blvd 4th Fl *Web:* www.sackstierney.com	Scottsdale	AZ	85251	480-425-2600		428
Sacks, Press & Lacher PC 600 Third Ave 18th Fl *Web:* spl-cpa.com	New York	NY	10016	212-682-6640		2
Sac-N-Pac Stores Inc 1405 United Dr *Web:* www.sacnpac.com	San Marcos	TX	78666	512-392-6484		297-8
Saco Industries Inc 17151 Morse St *Web:* www.sacoindustries.com	Lowell	IN	46356	219-696-2800		115
SACOG (Sacramento Area Council of Governments) 1415 L St Ste 300 *Web:* www.sacog.org	Sacramento	CA	95814	916-321-9000		48-6
Sacor Financial Inc 1911 Douglas Blvd 85-126 *TF:* 866-556-0231 ■ *Web:* www.sacor.net	Roseville	CA	95661	866-556-0231		393
Sacramento Area Council of Governments (SACOG) 1415 L St Ste 300 *Web:* www.sacog.org	Sacramento	CA	95814	916-321-9000		48-6
Sacramento Bag Manufacturing Co 440 N Pioneer Ave Ste 300 *TF:* 800-287-2247 ■ *Web:* www.sacbag.com	Woodland	CA	95776	530-662-6130	662-6381	67
Sacramento Ballet 1631 K St *Web:* www.sacballet.org	Sacramento	CA	95814	916-552-5800	552-5815	573-1
Sacramento Bee PO Box 15779 **Fax Area Code:* 916 ■ *TF:* 800-284-3233 ■ *Web:* www.sacbee.com	Sacramento	CA	95852	800-222-7463	321-1109*	532-2
Sacramento City College 3835 Freeport Blvd *TF:* 800-700-4144 ■ *Web:* www.scc.losrios.edu	Sacramento	CA	95822	916-558-2351	558-2190	162
Sacramento City Unified School District 5735 47th Ave *Web:* www.scusd.edu	Sacramento	CA	95824	916-643-7400		685
Sacramento Computer Power Inc 829 W Stadium Ln *TF:* 800-441-1412 ■ *Web:* www.sacpower.com	Sacramento	CA	95834	800-441-1412		518
Sacramento Container Corp 4841 Urbani Ave *Web:* www.saccontainer.biz	Mcclellan	CA	95652	916-614-0580		100
Sacramento Convention & Visitors Bureau 1608 'I' St *TF:* 800-292-2334 ■ *Web:* www.visitsacramento.com	Sacramento	CA	95814	916-808-7777	808-7788	206
Sacramento County Public Law Library (SCPLL) 609 9th St *Web:* www.saclaw.org	Sacramento	CA	95814	916-874-6012	244-0699	434-3
Sacramento Credit Union 800 H St *Web:* sactocu.org	Sacramento	CA	95814	916-444-6070		219
Sacramento Employment & Training Agency 925 Del Paso Blvd *Web:* www.seta.net	Sacramento	CA	95815	916-263-3000		721
Sacramento History Museum 101 'I' St *Web:* www.historicoldsac.org	Sacramento	CA	95814	916-808-7059		521
Sacramento International Airport System 6900 Airport Blvd *Web:* sacramento.aero	Sacramento	CA	95837	916-929-5411		27
Sacramento Metro Chamber of Commerce 1 Capital Mall Ste 300 *Web:* metrochamber.org	Sacramento	CA	95814	916-552-6800	443-2672	139
Sacramento Natural Foods Cooperative Inc 2820 R St *Web:* sacfood.coop	Sacramento	CA	95816	916-455-2667		345
Sacramento Public Library 828 'I' St *TF:* 800-561-4636 ■ *Web:* www.saclibrary.org	Sacramento	CA	95814	916-264-2700		434-3
Sacramento Regional Transit District 1400 29th St *Web:* www.sacrt.com	Sacramento	CA	95812	916-321-2877	444-2156	468
Sacramento School of Bartending 1447 Fulton Ave *Web:* www.sacramentobartendingschool.com	Sacramento	CA	95825	916-995-6518		685
Sacramento Stucco Co 1550 Parkway Blvd *Web:* www.westernblended.com	West Sacramento	CA	95691	916-372-7442	372-4836	500
Sacramento Theatre Co 1419 H St *Web:* www.sactheatre.org	Sacramento	CA	95814	916-443-6722	446-4066	573-4
Sacramento Zoo 3930 W Land Pk Dr *Web:* www.saczoo.org	Sacramento	CA	95822	916-808-5888		823
Sacred Currents 11 E 88th St *Web:* www.sacredcurrents.com	New York	NY	10128	212-410-1832		194
Sacred Heart HealthCare System 421 Chew St *Web:* www.shh.org	Allentown	PA	18102	610-776-4500		374-3
Sacred Heart Home 359 Summer St *Web:* www.dhfo.org	New Bedford	MA	02740	508-996-6751	996-5189	450
Sacred Heart Hospital 900 W Clairemont Ave *TF:* 888-445-4554 ■ *Web:* www.sacredhearteauclaire.org	Eau Claire	WI	54701	715-717-4121		374-3
Sacred Heart Monastery 8969 Hwy 10 *Web:* www.sacredheartmonastery.com	Richardton	ND	58652	701-974-2121	974-2124	48-20
Sacred Heart Seminary and School of Theology 7335 S Hwy 100 *Web:* shsst.edu	Franklin	WI	53132	414-425-8300	529-6999	167-3
Sacred Heart University 5151 Park Ave *Web:* www.sacredheart.edu	Fairfield	CT	06825	203-371-7999	365-7609	166
Sacred Heart University Edgerton Center for Performing Arts 5151 Park Ave *Web:* www.edgertoncenter.org	Fairfield	CT	06825	203-371-7908	365-4858	572
Sadat Associates Inc 1545 Lamberton Rd *Web:* www.sadat.com	Trenton	NJ	08611	609-826-9600		261
Sadco Inc 4552 Baldwin Ave *Web:* www.sadco-furniture.com	Montgomery	AL	36108	334-288-5103		38
SADD (Students Against Destructive Decisions) 255 Main St *Web:* www.sadd.org	Marlborough	MA	01752	508-481-3568	481-5759	48-6
Saddle Butte Pipeline LLC 858 Main Ave Ste 301 *Web:* www.sbpipeline.com	Durango	CO	81301	970-375-3150		539
Saddle Creek Corp 3010 Saddle Creek Rd *Web:* www.sclogistics.com	Lakeland	FL	33801	863-665-0966		449
Saddleback College 28000 Marguerite Pkwy *Web:* www.saddleback.edu	Mission Viejo	CA	92692	949-582-4500		162
Saddleback Educational Publishing 151 Kalmus Dr J-1 *TF:* 888-735-2225 ■ *Web:* sdlback.com	Costa Mesa	CA	92626	714-640-5200		96

Phone | Fax | Class

Sadie's 6230 Fourth St NW Albuquerque NM 87107 505-345-5339 671
Web: sadiessalsa.com

Sadler Consulting
409 Congress Ave Pacific Grove CA 93950 831-333-1337 196
Web: www.sadlerconsulting.net

Sadler Strategic Media Inc
12103 Viewcrest Rd Studio City CA 91604 818-506-5443 506-8444 194
Web: www.sadlerstrategic.com

Sadler's Smokehouse Ltd
1206 N Frisco PO Box 1088 Henderson TX 75653 903-655-7246 296-26
Web: www.sadlerssmokehouse.com

Sadlers Creek State Park
940 Sadlers Creek Rd Anderson SC 29626 864-226-8950 565
Web: southcarolinaparks.com

Sadoff & Rudoy Industries LLP
240 W Arndt St Fond du Lac WI 54936 920-921-2070 921-1283 686
TF: 877-972-3633 ■ *Web:* sadoff.com

SAE (Sigma Alpha Epsilon Fraternity)
1856 Sheridan Rd Evanston IL 60201 847-424-3031 475-2250 48-16
TF: 800-233-1856 ■ *Web:* www.sae.net

SAE (Society of Automotive Engineers Inc)
400 Commonwealth Dr Warrendale PA 15096 724-776-4841 776-0790 49-21
TF: 877-606-7323 ■ *Web:* www.sae.org

SAE Power Inc 130 Knowles Dr Los Gatos CA 95032 408-369-2200 369-4911 253
Web: www.saepower.com

Saebo Inc
2709 Water Ridge Pkwy
Ste 100 Six Lake Pointe Plz Charlotte NC 28217 888-284-5433 414-0037* 475
**Fax Area Code:* 855 ■ *TF:* 888-284-5433 ■ *Web:* www.saebo.com

SAEC (South Alabama Electric Co-op)
PO Box 449 Troy AL 36081 334-566-2060 566-8949 245
TF: 800-556-2060 ■ *Web:* www.southaec.com

Saelens Corp
100 Veterans Dr PO Box 499 Johnson Creek WI 53038 920-699-8800 699-8801 350
Web: www.diamondprecision.com

SAEM (Society for Academic Emergency Medicine)
1111 E Touhy Ave Ste 540 Des Plaines IL 60018 847-813-9823 813-5450 49-8
Web: www.saem.org

Saenger Theatre 22 E Intendencia St Pensacola FL 32502 850-595-3880 595-3886 572
Web: www.pensacolasaenger.com

Saenger Theatre 6 S Joachim St Mobile AL 36602 251-208-5600 572
Web: www.mobilesaenger.com

SAES Getters USA Inc
1122 E Cheyenne Mountain Blvd Colorado Springs CO 80906 719-576-3200 576-5025 386
TF: 855-265-6958 ■ *Web:* www.saesgetters.com

SAF (Santa Fe Municipal Airport)
121 Aviation Dr Santa Fe NM 87504 505-955-2900 955-2905 27
Web: www.santafenm.gov

SAF (Society of American Florists)
1601 Duke St Alexandria VA 22314 703-836-8700 836-8705 49-4
TF: 800-336-4743 ■ *Web:* safnow.org

SAF (Society of American Foresters)
10100 Laureate Way Bethesda MD 20814 301-897-8720 897-3690 48-2
TF: 866-897-8720 ■ *Web:* www.eforester.org

Safari Books Online LLC
1005 Gravenstein Hwy N Sebastopol CA 95472 707-827-4100 95
Web: my.safaribooksonline.com

Safari Circuits Inc 411 Washington St Otsego MI 49078 269-694-9471 692-2651 176
TF: 888-694-7230 ■ *Web:* www.safaricircuits.com

Safari Micro Inc 2185 W Pecos Rd Chandler AZ 85224 888-446-4770 196
TF: 888-446-4770 ■ *Web:* www.safarimicro.com

Safari Press Inc
15621 Chemical Ln Ste B Huntington Beach CA 92649 714-894-9080 894-4949 96
Web: www.safaripress.com

Safari West Wildlife Preserve & Tent Camp
3115 Porter Creek Rd Santa Rosa CA 95404 707-579-2551 579-8777 823
TF: 800-616-2695 ■ *Web:* www.safariwest.com

Safariland LLC
13386 International Pkwy Jacksonville FL 32218 904-741-5400 576
TF: 800-347-1200 ■ *Web:* www.safariland.com

Safas Corp 2 Ackerman Ave Clifton NJ 07011 973-772-5252 601
TF: 800-472-6854 ■ *Web:* www.safascorp.com

Safco Products Co
9300 West Research Center Rd New Hope MN 55428 888-971-6225 319-1
TF: 800-328-3020 ■ *Web:* www.safcoproducts.com

SAFE (Secure America's Future Economy)
214 N Spring Valley Rd Wilmington DE 19807 302-478-0676 48-7
Web: www.s-a-f-e.org

Safe & Civil Schools
2451 Willamette St Eugene OR 97405 541-345-1442 242
TF: 800-323-8819 ■ *Web:* www.safeandcivilschools.com

Safe 1 Credit Union
1400 Mill Rock Way Bakersfield CA 93303 661-327-3818 219
Web: www.safe1.org

Safe Auto Insurance Co
4 Easton Oval PO Box 182109 Columbus OH 43219 614-231-0200 391-4
TF: 800-723-3288 ■ *Web:* www.safeauto.com

Safe Credit Union
3720 Madison Ave North Highlands CA 95660 916-979-7233 219
TF: 800-733-7233 ■ *Web:* www.safecu.org

Safe Credit Union Convention Ctr
1515 J St Sacramento CA 95814 916-808-5291 205
Web: safecreditunionconventioncenter.com

Safe Federal Credit Union
201 N 12th St West Columbia SC 29169 800-763-8600 219
TF: 800-763-8600 ■ *Web:* www.safefed.org

Safe Flight Instrument Corp
20 New King St White Plains NY 10604 914-946-9500 946-7882 529
Web: www.safeflight.com

Safe Harbor Access Systems LLC
211 N Koppers Rd Florence SC 29506 843-679-6888 480
Web: www.safe-harbor.com

Safe Harbor Title Agency Ltd
1529 Main St Port Jefferson NY 11777 631-473-0800 473-7685 653
Web: safeharbor-title.com

Safe Harbor Water Power Corp
1 Powerhouse Rd Conestoga PA 17516 717-872-5441 787
Web: www.shwpc.com

Safe Harbour Group Ltd 91 S Main St New City NY 10956 845-634-6787 634-0022 390
Web: safeharbourgroup.com

Safe Home Security Inc
1125 Middle St Ste 201 Middletown CT 06457 800-833-3211 693
TF: 800-833-3211 ■ *Web:* www.safehomesecurityinc.com

Safe House 779 N Front St Milwaukee WI 53202 414-271-2007 671
Web: www.safe-house.com

Safe Kids Worldwide
1301 Pennsylvania Ave NW Ste 1000 Washington DC 20004 202-662-0600 393-2072 48-6
Web: www.safekids.org

Safe Passage International Inc
333 Metro Pk Rochester NY 14623 585-292-4910 177
Web: www.safe-passage.com

Safe Reflections Inc
3220 N Granada Ave Ste 100 Saint Paul MN 55128 651-773-8199 770-0273 745-3
TF: 800-773-8199 ■ *Web:* www.safereflections.com

Safe Security PO Box 3888 Ste A Silverdale WA 98383 360-698-9800 693
Web: safesecurity.us

Safe Systems Inc
11395 Old Roswell Rd Alpharetta GA 30009 770-752-0550 225
Web: www.safesystems.com

Safeamerica Credit Union
6001 Gibraltar Dr Pleasanton CA 94588 925-734-4111 219
TF: 800-972-0999 ■ *Web:* www.safeamerica.com

Safeco Insurance Company of America
1001 Fourth Ave Seattle WA 98154 206-545-5000 391-4
Web: www.safeco.com

Safeguard Business Systems Inc
8585 N Stemmons Fwy Ste 600 N Dallas TX 75247 855-778-3124 439-3423* 142
**Fax Area Code:* 800 ■ *TF:* 800-523-2422 ■ *Web:* www.gosafeguard.com

Safeguard Chemical Corp 411 Wales Ave Bronx NY 10454 718-585-3170 585-3657 280
TF: 800-536-3170 ■ *Web:* www.safeguardchemical.com

Safeguard Products Inc
2710 Division Hwy New Holland PA 17557 717-354-4586 237
TF: 800-433-1819 ■ *Web:* www.safeguardproducts.com

Safeguard Properties Inc
7887 Safeguard Cir Valley View OH 44125 800-852-8306 509
TF: 800-852-8306 ■ *Web:* www.safeguardproperties.com

Safeguard Scientifics Inc
170 N Radnor-Chester Rd Ste 200 Radnor PA 19087 610-293-0600 792
NYSE: SFE ■ *Web:* www.safeguard.com

Safeguards Technology LLC
75 Atlantic St Hackensack NJ 07601 201-488-1022 692
Web: www.safeguards.com

Safelite Group Inc 2400 Farmers Dr Columbus OH 43235 877-664-8931 62-2
TF: 877-664-8931 ■ *Web:* www.safelite.com

Safemark Systems LP
2101 Park Center Dr Ste 125 Orlando FL 32835 407-299-0044 350
Web: www.safemark.com

SafeNet Consulting Inc
5810 Baker Rd Minnetonka MN 55345 952-930-3636 177
Web: safenetconsulting.com

Safer Foundation 571 W Jackson Blvd Chicago IL 60661 312-922-2200 922-0839 48-6
Web: www.saferfoundation.org

Safer Systems LLC
4165 E Thousand Oaks Blvd Ste 145 Camarillo CA 91362 805-383-9711 177

Saferack Manufactoring 219 Safety Ave Andrews SC 29510 843-264-8096 697
Web: www.saferack.com

Safetec of America Inc
887 Kensington Ave Buffalo NY 14215 716-895-1822 895-2969 151
TF: 800-456-7077 ■ *Web:* safetec.com

Safe-T-Gard Corp
4975 Miller St Unit B Wheat Ridge CO 80033 303-763-8900 763-8071 576
TF: 800-356-9026 ■ *Web:* safetgard.myshopify.com

Safety & Ecology Corp (SEC)
2800 Solway Rd SEC Business Ctr Knoxville TN 37931 865-690-0501 539-9868 667
Web: www.sec-tn.com

Safety Advantage LLC
15201 E Fwy Ste 102 Channelview TX 77530 713-977-5690 977-5693 194
TF: 800-960-1239 ■ *Web:* www.safetyadvantage.com

Safety Analysis & Forensic Engineering
5665 Hollister Ave Goleta CA 93117 805-964-0676 964-7669 668
TF: 800-426-7866 ■ *Web:* www.saferesearch.com

Safety Center Inc 3909 Bradshaw Rd Sacramento CA 95827 916-366-7233 196
Web: safetycenter.org

Safety Components International Inc
40 Emery St Greenville SC 29605 864-240-2600 678
TF: 800-896-6926 ■ *Web:* www.safetycomponents.com

Safety Council of The Ozarks
LIII S Glenstone Ste 101 Springfield MO 65804 417-869-2121 48-21

Safety First Systems LLC 65 Rt 4 E River Edge NJ 07661 201-267-8900 41
Web: www.safetyfirst.com

Safety Harbor Resort & Spa
105 N Bayshore Dr Safety Harbor FL 34695 888-237-8772 669
TF: 888-237-8772 ■ *Web:* www.safetyharborspa.com

Safety Insurance Group Inc
20 Custom House St Boston MA 02110 617-951-0600 391-4
NASDAQ: SAFT ■ *TF:* 800-951-2100 ■ *Web:* www.safetyinsurance.com

Safety Management Systems Inc
2916 N University Ave LaFayette LA 70507 337-521-3400 41
TF: 800-252-5522 ■ *Web:* safetyms.com

Safety Products Inc
3517 Craftsman Blvd Lakeland FL 33803 863-665-3601 330-0395* 679
**Fax Area Code:* 800 ■ *TF:* 800-248-6860 ■ *Web:* www.spisafety.com

Safety Seal Piston Ring Co
4000 Airport Rd Marshall TX 75672 903-938-9241 938-9317 128
TF: 800-962-3631 ■ *Web:* www.sswesco.com

Safety Service Systems Inc
4036 N Nashville Ave Chicago IL 60634 773-282-4900 693
Web: safetyservicesystemsinc.com

Safety Services Co 2626 S Roosevelt St Tempe AZ 85282 877-754-9578 765
TF: 877-894-2566 ■ *Web:* www.safetyservicescompany.com

Safety Shoe Distributors of Oki
10156 Reading Rd Cincinnati OH 45241 513-563-4220 301
Web: www.safetyshoedistributors.com

Safety Speed Cut Manufacturing Company Inc
13943 Lincoln St NE Ham Lake MN 55304 763-755-1600 755-6080 821
TF: 800-772-2327 ■ *Web:* www.safetyspeed.com

	Phone	Fax	Class
Safety Technology International Inc 2306 Airport Rd . . . . . Waterford MI 48327 *TF:* 800-888-4784 ■ *Web:* www.sti-usa.com	248-673-9898		608
Safety Today I 3287 SW Blvd . . . . . Grove City OH 43123 **Fax Area Code:* 614 ■ *TF:* 800-837-5900 ■ *Web:* www.safetytoday.com	800-837-5900	409-7201*	358
Safety Training Seminars 598 Vermont St. . . . . San Francisco CA 94107 *TF:* 800-470-9026 ■ *Web:* m.safetytrainingseminars.com	415-437-1600		138
Safety-Kleen Corp 2600 N Central Expwy Ste 400 . . . . . Richardson TX 75080 *TF:* 800-669-5740 ■ *Web:* www.safety-kleen.com	972-265-2000		667
Safetywear PO Box 11283 . . . . . Fort Wayne IN 46857 *TF:* 800-853-3119 ■ *Web:* www.safety-wear.com	260-456-3630		45
Safeware Inc 4403 Forbes Blvd Lanham MD 20706 . . . . . Landover Hills MD 20785 *TF:* 800-331-6707 ■ *Web:* www.safewareinc.com	301-683-1234	683-1200	679
Safe-Way Bus Co 6030 Carmen Ave . . . . . Inver Grove Heights MN 55076 *Web:* www.safewaybus.com	651-451-1375	451-3525	109
Safeway Inc 5918 Stoneridge Mall Rd . . . . . Pleasanton CA 94588 *NYSE: SWY* ■ *Web:* www.safeway.com	925-467-3000	467-3323	345
Safeway Industrial Services LLC 308 E Air Depot Rd . . . . . Glencoe AL 35905 *Web:* www.safewayind.com	256-492-3704		196
Safeway Insurance Group 790 Pasquinelli Dr PO Box 291 . . . . . Westmont IL 60559 *TF:* 800-273-0300 ■ *Web:* www.safewayinsurance.com	630-887-8300		391-4
Safeway Sign Co 9875 Yucca Rd . . . . . Adelanto CA 92301 **Fax Area Code:* 760 ■ *TF:* 800-637-7233 ■ *Web:* www.safewaysign.com	800-637-7233	246-5512*	701
Safford City - Graham County Library 808 Seventh Ave. . . . . Safford AZ 85546 *Web:* www.cityofsafford.us	928-348-3202	348-3209	434-3
Safford Unified School District 1 734 W 11th St. . . . . Safford AZ 85546 *Web:* www.saffordusd.com	928-348-7000		685
Saffron Patch 20600 Chagrin Blvd Twr E Bldg . . . . . Shaker Heights OH 44122 *Web:* www.thesaffronpatch.com	216-295-0400		671
SAF-Holland USA 1950 Industrial Blvd . . . . . Muskegon MI 49442 *Web:* corporate.safholland.com	231-773-3271		60
Safra National Bank of New York 546 Fifth Ave. . . . . New York NY 10036 *Web:* www.safra.com	212-704-5500	704-9397	70
Safran Cabin 7330 Lincoln Way . . . . . Garden Grove CA 92841 *Web:* zodiacaerospace.com	714-891-1906		22
Safran USA Inc 2300 Clarendon Blvd Ste 607 . . . . . Arlington VA 22201 *Web:* www.safran-usa.com	703-351-9898		815
Safstrom & Company PS 1325 Fourth Ave Ste 1530 . . . . . Seattle WA 98101 *Web:* safstrom.com	206-622-6456	622-6461	734
Saft America Inc 313 Crescent St NE . . . . . Valdese NC 28690 *Web:* www.saftbatteries.com	828-874-4111		74
Saf-T Auto Centers 121 N Plains Industrial Rd . . . . . Wallingford CT 06492 *Web:* www.saftauto.com	203-599-4875		62-7
Saf-T-Co Supply 1300 E Normandy Pl. . . . . Santa Ana CA 92705 *Web:* saftco.com	714-547-9975		191-1
Saf-T-Gard International Inc 205 Huehl Rd . . . . . Northbrook IL 60062 *TF:* 800-548-4273 ■ *Web:* www.saftgard.com	847-291-1600	291-1610	679
SAG (Strategic Advisory Group Inc) PO Box 773 . . . . . Sag Harbor NY 11963 *Web:* www.strategicadvisorygroup.com	631-725-7746	725-7739	194
Sag Harbor Industries Inc 1668 Sag Harbor Tpke . . . . . Sag Harbor NY 11963 *TF:* 800-724-5952 ■ *Web:* www.sagharborind.com	631-725-0440	725-4234	518
Saga Communications Inc 73 Kercheval Ave . . . . . Grosse Pointe Farms MI 48236 *NYSE: SGA* ■ *Web:* sagacom.com	313-886-7070	886-7150	643
Saga Musical Instruments Inc 137 Utah Ave . . . . . South San Francisco CA 94080 *Web:* www.sagamusic.com	650-588-5558		526
Sagadahoc County 752 High St . . . . . Bath ME 04530 *Web:* www.sagcounty.com	207-443-8200	443-8213	338
Sagamore Health Network 11595 N Meridian St Ste 600 . . . . . Carmel IN 46032 *TF:* 800-521-6139 ■ *Web:* www.sagamorehn.com	317-573-2886		391-3
Sagamore Hill National Historic Site 20 Sagamore Hill Rd. . . . . Oyster Bay NY 11771 *Web:* www.nps.gov	516-922-4788	922-4792	564
Sagamore, The 110 Sagamore Rd. . . . . Bolton Landing NY 12814 *TF:* 866-384-1944 ■ *Web:* www.thesagamore.com	518-644-9400	743-6036	669
Sagarsoft Inc 78 Eastern Blvd . . . . . Glastonbury CT 06033 *Web:* sagarsoft.com	860-633-2025	633-2880	177
Sagat Burton LLP 245 Park Ave 39th Fl . . . . . New York NY 10167 *Web:* sagatburton.com	212-672-1840		41
Sage Advantage 9414 E San Salvador Dr Ste 250. . . . . Scottsdale AZ 85258 *TF:* 800-673-7191 ■ *Web:* sageadvantage.com	480-941-0094		737
Sage Advisory Services Limited Co 5900 SW Pkwy Bldg 1 Ste 100 . . . . . Austin TX 78735 *Web:* www.sageadvisory.com	512-327-5530		401
Sage Centers 1410 Monument Blvd Ste 100 . . . . . Concord CA 94520 *Web:* www.sagecenters.com	925-627-7243		794
Sage College 12125 Day St Ste L . . . . . Moreno Valley CA 92557 *Web:* my.sagecollege.edu	951-781-2727		166
Sage College of Albany 140 New Scotland Ave . . . . . Albany NY 12208 *TF:* 888-837-9724 ■ *Web:* www.sage.edu	518-292-1730	292-1912	166
Sage Computing Inc 11491 Sunset Hills Rd Ste 350. . . . . Reston VA 20190 *Web:* www.sagecomputing.com	703-742-7881		177
Sage Consulting Group 1623 Blake St Ste 400 . . . . . Denver CO 80202 *Web:* www.sageconsulting.com	303-571-0237		261
Sage Direct Inc 3400 Raleigh Dr SE . . . . . Grand Rapids MI 49512 *Web:* www.sagedirect.com	616-940-8311		5
Sage Financial Group 300 Barr Harbor Dr Five Tower Bridge Ste 200 . . . . . West Conshohocken PA 19428 *Web:* www.sagefinancial.com	484-342-4400		194
Sage French Cafe 2378 N Federal Hwy . . . . . Fort Lauderdale FL 33305 *Web:* www.sagecafe.net	954-565-2299		671
Sage Group LLC, The 11111 Santa Monica Blvd Ste 2200 . . . . . Los Angeles CA 90025 *Web:* www.sagellc.com	310-478-7899	478-6619	401
Sage Group PLC 271 17th St NW . . . . . Atlanta GA 30363 *TF:* 800-368-2405 ■ *Web:* www.sage.com	866-996-7243		178-1
Sage Hospitality Resources LLC 1575 Welton St Ste 300 . . . . . Denver CO 80202 *Web:* www.sagehospitality.com	303-595-7200		379
Sage Microsystems Inc 18 N Village Ave . . . . . Exton PA 19341 *TF:* 800-724-7400 ■ *Web:* www.sagesystem.com	610-524-1300		177
Sage Policy Group Inc 575 S Charles St Ste 505 . . . . . Baltimore MD 21201 *Web:* sagepolicy.com	410-522-7243	522-7244	194
Sage Publications Inc 2455 Teller Rd. . . . . Thousand Oaks CA 91320 *TF:* 800-818-7243 ■ *Web:* www.us.sagepub.com	805-499-9774	499-0871	637-2
Sage Rock 15 Broad St. . . . . Akron OH 44305 *Web:* www.sagerock.com	330-379-9000		225
Sage Room 81 Pope Ave . . . . . Hilton Head Island SC 29928 *Web:* thesageroom.com	843-785-5352		671
Sage Rutty & Company Inc 100 Corporate Woods Ste 300 . . . . . Rochester NY 14623 *Web:* www.sagerutty.com	585-232-3760		401
Sage Studio PO Box 77435 . . . . . Seattle WA 98177 *Web:* www.sagestudio.com	206-569-8261		177
Sage Technologies Ltd 1 Ivybrook Blvd Ste 190 . . . . . Warminster PA 18974 *TF:* 800-818-4215 ■ *Web:* www.goagc.com	215-658-0500		180
Sage Therapeutics 215 First St . . . . . Cambridge MA 02142 *Web:* www.sagerx.com	617-299-8380		85
Sage Truck Driving School Mohawk Valley Community College Academic Bldg. . . Rome NY 13440 *TF:* 866-878-2568 ■ *Web:* www.sageschools.com	315-334-7793		685
Sage V Foods LLC 1470 Walnut St Ste 202 . . . . . Boulder CO 80302 *Web:* www.sagevfoods.com	303-449-5626		345
Sage YMCA of Metro Chicago 701 Manor Rd. . . . . Crystal Lake IL 60014 *Web:* www.ymcachicago.org	815-459-4455		31
Sagebrush Steakhouse 129 Fast Ln . . . . . Mooresville NC 28117 *TF:* 877-704-5939 ■ *Web:* www.sagebrushsteakhouse.com	704-660-5939	799-6199	670
SageLogix Inc 9000 E Nichols Ave Ste 140 . . . . . Centennial CO 80112 *Web:* www.sagelogix.com	303-925-0100		177
Sagent Pharmaceuticals Inc 1901 N Roselle Rd Ste 450. . . . . Schaumburg IL 60195 *NASDAQ: SGNT* ■ *TF:* 866 625-1618 ■ *Web:* www.sagentpharma.com	847-908-1600	908-1601	582
SagePoint Financial Inc 2800 N Central Ave Ste 2100 . . . . . Phoenix AZ 85004 *TF:* 800-552-3319 ■ *Web:* www.sagepointfinancial.com	800-552-3319		690
Sager Electronics Inc 19 Lorena Dr . . . . . Middleboro MA 02346 *TF:* 800-724-3780 ■ *Web:* www.sager.com	508-947-8888	947-0869	246
Sager Metal Strip Company LLC 100 Boone Dr . . . . . Michigan City IN 46360 *Web:* www.sagermetal.com	219-874-3609		492
Sager's Seafood Plus Inc 4802 Bridal Wreath Dr . . . . . Richmond TX 77406 *TF:* 800-929-3474 ■ *Web:* www.sagersseafoodplus.com	800-929-3474		297-5
SageRider Inc 12950 S Kirkwood Ste 160. . . . . Stafford TX 77477 *TF:* 877-219-4730 ■ *Web:* www.sageriderinc.com	877-219-4730		539
SAGES (Society of American Gastrointestinal & Endoscopic Surgeons) 11300 W Olympic Blvd Ste 600 . . . . . Los Angeles CA 90064 *Web:* www.sages.org	310-437-0544	437-0585	49-8
Sagestone Spa & Salon *Red Mountain Resort* 1275 East Red Mtn Cir. . . . . Ivins UT 84738 *TF:* 877-246-4453 ■ *Web:* www.redmountainresort.com	435-673-4905		706
SageView Advisory Group LLC 1920 Main St Ste 800. . . . . Irvine CA 92614 *TF:* 800-814-8742 ■ *Web:* www.sageviewadvisory.com	949-955-1395	955-1991	194
Sagicor Life Insurance Co 4343 N Scottsdale Rd Ste 300 . . . . . Scottsdale AZ 85251 **Fax Area Code:* 480 ■ *TF:* 888-724-4267 ■ *Web:* www.sagicorlifeusa.com	888-724-4267	425-5150*	796
Sagient Research Systems 3655 Nobel Dr Ste 600 . . . . . San Diego CA 92122 *TF:* 888-670-8900 ■ *Web:* www.sagientresearch.com	858-623-1600	623-1601	401
Sagimet Biosciences 155 Bovet Rd Ste 303. . . . . San Mateo CA 94402 *Web:* sagimet.com	650-561-8600		231
Saginaw Bay Plastics Inc 2768 S Huron Rd . . . . . Kawkawlin MI 48631 *Web:* www.saginawbayplastics.com	989-686-7860	686-0628	604
Saginaw Chippewa Tribal College 2274 Enterprise Dr . . . . . Mount Pleasant MI 48858 *TF:* 800-225-8172 ■ *Web:* www.sagchip.org	989-775-4123	775-4528	165
Saginaw Control & Engineering Inc 95 Midland Rd . . . . . Saginaw MI 48638 *TF:* 800-234-6871 ■ *Web:* www.saginawcontrol.com	989-799-6871	799-4524	816
Saginaw Correctional Facility 9625 Pierce Rd . . . . . Freeland MI 48623 *Web:* www.michigan.gov	989-695-9880		213
Saginaw County 111 S Michigan Ave . . . . . Saginaw MI 48602 *Web:* www.saginawcounty.com	989-790-5200		338
Saginaw County Chamber of Commerce 515 N Washington Ave 2nd Fl . . . . . Saginaw MI 48607 *Web:* www.saginawchamber.org	989-752-7161	752-9055	139

				Phone	Fax	Class
Saginaw Machine Systems (SMS) 800 N Hamilton St — *Web:* saginawmachine.com	Saginaw	MI	48602	989-753-8465		455
Saginaw News 203 S Washington Ave — *TF:* 877-611-6397 ■ *Web:* www.mlive.com	Saginaw	MI	48607	989-752-7171		532-2
Saginaw Pipe Company Inc 1980 Hwy 31 S PO Box 8 — **Fax Area Code:* 717 ■ *TF:* 800-433-1374 ■ *Web:* www.saginawpipe.com	Saginaw	AL	35137	205-664-3670	838-8069*	492
Saginaw Valley State University 7400 Bay Rd — *TF:* 800-968-9500 ■ *Web:* www.svsu.edu	University Center	MI	48710	989-964-4200	790-0180	166
Sagitec Solutions LLC 422 County Rd D E — *Web:* www.sagitec.com	Little Canada	MN	55117	612-284-7130		180
Sagittarius Hair Designs Ltd 1136 Conrad Ct — *Web:* www.sagittariussalon.com	Hagerstown	MD	21740	301-797-8008		77
Sagon Phior 2107 Sawtelle Blvd — *Web:* sagon-phior.com	Los Angeles	CA	90025	310-575-4441		4
Saguache County 501 Fourth St PO Box 176 — *Web:* saguachecounty.net	Saguache	CO	81149	719-655-2512	655-2730	338
Saguaro Lake Ranch 13020 Bush Hwy — *TF:* 800-868-5617 ■ *Web:* www.saguarolakeranch.com	Mesa	AZ	85215	480-984-2194		669
Saguaro National Park 3693 S Old Spanish Trl — *Web:* www.nps.gov	Tucson	AZ	85730	520-733-5100	733-5183	564
Saguaro Resources Ltd 3000 500 - Fourth Ave SW — *TF:* 855-835-4434 ■ *Web:* saguaroresources.com	Calgary	AB	T2P2V6	403-453-3040		536
Saguenay Port Authority 6600 Quai-Marcel-Dionne Rd — *Web:* www.portsaguenay.ca	La Baie	QC	G7B3N9	418-697-0250	697-0243	618
Saguenay-Lac-Saint-Jean Integrated Health & Social Services Ctr 930 Jacques-Cartier St E — *TF:* 800-370-4980 ■ *Web:* santesaglac.gouv.qc.ca	Chicoutimi	QC	G7H7K9	418-545-4980	545-8791	374-2
Saguenay-Saint Lawrence Marine Park 182 Rue de l'Eglise — *Web:* www.pc.gc.ca	Tadoussac	QC	G0T2A0	418-235-4703	235-4686	563
SAH (Society of Architectural Historians) 1365 N Astor St — *Web:* www.sah.org	Chicago	IL	60610	312-573-1365	573-1141	48-13
Sahadi Fine Foods Inc 4215 First Ave — *Web:* www.sahadifinefoods.com	Brooklyn	NY	11232	718-369-0100		297-8
Sahara Energy Ltd 444-7th Ave Ste 400 — *Web:* www.saharaenergy.ca	Calgary	AB	T2P0X8	403-232-1359	232-1307	539
Sahara Restaurant 143 Highland St — *Web:* eatsahara.com	Worcester	MA	01609	508-798-2181		671
Sahlen Packing Company Inc 318 Howard St — *TF:* 800-466-8165 ■ *Web:* www.sahlen.com	Buffalo	NY	14206	716-852-8677		296-26
Sahlman Seafoods Inc 1601 Sahlman Dr PO Box 5009 — *Web:* www.sahlmanseafood.com	Tampa	FL	33605	813-248-5726	247-5787	285
Sahouri Insurance 8200 Grnsburg Dr Ste 1550 — **Fax Area Code:* 855 ■ *Web:* www.sahouri.com	McLean	VA	22102	703-883-0500	242-6660*	390
SAI (Sigma Alpha Iota) 1 Tunnel Rd — *Web:* www.sai-national.org	Asheville	NC	28805	828-251-0606	251-0644	48-16
SAI Ann International Inc 28428 Golf Pointe Blvd — *Web:* www.saiann-inc.com	Farmington Hills	MI	48331	248-324-1604		809
SAI Consulting Engineers Inc 1350 Penn Ave Ste 300 — *Web:* www.saiengr.com	Pittsburgh	PA	15222	412-392-8750	392-8785	261
SAI Engineering Inc 13662 Office Pl Ste 101 — *Web:* www.saimep.com	Woodbridge	VA	22192	703-590-8200		256
SAI Systems International Inc 5 Research Dr — *TF:* 877-724-4748 ■ *Web:* www.saisystems.com	Shelton	CT	06484	203-929-0790	929-6948	180
SAIC (Science Application International Corporation Inc) 1710 SAIC Dr — *TF:* 866-400-7242 ■ *Web:* www.saic.com	McLean	VA	22102	866-955-7242		178-5
Saiful/Bouquet Inc 155 N Lake Ave Ste 600 — *Web:* saifulbouquet.com	Pasadena	CA	91101	626-304-2616		261
Saigon 85 Clarence St	Ottawa	ON	K1N5P5	613-789-7934		671
Saigon 1904 Pacific Ave	Stockton	CA	95204	209-463-2274		671
Saigon Cafe 440 W 300 S — *Web:* saigoncafeprovo.biz	Provo	UT	84601	801-812-1173		671
Saigon on Fifth 3900 Fifth Ave — *Web:* saigononfifth.menutoeat.com	San Diego	CA	92103	619-220-8828		671
Saigon Rendezvous (Pho Na) 117 5th Ave SW — *Web:* phonaolympia.business.site	Olympia	WA	98501	360-352-1989		671
Sail Venture Partners LP 3161 Michelson Dr Ste 750 — *Web:* www.sailcapital.com	Irvine	CA	92612	949-398-5100	398-5101	792
Sailfish Club of Florida Inc, The 1338 N Lake Way — *Web:* www.sailfishclub.com	Palm Beach Gardens	FL	33480	561-844-0206		354
Sailing World Magazine 55 Hammarlund Way — *Web:* www.sailingworld.com	Middletown	RI	02842	401-845-5100	845-5180	457-4
Sailor's Creek Battlefield State Park 6541 Saylers Creek Rd — *Web:* www.dcr.virginia.gov	Rice	VA	23966	804-561-7510		565
Sain Construction Co 713 Vincent St — *Web:* sainconstruction.com	Manchester	TN	37355	931-728-7644		186
Sainergy Inc 1999 S Bascom Ave Ste 700 — *Web:* www.sainergy.net	Campbell	CA	95008	408-532-9800		624
Saint Agnes HealthCare 900 Caton Ave — *TF:* 800-875-8750 ■ *Web:* www.stagnes.org	Baltimore	MD	21229	410-368-6000		374-3
Saint Agnes Medical Ctr 1303 E Herndon Ave — *Web:* www.samc.com	Fresno	CA	93720	559-450-3000		374-3
Saint Albans School Mt St Alban — *Web:* www.stalbansschool.org	Washington	DC	20016	202-537-6435	537-6434	623
Saint Alexius Hospital *Broadway Campus* 3933 S Broadway — *TF:* 800-245-1431 ■ *Web:* www.stalexiushospital.com	Saint Louis	MO	63118	314-856-7000	865-7983	374-3
Saint Alphonsus Regional Medical Ctr 1055 N Curtis Rd — *TF:* 877-401-3627 ■ *Web:* www.saintalphonsus.org	Boise	ID	83706	208-367-2121		374-3
Saint Ambrose University 518 W Locust St — *TF:* 800-383-2627 ■ *Web:* www.sau.edu	Davenport	IA	52803	563-333-6000	333-6243	166
Saint Andrew's Abbey 31001 N Valyermo Rd — *Web:* www.saintandrewsabbey.com	Valyermo	CA	93563	661-944-2178	944-1076	673
Saint Andrew's College 15800 Yonge St — *TF:* 877-378-1899 ■ *Web:* www.sac.on.ca	Aurora	ON	L4G3H7	905-727-3178	727-9032	622
Saint Andrew's School 3900 Jog Rd — *Web:* www.saintandrews.net	Boca Raton	FL	33434	561-210-2000	210-2007	622
Saint Andrew's School 63 Federal Rd — *Web:* www.standrews-ri.org	Barrington	RI	02806	401-246-1230	246-0510	622
Saint Andrew's-Sewanee School (SAS) 290 Quintard Rd — *Web:* www.sasweb.org	Sewanee	TN	37375	931-598-5651		622
Saint Andrews State Park 4607 State Pk Ln — *Web:* www.floridastateparks.org	Panama City	FL	32408	850-708-6100		565
Saint Anne's-Belfield School 2132 Ivy Rd — *Web:* www.stab.org	Charlottesville	VA	22903	434-296-5106		622
Saint Anselm College 100 St Anselm Dr — *TF:* 888-426-7356 ■ *Web:* www.anselm.edu	Manchester	NH	03102	603-641-7000	641-7550	166
Saint Anthony Spirituality Ctr 300 E Fourth St — *Web:* www.sarcenter.com	Marathon	WI	54448	715-443-2236	443-2235	673
Saint Anthony's Catholic High School 3200 McCullough Ave — *Web:* www.sachs.org	San Antonio	TX	78212	210-832-5600	832-5633	622
Saint Anthony's Hospice 2410 S Green St — *TF:* 866-380-2326 ■ *Web:* stanthonyshospice.org	Henderson	KY	42420	270-826-2326	831-2169	371
Saint Anthony's Hospital Foundation 1200 Seventh Ave N — *Web:* www.stanthonysfoundation.org	Saint Petersburg	FL	33705	727-825-1086	825-1184	374-3
Saint Anthony's Memorial Hospital 503 N Maple St — *Web:* stanthonyshospital.org	Effingham	IL	62401	217-342-2121		374-3
Saint Augustine Alligator Farm 999 Anastasia Blvd — *Web:* www.alligatorfarm.com	Saint Augustine	FL	32080	904-824-3337		823
Saint Augustine City Hall PO Box 210 — *Web:* www.staugustinegovernment.com	Saint Augustine	FL	32085	904-825-1040	209-4286	337
Saint Augustine College 1345 W Argyle St — *Web:* www.staugustine.edu	Chicago	IL	60640	773-878-8756	878-0937	162
Saint Augustine Lighthouse & Museum 81 Lighthouse Ave — *Web:* www.staugustinelighthouse.org	Saint Augustine	FL	32080	904-829-0745	808-1248	520
Saint Augustine National Cemetery 104 Marine St — **Fax Area Code:* 352 ■ *Web:* www.cem.va.gov	Saint Augustine	FL	32084	904-766-5222	793-9560*	136
Saint Augustine's College 1315 Oakwood Ave — *TF:* 800-948-1126 ■ *Web:* st-aug.edu	Raleigh	NC	27610	919-516-4000	516-5805	166
Saint Basil Academy 711 Fox Chase Rd — *Web:* www.stbasilacademy.org	Jenkintown	PA	19046	215-885-3771	885-4025	685
Saint Bernard Parish Library 2600 Palmisano Blvd — *Web:* stbernard.lib.la.us	Chalmette	LA	70043	504-279-0448		434-3
Saint Bernard Preparatory School 1600 St Bernard Dr SE — *Web:* stbernardprep.com	Cullman	AL	35055	256-739-6682	734-2925	622
Saint Bernard State Park 501 St Bernard Pkwy — *TF:* 888-677-7823 ■ *Web:* crt.state.la.us	Braithwaite	LA	70040	504-682-2101		565
Saint Bernard's Medical Ctr 225 E Jackson Ave — *Web:* www.stbernards.info	Jonesboro	AR	72401	870-207-4100		374-3
Saint Bernard's School of Theology & Ministry 120 French Rd — *Web:* www.stbernards.edu	Rochester	NY	14618	585-271-3657	271-2045	167-3
Saint Brides Correctional Ctr 701 Sanderson Rd — *Web:* vadoc.virginia.gov	Chesapeake	VA	23322	757-421-6600		213
Saint Catherine of Siena Medical Ctr 50 NY 25 A — *Web:* stcatherines.chsli.org	Smithtown	NY	11787	631-862-3000		374-3
Saint Catherine's School 6001 Grove Ave — *Web:* www.st.catherines.org	Richmond	VA	23226	804-288-2804	285-8169	622
Saint Charles Borromeo Seminary 100 E Wynnewood Rd — *Web:* www.scs.edu	Wynnewood	PA	19096	610-667-3394		167-3
Saint Charles City County Library District 77 Boone Hill Dr — *Web:* www.mylibrary.org	Saint Peters	MO	63376	636-441-2300		434-3
Saint Charles County PO Box 1872 — *Web:* www.sccmo.org	Saint Charles	MO	63301	636-949-7900		338
Saint Charles Parish 15045 River Rd PO Box 302 — *Web:* www.stcharlesgov.net	Hahnville	LA	70057	985-783-5000	783-2067	338

Name / Address	City	State	ZIP	Phone	Fax	Class
Saint Charles Vision 8040 St Charles Ave *Web:* www.stcharlesvision.com	New Orleans	LA	70118	504-866-6311		543
Saint Clair County 165 Fifth Ave Ste 100 *Web:* www.stclairco.com	Ashville	AL	35953	205-594-2100	594-2110	338
Saint Clair County 10 Public Sq *Web:* www.stclaircounty.org	Belleville	IL	62220	618-233-0659		338
Saint Clair County Library System 210 McMorran Blvd *TF:* 877-987-7323 ■ *Web:* www.sccl.lib.mi.us	Port Huron	MI	48060	810-987-7323	987-7874	434-3
Saint Clair Square 134 St Clair Sq *Web:* www.stclairsquare.com	Fairview Heights	IL	62208	618-632-7567		460
Saint Claire Regional Medical Ctr 222 Medical Cir *Web:* www.st-claire.org	Morehead	KY	40351	606-783-6500		374-3
Saint Clare's Hospital 25 Pocono Rd *TF:* 888-808-1234 ■ *Web:* www.saintclares.com	Denville	NJ	07834	973-625-6000		374-3
Saint Cloud Area Convention & Visitors Bureau 1411 W St Germain St Ste 104 *TF:* 800-264-2940 ■ *Web:* www.visitstcloud.com	Saint Cloud	MN	56301	320-251-4170		206
Saint Cloud Hospital 1406 Sixth Ave N *Web:* www.centracare.com	Saint Cloud	MN	56303	320-251-2700		374-3
Saint Cloud Times 3000 Seventh St N *TF:* 877-424-4921 ■ *Web:* www.sctimes.com	Saint Cloud	MN	56303	320-255-8700		532-2
Saint Cloud/Greater Osceola Chamber of Commerce 1200 New York Ave *Web:* stcloudflchamber.com	Saint Cloud	FL	34769	407-892-3671	892-5289	139
Saint Croix County 3001 Hanley Rd *Web:* www.co.saint-croix.wi.us	Hudson	WI	54016	715-381-7333	381-4400	338
Saint Croix Electric Coop 1925 Ridgeway St PO Box 160 *TF:* 800-924-3407 ■ *Web:* www.scecnet.net	Hammond	WI	54015	715-796-7000	796-7070	245
Saint Croix Island International Historic Site PO Box 247 *Web:* www.nps.gov	Calais	ME	04619	207-454-3871	288-8813	564
Saint Croix National Scenic Riverway 401 N Hamilton St *Web:* www.nps.gov	Saint Croix Falls	WI	54024	715-483-2274	483-3288	564
Saint Croix Press Inc 1185 S Knowles Ave *TF:* 800-826-6622 ■ *Web:* www.stcroixpress.com	New Richmond	WI	54017	715-246-5811	246-2486	637-9
Saint Croix State Park 30065 St Croix Park Rd *Web:* www.dnr.state.mn.us	Hinckley	MN	55037	320-384-6591		565
Saint Croix Valley Chamber of Commerce 39 Union St *Web:* visitstcroixvalley.com	Calais	ME	04619	207-454-2308		139
Saint Dominic-Jackson Memorial Hospital 969 Lakeland Dr *Web:* www.stdom.com	Jackson	MS	39216	601-200-2000		374-3
Saint Edward State Park 14445 Juanita Dr NE *Web:* parks.state.wa.us	Kenmore	WA	98028	425-823-2992		565
Saint Elizabeth Home 1 St Elizabeth Way *Web:* www.stelizabethcommunity.org	East Greenwich	RI	02818	401-471-6060	471-6056	450
Saint Elizabeth University 2 Convent Rd *TF:* 800-210-7900 ■ *Web:* www.steu.edu	Morristown	NJ	07960	973-290-4700		166
Saint Elizabeths Hospital 1100 Alabama Ave SE *Web:* www.sehcommunity.org	Washington	DC	20032	202-299-5100		374-5
Saint Elmo Steak House 127 S Illinois St *Web:* www.stelmos.com	Indianapolis	IN	46225	317-635-0636		671
Saint Emilion 3617 W Seventh St *Web:* www.saint-emilionrestaurant.com	Fort Worth	TX	76107	817-737-2781		671
Saint Francis College 180 Remsen St *Web:* www.sfc.edu	Brooklyn	NY	11201	718-522-2300		166
Saint Francis County 313 S Izard St *Web:* stfranciscountyar.org	Forrest City	AR	72335	870-261-1700		338
Saint Francis Hospital 2122 Manchester Expy *Web:* www.mystfrancis.com	Columbus	GA	31904	706-596-4000		374-3
Saint Francis Hospital 5959 Park Ave *Web:* www.saintfrancishosp.com	Memphis	TN	38119	901-765-1000		374-3
Saint Francis Hospital 333 Laidley St *Web:* www.stfrancishospital.com	Charleston	WV	25301	304-347-6500		374-3
Saint Francis Medical Ctr 211 St Francis Dr *Web:* www.sfmc.net	Cape Girardeau	MO	63703	573-331-3000	331-5009	374-3
Saint Francis Retreat Ctr 549 Mission Vineyard Rd *Web:* stfrancisretreat.com	San Juan Bautista	CA	95045	831-623-4234	623-9046	673
Saint Francis University 117 Evergreen Dr PO Box 600 *Web:* www.francis.edu	Loretto	PA	15940	814-472-3000		166
Saint Francis Xavier University PO Box 5000 *TF:* 877-867-7839 ■ *Web:* www.stfx.ca	Antigonish	NS	B2G2W5	902-863-3300	867-2329	785
Saint Francois County 1 W Liberty St *Web:* www.sfcgov.org	Farmington	MO	63640	573-756-3623	431-6967	338
Saint George Library Ctr 5 Central Ave	Staten Island	NY	10301	718-442-8560		434-3
Saint George's Anglican Church 227 Wharncliffe Rd N *Web:* www.stgeorgeslondon.ca	London	ON	N6H2B6	519-438-2994	438-2995	50-1
Saint George's Church 2222 Brunswick St *Web:* roundchurch.ca	Halifax	NS	B3K2Z3	902-423-1059	423-0897	50-1
Saint Gobain 20 Moores Rd **Fax Area Code:* 855 ■ *TF:* 800-345-1145 ■ *Web:* www.saint-gobain-abrasives.com	Malvern	PA	19355	800-345-1145	639-6629*	1
Saint Innocent Winery 5657 Zena Rd NW *Web:* stinnocentwine.com	Salem	OR	97304	503-378-1526		50-7
Saint James Hotel 330 Magazine St *Web:* www.saintjameshotel.com	New Orleans	LA	70130	504-304-4000		379
Saint James Mercy Hospital 411 Canisteo St *TF:* 800-346-2211 ■ *Web:* www.stjamesmercy.org	Hornell	NY	14843	607-324-8000	324-8115	374-3
Saint James Parish 5800 Hwy 44 PO Box 106 *Web:* www.stjamesla.com	Convent	LA	70723	225-562-2286	562-2279	338
Saint James School 17641 College Rd *Web:* www.stjames.edu	Hagerstown	MD	21740	301-733-9330	739-1310	622
Saint Jerome's University 290 Westmount Rd N *Web:* www.sju.ca	Waterloo	ON	N2L3G3	519-884-8111		785
Saint Joe State Park 2800 Pimville Rd *Web:* mostateparks.com	Park Hills	MO	63601	573-431-1069		565
Saint John Hospital 3500 S Fourth St *Web:* www.stjohnleavenworth.com	Leavenworth	KS	66048	913-680-6000		374-3
Saint John of Kronstadt Press 1180 Orthodox Way *Web:* www.sjkp.org	Liberty	TN	37095	615-536-5239		637-2
Saint John Port Authority 111 Water St *Web:* www.sjport.com	Saint John	NB	E2L0B1	506-636-4869	636-4443	618
Saint John Regional Library 1 Market Sq *Web:* www.saintjohnlibrary.com	Saint John	NB	E2L4Z6	506-643-7220	643-7225	436
Saint John the Baptist Parish 1801 W Airline Hwy *Web:* www.sjbparish.com	LaPlace	LA	70068	985-652-9569	652-4131	338
Saint John Vianney Theological Seminary 1300 S Steele St *Web:* sjvdenver.edu	Denver	CO	80210	303-282-3427	715-2007	167-3
Saint John's Hospital 800 E Carpenter St *TF:* 855-228-4438 ■ *Web:* st-johns.org	Springfield	IL	62769	217-544-6464		374-3
Saint John's Northwestern Military Academy 1101 Genesee St *TF:* 800-752-2338 ■ *Web:* www.sjnma.org	Delafield	WI	53018	800-752-2338		622
Saint John's On the Lake 1840 N Prospect Ave *Web:* www.saintjohnsmilw.org	Milwaukee	WI	53202	414-831-7300		672
Saint John's Preparatory School 2280 Watertower Rd PO Box 4000 *TF:* 800-525-7737 ■ *Web:* sjprep.net	Collegeville	MN	56321	320-363-3315		622
Saint John's Restaurant 1278 Market St *Web:* stjohnsrestaurant.com	Chattanooga	TN	37402	423-266-4400		671
Saint John's Seminary 127 Lake St *Web:* www.sjs.edu	Brighton	MA	02135	617-254-2610		167-3
Saint John's Seminary 5012 Seminary Rd *Web:* stjohnsem.edu	Camarillo	CA	93012	805-482-2755		167-3
Saint John's University 8000 Utopia Pkwy *TF:* 888-978-5646 ■ *Web:* www.stjohns.edu	Queens	NY	11439	718-990-2000	990-2096	166
Saint John's University 2850 Abbey Plz PO Box 2000 *Web:* www.csbsju.edu	Collegeville	MN	56321	320-363-2196		166
Saint John's-Ravenscourt School 400 S Dr *Web:* www.sjr.mb.ca	Winnipeg	MB	R3T3K5	204-477-2485	477-2429	622
Saint Johns County Chamber of Commerce 1 News Pl *Web:* sjcchamber.com	Saint Augustine	FL	32084	904-829-5681		139
Saint Joseph Area Chamber of Commerce 3003 Frederick Ave *TF:* 800-748-7856 ■ *Web:* saintjoseph.com	Saint Joseph	MO	64506	816-232-4461	364-4873	139
Saint Joseph Cathedral 521 N Duluth Ave *Web:* www.stjosephcathedral.net	Sioux Falls	SD	57104	605-336-7390		50-1
Saint Joseph Convention & Visitors Bureau 911 Frederick Ave *TF:* 800-785-0360 ■ *Web:* stjomo.com	Saint Joseph	MO	64501	816-233-6688		206
Saint Joseph County 125 W Main St PO Box 189 *Web:* www.stjosephcountymi.org	Centreville	MI	49032	269-467-5500	467-5628	338
Saint Joseph County 101 S Main St *Web:* www.stjosephcountyindiana.com	South Bend	IN	46601	574-235-9635	235-9838	338
Saint Joseph County Public Library 304 S Main St *Web:* www.sjcpl.lib.in.us	South Bend	IN	46601	574-282-4630		434-3
Saint Joseph Hospital 172 Kinsley St *Web:* www.stjosephhospital.com	Nashua	NH	03060	603-882-3000		374-3
Saint Joseph Hospital 1100 W Stewart Dr *Web:* www.sjo.org	Orange	CA	92868	714-633-9111		374-3
Saint Joseph Hospital 700 Broadway *TF:* 800-258-0974 ■ *Web:* lutheranhealth.net	Fort Wayne	IN	46802	260-425-3000		374-3
Saint Joseph Medical Ctr 1401 St Joseph Pkwy *Web:* www.sjmctx.org	Houston	TX	77002	713-757-1000	657-7123	374-3
Saint Joseph Medical Ctr 2500 Bernville Rd *TF:* 800-969-5007 ■ *Web:* www.thefutureofhealthcare.org	Reading	PA	19605	610-378-2000		374-3
Saint Joseph Mercy Ann Arbor 5301 McAuley Dr *TF:* 866-522-8268 ■ *Web:* www.stjoeshealth.org	Ypsilanti	MI	48197	734-712-3456	712-3855	374-3
Saint Joseph Mercy Hospital Port Huron 2601 Electric Ave *Web:* www.mylakehuron.com	Port Huron	MI	48060	810-985-1500		374-3
Saint Joseph Mercy Oakland 44405 Woodward Ave *TF:* 800-396-1313 ■ *Web:* www.stjoesoakland.org	Pontiac	MI	48341	248-858-3000	858-3155	374-3

	Phone	Fax	Class
Saint Joseph Regional Medical Center Mishawaka 5215 Holy Cross Pkwy .... Mishawaka IN 46545 *TF:* 800-274-1314 ■ *Web:* www.sjmed.com	574-335-5000		374-3
Saint Joseph Regional Medical Ctr 415 Sixth St .... Lewiston ID 83501 *TF:* 800-678-2511 ■ *Web:* www.sjrmc.org	208-743-2511		374-3
Saint Joseph's College *Brooklyn* 245 Clinton Ave .... Brooklyn NY 11205 *Web:* www.sjcny.edu	718-940-5300	636-8303	166
Saint Joseph's College of Maine 278 Whites Bridge Rd........................ Standish ME 04084 *TF:* 800-338-7057 ■ *Web:* www.sjcme.edu	207-893-7746	893-7862	166
Saint Joseph's Health Care *London* 268 Grosvenor St PO Box 5777 Stn B .... London ON N6A4V2 *Web:* www.sjhc.london.on.ca	519-646-6100		374-2
Saint Joseph's Health Ctr *Guelph* 100 Westmount Rd .... Guelph ON N1H5H8 *Web:* www.sjhcg.ca	519-824-6000		374-2
Saint Joseph's Healthcare Hamilton 50 Charlton Ave E.......................... Hamilton ON L8N4A6 *TF:* 800-461-2156 ■ *Web:* stjoes.ca	905-522-1155	521-6140	374-2
Saint Joseph's Hospital 3001 W Dr Martin Luther King Jr Blvd .... Tampa FL 33607	813-870-4000	870-4132	374-3
Saint Joseph's Hospital Health Ctr 301 Prospect Ave .... Syracuse NY 13203 *TF:* 888-785-6371 ■ *Web:* www.sjhsyr.org	315-448-5111		374-3
Saint Joseph's Lifecare Ctr 99 Wayne Gretzky Pkwy .... Brantford ON N3S6T6 *TF:* 888-699-7817 ■ *Web:* www.sjlc.ca	519-751-7096	753-7996	374-2
Saint Joseph's Medical Ctr (SJMC) 127 S Broadway .... Yonkers NY 10701 *Web:* www.saintjosephs.org	914-378-7000		374-3
Saint Joseph's Regional Medical Ctr 703 Main St .... Paterson NJ 07503 *Web:* www.stjosephshealth.org	973-754-2000	754-2208	374-3
Saint Joseph's Seminary 201 Seminary Ave........................... Yonkers NY 10704 *Web:* www.archny.org	914-968-6200	968-6671	167-3
Saint Joseph's University 5600 City Ave.......................... Philadelphia PA 19131 *TF:* 888-232-4295 ■ *Web:* www.sju.edu	610-660-1000	660-1314	166
Saint Joseph's University Press 5600 City Ave.......................... Philadelphia PA 19131 *Web:* www.sjupress.com	610-660-3402	660-3412	637-2
Saint Jude Medical Ctr 101 E Valencia Mesa Dr .... Fullerton CA 92835 *TF:* 800-378-4189 ■ *Web:* www.stjudemedicalcenter.org	714-871-3280		374-3
Saint Jude The Apostle School 7171 Glenridge Dr NE......................... Atlanta GA 30328 *Web:* www.saintjude.net	770-394-2880	804-9248	685
Saint Lawrence County 48 Ct St................ Canton NY 13617 *Web:* www.stlawco.org	315-379-2240	379-9934	338
Saint Lawrence Rehabilitation Ctr 2381 Lawrenceville Rd .... Lawrenceville NJ 08648 *Web:* www.slrc.org	609-896-9500		374-6
Saint Lawrence Seaway Development Corp 1200 New Jersey Ave SE.................. Washington DC 20590 *TF:* 800-785-2779 ■ *Web:* www.seaway.dot.gov	202-366-0091	366-7147	340-17
Saint Lawrence State Park Golf Course 4955 State Hwy 37 .... Ogdensburg NY 13669 *Web:* parks.ny.gov	315-393-2286		565
Saint Lawrence University 23 Romoda Dr .... Canton NY 13617 *TF:* 800-285-1856 ■ *Web:* www.stlawu.edu	315-229-5261	229-5818	166
Saint Leo University 33701 State Rd 52 .... Saint Leo FL 33574 *TF:* 800-334-5532 ■ *Web:* www.saintleo.edu	352-588-8200	588-8257	166
Saint Louis Art Museum 1 Fine Arts Dr Forest Pk .... Saint Louis MO 63110 *Web:* www.slam.org	314-721-0072		520
Saint Louis Bride Magazine 1006 Olive St Ste 202..................... Saint Louis MO 63101 *Web:* www.bridestl.com	314-588-8313		457-22
Saint Louis Cathedral 615 Pere Antoine Alley .... New Orleans LA 70116 *Web:* www.stlouiscathedral.org	504-525-9585	525-9583	50-1
Saint Louis Children's Hospital 1 Children's Pl .... Saint Louis MO 63110 *TF:* 800-427-4626 ■ *Web:* www.stlouischildrens.org	314-454-6000		374-1
Saint Louis Christian College 1360 Grandview Dr......................... Florissant MO 63033 *TF:* 800-887-7522 ■ *Web:* stlchristian.edu	314-837-6777	837-8291	161
Saint Louis City Hall 1200 Market St........................... Saint Louis MO 63103 *Web:* www.stlouis-mo.gov	314-622-4800	622-4061	337
Saint Louis College of Pharmacy 4588 Parkview Pl .... Saint Louis MO 63110 *TF:* 800-278-5267 ■ *Web:* www.stlcop.edu	314-367-8700	446-8304	166
Saint Louis Community College (STLCC) 300 S Broadway .... Saint Louis MO 63102 *Web:* www.stlcc.edu	314-539-5000		162
Saint Louis Correctional Facility 8585 N Croswell Rd .... Saint Louis MI 48880 *Web:* www.michigan.gov	989-681-6444		213
Saint Louis County Library (SLCL) 1640 S Lindbergh Blvd..................... Saint Louis MO 63131 *Web:* www.slcl.org	314-994-3300		434-3
Saint Louis Music 1400 Ferguson Ave......................... Saint Louis MO 63133 *Web:* www.stlouismusic.com	314-727-4512		527
Saint Louis Paper & Box Co 3843 Garfield Ave......................... Saint Louis MO 63113 *TF:* 800-779-7901 ■ *Web:* www.stlpaper.com	314-531-7900	531-0968	559
Saint Louis Public Schools 801 N 11th St............................ Saint Louis MO 63101 *Web:* www.slps.org	314-231-3720	345-2650	685
Saint Louis Science Ctr 5050 Oakland Ave.......................... Saint Louis MO 63110 *TF:* 800-456-7572 ■ *Web:* www.slsc.org	314-289-4400	535-0104	520
Saint Louis Symphony Orchestra 718 N Grand Blvd........................ Saint Louis MO 63103 *TF:* 800-232-1880 ■ *Web:* www.slso.org	314-533-2500	286-4111	573-3
Saint Louis University 1 N Grand Blvd........................... Saint Louis MO 63103 *TF:* 800-758-3678 ■ *Web:* www.slu.edu	314-977-7288	977-7136	166
Saint Louis Zoological Park 1 Government Dr .... Saint Louis MO 63110 *TF:* 800-966-8877 ■ *Web:* www.stlzoo.org	314-781-0900		823
Saint Lucia *Consulate General* 800 Second Ave 5th Fl.................... New York NY 10017 *Web:* saintluciaconsulateny.org	212-697-9360	697-4993	257
Embassy 3216 New Mexico Ave NW .... Washington DC 20016 *Web:* www.state.gov	202-364-6792		257
Saint Lucie County Library System 2300 Virginia Ave......................... Fort Pierce FL 34982 *Web:* www.stlucieco.gov	772-462-1100		434-3
Saint Lucie Medical Ctr 1800 SE Tiffany Ave .... Port Saint Lucie FL 34952 *TF:* 800-382-3522 ■ *Web:* stluciemed.com	772-335-4000	398-3608	374-3
Saint Luke Institute Foundation Inc 8901 New Hampshire Ave................. Silver Spring MD 20903 *Web:* sli.org	301-445-7970		305
Saint Luke's Cardiovascular Consultants 4330 Wornall Rd Ste 2000 .... Kansas City MO 64111 *Web:* www.saintlukeskc.org	816-931-1883		582
Saint Luke's Cornwall Hospital *Cornwall Campus* 19 Laurel Ave.............. Cornwall NY 12518 *Web:* www.stlukescornwallhospital.org	845-534-7711		374-3
Saint Luke's Home Care & Hospice 3100 Broadway St Ste 1000 .... Kansas City MO 64111 *TF:* 888-303-7576 ■ *Web:* www.saintlukeskc.org	816-756-1160	756-0838	371
Saint Luke's Hospital 232 S Woods Mill Rd .... Chesterfield MO 63017 *Web:* www.stlukes-stl.com	314-434-1500		374-3
Saint Luke's Hospital 4401 Wornall Rd.......................... Kansas City MO 64111 *Web:* www.saintlukeshealthsystem.org	816-932-2000	932-5842	374-3
Saint Luke's Medical Ctr 1800 E Van Buren St......................... Phoenix AZ 85006 *TF:* 800-446-2279 ■ *Web:* www.stlukesmedcenter.org	602-251-8100	251-8207	374-3
Saint Luke's Rehabilitation Institute 711 S Cowley St............................ Spokane WA 99202 *Web:* www.st-lukes.org	509-473-6000	473-6978	374-6
Saint Mark Village 2655 Nebraska Ave...................... Palm Harbor FL 34684 *TF:* 800-706-4513 ■ *Web:* www.stmarkvillage.org	727-785-2580		672
Saint Mark's School 25 Marlborough Rd .... Southborough MA 01772 *Web:* www.stmarksschool.org	508-786-6000	786-6120	622
Saint Martin Parish Library 201 Porter St .... Saint Martinville LA 70582 *Web:* www.stmartinparishlibrary.org	337-394-2207	394-2248	434-3
Saint Martin's University 5300 Pacific Ave SE .... Lacey WA 98503 *TF:* 800-368-8803 ■ *Web:* www.stmartin.edu	360-438-4311	412-6189	166
Saint Martin's Wine Bistro 3020 Greenville Ave .... Dallas TX 75206 *Web:* www.stmartinswinebistro.com	214-826-0940	826-1229	671
Saint Mary Mercy Hospital 36475 Five-Mile Rd .... Livonia MI 48154 *TF:* 800-464-7492 ■ *Web:* www.stmarymercy.org	734-655-4800		374-3
Saint Mary Seminary & Graduate School of Theology 28700 Euclid Ave .... Wickliffe OH 44092 *Web:* www.stmarysem.edu	440-943-7600	943-7577	167-3
Saint Mary's Cathedral 203 E Tenth St .... Austin TX 78701 *Web:* www.smcaustin.org	512-476-6182	476-8799	50-1
Saint Mary's Catholic Church 111 Hampton Ave......................... Greenville SC 29601 *Web:* smcgvl.org	864-271-8422		50-1
Saint Mary's College Le Mans Hall .... Notre Dame IN 46556 *TF:* 800-551-7621 ■ *Web:* www.saintmarys.edu	574-284-4587	284-4841	166
Saint Mary's College of California 1928 St Mary's Rd .... Moraga CA 94556 *TF:* 800-800-4762 ■ *Web:* www.stmarys-ca.edu	925-631-4000	376-7193	166
Saint Mary's College of Maryland 47645 College Dr .... Saint Marys City MD 20686 *TF:* 800-492-7181 ■ *Web:* www.smcm.edu	240-895-2000		166
Saint Mary's Correctional Ctr 2880 N Pleasants Hwy .... Saint Marys WV 26170 *Web:* www.wvdoc.com	304-684-5500	684-5506	213
Saint Mary's County 41770 Baldridge St PO Box 653............ Leonardtown MD 20650 *Web:* www.co.saint-marys.md.us	301-475-4200	475-4935	338
Saint Mary's General Hospital 911 Queen's Blvd .... Kitchener ON N2M1B2 *Web:* www.smgh.ca	519-744-3311	749-6426	374-2
Saint Mary's Health Care System 1230 Baxter St .... Athens GA 30606 *TF:* 800-233-7864 ■ *Web:* www.stmaryshealthcaresystem.org	706-389-3000		374-3
Saint Mary's Hospice of Northern Nevada 690 Sierra Rose Dr............................. Reno NV 89511 *Web:* www.saintmarysreno.com	775-770-3081		371
Saint Mary's Hospital 1800 E Lake Shore Dr......................... Decatur IL 62521 *Web:* stmarysdecatur.com	217-464-2966		374-3
Saint Mary's Hospital Ctr 3830 Lacombe Ave........................... Montreal QC H3T1M5 *Web:* www.smhc.qc.ca	514-345-3511		374-2
Saint Mary's Hospital Medical Ctr 1726 Shawano Ave......................... Green Bay WI 54303 *Web:* stmgb.org	920-498-4200		374-3
Saint Mary's Medical Ctr 201 NW Rd Mize Rd .... Blue Springs MO 64014 *Web:* www.stmaryskc.com	816-228-5900	655-5408	374-3
Saint Mary's Regional Medical Ctr 1808 W Main St .... Russellville AR 72801 *Web:* www.saintmarysregional.com	479-968-2841		374-3

Name / Address	City	State	ZIP	Phone	Fax	Class
Saint Mary's Regional Medical Ctr 93 Campus Ave. *Web:* www.stmarysmaine.com	Lewiston	ME	04240	207-777-8100		374-3
Saint Mary's Regional Medical Ctr 305 S Fifth St *Web:* www.stmarysregional.com	Enid	OK	73701	580-233-6100		374-3
Saint Mary's School 900 Hillsborough St *Web:* www.sms.edu	Raleigh	NC	27603	919-424-4000	424-4122	622
Saint Mary's Seminary & University 5400 Roland Ave. *Web:* www.stmarys.edu	Baltimore	MD	21210	410-864-4000		167-3
Saint Mary's University 923 Robie St *Web:* www.smu.ca	Halifax	NS	B3H3C3	902-420-5756	420-5141	785
Saint Mary's University of Minnesota 700 Terr Hts *TF:* 800-635-5987 ■ *Web:* www.smumn.edu	Winona	MN	55987	507-452-4430		166
Saint Mary-Corwin Medical Ctr 1008 Minnequa Ave *TF:* 800-228-4039 ■ *Web:* www.stmarycorwin.org	Pueblo	CO	81004	719-557-4000		374-3
Saint Mary-of-the-Woods College 3301 St Mary Rd. *TF:* 800-926-7692 ■ *Web:* www.smwc.edu	Saint Mary of The Woods	IN	47876	812-535-5106	535-5010	166
Saint Marys Carbon Co 259 Eberl St *Web:* www.stmaryscarbon.com	Saint Marys	PA	15857	814-781-7333	834-9201	127
Saint Meinrad Archabbey 200 Hill Dr *TF:* 800-682-0988 ■ *Web:* www.saintmeinrad.edu	Saint Meinrad	IN	47577	812-357-6585	357-6325	673
Saint Michael's College 1 Winooski Pk *TF:* 800-762-8000 ■ *Web:* www.smcvt.edu	Colchester	VT	05439	802-654-2000	654-2906	166
Saint Michael's Hospital 30 Bond St *Web:* www.stmichaelshospital.com	Toronto	ON	M5B1W8	416-360-4000	864-5870	374-2
Saint Michael's Medical Ctr 111 Central Ave *Web:* www.smmcnj.com	Newark	NJ	07102	973-877-5000		374-3
Saint Michael's University School (SMUS) 3400 Richmond Rd *TF:* 800-661-5199 ■ *Web:* www.smus.ca	Victoria	BC	V8P4P5	250-592-2411	592-2812	622
Saint Michaels Harbour Inn & Marina 101 N Harbor Rd. *TF:* 800-955-9001 ■ *Web:* harbourinn.com	Saint Michaels	MD	21663	410-745-9001		379
Saint Norbert College 100 Grant St. *TF:* 800-236-4878 ■ *Web:* www.snc.edu	De Pere	WI	54115	920-403-3005	403-4072	166
Saint Patrick's Seminary & University 320 Middlefield Rd *Web:* www.stpsu.edu	Menlo Park	CA	94025	650-325-5621		167-3
Saint Paul Area Chamber of Commerce 401 N Robert St Ste 150 *Web:* www.saintpaulchamber.com	Saint Paul	MN	55101	651-223-5000	223-5119	139
Saint Paul Chamber Orchestra 408 St Peter St The Historic Hamm Bldg Third Fl *Web:* www.thespco.org	Saint Paul	MN	55102	651-291-1144		573-3
Saint Paul City Hall 15 W Kellogg Blvd *Web:* www.stpaul.gov	Saint Paul	MN	55102	651-266-8989	266-8521	337
Saint Paul College 235 Marshall Ave *TF:* 800-227-6029 ■ *Web:* www.saintpaul.edu	Saint Paul	MN	55102	651-846-1600	846-1703	800
Saint Paul Foundation, The 101 5th St E Ste 2400 *TF:* 800-875-6167 ■ *Web:* www.saintpaulfoundation.org	Saint Paul	MN	55101	651-224-5463	224-8123	303
Saint Paul Hotel 350 Market St. *TF:* 800-292-9292 ■ *Web:* www.saintpaulhotel.com	Saint Paul	MN	55102	651-292-9292		379
Saint Paul Linoleum & Carpet Co 2050 Center Ct *Web:* www.stpaullinocpt.com	Eagan	MN	55121	651-686-7770		290
Saint Paul Public Library 90 W Fourth St *Web:* sppl.org	Saint Paul	MN	55102	651-266-7000		434-3
Saint Paul River Ctr 175 W Kellogg Blvd *Web:* www.rivercentre.org	Saint Paul	MN	55102	651-265-4800	265-4899	205
Saint Paul School of Theology (SPST) 4370 W 109th St Ste 300 *Web:* www.spst.edu	Overland Park	KS	66211	913-253-5000		167-3
Saint Paul Stamp Works Inc 87 Empire Dr *Web:* www.stpaulstamp.com	Saint Paul	MN	55103	651-222-2100	228-1314	467
Saint Paul University 223 Main St. *TF:* 800-637-6859 ■ *Web:* ustpaul.ca	Ottawa	ON	K1S1C4	613-236-1393	782-3014	785
Saint Paul's Church National Historic Site 897 S Columbus Ave *Web:* www.nps.gov	Mount Vernon	NY	10550	914-667-4116		564
Saint Paul's College 115 College Dr *Web:* www.saintpaul.education	Lawrenceville	VA	23868	626-249-0807		166
Saint Paul's Episcopal Church 1430 J St *Web:* stpaulssacramento.org	Sacramento	CA	95814	916-446-2620		50-1
Saint Paul's Hospital 1702 20th St W. *Web:* www.stpaulshospital.org	Saskatoon	SK	S7M0Z9	306-655-5000		374-2
Saint Paul's School 325 Pleasant St *Web:* www.sps.edu	Concord	NH	03301	603-229-4600		622
Saint Peter's Seminary 1040 Waterloo St N. *TF:* 888-548-9649 ■ *Web:* www.stpetersseminary.ca	London	ON	N6A3Y1	519-432-1824	432-0964	167-3
Saint Peter's University Hospital 254 Easton Ave. *Web:* www.saintpetershcs.com	New Brunswick	NJ	08901	732-745-8600		374-3
Saint Petersburg Museum of History (SPMOH) 335 2nd Ave NE *Web:* www.spmoh.org	Saint Petersburg	FL	33701	727-894-1052		520
Saint Petersburg Public Library 3745 Ninth Ave N *Web:* www.splibraries.org	Saint Petersburg	FL	33713	727-893-7724		434-3

Name / Address	City	State	ZIP	Phone	Fax	Class
Saint Photios Greek Orthodox National Shrine 41 St George St *Web:* www.stphotios.org	Saint Augustine	FL	32085	904-829-8205	829-8707	50-1
Saint Regis Aspen Resort, The 315 E Dean St. *TF:* 888-627-7198 ■ *Web:* www.stregisaspen.com	Aspen	CO	81611	970-920-3300	925-8998	669
Saint Regis Culvert Inc 202 Morrell St *TF:* 800-527-4604 ■ *Web:* www.stregisculvert.com	Charlotte	MI	48813	517-543-3430	543-2313	697
Saint Regis Hotel 602 Dunsmuir St *TF:* 800-770-7929 ■ *Web:* www.stregishotel.com	Vancouver	BC	V6B1Y6	604-681-1135	683-1126	379
Saint Rose Hospital 27200 Calaroga Ave *Web:* www.strosehospital.org	Hayward	CA	94545	510-264-4000	887-7421	374-3
Saint Stanislaus College 304 S Beach Blvd *Web:* ststan.com	Bay Saint Louis	MS	39520	228-467-9057		622
Saint Stephen's & Saint Agnes School 1000 St Stephen's Rd *Web:* www.sssas.org	Alexandria	VA	22304	703-751-2700	683-5930	623
Saint Stephen's Episcopal School 6500 St Stephen's Dr *Web:* www.sstx.org	Austin	TX	78746	512-327-1213		622
Saint Tammany Parish Library 310 W 21st Ave. *Web:* www.sttammanylibrary.org	Covington	LA	70433	985-893-6280	871-1271	434-3
Saint Tammany Parish Tourist & Convention Commission 68099 Hwy 59 *TF:* 800-634-9443 ■ *Web:* www.louisiananorthshore.com	Mandeville	LA	70471	985-892-0520	892-1441	206
Saint Tammany West Chamber of Commerce 610 Hollycrest Blvd *Web:* www.sttammanychamber.org	Covington	LA	70433	985-892-3216		139
Saint Thomas Aquinas College 125 Rt 340 *TF:* 800-262-3257 ■ *Web:* www.stac.edu	Sparkill	NY	10976	845-398-4000	398-4114	166
Saint Thomas Choir School 202 W 58th St. *Web:* www.choirschool.org	New York	NY	10019	212-247-3311		622
Saint Thomas Hospital 444 N Main St *TF:* 800-237-8662 ■ *Web:* www.summahealth.org	Akron	OH	44310	330-375-3000		374-3
Saint Thomas University 51 Dineen Dr *Web:* www.stu.ca	Fredericton	NB	E3B5G3	506-452-0640		785
Saint Thomas University 16401 NW 37th Ave *TF:* 800-367-9010 ■ *Web:* www.stu.edu	Miami Gardens	FL	33054	305-628-6546	628-6591	166
Saint Thomas-Elgin General Hospital 189 Elm St *Web:* www.stegh.on.ca	Saint Thomas	ON	N5R5C4	519-631-2020	631-1825	374-2
Saint Tikhon's Orthodox Theological Seminary St Tikhon's Rd PO Box 130. *Web:* www.stots.edu	South Canaan	PA	18459	570-561-1818		167-3
Saint Timothy's School 8400 Greenspring Ave *Web:* www.stt.org	Stevenson	MD	21153	410-486-7400		622
Saint Vincent Charity Hospital (SVCH) 2322 E 22nd St Ste 102 *Web:* www.stvincentcharity.com	Cleveland	OH	44115	216-861-6200		374-3
Saint Vincent de Paul Regional Seminary 10701 S Military Trl *Web:* www.svdp.edu	Boynton Beach	FL	33436	561-732-4424	737-2205	167-3
Saint Vincent Hospital-Worcester Medical Ctr 123 Summer St. *TF:* 877-633-2368 ■ *Web:* www.stvincenthospital.com	Worcester	MA	01608	508-363-5000		374-3
Saint Vincent Medical Ctr 2131 W Third St *Web:* stvincent.verity.org	Los Angeles	CA	90057	213-484-7111		374-3
Saint Vincent Rehabilitation Hospital 2201 Wildwood Ave *Web:* stvincentrehabhospital.com	Sherwood	AR	72120	501-834-1800		374-6
Saint Vincent Seminary 300 Fraser Purchase Rd *Web:* www.saintvincentseminary.edu	Latrobe	PA	15650	724-532-6600	532-5052	167-3
Saint Vincent Women's Hospital 8111 Township Line Rd *TF:* 800-582-8258 ■ *Web:* www.stvincent.org	Indianapolis	IN	46260	317-415-8111		374-7
Saint Vincent's Hospital 810 St Vincent's Dr *TF:* 800-965-7231 ■ *Web:* healthcare.ascension.or	Birmingham	AL	35205	205-939-7000		374-3
Saint Vincent's Medical Ctr 2800 Main St *TF:* 877-255-7847 ■ *Web:* www.stvincents.org	Bridgeport	CT	06606	203-576-6000		374-3
Saint Vrain State Park 3525 State Hwy 119 *Web:* cpw.state.co.us	Firestone	CO	80504	303-678-9402	776-7320	565
Saint Xavier University 3700 W 103rd St *TF:* 800-462-9288 ■ *Web:* www.sxu.edu	Chicago	IL	60655	773-298-3000	298-3076	166
Sainte Genevieve County 55 S Third St *Web:* www.stegencounty.org	Sainte Genevieve	MO	63670	573-883-3000	883-5312	338
Sainte Marie among the Iroquois Museum 6680 Onondaga Lake Pkwy *Web:* ongov.net	Liverpool	NY	13088	315-453-6768		520
Saint-Gaudens National Historic Site 139 St Gaudens Rd *Web:* www.nps.gov	Cornish	NH	03745	603-675-2175	675-2701	564
Saint-Gobain Ceramics & Plastics Inc 1 New Bond St *Web:* www.ceramicmaterials.saint-gobain.com	Worcester	MA	01606	508-795-5000		751
Saint-Gobain High-Performance Refractories 4702 Rt 982 *TF:* 800-438-7237 ■ *Web:* www.refractories.saint-gobain.com	Latrobe	PA	15650	724-539-6000	539-6070	249
Saint-Jacques 6112 Falls of the Neuse Rd *Web:* saintjacquesfrenchcuisine.com	Raleigh	NC	27609	919-862-2770	862-2771	671
Saints Capital 2020 Union St *Web:* saintscapital.com	San Francisco	CA	94123	415-773-2080		792

Name / Address	City	State	Zip	Phone	Fax	Class
SAISD (San Antonio Independent School District) 141 Lavaca St *Web:* www.saisd.net	San Antonio	TX	78210	210-554-2200	299-5600	685
Sajak Broadcasting Corp 236 Admiral Dr *Web:* www.1430wnav.com	Annapolis	MD	21401	410-263-1430	268-5360	645-141
SAJE Technology LLC 765 Dixon Ct *Web:* www.saje-tech.com	Hoffman Estates	IL	60192	847-756-7603	496-4515	735
Saji-Ya 695 Grand Ave *Web:* www.sajiya.com	Saint Paul	MN	55105	651-292-0444		671
Sakana 2026 P St NW *Web:* www.sakana.juisyfood.com	Washington	DC	20036	202-887-0900		671
Sakata Farms Inc 384 E Bromley Ln PO Box 508	Brighton	CO	80601	303-659-1559		10-11
Sakata Seed America Inc 18095 Serene Dr *Web:* www.sakata.com	Morgan Hill	CA	95037	408-778-7758	778-7768	694
Sakatah Lake State Park 50499 Sakatah Lake State Park Rd *Web:* www.dnr.state.mn.us	Waterville	MN	56096	507-698-7850		565
Sake Cafe 2830 Magazine St *Web:* www.sakecafeonmagazine.com	New Orleans	LA	70115	504-894-0033		671
Saker Aviation Services Inc 20 South St *Web:* sakeraviation.com	New York	NY	10004	212-776-4046	363-6792	63
Sakki Computers Inc 22B Hempstead Tpke *Web:* sakki.com	Farmingdale	NY	11735	516-293-1609		180
Sakonnet Vineyards 162 W Main Rd *Web:* www.sakonnetwine.com	Little Compton	RI	02837	401-635-8486		50-7
Sakrete 8201 Arrowridge Blvd *Web:* www.sakrete.com	Charlotte	NC	28273	704-525-1621	529-5261	183
Sakshar Inc 980 Moraga Ave *Web:* www.sakshar.com	Piedmont	CA	94611	510-808-5176	653-8508	637-2
Sakura 7201 N Keystone Ave *Web:* www.indysakura.com	Indianapolis	IN	46240	317-259-4171		671
Sakura 5828 W Jefferson Blvd *Web:* www.sakurafortwayne.com	Fort Wayne	IN	46804	260-459-2022		671
Sakura Bana 4800 I-55 N *Web:* www.sakurabanajackson.com	Jackson	MS	39211	601-982-3035		671
Sakura Fine Japanese Dining 6194 Hwy 49 N	Hattiesburg	MS	39401	601-545-9393		671
Sakura Finetek USA Inc 1750 W 214th St *TF:* 800-725-8723 ■ *Web:* www.sakuraus.com	Torrance	CA	90501	310-972-7800	972-7888	419
Sakura Japanese Restaurant 350 St Peter St *Web:* www.sakurastpaul.com	Saint Paul	MN	55102	651-224-0185		671
Sakurabana 57 Broad St *Web:* www.sakurabanaboston.com	Boston	MA	02109	617-542-4311		671
Sal Deforte's 1400 Parkway Ave Serenity Plz *Web:* www.saldefortesristorante.com	Ewing	NJ	08628	609-406-0123		671
Sal's 1242 Richmond Rd *Web:* salsbyvictor.com	Williamsburg	VA	23185	757-220-2641		671
Salad Creations 4437 Lyons Rd *Web:* saladcreations.net	Coconut Creek	FL	33073	954-972-5237		670
Saladax Biomedical Inc 116 Research Dr *Web:* www.saladax.com	Bethlehem	PA	18015	610-419-6731		231
Saladino's Inc 3325 W Figarden Dr *TF:* 800-248-8089 ■ *Web:* www.saladinos.com	Fresno	CA	93711	559-271-3700		297
Saladmaster Inc 4300 Amon Carter Blvd Ste 100 *TF:* 800-765-5795 ■ *Web:* saladmaster.com	Arlington	TX	76018	817-633-3555	633-5544	486
Salamon, Gruber, Blaymore & Strenger PC 97 Powerhouse Rd Ste 102 *Web:* sgnblaw.com	Roslyn Heights	NY	11577	516-625-1700		41
Salamonie Lake 9214 Lost Bridge Rd W *Web:* www.in.gov	Andrews	IN	46702	260-468-2125		565
Salazar International Inc 23800 Commerce Park Rd *Web:* salazarinternational.com	Cleveland	OH	44122	216-464-2420	464-9084	61
Salazar Service & Trucking Corp 1360 S US 385 *Web:* www.salazarservice.com	Andrews	TX	79714	432-523-9658		539
Salcido Law Firm PLLC 43 West 9000 South Ste B *Web:* salcidolawfirm.com	Sandy	UT	84070	801-413-1753		41
Salco Products Inc 1385 101st St Ste A *Web:* www.salcoproducts.com	Lemont	IL	60439	630-685-4661	783-2590	650
Saleem Fish Supreme LLC 2198 Pio Nono Ave	Macon	GA	31206	478-788-8600		671
Saleen Automotive Inc 2735 Wardlow Rd *TF:* 800-888-8945 ■ *Web:* saleen.com	Corona	CA	92882	800-888-8945		59
Salem Academy (SA) 942 Lancaster Dr NE *Web:* salemacademy.org	Salem	OR	97301	503-378-1219		622
Salem Area Chamber of Commerce 1110 Commercial St NE *Web:* salemchamber.org	Salem	OR	97301	503-581-1466	581-0972	139
Salem Area Chamber of Commerce 713 E State St *Web:* www.salemohiochamber.org	Salem	OH	44460	330-337-3473	337-3474	139
Salem Associates Inc 7074 Peachtree Indus Blvd *Web:* www.salemassociates.com	Norcross	GA	30071	770-729-8089		196
Salem Athenaeum, The 337 Essex St *Web:* salemathenaeum.net	Salem	MA	01970	978-744-2540	744-7536	434-4
Salem Chamber of Commerce 265 Essex St *Web:* www.salem-chamber.org	Salem	MA	01970	978-744-0004	745-3855	139
Salem City Hall 555 Liberty St SE Rm 220 *Web:* www.cityofsalem.net	Salem	OR	97301	503-588-6255	588-6354	337
Salem College 601 S Church St *TF:* 800-327-2536 ■ *Web:* www.salem.edu	Winston-Salem	NC	27101	336-721-2600	917-5572	166
Salem Community College 460 Hollywood Ave *Web:* www.salemcc.edu	Carneys Point	NJ	08069	856-299-2100		162
Salem Conference Ctr 200 Commercial St SE *TF:* 877-589-1700 ■ *Web:* salemconventioncenter.org	Salem	OR	97301	503-589-1700		205
Salem Convention & Visitors Assn 181 High St NE *TF:* 800-874-7012 ■ *Web:* www.travelsalem.com	Salem	OR	97301	503-581-4325	581-4540	206
Salem County 94 Market St *Web:* www.salemcountynj.gov	Salem	NJ	08079	856-935-7510	935-6725	338
Salem Ctr 401 Center St NE *Web:* www.salemcenter.com	Salem	OR	97301	503-399-9676		460
Salem Electric 633 Seventh St NW *Web:* www.salemelectric.com	Salem	OR	97304	503-362-3601	371-2956	245
Salem Electric Company Inc 3933 Westpoint Blvd PO Box 26784 *Web:* www.salemelectriccoinc.com	Winston-Salem	NC	27114	336-765-0221	765-7286	189-4
Salem Equipment Inc 14440 SW Tltn Shrwd Rd *Web:* www.salemequip.com	Sherwood	OR	97140	503-581-8411	581-8951	821
Salem Farm Supply Inc 5109 State Rte 22 *TF:* 800-999-3276 ■ *Web:* www.salemfarmsupply.com	Salem	NY	12865	518-854-7424	854-3057	274
Salem Five & Savings Bank 210 Essex St *TF:* 800-850-5000 ■ *Web:* www.salemfive.com	Salem	MA	01970	978-745-5555	745-1073	70
Salem Group, The 2 Trans Am Plz Dr *Web:* www.saleminc.com	Oakbrook Terrace	IL	60181	630-932-7000		721
Salem Hospital 665 Winter St SE *TF:* 800-876-1718 ■ *Web:* www.salemhealth.org	Salem	OR	97301	800-876-1718		374-3
Salem House Press PO Box 249 *Web:* www.salemhousepress.com	Salem	MA	01970	978-578-9238		637-2
Salem International University 223 W Main St *TF:* 800-283-4562 ■ *Web:* www.salemu.edu	Salem	WV	26426	304-326-1109		166
Salem Maritime National Historic Site 160 Derby St *Web:* www.nps.gov	Salem	MA	01970	978-740-1650		564
Salem Media Group 4880 Santa Rosa Rd *Web:* www.salemmedia.com	Camarillo	CA	93012	805-987-0400		647
Salem Metal Fabricators Inc 21 Lonergan Rd *Web:* www.salemmetal.com	Middleton	MA	01949	978-774-2100	777-4597	697
Salem Museum 801 E Main St *Web:* www.salemmuseum.org	Salem	VA	24153	540-389-6760		520
Salem Music Network Inc 402 BNA Dr Ste 400 *Web:* www.salemmusicnetwork.com	Nashville	TN	37217	615-367-2210		647
Salem Radio Network 6400 N Beltline Rd Ste 210 **Fax Area Code:* 972 ■ *Web:* www.srnonline.com	Irving	TX	75063	212-419-4663	831-8626*	646
Salem Ready Mix Concrete Inc 2250 Salem Industrial Dr *Web:* salemreadymix.com	Salem	VA	24153	540-387-1171	389-5531	182
Salem State College 352 Lafayette St *Web:* www.salemstate.edu	Salem	MA	01970	978-542-6000	542-6893	166
Salem Technologies Inc 2580 Salem Point Ct *TF:* 888-872-3652 ■ *Web:* www.salemtech.net	Winston-Salem	NC	27103	336-777-3652	777-3654	604
Salem Tools Inc 1602 Midland Rd *TF:* 800-390-4348 ■ *Web:* www.salemtools.com	Salem	VA	24153	540-378-3500	375-3807	386
Salem Tube Inc 951 Fourth St *Web:* www.salemtube.com	Greenville	PA	16125	724-646-4301	646-4311	490
Salem Veterans Affairs Medical Ctr 1970 Roanoke Blvd *TF:* 888-982-2463 ■ *Web:* va.gov	Salem	VA	24153	540-982-2463		374-8
Salem Village Craftsmen Inc 14 S Pleasant St *TF:* 800-840-9121 ■ *Web:* www.shakerworkshops.com	Ashburnham	MA	01430	978-827-9900	827-6554	321
Salem Witch Museum 19 1/2 Washington Sq N *Web:* www.salemwitchmuseum.com	Salem	MA	01970	978-744-1692		520
Salem/Roanoke County Chamber of Commerce 611 E Main St *Web:* www.s-rcchamber.org	Salem	VA	24153	540-387-0267	387-4110	139
Salem-Keizer Public Schools 2450 Lancaster Dr NE *TF:* 877-293-1090 ■ *Web:* salkeiz.k12.or.us	Salem	OR	97305	503-399-3000		685
Salem-Republic Rubber Co 475 W California Ave **Fax Area Code:* 330 ■ *TF:* 800-686-4199 ■ *Web:* www.salem-republic.com	Sebring	OH	44672	877-425-5079	938-9809*	370
Salena's Mexican Restaurant At the Vlg Gate 302 N Goodman St *Web:* www.salenas.com	Rochester	NY	14607	585-256-5980		671
Salenger, Sack, Kimmel & Bavaro LLP 180 Froehlich Farm Blvd *Web:* sskblaw.com	Woodbury	NY	11797	516-677-0100		41
SalePoint Inc 9909 Huennekens St Ste 205 *Web:* www.salepoint.com	San Diego	CA	92121	858-546-9400		225
Sales & Marketing Management Magazine 27020 Noble Rd *Web:* salesandmarketing.com	Excelsior	MN	55331	952-401-1283	401-7899	457-5
Sales Benchmark Index 2021 McKinney Ave Ste 550 *TF:* 888-556-7338 ■ *Web:* salesbenchmarkindex.com	Dallas	TX	75201	888-556-7338		5
Sales Concepts Inc 610 Hembree Pkwy *TF:* 800-229-2328 ■ *Web:* salesconcepts.com	Roswell	GA	30076	678-624-9229		463
Sales Effectiveness Inc 570 W Crssvlle Rd *Web:* saleseffectiveness.com	Roswell	GA	30075	770-552-6612		463
Sales Evolution LLC 2837 Dogwood Ln *Web:* www.salesevolution.com	Broomall	PA	19008	610-662-3199		195
Sales Gauge 70 Constitution Rd *Web:* www.sales-gauge.com	Charlestown	MA	02129	781-910-0077		393
Sales Lead Management Assn 1770 Front St Ste 265 *Web:* www.salesleadmgmtassn.com	Lynden	WA	98264	360-933-1259		78

Phone | Fax | Class

Sales Loft
1180 W Peachtree St NW Ste 600 Atlanta GA 30309 770-756-8022 788
Web: www.salesloft.com

Sales Opportunity Services Inc
PO Box 951 Altoona PA 16603 814-949-3327 949-3339 387
TF: 800-225-6853 ■ *Web:* www.sossos.com

Sales Partnerships Inc
350 Interlocken Blvd Ste 280 Broomfield CO 80021 800-570-1652 449-7116* 192
**Fax Area Code:* 303 ■ *TF:* 800-570-1652 ■ *Web:* www.salespartnerships.com

Sales Performance International Inc
6201 Fairview Rd Ste 400 Charlotte NC 28210 704-227-6500 242
Web: www.spisales.com

Sales Readiness Group Inc
8015 SE 28th St Ste 200 Mercer Island WA 98040 206-905-8756 274-9219 195
TF: 800-490-0715 ■ *Web:* www.salesreadinessgroup.com

Sales Simplicity Software
325 E Elliot Rd Chandler AZ 85225 480-892-2500 177
Web: www.salessimplicity.net

Sales Systems Ltd 700 Florida Ave Portsmouth VA 23707 757-397-0763 393-3669 351
TF: 800-368-3711 ■ *Web:* catalogue.salessystemsltd.com

Sales Tax Resource Group
16882 Bolsa Chica St Ste 206 Huntington Beach CA 92649 714-377-2600 2
Web: www.salestaxresource.com

Salesforce East 415 Mission St San Francisco CA 94105 415-291-8880 178-2
NYSE: CRM ■ *Web:* www.salesforce.com

SalesforceCom Foundation
The Landmark @ One Market Ste 300 San Francisco CA 94105 800-667-6389 305
TF: 800-667-6389 ■ *Web:* www.salesforce.org

Salesian High School
2851 Salesian Ave Richmond CA 94804 510-234-4433 685
Web: www.salesian.com

Salford Systems Inc
9685 Via Excelencia Ste 208 San Diego CA 92126 619-543-8880 177
Web: www.salford-systems.com

Salice America Inc
2123 Crown Centre Dr Charlotte NC 28227 704-841-7810 350
TF: 800-222-9652 ■ *Web:* www.saliceamerica.com

Salida Union School District
4801 Sisk Rd Salida CA 95308 209-545-0339 780
Web: www.salida.k12.ca.us

Salient Corp 203 Colonial Dr Horseheads NY 14845 607-739-4511 466
Web: www.salient.com

Salina Area Chamber of Commerce
120 W Ash St Salina KS 67401 785-827-9301 827-9758 139
TF: 877-725-4625 ■ *Web:* www.salinakansas.org

Salina Concrete Products Inc
PO Box 136 Salina KS 67401 785-827-7281 182
Web: www.salinaconcreteproducts.com

Salina Journal PO Box 740 Salina KS 67402 785-823-6363 827-6363 532-2
TF: 800-827-6363 ■ *Web:* www.salina.com

Salina Public Library 301 W Elm St Salina KS 67401 785-825-4624 823-0706 434-3
TF: 800-362-2642 ■ *Web:* www.salinapubliclibrary.org

Salina Regional Health Ctr
400 S Santa Fe Ave Salina KS 67401 785-452-7000 374-3
Web: www.srhc.com

Salina Supply Co, The
302 N Santa Fe Ave Salina KS 67402 785-823-2221 823-3532 612
TF: 800-288-1231 ■ *Web:* www.salinasupply.com

Salina Vortex Corp 1725 Vortex Ave Salina KS 67401 888-829-7821 825-7194* 789
**Fax Area Code:* 785 ■ *TF:* 888-829-7821 ■ *Web:* www.vortexglobal.com

Salinas Tile Sales Inc 1 Spring St Salinas CA 93901 831-424-8046 424-9836 751
Web: www.salinastile.com

Salinas Valley Chamber of Commerce
119 E Alisal St Salinas CA 93901 831-751-7725 424-8639 139
Web: www.salinaschamber.com

Salinas Valley Memorial Hospital (SVMH)
450 E Romie Ln Salinas CA 93901 831-757-4333 374-3
Web: www.svmh.com

Salinas Valley State Prison
31625 Hwy 101 N Soledad CA 93960 831-678-5500 213
Web: cdcr.ca.gov

Salina-Spavinaw Telephone Company Inc (SST)
109 E Evanjoy St Salina OK 74365 918-434-5392 434-6960 224
TF: 800-722-3450 ■ *Web:* www.sstelco.com

Saline Area Schools
7265 Saline Ann Arbor Rd Saline MI 48176 734-429-8000 685
Web: www.salineschools.org

Saline County 200 N Main St Ste 117 Benton AR 72015 501-303-5630 338
TF: 800-438-6233 ■ *Web:* www.salinecounty.org

Saline County 10 E Poplar St Ste 17 Harrisburg IL 62946 618-253-5096 253-3904 338
Web: www.illinoiscourts.gov

Saline County PO Box 665 Marshall MO 65340 660-886-7777 886-2603 338
Web: www.salinecountymo.org

Saline County 300 W Ash Rm 215 Salina KS 67402 785-309-5820 309-5826 338
Web: www.saline.org

Saline County History and Heritage Society (SCHHS)
123 N Market St Benton AR 72015 501-778-3770 520
Web: www.schhs.us

Saline County Public Library
1800 Smithers Dr Benton AR 72015 501-778-4766 434-3
Web: www.salinecountylibrary.org

Saline County State Fish & Wildlife Area
85 Glen O Jones Rd Equality IL 62934 618-276-4405 565
Web: www.dnr.illinois.gov

Saline Courthouse
204 S High St PO Box 865 Wilber NE 68465 402-821-2374 821-3381 338
Web: co.saline.ne.us

Saline Memorial Hospital
1 Medical Pk Dr Benton AR 72015 501-776-6000 776-6019 374-3
Web: www.salinememorial.org

Salisbury Area Chamber of Commerce
144 E Main St PO Box 510 Salisbury MD 21803 410-749-0144 860-9925 139
Web: salisburyarea.com

Salisbury Bancorp Inc
5 Bissell St PO Box 1868 Lakeville CT 06039 860-435-9801 435-0631 360-2
NASDAQ: SAL ■ *TF:* 800-222-9801 ■ *Web:* www.salisburybank.com

Salisbury Beach State Reservation
Beach Rd Rt 1A Salisbury MA 01952 978-462-4481 565
Web: www.mass.gov

Phone | Fax | Class

Salisbury Management Inc (SMI)
120 Shrewsbury St Boylston MA 01505 508-869-0764 652
Web: salisburymanagement.com

Salisbury Motor Company Inc
700 W Innes St Salisbury NC 28144 704-636-1341 57
Web: www.salisburymotorcompany.com

Salisbury National Cemetery
501 Statesville Blvd Salisbury NC 28144 704-636-2661 636-1115 136
Web: www.cem.va.gov

Salisbury Ocean City-Wicomico County Regional Airport
5485 Airport Terminal Rd Salisbury MD 21804 410-548-4827 27
Web: flysbyairport.com

Salisbury School 251 Canaan Rd Salisbury CT 06068 860-435-5732 435-5750 622
Web: www.salisburyschool.org

Salisbury Scrap Metal Inc
909 Boundary St Salisbury MD 21801 410-546-1111 686
Web: salisburyscrap.com

Salisbury University
1200 Camden Ave Salisbury MD 21801 410-543-6000 546-6016 166
TF: 888-543-0148 ■ *Web:* www.salisbury.edu

Salisbury VA Medical Ctr
1601 Brenner Ave Salisbury NC 28144 704-638-9000 374-8
TF: 800-469-8262 ■ *Web:* www.salisbury.va.gov

Salisbury Zoological Park
755 S Pk Dr Salisbury MD 21804 410-548-3188 860-0919 823
Web: www.salisburyzoo.org

Salish Kootenai College PO Box 70 Pablo MT 59855 406-275-4800 275-4801 165
TF: 877-752-6553 ■ *Web:* www.skc.edu

Salish Lodge & Spa
6501 Railroad Ave SE Snoqualmie WA 98065 425-888-2556 888-9634 669
TF: 800-272-5474 ■ *Web:* www.salishlodge.com

Salishan Lodge & Golf Resort
7760 Hwy 101 N Gleneden Beach OR 97388 800-452-2300 764-3681* 669
**Fax Area Code:* 541 ■ *TF:* 800-452-2300 ■ *Web:* www.salishan.com

Salit Steel Ltd
7771 Stanley Ave Niagara Falls ON L2E6V6 905-354-5691 492
TF: 800-263-7110 ■ *Web:* www.salitsteel.com

Salix Pharmaceuticals Inc
8510 Colonnade Center Dr Raleigh NC 27615 919-862-1000 582
TF: 800-508-0024 ■ *Web:* www.salix.com

Salk Institute for Biological Studies
PO Box 85800 San Diego CA 92186 858-453-4100 668
Web: www.salk.edu

Sallee Horse Vans Inc 2053 Buck Ln Lexington KY 40511 859-255-9406 281-6257 780
Web: www.salleehorsevans.com

Salley Law Firm PA 129 E Main St Lexington SC 29072 803-356-5000 41
Web: salleylawfirm.com

Sallie Mae 12061 Bluemont Way Reston VA 20190 703-810-3000 848-1949* 217
**Fax Area Code:* 800 ■ *TF:* 888-272-5543 ■ *Web:* www.salliemae.com

Sallisaw Chamber of Commerce
301 E Cherokee Ave Sallisaw OK 74955 918-775-2558 775-4021 139
Web: www.sallisawchamber.com

Sally Beauty Company Inc
3001 Colorado Blvd Denton TX 76210 940-898-7500 76
TF: 800-777-5706 ■ *Web:* www.sallybeauty.com

Sally Corp 745 W Forsyth St Jacksonville FL 32204 904-355-7100 355-7170 239
Web: www.sallycorp.com

Sally Silver Cos PO Box 1265 Marblehead MA 01945 781-890-7272 663-4877* 260
**Fax Area Code:* 253 ■ *Web:* www.sallysilver.com

Sally's Flower Shop 325 Main St Ste 5 Winooski VT 05404 802-655-3894 292
TF: 800-392-4196 ■ *Web:* www.sallysflowers.org

Salmon Brook Veterinary Hospital PC
136 Salmon Brook St Granby CT 06035 860-653-7238 794
Web: salmonbrookvets.com

Salmon River Electric Co-opeartive Inc
1130 Main St PO Box 384 Challis ID 83226 208-879-2283 879-2596 245
TF: 877-806-2283 ■ *Web:* www.srec.org

Salmonier Nature Park PO Box 190 Holyrood NL A0A2R0 709-229-7888 229-7078 823
Web: www.env.gov.nl.ca

Salomon & Ludwin LLC 1401 Gaskins Rd Richmond VA 23238 804-592-4999 690
Web: salomonludwin.com

Salon 7 107 W Branch Ave Pine Hill NJ 08021 856-258-2072 77
Web: salon7nj.com

Salon Aria LLC 5260 Utica Ridge Rd Davenport IA 52807 563-359-5098 77
Web: salonaria.com

Salon Marrow Dyckman Newman & Broudy LLP
292 Madison Ave New York NY 10017 888-317-8676 445
TF: 888-317-8676 ■ *Web:* www.salonmarrow.com

Salon Professional Academy Altoona
415 D Orchard Ave Altoona PA 16601 814-944-4494 167-3
Web: www.tspaaltoona.com

Salon Professional Academy Anderson
5335 S Scatterfield Rd Anderson IN 46013 765-649-5555 167-3
Web: www.andersonsalonacademy.com

Salon Professional Academy Appleton
3355 W College Ave Appleton WI 54914 920-968-0433 167-3
Web: www.tspaappleton.com

Salon Professional Academy Buffalo
2309 Eggert Rd Tonawanda NY 14150 716-833-8772 167-3
Web: www.tspabuffalo.com

Salon Professional Academy Colorado Springs
4388 Austin Bluffs Pkwy Colorado Springs CO 80918 719-226-9400 167-3
Web: www.thesalonprofessionalacademycoloradosprings.com

Salon Professional Academy Dallas
Stemmons Fwy 2440 S Ste B Lewisville TX 75067 214-222-2436 167-3
Web: www.tspadallas.com

Salon Professional Academy Evansville
5545 Vogel Rd Evansville IN 47715 812-437-8772 167-3
Web: www.tspaevansville.com

Salon Professional Academy Fargo
4377 15th Ave S Fargo ND 58103 701-451-9100 167-3
Web: www.tspafargo.com

Salon Professional Academy Fort Myers
1388 Colonial Blvd Fort Myers FL 33907 239-208-3954 167-3
Web: www.tspaftmyers.com

Salon Professional Academy Iowa City
1550 S 1st Ave Iowa City IA 52240 319-248-2958 167-3
Web: www.tspaiowacity.com

	Phone	Fax	Class
Salon Professional Academy Little Rock 4619 JFK Blvd North Little Rock AR 72116 *Web:* www.littlerockbeautyschool.com	501-753-2400		167-3
Salon Professional Academy Nashville 2710 Old Lebanon Rd Ste 6 Nashville TN 37214 *Web:* www.nashvillebeautyschool.com	615-828-1866		167-3
Salon Professional Academy Onalaska 566 Theater Rd Onalaska WI 54650 *Web:* www.salonproacademy.com	608-783-7400		167-3
Salon Professional Academy Shorewood 335 Vertin Blvd Shorewood IL 60404 *Web:* www.tspashorewood.com	815-609-6880		167-3
Salon Professional Academy St Louis 3141 W Clay St Saint Charles MO 63301 *Web:* www.tspastlouis.com	636-542-4723		167-3
Salon Secrets Inc 1805 N Mason Rd Katy TX 77449 *Web:* salonsecretsinkaty.com	281-347-4887		77
Salon Service Group Inc 1520 E Evergreen Springfield MO 65803 *TF:* 800-933-5733 ■ *Web:* www.salonservicegroup.com	417-761-7309		77
Salon Services & Supplies Inc 740 SW 34th St Renton WA 98057 *TF:* 800-251-4247 ■ *Web:* www.salonservicesnw.com	425-251-8840		77
Salon Success Academy 1915 W Redlands Blvd Ste 111 Redlands CA 92373 *Web:* www.gotobeautyschool.com	909-307-0312		167-3
Salon Success Academy 16803 Arrow Blvd Fontana CA 92335 *Web:* www.gotobeautyschool.com	909-822-1149		77
Salon Success Academy 1385 E Foothill Blvd Upland CA 91786 *TF:* 877-987-4247 ■ *Web:* www.gotobeautyschool.com	909-982-4662		77
Saloncom 22 Fourth St 16th Fl San Francisco CA 94103 *Web:* www.salon.com	415-645-9200	645-9204	171
Salone De Bella 416 Washington St Holliston MA 01746 *Web:* salonedebella.com	508-429-2287		77
Saloon 750 S Seventh St Philadelphia PA 19147 *Web:* www.saloonrestaurant.net	215-627-1811		671
Salpicon 1252 N Wells St Chicago IL 60610 *Web:* salpicon.com	312-988-7811		671
Salsa 6 Patton Ave Asheville NC 28801 *Web:* www.salsasnc.com	828-252-9805		671
Salsa A la Salsa 1420 Nicollet Ave Minneapolis MN 55403 *Web:* www.salsaalasalsa.com	612-813-1970		671
Salsbury Industries Inc 1010 E 62nd St Los Angeles CA 90001 *TF:* 800-624-5299 ■ *Web:* www.mailboxes.com	323-846-6700	846-6800	286
Salt & Pepper 6515 Bowness Rd NW Calgary AB T3B0E8 *Web:* www.saltnpepper.ca	403-247-4402		671
Salt Branding LLC 1620 Montgomery St Ste 120 San Francisco CA 94111 *Web:* saltbranding.com	415-616-1500		195
Salt Cellar 550 N Hayden Rd Scottsdale AZ 85257 *Web:* saltcellarrestaurant.com	480-947-1963	941-0929	671
Salt Group, The 1845 Sidney Baker St Kerrville TX 78028 *TF:* 888-257-1266 ■ *Web:* www.thesaltgroup.com	830-257-1290		734
Salt Lake Cable & Harness Inc 421 W 900 N North Salt Lake UT 84054 *Web:* www.saltlakecable.com	801-292-4999		463
Salt Lake City - City Hall 451 S State St Salt Lake City UT 84111 *Web:* www.slcgov.com	801-535-7704	535-6331	337
Salt Lake City Chamber of Commerce 175 E University Blvd 400 S Ste 600 Salt Lake City UT 84111 *Web:* slchamber.com	801-364-3631	328-5098	139
Salt Lake City International Airport 776 N Terminal Dr PO Box 145550 Salt Lake City UT 84116 *TF:* 800-595-2442 ■ *Web:* slcairport.com	801-575-2400	575-2645	27
Salt Lake City Weekly 248 S Main St Salt Lake City UT 84101 *Web:* www.cityweekly.net	801-575-7003	575-6106	532-5
Salt Lake Community College Grand Theatre 1575 S State St Salt Lake City UT 84115 *TF:* 800-524-9400 ■ *Web:* www.slcc.edu	801-957-3322		572
Salt Lake County 2001 S State St Salt Lake City UT 84190 *Web:* slco.org	801-468-3000		338
Salt Lake County Library System 2197 E Ft Union Blvd Salt Lake City UT 84121 *Web:* www.slcolibrary.org	801-943-4636	942-6323	434-3
Salt Lake Mailing & Printing Inc 1841 S Pioneer Rd Salt Lake City UT 84104 *Web:* www.saltlakemailing.com	801-923-4800		627
Salt Lake Regional Medical Ctr 1050 E South Temple Salt Lake City UT 84102 *TF:* 866-431-9355 ■ *Web:* www.saltlakeregional.org	801-350-4111	350-4522	374-3
Salt Lake School District 440 East 100 South Salt Lake City UT 84111 *Web:* www.slcschools.org	801-578-8599	578-8689	685
Salt Lake Temple 50 W N Temple St Salt Lake City UT 84150 *Web:* www.lds.org	801-240-2640		50-1
Salt Lake Tribune 90 South 400 West Ste 700 Salt Lake City UT 84101 *Web:* www.sltrib.com	801-257-8742	257-8525	532-2
Salt Lick 18300 FM 1826 Driftwood TX 78619 *Web:* saltlickbbq.com	512-858-4959		671
Salt Palace Convention Ctr 100 W Temple Salt Lake City UT 84101 *Web:* www.visitsaltlake.com	385-468-2222		205
Salt Point State Park 25050 Hwy 1 Jenner CA 95450 *Web:* www.parks.ca.gov	707-847-3221		565
Salt Pond Coalition (SPC) PO Box 875 Charlestown RI 02813 *Web:* www.saltpondscoalition.org	401-322-3068		192
Salt River Bay National Historical Park & Ecological Preserve 2100 Church St Ste 100 Christiansted VI 00820 *Web:* www.nps.gov	340-773-1460		564
Salt River Electric Co-opeartive Corp 111 W Brashear Ave Bardstown KY 40004 *TF:* 800-221-7465 ■ *Web:* www.srelectric.com	502-348-3931		245
Salt River Project (SRP) 1521 N Project Dr Tempe AZ 85281 *TF:* 800-258-4777 ■ *Web:* srpnet.com	602-236-5900	236-2442	787
Salt Water Cowboy's 299 Dondanville Rd Saint Augustine FL 32084 *Web:* www.saltwatercowboys.com	904-471-2332		671
Saltech Systems Inc 137 Lynn Ave Ste 200 Ames IA 50014 *Web:* www.saltechsystems.com	515-520-8200		177
Salter Bus Lines Inc 212 Hudson Ave Jonesboro LA 71251 *TF:* 800-223-8056 ■ *Web:* www.salter.us	318-259-2522		107
Salter Labs 100 Sycamore Rd Arvin CA 93203 *TF:* 800-421-0024 ■ *Web:* www.salterlabs.com	661-854-3166	854-3850	476
Salter Mcgowan Sylvia & Leonard Inc 321 S Main St Providence RI 02903 *Web:* smsllaw.com	401-274-0300		41
Salter Mitchell Inc 117 S Gadsden St Tallahassee FL 32301 *Web:* www.saltermitchell.com	850-681-3200		636
Saltgrass Steak House 520 Meyerland Plaza Mall Houston TX 77096 *Web:* www.saltgrass.com	713-665-2226		671
Salton Sea State Recreation Area 100-225 State Park Rd North Shore CA 92254 *Web:* www.parks.ca.gov	760-393-3059		565
Saltwater State Park 25205 Eigth Pl S Des Moines WA 98198 *Web:* parks.state.wa.us	253-661-4956		565
Salty Dog Cafe, The 232 S Sea Pines Dr Hilton Head Island SC 29928 *Web:* saltydog.com	843-671-2233		671
Salty's on Alki Beach 1936 Harbor Ave SW Seattle WA 98126 *Web:* www.saltys.com	206-937-1600		671
Saltzman & Gordon LLC 1611 Pond Rd Ste 230 Allentown PA 18104 *Web:* saltzmangordonlaw.com	610-435-6300	435-7652	41
Saltzmans Watches & More Inc 1024 Reservoir Ave Cranston RI 02910 *Web:* saltzmans-watches.com	401-946-0930		411
Saluda Standard PO Box 668 Saluda SC 29138 *Web:* www.saludastandard-sentinel.com	864-445-2527	445-8679	532-2
Saluda's 751 Saluda Ave Columbia SC 29205 *Web:* www.saludas.com	803-799-9500		671
Saludos Hispanos 73-121 Fred Waring Dr Ste 100 Palm Desert CA 92260 *TF:* 800-371-4456 ■ *Web:* www.saludos.com	760-776-1206	776-1214	637-9
Salus Group Benefits Inc 37525 Mound Rd Sterling Heights MI 48310 *TF:* 866-991-9907 ■ *Web:* thesalusgroup.com	866-991-9907		260
Salute Homecare LLC 451 Meriden Rd Ste 5 Waterbury CT 06705 *Web:* salutehomecare.com	203-528-3417		363
Salva O'renick 107 S Main St Ste 200 Independence MO 64108	816-842-6996		4
Salvado, Salvado, & Salvado PC 5985 Columbia Pk Ste 302 Falls Church VA 22041 *Web:* salvadolaw.com	703-379-9446		41
Salvaggio Law Group LLC 65 Madison Ave Ste 210 Morristown NJ 07960 *Web:* salvaggiolaw.com	973-455-1220		41
Salvagnini America Inc 27 Bicentennial Ct Hamilton OH 45015 *Web:* www.salvagnini.com	513-874-8284	874-2229	386
Salvation Cafe 140 Broadway Newport RI 02840 *Web:* salvationcafe.com	401-847-2620		671
Salvatore's Hospitality 6461 Transit Rd Depew NY 14043 *TF:* 877-456-4097 ■ *Web:* salvatoreshospitality.com	716-635-9000		379
Salvatore's Restaurant 1333 Boston Rd Springfield MA 01119 *Web:* www.salvatoresrestaurant.net	413-782-9968	796-7601	671
Salve Regina University 100 Ochre Pt Ave Newport RI 02840 *Web:* www.salve.edu	401-847-6650	848-2823	166
Salver & Cook. LLP 2721 Executive Park Dr Ste 4 Weston FL 33331 *Web:* pscpas.com	954-389-1333	389-1397	2
Salvi & Schostok Pc 218 N Martin Luther King Jr Ave Waukegan IL 60085 *Web:* www.salvilaw.com	847-249-1227		428
Salvona Technologies LLC 65 Stults Rd Bldg 1 Dayton NJ 08810 *Web:* www.salvona.com	609-655-0173		479
Salyer Orthodontics PC 3415 E Lawrenceville St Duluth GA 30096 *Web:* salyersmiles.com	770-623-8520		363
Salzgitter Mannesmann International (USA) Inc 1770 St James Pl Ste 500 Houston TX 77056 *Web:* www.salzgitter-usa.com	713-386-7900	965-9330	492
Sam A. Baker State Park Rt 1 PO Box 18150 Patterson MO 63956 *Web:* www.mostateparks.com	573-856-4411		565
Sam Bell Maxey House State Historic Site 812 S Church St Paris TX 75460 *Web:* www.thc.texas.gov	903-785-5716		565
Sam Clar Office Furniture Inc 1221 Diamond Way Concord CA 94520 *TF:* 800-726-2527 ■ *Web:* www.samclar.com	800-726-2527		321
Sam Diego's 950 Iyanough Rd Rt 132 Hyannis MA 02601 *Web:* www.samdiegos.com	508-771-8816	771-0174	671
Sam Flax Inc 1800 E Colonial Dr Orlando FL 32803 *Web:* www.samflaxorlando.com	407-898-9785		320
Sam Hatfield Realty Inc 4470 Mansford Rd Winchester TN 37398 *TF:* 866-959-7474 ■ *Web:* www.samhatfield.com	931-968-0500		652
Sam Hausman Meat Packer Inc 4261 Beacon Corpus Christi TX 78403 *TF:* 800-364-5521 ■ *Web:* www.hausmanfoods.com	361-883-5521	883-1003	473

Listing	City	State	ZIP	Phone	Fax	Class
Sam Hawk 684 N Freedom Blvd *Web:* samhawkprovo.com	Provo	UT	84601	801-377-7766		671
Sam Houston Electric Co-opeartive Inc 1157 E Church St *TF:* 800-458-0381 ■ *Web:* www.samhouston.net	Livingston	TX	77351	936-327-5711	328-1244	245
Sam Houston Jones State Park 107 Sutherland Rd *TF:* 888-677-7264 ■ *Web:* crt.state.la.us	Lake Charles	LA	70611	337-855-2665		565
Sam Houston Race Park 7575 N Sam Houston Pkwy W *Web:* www.shrp.com	Houston	TX	77064	281-807-8700	807-8777	642
Sam Houston State University 1903 University Ave *TF:* 866-232-7528 ■ *Web:* www.shsu.edu	Huntsville	TX	77340	936-294-1040	294-3758	166
Sam Levitz Furniture 3430 E 36th St *Web:* www.samlevitz.com	Tucson	AZ	85713	520-624-7443		321
Sam Miller's Restaurant 1210 E Cary St *Web:* www.sammillers.com	Richmond	VA	23219	804-644-5465		671
Sam Moore Furniture Industries 1556 Dawn Dr *Web:* www.sammoore.com	Bedford	VA	24523	540-586-8253		319-2
Sam Parr State Fish & Wildlife Area 13225 E State Hwy 33 *Web:* www.dnr.illinois.gov	Newton	IL	62448	618-783-2661		565
Sam S. Accursio And Sons Farms Inc 1225 NW 2nd St	Homestead	FL	33030	305-246-3455		10-11
Sam S. Sloven Inc 3025 S Parker Rd Ste 733	Aurora	CO	80014	303-750-0050		734
Sam's Appliance & Television Rental Inc 5050 E Belknap St *Web:* www.samsfurniture.com	Fort Worth	TX	76117	817-665-5050		321
Sam's No 3 2580 S Havana St *Web:* samsno3.com	Aurora	CO	80014	303-751-0347		671
Sam's on the Waterfront 2020 Chesapeake Harbour Dr E *Web:* www.samsonthewaterfront.com	Annapolis	MD	21403	410-263-3600		671
Sam's Steakhouse 10205 Gravois Rd *Web:* www.samssteakhouse.com	Saint Louis	MO	63123	314-849-3033		671
Sam's Town Hotel & Casino Shreveport 315 Clyde Fant Pkwy *Web:* www.samstownshreveport.com	Shreveport	LA	71101	318-424-7777		133
Sam's Town Hotel & Gambling Hall 5111 Boulder Hwy *TF:* 800-897-8696 ■ *Web:* www.samstownlv.com	Las Vegas	NV	89122	702-456-7777		133
Sama Eye Wear 15120 Keswick St *TF:* 877-788-7262 ■ *Web:* www.samaeyewear.net	Van Nuys	CA	91405	323-822-3955	822-3963	237
Samanage Usa Inc 117 Edinburgh S *TF:* 888-250-8971 ■ *Web:* samanage.com	Cary	NC	27511	888-250-0971		177
Samani Marions Panyaught Consultancy 20-28 Parsons Blvd Whitestone Long Island **Fax Area Code:* 800 ■ *Web:* www.biostrategist.com	Beechhurst	NY	11357	718-939-8595	873-8939*	196
Samaritan Health Plans 2300 NW Walnut Blvd *TF:* 800-832-4580 ■ *Web:* www.samhealthplans.org	Corvallis	OR	97330	541-768-4550		353
Samaritan Hospice 5 Eves Dr Ste 300 *TF:* 800-229-8183 ■ *Web:* samaritannj.org	Marlton	NJ	08053	856-596-1600	596-7881	371
Samaritan Hospital 2215 Burdett Ave *Web:* www.nehealth.com	Troy	NY	12180	518-268-5060		374-3
Samaritan Medical Ctr 830 Washington St *TF:* 877-888-6138 ■ *Web:* www.samaritanhealth.com	Watertown	NY	13601	315-785-4000		374-3
Samaritan Pharmaceuticals Inc 101 Convention Center Dr Ste 310 *NASDAQ: LIV*	Las Vegas	NV	89109	702-735-7001	737-7016	85
Samaritan Village 138-02 Queens Blvd *TF:* 855-322-4357 ■ *Web:* samaritanvillage.org	Briarwood	NY	11435	718-206-2000		726
Sambatek Inc 12800 Whitewater Dr Ste 300 *Web:* www.sambatek.com	Minnetonka	MN	55343	763-476-6010	476-8532	194
Sambazon 209 Avenida Fabricante Ste 200 *TF:* 877-726-2296 ■ *Web:* www.sambazon.com	San Clemente	CA	92672	877-726-2296		297-7
Samco Capital Markets 6805 Capital of Texas Hwy Ste 350 *Web:* www.samcocapital.com	Austin	TX	78731	512-794-9100		401
SAME (Society of American Military Engineers) 607 Prince St *Web:* www.same.org	Alexandria	VA	22314	703-549-3800	684-0231	48-19
SAME Inc 2100 Ne Spaulding Ave *Web:* www.esam.com	Grants Pass	OR	97526	541-476-9162	476-0486	253
SameDay Security Inc 506 S Main St Ste 1000 10th Fl *Web:* www.electroniccaregiver.com	Las Cruces	NM	88001	575-522-4046		475
Samet Corp 309 Gallimore Dairy Rd Ste 102 PO Box 8050 *Web:* www.sametcorp.com	Greensboro	NC	27409	336-544-2600	544-2638	186
Sametz Blackstone Assoc Blackstone Sq 40 W Newton St *Web:* sametz.com	Boston	MA	02118	617-266-8577		344
Samford University 800 Lakeshore Dr *TF:* 800-888-7218 ■ *Web:* www.samford.edu	Birmingham	AL	35229	205-726-3673	726-2171	166
Samick Music Corp 1329 Gateway Dr *Web:* www.smcmusic.com	Gallatin	TN	37066	615-206-0077		527
Saminco Inc 10030 Amberwood Rd *TF:* 866-878-4279 ■ *Web:* www.samincoinc.com	Fort Myers	FL	33913	239-839-3470	561-1502	203
Sammons Center for the Arts 3630 Harry Hines Blvd *Web:* sammonsartcenter.org	Dallas	TX	75219	214-520-7788		572
Sammons Enterprises Inc 5949 Sherry Ln Ste 1900 *Web:* sammonsenterprises.com	Dallas	TX	75225	214-210-5000		185
Sammons Trucking PO Box 16050 *TF:* 800-548-9276 ■ *Web:* www.sammonstrucking.com	Missoula	MT	59808	406-728-2600	549-4989	780
Sammy G's 265 S Palm Canyon Dr *Web:* www.sammygsrestaurant.com	Palm Springs	CA	92262	760-320-8041		671
Sammy's Barbeque 2126 Leonard St *Web:* sammysbarbeque.com	Dallas	TX	75201	214-880-9064		671
Samon's Tiger Stores Inc 2511 Monroe NE **Fax Area Code:* 505 ■ *Web:* www.samons.biz	Albuquerque	NM	87110	575-526-3359	884-1725*	612
Samos 600 Oldham St *Web:* www.samosrestaurant.com	Baltimore	MD	21224	410-675-5292		671
Samoset Resort 220 Warrenton St *TF:* 800-341-1650 ■ *Web:* www.samosetresort.com	Rockport	ME	04856	207-594-2511	594-0722	669
Sampan 675 East 2100 South *Web:* www.esampan.com	Salt Lake City	UT	84106	801-467-3663		671
Sampco Inc 651 W Washington Blvd Ste 300 *TF:* 800-767-0689 ■ *Web:* www.sampcoinc.com	Chicago	IL	60661	312-346-1506	346-8302	297-9
SAMPE (Society for the Advancement of Material & Process Engineering) 21680 Gateway Center Dr Ste 300 *TF:* 800-562-7360 ■ *Web:* www.nasampe.org	Diamond Bar	CA	91765	626-521-9460		49-19
Sampers Financial Inc 79 Midland Ave *TF:* 877-536-1014 ■ *Web:* www.sampersfinancial.com	Montclair	NJ	07042	973-744-1014		401
Sampson Community College PO Box 318 *TF:* 844-319-3640 ■ *Web:* sampsoncc.edu	Clinton	NC	28329	910-592-8081	592-8048	162
Sampson Correctional Institution 700 NW Blvd Hwy 421N *TF:* 800-368-1985 ■ *Web:* www.ncdps.gov	Clinton	NC	28328	910-592-2151	592-2543	213
Sampson County Schools 437 Rowan Rd *TF:* 855-473-7529 ■ *Web:* www.sampson.k12.nc.us	Clinton	NC	28328	910-592-1401	590-2445	685
Sampson Regional Medical Ctr 607 Beaman St *TF:* 800-827-5312 ■ *Web:* www.sampsonrmc.org	Clinton	NC	28328	910-592-8511	590-2321	374-3
Sampson State Park 6096 Rt 96A *Web:* parks.ny.gov	Romulus	NY	14541	315-585-6392		565
Sampson-Bladen Oil Company Inc 510 Commerce St PO Box 469 *TF:* 800-849-4177 ■ *Web:* www.sboil.com	Clinton	NC	28329	910-592-4177		324
Samrat 2529 Apalachee Pkwy *Web:* samratindianrestaurantfl.com	Tallahassee	FL	32301	850-942-1993	942-8091	671
SAMS (Society of Accredited Marine Surveyors Inc) 7855 Argyle Forest Blvd Ste 203 *TF:* 800-344-9077 ■ *Web:* www.marinesurvey.org	Jacksonville	FL	32244	904-384-1494	388-3958	48-1
Sams Technical Publishing 9850 E 30th St *TF:* 800-428-7267 ■ *Web:* samswebsite.com	Indianapolis	IN	46229	800-428-7267	552-3910	637-2
SAMSA Inc 5560 Gratiot Ste D *TF:* 800-809-3254 ■ *Web:* www.samsa.com	Saginaw	MI	48638	989-790-0507		177
Samsara 350 Rhode Island St Ste 400s *Web:* samsara.com	San Francisco	CA	94103	415-985-2400		657
Samsill Corp 5740 Hartman Rd *TF:* 800-255-1100 ■ *Web:* www.samsill.com	Fort Worth	TX	76119	817-536-1906	535-6900	86
Samson Banking Co 2 W Main St *Web:* samsonbanking.com	Samson	AL	36477	334-898-7107		70
Samson Oil & Gas USA Inc 1726 Cole Blvd Ste 210 *Web:* www.samsonoilandgas.com	Lakewood	CO	80401	303-295-0344		536
Samson Plastic Pipe Inc 100 Industrial Pk *Web:* www.samsonplasticpipe.com	Samson	AL	36477	334-898-7124	898-2617	596
Samson Resources Corp 15 E Fifth St Ste 1000 *Web:* www.samson.com	Tulsa	OK	74103	918-591-1791	591-1796	539
Samson Rope Technologies Inc 2090 Thornton Rd **Fax Area Code:* 800 ■ *TF:* 800-227-7673 ■ *Web:* www.samsonrope.com	Ferndale	WA	98248	360-384-4669	299-9246*	208
Samson Technologies Inc 45 Gilpin Ave *TF:* 800-372-6766 ■ *Web:* www.samsontech.com	Hauppauge	NY	11788	631-784-2200		514
Samsung Austin Semiconductor LLC 12100 Sam Sung Blvd *Web:* cleanairforce.org	Austin	TX	78754	512-225-7780		186
Samsung Semiconductors Inc 3655 N First St *Web:* www.samsung.com	San Jose	CA	95134	408-544-4000	544-4980	696
Samtan Engineering Corp 127 Wyllis Ave *Web:* www.samtanengineering.com	Malden	MA	02148	781-322-7880		454
Samtec Inc 520 Park E Blvd PO Box 1147 *TF:* 800-726-8329 ■ *Web:* www.samtec.com	New Albany	IN	47151	812-944-6733	948-5047	253
Samuel A. Ramirez & Company Inc 61 Broadway Ste 2924 *TF:* 800-888-4086 ■ *Web:* www.ramirezco.com	New York	NY	10006	800-888-4086		690
Samuel Cabot Inc 100 Hale St *TF:* 800-877-8246 ■ *Web:* www.cabotstain.com	Newburyport	MA	01950	978-465-1900		550
Samuel Engineering Inc 8450 E Crescent Pkwy *Web:* www.samuelengineering.com	Greenwood Village	CO	80111	303-714-4840		261
Samuel Goldwyn Films 8675 Washington Blvd Ste 203 *Web:* www.samuelgoldwynfilms.com	Los Angeles	CA	90035	310-860-3100	872-5077	514
Samuel Mahelona Memorial Hospital 4800 Kawaihau Rd *Web:* smmh.hhsc.org	Kapaa	HI	96746	808-822-4961	823-4100	374-7
Samuel Merritt College 370 Hawthorne Ave *TF:* 800-607-6377 ■ *Web:* www.samuelmerritt.edu	Oakland	CA	94609	510-869-6576	869-6525	166
Samuel P. Taylor State Park PO Box 251 *Web:* www.parks.ca.gov	Lagunitas	CA	94938	415-488-9897		565
Samuel S. Lewis State Park 6000 Mt Pisgah Rd *Web:* www.dcnr.pa.gov	York	PA	17406	717-252-1134		565
Samuel Shapiro & Company Inc 100 N Charles St One Charles Ctr Ste 1200 *Web:* www.shapiro.com	Baltimore	MD	21201	410-539-0540		311
Samuel Steel Pickling Co 1400 Enterprise Pkwy *Web:* www.samuelsteel.com	Twinsburg	OH	44087	330-963-3777	963-0770	307
Samuel T. Wood Co 2704 Cedar Dr	Riva	MD	21140	410-798-7440		610

Name / Address	Phone	Fax	Class
Samuel Whitehorne House 416 Thames St. . . . . . . Newport RI 02840 *Web:* www.newportrestoration.org	401-847-8344		50-3
Samuels Diamonds 9607 Research Blvd Ste 100 Bldg F . . . . Austin TX 78759 *TF:* 877-388-1836 ■ *Web:* www.samuelsjewelers.com	877-388-1836		410
Samuels Glass Co 3011 NE Loop 410 Ste 120. . . . . San Antonio TX 78218 *Web:* www.samuelsglass.com	210-227-2481		191-2
Samuels Group Inc 311 Financial Way St 300. Wausau WI 54401 *Web:* www.samuelsgroup.net	715-842-2222		186
Samuels Public Library 330 E Criser Rd . . . . Front Royal VA 22630 *Web:* www.samuelslibrary.net	540-635-3153		434-3
Samuels, Miller, Schroeder, Jackson & Sly LLP 225 N Water St Ste 301 . . . . Decatur IL 62523 *Web:* www.samuelsmiller.com	217-429-4325		428
Samurai Grill & Sushi Bar 9500 Montgomery Blvd NE. . . . . Albuquerque NM 87111 *Web:* www.abqsamurai.com	505-275-6601		671
Samy's Camera Inc 431 S Fairfax Ave . . . . Los Angeles CA 90036 *TF:* 800-321-4726 ■ *Web:* www.samys.com	323-938-2420	692-0750	119
San Angelo Chamber of Commerce 418 W Ave B. . . . . San Angelo TX 76903 *TF:* 800-252-1381 ■ *Web:* www.sanangelo.org	325-655-4136	658-1110	206
San Angelo Community Medical Ctr 3501 Knickerbocker Rd. . . . . San Angelo TX 76904 *Web:* www.sacmc.com	325-949-9511	947-6550	374-3
San Angelo Federal Credit Union 235 W First St. . . . . San Angelo TX 76903 *Web:* safcu.com	325-653-8320		219
San Anselmo Public Library Collection 110 Tunstead Ave . . . . San Anselmo CA 94960 *Web:* www.townofsananselmo.org	415-258-4656	258-4666	434-3
San Antonio Botanical Garden & Lucile Halsell Conservatory 555 Funston Pl . . . . San Antonio TX 78209 *Web:* www.sabot.org	210-536-1400	207-3274	97
San Antonio Children's Museum 2800 Broadway . . . . San Antonio TX 78209 *Web:* www.thedoseum.org	210-212-4453		521
San Antonio City Hall PO Box 839966 . . . . San Antonio TX 78283 *Web:* www.sanantonio.gov	210-207-7040		337
San Antonio Community Hospital 999 San Bernardino Rd. . . . . Upland CA 91786 *Web:* www.sarh.org	909-985-2811		374-3
San Antonio Convention & Visitors Bureau 203 S St Marys St Ste 200 . . . . San Antonio TX 78205 *TF:* 800-447-3372 ■ *Web:* www.visitsanantonio.com	210-207-6700	207-6768	206
San Antonio Current 915 Dallas St . . . . San Antonio TX 78215 *Web:* www.sacurrent.com	210-227-0044		532-5
San Antonio Eye Bank 9150 Huebner Rd Ste 105. . . . . San Antonio TX 78240 *Web:* www.saeyebank.org	210-614-1209		269
San Antonio Independent School District (SAISD) 141 Lavaca St . . . . San Antonio TX 78210 *Web:* www.saisd.net	210-554-2200	299-5600	685
San Antonio International Airport (SAT) 9800 Airport Blvd Rm 2041 . . . . San Antonio TX 78216 *TF:* 800-237-6639 ■ *Web:* www.sanantonio.gov	210-207-3411	207-3500	27
San Antonio Lighthouse for The Blind 2305 Roosevelt Ave . . . . San Antonio TX 78210 *Web:* www.salighthouse.org	210-533-5195		586
San Antonio Livestock Exposition Inc PO Box 200230 . . . . San Antonio TX 78220 *Web:* www.sarodeo.com	210-225-0575		446
San Antonio Missions National Historical Park 2202 Roosevelt Ave . . . . San Antonio TX 78210 *Web:* www.nps.gov	210-534-8833		564
San Antonio Museum of Art 200 W Jones Ave . . . . San Antonio TX 78215 *Web:* www.samuseum.org	210-978-8100	978-8134	520
San Antonio Public Library 600 Soledad St. . . . . San Antonio TX 78205 *Web:* www.sanantonio.gov	210-207-2500		434-3
San Antonio Sam's Club 5565 Dezavala Rd . . . . San Antonio TX 78249 *Web:* www.samsclub.com	210-641-4810		671
San Antonio State Hospital 6711 S Braunfels Ave . . . . San Antonio TX 78223 *Web:* www.dshs.texas.gov	210-532-8811	531-7780	374-5
San Antonio Symphony 115 Auditorium Cir. . . . . San Antonio TX 78205 *Web:* sasymphony.org	210-554-1000	554-1008	573-3
San Antonio Wholesale Lumber (SAW) 17480 Judson Rd . . . . San Antonio TX 78247 *TF:* 877-834-3325 ■ *Web:* www.wholesalelumber.biz	210-655-3808		191-3
San Antonio Zoological Gardens & Aquarium 3903 N St Mary's St . . . . San Antonio TX 78212 *Web:* sazoo.org	210-734-7184	734-7291	823
San Augustine County 223 N Harrison . . . . San Augustine TX 75972 *Web:* www.co.san-augustine.tx.us	936-275-2452	275-2263	338
San Benito County 450 Fourth St . . . . Hollister CA 95023 *TF:* 800-503-9230 ■ *Web:* www.cosb.us	831-636-4029	636-2939	338
San Benito Public Library 401 N Sam Houston Blvd . . . . San Benito TX 78586 *Web:* www.cityofsanbenito.com	956-361-3860	361-3867	434-3
San Bernard Electric Co-opeartive Inc 309 W Main St . . . . Bellville TX 77418 *TF:* 800-364-3171 ■ *Web:* www.sbec.org	979-865-3171	865-9706	245
San Bernardino Area Chamber of Commerce PO Box 658 . . . . San Bernardino CA 92402 *TF:* 800-928-5091 ■ *Web:* www.sbachamber.org	909-885-7515	384-9979	139
San Bernardino City Hall 300 N 'D' St. . . . . San Bernardino CA 92418 *Web:* www.ci.san-bernardino.ca.us	909-384-7272	384-5158	337
San Bernardino County 777 E Rialto Ave . . . . San Bernardino CA 92415 *TF:* 888-818-8988 ■ *Web:* www.sbcounty.gov	909-387-8306		338
San Bernardino Valley College 701 S Mt Vernon Ave . . . . San Bernardino CA 92410 *Web:* www.valleycollege.edu	909-384-4400		162
San Bernardino Valley Genealogical Society (SBVGS) 555 W 6th St. . . . . San Bernardino CA 92410 *Web:* www.empirenet.com	909-381-8201		48-13
San Bruno Chamber of Commerce 618 San Mateo Ave. . . . . San Bruno CA 94066 *Web:* www.sanbrunochamber.com	650-588-0180	588-6473	139
San Bruno Public Library 701 Angus Ave W . . . . San Bruno CA 94066 *Web:* www.sanbruno.ca.gov	650-616-7078	876-0848	434-3
San Carlos Chamber of Commerce 610 Elm St Ste 206. . . . . San Carlos CA 94070 *Web:* sancarloschamber.org	650-593-1068	593-9108	139
San Carlos Hotel 150 E 50th St. . . . . New York NY 10022 *TF:* 800-722-2012 ■ *Web:* www.sancarloshotel.com	212-755-1800		379
San Chez 1709 Division Ave S . . . . Grand Rapids MI 49503 *Web:* www.sanchezbistro.com	616-774-8272		671
San Clemente Chamber of Commerce 1100 N El Camino Real. . . . . San Clemente CA 92672 *Web:* www.scchamber.com	949-492-1131	492-3764	139
San Damiano Retreat Ctr 710 Highland Dr PO Box 767 . . . . Danville CA 94526 *Web:* sandamiano.org	925-837-9141	837-0522	673
San Diego Air & Space Museum 2001 Pan American Plz. . . . . San Diego CA 92101 *Web:* sandiegoairandspace.org	619-234-8291	233-4526	520
San Diego Aircraft Carrier Museum 910 N Harbor Dr Navy Pier. . . . . San Diego CA 92101 *Web:* www.midway.org	619-544-9600	544-9188	520
San Diego Archaeological Ctr 16666 San Pasqual Valley Rd. . . . . Escondido CA 92027 *Web:* sandiegoarchaeology.org	760-291-0370	291-0371	520
San Diego Association of Governments-sandag 401 B St Ste 800. . . . . San Diego CA 92101 *Web:* www.sandag.org	619-699-1900		463
San Diego Automotive Museum 2080 Pan American Plz. . . . . San Diego CA 92101 *Web:* sdautomuseum.org	619-231-2886	231-9869	520
San Diego Ballet 2650 Truxtun Rd . . . . San Diego CA 92106 *Web:* sandiegoballet.org	619-294-7378		573-1
San Diego Botanic Garden 230 Quail Gardens Dr PO Box 230005 . . . . Encinitas CA 92023 *Web:* www.sdbgarden.org	760-436-3036	632-0917	97
San Diego Business Journal 4909 Murphy Canyon Rd Ste 200. . . . . San Diego CA 92123 *Web:* www.sdbj.com	858-277-6359		457-5
San Diego Chargers 4020 Murphy Canyon Rd . . . . San Diego CA 92123 *TF:* 877-242-7437 ■ *Web:* www.chargers.com	858-874-4500	292-2760	715-3
San Diego Christian College 200 Riverview Pkwy . . . . Santee CA 92071 *TF:* 800-676-2242 ■ *Web:* sdcc.edu	619-201-8700		166
San Diego City College 1313 Pk Blvd . . . . San Diego CA 92101 *Web:* www.sdcity.edu	619-388-3400	388-3241	162
San Diego City Hall 202 C St . . . . San Diego CA 92101 *TF:* 866-470-1308 ■ *Web:* www.sandiego.gov	619-533-4000	533-4045	337
San Diego Coastal Chamber of Commerce 1104 Camino Del Mar Ste 1 . . . . Del Mar CA 92014 *Web:* www.delmarchamber.org	858-793-5291		139
San Diego Community Newspaper 1621 Grand Ave 2nd Fl Ste C . . . . San Diego CA 92109 *Web:* www.sdnews.com	858-270-3103		532-3
San Diego Concierge 4379 30th St Ste 4 . . . . San Diego CA 92120 *TF:* 800-979-9091 ■ *Web:* www.sandiegoconcierge.com	619-280-4121		376
San Diego Convention & Visitors Bureau 750 B St Ste 1500. . . . . San Diego CA 92101 *Web:* www.sandiego.org	619-232-3101	696-9371	206
San Diego Convention Ctr 111 W Harbor Dr . . . . San Diego CA 92101 *Web:* visitsandiego.com	619-525-5000		205
San Diego County 1600 Pacific Hwy Rm 166. . . . . San Diego CA 92101 *Web:* www.sandiegocounty.gov	619-531-5413	531-5219	338
San Diego County Credit Union 6545 Sequence Dr . . . . San Diego CA 92121 **Fax Area Code:* 858 ■ *TF:* 877-732-2848 ■ *Web:* www.sdccu.com	877-732-2848	597-6509*	219
San Diego County Library System 5560 Overland Ave Ste 110 . . . . San Diego CA 92123 *Web:* www.sdcl.org	858-694-2415		434-3
San Diego County Office of Education 6401 Linda Vista Rd . . . . San Diego CA 92111 *Web:* www.sdcoe.net	858-292-3500	268-5864	685
San Diego County Psychiatric Hospital 3853 Rosecrans St . . . . San Diego CA 92110 *Web:* www.sandiegocounty.gov	619-692-8200		374-5
San Diego Culinary Institute (SDCI) 8024 La Mesa Blvd. . . . . La Mesa CA 91941 *Web:* sandiegoculinary.edu	619-644-2100	644-2106	163
San Diego Daily Transcript 2131 Third Ave . . . . San Diego CA 92101 *TF:* 800-697-6397 ■ *Web:* www.sddt.com	619-232-4381	236-8126	532-2
San Diego East County Chamber of Commerce 201 S Magnolia Ave . . . . El Cajon CA 92020 *TF:* 800-402-8765 ■ *Web:* eastcountychamber.org	619-440-6161	440-6164	139
San Diego Eye Bank (SDEB) 9246 Lightwave Ave Ste 120. . . . . San Diego CA 92123 *TF:* 800-393-2265 ■ *Web:* www.sdeb.org	858-694-0400	565-7368	269
San Diego Film Festival 2683 Via de la Valle Ste G210 . . . . Del Mar CA 92014 *Web:* sdfilmfest.com	619-818-2221		282
San Diego Firefighters Federal Credit Union 4926 La Cuenta Dr . . . . San Diego CA 92124 *Web:* sdffcu.org	619-283-5477		219

Name / Address	City	State	ZIP	Phone	Fax	Class
San Diego Foundation, The 2508 Historic Decatur Rd Ste 200 *Web:* www.sdfoundation.org	San Diego	CA	92106	619-235-2300	239-1710	303
San Diego Futures Foundation 4283 El Cajon Blvd Ste 220 *Web:* sdfutures.org	San Diego	CA	92105	619-269-1684		303
San Diego Gas & Electric Co 101 Ash St **Fax Area Code:* 858 ■ *TF:* 800-411-7343 ■ *Web:* www.sdge.com	San Diego	CA	92101	619-699-5064	654-1755*	787
San Diego Gold Exchange Inc 5859 Mission Gorge Rd *Web:* sdgoldrefinery.com	San Diego	CA	92120	619-516-4653		410
San Diego International Airport - Lindbergh Field 3225 N Harbor Dr County Regional Airport Authority Third Fl *Web:* www.san.org	San Diego	CA	92101	619-400-2404		27
San Diego Jewish Academy 11860 Carmel Creek Rd *Web:* www.sdja.com	San Diego	CA	92130	858-704-3700		685
San Diego Law Library 1105 Front St *Web:* sandiegolawlibrary.org	San Diego	CA	92101	619-531-3900	238-7716	434-3
San Diego Mesa College 7250 Mesa College Dr *Web:* sdmesa.edu	San Diego	CA	92111	619-388-2600		162
San Diego Miramar College 10440 Black Mountain Rd *Web:* www.sdmiramar.edu	San Diego	CA	92126	619-388-7844		162
San Diego Model Management 438 Camino del Rio S Ste 116 *Web:* www.sdmodel.com	San Diego	CA	92108	619-296-1018		506
San Diego Model Railroad Museum 1649 El Prado *Web:* sdmrm.org	San Diego	CA	92101	619-696-0199		520
San Diego Museum of Art 1450 El Prado Balboa Pk PO Box 122107 *Web:* www.sdmart.org	San Diego	CA	92112	619-232-7931	232-4504	520
San Diego Museum of Man 1350 El Prado Balboa Pk *Web:* www.museumofman.org	San Diego	CA	92101	619-239-2001	239-2749	520
San Diego Natural History Museum 1788 El Prado PO Box 121390 *TF:* 877-946-7797 ■ *Web:* www.sdnhm.org	San Diego	CA	92101	619-232-3821	232-0248	520
San Diego Opera 233 A St Ste 500 *Web:* www.sdopera.org	San Diego	CA	92101	619-232-7636	231-6915	573-2
San Diego Plastics Inc 2220 Mckinley Ave *TF:* 800-925-4855 ■ *Web:* www.sdplastics.com	National City	CA	91950	619-477-4855		603
San Diego Printers 9190 Camino Santa Fe *Web:* www.sdprinters.com	San Diego	CA	92121	858-684-5200		627
San Diego Public Library 820 E St *Web:* www.sandiego.gov	San Diego	CA	92101	619-236-5800		434-3
San Diego Regional Chamber of Commerce 402 W Broadway Ste 1000 *Web:* sdchamber.org	San Diego	CA	92101	619-544-1300		139
San Diego Repertory Theatre 79 Horton Plz *Web:* www.sdrep.org	San Diego	CA	92101	619-231-3586		573-4
San Diego State University 5500 Campanile Dr *Web:* www.sdsu.edu	San Diego	CA	92182	619-594-5200		166
San Diego State University *Imperial Valley* 720 Heber Ave *Web:* www.ivcampus.sdsu.edu	Calexico	CA	92231	760-768-5500	768-5589	166
San Diego State University-Library & Information Access-Media Ctr *Love Library Addition* 5500 Campanile Dr Lower Level Rm 61 *Web:* library.sdsu.edu	San Diego	CA	92182	619-594-6757		434-3
San Diego Supercomputer Ctr (SDSC) 9500 Gilman Dr *TF:* 800-451-4515 ■ *Web:* www.sdsc.edu	La Jolla	CA	92093	858-534-5000	534-5056	668
San Diego Symphony Orchestra 1245 Seventh Ave *Web:* www.sandiegosymphony.org	San Diego	CA	92101	619-235-0804	235-0005	573-3
San Diego Unified School District 4100 Normal St *Web:* www.sandiegounified.org	San Diego	CA	92103	619-725-8000		685
San Diego Voice & Viewpoint, The 3619 College Ave *Web:* www.sdvoice.info	San Diego	CA	92112	619-266-2233	266-0533	532-2
San Diego Wholesale Flowers and Bouquets 1205 Aviara Pky *Web:* www.sandiegowholesaleflowers.com	Carlsbad	CA	92011	858-505-0055		293
San Diego World Trade Ctr 1250 6th Ave 7th Fl *Web:* www.sandiegobusiness.org	San Diego	CA	92101	619-234-8484		822
San Diego Yacht Club Sailing Foundation 1011 Anchorage Ln *Web:* sdycsf.org	San Diego	CA	92106	619-221-8400		305
San Diego Zoo 2920 Zoo Dr *Web:* zoo.sandiegozoo.org	San Diego	CA	92101	619-231-1515		823
San Diego Zoo Safari Park 15500 San Pasqual Valley Rd *TF:* 877-363-6237 ■ *Web:* www.sdzsafaripark.org	Escondido	CA	92027	760-747-8702		823
San Dimas Chamber of Commerce 246 E Bonita Ave *Web:* sandimaschamber.com	San Dimas	CA	91773	909-592-3818	592-8178	139
San Dimas Community Hospital 1350 W Covina Blvd *Web:* www.sandimashospital.com	San Dimas	CA	91773	909-599-6811		374-3
San Domenico School 1500 Butterfield Rd *Web:* www.sandomenico.org	San Anselmo	CA	94960	415-258-1900	258-1901	622
San Felasco Hammock Preserve State Park 12720 NW 109 Ln *Web:* www.floridastateparks.org	Alachua	FL	32615	386-462-7905		565
San Francisco 49ers 4949 Centennial Blvd *Web:* www.49ers.com	Santa Clara	CA	95054	408-562-4949	727-4937	715-3
San Francisco Art Institute 800 Chestnut St *TF:* 800-345-7324 ■ *Web:* www.sfai.edu	San Francisco	CA	94133	415-771-7020		164
San Francisco Association Management Services 655 Beach St *Web:* sfams.com	San Francisco	CA	94109	415-561-8568		463
San Francisco Ballet 455 Franklin St *Web:* www.sfballet.org	San Francisco	CA	94102	415-865-2000	861-2684	573-1
San Francisco Bay Guardian 135 Mississippi St *Web:* www.sfbg.com	San Francisco	CA	94107	415-255-3100		532-5
San Francisco Botanical Garden 1199 Ninth Ave *Web:* www.sfbg.org	San Francisco	CA	94122	415-661-1316		97
San Francisco Chamber of Commerce 235 Montgomery St 12th Fl *Web:* www.sfchamber.com	San Francisco	CA	94104	415-392-4520	392-0485	139
San Francisco Chronicle 901 Mission St *TF:* 866-732-4766 ■ *Web:* www.sfgate.com	San Francisco	CA	94103	415-777-1111		532-2
San Francisco City & County 1 Dr Carlton B Goodlett Pl City Hall Rm 362 *Web:* sfgsa.org	San Francisco	CA	94102	415-554-4851	554-4849	338
San Francisco Conservatory of Music 50 Oak St *Web:* sfcm.edu	San Francisco	CA	94102	415-864-7326	503-6299	166
San Francisco Design Ctr (SFDC) 2 Henry Adams St Ste 2M-33 *Web:* www.sfdesigncenter.com	San Francisco	CA	94103	415-490-5800	490-5885	321
San Francisco Examiner 835 Market St Ste 550 *TF:* 888-822-7355 ■ *Web:* www.sfexaminer.com	San Francisco	CA	94103	415-359-2868	359-2766	532-2
San Francisco Federal Credit Union 770 Golden Gate Ave *TF:* 800-852-7598 ■ *Web:* www.sanfranciscofcu.com	San Francisco	CA	94102	415-775-5377	775-5340	219
San Francisco Film Society 39 Mesa St Ste 110 *Web:* www.sffilm.org	San Francisco	CA	94129	415-561-5000	440-1760	282
San Francisco Fire Department Museum 655 Presidio Ave *Web:* guardiansofthecity.org	San Francisco	CA	94115	415-715-4039		520
San Francisco Food Co 14054 Catalina St *Web:* www.sanfranciscofoods.com	San Leandro	CA	94577	510-357-7343		123
San Francisco Foundation 1 Embarcadero Ctr Ste 1400 *Web:* www.sff.org	San Francisco	CA	94111	415-733-8500	477-2783	303
San Francisco Herb Co 250 14th St *TF:* 800-227-4530 ■ *Web:* www.sfherb.com	San Francisco	CA	94103	415-861-7174		297-2
San Francisco International Airport PO Box 8097 *TF:* 800-435-9736 ■ *Web:* www.flysfo.com	San Francisco	CA	94128	650-821-8211	821-5005	27
San Francisco Law Library (SFLL) 1145 Market St 4th Fl *Web:* www.sflawlibrary.org	San Francisco	CA	94103	415-554-1772	863-4022	434-3
San Francisco Magazine 243 Vallejo St **Fax Area Code:* 415 ■ *TF:* 866-736-2499 ■ *Web:* sanfran.com	San Francisco	CA	94111	404-443-1180	398-6777*	457-22
San Francisco Maritime National Historical Park 2 Marina Blvd Bldg E *Web:* www.nps.gov	San Francisco	CA	94123	415-561-7000		564
San Francisco Mime Troupe, The (SFMT) 855 Treat Ave *Web:* www.sfmt.org	San Francisco	CA	94110	415-285-1717	285-1290	226
San Francisco Museum of Modern Art 151 Third St *TF:* 888-357-0037 ■ *Web:* www.sfmoma.org	San Francisco	CA	94103	415-357-4000	357-4037	520
San Francisco Music Box Co 5370 W 95th St *TF:* 800-227-2190 ■ *Web:* www.sanfranciscomusicbox.com	Prairie Village	KS	66207	800-227-2190		327
San Francisco Opera 301 Van Ness Ave *TF:* 800-308-2898 ■ *Web:* sfopera.com	San Francisco	CA	94102	415-861-4008		573-2
San Francisco Public Library 100 Larkin St *Web:* sfpl.org	San Francisco	CA	94102	415-557-4400	557-4239	434-3
San Francisco State University 1600 Holloway Ave *Web:* www.sfsu.edu	San Francisco	CA	94132	415-338-1111		166
San Francisco Study Ctr 1663 Mission St Ste 504 *Web:* www.studycenter.org	San Francisco	CA	94103	415-626-1650	626-7276	637-2
San Francisco Symphony 201 Van Ness Ave *Web:* www.sfsymphony.org	San Francisco	CA	94102	415-864-6000		573-3
San Francisco Theological Seminary 105 Seminary Rd *TF:* 800-447-8820 ■ *Web:* sfts.edu	San Anselmo	CA	94960	415-451-2800	451-2851	167-3
San Francisco Travel Assn 201 Third St Ste 900 *Web:* www.sftravel.com	San Francisco	CA	94103	415-974-6900	227-2602	206
San Francisco Unified School District 555 Franklin St *Web:* www.sfusd.edu	San Francisco	CA	94102	415-241-6000	241-6036	685
San Francisco VA Medical Ctr 4150 Clement St *TF:* 877-487-2838 ■ *Web:* www.sanfrancisco.va.gov	San Francisco	CA	94121	415-221-4810		374-8
San Francisco War Memorial & Performing Arts Ctr (SFWMPAC) 401 Van Ness Ave Rm 110 *Web:* www.sfwmpac.org	San Francisco	CA	94102	415-621-6600	621-5091	572
San Francisco Zoo 1 Zoo Rd *Web:* www.sfzoo.org	San Francisco	CA	94132	415-753-7080		823
San Gabriel Chamber of Commerce 620 W Santa Anita St *Web:* sangabrielchamber.org	San Gabriel	CA	91776	626-576-2525	289-2901	139

Name / Address	Phone	Fax	Class
San Gabriel Mission 428 S Mission Dr . . . . . San Gabriel CA 91776 *Web:* www.sangabrielmissionchurch.org	626-457-3035	282-5308	50-1
San Gabriel Nursery & Florist 632 S San Gabriel Blvd. . . . . San Gabriel CA 91776 *Web:* www.sgnurserynews.com	626-286-3782		323
San Gabriel Valley Medical Ctr 438 W Las Tunas Dr . . . . . San Gabriel CA 91776 *TF:* 888-214-3874 ■ *Web:* www.sgvmc.com	626-289-5454		374-3
San Isabel Electric inc 781 E Industrial Blvd . . . . . Pueblo CO 81007 *TF:* 800-279-7432 ■ *Web:* www.siea.com	719-547-2160	547-2229	245
San Jacinto College *North* 5800 Uvalde Rd . . . . . Houston TX 77049 *Web:* www.sanjac.edu	281-998-6150		162
San Jacinto County 1 State Hwy 150 Rm 2 . . . . . Coldspring TX 77331 *Web:* www.co.san-jacinto.tx.us	936-653-2324	653-5604	338
San Jacinto Mall 1496 San Jacinto Mall . . . . . Baytown TX 77521 *Web:* www.sanjacintomall.com	281-421-3908	421-7377	460
San Jacinto Museum of History 1 Monument Cir . . . . . La Porte TX 77571 *Web:* www.sanjacinto-museum.org	281-479-2421		520
San Jacinto River Authority 1577 Dam Site Rd. . . . . Conroe TX 77304 *Web:* www.sjra.net	936-588-3111		787
San Jacinto Valley Academy Inc 480 N San Jacinto Ave . . . . . San Jacinto CA 92583 *Web:* www.sjva.net	951-654-6113		685
San Jamar Inc 555 Koopman Ln . . . . . Elkhorn WI 53121 *TF:* 800-248-9826 ■ *Web:* www.sanjamar.com	262-723-6133		14
San Joaquin College of Law 901 Fifth St. . . . . Clovis CA 93612 *Web:* www.sjcl.edu	559-323-2100		166
San Joaquin County Fairgrounds 1658 S Airport Way. . . . . Stockton CA 95206 *Web:* sanjoaquinfairgrounds.com	209-466-5041	466-5739	642
San Joaquin County Historical Society & Museum 11793 N Micke Grove Rd . . . . . Lodi CA 95240 *Web:* www.sanjoaquinhistory.org	209-331-2055	331-2057	520
San Joaquin Delta College 5151 Pacific Ave. . . . . Stockton CA 95207 *TF:* 800-835-4611 ■ *Web:* www.deltacollege.edu	209-954-5151	954-5769	162
San Joaquin General Hospital (SJGH) 500 W Hospital Rd . . . . . French Camp CA 95231 *Web:* www.sjgeneral.org	209-468-6000		374-3
San Joaquin Helicopters 1408 S Lexington St . . . . . Delano CA 93215 *Web:* www.sjhelicopters.com	661-725-1898	725-5401	359
San Joaquin Hotel 1309 W Shaw Ave. . . . . Fresno CA 93711 *Web:* www.sjhotel.com	559-225-1309		379
San Joaquin Refining Company Inc 3129 Standard St . . . . . Bakersfield CA 93308 *Web:* www.sjr.com	661-327-4257	327-3236	580
San Joaquin Sulphur Company Inc 720 N Sacramento St . . . . . Lodi CA 95240 *Web:* www.sjsulphur.com	209-368-6676	367-4929	276
San Joaquin Valley National Cemetery 32053 W McCabe Rd . . . . . Santa Nella CA 95322 *Web:* www.cem.va.gov	209-854-1040	854-3944	136
San Joaquin Valley Rehabilitation Hospital 7173 N Sharon Ave. . . . . Fresno CA 93720 *Web:* www.vibrahealthcare.com	559-436-3600		374-6
San Jose Boiler Works Inc 1585 Schallenberger Rd . . . . . San Jose CA 95131 *Web:* sanjoseboiler.com	408-295-5235		612
San Jose Center for the Performing Arts 255 S Almaden Blvd . . . . . San Jose CA 95113 *TF:* 800-726-5673 ■ *Web:* www.sanjose.org	408-288-2800	277-3535	572
San Jose City College 2100 Moorpark Ave . . . . . San Jose CA 95128 *Web:* www.sjcc.edu	408-298-2181	298-1935	162
San Jose City Hall 200 Santa Clara St . . . . . San Jose CA 95113 *Web:* www.sanjoseca.gov	408-535-3500	292-6731	337
San Jose Delta Inc 482 Sapena Ct . . . . . Santa Clara CA 95054 *Web:* www.sanjosedelta.com	408-727-1448	727-6019	500
San Jose Downtown Assn 120 S Market St . . . . . San Jose CA 95113 *Web:* www.sjdowntown.com	408-279-1775		533
San Jose Film Festival - CineQuest PO Box 720040 . . . . . San Jose CA 95172 *Web:* www.cinequest.org	408-995-5033		282
San Jose Mailing & Printing 1445 Monterey Hwy . . . . . San Jose CA 95110 *Web:* sanjosemailing.com	408-971-1911		5
San Jose Museum of Art 110 S Market St . . . . . San Jose CA 95113 *Web:* www.sjmusart.org	408-271-6840	294-2977	520
San Jose Museum of Quilts & Textiles 520 S First St . . . . . San Jose CA 95113 *Web:* www.sjquiltmuseum.org	408-971-0323		520
San Jose Original Joe's 301 S First St . . . . . San Jose CA 95113 *TF:* 888-841-7030 ■ *Web:* www.sanjoseoriginaljoes.com	408-292-7030		671
San Jose Public Library 150 E San Fernando St . . . . . San Jose CA 95113 *Web:* www.sjpl.org	408-808-2000		434-3
San Jose Silicon Valley Chamber of Commerce (SJSVCC) 101 W Santa Clara St . . . . . San Jose CA 95113 *Web:* www.thesvo.com	408-291-5250	286-5019	139
San Jose Stage Co 490 S 1st St. . . . . San Jose CA 95113 *Web:* www.thestage.org	408-283-7142		573-4
San Jose State University 1 Washington Sq . . . . . San Jose CA 95192 *Web:* www.sjsu.edu	408-924-1000	924-2050	166
San Jose Surgical Supply Inc 902 S Bascom Ave . . . . . San Jose CA 95128 *Web:* www.sjsurgical.com	408-293-9033	293-0587	475
San Jose Unified School District 855 Lenzen Ave. . . . . San Jose CA 95126 *Web:* www.sjusd.org	408-535-6000		685
San Juan Airlines Co 4167 Mitchell Way . . . . . Bellingham WA 98226 *TF:* 800-874-4434 ■ *Web:* sanjuanairlines.com	800-874-4434		13
San Juan Capistrano Chamber of Commerce 31421 La Matanza St . . . . . San Juan Capistrano CA 92675 *Web:* www.sanjuanchamber.com	949-493-4700	489-2695	139
San Juan College 4601 College Blvd . . . . . Farmington NM 87402 *TF:* 866-426-1233 ■ *Web:* www.sanjuancollege.edu	505-326-3311	566-3500	162
San Juan County 100 S Oliver Dr . . . . . Aztec NM 87410 *Web:* www.sjcounty.net	505-334-9481	334-3168	338
San Juan County 350 Ct St 2nd Fl . . . . . Friday Harbor WA 98250 *TF:* 800-762-3716 ■ *Web:* www.sanjuanco.com	360-378-2163	378-3967	338
San Juan County PO Box 338. . . . . Monticello UT 84535 *Web:* www.sanjuancounty.org	435-587-3223	587-2425	338
San Juan County 1557 Greene St PO Box 466. . . . . Silverton CO 81433 *Web:* sanjuancounty.colorado.gov	970-387-8040	387-8043	338
San Juan Golf & Tennis Club 806 Golf Course Rd . . . . . Friday Harbor WA 98250 *Web:* www.sjgolfclub.com	360-378-2254		711
San Juan Island National Historical Park 4668 Cattle Point Rd PO Box 429. . . . . Friday Harbor WA 98250 *Web:* www.nps.gov	360-378-2240	378-2615	564
San Juan National Historic Site 501 Norzagaray St . . . . . San Juan PR 00901 *Web:* www.nps.gov	787-729-6960	289-7972	564
San Juan Regional Medical Ctr 801 W Maple St . . . . . Farmington NM 87401 *Web:* www.sanjuanregional.com	505-609-2000		374-3
San Juan Veterinary Clinic Inc 822 Spring Creek Rd . . . . . Montrose CO 81401 *Web:* sanjuanvetclinic.com	970-249-4490		794
San Leandro Adult School 835 E 14th St Ste 200. . . . . San Leandro CA 94577 *Web:* www.sanleandro.k12.ca.us	510-667-3500	667-6234	685
San Leandro Chamber of Commerce 120 Estudillo Ave . . . . . San Leandro CA 94577 *Web:* sanleandrochamber.com	510-317-1400		139
San Lorenzo Unified School District (SLZUSD) 15510 Usher St. . . . . San Lorenzo CA 94580 *Web:* www.slzusd.org	510-317-4600	278-3048	685
San Luis Butane Distributors Inc PO Box 3068 . . . . . Paso Robles CA 93447 *Web:* deltaliquidenergy.com	805-239-0616	239-1327	579
San Luis Garbage Co 4388 Old Santa Fe Rd. . . . . San Luis Obispo CA 93401 *Web:* www.wasteconnections.com	805-543-0875		804
San Luis Obispo Botanical Garden 3450 Dairy Creek Rd. . . . . San Luis Obispo CA 93405 *Web:* www.slobg.org	805-541-1400	541-1466	97
San Luis Obispo Chamber of Commerce 1039 Chorro St. . . . . San Luis Obispo CA 93401 *TF:* 800-634-1414 ■ *Web:* slochamber.org	805-781-2777	543-1255	139
San Luis Obispo City-County Library 995 Palm St . . . . . San Luis Obispo CA 93401 *Web:* slolibrary.org	805-781-5991		434-3
San Luis Obispo County 1055 Monterey St. . . . . San Luis Obispo CA 93408 *TF:* 800-834-4636 ■ *Web:* www.slocounty.ca.gov	805-781-5000		338
San Luis Obispo County Law Library (SLOCLL) 1050 Monterey St Rm 125 . . . . . San Luis Obispo CA 93408 *Web:* www.slocll.org	805-781-5855	781-4172	434-3
San Luis Obispo County Planning Department Technical Information Library County Government Ctr 976 Osos St . . . . . San Luis Obispo CA 93408 *Web:* www.slocounty.ca.gov	805-781-5600		434-3
San Luis Obispo Defenders, A Professional Law Corp 991 Osos St Ste A. . . . . San Luis Obispo CA 93401 *Web:* slodefend.com	805-541-5715		41
San Luis Obispo High School 1500 Lizzie St. . . . . San Luis Obispo CA 93401 *Web:* www.slcusd.org	805-596-4040		685
San Luis Obispo New Times 505 Higuera St . . . . . San Luis Obispo CA 93401 *Web:* www.newtimesslo.com	805-546-8208	546-8641	532-5
San Luis Resort Spa & Conference Ctr, The 5222 Seawall Blvd . . . . . Galveston TX 77551 *TF:* 800-445-0090 ■ *Web:* www.sanluisresort.com	409-744-1500	744-8452	669
San Luis Tallow Co 445 Prado Rd . . . . . San Luis Obispo CA 93401	805-543-8660		296-12
San Luis Valley Regional Medical Ctr 106 Blanca Ave. . . . . Alamosa CO 81101 *Web:* sanluisvalleyhealth.org	719-589-2511		374-3
San Luis Valley Rural Electric Co-op 3625 US Hwy 160 W . . . . . Monte Vista CO 81144 *TF:* 800-332-7634 ■ *Web:* www.slvrec.com	719-852-3538		245
San Luis Video Publishing PO Box 6715 . . . . . Los Osos CA 93412 *Web:* www.horticulturevideos.com	805-528-8322	528-7227	525
San Manuel Indian Bingo & Casino 777 San Manuel Blvd . . . . . Highland CA 92346 *TF:* 800-359-2464 ■ *Web:* www.sanmanuel.com	909-864-5050		133
San Marcos Academy 2801 Ranch Rd 12 . . . . . San Marcos TX 78666 *TF:* 800-428-5120 ■ *Web:* www.smabears.org	512-353-2400	753-8031	622
San Marcos Area Chamber of Commerce 202 N CM Allen Pkwy. . . . . San Marcos TX 78666 *Web:* sanmarcostexas.com	512-393-5900	393-5912	139
San Marcos Chamber of Commerce 904 W San Marcos Blvd . . . . . San Marcos CA 92078 *Web:* www.sanmarcoschamber.com	760-744-1270	744-5230	139
San Marcos de Apalache Historic State Park 148 Old Ft Rd . . . . . Saint Marks FL 32355 *Web:* www.floridastateparks.org	850-925-6216		565

	Phone	Fax	Class
San Marcos Public Library 625 E Hopkins St . . . San Marcos TX 78666 *Web:* www.sanmarcostx.gov	512-393-8200	754-8131	434-3
San Marino Ristorante 66 Charlton St . . . New York NY 10014 *Web:* www.sanmarinosoho.com	212-206-3766		784
San Mateo Area Chamber of Commerce 1700 S El Camino Real Ste 406 . . . San Mateo CA 94402 *TF:* 877-304-2441 ■ *Web:* sanmateochamber.org	650-401-2440		139
San Mateo County 455 County Ctr 4th Fl . . . Redwood City CA 94063 *Web:* www.smcgov.org	650-363-4020	599-1721	338
San Mateo County Convention & Visitors Bureau 111 Anza Blvd Ste 410 . . . Burlingame CA 94010 *TF:* 800-288-4748 ■ *Web:* www.smccvb.com	650-348-7600	348-7687	206
San Mateo County Medical Assn (SMCMA) 777 Mariners Island Blvd Ste 100 . . . San Mateo CA 94404 *Web:* www.smcma.org	650-312-1663	312-1664	49-19
San Mateo County Transit District 1250 San Carlos Ave PO Box 3006 . . . San Carlos CA 94070 *Web:* www.smctd.com	650-508-6200		468
San Miguel County PO Box 548 . . . Telluride CO 81435 *Web:* www.sanmiguelcountyco.gov	970-728-3954	728-4808	338
San Miguel Joint Un School Dst 1601 L St . . . San Miguel CA 93451 *Web:* www.sanmiguelschools.org	805-467-3216		685
San Miguel Mission 401 Old Santa Fe Trl . . . Santa Fe NM 87501 *Web:* www.sanmiguelchapel.org	505-983-3974		50-1
San Miguel Power Association Inc 170 W Tenth Ave . . . Nucla CO 81424 *TF:* 800-864-7256 ■ *Web:* www.smpa.com	970-864-7311	864-7257	245
San Miguel Produce Inc 4444 Naval Air Rd . . . Oxnard CA 93033 *Web:* www.cutnclean.com	805-488-0981		10-11
San Nicolas Michael F Q (Rep D - GU) 1632 Longworth House Office Bldg . . . Washington DC 20515 *Web:* www.sannicolas.house.gov	202-225-1188		342-2
San Pablo Chamber of Commerce 13925 San Pablo Ave . . . San Pablo CA 94806 *Web:* ci.san-pablo.ca.us	510-234-2067		139
San Pablo Lytton Casino 13255 San Pablo Ave . . . San Pablo CA 94806 *Web:* www.sanpablolytton.com	510-215-7888		452
San Pasqual Battlefield State Historic Park 15808 San Pasqual Valley Rd . . . Escondido CA 92027 *Web:* www.parks.ca.gov	760-737-2201		565
San Pasqual Fiduciary Trust Co 400 S Hope St Ste 1300 . . . Los Angeles CA 90071 *Web:* www.spftc.com	213-452-0500	489-4153	41
San Patricio Electric Co-opeartive Inc 402 E Sinton St . . . Sinton TX 78387 *TF:* 888-740-2220 ■ *Web:* www.sanpatricioelectric.org	361-364-2220	364-3467	245
San Pedro Bay Historical Society PO Box 1568 . . . San Pedro CA 90733 *Web:* sanpedrobayhistoricalsociety.com	310-548-3208		48-13
San Pedro Peninsula Chamber of Commerce 390 W Seventh St . . . San Pedro CA 90731 *Web:* www.sanpedrochamber.com	310-832-7272		139
San Rafael Chamber of Commerce 817 Mission Ave . . . San Rafael CA 94901 *Web:* srchamber.com	415-454-4163	454-7039	139
San Rafael Public Library 1400 Fifth Ave . . . San Rafael CA 94901 *Web:* www.cityofsanrafael.org	415-485-3323		434-3
San Rafael Ranch State Park 2036 Duquesne Rd . . . Patagonia AZ 85624 *Web:* azstateparks.com	520-394-2447		565
San Ramon Chamber of Commerce 2410 Camino Ramon Ste 125 . . . San Ramon CA 94583 *Web:* sanramon.org	925-242-0600	242-0603	139
San Ramon Insurance Agency Inc 2303 Camino Ramon Ste 210 . . . San Ramon CA 94583 *Web:* sanramoninsurance.com	925-277-0350		390
San Ramon Valley Conference Ctr 3301 Crow Canyon Rd . . . San Ramon CA 94583 *Web:* www.sanramonvalleyconferencecenter.com	925-866-7500		377
San Roque Pet Hospital Inc 3034 State St . . . Santa Barbara CA 93105 *Web:* sanroquepethospital.com	805-682-2647		794
San Saba County 500 E Wallace Ste 202 . . . San Saba TX 76877 *Web:* www.co.san-saba.tx.us	325-372-3614	372-6484	338
San Sebastian Winery 157 King St . . . Saint Augustine FL 32084 *TF:* 888-352-9463 ■ *Web:* www.sansebastianwinery.com	904-826-1594	826-1595	50-7
San Technology Inc 6210 Marindustry Dr . . . San Diego CA 92121 *Web:* www.santechnology.com	858-278-7300	278-7310	696
San Vicente Inn & Golf Course 24157 San Vicente Rd . . . Ramona CA 92065 *Web:* www.sdcea.net	760-789-3788		669
San Xavier Del Bac Mission 1950 W San Xavier Rd . . . Tucson AZ 85746 *Web:* www.sanxaviermission.org	520-294-2624		50-1
San Ysidro Chamber of Commerce 663 E San Ysidro Blvd . . . San Ysidro CA 92173 *Web:* www.sanysidrochamber.org	619-428-5200		139
San Ysidro Ranch 900 San Ysidro Ln . . . Santa Barbara CA 93108 *Web:* www.sanysidroranch.com	805-565-1700	565-1995	669
San Ysidro School District 4350 Otay Mesa Rd . . . San Ysidro CA 92173 *Web:* www.sysdschools.org	619-428-4476	428-9355	685
Sanaa's 401 E Eigth St Ste 100 . . . Sioux Falls SD 57103 *Web:* sanaacooks.com	605-275-2516		671
SanBio Inc 231 S Whisman Rd . . . Mountain View CA 94041 *Web:* www.san-bio.com	650-625-8965		668
SANBlaze Technology Inc 1 Monarch Dr Ste 204 . . . Littleton MA 01460 *Web:* www.sanblaze.com	978-679-1400		173-8

	Phone	Fax	Class
Sanborn Chevrolet Inc 1210 S Cherokee Ln . . . Lodi CA 95240 *Web:* www.sanbornchevrolet.com	209-642-4954		516
Sanborn Head & Associates Inc 20 Foundry St . . . Concord NH 03301 *Web:* sanbornhead.com	603-229-1900		261
Sanchez Blackner & Co 33305 First Way S Ste 107 . . . Federal Way WA 98003 *Web:* sanchezblackner.com	253-874-0320	874-9478	734
Sanchez Hayes & Associates LLC 1015 Tyrone Rd Bldg 600 Ste 620 . . . Tyrone GA 30290 *Web:* sanchezhayeslaw.com	770-692-5020		41
Sanchez Linda (Rep D - CA) 2329 Rayburn House Office Bldg . . . Washington DC 20515 *Web:* www.lindasanchez.house.gov	202-225-6676		342-2
Sancliff Inc 97 Temple St . . . Worcester MA 01604 *TF:* 800-332-0747 ■ *Web:* www.sancliff.com	508-795-0747	793-2984	757
Sanctuary Beach Resort Monterey Bay 3295 Dunes Rd . . . Marina CA 93933 *TF:* 855-693-6583 ■ *Web:* www.thesanctuarybeachresort.com	831-883-9478		707
Sanctuary for Families PO Box 1406 . . . New York NY 10268 *Web:* sanctuaryforfamilies.org	212-349-6009		428
Sanctuary Marketing Group Inc 219 E Maple St Ste 125 . . . North Canton OH 44720 *Web:* www.sanctuarymg.com	330-266-1188		5
Sanctuary on Camelback Mountain 5700 E McDonald Dr . . . Paradise Valley AZ 85253 *TF:* 855-245-2051 ■ *Web:* www.sanctuaryoncamelback.com	855-421-3522		669
Sand Assoc 3560 Green St . . . Harrisburg PA 17110 *Web:* www.sandassociates.com	717-238-5558	238-4626	184
Sand Bar State Park 1215 US Rt 2 . . . Milton VT 05468 *Web:* www.vtstateparks.com	802-893-2825		565
Sand Bridge State Park c/o R B Winter State Pk 17215 Buffalo Rd . . . Mifflinburg PA 17844 *Web:* www.dcnr.pa.gov	570-966-1455		565
Sand Cherry Associates Inc 8 Sand Cherry . . . Littleton CO 80127 *TF:* 877-933-9494 ■ *Web:* www.sandcherryassociates.com	303-933-9494	948-7788	463
Sand Creek Communications Co 6525 Sand Creek Hwy . . . Sand Creek MI 49279 *TF:* 866-380-5721 ■ *Web:* www.sandcreekcommunications.com	517-436-3750	436-3190	224
Sand Creek Massacre National Historic Site 910 Wansted . . . Eads CO 81036 *Web:* www.nps.gov	719-438-5916		564
Sand Creek Post & Beam 116 W First St . . . Wayne NE 68787 *TF:* 888-489-1680 ■ *Web:* www.sandcreekpostandbeam.com	402-833-5600	833-5602	106
Sand Island State Recreation Area PO Box 621 . . . Honolulu HI 96809 *Web:* dlnr.hawaii.gov	808-832-3781		565
Sand Lake Imaging 9350 Turkey Lake Rd . . . Orlando FL 32819 *Web:* www.sandlakeimaging.com	407-363-2772		415
Sand Mountain Electric Co-op 402 Main St W . . . Rainsville AL 35986 *TF:* 877-843-2512 ■ *Web:* www.smec.coop	256-638-2153		245
Sand Mountain Reporter 1603 Progress Dr . . . Albertville AL 35950 *Web:* www.sandmountainreporter.com	256-840-2987		532-3
Sand Pearl Resort LLC 500 Mandalay Ave . . . Clearwater Beach FL 33767 *TF:* 866-384-2995 ■ *Web:* www.sandpearl.com	727-441-2425		378
Sand Ridge State Forest PO Box 111 . . . Forest City IL 61532 *Web:* www.dnr.illinois.gov	309-597-2212		565
Sand Steel Building Co 101 Browell St . . . Emerado ND 58228 *Web:* www.sandsteelbuilding.com	701-594-4435	594-4438	189-1
Sandals Resorts Intl 4950 SW 72nd Ave . . . Miami FL 33155 *TF:* 888-726-3257 ■ *Web:* www.sandals.com	305-284-1300		669
Sandalwood Securities Inc 101 Eisenhower Pkwy . . . Roseland NJ 07068 *Web:* www.sandalwoodsecurities.com	973-233-8800		796
Sandata Technologies Inc 26 Harbor Park Dr . . . Port Washington NY 11050 *TF:* 800-544-7263 ■ *Web:* www.sandata.com	516-484-4400	484-6084	178-11
Sandbar Waterfront Restaurant 100 Spring Ave . . . Anna Maria FL 34216 *Web:* www.sandbardining.com	941-778-0444		671
Sandbox Industries Inc 1000 W Fulton Market Ste 213 . . . Chicago IL 60607 *Web:* sandboxindustries.com	312-243-4100		295
Sandcastle Water Park 1000 Sandcastle Dr . . . Homestead PA 15120 *Web:* www.sandcastlewaterpark.com	412-462-6666	462-0827	32
Sandel Avionics Inc 2401 Dogwood Way . . . Vista CA 92081 *Web:* www.sandel.com	760-727-4900	727-4899	21
Sandella's LLC 263 Farmington Ave . . . Farmington CT 06030 *Web:* www.sandellas.com	203-544-9984	544-9981	670
Sandelman & Assoc 257 La Paloma Ste 1 . . . San Clemente CA 92672 *TF:* 888-897-7881 ■ *Web:* www.sandelman.com	888-897-7881		668
Sanden International (USA) Inc 601 S Sanden Blvd . . . Wylie TX 75098 *Web:* www.sanden.com	972-442-8400		172
Sander Engineering Corp 2901 Wilcrest Ste 550 . . . Houston TX 77042 *Web:* sandereng.com	713-784-4830		261
Sanderling 400 S El Camino Real Ste 1200 . . . San Mateo CA 94402 *Web:* www.sanderling.com	650-401-2000		792
Sanderling Resort & Spa 1461 Duck Rd . . . Duck NC 27949 *TF:* 800-701-4111 ■ *Web:* www.sanderling-resort.com	855-412-7866		669
Sanders Bernard (Sen I - VT) 332 Dirksen Senate Office Bldg . . . Washington DC 20510 *Web:* www.sanders.senate.gov	202-224-5141	228-0776	342-2
Sanders County 1111 Main St W PO Box 519 . . . Thompson Falls MT 59873 *Web:* co.sanders.mt.us	406-827-6942	827-4388	338
Sanders Ford Inc 1135 Lejeune Blvd . . . Jacksonville NC 28540 *TF:* 888-897-8527 ■ *Web:* www.sandersfordsales.com	910-294-5016		516

Company / Address	City	State	ZIP	Phone	Fax	Class
Sanders Software Consulting Inc 3008 W 30th St *Web:* www.sanderssoftware.com	Lawrence	KS	66047	785-865-5111		175
Sanders/Wingo Adv Inc 303 N Oregon St Ste 1200 *Web:* www.sanderswingo.com	El Paso	TX	79901	915-533-9583		4
Sanderson Industries Inc 3550 Atlanta Industrial Pkwy	Atlanta	GA	30331	404-699-2022		489
Sanderson-MacLeod Inc PO Box 50 *TF:* 866-522-3481 ■ *Web:* www.sandersonmacleod.com	Palmer	MA	01069	413-283-3481	289-1919	103
Sandestin Golf & Beach Resort 9300 Emerald Coast Pkwy W *TF:* 800-277-0800 ■ *Web:* www.sandestin.com	Sandestin	FL	32550	850-267-8000		669
Sandhill Telephone Co-opeartive Inc PO Box 519 *Web:* shtc.net	Jefferson	SC	29718	843-658-3434	658-7700	736
Sandhills Community College 3395 Airport Rd *TF:* 800-338-3944 ■ *Web:* www.sandhills.edu	Pinehurst	NC	28374	910-692-6185	695-3981	162
Sandhills Publishing 120 W Harvest Dr *TF:* 800-331-1978 ■ *Web:* www.sandhills.com	Lincoln	NE	68521	402-479-2181	479-2195	637-9
Sandia National Laboratories - California (SNL) 7011 E Ave PO Box 969 *Web:* www.sandia.gov	Livermore	CA	94551	925-294-3000		668
Sandia National Laboratories - New Mexico (SNL) 1515 Eubank SE *TF:* 800-783-5337 ■ *Web:* www.sandia.gov	Albuquerque	NM	87123	505-844-8066		668
Sandia Resort & Casino 30 Rainbow Rd NE *TF:* 800-526-9366 ■ *Web:* www.sandiacasino.com	Albuquerque	NM	87113	505-796-7500		133
Sandiago's Grill at the Tram 40 Tramway Rd NE *Web:* sandiagos.com	Albuquerque	NM	87122	505-856-6692		671
SanDisk Corp 601 McCarthy Blvd *NASDAQ: SNDK* ■ *TF:* 866-726-3475 ■ *Web:* www.sandisk.com	Milpitas	CA	95035	408-801-1000	801-8657	288
Sandlapper Publishing Company Inc 1281 Amelia St *TF:* 800-849-7263 ■ *Web:* www.sandlapperpublishing.com	Orangeburg	SC	29115	803-531-1658	534-5223	637-2
Sandler Partners 1200 Artesia Blvd Ste 305 *TF:* 800-825-1055 ■ *Web:* www.sandlerpartners.com	Hermosa Beach	CA	90254	310-796-1393		224
Sandler Sales Institute 10411 Stevenson Rd *Web:* www.sandler.com	Stevenson	MD	21153	410-653-1993	358-7858	765
Sandlin Homes 5137 Davis Blvd *TF:* 800-821-4663 ■ *Web:* sandlinhomes.com	Fort Worth	TX	76180	817-281-3509	656-0719	187
Sandman Hotel Group 310-1755 W Broadway Ste 310 *Web:* www.sandmanhotels.com	Vancouver	BC	V6J4S5	604-730-6600	730-4645	379
Sandmeyer Steel Co 10001 Sandmeyer Ln *TF:* 800-523-3663 ■ *Web:* www.sandmeyersteel.com	Philadelphia	PA	19116	215-464-7100	677-1430	723
Sandor Development Co 5725 N Scottsdale Rd Ste C-195 *Web:* www.sandordev.com	Scottsdale	AZ	85250	480-949-9011		652
Sandoval County 1500 Idalia Rd Bldg D *TF:* 888-696-3473 ■ *Web:* www.sandovalcountynm.gov	Bernalillo	NM	87004	505-867-7500	867-7600	338
Sandoz Inc 100 College Rd W *TF:* 800-525-8747 ■ *Web:* www.us.sandoz.com	Princeton	NJ	08540	609-627-8500		582
Sandra Feinstein-Gamm Theatre 172 Exchange St *Web:* www.gammtheatre.org	Pawtucket	RI	02860	401-723-4266		573-4
Sandra Nelson Consulting 1906 Russell St *Web:* www.sandranelson.com	Nashville	TN	37206	615-227-7402		194
Sandridge Energy Inc 123 Robert S Kerr Ave *Web:* sandridgeenergy.com	Oklahoma City	OK	73102	405-429-5500		536
Sandridge Food Corp (SFC) 133 Commerce Dr *TF:* 800-627-2523 ■ *Web:* sandridge.com	Medina	OH	44256	330-725-2348	722-3998	296-33
Sands Publishing PO Box 46 *Web:* www.sandspublishing.com	Stockton	NJ	08559	267-714-8267		637-10
Sands Regency Casino Hotel 345 N Arlington Ave *TF:* 800-233-4939 ■ *Web:* sandsregency.com	Reno	NV	89501	775-348-2200		379
Sandstone Asset Management Inc 101 6 St SW *TF:* 866-318-6140 ■ *Web:* www.sandstoneam.com	Calgary	AB	T2P5K7	403-218-6125	263-2270	528
Sandstone Group Inc 223 N Water St Ste 500	Milwaukee	WI	53202	414-902-6700	902-6701	360-3
Sandt Products Inc 1275 Loop Rd *Web:* www.sandtproducts.com	Lancaster	PA	17601	717-299-4900		548
Sandusky County 622 Croghan St *Web:* www.sandusky-county.com	Fremont	OH	43420	419-334-6100	334-6104	338
Sandusky County Convention & Visitor's Bureau (SCCVB) 712 N St Ste 102 *TF:* 800-255-8070 ■ *Web:* www.sanduskycounty.org	Fremont	OH	43420	419-332-4470	332-4359	206
Sandusky International Inc 510 W Water St *Web:* sanduskyintl.com	Sandusky	OH	44870	419-626-5340	626-3339	307
Sandusky Lee Corp 16125 Widmere Rd PO Box 517 *TF:* 800-886-8688 ■ *Web:* www.sanduskycabinets.com	Arvin	CA	93203	661-854-5551	854-2003	286
Sandusky Packaging Corp 2016 George St *Web:* www.sanduskypackaging.com	Sandusky	OH	44870	419-626-8520	626-8522	557
Sandusky Register 314 W Market St *Web:* www.sanduskyregister.com	Sandusky	OH	44870	419-625-5500		532-2
Sandusky Speedway 614 W Perkins Ave *Web:* www.sanduskyspeedway.com	Sandusky	OH	44870	419-625-4084		515
Sandusky-Chicago Abrasive Wheel Company Inc 532 W Fourth St *Web:* www.sanduskychicago.com	Michigan City	IN	46360	219-879-6601		1
Sandvik Special Metals LLC 235407 E SR 397 *Web:* www.materials.sandvik	Kennewick	WA	99337	509-586-4131		485
Sandwich Glass Museum 129 Main St *Web:* www.sandwichglassmuseum.org	Sandwich	MA	02563	508-888-0251	888-4941	520
Sandwich Islands Publishing (SIP) PO Box 10669 *Web:* www.bestofmauiguide.com	Lahaina	HI	96761	808-665-9990		637-2
Sandwich Isle Pest Solutions Inc 96-1368 Waihona St *Web:* www.sandwichisle.com	Pearl City	HI	96782	808-456-7716		577
Sandwich Lodge & Resort 54 Rt 6A - Old King's Hwy *Web:* www.sandwichlodge.com	Sandwich	MA	02563	508-888-2275	888-8102	379
Sandy Alexander Inc 200 Entin Rd *TF:* 833-346-3832 ■ *Web:* sandyinc.com	Clifton	NJ	07014	973-470-8100		627
Sandy Area Chamber of Commerce 35 E 9270 *Web:* sandyoregonchamber.org	Sandy	UT	84070	801-566-0344	566-0346	139
Sandy Beach Resort 201 S Ocean Blvd *TF:* 800-844-6534 ■ *Web:* www.sandybeachoceanfrontresort.com	Myrtle Beach	SC	29577	800-844-6534		379
Sandy Farms 34500 SE Hwy 211 *Web:* www.sandyfarms.com	Boring	OR	97009	503-668-4525		315-1
Sandy Point State Park 1100 E College Pkwy *Web:* www.dnr.maryland.gov	Annapolis	MD	21409	410-974-2149		565
Sandy River Co 217 Commercial St PO Box 110 *Web:* www.sandyrivercompany.com	Portland	ME	04112	207-558-6053		652
Sandy Sansing Chevrolet 6200 Pensacola Blvd *TF:* 877-776-3459 ■ *Web:* www.sandysansingchevrolet.com	Pensacola	FL	32505	850-659-6923		57
Sandy Spring Bancorp Inc 17801 Georgia Ave *NASDAQ: SASR* ■ *TF:* 800-399-5919 ■ *Web:* www.sandyspringbank.com	Olney	MD	20832	301-774-6400		360-2
Sandy Spring Friends School 16923 Norwood Rd *Web:* www.ssfs.org	Sandy Spring	MD	20860	301-774-7455	924-1115	622
Sandy Valley Fasteners LLC 528 Broadway St *Web:* www.sandyvalleyfasteners.com	Paintsville	KY	41240	606-788-0222	788-7288	350
San-Ei Gen FFI Inc 630 5th Ave Ste 3201 *Web:* www.saneigen.com	New York	NY	10111	212-315-7850	974-2540	296-15
Sanexen Environmental Services Inc 9935 Rue de Chateauneuf Entrance 1 Ste 200 *TF:* 800-263-7870 ■ *Web:* sanexen.com	Brossard	QC	J4Z3V4	450-466-2123	466-2240	192
Sanford & Company PA 812 Dequeen *Web:* sanford-cpa.com	Mena	AR	71953	479-394-5414		2
Sanford Aircraft 701 Rod Sullivan Rd *TF:* 800-237-6902 ■ *Web:* www.sanfordaircraft.com	Sanford	NC	27330	919-708-5549		63
Sanford Area Chamber of Commerce 115 Chatham St Ste 4 PO Box 519 **Fax Area Code: 855* ■ *Web:* www.growsanfordnc.com	Sanford	NC	27330	919-775-7341	884-2547*	139
Sanford Bruker Banks & Tabb 931 Broad St *Web:* sanfordbrukerbanks.com	Augusta	GA	30901	706-724-2452		390
Sanford Chamber of Commerce 400 E First St *Web:* www.sanfordchamber.com	Sanford	FL	32771	407-322-2212	322-8160	139
Sanford Consortium For Regenerative Medicine 2880 Torrey Pines Scenic Dr *Web:* www.sanfordconsortium.org	La Jolla	CA	92037	858-246-1071		743
Sanford Correctional Ctr 417 Prison Camp Rd *Web:* www.ncdps.gov	Sanford	NC	27330	919-776-4325	774-1866	213
Sanford Herald, The 217 E First St *Web:* www.mysanfordherald.com	Sanford	FL	32771	407-322-2611	323-9408	532-2
Sanford Insurance Center Inc 1722 S Horner Blvd *Web:* sanfordinsurance.com	Sanford	NC	27330	919-775-7216		390
Sanford J. Greenburger Associates Inc 55 Fifth Ave *Web:* www.greenburger.com	New York	NY	10003	212-206-5600	463-8718	444
Sanford Museum & Planetarium 117 E Willow St *Web:* sanfordmuseum.org	Cherokee	IA	51012	712-225-3922		598
Sanford N. Groendyke Inc 295 County Rd 513 *Web:* groendyke.net	Califon	NJ	07830	908-638-8558		390
Sanford Organization, The (TSO) 1000 N Rand Rd Ste 214 *Web:* www.tso.net	Wauconda	IL	60084	847-526-2010	526-3993	47
Sanford Restaurant 1547 N Jackson St *Web:* sanfordrestaurant.com	Milwaukee	WI	53202	414-276-9608	278-8509	671
Sanford Rose Associates International Inc 6860 Dallas Pkwy Ste 302 *Web:* sanfordrose.net	Plano	TX	75024	972-616-7870		260
Sanford USD Medical Ctr 1305 W 18th St *Web:* www.sanfordhealth.org	Sioux Falls	SD	57117	605-333-1000		374-3
Sanford's Grub & Pub LLC 61 SE Wyoming Blvd *Web:* thegrubandpub.com	Casper	WY	82609	307-315-6040		671
Sanford-Brown 1345 Mendota Heights Rd *TF:* 888-247-4238 ■ *Web:* www.sanfordbrown.edu	Mendota Heights	MN	55120	651-905-3400		800
Sanford-Springvale Chamber of Commerce 917 Main St Ste B *Web:* www.sanfordmainechamber.org	Sanford	ME	04073	207-324-4280		139
Sangamo BioSciences Inc 501 Canal Blvd Ste A100 *NASDAQ: SGMO* ■ *TF:* 877-779-8683 ■ *Web:* www.sangamo.com	Richmond	CA	94804	510-970-6000	236-8951	85
Sangamon County 200 S Ninth St Rm 212 *Web:* co.sangamon.il.us	Springfield	IL	62701	217-753-6700		338
Sanganois State Fish & Wildlife Area 3594 County Rd 200 N *Web:* www.dnr.illinois.gov	Chandlerville	IL	62627	309-546-2628		565
Sangchris Lake State Park 9898 Cascade Rd *Web:* www.dnr.illinois.gov	Rochester	IL	62563	217-498-9208		565

Name / Address	City	State	ZIP	Phone	Fax	Class
Sanger & Eby Design LLC 501 Chestnut St *Web:* www.sangereby.com	Cincinnati	OH	45203	513-784-9046		344
Sangre de Cristo Arts & Conference Ctr 210 N Santa Fe Ave *Web:* www.sdc-arts.org	Pueblo	CO	81003	719-295-7200	295-7230	572
Sangre de Cristo Electric Assn 29780 US Hwy 24 *Web:* www.myelectric.coop	Buena Vista	CO	81211	719-395-2412		245
Sangre de Cristo Hospice 1207 Pueblo Blvd Way *Web:* socohospice.org	Pueblo	CO	81005	719-542-0032		371
Sanibel & Captiva Islands Chamber of Commerce 1159 Cswy Rd *TF:* 800-851-5088 ■ *Web:* sanibel-captiva.org	Sanibel	FL	33957	239-472-1080	472-1070	139
Sanibel Inn 937 E Gulf Dr *TF:* 866-565-5480 ■ *Web:* www.theinnsofsanibel.com	Sanibel	FL	33957	239-472-3181		379
Sanibel Packing Company Inc 2477 Periwinkle Way *Web:* baileys-sanibel.com	Sanibel	FL	33957	239-472-1516	472-8073	345
Sanilac County 60 W Sanilac Ave Rm 203 *Web:* sanilaccounty.net	Sandusky	MI	48471	810-648-3212	648-5466	338
San-I-Pak Pacific Inc 23535 S Bird Rd *Web:* www.sanipak.com	Tracy	CA	95378	209-836-2310	836-2336	91
SaniServ Inc 451 E County Line Rd *TF:* 800-733-8073 ■ *Web:* www.saniserv.com	Mooresville	IN	46158	317-831-7030	831-7036	298
Sanitary Services Company Inc 21 Bellwether Way Ste 404 *Web:* www.ssc-inc.com	Bellingham	WA	98225	360-734-3490	671-0239	804
Sanitation District 1 of Northern Kentucky 1045 Eaton Dr *Web:* www.sd1.org	Fort Wright	KY	41017	859-578-7450		804
Sanky Perlowin Associates Inc *Sanky Communications Inc* 599 11th Ave 6th Fl *Web:* sankyinc.com	New York	NY	10036	212-868-4300		317
Sanli Pastore & Hill Inc Sanli Pastore & Hill 1990 S Bundy Dr Ste 800 *Web:* www.sphvalue.com	Los Angeles	CA	90025	310-571-3400		194
Sanlo Inc 400 State Hwy 212 *TF:* 800-275-5408 ■ *Web:* www.sanlo.com	Michigan City	IN	46360	219-879-0241	879-5628	73
San-Mar Laboratories Inc 4 Warehouse Ln *Web:* www.processtechnologies.com	Elmsford	NY	10523	570-587-8326		231
Sanmina-Sci USA Inc 2700 N 1st St *NASDAQ: SANM* ■ *Web:* www.sanmina-sci.com	San Jose	CA	95134	801-588-1200		625
Sanocki Newman & Turret LLP 225 Broadway *Web:* sntlawfirm.com	New York	NY	10007	212-962-1190	964-1573	41
Sanofi Pasteur Inc Discovery Dr *TF:* 800-822-2463 ■ *Web:* www.sanofipasteur.us	Swiftwater	PA	18370	570-957-7187		85
Sanofi-Aventis Canada 2905 Pl Louis R Renaud *TF:* 800-265-7927 ■ *Web:* www.sanofi.ca	Laval	QC	H7V0A3	514-956-6200		85
Sanofi-Aventis US LLC 55 Corporate Dr *Web:* www.sanofi.us	Bridgewater	NJ	08807	908-981-5000		231
S-Anon International Family Groups Inc PO Box 111242 *TF:* 800-210-8141 ■ *Web:* www.sanon.org	Nashville	TN	37222	615-833-3152		48-21
Sanrio Company Ltd 570 Eccles Ave *Web:* www.sanrio.com	South San Francisco	CA	94080	650-952-2880		328
Sans Inc 10 White Wood Ln *Web:* www.sansinc.com	North Branford	CT	06471	718-335-1698		180
Sansei Seafood Restaurant & Sushi Bar *Waikiki Beach Marriot* 2552 Kalakauna Ave 3rd Fl *Web:* www.sanseihawaii.com	Honolulu	HI	96815	808-931-6286		671
Sansei Showa Company Ltd 31000 Bainbridge Rd *Web:* sanseishowa.com	Solon	OH	44139	440-248-4440	248-0272	201
Sansiveri Kimball & Company LLP 50 Holden St *Web:* sansiveri.com	Providence	RI	02908	401-331-0500	331-9040	2
Santa Ana Chamber of Commerce 1631 W Sunflower Ave Ste C35 *Web:* santaanachamber.com	Santa Ana	CA	92704	714-541-5353	541-2238	139
Santa Ana City Hall 20 Civic Center Plz *Web:* www.santa-ana.org	Santa Ana	CA	92701	714-647-6900	647-6954	337
Santa Ana College 1530 W 17th St *Web:* www.sac.edu	Santa Ana	CA	92706	714-564-6000	564-6455	162
Santa Ana Public Library 26 Civic Center Dr *Web:* www.santa-ana.org	Santa Ana	CA	92701	714-647-5250		434-3
Santa Ana Star Casino 54 Jemez Dam Rd *Web:* www.santaanastar.com	Bernalillo	NM	87004	505-867-0000		452
Santa Ana Zoo 1801 E Chestnut Ave *Web:* www.santaanazoo.org	Santa Ana	CA	92701	714-835-7484	550-0346	823
Santa Barbara Asset Management 2049 Century Park E 17th Fl *Web:* www.sbasset.com	Los Angeles	CA	90067	310-552-5100		401
Santa Barbara Botanic Garden 1212 Mission Canyon Rd *Web:* www.sbbg.org	Santa Barbara	CA	93105	805-682-4726		97
Santa Barbara City College 721 Cliff Dr *TF:* 877-232-3919 ■ *Web:* www.sbcc.edu	Santa Barbara	CA	93109	805-965-0581	963-7222	162
Santa Barbara Control Systems 5375 Overpass Rd *TF:* 800-621-2279 ■ *Web:* www.sbcontrol.com	Santa Barbara	CA	93111	805-683-8833		407
Santa Barbara Cottage Hospital PO Box 689 *TF:* 877-247-3260 ■ *Web:* www.cottagehealth.org	Santa Barbara	CA	93102	805-682-7111		374-3
Santa Barbara County PO Box 159 *Web:* www.countyofsb.org	Santa Barbara	CA	93102	805-568-2550	568-3247	338
Santa Barbara Independent 122 W Figueroa St *Web:* www.independent.com	Santa Barbara	CA	93101	805-965-5205	965-5518	532-5
Santa Barbara Infrared Inc 30 S Calle Cesar Chavez Ste D *Web:* www.sbir.com	Santa Barbara	CA	93103	805-965-3669		201
Santa Barbara Inn 901 E Cabrillo Blvd *TF:* 800-231-0431 ■ *Web:* www.santabarbarainn.com	Santa Barbara	CA	93103	800-231-0431		379
Santa Barbara International Film Festival 1528 Chapala St Ste 203 *Web:* sbiff.org	Santa Barbara	CA	93101	805-963-0023		282
Santa Barbara Metropolitan Transit District 550 Olive St *Web:* sbmtd.gov	Santa Barbara	CA	93101	805-963-3364		468
Santa Barbara Museum of Art 1130 State St *Web:* www.sbma.net	Santa Barbara	CA	93101	805-963-4364	966-6840	520
Santa Barbara Museum of Natural History 2559 Puesta Del Sol Rd *Web:* www.sbnature.org	Santa Barbara	CA	93105	805-682-4711	569-3170	520
Santa Barbara Public Library 40 E Anapamu St *TF:* 800-354-9660 ■ *Web:* www.santabarbaraca.gov	Santa Barbara	CA	93101	805-962-7653	564-5660	434-3
Santa Barbara Region Chamber of Commerce 924 Anacapa St Ste 1 *Web:* www.sbchamber.org	Santa Barbara	CA	93101	805-965-3023	966-5954	139
Santa Barbara Symphony 1330 State St Ste 102 *Web:* www.thesymphony.org	Santa Barbara	CA	93101	805-898-9386		573-3
Santa Barbara Teachers Federal Credit Union 3970 La Colina Rd *Web:* sbtfcu.org	Santa Barbara	CA	93110	805-682-2467		219
Santa Barbara Unified School District 720 Santa Barbara St *Web:* www.sbunified.org	Santa Barbara	CA	93101	805-963-4338	965-6872	685
Santa Barbara Visitors Bureau & Film Commission 1601 Anacapa St *TF:* 800-676-1266 ■ *Web:* santabarbaraca.com	Santa Barbara	CA	93101	805-966-9222	966-1728	206
Santa Barbara Zoological Gardens 500 Ninos Dr *Web:* www.sbzoo.org	Santa Barbara	CA	93103	805-962-5339	962-1673	823
Santa Cabrini Hospital 5655 Rue Saint-Zotique E *Web:* ciusss-estmtl.gouv.qc.ca	Montreal	QC	H1T1P7	514-252-1535		374-2
Santa Catalina Ranger District 5700 N Sabino Canyon Rd *Web:* www.fs.usda.gov	Tucson	AZ	85750	520-749-8700		50-5
Santa Catalina School 1500 Mark Thomas Dr *Web:* www.santacatalina.org	Monterey	CA	93940	831-655-9300	655-7535	622
Santa Clara Chamber of Commerce 1850 Warburton Ave *Web:* www.santaclarachamber.com	Santa Clara	CA	95050	408-800-7453	244-7830	139
Santa Clara City Library 2635 Homestead Rd *Web:* www.santaclaraca.gov	Santa Clara	CA	95051	408-615-2900		434-3
Santa Clara Convention Ctr 5001 Great America Pkwy *TF:* 800-272-6822 ■ *Web:* www.santaclara.org	Santa Clara	CA	95054	408-748-7000		205
Santa Clara County 70 W Hedding St 10th Fl East Wing *Web:* www.sccgov.org	San Jose	CA	95110	408-299-5688	295-2192	338
Santa Clara County Library 14600 Winchester Blvd *TF:* 800-286-1991 ■ *Web:* www.sccl.org	Los Gatos	CA	95032	408-293-2326	364-0161	434-3
Santa Clara Pet Hospital Inc 830 Kiely Blvd Ste 107 *Web:* santaclarapethospital.com	Santa Clara	CA	95051	408-296-5857	243-5434	794
Santa Clara University 500 El Camino Real *Web:* www.scu.edu	Santa Clara	CA	95053	408-554-4000	554-5255	166
Santa Clara Valley Medical Ctr 751 S Bascom Ave *TF:* 800-814-4351 ■ *Web:* www.scvmc.org	San Jose	CA	95128	408-885-5000		374-3
Santa Clara Valley Transportation Authority (VTA) 3331 N First St *TF:* 800-894-9908 ■ *Web:* www.vta.org	San Jose	CA	95134	408-321-2300		468
Santa Clarita Association Mana 27644 Newhall Ranch Rd Unit 45 *Web:* valencia.management	Valencia	CA	91355	661-295-9474		653
Santa Clarita Valley Chamber of Commerce 28494 Westinghouse Pl Ste 114 *Web:* www.scvchamber.com	Santa Clarita	CA	91355	661-702-6977		139
Santa Cruz Beach Boardwalk 400 Beach St *Web:* beachboardwalk.com	Santa Cruz	CA	95060	831-423-5590		32
Santa Cruz Chamber of Commerce 611 Ocean St Ste 1 *TF:* 866-282-5900 ■ *Web:* www.santacruzchamber.org	Santa Cruz	CA	95060	831-457-3713	423-1847	139
Santa Cruz Civic Auditorium 307 Church St *Web:* www.cityofsantacruz.com	Santa Cruz	CA	95060	831-420-5240	420-5261	572
Santa Cruz County 2150 N Congress Dr *Web:* www.santacruzcountyaz.gov	Nogales	AZ	85621	520-375-7800		338
Santa Cruz County Conference & Visitors Council 303 Water St Ste 100 *TF:* 800-833-3494 ■ *Web:* www.santacruz.org	Santa Cruz	CA	95060	831-425-1234		206
Santa Cruz County Fair & Rodeo 3142 Arizona 83 PO Box 85 *Web:* www.sonoitafairgrounds.com	Sonoita	AZ	85637	520-455-5553	455-5330	642
Santa Cruz Mission State Historic Park 303 Big Trees Park Rd *Web:* www.parks.ca.gov	Felton	CA	95018	831-335-6318	429-2870	565
Santa Cruz Nutritionals 2200 Delaware Ave *Web:* www.santacruznutritionals.com	Santa Cruz	CA	95060	831-457-3200		296-8

Name / Address	Phone	Fax	Class
Santa Cruz Sentinel Inc 207 Church St ....Santa Cruz CA 95060 *TF:* 800-952-2335 ■ *Web:* www.santacruzsentinel.com	831-423-4242		532-3
Santa Cruz Symphony 307 Church St ....Santa Cruz CA 95060 *Web:* santacruzsymphony.org	831-462-0553		573-3
Santa Fe Cafe 807 William Hilton Pkwy ....Hilton Head Island SC 29928 *Web:* santafehhi.com	843-785-3838		671
Santa Fe Chamber of Commerce 1644 St Michael's Dr....Santa Fe NM 87507 *Web:* www.santafechamber.com	505-988-3279	984-2205	139
Santa Fe Children's Museum 1050 Old Pecos Trl....Santa Fe NM 87505 *Web:* santafechildrensmuseum.org	505-989-8359	989-7506	521
Santa Fe City Hall 200 Lincoln Ave ....Santa Fe NM 87501 *TF:* 866-773-2587 ■ *Web:* www.santafenm.gov	505-955-6520	955-6829	337
Santa Fe Community College (SFCC) 6401 Richards Ave....Santa Fe NM 87508 *Web:* www.sfcc.edu	505-428-1000		162
Santa Fe Community College Teaching Zoo 3000 NW 83rd St....Gainesville FL 32606 *Web:* www.sfcollege.edu	352-395-5604		823
Santa Fe Convention Ctr 201 W Marcy St ....Santa Fe NM 87501 *TF:* 800-777-2489 ■ *Web:* santafe.org	505-955-6200	955-6222	206
Santa Fe County 102 Grant Ave ....Santa Fe NM 87501 *Web:* www.co.santa-fe.nm.us	505-986-6200	995-2740	338
Santa Fe Extruders & Printing 15315 Marquardt Ave....Santa Fe Springs CA 90670 **Fax Area Code:* 562 ■ *TF:* 800-645-0626 ■ *Web:* www.sigmaplasticsgroup.com	800-645-0626	926-3942*	596
Santa Fe Independent School District PO Box 370 ....Santa Fe TX 77510 *Web:* www.sfisd.org	409-925-3526		685
Santa Fe Institute Library 1399 Hyde Park Rd....Santa Fe NM 87501 *Web:* www.santafe.edu	505-984-8800	982-0565	434-3
Santa Fe Municipal Airport (SAF) 121 Aviation Dr....Santa Fe NM 87504 *Web:* www.santafenm.gov	505-955-2900	955-2905	27
Santa Fe National Cemetery 501 N Guadalupe St....Santa Fe NM 87501 *Web:* www.cem.va.gov	505-988-6400	988-6497	136
Santa Fe New Mexican, The 202 E Marcy St PO Box 2048....Santa Fe NM 87504 *Web:* www.santafenewmexican.com	505-983-3303		532-2
Santa Fe Opera, The 301 Opera Dr ....Santa Fe NM 87506 *TF:* 800-280-4654 ■ *Web:* www.santafeopera.org	505-986-5900		573-2
Santa Fe Performing Arts 1050 Old Pecos Trl....Santa Fe NM 87505 *Web:* www.sfperformingarts.org	505-982-7992		572
Santa Fe Playhouse 142 E DeVargas St....Santa Fe NM 87501 *Web:* santafeplayhouse.org	505-988-4262		572
Santa Fe Preparatory School 1101 Camino De Cruz Blanca....Santa Fe NM 87505 *Web:* www.sfprep.org	505-982-1829		685
Santa Fe Public Library 145 Washington Ave....Santa Fe NM 87501 *Web:* www.santafelibrary.org	505-955-6780		434-3
Santa Fe Reporter 132 E Marcy St....Santa Fe NM 87501 *Web:* www.sfreporter.com	505-988-5541		532-5
Santa Fe Rubber Products Inc 12306 E Washington Blvd....Whittier CA 90606 *Web:* www.santaferubber.com	562-693-2776	693-4936	326
Santa Fe Station 4949 N Rancho Dr....Las Vegas NV 89130 *TF:* 866-767-7770 ■ *Web:* santafestation.sclv.com	702-658-4900		133
Santa Fe Symphony Orchestra & Chorus Inc 551 W Cordova Rd Ste D ....Santa Fe NM 87505 *Web:* santafesymphony.org	505-983-3530		573-3
Santa Fe Trail Ctr 1349 K-156 Hwy ....Larned KS 67550 *Web:* santafetrailcenter.org	620-285-2054	285-7491	520
Santa Fe University of Art & Design 1600 St Michaels Dr....Santa Fe NM 87505 **Fax Area Code:* 505 ■ *TF:* 800-456-2673 ■ *Web:* santafeuniversity.edu	800-456-2673	473-6011*	166
Santa Gertrudis Breeders Intl PO Box 1257 ....Kingsville TX 78364 *Web:* www.santagertrudis.com	361-592-9357	592-8572	48-2
Santa Margarita Catholic High School 22062 Antonio Pkwy....Rancho Santa Margarita CA 92688 *Web:* www.eaglesfootball.com	949-766-6000		685
Santa Maria Ford Lincoln 1035 E Battles Rd....Santa Maria CA 93454 *Web:* www.santamariaford.net	805-925-2445		57
Santa Maria Inn 801 S Broadway ....Santa Maria CA 93454 *TF:* 800-462-4276 ■ *Web:* www.santamariainn.com	805-928-7777	928-5690	379
Santa Maria Museum of Flight Inc 3015 Airpark Dr ....Santa Maria CA 93455 *Web:* www.smmof.org	805-922-8758		522
Santa Maria Public Library 421 S McClelland St....Santa Maria CA 93454 *Web:* www.cityofsantamaria.org	805-925-0994		434-3
Santa Maria Software Inc 151 W Dana St Ste 202....Nipomo CA 93444 *TF:* 800-937-6590 ■ *Web:* www.counterman.net	805-929-8266	929-8267	178-1
Santa Maria Times PO Box 400....Santa Maria CA 93456 *Web:* santamariatimes.com	805-925-2691	928-5657	532-2
Santa Maria Tire Inc 249 Montgomery Ave....Oxnard CA 93036 *Web:* www.smtire.com	805-642-0174		57
Santa Maria Valley Chamber of Commerce 614 S Broadway....Santa Maria CA 93454 *Web:* santamaria.com	805-925-2403		139
Santa Maria Valley Historical Society 616 S Broadway....Santa Maria CA 93454 *Web:* santamariahistory.com	805-922-3130		48-13
Santa Maria-Bonita School Dist 708 S Miller St....Santa Maria CA 93454 *Web:* www.smbsd.org	805-928-1783		685
Santa Monica Amusements LLC 380 Santa Monica Pier....Santa Monica CA 90401 *Web:* www.pacpark.com	310-260-8744		32
Santa Monica Chamber of Commerce 610 Santa Monica Blvd Ste 213....Santa Monica CA 90401 *Web:* smchamber.com	310-393-9825	394-1868	139
Santa Monica Civic Auditorium 1855 Main St ....Santa Monica CA 90401 *TF:* 866-728-3229 ■ *Web:* www.smgov.net	310-458-8551		205
Santa Monica College 1900 Pico Blvd....Santa Monica CA 90405 *Web:* www.smc.edu	310-434-4000	434-3645	162
Santa Monica Convention & Visitors Bureau 1920 Main St Ste B....Santa Monica CA 90405 *TF:* 800-544-5319 ■ *Web:* www.santamonica.com	310-319-6263	319-6273	206
Santa Monica Mountains National Recreation Area 401 W Hillcrest Dr ....Thousand Oaks CA 91360 *TF:* 888-275-8747 ■ *Web:* www.nps.gov	805-370-2300		564
Santa Monica Public Library 601 Santa Monica Blvd....Santa Monica CA 90401 *Web:* www.smpl.org	310-458-8608		434-3
Santa Monica State Beach Pacific Coast Hwy....Santa Monica CA 90401 *Web:* www.parks.ca.gov	310-458-8300		565
Santa Monica Yoga 1640 Ocean Park Blvd ....Santa Monica CA 90405 *Web:* www.santamonicayoga.com	310-396-4040		810
Santa Paula Chamber of Commerce 200 N Tenth St ....Santa Paula CA 93060 *Web:* santapaulachamber.net	805-525-5561		139
Santa Rosa Chamber of Commerce 1260 N Dutton Ave Ste 272 ....Santa Rosa CA 95404 *Web:* www.santarosametrochamber.com	707-545-1414	545-6914	139
Santa Rosa Correctional Institution 5850 E Milton Rd ....Milton FL 32583 *Web:* dc.state.fl.us	850-983-5800	983-5907	213
Santa Rosa County 6495 Caroline St Ste M ....Milton FL 32570 *Web:* www.santarosa.fl.gov	850-983-1877		338
Santa Rosa County Chamber of Commerce 5247 Stewart St ....Milton FL 32570 *TF:* 800-239-8732 ■ *Web:* www.srcchamber.com	850-623-2339	623-4413	139
Santa Rosa Junior College 1501 Mendocino Ave ....Santa Rosa CA 95401 *Web:* www.santarosa.edu	707-527-4011	527-4798	162
Santa Rosa Memorial Hospital (SRMH) 1165 Montgomery Dr....Santa Rosa CA 95405 *TF:* 877-449-3627 ■ *Web:* www.stjosephhealth.org	707-546-3210		374-3
Santa Rosa Press Gazette 6576 Caroline St....Milton FL 32570 *Web:* www.srpressgazette.com	850-623-2120		532-2
Santa Rosa Symphony (SRS) 50 Santa Rosa Ave Ste 410....Santa Rosa CA 95404 *Web:* www.srsymphony.org	707-546-8742	546-0460	573-3
Santacafe 231 Washington Ave....Santa Fe NM 87501 *Web:* santacafe.com	505-984-1788		671
Santana Property Group Inc 350 5th Ave 59th Fl ....New York NY 10118 *Web:* www.santanapropertygroup.com	212-268-9322	327-2141	652
Santana Row 377 Santana Row....San Jose CA 95128 *Web:* www.santanarow.com	408-551-4611		50-6
Santander Bank NA PO Box 841003 ....Boston MA 02284 *TF:* 877-768-2265 ■ *Web:* www.sovereignbank.com	877-768-2265		70
Santander Performing Arts Ctr 136 N Sixth St ....Reading PA 19601 *Web:* santander-arena.com	610-898-7299		572
Santariello, Akl & Associates PLLC 200 Canal View Blvd Ste 206....Rochester NY 14623 *Web:* santariello.com	585-424-3769		653
Santec Inc 3501 Challenger St....Torrance CA 90503 *TF:* 800-284-4050 ■ *Web:* www.santecfaucet.com	310-542-0063		361
Santee Chamber of Commerce 10315 Mission Gorge Rd ....Santee CA 92071 *Web:* santeechamber.com	619-449-6572		139
Santee Electric Co-opeartive Inc 424 Sumter Hwy....Kingstree SC 29556 *TF:* 800-922-1604 ■ *Web:* www.santee.org	843-355-6187		245
Santee School District 9625 Cuyamaca St ....Santee CA 92071 *Web:* www.santeesd.net	619-258-2300		685
Santee State Park 251 State Park Rd....Santee SC 29142 *Web:* southcarolinaparks.com	803-854-2408		565
Santek Components 1060 Holland Ave ....Clovis CA 93612 *Web:* santekcomp.com	559-294-6015		246
Santen & Hughes 600 Vine St Ste 2700 ....Cincinnati OH 45202 *Web:* www.santenhughes.com	513-721-4450		41
Santen Inc 6401 Hollis St Ste 125....Emeryville CA 94608 *TF:* 855-772-6836 ■ *Web:* www.santenusa.com	415-268-9100		231
Santeon Group Inc 12110 Sunset Hills Rd Ste 630....Reston VA 20190 *Web:* www.santeon.com	703-970-9200		395
Santi & Associates PC 4010 Old Milton Pkwy Ste 100....Alpharetta GA 30005 *Web:* santicpa.com	770-623-4440	623-4009	2
Santiago Canyon College 8045 E Chapman Ave....Orange CA 92869 *Web:* www.sccollege.edu	714-628-4900	628-4723	162
Santie Oil Co 126 Larcel Dr....Sikeston MO 63801 *TF:* 800-748-7788 ■ *Web:* www.santiemidwest.com	314-436-3569		138
Santillana USA Publishing Co 2023 NW 84th Ave....Doral FL 33122 **Fax Area Code:* 888 ■ *TF:* 800-245-8584 ■ *Web:* www.santillanausa.com	305-591-9522	248-9518*	637-2
Santilli Oil Company Inc 240 Franklin St....Shoemakersville PA 19555 *Web:* santillioil.com	610-562-7557		316
Santinelli International Inc 325 Oser Ave ....Hauppauge NY 11788 *TF:* 800-644-3343 ■ *Web:* www.santinelli.com	800-644-3343		454

Name / Address	City	State	ZIP	Phone	Fax	Class
Santini Foods Inc 16505 Worthley Dr *Web:* www.santinifoods.com	San Lorenzo	CA	94580	510-317-8888		297-8
Santo Insurance & Financial Services Inc 224 Main St *Web:* santoinsurance.com	Salem	NH	03079	603-890-6439		390
Santora CPA Group 220 Continental Dr Ste 112 Christiana Executive Campus *TF:* 800-347-0116 ■ *Web:* www.santoracpagroup.com	Newark	DE	19713	302-737-6200		2
Santorini Greek Taverna 1502 Centre St N *Web:* www.santorinirestaurant.com	Calgary	AB	T2E2R9	403-276-8363		671
Santoro Oil Company Inc 101 Corliss St *Web:* www.santorooil.com	Providence	RI	02904	401-942-5000		316
Santos Family Enterprises Ltd 5400 Alameda *Web:* www.foodcityep.com	El Paso	TX	79905	915-779-3641	772-1461	345
Santos Precision Inc 2220 S Anne St *Web:* www.santosprecision.com	Santa Ana	CA	92704	714-957-0299	957-0949	22
SANUWAVE Health Inc 3360 Martin Farm Rd *Web:* www.sanuwave.com	Suwanee	GA	30024	770-419-7525	419-8634	476
Sanyo Denki America Inc 468 Amapola Ave *Web:* www.sanyodenki.com	Torrance	CA	90501	310-783-5400	212-6545	174
SAP America Inc 3999 W Chester Pk *Web:* www.sap.com	Newtown Square	PA	19073	610-661-1000		178-1
SAP USA Truck & Auto Parts Inc 5301 NW 74 Ave Ste 200 *Web:* sapcorp.net	Miami	FL	33166	305-594-2844	599-2351	54
Sapers & Wallack Inc 275 Washington St Ste 205 *Web:* sapers-wallack.com	Newton	MA	02458	617-225-2600	494-5485	401
SAPIEN Technologies Inc 841 Latour Ct Ste D *Web:* www.sapien.com	Napa	CA	94558	707-252-8700		177
Sapiens International Corp 4000 CentreGreen Way Ste 150 *NASDAQ: SPNS* ■ *TF:* 888-281-1167 ■ *Web:* www.sapiens.com	Cary	NC	27513	919-405-1500	405-1700	178-10
Sapient Capital Management LLC 545 Green Ln PO Box 1590 *Web:* www.sapientcapital.com	Wilson	WY	83014	307-733-3806		792
Sapient Private Wealth Management Services LLC 101 E Broadway Ste 480 *Web:* sapientprivatewealthmanagement.com	Eugene	OR	97401	541-762-0300		690
Sapient Razorfish 70 Birch Alley Ste 240 *Web:* www.sapientrazorfish.com	Beavercreek	OH	45440	937-723-2322		193
Sapio Sciences LLC 205 N George St *Web:* sapiosciences.com	York	PA	17401	410-800-4620		177
Sapona Mfg 2478 Cedar Falls Rd *Web:* www.saponamfg.com	Franklinville	NC	27248	336-625-2727	626-0876	745-9
Sapp Bros Petroleum Inc 9915 S 148th St *TF:* 800-233-4059 ■ *Web:* www.sappbros.net	Omaha	NE	68138	402-895-2202		579
Sapphire Grill 110 W Congress St *Web:* www.sapphiregrill.com	Savannah	GA	31401	912-443-9962	443-9964	671
Sapphire Scientific Inc 2604 Liberator *TF:* 800-932-3030 ■ *Web:* www.legendbrandscleaning.com	Prescott	AZ	86301	800-932-3030		427
Sappi Pulp Americas LP 925 Westchester Ave Ste 115 **Fax Area Code:* 914 ■ *Web:* www.sappi.com	West Harrison	NY	10604	207-776-5853	253-8671*	552-1
Sapporo Fantasy Japanese Steak 2939 C Battleground Ave *Web:* www.sapporofantasy.net	Greensboro	NC	27408	336-282-5345		671
Sapporo Restaurant 230 Commercial St *Web:* www.sappororestaurant.com	Portland	ME	04101	207-772-1233		671
Sapta Global Inc 200 Middlesex Esex Tpke Ste 306 E **Fax Area Code:* 877 ■ *Web:* www.saptanet.com	Iselin	NJ	08830	732-602-0240	397-1676*	809
Saputo Inc 6869 Boul Metropolitain *TSE: SAP* ■ *TF:* 800-387-7937 ■ *Web:* www.saputo.com	Saint-Leonard	QC	H1P1X8	514-328-6662		296-5
Sara Hightower Regional Library 205 Riverside Pkwy NE *Web:* rome.shrls.org	Rome	GA	30161	706-236-4600		434-3
Sarabande Books Inc 822 E Market St *Web:* www.sarabandebooks.org	Louisville	KY	40206	502-458-4028		637-2
Saracen Energy Partners LP 3033 W Alabama *Web:* www.saracenenergy.com	Houston	TX	77098	713-285-2900		579
Sarafinchin Associates Ltd 238 Galaxy Blvd *Web:* www.sarafinchin.com	Toronto	ON	M9W5R8	416-674-1770		261
Sarah Bush Lincoln Health Ctr (SBLHC) 1000 Health Center Dr PO Box 372 *TF:* 800-345-3191 ■ *Web:* www.sarahbush.org	Mattoon	IL	61938	217-258-2525	258-4117	374-3
Sarah House Inc 100 Roberts Ave *Web:* sarahsguesthouse.org	Syracuse	NY	13207	315-475-1747		372
Sarah Lawrence College 1 Mead Way *TF:* 800-888-2858 ■ *Web:* www.sarahlawrence.edu	Bronxville	NY	10708	914-337-0700	395-2515	166
Sarah P. Duke Gardens 420 Anderson St *Web:* gardens.duke.edu	Durham	NC	27708	919-684-3698	668-3610	97
Sarakem Corp 15 Buell St *Web:* sarakem.com	Hanover	NH	03755	603-643-5720		271
Saranac Glove Co 999 Lombardi Ave *TF:* 800-727-2622 ■ *Web:* www.saranacglove.com	Green Bay	WI	54304	920-435-3737		155-8
Saraphino's 3074 E Layton Ave *Web:* saraphinossaintfranciswi.com	Saint Francis	WI	53235	414-744-0303		671
Sarasota Ballet of Florida 5555 N Tamiami Trl *Web:* www.sarasotaballet.org	Sarasota	FL	34243	941-359-0099		573-1
Sarasota Classified/Teachers Assoc 4675 S Tamiami Trl *Web:* sctaonline.org	Sarasota	FL	34231	941-922-9022		414
Sarasota Film Festival 332 Cocoanut Ave *Web:* www.sarasotafilmfestival.com	Sarasota	FL	34236	941-364-9514	364-8411	282
Sarasota Herald-Tribune 1741 Main St *TF:* 866-284-7102 ■ *Web:* www.heraldtribune.com	Sarasota	FL	34236	941-953-7755		532-2
Sarasota Home Health Care Agency 678 S Tamiami Trl *Web:* www.sarasotahomehealthcare.com	Osprey	FL	34229	941-306-4347	866-7539	363
Sarasota Jungle Gardens 3701 Bay Shore Rd *TF:* 877-681-6547 ■ *Web:* www.sarasotajunglegardens.com	Sarasota	FL	34234	941-355-5305		823
Sarasota Kennel Club Inc 5400 Bradenton Rd *Web:* www.sarasotakennelclub.com	Sarasota	FL	34234	941-355-7744		642
Sarasota Memorial Hospital 1700 S Tamiami Trl *TF:* 800-764-8255 ■ *Web:* www.smh.com	Sarasota	FL	34239	941-917-9000		374-3
Sarasota Opera 61 N Pineapple Ave *TF:* 866-951-0111 ■ *Web:* www.sarasotaopera.org	Sarasota	FL	34236	941-366-8450	955-5571	573-2
Sarasota Orchestra 709 N Tamiami Trl *TF:* 866-508-0611 ■ *Web:* www.sarasotaorchestra.org	Sarasota	FL	34236	941-953-4252	953-3059	573-3
Sarasota-Bradenton International Airport 6000 Airport Cir *TF:* 800-711-1712 ■ *Web:* www.srq-airport.com	Sarasota	FL	34243	941-359-2770	359-5054	27
Sarasota-Manatee Jewish Housing Council Inc 1951 N Honore Ave *Web:* www.avivaseniorlife.org	Sarasota	FL	34235	941-379-3553		672
Saratoga Botanicals LLC 80 Henry St *Web:* saratogabotanicals.com	Saratoga Springs	NY	12866	518-306-4108		77
Saratoga Chamber of Commerce 14485 Big Basin Way *Web:* saratogachamber.org	Saratoga	CA	95070	408-867-0753		139
Saratoga Convention & Tourism Bureau 60 Railroad Pl Ste 301 *TF:* 855-424-6073 ■ *Web:* www.discoversaratoga.org	Saratoga Springs	NY	12866	518-584-1531	584-2969	206
Saratoga County 40 McMaster St *Web:* www.saratogacountyny.gov	Ballston	NY	12020	518-885-5381	884-4726	338
Saratoga County Chamber of Commerce 28 Clinton St *TF:* 855-765-7873 ■ *Web:* www.saratoga.org	Saratoga Springs	NY	12866	518-584-3255	798-0163	139
Saratoga Eagle Sales & Service Inc 45 Duplainville Rd	Saratoga Springs	NY	12866	518-581-7377	581-7777	81-1
Saratoga Food Specialties 771 W Crossroads Pky *TF:* 800-451-0407 ■ *Web:* www.saratogafs.com	Bolingbrook	IL	60490	800-451-0407		296-37
Saratoga Gaming & Raceway 342 Jefferson St PO Box 356 *TF:* 800-727-2990 ■ *Web:* saratogacasino.com	Saratoga Springs	NY	12866	518-584-2110		642
Saratoga Honda 3402 Rt 9 *TF:* 888-658-2303 ■ *Web:* www.saratogahonda.com	Saratoga Springs	NY	12866	888-658-2303		57
Saratoga Hospital 211 Church St *Web:* www.saratogahospital.org	Saratoga Springs	NY	12866	518-587-3222	580-4122	374-3
Saratoga Insurance Brokers 532 Baltimore Blvd Ste 306 *Web:* sarabrokers.com	Westminster	MD	21157	410-781-6396		390
Saratoga Liquor Company Inc 3215 James Day Ave *TF:* 800-472-6923 ■ *Web:* www.saratogaliquor.com	Superior	WI	54880	715-394-4487		443
Saratoga National Historical Park 648 Rt 32 *Web:* www.nps.gov	Stillwater	NY	12170	518-664-9821		564
Saratoga Performing Arts Ctr (SPAC) 108 Avenue of the Pines *Web:* spac.org	Saratoga Springs	NY	12866	518-584-9330	584-0809	572
Saratoga Race Course 267 Union Ave *Web:* www.saratogaracetrack.com	Saratoga Springs	NY	12866	518-584-6200		642
Saratoga Spa Co 33 Wade Rd *Web:* www.saratogaspas.com	Latham	NY	12110	518-786-1111		77
Saratoga Spa State Park 110 Avenue of the Pines *Web:* parks.ny.gov	Saratoga Springs	NY	12866	518-584-2535		565
Saratoga Springs City Ctr 522 Broadway *Web:* www.saratogacitycenter.org	Saratoga Springs	NY	12866	518-584-0027	584-0117	205
Saratoga Sun 116 E Bridge St *Web:* www.saratogasun.com	Saratoga	WY	82331	307-326-8311		532-2
Saratoga's Community Federal Credit Union 23 Division St *TF:* 866-322-2684 ■ *Web:* saratogafcu.org	Saratoga Springs	NY	12866	518-583-2323	583-9143	219
Sarbanes John P (Rep D - MD) 2370 Rayburn House Office Bldg *Web:* sarbanes.house.gov	Washington	DC	20515	202-225-4016	225-9219	342-2
Sarco Inc 50 Hilton St *Web:* www.e-sarcoinc.com	Easton	PA	18042	610-250-3960	250-3961	459
SARCOM Inc *AEP Colloids Div* 6299 Rt 9N *TF:* 800-848-0658 ■ *Web:* www.aepcolloids.com	Hadley	NY	12835	518-696-9900	696-9997	146
Sarcoma Foundation of America Inc, The 9899 Main St Ste 204 *Web:* www.curesarcoma.org	Damascus	MD	20872	301-253-8687	253-8690	305
Sardee Industries Inc 5100 Academy Dr Ste 400 *Web:* www.sardee.com	Lisle	IL	60532	630-824-4200	780-9915	358
Sardella's Restaurant 30 Memorial Blvd W *Web:* www.sardellas.com	Newport	RI	02840	401-849-6312		671
Sardello Inc 1000 Corporation Dr *Web:* www.sardello.com	Aliquippa	PA	15001	724-375-4101		770
Sardine Factory, The 701 Wave St *Web:* sardinefactory.com	Monterey	CA	93940	831-373-3775		671
Sarducci's 3 Main St *Web:* www.sarduccis.com	Montpelier	VT	05602	802-223-0229	223-6003	671
Sare Plastics 14600 Commerce St NE *Web:* www.sareplastics.com	Alliance	OH	44601	330-821-4299	821-3433	608
Sareen & Associates 10702 Vandor Ln *Web:* www.sareentax.com	Manassas	VA	20109	703-366-3444		2

Name / Address	City	State	ZIP	Phone	Fax	Class
Sares-Regis Group 18802 Bardeen Ave *Web:* www.sares-regis.com	Irvine	CA	92612	949-756-5959	756-5955	655
Saretsky, Katz, & Dranoff LLP 475 Park Ave S 26th Fl *Web:* skdllp.com	New York	NY	10016	212-973-9797		41
Sarfino & Rhoades LLP 11921 Rockville Pk Ste 501 *Web:* sarfinoandrhoades.com	Rockville	MD	20852	301-770-5500		2
Sargent & Greenleaf Inc 1 Security Dr *TF:* 800-826-7652 ■ *Web:* www.sargentandgreenleaf.com	Nicholasville	KY	40356	859-885-9411	885-3063	350
Sargent & Lundy LLC 55 E Monroe St *Web:* www.sargentlundy.com	Chicago	IL	60603	312-269-2000		261
Sargent Art Inc 100 E Diamond Ave **Fax Area Code:* 570 ■ *TF:* 800-424-3596 ■ *Web:* www.sargentart.com	Hazleton	PA	18201	800-424-3596	459-1752*	43
Sargent Controls & Aerospace 5675 W Burlingame Rd *TF:* 800-230-0359 ■ *Web:* www.sargentaerospace.com	Tucson	AZ	85743	520-744-1000	744-9494	223
Sargent Corp 378 Bennoch Rd *Web:* sargent-corp.com	Stillwater	ME	04489	207-827-4435	827-6150	188-4
Sargent County 355 Main St *Web:* sargentnd.com	Forman	ND	58032	701-724-6241	724-6244	338
Sargent Manufacturing Co 100 Sargent Dr *TF:* 800-727-5477 ■ *Web:* www.sargentlock.com	New Haven	CT	06511	800-727-5477		350
Sargento Foods Inc 1 Persnickety Pl *TF:* 800-243-3737 ■ *Web:* www.sargento.com	Plymouth	WI	53073	920-893-8484		296-5
Sargents Title Company LLC 625 S Grand Traverse *Web:* sargentstitle.com	Flint	MI	48502	810-767-2355		653
Sargis Associates Inc 25 Commerce Dr *Web:* sargisassociates.com	Cromwell	CT	06416	860-461-1544		261
Saria International Inc 1200 Industrial Rd Ste 2 *TF:* 800-719-7255 ■ *Web:* www.sariainternational.com	San Carlos	CA	94070	650-591-1440	591-1976	523
Sarkes Tarzian Inc 205 N College Ave Ste 800	Bloomington	IN	47404	812-332-7251		738
Sarlo Power Mowers Inc PO Box 1169 *Web:* www.sarlomower.com	Fort Myers	FL	33902	239-332-1955		273
Sarnoff Corp 201 Washington Rd PO Box 5300 *Web:* www.sri.com	Princeton	NJ	08543	609-734-2000		668
Sarofim Realty Advisors 8115 Preston Rd Ste 400 *Web:* www.sraco.com	Dallas	TX	75225	214-692-4200	692-4201	401
Sarpy County 1210 Golden Gate Dr Ste 1250 *Web:* www.sarpy.com	Papillion	NE	68046	402-593-2100	593-4360	338
Sarpy County Chamber of Commerce 7775 Olson Dr Ste 207 *TF:* 855-746-3784 ■ *Web:* www.sarpychamber.org	Papillion	NE	68046	402-339-3050		139
Sarreid Ltd 3905 Airport Dr NW *Web:* www.sarreid.com	Wilson	NC	27896	252-291-1414	237-1592	320
SARS Software Products Inc 2175 E Francisco Blvd Ste A-3 *TF:* 866-279-8373 ■ *Web:* www.sarsgrid.com	San Rafael	CA	94901	415-226-0040	226-0038	177
Sarstedt Inc 1025 St James Church Rd PO Box 468 *TF:* 800-257-5101	Newton	NC	28658	828-465-4000	465-4003	596
Sartek Industries Inc 17 Belle Meade Rd Building 1 Unit 4 *Web:* www.sarind.com	Setauket	NY	11733	631-473-3555	473-3558	647
Sartomer 502 Thomas Jones Way *Web:* www.sartomer.com	Exton	PA	19341	610-363-4100	363-4140	605-2
Sartori 107 Pleasant View Rd *TF:* 800-558-5888 ■ *Web:* www.sartoricheese.com	Plymouth	WI	53073	800-558-5888		296-5
Sartorius North America Inc 131 Heartland Blvd *TF:* 800-368-7178 ■ *Web:* www.sartorius.com	Brentwood	NY	11717	631-254-4249	254-4253	420
SAS (S Abraham & Sons Inc) 4001 3 Mile Rd NW PO Box 1768 *TF:* 800-477-5455 ■ *Web:* www.sasinc.com	Grand Rapids	MI	49534	616-453-6358	453-9259	297-8
SAS (Saint Andrew's-Sewanee School) 290 Quintard Rd *Web:* www.sasweb.org	Sewanee	TN	37375	931-598-5651		622
SAS (Scandinavian Airlines System) 301 Rt 17 N Ste 500 **Fax Area Code:* 201 ■ *TF:* 800-221-2350 ■ *Web:* www.flysas.com	Rutherford	NJ	07070	212-332-2520	896-3735*	25
SAS (Specialty Answering Service) 800 N Henderson Rd *TF:* 888-532-4794 ■ *Web:* www.specialtyansweringservice.net	King of Prussia	PA	19406	888-532-4794	644-4129	393
SAS Enterprises PO Box 21388 *Web:* sasenterprises.biz	Concord	CA	94521	925-685-8968		194
SAS Institute Inc 100 SAS Campus Dr *TF:* 800-727-0025 ■ *Web:* www.sas.com	Cary	NC	27513	919-677-8000	677-4444	178-1
SAS Safety Corp 3031 Gardenia Ave **Fax Area Code:* 800 ■ *TF:* 800-262-0200 ■ *Web:* sassafety.com	Long Beach	CA	90807	562-427-2775	244-1938*	477
SAS Shoemakers 1717 Sas Dr *TF:* 877-782-7463 ■ *Web:* sasshoes.com	San Antonio	TX	78224	877-782-7463		301
Sasaki Associates Inc 64 Pleasant St *Web:* www.sasaki.com	Watertown	MA	02472	617-926-3300	924-2748	261
Sasco Capital Inc 10 Sasco Hill Rd *Web:* www.sascocap.com	Fairfield	CT	06824	203-254-6800	259-3842	401
SASCO Electric 2750 Moore Ave *TF:* 800-477-4422 ■ *Web:* www.sasco.com	Fullerton	CA	92833	714-870-0217	738-3571	189-4
Sashco Inc 8150 Inspiration Dr Ste D *TF:* 800-600-3232 ■ *Web:* www.sashcoinc.com	Ontario	CA	91761	909-937-8222	937-8223	189-6
Saskatchewan Health Research Foundation 324-111 Research Dr *TF:* 800-975-1699 ■ *Web:* shrf.ca	Saskatoon	SK	S7N3R2	306-975-1680	975-1688	231
Saskatchewan Indian Gaming Authority 103 Aspen Pl *TF:* 800-306-6789 ■ *Web:* www.siga.sk.ca	Saskatoon	SK	S7N1K4	306-477-7777	477-7582	133
Saskatchewan Roughrider Football Club 1910 Piffles Taylor Way PO Box 1966 *TF:* 888-474-3377 ■ *Web:* www.riderville.com	Regina	SK	S4P3E1	306-569-2323	566-4280	715-2
Saskatchewan Sports Hall of Fame & Museum 2205 Victoria Ave *Web:* sasksportshalloffame.com	Regina	SK	S4P0S4	306-780-9232		522
Saskatoon 681 Halton Rd *Web:* saskatoonrestaurant.com	Greenville	SC	29607	864-297-7244		671
Saskatoon Business College Ltd 221 Third Ave N *TF:* 800-679-7711 ■ *Web:* www.sbccollege.ca	Saskatoon	SK	S7K2H7	306-244-6333		162
Saskatoon Inn Hotel & Conference Ctr 2002 Airport Dr *TF:* 800-667-8789 ■ *Web:* www.saskatooninn.com	Saskatoon	SK	S7L6M4	306-242-1440		378
Sasnak Management Corp 1877 N Rock Rd	Wichita	KS	67206	316-683-2611		670
SA-SO Co 525 N Great SW Pkwy *Web:* sa-so.com	Arlington	TX	76011	972-641-4911	660-3684	701
Sasol North America Inc 900 Threadneedle St Ste 100 *Web:* www.sasolnorthamerica.com	Houston	TX	77079	281-588-3000		144
Sasol Wax North America Corp 21325-B Cabot Blvd *Web:* www.sasolwax.com	Hayward	CA	94545	510-783-9295		146
Sassafraz 100 Cumberland St *Web:* www.sassafraz.ca	Toronto	ON	M5R1A6	416-964-2222	964-2402	671
Sasse Ben (Sen R - NE) 107 Russell Senate Office Bldg *Web:* www.sasse.senate.gov	Washington	DC	20510	202-224-4224		342-2
Sassi 10455 E Pinnacle Peak Pkwy *Web:* www.sassi.biz	Scottsdale	AZ	85255	480-502-9095		671
Sassoon Salons 399 Boylston St *Web:* www.sassoon-salon.com	Boston	MA	02116	617-536-5496		77
SAT (San Antonio International Airport) 9800 Airport Blvd Rm 2041 *TF:* 800-237-6639 ■ *Web:* www.sanantonio.gov	San Antonio	TX	78216	210-207-3411	207-3500	27
Satair USA Inc 525 Westpark Dr *Web:* www.satair.com	Peachtree City	GA	30269	404-675-6352	675-6311	770
Satake USA Inc 10905 Cash Rd *Web:* www.satake-usa.com	Stafford	TX	77477	281-276-3600	494-1427	547
Satay 3202 W Anderson Ln *Web:* www.satayusa.com	Austin	TX	78757	512-467-6731		671
Satay Sarinah 512A S Van Dorn St *Web:* www.sataysarinah.com	Alexandria	VA	22304	703-370-4313	370-9672	671
Satchidananda Ashram Yogaville 108 Yogaville Way *TF:* 800-858-9642 ■ *Web:* www.yogaville.org	Buckingham	VA	23921	434-969-3121		673
Satco Products Inc 110 Heartland Blvd *TF:* 800-437-2826 ■ *Web:* www.satco.com	Edgewood	NY	11717	631-243-2022	243-2027	437
Satcom Direct Inc 1901 Hwy A1A *Web:* www.satcomdirect.com	Satellite Beach	FL	32937	321-777-3000		177
Satcom Resources 101 Eagle Rd Bldg 7 *Web:* www.satcomresources.com	Avon	CO	81620	970-748-4250		177
Satelles Inc 360 Herndon Pkwy Ste 1400 *Web:* satellesinc.com	Herndon	VA	20170	703-723-4599		261
Satellite Broadcasting & Communications Assn (SBCA) 1730 M St NW Ste 600 *TF:* 800-541-5981 ■ *Web:* www.sbca.com	Washington	DC	20036	202-349-3620	349-3621	49-14
Satellite Hotel 411 Lakewood Cir *TF:* 800-423-8409 ■ *Web:* satellitehotel.net	Colorado Springs	CO	80910	719-596-6800		379
Satellite Industries Inc 2530 Xenium Ln N *TF:* 800-328-3332 ■ *Web:* www.satelliteindustries.com	Minneapolis	MN	55441	800-328-3332	328-3334	505
Satellite Logistics Group Inc 12621 Featherwood Ste 390 *TF:* 877-795-7540 ■ *Web:* www.slg.com	Houston	TX	77034	281-902-5500	902-5501	311
Satellite Management Services Inc 4529 E Broadway Rd Ste 100 *TF:* 800-788-8388 ■ *Web:* smstv.com	Phoenix	AZ	85040	602-386-4444		224
Satellite Receivers Limited/Cash Depot 1740 Cofrin Dr Ste 2 *TF:* 800-776-8834 ■ *Web:* www.cashdepotplus.com	Green Bay	WI	54302	920-432-1918		116
Satellite Shelters Inc 2530 Xenium Ln N *TF:* 800-453-1299 ■ *Web:* www.satelliteco.com	Plymouth	MN	55441	763-553-1900	551-7282	106
Satellite Systems Corp 101 Malibu Dr *Web:* www.satsyscorp.com	Virginia Beach	VA	23452	757-463-3553	463-3891	647
Satellite T.V. Supermarket 2924 N Ave *Web:* www.stsgj.com	Grand Junction	CO	81504	970-243-7237	241-1113	35
Sather Financial Group Inc 120 E Constitution St *Web:* www.satherfinancial.com	Victoria	TX	77901	361-570-1800		251
Sathre Bergquist Inc 150 Broadway Ave S *Web:* www.sathre.com	Wayzata	MN	55391	952-476-6000		261
Saticoy Lemon Assn 7560 E Bristol Rd *Web:* www.saticoylemon.com	Ventura	CA	93003	805-654-6500		315-2
Satin Fine Foods Inc 32 Leone Ln *Web:* satinice.com	Chester	NY	10918	845-469-1034	469-8345	297-8
SATISFYD 47 E Chicago Ave Ste 360 *TF:* 800-562-9557 ■ *Web:* satisfyd.com	Naperville	IL	60540	800-562-9557		196
Sato America Inc 10350A Nations Ford Rd *TF:* 888-871-8741 ■ *Web:* www.satoamerica.com	Charlotte	NC	28273	704-644-1650	644-1662	173-6
Satov Consultants Inc 250 The Esplanade Ste 200 *Web:* satovconsultants.com	Toronto	ON	M5A1J2	416-777-9000		463
Satriana & Biscan LLC 720 S Colorado Blvd Ste 452 - S *Web:* sbattys.com	Denver	CO	80246	303-468-5400		41
Satter Law Firm PLLC 217 S Salina St *Web:* satterlaw.com	Syracuse	NY	13202	315-471-0405		41
Satterfield & Pontikes Construction Inc 11000 Equity Dr Ste 100 *Web:* www.satpon.com	Houston	TX	77041	713-996-1300	996-1400	186
Satterlund Supply Company Inc 26277 Sherwood *TF:* 800-442-4343 ■ *Web:* www.satterlund.com	Warren	MI	48091	586-755-9700		492

Name / Address	City	State	ZIP	Phone	Fax	Class
Sattler Homes Inc 3535 S Platte River Dr Unit F *Web:* www.thomassattlerhomes.com	Englewood	CO	80110	303-771-5995		187
Sattre Press 2962 Middle Sattre Rd *Web:* sattre-press.com	Decorah	IA	52101	815-301-9638		637-2
Satuit Technologies Inc 100 Grossman Dr *Web:* www.satuit.com	Braintree	MA	02184	781-871-7788		177
Saturday Evening Post, The 1100 Waterway Blvd *TF:* 800-829-5576 ■ *Web:* www.saturdayeveningpost.com	Indianapolis	IN	46202	317-634-1100	637-0126	457-11
Saturn Electronics Corp 28450 Northline Rd *Web:* www.saturnelectronics.com	Romulus	MI	48174	734-941-8100	941-3707	625
Saturn Fasteners Inc 425 S Varney St *TF:* 800-947-9414 ■ *Web:* www.saturnfasteners.com	Burbank	CA	91502	818-846-7145		350
Saturn Freight Systems Inc PO Box 680308 *TF:* 866-722-9136 ■ *Web:* www.saturnfreight.com	Marietta	GA	30068	770-952-3490	693-5749	311
Saturn Industries Inc 157 Union Tpke *TF:* 800-775-1651 ■ *Web:* www.saturnedm.com	Hudson	NY	12534	518-828-9956	828-9868	127
Saturn Infotech Inc 1120 Welsh Rd Ste 110 *Web:* saturninfotech.com	North Wales	PA	19454	267-337-6779		196
Saturn Machine Inc 4815 Front St *Web:* www.saturnmachine.com	Brookshire	TX	77423	281-391-7800	375-8081	454
Saturn Overhead Equipment LLC 100 Apgar Dr *TF:* 800-631-4473 ■ *Web:* www.saturnoe.com	Somerset	NJ	08873	732-560-7210		470
Saturn Resource Management Inc 805 N Last Chance Gulch *TF:* 800-735-0577 ■ *Web:* www.srmi.biz	Helena	MT	59601	406-443-3433	442-1316	95
Saturn Systems Inc 314 W Superior St Ste 1015 *TF:* 888-638-4335 ■ *Web:* www.saturnsys.com	Duluth	MN	55802	218-623-7200		177
Saturna Capital Corp 1300 N State St *TF:* 888-732-6262 ■ *Web:* www.saturna.com	Bellingham	WA	98225	360-734-9900		401
Saturno Design 421 SW Hall St *Web:* www.saturnodesign.com	Portland	OR	97201	503-478-1830		180
Satya Jewelry Inc 330 Bleecker St *Web:* www.satyajewelry.com	New York	NY	10014	212-243-7313		410
Sauber Manufacturing Co 10 N Sauber Rd *TF:* 800-323-9147 ■ *Web:* saubermfg.com	Virgil	IL	60151	630-365-6600		190
Saucebox 214 SW Broadway *Web:* www.saucebox.com	Portland	OR	97205	503-241-3393		671
Saucon Technologies Inc 2455 Baglyos Cir *Web:* www.sauc ontds.com	Bethlehem	PA	18020	484-241-2514		180
Saucony Inc 191 Spring St *TF:* 800-282-6575 ■ *Web:* www.saucony.com	Lexington	MA	02420	800-282-6575		301
Sauder School of Business 2053 Main Mall *Web:* www.sauder.ubc.ca	Vancouver	BC	V6T1Z2	604-822-8399		685
Sauder Village 22611 SR 2 *Web:* saudervillage.org	Archbold	OH	43502	419-446-2541	445-5251	520
Sauder Woodworking Co 502 Middle St *TF:* 800-523-3987 ■ *Web:* www.sauder.com	Archbold	OH	43502	419-446-2711		319-2
Saudi Arabia *Consulate General* 5718 Westheimer Rd Ste 1500 *Web:* www.saudiembassy.net	Houston	TX	77057	713-785-5577	273-6937	257
Sauer Compressors USA Inc 64 Log Canoe Cir *Web:* www.sauerusa.com	Stevensville	MD	21666	410-604-3142		172
Sauer Holdings Inc 30 51st St *Web:* www.sauerholdings.com	Pittsburgh	PA	15201	412-687-4100	687-3576	256
Sauer Inc 11223 Phillips Pkwy Dr E *Web:* www.sauer-inc.com	Jacksonville	FL	32256	904-262-6444		189-10
Sauers Group Inc, The 1585 Roadhaven Dr *Web:* sauersgroup.com	Stone Mountain	GA	30083	770-621-8888		627
Saugatuck Capital Co 187 Danbury Rd *Web:* www.saugatuckcapital.com	Wilton	CT	06897	203-348-6669	324-6995	792
Saugus Free Public Library 295 Central St *Web:* www.sauguspubliclibrary.org	Saugus	MA	01906	781-231-4168	231-4169	434-3
Saugus High School 21900 Centurion Way *Web:* www.hartdistrict.org	Santa Clarita	CA	91350	661-297-3900		685
Saugus Iron Works National Historic Site 244 Central St *Web:* www.nps.gov	Saugus	MA	01906	781-233-0050		564
Saugus Speedway 22500 Soledad Canyon Rd *Web:* www.saugusspeedway.com	Saugus	CA	91350	661-259-3886	259-8534	515
Saugus Union School, The 24930 Ave Stanford *Web:* www.saugususd.org	Santa Clarita	CA	91355	661-294-5300		186
Sauk County 505 S Broadway St *Web:* www.co.sauk.wi.us	Baraboo	WI	53913	608-355-3286	355-3522	338
Sauk Rapids Recreation Program 901 First St S *Web:* www.isd47.org	Sauk Rapids	MN	56379	320-253-6631		564
Sauk Valley Community College 173 Illinois Rt 2 *Web:* www.svcc.edu	Dixon	IL	61021	815-288-5511	288-3190	162
Saul Centers Inc 7501 Wisconsin Ave Ste 1500E *NYSE:* BFS ■ *Web:* www.saulcenters.com	Bethesda	MD	20814	301-986-6200	986-6079	655
Saul Restaurant + Bar 200 Eastern Pkwy *Web:* www.saulrestaurant.com	Brooklyn	NY	11238	718-935-9842		671
Sault Area Chamber of Commerce 2581 I-75 Business Spur *Web:* saultstemarie.org	Sault Sainte Marie	MI	49783	906-632-3301	632-2331	139
Sault College 443 Northern Ave *TF:* 800-461-2260 ■ *Web:* www.saultcollege.ca	Sault Sainte Marie	ON	P6A5L3	705-759-6700		162
Sault Printing Company Inc 314 Osborn Blvd *TF:* 800-421-7727 ■ *Web:* www.saultprinting.com	Sault Sainte Marie	MI	49783	906-632-3369	635-3371	534
Sault Sainte Marie Convention 225 E Portage Ave *TF:* 800-647-2858 ■ *Web:* www.saultstemarie.com	Sault Sainte Marie	MI	49783	906-632-3366		206
Sault Star, The 145 Old Garden River Rd *Web:* www.saultstar.com	Sault Sainte Marie	ON	P6A5M5	705-759-3030		532-1
Sault Ste Marie Canal National Historic Site 1 Canal Dr *Web:* pc.gc.ca	Sault Sainte Marie	ON	P6A6W4	705-941-6262	941-6206	563
Saunders & Associates LLC 2520 E Rose Garden Ln *Web:* www.saunders-assoc.com	Phoenix	AZ	85050	602-971-9977		407
Saunders & Schmieler 5405 Twin Knolls Rd Ste 5 *Web:* sslawfirm.com	Columbia	MD	21045	301-588-7717		41
Saunders Archery Co 1874 14th Ave PO Box 1707 *TF:* 800-228-1408 ■ *Web:* www.sausa.com	Columbus	NE	68601	402-564-7176	564-3260	710
Saunders Brothers LLC 256 Main St *Web:* www.saundersbros.com	Locke Mills	ME	04255	207-875-2853	875-2857	820
Saunders Construction Inc 1705 17th St Ste 350 *Web:* www.saundersinc.com	Denver	CO	80202	303-699-9000		186
Saunders County PO Box 61 *Web:* saunderscounty.ne.gov	Wahoo	NE	68066	402-443-8101	443-8174	338
Saunders Electronics 192 Gannett Dr *Web:* saunderselectronics.com	South Portland	ME	04106	207-228-1888		767
Saunders Hotel Group Ltd 715 Bolyston Ste 310 *Web:* saundershotelgroup.com	Boston	MA	02116	617-861-9000		379
Saunders Manufacturing Co 65 Nickerson Hill Rd *TF:* 800-341-4674 ■ *Web:* www.saunders-usa.com	Readfield	ME	04355	207-512-2550		488
Saunders Veterinary Services 2801 Us Hwy 27 S *Web:* saundersvet.com	Avon Park	FL	33825	863-453-5700	453-2549	794
Sauper Associates Inc 1317 Rt 73 Ste 205 *Web:* sauper.com	Mount Laurel	NJ	08054	856-778-3800	778-3820	809
Sause Bros 3710 NW Front Ave *TF:* 800-488-4167 ■ *Web:* www.sause.com	Portland	OR	97210	503-222-1811	222-2010	465
Sauter Sullivan LLC 3415 Hampton Ave *Web:* sautersullivan.com	Saint Louis	MO	63139	314-768-6800	781-2726	41
Sava Transportation Inc 1200 Greenwood Ave *Web:* www.savatrans.com	Maywood	IL	60153	708-731-2400	731-2406	780
Savage & Associates Inc 4427 Talmadge Rd *Web:* savageandassociates.com	Toledo	OH	43623	419-475-8665		194
Savage Arms Inc 100 Springdale Rd **Fax Area Code:* 714 ■ *TF:* 800-243-3220 ■ *Web:* www.savagearms.com	Westfield	MA	01085	413-568-7001	378-4688*	284
Savage Design Group Inc 4203 Yoakum Blvd 4th Fl *Web:* savagebrands.com	Houston	TX	77006	713-522-1555		344
Savage IO Inc 8 S Lyon St *Web:* www.savageio.com	Batavia	NY	14020	585-250-4216		173-8
Savage Saws 31 Commerce St E Haven Industrial Pk *Web:* www.thermatool.com	East Haven	CT	06512	609-267-8501	267-1366	455
Savages Drug Inc 33 Plaza Dr *Web:* savagesdrug.com	Unity	ME	04988	207-948-3950		237
Savanna Animal Hospital Inc 1800 NE Savanna Rd *Web:* savannaanimalhospital.com	Jensen Beach	FL	34957	772-334-4454		794
Savanna Pallets Inc 41496 State Hwy 65 *Web:* www.savannapallets.com	McGregor	MN	55760	218-768-2077		551
Savanna Portage State Park 55626 Lake Pl *Web:* www.dnr.state.mn.us	McGregor	MN	55760	218-426-3271		565
Savanna Thomson State Bank 302 Main St *Web:* savannathomsonstatebank.com	Savanna	IL	61074	815-273-2261		70
Savannah Area Convention & Visitors Bureau 101 E Bay St *TF:* 877-728-2662 ■ *Web:* www.visitsavannah.com	Savannah	GA	31401	912-644-6400	644-6499	206
Savannah Blueprint Co 11 E York St *Web:* www.savannahblue.com	Savannah	GA	31401	912-232-2162		240
Savannah City Hall PO Box 1027 *Web:* savannahga.gov	Savannah	GA	31402	912-651-6441	651-4260	337
Savannah Civic Ctr 301 W Oglethorp Ave *TF:* 800-337-1101 ■ *Web:* www.savannahga.gov	Savannah	GA	31401	912-651-6550	651-6552	572
Savannah College of Art & Design 342 Bull St *TF:* 800-869-7223 ■ *Web:* www.scad.edu	Savannah	GA	31402	912-525-5100	525-5986	164
Savannah Distributing Company Inc 2425 W Gwinnett St *TF:* 800-551-0777 ■ *Web:* www.savdist.com	Savannah	GA	31415	912-233-1167	233-1557	81-1
Savannah ePASS 7000 LaRoche Ave *Web:* savannahepass.com	Savannah	GA	31406	912-352-8221		671
Savannah History Museum 303 ML King Jr Blvd *Web:* www.chsgeorgia.org	Savannah	GA	31401	912-651-6840		520
Savannah International Trade & Convention Ctr 1 International Dr *Web:* www.savtcc.com	Savannah	GA	31421	912-447-4000	447-4722	205
Savannah Magazine PO Box 1088 *Web:* www.savannahmagazine.com	Savannah	GA	31402	912-652-0423	525-0611	457-22
Savannah Mall 14045 Abercorn St *Web:* www.savannahmall.com	Savannah	GA	31419	912-927-7467		460

Name / Address	City	State	ZIP	Phone	Fax	Class
Savannah Morning News 1375 Chatham Pkwy *TF:* 800-533-1150 ■ *Web:* www.savannahnow.com	Savannah	GA	31405	912-236-9511	525-0795	532-2
Savannah River National Laboratory Savannah River Site *Web:* srnl.doe.gov	Aiken	SC	29808	803-725-5179		668
Savannah Suites 3421 Wrightsboro Rd *Web:* www.savannahsuites.com	Augusta	GA	30909	706-849-3100		132
Savannah Technical College 5717 White Bluff Rd *Web:* www.savannahtech.edu	Savannah	GA	31405	912-443-5700	443-5705	800
Savannah Tribune Inc 1805 Martin Luther King Jr Blvd *Web:* www.savannahtribune.com	Savannah	GA	31401	912-233-6128	233-6140	532-2
Savannah/Hilton Head International Airport 400 Airways Ave *Web:* savannahairport.com	Savannah	GA	31408	912-964-0514	964-0877	27
Savant Capital LLC 190 Buckley Dr *TF:* 866-489-0500 ■ *Web:* savantwealth.com	Rockford	IL	61107	815-227-0300		194
Savant Investment Group LLC 555 12th St Ste 925 *Web:* www.savantig.com	San Francisco	CA	94107	415-926-7200		401
Savant Manufacturing Inc 2930 Hwy 383 PO Box 520 *TF:* 800-326-6880 ■ *Web:* savantmfg.com	Kinder	LA	70648	337-738-5896	738-3215	350
Save - Suicide Awareness Voices of Education 8120 Penn Ave S Ste 470 *Web:* save.org	Bloomington	MN	55431	952-946-7998		49-15
Save America's Forests 4 Library Ct SE *TF:* 800-729-1363 ■ *Web:* www.saveamericasforests.org	Washington	DC	20003	202-544-9219	544-7462	48-13
Save Mart Supermarkets Inc 2100 Standiford Ave *Web:* www.savemart.com	Modesto	CA	95350	209-577-0545		345
Save More Products 1829 Wall Ave *Web:* www.savemoreproducts.com	Ogden	UT	84401	801-621-4213		183
Save the Manatee Club (SMC) 500 N Maitland Ave *TF:* 800-432-5646 ■ *Web:* www.savethemanatee.org	Maitland	FL	32751	407-539-0990	539-0871	48-3
Save-A-Lot Ltd 100 Corporate Office Dr *Web:* save-a-lot.com	Earth City	MO	63045	314-592-9100		345
Save-A-Patriot Fellowship PO Box 2464 *Web:* www.save-a-patriot.org	Westminster	MD	21157	410-857-4441	857-5249	48-6
SaveDailycom Inc 1503 S Coast Dr Ste 330 *Web:* www.savedaily.com	Seal Beach	CA	90740	562-795-7500		787
Savelli's Italian restaurant 3055 Sutherland Ave *Web:* www.savellisknoxville.com	Knoxville	TN	37919	865-521-9085		671
SaveMart Pharmacy 241 W Roseville Rd *Web:* www.savemartpa.com	Lancaster	PA	17601	717-569-7384		238
SaveOnResorts.com LLC 2173 Salk Ave Ste 300 *Web:* www.saveonresorts.com	Carlsbad	CA	92008	858-625-0630		775
Saver Group Inc 95 London Rd *Web:* www.savergroup.com	Campbellsville	KY	42718	270-465-8675	465-8187	297-8
Savers Inc 11400 SE 6th St Ste 220 *Web:* www.savers.com	Bellevue	WA	98004	425-462-1515	451-2250	229
Saveur Magazine 2 Park Ave *Web:* www.saveur.com	New York	NY	10016	212-219-7400		457-11
Savex Manufacturing Company Inc 170 Easy St *Web:* www.savex.us	Carol Stream	IL	60188	630-668-7219	668-7289	476
Savills Studley Inc 399 Park Ave 11th Fl *Web:* www.savills-studley.com	New York	NY	10022	212-326-1000	326-1034	652
Savin Engineers PC 3 Campus Dr *Web:* www.savinengineers.com	Pleasantville	NY	10570	914-769-3200	747-6686	261
Savings Bank Mutual Life Insurance Company of Massachusetts, The (SBLI) 1 Linscott Rd **Fax Area Code:* 781 ■ *TF:* 888-630-5000 ■ *Web:* www.sbli.com	Woburn	MA	01801	888-630-5000	994-4240*	391-2
Savino Del Bene USA Inc 1905 S Mt Prospect Rd Ste D *Web:* www.savinodelbene.com	Des Plaines	IL	60018	847-390-3600		194
Savio's 516 S Van Dorn St *Web:* www.saviosrestaurant.com	Alexandria	VA	22304	703-212-9651		671
Savis Inc 9 N Wabash Ave Ste 102 *Web:* www.savis-inc.com	Chicago	IL	60602	847-797-8857		196
Savitz Law Offices Pc 6 Beacon St *Web:* immigrationoptions.com	Boston	MA	02108	617-723-7111		41
Savko Plastic Pipe & Fittings Inc 683 E Lincoln Ave **Fax Area Code:* 614 ■ *TF:* 877-885-4445 ■ *Web:* www.savko.com	Columbus	OH	43229	877-885-4445	885-4470*	596
Sav-Mart Co 1729 N Wenatchee Ave *Web:* www.savmart.net	Wenatchee	WA	98801	509-663-1671		229
Sav-Mor Drug Stores 43155 W Nine-Mile Rd *Web:* www.sav-mor.com	Novi	MI	48376	248-348-1570		237
Savoir-Faire 40 Leveroni Ct *Web:* www.savoirfaire.com	Novato	CA	94949	415-884-8090		45
Savol Pools (SP) 91 Prestige Park Cir *TF:* 800-867-0098 ■ *Web:* www.savolpools.com	East Hartford	CT	06108	860-282-0878		146
Savon Plating & Powder Coating Inc 17 W Watkins Rd *Web:* sav-onplating.com	Phoenix	AZ	85003	602-252-4311		481
Savoy Medical Ctr 801 Poinciana Ave *Web:* www.savoymedical.com	Mamou	LA	70554	337-457-3135		374-3
Savoy Mountain State Forest 260 Central Shaft Rd *Web:* www.mass.gov	Florida	MA	01247	413-663-8469		565
Savran Benson LLP 146 Montgomery Ave Ste 300 *Web:* savranbenson.com	Bala Cynwyd	PA	19004	610-664-6400		2
SAW (San Antonio Wholesale Lumber) 17480 Judson Rd *TF:* 877-834-3325 ■ *Web:* www.wholesalelumber.biz	San Antonio	TX	78247	210-655-3808		191-3
Saw Mill River Audubon Inc 275 Millwood Rd *Web:* www.sawmillriveraudubon.org	Chappaqua	NY	10514	914-666-6503	666-7430	50-5
Saw Service & Supply Inc 11925 Zelis Rd *TF:* 800-735-5604 ■ *Web:* www.sawservicesupply.com	Cleveland	OH	44135	216-252-5600	252-7476	273
Saw Textiles Inc 3025 Appling Rd *TF:* 800-238-3304 ■ *Web:* www.sawtextiles.com	Memphis	TN	38133	901-377-2968	377-9567	155-14
Sawaddee Thai Restaurant 93 Hope St *Web:* www.sawaddeerestaurant.com	Providence	RI	02906	401-831-1122	831-1121	671
Sawasdee Thai 4250 Main St *Web:* www.sawasdeethairestaurant.com	Vancouver	BC	V5V3P9	604-876-4030		671
Sawatdee 607 Washington Ave S *Web:* www.sawatdee.com	Minneapolis	MN	55415	612-338-6451	338-6498	671
Sawatdee Thai Cuisine 10938 N 56th St *Web:* sawatdeethaioftampa.com	Tampa	FL	33617	813-985-2071		671
Sawbridge Studios 897 Green Bay Rd *Web:* sawbridge.com	Winnetka	IL	60093	847-441-2441		321
Sawbrook Steel Castings Co 425 Shepherd Ave *Web:* www.sawbrooksteel.com	Cincinnati	OH	45215	513-554-1700	554-0092	307
Sawmill Creek Resort 400 Sawmill Creek Dr *TF:* 800-729-6455 ■ *Web:* sawmillcreekresort.com	Huron	OH	44839	419-433-3800		669
Sawnee Electric Membership Corp 543 Atlantic Hwy *TF:* 800-635-9131 ■ *Web:* www.sawnee.com	Cumming	GA	30028	770-887-2363		245
Sawtooth Botanical Garden (SBG) 11 Gimlet Rd PO Box 928 *Web:* sbgarden.org	Ketchum	ID	83340	208-726-9358		97
Sawtooth Group 25 Bridge Ave Ste 203 *Web:* www.sawtoothgroup.com	Red Bank	NJ	07701	732-945-1004		4
Sawtooth Software Inc 1457 East 840 North **Fax Area Code:* 801 ■ *Web:* www.sawtoothsoftware.com	Orem	UT	84097	360-681-2300	337-7410*	809
Sawyer Aviation Flight Academy 14600 N Airport Dr 2nd Fl *TF:* 877-359-7299 ■ *Web:* www.sawyeraviation.com	Scottsdale	AZ	85260	480-922-5221		167-3
Sawyer County 10610 Main St Ste 10 *TF:* 877-699-4110 ■ *Web:* www.sawyercountygov.org	Hayward	WI	54843	715-634-4866	634-3666	338
Sawyer Free Library 2 Dale Ave *Web:* www.sawyerfreelibrary.org	Gloucester	MA	01930	978-281-9763		434-3
Sawyer Law Firm LLC 106 N Main St *Web:* sawyerfirm.com	Enterprise	AL	36330	334-475-3213		41
Sawyer Nursery Inc 5401 Port Sheldon St *TF:* 888-378-7800 ■ *Web:* sawyernursery.com	Hudsonville	MI	49426	888-378-7800		292
Sawyer Products Inc 605 Seventh Ave N *Web:* sawyer.com	Safety Harbor	FL	34695	727-725-1177		791
Sawyer School 101 Main St *TF:* 800-426-7975 ■ *Web:* www.sawyerschool.org	Pawtucket	RI	02860	401-272-8400		685
Sawyer Technical Materials LLC 35400 Lakeland Blvd *Web:* sawyerllc.com	Eastlake	OH	44095	440-951-8770	951-1480	253
Sax Benefits Group Inc 10825 Watson Rd Ste 160 *Web:* sbgstl.com	Saint Louis	MO	63127	314-822-6100	821-3746	390
Saxco International LLC 200 Gibraltar Rd Ste 101 *Web:* www.saxco.com	Horsham	PA	19044	215-443-8100		360-3
Saxe Doernberger & Vita PC 1952 Whitney Ave *Web:* www.sdvlaw.com	Hamden	CT	06517	203-287-2100		428
Saxe Real Estate Management Service 1999 Van Ness Ave *Web:* saxerealestate.com	San Francisco	CA	94109	415-474-2435	447-8652	655
Saxon Global Inc 1320 Greenway Dr *Web:* saxonglobal.com	Irving	TX	75038	972-363-1009		177
Saxon Group Inc, The 790 Brogdon Rd	Suwanee	GA	30024	770-271-2174		186
Saxton Incorporated Design Group 600 Third St SE Ste 300 *Web:* www.saxtoninc.com	Cedar Rapids	IA	52401	319-365-6967		320
Saxtons River Publications Inc 819 Monroe St *TF:* 800-932-4438 ■ *Web:* www.netique.com	Herndon	VA	20170	703-689-3700	689-3703	637-2
Saybrook Capital LLC 11400 W Olympic Blvd *Web:* www.saybrook.net	Los Angeles	CA	90064	310-899-9200		401
Saybrook Point Inn & Spa 2 Bridge St *Web:* www.saybrook.com	Old Saybrook	CT	06475	860-395-2000		669
Sayer Energy Advisors 1620 540 - Fifth Ave SW *Web:* www.sayeradvisors.com	Calgary	AB	T2P0M2	403-266-6133		528
Sayers Group LLC 825 Corporate Woods Pkwy *TF:* 800-323-5357 ■ *Web:* www.sayers.com	Vernon Hills	IL	60061	800-323-5357		180
Sayle Oil Company Inc 410 W Main *Web:* www.sayleoil.com	Charleston	MS	38921	662-647-5802		324
Saylent Technologies 116 Huntington Ave Ste 502 *Web:* www.saylent.com	Boston	MA	02116	508-570-2161		177
Saylor Beall Manufacturing Company Inc 400 N Kibbee St PO Box 40 *TF:* 800-248-9001 ■ *Web:* www.saylor-beall.com	Saint John	MI	48879	989-224-2371	224-8788	172
Sayre Assoc 216 S Duluth Ave *Web:* sayreassociates.com	Sioux Falls	SD	57104	605-332-7211		261
Sayville Ford 5686 Sunrise Hwy *Web:* www.sayvilleford.com	Sayville	NY	11782	631-589-4800		57
Saz's 5539 W State St *Web:* sazs.com	Milwaukee	WI	53208	414-453-2410		671
SB Ballard Construction Co 2828 Shipps Corner Rd *Web:* www.sbballard.com	Virginia Beach	VA	23453	757-440-5555	451-2873	189-3
SB International Inc 3626 N Hall St Ste 910 *Web:* sbisteel.com	Dallas	TX	75219	214-526-4423	526-1503	492

Name / Address	City	State	ZIP	Phone	Fax	Class
SB One Bank 100 Enterprise Dr Ste 700 *NASDAQ:* SBBX ■ *TF:* 800-511-9900 ■ *Web:* www.sbone.bank	Rockaway	NJ	07866	973-383-2211		360-2
SB Recommend Inc 606 S Blvd The Hillsborough County Medical Association Bldg. **Fax Area Code:* 813 ■ *TF:* 877-426-6320 ■ *Web:* www.sbrecommend.com	Tampa	FL	33606	877-426-6320	441-0477*	631
SB Whistler & Sons Inc PO Box 270 *TF:* 800-828-1010 ■ *Web:* www.sbwhistler.com	Medina	NY	14103	585-318-4630	798-5612	757
SBA (Small Business Administration) 409 Third St SW *Web:* www.sba.gov	Washington	DC	20416	202-205-6533	205-6802	340-20
SBA (Small Business Administration Regional Offices) *Region 1* 10 Causeway St Ste 265A *Web:* www.sba.gov	Boston	MA	02222	617-565-8416	565-8420	340-20
SBA Materials Inc 9430-H San Mateo Blvd NE *TF:* 800-498-9608 ■ *Web:* www.sbamaterials.com	Albuquerque	NM	87113	800-498-9608		601
SBB (Science & Behavior Books Inc) PO Box 60519 *TF:* 800-547-9982 ■ *Web:* www.sbbks.com	Palo Alto	CA	94306	650-965-0954	965-8998	637-2
SBC (Southern Baptist Convention) 901 Commerce St *TF:* 866-722-5433 ■ *Web:* www.sbc.net	Nashville	TN	37203	615-244-2355		48-20
SBCA (Satellite Broadcasting & Communications Assn) 1730 M St NW Ste 600 *TF:* 800-541-5981 ■ *Web:* www.sbca.com	Washington	DC	20036	202-349-3620	349-3621	49-14
SBCC (South Baldwin Chamber of Commerce) 112 W Laurel Ave PO Box 1117 *TF:* 877-461-3712 ■ *Web:* www.southbaldwinchamber.com	Foley	AL	36535	251-943-3291	943-6810	139
SBE (Society of Broadcast Engineers Inc) 9102 N Meridian St Ste 150 *Web:* www.sbe.org	Indianapolis	IN	46260	317-846-9000	846-9120	49-14
SBE (Small Business & Entrepreneurship Council) 301 Maple Ave W Ste 100 *Web:* sbecouncil.org	Vienna	VA	22180	703-242-5840		49-12
SBE Hotel Licensing LLC 5900 Wilshire Blvd 30th Fl *Web:* www.sbe.com	Los Angeles	CA	90036	323-655-8000		379
SB&F (Science Books & Films) 1200 New York Ave NW *Web:* www.sbfonline.com	Washington	DC	20005	202-326-6417		637-2
SBFC (Seven Bridges Field Club) 160 Seven Bridges Rd *Web:* www.sevenbridgesfieldclub.org	Chappaqua	NY	10514	914-242-1838		637-10
SBG (Sawtooth Botanical Garden) 11 Gimlet Rd PO Box 928 *Web:* sbgarden.org	Ketchum	ID	83340	208-726-9358		97
SBIA (Small Business Investor Alliance) 1100 H St NW Ste 1200 *TF:* 800-471-6153 ■ *Web:* www.sbia.org	Washington	DC	20005	202-628-5055		615
SBL (Society of Biblical Literature) The Luce Ctr 825 Houston Mill Rd *TF:* 866-727-9955 ■ *Web:* www.sbl-site.org	Atlanta	GA	30329	404-727-3100	727-3101	48-20
SBL (Silas Bronson Library) 267 Grand St *Web:* www.bronsonlibrary.org	Waterbury	CT	06702	203-574-8222	574-8055	434-3
SBLC (Small Business Legislative Council) 4800 Hampden Ln 6th Fl *Web:* www.sblc.org	Bethesda	MD	20814	301-652-8302		49-12
SBLHC (Sarah Bush Lincoln Health Ctr) 1000 Health Center Dr PO Box 372 *TF:* 800-345-3191 ■ *Web:* www.sarahbush.org	Mattoon	IL	61938	217-258-2525	258-4117	374-3
SBLI (Savings Bank Mutual Life Insurance Company of Massachusetts, The) 1 Linscott Rd **Fax Area Code:* 781 ■ *TF:* 888-630-5000 ■ *Web:* www.sbli.com	Woburn	MA	01801	888-630-5000	994-4240*	391-2
SBM (Society of Behavioral Medicine) 555 E Wells St Ste 1100 *Web:* www.sbm.org	Milwaukee	WI	53202	414-918-3156	276-3349	49-15
SBP Consulting 4900 38th Ave Ste 5 *Web:* www.sbpcorp.com	Moline	IL	61265	309-228-4600		196
SBPI Inc 13825 Parks Steed Dr *Web:* www.sbpigraphics.com	Earth City	MO	63045	314-423-2424	423-2802	627
SBS (Storage Battery Systems Inc) N56 W16665 Ridgewood Dr *TF:* 800-554-2243 ■ *Web:* www.sbsbattery.com	Menomonee Falls	WI	53051	262-703-5800	703-3073	246
SBS Industries LLC 1843 N 106th E Ave *Web:* www.sbsindustries.com	Tulsa	OK	74116	918-836-7756		351
SBS Transit Inc 3747 Colorado Ave *Web:* www.loraincounty.com	Sheffield Village	OH	44054	440-949-8121		107
SBSO (South Bend Symphony Orchestra) 127 N Michigan St *TF:* 800-537-6415 ■ *Web:* www.southbendsymphony.org	South Bend	IN	46601	574-232-6343	232-6627	573-3
SBT (Shannon Brothers Tile Inc) 1309 Putnam Dr NW *Web:* www.sbtile.com	Huntsville	AL	35816	256-837-6520		191-1
SBUH (Stony Brook University Hospital) 101 Nicolls Rd *Web:* www.stonybrookmedicine.edu	Stony Brook	NY	11794	631-444-4000		374-3
SBVGS (San Bernardino Valley Genealogical Society) 555 W 6th St *Web:* www.empirenet.com	San Bernardino	CA	92410	909-381-8201		48-13
SBW Consulting Inc 2820 Northup Way Ste 230 *Web:* www.sbwconsulting.com	Bellevue	WA	98004	425-827-0330		194
SC (Computer Source Inc) 2623 Wayne Sullivan Dr *Web:* www.computer-source.com	Paducah	KY	42003	270-442-9726	442-5058	179
SC & A Inc 1608 Spring Hill Rd Ste 400 *Web:* www.scainc.com	Vienna	VA	22182	703-893-6600	821-8236	668
SC & H Group LLC 910 Ridgebrook Rd *TF:* 800-832-3008 ■ *Web:* www.schgroup.com	Sparks	MD	21152	410-403-1500	403-1570	2
SC Anderson Inc PO Box 81747 *Web:* www.scanderson.com	Bakersfield	CA	93308	661-392-7000	391-9999	186
SC Builders Inc 910 Thompson Pl *Web:* www.scbuildersinc.com	Sunnyvale	CA	94085	408-328-0688		186
SC Engineers Inc 17075 Via Del Campo *Web:* scengineers.net	San Diego	CA	92127	858-946-0333	946-0334	261
SC Johnson & Son Inc 1525 Howe St *Web:* www.scjohnson.com	Racine	WI	53403	262-260-2154	260-6004	151
SCA (Society of Cardiovascular Anesthesiologists) 8735 W Higgins Rd Ste 300 **Fax Area Code:* 847 ■ *TF:* 800-283-6296 ■ *Web:* www.scahq.org	Chicago	IL	60631	855-658-2828	375-6323*	49-8
SCA (Shipbuilders Council of America Inc) 20 F St NW Ste 500 *Web:* www.shipbuilders.org	Washington	DC	20001	202-737-3234		49-21
SCA (Student Conservation Assn) 689 River Rd PO Box 550 *TF:* 888-722-9675 ■ *Web:* www.thesca.org	Charlestown	NH	03603	603-543-1700	543-1828	48-13
SCA Americas 2929 Arch St Ste 2600 *Web:* www.sca.com	Philadelphia	PA	19104	610-499-3700	499-3391	558
SCAA (Specialty Coffee Association of America) 117 W Fourth St Ste 300 *TF:* 800-995-9019 ■ *Web:* sca.coffee	Santa Ana	CA	92701	562-624-4100	624-4101	49-6
Scadaware Inc 2023 Eagle Rd. *Web:* scadaware.com	Normal	IL	61761	309-665-0135		177
Scaffs Inc 134 SE Colburn Ave *Web:* scaffs.com	Lake City	FL	32025	386-752-7344		204
Scala Inc 7 Great Valley Pkwy Ste 300 *TF:* 888-722-5296 ■ *Web:* scala.com	Malvern	PA	19355	610-363-3350	363-4010	177
Scala's Bistro 432 Powell St *Web:* www.scalasbistro.com	San Francisco	CA	94102	415-395-8555		671
Scalability Experts Inc 1203 Crestside Dr. *Web:* www.scalabilityexperts.com	Coppell	TX	75019	469-635-6200		177
Scalable Display Technologies Inc 585 Massachusetts Ave 4th Fl *Web:* www.scalabledisplay.com	Cambridge	MA	02139	617-864-9300		194
Scalable Software Inc 600 Congress Ave Ste C100 *TF:* 866-722-5225 ■ *Web:* www.scalable.com	Austin	TX	78701	713-501-2828	583-9266	177
Scalamandre Silks Inc 350 Wireless Blvd. *TF:* 800-932-4361 ■ *Web:* scalamandre.com	Hauppauge	NY	11788	631-467-8800	467-9448	745-1
Scale Models Unlimited 400 S Front St Ste 300 *Web:* www.smu.com	Memphis	TN	38103	901-577-5155		261
Scale Venture Partners 950 Tower Ln Ste 1150 *Web:* www.scalevp.com	Foster City	CA	94404	650-378-6000	378-6040	792
Scaled Composites Inc 1624 Flight Line Rd *Web:* www.scaled.com	Mojave	CA	93501	661-824-4541	824-4174	20
ScaleFactor 979 Springdale Rd Ste 110 *TF:* 877-892-0954 ■ *Web:* www.scalefactor.com	Austin	TX	78702	877-892-0954		216
ScaleGrid 2225 E Bayshore Rd *TF:* 866-449-2478 ■ *Web:* scalegrid.io	Palo Alto	CA	94303	866-449-2478		396
Scalehouse Inc, The 974 Rd E	Schuyler	NE	68661	402-352-3686		361
ScaleMatrix Inc 5775 Kearny Villa Rd *TF:* 888-349-9994 ■ *Web:* www.scalematrix.com	San Diego	CA	92123	888-349-9994		631
ScaleMP Inc 2175 Lemoine Ave Ste 401 *Web:* www.scalemp.com	Fort Lee	NJ	07024	201-429-9740		177
Scales & Shells Restaurant & Raw Bar 527 Thames St *Web:* www.scalesandshells.com	Newport	RI	02840	401-846-3474		671
Scales Air Compressor Corp 110 Voice Rd *TF:* 877-798-0454 ■ *Web:* www.scalesair.com	Carle Place	NY	11514	516-248-9096	248-9639	172
Scaletron Industries Ltd 53 Apple Tree Ln *Web:* www.scaletronscales.com	Plumsteadville	PA	18949	215-766-2670	766-2672	684
Scalini Fedeli 165 Duane St *Web:* www.scalinifedeli.com	New York	NY	10013	212-528-0400		671
Scalise Steve (Rep R - LA) 2049 Rayburn House Office Bldg *Web:* scalise.house.gov	Washington	DC	20515	202-225-3015		342-2
Scalley Reading Bates Hansen & Rasmussen PC 15 W South Temple Ste 600 *Web:* scalleyreading.com	Salt Lake City	UT	84101	801-531-7870		41
Scalo Northern Italian Grill 3500 Central Ave SE *Web:* www.scalonobhill.com	Albuquerque	NM	87106	505-255-8781	265-7850	671
SCAN Health Plan 3800 Kilroy Airport Way Ste 100 *TF:* 800-247-5091 ■ *Web:* www.scanhealthplan.com	Long Beach	CA	90806	562-989-5100		352
SCANA Corp 220 Operation Way *NYSE:* SCG ■ *Web:* www.scana.com	Cayce	SC	29033	803-217-9000		360-5
Scanbuy Inc 10 E 39th St 10th Fl *Web:* www.scanlife.com	New York	NY	10016	212-278-0178		180
Scandaglia Ryan LLP 55 E Monroe Ste 3440 *Web:* scandagliaryan.com	Chicago	IL	60603	312-580-2020		41
Scandent Group Inc 340 Interstate N Pkwy Ste 360 *Web:* www.scandent.com	Atlanta	GA	30339	770-303-4448	303-4434	396
Scandia Packaging Machinery Co 15 Industrial Rd *Web:* www.scandiapack.com	Fairfield	NJ	07004	973-473-6100	473-7226	547
Scandic Spring Inc 700 Montague St *Web:* scandic.com	San Leandro	CA	94577	510-352-3700		492
Scandinave Spa Mont-Tremblant 4280 Montee Ryan *TF:* 888-537-2263 ■ *Web:* www.scandinave.com	Mont-Tremblant	QC	J8E1S4	819-425-9595		354
Scandinavian Airlines System (SAS) 301 Rt 17 N Ste 500 **Fax Area Code:* 201 ■ *TF:* 800-221-2350 ■ *Web:* www.flysas.com	Rutherford	NJ	07070	212-332-2520	896-3735*	25
Scandrill Inc 11777 Katy Fwy Ste 470 *Web:* www.scandrill.com	Houston	TX	77079	281-496-5571		540
Scania USA Inc 121 Interpark Blvd Ste 601 *TF:* 800-272-2642 ■ *Web:* www.scania.com	San Antonio	TX	78216	210-403-0007		516
Scanics 723 S Neil St PO Box 2007 *Web:* scanics.com	Champaign	IL	61825	217-403-4000		175

Name / Address	City	State	Zip	Phone	Fax	Class
Scanlankemperbard Companies LLC 222 SW Columbia St Ste 700 *TF:* 877-795-4679 ■ *Web:* skbcos.com	Portland	OR	97201	503-220-2600		653
Scanline Vfx La Inc 12950 Culver Blvd *Web:* www.scanlinevfx.com	Los Angeles	CA	90066	310-827-1555		514
Scanlon Mary Gay (Rep D - PA) 1535 Longworth House Office Bldg *Web:* www.scanlon.house.gov	Washington	DC	20515	202-225-2011		342-2
Scannicchio's 2500 S Broad St *Web:* www.scannicchio.com	Philadelphia	PA	19145	215-468-3900		671
Scanning America Inc 1440 N Third St *Web:* www.scanningamerica.com	Lawrence	KS	66044	785-749-7471		317
Scan-Optics Inc 169 Progress Dr *TF:* 800-543-8681 ■ *Web:* www.scanoptics.com	Manchester	CT	06042	860-645-7878	645-7995	178-8
ScanSource Inc 6 Logue Ct *NASDAQ: SCSC* ■ *TF:* 800-944-2432 ■ *Web:* www.scansource.com	Greenville	SC	29615	864-286-4603		174
Scantek Infomanagement Solutions Inc 1100 Easton Rd *Web:* www.scantek.info	Willow Grove	PA	19090	215-882-5000		396
Scantibodies Laboratory Inc 9336 Abraham Way *TF:* 800-279-9181 ■ *Web:* www.scantibodies.com	Santee	CA	92071	619-258-9300	258-9366	231
Scantron Corp 34 Parker *TF:* 800-722-6876 ■ *Web:* www.scantron.com	Irvine	CA	92618	949-639-7500	639-7710	173-7
Scanwell Logistics (NYC) Inc 1995 Linden Blvd *Web:* www.scanwell.com	Elmont	NY	11003	516-285-8100	285-7763	314
Scap Auto Group 387 Tunxis Hill Rd *Web:* www.scapauto.com	Fairfield	CT	06825	203-384-9300		57
Scapa Tapes North America LLC 111 Great Pond Dr *Web:* www.scapa.com	Windsor	CT	06095	860-688-8000		552-1
Scarab Behavioral Health Services LLC 3203 Brick Church Pk *Web:* scarabhealth.com	Nashville	TN	37207	615-262-7822		363
Scaramouche Restaurant 1 Benvenuto Pl *Web:* www.scaramoucherestaurant.com	Toronto	ON	M4V2L1	416-961-8011		671
Scarantino's 1524 E Colorado St *Web:* www.scarantinos.com	Glendale	CA	91205	818-247-9777		671
Scarborough Downs 90 Payne Rd *Web:* www.scarboroughdowns.com	Scarborough	ME	04070	207-883-4331	883-2020	642
Scarborough Hospital Birchmount campus 3030 Birchmount Rd *Web:* www.tsh.to	Scarborough	ON	M1W3W3	416-495-2400	495-2562	374-2
Scarbrough International Ltd 10841 Ambassador Dr *Web:* www.scarbrough-intl.com	Kansas City	MO	64153	816-891-2400		311
Scariano Brothers LLC 11052 Scariano Ln **Fax Area Code:* 985 ■ *TF:* 800-256-1099 ■ *Web:* www.scarianobrothers.com	Hammond	LA	70403	800-256-1099	370-1550*	297-8
Scarlett Machinery Inc 4355 Airwest Dr SE *Web:* www.scarlettinc.com	Grand Rapids	MI	49512	616-871-9889	871-9879	385
Scarponi Textiles Inc 150 N Miller Rd Ste 300B *Web:* scartex.com	Fairlawn	OH	44333	330-864-0360	864-0214	41
Scarr Moving and Storage Inc 1353 Dayton St *TF:* 800-722-7784 ■ *Web:* www.scarrmoving.com	Salinas	CA	93901	831-424-2784		519
Scarritt Group Inc 7636 N Oracle Rd *Web:* www.scarrittgroup.com	Tucson	AZ	85704	520-529-0000	529-2960	463
Scarsdale Public Schools 2 Brewster Rd *Web:* www.scarsdaleschools.k12.ny.us	Scarsdale	NY	10583	914-721-2410		685
Scarsdale Security Systems Inc 132 Montgomery Ave *Web:* www.scarsdalesecurity.com	Scarsdale	NY	10583	914-722-2200	722-7272	693
Scarsin Corp 2 Brock St W Ste 201 *Web:* www.scarsin.com	Uxbridge	ON	L9P1P2	905-852-0086		195
Scat Enterprises Inc 1400 Kingsdale Ave *Web:* procarbyscat.com	Redondo Beach	CA	90278	310-370-5501	214-2285	57
Scattergood Friends School 1951 Delta Ave *Web:* scattergood.org	West Branch	IA	52358	319-519-1860	643-7485	622
SCB (Shipowners Claims Bureau) 1 Battery Park Plz 31st Fl *Web:* www.american-club.com	New York	NY	10004	212-847-4500	847-4599	49-21
SCB Marketing 5131 Industry Dr *Web:* scbmarketing.com	Melbourne	FL	32940	321-622-5986	622-8906	530
SCBG (South Coast Botanic Garden) 26300 Crenshaw Blvd *Web:* southcoastbotanicgarden.org	Palos Verdes Peninsula	CA	90274	310-544-1948		97
SCC (Society of Cosmetic Chemists) 120 Wall St Ste 2400 *Web:* www.scconline.org	New York	NY	10005	212-668-1500	668-1504	49-19
SCC (Stanridge Color Corp) PO Box 1086 *Web:* www.standridgecolor.com	Social Circle	GA	30025	770-464-3362		608
SCC (Superior Crane Corp) 208 Wilmont Dr PO Box 1464 *Web:* www.superiorcrane.com	Waukesha	WI	53189	262-542-0099	542-7767	386
SCC Inc 1250 Lunt Ave *TF:* 877-891-1605 ■ *Web:* scccombustion.com	Elk Grove Village	IL	60007	224-366-8445	366-8455	360-3
SCC Soft Computer Inc 5400 Tech Data Dr *TF:* 800-763-8352 ■ *Web:* www.softcomputer.com	Clearwater	FL	33760	727-789-0100	789-0124	180
SCCA (Sports Car Club of America) 6700 SW Topeka Blvd **Fax Area Code:* 785 ■ *TF:* 800-770-2055 ■ *Web:* www.scca.com	Topeka	KS	66619	800-770-2055	232-7228*	48-18
SCCM (Society of Critical Care Medicine) 500 Midway Dr *Web:* www.sccm.org	Mount Prospect	IL	60056	847-827-6869	439-7226	49-8
SCCVB (Sandusky County Convention & Visitor's Bureau) 712 N St Ste 102 *TF:* 800-255-8070 ■ *Web:* www.sanduskycounty.org	Fremont	OH	43420	419-332-4470	332-4359	206
SCDAA (Sickle Cell Disease Association of America) 3700 Koppers St Ste 570 *TF:* 800-421-8453 ■ *Web:* www.sicklecelldisease.org	Baltimore	MD	21202	410-528-1555		48-17
SCE (Soil Consultant Engineering) 9303 Center St *Web:* soilconsultants.net	Manassas	VA	20110	703-366-3000		261
Scelzi Enterprises 2286 E Date *TF:* 800-858-2883 ■ *Web:* www.seinc.com	Fresno	CA	93706	626-334-0573		516
Scene Publications 4642 Capital Ave SW *Web:* www.scenepub.com	Battle Creek	MI	49015	269-979-1411	979-3474	637-9
Scenic Airlines Inc 1265 Airport Rd *TF:* 800-634-6801 ■ *Web:* www.scenic.com	Boulder City	NV	89005	702-638-3300		760
Scenic Rivers Energy Co-op 231 N Sheridan St *TF:* 800-236-2141 ■ *Web:* www.sre.coop	Lancaster	WI	53813	608-723-2121		245
Scenic State Park 56956 Scenic Hwy 7 *Web:* www.dnr.state.mn.us	Bigfork	MN	56628	218-743-3362		565
Scenic Valley Coop 354 Morrow St **Fax Area Code:* 920 ■ *TF:* 800-686-1336 ■ *Web:* www.scenicvalleycoop.com	Seymour	WI	54165	800-686-1336	833-7332*	579
Scentair Inc 3810 Shutterfly Rd *Web:* www.scentair.com	Charlotte	NC	28217	704-504-2320		194
Scentations Inc 913 Plz Dr **Fax Area Code:* 870 ■ *TF:* 800-748-7648 ■ *Web:* www.scentations.com	Pocahontas	AR	72455	800-748-7648	892-2593*	322
Scentisphere LLC 97 Old Rt 6 Unit 2 *Web:* www.scentisphere.com	Carmel	NY	10512	845-225-3600		77
ScentSational Technologies LLC 425 York Rd *Web:* www.scentsationaltechnologies.com	Jenkintown	PA	19046	215-886-7777		393
Scepter Publishers PO Box 360694 *TF:* 800-322-8773 ■ *Web:* scepterpublishers.org	Strongsville	OH	44136	800-322-8773		637-2
SCF Partners 600 Travis Ste 6600 **Fax Area Code:* 832 ■ *Web:* www.scfpartners.com	Houston	TX	77002	713-227-7888	213-1313*	41
SCF Securities Inc 155 E Shaw Ave Ste 102 *Web:* www.scfsecurities.com	Fresno	CA	93710	559-456-6100		390
SCFM Compressor Systems 3701 S Maybelle Ave *Web:* www.scfm.com	Tulsa	OK	74107	918-663-1309		172
SCFTA (Segerstrom Center for the Arts) 600 Town Center Dr *Web:* www.scfta.org	Costa Mesa	CA	92626	714-636-7433	556-8984	572
SCG (Southern Connecticut Gas) 60 Marsh Hill Rd *TF:* 866-268-2887 ■ *Web:* www.soconngas.com	Orange	CT	06477	866-268-2887		787
SCG Governmental Affairs 111 N Calhoun St Ste 6 *Web:* www.scggov.com	Tallahassee	FL	32301	850-513-0004		636
SCH (Sunbury Community Hospital) 350 N 11th St *Web:* www.sunburyhospital.com	Sunbury	PA	17801	570-286-3333		374-3
Schaab Metal Products Inc 1216 N Harrison St *TF:* 800-343-3386 ■ *Web:* www.schaabmetals.com	Fort Wayne	IN	46808	260-423-3386	423-3389	492
Schaaf Equipment Co 8657 S Beloit Ave *Web:* schaafequipment.com	Bridgeview	IL	60455	708-598-9099		358
Schadegg Mechanical Inc 225 Bridgepoint Dr *Web:* schadegg-mech.com	South Saint Paul	MN	55075	651-292-9933		697
Schaefer Ambulance Service Inc 4627 Beverly Blvd *TF:* 800-582-2258 ■ *Web:* www.schaeferamb.com	Los Angeles	CA	90004	323-468-1600		30
Schaefer Brush Manufacturing Company Inc 1101 S Prairie Ave *TF:* 800-347-3501 ■ *Web:* schaeferbrush.com	Waukesha	WI	53186	262-547-3500		586
Schaefer Enterprises Inc 77 Chambers St 3rd Fl *TF:* 877-237-2481 ■ *Web:* seinewyork.com	New York	NY	10007	877-237-2481		390
Schaefer Marine Inc 158 Duchaine Blvd *Web:* www.schaefermarine.com	New Bedford	MA	02745	508-995-9511	995-4882	360-3
Schaefer Megomat USA Inc W233 N2830 Roundy Cir W *Web:* www.schaefer.biz	Pewaukee	WI	53072	262-524-1100	524-1133	494
Schaefer Mold Inc 2358 Blue Smoke Ct N *Web:* www.schaefermold.com	Fort Worth	TX	76105	817-534-7461	534-7466	757
Schaefer Pyrotechnics Inc 376 Hartman Bridge Rd	Ronks	PA	17572	717-687-0647		268
Schaefer Systems International Inc 10021 Westlake Dr *TF:* 800-876-6000 ■ *Web:* www.ssi-schaefer.com	Charlotte	NC	28241	704-944-4500	588-1862	199
Schaefers Market 411 Sinclair Lewis Ave *Web:* www.schaefersmarket.com	Sauk Centre	MN	56378	320-352-6490		473
Schaeffer & Associates Ltd 6 Ronrose Dr *Web:* www.schaeffers.com	Concord	ON	L4K4R3	905-738-6100		261
Schaeffer Manufacturing Company Inc 102 Barton St *TF:* 800-325-9962 ■ *Web:* www.schaefferoil.com	Saint Louis	MO	63104	314-865-4100	865-4107	541
Schaeffer Nassar Schneidegg Consulting Engineers LLC 1425 Cantillon Blvd *Web:* www.snsce.com	Mays Landing	NJ	08330	609-625-7400		261
Schaeperkoetter Sales and Service 2715 Hwy A *TF:* 888-437-5614 ■ *Web:* www.schaeperkoetter.com	Mount Sterling	MO	65062	573-943-6323	943-6358	274
SCHAERER MEDICAL USA Inc 675 Wilmer Ave *TF:* 800-755-6381 ■ *Web:* www.schaerermedicalusa.com	Cincinnati	OH	45226	513-561-2241	561-0195	475
Schafer Condon Carter Inc 1029 W Madison *Web:* www.schafercondoncarter.com	Chicago	IL	60607	312-464-1666		344
Schafer Corp 3811 N Fairfax Dr Ste 400 *Web:* www.schafercorp.com	Arlington	VA	22203	703-516-6000	516-6065	261

Name / Address	City	State	ZIP	Phone	Fax	Class
Schafer Gear Works Inc 4701 Nimtz Pkwy *Web:* schaferindustries.com	South Bend	IN	46628	574-234-4116	234-4115	709
Schafer State Park W 1365 Schafer Park Rd *Web:* parks.state.wa.us	Elma	WA	98541	360-482-3852		565
Schafer Veterinary Consultants LLC 800 Helena Ct *Web:* schaferveterinary.com	Fort Collins	CO	80524	970-224-5103		794
Schaff Piano Supply Co 451 Oakwood Rd *TF:* 800-747-4266 ■ *Web:* www.schaffpiano.com	Lake Zurich	IL	60047	847-438-4556	438-4615	527
Schaffer Consulting 707 Summer St *Web:* www.schafferresults.com	Stamford	CT	06901	203-322-1604		194
Schaffer Grinding Co 848 S Maple Ave *Web:* www.schaffergrinding.com	Montebello	CA	90640	323-724-4476	724-2635	454
Schaffer Manufacturing 109 Industrial Ave *Web:* www.schaffermfg.com	Milltown	WI	54858	715-825-2424		757
Schaffner Manufacturing Company Inc 21 Herron Ave *Web:* www.schaffnermfg.com	Pittsburgh	PA	15202	412-761-9902	761-8998	1
Schahet Hotels Inc 9333 N Meridian St *Web:* www.schahethotels.com	Indianapolis	IN	46260	317-848-9000		194
Schakowsky Jan (Rep D - IL) 2367 Rayburn House Office Bldg *Web:* schakowsky.house.gov	Washington	DC	20515	202-225-2111	226-6890	342-2
Schaller & Weber Inc 1654 Second Ave *Web:* schallerweber.com	New York	NY	10028	718-721-5480		296-26
Schaller Corp 49495 Gratiot Ave *Web:* www.schallergroup.com	Chesterfield	MI	48051	586-949-6000		488
Schaller Telephone Co 111 W Second St *Web:* www.schallertel.net	Schaller	IA	51053	712-275-4211		387
Schalmont Central School District 4 Sabre Dr *Web:* www.schalmont.org	Schenectady	NY	12306	518-355-9200	355-9203	685
Schanz Beverage 400 4th St *Web:* www.schanzbeverage.com	Watervliet	NY	12189	518-273-4045		81-1
Scharer Insurance Inc 454 E Center St *Web:* www.scharerinsurance.com	Marion	OH	43302	740-387-4311		390
Scharf Investments LLC 5619 Scotts Vly Dr Ste 140 *Web:* scharfinvestments.com	Scotts Valley	CA	95066	831-429-6513		401
Scharine Group, The 4213 N Scharine Rd *TF:* 800-472-2880 ■ *Web:* www.thescharinegroup.com	Whitewater	WI	53190	608-883-2880		186
Schatten Properties Management Company Inc 1514 S St *TF:* 800-892-1315 ■ *Web:* schattenproperties.com	Nashville	TN	37212	615-329-3011	327-2343	653
Schatz Bearing Corp 10 Fairview Ave *TF:* 800-554-1406 ■ *Web:* www.schatzbearing.com	Poughkeepsie	NY	12601	845-452-6000	452-1660	75
Schatz Brian (Sen D - HI) 722 Hart Senate Office Bldg *Web:* www.schatz.senate.gov	Washington	DC	20510	202-224-3934	228-1153	342-2
Schauer & Simank PC 615 N Upper Broadway Ste 700 *Web:* schauerandsimanklaw.com	Corpus Christi	TX	78401	361-884-2800		41
Schaumburg Park District 235 E Beech Dr *Web:* www.parkfun.com	Schaumburg	IL	60193	847-985-2115		31
Schaumburg Specialties Co 550 Albion Ave Unit 30 *TF:* 800-834-8125 ■ *Web:* shopcraftracks.com	Schaumburg	IL	60193	800-834-8125		111
Schaumburg Township District Library (STDL) 130 S Roselle Rd *Web:* www.schaumburglibrary.org	Schaumburg	IL	60193	847-985-4000		434-3
Schawbel Corp 26 Crosby Dr *TF:* 866-753-3837 ■ *Web:* www.thermacell.com	Bedford	MA	01730	781-541-6900		37
Schechner Lifson Corp 4 Chatham Rd *Web:* slcinsure.com	Summit	NJ	07901	908-598-7800		390
Schechter Dokken Kanter CPA'S 100 Washington Ave S Ste 1600 *Web:* www.sdkcpa.com	Minneapolis	MN	55401	612-332-5500		734
Schechter Wealth Strategies 251 Pierce St *Web:* www.schechterwealth.com	Birmingham	MI	48009	248-731-9500		401
Schecter Guitar Research Inc 10953 Pendleton St *TF:* 800-660-6621 ■ *Web:* www.schecterguitars.com	Sun Valley	CA	91352	818-846-2700		527
Schedel Arboretum & Gardens 19255 W Portage River S Rd *Web:* www.schedel-gardens.org	Elmore	OH	43416	419-862-3182		97
Schedulicity Inc 424 E Main Ste 201 *Web:* www.schedulicity.com	Bozeman	MT	59715	406-582-0494		177
Scheef & Stone LLP 500 N Akard St Ste 2700 *Web:* www.solidcounsel.com	Dallas	TX	75201	214-706-4200		428
Scheeser Buckley Mayfield Inc 1540 Corporate Woods Pkwy *TF:* 800-448-9338 ■ *Web:* www.sbmce.com	Uniontown	OH	44685	330-526-2700	896-9180	261
Scheflow Engineers PC 1814 Grandstand Pl *Web:* www.scheflоweng.com	Elgin	IL	60123	847-697-7095	697-7099	261
Scheibel Halaska 735 N Water St Ste 200 *Web:* trefoilgroup.com	Milwaukee	WI	53202	414-272-6898		463
Scheid & Company PC 101 Commonwealth Ave *Web:* scheidco.com	Concord	MA	01742	978-318-9600		2
Scheid Vineyards Inc 305 Hilltown Rd *TF:* 888-772-4343 ■ *Web:* www.scheidvineyards.com	Salinas	CA	93908	831-455-9990	455-9998	315-5
Scheig Assoc PO Box 2628 **Fax Area Code:* 800 ■ *TF:* 800-999-8582 ■ *Web:* www.scheig.com	Gig Harbor	WA	98335	253-858-3534	766-3533*	196

Name / Address	City	State	ZIP	Phone	Fax	Class
Scheinkman & Scheinkman CPA PA 18 NE Second Ave *Web:* www.954cpa.com	Dania Beach	FL	33004	954-920-6173	920-3347	2
Schemmer Associates Inc, The 1044 N 115th St Ste 300 *Web:* www.schemmer.com	Omaha	NE	68154	402-493-4800	493-7951	261
Schemper Corp 150 N Wilma Ave *Web:* schempersace.com	Ripon	CA	95366	209-599-2141		351
Schenck Business Solutions *Cliftonlarsonallen LLP* 200 E Washington St *TF:* 800-236-2246 ■ *Web:* www.schencksc.com	Appleton	WI	54911	920-731-8111	731-8037	2
Schenck Trebel Corp 535 Acorn St *TF:* 800-873-2357 ■ *Web:* www.schenck-usa.com	Deer Park	NY	11729	631-242-4010	242-5077	684
Schendel Pest Services 1035 SE Quincy St *TF:* 800-591-7378 ■ *Web:* www.schendelpest.com	Topeka	KS	66612	785-232-9357		577
Schenectady County 620 State St *Web:* www.schenectadycounty.com	Schenectady	NY	12305	518-388-4220	388-4224	338
Schenectady County Community College 78 Washington Ave *Web:* www.sunysccc.edu	Schenectady	NY	12305	518-381-1200		162
Schenectady County Public Library System 99 Clinton St *Web:* www.scpl.org	Schenectady	NY	12305	518-388-4500	386-2241	434-3
Schenectady Hardware & Electric Company Inc PO Box 338 *Web:* www.sheinc.com	Schenectady	NY	12301	518-346-2369	372-7549	189-4
Schenectady Museum & Suits-Bueche Planetarium 15 Nott Terr Hts *Web:* www.schenectadymuseum.org	Schenectady	NY	12308	518-382-7890	382-7893	520
Schenectady Steel Company Inc 18 Mariaville Rd *Web:* www.schenectadysteel.com	Schenectady	NY	12306	518-355-3220		480
Schenk Packing Company Inc 8204 288th St NW *Web:* www.schenkpacking.com	Stanwood	WA	98292	360-629-6290		473
SchenkelShultz Architects 200 E Robinson St Ste 300 *Web:* www.schenkelshultz.com	Orlando	FL	32801	407-872-3322	872-3303	261
Schenker Inc 1305 Executive Blvd Ste 200 *TF:* 800-225-5229 ■ *Web:* www.dbschenker.com	Chesapeake	VA	23310	800-225-5229		449
Schenker of Canada Ltd 5935 Airport Rd 10th Fl *TF:* 800-461-3686 ■ *Web:* www.dbschenker.com	Mississauga	ON	L4V1W5	905-676-0676		311
Scher Fabrics Inc 119 W 40th St	New York	NY	10018	212-382-2266		594
Schererville Chamber of Commerce 122 E Joliet St *Web:* scherervillechamber.org	Schererville	IN	46375	219-322-5412		139
Scherr Furniture Rental Inc 11910 Parklawn Dr Ste A *Web:* scherrfurniture.net	Rockville	MD	20852	301-881-8960		321
Schetky Northwest Sales Inc 8430 NE Killingsworth St *TF:* 800-255-8341 ■ *Web:* www.schetkynw.com	Portland	OR	97220	503-607-3137		516
Scheurer Hospital Inc 170 N Caseville Rd *Web:* www.scheurer.org	Pigeon	MI	48755	989-453-3223	856-2209	374-3
Schewel Furniture Company Inc 1031 Main St *Web:* schewels.com	Lynchburg	VA	24504	434-522-0200		321
SCHHS (Saline County History and Heritage Society) 123 N Market St *Web:* www.schhs.us	Benton	AR	72015	501-778-3770		520
Schiavone Construction Company Inc 150 Meadowlands Pkwy 3rd Fl *Web:* www.schiavoneconstruction.com	Secaucus	NJ	07094	201-867-5070	864-3196	188-4
Schibell & Mennie LLC 1806 Hwy 35 S PO Box 2237 *Web:* schibelllaw.com	Ocean City	NJ	07712	732-774-1000		41
Schick Shadel Hospital 12101 Ambaum Blvd SW *TF:* 800-272-8464 ■ *Web:* www.schickshadel.com	Seattle	WA	98146	800-272-8464		726
Schiefelbusch Institute for Life Span Studies *Life Span Institute at the University of Kansas* 1000 Sunnyside Ave Rm 1052 *Web:* www.lsi.ku.edu	Lawrence	KS	66045	785-864-4295	864-5323	668
Schiele Museum of Natural History & James H Lynn Planetarium 1500 E Garrison Blvd *Web:* www.schielemuseum.org	Gastonia	NC	28054	704-866-6908	866-6041	520
Schienke Products Inc 120 Mclean *Web:* www.schienkeproducts.com	Bruce Township	MI	48065	586-752-5454	752-0819	455
Schiff Adam (Rep D - CA) 2269 Rayburn House Office Bldg *Web:* schiff.house.gov	Washington	DC	20515	202-225-4176	225-5828	342-2
Schiff Hardin LLP 233 S Wacker Dr Ste 7100 *Web:* www.schiffhardin.com	Chicago	IL	60606	312-258-5500	258-5600	428
Schiff's Restaurant Service Inc 3410 N Main Ave *Web:* www.myschiffs.com	Scranton	PA	18508	570-343-1294		297-8
Schiffer Mason Contractors Inc 2190 Delhi St NE PO Box 250 *Web:* www.schiffermason.com	Holt	MI	48842	517-694-2566	694-1936	189-7
Schiffman Firm LLC 1300 Fifth Ave *Web:* schiffmanfirm.com	Pittsburgh	PA	15219	412-288-9444		41
Schiffman Law Office PC 4506 N 12th St *Web:* schiffmanlaw.com	Phoenix	AZ	85014	602-266-2667	266-0141	41
Schiffman Sheridan & Brown PC 2080 Linglestown Rd Ste 201 *TF:* 800-294-2889 ■ *Web:* ssbc-law.com	Harrisburg	PA	17110	717-540-9170	540-5481	428
Schifrin Gagnon & Dickey Inc 9171 Gazette Ave **Fax Area Code:* 619 ■ *TF:* 800-743-2524 ■ *Web:* sgdinc.com	Chatsworth	CA	91311	818-909-9090	546-8723*	390

	Phone	Fax	Class
Schildberg Construction Co 108 SE Sixth St PO Box 358 .... Greenfield IA 50849 *Web:* schildberg.com	641-743-2131	743-6264	440
Schiller & Knapp LLP 950 New Loudon Rd Ste 109 .... Latham NY 12110 *Web:* www.schillerknapp.com	518-786-9069	786-1246	428
Schiller & Pittenger PC 1771 Front St Ste D .... Scotch Plains NJ 07076 *Web:* sp-lawyers.com	908-490-0444		41
Schiller Ducanto & Fleck 225 E Deerpath Ste 270 .... Lake Forest IL 60045 *Web:* www.sdflaw.com	847-615-8300		41
Schiller Grounds Care Inc 1028 St Rd .... Southampton PA 18966 *TF:* 877-596-6337 ■ *Web:* www.littlewonder.com	215-357-5110		429
Schiller International University 8560 Ulmerton Rd .... Largo FL 33771 *TF:* 855-787-2262 ■ *Web:* www.schiller.edu	727-736-5082		786
Schilli Transportation Services Inc 6358 W US Hwy 24 .... Remington IN 47977 *Web:* www.schilli.com	219-261-2101		780
Schilling Bros Inc 5400 US Hwy 45 .... Mattoon IL 61938 *Web:* www.schillingbros.com	217-234-6478		274
Schilling Paper Co PO Box 369 .... La Crosse WI 54602 *TF:* 800-888-1885 ■ *Web:* www.schillingsupply.com	800-888-1885		559
Schilling-Douglas School of Hair Design L L C Shoppes at Louviers 211 Louviers Dr .... Newark DE 19711 *Web:* www.schillingdouglas.com	302-737-5100	737-4141	685
Schimenti Construction Co 650 Danbury Rd .... Ridgefield CT 06877 *Web:* www.schimenti.com	914-244-9100	244-9103	186
Schindler Cohen & Hochman LLP 100 Wall St 15th Fl .... New York NY 10005 *Web:* schlaw.com	212-277-6300		428
Schindler Elevator Corp 20 Whippany Rd .... Morristown NJ 07960 *TF:* 800-225-3123 ■ *Web:* www.schindler.com	973-397-6500	397-3619	256
Schippers & Crew Inc 5309 Shlshl Ave NW 100 .... Seattle WA 98107 *TF:* 877-263-4879 ■ *Web:* schippersandcrew.com	206-782-2325	782-2363	22
Schlachman, Belsky & Weiner PA 300 E Lombard St Ste 1100 .... Baltimore MD 21202 *TF:* 877-736-1845 ■ *Web:* www.sbwlaw.com	410-685-2022	783-4771	428
Schlage Lock Co 3899 Hancock Expy .... Colorado Springs CO 80911 *Web:* www.schlage.com	719-896-3000		350
Schlagel Inc 491 N Emerson .... Cambridge MN 55008 *TF:* 800-328-8002 ■ *Web:* www.schlagel.com	763-689-5991		273
Schlagel Long LLC 100 E Park St Ste 8 .... Olathe KS 66061 *Web:* schlagellong.com	913-782-5885		41
Schlager Group Inc 325 N St Paul Ste 3425 .... Dallas TX 75201 **Fax Area Code:* 214 ■ *TF:* 888-416-5727 ■ *Web:* www.schlagergroup.com	888-416-5727	347-9469*	94
Schlegel Systems Inc 1555 Jefferson Rd .... Rochester NY 14623 *TF:* 888-924-7694 ■ *Web:* www.amesbury.com	585-427-7200		326
Schlegel Villages Inc 325 Max Becker Dr Ste 201 .... Kitchener ON N2E4H5 *Web:* schlegelvillages.com	519-571-1873		371
Schleicher County 164 E US Hwy 190 .... Eldorado TX 76936 *Web:* www.schleichercountytexas.us	325-853-2593	853-2603	338
Schlenner Wenner & Co 630 Roosevelt Rd .... Saint Cloud MN 56301 *TF:* 877-616-0286 ■ *Web:* www.swcocpas.com	320-251-0286		2
Schlesinger's Chop House 1106 William Styron Sq S .... Newport News VA 23606 *Web:* schlesingerssteaks.com	757-599-4700		671
Schlessman Seed Co 11513 US Rt 250 .... Milan OH 44846 *TF:* 888-534-7333 ■ *Web:* www.schlessman-seed.com	419-499-2572	499-2574	694
Schleuniger Inc 87 Colin Dr .... Manchester NH 03103 *TF:* 877-902-1470 ■ *Web:* www.schleuniger.com	603-668-8117	668-8119	456
Schley County 14 S Broad .... Ellaville GA 31806 *Web:* www.schleycountyga.us	229-937-2609		338
Schlichter & Shonack LLP 2381 Rosecrans Ave Ste 326 .... El Segundo CA 90245 *Web:* sandsattorneys.com	310-643-0111		41
Schlichter, Bogard & Denton 100 S Fourth St Ste 900 .... Saint Louis MO 63102 *TF:* 800-873-5297 ■ *Web:* uselaws.com	314-621-6115		428
Schlitterbahn Waterpark Resort 381 E Austin St .... New Braunfels TX 78130 *Web:* www.schlitterbahn.com	830-625-2351		32
Schlitz Audubon Nature Ctr 1111 E Brown Deer Rd .... Bayside WI 53217 *Web:* www.schlitzaudubon.org	414-352-2880	352-6091	50-5
Schlossberg & Associates, A Law Corp 3050 Saturn St Ste 100 .... Brea CA 92821 *Web:* schlossberglaw.com	714-526-8460		41
Schlueter Co 320 N Main St .... Janesville WI 53545 *TF:* 800-359-1700 ■ *Web:* www.schlueterco.com	608-755-5444	755-5440	298
Schlumberger Ltd 5599 San Felipe 17th Fl .... Houston TX 77056 *NYSE: SLB* ■ *Web:* www.slb.com	713-513-2000	513-2006	538
Schlumberger Ltd 3600 Briar Park Dr .... Houston TX 77042 *Web:* www.connect.slb.com	281-285-4376		538
Schmeiser Olsen & Watts LLP 18 E University Dr Ste 101 .... Mesa AZ 85201 *Web:* www.iplawusa.com	480-655-0073	655-9536	445
Schmidt Associates PC 2530 S Grand Ave .... Carthage MO 64836 *Web:* www.schmidt-cpapc.com	417-358-6090		2
Schmidt Baking Company Inc 7801 Fitch Ln .... Baltimore MD 21236 *Web:* www.schmidtbaking.com	410-668-8200	558-3096	296-1
Schmidt Consulting Services Inc 405 McKnight Park Dr .... Pittsburgh PA 15237 *TF:* 888-887-4535 ■ *Web:* www.schmidtmr.com	412-367-1226	367-9316	195
Schmidt Custom Floors Inc N8 W22590 Johnson Dr .... Waukesha WI 53186 *Web:* www.schmidtflooring.com	262-547-8763		131
Schmidt Electric Coy L P 9701 FM 1625 .... Austin TX 78747 *Web:* www.schmidt-electric.com	512-243-1450		189-4
Schmidt Kramer Pc 209 State St .... Harrisburg PA 17101 *Web:* schmidtkramer.com	717-888-8888		41
Schmidt Machine Co 7013 Ohio 199 .... Upper Sandusky OH 43351 *TF:* 866-368-3814 ■ *Web:* www.schmidtmachine.com	419-294-3814	294-2607	274
Schmidt Westergard & Company PLLC 77 W University Dr .... Mesa AZ 85201 *Web:* sw-cpa.com	480-834-6030		2
Schmidt's Auto Inc 1621 Beld St .... Madison WI 53715 *Web:* www.schmidtsauto.com	608-257-0505		62-5
Schmidt's Sausage Haus 240 E Kossuth St .... Columbus OH 43206 *Web:* www.schmidthaus.com	614-444-6808	445-3072	671
Schmidt-Goodman Office Products 1920 N Broadway .... Rochester MN 55906 *TF:* 800-247-0663 ■ *Web:* www.schmidtgoodman.com	507-282-3870		321
Schmiede Corp 1865 Riley Creek Rd PO Box 1630 .... Tullahoma TN 37388 *TF:* 800-535-1851 ■ *Web:* www.schmiedecorp.com	931-455-4801		454
Schmitt Furniture Company Inc 101 E Main St .... New Albany IN 47150 *Web:* schmittfurniture.com	812-944-2285		321
Schmitt Industries Inc 2765 NW Nicolai St .... Portland OR 97210 *NASDAQ: SMIT* ■ *Web:* www.schmittindustries.com	503-227-7908	223-1258	472
Schmitt Music Co 2400 Fwy Blvd .... Brooklyn Center MN 55430 *TF:* 877-724-6488 ■ *Web:* www.schmittmusic.com	763-566-4560	566-5725	526
Schmittinger & Rodriguez PA 414 S State St .... Dover DE 19901 *Web:* schmittrod.com	302-674-0140		41
Schmitz Press 37 Loveton Cir .... Sparks MD 21152 *Web:* schmitzpress.net	410-329-3000		174
Schmitz Ready Mix Inc 5400 N 124th St .... Milwaukee WI 53225 *Web:* www.schmitzmix.com	414-831-2400	462-8812	182
Schmolz+Bickenbach USA 365 Village Dr .... Carol Stream IL 60188 *TF:* 800-323-1233 ■ *Web:* www.schmolz-bickenbach.us	800-323-1233		492
Schmuckal Oil Co 1516 Barlow St .... Traverse City MI 49686 *Web:* www.schmuckaloil.com	231-946-2800	941-7435	324
Schnabel Engineering Inc 9800 JEB Stuart Pkwy Ste 200 .... Glen Allen VA 23059 *Web:* www.schnabel-eng.com	804-264-3222		261
Schnabel Foundation Co 45240 Business Ct Ste 250 .... Sterling VA 20166 *Web:* www.schnabel.com	703-742-0020	742-3319	189-11
Schnadig International Corp 4200 Tudor Ln .... Greensboro NC 27410 *TF:* 800-468-8730 ■ *Web:* www.schnadig.com	800-468-8730		319-2
Schnake Turnbo Frank Inc 20 E Fifth St Ste 1500 .... Tulsa OK 74103 **Fax Area Code:* 405 ■ *Web:* www.schnake.com	918-582-9151	602-2029*	7
Schneck Medical Ctr 411 W Tipton St .... Seymour IN 47274 *TF:* 800-234-9222 ■ *Web:* www.schneckmed.org	812-522-2349		374-3
Schneeberger Inc 44 6th Rd .... Bedford MA 01730 *Web:* www.schneeberger.com	781-271-0140	275-4749	472
Schneider Bradley (Rep D - IL) 1432 Longworth House Office Bldg .... Washington DC 20515 *Web:* schneider.house.gov	202-225-4835		342-2
Schneider Capital Management Corp 460 E Swedesford Rd Ste 2000 .... Wayne PA 19087 *TF:* 888-520-3277 ■ *Web:* www.schneidercap.com	610-687-8080	687-9150	401
Schneider Company Inc 1112 W Seventh St .... Saint Paul MN 55102 *Web:* schneidercarpetonesaintpaul.com	651-760-7574		290
Schneider Corp 8901 Otis Ave .... Indianapolis IN 46216 **Fax Area Code:* 317 ■ *TF:* 866-973-7100 ■ *Web:* schneidercorp.com	866-973-7100	826-7200*	261
Schneider Downs & Company Inc 1133 Penn Ave .... Pittsburgh PA 15222 *Web:* www.schneiderdowns.com	412-261-3644	261-4876	2
Schneider Electric 10350 Ormsby Pk Pl Ste 400 .... Louisville KY 40223 *TF:* 866-907-8664 ■ *Web:* www.schneider-electric.us	502-429-3800		463
Schneider Electric Buildings LLC 1354 Clifford Ave .... Loves Park IL 61111 *TF:* 877-342-5173 ■ *Web:* www.schneider-electric.com	877-342-5173		186
Schneider Graphic's Inc 6082 NE 14th St .... Des Moines IA 50313 *Web:* www.schneidergraphics.com	515-289-4464	289-4468	62-4
Schneider Group 5400 Bosque Blvd Ste 680 .... Waco TX 76710 *Web:* www.sgmeet.com	254-776-3550	776-3767	184
Schneider Homes Inc 6510 Southcenter Blvd .... Tukwila WA 98188 *Web:* www.schneiderhomes.com	206-248-2471		187
Schneider Institute for Health Policy Brandeis University 415 S St .... Waltham MA 02454 *Web:* sihp.brandeis.edu	781-736-3964		634
Schneider Laboratories Inc 2512 W Cary St .... Richmond VA 23220 *TF:* 800-785-5227 ■ *Web:* www.slabinc.com	804-353-6778		743
Schneider Law Group PLLC 1201 Edwards Mill Rd Ste 130 .... Raleigh NC 27607 *Web:* schneiderlawgroup.com	919-324-3600		41
Schneider National Inc 3101 S Packerland Dr PO Box 2545 .... Green Bay WI 54306 *TF:* 800-558-6767 ■ *Web:* schneider.com	920-592-2000		449
Schneider Optics Century Div 7701 Haskell Ave .... Van Nuys CA 91406 *TF:* 800-228-1254 ■ *Web:* schneiderkreuznach.com	818-766-3715	505-9865	591
Schneider Packaging Equipment Company Inc 5370 Guy Young Rd .... Brewerton NY 13029 *TF:* 800-829-9266 ■ *Web:* www.schneiderpackaging.com	315-676-3035	676-2875	547

	City	State	ZIP	Phone	Fax	Class
Schneider's Dairy Inc 726 Frank St *Web:* www.schneidersdairypgh.com	Pittsburgh	PA	15227	412-881-3525	881-7722	296-27
Schneiderman & Sherman 23938 Research Dr Ste 300 *TF:* 866-867-7688 ■ *Web:* sspclegal.com	Farmington Hills	MI	48335	248-539-7400		428
Schnell & Hancock PC 5131 Utica Ridge Rd Ste B *Web:* shlawdav.com	Davenport	IA	52807	563-359-7112		41
Schneller Inc 6019 Powdermille Rd *Web:* www.schneller.com	Kent	OH	44240	330-673-1400		599
Schnitzer Steel Industries Inc 6241 SE 111th Ave *NASDAQ: SCHN* ■ *Web:* www.schnitzersteel.com	Portland	OR	97266	503-224-9900		723
Schnuck Markets Inc 11420 Lackland Rd *TF:* 800-264-4400 ■ *Web:* nourish.schnucks.com	Saint Louis	MO	63146	314-994-4400		345
Schober & Schober Pc 400 W 15th St Ste 1405 *Web:* schoberlegal.com	Austin	TX	78701	512-474-7678		41
Schoeffler Energy Group Inc 224 Rue De Jean *Web:* segland.com	LaFayette	LA	70508	337-232-1122		653
Schoeller-Bleckmann Energy Services LLC 712 St Etienne Rd *Web:* www.sbesllc.com	Broussard	LA	70518	337-837-2030		539
Schoeneck Containers Inc 2160 S 170th St *Web:* www.schoeneck.com	New Berlin	WI	53151	262-786-9360		98
Schoeneckers Inc 7630 Bush Lake Rd *Web:* www.biworldwide.com	Minneapolis	MN	55439	952-835-4800		113
Schoeneman's Building Materials Ctr 4000 S Western Ave *Web:* schoenemans.com	Sioux Falls	SD	57105	605-339-0745		191-3
Schoenmann Produce Company Inc 6950 Neuhaus St *Web:* www.schoenmannproduce.com	Houston	TX	77061	713-923-2728	923-5897	461
Schoepfle Garden 12882 Diagonal Rd *TF:* 800-526-7275 ■ *Web:* www.metroparks.cc	LaGrange	OH	44050	440-458-5121	458-8924	97
Schoharie County 284 Main St PO Box 429 *Web:* www.schohariecounty-ny.gov	Schoharie	NY	12157	518-295-8347	295-8482	338
Schoharie County Chamber of Commerce 256 Main St PO Box 143 *Web:* schohariechamber.com	Schoharie	NY	12092	518-295-8824	295-8826	139
Schoharie Crossing State Historic Site 129 Schoharie St PO Box 140 *Web:* parks.ny.gov	Fort Hunter	NY	12069	518-829-7516		565
Schoitz Engineering Inc 4901 Sergeant Rd Hwy 63 S *Web:* www.schoitz.com	Waterloo	IA	50704	319-234-6615		757
Scholar Hotel Syracuse 1060 E Genesee St *Web:* scholarhotels.com	Syracuse	NY	13210	315-476-4212		671
Scholarcraft Inc PO Box 170748 *Web:* www.scholarcraft.com	Birmingham	AL	35217	205-841-1922	841-1992	319-3
Scholarship America 1 Scholarship Way *TF:* 800-537-4180 ■ *Web:* scholarshipamerica.org	Saint Peter	MN	56082	507-931-1682		48-11
Scholarship Foundation of Santa Barbara 2253 Las Positas Rd *Web:* www.sbscholarship.org	Santa Barbara	CA	93105	805-687-6065		305
Scholastic Book Fairs Inc 1080 Greenwood Blvd *TF:* 800-874-4809 ■ *Web:* bookfairs.scholastic.com	Lake Mary	FL	32746	573-632-1687		96
Scholastic Coach & Athletic Director Magazine 557 Broadway *Web:* www.scholastic.com	New York	NY	10012	212-343-6100		457-8
Scholastic Inc 557 Broadway *TF:* 800-724-6527 ■ *Web:* www.scholastic.co.in	New York	NY	10012	800-724-6527		637-2
Schold Machine Corp 7201 W 64th Pl *Web:* www.schold.com	Chicago	IL	60638	708-458-3788		111
Scholl Lumber 6202 N Houston Rosslyn Rd *Web:* scholllumber.com	Houston	TX	77091	713-329-5300	329-5303	191-3
Schollnick Advertising LLC 2828 Metairie Ct **Fax Area Code:* 866 ■ *Web:* www.schollnickadvertising.com	Metairie	LA	70002	504-838-9615	977-4632*	4
Scholtz & Company LLC 107 Elm St 4 Stamford Plz 5th Fl *Web:* www.scholtzandco.com	Stamford	CT	06902	203-714-9900	588-9032	528
School Annual Publishing Co 2568 Park Center Blvd *TF:* 800-436-6030 ■ *Web:* schoolannual.com	State College	PA	16801	800-436-6030		637-2
School Board of Highlands County 426 School St *Web:* www.highlands.k12.fl.us	Sebring	FL	33870	863-471-5555	471-5673	685
School District of Cheltenham Township 2000 Ashbourne Rd *Web:* www.cheltenham.org	Elkins Park	PA	19027	215-886-9500		685
School District of Hartford 675 E Rossman St *Web:* www.hartfordjt1.k12.wi.us	Hartford	WI	53027	262-673-3155	673-3548	685
School District of Philadelphia 440 N Broad St *Web:* www.philasd.org	Philadelphia	PA	19130	215-400-4000		685
School District of The Chathams 58 Meyersville Rd *Web:* www.chatham-nj.org	Chatham	NJ	07928	973-457-2500		685
School Employees Retirement System of Ohio 300 E Broad St Ste 100 *TF:* 800-878-5853 ■ *Web:* ohsers.org	Columbus	OH	43215	614-222-5853		528
School Guide Publications 210 N Ave *Web:* www.schoolguides.com	New Rochelle	NY	10801	914-632-7771		637-2
School Health Alert PO Box 150127 *TF:* 866-370-7899 ■ *Web:* www.schoolnurse.com	Nashville	TN	37215	615-370-7899	370-9993	637-10
School Innovations & Advocacy Inc 5200 Golden Foothill Pkwy **Fax Area Code:* 888 ■ *TF:* 877-954-4357 ■ *Web:* www.sia-us.com	El Dorado Hills	CA	95762	800-487-9234	487-6441*	463
School Library Journal 123 William St Ste 802 *TF:* 800-588-1030 ■ *Web:* www.schoollibraryjournal.com	New York	NY	10038	646-380-0700	380-0756	457-8
School Nurse Supply Co 1690 Wright Blvd *TF:* 800-485-2737 ■ *Web:* www.schoolnursesupplyinc.com	Schaumburg	IL	60193	800-485-2737		685
School Nutrition Assn (SNA) 700 S Washington St Ste 300 *TF:* 800-877-8822 ■ *Web:* schoolnutrition.org	Alexandria	VA	22314	703-739-3900	739-3915	49-6
School of Advertising Art Inc 1725 E David Rd *TF:* 877-300-9866 ■ *Web:* saa.edu	Dayton	OH	45440	937-294-0592	294-5869	7
School of Self-Reliance PO Box 41834 *Web:* www.self-reliance.net	Los Angeles	CA	90041	323-255-9502		637-2
School of the Museum of Fine Arts 230 The Fenway **Fax Area Code:* 617 ■ *TF:* 800-643-6078 ■ *Web:* bigfuture.collegeboard.org	Boston	MA	02115	800-591-1474	369-4264*	166
School of Visual Arts 209 E 23rd St *TF:* 800-436-4204 ■ *Web:* www.sva.edu	New York	NY	10010	212-592-2000	592-2116	164
School Photo Marketing 200 D Campus Dr **Fax Area Code:* 877 ■ *TF:* 877-543-9742 ■ *Web:* www.schoolphotoonline.com	Morganville	NJ	07751	732-431-0440	543-9745*	195
School Specialty Inc PO Box 1579 *OTC: SCOO* ■ **Fax Area Code:* 920 ■ *TF:* 888-388-3224 ■ *Web:* www.schoolspecialty.com	Appleton	WI	54912	419-589-1600	882-5603*	243
School Systems Federal Credit Union 150 Defreest Dr *Web:* schoolfcu.com	Troy	NY	12180	518-286-1611		219
School Webmasters 2846 E Nora St *TF:* 888-750-4556 ■ *Web:* www.schoolwebmasters.com	Mesa	AZ	85213	888-750-4556		177
Schoolcraft College 18600 Haggerty Rd *Web:* www.schoolcraft.edu	Livonia	MI	48152	734-462-4400	462-4553	162
Schoolcraft County 300 Walnut St Rm 169 *Web:* www.schoolcraftcounty.net	Manistique	MI	49854	906-341-3630		338
SchoolDocs LLC 6044 Luther Ln Ste 600 *TF:* 866-311-2293 ■ *Web:* www.schooldocs.com	Dallas	TX	75225	800-311-2293		387
Schools Financial Credit Union 1485 Response Rd Ste 126 *TF:* 800-962-0990 ■ *Web:* www.schools.org	Sacramento	CA	95815	916-569-5400		219
School-Tech Inc 745 State Cir *TF:* 800-521-2832 ■ *Web:* www.school-tech.com	Ann Arbor	MI	48108	800-521-2832	654-4321	346
Schooner Surprise 1 Bayview St *Web:* schoonersurprise.com	Camden	ME	04843	207-236-4687		220
Schoox 701 Brazos St Ste 539 *Web:* www.schoox.com	Austin	TX	78701	517-965-3300		657
Schoppe Company Inc 352 Van Buren Ave	Salt Lake City	UT	84115	801-467-5466		189-10
Schorin Company Inc 1800 Penn Ave *Web:* www.schorin.com	Pittsburgh	PA	15222	412-281-0650	281-2880	559
Schostak Bros & Company Inc 17800 Laurel Pk Dr N Ste 200C *Web:* www.schostak.com	Livonia	MI	48152	248-262-1000	262-1814	653
Schott Magnetics 1401 Air Wing Rd *Web:* www.schottcorp.com	San Diego	CA	92154	507-223-5572	223-5055	253
SCHOTT North America Inc 615 Hwy 68 *Web:* www.us.schott.com	Sweetwater	TN	37874	423-337-3522	337-7979	329
Schott Textiles Inc 2850 Gilchrist Rd *TF:* 877-661-2121 ■ *Web:* schotttextiles.com	Akron	OH	44305	330-794-2121	794-2122	594
Schrader Kurt (Rep D - OR) 2431 Rayburn House Office Bldg *Web:* schrader.house.gov	Washington	DC	20515	202-225-5711	225-5699	342-2
Schramm Inc 800 E Virginia Ave *TF:* 888-737-9438 ■ *Web:* www.schramminc.com	West Chester	PA	19380	610-696-2500	696-6950	537
Schramm Park State Recreation Area 15810 Hwy 50 *Web:* www.nrtdatabase.org	Louisville	NE	68037	402-332-3901		565
Schramm, Williams & Associates Inc 512 C St NE *Web:* www.swaconsult.com	Washington	DC	20002	202-543-4455	543-4586	196
Schreiber Corp 29945 Beck Rd *Web:* www.schreiberroofing.com	Wixom	MI	48393	248-926-1500	926-1788	189-12
Schreiber Foods Inc 400 N Washington St *Web:* www.schreiberfoods.com	Green Bay	WI	54301	920-437-7601		296-5
Schreiber Foods International Inc 600 E Crescent Ave Ste 103 *TF:* 800-631-7070 ■ *Web:* www.ambrosia-foods.com	Upper Saddle River	NJ	07458	201-327-3535	327-2812	297-11
Schreiber LLC 100 Schreiber Dr *Web:* www.schreiberwater.com	Trussville	AL	35173	205-655-7466	655-7669	806
Schreiber Translations Inc 51 Monroe St Ste 101 *TF:* 800-822-3213 ■ *Web:* www.schreibernet.com	Rockville	MD	20850	301-424-7737		768
Schreimann, Rackers & Francka LLC 931 Wildwood Dr Ste 201 *Web:* srfblaw.com	Jefferson City	MO	65109	573-634-7580	635-6034	41
Schreiner University 2100 Memorial Blvd *TF:* 800-343-4919 ■ *Web:* www.schreiner.edu	Kerrville	TX	78028	830-792-7217	792-7226	166
Schreiner's Iris Gardens 3625 Quinaby Rd NE *TF:* 800-525-2367 ■ *Web:* schreinersgardens.com	Salem	OR	97303	503-393-3232	393-5590	97
Schrickel Rollins & Associates Inc 1161 Corporate Dr W Ste 200 *Web:* www.sradesign.com	Arlington	TX	76006	817-649-3216	649-7645	422
Schrier Kim (Rep D - WA) 1123 Longworth House Office Bldg *Web:* www.schrier.house.gov	Washington	DC	20515	202-225-7761		342-2
Schroder 875 Third Ave *Web:* www.schroders.com	New York	NY	10022	212-641-3800		690
Schroder, Joseph & Associates LLP 392 Pearl St Ste 301 *Web:* sjalegal.com	Buffalo	NY	14202	716-881-4900		41
Schroeder & Bogardus Die Company Inc 1130 Red Gum St	Anaheim	CA	92806	714-630-2270	630-1739	757

Company / Address	City	State	Zip	Phone	Fax	Class
Schroeder Industries LLC 580 W Park Rd *TF:* 800-722-4810 ■ *Web:* www.schroederindustries.com	Leetsdale	PA	15056	724-318-1100	318-1200	207
Schroeder Measurement Technologies Inc 25400 Hgwy 19 Ste 285 *TF:* 800-556-0484 ■ *Web:* home.smttest.com	Clearwater	FL	33763	727-738-8727		463
Schroeder's Book Haven 104 Michigan Ave *TF:* 800-894-5032 ■ *Web:* www.bookhaventexas.com	League City	TX	77573	281-332-5226		95
Schroeder's Cafe 240 Front St *Web:* www.schroederssf.com	San Francisco	CA	94111	415-421-4778		671
Schroeder's Flowerland Inc 1530 S Webster Ave *TF:* 800-236-4769 ■ *Web:* www.schroederflowers.com	Green Bay	WI	54301	920-436-6363		292
Schroer & Associates PC 42 N Second St *Web:* schroer-cpa.com	Council Bluffs	IA	51503	712-322-8734	322-4699	2
Schroer Manufacturing Co 511 Osage Ave *TF:* 800-444-1579 ■ *Web:* www.shor-line.com	Kansas City	KS	66105	913-281-1500		419
Schroeter Goldmark & Bender Ps 810 Third Ave *TF:* 800-809-2234 ■ *Web:* sgb-law.com	Seattle	WA	98104	206-622-8000		445
Schroth & Lorensons Jewelers 446 Springfield Ave *Web:* schrothlorenson.com	Summit	NJ	07901	908-273-1676		410
Schrudder Performance Group LLC 7723 Tylers Place Blvd Ste 141	West Chester	OH	45069	513-666-4578		463
SCHS (Schuylkill County Historical Society) 305 N Centre St *Web:* schuylkillhistory.org	Pottsville	PA	17901	570-622-7540		48-13
Schu Industries Inc 453 5th St *TF:* 800-967-3688 ■ *Web:* www.schuindustries.com	Random Lake	WI	53075	800-967-3688		319-1
Schubert Club Museum, The 75 W Fifth St 302 Landmark Ctr *Web:* schubert.org	Saint Paul	MN	55102	651-292-3267	292-4317	520
Schubert Communications Inc 112 Schubert Dr *Web:* www.schubertb2b.com	Downingtown	PA	19335	610-269-2100		7
Schuco USA L.LLP 240 Pane Rd *Web:* www.schueco.com	Newington	CT	06111	860-666-0505	665-0137	499
Schuette Manufacturing & Steel Sales Inc 5028 Hwy 42 *TF:* 800-626-6409 ■ *Web:* www.schuettemfg.com	Manitowoc	WI	54220	920-758-2491	758-2599	273
Schuff International Inc 420 S 19th Ave *OTC:* SHFK ■ *Web:* www.schuff.com	Phoenix	AZ	85009	602-252-7787		360-3
Schuff Steel Co 1971 W 700 N Ste 101 *Web:* www.mssteel.com	Lindon	UT	84042	801-648-5015		492
Schukei Chevrolet Inc 721 S Monroe *TF:* 877-288-0063 ■ *Web:* www.schukeichevy.com	Mason City	IA	50401	641-423-5402		57
Schulenburg Printing & Office Supplies Inc 705 Upton Ave *TF:* 800-874-9621 ■ *Web:* schulenburgprinting.com	Schulenburg	TX	78956	979-743-4511	743-4230	627
Schuler & Shook 750 N Orleans St Ste 400 *Web:* schulershook.com	Chicago	IL	60654	312-944-8230		722
Schuler Books & Music Inc 2660 28th St SE *Web:* www.schulerbooks.com	Grand Rapids	MI	49512	616-942-2561		95
Schuler, Halvorson, Weisser & Zoeller PA 1615 Forum Pl Ste 4-D *TF:* 800-689-8180 ■ *Web:* shw-law.com	West Palm Beach	FL	33401	561-689-8180	684-9683	41
Schulich School of Medicine & Dentistry Western University *Web:* www.schulich.uwo.ca	London	ON	N6A5C1	519-661-3459	661-3797	167-2
Schulmerich Carillons Inc Carillon Hill *TF:* 800-772-3557 ■ *Web:* schulmerichbells.com	Sellersville	PA	18960	215-257-2771	257-1910	527
Schulte Building Systems Inc 17600 Badtke Rd *TF:* 877-257-2534 ■ *Web:* sbslp.com	Hockley	TX	77447	281-304-6111		106
Schulte Roth & Zabel LLP 919 Third Ave *Web:* www.srz.com	New York	NY	10022	212-756-2000	593-5955	428
Schultz & Chez LLP 141 W Jackson Blvd Ste 2900 *Web:* schultzchez.com	Chicago	IL	60604	312-332-1912	332-3635	2
Schultz & Kellar PLLC 1100 E Southlake Blvd Ste 300 *Web:* independencetitle.com	Southlake	TX	76092	817-329-6470		41
Schultz Collins Lawson Chambers Inc 455 Market St Ste 1250 *TF:* 877-291-2205 ■ *Web:* www.schultzcollins.com	San Francisco	CA	94105	415-291-3000		401
Schultz Lubricants Inc 164 Shrewsbury St *TF:* 800-262-3962 ■ *Web:* www.schultzlubricants.com	West Boylston	MA	01583	508-835-4446		541
Schultz Veterinary Clinic 2770 Bennett *Web:* schultzvetclinic.com	Okemos	MI	48864	517-337-4800		794
Schultze Asset Management LP 800 Westchester Ave S-632 *Web:* www.samco.net	Rye Brook	NY	10573	914-701-5260		401
Schulweis Realty Inc 590 Madison Ave Ste 2100 *Web:* www.schulweisrealty.com	New York	NY	10022	212-407-2170		792
Schulz Electric Co 30 Gando Dr *TF:* 800-826-1425 ■ *Web:* schulzelectric.com	New Haven	CT	06513	203-562-5811		45
Schulz of America Inc 3420 Novis Pointe *Web:* www.schulzamerica.com	Acworth	GA	30101	770-529-4731	529-4733	172
Schulze & Burch Biscuit Co 1133 W 35th St *Web:* www.schulzeburch.com	Chicago	IL	60609	773-927-6622		68
Schumacher & Seiler Inc 10 W Aylesbury Rd *TF:* 800-992-9356 ■ *Web:* schumacherseiler.com	Timonium	MD	21093	410-465-7000		612
Schumacher Clinical Partners 200 Corporate Blvd *TF:* 800-893-9698 ■ *Web:* www.scp-health.com	LaFayette	LA	70508	800-893-9698		353
Schumacher Companies Inc, The 392 Pleasant St *Web:* www.dschumacher.com	West Bridgewater	MA	02379	508-427-7707		422
Schumacher Electric Corp 801 E Business Center Dr *TF:* 800-621-5485 ■ *Web:* www.batterychargers.com	Mount Prospect	IL	60056	800-621-5485		253
Schumacher Elevator Co 1 Schumacher Way *TF:* 800-779-5438 ■ *Web:* www.schumacherelevator.com	Denver	IA	50622	319-984-5676	984-6316	256
Schumacher European Ltd 18530 N Scottsdale Rd *Web:* www.schumachermb.com	Phoenix	AZ	85054	480-991-1155		57
Schumacher, Smejkal, Brockhaus & Herley PC 3403 27th St *Web:* gotcpas.com	Columbus	NE	68601	402-564-1366	564-1360	2
Schumann Printers Inc 701 S Main St *Web:* www.spiweb.com	Fall River	WI	53932	920-484-3348		627
Schumer Charles E (Sen D - NY) 322 Hart Senate Office Bldg *Web:* www.schumer.senate.gov	Washington	DC	20510	202-224-6542	228-3027	342-2
Schundler Co, The 150 Whitman Ave *Web:* www.schundler.com	Edison	NJ	08817	732-287-2244	287-4185	500
Schunk GmbH & Company KG 211 Kitty Hawk Dr *Web:* www.schunk.com	Morrisville	NC	27560	919-572-2705		127
Schurman Fine Papers 500 Chadbourne Rd *Web:* www.papyrusonline.com	Fairfield	CA	94533	707-428-0200		552-2
Schurz Communications Inc 1301 E Douglas Rd Ste 200 *Web:* www.schurz.com	Mishawaka	IN	46545	574-247-7237		532-3
Schuster Electronics Inc 11320 Grooms Rd *TF:* 800-521-1358 ■ *Web:* www.schusterusa.com	Cincinnati	OH	45242	800-521-1358		246
Schutt Industries Inc 185 Industrial Ave *Web:* www.schuttindustries.com	Clintonville	WI	54929	715-823-8025		779
Schutte & Koerting LLC 2510 Metropolitan *Web:* www.s-k.com	Trevose	PA	19053	215-639-0900	639-1597	386
Schutte Lumber Co 3001 SW Blvd *Web:* schuttelumber.com	Kansas City	MO	64108	816-753-6262		821
Schuur Solutions 2500 E Imperial Hwy Ste 201 *Web:* www.schuur.com	Brea	CA	92821	714-986-9990		180
Schuyler County PO Box 200 *TF:* 800-795-3272 ■ *Web:* www.schuylercountyillinois.com	Rushville	IL	62681	217-322-4734	322-6164	338
Schuyler County 105 Ninth St *Web:* www.schuylercounty.us	Watkins Glen	NY	14891	607-535-8133	535-8130	338
Schuyler Mansion State Historic Site 32 Catherine St *Web:* parks.ny.gov	Albany	NY	12202	518-434-0834		565
Schuylerville Central School District 14 Spring St *Web:* www.schuylervilleschools.org	Schuylerville	NY	12871	518-695-3255	695-6491	610
Schuylkill Capital Management Ltd 1631 Locust St 3rd Fl *Web:* www.schuylkillcap.com	Philadelphia	PA	19103	215-735-0299	735-3545	401
Schuylkill Center For Environmental Education 8480 Hagy'S Mill Rd *Web:* schuylkillcenter.org	Philadelphia	PA	19128	215-482-7300	482-8158	302
Schuylkill Chamber of Commerce 91 S Progress Ave *TF:* 800-755-1942 ■ *Web:* www.schuylkillchamber.com	Pottsville	PA	17901	570-622-1942	622-1638	139
Schuylkill County 401 N Ctr St *Web:* www.city.pottsville.pa.us	Pottsville	PA	17901	570-622-1234	628-1210	338
Schuylkill County Historical Society (SCHS) 305 N Centre St *Web:* schuylkillhistory.org	Pottsville	PA	17901	570-622-7540		48-13
Schuylkill Technology Center - North Campus 101 Technology Dr *Web:* www.stcenters.org	Frackville	PA	17931	570-874-1034		167-3
Schuylkill Valley School District 929 Lakeshore Dr *Web:* www.schuylkillvalley.org	Leesport	PA	19533	610-926-1706		685
Schwaab Inc 11415 W Burleigh St *Fax Area Code: 800 ■ *TF:* 800-935-9877 ■ *Web:* www.schwaab.com	Milwaukee	WI	53222	414-771-4150	935-9866*	467
Schwabe & Associates Inc 8525 SW 92nd St Ste B6 *Web:* www.schwabebenefitsgroup.com	Miami	FL	33156	954-889-0007		690
Schwabe Williamson & Wyatt PC 1211 SW Fifth Ave Ste 1900 *Web:* www.schwabe.com	Portland	OR	97204	503-222-9981		445
Schwan's Co 115 W College Dr *TF:* 800-533-5290 ■ *Web:* www.schwanscompany.com	Marshall	MN	56258	507-532-3274		296-36
Schwank Infrared Radiant Heaters 2 Schwank Way at Hwy 56N *TF:* 877-446-3727 ■ *Web:* www.schwankgroup.com	Waynesboro	GA	30830	877-446-3727		357
Schwant Tractor and Service Inc 13552 SW K-4 Hwy *Web:* www.schwanttractor.com	Dover	KS	66420	785-256-6242	256-6199	274
Schwartz & Stafford Pa 8625 Crown Crescent Ct Ste 110 *TF:* 866-254-4433 ■ *Web:* pss-law.com	Charlotte	NC	28227	704-708-5176		41
Schwartz Farms Inc 32296 190th St *Web:* schwartzfarms.com	Sleepy Eye	MN	56085	507-794-5779		10-6
Schwartz Hannum PC 11 Chestnut St *Web:* www.shpclaw.com	Andover	MA	01810	978-623-0900	623-0908	428
Schwartz Heslin Group Inc (SHG) 8 Airport Park Blvd *Web:* www.shggroup.com	Latham	NY	12110	518-786-7733		463
Schwartz Industries Inc 4719 Summer Hill	Brighton	MI	48116	586-759-1777	759-0808	454
Schwartz Investment Counsel Inc 801 W Ann Arbor Trl Ste 244 *Web:* www.schwartzinvest.com	Plymouth	MI	48170	734-455-7777	455-7720	528

	Phone	Fax	Class
Schwartz Lasson Harris Ltd 2 Walnut Grove Dr . . . . . Horsham PA 19044 *Web:* slhcpas.com	215-956-9700		2
Schwartz Levine & Kaplan 7 Penn Plz Ste 210 . . . . . New York NY 10001 *Web:* slklawfirm.com	646-518-7273		41
Schwartz Levitsky Feldman Ch A 2300 Yonge St Ste 1500 PO Box 2434 . . . . . Toronto ON M4P1E4 *Web:* www.slf.ca	416-785-5353		445
Schwartz Machine Co 4441 E 8 Mile Rd . . . . . Warren MI 48091 *Web:* www.schwartzmachine.com	586-756-2300	756-3792	454
Schwartz Semerdjian Ballard & Cauley LLP 101 W Broadway Ste 810 . . . . . San Diego CA 92101 *Web:* www.schwartzsemerdjian.com	619-236-8821		428
Schwarz 8338 Austin Ave . . . . . Morton Grove IL 60053 **Fax Area Code:* 847 ■ *TF:* 800-323-4903 ■ *Web:* www.schwarz.com	800-323-4903	966-1271*	559
Schwarz Gallery 1806 Chestnut St . . . . . Philadelphia PA 19103 *Web:* www.schwarzgallery.com	215-563-4887	561-5621	42
Schwarze Industries Inc 1055 Jordan Rd . . . . . Huntsville AL 35811 *TF:* 800-879-7933 ■ *Web:* www.schwarze.com	800-879-7933		59
Schwebel Baking Co PO Box 6018 . . . . . Youngstown OH 44501 *TF:* 800-860-2867 ■ *Web:* schwebels.com	330-783-2860	782-1774	296-1
Schweikert David (Rep R - AZ) 1526 Longworth House Office Bldg . . . . . Washington DC 20515 *Web:* schweikert.house.gov	202-225-2190	225-0096	342-2
Schweitzer E. O. Manufacturing Company Inc 450 Enterprise Pkwy . . . . . Lake Zurich IL 60047 **Fax Area Code:* 509 ■ *Web:* selinc.com	847-362-8304	332-7990*	248
Schweitzer-Mauduit International Inc (SWM) 100 N Point Ctr E Ste 600 . . . . . Alpharetta GA 30022 *NYSE: SWM* ■ *Web:* www.swmintl.com	770-569-4200		557
Schweizer Dipple Inc 7227 Div St . . . . . Oakwood OH 44146 *Web:* www.schweizer-dipple.com	440-786-8090	786-8099	189-10
Schweizer Emblem Co 1022 Busse Hwy . . . . . Park Ridge IL 60068 *TF:* 800-942-5215 ■ *Web:* schweizer-emblem.com	847-292-1022	292-1028	258
Schwend Inc 28945 Johnston Rd . . . . . Dade City FL 33523 *TF:* 800-243-7757 ■ *Web:* www.schwendinc.com	352-588-2220	588-2221	779
Schwerdtle Stamp Co 166 Elm St . . . . . Bridgeport CT 06601 *TF:* 800-535-0004 ■ *Web:* schwerdtle.com	203-330-2750	330-2700	407
Schwing America Inc 5900 Centerville Rd . . . . . Saint Paul MN 55127 *Web:* schwing.com	651-429-0999		190
Schwing Bioset Inc 350 SMC Dr . . . . . Somerset WI 54025 *Web:* www.schwingbioset.com	715-247-3433		791
SCI (Sister Cities Intl) 1301 Pennsylvania Ave NW Ste 850 . . . . . Washington DC 20004 *Web:* sistercities.org	202-347-8630	393-6524	48-7
SCI (Smart Card Integrators Inc) 2424 N Ontario St . . . . . Burbank CA 91504 *Web:* www.sci-s.com	818-847-1022		178-12
SCI 180 Attwell Dr Ste 600 . . . . . Toronto ON M9W6A9 *TF:* 866-773-7735 ■ *Web:* www.sci.ca	416-401-3011		314
SCI (Service Communications Inc) 15223 NE 90th St . . . . . Redmond WA 98052 *TF:* 800-488-0468 ■ *Web:* www.servicecommunications.com	425-278-0300		179
SCI (Synergy Concepts Inc) PO Box 803088 . . . . . Dallas TX 75380 *TF:* 888-311-4499 ■ *Web:* www.synergyconcepts.com	972-385-3874		681
SCI Albion 10745 Rt 18 . . . . . Albion PA 16475 *Web:* www.cor.pa.gov	814-756-5778		213
SCI Global Structural Contours Inc PO Box 4970 . . . . . Greenwich CT 06830 *Web:* www.sciglobal.com	203-531-4400	531-4403	189-1
SCI Infrastructure LLC 2825 S 154th St . . . . . SeaTac WA 98188 *TF:* 800-255-0633 ■ *Web:* www.sciinfrastructure.com	206-242-0633	588-0494	191
SCI Solutions Inc 655 Campbell Technology Pky . . . . . Campbell CA 95008 *TF:* 800-472-4338 ■ *Web:* www.scisolutions.com	866-472-4338		178-1
Sciaky Inc 4915 W 67th St . . . . . Chicago IL 60638 *TF:* 877-450-2518 ■ *Web:* www.sciaky.com	708-594-3800	594-9213	811
Sciarabba Walker & Company LLP 410 E Upland Rd . . . . . Ithaca NY 14850 *Web:* swcllp.com	607-272-5550		2
SciCan Ltd 701 Technology Dr . . . . . Canonsburg PA 15317 *TF:* 800-572-1211 ■ *Web:* www.scicanusa.com	724-820-1600	820-1479	475
SciClone Pharmaceuticals Inc 950 Tower Ln Ste 900 . . . . . Foster City CA 94404 *NASDAQ: SCLN* ■ *TF:* 800-724-2566 ■ *Web:* www.sciclone.com	650-358-3456	358-3469	582
SCI-Coal Township 1 Kelley Dr . . . . . Coal Township PA 17866 *Web:* www.cor.pa.gov	570-644-7890		213
Scicom Data Services Ltd 10101 Bren Rd E . . . . . Minnetonka MN 55343	952-933-4200	936-4132	225
Scicom Infrastructure Services Inc 2250 N Druid Hills Rd NE Ste 238 . . . . . Atlanta GA 30329 *Web:* scicominfra.com	404-636-9882	636-9885	177
Scicon Technologies Corp 27525 Newhall Ranch Rd . . . . . Valencia CA 91355 *Web:* scicontech.com	661-295-8630		454
SCI-Dallas 1000 Follies Rd . . . . . Dallas PA 18612 *Web:* www.cor.pa.gov	570-675-1101		213
Sciemetric Instruments Inc 359 Terry Fox Dr Ste 100 . . . . . Ottawa ON K2K2E7 *Web:* www.sciemetric.com	613-254-7054		246
Science & Behavior Books Inc (SBB) PO Box 60519 . . . . . Palo Alto CA 94306 *TF:* 800-547-9982 ■ *Web:* www.sbbks.com	650-965-0954	965-8998	637-2
Science & Engineering Services 6992 Columbia Gateway Dr . . . . . Columbia MD 21046 *Web:* www.sesi-md.com	443-539-0139		544
Science and Humanities Press PO Box 7151 . . . . . Chesterfield MO 63006 *Web:* www.sciencehumanitiespress.com	636-394-4950		637-2
Science and Technology Associates Inc 4100 Fairfax Dr Ste 910 . . . . . Arlington VA 22203 *Web:* stassociates.com	703-522-5123	522-0367	463
Science Application International Corporation Inc (SAIC) 1710 SAIC Dr . . . . . McLean VA 22102 *TF:* 866-400-7242 ■ *Web:* www.saic.com	866-955-7242		178-5
Science Books & Films (SB&F) 1200 New York Ave NW . . . . . Washington DC 20005 *Web:* www.sbfonline.com	202-326-6417		637-2
Science Center of Iowa 401 W Martin Luther King Jr Pkwy . . . . . Des Moines IA 50309 *Web:* www.sciowa.org	515-274-6868	274-3404	520
Science Central 1950 N Clinton St . . . . . Fort Wayne IN 46805 *Web:* www.sciencecentral.org	260-424-2400	422-2899	520
Science Club for Girls Inc 136 Magazine St . . . . . Cambridge MA 02139 *Web:* www.scienceclubforgirls.org	617-391-0361		148
Science Factory Children's Museum & Planetarium 2300 Leo Harris Pkwy . . . . . Eugene OR 97401 *Web:* www.sciencefactory.org	541-682-7888		521
Science Fiction Continuum PO Box 154 . . . . . Colonia NJ 07067 *Web:* www.sfcontinuum.com	908-412-1800		95
Science Magazine 1200 New York Ave NW . . . . . Washington DC 20005 *TF:* 866-434-2227 ■ *Web:* www.sciencemag.org	202-326-6500	842-1065	457-19
Science Museum of Minnesota 120 W Kellogg Blvd . . . . . Saint Paul MN 55102 *TF:* 800-221-9444 ■ *Web:* new.smm.org	651-221-9444	221-4777	520
Science Museum of Viriginia 2500 W Broad St . . . . . Richmond VA 23220 *Web:* www.smv.org	804-864-1400		598
Science Museum Oklahoma 2020 Remington Pl . . . . . Oklahoma City OK 73111 *Web:* sciencemuseumok.org	405-602-6664		520
Science News 1719 North St NW . . . . . Washington DC 20036 *TF:* 800-552-4412 ■ *Web:* www.sciencenews.org	202-785-2255		457-19
Science Park Federal Credit Union 2 Amity Rd . . . . . New Haven CT 06510 *Web:* scienceparkfcu.org	203-786-5885		219
Science Publishers Inc 234 May St . . . . . Enfield NH 03748 *Web:* www.scipub.net	603-632-7377	632-5611	637-2
Science Spectrum-Omni Theater 2579 S Loop 289 . . . . . Lubbock TX 79423 *Web:* www.sciencespectrum.org	806-745-2525		520
ScienceCare Inc 21410 N 19th Ave Ste 126 . . . . . Phoenix AZ 85027 **Fax Area Code:* 602 ■ *TF:* 800-417-3747 ■ *Web:* www.sciencecare.com	800-417-3747	331-4344*	545
ScienceMedia Inc 6256 Greenwich Dr Ste 515 . . . . . San Diego CA 92122 *Web:* sciencemedia.com	858-625-9261	625-9262	344
Scienscope Inc 5751 Schaefer Ave . . . . . Chino CA 91710 *TF:* 800-216-1800 ■ *Web:* www.scienscope.com	909-590-7273	494-5513	201
Scientech Inc 5649 Arapahoe Ave . . . . . Boulder CO 80303 *TF:* 800-525-0522 ■ *Web:* scientech-inc.com	303-444-1361	444-9229	684
Scientia Global Inc 2210 Front St Ste 204 . . . . . Melbourne FL 32901 *Web:* www.scientiaglobal.com	321-733-1971		195
Scientific Brake and Equipment Co 314 W Genesee Ave . . . . . Saginaw MI 48602 *TF:* 800-292-0235 ■ *Web:* www.scientificbrake.com	989-755-4411	755-4469	61
Scientific Drilling Controls Inc 16701 Greenspoint Pk Dr Ste 200 . . . . . Houston TX 77060 *Web:* scientificdrilling.com	281-443-3300		540
Scientific Equipment & Furniture Assn (SEFA) 65 Hilton Ave . . . . . Garden City NY 11530 *TF:* 877-294-5424 ■ *Web:* www.sefalabs.com	516-294-5424	294-2758	49-19
Scientific Games Corp 6601 Bermuda Rd . . . . . Las Vegas NV 89119 *Web:* www.scientificgames.com	702-584-7700		52
Scientific Industries Inc 70 Orville Dr . . . . . Bohemia NY 11716 *TF:* 888-850-6208 ■ *Web:* www.scientificindustries.com	631-567-4700		419
Scientific Learning Corp 300 Frank H Ogawa Plz Ste 600 . . . . . Oakland CA 94612 *OTC: SCIL* ■ *TF:* 888-665-9707 ■ *Web:* www.scilearn.com	510-444-3500	444-3580	178-3
Scientific Marketing Services Inc 145 E Weymouth Rd . . . . . Landisville NJ 08326 *Web:* www.smsmktg.com	856-697-2341		4
Scientific Materials Corp 31948 Frontage Rd . . . . . Bozeman MT 59715 *Web:* www.scientificmaterials.com	406-585-3772	585-8606	425
Scientific Molding Corporation Ltd 330 SMC Dr . . . . . Somerset WI 54025 *Web:* www.smcltd.com	715-247-3500	247-3611	418
Scientific Polymer Products Inc 6265 Dean Pkwy . . . . . Ontario NY 14519 *Web:* www.scientificpolymer.com	585-265-0413	265-1390	605-2
Scientific Protein Laboratories Inc 700 E Main St . . . . . Waunakee WI 53597 *TF:* 800-334-4775 ■ *Web:* spl-pharma.com	608-849-5944		479
Scientific Software Tools Inc 1023 E Baltimore Pke Ste 100 . . . . . Media PA 19063 *Web:* www.sstnet.com	610-891-1640	891-8556	178-1
Scientific Systems Company Inc 500 W Cummings Pk Ste 3000 . . . . . Woburn MA 01801 *Web:* www.ssci.com	781-933-5355		256
Scientific Technologies Corp 4400 E Broadway Blvd Ste 705 . . . . . Tucson AZ 85711 *Web:* stchealth.com	520-202-3333		356
Scientist, The 478 Bay St Ste A213 . . . . . Midland ON L4R1K9 *TF:* 888-781-0328 ■ *Web:* www.the-scientist.com	705-528-6888		457-19
Sciforma Corp 4880 Stevens Creek Blvd Ste 102 . . . . . San Jose CA 95129 *TF:* 800-533-9876 ■ *Web:* www.sciforma.com	408-354-0144		178-1
SCI-Graterford PO Box 246 . . . . . Graterford PA 19426 **Fax Area Code:* 484 ■ *Web:* www.cor.pa.gov	610-489-4151	961-7907*	213
SCI-Greene 169 Progress Dr Staff . . . . . Waynesburg PA 15370 *Web:* www.cor.pa.gov	724-852-2902		213
SCI-Houtzdale PO Box 1000 . . . . . Houtzdale PA 16698 *Web:* www.cor.pa.gov	814-378-1000		213
SCI-Huntingdon 1100 Pike St . . . . . Huntingdon PA 16654 *Web:* www.cor.pa.gov	814-643-2400		213
SciImage Inc 4916 El Camino Real . . . . . Los Altos CA 94022 *Web:* scimage.com	650-694-4861		809

	Phone	Fax	Class
SCI-Mahanoy 301 Morea Rd ... Frackville PA 17932 *Web:* www.cor.pa.gov	570-773-2158		213
SCIMEDX Corp 100 Ford Rd ... Denville NJ 07834 *TF:* 800-221-5598 ■ *Web:* www.scimedx.com	973-625-8822	625-8796	231
SCI-Muncy PO Box 180 ... Muncy PA 17756 *Web:* www.cor.pa.gov	570-546-3171		213
Scio Mutual Telephone Assn 38770 N Main St PO Box 1100 ... Scio OR 97374 *Web:* smta.coop	503-394-3366		116
Scion Aviation LLC 3693 E County Rd 30 ... Fort Collins CO 80528 *Web:* www.scionaviation.com	970-207-1720		127
Scion Medical Technologies LLC 90 Oak St ... Newton MA 02464 *TF:* 888-582-6211 ■ *Web:* scionmedtech.com	888-582-6211		743
Scion Steel Inc 21555 Mullin Ave ... Warren MI 48089 *TF:* 800-288-2127 ■ *Web:* www.scionsteel.com	586-755-4000	757-5210	723
Scioto County 602 Seventh St Rm 103 ... Portsmouth OH 45662 *Web:* www.sciotocountydirectory.net	740-355-8313	353-7358	338
Scioto Downs Inc 6000 S High St ... Columbus OH 43207 *TF:* 800-589-9966 ■ *Web:* www.sciotodowns.com	614-295-4700	295-8871	642
Scioto Sign Company Inc 6047 US Rt 68 N ... Kenton OH 43326 *TF:* 800-572-4686 ■ *Web:* www.sciotosigns.com	419-673-1261	675-3298	701
Scioto Trail State Park 144 Lake Rd ... Chillicothe OH 45601 *Web:* trails.ohiodnr.gov	740-887-4818		565
SCIP (Strategic & Competitive Intelligence Professional) 7550 IH 10 W Ste 400 ... San Antonio TX 78229 *Web:* www.scip.org	703-739-0696	739-2524	49-12
Sci-Port Discovery Ctr 820 Clyde Fant Pkwy ... Shreveport LA 71101 *TF:* 877-724-7678 ■ *Web:* www.sci-port.org	318-424-3466	222-5592	520
Scireg Inc 12733 Directors Loop ... Woodbridge VA 22192 *Web:* scireg.com	703-494-6500		196
SCI-Retreat 660 SR 11 ... Hunlock Creek PA 18621 *Web:* www.cor.pa.gov	570-735-8754	733-1041	213
Sciro & Marotta PC 66 Hamilton St Ste 103 ... Paterson NJ 07505 *Web:* sciromarottalaw.com	973-279-7712		41
SCI-Rockview 1 Rockview Pl Rte 26 PO Box A ... Bellefonte PA 16823 *Web:* www.cor.pa.gov	814-355-4874		213
SCI-Smithfield 1120 Pike St PO Box 999 ... Huntingdon PA 16652 *Web:* www.cor.pa.gov	814-643-6520		213
SCI-Somerset 1590 Walters Mill Rd ... Somerset PA 15510 *Web:* www.cor.pa.gov	814-443-8100		213
Sci-Tek Consultants Inc 655 Rodi Rd Ste 303 ... Pittsburgh PA 15235 *Web:* scitekanswers.com	412-371-4460		261
Scitent Inc 400 Preston Ave Ste 300 ... Charlottesville VA 22903 *TF:* 844-571-4837 ■ *Web:* scitent.com	844-571-4837		180
Scivantage Inc 499 Washington Blvd 11th Fl ... Jersey City NJ 07310 *TF:* 866-724-8268 ■ *Web:* www.scivantage.com	646-452-0050	452-0049	174
SCI-Waymart PO Box 256 Ste 6 ... Waymart PA 18472 *Web:* www.cor.pa.gov	570-488-5811		213
SCL (Sumitomo Canada Ltd) 150 King St W Ste 2304 ... Toronto ON M5H1J9 *Web:* www.sumitomocanada.com	416-860-3800	365-3141	360-3
SCL Health 500 Eldorado Blvd Ste 4300 ... Broomfield CO 80021 *TF:* 866-877-4325 ■ *Web:* www.sclhealth.org	866-877-4325		353
SCLA (South Carolina Library Assn) PO Box 1763 ... Columbia SC 29202 *Web:* www.scla.org	803-252-1087	252-0589	435
Scleroderma Foundation 300 Rosewood Dr Ste 105 ... Danvers MA 01923 *TF:* 800-722-4673 ■ *Web:* www.scleroderma.org	978-463-5843	463-5809	48-17
SCM Elderbus Inc 124 Southbridge Rd ... Charlton MA 01507 *TF:* 800-321-0243 ■ *Web:* scmelderbus.org	800-321-0243		107
SCMS Inc 10201 Rodney Blvd ... Pineville NC 28134 *TF:* 800-438-6040 ■ *Web:* www.scmsinc.com	704-889-4508	889-4540	225
SCNA (South Carolina Nurses Assn) 1821 Gadsden St ... Columbia SC 29201 *Web:* www.scnurses.org	803-252-4781	779-3870	533
Scobre Educational 2255 Calle Clara ... La Jolla CA 92037 **Fax Area Code:* 858 ■ *TF:* 877-726-2734 ■ *Web:* www.scobre.com	877-726-2734	551-1232*	423
SCOLA 21557 270th St ... McClelland IA 51548 *Web:* scola.org	712-566-2202	566-2502	740
Scolaro, Shulman, Cohen, Fetter & Burstein PC Franklin Sq 507 Plum St Ste 300 ... Syracuse NY 13204 *Web:* www.scolaro.com	315-471-8111		428
Scoliosis Research Society 555 E Wells St Ste 1100 ... Milwaukee WI 53202 *Web:* www.srs.org	414-289-9107		138
Sconyer's Bar-B-Que 2250 Sconyers Way ... Augusta GA 30906 *Web:* sconyersbar-b-que.com	706-790-5411	790-1505	671
Sconza 1 Sconza Candy Ln ... Oakdale CA 95361 *Web:* sconza.com	209-845-3700	845-3737	296-8
Scope Infotech Inc 10420 Little Patuxent Pkwy Ste 550 ... Columbia MD 21044 *Web:* scopeinfotechinc.com	443-741-2680		180
Scope Services Inc 2095 Niles Rd ... Saint Joseph MI 49085 *Web:* www.scope-services.com	269-982-2888	983-8040	631
Scope Seven Inc 2201 Park Pl Ste 100 ... El Segundo CA 90245 *Web:* www.zoodigital.com	310-220-3939		514
Scopelitis, Garvin, Light, Hanson & Feary PLC 600 Republic Centre 633 Chestnut St ... Chattanooga TN 37450 **Fax Area Code:* 615 ■ *Web:* www.scopelitis.com	423-266-2769	247-9950*	428
Score 726 E Anaheim St ... Wilmington CA 90744 *TF:* 800-626-7774 ■ *Web:* scoresports.com	800-626-7774		155-19
Score a Goal in The Classroom 575 Diamond Bar Trl ... Aledo TX 76008 *Web:* scoreagoal.org	817-429-4024	882-9393	196
Score Assn 1175 Herndon Pkwy Ste 900 ... Herndon VA 20170 **Fax Area Code:* 703 ■ *TF:* 800-634-0245 ■ *Web:* www.score.org	800-634-0245	487-3066*	49-12
Score Technologies Inc 1221 Venture Dr ... Forest VA 24551 *Web:* www.scoretechnologies.com	949-232-5478		396
Scorpion Design Inc 27750 Entertainment Dr Ste 100 ... Valencia CA 91355 *TF:* 866-622-5648 ■ *Web:* www.scorpion.co	866-622-5648		180
Scorr Marketing 2201 Central Ave Ste A ... Kearney NE 68847 *Web:* www.scorrmarketing.com	308-237-5567	236-8208	636
Scosche Industries Inc PO Box 2901 ... Oxnard CA 93034 **Fax Area Code:* 805 ■ *TF:* 800-363-4490 ■ *Web:* www.scosche.com	800-363-4490	486-9996*	253
Scot Forge Co 8001 Winn Rd PO Box 8 ... Spring Grove IL 60081 *TF:* 800-435-6621 ■ *Web:* www.scotforge.com	847-587-1000	587-2000	483
Scot Pump 6437 Pioneer Rd PO Box 286 ... Cedarburg WI 53012 *Web:* www.scotpump.com	262-377-7000	377-7330	641
Scotch 'N Sirloin, The 3999 Maple ... Amherst NY 14226 *Web:* scotchnsirloinrestaurant.net	716-837-4900		671
Scotch Lumber Co 119 W Main St PO Box 38 ... Fulton AL 36446 *Web:* scotchplywood.com	334-636-4424		683
Scotch Malt Whiskey Society 261 Madison Ave 9th Fl ... New York NY 10016 *Web:* www.smwsa.com	646-844-1154		354
Scotch Plains-Fanwood Board of Education 667 Westfield Rd ... Scotch Plains NJ 07076 *Web:* www.spfk12.org	908-889-5331		685
Scotchman Industries Inc 180 E Hwy 14 ... Philip SD 57567 *TF:* 800-843-8844 ■ *Web:* www.scotchman.com	605-859-2542	859-2499	493
Scotiabank 250 Vesey St 23rd & 24th Fl ... New York NY 10281 *TF:* 877-294-3435 ■ *Web:* www.gbm.scotiabank.com	212-225-5000	225-5090	690
Scotland County PO Box 489 ... Laurinburg NC 28353 *TF:* 800-913-6109 ■ *Web:* www.scotlandcounty.org	910-277-2406	277-2411	338
Scotland County 117 S Market St ... Memphis MO 63555 *Web:* www.scotlandcountymo.org	660-465-8605		338
Scotland Manufacturing Inc 22261 Skyway Church Rd ... Laurinburg NC 28353 *Web:* www.scotlandmanufacturing.com	910-844-3956		488
Scotland Memorial Hospital 500 Lauchwood Dr ... Laurinburg NC 28352 *TF:* 800-557-9249 ■ *Web:* www.scotlandhealth.org	910-291-7000		374-3
Scotland Yard Store 802 Magnolia Ave ... Shelbyville KY 40065 *TF:* 800-636-0116 ■ *Web:* www.scotyard.com	502-633-9288		594
Scotsman Ice Systems 775 Corporate Woods Pkwy ... Vernon Hills IL 60061 *TF:* 800-726-8762 ■ *Web:* www.scotsman-ice.com	847-215-4500	913-9844	664
Scott & Company LLC 1441 Main St Ste 800 ... Columbia SC 29202 *Web:* scottandco.com	803-256-6021		2
Scott & Shuman PA 33292 Coastal Hwy Ste 3 ... Bethany Beach DE 19930 *Web:* scottshumanlaw.com	302-537-1147	537-1174	41
Scott + Hespen Law PLLC 2356 University Ave W Ste 400 ... Saint Paul MN 55114 *TF:* 866-442-3092 ■ *Web:* www.scotthespenlaw.com	651-968-1457	647-9544	428
Scott Air Force Base 101 Heritage Dr Ste 210 ... Scott AFB IL 62225 *Web:* www.scott.af.mil	618-256-6311		497-1
Scott Arboretum of Swarthmore College 500 College Ave ... Swarthmore PA 19081 *Web:* www.scottarboretum.org	610-328-8025		97
Scott Austin (Rep R - GA) 2417 Rayburn House Office Bldg ... Washington DC 20515 *Web:* austinscott.house.gov	202-225-6531	225-3013	342-2
Scott Brown Media Group 645 Pressley Rd Ste D ... Charlotte NC 28217 *TF:* 800-760-1870 ■ *Web:* www.sbmg.com	800-760-1870		7
Scott Builders Inc 8105 - 49 Ave Close ... Red Deer AB T4P2V5 *TF:* 877-343-5232 ■ *Web:* www.scottbuilders.com	403-343-7270	346-4310	186
Scott C. Gottlieb 29 Riverside Dr ... Binghamton NY 13905 *Web:* scottgottlieblaw.com	607-724-7700		2
Scott College of Cosmetology 1502 Market St ... Wheeling WV 26003 *Web:* www.scott-college.com	304-232-7798		167-3
Scott Construction Inc 560 Munroe Ave ... Lake Delton WI 53940 *TF:* 800-843-1556 ■ *Web:* www.scottconstructioninc.com	608-254-2555	254-2249	188-4
Scott County 131 S Winchester St PO Box 188 ... Benton MO 63736 *Web:* www.scottcountymo.com	573-545-3549	545-3540	338
Scott County 416 W 4th St ... Davenport IA 52801 *Web:* www.scottcountyiowa.com	563-326-8647	326-8298	338
Scott County 151 Erle Johnston Dr ... Forest MS 39074 *Web:* cityofforest.com	601-469-2928		338
Scott County 336 Water St ... Gate City VA 24251 *Web:* www.scottcountyva.com	276-386-6521	386-9198	338
Scott County 101 E Main St Ste 210 ... Georgetown KY 40324 *Web:* scottky.gov	502-863-7850	863-7852	338
Scott County 282 Ct St ... Huntsville TN 37756 *Web:* www.scottcounty.com	423-663-2588		338
Scott County 210 W Fourth S Ste 1 ... Scott City KS 67871 *Web:* www.scott.k-state.edu	620-872-2640		338
Scott County 200 Fourth Ave W ... Shakopee MN 55379 *Web:* www.co.scott.mn.us	952-445-7750		338
Scott County 207 Washington St ... Waldron AR 72958 *Web:* scottcountyar.com	479-637-2642	637-0124	338
Scott County 35 E Market St ... Winchester IL 62694 *Web:* www.illinoiscourts.gov	217-742-5217	742-5853	338
Scott County Animal Hospital PC 115 S 16th Ave ... Eldridge IA 52748 *Web:* scottcountyanimalhospital.com	563-285-8624		794
Scott County Library System 1615 Weston Ct ... Shakopee MN 55379 *TF:* 877-772-8346 ■ *Web:* www.scottlib.org	952-707-1770		434-3

	Phone	Fax	Class
Scott County Library System 200 N 6th Ave ... Eldridge IA 52748 *Web:* www.scottcountylibrary.org	563-285-4794	285-4743	434-3
Scott Danahy Naylon Company Inc (SDN) 300 Spindrift Dr ... Williamsville NY 14221 *TF:* 800-728-6362 ■ *Web:* www.sdnins.com	716-633-3400	633-4306	390
Scott David (Rep D - GA) 225 Cannon House Office Bldg ... Washington DC 20515 *Web:* davidscott.house.gov	202-225-2939	225-4628	342-2
Scott E. Grosser PSC 9 Highland Ave ... Fort Thomas KY 41075 *Web:* scottgrossercpas.com	859-781-7982		2
Scott Electric 1000 S Main St PO Box S ... Greensburg PA 15601 **Fax Area Code:* 800 ■ *TF:* 800-442-8045 ■ *Web:* www.scottelectricusa.com	724-834-4321	426-9598*	246
Scott Enterprises Inc 2225 Downs Dr 6th Fl Executive Stes ... Erie PA 16509 *TF:* 877-866-3445 ■ *Web:* www.visitscott.com	814-868-9500		387
Scott Equipment Co 605 Fourth Ave NW ... New Prague MN 56071 *Web:* www.scottequipment.com	952-758-2591		298
Scott Family of Dealerships 3333 Lehigh St ... Allentown PA 18103 *TF:* 888-884-0318 ■ *Web:* www.scottcars.com	888-884-0318		57
Scott Fetzer Co 28800 Clemens Rd ... Westlake OH 44145 *Web:* www.scottfetzer.com	440-892-3000	892-3033	386
Scott Fetzer Co *Scot Laboratories Div* 16841 Pk Cir Dr ... Chagrin Falls OH 44023 *TF:* 800-486-7268 ■ *Web:* www.scotlabs.com	440-543-3033		151
Scott Fly Rod Co 2355 Air Pk Way ... Montrose CO 81401 *TF:* 800-728-7208 ■ *Web:* www.scottflyrod.com	970-249-3180	249-4172	710
Scott H. Marcus & Assoc 121 Johnson Rd ... Turnersville NJ 08012 *Web:* marcuslaw.net	856-227-0800	227-7939	445
Scott Health & Safety *3M Scott Fire & Safety* 4320 Goldmine Rd PO Box 569 ... Monroe NC 28110 *TF:* 800-247-7257 ■ *Web:* www.3mscott.com	704-291-8300	291-8340	576
Scott Howell & Company Inc 3900 Willow St Ste 200 ... Dallas TX 75226 *Web:* www.scotthowell.com	214-951-9494	688-0555	4
Scott Hulse Marshall Feuille Finger & Thurmond Library 1100 Chase Twr 201 E Main Dr ... El Paso TX 79901 *Web:* www.scotthulse.com	915-533-2493	546-8333	434-3
Scott Industrial Systems Inc 4433 Interpoint Blvd ... Dayton OH 45424 **Fax Area Code:* 800 ■ *Web:* www.scottindustrialsystems.com	937-233-8146	416-6023*	470
Scott Industries Inc 1573 Hwy 136 W PO Box 7 ... Henderson KY 42419 *TF:* 800-951-9276 ■ *Web:* www.scott-mfg.com	270-831-2037	831-2039	389
Scott Insurance 1301 Old Graves Mill Rd ... Lynchburg VA 24502 *TF:* 800-365-0101 ■ *Web:* scottins.com	434-832-2100		391-4
Scott Joplin House State Historic Site 2658 Delmar Blvd ... Saint Louis MO 63103 *Web:* mostateparks.com	314-340-5790		565
Scott Logistics Corp PO Box 391 ... Rome GA 30162 *TF:* 800-893-6689 ■ *Web:* www.scottlogistics.com	706-234-1184		311
Scott M. Sandler PA 75 Valencia Ave Ste 400 ... Miami FL 33134 *Web:* scottsandlerlawoffice.com	305-858-1622		41
Scott Machine Inc 4025 Morrill Rd ... Jackson MI 49201 *Web:* www.scottmachineinc.com	517-787-6616	787-6632	22
Scott Madden & Associates Inc 2626 Glenwood Ave Ste 480 ... Raleigh NC 27608 *Web:* www.scottmadden.com	919-781-4191		194
Scott Memorial Library 1020 Walnut St ... Philadelphia PA 19107 *Web:* library.jefferson.edu	215-503-6994	923-3203	434-1
Scott Petroleum Corporation Inc 102 Main St ... Itta Bena MS 38941 *Web:* www.scottpetroleuminc.com	662-254-9024		581
Scott Powers Stuidos Inc 381 Park Ave S Ste 809 ... New York NY 10016 *Web:* scottpowers.com	212-242-4700		514
Scott Public Relations 21201 Victory Blvd Ste 270 ... Canoga Park CA 91303 *Web:* scottpublicrelations.com	818-610-0270		636
Scott Resort & Spa, The 4925 N Scottsdale Rd ... Scottsdale AZ 85251 **Fax Area Code:* 480 ■ *TF:* 800-528-7867 ■ *Web:* www.thescottresort.com	800-528-7867	946-4056*	707
Scott Rice Office Works 14720 W 105th St ... Lenexa KS 66215 *Web:* www.scottrice.com	913-888-7600		321
Scott Rick (Sen R - FL) 716 Hart Senate Office Bldg ... Washington DC 20510 *Web:* www.rickscott.senate.gov	202-224-5274		342-2
Scott Robert C (Rep D - VA) 1201 Longworth House Office Bldg ... Washington DC 20515 *Web:* bobbyscott.house.gov	202-225-8351	225-8354	342-2
Scott S. Loomis 4439 Spencer Hwy ... Pasadena TX 77504 *Web:* scottloomis.net	713-477-1151		390
Scott Safety Supply Services Inc 5012 Caxton St W PO Box 1983 ... Whitecourt AB T7S1P7 *TF:* 888-517-3389 ■ *Web:* www.scottsafety.ca	780-778-3389		538
Scott Sheldon LLC 1375 S Main St Ste 203 ... North Canton OH 44720 *TF:* 844-835-2527 ■ *Web:* www.scott-sheldon.com	234-347-0689	347-0919	463
Scott Swimming Pools Inc 75 Washington Rd ... Woodbury CT 06798 *Web:* www.scottpools.com	203-263-2108		186
Scott Tim (Sen R - SC) 104 Hart Senate Office Bldg ... Washington DC 20510 *TF:* 855-425-6324 ■ *Web:* www.scott.senate.gov	202-224-6121	228-5143	342-2
Scott Transportation Inc 400 SW Bluff Dr Ste 101 ... Bend OR 97702 *TF:* 888-536-6555 ■ *Web:* scotttransport.com	541-536-3636	536-8500	780
Scott Turbon Mixer Inc 9351 Industrial Way ... Adelanto CA 92301 *Web:* www.haywardgordon.com	760-246-3430		298
Scott USA Inc PO Box 2030 ... Sun Valley ID 83353 *TF:* 800-292-5874 ■ *Web:* www.scott-sports.com	208-622-1000	622-1005	710
Scott Yaw Associates LLC 1074 Park Ave ... Newtown PA 18940 *Web:* www.scottyaw.com	215-598-9977		195
Scott Yuill Insurance & Financial 2160 Sunset Blvd Ste 504 ... Rocklin CA 95765 *Web:* scottyuillagency.net	916-772-2131		390
Scott's Liquid Gold Inc 4880 Havana St ... Denver CO 80239 *OTC: SLGD* ■ *TF:* 800-447-1919 ■ *Web:* www.scottsliquidgold.com	303-373-4860		151
Scott's Seafood Grill & Bar 4800 Riverside Blvd ... Sacramento CA 95822 *Web:* www.scottsseafood.net	916-379-5959		671
Scott's Seafood Grill & Bar *Jack London Square* 2 Broadway ... Oakland CA 94607 *Web:* scottsjls.com	510-444-3456		671
Scott, Sullivan, Streetman & Fox PC 2450 Valleydale Rd ... Birmingham AL 35244 *Web:* sssandf.com	205-967-9675		41
Scottdale Bank & Trust 125 S Arch St ... Connellsville PA 15425 *Web:* www.midpennbank.com	724-628-3200		70
Scottdel Inc 400 Church St ... Swanton OH 43558 *TF:* 800-446-2341 ■ *Web:* www.scottdel.com	419-825-2341	825-1523	131
Scott-Hourigan Co 164 W Nobes Rd ... York NE 68467 *TF:* 800-284-7066 ■ *Web:* www.scotthourigan.com	800-284-7066		274
Scottish Heritage USA 315 Page Rd Ste 10 ... Pinehurst NC 28374 *Web:* scottishheritageusa.org	910-295-4448	295-3147	48-14
Scottish Re Inc 14120 Ballantyne Corporate Pl Ste 300 ... Charlotte NC 28277 *Web:* www.scottishre.com	704-542-9192	542-5744	360-4
Scottish Rite Cathedral 160 S Scott Ave ... Tucson AZ 85701 *Web:* tucsonscottishrite.org	520-622-8364		50-1
Scotts Bluff County 1825 10th St ... Gering NE 69341 *Web:* www.scottsbluffcounty.org	308-436-6600		338
Scotts Miracle-Gro Co 14111 Scottslawn Rd ... Marysville OH 43041 *NYSE: SMG* ■ *TF:* 800-543-8873 ■ *Web:* www.scotts.com	937-644-0011		280
Scotts Valley Unified School District Inc 4444 Scotts Valley Dr Ste 5b ... Scotts Valley CA 95066 *Web:* www.svusd.santacruz.k12.ca.us	831-438-1820	438-2314	685
Scottsdale Area Chamber of Commerce 7501 E McCormick Pkwy Ste 202-N ... Scottsdale AZ 85258 *Web:* www.scottsdalechamber.com	480-355-2700	355-2710	139
Scottsdale Camelback Resort 6302 E Camelback Rd ... Scottsdale AZ 85251 *TF:* 800-891-8585 ■ *Web:* www.scottsdalecamelback.com	480-947-3300		669
Scottsdale Center for the Performing Arts 7380 E Second St ... Scottsdale AZ 85251 *Web:* www.scottsdaleperformingarts.org	480-994-2787	874-4699	572
Scottsdale City Hall 7447 E Indian School Rd ... Scottsdale AZ 85251 *Web:* www.scottsdaleaz.gov	480-312-3111	312-2888	337
Scottsdale Community College 9000 E Chaparral Rd ... Scottsdale AZ 85256 *TF:* 800-784-2433 ■ *Web:* www.scottsdalecc.edu	480-423-6000	423-6200	162
Scottsdale Community Partners 5340 W Luke Ave ... Glendale AZ 85301 *Web:* scottsdalecommunitypartners.org	623-931-9131		194
Scottsdale Convention & Visitors Bureau 4343 N Scottsdale Rd Ste 170 ... Scottsdale AZ 85251 *TF:* 800-782-1117 ■ *Web:* www.experiencescottsdale.com	480-421-1004	421-9733	206
Scottsdale Gun Club 14860 N Northsight Blvd ... Scottsdale AZ 85260 *Web:* www.scottsdalegunclub.com	480-348-1111		711
Scottsdale Historical Museum 7333 E Scottsdale Mall ... Scottsdale AZ 85251 *Web:* www.scottsdalemuseum.com	480-945-4499		520
Scottsdale Museum of Contemporary Art (SMOCA) 7374 E Second St ... Scottsdale AZ 85251 *Web:* smoca.org	480-874-4666		520
Scottsdale Plaza Resort 7200 N Scottsdale Rd ... Scottsdale AZ 85253 *TF:* 800-832-2025 ■ *Web:* www.scottsdaleplaza.com	480-948-5000	998-5971	669
Scottsdale Stadium 7408 E Osborn Rd ... Scottsdale AZ 85251 *TF:* 877-229-5042 ■ *Web:* www.scottsdaleaz.gov	480-312-2586	312-7729	720
Scotty's Fashions Inc 636 Pen Argyl St ... Pen Argyl PA 18072 *Web:* www.scottysfashions.com	610-863-6454	863-6490	155-21
Scoular Co 2027 Dodge St ... Omaha NE 68102 *Web:* www.scoular.com	402-342-3500		275
Scout Boats Inc 2531 US 78 ... Summerville SC 29483 *Web:* www.scoutboats.com	843-821-0068	821-4786	90
Scout shop PO Box 7143 ... Charlotte NC 28241 *TF:* 800-323-0736 ■ *Web:* www.scoutshop.org	800-323-0736		791
Scouting Magazine 1325 W Walnut Hill Ln PO Box 152079 ... Irving TX 75015 **Fax Area Code:* 972 ■ *TF:* 866-584-6589 ■ *Web:* scoutingmagazine.org	866-584-6589	580-2079*	457-10
Scouts Canada 1345 Baseline Rd ... Ottawa ON K2C0A7 *TF:* 888-855-3336 ■ *Web:* www.scouts.ca	613-224-5134		775
Scovill Fasteners Inc 1802 Scovill Dr ... Clarkesville GA 30523 *TF:* 888-726-8455 ■ *Web:* www.scovill.com	706-754-1000	754-4000	594
Scovill Zoo 2450 US-Business Rt 51 ... Decatur IL 62521 *Web:* www.decatur-parks.org	217-421-7435		823
SCP (Standard Concrete Products Inc) PO Box 1360 ... Columbus GA 31902 *Web:* www.standardconcrete.net	706-322-3274		188-4
SCP (Odyssey Press) 1842 Santa Margarita Dr ... Fallbrook CA 92028 *Web:* www.roadtripeurope.com	760-826-3182		637-2

Name / Address	City	State	ZIP	Phone	Fax	Class
SCP Private Equity Partners 1200 Liberty Ridge Dr. *Web:* www.scppartners.com	Chesterbrook	PA	19087	610-995-2900	975-9546	405
SCPL (Switzerland County Public Library) 205 Ferry St *Web:* scpl.us	Vevay	IN	47043	812-427-3363	427-3654	434-3
SCPLL (Sacramento County Public Law Library) 609 9th St. *Web:* www.saclaw.org	Sacramento	CA	95814	916-874-6012	244-0699	434-3
SCPPA (Southern California Public Power Authority) 225 S Lake Ave Ste 1250 *Web:* www.scppa.org	Pasadena	CA	91101	626-793-9364	793-9461	787
SCPPD (South Central Public Power District) 275 S Main St PO Box 406 *TF:* 800-557-5254 ■ *Web:* southcentralppd.com	Nelson	NE	68961	402-225-2351		245
SCR Civil Construction LLC 5420 FM 2218 Rd. *Web:* www.scrconstruction.com	Richmond	TX	77469	281-344-0700	344-0099	186
SCR Molding Inc 2340 Pomona Rincon Rd. *Web:* www.scrmolding.com	Corona	CA	92880	951-736-5490		604
SC&RA (Specialized Carriers & Rigging Assn) 5870 Trinity Pkwy Ste 200 *Web:* www.scranet.org	Centreville	VA	20120	703-698-0291	698-0297	49-21
Scranton City Hall 340 N Washington Ave *Web:* www.scrantonpa.gov	Scranton	PA	18503	570-348-4100	348-4207	337
Scranton Counseling Center Inc 326 Adams Ave. *Web:* www.scrantonscc.org	Scranton	PA	18503	570-348-6100		353
Scranton Cultural Ctr 420 N Washington Ave *Web:* www.scrantonculturalcenter.org	Scranton	PA	18503	570-346-7369	346-7365	572
Scranton Motors Inc 777 Talcottville Rd *Web:* www.scrantonmotors.com	Vernon	CT	06066	860-375-8539		57
Scranton Products Inc 801 E Corey St *Web:* www.scrantonproducts.com	Scranton	PA	18505	570-348-0997		600
Scranton School District 425 N Washington Ave *Web:* www.scrsd.org	Scranton	PA	18503	570-348-3474	348-3563	685
Scranton Times-Tribune 149 Penn Ave. *TF:* 800-228-4637 ■ *Web:* thetimes-tribune.com	Scranton	PA	18503	570-348-9100	348-9135	532-2
Scrapbook Factory Inc 2004 W Hwy 50 Ste C.	O'Fallon	IL	62269	618-628-8877		270
Scratch Off Works 19537 Lake Rd *Web:* scratchoffworks.com	Cleveland	OH	44116	440-333-4302		627
Scream Agency LLC 1501 Wazee St Ste 1b *Web:* www.screamagency.com	Denver	CO	80202	303-893-8608		7
Screamer Co 419 W Johanna St 2nd Fl *Web:* screamerco.com	Austin	TX	78704	512-691-7894	691-7895	7
SCREC (Sullivan County Rural Electric Co-opeartive Inc) 5675 Rt 87 PO Box 65 *TF:* 800-570-5081 ■ *Web:* www.screc.com	Forksville	PA	18616	570-924-3381		245
Screen Graphics of Florida Inc 1801 N Andrews Ave. *TF:* 800-346-4420 ■ *Web:* www.screen-graphics.com	Pompano Beach	FL	33069	800-346-4420		687
Screen Media Ventures LLC 800 3rd Ave 3rd Fl *Web:* screenmedia.net	New York	NY	10022	212-308-1790	308-1791	511
Screen Tech Inc 470 Needles Dr. *Web:* screentechinc.com	San Jose	CA	95112	408-885-9750	885-8756	295
Screen Works 2201 W Fulton St *TF:* 800-294-8111 ■ *Web:* www.thescreenworks.com	Chicago	IL	60612	312-243-8265		722
Screenco Enterprises 9 Bell Rd. *Web:* www.screenco.biz	Selma	AL	36701	334-872-0051		627
Screeningone Inc 2233 W 190th St *TF:* 888-327-6511 ■ *Web:* www.screeningone.com	Torrance	CA	90504	888-327-6511		218
Screenmobile Corp 72-050A Corporate Way *Web:* www.screenmobile.com	Thousand Palms	CA	92276	760-343-3500		310
ScreenPlay Inc 3411 Thorndyke Ave W *Web:* www.screenplayinc.com	Seattle	WA	98119	206-625-9901		5
ScreenScape Networks Inc 133 Queen St 3rd Fl *Fax Area Code: 902 ■ *TF:* 877-666-1975 ■ *Web:* www.screenscape.com	Charlottetown	PE	C1A4B3	877-666-1975	368-3706*	7
Screven County 101 S Main St *Web:* screvencounty.com	Sylvania	GA	30467	912-564-7878		338
Screw Conveyor Corp 700 Hoffman St. *Web:* www.screwconveyor.com	Hammond	IN	46327	219-931-1450	931-0209	207
SCRI International Inc 2023 N Atlantic Ave Ste 310 *Web:* scri.com	Cocoa Beach	FL	32931	321-868-8273	799-3052	466
Scribe Inc 842 S Second St *Web:* scribenet.com	Philadelphia	PA	19147	215-336-5094		196
Scribe Media PO Box 6293 *Web:* www.radioscribe.com	Madison	WI	53716	608-628-8609		96
Scribendi Inc 405 Riverview Dr Ste 304 *TF:* 877-351-1626 ■ *Web:* www.scribendi.com	Chatham-Kent	ON	N7M0N3	519-351-1626		393
Scribner Associates Inc 150 E Connecticut Ave *TF:* 800-566-8228 ■ *Web:* www.scribner.com	Southern Pines	NC	28387	910-695-8884	695-8886	757
Scribner Cohen & Company SC 400 E Mason St Ste 300 *TF:* 888-730-0045 ■ *Web:* scribnercohen.com	Milwaukee	WI	53202	414-271-1700		2
Scribner, Hall & Thompson LLP 1030 15th St NW Ste 700 E *Web:* scribnerhall.com	Washington	DC	20005	202-331-8585		41
Scripps College 1030 Columbia Ave. *TF:* 800-770-1333 ■ *Web:* www.scrippscollege.edu	Claremont	CA	91711	909-621-8149	607-7508	166
Scripps Howard Foundation 312 Walnut St Ste 2800 *Web:* www.scripps.com	Cincinnati	OH	45202	513-977-3035		304
Scripps Institution of Oceanography (SIO) 8622 Kennel Way 9500 Gilman Dr MC 0210 *Web:* scripps.ucsd.edu	La Jolla	CA	92037	858-534-3624		668
Scripps Laboratories Inc 6838 Flanders Dr *Web:* www.scrippslabs.com	San Diego	CA	92121	858-546-5800	546-5812	231
Scripps Media 1090 Vermont Ave NW Ste 1000. *Web:* www.shns.com	Washington	DC	20005	202-408-1484	408-2062	530
Scripps Networks LLC 9721 Sherrill Blvd. *Web:* www.diynetwork.com	Knoxville	TN	37932	865-694-2700		740
Scripps Ranch Swim & Racquet Club 9875 Aviary Dr *Web:* www.srsrc.com	San Diego	CA	92131	858-271-6222		354
Scripps Research Institute 10550 N Torrey Pines Rd *Web:* www.scripps.edu	La Jolla	CA	92037	858-784-1000	784-2802	668
Script to Screen Productions 200 N Tustin Ave Ste 200 *Web:* www.scripttoscreen.com	Santa Ana	CA	92705	714-558-3971		514
Scriptorium Publishing Services Inc 2605 Meridian Pky Ste 110 *Fax Area Code: 815 ■ *TF:* 866-605-9677 ■ *Web:* www.scriptorium.com	Durham	NC	27713	919-481-2701	331-0695*	177
ScripType Publishing Inc 4300 W Streetsboro Rd. *Web:* www.scriptype.com	Richfield	OH	44286	330-659-0303	659-9488	637-9
SCRMC (South Central Regional Medical Ctr) 1220 Jefferson St *Web:* scrmc.com	Laurel	MS	39440	601-426-4000		374-3
ScrubaDub Auto Wash Centers Inc 172 Worcester Rd *Web:* www.scrubadub.com	Natick	MA	01760	508-650-1155	655-9261	62-1
Scrugg's Barbeque 7529 Moores Mill Rd *Web:* www.scruggsbbq.com	Huntsville	AL	35811	256-859-6800		671
Scruggs Company Inc PO Box 2065 *TF:* 800-230-7263 ■ *Web:* scruggscompany.com	Valdosta	GA	31604	229-242-2388	242-7109	188-4
Scruggs Equipment Co 1940 Channel Ave *TF:* 888-942-9311 ■ *Web:* www.scruggsequipment.net	Memphis	TN	38113	901-942-9311		61
SCS (Structural Component Systems Inc) 1255 Front St *TF:* 800-844-5622 ■ *Web:* www.scstruss.com	Fremont	NE	68026	402-721-5622		187
SCS Engineers 3900 Kilroy Airport Way Ste 100 *TF:* 800-326-9544 ■ *Web:* www.scsengineers.com	Long Beach	CA	90806	562-426-9544	427-0805	261
SCSD (Sweetwater County School District 1) 3550 Foothill Blvd *Fax Area Code: 888 ■ *TF:* 888-503-5671 ■ *Web:* www.sweetwater1.org	Rock Springs	WY	82901	307-352-3400	503-7562*	780
SCSK USA Inc 300 Madison Ave 4th Fl *Web:* www.scskusa.com	New York	NY	10017	212-419-6500	297-2501	180
Scst Inc 6280 Riverdale St *Web:* www.scst.com	San Diego	CA	92120	619-280-4321	280-4717	743
SCT (Stockton Civic Theatre) 2312 Rose Marie Ln *Web:* www.sctlivetheatre.com	Stockton	CA	95207	209-473-2400	473-1502	573-4
SCTA (Springville Cooperative Telephone Association Inc) 207 Broadway *Web:* www.springvilletelephone.com	Springville	IA	52336	319-854-9960		224
SCTC (Society of Communications Technology Consultants) 230 Washington Ave Ext Ste 101 *TF:* 800-782-7670 ■ *Web:* www.sctcconsultants.org	Albany	NY	12203	800-782-7670	859-3205	49-20
SCTC (Southern California Trophy Co) 2515 S Broadway *Web:* www.socaltrophy.com	Los Angeles	CA	90007	213-746-8046	746-9180	45
SCTE (Society of Cable Telecommunications Engineers) 140 Philips Rd *TF:* 800-542-5040 ■ *Web:* www.scte.org	Exton	PA	19341	610-363-6888	363-5898	49-19
SCTELCOM (South Central Telephone Association Inc) 215 S Iliff *TF:* 877-723-6875 ■ *Web:* www.sctelcom.net	Medicine Lodge	KS	67104	620-930-1000		224
Scuba Centers of Michigan 3280 Fort St *Web:* www.scubacenters.com	Lincoln Park	MI	48146	313-388-3483		167-3
Scuba Com Inc 1752 Langley Ave *TF:* 800-347-2822 ■ *Web:* www.scuba.com	Irvine	CA	92614	949-221-9300		711
Scuba Emporium 16336 S 104th Ave *Web:* www.scubaemporium.com	Orland Park	IL	60467	708-226-1614	403-5447	167-3
Scully Capital Services Inc 1730 M St NW Ste 204 *Web:* www.scullycapital.com	Washington	DC	20036	202-775-3434		251
Scully Oil Company Inc 150 E Flint St PO Box 398 *Web:* scullyoil.com	Lyndon Station	WI	53944	608-666-2662	666-2239	449
Scully Signal Co 70 Industrial Way *TF:* 800-272-8559 ■ *Web:* www.scully.com	Wilmington	MA	01887	617-692-8600	692-8620	201
Sculpt Nouveau PO Box 460459 *TF:* 800-728-5787 ■ *Web:* www.sculptnouveau.com	Escondido	CA	92046	800-728-5787		192
Sculptimage Studio 406 Milton St. *Web:* www.sculptimage.com	Valparaiso	IN	46385	219-707-0012		192
SCUP (Society for College & University Planning) 339 E Liberty St Ste 300 *Web:* www.scup.org	Ann Arbor	MI	48104	734-669-3270	998-6532	49-5
Scurlock Industries of Springfield Inc 3401 W Commercial St. *Web:* www.scurlockindustries.com	Springfield	MO	65803	417-862-5088		183
Scurry County 1806 25th St Ste 300 *Web:* www.co.scurry.tx.us	Snyder	TX	79549	325-573-5332	573-7396	338
Scusset Beach State Reservation 20 Scusset Beach Rd *Web:* www.mass.gov	Sandwich	MA	02563	508-888-0859		565
SD Ireland Co 193 Industrial Ave *TF:* 800-339-4565 ■ *Web:* www.sdireland.com	Williston	VT	05495	802-863-6222		183
SD Richman Sons Inc 2435 Wheatsheaf Ln *Web:* www.sdrichmansons.com	Philadelphia	PA	19137	215-535-5100	288-1043	686
SDA Consulting Inc 3011 183rd St Ste 377 *TF:* 800-823-2990 ■ *Web:* www.sdaci.com	Homewood	IL	60430	800-823-2990		180
SDB Inc 1001 S Edward Dr *Web:* www.sdb.com	Tempe	AZ	85281	480-967-5810	967-5841	186
SDB Trade International LP 11200 Richmond Ave Ste 180 *Web:* www.thesdbgroup.com	Houston	TX	77082	713-475-0048		791

Name / Address	City	State	Zip	Phone	Fax	Class
SDC (Stainless Design Concepts Ltd) 1117 Kings Hwy *Web:* www.stainlessdesign.com	Saugerties	NY	12477	845-246-3631	246-1595	695
SDC (Seattle Design Ctr) 5701 6th Ave S Ste 378 *Web:* www.seattledesigncenter.com	Seattle	WA	98108	206-957-7016		361
SDC Technologies Inc 45 Parker Ste 100 *Web:* www.sdctech.com	Irvine	CA	92618	714-939-8300	939-8330	481
SDCC (Selkirk & District Chamber of Commerce) 200 Eaton Ave *Web:* www.selkirkanddistrictchamber.ca	Selkirk	MB	R1A0W6	204-482-7176	482-5448	137
SDCI (San Diego Culinary Institute) 8024 La Mesa Blvd *Web:* sandiegoculinary.edu	La Mesa	CA	91941	619-644-2100	644-2106	163
SDEB (San Diego Eye Bank) 9246 Lightwave Ave Ste 120 *TF:* 800-393-2265 ■ *Web:* www.sdeb.org	San Diego	CA	92123	858-694-0400	565-7368	269
SDG (Solution Design Group Inc) 7500 Olson Memorial Hwy *Web:* solutiondesign.com	Golden Valley	MN	55427	952-278-2500		809
SDG Advisors LLC 3369B S Wakefield St *Web:* sdgadvisors.org	Arlington	VA	22206	216-262-1669		194
SDG Corp 55 N Water St *Web:* www.sdgc.com	Norwalk	CT	06854	203-866-8886		317
SDG Inc 200 N Broadway St *Web:* www.sharpeclothing.com	Checotah	OK	74426	918-473-2233		157-2
SDG Systems LLC 330 Perry Hwy Ste 200 *Web:* sdgsystems.com	Harmony	PA	16037	724-452-9366		179
SDGFA (South Dakota Grain and Feed Assn) 320 E Capitol Ave *Web:* www.sdgfa.org	Pierre	SD	57501	605-224-2445	224-9913	139
SDI (System Dynamics International Inc) 560 Discovery Dr NW *Web:* www.sdi-inc.com	Huntsville	AL	35806	256-895-9000		261
SDI (Symbolic Displays Inc) 1917 E St Andrew Pl E *Web:* www.symbolicdisplays.com	Santa Ana	CA	92705	714-258-2811	258-2810	22
SDI 330 N Wabash Ave Ste 2000 *Web:* www.sditravel.com	Chicago	IL	60611	312-587-8200	587-7111	772
SDI Industries Inc 13000 Pierce St *Web:* sdi.systems	Pacoima	CA	91331	818-890-6002	890-2858	207
SDI Media 6060 Center Dr Ste 100 *Web:* www.sdimedia.com	Los Angeles	CA	90045	310-388-8800	388-8950	512
SDI Presence LLC 33 W Monroe Ste 400 *TF:* 888-968-7734 ■ *Web:* www.sdipresence.com	Chicago	IL	60603	312-580-7500	580-7600	693
SDI Technologies Inc 1299 Main St *TF:* 800-333-3092 ■ *Web:* sditechnologies.com	Rahway	NJ	07065	800-333-3092		52
SDK Laboratories 1000 Corey Rd *TF:* 877-464-0623 ■ *Web:* www.sdklabs.com	Hutchinson	KS	67501	620-665-5661		743
SDK Software Inc 11322 86th Ave N *Web:* www.sdksoft.com	Maple Grove	MN	55369	763-657-1189	657-1890	177
SDL Capital LP 4984 El Camino Real Ste 230 *Web:* www.sdlventures.com	Los Altos	CA	94022	650-559-9355	559-9353	401
SDLC Partners LP 1 PPG Pl Ste 3200 *Web:* www.sdlcpartners.com	Pittsburgh	PA	15222	412-251-0848		196
SDML (South Dakota Municipal League) 208 Island Dr *Web:* www.sdmunicipalleague.org	Fort Pierre	SD	57532	605-224-8654	224-8655	48-13
SDMS (Society of Diagnostic Medical Sonography) 2745 Dallas Pkwy *TF:* 800-229-9506 ■ *Web:* www.sdms.org	Plano	TX	75093	214-473-8057	473-8563	49-8
SDN (Scott Danahy Naylon Company Inc) 300 Spindrift Dr *TF:* 800-728-6362 ■ *Web:* www.sdnins.com	Williamsville	NY	14221	716-633-3400	633-4306	390
SDN Global Inc 11702 Blalock Forest *TF:* 800-555-6789 ■ *Web:* sdn.global	Houston	TX	77024	732-588-8996		177
SDNA (South Dakota Nurses Assn) PO Box 1015 **Fax Area Code:* 888 ■ *Web:* www.sdnursesassociation.org	Pierre	SD	57501	605-945-4265	600-1232*	533
SDPB (South Dakota Public Broadcasting) 555 N Dakota St PO Box 5000 *TF:* 800-456-0766 ■ *Web:* www.sdpb.org	Vermillion	SD	57069	605-677-5861	677-5010	632
SDR Plastics Inc 1 Plastics Ave *Web:* www.starplastics.com	Ravenswood	WV	26164	304-273-5326	273-5325	686
SDR Ventures Inc 5613 DTC Pkwy Ste 830 *Web:* sdrventures.com	Greenwood Village	CO	80111	720-221-9220		796
SDS Consulting Corp 3115 12 St NE Ste 310 *Web:* www.sdsconsulting.ca	Calgary	AB	T2E7J2	403-221-8077		449
SDS Lumber Co 123 Industrial Rd PO Box 266 *Web:* sdslumber.com	Bingen	WA	98605	509-493-2155	493-2535	613
SDS Pro LLC 1300 E 68th Ave Ste 208A *TF:* 888-673-7776 ■ *Web:* www.msdspro.com	Anchorage	AK	99518	907-272-6635	274-6635	178-1
SDSC (San Diego Supercomputer Ctr) 9500 Gilman Dr *TF:* 800-451-4515 ■ *Web:* www.sdsc.edu	La Jolla	CA	92093	858-534-5000	534-5056	668
SDSMA (South Dakota State Medical Assn) 2600 W 49th St Ste 200 *Web:* www.sdsma.org	Sioux Falls	SD	57105	605-336-1965	274-3274	457-16
SDSol Technologies 999 Ponce de Leon Blvd Ste 730 *Web:* www.sdsol.com	Coral Gables	FL	33134	305-274-2147		180
SDT North America Inc 1532 Ontario St *TF:* 800-667-5325 ■ *Web:* www.sdtnorthamerica.com	Cobourg	ON	K9A4R5	905-377-1313		358
SDV Construction Inc 6436 Edith Blvd NE *Web:* sdvconstruction.com	Albuquerque	NM	87107	505-883-3176		186
SDV Solutions Inc 5400 Discovery Park Blvd Ste 104 *Web:* sdvsolutions.us	Williamsburg	VA	23188	757-903-2068	282-7650	174
SE C Inc 91 Simmons Industrial Pl *Web:* www.simmonsengineeringcompany.com	Dallas	GA	30132	770-445-6085	443-9058	298
SE Technologies LLC 98 Vanadium Rd Bldg D *Web:* www.se-env.com	Bridgeville	PA	15017	412-221-1100	257-6103	261
SEA (Software Engineering of America Inc) 1230 Hempstead Tpke *TF:* 800-272-7322 ■ *Web:* seasoft.com	Franklin Square	NY	11010	516-328-7000	354-4015	178-12
Sea Blue 503 Hwy 17 N *Web:* www.seabluerestaurant.com	North Myrtle Beach	SC	29582	843-249-8800		671
Sea Box Inc 1 Sea Box Dr *Web:* www.seabox.com	Cinnaminson	NJ	08077	856-303-1101		770
Sea Breeze Inc 441 Rt 202 **Fax Area Code:* 973 ■ *TF:* 800-732-2733 ■ *Web:* www.seabreezesyrups.com	Towaco	NJ	07082	800-732-2733	334-2617*	296-15
Sea Cat Boats Inc 1005 Marina Rd *Web:* www.seacatboats.com	Titusville	FL	32796	321-268-2628		90
Sea Catch 1054 31st St NW *Web:* www.seacatchrestaurant.com	Washington	DC	20007	202-337-8855		671
Sea Chambers Motel 67 Shore Rd *Web:* www.seachambers.com	Ogunquit	ME	03907	207-646-9311		379
Sea Cloud Cruises Inc 282 Grand Ave Ste 3 *TF:* 888-732-2568 ■ *Web:* www.seacloud.com	Englewood	NJ	07631	201-227-9404	227-9424	220
Sea Com Corp 7030 220th St SW *Web:* www.seacomcorp.com	Mountlake Terrace	WA	98043	425-771-2182	771-2650	647
Sea Crest Resort & Conference Ctr 350 Quaker Rd *TF:* 800-225-3110 ■ *Web:* www.seacrestbeachhotel.com	North Falmouth	MA	02556	508-540-9400		669
Sea Eagle Boats Inc 19 N Columbia St Ste 1 *TF:* 800-748-8066 ■ *Web:* www.seaeagle.com	Port Jefferson	NY	11777	631-791-1799	473-7398	710
Sea Engineering Inc 863 N Nimitz *Web:* seaengineering.com	Honolulu	HI	96817	808-536-3603	536-3703	261
Sea Fare Expositions Inc 5350 30th Ave NW Ste D *Web:* chinaseafoodexpo.com	Seattle	WA	98107	206-789-5741	789-0504	466
Sea Fox Boat Company Inc 2550 Hwy 52 *Web:* www.seafoxboats.com	Moncks Corner	SC	29461	843-761-6090	761-6139	90
Sea Fresh USA Inc 45 All American Way *Web:* www.seafreshusa.com	North Kingstown	RI	02852	401-583-0200		296-14
Sea Gardens Beach & Tennis Resort 615 N Ocean Blvd *Web:* www.seagardens.com	Pompano Beach	FL	33062	954-943-6200		669
Sea Grant Assn (SGA) 5784 York Complex PO Box 1950 *Web:* www.sga.seagrant.org	Ocean Springs	MS	39566	207-581-1435	581-1426	48-13
Sea Gull Lighting Products LLC A Generations Brands Co 301 W Washington St *TF:* 800-347-5483 ■ *Web:* www.seagulllighting.com	Riverside	NJ	08075	800-519-4092		439
Sea Harvest Packing Co 4270 Us Hwy 17 N	Brunswick	GA	31525	912-264-3212	264-2749	296-14
Sea Island 100 Cloister Dr *TF:* 855-572-4975 ■ *Web:* seaisland.com	Sea Island	GA	31561	912-638-3611	638-5805	655
Sea Launch Company LLC 2700 Nimitz Rd *Web:* www.sea-launch.com	Long Beach	CA	90802	562-951-7000		504
Sea Life Minnesota LLC Mall of America 120 E Broadway *Web:* www.visitsealife.com	Bloomington	MN	55425	952-883-0202		823
Sea Life Park 41-202 Kalanianaole Hwy *Web:* www.sealifeparkhawaii.com	Waimanalo	HI	96795	808-259-2500		40
Sea Lion Caves 91560 Hwy 101 *Web:* www.sealioncaves.com	Florence	OR	97439	541-547-3111	547-3545	50-5
Sea Ltd 7349 Worthington-Galena Rd *TF:* 800-782-6851 ■ *Web:* sealimited.com	Columbus	OH	43085	800-782-6851		463
Sea Mar Community Health Ctr 1040 S Henderson St *TF:* 855-289-4503 ■ *Web:* www.seamar.org	Seattle	WA	98108	206-763-5277	788-3204	353
Sea Mist Resort 1200 S Ocean Blvd *TF:* 800-793-6507 ■ *Web:* www.myrtlebeachseamist.com	Myrtle Beach	SC	29577	843-448-1551		669
Sea Mountain Insurance Brokers Inc 19630 76th Ave W *TF:* 800-553-3624 ■ *Web:* sea-mountain.com	Lynnwood	WA	98036	425-775-1410	774-4177	390
Sea Palms Golf & Tennis Resort 5445 Frederica Rd *TF:* 800-841-6268 ■ *Web:* www.seapalms.com	Saint Simons Island	GA	31522	912-638-3351	634-8029	669
Sea Pearl Seafood Company Inc 14120 Shell Belt Rd *TF:* 800-872-8804 ■ *Web:* sea-pearl.com	Bayou La Batre	AL	36509	251-824-2129		393
Sea Pines Resort, The 32 Greenwood Dr *TF:* 866-561-8802 ■ *Web:* www.seapines.com	Hilton Head Island	SC	29928	843-785-3333		653
Sea Ranch Lodge 60 Sea Walk Dr PO Box 44 *TF:* 800-732-7262 ■ *Web:* www.searanchlodge.com	The Sea Ranch	CA	95497	707-785-2371		379
Sea Raven Press (SRP) PO Box 1484 *TF:* 800-925-1563 ■ *Web:* www.searavenpress.com	Spring Hill	TN	37174	800-925-1563		637-2
Sea Rim State Park PO Box 356 *Web:* tpwd.texas.gov	Sabine Pass	TX	77655	409-971-2559		565
Sea School 8440 4th St N *TF:* 800-237-8663 ■ *Web:* www.seaschool.com	Saint Petersburg	FL	33702	800-237-8663		685
Sea Sense Inc PO Box 48847 *Web:* www.seasenseboating.com	Saint Petersburg	FL	33743	727-289-6917		239
Sea Shepherd Conservation Society 1225 Wold Rd *Web:* seashepherd.org	Friday Harbor	WA	98250	360-370-5650		196
Sea Tow Services International Inc 1560 Youngs Ave PO Box 1178 *TF:* 800-473-2869 ■ *Web:* www.seatow.com	Southold	NY	11971	877-568-1672		465
Sea Trail Corp 75A Clubhouse Rd *TF:* 888-321-9048 ■ *Web:* www.seatrail.com	Sunset Beach	NC	28468	910-287-1100		653
Sea Venture Resort 100 Ocean View Ave *Web:* www.seaventure.com	Pismo Beach	CA	93449	805-773-4994	773-0924	669
Sea View Hotel 9909 Collins Ave *TF:* 800-447-1010 ■ *Web:* seaview-hotel.com	Bal Harbour	FL	33154	305-866-4441	866-1898	379
Sea Vision USA 4399 35th St N **Fax Area Code:* 800 ■ *TF:* 800-732-6275 ■ *Web:* www.seavisionusa.com	Saint Petersburg	FL	33714	727-525-6906	659-0284*	542

	Phone	Fax	Class
Sea Watch International Ltd 8978 Glebe Pk Dr ... Easton MD 21601 *Web:* www.seawatch.com	410-822-7500	822-1266	296-14
Sea Watch Restaurant 6002 N Ocean Blvd ... Fort Lauderdale FL 33308 *Web:* www.seawatchontheocean.com	954-781-2200		671
Seabee Corp 712 First St NW ... Hampton IA 50441 *Web:* www.seabeecylinders.com	641-456-4871	456-2387	223
Seaberg Industries Inc 2395 W Lake Blvd ... Davenport IA 52804 *Web:* www.seaberginc.com	563-445-2130	381-5031	454
Sea-Bird Scientific 620 Applegate St ... Philomath OR 97370 *Web:* www.seabird.com	541-929-5650		668
Seaboard Asphalt Products Co 3601 Fairfield Rd ... Baltimore MD 21226 *TF:* 800-536-0332 ■ *Web:* www.seaboardasphalt.com	410-355-0330	355-5864	46
Seaboard Corp 9000 W 67th St ... Shawnee Mission KS 66202 *NYSE: SEB* ■ *Web:* www.seaboardcorp.com	913-676-8800	676-8872	185
Seaboard Folding Box Company Inc 100 Simplex Dr PO Box 650 ... Westminster MA 01473 *TF:* 800-225-6313 ■ *Web:* www.seaboardbox.com	978-342-8921	342-1105	101
Seaboard Foods 9000 W 67th St Ste 200 ... Shawnee Mission KS 66202 *TF:* 800-262-7907 ■ *Web:* www.seaboardfoods.com	913-261-2600		10-6
Seaboard International Forest Products LLC 22F Cotton Rd ... Nashua NH 03063 *TF:* 800-669-6800 ■ *Web:* www.sifp.com	603-881-3700		191-3
Seaboard Marine 8001 NW 79th Ave ... Miami FL 33166 *TF:* 866-676-8886 ■ *Web:* www.seaboardmarine.com	305-863-4444	863-4400	313
Seaborn Health Care 8918 78th Ave ... Seminole FL 33777 *TF:* 800-335-6176 ■ *Web:* www.seabornhc.com	727-398-1710	392-0321	393
Seabridge Gold Inc 106 Front St E Ste 400 ... Toronto ON M5A1E1 *TSX: SEA* ■ *Web:* seabridgegold.net	416-367-9292	367-2711	502
Seabrook Bros & Sons Inc 85 Finley Rd ... Bridgeton NJ 08302 *Web:* www.seabrookfarms.com	856-455-8080	455-9282	296-21
Seabrook Island 3772 Seabrook Island Rd ... Seabrook Island SC 29455 *TF:* 866-650-7918 ■ *Web:* www.discoverseabrook.com	843-768-2500		669
Seabury Venture Partners PO Box 2249 ... Redwood City CA 94064 *Web:* seaburypartners.com	650-373-1030		528
SeaChange International Inc 50 Nagog Pk ... Acton MA 01720 *NASDAQ: SEAC* ■ *Web:* www.schange.com	978-897-0100	897-0132	647
Seacoast Banking Corporation of Florida PO Box 9012 ... Stuart FL 34995 *NASDAQ: SBCF* ■ *TF:* 800-706-9991 ■ *Web:* www.seacoastbanking.com	772-287-4000	288-6012	360-2
Seacoast Capital Partners 55 Ferncroft Rd ... Danvers MA 01923 *Web:* www.seacoastcapital.com	978-750-1300		402
Seacoast Commerce Bank 11939 Rancho Bernardo Rd Ste 200 ... San Diego CA 92128 **Fax Area Code: 760* ■ *TF:* 877-531-5745 ■ *Web:* sccombank.com	858-432-7000	448-2858*	70
Seacoast Laboratory Data Systems Inc 195 New Hampshire Ave Ste 140 ... Portsmouth NH 03801 *Web:* www.sldsi.com	603-431-4114		177
Seacoast Media Group 111 New Hampshire Ave ... Portsmouth NH 03801 *TF:* 800-439-0303 ■ *Web:* www.seacoastonline.com	800-439-0303		532-3
Seacoast School of Technology 40 Linden St ... Exeter NH 03833 *Web:* www.seacoasttech.com	603-775-8461	775-8983	685
Seacoast Science Center Inc 570 Ocean Blvd ... Rye NH 03870 *Web:* www.seacoastsciencecenter.org	603-436-8043	433-2235	520
Seacoast Suites Hotel 5101 Collins Ave ... Miami Beach FL 33140 *Web:* www.seacoastsuites.com	305-865-5152		379
Seacomm Erectors Inc 32527 SR 2 PO Box 1740 ... Sultan WA 98294 *Web:* www.seacomm.com	360-793-6564	793-4402	188-1
Seacon Engineering Associates Inc 716B Lakeside Dr W ... Mobile AL 36693 *Web:* www.seaconeng.com	251-662-0300		261
SEACOR Holdings Inc 2200 Eller Dr PO Box 13038 ... Fort Lauderdale FL 33316 *NYSE: CKH* ■ *TF:* 800-516-6203 ■ *Web:* www.seacorholdings.com	954-523-2200	524-9185	667
Seacrest Oceanfront Resort on the South Beach 803 S Ocean Blvd ... Myrtle Beach SC 29577 *TF:* 888-889-4037 ■ *Web:* www.myrtlebeach-resorts.com	888-889-4037		669
Seacrest Village 1001 Center St ... Little Egg Harbor Township NJ 08087 *Web:* www.seacrestvillagenj.com	609-296-9292		793
Sea-Dog Corp 3402 Smith Ave ... Everett WA 98201 *Web:* www.sea-dog.com	425-259-0194		770
SeaDream Yacht Club 601 Brickell Key Dr Ste 1050 ... Miami FL 33131 *TF:* 800-707-4911 ■ *Web:* seadream.com	305-631-6110		220
Seadrill Americas Inc 11210 Equity Dr Ste 150 ... Houston TX 77041 *Web:* www.seadrill.com	713-329-1150		540
Seafare of Williamsburg 1632 Richmond Rd ... Williamsburg VA 23185 *Web:* www.seafareofwilliamsburg.com	757-229-0099		671
Seafarer Motel 2079 Main St ... Chatham MA 02633 *Web:* www.chathamseafarer.com	508-432-1739		379
Seafood Producers Co-op 2875 Roeder Ave ... Bellingham WA 98225 *Web:* www.spcsales.com	360-733-0120	733-0513	296-14
Seafood Supply Co 1500 Griffin St E ... Dallas TX 75215 *Web:* www.seafoodsupplycompany.com	214-565-1851	421-2831	297-5
SeaGate Convention Ctr 401 Jefferson Ave ... Toledo OH 43604 *Web:* www.toledo-seagate.com	419-255-3300	255-7731	205
Seaglass Publishing PO Box 156 ... Bishopville MD 21813 *Web:* www.seaglasspublishing.com	410-778-4999	778-2365	637-2
Seagrave Fire Apparatus LLC 105 E 12th St ... Clintonville WI 54929 *Web:* seagrave.com	715-823-2141	823-5768	516
Seagull Book & Tape Inc 1720 S Redwood Rd ... Salt Lake City UT 84104 *TF:* 800-999-6257 ■ *Web:* www.seagullbook.com	877-324-8551		95
Seagull Environmental Training 900 NW 5th Ave ... Fort Lauderdale FL 33311 *TF:* 800-966-9933 ■ *Web:* seagull.comcastbiz.net	954-524-7208	524-2430	192
Seagull Printing Services Inc 6969 High Tech Dr ... Midvale UT 84047 *Web:* www.seagullprinting.com	801-565-1393		627
Seagull Scientific Inc 15325 SE 30th Pl Ste 100 ... Bellevue WA 98007 *TF:* 800-758-2001 ■ *Web:* seagullscientific.com	425-641-1408	641-1599	225
Seahorse Fitness Inc 69 Columbia St ... New York NY 10002 *Web:* www.seahorseswimclub.com	212-254-3651		354
Seal Beach Chamber & Business Assn 201 Eigth St Ste 110 ... Seal Beach CA 90740 *Web:* sealbeachchamber.org	562-799-0179	795-5637	139
Seal Methods Inc 11915 Shoemaker Ave ... Santa Fe Springs CA 90670 *TF:* 800-423-4777 ■ *Web:* sealmethodsinc.com	562-944-0291	946-9439	326
Seal Systems Inc 17505 N 79th Ave ... Glendale AZ 85308 **Fax Area Code: 602* ■ *Web:* www.sealsystems.com	865-380-0005	324-9658*	809
Sea-Land Chemical Co 821 Westpoint Pkwy ... Westlake OH 44145 *Web:* www.sealandchem.com	440-871-7887		146
Sealaska Corp 1 Sealaska Plz Ste 400 ... Juneau AK 99801 *TF:* 800-848-5921 ■ *Web:* www.sealaska.com	907-586-1512	586-2304	448
Sealco Commercial Vehicle Products Inc 215 E Watkins St ... Phoenix AZ 85004 **Fax Area Code: 800* ■ *Web:* www.sealcocvp.com	602-253-1007	222-2334*	60
Sealco Data Center Services Ltd 1751 International Pkwy Ste 115 ... Richardson TX 75081 *TF:* 800-283-5567 ■ *Web:* sealco.net	972-234-5567		104
Sea-Lect Plastic Corp 3420 Smith Ave ... Everett WA 98201 *Web:* sealectplastics.com	425-339-0288	339-1345	757
Sealed Air 100 Rogers Bridge Rd ... Duncan SC 29334 *TF:* 800-391-5645 ■ *Web:* www.sealedair.com	800-391-5645		548
Sealed Air Corp 200 Riverfront Blvd ... Elmwood Park NJ 07407 *NYSE: SEE* ■ *Web:* sealedair.com	201-791-7600		88
Sealed Unit Parts Company Inc 2230 Landmark Pl ... Allenwood NJ 08720 *TF:* 800-333-9125 ■ *Web:* www.supco.com	732-223-6644	223-1617	14
Sealeze 8000 Whitepine Rd ... North Chesterfield VA 23237 **Fax Area Code: 800* ■ *TF:* 800-787-7325 ■ *Web:* www.sealeze.com	804-743-0982	448-2908*	103
Sealift Inc 68 W Main St ... Oyster Bay NY 11771 *Web:* www.sealiftinc.com	516-922-1000		313
Sealing Devices Inc 4400 Walden Ave ... Lancaster NY 14086 *TF:* 800-727-3257 ■ *Web:* www.sealingdevices.com	716-684-7600	684-0760	326
Seals Unlimited Inc 6410 NE Jacobson St ... Hillsboro OR 97124 *TF:* 800-423-6644 ■ *Web:* www.sealsunlimited.com	503-690-6644	690-6688	326
Seals-Eastern Inc 134 Pearl St ... Red Bank NJ 07701 *Web:* www.sealseastern.com	732-747-9200		326
Seaman Corp 1000 Venture Blvd ... Wooster OH 44691 *TF:* 800-927-8578 ■ *Web:* www.seamancorp.com	330-262-1111	263-6950	745-2
Seaman Paper Company of Massachusetts 51 Main St ... Otter River MA 01436 *TF:* 800-784-7783 ■ *Web:* www.seamanpaper.com	978-632-1513	632-6319	557
Seaman Unified School District 345 901 NW Lyman Rd ... Topeka KS 66608 *Web:* www.seamanschools.org	785-575-8600		685
Seamans Capital Management LLC 80 Hayden Ave Ste 110 ... Lexington MA 02421 *Web:* www.seamanscapital.com	781-890-5225		401
Seamar Holdings LLC 13715 N Promenade Blvd ... Stafford TX 77477 *Web:* www.seamardivers.com	281-208-2522	208-2524	536
SEAMARK Asset Management Ltd 810-1801 Hollis St ... Halifax NS B3J3N4 *TF:* 888-303-5055 ■ *Web:* www.seamark.ca	902-423-9367	423-0726	528
SeaMates International Inc 316 Main St PO Box 436 ... East Rutherford NJ 07073 *TF:* 800-541-4538 ■ *Web:* seamates.com	201-896-8899		194
Seamen's Bank 221 Commercial St PO Box 659 ... Provincetown MA 02657 *TF:* 855-227-5347 ■ *Web:* www.seamensbank.com	508-487-0035	487-8421	70
Seamen's Church Institute 50 Broadway 26th Fl ... New York NY 10004 *TF:* 800-708-1998 ■ *Web:* www.seamenschurch.org	212-349-9090		167-3
Seamless Technologies Inc 35 Airport Rd ... Morristown NJ 00796 *Web:* www.seamlessti.com	973-326-8900		111
Seaport Capital LLC 40 Fulton St 27th Fl ... New York NY 10038 *Web:* www.seaportcapital.com	212-847-8900	320-0270	401
Seaport Group LLC, The *Research Div* 360 Madison Ave 22nd Fl ... New York NY 10017 *Web:* seaportglobal.com	212-616-7700		401
Seaport Hotel & World Trade Ctr 1 Seaport Ln ... Boston MA 02210 *TF:* 877-732-7678 ■ *Web:* www.seaportboston.com	617-385-4000	385-4001	379
Seaport Marina Hotel 6400 E Pacific Coast Hwy ... Long Beach CA 90803 *Web:* www.seaportmarinahotel.com	562-434-8451	598-6028	379
Seaport Meat Co 2533 Folex Way ... Spring Valley CA 91978 *Web:* www.seaportmeat.com	619-713-2278	713-2285	297-9
Seaport Securities Corp 60 Broad St Ste 3101 ... New York NY 10004 *Web:* seaportsecurities.com	212-482-8689	809-1107	691
Seaport Village 849 W Harbor Dr ... San Diego CA 92101 *Web:* www.seaportvillage.com	619-235-4014	696-0025	50-6
Seaquest State Park 3029 Spirit Lake Hwy ... Castle Rock WA 98611 *Web:* parks.state.wa.us	360-274-8633		565

Name / Address	City	State	ZIP	Phone	Fax	Class
SEARAC (Southeast Asia Resource Action Ctr) 1628 16th St NW	Washington	DC	20009	202-601-2960	667-6449	48-5
Web: www.searac.org						
Search Company Intl 7700 E Arapahoe Rd Ste 220	Centennial	CO	80112	303-863-1800	863-7767	635
TF: 800-727-2120 ■ *Web:* www.searchcompanyintl.com						
SEARCH Group Incorporated Library 7311 Greenhaven Dr Ste 270	Sacramento	CA	95831	916-392-2550	392-8440	434-3
Web: www.search.org						
Search Guru Inc, The 21887 Lorain Rd Ste 71	Cleveland	OH	44126	440-306-2418		260
Web: thesearchguru.com						
Search Network Ltd 1503 42nd St Ste 210	West Des Moines	IA	50266	515-223-1153		635
TF: 800-383-5050 ■ *Web:* www.searchnetworkltd.com						
Search Wizards Inc 15 Paradise Plz Ste 261	Sarasota	FL	34239	941-960-8815		260
Web: www.searchwizards.net						
SearchDex 17330 Preston Rd Ste 240B	Dallas	TX	75252	214-999-0889		463
Web: www.searchdex.com						
Searchlight Group Inc 708 Third Ave 44th St-Grand Central Fifth Fl	New York	NY	10017	212-425-4800		260
Web: www.searchlightjobs.com						
SearchLogix Group, The 2950 Cherokee St Bldg 1000	Kennesaw	GA	30144	770-517-2660		193
Web: www.searchlogixgroup.com						
Searchpros Staffing 6363 Auburn Blvd	Citrus Heights	CA	95621	916-721-6000		260
Web: spstaffing.com						
SearchTec Inc 314 N 12th St Ste 100	Philadelphia	PA	19107	215-963-0888	851-8775	635
TF: 800-528-8790 ■ *Web:* www.searchtec.com						
Searchwide Inc 680 Commerce Dr Ste 220	Woodbury	MN	55125	651-275-1370	275-1367	193
TF: 888-386-6390 ■ *Web:* searchwide.com						
Searchwright Inc 505 Montgomery St 10th Fl	San Francisco	CA	94111	415-538-1500	538-1501	260
Web: searchwright.com						
Searcy Beauty College 1004 S Main St	Searcy	AR	72143	501-268-6300		167-3
Web: www.searcybeautycollege.com						
Searcy County, Arkansas PO Box 1385	Marshall	AR	72650	870-448-2557		338
TF: 800-355-6111 ■ *Web:* searcycountyarkansas.org						
Searcy Denney Scarola Barnhart PO Box 3626	West Palm Beach	FL	33402	561-686-6300		428
TF: 800-780-8607 ■ *Web:* www.searcylaw.com						
Searing Industries Inc 8901 Arrow Rt	Rancho Cucamonga	CA	91730	909-948-3030		492
TF: 800-874-4412 ■ *Web:* www.searingindustries.com						
SEARK (Southeast Arkansas College) 1900 Hazel St	Pine Bluff	AR	71603	870-543-5900		162
TF: 888-732-7582 ■ *Web:* www.seark.edu						
Searles Valley Minerals 9401 Indian Creek Pkwy Ste 1000	Overland Park	KS	66210	913-344-9500		503-1
TF: 800-637-2775 ■ *Web:* www.svminerals.com						
Sears Imported Autos Inc 13500 Wayzata Blvd	Minnetonka	MN	55305	952-546-5301	546-2899	57
TF: 888-580-8791 ■ *Web:* www.searsimports.com						
Sears Manufacturing Co PO Box 3667	Davenport	IA	52808	563-383-2800	383-2819	689
TF: 800-553-3013 ■ *Web:* www.searsseating.com						
Sears Roebuck & Co 3333 Beverly Rd	Hoffman Estates	IL	60179	847-286-2500		229
TF: 800-349-4358 ■ *Web:* www.sears.com						
SEAS Education 955 Wallace Knob Ste 1	Mountain Home	AR	72654	877-221-7327	425-6968*	525
**Fax Area Code:* 870 ■ *TF:* 877-221-7327 ■ *Web:* seaseducation.com						
Seashore Food Distributors Inc 1 Satt Blvd PO Box 235	Rio Grande	NJ	08242	609-886-3100	886-7262	345
Web: www.seashorefood.com						
Seaside Civic & Convention Ctr 415 First Ave	Seaside	OR	97138	503-738-8585	738-0198	205
TF: 800-394-3303 ■ *Web:* www.seasideconvention.com						
Seaside Golf Vacations 218 Main St	North Myrtle Beach	SC	29582	877-732-6999		771
TF: 877-732-6999 ■ *Web:* www.seasidegolf.com						
Seasoned Chef Cooking School 999 Jasmine St Ste 100	Denver	CO	80220	303-377-3222		685
Web: www.theseasonedchef.com						
Seasons 52 7700 Sand Lake Rd	Orlando	FL	32819	407-354-5212		671
Web: www.seasons52.com						
Seasons Restaurant at Highland Lake Inn 86 Lilly Pad Ln	Flat Rock	NC	28731	828-696-9094		707
TF: 800-635-5101 ■ *Web:* www.hliresort.com						
Seasons Rotisserie & Grill 2031 Mountain Rd NW	Albuquerque	NM	87104	505-766-5100	766-5252	671
Web: seasonsabq.com						
Seasons-4 Inc 4500 Industrial Access Rd	Douglasville	GA	30134	770-489-0716	489-2938	14
Web: www.seasons4.net						
SeaSpace Corp 13000 Gregg St	Poway	CA	92064	858-746-1100	746-1199	647
Web: www.seaspace.com						
Seastrom Manufacturing Company Inc 456 Seastrom St	Twin Falls	ID	83301	208-737-4300		350
TF: 800-634-2356 ■ *Web:* www.seastrom-mfg.com						
Seat of the Soul Foundation PO Box 3310	Ashland	OR	97520	541-482-1515	482-9417	48-20
TF: 877-733-4279 ■ *Web:* seatofthesoul.com						
SeatGeek Stadium 7000 S Harlem Ave	Bridgeview	IL	60455	708-594-7200	496-6050	717
TF: 888-657-3473 ■ *Web:* www.seatgeekstadium.com						
Seatile Distributors Inc 800 Capital Circle SE Ste 11	Tallahassee	FL	32301	850-562-2888		191-1
Web: seatiledistributors.com						
Seats Inc 1515 Industrial St	Reedsburg	WI	53959	608-524-8261		689
TF: 800-443-0615 ■ *Web:* www.seatsinc.com						
Seattle Aquarium 1483 Alaskan Way Pier 59	Seattle	WA	98101	206-386-4300	386-4328	40
TF: 800-853-1964 ■ *Web:* www.seattleaquarium.org						
Seattle Art Museum 1300 First Ave	Seattle	WA	98101	206-654-3100	654-3135	520
Web: www.seattleartmuseum.org						
Seattle Athletic Club 2020 Western Ave	Seattle	WA	98121	206-443-1111		354
Web: www.sacdt.com						
Seattle Cancer Care Alliance 825 Eastlake Ave E PO Box 19023	Seattle	WA	98109	206-606-7222		769
TF: 800-804-8824 ■ *Web:* www.seattlecca.org						
Seattle Central College 1701 Broadway	Seattle	WA	98122	206-934-3800		167-3
Web: www.seattlecentral.edu						
Seattle Children's Hospital 4800 Sand Pt Way NE	Seattle	WA	98105	206-987-2000	987-5060	374-1
TF: 866-987-2000 ■ *Web:* www.seattlechildrens.org						
Seattle Chinese Post Inc 412 Maynard Ave S	Seattle	WA	98104	206-223-0623	223-0626	532-2
Web: www.nwasianweekly.com						
Seattle City Hall 600 Fourth Ave 2nd Fl	Seattle	WA	98104	206-684-8888	684-8587	337
Web: www.seattle.gov						
Seattle Daily Journal of Commerce PO Box 11050	Seattle	WA	98111	206-622-8272	622-8416	532-2
Web: www.djc.com						
Seattle Design Ctr (SDC) 5701 6th Ave S Ste 378	Seattle	WA	98108	206-957-7016		361
Web: www.seattledesigncenter.com						
Seattle Fish Co 6211 E 42nd Ave	Denver	CO	80216	303-329-9595		297-5
TF: 800-766-3787 ■ *Web:* www.seattlefish.com						
Seattle Foundation 1200 Fifth Ave Ste 1300	Seattle	WA	98101	206-622-2294	622-7673	303
Web: www.seattlefoundation.org						
Seattle Genetics Inc 21823 30th Dr SE	Bothell	WA	98021	425-527-4000	527-4001	85
NASDAQ: SGEN ■ *Web:* www.seattlegenetics.com						
Seattle Hospitality Group 100 W Harrison St Ste S-370	Seattle	WA	98119	206-623-2540		184
Web: www.shworldwide.com						
Seattle International Film Festival 305 Harrison St	Seattle	WA	98109	206-464-5830	264-7919	282
Web: www.siff.net						
Seattle Lighting Fixture Co 222 Second Ave Ext S	Seattle	WA	98104	206-622-4736		362
TF: 800-689-1000 ■ *Web:* www.seattlelighting.com						
Seattle Mailing Bureau Inc 21319 68th Ave S	Kent	WA	98032	206-431-5700		5
Web: seattlemailing.com						
Seattle Manufacturing Corp 6930 Salashan Pkwy	Ferndale	WA	98248	360-366-5534	366-5723	576
TF: 800-426-6251 ■ *Web:* smcgear.com						
Seattle Marathon Assn 1500 Westlake Ave N Ste 008	Seattle	WA	98109	206-729-3660		78
Web: www.seattlemarathon.org						
Seattle Mariners PO Box 4100	Seattle	WA	98194	206-346-4000		714-1
Web: www.seattle.mariners.mlb.com						
Seattle Metaphysical Library 2220 NW Market St L-05	Seattle	WA	98107	206-329-1794		434-3
Web: www.seattlemetaphysicallibrary.org						
Seattle Musical Theatre 7400 Sand Pt Way NE Ste 101-N	Seattle	WA	98115	206-363-2809		573-2
Web: www.seattlemusicaltheatre.org						
Seattle Opera 1020 John St	Seattle	WA	98109	206-389-7600	389-7651	573-2
TF: 800-426-1619 ■ *Web:* www.seattleopera.org						
Seattle Pacific University 3307 Third Ave W	Seattle	WA	98119	206-281-2000	281-2544	166
TF: 800-366-3344 ■ *Web:* www.spu.edu						
Seattle Post-Intelligencer 200 First Ave W Ste 230	Seattle	WA	98119	206-448-8030	448-8166	532-2
TF: 800-542-0820 ■ *Web:* www.seattlepi.com						
Seattle Public Library 1000 Fourth Ave	Seattle	WA	98104	206-386-4636	386-4119	434-3
Web: www.spl.org						
Seattle Public Schools Seattle Public Schools MS 32-149	Seattle	WA	98124	206-252-0000		685
Web: www.seattleschools.org						
Seattle Repertory Theatre (SRT) 155 Mercer St PO Box 900923	Seattle	WA	98109	206-443-2210	443-2379	573-4
TF: 877-900-9285 ■ *Web:* www.seattlerep.org						
Seattle Seahawks 12 Seahawks Way	Renton	WA	98056	888-635-4295		715-3
TF: 888-635-4295 ■ *Web:* www.seahawks.com						
Seattle Service Bureau Inc 18912 N Creek PKWY Ste 205	Seattle	WA	98133	206-533-0877	542-8994	160
Web: www.nsbi.net						
Seattle Snohomish Mill Company Inc 9525 Airport Way	Snohomish	WA	98296	360-568-2171		683
Seattle Sport Sciences Inc 24066 NE 53rd Pl	Redmond	WA	98053	425-939-0015		526
Web: www.seattlesportsciences.com						
Seattle Symphony 200 University St	Seattle	WA	98101	206-215-4700	215-4701	573-3
TF: 866-833-4747 ■ *Web:* seattlesymphony.org						
Seattle Tennis Club 922 Mcgilvra Blvd E	Seattle	WA	98112	206-324-3200		354
Web: seattletennisclub.org						
Seattle Theatre Group 911 Pine St	Seattle	WA	98101	206-467-5510		720
TF: 877-784-4849 ■ *Web:* www.stgpresents.org						
Seattle Times 1120 John St	Seattle	WA	98109	206-464-2111	464-2261	532-2
Web: www.seattletimes.com						
Seattle University 901 12th Ave	Seattle	WA	98122	206-296-6000	296-5656	166
TF: 800-426-7123 ■ *Web:* www.seattleu.edu						
Seattle University School of Law 901 12th Ave PO Box 222000	Seattle	WA	98122	206-398-4200	398-4058	167-1
Web: law.seattleu.edu						
Seattle Weekly 307 Third Ave S Ste 2	Seattle	WA	98104	206-623-0500	467-4338	532-5
Web: www.seattleweekly.com						
Seattle's Best Coffee LLC PO Box 3717	Seattle	WA	98124	800-611-7793		159
TF: 800-611-7793 ■ *Web:* seattlesbest.com						
Seattle's Convention & Visitors Bureau 701 Pike St Ste 800	Seattle	WA	98101	206-461-5800	461-5855	206
TF: 866-732-2695 ■ *Web:* www.visitseattle.org						
Seavin Inc 19239 US Hwy 27	Clermont	FL	34715	352-394-8627	394-7490	80-3
TF: 800-768-9463 ■ *Web:* lakeridgewinery.com						
Seaway Bank & Trust Co 645 E 87th St	Chicago	IL	60619	773-487-4800		70
TF: 877-369-2828 ■ *Web:* www.self-helpfcu.org						

Name / Address	City	State	ZIP	Phone	Fax	Class
Seaway Manufacturing Corp 2250 E 33rd St *TF:* 800-458-2244 ■ *Web:* www.seawaymfg.com	Erie	PA	16510	814-898-2255		234
Seaway Plastics Engineering LLC 6006 Siesta Ln *Web:* www.seawayplastics.com	Port Richey	FL	34668	727-845-3235		604
Seaway Printing Company Inc 1609 Western Ave *TF:* 800-622-3255 ■ *Web:* www.seawayprinting.com	Green Bay	WI	54303	920-468-1500		627
Seaways Publishing Inc PO Box 525 *TF:* 888-798-2194 ■ *Web:* www.seaways.com	Niwot	CO	80544	888-798-2194		637-9
SeaWorld Orlando 7007 Sea World Dr *Web:* seaworldparks.com	Orlando	FL	32821	407-545-5550		32
Seaworthy Publications Inc 2023 N Atlantic Ave Unit No 226 *Web:* www.seaworthy.com	Cocoa Beach	FL	32931	321-610-3634		637-2
Seay Oil Company Inc 700 W 15th St *Web:* www.seayoil.com	Hopkinsville	KY	42240	270-885-5488		579
Sebacia Inc 2905 Premiere Pkwy Ste 150 *Web:* www.sebacia.com	Duluth	GA	30097	678-417-7626	417-7325	475
Sebago Lake State Park 11 Pk Access Rd *Web:* www.maine.gov	Casco	ME	04015	207-693-6231		565
Sebago Lakes Region Chamber of Commerce (SLRCC) 909A Roosevelt Trl *Web:* www.sebagolakeschamber.com	Windham	ME	04062	207-892-8265	893-0110	139
Sebago Technics Inc 75 John Roberts Rd Ste 1A *Web:* sebago-technics.com	South Portland	ME	04106	207-200-2100		261
Sebago USA LLC 9341 Courtland Dr *TF:* 866-699-7367 ■ *Web:* www.sebago.com	Rockford	MI	49351	866-699-7367		301
Sebaly Shillito & Dyer 1900 Kettering Tower 40 N Main St *Web:* ssdlaw.com	Dayton	OH	45423	937-222-2500		428
Sebasco Harbor Resort 29 Keynon Rd **Fax Area Code: 207* ■ *TF:* 800-225-3819 ■ *Web:* www.sebasco.com	Phippsburg	ME	04562	877-389-1161	389-2004*	669
Sebastian 23990 Foresthill Rd *TF:* 800-450-1595 ■ *Web:* www.sebastiancorp.com	Foresthill	CA	95631	530-367-2222	367-3600	224
Sebastian County 35 S Sixth St Rm 105 *TF:* 800-637-9314 ■ *Web:* sebastiancountyar.gov	Fort Smith	AR	72901	479-782-5065	784-1567	338
Sebastian Inlet State Park 9700 S A1A *Web:* www.floridastateparks.org	Melbourne Beach	FL	32951	321-984-4852		565
Sebastian River Area Chamber of Commerce 700 Main St *Web:* www.sebastianchamber.com	Sebastian	FL	32958	772-589-5969	589-5993	139
Sebastian River Medical Ctr 13695 US Hwy 1 *Web:* www.sebastianrivermedical.org	Sebastian	FL	32958	772-589-3186		374-3
Sebastiani Vineyards Inc 389 Fourth St E *TF:* 855-232-2338 ■ *Web:* www.sebastiani.com	Sonoma	CA	95476	707-933-3230		80-3
Sebastopol Area Chamber of Commerce 265 S Main St *Web:* www.sebastopol.org	Sebastopol	CA	95472	707-823-3032		139
Sebastopol State Historic Site 704 Zorn St *Web:* www.seguintexas.gov	Seguin	TX	78155	830-379-4833		565
Sebewaing Tool & Engineering Co 415 Union St *TF:* 800-453-2207 ■ *Web:* www.sebewaingtool.com	Sebewaing	MI	48759	989-883-2000		350
Sebis Direct Inc 6516 W 74th St *Web:* www.sebis.com	Bedford Park	IL	60638	312-243-9300		5
Sebright Products Inc 127 N Water St *TF:* 800-253-0532 ■ *Web:* www.sebrightproducts.com	Hopkins	MI	49328	269-793-7183	793-4022	806
Sebring International Raceway 113 Midway Dr *TF:* 800-626-7223 ■ *Web:* www.sebringraceway.com	Sebring	FL	33870	863-655-1442	655-1777	515
Sebring Software Inc 1400 Cattlemen Rd Ste D *Web:* sebringsoft.com	Sarasota	FL	34232	941-377-0715	377-0719	195
SEC (Shelby Electric Co-op) 1355 IL-128 State PO Box 560 *TF:* 800-677-2612 ■ *Web:* www.shelbyelectric.coop	Shelbyville	IL	62565	217-774-3986		245
SEC (Securities & Exchange Commission) 100 F St NE **Fax Area Code: 202* ■ *TF:* 800-732-0330 ■ *Web:* www.sec.gov	Washington	DC	20549	855-215-3032	772-9295*	340-20
SEC (Safety & Ecology Corp) 2800 Solway Rd SEC Business Ctr *Web:* www.sec-tn.com	Knoxville	TN	37931	865-690-0501	539-9868	667
SEC (Special Energy Corp) 4815 Perkins Rd PO Box 369 *Web:* www.specialenergycorp.com	Stillwater	OK	74074	405-377-1177	743-1617	536
SEC Energy Products & Services LP 9523 Fairbanks N *Web:* www.sec-ep.com	Houston	TX	77064	281-890-9977		539
SECA (Southern Early Childhood Assn) 1123 S University Ave Ste 255 *TF:* 800-305-7322 ■ *Web:* www.southernearlychildhood.org	Little Rock	AR	72204	800-305-7322		49-19
Sechrist Industries Inc 4225 E La Palma Ave *TF:* 800-732-4747 ■ *Web:* www.sechristusa.com	Anaheim	CA	92807	714-579-8400	579-0814	476
Sechrist-Hall Co 102 Omaha Dr	Corpus Christi	TX	78408	361-884-5264		189-12
SECNAP Network Security Corp 3250 W Commercial Blvd Ste 345 *TF:* 844-638-7328 ■ *Web:* www.secnap.com	Fort Lauderdale	FL	33309	561-999-5000		809
SECO (Southeast Electric Co-opeartive Inc) 110 S Main St *TF:* 888-485-8762 ■ *Web:* www.seecoop.com	Ekalaka	MT	59324	406-775-8762		245
SECO Manufacturing Company Inc 4155 Oasis Rd *Web:* www.surveying.com	Redding	CA	96003	530-225-8155		407
Seco Tools 2805 Bellingham Dr *Web:* www.secotools.com	Troy	MI	48083	248-528-5200	528-5600	493
SECO/Warwick Corp 180 Mercer St *Web:* www.secowarwick.com	Meadville	PA	16335	814-332-8400	724-1407	318
Seco-Larm USA Inc 16842 Millikan Ave *TF:* 800-662-0800 ■ *Web:* www.seco-larm.com	Irvine	CA	92606	949-857-0811	261-7326	692
Secom Intl 9610 Bellanca Ave *Web:* www.secomintl.com	Los Angeles	CA	90045	310-641-1290		693
Secon Rubber & Plastics Inc 240 Kaskaskia Dr *TF:* 877-282-7750 ■ *Web:* www.seconrubber.com	Red Bud	IL	62278	618-282-7700		326
Second Amendment Foundation 12500 NE Tenth Pl *TF:* 800-426-4302 ■ *Web:* www.saf.org	Bellevue	WA	98005	425-454-7012	451-3959	48-8
Second City Chicago 1608 N Wells St *Web:* www.secondcity.com	Chicago	IL	60614	312-664-4032	664-9837	573-4
Second Cup Ltd 6303 Airport Rd *TF:* 877-212-1818 ■ *Web:* www.secondcup.com	Mississauga	ON	L4V1R8	877-212-1818		159
Second Empire 330 Hillsborough St *Web:* www.second-empire.com	Raleigh	NC	27603	919-829-3663	829-9519	671
Second Harvest Food Bank of Central Florida 411 Mercy Dr *Web:* www.feedhopenow.org	Orlando	FL	32805	407-295-1066		48-5
Second Measure 201 S B St Ste 200 *Web:* secondmeasure.com	San Mateo	CA	94401	415-214-8383		657
Second Nature 333 Fayetteville St Ste 600 *TF:* 800-308-1186 ■ *Web:* www.secondnature.com	Raleigh	NC	27601	800-308-1186		23
Second Sense 65 E Wacker Pl Ste 1010 *Web:* www.second-sense.org	Chicago	IL	60601	312-236-8569	236-8128	637-2
Second Street Restaurant & Tavern 140 Second St *Web:* secondst.com	Williamsburg	VA	23185	757-220-2286		671
Second Time Around Watch Company Inc 160 S Beverly Dr *TF:* 800-977-7615 ■ *Web:* secondtimearoundwatchco.com	Beverly Hills	CA	90212	310-271-6615	271-1473	410
Secord Contracting Corp 4812 Coolidge Ave N *Web:* secord.us	Tampa	FL	33622	813-870-0630		414
Secova Inc 3090 Bristol St Ste 200 *TF:* 877-632-8122 ■ *Web:* secova.com	Costa Mesa	CA	92626	877-632-8122		194
SECPA (Southeast Colorado Power Assn) 27850 Harris Rd *TF:* 800-332-8634 ■ *Web:* secpa.com	La Junta	CO	81050	719-384-2551	384-7320	245
Secrest Wardle 2600 Troy Center Dr *Web:* www.secrestwardle.com	Troy	MI	48007	248-851-9500	538-1223	428
Secret Location Inc 134 Peter St Ste 700 *Web:* secretlocation.com	Toronto	ON	M5V2H2	416-646-2400		5
Secret Weapon Marketing 5870 W Jefferson Blvd *Web:* secretweapon.net	Los Angeles	CA	90016	310-656-5999		7
Secretariat PO Box 3509 *Web:* www.secevents.com	Wilmington	DE	19807	302-654-4479	654-4117	184
Secretary of Agriculture 1400 Independence Ave SW *Web:* www.usda.gov	Washington	DC	20250	202-720-3631	720-2166	340-1
Secretary of Commerce 1401 Constitution Ave NW *Web:* www.commerce.gov	Washington	DC	20230	202-482-2000		340-2
Secretary of Education 400 Maryland Ave SW *Web:* www.ed.gov	Washington	DC	20202	202-401-0113		340-8
Secretary of Homeland Security Naval Security Stn *Web:* www.dhs.gov	Washington	DC	20528	202-282-8000		340-11
Secretary of Labor 200 Constitution Ave NW Rm N-4123 *Web:* www.dol.gov	Washington	DC	20210	202-693-6000		340-15
Secretary of State *Office of the Coordinator for Counterterrorism* 2201 C St NW Rm 2206 *Web:* www.state.gov	Washington	DC	20520	202-647-2200		340-16
Secs Inc 550 S Columbus Ave *TF:* 800-533-7327 ■ *Web:* www.secsinc.com	Mount Vernon	NY	10550	914-667-5600	699-0377	709
Section Pharmacy Inc 5295 Tammy Little Dr PO Box 108 *Web:* sectionpharmacy.com	Section	AL	35771	256-228-7179		237
Sector 5 Digital 4300 Amon Carter Blvd Ste 104 *Web:* www.sector5digital.com	Fort Worth	TX	76155	817-886-0485		195
Sector Micro Computers Inc 399 Hoover Ave Ste 7 *Web:* sectormicro.com	Bloomfield	NJ	07003	973-429-1113		179
Sector3 Appraisals Inc 8802 69th Rd *Web:* www.sector3appraisals.com	Forest Hills	NY	11375	718-268-4376	425-9784	41
SECU (State Employees' Credit Union) PO Box 29606 **Fax Area Code: 919* ■ *TF:* 888-732-8562 ■ *Web:* www.ncsecu.org	Raleigh	NC	27626	888-732-8562	857-2000*	219
SecuGen Corp 2065 Martin Ave Ste 108 *Web:* secugen.com	Santa Clara	CA	95050	408-727-7787	834-7762	84
Secular Organizations for Sobriety (SOS) 4773 Hollywood Blvd *Web:* www.cfiwest.org	Hollywood	CA	90027	323-666-4295		48-21
Secura Insurance Cos PO Box 819 *TF:* 800-558-3405 ■ *Web:* www.secura.net	Appleton	WI	54912	920-739-3161		391-4
Securacell Inc PO Box 35729 *TF:* 866-836-2355 ■ *Web:* www.securacell.com	Canton	OH	44708	866-836-2355		352
Securance Consulting 13904 Monroes Business Pk **Fax Area Code: 813* ■ *TF:* 877-578-0215 ■ *Web:* www.securanceconsulting.com	Tampa	FL	33635	877-578-0215	328-4465*	180
Securboration Inc 1050 W Nasa Blvd Ste 155 *Web:* www.securboration.com	Melbourne	FL	32901	321-409-5252		809
Secure America's Future Economy (SAFE) 214 N Spring Valley Rd *Web:* www.s-a-f-e.org	Wilmington	DE	19807	302-478-0676		48-7
Secure Care Products LLC 39 Chenell Dr *TF:* 800-451-7917 ■ *Web:* www.securecare.com	Concord	NH	03301	603-223-0745	227-0200	475
Secure Health 577 Mulberry St Ste 1000 *TF:* 800-648-7563 ■ *Web:* www.shpg.com	Macon	GA	31201	478-314-2400		391-3

	Phone	Fax	Class

Secure Mentem Inc
1910 Towne Centre Blvd Ste 250 . . . . Annapolis MD 21401 | 443-603-0200 | | 693
Web: www.securementem.com

Secure Network Systems LLC
4282 York St. . . . . Dacono CO 80514 | 303-637-7617 | | 41

Secure Planning Inc 42 Middle St. . . . . Portsmouth NH 03801 | 603-433-5515 | 433-6023 | 690
Web: secureplanninginc.com

Secure Resolutions Inc
1921 S Alma School Rd Ste 201. . . . . Mesa AZ 85210 | 480-491-7016 | | 226

Secure Retirement Financial & Insurance Services
18 Crow Canyon Ct Ste 325 . . . . San Ramon CA 94583 | 925-855-4300 | | 390
Web: secureretire.com

Secure Technology Alliance
191 Clarkville Rd . . . . .Princeton Junction NJ 08550 | 800-556-6828 | 799-7032* | 49-2
**Fax Area Code:* 609 ■ *TF:* 800-556-6828 ■ *Web:* www.securetechalliance.org

SecureCare Dental
3625 N 16th St Ste 206 . . . . .Phoenix AZ 85016 | 602-234-3266 | 285-0121* | 390
**Fax Area Code:* 888 ■ *TF:* 888-256-3266 ■ *Web:* www.securecaredental.com

SecureUSA Inc
4250 Keith Bridge Rd Ste 160. . . . . .Cumming GA 30041 | 770-205-0789 | 889-7939 | 692
Web: secureusa.net

Securian Financial Group Inc
400 & 401 Robert St N . . . . Saint Paul MN 55101 | 651-665-3500 | 665-4488 | 360-4
Web: www.securian.com

Securiguard Inc
6858 Old Dominion Dr Ste 307 . . . . McLean VA 22101 | 703-821-6777 | 790-1696 | 693
Web: securiguardinc.com

Securisyn Medical LLC
9150 Commerce Center Cir Ste 135. . . . . . Highlands Ranch CO 80129 | 303-952-4551 | | 475
Web: www.securisyn.com

Securitas Security Services USA Inc
2 Campus Dr . . . . .Parsippany NJ 07054 | 973-267-5300 | | 692
TF: 800-555-0906 ■ *Web:* www.securitas.com

Securitech Inc
8230 E Broadway Blvd Ste E-10. . . . . .Tucson AZ 85710 | 520-721-0305 | | 635
TF: 888-792-4473 ■ *Web:* www.localscreening.com

Securities & Exchange Commission (SEC)
100 F St NE . . . . .Washington DC 20549 | 855-215-3032 | 772-9295* | 340-20
**Fax Area Code:* 202 ■ *TF:* 800-732-0330 ■ *Web:* www.sec.gov

Securities & Exchange Commission
Office of Investor Education & Advocacy
100 F St NE. . . . . .Washington DC 20549 | 202-942-8088 | 772-9295 | 340-20
Web: www.investor.gov
Salt Lake Regional Office
351 S W Temple St Ste 6 . . . . .Salt Lake City UT 84101 | 801-524-5796 | 524-3558 | 340-20
Web: www.sec.gov
San Francisco Regional Office
44 Montgomery St Ste 2800 . . . . San Francisco CA 94104 | 415-705-2500 | | 340-20
Web: sec.gov

Securities & Exchange Commission Regional Offices
Atlanta Regional Office
3475 Lenox Rd NE Ste 1000 . . . . Atlanta GA 30326 | 404-842-7600 | | 340-20
Web: www.sec.gov
Boston Regional Office
33 Arch St 23rd Fl. . . . . .Boston MA 02110 | 617-573-8900 | | 340-20
Web: www.sec.gov
Chicago Regional Office
175 W Jackson Blvd Ste 900. . . . . .Chicago IL 60604 | 312-353-7390 | 353-7398 | 340-20
Web: www.sec.gov
Denver Regional Office
1801 California St Ste 1500. . . . . .Denver CO 80202 | 303-844-1000 | 844-1010 | 340-20
Web: www.sec.gov
Fort Worth Regional Office
Burnett Plz 801 Cherry St
Unit 18 Ste 1900 . . . . Fort Worth TX 76102 | 817-978-3821 | | 340-20
Web: www.sec.gov
Los Angeles Regional Office
5670 Wilshire Blvd 11th Fl . . . . .Los Angeles CA 90036 | 323-965-3998 | 965-3815 | 340-20
Web: www.sec.gov
Miami Regional Office
801 Brickell Ave Ste 1800 . . . . Miami FL 33131 | 305-982-6300 | | 340-20
Web: www.sec.gov
New York Regional Office
200 Vesey St Ste 400. .New York NY 10281 | 212-336-1100 | | 340-20
Web: www.sec.gov
Philadelphia Regional Office
1617 JFK Blvd Ste 520 . . . . .Philadelphia PA 19103 | 215-597-3100 | | 340-20
Web: www.sec.gov

Securities Center Inc, The
245 E St . . . . Chula Vista CA 91910 | 619-426-3550 | | 690
TF: 800-244-1718 ■ *Web:* www.securitiescenter.com

Securities Industry & Financial Markets Assn (SIFMAA)
120 Broadway 35th Fl. . . . . .New York NY 10271 | 212-313-1200 | | 49-2
Web: www.sifma.org

Securities Service Network Inc
9729 Cogdill Rd Ste 301 . . . . Knoxville TN 37932 | 866-843-4635 | | 690
TF: 866-843-4635 ■ *Web:* www.ssnetwork.com

Securitron Magnalock Corp
10027 S 51st St Ste 102. . . . . Phoenix AZ 85044 | 623-582-4626 | 582-4641* | 350
**Fax Area Code:* 866 ■ *TF:* 800-624-5625 ■ *Web:* www.assaabloyesh.com

Security & Access Systems
3811 Rutledge Rd NE . . . . Albuquerque NM 87109 | 505-823-1561 | | 693
Web: www.securityandaccess.com

Security 101 LLC
2465 Mercer Ave Ste 101 . . . . .West Palm Beach FL 33401 | 888-909-4101 | | 693
TF: 888-909-4101 ■ *Web:* www.security101.com

Security America Inc
3412 Chesterfield Ave. . . . . .Charleston WV 25304 | 304-925-4747 | | 693
TF: 888-832-6732 ■ *Web:* www.securityamerica.com

Security and Fire Electronics Inc
2590 Dobbs Rd. . . . . Saint Augustine FL 32086 | 904-844-0964 | 824-7771 | 425
Web: www.safeinc.com

Security Aviation
12016 S Praire Ave. . . . . Hawthorne CA 90250 | 310-978-1095 | 978-1191 | 167-3
Web: www.securityaviation.net

Security Bank & Trust Co
735 11th St E . . . . Glencoe MN 55336 | 320-864-3171 | 864-5133 | 685
Web: www.security-banks.com

Security Bank NA 10727 E 51st St . . . . Tulsa OK 74146 | 918-664-6100 | | 70
Web: sbtulsa.bank

Security Bank of Pulaski County
110 Lynn St PO Box S . . . . Waynesville MO 65583 | 573-774-6417 | 774-6465 | 70
Web: www.sbpc.com

Security Bank Usa
1025 Paul Bunyan Dr PO Box 1630 . . . . Bemidji MN 56601 | 218-751-1510 | | 70
Web: securitybankusa.com

Security Benefit Group of Cos
1 Security Benefit Pl . . . . Topeka KS 66636 | 785-438-3000 | 368-1772 | 360-4
TF: 800-888-2461 ■ *Web:* www.securitybenefit.com

Security Corp 22325 Roethel Dr . . . . .Novi MI 48375 | 877-374-5700 | | 692
TF: 877-374-5700 ■ *Web:* www.securitycorp.com

Security Credit Services LLC
2653 W Oxford Loop Ste 108 . . . . Oxford MS 38655 | 866-699-7889 | | 403
TF: 866-699-7889 ■ *Web:* securitycreditservicesllc.com

Security Defense Systems Corp
160 Park Ave. . . . . Nutley NJ 07110 | 800-325-6339 | 235-0132* | 692
**Fax Area Code:* 973 ■ *TF:* 800-325-6339 ■ *Web:* www.securitydefense.com

Security Door Controls Inc
801 Avenida Acaso . . . . .Camarillo CA 93012 | 805-494-0622 | | 350
TF: 800-413-8783 ■ *Web:* www.sdcsecurity.com

Security Engineered Machinery Company Inc
5 Walkup Dr PO Box 1045 . . . . .Westborough MA 01581 | 508-366-1488 | 836-4154 | 111
TF: 800-225-9293 ■ *Web:* www.semshred.com

Security Escrow & Title Insurance Agency
337 S Main St. . . . . Cedar City UT 84720 | 435-867-0402 | | 390
Web: securityescrowutah.com

Security Federal Corp (SFB)
238 Richland Ave NW PO Box 810. . . . . Aiken SC 29802 | 803-641-3000 | | 71
TF: 866-851-3000 ■ *Web:* www.securityfederalbank.com

Security Finance Corp
181 Security Pl PO Box 3146 . . . . .Spartanburg SC 29304 | 864-582-8193 | | 217
TF: 866-281-7043 ■ *Web:* www.securityfinance.com

Security Fire Protection Company Inc
4495 Mendenhall Rd S . . . . Memphis TN 38141 | 901-362-6250 | 366-7869 | 189-13
Web: www.securityfire.com

Security First Corp
29811 Santa Margarita Pkwy
Ste 600. . . . . .Rancho Santa Margarita CA 92688 | 888-884-7152 | | 84
TF: 888-884-7152 ■ *Web:* securityfirstcorp.com

Security First Insurance Agency Inc
7851 S Elati St Ste 100. . . . . Littleton CO 80120 | 303-730-2327 | | 390
Web: securityfirstia.com

Security Horizon Inc
5350 Tomah Dr Ste 3200 . . . . Colorado Springs CO 80918 | 719-488-4500 | | 693
Web: www.securityhorizon.com

Security Industry Assn (SIA)
8405 Colesville Rd Ste 500 . . . . Silver Spring MD 20910 | 301-804-4700 | 683-2469* | 49-4
**Fax Area Code:* 703 ■ *TF:* 866-817-8888 ■ *Web:* www.securityindustry.org

Security Information Systems Inc
6314 Kingspointe Pkwy Ste 3. . . . . Orlando FL 32819 | 407-345-1550 | | 693
Web: www.securitysoftware.com

Security Instrument Corporation of Delaware
309 W Newport Pk . . . . Wilmington DE 19804 | 302-633-5621 | | 693
Web: www.securityinstrument.com

Security Life Insurance Company of America
10901 Red Cir Dr . . . . Minnetonka MN 55343 | 717-397-2751 | 945-3419* | 391-2
**Fax Area Code:* 952 ■ *TF:* 800-328-4667 ■ *Web:* www.securitylife.com

Security Management Systems Inc
225 Community Dr Ste 150 . . . . .Great Neck NY 11021 | 516-450-3120 | | 693
Web: www.securitymgt.com

Security Metal Products Corp
5700 Hannum Ave Ste 250. . . . . .Culver City CA 90230 | 310-641-6690 | | 480
Web: www.secmet.com

Security Mutual Insurance Co
2417 N Triphammer Rd PO Box 4620. . . . . .Ithaca NY 14852 | 607-257-5000 | 257-5003 | 391-6
Web: www.securitymutual.com

Security Mutual Life Insurance Company of New York
100 Court St PO Box 1625 . . . . .Binghamton NY 13901 | 800-346-7171 | 723-8665* | 391-2
**Fax Area Code:* 607 ■ *TF:* 800-927-8846 ■ *Web:* www.smlny.com

Security National Bank
40 S Limestone St . . . . .Springfield OH 45502 | 937-324-6800 | | 70
TF: 800-836-1557 ■ *Web:* parknationalbank.com

Security National Bank
1 W Broadway St PO Box 427. . . . . Witt IL 62094 | 217-594-2221 | 594-2255 | 70
TF: 800-594-0242 ■ *Web:* securitynb.com

Security National Bank of Enid
201 W Maine Ave . . . . .Enid OK 73701 | 580-234-5151 | | 70
Web: www.snbenid.com

Security National Bank of Omaha (Inc)
1120 S 101st St PO Box 31400 . . . . .Omaha NE 68124 | 402-344-7300 | | 70
Web: www.snbconnect.com

Security National Bank of Sioux City Iowa
601 Pierce St . . . . Sioux City IA 51101 | 712-277-6500 | | 70
Web: www.snbonline.com

Security National Financial Corp (SNFC)
121 W Election Dr Ste 100 . . . . Draper UT 84020 | 801-264-1060 | | 391-2
NASDAQ: SNFCA ■ *Web:* www.securitynational.com

Security Personnel Inc
12521 W Hampton Ave. . . . . .Butler WI 53007 | 262-252-2500 | 252-8494 | 693
Web: www.securitypersonnel.com

Security Resource Group Inc
300-1914 Hamilton St . . . . Regina SK S4P3N6 | 306-522-0135 | | 693
TF: 888-951-3388 ■ *Web:* www.securityresourcegroup.com

Security Risk Management Consultants LLC
150 E Mound St Ste 308. Columbus OH 43215 | 614-224-3100 | 224-3252 | 194
Web: srmcllc.com

Security Risk Solutions Inc
698 Fishermans Bend. . . . . Mount Pleasant SC 29464 | 843-647-1556 | | 463
Web: www.securityrisksolutions.com

Security Service Federal Credit Union
16211 La Cantera Pkwy .San Antonio TX 78256 | 210-476-4000 | 444-3000 | 219
TF: 800-527-7328 ■ *Web:* www.ssfcu.org

Security Signal Devices Inc
1740 N Lemon St . . . . Anaheim CA 92801 | 800-888-0444 | | 692
TF: 800-888-0444 ■ *Web:* www.ssdalarm.com

Security Signals Inc 9509 Macon Rd. . . . . .Cordova TN 38016 | 901-754-7228 | | 621
Web: www.securitysignalsinc.com

	City	State	ZIP	Phone	Fax	Class
Security Solutions Intl 13155 SW 134th St *Fax Area Code: 866 ■ TF: 866-573-3999 ■ Web: www.homelandsecurityssi.com	Miami	FL	33186	786-573-3999	573-2090*	637-9
Security Square Mall 6901 Security Blvd TF: 800-977-2769 ■ Web: www.securitysquare.com	Baltimore	MD	21244	410-265-6000	281-1473	460
Security State Bank & Trust (Inc) 201 W Main St PO Box 471 Web: www.ssbtexas.com	Fredericksburg	TX	78624	830-997-7575	997-7994	70
Security State Bank of Wanamingo 232 Main St TF: 800-879-6854 ■ Web: ssbwanamingo.com	Wanamingo	MN	55983	507-824-2265	824-2960	70
Security Steel Sales Inc 14321 Vimy Ridge Rd TF: 800-465-5449 ■ Web: www.pieceometal.com	Alexander	AR	72002	501-455-5083	455-0309	492
Security Supply Corp 196 Maple Ave Web: www.secsupply.com	Selkirk	NY	12158	518-767-2226	767-2065	612
Security Traders Assn 1115 Broadway *Fax Area Code: 202 ■ Web: securitytraders.org	New York	NY	10010	646-699-5996	659-5249*	49-2
Security Van Lines LLC 100 W Airline Dr TF: 800-794-5961 ■ Web: www.securitymayflower.com	Kenner	LA	70062	800-794-5961		780
SecurLinx 39555 Orchard Hill Pl Ste 600 Web: www.securlinx.com	Novi	MI	48375	248-374-5017		809
SecurTek Monitoring Solutions Inc 70-1st Ave N TF: 844-321-2712 ■ Web: www.securtek.com	Yorkton	SK	S3N1J7	877-777-7591		693
Securus Technologies Inc 4000 International Pkwy Web: www.securustech.net	Dallas	TX	75254	972-734-1111	277-0301	736
SED Systems 18 Innovation Blvd Web: www.sedsystems.ca	Saskatoon	SK	S7N3R1	306-931-3425	933-1486	246
SEDA Construction Co 2120 Corporate Sq Blvd Ste 3 Web: sedaconstruction.com	Jacksonville	FL	32216	904-724-7800	727-9500	653
Seda France Inc 10200 McKalla Pl Ste 400 TF: 800-474-0854 ■ Web: www.sedafrance.com	Austin	TX	78758	512-206-0105		96
SEDALCO Construction Services 4100 Fossil Creek Blvd Web: www.sedalco.com	Fort Worth	TX	76137	817-831-2245	831-2248	186
Sedalia Area Chamber of Commerce 600 E Third St Web: www.sedaliachamber.com	Sedalia	MO	65301	660-826-2222	826-2223	139
Sedan Floral Inc 406 S School St PO Box 339 Web: www.sedanfloral.com	Sedan	KS	67361	620-725-3111	725-5257	369
Sedano's Supermarkets 3140 W 76 St Web: sedanos.com	Hialeah	FL	33018	305-364-2303	556-6981	345
Sedco 2304 W Beecher Rd PO Box 624 Web: www.sedco-prv.com	Adrian	MI	49221	517-263-2220	265-6160	790
Seder & Chandler 339 Main St Burnside Bldg Web: www.sederlaw.com	Worcester	MA	01608	508-757-7721	831-0955	428
Sedgewick Industries 667 W Ward Ave Web: www.sedgewick.com	High Point	NC	27260	336-885-9300	885-9174	319-1
Sedgwick County 525 N Main St Ste 211 TF: 800-527-0709 ■ Web: sedgwickcounty.org	Wichita	KS	67203	316-660-9222	383-7961	338
Sedgwick County Electric Co-op 1355 S 383rd St W TF: 866-542-4732 ■ Web: www.sedgwickcountyelectric.coop	Cheney	KS	67025	316-542-3131	542-3943	245
Sedgwick County Zoo 5555 W Zoo Blvd Web: scz.org	Wichita	KS	67212	316-660-9453	942-3781	823
Sedgwick Pharmacy Inc 3887 Sedgwick Ave Web: sedgwickpharmacy.com	Bronx	NY	10463	718-543-3116		237
SEDL 4700 Mueller Blvd TF: 800-476-6861 ■ Web: www.sedl.org	Austin	TX	78723	512-476-6861	476-2286	668
Sedlak Interiors Inc 34300 Solon Rd Web: www.sedlakinteriors.com	Solon	OH	44139	440-248-2424		321
Sedlak Management Consultants Inc Metropolitan Plz 22901 Millcreek Blvd Ste 600 Web: www.jasedlak.com	Highland Hills	OH	44122	216-206-4700	206-4840	194
Sedocom LLC 161 First St 4th Fl Web: www.sedo.com	Cambridge	MA	02142	617-499-7200		387
SEDONA Corp 1003 W Ninth Ave 2nd Fl TF: 800-815-3307 ■ Web: www.sedonacorp.com	King of Prussia	PA	19406	610-337-8400		177
Sedona Rouge Hotel & Spa 2250 W SR- 89A TF: 866-312-4111 ■ Web: www.sedonarouge.com	Sedona	AZ	86336	928-203-4111		379
Sedona Staffing 7380 Clairemont Mesa Blvd Ste 209 Web: www.sedonastaffing.com	San Diego	CA	92111	858-268-9844		41
SEE Science Ctr 200 Bedford St Web: www.see-sciencecenter.org	Manchester	NH	03101	603-669-0400		520
See The Trainer 1250 NW 128th St Ste160 Web: seethetrainer.com	Clive	IA	50325	515-274-0055		363
See Water Inc 22220 Opportunity Way Ste 101 TF: 888-733-9283 ■ Web: www.seewaterinc.com	Riverside	CA	92518	951-487-8073	487-0557	201
See World Satellites Inc 1321 Wayne Ave TF: 800-435-2808 ■ Web: www.seeworld.biz	Indiana	PA	15701	724-463-3200		116
See's Candies Inc 210 El Camino Real TF: 800-877-7337 ■ Web: www.sees.com	South San Francisco	CA	94080	650-761-2490		296-8
SeeClickFix Inc 746 Chapel St Ste 207 Web: seeclickfix.com	New Haven	CT	06510	203-752-0777		387
Seed Mackall & Cole LLP 1332 Anacapa St Ste 200 Web: www.seedmackall.com	Santa Barbara	CA	93101	805-963-0669		428
Seedling Continental Press 520 E Bainbridge St *Fax Area Code: 888 ■ TF: 800-233-0759 ■ Web: www.continentalpress.com	Elizabethtown	PA	17022	800-233-0759	834-1303*	637-2
Seedorff Masonry Inc (SMI) 408 W Mission St Web: www.seedorff.com	Strawberry Point	IA	52076	563-933-2296		189-7
Seeds of Peace 183 Powhatan Rd Web: www.seedsofpeace.org	Otisfield	ME	04270	212-573-8040		239
Seedspark LLC 5970 Fairview Rd Ste 400 TF: 888-681-2855 ■ Web: seedspark.com	Charlotte	NC	28210	704-246-5052		180
Seedway LLC 1734 Railroad Pl TF: 800-836-3710 ■ Web: www.seedway.com	Hall	NY	14463	585-526-6391	526-6832	694
SEEK Careers/Staffing Inc 1160 Opportunity Dr Web: www.seekcareers.com	Grafton	WI	53024	262-377-8888	375-6677	721
Seeker Rod Co 700 N Batavia Unit B TF: 800-373-3537 ■ Web: seekerrods.com	Orange	CA	92868	714-769-1700		710
Seekins Ford Lincoln Inc 1625 Seekins Ford Dr Web: www.seekins.com	Fairbanks	AK	99701	907-459-4000		57
Seekirk Inc 2420 Scioto Harper Dr Web: www.seekirk.com	Columbus	OH	43204	614-278-9200	278-9257	201
Seelbach Hilton Louisville 500 S Fourth St TF: 800-333-3399 ■ Web: www.seelbachhilton.com	Louisville	KY	40202	502-585-3200	585-9239	379
Seelig & Co 330 S Midway St Ste 101 Web: www.seeligs.com	Campbell	CA	95008	408-377-0123		196
Seelig Law Offices LLC 299 Broadway Ste 1600 Web: pseeliglaw.com	New York	NY	10007	212-766-0600		41
Seelye Craftsmen Co 2220 Fernbrook Ln TF: 877-413-7156 ■ Web: www.seelyecraftsmen.com	Minneapolis	MN	55447	763-577-0700	577-0777	697
Seelye Plastics Inc 9700 Newton Ave S *Fax Area Code: 952 ■ TF: 800-328-2728 ■ Web: seelyeplastics.com	Bloomington	MN	55431	800-328-2728	881-3503*	603
Seemann Composites Inc 12481 Glascock Dr Web: www.seemanncomposites.com	Gulfport	MS	39503	228-314-8000	314-8001	604
SeeMore Putter Co, The 277 Mallory Sta Ste 119 TF: 800-985-8170 ■ Web: www.seemore.com	Franklin	TN	37067	615-435-8015		711
Seepex Inc 511 Speedway Dr Web: www.seepex.com	Enon	OH	45323	937-864-7150	864-7157	641
SeePoint Technology LLC 2619 Manhattan Beach Blvd TF: 888-587-1777 ■ Web: www.seepoint.com	Redondo Beach	CA	90278	310-725-9660	535-9234	614
Seer Capital Management LP 1177 Avenue of the Americas 34th Fl Web: seercap.com	New York	NY	10036	212-850-9000	850-9011	690
SEER Technology Inc 2681 Parleys Way Ste 201 TF: 877-505-7337 ■ Web: www.seertechnology.com	Salt Lake City	UT	84109	801-746-7888		419
Sef Inc 500 Saint Francis St Web: www.seforms.com	Mobile	AL	36602	251-432-2936	432-7759	110
SEFA (Scientific Equipment & Furniture Assn) 65 Hilton Ave TF: 877-294-5424 ■ Web: www.sefalabs.com	Garden City	NY	11530	516-294-5424	294-2758	49-19
Sefar Printing Solutions Inc 111 Calumet St TF: 800-995-0531 ■ Web: www.sefar.com	Depew	NY	14043	716-683-4050	685-9469	745-3
Sefcor Inc 1150 Uniform Rd Web: www.sefcor.com	Griffin	GA	30224	770-227-8297	229-5120	567
SEFCU Insurance Agency 469 State St TF: 888-250-6689 ■ Web: www.sefcuinsuranceagency.com	Schenectady	NY	12305	518-786-9905		390
SEFCU Mortgage Services 700 Patroon Creek Blvd Ste 301 TF: 800-444-6313 ■ Web: www.sefcumortgageservices.com	Albany	NY	12206	518-783-1234		509
SEG (Society of Exploration Geophysicists) 8801 S Yale Ave Ste 500 PO Box 702740 Web: seg.org	Tulsa	OK	74137	918-497-5500	497-5557	48-12
Segal Co 333 W 34th St Web: www.segalco.com	New York	NY	10001	212-251-5000		193
Segall Bryant & Hamill 540 W Madison St Ste 1900 TF: 800-836-4265 ■ Web: www.sbhic.com	Chicago	IL	60661	312-474-1222		401
SEGEPO-FSM Inc 1188 Industrial Rd Web: www.segepofsm.com	Cold Spring	KY	41076	859-781-1400	781-4702	621
Segerstrom Center for the Arts (SCFTA) 600 Town Center Dr Web: www.scfta.org	Costa Mesa	CA	92626	714-636-7433	556-8984	572
Segment 100 California St Ste 700 Web: segment.com	San Francisco	CA	94111	415-603-6900		570
Seguin Area Chamber of Commerce 116 N Camp St Web: www.seguinchamber.com	Seguin	TX	78155	830-379-6382	379-6971	139
Seguin Independent School District 1221 E Kingsbury St Web: www.seguin.k12.tx.us	Seguin	TX	78155	830-401-8600	379-0392	685
Seguin Moreau Napa Cooperage Inc 151 Camino Dorado Web: seguinmoreaunapa.com	Napa	CA	94558	707-252-3408		200
Segway Inc 14 Technology Dr TF: 866-473-4929 ■ Web: www.segway.com	Bedford	NH	03110	603-222-6000	222-6001	516
SEI 1 Freedom Vly Dr NASDAQ: SEIC ■ TF: 800-342-5734 ■ Web: seic.com	Oaks	PA	19456	610-676-1000		528
SEI (Software Engineering Institute) 4500 Fifth Ave TF: 888-201-4479 ■ Web: www.sei.cmu.edu	Pittsburgh	PA	15213	412-268-5800	268-6257	668
SEI (Stephenson Equipment Inc) 7201 Paxton St TF: 800-325-6455 ■ Web: stephensonequipment.com	Harrisburg	PA	17111	717-564-3434		264-3
SEI (System Engineering International Inc) 5115 Pegasus Ct Ste Q TF: 800-765-4734 ■ Web: www.seipower.com	Frederick	MD	21704	301-694-9601	694-9608	787
SEI (Steel Edge Inc) 716 W Mesquite Ave Web: www.steeledgeinc.com	Las Vegas	NV	89106	702-386-0023	795-8263	492

	Phone	Fax	Class
SEI Group Inc 689 Discovery Dr Ste 310 .... Huntsville AL 35806 *Web:* www.seigroupinc.com	256-533-0500		261
SEIA (Solar Energy Industries Assn) 600 14th St NW Ste 400 .... Washington DC 20005 *Web:* www.seia.org	202-682-0556	682-0559	48-12
SEIA (Signature Estate & Investment Advisors LLC) 2121 Avenue of the Stars Ste 1600 .... Los Angeles CA 90067 *TF:* 800-723-5115 ■ *Web:* www.seia.com	310-712-2323	712-2345	401
Seibel & Katz CPAS 3814 West St Ste 311 .... Cincinnati OH 45227 *Web:* seibelkatzcpa.com	513-271-7835		2
Seico Security Systems 132 Court St .... Pekin IL 61554 *TF:* 800-272-0316 ■ *Web:* www.seicosecurity.com	309-347-3200		693
Seidcon Inc 1911 Riviera Dr .... Vista CA 92084 *Web:* www.seidcon.com	760-510-9800	510-9806	809
Seidel Schroeder & Co 304 E Blue Bell Rd .... Brenham TX 77833 *Web:* www.ssccpa.com	979-836-6131	830-8131	2
Seidel Tanning Corp 1306 E Meinecke Ave .... Milwaukee WI 53212 *TF:* 800-826-6379 ■ *Web:* www.seideltanning.com	414-562-4030	562-4445	432
Seiden 112 Madison Ave 9th Fl .... New York NY 10016 *Web:* seidenadvertising.com	212-223-8700		4
Seiden Family Law LLC 1130 Raritan Rd Ste 3 .... Cranford NJ 07016 *Web:* seidenfamilylaw.com	908-324-5400		41
Seidl Law Office, A Professional Corp 121 SW Morrison St Ste 475 .... Portland OR 97204 *Web:* seidl-law.com	503-224-7840		41
Seidler Equity Partners 4640 Admiralty Way Ste 1200 .... Marina del Rey CA 90292 *Web:* www.sepfunds.com	213-683-4622	624-0691	792
Seifer Flatow PLLC 2319 Crescent Ave .... Charlotte NC 28207 *Web:* seiferflatowlaw.com	704-512-0606		41
Seifert's Farm Supply 108 E Maple St .... Three Oaks MI 49128 *Web:* seifertsfarmsupply.webs.com	269-756-9592	756-2401	276
Seigfreid Bingham PC 2323 Grand Blvd Ste 1000 .... Kansas City MO 64108 *Web:* sb-kc.com	816-421-4460		41
Seigle's 1331 Davis Rd .... Elgin IL 60123 *Web:* www.seigles.com	847-742-2000		364
Seiko Corporation of America 1111 MacArthur Blvd .... Mahwah NJ 07430 *TF:* 800-545-2783 ■ *Web:* seikousa.com	201-529-5730		153
Seiko Instruments USA Inc 21221 S Western Ave Ste 250 .... Torrance CA 90501 *TF:* 800-688-0817 ■ *Web:* www.seikoinstruments.com	310-517-7700	517-7709	153
Seiler Instrument & Manufacturing Company Inc 3433 Tree Court Industrial Blvd .... Saint Louis MO 63122 *TF:* 800-489-2282 ■ *Web:* www.seilerinst.com	314-968-2282		544
Seiler LLP 3 Lagoon Dr Ste 400 .... Redwood City CA 94065 *Web:* seiler.com	650-365-4646	368-4055	2
Seilevel Inc 3410 Far W Blvd .... Austin TX 78731 *Web:* www.seilevel.com	512-527-9952		177
SEIMAX Technologies LP 4805 Westway Park Bouvelard Ste 100 .... Houston TX 77041 *Web:* www.seismicventures.com	832-554-4301		536
Seismic 12390 El Camino Real .... San Diego CA 92130 *TF:* 855-466-8748 ■ *Web:* seismic.com	855-466-8748		178-1
Seismic Energy Products LP (SEP) 518 Progress Way .... Athens TX 75751	903-675-8571		676
Seismic Productions LLC 7010 Santa Monica Blvd .... Los Angeles CA 90038 *Web:* www.seismicproductions.com	323-957-3350		7
Seismic Source Co 9425 E Tower Rd .... Ponca City OK 74604 *Web:* seismicsource.com	580-362-3402		539
Seitel Inc 10811 S Westview Cir Dr Bldg C Ste 100 .... Houston TX 77043 *Web:* www.seitel.com	713-881-8900		538
Seitel Systems LLC 1200 Westlake Ave N Ste 100 .... Seattle WA 98101 *Web:* seitelsystems.com	206-832-2875		180
Seitz Insurance Agency 114 Second Ave SE .... Sidney MT 59270 *Web:* seitzinsure.com	406-433-1411		390
Seitz LLC 212 Industrial Ln .... Torrington CT 06790 *TF:* 800-261-2011 ■ *Web:* www.seitzllc.com	860-489-0476		604
Seiu Local 503 488 E 11th Ave Ste B100 .... Eugene OR 97401 *TF:* 800-452-2146 ■ *Web:* seiu503.org	541-342-1055		414
Seize The Deal LLC 1851 N Greenville Ave Ste 100 .... Richardson TX 75081 *TF:* 866-210-0881 ■ *Web:* www.seizethedeal.com	866-210-0881		387
SEJ (Society of Environmental Journalists) 1629 K St NW Ste 300 .... Washington DC 20006 **Fax Area Code:* 215 ■ *Web:* www.sej.org	202-558-2300	884-8175*	49-14
SEK Genetics 9525 70th Rd .... Galesburg KS 66740 **Fax Area Code:* 620 ■ *TF:* 800-443-6389 ■ *Web:* sekgenetics.com	800-443-6389	763-2231*	11-2
SEKAI Electronics Inc 14600 Industry Cir .... La Mirada CA 90638 *Web:* www.sekai-electronics.com	714-736-4180		647
Sekan Printing Company Inc 2210 S Main St .... Fort Scott KS 66701 *TF:* 800-243-6411 ■ *Web:* www.sekan.com	620-223-5190	223-6955	627
Sekas International Ltd 345 Seventh Ave 9th Fl .... New York NY 10001 *Web:* sekasinternational.com	212-629-6095	629-6097	155-7
Sekisui 25 S Belvedere Blvd .... Memphis TN 38104 *Web:* www.sekisuiusa.com	901-725-0005		671
Sekisui America Corp 333 Meadowlands Pkwy .... Secaucus NJ 07094 *Web:* www.sekisui-corp.com	201-423-7960	423-7979	603
Sekisui Diagnostics LLC 4 Hartwell Pl .... Lexington MA 02421 *Web:* www.sekisuidiagnostics.com	781-652-7800		476
Sekisui of Chattanooga 1120 Houston St .... Chattanooga TN 37402 *Web:* www.sekisuichattanooga.com	423-267-4600		671
Sekisui Voltek LLC 100 Shepard St .... Lawrence MA 01843 *TF:* 800-225-0668 ■ *Web:* www.sekisuivoltek.com	978-685-2557	685-9861	601
SEKO Logistics 1100 Arlington Heights Rd Ste 600 .... Itasca IL 60143 *TF:* 800-228-2711 ■ *Web:* www.sekologistics.com	630-919-4800	773-9219	449
Selamat Designs 231 S Maple Ave .... South San Francisco CA 94080 *Web:* www.selamatdesigns.com	650-243-4840		96
Selbert Perkins Design 432 Culver Blvd .... Playa Del Rey CA 90293 *Web:* selbertperkins.com	310-822-5223		344
Selby Furniture Hardware Company Inc 321 Rider Ave .... Bronx NY 10451 *Web:* www.selbyhardware.com	718-993-3700	993-3143	350
Selby Public Library 1331 First St .... Sarasota FL 34236 *Web:* www.selbylibraryfriends.org	941-365-5228		434-3
Selby Venture Partners PO Box Q .... Menlo Park CA 94026 *Web:* selbyventures.com	650-300-5882		792
Selbysoft Inc 8326 Woodland Ave E .... Puyallup WA 98371 *TF:* 800-454-4434 ■ *Web:* www.selbysoft.com	800-454-4434		177
Selco Community Credit Union 299 E 11th Ave .... Eugene OR 97401 *TF:* 800-445-4483 ■ *Web:* www.selco.org	541-686-8000		219
Selden Fox Ltd 619 Enterprise Dr .... Oak Brook IL 60523 *Web:* www.seldenfox.com	630-954-1400		2
Selden's Home Furnishings 1802 62nd Ave E .... Tacoma WA 98424 *Web:* www.seldens.com	253-922-5700		321
Seldovia Native Association Inc 101 W Benson Blvd Ste 302 .... Anchorage AK 99503 *TF:* 844-868-8006 ■ *Web:* snai.com	907-868-8006	868-8042	48-13
Select Computing Inc 3001 Broadway St NE Ste 655 .... Minneapolis MN 55413 *Web:* www.selectcomputing.com	612-331-5535		180
Select Design 208 Flynn Ave .... Burlington VT 05401 *Web:* www.selectdesign.com	802-864-9075		687
Select Engineered Systems 7991 W 26th Ave .... Hialeah FL 33016 *TF:* 800-342-5737 ■ *Web:* www.selectses.com	305-823-5410		693
Select Group LLC, The 5520 Capital Center Dr .... Raleigh NC 27606 *Web:* www.selectgroup.com	919-459-1400		260
Select Group Real Estate Inc 409 Century Park Dr .... Yuba City CA 95991 *TF:* 800-992-3883 ■ *Web:* selectgroupre.com	800-992-3883		652
Select Medical Corp 4714 Gettysburg Rd .... Mechanicsburg PA 17055 *TF:* 888-735-6332 ■ *Web:* www.selectmedical.com	717-972-1100		463
Select Portfolio Management Inc 120 Vantis .... Aliso Viejo CA 92656 *TF:* 800-445-9822 ■ *Web:* www.selectportfolio.com	949-975-7900		401
Select Portfolio Servicing Inc PO Box 65250 .... Salt Lake City UT 84165 *TF:* 800-258-8602 ■ *Web:* www.spservicing.com	800-258-8602		217
Select Properties Ltd 6620 Riverside Dr .... Metairie LA 70033 *Web:* www.selectpropertiesltdrealty.com	504-833-0044		652
Select Publishing Inc 6417 Normandy Ln .... Madison WI 53719 *TF:* 800-278-5670 ■ *Web:* selectpub.com	608-277-5787		366
Select Restaurants Inc 1 Chagrin Highlands 2000 Auburn Dr .... Cleveland OH 44122 *Web:* selectrestaurants.com	216-464-6606	464-8565	670
Select Sewing Service Inc 2415 E 65th St .... Indianapolis IN 46220 *Web:* selectsewingservice.com	317-255-6332		35
Select Sires Inc 11740 US Hwy 42 N .... Plain City OH 43064 *Web:* www.selectsires.com	614-873-4683	873-5751	11-2
Select Specialty Hospital - Wichita Inc 929 N Saint Francis St North Tower 6th Fl .... Wichita KS 67214 *Web:* wichita.selectspecialtyhospitals.com	316-261-8303	291-7524	371
Select Specialty Hospital-Danville Inc 100 N Academy Ave Internal MC 42-10 .... Danville PA 17822 *Web:* danville.selectspecialtyhospitals.com	570-214-9653	214-9616	371
Select Specialty Hospital-Fort Smith Inc 1001 Towson Ave .... Fort Smith AR 72901 *Web:* fortsmith.selectspecialtyhospitals.com	479-441-3980		374-3
Select Specialty Hospital-Oklahoma City Inc 3524 NW 56th St .... Oklahoma City OK 73112 *Web:* oklahomacity.selectspecialtyhospitals.com	405-606-6900	606-6110	374-3
Select Specialty Hospital-Orlando Inc 5579 S Orange Ave .... Edgewood FL 32809 *Web:* orlandosouth.selectspecialtyhospitals.com	407-241-4800	241-0324	371
Select Specialty Hospital-Pittsburgh/UPMC Inc 200 Lothrop MUH E824 3485 Fifth Avenue for FedEx .... Pittsburgh PA 15213 *Web:* pittsburghupmc.selectspecialtyhospitals.com	412-586-9805	586-9828	371
Select Specialty Hospital-TriCities Inc 1 Medical Pk Blvd 5 W .... Bristol TN 37620 *Web:* tricities.selectspecialtyhospitals.com	423-844-5916		371
Select Staffing 1019 Chapala St .... Santa Barbara CA 93101 *TF:* 844-864-0634 ■ *Web:* www.select.com	805-687-1200		721
Select Stainless LLC 11145 Monroe Rd .... Matthews NC 28105 *Web:* selectstainless.com	704-841-1090		697
Select Technical Staffing Inc 1025 S 108th St .... West Allis WI 53214 *TF:* 888-476-9331 ■ *Web:* selecttechnicalstaffing.com	414-476-9331	476-9340	260
Select-A-Ticket Inc 25 Rt 23 S .... Riverdale NJ 07457 *TF:* 800-735-3288 ■ *Web:* www.selectaticket.com	973-839-6100	839-0870	750
Selectech Inc 33 Wales Ave Ste F .... Avon MA 02322 *Web:* www.selectechinc.com	508-583-3200		604
Selected Funds PO Box 8243 .... Boston MA 02266 *TF:* 800-243-1575 ■ *Web:* www.selectedfunds.com	800-243-1575		528
Selected Funeral & Life Insurance Co 119 Convention Blvd .... Hot Springs AR 71902 *TF:* 800-272-2087 ■ *Web:* sflic.net	501-624-2172		391-2

Name / Address	City	State	ZIP	Phone	Fax	Class
Selected Independent Funeral Homes 500 Lake Cook Rd Ste 205 **Fax Area Code: 847* ■ *TF:* 800-323-4219 ■ *Web:* www.selectedfuneralhomes.org	Deerfield	IL	60015	800-323-4219	236-9968*	49-4
Selection Management Systems Inc 155 Tri County Pkwy Ste 150 *TF:* 800-325-3609 ■ *Web:* selection.com	Cincinnati	OH	45246	800-325-3609		193
Selective Enterprises Inc 10701 Texland Blvd *TF:* 800-334-1207 ■ *Web:* www.unitedsupplyco.com	Charlotte	NC	28273	704-588-3310		361
Selective First Realty 4110 Main St *Web:* www.selectivefirstrealty.com	Flushing	NY	11355	718-461-2510		652
Selective Insurance Group Inc 40 Wantage Ave *NASDAQ: SIGI* ■ *TF:* 800-777-9656 ■ *Web:* www.selective.com	Branchville	NJ	07890	973-948-3000		360-4
Selective Service System 1515 Wilson Blvd *TF:* 888-655-1825 ■ *Web:* www.sss.gov	Arlington	VA	22209	847-688-6888		340-20
Select-O-Hits Inc 1981 Fletcher Creek Dr *TF:* 800-346-0723 ■ *Web:* www.selectohits.com	Memphis	TN	38133	901-388-1190		523
Selectpath Benefits & Financial Inc 310-700 Richmond St *TF:* 888-327-5777 ■ *Web:* www.selectpath.ca	London	ON	N6A5C7	519-675-1177		390
SelecTransportation Resources LLC 9550 N Loop E *TF:* 800-299-4200 ■ *Web:* www.selectransportation.com	Houston	TX	77029	713-672-4115		791
SelectResources Intl (SRI) 10940 Wilshire Blvd Ste 925 *Web:* www.selectresources.com	Los Angeles	CA	90024	310-824-8999		196
Selectric Signs 3055 State St *TF:* 800-489-2263 ■ *Web:* www.selectricsigns.com	Columbus	IN	47201	812-378-6129	376-0556	9
Selectron Technologies Inc 12323 SW 66th Ave *Web:* www.selectrontechnologies.com	Portland	OR	97223	503-443-1400		179
Selectronix Inc 16419 199th Ct NE *Web:* www.selectronix.us	Woodinville	WA	98077	425-788-2979		201
Selectus Consulting LLC 17875 Kandel Rd *Web:* selectusconsulting.com	Marysville	OH	43040	937-644-8562		196
Selectx Pharmaceuticals Inc 1 Innovation Dr *Web:* www.selectxpharm.com	Worcester	MA	01605	508-798-0216		583
Selee Corp 700 Shepherd St *TF:* 800-842-3818 ■ *Web:* selee.com	Hendersonville	NC	28792	828-697-2411	693-1868	144
Selerity Technologies Inc 1950 South 900 West Ste S3 *Web:* www.selerity.com	Salt Lake City	UT	84104	801-978-2295		743
Selerix Systems Inc 2851 Craig Dr Ste 300 *Web:* www.selerix.com	Mckinney	TX	75070	469-452-7076		194
SELEX Inc 11300 W 89th St *TF:* 800-765-0861 ■ *Web:* www.us.selex-es.com	Overland Park	KS	66214	913-495-2600	492-0870	529
Self Industries Inc 3491 Mary Taylor Rd *Web:* selfindustries.com	Birmingham	AL	35235	205-655-3284	655-3288	198
Self Opportunity Inc 808 Office Park Cir *TF:* 800-594-7036 ■ *Web:* www.selfopportunity.com	Lewisville	TX	75057	214-222-1500		194
Self Regional Hospital 1325 Spring St *Web:* www.selfregional.org	Greenwood	SC	29646	864-725-4111		374-3
Self Storage Assn (SSA) 1901 N Beauregard St Ste 106 *TF:* 888-735-3784 ■ *Web:* www.selfstorage.org	Alexandria	VA	22311	703-575-8000	575-8901	49-21
Self-Direct Inc 43 Oswego St *Web:* selfdirectinc.com	Baldwinsville	NY	13027	315-635-5374		363
Self-Employed America Magazine PO Box 241 *TF:* 800-649-6273 ■ *Web:* www.nase.org	Annapolis Junction	MD	20701	800-649-6273		457-5
Selfhelp Community Services 520 Eigth Ave 5th Fl *TF:* 866-735-1234 ■ *Web:* selfhelp.net	New York	NY	10018	212-971-7600		363
Selflock Screw Products Company Inc 461 E Brighton Ave *Web:* sspmfg.com	Syracuse	NY	13210	315-541-4464	475-1093	621
Self-Realization Fellowship Publishers 3880 San Rafael Ave *TF:* 888-773-8680 ■ *Web:* www.yogananda-srf.org	Los Angeles	CA	90031	323-276-6002	927-1624	637-2
Self-Seal Container Corp 315-329 E Second St PO Box 431 **Fax Area Code: 484* ■ *Web:* www.selfsealtubes.com	Boyertown	PA	19512	610-275-2300	624-5658*	125
Selig Enterprises Inc 1100 Spring St NW Ste 550 *Web:* www.seligenterprises.com	Atlanta	GA	30309	404-876-5511	875-2629	655
Selig Group Inc 342 E Wabash Ave *Web:* www.seligsealing.com	Forrest	IL	61741	815-785-2100		295
Seligman & Assoc 1 Town Sq 26100 NW Hwy Ste 1913 *Web:* www.seligmangroup.com	Southfield	MI	48076	248-862-8000		655
Seligsohn Soens Hess Co 123 S Broad St 8th Fl Ste 850 *Web:* sshrealestate.com	Philadelphia	PA	19103	215-893-3000		652
Selkirk & District Chamber of Commerce (SDCC) 200 Eaton Ave *Web:* www.selkirkanddistrictchamber.ca	Selkirk	MB	R1A0W6	204-482-7176	482-5448	137
Selkirk Canada Corp 375 Green Rd *TF:* 800-263-9308 ■ *Web:* www.selkirkcorp.com	Stoney Creek	ON	L8E4A5	905-662-6600		183
Selkirk College 301 Frank Beinder Way *TF:* 888-953-1133 ■ *Web:* www.selkirk.ca	Castlegar	BC	V1N4L3	250-365-7292	365-6568	166
Selkirk Shores State Park 7101 SR-3 *Web:* parks.ny.gov	Pulaski	NY	13142	315-298-5737		565
Sell My Timeshare Now LLC 383 Central Ave Ste 260 *TF:* 877-815-4227 ■ *Web:* www.sellmytimesharenow.com	Dover	NH	03820	603-516-0200		387
Sellars 6565 N 60th St **Fax Area Code: 414* ■ *TF:* 800-237-8454 ■ *Web:* sellarscompany.com	Milwaukee	WI	53223	800-237-8454	353-5707*	745-6
Sellen Construction 227 Westlake Ave N *Web:* www.sellen.com	Seattle	WA	98109	206-682-7770		186
Sellers Publishing Inc 161 John Roberts Rd *TF:* 800-778-7266 ■ *Web:* www.rsvp.com	South Portland	ME	04106	207-772-6833	772-6814	637-2
Sellex International Corp 88 E Broad St Ste 1220 *Web:* www.sellexinternational.com	Columbus	OH	43215	614-463-1986	463-1987	463
Selling Power Magazine 1140 International Pkwy *TF:* 800-752-7355 ■ *Web:* www.sellingpower.com	Fredericksburg	VA	22406	540-752-7000	752-7001	457-5
Selling Simplified Inc 7400 E Orchard Rd Ste 350S *Web:* sellingsimplified.com	Greenwood Village	CO	80111	720-638-8500		195
Sellmore Industries Inc 815 Smith St *Web:* www.sellmoreind.com	Buffalo	NY	14206	716-854-1600		234
Sellstrom Manufacturing Co 2050 Hammond Dr *TF:* 800-323-7402 ■ *Web:* www.sellstrom.com	Schaumburg	IL	60173	847-358-2000		576
Selltis LLC 9990 Richmond Ave Ste 250 N *Web:* selltis.com	Houston	TX	77042	985-727-3455		177
Selma University 1501 Lapsley St *Web:* selmauniversity.org	Selma	AL	36701	334-872-2533		166
Selma-Dallas County Chamber of Commerce 912 Selma Ave *Web:* www.selmaalabama.com	Selma	AL	36701	334-875-7241	875-7142	139
Selman Breitman LLP 11766 Wilshire Blvd *Web:* www.selmanlaw.com	Los Angeles	CA	90025	310-445-0800	473-2525	428
Selmer Co 2200 Woodale Ave *Web:* www.theboldtcompany.com	Green Bay	WI	54313	920-434-0230		187
Selmet Inc 33992 SE 7 Mile Ln PO Box 689 *Web:* selmetinc.com	Albany	OR	97322	541-926-7731		308
Selrico Services Inc 717 W Ashby Pl *Web:* www.selricoservices.com	San Antonio	TX	78212	210-737-8220	737-7994	670
Selsoft Inc 303 S Jupiter Ste 110 *Web:* www.selsoftinc.com	Allen	TX	75002	217-721-3186		177
Seltzer Caplan Mcmahon Vitek 2100 Symphony Towers 750 B St *Web:* www.scmv.com	San Diego	CA	92101	619-685-3003		428
Seltzer Firm Pllc, The 1115 Broadway *Web:* theseltzerfirm.com	New York	NY	10010	212-796-8844		41
Selva Grill 1345 Main St *Web:* www.selvagrill.com	Sarasota	FL	34236	941-362-4427		671
Selway Corp PO Box 287 *Web:* selwaycorp.com	Stevensville	MT	59870	406-777-5471	777-5473	821
SEM (Society for Experimental Mechanics Inc) 7 School St *TF:* 800-627-8258 ■ *Web:* sem.org	Bethel	CT	06801	203-790-6373	790-4472	49-19
SEM (Society for Ethnomusicology) Indiana University 800 E Third St *TF:* 800-933-9330 ■ *Web:* www.ethnomusicology.org	Bloomington	IN	47405	812-855-6672	855-6673	48-4
SEMA (Specialty Equipment Market Assn) 1575 S Vly Vista Dr *Web:* www.sema.org	Diamond Bar	CA	91765	909-396-0289	860-0184	49-21
SEMA Equipment Inc 11555 Hwy 60 Blvd *TF:* 800-569-1377 ■ *Web:* www.semaequip.com	Wanamingo	MN	55983	507-824-2256	824-2668	274
Se-Ma-No Electric Co-op 601 N Business 60 *Web:* www.semano.com	Mansfield	MO	65704	417-924-3243		245
Semantic Research Inc 4922 N Harbor Dr *Web:* www.semanticresearch.com	San Diego	CA	92106	619-222-4050		637-10
Semasys Inc 4480 Blalock Rd *TF:* 800-231-1425 ■ *Web:* semasys.com	Houston	TX	77041	800-231-1425		286
Sematco Inc 275 Eastpark Dr *Web:* www.sematco.com	Roanoke	VA	24019	540-977-3200	977-0660	454
Sembler Co, The 5858 W Central Ave *TF:* 800-940-6000 ■ *Web:* sembler.com	Saint Petersburg	FL	33707	727-384-6000		653
Semcasting Inc 41 High St *Web:* www.semcasting.com	North Andover	MA	01845	978-684-7580		387
Semco Duct and Acoustical Products Inc 1800 E Pointe Dr *TF:* 888-473-6264 ■ *Web:* semcohvac.com	Columbia	MO	65201	573-443-1481	443-6921	697
Semco Energy Gas Co 1411 3rd St Ste A *TF:* 800-624-2019 ■ *Web:* www.semcoenergygas.com	Port Huron	MI	48060	800-624-2019		580
Semco Manufacturing Co 705 E Business 83 *Web:* semcoice.com	Pharr	TX	78577	956-683-1411		664
Semco Plastic Co 5301 Old Baumgartner Rd *Web:* www.semcoplastics.com	Saint Louis	MO	63129	314-487-4557		608
Semco Productions 295 W Crossville Rd Bldg 200 **Fax Area Code: 770* ■ *Web:* www.semcoproductions.com	Roswell	GA	30075	678-822-9806	642-4715*	393
Seme & Son Automotive Inc 1320 E 260th St *TF:* 800-282-0991 ■ *Web:* www.semeandson.com	Euclid	OH	44132	216-261-0066		454
Semi Dice Inc PO Box 3002 *Web:* www.semidice.com	Los Alamitos	CA	90720	562-594-4631	430-5942	246
Semiconductor Circuits Inc 49 Range Rd *Web:* www.dcdc.com	Windham	NH	03087	603-893-2330	893-6280	253
Semiconductor Equipment & Materials Intl 3081 Zenker Rd *TF:* 877-746-7788 ■ *Web:* www.semi.org	San Jose	CA	95134	408-943-6900	428-9600	49-19
Semiconductor Process Equipment Corp 27963 Franklin Pkwy *Web:* www.team-spec.com	Valencia	CA	91355	661-257-0934		696
Semifab Inc 150 Great Oaks Blvd *Web:* www.semifab.com	San Jose	CA	95119	408-414-5928		696

Name / Address	City	State	ZIP	Phone	Fax	Class
Semifreddis Inc 1980 N Loop Rd *TF:* 877-568-7364 ■ *Web:* www.semifreddis.com	Alameda	CA	94502	510-596-9930		297-2
Semi-Kinetics Inc 20191 Windrow Dr Ste A *Web:* www.semi-kinetics.com	Lake Forest	CA	92630	949-830-7364	830-7385	695
Semikron Inc 11 Executive Dr *Web:* www.semikron.com	Hudson	NH	03051	603-883-8102		696
Seminary Co-opeartive Bookstore 5757 S University Ave. *Web:* www.semcoop.com	Chicago	IL	60637	773-752-4381	752-8507	95
Seminary Extension Independent Study Institute 901 Commerce St Ste 500 *Web:* www.seminaryextension.org	Nashville	TN	37203	615-242-2453	782-4822	167-3
Seminary of the Immaculate Conception 440 W Neck Rd. *Web:* icseminary.edu	Huntington	NY	11743	631-423-0483		167-3
Seminary of the southwest (SSW) 501 E 32nd PO Box 2247 *TF:* 800-252-5400 ■ *Web:* ssw.edu	Austin	TX	78705	512-472-4133	472-3098	167-3
Seminole Canyon State Park & Historic Site PO Box 820 *Web:* tpwd.texas.gov	Comstock	TX	78837	432-292-4464		565
Seminole Casino Hollywood 4150 N State Rd 7 *Web:* www.seminolehollywoodcasino.com	Hollywood	FL	33021	954-961-3220		133
Seminole Casino Immokalee 506 S First St *TF:* 800-218-0007 ■ *Web:* www.seminoleimmokaleecasino.com	Immokalee	FL	34142	800-218-0007		133
Seminole Coconut Creek Casino 5550 NW 40th St *Web:* www.seminolecoconutcreekcasino.com	Coconut Creek	FL	33073	954-977-6700		133
Seminole County 1101 E First St *Web:* www.seminolecountyfl.gov	Sanford	FL	32771	407-665-7945	665-7939	338
Seminole County Public Library 215 N Oxford Rd. *Web:* www.seminolecountyfl.gov	Casselberry	FL	32707	407-665-1500		434-3
Seminole County Public Library - North Branch 150 N Palmetto Ave *Web:* www.seminolecountyfl.gov	Sanford	FL	32771	407-665-0000		434-3
Seminole Electric Cooperative Inc 16313 N Dale Mabry Hwy. *Web:* www.seminole-electric.com	Tampa	FL	33618	813-963-0994	264-7906	245
Seminole Energy Services LLC 1323 E 71st St Ste 300 *Web:* www.seminoleenergy.com	Tulsa	OK	74136	918-492-2840	492-3075	325
Seminole Feed 335 NE Watula Ave PO Box 940 *TF:* 800-683-1881 ■ *Web:* seminolefeed.com	Ocala	FL	34470	352-732-4143		447
Seminole Hard Rock Hotel & Casino Hollywood 1 Seminole Way *TF:* 866-502-7529 ■ *Web:* www.theseminolecasinos.com	Hollywood	FL	33314	866-502-7529		669
Seminole Hard Rock Hotel & Casino Tampa (SHRH&C) 5223 N Orient Rd **Fax Area Code:* 954 ■ *TF:* 866-388-4263 ■ *Web:* www.seminolehardrocktampa.com	Tampa	FL	33610	813-627-7625	983-0242*	133
Seminole Marine 2501 Industrial Park Dr. *Web:* www.sailfishboats.com	Cairo	GA	39828	229-377-2125	377-1855	90
Seminole Precast Manufacturing Inc 331 Benson Junction Rd. *Web:* www.seminoleprecast.com	Debary	FL	32713	386-668-7323		183
Seminole Public Schools Federal Credit Union 207 SW Sixth St *Web:* seminoleisd.net	Seminole	TX	79360	432-758-3662		219
Seminole State College 100 Weldon Blvd *Web:* www.seminolestate.edu	Sanford	FL	32773	407-708-4722		162
Seminole State College 2701 Boren Blvd PO Box 351 *TF:* 877-738-6365 ■ *Web:* sscok.edu	Seminole	OK	74868	405-382-9950		162
Seminole State Park 7870 State Pk Dr. *Web:* gastateparks.org	Donalsonville	GA	39845	229-861-3137		565
Seminole Towne Ctr 200 Towne Center Cir *Web:* seminoletownecenter.com	Sanford	FL	32771	407-323-2262		460
Seminole Tribe of Florida Inc, The 6300 Stirling Rd *TF:* 800-683-7800 ■ *Web:* www.semtribe.com	Hollywood	FL	33024	954-966-6300		653
Seminole Valley Farm 1400 Seminole Valley Rd NE *Web:* www.seminolevalleyfarmmuseum.net	Cedar Rapids	IA	52411	319-378-9240		50-3
SemiProbe Inc 276 E Allen St *Web:* www.semiprobe.com	Winooski	VT	05404	802-860-7000		246
SemiTorr Inc 10655 Manhasset Dr. *TF:* 877-318-9275 ■ *Web:* www.semitorrinc.com	Tualatin	OR	97062	503-682-7052		196
Semler Industries Inc (SI) 3800 N Carnation St *Web:* www.semlerindustries.com	Franklin Park	IL	60131	847-671-5650	671-7686	770
Semling-Menke Company Inc PO Box 378 *TF:* 800-333-2206 ■ *Web:* www.semcowindows.com	Merrill	WI	54452	715-536-9411	536-3067	236
SEMO Electric Coop 1505 S Main *TF:* 800-813-5230 ■ *Web:* gosemo.com	Sikeston	MO	63801	800-813-5230		245
Semonin Realtors 600 N Hurstbourne Pkwy Ste 200 *TF:* 800-548-1650 ■ *Web:* www.semonin.com	Louisville	KY	40222	502-425-4760		652
Semple Brown 1160 Santa Fe Dr. *Web:* semplebrown.com	Denver	CO	80204	303-571-4137		708
Semple, Farrington & Everall PC 1120 Lincoln St Ste 1308 *Web:* smmpc.com	Denver	CO	80203	303-595-0941		41
Sempra Energy Corp 101 Ash St *NYSE: SRE* ■ *Web:* www.sempra.com	San Diego	CA	92101	619-696-2000		360-5
Semprex Corp 782 Camden Ave *Web:* www.semprex.com	Campbell	CA	95008	408-374-1843		248
Semtech Corp 200 Flynn Rd *NASDAQ: SMTC* ■ *Web:* www.semtech.com	Camarillo	CA	93012	805-498-2111	498-3804	696
SEMTORQ Inc 1953 Case Pky *Web:* www.semtorq.com	Twinsburg	OH	44087	330-487-0600	487-0646	674
SemWare Corp 730 Elk Cove Ct *Web:* www.semware.com	Kennesaw	GA	30152	678-355-9810	355-9812	178-2
Sen Plex Corp 938 Kohou St *Web:* www.senplex.com	Honolulu	HI	96817	808-848-0111		655
Senate Engineering Co 420 William Pitt Way *Web:* senateengineering.com	Pittsburgh	PA	15238	412-826-5454		261
Senate House State Historic Site 296 Fair St *Web:* parks.ny.gov	Kingston	NY	12401	845-338-2786		565
Senate Luxury Suites 900 SW Tyler St. *Web:* www.senatesuites.com	Topeka	KS	66612	785-233-5050		379
Senator Frank S Farley State Marina 600 Huron Ave *Web:* www.njparksandforests.org	Atlantic City	NJ	08401	609-441-8482		565
Senator Inn & Spa of Augusta 284 Western Ave. *TF:* 877-772-2224 ■ *Web:* www.senatorinn.com	Augusta	ME	04330	207-622-5804		707
Senator International Inc 1630 Holland Rd. *Web:* www.thesenatorgroup.com	Maumee	OH	43537	419-887-5806		321
Senator John Heinz Pittsburgh Regional History Ctr 1212 Smallman St *Web:* www.heinzhistorycenter.org	Pittsburgh	PA	15222	412-454-6000		520
SENCO 4270 Ivy Pointe Blvd **Fax Area Code:* 513 ■ *TF:* 800-543-4596 ■ *Web:* www.senco.com	Cincinnati	OH	45245	800-543-4596	388-3100*	759
Sencore Inc 3200 W Sencore Dr *Web:* www.sencore.com	Sioux Falls	SD	57107	605-978-4600	335-6379	248
SencorpWhite Inc 400 Kidds Hill Rd *TF:* 800-571-8822 ■ *Web:* www.whitesystems.com	Hyannis	MA	02601	508-771-9400	790-0002	207
Send Out Cards LLC 1825 W Research Way *Web:* www.sendoutcards.com	Salt Lake City	UT	84119	801-463-3800	463-3900	130
Send.com 100 Canal Pointe Blvd Ste 204 *TF:* 800-393-2181 ■ *Web:* www.send.com	Princeton	NJ	08540	609-720-0300		241
Senderex Cargo Inc 17022 Montanero Ave Ste 6 *Web:* www.senderex.com	Carson	CA	90746	310-342-2900		311
Sendio Inc 4911 Birch St Ste 150 *Web:* sendio.com	Newport Beach	CA	92660	949-274-4375		100
Sendoso 447 Battery St 2nd Fl *TF:* 888-717-3287 ■ *Web:* sendoso.com	San Francisco	CA	94111	888-717-3287		657
Sen-Dure Products Inc 6785 NW 17th Ave *TF:* 800-394-5112 ■ *Web:* www.sen-dure.net	Fort Lauderdale	FL	33309	954-973-1260		91
Seneca Biopharma Inc 20271 Goldenrod Ln Ste 2024 *Web:* senecabio.com	Germantown	MD	20876	301-366-4960		85
Seneca College 1750 Finch Ave E *Web:* www.senecacollege.ca	Toronto	ON	M2J2X5	416-491-5050		165
Seneca Consulting Group Inc 111 Smithtown Byp Ste 112 *TF:* 866-487-4157 ■ *Web:* www.senecaconsulting.com	Hauppauge	NY	11788	631-577-4092		466
Seneca County 111 Madison St *Web:* www.seneca-county.com	Tiffin	OH	44883	419-447-4550		338
Seneca County 1 DiPronio Dr. *Web:* www.co.seneca.ny.us	Waterloo	NY	13165	315-539-1945	539-3789	338
Seneca County Chamber of Commerce 2020 Rt 5 & 20 W. *TF:* 800-732-1848 ■ *Web:* fingerlakesgateway.com	Seneca Falls	NY	13148	315-568-2906		139
Seneca Creek State Park 11950 Clopper Rd *Web:* www.dnr.maryland.gov	Gaithersburg	MD	20878	301-924-2127		565
Seneca Falls Central School District 98 Clinton St *Web:* www.senecafallscsd.org	Seneca Falls	NY	13148	315-568-5818		685
Seneca Falls Technology Group 314 Fall St *Web:* www.sftg.com	Seneca Falls	NY	13148	315-568-5804	568-5800	455
Seneca Flight Operations 2262 Airport Dr. *Web:* www.senecaflight.com	Penn Yan	NY	14527	315-536-4471	536-4558	13
Seneca Foods Corp 3736 S Main St. *NASDAQ: SENEA* ■ *TF:* 800-622-6757 ■ *Web:* www.senecafoods.com	Marion	NY	14505	315-926-8100	926-8300	296-20
Seneca Foundry Inc 240 Mackinlay Kantor Dr *Web:* www.senecafoundry.com	Webster City	IA	50595	515-832-1722	832-2579	492
Seneca Highlands Career & Technical Ctr 219 Edison Bates Dr *Web:* www.iu9.org	Port Allegany	PA	16743	814-642-2573		48-11
Seneca Lake State Park 1 Lakefront Dr *Web:* parks.ny.gov	Geneva	NY	14456	315-789-2331		565
Seneca Larkin 701 LLC 701 Seneca St Ste 200 *Web:* larkincenter.com	Buffalo	NY	14210	716-856-0810	852-2292	653
Seneca Nation of Indians Federal Credit Union 12837 Rt 438 *Web:* sni.org	Irving	NY	14081	716-532-4900		219
Seneca Niagara Casino 310 Fourth St *TF:* 877-873-6322 ■ *Web:* senecaniagaracasino.com	Niagara Falls	NY	14303	716-299-1100		133
Seneca Park Zoo 2222 St Paul St. *Web:* senecaparkzoo.org	Rochester	NY	14621	585-336-7200	342-1477	823
Seneca Partners Inc 300 Park St Ste 400 *Web:* senecapartners.com	Birmingham	MI	48009	248-723-6650		194
Seneca Resources Corp 1201 Louisiana St Ste 400 *Web:* natfuel.com	Houston	TX	77002	713-654-2600		536
Seneca Sawmill Co 90201 Hwy 99. *Web:* senecasawmill.com	Eugene	OR	97440	541-689-1011		683
Seneca State Forest 10135 Browns Creek Rd *Web:* wvstateparks.com	Dunmore	WV	24934	304-799-6213		565
Seneca Tank Inc 5585 NE 16th St *TF:* 800-362-2910 ■ *Web:* www.senecatank.com	Des Moines	IA	50313	515-262-5900		57
Senergy Petroleum LLC 622 S 56th Ave *TF:* 800-964-0076 ■ *Web:* www.brownevans.com	Phoenix	AZ	85043	602-272-6795		579

Company	City	State	Zip	Phone	Fax	Class
Senes Oak Ridge Center for Risk Analysis Inc 102 Donner Dr *Web:* senes.com	Oak Ridge	TN	37830	865-483-6111		196
Senesco Marine LLC 10 Macnaught St *Web:* www.senescomarine.com	North Kingstown	RI	02852	401-295-0373		698
Senet Inc 100 Market St Ste 302 *TF:* 877-807-5755 ■ *Web:* www.senetco.com	Portsmouth	NH	03801	877-807-5755		407
Senex Explosives Inc 719 Millers Run Rd	Cuddy	PA	15031	412-221-3218		268
Senga Engineering 1525 E Warner Ave *Web:* www.senga-eng.com	Santa Ana	CA	92705	714-549-8011		261
Sengen Inc 9001 Highland Woods Blvd Ste 203 *Web:* sengen.com	Bonita Springs	FL	34134	239-908-6700		809
Senior Aerospace AMT 20100 71st Ave NE *Web:* www.amtnw.com	Arlington	WA	98223	360-435-1119		454
Senior Aerospace Jet Products 9106 Balboa Ave *Web:* www.seniorplc.com	San Diego	CA	92123	858-430-2203	278-8768	621
Senior Aerospace Ketema Div 790 Greenfield Dr *Web:* www.sfketema.com	El Cajon	CA	92021	619-442-3451	440-1456	21
Senior Aerospace Metal Bellows 1075 Providence Hwy *TF:* 800-267-1975 ■ *Web:* www.metalbellows.com	Sharon	MA	02067	781-784-1400	784-1405	386
Senior Alternatives For Living 26211 Central Park Blvd *TF:* 800-350-0770 ■ *Web:* www.alternativesforseniors.com	Southfield	MI	48076	800-350-0770		5
Senior Benefit Services Inc 13511 Label Ln Ste 204 *TF:* 800-924-4727 ■ *Web:* seniorbenefitclient.com	Hagerstown	MD	21740	301-733-0085		390
Senior Care Pharmacy 4455 Morris Park Dr Ste A *Web:* star848.wixsite.com	Charlotte	NC	28227	704-545-8641		237
Senior Flexonics GA Precision 5215 W Airways Ave *Web:* www.seniorflexonicsgaprecision.com	Franklin	WI	53132	414-423-6400		621
Senior Flexonics Inc 300 E Devon Ave *Web:* seniorflexonics.com	Bartlett	IL	60103	630-837-1811		480
Senior Flexonics Inc 2400 Longhorn Industrial Dr *Web:* www.sfpathway.com	New Braunfels	TX	78130	830-629-6899		480
Senior Housing Cos 208 35th St Dr SE Ste 500 **Fax Area Code:* 319 ■ *TF:* 800-366-6716 ■ *Web:* www.seniorhousingcompanies.com	Cedar Rapids	IA	52403	800-366-6716	363-6145*	193
Senior Housing Properties Trust 255 Washington St *NASDAQ: SNH* ■ *Web:* www.snhreit.com	Newton	MA	02458	617-796-8350	796-8349	655
Senior Lifestyle 303 E Upper Wacker Dr Ste 2400 *TF:* 877-315-0914 ■ *Web:* www.seniorlifestyle.com	Chicago	IL	60601	877-315-0914		672
Senior Market Sales Inc (SMS) 8420 W Dodge Rd Ste 510 *TF:* 800-786-5566 ■ *Web:* www.seniormarketsales.com	Omaha	NE	68114	402-397-3311	397-0455	390
Senior Marketing Specialist 801 Gray Oak Dr *TF:* 800-689-2800 ■ *Web:* www.smsteam.net	Columbia	MO	65201	800-689-2800		195
Senior Settlements LLC 1000 S Lenola Rd Bldg 1 Ste 202 *Web:* www.seniorsettlementsllc.com	Maple Shade	NJ	08052	856-235-2133	235-1294	796
Senior Softball USA 9823 Old Winery Pl Ste 12 *TF:* 800-327-0074 ■ *Web:* seniorsoftball.com	Sacramento	CA	95827	916-326-5303	326-5304	48-22
Senior Whole Health LLC (SWH) 58 Charles St *TF:* 888-794-7268 ■ *Web:* www.seniorwholehealth.com	Cambridge	MA	02141	617-494-5353	494-5599	353
Seniority Benefit Group 6365 Riverside Dr *Web:* www.senioritybenefitgroup.com	Dublin	OH	43017	614-799-1403		390
Seniors First Foundation Inc 5395 L B Mcleod Rd *Web:* seniorsfirstinc.org	Orlando	FL	32811	407-292-0177		305
Seniors Plus 8 Falcon Rd *TF:* 800-427-1241 ■ *Web:* seniorsplus.org	Lewiston	ME	04240	207-795-4010	795-4009	672
Senn Visciano Canges PC 1700 Lincoln St Ste 4300 *Web:* sennlaw.com	Denver	CO	80203	303-298-1122		41
Senn-Delaney Leadership Consulting Group LLC 7755 Center Ave Ste 900 *Web:* www.senndelaney.com	Huntington Beach	CA	92647	562-426-5400	426-5174	196
Senne Company Inc 33 Church St *Web:* sennere.com	Cambridge	MA	02138	617-314-9400		652
Sennheiser Electronics Corp 1 Enterprise Dr *TF:* 877-736-6434 ■ *Web:* en-us.sennheiser.com	Old Lyme	CT	06371	860-434-9190	434-1759	246
Seno Medical Instruments Inc 5253 Prue Rd Ste 315 *Web:* senomedical.com	San Antonio	TX	78240	210-615-6501		475
Senor Fish 9530 Viscount Blvd Ste 1A	El Paso	TX	79925	915-598-3630		671
Senor Frogs 1304 Celebrity Cir R-8 *Web:* www.senorfrogs.com	Myrtle Beach	SC	29577	843-444-5506		671
Senor Ric's 13200 E Mississippi Ave *Web:* www.senorrics.net	Aurora	CO	80012	303-750-9000		671
SenovvA Inc 1401 E 3rd St *Web:* www.senovva.com	Los Angeles	CA	90033	213-689-6900		23
Sensato Investors LLC 1 Sansome St Ste 3430 *Web:* www.sensatoinvestors.com	San Francisco	CA	94104	415-391-4600		528
Senscio Systems Inc 1740 Massachusetts Ave *Web:* www.sensciosystems.com	Boxborough	MA	01719	978-635-9090		177
Sense Corp 2731 Sutton Blvd Ste 200 *Web:* sensecorp.com	Saint Louis	MO	63143	314-266-3700		180
Sensei Lanai, A Four Seasons Resort 1 Keomoku Hwy PO Box 631380 **Fax Area Code:* 808 ■ *Web:* secure.fourseasons.com	Lanai City	HI	96763	800-505-2624	565-4577*	669
Sensenbrenner F. James (Rep R - WI) 2449 Rayburn House Office Bldg *Web:* sensenbrenner.house.gov	Washington	DC	20515	202-225-5101		342-2
Senseonics Inc 20451 Seneca Meadows Pky *Web:* www.senseonics.com	Germantown	MD	20876	301-515-7260	515-0988	634
Sensi Media Group LLC 512 17th St *Web:* sensimag.com	Denver	CO	80202	720-486-9062		568
Sensible Vision Inc 40376 Blue Star Hwy Ste 11 *Web:* www.sensiblevision.com	Covert	MI	49043	269-932-4548		809
Sensical Incorporated Decals 31115 Aurora Rd *Web:* sensical.com	Solon	OH	44139	216-641-1141		687
Sensidyne Inc 16333 Bay Vista Dr *TF:* 800-451-9444 ■ *Web:* www.sensidyne.com	Clearwater	FL	33760	727-530-3602	539-0550	201
Sensient Colors Inc 2515 N Jefferson Ave *TF:* 800-325-8110 ■ *Web:* sensientfoodcolors.com	Saint Louis	MO	63106	314-889-7600		296-15
Sensient Technologies Corp 777 E Wisconsin Ave Ste 1100 *NYSE: SXT* ■ *TF:* 800-558-9892 ■ *Web:* www.sensient.com	Milwaukee	WI	53202	414-271-6755	347-3785	296-15
Sensis 818 S Broadway Ste 1100 *Web:* www.sensisagency.com	Los Angeles	CA	90014	231-341-0171		4
Sensitech Inc 800 Cummings Ctr Ste 258x *TF:* 800-843-8367 ■ *Web:* www.sensitech.com	Beverly	MA	01915	978-927-7033		171
Sensitile Systems 1735 Holmes Rd *Web:* sensitile.com	Ypsilanti	MI	48198	313-872-6314		499
Sensitron Semiconductor 221 W Industry Ct *Web:* www.sensitron.com	Deer Park	NY	11729	631-586-7600		695
Senske Services 400 N Quay St *TF:* 877-944-4007 ■ *Web:* senske.com	Kennewick	WA	99336	509-374-5000		577
Sensor Dynamics Inc 4568 Enterprise St *Web:* sensordynamics.com	Fremont	CA	94538	510-623-1459		354
Sensor Geophysical Ltd 736-6 Ave SW Ste 1300 *Web:* sensorseismic.com	Calgary	AB	T2P3T7	403-237-7711		41
Sensor Platforms Inc 2860 Zanker Rd Ste 210 *Web:* www.sensorplatforms.com	San Jose	CA	95134	408-850-9350		696
Sensor Systems Inc 8929 Fullbright Ave *Web:* www.sensorantennas.com	Chatsworth	CA	91311	818-341-5366	341-9059	647
Sensor Systems LLC 2800 Anvil St N *Web:* www.sensorsllc.com	Saint Petersburg	FL	33710	727-347-2181	347-7520	472
Sensorlink Corp 1360 Stonegate Way *Web:* sensorlink.com	Ferndale	WA	98248	360-595-1000	595-1001	246
Sensormatic Electronics Corp 6600 Congress Ave *TF:* 800-327-1765 ■ *Web:* www.sensormatic.com	Boca Raton	FL	33487	561-912-6000		692
Sensors Unlimited Inc 330 Carter Rd *Web:* www.sensorsinc.com	Princeton	NJ	08540	609-333-8000	333-8103	529
Sensortags Inc 5660 Roberts Rd *TF:* 800-934-7080 ■ *Web:* www.sensortags.com	Terre Haute	IN	47805	812-877-9930		246
Sensorwise Inc 2908 Rogerdale Rd *Web:* www.sensorwise.com	Houston	TX	77042	713-952-3350		261
Sensory Analytics 4413-C W Market St *Web:* www.specmetrix.com	Greensboro	NC	27407	336-315-6090	315-6030	201
Senspex Inc 9798 Coors Blvd NW Bldg B *Web:* www.senspex.com	Albuquerque	NM	87114	505-891-0034		696
Senstar Corp 119 John Cavanaugh Dr *Web:* senstar.com	Ottawa	ON	K0A1L0	613-839-5572		693
Sensus 8601 Six Forks Rd Ste 700 *TF:* 800-638-3748 ■ *Web:* sensus.com	Raleigh	NC	27615	919-845-4000		201
Sentara College of Health Sciences Crossways I Ste 105 *TF:* 877-609-8870 ■ *Web:* www.sentara.edu	Chesapeake	VA	23320	757-388-2900		167-3
Sentara Healthcare 6015 Poplar Hall Dr *Web:* www.sentara.com	Norfolk	VA	23502	757-455-7976		353
Sentech Inc 2851 Limekiln Pke *TF:* 888-461-8324 ■ *Web:* www.sentechlvdt.com	Glenside	PA	19038	215-887-8665	887-8449	248
Sentencing Project 1705 DeSales St NW 8th Fl *Web:* www.sentencingproject.org	Washington	DC	20036	202-628-0871	628-1091	48-8
Senterra Real Estate Group LLC 11 Greenway Plz Ste 3100 *Web:* www.senterrarealestategroup.com	Houston	TX	77046	713-965-2940		652
Sentient Energy Inc 880 Mitten Rd *Web:* www.sentient-energy.com	Burlingame	CA	94010	650-523-6680	239-9048	407
Sentient Jet 100 Grossman Dr 4th Fl **Fax Area Code:* 781 ■ *TF:* 866-602-0044 ■ *Web:* www.sentient.com	Braintree	MA	02184	866-602-0044	871-8002*	13
Sentient Publications LLC 1113 Spruce St *TF:* 866-588-9846 ■ *Web:* www.sentientpublications.com	Boulder	CO	80302	303-443-2188	381-2538	637-2
Sentinel 12100 E Iliff Ave Ste 102 *TF:* 855-269-4484 ■ *Web:* aurorasentinel.com	Aurora	CO	80014	303-750-7555	750-7699	532-4
Sentinel & Enterprise PO Box 730 *Web:* www.sentinelandenterprise.com	Fitchburg	MA	01420	978-343-6911		532-2
Sentinel Benefits & Financial Group 100 Quannapowitt Pky Ste 300 *TF:* 888-762-6088 ■ *Web:* www.sentinelgroup.com	Wakefield	MA	01880	781-914-1200	213-6770	401
Sentinel Brokers Company Inc 20 Broadway *Web:* www.sentinelbrokers.com	Massapequa	NY	11758	516-541-9100	541-6413	690
Sentinel Building Systems Inc 237 S 4th St PO Box 348 *TF:* 800-327-0790 ■ *Web:* sentinelbuildings.com	Albion	NE	68620	402-395-5076		307
Sentinel Development Solutions Inc 4015 Beltline Rd Ste 100 **Fax Area Code:* 972 ■ *TF:* 877-395-8976 ■ *Web:* ecollections.com	Addison	TX	75001	515-564-0585	692-8415*	809
Sentinel Fence LLC 1527 NC Hwy 711 *Web:* www.sentinelmfg.com	Lumberton	NC	28360	910-735-1351		567

Name / Address	City	State	Zip	Phone	Fax	Class
Sentinel Hotel 614 SW 11th Ave *TF:* 888-246-5631 ■ *Web:* www.sentinelhotel.com	Portland	OR	97205	503-224-3400		379
Sentinel Integrity Solutions Inc 6606 Miller Rd 2 *Web:* sentinelintegrity.com	Houston	TX	77049	281-457-2225	457-0225	743
Sentinel Lubricants Inc 15755 Nw 15th Ave *Web:* www.sentinelsynthetic.com	Miami	FL	33169	305-625-6400	625-6565	541
Sentinel Offender Services LLC 201 Technology Dr *Web:* www.sentineladvantage.com	Irvine	CA	92618	949-453-1550		693
Sentinel Power Services Inc 7517 E Pine St *TF:* 800-831-9550 ■ *Web:* sentinelpowerservices.com	Tulsa	OK	74115	918-359-0350		532-3
Sentinel Process Systems 3265 Sunset Ln *TF:* 800-345-3569 ■ *Web:* www.sentinelprocess.com	Hatboro	PA	19040	888-329-9669		330
Sentinel Real Estate Corp 1251 Avenue of the Americas *Web:* www.sentinelcorp.com	New York	NY	10020	212-408-5035	603-8253	655
Sentinel Structures Inc 477 S Peck Ave *Web:* www.sentinelstructures.com	Peshtigo	WI	54157	715-582-4544	582-4932	817
Sentinel Systems Corp 1620 Kipling St *TF:* 800-456-9955 ■ *Web:* www.sentinelsystems.com	Lakewood	CO	80215	303-242-2000		532-3
Sentinel Technologies Inc 2550 Warrenville Rd *TF:* 800-769-4343 ■ *Web:* www.sentinel.com	Downers Grove	IL	60515	800-769-4343		175
Sentinel Transportation LLC 3521 Silverside Rd Ste 2A *TF:* 855-496-7572 ■ *Web:* www.sentineltrans.com	Wilmington	DE	19810	302-477-1640	477-1652	532-3
Sentinel Wealth Management Inc 11710 Plaza America Dr Ste 130 *Web:* www.sentinelwealth.com	Reston	VA	20190	703-787-5770		401
Sentinel, The 457 E N St *TF:* 800-829-5570 ■ *Web:* www.cumberlink.com	Carlisle	PA	17013	717-243-2611		532-2
Sentinel, The 300 W Sixth St *TF:* 888-606-0605 ■ *Web:* hanfordsentinel.com	Hanford	CA	93230	559-582-0471		532-2
Sentinel-Record 300 Spring St *Web:* www.hotsr.com	Hot Springs	AR	71902	501-623-7711		532-2
Sentran LLC 4355 Lowell St *TF:* 888-545-8988 ■ *Web:* www.sentranllc.com	Ontario	CA	91761	909-605-1544	605-6305	362
Sentry 360 Security Inc 23807 W Andrew Rd Ste B *Web:* sentry360.com	Plainfield	IL	60585	630-355-3440		693
Sentry Alarm Systems of America Inc 8 Thomas Owens Way *Web:* www.sentryalarm.com	Monterey	CA	93940	831-375-2727		693
Sentry BioPharma Services Inc 4605 Decatur Blvd Ameriplex Pk *TF:* 866-757-7400 ■ *Web:* sentrybps.com	Indianapolis	IN	46241	317-856-5889		583
Sentry Communications and Security 60 Bethpage Rd *TF:* 866-573-6879 ■ *Web:* www.sentryprotectsyou.com	Hicksville	NY	11801	866-573-6879		692
Sentry Electric 185 Buffalo Ave *Web:* www.sentrylighting.com	Freeport	NY	11520	516-379-4660	378-0624	439
Sentry Equipment & Erectors Inc 13150 E Lynchburg Salem Tpke *Web:* www.sentryequipment.com	Forest	VA	24551	434-525-0769	525-1701	386
Sentry Equipment Corp 966 Blue Ribbon Cir N *Web:* sentry-equip.com	Oconomowoc	WI	53066	262-567-7256	567-4523	419
Sentry Group 900 Linden Ave *TF:* 800-828-1438 ■ *Web:* www.sentrysafe.com	Rochester	NY	14625	585-381-4900	381-2940	692
Sentry Hospitality Ltd 136 E 57th St Ste 1003 *Web:* www.sentryhospitality.com	New York	NY	10022	212-753-5347		463
Sentry Insurance A Mutual Co 1800 N Point Dr PO Box 8032 *TF:* 800-473-6879 ■ *Web:* www.sentry.com	Stevens Point	WI	54481	800-473-6879		391-4
Sentry Products Inc 2378 B Walsh Ave *TF:* 800-899-1940 ■ *Web:* www.sentryproducts.net	Santa Clara	CA	95051	408-727-1866	727-2129	692
Sentry Security LLC 339 Egidi Dr *TF:* 888-272-7080 ■ *Web:* www.sentrysecurity.com	Wheeling	IL	60090	847-353-7200		693
Sentry Technology Corp 1881 Lakeland Ave *OTC:* SKVY ■ **Fax Area Code:* 631 ■ *TF:* 800-645-4224 ■ *Web:* www.sentrytechnology.com	Ronkonkoma	NY	11779	800-645-4224	739-2124*	692
Sentry Watch Inc 1705 Holbrook St *TF:* 800-632-4961 ■ *Web:* www.sentrywatch.com	Greensboro	NC	27403	800-632-4961		693
Senture LLC 460 Industrial Blvd *Web:* www.senture.com	London	KY	40741	606-877-6670	877-6672	624
Senvoy LLC 18055 NE San Rafael St *TF:* 866-373-6869 ■ *Web:* www.senvoy.com	Portland	OR	97230	503-234-7722	230-7061	311
SEO com LLC 14870 S Pony Express Rd Ste 100 *TF:* 800-351-9081 ■ *Web:* www.seo.com	Bluffdale	UT	84065	800-351-9081		7
SEOP 1621 Alton Pkwy Ste 150 *TF:* 877-231-1557 ■ *Web:* seop.com	Irvine	CA	92606	877-231-1557		7
SEP (Seismic Energy Products LP) 518 Progress Way	Athens	TX	75751	903-675-8571		676
SEP Communications 90 SE Fourth Ave Ste 2 *Web:* www.sepcommunications.com	Delray Beach	FL	33483	561-998-0870	998-0463	627
Separation Processes Inc 3156 Lionshead Ave Ste 2 *Web:* spi-engineering.com	Carlsbad	CA	92010	760-400-3660	400-3661	261
Sephora USA Inc 525 Market St 1st Market Twr 32nd Fl *TF:* 877-737-4672 ■ *Web:* www.sephora.com	San Francisco	CA	94105	877-737-4672		214
SEPLSO (Southeastern Public Library System of Oklahoma) 401 N 2nd St **Fax Area Code:* 866 ■ *TF:* 800-562-9520 ■ *Web:* oklibrary.net	McAlester	OK	74501	918-426-0456	569-8188*	434-3
Sepp Leaf Products Inc 381 Park Ave S Ste 1301 *TF:* 800-971-7377 ■ *Web:* www.seppleaf.com	New York	NY	10016	212-683-2840	725-0308	44
SEPTA (Southeastern Pennsylvania Transportation Authority) 1234 Market St *TF:* 877-737-8248 ■ *Web:* www.septa.org	Philadelphia	PA	19107	215-580-7800		468
Septagon Construction 113 E Third St *TF:* 800-733-5999 ■ *Web:* www.septagon.com	Sedalia	MO	65301	660-827-2115		186
Sept-Iles *Chamber of Commerce* 700 Laure Blvd Ste 237 *Web:* www.ccseptiles.com	Sept-Iles	QC	G4R1Y1	418-968-3488	968-3432	137
Sequa Corp *Precoat Metals Div* 1310 Papin St 3rd Fl *Web:* precoatmetals.com	Saint Louis	MO	63103	314-436-7010	436-7050	481
Sequachee Valley Electric Co-op 512 Cedar Ave PO Box 31 *TF:* 800-923-2203 ■ *Web:* www.svalleyec.com	South Pittsburg	TN	37380	423-837-8605	837-9836	245
Sequatchie Concrete Service Inc 406 Cedar Ave *TF:* 800-824-0824 ■ *Web:* www.seqconcrete.com	South Pittsburg	TN	37380	423-837-7913		183
Sequatchie County 22 Cherry St PO Box 595 *Web:* sequatchiegov.com	Dunlap	TN	37327	423-949-3479	949-2579	338
Sequel Data Systems Inc 11824 Jollyville Rd Ste 400 *Web:* www.sequeldata.com	Austin	TX	78759	512-918-8841	519-7868	196
Sequel Energy LLC 8101 E Prentice Ave Ste 1175 *Web:* sequelenergy.com	Greenwood Village	CO	80111	303-468-2106		536
Sequel Studio LLC 12 W 27th St *Web:* sequelstudio.com	New York	NY	10001	212-994-4320		344
Sequel Venture Partners 4430 Arapahoe Ave Ste 220 *Web:* www.sequelvc.com	Boulder	CO	80303	303-546-0400	546-9728	792
Sequence Controls Inc 150 Rosamond St *TF:* 800-663-1833 ■ *Web:* www.sequencecontrols.com	Carleton	ON	K7C1V2	613-257-7356		203
Sequent Energy Management 1200 Smith St *TF:* 866-581-8074 ■ *Web:* www.sequentenergy.com	Houston	TX	77002	832-397-1700	397-3713	104
Sequim Bay State Park 269035 Hwy 101 *Web:* parks.state.wa.us	Sequim	WA	98382	360-683-4235		565
Sequins International Inc 60-01 31st Ave *TF:* 800-221-5801 ■ *Web:* www.sequinsdirect.com	Woodside	NY	11377	718-204-0002	204-0999	745-5
Sequoia 1777 Botelho Dr Ste 300 *Web:* www.elevatetosequoia.com	Walnut Creek	CA	94596	925-945-0900		405
Sequoia 2800 Sand Hill Rd Ste 101 *Web:* www.sequoiacap.com	Menlo Park	CA	94025	650 854 3927		792
Sequoia & Kings Canyon National Parks 47050 Generals Hwy *Web:* www.nps.gov	Three Rivers	CA	93271	559-565-3341	565-3730	564
Sequoia Brewing Co 777 E Olive St *Web:* sequoiabrewing.com	Fresno	CA	93728	559-264-5521		671
Sequoia Equipment Company Inc PO Box 2747 *Web:* www.sequoiaequipment.com	Fresno	CA	93745	559-441-1122	441-0454	358
Sequoia Living 1525 Post St *Web:* www.sequoialiving.org	San Francisco	CA	94109	415-202-7800		672
Sequoia Park Zoo 3414 W St *Web:* www.sequoiaparkzoo.net	Eureka	CA	95503	707-441-4263		823
Sequoia Scientific Inc 2700 Richards Rd Ste 107 *TF:* 866-212-2226 ■ *Web:* www.sequoiasci.com	Bellevue	WA	98005	425-641-0944	643-0595	668
Sequoias Portola Valley, The *Northern California Presbyterian Homes & Services* 501 Portola Rd *Web:* www.ncphs.org	Portola Valley	CA	94028	650-851-1601	851-5007	672
Sequoyah Bay State Park 6237 E 100th St N *Web:* www.travelok.com	Wagoner	OK	74467	918-683-0878	687-6797	565
Sequoyah State Park & Western Hills Guest Ranch 17131 Pk 10 *Web:* www.travelok.com	Hulbert	OK	74441	918-772-2046	772-3042	565
Sequoyah Technologies LLC 201 E Hobson Ave *Web:* www.seqtek.com	Sapulpa	OK	74066	918-493-7200		809
Sera Prognostics Inc 2749 E Parleys Way Ste 200 *Web:* seraprognostics.com	Salt Lake City	UT	84109	801-990-0520		261
Seraaj Family Homes Inc 400 Cotton Gin Rd *TF:* 877-656-2638 ■ *Web:* seraajfh.com	Montgomery	AL	36117	334-271-2402	271-2405	260
Sera-Brynn LLC 5806 Harbour View Blvd Ste 204 *Web:* sera-brynn.com	Suffolk	VA	23435	757-243-1257		196
SeraCare Life Sciences Inc 37 Birch St *NASDAQ:* SRLS ■ *TF:* 800-676-1881 ■ *Web:* www.seracare.com	Milford	MA	01757	508-244-6400	634-3394	89
Serafina 2043 Eastlake Ave E *Web:* serafinaseattle.com	Seattle	WA	98102	206-323-0807		671
Serapid Inc 34100 Mound Rd *Web:* www.serapid.com	Sterling Heights	MI	48310	586-274-0774		757
Serbia *Consulate General* 201 E Ohio St Ste 200 *Web:* www.scgchicago.org	Chicago	IL	60611	312-670-6707		257
Sercel Inc 17200 Pk Row *Web:* www.sercel.com	Houston	TX	77084	281-492-6688	579-6555	472
Serco Group Inc 1818 Library St Ste 1000 *Web:* www.serco.com	Reston	VA	20190	703-939-6000	939-6001	271
Serendipity Interactive 181 N Main St *Web:* serendipityinteractive.com	Mooresville	NC	28115	704-230-2352		195
Serengeti Systems Inc 1108 Lavaca St Ste 110 PMB 431 *TF:* 800-634-3122 ■ *Web:* www.serengeti.com	Austin	TX	78701	512-345-2211		178-12

Name / Address	City	State	Zip	Phone	Fax	Class
Serenity Hospice and Palliative Care 2999 N 44th St Ste 225 *Web:* www.serenityhospiceaz.com	Phoenix	AZ	85018	602-216-2273	443-5398	450
Serenity Lane 1 Serenity Ln PO Box 8549 *TF:* 800-543-9905 ■ *Web:* serenitylane.org	Coburg	OR	97408	541-687-1110	683-9061	726
Serenity Mental Health Services 6613 Eastridge Rd *TF:* 888-347-7560 ■ *Web:* www.serenitymentalhealth.com	Black Hawk	SD	57718	605-431-8595		374-5
Serenity Packaging Corp 1601 E Main St Ste 2E *TF:* 866-219-3651 ■ *Web:* www.serenitypkg.com	Saint Charles	IL	60174	630-762-9870	762-9873	385
Sereno Group Real Estate 369 S San Antonio Rd *Web:* www.serenogroup.com	Los Altos	CA	94022	650-947-2900		652
Sererra Consulting Group LLC 4590 MacArthur Blvd Ste 500 *TF:* 877-276-3774 ■ *Web:* sererra.com	Newport Beach	CA	92660	877-276-3774		196
Seret and Sons Inc 224 Galisteo St *Web:* seretandsons.org	Santa Fe	NM	87501	505-988-9151	982-3027	320
Seretta Construction Inc 2604 Clark St *Web:* www.seretta.com	Apopka	FL	32703	407-290-9440	290-9372	189-3
Serfco Termite & Pest Control Inc 1701 S Walton Blvd *TF:* 800-495-2220 ■ *Web:* www.serfcopest.com	Bentonville	AR	72712	479-273-2220		577
Serfilco Ltd 2900 MacArthur Blvd *TF:* 800-323-5431 ■ *Web:* www.serfilco.com	Northbrook	IL	60062	847-559-1777	559-1141	641
Sergeant Alvin C York State Historic Park 2609 N York Hwy *Web:* tnstateparks.com	Pall Mall	TN	38577	931-879-6456		565
Sergenian's Residential Flooring 2805 W Beltline Hwy *Web:* www.sergenians.com	Madison	WI	53713	608-271-1111		290
SERI (Society for Ecological Restoration Intl) 1017 O St NW **Fax Area Code:* 270 ■ *Web:* www.ser.org	Washington	DC	20001	202-299-9518	626-5485*	48-13
Serigraph Inc 3801 E Decorah Rd *TF:* 800-279-6060 ■ *Web:* www.serigraph.com	West Bend	WI	53095	262-335-7200	335-7699	687
Serino Coyne Inc 1285 Ave of the Americas 5th Fl *Web:* www.serinocoyne.com	New York	NY	10022	212-626-2700		4
SeriousFun Children's Network 228 Saugatuck Ave *Web:* seriousfun.org	Westport	CT	06880	203-562-1203	562-1207	48-5
Serna & Company PC 6031 W I-20 Ste 251 *Web:* www.serna.com	Arlington	TX	76017	817-483-3884		2
Seroka 200 S Executive Dr *TF:* 866-379-0400 ■ *Web:* www.seroka.com	Brookfield	WI	53005	866-379-0400		195
Serpe & Sons Inc 1411 Kirkwood Hwy *Web:* www.serpesbakery.com	Elsmere	DE	19805	302-994-1868	904-7355	296-1
Serra Automotive 102 W Silver Lake Rd *Web:* www.serrausa.com	Grand Blanc	MI	48439	810-694-1720		57
Serra Corp 4468 Technology Dr	Fremont	CA	94538	510-651-7333	657-5860	697
Serra High School 31422 Camino Capistrano *Web:* serra-capousd-ca.schoolloop.com	San Juan Capistrano	CA	92675	949-489-7216		685
Serra International Inc 75 Montgomery St Ste 300 *Web:* www.serraintl.com	Jersey City	NJ	07302	201-860-9600		311
Serra Retreat Ctr 3401 Serra Rd *Web:* www.serraretreat.com	Malibu	CA	90265	310-456-6631	456-9417	673
Serrano Jose E (Rep D - NY) 2354 Rayburn House Office Bldg *Web:* www.serrano.house.gov	Washington	DC	20515	202-225-4361		342-2
Serta Mattress 3 Golf Ctr Ste 392 *TF:* 888-557-3782 ■ *Web:* www.serta.com	Hoffman Estates	IL	60169	888-708-1466		471
Sertco Industries Inc 600 S Sertco Rd *Web:* www.sertco.com	Okemah	OK	74859	918-623-0526	623-0527	22
Serti Informatique Inc 7555 Beclard St *TF:* 800-361-6615 ■ *Web:* www.serti.com	Montreal	QC	H1J2S5	514-493-1909		196
Sertoma Intl 1912 E Meyer Blvd *TF:* 800-593-5646 ■ *Web:* sertoma.org	Kansas City	MO	64132	816-333-8300	333-4320	48-5
Serva Group LLC 1045 Keystone Ave *Web:* www.servagroup.com	Catoosa	OK	74015	918-266-0700		538
Servaas Laboratories Inc 5240 Walt Pl *TF:* 800-433-5818 ■ *Web:* www.barkeepersfriend.com	Indianapolis	IN	46254	317-636-7760		151
Servant Systems Inc 13770 Is Lake Rd *Web:* www.servantsystems.com	Chelsea	MI	48118	734-475-1619		809
Servco Pacific Inc 2850 Pukoloa Ste 300 *Web:* www.servco.com	Honolulu	HI	96819	808-564-1300	523-3937	57
Serve 5900 Summit Ave Ste 201 *TF:* 800-755-3277 ■ *Web:* www.serveincstore.org	Browns Summit	NC	27214	336-315-7400	315-7457	668
Serve You RX 10201 W Innovation Dr Ste 600 *TF:* 800-759-3203 ■ *Web:* www.serve-you-rx.com	Milwaukee	WI	53226	800-759-3203		586
Server Products Inc 3601 Pleasant Hill Rd PO Box 98 *TF:* 800-558-8722 ■ *Web:* www.server-products.com	Richfield	WI	53076	262-628-5100	628-5110	298
Server Technology Inc 1040 Sandhill Dr *TF:* 800-835-1515 ■ *Web:* www.servertech.com	Reno	NV	89521	775-284-2000	284-2065	176
ServerCentral Turing Group 111 W Jackson Blvd Ste 1600 *Web:* www.servercentral.com	Chicago	IL	60604	312-829-1111		180
ServerLift Corp 17453 N 25th Ave *TF:* 844-802-6532 ■ *Web:* serverlift.com	Phoenix	AZ	85023	602-254-1557		196
ServerLogic Corp 2800 Northup Way Ste 110 *Web:* www.serverlogic.com	Bellevue	WA	98004	425-803-0378	803-0349	177
Service 800 2190 W Wayzata Blvd *TF:* 800-475-3747 ■ *Web:* www.service800.com	Long Lake	MN	55356	952-475-3747	475-3773	466
Service By Air Inc 222 Crossways Park Dr *TF:* 877-817-5535 ■ *Web:* www.servicebyair.com	Woodbury	NY	11797	516-239-0241	576-0535	311
Service Champ Inc 180 New Britain Blvd *Web:* www.servicechamp.com	Chalfont	PA	18914	215-822-8500		61
Service Communications Inc (SCI) 15223 NE 90th St *TF:* 800-488-0468 ■ *Web:* www.servicecommunications.com	Redmond	WA	98052	425-278-0300		179
Service Companies Inc, The 14750 NW 77th Ct Ste 100 *TF:* 800-385-8800 ■ *Web:* www.theservicecompanies.com	Miami Lakes	FL	33016	305-681-8800		393
Service Construction Supply Inc PO Box 13405 *TF:* 866-729-4968 ■ *Web:* www.serviceconstructionsupply.com	Birmingham	AL	35202	205-252-3158	252-5720	191-3
Service Corporation Intl 1929 Allen Pkwy *NYSE: SCI* ■ *TF:* 800-758-5804 ■ *Web:* www.sci-corp.com	Houston	TX	77019	713-522-5141		510
Service Electric Cable TV & Communications 2260 Ave A *TF:* 800-232-9100 ■ *Web:* www.sectv.com	Bethlehem	PA	18017	610-865-9100	865-7888	116
Service Electric Supply Inc 15424 Oakwood Dr *TF:* 800-426-7575 ■ *Web:* www.servelectric.com	Romulus	MI	48174	734-229-9100	229-9101	246
Service Elements Inc 15029 N Thompson Peak Pkwy Ste B111-444 *Web:* serviceelements.com	Scottsdale	AZ	85260	480-538-0123		256
Service Employees Int L Union Local 49 3536 SE 26th Ave *Web:* seiu49.org	Portland	OR	97202	503-236-4949		414
Service Employees International Union 1800 Massachusetts Ave NW *TF:* 800-424-8592 ■ *Web:* www.seiu.org	Washington	DC	20036	202-730-7000		414
Service Engineering Co 16 Pearl St *Web:* www.serviceengineeringwnc.com	Asheville	NC	28801	828-252-6297	253-0849	475
Service Engineering Inc 2190 W Main St *TF:* 877-727-8333 ■ *Web:* www.serviceengineering.com	Greenfield	IN	46140	317-467-2000	467-2001	695
Service Express Inc 3854 Broadmoor Ave SE *TF:* 800-940-4484 ■ *Web:* serviceexpress.com	Grand Rapids	MI	49512	800-940-5585		175
Service General ' 13 E Laurel St *Web:* www.servicegeneral.net	Georgetown	DE	19947	302-858-4973		141
Service Graphics LLC 8350 Allison Ave *TF:* 800-884-9876 ■ *Web:* www.mysgi.com	Indianapolis	IN	46268	317-471-8246		687
Service Ideas Inc 2354 Ventura Dr *TF:* 800-328-4493 ■ *Web:* www.serviceideas.com	Woodbury	MN	55125	651-730-8800		300
Service Industry Assn (SIA) 2164 Historic Decatur Rd *Web:* www.servicenetwork.org	San Diego	CA	92106	619-221-9200		49-12
Service King Collision Repair Centers 2375 N Glenville Dr *TF:* 844-611-5068 ■ *Web:* www.serviceking.com	Richardson	TX	75080	972-960-7595	980-4266	62-4
Service Linen Supply Inc 903 S Fourth St *Web:* www.servicelinen.com	Renton	WA	98057	425-255-8686		442
Service Machine Specialties Inc 1519 Aymond St *Web:* www.servicems.com	Eunice	LA	70535	337-457-8712	457-8764	454
Service Management Systems 7135 Charlotte Pk Ste 100 *Web:* www.smsclean.com	Nashville	TN	37209	615-399-1839		152
Service Motor Co W9614 State Hwy 96 *Web:* www.servicemotor.com	Dale	WI	54931	920-779-4311		385
Service Objects Inc 27 E Cota St Ste 500 *TF:* 800-694-6269 ■ *Web:* serviceobjects.com	Santa Barbara	CA	93101	800-694-6269		177
Service Oil Inc 1718 E Main Ave *Web:* www.stamart.com	West Fargo	ND	58078	701-277-1050	277-1723	324
Service Performance Insight LLC 6260 Winter Hazel Dr *Web:* spiresearch.com	Liberty Township	OH	45044	513-759-5443		466
Service Plus Transport Inc 3686 Flowerfield Rd *TF:* 800-315-9152 ■ *Web:* www.sptransport.com	Blaine	MN	55014	763-571-8786	571-8922	311
Service Products Inc 5900 W 51st St **Fax Area Code:* 708 ■ *Web:* www.serviceproductsinc.com	Chicago	IL	60638	773-767-2360	496-1818*	233
Service Properties Trust 255 Washington St *NASDAQ: HPT* ■ *Web:* www.svcreit.com	Newton	MA	02458	617-964-8389	969-5730	655
Service Roundtable 131 W Main St *Web:* www.serviceroundtable.com	Lewisville	TX	75057	817-416-0978		610
Service Steel Aerospace Corp 4609 70th St E *TF:* 800-426-9794 ■ *Web:* www.ssa-corp.com	Fife	WA	98424	253-627-2910		492
Service Steel Inc 4208 E Schrimsher Ln SW Ste 2B7 *Web:* www.servicesteelinc.com	Huntsville	AL	35805	256-883-1190	882-0918	492
Service Systems Associates Inc 4699 Marion St *Web:* www.kmssa.com	Denver	CO	80216	303-322-3031		328
Service Transport Co 7900 Almeda Genoa Rd *TF:* 800-749-4285 ■ *Web:* www.svtn.com	Houston	TX	77075	713-209-2500		780
Service Trucking Inc 2815 Hwy 44 W *TF:* 800-899-1300 ■ *Web:* www.servicetrucking.com	Eustis	FL	32726	352-357-1300		780
ServiceMaster Clean 4395 South Mendenhall *TF:* 844-319-5401 ■ *Web:* www.servicemasterclean.com	Memphis	TN	38125	844-319-5401		152
Servicengine Corp 100 Danbury Rd Ste 202 *Web:* servicengine.com	Ridgefield	CT	06877	203-438-7880		180
Serviko Inc 2670 Rue Duchesne *Web:* www.serviko.com	Saint-Laurent	QC	H4R1J3	514-332-2600		260
Servilla Whitney LLC 33 Wood Ave S Ste 830 *Web:* dsiplaw.com	Iselin	NJ	08830	732-815-0404		41
Serving by Irving Inc 233 Broadway Ste 2201 *Web:* www.servingbyirving.com	New York	NY	10279	212-233-3346	349-0338	393

Name / Address	City	State	ZIP	Phone	Fax	Class
ServIT Inc 3721 Cherokee St *TF:* 800-336-0374 ■ *Web:* www.servit.net	Kennesaw	GA	30144	770-499-6300		196
Servo Corporation of America 123 Frost St *Web:* www.servo.com	Westbury	NY	11590	516-938-9700	938-9644	544
Servo Products Co 34940 Lakeland Blvd *TF:* 800-521-7359 ■ *Web:* www.servoproductsco.com	Eastlake	OH	44095	440-942-9999	942-9100	455
Servotronics Inc 1110 Maple St PO Box 300 *NYSE: SVT* ■ *Web:* www.servotronics.com	Elma	NY	14059	716-655-5990	655-6012	789
Servpro Industries Inc 801 Industrial Blvd *TF:* 800-826-9586 ■ *Web:* www.servpro.com	Gallatin	TN	37066	615-451-0200	451-0291	152
Servsteel Inc 214 Westbridge Dr **Fax Area Code:* 412 ■ *TF:* 888-737-8783 ■ *Web:* www.servsteelinc.com	Morgan	PA	15064	888-737-8783	221-2810*	492
Serv-U-Clean 207 Edgeley Blvd *Web:* www.servuclean.com	Concord	ON	L4K4B5	416-667-0696		152
SERVUS 4201 Mannheim Rd Ste A *Web:* www.greatservus.com	Jasper	IN	47546	812-482-3212		670
SES Advisors Inc 10 Shurs Ln Ste 102 *Web:* sesadvisors.com	Philadelphia	PA	19127	215-508-1600		194
SES World Skies 4 Research Way *Web:* www.ses.com	Princeton	NJ	08540	609-987-4000		681
SESAC Inc 55 Music Sq E *TF:* 800-826-9996 ■ *Web:* www.sesac.com	Nashville	TN	37203	615-320-0055	321-6290	48-4
Sesame Inn 715 Washington Rd *Web:* sesameinn.com	Pittsburgh	PA	15228	412-341-2555		671
Sesame Place 100 Sesame Rd *Web:* sesameplace.com	Langhorne	PA	19047	215-702-3566	741-5307	32
Sesame Software 5201 Great America Pkwy Ste 320 *TF:* 866-474-7575 ■ *Web:* www.sesamesoftware.com	Santa Clara	CA	95054	408-550-7999		178-5
Sesame Workshop 1 Lincoln Plz *Web:* www.sesameworkshop.org	New York	NY	10023	212-595-3456		514
Sesco Lighting Inc 222 W Maitland Blvd *Web:* www.sescolighting.com	Maitland	FL	32751	407-629-6100	629-6168	439
Sesquicentennial State Park 9564 Two Notch Rd *Web:* southcarolinaparks.com	Columbia	SC	29223	803-788-2706		565
SESRC (Social & Economic Sciences Research Ctr) *Washington State University* Wilson Hall Rm 133 PO Box 644014 *TF:* 800-932-5393 ■ *Web:* sesrc.wsu.edu	Pullman	WA	99164	509-335-1511	335-0116	668
Sessions Specialty Co 5090 Styers Ferry Rd **Fax Area Code:* 800 ■ *TF:* 800-763-0077 ■ *Web:* sessionsusa.com	Lewisville	NC	27023	336-766-2880	723-0055*	146
Set & Service Resources LLC 5400 Glenwood Ave Ste 310 *TF:* 866-867-5571 ■ *Web:* www.sasrlink.com	Raleigh	NC	27615	866-867-5571		260
SET Consulting Inc 5821 Windermere Ln *Web:* www.setconsulting.com	Fairfield	OH	45014	240-296-0800		463
Set Shop Inc 36 W 20th St *TF:* 800-422-7381 ■ *Web:* www.setshop.com	New York	NY	10011	212-255-3500	229-9600	628
Set Solutions Inc 1800 W Loop S Ste 700 *TF:* 888-353-0574 ■ *Web:* www.setsolutions.com	Houston	TX	77027	713-956-6600	956-9678	174
Seta Corp 6400 E Rogers Cir *Web:* www.setacorporation.com	Boca Raton	FL	33499	561-994-2660		459
SETAC (Society of Environmental Toxicology & Chemistry) 1010 N 12th Ave *Web:* www.setac.org	Pensacola	FL	32501	850-469-1500	469-9778	49-19
Setai, The 2001 Collins Ave *TF:* 888-625-7500 ■ *Web:* www.thesetaihotel.com	Miami Beach	FL	33139	305-520-6000	520-6600	379
Setaro Law Firm LLC 2 Terrace Pl *Web:* setarolaw.com	Danbury	CT	06810	203-826-9593	942-2523	41
Setco Sales Co 5880 Hillside Ave *TF:* 800-543-0470 ■ *Web:* www.setco.com	Cincinnati	OH	45233	513-941-5110	941-6913	455
Setcom Corp 3019 Alvin DeVane Blvd Ste 560 *TF:* 800-645-1285 ■ *Web:* www.setcomcorp.com	Austin	TX	78741	650-965-8020		647
Setec Investigations 8391 Beverly Blvd Ste 167 *TF:* 800-748-5440 ■ *Web:* www.setecinvestigations.com	Los Angeles	CA	90048	323-939-5598		194
Setel 1165 S 6th St *TF:* 800-662-0716 ■ *Web:* www.setel.solutions	Macclenny	FL	32063	904-259-1300		387
SETEL UC 109 Westpark Dr Ste 240 *TF:* 800-743-1340 ■ *Web:* seteluc.com	Brentwood	TN	37027	615-874-6000		787
Setex Inc 1111 Mckinley Rd *Web:* www.setexinc.com	Saint Marys	OH	45885	419-394-7800	394-7193	319-3
Seton Hall University 400 S Orange Ave *TF:* 800-992-4723 ■ *Web:* www.shu.edu	South Orange	NJ	07079	973-761-9332	275-2321	166
Seton Hill University 1 Seton Hill Dr *TF:* 800-826-6234 ■ *Web:* www.setonhill.edu	Greensburg	PA	15601	724-838-4255	830-1294	166
Seton Home Study School 1350 Progress Dr *TF:* 800-542-1066 ■ *Web:* www.setonhome.org	Front Royal	VA	22630	540-636-9990		685
Seton Hotel 144 E 40th St *TF:* 866-697-3866 ■ *Web:* www.setonhotelny.com	New York	NY	10016	212-889-5301		463
Seton Imaging 2950 Elmwood Ave *Web:* www.setonimaging.com	Buffalo	NY	14217	716-447-6856		592
Seton Medical Center Coastside 600 Marine Blvd *Web:* verity.org	Moss Beach	CA	94038	650-563-7100		450
Seton Medical Ctr 1900 Sullivan Ave *TF:* 833-427-7436 ■ *Web:* seton.verity.org	Daly City	CA	94015	650-992-4000		374-3
Setpoint Systems Inc 2835 Commerce Way *Web:* www.setpointusa.com	Ogden	UT	84401	801-621-4117		194
Setra Systems Inc 159 Swanson Rd *TF:* 800-257-3872 ■ *Web:* www.setra.com	Boxborough	MA	01719	978-263-1400	264-0292	472
Settle & Pou PC 3333 Lee Pkwy 8th Fl *TF:* 800-538-4661 ■ *Web:* www.settlepou.com	Dallas	TX	75219	214-520-3300		428
Settlers 1424 W Jefferson Blvd *Web:* www.settlersinc.org	Fort Wayne	IN	46802	260-424-7212		50-3
Setton Pistachio of Terra Bella Inc 9370 Rd 234 PO Box 11089 *Web:* www.settonfarms.com	Terra Bella	CA	93270	559-535-6050	535-6089	297-11
Setzer Pharmacy Inc 1685 Rice St *Web:* setzerrx.com	Saint Paul	MN	55113	651-488-0251		237
Setzler & Scott PA 1708 Augusta Rd *Web:* setzler-scott.com	West Columbia	SC	29171	803-796-1285		41
Seubert Excavators Inc 604 King St	Cottonwood	ID	83522	208-962-3501		189-5
Seva Foundation 1786 Fifth St *TF:* 877-764-7382 ■ *Web:* www.seva.org	Berkeley	CA	94710	510-845-7382		305
Seva Technologies LLC 1618 Mahan Center Blvd *Web:* www.sevatechnologies.com	Tallahassee	FL	32308	850-391-4832	219-8979	226
Sevatec Inc 3112 Fairview Park Dr *Web:* www.sevatec.com	Falls Church	VA	22042	571-766-1300		196
Sevcon 155 Northboro Rd *NASDAQ: SEV* ■ *Web:* www.sevcon.com	Southborough	MA	01772	508-281-5500		203
Seven Arrows Elementary School Inc 15240 La Cruz Dr *Web:* www.sevenarrows.org	Pacific Palisades	CA	90272	310-230-0257		685
Seven Bridges Field Club (SBFC) 160 Seven Bridges Rd *Web:* www.sevenbridgesfieldclub.org	Chappaqua	NY	10514	914-242-1838		637-10
Seven Buffaloes Press PO Box 249 *Web:* www.artcoelho.com	Big Timber	MT	59011	406-932-5564		637-2
Seven Days 255 S Champlain St Ste 5 PO Box 1164 *Web:* www.sevendaysvt.com	Burlington	VT	05401	802-864-5684		532-5
Seven Degrees 891 Laguna Canyon Rd *Web:* seven-degrees.com	Laguna Beach	CA	92651	949-376-1555		196
Seven Dials Media 2449 Wendover Dr	Naperville	IL	60565	630-355-6199		4
Seven Gables Inn 26 N Meramec Ave *Web:* sevengablesinn.com	Saint Louis	MO	63105	314-863-8400	863-8846	379
Seven Glaciers Restaurant 1000 Arlberg Ave *Web:* www.alyeskaresort.com	Girdwood	AK	99587	907-754-2237		671
Seven Hills 1550 Hyde St *Web:* sevenhillssf.com	San Francisco	CA	94109	415-775-1550		671
Seven Hills Preparatory Academy 1401 W 76th St *TF:* 800-752-4223 ■ *Web:* www.sevenhillspreparatoryacademy.org	Richfield	MN	55423	612-314-7600	314-7609	685
Seven Lakes State Park 14390 Fish Lake Rd *Web:* www.michigan.gov	Holly	MI	48442	248-634-7271		565
Seven Lazy P Guest Ranch 891 Teton Canyon Rd *Web:* sevenlazyp.com	Choteau	MT	59422	406-466-2245		239
Seven Oaks Capital Associates LLC 7854 Anselmo Ln PO Box 82360 *TF:* 800-511-4588 ■ *Web:* www.sevenoakscapital.com	Baton Rouge	LA	70810	225-757-1919	757-1916	272
Seven Oaks General Hospital 2300 McPhillips St *Web:* sogh.ca	Winnipeg	MB	R2V3M3	204-632-7133	697-2106	374-2
Seven Peaks Water Park 1330 East 300 North *Web:* www.sevenpeaks.com	Provo	UT	84606	801-373-8777		32
Seven R Transportation Inc 2818 Queen City Dr Ste G **Fax Area Code:* 336 ■ *Web:* www.sevenr.com	Charlotte	NC	28266	704-391-0694	482-2932*	311
Seven Seventeen Credit Union Inc 3181 Larchmont Ave NE *Web:* www.717cu.com	Warren	OH	44483	330-372-8100		219
Seven Simple Machines (7SM) 5429 Russell Ave NW No 201 *Web:* www.7simplemachines.com	Seattle	WA	98107	206-545-4850		177
Seven Springs Mountain Resort 777 Waterwheel Dr *Web:* www.7springs.com	Champion	PA	15622	814-352-7777		669
Seven Step RPO 1 Center Plz 4 th Fl *Web:* www.sevensteprpo.com	Boston	MA	02108	857-239-5546		260
Seven Tablets Inc 5080 Spectrum Dr Ste 1100E *Web:* seventablets.com	Addison	TX	75001	214-299-5100		177
Seven-Eleven Hawaii Inc 1755 Nuuanu Ave *Web:* www.7elevenhawaii.com	Honolulu	HI	96817	808-526-1711		204
Sevenrooms Inc 127 W 24th St 5th Fl *Web:* sevenrooms.com	New York	NY	10011	212-242-5607		393
Sevenson Environmental Services Inc 2749 Lockport Rd *Web:* sevenson.com	Niagara Falls	NY	14305	716-284-0431	284-7645	667
Seventh Generation Inc 60 Lake St *TF:* 800-456-1191 ■ *Web:* www.seventhgeneration.com	Burlington	VT	05401	802-658-3773	658-1771	151
Seventh Mountain Resort 18575 SW Century Dr *TF:* 877-765-1501 ■ *Web:* www.seventhmountain.com	Bend	OR	97702	541-382-8711	382-3517	669
Seventh Star Press 529 Fogo Ct *Web:* www.seventhstarpress.com	Lexington	KY	40503	859-223-1560		637-2
Seventh Street Medical Supply Inc 307 E Pennsylvania Blvd *TF:* 800-723-8110 ■ *Web:* www.seventhstreetmedicalsupply.com	Feasterville-Trevose	PA	19053	215-396-2450	396-2454	475
Seventh-day Adventist World Church 12501 Old Columbia Pk *TF:* 800-226-1119 ■ *Web:* www.adventist.org	Silver Spring	MD	20904	301-680-6000		48-20
Seventrees Corp 2181 M-139 S *Web:* www.7trees.com	Benton Harbor	MI	49022	269-925-8111		400
SevenTwenty Strategies 1220 19th St NW Ste 300 *Web:* 720strategies.com	Washington	DC	20036	202-962-3955		225
Severance Foods Inc 3478 Main St *Web:* www.pandeoro.com	Hartford	CT	06120	860-724-7063		296-35
Severance Trucking Company Inc 49 McGrath Rd *TF:* 800-225-1111 ■ *Web:* severance.acordex.com	Dracut	MA	01826	978-423-0971	275-3811	780

Name / Address	City	State	ZIP	Phone	Fax	Class
Severn Bancorp Inc 200 Westgate Cir Ste 200 *NASDAQ: SVBI* ■ *TF:* 800-752-5854 ■ *Web:* severnbank.com	Annapolis	MD	21401	410-260-2000	841-6296	70
Severn Engineering Company Inc 555 Old Stage Rd Ste 1a *Web:* severnengineering.com	Auburn	AL	36830	334-821-8995	821-7995	495
Severson Dells Nature Ctr 8786 Montague Rd *Web:* www.seversondells.com	Rockford	IL	61102	815-335-2915	335-2471	50-5
Sevier County 115 N Third St Rm 102 *Web:* www.seviercountyar.com	De Queen	AR	71832	870-642-2852	642-3896	338
Sevier County 125 Ct Ave Ste 210 W *Web:* www.seviercountytn.org	Sevierville	TN	37862	865-453-3242	774-3957	338
Sevier County Public Library 408 High St *Web:* www.sevierlibrary.org	Sevierville	TN	37862	865-453-3532	365-1667	434-3
Sevilla Riverside 3252 Mission Inn Ave *Web:* www.cafesevilla.com	Riverside	CA	92507	951-778-0611		671
Sevin Rosen Funds PO Box 192128 *Web:* www.srfunds.com	Dallas	TX	75219	972-702-1100	702-1103	792
Seviroli Foods 601 Brook St *Web:* www.seviroli.com	Garden City	NY	11530	516-222-6220	222-0534	296-36
Sevy's Grill 8201 Preston Rd Ste 100 *Web:* sevys.com	Dallas	TX	75225	214-265-7389		671
Seward & Kissel 1 Battery Park Plz *Web:* www.sewkis.com	New York	NY	10004	212-574-1200	480-8421	428
Seward & Monde 296 State St *Web:* www.sewardmonde.com	North Haven	CT	06473	203-248-9341	248-5813	2
Seward Community Library 239 6th Ave *Web:* www.cityofseward.us	Seward	AK	99664	907-224-4082	224-3521	434-3
Seward Convention & Visitors Bureau 2001 Seward Hwy *TF:* 800-257-7760 ■ *Web:* www.seward.com	Seward	AK	99664	907-224-8051	224-5353	206
Seward County 515 N Washington *Web:* www.sewardcountyks.org	Liberal	KS	67901	620-626-3212		338
Seward County 616 Bradford *Web:* www.connectseward.org	Seward	NE	68434	402-643-2883		338
Seward County Community College 1801 N Campus Ave PO Box 1137 *TF:* 800-373-9951 ■ *Web:* www.sccc.edu	Liberal	KS	67905	620-624-1951		162
Seward Motor Freight PO Box 126 *TF:* 800-786-4469 ■ *Web:* www.sewardmotor.com	Seward	NE	68434	402-643-4503	643-3199	780
Sewell & Neal PLLC 220 W Main St LG&E Ctr Ste 1800 *Web:* sonlegal.com	Louisville	KY	40202	502-582-2030	561-0766	41
Sewell C. Biggs Museum of American Art 406 Federal St *Web:* www.biggsmuseum.org	Dover	DE	19901	302-674-2111	674-5133	520
Sewell Printing Service Inc 2697 Apple Valley Rd NE *Web:* www.sewellprinting.com	Atlanta	GA	30319	404-237-2553		627
Sewell Terri A (Rep D - AL) 2201 Rayburn House Office Bldg *Web:* sewell.house.gov	Washington	DC	20515	202-225-2665	226-9567	342-2
Sewer Equipment Company of America 1590 Dutch Rd *TF:* 800-323-1604 ■ *Web:* www.sewerequipment.com	Dixon	IL	61021	815-835-5566	284-0452	806
Sewerage & Water Board Efcu 625 St Joseph St Rm B-13 *Web:* swbfcu.com	New Orleans	LA	70130	504-585-2008		219
SEW-Eurodrive Inc 1295 Old Spartanburg Hwy *Web:* www.seweurodrive.com	Lyman	SC	29365	864-439-8792	949-3039	709
Sewn Products Equipment Suppliers Assn (SPESA) 9650 Strickland Rd Ste 103-324 *Web:* www.spesa.org	Raleigh	NC	27615	919-872-8909		49-13
Sewon America Inc 1000 Sewon Blvd *Web:* www.se-won.com	LaGrange	GA	30240	706-298-5800		186
Sex & Love Addicts Anonymous (SLAA) 1550 NE Loop 410 Ste 118 *Web:* slaafws.org	San Antonio	TX	78209	210-828-7900	828-7922	48-21
Sex Addicts Anonymous (SAA) PO Box 70949 *TF:* 800-477-8191 ■ *Web:* saa-recovery.org	Houston	TX	77270	713-869-4902	692-0105	48-21
Sexaholics Anonymous (SA) PO Box 3565 *TF:* 866-424-8777 ■ *Web:* www.sa.org	Brentwood	TN	37024	615-370-6062	370-0882	48-21
Seyer Industries Inc 66 Patmos Ct *Web:* www.seyerind.com	Saint Peters	MO	63376	636-928-1190	928-8945	697
Seyfarth Shaw LLP 131 S Dearborn St Ste 2400 *Web:* www.seyfarth.com	Chicago	IL	60603	312-460-5000	460-7000	428
Seyferth & Associates Inc 40 Monroe Ctr NW *Web:* www.seyferthpr.com	Grand Rapids	MI	49503	616-776-3511		636
Seyler Favaloro Ltd 1615 Poydras St Ste 1040 *Web:* sflrehab.com	New Orleans	LA	70112	504-524-3378		390
Seymour Duncan Inc 5427 Hollister Ave *Web:* www.seymourduncan.com	Santa Barbara	CA	93111	805-964-9610		526
Seymour Family Law 10585 165th St W *Web:* seymourfamilylaw.com	Lakeville	MN	55044	952-255-8735	255-8739	41
Seymour Johnson Air Force Base 1510 Wright Bros Ave Ste 200 *Web:* www.seymourjohnson.af.mil	Goldsboro	NC	27531	919-722-0027		497-1
Seymour Manufacturing Company Inc PO Box 248 *Web:* seymourmidwest.com	Seymour	IN	47274	812-522-2900		758
Seymour of Sycamore Inc 917 Crosby Ave *TF:* 800-435-4482 ■ *Web:* www.seymourpaint.com	Sycamore	IL	60178	815-895-9101	895-8475	550
Seyon Lodge State Park 1 National Life Dr *Web:* www.vtstateparks.com	Groton	VT	05602	802-584-3829		565
Sezzle 251 N 1st Ave *TF:* 888-540-1867 ■ *Web:* sezzle.com	Minneapolis	MN	55401	888-540-1867		113
SF Weekly 185 Berry St Ste 3800 *Web:* www.sfweekly.com	San Francisco	CA	94107	415-536-8130		532-5

Name / Address	City	State	ZIP	Phone	Fax	Class
SFAA (Surety & Fidelity Association of America) 1140 19th St NW Ste 500 *Web:* www.surety.org	Washington	DC	20036	202-463-0600	463-0606	49-9
SFB (Security Federal Corp) 238 Richland Ave NW PO Box 810 *TF:* 866-851-3000 ■ *Web:* www.securityfederalbank.com	Aiken	SC	29802	803-641-3000		71
SFC (Sandridge Food Corp) 133 Commerce Dr *TF:* 800-627-2523 ■ *Web:* sandridge.com	Medina	OH	44256	330-725-2348	722-3998	296-33
SFC (Smith Floor Covering Distributors Inc) 1118 Smith St *Web:* www.sfc-wv.com	Charleston	WV	25330	304-344-2493	344-2475	191-1
SFC Engineering Partnership Inc 1 Industrial Dr *Web:* sfceng.com	Windham	NH	03087	603-647-8700		261
SFC Graphics 110 E Woodruff Ave *Web:* www.sfcgraphics.com	Toledo	OH	43604	419-255-1283		701
SFCC (Santa Fe Community College) 6401 Richards Ave *Web:* www.sfcc.edu	Santa Fe	NM	87508	505-428-1000		162
SFCC Inc 12600 Preston Rd *Web:* www.sfccinc.net	Frisco	TX	75033	214-387-7987		186
SFDC (San Francisco Design Ctr) 2 Henry Adams St Ste 2M-33 *Web:* www.sfdesigncenter.com	San Francisco	CA	94103	415-490-5800	490-5885	321
SFE Investment Counsel Inc 801 S Figueroa St Ste 2100 *TF:* 800-445-6320 ■ *Web:* www.sfeic.com	Los Angeles	CA	90017	213-612-0220		690
SFFC (South Fork Forest Camp) 48300 Wilson River Hwy *Web:* www.oregon.gov	Tillamook	OR	97141	503-842-2811	842-7943	213
SFHCC (Elmwood Healthcare Center & Specialty Hospital) 401 N Broadway *Web:* www.elmwoodcommunities.com	Green Springs	OH	44836	419-639-2626		374-7
SFI Electronics Inc 400A Clanton Rd *Web:* www.sfi-electronics.com	Charlotte	NC	28217	704-522-0800		693
SFI of Tennessee LLC 4768 Hungerford Rd *TF:* 844-257-6866 ■ *Web:* www.sfifab.com	Memphis	TN	38118	844-257-6866		803-1
SFI-Gray Steel Ltd 3511 W 12th St *TF:* 844-767-8068 ■ *Web:* www.sfigray.com	Houston	TX	77008	713-864-6450	864-6459	480
SFLL (San Francisco Law Library) 1145 Market St 4th Fl *Web:* www.sflawlibrary.org	San Francisco	CA	94103	415-554-1772	863-4022	434-3
SFMT (San Francisco Mime Troupe, The) 855 Treat Ave *Web:* www.sfmt.org	San Francisco	CA	94110	415-285-1717	285-1290	226
SFN (Society for Neuroscience) 1121 14th St NW Ste 1010 *Web:* www.sfn.org	Washington	DC	20005	202-962-4000	962-4941	49-8
SFPA (Southern Forest Products Assn) 6660 Riverside Dr Ste 212 *Web:* www.sfpa.org	Metairie	LA	70003	504-443-4464		48-2
SFRi LLC 284 W 11th St *Web:* www.sfrillc.com	New York	NY	10014	415-394-3900		693
SFS (Special Fleet Service Inc) 875 Waterman Dr *TF:* 800-395-2152 ■ *Web:* www.specialfleet.com	Harrisonburg	VA	22802	540-434-4488	434-2244	188-10
SFS intec Inc Spring St & Van Reed Rd *TF:* 800-234-4533 ■ *Web:* www.sfsintecusa.com	Wyomissing	PA	19610	610-376-5751		621
SFSA (Steel Founders' Society of America) 780 McArdle Dr Ste G *Web:* www.sfsa.org	Crystal Lake	IL	60014	815-455-8240	455-8241	49-13
SFSP (Society of Financial Service Professionals) 19 Campus Blvd Ste 100 *Web:* www.financialpro.org	Newtown Square	PA	19073	610-526-2500	527-4010	49-9
SFWMPAC (San Francisco War Memorial & Performing Arts Ctr) 401 Van Ness Ave Rm 110 *Web:* www.sfwmpac.org	San Francisco	CA	94102	415-621-6600	621-5091	572
SG Footwear Inc 3 University Plz Ste 400 *Web:* www.thesgcompanies.com	Hackensack	NJ	07601	201-342-1200		301
SG360 Inc 1351 S Wheeling Rd *Web:* www.sg360.com	Wheeling	IL	60090	847-541-1080		627
SGA (Sea Grant Assn) 5784 York Complex PO Box 1950 *Web:* www.sga.seagrant.org	Ocean Springs	MS	39566	207-581-1435	581-1426	48-13
SGB Enterprises Inc Unit A & B 24844 Anza Dr *Web:* sgbent.com	Santa Clarita	CA	91355	661-294-8306	294-8309	21
SGC World Inc 13737 SE 26th St *Web:* www.sgcworld.com	Bellevue	WA	98005	425-746-6310	746-6384	647
SGCD (Society of Glass & Ceramic Decorators) PO Box 2489 *Web:* www.sgcd.org	Zanesville	OH	43702	740-588-9882		48-4
SGH (Southwest General Hospital) 7400 Barlite Blvd *Web:* www.southwestgeneralhospital.org	San Antonio	TX	78224	210-921-2000		374-3
SGH Golf Inc 6805 Mt Vernon Ave *TF:* 800-284-8884 ■ *Web:* www.sghgolf.com	Cincinnati	OH	45227	513-984-0414	984-9648	771
SGI Delivery Solutions 250 A Lyon Ln *TF:* 800-941-2575 ■ *Web:* sgi-solutions.com	Birmingham	AL	35211	205-941-2575	941-2579	317
SGIA (Specialty Graphic Imaging Assn) 10015 Main St *TF:* 888-385-3588 ■ *Web:* www.sgia.org	Fairfax	VA	22031	703-385-1335	273-0456	49-16
SGL Carbon LLC 307 Jamestown Rd *Web:* www.sglgroup.com	Morganton	NC	28655	828-437-3221	432-5885	127
SGMC (South Georgia Medical Ctr) 2501 N Patterson St *Web:* www.sgmc.org	Valdosta	GA	31602	229-333-1000		374-3
SGNA (Society of Gastroenterology Nurses & Associates Inc) 401 N Michigan Ave *TF:* 800-245-7462 ■ *Web:* www.sgna.org	Chicago	IL	60611	312-321-5165	673-6694	49-8
SGS 291 Fairfield Ave *Web:* www.sgsgroup.us.com	Fairfield	NJ	07004	973-575-5252	575-7175	743
SGS Architects Engineers Inc 1 Tyler Ct *Web:* www.sgsarchitects.com	Carlisle	PA	17015	717-249-4569		261

Name / Address	City	State	ZIP	Phone	Fax	Class
SGS Canada Inc 6490 Vipond Dr. *Web:* www.sgs.ca	Mississauga	ON	L5T1W8	905-364-3757	364-0344	743
SGS Technologie LLC 6817 Southpoint Pkwy Ste 2104 *Web:* www.sgstechnologies.net	Jacksonville	FL	32216	904-332-4534		180
SGV International LLC 575 N Dairy Ashford Ste 230 *Web:* www.sgvinternational.com	Houston	TX	77079	713-647-7555	647-7558	463
SGW Integrated Marketing Communications Inc 219 Changebridge Rd *Web:* www.sgw.com	Montville	NJ	07045	973-299-8000		7
SH (Sherrill House) 135 S Huntington Ave *Web:* www.sherrillhouse.org	Jamaica Plain	MA	02130	617-731-2400	731-8671	450
SH (Shive-Hattery Inc) 316 Second St SE Ste 500 PO Box 1599 *TF:* 800-798-0227 ■ *Web:* www.shive-hattery.com	Cedar Rapids	IA	52406	319-362-0313		261
SH Enterprises Inc 4000 Central Dr *Web:* www.shenter.com	Wausau	WI	54401	715-848-1200		492
SHA (Sight & Hearing Assn) 1246 University Ave W Ste 226 *Web:* www.sightandhearing.org	Saint Paul	MN	55104	651-645-2546	645-2742	637-2
Shaan Seet Inc 501 Main St *Web:* www.shaanseet.com	Craig	AK	99921	907-826-3251	826-3980	448
ShabaShabu 3080 Wake Forest Rd *Web:* www.shabashabu.wixsite.com	Raleigh	NC	27609	919-501-7755	501-7479	671
Shabbona Lake State Park 4201 Shabbona Grove Rd *Web:* shabbonalake.com	Shabbona	IL	60550	815-824-2106		565
Shabu Shabu House 127 Japanese Village Plz Mall *Web:* shabushabuhouse.menutoeat.com	Los Angeles	CA	90012	213-680-3890		671
Shackelford County PO Box 1886 *Web:* shackelfordcounty.org	Albany	TX	76430	325-762-2232		338
Shackleton Group Inc 777 Wadsworth Blvd Ste 2-209 *Web:* www.shkgrp.com	Lakewood	CO	80226	303-482-2370		94
Shade Inc 6211 O St *Web:* www.shadeinc.com	Lincoln	NE	68510	402-805-4163	423-5805	463
Shade Systems Inc 4150 SW 19th St *TF:* 800-609-6066 ■ *Web:* shadesystemsinc.com	Ocala	FL	34474	352-237-0135		295
Shade Tree Service Company Inc 520 S Hwy Dr *Web:* www.stsco.net	Fenton	MO	63026	636-343-1212	343-5660	776
Shader Bros Corp 6325 Edgewater Dr *TF:* 866-762-4888 ■ *Web:* www.personalministorage.com	Orlando	FL	32810	866-762-4888		803-3
Shades of Green on Walt Disney World Resort 1950 W Magnolia Palm Dr *TF:* 888-593-2242 ■ *Web:* www.shadesofgreen.org	Lake Buena Vista	FL	32830	407-824-3400	824-3665	379
Shadin LP 6831 Oxford St *TF:* 800-328-0584 ■ *Web:* www.shadin.com	Saint Louis Park	MN	55426	952-927-6500		529
Shadow Beverages & Snacks LLC 4650 E Cotton Center Blvd Ste 240 *Web:* www.shadowbev.com	Phoenix	AZ	85040	480-371-1100		406
Shadow Financial Systems Inc 1551 S Washington Ave *Web:* www.shadowfinancial.com	Piscataway	NJ	08854	732-225-6800		180
Shadow Mountain Resort & Club 45-750 San Luis Rey *TF:* 800-472-3713 ■ *Web:* www.shadowmountainresort.com	Palm Desert	CA	92260	760-346-6123		669
Shadow-soft LLC 8302 Dunwoody Pl Ste 100 *Web:* shadow-soft.com	Atlanta	GA	30350	770-546-0077		177
Shady Maple Farm Market Inc 1324 Main St *Web:* www.shady-maple.com	East Earl	PA	17519	717-354-4981		345
Shady Side Academy 423 Fox Chapel Rd *Web:* www.shadysideacademy.org	Pittsburgh	PA	15238	412-968-3000	968-3213	622
Shafer Insurance Agency Inc 1100 Marion St Ste 200 *Web:* shaferinsurance.com	Knoxville	TN	37921	865-546-0761		390
Shafer Vineyards 6154 Silverado Trl *Web:* www.shafervineyards.com	Napa	CA	94558	707-944-2877		443
Shafer's Tour & Charter 500 N St *TF:* 800-287-8986 ■ *Web:* shaferbus.com	Endicott	NY	13760	607-797-2006		107
Shaffer & Engle Law Offices LLC 2205 Forest Hills Dr Ste 10 *Web:* shafferengle.com	Harrisburg	PA	17112	717-268-4287		41
Shaffstall Corp 8531 Bash St *TF:* 800-357-6250 ■ *Web:* www.shaffstall.com	Indianapolis	IN	46250	317-842-2077		173-8
Shaft Grounding Systems Inc PO Box 41000 *Web:* www.shaftgroundingsystems.com	Florence	OR	97439	541-997-4068	997-7278	246
Shafter Press 336 Pacific Ave *Web:* www.shafter.com	Shafter	CA	93263	661-746-5001		532-2
Shaftesbury Films Inc 18 Logan Ave *Web:* shaftesbury.ca	Toronto	ON	M4M2M8	416-363-1411	363-1428	514
Shah & Associates Inc 416 N Frederick Ave *Web:* www.shahpe.com	Gaithersburg	MD	20877	301-926-2797		261
Shah Smith & Associates Inc 2825 Wilcrest Ste 350 *Web:* shahsmith.com	Houston	TX	77042	713-780-7563		261
Shah Software Inc 13601 Preston Rd Ste E450 *TF:* 800-968-2748 ■ *Web:* www.shahsoftware.com	Dallas	TX	75240	800-968-2748		177
Shaheen Bros Inc PO Box 897 *Web:* www.shaheenbros.com	Amesbury	MA	01913	978-388-6776	388-6617	297-8
Shaheen Carpet Mills Inc 3742 US Hwy 41 NW PO Box 167 *Web:* temp.shaheencarpet.com	Resaca	GA	30735	706-629-9544	625-5341	361
Shaheen Jeanne (Sen D - NH) 506 Hart Senate Office Bldg *Web:* www.shaheen.senate.gov	Washington	DC	20510	202-224-2841	228-3194	342-2
Shahrazad 2847 N Oakland Ave *Web:* shahrazadrestaurant.com	Milwaukee	WI	53211	414-964-5475	964-5471	671
Shajani LLP 5212 48 St *Web:* shajani.ca	Red Deer	AB	T4N7C3	403-347-1384		2
Shakamak State Park 6265 W State Rd 48 *Web:* www.in.gov	Jasonville	IN	47438	812-665-2158		565
Shaker Group Inc, The 862 Albany Shaker Rd *TF:* 800-267-0314 ■ *Web:* theshakergroup.com	Latham	NY	12110	518-786-9286		449
Shaker Heights Public Library 16500 Van Aken Blvd *Web:* shakerlibrary.org	Cleveland	OH	44120	216-991-2030		434-3
Shaker Museum 88 Shaker Museum Rd *Web:* www.shakerml.org	Old Chatham	NY	12136	518-794-9100		637-2
Shaker Recruitment Adv & Communications 1100 Lake St *Web:* shaker.com	Oak Park	IL	60301	708-383-5320		4
Shaker Village of Pleasant Hill 3501 Lexington Rd *TF:* 800-734-5611 ■ *Web:* shakervillageky.org	Harrodsburg	KY	40330	859-734-5411		520
Shakespeare & Company Inc 70 Kemble St *Web:* www.shakespeare.org	Lenox	MA	01240	413-637-1199		749
Shakespeare Fishing Tackle Co 7 Science Ct *TF:* 800-466-5643 ■ *Web:* www.shakespeare-fishing.com	Columbia	SC	29203	803-754-7000		710
Shakespeare Machine Stamping of Wisconsin Inc 2801 S Memorial Dr **Fax Area Code:* 262 ■ *TF:* 888-399-7117 ■ *Web:* www.smsales.com	Racine	WI	53403	888-399-7117	635-2449*	1
Shakespeare Theatre 516 Eigth St SE *TF:* 877-487-8849 ■ *Web:* www.shakespearetheatre.org	Washington	DC	20003	202-547-3230	547-0226	573-4
Shakey's USA 2200 W Valley Blvd *Web:* www.shakeys.com	Alhambra	CA	91803	626-576-0616		670
Shaklee Corp 4747 Willow Rd *TF:* 800-742-5533 ■ *Web:* www.shaklee.com	Pleasanton	CA	94588	925-924-2000		366
Shalako Press PO Box 371 *Web:* shalakopress.com	Oakdale	CA	95361	209-606-4154		637-2
Shalala Donna E (Rep D - FL) 1320 Longworth House Office Bldg *Web:* www.shalala.house.gov	Washington	DC	20515	202-225-3931		342-2
Shales McNutt Construction 425 Renner Dr *Web:* shalesmcnutt.com	Elgin	IL	60123	847-622-1214		186
Shalimar 307 S Main St *Web:* www.shalimarrestaurant.com	Ann Arbor	MI	48104	734-663-1500	929-9129	671
Shalimar 3711 Hillsboro Pk *Web:* shalimarfinedining.com	Nashville	TN	37215	615-269-8577	292-0330	671
Shallco Inc 308 Components Dr *TF:* 800-876-3135 ■ *Web:* www.shallco.com	Smithfield	NC	27577	919-934-3135	934-3298	246
Shallowford Farms Popcorn Inc 3732 Hartman Rd *Web:* shallowfordfarmspopcorn.com	Yadkinville	NC	27055	336-463-5938		123
Shalon Ventures 155 Island Dr *Web:* www.shalon.com	Palo Alto	CA	94301	650-566-8200		111
Shamaley Buick GMC 955 Crockett Way *Web:* www.shamaleybuickgmc.com	El Paso	TX	79922	915-317-5958		57
Shambaugh & Son LP 7614 Opportunity Dr *Web:* shambaugh.com	Fort Wayne	IN	46825	260-487-7777	487-7701	189-10
Shamberg, Johnson, Bergman, Chartered 2600 Grand Blvd Ste 550 *Web:* sjblaw.com	Kansas City	MO	64108	816-474-0004		41
Shambhala Mountain Ctr 151 Shambhala Wy *TF:* 888-788-7221 ■ *Web:* www.shambhalamountain.org	Red Feather Lakes	CO	80545	970-881-2184	881-2909	673
Shamin Hotels Inc 2000 Ware Bottom Spring Rd *Web:* www.shaminhotels.com	Chester	VA	23836	804-777-9000		378
Shamokin Filler Company Inc PO Box 568 *TF:* 800-577-8008 ■ *Web:* www.shamokinfiller.com	Shamokin	PA	17872	570-644-0437		190
Shamokin Valley Railroad Co 356 Priestley Ave *Web:* www.nshr.com	Northumberland	PA	17857	570-473-7949		649
Shamrock Cabinet & Fixture Corp 10201 E 65th St *Web:* shamrockcabinet.com	Raytown	MO	64133	816-737-2300	356-7835	115
Shamrock Companies Inc, The 24090 Detroit Rd *Web:* www.shamrockcompanies.net	Westlake	OH	44145	440-899-9510	250-2180	360-3
Shamrock Farms Co 40034 W Clayton Rd *Web:* www.shamrockfarms.net	Stanfield	AZ	85172	602-477-2462		10-3
Shamrock Foods 3900 E Camelback Rd Ste 300 *TF:* 800-289-3663 ■ *Web:* www.shamrockfoods.com	Phoenix	AZ	85018	602-477-2500		296-27
Shamrock Holdings Inc 3500 W Olive Ave *Web:* www.shamrock.com	Burbank	CA	91505	818-845-4444		360-3
Shamrock ISD 100 S Illinois St *Web:* www.shamrockisd.net	Shamrock	TX	79079	806-256-3492	256-3628	685
Shamrock Office Solutions Inc 6908 Sierra Ct Ste A *Web:* www.shamrockoffice.com	Dublin	CA	94568	925-875-0480		179
Shamrock Pipe Tools LLC 11210 S Choctaw Dr *TF:* 800-633-7696 ■ *Web:* www.shamrocktools.com	Baton Rouge	LA	70815	800-633-7696		806
Shamrock Scientific Specialty Systems Inc 34 Davis Dr *TF:* 800-323-0249 ■ *Web:* www.shamrocklabels.com	Bellwood	IL	60104	800-323-0249	248-1907	413
Shamrock Steel Sales Inc 238 W County Rd S *TF:* 800-299-2317 ■ *Web:* www.shamrocksteelsales.com	Odessa	TX	79763	432-337-2317	337-5049	492
Shamrock Structures LLC 1440 Davey Rd *Web:* www.shamrockstructures.com	Woodridge	IL	60517	630-739-3215		668
Shamrock Technologies Inc Foot of Pacific St *Web:* shamrocktechnologies.com	Newark	NJ	07114	973-242-2999		146
Shandon Baptist Church 5250 Forest Dr *Web:* shandon.org	Columbia	SC	29206	803-782-1300		48-20

Name / Address	City	State	ZIP	Phone	Fax	Class
Shands Hospital at the University of Florida 1600 SW Archer Rd *TF:* 855-483-7546 ■ *Web:* ufhealth.org	Gainesville	FL	32608	352-265-0111	627-4173	374-3
Shane Co 9790 E Arapahoe Rd *TF:* 866-467-4263 ■ *Web:* www.shaneco.com	Greenwood Village	CO	80112	303-799-4700		410
Shane Homes Ltd 5661 Seventh St NE *Web:* www.shanehomes.com	Calgary	AB	T2E8V3	403-536-2200		364
Shane's Rib Shack 9404 W Westgate Blvd Ste C101 *Web:* www.shanesribshack.com	Glendale	AZ	85305	623-877-7427		378
Shanelaris & Schirch PLLC 35 E Pearl St *Web:* sandslawfirm.com	Nashua	NH	03060	603-594-8300		41
Shaner Hotel Group 1965 Waddle Rd *Web:* www.shanercorp.com	State College	PA	16803	814-234-4460	278-7295	379
Shang Hai 3051 25th St SW *Web:* www.fargoshanghai.com	Fargo	ND	58103	701-280-5818		671
Shanghai Commercial Bank Limited New York Branch 125 E 56th St *Web:* www.shacombank.com.hk	New York	NY	10022	212-699-2800	699-2818	70
Shanghai Mama's 216 E Sixth St *Web:* shanghaimamas.com	Cincinnati	OH	45202	513-241-7777		671
Shanghai Restaurant 3433 Hillsborough Rd *Web:* www.shanghaidurham.com	Durham	NC	27705	919-383-7581		671
Shanghai Restaurant 651 Somerset St W *Web:* www.theshang.wordpress.com	Ottawa	ON	K1R5K3	613-233-4001		671
Shangri La Botanical Gardens & Nature Ctr 2111 W Park Ave *Web:* starkculturalvenues.org	Orange	TX	77630	409-670-9113		97
Shangri La Chinese Gourmet 4248 Buena Vista Rd *Web:* www.shangrilacolumbus.com	Columbus	GA	31907	706-568-7554		671
Shangri-La Hotel Toronto 188 University Ave *Web:* www.shangri-la.com	Toronto	ON	M5H0A3	647-788-8888		379
Shangri-La Publications Coburn Hill Rd Ste 3 **Fax Area Code:* 413 ■ *TF:* 866-966-6288 ■ *Web:* www.shangri-la.0catch.com	Warren Center	PA	18851	570-395-3423	683-4831*	637-2
Shank Constructors Inc 3501 85th Ave N *Web:* www.shankconstructors.com	Brooklyn Park	MN	55443	763-424-8300		610
Shank Public Relations Counselors Inc 5310 Hallwood Ct Ste 101 *Web:* shankpr.com	Indianapolis	IN	46254	317-293-5590	293-5706	636
Shank Wealth Management LLC 2627 Chestnut Ridge Dr Ste 110 *Web:* shankwm.com	Kingwood	TX	77339	281-359-3133		690
Shanks Extracts Inc 350 Richardson Dr *TF:* 800-346-3135 ■ *Web:* shanks.com	Lancaster	PA	17603	717-393-4441		297-8
Shanley Pump & Equipment Inc 2525 S Clearbrook Dr *Web:* www.shanleypump.com	Arlington Heights	IL	60005	847-439-9200		641
Shannahan Crane & Hoist Inc 11695 Wakeside Crossing Ct *Web:* www.shannahancrane.com	Saint Louis	MO	63146	314-965-2800	291-0408	358
Shannon & Associates LLP 1851 Central Pl S Ste 225 *Web:* www.shannon-cpas.com	Kent	WA	98030	253-852-8500		2
Shannon Airport 3380 Shannon Airport Cir *Web:* www.shannonezf.com	Fredericksburg	VA	22408	540-373-4431		63
Shannon Brothers Tile Inc (SBT) 1309 Putnam Dr NW *Web:* www.sbtile.com	Huntsville	AL	35816	256-837-6520		191-1
Shannon County 18529 Main St PO Box 187 *Web:* www.shannon-county.com	Eminence	MO	65466	573-226-3414	226-5325	338
Shannon Diversified Inc 1360 E Locust St *TF:* 800-794-2345 ■ *Web:* sdiquality.com	Ontario	CA	91761	800-794-2345		104
Shannon Medical Ctr (SMC) 120 E Harris Ave *Web:* www.shannonhealth.com	San Angelo	TX	76903	325-653-6741	658-8295	374-3
Shannon Precision Fastener LLC 31600 Stephenson Hwy *Web:* www.shannonpf.com	Madison Heights	MI	48071	248-589-9670		492
Shannon Systems LLC 173 Spark St *Web:* www.b2bgateway.net	Brockton	MA	02302	401-491-9595		636
Shannon, Banks, & Smith Inc 200 Chestnut St Ste B *Web:* shannonbanks.com	Gadsden	AL	35901	256-543-1424		390
Shanor Electric Supply Inc 1276 Military Rd *Web:* www.shanorelectric.com	Kenmore	NY	14217	716-876-0711	876-7375	246
Shan-Rod Inc 7308 Drr Rd PO Box 380 *Web:* shanrodinc.com	Berlin Heights	OH	44814	419-588-2066	588-3310	789
Shanti Bithi Nursery Inc 3047 High Ridge Rd *Web:* www.shantibithi.com	Stamford	CT	06903	203-329-0768		323
Shanty Creek Resort 5780 Shanty Creek Rd *TF:* 800-678-4111 ■ *Web:* www.shantycreek.com	Bellaire	MI	49615	231-533-8621		669
Shapard Research LLC 820 NE 63rd St Uppr E *Web:* www.shapard.com	Oklahoma City	OK	73105	405-607-4664	286-1992	466
Shapco Inc 1666 20th St Ste 100	Santa Monica	CA	90404	310-264-1666		352
Shape Corp 1900 Hayes St *Web:* www.shapecorp.com	Grand Haven	MI	49417	616-846-8700	846-3464	480
Shape LLC 2105 Corporate Dr *TF:* 800-367-5811 ■ *Web:* www.shapellc.com	Addison	IL	60101	630-620-8394	620-0784	767
Shape-Master Tool Co 801 W Main St *Web:* www.shapemastertool.com	Kirkland	IL	60146	815-522-6186	522-6229	493
Shapemasters Inc PO Box 11128 *Web:* www.shapemasters.com	Southport	NC	28461	910-278-1434	278-1944	188-3
Shapiro & Appleton PC 1294 Diamond Springs Rd *TF:* 800-752-0042 ■ *Web:* hsinjurylaw.com	Virginia Beach	VA	23455	757-460-7776	460-3428	41
Shapiro Wholesale 740 Tollgate Rd *Web:* www.shapirowholesale.com	Elgin	IL	60123	847-741-6465	741-4540	157-4
Shapiro, Galvin, Shapiro & Moran, A Professional Corp 640 Third St 2nd Fl *Web:* shapirogalvinlaw.com	Santa Rosa	CA	95404	707-544-5858		41
SHAR Music 2465 S Industrial *TF:* 800-997-8723 ■ *Web:* www.sharmusic.com	Ann Arbor	MI	48104	800-997-8723		523
Shar Systems Inc 3210 Freeman St *Web:* www.sharsystems.com	Fort Wayne	IN	46802	260-432-5312		695
Share Corp 7821 N Faulkner Rd **Fax Area Code:* 414 ■ *TF:* 800-776-7192 ■ *Web:* www.sharecorp.com	Milwaukee	WI	53224	800-776-7192	355-0516*	151
SHARE El Salvador 2425 College Ave *Web:* www.share-elsalvador.org	Berkeley	CA	94704	510-848-8487		48-5
Share Our Strength 1730 M St NW Ste 700 *TF:* 800-969-4767 ■ *Web:* nokidhungry.org	Washington	DC	20036	202-393-2925		48-5
Share Pregnancy & Infant Loss Support Inc 402 Jackson St *TF:* 800-821-6819 ■ *Web:* www.nationalshare.org	Saint Charles	MO	63301	636-947-6164		48-21
ShareASalecom Inc 15 W Hubbard St Ste 500 *Web:* www.shareasale.com	Chicago	IL	60654	312-321-0487		393
Shared Imaging LLC 801 Phoenix Lake Ave *Web:* sharedimaging.com	Streamwood	IL	60107	630-483-3980		475
Shared Logic Group inc, The 6904 Spring Vly Dr Ste 305 *TF:* 877-865-0083 ■ *Web:* www.sharedlogic.com	Holland	OH	43528	419-865-0083		177
Shared Service Systems Inc 1725 S 20th St *TF:* 800-228-9976 ■ *Web:* b2b.sharedomaha.com	Omaha	NE	68108	402-536-5300		475
Sharefax Credit Union Inc 1147 Old SR- 74 *Web:* www.sharefax.org	Batavia	OH	45103	513-753-2440		219
Shareintel 151 Rowayton Ave *Web:* www.shareintel.com	Rowayton	CT	06853	203-838-5471		317
ShareSquared Inc 2155 Verdugo Blvd *TF:* 800-445-1279 ■ *Web:* sharesquared.com	Montrose	CA	91020	800-445-1279		180
ShareTracker PO Box 20 *TF:* 888-628-3088 ■ *Web:* www.sharetracker.net	Ashland	MO	65010	888-628-3088		466
Sharf Woodward & Associates Inc 5900 Sepulveda Blvd *TF:* 877-482-6687 ■ *Web:* swjobs.com	Van Nuys	CA	91411	818-989-2200		260
Shari's Restaurant & Pies 9400 SW Gemini Dr *TF:* 800-433-5334 ■ *Web:* www.sharis.com	Beaverton	OR	97008	503-605-4299	605-4260	670
Sharian Inc 368 W Ponce de Leon Ave *Web:* www.sharian.com	Decatur	GA	30030	404-373-2274		152
Sharif Designs Ltd 34-12 36th Ave	Long Island City	NY	11106	718-472-1100		430
Shark Industries Ltd 6700 Bleck Dr *TF:* 800-537-4275 ■ *Web:* sharkind.com	Rockford	MN	55373	763-565-1900	565-1901	1
Sharkey County PO Box 218 *Web:* www.sharkey.msghn.org	Rolling Fork	MS	39159	662-873-2755		338
Sharkey Howes & Javer Inc 720 S Colorado Blvd Ste 600 S Twr *TF:* 800-557-9380 ■ *Web:* www.shwj.com	Denver	CO	80246	303-639-5100		194
Sharkey's Cuts For Kids 1568 Post Rd E *Web:* sharkeyscutsforkids.com	Westport	CT	06880	203-557-8700		77
Sharks Success Marketing Ent 1532 Pickwood Ave *Web:* www.sharkssuccess.com	Fern Park	FL	32730	407-260-9780		195
Sharlot Hall Museum Library/Archives 115 S McCormick St *Web:* www.sharlot.org	Prescott	AZ	86303	928-445-3122		434-3
Sharon Coating LLC 277 Sharpsville Ave *Web:* www.us.nlmk.com	Sharon	PA	16146	724-981-3545	981-3009	307
Sharon Health Care Ctr 27 Hospital Hill Rd PO Box 1268 *Web:* athenahealthcare.com	Sharon	CT	06069	860-364-1002	364-0237	450
Sharon Piping and Equipment Inc 1260 Garnet Dr *Web:* sharpevalves.com	Northlake	IL	60164	708-562-9221		789
Sharon Public Library 90 S Main St *TF:* 800-825-3260 ■ *Web:* www.townofsharon.net	Sharon	MA	02067	781-784-1578		434-3
Sharon Regional Health System 740 E State St *Web:* www.sharonregionalmedical.org	Sharon	PA	16146	724-983-3911	983-3842	374-3
Sharon Towers 5100 Sharon Rd *Web:* sharontowers.org	Charlotte	NC	28210	704-553-1670		672
Sharons Wig Salon 13723 W Capitol Dr *Web:* sharonswigsalon.com	Milwaukee	WI	53005	262-783-6900		671
Sharonville Convention Ctr 11355 Chester Rd *TF:* 800-294-3179 ■ *Web:* sharonvilleconventioncenter.com	Cincinnati	OH	45246	513-771-7744	772-5745	205
Sharp & Cobos PC 4705 Spicewood Springs Rd Ste 100 *Web:* sharpcobos.com	Austin	TX	78759	512-473-2265	473-8525	428
Sharp Bros Seed Co 1005 S Sycamore *TF:* 800-462-8483 ■ *Web:* www.sharpseed.com	Healy	KS	67850	620-398-2231	398-2220	694
Sharp Bus Lines Ltd 567 Oak Park Rd *TF:* 855-242-5726 ■ *Web:* www.sharpbus.com	Brantford	ON	N3T5L8	519-751-3434		107
Sharp Communication Inc 3403 Governors Dr *TF:* 800-548-2484 ■ *Web:* www.sharpcom.com	Huntsville	AL	35805	256-533-2484		246
Sharp County 718 Ash Flat Dr *Web:* www.ark.org	Ash Flat	AR	72513	870-994-7334		338
Sharp Decisions Inc 1040 Avenue of the A *TF:* 800-742-7792 ■ *Web:* www.sharpdecisions.com	New York	NY	10018	212-481-5533	481-8751	113
Sharp Electronics Corp 1 Sharp Plz *TF:* 800-237-4277 ■ *Web:* www.sharpusa.com	Mahwah	NJ	07430	201-529-8200		52
Sharp End Publishing PO Box 1613 *Web:* stores.sharpendbooks.com	Boulder	CO	80306	303-444-2698		637-2

Phone | Fax | Class

Sharp Energy Inc 648 Ocean Hwy......... Pocomoke City MD 21851 888-742-7740 316
TF: 888-742-7740 ■ *Web:* www.sharpenergy.com

Sharp Health Plan
4305 University Ave Ste 200................. San Diego CA 92105 619-228-2300 391-3
TF: 800-359-2002 ■ *Web:* www.sharphealthplan.com

Sharp Healthcare
8695 Spectrum Center Blvd................. San Diego CA 92123 858-499-4000 499-5237 353
TF: 800-827-4277 ■ *Web:* www.sharp.com

Sharp Innovations Inc
3113 Main St Bldg B Main Level.............Conestoga PA 17516 717-290-6760 290-6877 809
TF: 888-575-8977 ■ *Web:* www.sharpinnovations.com

Sharp Laboratories of America
5750 NW Pacific Rim Blvd.....................Camas WA 98607 360-817-8400 668
Web: www.sharplabs.com

Sharp Mcqueen PA
419 N Kansas Ave PO Box 2619.................Liberal KS 67905 620-624-2548 41
Web: sharpmcqueen.com

Sharp Microelectronics of the Americas
5700 NW Pacific Rim Blvd.....................Camas WA 98607 360-834-8700 253
Web: www.sharpsma.com

Sharp Shopper Inc 1100 Sharp Ave............. Ephrata PA 17522 717-733-9555 345
Web: sharpshopper.net

Sharp Sky Partners
520 Baker Bldg 706 Second Ave S...........Minneapolis MN 55402 612-339-3444 339-3344 193
Web: www.sharpsky.com

Sharp Tooling Solutions Inc
70745 Powell Rd.....................Bruce Township MI 48065 586-752-3099 752-1820 757
Web: www.sharptoolingsolutions.com

Sharp Transportation Inc
390 N 900 E..............................Wellsville UT 84339 435-245-6053 780
TF: 800-258-2074 ■ *Web:* www.sharptrucking.com

Sharp Water Culligan
129 Columbia Rd..........................Salisbury MD 21801 410-220-6493 806
Web: sharpwater.com

Sharpe Consulting LLC
1802 NJ-31 Ste 389..........................Clinton NJ 08809 908-319-3650 463
Web: www.sharpeconsulting.biz

Sharphat Inc
333 Sylvan Ave Ste 324...............Englewood Cliffs NJ 07632 201-503-0020 100
Web: www.sharphat.com

Sharpless McClearn Lester Duffy PA
200 S Elm St Ste 400.....................Greensboro NC 27401 336-333-6400 333-6399 41
Web: sharpless-stavola.com

Sharprint Silkscreen & Graphics Inc
4200 W Wrightwood Ave.....................Chicago IL 60639 773-862-9300 627
Web: www.sharprint.com

Sharpsville Container Corp
600 Main St............................Sharpsville PA 16150 724-962-1100 100
Web: sharpsvillecontainer.com

Sharrard McGee & Company PA
1321 Long St............................High Point NC 27262 336-884-0410 2
Web: www.sharrardmcgee.com

Shartsis Friese LLP
1 Maritime Plz 18th Fl..................San Francisco CA 94111 415-421-6500 421-2922 428
Web: www.sflaw.com

Sharut Furniture Inc 220 Passaic St............ Passaic NJ 07055 973-473-1000 473-4416 820
Web: www.furnitureinmotion.com

Sharzer Associates Inc
275 W 96th St Ste 11.......................New York NY 10025 212-222-5721 96
Web: sharzer.com

Shasta Abbey Buddhist Monastery
c/o Shasta Abbey 3724 Summit Dr......... Mount Shasta CA 96067 530-926-4208 926-0428 48-20
Web: shastaabbey.org

Shasta Beverages Inc
26901 Industrial Blvd........................Hayward CA 94545 510-783-4070 80-2
TF: 800-834-9980 ■ *Web:* www.shastapop.com

Shasta Bible College & Graduate School
2951 Goodwater Ave.........................Redding CA 96002 530-221-4275 221-6929 685
TF: 800-800-4722 ■ *Web:* www.shasta.edu

Shasta College
11555 Old Oregon Trl PO Box 496006...........Redding CA 96049 530-242-7500 800
Web: www.shastacollege.edu

Shasta County 1643 Market St.................Redding CA 96099 530-225-5730 225-5454 338
TF: 800-735-2922 ■ *Web:* www.co.shasta.ca.us

Shasta Inc 300 Steel St......................Aliquippa PA 15001 724-378-8280 378-5217 723
Web: shastainc.com

Shasta Public Library
1100 Parkview Ave..........................Redding CA 96001 530-245-7250 434-3
Web: www.shastalibraries.org

Shasta Qa 1538 Market St.....................Redding CA 96001 530-242-5799 177
Web: www.shastaqa.com

Shasta Regional Medical Ctr (SRMC)
1100 Butte St..............................Redding CA 96001 530-244-5400 374-3
TF: 866-800-2987 ■ *Web:* www.shastaregional.com

Shasta State Historic Park
c/o Northern Buttes District Ofc
400 Glen Dr............................... Oroville CA 95966 530-243-8194 565
Web: www.parks.ca.gov

Shasta Ventures
2440 Sand Hill Rd Ste 300................. Menlo Park CA 94025 650-543-1700 792
Web: shastaventures.com

Shasteen & Morris Pc 7441 O St Ste 105........ Lincoln NE 68510 402-464-0064 41
Web: shasteenandmorris.com

Shattered Wig Review 425 E 31st St...........Baltimore MD 21218 410-243-6888 637-9
Web: www.normals.com

Shattuck-Saint Mary's School
1000 Shumway Ave........................ Faribault MN 55021 507-333-1500 622
TF: 800-421-2724 ■ *Web:* www.s-sm.org

Shaunna L. Browne Law PLLC
102 Bay St Ste 2......................... Manchester NH 03104 603-626-8080 41
Web: shaunnabrownelaw.com

Shavel Assoc 13 Roszel Rd...................Princeton NJ 08540 609-452-1800 361
Web: www.shavel.com

Shaver Lake Real Estate Inc
41593 Tollhouse Rd......................Shaver Lake CA 93664 800-841-8919 652
TF: 800-841-8919 ■ *Web:* shaverlake.com

Shaver Properties Inc
1872 Commerce Ave Ste K................. Vero Beach FL 32967 772-569-3466 499
Web: www.shavermillwork.com

Phone | Fax | Class

Shaw & Sullivan P C
1221 Cameron St.........................Alexandria VA 22314 703-548-2776 548-7988 2
Web: shawcpa.com

Shaw Air Force Base
20 FW/SEF 517 Lance Ave Ste 215........... Shaw AFB SC 29152 803-895-1971 497-1
TF: 800-235-7776 ■ *Web:* www.shaw.af.mil

Shaw Communications Inc
2421 37 Ave NE............................ Calgary AB T2P4L4 403-750-4500 116
TSE: SJR.B ■ *TF:* 888-472-2222 ■ *Web:* www.shaw.ca

Shaw Construction LLC 300 Kalamath St.........Denver CO 80223 303-825-4740 825-6403 187
Web: www.shawconstruction.net

Shaw Electric Co
22100 Telegraph Rd....................... Southfield MI 48033 248-228-2000 228-2080 189-4
Web: www.shawelectric.com

Shaw Glass Company Inc
55 Bristol Dr...........................South Easton MA 02375 800-225-0430 238-0103* 330
**Fax Area Code:* 508 ■ *TF:* 800-225-0430 ■ *Web:* www.solarseal.com

Shaw Industries Inc 616 E Walnut Ave........... Dalton GA 30722 800-441-7429 131
TF: 800-441-7429 ■ *Web:* shawfloors.com

Shaw Institute
55 Main St PO Box 1652....................Blue Hill ME 04614 207-374-2135 668
Web: www.meriresearch.org

Shaw media 7717 S Illinois Rt 31............Crystal Lake IL 60014 630-845-5233 532-3
Web: www.shawmedia.com

Shaw Pipeline Services Inc
4250 N Sam Houston Pkwy E Ste 180...........Houston TX 77032 832-601-0850 539
Web: www.shawpipeline.com

Shaw Satellite Services Inc
2055 Flavelle Blvd...................... Mississauga ON L5K1Z8 888-554-7827 681
TF: 888-554-7827 ■ *Web:* www.shawdirect.ca

Shaw Systems Associates Inc
6200 Savoy Dr Ste 1000......................Houston TX 77036 713-782-7730 177
Web: www.shawsystems.com

Shaw University 118 E S St.................... Raleigh NC 27601 919-546-8275 546-8271 166
TF: 800-214-6683 ■ *Web:* www.shawu.edu

Shaw's Crab House Chicago
21 E Hubbard St............................Chicago IL 60611 312-527-2722 671
Web: www.shawscrabhouse.com

Shaw/Stewart Lumber Co
645 Johnson St NE.......................Minneapolis MN 55413 612-378-1520 499
TF: 800-233-0101 ■ *Web:* www.shawstewart.com

Shawano Country Chamber of Commerce
1263 S Main St............................ Shawano WI 54166 715-524-2139 524-3127 139
TF: 800-235-8528 ■ *Web:* www.shawanocountry.com

Shawano County 311 N Main St............... Shawano WI 54166 715-526-9150 524-5157 338
Web: www.co.shawano.wi.us

ShawCor Ltd 25 Bethridge Rd.................. Toronto ON M9W1M7 416-743-7111 743-7199 537
TSX: SCL ■ *TF:* 800-845-6808 ■ *Web:* www.shawcor.com

Shawe & Rosenthal LLP
1 S St Ste 1800............................Baltimore MD 21202 410-752-1040 752-8861 445
Web: shawe.com

Shaw-Lundquist Associates Inc
2757 W Service Rd........................ Saint Paul MN 55121 651-454-0670 454-7982 186
Web: www.shawlundquist.com

Shawmut Advertising Inc
33 Cherry Hill Dr..........................Danvers MA 01923 978-762-7500 627
Web: www.shawmutdelivers.com

Shawmut Design & Construction
560 Harrison Ave...........................Boston MA 02118 617-622-7000 186
TF: 877-342-7233 ■ *Web:* www.shawmut.com

Shawmut Mills 2770 Dove St.................Port Huron MI 48060 810-987-2222 113
Web: www.shawmutcorporation.com

Shawn Harrison Associates PLLC
1010 N Florida Ave......................... Tampa FL 33602 813-337-6683 41
Web: sha-law.com

Shawnee Chamber of Commerce
15100 W 67th St Ste 202..................... Shawnee KS 66217 913-631-6545 631-9628 139
Web: www.shawneekschamber.com

Shawnee Chemical Company Inc
136 Main St Ste 300........................Princeton NJ 08540 609-799-3930 799-6576 601
Web: www.shawchem.com

Shawnee Community College
8364 Shawnee College Rd.......................Ullin IL 62992 618-634-3200 634-3300 162
TF: 800-481-2242 ■ *Web:* www.shawneecc.edu

Shawnee Correctional Ctr 6665 SR-146 E........ Vienna IL 62995 618-658-8331 658-4014 213
Web: www.illinois.gov

Shawnee County 200 SE Seventh St Rm 100....... Topeka KS 66603 785-251-4042 251-4902 338
Web: www.snco.us

Shawnee forward 231 N Bell................. Shawnee OK 74801 405-273-6092 275-9851 139
Web: www.shawneechamber.com

Shawnee Milling Company Inc
201 S Broadway PO Box 1567................ Shawnee OK 74802 405-273-7000 273-7333 296-23
TF: 800-654-2600 ■ *Web:* shawneemilling.com

Shawnee Mission Medical Ctr
9100 W 74th St.................... Shawnee Mission KS 66204 913-676-2000 374-3
Web: www.shawneemission.org

Shawnee Mountain Ski Area
401 Hollow Rd......................East Stroudsburg PA 18301 570-421-7231 31
TF: 800-233-4218 ■ *Web:* www.shawneemt.com

Shawnee State Park
132 State Park Rd........................Schellsburg PA 15559 814-733-4218 565
Web: www.dcnr.pa.gov

Shawnee State University
940 Second St........................... Portsmouth OH 45662 740-351-3221 351-3111 166
TF: 800-959-2778 ■ *Web:* www.shawnee.edu

Shawnee Steel & Welding Inc
6124 Merriam Dr...........................Merriam KS 66203 913-432-8046 432-0819 567
Web: shawnee-steel.com

Shawnee Telephone Co 120 W Lane St.......... Equality IL 62934 618-276-4211 736
TF: 800-461-3956 ■ *Web:* www.myshawnee.net

Shawnee Tva Employees Federal Credit Union
7755 Metropolis Lake Rd................ West Paducah KY 42086 270-442-6479 219
Web: stvafcu.virtualcu.net

Shawnigan Lake School (SLS)
1975 Renfrew Rd....................Shawnigan Lake BC V0R2W1 250-743-5516 622
Web: www.shawnigan.ca

Shaw-Ross International Inc
2900 SW 149 Ave Ste 200....................Miramar FL 33027 954-443-5650 430-5045 81-3
TF: 800-255-1350 ■ *Web:* www.shawross.com

Phone | Fax | Class

Shawvver & Associates LLC
5959 S Staples Ste 206 ... Corpus Christi TX 78413 361-880-8968 880-8971 400
Web: www.stxpi.com

Shawvver & Son Inc
144 NE 44th St ... Oklahoma City OK 73105 405-525-9451 525-6136 189-4
Web: www.shawver.net

Shaw-Winkler Inc 4910 Dawn Ave ... East Lansing MI 48823 517-351-5720 189-10
Web: shawwinkler.com

Shayne, Dachs, Sauer & Dachs LLP
114 Old Country Rd Ste 410 ... Mineola NY 11501 516-747-1100 41
Web: shaynedachs.com

SHAZAM Inc 6700 Pioneer Pkwy ... Johnston IA 50131 515-288-2828 225
Web: www.shazam.net

SHC International Inc
225 Lisburn Way ... Vacaville CA 95688 707-448-6076 360-3
Web: www.shc-intl.com

SHDR (Stanley Hunt DuPree & Rhine)
McGriff Insurance Services Inc
7701 Airport Center Dr ... Greensboro NC 27409 336-291-1133 293-9048* 193
**Fax Area Code:* 252 ■ *TF:* 800-930-2441 ■ *Web:* www.shdr.com

Shea Brothers Inc 65 Innerbelt Rd ... Somerville MA 02143 617-623-2001 623-0939 627
Web: www.sheabrothers.com

Shea Concrete Products Inc
87 Haverhill Rd ... Amesbury MA 01913 978-388-1509 770
TF: 800-696-7432 ■ *Web:* sheaconcrete.com

Shea's Performing Arts Ctr
646 Main St ... Buffalo NY 14202 716-847-1410 847-1644 572
Web: www.sheas.org

Sheaff Brock Investment Advisors LLC
8801 River Crossing Blvd Ste 100 ... Indianapolis IN 46240 317-705-5700 705-5110 401
TF: 866-575-5700 ■ *Web:* sheaffbrock.com

Shealy Wellness 5607 S 222nd Rd ... Fair Grove MO 65648 417-467-2124 637-2
TF: 855-329-2124 ■ *Web:* www.normshealy.com

Shealy's Truck Center Inc
1340 Bluff Rd ... Columbia SC 29201 803-771-0176 771-4879 516
TF: 800-951-8580 ■ *Web:* shealytruck.com

Shear Ego International School of Hair Design
525 Titus Ave ... Rochester NY 14617 585-342-0070 342-0863 685
TF: 800-726-1498 ■ *Web:* www.shearegoschool.com

Shearer & Associates Inc
4960 Corporate Dr Ste 100 ... Huntsville AL 35805 256-830-1031 196
Web: shearerassociates.us

Shearer Printing Service Inc
107 W Markland Ave ... Kokomo IN 46901 765-457-3274 457-1639 627
Web: www.shearerpos.com

Shearman & Sterling
599 Lexington Ave ... New York NY 10022 212-848-4000 428
Web: www.shearman.com

Sheboygan Area Credit Union
1707 Indiana Ave ... Sheboygan WI 53081 920-459-5151 219
Web: shebareacu.com

Sheboygan County 615 N Sixth St ... Sheboygan WI 53081 920-459-3068 459-3921 338
Web: www.sheboygancounty.com

Sheboygan County Chamber of Commerce
621 S Eigth St ... Sheboygan WI 53081 920-457-9491 457-6269 139
Web: www.sheboygan.org

Sheboygan Paint Co (SPC)
1439 N 25th St PO Box 417 ... Sheboygan WI 53081 920-458-2157 458-5620 550
TF: 800-773-7801 ■ *Web:* shebpaint.com

Sheboygan Paper Box Co
716 Clara Ave PO Box 326 ... Sheboygan WI 53082 920-458-8373 458-2901 101
Web: www.spbox.com

Sheboygan Press 632 Center Ave ... Sheboygan WI 53081 920-457-7711 532-2
TF: 800-686-3900 ■ *Web:* www.sheboyganpress.com

Shed, The 113 1/2 E Palace Ave ... Santa Fe NM 87501 505-982-9030 671
Web: www.sfshed.com

Shee Atika Inc 315 Lincoln St Ste 300 ... Sitka AK 99835 907-747-3534 747-5727 113
TF: 800-478-3534 ■ *Web:* www.sheeatika.com

Sheedy Drayage Company Inc
1215 Michigan St ... San Francisco CA 94107 415-648-7171 648-1535 780
Web: sheedydrayage.com

Sheehan Pipe Line Construction Co
2431 E 61st St Ste 700 ... Tulsa OK 74136 918-747-3471 747-9888 188-10

Sheehy & Assoc 2297 Lexington Rd ... Louisville KY 40206 502-456-9007 4
Web: sheehy1.com

Sheehy Auto Stores
12701 Fair Lakes Cir ... Fairfax VA 22033 703-802-3480 57
Web: www.sheehy.com

Sheely's Furniture & Appliance Company Inc
11450 S Ave ... North Lima OH 44452 330-549-3901 321
Web: www.sheelys.com

SheerID 2451 Willamette St ... Eugene OR 97405 541-654-4589 178-1
Web: www.sheerid.com

SheerVision Inc(NDA)
4030 Palos Verdes Dr N Ste 104 ... Rolling Hills Estates CA 90274 310-265-8918 544
Web: www.sheervision.com

Sheet Metal & Air Conditioning Contractors' NA (SMACNA)
4201 Lafayette Center Dr ... Chantilly VA 20151 703-803-2980 803-3732 49-3
Web: www.smacna.org

Sheet Metal Automation Inc
515 17th St SE ... Independence IA 50644 319-334-7081 334-2753 456
Web: www.smaemm.com

Sheet Metal Connectors Inc
5850 Main St NE ... Minneapolis MN 55432 763-572-0000 572-1100 697
TF: 800-328-1966 ■ *Web:* www.smcduct.com

Sheet Metal Engineers Inc
383 Tower Rd ... Martinez GA 30907 706-863-6575 697

Sheetz Inc 5700 6th Ave ... Altoona PA 16602 814-946-3611 941-5105 204
TF: 800-487-5444 ■ *Web:* www.sheetz.com

Sheffer Corp 6990 Cornell Rd ... Cincinnati OH 45242 513-489-9770 489-3034 223
Web: www.sheffercorp.com

Sheffield Cutting Equipment
4561 Mission Gorge Pl ... San Diego CA 92120 619-280-0011 806
Web: www.sheffieldcuttingequip.com

Sheffield Institute for the Recording Arts
13816 Sunnybrook Rd ... Phoenix MD 21131 410-628-7260 628-1977 167-3
TF: 800-355-6613 ■ *Web:* www.sheffieldav.com

Sheffield Metals International Inc
5467 Evergreen Pkwy ... Sheffield Village OH 44054 440-934-8500 492
TF: 800-283-5262 ■ *Web:* www.sheffieldmetals.com

Sheffield Publishing Co (SPC)
9009 Antioch Rd ... Salem WI 53168 262-843-2281 843-3683 637-2
Web: www.spcbooks.com

Sheffield Resource Network
2239 N Hayden Rd ... Scottsdale AZ 85257 480-968-6199 463
Web: www.sheffieldnet.com

Shefield Group 2265 W Railway St ... Abbotsford BC V2S2E3 604-859-1014 859-1711 159
Web: shefield.com

Sheila Greco Associates LLC
174 State Hwy 67 ... Amsterdam NY 12010 518-843-4611 393
Web: www.sheilagreco.com

Sheiness, Glover & Grossman LLP
4544 Post Oak Pl Dr Ste 270 ... Houston TX 77027 713-374-7000 374-7049 466
Web: www.sgglawyers.com

Sheladia Associates Inc
15825 Shady Grove Rd Ste 100 ... Rockville MD 20850 301-590-3939 261
Web: www.sheladia.com

Shelba D. Johnson Trucking Inc
PO Box 7287 ... High Point NC 27264 336-476-2000 476-0187 780
TF: 800-777-2583 ■ *Web:* www.sdjtrucking.com

Shelborne South Beach
1801 Collins Ave ... Miami Beach FL 33139 305-531-1271 531-2206 379
Web: www.shelborne.com

Shelburne Farms 1611 Harbor Rd ... Shelburne VT 05482 802-985-8686 985-8123 48-13
TF: 800-286-6022 ■ *Web:* shelburnefarms.org

Shelburne Museum 5555 Shelburne Rd ... Shelburne VT 05482 802-985-3346 985-2331 520
Web: www.shelburnemuseum.org

Shelby County 100 Hurst St ... Center TX 75935 936-598-5600 598-3701 338
Web: www.co.shelby.tx.us

Shelby County 612 Ct St ... Harlan IA 51537 712-755-3831 755-3200 338
TF: 800-735-3942 ■ *Web:* www.shco.org

Shelby County 25 W Polk St ... Shelbyville IN 46176 317-392-6330 392-6393 338
Web: www.co.shelby.in.us

Shelby County 1000 Detention Rd ... Shelbyville KY 40065 502-633-2343 647-1457 338
Web: www.shelbycounty.ky.gov

Shelby County 202 W Poplar St ... Sidney OH 45365 937-498-7226 498-1293 338
TF: 800-553-6763 ■ *Web:* co.shelby.oh.us

Shelby County
Lake Shelbyville 315 E Main ... Shelbyville IL 62565 217-774-2244 206
Web: www.lakeshelbyville.com

Shelby County Alabama PO Box 326 ... Columbiana AL 35051 205-670-6550 338
TF: 800-272-4263 ■ *Web:* www.shelbyal.com

Shelby County Chamber of Commerce
501 N Harrison St ... Shelbyville IN 46176 317-398-6647 392-3901 139
TF: 800-318-4083 ■ *Web:* shelbychamber.net

Shelby County Chamber of Commerce
316 Main St ... Shelbyville KY 40065 502-633-1636 139
Web: www.shelbycountykychamber.com

Shelby County Missouri 204-B N Ctr ... Shelbina MO 63468 573-822-9651 338
Web: shelbycountymo.com

Shelby County Reporter
115 N Main St ... Columbiana AL 35051 205-669-3131 669-4217 532-4
Web: www.shelbycountyreporter.com

Shelby Electric Co-op (SEC)
1355 IL-128 State PO Box 560 ... Shelbyville IL 62565 217-774-3986 245
TF: 800-677-2612 ■ *Web:* www.shelbyelectric.coop

Shelby Energy Co-opeartive Inc
620 Old Finchville Rd ... Shelbyville KY 40065 502-633-4420 245
TF: 800-292-6585 ■ *Web:* www.shelbyenergy.com

Shelby Engineering Ltd
9632 54 Ave NW ... Edmonton AB T6E5V1 780-438-2540 261
Web: shelbyeng.ca

Shelby Materials
157 E Rampart St PO Box 242 ... Shelbyville IN 46176 800-548-9516 182
TF: 800-548-9516 ■ *Web:* www.shelbymaterials.com

Shelby Richard C (Sen R - AL)
304 Russell Senate Office Bldg ... Washington DC 20510 202-224-5744 224-3416 342-2
Web: www.shelby.senate.gov

Shelby State Bank 242 N Michigan Ave ... Shelby MI 49455 231-861-2123 70
Web: www.shelbybank.com

Shelby Systems Inc
7345 Goodlett Farms Pkwy ... Cordova TN 38016 901-757-2372 177
TF: 800-877-0222 ■ *Web:* www.shelbysystems.com

Shelby Township Library
51680 Van Dyke Hwy ... Shelby Township MI 48316 586-739-7414 726-0535 434-3
Web: www.shelbytwplib.org

Shelby Williams Industries Inc
810 W Hwy 25/70 ... Newport TN 37821 423-623-0031 319-9371* 319-3
**Fax Area Code:* 866 ■ *TF:* 800-873-3252 ■ *Web:* www.shelbywilliams.com

Shelbyville Daily Union
100 W Main St ... Shelbyville IL 62565 217-774-2161 774-5732 532-2
Web: www.shelbyvilledailyunion.com

Shelbyville State Fish & Wildlife Area
562 State Hwy 121 PO Box 42A ... Bethany IL 61914 217-665-3112 565
Web: dnr.illinois.gov

Shelbyville-Bedford County Chamber of Commerce
100 N Cannon Blvd ... Shelbyville TN 37160 931-684-3482 684-3483 139
Web: www.shelbyvilletn.com

Shelbyville-Shelby County Public Library
57 W Broadway ... Shelbyville IN 46176 317-398-7121 421-2758 434-3
Web: www.myshelbylibrary.org

Sheldahl Corp 1150 Sheldahl Rd ... Northfield MN 55057 507-663-8000 696
TF: 800-927-3580 ■ *Web:* www.sheldahl.com

Sheldon Gross Realty Inc
80 Main St ... West Orange NJ 07052 973-325-6200 652
Web: www.sheldongrossrealty.com

Sheldon Jackson Museum 104 College Dr ... Sitka AK 99835 907-747-6233 747-3004 520
Web: museums.alaska.gov

Sheldon Laboratory Systems Inc
102 Kirk St ... Crystal Springs MS 39059 601-892-2731 892-3316 419
TF: 800-531-7604 ■ *Web:* www.sheldonlabs.com

Sheldon Lake State Park & Environmental Learning Ctr
14140 Garrett Rd ... Houston TX 77049 281-456-2800 565
Web: tpwd.texas.gov

Name	Address	City	State	Zip	Phone	Fax	Class	Other
Sheldon Manufacturing Inc	300 N 26th Ave	Cornelius	OR	97113	503-640-3000	640-1366	697	TF: 888-227-1410 ■ Web: www.sheldonmanufacturing.com
Sheldon Museum of Art	PO Box 880300	Lincoln	NE	68588	402-472-2461		520	Web: www.sheldonartmuseum.org
Sheldon's Express Pharmacy Inc	843 Fairview Ave	Bowling Green	KY	42101	270-842-4515		238	Web: sheldonsrx.com
Sheldons' Inc	626 Center St	Antigo	WI	54409	715-623-2382	623-3001	710	Web: www.mepps.com
Shell Canada Ltd	400 Fourth Ave SW	Calgary	AB	T2P0J4	403-691-3111		536	TF: 877-656-3111 ■ Web: www.shell.ca
Shell Chemical Co	910 Louisiana St	Houston	TX	77002	855-697-4355		144	TF: 855-697-4355 ■ Web: www.shell.us
Shell Education	5301 Oceanus Dr	Huntington Beach	CA	92649	714-891-2273	230-7070	637-10	TF: 800-858-7339 ■ Web: www.teachercreatedmaterials.com
Shell Engineering and Associates Inc	2403 W Ash St	Columbia	MO	65203	573-445-0106	445-0137	261	Web: www.shellengr.com
Shell Horizons Inc	14191 63rd Way	Clearwater	FL	33760	727-536-3333	536-8888	594	Web: www.shellhorizons.com
Shell House Restaurant, The	8 Gateway Blvd	Savannah	GA	31419	912-927-3280		671	Web: shellhouseseafoodsavannah.com
Shell Island Ocean Front Suites	2700 N Lumina Ave	Wrightsville Beach	NC	28480	910-256-8696		707	TF: 800-689-6765 ■ Web: www.shellisland.com
Shell Lumber & Hardware Co	2733 SW 27th Ave	Miami	FL	33133	305-856-6401		752	Web: www.shelllumber.com
Shell Machine Works Inc	5317 Agnes St	Corpus Christi	TX	78405	361-883-7073		567	Web: www.shellmachineworks.com
Shell Point Village	15101 Shell Pt Blvd	Fort Myers	FL	33908	239-466-1131		672	TF: 800-780-1131 ■ Web: www.shellpoint.org
Shell Vacations Club	40 Skokie Blvd Ste 350	Northbrook	IL	60062	847-564-4600		753	Web: www.shellvacationsclub.com
Shelley Electric Inc	3619 W 29th St S	Wichita	KS	67217	316-945-8311		189-4	Web: www.shelleyelectric.com
Shelly and Sands Inc	3570 S River Rd	Zanesville	OH	43701	740-453-0721	455-3144	188-4	Web: www.shellyandsands.com
Shelly Associates Inc	17171 Murphy Ave	Irvine	CA	92614	949-417-8070	417-8075	253	Web: shellyinc.com
Shelly Automotive Group	*Irvine BMW* 9881 Research Dr	Irvine	CA	92618	888-853-7429		57	TF: 888-853-7429 ■ Web: www.shellygroup.com
Shelly Co	80 Pk Dr	Thornville	OH	43076	740-246-6315		188-4	TF: 888-743-5590 ■ Web: www.shellyco.com
Shelly Enterprises	3120 Old State Rd	Telford	PA	18969	215-723-5108		499	Web: www.shellyssupply.com
Shelly Law Offices LLC	70 W Oakland Ave Ste 208	Doylestown	PA	18901	866-214-3323	454-7941*	41	*Fax Area Code: 267 ■ TF: 866-214-3323 ■ Web: shelly-law.com
Shelmark Engineering LLC	921 Fm 517 Rd E	Dickinson	TX	77539	409-935-9986		261	Web: shelmark.net
SheltAir Aviation Services Fort Lauderdale	4860 NE 12th Ave	Fort Lauderdale	FL	33334	954-771-2210	771-3745	63	TF: 800-700-2210 ■ Web: sheltairaviation.com
Shelter Canadian Properties Ltd	2600 Seven Evergreen Pl	Winnipeg	MB	R3L2T3	204-475-9090		652	Web: www.scpl.com
Shelter Enterprises	8 Saratoga St	Cohoes	NY	12047	518-237-4100		234	TF: 800-836-0719 ■ Web: www.shelter-ent.com
Shelter Institute	873 US Route 1	Woolwich	ME	04579	207-442-7938	442-7939	167-3	Web: www.shelterinstitute.com
Shelter Island State Marine Park	PO Box 111071	Juneau	AK	99811	907-465-2482		565	Web: dnr.alaska.gov
Shelter Mortgage Company LLC	4000 W Brown Deer Rd	Milwaukee	WI	53209	414-716-2800		77	Web: www.sheltermortgage.com
Shelter Mutual Insurance Co	1817 W Broadway	Columbia	MO	65218	573-445-8441		391-4	TF: 800-743-5587 ■ Web: www.shelterinsurance.com
Shelter Systems Ltd	1025 Meadow Branch Rd	Westminster	MD	21158	410-876-3900	857-5754	817	Web: www.sheltersystems.com
ShelterLogic Corp	150 Callendar Rd	Watertown	CT	06795	800-560-8383		105	TF: 800-560-8383 ■ Web: www.shelterlogic.com
Shelton City School District	382 Long Hill Ave	Shelton	CT	06484	203-924-1023		685	Web: www.sheltonpublicschools.org
Shelton Group	12400 Coit Rd Ste 650	Dallas	TX	75251	972-239-5119		636	Web: www.sheltongroup.com
Shelton State *Community College*	9500 Old Greensboro Rd	Tuscaloosa	AL	35405	205-391-2211	391-3910	162	TF: 877-838-2778 ■ Web: www.sheltonstate.edu
Shelton-Mason County Chamber of Commerce	215 W Railroad Ave PO Box 2389	Shelton	WA	98584	360-426-2021	426-8678	139	TF: 800-576-2021 ■ Web: www.sheltonchamber.org
Shelton-McMurphey-Johnson House	303 Willamette St	Eugene	OR	97401	541-484-0808		50-3	Web: www.smjhouse.org
Shelving Inc	32 S Squirrel Rd	Auburn Hills	MI	48326	248-852-8600		361	Web: www.shelving.com
Shemer Arts Center & Museum Association Inc (SACAMA)	5005 E Camelback Rd	Phoenix	AZ	85018	602-262-4727		520	Web: shemerartcenter.org
Shenandoah at the Arbor	10631 Los Alamitos Blvd	Los Alamitos	CA	90720	562-431-1990		671	Web: eatatthearbor.com
Shenandoah County	600 N Main St Ste 102	Woodstock	VA	22664	540-459-6167	459-6192	338	Web: shenandoahcountyva.us
Shenandoah Furniture Inc	225 Beaver Creek Dr	Martinsville	VA	24112	276-632-0502		321	
Shenandoah National Park	3655 US Hwy 211E	Luray	VA	22835	540-999-3500		564	Web: www.nps.gov
Shenandoah Telecommunications Co	500 Shentel Way	Edinburg	VA	22824	540-984-5224	984-3438	360-3	NASDAQ: SHEN ■ TF: 800-743-6835 ■ Web: www.shentel.com
Shenandoah University	1460 University Dr	Winchester	VA	22601	540-665-4581		166	TF: 800-432-2266 ■ Web: www.su.edu
Shenandoah Valley Westminster-Canterbury	300 Westminster-Canterbury Dr	Winchester	VA	22603	540-665-5914		672	TF: 800-492-9463 ■ Web: www.svwc.org
Shenango Valley Chamber of Commerce	41 Chestnut Ave	Sharon	PA	16146	724-981-5880	981-5480	139	Web: svchamber.com
Shenehon Co	88 S 10th St Ste 400	Minneapolis	MN	55403	612-333-6533	344-1635	652	Web: www.shenehon.com
Shenker Zacarese & Marks LLP	53 N Park Ave Ste 51	Rockville Centre	NY	11570	516-536-7100	536-6829	2	Web: rszm-cpa.com
Shenkman Capital Management Inc	461 Fifth Ave 22nd Fl	New York	NY	10017	212-867-9090		194	Web: www.shenkmancapital.com
Shenvalee Golf Resort	9660 Fairway Dr	New Market	VA	22844	540-740-3181		669	TF: 888-339-3181 ■ Web: www.shenvalee.com
Shepard Exposition Services	1531 Carroll Dr NW	Atlanta	GA	30318	404-720-8600	720-8750	184	Web: www.shepardes.com
Shepard State Park	1034 Graveline Rd	Gautier	MS	39553	228-497-2244		565	Web: www.mdwfp.com
Shepard Steel Company Inc	110 Meadow St	Hartford	CT	06114	860-525-4446		480	Web: www.shepardsteel.com
Shepeard Community Blood Ctr	1533 Wrightsboro Rd	Augusta	GA	30904	706-737-4551		89	Web: www.shepeardblood.org
Shephard's Beach Resort	619 S Gulfview Blvd	Clearwater Beach	FL	33767	727-441-6875		379	Web: www.shephards.com
Shepherd Canyon Books	25 Southwood Ct	Oakland	CA	94611	866-219-8260		637-2	TF: 866-219-8260 ■ Web: www.backpack45.com
Shepherd Caster	203 Kerth St	Saint Joseph	MI	49085	269-983-7351		350	Web: www.shepherdcasters.com
Shepherd CE Company Inc	2221 Canada Dry St	Houston	TX	77023	713-924-4300	928-2324	600	TF: 800-324-6733 ■ Web: ceshepherd.com
Shepherd Chemical Co	4900 Beech St	Cincinnati	OH	45212	513-731-1110		143	Web: www.shepchem.com
Shepherd Ctr	2020 Peachtree Rd NE	Atlanta	GA	30309	404-352-2020		374-6	Web: www.shepherd.org
Shepherd Electric Supply	7401 Pulaski Hwy	Baltimore	MD	21237	410-866-6000	866-6001	246	TF: 800-253-1777 ■ Web: www.shepherdelec.com
Shepherd Express	207 E Buffalo St Ste 410	Milwaukee	WI	53202	414-292-3830	276-3312	532-5	Web: shepherdexpress.com
Shepherd of the Hills Homestead & Outdoor Theatre	5586 W Hwy 76	Branson	MO	65616	417-334-4191		572	Web: theshepherdofthehills.com
Shepherd Oil Company LP	1831 S Main	Blackwell	OK	74631	580-363-4280	363-0319	324	TF: 800-420-4280 ■ Web: www.shepherdoil.com
Shepherd University	301 N King St	Shepherdstown	WV	25443	304-876-5000	876-5165	166	TF: 800-344-5231 ■ Web: www.shepherd.edu
Shepherd Valley Waldorf School	6500 Dry Creek Pkwy	Niwot	CO	80503	303-652-0130	568-7581	685	Web: bvwaldorf.org
Shepherd Ventures	11526 Sorrento Valley Rd Ste F	San Diego	CA	92121	858-509-4744		792	Web: www.shepherdventures.com
Shepherd's Cove Hospice	408 Martling Rd	Albertville	AL	35951	256-891-7724	891-7754	371	TF: 888-334-9336 ■ Web: www.shepherdscove.org
Shepherd's Home Hardware Ltd	3525 Mill St	Armstrong	BC	V0E1B0	250-546-3002		350	TF: 888-546-3002 ■ Web: www.shepherdshardware.ca
Shepherd, Finkelman, Miller & Shah LLP	65 Main St	Chester	CT	06412	860-526-1100		428	Web: www.sfmslaw.com
Shepherdsville-Bullitt County Tourist & Convention Commission	395 Paroquet Springs Dr	Shepherdsville	KY	40165	502-543-8687	543-4889	206	TF: 800-526-2068 ■ Web: www.travelbullitt.org
Sheplers Inc	6501 W Kellogg Dr	Wichita	KS	67209	316-946-3786	946-3646	157-5	TF: 888-835-4004 ■ Web: www.sheplers.com
Shepley Bulfinch	2 Seaport Ln	Boston	MA	02210	617-423-1700	451-2420	261	Web: shepleybulfinch.com
Sheppard Air Force Base	419 G Ave Ste 1	Sheppard AFB	TX	76311	940-676-2511	676-4245	497-1	TF: 877-676-1847 ■ Web: www.sheppard.af.mil
Sheppard Motors	2300 W Seventh Ave	Eugene	OR	97402	541-343-8811		57	TF: 877-362-1865 ■ Web: www.sheppardmotors.com
Sheppard Mullin Richter & Hampton LLP	333 S Hope St 48th Fl	Los Angeles	CA	90071	213-620-1780	620-1398	428	Web: www.sheppardmullin.com
Sheppard Pratt Health System (SPHS)	6501 N Charles St	Baltimore	MD	21285	410-938-3000		374-5	TF: 800-627-0330 ■ Web: www.sheppardpratt.org
Sheppard T. Powell Associates LLC	1915 Aliceanna St	Baltimore	MD	21231	410-327-3500		256	Web: www.stpa.com
Shepstone Management Co (SMC)	100 4th St Ste 32	Honesdale	PA	18431	570-251-9550	251-9551	196	Web: www.shepstone.net

				Phone	Fax	Class
Sheraton Agoura Hills Hotel 30100 Agoura Rd	Agoura Hills	CA	91301	818-707-1220		707
TF: 866-716-8134 ■ *Web:* www.sheratonagourahills.com						
Sheraton Atlanta 165 Courtland St NE	Atlanta	GA	30303	404-659-6500	524-1259	378
TF: 800-833-8624 ■ *Web:* www.sheratonatlanta.com						
Sheraton Colonial Hotel & Golf Club Boston North 1 Audubon Rd	Wakefield	MA	01880	781-245-9300		379
TF: 866-716-8133 ■ *Web:* www.fourpointswakefieldboston.com						
Sheraton Crescent Hotel 2620 W Dunlap Ave	Phoenix	AZ	85021	602-943-8200		378
Web: www.sheratoncrescent.com						
Sheraton Denver Tech Center Hotel 7007 S Clinton St	Greenwood Village	CO	80112	303-799-6200		707
TF: 800-525-3177 ■ *Web:* www.sheratondenvertech.com						
Sheraton Gateway Hotel Los Angeles 6101 W Century Blvd	Los Angeles	CA	90045	310-642-1111		379
TF: 888-627-7104 ■ *Web:* www.sheratonlax.com						
Sheraton Gunter Hotel 205 E Houston St	San Antonio	TX	78205	210-554-1409		707
Web: www.sheratongunter.com						
Sheraton Kauai Resort 2440 Hoonani Rd	Koloa	HI	96756	808-742-1661		669
Web: www.sheraton-kauai.com						
Sheraton Lake Buena Vista 12205 S Apopka Vineland Rd	Orlando	FL	32836	407-239-0444		707
Web: www.sheratonlakebuenavistaresort.com						
Sheraton Maui Resort 2605 Kaanapali Pkwy	Lahaina	HI	96761	808-661-0031	661-0458	669
Web: www.sheraton-maui.com						
Sheraton Music City Hotel (Nashville Tenn) 777 McGavock Pk	Nashville	TN	37214	615-885-2200		378
Web: www.starwoodhotels.com						
Sheraton Nashville Downtown Hotel 623 Union St	Nashville	TN	37219	615-259-2000		378
Web: www.sheratonnashvilledowntown.com						
Sheraton New York Hotel & Towers 811 7th Ave	New York	NY	10019	212-581-1000	262-4410	377
TF: 888-236-2427 ■ *Web:* www.sheratonnewyork.com						
Sheraton Oklahoma City Hotel 1 N Broadway	Oklahoma City	OK	73102	405-235-2780		378
TF: 888-627-8416 ■ *Web:* www.sheratonokc.com						
Sheraton Old San Juan Hotel 100 Brumbaugh St	San Juan	PR	00901	787-289-1914		377
TF: 888-627-8185 ■ *Web:* www.sheratonoldsanjuan.com						
Sheraton Phoenix Downtown Hotel 340 N 3rd St	Phoenix	AZ	85004	602-262-2500		707
Web: www.sheratonphoenixdowntown.com						
Sheraton Raleigh Hotel 421 S Salisbury St	Raleigh	NC	27601	919-834-9900		707
TF: 888-627-8319 ■ *Web:* www.sheratonraleigh.com						
Sheraton Sand Key Resort 1160 Gulf Blvd	Clearwater Beach	FL	33767	727-595-1611		669
TF: 800-456-7263 ■ *Web:* www.sheratonsandkey.com						
Sheraton Suites Calgary Eau Claire 255 Barclay Parade SW	Calgary	AB	T2P5C2	403-266-7200		379
Web: www.sheratonsuites.com						
Sheraton Universal Hotel 333 Universal Hollywood Dr	Universal City	CA	91608	818-980-1212	985-4980	378
TF: 888-627-7186 ■ *Web:* www.sheratonuniversal.com						
Sheraton Waikiki 2255 Kalakaua Ave	Honolulu	HI	96815	808-922-4422		669
Web: www.sheraton-waikiki.com						
Sheraton Washington North Hotel 4095 Powder Mill Rd	Beltsville	MD	20705	301-937-4422		707
TF: 888-627-8646 ■ *Web:* www.sheratoncollegeparknorth.com						
Sheraton Wild Horse Pass Resort & Spa 5594 W Wild Horse Pass Blvd	Phoenix	AZ	85048	602-225-0100	225-0300	669
TF: 866-837-4156 ■ *Web:* www.wildhorsepassresort.com						
Sheridan College 3059 Coffeen Ave PO Box 1500	Sheridan	WY	82801	307-674-6446	674-7205	162
TF: 800-913-9139 ■ *Web:* www.sheridan.edu						
Sheridan County 100 W Laurel Ave	Plentywood	MT	59254	406-765-1660	765-2609	338
Web: www.co.sheridan.mt.us						
Sheridan County PO Box 39	Rushville	NE	69360	308-327-5650		338
Web: sheridancountyne.com						
Sheridan County 224 S Main St Ste B-2	Sheridan	WY	82801	307-674-2500		338
TF: 800-565-4502 ■ *Web:* www.sheridancounty.com						
North Dakota 215 E Second St	McClusky	ND	58463	701-363-2207		338
Web: www.co.sheridan.nd.us						
Sheridan County Chamber of Commerce 1898 Fort Rd	Sheridan	WY	82801	307-672-2485	672-7321	139
TF: 800-453-3650 ■ *Web:* www.sheridanwyomingchamber.org						
Sheridan Electric Co-opeartive Inc PO Box 227	Medicine Lake	MT	59247	406-789-2231	789-2234	245
Web: www.sheridanelectric.coop						
Sheridan Group 11311 McCormick Rd Ste 260	Hunt Valley	MD	21031	410-785-7277	785-7217	626
TF: 800-352-2210 ■ *Web:* www.sheridan.com						
Sheridan Group Inc, The 2045 Pontius Ave	Los Angeles	CA	90025	310-575-0664		321
Web: www.sheridaninc.com						
Sheridan Headlights PO Box 539	Sheridan	AR	72150	870-942-2142	942-8823	532-2
Web: www.thesheridanheadlight.com						
Sheridan Healthcare Inc 1613 NW 136th Ave Ste 200	Sunrise	FL	33323	800-437-2672		463
TF: 800-437-2672 ■ *Web:* www.sheridanhealthcare.com						
Sheridan Legacy Group 400 N Michigan Ave Ste 900	Chicago	IL	60611	312-548-7064		528
Web: sheridancp.com						
Sheridan Livestock Auction Company Inc Sale Barn Rd	Rushville	NE	69360	308-327-2406		446
Web: www.sheridanlivestock.com						
Sheridan Memorial Hospital 1401 W Fifth St	Sheridan	WY	82801	307-672-1000		374-3
Web: www.sheridanhospital.org						
Sheridan Pond 8130 S Lakewood Pl	Tulsa	OK	74137	918-602-4709		379
Web: www.sheridanpondapartmentstulsa.com						
Sheridan Technical College 5400 Sheridan St	Hollywood	FL	33021	754-321-5400	321-5680	167-3
Web: www.sheridantechnicalcollege.edu						
Sherinian & Hasso Law Firm 521 E Locust Ste 300	Des Moines	IA	50309	515-224-2079	224-2321	41
Web: sherinianlaw.com						
Shermag Inc 3035 Boul Industriel	Sherbrooke	QC	J1L2T9	819-566-1515	566-7323	319-2
TF: 800-567-3419 ■ *Web:* www.shermag.com						
Sherman & Armbruster LLP 609 Treybourne Dr	Greenwood	IN	46142	317-881-6670		2
Web: www.shermanandarmbruster.com						
Sherman & Patterson Ltd 1613 Maple Ave	Maple Plain	MN	55359	763-479-2699		41
Web: splawfirm.net						
Sherman & Reilly Inc 400 W 33rd St	Chattanooga	TN	37410	423-756-5300	756-2948	470
TF: 800-251-7780 ■ *Web:* sherman-reilly.com						
Sherman and Howard LLC 633 17th St Ste 3000	Denver	CO	80202	303-297-2900	298-0940	41
Web: shermanhoward.com						
Sherman Asher Publishing 126 Candelario St	Santa Fe	NM	87501	505-988-7214		637-2
Web: www.shermanasher.com						
Sherman Brad (Rep D - CA) 2181 Rayburn House Office Bldg	Washington	DC	20515	202-225-5911	225-5879	342-2
Web: sherman.house.gov						
Sherman Bros Trucking 32921 Diamond Hill Dr PO Box 706	Harrisburg	OR	97446	541-995-7751		780
TF: 800-547-8980 ■ *Web:* www.shermantrucking.com						
Sherman Clay & Company Inc 1111 Bayhill Dr Ste 450	San Bruno	CA	94066	888-562-4069		526
TF: 888-562-4069 ■ *Web:* www.shermanclay.com						
Sherman County 1004 W 8th St Rm 103	Goodland	KS	67735	785-890-4810	890-4844	338
Sherman County PO Box 456	Loup City	NE	68853	308-745-1513	745-0297	338
Web: www.co.sherman.ne.us						
Sherman County PO Box 270	Stratford	TX	79084	806-366-2371	366-5670	338
Web: www.co.sherman.tx.us						
Sherman Financial Group LLC 335 Madison Ave	New York	NY	10017	212-922-1616		69
Web: sfg.com						
Sherman Insurance Agency Inc 120 Bridgepoint Way Ste C	South Saint Paul	MN	55075	651-451-1758		390
Web: shermanins.com						
Sherman International Corp 367 Mansfield Ave	Pittsburgh	PA	15220	412-928-2880	928-2881	194
Web: www.shermaninternational.com						
Sherman Library & Gardens 2647 E Coast Hwy	Corona Del Mar	CA	92625	949-673-2261	675-5458	97
Web: www.slgardens.org						
Sherman Machine Inc 1622 S First St	Sherman	TX	75090	903-892-2889	868-2034	454
Web: www.shermanmachine.com						
Sherman Mechanical Inc 1075 Alexander Ct	Cary	IL	60013	847-462-1020	462-0063	35
Web: www.shermanmech.com						
Sherman Oaks Hospital & Health Ctr 4929 Van Nuys Blvd	Sherman Oaks	CA	91403	818-981-7111		374-3
Web: www.shermanoakshospital.org						
Sherman Public Library 421 N Travis St	Sherman	TX	75090	903-892-7240	892-7101	434-3
Web: www.ci.sherman.tx.us						
Sherman West Court *Avantara Elgin* 1950 Larkin Ave	Elgin	IL	60123	847-742-7070		450
Web: www.avantaraelgin.com						
Sherman, Spero, Safarino & Company CPAS PC 760 Lynnhaven Pkwy Ste 108	Virginia Beach	VA	23452	757-468-2279	468-2196	2
Web: ssscompany-cpa.com						
Shermco Industries Inc 2425 E Pioneer Dr	Irving	TX	75061	972-793-5523		261
Web: www.shermco.com						
Shermeta, Adams & Von Allmen PC 1030 Doris Rd Ste 200	Auburn Hills	MI	48326	248-519-1700		428
TF: 800-451-7992 ■ *Web:* www.shermeta.com						
Shermoenjaksa Law PLLC 345 Sixth Ave	International Falls	MN	56649	218-283-4494		41
Web: shermoenjaksa.com						
Shernoff Bidart Darras & Echeverria LLP 600 S Indian Hill Blvd	Claremont	CA	91711	909-621-4935		428
TF: 800-458-3386 ■ *Web:* shernoff.com						
Sheron Enterprises Inc 1035 S Carley Ct	North Bellmore	NY	11710	516-783-5885		637-2
Web: www.mah-jonggsets.com						
Sherpa Adventure Gear Inc 7857 S 180th St	Kent	WA	98032	425-251-0760		157-6
Web: www.sherpaadventuregear.com						
Sherpa Digital Media Inc 509 Seaport Ct	Redwood City	CA	94063	866-989-7794		5
TF: 866-989-7794 ■ *Web:* www.sherpadigitalmedia.com						
Sherpalo Ventures 2725 Sand Hill Rd Ste 120	Menlo Park	CA	94025	650-319-2220	319-2221	463
Web: www.sherpalo.com						
Sherrard Kuzz LLP 155 University Ave	Toronto	ON	M5H3B7	416-603-0700		428
Web: www.sherrardkuzz.com						
Sherrard Roe Voigt & Harbison PLC 150 Third Ave S Ste 1100	Nashville	TN	37201	615-742-4200		445
Web: srvhlaw.com						
Sherrard, German & Kelly PC 535 Smithfield St Ste 300	Pittsburgh	PA	15222	412-355-0200	261-6221	41
Web: sgkpc.com						
Sherrets Bruno & Vogt LLC 260 Regency Parkway Dr Ste 200	Omaha	NE	68114	402-390-1112		41
Web: sherretslaw.com						
Sherrill Furniture Co 2405 Highland Ave NE	Hickory	NC	28601	828-322-2640		319-2
Web: www.sherrillfurniture.com						
Sherrill House (SH) 135 S Huntington Ave	Jamaica Plain	MA	02130	617-731-2400	731-8671	450
Web: www.sherrillhouse.org						
Sherrill Mikie (Rep D - NJ) 1208 Longworth House Office Bldg	Washington	DC	20515	202-225-5034		342-2
Web: www.sherrill.house.gov						
Sherrill-Lubinski Corp 240 Tamal Vista Blvd	Corte Madera	CA	94925	415-927-8400		177
TF: 800-548-6881 ■ *Web:* sl.com						

Company / Address	City	State	ZIP	Phone	Fax	Class
Sherritt International Corp 1133 Yonge St TSE: S ■ TF: 800-704-6698 ■ Web: www.sherritt.com	Toronto	ON	M4T2Y7	416-924-4551	924-5015	502
Sherrod Vans Inc 3151 Industrial Blvd TF: 800-824-6333 ■ Web: sherrodvans.com	Waycross	GA	31503	800-824-6333		62-7
Sherry Manufacturing Company Inc 3287 NW 65th St TF: 800-741-4750 ■ Web: www.sherrymfg.com	Miami	FL	33147	305-693-7000	691-6132	155-3
Sherry Matthews Inc 200 S Congress Ave TF: 877-478-4397 ■ Web: www.sherrymatthews.com	Austin	TX	78704	512-478-4397		4
Sherry-Lehmann Wine & Spirits 505 Park Ave. Web: www.sherry-lehmann.com	New York	NY	10022	212-838-7500	838-9285	443
Sherry-Netherland Hotel 781 Fifth Ave. TF: 877-743-7710 ■ Web: www.sherrynetherland.com	New York	NY	10022	212-355-2800	319-4306	379
Sherwin Manor Nursing Ctr 7350 N Sheridan Rd Web: www.sherwinmanor.com	Chicago	IL	60626	773-274-1000		450
Sherwin Miller Museum of Jewish Art 2021 E 71st St Web: www.jewishmuseum.net	Tulsa	OK	74136	918-492-1818	492-1888	520
Sherwin-Williams Automotive Finishes 4440 Warrensville Center Rd TF: 800-798-5872 ■ Web: www.sherwin-automotive.com	Warrensville Heights	OH	44128	800-798-5872		550
Sherwood 1000 Washington Rd TF: 888-508-2583 ■ Web: www.sherwoodvalve.com	Washington	PA	15301	724-225-8000	225-6188	789
Sherwood America 6120 Valley View Buena Pk Web: www.sherwoodamerica.com	Buena Park	CA	90620	714-739-2000		52
Sherwood Construction Company Inc 3219 W May St Web: www.sherwoodcompanies.com	Wichita	KS	67213	316-943-0211	943-3772	188-4
Sherwood Design Engineers 58 Maiden Ln 3rd Fl Web: www.sherwoodengineers.com	San Francisco	CA	94108	415-677-7300		261
Sherwood Food Distributors 12499 Evergreen Web: www.sherwoodfoods.com	Detroit	MI	48228	313-659-7300		805
Sherwood Forest Plantation 14501 John Tyler Memorial Hwy Web: www.sherwoodforest.org	Charles City	VA	23030	804-829-5377		520
Sherwood Fox Arboretum *University of Western Ontario* 1151 Richmond St Web: uwo.ca	London	ON	N6A5B7	519-850-2542	661-3935	97
Sherwood Island State Park PO Box 188 Web: portal.ct.gov	Greens Farms	CT	06838	203-226-6983		565
Sherwood Mutual Telephone Association Inc 105 W Vine St Web: smta.cc	Sherwood	OH	43556	419-899-2121	899-4567	224
Sherwood Oaks 100 Norman Dr TF: 800-642-2217 ■ Web: sherwood-oaks.com	Cranberry Township	PA	16066	724-776-8100	776-8468	672
Sherwood Windows Ltd 37 Iron St TF: 800-770-5256 ■ Web: www.sherwoodwindows.com	Toronto	ON	M9W5E3	416-675-3262		350
Sherwood-Logan & Associates Inc 2140 Renard Ct Web: www.sherwoodlogan.com	Annapolis	MD	21401	410-841-6810		806
Sherzer & Associates Insurance Inc 110 Stony Point Rd Ste 120 Web: www.sherzer.com	Santa Rosa	CA	95401	707-573-1010		390
Shesam Inc 15401 Mcmullen Hwy SW Web: www.wilsonsupply.net	Cumberland	MD	21502	301-729-2515	729-1732	146
Shetakis Wholesalers Inc 3840-A North Civic Center Dr Web: www.shetakis.com	North Las Vegas	NV	89030	702-940-3663		297-2
Shetler Moving & Storage Inc 1253 E Diamond Ave TF: 800-321-5069 ■ Web: shetlermoving.com	Evansville	IN	47711	812-421-7750	421-7759	780
Sheyenne Tooling & Mfg 701 Lenham Ave SW Web: www.sheyennemfg.com	Cooperstown	ND	58425	701-797-2700		454
SHI (Software House Intl) 290 Davidson Ave TF: 888-764-8888 ■ Web: www.shi.com	Somerset	NJ	08873	888-764-8888		174
Shiao Lan Kung 930 Race St Web: www.shiaolankung.com	Philadelphia	PA	19107	215-928-0282		671
Shiatsu School of Canada Inc *SSC Acupuncture Institute* 455 Spadina Ave Ste 300 TF: 800-263-1703 ■ Web: aim-academy.ca	Toronto	ON	M5S2G8	416-323-1818	323-1681	685
Shiawassee County, Michigan 208 N Shiawassee St Web: www.shiawassee.net	Corunna	MI	48817	989-743-2242	743-2241	338
Shibata Floral Company Supplies 620 Brannan St Web: www.shibatafc.com	San Francisco	CA	94107	415-495-8611		292
Shibuya Hoppmann Corp 13129 Airpark Dr Ste 120 TF: 800-368-3582 ■ Web: www.shibuyahoppmann.com	Elkwood	VA	22718	540-829-2564	829-1726	547
Shidlofsky Law Firm PLLC 7200 N Mopac Expy Ste 430 Web: shidlofskylaw.com	Austin	TX	78731	512-685-1400		41
Shie Law Office PC 601 Brady St Ste 220 Web: shielaw.com	Davenport	IA	52803	563-324-8244		41
Shiel Medical Laboratory Inc 63 Flushing Avenue Unit Ste 336 TF: 800-553-0873 ■ Web: www.radcliffecardiology.com	Brooklyn	NY	11205	718-552-1000	552-1026	415
Shiel Sexton Company Inc 902 N Capitol Ave Web: www.shielsexton.com	Indianapolis	IN	46204	317-423-6000	423-6300	186
Shield AI 600 W Broadway Ste 250 Web: shield.ai	San Diego	CA	92101	619-719-5740		178-8
Shield Air Solutions Inc 3708 Greenhouse Rd TF: 800-237-2095 ■ Web: www.shieldair.com	Houston	TX	77084	281-944-4300		14
Shield Engineering Inc 4301 Taggart Creek Rd TF: 800-395-5220 ■ Web: www.shieldengineering.com	Charlotte	NC	28208	704-394-6913		261
Shields & Company Inc 890 Winter St Ste 160 Web: www.shieldsco.com	Waltham	MA	02451	781-890-7033	890-7034	401
Shields Bag & Printing Co 1009 Rock Ave *Fax Area Code: 509 ■ TF: 800-541-8630 ■ Web: www.shieldsbag.com	Yakima	WA	98902	800-541-8630	248-6304*	66
SHIELDS Electronics Supply Inc 4722 Middlebrook Pk Web: shieldselectronics.com	Knoxville	TN	37921	865-588-2421		179
Shields Inc 2625 Hope Church Rd Web: www.shieldsinc.com	Winston-Salem	NC	27103	336-765-9040	765-3715	189-9
Shields Insurance Agency Inc 221 W Mahoning St TF: 800-242-9291 ■ Web: shieldsinsurance.com	Punxsutawney	PA	15767	814-938-5291	938-5870	390
Shields Law Offices 1920 Main St Ste 1080 Web: shieldslawoffices.com	Irvine	CA	92614	949-724-7900	724-7905	41
Shields Publications PO Box 669 Web: www.wormbooks.com	Eagle River	WI	54521	715-479-4810	479-3905	637-2
Shifamed LLC 590 Divisin St Web: www.shifamed.com	Campbell	CA	95008	408-560-2500	903-4095	475
Shiffler Equipment Sales Inc 745 S St Web: www.chairglides.com	Chardon	OH	44024	440-285-9175		362
SHIFT Communications LLC 120 St James Ave 6th Fl Web: www.shiftcomm.com	Boston	MA	02116	617-779-1800	779-1899	636
SHIFT Energy Inc 1 Germain St 18th Fl *Fax Area Code: 506 ■ TF: 855-744-3860 ■ Web: shiftenergy.com	Saint John	NB	E2L4V1	855-744-3860	642-3487*	192
ShiftWise Inc 200 SW Market St Ste 700 TF: 866-399-2220 ■ Web: www.shiftwise.com	Portland	OR	97201	866-399-2220		809
Shikatani Lacroix Design Inc 387 Richmond E Web: www.sld.com	Toronto	ON	M5A1P6	416-367-1999		5
Shikellamy School District 200 Island Blvd Web: www.shikbraves.org	Sunbury	PA	17801	570-286-3721		685
Shiki Hana 222 Post Rd Web: www.shikihanafairfield.com	Fairfield	CT	06824	203-259-5950		671
Shiki Sushi 207 N Carolina 54 Web: shikitasu.com	Durham	NC	27713	919-484-4108		671
Shiley-Marcos Alzheimer's Disease Research Ctr 8950 Villa La Jolla Dr Ste C129 Web: www.adrc.ucsd.edu	La Jolla	CA	92037	858-622-5800	622-1012	668
Shillington Box Company LLC 3501 Tree Ct Industrial Web: www.shillingtonbox.com	Saint Louis	MO	63122	636-225-5353	225-5306	100
Shilo Inn Suites Salem 3304 Market St TF: 800-222-2244 ■ Web: www.shiloinns.com	Salem	OR	97301	503-581-4001		379
Shiloh Industries Corp 880 Steel Dr TF: 800-414-3627 ■ Web: shiloh.com	Valley City	OH	44280	330-558-2600		489
Shiloh National Military Park 1055 Pittsburg Landing Rd Web: www.nps.gov	Shiloh	TN	38376	731-689-5696		564
Shiloh Service Inc 85 Mtn View Pl Web: shilohservice.com	North Huntingdon	PA	15642	724-863-0190		175
Shim Gum Do Assn 203 Chestnut Hill Ave Web: www.shimgumdo.org	Boston	MA	02135	617-787-1506	787-2708	637-2
Shimadzu Medical Systems 20101 S Vermont Ave TF: 800-477-1227 ■ Web: www.shimadzu.com	Torrance	CA	90502	310-217-8855	217-0661	382
Shimadzu Scientific Instruments Inc 7102 Riverwood Dr Web: www.ssi.shimadzu.com	Columbia	MD	21046	410-381-1227	381-1222	419
Shimano American Corp 1 Holland Dr TF: 877-577-0600 ■ Web: www.shimano.com	Irvine	CA	92618	949-951-5003		82
Shimanovsky & Moscardini LLP 130 S Jefferson St Ste 350 Web: elsm.com	Chicago	IL	60661	312-876-0600		41
Shimek State Forest 33653 Rt J56 Web: www.iowadnr.gov	Farmington	IA	52626	319-878-3811		565
Shimkus John (Rep R - IL) 2217 Rayburn House Office Bldg Web: shimkus.house.gov	Washington	DC	20515	202-225-5271	225-5880	342-2
Shimmick Construction 8201 Edgewater Dr Ste 202 Web: www.shimmick.com	Oakland	CA	94621	510-777-5000	777-5099	194
Shimokaji & Associates Pc 8911 Research Dr Web: www.shimokaji.com	Irvine	CA	92618	949-788-9961		445
Shimpo 1701 Glenlake Ave TF: 800-842-1479 ■ Web: www.nidec-shimpo.com	Itasca	IL	60143	630-924-7138		190
Shinano Kenshi Corp 6065 Bristol Pkwy Web: shinano.com	Culver City	CA	90230	310-693-7600	693-7599	518
Shindengen America Inc 2333 Waukegan Rd Ste E250 TF: 800-543-6525 ■ Web: www.shindengen.com	Bannockburn	IL	60015	847-444-1363		246
Shindler, Anderson, Goplerud & Weese PC 5015 Grand Ridge Dr Ste 100 Web: www.sagwlaw.com	West Des Moines	IA	50265	515-223-4567	223-8887	428
Shine Investment Advisory Services Inc 9892 Rosemont Ave Ste 100 Web: shineinvestments.com	Lone Tree	CO	80124	303-740-8600		401
Shine Medical Technologies Inc 101 E Milwaukee St Ste 600 TF: 877-512-6554 ■ Web: shinemed.com	Janesville	WI	53545	608-210-1060		743
Shine Systems & Technologies 1 Morton Dr Ste 100 Web: shinesystems.com	Charlottesville	VA	22903	434-422-4220		180

Name / Address	City	State	Zip	Phone	Fax	Class
Shine Tidelands State Park 202 NE Park St *Web:* parks.state.wa.us	Poulsbo	WA	98370	360-779-3205		565
Shine United LLC 202 N Henry St *Web:* shineunited.com	Madison	WI	53703	608-442-7373		7
Shin-Etsu Handotai America Inc 4111 NE 112th Ave *Web:* www.sehamerica.com	Vancouver	WA	98682	360-883-7053	883-7074	696
Shin-Etsu Magnetics Inc 2372 Qume Dr Ste B *Web:* www.shinetsu-rare-earth-magnet.jp	San Jose	CA	95131	408-383-9240	383-9245	146
Shin-Etsu Microsi Inc 10028 S 51st St *TF:* 888-642-7674 ■ *Web:* www.microsi.com	Phoenix	AZ	85044	480-893-8898	893-8637	695
Shin-Etsu Silicones of America 1150 Damar Dr *TF:* 800-544-1745 ■ *Web:* www.shinetsusilicones.com	Akron	OH	44305	330-630-9860	630-9855	144
Shingle Belting 420 Drew Ct *TF:* 800-345-6294 ■ *Web:* www.shinglebelting.com	King of Prussia	PA	19406	610-239-6667	239-6668	207
Shingle Springs/Cameron Park Chamber of Commerce 4095 Cameron Park Dr *Web:* www.sscpchamber.org	Shingle Springs	CA	95682	530-677-8000	676-8313	139
Shingler Lewis LLC 1230 Peachtree St NE Ste 1075 *Web:* shinglerlewis.com	Atlanta	GA	30309	404-907-1999		41
Shingobee Builders Inc PO Box 8 *Web:* www.shingobee.com	Loretto	MN	55357	763-479-1300	479-3267	186
Shinoda Design Ctr 601 W Dyer Rd *Web:* www.shinodadesigncenter.net	Santa Ana	CA	92707	714-541-4444	541-0282	293
Shinsei Corp 1001 Southpark Dr *Web:* www.shinseiusa.com	Peachtree City	GA	30269	770-487-2294		596
Shintech Inc 3 Greenway Plz Ste 1150 *Web:* www.shintechinc.com	Houston	TX	77046	713-965-0713	965-0629	605-2
Shioi Construction Inc 98-724 Kuaho Pl *Web:* shioihawaii.com	Pearl City	HI	96782	808-487-2441		186
Ship & Shore Environmental Inc 2474 N Palm Dr *Web:* www.shipandshore.com	Signal Hill	CA	90755	562-997-0233	997-0604	697
Shipbuilders Council of America Inc (SCA) 20 F St NW Ste 500 *Web:* www.shipbuilders.org	Washington	DC	20001	202-737-3234		49-21
Shipcom Wireless Inc 11200 Richmond Ave Ste 552 *Web:* www.shipcomwireless.com	Houston	TX	77082	281-558-5252		225
Shipley Associates Inc 532 N 900 W *Web:* www.shipleywins.com	Kaysville	UT	84037	801-544-9787		463
Shipley Energy Company Inc 415 Norway St *TF:* 800-839-1849 ■ *Web:* www.shipleyenergy.com	York	PA	17403	717-848-4100	854-5496	316
Shipley Snell Montgomery LLP 712 Main St Ste 1400 *Web:* shipleysnell.com	Houston	TX	77002	713-652-5920		41
Shipowners Claims Bureau (SCB) 1 Battery Park Plz 31st Fl *Web:* www.american-club.com	New York	NY	10004	212-847-4500	847-4599	49-21
Shippensburg Area Chamber of Commerce 53 W King St *Web:* shippensburg.org	Shippensburg	PA	17257	717-532-5509	532-7501	139
Shippensburg Pump Company Inc PO Box 279 *Web:* www.shipcopumps.com	Shippensburg	PA	17257	717-532-7321		641
Shippensburg University 1871 Old Main Dr *TF:* 800-822-8028 ■ *Web:* www.ship.edu	Shippensburg	PA	17257	717-477-1231	477-4016	166
Shippers Express INC 1651 Kerr Dr *TF:* 800-647-2480 ■ *Web:* www.shippersexpressinc.com	Jackson	MS	39204	601-948-4251	948-5232	780
Shippers Group, The 8901 Forney Rd *Web:* www.shipperswarehouse.com	Dallas	TX	75227	214-381-5050		803-1
Ship-Right Solutions LLC 165 Pleasant Ave *TF:* 855-249-5621 ■ *Web:* www.shiprightsolutions.com	South Portland	ME	04106	207-321-3500		317
Ships of the Sea Maritime Museum 41 Martin Luther King Junior Blvd *Web:* www.shipsofthesea.org	Savannah	GA	31401	912-232-1511		520
Shipshewana/LaGrange County Convention & Visitors Bureau 350 S Van Buren St Ste H *TF:* 800-254-8090 ■ *Web:* visitshipshewana.org	Shipshewana	IN	46565	260-768-4008		206
Shipside Crating Company Lp 16400 Jacinto Port Blvd *Web:* www.shipsidecrating.com	Houston	TX	77015	281-457-2647		549
Shipwell 515 Congress Ave Ste 2650 *Web:* shipwell.com	Austin	TX	78701	512-333-0898		178-1
Shira Accessories Ltd 28 W 36th St *Web:* www.shiraaccessories.com	New York	NY	10018	212-594-4455		408
Shiraz Specialty Pharmacy 6007 244th St SW Ste A2 *Web:* www.axispharmacynw.com	Mountlake Terrace	WA	98043	425-356-3276	356-3101	237
Shirl K. Floral Designs 2701 Pontoon Rd *Web:* www.shirlkfloral.com	Granite City	IL	62040	618-797-6210		292
Shirley Contracting Corp 8435 Backlick Rd *Web:* www.shirleycontracting.com	Lorton	VA	22079	703-550-8100	550-7897	188-4
Shirley Plantation 501 Shirley Plantation Rd *Web:* www.shirleyplantation.com	Charles City	VA	23030	804-829-5121		50-3
Shirley's Cookie Company Inc 153 William Ward Dr *Web:* www.shirleyscookies.com	Claysburg	PA	16625	814-239-2208		296-9
Shiro's Sushi Restaurant 2401 Second Ave *Web:* shiros.com	Seattle	WA	98121	206-443-9844		671
Shiroki North America Inc 1111 W Broad St *Web:* www.shiroki-na.com	Smithville	TN	37166	615-395-3850	395-3840	567
Shirtcliff Oil Co PO Box 6003 *TF:* 800-422-0536 ■ *Web:* www.shirtcliffoil.com	Myrtle Creek	OR	97457	541-863-5268	863-5144	324
Shiva 2514 Times Blvd *Web:* www.shivarestaurant.com	Houston	TX	77005	713-523-4753	523-4754	671
Shive-Hattery Inc (SH) 316 Second St SE Ste 500 PO Box 1599 *TF:* 800-798-0227 ■ *Web:* www.shive-hattery.com	Cedar Rapids	IA	52406	319-362-0313		261
Shively Bros Inc 2919 S Grand Travers St PO Box 1520 *TF:* 800-530-9352 ■ *Web:* www.shivelybros.com	Flint	MI	48501	810-232-7401	232-3219	385
Shively Labs 188 Harrison Rd PO Box 389 *TF:* 888-744-8359 ■ *Web:* www.shively.com	Bridgton	ME	04009	207-647-3327	647-8273	647
Shivvers Inc 614 W English St *TF:* 800-245-9093 ■ *Web:* www.shivvers.com	Corydon	IA	50060	641-872-1005	872-1593	273
Shlesinger, Arkwright & Garvey LLP 5845 Richmond Hwy Ste 415 *Web:* saglIp.com	Alexandria	VA	22303	703-684-5600	836-5288	41
SHLP (Simpson Housing LLLP) 8110 E Union Ave Ste 200 *Web:* www.simpsonhousing.com	Denver	CO	80237	303-283-4100		653
SHN Consulting Engineers & Geologists Inc 812 W Wabash *Web:* www.shn-engr.com	Eureka	CA	95501	707-441-8855	441-8877	261
Sho-Air Intl 5401 Argosy Ave *TF:* 800-227-9111 ■ *Web:* www.shoair.com	Huntington Beach	CA	92649	949-476-9111	476-9991	311
Shoal Creek Living History Museum 7000 NE Barry Rd *Web:* www.shoalcreeklivinghistorymuseum.com	Kansas City	MO	64156	816-792-2655		520
Shoal Point Energy Ltd 1060-1090 Georgia St W *Web:* www.shoalpointenergy.com	Vancouver	BC	V6E3V7	416-637-2181		536
Shoals Chamber of Commerce 20 Hightower Pl *Web:* shoalschamber.com	Florence	AL	35630	256-764-4661	766-9017	139
Shoalwater Bay Casino 4112 State Hwy 105 *TF:* 866-992-3675 ■ *Web:* www.swbcasino.com	Tokeland	WA	98590	360-267-2048		132
Shock Tech Inc 360 Rt 59 *Web:* www.shocktech.com	Airmont	NY	10952	845-368-8600		22
Shock Trauma Air Rescue Society (STARS) 1441 Aviation Pk NE *Web:* www.stars.ca	Calgary	AB	T2E8M7	403-295-1811	275-4891	30
Shockoe Commerce Group LLC 11 S 12th St 4th Fl *Web:* www.shockoecommerce.com	Richmond	VA	23219	804-343-3441		354
Shoco Oil Inc 5135 E 74th Ave *TF:* 800-854-5553 ■ *Web:* shocooil.com	Commerce City	CO	80037	303-289-1677		579
Shodeen Inc 77 N First St *Web:* www.shodeen.com	Geneva	IL	60134	630-232-0300		653
Shoe Carnival Inc 7500 E Columbia St *NASDAQ: SCVL* ■ *TF:* 800-430-7463 ■ *Web:* www.shoecarnival.com	Evansville	IN	47715	812-867-6471		301
Shoe Sensation Inc 253 America Pl **Fax Area Code:* 812 ■ *TF:* 844-891-3070 ■ *Web:* www.shoesensation.com	Jeffersonville	IN	47130	844-891-3070	288-7747*	301
Shoe Service Institute of America (SSIA) 1013 Beards Hill Rd Ste 101 *Web:* www.ssia.info	Aberdeen	MD	21001	410-569-3425	569-8333	49-4
Shoei Foods (USA) Inc 1900 Feather River Blvd *Web:* www.shoeiyj.com.cn	Olivehurst	CA	95961	530-742-7866		805
Shoemaker & Dart PS Inc 6706 24th St W Ste A *TF:* 800-269-5019 ■ *Web:* shoedartlaw.com	Tacoma	WA	98466	253-365-6363		41
Shoemaker Construction Co 100 Front St Ste 365 *Web:* www.shoemakerco.com	West Conshohocken	PA	19428	610-941-5500	941-5525	186
Shofer's Furniture Company LLC 930 S Charles St *Web:* www.shofers.com	Baltimore	MD	21230	410-752-4212		321
Shoffner Mechanical Industrial & Service Company Inc 3600 Papermill Dr *Web:* skmes.com	Knoxville	TN	37909	865-523-1129		610
Shofu Dental Corp 1225 Stone Dr *TF:* 800-827-4638 ■ *Web:* www.shofu.com	San Marcos	CA	92078	760-736-3277		476
Shogun 821 E 3rd Ave *Web:* shogunspokane.com	Spokane	WA	99202	509-534-7777		671
Shogun Japanese Steak House 2815 Cantrell Rd *Web:* www.shogunlr.com	Little Rock	AR	72202	501-666-7070		671
Shogyo International Corp 6851 Jericho Tpke *Web:* www.shogyo.com	Syosset	NY	11791	516-921-9111	921-3777	253
Shollenberger Januzzi & Wolfe LLP 2225 Millennium Way *Web:* sholljanlaw.com	Enola	PA	17025	717-728-3200		41
Sho-Me Power Electric Coop 301 W Jackson St *TF:* 888-468-2615 ■ *Web:* www.shomepower.com	Marshfield	MO	65706	888-859-2615		245
ShoMi Japanese Restaurant 419 Lincoln Ctr *Web:* shomi-restaurant.com	Stockton	CA	95207	209-951-3525		671
Shoney's Restaurants Inc 1717 Elm Hill Pk Ste B1 *TF:* 800-708-3558 ■ *Web:* www.shoneys.com	Nashville	TN	37210	800-708-3558		670
Shook & Fletcher Insulation Co 4625 Valleydale Rd *TF:* 888-829-2575 ■ *Web:* www.shookandfletcher.com	Birmingham	AL	35242	205-991-7606	991-7745	191-4
Shook & Fletcher Mechanical Contractors Inc 2915 Richard Arrington Jr Blvd N *Web:* shook-fletcher.com	Birmingham	AL	35203	205-252-9400		189-10
Shook & Stone Attorneys at Law 710 S Fourth St *TF:* 888-662-2013 ■ *Web:* www.shookandstone.com	Las Vegas	NV	89101	702-385-2220		428
Shook Builder Supply Co 1400 16th St NE *Web:* shookbuildersupply.com	Hickory	NC	28601	828-328-2051		817
Shook Construction 4977 Northcutt Pl *Web:* www.shookconstruction.com	Dayton	OH	45414	937-276-6666	276-6676	188-7
Shook Hardy & Bacon LLP 2555 Grand Blvd *TF:* 855-380-7584 ■ *Web:* www.shb.com	Kansas City	MO	64108	816-474-6550	421-5547	428

	Phone	Fax	Class
Shoosmith Bros Inc 11800 Lewis Rd .... Chester VA 23831 *Web:* www.shoosmith.com	804-748-5823	748-8482	189-5
Shooter McGees 5239 Duke St.............. Alexandria VA 22304 *Web:* www.shootermcgees.com	703-751-9266		671
Shooters International Inc 63 Berkeley St............................. Toronto ON M5A2W5 *Web:* www.shootersfilm.com	416-862-1959		514
Shooting Star Casino 777 SE Casino Rd...................... Mahnomen MN 56557 *TF:* 800-453-7827 ■ *Web:* www.starcasino.com	800-453-7827		452
Shop 'n Save 10461 Manchester Rd .... Kirkwood MO 63122 *TF:* 800-428-6974 ■ *Web:* www.shopnsave.com	314-984-0322		345
Shop 'N Save Liquors 20 Independence Ave ....Quincy MA 02169 *Web:* www.shopnsaveliquors.com	617-773-2060	786-9797	443
Shop at North Bridge, The 520 N Michigan Ave.........................Chicago IL 60611 *TF:* 800-977-6255 ■ *Web:* www.theshopsatnorthbridge.com	312-327-2300		460
Shop Floor Automations Inc 5360 Jackson Dr............................La Mesa CA 91942 *TF:* 877-611-5825 ■ *Web:* www.shopfloorautomations.com	619-461-4000		225
ShopHQ 6740 Shady Oak Rd................ Eden Prairie MN 55344 *TF:* 800-676-5523 ■ *Web:* www.shophq.com	800-676-5523		740
Shopko LLC 700 Pilgrim Way.............. Green Bay WI 54304 *TF:* 800-791-7333 ■ *Web:* www.shopko.com	920-497-2211		229
Shopletcom 39 Broadway Ste 2030............New York NY 10006 **Fax Area Code:* 212 ■ *TF:* 800-757-3015 ■ *Web:* www.shoplet.com	800-757-3015	617-3389*	791
Shoppa's Material Handling Ltd 15217 Grand River Rd ....Fort Worth TX 76155 *Web:* www.shoppas.com	817-359-1100		112
Shopper Local 104 South Estes Dr Stes 202 & 204.............Durham NC 27713 *TF:* 877-251-4592 ■ *Web:* shopperlocal.com	877-251-4592		414
Shoppers Food & Pharmacy 10501 Martin Luther King Jr Hwy.................Bowie MD 20720 *Web:* www.shoppersfood.com	240-544-0180	544-0187	345
Shoppes at Bel Air, The 3299 Bel Air Mall ....Mobile AL 36606 *Web:* www.theshoppesatbelair.com	251-478-1893		460
Shopping Ch, The 59 Ambassador Dr........ Mississauga ON L5T2P9 *Web:* www.theshoppingchanneldirect.com	647-201-3448		740
Shopping Channel, The 59 Ambassador Dr .... Mississauga ON L5T2P9 *Web:* theshoppingchanneldirect.com	905-362-2020		195
Shopping.com 8000 Marina Blvd 5th Fl .... Brisbane CA 94005 *Web:* www.shopping.com	650-616-6500	616-6510	114
ShoppingSpot 1840 Oak Ave.................. Evanston IL 60201 *Web:* www.shoppingspot.com	847-866-1830	866-1880	397
ShoppingTown Mall 3649 Erie Blvd E............. DeWitt NY 13214 *Web:* www.shoppingtownmall.com	315-446-9159		460
ShopRite PO Box 7812.......................... Edison NJ 08818 **Fax Area Code:* 732 ■ *TF:* 800-746-7748 ■ *Web:* www.shoprite.com	800-746-7748	251-9519*	345
Shops at Briargate 1885 Briargate Pkwy................. Colorado Springs CO 80920 *Web:* www.thepromenadeshopsatbriargate.com	719-265-6264		460
Shops at Carolina Furniture of Williamsburg 5425 Richmond Rd......................Williamsburg VA 23188 *Web:* carolina-furniture.com	757-565-3000	565-4476	321
Shops at Columbus Circle, The 10 Columbus Cir ....New York NY 10019 *Web:* www.theshopsatcolumbuscircle.com	212-823-6300		50-6
Shops at Hilltop North East & West Laskin Rd ....Virginia Beach VA 23451 *Web:* www.hilltopshops.com	757-428-2224		460
Shops at Hilltop, The 2200 Hilltop Mall Rd .... Richmond CA 94806 *Web:* hilltopbythebaysf.com	510-223-6900		460
Shops at Houston Ctr 1200 Mckinney Ste 545 ....Houston TX 77010 *Web:* www.shopsathc.com	713-759-1442		460
Shops at La Cantera 15900 La Cantera Pkwy Ste 6698............San Antonio TX 78256 *Web:* theshopsatlacantera.com	210-582-6255		460
Shops at Liberty Place 1625 Chestnut St ....Philadelphia PA 19103 *Web:* www.shopsatliberty.com	215-851-9055		460
Shops at Riverwoods 4801 N University Ave ....Provo UT 84604 *Web:* www.shopsatriverwoods.com	801-802-8430		460
Shops at Tanforan, The 1150 El Camino Real .... San Bruno CA 94066 *Web:* www.theshopsattanforan.com	650-873-2000	873-4210	460
Shops at Willow Bend 6121 W Pk Blvd Ste 1000.......................Plano TX 75093 *Web:* www.shopwillowbend.com	972-202-4900		460
Shopsmith Inc 6530 Poe Ave....................Dayton OH 45414 *OTC: SSMH* ■ **Fax Area Code:* 800 ■ *TF:* 800-543-7586 ■ *Web:* www.shopsmith.com	937-898-6070	722-3965*	759
Shoptology Inc 7800 N Dallas Pkwy Ste 600.....................Plano TX 75024 *Web:* goshoptology.com	469-287-1200		195
Shop-Vac Corp 2323 Reach Rd PO Box 3307 .... Williamsport PA 17701 *TF:* 844-807-7711 ■ *Web:* www.shopvac.com	570-326-0502	326-7185	386
Shorcan Brokers Ltd 20 Adelaide St E Ste 1000 .... Toronto ON M5C2T6 *Web:* www.shorcan.com	416-360-2500		690
Shore Acres State Park 725 Summer St NE Ste C .... Salem OR 97301 *Web:* oregonstateparks.org	541-888-3732		565
Shore Bancshares Inc 18 E Dover St............. Easton MD 21601 *NASDAQ: SHBI* ■ *Web:* www.shoreunitedbank.com	410-822-1400		360-2
Shore Beauty School English Creek Shopping Ctr 3003 English Creek Ave .... Egg Harbor Township NJ 08234 *TF:* 888-237-4673 ■ *Web:* www.shorebeautyschool.com	609-645-3635	645-0024	685
Shore Capital Partners LLC 1 E Wacker Dr Ste 400 ....Chicago IL 60601 *Web:* shorecp.com	312-348-7580		528
Shore Crest Vacation Villas 4709 S Ocean Blvd................. North Myrtle Beach SC 29582 *Web:* www.bluegreenrentals.com	843-361-3600		669
Shore Distributors Inc 807 Brown St........... Salisbury MD 21804 *Web:* www.shoredist.com	410-749-3121	524-0230	612
Shore Drugs Inc 30 E Main St................ Bay Shore NY 11706 *Web:* www.shoredrug.com	631-665-3000	206-1246	237
Shore Line Trolley Museum 17 River St ....East Haven CT 06512 *Web:* www.bera.org	203-467-6927		520
Shore Memorial Hospital 1 E New York Ave ....Somers Point NJ 08244 *Web:* shoremedicalcenter.org	609-653-3500		374-3
Shore Memorial Hospital 20480 Market St PO Box 430.................Onancock VA 23417 *TF:* 800-834-7035 ■ *Web:* www.riversideonline.com	757-302-2100		374-3
Shore Morgan Young 300 W Wilson Bridge Rd ....Worthington OH 43085 *TF:* 800-288-2117 ■ *Web:* www.shoremorganyoung.com	614-888-2117		690
Shore Trucking Company Inc 3501 Central Park Blvd......................Louisville TN 37777 *Web:* shoretrucking.com	865-984-4252		311
Shoreland Inc 933 N Mayfair Rd Ste 208................... Milwaukee WI 53226 *TF:* 800-433-5256 ■ *Web:* www.shoreland.com	414-290-1900		177
Shoreline Amphitheatre 1 Amphitheatre Pkwy ....Mountain View CA 94043 *Web:* www.mountainviewamphitheater.com	650-967-4040		572
Shoreline Chamber of Commerce 18560 First Ave NE.........................Shoreline WA 98155 *Web:* shorelinechamber.org	206-361-2260		139
Shoreline Chamber of Commerce 764 E Main St..............................Branford CT 06405 *Web:* www.shorelinechamberct.com	203-488-5500		139
Shoreline Community College 16101 Greenwood Ave N ....Shoreline WA 98133 *Web:* www.shoreline.edu	206-546-4101	546-5835	162
Shoreline Container Inc 4450 N 136th Ave PO Box 1993................ Holland MI 49422 *TF:* 800-968-2088 ■ *Web:* shorelinecontainer.com	616-399-2088	399-7240	100
Shoreline Partners LLC 6310 Greenwich Dr Ste 120 .... San Diego CA 92122 *Web:* www.shoreline.com	858-587-9800		194
Shoreline Publishing Group 125 Santa Rosa Pl .... Santa Barbara CA 93109 **Fax Area Code:* 800 ■ *Web:* www.shorelinepublishing.com	805-564-1004	840-6713*	94
Shoreline Village 429 Shoreline Village Dr Ste 100 .... Long Beach CA 90802 *Web:* shorelinevillage.com	562-435-2668		50-6
Shores Resort & Spa, The 2637 S Atlantic Ave.....................Daytona Beach FL 32118 *Web:* www.shoresresort.com	386-767-7350		379
Shorewest Real Estate Institute 11622 W North Ave....................... Wauwatosa WI 53226 *Web:* www.shorewest.com	414-476-1231		167-3
Shorewood-Troy Public Library District 650 Deerwood Dr .... Shorewood IL 60404 *Web:* www.shorewoodtroylibrary.org	815-725-1715	725-1722	434-3
Shorr Packaging Inc 800 N Commerce St......... Aurora IL 60504 *TF:* 888-885-0055 ■ *Web:* www.shorr.com	630-978-1000		559
Short Freight Lines Inc 459 S River Rd PO Box 357 ....Bay City MI 48707 *TF:* 800-248-0625 ■ *Web:* www.shortfreightlines.com	989-893-3505	893-3151	780
Short Hills Tours 46 Chatham Rd .... Short Hills NJ 07078 *TF:* 800-348-6871 ■ *Web:* www.shorthillstours.com	973-467-2113	467-3353	760
Short Order Lp 12521 Amherst Dr................ Austin TX 78727 *TF:* 800-262-4313 ■ *Web:* www.shortordor.com	800-262-4313		45
Short Stop 105 Olive Rd....................Fayetteville NC 28305 *Web:* www.shortstopfoodmarts.com	910-486-5058		204
Short-Elliott-Hendrickson Inc 3535 Vadnais Center Dr .... Saint Paul MN 55110 *TF:* 800-325-2055 ■ *Web:* www.sehinc.com	651-490-2000	490-2150	261
Shorter College 604 N Locust St .... North Little Rock AR 72114 *Web:* www.shortercollege.edu	501-374-6305		162
Shorter University 315 Shorter Ave ....Rome GA 30165 *TF:* 800-868-6980 ■ *Web:* www.shorter.edu	706-233-7319	233-7224	166
Shortridge Instruments Inc 7855 E Redfield Rd........................ Scottsdale AZ 85260 *Web:* www.shortridge.com	480-991-6744	443-1267	472
Shorty Small's Great American Restaurant 11100 N Rodney Parham Rd................. Little Rock AR 72212 *Web:* shortysmalls.com	501-224-3344		671
Shorty's 1050 Bicentennial Dr................ Manchester NH 03104 *Web:* shortysmex.com	603-625-1730		671
Shorty's Bar-B-Q 9150 SW 87th Ave Ste 205..................... Miami FL 33176 *Web:* shortys.com	305-595-1622	279-2159	671
Shoshone County 700 Bank St .... Wallace ID 83873 *Web:* shoshonecounty.id.gov	208-752-3331	752-4304	338
Shot Tower Historical State Park 176 Orphanage Dr .... Foster Falls VA 24360 *Web:* www.dcr.virginia.gov	276-699-6778		565
Shotking LLC 302 Railroad Ave ....Adel GA 31620 *Web:* www.shotking.com	229-242-6824		358
Shotmeyer Brothers Petroleum Corp 10 Wagaraw Rd.........................Hawthorne NJ 07506 *Web:* shotmeyerbros.com	973-427-1000		316
Shoulder 2 Shoulder Inc 33735 Snickersville Tpke Ste 201..............Bluemont VA 20135 *Web:* shoulder2shoulderinc.com	540-554-2680	554-2681	177
Shout Mouse Press 1735 17th St NW .... Washington DC 20009 *Web:* www.shoutmousepress.org	240-772-1545		637-2
Show Management Services Inc 1963 University Ln.............................Lisle IL 60532 *Web:* www.rocexhibitions.com	630-271-8210		317
Show Me Ctr 1333 N Sprigg St .... Cape Girardeau MO 63701 *Web:* www.showmecenter.biz	573-651-2297	651-5054	720

Company / Address	City	State	Zip	Phone	Fax	Class
Show Media 6623 Las Vegas Blvd S Ste 370	Las Vegas	NV	89119	702-778-5313		396
Show Pros Entertainment Services Inc PO Box 12599 *Web:* www.showprostaff.com	Charlotte	NC	28220	704-525-3784	525-3785	721
SHOWA 579 Edison St **Fax Area Code:* 888 ■ *TF:* 800-241-0323 ■ *Web:* www.showagroup.com	Menlo	GA	30731	800-241-0323	393-2666*	432
Showa Aluminum Inc 10500 O'Day-Harrison Rd	Mount Sterling	OH	43143	740-869-3333		247
Showa Denko America 420 Lexington Ave Ste 2335A *Web:* www.showadenko.us	New York	NY	10170	212-370-0033	370-4566	696
Showa Denko Carbon Inc 478 Ridge Rd *TF:* 800-525-7031 ■ *Web:* www.sdkc.com	Ridgeville	SC	29472	843-875-3200	875-2640	127
Showalter Flying Service 600 Herndon Ave *Web:* www.showalter.com	Orlando	FL	32803	407-326-6062		63
Showbest Fixture Corp 4112 Sarellen Rd *Web:* www.showbest.com	Henrico	VA	23231	804-222-5535		286
Showcase Honda 1333 E Camelback Rd *TF:* 844-880-3581 ■ *Web:* www.showcasehonda.com	Phoenix	AZ	85014	844-880-3581		57
Showcase of Citrus 5010 US Hwy 27 *Web:* www.showcaseofcitrus.com	Clermont	FL	34714	352-394-4377		297-7
Show-me Publishing Inc 2049 Wyandotte St *Web:* ingrams.com	Kansas City	MO	64108	816-842-9994	474-1111	532-3
Showplace Wood Products Inc 1 Enterprise St *TF:* 877-512-2500 ■ *Web:* www.showplacecabinetry.com	Harrisburg	SD	57032	605-743-2200		115
Showtime Concession Supply Inc 200 SE 19th St *Web:* www.showplacemarket.com	Moore	OK	73160	405-895-9902		297-3
Showtime Networks Inc 1633 Broadway *Web:* www.sho.com	New York	NY	10019	212-708-1600		740
Showtime Pictures LLC 281 S Vineyard Rd Ste 108 *Web:* www.showtimepictures.com	Orem	UT	84058	954-449-8844	449-8858	592
Showtime Tv 2465 S E Hwy 484 *Web:* showtimetvservice.com	Belleview	FL	34420	352-401-1800		35
SHP (Sydney Harbour Paints Inc) 1520 Cotner Ave *Web:* www.shpcompany.com	Los Angeles	CA	90025	310-444-2882		44
SHPTV (Smoky Hills Public Television) 604 Elm St *TF:* 800-337-4788 ■ *Web:* www.shptv.org	Bunker Hill	KS	67626	785-483-6990	483-4605	632
Shred Works Inc 1601 Bayshore Hwy Ste 211 *Web:* shredworks.com	Burlingame	CA	94010	510-729-7110		317
Shred-Pac Inc 2982 22nd St *TF:* 800-592-5959 ■ *Web:* bestcompactors.com	Hopkins	MI	49328	269-793-3232	793-7451	806
Shreve Crump & Low Inc 39 Newbury St *Web:* www.shrevecrumpandlow.com	Boston	MA	02116	617-267-9100		410
Shreve Land Company Inc 624 Travis St Ste 100 *Web:* www.shreveland.com	Shreveport	LA	71101	318-226-0056	226-0064	187
Shreve Memorial Library 424 Texas St *Web:* www.shreve-lib.org	Shreveport	LA	71101	318-226-5897	226-4780	434-3
Shreveport City Hall PO Box 31109 *Web:* www.shreveportla.gov	Shreveport	LA	71130	318-673-5420	673-5099	337
Shreveport Convention Ctr 400 Caddo St *Web:* www.shreveportcenter.com	Shreveport	LA	71101	318-841-4000		184
Shreveport Opera 212 Texas St Ste 101 *Web:* www.shreveportopera.org	Shreveport	LA	71101	318-227-9503	227-9518	573-2
Shreveport Regional Airport 5103 Hollywood Ave *Web:* www.shreveportla.gov	Shreveport	LA	71109	318-673-5370		27
Shreveport Symphony Orchestra 619 Louisiana Ave *Web:* www.shreveportsymphony.com	Shreveport	LA	71101	318-222-7496	222-7490	573-3
Shreveport-Bossier Convention & Tourist Bureau 629 Spring St *TF:* 800-551-8682 ■ *Web:* www.shreveport-bossier.org	Shreveport	LA	71101	318-222-9391	222-0056	206
SHRH&C (Seminole Hard Rock Hotel & Casino Tampa) 5223 N Orient Rd **Fax Area Code:* 954 ■ *TF:* 866-388-4263 ■ *Web:* www.seminolehardrocktampa.com	Tampa	FL	33610	813-627-7625	983-0242*	133
Shrine Auditorium & Exposition Ctr 665 W Jefferson Blvd *Web:* www.shrineauditorium.com	Los Angeles	CA	90007	213-748-5116		205
Shrine of Our Lady of La Leche 27 Ocean Ave *TF:* 800-342-6529 ■ *Web:* www.missionandshrine.org	Saint Augustine	FL	32084	904-824-2809		50-1
Shrine of Saint John Neumann 1019 N Fifth St *Web:* stjohnneumann.org	Philadelphia	PA	19123	215-627-3080	627-3296	50-1
Shriners Hospitals for Children Cincinnati 3229 Burnet Ave *Web:* shrinershospitalcincinnati.org	Cincinnati	OH	45229	513-872-6000	872-6999	374-1
Shriners Intl 2900 Rocky Point Dr *Web:* www.shrinersinternational.org	Tampa	FL	33607	813-281-0300		50-5
Shriver House Museum 309 Baltimore St *Web:* www.shriverhouse.org	Gettysburg	PA	17325	717-337-2800		520
SHSMD (Society for Healthcare Strategy & Market Development) 155 N Wacker Dr Ste 400 *TF:* 800-242-2626 ■ *Web:* www.shsmd.org	Chicago	IL	60606	312-422-3888	278-0883	49-8
Shubert Foundation Inc, The 234 W 44th St *Web:* www.shubertfoundation.org	New York	NY	10036	212-944-3777		305
Shubert Theater 247 College St *Web:* www.shubert.com	New Haven	CT	06510	203-624-1825	789-2286	572
Shuert Technologies LLC 6600 Dobry Rd *TF:* 877-748-3781 ■ *Web:* www.shuert.com	Sterling Heights	MI	48314	586-254-4590		386
Shugart Enterprises LLC 221 Jonestown Rd *Web:* buyshugart.com	Winston-Salem	NC	27104	336-765-9661	765-1295	187
Shugart Studios Inc 812 College Ave PO Box 580	Levelland	TX	79336	806-897-1754		590
Shuhei Inc 23360 Chagrin Blvd *Web:* shuheirestaurant.com	Beachwood	OH	44122	216-464-1720		670
Shui Spa at Crowne Pointe Historic Inn 82 Bradford St *TF:* 877-276-9631 ■ *Web:* crownepointe.com	Provincetown	MA	02657	508-487-6767		707
Shukat Arrow Hafer Weber & Herbsman LLP 494 Eighth Ave 6th Fl *Web:* musiclaw.com	New York	NY	10001	212-245-4580		41
Shula's Steak 2 6842 Main St *Web:* www.shulas.com	Miami Lakes	FL	33014	305-820-8047		671
Shula's Steak House 5111 Tamiami Trl N *Web:* shulasnaples.com	Naples	FL	34103	239-430-4999		671
Shular Hospitality 9475 Hwy 49 *Web:* www.shularhospitality.com	Gulfport	MS	39503	228-868-1888	867-2983	656
Shults Management Group Inc 181 E Fairmount Ave *Web:* www.shultsauto.com	Lakewood	NY	14750	716-763-1551		57
Shultz & Rollins Ltd 1980 E Fort Lowell Rd Ste 200 *Web:* shultz-rollins.com	Tucson	AZ	85719	520-577-7777		41
Shultz Steel Company Inc 5321 Firestone Blvd *Web:* www.shultzsteel.com	South Gate	CA	90280	323-564-3281	564-4105	492
Shumaker Consulting Engineer PC 143 Court St *Web:* www.shumakerengineering.com	Binghamton	NY	13901	607-798-8081	798-8186	261
Shuman Plastics Inc 35 Neoga St *TF:* 800-803-6242 ■ *Web:* www.shuman-plastics.com	Depew	NY	14043	716-685-2121	685-3236	605-2
Shumate, Flaherty, Eubanks & Baechtold, Psc 225 W Irvine St *TF:* 800-494-9916 ■ *Web:* eblawfirm.com	Richmond	KY	40475	859-623-3049	623-6406	41
Shumsky Enterprises Inc 811 E Fourth St *TF:* 800-223-2203 ■ *Web:* www.shumsky.com	Dayton	OH	45402	800-223-2203		4
Shun Fat Supermarket 4562 Mack Rd *Web:* www.shunfatsupermarket.com	Sacramento	CA	95823	916-395-6868	395-8788	345
Shun Lee Palace 155 E 55th St *Web:* www.shunleepalace.com	New York	NY	10022	212-371-8844		671
Shur-Co Inc 2309 Shur-Lok St PO Box 713 *TF:* 800-474-8756 ■ *Web:* www.shurco.com	Yankton	SD	57078	605-665-6000	665-0501	733
Shure Inc 5800 W Touhy Ave *TF:* 800-257-4873 ■ *Web:* www.shure.com	Niles	IL	60714	847-600-2000	600-1212	52
Shure Manufacturing Corp 1901 W Main St *TF:* 800-227-4873 ■ *Web:* shureusa.com	Washington	MO	63090	636-390-7100	390-7171	319-1
Shure-line Construction Inc PO Box 249 *Web:* www.shure-line.com	Kenton	DE	19955	302-653-4610	653-4752	480
SHURflo Pump Manufacturing Company Inc 5900 Katella Ave *TF:* 800-854-3218 ■ *Web:* www.shurflo.com	Cypress	CA	90630	562-795-5200	795-7554	641
Shur-Lok Corp 2541 White Rd *Web:* www.shur-lok.com	Irvine	CA	92614	949-474-6000		21
Shurtape Technologies LLC 1712 Eigth St Dr SE **Fax Area Code:* 800 ■ *TF:* 888-442-8273 ■ *Web:* www.shurtape.com	Hickory	NC	28602	828-322-2700	335-7651*	732
ShurTech Brands 32150 Just Imagine Dr *TF:* 800-321-1733 ■ *Web:* www.shurtapetech.com	Avon	OH	44011	440-937-7000	937-7077	535
Shurtleff & Andrews Corp 1875 West 500 South *Web:* www.shurtleff-slc.com	Salt Lake City	UT	84104	801-973-9096		189-14
Shuster Corp 55 Samuel Barnet Blvd *Web:* www.shustercorp.com	New Bedford	MA	02745	508-999-3261	990-2157	370
Shuster's Building Components 2920 Clay Pk **Fax Area Code:* 800 ■ *TF:* 800-735-9899 ■ *Web:* www.shusters.com	Irwin	PA	15642	724-446-7000	676-0640*	499
Shuster's Transportation Inc 750 E Valley St	Willits	CA	95490	707-459-4131		780
Shutler Consulting Engineers Inc 12503 Bel Red Rd *Web:* shutler.com	Bellevue	WA	98005	425-450-4075		261
Shutter Mill Inc 8517 S Perkins Rd *TF:* 800-416-6455 ■ *Web:* www.kirtz.com	Stillwater	OK	74074	405-377-6455	377-1010	699
Shutterbug Magazine 1419 Chaffee Dr Ste 1 *TF:* 800-829-9153 ■ *Web:* www.shutterbug.com	Titusville	FL	32780	321-269-3212		457-14
Shutterfly Inc 2800 Bridge Pkwy Ste 101 *Web:* www.shutterfly.com	Redwood City	CA	94065	650-610-5200	654-1299	588
Shutters on the Beach 1 Pico Blvd *TF:* 866-527-6612 ■ *Web:* www.shuttersonthebeach.com	Santa Monica	CA	90405	310-458-0030		379
Shutterstock Inc 350 Fifth Ave 2nd Fl **Fax Area Code:* 347 ■ *TF:* 866-663-3954 ■ *Web:* www.shutterstock.com	New York	NY	10118	646-419-4452	402-0710*	592
Shuttle Computer Group Inc 17068 Evergreen Pl *TF:* 888-972-1818 ■ *Web:* www.us.shuttle.com	City of Industry	CA	91745	626-820-9000	820-5060	173-2
Shuttleworth Inc 10 Commercial Rd *TF:* 800-444-7412 ■ *Web:* www.shuttleworth.com	Huntington	IN	46750	260-356-8500	359-7810	207
Shwiff Levy & Polo LLP 433 California St Ste 1000 *Web:* www.slpconsults.com	San Francisco	CA	94104	415-291-8600		734
SI (Semler Industries Inc) 3800 N Carnation St *Web:* www.semlerindustries.com	Franklin Park	IL	60131	847-671-5650	671-7686	770
SI Group Inc 2750 Balltown Rd *TF:* 800-962-8641 ■ *Web:* www.siigroup.com	Schenectady	NY	12301	518-347-4200		605-2
SI Holdings 3267 Bee Caves Rd Ste 107 *TF:* 866-551-4646 ■ *Web:* sysinformation.com	Austin	TX	78746	866-551-4646		396
SI Jacobson Manufacturing Co 1414 Jacobson Dr *Web:* www.sij.com	Waukegan	IL	60085	847-623-1414		548

	Phone	Fax	Class
Si Senor Restaurant 1551 E Amador Ave .... Las Cruces NM 88001 *Web:* www.sisenor.com	575-527-0817		671
SI Systems LLC 101 Larry Holmes Dr Ste 500 .... Easton PA 18042 *TF:* 800-523-9464 ■ *Web:* www.sihs.com	610-252-7321	250-9677	581
SI Video Sales Group PO Box 63754 .... Philadelphia PA 19147 *Web:* www.sivideo.com	267-519-2222		511
SIA (Service Industry Assn) 2164 Histroic Decatur Rd .... San Diego CA 92106 *Web:* www.servicenetwork.org	619-221-9200		49-12
SIA (Survivors of Incest Anonymous) PO Box 190 .... Benson MD 21018 *TF:* 877-742-9761 ■ *Web:* www.siawso.org	877-742-9761		48-21
SIA (SnowSports Industries America) 1918 Prospector Ave .... Park City UT 84060 *Web:* www.snowsports.org	435-657-5140	659-3434	49-4
SIA (Security Industry Assn) 8405 Colesville Rd Ste 500 .... Silver Spring MD 20910 *Fax Area Code: 703 ■ *TF:* 866-817-8888 ■ *Web:* www.securityindustry.org	301-804-4700	683-2469*	49-4
SIAM (Society for Industrial & Applied Mathematics) 3600 Market St 6th Fl .... Philadelphia PA 19104 *TF:* 800-447-7426 ■ *Web:* www.siam.org	215-382-9800	386-7999	49-19
Siam Cafe 3951 St Clair Ave NE .... Cleveland OH 44114	216-361-2323		671
Siam Cafe Inc 316 McCall St .... Nashville TN 37211	615-834-3181		671
Siam Garden Thai Restaurant 3125 Ninth St N .... Saint Petersburg FL 33704 *Web:* siamgardenthai.com	727-822-0613	898-2933	671
Siam Orchid 12 N Main St .... Concord NH 03301 *Web:* www.siamorchid.net	603-228-1529		671
Siamab Therapeutics Inc 90 Bridge St Ste 100 .... Newton MA 02458 *Web:* www.siamab.com	617-714-9773	752-3653	743
Siano Appliance Distributors Inc 5372 Pleasant View Rd .... Memphis TN 38134 *Web:* www.siano-appliance.com	901-382-5833		38
SIB Development & Consulting Inc 796 Meeting St .... Charleston SC 29403 *Web:* www.aboutsib.com	843-576-3606		403
Sibel Ayse Halac Iron Works Inc 21675 Ashgrove Ct .... Sterling VA 20166 *Web:* www.sahalac.com	703-406-4766		492
Siben & Siben LLP 90 E Mn St .... Bay Shore NY 11706 *Web:* www.sibensiben.com	631-665-3400		428
Sibley County 400 Court St PO Box H .... Gaylord MN 55334 *Web:* www.co.sibley.mn.us	507-647-5377	237-4062	338
Sibley State Park 800 Sibley Park Rd .... New London MN 56273 *Web:* www.willmarlakesarea.com	320-354-2055		565
Sibridge 2275 E Continental Blvd .... Southlake TX 76092 *Web:* www.sibridge.com	817-756-6231		463
SIC (Stamford Innovation Ctr) 175 Atlantic St .... Stamford CT 06901 *Web:* stamfordicenter.com	203-226-8701		393
Siciliano Inc 3601 Winchester Rd .... Springfield IL 62707 *Web:* www.sicilianoinc.com	217-585-1200	585-1211	188-10
Sickle Cell Disease Association of America (SCDAA) 3700 Koppers St Ste 570 .... Baltimore MD 21202 *TF:* 800-421-8453 ■ *Web:* www.sicklecelldisease.org	410-528-1555		48-17
SICO America Inc 7525 Cahill Rd .... Minneapolis MN 55439 *TF:* 800-328-6138 ■ *Web:* www.sicoinc.com	952-941-1700	941-6737	319-3
Sicpa Securink Corp 8000 Research Way .... Springfield VA 22153 *Web:* www.sicpa.com	703-455-8050		388
SID (Society for Information Display) 1475 S Bascom Ave Ste 114 .... Campbell CA 95008 *TF:* 800-350-0111 ■ *Web:* www.sid.org	408-879-3901	879-3833	48-9
SID (Society for Investigative Dermatology Inc) 526 Superior Ave E Ste 340 .... Cleveland OH 44114 *Web:* www.sidnet.org	216-579-9300	579-9333	49-8
Sid Birzon Inc 1376 Niagara Falls Blvd .... Tonawanda NY 14150 *Web:* www.birzonjewelers.com	716-856-8255		411
Sid Factor 1537 Pearl St .... Boulder CO 80302 *Web:* sidfactor.com	303-449-5323		195
Sid Goldstien - Civil Engineer Inc 2030 Dermanak Dr .... Solvang CA 93463 *Web:* sjgce.com	805-688-1526		261
Sid Harvey Industries Inc 605 Locust St .... Garden City NY 11530 *TF:* 800-342-7839 ■ *Web:* www.sidharvey.com	516-745-9200	222-9027	612
Sid Lee Inc 75 Queen St Ste 1400 .... Montreal QC H3C2N6 *Web:* sidlee.com	514-282-2200		195
Sid Richardson Carbon & Energy Cos 201 Main St .... Fort Worth TX 76102 *Web:* www.sidrich.com	817-390-8600		145
Siddall Communications LLC 715 E 4th St Ste 9 .... Richmond VA 23224 *Web:* www.siddall.com	804-788-8011	782-9792	4
SIDDHA Yoga Publications 371 Brickman Rd .... South Fallsburg NY 12779 *Web:* www.siddhayoga.org	845-434-2000		637-2
Side Effects Software Inc 123 Front St W Ste 1401 .... Toronto ON M5J2M2 *TF:* 888-504-9876 ■ *Web:* www.sidefx.com	416-504-9876		179
Side Street Inn 1225 Hopaka St .... Honolulu HI 96814 *Web:* sidestreetinn.com	808-591-0253	732-7333	671
Sidehill Copper Works Inc 12 Port Access Rd .... Erie PA 16507 *Web:* www.sidehillcopper.com	814-451-0400	451-0294	91
Sidel Inc 5600 Sun Ct .... Norcross GA 30092 *Fax Area Code: 770 ■ *Web:* www.sidel.com	678-221-3000	447-0084*	547
Sidel Systems Usa Inc 12500 El Camino Real .... Atascadero CA 93422 *TF:* 800-668-5003 ■ *Web:* www.sidelsystems.com	805-462-1250		358
SIDES & Associates Inc 222 Jefferson St Ste B .... LaFayette LA 70501 *Web:* sides.com	337-233-6473		4
Sideshow Media LLC 611 Broadway Ste 611 .... New York NY 10012 *Web:* sideshowbooks.com	212-674-5335		94
Sidewalk Film Center & Cinema festival 310 18th St N Ste 100 .... Birmingham AL 35203 *Web:* www.sidewalkfest.com	205-324-0888		282
Sidewinder Conversions 44658 Yale Rd W .... Chilliwack BC V2R0G5 *TF:* 888-266-2299 ■ *Web:* www.sidewinder-conversions.com	604-792-2082	792-8920	62-7
Sidley Austin LLP 787 Seventh Ave .... New York NY 10019 *Web:* www.sidley.com	212-839-5300	839-5599	428
Sidley Diamond Tool Co 32320 Ford Rd .... Garden City MI 48135 *Web:* www.sidleydiamond.com	734-261-7970	261-2028	1
Sidney Lanier Cottage 935 High St .... Macon GA 31201 *Web:* www.historicmacon.org	478-743-3851		50-3
Sidney Manufacturing Company Inc 405 N Main Ave .... Sidney OH 45365 *Web:* www.sidneymanufacturing.com	937-492-4154	492-0919	298
Sidney Scheinert & Son Inc (SSS) 404 Midland Ave .... Saddle Brook NJ 07663 *Web:* www.scheinertscrews.com	201-791-4600	791-8551	278
Sidney State Bank 3016 W Sidney Rd .... Sidney MI 48885 *Web:* sidneybank.com	989-328-2501		70
Sidney Street Cafe 2000 Sidney St .... Saint Louis MO 63104 *Web:* www.sidneystreetcafestl.com	314-771-5777		671
Sidney Tax Service Inc 115 2nd St NE .... Sidney MT 59270	406-433-3131		734
Sidney Transportation Services 777 W Russell Rd PO Box 946 .... Sidney OH 45365 *TF:* 800-743-6391 ■ *Web:* www.sidneytransportationservices.com	937-498-2323		685
Sidney's Hairdressing College Inc 200 E 3rd Ave .... Hutchinson KS 67501 *Web:* www.sidneyshair.com	620-662-5481		167-3
Sidney-Shelby County Chamber of Commerce 101 S Ohio Ave 2nd Fl .... Sidney OH 45365 *Web:* www.sidneyshelbychamber.com	937-492-9122	498-2472	139
Sidran Inc 1050 Venture Ct Ste 100 .... Carrollton TX 75006 *TF:* 800-969-5015 ■ *Web:* www.sidraninc.com	214-352-7979	352-0439	155-20
Sidus Investment Management LLC 767 Third Ave 15th Fl .... New York NY 10017 *Web:* www.sidusfunds.com	212-751-6644		401
Sidwell Company Inc 2570 Foxfield Rd Ste 300 .... Saint Charles IL 60174 *TF:* 877-743-9355 ■ *Web:* www.sidwellco.com	630-549-1000	549-1111	727
Sidwell Friends School 3825 Wisconsin Ave NW .... Washington DC 20016 *Web:* www.sidwell.edu	202-537-8100		623
SIE Computing Solutions Inc 10 Mupac Dr .... Brockton MA 02301 *Web:* www.atrenne.com	508-588-6110		407
Sieben Polk PA 2600 Eagan Woods Dr Ste 50 .... Eagan MN 55121 *TF:* 800-620-1829 ■ *Web:* www.siebenpolklaw.com	651-304-6708	437-2732	428
Siebenthaler Co 2074 Beaver Valley Rd .... Beavercreek OH 45434 *Web:* www.siebenthaler.com	937-274-1154		323
Sieck 311 E Chase St .... Baltimore MD 21202 *Web:* www.sieck.com	410-685-4660	685-1547	293
Siefert Associates LLC 180 Church St .... Naugatuck CT 06770 *Web:* siefertassociates.com	203-723-1477		261
Siegal Steel Co 4747 S Kedzie Ave .... Chicago IL 60632 *Web:* www.siegalsteel.com	773-927-7600	927-7621	492
Siegel & Gale 625 Avenue of the Americas 4th Fl .... New York NY 10011 *Web:* www.siegelgale.com	212-453-0400		7
Siegel & Stockman USA 126 W 25th St .... New York NY 10001 *Web:* www.siegel-stockman.com	212-633-0138		464
Siegel Insurance Inc 2987 Clairmont Rd NE Ste 425 .... Atlanta GA 30329 *TF:* 888-275-0553 ■ *Web:* siegelinsurance.com	404-633-6332	633-9388	390
Siegel Suites Tropicana 3890 Graphic Center Dr .... Las Vegas NV 89118 *Web:* www.siegelsuites.com	702-507-9999		378
Siegel, Reilly & Kaufman LLC 1266 E Main St 6th Fl .... Stamford CT 06902 *Web:* srkfamlaw.com	203-326-5145		41
Siegeler Insurance Agency Inc 172 W Austin St .... Giddings TX 78942 *TF:* 800-283-4086 ■ *Web:* siegins.com	979-542-3449	542-0469	390
Siegers Seed Co 13031 Reflections Dr .... Holland MI 49424 *TF:* 800-962-4999 ■ *Web:* www.siegers.com	616-786-4999	994-0333	276
Siegfried Group LLP, The 1201 Market St .... Wilmington DE 19801 *Web:* www.siegfriedgroup.com	302-984-1800		2
Siegfried USA LLC 33 Industrial Park Rd .... Pennsville NJ 08070 *TF:* 877-763-8630 ■ *Web:* www.siegfried.ch	856-678-3601	678-8201	479
Siegwerk USA Co 3535 SW 56th St .... Des Moines IA 50321 *TF:* 800-728-8200 ■ *Web:* www.siegwerk.com	515-471-2100	471-2200	388
Sielc Technologies 804 Seton Ct .... Wheeling IL 60090 *Web:* www.sielc.com	847-229-2629	655-6079	358
Sielox LLC 170 E Ninth Ave .... Runnemede NJ 08078 *TF:* 800-424-2126 ■ *Web:* www.sielox.com	856-939-9300		692
Siemens Corp 300 New Jersey Ave Ste 1000 .... Washington DC 20001 *Fax Area Code: 678 ■ *TF:* 800-743-6367 ■ *Web:* www.siemens.com	800-743-6367	867-7450*	185
Siemens Manufacturing Company Inc 410 W Washington St .... Freeburg IL 62243 *Web:* siemensmfg.com	618-539-3000	539-6172	625
Siemer Milling Co 111 W Main St .... Teutopolis IL 62467 *TF:* 800-826-1065 ■ *Web:* www.siemermilling.com	217-857-3131	857-3092	296-23
Siemion Huckabay PC 1 Towne Sq Ste 1400 .... Southfield MI 48076 *Web:* siemion-huckabay.com	248-357-1400		41
Siemon Co 101 Siemon Co Dr .... Watertown CT 06795 *TF:* 866-548-5814 ■ *Web:* www.siemon.com	860-945-4200	945-4225	814

	Phone	Fax	Class
Siemon Law Firm PC, The 347 Dahlonega St. Cumming GA 30040 *Web:* siemonlawfirm.com	770-888-5120		41
Siena College 515 Loudon Rd. Loudonville NY 12211 *Web:* www.siena.edu	518-783-2300	783-2436	166
Siena Ctr 5635 Erie St. Racine WI 53402 *Web:* www.racinedominicans.org	262-639-4100		673
Siena Engineering Group Inc 50 Mall Rd Ste 203. Burlington MA 01803 *Web:* sienaengineeringgroup.com	781-221-8400		226
Siena Heights University 1247 E Siena Heights Dr. Adrian MI 49221 *TF:* 800-521-0009 ■ *Web:* www.sienaheights.edu	517-263-0731	264-7745	166
Siena Hotel 1505 E Franklin St. Chapel Hill NC 27514 *TF:* 800-223-7379 ■ *Web:* www.sienahotel.com	919-929-4000	968-8527	379
Sienko Precision Inc 10102 Sussex Ln. Houston TX 77041 *Web:* www.sienkoprecision.com	713-462-7482		454
Siepert & Company LLP 1920 W Hart Rd. Beloit WI 53511 *Web:* www.siepert.com	608-365-2266		2
Sierra Academy of Aeronautics 2305 Jetlift Dr. Atwater CA 95301 *Web:* www.sierraacademy.com	209-722-7522		167-3
Sierra Bancorp 86 N Main St PO Box 1930. Porterville CA 93257 *NASDAQ: BSRR* ■ *TF:* 888-454-2265 ■ *Web:* www.bankofthesierra.com	888-454-2265		360-2
Sierra Bullets LLC 1400 W Henry St. Sedalia MO 65301 *Web:* www.sierrabullets.com	660-827-6300		711
Sierra Business Council 10183 Truckee Airport Rd Ste 202 Truckee CA 96161 *Web:* sierrabusiness.org	530-582-4800	582-1230	196
Sierra Club 85 Second St 2nd Fl San Francisco CA 94105 *Web:* www.sierraclub.org	415-977-5500	977-5799	48-13
Sierra Club Canada 412-1 Nicholas St. Ottawa ON K1N7B7 *TF:* 888-810-4204 ■ *Web:* www.sierraclub.ca	613-241-4611	241-2292	48-13
Sierra Club of Canada Bc Chapter 301 - 2994 Douglas St. Victoria BC V8T4N4 *Web:* sierraclub.bc.ca	250-386-5255		138
Sierra Community College 5100 Sierra College Blvd Rocklin CA 95677 *TF:* 800-242-4004 ■ *Web:* sierracollege.edu	916-624-3333		162
Sierra Computer Group 1900 Vassar St. Reno NV 89502 *Web:* www.sierracomputergroup.com	775-322-6455		177
Sierra Converting Corp 1400 Kleppe Ln Sparks NV 89431 *TF:* 800-332-8221 ■ *Web:* www.sierraconverting.com	800-332-8221		557
Sierra County 100 Courthouse Sq Rm 11. Downieville CA 95936 *Web:* www.sierracounty.ca.gov	530-289-3295	289-2830	338
Sierra Creative Systems Inc 15700 Texaco Ave. Paramount CA 90723 *TF:* 800-961-4877 ■ *Web:* www.theaddressers.com	562-232-8100		809
Sierra Donor Services 3940 Industrial Blvd West Sacramento CA 95691 *TF:* 877-401-2546 ■ *Web:* sierradonor.org	877-401-2546		545
Sierra Electric Co-opeartive Inc 610 Hwy 195 PO Box 290. Elephant Butte NM 87935 *TF:* 888-336-3380 ■ *Web:* www.sierraelectric.org	575-744-5231		245
Sierra Electronics 690 E Glendale Ave Ste 9B PO Box 1545 Sparks NV 89432 *TF:* 800-874-7515 ■ *Web:* www.sierraelectronics.com	775-359-1121		246
Sierra Energy 1020 Winding Creek Rd Ste 100. Roseville CA 95678 *TF:* 800-576-2264 ■ *Web:* www.sierraenergyexpress.com	916-218-1600		579
Sierra Forest Products 13575 Benson Ave Chino CA 91710 *TF:* 800-548-3975 ■ *Web:* www.sierrafp.com	909-591-9442	591-9449	683
Sierra Group, The 588 N Gulph Rd Ste 110. King of Prussia PA 19406 *TF:* 800-973-7687 ■ *Web:* www.thesierragroup.com	610-992-0288		194
Sierra Health Foundation 1321 Garden Hwy. Sacramento CA 95833 *Web:* www.sierrahealth.org	916-922-4755		305
Sierra Hospice 150 Brentwood Dr. Chester CA 96020 *Web:* www.sierrahospice.com	530-258-3412	258-3001	450
Sierra Hr Partners Inc 7112 N Fresno St Ste 450. Fresno CA 93720 *TF:* 844-431-4748 ■ *Web:* sierrahr.com	559-431-8090		193
Sierra Infosys Inc 6001 Savoy Dr Ste 210. Houston TX 77036 *Web:* www.sierratec.com	713-747-9693	222-2434	463
Sierra Instruments Inc 5 Harris Ct Bldg L. Monterey CA 93940 *TF:* 800-866-0200 ■ *Web:* www.sierrainstruments.com	831-373-0200	373-4402	201
Sierra Ip Law PC 7030 N Fruit Ste 110. Fresno CA 93711 *Web:* sierraiplaw.com	559-436-3800		41
Sierra Land Group Inc 801 N Brand Blvd Ste 1010 Glendale CA 91203	818-247-3681		379
Sierra Machinery Inc 1651 Glendale Ave Sparks NV 89431 *Web:* www.sierramachinery.com	775-358-6721	358-6739	386
Sierra Monitor Corp 1991 Tarob Ct. Milpitas CA 95035 *OTC: SRMC* ■ *TF:* 888-509-1970 ■ *Web:* www.sierramonitor.com	408-262-6611	262-9042	472
Sierra Nevada Brewing Co 1075 E 20th St. Chico CA 95928 *Web:* www.sierranevada.com	530-893-3520		102
Sierra Nevada College 999 Tahoe Blvd. Incline Village NV 89451 *TF:* 866-412-4636 ■ *Web:* www.sierranevada.edu	775-831-1314		166
Sierra Nevada Corp (SNC) 444 Salomon Cir. Sparks NV 89434 *Web:* www.sncorp.com	775-331-0222	331-0370	253
Sierra Outdoor Products LLC 4272 Caughlin Pky Dept WS Reno NV 89519 *Web:* www.sierraoutdoorproducts.com	775-747-8820	747-8823	96
Sierra Pacific Industries 19794 Riverside Ave. Anderson CA 96007 *Web:* spi-ind.com	530-378-8000	378-8109	683
Sierra Pacific West 2125 La Mirada Dr. Vista CA 92081 *Web:* www.sierrapacificwest.com	760-599-0755		261
Sierra Pacific Windows 11605 Reading Rd PO Box 8489 Red Bluff CA 96080 *TF:* 800-433-4873 ■ *Web:* www.sierrapacificwindows.com	530-527-9620	527-4438	499
Sierra Ready Mix LLC 4150 Smiley Rd North Las Vegas NV 89081 *Web:* www.sierrareadymix.com	702-644-8700		182
Sierra Receivables Management Inc 2500 Goodwater Ave. Redding CA 96002 *TF:* 800-237-3205 ■ *Web:* www.sierrareceivables.com	530-224-1360		160
Sierra Safari Zoo *Sierra Nevada Zoological Park* 10200 N Virgina St PO Box 600223 Reno NV 89506 *Web:* www.snzp.org	775-677-1101		823
Sierra Select Distributors 4320 Roseville Rd. North Highlands CA 95660 *TF:* 800-793-7334 ■ *Web:* sierraselect.com	800-793-7334		50-6
Sierra Tech Computers 8674 SW Ave Fresno CA 93706 *TF:* 888-253-9560 ■ *Web:* sierra-tech.net	559-348-3278		180
Sierra Tel 49150 Rd 426. Oakhurst CA 93644 *TF:* 877-658-4611 ■ *Web:* www.sierratel.com	559-683-4611		224
Sierra Trading Post Inc 5025 Campstool Rd Cheyenne WY 82007 *Web:* www.sierratradingpost.com	307-775-8090		229
Sierra Tucson Inc 39580 S Lago Del Oro Pkwy. Tucson AZ 85739 *TF:* 800-842-4487 ■ *Web:* www.sierratucson.com	520-624-4000		726
Sierra Ventures 1400 Fashion Island Blvd Ste 1010 San Mateo CA 94404 *Web:* www.sierraventures.com	650-854-1000		792
Sierra View Company Inc 4202 Douglas Blvd Ste 100 Granite Bay CA 95746 *Web:* www.sierraview.com	916-774-7000	774-7010	186
Sierra View District Hospital (SVDH) 465 W Putnam Ave. Porterville CA 93257 *Web:* www.sierra-view.com	559-784-1110		374-3
Sierra Vista Area Chamber of Commerce 21 E Wilcox Dr Sierra Vista AZ 85635 *Web:* sierravistachamber.org	520-458-6940	452-0878	139
Sierra Vista Herald 102 Fab Ave Sierra Vista AZ 85635 *Web:* www.svherald.com	520-458-9440	459-0120	532-2
Sierra Vista Mall 1050 Shaw Ave. Clovis CA 93612 *Web:* www.sierravistamall.com	559-299-5070		460
Sierra Vista Regional Medical Ctr (SVRMC) 1010 Murray Ave San Luis Obispo CA 93405 *Web:* www.sierravistaregional.com	805-546-7600		374-3
Sierra Volkswagen Inc 510 E Norris Dr. Ottawa IL 61350 *TF:* 877-854-2771 ■ *Web:* www.sierravw.com	855-316-8246		57
Sierra W/O Wires Inc 2 Robinson Plz Ste 300 Pittsburgh PA 15205 *Web:* sierraexperts.com	412-722-0707		225
Sierra Wireless Inc 13811 Wireless Way. Richmond BC V6V3A4 *Web:* www.sierrawireless.com	604-231-1100	231-1109	173-3
Sievers Equipment Co 406 N Old Rte 66. Hamel IL 62046 *Web:* www.sieversequipment.com	618-633-2622	633-2456	274
Siewert Cabinet & Fixture Manufacturing Inc 2640 Minnehaha Ave Minneapolis MN 55406 *Web:* www.siewertcabinet.com	612-721-4456		499
Sifco Asc 5708 E Schaaf Rd. Independence OH 44131 *TF:* 800-765-4131 ■ *Web:* www.sifcoasc.com	216-524-0099	524-6331	21
Sifco Industries Inc 970 E 64th St. Cleveland OH 44103 *NYSE: SIF* ■ *Web:* sifco.com	216-881-8600	432-6281	24
Siferd & Mccluskey 212 N Elizabeth St. Lima OH 45801 *Web:* siferd.com	419-222-5045	222-0473	41
SIFMAA (Securities Industry & Financial Markets Assn) 120 Broadway 35th Fl. New York NY 10271 *Web:* www.sifma.org	212-313-1200		49-2
Sift Media (US) Inc 120 E 23rd St 4th Fl New York NY 10010 *TF:* 855-253-8392 ■ *Web:* www.accountingweb.com	855-253-8392		530
SIG (Susquehanna International Group LLP) 401 City Ave. Bala Cynwyd PA 19004 *Web:* sig.com	610-617-2600		690
SIG Manufacturing Company Inc 401 S Front St Montezuma IA 50171 *TF:* 800-247-5008 ■ *Web:* sigmfg.com	641-623-5154	623-3922	762
SIG SAUER Inc 72 Pease Blvd Newington NH 03801 *TF:* 866-345-6744 ■ *Web:* www.sigsauer.com	603-610-3000	610-3001	284
Sigel's Beverages LP 2960 Anode Ln Dallas TX 75220 *Web:* www.sigels.com	214-350-1271	357-3490	443
Sight & Hearing Assn (SHA) 1246 University Ave W Ste 226 Saint Paul MN 55104 *Web:* www.sightandhearing.org	651-645-2546	645-2742	637-2
Sight Society of Northeastern New York Inc *Lions Eye Bank at Albany* 6 Executive Pk Dr. Albany NY 12203 *Web:* www.lionseyebankalbany.org	518-489-7606	489-7607	269
SightLife 221 Yale Ave N Ste 450. Seattle WA 98109 *TF:* 800-847-5786 ■ *Web:* www.sightlife.org	206-682-8500	682-4666	269
SightLine Systems Corp 4035 Ridge Top Rd Ste 510 Fairfax VA 22030 *Web:* sightline.com	703-563-3000		624
Sightly Enterprises Inc 11848 Bernardo Plz Ct Ste 110. San Diego CA 92128 *Web:* www.sightly.com	951-225-7000		393
Sights Productions 15130 Black Ankle Rd. Mount Airy MD 21771 *Web:* www.sights-productions.com	410-795-4582		637-2
SightSound Technologies Inc 311 S Craig St Ste 104. Pittsburgh PA 15213 *Web:* www.sightsound.com	412-621-6100	621-0103	525
SightWorks Inc 2505 SE 11th Ave Ste 250 Portland OR 97202 *Web:* www.sightworks.com	503-223-4184		5
Sigit Automation Inc 840 Seventh Ave SW Ste 1710. Calgary AB T2P3G2 *Web:* www.sigit.com	403-723-4256		261
Sigler 3100 S Riverside Dr PO Box 887 Ames IA 50010 *TF:* 800-750-6997 ■ *Web:* www.sigler.com	515-232-6997		627
SIGMA (Society of Independent Gasoline Marketers of America) 3930 Pender Dr Ste 340. Fairfax VA 22030 *Web:* www.sigma.org	703-709-7000	709-7007	49-18

Name / Address	City	State	ZIP	Phone	Fax	Class
Sigma Alpha Epsilon Fraternity (SAE)						
1856 Sheridan Rd.	Evanston	IL	60201	847-424-3031	475-2250	48-16
TF: 800-233-1856 ■ *Web:* www.sae.net						
Sigma Alpha Iota (SAI) 1 Tunnel Rd.	Asheville	NC	28805	828-251-0606	251-0644	48-16
Web: www.sai-national.org						
Sigma Analysis & Management Ltd						
Mars Ctr W Tower 661 University Ave Ste 1120	Toronto	ON	M5G1M1	416-260-6291	260-6297	401
Web: www.sigmanalysis.com						
Sigma Associates Inc						
1900 St Antoine St Ste 500	Detroit	MI	48226	313-963-9700	963-7626	186
Web: www.sigmaassociates.com						
Sigma Breakthrough Technologies Inc						
123 N Edward Gary 2nd Fl	San Marcos	TX	78666	512-353-7489		463
TF: 888-752-7070 ■ *Web:* www.sbtionline.com						
Sigma Business Solutions Inc						
55 York St.	Toronto	ON	M5J1R7	855-594-1991		809
TF: 855-594-1991 ■ *Web:* sigma-sbs.com						
Sigma Chi Fraternity 1714 Hinman Ave.	Evanston	IL	60201	877-471-5410	869-4906*	48-16
**Fax Area Code:* 847 ■ *TF:* 877-471-5410 ■ *Web:* www.sigmachi.org						
Sigma Corporation of America						
15 Fleetwood Ct	Ronkonkoma	NY	11779	631-585-1144		542
Web: www.sigmaphoto.com						
Sigma Delta Tau 714 Adams St.	Carmel	IN	46032	317-846-7747	575-5562	48-16
Web: sigmadeltatau.org						
Sigma Design 5521 Jackson St	Alexandria	LA	71303	318-449-9900		178-8
TF: 888-990-0900 ■ *Web:* www.arriscad.com						
Sigma Designs Inc 1778 Mcarthy Blvd.	Milpitas	CA	95035	408-957-9847		696
NASDAQ: SIGM ■ *Web:* www.sigmadesigns.com						
Sigma Electronics Inc						
1027 Commercial Ave.	East Petersburg	PA	17520	717-569-2926	569-4056	253
TF: 866-569-2681 ■ *Web:* www.sigmatechsys.com						
Sigma Environmental Services Inc						
1300 W Canal St.	Milwaukee	WI	53233	414-643-4200	643-4210	667
Web: www.thesigmagroup.com						
Sigma Financial Corp						
300 Parkland Plz.	Ann Arbor	MI	48103	734-663-1611		690
TF: 888-744-6264 ■ *Web:* www.sigmafinancial.com						
Sigma Gamma Rho Sorority Inc						
1000 Southhill Dr Ste 200	Cary	NC	27513	919-678-9720	678-9721	48-16
TF: 888-747-1922 ■ *Web:* www.sgrho1922.org						
Sigma Inc 711 Park Ave	Medina	NY	14103	800-356-3454		476
TF: 800-356-3454 ■ *Web:* www.sigmapumps.com						
Sigma Kappa Sorority						
695 Pro-Med Ln Ste 300	Carmel	IN	46032	317-872-3275	872-0716	48-16
Web: sigmakappa.org						
Sigma Nu Fraternity Inc						
9 N Lewis St PO Box 1869	Lexington	VA	24450	540-463-1869	463-1669	48-16
Web: www.sigmanu.org						
Sigma Partners						
2105 S Bascom Ave Ste 370.	Campbell	CA	95008	650-853-1700	853-1717	792
Web: www.sigmapartners.com						
Sigma Phi Epsilon Fraternity						
310 S Blvd	Richmond	VA	23220	804-353-1901	359-8160	48-16
TF: 800-767-1901 ■ *Web:* sigep.org						
Sigma Plastics Group PO Box 808	Lyndhurst	NJ	07071	201-933-6000	933-6429	600
Web: www.sigmaplasticsgroup.com						
Sigma Resources & Technologies Inc						
1605 S Main St Ste 117	Milpitas	CA	95035	408-748-0070		177
Web: sigma-rt.com						
Sigma Resources LLC						
7950 Saltsburg Rd	Pittsburgh	PA	15239	412-712-1070		196
Web: www.sigma-resources.com						
Sigma Sigma Sigma Foundation						
225 N Muhlenberg St	Woodstock	VA	22664	540-459-4212		379
Web: www.trisigma.org						
Sigma Space Corp 4600 Forbes Blvd	Lanham	MD	20706	301-552-6000	552-6411	256
Web: www.sigmaspace.com						
Sigma Stretch Film Corp						
Page & Schuyler Aves Bldg 8	Lyndhurst	NJ	07071	201-507-9100		601
TF: 800-672-9727 ■ *Web:* www.sigmastretchtools.com						
Sigma Systems Inc						
201 Boston Post Rd Ste 201	Marlborough	MA	01752	508-925-3200		721
Web: www.sigmainc.com						
Sigma Tau Gamma 8741 Founders Rd	Indianapolis	IN	46268	317-644-1920		48-16
Web: sigtau.org						
Sigma Tek Inc 1001 Industrial Rd	Augusta	KS	67010	316-775-6373	775-1416	22
Web: www.sigmatek.com						
Sigma Test Labs 1480 W 178th St	Gardena	CA	90248	310-324-9465	532-6216	743
Web: www.sigmatestlabs.com						
Sigma Theta Tau Intl 550 W N St.	Indianapolis	IN	46202	317-634-8171	634-8188	48-16
TF: 888-634-7575 ■ *Web:* www.sigmanursing.org						
Sigma Xi Scientific Research Society						
3106 E NC Hwy 54 PO Box 13975	Research Triangle Park	NC	27709	919-549-4691	549-0090	48-16
TF: 800-243-6534 ■ *Web:* www.sigmaxi.org						
Sigma-Aldrich Corp 3050 Spruce St.	Saint Louis	MO	63103	314-771-5765	325-5052*	145
NASDAQ: SIAL ■ **Fax Area Code:* 800 ■ *TF:* 800-325-3010 ■ *Web:* www.sigmaaldrich.com						
SigmaBleyzer LLC						
123 N Post Oak Ln Ste 410	Houston	TX	77024	713-621-3111		194
Web: www.sigmableyzer.com						
Sigman Heating & Air Conditioning						
6200 Old St Louis Rd	Belleville	IL	62223	618-234-4343	234-9300	189-10
Web: sigmanhvacr.com						
Sigman Janssen Stack Sewall & Pitz						
303 S Memorial Dr	Appleton	WI	54911	920-731-5201		428
TF: 800-775-1441 ■ *Web:* www.sigmanlegal.com						
Sigma-Netics Inc 2 N Corporate Dr	Riverdale	NJ	07457	973-227-6372		729
Web: www.sigmanetics.com						
Sigmatech Inc 4901-C Corporate Dr.	Huntsville	AL	35805	256-382-1188		242
Web: www.sigmatech.com						
SigmaTEK Systems LLC						
1445 Kemper Meadow Dr	Cincinnati	OH	45240	513-674-0005		174
Web: www.sigmanest.com						
SigmaTron International Inc						
2201 Landmeier Rd	Elk Grove Village	IL	60007	847-956-8000		625
NASDAQ: SGMA ■ *TF:* 800-700-9095 ■ *Web:* www.sigmatronintl.com						
Sigmetrix 2240 Bush Dr Ste 200	Mckinney	TX	75070	972-542-7517		809
Web: www.sigmetrix.com						
Sign Biz Inc 24681 La Plz Ste 270	Dana Point	CA	92629	949-234-0408		196
TF: 800-633-5580 ■ *Web:* www.signbiz.com						

Name / Address	City	State	ZIP	Phone	Fax	Class
Sign Builders Inc						
4800 Jefferson Ave PO Box 28380	Birmingham	AL	35228	800-222-7330	923-2124*	701
**Fax Area Code:* 205 ■ *TF:* 800-222-7330 ■ *Web:* www.signbuilders.com						
Sign Designs Inc 204 Campus Way	Modesto	CA	95352	209-524-4484	521-0272	701
TF: 800-421-7446 ■ *Web:* www.signdesigns.com						
Sign Resource Inc 6135 District Blvd.	Maywood	CA	90270	323-771-2098		701
TF: 800-423-4283 ■ *Web:* www.signresource.com						
Signa Engineering Corp						
2 Northpoint Dr Ste 700	Houston	TX	77060	281-774-1000		261
TF: 800-987-3331 ■ *Web:* www.signa.net						
Signal Communication System						
4325 W Shaw Ave.	Fresno	CA	93722	559-275-8500	275-1911	224
TF: 888-275-4560 ■ *Web:* www.signalcommunication.com						
Signal Hill Equity Partners						
2 Carlton St Ste 1700	Toronto	ON	M5B1J3	416-847-1168		528
Web: www.signalhillequity.com						
Signal Industrial Products Corp						
1601 Cowart St.	Chattanooga	TN	37408	423-756-4980		351
TF: 800-728-1326 ■ *Web:* www.signalproducts.com						
Signal Mountain Lodge PO Box 50	Moran	WY	83013	307-543-2831	543-2569	669
Web: www.signalmountainlodge.com						
Signal Peak						
2755 E Cottonwood Pkwy Ste 520	Salt Lake City	UT	84121	801-942-8999	942-1636	792
Web: www.spv.com						
Signal Point Systems Inc						
1270 Shiloh Rd Ste 100	Kennesaw	GA	30144	770-499-0439		186
TF: 800-814-6502 ■ *Web:* www.sigpoint.com						
Signal Processing Consultants Inc						
25536 Quits Pond Ct	South Riding	VA	20152	703-477-5399		647
Web: www.signalprocessing.com						
Signal Securities Inc						
700 Throckmorton St	Fort Worth	TX	76102	817-877-4256		196
TF: 800-957-4256 ■ *Web:* www.signalsecurities.com						
Signal Travel & Tours Inc 219 E Main St	Niles	MI	49120	269-684-2880		772
TF: 800-811-1522 ■ *Web:* www.signaltravel.com						
Signalert Asset Management LLC						
525 Northern Blvd Ste 210	Great Neck	NY	11021	516-829-6444		401
Web: www.systemsandforecasts.com						
Signalfire Wireless Telemetry Inc						
43 Broad St.	Hudson	MA	01749	978-212-2868		645-11
TF: 800-772-0878 ■ *Web:* www.signal-fire.com						
SignalFx 270 Brannan St	San Francisco	CA	94107	650-539-8650		178-8
Web: www.signalfx.com						
Signalisation Ver-Mac Inc						
1781 Bresse	Quebec City	QC	G2G2V2	418-654-1303	654-0517	407
TF: 888-488-7446 ■ *Web:* www.ver-mac.com						
Signal-Tech 4985 Pittsburgh Ave.	Erie	PA	16509	814-835-3000		196
TF: 877-547-9900 ■ *Web:* www.signal-tech.com						
Sign-A-Rama 2121 Vista Pkwy.	West Palm Beach	FL	33411	561-640-5570	640-5580	701
Web: www.signarama.com						
Signature Bank 565 Fifth Ave 12th Fl	New York	NY	10017	646-822-1500		70
NASDAQ: SBNY ■ *TF:* 866-744-5463 ■ *Web:* www.signatureny.com						
Signature Breads Inc 100 Justin Dr.	Chelsea	MA	02150	888-602-6533		296-1
TF: 888-602-6533 ■ *Web:* www.signaturebreads.com						
Signature Capital LLC						
100 Commercial St.	Portland	ME	04101	207-887-1517		792
Web: www.signaturecapital.com						
Signature Control Systems Inc						
738 E Main St.	Ravenna	OH	44266	720-641-1131		201
Web: www.signaturecontrol.com						
Signature Custom Cabinetry Inc						
434 Springville Rd	Ephrata	PA	17522	717-738-4884		115
Web: www.signaturecab.com						
Signature Estate & Investment Advisors LLC (SEIA)						
2121 Avenue of the Stars Ste 1600	Los Angeles	CA	90067	310-712-2323	712-2345	401
TF: 800-723-5115 ■ *Web:* www.seia.com						
Signature Flight Support						
201 S Orange Ave Ste 1100-S	Orlando	FL	32801	407-648-7200		63
Web: www.signatureflight.com						
Signature Graphics Inc						
1000 Signature Dr	Porter	IN	46304	219-926-4994	926-7231	344
TF: 800-356-3235 ■ *Web:* signaturegraphicsinc.com						
Signature Hardware						
2700 Crescent Spring Pk	Erlanger	KY	41017	866-855-2284	431-4012*	350
**Fax Area Code:* 859 ■ *TF:* 866-855-2284 ■ *Web:* www.signaturehardware.com						
Signature Health Care LLC						
12201 Bluegrass Pkwy	Louisville	KY	40299	502-568-7800		450
Web: www.ltcrevolution.com						
Signature Homes						
4670 Willow Rd Ste 200	Pleasanton	CA	94588	925-463-1122	463-0832	656
Web: sighomes.com						
Signature Housewares Inc						
671 Via Alondra Ste 801	Camarillo	CA	93012	805-484-6666	987-6637	361
Web: www.sighouse.com						
Signature Inc 5115 Parkcenter Ave	Dublin	OH	43017	614-766-5101		194
TF: 800-398-0518 ■ *Web:* www.signatureworldwide.com						
Signature Kitchen & Bath Desig						
1471 S De Anza Blvd	Cupertino	CA	95014	408-252-8011		362
Web: sigkb.com						
Signature Press 11508 Green Rd	Wilton	CA	95693	800-305-7942	939-1960*	637-2
**Fax Area Code:* 916 ■ *TF:* 800-305-7942 ■ *Web:* www.signaturepress.com						
Signature Print Services						
825a S 5th St	San Jose	CA	95112	408-213-3393	213-3399	393
Web: www.signatureprint.com						
Signature Printing Inc						
5 Almeida Ave.	East Providence	RI	02914	401-438-1200		627
Web: www.signatureprinters.com						
Signature Resources Inc						
1620 SW Magazine Rd Ste A	Ankeny	IA	50023	515-963-1040		652
Web: iowac21.com						
Signature Services Corp 2705 Hawes Ave	Dallas	TX	75235	214-353-2661		299
TF: 800-929-5519 ■ *Web:* www.signatureservices.com						
Signature Theatre 4200 Campbell Ave.	Arlington	VA	22206	703-820-9771	820-7790	573-4
Web: www.sigtheatre.org						
Signatures 220 Bloor St W.	Toronto	ON	M5S1T8	416-960-5200	960-8269	671
Web: www.toronto.intercontinental.com						
Signcraft Screenprint Inc						
100 A J Harle Dr.	Galena	IL	61036	815-777-3030		687
TF: 800-733-5150 ■ *Web:* www.signcraftinc.com						

Phone Fax Class

Signe's Bakery & Cafe
93 Arrow Rd ... Hilton Head Island SC 29928 843-785-9118 785-6144 671
TF: 866-807-4463 ■ *Web:* www.signesbakery.com

Signet Armorlite 1001 Armorlite Dr ... San Marcos CA 92069 760-481-3360 542
Web: www.signetarmorlite.com

Signet Inc 1801 Shelby Oaks Dr Ste 12 ... Memphis TN 38134 800-654-3889 387-5544* 195
**Fax Area Code:* 901 ■ *TF:* 800-654-3889 ■ *Web:* www.gosignet.com

Signet Marking Devices
3121 Red Hill Ave ... Costa Mesa CA 92626 800-421-5150 467
TF: 800-421-5150 ■ *Web:* www.signetmarking.com

Signia Capital Management LLC
111 N Post St Ste 301 ... Spokane WA 99201 509-789-8970 401
Web: www.signiacapital.com

Signiant Inc 152 Middlesex Tpke ... Burlington MA 01803 781-221-4000 177
Web: www.signiant.com

Signifi Solutions Inc
2100 Matheson Blvd E Ste 100 ... Mississauga ON L4W5E1 905-602-7707 177
TF: 877-744-6434 ■ *Web:* signifi.com

Signix Inc 1110 Market St Ste 402 ... Chattanooga TN 37402 877-890-5350 525
TF: 877-890-5350 ■ *Web:* www.signix.com

Signs by Tomorrow USA Inc
8681 Robert Fulton Dr ... Columbia MD 21046 410-312-3600 312-3520 701
TF: 800-765-7446 ■ *Web:* www.signsbytomorrow.com

Signs Now 5368 Dixie Hwy Ste 1 ... Waterford MI 48329 248-596-8600 596-8601 701
TF: 800-356-3373 ■ *Web:* www.signsnow.com

Signs of All Kinds LLC
227 Progress Dr ... Manchester CT 06042 860-649-1989 649-2256 9
TF: 800-214-4449 ■ *Web:* www.signsofallkinds.com

Signtech Electrical Adv Inc
4444 Federal Blvd ... San Diego CA 92102 619-527-6100 275-6115* 701
**Fax Area Code:* 866 ■ *TF:* 877-885-1135 ■ *Web:* www.signtech.com

Signtronix 1445 W Sepulveda Blvd ... Torrance CA 90501 800-729-4853 539-3554* 701
**Fax Area Code:* 310 ■ *TF:* 800-729-4853 ■ *Web:* www.signtronix.com

Signum Group LLC 1200 Stephenson Hwy ... Troy MI 48083 844-854-3282 463
TF: 844-854-3282 ■ *Web:* www.signumgroup.com

Sign-ups & Banners Corp
2764 W T C Jester Blvd ... Houston TX 77018 713-682-7979 627
TF: 877-682-7979 ■ *Web:* www.signupsandbanners.com

Siguler Guff & Company LLC
825 Third Ave 10th Fl ... New York NY 10022 212-332-5100 332-5120 792
Web: www.sigulerguff.com

SIHI (Strategic Investments & Holdings Inc)
4445 N A1A Ste 247 ... Vero Beach FL 32963 716-857-6000 857-6490 792
Web: www.sihi.net

SII Investments Inc
5555 W Grande Market Dr ... Appleton WI 54913 920-996-2600 775-8575* 690
**Fax Area Code:* 866 ■ *TF:* 800-426-5975 ■ *Web:* www.siionline.com

SIIA (Software & Information Industry Assn)
1090 Vermont Ave NW 6th Fl ... Washington DC 20005 202-289-7442 289-7097 48-9
Web: www.siia.net

SIIG Inc 6078 Stewart Ave ... Fremont CA 94538 510-657-8688 625
Web: www.siig.com

Sika Corp 201 Polito Ave ... Lyndhurst NJ 07071 201-933-8800 145
TF: 800-933-7452 ■ *Web:* usa.sika.com

Sikeston Career & Technology Ctr
200 Pine St ... Sikeston MO 63801 573-471-5442 472-8861 230
Web: www.ct.sikestonr6.org

Sikich LLP 1415 W Diehl Rd Ste 400 ... Naperville IL 60563 630-566-8400 566-8401 2
TF: 877-279-1900 ■ *Web:* www.sikich.com

Sikkema Jenkins & Co 530 W 22nd St ... New York NY 10011 212-929-2262 42
Web: www.sikkemajenkinsco.com

Siko Products Inc 2155 Bishop Cir E ... Dexter MI 48130 734-426-3476 426-3453 472
Web: www.siko-global.com

Sila Nanotechnologies
2450 Mariner Square Loop ... Alameda CA 94501 408-475-7452 49-13
Web: www.silanano.com

Silas Bronson Library (SBL)
267 Grand St ... Waterbury CT 06702 203-574-8222 574-8055 434-3
Web: www.bronsonlibrary.org

Silber & Davis LLC
1806 Old Okeechobee Rd ... West Palm Beach FL 33409 561-615-6262 615-6263 41
Web: silberdavis.com

Silberline Manufacturing Company Inc
130 Lincoln Dr PO Box B ... Tamaqua PA 18252 570-668-6050 668-0197 143
TF: 800-348-4824 ■ *Web:* www.silberline.com

Silberman Langner Assoc
6050 Santo Rd ... San Diego CA 92124 858-268-3330 2
Web: silbermanlangner.com

Silbrico Corp 6300 River Rd ... Hodgkins IL 60525 708-354-3350 354-6698 500
TF: 800-323-4287 ■ *Web:* www.silbrico.com

Silencerco LLC 5511 S 6055 W ... West Valley City UT 84118 801-417-5384 807
Web: silencerco.com

Silent Knight
7550 Meridian Cir Ste 100 ... Maple Grove MN 55369 763-493-6400 493-6475 283
TF: 800-328-0103 ■ *Web:* www.silentknight.com

Silent Solutions 8704 Lee Hwy Ste 300 ... Fairfax VA 22031 703-849-8246 809
Web: www.silentsolutions.com

Silestone 2245 Texas Dr Ste 600 ... Sugar Land TX 77479 281-494-7277 607
TF: 877-532-6394 ■ *Web:* www.silestoneusa.com

Silex Technology America Inc
167 W 7065 S Ste 330 ... Midvale UT 84047 801-748-1199 748-0730 396
TF: 866-765-8761 ■ *Web:* silextechnology.com

Silgan Containers Corp
21600 Oxnard St Ste 1600 ... Woodland Hills CA 91367 818-710-3700 593-6940 124
Web: www.silgancontainers.com

Silgan Holdings Inc
4 Landmark Sq Ste 400 ... Stamford CT 06901 203-975-7110 975-7902 124
NASDAQ: SLGN ■ *Web:* www.silganholdings.com

Silgan Plastics Corp
14515 N Outer Forty Ste 210 ... Chesterfield MO 63017 800-274-5426 469-5387* 98
**Fax Area Code:* 314 ■ *TF:* 800-274-5426 ■ *Web:* www.silganplastics.com

Silhouette Optical Ltd
260 Cannon St ... Green Island NY 12183 800-223-0180 542
TF: 800-223-0180 ■ *Web:* silhouettelab.com

Silicon Alley Group 1 Austin Ave 2nd Fl ... Iselin NJ 08830 732-326-1600 195
Web: www.sag-inc.com

Silicon Drafting Institute
1879 Lundy Ave Ste 189 ... San Jose CA 95131 408-828-2323 167-3
Web: www.silicondrafting.com

Silicon Laboratories Inc
400 W Cesar Chavez St ... Austin TX 78701 512-416-8500 416-9669 696
NASDAQ: SLAB ■ *TF:* 877-444-3032 ■ *Web:* www.silabs.com

Silicon Microstructures Inc
1701 Mccarthy Blvd ... Milpitas CA 95035 408-577-0100 696
Web: www.si-micro.com

Silicon Valley Association of Realtors
19400 Stevens Creek Blvd Ste 100 ... Cupertino CA 95014 408-200-0100 200-0101 652
TF: 877-699-6787 ■ *Web:* www.silvar.org

Silicon Valley Bank (SVB)
3003 Tasman Dr ... Santa Clara CA 95054 408-654-7400 70
Web: www.svb.com

Silicon Valley Staffing
2336 Harrison St ... Oakland CA 94612 480-730-1516 923-9313* 721
**Fax Area Code:* 510 ■ *TF:* 877-660-6000 ■ *Web:* www.svsjobs.com

Silicon Valley University
2160 Lundy Ave Ste 110 ... San Jose CA 95131 408-435-8989 166
Web: www.svuca.edu

Silicone Plastics Inc 97 W 300 S ... Millville UT 84326 435-753-7307 753-2207 604
Web: www.siliconeplastics.com

Silicone Solutions
338 Remington Rd ... Cuyahoga Falls OH 44224 330-920-3125 920-3126 192
Web: siliconesolutions.com

Silicone Specialties Inc
430 S Rockford Ave ... Tulsa OK 74120 918-587-5567 351
TF: 888-243-0672 ■ *Web:* www.ssicm.com

Silicones Inc 211 Woodbine St ... High Point NC 27261 336-886-5018 886-7122 493
Web: www.silicones-inc.com

Siliconix Inc 2201 Laurelwood Rd ... Santa Clara CA 95054 408-988-8000 567-8950 696
Web: www.vishay.com

Silipos Inc 7049 Williams Rd ... Niagara Falls NY 14304 716-283-0700 582
TF: 800-229-4404 ■ *Web:* www.silipos.com

Silitronics Inc 1957 Concourse Dr ... San Jose CA 95131 408-954-8301 253
Web: www.silitronics.com

Silk Flower Depot 5110 W Knox St ... Tampa FL 33634 813-889-9095 889-9176 361
Web: www.e-silkflowerdepot.com

Silk Purse Consignment Boutique
213 Rte 37 E ... Toms River NJ 08753 732-914-1414 637-9
Web: silkpurseconsignment.com

Silk Road Transport Inc
8781 State Rte 36 ... Arkport NY 14807 800-451-3879 780
TF: 800-451-3879 ■ *Web:* www.silkroadtrans.com

Silk Software Corp
15440 Laguna Canyon Rd Ste 210 ... Irvine CA 92618 949-748-3700 177
Web: www.silksoftware.com

Silke Communications Inc 680 Tyler St ... Eugene OR 97402 541-687-1611 179
Web: www.silkecom.com

Silko & Associates PC
80 Emerson Ln ... Bridgeville PA 15017 412-914-0144 41
Web: silkolaw.com

Silkroute Global 950 Stephenson Hwy ... Troy MI 48083 248-854-3409 180
Web: silkrouteglobal.com

Silkscreening by Classic Graphix
12152 Woodruff Ave ... Downey CA 90241 562-940-0806 258
Web: www.classicgraphix.com

Silktown Roofing Inc
27 Pleasant St ... Manchester CT 06040 860-647-0198 189-12
Web: www.silktownroofing.com

Silkworm Inc 102 S Sezmore Dr ... Murphysboro IL 62966 618-687-4077 687
TF: 800-826-0577 ■ *Web:* www.silkwormink.com

Silky O'sullivan's 183 Beale St ... Memphis TN 38103 901-522-9596 522-8462 671
Web: www.silkyosullivans.com

Sill Technical Assn
21 Edgewood Dr ... Mechanicsburg PA 17055 717-691-6730 260
Web: www.sillandassociates.com

Silliman Associates Incorporated Thomas
425 N Lee St ... Alexandria VA 22314 703-548-4100 463
TF: 800-454-5554 ■ *Web:* www.tsilliman.com

Sills Cummis & Gross PC
1 Riverfront Plz The Legal Ctr ... Newark NJ 07102 973-643-7000 428
Web: www.sillscummis.com

SILLY STRING Products PO Box 719 ... Watertown NY 13601 315-788-3431 788-7467 145
Web: www.silly-string.com

Silo 1604 1133 Austin Hwy ... San Antonio TX 78209 210-824-8686 671
Web: siloelevatedcuisine.com

Silo Cooking School 44 Upland Rd ... New Milford CT 06776 860-355-0300 685
Web: www.hunthillfarmtrust.org

Siloam Springs State Park
938 E 3003rd Ln ... Clayton IL 62324 217-894-6205 565
Web: www.dnr.illinois.gov

SilTerra USA Inc
2880 Zanker Rd Ste 203 ... San Jose CA 95134 408-530-0888 530-0877 696
Web: www.silterra.com

Siltronic Corp 7200 NW Front Ave ... Portland OR 97210 503-243-2020 564-3219* 696
**Fax Area Code:* 898 ■ *Web:* www.siltronic.com

SiltShield LLC
6220 18 1/2 Mile Rd ... Sterling Heights MI 48314 586-731-5577 731-1148 189-11
Web: www.siltshield.com

Silva International Inc 523 N Ash St ... Momence IL 60954 815-472-3535 345
Web: silva-intl.com

Silvaco Inc
4701 Patrick Henry Dr Bldg 2 ... Santa Clara CA 95054 408-567-1000 225
Web: www.silvaco.com

Silvan Ridge/Hinman Vineyards
27012 Briggs Hill Rd ... Eugene OR 97405 541-345-1945 50-7
Web: silvanridge.com

Silvanus Products
40 Merchant St ... Sainte Genevieve MO 63670 800-822-2788 596
TF: 800-822-2788 ■ *Web:* www.silvanusproducts.com

Silvas Oil Company Inc
3217 E Lorena Ave ... Fresno CA 93725 559-233-5171 589-2883* 579
**Fax Area Code:* 661 ■ *Web:* www.silvasoil.com

Silver & Archibald LLP
997 S Milledge Ave ... Athens GA 30605 706-548-8122 428
TF: 877-526-6281 ■ *Web:* silverandarchibald.com

Silver Airways Corp
1100 Lee Wagener Blvd Ste 201 ... Fort Lauderdale FL 33315 801-401-9100 25
TF: 844-674-5837 ■ *Web:* www.silverairways.com

Name / Address	City	State	Zip	Phone	Fax	Class
Silver Bullet Technology Inc 25 W Cedar St Ste 440 *Web:* sbullet.com	Pensacola	FL	32502	850-437-5880		179
Silver City-Grant County Chamber of Commerce 201 N Hudson St *TF:* 800-548-9378 ■ *Web:* www.silvercity.org	Silver City	NM	88061	575-534-1700		139
Silver Cloud Hotel Seattle Broadway 1100 Broadway *TF:* 800-590-1801 ■ *Web:* www.silvercloud.com	Seattle	WA	98122	206-325-1400	324-1995	379
Silver Cos 1001 E Telecom Dr *Web:* www.silvercompanies.com	Boca Raton	FL	33431	561-981-5252		528
Silver Creative Group 50 Washington St 7th Fl *Web:* silvercreativegroup.com	Norwalk	CT	06854	203-855-7705		7
Silver Creek Financial ServicesInc 175 Hwy 82 *TF:* 866-569-0020 ■ *Web:* www.silvercreekteam.com	Lostine	OR	97857	541-569-2272		734
Silver Creek Industries Inc 2830 Barrett Ave *Web:* silver-creek.net	Perris	CA	92571	951-943-5393		189-14
Silver Creek Specialty Meats Inc 153 W 28th Ave *Web:* www.silvercreekspecialtymeats.com	Oshkosh	WI	54902	920-232-3581		296-26
Silver Diner Development LLC 12276 Rockville Pk *TF:* 866-561-0518 ■ *Web:* silverdiner.com	Rockville	MD	20852	301-770-0333	770-2832	670
Silver Dragon Restaurant 106 Third Ave SE *Web:* www.silverdragoncalgary.ca	Calgary	AB	T2G0B6	403-264-5326		671
Silver Eagle Distributors LP 7777 Washington Ave *TF:* 855-332-2110 ■ *Web:* silvereagle.com	Houston	TX	77007	713-869-4361	867-8112	81-1
Silver Eagle Manufacturing Company Inc 5825 NE Skyport Way *Web:* silvereaglemfg.com	Portland	OR	97218	503-281-0727		247
Silver Edge Co-op 39999 Hilton Rd *TF:* 800-632-5953 ■ *Web:* www.silveredgecoop.com	Edgewood	IA	52042	563-928-6419		276
Silver Engineering Inc 255 East Dr Ste A *Web:* silvereng.com	Melbourne	FL	32904	321-676-7596		261
Silver Eye Center for Photography 1015 E Carson St *Web:* www.silvereye.org	Pittsburgh	PA	15203	412-431-1810	431-5777	50-2
Silver Falls State Park 20024 Silver Falls Hwy SE *Web:* oregonstateparks.org	Sublimity	OR	97385	503-873-8681		565
Silver Fox Restaurant & Lounge 3422 S Energy Ln *Web:* www.silverfoxcasper.com	Casper	WY	82604	307-235-3000		671
Silver Fox Steakhouse 1651 S University Dr *Web:* www.silverfoxcafe.com	Fort Worth	TX	76107	817-332-9060		671
Silver Fox Tours & Motorcoaches 3 Silver Fox Dr *TF:* 800-342-5998 ■ *Web:* www.silverfoxcoach.com	Millbury	MA	01527	508-865-6000	865-4660	760
Silver Freedman Taff & Tiernan LLP 3299 K St NW Ste 100 *Web:* sfttlaw.com	Washington	DC	20007	202-295-4500	337-5502	734
Silver Golub & Teitell LLP 184 Atlantic St *TF:* 866-248-8744 ■ *Web:* www.sgtlaw.com	Stamford	CT	06901	203-325-4491	325-3769	428
Silver Heights Capital Management Inc 333 Bay St Ste 1140 *Web:* silverheights.com	Toronto	ON	M5H2R2	416-342-5626		528
Silver Institute, The 1400 I St NW Ste 550 *Web:* www.silverinstitute.org	Washington	DC	20005	202-835-0185		49-4
Silver King Refrigeration Inc 1600 Xenium Ln N *TF:* 800-328-3329 ■ *Web:* www.silverking.com	Minneapolis	MN	55441	763-923-2441		664
Silver Lake College 2406 S Alverno Rd *TF:* 800-236-4752 ■ *Web:* www.sl.edu	Manitowoc	WI	54220	920-686-6175	684-7082	166
Silver Lake Resort Ltd 7751 Black Lake Rd *TF:* 800-226-6090 ■ *Web:* silverlakeresort.com	Kissimmee	FL	34747	407-397-2828		378
Silver Lake State Park 138 Silver Lake Rd *Web:* www.nhstateparks.org	Hollis	NH	03049	603-465-2342		565
Silver Lake Technology Management LLC 2775 Sand Hill Rd Ste 100 *Web:* www.silverlake.com	Menlo Park	CA	94025	650-233-8120	233-8125	401
Silver Legacy Resort & Casino 407 N Virginia St *TF:* 800-687-8733 ■ *Web:* www.silverlegacyreno.com	Reno	NV	89501	775-325-7401	325-7474	133
Silver Lerner Schwartz Fertel 8707 N Skokie Blvd Ste 400 *Web:* www.slsf.com	Skokie	IL	60077	847-779-6200		734
Silver Lightning Home Health Care LLC 2880 W Oakland Park Blvd Ste 221 *Web:* www.silverlightninghhc.com	Oakland Park	FL	33311	954-677-2220	677-2272	363
Silver Oaks Communications 824 17th St *Web:* silveroaks.com	Moline	IL	61265	309-797-9898		344
Silver Oven Studios Inc 953 Islington St *Web:* www.silveroven.com	Portsmouth	NH	03801	603-570-7300	431-7844	177
Silver Palate 211 Knickerbocker Rd *Web:* silverpalate.com	Dumont	NJ	07628	201-568-0110		296-41
Silver Reef Casino 4876 Haxton Way *TF:* 866-383-0777 ■ *Web:* www.silverreefcasino.com	Ferndale	WA	98248	360-383-0777		132
Silver Research Consortium (SRC) 2525 Meridian Pkwy Ste 100 *Web:* www.ilzro.org	Durham	NC	27713	919-361-4647	361-1957	49-19
Silver River State Park 1425 NE 58th Ave *Web:* www.floridastateparks.org	Ocala	FL	34470	352-236-7148		565
Silver Saddle Ranch & Club Inc 20751 Aristotle Dr *TF:* 888-430-8728 ■ *Web:* silversaddleranch.life	California City	CA	93505	760-373-8617		653
Silver Smith Hotel & Suites 10 S Wabash Ave *TF:* 800-979-0084 ■ *Web:* www.silversmithchicagohotel.com	Chicago	IL	60603	312-372-7696	372-7320	379
Silver Springs Bottled Water Company Inc PO Box 926 *TF:* 800-556-0334 ■ *Web:* www.ssbwc.com	Silver Springs	FL	34489	800-556-0334		297-11
Silver Springs Citrus Inc 3810 SE 11th Pl *Web:* silverspringscitrus.com	Howey in the Hills	FL	34737	352-324-2101		315-2
Silver Springs Farminc 640 Meetinghouse Rd *Web:* www.silverspringsfarminc.com	Harleysville	PA	19438	215-256-4321		473
Silver Springs State Fish & Wildlife Area 13608 Fox Rd *Web:* www.dnr.illinois.gov	Yorkville	IL	60560	630-553-6297		565
Silver Springs State Park 5656 E Silver Springs Blvd *Web:* www.floridastateparks.org	Silver Springs	FL	34488	352-261-5840		32
Silver Springs-Martin Luther School 512 W Township Line Rd *Web:* www.silver-springs.org	Plymouth Meeting	PA	19462	610-825-4440		685
Silver Spur Corp 16010 Shoemaker Ave *Web:* www.silverspurcorp.com	Cerritos	CA	90703	562-921-6880		238
Silver Star Cadillac 3601 Auto Mall Dr *TF:* 877-813-1334 ■ *Web:* www.silverstarcadillac.com	Thousand Oaks	CA	91362	805-267-3200		57
Silver Star Communications 570 S Washington St *TF:* 877-883-2411 ■ *Web:* www.silverstar.com	Afton	WY	83110	307-883-2411	883-2575	224
Silver Star Meats Inc 1720 Middletown Rd *TF:* 800-548-1321 ■ *Web:* silverstarmeats.com	McKees Rocks	PA	15136	412-777-4460	771-0568	296-26
Silver State Inc 1010 W 2610 S *TF:* 800-473-5777 ■ *Web:* www.silverstatetextiles.com	Salt Lake City	UT	84119	801-972-6770	972-5005	745-3
Silver State Industries 3955 W Russell Rd *Web:* silverstatecu.com	Las Vegas	NV	89118	702-486-6491	486-9908	630
Silver State Materials LLC 4025 W Nevso Dr Ste 2	Las Vegas	NV	89103	702-650-5000		183
Silver State Post PO Box 111 *Web:* www.sspmt.com	Deer Lodge	MT	59722	406-846-2424		532-2
Silver Strand State Beach 5000 Hwy 75 *Web:* www.parks.ca.gov	Coronado	CA	92118	619-435-5184		565
Silver Strong & Assoc 3 Tice Rd **Fax Area Code: 201* ■ *TF:* 800-962-4432 ■ *Web:* thoughtfulclassroom.com	Franklin Lakes	NJ	07417	800-962-4432	652-1127*	244
Silver Sun Wholesale Inc 116 San Felipe St NW (Old Town) *TF:* 800-662-3220 ■ *Web:* www.silversunalbuquerque.com	Albuquerque	NM	87104	505-246-9692		411
Silver Terrace Nurseries Inc 501 N St	Pescadero	CA	94060	650-879-2110		369
Silver Towne LP 120 E Union City Pk PO Box 424 *TF:* 800-788-7481 ■ *Web:* www.silvertowne.com	Winchester	IN	47394	765-584-7481	584-1246	327
Silverado Cable Co 1840 W First Ave *Web:* www.silveradocable.com	Mesa	AZ	85202	480-655-8751		116
Silverado Resort & Spa 1600 Atlas Peak Rd *TF:* 800-532-0500 ■ *Web:* www.silveradoresort.com	Napa	CA	94558	707-257-0200		669
SilverBirch Hotels & Resorts 1640 - 1188 W Georgia St *TF:* 800-431-0070 ■ *Web:* www.silverbirchhotels.com	Vancouver	BC	V6E4A2	604-646-2447	646-2404	379
Silverblatt & Assoc 15 Public Sq Ste 506 *Web:* silverblattandassociates.com	Wilkes-Barre	PA	18701	570-820-9800		41
Silverchair Science + Communications LLC 316 E Main St Ste 300 *Web:* www.silverchair.com	Charlottesville	VA	22902	434-296-6333	220-8080	637-9
Silvercrest Asset Management Group LLC 1330 Avenue of the Americas 38th Fl *Web:* www.silvercrestgroup.com	New York	NY	10019	212-649-0600		401
Silvercup Studios 3402 Starr Ave *Web:* www.silvercupstudios.com	Long Island City	NY	11101	718-906-3000		657
Silverdale Beach Hotel 3073 NW Bucklin Hill Rd *TF:* 800-544-9799 ■ *Web:* www.silverdalebeachhotel.com	Silverdale	WA	98383	360-698-1000	692-0932	379
Silverhawk Aviation Inc 1751 W Kearney Ave *TF:* 800-479-5851 ■ *Web:* silverhawkaviation.com	Lincoln	NE	68524	402-475-8600		63
Silverleaf Resorts Inc 1221 Riverbend Dr Ste 120 *TF:* 800-544-8468 ■ *Web:* www.silverleafresorts.com	Dallas	TX	75247	214-631-1166	689-8671	753
Silver-Line Plastics 900 Riverside Dr *TF:* 800-438-9020 ■ *Web:* www.slpipe.com	Asheville	NC	28804	828-252-8755	252-9934	596
Silverman & Light Inc 1201 Park Ave Ste 100 *Web:* www.silvermanlight.com	Emeryville	CA	94608	510-655-1200	655-1344	261
Silverman McGovern Staffing & Recruiting 284 W Exchange St *Web:* silvermanmcgovern.com	Providence	RI	02903	401-632-0580		260
Silvermine Arts Ctr 1037 Silvermine Rd *Web:* www.silvermineart.org	New Canaan	CT	06840	203-966-9700	966-2763	50-2
Silveron Industries Inc 182 S Brent Cir *Web:* www.silveron.co.kr	City of Industry	CA	91789	909-598-4533	594-9234	203
SilverRail Technologies Inc 300 Trade Ctr Ste 6700 *Web:* silverrailtech.com	Woburn	MA	01801	617-934-6786		387
SilverSky 1155 Kelly Johnson Blvd Ste 305 *TF:* 800-653-0179 ■ *Web:* www.usa.net	Colorado Springs	CO	80920	719-265-2930		180
SilverSun Technologies Inc 5 Regent St Ste 520 *TF:* 877-979-5462 ■ *Web:* www.silversuntech.com	Livingston	NJ	07039	973-758-6108		787

Company	City	State	Zip	Phone	Fax	Class
SilverTech Inc 196 Bridge St *Web:* www.silvertech.com	Manchester	NH	03104	603-669-6600		195
Silvertip Inc 600 St Mary St *Web:* www.silvertip-inc.com	Lewisburg	PA	17837	570-523-1206	523-1484	189-10
Silverton Hotel & Casino 9620 Las Vegas Blvd S Ste E9 *TF:* 866-722-4608 ■ *Web:* silvertoncasino.com	Las Vegas	NV	89139	702-263-7777		133
SilverTribe PO Box 481 *TF:* 888-659-2227 ■ *Web:* www.silvertribe.com	Scottsdale	AZ	85252	888-659-2227		411
Silverwood Partners LLC Silverwood Farm Pl 32 Pleasant St *Web:* silverwoodpartners.com	Sherborn	MA	01770	508-651-2194		690
Silvestri Studio Inc 8125 Beach St *TF:* 800-647-8874 ■ *Web:* www.silvestricalifornia.com	Los Angeles	CA	90001	323-277-4420		464
Silvi Concrete Products Inc 355 Newbold Rd *TF:* 800-426-6273 ■ *Web:* www.silvi.com	Fairless Hills	PA	19030	215-295-0777		182
Silvon Software Inc 900 Oakmont Ln Ste 400 *TF:* 800-874-5866 ■ *Web:* www.silvon.com	Westmont	IL	60559	630-655-3313	655-3377	178-1
Silynx Communications Inc 9901 Belward Campus Dr Ste 150 *Web:* www.silynxcom.com	Rockville	MD	20850	301-217-9223		647
SIM (Society for Information Management) 1120 Rte 73 Ste 200 **Fax Area Code:* 856 ■ *TF:* 800-387-9746 ■ *Web:* www.simnet.org	Mount Laurel	NJ	08054	312-527-6734	439-0525*	48-9
Sim USA Inc PO Box 7900 *TF:* 800-521-6449 ■ *Web:* www.simusa.org	Charlotte	NC	28241	800-521-6449		48-20
Sima Financial Group Inc 6802 Paragon Pl Ste 440 *Web:* simafinancialgroup.com	Richmond	VA	23230	804-285-5700		2
Sima Products 125 Commerce Dr *Web:* www.simaproducts.com	Hauppauge	NY	11788	631-435-0200		52
Simacor LLC 10700 Hwy 55 Ste 170 *TF:* 888-284-4415 ■ *Web:* www.simacor.com	Plymouth	MN	55441	763-544-4415		180
Simantel Group 321 SW Water St *Web:* www.simantel.com	Peoria	IL	61602	309-674-7747		7
Simard 1212 32nd Ave *TF:* 888-282-9321 ■ *Web:* www.simard.ca	Lachine	QC	H8T3K7	905-670-2005		393
Simark Controls Ltd 10509 46 St SE *TF:* 800-565-7431 ■ *Web:* www.simarkcontrols.com	Calgary	AB	T2C5C2	403-236-0580		358
Simasko, Simasko & Simasko Pc 319 N Gratiot *Web:* simaskolaw.com	Mount Clemens	MI	48043	586-468-6793		41
Simba Information 6116 Executive Blvd Ste 550 **Fax Area Code:* 240 ■ *Web:* www.simbainformation.com	Rockville	MD	20852	888-297-4622	747-3004*	6
Simba Technologies Inc 938 W Eigth Ave *Web:* www.simba.com	Vancouver	BC	V5Z1E5	604-633-0008		177
Simbex LLC 10 Water St Ste 410 *Web:* simbex.com	Lebanon	NH	03766	603-448-2367		476
Simbionix USA Corp 5381 S Alkire Cir *Web:* simbionix.com	Littleton	CO	80127	720-643-1001		475
Simco Drilling Equipment Inc PO Box 448 *TF:* 800-338-9925 ■ *Web:* simcodrill.com	Osceola	IA	50213	641-342-2166	342-6764	190
Simco Electronics 3131 Jay St *TF:* 866-299-6029 ■ *Web:* www.simco.com	Santa Clara	CA	95054	408-734-9750	734-9780	743
Simco Leather Corp 99 Pleasant Ave *Web:* simcoleather.com	Johnstown	NY	12095	518-762-7100		432
Simco Sales Service of Pennsylvania Inc 101 Commerce Dr *Web:* www.jjicc.com	Moorestown	NJ	08057	856-813-2300		297-4
Simcoe & District Chamber of Commerce 10 Argyle St *Web:* www.simcoechamber.on.ca	Simcoe	ON	N3Y1V5	519-426-5867	428-7718	137
Simcoe Parts Service Inc 6795 Industrial Pkwy *Web:* www.simcoeparts.com	Alliston	ON	L9R1W1	705-435-7814		311
Simcrest Inc 1914 Skillman St Ste 110-319 *Web:* www.simcrest.com	Dallas	TX	75206	214-644-4000		177
Simek's Inc 940 Hastings Ave *TF:* 877-874-6357 ■ *Web:* www.simeks.com	Saint Paul Park	MN	55071	651-459-5578		345
Simen, Figura & Parker PLC 5206 Gateway Centre *Web:* sfplaw.com	Flint	MI	48507	810-235-9000		41
Simeri's Old Town Tap 1505 W Indiana Ave *Web:* simerisoldtowntap.weebly.com	South Bend	IN	46613	574-289-1361		671
Simetri Inc 7005 University Blvd *Web:* simetri.us	Winter Park	FL	32792	321-972-9980		177
Simflo Pumps Inc 754 E Maley St *Web:* simflo.com	Willcox	AZ	85644	520-384-2273	384-4042	641
Simi Valley Chamber of Commerce 40 W Cochran St Ste 100 *Web:* www.simivalleychamber.org	Simi Valley	CA	93065	805-526-3900	526-6234	139
Simi Valley Historical Society Strathearn Historical Pk 137 Strathearn Pl *Web:* www.simihistory.com	Simi Valley	CA	93065	805-526-6453		49-19
Simione Healthcare Consultants LLC 4130 Whitney Ave *Web:* www.simione.com	Hamden	CT	06518	203-287-9288		463
Simkar Corp 700 Ramona Ave *TF:* 800-523-3602 ■ *Web:* www.simkar.com	Philadelphia	PA	19120	215-831-7700	831-7703	439
Simmons Bank Arena 1 Verizon Arena Way *Web:* simmonsbankarena.com	North Little Rock	AR	72114	501-340-5660		720
Simmons Co 1 Concourse Pkwy Ste 800 *Web:* www.simmons.com	Atlanta	GA	30328	770-206-2750	613-8575	471
Simmons College 300 The Fenway *TF:* 800-345-8468 ■ *Web:* www.simmons.edu	Boston	MA	02115	617-521-2000	521-3190	166
Simmons Farm Raised Catfish Inc 2628 Erickson Rd *Web:* www.simmonscatfish.com	Yazoo City	MS	39194	662-746-5687	746-8625	296-14
Simmons First National Corp 501 S Main St PO Box 7009 *NASDAQ: SFNC* ■ *Web:* simmonsbank.com	Pine Bluff	AR	71601	817-298-5600		360-2
Simmons Foods Inc 601 N Hico St *Web:* simmonsfoods.com	Siloam Springs	AR	72761	479-524-8151		619
Simmons Hanly Conroy LLC 230 W Monroe Ste 2221 *TF:* 877-438-6610 ■ *Web:* www.simmonsfirm.com	Chicago	IL	60606	877-438-6610		445
Simmons Investigative & Security Agency Inc 76 S Winter Park Dr *Web:* www.simmonssecurity.com	Casselberry	FL	32707	407-699-5308		693
Simmons Knife & Saw 400 Regency Dr **Fax Area Code:* 630 ■ *TF:* 800-252-3381 ■ *Web:* simcut.com	Glendale Heights	IL	60139	800-252-3381	912-2890*	261
Simmons Machine Tool Corp 1700 N Broadway *Web:* smtgroup.com	Albany	NY	12204	518-462-5431	462-0371	455
Simmons Perrine Moyer Bergman PLC 115 Third St SE Ste 1200 *Web:* www.spmblaw.com	Cedar Rapids	IA	52401	319-366-7641		428
Simmons Scientific Products PO Box 10057 *Web:* www.simmonsscientificproducts.com	Wilmington	NC	28404	910-686-1656		472
Simmons-Boardman Books Inc 1809 Capitol Ave *TF:* 800-228-9670 ■ *Web:* www.transalert.com	Omaha	NE	68102	402-346-4300	346-1783	637-2
Simmons-Boardman Publishing Corp 55 Broad St 26th Fl *TF:* 800-257-5091 ■ *Web:* www.simmonsboardman.com	New York	NY	10004	212-620-7200	633-1165	637-9
Simmons-rockwell Inc 784 County Rd 64 *TF:* 888-520-2213 ■ *Web:* www.simmons-rockwell.com	Elmira	NY	14903	607-796-5555		57
Simms Fishing Products Corp 101 Evergreen Dr *TF:* 800-217-4667 ■ *Web:* www.simmsfishing.com	Bozeman	MT	59715	406-585-3557	585-3562	710
Simon & Arrington Inc 11825 Via Cassina Ct *Web:* www.s-a.us	Miromar Lakes	FL	33913	305-718-0630		525
Simon & Associates Inc 3200 Commerce St *TF:* 800-763-4234 ■ *Web:* simonassoc.com	Blacksburg	VA	24060	540-951-4234		261
Simon & Geherin PLLC 1310 S Main St Ste 11 *Web:* www.simongeherin.com	Ann Arbor	MI	48104	734-997-0870		428
Simon & Seafort's Saloon & Grill 420 L St *Web:* simonandseaforts.com	Anchorage	AK	99501	907-274-3502		671
Simon Consulting LLC 3200 N Central Ave Ste 2460 *Web:* simonconsulting.net	Phoenix	AZ	85012	602-279-7500	279-7510	196
Simon Foundation for Incontinence PO Box 815 *Web:* simonfoundation.org	Wilmette	IL	60091	847-864-3913	864-9758	48-17
Simon Fraser University *Harbour Centre* 515 W Hastings St *Web:* www.sfu.ca	Vancouver	BC	V6B5K3	778-782-5029		785
Simon G. Jewelry Inc 528 State St *Web:* www.simongjewelry.com	Glendale	CA	91203	818-500-9697		410
Simon Group Inc, The 1506 Old Bethlehem Pk *Web:* www.simongroup.com	Sellersville	PA	18960	215-453-8700		4
Simon Hegele Healthcare Solutions LLC 1001 Mittel Dr *Web:* www.simonhegele.com	Wood Dale	IL	60191	847-690-0430		475
Simon Law Group PC 720 Olive St Ste 1720 *Web:* simongrouppc.com	Saint Louis	MO	63101	314-621-2828	621-4646	41
Simon Lever & Co 147 W Airport Rd *Web:* www.simonlever.com	Lititz	PA	17543	717-569-7081		2
Simon Printing Co 10810 Craighead Dr *Web:* www.simonprinting.com	Houston	TX	77025	713-666-1296	666-4111	627
Simon Property Group Inc 225 W Washington St *NYSE: SPG* ■ *Web:* www.simon.com	Indianapolis	IN	46204	317-636-1600		655
Simon Roofing & Sheet Metal Corp 4654 Kenny Rd *TF:* 800-523-7714 ■ *Web:* simonroofing.com	Youngstown	OH	44512	330-629-7663	629-7399	46
Simon's Rock College of Bard 84 Alford Rd *Web:* simons-rock.edu	Great Barrington	MA	01230	413-644-4400		166
Simoncomputing Inc 5350 Shawnee Rd Ste 200 *Web:* simoncomputing.com	Alexandria	VA	22312	703-914-5454	914-1133	177
Simondavis Inc 730 17th St Ste 107 *Web:* simon-davis.com	Denver	CO	80202	303-837-1119		390
Simonds Inc 248 Elm St *Web:* www.simonds-inc.com	Southbridge	MA	01550	508-764-3235	765-5125	759
Simonds Intl 135 Intervale Rd *TF:* 800-343-1616 ■ *Web:* www.simondsint.com	Fitchburg	MA	01420	800-343-1616	541-6224	682
Simonian Fruit Co 511 N Seventh St PO Box 340 *Web:* simonianfruit.com	Fowler	CA	93625	559-834-5921	834-1580	297-7
Simonini Homes 501 E Morehead Ste 4 *Web:* simonini.com	Charlotte	NC	28202	704-333-8999	896-3630	187
Simoniz Car Wash 435 Eastern Ave *Web:* www.washdepot.com	Malden	MA	02148	781-321-1900		62-1
Simoniz USA 201 Boston Tpke **Fax Area Code:* 860 ■ *TF:* 800-227-5536 ■ *Web:* www.simoniz.com	Bolton	CT	06043	800-227-5536	645-6070*	151
Simonmed Imaging 6900 E Camelback Rd Ste 700 *TF:* 866-614-8555 ■ *Web:* www.simonmed.com	Scottsdale	AZ	85251	480-614-8555		415
Simons Bitzer & Associates PC 8350 S Emerson Ave Ste 100 *Web:* simonsbitzer.com	Indianapolis	IN	46237	317-782-3070		2
Simons Trucking Inc 920 Simon Dr PO Box 8 *TF:* 800-373-2580 ■ *Web:* www.simonstrucking.com	Farley	IA	52046	563-744-3304	744-3726	780
Simonsen Industries Inc 500 Iowa 31 *TF:* 800-831-4860 ■ *Web:* www.simonsen-industries.com	Quimby	IA	51049	712-445-2211	445-2626	273

Company / Address	City	State	ZIP	Phone	Fax	Class
Simonsen Laboratories Inc 1180-C Day Rd *Web:* www.simlab.com	Gilroy	CA	95020	408-847-2002	847-4176	11-2
Simonson Properties Co 535 First St NE *TF:* 888-843-8789 ■ *Web:* www.simonson-lumber.com	Saint Cloud	MN	56304	320-252-9385		364
Simonton Court Historic Inn & Cottages 320 Simonton St *TF:* 800-944-2687 ■ *Web:* www.simontoncourt.com	Key West	FL	33040	800-944-2687		379
Simonton Windows Inc 5020 Weston Pkwy Ste 400 *TF:* 800-746-6686 ■ *Web:* www.simonton.com	Cary	NC	27513	800-746-6686		608
SimPak International LLC 2107 Production Dr *Web:* simpakinternational.com	Louisville	KY	40299	502-671-8250		601
Simpay 1210 Northbrook Dr *TF:* 866-253-2227 ■ *Web:* www.alphacardservices.com	Feasterville-Trevose	PA	19053	866-253-2227	289-6600	251
SimPhonics Inc 3226 N Falkenburg Rd *Web:* www.simphonics.com	Tampa	FL	33619	813-623-9917		703
Simple Computer Repair 1000 N Green Valley Pkwy *Web:* simplecomputerrepair.com	Henderson	NV	89074	702-483-5464		196
Simple Practice 11801 Mississippi Ave 2nd Fl *TF:* 800-559-6087 ■ *Web:* www.simplepractice.com	Los Angeles	CA	90025	800-559-6087		39
Simple Siphon PLUS 684 Divide So Dr *Web:* www.simplesiphon.com	Divide	CO	80814	719-687-0928		612
Simple Verity Inc 1218 3rd Ave **Fax Area Code:* 206 ■ *TF:* 855-583-7489 ■ *Web:* www.simpleverity.com	Seattle	WA	98101	617-905-7467	512-3480*	393
Simplegrid Technology Inc 40 Baldwin Rd *Web:* www.simplegrid.com	Parsippany	NJ	07054	973-265-2838		393
Simpler Gifts Press 1050 Rosecrans St Ste D *TF:* 800-688-1209 ■ *Web:* www.simplergifts.com	San Diego	CA	92106	619-226-7393	226-2988	637-2
SimpleSignal Inc 34232 Pacific Coast Hwy *TF:* 866-434-4404 ■ *Web:* www.simplesignal.com	Dana Point	CA	92629	866-434-4404		224
Simplesoft Inc 257 Castro St Ste 220 *Web:* www.smplsft.com	Mountain View	CA	94041	650-965-4515		177
SimpleSolve Inc 33 Airport Center Dr Ste 104 *Web:* www.simplesolve.com	Princeton	NJ	08540	609-452-2323		809
SimpleTuition Inc 268 Summer St Ste 502 *Web:* www.simpletuition.com	Boston	MA	02210	617-747-2222	630-1104	509
Simplex Diam Inc 50 W 47th St Ste 20N *Web:* simplexdiam.com	New York	NY	10036	212-883-0888		411
Simplex Engine & Machine Inc 1011 Westminster St *Web:* www.simplexengine.com	Providence	RI	02903	401-331-3500	331-4130	62-7
Simplex Equipment Rental 9740 Boul de l'Acadie *Web:* www.simplex.ca	Montreal	QC	H4N1L8	514-331-7777		23
Simplex Homes 1 Simplex Dr *Web:* www.simplexind.com	Scranton	PA	18504	570-346-5113		106
Simplex Inc 5300 Rising Moon Rd **Fax Area Code:* 217 ■ *TF:* 800-637-8603 ■ *Web:* www.simplexdirect.com	Springfield	IL	62711	800-637-8603	483-1616*	253
Simplex Manufacturing Co 13340 NE Whitaker Way *Web:* simplex.aero	Portland	OR	97230	503-257-3511		22
Simpli 1437 E Ft Ave *TF:* 800-931-1702 ■ *Web:* simpliengage.com	Baltimore	MD	21230	410-727-4569	727-2436	260
Simplicity Consulting Inc 6710 108th Ave NE Ste 354 *TF:* 888-252-0385 ■ *Web:* www.simplicityci.com	Kirkland	WA	98033	888-252-0385		196
Simplicity Manufacturing Inc N363 US Highway 14 *TF:* 800-837-6836 ■ *Web:* www.simplicitymfg.com	Milwaukee	WI	53201	800-837-6836		429
Simplified Logistics LLC 28915 Clemens Rd *Web:* www.simplifiedlogistics.com	Westlake	OH	44145	440-250-8912		192
Simplifile 5072 N 300 W *TF:* 800-460-5657 ■ *Web:* simplifile.com	Provo	UT	84604	800-460-5657		225
Simplion Technologies Inc 1525 McCarthy Blvd Ste 228 *Web:* www.simplion.com	Milpitas	CA	95035	408-935-8686		196
Simply Fondue 2108 Greenville Ave *Web:* simplyfondue.com	Dallas	TX	75206	214-827-8878		671
Simply Fresh Foods Inc 6535 Caballero Blvd Bldg C *Web:* www.ffci.us	Buena Park	CA	90620	714-562-5000		297-8
Simply Fun LLC 11245 SE Sixth St Ste 110 **Fax Area Code:* 425 ■ *TF:* 877-557-7767 ■ *Web:* simplyfun.com	Bellevue	WA	98004	877-557-7767	289-0865*	366
Simply Healthcare Plans Inc 1701 Ponce De Leon Blvd Ste 300 *TF:* 877-577-9042 ■ *Web:* www.simplyhealthcareplans.com	Coral Gables	FL	33134	305-408-5890		194
Simply Home PO Box 1155 *TF:* 877-684-3581 ■ *Web:* www.simply-home.com	Arden	NC	28704	877-684-3581		745-1
Simply Orange Juice Co 2659 Orange Ave *TF:* 800-871-2653 ■ *Web:* www.simplyorangejuice.com	Apopka	FL	32703	800-871-2653		296-20
Simply Whispers 50 Perry Ave **Fax Area Code:* 774 ■ *TF:* 800-451-5700 ■ *Web:* www.simplywhispersstore.com	Attleboro	MA	02703	508-455-0864	203-3974*	415
Simpson College 701 N 'C' St *TF:* 800-362-2454 ■ *Web:* www.simpson.edu	Indianola	IA	50125	515-961-6251	961-1870	166
Simpson County PO Box 459 *Web:* www.simpsontax.com	Mendenhall	MS	39114	601-847-1744	847-2119	338
Simpson County Development Foundation 176 W Court St *Web:* simpsoncounty.biz	Mendenhall	MS	39114	601-847-2375	847-2380	187
Simpson Door Co 400 Simpson Ave *TF:* 800-746-7766 ■ *Web:* www.simpsondoor.com	Mccleary	WA	98557	800-746-7766		683
Simpson Electric Co 520 Simpson Ave *Web:* simpsonelectric.com	Lac Du Flambeau	WI	54538	715-588-3311	588-1248	248
Simpson Gumpertz & Heger Inc 41 Seyon St Bldg 1 Ste 500 *TF:* 800-729-7429 ■ *Web:* www.sgh.com	Waltham	MA	02453	781-907-9000	907-9009	261
Simpson House 2101 Belmont Ave *Web:* www.simpsonhouse.org	Philadelphia	PA	19131	215-878-3600		672
Simpson Housing LLLP (SHLP) 8110 E Union Ave Ste 200 *Web:* www.simpsonhousing.com	Denver	CO	80237	303-283-4100		653
Simpson Mike (Rep R - ID) 2084 Rayburn House Office Bldg *Web:* simpson.house.gov	Washington	DC	20515	202-225-5531	225-8216	342-2
Simpson Norton Corp 4144 S Bullard Ave *TF:* 877-859-8676 ■ *Web:* www.simpsonnorton.com	Goodyear	AZ	85338	623-932-5116	932-5299	274
Simpson Performance Products Inc 328 FM 306 *TF:* 800-654-7223 ■ *Web:* simpsonraceproducts.com	New Braunfels	TX	78130	830-625-1774	625-3269	60
Simpson Strong-Tie Company Inc 5956 W Las Positas Blvd *TF:* 800-925-5099 ■ *Web:* www.strongtie.com	Pleasanton	CA	94588	925-560-9000	847-1597	350
Simpson Thacher & Bartlett LLP 425 Lexington Ave *Web:* www.stblaw.com	New York	NY	10017	212-455-2000	455-2502	428
Simpson University 2211 College View Dr *TF:* 888-974-6776 ■ *Web:* www.simpsonu.edu	Redding	CA	96003	530-224-5600	226-4861	166
Simpson's Eggs Inc 5015 Hwy 218 E *TF:* 800-726-1330 ■ *Web:* simpsonseggs.com	Monroe	NC	28110	704-753-1478	753-4762	10-8
Simpsonville Animal Hospital Inc 1233 W Georgia Rd *Web:* simpsonvilleah.com	Simpsonville	SC	29680	864-757-0850	757-0852	794
Simrex Corp 5490 Broadway St *Web:* www.simrex.com	Lancaster	NY	14086	480-926-6069		647
Sims & Guess Real Estate Inc 4526 E University Blvd Ste 1 *Web:* simsguessrealtors.com	Odessa	TX	79761	432-368-6800		652
Sims & Steele Consulting PO Box 8305 *Web:* www.simsandsteele.com	Asheville	NC	28814	828-254-9004		196
Sims Bark Company Inc 1765 Spring Valley Rd *TF:* 800-346-3216 ■ *Web:* www.simsbark.com	Tuscumbia	AL	35674	256-381-8323		683
Sims Brothers Recycling 1011 S Prospect St *TF:* 800-536-7465 ■ *Web:* www.simsbros.com	Marion	OH	43302	740-387-9041		686
Sims Cab Depot 200 Moulinette Rd *TF:* 800-225-7290 ■ *Web:* www.cabdepot.com	Long Sault	ON	K0C1P0	613-534-2289		480
Sims Recycling Solutions Holdings Inc 1600 Harvester Rd *TF:* 800-270-8220 ■ *Web:* www.simsrecycling.com	West Chicago	IL	60185	630-231-6060		787
Simsbury Public Library 725 Hopmeadow St *Web:* www.simsburylibrary.info	Simsbury	CT	06070	860-658-7663	658-6732	434-3
Simtech Inc 66A Floydville Rd *Web:* www.simtech-inc.com	East Granby	CT	06026	860-653-2408	653-3857	770
Sim-Tex LP 20880 FM 362 Rd *TF:* 866-829-8939 ■ *Web:* www.sim-tex.com	Waller	TX	77484	713-450-3940		492
Simulaids 16 Simulaids Dr PO Box 1289 *Web:* www.simulaids.com	Saugerties	NY	12477	845-679-2475	679-8996	678
Simulations Plus Inc 42505 Tenth St W *NASDAQ: SLP* ■ *TF:* 888-266-9294 ■ *Web:* www.simulations-plus.com	Lancaster	CA	93534	661-723-7723	723-5524	178-10
Simulent Inc 203 College St Ste 302 *Web:* simulent.com	Toronto	ON	M5T1P9	416-979-5544		261
SimulTrans LLC 155 N Whisman Rd Ste 400 *Web:* www.simultrans.com	Mountain View	CA	94043	650-605-1300		768
Simulyze Inc 12020 Sunrise Valley Dr Ste 300 *Web:* simulyze.com	Reston	VA	20191	703-391-7001		177
Simunition Ltd 65 Sandscreen Rd *TF:* 800-465-8255 ■ *Web:* www.simunition.com	Avon	CT	06001	860-404-0162		463
Simutek Inc 3136 E Ft Lowell Rd *Web:* www.simutek.com	Tucson	AZ	85716	520-321-9077		35
Sinai Hospital of Baltimore 2401 W Belvedere Ave *TF:* 800-876-1175 ■ *Web:* www.sinai-balt.com	Baltimore	MD	21215	410-601-9000		374-3
Sinaloa Hawaiian Tortillas Inc 3240 Ualena St *Web:* www.sinaloahawaii.com	Honolulu	HI	96818	808-833-3695	833-4270	296-37
Sinars Rollins LLC 55 W Monroe Ste 4000 *Web:* sinarsrollins.com	Chicago	IL	60603	312-767-9790	767-9780	41
Sincera Consulting LLC Address on File with BBB *Web:* www.sincera.net	Charlevoix	MI	49720	231-547-0478		809
Sincere Design 103 Santa Fe Ave *Web:* www.sinceredesign.com	Point Richmond	CA	94801	510-215-1139		393
Sinclair & Rush Inc 123 Manufacturers Dr *TF:* 800-526-6273 ■ *Web:* www.sinclair-rush.com	Arnold	MO	63010	636-282-6800	282-6888	600
Sinclair Broadcast Group Inc 3500 Myer Lee Dr *Web:* www.abc45.com	Winston-Salem	NC	27101	336-722-4545	723-8217	632
Sinclair Broadcast Group Inc 10706 Beaver Dam Rd *NASDAQ: SBGI* ■ *Web:* www.sbgi.net	Hunt Valley	MD	21030	410-568-1500		738
Sinclair Community College 444 W Third St *TF:* 800-315-3000 ■ *Web:* www.sinclair.edu	Dayton	OH	45402	937-512-3000		162
Sinclair Dental Company Ltd 900 Harbourside Dr *Web:* www.sinclairdental.com	North Vancouver	BC	V7P3T8	604-986-1544		475
Sinclair Insurance Group Inc 4 Tower Dr Ste 200 *Web:* srfm.com	Wallingford	CT	06492	203-265-0996		390

	Phone	Fax	Class
Sinclair Law Office 300 Frank H Ogawa Plz Rotunda Bldg Ste 160 ..... Oakland CA 94612 *Web:* sinclairlawoffice.com	510-465-5300	465-5356	41
Sinclair Oil Corp PO Box 30825 .... Salt Lake City UT 84130 *Web:* www.sinclairoil.com	801-524-2700	524-2880	580
Sinclair Pratt Cameron PC 1630 Donna Dr Ste 103 .... Virginia Beach VA 23451 *Web:* www.spc-eng.com	757-417-0565	417-0568	261
Sinclair Printing Co 4005 Whiteside St .... Los Angeles CA 90063 *Web:* www.sinclairprinting.com	323-264-4000		627
Sindel, Sindel & Noble PC 8000 Maryland Ave Ste 910 .... Saint Louis MO 63105 *TF:* 866-489-5504 ■ *Web:* www.sindellaw.com	314-499-1282		428
Sine Irish Pub & Restaurant 1327 E Cary St .... Richmond VA 23218 *Web:* www.sineirishpub.com	804-649-7767	649-0661	671
Sinema Kyrsten (Sen D - AZ) 317 Hart Senate Office Bldg .... Washington DC 20510 *Web:* www.sinema.senate.gov	202-224-4521		342-2
Sing Sing Correctional Facility 354 Hunter St .... Ossining NY 10562 *Web:* www.doccs.ny.gov	914-941-0108		213
Singapore			
Consulate General 710 N McDonald Rd 2nd Fl Ste 2450 .... San Francisco CA 94105 *Web:* www.mfa.gov.sg	415-543-4775	543-4788	257
Embassy 650 East Swedesford Rd 2nd Fl .... Washington DC 20008 *Web:* www.mfa.gov.sg	202-537-3100	537-0876	257
Singapore Airlines KrisFlyer 380 World Way Ste 336B .... Los Angeles CA 90045 *TF:* 800-742-3333 ■ *Web:* www.singaporeair.com	310-647-6144	615-0373	26
Singapore Sam's 11th Ave SW Unit101-555 .... Calgary AB T2R1P6 *Web:* singaporesams.com	403-234-8088	266-6883	671
Singer & Levick Pc 16200 Addison Rd Ste 140 .... Addison TX 75001 *Web:* www.singerlevick.com	972-380-5533		428
Singer & Lusardi 370 Main St .... Worcester MA 01608 *Web:* singerlusardi.com	508-756-4657		2
Singer Lewak Greenbaum & Goldstein LLP 10960 Wilshire Blvd 7th Fl .... Los Angeles CA 90024 *TF:* 877-754-4557 ■ *Web:* www.singerlewak.com	310-477-3924	478-6070	2
Singer Optical Company Inc 1401 N Royal Ave .... Evansville IN 47715 *TF:* 800-431-6267 ■ *Web:* www.singeroptical.com	800-431-6267	447-5246	542
Singer Sewing Co 1714 Heil Quaker Blvd Ste 130 .... La Vergne TN 37086 *TF:* 800-474-6437 ■ *Web:* www.singerco.com	615-213-0880		37
Singer Specs 123 W Lincoln Hwy .... Exton PA 19341 *Web:* www.sterlingoptical.com	610-524-8886		543
Singer Steel Co 1 Singer Dr .... Streetsboro OH 44241 *Web:* scsprocess.com	330-562-7200	562-7557	492
Singer, Berger, Press & Co 23500 Mercantile Rd Ste A .... Beachwood OH 44122 *Web:* sbp-cpas.com	216-595-9400	595-9442	2
Singh Homes Inc 7125 Orchard Lake Rd Ste 200 .... West Bloomfield MI 48322 *Web:* www.singhweb.com	248-865-1620	865-1630	653
Singha Thai 2237 S 108th St .... Milwaukee WI 53227 *Web:* www.singhathaimilwaukee.com	414-541-1234		671
Singh-Ray Filters 2721 SE Hwy 31 .... Arcadia FL 34266 *Web:* www.singh-ray.com	863-993-4100		628
Singing Machine Company Inc, The 6601 Lyons Rd Bldg A-7 .... Coconut Creek FL 33073 *OTC:* SMDM ■ *TF:* 866-670-6888 ■ *Web:* singingmachine.com	954-596-1000	596-2000	246
Singing River Electric Power Association Inc 11187 Old Hwy 63 PO Box 767 .... Lucedale MS 39452 *Web:* www.singingriver.com	601-947-4211	947-6548	245
Singing River Federal Credit Union 6006 Hwy 63 .... Moss Point MS 39563 *Web:* srfcu.org	228-475-9531	475-5919	219
Singing River Hospital 2809 Denny Ave .... Pascagoula MS 39581 *Web:* www.singingriverhealthsystem.com	228-809-5000		374-3
Single Mothers by Choice Inc (SMC) PO Box 1642 .... New York NY 10028 *Web:* www.singlemothersbychoice.org	212-988-0993		48-21
Single Pebble 133 Bank St .... Burlington VT 05401 *Web:* asinglepebble.com	802-865-5200		671
Single Source Technologies Inc 2600 Superior Ct .... Auburn Hills MI 48326 *TF:* 800-336-7283 ■ *Web:* www.singlesourcetech.com	248-232-6232		358
SinglePoint Solutions 210 Townepark Cir Ste 200 .... Louisville KY 40243 *TF:* 877-774-4840 ■ *Web:* sptsolutions.com	502-212-4017	515-4917	196
Singletary Lake State Park 6707 NC 53 Hwy E .... Kelly NC 28448 *Web:* www.ncparks.gov	910-669-2928		565
Singlewire Software LLC 1002 Deming Way PO Box 46218 .... Madison WI 53717 *Web:* www.singlewire.com	608-661-1140		41
Singular Solutions 448 S Santa Anita Ave .... Pasadena CA 91107 *TF:* 800-300-7066 ■ *Web:* www.singular.com	626-792-9567		177
Sinister Cinema PO Box 4369 .... Medford OR 97501 *Web:* www.sinistercinema.com	541-773-6860	779-8650	459
SinJu 7339 Sw Bridgeport Rd .... Portland OR 97209 *Web:* sinjurestaurant.com	503-223-6535		671
Sinkyone Wilderness State Park PO Box 245 .... Whitethorn CA 95589 *Web:* www.parks.ca.gov	707-986-7711		565
Sinn- Tech Industries Inc 48 Gleam St .... West Babylon NY 11704 *Web:* www.sinn-tech.com	631-643-1171	643-1176	493
Sinnemahoning State Park 8288 First Fork Rd .... Austin PA 16720 *Web:* www.dcnr.pa.gov	814-647-8401		565

	Phone	Fax	Class
Sinopec Daylight Energy Ltd 112-4th Ave SW Sun Life Plz E Tower Ste 2700 .... Calgary AB T2P0H3 *TF:* 877-266-6901 ■ *Web:* www.sinopeccanada.com	403-266-6900		536
Sinte Gleska University 101 Antelope Lake Cir Dr PO Box 105 .... Mission SD 57555 *Web:* www.sintegleska.edu	605-856-8100	856-4135	165
Sintel Inc 18437 171st Ave .... Spring Lake MI 49456 *TF:* 800-394-8276 ■ *Web:* sintelinc.com	616-842-6960		454
Sinton Dairy Foods Company LLC 5301 Alpha Rd Ste 80-300 .... Dallas TX 75240 *Web:* www.lala-us.com	719-633-3821	667-7470	296-10
SinuSys Corp 4030 Fabian Way .... Palo Alto CA 94303 *Web:* sinusys.com	650-213-9988		475
SIO (Scripps Institution of Oceanography) 8622 Kennel Way 9500 Gilman Dr MC 0210 ...... La Jolla CA 92037 *Web:* scripps.ucsd.edu	858-534-3624		668
SIOR (Society of Industrial & Office Realtors) 1201 New York Ave NW Ste 350 .... Washington DC 20005 *Web:* www.sior.com	202-449-8200	216-9325	49-17
Sioux Automation Center Inc 877 First Ave NW .... Sioux Center IA 51250 *TF:* 866-722-1488 ■ *Web:* www.siouxautomation.com	712-722-1488		274
Sioux Center Shopper 303 N Main Ave .... Sioux Center IA 51250 *Web:* www.siouxcenterchamber.com	712-722-3457	722-3465	139
Sioux Chief Manufacturing Company Inc 14940 Thunderbird Rd .... Kansas City MO 64147 **Fax Area Code:* 816 ■ *TF:* 800-821-3944 ■ *Web:* www.siouxchief.com	800-821-3944	348-7502*	612
Sioux City Art Ctr 225 Nebraska St .... Sioux City IA 51101 *Web:* siouxcityartcenter.org	712-279-6272	255-2921	520
Sioux City Convention Ctr 801 Fourth St .... Sioux City IA 51101 *TF:* 800-593-2228 ■ *Web:* www.visitsiouxcity.org	712-279-4800	279-4900	205
Sioux City Foundry Co 801 Div St .... Sioux City IA 51102 *TF:* 800-831-0874 ■ *Web:* www.siouxcityfoundry.com	712-252-4181	252-4197	307
Sioux City Journal 515 Pavonia St .... Sioux City IA 51101 *TF:* 800-397-3530 ■ *Web:* www.siouxcityjournal.com	712-293-4300	279-5059	532-2
Sioux City Public Library 529 Pierce St .... Sioux City IA 51101 *Web:* www.siouxcitylibrary.org	712-255-2933		434-3
Sioux City Public Museum 2901 Jackson St .... Sioux City IA 51104 *Web:* www.sioux-city.org	712-279-6174		520
Sioux City Symphony Orchestra 518 Pierce St .... Sioux City IA 51101 *Web:* www.siouxcitysymphony.org	712-277-2111	252-0224	573-3
Sioux Empire Medical Museum 1305 W 18th St .... Sioux Falls SD 57104 *Web:* www.experiencesiouxfalls.com	605-333-6397		520
Sioux Falls Arena 1201 NW Ave .... Sioux Falls SD 57104 *TF:* 800-338-3177 ■ *Web:* www.sfarena.com	605-367-7288	338-1463	720
Sioux Falls City Hall 224 W Ninth St .... Sioux Falls SD 57104 *Web:* siouxfalls.org	605-367-8000	367-7801	337
Sioux Falls Construction Company Inc 800 S Seventh Ave .... Sioux Falls SD 57101 *Web:* journeyconstruction.com	605-332-5968	334-9342	188-4
Sioux Falls Convention & Visitors Bureau 200 N Phillips Ave Ste 102 .... Sioux Falls SD 57104 *TF:* 800-333-2072 ■ *Web:* visitsiouxfalls.com	605-275-6060	336-6499	206
Sioux Falls Regional Airport 2801 Jaycee Ln .... Sioux Falls SD 57104 *Web:* www.sfairport.com	605-336-0762	367-7374	27
Sioux Falls School District 201 E 38th St .... Sioux Falls SD 57105 *Web:* www.sf.k12.sd.us	605-367-7900	367-4637	685
Sioux Falls Seminary 2100 S Summit .... Sioux Falls SD 57105 *TF:* 800-440-6227 ■ *Web:* sfseminary.edu	605-336-6588	335-9090	167-3
Sioux Honey Association Co-op 301 Lewis Blvd .... Sioux City IA 51101 *Web:* siouxhoney.com	712-258-0638		296-24
Sioux Steel Co 196 1/2 E Sixth St .... Sioux Falls SD 57104 *TF:* 800-557-4689 ■ *Web:* www.siouxsteel.com	605-336-1750	336-2528	273
Sioux Tools Inc 250 Snap-on Dr .... Murphy NC 28906 *TF:* 800-722-7290 ■ *Web:* www.siouxtools.com	828-835-9765	835-9685	759
Sioux Valley-Southwestern Electric Co-opeartive Inc 47092 SD Hwy 34 PO Box 216 .... Colman SD 57017 *TF:* 800-234-1960 ■ *Web:* www.siouxvalleyenergy.com	605-534-3535		245
Siouxland Chamber of Commerce 101 Pierce St .... Sioux City IA 51101 *TF:* 800-228-7903 ■ *Web:* siouxlandchamber.com	712-255-7903	258-7578	139
Sioux-Preme Packing Co 4241 US 75th Ave .... Sioux Center IA 51250 *TF:* 800-735-7675 ■ *Web:* siouxpreme.com	800-735-7675		473
SIP (Sandwich Islands Publishing) PO Box 10669 .... Lahaina HI 96761 *Web:* www.bestofmauiguide.com	808-665-9990		637-2
Sipi Metals Corp 1720 N Elston Ave .... Chicago IL 60642 *TF:* 800-621-8013 ■ *Web:* www.sipimetals.com	773-276-0070		485
SIR (Society of Interventional Radiology) 3975 Fair Rdige Dr Ste 400 N .... Fairfax VA 22033 *Web:* www.sirweb.org	703-691-1805	691-1855	49-8
Sir Benedict's Tavern 805 E Superior St .... Duluth MN 55802 *Web:* www.sirbens.com	218-728-1192		671
Sir Francis Drake Hotel 450 Powell St .... San Francisco CA 94102 *TF:* 800-795-7129 ■ *Web:* www.sirfrancisdrake.com	415-392-7755	391-8719	379
SIRCHIE Finger Print Laboratories Inc 100 Hunter Pl .... Youngsville NC 27596 *TF:* 800-356-7311 ■ *Web:* www.sirchie.com	919-554-2244	554-2266	84
Siren Star Publishing PO Box 5183 .... Los Angeles CA 90055 *Web:* www.sirenstar.net	310-804-2590		637-2
Siren Telephone Company Inc 7723 W Main St .... Siren WI 54872 *Web:* sirentel.com	715-349-2224		224

Name / Address	City	State	Zip	Phone	Fax	Class
Sires Albio (Rep D - NJ) 2268 Rayburn House Office Bldg *Web:* www.sires.house.gov	Washington	DC	20515	202-225-7919	226-0792	342-2
Sirius Solution LLC 1233 W Loop S *Web:* www.sirsol.com	Houston	TX	77027	713-888-0488		194
Sirius Technical Services Inc 6215 Rangeline Rd Ste 102 *Web:* www.siriustechnical.com	Theodore	AL	36582	251-443-1166		260
Sirius XM Canada Inc 135 Liberty St 4th Fl *TF:* 888-539-7474 ■ *Web:* www.siriusxm.ca	Toronto	ON	M6K1Y7	416-408-6000	513-7489	736
SiriusDecisions Inc 187 Danbury Rd *Web:* www.siriusdecisions.com	Wilton	CT	06897	203-665-4000		194
Sirko Associates Inc 12130 N Pennsylvania St Ste 102 *Web:* sirko.com	Denver	CO	80241	303-428-0901		261
Sirmilik National Park PO Box 300 *Web:* www.pc.gc.ca	Pond Inlet	NU	X0A0S0	867-899-8092		563
Sirois Tool Company Inc 169 White Oak Dr *TF:* 800-864-2652 ■ *Web:* siroistool.com	Berlin	CT	06037	860-828-5327	828-5367	757
Sirote & Permutt Pc 2311 Highland Ave S *Web:* www.sirote.com	Birmingham	AL	35205	205-930-5100	930-5101	428
Sirsi Corp 3300 N Ashton Blvd Ste 500 *TF:* 800-288-8020 ■ *Web:* www.sirsidynix.com	Lehi	UT	84043	800-288-8020		177
Sirus Inc 675 E 16th St Ste 200 *Web:* www.sirus.com	Holland	MI	49423	616-394-0558	394-9228	225
SIRVA Inc 1 Parkview Plz *TF:* 800-341-5648 ■ *Web:* www.sirva.com	Oakbrook Terrace	IL	60181	630-570-3050		666
SIS (Software Information Systems Inc) 165 Barr St *TF:* 800-337-6914 ■ *Web:* www.thinksis.com	Lexington	KY	40507	859-977-4747	977-4750	180
SIS International Research Inc 11 E 22nd St 2nd Fl *Web:* www.sisinternational.com	New York	NY	10010	212-505-6805		668
Sisbarro Dealerships 425 W Boutz Rd *TF:* 800-215-8021 ■ *Web:* www.sisbarro-buickgmc.com	Las Cruces	NM	88005	575-524-7707		57
Sisemore Weisz & Associates Inc 6111 E 32nd Pl *Web:* sw-assoc.com	Tulsa	OK	74135	918-665-3600	665-8668	261
Sisense 1359 Broadway 4th Fl *Web:* www.sisense.com	New York	NY	10018	646-432-1507		178-1
Sisk Fulfillment Service Inc 1900 Industrial Park Rd *Web:* www.siskfulfillment.com	Federalsburg	MD	21632	410-754-8141	754-8223	393
Siskin Hospital for Physical Rehabilitation 1 Siskin Plz *Fax Area Code: 630 ■ *Web:* www.siskinrehab.org	Chattanooga	TN	37403	423-634-1200	792-5636*	374-6
Siskin Steel & Supply Company Inc 1901 Riverfront Pkwy *TF:* 800-756-3671 ■ *Web:* www.siskin.com	Chattanooga	TN	37408	423-756-3671		492
Siskinds LLP 680 Waterloo St PO Box 2520 *TF:* 877-672-2121 ■ *Web:* www.siskinds.com	London	ON	N6A3V8	519-672-2121		428
Siskiyou Central Credit Union 845 Fourth St *Web:* siskiyoucu.org	Yreka	CA	96097	530-842-1694		219
Siskiyou Corp 110 SW Booth St *TF:* 877-313-6418 ■ *Web:* www.siskiyou.com	Grants Pass	OR	97526	541-479-8697		419
Siskiyou County 609 S Gold St *Web:* www.co.siskiyou.ca.us	Yreka	CA	96097	530-842-8005	842-8013	338
Siskiyou Development Company Inc 79 S Weed Blvd *Web:* www.sisdevco.com	Weed	CA	96094	530-938-3468	938-3610	378
Siskiyou Veterinary Hospital 100 W Stewart Ave *Web:* siskiyouvet.com	Medford	OR	97501	541-773-1335		701
Sisseton Wahpeton College 12572 BIA Hwy 700 *Web:* www.swc.tc	Sisseton	SD	57262	605-698-3966	742-0394	165
Sister Cities Intl (SCI) 1301 Pennsylvania Ave NW Ste 850 *Web:* sistercities.org	Washington	DC	20004	202-347-8630	393-6524	48-7
Sisters Network Inc 2922 Rosedale St *TF:* 866-781-1808 ■ *Web:* www.sistersnetworkinc.org	Houston	TX	77004	713-781-0255	780-8998	48-21
Sisters of Charity of Saint Augustine Health System 2475 E 22nd St *Web:* www.sistersofcharityhealth.org	Cleveland	OH	44115	216-696-5560	696-2204	353
Sisters of Mary of the Presentation Health System 1202 Page Dr SW PO Box 10007 *Web:* www.smphs.org	Fargo	ND	58106	701-237-9290	235-0906	353
Sisters of Notre Dame de Namur (SNDDEN) Congregational Mission Office 30 Jeffreys Neck Rd *Web:* www.sndden.org	Ipswich	MA	01938	978-356-2159	356-1034	637-10
Sisters of Saint Francis 1545 S Layton Blvd *Web:* www.lbwn.org	Milwaukee	WI	53215	414-383-9038	385-5206	48-20
Sisters of st Francis of Assisi of 3221 S Lake Dr *Web:* www.lakeosfs.org	Saint Francis	WI	53235	414-744-1160		48-20
Sisters of the Holy Family of Nazareth Sacred Heart Province 310 N River Rd *Web:* www.nazarethcsfn.org	Des Plaines	IL	60016	847-298-6760		353
Sisters of The Presentation 281 Masonic Ave *Web:* www.presentationsistersf.org	San Francisco	CA	94118	415-422-5001		48-20
Sisters' Choice 704 Gilman St *Fax Area Code: 530 ■ *Web:* www.sisterschoice.com	Berkeley	CA	94710	510-843-0533	544-8811*	637-2
Sisto CPA Group Inc 919 Reserve Dr *Web:* sistoadvisory.com	Roseville	CA	95678	916-724-1693		2
SISU Inc 7635 N Fraser Way Ste 102 *TF:* 800-663-4163 ■ *Web:* www.sisu.com	Burnaby	BC	V5J0B8	604-420-6610		582
SIS-USA Inc 55 Wentworth Ave *Web:* www.sisergo.com	Londonderry	NH	03053	603-432-4495	434-8456	320
Sit 'n Sleep 14300 S Main St *TF:* 877-262-4006 ■ *Web:* www.sitnsleep.com	Gardena	CA	90248	310-604-8903		321
Sit Investment Associates Inc 80 S Eigth St 3300 IDS Ctr *Web:* www.sitinvest.com	Minneapolis	MN	55402	612-332-3223		401
Sita Tile Distributors Inc 8510 Truck Way *Web:* www.sitatile.com	Capitol Heights	MD	20743	301-336-0450	336-1526	191-1
Sita World Travel Inc 16250 Ventura Blvd *TF:* 800-421-5643 ■ *Web:* www.sitatours.com	Encino	CA	91436	818-990-9530		771
Sitar Indian Cuisine 6004 Kingston Pk *Web:* sitarknoxville.com	Knoxville	TN	37919	865-588-1828		671
Sitar Indian Cuisine 116 21st Ave N *Web:* www.sitarnashville.com	Nashville	TN	37203	615-321-8889	321-2688	671
Sitar of India 702 Lee St E *Web:* sitarofindia.org	Charleston	WV	25301	304-346-3745	720-6260	671
SITE 120 Pembina Rd Ste 170 *TF:* 800-801-3740 ■ *Web:* siterg.com	Sherwood Park	AB	T8H0M2	780-400-7483		540
SITE (Society of Incentive & Travel Executives) 330 N Wabash Ste 2000 *Web:* www.siteglobal.com	Chicago	IL	60611	312-321-5148		48-23
Site Centers Corp 3300 Enterprise Pkwy *Web:* www.sitecenters.com	Beachwood	OH	44122	216-755-5500		653
Site Design Concepts Inc 127 W Market St Ste 200 *Web:* sitedc.com	York	PA	17401	717-757-9414		261
Site Engineering Inc 650 Albertson Pkwy *Web:* site-eng.com	Broussard	LA	70518	337-981-1414		261
Site Inc 10215 Technology Dr Ste 304 *Web:* site-incorporated.com	Knoxville	TN	37932	865-777-4160		261
Site Santa Fe 1606 Paseo de Peralta *Web:* sitesantafe.org	Santa Fe	NM	87501	505-989-1199	989-1188	48-4
Site Strategics Inc 1317 N Pennsylvania St Ste A *Web:* sitestrategics.com	Indianapolis	IN	46202	317-882-8500		180
Site Tech Systems 2513 N Oak St Ste 305 *TF:* 800-470-2895 ■ *Web:* www.sitetechsystems.com	Myrtle Beach	SC	20577	843-000-0710		403
Sitegoal LLC 4812 Trail Crest Cir *Web:* sitegoals.com	Austin	TX	78735	512-474-2025		180
Sitel Corp 3102 W End Ave Two American Ctr Ste 1000 *Web:* www.sitel.com	Nashville	TN	37203	615-301-7100		737
Siteman Cancer Ctr 4921 Parkview Pl *TF:* 800-600-3606 ■ *Web:* siteman.wustl.edu	Saint Louis	MO	63110	314-362-5196		668
SiteMaster Inc 6914 S Yorktown Ave Ste 210 *Web:* www.sitemaster.com	Tulsa	OK	74136	918-663-2232	663-2291	480
SiteOne Landscape Supply 31691 Dequindre Rd *TF:* 800-347-4272 ■ *Web:* www.siteone.com	Madison Heights	MI	48071	248-588-2990		274
SiteTech Inc 8061 Church St *Web:* www.sitetechinc.com	Highland	CA	92346	909-864-3180		261
SiteTuners com Inc 4420 Hotel Circle Ct Ste 330 *Web:* sitetuners.com	San Diego	CA	92108	619-223-8020		196
Sitex Corp 1300 Commonwealth Dr *TF:* 800-278-3537 ■ *Web:* sitex-corp.com	Henderson	KY	42420	270-827-3537		442
SiTime Corp 990 Almanor Ave *Web:* www.sitime.com	Sunnyvale	CA	94085	408-328-4400		177
Sitka Harbor 100 Lincoln St *Web:* cityofsitka.com	Sitka	AK	99835	907-747-3439	747-6278	618
Sitka National Historical Park 106 Metlakatla St *Web:* www.nps.gov	Sitka	AK	99835	907-747-6281	747-5938	564
Sitkins Group Inc 6700 Winkler Rd Ste 4 *Web:* www.sitkins.com	Fort Myers	FL	33919	239-337-2555		195
Sitonit Seating 6415 Katella Ave *Web:* www.sitonit.net	Cypress	CA	90630	714-995-4800		321
Sitrick & Co 11999 San Vicente Blvd PH *TF:* 800-288-8809 ■ *Web:* www.sitrick.com	Los Angeles	CA	90049	310-788-2850	788-2855	636
Sittercity Inc 20 W Kinzie St Ste 1500 *TF:* 877-494-1014 ■ *Web:* www.sittercity.com	Chicago	IL	60654	877-494-1014		189-11
Sitters & More Inc 125 A Stonebridge Blvd *Web:* sittersandmore.com	Jackson	TN	38305	731-660-0001		363
Sitting Bull College 9299 Hwy 24 *Web:* sittingbull.edu	Fort Yates	ND	58538	701-854-8000	854-3403	165
Sittner & Nelson LLC 497 Oakway Rd Ste 300 *Web:* sittnerandnelson.com	Eugene	OR	97401	541-636-4001		690
Sitton Buick GMC 2640 Laurens Rd *Web:* www.sittongm.com	Greenville	SC	29607	864-288-5600		57
Situation Management Systems Inc 98 Spit Brook Rd Ste 201 *Web:* situationmanagementsystems.com	Nashua	NH	03062	603-897-1200		765
SIU (Southern Illinois University School of Medicine Medical Library) 801 N Rutledge St *TF:* 800-342-5748 ■ *Web:* www.siumed.edu	Springfield	IL	62702	217-545-2122		434-1
SIU University Museum 1000 Faner Dr Faner Hall Door 12 MC 4508 *Web:* museum.siu.edu	Carbondale	IL	62901	618-453-5388	453-7409	520
SIU's Advanced Coal & Energy Research Ctr 405 W Grand Ave *Web:* energy.siu.edu	Carbondale	IL	62901	618-536-5521	453-7346	668
Siuslaw School District 97j 2111 Oak St *Web:* www.greatschools.org	Florence	OR	97439	541-997-2651		685
Sivaco Wire Group 800 Rue Ouellette *TF:* 800-876-9473 ■ *Web:* www.sivaco.com	Marieville	QC	J3M1P5	450-658-8741	460-2744	813
Sivad Business Solutions 6400 Head Rd *Web:* www.sivadsolutions.com	Wilmington	NC	28409	678-215-1705		196

Company	City	State	Zip	Phone	Fax	Class
Sivalls Inc 2200 E Second St *Web:* www.sivalls.com	Odessa	TX	79761	432-337-3571	337-2624	91
Sivananda Yoga Vedanta Ctr 1185 Vicente St *Web:* www.sivananda.org	San Francisco	CA	94116	415-681-2731		148
Siver Insurance Consultants 805 Executive Center Dr W Ste 110 *Web:* www.siver.com	Saint Petersburg	FL	33702	727-577-2780	579-8692	466
Sivyer Steel Corp 225 S 33rd St *Web:* www.sivyersteel.com	Bettendorf	IA	52722	563-355-1811		307
Siwel Consulting Inc 15 W 24th St Ste 9E *Web:* www.siwel.com	New York	NY	10010	212-691-9326	929-6815	178-1
Six & Geving Insurance Inc 3630 Sinton Rd Ste 200 *Web:* six-geving.com	Colorado Springs	CO	80907	719-590-9990		390
Six Consulting 5900 Windwood Pky Ste 410 *Web:* www.sixconsultingcorp.com	Alpharetta	GA	30005	470-395-0200		180
Six Degrees LLC 8040 E Gelding Dr *Web:* www.six-degrees.com	Scottsdale	AZ	85260	480-627-9850		708
Six Financial Information USA Inc 1 Omega Dr River Bend Centre Bldg 3 *Web:* www.six-group.com	Stamford	CT	06907	203-353-8100		624
Six Flags Entertainment Corp 924 Avenue J E *NYSE: SIX* ■ *Web:* www.sixflags.com	Grand Prairie	TX	75050	972-595-5000		564
Six Pence Pub 245 Bull St *Web:* www.sixpencepub.com	Savannah	GA	31401	912-233-3151		671
Six Red Marbles LLC 10 City Sq 3rd Fl Charlestown *TF:* 866-632-6623 ■ *Web:* sixredmarbles.com	Boston	MA	02129	857-588-9000		225
Six Robblees' Inc 11010 Tukwila International Blvd *TF:* 800-275-7499 ■ *Web:* sixrobblees.com	Tukwila	WA	98168	206-767-7970	763-7416	61
Six States Distributors Inc 247 West 1700 South *TF:* 800-453-5703 ■ *Web:* www.sixstates.com	Salt Lake City	UT	84115	801-488-4666	488-4676	61
Sixteen Rivers Press PO Box 640663 *Web:* www.sixteenrivers.org	San Francisco	CA	94164	415-273-1303	221-5116	637-2
Sixteenth Street Baptist Church 1530 Sixth Ave N *Web:* 16thstreetbaptist.org	Birmingham	AL	35203	205-251-9402		50-1
Sixth & i Historic Synagogue 600 I St NW *Web:* www.sixthandi.org	Washington	DC	20001	202-408-3100		48-20
Sixth Floor Museum 411 Elm St *TF:* 888-485-4854 ■ *Web:* www.jfk.org	Dallas	TX	75202	214-747-6660		520
Sixth Sense Media 4220 NC Hwy 55 Ste 340 *Web:* sixthsensemedia.com	Durham	NC	27713	919-484-2442		195
Sixth Star Entertainment & Marketing Inc 21 NW Fifth St *Web:* www.sixthstar.com	Fort Lauderdale	FL	33301	954-462-6760		195
Sixth Street Grill 55 W 6th Ave *Web:* www.sixthstreetgrill.com	Eugene	OR	97401	541-485-2961		671
Sixthman LTD 437 Memorial Dr SE Ste A10 *TF:* 877-749-8462 ■ *Web:* www.sixthman.net	Atlanta	GA	30312	404-525-0222		760
Sixty Hotels 206 Spring St 4th Fl *TF:* 877-431-0400 ■ *Web:* sixtyhotels.com	New York	NY	10012	877-431-0400		707
Sizemore Inc 2116 Walton Way *TF:* 800-445-1748 ■ *Web:* www.sizemoreinc.com	Augusta	GA	30904	706-736-1456		692
Sizerville State Park 199 E Cowley Run Rd *Web:* www.dcnr.pa.gov	Emporium	PA	15834	814-486-5605		565
Sizzler Restaurants 25910 Acero Rd Ste 350 *Web:* www.sizzler.com	Mission Viejo	CA	92691	949-273-4497		670
SJ Amoroso Construction Company Inc 390 Bridge Pkwy *Web:* www.sjamoroso.com	Redwood City	CA	94065	650-654-1900	654-9002	188-7
SJ Transportation Company Inc PO Box 169 *TF:* 800-524-2552 ■ *Web:* sjtransportation.com	Woodstown	NJ	08098	856-769-2741	769-9811	780
SJB Group 8377 Picardy Ave *Web:* www.sjbgroup.com	Baton Rouge	LA	70809	225-769-3400	769-3596	261
SJCA PC 9102 N Meridian St Ste 200 *Web:* sjca-pc.com	Indianapolis	IN	46260	317-566-0629		261
SJE-Rhombus 22650 County Hwy 6 PO Box 1708 *TF:* 800-746-6287 ■ *Web:* www.sjerhombus.com	Detroit Lakes	MN	56502	218-847-1317	847-4617	201
SJF Material Handling Equipment 211 Baker Ave *TF:* 800-598-5532 ■ *Web:* www.sjf.com	Winsted	MN	55395	320-485-2824	485-2832	386
SJGH (San Joaquin General Hospital) 500 W Hospital Rd *Web:* www.sjgeneral.org	French Camp	CA	95231	209-468-6000		374-3
SJI (State Justice Institute) 11951 Freedom Dr Ste 1020 *Web:* www.sji.gov	Reston	VA	20190	571-313-8843	313-1173	340-20
SJMC (Saint Joseph's Medical Ctr) 127 S Broadway *Web:* www.saintjosephs.org	Yonkers	NY	10701	914-378-7000		374-3
SJMH (Stonewall Jackson Memorial Hospital) 230 Hospital Plz *TF:* 866-637-0471 ■ *Web:* www.stonewalljacksonhospital.com	Weston	WV	26452	304-269-8000	269-8090	374-3
Sjoberg & Votta 200 Centerville Rd Ste 4 *Web:* sjoberglaw.com	Warwick	RI	02886	401-737-9696		41
Sjogren Industries Inc 982 Southbridge St *Web:* www.sjogren.com	Worcester	MA	01610	508-987-3206		454
Sjostrom & Sons Inc PO Box 5766 *Web:* www.sjostromconstruction.com	Rockford	IL	61125	815-226-0330	226-8868	186
SJP (St Johann Press) PO Box 241 *Web:* www.stjohannpress.com	Haworth	NJ	07641	201-387-1529	501-0698	637-2
SJSVCC (San Jose Silicon Valley Chamber of Commerce) 101 W Santa Clara St *Web:* www.thesvo.com	San Jose	CA	95113	408-291-5250	286-5019	139
SJW Corp 110 W Taylor St *NYSE: SJW* ■ *Web:* www.sjwater.com	San Jose	CA	95110	408-279-7900		360-5
SK Food Group Inc 4600 37th Ave SW *TF:* 800-722-6290 ■ *Web:* www.skfoodgroup.com	Seattle	WA	98126	206-935-8100		366
SK Food International Inc 4666 Amber Vly Pkwy *Web:* www.skfood.com	Fargo	ND	58104	701-356-4106	356-4102	297-11
SK Hynix Memory Solutions 3103 N First St *Web:* www.skhms.com	San Jose	CA	95134	408-514-3500	514-3501	696
SK Plastic Molding Inc 1608 4th Ave W *Web:* www.skplasticmolding.com	Monroe	WI	53566	608-325-6004	325-4916	604
SK Publications 4105 Naperville Rd *Web:* www.sos.org	Lisle	IL	60532	630-955-1200	955-1205	637-2
SK Textile Inc 1 Knollcrest Dr **Fax Area Code: 888* ■ *TF:* 800-888-9112 ■ *Web:* www.sktextile.com	Cincinnati	OH	45237	800-888-9112	415-0854*	258
SKA Brewing Co 225 Girard St *Web:* skabrewing.com	Durango	CO	81303	970-247-5792		102
SKA Consulting Engineers Inc 300 Pomona Dr *Web:* www.skaeng.com	Greensboro	NC	27407	336-855-0993		261
Skach Manufacturing Company Inc 950 Anita Ave *Web:* www.skachcoldform.com	Antioch	IL	60002	847-395-3560	395-9123	278
Skadden, Arps, Slate, Meagher & Flom LLP 4 Times Sq *Web:* www.skadden.com	New York	NY	10036	212-735-3000	735-2000	428
Skaggs Family Records PO Box 2478 *Web:* skaggsfamilyrecords.com	Hendersonville	TN	37077	615-264-8877	264-8899	657
Skagit Farmers Supply 1833 Pk Ln PO Box 266 *TF:* 888-757-6053 ■ *Web:* www.skagitfarmers.com	Burlington	WA	98233	360-757-6053	757-4143	48-2
Skagit Transportation Inc 16159 McLean Rd *TF:* 800-562-3218 ■ *Web:* www.skagittrans.com	Mount Vernon	WA	98273	360-424-4214	428-4851	519
Skagit Valley Casino Resort 5984 N Darrk Ln *TF:* 877-275-2448 ■ *Web:* www.theskagit.com	Bow	WA	98232	877-275-2448		133
Skagit Valley College 2405 E College Way *TF:* 877-385-5360 ■ *Web:* www.skagit.edu	Mount Vernon	WA	98273	360-416-7600	416-7890	162
Skagit Valley Herald 1000 E College Way *TF:* 800-683-3300 ■ *Web:* www.goskagit.com	Mount Vernon	WA	98273	360-424-4567	424-5300	532-2
Skagit Valley Hospital 300 Hospital Pkwy *Web:* www.skagitvalleyhospital.org	Mount Vernon	WA	98273	360-424-4111		374-3
Skagway Chamber of Commerce PO Box 194 *Web:* www.skagwaychamber.org	Skagway	AK	99840	907-983-1898	983-2031	139
Skagway Visitor Information 245 Broadway PO Box 1029 *TF:* 888-762-1898 ■ *Web:* skagway.com	Skagway	AK	99840	907-983-2854	983-3854	206
Skamania County 240 NW Vancouver Ave PO Box 790 *TF:* 800-375-5283 ■ *Web:* www.skamaniacounty.org	Stevenson	WA	98648	509-427-3770	427-3777	338
Skane Wilcox LLP 1055 W Seventh St Ste 1700 *Web:* skanewilcox.com	Los Angeles	CA	90017	213-452-1200		41
Skanska USA Inc 350 Fifth Ave *Web:* www.skanska.com	New York	NY	10118	718-767-2600		186
Skarstedt Gallery Ltd 20 E 79th St *Web:* skarstedt.com	New York	NY	10075	212-737-2060		42
Skasol Inc 1696 W Grand Ave *Web:* www.skasol.com	Oakland	CA	94607	510-839-1000	839-1090	145
Skate One 30 S La Patera Ln *TF:* 800-288-7528 ■ *Web:* www.skateone.com	Santa Barbara	CA	93117	805-964-1330	964-0511	710
Skaug Law PC 1226 E Karcher Rd *TF:* 800-944-1210 ■ *Web:* skauglaw.com	Nampa	ID	83687	208-466-0030	466-8903	41
Skaug Truck Body Works Inc 1404 1st St	San Fernando	CA	91340	818-365-9123		516
SKB Corp 434 W Levers Pl *TF:* 800-410-2024 ■ *Web:* www.skbcases.com	Orange	CA	92867	714-637-1252	637-0491	453
SKBA Capital Management 44 Montgomery St Ste 3500 *Web:* www.skba.com	San Francisco	CA	94104	415-989-7852	989-2114	401
SKC & Company CPAS LLC 1 Mars Ct Ste 1 *Web:* skcandco.com	Boonton Township	NJ	07005	973-335-1112	335-7976	2
SKC Inc 863 Vly View Rd *TF:* 800-752-8472 ■ *Web:* www.skcinc.com	Eighty Four	PA	15330	724-941-9701	941-1369	420
Skechers USA Inc 228 Manhattan Beach Blvd *NYSE: SKX* ■ *TF:* 800-746-3411 ■ *Web:* www.skechers.com	Manhattan Beach	CA	90266	310-318-3100		301
Skeele Agency Inc 1715 Albany St PO Box 459 *Web:* skeele.com	Deruyter	NY	13052	315-852-6180	682-5143	390
Skeeter Products Inc 1 Skeeter Rd *Web:* www.skeeterboats.com	Kilgore	TX	75662	903-984-0541		90
Skeleton Key 3260 Hampton Ave Ste 200 *Web:* www.skeletonkey.com	Saint Louis	MO	63139	314-353-4300		180
Skelton, Brumwell & Associates Inc 93 Bell Farm Rd Ste 107 *Web:* www.skeltonbrumwell.ca	Barrie	ON	L4M5G1	705-726-1141		261
Skernkraft Inc 281 E Water St *Web:* www.vology.com	Rockland	MA	02370	781-384-2023		226
SKF Books Inc 1050 Larrabee Ave Ste 104-357 *TF:* 800-927-8178 ■ *Web:* www.skfbooks.com	Bellingham	WA	98225	360-202-4567	734-9527	637-2
SKF USA Inc *Roller Bearing Div* 20 Industrial Dr *Web:* www.skf.com	Hanover	PA	17331	717-637-8981		75
SKI Bromont 150 Champlain *TF:* 866-276-6668 ■ *Web:* skibromont.com	Bromont	QC	J2L1A2	450-534-2200		379

				Phone	Fax	Class
SKI Magazine 5720 Flatiron Pkwy *TF:* 800-678-0817 ■ *Web:* www.skimag.com	Boulder	CO	80301	303-253-6300		457-20
SKI Pro 1924 W Eigth St *TF:* 888-754-7761 ■ *Web:* skipro.com	Mesa	AZ	85201	480-962-6910		711
Skidata Inc 120 Albany St Tower II - Ste 750 *Web:* www.skidata.com	New Brunswick	NJ	08901	908-243-0000	243-0660	196
Skidaway Island State Park 52 Diamond Cswy *Web:* www.gastateparks.org	Savannah	GA	31411	912-598-2300	598-2365	565
Skidmore College 815 N Broadway *TF:* 800-867-6007 ■ *Web:* www.skidmore.edu	Saratoga Springs	NY	12866	518-580-5000	580-5584	166
Skidmore Owings & Merrill LLP (SOM) 224 S Michigan Ave Ste 1000 *TF:* 866-296-2688 ■ *Web:* www.som.com	Chicago	IL	60604	312-554-9090	360-4545	261
Skidmore Studio 1555 Broadway *Web:* www.skidmorestudio.com	Detroit	MI	48226	313-446-8200		344
Skier's Choice Inc 1717 Henry G Ln St *TF:* 800-320-2779 ■ *Web:* www.supraboats.com	Maryville	TN	37801	865-983-9924	983-9950	90
Skilcraft LLC 5184 Limaburg Rd *TF:* 800-888-2122 ■ *Web:* skilcraft.com	Burlington	KY	41005	859-371-0799	371-2627	697
Skill Creations Inc 2101 Royall Ave PO Box 10628 **Fax Area Code:* 252 ■ *Web:* www.skillcreations.com	Goldsboro	NC	27532	919-734-7398	442-0836*	48-15
Skilled Care Pharmacy Inc 6175 HI Tek Ct *TF:* 800-334-1624 ■ *Web:* www.skilledcare.com	Mason	OH	45040	513-459-7455		583
Skillern Law 701 N Post Oak Ste 207 *Web:* skillernfirm.com	Houston	TX	77024	713-597-5802		41
Skillforce Inc 405 Williams Ct Ste 106 *TF:* 866-581-8989 ■ *Web:* www.skillforce.com	Baltimore	MD	21220	866-581-8989		260
Skillman Corp, The 3834 S Emerson Ave Bldg A *Web:* www.skillman.com	Indianapolis	IN	46203	317-783-6151		194
Skillpath Seminars 6900 Squibb Rd **Fax Area Code:* 913 ■ *TF:* 800 873 7545 ■ *Web:* www.skillpath.com	Mission	KS	66202	800-873-7545	362-4241*	195
Skillpoint Alliance 201 E Second St Ste B *Web:* skillpointalliance.org	Austin	TX	78701	512-323-6773	323-5884	765
Skills Career Education Ctr 150 Fearing St *Web:* www.skillsamherst.com	Amherst	MA	01002	413-549-2686		167-3
Skillshare Inc 35 E 21st St 5th Fl *Web:* www.skillshare.com	New York	NY	10010	202-996-8412		178-8
SkillSoft PLC 300 Innovative Way Ste 201 *TF:* 877-545-5763 ■ *Web:* www.skillsoft.com	Nashua	NH	03062	603-324-3000		765
SkillStorm Commercial Services LLC 6414 NW Fifth Way *Web:* skillstorm.com	Fort Lauderdale	FL	33309	954-566-4647		260
SkillsUSA 14001 James Monroe Hwy *TF:* 800-321-8422 ■ *Web:* www.skillsusa.org	Leesburg	VA	20176	703-777-8810	777-8999	48-11
SkinMedica Inc 5770 Armada Dr *TF:* 877-944-1412	Carlsbad	CA	92008	877-944-1412		214
Skinner & Kennedy Co 9451 Natural Bridge Rd *TF:* 800-426-3094 ■ *Web:* www.skinnerkennedy.com	Saint Louis	MO	63134	314-426-2800		627
Skinner Transfer Corp PO Box 438 *TF:* 800-356-9350 ■ *Web:* skinnertransfer.com	Reedsburg	WI	53959	608-524-2326	524-9660	780
Skinner Transportation Inc 850 Ed Bluestein Blvd *Web:* www.skinnertrans.com	Austin	TX	78721	512-389-3311	389-0084	780
Skinworks School of Advanced Skincare 2121 Nowell Cir *Web:* www.skin-works.com	Salt Lake City	UT	84115	801-530-0001		685
Skipping Stone Inc 83 Pine St Ste 101 *Web:* skippingstone.com	West Peabody	MA	01960	978-717-6100	717-6199	196
Skirball Cultural Ctr 2701 N Sepulveda Blvd *Web:* www.skirball.org	Los Angeles	CA	90049	310-440-4500		50-2
Skitter TV 3230 Peachtree Corners Cir Ste H *Web:* skitter.tv	Norcross	GA	30092	678-894-8808		647
Skjonberg Controls Inc 1363 Donlon St Ste 6 *Web:* www.skjonberg.com	Ventura	CA	93003	805-650-0877	650-0360	203
Sklar Exploration Company LLC 401 Edwards St Ste 1601 *Web:* www.sklarexploration.com	Shreveport	LA	71101	318-227-8668		539
Sklar Surgical Instruments 889 S Matlack St *TF:* 800-221-2166 ■ *Web:* www.sklarcorp.com	West Chester	PA	19382	610-756-7863	430-3941	476
SKO (Stoll Keenon Ogden PLLC) 300 W Vine St Ste 2100 *Web:* www.skofirm.com	Lexington	KY	40507	859-231-3000	253-1093	41
Skoah Inc 4800 Kingsway Ave Ste 309 *TF:* 888-697-5624 ■ *Web:* www.skoah.com	Burnaby	BC	V5H4J2	604-433-0200		354
Skoda Minotti 6685 Beta Dr *TF:* 888-201-4484 ■ *Web:* skodaminotti.com	Cleveland	OH	44143	440-449-6800		734
Skody Scot & Company CPA PC 520 Eighth Ave Ste 2200 *Web:* skodyscot.com	New York	NY	10018	212-967-1100		2
Skoflo Industries Inc 14241 NE 200th Ste A *Web:* www.skoflo.com	Woodinville	WA	98072	425-485-7816		789
Skogman Construction Company Inc 411 First Ave *Web:* www.skogman.com	Cedar Rapids	IA	52401	319-363-8285	366-7257	187
Skokie Chamber of Commerce 5002 Oakton St PO Box 106 *TF:* 800-526-8441 ■ *Web:* skokiechamber.org	Skokie	IL	60077	847-673-0240	673-0249	139
Skokie Public Library 5215 Oakton St *Web:* skokielibrary.info	Skokie	IL	60077	847-673-7774	673-7797	434-3
Skol Manufacturing Co 4444 N Ravenswood Ave *Web:* www.skolmfg.com	Chicago	IL	60640	773-878-5959	878-0320	492
Skoler, Abbott & Presser PC 1 Monarch Pl Ste 2000 *TF:* 800-274-6774 ■ *Web:* skoler-abbott.com	Springfield	MA	01144	413-737-4753	787-1941	428
Skolnik Industries Inc 4900 S Kilbourn Ave *TF:* 800-441-8780 ■ *Web:* www.skolnik.com	Chicago	IL	60632	773-735-0700		198
Skoloff & Wolfe PC 293 Eisenhower Pkwy *Web:* skoloffwolfe.com	Livingston	NJ	07039	973-992-0900		41
Skotdal Real Estate 2707 Colby Ave Ste 1200 *Web:* www.skotdal.com	Everett	WA	98201	425-252-5400	258-2473	78
SKRL Die Casting Inc 34580 Lakeland Blvd *Web:* www.skrltool.com	Willoughby	OH	44095	440-946-7200	946-2929	757
SKS Bottle & Packaging Inc 2600 Seventh Ave Bldg 60 W *TF:* 800-880-6990 ■ *Web:* www.sks-bottle.com	Watervliet	NY	12189	518-880-6980		385
SKS Engineers LLC 2900 N Martin Luther King Jr Dr *Web:* www.sksengineers.com	Decatur	IL	62526	217-877-2100	877-4816	261
Skuld North America Inc 757 3rd Ave 25th Fl *Web:* www.skuld.com	New York	NY	10017	212-758-9200	758-9935	391-4
Skupin & Lucas PC 155 W Congress Ste 350 *TF:* 800-710-4811 ■ *Web:* skupinlucas.com	Detroit	MI	48226	313-961-0425	961-1033	41
Skupos 1462 Pine St *TF:* 800-559-1358 ■ *Web:* www.skupos.com	San Francisco	CA	94109	800-559-1358		113
Skurka Aerospace Inc 4600 Calle Bolero *Web:* www.skurka-aero.com	Camarillo	CA	93012	805-484-8884	482-7771	518
Skuttle Manufacturing Co 101 Margaret St *TF:* 800-848-9786 ■ *Web:* www.skuttle.com	Marietta	OH	45750	740-373-9169	373-9565	14
Skwiercky, Alpert & Bressler LLP 462 Seventh Ave 23rd Fl *Web:* sabllp.com	New York	NY	10018	212-714-0462		2
Sky & Telescope Magazine 90 Sherman St **Fax Area Code:* 617 ■ *TF:* 800-253-0245 ■ *Web:* skyandtelescope.org	Cambridge	MA	02140	855-638-5388	864-6117*	457-19
Sky Adv Inc 14 E 33rd St *Web:* www.skyad.com	New York	NY	10016	212-677-2500		4
Sky Bird Travel & Tours 24701 Swanson *TF:* 888-759-2473 ■ *Web:* www.skybirdtravel.com	Southfield	MI	48033	240-372-4800	372-4810	16
Sky Bright 65 Aviation Dr *TF:* 800-639-6012 ■ *Web:* www.skybright.com	Gilford	NH	03249	603-528-6818		63
Sky Climber LLC 1800 Pittsburgh Dr *TF:* 800-255-4629 ■ *Web:* skyclimber.com	Delaware	OH	43015	740-203-3900	203-3901	393
Sky Cylinder Testing 2220 Lexington Rd *Web:* www.skycylinder.com	Evansville	IN	47720	812-423-1759		743
SKY Foundation 339 Fitzwater St *Web:* www.skyfoundation.org	Philadelphia	PA	19147	215-574-9180	247-8054	637-2
Sky Helicopters Inc 2559 S Jupiter Rd *Web:* www.skyhelicopters.com	Garland	TX	75041	214-349-7000	342-8616	24
Sky High Marketing 3550 E Post Rd *TF:* 800-246-7447 ■ *Web:* www.skyhighmarketing.com	Las Vegas	NV	89120	702-436-0867	436-0905	195
Sky I. T. Group LLC 330 Seventh Ave *TF:* 866-641-6017 ■ *Web:* www.skyitgroup.com	New York	NY	10001	212-868-7800		196
Sky Lakes Medical Ctr 2865 Daggett Ave *Web:* www.skylakes.org	Klamath Falls	OR	97601	541-882-6311		374-3
Sky Meadows State Park 11012 Edmonds Ln *Web:* www.dcr.virginia.gov	Delaplane	VA	20144	540-592-3556		565
Sky Publishing Corp 90 Sherman St *Web:* www.skyandtelescope.com	Cambridge	MA	02140	617-864-7360	864-6117	637-9
Sky Ranch 24657 CR 448 *TF:* 800-962-2267 ■ *Web:* skyranch.org	Van	TX	75790	800-962-2267		148
Sky U LLC 33 W 19th St *Web:* www.skyu.tv	New York	NY	10011	212-385-9500	385-9505	741-99
Sky Ute Casino 14324 US Hwy 172 N *TF:* 888-842-4180 ■ *Web:* www.skyutecasino.com	Ignacio	CO	81137	970-563-7777		133
Sky Valley Golf Club 568 Sky Vly Way *Web:* skyvalleycountryclub.com	Sky Valley	GA	30537	706-746-5303		669
Skybank Financial Services Corp 1444 Biscayne Blvd Ste 309 *TF:* 800-617-9980 ■ *Web:* skybankfinancial.com	Miami	FL	33132	800-617-9980		225
SkyBox Inc 8601 Nw 27th St *Web:* www.skybox.net	Doral	FL	33172	786-265-4880		459
Skybox Security Inc 2099 Gateway Pl Ste 450 *TF:* 866-675-9269 ■ *Web:* www.skyboxsecurity.com	San Jose	CA	95110	408-441-8060		177
Skybridge Global Inc Northridge Ctr II 375 Northridge Rd Ste 400 *Web:* skybridgeglobal.com	Atlanta	GA	30350	770-373-2300	984-2662	178-1
Skycasters LLC 1520 S Arlington St Ste 100 *Web:* www.skycasters.com	Akron	OH	44306	330-785-2100		224
Skycom Avionics Inc 2441 Aviation Rd *TF:* 800-443-4490 ■ *Web:* www.skycomavionics.com	Waukesha	WI	53188	262-521-8180		20
Skycraft Parts & Surplus Inc 2245 W Fairbanks Ave *Web:* www.skycraftsurplus.com	Winter Park	FL	32789	407-628-5634		791
Skye Biologics Inc 2629 Manhattan Beach Blvd *Web:* static1.squarespace.com	Redondo Beach	CA	90266	310-796-5680		476
Skyemed Pharmacy 1332 N Federal Hwy	Pompano Beach	FL	33062	954-580-0170		237
Skyfold Inc *Railtech Ltd* 325 Lee Ave *Web:* www.railtech.ca	Montreal	QC	H9X3S3	514-457-4760	457-7111	770

Company	City	State	ZIP	Phone	Fax	Class
SkyFuel Inc 200 Union Blvd Ste 590 *Web:* www.skyfuel.com	Lakewood	CO	80228	303-330-0276		696
Skygone Inc 700 E Redlands Blvd Ste 343 **Fax Area Code:* 909 ■ *TF:* 888-759-4471	Redlands	CA	92373	888-759-4471	363-4076*	196
Skyhawks Sports Academy Inc 9425 N Nevada Ste 210 *TF:* 800-804-3509 ■ *Web:* www.skyhawks.com	Spokane	WA	99218	509-466-6590		239
Skyjack Inc 55 Campbell Rd *TF:* 800-265-2738 ■ *Web:* www.skyjack.com	Guelph	ON	N1H1B9	800-265-2738		111
Skyland Travel Inc 100-445 6th Ave W *TF:* 888-685-6888 ■ *Web:* www.escapes.ca	Vancouver	BC	V5Y1L3	604-685-6885		775
Skylight Books 1818 N Vermont Ave *Web:* www.skylightbooks.com	Los Angeles	CA	90027	323-660-1175	660-0232	95
Skylight Opera Theatre 158 N Broadway *Web:* www.skylightmusictheatre.org	Milwaukee	WI	53202	414-291-7811	291-7815	573-2
Skyline 3355 Discovery Rd *TF:* 800-328-2725 ■ *Web:* www.skyline.com	Saint Paul	MN	55121	651-234-6592		393
Skyline Asset Management LP 120 S Lasalle St Ste 1400 *Web:* www.skylinelp.com	Chicago	IL	60603	312-913-0900	750-0698	528
Skyline Assisted & Independent Living 7350 Graceland Dr *Web:* keystonevillasliving.com	Omaha	NE	68134	402-572-5750		672
Skyline Chili Inc 4180 Thunderbird Ln *TF:* 800-443-4371 ■ *Web:* www.skylinechili.com	Fairfield	OH	45014	513-874-1188		670
Skyline College 3300 College Dr *Web:* www.skylinecollege.edu	San Bruno	CA	94066	650-738-4100		162
Skyline Construction 505 Sansome St 7th Fl *Web:* www.skylineconstruction.build	San Francisco	CA	94111	415-908-1020		186
Skyline Corp 2520 By-Pass Rd *NYSE: SKY* ■ *TF:* 800-348-7469 ■ *Web:* www.skylinecorp.com	Elkhart	IN	46514	574-294-6521		120
Skyline Hotel 725 Tenth Ave *Web:* www.skylinehotelny.com	New York	NY	10019	212-586-3400		379
Skyline Medical Inc 2915 Commers Dr Ste 900 *Web:* www.skylinemedical.com	Eagan	MN	55121	651-389-4800		476
Skyline Membership Corp 1200 NC Hwy 194 N *TF:* 800-759-2226 ■ *Web:* www.skybest.com	West Jefferson	NC	28694	800-759-2226		736
Skyline Network Engineering LLC 6956-F Aviation Blvd *Web:* www.skylinenet.net	Glen Burnie	MD	21061	410-795-2700		176
Skyline Pest Solutions Inc 1745 Pennsylvania Ave *Web:* www.skylinepest.com	Mcdonough	GA	30253	678-432-5464		577
Skyline Products 2903 Delta Dr *TF:* 800-759-9046 ■ *Web:* www.skylineproducts.com	Colorado Springs	CO	80910	800-759-9046		697
Skyline Properties South Inc 50 116th Ave SE Ste 120 *TF:* 800-753-6156 ■ *Web:* www.skylineproperties.com	Bellevue	WA	98004	425-455-2065		652
Skyline Steel LLC 8 Woodhollow Rd Ste 102 *Web:* www.skylinesteel.com	Parsippany	NJ	07054	973-428-6100		492
Skyline Technologies Inc 1400 Lombardi Ave *Web:* www.skylinetechnologies.com	Green Bay	WI	54304	920-437-1360		177
Skyline Ultd Inc 427 N Lee St *Web:* www.skyline-ultd.com	Alexandria	VA	22314	703-373-2330	373-1714	180
Skylink Travel 980 Avenue of the Americas *TF:* 800-247-6659 ■ *Web:* www.skylinkus.com	New York	NY	10018	212-380-2433	573-8878	16
Skymicro Inc 2060 E Avenida De Los Arboles Ste D344 *Web:* www.skymicro.com	Thousand Oaks	CA	91362	805-491-8995		52
Skyservice Airlines Inc 9785 Ryan Ave *TF:* 888-985-1402 ■ *Web:* www.skyservice.com	Dorval	QC	H9P1A2	514-636-3300	636-4855	13
Sky-Skan Inc 51 Lake St *TF:* 800-880-8500 ■ *Web:* www.skyskan.com	Nashua	NH	03060	603-880-8500	882-6522	393
Skyspares Parts Inc 6640 View Park Ct *Web:* www.machininglogistics.com	Riverside	CA	92503	951-351-0770	351-1741	22
Skystone Partner 635 W Seventh St Ste 107 *TF:* 800-883-0801 ■ *Web:* www.skystonepartners.com	Cincinnati	OH	45203	513-241-6778		317
SkyTech Inc 701 Wilson Pt Rd Ste 3 PO Box 4942 *Web:* www.skytechinc.com	Baltimore	MD	21220	410-574-4144		770
SkyTel Corp PO Box 2469 *TF:* 800-759-8737 ■ *Web:* www.skytel.com	Jackson	MS	39225	800-759-8737		736
Skytop Lodge 1 Skytop Meadows *TF:* 800-345-7759 ■ *Web:* www.skytop.com	Skytop	PA	18357	855-345-7759		669
Skyview Memorial Lawn 200 Rollingwood Dr *Web:* www.skyviewmemorial.com	Vallejo	CA	94591	707-644-7474		510
Skywalker AV Supply 1760 W Terra Ln *TF:* 800-844-9555 ■ *Web:* www.skywalker.com	O'Fallon	MO	63366	636-272-8025		246
Skyward Inc 5233 Coye Dr *TF:* 800-236-7274 ■ *Web:* www.skyward.com	Stevens Point	WI	54481	800-236-7274		178-12
Skyway Precision Inc 41225 Plymouth Rd *Web:* www.skywayprecision.com	Plymouth	MI	48170	734-454-3550		621
Skyway Towers LLC 3637 Madaca Ln *Web:* www.skywaytowers.com	Tampa	FL	33618	813-960-6200		246
Skyway West 3644 Beach Ave *TF:* 877-771-1077 ■ *Web:* www.skywaywest.com	Roberts Creek	BC	V0N2W2	604-482-1228		224
Skyweb Networks 2710 State St *TF:* 866-575-9932 ■ *Web:* www.skywebonline.com	Saginaw	MI	48602	989-792-8681		180
SkyWest Airlines 444 S River Rd *Web:* www.skywest.com	Saint George	UT	84790	435-634-3000	634-3105	25
Skyworks LLC 100 Thielman Dr *TF:* 877-601-5438 ■ *Web:* www.skyworksllc.com	Buffalo	NY	14206	716-822-5438		264-3
Skyworks Solutions Inc 20 Sylvan Rd *NASDAQ: SWKS* ■ *Web:* www.skyworksinc.com	Woburn	MA	01801	781-376-3000		696
Skyy Consulting Inc 1335 Fourth St Ste 200 **Fax Area Code:* 310 ■ *TF:* 877-897-3473 ■ *Web:* www.callfire.com	Santa Monica	CA	90401	877-897-3473	943-0415*	224
SL Green Realty Corp 420 Lexington Ave *NYSE: SLG* ■ *Web:* www.slgreen.com	New York	NY	10170	212-594-2700		655
SL Power Electronics Inc 6050 King Dr Bldg A **Fax Area Code:* 858 ■ *TF:* 800-235-5929 ■ *Web:* www.slpower.com	Ventura	CA	93003	805-486-4565	712-2040*	253
SLA (Special Libraries Assn) 331 S Patrick St *TF:* 866-446-6069 ■ *Web:* www.sla.org	Alexandria	VA	22314	703-647-4900	647-4901	49-11
SLAA (Sex & Love Addicts Anonymous) 1550 NE Loop 410 Ste 118 *Web:* slaafws.org	San Antonio	TX	78209	210-828-7900	828-7922	48-21
SLAC (Stanford Linear Accelerator Ctr) 2575 Sand Hill Rd *Web:* www.slac.stanford.edu	Menlo Park	CA	94025	650-926-3300	926-4999	668
Slack & Davis LLP 2705 Bee Caves Rd Ste 220 *TF:* 800-455-8686 ■ *Web:* www.slackdavis.com	Austin	TX	78746	512-795-8686		428
Slack Auto Parts 404 Main St SW *Web:* www.slackautoparts.com	Gainesville	GA	30501	770-535-6000		791
Slack Chemical Company Inc 465 S Clinton St *TF:* 800-479-0430 ■ *Web:* www.slackchem.com	Carthage	NY	13619	315-493-0430	493-3931	146
Slack Inc 6900 Grove Rd *TF:* 800-257-8290 ■ *Web:* www.slackinc.com	Thorofare	NJ	08086	856-848-1000	848-6091	637-9
Slacktronics LLC 682 Lambert Rd *Web:* www.slacktronics.com	Orange	CT	06477	203-795-5955		177
Slade Gorton Company Inc 225 Southampton St *TF:* 800-225-1573 ■ *Web:* www.sladegorton.com	Boston	MA	02118	617-442-5800	442-9090	297-5
Slade Quilty & Associates CPAs LLP 26619 Carmel Center Pl Ste 102 *Web:* sladequiltyandassoccarmelca.com	Carmel By The Sea	CA	93923	831-625-8740		2
Slade Veterinary Hospital Inc 334 Concord St *Web:* sladevet.com	Framingham	MA	01702	508-875-7086		794
Slam Dunk Networks Inc 2600 S El Camino Real Ste 220	San Mateo	CA	94403	650-525-3902		174
Slane Hosiery Mills Inc 313 S Centennial St *Web:* www.slanehosiery.com	High Point	NC	27261	336-883-4136		155-10
Slant Fin Corp 100 Forest Dr *TF:* 800-875-2389 ■ *Web:* www.slantfin.com	Greenvale	NY	11548	516-484-2600		14
Slanted Door 1 Ferry Bldg Ste 3 *Web:* www.slanteddoor.com	San Francisco	CA	94111	415-861-8032		671
Slash Pine Electric Membership Corp 794 W Dame Ave Ste 356 *Web:* slashpineemc.com	Homerville	GA	31634	912-487-5201	487-2948	245
Slate Group 6024 45th St *TF:* 800-794-5594 ■ *Web:* slategroup.com	Lubbock	TX	79407	806-794-7752	798-8190	627
Slate Magazine 1707 L St NW Ste 800 *Web:* slate.com	Washington	DC	20036	212-445-5330		457-17
Slate Professional Resources Inc 800 W Main St Ste 204 *Web:* www.slateprofessional.com	Freehold	NJ	07728	732-303-6329		631
Slate Properties Inc 121 King St W Ste 200 *Web:* www.slateam.com	Toronto	ON	M5H3T9	416-644-4264	947-9366	653
Slater Inc 4712 68th Ave *Web:* www.slater-inc.com	Kenosha	WI	53144	262-658-8626	658-8628	454
Slater Memorial Museum 108 Crescent St *Web:* www.slatermuseum.org	Norwich	CT	06360	860-887-2506		520
Slater Partners LLC *Bulldog Ventures Media LLC* 204 Galway Dr *Web:* www.slaterpartners.com	Chapel Hill	NC	27517	919-933-6883	969-1970	463
Slater Technology Fund 3 Davol Sq Ste A340 *Web:* www.slaterfund.com	Providence	RI	02903	401-831-6633		415
Slaton Independent School District 140 E Panhandle St *Web:* www.slatonisd.net	Slaton	TX	79364	806-828-6591		685
Slave Haven Underground Railroad Museum 826 N Second St *Web:* www.slavehavenundergroundrailroadmuseum.org	Memphis	TN	38173	901-527-3427		520
Slawson Companies Inc 727 N Waco St Ste 400 *Web:* www.slawsoncompanies.com	Wichita	KS	67203	316-263-3201		536
Slay Industries Inc 1441 Hampton Ave *TF:* 800-852-7529 ■ *Web:* www.slay.com	Saint Louis	MO	63139	314-647-7529	647-5240	449
Slayton Public Library 2451 Broadway Ave *Web:* www.plumcreeklibrary.org	Slayton	MN	56172	507-836-8778		434-3
SLB (South Louisiana Bank) 1362 W Tunnel Blvd PO Box 1718 *Web:* ayeee.com	Houma	LA	70361	985-851-3434	879-3095	70
SLC Meter LLC 595 Bradford St *TF:* 800-433-4332 ■ *Web:* slcmeterllc.com	Pontiac	MI	48340	248-625-0667	625-8650	385
SLCHA (St Lawrence County Historical Assn) 3 E Main St *Web:* www.slcha.org	Canton	NY	13617	315-386-8133		637-2
SLCL (Saint Louis County Library) 1640 S Lindbergh Blvd *Web:* www.slcl.org	Saint Louis	MO	63131	314-994-3300		434-3
Sledge Telephone Company Inc 124 Delta Ave *TF:* 888-655-7707 ■ *Web:* www.deltaland.net	Sunflower	MS	38778	662-569-3311		224
Sleep America Inc 1202 N 54th Ave Ste 111	Phoenix	AZ	85043	602-269-7000		321
Sleep Country Canada LP 140 Wendell Ave *Web:* www.sleepcountry.ca	North York	ON	M9N3R2	289-748-0206		364
Sleep Designs 5808 Berry Brook Dr *Web:* www.sleep-designs.com	Houston	TX	77017	713-227-0121		471

	Phone	Fax	Class
Sleep Unlimited Inc - Cordova 320 S Walnut Bend Rd Ste 6 . . . Cordova TN 38018 *Web:* www.willwork4sleep.com	901-737-9196	432-6230	152
Sleeping Bear Dunes National Lakeshore 9922 Front St . . . Empire MI 49630 *Web:* www.nps.gov	231-326-5134	326-5382	564
Sleeping Giant State Park 200 Mt Carmel Ave . . . Hamden CT 06518 *Web:* portal.ct.gov	203-582-8200		565
Sleepless Warrior Publishing 14989 Grassy Knoll Ct . . . Woodbridge VA 22193 *Web:* www.sleeplesswarrior.com	703-897-9394		637-2
Sleepy Hollow Cemetery 540 N Broadway . . . Sleepy Hollow NY 10591 *Web:* sleepyhollowcemetery.org	914-631-0081		50-3
Sleepy Hollow State Park 7835 E Price Rd . . . Laingsburg MI 48848 *Web:* www.michigan.org	517-651-6217		565
Slepian Law Office Pllc, The 3737 N Seventh St Ste 106 . . . Phoenix AZ 85014 *Web:* slepian.com	602-842-6740		41
Sletten Construction Company Inc 1000 25th St N . . . Great Falls MT 59401 *Web:* www.slettencompanies.com	406-761-7920	761-0923	186
Slevin & Hart PC 1625 Massachusetts Ave NW Ste 450 . . . Washington DC 20036 *Web:* www.slevinhart.com	202-797-8700		428
SLG Books PO Box 9465 . . . Berkeley CA 94709 *TF:* 800-603-9903 ■ *Web:* www.slgbooks.com	510-525-1134		637-2
SlickData 252 Nassau St 2nd Fl . . . Princeton NJ 08542 *Web:* www.slickdata.com	609-736-0036		196
SlickEdit Inc 3000 Aerial Center Pkwy Ste 120 . . . Morrisville NC 27560 *TF:* 800-934-3348 ■ *Web:* www.slickedit.com	919-473-0070	473-0080	178-2
Slide Inn, The 2348 SE Ankeny . . . Portland OR 97214 *Web:* www.slideinnpdx.com	503-236-4997		671
Slidell Memorial Hospital (SMH) 1001 Gause Blvd . . . Slidell LA 70458 *Web:* slidellmemorial.org	985-280-2200		374-3
Slidematic Products Co 4520 W Addison St . . . Chicago IL 60641 *Web:* www.slidematicproducts.com	773-545-4213	545-0797	488
Slifer Designs 216 Main St Ste C-100 . . . Edwards CO 81632 *TF:* 866-926-8200 ■ *Web:* www.sliferdesigns.com	970-926-8200		393
Sligh Cabinets Inc 105 Calle Propano . . . Paso Robles CA 93446 *Web:* www.slighcabinets.com	805-239-2550		115
Slightly North of Broad 192 E Bay St . . . Charleston SC 29401 *Web:* snobcharleston.com	843-723-3424	724-3811	671
Slingshot LLC 208 N Market St Ste 500 . . . Dallas TX 75202 *Web:* www.slingshot.com	214-634-4411	634-5511	4
Slippery Rock University 1 Morrow Way . . . Slippery Rock PA 16057 *TF:* 800-929-4778 ■ *Web:* www.sru.edu	724-738-9000	738-2913	166
Sliqua Enterprise Hosting 340 S Lemon Ave No 2450 . . . Walnut CA 91789 *TF:* 877-475-4782 ■ *Web:* www.sliqua.com	877-475-4782		225
Sliters Lumber & Building Supply 55 Somers Rd . . . Somers MT 59932 *Web:* www.sliters.com	406-857-3306		364
SLM Manufacturing Corp 215 Davidson Ave . . . Somerset NJ 08873 *TF:* 800-526-3708 ■ *Web:* www.slmcorp.com	732-469-7500	469-5546	600
SL-Montevideo Technology Inc 2002 Black Oak Ave . . . Montevideo MN 56265 *Web:* www.slmti.com	320-269-6562	269-7662	518
SLMP LLC 407 Interchange St . . . Mckinney TX 75071 *TF:* 800-442-3573 ■ *Web:* www.statlab.com	972-436-1010		475
Sloan & Co 49 Bloomfield Ave Ste 101 . . . Mountain Lakes NJ 07046 *Web:* www.sloanandcompany.com	973-227-3555	227-8731	393
Sloan Construction Company Inc 250 Plemmons Rd . . . Duncan SC 29334 *Web:* www.sloan-construction.com	864-968-2250	968-2255	188-4
Sloan Implement Co 120 N Business 51 . . . Assumption IL 62510 *TF:* 800-745-4020 ■ *Web:* www.sloans.com	217-226-4411	226-3351	274
Sloan Management Review 77 Massachusetts Ave E60-100 . . . Cambridge MA 02139 *TF:* 800-876-5764 ■ *Web:* sloanreview.mit.edu	617-253-7170	258-9739	457-5
Sloan Miyasato 2 Henry Adams St Ste 300 . . . San Francisco CA 94103 *Web:* www.sloanm.com	415-431-1465	431-1397	361
Sloan Valve Co 10500 Seymour Ave . . . Franklin Park IL 60131 *TF:* 800-982-5839 ■ *Web:* www.sloan.com	847-671-4300	671-6944	609
Sloane & Co 7 Times Sq 17th Fl . . . New York NY 10036 *Web:* www.sloanepr.com	212-486-9500		636
Sloat Garden Center Inc 420 Coloma St . . . Sausalito CA 94965 *Web:* www.sloatgardens.com	415-332-0657		323
SLOCLL (San Luis Obispo County Law Library) 1050 Monterey St Rm 125 . . . San Luis Obispo CA 93408 *Web:* www.slocll.org	805-781-5855	781-4172	434-3
Slocum and Sons Inc 30 Corporate Dr . . . North Haven CT 06473 *TF:* 800-922-2956 ■ *Web:* www.slocumandsons.com	203-239-8000		81-3
Slomin's Inc 125 Lauman Ln . . . Hicksville NY 11801 *TF:* 800-252-7663 ■ *Web:* www.slomins.com	516-932-7000		692
Slone Melhuish & Co 306 Spring St . . . Jamestown NY 14701 *Web:* slonemelhuish.com	716-483-1591		390
Slope Drugs & Surgical Supply Inc 406 5th Ave . . . Brooklyn NY 11215	718-788-8899		237
Slope Electric Co-opeartive Inc 116 E 12th St PO Box 338 . . . New England ND 58647 *TF:* 800-559-4191 ■ *Web:* www.slopeelectric.coop	701-579-4191		245
Sloss Furnaces National Historic Landmark 20 32nd St N . . . Birmingham AL 35222 *Web:* www.slossfurnaces.com	205-254-2025		520
Slosson Educational Publications Inc 538 Buffalo Rd . . . East Aurora NY 14052 *TF:* 888-756-7766 ■ *Web:* www.slosson.com	716-652-0930		637-2
Slotkin Elissa (Rep D - MI) 1531 Longworth House Office Bldg . . . Washington DC 20515 *Web:* www.slotkin.house.gov	202-225-4872		342-2
Slovak Baron Empey Murphy & Pinkney LLP 1800 E Tahquitz Canyon Way . . . Palm Springs CA 92262 *Web:* sbemp.com	760-322-2275	322-2107	41
Slovak Institute and Reference Library 10510 Buckeye Rd . . . Cleveland OH 44104 *Web:* www.slovakinstitute.com	216-721-5300	791-8268	434-3
Slovene National Benefit Society 247 W Allegheny Rd . . . Imperial PA 15126 *TF:* 800-843-7675 ■ *Web:* www.snpj.org	724-695-1100	695-1555	391-2
Slovenia			
Consulate General 120 E 56th St Ste 320 . . . New York NY 10022 *Web:* www.culture.si	212-370-3006	370-3581	257
Embassy 2410 California St NW . . . Washington DC 20008 *Web:* www.washington.embassy.si	202-386-6601	386-6633	257
Slover & Loftus LLP 1224 17th St NW . . . Washington DC 20036 *Web:* www.sloverandloftus.com	202-347-7170		428
SLR Contracting & Service Company Inc 260 Michigan Ave . . . Buffalo NY 14203 *Web:* www.slrcontracting.com	716-896-8148		186
SLRCC (Sebago Lakes Region Chamber of Commerce) 909A Roosevelt Trl . . . Windham ME 04062 *Web:* www.sebagolakeschamber.com	207-892-8265	893-0110	139
SLS (Society of Laparoendoscopic Surgeons) 7330 SW 62nd Pl Ste 410 . . . Miami FL 33143 *Web:* www.sls.org	305-665-9959	667-4123	49-8
SLS (Shawnigan Lake School) 1975 Renfrew Rd . . . Shawnigan Lake BC V0R2W1 *Web:* www.shawnigan.ca	250-743-5516		622
SLS South Beach 1701 Collins Ave . . . Miami Beach FL 33139 *TF:* 855-757-7623 ■ *Web:* slshotels.com	305-674-1701		707
SLT (Spirit Lake Tribe) PO Box 359 . . . Fort Totten ND 58335 *Web:* www.spiritlakenation.com	701-766-4221	766-4126	804
Sluice Boxes State Park 4600 Giant Springs Rd . . . Great Falls MT 59405 *Web:* www.fwp.mt.gov	406-454-5840		565
Slumberland Inc 3060 Centerville Rd . . . Little Canada MN 55117 *TF:* 888-957-5862 ■ *Web:* www.slumberland.com	888-957-5862		321
Slutzky Wolfe & Bailey LLP 2255 Cumberland Pkwy SE Bldg 1300 . . . Atlanta GA 30339 *Web:* swbatl.com	770-438-8000	438-9657	428
Sly Inc 8300 Dow Cir . . . Strongsville OH 44136 *TF:* 800-334-2957 ■ *Web:* www.slyinc.com	440-891-3200	891-3210	18
SLZUSD (San Lorenzo Unified School District) 15510 Usher St . . . San Lorenzo CA 94580 *Web:* www.slzusd.org	510-317-4600	278-3048	685
SM & A 18400 Von Karman Ave Ste 500 . . . Irvine CA 92612 *Web:* www.smawins.com	949-975-1550	975-1624	178-10
SM Arnold Inc 7901 Michigan Ave . . . Saint Louis MO 63111 *TF:* 800-325-7865 ■ *Web:* www.smarnold.com	314-544-4103	544-3159	103
SM Engineering Co 9 Ninth Ave N . . . Hopkins MN 55343 *Web:* www.smeng.com	952-938-7407		261
SMA (SMA Services Inc) 3500 Blue Lake Dr Ste 360 . . . Birmingham AL 35243 *Web:* smaservicesinc.com	205-945-1840		49-8
SMA (Steel Manufacturers Assn) 1150 Connecticut Ave NW Ste 1125 . . . Washington DC 20036 *Web:* steelnet.org	202-296-1515	296-2506	49-13
SMA Services Inc (SMA) 3500 Blue Lake Dr Ste 360 . . . Birmingham AL 35243 *Web:* smaservicesinc.com	205-945-1840		49-8
Smaato Inc 240 Stockton St 10th Fl . . . San Francisco CA 94108 *Web:* www.smaato.com	650-286-1198	240-0708	7
SMAC (SMAC Corp) 5807 Van Allen Way . . . Carlsbad CA 92008 *Web:* www.smac-mca.com	760-929-7575		203
SMAC Corp (SMAC) 5807 Van Allen Way . . . Carlsbad CA 92008 *Web:* www.smac-mca.com	760-929-7575		203
SMACNA (Sheet Metal & Air Conditioning Contractors' NA) 4201 Lafayette Center Dr . . . Chantilly VA 20151 *Web:* www.smacna.org	703-803-2980	803-3732	49-3
Smaha Law Group Aplc 2398 San Diego Ave . . . San Diego CA 92110 *Web:* smaha.com	619-688-1557		41
Small Batch Books 493 S Pleasant St . . . Amherst MA 01002 *Web:* www.smallbatchbooks.com	413-230-3943		637-2
Small Beer Press 150 Pleasant St Ste 306 . . . Easthampton MA 01027 *Web:* smallbeerpress.com	413-203-1636		637-2
Small Business & Entrepreneurship Council (SBE) 301 Maple Ave W Ste 100 . . . Vienna VA 22180 *Web:* sbecouncil.org	703-242-5840		49-12
Small Business Administration (SBA) 409 Third St SW . . . Washington DC 20416 *Web:* www.sba.gov	202-205-6533	205-6802	340-20
Small Business Administration *National Women's Business Council* 409 Third St SW 5th Fl . . . Washington DC 20416 *Web:* www.nwbc.gov	202-205-3850		340-20
Small Business Administration Regional Offices (SBA)			
Region 1 10 Causeway St Ste 265A . . . Boston MA 02222 *Web:* www.sba.gov	617-565-8416	565-8420	340-20
Region 3 1150 First Ave Ste 1001 . . . King of Prussia PA 19406 *Web:* www.sba.gov	610-382-3092		340-20
Region 4 233 Peachtree St NE Ste 1800 . . . Atlanta GA 30303 *Web:* www.sba.gov	404-331-4999	331-2354	340-20

	Phone	Fax	Class
Region 5 500 W Madison St Ste 1150.......... Chicago IL 60661 *Web:* www.sba.gov	312-353-0357	353-3426	340-20
Region 6 4300 Amon Carter Blvd Ste 108 .... Fort Worth TX 76155 *TF:* 800-274-2812 ■ *Web:* www.sba.gov	817-684-5581	684-5588	340-20
Region 6 1301 Young St .... Dallas TX 75202 *Web:* www.ssa.gov	214-767-9401	767-8986	340-20
Region 7 1000 Walnut Ste 530 .... Kansas City MO 64106 *Web:* www.sba.gov	816-426-4840	426-4848	340-20
Region 8 721 19th St Ste 426 .... Denver CO 80202 *Web:* www.sba.gov	303-844-2607		340-20
Region 9 330 N Brand Blvd Ste 1200 .... Glendale CA 91203 **Fax Area Code:* 202 ■ *Web:* www.sba.gov	818-552-3437	481-0344*	340-20
Region 10 2401 Fourth Ave Ste 400 .... Seattle WA 98121 *Web:* www.sba.gov	206-553-5676	553-4155	340-20
Region 10 701 Fifth Ave Ste 2900.......... Seattle WA 98104 *Web:* www.ssa.gov	206-615-2236		340-20
Small Business Investor Alliance (SBIA) 1100 H St NW Ste 1200 .... Washington DC 20005 *TF:* 800-471-6153 ■ *Web:* www.sbia.org	202-628-5055		615
Small Business Legislative Council (SBLC) 4800 Hampden Ln 6th Fl .... Bethesda MD 20814 *Web:* www.sblc.org	301-652-8302		49-12
Small Business Times 126 N Jefferson St Ste 403.......... Milwaukee WI 53202 *Web:* www.biztimes.com	414-277-8181		532-3
Small Changes Inc 1418 NW 53rd St.......... Seattle WA 98107 *Web:* www.smallchanges.com	206-382-1980	382-1514	96
Small Mine Development LLC 967 E Parkcenter Blvd.......... Boise ID 83706 *Web:* www.undergroundmining.com	208-338-8880	338-8881	186
Small Parts Inc 600 Humphrey St.......... Logansport IN 46947 *Web:* www.smallpartsinc.com	574-753-6323	753-6660	488
Small Plates 1521 Broadway St.......... Detroit MI 48226 *Web:* www.smallplates.com	313-963-0702		671
Small Precision Tools Inc 1330 Clegg St.......... Petaluma CA 94954 *Web:* www.smallprecisiontools.com	707-762-5880	559-2072	695
Small Tube Products PO Box 1017 .... Duncansville PA 16635 *Web:* www.smalltubeproducts.com	814-695-4491		490
Small Wonders Enterprises 12210 Fairfax Towne Ctr.......... Fairfax VA 22033 *Web:* www.snickerdoodleforkids.com	703-352-0226		478
Small World Productions PO Box 28369 .... Seattle WA 98122 *Web:* www.smarttravels.tv	206-329-7167		741-99
Small, Henstridge & Cabodi 25411 Cabot Rd Ste 202.......... Laguna Hills CA 92653 *Web:* shcplaw.com	949-364-3700		41
Smallfellow Press 9454 Wilshire Blvd Ste 550 .... Beverly Hills CA 90212 *Web:* www.smallfellow.com	310-203-3837	203-3893	637-9
Smalls Electrical Construction Inc Brooklyn Navy Yard 63 Flushing Ave Ste 338 Bldg 3 Ste 1107.......... Brooklyn NY 11205 *Web:* www.smallselectrical.com	718-254-0009	254-0110	189-4
Smallwood & Stewart Inc 5 E 20th St.......... New York NY 10003 *Web:* www.smallwoodandstewart.com	212-505-3268		94
Smallwood Reynolds Stewart Stewart & Associates Inc (SRSSA) 1 Piedmont Ctr 3565 Piedmont Rd Ste 303 .... Atlanta GA 30305 *Web:* www.srssa.com	404-233-5453	264-0929	261
Smallwood State Park 2750 Sweden Pt Rd .... Marbury MD 20658 *Web:* www.dnr.maryland.gov	301-743-7613		565
SMAR International Corp 6001 Stonington Ste 100 .... Houston TX 77040 *Web:* www.smar.com	713-690-3808		246
Smardan-Hatcher Company Inc 810 E Mason St .... Santa Barbara CA 93103 *Web:* www.smardan.com	805-963-8991		612
Smardt Inc 1840 Trans Canada Hwy.......... Dorval QC H9P1H7 *Web:* www.smardt.com	514-426-8989	426-5757	480
SMART (Special Military Active Retired Travel Club) 600 University Office Blvd Ste 1A.......... Pensacola FL 32504 *TF:* 800-354-7681 ■ *Web:* www.smartrving.org	850-478-1986		48-23
SMART (Suburban Mobility Authority for Regional Transportation) 535 Griswold St Ste 600.......... Detroit MI 48226 *TF:* 866-962-5515 ■ *Web:* www.smartbus.org	313-223-2100		468
Smart & Final Inc 600 Citadel Dr.......... Commerce CA 90040 *TF:* 800-894-0511 ■ *Web:* www.smartandfinal.com	323-869-7500		345
Smart Alabama LLC 121 Shin Young Dr.......... Luverne AL 36049 *Web:* www.smart-alabama.com	334-335-5800		247
Smart Business Network Inc 835 Sharon Dr Ste 200.......... Cleveland OH 44145 *TF:* 800-988-4726 ■ *Web:* www.sbnonline.com	800-988-4726		532-3
Smart Cabling Solutions Inc 1250 N Winchester St.......... Olathe KS 66061 *TF:* 877-390-9501 ■ *Web:* www.thinkscs.com	913-390-9501		224
Smart Card Integrators Inc (SCI) 2424 N Ontario St.......... Burbank CA 91504 *Web:* www.sci-s.com	818-847-1022		178-12
Smart Care Equipment Solutions 370 Wabasha St N .... Saint Paul MN 55102 *TF:* 800-822-2302 ■ *Web:* smartcaresolutions.com	651-250-5555		393
Smart Choice Communications LLC 56 W 45th St Fl 2 .... New York NY 10036 *TF:* 800-217-3096 ■ *Web:* smartchoiceus.com	212-660-7300		387
Smart City Networks 5795 W Badura Ave Ste 110.......... Las Vegas NV 89118 *TF:* 888-446-6911 ■ *Web:* www.smartcity.com	702-943-6000	943-6001	736
Smart Creations Inc 1799 St Johns Ave .... Highland Park IL 60035	847-433-3451		410
Smart Dolphins It Solutions Inc 303-3995 Quadra St.......... Victoria BC V8X1J8 *Web:* smartdolphins.com	250-721-2499		175
Smart Eye Care Ctr 255 Western Ave.......... Augusta ME 04330 *TF:* 800-459-5800 ■ *Web:* www.smarteyecare.com	207-622-5800		237
Smart Furniture Inc 430 Market St.......... Chattanooga TN 37402 *TF:* 888-467-6278 ■ *Web:* www.smartfurniture.com	423-267-7007		321

	Phone	Fax	Class
Smart Imaging Technologies Inc 1770 St James Pl Ste 414.......... Houston TX 77056 *Web:* smartimtech.com	713-589-3500		419
Smart Industries Corp 1626 Delaware Ave.......... Des Moines IA 50317 *TF:* 800-553-2442 ■ *Web:* www.smartind.com	515-265-9900	265-3148	322
Smart Interiors Inc 5141 Mariner Blvd .... Spring Hill FL 34609 *Web:* smartinteriorsfurn.com	352-688-4633		321
Smart IT Services Inc 34715 Van Dyke Ave.......... Sterling Heights MI 48312 *Web:* smartservices.com	586-258-0650		387
Smart Levels Media Inc 16 Hammond .... Irvine CA 92618 *Web:* www.smartlevels.com	949-540-0500		179
Smart Luck Publishers PO Box 81770 .... Las Vegas NV 89180 **Fax Area Code:* 800 ■ *TF:* 800-945-4245 ■ *Web:* www.smartluck.com	727-441-8906	876-4245*	637-2
Smart Machine Technologies Inc 650 Frith Dr .... Ridgeway VA 24148 *Web:* www.smartmachine.com	276-632-9853		295
Smart Modular Technologies Inc 39870 Eureka Dr.......... Newark CA 94560 *NASDAQ: SMOD* ■ *TF:* 800-956-7627 ■ *Web:* www.smartm.com	510-623-1231	623-1434	173-1
Smart MultiMedia Inc 1113 Vine St Ste 239 .... Houston TX 77002 **Fax Area Code:* 281 ■ *Web:* www.smartmm.com	713-574-6690	247-9823*	738
Smart Pipe Company Inc 1319 W Sam Houston Pkwy Ste 100 .... Houston TX 77043 **Fax Area Code:* 713 ■ *Web:* smart-pipe.com	281-945-5700	492-2432*	595
Smart Power Systems Inc 1760 Stebbins Dr .... Houston TX 77043 *TF:* 800-882-8285 ■ *Web:* smartpowersystems.com	713-464-8000		253
Smart Recovery 7304 Mentor Ave Ste F.......... Mentor OH 44060 *TF:* 866-951-5357 ■ *Web:* www.smartrecovery.org	440-951-5357	951-5358	48-21
Smart Recruiters 225 Bush St .... San Francisco CA 94104 *Web:* www.smartrecruiters.com	415-659-9130		788
Smart Safety Group 2535 Camino Del Rio S Ste 125.......... San Diego CA 92108 *Web:* www.smartsafetygroup.com	619-491-3099		196
Smart Staffing Service 132 Central St Ste 210.......... Foxborough MA 02035 *Web:* www.smart-tek.net	508-698-9988		260
Smart Union 1750 New York Ave NW 6th Fl .... Washington DC 20006 *TF:* 800-457-7694 ■ *Web:* smart-union.org	202-662-0800	662-0894	49-3
Smart Warehousing LLC 18905 Kill Creek Rd .... Edgerton KS 66021 *TF:* 800-591-2097 ■ *Web:* smartwarehousing.com	800-591-2097		803-1
Smart Work Network Inc 135 S Main St Ste 402 .... Greenville SC 29601 *Web:* www.smartworknetwork.com	864-233-3007		463
Smartcat 179 S St 6th Fl .... Boston MA 02111 *TF:* 888-794-8856 ■ *Web:* www.smartcat.ai	888-794-8856		39
Smartech Systems Inc 500 E Brighton Ave.......... Syracuse NY 13210 *Web:* www.s2ieng.com	315-701-2316	701-2317	180
SmarTek21 LLC 12910 Totem Lake Blvd NE Ste 200 .... Kirkland WA 98034 **Fax Area Code:* 425 ■ *TF:* 888-221-9578 ■ *Web:* www.smartek21.com	888-221-9578	823-5325*	196
SmarterTools Inc 1903 W Parkside Ln Ste 106 .... Phoenix AZ 85027 *TF:* 877-357-6278 ■ *Web:* www.smartertools.com	623-434-8050		177
Smarthome Inc 16542 Millikan Ave .... Irvine CA 92606 *TF:* 800-762-7846 ■ *Web:* www.smarthome.com	800-762-7846		35
Smarties Candy Co 1091 Lousons Rd .... Union NJ 07083 *Web:* www.smarties.com	908-964-0660		296-8
Smart-IS Intl 1302 S Main ST .... Oshkosh WI 54902 *Web:* www.smart-is.com	920-303-0470		180
SmartIT Staffing Inc 6500 Technology Center Dr Ste 300.......... Indianapolis IN 46278 *TF:* 800-336-4466 ■ *Web:* onebridge.tech	317-634-0211		260
Smartleaf Inc 210 Broadway 4th Fl.......... Cambridge MA 02139 *Web:* www.smartleaf.com	617-453-0714	491-5556	809
SmartLink 18401 Von Karman Ave Ste 450 .... Irvine CA 92612 *TF:* 800-256-4814 ■ *Web:* www.smartlinkcorp.com	949-552-1599	552-1699	179
SmartLink Internet Strategies Inc 8895 N Military Trl Ste B202 .... Palm Beach Gardens FL 33410 *Web:* www.thinksmartlink.com	561-688-8155		631
Smartorg Inc 855 Oak Grove Ave.......... Menlo Park CA 94025 *Web:* smartorg.com	650-328-1612		225
Smartpak Equine LLC 40 Grissom Rd Ste 500.......... Plymouth MA 02360 *TF:* 888-752-5171 ■ *Web:* www.smartpakequine.com	774-773-1445		366
SmartProcure LLC 700 W Hillsboro Blvd Ste 4-100.......... Deerfield Beach FL 33441 *Web:* www.smartprocure.us	954-420-9900		387
Smartronix Inc 44150 Smartronix Way .... Hollywood MD 20636 *TF:* 866-442-7767 ■ *Web:* www.smartronix.com	301-373-6000	373-7171	177
SmarTrunk Systems Inc 867 Bowsprit Rd.......... Chula Vista CA 91914 *Web:* www.smartrunk.com	619-426-3781	426-3788	735
Smartsat Inc 8222 118th Ave Ste 600.......... Largo FL 33773 *Web:* www.smartsat.com	727-535-6880		387
SmartScrubs LLC 3400 E Mcdowell Rd.......... Phoenix AZ 85008 *TF:* 800-800-5788 ■ *Web:* www.smartscrubs.com	800-800-5788		475
Smartsearch Marketing 4450 Arapahoe Ave Ste 100 .... Boulder CO 80303 *Web:* smartsearchmarketing.com	303-444-3134		195
Smartware Computer Services 2821 S Bay St Ste B.......... Eustis FL 32726 *TF:* 800-796-5000 ■ *Web:* smartwareonline.com	352-483-4350		175
Smashbox Beauty Cosmetics Inc 8549 Higuera St.......... Culver City CA 90232 *TF:* 888-763-1361 ■ *Web:* www.smashbox.com	888-763-1361		238
Smashing Ideas Inc 2211 Elliott Ave Ste 110 .... Seattle WA 98121 *Web:* smashingideas.com	206-378-0100		33
SMBC (Sumitomo Mitsui Banking Corp) 277 Park Ave.......... New York NY 10172 *Web:* www.smbcgroup.com	212-224-4000	593-9522	70

	Phone	Fax	Class
SMC (Single Mothers by Choice Inc) PO Box 1642 .... New York NY 10028 *Web:* www.singlemothersbychoice.org	212-988-0993		48-21
SMC (Southwestern Michigan College) 58900 Cherry Grove Rd .... Dowagiac MI 49047 *Fax Area Code: 269 ■ *TF:* 800-456-8675 ■ *Web:* www.swmich.edu	800-456-8675	782-1331*	162
SMC (Shannon Medical Ctr) 120 E Harris Ave .... San Angelo TX 76903 *Web:* www.shannonhealth.com	325-653-6741	658-8295	374-3
SMC (Save the Manatee Club) 500 N Maitland Ave .... Maitland FL 32751 *TF:* 800-432-5646 ■ *Web:* www.savethemanatee.org	407-539-0990	539-0871	48-3
SMC (Sound Marketing Concepts) 6 Cooper Pond Rd .... Rowley MA 01969 *Web:* www.soundmarketingconcepts.com	978-948-7688		7
SMC (Southern Metals Company Inc) 2200 Donald Ross Rd .... Charlotte NC 28208 *Web:* www.southernmetalscompany.com	704-394-3161	394-3163	686
SMC (Shepstone Management Co) 100 4th St Ste 32 .... Honesdale PA 18431 *Web:* www.shepstone.net	570-251-9550	251-9551	196
SMC (Southern Machinery Company Inc) 3735 Vulcan Dr .... Nashville TN 37211 *Web:* somachinery.com	615-832-3365	834-9016	385
SMC Consulting Engineers PC 815 W Main .... Oklahoma City OK 73106 *Web:* smcokc.com	405-232-7715		261
SMC Corporation of America 10100 SMC Blvd .... Noblesville IN 46060 *Web:* www.smcusa.com	317-899-4440		223
SMC Electrical Products Inc PO Box 880 .... Barboursville WV 25504 *Web:* www.beckersmc.com	304-736-8933		729
SMC Metal Fabricators Inc 2100 S Oakwood Rd .... Oshkosh WI 54904 *Web:* www.smcmetal.com	920-426-6080		492
SMC Technologies Inc 1517 Ocama Blvd .... Midwest City OK 73110 *TF:* 800-727-2740 ■ *Web:* www.smc-technologies.com	405-737-3740	737-3759	145
SMCC (Southern Maine Community College) 2 Fort Rd .... South Portland ME 04106 *TF:* 877-282-2182 ■ *Web:* www.smccme.edu	207-741-5500	741-5760	800
SMCI (Supermicro Computer Inc) 980 Rock Ave .... San Jose CA 95131 *NASDAQ: SMCI* ■ *Web:* www.supermicro.com	408-503-8000	503-8008	625
SMCMA (San Mateo County Medical Assn) 777 Mariners Island Blvd Ste 100 .... San Mateo CA 94404 *Web:* www.smcma.org	650-312-1663	312-1664	49-19
SMD (SMD Inc) 1 Oldfield .... Irvine CA 92618 *Web:* www.smdinc.com	949-470-7700	470-7777	246
SMD Inc (SMD) 1 Oldfield .... Irvine CA 92618 *Web:* www.smdinc.com	949-470-7700	470-7777	246
SME (Soil & Materials Engineers Inc) 1501 W Thomas St .... Bay City MI 48706 *Web:* www.sme-usa.com	989-684-6050	684-0210	261
SME (Society of Manufacturing Engineers) 1 SME Dr .... Dearborn MI 48128 *TF:* 800-733-4763 ■ *Web:* www.sme.org	313-425-3000	425-3400	49-13
SME (Society for Mining Metallurgy & Exploration Inc) 12999 E Adam Aircraft Cir .... Englewood CO 80112 *TF:* 800-763-3132 ■ *Web:* www.smenet.org	303-948-4200	973-3845	49-13
SME (Star Middle East USA Inc) 2 Riverway Ste 1060 .... Houston TX 77056 *Web:* www.drillequip.com	713-871-1121	871-0327	385
Smeal Fire Apparatus Co 610 W 4th St PO Box 8 .... Snyder NE 68664 *Web:* www.smeal.com	402-568-2224		283
SMF Inc 1550 Industrial Pk .... Minonk IL 61760 *Web:* www.smf-inc.com	309-432-2586	432-2390	454
SMG 300 Conshohocken State Rd Ste 770 .. West Conshohocken PA 19428 *Web:* www.jaxevents.com	610-729-7900	729-1590	271
SMH (Slidell Memorial Hospital) 1001 Gause Blvd .... Slidell LA 70458 *Web:* slidellmemorial.org	985-280-2200		374-3
SMH (Southeast Missouri Hospital) 1701 Lacey St .... Cape Girardeau MO 63701 *TF:* 800-800-5123 ■ *Web:* www.sehealth.org	573-334-4822		374-3
SMI (Speedway Motorsports Inc) 5555 Concord Pkwy S .... Concord NC 28027 *NYSE: TRK* ■ *Web:* www.speedwaymotorsports.com	704-455-3239		181
SMI (Spring Manufacturers Institute) 2001 Midwest Rd Ste 106 .... Oak Brook IL 60523 *TF:* 866-482-5569 ■ *Web:* www.smihq.org	630-495-8588	495-8595	49-13
SMI (Seedorff Masonry Inc) 408 W Mission St .... Strawberry Point IA 52076 *Web:* www.seedorff.com	563-933-2296		189-7
SMI (Salisbury Management Inc) 120 Shrewsbury St .... Boylston MA 01505 *Web:* salisburymanagement.com	508-869-0764		652
SMI (Starr Manufacturing Inc) 4175 Warren Sharon Rd .... Vienna OH 44473 *Web:* www.starrmfg.com	330-394-9891	394-9890	480
SMI (Solberg Manufacturing Inc) 1151 Ardmore Ave .... Itasca IL 60143 *Web:* www.solbergmfg.com	630-773-1363	773-0727	18
SMI Cos 1456 Hwy 317 S .... Franklin LA 70538 *Web:* smicompanies.com	337-836-9894		317
SMI properties 5239 zMax Blvd .... Harrisburg NC 28075 *Web:* www.smiproperties.com	704-455-9453	455-9317	656
SMI Travel Inc 1170 Nikki View Dr .... Brandon FL 33511 *Web:* smitrav.com	813-315-9840	315-9844	226
Smile Direct Club 414 Union St .... Nashville TN 37219 *TF:* 800-688-4010 ■ *Web:* smiledirectclub.com	800-688-4010		48-17
Smile Train Inc 633 Third Ave 9th Fl .... New York NY 10017 *TF:* 800-932-9541 ■ *Web:* www.smiletrain.org	212-689-9199	689-9299	48-5
Smilebox Inc 15809 Bear Creek Pkwy .... Redmond WA 98052 *Web:* www.smilebox.com	360-797-5269		225

	Phone	Fax	Class
Smiley Technologies Inc 11500 Fairview Rd .... Little Rock AR 72212 *Web:* sibanking.com	501-219-2922		225
Smith 5306 Hollister Rd .... Houston TX 77040 *Fax Area Code: 713 ■ *TF:* 800-468-7866 ■ *Web:* www.sourcetoday.com	800-468-7866	430-3099*	246
Smith & Butterfield Company Inc 2800 Lynch Rd .... Evansville IN 47711 *TF:* 800-321-6543 ■ *Web:* www.smithbutterfield.com	812-422-3261	429-0532	535
Smith & Cashion PLC 231 Third Ave N .... Nashville TN 37201 *Web:* smithcashion.com	615-742-8555		41
Smith & DeShields Inc 165 NW 20th St .... Boca Raton FL 33431 *Web:* smithanddeshields.com	561-395-0808		234
Smith & Greene Co 19015 66th Ave S .... Kent WA 98032 *TF:* 800-232-8050 ■ *Web:* smithandgreene.com	800-232-8050		300
Smith & Howard PC 271 17th St NW Ste 1600 .... Atlanta GA 30363 *Web:* www.smith-howard.com	404-874-6244	874-1658	2
Smith & Keene Electric Service Inc 833 Live Oak Dr .... Chesapeake VA 23320 *Web:* smithandkeene.com	757-420-1231		189-4
Smith & Loveless Inc 14040 Santa Fe Trail Dr .... Lenexa KS 66215 *TF:* 800-922-9048 ■ *Web:* www.smithandloveless.com	913-888-5201		427
Smith & Nephew Inc *Endoscopy Div* 130 Forbes Blvd .... Andover MA 01810 *TF:* 800-343-5717 ■ *Web:* www.smith-nephew.com	978-749-1000	749-1599	476
Smith & Oby Company Inc 7676 Northfield Rd .... Walton Hills OH 44146 *Web:* smithandoby.com	440-735-5333	735-5334	189-10
Smith & Richardson Manufacturing Co PO Box 589 .... Geneva IL 60134 *TF:* 800-426-0876 ■ *Web:* www.smithandrichardson.com	630-232-2581	232-2610	621
Smith & Smith CPA PC 1150 Executive Cir Ste 5 .... Cary NC 27511 *Web:* smithandsmithcpa.com	919-380-0600		2
Smith & Smith CPAs PC 2423 US Hwy 2 E .... Kalispell MT 59901	406-755-4567		2
Smith & Stephens PC 315 W Pine St .... Missoula MT 59802 *Web:* smithandstephenspc.com	406-721-0300		41
Smith & Wesson 2100 Roosevelt Ave .... Springfield MA 01104 *Fax Area Code: 413 ■ *TF:* 800-331-0852 ■ *Web:* www.smith-wesson.com	800-331-0852	747-3317*	678
Smith & Wollensky 101 Station Landing Ste 100 .... Medford MA 02155 *Web:* www.smithandwollensky.com	617-600-3500		671
Smith Adam (Rep D - WA) 2264 Rayburn House Office Bldg .... Washington DC 20515 *Web:* www.adamsmith.house.gov	202-225-8901	225-5893	342-2
Smith Adrian (Rep R - NE) 502 Cannon House Office Bldg .... Washington DC 20515 *Web:* www.adriansmith.house.gov	202-225-6435	225-0207	342-2
Smith Affiliated Capital (SAC) 800 Third Ave 12th Fl .... New York NY 10022 *TF:* 888-387-3298 ■ *Web:* www.smithcapital.com	212-644-9440	644-1079	403
Smith Alling PS 1501 Dock St .... Tacoma WA 98402 *Web:* smithalling.com	253-627-1091		41
Smith Anglin Financial LLC 14755 Preston Rd Ste 700 .... Dallas TX 75254 *TF:* 800-301-8486 ■ *Web:* www.smithanglin.com	972-267-1244	267-1243	2
Smith Animal Hospital PA 991 Asheville Hwy .... Spartanburg SC 29303 *Web:* smithanimalhospital.net	864-585-3401		794
Smith Bovill Pc 200 St Andrews Rd .... Saginaw MI 48638 *Web:* smithbovill.com	989-792-9641	652-3607	428
Smith Brooks Bolshoun & CoLLP 5840 E Evans Ave .... Denver CO 80222 *Web:* www.sbbllp.com	303-480-1200	480-0022	2
Smith Bros Construction 444 S Cedros Ave .... Solana Beach CA 92075 *Web:* smithbrothersconstruction.com	858-350-1445		187
Smith Brothers Restaurant Corp 100 E Corson St Ste 320 .... Pasadena CA 91103 *Web:* www.smithbrothersrestaurants.com	626-577-2400	577-8330	670
Smith Burial and Life Insurance Co 310 Church St .... Stamps AR 71860 *Web:* www.aosmithfuneralhome.com	870-533-2070		796
Smith Cast Iron Boilers 260 N Elm St .... Westfield MA 01085 *Web:* www.westcastboilers.com	413-562-9631	562-3799	357
Smith Chapel Free Will Baptist Church 713 Pineview Cemetery Rd .... Mount Olive NC 28365	910-483-4437		48-20
Smith Chris (Rep R - NJ) 2373 Rayburn House Office Bldg .... Washington DC 20515 *Web:* www.chrissmith.house.gov	202-225-3765	225-7768	342-2
Smith College 7 College Ln .... Northampton MA 01063 *TF:* 800-383-3232 ■ *Web:* www.smith.edu	413-584-2700	585-2527	166
Smith Control Systems Inc 1839 Rte 9h .... Hudson NY 12534 *Web:* smithcontrols.net	518-828-7646	828-2845	729
Smith County 939 Upper Ferry Rd .... Carthage TN 37030 *Web:* www.smithcountychamber.org	615-735-2093	735-9904	338
Smith County 218 S Grant St .... Smith Center KS 66967 *Web:* www.smithcoks.com	785-282-5110	686-4014	338
Smith Crossing 10501 Emilie Ln Ofc .... Orland Park IL 60467 *Web:* www.smithcrossing.org	708-326-2308		371
Smith Dray Line 320 Frontage Rd .... Greenville SC 29611 *TF:* 877-203-7048 ■ *Web:* smithdray.com	877-203-7048		519
Smith Drug & Compounding Inc 1629 Airport Rd Ste D .... Hot Springs AR 71913 *Web:* smithdrugandcompounding.com	501-767-2220		237
Smith Engineering Co 2201 San Pedro Dr NE 4-200 .... Albuquerque NM 87110 *Web:* www.smithengineering.pro	505-884-0700		261
Smith Falls State Park 90165 Smith Falls Rd .... Valentine NE 69201 *Web:* outdoornebraska.gov	402-376-1306		565
Smith Fastener Co 3613 Florence Ave .... Bell CA 90201 *Web:* www.smithfast.com	323-587-0382	587-8712	350

Phone | Fax | Class

Smith Floor Covering Distributors Inc (SFC)
1118 Smith St. Charleston WV 25330 304-344-2493 344-2475 191-1
Web: www.sfc-wv.com

Smith Flooring Inc
1501 W Hwy 60 PO Box 99 Mountain View MO 65548 417-934-2291 934-2295 683
Web: www.smithflooring.com

Smith Food Machinery Inc
1133 N Broadway Ave. Stockton CA 95205 209-465-3688 298
Web: www.smithfoodmachinery.com

Smith Fork Ranch
45362 Needle Rock Rd Crawford CO 81415 970-921-3454 921-3475 239
TF: 855-539-1492 ■ *Web:* www.smithforkranch.com

Smith Foundry Co 1855 E 28th St. Minneapolis MN 55407 612-729-9395 729-2519 307
Web: www.smithfoundry.com

Smith Frozen Foods Inc 101 Depot St. Weston OR 97886 541-566-3515 296-21
Web: www.smithfrozenfoods.com

Smith Gambrell & Russell LLP
1230 Peachtree St NE Promenade II Ste 3100 Atlanta GA 30309 404-815-3500 41
Web: www.sgrlaw.com

Smith Gardens Inc
4164 Meridian St Ste 400. Bellingham WA 98226 360-733-4671 369
TF: 800-755-6256 ■ *Web:* www.smithgardens.com

Smith Graham & Co
600 Travis St 6900 JPMorgan Chase Tower Houston TX 77002 713-227-1100 227-0912 401
TF: 800-739-4470 ■ *Web:* smithgraham.com

Smith Hartvigsen PLLC
257 E 200 S Ste 500. Salt Lake City UT 84111 801-413-1600 413-1620 428
TF: 877-825-2064 ■ *Web:* www.smithhartvigsen.com

Smith Hulsey & Busey
225 Water St Ste 1800 Jacksonville FL 32202 904-359-7700 359-7708 428
Web: www.smithhulsey.com

Smith Industries Inc
2781 Gunter Park Dr E Montgomery AL 36109 334-277-8520 198
Web: www.jrsmith.com

Smith Inland Environmental Services Inc
PO Box 23756 Waco TX 76702 940-783-1732 192
Web: www.smithinland.com

Smith Jason (Rep R - MO)
2418 Rayburn House Office Bldg Washington DC 20515 202-225-4404 226-0326 342-2
Web: www.jasonsmith.house.gov

Smith Jewelers C W
603 Wisconsin Ave. North Fond Du Lac WI 54937 920-922-6259 410
Web: www.cwsmithjewelers.com

Smith Koelling Dykstra & Ohm PC
1605 N Convent Bourbonnais IL 60914 815-937-1997 2
Web: www.skdocpa.com

Smith Landscape Services Inc
10700 47th St N Clearwater FL 33762 727-440-6565 422
Web: smithlandscapeservices.com

Smith Leonard PLLC
4035 Premier Dr Ste 300 High Point NC 27265 336-883-0181 2
Web: smith-leonard.com

Smith Management Group
1860b Williamson Ct Louisville KY 40223 502-587-6482 196
Web: www.smithmanage.com

SMITH Manufacturing Company Inc
1610 S Dixie Hwy. Pompano Beach FL 33060 954-941-9744 545-0348 82
TF: 800-653-9311 ■ *Web:* www.smithmfg.com

Smith Marion & Company LLP
1940 Orange Tree Ln Ste 100 Redlands CA 92374 909-307-2323 2
Web: smcocpa.com

Smith Mazure Director Wilkins Young & Yagerman PC
111 John St 20th Fl New York NY 10038 212-964-7400 374-1935 428
Web: www.smithmazure.com

Smith McDonald Corp 1270 Niagara St. Buffalo NY 14213 800-753-8548 608
TF: 800-753-8548 ■ *Web:* www.smithmcdonald.com

Smith McDowell House Museum
283 Victoria Rd. Asheville NC 28801 828-253-9231 520
Web: www.wnchistory.org

Smith Micro Software Inc
51 Columbia St. Aliso Viejo CA 92656 949-362-5800 362-2300 178-7
NASDAQ: SMSI ■ *Web:* www.smithmicro.com

Smith Motors Incorporated of Hammond
6405 Indianapolis Blvd. Hammond IN 46320 219-845-4000 57
TF: 877-392-2689 ■ *Web:* www.smithchevyusa.com

Smith Mountain Industries Inc
1000 Dillard Dr. Forest VA 24551 434-385-1305 96

Smith Nadenbousch Insurance Inc
132 S Queen St. Martinsburg WV 25401 304-263-3388 390
Web: smnains.com

Smith Packing Company Inc
105-125 Washington St Utica NY 13503 315-732-5125 296-26
Web: www.smithpacking.com

Smith Peterson Law Office
133 W Broadway PO Box 249. Council Bluffs IA 51503 712-328-1833 428
Web: smithpeterson.com

Smith Plantation Home
935 Alpharetta St Roswell GA 30075 770-641-3978 50-3
Web: www.roswellgov.com

Smith Power Products Inc
3065 W California Ave Salt Lake City UT 84104 801-415-5000 415-5700 385
TF: 800-658-5352 ■ *Web:* smithpowerproducts.com

Smith Precision Products Co
1299 Lawrence Dr. Newbury Park CA 91320 805-498-6616 499-2867 641
Web: www.smithpumps.com

Smith Protective Services Inc
1801 Royal Ln Ste 250 Dallas TX 75229 214-631-4444 693
TF: 800-631-1384 ■ *Web:* smith1903.com

Smith Pump Company Inc
301 M B Industrial Woodway TX 76712 254-776-0377 776-0023 641
Web: smithpump.com

Smith Ranch Homes
400 Deer Valley Rd San Rafael CA 94903 415-491-4918 491-0254 672
TF: 800-772-6264 ■ *Web:* www.smithranchhomes.com

Smith Ready Mix Inc
251 W Lincolnway Valparaiso IN 46383 219-462-3191 465-4025 182
Web: www.smithreadymix.com

Smith Research Inc 710 Estate Dr Deerfield IL 60015 847-948-0440 463
TF: 866-783-9894 ■ *Web:* www.smithresearch.com

Phone | Fax | Class

Smith Reynolds Airport
3801 N Liberty St Winston-Salem NC 27105 336-767-6361 767-8556 27
Web: www.smithreynolds.org

Smith Richardson Foundation Inc
60 Jesup Rd Westport CT 06880 203-222-6222 305
Web: srf.org

Smith Robertson Museum & Cultural Ctr
528 Bloom St Jackson MS 39202 601-960-1457 520
Web: www.jacksonms.gov

Smith Rock State Park
9241 NE Crooked River Dr Terrebonne OR 97760 541-548-7501 565
Web: oregonstateparks.org

Smith Schafer & Associates Ltd
220 S Broadway Ste 102. Rochester MN 55904 507-288-3277 2
Web: www.smithschafer.com

Smith Seckman Reid Inc
2995 Sidco Dr Nashville TN 37204 615-383-1113 261
Web: www.ssr-inc.com

Smith Services Inc 1306 29th St Vero Beach FL 32960 866-592-8268 14
TF: 866-592-8268 ■ *Web:* www.smith-hvac.com

Smith Southwestern Inc 1850 N Rosemont Mesa AZ 85205 480-854-9545 292
TF: 800-783-3909 ■ *Web:* www.smith-southwestern.com

Smith State Prison 9676 Hwy 301 N Glennville GA 30427 912-654-5000 654-5131 213
Web: www.dcor.state.ga.us

Smith System Driver Improvement Institute Inc
2301 E Lamar Blvd Ste 250 Arlington TX 76006 817-652-6969 162
TF: 800-777-7648 ■ *Web:* www.drivedifferent.com

Smith Tank & Steel Inc 42422 Hwy 30 Gonzales LA 70737 225-644-8747 186
Web: www.smith-tank.com

Smith Tina (Sen D - MN)
720 Hart Senate Office Bldg Washington DC 20510 202-224-5641 342-2
Web: www.smith.senate.gov

Smith Transport Inc
153 Smith Transport Rd Roaring Spring PA 16673 800-877-1173 224-5319* 780
**Fax Area Code:* 814 ■ *TF:* 800-877-1173 ■ *Web:* www.smithtransport.com

Smith Travel Research Inc
735 E Main St. Hendersonville TN 37075 615-824-8664 466
Web: www.str.com

Smith Village Home Furnishings
34 N Main St Jacobus PA 17407 717-428-1921 321
TF: 800-242-1921 ■ *Web:* www.smithvillage.com

Smith's Machine and Grinding Inc
203 E Battle Creek St Galesburg MI 49053 269-665-4231 665-4234 454
Web: www.smithsmachinegrinding.com

Smith, Anderson, Blount, Dorsett, Mitchell & Jernigan LLP
150 Fayetteville St Ste 2300 Raleigh NC 27601 919-821-1220 821-6800 428
Web: www.smithlaw.com

Smith, Brown & Groover Inc
4001 Vineville Ave Macon GA 31210 478-474-7004 690
Web: smithbrownandgroover.com

Smith, Kaplan, Allen & Reynolds Advertising Agency Inc
111 S 108th Ave Omaha NE 68154 402-330-0110 7
Web: skar.com

Smith, Katzenstein & Jenkins LLP
1000 West St Ste 1501 Wilmington DE 19801 302-652-8400 652-8405 428
Web: www.skjlaw.com

Smith, Miner, O'shea & Smith LLP
69 Delaware Ave Rm 1212 Buffalo NY 14202 716-855-3611 855-3250 428
Web: www.smithminerlaw.com

Smith, Sovik, Kendrick & Sugnet PC
250 S Clinton St Ste 600 Syracuse NY 13202 315-474-2911 428
TF: 800-675-0011 ■ *Web:* smithsovik.com

Smith, Von Schleicher & Associates PC
180 N Lasalle St Ste 3130 Chicago IL 60601 312-541-0300 41
Web: svs-law.com

Smithahn Company Inc 836 E N St Bethlehem PA 18017 610-866-4461 492
Web: smithahn.com

SmithAmundsen LLC
308 W State St Ste 320. Rockford IL 61101 815-987-0441 987-9891 428
Web: salawus.com

Smith-Berclair Insurance Inc
855 Ridge Lake Blvd Ste 400 Memphis TN 38120 901-753-4323 390
Web: smithberclair.com

Smithbilt Industries Inc
1061 US 92 Auburndale FL 33823 863-665-3767 665-0159 105
Web: www.smithbilt.com

Smith-Cairns Ford
900 Central Park Ave Yonkers NY 10704 914-377-8100 516
Web: www.smith-cairns.com

SmithCFI 620 NE 19th Ave Portland OR 97232 503-226-4151 226-9233 321
Web: www.smithcfi.com

Smithco Engineering Inc
6312 S 39th W Ave Tulsa OK 74132 918-446-4406 445-2857 91
Web: www.smithco-eng.com

Smithco Inc 34 W Ave Wayne PA 19087 610-688-4009 429
TF: 877-833-7648 ■ *Web:* www.smithco.com

Smith-Cooper Intl 2867 Vail Ave Commerce CA 90040 323-890-4455 890-4456 492
Web: www.smithcooper.com

Smith-Edwards-Dunlap Co
2867 E Allegheny Ave Philadelphia PA 19134 215-425-8800 626
TF: 800-829-0020 ■ *Web:* www.sed.com

Smithereen Pest Management Services
7400 N Melvina Ave Niles IL 60714 847-647-0010 647-0606 577
TF: 800-336-3500 ■ *Web:* www.smithereen.com

Smithers Group Inc, The
121 S Main St Ste 300 Akron OH 44308 330-762-7441 743
Web: www.smithers.com

Smithfield Foods Inc
200 Commerce St. Smithfield VA 23430 757-365-3000 473
NYSE: SFD ■ *Web:* www.smithfieldfoods.com

Smithfield Manufacturing Inc
237 Kraft St. Clarksville TN 37040 931-552-4327 648-4460 621
Web: www.smithfieldmfg.com

SmithFoods Inc 1381 Dairy Ln Orrville OH 44667 330-683-8710 296-27
Web: www.smithsbrand.com

Smithgall Woods Conservation Area & Lodge
61 Tsalaki Trl. Helen GA 30545 706-878-3087 565
Web: www.gastateparks.org

Name / Address	City	State	ZIP	Phone	Fax	Class
Smithgeiger LLC 31365 Oak Crest Dr Ste 150 *Web:* www.smithgeiger.com	Westlake Village	CA	91361	818-874-2000	874-2020	195
SmithGifford Inc 106 W Jefferson St *Web:* www.smithgifford.com	Falls Church	VA	22046	703-532-5992		5
Smithgroup Communications Inc 267 SE 33rd Ave *Web:* smithgrp.com	Portland	OR	97214	503-239-4215		514
SmithGroup Inc 500 Griswold St Ste 1700 *Web:* www.smithgroupjjr.com	Detroit	MI	48226	313-983-3600	983-3636	261
Smith-Kettlewell Eye Research Institute 2318 Fillmore St *Web:* www.ski.org	San Francisco	CA	94115	415-345-2000	345-8455	668
Smithlain Enterprises Inc 1300 Meridian St Ste 15 *Web:* www.smithlain.com	Huntsville	AL	35801	256-704-7880		196
Smith-Midland Corp 5119 Catlett Rd PO Box 300 *OTC:* SMID ■ *Web:* smithmidland.com	Midland	VA	22728	540-439-3266	439-1232	183
Smiths Detection 2202 Lakeside Blvd *TF:* 800-297-0955 ■ *Web:* www.smithsdetection.com	Edgewood	MD	21040	410-510-9100		472
Smiths Interconnect 1725 N Salisbury Blvd *Web:* www.smithsinterconnect.com	Salisbury	MD	21802	800-780-2169		253
Smiths Interconnect Microwave Components Inc 8851 SW Old Kansas Ave *Web:* www.smithsinterconnect.com	Stuart	FL	34997	772-286-9300		767
Smiths Medical 5200 Upper Metro Pl Ste 200 **Fax Area Code:* 614 ■ *TF:* 800-258-5361 ■ *Web:* www.smiths-medical.com	Dublin	OH	43017	800-258-5361	734-0254*	356
Smithsonian Air & Space Magazine PO Box 37012 **Fax Area Code:* 202 ■ *TF:* 800-766-2149 ■ *Web:* www.airspacemag.com	Washington	DC	20013	800-766-2149	633-6085*	457-19
Smithsonian Enterprises 600 Maryland Ave SW Ste 5060 *Web:* si.edu	Washington	DC	20024	202-633-6080		637-9
Smithsonian Environmental Research Ctr 647 Contees Wharf Rd *Web:* serc.si.edu	Edgewater	MD	21037	443-482-2200	482-2380	668
Smithsonian Folkways Recordings 600 Maryland Ave SW Ste 200 *TF:* 800-410-9815 ■ *Web:* folkways.si.edu	Washington	DC	20024	202-633-6450	633-6477	657
Smithsonian Libraries 10th St and Constitution Ave NW Natural History Bldg *Web:* www.library.si.edu	Washington	DC	20560	202-633-2240		434-4
Smithsonian Magazine 600 Maryland Ave Ste 6001 *Web:* www.smithsonianmag.com	Washington	DC	20024	202-633-6090		457-11
Smithsonian National Museum of African Art 950 Independence Ave SW *Web:* africa.si.edu	Washington	DC	20560	202-633-4600	357-4879	520
Smithsonian Tropical Research Institute (STRI) 1100 Jefferson Dr Ste 3123 MRC 705 *Web:* stri.si.edu	Washington	DC	20013	202-633-4014	786-2557	668
Smithtown Chamber of Commerce 79 E Main St Ste E *Web:* smithtownchamber.org	Smithtown	NY	11787	631-979-8069	979-2206	139
Smithville Communications Inc 1600 W Temperance St *TF:* 800-742-4084 ■ *Web:* smithville.com	Ellettsville	IN	47429	812-876-2211		736
Smithway Inc PO Box 188 *Web:* www.smithwayinc.com	Fairview	NC	28730	828-628-1756		779
Smithwick & Mariners Insurance Inc 366 US Route 1 *Web:* smithwick-ins.com	Falmouth	ME	04105	207-781-5553		300
Smitty Bilt Inc 400 W Artesia Blvd *Web:* www.smittybilt.com	Compton	CA	90220	310-762-9944	762-2297	60
Smitty's Canada Inc 501 18th Ave SW Ste 500 *TF:* 800-927-0366 ■ *Web:* smittys.ca	Calgary	AB	T2S0C7	403-229-3838	229-3899	670
Smitty's Supply Inc 63399 Hwy 51 N PO Box 530 *TF:* 800-256-7575 ■ *Web:* www.smittysinc.net	Roseland	LA	70456	985-748-6572		541
SMK Electronics Corporation USA 1055 Tierra Del Rey *Web:* www.smk.co.jp	Chula Vista	CA	91910	619-216-6400	216-6498	253
SMK Soft Inc 2201 Cooperative Way Ste 600 *Web:* smksoftinc.com	Herndon	VA	20171	703-542-9881		177
SML Intelligent Inventory Solutions LLC 6400 International Pky Ste 1550 *Web:* sml-rfid.com	Plano	TX	75093	972-690-9460		253
SMMA (Symmes Maini & McKee Assoc) 1000 Massachusetts Ave **Fax Area Code:* 800 ■ *Web:* www.smma.com	Cambridge	MA	02138	617-547-5400	648-4920*	261
SMO (Southern Maryland Oil Company Inc) 109 N Maple Ave *TF:* 888-222-3720 ■ *Web:* smoenergy.com	La Plata	MD	20646	888-222-3720		579
Smoak Davis & Nixon LLP 5011 Gate Pkwy Bldg 100 Ste 300 *Web:* www.sdnllp.com	Jacksonville	FL	32256	904-396-5831		2
SMOCA (Scottsdale Museum of Contemporary Art) 7374 E Second St *Web:* smoca.org	Scottsdale	AZ	85251	480-874-4666		520
Smock Fansler Corp 2910 W Minnesota St *Web:* www.smockfansler.com	Indianapolis	IN	46241	317-248-8371	244-4507	189-3
Smoke Magazine 26 Broadway **Fax Area Code:* 212 ■ *TF:* 800-766-2633 ■ *Web:* www.smokemag.com	New York	NY	10004	800-766-2633	827-0945*	457-14
Smokehouse, The 34 Palmetto Bay Rd *Web:* www.smokehousehhi.com	Hilton Head Island	SC	29928	843-842-4227		671
Smoker Craft PO Box 65 *TF:* 866-719-7873 ■ *Web:* www.smokercraft.com	New Paris	IN	46553	866-719-7873		90
Smoker Smith & Associates Pc 339 W Governor Rd Ste 202 *TF:* 888-277-1040 ■ *Web:* www.smokersmith.com	Hershey	PA	17033	717-533-5154		2
Smokey Bones BBQ 2074 Interchange Rd *Web:* smokeybones.com	Erie	PA	16565	814-868-3388		671
Smokin Joes Cigars LLC 2293 Saunders Settlement Rd *Web:* www.smokinjoes.com	Sanborn	NY	14132	716-261-9327		156
Smokin' Guns BBQ 1218 Swift Ave *Web:* www.smokingunsbbq.com	Kansas City	MO	64116	816-221-2535	221-2606	671
Smoky Hills Public Television (SHPTV) 604 Elm St *TF:* 800-337-4788 ■ *Web:* www.shptv.org	Bunker Hill	KS	67626	785-483-6990	483-4605	632
Smoky Mountain Knife Works Inc 2320 Winfield Dunn Pkwy PO Box 4430 *TF:* 800-251-9306 ■ *Web:* www.smkw.com	Sevierville	TN	37876	800-251-9306		362
Smoky Mountain Pizzeria Grill 408 E 41st St *Web:* www.smokymountainpizza.com	Boise	ID	83714	208-433-9596	433-9588	671
Smoky Mountain Visitors Bureau 7906 E Lamar Alexander Pkwy *Web:* www.smokymountains.org	Townsend	TN	37882	865-448-6134		206
Smoky Shadows Motel & Conference Ctr 4215 Pkwy *Web:* www.smokyshadows.com	Pigeon Forge	TN	37863	865-453-7155		379
Smoky's Club 3005 University Ave *Web:* www.smokysclub.com	Madison	WI	53705	608-233-2120		671
Smolin, Lupin & Company PA 165 Passaic Ave 4th Fl *Web:* smolin.com	Fairfield	NJ	07004	973-439-7200		2
Smoll & Banning CPAs LLC 2410 Central Ave *TF:* 800-499-8881 ■ *Web:* smollbanning.com	Dodge City	KS	67801	620-225-6100		2
Smoot Construction Co 1907 Leonard Ave *Web:* smootconstruction.com	Columbus	OH	43219	614-253-9000		186
Smooth Fusion Inc 5502 58th St Ste 500 *Web:* www.smoothfusion.com	Lubbock	TX	79414	806-771-3873		177
Smooth Solutions Inc 300 2 Rt 17 S *Web:* smoothsolutions.com	Lodi	NJ	07644	973-249-6666		180
Smooth-On Inc 2000 St John St *TF:* 800-762-0744 ■ *Web:* www.smooth-on.com	Easton	PA	18042	610-252-5800	252-6200	43
SMP Architecture 40 Palafox Pl Ste 202 *Web:* www.smp-arch.com	Pensacola	FL	32502	850-432-7772		194
SMP Asset Management LLC 1865 Palmer Ave *Web:* www.smplp.com	Larchmont	NY	10538	914-833-0958	833-1068	2
SMP Communications Corp 7626 E Greenway Rd Ste 100 *TF:* 888-796-3342 ■ *Web:* smpcom.com	Scottsdale	AZ	85260	480-905-4100		514
SMPS (Society for Marketing Professional Services) 123 N Pitt St Ste 400 *Web:* www.smps.org	Alexandria	VA	22314	703-549-6117	549-2498	49-18
SMPTE (Society of Motion Picture & Television Engineers) 3 Barker Ave *Web:* www.smpte.org	White Plains	NY	10601	914-761-1100	761-3115	48-4
SMR Technologies Inc 93 Nettie Fenwick Rd *TF:* 800-767-6899 ■ *Web:* www.smrtech.com	Fenwick	WV	26202	304-846-6636		676
SMRC (Southwestern Mission Research Ctr) PO Box 41962 *Web:* southwestmissions.org	Tucson	AZ	85721	520-621-6278		637-2
SMS (Senior Market Sales Inc) 8420 W Dodge Rd Ste 510 *TF:* 800-786-5566 ■ *Web:* www.seniormarketsales.com	Omaha	NE	68114	402-397-3311	397-0455	390
SMS (Saginaw Machine Systems) 800 N Hamilton St *Web:* saginawmachine.com	Saginaw	MI	48602	989-753-8465		455
SMS (Superior Metal Systems) 68 Industrial Dr Napier Field *Web:* www.superiormetals.com	Dothan	AL	36303	334-983-9632	983-1201	697
SMS (SMS Integration Inc) 19 Smoky Mountain Dr *Web:* www.smsintegration.net	Franklin	NC	28734	828-369-6067	369-5909	681
SMS Concast America Inc 100 Sandusky St *Web:* www.sms-concast.ch	Pittsburgh	PA	15212	412-237-8950		261
SMS Data Products Group Inc 1751 Pinnacle Dr 12th Fl **Fax Area Code:* 703 ■ *TF:* 800-331-1767 ■ *Web:* www.sms.com	McLean	VA	22102	800-331-1767	356-4831*	180
SMS Datacenter 2525 Main St Ste 120 *Web:* www.smsdatacenter.com	Irvine	CA	92614	949-223-9240		177
SMS Direct Inc 7540 Mason King Ct *Web:* www.smsdirect.com	Manassas	VA	20109	703-392-0123		195
SMS Financial LLC 6829 N 12th St *Web:* smsfinancial.net	Phoenix	AZ	85014	602-944-0624		401
SMS group 100 Sandusky St *Web:* sms-group.us	Pittsburgh	PA	15212	412-231-1200	231-3995	261
SMS Integration Inc (SMS) 19 Smoky Mountain Dr *Web:* www.smsintegration.net	Franklin	NC	28734	828-369-6067	369-5909	681
SMS Productions Inc 10555 Guilford Rd Ste 114 *TF:* 800-289-7671 ■ *Web:* www.smsproductions.com	Hanover	MD	21076	301-953-0011		627
SMS proTECH 1089 Fairington Dr *Web:* www.perryprotech.com	Sidney	OH	45365	937-498-7080		624
SMT Farms 8420 E US Hwy 95	Yuma	AZ	85365	928-341-9616		10-11
SMT Inc 7300 ACC Blvd *TF:* 888-214-4804 ■ *Web:* www.smtcoinc.com	Raleigh	NC	27617	919-782-4804	781-1498	697
SMTBUSA (Sumitomo Mitsui Trust Bank (USA)) 111 River St *Web:* www.smtb.jp	Hoboken	NJ	07030	201-420-9470		70
SMTC Corp 635 Hood Rd *NASDAQ:* SMTX ■ *Web:* www.smtc.com	Markham	ON	L3R4N6	905-479-1810	479-1877	253
SMU (Spencer Municipal Utilities) 520 Second Ave E Ste 1 *Web:* smunet.net	Spencer	IA	51301	712-580-5800	580-5336	116

Phone | Fax | Class

Smucker Lloyd (Rep R - PA)
127 Cannon House Office Bldg. Washington DC 20515 202-225-2411 225-2013 342-2
Web: smucker.house.gov

Smuggler's Inn 6920 MacLeod Trl S Calgary AB T2H0L3 403-253-5355 671
Web: www.smugglers.ca

Smugglers Notch State Park
6443 Mountain Rd Stowe VT 05672 802-253-4014 565
Web: www.vtstateparks.com

Smugglers' Notch Resort
4323 Vermont Rt 108 S. Jeffersonville VT 05464 802-644-8851 644-1230 669
TF: 800-451-8752 ■ *Web:* www.smuggs.com

Smurfit Kappa North America LLC
13400 Nelson Ave. City of Industry CA 91746 800-306-8326 100
Web: www.smurfitkappa.com

SMUS (Saint Michael's University School)
3400 Richmond Rd. Victoria BC V8P4P5 250-592-2411 592-2812 622
TF: 800-661-5199 ■ *Web:* www.smus.ca

SMW Autoblok Corp 285 Egidi Dr Wheeling IL 60090 847-215-0591 215-0594 358
Web: www.smwautoblok.com

Smyrna Truck Equipment 2158 Atlanta Rd Smyrna GA 30080 770-433-0112 438-1504 62-7
TF: 855-269-5347 ■ *Web:* www.smyrnatruck.com

Smyth Companies Inc
1085 Snelling Ave N. Saint Paul MN 55108 651-646-4544 413
TF: 800-473-3464 ■ *Web:* www.smythco.com

Smyth County 109 W Main St Rm 144 Marion VA 24354 276-782-4044 782-4045 338
Web: www.smythcounty.org

Smythe 700 - 355 Burrard St Vancouver BC V6C2G8 604-687-1231 2
Web: www.smythecpa.com

Smythe Volvo Cars 40 River Rd Summit NJ 07901 908-273-4200 57
Web: www.smythevolvocars.com

SN Precision Enterprises Inc
145 Jordan Rd Troy NY 12180 518-283-8002 283-8032 75
Web: www.pacamor.com

SNA (School Nutrition Assn)
700 S Washington St Ste 300. Alexandria VA 22314 703-739-3900 739-3915 49-6
TF: 800-877-8822 ■ *Web:* schoolnutrition.org

SNAC (St Norbert Arts Ctr)
100 Rue des Ruines du Monastere Winnipeg MB R3V0A8 204-269-0564 261-1927 50-2
Web: snac.mb.ca

SNAC international
1600 Wilson Blvd Ste 650 Arlington VA 22209 703-836-4500 49-6
TF: 800-628-1334 ■ *Web:* snacintl.org

SNAFU Designs
2500 University Ave W Ste E4 Saint Paul MN 55114 651-698-8581 698-8661 534
TF: 800-766-5786 ■ *Web:* www.snafudesigns.com

Snake Den State Park
2321 Hartford Ave. Johnston RI 02919 401-222-2632 565
Web: www.riparks.com

Snake River Brewing Co
265 S Millward St. Jackson WY 83001 307-739-2337 671
Web: www.snakeriverbrewing.com

Snake River Correctional Institution
777 Stanton Blvd Ontario OR 97914 541-881-5460 881-5009 213
Web: www.oregon.gov

Snake River Grill 84 E Broadway Jackson WY 83001 307-733-0557 671
Web: www.snakerivergrill.com

Snake River Heritage Ctr
2295 Paddock Ave Weiser ID 83672 208-549-0205 423
Web: www.weisermuseum.com

Snake River Lodge & Spa
7710 Granite Loop Rd. Teton Village WY 83025 307-732-6000 732-6009 378
TF: 855-342-4712 ■ *Web:* www.snakeriverlodge.com

SNAME (Society of Naval Architects & Marine Engineers)
601 Pavonia Ave. Jersey City NJ 07306 201-798-4800 798-4975 49-21
TF: 800-798-2188 ■ *Web:* www.sname.org

SNAP (Survivors Network of Those Abused by Priests)
PO Box 6416 Chicago IL 60680 312-455-1499 48-21
TF: 877-762-7432 ■ *Web:* www.snapnetwork.org

SNAP (Spokane Neighborhood Action Partners)
3102 W Fort George Wright Dr. Spokane WA 99224 509-456-7627 534-5874 196
Web: www.snapwa.org

Snap Inc
4080 Lafayette Center Dr Ste 340 Chantilly VA 20151 703-393-6400 180
Web: www.snapinc.net

Snap Surveys Ltd
210 Commerce Way Ste 200 Portsmouth NH 03801 603-610-8700 809
Web: www.snapsurveys.com

Snapdragon Associates LLC
8 Commerce Dr Ste 102A. Bedford NH 03110 603-621-9037 260
Web: www.snapdragonassociates.com

Snapfinger
3025 Windward Plz Ste 150 Alpharetta GA 30005 678-739-4650 387
Web: www.snapfinger.com

SnapGoods Inc 155 Water St. Brooklyn NY 11201 347-651-0845 387
Web: snapgoods.com

Snap-on Credit LLC
950 Technology Way Ste 301 Libertyville IL 60048 877-777-8455 777-9375 216
TF: 877-777-8455 ■ *Web:* www.snaponcredit.com

Snap-on Diagnostics
420 Barclay Blvd. Lincolnshire IL 60069 847-478-0700 248
Web: www.snapon.com

SnapOne Inc 3490 Rt 1 Ste 16. Princeton NJ 08540 609-720-1900 736

Snapp & Associates Insurance Services Inc
438 Camino Del Rio S Ste 112-B. San Diego CA 92108 619-908-3100 908-3110 390
Web: snappassociates.com

Snapp & Son Insurance Inc
221 First Ave W Ste 200. Seattle WA 98119 206-282-3425 390
Web: snapp.com

Snapping Shoals Electric Membership Corp
14750 Brown Bridge Rd Covington GA 30016 770-786-3484 245
Web: ssemc.com

Snappy Tomato Pizza Co
6111 A Burgundy Hill Dr Burlington KY 41005 859-525-4680 525-4686 670
Web: www.snappytomato.com

Snap-Tite Inc
Snap-Tite Autoclave Engineers Div
8325 Hessinger Dr. Erie PA 16509 814-838-5700 91
TF: 800-458-0409 ■ *Web:* snap-tite.com

Snaptron Inc 960 Diamond Valley Dr. Windsor CO 80550 970-686-5682 203
Web: www.snaptron.com

Snavely Associates Ltd
112 W Foster Ave Ste 401 State College PA 16804 814-234-3672 344
Web: www.snavelyassociates.com

Snavely Forest Products Inc
600 Delwar Rd Pittsburgh PA 15236 412-885-4005 885-6050 364
Web: www.snavelyforest.com

SNC (Sierra Nevada Corp) 444 Salomon Cir Sparks NV 89434 775-331-0222 331-0370 253
Web: www.sncorp.com

SNC (Strategic Network Consulting)
5555 W Loop S Ste 450 Bellaire TX 77401 713-366-3412 871-0057 180
Web: www.snc.net

SNC (Southeast Nebraska Communications)
110 W 17th St. Falls City NE 68355 402-245-4451 245-4770 224
Web: www.sentco.net

SNC Lavalin Group Inc
455 Rene-Levesque Blvd W Montreal QC H2Z1Z3 514-393-1000 866-0795 261
TSE: SNC ■ *Web:* www.snclavalin.com

SNC Manufacturing Company Inc
101 W Waukau Ave. Oshkosh WI 54902 920-231-7370 231-1090 253
TF: 800-558-3325 ■ *Web:* www.sncmfg.com

SND (Society for News Design)
424 E Central Blvd Ste 406. Orlando FL 32801 407-420-7748 420-7697 49-14
Web: www.snd.org

SNDDEN (Sisters of Notre Dame de Namur)
Congregational Mission Office
30 Jeffreys Neck Rd Ipswich MA 01938 978-356-2159 356-1034 637-10
Web: www.sndden.org

Snead State Community College
220 N Walnut St PO Box 734 Boaz AL 35957 256-593-5120 593-7180 162
Web: www.snead.edu

Sneed Elementary School
9855 Pagewood Ln. Houston TX 77042 713-789-6979 260-7307 685
Web: www.aliefisd.net

Snell & Wilmer LLP
1 Arizona Ctr 400 E Van Buren St Ste 1900 Phoenix AZ 85004 602-382-6000 382-6070 428
TF: 800-322-0430 ■ *Web:* www.swlaw.com

Snell House 21 Atlantic Ave Bar Harbor ME 04609 207-288-8004 379
Web: www.snellhouse.com

Snell MotorsInc 1900 Madison Ave Mankato MN 56001 507-345-4626 57
Web: www.snellmotors.com

Snelling Co 1400 Concordia Ave Saint Paul MN 55104 651-646-7381 189-10
Web: www.snellingcompany.com

Snellings Walters Insurance Agency
1117 Perimeter Ctr W W101. Atlanta GA 30338 770-396-9600 390
Web: snellingswalters.com

Snelson Company Inc
601 W State St Sedro-Woolley WA 98284 360-856-6511 856-5816 188-10
Web: www.snelsonco.com

Snethkamp Chrysler Dodge Jeep Ram
11600 Telegraph Rd Redford MI 48239 313-405-7585 516
TF: 888-455-6146 ■ *Web:* www.snethkampchryslerjeep.net

SNFC (Security National Financial Corp)
121 W Election Dr Ste 100 Draper UT 84020 801-264-1060 391-2
NASDAQ: SNFCA ■ *Web:* www.securitynational.com

SNG Engineering Inc
344 Main St Ste 200. Gaithersburg MD 20878 301-548-0055 548-1840 261
Web: sngeng.com

SNI (Southern Newspapers Inc)
5701 Woodway Dr Houston TX 77057 713-266-5481 266-1847 637-8
Web: sninews.com

Snider Industries LLP
3311 Sue Belle Lake Rd Marshall TX 75670 903-938-9221 683
Web: www.sniderindustries.com

Snider Mold Company Inc
6303 W Industrial Dr Mequon WI 53092 262-242-0870 757
Web: www.snidermold.com

Snipes Insurance Service Inc
105 N Wilson Ave. Dunn NC 28334 910-892-2121 390
Web: snipesinsurance.com

Snipp Interactive Inc
530 Richmond St W Rear Lower Level Toronto ON M5V1K4 888-997-6477 195
TF: 888-997-6477 ■ *Web:* www.snipp.com

Snite Museum of Art
100 Moose Krause Cir Notre Dame IN 46556 574-631-5466 631-8501 520
Web: sniteartmuseum.nd.edu

SNK America Inc
1150 Feehanville Dr Mount Prospect IL 60056 847-364-0801 364-4363 455
Web: snkamerica.com

SNL (Sandia National Laboratories - California)
7011 E Ave PO Box 969 Livermore CA 94551 925-294-3000 668
Web: www.sandia.gov

SNL (Sandia National Laboratories - New Mexico)
1515 Eubank SE. Albuquerque NM 87123 505-844-8066 668
TF: 800-783-5337 ■ *Web:* www.sandia.gov

SNM (Society of Nuclear Medicine)
1850 Samuel Morse Dr. Reston VA 20190 703-708-9000 708-9015 49-8
Web: www.snmmi.org

SNMP Research International Inc
3001 Kimberlin Heights Rd. Knoxville TN 37920 865-579-3311 579-6565 178-12
Web: www.snmp.com

Snocope Credit Union
3130 Rockefeller Ave Everett WA 98201 425-405-9973 219
TF: 844-766-2673 ■ *Web:* snocope.org

Snodgrass & Son's Construction Company Inc
2700 S George Washington Bldg Wichita KS 67210 316-687-3110 687-5853 685
Web: www.snodgrassconstruction.com

Snohomish County 3000 Rockefeller Ave Everett WA 98201 425-388-3411 338
TF: 800-584-3578 ■ *Web:* snohomishcountywa.gov

Snohomish Flying Service Inc
9900 Airport Way Snohomish WA 98296 360-568-1541 568-6034 63
Web: www.snohomishflying.com

Snoopy's Pier
13313 S Padre Island Dr. Corpus Christi TX 78418 361-949-8815 671
Web: snoopyspier.com

Snooth Inc 33 W 19th St 4th Fl New York NY 10011 646-723-4328 387
Web: www.snooth.com

Name / Address	City	State	ZIP	Phone	Fax	Class
Snoqualmie Entertainment Authority						
37500 SE N Bend Way	Snoqualmie	WA	98065	425-888-1234		133
Web: www.snocasino.com						
Snoqualmie Valley Record						
8124 Falls Ave SE	Snoqualmie	WA	98065	425-888-2311	888-2427	532-2
Web: www.valleyrecord.com						
Snorkel 2009 Roseport Rd	Elwood	KS	66024	785-989-3000	989-3070	470
TF: 800-255-0317 ■ *Web:* www.snorkellifts.com						
Snow Christensen & Martineau						
10 Exchange Pl	Salt Lake City	UT	84111	801-521-9000		428
Web: www.scmlaw.com						
Snow College						
150 College Ave PO Box 1037	Ephraim	UT	84627	435-283-7000	283-7157	162
TF: 800-848-3399 ■ *Web:* www.snow.edu						
Snow Hill Chamber of Commerce						
5485 Airport Terminal Rd	Salisbury	MD	21804	410-632-2080		139
Web: www.snowhillmd.com						
Snow Jr & King Inc 2415 Church St	Norfolk	VA	23504	757-627-8621		189-7
Web: www.snowjrandking.com						
Snow King Resort & Grand View Lodge						
400 E Snow King Ave	Jackson	WY	83001	307-733-5200	733-4086	669
Web: www.snowking.com						
Snow Tree Books 294 Lynn St	Peabody	MA	01960	781-592-9866		637-2
Web: www.snowtreebooks.com						
Snow Valley Mountain Resort						
35100 State Hwy 18 PO Box 2337	Running Springs	CA	92382	909-867-2751	867-7687	669
Web: www.snow-valley.com						
Snowbasin Ski Resort						
3925 E Snowbasin Rd	Huntsville	UT	84317	801-620-1100		669
TF: 888-437-5488 ■ *Web:* www.snowbasin.com						
SnowBear Ltd						
259 Third Concession Rd	Princeton	ON	N0J1V0	800-337-2327		480
TF: 800-337-2327 ■ *Web:* www.snowbear.com						
Snowbird Mountain Lodge						
4633 Santeetlah Rd	Robbinsville	NC	28771	828-479-3433	479-3473	379
TF: 800-941-9290 ■ *Web:* snowbirdlodge.com						
Snowbound Software						
309 Waverley Oaks Rd Ste 401	Waltham	MA	02452	617-607-2000	607-2002	178-10
Web: www.snowbound.com						
Snowdale State Park 501 S 439	Salina	OK	74365	918-434-2651	435-2101	565
Web: www.travelok.com						
Snowfire 100 Us Rt 2	Waterbury	VT	05676	802-244-5606		57
TF: 800-287-5606 ■ *Web:* snowfireauto.com						
Snowflake Inc 450 Concar Dr	San Mateo	CA	94402	844-766-9355		225
TF: 844-766-9355 ■ *Web:* www.snowflake.com						
Snowline Engineering						
4261 Business Dr	Cameron Park	CA	95682	530-677-2675		261
TF: 800-361-6083 ■ *Web:* www.snowlineengineering.com						
Snowmass Club PO Box G-2	Snowmass Village	CO	81615	970-923-5600	923-6944	669
Web: www.snowmassclub.com						
Snowshoe Mountain Resort						
10 Snowshoe Dr	Snowshoe	WV	26209	877-441-4386		669
TF: 877-441-4386 ■ *Web:* www.snowshoemtn.com						
SnowSports Industries America (SIA)						
1918 Prospector Ave	Park City	UT	84060	435-657-5140	659-3434	49-4
Web: www.snowsports.org						
Snowy Owl Inn 41 Village Rd	Waterville Valley	NH	03215	603-236-8383		379
TF: 800-766-9969 ■ *Web:* www.snowyowlinn.com						
SNPRC (Southwest National Primate Research Ctr)						
Texas Biomedical Research Institute						
PO Box 760549	San Antonio	TX	78245	210-258-9400		668
Web: snprc.org						
SNtial Technologies Inc						
150 N Michigan Ave Ste 2800	Chicago	IL	60601	312-863-8633	929-8535*	317
**Fax Area Code:* 630 ■ *Web:* www.sntialtech.com						
Snug Harbor Cultural Ctr						
1000 Richmond Ter Bldg P	Staten Island	NY	10301	718-425-3504		572
Web: www.snug-harbor.org						
Snuggle Bugz 3245 Fairview St	Burlington	ON	L7N3L1	905-631-0005		321
Web: www.snugglebugz.ca						
SNUPI Technologies Inc						
4512 University Way NE	Seattle	WA	98105	206-673-2707		693
Web: www.wallyhome.com						
Snyder & Associates Inc PO Box 1159	Ankeny	IA	50023	515-964-2020		261
Web: www.snyder-associates.com						
Snyder & Co 129 W Chestnut St	Lancaster	OH	43130	740-654-9989		2
Web: snydercpas.com						
Snyder & Staley Engineering PLC						
3085 Bay Rd Ste 6	Saginaw	MI	48603	989-797-1710	797-1715	261
TF: 877-223-6805 ■ *Web:* ssengineering.com						
Snyder Brothers Inc						
1 Glade Park Dr	Kittanning	PA	16201	724-548-8101		536
Web: www.snyderbrothersinc.com						
Snyder Chevrolet 524 N Perry St	Napoleon	OH	43545	567-341-4132		57
TF: 800-569-3957 ■ *Web:* www.snyderchevrolet.com						
Snyder County 9 W Market St	Middleburg	PA	17842	570-837-4207	837-4282	338
Web: www.snydercounty.org						
Snyder Industries Inc						
6940 O St Ste 100	Lincoln	NE	68504	402-467-5221	465-1220	199
TF: 888-422-8683 ■ *Web:* www.snydernet.com						
Snyder Langston Inc 17962 Cowan St	Irvine	CA	92614	949-863-9200	863-1087	186
Web: www.snyderlangston.com						
Snyder Manufacturing Corp						
1541 W Cowles St	Long Beach	CA	90813	562-432-2038		151
TF: 800-395-6478 ■ *Web:* www.snydermanufacturing.com						
Snyder of Berlin 1313 Stadium Dr	Berlin	PA	15530	330-854-0818		296-35
TF: 888-257-8042 ■ *Web:* www.snyderofberlin.com						
Snyder Paper Corp						
250 26th St Dr SE PO Box 758	Hickory	NC	28603	828-328-2501		559
TF: 800-222-8562 ■ *Web:* snydersolutions.com						
Snyder Roofing & Sheet Metal Inc						
20203 Broadway Ave	Tigard	OR	97223	503-620-5252	684-3310	189-12
Web: snyder-builds.com						
Snyder Tire 401 Cadiz Rd	Steubenville	OH	43953	740-264-5543		755
TF: 800-967-8473 ■ *Web:* www.snydertire.com						
Snyder's of Hanover						
1250 York St PO Box 6917	Hanover	PA	17331	717-632-4477	632-7207	296-9
TF: 800-233-7125 ■ *Web:* snyderslance.com						

Name / Address	City	State	ZIP	Phone	Fax	Class
So Cal Sandbags Inc 12620 Bosley Ln	Corona	CA	92883	951-277-3404		385
TF: 800-834-8682 ■ *Web:* www.socalsandbags.com						
So Low Environmental Equipment Company Inc						
10310 Spartan Dr	Cincinnati	OH	45215	513-772-9410	772-0570	14
Web: www.so-low.com						
SOA (Society of Actuaries)						
475 N Martingale Rd Ste 600	Schaumburg	IL	60173	847-706-3500	706-3599	49-9
Web: www.soa.org						
Soap Plant 4633 Hollywood Blvd	Los Angeles	CA	90027	323-663-0122		327
Web: www.soapplant.com						
SOAProjects Inc						
495 N Whisman Rd Ste 100	Mountain View	CA	94043	650-960-9900		196
Web: soaprojects.com						
Soar with Eagles						
2809 Laurel Crossing Cir	Rogers	AR	72756	479-903-0208		637-2
Web: www.soarhigher.com						
Soaring Eagle Casino & Resort						
6800 E Soaring Eagle Blvd	Mount Pleasant	MI	48858	888-732-4537		133
TF: 888-732-4537 ■ *Web:* www.soaringeaglecasino.com						
Soaring Society of America						
Jack Gomez Blvd	Hobbs	NM	88240	575-392-1177		533
Web: www.ssa.org						
Soaring Software Solutions Inc						
128 N Main St Ste 6	Swanton	OH	43558	419-826-0444		177
Web: soaringsoftware.com						
Soave Enterprises LLC						
3400 E Lafayette St	Detroit	MI	48207	313-567-7000		686
Web: www.soave.com						
Sobel & Company LLC						
293 Eisenhower Pkwy Ste 290	Livingston	NJ	07039	973-994-9494		2
TF: 800-471-2468 ■ *Web:* sobelcollc.com						
Sobel Weber Associates Inc						
146 E 19th St	New York	NY	10003	212-420-8585		637-2
Web: www.sobelweber.com						
Sobel Westex Inc 2670 Western Ave	Las Vegas	NV	89109	855-697-6235		361
TF: 855-697-6235 ■ *Web:* www.sobelathome.com						
Sobeys Inc 115 King St	Stellarton	NS	B0K1S0	902-752-8371		345
TF: 800-723-3929 ■ *Web:* www.sobeys.com						
Soboba Casino 23333 Soboba Rd	San Jacinto	CA	92583	951-665-1000		452
TF: 866-476-2622 ■ *Web:* www.soboba.com						
Soby's 207 S Main St	Greenville	SC	29601	864-232-7007		671
Web: www.sobys.com						
Socal Ip Law Group LLP						
310 N Westlake Blvd	Westlake Village	CA	91361	805-230-1350	230-1355	41
Web: socalip.com						
SOCAN 41 Valleybrook Dr	Toronto	ON	M3B2S6	416-445-8700		138
TF: 866-307-6226 ■ *Web:* www.socan.ca						
SOCAP Intl						
625 N Washington St Ste 304	Alexandria	VA	22314	703-519-3700	549-4886	48-10
Web: www.socap.org						
Soccer 4 All						
1306 Fm 1092 Rd Ste 101	Missouri City	TX	77459	281-499-6665		711
Web: soccer4all.com						
Soccer City LLC 5770 Springdale Rd	Cincinnati	OH	45247	513-741-8480		720
Web: indoorsoccercity.com						
Soccer Magic LLC 1050 Schadt Ave	Whitehall	PA	18052	610-443-2300	443-2302	459
Web: www.soccermagicdiscounts.com						
Social & Economic Sciences Research Ctr (SESRC)						
Washington State University						
Wilson Hall Rm 133 PO Box 644014	Pullman	WA	99164	509-335-1511	335-0116	668
TF: 800-932-5393 ■ *Web:* sesrc.wsu.edu						
Social & Scientific Systems Inc						
8757 Georgia Ave 12th Fl	Silver Spring	MD	20910	301-628-3000	628-3001	180
Web: www.s-3.com						
Social Communications Co						
650 Castro St Ste 100	Mountain View	CA	94041	650-425-7801		194
Web: www.sococo.com						
Social Science Research Council (SSRC)						
810 Seventh Ave	New York	NY	10019	212-377-2700	377-2727	634
Web: www.ssrc.org						
Social Security Administration (SSA)						
6401 Security Blvd	Baltimore	MD	21235	410-965-8904		340-20
Web: www.ssa.gov						
Social Security Administration Regional Offices						
Region 2 26 Federal Plz Rm 40-102	New York	NY	10278	212-264-4036		340-20
Web: www.ssa.gov						
Region 4 61 Forsyth St SW Ste 23T29	Atlanta	GA	30303	800-772-1213		340-20
TF: 800-772-1213 ■ *Web:* www.ssa.gov						
Region 5 600 W Madison St PO Box 8280	Chicago	IL	60680	312-575-4050		340-20
Web: www.ssa.gov						
Social Security Advisory Board						
400 Virginia Ave SW Ste 625	Washington	DC	20024	202-475-7700	475-7715	340-20
Web: www.ssab.gov						
Social Strategy1						
5000 Sawgrass Village Cir Ste 30	Ponte Vedra Beach	FL	32082	877-771-3366		387
TF: 877-771-3366 ■ *Web:* www.socialstrategy1.com						
Social Studies School Service						
PO Box 802	Culver City	CA	90232	310-839-2436	944-5432*	95
**Fax Area Code:* 800 ■ *TF:* 800-421-4246 ■ *Web:* www.socialstudies.com						
Social Survey						
12677 Alcosta Blvd Ste 250	San Ramon	CA	94583	888-701-4512		39
TF: 888-701-4512 ■ *Web:* www.socialsurvey.com						
Social Work Pr.n. Inc						
10680 Barkley Ste 100	Overland Park	KS	66212	913-648-2984		260
TF: 800-595-9648 ■ *Web:* www.socialworkprn.com						
SocialChorus Inc						
123 Mission St 25th Fl	San Francisco	CA	94105	415-655-2700		387
Web: www.socialchorus.com						
SocialCode LLC 151 W 26th St 9th Fl	New York	NY	10001	844-608-4610		5
TF: 844-608-4610 ■ *Web:* socialcode.com						
Sociale 3665 Sacramento St	San Francisco	CA	94118	415-921-3200		671
Web: sfsociale.com						
SocialFlow Inc						
52 Vanderbilt Ave 12th Fl	New York	NY	10017	212-883-9844		387
Web: www.socialflow.com						
Societe Des Traversiers Du Quebec						
250 Rue Saint-Paul	Quebec City	QC	G1K9K9	418-643-2019		342
TF: 877-787-7483 ■ *Web:* www.traversiers.com						

				Phone	Fax	Class
Societe Generale USA 245 Park Ave *Web:* www.cib.societegenerale.com	New York	NY	10167	212-278-6000		70
Societe Grics 5100 Rue Sherbrooke E. *Web:* grics.ca	Montreal	QC	H1V3R9	514-251-3700		225
Society for Academic Emergency Medicine (SAEM) 1111 E Touhy Ave Ste 540 *Web:* www.saem.org	Des Plaines	IL	60018	847-813-9823	813-5450	49-8
Society for American Archaeology (SAA) 900 Second St NE Ste 12 *Web:* www.saa.org	Washington	DC	20002	202-789-8200	789-0284	49-5
Society for Biomaterials 1120 Rte 73 Ste 200 *Web:* www.biomaterials.org	Mount Laurel	NJ	08054	856-439-0826		49-19
Society for College & University Planning (SCUP) 339 E Liberty St Ste 300 *Web:* www.scup.org	Ann Arbor	MI	48104	734-669-3270	998-6532	49-5
Society for Ecological Restoration Intl (SERI) 1017 O St NW **Fax Area Code:* 270 ■ *Web:* www.ser.org	Washington	DC	20001	202-299-9518	626-5485*	48-13
Society for Ethnomusicology (SEM) Indiana University 800 E Third St *TF:* 800-933-9330 ■ *Web:* www.ethnomusicology.org	Bloomington	IN	47405	812-855-6672	855-6673	48-4
Society for Experimental Mechanics Inc (SEM) 7 School St *TF:* 800-627-8258 ■ *Web:* sem.org	Bethel	CT	06801	203-790-6373	790-4472	49-19
Society for Healthcare Epidemiology of America 1300 Wilson Blvd Ste 300 *Web:* www.shea-online.org	Arlington	VA	22209	703-684-1006	684-1009	49-8
Society for Healthcare Strategy & Market Development (SHSMD) 155 N Wacker Dr Ste 400 *TF:* 800-242-2626 ■ *Web:* www.shsmd.org	Chicago	IL	60606	312-422-3888	278-0883	49-8
Society for Imaging Science & Technology (IS&T) 7003 Kilworth Ln *TF:* 800-654-2240 ■ *Web:* www.imaging.org	Springfield	VA	22151	703-642-9090	642-9094	49-16
Society for Industrial & Applied Mathematics (SIAM) 3600 Market St 6th Fl *TF:* 800-447-7426 ■ *Web:* www.siam.org	Philadelphia	PA	19104	215-382-9800	386-7999	49-19
Society for Information Display (SID) 1475 S Bascom Ave Ste 114 *TF:* 800-350-0111 ■ *Web:* www.sid.org	Campbell	CA	95008	408-879-3901	879-3833	48-9
Society for Information Management (SIM) 1120 Rte 73 Ste 200 **Fax Area Code:* 856 ■ *TF:* 800-387-9746 ■ *Web:* www.simnet.org	Mount Laurel	NJ	08054	312-527-6734	439-0525*	48-9
Society for Investigative Dermatology Inc (SID) 526 Superior Ave E Ste 340 *Web:* www.sidnet.org	Cleveland	OH	44114	216-579-9300	579-9333	49-8
Society for Manitobans with Disabilities Library 825 Sherbrook St *TF:* 866-282-8041 ■ *Web:* www.smd.mb.ca	Winnipeg	MB	R3A1M5	204-975-3010	975-3073	434-3
Society for Marketing Professional Services (SMPS) 123 N Pitt St Ste 400 *Web:* www.smps.org	Alexandria	VA	22314	703-549-6117	549-2498	49-18
Society for Medical Decision Making 390 Amwell Rd Ste 402 *Web:* www.smdm.org	Hillsborough	NJ	08844	908-359-1184	450-1119	49-8
Society for Mining Metallurgy & Exploration Inc (SME) 12999 E Adam Aircraft Cir *TF:* 800-763-3132 ■ *Web:* www.smenet.org	Englewood	CO	80112	303-948-4200	973-3845	49-13
Society for Modeling & Simulation Intl 11315 Rancho Bernardo Rd Ste 139 *Web:* www.scs.org	San Diego	CA	92127	858-277-3888	277-3930	48-9
Society for Neuroscience (SFN) 1121 14th St NW Ste 1010 *Web:* www.sfn.org	Washington	DC	20005	202-962-4000	962-4941	49-8
Society for News Design (SND) 424 E Central Blvd Ste 406 *Web:* www.snd.org	Orlando	FL	32801	407-420-7748	420-7697	49-14
Society for Protective Coatings (SSPC) 40 24th St 6th Fl *TF:* 877-281-7772 ■ *Web:* www.sspc.org	Pittsburgh	PA	15222	412-281-2331	281-9995	49-13
Society for Research in Child Development (SRCD) 2950 S State St Ste 401 *Web:* www.srcd.org	Ann Arbor	MI	48104	734-926-0600	926-0601	49-5
Society for Scholarly Publishing (SSP) 10200 W 44th Ave Ste 304 *Web:* www.sspnet.org	Wheat Ridge	CO	80033	303-422-3914		49-16
Society for Sedimentary Geology 4111 S Darlington Ste 100 *TF:* 800-865-9765 ■ *Web:* www.sepm.org	Tulsa	OK	74135	918-610-3361	621-1685	49-19
Society for Social Work Leadership in Health Care 100 N 20th St 4th Fl **Fax Area Code:* 215 ■ *TF:* 866-237-9542 ■ *Web:* www.sswlhc.org	Philadelphia	PA	19103	866-237-9542	564-2175*	49-15
Society for Surgery of the Alimentary Tract (SSAT) 900 Cummings Ctr Ste 221-U *Web:* www.ssat.com	Beverly	MA	01915	978-927-8330	524-8890	49-8
Society for Technical Communication (STC) 9401 Lee Hwy Ste 300 *Web:* www.stc.org	Fairfax	VA	22031	703-522-4114	522-2075	49-14
Society for the Advancement of Material & Process Engineering (SAMPE) 21680 Gateway Center Dr Ste 300 *TF:* 800-562-7360 ■ *Web:* www.nasampe.org	Diamond Bar	CA	91765	626-521-9460		49-19
Society for Vascular Surgery (SVS) 633 N St Clair St 22nd Fl *TF:* 800-258-7188 ■ *Web:* vascular.org	Chicago	IL	60611	312-334-2300	334-2320	49-8
Society for Women's Health Research (SWHR) 1025 Connecticut Ave NW Ste 601 *Web:* swhr.org	Washington	DC	20036	202-223-8224	833-3472	48-17
Society Hill Playhouse 507 S Eigth St *Web:* www.societyhillplayhouse.org	Philadelphia	PA	19147	215-923-0210		572
Society of Accredited Marine Surveyors Inc (SAMS) 7855 Argyle Forest Blvd Ste 203 *TF:* 800-344-9077 ■ *Web:* www.marinesurvey.org	Jacksonville	FL	32244	904-384-1494	388-3958	48-1
Society of Actuaries (SOA) 475 N Martingale Rd Ste 600 *Web:* www.soa.org	Schaumburg	IL	60173	847-706-3500	706-3599	49-9
Society of American Archivists (SAA) 17 N State St Ste 1425 *TF:* 866-722-7858 ■ *Web:* www2.archivists.org	Chicago	IL	60602	312-606-0722	606-0728	48-4
Society of American Florists (SAF) 1601 Duke St *TF:* 800-336-4743 ■ *Web:* safnow.org	Alexandria	VA	22314	703-836-8700	836-8705	49-4
Society of American Foresters (SAF) 10100 Laureate Way *TF:* 866-897-8720 ■ *Web:* www.eforester.org	Bethesda	MD	20814	301-897-8720	897-3690	48-2
Society of American Gastrointestinal & Endoscopic Surgeons (SAGES) 11300 W Olympic Blvd Ste 600 *Web:* www.sages.org	Los Angeles	CA	90064	310-437-0544	437-0585	49-8
Society of American Military Engineers (SAME) 607 Prince St *Web:* www.same.org	Alexandria	VA	22314	703-549-3800	684-0231	48-19
Society of Animal Artists Inc 5451 Sedona Hills Dr *Web:* www.societyofanimalartists.com	Berthoud	CO	80513	970-532-3127		48-4
Society of Architectural Historians (SAH) 1365 N Astor St *Web:* www.sah.org	Chicago	IL	60610	312-573-1365	573-1141	48-13
Society of Automotive Engineers Inc (SAE) 400 Commonwealth Dr *TF:* 877-606-7323 ■ *Web:* www.sae.org	Warrendale	PA	15096	724-776-4841	776-0790	49-21
Society of Behavioral Medicine (SBM) 555 E Wells St Ste 1100 *Web:* www.sbm.org	Milwaukee	WI	53202	414-918-3156	276-3349	49-15
Society of Biblical Literature (SBL) The Luce Ctr 825 Houston Mill Rd *TF:* 866-727-9955 ■ *Web:* www.sbl-site.org	Atlanta	GA	30329	404-727-3100	727-3101	48-20
Society of Broadcast Engineers Inc (SBE) 9102 N Meridian St Ste 150 *Web:* www.sbe.org	Indianapolis	IN	46260	317-846-9000	846-9120	49-14
Society of Cable Telecommunications Engineers (SCTE) 140 Philips Rd *TF:* 800-542-5040 ■ *Web:* www.scte.org	Exton	PA	19341	610-363-6888	363-5898	49-19
Society of California Pioneers 101 Montgomery Ste 150 *Web:* www.californiapioneers.org	San Francisco	CA	94129	415-957-1849		520
Society of Cardiovascular Anesthesiologists (SCA) 8735 W Higgins Rd Ste 300 **Fax Area Code:* 847 ■ *TF:* 800-283-6296 ■ *Web:* www.scahq.org	Chicago	IL	60631	855-658-2828	375-6323*	49-8
Society of Communications Technology Consultants (SCTC) 230 Washington Ave Ext Ste 101 *TF:* 800-782-7670 ■ *Web:* www.sctcconsultants.org	Albany	NY	12203	800-782-7670	859-3205	49-20
Society of Corporate Secretaries & Governance Professionals 240 W 35th St Ste 400 *Web:* www.main.societycorpgov.org	New York	NY	10001	212-681-2000	681-2005	49-12
Society of Cosmetic Chemists (SCC) 120 Wall St Ste 2400 *Web:* www.scconline.org	New York	NY	10005	212-668-1500	668-1504	49-19
Society of Critical Care Medicine (SCCM) 500 Midway Dr *Web:* www.sccm.org	Mount Prospect	IL	60056	847-827-6869	439-7226	49-8
Society of Decorative Painters 1220 E First St *Web:* www.decorativepainters.org	Wichita	KS	67214	316-269-9300	269-9191	48-18
Society of Diagnostic Medical Sonography (SDMS) 2745 Dallas Pkwy *TF:* 800-229-9506 ■ *Web:* www.sdms.org	Plano	TX	75093	214-473-8057	473-8563	49-8
Society of Environmental Journalists (SEJ) 1629 K St NW Ste 300 **Fax Area Code:* 215 ■ *Web:* www.sej.org	Washington	DC	20006	202-558-2300	884-8175*	49-14
Society of Environmental Toxicology & Chemistry (SETAC) 1010 N 12th Ave *Web:* www.setac.org	Pensacola	FL	32501	850-469-1500	469-9778	49-19
Society of Exploration Geophysicists (SEG) 8801 S Yale Ave Ste 500 PO Box 702740 *Web:* seg.org	Tulsa	OK	74137	918-497-5500	497-5557	48-12
Society of Financial Service Professionals (SFSP) 19 Campus Blvd Ste 100 *Web:* www.financialpro.org	Newtown Square	PA	19073	610-526-2500	527-4010	49-9
Society of Gastroenterology Nurses & Associates Inc (SGNA) 401 N Michigan Ave *TF:* 800-245-7462 ■ *Web:* www.sgna.org	Chicago	IL	60611	312-321-5165	673-6694	49-8
Society of Glass & Ceramic Decorators (SGCD) PO Box 2489 *Web:* www.sgcd.org	Zanesville	OH	43702	740-588-9882		48-4
Society of Hospital Medicine 190 N Independence Mall W. *TF:* 800-843-3360 ■ *Web:* www.hospitalmedicine.org	Philadelphia	PA	19106	800-843-3360		78
Society of Incentive & Travel Executives (SITE) 330 N Wabash Ste 2000 *Web:* www.siteglobal.com	Chicago	IL	60611	312-321-5148		48-23
Society of Independent Gasoline Marketers of America (SIGMA) 3930 Pender Dr Ste 340 *Web:* www.sigma.org	Fairfax	VA	22030	703-709-7000	709-7007	49-18
Society of Industrial & Office Realtors (SIOR) 1201 New York Ave NW Ste 350 *Web:* www.sior.com	Washington	DC	20005	202-449-8200	216-9325	49-17
Society of Interventional Radiology (SIR) 3975 Fair Rdige Dr Ste 400 N. *Web:* www.sirweb.org	Fairfax	VA	22033	703-691-1805	691-1855	49-8
Society of Laparoendoscopic Surgeons (SLS) 7330 SW 62nd Pl Ste 410 *Web:* www.sls.org	Miami	FL	33143	305-665-9959	667-4123	49-8
Society of Manufacturing Engineers (SME) 1 SME Dr *TF:* 800-733-4763 ■ *Web:* www.sme.org	Dearborn	MI	48128	313-425-3000	425-3400	49-13
Society of Motion Picture & Television Engineers (SMPTE) 3 Barker Ave *Web:* www.smpte.org	White Plains	NY	10601	914-761-1100	761-3115	48-4
Society of Naval Architects & Marine Engineers (SNAME) 601 Pavonia Ave *TF:* 800-798-2188 ■ *Web:* www.sname.org	Jersey City	NJ	07306	201-798-4800	798-4975	49-21
Society of Nuclear Medicine (SNM) 1850 Samuel Morse Dr *Web:* www.snmmi.org	Reston	VA	20190	703-708-9000	708-9015	49-8
Society of Petroleum Engineers (SPE) 222 Palisades Creek Dr *TF:* 800-456-6863 ■ *Web:* www.spe.org	Richardson	TX	75080	972-952-9393	952-9435	48-12

	Phone	Fax	Class
Society of Petrophysicists & Well Log Analysts (SPWLA) 8866 Gulf Fwy Ste 320 .... Houston TX 77017 *Web:* spwla.org	713-947-8727	947-7181	48-12
Society of Plastics Engineers (SPE) 13 Church Hill Rd .... Newtown CT 06470 *Web:* www.4spe.org	203-775-0471	775-8490	49-13
Society of Professional Benefit Administrators (SPBA) 2 Wisconsin Cir Ste 670 .... Chevy Chase MD 20815 *Web:* spbatpa.org	301-718-7722	718-9440	49-12
Society of Professional Journalists (SPJ) 3909 N Meridian St .... Indianapolis IN 46208 *Web:* www.spj.org	317-927-8000	920-4789	49-14
Society of Saint Andrew (SOSA) 3383 Sweet Hollow Rd .... Big Island VA 24526 *TF:* 800-333-4597 ■ *Web:* endhunger.org	434-299-5956	299-5949	48-5
Society of Teachers of Family Medicine (STFM) 11400 Tomahawk Creek Pkwy Ste 240 .... Leawood KS 66211 **Fax Area Code:* 913 ■ *TF:* 800-274-7928 ■ *Web:* www.stfm.org	800-274-7928	906-6096*	49-8
Society of Thoracic Surgeons (STS) 633 N St Clair St Ste 2320 .... Chicago IL 60611 *TF:* 877-865-5321 ■ *Web:* www.sts.org	312-202-5800	202-5801	49-8
Society of Toxicology (SOT) 1821 Michael Faraday Dr Ste 300 .... Reston VA 20190 *Web:* www.toxicology.org	703-438-3115	438-3113	49-8
Society of Tribologists & Lubrication Engineers (STLE) 840 Busse Hwy .... Park Ridge IL 60068 *Web:* www.stle.org	847-825-5536	825-1456	49-13
Society of Vacuum Coaters (SVC) 71 Pinon Hill Pl NE .... Albuquerque NM 87122 *TF:* 800-443-8817 ■ *Web:* www.svc.org	505-856-7188	856-6716	49-13
Society's Assets Inc 5200 Washington Ave Ste 225 .... Racine WI 53406 *TF:* 800-378-9128 ■ *Web:* societysassets.org	262-637-9128		363
Sockwell Partners Inc 800 E Blvd Ste 200 .... Charlotte NC 28203 *Web:* www.sockwell.com	704-372-1865		260
Soco Thornton Park 629 E Central Blvd .... Orlando FL 32801 *Web:* socothorntonpark.com	407-849-1800		671
Socorro County 101 Plaza St .... Socorro NM 87801 *Web:* www.socorrochamber.org	575-835-0424		338
Socorro Electric Co-opeartive Inc 215 Manzanares Ave PO Box H .... Socorro NM 87801 *TF:* 800-351-7575 ■ *Web:* www.socorroelectric.com	575-835-0560		245
Socrates Academy 3909 Weddington Rd .... Matthews NC 28105 *Web:* www.socratesacademy.us	704-321-1711	321-1714	685
Socratic Technologies Inc 2505 Mariposa St .... San Francisco CA 94110 *TF:* 800-576-2728 ■ *Web:* www.sotech.com	415-430-2200		668
Socure Inc 330 7th Ave Ste 201 .... New York NY 10001 *TF:* 866-932-9013 ■ *Web:* www.socure.com	866-932-9013		178-1
Soderberg Manufacturing Company Inc 20821 Currier Rd .... Walnut CA 91789 *Web:* www.soderberg.aero	909-595-1291		438
Sodelle K-M Plunkett PC 512 Westminster Ave .... Elizabeth NJ 07208 *Web:* skmplaw.com	908-629-1120		41
Sodexho 9801 Washingtonian Blvd .... Gaithersburg MD 20878 *TF:* 888-763-3967 ■ *Web:* www.sodexousa.com	301-987-4000		299
Sodexo | Roth 3847 Crum Rd .... Youngstown OH 44515 *TF:* 800-872-7684 ■ *Web:* www.sodexoroth.com	800-872-7684		612
Sodexo Canada Ltd 5420 N Service Rd Ste 501 .... Burlington ON L7L6C7 *Web:* www.ca.sodexo.com	905-632-8592		671
Sodoro Daly Shomaker & Selde Pc Llo 7000 Spring St .... Omaha NE 68106 *Web:* sodorolaw.com	402-397-6200		41
Sof Tec Solutions Inc 384 Inverness Pkwy Ste 211 .... Englewood CO 80112 *Web:* softecinc.com	303-662-1010	662-1060	225
Sofcom Inc 1431 Opus Pl Ste 110 .... Downers Grove IL 60515 *Web:* www.sofcom.net	630-796-3900		178-1
Sofec Inc 14741 Yorktown Plz .... Houston TX 77040 *Web:* www.sofec.com	713-510-6600	510-6601	261
Soffa Electric Inc 5901 Corvette St .... Commerce CA 90040 *Web:* www.soffaelectric.com	323-728-0230	724-5513	261
Soffront Software Inc 45437 Warm Springs Blvd .... Fremont CA 94539 *Web:* soffront.com	510-413-9000		178-1
Sofia Hotel 150 W Broadway .... San Diego CA 92101 *TF:* 800-826-0009 ■ *Web:* thesofiahotel.com	619-234-9200		379
Sofinnova Ventures Inc 3000 Sand Hill Rd Bldg 4 Ste 250 .... Menlo Park CA 94025 *Web:* www.sofinnova.com	650-681-8420	322-2037	792
Sofitel Philadelphia Hotel 120 S 17th St .... Philadelphia PA 19103 *Web:* www.sofitel.com	215-569-8300		707
Sofradir EC Inc 373 US-46W .... Fairfield NJ 07004 *Web:* www.sofradir-ec.com	973-882-0211	882-0997	692
Soft Pretzel Franchise Systems Inc 7368 Frankford Ave .... Philadelphia PA 19136 *TF:* 800-679-4221 ■ *Web:* phillypretzelfactory.com	215-338-4606		296-1
Soft Science 2101 CityWest Blvd .... Houston TX 77042 **Fax Area Code:* 800 ■ *TF:* 888-507-6387 ■ *Web:* soft-science.com	281-861-0832	466-2902*	177
Soft Stone Publishing PO Box 2755 .... Los Angeles CA 90001 *Web:* www.askkrs.com	323-851-8623		637-2
Soft Surroundings 1100 N Lindbergh Blvd Ste 100 .... Saint Louis MO 63146 *TF:* 800-240-7076 ■ *Web:* www.softsurroundings.com	800-240-7076		157-6
Soft Touch Medical LLC 1800 Sandy Plains Pky .... Marietta GA 30066 *TF:* 800-926-1103 ■ *Web:* www.softtouchmedical.com	770-590-7383		363
Softassist Inc 700 American Ave .... King of Prussia PA 19406 *Web:* www.softassist.com	610-265-8484		180
Softbank Telecom America Corp 21250 Hawthorne Blvd Ste 570 .... Torrance CA 90503 *Web:* www.jt-america.com	212-422-4650	422-4653	736
Softcare Software Inc 12223 Highland Ave Ste 106-518 .... Rancho Cucamonga CA 91739 *Web:* www.softcare.net	909-987-6693		178-1
Softchalk LLC 22 S Auburn Ave .... Richmond VA 23221 *TF:* 877-638-2425 ■ *Web:* softchalk.com	877-638-2425		177
Soft-Con Enterprises Inc 6505 Belcrest Rd Ste 120 .... Hyattsville MD 20782 *Web:* softcon1.com	301-429-0075		180
Softcrylic LLC 718 Washington Ave Ste 208 .... Minneapolis MN 55401 *Web:* softcrylic.com	612-338-2633	677-3860	177
Softdocs Inc 807 Bluff Rd .... Columbia SC 29201 *TF:* 888-457-8879 ■ *Web:* www.softdocs.com	803-695-6044		177
Softech & Associates Inc 1570 Corporate Dr Ste B .... Costa Mesa CA 92626 *TF:* 877-638-3241 ■ *Web:* www.softechis.com	714-427-1122		180
Softech Inc 28104 Orchard Lake Rd Ste 100 .... Farmington Hills MI 48334 *TF:* 800-233-4998 ■ *Web:* dentech.com	800-233-4998		177
Softechnologies Inc 1504 W Northwest Blvd .... Spokane WA 99205 *TF:* 866-873-9799 ■ *Web:* www.softechnologies.com	866-873-9799		179
Softek International Inc 242 Old New Brunswick Rd Ste 320 .... Piscataway NJ 08854 *Web:* www.softekintl.com	732-287-3337		180
Softek Service Inc 1101 14th St NW Ste 850 .... Washington DC 20005 *Web:* www.softekdc.com	202-747-5000		177
Softek Solutions Inc 4500 W 89th St .... Prairie Village KS 66207 *Web:* www.softekinc.com	913-649-1024	648-0128	525
Softengine Inc 21800 Oxnard St Ste 1060 .... Woodland Hills CA 91367 *Web:* softengine.com	818-704-7000	884-3900	180
Softeq Development Corp 1155 Dairy Ashford Ste 125 .... Houston TX 77079 *TF:* 888-552-5001 ■ *Web:* www.softeq.com	281-552-5000		177
Softerware Inc 132 Welsh Rd Ste 140 .... Horsham PA 19044 *TF:* 800-220-8111 ■ *Web:* www.softerware.com	215-628-0400	628-0585	177
Softex Inc 9300 Jollyville Rd Ste 201 .... Austin TX 78759 *Web:* www.softexinc.com	512-452-8836	795-8702	809
Softlayer Technologies Inc 4849 Alpha Rd .... Dallas TX 75244 *TF:* 866-398-7638 ■ *Web:* www.softlayer.com	214-442-0600	442-0601	225
Soft-Lite LLC 10250 Philipp Pkwy .... Streetsboro OH 44241 *TF:* 800-551-1953 ■ *Web:* www.soft-lite.com	330-528-3400	528-3501	235
Softman Products LLC 13470 Washington Blvd Ste 300 .... Marina CA 90292	310-305-3644		177
SoftNice Inc 5050 Tilghman St Ste 115 .... Allentown PA 18104 *Web:* www.softnice.com	610-871-0400		196
Softomate LLC 901 N Pitt St Ste 325 .... Alexandria VA 22314 *TF:* 877-243-8735 ■ *Web:* www.softomate.com	877-243-8735		530
Softplan Systems Inc 8118 Isabella Ln .... Brentwood TN 37027 *TF:* 800-248-0164 ■ *Web:* softplan.com	615-370-1121		177
Softplc Corp 25603 Red Brangus Rd .... Spicewood TX 78669 *Web:* www.softplc.com	512-264-8390	264-8399	177
SoftPress Systems Inc 3020 Bridgeway Ste 408 .... Sausalito CA 94965 *TF:* 800-853-6454 ■ *Web:* www.softpress.com	415-331-4820	331-4824	178-8
Softrek Corp 30 Bryant Woods N .... Amherst NY 14228 *TF:* 855-378-2961 ■ *Web:* softrek.com	855-378-2961		177
Softresources LLC 11411 NE 124th St Ste 270 .... Kirkland WA 98034 *Web:* www.softresources.com	425-216-4030		195
Softrim 9210 Estero Park Commons Blvd Ste 5 .... Estero FL 33928 *Web:* www.softrim.com	239-449-4444	449-4445	180
Softrisc Communication Solutions Inc 575 N Pastoria Ave .... Sunnyvale CA 94085 *Web:* www.softrisc.com	408-333-9775	884-2317	177
SoftSol Resources Inc 46755 Fremont Blvd .... Fremont CA 94538 *Web:* www.softsol.com	510-824-2000		177
SoftThinks USA Inc 11940 Jollyville Rd Ste 225-S .... Austin TX 78759 *TF:* 800-305-1754 ■ *Web:* www.softthinks.com	800-305-1754		809
Software & Information Industry Assn (SIIA) 1090 Vermont Ave NW 6th Fl .... Washington DC 20005 *Web:* www.siia.net	202-289-7442	289-7097	48-9
Software & Services of Louisiana LLC 1120 S Pointe Pkwy .... Shreveport LA 71105 *Web:* softwareservices.net	318-865-1505		177
Software AG USA 11700 Plaza America Dr Ste 700 .... Reston VA 20190 *TF:* 877-724-4965 ■ *Web:* www.softwareag.com	703-860-5050	391-6975	178-1
Software and Systems Design Inc 3 Broadview Rd .... Acton MA 01720 *Web:* www.softwaresystemsdesign.com	978-760-0313		180
Software Answers Inc 6770 W Snowville Rd Ste 200 .... Cleveland OH 44141 *TF:* 800-638-5212 ■ *Web:* www.software-answers.com	440-526-0095	526-2557	764
Software Business Systems Inc 7401 Metro Blvd Ste 550 .... Minneapolis MN 55439 *Web:* sbsweb.com	952-835-0100		525
Software Concepts International LLC 57 Technology Way .... Nashua NH 03060 *Web:* sciinc.com	603-879-9022		177
Software Consulting Services LLC 630 Municipal Dr Ste 420 .... Nazareth PA 18064 *Web:* www.newspapersystems.com	610-746-7700	746-7900	178-10
Software Design Group Inc 10564 Progress Way Ste A .... Cypress CA 90630 *Web:* www.sdgi.com	714-761-3849	766-8448	180
Software Engineering Institute (SEI) 4500 Fifth Ave .... Pittsburgh PA 15213 *TF:* 888-201-4479 ■ *Web:* www.sei.cmu.edu	412-268-5800	268-6257	668

Company / Address	City	State	ZIP	Phone	Fax	Class
Software Engineering of America Inc (SEA) 1230 Hempstead Tpke — *TF:* 800-272-7322 ■ *Web:* seasoft.com	Franklin Square	NY	11010	516-328-7000	354-4015	178-12
Software Engineering Services Corp 1311 Ft Crook Rd S — *TF:* 800-244-1278 ■ *Web:* www.sessolutions.com	Bellevue	NE	68005	402-292-8660		668
Software Enterprises Inc 5380 Twin Hickory Rd — *Web:* softent.com	Glen Allen	VA	23059	804-747-6436	747-6559	179
Software Folks Inc 212 Carnegie Ctr Ste 206 — *Web:* www.softwarefolks.com	Princeton	NJ	08540	609-919-6327		809
Software Generation 124 Hillcrest Dr — *Web:* www.softgen.com	Denville	NJ	07834	973-627-4334		180
Software House Intl (SHI) 290 Davidson Ave — *TF:* 888-764-8888 ■ *Web:* www.shi.com	Somerset	NJ	08873	888-764-8888		174
Software Images Inc 1765 Landess Ave Ste 156 — *Web:* www.software-images.com	Milpitas	CA	95035	408-946-6017	946-9008	180
Software Information Systems Inc (SIS) 165 Barr St — *TF:* 800-337-6914 ■ *Web:* www.thinksis.com	Lexington	KY	40507	859-977-4747	977-4750	180
Software Integrators Inc 255 Comfort Ln — *TF:* 800-547-2349 ■ *Web:* www.si87.com	Bozeman	MT	59718	406-586-8866	585-0028	173-1
Software Interphase Inc 82 Cucumber Hill Rd — *Web:* www.sinterphase.com	Foster	RI	02825	401-397-4540	397-6814	177
Software Methods Inc 770 E Market St — *Web:* www.software-methods.com	West Chester	PA	19382	610-430-8956		177
Software Partners Inc 447 Old Boston Rd Rt 1 — *Web:* www.softwarepartners.com	Topsfield	MA	01983	978-887-6409		88
Software Professionals Inc 1029 Long Prairie Rd Ste A — **Fax Area Code:* 214 ■ *Web:* www.spius.net	Flower Mound	TX	75022	972-518-0198	260-1112*	177
Software Pursuits Inc 1900 S Norfolk St Ste 330 — *TF:* 800-367-4823 ■ *Web:* www.softwarepursuits.com	San Mateo	CA	94403	650-372-0900	372-2912	178-12
Software Revolution Inc, The 11410 NE 122nd Way Ste 105 — *Web:* tsri.com	Kirkland	WA	98034	425-284-2770		177
Software Science Inc 7 Mt Lassen Dr — *Web:* www.softsci.com	San Rafael	CA	94903	415-479-7286		180
Software Solutions Inc (SSI) 10570 Justin Dr — **Fax Area Code:* 888 ■ *Web:* www.ssicomputing.com	Urbandale	IA	50322	515-221-9922	400-3260*	178-1
Software Solutions Inc 420 E Main St — *TF:* 800-686-9578 ■ *Web:* www.mysoftwaresolutions.com	Lebanon	OH	45036	513-932-6667		177
Software Solutions Unlimited Inc 9595 SW Gemini Dr — *Web:* ssui.com	Beaverton	OR	97008	971-249-5400		251
Software Synergy Inc 151 NJ-33 — *Web:* ssi-corp.com	Manalapan	NJ	07726	732-617-9300		261
Software Systems Quality Consulting (SSQC) 2269 Sunny Vista Dr — *Web:* www.ssqc.com	San Jose	CA	95128	408-985-4476	248-7772	194
Software Technology Group 555 S 300 E — *TF:* 888-595-1001 ■ *Web:* stgconsulting.com	Salt Lake City	UT	84111	801-595-1000	595-1080	180
Software Toolbox 148A E Charles St — *TF:* 888-665-3678 ■ *Web:* www.softwaretoolbox.com	Matthews	NC	28105	704-849-2773		177
Software Tree LLC 2953 Bunker Hill Ln Ste 400 — *Web:* www.softwaretree.com	Santa Clara	CA	95054	408-282-3606		178-1
Softworks Systems Inc 6311 Westerly Ter — *Web:* softworkssystems.com	Jamesville	NY	13078	315-251-1244		177
Softworld Inc 281 Winter St Ste 301 — *TF:* 877-899-1166 ■ *Web:* www.softworldinc.com	Waltham	MA	02451	877-899-1166		721
Softwyre Inc 14916 Wade Blvd — *TF:* 866-363-7638 ■ *Web:* www.softwyre.com	Maumelle	AR	72113	501-734-0017		809
SOG Specialty Knives & Tools LLC 6521 212th St SW — *TF:* 888-405-6433 ■ *Web:* www.sogknives.com	Lynnwood	WA	98036	425-771-6230		361
Sogetel Inc 111 Rue du 12-Novembre — *TF:* 866-764-3835 ■ *Web:* www.sogetel.com	Nicolet	QC	J3T1S3	819-293-6125		387
Sohar Inc 400 Corporate Pointe Ste 300 — *Web:* www.sohar.com	Culver City	CA	90230	323-410-0992		809
Sohn Manufacturing Inc 544 Sohn Dr — *Web:* www.sohnmanufacturing.com	Elkhart Lake	WI	53020	920-876-3361	876-2952	413
Sohnen-Moe Associates Inc PO Box 86913 — *TF:* 800-786-4774 ■ *Web:* sohnen-moe.com	Tucson	AZ	85754	520-743-3936	743-3656	637-10
Soho Beach House 4385 Collins Ave — *Web:* www.sohobeachhouse.com	Miami Beach	FL	33140	786-507-7900		707
SoHo Grand Hotel 310 W Broadway — *Web:* www.sohogrand.com	New York	NY	10013	212-965-3000		379
SoHo Metropolitan Hotel 318 Wellington St W — *TF:* 866-764-6638 ■ *Web:* www.metropolitan.com	Toronto	ON	M5V3T4	416-599-8800	599-8801	379
SOHO Prospecting Inc 55 S Glenn Dr — *TF:* 866-644-7646 ■ *Web:* www.sohoprospecting.com	Camarillo	CA	93010	805-482-2170	482-2176	180
Sohum Inc 1055 Minnesota Ave Ste 6 — *Web:* www.sohum.biz	San Jose	CA	95125	408-265-2391		177
Soi 4 *Bangkok Eatery* 5421 College Ave — *Web:* soifour.com	Oakland	CA	94618	510-655-0889		671
Soil & Materials Engineers Inc (SME) 1501 W Thomas St — *Web:* www.sme-usa.com	Bay City	MI	48706	989-684-6050	684-0210	261
Soil & Water Conservation Society (SWCS) 945 SW Ankeny Rd — *TF:* 800-843-7645 ■ *Web:* www.swcs.org	Ankeny	IA	50023	515-289-2331	289-1227	48-13
Soil Consultant Engineering (SCE) 9303 Center St — *Web:* soilconsultants.net	Manassas	VA	20110	703-366-3000		261
Soil Engineering Construction Inc 927 Arguello St — *Web:* soilengineeringconstruction.com	Redwood City	CA	94063	650-367-9595	367-8139	189-5
Soil Retention Systems Inc 2501 State St — *TF:* 800-346-7995 ■ *Web:* soilretention.com	Carlsbad	CA	92008	800-346-7995		422
Soilmoisture Equipment Corp 801 S Kellogg Ave — *Web:* www.soilmoisture.com	Goleta	CA	93117	805-964-3525		419
Sojitz Aerospace America Corp 1120 Avenue of the Americas — *Web:* www.sojitz.com	New York	NY	10036	212-704-6500	704-6543	791
Sokol & Co 5315 Dansher Rd — *TF:* 800-328-7656 ■ *Web:* www.solofoods.com	Countryside	IL	60525	800-328-7656		296-1
Sol Azteca 1360 Montgomery Hwy Ste 128 — *Web:* solaztecamexicanrestaurant.business.site	Vestavia Hills	AL	35216	205-979-4902		671
Sol Jewelry Designs Inc 550 S Hill St Ste 1020 — *TF:* 888-323-7772 ■ *Web:* soljewelry.com	Los Angeles	CA	90013	213-622-7772		410
Sol Schwartz & Assoc 8000 IH-10 W Ste 1100 — *Web:* www.ssacpa.com	San Antonio	TX	78229	210-384-8000	384-8011	2
Solacom Technologies Inc 84 Jean-Proulx — *TF:* 888-765-2266 ■ *Web:* www.solacom.com	Gatineau	QC	J8Z1W1	888-765-2266		529
Solai & Cameron Technologies 3410 W Van Buren — *Web:* solcam.com	Chicago	IL	60624	773-506-2720		177
Solairus Aviation 201 1st St — **Fax Area Code:* 866 ■ *TF:* 800-359-7861 ■ *Web:* www.solairus.aero	Petaluma	CA	94952	800-359-7861	359-7862*	24
Solanbridge Group Inc 3431 Rayford Rd — *Web:* www.solanbridgegroup.com	Spring	TX	77386	913-222-2977		652
Solanco School District 211 S Hess St — *Web:* www.solanco.k12.pa.us	Quarryville	PA	17566	717-786-8401	786-8245	685
Solano Coalition for Better Health 744 Empire St Ste 210 — *TF:* 800-978-7547 ■ *Web:* solanocoalition.org	Fairfield	CA	94533	800-978-7547		363
Solano Community College 4000 Suisun Valley Rd — *Web:* www.solano.edu	Fairfield	CA	94534	707-864-7171	864-7175	162
Solano County 675 Texas St Ste 2700 — *Web:* www.solanocounty.com	Fairfield	CA	94533	707-784-6200	784-6209	338
Solano County Fair 900 Fairgrounds Dr — *Web:* www.scfair.com	Vallejo	CA	94589	707-551-2000	642-7947	642
Solano Press Books PO Box 773 — *TF:* 800-931-9373 ■ *Web:* www.solano.com	Point Arena	CA	95468	707-884-4508	884-4109	637-2
Solar Atmospheres Inc 1969 Clearview Rd — *TF:* 800-347-3236 ■ *Web:* solaratm.com	Souderton	PA	18964	215-721-1502		484
Solar Bat Enterprises Inc 3628 E County Rd 600 N — *Web:* www.solarbat.com	Brazil	IN	47834	812-986-3551		543
Solar Compounds Corp 1201 W Blancke St — *Web:* www.solarcompounds.com	Linden	NJ	07036	908-862-2813	862-8061	3
Solar Electric Systems 742 Hampshire Rd Ste A — *Web:* www.gogreensolarsolutions.com	Westlake Village	CA	91361	805-497-9808		610
Solar Energy Industries Assn (SEIA) 600 14th St NW Ste 400 — *Web:* www.seia.org	Washington	DC	20005	202-682-0556	682-0559	48-12
Solar Energy Systems LLC 1205 Manhattan Ave Ste 1210 — *Web:* www.solaresystems.com	Brooklyn	NY	11222	718-389-1545		612
Solar Graphics Inc 12167 49th Ave N Ste 100 — *TF:* 800-869-8468 ■ *Web:* www.solargraphics.com	Clearwater	FL	33762	727-327-4288		189-6
Solar Industries Inc 4940 S Alvernon Way PO Box 27337 — *TF:* 800-449-2323 ■ *Web:* solarindustriesinc.com	Tucson	AZ	85706	520-519-8258	519-8281	191-3
Solar Light Company Inc 100 E Glenside Ave — *Web:* solarlight.com	Glenside	PA	19038	215-517-8700		610
Solar Plastics Inc 860 Johnson Dr — *Web:* www.solarplastics.com	Delano	MN	55328	763-972-5600		596
Solar Products Inc 228 Wanaque Ave — *Web:* www.solarproducts.com	Pompton Lakes	NJ	07442	973-248-9370		318
Solar Store Sustainable energy solutions 2833 N Country Club Rd — *Web:* www.solarstore.com	Tucson	AZ	85716	520-332-6535		610
Solar Technologies Inc 26180 Enterprise Way Bldg 100	Lake Forest	CA	92630	949-458-1080		180
Solar Turbines Inc 2200 Pacific Hwy — *Web:* www.solarturbines.com	San Diego	CA	92101	619-544-5000	544-5825	262
Solarbos Inc 310 Stealth Ct — *Web:* www.solarbos.com	Livermore	CA	94551	925-456-7744		153
Solari Enterprises Inc 1572 N Main St — *Web:* solari-ent.com	Orange	CA	92867	714-282-2520		652
Solaria Corp 6200 Paseo Padre Pkwy — *Web:* www.solaria.com	Fremont	CA	94555	510-270-2500		620
Solaris Paper Inc 13415 Carmenita Rd — *TF:* 888-998-4778 ■ *Web:* www.solarispaper.com	Santa Fe Springs	CA	90670	888-998-4778		558
Solarity Credit Union 110 N Fifth Ave — *TF:* 800-347-9222 ■ *Web:* www.solaritycu.org	Yakima	WA	98902	509-248-1720		219
Solarus 440 E Grand Ave — *TF:* 800-421-9282 ■ *Web:* www.solarus.net	Wisconsin Rapids	WI	54494	715-421-8111	421-6081	736
SOLAS Press 4627 Shetland Way — *Web:* www.solaspress.com	Antioch	CA	94531	925-281-3095		637-2
Solatech Inc 1560 N Main St Ste 102 — *TF:* 877-994-8324 ■ *Web:* solatech.com	High Point	NC	27262	336-889-2455		525
Solatube International Inc 2210 Oak Ridge Way — *TF:* 888-765-2882 ■ *Web:* www.solatube.com	Vista	CA	92081	760-477-1120		696

Name / Address	City	State	ZIP	Phone	Fax	Class
Solazyme Inc 225 Gateway Blvd *NASDAQ: SZYM* ■ *Web:* solazymeindustrials.com	South San Francisco	CA	94080	650-780-4777		470
Solberg Manufacturing Inc (SMI) 1151 Ardmore Ave *Web:* www.solbergmfg.com	Itasca	IL	60143	630-773-1363	773-0727	18
Solco Plumbing Supply Inc 413 Liberty Ave *TF:* 800-273-6632 ■ *Web:* www.solco.com	Brooklyn	NY	11207	800-273-6632		612
Soldier Field 1410 S Museum Campus Dr *Web:* soldierfield.net	Chicago	IL	60605	312-235-7000	235-7030	720
Soldier of Fortune Magazine 2135 11th St *Web:* www.sofmag.com	Boulder	CO	80302	303-449-3750		457-12
Soldiers & Sailors Memorial Auditorium 501 W 12th St *Web:* www.chattanooga.gov	Chattanooga	TN	37402	423-643-6601		572
Soldiers & Sailors National Military Museum & Memorial 4141 Fifth Ave *Web:* soldiersandsailorshall.org	Pittsburgh	PA	15213	412-621-4253	683-9339	520
Soldream Inc 203 Hartford Tpke *Web:* www.soldream.com	Tolland	CT	06084	860-871-6883		697
Sole East LLC 90 Second House Rd *Web:* www.soleeast.com	Montauk	NY	11954	631-668-2105	668-0171	707
Sole Proprietor, The 118 Highland St *Web:* www.thesole.com	Worcester	MA	01609	508-798-3474	753-4889	671
Sole Solutions Inc 9 S Royal Ste A *Web:* ssinc.com	Front Royal	VA	22630	540-631-9166		177
Solebury School 6832 Phillips Mill Rd *TF:* 800-675-6900 ■ *Web:* www.solebury.org	New Hope	PA	18938	215-862-5261	862-3366	622
Solectek Corp 8375 Camino Santa Fe Ste A *Web:* www.solectek.com	San Diego	CA	92121	858-450-1220		176
Solem, Mack & Steinhoff PC 3333 S Bannock St Ste 900 *Web:* www.solemlaw.com	Englewood	CO	80110	303-761-4900		428
Soleno Inc 1160 Rt 133 CP 837 *Web:* soleno.com	Saint-Jean-sur-Richelieu	QC	J2X4J5	450-347-7855		492
Solenture Inc 2 Gateway Ctr Ste 1600 *Web:* www.solenture.com	Pittsburgh	PA	15222	412-281-5472		193
Soleo Communications Inc 209 High Point Dr Ste 300 *Web:* www.soleo.com	Victor	NY	14564	585-641-4300		224
Solera 5410 E Colfax Ave *Web:* solerarestaurant.com	Denver	CO	80220	303-388-8429		671
Soleratec LLC 2430 Auto Park Way Ste 205 *Web:* www.soleratec.com	Escondido	CA	92029	760-743-7200		177
Solex College 350 E Dundee Rd Ste 200 *Web:* www.solex.edu	Wheeling	IL	60090	847-229-9595	229-1919	685
Solexx Greenhouses 3740 Brooklake Rd NE *TF:* 800-825-1925 ■ *Web:* www.farmwholesale.com	Salem	OR	97303	503-393-3973	393-3119	276
Solheim Senior Community 2236 Merton Ave *Web:* www.solheimsenior.org	Los Angeles	CA	90041	323-257-7518		672
Soliant Consulting Inc 14 N Peoria St 2H *TF:* 800-582-0170 ■ *Web:* www.soliantconsulting.com	Chicago	IL	60607	312-850-3830		177
Solid Border 1806 Turnmill St *TF:* 800-213-8175 ■ *Web:* www.solidborder.com	San Antonio	TX	78248	800-213-8175	887-9974	180
Solid Concepts Inc 28309 Ave Crocker *TF:* 888-311-1017 ■ *Web:* www.stratasysdirect.com	Valencia	CA	91355	661-295-4400		454
Solid Gospel 1270 PO Box 307 *TF:* 800-522-0370 ■ *Web:* solidgospel1270.com	Elkhart	IN	46515	574-875-5166	875-6662	645
Solid Light Inc 800 S Fifth St *Web:* www.solidlight-inc.com	Louisville	KY	40203	502-562-0060	562-0055	344
Solid State Devices Inc 14701 Firestone Blvd *Web:* www.ssdi-power.com	La Mirada	CA	90638	562-404-4474		696
Solid State Scientific Corp 27-2 Wright Rd *Web:* www.solidstatescientific.com	Hollis	NH	03049	603-598-1194		178-4
Solid State Testing Inc 780 Boston Rd *Web:* www.solidstatetesting.com	Billerica	MA	01821	978-670-7300	670-7450	253
Solid Waste Association of North America (SWANA) 1100 Wayne Ave Ste 700 *TF:* 800-467-9262 ■ *Web:* www.swana.org	Silver Spring	MD	20910	301-585-2898	589-7068	531-5
Solidarity Community Federal Credit Union 201 E Southway Blvd *Web:* solfcu.org	Kokomo	IN	46902	765-453-4020		219
SolidBoss Worldwide Inc 200 Veterans Blvd *TF:* 888-258-7252 ■ *Web:* www.solidboss.com	South Haven	MI	49090	269-637-6356		754
Solidia Technologies Inc 11 Colonial Dr **Fax Area Code:* 732 ■ *Web:* solidiatech.com	Piscataway	NJ	08854	908-315-5901	981-0273*	724
Solidifi Inc 701 Seneca St Ste 660 **Fax Area Code:* 716 ■ *TF:* 866-781-0184 ■ *Web:* www.solidifi.com	Buffalo	NY	14210	866-781-0184	800-4591*	509
Solidiform Inc 3928 Lawnwood St *Web:* www.solidiform.com	Fort Worth	TX	76111	817-831-2626	831-8258	492
Solidscape Inc 316 Daniel Webster Hwy *Web:* www.solidscape.com	Merrimack	NH	03054	603-429-9700		494
Solidus Technical Solutions Inc 17 Forsythia Rd *Web:* www.solidus-ts.com	Leominster	MA	01453	978-534-8363		809
SolidWorks Corp 300 Baker Ave *TF:* 800-693-9000 ■ *Web:* www.solidworks.com	Concord	MA	01742	978-371-5011		178-10
Solien Technology 510 Arizona Ave Ste 200 *Web:* www.solien.com	Santa Monica	CA	90401	310-576-2727	984-6952	180
Soligenix Inc 29 Emmons Dr Ste B-10 *OTC: SNGX* ■ *Web:* www.soligenix.com	Princeton	NJ	08540	609-538-8200	452-6467	85
Solis Capital Partners LLC 23 Corporate Plaza Dr Ste 215 *Web:* www.soliscapital.com	Newport Beach	CA	92660	949-296-2440		360-3
Solisco Inc 120 10e Rue *TF:* 800-463-4188 ■ *Web:* solisco.com	Scott	QC	G0S3G0	418-387-8908		627
Solitron Devices Inc 3301 Electronics Way *OTC: SODI* ■ *Web:* www.solitrondevices.com	West Palm Beach	FL	33407	561-848-4311	863-5946	696
Solitude Mountain 12000 Big Cottonwood Canyon *TF:* 800-748-4754 ■ *Web:* solitudemountain.com	Solitude	UT	84121	801-534-1400	517-7705	669
Solix Inc 30 Lanidex Plz W PO Box 685 *TF:* 800-200-0818 ■ *Web:* www.solixinc.com	Parsippany	NJ	07054	973-581-6700		708
Solix Technologies Inc 4701 Patrick Henry Dr Bldg 20 *Web:* www.solix.com	Santa Clara	CA	95054	408-654-6400		177
Solmax International Inc 2801 Marie-Victorin Blvd *TF:* 800-571-3904 ■ *Web:* www.solmax.com	Varennes	QC	J3X1P7	450-929-1234		146
Solmet Technologies Inc 2716 Shepler Church Ave SW *Web:* www.solmet.net	Canton	OH	44706	330-455-4328	580-5199	483
Solmetric Corp 117 Morris St Ste 100 *Web:* www.solmetric.com	Sebastopol	CA	95472	707-823-4600		407
Solo Printing Inc 7860 NW 66th St *TF:* 800-325-0118 ■ *Web:* www.soloprinting.com	Miami	FL	33166	305-594-8699	599-5245	627
Soloflex Inc 1281 NE 25th Ave Ste I *TF:* 800-547-8802 ■ *Web:* soloflex.com	Hillsboro	OR	97124	800-547-8802		267
Soloflight Design 3340 Peachtree Rd NE Ste 1010 *Web:* soloflightdesign.com	Atlanta	GA	30326	770-925-1115		5
SOLOMO Technology Inc 222 W Washington Ave Ste 705 *Web:* www.solomotechnology.com	Madison	WI	53703	608-620-4285		387
Solomon Corp 103 W Main *TF:* 800-234-2867 ■ *Web:* www.solomoncorp.com	Solomon	KS	67480	785-655-2191		620
Solomon Group 825 Girod St *Web:* www.solomongroup.com	New Orleans	LA	70113	504-252-4500		226
Solomon Hardwick & Associates LLC 1160 Folly Rd *Web:* www.solomonhardwick.com	Charleston	SC	29412	843-406-6680		463
Solomon Publications PO Box 2124 *Web:* www.solomonpublications.com	Rockville	MD	20847	301-816-1025		96
Solon Manufacturing Co 425 Center St *TF:* 800-323-9717 ■ *Web:* www.solonmfg.com	Chardon	OH	44024	440-286-7149		492
Solon State Bank 126 S Market St *Web:* solonstatebank.com	Solon	IA	52333	319-624-3405	624-3407	70
Solstice Capital 81 Washington St Ste 303 *Web:* www.solcap.com	Salem	MA	01970	617-523-7733		792
Solta Medical Inc 25881 Industrial Blvd **Fax Area Code:* 510 ■ *TF:* 877-782-2286 ■ *Web:* www.solta.com	Hayward	CA	94545	877-782-2286	786-6895*	250
Solterra Renewable Technologies Inc 7700 S River Pky *Web:* www.solterrasolarcells.com	Tempe	AZ	85284	604-569-3184		696
Soltrix Technology Solutions Inc 16 Thomas Newton Dr *Web:* soltrixsolutions.com	Westborough	MA	01581	774-293-1293		809
Solusia Inc 3343 Peachtree Rd *Web:* www.solusia.com	Atlanta	GA	30326	404-601-1100		256
Solutek Corp 94 Shirley St *TF:* 800-403-0770 ■ *Web:* www.solutekcorporation.com	Boston	MA	02119	617-445-5335	445-9623	145
Solutia Consulting Inc 1241 Amundson Cir *Web:* www.solutiaconsulting.com	Stillwater	MN	55082	651-351-0123		180
Solution Beacon LLC 14419 Greenwood Ave N Ste 332 *Web:* www.solutionbeacon.com	Seattle	WA	98133	206-366-6606	299-3528	180
Solution Design Group Inc (SDG) 7500 Olson Memorial Hwy *Web:* solutiondesign.com	Golden Valley	MN	55427	952-278-2500		809
Solution Partners Inc 1770 N Park St Ste 100 *Web:* www.solpart.com	Naperville	IL	60563	630-416-1335		194
Solution Sources Programming Inc 1600 N Fourth St *Web:* ssprog.com	San Jose	CA	95112	408-487-0270		177
Solution Systems Inc 3201 Tollview Dr *Web:* www.solsyst.com	Rolling Meadows	IL	60008	847-590-3000		174
Solutioninc Technologies Ltd 5692 Bloomfield St *TF:* 888-496-2221 ■ *Web:* www.solutioninc.com	Halifax	NS	B3K1T2	902-420-0077		364
SolutionPoint International Inc 415 Madison Ave 11th Fl *Web:* www.guidepostsolutions.com	New York	NY	10017	212-817-6700		692
Solutions 21 152 Wabash St *TF:* 866-765-2121 ■ *Web:* solutions21.com	Pittsburgh	PA	15220	866-765-2121		463
Solutions AE Inc 236 Auburn Ave *TF:* 888-562-4441 ■ *Web:* solutionsae.com	Atlanta	GA	30303	888-562-4441		463
Solutions Development Corp 12220 Charles St *Web:* www.sdc-world.com	La Plata	MD	20646	301-638-3040		177
Solutions Financial Mortgage Co 1701 E Lake Ave Ste 280 *Web:* solutionsfn.com	Glenview	IL	60025	847-834-0100		217
Solutions for Associations Inc 140 N Bloomingdale Rd *Web:* www.sfainc.biz	Bloomingdale	IL	60108	630-351-8669		47
Solutions Inc 55 S Judd St PH-2 *TF:* 877-394-1213 ■ *Web:* www.drakebeil.com	Honolulu	HI	96817	808-483-0022		194
Solutions Management Inc 138 Montauk Hwy *TF:* 800-508-5884 ■ *Web:* smi247.com	East Moriches	NY	11940	800-508-5884		104
Solutions Plus 35583 Atlantic Ave *Web:* www.splus.net	Millville	DE	19967	302-539-6421		196

Company	Phone	Fax	Class
SolutionsIQ Inc 6801 185th Ave NE Ste 200 .... Redmond WA 98052 TF: 800-235-4091 ■ Web: www.solutionsiq.com	425-451-2727		180
SolutionStream 249 N 1200 E..................... Lehi UT 84043 TF: 800-314-3451 ■ Web: www.solutionstream.com	800-314-3451		396
Solvang Bakery 438 Alisal Rd.................. Solvang CA 93463 Web: www.solvangbakery.com	805-688-4939		68
Solvate com Inc 405 Greenwich St Ste 2A .... New York NY 10013 Web: www.solvate.com	646-720-7110	308-1128	260
Solvay Bank 1537 Milton Ave .... Solvay NY 13209 Web: www.solvaybank.com	315-468-1661	635-6838	70
Solvents & Chemicals Inc 2505 Collingsworth St .... Pearland TX 77581 TF: 800-622-3990 ■ Web: www.solvchem.com	281-485-5377		146
Solver Inc 10780 Santa Monica Blvd Ste 370 .... Los Angeles CA 90025 Web: solverglobal.com	310-691-5300		180
Solvera Solutions Inc 201 - 1853 Hamilton St .... Regina SK S4P2C1 Web: www.solvera.ca	306-757-3510		196
Solvere LLC 69 Mcadenville Rd .... Belmont NC 28012 Web: www.solvere.net	704-829-1015		180
SOM (Skidmore Owings & Merrill LLP) 224 S Michigan Ave Ste 1000 .... Chicago IL 60604 TF: 866-296-2688 ■ Web: www.som.com	312-554-9090	360-4545	261
SOM Publishing 163 Moon Valley Rd .... Windyville MO 65783 Web: www.som.org	417-345-8411		637-2
SOMA Medical Assessments 8800 Dufferin St Ste 105 .... Vaughan ON L4K0C5 TF: 877-664-7662 ■ Web: www.somamedical.com	905-881-8855	881-7887	41
Somach Simmons & Dunn 500 Capitol Mall Ste 1000 .... Sacramento CA 95814 Web: somachlaw.com	916-446-7979	446-8199	428
Somagen Diagnostics Inc 9220 25th Ave. .... Edmonton AB T6N1E1 TF: 800-661-9993 ■ Web: www.somagen.com	780-702-9500	438-6595	475
Somarakis Inc 552 Hendrickson Dr. .... Kalama WA 98625 TF: 800-255-7113 ■ Web: www.somarakis.com	360-574-6722	673-3978	385
Somat Engineering Inc 660 Woodward Ave Ste 2430 .... Detroit MI 48226 Web: www.somateng.com	313-963-2721	769-2761	261
Somatherapy Institute 70-225 Hwy 111 Ste B & C .... Rancho Mirage CA 92270 Web: www.somatherapy.com	760-321-9214		167-3
SOMC (Southern Ohio Medical Ctr) 1805 27th St. .... Portsmouth OH 45662 Web: www.somc.org	740-356-5000		374-3
Some's Uniforms Inc 314 Main St .... Hackensack NJ 07601 Web: www.somes.com	201-843-1199		157-4
Somers Agency LLC 5311 Leavitt Rd Ste 100 .... Lorain OH 44053 Web: somersagency.com	440-324-3447		390
Somers Cove Marina 715 Broadway .... Crisfield MD 21817 TF: 800-967-3474 ■ Web: www.somerscovemarina.com	410-968-0925		565
Somers Historical Society PO Box 336 Elephant Hotel.................... Somers NY 10589 Web: www.hrvh.org	914-277-4977		49-19
Somers Mansion State Historic Site 1000 Shore Rd .... Somers Point NJ 08244 Web: www.njparksandforests.org	609-927-2212		565
Somerset Capital Group Ltd 612 Wheelers Farms Rd .... Milford CT 06461 *Fax Area Code: 203 ■ TF: 877-282-9922 ■ Web: somersetcapital.com	877-282-9922	301-3253*	264-2
Somerset Community College 808 Monticello St. .... Somerset KY 42501 TF: 877-629-9722 ■ Web: somerset.kctcs.edu	606-679-8501	676-9065	162
Somerset Consulting Group Inc 3445 Executive Center Dr Ste 110 .... Austin TX 78731 Web: www.somersetcg.com	512-327-0090		196
Somerset County 11440 Ocean Hwy PO Box 243............ Princess Anne MD 21853 TF: 800-521-9189 ■ Web: www.visitsomerset.com	410-651-2968		338
Somerset County 3 Milburn St.............. Skowhegan ME 04976 Web: www.somersetcounty-me.org	207-474-9861	474-7405	338
Somerset County 300 N Center Ave .... Somerset PA 15501 Web: www.co.somerset.pa.us	814-445-1400		338
Somerset County 20 Grove St PO Box 3000.................. Somerville NJ 08876 TF: 800-246-0527 ■ Web: www.co.somerset.nj.us	908-231-7000	253-8853	338
Somerset County Business Partnership 360 Grove St. .... Bridgewater NJ 08807 Web: www.scbp.org	908-218-4300	722-7823	139
Somerset County Chamber of Commerce 601 N Center Ave .... Somerset PA 15501 Web: somersetcountychamber.com	814-445-6431	443-4313	139
Somerset County Library 1 Vogt Dr .... Bridgewater NJ 08807 Web: www.somerset.lib.nj.us	908-526-4016	526-5221	434-3
Somerset CPAs PC 3925 River Crossing Pkwy Ste 300........... Indianapolis IN 46240 Web: somersetcpas.com	317-472-2200		2
Somerset Door & Column Co 174 Sagamore St .... Somerset PA 15501 TF: 800-242-7916 ■ Web: doorandcolumn.com	814-444-9427	443-1658	499
Somerset Door and Column Co 1123 S Edgewood Ave .... Somerset PA 15501 Web: www.sdcbuildingcenter.com	814-445-9608		499
Somerset Hills Hotel 200 Liberty Corner Rd .... Warren NJ 07059 Web: www.thesomersethillshotel.com	908-647-6700	647-8053	379
Somerset Hospital 225 S Center Ave .... Somerset PA 15501 Web: www.somersethospital.com	814-443-5000		374-3
Somerset Inn 2601 W Big Beaver Rd................ Troy MI 48084 TF: 800-228-8769 ■ Web: www.somersetinn.com	248-643-7800	643-2296	379
Somerset Management Group LLC 1215 Livingston Ave Ste 306 .... North Brunswick NJ 08902 Web: www.somersetmgmt.com	732-228-8200		195
Somerset Patriots Baseball Club 1 Patriots Pk............................ Bridgewater NJ 08807 Web: somersetpatriots.com	908-252-0700		354
Somerset Rural Electric Co-op 223 Industrial Park Rd .... Somerset PA 15501 TF: 800-443-4255 ■ Web: www.somersetrec.com	814-445-4106		245
Somerset Telephone Company Inc 300 Spring St............................. Somerset WI 54025 Web: www.nwcomm.net	715-247-5545		224
Somerset Trust Co 151 W Main St PO Box 777 .... Somerset PA 15501 TF: 800-972-1651 ■ Web: www.somersettrust.com	814-443-9200		70
Somerset Valley Ymca 2 Green St. .... Somerville NJ 08876 Web: www.somersetcountyymca.org	908-722-4567		354
Somerset Welding & Steel Inc 10558 Somerset Pk .... Somerset PA 15501 TF: 800-777-2671 ■ Web: www.jjbodies.com	814-444-3400	443-2621	516
Somerset-Pulaski County Chamber of Commerce 445 S Hwy 27 Ste 101 .... Somerset KY 42501 Web: somersetpulaskichamber.com	606-679-7323	679-1744	139
Somerville Chamber of Commerce 2 Alpine St PO Box 44034 .... Somerville MA 02144 Web: somervillechamber.org	617-776-4100		139
Somerville Public Library (SPL) 79 Highland Ave.......................... Somerville MA 02143 Web: www.somervillepubliclibrary.org	617-623-5000		434-3
Somethingcoolcom LLC 121a E High St .... Potosi MO 63664 Web: somethingcool.com	573-436-2665		180
Somewhere Dine Bar 110 Murray St .... Ottawa ON K1N5M6 Web: www.somewheredinebar.com	613-562-7244		671
Somic America Inc 6 Baker Blvd .... Brewer ME 04412 Web: www.somicamerica.com	207-989-1759		60
Somma Tool Company Inc 109 Scott Rd....... Waterbury CT 06705 Web: www.sommatool.com	203-753-2114	756-5489	493
Sommer Electric Corp 818 Third St NE........... Canton OH 44704 TF: 800-766-6373 ■ Web: www.sommerelectric.com	800-766-6373		246
Sommer's Automotive 7211 W Meq .... Mequon WI 53092 Web: www.sommerscars.com	262-242-0100		57
Sommermaid Creamery Inc PO Box 350 ..... Doylestown PA 18901 Web: www.sommermaid.com	215-345-6160	345-4945	296-3
Somnus Therapeutics Inc 135 US Hwy 202/206 Ste 9 .... Bedminster NJ 07921	908-901-0300		668
SONA (Symphony of Northwest Arkansas) 217 E Dickson St Ste 106 PO Box 1243........ Fayetteville AR 72701 Web: www.sonamusic.org	479-521-4166		573-3
Sonalysts Inc 215 Waterford Pkwy N............ Waterford CT 06385 TF: 800-526-8091 ■ Web: www.sonalysts.com	860-442-4355	447-8883	261
Sonar Entertainment 2121 Avenue of the Stars Ste 2150........... Los Angeles CA 90067 Web: sonarent.com	424-230-7140		514
SonarMed Inc 12220 N Meridian St Ste 150................... Carmel IN 46032 TF: 866-853-3684 ■ Web: www.sonarmed.com	317-489-3161		250
Sonas Consulting 17905 Apricot Way...................... Castro Valley CA 94546 Web: www.sonasconsulting.com	650-619-4853		196
Sonata Capital Group Inc 2001 Sixth Ave Ste 3410 .... Seattle WA 98121 Web: sonatacap.com	206-256-4400		401
Sonatech Inc 879 Ward Dr .... Santa Barbara CA 93111 Web: www.sonatech.com	805-683-1431	690-5388	529
Sonatype Inc 12501 Prosperity Dr Ste 350 .... Silver Spring MD 20904 Web: www.sonatype.com	301-684-8080		177
Sonavation Inc 3970 RCA Blvd Ste 7003 .... Palm Beach Gardens FL 33410 Web: www.sonavation.com	561-209-1201		693
Sonepar USA 510 Walnut St Ste 400 .... Philadelphia PA 19106 Web: sonepar-us.com	215-399-5900		246
Sonesta International Hotels Corp 255 Washington St.......................... Newton MA 02458 TF: 800-766-3782 ■ Web: www.sonesta.com	800-766-3782		379
Sonetics Corp 7340 SW Durham Rd............. Portland OR 97224 TF: 800-833-4558 ■ Web: www.firecom.com	800-833-4558		647
Sonetronics Inc PO Box L................. West Belmar NJ 07719 Web: www.sonetronics.com	732-681-5016	681-5216	735
Song of the Morning Yoga Retreat Ctr 9607 Sturgeon Valley Rd .... Vanderbilt MI 49795 Web: www.songofthemorning.org	989-983-4107		673
Songkran Inc 2309 S Ridgewood Ave.................. South Daytona FL 32119	386-760-0300		671
Songwriters Guild of America 210 Jamestown Park Rd Ste 100 .... Brentwood TN 37027 TF: 800-524-6742 ■ Web: www.songwritersguild.com	615-742-9945		48-4
Soniat House 1133 Chartres St .... New Orleans LA 70116 TF: 800-544-8808 ■ Web: www.soniathouse.com	504-522-0570		379
Sonic Air Systems Inc 1050 Beacon St .... Brea CA 92821 TF: 800-827-6642 ■ Web: www.sonicairsystems.com	714-255-0124	255-8366	18
Sonic Automotive Inc 4401 Colwick Rd .... Charlotte NC 28211 NYSE: SAH ■ Web: www.sonicautomotive.com	704-566-2400		57
Sonic Corp 300 Johnny Bench Dr. .... Oklahoma City OK 73104 NASDAQ: SONC ■ TF: 877-828-7868 ■ Web: www.sonicdrivein.com	405-225-5000		670
Sonic Corp 1 Research Dr...................... Stratford CT 06615 Web: www.sonicmixing.com	203-375-0063	378-4079	298
Sonic Healthcare USA Inc 12357-A Riata Trace Pkwy Ste 210.............. Austin TX 78727 Web: www.sonichealthcareusa.com	512-439-1600		415
Sonic Innovations Inc 2501 Cottontail Ln .... Somerset NJ 08873 TF: 888-678-4327 ■ Web: www.sonici.us	888-423-7834		477
Sonic Manufacturing Corp 950 Lee St .... Elk Grove Village IL 60007 Web: www.sonicmfgcorp.com	847-228-0015	593-6763	454
Sonic power boats 309 Angle Rd............ Fort Pierce FL 34947 Web: www.sonicpowerboats.com	772-429-8888		90
Sonicor Inc 82 Otis St .... West Babylon NY 11704 TF: 800-864-5022 ■ Web: www.sonicor.com	631-920-6555	920-6080	782

Name / Address	City	State	ZIP	Phone	Fax	Class
Sonics & Materials Inc 53 Church Hill Rd *OTC: SIMA* ■ *TF:* 800-745-1105 ■ *Web:* www.sonics.com	Newtown	CT	06470	203-270-4600	270-4610	782
SonicWALL Inc 2001 Logic Dr *TF:* 888-557-6642 ■ *Web:* www.sonicwall.com	San Jose	CA	95124	408-745-9600	745-9300	176
Sonit Systems LLC 130 W Field Dr *Web:* sonit.com	Archbold	OH	43502	419-446-2151		180
Sonivate Medical Inc 4640 SW Macadam Ave Ste 200 *Web:* sonivate.com	Portland	OR	97239	503-616-4357	378-4381	743
Soniya Technology International inc 3130 De La Cruz Blvd Ste 101 *Web:* www.soniyatechnology.com	Santa Clara	CA	95054	408-493-0310	567-9827	177
Sonjara Inc 207 Park Ave *Web:* www.sonjara.com	Falls Church	VA	22046	571-297-6383	297-6384	344
Sonnabend & Shu CPAs Inc 5832 Melvin Ave	Tarzana	CA	91356	818-776-0060		2
Sonnenalp Resort of Vail 20 Vail Rd *TF:* 800-654-8312 ■ *Web:* sonnenalp.com	Vail	CO	81657	970-476-5656	476-1639	669
Sonnenberg Gardens 151 Charlotte St *Web:* www.sonnenberg.org	Canandaigua	NY	14424	585-394-4922	394-2192	97
Sonnet Software Inc 100 Elwood Davis Rd *Web:* sonnetsoftware.com	Syracuse	NY	13212	315-453-3096		177
Sonnhalter 1320 Sumner Ave Ste 200 *Web:* www.sonnhalter.com	Cleveland	OH	44115	216-242-0420		7
Sonny Bryan's Smoke House 12720 Hillcrest Rd Ste 910 *Web:* www.sonnybryans.com	Dallas	TX	75230	214-350-1800	350-3738	671
Sonny Williams' Steak Room 500 President Clinton Ave *Web:* www.sonnywilliamssteakroom.com	Little Rock	AR	72201	501-324-2999		671
Sonny's Franchise Co 2605 Maitland Center Pkwy Ste C *Web:* www.sonnysbbq.com	Maitland	FL	32751	407-660-8888		310
Sonobana Japanese Restaurant & Grocery 40 White Bridge Rd *Web:* www.sonobananashville.com	Nashville	TN	37205	615-356-6600		671
Sonobi 444 W New England Ave Ste 215 *Web:* www.sonobi.com	Winter Park	FL	32789	386-320-5400		5
Sonobond Ultrasonics Inc 1191 McDermott Dr *TF:* 800-323-1269 ■ *Web:* www.sonobondultrasonics.com	West Chester	PA	19380	610-696-4710	692-0674	811
Sonoco 1 N Second St *NYSE: SON* ■ *TF:* 800-377-2692 ■ *Web:* www.sonoco.com	Hartsville	SC	29550	800-377-2692		601
Sonoma County 2615 Paulin Dr *Web:* www.sonomacounty.ca.gov	Santa Rosa	CA	95403	707-565-2431	565-3778	338
Sonoma County Fairgrounds 1350 Bennett Valley Rd *Web:* www.sonomacountyfair.com	Santa Rosa	CA	95404	707-545-4200	573-9342	642
Sonoma County Library Third & E Sts *Web:* sonomalibrary.org	Santa Rosa	CA	95404	707-545-0831		434-3
Sonoma County Transit 355 W Robles Ave *TF:* 800-345-7433 ■ *Web:* sctransit.com	Santa Rosa	CA	95407	707-576-7433		468
Sonoma Developmental Ctr 15000 Arnold Dr *TF:* 800-862-0007 ■ *Web:* www.dds.ca.gov	Eldridge	CA	95431	707-938-6000	938-3605	230
Sonoma Electrical Engineering Inc 1125 Shady Oak Pl *Web:* sonomaee.com	Santa Rosa	CA	95404	707-483-8829		261
Sonoma Graphic Products Inc 961 Stockton Ave *TF:* 800-250-4252 ■ *Web:* www.sgpweb.com	San Jose	CA	95110	408-294-2072		601
Sonoma Home Health Care Inc 6225 Dean Martin Dr *Web:* sonomahomehealth.com	Las Vegas	NV	89118	702-222-0733	222-0766	363
Sonoma Index-Tribune Inc 117 W Napa St *Web:* www.sonomanews.com	Sonoma	CA	95476	707-938-2111	938-1600	637-8
Sonoma Outfitters 2412 Magowan Dr *TF:* 800-290-1920 ■ *Web:* www.sonomaoutfitters.com	Santa Rosa	CA	95405	800-290-1920		711
Sonoma Overhead Doors 21600 8th St E *TF:* 800-696-4132 ■ *Web:* www.sonomaoverheaddoors.com	Sonoma	CA	95476	707-996-4132		364
Sonoma Raceway 29355 Arnold Dr Hwy 37 & 121 *TF:* 800-870-7223 ■ *Web:* www.sonomaraceway.com	Sonoma	CA	95476	707-938-8448	938-8430	515
Sonoma Scientific Inc 2236A Park Pl *Web:* www.sonomascientific.com	Minden	NV	89423	775-783-9100	783-9098	253
Sonoma State Historic Park 5729 20 E Spain St *Web:* www.parks.ca.gov	Sonoma	CA	95476	707-935-6832		565
Sonoma State University 1801 E Cotati Ave *Web:* www.sonoma.edu	Rohnert Park	CA	94928	707-664-2880	664-2060	166
Sonoma Technical Support Services 505-8840 210th St Ste 342 *TF:* 866-898-3123 ■ *Web:* www.sonomaservices.com	Langley	BC	V1M2Y2	866-898-3123		196
Sonoma Valley Chamber of Commerce 651A Broadway *Web:* www.sonomachamber.org	Sonoma	CA	95476	707-996-1033	996-9402	139
Sonoma Valley Film Festival 103 E Napa St Ste A *Web:* www.sonomafilmfest.org	Sonoma	CA	95476	707-933-2600	933-2602	282
Sonoma West Holdings Inc 2064 Hwy 116 N *Web:* sonomawestholdings.com	Sebastopol	CA	95472	707-824-2534	829-4630	655
Sonoma West Publishers Inc PO Box 518 *Web:* www.sonomawest.com	Healdsburg	CA	95448	707-823-7845		532-2
Sonoma Wire Works 101 First St Ste 587 *Web:* www.sonomawireworks.com	Los Altos	CA	94022	650-948-2003		177
Sonometrics Corp 500 Nottinghill Rd *Web:* www.sonometrics.com	London	ON	N6K3P1	519-474-6464	474-6426	261
SonoPlot Inc 3030 Laura Ln Ste 120 *Web:* www.sonoplot.com	Middleton	WI	53562	608-824-9311		419
Sonora Behavioral Health Hospital 6050 N Corona Rd *TF:* 800-469-8700 ■ *Web:* www.sonorabehavioral.com	Tucson	AZ	85704	520-349-0083		374-5
Sonoran Science Academy 5741 E Ironwood St *Web:* www.sonoranschools.org	Tucson	AZ	85708	520-300-5699	207-7698	685
Sonos 614 Chapala St *TF:* 800-680-2345 ■ *Web:* sonos.com	Santa Barbara	CA	93101	805-965-3001		180
Sonoscan Inc 2149 Pratt Blvd *Web:* sonoscan.com	Elk Grove Village	IL	60007	847-437-6400	437-1550	743
SonoSite Inc 21919 30th Dr SE *NASDAQ: SONO* ■ *TF:* 888-482-9449 ■ *Web:* www.sonosite.com	Bothell	WA	98021	425-951-1200	951-1201	382
Sonoted LLC 3610 Commerce Dr Ste 809 *Web:* www.sonoted.com	Baltimore	MD	21227	410-744-3950		396
Sonotronics Inc 3169 S Chrysler Ave *Web:* www.sonotronics.com	Tucson	AZ	85713	520-746-3322	294-2040	472
Sons of Norway 1455 W Lake St *TF:* 800-945-8851 ■ *Web:* www.sofn.com	Minneapolis	MN	55408	612-827-3611	827-0658	48-14
Sons Tool Inc 460 Thompson Rd *Web:* www.sonstool.com	Woodville	WI	54028	715-698-2471	698-2335	488
Sonsie 327 Newbury St *Web:* sonsieboston.com	Boston	MA	02115	617-351-2500		671
Sonsray Machinery LLC 1475 Pioneer Way *Web:* www.sonsraymachinery.com	El Cajon	CA	92020	619-873-0123		23
Sonstegard Foods Co 5005 S Bur Oak Pl *TF:* 800-533-3184 ■ *Web:* www.sonstegard.com	Sioux Falls	SD	57108	800-533-3184		619
Sony Computer Entertainment America Inc 919 E Hillsdale Blvd *Web:* www.playstation.com	Foster City	CA	94404	650-655-8000		762
Sony Corporation of America 25 Madison Ave *Web:* www.sony.com	New York	NY	10010	212-833-8800		525
Sony Creative Software 8215 Greenway Blvd Ste 400 *TF:* 800-577-6642 ■ *Web:* www.sonycreativesoftware.com	Middleton	WI	53562	608-203-7620	250-1745	178-9
Sony DADC US INC 1800 N Fruitridge Ave *Web:* sonydadc.com	Terre Haute	IN	47804	812-462-8100		658
Sony Music Entertainment 550 Madison Ave *Web:* www.sonymusic.com	New York	NY	10022	212-833-8000		657
Sony Music Nashville 1201 Demonbreun St Ste 1300 *Web:* www.sonymusicnashville.com	Nashville	TN	37212	615-301-4300		657
Sony Pictures Animation 9050 W Washington Blvd *Web:* www.sonypicturesanimation.com	Culver City	CA	90232	310-840-8000		33
Sony Pictures Entertainment Inc 10202 W Washington Blvd *Web:* www.sonypictures.com	Culver City	CA	90232	310-244-4000	244-1411	514
Sony/ATV Music Publishing LLC 25 Madison Ave 24th Fl *Web:* www.sonyatv.com	New York	NY	10010	212-833-7730		637-7
Sooner Pipe LLC 1331 Lamar St Ste 970 *TF:* 800-888-9161 ■ *Web:* www.soonerpipe.com	Houston	TX	77010	713-759-1200	759-0442	385
Sooner Scale Inc 2428 SW 14th St *Web:* www.soonerscale.com	Oklahoma City	OK	73108	405-236-3566		684
SOPAKCO Inc 118 S Cypress St *Web:* sopakco.com	Mullins	SC	29574	843-464-7851		803-1
Sopark Corp 3300 S Park Ave *TF:* 866-576-7275 ■ *Web:* sopark.com	Buffalo	NY	14218	716-822-0434	822-5062	625
Sopheon Corp 3001 Metro Dr *Web:* www.sopheon.com	Bloomington	MN	55425	952-851-7500	851-7599	387
Sophia Spirituality Ctr 751 S Eigth St *Web:* www.mountosb.org	Atchison	KS	66002	913-360-6173		673
Sophienburg Museum and Archives 401 W Coll St *Web:* sophienburg.com	New Braunfels	TX	78130	830-629-1572	629-3906	637-2
SophLogic Global LLC 8374 Market St Ste 133 *Web:* sophlogic.com	Bradenton	FL	34202	941-932-8570		260
Sophos Inc 3 Van de Graaff Dr 2nd Fl **Fax Area Code: 781* ■ *TF:* 866-866-2802 ■ *Web:* www.sophos.com	Burlington	MA	01803	866-866-2802	494-5801*	178-1
Sophos Software Ltd 3449 N Druid Hills Rd Ste H *TF:* 888-767-4671 ■ *Web:* www.sophosoft.com	Decatur	GA	30033	404-325-9494		178-1
Soquelec Ltd 5524 Rue St Patrick Ste 405 *Web:* www.soquelec.com	Montreal	QC	H4E1A8	514-482-6427	482-1929	419
SOR Inc 14685 W 105th St *TF:* 800-676-6794 ■ *Web:* www.sorinc.com	Lenexa	KS	66215	913-888-2630	888-0767	201
Sorabol Korean Restaurant 805 Keeaumoku St *Web:* www.sorabolhawaii.com	Honolulu	HI	96814	808-947-3113		671
Sorbee International Ltd 9990 Global Rd *Web:* www.sorbee.com	Philadelphia	PA	19115	215-677-5200	677-7736	296-8
Sorbothane Inc 2144 SR-59 *TF:* 800-838-3906 ■ *Web:* www.sorbothane.com	Kent	OH	44240	330-678-9444		326
Sordoni Construction Co 1 Pluckemin Way 2nd Fl *Web:* sordoniconstruction.com	Bedminster	NJ	07921	908-879-1130	879-1147	186
Sordoni Construction Services Inc 45 Owen St *Web:* www.sordoni.com	Forty Fort	PA	18704	570-287-3161		186
Sorensen Craig F Construction Inc 918 S 2000 W *Web:* gosci.com	Syracuse	UT	84075	801-773-4390		540
Sorensen Vance & Company PC 3115 E Lion Ln Ste 220 *Web:* www.sorensenvance.com	Salt Lake City	UT	84121	801-733-5055	733-6783	2
Sorenson Bioscience 6507 S 400 W *Web:* www.sorbio.com	Murray	UT	84107	801-266-9334		596

	City	State	ZIP	Phone	Fax	Class
Sorenson Communications Inc 4192 Riverboat Rd Ste 100 *Web:* www.sorenson.com	Salt Lake City	UT	84123	801-287-9400	287-9401	253
Sorenson Engineering Inc 32032 Dunlap Blvd *Web:* www.sorensoneng.com	Yucaipa	CA	92399	909-795-2434	795-7190	621
Sorenson Media Inc 25 E Scenic Pointe Dr Ste 100 *TF:* 888-767-3676 ■ *Web:* www.sorensonmedia.com	Draper	UT	84020	801-501-8650		544
Soreo In Home Support Services LLC 2475 E Water St *Web:* soreo.com	Tucson	AZ	85719	520-881-4477		363
Sorgente Asset Management Inc 66 White St 5th Fl *Web:* sorgentegroupofamerica.com	New York	NY	10013	212-542-4290	542-4291	653
Sorin Books PO Box 428 *TF:* 800-282-1865 ■ *Web:* www.avemariapress.com	Notre Dame	IN	46556	800-282-1865	282-5681	637-2
Sorin Group USA Inc 14401 W 65th Way **Fax Area Code:* 303 ■ *TF:* 800-289-5759 ■ *Web:* www.livanova.sorin.com	Arvada	CO	80004	800-221-7943	467-6584*	476
Sorling Northrup 1 N Old State Capitol Plz Ste 200 PO Box 5131 *Web:* www.sorlinglaw.com	Springfield	IL	62705	217-544-1144	522-3173	428
Sorman & Frankel Ltd 180 N La Salle St Ste 2700 *Web:* sormanfrankel.com	Chicago	IL	60601	312-332-3535	332-3545	41
Sorna Corp 2020 Silver Bell Rd Ste 17 *TF:* 866-767-6226 ■ *Web:* sorna.com	Eagan	MN	55122	651-406-9900	406-9904	476
Soroc Products Inc *Plastics Div* 4349 S Dort Hwy *Web:* www.sorocproducts.com	Burton	MI	48529	810-743-2660	743-5922	602
Soroc Technology Inc 607 Chrislea Rd *Web:* www.soroc.com	Woodbridge	ON	L4L8A3	905-265-8000		174
Soroptimist International of the Americas 1709 Spruce St *Web:* www.soroptimist.org	Philadelphia	PA	19103	215-893-9000	893-5200	48-5
Sorrento Hotel 900 Madison St *TF:* 800-426-1265 ■ *Web:* www.hotelsorrento.com	Seattle	WA	98104	206-622-6400		671
Sorteo Games 6725 Mesa Ridge Rd Ste 102	San Diego	CA	92121	858-554-0297		225
Sortimat Technology 5655 Meadowbrook Industrial Ct *TF:* 800-385-6805 ■ *Web:* www.sortimat.com	Rolling Meadows	IL	60008	847-925-1234	640-2851	393
Sort-Rite International Inc 825 W Jefferson Ave *Web:* www.sort-rite.com	Harlingen	TX	78550	956-423-2427	423-2543	298
SOS (Store Opening Solutions) 800 Middle Tennessee Blvd *TF:* 877-388-9262 ■ *Web:* www.store-solutions.com	Murfreesboro	TN	37129	877-388-9262		449
SOS (Secular Organizations for Sobriety) 4773 Hollywood Blvd *Web:* www.cfiwest.org	Hollywood	CA	90027	323-666-4295		48-21
SOS Alarm 3273 Biddle Rd *Web:* www.sosasap.com	Medford	OR	97504	541-773-3900	776-2819	692
SOS Children's Villages-USA 1620 I St NW Ste 900 *TF:* 888-767-4543 ■ *Web:* www.sos-usa.org	Washington	DC	20006	202-347-7920		48-6
SOS Global Express Inc 2803 Trent Rd *TF:* 800-628-6363 ■ *Web:* sosglobal.com	New Bern	NC	28562	252-635-1400		311
SOSA (Society of Saint Andrew) 3383 Sweet Hollow Rd *TF:* 800-333-4597 ■ *Web:* endhunger.org	Big Island	VA	24526	434-299-5956	299-5949	48-5
Soshin Electronics of America Inc 2520 Micaion College Bl104 Ste 104 *Web:* soshin-ele.com	Santa Clara	CA	95054	408-748-6928	748-6936	246
SOT (Society of Toxicology) 1821 Michael Faraday Dr Ste 300 *Web:* www.toxicology.org	Reston	VA	20190	703-438-3115	438-3113	49-8
Sotax Corp 2400 Computer Dr *Web:* www.sotax.com	Westborough	MA	01581	508-417-1112		407
Sotech Nitram Inc 1695 Boulevard Laval *TF:* 877-664-8726 ■ *Web:* www.sotechnitram.com	Laval	QC	H7S2M2	450-975-2100		311
Sotek Inc 3590 Jeffrey Blvd *Web:* www.sotek.com	Buffalo	NY	14219	716-821-5961	821-5965	454
Sotheby's Inc 1334 York Ave *Web:* www.sothebys.com	New York	NY	10021	212-606-7000		51
Sotheby's International Realty 38 E 61st St *TF:* 866-899-4747 ■ *Web:* www.sothebysrealty.com	New York	NY	10065	212-606-7660		652
Sothys USA Inc 1500 NW 94th Ave *TF:* 800-325-0503 ■ *Web:* www.sothys-usa.com	Miami	FL	33172	305-594-4222	592-5785	238
Soto Darren (Rep D - FL) 1507 Longworth House Office Bldg *Web:* soto.house.gov	Washington	DC	20515	202-225-9889	225-9742	342-2
Sotto Sopra 405 N Charles St *Web:* www.sottosoprainc.com	Baltimore	MD	21201	410-625-0534		671
Sotto Sotto Cucina Italiana 313 N Highland Ave *Web:* www.sottosottoatl.com	Atlanta	GA	30307	404-523-6678		671
Soucy Holding Inc 5450 Saint-Roch St *TF:* 844-474-4740 ■ *Web:* www.soucy-group.com	Drummondville	QC	J2B6W3	819-474-9008		60
Soudan Underground Mine State Park 1302 McKinley Park Rd *Web:* www.dnr.state.mn.us	Soudan	MN	55782	218-300-7000	753-2246	565
Souders Financial Group Inc 5968 Bridgetown Rd *Web:* soudersfinancial.com	Cincinnati	OH	45248	513-598-2400		690
Souderton Area School District 760 Lower Rd *Web:* www.soudertonsd.org	Souderton	PA	18964	215-723-6061	723-8897	685
Souhegan Valley Chamber of Commerce 69 New Hampshire 101A *Web:* www.souhegan.net	Amherst	NH	03031	603-673-4360		139
Soukup Bush & Associates CPAs PC 2032 Caribou Dr Ste 200 *Web:* soukupbush.com	Fort Collins	CO	80525	970-223-2727		2
Soule Software Inc 25350 Magic Mountain Pky Ste 300 *Web:* www.soulesoftware.com	Valencia	CA	91355	818-303-1364		177
Soulman's Barbeque 3410 Broadway Blvd *Web:* soulmans.com	Garland	TX	75043	972-271-6885		671
SoulSource PO Box 877 *Web:* soul-source.org	Fairfax	CA	94978	415-459-1442		637-2
Sound & Cellular Inc 824 W Yellowstone Hwy *TF:* 800-689-7256 ■ *Web:* www.soundandcellular.com	Casper	WY	82601	800-689-7256		539
Sound Around USA 1600 63rd St *Web:* www.soundaroundusa.com	Brooklyn	NY	11204	718-535-1800		246
Sound Brokerage International LLC 3600 Port of Tacoma Rd Ste 301 *Web:* www.soundbrokerage.com	Tacoma	WA	98424	253-922-7718	922-7216	311
Sound Com Corp 227 Depot St *TF:* 800-628-8739 ■ *Web:* www.soundcom.net	Berea	OH	44017	440-234-2604	234-2614	52
Sound Delivery Service 13505 Pioneer Way E *TF:* 800-562-7014 ■ *Web:* www.sounddeliveryservice.com	Puyallup	WA	98372	253-200-2208	200-2235	311
Sound Financial Management Inc 15224 Main St Ste 200 *Web:* www.soundfinancialplanning.net	Mill Creek	WA	98012	425-745-4997		690
Sound Glass Sales Inc 5501 75th St W *TF:* 800-468-9949 ■ *Web:* soundglass.com	Tacoma	WA	98499	253-473-7477		189-6
Sound Hospitality Management LLC 3850 Bird Rd Ste 302 *Web:* www.soundhospitality.com	Miami	FL	33146	305-448-2898	448-2958	463
Sound Image 2425 Auto Park Way *Web:* www.sound-image.com	Escondido	CA	92029	760-737-3900		23
Sound Imaging Inc 7580 Trade St *TF:* 866-530-7850 ■ *Web:* soundimaging.com	San Diego	CA	92121	866-530-7850		476
Sound Inc 1550 Shore Rd *Web:* www.soundinc.com	Naperville	IL	60563	630-369-2900		246
Sound Marketing Concepts (SMC) 6 Cooper Pond Rd *Web:* www.soundmarketingconcepts.com	Rowley	MA	01969	978-948-7688		7
Sound Propeller Services Inc 7916 Eighth Ave S *Web:* www.soundprop.com	Seattle	WA	98108	206-788-4202		454
Sound Publishing Inc 11323 Commando Rd W Unit Main *Web:* www.soundpublishing.com	Everett	WA	98204	360-394-5800	394-5829	637-8
Sound Shore Fund 3 Canal Plz *TF:* 800-754-8758 ■ *Web:* www.soundshorefund.com	Portland	ME	04101	800-754-8758		528
Sound Shore Management Inc 8 Sound Shore Dr Ste 180 *TF:* 800-551-1980 ■ *Web:* www.soundshore.com	Greenwich	CT	06830	203-629-1980		401
Sound Sleep Products 14901 Puyallup St E *Web:* soundsleep.com	Sumner	WA	98390	253-891-1293		321
Sound Specialists Inc 1661 N Elston Ave *Web:* soundspecialists.com	Chicago	IL	60642	773-278-1650		794
Soundair Inc 1826 Bickford Ave *Web:* www.soundair.com	Snohomish	WA	98290	360-453-2300		22
Soundcoat Co 1 Burt Dr *TF:* 800-394-8913 ■ *Web:* www.soundcoat.com	Deer Park	NY	11729	631-242-2200	242-2246	389
Soundearth 2811 Fairview Ave E *Web:* www.soundearthinc.com	Seattle	WA	98102	206-306-1900		196
SoundTraxx 210 Rock Point Dr *TF:* 888-789-7637 ■ *Web:* www.soundtraxx.com	Durango	CO	81301	970-259-0690	259-0691	38
Soundview Executive Book Summaries 511 School House Rd Ste 300 **Fax Area Code:* 800 ■ *TF:* 800-786-6279 ■ *Web:* www.summary.com	Kennett Square	PA	19348	484-730-1270	453-5062*	196
Soundview Preparatory School 370 Underhill Ave *Web:* www.soundviewprep.org	Yorktown Heights	NY	10598	914-962-2780		685
Soundwich Inc 881 Wayside Rd *Web:* soundwich.com	Cleveland	OH	44110	216-486-2666		247
Souplantation 15822 Bernardo Center Dr Ste A *Web:* souplantation.com	San Diego	CA	92127	858-675-1600		670
Source Audio LLC 120 Cummings Pk *Web:* www.sourceaudio.net	Woburn	MA	01801	781-932-8080		527
Source Brokerage Inc 9535 E 59th St Ste C *TF:* 800-925-3898 ■ *Web:* sourcebrokeragedi.com	Indianapolis	IN	46216	317-803-3330	803-3370	690
Source Communications Inc 433 Hackensack Ave *Web:* www.sourcead.com	Hackensack	NJ	07601	201-343-5222		4
Source Data Products Inc 18350 Mt Langley St *TF:* 800-333-2669 ■ *Web:* www.source-data.com	Fountain Valley	CA	92708	714-593-0387		196
Source Dynamics Inc 22525 SE 64th Pl Ste 260 *TF:* 800-552-2231 ■ *Web:* www.sourcedyn.com	Issaquah	WA	98027	425-557-3630	557-3631	178-1
Source Fluid Power Inc 331 Lake Hazeltine Dr *Web:* www.sourcefp.com	Chaska	MN	55318	952-368-3866	448-3392	790
Source Group Inc, The 3478 Buskirk Ave Ste 100 *Web:* www.thesourcegroup.net	Pleasant Hill	CA	94523	925-944-2856		193
Source Intelligence LLC 1921 Palomar Oaks Way Ste 205 *TF:* 877-916-6337 ■ *Web:* www.sourceintelligence.com	Carlsbad	CA	92008	877-916-6337		192
Source Marketing LLC 761 Main Ave *Web:* www.sourcecxm.com	Norwalk	CT	06859	203-291-4000		7
Source Media Inc 1 State St Plz 27th Fl *TF:* 800-221-1809 ■ *Web:* www.sourcemedia.com	New York	NY	10004	212-803-8200		637-9
Source Medical 100 Grandview Pl Ste 400 *TF:* 866-687-2300 ■ *Web:* www.sourcemed.net	Birmingham	AL	35243	866-687-2300		178-1
Source North America Corp 510 S Westgate *TF:* 800-621-5524 ■ *Web:* www.sourcena.com	Addison	IL	60101	847-364-1744		580

Name / Address	City	State	ZIP	Phone	Fax	Class
Source One Communications Inc 1832 Soscol Ave No 112 *Web:* www.sourceonecom.com	Napa	CA	94559	707-258-2942		224
Source One Distribution Services 1220 Morse Ave *Web:* www.sourceone-dist.com	Royal Oak	MI	48067	248-399-5060		5
Source One Personnel Inc 2 Carnegie Rd *Web:* www.source1-financial.com	Lawrenceville	NJ	08648	609-895-9700		260
Source One Solutions 2135 Spy Run Ave *Web:* s1sonline.com	Fort Wayne	IN	46805	260-482-2399	484-9842	180
Source One Spares Inc 12141 Wickchester Ln Ste 600 *Web:* www.sourceonespares.com	Houston	TX	77079	832-364-6800	384-9438	770
Source One Technical Solutions LLC 1952 Rt 22 E *Web:* source1tek.com	Bound Brook	NJ	08805	732-748-8643		196
Source Photonics Inc 8521 Fallbrook Ave Ste 200 *Web:* www.sourcephotonics.com	West Hills	CA	91304	818-773-9044	773-0261	177
Source Production & Equipment Company Inc 113 Teal St *Web:* www.spec150.com	Saint Rose	LA	70087	504-464-9471		407
Source Technologies 4205B Westinghouse Commons Dr *TF:* 800-922-8501 ■ *Web:* www.sourcetech.com	Charlotte	NC	28273	704-969-7500	969-7595	178-1
Source2 1245 W Fairbanks Ave *TF:* 800-557-6704 ■ *Web:* www.source2.com	Winter Park	FL	32789	407-893-3711		260
Source4 3473 Brandon Ave SW *Web:* www.source4.com	Chicago	IL	60609	773-247-4141	247-1313	110
Sourcebook Project PO Box 107 *Web:* www.science-frontiers.com	Parkville	MD	21234	410-668-6047		637-2
Sourcebooks Inc 1935 Brookdale Rd Ste 139 *TF:* 800-432-7444 ■ *Web:* www.sourcebooks.com	Naperville	IL	60563	630-961-3900	961-2168	637-2
SourceGear LLC 115 N Neil St Ste 408 *Web:* www.sourcegear.com	Champaign	IL	61820	217-356-0105		631
SourceLink LLC 500 Pk Blvd Ste 1425 *TF:* 866-947-6872 ■ *Web:* www.sourcelink.com	Itasca	IL	60143	866-947-6872		5
SourceN Inc 4848 San Filipe Rd Ste 150 116 *Web:* sourcen.com	San Jose	CA	95135	831-297-2838		196
Sourcentra Inc 111 Speen St Ste LL 003 *Web:* www.sourcentra.com	Framingham	MA	01701	508-405-2605	302-4793	88
SourcePoint Staffing LLC 12745 W Capitol Dr *Web:* sourcepointstaffing.com	Brookfield	WI	53005	414-755-8600		260
Sourcery, The 450 Mission St Ste 101 *Web:* www.thesourcery.com	San Francisco	CA	94105	415-418-7156		260
Sourcing Interests Group (SIG) 221 N Hogan St Ste 389 *Web:* www.sig.org	Jacksonville	FL	32202	904-310-9560		721
Sourdough Studio (SS) PO Box 92205 *Web:* www.douglindstrand.com	Anchorage	AK	99509	907-563-2568	563-4456	637-2
Souris Valley Extended Care Centre Health Sciences Library PO Box 2003 *Web:* www.suncountry.sk.ca	Weyburn	SK	S4H2Z9	306-842-8399		434-3
Sousa Archives & Center for American Music (SACAM) 1103 S Sixth St Harding Band Bldg *Web:* archives.library.illinois.edu	Champaign	IL	61820	217-333-2290	244-8695	520
Sousa Court Reporters 1013 Garces Ave *Web:* www.sousa.com	Las Vegas	NV	89101	702-765-7100		196
Sousley Sound & Communications 1006 Tieton Dr *TF:* 800-876-3369 ■ *Web:* www.sousley.com	Yakima	WA	98902	509-248-4848		246
Soutex Inc 357 Rue Jackson *TF:* 800-463-2839 ■ *Web:* www.soutex.ca	Quebec City	QC	G1N4C4	418-871-2455		261
South Africa						
Consulate General 200 S Michigan Ave Ste 600 *Web:* www.sachicago.pwpsystems.com	Chicago	IL	60604	312-939-7929	939-2588	257
Consulate General 333 E 38th St 9th Fl *Web:* www.southafrica-newyork.net	New York	NY	10016	212-213-4880	213-0102	257
Embassy 3051 Massachusetts Ave NW *Web:* www.saembassy.org	Washington	DC	20008	202-232-4400		257
South African						
Consulate-General 6300 Wilshire Blvd Ste 600 *Web:* www.dirco.gov.za	Los Angeles	CA	90048	323-651-0902		257
South African Airways 1200 S Pine Island Rd Ste 650 *TF:* 800-722-9675 ■ *Web:* www.flysaa.com	Plantation	FL	33324	954-769-5000	769-5079	25
South Alabama Electric Co-op (SAEC) PO Box 449 *TF:* 800-556-2060 ■ *Web:* www.southaec.com	Troy	AL	36081	334-566-2060	566-8949	245
South Alabama Regional Planning Commission 110 Beauregard St *Web:* sarpc.org	Mobile	AL	36633	251-433-6541		196
South Arkansas Community College PO Box 7010 *TF:* 800-955-2289 ■ *Web:* www.southark.edu	El Dorado	AR	71731	870-862-8131		162
South Atlantic Capital Inc 1900 E wood Rd Ste 14 *Web:* www.southatlantic.com	Tampa	FL	33606	813-253-2500		792
South Atlantic Packaging Corp 3932 Westpoint Blvd *Web:* southatlanticpackaging.com	Winston-Salem	NC	27103	336-774-3122		317
South Atlantic Services Inc PO Box 1886 *Web:* www.southatlanticservices.com	Wilmington	NC	28402	910-763-3496	251-1103	393
South Baldwin Chamber of Commerce (SBCC) 112 W Laurel Ave PO Box 1117 *TF:* 877-461-3712 ■ *Web:* www.southbaldwinchamber.com	Foley	AL	36535	251-943-3291	943-6810	139

Name / Address	City	State	ZIP	Phone	Fax	Class
South Bay Construction 1711 Dell Ave *Web:* www.sbci.com	Campbell	CA	95008	408-379-5500	379-3256	186
South Bay Correctional Facility 600 US Hwy 27 S *Web:* dc.state.fl.us	South Bay	FL	33493	561-992-9505	992-9551	213
South Bay Expressway LP 1129 La Media Rd *TF:* 888-889-1515 ■ *Web:* www.southbayexpressway.com	San Diego	CA	92154	619-661-7070		415
South Bay Galleria 1815 Hawthorne Blvd Ste 201 *Web:* www.southbaygalleria.com	Redondo Beach	CA	90278	310-371-7546		460
South Bay Hospital 4016 Sun City Center Blvd *TF:* 888-499-1293 ■ *Web:* southbayhospital.com	Sun City Center	FL	33573	813-634-3301		374-3
South Bay Union School District 601 Elm Ave *Web:* www.sbusd.org	Imperial Beach	CA	91932	619-628-1600		685
South Baylo University 1126 N Brookhurst St *TF:* 888-642-2956 ■ *Web:* www.southbaylo.edu	Anaheim	CA	92801	714-533-1495	533-6040	166
South Beach Grill 45 Cubbedge Rd *Web:* www.southbeachgrill.net	Saint Augustine	FL	32080	904-471-8700		671
South Beach Marina Inn & Vacation Rentals 232 S Sea Pines Dr *TF:* 800-367-3909 ■ *Web:* www.sbinn.com	Hilton Head Island	SC	29928	843-671-6498	671-7495	379
South Beach Psychiatric Ctr 777 Seaview Ave *Web:* omh.ny.gov	Staten Island	NY	10305	718-667-2300		374-5
South Belt-Ellington Chamber of Commerce 10500 Scarsdale Blvd *Web:* southbeltchamber.com	Houston	TX	77089	281-481-5516		139
South Bend City Hall 227 W Jefferson Blvd Ste 1316 *Web:* www.southbendin.gov	South Bend	IN	46601	574-235-9221	235-9173	337
South Bend Firefighters FCU 1122 S Main St *Web:* sbfcu.org	South Bend	IN	46601	574-287-6161		219
South Bend Medical Foundation 530 N Lafayette Blvd *TF:* 800-544-0925 ■ *Web:* www.sbmf.org	South Bend	IN	46601	574-234-4176		418
South Bend Modern Molding Inc 605 Laurel St *Web:* www.sbmm.com	Mishawaka	IN	46544	574-255-0711		677
South Bend Museum of Art 120 S St Joseph St *Web:* southbendart.org	South Bend	IN	46601	574-235-9102	235-5782	520
South Bend Regional Airport 4477 Progress Dr *Web:* www.flysbn.com	South Bend	IN	46628	574-282-4590		27
South Bend Symphony Orchestra (SBSO) 127 N Michigan St *TF:* 800-537-6415 ■ *Web:* www.southbendsymphony.org	South Bend	IN	46601	574-232-6343	232-6627	573-3
South Bend Tribune 225 W Colfax Ave *TF:* 800-220-7378 ■ *Web:* www.southbendtribune.com	South Bend	IN	46626	574-235-6464		532-2
South Bend/Mishawaka Convention & Visitors Bureau 101 N Michigan St Ste 300 *TF:* 800-519-0577 ■ *Web:* visitsouthbend.com	South Bend	IN	46601	800-519-0577		206
South Boston News Inc 511 Broad St *Web:* www.sovanow.com	South Boston	VA	24592	434-572-2928	572-2920	532-2
South Boston Speedway 1188 James D Hagood Hwy PO Box 1066 *TF:* 877-440-1540 ■ *Web:* www.southbostonspeedway.com	South Boston	VA	24592	434-572-4947	575-8992	515
South Broadway Cultural Ctr 1025 Broadway Blvd SE *Web:* www.cabq.gov	Albuquerque	NM	87102	505-848-1320	848-1329	50-2
South Brunswick Public Schools 231 Black Horse Ln PO Box 181 *Web:* www.sbschools.org	Monmouth Junction	NJ	08852	732-297-7800		186
South by Southwest Film Festival 500 E Cesar Chavez St *Web:* www.sxsw.com	Austin	TX	78701	512-467-7979	451-0754	282
South Cape Beach State Park Great Oak Rd *Web:* www.mass.gov	Mashpee	MA	02649	508-457-0495		565
South Carolina						
Adoption Services Div PO Box 1520 *Web:* dss.sc.gov	Columbia	SC	29202	803-898-7561		339-41
Agriculture Dept 1200 Senate St 5th Fl Wade Hampton Bldg *Web:* agriculture.sc.gov	Columbia	SC	29201	803-734-2210	734-2192	339-41
Arts Commission 1026 Sumter St Ste 200 *Web:* www.southcarolinaarts.com	Columbia	SC	29201	803-734-8696	734-8526	339-41
Attorney General 1000 Assembly St Rembert Dennis Bldg Rm 519 *Web:* www.scag.gov	Columbia	SC	29201	803-734-3970	253-6283	339-41
Child Support Enforcement Office 3150 Harden St Ext PO Box 1469 *Web:* www.dss.sc.gov	Columbia	SC	29203	803-898-9282	898-9465	339-41
Commerce Dept 1201 Main St Ste 1600 *TF:* 800-868-7232 ■ *Web:* www.sccommerce.com	Columbia	SC	29201	803-737-0400	737-0418	339-41
Commission on Higher Education 1122 Lady St Ste 300 *Web:* www.che.sc.gov	Columbia	SC	29201	803-737-2260	737-2297	339-41
Corrections Dept 4444 Broad River Rd *Web:* www.doc.sc.gov	Columbia	SC	29210	803-896-8500		339-41
Education Lottery PO Box 11949 *TF:* 866-736-9819 ■ *Web:* www.sceducationlottery.com	Columbia	SC	29211	803-737-2002		452
Emergency Management Div (SCEMD) 2779 Fish Hatchery Rd *Web:* scemd.org	West Columbia	SC	29172	803-737-8500	737-8570	339-41
Ethics Commission 5000 Thurmond Mall Ste 250 *Web:* www.ethics.sc.gov	Columbia	SC	29201	803-253-4192	253-7539	265

				Phone	Fax	Class
Health & Environmental Control Dept 2600 Bull St TF: 877-284-1008 ■ Web: www.scdhec.gov	Columbia	SC	29201	803-898-4123		339-41
Health & Human Services Dept 1717 Gervais St PO Box 192	Columbia	SC	29201	803-929-6000		339-41
Higher Education Tuition Grants Commission 115 Atrium Wy Ste 102 Web: sctuitiongrants.org	Columbia	SC	29203	803-896-1120	896-1126	725
Highway Patrol 5400 Broad River Rd Bldg 12 Web: www.scdps.gov	Columbia	SC	29212	803-896-9689	896-9685	339-41
Historic Preservation Office 8301 Parklane Rd Web: www.scdah.sc.gov	Columbia	SC	29223	803-896-6196		339-41
Insurance Dept (SCDOI) 1201 Main St Ste 1000 PO Box 100105 Web: www.doi.sc.gov	Columbia	SC	29201	803-737-6160	737-6231	339-41
Labor Licensing & Regulation Dept 110 Centerview Dr Web: www.llr.state.sc.us	Columbia	SC	29210	803-896-4300		339-41
Law Enforcement Div 4400 Broad River Rd PO Box 21398 Web: www.sled.sc.gov	Columbia	SC	29210	803-737-9000		339-41
Legislature 1105 Pendleton St 223 Blatt Bldg Web: www.scstatehouse.gov	Columbia	SC	29201	803-212-4490		339-41
Mental Health Dept 2414 Bull St PO Box 485 Web: scdmh.org	Columbia	SC	29202	803-898-8581		339-41
Motor Vehicles Div 10311 Wilson Blvd PO Box 1498 Web: www.scdmvonline.com	Blythewood	SC	29016	803-896-5500	896-2698	339-41
Natural Resources Dept 1000 Assembly St Web: www.dnr.sc.gov	Columbia	SC	29201	803-734-4006	734-4300	339-41
Parks Recreation & Tourism Dept 1205 Pendleton St Web: southcarolinaparks.com	Columbia	SC	29201	803-734-0156		339-41
Probation Parole & Pardon Services Dept 2221 Devine St Ste 600 PO Box 50666 TF: 888-551-4118 ■ Web: www.dppps.sc.gov	Columbia	SC	29250	803-734-9220	734-5664	339-41
Secretary of State 1205 Pendleton St Ste 525 Web: www.scsos.com	Columbia	SC	29201	803-734-2170		339-41
Securities Div 1000 Assembly St PO Box 11549 Web: www.scag.gov	Columbia	SC	29211	803-734-9916		339-41
Social Services Dept 1535 Confederate Ave TF: 800-616-1309 ■ Web: dss.sc.gov	Columbia	SC	29202	803-898-7601		339-41
State Housing Finance & Development Authority 300 Outlet Pointe Blvd Ste C TF: 800-476-0412 ■ Web: www.schousing.com	Columbia	SC	29210	803-896-9001	896-8592	339-41
State Ports Authority 176 Concord St TF: 800-845-7106 ■ Web: www.scspa.com	Charleston	SC	29401	843-723-8651	577-8710	618
Supreme Court 300 Outlet Pointe Blvd Supreme Court Bldg Ste A Web: dss.sc.gov	Columbia	SC	29201	803-734-1080	734-1499	339-41
Transportation Dept 955 Park St PO Box 191 Web: www.scdot.org	Columbia	SC	29202	803-737-1302	737-2038	339-41
Treasurer Wade Hampton Bldg 1200 Senate St Ste 214 Web: treasurer.sc.gov	Columbia	SC	29201	803-734-2101	734-2690	339-41
Veterans Affairs Div 1205 Pendleton St Ste 463 Web: www.va.gov	Columbia	SC	29201	803-734-0200	734-4014	339-41
Victim Assistance Div 1205 Pendleton St TF: 800-220-5370 ■ Web: www.sova.sc.gov	Columbia	SC	29201	803-734-1900	734-1708	339-41
Vocational Rehabilitation Dept 1410 Boston Ave PO Box 15 TF: 800-832-7526 ■ Web: scvrd.net	West Columbia	SC	29171	803-896-6500		339-41
Wildlife & Freshwater Fisheries Div 1000 Assembly St PO Box 167 Web: www.dnr.sc.gov	Columbia	SC	29202	803-734-3886	734-6020	339-41
South Carolina Aquarium 100 Aquarium Wharf *Fax Area Code: 866 ■ TF: 800-722-6455 ■ Web: www.scaquarium.org	Charleston	SC	29401	843-577-3474	210-1059*	40
South Carolina Association of Realtors 3780 Fernandina Rd TF: 800-233-6381 ■ Web: www.screaltors.org	Columbia	SC	29210	803-772-5206	798-6650	656
South Carolina Association of Veterinarians PO Box 11766 TF: 800-441-7228 ■ Web: www.scav.org	Columbia	SC	29211	803-254-1027	254-3773	795
South Carolina Bar 950 Taylor St TF: 877-797-2227 ■ Web: www.scbar.org	Columbia	SC	29201	803-799-6653	799-4118	72
South Carolina Book Festival PO Box 5287 Web: schumanities.org	Columbia	SC	29250	803-771-2477	771-2487	281
South Carolina Chamber of Commerce 1301 Gervais St Ste 1100 TF: 800-799-4601 ■ Web: www.scchamber.net	Columbia	SC	29201	803-799-4601	779-6043	140
South Carolina Children's Theatre 153 Augusta St Web: scchildrenstheatre.org	Greenville	SC	29601	864-235-2885	235-0208	573-4
South Carolina Civil War Museum 4857 Hwy 17 Bypass S Web: scmuseum.org	Myrtle Beach	SC	29577	843-293-3377		520
South Carolina Democratic Party, The 915 Lady St Ste 111 Web: scdp.org	Columbia	SC	29201	803-799-7798	765-1692	616-1
South Carolina Dental Assn 120 Stonemark Ln TF: 800-327-2598 ■ Web: www.scda.org	Columbia	SC	29210	803-750-2277	750-1644	227
South Carolina Education Assn, The 421 Zimalcrest Dr TF: 800-422-7232 ■ Web: www.thescea.org	Columbia	SC	29210	803-772-6553		533
South Carolina Elastic Co 201 S Carolina Elastic Rd TF: 800-845-6700 ■ Web: scelastic.com	Landrum	SC	29356	800-845-6700		745-5
South Carolina Federal Credit Union PO Box 190012 TF: 800-845-0432 ■ Web: www.scfederal.org	North Charleston	SC	29419	843-797-8300		219
South Carolina Library Assn (SCLA) PO Box 1763 Web: www.scla.org	Columbia	SC	29202	803-252-1087	252-0589	435
South Carolina Medical Assn 132 Westpark Blvd TF: 800-327-1021 ■ Web: www.scmedical.org	Columbia	SC	29210	803-798-6207	772-6783	474
South Carolina Nurses Assn (SCNA) 1821 Gadsden St Web: www.scnurses.org	Columbia	SC	29201	803-252-4781	779-3870	533
South Carolina Pharmacy Assn 1350 Browning Rd Web: www.scrx.org	Columbia	SC	29210	803-354-9977	354-9207	585
South Carolina Philharmonic 721 Lady St Web: www.scphilharmonic.com	Columbia	SC	29201	803-251-2222	771-0268	573-3
South Carolina Press Assn 106 Outlet Pointe Blvd PO Box 11429 TF: 888-727-7377 ■ Web: www.scpress.org	Columbia	SC	29210	803-750-9561	551-0903	624
South Carolina Public Radio 1041 George Rogers Blvd Web: www.southcarolinapublicradio.org	Columbia	SC	29201	803-737-3200		645-38
South Carolina Republican Party, The 1913 Marion St Web: www.sc.gop	Columbia	SC	29201	803-988-8440	988-8444	616-2
South Carolina State Library 1500 Senate St TF: 888-221-4643 ■ Web: www.statelibrary.sc.gov	Columbia	SC	29201	803-734-8666	734-8676	434-5
South Carolina State Museum 301 Gervais St Web: www.scmuseum.org	Columbia	SC	29201	803-898-4921	898-4969	520
South Carolina State University 300 College St NE TF: 800-260-5956 ■ Web: www.scsu.edu	Orangeburg	SC	29117	803-536-7000	536-8990	166
South Cedar Greenhouses 23111 Cedar Ave S Web: www.southcedar.com	Farmington	MN	55024	952-469-3202	469-5335	293
South Central Arkansas Electric Co-op 4818 Hwy 8 W PO Box 476 TF: 800-814-2931 ■ Web: www.scaec.com	Arkadelphia	AR	71923	870-246-6701		245
South Central College *Faribault* 1225 Third St TF: 800-422-0391 ■ Web: southcentral.edu	Faribault	MN	55021	507-332-5800	332-5888	162
South Central Correctional Facility 555 Forest Ave PO Box 279 Web: www.tn.gov	Clifton	TN	38425	931-676-5372	676-5104	213
South Central Electric Assn 71176 Tiell Dr PO Box 150 TF: 888-805-7232 ■ Web: www.southcentralelectric.com	Saint James	MN	56081	507-375-3164	375-3166	245
South Central Indiana Rural Electric Membership Corp 300 Morton Ave TF: 800-264-7362 ■ Web: www.sciremc.com	Martinsville	IN	46151	765-342-3344		245
South Central Library System 4610 S Biltmore Ln TF: 855-516-7257 ■ Web: www.scls.info	Madison	WI	53718	608-246-7970		434-3
South Central Oil Company Inc 2121 W Main St Web: www.southcentraloil.com	Albemarle	NC	28001	704-982-2173		579
South Central Power Company Inc 2780 Coon Path Rd TF: 800-282-5064 ■ Web: www.southcentralpower.com	Lancaster	OH	43130	740-653-4422	681-4488	245
South Central Preferred 3421 Concord Rd TF: 800-842-1768 ■ Web: www.scp-ppo.com	York	PA	17402	717-851-6800	851-6775	390
South Central Public Power District (SCPPD) 275 S Main St PO Box 406 TF: 800-557-5254 ■ Web: southcentralppd.com	Nelson	NE	68961	402-225-2351		245
South Central Regional Medical Ctr (SCRMC) 1220 Jefferson St Web: scrmc.com	Laurel	MS	39440	601-426-4000		374-3
South Central Telephone Association Inc (SCTELCOM) 215 S Iliff TF: 877-723-6875 ■ Web: www.sctelcom.net	Medicine Lodge	KS	67104	620-930-1000		224
South Central Wisconsin Mls Corp 4801 Forest Run Rd Ste 101 Web: rascw.org	Madison	WI	53704	608-240-2800		653
South Charlotte Nissan 9215 S Blvd TF: 888-411-1423 ■ Web: www.scottclarknissan.com	Charlotte	NC	28273	704-552-9191		57
South City Kitchen 233 Peachtree St NE Ste 2600 Web: fifthgroup.com	Atlanta	GA	30309	404-873-7358		671
South Coast Botanic Garden (SCBG) 26300 Crenshaw Blvd Web: southcoastbotanicgarden.org	Palos Verdes Peninsula	CA	90274	310-544-1948		97
South Coast Construction Services Inc 3235 Fuqua St Web: sccsi.net	Houston	TX	77047	713-222-2308		186
South Coast Plaza 3333 Bristol St TF: 800-782-8888 ■ Web: www.southcoastplaza.com	Costa Mesa	CA	92626	800-782-8888		460
South Coast Repertory 655 Town Center Dr Web: www.scr.org	Costa Mesa	CA	92626	714-708-5500	708-5576	749
South Coast Terminals Inc 7401 Wallisville Rd Web: www.scterm.com	Houston	TX	77020	713-672-2401		541
South Coast Water District 31592 W St Web: www.scwd.org	Laguna Beach	CA	92651	949-499-4555	499-4256	787
South College 3904 Lonas Dr TF: 877-557-2575 ■ Web: www.south.edu	Knoxville	TN	37909	865-251-1800		800

Name / Address	City	State	ZIP	Phone	Fax	Class
South County Ctr 18 S County Centerway *Web:* www.shopsouthcountycenter.com	Saint Louis	MO	63129	314-892-8954		460
South County Hospital 100 Kenyon Ave *Web:* www.southcountyhealth.org	Wakefield	RI	02879	401-782-8000	783-6330	374-3
South Cumberland State Park 11745 US 41 *Web:* tnstateparks.com	Monteagle	TN	37356	931-924-2980		565
South Dade Electrical Supply 13100 SW 87th Ave *Web:* www.south-dade.com	Miami	FL	33176	305-238-7131	251-5254	246
South Dade Nursing & Rehabilitation Ctr 17475 S Dixie Hwy *Web:* www.floridahealthfinder.gov	Miami	FL	33157	305-255-1045		371
South Dakota						
Agriculture Dept 523 E Capitol Ave Joe Foss Bldg 3rd Fl *TF:* 800-228-5254 ■ *Web:* sdda.sd.gov	Pierre	SD	57501	605-773-5425	773-3481	339-42
Arts Council 711 E Wells Ave **Fax Area Code:* 605 ■ *TF:* 800-952-3625 ■ *Web:* artscouncil.sd.gov	Pierre	SD	57501	800-952-3625	773-5977*	339-42
Attorney General 1302 E Hwy 14 Ste 1 *Web:* sd.gov	Pierre	SD	57501	605-773-3215	773-4106	339-42
Banking Div 1601 N Harrison Ave Ste 1 *Web:* dlr.sd.gov	Pierre	SD	57501	605-773-3421		339-42
Career Ctr Div 116 W Missouri Ave *Web:* dlr.sd.gov	Pierre	SD	57501	605-773-3372	773-6680	259
Consumer Protection Div 1302 E Hwy 14 Ste 3 *TF:* 800-300-1986 ■ *Web:* sd.gov	Pierre	SD	57501	605-773-4400	773-7163	339-42
Department of Health 600 E Capitol Ave Robert Hayes Bldg *TF:* 800-738-2301 ■ *Web:* sd.gov	Pierre	SD	57501	605-773-3361	773-5683	339-42
Department of Tribal Relations 302 E Dakota *Web:* www.sdtribalrelations.com	Pierre	SD	57501	605-773-3415	773-6592	339-42
Education Dept 800 Governors Dr *Web:* www.doe.sd.gov	Pierre	SD	57501	605-773-3134		339-42
Emergency Management Office 118 W Capitol Ave *Web:* dps.sd.gov	Pierre	SD	57501	605-773-3231		339-42
Environment & Natural Resources Dept 523 E Capitol Ave *Web:* denr.sd.gov	Pierre	SD	57501	605-773-3151	773-6035	339-42
Finance & Management Bureau 500 E Capitol Ave *Web:* bfm.sd.gov	Pierre	SD	57501	605-773-3411		339-42
Highway Patrol Div 118 W Capitol Ave *Web:* dps.sd.gov	Pierre	SD	57501	605-773-3105	773-6046	339-42
Housing Development Authority PO Box 1237 *Web:* www.sdhda.org	Pierre	SD	57501	605-773-3181	773-5154	339-42
Insurance Div 124 S Euclid Ave 2nd Fl *Web:* dlr.sd.gov	Pierre	SD	57501	605-773-3563	773-5369	339-42
Labor Dept 123 W Missouri Ave *Web:* www.sdjobs.org	Pierre	SD	57501	605-773-3101	773-6184	339-42
Lake Cochrane Recreation Area 3454 Edgewater Dr *Web:* gfp.sd.gov	Gary	SD	57237	605-882-5200		565
Legislature Capitol Bldg 500 E Capitol Ave 3rd Fl *Web:* sdlegislature.gov	Pierre	SD	57501	605-773-3251	773-4576	339-42
Military & Veterans Affairs Dept 2525 W Main St Ste 303A *Web:* vetaffairs.sd.gov	Rapid City	SD	57702	605-593-7781		339-42
Pardons & Parole Board 1600 N Dr PO Box 5911 *Web:* doc.sd.gov	Sioux Falls	SD	57117	605-367-5040		339-42
Real Estate Commission 221 W Capitol Ave Ste 101 *Web:* sd.gov	Pierre	SD	57501	605-773-3600	773-7175	339-42
Regents Board 306 E Capitol Ave Ste 200 *Web:* www.sdbor.edu	Pierre	SD	57501	605-773-3455		339-42
Rehabilitation Services Div 500 E Capitol Ave *TF:* 877-873-8500 ■ *Web:* dhs.sd.gov	Pierre	SD	57501	605-773-5990		339-42
Revenue 445 E Capitol Ave *Web:* dor.sd.gov	Pierre	SD	57501	605-773-3311		339-42
Secretary of State 500 E Capitol Ave Capitol Bldg Ste 204 *Web:* www.sdsos.gov	Pierre	SD	57501	605-773-3537	773-6580	339-42
Social Services Dept 700 Governors Dr *TF:* 800-597-1603 ■ *Web:* dss.sd.gov	Pierre	SD	57501	605-773-3165	773-4855	339-42
State Historical Society 900 Governors Dr *Web:* history.sd.gov	Pierre	SD	57501	605-773-3458	773-6041	339-42
Supreme Court 500 E Capitol Ave *Web:* ujs.sd.gov	Pierre	SD	57501	605-773-3511	773-6128	339-42
Tourism Office 711 E Wells Ave *TF:* 800-732-5682 ■ *Web:* www.travelsouthdakota.com	Pierre	SD	57501	605-773-3301		339-42
Treasurer 500 E Capitol Ave Ste 212 *TF:* 866-357-2547 ■ *Web:* sdtreasurer.gov	Pierre	SD	57501	605-773-3379	773-3115	339-42
Weights & Measures Office 118 W Capitol Ave *Web:* dps.sd.gov	Pierre	SD	57501	605-773-3697	773-6631	339-42
South Dakota Association of Realtors 204 N Euclid Ave *TF:* 800-227-5877 ■ *Web:* www.sdrealtor.org	Pierre	SD	57501	605-224-0554	224-8975	656
South Dakota Bankers Association Inc 109 W Missouri Ave *Web:* sdba.com	Pierre	SD	57501	605-224-1653		70
South Dakota Chamber of Commerce & Industry 222 E Capitol Ave Ste 15 *TF:* 800-742-8112 ■ *Web:* sdchamber.biz	Pierre	SD	57501	605-224-6161	224-7198	140
South Dakota Democratic Party 335 N Main Ave Ste 200 *Web:* www.sddp.org	Sioux Falls	SD	57104	605-271-5405		616-1

Name / Address	City	State	ZIP	Phone	Fax	Class
South Dakota Dental Assn 804 N Euclid Ave Ste 103 *TF:* 866-551-8023 ■ *Web:* www.sddental.org	Pierre	SD	57501	605-224-9133	224-9168	227
South Dakota Discovery Center & Aquarium 805 W Sioux Ave *Web:* sd-discovery.org	Pierre	SD	57501	605-224-8295		520
South Dakota Family Connection 303 N Minnesota Ave *Web:* www.sdfamilyconnection.org	Sioux Falls	SD	57104	605-357-0777		637-2
South Dakota Grain and Feed Assn (SDGFA) 320 E Capitol Ave *Web:* www.sdgfa.org	Pierre	SD	57501	605-224-2445	224-9913	139
South Dakota Municipal League (SDML) 208 Island Dr *Web:* www.sdmunicipalleague.org	Fort Pierre	SD	57532	605-224-8654	224-8655	48-13
South Dakota National Guard Museum 425 E Capitol Ave *Web:* www.military.sd.gov	Pierre	SD	57501	605-773-3269		520
South Dakota Newspaper Services 1125 32nd Ave *TF:* 800-658-3697 ■ *Web:* www.sdna.com	Brookings	SD	57006	800-658-3697		624
South Dakota Nurses Assn (SDNA) PO Box 1015 **Fax Area Code:* 888 ■ *Web:* www.sdnursesassociation.org	Pierre	SD	57501	605-945-4265	600-1232*	533
South Dakota Pharmacists Assn PO Box 518 *Web:* www.sdpha.org	Pierre	SD	57501	605-224-2338	224-1280	585
South Dakota Public Broadcasting (SDPB) 555 N Dakota St PO Box 5000 *TF:* 800-456-0766 ■ *Web:* www.sdpb.org	Vermillion	SD	57069	605-677-5861	677-5010	632
South Dakota Republican State Central Committee 120 W Pleasant Ave PO Box 1099 *Web:* southdakotagop.com	Pierre	SD	57501	605-610-1479		616-2
South Dakota Rural Electric Assn 222 W Pleasant Dr *Web:* www.sdrea.coop	Pierre	SD	57501	605-224-8823		48-13
South Dakota State Library 800 Governors Dr *TF:* 800-423-6665 ■ *Web:* www.library.sd.gov	Pierre	SD	57501	605-773-3131	773-4950	434-5
South Dakota State Medical Assn (SDSMA) 2600 W 49th St Ste 200 *Web:* www.sdsma.org	Sioux Falls	SD	57105	605-336-1965	274-3274	457-16
South Dakota State University PO Box 2201 *TF:* 800-952-3541 ■ *Web:* www.sdstate.edu	Brookings	SD	57007	605-688-4121	688-6891	166
South Dakota Symphony Orchestra 301 S Main Ave *Web:* www.sdsymphony.org	Sioux Falls	SD	57104	605-335-7933		573-3
South Davis Community Hospital 401 S 400 E *Web:* www.sdch.com	Bountiful	UT	84010	801-295-2361		450
South Division Credit Union 9122 S Kedzie Ave *Web:* sdcu.org	Evergreen Park	IL	60805	708-857-7070		219
South East Health Integration Network 71 Adam St *Web:* www.southeastlhin.on.ca	Belleville	ON	K8N5K3	613-967-0196		474
South Florida Community College 600 W College Dr *Web:* www.southflorida.edu	Avon Park	FL	33825	863-453-6661	453-2365	162
South Florida Federal Credit Union 1902 NW 14th Ave *Web:* southfloridafcu.com	Miami	FL	33125	305-545-0744		219
South Florida Museum 201 10th St W *Web:* www.southfloridamuseum.org	Bradenton	FL	34205	941-746-4131	747-2556	520
South Florida Science Museum 4801 Dreher Trail N *Web:* www.sfsciencecenter.org	West Palm Beach	FL	33405	561-832-1988	833-0551	520
South Florida State Hospital 800 E Cypress Dr *Web:* wellpathcare.com	Pembroke Pines	FL	33025	954-392-3000		374-5
South Fork Forest Camp (SFFC) 48300 Wilson River Hwy *Web:* www.oregon.gov	Tillamook	OR	97141	503-842-2811	842-7943	213
South Fork Industries Inc 535 Elm Grove Rd *Web:* www.southforkind.com	Lincolnton	NC	28092	704-732-6946	732-2352	745-7
South Fork State Recreation Area 353 Lower S Fork Unit 8 *Web:* parks.nv.gov	Spring Creek	NV	89815	775-744-4346		565
South Gate Chamber of Commerce 3350 Tweedy Blvd *Web:* www.sgchamber.org	South Gate	CA	90280	323-567-1203		139
South Georgia Medical Ctr (SGMC) 2501 N Patterson St *Web:* www.sgmc.org	Valdosta	GA	31602	229-333-1000		374-3
South Georgia Pecan Co 309 S Lee St *Web:* georgiapecan.com	Valdosta	GA	31601	229-244-1321		296-28
South Georgia Regional Library 300 Woodrow Wilson Dr *Web:* www.sgrl.org	Valdosta	GA	31602	229-333-0086	333-7669	434-3
South Haven Public Schools Inc 554 Green St *Web:* www.shps.org	South Haven	MI	49090	269-637-0520		685
South Higgins Lake State Park 106 State Pk Dr *Web:* www.michigan.org	Roscommon	MI	48653	989-821-6374		565
South Hills Chamber of Commerce 61 McMurray Rd Ste 105 *Web:* www.shchamber.org	Pittsburgh	PA	15241	412-306-8090	221-4205	139
South Hills Country Club Golf Shop 2655 S Citrus St *Web:* www.southhillscountryclub.org	West Covina	CA	91791	626-339-1231		326
South Hills School of Business & Technology 480 Waupelani Dr *TF:* 888-282-7427 ■ *Web:* www.southhills.edu	State College	PA	16801	814-234-7755	234-0926	166
South Holland Public Library 16250 Wausau Ave *Web:* shlibrary.org	South Holland	IL	60473	708-527-3150	331-6557	435

Name / Address	City	State	Zip	Phone	Fax	Class
South Jersey Port Corp						
101 Joseph A Balzano Blvd	Camden	NJ	08103	856-757-4969	757-4903	618
Web: southjerseyport.com						
South Jersey Radiology Associates PA						
100 Carnie Blvd	Voorhees	NJ	08043	856-751-5522	751-0535	415
TF: 888-909-7572 ■ *Web:* www.sjra.com						
South Kansas City Chamber of Commerce						
406 E Bannister Rd Ste F	Kansas City	MO	64131	816-761-7660	761-7340	139
Web: southkcchamber.com						
South Kent School						
40 Bulls Bridge Rd	South Kent	CT	06785	860-927-3539	803-0040*	622
**Fax Area Code:* 888 ■ *Web:* southkentschool.org						
South Kentucky Rural Electrical Co-op						
925 N Main St PO Box 910	Somerset	KY	42502	606-678-4121	679-8279	245
TF: 800-264-5112 ■ *Web:* www.skrecc.com						
South Kitsap School District						
2689 Hoover Ave SE	Port Orchard	WA	98366	360-874-7000	874-7068	685
Web: www.skschools.org						
South Lake Associates Inc						
1333 N Northlake Way Ste H	Seattle	WA	98103	206-225-6786		653
Web: southlakeassociates.com						
South Llano River State Park						
1927 Park Rd 73	Junction	TX	76849	325-446-3994		565
Web: tpwd.texas.gov						
South Louisiana Bank (SLB)						
1362 W Tunnel Blvd PO Box 1718	Houma	LA	70361	985-851-3434	879-3095	70
Web: ayeee.com						
South Louisiana Electric Cooperative Assn						
2028 Coteau Rd	Houma	LA	70364	985-876-6880	851-3644	245
TF: 800-256-8826 ■ *Web:* www.sleca.com						
South Mall 3300 Lehigh St	Allentown	PA	18103	610-791-0606		460
Web: www.shopsouthmall.com						
South Metro Denver Chamber of Commerce						
2154 E Commons Ave	Centennial	CO	80122	303-795-0142	795-7520	139
Web: www.bestchamber.com						
South Metro Regional Chamber of Commerce						
7887 Washington Village Dr Ste 265	Dayton	OH	45459	937-433-2032		139
Web: www.smrcoc.org						
South Miami Audiology Consultants						
7000 SW 62nd Ave Ste 315	South Miami	FL	33143	305-663-0505	663-0170	352
Web: www.southmiamiaudiology.com						
South Mississippi Correctional Institution						
22689 Hwy 63 N PO Box 1419	Leakesville	MS	39451	601-394-5600	394-4451	213
Web: www.mdoc.ms.gov						
South Montgomery County Woodlands Chamber of Commerce						
1400 Woodloch Forest Dr Ste 300	The Woodlands	TX	77380	281-367-5777	292-1655	139
Web: www.woodlandschamber.org						
South Motors Infiniti 16915 S Dixie Hwy	Miami	FL	33157	844-490-1671		57
TF: 844-490-1671 ■ *Web:* www.southinfiniti.com						
South Mountain Community College						
7050 S 24th St	Phoenix	AZ	85042	602-243-8000	243-8199	162
TF: 855-622-2332 ■ *Web:* www.southmountaincc.edu						
South Mountain Restoration Ctr						
10058 S Mountain Rd	South Mountain	PA	17261	717-749-3121		450
Web: www.dhs.pa.gov						
South Mountains State Park						
3001 S Mtns State Park Ave	Connelly Springs	NC	28612	828-433-4772		565
Web: www.ncparks.gov						
South Oaks Hospital						
400 Sunrise Hwy	Amityville	NY	11701	631-608-5610		374-5
Web: southoaks.northwell.edu						
South of the Border Tours						
7937 E Coronado Ridge	Tucson	AZ	85750	520-760-4000		760
South Oklahoma City Chamber of Commerce						
701 SW 74 St	Oklahoma City	OK	73139	405-634-1436	634-1462	139
Web: southokc.com						
South Orangetown School District (Inc), The						
160 Van Wyck Rd	Blauvelt	NY	10913	845-680-1000		685
Web: www.socsd.org						
South Pacific Wholesale Co						
114 River St	Montpelier	VT	05602	800-338-2162	223-4044*	410
**Fax Area Code:* 802 ■ *TF:* 800-338-2162 ■ *Web:* www.beading.com						
South Padre Island Convention & Visitors Bureau						
7355 Padre Blvd	South Padre Island	TX	78597	956-761-6433		206
TF: 800-767-2373 ■ *Web:* www.sopadre.com						
South Park Mall						
2310 SW Military Dr	San Antonio	TX	78224	210-921-0534		460
Web: www.visitsouthpark.com						
South Penn Eye Care 250 E Walnut St	Hanover	PA	17331	717-632-6063		798
Web: www.southpenneyecare.com						
South Piedmont Community College						
680 Hwy 74	Polkton	NC	28135	704-272-5300	272-5303	162
Web: spcc.edu						
South Pier Inn on the Canal						
701 Lake Ave S	Duluth	MN	55802	218-786-9007		379
TF: 800-430-7437 ■ *Web:* southpierinn.com						
South Pinellas Medical Management C						
341 Third St S	Saint Petersburg	FL	33701	727-822-4600		390
Web: pinellastrust.com						
South Plains College						
1401 S College Ave	Levelland	TX	79336	806-894-9611	897-3167	162
Web: www.southplainscollege.edu						
South Plains Electric Co-opeartive Inc						
PO Box 1830	Lubbock	TX	79408	806-775-7766	775-7796	245
TF: 800-658-2655 ■ *Web:* www.spec.coop						
South Plains Implement						
1645 FM 403 PO Box 752	Brownfield	TX	79316	806-637-3594	637-8992	274
TF: 800-725-5435 ■ *Web:* www.southplainsimplement.com						
South Plains Mall 6002 Slide Rd	Lubbock	TX	79414	806-792-4653		460
Web: www.southplainsmall.com						
South Plains Public Health District						
919 E Main	Brownfield	TX	79316	806-637-2164		363
Web: southplainshealth.org						
South Plains Telephone Cooperative Inc (SPTC)						
2425 Marshall St	Lubbock	TX	79415	806-763-2301		224
Web: www.sptc.net						
South Platte Press (SPP) PO Box 163	David City	NE	68632	402-367-3554		637-2
Web: www.southplattepress.com						
South Point Systems Inc 1019 US Hwy 431	Boaz	AL	35957	256-593-1337	593-7168	225
Web: www.southpoint.net						
South Pole 222 Bridge Plz S	Fort Lee	NJ	07024	201-242-5900		157-4
Web: www.southpole-usa.com						
South Puget Sound Community College						
2011 Mottman Rd SW	Olympia	WA	98512	360-754-7711	596-5709	162
Web: spscc.edu						
South River Electric Membership Corp						
17494 US 421 S PO Box 931	Dunn	NC	28335	910-892-8071	230-2981	245
TF: 800-338-5530 ■ *Web:* www.sremc.com						
South River Technologies Inc						
1910 Towne Centre Blvd Ste 250	Annapolis	MD	21401	410-266-0667		177
TF: 866-861-9483 ■ *Web:* southrivertech.com						
South Salt Lake Chamber of Commerce						
220 E Morris Ave Ste 150	Salt Lake City	UT	84115	801-466-3377		139
Web: sslchamber.com						
South San Antonio Chamber of Commerce						
3315 Sidney Brooks Dr Ste 200	San Antonio	TX	78235	210-533-1600	314-2769	139
Web: www.southsachamber.org						
South San Antonio Independent School District						
5622 Ray Ellison	San Antonio	TX	78242	210-977-7000		685
Web: www.southsanisd.net						
South San Francisco Chamber of Commerce						
213 Linden Ave	South San Francisco	CA	94080	650-588-1911	588-2534	139
Web: www.ssfchamber.com						
South San Francisco Conference Ctr						
255 S Airport Blvd	South San Francisco	CA	94080	650-877-8787	877-5356	624
Web: ssfconf.com						
South San Francisco Public Library						
400 Grand Ave	South San Francisco	CA	94080	650-877-8500	829-3866	434-3
Web: www.ssf.net						
South San Francisco Unified School District						
398 B St	South San Francisco	CA	94080	650-877-8700		685
Web: www.ssfusd.org						
South Seas Island Resort						
5400 Plantation Rd	Captiva	FL	33924	239-472-5111	472-7541	669
TF: 866-565-5089 ■ *Web:* www.southseas.com						
South Seattle Community College						
6000 16th Ave SW	Seattle	WA	98106	206-934-5300		162
Web: www.southseattle.edu						
South Shore Chamber of Commerce						
1050 Hingham St	Rockland	MA	02370	781-421-3900	479-9274*	139
**Fax Area Code:* 617 ■ *Web:* www.southshorechamber.org						
South Shore Controls Inc						
4485 N Ridge Rd	Perry	OH	44081	440-259-2500	259-5015	203
Web: southshorecontrols.com						
South Shore Cultural Ctr						
7059 S Shore Dr	Chicago	IL	60649	773-256-0149		50-2
Web: www.chicagoparkdistrict.com						
South Shore Educational Collaborative						
75 Abington St	Hingham	MA	02043	781-749-7518	740-0784	166
Web: www.ssec.org						
South Shore Harbour Resort & Conference Ctr						
2500 S Shore Blvd	League City	TX	77573	281-334-1000	334-1157	653
TF: 800-442-5005 ■ *Web:* www.sshr.com						
South Shore Hospital (SSH)						
8012 S Crandon Ave	Chicago	IL	60617	773-356-5000		374-3
Web: www.southshorehospital.com						
South Shore Music Circus						
130 Sohier St	Cohasset	MA	02025	781-383-9850	383-9804	572
TF: 800-514-3849 ■ *Web:* www.themusiccircus.org						
South Shore Transportation						
4010 Columbus Ave	Sandusky	OH	44870	419-626-6267	626-9640	780
Web: www.sshoretrans.com						
South Side Chamber of Commerce						
1100 E Carson St	Pittsburgh	PA	15203	412-431-3360		139
Web: www.southsidechamber.org						
South Side Control Supply Co						
488 N Milwaukee Ave	Chicago	IL	60654	312-226-4900	226-3484	665
TF: 800-572-3389 ■ *Web:* www.southsidecontrol.com						
South Side Machine Works Inc						
3761 Eiler St	Saint Louis	MO	63116	314-481-7171	481-9271	454
Web: www.southsidemachine.net						
South Sioux City Convention & Visitors Bureau						
4401 Dakota Ave	South Sioux City	NE	68776	402-494-1307		206
TF: 866-494-1307 ■ *Web:* visitsouthsiouxcity.com						
South Slope Cooperative Communications						
980 N Front St	North Liberty	IA	52317	319-626-2211	665-7000	224
TF: 800-272-6449 ■ *Web:* www.southslope.com						
South Sound Speedway						
3730 183rd Ave SW	Rochester	WA	98579	360-273-6420		515
Web: www.southsoundspeedway.com						
South st Paul Steel Supply Company Inc						
200 Hardman Ave N	South Saint Paul	MN	55075	651-451-6666		492
TF: 800-456-7777 ■ *Web:* sspss.com						
South State Inc						
202 Reeves Rd PO Box 68	Bridgeton	NJ	08302	856-451-5300	455-3461	46
TF: 877-391-1436 ■ *Web:* southstateinc.com						
South Street Seaport 19 Fulton St	New York	NY	10038	212-732-8257		50-6
Web: www.seaportdistrict.nyc						
South Street Seaport Museum						
12 Fulton St	New York	NY	10038	212-748-8600		520
Web: southstreetseaportmuseum.org						
South Street Securities LLC						
825 Third Ave 35th Fl	New York	NY	10022	212-824-0738		690
Web: www.southstreetsecurities.com						
South Suburban College						
15800 S State St	South Holland	IL	60473	708-596-2000	225-5806	162
TF: 800-609-8056 ■ *Web:* ssc.edu						
South Summit School District						
285 E 400 S	Kamas	UT	84036	435-783-4301	783-4501	685
Web: www.ssummit.org						
South Tacoma Honda 7802 S Tacoma Way	Tacoma	WA	98409	888-746-4905		57
TF: 888-746-4905 ■ *Web:* www.southtacomahonda.com						
South Tahoe Refuse Co						
2140 Ruth Ave	South Lake Tahoe	CA	96150	530-541-5105	544-2608	804
Web: www.southtahoerefuse.com						

Name / Address	City	State	Zip	Phone	Fax	Class
South Texas Blood & Tissue Ctr 6211 IH-10 W *TF:* 800-292-5534 ■ *Web:* southtexasblood.org	San Antonio	TX	78201	210-731-5555		89
South Texas Botanical Gardens & Nature Ctr 8545 S Staples St *Web:* www.stxbot.org	Corpus Christi	TX	78413	361-852-2100	852-7875	97
South Texas College of Law 1303 San Jacinto St *Web:* www.stcl.edu	Houston	TX	77002	713-659-8040		167-1
South Texas Institute for the Arts 1902 N Shoreline Blvd *Web:* www.artmuseumofsouthtexas.org	Corpus Christi	TX	78401	361-825-3500	825-3520	520
South Texas Money Management Ltd 700 N St Mary's St Ste 100 *TF:* 800-805-1385 ■ *Web:* www.captrust.com	San Antonio	TX	78205	210-824-8916		401
South Texas Veterans Health Care System 7400 Merton Minter St *TF:* 800-209-7377 ■ *Web:* www.southtexas.va.gov	San Antonio	TX	78229	210-617-5300		374-8
South Toledo Bend State Park 120 Bald Eaglel Rd *TF:* 888-398-4770 ■ *Web:* crt.state.la.us	Anacoco	LA	71403	337-286-9075		565
South Towns Community Federal Credit Union 3040 S Park Ave *Web:* stownsfcu.com	Lackawanna	NY	14218	716-827-7788		219
South Trust Bank NA 601 Guadalupe St *Web:* southtrust.com	George West	TX	78022	361-449-1571		70
South University *Montgomery* 5355 Vaughn Rd *TF:* 866-629-2962 ■ *Web:* www.southuniversity.edu	Montgomery	AL	36116	334-395-8800		166
South Valley Drywall Inc 8101 Midway Dr *Web:* www.southvalleydrywall.com	Littleton	CO	80125	303-791-7212	470-0116	189-9
South Valley Internet Inc (SVI) 95 E San Martin Ave *TF:* 800-899-4125 ■ *Web:* www.garlic.net	San Martin	CA	95046	408-683-4533	681-1528	681
South Valley Specialties 547 W 9320 S *Web:* www.svsco.com	Sandy	UT	84070	801-566-3977	566-3978	677
South Western Communications Inc 4871 Rosebud Ln *TF:* 800-903-8432 ■ *Web:* www.swc.net	Newburgh	IN	47630	812-477-6495		246
South Whidbey Island State Park 4128 Smugglers Cove Rd *Web:* parks.state.wa.us	Freeland	WA	98249	360-331-4559		565
South Whidbey School District 5520 Maxwelton Rd *Web:* www.sw.wednet.edu	Langley	WA	98260	360-221-6100	221-3835	685
South Woods State Prison 215 Burlington Rd S *Web:* state.nj.us	Bridgeton	NJ	08302	856-459-7000	459-7140	213
South Yuba River State Park 17660 Pleasant Valley Rd *Web:* www.parks.ca.gov	Penn Valley	CA	95946	530-432-2546		565
South49 Solutions 46040 Center Oak Plz Ste 160 *TF:* 800-961-5203 ■ *Web:* www.south49.com	Sterling	VA	20166	800-961-5203		178-1
Southampton Chamber of Commerce 76 Main St *Web:* southamptonchamber.com	Southampton	NY	11968	631-283-0402		139
Southampton County 22350 Main St *Web:* www.southamptoncounty.org	Courtland	VA	23837	757-653-2200	653-2547	338
Southampton Hospital 240 Meeting House Ln *Web:* southampton.stonybrookmedicine.edu	Southampton	NY	11968	631-726-8200	283-5730	374-3
Southampton Inn 91 Hill St *TF:* 800-832-6500 ■ *Web:* www.southamptoninn.com	Southampton	NY	11968	631-283-6500	283-6559	379
Southampton Memorial Hospital 100 Fairview Dr *Web:* www.smhfranklin.com	Franklin	VA	23851	757-569-6100		374-3
Southampton Press, The 135 Windmill Ln *Web:* 27east.com	Southampton	NY	11968	631-283-4100		532-3
Southard Freeman Communications 111 John St Ste 630 *Web:* www.southardinc.com	New York	NY	10038	212-777-2220		636
Southard Supply Inc (SSI) 236 N 3rd St *TF:* 800-313-7652 ■ *Web:* www.southardsupply.com	Columbus	OH	43215	614-221-3323	221-5130	612
Southaven Chamber of Commerce 500 Main St *Web:* southavenchamber.com	Southaven	MS	38671	662-342-6114	342-6365	139
Southbay Foundry Inc 9444 Abraham Way *Web:* www.southbayfoundry.com	Santee	CA	92071	619-956-2780	956-2788	492
Southbend Inc 1100 Old Honeycutt Rd *TF:* 800-755-4777 ■ *Web:* www.southbendnc.com	Fuquay-Varina	NC	27526	919-762-1000	762-1121	298
Southboro Medical Group Inc 24 Newton St *TF:* 800-283-2556 ■ *Web:* www.reliantmedicalgroup.org	Southborough	MA	01772	508-481-5500		374-3
Southbridge Credit Union 205 Main St *Web:* sbgecu.org	Southbridge	MA	01550	508-765-5454		219
Southbridge Sheet Metal Works Inc 441 Main St PO Box 517 *Web:* ssmwusa.com	Sturbridge	MA	01566	508-347-7800	347-9118	697
Southbridge Tool & Manufacturing Inc 181 Southbridge Rd *Web:* www.southbridgetool.com	Dudley	MA	01571	508-764-2779		454
Southcentral Kentucky Community & Technical College 1845 Loop Dr *TF:* 855-246-2482 ■ *Web:* www.southcentral.kctcs.edu	Bowling Green	KY	42101	270-901-1000	901-1144	165
Southco 210 N Brinton Lake Rd *TF:* 877-821-0666 ■ *Web:* www.southco.com	Concordville	PA	19331	610-459-4000	459-4012	350
Southco Distributing Co 2201 S John St *TF:* 800-969-3172 ■ *Web:* www.southcodistributing.com	Goldsboro	NC	27530	919-735-8012		297-8
Southco Incorporated of North Carolina 3125 N Kerr Ave *Web:* www.southcoinc.com	Wilmington	NC	28405	910-763-3451		492
Southco Industries Inc 1840 E Dixon Blvd *Web:* www.southcoindustries.net	Shelby	NC	28152	704-482-1477	482-2015	516
Southcoast Cabinet Co 755 Pinefall Ave *Web:* www.southcoastcabinet.com	Walnut	CA	91789	909-594-3089		115
Southdale Pet Hospital PLLC 3910 W 70th St *Web:* southdalepethospital.com	Edina	MN	55435	952-926-1831		794
Southdata Inc 201 Technology Ln *TF:* 800-549-4722 ■ *Web:* www.southdata.com	Mount Airy	NC	27030	800-549-4722		177
Southeast Alabama Medical Ctr 1108 Ross Clark Cir Ste 302 *Web:* www.samc.org	Dothan	AL	36301	334-793-8111		374-3
Southeast Apothecary Inc 2032 Poplar St *Web:* southeastapothecary.com	Montgomery	AL	36106	334-262-2625		237
Southeast Arkansas College (SEARK) 1900 Hazel St *TF:* 888-732-7582 ■ *Web:* www.seark.edu	Pine Bluff	AR	71603	870-543-5900		162
Southeast Asia Resource Action Ctr (SEARAC) 1628 16th St NW *Web:* www.searac.org	Washington	DC	20009	202-601-2960	667-6449	48-5
Southeast Career Technical Academy 5710 Mountain Vista St *Web:* www.secta.us	Las Vegas	NV	89120	702-799-7500	799-2007	167-3
Southeast Climate Care 1801 Asheville Hwy *Web:* www.southeastclimatecare.com	Arden	NC	28704	828-585-5535		189-10
Southeast Colorado Power Assn (SECPA) 27850 Harris Rd *TF:* 800-332-8634 ■ *Web:* secpa.com	La Junta	CO	81050	719-384-2551	384-7320	245
Southeast Community College *Milford* 600 State St *TF:* 800-933-7223 ■ *Web:* www.southeast.edu	Milford	NE	68405	402-761-2131	761-2324	800
Southeast Computer Solutions Inc 15165 NW 77th Ave Ste 2009 *TF:* 888-773-2161 ■ *Web:* www.southeastcomputers.com	Miami	FL	33014	305-556-4697		177
Southeast Connections LLC 2720 Dogwood Dr SE *Web:* www.seconnections.com	Conyers	GA	30013	404-659-1422	659-1425	186
Southeast Culvert Inc 1094 Bankhead Hwy *Web:* southeastculvert.com	Winder	GA	30680	770-868-5599	868-5735	595
Southeast Dallas Chamber of Commerce 802 S Buckner Blvd *Web:* www.sedallaschamber.org	Dallas	TX	75217	214-398-9590		139
Southeast Delco School District 1560 Delmar Dr *Web:* www.sedelco.org	Folcroft	PA	19032	610-522-4300		449
Southeast Electric Co-opeartive Inc (SECO) 110 S Main St *TF:* 888-485-8762 ■ *Web:* www.seecoop.com	Ekalaka	MT	59324	406-775-8762		245
Southeast Fabricators Inc 7301 University Blvd E *TF:* 800-932-3227 ■ *Web:* www.sefab.com	Cottondale	AL	35453	205-556-3227		480
Southeast Fisheries Science Ctr 75 Virginia Beach Dr *Web:* www.sefsc.noaa.gov	Miami	FL	33149	305-361-4200	361-4219	668
Southeast Fuels Inc 620 Green Valley Rd Ste 303 *Web:* www.southeastfuels.com	Greensboro	NC	27408	336-854-1106		316
Southeast Georgia Health System Brunswick Campus 2415 Parkwood Dr *TF:* 800-537-5142 ■ *Web:* www.sghs.org	Brunswick	GA	31520	912-466-7000	466-7013	374-3
Southeast Industrial Equipment Inc 12200 Steele Creek Rd *TF:* [illegible] ■ *Web:* sielift.com	Charlotte	NC	28273	704-399-9700	393-1714	470
Southeast Kentucky Community & Technical College *Whitesburg* 2 Long Ave *TF:* 888-274-7322 ■ *Web:* southeast.kctcs.edu	Whitesburg	KY	41858	606-633-0279		162
Southeast Law Group Pa 1825 Business Park Blvd Ste A *Web:* southeastlaw.com	Daytona Beach	FL	32114	386-274-1700		41
Southeast Milk Inc PO Box 3790 **Fax Area Code:* 352 ■ *TF:* 800-598-7866 ■ *Web:* www.southeastmilk.org	Belleview	FL	34420	800-598-7866	245-9434*	296-27
Southeast Missouri Hospital (SMH) 1701 Lacey St *TF:* 800-800-5123 ■ *Web:* www.sehealth.org	Cape Girardeau	MO	63701	573-334-4822		374-3
Southeast Missouri Mental Health Ctr 1010 W Columbia St *Web:* dmh.mo.gov	Farmington	MO	63640	573-218-6792		374-5
Southeast Missouri State University 1 University Plz *Web:* www.semo.edu	Cape Girardeau	MO	63701	573-651-2000	651-5936	166
Southeast Missourian 301 Broadway St *TF:* 800-879-1210 ■ *Web:* www.semissourian.com	Cape Girardeau	MO	63701	573-335-6611	334-7288	532-2
Southeast Modular Mfg 2500 Industrial St *Web:* www.southeastmodular.net	Leesburg	FL	34748	352-728-2930	728-3093	106
Southeast Museum of Photography 1200 Int'l Speedway Blvd *Web:* www.smponline.org	Daytona Beach	FL	32114	386-506-4475		520
Southeast Nebraska Communications (SNC) 110 W 17th St *Web:* www.sentco.net	Falls City	NE	68355	402-245-4451	245-4770	224
SouthEast Personnel Leasing Inc 2739 US Hwy 19 N *TF:* 866-800-0785 ■ *Web:* www.southeastpersonnel.com	Holiday	FL	34691	727-938-5562	937-2138	260
Southeast Pet 7775 The Bluffs Ste H **Fax Area Code:* 800 ■ *TF:* 800-394-3900 ■ *Web:* www.southeastpet.com	Austell	GA	30168	770-948-7600	503-9452*	45
Southeast Regional Library 49 Bison Ave *Web:* southeastlibrary.ca	Weyburn	SK	S4H0H9	306-848-3100	842-2665	436
Southeast Steuben County Library 300 Nasser Civic Center Plz Ste 101 *Web:* www.ssclibrary.org	Corning	NY	14830	607-936-3713	936-1714	434-3

Name / Address	Phone	Fax	Class
Southeast Technical Institute 2320 N Career Ave .... Sioux Falls SD 57107 *TF:* 800-247-0789 ■ *Web:* southeasttech.edu	605-367-8355	367-4372	800
Southeast Valley Regional Association of Realtors 1363 S Vineyard .... Mesa AZ 85210 *Web:* www.sevrar.com	480-833-7510		533
Southeast Veterinary Dermatology & Ear Clinic LLC 804 Johnnie Dodds Blvd .... Mount Pleasant SC 29464 *Web:* southeastvetderm.com	843-849-7770		794
Southeast Volusia Chamber of Commerce 115 Canal St .... New Smyrna Beach FL 32168 *Web:* www.sevchamber.com	386-428-2449	423-3512	139
Southeastern Aluminum Products Inc 4925 Bulls Bay Hwy .... Jacksonville FL 32219 *TF:* 800-243-8200 ■ *Web:* www.southeasternaluminum.com	904-781-8200	224-8068	234
Southeastern Asset Management Inc 6410 Poplar Ave Ste 900 .... Memphis TN 38119 *TF:* 800-445-9469 ■ *Web:* www.southeasternasset.com	901-761-2474		401
Southeastern Baptist College 4229 Hwy 15 N .... Laurel MS 39440 *Web:* southeasternbaptist.edu	601-426-6346	426-6347	161
Southeastern Baptist Theological Seminary 120 S Wingate St .... Wake Forest NC 27587 *TF:* 800-284-6317 ■ *Web:* www.sebts.edu	919-761-2100		167-3
Southeastern Center for Contemporary Art 750 Marguerite Dr .... Winston-Salem NC 27106 *Web:* www.secca.org	336-725-1904		50-2
Southeastern College 6700 S Point Pkwy Ste 400 .... Jacksonville FL 32216 *Web:* www.sec.edu	904-448-9499		166
Southeastern Community College 1500 W Agency Rd .... West Burlington IA 52655 *Web:* www.scciowa.edu	319-208-5375	752-4957	162
Southeastern Community College PO Box 151 .... Whiteville NC 28472 *Web:* www.sccnc.edu	910-642-7141	642-1267	162
Southeastern Computer Consultants Inc 5166 Potomac Dr Ste 400 .... King George VA 22485 *Web:* www.teamscci.com	301-695-5311	695-6101	180
Southeastern Construction & Maintenance Company Inc 1150 Pebbledale Rd PO Box 1055 .... Mulberry FL 33860 *Web:* www.southeasternconst.com	863-428-1511	428-1110	189-14
Southeastern Container Inc 1250 Sand Hill Rd .... Enka NC 28728 *Web:* www.secontainer.com	828-350-7200	667-0122	98
Southeastern Correctional Institution 5900 B I S Rd .... Lancaster OH 43130 *TF:* 800-237-3454 ■ *Web:* ohio.gov	740-653-4324	653-0779	213
Southeastern Electric Co-opeartive Inc 1514 E Hwy 70 PO Box 1370 .... Durant OK 74702 *TF:* 866-924-1315 ■ *Web:* www.se-coop.com	580-924-2170		245
Southeastern Electric Cooperative Inc 501 S Broadway .... Marion SD 57043 *TF:* 800-333-2859 ■ *Web:* www.southeasternelectric.com	605-648-3619	648-3778	245
Southeastern Electronic Assembly Services Inc 2531 Broad St .... Camden SC 29020 *Web:* www.seaselectronics.com	803-425-4258		253
Southeastern Equipment Company Inc 10874 E Pike Rd .... Cambridge OH 43725 *TF:* 800-798-5438 ■ *Web:* www.southeasternequip.com	740-432-6303	432-3303	358
Southeastern Freight Lines Inc 420 Davega Rd .... Lexington SC 29073 *TF:* 800-637-7335 ■ *Web:* www.sefl.com	803-794-7300	939-3462	780
Southeastern Home Care 875 E Main St .... Barnesville OH 43713 *TF:* 800-320-9355 ■ *Web:* www.southeasternhomecare.com	740-425-5117		363
Southeastern Home Oxygen Service Inc 1112 15th St .... Columbus GA 31901 *Web:* www.seho.us	706-327-8993	327-0254	352
Southeastern Illinois College 3575 College Rd .... Harrisburg IL 62946 *TF:* 866-338-2742 ■ *Web:* www.sic.edu	618-252-5400	252-3062	162
SouthEastern Illinois Electric Cooperative Inc 100 Cooperative Way PO Box 1001 .... Carrier Mills IL 62917 *TF:* 800-833-2611 ■ *Web:* www.seiec.com	618-273-2611	273-3886	245
Southeastern Indiana Rural Electric Membership Corp 712 S Buckeye St .... Osgood IN 47037 *TF:* 800-737-4111 ■ *Web:* www.seiremc.com	812-689-4111	689-6987	245
Southeastern Industrial Inc 4977 Steele Village Rd .... Rock Hill SC 29730 *Web:* www.siincorp.com	803-327-3171		454
Southeastern Institute 5250 77 Center Dr Ste 100 .... Charlotte NC 28217 *TF:* 800-420-4263 ■ *Web:* www.southeasterninstitute.edu	704-527-4979	527-3104	167-3
Southeastern Louisiana University 500 Western Ave .... Hammond LA 70402 *TF:* 800-222-7358 ■ *Web:* www.southeastern.edu	985-549-2062	549-5632	166
Southeastern Metal Products LLC 1420 Metals Dr .... Charlotte NC 28206 *Web:* sempllc.com	704-596-4017	596-3844	697
Southeastern Metals Manufacturing Company Inc 11801 Industry Dr .... Jacksonville FL 32218 *TF:* 800-874-0335 ■ *Web:* www.semetals.com	904-757-4200		234
Southeastern Ohio Regional Medical Ctr 1341 Clark St .... Cambridge OH 43725 *Web:* www.seormc.org	740-439-8000		374-3
Southeastern Oklahoma State University 1405 N Fourth St .... Durant OK 74701 *TF:* 800-435-1327 ■ *Web:* www.se.edu	580-745-2000	745-7502	166
Southeastern Paperboard Inc 100 S Harris Rd .... Piedmont SC 29673 *TF:* 800-229-7372 ■ *Web:* www.southeasternpaperboard.com	864-277-7353		554
Southeastern Pennsylvania Transportation Authority (SEPTA) 1234 Market St .... Philadelphia PA 19107 *TF:* 877-737-8248 ■ *Web:* www.septa.org	215-580-7800		468
Southeastern Plastics Corp 15 Home News Row .... New Brunswick NJ 08901 *Web:* www.sigmaplasticsgroup.com	732-846-8500		596
Southeastern Printing Company Inc 3601 SE Dixie Hwy .... Stuart FL 34997 *Web:* www.seprint.com	772-287-2141		781
Southeastern Public Library System of Oklahoma (SEPLSO) 401 N 2nd St .... McAlester OK 74501 **Fax Area Code:* 866 ■ *TF:* 800-562-9520 ■ *Web:* oklibrary.net	918-426-0456	569-8188*	434-3
Southeastern Regional Medical Ctr 300 W 27th St .... Lumberton NC 28358 *Web:* www.srmc.org	910-671-5000	671-5200	374-3
Southeastern Stages Inc 260 University Ave SW .... Atlanta GA 30315 *Web:* www.southeasternstages.com	404-591-2780	591-2745	108
Southeastern Technical Institute 250 Foundry St .... South Easton MA 02375 *Web:* www.stitech.edu	508-230-1297		167-3
Southeastern University 1000 Longfellow Blvd .... Lakeland FL 33801 *TF:* 800-500-8760 ■ *Web:* www.seu.edu	863-667-5000	667-5200	166
Southeastern Wholesale Tire Co 4721 Trademark Dr .... Raleigh NC 27610 **Fax Area Code:* 919 ■ *TF:* 800-849-9215 ■ *Web:* www.southeasterntireonline.com	800-849-9215	861-4357*	755
Southern Accent 839 College St .... Toronto ON M6H1A1 *Web:* www.southernaccent.com	416-901-3211		671
Southern Adirondack Library System 22 Whitney Pl .... Saratoga Springs NY 12866 *Web:* www.sals.edu	518-584-7300	587-5589	434-3
Southern Adventist University 4881 Taylor Cir .... Collegedale TN 37315 *TF:* 800-768-8437 ■ *Web:* www.southern.edu	423-236-2000	236-1000	166
Southern Air Inc 2655 Lakeside Dr .... Lynchburg VA 24501 *TF:* 800-743-1214 ■ *Web:* www.southern-air.com	434-385-6200	385-9081	189-10
Southern Alberta Institute of Technology 1301 16th Ave NW .... Calgary AB T2M0L4 *TF:* 877-284-7248 ■ *Web:* www.sait.ca	403-284-7248	284-7112	167-3
Southern Alloy Corp 36280 US Hwy 280 .... Sylacauga AL 35150 *Web:* www.southernalloy.com	256-245-5237	245-4992	307
Southern Arizona Veterans Healthcare System 3601 S Sixth Ave .... Tucson AZ 85723 *TF:* 800-470-8262 ■ *Web:* tucson.va.gov	520-792-1450		374-8
Southern Arkansas University 100 E University St .... Magnolia AR 71753 *TF:* 800-332-7286 ■ *Web:* web.saumag.edu	870-235-4050	235-5005	166
Southern Association of Colleges & Schools 1866 Southern Ln .... Decatur GA 30033 *Web:* www.sacs.org	404-679-4500	679-4558	49-5
Southern Audio Services 14763 Florida Blvd .... Baton Rouge LA 70819 **Fax Area Code:* 225 ■ *TF:* 800-843-8823 ■ *Web:* www.bazooka.com	888-651-1203	272-9844*	52
Southern Avionics Co 5055 Belmont St .... Beaumont TX 77707 *Web:* www.southernavionics.com	409-842-1717	842-2987	529
Southern Banc Company Inc 221 S Sixth St .... Gadsden AL 35901 *OTC: SRNN* ■ *Web:* sobanco.com	256-543-3860		360-2
Southern Baptist Convention (SBC) 901 Commerce St .... Nashville TN 37203 *TF:* 866-722-5433 ■ *Web:* www.sbc.net	615-244-2355		48-20
Southern Baptist Theological Seminary 2825 Lexington Rd .... Louisville KY 40280 **Fax Area Code:* 502 ■ *TF:* 800-626-5525 ■ *Web:* www.sbts.edu	800-626-5525	897-4723*	167-3
Southern Beverage Company Inc 1939 Davis Johnson Dr .... Richland MS 39218 *Web:* www.southernbeverage.com	601-933-6900		81-1
Southern Biotechnology Associates Inc 160A Oxmoor Blvd .... Birmingham AL 35209 *TF:* 800-722-2255 ■ *Web:* www.southernbiotech.com	205-945-1774	945-8768	231
Southern Bleacher Company Inc 801 Fifth St .... Graham TX 76450 *TF:* 800-433-0912 ■ *Web:* www.southernbleacher.com	940-549-0733		106
Southern Bowl 1010 US Hwy 31 S .... Greenwood IN 46143 *TF:* 888-960-9653 ■ *Web:* www.royalpin.com	317-881-8686		99
Southern California Boiler Inc 5331 Business Dr .... Huntington Beach CA 92649 *TF:* 800-775-2645 ■ *Web:* www.californiaboiler.com	714-891-0701		187
Southern California Earthquake Ctr 3651 Trousdale Pkwy Ste 169 .... Los Angeles CA 90089 *Web:* www.scec.org	213-740-5843	740-0011	668
Southern California Gas Co 555 W Fifth St .... Los Angeles CA 90013 **Fax Area Code:* 213 ■ *TF:* 800-427-2200 ■ *Web:* www.socalgas.com	909-305-8261	244-8293*	787
Southern California Grading Inc 16291 Construction Cir E Ste A .... Irvine CA 92606 *Web:* www.socalgrading.com	949-551-6655	551-4237	189-5
Southern California Institute of Architecture 960 E Third St .... Los Angeles CA 90013 *Web:* sciarc.edu	213-613-2200	613-2260	166
Southern California Public Power Authority (SCPPA) 225 S Lake Ave Ste 1250 .... Pasadena CA 91101 *Web:* www.scppa.org	626-793-9364	793-9461	787
Southern California Public Radio 474 S Raymond Ave .... Pasadena CA 91105 *Web:* www.scpr.org	626-583-5100	583-5101	645
Southern California Regional Rail Authority 700 S Flower St Ste 2600 .... Los Angeles CA 90017 *TF:* 800-371-5465 ■ *Web:* www.metrolinktrains.com	213-452-0200		468
Southern California Seminary 2075 E Madison Ave .... El Cajon CA 92019 *TF:* 888-389-7244 ■ *Web:* www.socalsem.edu	888-389-7244		166
Southern California Trophy Co (SCTC) 2515 S Broadway .... Los Angeles CA 90007 *Web:* www.socaltrophy.com	213-746-8046	746-9180	45
Southern Carbide Specialists Inc 901 N Highland St .... Quitman GA 31643 *TF:* 800-343-1573 ■ *Web:* www.socarb.com	229-263-8927	263-9268	351
Southern Care Lawn & Landscape Inc 289 N Price Rd .... Sugar Hill GA 30518	678-248-5410		776
Southern Careers Institute 238 SW Military Dr Ste 101 .... San Antonio TX 78221 *Web:* www.scitexas.edu	210-802-2230		167-3

Name / Address	City	State	ZIP	Phone	Fax	Class
Southern Cellulose Products Inc 105 W 45th St	Chattanooga	TN	37410	423-821-1561		638
Southern Chautauqua Federal Credit Union 168 E Fairmount Ave *Web:* 665-7000.com	Lakewood	NY	14750	716-665-7000		219
Southern Chester County Chamber of Commerce 217 W State St *Web:* www.scccc.com	Kennett Square	PA	19348	610-444-0774	444-5105	139
Southern Co 30 Ivan Allen Jr Blvd NW *TF:* 800-754-9452 ■ *Web:* www.southerncompany.com	Atlanta	GA	30308	404-506-5000	506-3076	787
Southern Coastal Cable 2101 S Fraser St *Web:* www.southerncoastalcable.com	Georgetown	SC	29440	843-546-2200		116
Southern Columbiana County Regional Chamber of Commerce 529 Market St PO Box 94 *TF:* 800-804-0468 ■ *Web:* www.sccregionalchamber.org	East Liverpool	OH	43920	330-385-0845	385-0581	139
Southern Communications Services Inc 5555 Glenridge Connector Ste 500 *TF:* 800-818-5462 ■ *Web:* southernlinc.com	Atlanta	GA	30342	800-818-5462		736
Southern Company Inc 3101 Carrier St *TF:* 800-264-7626 ■ *Web:* www.socomemphis.com	Memphis	TN	38116	901-345-2531		537
Southern Company of NLR Inc, The 1201 N Cypress St *TF:* 800-482-5493 ■ *Web:* www.thesoco.com	North Little Rock	AR	72114	501-376-6333		791
Southern Components Inc 7360 Julie Frances Dr *TF:* 800-256-2144 ■ *Web:* www.socomp.com	Shreveport	LA	71129	318-687-3330		817
Southern Concrete Products Inc 380 Pierce Rd *Web:* www.southernconcrete.com	Lexington	TN	38351	731-968-8394		539
Southern Connecticut Gas (SCG) 60 Marsh Hill Rd *TF:* 866-268-2887 ■ *Web:* www.soconngas.com	Orange	CT	06477	866-268-2887		787
Southern Connecticut State University 501 Crescent St *TF:* 888-500-7278 ■ *Web:* www.southernct.edu	New Haven	CT	06515	203-392-5200	392-5727	166
Southern Container Ltd 10410 Papalote St Ste 130 *Web:* www.southerncontainer.com	Houston	TX	77041	713-466-5661	466-4223	100
Southern Controls Inc 3511 Wetumpka Hwy *TF:* 800-392-5770 ■ *Web:* www.southerncontrols.com	Montgomery	AL	36110	800-392-5770		246
Southern Copper & Supply Company Inc 875 Yeager Pkwy *TF:* 800-289-2728 ■ *Web:* southerncopper.com	Pelham	AL	35124	205-664-9440		492
Southern Correctional Institution 272 Glen Rd *Web:* www.ncdps.gov	Troy	NC	27371	910-572-3784		213
Southern Crescent Technical College 501 Varsity Dr *TF:* 877-897-0006 ■ *Web:* www.sctech.edu	Griffin	GA	30223	770-228-7348		167-3
Southern Cross Corp 3175 Corners N Ct **Fax Area Code:* 770 ■ *TF:* 800-241-5057 ■ *Web:* www.southerncrossinc.com	Peachtree Corners	GA	30071	800-241-5057	368-8014*	472
Southern Data Systems Inc 1245 Land O Lakes Dr *TF:* 888-425-6151 ■ *Web:* www.southern-data.com	Roswell	GA	30075	770-993-7103		225
Southern Development Co 8132 Old Federal Rd *TF:* 800-499-3034 ■ *Web:* sdcinc.org	Montgomery	AL	36117	334-244-1801	244-1421	648
Southern District of West Virginia 300 Virginia St E Ste 2400 *Web:* www.wvsd.uscourts.gov	Charleston	WV	25301	304-347-3000		341-3
Southern Door & Plywood Co 3686 Moreland Ave *TF:* 800-227-4086 ■ *Web:* www.southerndoorply.com	Conley	GA	30288	404-361-7800	366-6366	499
Southern Duchess News 84 E Main St *Web:* sdutchessnews.com	Wappingers Falls	NY	12590	845-297-3723		532-4
Southern Early Childhood Assn (SECA) 1123 S University Ave Ste 255 *TF:* 800-305-7322 ■ *Web:* www.southernearlychildhood.org	Little Rock	AR	72204	800-305-7322		49-19
Southern Electrical Equipment Company Inc 4045 Hargrove Ave *Web:* www.seecoswitch.com	Charlotte	NC	28208	704-392-1396		729
Southern Environmental Inc 6690 W Nine Mile Rd *Web:* www.southernenvironmental.com	Pensacola	FL	32526	850-944-4475	944-8270	202
Southern Environmental Law Ctr 201 W Main St Ste 14 *Web:* www.southernenvironment.org	Charlottesville	VA	22902	434-977-4090		428
Southern Equine Services LLC 1258 Banks Mill Rd *Web:* southernequineservice.com	Aiken	SC	29803	803-644-1544		794
Southern Eye Bank 2701 Kingman St Ste 200 *Web:* southerneyebank.org	Metairie	LA	70006	504-891-3937	891-2401	269
Southern Fabricators Inc 8188 Hwy 74 W *TF:* 866-930-0236 ■ *Web:* www.southernfabricators.net	Polkton	NC	28135	704-272-7615	272-7806	697
Southern Farm Bureau Casualty Insurance Co 1800 E County Line Rd *Web:* w3.sfbcic.com	Ridgeland	MS	39157	601-957-7777		391-4
Southern Farm Bureau Life Insurance Co PO Box 78 *TF:* 800-457-9611 ■ *Web:* www.sfbli.com	Jackson	MS	39205	601-981-7422		391-2
Southern Festival of Books Humanities Tennessee 807 Main St *Web:* humanitiestennessee.org	Nashville	TN	37201	615-770-0006	770-0007	281
Southern Filter Media LLC 2401 Bachman St PO Box 2170 *Web:* www.southernfiltermedia.com	Hixson	TN	37343	423-698-8988	624-0274	820
Southern Financial Exchange 1340 Poydras St Ste 2010 *Web:* www.sfe.org	New Orleans	LA	70112	504-525-6779		507
Southern Financial Insurance 105 Public Sq *TF:* 800-736-9676 ■ *Web:* southernfinancialinsurance.com	Scottsville	KY	42164	800-736-9676		390
Southern Finishing 801 E Church St *Web:* www.southernfinishing.com	Martinsville	VA	24112	276-632-4901		321
Southern First Bancshares Inc 100 Verdae Blvd Ste 100 *TF:* 877-679-9646 ■ *Web:* www.southernfirst.com	Greenville	SC	29607	864-679-9000		70
Southern Floral Co 1313 W 20th St *TF:* 800-833-0142 ■ *Web:* www.sofloco.com	Houston	TX	77008	713-880-1300	880-4937	293
Southern Folger Detention Equipment Co 4634 S Presa St *TF:* 888-745-0530 ■ *Web:* www.southernfolger.com	San Antonio	TX	78223	210-533-1231	533-2211	692
Southern Foods Inc 3500 Old Battleground Rd *TF:* 800-642-3768 ■ *Web:* www.southernfoods.com	Greensboro	NC	27410	800-642-3768		297-9
Southern Forest Products Assn (SFPA) 6660 Riverside Dr Ste 212 *Web:* www.sfpa.org	Metairie	LA	70003	504-443-4464		48-2
Southern FS Inc 2002 E Main St PO Box 728 *TF:* 800-492-7684 ■ *Web:* www.southernfs.com	Marion	IL	62959	618-993-2833	997-2526	276
Southern Fulfillment Services LLC 1650 90th Ave *TF:* 800-891-2120 ■ *Web:* www.southernfulfillment.com	Vero Beach	FL	32966	772-226-3500		459
Southern Furniture Company of Conover Inc 2220 US Hwy 70 SE Ste 421 *Web:* www.southernstylefinefurniture.com	Conover	NC	28613	828-464-0311		321
Southern Gardens Citrus 1820 Country Rd 833 *Web:* www.ussugar.com	Clewiston	FL	33440	863-983-3030		315-2
Southern Georgia Bay Chamber of Commerce 208 King St *Web:* southerngeorgianbay.ca	Midland	ON	L4R3L9	705-526-7884	526-1744	137
Southern Glove Manufacturing Company Inc 749 AC Little Dr *TF:* 800-222-1113 ■ *Web:* www.southernglove.com	Newton	NC	28658	828-464-4884	464-7968	155-8
Southern Graphics Systems 626 W Main St Ste 500 *Web:* www.sgsintl.com	Louisville	KY	40202	502-637-5443		781
Southern Grouts & Mortars Inc 1502 SW Second Pl **Fax Area Code:* 954 ■ *TF:* 800-641-9247 ■ *Web:* www.sgm.cc	Pompano Beach	FL	33069	800-641-9247	943-2402*	3
Southern Healthcare Agency Inc PO Box 320999 *TF:* 800-880-2772 ■ *Web:* www.southernhealthcare.com	Flowood	MS	39232	601-933-0037		260
Southern Heat Exchanger Corp 6100 Old Montgomery Hwy *Web:* www.sheco.com	Tuscaloosa	AL	35405	205-345-5335		488
Southern Hens Inc 329 Moselle-Seminary Rd *Web:* www.southernhensmississippi.com	Moselle	MS	39459	601-582-2262		619
Southern Hydraulic Cylinder Inc 3020 Lee Hwy **Fax Area Code:* 423 ■ *TF:* 800-737-8988 ■ *Web:* www.southhydcyl.com	Athens	TN	37303	800-737-8988	744-8974*	223
Southern Illinois Electric Co-op 7420 US Hwy 51 S *TF:* 800-762-1400 ■ *Web:* siec.coop	Dongola	IL	62926	618-827-3555		245
Southern Illinois University *Edwardsville* 1 Hairpin Dr *TF:* 888-328-5168 ■ *Web:* www.siue.edu	Edwardsville	IL	62026	618-650-5555	650-5013	166
Southern Illinois University Carbondale 1263 Lincoln Dr *Web:* siu.edu	Carbondale	IL	62901	618-453-2121	453-4562	166
Southern Illinois University Carbondale Morris Library 605 Agriculture Dr MC 6632 *Web:* www.lib.siu.edu	Carbondale	IL	62901	618-453-2522	453-3440	434-6
Southern Illinois University Press 1915 University Press Dr **Fax Area Code:* 800 ■ *Web:* www.siupress.com	Carbondale	IL	62901	618-453-2281	621-8476*	637-2
Southern Illinois University School of Law 1209 W Chautauqua Rd *TF:* 800-739-9187 ■ *Web:* www.law.siu.edu	Carbondale	IL	62901	618-453-8858	453-8921	167-1
Southern Illinois University School of Medicine Medical Library (SIU) 801 N Rutledge St *TF:* 800-342-5748 ■ *Web:* www.siumed.edu	Springfield	IL	62702	217-545-2122		434-1
Southern Illinoisan 710 N Illinois Ave *TF:* 800-228-0429 ■ *Web:* thesouthern.com	Carbondale	IL	62901	618-529-5454	457-2935	532-2
Southern Imperial Inc 1400 Eddy Ave *TF:* 800-747-4665 ■ *Web:* www.southernimperial.com	Rockford	IL	61103	815-877-7041		286
Southern Implants Inc 5 Holland Bldg 209 *Web:* southernimplants.us	Irvine	CA	92618	949-273-8505		228
Southern Indiana Rehabilitation Hospital 3104 Blackiston Blvd *TF:* 800-737-7090 ■ *Web:* sirh.org	New Albany	IN	47150	812-941-8300		374-6
Southern Indiana Rural Electric Co-opeartive Inc 1776 Tenth St PO Box 219 *TF:* 800-323-2316 ■ *Web:* www.sinpwr.com	Tell City	IN	47586	812-547-2316	547-6853	245
Southern Industrial Constructors Inc 6101 Triangle Dr *TF:* 800-851-0868 ■ *Web:* www.southernindustrial.com	Raleigh	NC	27617	919-782-4600	782-2935	189-10
Southern Insurance Services Inc 244 Pulaski St PO Box 825 *TF:* 800-633-6599 ■ *Web:* thesoutherninsurancegroup.com	Lawrenceburg	TN	38464	931-762-0880	762-1500	390
Southern Intermodal Xpress Inc 620 Bay Bridge Rd *Web:* sixllc.net	Mobile	AL	36610	251-438-2749	438-4749	780
Southern Ionics Inc 201 Commerce St **Fax Area Code:* 662 ■ *TF:* 800-953-3585 ■ *Web:* www.southernionics.com	West Point	MS	39773	912-647-0301	495-2590*	143
Southern Iowa Electric Co-opeartive Inc 22458 Hwy 2 PO Box 70 *TF:* 800-607-2027 ■ *Web:* www.sie.coop	Bloomfield	IA	52537	641-664-2277	664-3502	245
Southern Iron Works Inc 6600 Electronic Dr	Springfield	VA	22151	703-354-5500		480
Southern Jersey Family Medical Centers Inc 860 S White Horse Pke *Web:* www.sjfmc.org	Hammonton	NJ	08037	609-567-0200	567-1951	374-3

				Phone	Fax	Class
Southern Kentucky Book Fest 2355 Nashville Rd Ste 11067 *Web:* sokybookfest.org	Bowling Green	KY	42101	270-745-4502		281
Southern Kentucky Rehabilitation Hospital 1300 Campbell Ln *TF:* 800-989-5775 ■ *Web:* www.vibrahealthcare.com	Bowling Green	KY	42104	270-782-6900		374-6
Southern Kitchen 1716 Sixth Ave *Web:* www.southernkitchen-tacoma.com	Tacoma	WA	98405	253-627-4282		671
Southern Landscape Professionals Inc 8625 Mt Pleasant Church Rd *Web:* www.southernlandscapepros.com	Willow Spring	NC	27592	919-552-1156	552-5944	192
Southern Leather Co 677 Phelan Ave **Fax Area Code:* 901 ■ *TF:* 800-844-6767 ■ *Web:* www.southernleatherco.com	Memphis	TN	38126	800-844-6767	946-1059*	76
Southern Lehigh School District 5775 Main St *Web:* www.slsd.org	Center Valley	PA	18034	610-282-3121	282-0193	685
Southern Lights 2415 Lawndale Dr *Web:* www.southernlightsbistro.com	Greensboro	NC	27408	336-379-9414		671
Southern Living Magazine 2100 Lakeshore Dr **Fax Area Code:* 205 ■ *TF:* 866-772-7083 ■ *Web:* www.southernliving.com	Birmingham	AL	35209	866-772-7083	445-6700*	457-22
Southern Machine & Fabrication Company Inc 18 Commerce Dr *Web:* www.smfco.org	Cartersville	GA	30120	770-386-0194	386-6881	454
Southern Machinery Company Inc (SMC) 3735 Vulcan Dr *Web:* somachinery.com	Nashville	TN	37211	615-832-3365	834-9016	385
Southern Maid Donut Flour Co 3615 Cavalier Dr *Web:* www.southernmaiddonuts.com	Garland	TX	75042	972-272-6425	276-3549	68
Southern Maine Community College (SMCC) 2 Fort Rd *TF:* 877-282-2182 ■ *Web:* www.smccme.edu	South Portland	ME	04106	207-741-5500	741-5760	800
Southern Maryland Hospital Ctr 7503 Surratts Rd *TF:* 800-862-2166 ■ *Web:* www.medstarsouthernmaryland.org	Clinton	MD	20735	301-868-8000		374-3
Southern Maryland Oil Company Inc (SMO) 109 N Maple Ave *TF:* 888-222-3720 ■ *Web:* smoenergy.com	La Plata	MD	20646	888-222-3720		579
Southern Metals Company Inc (SMC) 2200 Donald Ross Rd *Web:* www.southernmetalscompany.com	Charlotte	NC	28208	704-394-3161	394-3163	686
Southern Methodist University 6425 Boaz Ln *TF:* 800-323-0672 ■ *Web:* www.smu.edu	Dallas	TX	75205	214-768-2033	768-0202	166
Southern Michigan Bank & Trust 51 W Pearl St PO Box 309 *TF:* 800-379-7628 ■ *Web:* www.smb-t.com	Coldwater	MI	49036	517-279-5500		70
Southern Midcoast Maine Chamber 8 Venture Ave PO Box 33 *Web:* www.midcoastmaine.com	Brunswick	ME	04011	207-725-8797		139
Southern Minnesota Beet Sugar Co-op 83550 CR 21 PO Box 500 *Web:* www.smbsc.com	Renville	MN	56284	320-329-8305	329-3252	296-38
Southern Minnesota Municipal Power Agency 500 First Ave SW *Web:* smmpa.com	Rochester	MN	55902	507-285-0478	292-6414	245
Southern Missouri Bancorp Inc 2991 Oak Grove Rd *NASDAQ: SMBC* ■ *TF:* 855-452-7272 ■ *Web:* www.bankwithsouthern.com	Poplar Bluff	MO	63901	573-778-1800		360-2
Southern Motion Inc 195 Henry Southern Dr *Web:* www.southernmotion.com	Pontotoc	MS	38863	662-488-4007		319-2
Southern Motor Carriers Rate Conference Inc 500 Westpark Dr *TF:* 800-845-8090 ■ *Web:* www.smc3.com	Peachtree City	GA	30269	770-486-5800		478
Southern Motorcycle Supply Inc 3670 Ruffin Rd *Web:* www.southernms.com	San Diego	CA	92123	858-560-5005	560-4626	61
Southern Multifoods Inc 101 E Cherokee St *Web:* www.smi-tex.com	Jacksonville	TX	75766	903-586-1524		670
Southern Museum of Flight 4343 73rd St N *Web:* www.southernmuseumofflight.org	Birmingham	AL	35206	205-833-8226	836-2439	520
Southern Nazarene University 6729 NW 39th Expy *TF:* 800-648-9899 ■ *Web:* www.snu.edu	Bethany	OK	73008	405-789-6400	491-6320	166
Southern Nebraska Register PO Box 80328 *Web:* www.lincolndiocese.org	Lincoln	NE	68501	402-488-0090	488-3569	532-2
Southern New Hampshire Medical Ctr 8 Prospect St PO Box 2014 *Web:* www.snhhealth.org	Nashua	NH	03061	603-577-2000		374-3
Southern New Hampshire University 2500 N River Rd **Fax Area Code:* 802 ■ *TF:* 800-668-1249 ■ *Web:* www.snhu.edu	Manchester	NH	03106	603-668-2211	655-0236*	166
Southern New Mexico Correctional Facility 1983 Joe R Silva Blvd *Web:* cd.nm.gov	Las Cruces	NM	88004	575-523-3200		213
Southern Newspapers Inc (SNI) 5701 Woodway Dr *Web:* sninews.com	Houston	TX	77057	713-266-5481	266-1847	637-8
Southern Ocean County Chamber of Commerce 265 W Ninth St *TF:* 800-292-6372 ■ *Web:* visitlbiregion.com	Ship Bottom	NJ	08008	609-494-7211	494-5807	139
Southern Ohio Correctional Facility 1724 St Rt 728 PO Box 45699 *Web:* drc.ohio.gov	Lucasville	OH	45699	740-259-5544	259-2882	213
Southern Ohio Medical Ctr (SOMC) 1805 27th St *Web:* www.somc.org	Portsmouth	OH	45662	740-356-5000		374-3
Southern Oklahoma Technology Ctr 2610 Sam Noble Pkwy *TF:* 800-989-4599 ■ *Web:* www.sotech.edu	Ardmore	OK	73401	580-223-2070		167-3
Southern Oregon University Britt Hall 1250 Siskiyou Blvd *TF:* 800-482-7672 ■ *Web:* www.sou.edu	Ashland	OR	97520	541-552-6411	552-8403	166
Southern Oregon University Hannon Library 1250 Siskiyou Blvd *Web:* hanlib.sou.edu	Ashland	OR	97520	541-552-6442		434-6
Southern Pan Services Co (SPS) 2385 Lithonia Industrial Blvd *Web:* www.southernpan.com	Lithonia	GA	30058	678-301-2400		780
Southern Petroleum Lab Inc 8850 Interchange Dr **Fax Area Code:* 225 ■ *TF:* 877-775-5227 ■ *Web:* www.spl-inc.com	Houston	TX	77054	713-660-0901	219-3309*	743
Southern Pine Electric Co-op 2134 S Blvd *Web:* www.billing.southernpine.org	Brewton	AL	36426	251-867-5415		245
Southern Pine Electric Power Assn 110 Risher St PO Box 60 *TF:* 800-231-5240 ■ *Web:* www.southernpine.coop	Taylorsville	MS	39168	601-785-6511	785-4980	245
Southern Pine Timber Products (SPTP) 6910 Lithia Pinecrest Rd *TF:* 800-229-7463 ■ *Web:* southernpinetimber.co	Lithia	FL	33547	813-681-7600	681-7601	191-3
Southern Pines Nursing Ctr 6140 Congress St *Web:* southernpineshealthcare.com	New Port Richey	FL	34653	727-842-8402	841-8060	450
Southern Precision Spring Company Inc 2200 Old Steele Creek Rd *Web:* www.spspring.com	Charlotte	NC	28208	704-392-4393		492
Southern Prestige Industries Inc 113 Hatfield Rd *Web:* www.southernprestige.com	Statesville	NC	28625	704-872-9524		454
Southern Public Power District (SPPD) 4550 W Husker Hwy PO Box 1687 *TF:* 800-652-2013 ■ *Web:* southernpd.com	Grand Island	NE	68803	308-384-2350	384-5018	245
Southern Pump & Filter Inc 1682 N Shelby Oaks Dr Ste 4 *TF:* 800-490-3290 ■ *Web:* www.southernfountains.com	Memphis	TN	38134	901-493-4727		385
Southern Pump & Tank Co 4800 N Graham St *TF:* 800-477-2826 ■ *Web:* spatco.com	Charlotte	NC	28269	704-596-4373		385
Southern Railway of British Columbia Ltd 2102 River Dr *Web:* www.sryraillink.com	New Westminster	BC	V3M6S3	604-521-1966		650
Southern Refrigeration Corp 3140 Shenandoah Ave NW PO Box 12646 *TF:* 800-763-4433 ■ *Web:* srcusa.com	Roanoke	VA	24027	540-342-3493	343-2163	665
Southern Regional High School District Board of Education 600 N Main St *Web:* www.srsd.net	Manahawkin	NJ	08050	609-597-9481	978-0298	685
Southern Regional Medical Ctr 11 Upper Riverdale Rd SW *Web:* www.southernregional.org	Riverdale	GA	30274	770-991-8000		374-3
Southern Regional Research Ctr (SRRC) 1100 Robert E Lee Blvd **Fax Area Code:* 504 ■ *Web:* www.ars.usda.gov	New Orleans	LA	70124	706-546-3527	286-4419*	668
Southern Reprographics Inc 901 W 7th St *Web:* www.southernrepro.com	Little Rock	AR	72201	501-372-4011		627
Southern Research 2000 Ninth Ave S *TF:* 800-967-6774 ■ *Web:* southernresearch.org	Birmingham	AL	35205	205-581-2000	581-2726	668
Southern Research Company Inc 2850 Centenary Blvd *TF:* 888-772-6952 ■ *Web:* www.southernresearchinc.com	Shreveport	LA	71104	318-227-9700	424-1801	400
Southern Research Station 200 WT Weaver Blvd *Web:* www.srs.fs.usda.gov	Asheville	NC	28804	828-257-4832	257-4840	668
Southern Rhode Island Chamber of Commerce 230 Old Tower Hill Rd *Web:* www.srichamber.com	Wakefield	RI	02879	401-783-2801	789-3120	139
Southern Rubber Company Inc 2209 Patterson St *TF:* 800-333-7325 ■ *Web:* southernrubber.com	Greensboro	NC	27407	336-299-2456		326
Southern School of Beauty 140 W Main St *Web:* southernschoolbeauty.com	Durant	OK	74701	580-924-1049	924-4841	685
Southern Software Inc 150 Perry Dr *TF:* 800-842-8190 ■ *Web:* www.southernsoftware.com	Southern Pines	NC	28387	910-695-0005	695-0251	177
Southern Solutions Group Inc 4305 Poplar Creek Ln *TF:* 866-581-6055 ■ *Web:* www.ssg-nc.com	High Point	NC	27265	866-581-6055		463
Southern Spring & Stamping Inc 401 Sub Stn Rd *TF:* 800-450-5882 ■ *Web:* www.southernspring.com	Venice	FL	34285	941-488-2276	485-9156	718
Southern Stainless Equip Co 1400 Hopeman Pkwy *Web:* www.southernstainless.net	Waynesboro	VA	22980	540-943-8000		14
Southern Staircase Inc 6025 Shiloh Rd Ste E *TF:* 888-510-0342 ■ *Web:* artisticstairs-us.com	Alpharetta	GA	30005	770-888-7333		499
Southern Standard Cartons Inc 2415 Plantside Dr *Web:* thestandardgroup.com	Louisville	KY	40299	502-491-2760	491-2767	101
Southern Star 1300 Broad St *Web:* www.southernstarrestaurant.com	Chattanooga	TN	37402	423-267-8899		671
Southern State Community College 12681 US Rt 62 *TF:* 877-644-6562 ■ *Web:* www.sscc.edu	Sardinia	OH	45171	937-695-0307		162
Southern State Correctional Facility 4295 Rte 47 *Web:* www.njdoc.gov	Delmont	NJ	08314	856-785-1300		213
Southern States Chemical Co 1600 E President St *TF:* 888-337-8922 ■ *Web:* www.sschemical.com	Savannah	GA	31404	912-232-1101	232-1103	280
Southern States Co-opeartive Inc 6606 W Broad St *TF:* 866-372-8272 ■ *Web:* www.southernstates.com	Richmond	VA	23230	804-281-1000		276
Southern States LLC 30 Georgia Ave *TF:* 866-394-3661 ■ *Web:* www.southernstatesllc.com	Hampton	GA	30228	770-946-4562		767
Southern States Packaging Co PO Box 650 *TF:* 800-621-2051 ■ *Web:* www.sspc.biz	Spartanburg	SC	29304	800-621-2051		549

Name / Address	Phone	Fax	Class
Southern Systems Inc 4101 Viscount Ave Memphis TN 38118 *Web:* www.ssiconveyors.com	901-362-7340		207
Southern Tank & Manufacturing Inc 1501 Haynes Ave Owensboro KY 42303 *Web:* www.southerntank.net	270-684-2321		492
Southern Technical College 298 Havendale Blvd Auburndale FL 33823 *TF:* 877-347-5492 ■ *Web:* www.southerntech.edu	863-551-1112		166
Southern Theatres LLC 305 Baronne St Ste 900 New Orleans LA 70112 *Web:* www.thegrandtheatre.com	504-297-1133		748
Southern Tier Brewing Co 2072 Stoneman Cir Lakewood NY 14750 *Web:* www.stbcbeer.com	716-763-5479	763-5489	102
Southern Tile Distributors Inc 4590 Village Ave Norfolk VA 23502 *Web:* www.wmbird.com	757-855-8041		361
Southern Tioga School District 310 Morris St Blossburg PA 16912 *Web:* www.southerntioga.org	570-638-2183	638-3512	685
Southern Tire Mart LLC 1010 Hardy St Columbia MS 39429 *Web:* www.stmtires.com	601-424-3200		755
Southern Title Inc 2325 Manhattan Blvd Harvey LA 70058 *Web:* southerntitleonline.com	504-363-4634		653
Southern Union Conference Association of The Seventh Day Adventist Church 302 Research Dr Norcross GA 30092 *Web:* www.southernunion.com	770-408-1800		50-1
Southern Union State Community College *Opelika* 301 Lake Condy Rd Opelika AL 36801 *Web:* www.suscc.edu	334-745-6437	742-9418	162
Southern University & A & M College 156 Elton C Harrison Dr PO Box 9757 Baton Rouge LA 70813 *TF:* 800-256-1531 ■ *Web:* www.subr.edu	225-771-5180	771-4762	166
Southern University Law Ctr 2 Roosevelt Steptoe Dr Baton Rouge LA 70813 *TF:* 800-537-1135 ■ *Web:* www.sulc.edu	225-771-6297	771-2121	167-1
Southern University Museum of Art 801 Harding Blvd Baton Rouge LA 70807 *Web:* www.sus.edu	225-771-4500		520
Southern University Museum of Art 3050 Martin Luther King Jr Dr Shreveport LA 71107 *TF:* 800-458-1472 ■ *Web:* www.susla.edu	318-670-6000		520
Southern Utah University 351 W Center St Cedar City UT 84720 *Web:* www.suu.edu	435-586-7700	865-8223	166
Southern Utah Wilderness Alliance (SUWA) 425 East 100 South Salt Lake City UT 84111 *Web:* suwa.org	801-486-3161		48-13
Southern Ute Indian Tribe 356 Ouray Dr PO Box 737 Ignacio CO 81137 *Web:* www.southernute-nsn.gov	970-563-4401		50-2
Southern Vermont Cable Co PO Box 166 Bondville VT 05340 *TF:* 800-544-5931 ■ *Web:* www.svcable.net	800-544-5931		116
Southern Vermont College 982 Mansion Dr Bennington VT 05201 *TF:* 800-378-2782 ■ *Web:* svc.edu	802-442-5427	447-4695	166
Southern Virginia Regional Medical Ctr 727 N Main St Emporia VA 23847 *Web:* www.svrmc.com	434-348-4410		374-3
Southern Virginia University 1 University Hill Dr Buena Vista VA 24416 *TF:* 800-229-8420 ■ *Web:* www.svu.edu	540-261-8400	261-8559	166
Southern Wall Products Inc 1827 Fellowship Rd Tucker GA 30084 *Web:* www.ruco.com	770-621-3065		347
Southern Warehousing & Distribution Inc 3232 N Pan Am Expy San Antonio TX 78219 *TF:* 877-640-4058 ■ *Web:* www.southernwd.com	210-224-7771	226-9485	803-1
Southern Wayne County Chamber of Commerce 20904 Northline Rd Taylor MI 48180 *Web:* www.swcrc.com	734-284-6000	284-0198	139
Southern Weaving Co 1005 W Bramlett Rd Greenville SC 29611 *Web:* www.southernweaving.com	864-233-1635	240-9302	745-5
Southern Wesleyan University 907 Wesleyan Dr Central SC 29630 *TF:* 800-282-8798 ■ *Web:* www.swu.edu	864-644-5000		166
Southern West Virginia Community & Technical College *Logan* 2900 Dempsey Branch Rd Mount Gay WV 25637 *Web:* www.southernwv.edu	304-792-7098	792-7028	162
Southern West Virginia Convention & Visitors Bureau 1406 Harper Rd Beckley WV 25801 *TF:* 800-847-4898 ■ *Web:* visitwv.com	304-252-2244		206
Southern Wholesale Flooring Company Inc 955B Cobb Pl Blvd Kennesaw GA 30144 *Web:* www.swfloor.com	770-514-7110		362
Southern Wire 8045 Metro Rd Olive Branch MS 38654 **Fax Area Code:* 662 ■ *TF:* 800-238-0333 ■ *Web:* www.southernwire.com	800-238-0333	893-4732*	492
Southern Woodsmith Inc 20 Monroe Dr Pelham AL 35124 *Web:* www.southernwoodsmith.com	205-663-5299		499
Southern Yarn Dyers Inc 101 Conyers Industrial Dr Cartersville GA 30120 *Web:* www.southernyarn.com	770-382-3800		745-9
Southernmost Beach Resort 1319 Duval St Key West FL 33040 *TF:* 800-354-4455 ■ *Web:* www.southernmostbeachresort.com	305-296-6577		379
Southernmost Illinois Tourism Bureau PO Box 378 Anna IL 62906 *TF:* 800-248-4373 ■ *Web:* southernmostillinois.com	618-833-9928		206
SouthernSun Asset Management LLC 6000 Poplar Ste 220 Memphis TN 38103 *Web:* southernsunam.com	901-341-2700	341-2701	401
Southfield Chamber of Commerce 24300 Southfield Rd Ste 101 Southfield MI 48075 *Web:* www.southfieldchamber.com	248-557-6661	557-3931	139
Southfield Dodge Chrysler Jeep Ram 28100 Telegraph Rd Southfield MI 48034 *TF:* 888-714-1015 ■ *Web:* www.southfieldchryslerdodgejeepram.com	248-331-9937		57
Southfield Public Library 26300 Evergreen Rd Southfield MI 48076 *Web:* southfieldlibrary.org	248-796-4200		434-3
SouthFirst Bancshares Inc 126 N Norton Ave PO Box 167 Sylacauga AL 35150 *OTC: SZBI* ■ *TF:* 800-239-1492 ■ *Web:* www.southfirst.com	256-245-4365	245-6341	360-2
Southford Falls State Park Quaker Farms Rd Rt 188 Southbury CT 06488 *Web:* portal.ct.gov	203-264-5169		565
Southgate Coins 5032 S Virginia St Reno NV 89502 *Web:* www.southgatecoins.com	775-322-4455		45
Southgate Community School District 14600 Dix Toledo Rd Southgate MI 48195 *Web:* www.southgateschools.com	734-246-4600	283-6791	685
Southgroup & Financial Services Inc 795 Woodlands Pkwy Ste 101 Ridgeland MS 39157 *Web:* southgroup.net	601-914-3220		216
Southington Public Library 255 Main St Southington CT 06489 *Web:* www.southingtonlibrary.org	860-628-0947		434-3
Southlake Chamber of Commerce 1501 Corporate Circle Southlake TX 76092 *Web:* www.southlakechamber.com	817-481-8200	749-8202	139
Southlake Mall 1000 Southlake Mall Morrow GA 30260 *Web:* www.southlakemall.com	770-961-1050	961-1113	460
Southlake Regional Health Ctr 596 Davis Dr Newmarket ON L3Y2P9 *TF:* 800-445-1822 ■ *Web:* www.southlakeregional.org	905-895-4521	830-5972	374-2
Southland Box Co 4201 Fruitland Ave Vernon CA 90058 *Web:* www.southlandbox.com	323-583-2231	584-2095	548
South-Land Carbon Products Inc 321 Fleming Rd Birmingham AL 35217 **Fax Area Code:* 800 ■ *TF:* 800-476-7524 ■ *Web:* www.southlandcarboninc.com	205-841-8799	841-3092*	127
Southland Industries 7421 Orangewood Ave Garden Grove CA 92841 *Web:* www.southlandind.com	714-901-5800		189-10
Southland Log Homes 7521 Broad River Rd Irmo SC 29063 *Web:* www.southlandloghomes.com	803-407-4650		106
Southland Mall 1 Southland Mall Dr Hayward CA 94545 *Web:* www.southlandmall.com	510-782-3527		460
Southland Mall 20505 S Dixie Hwy Miami FL 33189 *Web:* www.mysouthlandmall.com	305-235-8880	235-7956	460
Southland National Insurance Corp 2200 Jack Warner Pky Ste 150 Tuscaloosa AL 35401 *TF:* 800-277-8762 ■ *Web:* www.southlandnational.com	205-345-7410		796
Southland Oil Co 5170 Galaxie Dr Jackson MS 39206 *Web:* petroleum-oil-wholesalers.cmac.ws	601-981-4151		580
Southland Printing Company Inc 213 Airport Dr Shreveport LA 71107 *TF:* 800-241-8662 ■ *Web:* www.southlandprinting.com	318-221-8662		627
Southland Printing Inc 1079 Majaun Rd Lexington KY 40511 *Web:* www.southlandprint.com	859-276-1965	225-3341	627
Southland Safety LLC 1409 Kilgore Dr Henderson TX 75652 *TF:* 866-723-3719 ■ *Web:* southlandsafety.com	903-657-8669		196
Southland Steel Fabricators Inc 251 Greensburg St Greensburg LA 70441 *TF:* 800-738-7734 ■ *Web:* www.southlandsteel.com	225-222-4141		480
Southland Title LLC 6710 Stewart Rd Ste 200 Galveston TX 77551 *Web:* www.southlandtitle.net	409-744-0727	744-3909	391-6
Southland Tube Inc 3525 Richard Arrington Blvd N Birmingham AL 35234 *TF:* 800-543-9024 ■ *Web:* www.southlandtube.com	205-251-1884	251-1553	490
Southmedic Inc 50 Alliance Blvd Barrie ON L4M5K3 *TF:* 800-463-7146 ■ *Web:* www.southmedic.com	705-726-9383		477
Southold Pharmacy Inc 53895 Main Rd Southold NY 11971 *Web:* southoldpharmacy.com	631-765-3434		237
Southpark Seafood Grill & Wine Bar 901 SW Salmon St Portland OR 97205 *Web:* southparkseafood.com	503-326-1300		671
Southpaw Asset Management LP 2 W Greenwich Office Pk Greenwich CT 06831 *Web:* www.southpawassetmanagement.com	203-862-6200		528
SouthPointe Pavilions 2910 Pine Lake Rd Ste Q Lincoln NE 68516 *Web:* www.southpointeshopping.com	402-421-2114	421-2191	460
Southport Antique Mall 2028 E Southport Rd Indianapolis IN 46227 *Web:* www.southportantiquemall.net	317-786-8246		460
Southport Correctional Facility 236 Bob Masia Dr PO Box 2000 Pine City NY 14871 *Web:* www.doccs.ny.gov	607-737-0850		213
Southport Veterinary Ctr 2131 Post Rd Fairfield CT 06824 *Web:* southportveterinarycenter.com	203-259-5295		794
Southridge LLC 90 Grove St Ridgefield CT 06877 *Web:* www.southridge.com	203-431-8300	431-8301	528
Southridge Mall 1111 E Army Post Rd Des Moines IA 50315 *Web:* www.shopsouthridgemall.com	515-287-3881		460
SouthShore Chamber of Commerce 137 Harbor Village Ln Apollo Beach FL 33572 *Web:* www.southshorechamberofcommerce.org	813-645-1366	645-2099	139
Southside 815 815 S Washington St Alexandria VA 22314 *Web:* www.southside815.com	703-836-6222		671
Southside Bancshares Inc 1201 S Beckham Ave Tyler TX 75701 *NASDAQ: SBSI* ■ *TF:* 877-639-3511 ■ *Web:* www.southside.com	903-531-7111		360-2
Southside Bistro 1320 Huffman Pk Dr Anchorage AK 99515 *Web:* www.southsidebistro.com	907-348-0088	348-0089	671
Southside Electric Co-opeartive Inc 2000 W Virgina Ave Crewe VA 23930 *TF:* 800-552-2118 ■ *Web:* www.sec.coop	434-645-7721	645-1147	245

Name / Address	Phone	Fax	Class
Southside Regional Medical Ctr 200 Medical Park Blvd .... Petersburg VA 23805 *Web:* www.srmconline.com	804-765-5000		374-3
Southside Virginia Community College 109 Campus Dr .... Alberta VA 23821 *TF:* 888-220-7822 ■ *Web:* www.southside.edu	434-949-1000	949-7863	162
Southview Acres Health Care Ctr 2000 Oakdale Ave........................ Saint Paul MN 55118 *Web:* www.southviewacres.com	651-554-9500		371
Southwark Metal Manufacturing Company Inc 2800 Red Lion Rd....................... Philadelphia PA 19114 *TF:* 800-523-1052 ■ *Web:* www.southwarkmetal.com	215-735-3401	735-0411	697
Southwell & Orourke PS 421 W Riverside Ste 960 .... Spokane WA 99201 *Web:* southwellorourke.com	509-624-0159		41
Southwest Acupuncture College 1622 Galisteo St........................... Santa Fe NM 87505 *Web:* www.acupuncturecollege.edu	505-888-8898		167-3
Southwest Airlines Air Cargo 2702 Love Field Dr.......................... Dallas TX 75235 *TF:* 800-533-1222 ■ *Web:* www.swacargo.com	800-533-1222		12
Southwest Airlines Co 2702 Love Field Dr PO Box 36611 .... Dallas TX 75235 *NYSE:* LUV ■ *TF:* 800-435-9792 ■ *Web:* www.southwest.com	214-792-4000		25
Southwest Arkansas Electric Co-op 2904 E Ninth St .... Texarkana AR 71854 *TF:* 888-265-2743 ■ *Web:* www.swrea.com	870-772-2743		245
Southwest Art Magazine 10901 W 120th Ave Ste 340................ Broomfield CO 80021 *TF:* 877-212-1938 ■ *Web:* www.southwestart.com	303-442-0427	449-0279	457-2
Southwest Baptist University 1600 University Ave .... Bolivar MO 65613 **Fax Area Code: 417* ■ *TF:* 800-526-5859 ■ *Web:* sbuniv.edu	800-526-5859	328-1808*	166
Southwest Behavioral Health Services Inc 3450 N Third St .... Phoenix AZ 85012 *Web:* www.sbhservices.org	602-265-8338		374-5
Southwest Binding & Laminating 109 Millwell Ct..................... Maryland Heights MO 63043 *TF:* 800-325-3628 ■ *Web:* www.swbindinglaminating.com	314-739-4400		86
Southwest Business Corp 9311 San Pedro Ave Ste 600 .... San Antonio TX 78216 *Web:* www.swbc.com	210-525-1241		390
SouthWest Capital Bank 622 Douglas Ave.......................... Las Vegas NM 87701 *TF:* 800-748-2406 ■ *Web:* www.southwestcapital.com	505-425-7565		70
Southwest Center Mall 3662 W Camp Wisdom Rd.................... Dallas TX 75237 *Web:* swcmall.com	972-296-1491	861-5798	460
Southwest Cheese Company LLC 1141 Curry County Rd Ste 4.................... Clovis NM 88101 *TF:* 800-336-2183 ■ *Web:* www.southwestcheese.com	575-742-9200		296-25
Southwest Conservation Corps 701 Camino Del Rio Ste 101 .... Durango CO 81301 *Web:* sccorps.org	970-403-1149		302
Southwest Copy Systems 4545 McLeod Rd NE..................... Albuquerque NM 87109 *Web:* www.southwestcopy.com	505-344-8211		627
Southwest Cyberport Inc 5021 Indian School Rd NE Ste 600.......... Albuquerque NM 87110 *Web:* www.swcp.com	505-232-7992	232-7975	224
Southwest Electric Co PO Box 82639 .... Oklahoma City OK 73148 *Web:* www.swelectric.com	405-869-1100		729
Southwest Fabrication LLC 22233 N 23rd Ave........................... Phoenix AZ 85027 *Web:* www.sw-fab.com	623-587-4648	492-0393	480
Southwest Florida International Airport 11000 Terminal Access Rd Ste 8671 .... Fort Myers FL 33913 *TF:* 800-359-6786 ■ *Web:* flylcpa.com	239-590-4800	590-4511	27
Southwest Forest Products Inc 2020 N Central Ave Ste 720 .... Phoenix AZ 85004 *Web:* www.southwestforestproducts.com	602-278-3493		200
Southwest Freight Inc 9005 Spikewood Dr .... Houston TX 77078 *Web:* www.southwestfreight.com	713-633-8889	633-1845	780
Southwest Freightlines 11991 Transpark Dr .... El Paso TX 79927 *TF:* 800-776-5799 ■ *Web:* www.swflines.com	915-860-8592	860-9606	780
Southwest Funding LP 13150 Coit Rd Ste 100......................... Dallas TX 75240 *TF:* 877-878-8989 ■ *Web:* www.southwestfunding.com	877-878-8989		509
Southwest General Health Ctr 18697 Bagley Rd .... Middleburg Heights OH 44130 *Web:* www.swgeneral.com	440-816-8000		374-3
Southwest General Hospital (SGH) 7400 Barlite Blvd .... San Antonio TX 78224 *Web:* www.southwestgeneralhospital.org	210-921-2000		374-3
Southwest Geophysics Inc 8057 Raytheon Rd Ste 9.................... San Diego CA 92111 *Web:* southwestgeophysics.com	858-527-0849		727
Southwest Georgia Financial Corp 201 1st St SE .... Moultrie GA 31768 *NYSE:* SGB ■ *TF:* 888-683-2265 ■ *Web:* www.sgb.bank	229-985-1120		360-2
Southwest Hazard Control Inc 1953 W Grant Rd .... Tucson AZ 85745 *Web:* swhaz.com	520-622-3607		192
Southwest Health Center Inc 1400 Eastside Rd .... Platteville WI 53818 *Web:* www.southwesthealth.org	608-348-2331		374-3
Southwest Heat Treat 1733 Lauder Rd .... Houston TX 77039 *Web:* swheattreat.com	281-442-6694		484
Southwest Hide Co 250 S Beechwood Ste 180 .... Boise ID 83709	208-378-8000		432
Southwest Import Co PO Box 180247 .... Dallas TX 75218 *TF:* 800-521-8091 ■ *Web:* www.swimport.com	800-521-8091		328
Southwest Inspection & Testing 441 Commercial Way .... La Habra CA 90631 *Web:* www.southwesttesting.com	562-941-2990		365
Southwest Institute of Healing Arts 1100 E Apache Blvd .... Tempe AZ 85281 *TF:* 888-504-9106 ■ *Web:* www.swiha.edu	480-994-9244		800
Southwest Iowa Rural Electric Co-op 1801 Grove Ave .... Corning IA 50841 *TF:* 888-220-4869 ■ *Web:* www.swiarec.coop	641-322-3165	322-5274	245
Southwest Journal 1115 Hennepin Ave S.................... Minneapolis MN 55403 *Web:* www.southwestjournal.com	612-825-9205		532-4
Southwest Local School District 230 S Elm St................................ Harrison OH 45030 *Web:* www.southwestschools.org	513-367-4139		685
Southwest Louisiana Convention & Visitors Bureau 1205 N Lakeshore Dr .... Lake Charles LA 70601 *TF:* 800-456-7952 ■ *Web:* www.visitlakecharles.org	337-436-9588		206
Southwest Louisiana Electric Membership Corp 3420 NE Evangeline Thwy .... LaFayette LA 70509 *TF:* 888-275-3626 ■ *Web:* www.slemco.com	337-896-5384	896-2533	245
Southwest LTC 5560 Tennyson Pkwy Ste 210........ Plano TX 75024 *Web:* www.swltc.com	469-916-6100	916-6105	371
Southwest Materials Handling Company Inc 4719 Almond St .... Dallas TX 75247 *TF:* 866-674-6067 ■ *Web:* www.swmhc.com	214-630-1375		358
Southwest Medical Associates Inc 638 E Market St PO Box 2168 .... Rockport TX 78382 *TF:* 800-929-4854 ■ *Web:* www.swmed.com	361-729-0646	729-8854	721
Southwest Metalsmiths Inc 5026 E Beverly Rd .... Phoenix AZ 85044 *Web:* www.swmetalsmiths.com	602-438-8577		492
Southwest Minnesota State University 1501 State St .... Marshall MN 56258 *TF:* 800-642-0684 ■ *Web:* smsumustangs.com	800-642-0684		166
Southwest Mississippi Community College 1156 College Dr........................... Summit MS 39666 *Web:* www.smcc.edu	601-276-2000	276-3888	162
Southwest Mississippi Electric Power Assn 18671 Hwy 61 PO Box 5...................... Lorman MS 39096 *TF:* 800-287-8564 ■ *Web:* www.southwestepa.com	800-287-8564		245
Southwest Mississippi Regional Medical Ctr 215 Marion Ave .... McComb MS 39648 *Web:* www.smrmc.com	601-249-5500	249-1397	374-3
Southwest Missouri Bank 2417 S Grand Ave.......................... Carthage MO 64836 *TF:* 800-943-8488 ■ *Web:* www.smbonline.com	417-358-1770	358-4081	70
Southwest Montana Community Federal Credit Union 1035 W Pk .... Anaconda MT 59711 *Web:* swmcfcu.org	406-563-8484		219
Southwest National Primate Research Ctr (SNPRC) *Texas Biomedical Research Institute* PO Box 760549 .... San Antonio TX 78245 *Web:* snprc.org	210-258-9400		668
Southwest Networks Inc 73-700 Dinah Shore Dr Ste 404 .... Palm Desert CA 92211 *Web:* www.southwest-networks.com	760-770-5200		196
Southwest Offset Printing Company Inc 13650 Gramercy Pl.......................... Gardena CA 90249 *Web:* southwestoffset.com	310-323-0112		627
Southwest Oilfield Products Inc 10340 Wallisville Rd......................... Houston TX 77013 *TF:* 800-392-4600 ■ *Web:* www.swoil.com	713-675-7541		537
Southwest Oklahoma Federal Credit Union 1806 NW Liberty Ave .... Lawton OK 73507 *TF:* 866-353-0490 ■ *Web:* swofcu.com	580-353-0490	248-8149	219
Southwest Oklahoma Juvenile Ctr 320 S Broadway Avw .... Manitou OK 73555 *Web:* ok.gov	580-397-3511	397-3491	412
Southwest Paper Company Inc 3930 N Bridgeport Cir .... Wichita KS 67219 *Web:* www.swpaper.com	316-838-7755	838-7864	559
Southwest Plaza Mall 8501 W Bowles Ave .... Littleton CO 80123 *Web:* www.southwestplaza.com	303-973-5300		460
Southwest Precision Printers Inc 1055 Conrad Sauer Dr .... Houston TX 77043 *TF:* 800-437-3337 ■ *Web:* www.swpp.com	713-777-3333		627
Southwest Property Management Corp 1044 Castello Dr Ste 206 .... Naples FL 34103 *Web:* www.swpropmgt.com	239-261-3440		652
Southwest Public Power District 221 S Main St PO Box 289.................. Palisade NE 69040 *TF:* 800-379-7977 ■ *Web:* www.swppd.com	308-285-3295		245
Southwest Publishing & Mailing Corp 2600 NW Topeka Blvd........................ Topeka KS 66617 *TF:* 800-258-1491 ■ *Web:* www.swpks.com	785-233-5662	233-7258	626
Southwest Regional Medical Ctr 350 Bonar Ave .... Waynesburg PA 15370 *Web:* www.southwestregionalmedical.com	724-627-3101	627-8653	374-3
Southwest Research Institute (SWRI) 6220 Culebra Rd......................... San Antonio TX 78238 *Web:* www.swri.org	210-684-5111	522-3496	668
Southwest Rural Electric Assn 700 N Broadway PO Box 310 .... Tipton OK 73570 *TF:* 800-256-7973 ■ *Web:* www.swre.com	580-667-5281	667-5284	245
Southwest School of Art & Craft 300 Augusta St.......................... San Antonio TX 78205 *Web:* www.swschool.org	210-200-8200	224-9337	685
Southwest Service Life Insurance Co PO Box 982005 .... Fort Worth TX 76182 *TF:* 800-966-7491 ■ *Web:* www.southwestservicelife.com	817-284-4888	284-4474	796
Southwest Shipyard L P 18310 Market St.......................... Channelview TX 77530 *Web:* www.swslp.com	281-860-3200	860-3215	698
Southwest Steel Casting Co 600 Foundry Dr .... Longview TX 75604 *Web:* www.swscc.com	903-759-3946		492
Southwest Technical College 757 W 800 South .... Cedar City UT 84720 *Web:* stech.edu	435-586-2899		507

	Phone	Fax	Class
Southwest Technologies Inc 1746 Levee Rd North Kansas City MO 64116 *TF:* 800-247-9951 ■ *Web:* elastogel.com	816-221-2442	221-3995	477
Southwest Tel-Supply Inc 118 Buckskin Dr San Angelo TX 76906 *TF:* 866-618-4893 ■ *Web:* www.southwesttelsupply.com	325-658-1228	655-0361	45
Southwest Tennessee Community College 5983 Macon Cove PO Box 780 Memphis TN 38134 *TF:* 877-717-7822 ■ *Web:* www.southwest.tn.edu	901-333-5000	333-4473	162
Southwest Tennessee Electric Membership Corp 1009 E Main St Brownsville TN 38012 *TF:* 800-772-0472 ■ *Web:* www.stemc.com	731-772-1322	772-1037	245
Southwest Texas Electric Co-opeartive Inc 101 E Gillis St PO Box 677 Eldorado TX 76936 *TF:* 800-643-3980 ■ *Web:* www.swtec.com	325-853-2544	853-3141	245
Southwest Texas Junior College 2401 Garner Field Rd Uvalde TX 78801 *Web:* www.swtjc.edu	830-278-4401	591-7396	162
Southwest Texas Telephone Co (SWTTC) 939 S Texas Hwy 55 Rocksprings TX 78880 *TF:* 800-752-4753 ■ *Web:* www.swtexas.com	830-683-2111	683-4190	224
Southwest Trails Inc 19203 S Figueroa St Gardena CA 90248 *TF:* 800-331-1820 ■ *Web:* www.southwesttrails.com	800-331-1820		780
Southwest Training Schools Inc 4907 15th St Lubbock TX 79416 *TF:* 866-959-6230 ■ *Web:* www.swts.com	866-959-6230		685
Southwest University of Visual Arts 2525 N Country Club Rd Tucson AZ 85716 *TF:* 800-825-8753 ■ *Web:* www.suva.edu	520-325-0123		786
Southwest Valley Chamber of Commerce 289 N Litchfield Rd Goodyear AZ 85338 *Web:* www.southwestvalleychamber.org	623-932-2260	932-9057	139
Southwest Vermont Career Development Ctr 321 Park St Bennington VT 05201 *Web:* www.svcdc.org	802-447-0220		167-3
Southwest Veterinary Services Sc 37460 Hwy 18 Prairie du Chien WI 53804 *Web:* swvetservices.com	608-326-6464		794
Southwest Virginia Community College 724 Community College Rd Cedar Bluff VA 24609 *TF:* 855-877-3944 ■ *Web:* sw.edu	276-964-2555	964-7716	162
Southwest Washington Convention & Visitors Bureau 1220 Main S Ste 220 Vancouver WA 98660 *TF:* 877-600-0800 ■ *Web:* www.visitvancouverusa.com	360-750-1553		206
Southwest Water Co 12535 Reed Rd Sugar Land TX 77478 *TF:* 866-674-7992 ■ *Web:* www.swwc.com	281-207-5800		787
Southwest Wisconsin Library System (SWLS) 1300 Industrial Dr Ste 2 Fennimore WI 53809 *Web:* www.swls.org	608-822-3393		434-3
Southwest Wisconsin Technical College (SWTC) 1800 Bronson Blvd Fennimore WI 53809 *TF:* 800-362-3322 ■ *Web:* swtc.edu	608-822-3262	822-6019	800
Southwestern Academy 2800 Monterey Rd San Marino CA 91108 *Web:* www.southwesternacademy.edu	626-799-5010	799-0407	622
Southwestern Adventist University 100 W Hillcrest Dr Keene TX 76059 *TF:* 800-433-2240 ■ *Web:* www.swau.edu	817-645-3921		166
Southwestern Assemblies of God University 1200 Sycamore St Waxahachie TX 75165 *TF:* 888-937-7248 ■ *Web:* www.sagu.edu	972-937-4010		166
Southwestern Baptist Theological Seminary PO Box 22740 Fort Worth TX 76122 *TF:* 877-467-9287 ■ *Web:* swbts.edu	817-923-1921	921-8758	167-3
Southwestern Central School District 600 Hunt Rd WE Jamestown NY 14701 *Web:* www.swcsk12.org	716-484-6800	488-2442	685
Southwestern Christian College PO Box 10 Terrell TX 75160 *TF:* 800-925-9357 ■ *Web:* www.swcc.edu	972-524-3341	563-7133	166
Southwestern Christian University 7210 NW 39th Expy PO Box 340 Bethany OK 73008 *TF:* 888-418-9272 ■ *Web:* swcu.edu	405-789-7661	495-0078	166
Southwestern College 900 Otay Lakes Rd Chula Vista CA 91910 *TF:* 866-262-9881 ■ *Web:* swccd.edu	619-421-6700	482-6489	162
Southwestern College 100 College St Winfield KS 67156 **Fax Area Code:* 620 ■ *TF:* 800-846-1543 ■ *Web:* www.sckans.edu	800-846-1543	229-6344*	166
Southwestern College 100 Campus Dr Weatherford OK 73096 *Web:* www.swosu.edu	580-772-6611	774-3795	166
Southwestern Community College 1501 W Townline St Creston IA 50801 *TF:* 800-247-4023 ■ *Web:* www.swcciowa.edu	641-782-7081	782-3312	162
Southwestern Community College 447 College Dr Sylva NC 28779 *TF:* 800-447-4091 ■ *Web:* southwesterncc.edu	828-339-4000	339-4613	162
Southwestern Controls 6720 Sands Point Dr Ste 100 Houston TX 77074 *TF:* 800-444-9368 ■ *Web:* www.swcontrols.com	713-777-2626	988-1750	223
Southwestern Correctional Ctr 950 Kings Hwy East Saint Louis IL 62203 *Web:* www.illinois.gov	618-394-2200	394-2228	213
Southwestern Electric Cooperative Inc 525 US Rt 40 Greenville IL 62246 **Fax Area Code:* 618 ■ *TF:* 800-637-8667 ■ *Web:* www.sweci.com	800-637-8667	664-4179*	245
Southwestern Energy Co 10000 Energy Dr Spring TX 77389 *NYSE:* SWN ■ *TF:* 866-322-0801 ■ *Web:* www.swn.com	832-796-1000	796-4818	787
Southwestern Eye Ctr 2610 E University Dr Mesa AZ 85213 *Web:* www.sweye.com	480-892-8400		798
Southwestern Gold Inc 6909 Menaul Blvd NE Ste F Albuquerque NM 87110 *TF:* 800-545-6575 ■ *Web:* www.southwesterngold.com	505-881-3636	883-8957	241
Southwestern Illinois College 2500 Carlyle Ave Belleville IL 62221 *TF:* 800-222-5131 ■ *Web:* www.swic.edu	618-235-2700	222-9768	162
Southwestern Indian Polytechnic Institute 9169 Coors Blvd NW Albuquerque NM 87120 *Web:* www.sipi.edu	505-346-2306		165
Southwestern Industries Inc 2615 Homestead Pl Rancho Dominguez CA 90220 *TF:* 800-421-6875 ■ *Web:* www.southwesternindustries.com	310-608-4422	764-2668	455
Southwestern Manitoba Regional Library 149 Main St PO Box 670 Melita MB R0M1L0 *Web:* southwestern.mb.libraries.coop	204-522-3923		436
Southwestern Medical Ctr (SWMC) 5602 SW Lee Blvd Lawton OK 73505 *Web:* swmconline.com	580-531-4700		374-3
Southwestern Michigan College (SMC) 58900 Cherry Grove Rd Dowagiac MI 49047 **Fax Area Code:* 269 ■ *TF:* 800-456-8675 ■ *Web:* www.swmich.edu	800-456-8675	782-1331*	162
Southwestern Michigan Tourism Council 2300 Pipestone Rd Benton Harbor MI 49022 *TF:* 800 764 2836 ■ *Web:* www.swmichigan.org	269-925-6301	925-7540	206
Southwestern Mission Research Ctr (SMRC) PO Box 41962 Tucson AZ 85721 *Web:* southwestmissions.org	520-621-6278		637-2
Southwestern Motor Transport Inc 4600 Goldfield San Antonio TX 78218 *Web:* www.smtl.com	210-661-6791	662-3295	780
Southwestern Oregon Community College 1988 Newmark Ave Coos Bay OR 97420 *TF:* 800-962-2838 ■ *Web:* www.socc.edu	541-888-2525		162
Southwestern Oregon Publishing Co 1185 Baltimore Ave Bandon OR 97411 *Web:* theworldlink.com	541-347-2423		532-2
Southwestern Petroleum Corp PO Box 961005 Fort Worth TX 76161 **Fax Area Code:* 817 ■ *TF:* 800-877-9372 ■ *Web:* www.swepcousa.com	800-877-9372	877-4047*	541
SouthWestern Power Group II LLC 3610 N 44th St Ste 250 Phoenix AZ 85018 *TF:* 888-332-4599 ■ *Web:* www.southwesternpower.com	602-808-2004	808-2099	245
Southwestern Scale Company Inc 2535 W Broadway Rd Phoenix AZ 85041 *Web:* www.swscale.com	602-243-3951	243-0435	300
Southwestern Suppliers Inc 6815 E 14th Ave Tampa FL 33619 *Web:* www.sowes.com	813-626-2193		492
Southwestern University PO Box 770 Georgetown TX 78627 *TF:* 800-252-3166 ■ *Web:* www.southwestern.edu	512-863-1200	863-9601	166
Southwestern University Hospital 5151 Harry Hines Blvd Dallas TX 75390 *Web:* utswmed.org	214-645-5555		374-3
Southwestern University School of Law 3050 Wilshire Blvd Los Angeles CA 90010 *Web:* www.swlaw.edu	213-738-6700		167-1
Southwestern Vermont Medical Ctr 100 Hospital Dr Bennington VT 05201 *Web:* svhealthcare.org	802-442-6361		374-3
Southwestern Virginia Mental Health Institute 340 Bagley Cir Marion VA 24354 *Web:* www.swvmhi.dbhds.virginia.gov	276-783-1200		374-5
Southwestern Wire Inc PO Box CC Norman OK 73070 *TF:* 800-348-9473 ■ *Web:* swwire.com	405-447-6900	447-2830	813
Southwestern/Great American 2451 Atrium Way Nashville TN 37214 *TF:* 888-602-7867 ■ *Web:* www.southwestern.com	615-391-2500		96
Southwick Beach State Park 8119 Southwicks Pl Henderson NY 13650 *Web:* parks.ny.gov	315-846-5338		565
Southwick Clothing LLC 25 Computer Dr Haverhill MA 01832 *Web:* southwick.com	978-686-3833		155-12
Southwick Inc 2400 Shattuck Ave Berkeley CA 94704 *Web:* www.toyotaofberkeley.com	510-845-2530		57
Southwick Tolland Regional SD 86 Powder Mill Rd Southwick MA 01077 *Web:* www.stgrsd.org	413-569-5391		685
Southwind Bank 436 N Main Russell KS 67665 *Web:* southwindbank.net	785-483-2300		70
Southwind Carpet Mills 601 Callahan Rd SE PO Box 3577 Dalton GA 30719 *TF:* 800-272-2808 ■ *Web:* www.cherokeecarpet.com	800-272-2808		131
Southwire Co 1 Southwire Dr Carrollton GA 30119 *TF:* 800-444-1700 ■ *Web:* southwire.com	770-832-4242		485
Southworth Products Corp PO Box 1380 Portland ME 04104 *TF:* 800-743-1000 ■ *Web:* www.southworthproducts.com	207-878-0700	797-4734	470
Souza Agency Inc, The 2547 Housley Rd Annapolis MD 21401 *Web:* www.souza.com	410-573-1300		7
Souza-Baranowski Correctional Ctr 1 Harvard Rd PO Box Shirley MA 01464 *Web:* mass.gov	978-368-4816		213
Sova Pharmaceuticals Inc 11099 N Torrey Pines Rd Ste 290 La Jolla CA 92037 *Web:* www.sovapharma.com	858-750-4700	750-4701	238
Sovereign Pharmaceuticals Ltd 7590 Sand St Fort Worth TX 76118 *TF:* 877-248-0228 ■ *Web:* www.sovpharm.com	817-284-0429	284-0531	582
Sovereign Technologies LLC 11414 Gravois Rd Ste 301 Saint Louis MO 63126 *Web:* sovereigntec.com	314-537-5739		809
Sowell and Co 1601 Elm St Ste 3500 Thanksgiving Twr Dallas TX 75201 *Web:* www.sowellco.com	214-871-3320	871-1620	690
Sowell Gray Stepp & Laffitte LLC 1310 Gadsden St PO Box 11449 Columbia SC 29211 *Web:* robinsongray.com	803-929-1400	929-0300	428
Soybean Digest 7900 International Dr Ste 300 Minneapolis MN 55425 *Web:* www.cornandsoybeandigest.com	952-851-4667		457-1
SP (Savol Pools) 91 Prestige Park Cir East Hartford CT 06108 *TF:* 800-867-0098 ■ *Web:* www.savolpools.com	860-282-0878		146

Phone | Fax | Class

SP Kish Industries Inc
600 W Seminary St . . . Charlotte MI 48813 517-543-2650 550
Web: www.kishindustries.com

SP Mount 1306 E 55th St . . . Cleveland OH 44103 216-881-3316 627
Web: www.spmount.com

SP Scientific 935 Mearns Rd. . . . Warminster PA 18974 845-255-5000 672-7807* 420
**Fax Area Code:* 215 ■ *TF:* 800-431-8232 ■ *Web:* www.spscientific.com

SPA (Systems Planning & Analysis Inc)
2001 N Beauregard St. . . . Alexandria VA 22311 703-399-7550 261
Web: www.spa.com

Spa at Eagle Crest Resort
1522 Cline Falls Hwy . . . Redmond OR 97756 541-923-9647 707
TF: 855-682-4786 ■ *Web:* www.eagle-crest.com

Spa at the Diplomat Country Club
501 Diplomat Pkwy. . . . Hallandale Beach FL 33009 954-883-4900 707
Web: www.diplomatresort.com

Spa at the Hotel Hershey 100 Hotel Rd . . . Hershey PA 17033 717-520-5888 707
TF: 877-772-9988 ■ *Web:* www.chocolatespa.com

Spa at the Norwich Inn
607 W Thames St . . . Norwich CT 06360 860-425-3500 707
TF: 800-275-4772 ■ *Web:* www.thespaatnorwichinn.com

Spa at the Ponte Vedra Inn & Club
302 Ponte Vedra Blvd . . . Ponte Vedra Beach FL 32082 904-273-7700 273-7706 707
Web: www.pvspa.com

Spa at the Saddlebrook Resort
5700 Saddlebrook Way. . . . Wesley Chapel FL 33543 813-907-4419 707
TF: 800-729-8383 ■ *Web:* www.saddlebrook.com

Spa at The Setai 2001 Collins Ave . . . Miami Beach FL 33139 844-662-8387 706
TF: 844-662-8387 ■ *Web:* www.thesetaihotels.com

Spa at White Oaks Conference Resort
253 Taylor Rd . . . Niagara-on-the-Lake ON L0S1J0 905-641-2599 707
TF: 800-263-5766 ■ *Web:* www.whiteoaksresort.com

Spa Douce Heure 110 338 Rte . . . Les Coteaux QC J7X1A2 450-267-4949 226
Web: www.spadouceheure.com

Spa Manufacturers 6060 Ulmerton Rd. . . . Clearwater FL 33760 727-530-9493 539-8151 375
TF: 877-530-9493 ■ *Web:* www.spamanufacturers.com

Spa Moana at the Hyatt Regency Maui Resort & Spa
200 Nohea Kai Dr . . . Lahaina HI 96761 808-667-4725 707
Web: www.maui.regency.hyatt.com

Spa Radiance 3011 Fillmore St. . . . San Francisco CA 94123 415-346-6281 706
Web: www.sparadiance.com

Spa Resort Casino 401 E Amado Rd. . . . Palm Springs CA 92262 888-999-1995 133
TF: 888-999-1995 ■ *Web:* www.sparesortcasino.com

Spa Shiki at the Lodge of Four Seasons
PO Box 215 . . . Lake Ozark MO 65049 573-365-8108 707
Web: spashiki.com

Spa Tech Institute 126 High St . . . Ipswich MA 01938 978-356-0414 668
TF: 800-262-8530 ■ *Web:* www.spatech.edu

Spa Terre at Paradise Point Resort
1404 Vacation Rd . . . San Diego CA 92109 858-581-5998 707
Web: paradisepoint.com

SPAAN Tech Inc
311 S Wacker Dr Ste 2400 . . . Chicago IL 60606 312-277-8800 277-8808 390
Web: www.spaantech.com

Spaans Cookie Company Inc 456 C St. . . . Galt CA 95632 209-745-1974 745-5829 296-9
Web: www.spaanscookies.com

SPAC (Saratoga Performing Arts Ctr)
108 Avenue of the Pines . . . Saratoga Springs NY 12866 518-584-9330 584-0809 572
Web: spac.org

Space Age Tulsa Federal Credit Union
11310 E Pine St . . . Tulsa OK 74116 918-438-0140 219
Web: spaceagetulsafcu.com

Space Aliens Grill & Bar
1304 E Century Ave . . . Bismarck ND 58503 701-223-6220 671
Web: spacealiens.com

Space Center Houston 1601 Nasa Rd 1. . . . Houston TX 77058 281-244-2100 283-7724 520
Web: www.spacecenter.org

Space Coast Credit Union
8045 N Wickham Rd PO Box 419001 . . . Melbourne FL 32941 321-752-2222 219
TF: 800-447-7228 ■ *Web:* www.sccu.com

Space Coast Jet Ctr
7003 Challenger Ave. . . . Titusville FL 32780 321-267-8355 267-0129 63
TF: 800-559-5473 ■ *Web:* www.spacecoastjetcenter.com

Space Dynamics Laboratory
1695 N Research Pkwy . . . North Logan UT 84341 435-713-3400 713-3430 668
Web: www.sdl.usu.edu

Space Electronics LLC 81 Fuller Way . . . Berlin CT 06037 860-829-0001 829-0005 61
Web: www.space-electronics.com

Space Ground System Solutions
4343 Fortune Pl Ste C . . . Melbourne FL 32904 321-956-8200 728-1833 177
Web: sgss.com

Space Machine & Engineering Corp
2327 16 Ave N . . . Saint Petersburg FL 33713 727-323-2221 261
Web: space-machine.com

Space Micro Inc 10237 Flanders Ct . . . San Diego CA 92121 858-332-0700 647
Web: www.spacemicro.com

Space Murals Museum 12450 Hwy 70 E. . . . Las Cruces NM 88011 575-382-0977 520
Web: spacemurals.net

Space Needle 400 Broad St. . . . Seattle WA 98109 206-905-2100 671
Web: www.spaceneedle.com

Space Optics Research Labs LLC
15 Caron St . . . Merrimack NH 03054 978-250-8640 407
TF: 800-552-7675 ■ *Web:* www.sorl.com

Space Physics Research Laboratory
University of Michigan 2455 Hayward St . . . Ann Arbor MI 48109 734-936-7775 668
Web: www.sprl.umich.edu

Space Science & Engineering Ctr
University of Wisconsin-Madison 1225 W Dayton St
. . . Madison WI 53706 608-263-6750 262-5974 668
TF: 866-391-1753 ■ *Web:* www.ssec.wisc.edu

Space Systems/Loral 3825 Fabian Way . . . Palo Alto CA 94303 650-852-4000 647
TF: 800-332-6490 ■ *Web:* sslmda.com

Space Telescope Science Institute
3700 San Martin Dr . . . Baltimore MD 21218 410-338-4700 338-4767 668
Web: www.stsci.edu

Space Vector Corp 9174 Deering Ave . . . Chatsworth CA 91311 818-734-2600 428-6249 504
Web: www.spacevector.com

Space within 3142 Vantage Point Dr . . . Midland MI 48642 989-835-5151 835-5357 393
Web: spacewithin.net

SpaceAge Control Inc 38850 20th St E . . . Palmdale CA 93550 661-273-3000 273-4240 256
Web: spaceagecontrol.com

SPACECO Inc 9575 W Higgins Rd Ste 700. . . . Rosemont IL 60018 847-696-4060 696-4065 261
Web: www.spacecoinc.com

SPACECONNECTION Inc, The
10530 Victory Blvd . . . North Hollywood CA 91606 818-754-1100 387
Web: www.thespaceconnection.com

Spaceflight Systems
47 Constitution Dr . . . Bedford NH 03110 603-472-4934 472-4938 180
Web: ssc-nh.com

SpaceGuard Products Inc
711 S Commerce Dr . . . Seymour IN 47274 812-523-3044 428-5758* 286
**Fax Area Code:* 800 ■ *TF:* 800-841-0680 ■ *Web:* www.spaceguardproducts.com

Spacelabs Health Care
35301 SE Center St . . . Snoqualmie WA 98065 425-396-3300 396-3301 250
TF: 800-522-7025 ■ *Web:* www.spacelabshealthcare.com

Spacesaver Corp
1450 Janesville Ave . . . Fort Atkinson WI 53538 800-255-8170 563-2702* 286
**Fax Area Code:* 920 ■ *TF:* 800-255-8170 ■ *Web:* www.spacesaver.com

Spackenkill Union Free School Districts (Inc)
15 Croft Rd . . . Poughkeepsie NY 12603 845-463-7800 685
Web: www.spackenkillschools.org

Spader Business Management
2101 W 41st St Ste 49 . . . Sioux Falls SD 57105 800-772-3377 196
TF: 800-772-3377 ■ *Web:* spader.com

Spaghetti Warehouse Inc 1255 W I-20 . . . Arlington TX 76017 817-557-0321 550-0908* 670
**Fax Area Code:* 972 ■ *Web:* www.meatballs.com

Spagnuolo & Associates LLC
3057 W Market St Ste 201 . . . Fairlawn OH 44333 330-836-6661 261
Web: spagnuoloassoc.com

Spahn & Rose Lumber Co
2175 Southpark Ct . . . Dubuque IA 52003 563-582-3606 582-3749 364
Web: www.spahnandrose.com

Spaide, Kuipers & Co 3 Willow St. . . . Newport RI 02840 610-668-8296 194
Web: www.spaidekuipers.com

Spain 245 E 47th St 36th Fl. . . . New York NY 10017 212-661-1050 949-7247 784
Web: www.spainun.org

Spain
Consulate General
150 E 58th St 30th Fl. . . . New York NY 10155 212-355-4080 644-3751 257
Web: www.spainculture.us
Embassy 2375 Pennsylvania Ave NW . . . Washington DC 20037 202-452-0100 257
Web: www.exteriores.gob.es

Spain Restaurant 419 Market St. . . . Newark NJ 07105 973-344-0994 344-2669 671
Web: www.spainrestaurant.com

Spain-US Chamber of Commerce
80 Broad St Ste 2103 . . . New York NY 10004 212-967-2170 564-1415 138
Web: www.spainuscc.org

Spalding PO Box 90015 . . . Bowling Green KY 42103 855-253-4533 729-4800* 710
**Fax Area Code:* 877 ■ *TF:* 855-253-4533 ■ *Web:* www.spalding.com

Spalding Automotive Inc
4529 Adams Cir . . . Bensalem PA 19020 215-826-4000 550-9035* 60
**Fax Area Code:* 267 ■ *Web:* www.spaldingautomotive.com

Spalding County 119 E Solomon St . . . Griffin GA 30223 770-467-4233 467-4227 338
Web: www.spaldingcounty.com

Spalding Dedecker Associates Inc
905 S Blvd E. . . . Rochester Hills MI 48307 248-844-5400 261
Web: www.sda-eng.com

Spalding Hardware Ltd 1616 10 Ave SW. . . . Calgary AB T3C0J5 800-837-0850 350
TF: 800-837-0850 ■ *Web:* spaldinghardware.com

Spalding Rehabilitation Hospital
900 Potomac St . . . Aurora CO 80011 303-367-1166 374-6
TF: 800-367-3309 ■ *Web:* spaldingrehab.com

Spalding University
851 S Fourth St . . . Louisville KY 40203 502-585-9911 166
TF: 800-896-8941 ■ *Web:* spalding.edu

Spalon Montage
600 Market St Ste 270 . . . Chanhassen MN 55317 952-915-2900 354
Web: spalon.com

Spal-Usa Inc 1731 SE Oralabor Rd . . . Ankeny IA 50021 800-345-0327 54
TF: 800-345-0327 ■ *Web:* www.spalusa.com

Span Inc 1800 Malone St . . . Denton TX 76201 940-382-2224 108
Web: span-transit.org

SpanaFlight 16705 103rd Ave Ct E . . . Puyallup WA 98374 253-848-2020 840-5843 63
Web: www.spanaflight.com

Span-America Medical Systems Inc
70 Commerce Ctr . . . Greenville SC 29615 864-288-8877 288-8692 477
NASDAQ: SPAN ■ *TF:* 800-888-6752 ■ *Web:* www.spanamerica.com

Spanberger Abigail (Rep D - VA)
1239 Longworth House Office Bldg . . . Washington DC 20515 202-225-2815 342-2
Web: www.spanberger.house.gov

Spancrete Industries Inc
N 16 W 23415 Stone Ridge Dr PO Box 828 . . . Waukesha WI 53187 414-290-9000 290-9130 183
TF: 855-900-7726 ■ *Web:* www.spancrete.com

Spang & Co 110 Delta Dr . . . Pittsburgh PA 15238 412-963-9363 253
Web: www.spang.com

Spangler & Boyer Mechanical
5175 Commerce Dr . . . York PA 17408 717-792-8854 610
Web: www.spanglerboyer.com

Spangler Candy Co
400 N Portland St PO Box 71 . . . Bryan OH 43506 419-636-4221 636-3695 296-8
TF: 888-636-4221 ■ *Web:* www.spanglercandy.com

Spangler, Jennings & Dougherty PC
8396 Mississippi St . . . Merrillville IN 46410 219-769-2323 571-7686* 428
**Fax Area Code:* 317 ■ *Web:* www.sjdlaw.com

Spangles Inc 437 N Hillside St . . . Wichita KS 67214 316-685-8817 670
Web: www.spanglesinc.com

Spanish Cove 11 Palm Ave . . . Yukon OK 73099 800-965-2683 672
TF: 800-965-2683 ■ *Web:* www.spanishcove.com

Spanish Flower 4701 N Main St . . . Houston TX 77009 713-869-1706 671
Web: www.spanishflowersrestaurants.com

Spanish Kitchen 2960 N Main St . . . Las Cruces NM 88001 575-526-4275 671

Spanish Tavern 103 McWhorter St . . . Newark NJ 07105 973-589-4959 671
Web: spanishtavernnewark.com

Spanish Trail Pet Clinic Pc
9431 E 22nd St Ste 121 . . . Tucson AZ 85710 520-722-2771 794
Web: spanishtrailvet.com

Name / Address	City	State	ZIP	Phone	Fax	Class
Spanish-American Translating 330 Eagle Ave *TF:* 800-870-5790 ■ *Web:* arleneboas.com	West Hempstead	NY	11552	516-481-3339		768
Spano Ross (Rep R - FL) 224 Cannon House Office Bldg *Web:* www.spano.house.gov	Washington	DC	20515	202-225-1252		342-2
Spanos Przetak 475 14th St Ste 550 *Web:* spanos-przetak.business.site	Oakland	CA	94610	510-250-0200		428
Spanset Inc 3125 Industrial Dr *Web:* www.spanset.com	Sanford	NC	27332	919-774-6316		208
SpanTech LLC 1115 Cleveland Ave PO Box 369 *TF:* 866-851-5041 ■ *Web:* spantechconveyors.com	Glasgow	KY	42141	866-851-5041		358
SPAP Company LLC PO Box 680 *Web:* www.spapcompanyllc.com	Huntington Beach	CA	92648	714-960-0586		463
SPAR Group Inc 560 White Plains Rd *NASDAQ: SGRP* ■ *Web:* sparinc.com	Tarrytown	NY	10591	914-332-4100	332-0741	4
Spark Creations Inc 10 W 46th St *Web:* www.sparkcreations.com	New York	NY	10036	212-575-8385		410
Spark Energy Gas LP 2105 Citywest Blvd *TF:* 877-547-7275 ■ *Web:* www.sparkenergy.com	Houston	TX	77042	877-547-7275	374-8007	325
Spark Experience Design LLC *Spark Neuro Inc* 80 8th Ave Ste 202 *Web:* sparkneuro.com	New York	NY	10011	212-201-9292		631
Spark Labs 833 Broadway *Web:* www.spark-labs.co	New York	NY	10003	646-491-6423		393
Spark Museum of Electrical Invention 1312 Bay St *Web:* www.sparkmuseum.org	Bellingham	WA	98225	360-738-3886		520
Spark Networks PLC 8383 Wilshire Blvd Ste 800 *NYSE: LOV* ■ *Web:* www.spark.net	Beverly Hills	CA	90211	323-836-3000		226
Spark Plug Games LLC 1011 Passport Way *Web:* www.sparkpluggames.com	Cary	NC	27513	919-651-0792		809
Spark Technologies Inc 150 Railroad St *Web:* www.spark-tech.com	Schenley	PA	15682	724-295-3860	295-0157	757
SparkFun Electronics Inc 6175 Longbow Dr Ste 200 *Web:* www.sparkfun.com	Boulder	CO	80301	303-284-0979	443-0048	246
Sparkhound Inc 11207 Proverbs Ave *TF:* 866-217-1500 ■ *Web:* www.sparkhound.com	Baton Rouge	LA	70816	225-216-1500		180
Sparkle Solutions LP 100 Courtland Ave *TF:* 866-660-2282 ■ *Web:* www.sparklesolutions.ca	Concord	ON	L4K3T6	905-660-2282	660-2268	35
SparkPress 80 E Rio Salado Pky Ste 511 *Web:* gosparkpress.com	Tempe	AZ	85281	480-275-4280		637-2
Sparks Belting Co 3800 Stahl Dr SE *TF:* 800-451-4537 ■ *Web:* www.sparksbelting.com	Grand Rapids	MI	49546	616-949-2750	949-8518	370
Sparks Heritage Museum 814 Victorian Ave *Web:* sparksmuseum.org	Sparks	NV	89431	775-355-1144		520
Sparks Insurance 25103 Fm 2100 *Web:* johnwsparks.com	Huffman	TX	77336	281-324-9119		390
Sparks Marketing Corp 2828 Charter Rd *TF:* 800-925-7727 ■ *Web:* wearesparks.com	Philadelphia	PA	19154	215-676-1100		286
Sparks Personnel Services Inc 1775 Greensboro Sta Pl Tower II Ste 300 *Web:* sparksgroupinc.com	McLean	VA	22102	703-821-2650		260
Sparks Regional Medical Ctr (SRMC) 1001 Towson Ave *Web:* www.sparkshealth.com	Fort Smith	AR	72901	479-441-4000	441-5397	374-3
Sparks Steak House 210 E 46th St *Web:* www.sparkssteakhouse.com	New York	NY	10017	212-687-4855		671
Sparks Willson Borges Brandt & Johnson PC 24 S Weber St Ste 400 *Web:* sparkswillson.com	Colorado Springs	CO	80903	719-634-5700		41
Sparksight Inc 7718 Wood Hollow Dr Ste G100 Cross Bldg *Web:* sparksight.com	Austin	TX	78731	512-493-2070		636
Sparktech Inc 1308 Chisholm Trl Ste 105 *Web:* sparktechinc.com	Round Rock	TX	78681	512-716-3131		358
Sparkworks Media 2400 Airport Way S *Web:* www.sparkworksmedia.com	Seattle	WA	98134	206-284-5500	284-6611	514
Sparling Instruments Company Inc 4097 N Temple City Blvd *TF:* 800-800-3569 ■ *Web:* www.sparlinginstruments.com	El Monte	CA	91731	626-444-0571	444-2314	495
Sparqtron Corp 5079 Brandin Ct *Web:* sparqtron.com	Fremont	CA	94538	510-657-7198	683-0892	177
Sparrow Health System 1215 E Michigan Ave *TF:* 800-772-7769 ■ *Web:* www.sparrow.org	Lansing	MI	48912	517-364-1000		374-3
Sparrowk Livestock 18780 E Hwy 88 *Web:* www.sparrowk.com	Clements	CA	95227	209-759-3530	759-3831	10-1
Sparta Area Schools 465 S Union St *Web:* www.spartaschools.org	Sparta	MI	49345	616-887-8253	887-9958	685
Sparta Capital Ltd 390 Bay St Ste 1202 *Web:* www.spartacapital.com	Toronto	ON	M5H2Y2	587-318-3408		767
Sparta Chevrolet 8955 Sparta Ave NW *Web:* www.spartachevy.com	Sparta	MI	49345	616-887-1791		57
Sparta Steel & Equipment Corp 9875 Chestnut Ave SE *Web:* www.spartasteel.com	East Sparta	OH	44626	330-866-9621		480
Sparta Systems Inc 2000 Waterview Dr Ste 300 *TF:* 888-261-5948 ■ *Web:* www.spartasystems.com	Hamilton Township	NJ	08691	609-807-5100		177
Spartan Carbide 34110 Riviera *Web:* www.spartancarbide.com	Fraser	MI	48026	586-285-9786		697
Spartan Chemical Company Inc 1110 Spartan Dr *TF:* 800-537-8990 ■ *Web:* www.spartanchemical.com	Maumee	OH	43537	419-531-5551	536-8423	145
Spartan College of Aeronautics & Technology 8820 E Pine St *TF:* 800-331-1204 ■ *Web:* www.spartan.edu	Tulsa	OK	74115	918-836-6886	831-5287	800
Spartan Controls Ltd 305 - 27 St SE *Web:* www.spartancontrols.com	Calgary	AB	T2A7V2	403-207-0700		111
Spartan Distributors 487 W Division St *TF:* 800-822-2216 ■ *Web:* www.spartandistributors.com	Sparta	MI	49345	616-887-7301		274
Spartan Energy Corp 850 - Second St SW Ste 500 *TF:* 866-567-3105 ■ *Web:* www.spartanenergy.ca	Calgary	AB	T2P0R8	403-355-8920		536
Spartan Graphics Inc 200 Applewood Dr *TF:* 800-747-4477 ■ *Web:* spartangraphics.com	Sparta	MI	49345	616-887-8243		627
Spartan Insurance Agency LLC 125 S Pine River *TF:* 800-888-2767 ■ *Web:* spartancrop.com	Ithaca	MI	48847	800-888-2767		390
Spartan Light Metal Products Inc 3668 S Geyer Rd Ste 210 *Web:* www.spartanlmp.com	Saint Louis	MO	63127	314-620-2500		295
Spartan Logistics 4140 Lockbourne Rd *Web:* www.spartanwarehouse.com	Columbus	OH	43207	614-497-1777		311
Spartan Motors Inc 1541 Reynolds Rd *NASDAQ: SPAR* ■ *Web:* www.spartanmotors.com	Charlotte	MI	48813	517-543-6400		516
Spartan Offshore Drilling LLC 516 JF Smith Ave *Web:* www.spartanoffshore.com	Slidell	LA	70460	504-885-7449		536
Spartan Printing Inc 320 109th St *Web:* www.spartanprinting.com	Arlington	TX	76011	817-640-6341		627
Spartan Securities Group Ltd 15500 Roosevelt Blvd Ste 303 *Web:* www.spartansecurities.com	Clearwater	FL	33760	727-502-0508		690
Spartan Technology 125 Venture Blvd *TF:* 877-727-8260 ■ *Web:* www.spartantechnology.com	Spartanburg	SC	29306	877-727-8260		177
Spartanburg Area Chamber of Commerce 105 N Pine St *Web:* www.spartanburgchamber.com	Spartanburg	SC	29302	864-594-5000	594-5055	139
Spartanburg Community College 800 Brisack Rd PO Box 4386 *TF:* 866-591-3700 ■ *Web:* www.sccsc.edu	Spartanburg	SC	29305	864-592-4800	592-4564	800
Spartanburg Convention & Visitors Bureau 298 Magnolia St *TF:* 800-374-8326 ■ *Web:* www.visitspartanburg.com	Spartanburg	SC	29306	864-594-5050		206
Spartanburg County 180 Magnolia St *Web:* www.spartanburgcounty.org	Spartanburg	SC	29306	864-596-2591		338
Spartanburg County Public Library 151 S Church St *Web:* www.spartanburglibraries.org	Spartanburg	SC	29306	864-596-3507	596-3518	434-3
Spartanburg Herald-Journal 189 W Main St *Web:* www.goupstate.com	Spartanburg	SC	29306	864-582-4511	594-6350	532-2
Spartanburg Methodist College 1000 Powell Mill Rd *TF:* 800-772-7286 ■ *Web:* www.smcsc.edu	Spartanburg	SC	29301	864-587-4000	587-4355	162
Spartanburg Regional Medical Ctr (SRMC) 101 E Wood St *TF:* 800-318-2596 ■ *Web:* www.spartanburgregional.com	Spartanburg	SC	29303	864-560-6000		374-3
Spartanburg Steel Products Inc 1290 New Cut Rd PO Box 6428 *TF:* 888-974-7500 ■ *Web:* www.ssprod.com	Spartanburg	SC	29304	864-585-5211	583-5641	489
Spartek Inc 300 Milwaukee St *Web:* www.spartekinc.com	Sparta	WI	54656	608-269-3154	269-8369	604
Spartek Systems Inc 1 Thevenaz Industrial Trl *Web:* www.sparteksystems.com	Sylvan Lake	AB	T4S2J6	403-887-2443		539
Sparton 27 Hale Spring Rd *TF:* 800-772-7866 ■ *Web:* sparton.com	Plaistow	NH	03865	603-382-3840		203
Spates Fabricators 85435 Middleton *Web:* spates.com	Thermal	CA	92274	760-397-4122		191-2
Spatial Corp 8310 Interlocken Pkwy Ste 200 *TF:* 888-715-9109 ■ *Web:* www.spatial.com	Broomfield	CO	80021	303-544-2900	544-3000	178-8
Spatial Insights Inc 4938 Hampden Ln *TF:* 800-347-5291 ■ *Web:* spatialinsights.com	Bethesda	MD	20814	800-347-5291		539
Spaulding Composites Co 55 Nadeau Dr *TF:* 800-801-0560 ■ *Web:* spauldingcom.com	Rochester	NH	03867	603-332-0555	332-5357	599
Spaulding Equipment Co 75 Paseo Adelanto *Web:* www.spauldingparts.com	Perris	CA	92570	951-943-4531		190
Spaulding for Children 16250 Northland Dr Ste 120 *Web:* spaulding.org	Southfield	MI	48075	248-443-0300	443-7099	48-6
Spaulding Group Inc, The 33 Clyde Rd Ste 103 *Web:* www.spauldinggrp.com	Somerset	NJ	08873	732-873-5700	873-3997	463
Spaulding Rehabilitation Hospital 125 Nashua St *TF:* 888-774-0055 ■ *Web:* www.spauldingrehab.org	Boston	MA	02114	617-573-7000		374-6
SPAWAR 53560 Hull St *Web:* www.public.navy.mil	San Diego	CA	92152	619-553-2717		668
SpawGlass 13800 W Rd *Web:* www.spawglass.com	Houston	TX	77041	281-970-5300		463
Spawn Ideas Inc 510 L St *Web:* www.spawnideas.com	Anchorage	AK	99501	907-274-9553		4
SPBA (Society of Professional Benefit Administrators) 2 Wisconsin Cir Ste 670 *Web:* spbatpa.org	Chevy Chase	MD	20815	301-718-7722	718-9440	49-12
SPBA (Stein + Partners Brand Activation) 432 Park Ave S *Web:* www.steinias.com	New York	NY	10016	212-213-1112		7
SPC (St Petersburg College) PO Box 13489 *Web:* www.spcollege.edu	Saint Petersburg	FL	33733	727-341-4772		598
SPC (Sheboygan Paint Co) 1439 N 25th St PO Box 417 *TF:* 800-773-7801 ■ *Web:* shebpaint.com	Sheboygan	WI	53081	920-458-2157	458-5620	550
SPC (Sheffield Publishing Co) 9009 Antioch Rd *Web:* www.spcbooks.com	Salem	WI	53168	262-843-2281	843-3683	637-2
SPC (Salt Pond Coalition) PO Box 875 *Web:* www.saltpondscoalition.org	Charlestown	RI	02813	401-322-3068		192

	Phone	Fax	Class
SPC (Syracuse Peace Council) 2013 E Genesee St 2nd Fl .... Syracuse NY 13210 *Web:* www.peacecouncil.net	315-472-5478		637-2
Spco Credit Union 12755 N Houston Rosslyn Rd .... Houston TX 77086 *Web:* spcocu.org	713-455-8586		219
SPD Electrical Systems 13500 Roosevelt Blvd .... Philadelphia PA 19116 *Web:* www.l-3mps.com	215-677-4900		729
SPDI (Superior Products Distributors Inc) 1403 Meriden-Waterbury Rd Rte 322 .... Milldale CT 06467 *TF:* 800-937-7734 ■ *Web:* www.spdionline.com	860-621-3621	621-7922	612
SPE (Society of Petroleum Engineers) 222 Palisades Creek Dr .... Richardson TX 75080 *TF:* 800-456-6863 ■ *Web:* www.spe.org	972-952-9393	952-9435	48-12
SPE (Society of Plastics Engineers) 13 Church Hill Rd .... Newtown CT 06470 *Web:* www.4spe.org	203-775-0471	775-8490	49-13
SPE Federal Credit Union 650 Science Park Rd .... State College PA 16803 *Web:* spefcu.org	814-237-5458		219
Speak Easy 1001 30th Ave S .... Moorhead MN 56560 *Web:* speakeasyrestaurant.com	218-233-1326		671
Speak Incorporated Speakers Bureau 10680 Treena St Ste 230 .... San Diego CA 92131 *TF:* 800-677-3324 ■ *Web:* www.speakinc.com	858-228-3771	228-3989	708
Speakeasy Inc 3438 Peachtree Rd Ste 1000 Phipps Twr .... Atlanta GA 30326 *Web:* www.speakeasyinc.com	404-541-4800	541-4848	765
Speakers Unlimited PO Box 27225 .... Columbus OH 43227 *TF:* 888-333-6676 ■ *Web:* www.speakersunlimited.com	614-864-3703	864-3876	708
Speakers.com 1125 West St Ste 200 .... Annapolis MD 21401 *Web:* www.speakers.com	410-897-1970		708
Speaking Rock 122 S Old Pueblo Rd .... El Paso TX 79907 *Web:* www.speakingrock.com	915-860-7777		133
Speakman Co 400 Anchor Mill Rd .... New Castle DE 19720 *TF:* 800-537-2107 ■ *Web:* speakman.com	800-537-2107	977-2747	609
Spear Inc 5510 Courseview Dr .... Mason OH 45040 *Web:* www.spearinc.com	513-459-1100		413
Spear Marketing Group 1630 N Main St Ste 200 .... Walnut Creek CA 94596 *Web:* www.spearmarketing.com	925-891-9050		7
Speare Memorial Hospital Assn 16 Hospital Rd .... Plymouth NH 03264 *Web:* spearehospital.com	603-536-1120		374-3
Spearfish Canyon Resort 10619 Roughlock Falls Rd .... Lead SD 57754 *TF:* 877-975-6343 ■ *Web:* www.spfcanyon.com	605-584-3435	584-3990	669
Spearhead Staffing LLC 991 US 22 Ste 200 .... Bridgewater NJ 08807 *Web:* www.spearheadstaffing.com	908-864-8081		196
Spears Furniture Co 7004 Salem Ave .... Lubbock TX 79424 *Web:* www.spearsfurniture.com	806-747-3401		321
Spears Manufacturing Co PO Box 9203 .... Sylmar CA 91392 *TF:* 800-862-1499 ■ *Web:* www.spearsmfg.com	818-364-1611		608
Spears-Votta & Associates Inc 7526 Harford Rd .... Baltimore MD 21234 *Web:* www.spearsvotta.com	410-254-5800		261
Speastech Inc 1527 Bowman Rd Ste F .... Little Rock AR 72211 *TF:* 888-377-6766 ■ *Web:* speastech.com	501-219-9992	219-9995	180
SPEC (Systems & Processes Engineering Corp) 4120 Commercial Center Dr Ste 500 .... Austin TX 78744 *TF:* 800-789-7732 ■ *Web:* www.spec.com	512-479-7732	494-0756	261
SPEC Building Materials Corp 2840 Roe Ln .... Kansas City KS 66103 *TF:* 866-585-7785 ■ *Web:* speccorp.com	913-384-0804		191-4
SPEC Personnel LLC 25 Walls Dr .... Fairfield CT 06824 *TF:* 888-788-7732 ■ *Web:* speconthejob.com	888-788-7732		8
SPEC Services Inc 10540 Talbert Ave .... Fountain Valley CA 92708 *Web:* www.specservices.com	714-963-8077	963-0364	261
Spec's Wines Spirits & Finer Foods 2410 Smith St .... Houston TX 77006 *TF:* 888-526-8787 ■ *Web:* specsonline.com	713-526-8787	526-6129	443
Specchem 444 Richmond Ave .... Kansas City KS 66101 *Web:* www.specchemllc.com	816-968-5600		183
Specco Industries Inc 13087 Main St .... Lemont IL 60439 *TF:* 800-441-6646 ■ *Web:* specco.com	630-257-5060		145
Specht Newspapers Inc 203 Gleason St .... Minden LA 71055	318-377-1866	377-1895	532-3
Special Audience Marketing Inc 6700 Manchaca Rd .... Austin TX 78745 *Web:* specialaudience.com	512-441-6484		195
Special Care Dentistry Assn 330 N Wabash Ave Ste 2000 .... Chicago IL 60611 *Web:* www.scdaonline.org	312-527-6764		49-8
Special Care Medical Inc 3465 Leaphart Rd .... West Columbia SC 29169 *TF:* 800-326-3609 ■ *Web:* specialcaremedical.net	803-926-0161	926-0345	475
Special Counsel Inc 10151 Deerwood Park Blvd Bldg 400 Third Fl .... Jacksonville FL 32256 *TF:* 800-737-3436 ■ *Web:* www.specialcounsel.com	904-737-3436	360-2307	721
Special Design Products Inc 500 Industrial Mile Rd .... Columbus OH 43228 *Web:* www.sdpinc.net	614-272-6700	272-6844	601
Special Devices Inc 14370 White Sage Rd .... Moorpark CA 93021 *Web:* www.specialdevices.com	805-553-1200	387-1001	268
Special Energy Corp (SEC) 4815 Perkins Rd PO Box 369 .... Stillwater OK 74074 *Web:* www.specialenergycorp.com	405-377-1177	743-1617	536
Special Fab & Machine Inc 4133 Old Salisbury Rd .... Lexington NC 27295 *Web:* www.specialfabinc.com	336-956-2121	956-1485	454
Special Fleet Service Inc (SFS) 875 Waterman Dr .... Harrisonburg VA 22802 *TF:* 800-395-2152 ■ *Web:* www.specialfleet.com	540-434-4488	434-2244	188-10
Special Ideas Inc PO Box 9 .... Heltonville IN 47436 *TF:* 800-326-1197 ■ *Web:* www.bahairesources.com	812-834-5691		637-2
Special Journeys LLC 422 S 153rd Cir .... Omaha NE 68154 *Web:* www.specialjourneys.org	402-884-1014		317
Special Libraries Assn (SLA) 331 S Patrick St .... Alexandria VA 22314 *TF:* 866-446-6069 ■ *Web:* www.sla.org	703-647-4900	647-4901	49-11
Special Materials Co 70 W 40th St 2nd Fl .... New York NY 10018 *Web:* www.smc-global.com	646-366-0400	366-0595	146
Special Metals Corp 4317 Middle Settlement Rd .... New Hartford NY 13413 *TF:* 800-334-8351 ■ *Web:* www.specialmetals.com	315-798-2900	798-2016	485
Special Metals Inc 2009 S Broadway .... Moore OK 73160 **Fax Area Code:* 405 ■ *TF:* 800-727-7177 ■ *Web:* www.specialmetalsinc.com	800-727-7177	703-8100*	492
Special Military Active Retired Travel Club (SMART) 600 University Office Blvd Ste 1A .... Pensacola FL 32504 *TF:* 800-354-7681 ■ *Web:* www.smartrving.org	850-478-1986		48-23
Special Mine Services Inc PO Box 188 .... West Frankfort IL 62896 *Web:* www.smsconnectors.com	618-932-2151	937-2715	815
Special Olympics Inc 1133 19th St NW .... Washington DC 20036 *TF:* 800-700-8585 ■ *Web:* www.specialolympics.org	202-628-3630	824-0200	48-22
Special Products & Manufacturing Inc 2625 Discovery Blvd .... Rockwall TX 75032 *Web:* spmfg.com	972-771-8851	771-8563	697
Special Technical Services Inc 11 Carlton Rd .... Flanders NJ 07836 *Web:* www.specialtechnicalservices.com	609-259-2626	259-0044	203
Special Tool & Engineering Inc 33910 James J Pompo Dr .... Fraser MI 48026 *Web:* www.specialtool.net	586-285-5900	285-5901	757
Special Wish Foundation Inc 1250 Memory Ln N .... Columbus OH 43209 *Web:* www.spwish.org	614-258-3186		48-5
SpecialCare Hospital Management Corp 1551 Wall St Ste 210 .... Saint Charles MO 63303 *Web:* www.specialcarecorp.com	314-770-2212		535
Specialist Printing & Direct Mail Services 4974 Mercury St .... San Diego CA 92111 *Web:* www.specialistonline.com	760-208-2240		463
Specialists Marketing Services Inc 777 Terrace Ave Ste 401 .... Hasbrouck Heights NJ 07604 *Web:* www.sms-inc.com	201-865-5800		5
Specialized Bicycle Components 15130 Concord Cir .... Morgan Hill CA 95037 *TF:* 877-808-8154 ■ *Web:* www.specialized.com	408-779-6229		82
Specialized Business Software Inc 6325 Cochran Rd Unit 1 .... Solon OH 44139 *TF:* 866-328-4936 ■ *Web:* specializedbusinesssoftware.com	440-542-9145	542-9143	177
Specialized Carriers & Rigging Assn (SC&RA) 5870 Trinity Pkwy Ste 200 .... Centreville VA 20120 *Web:* www.scranet.org	703-698-0291	698-0297	49-21
Specialized Manufacturing Inc 12875 S Minuteman Dr .... Draper UT 84020 *TF:* 866-572-6690 ■ *Web:* www.specializedmfg.com	801-572-6690	572-7790	253
Specialized Printed Forms Inc 352 Center St .... Caledonia NY 14423 *TF:* 800-688-2381 ■ *Web:* www.spforms.com	585-538-2381	538-4922	110
Specialized Products Ltd 200 Summer St .... Clintonville WI 54929 *Web:* www.specializedproductsltd.com	715-823-3727		757
Specialized Rail Service Inc 4740 E Tropical Pky .... Las Vegas NV 89115 **Fax Area Code:* 402 ■ *TF:* 800-233-3978 ■ *Web:* www.specializedrail.com	702-388-9277	591-2570*	780
Specialized Technology Resources Inc 10 Water St .... Enfield CT 06082 *Web:* www.strsolar.com	860-758-7300		794
Specialized Transportation Services Inc 225 Sam Griffin Rd .... Smyrna TN 37167 *TF:* 855-787-7297 ■ *Web:* www.shipsts.com	855-787-7297		780
Specialized Vehicles Inc 2468 Industrial Row Dr .... Troy MI 48084 *Web:* www.svi-results.com	248-709-5736		743
Special-Lite Inc PO Box 6 .... Decatur MI 49045 *Web:* special-lite.com	269-423-7068	423-7610	234
Specialty Answering Service (SAS) 800 N Henderson Rd .... King of Prussia PA 19406 *TF:* 888-532-4794 ■ *Web:* www.specialtyansweringservice.net	888-532-4794	644-4129	393
Specialty Bakers Inc 450 S State Rd .... Marysville PA 17053 *Web:* www.sbiladyfingers.com	717-957-2131	957-0156	296-1
Specialty Bolt & Screw Inc 235 Bowles Rd .... Agawam MA 01001 *TF:* 800-322-7878 ■ *Web:* www.specialtybolt.com	413-789-6700		351
Specialty Cable Corp 2 Tower Dr .... Wallingford CT 06492 *Web:* www.specialtycable.com	203-265-7126	269-5293	116
Specialty Catalog Corp 400 Manley St .... West Bridgewater MA 02379 *Web:* www.scdirect.com	508-638-7000		459
Specialty Coating Systems Inc 7645 Woodland Dr .... Indianapolis IN 46278 *TF:* 800-369-3505 ■ *Web:* scscoatings.com	317-451-8549	240-2739	481
Specialty Coffee Association of America (SCAA) 117 W Fourth St Ste 300 .... Santa Ana CA 92701 *TF:* 800-995-9019 ■ *Web:* sca.coffee	562-624-4100	624-4101	49-6
Specialty Design & Manufacturing Co PO Box 4039 .... Reading PA 19606 *TF:* 800-720-0867 ■ *Web:* www.specialtydesign.com	610-779-1357	370-0269	757
Specialty Equipment Market Assn (SEMA) 1575 S Vly Vista Dr .... Diamond Bar CA 91765 *Web:* www.sema.org	909-396-0289	860-0184	49-21
Specialty Fabrications Inc 2674 Westhills Ct .... Simi Valley CA 93065 *Web:* www.specfabinc.com	805-579-9730	579-9745	697
Specialty Finishes Inc 1545 Marietta Blvd NW .... Atlanta GA 30318 *Web:* www.specialtyfinishes.com	404-351-1062	351-0535	189-8

	Phone	Fax	Class
Specialty Foods Group Inc 6 Dublin Ln. Owensboro KY 42301 *TF:* 800-238-0020 ■ *Web:* specialtyfoodsgroup.com	270-926-2324		296-26
Specialty Granules Inc 13424 Pennsylvania Ave Ste 303 Hagerstown MD 21742 *TF:* 866-266-8504 ■ *Web:* www.specialtygranules.com	301-733-4000	733-4003	144
Specialty Graphic Imaging Assn (SGIA) 10015 Main St Fairfax VA 22031 *TF:* 888-385-3588 ■ *Web:* www.sgia.org	703-385-1335	273-0456	49-16
Specialty Hearse & Ambulance Sale Corp 60 Engineers Ln E. Farmingdale NY 11735 *TF:* 800-349-6102 ■ *Web:* specialtyhearse.com	516-349-7700		57
Specialty Home Health Care Inc 331 Kimber Ln Evansville IN 47715 *Web:* specialhealthcare.com	812-476-5404	476-5766	363
Specialty Hospital Jacksonville *Curahealth Hospitals and Cobalt Rehabilitation* 4901 Richard St. Jacksonville FL 32207 *Web:* curahealth.com	904-737-3120		374-7
Specialty Imports Inc 4119 Ingra St Anchorage AK 99503 *TF:* 800-478-9463 ■ *Web:* www.specialtyimports.com	907-563-9100	563-9463	81-3
Specialty Industries Inc 175 Walnut St. Red Lion PA 17356 *TF:* 800-726-3601 ■ *Web:* www.specialtyindustries.com	717-246-1661	246-1660	100
Specialty Insurance Agency Inc 1610 Rt 88 Ste 102 Brick NJ 08724 *Web:* specialtyagencyonline.com	732-701-8945		390
Specialty Insurance Partners LLC 1221 Lake Plaza Dr Ste D Colorado Springs CO 80906 *Web:* specialtyinsurancepartners.com	719-313-5600		390
Specialty Laboratories Inc 27027 Tourney Rd. Valencia CA 91355 *TF:* 800-421-7110 ■ *Web:* www.specialtylabs.com	661-799-6543		418
Specialty Loose Leaf Inc 1 Cabot St. Holyoke MA 01040 *TF:* 800-227-3623 ■ *Web:* www.specialtyll.com	413-532-0106		552-2
Specialty Manufacturing Co 5858 Centerville Rd Saint Paul MN 55127 *TF:* 800-549-4473 ■ *Web:* www.specialtymfg.com	651-653-0599	653-0989	790
Specialty Manufacturing LLC 6001 San Francisco NE Albuquerque NM 87109	505-823-1832		480
Specialty Metals Corp 8300 S 206th St Kent WA 98032 *Web:* www.specialtymetalscorp.com	253-398-1730	872-0437	492
Specialty Metals Supply Inc 250 Commerce Park Dr Jackson MS 39213 *TF:* 800-423-4958 ■ *Web:* specialtymetalssupply.com	601-956-8555		492
Specialty Motors Inc 25060 Ave Tibbitts Valencia CA 91355 *TF:* 800-232-2612 ■ *Web:* www.specialtymotors.com	661-257-7388	257-7389	518
Specialty Pipe & Tube Inc PO Box 516 Mineral Ridge OH 44440 *TF:* 800-842-5839 ■ *Web:* specialtypipe.com	330-505-8262	505-8260	492
Specialty Plastic Fabricators Inc 1000 W National Ave Mokena IL 60448 *TF:* 800-747-9509 ■ *Web:* www.spfinc.com	708-479-5501	479-5598	199
Specialty Products & Insulation Co (SPI) 1650 Manheim Pk Ste 202 Lancaster PA 17601 **Fax Area Code:* 717 ■ *TF:* 800-788-7764 ■ *Web:* www.spi-co.com	855-519-4044	519-4046*	191-4
Specialty Restaurants Corp 8191 E Kaiser Blvd Anaheim CA 92808 *Web:* www.specialtyrestaurants.com	714-279-6100	998-7574	670
Specialty Roll Products Inc 601 25th Ave. Meridian MS 39302 *TF:* 800-647-6267 ■ *Web:* www.specialtyroll.com	601-693-1771	693-6211	561
Specialty Sales & Marketing Inc 6725 Millcreek Dr Ste 5 Mississauga ON L5N5V3 *Web:* www.specialtysales.ca	905-816-0011		194
Specialty Sleep Assn (SSA) 46639 Jones Ranch Rd. Friant CA 93626 *Web:* www.sleepinformation.org	559-868-4187		49-4
Specialty Steel Treating Inc 34501 Commerce Rd Fraser MI 48026 *Web:* www.sst.net	586-293-5355	293-5390	484
Specialty Surgical Products Inc 1131 US Hwy 93 N. Victor MT 59875 *TF:* 888-878-0811 ■ *Web:* ssp-inc.com	406-961-0102		475
Specialty Systems 11901 Riverwood Dr. Burnsville MN 55337 *Web:* www.specialtysystems.com	952-894-5111		697
Specialty Tires of America Inc 1600 Washington St. Indiana PA 15701 *TF:* 800-622-7327 ■ *Web:* www.stausaonline.com	724-349-9010	349-8192	754
Specialty Tools & Fasteners Distributors Assn (STAFDA) 500 Elm Grove Rd Ste 210 PO Box 44 Elm Grove WI 53122 *TF:* 800-352-2981 ■ *Web:* www.stafda.org	262-784-4774	784-5059	49-18
Specialty Trade Shows Inc 3939 Hardie Rd. Coconut Grove FL 33133 *Web:* spectrade15.weebly.com	305-663-6635	661-8118	393
Specialty Vehicle Institute of America (SVIA) 2 Jenner St Ste 150 Irvine CA 92618 *TF:* 800-887-2887 ■ *Web:* atvsafety.org	949-727-3727	727-4216	49-21
Specialty Welding & Fabing of NY Inc 1025 Hiawatha Blvd Syracuse NY 13208 *Web:* www.specweld.com	315-426-1807		697
Specific Impulse Inc 2601 Blanding Ave Ste 401 Alameda CA 94501 *TF:* 800-470-0043 ■ *Web:* www.si9.com	510-251-2330		180
Specific Solutions Inc 475 International Dr Williamsville NY 14221 *TF:* 800-873-2345 ■ *Web:* specificsolutions.com	716-632-7777	632-6051	390
Specific Systems Ltd 7655 E 41st St. Tulsa OK 74145 *Web:* specificsystems.com	918-663-9321		664
Specification Rubber Products Inc 1568 First St N Alabaster AL 35007 *TF:* 800-633-3415 ■ *Web:* specrubber.com	205-663-2521	663-1875	326
Specified Technologies Inc 210 Evans Way Somerville NJ 08876 *TF:* 800-992-1180 ■ *Web:* www.stifirestop.com	908-526-8000	526-9623	146

	Phone	Fax	Class
Specified Woodworking Corporation Inc 9327 Washington Blvd N Laurel MD 20723 *Web:* www.specifiedwoodworking.com	301-598-8200		321
Speck Plastics Inc 490 Belfast Rdac PO Box 421 Nazareth PA 18064 *Web:* www.speckplastics.com	610-759-1807	759-3916	602
Specmo Enterprises 1200 E Avis Dr Madison Heights MI 48071 *TF:* 800-545-7910 ■ *Web:* specmo.com	800-545-7910		54
Speco Inc 3946 Willow Rd Schiller Park IL 60176 *TF:* 800-541-5415 ■ *Web:* speco.com	847-678-4240		358
Speco Technologies 200 New Hwy Amityville NY 11701 *TF:* 800-645-5516 ■ *Web:* www.specotech.com	631-957-8700	957-9142	38
Specs Howard School of Media Arts 19900 W 9 Mile Rd. Southfield MI 48075 *TF:* 866-617-7327 ■ *Web:* www.specshoward.edu	248-358-9000		685
Spectator, The 44 Frid St Hamilton ON L8N3G3 *TF:* 800-263-6902 ■ *Web:* www.thespec.com	905-526-3333	526-1395	532-1
Spectec 9 Polaris Way Emigrant MT 59027 *Web:* www.spectecsensors.com	406-333-4967	333-4259	639
SpecTec Inc 22500 SE 64th Pl Ste 115 Issaquah WA 98029 *Web:* www.spectec.net	425-313-0154		809
Spectech 106 Union Valley Rd. Oak Ridge TN 37830 *Web:* www.spectrumtechniques.com	865-482-9948		419
Spectera Inc 6220 Old Dobbin Ln Liberty 6 Ste 200 Columbia MD 21045 *TF:* 800-638-3120 ■ *Web:* www.spectera.com	800-638-3120		391-3
Spector Gadon & Rosen PC 1635 Market St. Philadelphia PA 19103 *Web:* www.lawsgr.com	215-241-8888	241-8844	428
Spector Rubin PA 3250 Mary St Ste 405 Miami FL 33133 *Web:* spectorrubin.com	305-537-2000	537-2001	41
Spector Textile Products Inc 10 Embankment St Lawrence MA 01842 *TF:* 800-533-3501 ■ *Web:* www.spectortextile.com	800-533-3501		745-3
Spectra Aluminum Products Inc 95 Reagens Industrial Pkwy Bradford ON L3Z2A4 *Web:* www.spectraaluminum.com	905-778-8093		492
Spectra Analysis Inc 257 Simarano Dr Marlborough MA 01752 *Web:* www.spectra-analysis.com	508-281-6232		419
Spectra Co 2510 Supply St Pomona CA 91767 *TF:* 800-375-1771 ■ *Web:* spectracompany.com	800-375-1771		378
Spectra Color Inc 9116 Stellar Ct. Corona CA 92883	951-277-0200		388
Spectra Colors Corp 25 Rizzolo Rd Kearny NJ 07032 *TF:* 800-527-8588 ■ *Web:* spectracolors.com	201-997-0606		146
Spectra Equipment Inc 23807 Aliso Creek Rd Ste 220 Laguna Niguel CA 92677 *TF:* 800-745-1233 ■ *Web:* www.spectra.com	714-970-7000	970-7095	174
Spectra Integrated Systems Inc 8100 Arrowridge Blvd. Charlotte NC 28273 *TF:* 800-443-7561 ■ *Web:* www.sitechma.com	704-525-7099		246
Spectra Laboratories Inc 2221 Ross Way Tacoma WA 98421 *Web:* www.spectra-labs.com	360-779-5141		794
Spectra Merchandising International Inc 4230 N Normandy Ave Chicago IL 60634 *TF:* 800-777-5331 ■ *Web:* www.spectraintl.com	773-202-8408		246
Spectra Plus Inc 638 Goodwin Dr Richardson TX 75081	972-437-5705		787
Spectra Precision Inc 10368 Westmoor Dr Westminster CO 80021 *TF:* 888-527-3771 ■ *Web:* www.spectraprecision.com	888-527-3771		203
Spectra Print Corp 2301 Country Club Dr PO Box 247 Stevens Point WI 54481 *Web:* www.spectraprint.com	715-344-5175		393
Spectra Services Inc 6359 Dean Pkwy Ontario NY 14519 *TF:* 800-955-7732 ■ *Web:* spectraservices.com	800-955-7732		419
Spectrachem 10 Dell Glen Ave Lodi NJ 07644 *TF:* 800-524-2806 ■ *Web:* www.spectrachem.net	973-253-3553	253-3663	388
Spectragraphic Inc 4 Brayton Ct Commack NY 11725 *Web:* www.spectragraphic.com	631-499-3100	499-5255	781
Spectra-Kote Corp 301 E Water St. Gettysburg PA 17325 *TF:* 800-241-4626 ■ *Web:* www.spectra-kote.com	717-334-3177		554
Spectral Sciences Inc 4 Fourth Ave Burlington MA 01803 *Web:* www.spectral.com	781-273-4770	270-1161	196
SpectraLink Corp 2560 55th St. Boulder CO 80301 *Web:* www.spectralink.com	303-440-5330		647
Spectralux Corp 12335 134th Ct NE. Redmond WA 98052 *Web:* www.spectralux.com	425-285-3000		529
Spectralytics Inc 145 3rd St. Dassel MN 55325 *Web:* www.spectralytics.com	320-275-2118	275-2993	425
Spectra-Mat Inc 100 Westgate Dr. Watsonville CA 95076 *Web:* www.spectramat.com	831-722-4116	722-4172	482
Spectranetics Corp 9965 Federal Dr Colorado Springs CO 80921 *NASDAQ: SPNC* ■ *TF:* 800-231-0978 ■ *Web:* www.spectranetics.com	719-447-2000	447-2022	424
SpectraScience Inc 11568 Sorrento Valley Rd Ste 11 San Diego CA 92121 *Web:* www.spectrascience.com	858-847-0200		250
SpectraSensors Inc 4333 W Sam Houston Pkwy N Houston TX 77043 *TF:* 800-619-2861 ■ *Web:* www.spectrasensors.com	713-300-2700		201
Spectraserv Inc 75 Jacobus Ave. South Kearny NJ 07032 *Web:* www.spectraserv.com	973-589-0277	589-0415	780
Spectrasonics Inc 440 Woodcrest Rd Wayne PA 19087 *Web:* www.spectrasonics.com	610-220-6070		743
Spectratek Technologies Inc 9834 Jordan Cir Santa Fe Springs CA 90670 *Web:* www.spectratek.net	310-822-2400		601
Spectrio LLC 4033 Tampa Rd Ste 103 Oldsmar FL 34677 **Fax Area Code:* 727 ■ *TF:* 800-584-4653 ■ *Web:* www.spectrio.com	800-584-4653	785-7659*	393
Spectro Alloys Corp 13220 Doyle Path E Rosemount MN 55068 *Web:* www.spectroalloys.com	651-437-2815	438-3714	485
Spectro Associates Inc 734 Kent Oaks Way Ste 302 Gaithersburg MD 20878 *Web:* www.spectrosales.com	410-321-7890		180
Spectro Coating Corp 101 Scott Dr Leominster MA 01453 *Web:* www.spectrocoating.com	978-534-1800		745-8

Name / Address	City	State	ZIP	Phone	Fax	Class
Spectro Scientific 1 Executive Dr Ste 101 *Web:* www.spectrosci.com	Chelmsford	MA	01824	978-486-0123	486-0030	419
Spectrolab Inc 12500 Gladstone Ave *TF:* 800-936-4888 ■ *Web:* www.spectrolab.com	Sylmar	CA	91342	818-365-4611	361-5102	696
Spectron Glass & Electronics Inc 595 Old Willets Path A *Web:* www.spectronsensors.com	Hauppauge	NY	11788	631-582-5600	582-5671	253
Spectronics Corp 956 Brush Hollow Rd **Fax Area Code:* 800 ■ *TF:* 800-274-8888 ■ *Web:* www.spectroline.com	Westbury	NY	11590	516-333-4840	491-6868*	201
Spectrum Aerospace Inc 609 W Knox Rd *Web:* www.spectrum-aero.com	Tempe	AZ	85284	480-966-0077	752-0036	22
Spectrum Associates Inc 183 Plains Rd *Web:* www.spectrumct.com	Milford	CT	06461	203-878-4618	877-6927	128
Spectrum Bags Inc 12850 Midway Pl *TF:* 800-456-6935 ■ *Web:* www.spectrumbags.com	Cerritos	CA	90703	562-623-2555		601
Spectrum Beauty Academy 25 S Quaker Ln Ste 15 *Web:* www.learnatspectrum.com	Alexandria	VA	22314	703-370-9700	370-9773	167-3
Spectrum Brands 3001 Deming Way *TF:* 800-566-7899 ■ *Web:* www.spectrumbrands.com	Middleton	WI	53562	608-275-3340		280
Spectrum Community Service 2621 Barrington Ct *Web:* www.spectrumcs.org	Hayward	CA	94545	510-881-0300	537-3340	167-3
Spectrum Controls Inc PO Box 5533 *Web:* www.spectrumcontrols.com	Bellevue	WA	98006	425-746-9481	641-9473	201
Spectrum Corp 10048 Easthaven Blvd *Web:* www.specorp.com	Houston	TX	77075	713-944-6200		701
Spectrum Data Inc 131 N Third St *TF:* 800-733-6567 ■ *Web:* www.spectrumdata.org	Oregon	IL	61061	800-733-6567		225
Spectrum Diversified Designs Inc 675 Mondial Pkwy *Web:* www.spectrumdiversified.com	Streetsboro	OH	44241	330-422-1840		549
Spectrum Equity Investors LP 1 International Pl 35th Fl *Web:* www.spectrumequity.com	Boston	MA	02110	617-464-4600	464-4601	792
Spectrum Glass Co PO Box 646 *TF:* 800-426-3120 ■ *Web:* www.spectrumglass.com	Woodinville	WA	98072	425-483-6699	483-9007	329
Spectrum Health Lakeland 1234 Napier Ave *Web:* www.spectrumhealthlakeland.org	Saint Joseph	MI	49085	269-983-8300		352
Spectrum Health Systems Inc 10 Mechanic St Ste 302 *TF:* 800-464-9555 ■ *Web:* www.spectrumhealthsystems.org	Worcester	MA	01608	508-792-5400		48-15
Spectrum Healthcare Resources Inc 12647 Olive Blvd Ste 600 *TF:* 800-325-3982 ■ *Web:* spectrumhealth.com	Saint Louis	MO	63141	800-325-3982		463
Spectrum Industries Inc 925 First Ave **Fax Area Code:* 800 ■ *TF:* 800-235-1262 ■ *Web:* www.spectrumfurniture.com	Chippewa Falls	WI	54729	715-723-6750	335-0473*	286
Spectrum Industries Inc 700 Wealthy St SW *Web:* www.spectrumindustries.com	Grand Rapids	MI	49504	616-451-0784		481
Spectrum Kitchens 38 E 29th St 3rd Fl S *Web:* www.spectrumkitchens.com	New York	NY	10016	212-829-0500		115
Spectrum Label Corp 30803 San Clemente St *Web:* www.spectrumlabel.com	Hayward	CA	94544	510-477-0707		413
Spectrum Laboratories Inc 18617 S Broadwick St *TF:* 800-634-3300 ■ *Web:* www.spectrumlabs.com	Rancho Dominguez	CA	90220	310-885-4600	885-4666	419
Spectrum Laboratory Products Inc 14422 S San Pedro St *TF:* 800-772-8786 ■ *Web:* www.spectrumchemical.com	Gardena	CA	90248	310-516-8000	516-7512	479
Spectrum Litho 4300 Business Center Dr *Web:* www.spectrumlithograph.com	Fremont	CA	94538	510-438-9192		627
Spectrum Paint Company Inc 65 Brewer Rd *Web:* www.spectrumpaint.co	Sedona	AZ	86336	928-204-1706		802
Spectrum Pharmaceuticals Inc 11500 S Eastern Ave Ste 240 *NASDAQ: SPPI* ■ *Web:* www.sppirx.com	Henderson	NV	89052	702-835-6300	260-7405	85
Spectrum Plastics Group 1000 Calle Recodo *Web:* www.spectrumplastics.com	San Clemente	CA	92673	949-361-0774		608
Spectrum Printing Company LLC 4651 S Butterfield Dr *Web:* www.spectrumprintingcompany.com	Tucson	AZ	85714	520-571-1114	571-1395	627
Spectrum Products 7100 Spectrum Ln *TF:* 800-791-8056 ■ *Web:* www.spectrumproducts.com	Missoula	MT	59808	800-791-8056		480
Spectrum Programs 6100 Blue Lagoon Dr Ste 400	Miami	FL	33126	305-757-6100		726
Spectrum Signal Processing by Vecima 2700 Production Way Ste 300 *TF:* 800-663-8986 ■ *Web:* www.spectrumsignal.com	Burnaby	BC	V5A4X1	604-676-6700	421-1764	625
Spectrum Software 1021 S Wolfe Rd Ste 130 *Web:* www.spectrum-soft.com	Sunnyvale	CA	94086	408-738-4387	738-4702	178-1
Spectrum Software Technology Inc (SST) Atlantic City International Airport Ste 114 *Web:* sst-it.com	Egg Harbor Township	NJ	08234	609-910-0190	645-6864	177
Spectrum Solutions Inc 114 Castle Dr *Web:* www.spectrumsi.com	Madison	AL	35758	256-830-9759	722-0394	261
Spectrum Systems Inc 3410 W Nine-Mile Rd *TF:* 800-432-6119 ■ *Web:* spectrumsystems.com	Pensacola	FL	32526	850-944-3392	944-1011	419
Spectrum, The 275 E St George Blvd *Web:* www.thespectrum.com	Saint George	UT	84770	435-674-6200		532-2
Spede Technologies 24864 Detroit Rd **Fax Area Code:* 440 ■ *TF:* 888-808-4237 ■ *Web:* www.spede.com	Cleveland	OH	44145	888-808-4237	808-8086*	178-1
SPEEA 15205 52nd Ave S *Web:* speea.org	Tukwila	WA	98188	206-433-0991	248-3990	414
Speece Thorson Capital Group Inc 225 S Sixth St Ste 2575 *Web:* www.stcapital.com	Minneapolis	MN	55402	612-338-4649	338-7451	401
Speech & Language Development Ctr 8699 Holder St *Web:* sldc.net	Buena Park	CA	90620	714-821-3620		685
SPEECH Morphing SYSTEMS Inc 1245 S Winchester Blvd Ste 216 *Web:* speechmorphing.com	San Jose	CA	95128	408-642-1021		138
Speech-Language & Audiology Canada 1 Nicholas St Ste 1000 *TF:* 800-259-8519 ■ *Web:* www.sac-oac.ca	Ottawa	ON	K1N7B7	613-567-9968	567-2859	48-1
SpeechSoft Inc 49 The Xing *TF:* 800-878-8117 ■ *Web:* www.speechsoft.com	Armonk	NY	10504	914-273-5560		178-1
Speed Art Museum, The 2035 S Third St *Web:* www.speedmuseum.org	Louisville	KY	40208	502-634-2700		520
Speed Check Conveyor Company Inc 5345 Truman Dr *Web:* www.speedcheckconveyor.com	Decatur	GA	30035	770-981-5490		207
Speed Consulting LLC 500 Cantrell St *TF:* 800-256-7140 ■ *Web:* www.speedconsulting.com	Waxahachie	TX	75165	800-256-7140		463
Speed Fab Crete 1150 E Kennedale Pkwy *Web:* www.speedfab-crete.com	Kennedale	TX	76060	817-478-1153	561-2544	183
Speed Selector Inc 17050 Munn Rd *Web:* speedselector.com	Chagrin Falls	OH	44023	440-543-8233	543-8527	620
Speed Skating Canada 2781 Lancaster Rd *TF:* 877-572-4772 ■ *Web:* www.speedskating.ca	Ottawa	ON	K1B1A7	902-425-5450		138
Speed Sport 142 F S Cardigan Way *TF:* 866-455-2531 ■ *Web:* speedsport.com	Mooresville	NC	28117	704-790-0136		457-3
Speed Trader 1717 Rt 6 *TF:* 800-874-3039 ■ *Web:* speedtrader.com	Carmel	NY	10512	845-531-2487	622-4878	690
Speedemissions Inc 220 1015 Tyrone Rd Ste 710 *Web:* www.speedemissions.com	Tyrone	GA	30290	770-306-7667		62
Speedflo Inc 499 Conway Ct *Web:* www.speedflo-ky.com	Lexington	KY	40511	859-233-3070	253-3013	110
Speedgrip Chuck Inc 2000 E Industrial Pkwy *Web:* speedgrip.com	Elkhart	IN	46516	574-294-1506	294-2465	759
Speedhorse Inc PO Box 1000 *Web:* www.speedhorse.com	Norman	OK	73070	405-288-2145	288-2151	637-9
Speedie & Associates Inc 3331 E Wood St *TF:* 800-628-6221 ■ *Web:* www.speedie.net	Phoenix	AZ	85040	602-997-6391	943-5508	743
SpeedInfo 100 W San Fernando St Ste 475 *Web:* speedinfo.com	San Jose	CA	95113	408-446-7660	289-9171	224
Speeding Star 29 E 21st St *TF:* 800-398-2504 ■ *Web:* www.speedingstar.com	New York	NY	10010	908-771-9400	771-0925	637-2
Speedling Inc 4447 Old 41 Hwy S **Fax Area Code:* 813 ■ *TF:* 800-881-4769 ■ *Web:* www.speedling.com	Ruskin	FL	33570	800-881-4769	645-8123*	369
Speed-Mat Inc 374 S St *TF:* 800-882-7017 ■ *Web:* www.speed-mat.com	Biddeford	ME	04005	207-294-4358	294-4359	131
Speedway Digital Printing Inc 475 Fourth St *Web:* speedwayprinting.com	San Francisco	CA	94107	415-543-5928		627
Speedway LLC 500 Speedway Dr *TF:* 800-643-1948 ■ *Web:* www.speedway.com	Enon	OH	45323	937-864-3000		324
Speedway Motors 340 Victory Ln *TF:* 800-736-3733 ■ *Web:* www.speedwaymotors.com	Lincoln	NE	68528	800-979-0122		791
Speedway Motorsports Inc (SMI) 5555 Concord Pkwy S *NYSE: TRK* ■ *Web:* www.speedwaymotorsports.com	Concord	NC	28027	704-455-3239		181
Speedway Motorsports Inc c/o US Legend Cars 5245 NC Hwy 49 S *Web:* www.uslegendcars.com	Harrisburg	NC	28075	704-455-3896	455-3820	515
Speedway Printing & Copy Center Inc 2575 N Causeway Blvd *Web:* speedwayprinting.net	Mandeville	LA	70471	985-626-0032		113
Speedway Redi Mix Inc 1201 N Taylor Rd *TF:* 800-227-5649 ■ *Web:* www.speedwaycp.com	Garrett	IN	46738	260-357-6885	357-0238	182
Speedway Steel 501 N Truman Blvd PO Box 8 *Web:* www.speedwaysteel.net	Crystal City	MO	63019	636-931-6500	931-6050	480
Speedy Automated Mailers Inc 2200 Queen St Ste 15 *TF:* 800-678-4775 ■ *Web:* speedy-inc.com	Bellingham	WA	98229	360-676-4775		5
Speedy Glass 2422 Arctic Blvd *Web:* www.speedyglass.com	Anchorage	AK	99503	907-272-1435		62-2
Speedy Litho Inc 403 Catlin *Web:* speedylitho.com	Kelso	WA	98626	360-425-3610	636-5233	627
Speegle Construction Inc 210 Government Ave *Web:* www.speegleconstruction.com	Niceville	FL	32578	850-729-2484		449
Speer Memorial Library 801 E 12th St *Web:* www.mission.lib.tx.us	Mission	TX	78572	956-580-8750	580-8756	434-3
Speidel 34 Branch Ave *TF:* 800-441-2200 ■ *Web:* www.speidel.com	Providence	RI	02904	401-519-2000		408
Speier Jackie (Rep D - CA) 2465 Rayburn House Office Bldg *Web:* speier.house.gov	Washington	DC	20515	202-225-3531	226-4183	342-2
Spell Capital Partners LLC 222 S Ninth St Ste 2880 *Web:* spellcapital.com	Minneapolis	MN	55402	612-371-9650	371-9651	405
Spellman Hardwoods Inc 4645 N 43rd Ave **Fax Area Code:* 623 ■ *TF:* 800-624-5401 ■ *Web:* www.spellmanhardwoods.com	Phoenix	AZ	85031	602-272-2313	930-7668*	191-3
Spellman High Voltage Electronics Corp 475 Wireless Blvd *Web:* www.spellmanhv.com	Hauppauge	NY	11788	631-630-3000	435-1620	253
Spelman College 350 Spelman Ln SW *TF:* 800-982-2411 ■ *Web:* spelman.edu	Atlanta	GA	30314	404-681-3643	270-5201	166
Spence & Company Ltd 76 Campanelli Indus Dr *Web:* www.spenceltd.com	Brockton	MA	02301	508-427-5577		296-13

				Phone	Fax	Class
Spence Asset Management Inc 3529 Foothills Rd *TF:* 800-230-1840 ■ *Web:* www.spenceassetmanagement.com	Las Cruces	NM	88011	575-556-8500	556-8510	690
Spence Engineering Company Inc 150 Coldenham Rd *TF:* 800-398-2493 ■ *Web:* www.spenceengineering.com	Walden	NY	12586	845-778-5566	778-1072	789
Spence Law Firm LLC 15 S Jackson St *TF:* 800-967-2117 ■ *Web:* www.spencelawyers.com	Jackson	WY	83001	307-733-7290	733-5248	428
Spencer Calahan LLC 827 St Louis St *Web:* calahanlaw.com	Baton Rouge	LA	70802	225-387-2323	387-2324	41
Spencer Clarke LLC 555 Madison Ave *Web:* spencerclarke.com	New York	NY	10005	212-446-6100		690
Spencer Companies Inc 2600 Memorial Pkwy S *TF:* 800-633-2910 ■ *Web:* www.spencercos.com	Huntsville	AL	35801	256-533-1150	535-2910	579
Spencer County 200 Main St PO Box 12 *Web:* spencercounty.in.gov	Rockport	IN	47635	812-649-6028	649-6030	338
Spencer County 2 W Main St PO Box 544 *TF:* 888-497-9341 ■ *Web:* www.spencercountyky.gov	Taylorsville	KY	40071	502-477-8369	477-3216	338
Spencer Fabrications Inc 29511 County Rd 561 *TF:* 866-277-3623 ■ *Web:* www.spenfab.com	Tavares	FL	32778	352-343-0014		697
Spencer Fane Britt & Browne LLP 1000 Walnut St Ste 1400 *Web:* www.spencerfane.com	Kansas City	MO	64106	816-292-8881	474-3216	428
Spencer Foundation 625 N Michigan Ave Ste 1600 *Web:* www.spencer.org	Chicago	IL	60611	312-337-7000	337-0282	305
Spencer Gifts LLC 6826 Black Horse Pk *Web:* www.spencersonline.com	Egg Harbor Township	NJ	08234	609-645-3300		327
Spencer Gray LLC 1565 Hotel Cir S Ste 300 *Web:* spencergray.com	San Diego	CA	92108	619-281-3900		260
Spencer Hall Inc 11321 Torwilligorscrook Dr *TF:* 888-883-4332 ■ *Web:* www.spencerhall.com	Cincinnati	OH	45249	513-683-9724		195
Spencer Insurance Agency 2626 N Josey Ln Ste 104 *Web:* spencerinsurancedfw.com	Carrollton	TX	75007	972-242-1756		390
Spencer Municipal Utilities (SMU) 520 Second Ave E Ste 1 *Web:* smunet.net	Spencer	IA	51301	712-580-5800	580-5336	116
Spencer Museum of Art University of Kansas 1301 Mississippi St *Web:* spencerart.ku.edu	Lawrence	KS	66045	785-864-4710	864-3112	520
Spencer Oil Company Inc 16410 Common Rd *Web:* spenceroil.com	Roseville	MI	48066	586-775-5022		316
Spencer Plastics Inc 2300 Gary E Schwach St *Web:* spencerplastics.com	Cadillac	MI	49601	231-942-7100	775-4615	608
Spencer Recovery Centers Inc 1316 S Coast Hwy *TF:* 800-334-0394 ■ *Web:* spencerrecovery.com	Laguna Beach	CA	92651	800-334-0394		726
Spencer Reed Group Inc 5700 W 112th St Ste 110 *TF:* 800-477-5035 ■ *Web:* www.spencerreed.com	Overland Park	KS	66211	913-663-4400		266
Spencer Savings Bank SLA 611 River Dr *TF:* 800-363-8115 ■ *Web:* www.spencersavings.com	Elmwood Park	NJ	07407	973-772-6700		70
Spencer Shenk Capers & Assoc 1515 W 190th St *Web:* www.ssca.com	Gardena	CA	90248	310-515-7555		463
Spencer Turbine Co 600 Day Hill Rd *TF:* 800-232-4321 ■ *Web:* www.spencerturbine.com	Windsor	CT	06095	860-688-8361	688-0098	18
Spencer's Restaurant 701 W Barista Rd *Web:* www.spencersrestaurant.com	Palm Springs	CA	92262	760-327-3446		671
Spenco Medical Corp 6301 Imperial Dr *TF:* 800-877-3626 ■ *Web:* spenco.implus.com	Waco	TX	76702	800-877-3626		477
SpenDifference LLC 2000 Clay St 3rd Fl *Web:* www.spendifference.com	Denver	CO	80211	303-531-2680	531-2700	194
Spengler Company Inc 1402 Frontage Rd *Web:* www.spenglerco.com	O'Fallon	IL	62269	618-206-0022		189-10
Sperone Westwater 257 Bowery *Web:* www.speronewestwater.com	New York	NY	10002	212-999-7337	999-7338	42
Sperro Metal Products Inc 2 Skyline Dr *Web:* sperro.com	Montville	NJ	07045	973-335-2000		697
Sperry & Rice Manufacturing Company LLC 9146 US Hwy 52 *TF:* 800-541-9277 ■ *Web:* www.sperryrice.com	Brookville	IN	47012	765-647-4141	647-3302	677
Sperry Automatics Company Inc 1372 New Haven Rd PO Box 717 *TF:* 800-923-3709 ■ *Web:* www.sperryautomatics.com	Naugatuck	CT	06770	203-729-4589	729-7787	621
Sperry Marine Northrop Grumman 1070 Seminole Trl *Web:* www.sperrymarine.com	Charlottesville	VA	22901	434-974-2000		529
Sperry Rail Inc 46 Shelter Rock Rd *TF:* 800-525-8913 ■ *Web:* www.sperryrail.com	Danbury	CT	06810	203-791-4500		41
Sperry Software Inc 833 Pheasant Ct Ste 503 *TF:* 800-878-1645 ■ *Web:* www.sperrysoftware.com	Jacksonville	FL	32223	800-878-1645		525
Sperry's 5109 Harding Pk *Web:* www.sperrys.com	Nashville	TN	37205	615-353-0809		671
Sperry, Mitchell & Company Inc 595 Madison Ave 35th Fl *Web:* www.sperrymitchell.com	New York	NY	10022	212-832-6628	753-0757	401
Spertus Museum 610 S Michigan Ave *Web:* spertus.edu	Chicago	IL	60605	312-322-1700	922-6406	520
SPESA (Sewn Products Equipment Suppliers Assn) 9650 Strickland Rd Ste 103-324 *Web:* www.spesa.org	Raleigh	NC	27615	919-872-8909		49-13
Spesia Ayers Attorneys At Law 1415 Black Rd *Web:* www.spesia-taylor.com	Joliet	IL	60435	815-726-4311	846-2410	445
Spevcoinc 8118 Reynolda Rd *Web:* spevco.com	Pfafftown	NC	27040	336-924-8100		120
Spex Precision Machine Technology 85 Excel Dr *Web:* www.spex1.com	Rochester	NY	14621	585-467-0520		454
SPFPA (International Union Security Police & Fire Professionals of America) 25510 Kelly Rd *TF:* 800-228-7492 ■ *Web:* www.spfpa.org	Roseville	MI	48066	586-772-7250	772-9644	414
SPG Intl 11230 Harland Dr *TF:* 877-503-4774 ■ *Web:* www.spgusa.com	Covington	GA	30014	770-787-9830		286
Sphere 3D Corp 240 Matheson Blvd E *TF:* 800-406-7325 ■ *Web:* sphere3d.com	Mississauga	ON	L4Z1X1	416-749-5999		180
Spherexx LLC 9142 S Sheridan *Web:* www.spherexx.com	Tulsa	OK	74133	918-491-7500		180
Spherix Inc *Alkido Pharma Inc* 6430 Rockledge Dr Ste 503 *NASDAQ: SPEX* ■ *Web:* aikidopharma.com	Bethesda	MD	20817	301-897-2540	897-2567	192
Sphinx Home Health Care 4415 Metropolitan Pky Ste 200 *TF:* 855-271-6311 ■ *Web:* www.sphinxhomecare.com	Sterling Heights	MI	48310	586-264-2400	264-2919	363
SPHS (Sheppard Pratt Health System) 6501 N Charles St *TF:* 800-627-0330 ■ *Web:* www.sheppardpratt.org	Baltimore	MD	21285	410-938-3000		374-5
SPI (Specialty Products & Insulation Co) 1650 Manheim Pk Ste 202 **Fax Area Code:* 717 ■ *TF:* 800-788-7764 ■ *Web:* www.spi-co.com	Lancaster	PA	17601	855-519-4044	519-4046*	191-4
SPI Health & Safety inc 60 Rue Gaston-Dumoulin *Web:* www.spi-s.com	Blainville	QC	J7C0A3	450-420-2012		358
SPI Lasers 4000 Burton Dr *Web:* www.spilasers.com	Santa Clara	CA	95054	408-454-1170		466
SPI Lighting Inc 10400 N Enterprise Dr **Fax Area Code:* 414 ■ *Web:* www.spilighting.com	Mequon	WI	53092	262-242-1420	242-6414*	439
SPI Pharma Rockwood Office Pk 503 Carr Rd Ste 210 *TF:* 800-789-9755 ■ *Web:* www.spipharma.com	Wilmington	DE	19809	302-576-8567		479
SPI/Mobile Pulley Works Inc 905 S Ann St *TF:* 866-334-6325 ■ *Web:* www.spimpw.com	Mobile	AL	36605	251-653-0606	653-0668	261
Spiaggia 980 N Michigan Ave *Web:* www.spiaggiarestaurant.com	Chicago	IL	60611	312-280-2750		671
Spic & Span Inc 4301 N Richards St *Web:* www.splcandspan.com	Milwaukee	WI	53212	414-964-5050	964-5042	426
Spice Hunter Inc 2000 W Broad St *TF:* 800-444-3061 ■ *Web:* www.spicehunter.com	Richmond	VA	23220	800-444-3061		296-37
Spice Island Tea House 253 Atwood St *Web:* www.spiceislandteahouse.com	Pittsburgh	PA	15213	412-687-8821		671
Spice World Inc 8101 Presidents Dr *TF:* 800-433-4979 ■ *Web:* www.spiceworldinc.com	Orlando	FL	32809	407-851-9432		296-37
Spiced Pear 117 Memorial Blvd *TF:* 866-793-5664 ■ *Web:* www.thechanler.com	Newport	RI	02840	401-847-2244		671
Spicer Jeffries & Company LLP 5251 S Quebec St Ste 200 *Web:* spicerjeffries.com	Greenwood Village	CO	80111	303-753-1959		2
Spicers Canada Ltd 200 Galcat Dr *Web:* www.spicers.ca	Vaughan	ON	L4L0B9	905-265-5000		557
Spicers Paper Inc 12310 Slauson Ave *TF:* 800-774-2377 ■ *Web:* www.spicers.com	Santa Fe Springs	CA	90670	562-698-1199	945-2597	553
Spidell Publishing Inc PO Box 61044 *TF:* 800-277-2257 ■ *Web:* www.spidell.com	Anaheim	CA	92801	714-776-7850	776-9906	637-2
Spider Company Inc 2340 11th St *Web:* www.spidercompany.com	Rockford	IL	61104	815-961-8200		567
Spider Staging Corp 365 Upland Dr *TF:* 877-774-3370 ■ *Web:* www.spiderstaging.com	Tukwila	WA	98188	206-575-6445	575-6240	491
SPIE 1000 20th St *Web:* spie.org	Bellingham	WA	98225	360-676-3290	647-1445	49-19
Spiegel, Brown & Fichera LLP 272 Mill St *Web:* sbflawyers.com	Poughkeepsie	NY	12601	845-452-7400		41
Spike 1352 W Main **Fax Area Code:* 435 ■ *TF:* 800-821-4474 ■ *Web:* www.gspike.com	Tremonton	UT	84337	800-821-4474	257-5719*	274
Spike TV 345 Hudson St *Web:* www.spike.com	New York	NY	10014	212-846-8000	767-8891	647
Spiller Furniture 5605 Mcfarland Blvd *Web:* www.spillerfurniture.com	Northport	AL	35476	205-333-2030		321
Spiller's Reprographics 34 Lexington St Lewiston Industrial Pk *Web:* www.spillersrepro.com	Lewiston	ME	04241	207-784-1571		534
Spillman Co, The 1701 Moler Rd *Web:* www.spillmanform.com	Columbus	OH	43207	614-444-2184		697
Spillman Technologies Inc *Motorola Solutions Inc* 4625 Lake Pk Blvd *Web:* www.spillman.com	Salt Lake City	UT	84120	801-902-1200	902-1210	178-10
Spilltech Environmental Inc 1627 Odonoghue St *TF:* 800-228-3877 ■ *Web:* www.spilltech.com	Mobile	AL	36615	800-228-3877		608
Spilman Thomas & Battle PLLC 300 Kanawha Blvd E *TF:* 800-967-8251 ■ *Web:* www.spilmanlaw.com	Charleston	WV	25301	304-340-3800		428
Spin Games LLC 100 Washington St Ste 100 & 250 *TF:* 866-890-6448 ■ *Web:* www.spingames.net	Reno	NV	89503	775-420-3550		224
Spin Master Ltd 450 Front St W *TF:* 800-622-8339 ■ *Web:* www.spinmaster.com	Toronto	ON	M5V1B6	416-364-6002		762
Spin Sucks PO Box 13013 Ste 4n *Web:* spinsucks.com	Chicago	IL	60613	312-878-6406		636
Spina Bifida Assn 1600 Wilson Blvd Ste 800 *TF:* 800-621-3141 ■ *Web:* spinabifidaassociation.org	Arlington	VA	22209	202-944-3285	944-3295	48-17

Name / Address	City	State	ZIP	Phone	Fax	Class
Spinco Metal Products Inc 1 Country Club Dr *Web:* spincometal.com	Newark	NY	14513	315-331-6285		295
Spindler Co 4430 Portage St NW *TF:* 800-269-2560 ■ *Web:* thespindlercompany.com	North Canton	OH	44720	330-499-2560		297-2
Spindrift Inn 652 Cannery Row *TF:* 800-841-1879 ■ *Web:* www.spindriftinn.com	Monterey	CA	93940	831-646-8900	655-8174	379
Spindustries LLC 1301 La Salle St *Web:* www.lgspin.com	Lake Geneva	WI	53147	262-248-6601	248-1277	488
Spindustry Systems Inc 1370 NW 114th St Ste 300 *TF:* 877-225-4200 ■ *Web:* www.spindustry.com	Des Moines	IA	50325	515-225-0920	225-1785	809
Spine Align Inc 741 Chicago Dr *Web:* www.chirobed.com	Holland	MI	49423	616-392-4565		321
Spinesmith Partners 4719 S Congress Ave *Web:* spinesmithusa.com	Austin	TX	78701	512-206-0770		476
SpinGo Solutions Inc 14193 S Minuteman Dr Ste 100 *TF:* 877-377-4646 ■ *Web:* www.spingo.com	Draper	UT	84020	877-377-4646		387
Spiniello Cos 354 Eisenhower Pkwy *Web:* www.spiniello.com	Livingston	NJ	07039	973-808-8383	808-9591	188-10
Spinnaker Coating Inc 518 E Water St *TF:* 800-543-9452 ■ *Web:* www.spinnakercoating.com	Troy	OH	45373	937-332-6500	332-6518	554
Spinner Publications Inc 164 William St *TF:* 800-292-6062 ■ *Web:* www.spinnerpub.com	New Bedford	MA	02740	508-994-4564	994-6925	637-2
SPINS Inc 222 W Hubbard St Ste 300 **Fax Area Code:* 847 ■ *Web:* www.spins.com	Chicago	IL	60654	312-281-5100	517-1170*	668
Spintrac Systems Inc 690 Aldo Ave *Web:* www.spintrac.com	Santa Clara	CA	95054	408-980-1155	980-1267	695
SPINVI 1940 Duke St *Web:* www.spinvi.com	Alexandria	VA	22314	703-684-4464		788
Spira Data Corp 707 7th Ave SW Ste 1000 *TF:* 855-666-6353 ■ *Web:* www.spiradata.com	Calgary	AB	T2P0Z3	403-263-6475		387
Spiral Binding Company Inc 1 Maltese Dr **Fax Area Code:* 973 ■ *TF:* 800-631-3572 ■ *Web:* spiralbinding.com	Totowa	NJ	07511	800-631-3572	256-5981*	86
Spiral Diner 1314 W Magnolia *Web:* spiraldiner.com	Fort Worth	TX	76104	817-332-8834		671
Spiral-Matic Corp 7772 Park Pl *Web:* www.spiralmatic.com	Brighton	MI	48116	248-486-9700	486-5081	298
Spiratex Company Inc 1916 Frenchtown Center Dr *Web:* www.spiratex.com	Monroe	MI	48162	734-289-4800	289-4804	608
Spiration Inc 6675 185th Ave NE *Web:* www.spiration.com	Redmond	WA	98052	425-497-1700		250
Spirax Sarco Inc 1150 Northpoint Blvd *TF:* 800-883-4411 ■ *Web:* www.spiraxsarco.com	Blythewood	SC	29016	803-714-2000	714-2222	201
Spire 2828 Dauphin St *Web:* www.spireenergy.com	Mobile	AL	36606	251-476-8052	471-2588	787
Spire Capital Partners LLC 30 Rockefeller Plz Ste 4200 *Web:* www.spirecapital.com	New York	NY	10112	212-218-5454	218-5455	792
Spire Consulting Group LLC 114 W Seventh St Ste 1300 *TF:* 855-216-0812 ■ *Web:* www.spireconsultinggroup.com	Austin	TX	78701	512-637-0845		196
Spire Hospitality LLC 111 S Pfingsten Rd Ste 425 *Web:* www.spirehotels.com	Deerfield	IL	60015	847-498-6650		707
Spire Inc 65 Bay St *TF:* 877-350-8837 ■ *Web:* www.spire.net	Boston	MA	02125	617-350-8837	350-9951	344
Spire Integrated Solutions 8719 S 135th St Ste 300 **Fax Area Code:* 402 ■ *Web:* www.spire-is.com	Omaha	NE	68138	877-679-7800	344-4242*	228
Spire Investment Partners LLC 7901 Jones Branch Dr *TF:* 888-737-8907 ■ *Web:* www.spireip.com	McLean	VA	22102	703-748-5800		401
Spire Technologies Inc 2140 SW Jefferson St Ste 300 *TF:* 800-481-7332 ■ *Web:* www.spiretech.com	Portland	OR	97201	503-222-3086		196
Spirit 106.3 6420 S Zero St *Web:* www.kzkzfm.com	Fort Smith	AR	72903	479-646-6700	646-1373	645-59
Spirit AeroSystems Inc 3801 S Oliver St *TF:* 800-501-7597 ■ *Web:* www.spiritaero.com	Wichita	KS	67210	316-526-9000		20
Spirit Airlines Inc 2800 Executive Way *NASDAQ: SAVE* ■ *TF:* 800-772-7117 ■ *Web:* www.spirit.com	Miramar	FL	33025	954-447-7828		25
Spirit Financial Credit Union 8535 New Falls Rd *TF:* 800-437-9392 ■ *Web:* spiritfinancialcu.org	Levittown	PA	19054	267-580-0230	580-0239	219
SPIRIT Global Energy Solutions Inc 3406 S State Hwy 349 *Web:* www.apergyals.com	Midland	TX	79706	432-522-2288		538
Spirit Human Resources LLC 3030 Northwest Expy Ste 705 *Web:* spirithr.com	Oklahoma City	OK	73112	405-951-5300		570
Spirit Lake Casino & Resort 7889 Hwy 57 *TF:* 800-946-8238 ■ *Web:* spiritlakecasino.com	Saint Michael	ND	58370	701-766-4747		452
Spirit Lake Tribe (SLT) PO Box 359 *Web:* www.spiritlakenation.com	Fort Totten	ND	58335	701-766-4221	766-4126	804
Spirit Manufacturing Inc 3000 Nestle Rd *TF:* 800-258-4555 ■ *Web:* www.spiritfitness.com	Jonesboro	AR	72401	870-935-1107	935-7611	267
Spirit Publishing Co 510 Pine St *Web:* www.punxsutawneyspirit.com	Punxsutawney	PA	15767	814-938-8740		532-2
Spirit Rock Meditation Ctr 5000 Sir Francis Drake Blvd *Web:* www.spiritrock.org	Woodacre	CA	94973	415-488-0164		148
Spirit Truck Lines Inc 200 W Nolana *TF:* 800-726-7515 ■ *Web:* www.spirittrucklines.com	San Juan	TX	78589	956-781-7715	781-7211	780
Spirit Trucking Co 5400 W 47th St *Web:* www.spirittrucking.com	Chicago	IL	60638	708-496-8888	496-9770	780
Spirit Winds School of Thai Massage & International Healing Ctr PO Box 2326 *Web:* www.spiritwinds.net	Nevada City	CA	95959	530-263-3181		685
Spiritan Ctr 6230 Brush Run Rd *Web:* www.spiritans.org	Bethel Park	PA	15102	412-831-0302		637-2
Spiritual Life Ctr 7100 E 45th St N *Web:* catholicdioceseofwichita.org	Wichita	KS	67226	316-744-0167	744-8072	673
Spiro's 1054 N Woods Mill Rd *Web:* spiros-restaurant.com	Chesterfield	MO	63017	314-878-4449	878-1090	671
Spiroflow Systems Inc 2806 Gray Fox Rd *Web:* www.spiroflow.com	Monroe	NC	28110	704-291-9595		207
Spirol International Corp 30 Rock Ave *Web:* www.spirol.com	Danielson	CT	06239	860-774-8571	774-2048	487
Spirometrics Medical Equipment Co 22 Shaker Rd *TF:* 800-767-0004 ■ *Web:* www.spirometrics.com	Gray	ME	04039	207-657-6700	657-4123	476
Spitfire Aviation Flight School 300 Moffett Pl *Web:* www.spitfireaviationsb.com	Santa Barbara	CA	93117	805-967-4373		685
Spitfire Strategies LLC 2300 N Street NW Ste 610 *Web:* spitfirestrategies.com	Washington	DC	20037	202-293-6200	293-6201	636
Spitler Woods State Natural Area 705 Spitler Pk Dr *Web:* www.dnr.illinois.gov	Mount Zion	IL	62549	217-864-3121		565
Spitz Inc 700 Brandywine Dr *Web:* www.spitzinc.com	Chadds Ford	PA	19317	610-459-5200		628
Spitzer Engineering LLC 555 Madison Ave 18 th Fl	New York	NY	10022	212-765-5170		261
Spitzer Herriman Stephenson Holderead Conner 122 E Fourth St PO Box 927 *Web:* shshlaw.com	Marion	IN	46952	765-664-7307	662-0574	41
Spitzer Industries Inc 12141 Wickchester Ln Ste 750 *Web:* www.spitzerind.com	Houston	TX	77079	832-783-7000		595
Spitzer Management Inc 150 E Bridge St *Web:* www.spitzer.com	Elyria	OH	44035	440-323-4671		360-2
Spivey Enterprises Inc 6148 Brookshire Blvd *Web:* www.quikshoppe.com	Charlotte	NC	28216	704-399-4802	393-1940	345
Spivey Lemonik Swenor Pc 3868 Main St PO Box 1349 *Web:* slsvt.com	Manchester Center	VT	05255	802-362-1946		2
SPJ (Society of Professional Journalists) 3909 N Meridian St *Web:* www.spj.org	Indianapolis	IN	46208	317-927-8000	920-4789	49-14
SPL (Somerville Public Library) 79 Highland Ave *Web:* www.somervillepubliclibrary.org	Somerville	MA	02143	617-623-5000		434-3
SPL (Sunnyvale Public Library) 665 W Olive Ave *Web:* sunnyvale.ca.gov	Sunnyvale	CA	94086	408-730-7300		434-3
Splan Inc 5500 Stewart Ave Ste 102 *Web:* www.splan.com	Fremont	CA	94538	510-320-3305		178-1
Splash Lagoon Water Pk Resort 8091 Peach St *TF:* 866-377-5274 ■ *Web:* www.splashlagoon.com	Erie	PA	16509	866-377-5274		31
Splash Omnimedia 711 E Main St Ste J2 *Web:* www.splashomnimedia.com	Lexington	SC	29072	803-785-5656		195
Splash!events Inc 210 Hillsdale Ave *TF:* 866-204-6000 ■ *Web:* www.splashevents.com	San Jose	CA	95136	408-287-8600		184
Splashdot Inc 609 W Hastings St Ste 888 *Web:* www.splashdot.com	Vancouver	BC	V6B4W4	604-899-0597		225
Splashtown Water Park 21300 IH-45 N *Web:* www.wetnwildsplashtown.com	Spring	TX	77373	281-355-3300	353-7946	32
Splendora Independent School District 23419 FM 2090 Rd *Web:* www.splendoraisd.org	Splendora	TX	77372	281-689-3128	689-7509	685
SPLICE Software Inc 425 78 Ave SW *TF:* 855-677-5423 ■ *Web:* www.splicesoftware.com	Calgary	AB	T2V5K5	403-720-8326	720-5718	179
Splish Splash 2549 Splish Splash Dr *Web:* www.splishsplash.com	Calverton	NY	11933	631-727-3600		32
Split Oak Press 413 Smiddy Hall 953 Danby Rd *Web:* splitoakpress.net	Ithaca	NY	14850	607-274-5145		637-2
Split Rock Creek State Park 50th Ave *Web:* www.dnr.state.mn.us	Jasper	MN	56144	507-348-7908	348-8940	565
Split Rock Lighthouse State Park 3755 Split Rock Lighthouse Rd *Web:* www.dnr.state.mn.us	Two Harbors	MN	55616	218-595-7625		565
Split Rock Partners 16526 W 78th St Ste 504 *Web:* splitrock.com	Eden Prairie	MN	55346	952-995-7474		792
Split Rock Resort 100 Moseywood Rd *TF:* 800-255-7625 ■ *Web:* www.splitrockresort.com	Lake Harmony	PA	18624	570-722-9111		669
SPM Industries Inc 2455 E 10 Mile Rd *Web:* www.spmind.com	Warren	MI	48091	586-758-1100	757-8340	454
SPM Marketing & Communications 15 W Harris Ave Ste 300 *Web:* www.spmmarketing.com	LaGrange	IL	60525	708-246-7700		4
SPM Technology Inc 300 Park Central Blvd *Web:* www.spmtechnology.com	Georgetown	TX	78626	512-931-0201		454
SPMOH (Saint Petersburg Museum of History) 335 2nd Ave NE *Web:* www.spmoh.org	Saint Petersburg	FL	33701	727-894-1052		520
SPN Services Inc 5851 43rd Ave *Web:* www.spnservices.com	Flushing	NY	11377	718-565-5954		809
SPN Well Services 4727 Gaillardia Pkwy *Web:* spnws.com	Oklahoma City	OK	73142	405-748-2200		538
Spok Inc 6850 Versar Ctr Ste 420 **Fax Area Code:* 703 ■ *TF:* 888-878-5009 ■ *Web:* www.usamobility.com	Springfield	VA	22151	800-611-8488	660-6994*	736

	Phone	Fax	Class
Spokane Art Supply Inc 1303 N Monroe St .... Spokane WA 99201 *TF:* 800-556-5568 ■ *Web:* www.spokaneartsupply.com	509-327-6622		45
Spokane Association of Realtors 1924 N Ash St .... Spokane WA 99205 *Web:* spokanerealtor.com	509-326-9222		653
Spokane Civic Theatre 1020 N Howard St .... Spokane WA 99201 *Web:* spokanecivictheatre.com	509-325-2507		572
Spokane Community College 1810 N Greene St .... Spokane WA 99217 *TF:* 800-248-5644 ■ *Web:* www.scc.spokane.edu	509-533-7000	533-8181	162
Spokane Convention & Visitors Bureau Main Level River Park Sq 808 W Main Ave .... Spokane WA 99201 *TF:* 800-662-0084 ■ *Web:* www.visitspokane.com	509-624-1341	623-1297	206
Spokane County 1116 W Broadway Ave .... Spokane WA 99260 *TF:* 800-562-6000 ■ *Web:* www.spokanecounty.org	509-477-2265	477-2274	338
Spokane Ctr 720 W Mallon Ave .... Spokane WA 99201 *Web:* www.spokanecenter.com	509-279-7000	279-7050	205
Spokane Falls Community College 3410 W Ft George Wright Dr .... Spokane WA 99224 *TF:* 888-509-7944 ■ *Web:* sfcc.spokane.edu	509-533-3500	533-3237	162
Spokane Hardware Supply Inc 2001 E Trent Ave .... Spokane WA 99202 *TF:* 800-888-1663 ■ *Web:* www.spokane-hardware.com	509-535-1663		350
Spokane International Airport 9000 W Airport Dr .... Spokane WA 99224 *TF:* 800-776-5263 ■ *Web:* www.spokaneairports.net	509-455-6455	624-6633	27
Spokane Neighborhood Action Partners (SNAP) 3102 W Fort George Wright Dr .... Spokane WA 99224 *Web:* www.snapwa.org	509-456-7627	534-5874	196
Spokane Public Library 906 W Main Ave .... Spokane WA 99201 *Web:* www.spokanelibrary.org	509-444-5300		434-3
Spokane Public Radio 2319 N Monroe St .... Spokane WA 99201 *TF:* 800-328-5729 ■ *Web:* spokanepublicradio.org	509-328-5729	328-5764	645-151
Spokane Software Systems Inc PO Box 14930 .... Spokane WA 99214 *Web:* www.spokane.ag	509-872-5000	651-4455	809
Spokane Steel Foundry Co 3808 N Sullivan Rd Bldg 1 .... Spokane WA 99216 *TF:* 800-541-3601 ■ *Web:* www.spokaneindustries.com	509-924-0440	924-9448	307
Spokane Symphony PO Box 365 .... Spokane WA 99210 *TF:* 800-899-1482 ■ *Web:* www.spokanesymphony.org	509-624-1200	252-2637	573-3
Spokane Transit 701 W Riverside Ave .... Spokane WA 99201 *Web:* www.spokanetransit.com	509-456-7277		108
Spokane Valley Chamber of Commerce 1421 N Meadowwood Ln Ste 10 .... Spokane Valley WA 99206 *TF:* 866-475-1436 ■ *Web:* spokanevalleychamber.org	509-924-4994	924-4992	139
Spokane Valley Mall 14700 E Indiana Ave .... Spokane WA 99216 *Web:* www.spokanevalleymall.com	509-926-3700		460
Spoken Translation Inc 1100 W View Dr .... Berkeley CA 94705 *Web:* www.spokentranslation.com	510-843-9900		177
Spokes Etc Inc 1545 N Quaker Ln .... Alexandria VA 22302 *Web:* spokesetc.com	703-820-2200		711
Spongex LLC 3002 Anaconda Rd .... Tarboro NC 27886 *Web:* www.spongexfoam.com	252-824-0015		601
Sponseller Group Inc 1600 Timberwolf Dr .... Holland OH 43528 *TF:* 800-776-1625 ■ *Web:* sponsellergroup.com	419-861-3000		261
Spooky Cheetah Press 33 Glendale Dr .... Stamford CT 06906 *Web:* www.spookycheetah.com	203-357-1160		637-2
Spooltech Inc 9325 Hwy 6 N .... Houston TX 77095 *Web:* www.spooltech.com	281-861-6800		200
Spoon River College (SRC) 23235 N County Hwy 22 .... Canton IL 61520 *TF:* 800-334-7337 ■ *Web:* www.src.edu	309-647-4645	649-6393	162
Spoon River Electric Co-opeartive Inc (SREC) 930 S Fifth Ave PO Box 340 .... Canton IL 61520 *TF:* 877-404-2572 ■ *Web:* srecoop.org	309-647-2700		245
Spoons Grill & Bar 2601 Hotel Terr .... Santa Ana CA 92705 *Web:* www.spoonsoc.com	714-556-0700		671
Sport & Health 1800 Old Meadow Rd Ste 300 .... McLean VA 22102 *Web:* sportandhealth.com	703-556-6550		354
Sport Chevrolet 3101 Automobile Blvd .... Silver Spring MD 20904 *Web:* www.sportautomotive.com	301-890-6000		57
Sport Clips Inc 110 Briarwood Dr .... Georgetown TX 78628 *Web:* www.sportclips.com	512-869-1201		310
Sport Fishing Magazine 460 N Orlando Ave Ste 200 .... Winter Park FL 32789 *TF:* 800-879-0496 ■ *Web:* sportfishingmag.com	800-879-0496		457-20
Sport Fit Bowie Racquet & Fitness Club Inc 100 Whitemarsh Park Dr .... Bowie MD 20715 *Web:* sportfitclubs.com	301-262-4553		354
Sport Graphics PO Box 95 .... Shrewsbury MA 01545 *Web:* www.sportgraphics.com	508-925-0406		592
Sport Graphics Inc 3423 Park Davis Cir .... Indianapolis IN 46235 *Web:* www.sportg.com	317-899-7000		627
Sport Horse Publications 3145 Sandhill Rd .... Mason MI 48854 *Web:* www.sporthorsepublications.com	517-333-3833		637-2
Sport Obermeyer Limited USA Inc 115 AABC .... Aspen CO 81611 *TF:* 800-525-4203 ■ *Web:* www.obermeyer.com	970-925-5060		155-5
Sport Parachutist's Safety Journal (SPSJ) PO Box 2581 .... Hemet CA 92546 *Web:* www.makeithappen.com	909-658-3526		637-2
Sport Rx LLC 5076 Santa Fe St Ste A .... San Diego CA 92109 *TF:* 888-831-5817 ■ *Web:* sportrx.com	858-571-0240		543
Sport Seasons 539 Cool Springs Blvd Ste 120 .... Franklin TN 37067 *TF:* 855-354-3863 ■ *Web:* sport-seasons.com	615-778-1638		711
Sport Supply Group Inc 1901 Diplomat Dr .... Dallas TX 75234 *Web:* www.sportsupplygroup.com	972-484-9484		710
Sportco Sporting Goods Inc 2580 E Sunset Rd .... Las Vegas NV 89120 *Web:* sportcolasvegas.com	702-739-9750	739-9021	710
Sportech Inc 10800 175th Ave NW .... Elk River MN 55330 *Web:* www.sportechinc.com	763-712-3965		247
Sport-Haley Inc 10367 Brockwood Rd .... Dallas TX 75238 *TF:* 800-627-9211 ■ *Web:* sporthaley.com	800-627-9211		155-3
Sportika Export Inc 225 Episcopal Rd .... Berlin CT 06037 *Web:* www.sportika.com	860-828-9000	828-5962	799
Sporting Goods Intelligence Inc 442 Featherbed Ln .... Glen Mills PA 19342 *TF:* 800-328-6397 ■ *Web:* www.sginews.com	610-459-4040	459-4010	711
Sportology Publications N2689 Spring Ln .... Marinette WI 54143 *Web:* www.supershooting.com	715-735-3845		637-2
SportPharma Inc 3 Terminal Rd .... New Brunswick NJ 08901 *TF:* 800-872-0101 ■ *Web:* www.sportpharma.com	732-545-3130	509-0458	799
Sports & Fitness Industry Assn, The 1150 17th St NW Ste 850 .... Washington DC 20036 *Web:* www.sfia.org	202-775-1762	296-7462	49-4
Sports Afield Magazine 15621 Chemical Ln .... Huntington Beach CA 92649 *TF:* 800-451-4788 ■ *Web:* www.sportsafield.com	714-373-4910	894-4949	457-20
Sports Authority Field at Mile High 1701 Bryant St .... Denver CO 80204 *Web:* www.sportsauthorityfieldatmilehigh.com	720-258-3000	258-3050	720
Sports Business Daily 120 W Morehead St Ste 310 .... Charlotte NC 28202 *TF:* 800-829-9839 ■ *Web:* www.sportsbusinessdaily.com	704-973-1401		457-20
Sports Business Research Network Inc PO Box 2378 .... Princeton NJ 08543 *Web:* www.sbrnet.com	609-896-1996		637-2
Sports Byline USA 300 Broadway Ste 8 .... San Francisco CA 94133 *Web:* www.sportsbyline.com	415-434-8300		393
Sports Car Club of America (SCCA) 6700 SW Topeka Blvd .... Topeka KS 66619 *Fax Area Code: 785 ■ *TF:* 800-770-2055 ■ *Web:* www.scca.com	800-770-2055	232-7228*	48-18
Sports Empire PO Box 6169 .... Lakewood CA 90714 *TF:* 800-255-5258 ■ *Web:* www.sports-empire.com	562-920-2350	920-1828	771
Sports Excellence Corporation Inc 151 Alston Bureau 100 .... Pointe-Claire QC H9R5V9 *Web:* www.sportsexcellence.com	514-782-0400		711
Sports Haven Bar & Grille 600 Long Wharf Dr .... New Haven CT 06511 *TF:* 800-468-2260 ■ *Web:* www.sportshavenbarandgrille.com	203-946-3252		133
Sports Immortals Museum 6830 N Federal Hwy .... Boca Raton FL 33487 *Web:* www.sportsimmortals.com	561-997-2575	997-6949	522
Sports Imports Inc 4000 Pkwy Ln .... Hilliard OH 43026 *TF:* 800-556-3198 ■ *Web:* www.sportsimports.com	800-556-3198		711
Sports Inc 333 Second Ave N .... Lewistown MT 59457 *Web:* www.sportsinc.com	406-538-3496		138
Sports Leisure Vacations 9812 Old Winery Pl Ste 1 .... Sacramento CA 95827 *TF:* 800-951-5556 ■ *Web:* www.sportsleisure.com	916-361-2051		760
Sports Management Network Inc 131 W Long Lake Rd Ste 250 .... Troy MI 48098 *Web:* www.sportsmanagementnetwork.com	248-335-3535	335-3352	41
Sports Mania 924 N 3rd St .... Jacksonville Beach FL 32250 *Web:* sportsmaniausa.com	904-242-0640		711
Sports Med Properties LLC 4530 Park Rd Ste 220 .... Charlotte NC 28209 *Web:* sportsmedproperties.com	704-815-0297		653
Sports Molding Inc Freeport Ctr Bldg Z13 .... Clearfield UT 84016 *Web:* www.smimolding.com	801-776-4233	825-0982	604
Sports Museum, The 100 Legends Way .... Boston MA 02114 *Web:* www.sportsmuseum.org	617-624-1234		522
Sports Plus Inc 200 E Main St .... Greenwood IN 46143 *Web:* www.sportsplusinc.net	317-888-6441	887-1054	155-3
Sports Promotion Network 2895 113th St .... Grand Prairie TX 75050 *TF:* 800-460-9989 ■ *Web:* www.gotospn.com	866-780-6151		711
Sports Reference LLC 6757 Greene St Ste 315 .... Philadelphia PA 19119 *Fax Area Code: 800 ■ *TF:* 888-512-8907 ■ *Web:* www.sports-reference.com	215-301-9181	660-5292*	387
Sports Spectrum Magazine 640 Plaza Dr Ste 110 .... Highlands Ranch CO 80129 *TF:* 866-821-2971 ■ *Web:* sportsspectrum.com	866-821-2971		457-20
Sports Talk 1050 WTKA 1100 Victors Way Ste 100 .... Ann Arbor MI 48108 *Web:* www.wtka.com	734-302-8100		645-8
Sports Travel Inc 60 Main St PO Box 50 .... Hatfield MA 01038 *TF:* 800-662-4424 ■ *Web:* www.sportstravelandtours.com	413-247-7678	247-5700	760
Sports Turf Managers Assn (STMA) 805 New Hampshire Ste E .... Lawrence KS 66044 *TF:* 800-323-3875 ■ *Web:* www.stma.org	785-843-2549	843-2977	48-22
Sports Warehouse Inc 181 Suburban Rd .... San Luis Obispo CA 93401 *TF:* 800-883-6647 ■ *Web:* www.tennis-warehouse.com	805-781-6464	781-6476	711
SportsEngine Inc 807 Broadway St NE Ste 300 .... Minneapolis MN 55413 *TF:* 888-379-1035 ■ *Web:* www.sportsengine.com	888-379-1035		387
Sportsman's Warehouse 165 W 7200 S .... Midvale UT 84047 *Web:* www.sportsmanswarehouse.com	801-566-6681		711
Sportsmen on Film 231 Earl Garrett Ste 300 .... Kerrville TX 78028 *TF:* 800-910-4868 ■ *Web:* www.sportsmenonfilm.com	830-792-4200	792-4224	637-10
Sportsmen's Lodge Hotel 12825 Ventura Blvd .... Studio City CA 91604 *TF:* 800-821-8511 ■ *Web:* sportsmenslodge.com	818-769-4700		707
SportsPlay Equipment Inc 5642 Natural Bridge Ave .... Saint Louis MO 63120 *TF:* 800-727-8180 ■ *Web:* www.sportsplayinc.com	314-389-4140	389-9034	346
Sportsprint Inc 6197 Bermuda Dr .... Saint Louis MO 63135 *TF:* 800-325-4858 ■ *Web:* www.sportsprint.com	314-521-9000	521-0395	157-4

				Phone	Fax	Class
SpotHero Inc 2801 N Seminary Ave. *Web:* spothero.com	Chicago	IL	60657	312-566-7768		192
Spot-Hogg Archery Products 125 Smith St. *Web:* spot-hogg.com	Harrisburg	OR	97446	541-995-3702		711
Spotless Cleaners 311 S Blakely St	Dunmore	PA	18512	570-346-7577		426
Spotlight 29 Casino 46-200 Harrison Pl. *Web:* www.spotlight29.com	Coachella	CA	92236	760-775-5566	775-7677	133
Spotlight on Kids 408 S Main St *Web:* www.janesvillepac.org	Janesville	WI	53545	608-289-5021		749
Spotlight Promotions Inc 2000 Van Ness Ave Ste 101 *Web:* www.spotlightsf.com	San Francisco	CA	94109	415-202-7100	202-7110	701
Spotnails 1100 Hicks Rd *TF:* 800-873-2239 ■ *Web:* www.spotnails.com	Rolling Meadows	IL	60008	847-259-1620		813
SpotOn Inc 300 California St 4th Fl. *TF:* 877-814-4102 ■ *Web:* www.spoton.com	San Francisco	CA	94104	877-814-4102		387
Spotsylvania Career & Technical Ctr 6713 Smith Station Rd *Web:* www.spotsylvania.k12.va.us	Spotsylvania	VA	22553	540-898-2655	891-1784	230
Spotsylvania County 9104 Courthouse Rd PO Box 99 *Web:* www.spotsylvania.va.us	Spotsylvania	VA	22553	540-507-7010	507-7019	338
Spotts Fain PC 411 E Franklin St Ste 600 *TF:* 866-788-1190 ■ *Web:* www.spottsfain.com	Richmond	VA	23219	804-697-2000		41
Spotwave Wireless Inc 500 Van Buren St PO Box 550 *TF:* 866-704-9750 ■ *Web:* www.spotwave.com	Kemptville	ON	K0G1J0	613-591-1662		736
SPP (South Platte Press) PO Box 163 *Web:* www.southplattepress.com	David City	NE	68632	402-367-3554		637-2
SPPD (Southern Public Power District) 4550 W Husker Hwy PO Box 1687 *TF:* 800-652-2013 ■ *Web:* southernpd.com	Grand Island	NE	68803	308-384-2350	384-5018	245
SPR (Sumner Peck Ranch Inc) 14860 N Hwy 41 *Web:* sumnerpeckranch.com	Madera	CA	93636	559-822-3301		10-4
SPR Consulting Sears Tower 233 S Wacker Dr Ste 3500 *Web:* spr.com	Chicago	IL	60606	312-756-1760		631
Spradling International Inc 200 Cahaba Vly Pkwy PO Box 1668 *TF:* 800-333-0955 ■ *Web:* spradlingvinyl.com	Pelham	AL	35124	205-985-4206	985-9176	594
Spraggins Inc 3815 Silver Star Rd. *Web:* spragginsinc.com	Orlando	FL	32808	407-295-4150		290
Sprague & Curtis Inc 75 Western Ave *Web:* spragueandcurtis.com	Augusta	ME	04330	207-623-1123		652
Sprague & Janowsky Inc 121 E Seneca St *Web:* sprjan.com	Ithaca	NY	14850	607-273-5322		734
Sprague Energy 185 International Dr Ste 200 *TF:* 800-225-1560 ■ *Web:* www.spragueenergy.com	Portsmouth	NH	03801	603-431-1000		579
Sprague Pest Solutions 2725 Pacific Ave Ste 200 *TF:* 800-272-4988 ■ *Web:* www.spraguepest.com	Tacoma	WA	98402	253-272-4400	272-9676	577
Sprague's Sports LLC 345 W 32nd St *Web:* spragues.com	Yuma	AZ	85364	928-726-0022		711
Spray Enclosure Technologies 1427 N Linden Ave *Fax Area Code: 909 ■ *TF:* 800-535-8196 ■ *Web:* spraytech.com	Rialto	CA	92376	800-535-8196	419-7020*	697
Sprayglo USA Inc 1612 Hwy 138 NE *Web:* www.sprayglo.com	Conyers	GA	30012	770-918-9638		62-4
Spraying Systems Co PO Box 7900 *TF:* 800-800-6509 ■ *Web:* www.spray.com	Wheaton	IL	60189	630-665-5000	260-0842	487
Sprayway Inc 1005 S Westgate Ave *TF:* 800-332-9000 ■ *Web:* www.spraywayinc.com	Addison	IL	60101	630-628-3000	543-7797	145
SPRC (Stanford Prevention Research Ctr) 1070 Arastradero Rd Ste 100 & 300 *Web:* prevention.stanford.edu	Stanford	CA	94305	650-723-6254	725-6247	668
Spread the News PR Inc 1236 Inverness Dr *Web:* www.spreadthenewspr.com	Lawrence	KS	66049	785-842-8909		636
Sprecher + Schuh 15910 International Plaza Dr. *TF:* 877-721-5913 ■ *Web:* www.sprecherschuh.com	Houston	TX	77032	281-442-9000	442-1570	203
Spredfast Inc *Khoros LLC* 7300 Ranch Rd 2222 Bldg 1 *TF:* 800-212-2216 ■ *Web:* www.spredfast.com	Austin	TX	78701	512-649-3286		387
Spreedly Inc 733 Foster St. *TF:* 888-727-7750 ■ *Web:* www.spreedly.com	Durham	NC	27701	888-727-7750		387
Spreengs LLC 1441 Broadway 5th Fl *Web:* www.spreengs.com	New York	NY	10018	929-999-2999	999-1999	637-10
Sprenger Midwest Inc 523 E 14th St *Web:* www.sprengermidwest.com	Sioux Falls	SD	57104	605-334-7705		191-3
Sprig Electric Co 1860 S Tenth St *Web:* www.sprigelectric.com	San Jose	CA	95112	408-298-3134	298-2132	189-4
Spring Arbor Distributors 1 Ingram Blvd. *TF:* 800-395-4340 ■ *Web:* www.ingramcontent.com	La Vergne	TN	37086	615-793-5000		96
Spring Arbor University 106 E Main St. *TF:* 800-968-9103 ■ *Web:* www.saucougars.com	Spring Arbor	MI	49283	517-750-6504	750-2745	166
Spring Bar 4026 S W Temple *TF:* 800-453-7756 ■ *Web:* springbar.com	Millcreek	UT	84107	801-486-4161		711
Spring Capital Partners LP 2330 W Joppa Rd The Foxleigh Bldg Ste 340 *Web:* www.springcap.com	Lutherville	MD	21093	410-685-8000	545-0015	792
Spring City Electrical Manufacturing Co 1 S Main St PO Box 19 *Web:* www.springcity.com	Spring City	PA	19475	610-948-4000	948-5577	439
Spring Creek Animal Hospital 14837 Nacogdoches Rd *Web:* springcreekvet.com	San Antonio	TX	78247	210-599-2131		794
Spring Creek Barbeque 2340 W I- 20 Ste 100 *TF:* 888-467-0505 ■ *Web:* springcreekbarbeque.com	Arlington	TX	76017	817-467-0505		671
Spring Creek Correctional Ctr 3600 Bette Cato *Web:* www.correct.state.ak.us	Seward	AK	99664	907-224-8200	224-8062	213
Spring Creek Ranch 1600 N East Butte Rd PO Box 4780 *TF:* 800-443-6139 ■ *Web:* www.springcreekranch.com	Jackson	WY	83001	307-733-8833		379
Spring Creek Resort 28229 Spring Creek Pl *Web:* www.springcreekventure.com	Pierre	SD	57501	605-224-8336		669
Spring Creek Sun 1540 Van Siclen Ave. *Web:* springcreeksunonline.com	Brooklyn	NY	11239	718-642-2718	642-7301	532-2
Spring Creek Youth Services Ctr 3190 E Las Vegas St. *Web:* www.colorado.gov	Colorado Springs	CO	80906	719-390-2700		412
Spring Dynamics Inc 7378 Research Dr. *TF:* 888-274-8432 ■ *Web:* springdynamics.com	Almont	MI	48003	810-798-2622		719
Spring Engineers Inc 9740 Tanner Rd *TF:* 800-899-9488 ■ *Web:* www.springhouston.com	Houston	TX	77041	713-690-9488	690-1199	719
Spring Glen Animal Hospital LLC 1632 Whitney Ave. *Web:* springglenvetclinic.com	Hamden	CT	06517	203-248-2104		794
Spring Glen Fresh Foods Inc 314 Spring Glen Dr. *TF:* 800-641-2853 ■ *Web:* springglen.com	Ephrata	PA	17522	717-733-2201	721-6720	296-19
Spring Grove Cemetery 4521 Spring Grove Ave. *Fax Area Code: 513 ■ *TF:* 888-853-2230 ■ *Web:* www.springgrove.org	Cincinnati	OH	45232	888-853-2230	853-6802*	510
Spring Grove Hospital Ctr 55 Wade Ave. *Web:* health.maryland.gov	Catonsville	MD	21228	410-402-6000		374-5
Spring Hill College 4000 Dauphin St *TF:* 800-742-6704 ■ *Web:* www.badgerweb.shc.edu	Mobile	AL	36608	251-460-2112		166
Spring Hill Mall 1072 Spring Hill Mall *TF:* 800-718-8788 ■ *Web:* www.springhillmall.com	West Dundee	IL	60118	847-428-2200		460
Spring Hill Press LLC 16300 Law 2130 *Fax Area Code: 417 ■ *TF:* 800-627-8141 ■ *Web:* www.springhillpressmaps.com	Mount Vernon	MO	65712	800-627-8141	466-7013*	7
Spring Institute for Intercultural Learning 1373 Grant St *Web:* www.springinstitute.org	Denver	CO	80203	303-863-0188		685
Spring Lake State Fish & Wildlife Area 7982 S Park Rd. *Web:* www.dnr.illinois.gov	Manito	IL	61546	309-968-7135		565
Spring Manufacturers Institute (SMI) 2001 Midwest Rd Ste 106 *TF:* 866-482-5569 ■ *Web:* www.smihq.org	Oak Brook	IL	60523	630-495-8588	495-8595	49-13
Spring Meadows Golf Cntry Clb 59 Lewiston Rd. *Web:* www.springmeadowsgolf.com	Gray	ME	04039	207-657-2586		226
Spring Mill Partners LLC 2200 Renaissance Blvd Ste 320 *Web:* springmillpartners.com	King of Prussia	PA	19406	484-530-1230		734
Spring Mill State Park PO Box 376 *Web:* www.in.gov	Mitchell	IN	47446	812-849-4129		565
Spring Mountain Ranch State Park 6375 Hwy 159 *Web:* parks.nv.gov	Blue Diamond	NV	89004	702-875-4141		565
Spring Mountain Vineyards 2805 Spring Mtn Rd. *TF:* 877-769-4637 ■ *Web:* www.springmtn.com	Saint Helena	CA	94574	707-967-4188	963-2753	315-5
Spring River Park & Zoo 1306 E College Blvd PO Box 1838 *Web:* www.museumsusa.org	Roswell	NM	88201	575-624-6760		823
Spring Street Historical Museum 525 Spring St *Web:* www.springstreetmuseum.org	Shreveport	LA	71101	318-424-0964		520
Spring Valley Chamber of Commerce 3322 Sweetwater Springs Blvd Ste 202 *Web:* www.springvalleychamber.org	Spring Valley	CA	91977	619-670-9902	670-9924	139
Spring Valley City Bank 315 N Cornelia St *Web:* svcb.com	Spring Valley	IL	61362	815-663-2211		70
Spring Valley State Park HC 74 PO Box 201 *Web:* www.parks.nv.gov	Pioche	NV	89043	775-962-5102		565
Spring Venture Group LLC 120 W 12th St Ste 1700 *Web:* www.springventuregroup.com	Kansas City	MO	64105	816-888-7900		5
Springboard 22 Battery St Ste 1100 *Web:* www.springboard.com	San Francisco	CA	94111	415-857-4459		242
Springboard Biodiesel LLC 2282 Ivy St *Web:* www.springboardbiodiesel.com	Chico	CA	95928	530-894-1793	894-1048	362
Springboard Nonprofit Consumer Credit Management 4351 Latham St *TF:* 888-425-3453 ■ *Web:* www.bkhelp.org	Riverside	CA	92501	888-425-3453		393
Springbox 708 Colorado St *Web:* www.springbox.com	Austin	TX	78701	512-391-0065		7
Springbrook Software Inc 1000 SW Broadway Ste 1900 *TF:* 866-256-7661 ■ *Web:* www.springbrooksoftware.com	Portland	OR	97205	866-256-7661		178-1
Springbrook State Park 2437 160th Rd *Web:* www.iowadnr.gov	Guthrie Center	IA	50115	641-747-3591	747-8401	565
Springco Metal Coating 12500 Elmwood Ave. *Web:* www.springco-coatings.com	Cleveland	OH	44111	216-941-0020		481
Springdale Chamber of Commerce 202 W Emma Ave PO Box 166 *Web:* springdale.com	Springdale	AR	72764	479-872-2222		139
Springdot Inc 2611 Colerain Ave. *Web:* www.springdot.com	Cincinnati	OH	45214	513-542-4000		627
Springer & Steinberg PC 1600 Broadway Ste 1200 *TF:* 877-342-1230 ■ *Web:* springersteinberg.com	Denver	CO	80202	877-342-1230		41

Name	Address	City	State	Zip	Phone	Fax	Class
Springer Electric Co-opeartive Inc	408 Maxwell Ave PO Box 698 *TF:* 800-288-1353 ■ *Web:* www.springercoop.com	Springer	NM	87747	575-483-2421		245
Springer Marketing & Adv	65 Wilkie Way *Web:* www.springermktadv.com	Fletcher	NC	28732	828-687-0334		4
Springer Opera House	103 Tenth St *Web:* springeroperahouse.org	Columbus	GA	31901	706-327-3688		572
Springfield Area Chamber of Commerce	202 S John Q Hammons Pkwy *Web:* www.springfieldchamber.com	Springfield	MO	65806	417-862-5567	862-1611	139
Springfield Armory	420 W Main St *TF:* 800-680-6866 ■ *Web:* www.springfield-armory.com	Geneseo	IL	61254	309-944-5631	944-3676	284
Springfield Armory National Historic Site	1 Armory Sq Ste 2 *Web:* www.nps.gov	Springfield	MA	01105	413-734-8551	747-8062	564
Springfield Art Museum	1111 E Brookside Dr *Web:* www.sgfmuseum.org	Springfield	MO	65807	417-837-5700	837-5704	520
Springfield Beauty Academy	4223 Annandale Rd *Web:* www.springfieldbeautyacademy.com	Annandale	VA	22003	703-256-5662	256-9164	167-3
Springfield Brewing Co	305 S Market Ave *Web:* www.springfieldbrewingco.com	Springfield	MO	65806	417-832-8277		671
Springfield Business Journal	313 Pk Central W *Web:* www.sbj.net	Springfield	MO	65806	417-831-3238	864-4901	457-5
Springfield Chamber of Commerce	1011 S 2nd St *Web:* www.springfield-chamber.org	Springfield	OR	97477	541-746-1651	726-4727	139
Springfield City Library	220 State St *TF:* 800-852-3133 ■ *Web:* www.springfieldlibrary.org	Springfield	MA	01103	413-263-6828		434-3
Springfield College	263 Alden St *TF:* 800-343-1257 ■ *Web:* springfield.edu	Springfield	MA	01109	413-748-3136	748-3694	166
Springfield Conservation Nature Ctr	4600 S Chrisman Ave *Web:* mdc.mo.gov	Springfield	MO	65804	417-888-4237	888-4241	50-5
Springfield Convention & Visitors Bureau	109 N Seventh St *TF:* 800-545-7300 ■ *Web:* www.visitspringfieldillinois.com	Springfield	IL	62701	217-789-2360	544-8711	206
Springfield Creamery Inc	29440 Airport Rd *Web:* nancysyogurt.com	Eugene	OR	97402	541-689-2911		296-27
Springfield Electric Supply Co	700 N Ninth St *TF:* 800-747-2101 ■ *Web:* www.springfieldelectric.com	Springfield	IL	62702	217-351-7600	788-2134	246
Springfield Exposition Ctr	635 E St Louis St *Web:* springfieldexpo.com	Springfield	MO	65806	417-869-5588		205
Springfield Hospital	25 Ridgewood Rd *Web:* springfieldhospital.org	Springfield	VT	05156	802-885-2151	885-7357	374-3
Springfield Hospital Ctr	6655 Sykesville Rd *TF:* 800-333-7564 ■ *Web:* www.health.maryland.gov	Sykesville	MD	21784	410-970-7000		374-5
Springfield (IL) City Hall	800 E Monroe *Web:* www.springfield.il.us	Springfield	IL	62701	217-789-2200	789-2109	337
Springfield Little Theatre	311 E Walnut St *Web:* www.springfieldlittletheatre.org	Springfield	MO	65806	417-869-1334	869-4047	573-4
Springfield (MA) City Hall	36 Court St *Web:* www.springfield-ma.gov	Springfield	MA	01103	413-736-3111		337
Springfield Missouri Convention & Visitors Bureau	815 E St Louis St Ste 100 *TF:* 800-678-8767 ■ *Web:* www.springfieldmo.org	Springfield	MO	65806	417-881-5300	881-2231	206
Springfield (MO) City Hall	840 Boonville Ave *Web:* www.springfieldmo.gov	Springfield	MO	65802	417-864-1000	864-1649	337
Springfield Museum	590 Main St *Web:* www.springfield-museum.com	Springfield	OR	97477	541-726-2300		520
Springfield Museums	21 Edwards St *TF:* 800-625-7738 ■ *Web:* springfieldmuseums.org	Springfield	MA	01103	413-263-6800		520
Springfield National Cemetery	1702 E Seminole St *Web:* www.cem.va.gov	Springfield	MO	65804	417-881-9499	881-7862	136
Springfield News Leader	651 N Boonville Ave *Web:* www.news-leader.com	Springfield	MO	65806	417-836-1100		532-2
Springfield News-Sun	202 N Limestone St *TF:* 800-441-6397 ■ *Web:* www.springfieldnewssun.com	Springfield	OH	45503	937-328-0300		532-2
Springfield Paper Co	412 N National Ave *TF:* 800-862-5061 ■ *Web:* springfieldpaperonline.com	Springfield	MO	65802	417-862-5061	865-3711	559
Springfield Park District	2500 S 11th St *Web:* www.springfieldparks.org	Springfield	IL	62703	217-544-1751		565
Springfield Public Library	225 5th St *Web:* whereemindsgrow.org	Springfield	OR	97477	541-726-3766	726-3747	434-3
Springfield Public School District #186	1900 W Monroe St *TF:* 877-632-7753 ■ *Web:* www.sps186.org	Springfield	IL	62704	217-525-3006	525-3005	685
Springfield Public Schools	1550 Main St *Web:* www.springfieldpublicschools.com	Springfield	MA	01103	413-787-7100	787-7171	685
Springfield Public Schools	1359 E St Louis St *Web:* www.sps.org	Springfield	MO	65802	417-523-0000	523-0196	685
Springfield ReManufacturing Corp	4727 E Kearney *TF:* 800-531-7134 ■ *Web:* www.srcreman.com	Springfield	MO	65803	800-531-7134		262
Springfield Spring Corp	311 Shaker Rd *TF:* 800-637-3033 ■ *Web:* www.springfieldspring.com	East Longmeadow	MA	01028	413-525-6837		718
Springfield Symphony Orchestra	1350 Main St *Web:* www.springfieldsymphony.org	Springfield	MA	01103	413-733-0636	781-4129	573-3
Springfield Symphony Orchestra	411 N Sherman Pkwy *Web:* www.springfieldmosymphony.org	Springfield	MO	65802	417-864-6683	864-8967	573-3
Springfield Technical Community College	1 Armory Sq PO Box 900 *Web:* www.stcc.edu	Springfield	MA	01102	413-781-7822	755-6306	162
Springfield Theatre Ctr	420 S Sixth St *Web:* springfieldtheatrecentre.com	Springfield	IL	62701	217-523-0878		572
Springfield-Branson National Airport	2300 N Airport Blvd *Web:* www.flyspringfield.com	Springfield	MO	65802	417-868-0500	868-0501	27
Springfield-Clark Career Technology Ctr	1901 Selma Rd *Web:* www.scctc.org	Springfield	OH	45505	937-325-7368	325-7452	167-3
Spring-Ford Area School District	857 S Lewis Rd *Web:* www.spring-ford.net	Royersford	PA	19468	610-705-6000	705-6245	685
Spring-Green Lawn Care Corp	11909 Spaulding School Dr *TF:* 800-435-4051 ■ *Web:* www.spring-green.com	Plainfield	IL	60585	815-436-8777	436-9056	577
Springhill Medical Ctr	3719 Dauphin St *Web:* www.springhillmedicalcenter.com	Mobile	AL	36608	251-344-9630		374-3
Springmoor Life Care Retirement Community	1500 Sawmill Rd *Web:* www.springmoor.org	Raleigh	NC	27615	919-848-7000		672
Springport Telephone Co	400 E Main St *TF:* 877-820-7976 ■ *Web:* springcom.com	Springport	MI	49284	517-857-3500	857-3329	224
Springs Baptist Academy	3500 N Nevada Ave *Web:* www.sbasprings.com	Colorado Springs	CO	80907	719-593-7887		166
Springs Fabrication Inc	850 Aeroplaza Dr *TF:* 800-466-5896 ■ *Web:* www.springsfab.com	Colorado Springs	CO	80916	719-596-8830	596-1836	567
Springs Memorial Hospital	800 W Meeting St *Web:* www.springsmemorial.com	Lancaster	SC	29720	803-286-1214		374-3
Springs Window Fashions	2669 Industrial Dr *Web:* www.swfcontract.com	Grayling	MI	49738	989-348-2871		683
Springs Window Fashions LP	7549 Graber Rd *TF:* 877-792-0002 ■ *Web:* www.springswindowfashions.com	Middleton	WI	53562	608-836-1011		361
Springtown Chamber of Commerce	112 S Main St *Web:* www.springtowntexas.com	Springtown	TX	76082	817-220-7828		139
Springvale Terrace	8505 Springvale Rd *Web:* www.seaburyresources.org	Silver Spring	MD	20910	301-587-0190		401
Springville Cooperative Telephone Association Inc (SCTA)	207 Broadway *Web:* www.springvilletelephone.com	Springville	IA	52336	319-854-9960		224
Springville Museum of Art	126 E 400 S *TF:* 800-833-6667 ■ *Web:* www.smofa.org	Springville	UT	84663	801-489-2727		520
Sprinkles Cupcakes Inc	9635 S Santa Monica Blvd *Web:* sprinkles.com	Beverly Hills	CA	90210	310-274-8765		68
Sprinklr Inc	29 W 35th St 8th Fl *Web:* www.sprinklr.com	New York	NY	10001	917-933-7800		180
Sprint Copy Ctr	175 N Main St *Web:* sprintcopycenter.com	Sebastopol	CA	95472	707-823-3900		627
Sprint Multimedia Inc	3853 Northdale Blvd Ste 203	Tampa	FL	33624	813-971-0531		592
Sprint Quality Printing Inc	3609 Silverside Rd *Web:* www.sprintqp.com	Wilmington	DE	19810	302-478-0720		627
Sprintz Furniture Showroom Inc	325 White Bridge Pike *Web:* www.sprintz.com	Nashville	TN	37209	615-234-3200		321
Spris Pizza	731 Lincoln Rd *Web:* www.sprispizza.com	Miami Beach	FL	33139	305-673-2020		671
Spritzer Kaufman LLP	19 W 44th St Ste 312 *Web:* spritzerkaufman.com	New York	NY	10036	212-593-1040	593-4638	2
Sprocket Express LLC	23 W Bacon St *Web:* www.sprocketexpress.com	Plainville	MA	02762	508-695-3780		809
Sproles- Woodard- & Co	777 Main St Ste 3250 *Web:* www.sproles.com	Fort Worth	TX	76102	817-332-1328		2
Sprott Global Resource Investments Ltd	1910 Palomar Point Way Ste 200 *TF:* 800-477-7853 ■ *Web:* www.sprottglobal.com	Carlsbad	CA	92008	800-477-7853		691
Sprott Inc	Royal Bank Plz South Twr 200 Bay St Ste 2600 *TF:* 855-943-8099 ■ *Web:* www.sprott.com	Toronto	ON	M5J2J1	416-943-8099		528
Sproule Associates Ltd	900 N Tower Sun Life Plz 140 Fourth Ave SW *TF:* 877-777-6135 ■ *Web:* sproule.com	Calgary	AB	T2P3N3	403-294-5500		539
Sprout Pharmaceuticals Inc	4208 Six Forks Rd *TF:* 844-746-5745 ■ *Web:* addyi.com	Raleigh	NC	27609	919-882-0850		238
SPROUT Wellness Solutions Inc	366 Adelaide St W Ste 301 *TF:* 866-535-5027 ■ *Web:* www.sproutatwork.com	Toronto	ON	M5V1R9	866-535-5027		224
SproutLoud Media Networks LLC	15431 SW 14th St *Web:* sproutloud.com	Sunrise	FL	33326	954-476-6211		5
Sproutman Publications	PO Box 1100 *TF:* 800-777-6881 ■ *Web:* www.sproutman.com	Great Barrington	MA	01230	413-528-5200		637-2
Sproxil Inc	1035 Cambridge St Ste 21E *Web:* fightthefakes.org	Cambridge	MA	02141	209-877-7694		809

Name / Address	City	State	ZIP	Phone	Fax	Class
Spruce 2115 13th St *Web:* www.sprucebouldera do.com	Boulder	CO	80302	303-442-4880		671
Spruce 9 Cornell Rd *TF:* 800-777-8231 ■ *Web:* www.ecisolutions.com	Latham	NY	12110	800-777-8231		174
Spruce Pine Mica Co PO Box 219 *Web:* www.spruce-pine-mica.com	Spruce Pine	NC	28777	828-765-4241		253
Spruce Point Inn 88 Grandview Ave *TF:* 800-553-0289 ■ *Web:* www.sprucepointinn.com	Boothbay Harbor	ME	04538	207-633-4152	633-6347	669
Spruceland Millworks Inc 10383 - 283 St *Web:* www.spruceland.ab.ca	Acheson	AB	T7X6A7	780-962-6333	962-8259	499
SPS (Southern Pan Services Co) 2385 Lithonia Industrial Blvd *Web:* www.southernpan.com	Lithonia	GA	30058	678-301-2400		780
SPS (Systems Products & Solutions Inc) 307 Wynn Dr *Web:* www.services-sps.com	Huntsville	AL	35805	256-319-2135		177
SPS Companies Inc 6363 Minnesota 7 *Web:* www.spscompanies.com	Minneapolis	MN	55416	952-929-1377	929-1862	612
SPS Corp 1100 Perry Rd *Web:* www.spscorporation.com	Apex	NC	27502	919-367-8885		186
SPS Technologies Inc 301 Highland Ave *Web:* www.spstech.com	Jenkintown	PA	19046	215-572-3000	572-3790	278
SPSJ (Sport Parachutist's Safety Journal) PO Box 2581 *Web:* www.makeithappen.com	Hemet	CA	92546	909-658-3526		637-2
SPST (Saint Paul School of Theology) 4370 W 109th St Ste 300 *Web:* www.spst.edu	Overland Park	KS	66211	913-253-5000		167-3
SPTC (South Plains Telephone Cooperative Inc) 2425 Marshall St *Web:* www.sptc.net	Lubbock	TX	79415	806-763-2301		224
SPTP (Southern Pine Timber Products) 6910 Lithia Pinecrest Rd *TF:* 800-229-7463 ■ *Web:* southernpinetimber.co	Lithia	FL	33547	813-681-7600	681-7601	191-3
Spud Software Inc 9478 S Saginaw Rd *Web:* www.spudsoftware.com	Grand Blanc	MI	48439	810-695-0001	695-4004	177
Spudder, The 6536 E 50th St *Web:* www.thespudder.com	Tulsa	OK	74145	918-665-1416		671
Spudnik Equipment Co 584 W 100 N Rd *Web:* www.spudnik.com	Blackfoot	ID	83221	208-785-0480	785-1497	273
Spuncast Inc 6499 W Rhine Rd *TF:* 800-394-5798 ■ *Web:* www.spuncast.com	Watertown	WI	53098	920-261-7853	261-7977	307
Spurlock Museum *University of Illinois at Urbana* 600 S Gregory St *Web:* www.spurlock.illinois.edu	Urbana	IL	61801	217-333-2360	244-9419	520
SPWLA (Society of Petrophysicists & Well Log Analysts) 8866 Gulf Fwy Ste 320 *Web:* spwla.org	Houston	TX	77017	713-947-8727	947-7181	48-12
SPX Cooling Technologies 7401 W 129th St *TF:* 800-462-7539 ■ *Web:* www.spxcooling.com	Overland Park	KS	66213	913-664-7400	664-7439	91
SPX Flow 611 Sugar Creek Rd *TF:* 800-252-5200 ■ *Web:* www.spxflow.com	Delavan	WI	53115	800-252-5200		567
SPX Transformer Solutions Inc 400 S Prairie Ave *TF:* 800-835-2732 ■ *Web:* www.spxtransformersolutions.com	Waukesha	WI	53186	800-835-2732		767
SPY Inc 2070 Las Palmas Dr *TF:* 800-779-3937 ■ *Web:* www.spyoptic.com	Carlsbad	CA	92011	800-779-3937		543
Spycher Bros Farms 14827 W Harding Rd *Web:* www.spycherbros.com	Turlock	CA	95380	209-668-2471	668-4988	10-10
Spyder Byte Media Inc 47935 Ben Franklin Dr *Web:* spyderbytemedia.com	Shelby Township	MI	48315	586-260-1344		180
Spyder Ii 65 Pier Ave *Web:* www.spydersurf.com	Hermosa Beach	CA	90254	310-374-2494		711
Spyglass Creative 1639 Hennepin Ave *Web:* spyglasscreative.com	Minneapolis	MN	55403	612-486-5959		344
Spyglass Entertainment 245 N Beverly Dr *Web:* www.spyglassent.com	Beverly Hills	CA	90210	310-443-5800	443-5912	514
Spyglass Resources Corp 1700 - 250 2nd St SW *Web:* www.spyglassresources.com	Calgary	AB	T2P0C1	403-303-8500	264-0085	536
Spyratosdavis LLC 1001 Warrenville Rd Ste 210 *Web:* spydavlaw.com	Lisle	IL	60532	630-810-8881		41
Spyre Solutions Inc 91 Rylander Blvd Ste 7-250 *Web:* www.spyresolutions.com	Toronto	ON	M1B5M5	416-444-4924		393
SQA LABS Inc 16880 N 73rd Ave *Web:* www.sqalabs.com	Peoria	AZ	85382	602-439-5501		180
SQAD Inc 303 S Broadway Ste 130 *Web:* sqad.com	Tarrytown	NY	10591	914-524-7600		225
SQI Diagnostics Inc 36 Meteor Dr *Web:* sqidiagnostics.com	Toronto	ON	M9W1A4	416-674-9500		250
Sql Data Solutions Inc 43 Herkomer St *Web:* www.sqldatasolutionsinc.com	New Hyde Park	NY	11040	516-358-1998		177
SQN Banking Systems Inc 65 Indel Ave *Web:* www.sqnbankingsystems.com	Rancocas	NJ	08073	609-261-5500	265-9517	173-1
Squaglia Manufacturing 275 Polaris Ave *Web:* www.squaglia.com	Mountain View	CA	94043	650-965-9644	965-4999	454
Squantz Pond State Park 178 Shortwoods Rd *Web:* portal.ct.gov	New Fairfield	CT	06812	203-312-5023		565
Squar Milner Peterson Miranda & Williamson LLP 4100 Newport Pl Dr Ste 600 *Web:* squarmilner.com	Newport Beach	CA	92660	949-222-2999	222-2989	2
Square 1 Art LLC 5470 Oakbrook Pkwy Ste E *TF:* 888-332-3294 ■ *Web:* www.square1art.com	Norcross	GA	30093	678-906-2291		627
Square 2 Marketing 555 N Ln Ste 5050 *Web:* www.square2marketing.com	Conshohocken	PA	19428	215-491-0100		5
Square 3 221 Parking Way *Web:* square3it.com	Lake Jackson	TX	77566	979-297-1117		180
Square Books 160 Courthouse Sq *TF:* 800-648-4001 ■ *Web:* www.squarebooks.com	Oxford	MS	38655	662-236-2262		95
Square Mile Capital Management LLC 350 Park Ave 15th Fl *Web:* squaremilecapital.com	New York	NY	10022	212-605-1000		653
Square One Publishers Inc 115 Herricks Rd *Web:* www.squareonepublishers.com	Garden City Park	NY	11040	516-535-2010	535-2014	637-2
Square Root Inc 508 Oakland Ave *Web:* square-root.com	Austin	TX	78703	512-693-9232		177
Square-H Brands Inc 2731 S Soto St *Web:* www.squarehbrands.com	Los Angeles	CA	90058	323-267-4600		473
Squarei Technologies Inc 1315 Oakridge Dr Ste 100 *Web:* www.squarei.com	Fort Collins	CO	80525	970-377-0077		177
Squaremouth Inc 4355 Central Ave *TF:* 800-240-0369 ■ *Web:* squaremouth.com	Saint Petersburg	FL	33713	727-564-9203		652
Squatters Pub Brewery 147 W Broadway 300 S *Web:* www.squatters.com	Salt Lake City	UT	84101	801-363-2739		671
Squaw Valley USA PO Box 2007 *TF:* 800-403-0206 ■ *Web:* squawalpine.com	Olympic Valley	CA	96146	800-403-0206		669
Squire & Company PC 1329 S 800 E *Web:* www.squire.com	Orem	UT	84097	801-225-6900		2
Squire Corrugated Container Corp 111 Somogyi Ct	South Plainfield	NJ	07080	908-561-8550		100
Squire Patton Boggs 127 Public Sq 4900 Key Twr *Web:* www.squirepattonboggs.com	Cleveland	OH	44114	216-479-8500	479-8780	428
Squire Tech Solutions LLC 6304 Fallwater Trl Ste 100 **Fax Area Code: 469* ■ *Web:* www.squiretechsolutions.com	The Colony	TX	75056	214-306-6704	362-1432*	387
Squires Group Inc, The 608 Melvin Ave Ste 101 *Web:* www.squiresgroup.com	Annapolis	MD	21401	410-224-7779	224-5755	180
SqWire's 1415 S 18th St *Web:* sqwires.com	Saint Louis	MO	63104	314-865-3522		671
SR Metals Inc 2249 Manor Ave *Web:* www.delawarevalleysteel.com	Upper Darby	PA	19082	610-449-6100	449-4337	492
SR2020 Inc 3 Pointe Dr Ste 212	Brea	CA	92821	714-482-1922		536
SRA OSS Inc 5201 Great America Pkwy Ste 419 *Web:* www.sraoss.com	Santa Clara	CA	95054	408-855-8200	855-8206	225
SRAM Corp 1333 N Kingsbury St 4th Fl *TF:* 800-346-2928 ■ *Web:* www.sram.com	Chicago	IL	60622	312-664-8800	664-8826	82
SRAM LLC 3100 1st Ave *TF:* 800-660-6853 ■ *Web:* www.sram.com	Spearfish	SD	57783	605-642-2226		711
SRC (Spoon River College) 23235 N County Hwy 22 *TF:* 800-334-7337 ■ *Web:* www.src.edu	Canton	IL	61520	309-647-4645	649-6393	162
SRC (Silver Research Consortium) 2525 Meridian Pkwy Ste 100 *Web:* www.ilzro.org	Durham	NC	27713	919-361-4647	361-1957	49-19
SRC (Syracuse Research Corp) 7502 Round Pond Rd *TF:* 800-724-0451 ■ *Web:* www.srcinc.com	North Syracuse	NY	13212	315-452-8000		668
SRC (Strategic Research Corp) PO Box 5365 *Web:* www.sresearch.com	Santa Barbara	CA	93150	805-201-3178		196
SRC Computers LLC 4240 N Nevada Ave *Web:* www.srccomputers.com	Colorado Springs	CO	80907	719-262-0213	262-0223	173-2
SRC Holdings Corp 531 S Union Ave *TF:* 800-327-2253 ■ *Web:* www.srcholdings.com	Springfield	MO	65802	417-862-2337		262
SRC Logistics Inc 2065 E Pythian *Web:* www.srclogisticsinc.com	Springfield	MO	65802	417-864-4946		803-1
Src Medical Inc 263 Winter St *Web:* www.srcmedical.com	Hanover	MA	02339	781-826-9100		596
SRCD (Society for Research in Child Development) 2950 S State St Ste 401 *Web:* www.srcd.org	Ann Arbor	MI	48104	734-926-0600	926-0601	49-5
SREC (Spoon River Electric Co-opeartive Inc) 930 S Fifth Ave PO Box 340 *TF:* 877-404-2572 ■ *Web:* srecoop.org	Canton	IL	61520	309-647-2700		245
Sree Hotels LLC 5113 Piper Sta Dr Ste 300 *Web:* www.sree.com	Charlotte	NC	28277	704-364-6008	364-9293	378
SRF Consulting Group Inc 1 Carlson Pkwy N Ste 150 *TF:* 866-870-0773 ■ *Web:* www.srfconsulting.com	Minneapolis	MN	55447	763-475-0010		261
SRG (Station Resource Group) 24519 Peach Tree Rd PO Box 1858 *Web:* www.srg.org	Clarksburg	MD	20871	301-270-2617	270-2618	632
SRG (Sterling-Rice Group, The) 1801 13th St Ste 400 *Web:* www.srg.com	Boulder	CO	80302	303-381-6400		4
SRI (SelectResources Intl) 10940 Wilshire Blvd Ste 925 *Web:* www.selectresources.com	Los Angeles	CA	90024	310-824-8999		196
Sri Aurobindo Center of Los Angeles 12329 Marshall St *Web:* www.sriaurobindocenter-la.org	Culver City	CA	90230	310-390-9083		48-20
Sri Instruments 20720 Earl St *Web:* www.srigc.com	Torrance	CA	90503	310-214-5092	214-5097	253
Sri Lanka *Consulate General* 3250 Wilshire Blvd Ste 2180 *Web:* www.srilankaconsulatela.com	Los Angeles	CA	90010	213-387-0210		257
Embassy 3025 Whitehaven St NW *Web:* slembassyusa.org	Washington	DC	20008	202-483-4025		257
SRI Newspapers Inc 187 Main St *Web:* www.ricentral.com	Wakefield	RI	02879	401-789-9744	789-1550	532-2

Name / Address	City	State	Zip	Phone	Fax	Class
Sri Quality Sys 300 Northpointe Cir Ste 304 — *TF:* 800-549-6709 ■ *Web:* www.sriregistrar.com	Seven Fields	PA	16046	724-934-9000		196
SriLankan Airlines 379 Thornall St 6th Fl — *TF:* 877-915-2652 ■ *Web:* www.srilankanusa.com	Edison	NJ	08837	732-205-0017	205-0299	25
Srinsoft Inc 7243 Sawmill Rd Ste 205 — *Web:* srinsofttech.com	Dublin	OH	43016	614-333-5277		177
Sripraphai 64-13 39th Ave — *Web:* www.sripraphai.com	Woodside	NY	11377	718-899-9599		671
SRK Consulting Inc Oceanic Plz 1066 W Hastings St 22nd Fl — *Web:* www.na.srk.com	Vancouver	BC	V6E3X2	604-681-4196	687-5532	261
SRMC (Sparks Regional Medical Ctr) 1001 Towson Ave — *Web:* www.sparkshealth.com	Fort Smith	AR	72901	479-441-4000	441-5397	374-3
SRMC (Spartanburg Regional Medical Ctr) 101 E Wood St — *TF:* 800-318-2596 ■ *Web:* www.spartanburgregional.com	Spartanburg	SC	29303	864-560-6000		374-3
SRMC (Shasta Regional Medical Ctr) 1100 Butte St — *TF:* 866-800-2987 ■ *Web:* www.shastaregional.com	Redding	CA	96001	530-244-5400		374-3
SRMH (Santa Rosa Memorial Hospital) 1165 Montgomery Dr — *TF:* 877-449-3627 ■ *Web:* www.stjosephhealth.org	Santa Rosa	CA	95405	707-546-3210		374-3
SRN Broadcasting 307 E Washington — *Web:* internetfm.com	Lake Bluff	IL	60044	847-735-1995		644
Sroka Industries Inc 21265 Westwood Dr — *Web:* www.srokausa.com	Strongsville	OH	44149	440-572-1525		454
Srose Publishing Co PO Box 2821 — *Web:* www.srosepublishing.org	Southfield	MI	48037	248-208-7073		637-10
SRP (Salt River Project) 1521 N Project Dr — *TF:* 800-258-4777 ■ *Web:* srpnet.com	Tempe	AZ	85281	602-236-5900	236-2442	787
SRP (Sea Raven Press) PO Box 1484 — *TF:* 800-925-1563 ■ *Web:* www.searavenpress.com	Spring Hill	TN	37174	800-925-1563		637-2
SRP Environmental LLC 348 Aero Dr — *Web:* srpenvironmental.com	Shreveport	LA	71107	318-222-2364		85
SRP Federal Credit Union 1267 Augusta W Pkwy — *Web:* www.srpfcu.org	Augusta	GA	30909	803-278-4851		219
SRRC (Southern Regional Research Ctr) 1100 Robert E Lee Blvd — **Fax Area Code:* 504 ■ *Web:* www.ars.usda.gov	New Orleans	LA	70124	706-546-3527	286-4419*	668
SRS (Santa Rosa Symphony) 50 Santa Rosa Ave Ste 410 — *Web:* www.srsymphony.org	Santa Rosa	CA	95404	707-546-8742	546-0460	573-3
SRS Inc 106 Public Sq Ste 203PBM 170 — *Web:* www.srsincorp.com	Gallatin	TN	37066	615-230-2966		106
SRS Medical Systems Inc 76 Treble Cove Rd Bldg 3 — *TF:* 800-345-5642 ■ *Web:* www.srsmedical.com	North Billerica	MA	01862	978-663-2800	663-0999	743
SRSSA (Smallwood Reynolds Stewart Stewart & Associates Inc) 1 Piedmont Ctr 3565 Piedmont Rd Ste 303 — *Web:* www.srssa.com	Atlanta	GA	30305	404-233-5453	264-0929	261
SRT (Seattle Repertory Theatre) 155 Mercer St PO Box 900923 — *TF:* 877-900-9285 ■ *Web:* www.seattlerep.org	Seattle	WA	98109	206-443-2210	443-2379	573-4
SRT Securities LLC 1120 Ave of the Americas Ste 1512 — *Web:* iaenglander.com	New York	NY	10036	212-841-4500		690
Sru Inc 4116 W 5800 N Mountain Green — *TF:* 866-699-5918 ■ *Web:* www.semcomotion.com	Morgan	UT	84050	801-876-2111	876-2115	518
SS (Sourdough Studio) PO Box 92205 — *Web:* www.douglindstrand.com	Anchorage	AK	99509	907-563-2568	563-4456	637-2
SS & C Technologies Inc 80 Lamberton Rd — *TF:* 800-234-0556 ■ *Web:* www.ssctech.com	Windsor	CT	06095	800-234-0556		178-11
SS Cyril & Methodius Seminary 3535 Indian Trl — *Web:* sscms.edu	Orchard Lake	MI	48324	248-683-0310	738-6735	167-3
SS Nesbitt & Company Inc *Valent Group* 3500 Blue Lake Dr Ste 120 — *TF:* 800-422-3223 ■ *Web:* www.ssnesbitt.com	Birmingham	AL	35243	205-262-2700		391-4
SS Steele & Company Inc 4951 Government Blvd — *Web:* www.steelehomes.cc	Mobile	AL	36693	251-661-9600		187
SS White Burs Inc 1145 Towbin Ave — *TF:* 800-535-2877 ■ *Web:* www.sswhitedental.com	Lakewood	NJ	08701	732-905-1100		228
SS8 Networks Inc 750 Tasman Dr — *Web:* www.ss8.com	Milpitas	CA	95035	408-944-0250		681
SSA (Self Storage Assn) 1901 N Beauregard St Ste 106 — *TF:* 888-735-3784 ■ *Web:* www.selfstorage.org	Alexandria	VA	22311	703-575-8000	575-8901	49-21
SSA (Social Security Administration) 6401 Security Blvd — *Web:* www.ssa.gov	Baltimore	MD	21235	410-965-8904		340-20
SSA (Specialty Sleep Assn) 46639 Jones Ranch Rd — *Web:* www.sleepinformation.org	Friant	CA	93626	559-868-4187		49-4
SSA (Steve Smith Autosports) 239 S Glassell St — *Web:* www.ssapubl.com	Orange	CA	92866	714-639-7681	639-9741	637-2
SSA Consultants Inc 9331 Bluebonnet Blvd — *TF:* 800-634-2758 ■ *Web:* www.consultssa.com	Baton Rouge	LA	70810	225-769-2676		463
SSA Marine 1131 SW Klickitat Way — *TF:* 800-422-3505 ■ *Web:* www.ssamarine.com	Seattle	WA	98134	206-623-0304	623-0179	465
SSAI (Support Systems Associates Inc) Marina Towers 709 S Harbor City Blvd Ste 350 — *TF:* 877-234-7724 ■ *Web:* www.ssai.org	Melbourne	FL	32901	877-234-7724		261
SSAT (Society for Surgery of the Alimentary Tract) 900 Cummings Ctr Ste 221-U — *Web:* www.ssat.com	Beverly	MA	01915	978-927-8330	524-8890	49-8
SSCS (IEEE Solid State Circuits Society) 445 Hoes Ln — *Web:* sscs.ieee.org	Piscataway	NJ	08854	732-981-3400		49-19
Ssg Ltd 801 E Campbell Rd Ste 350 — *Web:* www.ssglimited.com	Richardson	TX	75081	214-333-2000	343-1107	196
SSH (South Shore Hospital) 8012 S Crandon Ave — *Web:* www.southshorehospital.com	Chicago	IL	60617	773-356-5000		374-3
SSI (Street Solutions Inc) 2930 Plz Five — *Web:* www.streetsolutions.com	Jersey City	NJ	07311	201-763-9500		196
SSI (Software Solutions Inc) 10570 Justin Dr — **Fax Area Code:* 888 ■ *Web:* www.ssicomputing.com	Urbandale	IA	50322	515-221-9922	400-3260*	178-1
SSI (Strategic Solutions Inc) 16W231 S Frontage Rd Ste 1 — *Web:* www.ssichicago.com	Burr Ridge	IL	60527	630-834-5330		180
SSI (Southard Supply Inc) 236 N 3rd St — *TF:* 800-313-7652 ■ *Web:* www.southardsupply.com	Columbus	OH	43215	614-221-3323	221-5130	612
SSI Express Inc 150 S Larch Ave — *Web:* ssiexpressinc.com	Rialto	CA	92376	909-874-3072		311
SSI Investment Management Inc 9440 Santa Monica Blvd 8th Fl — *Web:* www.ssi-invest.com	Beverly Hills	CA	90210	310-595-2000	595-2089	690
SSI Micro Ltd 356B Old Airport Rd — *Web:* www.ssimicro.com	Yellowknife	NT	X1A3T4	867-669-7500		224
SSI Technologies Inc PO Box 5011 — *Web:* www.ssi-sensors.com	Janesville	WI	53547	608-757-2000		203
SSI Technology Inc 35715 Stanley Dr — *Web:* www.ssi-tek.com	Sterling Heights	MI	48312	248-582-0600	545-8826	472
SSIA (Shoe Service Institute of America) 1013 Beards Hill Rd Ste 101 — *Web:* www.ssia.info	Aberdeen	MD	21001	410-569-3425	569-8333	49-4
SSJCPL (Stockton-San Joaquin County Public Library) 605 N El Dorado St — *TF:* 866-805-7323 ■ *Web:* www.ssjcpl.org	Stockton	CA	95202	209-937-8416		434-3
SSM Health 10101 Woodfield Ln — *Web:* www.ssmhealth.com	Saint Louis	MO	63132	314-944-7800	768-7451	374-3
Ssm Industries Inc 3401 Grand Ave — *Web:* www.ssmi.biz	Pittsburgh	PA	15225	412-777-5100		595
SSMB Pacific Holding Company Inc 1755 Adams Ave — *TF:* 866-572-2525 ■ *Web:* www.norcalkw.com	San Leandro	CA	94577	510-836-6100	836-2551	360-2
SSN (Straight Spouse Network) PO Box 4985 — *Web:* www.straightspouse.org	Chicago	IL	60680	773-413-8213		48-21
SSNet Inc 1905 S Clarkson St — *TF:* 800-697-9997 ■ *Web:* www.softwaresolutions.net	Denver	CO	80210	303-979-6019		174
SSOE 1001 Madison Ave — *Web:* www.ssoe.com	Toledo	OH	43604	419-255-3830	255-6101	261
SSP (Society for Scholarly Publishing) 10200 W 44th Ave Ste 304 — *Web:* www.sspnet.org	Wheat Ridge	CO	80033	303-422-3914		49-16
SSP (Sunshine Media) 1 Galleria Blvd Ste 1900 — *TF:* 800-259-9835 ■ *Web:* www.sunshinepages.com	Metairie	LA	70001	504-832-9835		637-9
SSPC (Society for Protective Coatings) 40 24th St 6th Fl — *TF:* 877-281-7772 ■ *Web:* www.sspc.org	Pittsburgh	PA	15222	412-281-2331	281-9995	49-13
SSPC (Survival Series Publishing Co) PO Box 77313 — *TF:* 800-200-7110 ■ *Web:* www.survival-series.com	San Francisco	CA	94107	415-979-6785		637-2
SSPR Public Relations Agency 150 N Upper Wacker Dr Ste 2010 — *TF:* 800-287-2279 ■ *Web:* sspr.com	Chicago	IL	60606	800-287-2279		636
SSQC (Software Systems Quality Consulting) 2269 Sunny Vista Dr — *Web:* www.ssqc.com	San Jose	CA	95128	408-985-4476	248-7772	194
SSR Engineering inc 950 Fee Ana Ste A — *Web:* ssreng.com	Placentia	CA	92870	714-229-9020	229-9015	529
SSR Mining Inc 999 W Hastings St Ste 1180 — *NASDAQ: SSRM* ■ *TF:* 888-338-0046 ■ *Web:* www.ssrmining.com	Vancouver	BC	V6C2W2	604-689-3846	689-3847	502
SSR Pump Co 105 Jeanette Ave N — *Web:* www.ssrpump.com	Michigan	ND	58259	701-259-2331		770
SSRC (Social Science Research Council) 810 Seventh Ave — *Web:* www.ssrc.org	New York	NY	10019	212-377-2700	377-2727	634
SSRL (Stanford Synchrotron Radiation Lightsource) 2575 Sand Hill Rd MS 69 — *TF:* 877-447-7522 ■ *Web:* www-ssrl.slac.stanford.edu	Menlo Park	CA	94025	650-926-2079	926-3600	668
SSS (Sidney Scheinert & Son Inc) 404 Midland Ave — *Web:* www.scheinertscrews.com	Saddle Brook	NJ	07663	201-791-4600	791-8551	278
SSS Co 71 University Ave — *TF:* 800-237-3843 ■ *Web:* www.ssspharmaceuticals.com	Atlanta	GA	30315	404-521-0857		582
SSSECO (Stockton Service Station Equipment Company Inc) 808 N Union St — *Web:* www.ssseco.com	Stockton	CA	95205	209-464-8333	464-8349	76
SST (Spectrum Software Technology Inc) Atlantic City International Airport Ste 114 — *Web:* sst-it.com	Egg Harbor Township	NJ	08234	609-910-0190	645-6864	177
SST (Salina-Spavinaw Telephone Company Inc) 109 E Evanjoy St — *TF:* 800-722-3450 ■ *Web:* www.sstelco.com	Salina	OK	74365	918-434-5392	434-6960	224
SST Corp 635 Brighton Rd — *TF:* 844-476-8200 ■ *Web:* www.sst-corp.com	Clifton	NJ	07012	973-473-4300	473-4326	479
SST Energy Corp 8901 W Yellowstone Hwy — *Web:* sstenergy.com	Casper	WY	82604	307-235-3529	473-1650	540
SST Group Inc 309 Laurelwood Rd Ste 20 — *TF:* 800-944-6281 ■ *Web:* www.sstgroup-inc.com	Santa Clara	CA	95054	408-350-3450		475
SST Planners 1615 M St NW Ste 700 — *Web:* www.sstplanners.com	Washington	DC	20036	202-909-4942		463
SSW (Seminary of the southwest) 501 E 32nd PO Box 2247 — *TF:* 800-252-5400 ■ *Web:* ssw.edu	Austin	TX	78705	512-472-4133	472-3098	167-3

Phone Fax Class

SSW Mechanical Incorporated Air Cond
670 S Oleander Rd . . . . . Palm Springs CA 92264 760-325-6007 610
Web: sswmechanical.com

St Agnes Home 10341 Manchester Rd . . . . . Kirkwood MO 63122 314-965-7616 965-3179 371
Web: www.stagneshome.com

St Agnes Hospital 430 E Div St . . . . . Fond du Lac WI 54935 920-929-2300 374-3
TF: 800-922-3400 ■ *Web:* www.agnesian.com

St Albert & District Chamber of Commerce
71 St Albert Trl . . . . . Saint Albert AB T8N6L5 780-458-2833 458-6515 137
TF: 800-207-9410 ■ *Web:* stalbertchamber.com

St Albert Public Library
5 St Anne St . . . . . Saint Albert AB T8N3Z9 780-459-1530 458-5772 435
Web: www.sapl.ca

St Alexius Medical Center School of Radiologic Technology
900 E Broadway Ave PO Box 5510 . . . . . Bismarck ND 58501 701-530-7751 685
Web: www.st.alexius.org

St Anastasia School
8631 Stanmoor Dr . . . . . Los Angeles CA 90045 310-645-8816 685
Web: www.st-anastasia.org

St Andrews University
1700 Dogwood Mile . . . . . Laurinburg NC 28352 910-277-5555 277-5020 166
TF: 800-763-0198 ■ *Web:* www.sa.edu

St Ann Catholic School
365 N Cool Spring St . . . . . Fayetteville NC 28301 910-483-3902 483-3195 685
Web: www.stanncatholicschool.net

St Ann Transportation Inc
11340 State Rte 149 . . . . . Fort Ann NY 12827 800-336-7826 639-8501* 780
*Fax Area Code: 518 ■ *TF:* 800-336-7826 ■ *Web:* www.stanngroup.com

St Ann's Warehouse 45 Water St . . . . . Brooklyn NY 11201 718-834-8794 522-2470 303
TF: 866-811-4111 ■ *Web:* stannswarehouse.org

St Anne's Credit Union of Fall River
286 Oliver St. . . . . . Fall River MA 02724 508-324-7300 673-1542 219
Web: www.stannes.com

St Anthony Riverwalk Wyndham Hotel, The
300 E Travis St . . . . . San Antonio TX 78205 210-227-4392 378
Web: www.thestanthonyhotel.com

St Athanasius Rectory
2050 E Walnut Ln . . . . . Philadelphia PA 19138 215-548-2700 48-20
Web: stathanasiuschurch.us

St Augustine Health Ministries
7801 Detroit Ave . . . . . Cleveland OH 44102 216-634-7400 450
Web: staugministries.org

St Augustine's Press Inc
17917 Killington Way . . . . . South Bend IN 46614 574-291-3500 291-3700 637-2
Web: www.staugustine.net

St Barnabas Episcopal Church in The City of Lafayette
400 Camellia Blvd . . . . . LaFayette LA 70503 337-984-3848 48-20
Web: saintbarnabas.us

St Benedict's Monastery
104 Chapel Ln . . . . . Saint Joseph MN 56374 320-363-7100 48-20
Web: sbm.osb.org

St Bernard Hospital & Health Care Ctr
326 W 64th St. . . . . . Chicago IL 60621 773-962-3900 374-3
Web: www.stbh.org

St Bernard Sports
5570 W Lovers Ln Ste 388 . . . . . Dallas TX 75209 214-357-9700 711
TF: 800-461-4450 ■ *Web:* www.saintbernard.com

St Brendans Church 333 E 206th St. . . . . . Bronx NY 10467 718-547-6655 48-20
Web: saintbrendanchurch.org

St Cecilia Catholic School
1310 Madison Ave N . . . . . Bainbridge Island WA 98110 206-842-2017 842-6988 685
Web: www.saintceciliaschool.org

St Charles Inc 151 S 84th St. . . . . . Milwaukee WI 53214 414-476-3710 685
Web: stcharlesinc.org

St Charles Nissan Inc
5625 Veterans Memorial Pkwy . . . . . Saint Peters MO 63376 636-441-4481 57
TF: 888-375-3511 ■ *Web:* www.stcharlesauto.com

St Charles Public Library
1 S 6th Ave . . . . . Saint Charles IL 60174 630-584-0076 584-9262 434-3
Web: www.stcharleslibrary.org

St Charles Town Company LLC
Equitable Building
1850 Platte St 2nd Fl . . . . . Denver CO 80202 720-598-1300 205
Web: www.stcharlestown.com

St Clair College of Applied Arts & Technology, The
2000 Talbot Rd W . . . . . Windsor ON N9A6S4 519-966-1656 162
Web: www.stclaircollege.ca

St Clair County Regional Educational Service Agency
499 Range Rd PO Box 1500 . . . . . Marysville MI 48040 810-364-8990 364-7474 685
TF: 800-294-9229 ■ *Web:* sccresa.org

St Clair Foods Inc 3100 Bellbrook Dr. . . . . . Memphis TN 38116 901-396-8680 297-8
Web: www.stclair.com

St Clair Service Co
1036 S Green Mount Rd . . . . . Belleville IL 62222 618-233-1248 233-7724 276
Web: www.stclairfs.com

St Cloud Technical & Community College
1540 Northway Dr. . . . . . Saint Cloud MN 56303 320-308-5000 165
TF: 800-222-1009 ■ *Web:* www.sctcc.edu

St Coletta's of Illinois Inc
18350 Crossing Dr . . . . . Tinley Park IL 60487 708-342-5200 342-2579 685
Web: www.stcil.org

ST Croix Forge 5195 Scandia Trl . . . . . Forest Lake MN 55025 651-287-8289 483
TF: 866-668-7642 ■ *Web:* stcroixforge.com

ST Croix Valley Foundation
516 Second St Ste 214 . . . . . Hudson WI 54016 715-386-9490 305
Web: scvfoundation.org

St David's Episcopal Church & School
1300 Wiltshire Ave . . . . . San Antonio TX 78209 210-824-2481 48-20
Web: www.saintdavids.net

St Edwards High School
13500 Detroit Ave . . . . . Lakewood OH 44107 216-221-3776 685
Web: www.sehs.net

ST Engineering
99 Canal Center Plz Ste 220 . . . . . Alexandria VA 22314 703-739-2610 21
Web: www.vt-systems.com

St Francis Animal Clinic PA
5380 Trail Blvd . . . . . Naples FL 34108 239-597-3108 794
Web: stfrancisanimalclinicnaples.com

St Francis De Sales High School
2323 W Bancroft St. . . . . . Toledo OH 43607 419-531-1618 685
Web: www.sfstoledo.org

St Francis Healthcare Systems
2226 Liliha St PO Box 29700 . . . . . Honolulu HI 96820 808-547-6883 371
Web: www.stfrancishawaii.org

St Francis High School
1885 Miramonte Ave. . . . . . Mountain View CA 94040 650-968-1213 685
Web: www.sfhs.com

St Francis Medical Ctr
3421 Medical Pk Dr . . . . . Monroe LA 71203 318-966-4000 374-3
Web: www.stfran.com

St Francis Xavier High School
15 School St. . . . . . Sumter SC 29150 803-773-0210 685
Web: www.sfxhs.com

St George Area
Chamber of Commerce
136 North 100 East . . . . . Saint George UT 84770 435-628-1650 673-1587 139
Web: www.stgeorgechamber.com

St George Greek Orthodox Church
1200 Klockner Rd . . . . . Trenton NJ 08619 609-586-4448 48-20
Web: www.stgeorgehamilton.com

St George Steel Fabrication Inc
1301 East 700 North . . . . . Saint George UT 84770 435-673-4856 628-4139 454
Web: www.stgeorgesteel.com

St Giles Hotels LLC
120-130 E 39th St . . . . . New York NY 10016 212-685-1100 377
Web: www.stgileshotels.com

St Gregory Group
9435 Waterstone Blvd Ste 180 . . . . . Cincinnati OH 45249 513-769-8440 7
Web: stgregory.com

St Gregory Hotel Dupont Circle
2033 M St NW . . . . . Washington DC 20036 202-530-3600 379
Web: www.stgregoryhotelwdc.com

St Henry District High School
3755 Scheben Dr . . . . . Erlanger KY 41018 859-525-0255 685
Web: shdhs.org

St Hope Foundation
6800 W Loop S Ste 560 . . . . . Bellaire TX 77401 713-839-7111 839-7156 305
Web: offeringhope.org

St Ignatius College Prep
2001 37th Ave. . . . . . San Francisco CA 94116 415-731-7500 685
TF: 888-225-5427 ■ *Web:* www.siprep.org

S-T Industries Inc
301 Armstrong Blvd N PO Box 517 . . . . . Saint James MN 56081 507-375-3211 375-4503 493
TF: 800-326-2039 ■ *Web:* www.stindustries.com

St James Academy 3100 Monkton Rd . . . . . Monkton MD 21111 410-771-4816 685
Web: www.saintjamesacademy.org

St James Episcopal School
602 S Carancahua St . . . . . Corpus Christi TX 78401 361-883-0835 685
Web: www.sjes.org

St James Hotel 406 Main St . . . . . Red Wing MN 55066 800-252-1875 379
TF: 800-252-1875 ■ *Web:* www.st-james-hotel.com

St James House of Baytown
5800 W Baker Rd . . . . . Baytown TX 77520 281-425-1200 424-1922 371
Web: www.stjameshouse.org

St James Security Services LLC
St James Bldg 1604 Ponce de Leon Ave Urb Caribe
. . . . . San Juan PR 00926 787-754-8448 281-6254 693
Web: stjamessecurity.com

St Jo Frontier Casino
777 Winners Cir . . . . . Saint Joseph MO 64505 816-279-5514 133
Web: www.stjofrontiercasino.com

St Joe Petroleum Co
2520 S Second St . . . . . Saint Joseph MO 64501 816-279-0770 297-8
Web: www.stjoepetroleum.com

St Johann Press (SJP) PO Box 241 . . . . . Haworth NJ 07641 201-387-1529 501-0698 637-2
Web: www.stjohannpress.com

St John Diakon Hospice
1201 N Church St. . . . . . Hazleton PA 18202 877-666-5784 371
TF: 877-666-5784 ■ *Web:* www.diakon.org

St John Lutheran Church
1140 W River Rd N. . . . . . Elyria OH 44035 440-324-4070 48-20
Web: stjohnlutheran-elyria.org

St John Medical Ctr
1923 S Utica Ave PO Box 4939 . . . . . Tulsa OK 74104 918-744-2345 353
Web: www.tulsarad.com

St John Neumann Regional Catholic School
791 Tom Smith Rd . . . . . Lilburn GA 30047 770-381-0557 685
Web: www.sjnrcs.org

St John The Apostle School
7421 Glenview Dr . . . . . Richland Hills TX 76180 817-284-2228 685
Web: stjs.org

St John Vianney High School
540A Line Rd . . . . . Holmdel NJ 07733 732-739-0800 739-0824 685
Web: www.sjvhs.com

St John's Buffalo Federal Credit Union
2322 Seneca St. . . . . . Buffalo NY 14210 716-823-1527 823-1158 219
Web: stjohnscreditunion.com

St John's Food Service Inc
4 Louise St . . . . . Saint Augustine FL 32084 904-824-0493 824-6527 297-6
Web: www.stjohnsfoods.com

St John-Mittelhauser & Assoc
1401 Branding Ave Ste 315 . . . . . Downers Grove IL 60515 630-427-8100 427-8129 261
Web: st-ma.com

St Johns County Public Library
1960 N Ponce de Leon Blvd . . . . . Saint Augustine FL 32084 904-827-6940 827-6945 434-3
Web: www.sjcpls.org

St Johns Ev Lutheran Church & School
4705 Brockway Rd . . . . . Saginaw MI 48638 989-799-0935 48-20
Web: www.stjohnsbrockway.org

St Johns River State College
5001 St Johns Ave . . . . . Palatka FL 32177 386-312-4200 162
TF: 888-757-2293 ■ *Web:* www.sjrstate.edu

St Johns Unified District
450 S 13th St W . . . . . Saint John AZ 85936 928-337-2255 337-2263 685
Web: www.sjusd.net

St Johnson Co 925 Stanford Ave . . . . . Oakland CA 94608 510-652-6000 652-4302 318
Web: www.stjohnson.com

Name / Address	City	State	ZIP	Phone	Fax	Class
St Joseph & St Mary's Medical Centers 1000 Carondelet Dr *Web:* www.carondelethealth.org	Kansas City	MO	64114	816-942-4400		374-3
St Joseph Communications 50 MacIntosh Blvd *Web:* stjoseph.com	Concord	ON	L4K4P3	905-660-3111		627
St Joseph Health 2700 Dolbeer St *Web:* www.stjoehumboldt.org	Eureka	CA	95501	707-445-8121		374-3
St Joseph Healthcare 360 Broadway PO Box 403 *Web:* www.stjoeshealing.org	Bangor	ME	04402	207-907-1000		374-3
St Joseph Residence 107 E Beckert Rd *Web:* stjosephresidence.com	New London	WI	54961	920-982-5354	982-5420	371
St Joseph's Health Ctr *Toronto* 30 The Queensway *Web:* stjoestoronto.ca	Toronto	ON	M6R1B5	416-530-6000		374-2
St Joseph's Wayne Hospital 224 Hamburg Tpke *Web:* stjosephshealth.org	Wayne	NJ	07470	973-942-6900		374-3
St Julien Hotel & Spa 900 Walnut St *TF:* 877-303-0900 ■ *Web:* www.stjulien.com	Boulder	CO	80302	720-406-9696		379
St Landry Bank & Trust Co 132 E Landry St *TF:* 800-369-4887 ■ *Web:* stlandrybank.com	Opelousas	LA	70570	337-942-7516	948-2449	70
St Lawrence County Chamber of Commerce 101 Main St 1st Flr *TF:* 877-228-7810 ■ *Web:* www.northcountryguide.com	Canton	NY	13617	315-386-4000	379-0134	139
St Lawrence County Historical Assn (SLCHA) 3 E Main St *Web:* www.slcha.org	Canton	NY	13617	315-386-8133		637-2
St Lawrence Seaway Management Corp 202 Pitt St *Web:* www.seaway.ca	Cornwall	ON	K6J3P7	613-932-5170		314
St Lawrence-Lewis BOCES 40 W Main St *Web:* www.sllboces.org	Canton	NY	13617	315-386-4504	379-0241	507
St Louis Antique Lighting Company Inc 801 N Skinker *Web:* www.slalco.com	Saint Louis	MO	63130	314-863-1414		439
St Louis Area Business Health Coalition 8888 Ladue Rd Ste 250	Saint Louis	MO	63124	314-721-7800		474
St Louis Association of Realtors 12777 Olive Blvd *Web:* www.stlrealtors.com	Saint Louis	MO	63141	314-576-0033		138
St Louis Cold Drawn Inc 1060 Pershall Rd *Web:* www.stlcd.com	Saint Louis	MO	63137	314-867-4301		492
St Louis County 100 N 5th Ave W Ste 103 *TF:* 800-450-9278 ■ *Web:* www.stlouiscountymn.gov	Duluth	MN	55802	218-726-2450	726-2469	338
St Louis County Historical Society 506 W Michigan St *Web:* www.thehistorypeople.org	Duluth	MN	55802	218-733-7586	733-7585	48-13
St Louis Hills Pharmacy LLC 4365 Chippewa St Ste 100 *Web:* stlhillsrx.com	Saint Louis	MO	63116	314-832-2480		237
St Louis Outlet Mall Hwy 370 Exit 11 *Web:* www.stlouisoutletmall.com	Hazelwood	MO	63042	314-227-5900	227-5901	460
St Louis Parking Co 505 N Seventh St Ste 2405 *Web:* stlouisparking.com	Saint Louis	MO	63101	314-241-7777	241-4960	562
St Louis Pipe & Supply Inc 17740 Edison Ave *TF:* 800-737-7473 ■ *Web:* www.stlpipesupply.com	Chesterfield	MO	63005	636-391-2500		492
St Louis Testing Laboratories 2810 Clark Ave *Web:* www.labinc.com	Saint Louis	MO	63103	314-531-8080	531-8085	743
St Luke Community Hospital (Inc) 107 Sixth Ave SW *Web:* www.stlukehealthnet.org	Ronan	MT	59864	406-676-4441		374-3
St Luke's College 2800 Pierce St Ste 410 *TF:* 800-352-4660 ■ *Web:* www.stlukescollege.edu	Sioux City	IA	51104	712-279-3149		507
St Luke's Health System 190 E Bannock St *Web:* www.stlukesonline.org	Boise	ID	83712	208-381-2222		186
St Luke's Home Care Services 220 N 6th Ave E *TF:* 800-321-3790 ■ *Web:* www.slhduluth.com	Duluth	MN	55805	212-249-6111		363
St Luke's Lehighton 211 N 12th St *Web:* www.slhn.org	Lehighton	PA	18235	610-377-1300		374-3
St Lukes Episcopal Day School 8833 Goodwood Blvd *Web:* www.stlukesbr.org	Baton Rouge	LA	70806	225-926-5343		685
St Margaret's School 1080 Lucas Ave *Web:* www.stmarg.ca	Victoria	BC	V8X3P7	250-479-7171		685
St Mark Coptic Orthodox Church 3603 Livernois Rd *Web:* www.stmarkmi.org	Troy	MI	48083	248-689-9099		637-2
St Mark's Episcopal Church Parish Library 680 Calder St *Web:* www.stmarksbeaumont.org	Beaumont	TX	77701	409-832-3405	832-8045	434-3
St Marks Evangelical Lutheran Church of North 2499 Helen St N *Web:* www.stmarks-nsp.org	Saint Paul	MN	55109	651-777-7451		48-20
St Mary Missionary Baptist Church of Plant City 1840 E State Rd 60	Plant City	FL	33567	813-737-3668		48-20
St Mary Parish Library 206 Iberia St *Web:* stmarylibrary.org	Franklin	LA	70538	337-828-5364	828-2329	434-3
St Mary School 422 - 20 St S *Web:* esm.holyspirit.ab.ca	Lethbridge	AB	T1J2V5	403-327-3098		623
St Mary's County Maryland Libraries 23250 Hollywood Rd *Web:* www.stmalib.org	Leonardtown	MD	20650	301-475-2846	884-4415	434-3
St Mary's Dominican High School Corp 7701 Walmsley Ave *Web:* www.stmarysdominican.org	New Orleans	LA	70125	504-865-9401	866-5958	685
St Mary's Healthcare System for Children 29-01 216th St *TF:* 888-543-7697 ■ *Web:* stmaryskids.org	Bayside	NY	11360	718-281-8800		450
St Mary's Home for Children 420 Fruit Hill Ave *Web:* www.smhfc.org	North Providence	RI	02911	401-353-3900	354-7986	685
St Mary's Hospital 427 Guy Park Ave *Web:* www.smha.org	Amsterdam	NY	12010	518-842-1900		374-3
St Mary's University San Antonio 1 Camino Santa Maria *TF:* 800-367-7868 ■ *Web:* www.stmarytx.edu	San Antonio	TX	78228	210-436-3011		162
St Marys Area Senior High School 977 S St Marys Rd *Web:* www.smasd.org	Saint Marys	PA	15857	814-834-7831		623
St Marys Foundry 405 E South St *Web:* www.stmfoundry.com	Saint Marys	OH	45885	419-394-3346	394-6482	492
St Matthew Catholic School 11525 Elm Ln *Web:* charlottediocese.org	Charlotte	NC	28277	704-544-2070		685
St Matthews Parish School 1031 Bienveneda Ave *Web:* www.stmatthewsschool.com	Pacific Palisades	CA	90272	310-454-1350	573-7423	48-20
St Meyer & Hubbard Inc 10N865 Williamsburg Dr *Web:* www.stmeyerandhubbard.com	Elgin	IL	60124	847-717-4322		195
St Michael's Inc 3310 Noble Pond Way *Web:* www.stmichaelsinc.com	Woodbridge	VA	22193	703-463-9463		463
St Moritz Building Services Inc 4616 Clairton Blvd *TF:* 800-218-9159 ■ *Web:* www.bsinc.com	Pittsburgh	PA	15236	412-885-2100		152
St Moritz Security Services Inc 4600 Clairton Blvd *TF:* 800-218-9156 ■ *Web:* www.smssi.com	Pittsburgh	PA	15236	412-885-3144	885-3740	693
St Norbert Arts Ctr (SNAC) 100 Rue des Ruines du Monastere *Web:* snac.mb.ca	Winnipeg	MB	R3V0A8	204-269-0564	261-1927	50-2
St Olivier School 325 Beckwell Ave *Web:* www.holyfamilyrcssd.ca	Radville	SK	S0C2G0	306-869-3221		685
St Onge Co 1400 Williams Rd *Web:* www.stonge.com	York	PA	17402	717-840-8181		463
St Onge Steward Johnston & Reens LLC 986 Bedford St *Web:* www.ssjr.com	Stamford	CT	06905	203-324-6155		428
St Patrick Catholic School 9040 Hutchins St *Web:* stpwl-school.org	White Lake	MI	48386	248-698-3240		685
St Paul Area Association of Realtors Inc 325 E Roselawn Ave *Web:* spaar.com	Saint Paul	MN	55117	651-776-6000		653
St Paul Education Regional Division No 1 4313 48 Ave *Web:* www.stpauleducation.ab.ca	Saint Paul	AB	T0A3A3	780-645-3323	645-5789	685
St Paul Flight Ctr 270 Airport Rd *TF:* 800-368-0107 ■ *Web:* www.stpaulflight.com	Saint Paul	MN	55107	651-227-8108	227-6195	63
St Paul Grill, The 350 Market St *Web:* www.stpaulgrill.com	Saint Paul	MN	55102	651-224-7455		671
St Paul High School 9635 Greenleaf Ave *Web:* www.stpaulhs.org	Santa Fe Springs	CA	90670	562-698-6246	696-8396	685
St Paul Saints Baseball Club Inc 360 Broadway St *Web:* saintsbaseball.com	Saint Paul	MN	55108	651-644-6659		713
St Petersburg College (SPC) PO Box 13489 *Web:* www.spcollege.edu	Saint Petersburg	FL	33733	727-341-4772		598
St Petersburg General Hospital 6500 38th Ave N *TF:* 800-733-0610 ■ *Web:* stpetegeneral.com	Saint Petersburg	FL	33710	727-384-1414		374-3
St Raphael Academy 123 Walcott St *TF:* 800-498-0045 ■ *Web:* www.saintrays.org	Pawtucket	RI	02860	401-723-8100	723-8740	148
St Renatus LLC 101 E Harmony Rd *TF:* 888-686-2314 ■ *Web:* www.st-renatus.com	Fort Collins	CO	80525	970-282-0156		231
St Rose Health Ctr 3515 Broadway Ave *Web:* www.strosehc.com	Great Bend	KS	67530	620-792-2511		374-3
St Sebastian's School 815 Broad Ave *Web:* www.stsebs.org	Belle Vernon	PA	15012	781-449-5200		685
St Stephen's Catholic School 16701 S St *Web:* stephen.org	Omaha	NE	68135	402-896-0754		685
St Stephens Episcopal Church 351 Main St *Web:* ststephensridgefield.org	Ridgefield	CT	06877	203-438-3789		48-20
St Tammany Parish Hospital 1202 S Tyler St *Web:* www.stph.org	Covington	LA	70433	985-898-4000	898-4394	374-3
St Thomas Aquinas Catholic Newman Center at Unlv 4765 Brussels St *Web:* www.unlvnewman.com	Las Vegas	NV	89119	702-736-0887		48-20
St Thomas Aquinas High School 1 Tingley Ln *Web:* www.stahs.net	Edison	NJ	08820	732-549-1108	494-2229	685
St Thomas Credit Union 4230 Harding Rd Ste 103 *TF:* 833-292-7828 ■ *Web:* stthomascu.org	Nashville	TN	37205	615-292-7828	463-2741	219
St Vincent's College 2800 Main St *TF:* 800-873-1013 ■ *Web:* www.stvincentscollege.edu	Bridgeport	CT	06606	800-873-1013		166
St Vrain Arbor Care 140 Gay St *Web:* www.stvrainarborcare.com	Longmont	CO	80501	303-772-3136	682-0399	192
STA (Student Transportation Inc) *Student Transportation of America* 3349 Hwy 138 Bldg A Ste C *TF:* 888-942-2250 ■ *Web:* www.ridestbus.com	Wall	NJ	07719	732-280-4200	280-4214	109
STA Intl 1400 Old Country Rd Ste 411 *TF:* 866-970-9882 ■ *Web:* www.stacollect.com	Westbury	NY	11590	866-970-9882		216
Staab Battery Manufacturing Co 931 S 11th St *TF:* 800-252-8625 ■ *Web:* www.staabbattery.com	Springfield	IL	62703	800-252-8625		74

Name / Address	City	State	ZIP	Phone	Fax	Class
STAAR Surgical Co 1911 Walker Ave *NASDAQ: STAA* ■ *TF:* 800-352-7842 ■ *Web:* www.staar.com	Monrovia	CA	91016	626-303-7902		542
Staatsburgh State Historic Site 75 Mills Mansion Rd *Web:* www.parks.ny.gov	Staatsburg	NY	12580	845-889-8851		565
Stabbert Mantime Management 2629 NW 54th St Ste 201 *Web:* www.stabbertmaritime.com	Seattle	WA	98107	206-547-6161		698
Stabenow Debbie (Sen D - MI) 731 Hart Senate Office Bldg *Web:* www.stabenow.senate.gov	Washington	DC	20510	202-224-4822		342-2
Stabil Drill Specialties LLC 110 Consolidate Dr *Web:* stabildrill.com	LaFayette	LA	70508	337-837-3001		539
Stabila Inc 332 Industrial Dr PO Box 402 **Fax Area Code:* 847 ■ *TF:* 800-869-7460 ■ *Web:* www.stabila.com	South Elgin	IL	60177	800-869-7460	488-0051*	758
Stabile Companies, The 20 Cotton Rd Ste 200 *Web:* www.stabilecompanies.com	Nashua	NH	03063	603-889-0318	595-2571	187
Stabilit America Inc *Glasteel* 285 Industrial Dr *TF:* 800-238-5546 ■ *Web:* www.glasteel.com	Moscow	TN	38057	901-877-3010		608
Stabinski & Funt PA 757 NW 27th Ave 3rd Fl *Web:* www.stabinskilaw.com	Miami	FL	33125	305-964-8644		445
Stablex Canada Inc 760 Blvd Industriel *Web:* www.stablex.com	Blainville	QC	J7C3V4	450-430-9230		194
Stacey Braun Associates Inc 377 Broadway *TF:* 888-949-1925 ■ *Web:* www.staceybraun.com	New York	NY	10013	212-226-7707		41
Stack & Co 6100 4th Ave Ste 281 *Web:* www.stackco.com	Seattle	WA	98108	206-762-7607	762-8731	44
Stack Plastics 3525 Haven Ave *Web:* www.stackplastics.com	Menlo Park	CA	94025	650-361-8600		608
Stackbin Corp 29 Powderhill Rd **Fax Area Code:* 401 ■ *TF:* 800-333-1603 ■ *Web:* www.stackbin.com	Lincoln	RI	02865	800-333-1603	333-1952*	198
Stackframe 114 W First St Ste 246 **Fax Area Code:* 321 ■ *Web:* www.stackframe.com	Sanford	FL	32771	407-543-2265	348-5853*	177
Stackhouse Bensinger Inc 330 Revere Blvd *Web:* stackhousebensinger.com	Sinking Spring	PA	19608	610-777-8000		261
Stack-On Products Co 1360 N Old Rand Rd *TF:* 800-323-9601 ■ *Web:* www.stack-on.com	Wauconda	IL	60084	800-323-9601		488
Stackpole & Partners Ltd 222 Merrimac St *Web:* stackpolepartners.com	Newburyport	MA	01950	978-463-6600		4
Stacy Cole Law PC 7929 Brookriver Dr Ste 605 *Web:* stacycolelaw.com	Dallas	TX	75247	214-800-5199		41
Stacy Furniture & Design 1900 S Main St *TF:* 800-403-6077 ■ *Web:* stacyfurniture.com	Grapevine	TX	76051	817-424-8800		321
Stadco Corp 107 South Ave 20 *Web:* www.stadco.com	Los Angeles	CA	90031	323-227-8888	221-1705	621
Stadelman Fruit LLC 200 W Northstone Pkwy *Web:* stadelmanfruit.com	Zillah	WA	98953	509-829-5145		315-3
Stadion Publishing Company Inc 135 Fitzgerald Ave *TF:* 800-873-7117 ■ *Web:* www.stadion.com	Island Pond	VT	05846	802-723-6175	723-6171	637-2
Stadium International Trucks Inc 105 Seventh North St *Web:* www.stadiumtrucks.com	Liverpool	NY	13088	315-475-8471	475-4150	57
Stadium Law Group LLC 705 S Ninth St Ste 106 *Web:* snlawllc.com	Tacoma	WA	98405	253-327-1040		41
Stadium Toyota 5088 N Dale Mabry Hwy *Web:* www.stadiumtoyota.com	Tampa	FL	33614	813-872-4881		57
Stafast Products Inc 505 Lake Shore Blvd *TF:* 800-782-3278 ■ *Web:* shop.stafast.com	Painesville	OH	44077	440-357-5546	357-7137	278
STAFDA (Specialty Tools & Fasteners Distributors Assn) 500 Elm Grove Rd Ste 210 PO Box 44 *TF:* 800-352-2981 ■ *Web:* www.stafda.org	Elm Grove	WI	53122	262-784-4774	784-5059	49-18
Staff Ciampino & Company CPAS PC 10 Colvin Ave *Web:* staffciampino.com	Albany	NY	12206	518-459-9205	459-1395	2
Staff Electric Company Inc W 133 N 5030 Campbell Dr *Web:* www.staffelectric.com	Menomonee Falls	WI	53051	262-781-8230		189-4
Staff Force Inc 13240 Hempstead Rd Ste 224 *Web:* www.staff-force.com	Houston	TX	77040	713-690-9696		260
Staff Leasing 149 Northern Concourse *Web:* staffleasing-peo.com	North Syracuse	NY	13212	315-641-3600		463
Staff Management Inc 5919 Spring Creek Rd *Web:* www.staffmgmt.com	Rockford	IL	61114	815-282-3900	282-0515	631
Staff One Inc 8111 LBJ Fwy **Fax Area Code:* 214 ■ *TF:* 800-771-7823 ■ *Web:* www.staffone.com	Dallas	TX	75251	800-771-7823	461-1141*	631
Staffcentrix LLC 33 Woodstock Meadows *Web:* www.staffcentrix.com	Woodstock	CT	06281	860-928-6969		196
Staffelbach Design Associates Inc 2525 McKinnon Ste 800 *Web:* www.staffelbach.com	Dallas	TX	75201	214-747-2511	855-5316	393
Staffing 360 Solutions Inc 641 Lexington Ave 27th Fl *Web:* www.staffing360solutions.com	New York	NY	10022	646-507-5710		260
Staffing Partners 2888 Crescent Ave *Web:* www.staffingoregon.com	Eugene	OR	97408	541-345-9675	242-1137	193
Staffing Resource Group Inc, The 405 Reo St Ste 255 *TF:* 877-774-7742 ■ *Web:* srg-us.com	Tampa	FL	33609	877-774-7742		260
Staffing Solutions 4951 E Grant Rd Ste 105 *Web:* www.staffingsolutions.com	Tucson	AZ	85716	520-881-3200		734
Staffing Technologies 221 Roswell St *Web:* www.staffingtechnologies.com	Alpharetta	GA	30009	678-338-2051		180
Staffingorg Inc 10 Burchard Ln *Web:* www.staffing.org	Rowayton	CT	06853	203-227-0186		463
StaffMark Inc 10164 Princeton-Glendale Rd *Web:* www.staffmark.com	Cincinnati	OH	45246	513-682-2800	682-2807	260
Stafford Communications Group 309 South St *Web:* staffcom.com	New Providence	NJ	07974	908-464-7740	464-7743	195
Stafford County 209 N Broadway St PO Box 296 *Web:* staffordcounty.org	Saint John	KS	67576	620-549-3295	549-3298	338
Stafford County 1300 Ct House Rd *Web:* staffordcountyva.gov	Stafford	VA	22554	540-658-8600		338
Stafford Motor Speedway 55 W St PO Box 105 *Web:* www.staffordmotorspeedway.com	Stafford Springs	CT	06076	860-684-2783	684-6236	515
Stafford Printing Co 2707 Jefferson Davis Hwy *TF:* 800-774-6831 ■ *Web:* www.staffordprinting.com	Stafford	VA	22554	540-659-4554		627
Stafford-Smith Inc 3414 S Burdick St *TF:* 800-968-2442 ■ *Web:* www.staffordsmith.com	Kalamazoo	MI	49001	269-343-1240	343-2509	665
Staffworks Group 25227 Dequindre Rd *Web:* staffworksgroup.com	Madison Heights	MI	48071	248-416-1150		260
Stage 2 Networks LLC 70 W 40th St 7th Fl *Web:* stage2networks.com	New York	NY	10018	212-497-8000	497-8001	387
Stage 4 Solutions inc 4701 Patrick Henry Dr Bldg 19 *Web:* www.stage4solutions.com	Santa Clara	CA	95054	408-868-9739		195
Stage Coach Theatre 4802 W Emerald *Web:* www.stagecoachtheatre.com	Boise	ID	83706	208-342-2000		573-4
Stage Directors & Choreographers Society Inc 321 W 44th St *TF:* 800-541-5204 ■ *Web:* sdcweb.org	New York	NY	10036	212-391-1070	302-6195	414
Stage Fright Productions PO Box 373 *Web:* www.stagefrightproductions.com	Geneva	IL	60134	630-485-9458		514
Stage III Community Theatre 900 N Center St *Web:* www.stageiiitheatre.org	Casper	WY	82601	307-234-0946		572
Stage Neck Inn 8 Stage Neck Rd PO Box 70 *TF:* 800-222-3238 ■ *Web:* stageneckinn.com	York Harbor	ME	03911	207-363-3850	363-2221	669
Stage One The Hair School 209 W College St *Web:* www.stageoneinc.com	Lake Charles	LA	70605	337-474-0533	474-9586	685
Stage Restaurant 1250 Kapiolani Blvd 2nd Fl *Web:* stagerestauranthawaii.com	Honolulu	HI	96814	808-237-5429		671
Stagecoach State Park 25500 County Rd 14 *Web:* cpw.state.co.us	Oak Creek	CO	80467	970-736-2436		565
Stagecraft Costuming Inc 3950 Spring Grove Ave *Web:* www.stagecraft.on-rev.com	Cincinnati	OH	45223	513-541-7150	541-7159	155-6
Stagecraft Industries Inc 5051 N Lagoon Ave *TF:* 800-727-2673 ■ *Web:* www.stagecraftindustries.com	Portland	OR	97217	503-286-1600		45
Stagepost 255 French Landing Dr *Web:* stagepost.com	Nashville	TN	37228	615-248-1978		514
Stageright Corp 495 Pioneer Pkwy *TF:* 800-438-4499 ■ *Web:* www.stageright.com	Clare	MI	48617	800-438-4499		321
Stages Repertory Theatre 3201 Allen Pkwy Ste 101 *Web:* www.stagestheatre.com	Houston	TX	77019	713-527-0220	527-8669	573-4
StageStruck 121 W Chestnut St *Web:* stagestruck.org	Goldsboro	NC	27530	919-736-4530	736-8584	749
Staggs & Fisher Consulting Engineers Inc 3264 Lochness Dr *Web:* www.sfengineering.com	Lexington	KY	40517	859-271-3246		261
Stagnaro Distributing LLC 351 Wilmer Ave *Web:* stagnarodistributing.com	Cincinnati	OH	45226	513-871-7272	871-4432	81-1
Stahancyk Kent & Hook 2400 SW Fourth Ave *TF:* 877-673-7632 ■ *Web:* www.stahancyk.com	Portland	OR	97201	503-222-9115	222-4037	445
Stahl Peterbilt Inc 18020-118 Ave *Web:* www.stahlpeterbilt.com	Edmonton	AB	T5S2G2	780-483-6666		791
Stahl Specialty Co 111 E Pacific *TF:* 800-821-7852 ■ *Web:* stahlspecialty.com	Kingsville	MO	64061	816-597-3322		308
Stahl USA 13 Corwin St *Web:* www.stahl.com	Peabody	MA	01960	978-532-0242		432
STAHL/A Scott Fetzer Co 3201 W Old Lincoln Way *TF:* 800-277-8245 ■ *Web:* www.stahltruckbodies.com	Wooster	OH	44691	330-264-7441	264-3319	516
Stahlin Non-Metallic Enclosure 505 W Maple St *Web:* stahlin.com	Belding	MI	48809	616-794-0700	794-3378	254
Stahls Inc 6353 14 Mile Rd *TF:* 800-521-5255 ■ *Web:* www.stahls.com	Sterling Heights	MI	48312	800-521-5255		258
Stailey Insurance Corp 2084 S Milwaukee St *Web:* www.staileycorp.com	Denver	CO	80210	303-759-2796		390
Staiman Design 17 Warren Rd 23b *Web:* staimanmedia.com	Pikesville	MD	21208	410-580-0100		344
Stained Glass Theatre 1996 W Evangel *Web:* www.sgtheatre.com	Ozark	MO	65721	417-581-9192		572
Stainless Design Concepts Ltd (SDC) 1117 Kings Hwy *Web:* www.stainlessdesign.com	Saugerties	NY	12477	845-246-3631	246-1595	695

Name / Address	City	State	Zip	Phone	Fax	Class
Stainless Fabrication Inc 4455 W Kearney St	Springfield	MO	65803	417-865-5696	865-7863	91
Web: www.stainlessfab.com						
Stainless Foundry & Engineering Inc 5110 N 35th St	Milwaukee	WI	53209	414-462-7400	462-7303	306
Web: www.stainlessfoundry.com						
Stainless Metals Inc 60-01 31st Ave	Woodside	NY	11377	718-784-1454		198
Web: www.stainlessmetals.com						
Stainless Specialists Inc T7441 Steel Ln	Wausau	WI	54403	715-675-4155	675-9096	189-12
TF: 800-236-4155 ■ *Web:* www.ssi-wis.com						
Stairways Inc 4166 Pinemont Dr	Houston	TX	77018	713-680-3110	680-2571	491
Web: www.stairwaysinc.com						
Staker Floral 1695 Ponderosa Dr	Idaho Falls	ID	83404	208-523-7950		293
TF: 888-821-2426 ■ *Web:* www.stakerfloral.com						
Staley Inc 6101 S Shackleford Rd	Little Rock	AR	72209	800-280-9675	565-9674*	189-4
**Fax Area Code:* 501 ■ *TF:* 877-708-7532 ■ *Web:* www.staleyinc.com						
Stallings Crop Insurance Corp PO Box 6100	Lakeland	FL	33807	863-647-2747		390
TF: 800-721-7099 ■ *Web:* www.stallingscrop.com						
Stallion Oilfield Services Inc 950 Corbindale Rd	Houston	TX	77024	713-528-5544		539
Web: www.stallionoilfield.com						
Stalnaker, Becker & Buresh PC 1111 N 102nd Ct Ste 330	Omaha	NE	68124	402-393-5421	393-2374	41
Web: sbblawfirm.com						
Stamas Yacht Inc 300 Pampas Ave	Tarpon Springs	FL	34689	727-937-4118		90
Web: www.stamas.com						
Stamats Communications Inc 615 Fifth St SE	Cedar Rapids	IA	52401	319-364-6167		637-9
TF: 800-553-8878 ■ *Web:* www.stamats.com						
Stambaugh Auditorium 1000 Fifth Ave	Youngstown	OH	44504	330-747-5175	747-1981	572
TF: 866-516-2269 ■ *Web:* www.stambaughauditorium.com						
Stambaugh Ness Inc 2600 Eastern Blvd Ste 101	York	PA	17402	717-757-6999		2
Web: stambaughness.com						
Stamco Industries Inc 26650 Lakeland Blvd	Euclid	OH	44132	216-731-9333		488
Web: stamcoind.com						
Stamey's Barbecue 2206 W Gate City Blvd	Greensboro	NC	27403	336-299-9888		671
Web: stameys.com						
Stamford Center for the Arts 61 Atlantic St	Stamford	CT	06901	203-325-4466	358-2313	572
Web: www.palacestamford.org						
Stamford Chamber of Commerce 970 Summer St	Stamford	CT	06901	203-359-4761	363-5069	139
Web: stamfordchamberofcommerce.com						
Stamford Federal Credit Union 888 Washington Blvd	Stamford	CT	06901	203-977-4701		219
Web: stamfordcu.org						
Stamford Hospital 1 Hospital Pl	Stamford	CT	06904	203-276-1000		374-3
Web: www.stamfordhealth.org						
Stamford Innovation Ctr (SIC) 175 Atlantic St	Stamford	CT	06901	203-226-8701		393
Web: stamfordicenter.com						
Stamford Insurance Group Inc 25 Crescent St Ste 105	Stamford	CT	06906	203-359-0880		390
TF: 866-346-3744 ■ *Web:* findsig.com						
Stamford Museum & Nature Ctr 39 Scofieldtown Rd	Stamford	CT	06903	203-322-1646	322-0408	520
Web: www.stamfordmuseum.org						
Stamford Scientific International Inc 4 Tucker Dr	Poughkeepsie	NY	12603	845-454-8171		358
Web: www.ssiaeration.com						
Stamford Suites 720 Bedford St	Stamford	CT	06901	203-359-7300	359-7304	379
TF: 866-394-4365 ■ *Web:* www.stamfordsuites.com						
Stamos & Trucco LLP 1 E Wacker Dr 3rd Fl	Chicago	IL	60601	312-630-7979	630-1183	41
Web: stamostrucco.com						
Stamped Products Inc 201 Industrial Pkwy	Gadsden	AL	35903	256-492-8890		488
Web: spi-al.com						
Stampede Meat Inc 7351 S 78th Ave	Bridgeview	IL	60455	800-353-0933		296-26
TF: 800-353-0933 ■ *Web:* stampedemeat.com						
Stamper Rubens PS 720 W Boone Ste 200	Spokane	WA	99201	509-326-4800		41
Web: stamperlaw.com						
Stampin Up 12907 S 3600 W	Riverton	UT	84065	800-782-6787		366
TF: 800-782-6787 ■ *Web:* stampinup.com						
Stampscom Inc 1990 E Grand Ave	El Segundo	CA	90245	855-889-7867		178-1
NASDAQ: STMP ■ *TF:* 855-889-7867 ■ *Web:* www.stamps.com						
Stamtex Metal Stampings 112 Erie St	Niles	OH	44446	330-652-2558	652-7369	488
Web: www.stamtexmp.com						
Stan Houston Equipment Co 501 S Marion Rd	Sioux Falls	SD	57106	605-336-3727	336-7860	358
TF: 800-952-3033 ■ *Web:* www.stanhouston.com						
Stan Hywet Hall & Gardens 714 N Portage Path	Akron	OH	44303	330-836-5533		520
TF: 888-836-5533 ■ *Web:* www.stanhywet.org						
Stan Johnson Company Inc 6120 S Yale Ave Ste 813	Tulsa	OK	74136	918-494-2690	494-2692	652
Web: www.stanjohnsonco.com						
Stan White Realty & Construction 2506 S Croatan Hwy	Nags Head	NC	27959	252-441-1515		652
TF: 800-338-3233 ■ *Web:* outerbanksrentals.com						
Stan'S Sport Center Inc 528 Washington St	Hoboken	NJ	07030	201-798-4466		711
Web: stanssportsctr.com						
Stanadyne Corp 92 Deerfield Rd	Windsor	CT	06095	860-525-0821	687-4235	60
TF: 888-336-3473 ■ *Web:* www.stanadyne.com						
Stanard & Associates Inc 309 W Washington St Ste 1000	Chicago	IL	60606	312-553-0213	553-0218	196
TF: 800-367-6919 ■ *Web:* www.stanard.com						
Stanbee Company Inc 70 Broad St	Carlstadt	NJ	07072	201-933-9666	933-7985	301
Web: www.stanbee.com						

Name / Address	City	State	Zip	Phone	Fax	Class
Stanbridge College 2041 Business Center Dr Ste 107	Irvine	CA	92612	949-794-9090	794-9094	167-3
Web: www.stanbridge.edu						
Stanbury Uniforms Inc 108 Stanbury Industrial Dr PO Box 100	Brookfield	MO	64628	800-826-2246	258-5781*	155-19
**Fax Area Code:* 660 ■ *TF:* 800-826-2246 ■ *Web:* stanbury.com						
Stancil Corp 2644 S Croddy Way	Santa Ana	CA	92704	714-546-2002	546-2092	52
Web: www.stancilcorp.com						
Stancills Inc 499 Mountain Hill Rd	Perryville	MD	21903	410-939-2224		503-4
TF: 877-536-9572 ■ *Web:* www.stancills.com						
Stanco Metal Prod Inc 2101 168th Ave	Grand Haven	MI	49417	616-842-5000		488
Web: stancometal.com						
Stancorp Mortgage Investors LLC 1100 SW 6th Ave	Portland	OR	97204	800-247-6888	878-3686*	509
**Fax Area Code:* 888 ■ *TF:* 800-247-6888 ■ *Web:* www.standard.com						
Standard & Poor's Corp 55 Water St	New York	NY	10041	212-438-1000		637-2
TF: 877-772-5436 ■ *Web:* www.standardandpoors.com						
Standard Air & Lite Corp 2406 Woodmere Dr	Pittsburgh	PA	15205	412-920-6505		612
TF: 800-472-2458 ■ *Web:* www.stdair.com						
Standard Analytical Service Inc 111 Westport Plaza Dr Ste 600	Saint Louis	MO	63146	314-731-5455	731-5007	637-10
Web: www.standardanalytical.com						
Standard Armament Inc 631 Allen Ave	Glendale	CA	91201	818-842-6144	848-6970	807
Web: www.standardarmament.com						
Standard Auto Parts Corp 2020 Hollins Ferry Rd	Baltimore	MD	21230	410-659-5400		54
Web: www.standardautoparts.com						
Standard Bag Manufacturing Co 1800 SW Merlo Dr	Beaverton	OR	97006	800-654-1395	642-9335*	557
**Fax Area Code:* 503 ■ *TF:* 800-654-1395 ■ *Web:* www.standardbag.com						
Standard Bank PaSB 4785 Old William Penn Hwy	Murrysville	PA	15668	877-856-2265		70
TF: 877-856-2265 ■ *Web:* www.standardbankpa.com						
Standard Banner, The 122 W Andrew Johnson Hwy	Jefferson City	TN	37760	865-475-2081	475-8539	532-2
Web: www.standardbanner.com						
Standard Bellows Co 375 Ella Grasso Tpke	Windsor Locks	CT	06096	860-623-2307	623-0398	454
Web: www.std-bellows.com						
Standard Beverage Corp 2416 E 37th St N	Wichita	KS	67219	800-999-8797		81-3
TF: 800-999-8797 ■ *Web:* www.standardbeverage.com						
Standard Candy Company Inc 715 Massman Dr	Nashville	TN	37210	615-889-6360		296-8
Web: googoo.com						
Standard Car Truck Co 865 Busse Hwy	Park Ridge	IL	60068	847-692-6050		650
Web: www.sctco.com						
Standard Change-Makers Inc 3130 N Mitthoeffer Rd	Indianapolis	IN	46235	317-899-6966	899-6977	427
Web: www.standardchange.com						
Standard Chartered Bank 1 Madison Ave	New York	NY	10010	212-667-0700		70
Web: www.sc.com						
Standard Commercial Systems 250 Walnut St	Englewood	NJ	07631	800-971-3663		178-1
TF: 800-971-3663 ■ *Web:* www.foodman123.com						
Standard Companies Inc, The 2601 S Archer Ave	Chicago	IL	60608	312-225-2777	225-2964	406
Web: www.thestandardcompanies.com						
Standard Concrete Products Inc (SCP) PO Box 1360	Columbus	GA	31902	706-322-3274		188-4
Web: www.standardconcrete.net						
Standard Construction Company Inc 7434 Raleigh Lagrange Rd	Cordova	TN	38018	901-754-5181	753-4935	188-4
Web: www.stdconst.com						
Standard Data Corp 26 Journal Sq	Jersey City	NJ	07306	201-533-4433		225
Web: www.standarddata.com						
Standard Die & Fabricating Inc 12980 Wayne Rd	Livonia	MI	48150	734-422-4430		757
TF: 800-838-5464 ■ *Web:* www.standarddie.com						
Standard Digital Imaging 4426 S 108th St	Omaha	NE	68137	402-592-1292	592-8003	240
TF: 800-642-8062 ■ *Web:* www.standardsharev3.com						
Standard Duplicating Machines Corp 10 Connector Rd	Andover	MA	01810	978-470-1920		112
TF: 800-526-4774 ■ *Web:* www.sdmc.com						
Standard Electric Co 2650 Trautner Dr	Saginaw	MI	48603	989-497-2100	497-2101	246
Web: www.standardelectricco.com						
Standard Electric Supply Co 222 N Emmber Ln PO Box 651	Milwaukee	WI	53233	414-272-8100	272-8111	246
TF: 800-776-8222 ■ *Web:* www.standardelectricsupply.com						
Standard Engineering Group 3516 Highland Park St NW	North Canton	OH	44720	330-494-4300	494-4303	261
Web: standardengineeringgroup.com						
Standard Equipment Company Inc 75 Beauregard St	Mobile	AL	36602	251-432-1705		770
TF: 800-239-3442 ■ *Web:* www.standardequipmentco.com						
Standard Filter Corp 5928 Balfour Ct	Carlsbad	CA	92008	760-929-8559	929-1901	18
TF: 800-634-5837 ■ *Web:* www.standardfilter.com						
Standard Forged Products Inc 75 Nichol Ave	McKees Rocks	PA	15136	412-778-2033		61
Web: standardforgedproductsinc.com						
Standard Furniture Manufacturing Company Inc 801 Hwy 31 S	Bay Minette	AL	36507	251-937-6741		319-2
TF: 877-788-1899 ■ *Web:* www.standardfurniture.com						
Standard Golf Co 6620 Nordic Dr	Cedar Falls	IA	50613	319-266-2638		710
TF: 866-743-9773 ■ *Web:* www.standardgolf.com						
Standard Heating & Air Conditioning 1082 Payne Ave	Saint Paul	MN	55130	651-772-2449		610
Web: www.standardheating.com						
Standard Imaging Inc 3120 Deming Way	Middleton	WI	53562	608-831-0025		639
TF: 800-261-4446 ■ *Web:* www.standardimaging.com						
Standard Industrial Manufacturing Partners Ltd 901 W 3rd St	Odessa	TX	79763	432-332-5955	332-6806	641
Web: www.standardpumpparts.com						

Company	Address	City	State	Zip	Phone	Fax	Class
Standard Insurance Agency Corp	8190 Precinct Line Rd Ste 101 *Web:* www.siatexas.com	Hurst	TX	76053	817-285-1800		390
Standard Iron & Wire Works Inc	524 Pine St *Web:* www.std-iron.com	Monticello	MN	55362	763-295-8700	295-8701	697
Standard Knapp Inc	63 Pickering St *TF:* 800-628-9565 ■ *Web:* www.standard-knapp.com	Portland	CT	06480	860-342-1100	342-0782	547
Standard Laboratories Inc	147 11th Ave Ste 100 *TF:* 888-216-0239 ■ *Web:* www.standardlabs.com	South Charleston	WV	25303	304-744-6800	744-6899	743
Standard Life Insurance Company of Indiana	8365 Keystone Crossing Ste 200 *Web:* www.standardlifeofindiana.com	Indianapolis	IN	46280	317-574-6201		391-2
Standard Life Investments	*Aberdeen Standard Investments* 1 Beacon St 34th Fl *Web:* www.us.standardlifeinvestments.com	Boston	MA	02108	617-720-7900		390
Standard Locknut Inc	*Standard Locknut LLC* 1045 E 169th St *TF:* 800-783-6887 ■ *Web:* www.miether.com	Westfield	IN	46074	317-867-0100		454
Standard Lumber Co	1912 Lehigh Ave *Web:* www.standardlumberco.com	Glenview	IL	60026	847-729-7800	729-8500	499
Standard Machine Inc	1952 W 93rd St *Web:* www.standardmachineinc.com	Cleveland	OH	44102	216-631-4440	631-2837	454
Standard Machine Ltd	868-60th St E *Web:* www.standardmachine.ca	Saskatoon	SK	S7K8G8	306-931-3343		709
Standard Management Co	9841 Airport Blvd Ste 1010 *Web:* www.standardmanagement.com	Los Angeles	CA	90045	310-410-2300		217
Standard Manufacturing Company Inc	750 Second Ave *Web:* www.sportsmaster.com	Troy	NY	12182	518-235-2200		155-5
Standard Meat Company LP	5105 Investment Dr *TF:* 866-859-6313 ■ *Web:* www.standardmeat.com	Dallas	TX	75236	214-561-0561	561-0560	296-26
Standard Metal Products	1541 W 132nd St *Web:* sheet-metal.com	Gardena	CA	90249	310-532-9861		697
Standard Metals Inc	440 Ledyard St *TF:* 800-243-2224 ■ *Web:* www.standardmetals.com	Hartford	CT	06114	860-296-5663	296-9877	492
Standard Motor Products Inc	37-18 Northern Blvd *NYSE: SMP* ■ *TF:* 800-895-1085 ■ *Web:* www.smpcorp.com	Long Island City	NY	11101	718-392-0200		247
Standard Motors Ltd	44 Second Ave NW *TF:* 866-334-8985 ■ *Web:* www.standardmotors.ca	Swift Current	SK	S9H3V6	866-334-8985		57
Standard Office Systems	2475 Meadowbrook Pkwy *Web:* soscanhelp.com	Duluth	GA	30096	770-449-9100	449-0828	366
Standard Oil of Connecticut Inc	299 Bishop Ave *TF:* 800-822-3835 ■ *Web:* www.standardsecurity.com	Bridgeport	CT	06610	800-822-3835		316
Standard Optical Company Inc	1901 W Parkway Blvd *Web:* standardoptical.net	Salt Lake City	UT	84119	801-886-2020		543
Standard Pacific Capital LLC	101 California St 36th Fl *Web:* standardpacific.com	San Francisco	CA	94111	415-352-7100		401
Standard Parking Corp	200 E Randolph St Ste 7700 *TF:* 888-700-7275 ■ *Web:* www.spplus.com	Chicago	IL	60611	312-274-2000	640-6169	562
Standard Press Inc	1210 Menlo Dr Nw *Web:* www.stpress.com	Atlanta	GA	30318	404-351-6780	351-7139	627
Standard Process Inc	1200 W Royal Lee Dr *Web:* www.standardprocess.com	Palmyra	WI	53156	262-495-2122		123
Standard Publishing Co	4050 Lee Vance Dr **Fax Area Code:* 877 ■ *TF:* 800-323-7543 ■ *Web:* www.standardpub.com	Colorado Springs	CO	80918	800-323-7543	867-5751*	637-9
Standard Roofing Co	516 N McDonough St PO Box 1309 *TF:* 800-239-5705 ■ *Web:* standardexteriorsolutions.com	Montgomery	AL	36102	334-265-1262	834-0239	189-12
Standard Rubber Products Co	120 Seegers Ave *Web:* www.srpco.com	Elk Grove Village	IL	60007	847-593-5630	593-5634	676
Standard Sales Company Inc	4800 E 42nd St Ste 400 *Web:* www.standardsalescompanylp.com	Odessa	TX	79762	432-367-7662		81-1
Standard Sand & Silica Co	1850 US Hwy 17-92 N *TF:* 877-444-7263	Davenport	FL	33837	877-444-7263		503-4
Standard Security Life Insurance Company of New York	485 Madison Ave 14th Fl *TF:* 800-477-0087 ■ *Web:* www.sslicny.com	New York	NY	10022	212-355-4141	644-5786	391-2
Standard Steel LLC	500 N Walnut St *Web:* www.standardsteel.com	Burnham	PA	17009	717-248-4911	248-8050	723
Standard Supply & Distributing Co	1431 Regal Row *Web:* www.ssdhvac.com	Dallas	TX	75247	214-630-7800	630-1894	351
Standard Tap	901 N 2nd St *Web:* news.standardtap.com.s86406.gridserver.com	Philadelphia	PA	19123	215-238-0630		671
Standard Testing Equipment Co	744 Noah Dr Ste 113 *Web:* www.standardtestingequipment.com	Jasper	GA	30143	706-692-2828	692-2829	472
Standard Textile Company Inc	1 Knollcrest Dr *TF:* 800-999-0400 ■ *Web:* www.standardtextile.com	Cincinnati	OH	45237	513-761-9255	761-0467	477
Standard Tool & Die Inc	2950 Johnson Rd *Web:* www.standardtool.net	Stevensville	MI	49127	269-465-6004	465-5301	757
Standard Washer & Mat Inc	299 Progress Dr *Web:* www.standardwasher.com	Manchester	CT	06042	860-643-5125	647-7964	676
Standard Waterproofing Corp	701 E 134th St *Web:* standardwaterproofing.com	Bronx	NY	10454	718-292-2800		186
Standard Wire & Steel Works	16255 Vincennes Ave *Web:* www.standardwiresteel.com	South Holland	IL	60473	708-333-8300		492
Standard, The	40 Island Ave *Web:* standardhotels.com	Miami Beach	FL	33139	305-673-1717		669
Standard-Examiner	332 Standard Way *TF:* 888-221-7070 ■ *Web:* www.standard.net	Ogden	UT	84404	801-625-4200		532-2
Standards Council of Canada	270 Albert St Ste 200 *TF:* 800-844-6790 ■ *Web:* www.scc.ca	Ottawa	ON	K1P6N7	613-238-3222		466
Standby Screw Machine Products Company Inc	1122 W Bagley Rd *Web:* www.standbyscrew.com	Berea	OH	44017	440-243-8200		621
Standex Electronics Inc	4538 Camberwell Rd *TF:* 866-782-6339 ■ *Web:* standexelectronics.com	Cincinnati	OH	45209	513-871-3777	871-3779	253
Standex International Corp	23 Keewaydin Dr *Web:* standex.com	Salem	NH	03079	603-893-9701	893-7324	481
Standex International Corp	*Custom Hoists Div* 771 County Rd 30A W *TF:* 800-837-4668 ■ *Web:* www.customhoists.com	Ashland	OH	44805	419-368-4721	368-4209	223
	Mullen Testers Div 939 Chicopee St *Web:* www.mullentesters.com	Chicopee	MA	01013	413-536-1311	536-1367	744
Standing Stone Inc	49 Richmondville Ave **Fax Area Code:* 203 ■ *TF:* 800-648-9877 ■ *Web:* www.standingstoneinc.com	Westport	CT	06880	800-648-9877	227-8982*	582
Standing Stone State Park	1674 Standing Stone Pk Hwy *Web:* www.state.tn.us	Hilham	TN	38568	931-823-6347		565
Standish Mellon	*BNY Mellon Center* 1 Boston Pl 201 Washington St *Web:* www.mellon.com	Boston	MA	02108	617-722-7250		401
Standley Batch Systems Inc	505 Aquamsi St *Web:* www.standleybatch.com	Cape Girardeau	MO	63703	573-334-3704		697
Stanfield & Odell Pc	1350 S Boulder Ave Ste 800 *Web:* stanfieldodell.com	Tulsa	OK	74119	918-628-0500		2
Stanfield Systems Inc	718 Sutter St Ste 108 *Web:* www.stanfieldsystems.com	Folsom	CA	95630	916-608-8006		196
Stanford Alumni Assn	Frances C Arrillaga Alumni Ctr 326 Galvez St *TF:* 800-786-2586 ■ *Web:* alumni.stanford.edu	Stanford	CA	94305	650-723-2021		138
Stanford Blood & Marrow Transplant Program	300 Pasteur Dr Rm H0101 *Web:* bmt.stanford.edu	Stanford	CA	94305	650-723-0822		769
Stanford Business Software Inc	2672 Bayshore Pky Ste 1020 *Web:* www.sbsi-sol-optimize.com	Mountain View	CA	94043	650-856-1695		174
Stanford Carr Development LLC	1100 Alakea St 27th Fl *Web:* www.stanfordcarr.com	Honolulu	HI	96813	808-537-5220	537-1801	516
Stanford Court Hotel	905 California St Nob Hill *Web:* www.stanfordcourt.com	San Francisco	CA	94108	415-989-3500		379
Stanford Daily Publishing Corp, The	456 Panama Mall *Web:* www.stanforddaily.com	Stanford	CA	94305	650-725-2100	725-1329	532-2
Stanford Federal Credit Union	1860 Embarcadero Rd **Fax Area Code:* 866 ■ *TF:* 888-723-7328 ■ *Web:* www.sfcu.org	Palo Alto	CA	94303	650-723-2509	579-9764*	219
Stanford Home Centers	2001 Rte 286 *Web:* www.stanfordhome.com	Plum	PA	15239	724-327-6800		191-3
Stanford Linear Accelerator Ctr (SLAC)	2575 Sand Hill Rd *Web:* www.slac.stanford.edu	Menlo Park	CA	94025	650-926-3300	926-4999	668
Stanford Prevention Research Ctr (SPRC)	1070 Arastradero Rd Ste 100 & 300 *Web:* prevention.stanford.edu	Stanford	CA	94305	650-723-6254	725-6247	668
Stanford Synchrotron Radiation Lightsource (SSRL)	2575 Sand Hill Rd MS 69 *TF:* 877-447-7522 ■ *Web:* www-ssrl.slac.stanford.edu	Menlo Park	CA	94025	650-926-2079	926-3600	668
Stanford University	450 Serra Mall *TF:* 877-407-9529 ■ *Web:* www.stanford.edu	Stanford	CA	94305	650-723-1941	725-2846	166
Stanford University Green Library	557 Escondido Mall *TF:* 800-521-0600 ■ *Web:* library.stanford.edu	Stanford	CA	94305	650-723-1493	725-0743	434-6
Stanford University Law School	559 Nathan Abbott Way *Web:* law.stanford.edu	Stanford	CA	94305	650-723-2465	725-0253	167-1
Stanford University Press	500 Broadway St *Web:* www.sup.org	Redwood City	CA	94063	650-723-9434	725-3457	637-4
Stanford University School of Medicine	291 Campus Dr Rm LK3C02 *Web:* med.stanford.edu	Stanford	CA	94305	650-725-3900	725-7368	167-2
Stanford's Restaurant & Bar	913 Lloyd Ctr *Web:* stanfords.com	Portland	OR	97232	503-335-0811		670
Stanfordville Machine & Manufacturing Inc	29 Victory Ln *Web:* www.stanfordville.com	Poughkeepsie	NY	12603	845-868-2266		757
Stange Agency Inc	120 E Felton St *Web:* stangeagency.com	North Tonawanda	NY	14120	716-692-0018		390
Stanion Wholesale Electric Co	812 S Main St PO Box F *TF:* 866-782-6466 ■ *Web:* www.stanion.com	Pratt	KS	67124	620-672-5678	672-6220	246
Stanisky & Co	2550 Leechburg Rd *Web:* stanisky.com	Lower Burrell	PA	15068	724-339-7340		2
Stanislaus County	800 11th St *Web:* www.stanct.org	Modesto	CA	95354	209-530-3100		434-3
Stanislaus County	1021 I St Ste 101 *TF:* 877-227-7478 ■ *Web:* www.stancounty.com	Modesto	CA	95354	209-525-5250	525-5804	338

Name / Address	City	State	Zip	Phone	Fax	Class
Stanislaus Farm Supply Co 624 E Service Rd *TF:* 800-323-0725 ■ *Web:* www.farmsupply.coop	Modesto	CA	95358	209-538-7070	541-3191	276
Stanislaus Food Products Co 1202 D St *TF:* 800-327-7201 ■ *Web:* www.stanislaus.com	Modesto	CA	95354	800-327-7201		296-20
Stanislaus Imports Inc 1415 Van Dyke Ave *Web:* www.lasioux.com	San Francisco	CA	94124	415-431-7122	431-4365	44
Stanker & Galetto Inc 317 W Elmer Rd *Web:* stankergaletto.com	Vineland	NJ	08360	856-692-8098		186
Stanley & Seafort's 115 E 34th St *Web:* stanleyandseaforts.com	Tacoma	WA	98404	253-473-7300		671
Stanley Access Technologies 65 Scott Swamp Rd **Fax Area Code:* 877 ■ *TF:* 800-722-2377 ■ *Web:* www.stanleyaccess.com	Farmington	CT	06032	860-677-2861	339-7923*	234
Stanley Benefit Services Inc 7800 McCloud Rd Ste 200 *Web:* www.stanleybenefits.com	Greensboro	NC	27409	336-271-4450		2
Stanley Center for the Arts 259 Genesee St *Web:* www.thestanley.org	Utica	NY	13501	315-724-1113	624-2926	572
Stanley Consultants Inc 225 Iowa Ave *TF:* 800-553-9694 ■ *Web:* www.stanleyconsultants.com	Muscatine	IA	52761	563-264-6600	264-6658	261
Stanley County Auditor 8 E Second Ave *Web:* stanleycounty.org	Fort Pierre	SD	57532	605-223-7780		338
Stanley Creations Inc 1414 Willow Ave *TF:* 800-220-1414 ■ *Web:* www.stanleycreations.com	Melrose Park	PA	19027	215-635-6200	635-2708	409
Stanley Electric US Company Inc 420 E High St *Web:* www.stanleyelectricus.com	London	OH	43140	740-852-5200	852-5201	815
Stanley Furniture Company Inc 200 N Hamilton St *TF:* 877-772-4858 ■ *Web:* www.stanleyfurniture.com	High Point	NC	27260	877-772-4858		319-2
Stanley Hotel 333 Wonderview Ave *TF:* 800-976-1377 ■ *Web:* www.stanleyhotel.com	Estes Park	CO	80517	970-577-4000	586-4964	379
Stanley Hunt DuPree & Rhine (SHDR) *McGriff Insurance Services Inc* 7701 Airport Center Dr **Fax Area Code:* 252 ■ *TF:* 800-930-2441 ■ *Web:* www.shdr.com	Greensboro	NC	27409	336-291-1133	293-9048*	193
Stanley Hydraulic Tools 3810 SE Naef Rd *TF:* 800-972-2647 ■ *Web:* www.stanleyinfrastructure.com	Milwaukie	OR	97267	503-659-5660	652-1780	759
Stanley Industries Inc 19120 Cranwood Pky *Web:* www.stanley-industries.com	Cleveland	OH	44128	216-475-4000		454
Stanley Jay s & Assoc 5313 Mcclanahan Dr Ste G5 *TF:* 888-758-4728 ■ *Web:* www.jaystanley.com	North Little Rock	AR	72116	501-758-8029		509
Stanley Korshak 500 Crescent Ct Ste 100 *TF:* 855-479-9539 ■ *Web:* www.stanleykorshak.com	Dallas	TX	75201	855-479-9539		157-4
Stanley M. Proctor Co 2016 Midway Dr *Web:* www.stanleyproctor.com	Twinsburg	OH	44087	330-425-7814		385
Stanley Machining & Tool Corp 425 Maple Ave *Web:* www.stanleymachining.com	Carpentersville	IL	60110	847-426-4560		757
Stanley Martin Cos 11111 Sunset Hills Rd Ste 200 *TF:* 800-446-4807 ■ *Web:* www.stanleymartin.com	Reston	VA	20190	703-964-5000		653
Stanley Mcdonald Agency of Illinois Inc 1101 Main St *Web:* armitageinconline.com	Onalaska	WI	54650	608-788-6162		390
Stanley Security Solutions Inc 14670 Cumberland Rd *Web:* www.stanleysecuritysolutions.com	Noblesville	IN	46060	317-776-3600		603
Stanley Spring & Stamping Corp 5050 W Foster Ave *Web:* www.stanleyspring.com	Chicago	IL	60630	773-777-2600		718
Stanley Stephens Company Inc 2565 Pearl Buck Rd **Fax Area Code:* 215 ■ *TF:* 800-523-5200 ■ *Web:* www.sstfloor.com	Bristol	PA	19007	800-523-5200	788-8535*	361
Stanley Tools Inc 701 E Joppa Rd *TF:* 800-262-2161 ■ *Web:* www.stanleytools.com	Towson	MD	21286	800-262-2161		758
Stanley Vidmar Storage Technologies 11 Grammes Rd *TF:* 800-523-9462 ■ *Web:* www.stanleyvidmar.com	Allentown	PA	18103	800-523-9462	523-9934	286
Stanley W. Bowles Corp 3375 Joseph Martin Hwy PO Box 4706 *Web:* www.bowlesproperties.com	Martinsville	VA	24115	276-632-3446	956-7038	264-3
Stanley's Tavern 2038 Foulk Rd *Web:* stanleys-tavern.com	Wilmington	DE	19810	302-475-1887	475-0904	671
Stanley, Lande & Hunter A Professional Corp 119 Sycamore St *Web:* slhlaw.com	Muscatine	IA	52761	563-264-5000		428
Stanley-Laman Group Ltd 1235 Westlakes Dr Ste 295 *Web:* www.stanleylaman.com	Berwyn	PA	19312	610-993-9100		194
Stanly Community College 141 College Dr *TF:* 877-275-4219 ■ *Web:* www.stanly.edu	Albemarle	NC	28001	704-982-0121	982-0819	800
Stanly County 201 S 2nd St PO Box 668 *Web:* www.nccourts.gov	Albemarle	NC	28002	704-986-7000		338
Stanly County Chamber of Commerce 116 E N St *Web:* stanlychamber.org	Albemarle	NC	28001	704-982-8116	983-5000	139
Stanly Fixtures Company Inc 11635 NC 138 Hwy PO Box 616 *Web:* www.stanlyfixtures.com	Norwood	NC	28128	704-474-3184	474-3011	286
Stanly Memorial Hospital *Atrium Health Stanly* 301 Yadkin St *Web:* www.carolinashealthcare.org	Albemarle	NC	28001	704-984-4000	983-3562	374-3
Stanmar Inc 321 Commonwealth Rd Ste 201 *Web:* www.stanmar-inc.com	Wayland	MA	01778	508-310-9922		655
Stanridge Color Corp (SCC) PO Box 1086 *Web:* www.standridgecolor.com	Social Circle	GA	30025	770-464-3362		608
Stansberry & Associates Investment Research LLC 1217 St Paul St *TF:* 888-261-2693 ■ *Web:* stansberryresearch.com	Baltimore	MD	21202	888-261-2693		401
Stanstead College 450 Dufferin St *Web:* www.stansteadcollege.com	Stanstead	QC	J0B3E0	819-876-2223		622
Stansteel Asphalt Plant Products 12700 Shelbyville Rd *TF:* 800-826-0223 ■ *Web:* www.stansteel.com	Louisville	KY	40243	502-245-1977		641
Stant Corp 1620 Columbia Ave *TF:* 800-822-3121 ■ *Web:* www.stant.com	Connersville	IN	47331	765-825-3121	825-2875	608
Stantec Inc 10160-112 St *TSE: STN* ■ *Web:* www.stantec.com	Edmonton	AB	T5K2L6	780-917-7000	917-7330	261
Stanton Carpet Corp 211 Robbins Ln *Web:* www.stantoncarpet.com	Syosset	NY	11791	516-822-5878	933-8890	364
Stanton Chase Intl 400 E Pratt St Ste 420 *Web:* www.stantonchase.com	Baltimore	MD	21202	410-528-8400		266
Stanton County 201 N Main St PO Box 190 *Web:* stantoncountyks.com	Johnson	KS	67855	620-492-2140	492-2688	338
Stanton County 804 Ivy St PO Box 347 *Web:* www.co.stanton.ne.us	Stanton	NE	68779	402-439-2222	439-2200	338
Stanton County Public Power District 807 Douglas St *TF:* 877-439-2300 ■ *Web:* www.scppd.net	Stanton	NE	68779	402-439-2228		245
Stanton Greg (Rep D - AZ) 128 Cannon House Office Bldg *Web:* www.stanton.house.gov	Washington	DC	20515	202-225-9888		342-2
Stanton Insurance Agency Inc 230 Second Ave Ste 105 *Web:* www.stantonins.com	Waltham	MA	02451	781-893-3200		390
Stanton Magnetics Inc 772 S Military Trl *Web:* www.stantondj.com	Deerfield Beach	FL	33442	954-949-9600		658
Stanton Public Relations & Marketing 880 Third Ave *Web:* www.stantonprm.com	New York	NY	10022	212-300-5300		030
Stanton Telecom Inc 1004 Ivy St *TF:* 800-411-2264 ■ *Web:* www.stantontelecom.com	Stanton	NE	68779	402-439-2264		224
Stanton Territorial Health Authority (STHA) 550 Byrne Rd PO Box 10 *Web:* www.nthssa.ca	Yellowknife	NT	X1A2N1	867-669-4111	669-4128	374-2
Stanton's Sheet Music 330 S Fourth St *TF:* 800-426-8742 ■ *Web:* www.stantons.com	Columbus	OH	43215	614-224-4257	224-5929	526
Stanwich Advisors LLC 1 Dock St Ste 600 *Web:* www.stanwichadvisors.com	Stamford	CT	06902	203-406-1099	406-1098	401
Stanyan Park Hotel 750 Stanyan St *Web:* www.stanyanpark.com	San Francisco	CA	94117	415-751-1000	668-5454	379
Stanz Cheese Company Inc 1840 Commerce Dr *TF:* 800-342-5664 ■ *Web:* www.stanz.com	South Bend	IN	46628	574-232-6666	236-4169	297-8
Staplcotn Cooperative Association Inc 214 W Market St *TF:* 800-293-6231 ■ *Web:* www.staplcotn.com	Greenwood	MS	38930	662-453-6231	453-6274	275
Staples Business Advantage 500 Staples Dr *TF:* 877-826-7755 ■ *Web:* www.staplesadvantage.com	Framingham	MA	01702	877-888-8248		534
Staples Construction Company Inc 1501 Eastman Ave *Web:* staplesconstruction.com	Ventura	CA	93003	805-658-8786	658-8785	463
Staples Ctr 1111 S Figueroa St *TF:* 888-929-7849 ■ *Web:* www.staplescenter.com	Los Angeles	CA	90015	888-929-7849		720
Staples Promotional Products 7500 W 110th St *TF:* 800-369-4669 ■ *Web:* www.staplespromotionalproducts.com	Overland Park	KS	66210	913-319-3100		9
Staples World 224 4th St Ne *TF:* 888-894-1112 ■ *Web:* staplesworld.com	Staples	MN	56479	218-894-1112	894-3570	532-2
Stapleton Technologies Inc 1350 W 12th St *TF:* 800-266-0541 ■ *Web:* www.stapletontech.com	Long Beach	CA	90813	562-437-0541	437-8632	145
Stapleton-Spence Packing Co 1530 The Alameda Ste 320 *TF:* 800-297-8815 ■ *Web:* www.stapleton-spence.com	San Jose	CA	95126	408-297-8815	297-0611	296-20
Staplex Co 777 Fifth Ave *TF:* 800-221-0822 ■ *Web:* www.staplex.com	Brooklyn	NY	11232	718-768-3333	965-0750	111
STAR 6688 93rd Ave N *TF:* 800-419-7827 ■ *Web:* engagestar.com	Minneapolis	MN	55445	763-561-4655	561-4688	393
Star 101.9 650 Iwilei Rd Ste 400 *Web:* star1019.iheart.com	Honolulu	HI	96817	808-550-9200		645-70
Star 21 Inc PO Box 21600 *Web:* www.star21online.com	Keizer	OR	97307	503-393-2600		264-4
Star 929 265 Hegeman Ave *TF:* 866-865-7827 ■ *Web:* www.star929.com	Colchester	VT	05446	802-655-0093	655-0478	645
Star 94.7FM 624 14th St E *TF:* 866-727-7827 ■ *Web:* www.starfmradio.com	Brandon	MB	R7A7E1	204-726-8888		647
Star Academy 12279 Brady Dr *TF:* 800-265-9684 ■ *Web:* www.doc.sd.gov	Custer	SD	57730	605-673-2521	673-5489	412
Star Asia International Inc 208 Church St *Web:* www.star-asia.com	Decatur	GA	30030	404-761-6900		311
Star Automation Inc N90 W 14401 Commerce Dr **Fax Area Code:* 414 ■ *Web:* www.starautomation.com	Menomonee Falls	WI	53051	262-253-3550	253-3559*	386
Star Bank 201 Second Ave NW PO Box 188 *Web:* www.starbank.net	Bertha	MN	56437	218-924-4055	924-2265	70
Star Beacon PO Box 2100 *TF:* 800-554-6768 ■ *Web:* www.starbeacon.com	Ashtabula	OH	44005	440-998-2323	998-7938	532-2
Star Building Systems 8600 S I-35 **Fax Area Code:* 405 ■ *TF:* 800-879-7827 ■ *Web:* www.starbuildings.com	Oklahoma City	OK	73149	800-879-7827	636-2419*	105
Star Casualty Insurance Company Inc PO Box 451037 *TF:* 877-782-7210 ■ *Web:* www.starcasualty.com	Miami	FL	33134	877-782-7210		390

Company	Phone	Fax	Class
Star Clippers Inc 760 NW 107th Ave, Miami FL 33172 *Web:* www.starclippers.com	305-442-0550		220
Star CNC Machine Tool Corp 123 Powerhouse Rd, Roslyn Heights NY 11577 *Web:* www.starcnc.com	516-484-0500	484-5820	385
Star Collaborative LLC 18120 46th Ave N, Plymouth MN 55446 *Web:* www.starcollaborative.com	763-515-7838		463
Star Consultants Inc 1910 Bethel Rd, Columbus OH 43235 *Web:* starconsultants.org	614-538-8445		186
Star Cutter Co 23461 Industrial Pk Dr, Farmington MI 48335 *TF:* 877-635-3488 ■ *Web:* www.starcutter.com	248-474-8200	474-9518	493
Star Democrat 29088 Airpark Dr PO Box 600, Easton MD 21601 *TF:* 800-220-1230 ■ *Web:* www.stardem.com	410-822-1500	770-4064	532-2
Star Die Molding Inc 2741 Katherine Way, Elk Grove Village IL 60007 *Web:* www.stardie.com	847-766-7952		608
Star Displays Inc 38w636 US Hwy 20, Elgin IL 60124 *Web:* www.starincorporated.com	847-695-2040	695-1108	393
Star Distributors Inc 10 Eder Rd, West Haven CT 06516 *TF:* 877-922-3501 ■ *Web:* www.stardistributors.com	203-932-3636	932-5977	81-1
Star Dynamics Corp 100 Outwater Ln, Garfield NJ 07026 *Web:* www.stardynamic.com	973-340-3883	340-1530	735
Star Engineering Services Inc 14350 W Sylvanfield Dr, Houston TX 77014 *Web:* starengr.com	281-453-7300		261
Star Extruded Shapes Inc 7055 Herbert Rd, Canfield OH 44406 *Web:* www.starext.com	330-533-9863		361
Star Financial Group Inc PO Box 11409, Fort Wayne IN 46858 *OTC: SFIGA* ■ *TF:* 888-395-2447 ■ *Web:* www.starfinancial.com	888-395-2447		70
Star Fine Foods 2680 W Shaw Ln, Fresno CA 93711 *Web:* www.starfinefoods.com	559-498-2900		296-30
Star Fleet Inc 915 S Main St, Middlebury IN 46540 *TF:* 877-805-9547 ■ *Web:* www.starfleettrucking.com	877-805-9547		780
Star Forge Inc 1801 S Ihm Blvd, Freeport IL 61032 *Web:* starmfg.com	815-235-7750	235-4813	273
Star Furniture Company Inc 16666 Barker Springs Rd, Houston TX 77084 *TF:* 800-364-6661 ■ *Web:* www.starfurniture.com	281-492-5424		321
Star Gold Cleaners Inc 200 Wilson St, Brewer ME 04412 *Web:* www.goldstarcleaners.com	207-989-5170	989-8683	426
Star Group LP 2187 Atlantic St, Stamford CT 06902 *NYSE: SGU* ■ *TF:* 800-960-7546 ■ *Web:* www.stargrouplp.com	203-328-7310	328-7470	316
Star Insurance Co 26255 American Dr, Southfield MI 48034 *Web:* www.starinsco.com	248-358-4020	358-1614	391-4
Star Island Corp, The 30 Middle St, Portsmouth NH 03801 *TF:* 800-441-4620 ■ *Web:* starisland.org	603-430-6272		239
Star Island Resort 5000 Avenue of the Stars, Kissimmee FL 34746 *TF:* 800-513-2820 ■ *Web:* www.star-island.com	407-997-8000		379
Star Leasing Co 4080 Business Pk Dr, Columbus OH 43204 *TF:* 888-771-1004 ■ *Web:* www.starleasing.com	614-278-9999	340-3137	778
Star Line Trucking Corp 18480 W Lincoln Ave, New Berlin WI 53146 *Web:* www.starlinetrucking.com	262-786-8280	786-0071	449
Star Lumber & Supply 325 S W St, Wichita KS 67213 *TF:* 800-797-9556 ■ *Web:* www.starlumber.com	316-942-2221		364
Star Manufacturing Intl 10 Sunnen Dr, Maplewood MO 63143 *Web:* star-mfg.com	314-781-2777		298
Star Market Inc 702 Pratt Ave NW, Huntsville AL 35801 *Web:* www.huntsvillestarmarket.com	256-534-4509		297-8
Star Micronics America Inc 1150 King George's Post Rd, Edison NJ 08837 *TF:* 800-782-7636 ■ *Web:* www.starmicronics.com	732-623-5500	623-5590	173-6
Star Middle East USA Inc (SME) 2 Riverway Ste 1060, Houston TX 77056 *Web:* www.drillequip.com	713-871-1121	871-0327	385
Star Milling Co 24067 Water St, Perris CA 92570 *TF:* 800-733-6455 ■ *Web:* www.starmilling.com	951-657-3143	657-3114	447
Star Moulding & Trim Co 6606 W 74th St, Chicago IL 60638 *Web:* www.starmoulding.com	708-458-1040		499
Star Multi Care Services Inc 115 Broad Hollow Rd Ste 275, Melville NY 11747 *TF:* 877-920-0600 ■ *Web:* www.starmulticare.com	631-424-7827	427-5466	363
Star Nail Products Inc 29120 Ave Paine, Valencia CA 91355 *TF:* 800-762-6245 ■ *Web:* www.starnail.com	661-257-7827	257-5856	214
Star News 296 Third Ave, Chula Vista CA 91910 *Web:* www.thestarnews.com	619-427-3000	426-6346	637-8
Star of India 1492 N Harbor Dr, San Diego CA 92101 *Web:* lrstarofindia.com	501-227-9900		671
Star of India 2900 W Anderson Ln Ste 12D, Austin TX 78757 *Web:* www.starofindiaaustin.com	512-452-8199		671
Star of the West Milling Co 121 E Tuscola St, Frankenmuth MI 48734 *Web:* www.starofthewest.com	989-652-9971	652-6358	10-4
Star One Federal Credit Union 1306 Bordeaux Dr, Sunnyvale CA 94088 *TF:* 866-543-5202 ■ *Web:* starone.org	408-543-5202	543-5203	219
Star Pipe LLC 4018 Westhollow Pkwy, Houston TX 77082 *TF:* 800-999-3009 ■ *Web:* www.starpipeproducts.com	281-558-3000		595
Star Plastic Design 25914 President Ave, Harbor City CA 90710 *Web:* www.starplastic.com	310-530-7119		601
Star Precision LLC 7300 Miller Dr, Longmont CO 80504 *Web:* www.starprecision.com	303-926-0559	926-8577	697
Star Rentals Inc 1919 Fourth Ave S, Seattle WA 98134 *TF:* 800-825-7880 ■ *Web:* www.starrentals.com	206-622-7880		264-3
Star Sales & Distributing Corp 29 Commerce Way, Woburn MA 01801 *TF:* 800-222-8118 ■ *Web:* www.starsales.com	781-933-8830	933-2145	191-2
Star Services 4663 Halls Mill Rd, Mobile AL 36693 *TF:* 800-661-9050 ■ *Web:* star-service.com	251-661-4050		610
Star Shuttle & Charter 1343 Hallmark Dr, San Antonio TX 78216 *Web:* starshuttle.com	210-341-6000		108
Star Signs LLC 801 E Ninth St, Lawrence KS 66044 *Web:* starsignsllc.com	785-842-4892		187
Star Stainless Screw Co 30 W End Rd, Totowa NJ 07512	973-256-2300		351
Star Su Company LLC 5200 Prairie Stone Pkwy Ste 100, Hoffman Estates IL 60192 *Web:* www.star-su.com	847-649-1450	649-0112	190
Star Tech Glass Inc 1835 N Major Ave, Chicago IL 60639 *Web:* startechglass.com	773-745-0800	745-0889	361
Star Tex Distributors Inc 12705 S Kirkwood Ste 218, Stafford TX 77477 *Web:* www.startexoil.com	281-277-0077	277-0707	580
Star Track Inc 258 Rte 110, Farmingdale NY 11735 *Web:* www.startrackinc.com	631-293-6654	293-5202	76
Star Transportation LLC 3201 E Highland Dr, Jonesboro AR 72402 *Web:* www.starcompanies.net	870-932-6679	932-2925	780
Star Trax Inc 1200 Woodwards Hts, Ferndale MI 48220 *Web:* www.startrax.com	248-263-6300		196
Star Tribune 425 Portland Ave, Minneapolis MN 55488 *Web:* www.startribune.com	612-673-4000		532-2
Star Truck Rentals Inc 3940 Eastern Ave SE, Grand Rapids MI 49508 *TF:* 800-748-0468 ■ *Web:* startruckrentals.com	616-243-7033	243-7498	778
Star Video Duplicating 6910 E 5th Ave, Scottsdale AZ 85251 *TF:* 800-238-7827 ■ *Web:* www.starvideo.com	800-238-7827		658
Staradio Corp 1300 Central Ave W, Great Falls MT 59404 *Web:* www.staradio.com	406-761-2800		645-141
Starboard Advertising Group 111 Center St, Saint Simons Island GA 31522 *Web:* starboardadgroup.com	912-638-8885		7
Starboard Cruise Services Inc 8400 NW 36th St, Miami FL 33166 *TF:* 800-540-4785 ■ *Web:* www.starboardcruise.com	786-845-7300	845-1112	241
Starboard Restaurant 2009 Hwy 1, Dewey Beach DE 19971 *Web:* www.thestarboard.com	302-227-4600		671
Starboard Value 777 3rd Ave, New York NY 10017 *Web:* www.starboardvalue.com	212-845-7977		401
Starborn Industries Inc 45 Mayfield Ave, Edison NJ 08837 *TF:* 800-596-7747 ■ *Web:* www.starbornindustries.com	800-596-7747		350
Starbridge Media Group Inc 1390 Chain Bridge Rd Ste 600, McLean VA 22101 *Web:* www.starbridgemedia.com	703-760-0051	883-1180	194
Starbucks Coffee Co 2401 Utah Ave S, Seattle WA 98134 *TF:* 800-782-7282 ■ *Web:* www.starbucks.com	206-447-1575	318-3432	159
StarCare Lubbock 1950 Aspen Ave, Lubbock TX 79408 *TF:* 800-687-7581 ■ *Web:* www.starcarelubbock.org	806-766-0310	744-9580	371
Starco Impex 2710 S 11th St, Beaumont TX 77701 **Fax Area Code: 888* ■ *TF:* 866-740-9601 ■ *Web:* www.starcoimpex.com	866-740-9601	842-5650*	345
Stardock Systems Inc 15090 N Beck Rd Ste 300, Plymouth MI 48170 *Web:* www.stardock.com	734-927-0677	927-0678	174
StarDot Technologies 6820 Orangethorpe Ave Bldg H, Buena Park CA 90620 *TF:* 888-782-7368 ■ *Web:* www.stardot-tech.com	714-228-9282	228-9283	628
Stardust Cruisers Inc 6775 E Hwy 90, Monticello KY 42633 *Web:* trifectahouseboats.com	606-340-3191		90
Starfish Junction Productions Llc 226 N Fehr Way, Bay Shore NY 11706 *Web:* www.starfishjunction.com	631-940-7290		366
Starflex Fabrication Inc 453 85 Cir, College Park GA 30349 *Web:* www.starflexfab.com	770-471-2111		296
Stargate Digital 1001 El Centro St, South Pasadena CA 91030 *Web:* stargatestudios.net	626-403-8403		530
Star-Gazette 310 E Church St PO Box 285, Elmira NY 14902 *TF:* 800-836-8970 ■ *Web:* www.stargazette.com	607-734-5151		532-2
Star-Glo Industries LLC 2 Carlton Ave, East Rutherford NJ 07073 *Web:* www.starglo.com	201-939-6162	939-4054	676
Stark & Knoll Company LPA 3475 Ridgewood Rd, Akron OH 44333 *Web:* www.stark-knoll.com	330-376-3300	376-6237	428
Stark & Stark 993 Lenox Dr Bldg 2, Lawrenceville NJ 08648 *TF:* 800-535-3425 ■ *Web:* www.stark-stark.com	609-896-9060	896-0629	428
Stark Aerospace Inc 319 Charleigh D Ford Jr Dr, Columbus MS 39701 *Web:* starkaerospace.com	662-798-4075	368-1329	529
Stark Co 2900 Grant Ave, Philadelphia PA 19114 *TF:* 888-779-2247 ■ *Web:* www.starkcompany.com	888-779-2247		112
Stark County 225 Fourth St NE, Canton OH 44702 *Web:* starkcountyohio.gov	330-451-7432	451-7190	338
Stark County PO Box 130, Dickinson ND 58602 *Web:* www.starkcountynd.gov	701-456-7630	456-7634	338
Stark County 130 W Main PO Box 426, Toulon IL 61483 *Web:* www.starkcountyillinois.com	309-286-5941	286-4039	338
Stark County District Library 715 Market Ave N, Canton OH 44702 *Web:* starklibrary.org	330-452-0665	452-0403	434-3
Stark Electronic 444 Franklin St, Worcester MA 01604 *Web:* www.starkelectronic.com	508-756-7136		246
Stark Manufacturing Inc 310 Pennington Dr, Paris AR 72855 *Web:* www.starkmfg.com	479-963-3046		595
Stark Services 12444 Victory Blvd 3rd Fl, North Hollywood CA 91606 *Web:* www.starkservices.com	818-985-2003		225
Stark State College of Technology 6200 Frank Ave NW, North Canton OH 44720 *TF:* 800-797-8275 ■ *Web:* www.starkstate.edu	330-494-6170	497-6313	800

Phone | Fax | Class

Starke County
County Courthouse 53 E Washington St. . . . . Knox IN 46534 574-772-9128 772-9169 338
Web: www.co.starke.in.us

Starker Forests Inc
7240 SW Philomath Blvd . . . . Corvallis OR 97333 541-929-2477 929-2178 752
Web: www.starkerforests.com

Starkey Hearing Technologies
6700 Washington Ave S . . . . .Eden Prairie MN 55344 888-251-9340 477
TF: 800-328-8602 ■ Web: www.starkey.com

Starkey Hearing Trechnologies
2476 Argentia Rd Ste 301. . . . . Mississauga ON L5N6M1 888-282-1086 250
TF: 888-282-1086 ■ Web: www.starkeycanada.ca

Starkey International Institute for Household Management
1350 Logan St . . . . .Denver CO 80203 303-832-5510 149
TF: 800-888-4904 ■ Web: www.starkeyintl.com

Starkey Machinery Inc
254 S Washington St . . . . Galion OH 44833 419-468-2560 468-1698 695
Web: www.starkeymachinery.com

Starkville Public Library
326 University Dr . . . . Starkville MS 39759 662-323-2766 323-9140 434-3
Web: starkville.lib.ms.us

Starkweather & Shepley Inc
60 Catamore Blvd. .East Providence RI 02914 401-435-3600 390
TF: 800-854-4625 ■ Web: www.starshep.com

Starlight Casino
2710 8882-170th St
Ste 2710 W Edmonton Mall . . . . Northwest Edmonton AB T5T3J7 780-444-2112 444-1155 133
Web: edmonton.starlightcasino.ca

Starlight Theatre
4600 Starlight Rd . . . . Kansas City MO 64132 816-363-7827 572
TF: 800-776-1730 ■ Web: www.kcstarlight.com

Starline Inc 1300 W Henry St . . . . .Sedalia MO 65301 660-827-6640 711
TF: 800-280-6660 ■ Web: www.starlinebrass.com

Starline Printing Inc
7111 Pan American W Svc NE . . . . Albuquerque NM 87109 505-345-8900 687
Web: www.starlineprinting.com

Starlite Limousines LLC
14747 N Northsight Blvd Ste 111-223 . . . . Scottsdale AZ 85267 480-422-3619 671-0522* 441
*Fax Area Code: 617 ■ TF: 877-474-4847 ■ Web: www.charterbuslimousines.com

Starmark Cabinetry
600 E 48th St N . . . . .Sioux Falls SD 57104 800-594-9444 115
TF: 800-594-9444 ■ Web: www.starmarkcabinetry.com

Starmark International Inc
210 S Andrews Ave. . . . . Fort Lauderdale FL 33301 954-874-9000 874-9010 195
TF: 888-280-9630 ■ Web: www.starmark.com

Starnes Aycock Haire Hogan Saunders & Rigsbee PLLC
118 N Sterling St . . . . .Morganton NC 28655 828-437-3335 41
Web: starneslawfirm.com

Starnet Data Design Inc
2659 Townsgate Rd Ste 227 . . . . Westlake Village CA 91361 805-371-0585 196
TF: 800-779-0587 ■ Web: www.starnetdata.com

Star-News Newspapers
1003 S 17th St . . . . Wilmington NC 28401 910-343-2000 343-2210 637-8
Web: www.starnewsonline.com

Starplex Scientific Inc
50 A Steinway Blvd. . . . . .Etobicoke ON M9W6Y3 416-674-7474 476
TF: 800-665-0954 ■ Web: www.starplexscientific.com

Starpoint Solutions
22 Cortlandt St 14th Fl . . . . New York NY 10007 212-962-1550 962-7175 180
Web: www.starpoint.com

StarQuest Software Inc 1288 Ninth St . . . . .Berkeley CA 94710 510-528-2900 387
Web: www.starquest.com

Starr Commonwealth
13725 Starr Commonwealth Rd . . . . Albion MI 49224 517-629-5591 630-2400 48-15
TF: 800-837-5591 ■ Web: www.starr.org

Starr Electric Company Inc
6 Battleground Ct . . . . Greensboro NC 27408 336-275-0241 273-0734 189-4
Web: www.starrelectric.net

Starr Foundation 399 Park Ave 3rd Fl . . . . New York NY 10022 212-909-3600 750-3237 305
Web: www.starrfoundation.org

Starr Group, The 5005 W Loomis Rd . . . . Greenfield WI 53220 414-421-3800 390
Web: www.starrgroup.com

Starr Instrument
1101 W Lawrence Hwy . . . . Charlotte MI 48813 517-543-8089 543-6166 201
Web: www.starrinstrument.com

Starr King School for the Ministry
2441 LeConte Ave. . . . . .Berkeley CA 94709 510-845-6232 845-6273 167-3
Web: www.sksm.edu

STARR Life Sciences Corp
333 Allegheney Ave Ste 300 . . . . Oakmont PA 15139 866-978-2779 419
TF: 866-978-2779 ■ Web: www.starrlifesciences.com

Starr Manufacturing Inc (SMI)
4175 Warren Sharon Rd . . . . Vienna OH 44473 330-394-9891 394-9890 480
Web: www.starrmfg.com

Starr Ranch 1 Oneonta Dr . . . . Wenatchee WA 98801 509-663-2191 297-7
Web: starranch.com

Starr Security Services
358 5th Ave Ste 1003 . . . . New York NY 10001 212-767-1110 693

Starr Transit Inc 2531 E State St. . . . . .Trenton NJ 08619 609-587-0626 107
TF: 800-782-7703 ■ Web: www.starrtours.com

Starrco Company Inc
11700 Fairgrove Industrial Blvd . . . . Maryland Heights MO 63043 314-567-5533 106
TF: 800-325-4259 ■ Web: www.starrco.com

Starrett Webber Gage Division
24500 Detroit Rd . . . . .Cleveland OH 44145 440-835-0001 892-9555 493
TF: 800-255-3924 ■ Web: www.starrett-webber.com

Starry Inc 38 Chauncy St 2nd Fl . . . . .Boston MA 02111 617-861-8300 657
Web: starry.com

STARS (Shock Trauma Air Rescue Society)
1441 Aviation Pk NE. . . . . Calgary AB T2E8M7 403-295-1811 275-4891 30
Web: www.stars.ca

Stars 712 E Villa St . . . . .Pasadena CA 91101 626-817-4506 305
Web: gostars.org

Star-Seal 6596 New Peachtree Rd . . . . Atlanta GA 30340 770-455-6551 580
TF: 800-779-6066 ■ Web: www.herculessealcoat.com

Starshak Winzenburg
55 W Monroe St Ste 2530 .Chicago IL 60603 312-444-9367 444-9519 690
Web: www.swandco.com

Starshot Ventures Inc
3555 Lakeshore Blvd W . . . . Toronto ON M8W1P4 416-503-8362 5
Web: starshot.com

Starside Security & Investigation Inc
1930 S Brea Canyon Rd Ste 220. . . . . Diamond Bar CA 91765 909-396-9999 400
TF: 888-478-2774 ■ Web: www.starside.com

Starsound Audio Inc 2679 Oddie Blvd. . . . . Reno NV 89512 775-331-1010 35
Web: starsound.com

Star-Spangled Banner Flag House, The
844 E Pratt St . . . . .Baltimore MD 21202 410-837-1793 520
Web: www.flaghouse.org

Starta Accelerator
220 E 23rd St Ste 500. . . . . .New York NY 10010 929-251-5142 393
Web: www.startaaccelerator.com

Startec Global Communications Corp
11300 Rockville Pk Ste 900 . . . . Rockville MD 20852 301-610-4300 329-2882* 736
*Fax Area Code: 877 ■ TF: 800-827-3374 ■ Web: www.startec.com

Startech Computing Inc
1755 Old W Main St. . . . . .Red Wing MN 55066 651-385-0607 180
TF: 888-385-0607 ■ Web: www.startech-comp.com

STARTEL 16 Goodyear B-125 . . . . Irvine CA 92618 800-782-7835 863-8775* 396
*Fax Area Code: 949 ■ TF: 800-782-7835 ■ Web: startel.com

Star-Tribune 170 Star Ln . . . . .Casper WY 82604 307-266-0500 532-2
TF: 866-981-6397 ■ Web: www.trib.com

StartSpot Mediaworks Inc
820 Davis St Ste 403 . . . . Evanston IL 60201 847-475-0354 658
Web: www.startspot.com

StartWire 10 Water St Ste 150 . . . . .Lebanon NH 03766 800-572-9470 260
TF: 800-572-9470 ■ Web: www.startwire.com

Starvaggi Industries Inc
224 Canton Rd . . . . Weirton WV 26062 304-748-1400 797-5208 182
Web: www.starvaggi.com

Starvation Creek State Park
Historic Columbia River Hwy State Trl . . . . . .Cascade Locks OR 97014 541-387-4010 565
Web: oregonstateparks.org

Starve Hollow State Recreation Area
4345 S County Rd 275 W. . . . . Vallonia IN 47281 812-358-3464 565
Web: www.in.gov

Starved Rock State Park PO Box 570. . . . . Utica IL 61373 815-667-4726 565
TF: 800-868-7625 ■ Web: www.starvedrocklodge.com

Starvin' Artist Supplies
802 S Oak Pk . . . . Oak Park IL 60304 708-358-3600 45
Web: www.starvinartistsupply.com

Starving Students Moving & Storage Co
1850 Sawtelle Blvd Ste 300 . . . . .Los Angeles CA 90025 888-931-6683 519
TF: 888-931-6683 ■ Web: www.ssmovers.com

Starwest Botanicals Inc
161 Main Ave . . . . Sacramento CA 95838 916-638-8100 853-9673 479
TF: 800-800-4372 ■ Web: www.starwest-botanicals.com

Starz Encore Group LLC
8900 Liberty Cir . . . . .Englewood CO 80112 720-852-7700 740
Web: www.starz.com

StarZen Technologies Inc
3340 SE Fed Hwy . . . . .Stuart FL 34997 561-329-2598 177
Web: www.starzen.com

Stason Pharmaceuticals Inc 11 Morgan . . . . Irvine CA 92618 949-380-4327 231
Web: www.stason.com

STAT Association Marketing & Management Inc
11240 Waples Mill Rd Ste 200. . . . . Fairfax VA 22030 703-934-0160 359-7562 47
Web: www.statmarketing.com

StataCorp LP 4905 Lakeway Dr . . . . College Station TX 77845 979-696-4600 696-4601 387
Web: www.stata.com

Stat-Chek Co PO Box 9636 . . . . Bend OR 97708 541-322-2870 322-1890 475
TF: 800-248-6618 ■ Web: www.statchek.com

Statco 8870 Business Park Dr . . . . Austin TX 78759 512-795-5000 225
Web: www.statco.com

State & Federal Communications Inc
80 S Summit St Ste 100 . . . . .Akron OH 44308 330-761-9960 761-9965 781
TF: 888-452-9669 ■ Web: stateandfed.com

State Auto Property & Casualty Insurance Co
518 E Broad St . . . . Columbus OH 43215 614-464-5000 391-4
TF: 800-444-9950 ■ Web: stateauto.com

State Ballet of Rhode Island, The
52 Sherman Ave . . . . Lincoln RI 02865 401-334-2560 334-0412 573-1
Web: www.stateballet.com

State Bank 175 N Leroy St. . . . . Fenton MI 48430 810-629-2263 70
TF: 800-535-0517 ■ Web: www.thestatebank.com

State Bank & Trust
Bell Bank 3100 13th Ave S PO Box 10877 . . . . .Fargo ND 58103 701-298-1500 70
TF: 800-450-8949 ■ Web: bellbanks.com

State Bank & Trust Co 1025 Sixth St. . . . . .Nevada IA 50201 515-382-2191 382-3826 70
Web: www.banksbt.com

State Bank of Blue Rapids
21 Public Sq. . . . . Blue Rapids KS 66411 785-363-7721 562-5526 70
Web: firstcommercebankonline.com

State Bank of Bottineau
105 11th St E . . . . Bottineau ND 58318 701-228-2204 70
Web: statebankofbottineau.com

State Bank of Cross Plains
1205 Main St PO Box 218 . . . . Cross Plains WI 53528 608-798-3961 798-3591 70
Web: www.crossplainsbank.com

State Bank of Southwest Missouri
3310 E Sunshine . . . . .Springfield MO 65804 417-882-1400 70
Web: statebankonline.net

State Bank of Spring Hill
201 S Webster . . . . .Spring Hill KS 66083 913-592-3326 70
Web: sbsh-ks.com

State Bank of Texas
11950 Webb Chapel Rd . . . . Dallas TX 75234 972-252-6000 70
Web: statebnk.com

State Bank of Toledo
100 E High St PO Box 309 . . . . Toledo IA 52342 641-484-2980 70
Web: www.banktoledo.com

State Bank of Waterloo PO Box 148. . . . . Waterloo IL 62298 618-939-7194 939-4140 70
Web: www.sbw.bank

State Bar Association of North Dakota
504 N Washington St PO Box 2136 . . . . Bismarck ND 58502 701-255-1404 224-1621 72
TF: 800-472-2685 ■ Web: www.sband.org

	City	State	ZIP	Phone	Fax	Class
State Bar of Arizona 4201 N 24th St Ste 100 *TF:* 866-482-9227 ■ *Web:* www.azbar.org	Phoenix	AZ	85016	602-252-4804	271-4930	72
State Bar of California 180 Howard St *Web:* www.calbar.ca.gov	San Francisco	CA	94105	415-538-2000	538-2304	72
State Bar of Michigan 306 Townsend St *TF:* 800-968-1442 ■ *Web:* www.michbar.org	Lansing	MI	48933	517-346-6300	482-6248	72
State Bar of Montana PO Box 577 *TF:* 877-880-1335 ■ *Web:* www.montanabar.org	Helena	MT	59624	406-442-7660	442-7763	72
State Bar of Nevada 1211 S Maryland Pkwy *TF:* 800-254-2797 ■ *Web:* www.nvbar.org	Las Vegas	NV	89104	702-382-2200	385-2878	72
State Bar of New Mexico 5121 Masthead St NE PO Box 92860 *TF:* 800-876-6227 ■ *Web:* nmbar.org	Albuquerque	NM	87109	505-797-6000	828-3765	72
State Bar of South Dakota 222 E Capitol Ave Ste 3 *Web:* statebarofsouthdakota.com	Pierre	SD	57501	605-224-7554	224-0282	72
State Bar of Texas Texas Law Ctr 1414 Colorado St *TF:* 800-204-2222 ■ *Web:* texasbar.com	Austin	TX	78701	512-427-1463	427-4100	72
State Bar of Wisconsin 5302 Eastpark Blvd *TF:* 800-728-7788 ■ *Web:* www.wisbar.org	Madison	WI	53718	608-257-3838		72
State Beauty Supply 1522 Cerrillos Rd *Web:* www.statebeautystores.com	Santa Fe	NM	87505	505-988-4152		77
State Botanical Garden of Georgia 2450 S Milledge Ave *Web:* botgarden.uga.edu	Athens	GA	30605	706-542-1244		97
State Center Community College District 1525 E Weldon Ave *Web:* www.scccd.edu	Fresno	CA	93704	559-226-0720		162
State Chamber of Oklahoma 330 NE Tenth St *Web:* www.okstatechamber.com	Oklahoma City	OK	73104	405-235-3669	235-3670	140
State College of Florida 5840 26th St W *Web:* www.scf.edu	Bradenton	FL	34207	941-752-5000	727-6380	162
State Compensation Insurance Fund 333 Bush St *TF:* 866-721-3498 ■ *Web:* www.statefundca.com	San Francisco	CA	94104	866-721-3498		391-4
State Education Resource Ctr 25 Industrial Park Rd *TF:* 800-842-8678 ■ *Web:* ctserc.org	Middletown	CT	06457	860-632-1485		435
State Electric Supply Company Inc 2010 Second Ave *TF:* 800-624-3417 ■ *Web:* www.stateelectric.com	Huntington	WV	25703	304-523-7491	525-8917	246
State Employees Association of New Hamsphire Inc 207 N Main St *Web:* seiu1984.org	Concord	NH	03301	603-271-3411		414
State Employees Credit Union of Maryland Inc 971 Corporate Blvd *TF:* 800-879-7328 ■ *Web:* www.secumd.org	Linthicum Heights	MD	21090	410-487-7328		219
State Employees Federal Credit Union Patroon Creek Corporate Ctr 700 Patroon Creek Blvd *TF:* 800-727-3328 ■ *Web:* www.sefcu.com	Albany	NY	12206	518-452-8234		219
State Employees' Credit Union (SECU) PO Box 29606 **Fax Area Code:* 919 ■ *TF:* 888-732-8562 ■ *Web:* www.ncsecu.org	Raleigh	NC	27626	888-732-8562	857-2000*	219
State Fair & Exposition 1001 Beulah Ave *TF:* 800-876-4567 ■ *Web:* www.coloradostatefair.com	Pueblo	CO	81004	719-404-2018		720
State Fair Community College 3201 W 16th St *TF:* 877-311-7322 ■ *Web:* www.sfccmo.edu	Sedalia	MO	65301	660-530-5800		162
State Fair of Texas Inc 3921 Martin Luther King Blvd *Web:* www.bigtex.com	Dallas	TX	75201	214-565-9931	421-8710	239
State Farm 7171 W Craig Rd Ste 109 *Web:* sedpoche.com	Las Vegas	NV	89129	702-396-0111		390
State Farm Financial Services FSB 1 State Farm Plz *TF:* 877-734-2265 ■ *Web:* www.statefarm.com	Bloomington	IL	61702	877-734-2265		70
State Farm Insurance 333 First Commerce Dr *TF:* 877-659-1570 ■ *Web:* www.statefarm.ca	Aurora	ON	L4G8A4	877-370-3276		391-4
State Farm Stadium 1 Cardinals Dr *Web:* www.universityofphoenixstadium.com	Glendale	AZ	85305	623-433-7101	433-7199	720
State Forest State Park 56750 Hwy 14 *Web:* cpw.state.co.us	Walden	CO	80480	970-723-8366	723-8325	565
State Historical Society of Missouri, The 1020 Lowry St *TF:* 800-747-6366 ■ *Web:* shsmo.org	Columbia	MO	65201	573-882-1187	884-4950	520
State Industrial Products 3100 Hamilton Ave *TF:* 877-747-6986 ■ *Web:* www.stateindustrial.com	Cleveland	OH	44114	216-861-7114		151
State Information Bureau 842 E Park Ave *Web:* stateinformationbureau.com	Tallahassee	FL	32301	850-561-3990		400
State Janitorial Supply Co 525 Otis Dr *Web:* www.statejanitorial.com	Dover	DE	19901	302-734-4814	734-8362	76
State Journal, The 1216 Wilkinson Blvd *Web:* www.state-journal.com	Frankfort	KY	40601	502-227-4556	227-2831	532-2
State Journal-Register PO Box 219 *Web:* www.sj-r.com	Springfield	IL	62705	217-788-1300	788-1551	532-2
State Justice Institute (SJI) 11951 Freedom Dr Ste 1020 *Web:* www.sji.gov	Reston	VA	20190	571-313-8843	313-1173	340-20
State Legislative Leaders Foundation 481 Main St *Web:* www.sllf.org	Centerville	MA	02632	508-771-3821		242
State Library of Louisia, The 701 N 4th St *Web:* www.state.lib.la.us	Baton Rouge	LA	70802	225-342-4913	219-4804	434-5
State Library of Ohio 274 E 1st Ave Ste 100 *TF:* 800-686-1532 ■ *Web:* library.ohio.gov	Columbus	OH	43201	614-644-7061	466-3584	434-5
State Museum of Pennsylvania, The 300 N St *TF:* 800-654-5984 ■ *Web:* www.statemuseumpa.org	Harrisburg	PA	17120	717-787-4980	783-4558	520
State Mutual Insurance Co 210 E Second Ave *TF:* 877-872-5500 ■ *Web:* statemutualinsurance.com	Rome	GA	30161	706-291-1054		390
State Narrow Fabrics Inc 2902 Borden Ave *Web:* www.statenarrow.com	Long Island City	NY	11101	718-392-8787	392-9421	745-5
State National Bank & Trust Co 122 Main St PO Box 130 *Web:* www.state-national-bank.com	Wayne	NE	68787	402-375-1130		70
State News 435 E Grand River Ave *Web:* statenews.com	East Lansing	MI	48823	517-295-1680		532-3
State of Hawaii World Trade Ctr 250 S Hotel St PO Box 2359 *Web:* hawaii.gov	Honolulu	HI	96813	808-587-2750		822
State of Nebraska PO Box 3395 *TF:* 877-713-4002 ■ *Web:* www.nebraska.gov	Omaha	NE	68103	877-713-4002		339-28
State of South Dakota 523 East Capitol Ave *Web:* www.gfp.sd.gov	Pierre	SD	57501	605-223-7660		339-42
State of the Heart Hospice 1350 N Broadway *TF:* 800-417-7535 ■ *Web:* stateoftheheartcare.org	Greenville	OH	45331	937-548-2999		371
State Pipe & Supply Inc 9615 S Norwalk Blvd *TF:* 800-733-6410 ■ *Web:* www.statepipe.com	Santa Fe Springs	CA	90670	562-695-5555	692-1054	492
State Plaza Hotel 2117 E St NW *TF:* 866-868-7774 ■ *Web:* www.stateplaza.com	Washington	DC	20037	202-861-8200		379
State Port Pilot 114 E Moore St *Web:* stateportpilot.com	Southport	NC	28461	910-457-4568		627
State Restaurant Equipment Co 3163 S Highland Dr *Web:* www.staterestaurant.com	Las Vegas	NV	89109	702-733-1515	733-0814	300
State Science & Technology Institute 5015 Pine Creek Dr *Web:* ssti.org	Westerville	OH	43081	614-901-1690		393
State Steel Supply Co 208 Ct St *TF:* 800-831-0862 ■ *Web:* statesteel.com	Sioux City	IA	51101	712-277-4000		492
State Street Brats 603 State St *Web:* statestreetbrats.com	Madison	WI	53703	608-255-5544		671
State Street Corp 1 Lincoln St *NYSE:* STT ■ *Web:* www.statestreet.com	Boston	MA	02111	617-786-3000		70
State Supply Co 597 Seventh St E *TF:* 877-775-7705 ■ *Web:* www.statesupply.com	Saint Paul	MN	55130	651-774-5985		610
State Teachers Retirement System of Ohio 275 E Broad St *TF:* 888-227-7877 ■ *Web:* www.strsoh.org	Columbus	OH	43215	888-227-7877		528
State Technical College of Missouri 1 Technology Dr *Web:* www.statetechmo.edu	Linn	MO	65051	573-897-5000	897-5026	167-3
State Theatre 15 Livingston Ave *TF:* 800-432-9382 ■ *Web:* www.stnj.org	New Brunswick	NJ	08901	732-247-7200	247-4005	572
State Theatre 1307 J St PO Box 1492 *Web:* www.thestate.org	Modesto	CA	95354	209-527-4697		572
State Tool & Manufacturing Co 1650 E Empire Ave *Web:* www.statetool.com	Benton Harbor	MI	49022	269-927-3153	927-4230	815
State Training School 3211 Edgington Ave *Web:* dhs.iowa.gov	Eldora	IA	50627	641-858-5402	858-2416	412
State Universities Retirement System of Illinois 1901 Fox Dr *Web:* www.surs.com	Champaign	IL	61820	217-378-8800		401
State University of New York						
Brockport 350 New Campus Dr *TF:* 888-800-0029 ■ *Web:* www.brockport.edu	Brockport	NY	14420	585-395-2751	395-5452	166
Canton 34 Cornell Dr *TF:* 800-388-7123 ■ *Web:* www.canton.edu	Canton	NY	13617	315-386-7011	386-7929	162
College at Old Westbury, The PO Box 210 *Web:* www.oldwestbury.edu	Old Westbury	NY	11568	516-876-3000	876-3307	166
College at Oneonta Ravine Pkwy *Web:* www.oneonta.edu	Oneonta	NY	13820	607-436-3500	436-3074	166
College of Agriculture & Technology at Cobleskill 106 Suffolk Cir *TF:* 800-295-8988 ■ *Web:* www.cobleskill.edu	Cobleskill	NY	12043	518-255-5525	255-6769	166
College of Environmental Science & Forestry 1 Forestry Dr *TF:* 800-777-7373 ■ *Web:* www.esf.edu	Syracuse	NY	13210	315-470-6500	470-6933	166
College of Technology at Alfred 10 Upper College Dr *TF:* 800-425-3733 ■ *Web:* www.alfredstate.edu	Alfred	NY	14802	607-587-4215	587-4299	162
Delhi 2 Main St *TF:* 800-963-3544 ■ *Web:* www.delhi.edu	Delhi	NY	13753	607-746-4000	746-4104	162
Empire State College 1 Union Ave *TF:* 800-847-3000 ■ *Web:* esc.edu	Saratoga Springs	NY	12866	518-587-2100	587-9759	166
Geneseo 1 College Cir *TF:* 866-245-5211 ■ *Web:* www.geneseo.edu	Geneseo	NY	14454	585-245-5571	245-5550	166
Institute of Technology 100 Seymour Rd *Web:* sunypoly.edu	Utica	NY	13504	315-792-7500		166
Maritime College 6 Pennyfield Ave Fort Schuyler *Web:* www.sunymaritime.edu	Bronx	NY	10465	718-409-7200	409-7465	166
New Paltz 1 Hawk Dr *TF:* 877-696-7411 ■ *Web:* www.newpaltz.edu	New Paltz	NY	12561	845-257-3212	257-3209	166
Oswego 7060 SR 104 *Web:* www.oswego.edu	Oswego	NY	13126	315-312-2500	312-3260	166
Potsdam 44 Pierrpont Ave *TF:* 877-768-7326 ■ *Web:* www.potsdam.edu	Potsdam	NY	13676	315-267-2180	267-2163	166
SUNY Plattsburgh 101 Broad St *TF:* 888-673-0012 ■ *Web:* www.plattsburgh.edu	Plattsburgh	NY	12901	518-564-2040	564-2045	166

Name / Address	City	State	ZIP	Phone	Fax	Class
State University of New York Press (SUNY) 22 Corporate Woods Blvd 3rd Fl *TF:* 866-430-7869 ■ *Web:* www.sunypress.edu	Albany	NY	12211	518-472-5000	472-5038	637-4
State University of New York Upstate Medical University 766 Irving Ave *TF:* 800-736-2171 ■ *Web:* www.upstate.edu	Syracuse	NY	13210	315-464-4570	464-8867	167-2
State University of New York, The (SUNY) State University Plz *TF:* 800-342-3811 ■ *Web:* www.suny.edu	Albany	NY	12246	518-320-1888		786
State University System of Florida 325 W Gaines St Ste 1614 *Web:* www.flbog.edu	Tallahassee	FL	32399	850-245-0466	245-9685	786
State Volunteer Mutual Insurance Co (SVMIC) 101 W Pk Dr Ste 300 *TF:* 800-342-2239 ■ *Web:* svmic.com	Brentwood	TN	37027	615-377-1999	370-1343	391-5
State Wide Accounting Taxes Inc 17625 Crenshaw Blvd Ste 301 *Web:* swatax.com	Torrance	CA	90504	310-515-7254	323-6634	734
State Wide Aluminum Inc 3518 County Rd 6 E *TF:* 800-860-2594 ■ *Web:* www.state-wide.com	Elkhart	IN	46514	574-262-2594	262-4125	60
State Wide Distributors Inc 14 Harlow St *Web:* www.statewidedist.com	Bangor	ME	04401	207-947-2000	947-1000	76
Stat-Ease Inc 2021 E Hennepin Ave Ste 480 *Web:* statease.com	Minneapolis	MN	55413	612-378-9449		225
Statehouse Convention Ctr 101 S Spring St PO Box 3232 *TF:* 800-844-4781 ■ *Web:* littlerockmeetings.com	Little Rock	AR	72201	501-376-4781		205
Statek Corp 512 N Main St *Web:* statek.com	Orange	CA	92868	714-639-7810	997-1256	203
Stately Oaks Plantation 100 Carriage Ln *Web:* historicaljonesboro.org	Jonesboro	GA	30236	770-473-0197	473-9855	50-3
Statement Systems Inc 1900 Diplomat Dr *Web:* www.statementsystems.com	Farmers Branch	TX	75234	214-210-0880		396
Staten Island Advance 950 W Fingerboard Rd *TF:* 800-675-8645 ■ *Web:* www.silive.com	Staten Island	NY	10305	718-981-1234		532-2
Staten Island Chamber of Commerce 130 Bay St *Web:* www.sichamber.com	Staten Island	NY	10301	718-727-1900	727-2295	139
Staten Island Children's Museum 1000 Richmond Ter *Web:* sichildrensmuseum.org	Staten Island	NY	10301	718-273-2060	273-2836	521
Staten Island Hotel 1415 Richmond Ave *Web:* esplanadesi.com	Staten Island	NY	10314	718-698-5000	737-7294	379
Staten Island Mall 2655 Richmond Ave *Web:* www.statenislandmall.com	Staten Island	NY	10314	718-761-6800		460
Staten Island Zoo 614 Broadway *Web:* www.statenislandzoo.org	Staten Island	NY	10310	718-442-3101	981-8711	823
Stater Bros Markets Inc 301 S Tippecanoe Ave *Web:* www.staterbros.com	San Bernardino	CA	92408	909-733-5000		345
States Industries LLC PO Box 41150 *TF:* 800-626-1981 ■ *Web:* statesind.com	Eugene	OR	97404	541-688-7871		613
States Logistics Services Inc 5650 Dolly Ave *Web:* www.stateslogistics.com	Buena Park	CA	90621	714-521-6520	521-6944	803-1
States Parks & Watercraft 2045 Morse Rd Bldg C *Web:* ohiodnr.gov	Columbus	OH	43229	614-265-6565		565
States Recovery Systems Inc 2491 Sunrise Blvd *TF:* 800-211-1435 ■ *Web:* www.statesrecovery.com	Rancho Cordova	CA	95670	916-631-7085		160
States Title Inc 101 Mission St Ste 740 *Web:* www.statestitle.com	San Francisco	CA	94105	650-419-3827		391-2
Statesboro-Bulloch Chamber of Commerce 102 S Main St *Web:* www.statesboro-chamber.org	Statesboro	GA	30458	912-764-6111		139
Statesman Journal 280 Church St NE *Web:* www.statesmanjournal.com	Salem	OR	97301	503-399-6611		532-2
Statesville Brick Co 391 Brickyard Rd *TF:* 800-522-4716 ■ *Web:* www.statesvillebrick.com	Statesville	NC	28677	704-872-4123	872-4125	150
Statesville Flying Service 116 N Center St *Web:* statesvilleregion.com	Statesville	NC	28677	704-871-0062		63
Stateville Correctional Ctr 16830 S Broadway St PO Box 112 *Web:* www2.illinois.gov	Joliet	IL	60434	815-727-3607	727-5511	213
Statewide Express Inc 5231 Engle Rd *TF:* 800-627-4600 ■ *Web:* www.swxe.net	Cleveland	OH	44142	216-676-4600	433-9944	780
Statewide Remodeling Inc 2450 Esters Blvd Ste 200 *Web:* www.statewideremodeling.com	Grapevine	TX	76051	214-238-9863		235
Static Control Components Inc 3010 Lee Ave PO Box 152 *TF:* 800-488-2426 ■ *Web:* www.scc-inc.com	Sanford	NC	27331	919-774-3808	774-1287	174
Static Controls Corp 30460 S Wixom Rd *Web:* www.scccontrols.com	Wixom	MI	48393	248-926-4400	926-4412	203
Staticworx Inc 124 Watertown St *TF:* 888-782-8429 ■ *Web:* www.StaticWorx.com	Watertown	MA	02472	617-923-2000		189-2
Station Casinos Inc 1505 S Pavilion Center Dr *TF:* 800-634-3101 ■ *Web:* www.sclv.com	Las Vegas	NV	89135	702-495-3000		132
Station Hill of Barrytown 120 Station Hill Rd *Web:* www.stationhill.org	Barrytown	NY	12507	845-758-5293		637-2
Station Resource Group (SRG) 24519 Peach Tree Rd PO Box 1858 *Web:* www.srg.org	Clarksburg	MD	20871	301-270-2617	270-2618	632
Station Square Restaurant 4250 Belmont Ave *Web:* www.thestationsquare.com	Youngstown	OH	44505	330-759-8802		671
Station Theatre 223 N Broadway Ave *Web:* www.stationtheatre.com	Urbana	IL	61801	217-384-4000		572
Stationers Inc 100 Industrial Ln *TF:* 800-862-7200 ■ *Web:* www.stationers-wv.com	Huntington	WV	25702	304-528-2780	528-2795	535
Statler Body Works Inc 1266 N Franklin St *Web:* www.statlerbody.com	Chambersburg	PA	17201	717-261-5936		62-4
Statlistics Inc 69 Kenosia Ave *Web:* www.statlistics.com	Danbury	CT	06810	203-778-8700		5
Statmon Technologies Corp 385 736 N Western Ave *TF:* 888-418-3646 ■ *Web:* www.statmon.com	Lake Forest	IL	60045	847-604-5366		736
Statoil Marketing & Trading 120 Long Ridge Rd Ste 3E01 *Web:* www.equinor.com	Stamford	CT	06902	203-978-6900		538
STATS ChipPAC Test Services Inc 46429 Landing Pkwy *Web:* www.statschippac.com	Fremont	CA	94538	510-979-8000	979-8001	253
STATS Inc 2775 Shermer Rd *Web:* www.stats.com	Northbrook	IL	60062	847-583-2100		225
Statue of Liberty Liberty Is *Web:* www.nps.gov	New York	NY	10004	212-363-3200		564
Statue of Liberty-Ellis Island Foundation Inc, The 17 Battery Pl Ste 210 *Web:* libertyellisfoundation.org	New York	NY	10004	212-561-4500		48-23
Staub Metals Corp 7747 E Rosecrans Ave *Web:* www.staubmetals.com	Paramount	CA	90723	562-602-2200	633-1456	492
Stauber Pete (Rep R - MN) 126 Cannon House Office Bldg *Web:* www.stauber.house.gov	Washington	DC	20515	202-225-6211		342-2
Staubli Corp 201 Pkwy W Hillside Pk *Web:* www.staubli.com	Duncan	SC	29334	864-433-1980		358
Staubus & Randall LLP 8401 N Central Expy *Web:* srllp.com	Dallas	TX	75225	214-691-3411		41
Stauder Technologies Inc 114 Mexico Ct *Web:* www.staudertech.com	Saint Peters	MO	63376	636-498-6658		809
Staufer Team Real Estate 932 Main St *Web:* stauferteam.com	Louisville	CO	80027	303-664-0000		652
Stauffer Diesel Inc 34 Stauffer Ln *Web:* www.staufferdiesel.com	Ephrata	PA	17522	717-738-2500		518
Stauffer Glove & Safety PO Box 45 *Web:* www.stauffersafety.com	Red Hill	PA	18076	215-679-4446	679-5053	679
Staunton Foods LLC 10 Morris Mill Rd *TF:* 800-932-2228 ■ *Web:* www.stauntonfoods.com	Staunton	VA	24401	540-885-1214	885-0021	297-2
Staunton (Independent City) 113 E Beverley St *Web:* www.ci.staunton.va.us	Staunton	VA	24401	540-332-3874	332-3970	338
Staunton River State Park 1170 Staunton Tr *Web:* www.dcr.virginia.gov	Scottsburg	VA	24589	434-572-4623		565
Staunton School of Cosmetology 128 E Beverly St *TF:* 800-296-5853 ■ *Web:* www.hairstylingschool.com	Staunton	VA	24401	540-885-0808		685
Staunton Star Times 108 W Main St *Web:* www.stauntonstartimes.com	Staunton	IL	62088	618-635-2000		532-3
Stautzenberger College 1796 Indian Wood Cir *TF:* 888-859-8225 ■ *Web:* www.sctoday.edu	Maumee	OH	43537	419-866-0261	867-9821	167-3
Staver Law Group PC 120 W Madison St Ste 400 *Web:* chicagolawyer.com	Chicago	IL	60602	312-236-2900		41
Stavis Seafoods Inc 212 Northern Ave Ste 305 *TF:* 800-390-5103 ■ *Web:* www.stavis.com	Boston	MA	02210	617-897-1200		297-5
Stavola Contracting PO Box 482 *TF:* 800-359-1424 ■ *Web:* www.stavola.com	Red Bank	NJ	07701	732-542-2328	389-6083	46
Stay Aspen Snowmass 255 Gold Rivers Ct Ste 300 *TF:* 888-649-5982 ■ *Web:* www.stayaspensnowmass.com	Basalt	CO	81621	970-429-5037	925-9008	376
StayClassy Productions Inc 533 F St Ste 300 *Web:* www.classy.org	San Diego	CA	92101	617-694-7963		305
StayinFront Inc 107 Little Falls Rd *TF:* 800-422-4520 ■ *Web:* stayinfront.com	Fairfield	NJ	07004	973-461-4800	461-4801	177
Stayner Bates PC 510 South 200 West Ste 200 *Web:* stayner.com	Salt Lake City	UT	84101	801-531-9100		2
staySky Resort Management 7055 S Kirkman Rd Ste 104 *Web:* www.skyresortmanagement.com	Orlando	FL	32819	407-992-0430	992-0431	656
StayTop Systems Inc 1525 McCarthy Blvd Ste 1133 *Web:* www.staytop.com	Milpitas	CA	95035	408-538-5990	987-9609	260
St-Boniface Hospital 409 Tache Ave *Web:* stbonifacehospital.ca	Winnipeg	MB	R2H2A6	204-233-8563	231-0041	374-2
STC (Society for Technical Communication) 9401 Lee Hwy Ste 300 *Web:* www.stc.org	Fairfax	VA	22031	703-522-4114	522-2075	49-14
STC Business Solutions 1283 Azalea Rd *Web:* www.stc360.com	Mobile	AL	36693	251-661-7130		180
STC Netcom Inc 11611 Industry Ave *Web:* www.stcnetcom.com	Fontana	CA	92337	951-685-8181		179
St-Damase Hotel Furniture 246 Rue Principale *Web:* www.st-damase.com	Saint-Damase	QC	J0H1J0	450-797-3702	797-3455	361
STDL (Schaumburg Township District Library) 130 S Roselle Rd *Web:* www.schaumburglibrary.org	Schaumburg	IL	60193	847-985-4000		434-3
Steadfast Networks Inc 800 S Wells St Ste 190 *Web:* www.steadfast.net	Chicago	IL	60616	312-602-2689		225

Name	Address	City	State	ZIP	Phone	Fax	Class	Other
Steadman Law Office PC	24 Main St E PO Box 87	Girard	PA	16417	814-774-2628		41	*Web:* steadmanlaw.com
SteadmanTech	1153 Powderhouse Rd	Vestal	NY	13850	607-772-0882		177	*Web:* www.steadmantech.com
Steadyhand Investment Funds LP	1747 W Third Ave	Vancouver	BC	V6J1K7	888-888-3147		528	*TF:* 888-888-3147 ■ *Web:* www.steadyhand.com
Steak N. Shake Co	107 S Pennsylvania St	Indianapolis	IN	46241	317-241-0483		670	*Web:* www.steaknshake.com
Steal Network LLC	2181 California Ave Ste 400	Salt Lake City	UT	84104	801-210-0304		492	*Web:* www.stealnetwork.com
Stealth	1617 Locust St	Saint Louis	MO	63103	314-480-3606		513	*Web:* stealthcreative.com
Stealth Monitoring Inc	15182 Marsh Ln	Addison	TX	75001	214-341-0123		693	*Web:* stealthmonitoring.com
STEALTHbits Technologies Inc	200 Central Ave	Hawthorne	NJ	07506	201-447-9300	447-1818	179	*Web:* www.stealthbits.com
StealthMachines LLC	136 S Lincoln Ave Bldg 1/2	Loveland	CO	80537	970-631-4474		179	*TF:* 888-273-2440 ■ *Web:* www.stealthmachines.com
Steam Bros Inc	2400 Vermont Ave	Bismarck	ND	58504	701-222-1263	222-1372	152	*TF:* 800-767-5064 ■ *Web:* www.steambrothers.com
Steamatic Inc	3333 Quorum Dr Ste 280	Fort Worth	TX	76137	817-632-1555		152	*Web:* www.steamatic.com
Steamboat Grand Resort Hotel & Conference Ctr	2300 Mt Werner Cir	Steamboat Springs	CO	80487	970-871-5500		669	*TF:* 877-269-2628 ■ *Web:* steamboatgrand.com
Steamboat Rock State Park	51052 Hgwy 155	Electric City	WA	99123	509-633-1304		565	*Web:* parks.state.wa.us
Steamboat Ski & Resort Corp	2305 Mt Werner Cir	Steamboat Springs	CO	80487	970-879-6111		669	*TF:* 877-237-2628 ■ *Web:* www.steamboat.com
Steamboat Ventures	801 N Brand Blvd Ste 665	Glendale	CA	91203	818-858-1890	696-2686	792	*Web:* steamboatvc.com
Steamer Seafood Co	17 Lagoon Rd	Hilton Head Island	SC	29928	843-785-2070		671	*Web:* www.steamerseafood.com
Steamist Inc	25 E Union Ave	East Rutherford	NJ	07073	201-933-0746		386	*TF:* 800-577-6478 ■ *Web:* www.steamist.com
Steamship Authority	1 Cowdry Rd PO Box 284	Woods Hole	MA	02543	508-548-3788		468	*Web:* www.steamshipauthority.com
Steamtown National Historic Site	150 S Washington Ave	Scranton	PA	18503	570-340-5200		564	*TF:* 888-693-9391 ■ *Web:* www.nps.gov
Steamworks Brewing Co	801 E 2nd Ave	Durango	CO	81301	970-259-9200		670	*TF:* 877-372-9200 ■ *Web:* www.steamworksbrewing.com
Stearns County	705 Courthouse Sq Rm 121	Saint Cloud	MN	56303	320-656-3601	656-6393	338	*Web:* co.stearns.mn.us
Stearns ElectricAssn	900 E Kraft Dr	Melrose	MN	56352	320-256-4241	256-3618	245	*TF:* 800-962-0655 ■ *Web:* www.stearnselectric.org
Stearns Packaging Corp	4200 Sycamore Ave	Madison	WI	53714	608-246-5150	246-5149	151	*TF:* 800-655-5008 ■ *Web:* stearnspkg.com
Stearns Weaver Miller Weissler Alhadeff & Sitterson PA	150 W Flagler St Ste 2200	Miami	FL	33130	305-789-3200	789-3395	428	*Web:* www.stearnsweaver.com
Stearnswood Inc	320 Third Ave NW PO Box 50	Hutchinson	MN	55350	320-587-2137	587-7646	200	*Web:* www.stearnswood.com
Steel & Pipe Supply Co	555 Poyntz Ave	Manhattan	KS	66502	785-587-5100		492	*Web:* www.spsci.com
Steel Ceilings Inc	451 E Coshocton St	Johnstown	OH	43031	740-967-1063	967-1478	491	*TF:* 800-848-0496 ■ *Web:* steelceilings.com
Steel Center for Career & Technical Education	565 N Lewis Run Rd	Jefferson Hills	PA	15025	412-469-3200	469-2196	800	*Web:* www.steelcentertech.com
Steel Cities Steels Inc	395 Melton Rd	Burns Harbor	IN	46304	219-787-9500	787-9501	492	*TF:* 800-228-2026 ■ *Web:* www.scsmetals.com
Steel City Corp	190 N Meridian Rd	Youngstown	OH	44501	330-792-7663	797-2947	488	*TF:* 800-321-0350 ■ *Web:* www.scity.com
Steel Craft Technologies Inc	8057 Graphic Dr NE	Belmont	MI	49306	616-866-4400	866-4545	295	*TF:* 877-866-4402 ■ *Web:* www.steelcrafttech.com
Steel Dynamics Inc	7575 W Jefferson Blvd	Fort Wayne	IN	46804	260-969-3500	969-3590	723	*NASDAQ: STLD* ■ *Web:* www.steeldynamics.com
Steel Edge Inc (SEI)	716 W Mesquite Ave	Las Vegas	NV	89106	702-386-0023	795-8263	492	*Web:* www.steeledgeinc.com
Steel Electric Products Company Inc	6301 New Utrecht Ave	Brooklyn	NY	11219	718-259-6100	331-1874	816	*Web:* www.sepco-usa.com
Steel Encounters Inc	525 East 300 South	Salt Lake City	UT	84102	801-478-8100		492	*Web:* www.steelencounters.com
Steel Equipment Specialist	1507 Beeson St NE	Alliance	OH	44601	330-821-3322		480	*Web:* seseng.com
Steel Fabricators LLC	721 NE 44th St	Fort Lauderdale	FL	33334	954-772-0440	938-7527	480	*Web:* www.sfab.com
Steel Fabricators of Monroe LLC	2101 Booth St	Monroe	LA	71201	318-387-9426		480	*Web:* www.steelfab.com
Steel Founders' Society of America (SFSA)	780 McArdle Dr Ste G	Crystal Lake	IL	60014	815-455-8240	455-8241	49-13	*Web:* www.sfsa.org
Steel Framing Alliance	25 Massachusetts Ave NW Ste 800	Washington	DC	20001	202-452-1039		49-3	*TF:* 800-797-8335 ■ *Web:* www.steelframing.org
Steel Grip Inc	1501 E Voorhees St	Danville	IL	61832	217-442-6240		576	*TF:* 800-223-1595 ■ *Web:* www.steelgripinc.com
Steel House Inc	3644 Eastham Dr	Culver City	CA	90232	888-978-3354		5	*TF:* 888-978-3354 ■ *Web:* steelhouse.com
Steel King Industries Inc	2700 Chamber St	Stevens Point	WI	54481	715-341-3120	341-8792	470	*TF:* 800-826-0203 ■ *Web:* www.steelking.com
Steel LLC	405 N Clarendon Ave	Scottdale	GA	30079	404-292-7373		492	*Web:* www.steelincga.com
Steel Manufacturers Assn (SMA)	1150 Connecticut Ave NW Ste 1125	Washington	DC	20036	202-296-1515	296-2506	49-13	*Web:* steelnet.org
Steel of West Virginia Inc	17th St & Second Ave	Huntington	WV	25703	304-696-8200	529-1479	723	*TF:* 800-624-3492 ■ *Web:* www.swvainc.com
Steel Parts Corp	801 Berryman Pk	Tipton	IN	46072	765-675-2191	675-4232	489	*Web:* www.steelparts.com
Steel Plant Museum	Heritage Discovery Ctr 100 Lee St	Buffalo	NY	14210	716-821-9361		520	*Web:* steelplantmuseumwny.org
Steel Restaurant & Lounge	3180 Welborn St	Dallas	TX	75219	214-219-9908		671	*Web:* www.steelsushi.com
Steel Service Corp	2260 Flowood Dr PO Box 321425	Jackson	MS	39232	601-939-9222	939-9359	307	*TF:* 800-844-9222 ■ *Web:* www.steelservice.com
Steel Services Inc	9800 Mayland Dr	Richmond	VA	23233	804-673-3810		492	*Web:* www.steelservicesinc.com
Steel Smart Inc	1042 Airport Rd	Pikeville	NC	27863	919-736-0681		480	
Steel Structures Technology Center Inc	5277 Leelanau Ct	Howell	MI	48843	734-878-9560	878-9571	194	*Web:* www.steelstructures.com
Steel Supply Co, The	5101 Newport Dr	Rolling Meadows	IL	60008	800-323-7571	828-1553	492	*TF:* 800-323-7571 ■ *Web:* www.steelsupply.com
Steel Tank Institute / Steel Plate Fabricators Assn	944 Donata Ct	Lake Zurich	IL	60047	847-438-8265	438-8766	48-5	*Web:* www.steeltank.com
Steel Technologies Inc	700 North Hurstbourne Pkwy Ste 400	Louisville	KY	40245	502-245-2110		492	*Web:* steeltechnologies.com
Steel Unlimited Inc	456 W Valley Blvd	Rialto	CA	92376	909-873-1222		492	*TF:* 800-544-6453 ■ *Web:* www.steelunlimited.com
Steel Ventures LLC	1000 N Burlington St	North Kansas City	MO	64116	816-474-5210		723	*TF:* 866-751-8823 ■ *Web:* exltube.com
Steel Warehouse Company Inc	2722 W Tucker Dr	South Bend	IN	46619	574-236-5100	236-5154	492	*TF:* 800-348-2529 ■ *Web:* www.steelwarehouse.com
Steel Works LLC, The	1020 Niedringhaus Ave	Granite City	IL	62040	618-452-2833	452-8780	492	*TF:* 800-234-5828 ■ *Web:* tswllc.com
Steelcase Inc	901 44th St SE	Grand Rapids	MI	49508	800-333-9939		319-1	*NYSE: SCS* ■ *TF:* 888-783-3522 ■ *Web:* www.steelcase.com
SteelCloud Inc	20110 Ashbrook Pl Ste 270	Ashburn	VA	20147	703-674-5500	674-5506	176	*OTC: SCLD* ■ *TF:* 800-296-3866 ■ *Web:* www.steelcloud.com
Steelco Inc	1020 Commercial Dr	Matthews	NC	28104	405-484-7115		480	*Web:* steelcoinc.com
SteelCon Supply Co	265 Industrial Dr	Beckley	WV	25801	304-255-1416	255-6799	791	*Web:* www.steelconsupply.com
Steelcraft Tool Company Inc	12930 Wayne Rd	Livonia	MI	48150	734-522-7130	522-1134	493	*Web:* www.steelcrafttool.com
Steele Canvas Basket Corp	201 William St PO Box 6267 IMCN	Chelsea	MA	02150	617-889-0202	889-0524	733	*TF:* 800-541-8929 ■ *Web:* www.steelecanvas.com
Steele Capital Management Inc	788 Main St Ste 200	Dubuque	IA	52001	563-588-2097		528	*TF:* 800-397-2097 ■ *Web:* www.steelecapital.com
Steele County	PO Box 296	Finley	ND	58230	701-524-2152		338	*TF:* 800-584-7077 ■ *Web:* www.co.steele.nd.us
Steele County	111 E Main St	Owatonna	MN	55060	507-444-7700		338	*Web:* www.co.steele.mn.us
Steele Financial Inc	131 N Pendleton Ave	Pendleton	IN	46064	765-778-8878	778-6900	690	*Web:* steelefinancialinc.com
Steele Group LLC, The	PO Box 30996	Indianapolis	IN	46230	317-824-1414	824-0404	194	*TF:* 877-824-0544 ■ *Web:* www.thesteelegroup.us
Steele Law Firm PC, The	949 County Rt 53	Oswego	NY	13126	315-216-4721		428	*TF:* 877-496-2687 ■ *Web:* www.thesteelelawfirm.com
Steele Memorial Library	101 E Church St	Elmira	NY	14901	607-733-9173	733-9176	434-3	*Web:* www.steele.lib.ny.us
Steele Realty & Investment Company Inc	8900 Grant Line Rd	Elk Grove	CA	95624	916-686-6670		652	*Web:* www.steelerealtyinc.com
Steele Solutions Inc	9909 S 57th St	Franklin	WI	53132	414-367-5099		480	*TF:* 888-542-5099 ■ *Web:* steelesolutions.com
Steeler Inc	10023 Martin Luther King Jr Way S	Seattle	WA	98178	206-725-2500	725-1300	351	*TF:* 800-275-2279 ■ *Web:* www.steeler.com
Steele-Waseca Co-opeartive Electric (SWCE)	2411 W Bridge St PO Box 485	Owatonna	MN	55060	507-451-7340		245	*TF:* 800-526-3514 ■ *Web:* swce.coop
SteelFab Inc	8623 Old Dowd Rd	Charlotte	NC	28214	704-394-5376		480	*Web:* www.steelfab-inc.com
Steelhead Brewery & Cafe	199 E Fifth Ave	Eugene	OR	97401	541-686-2739		671	*Web:* steelheadbrewery.com
Steelhead Inc	10322 Moursund Blvd	San Antonio	TX	78221	210-628-1066		385	*TF:* 800-966-7471 ■ *Web:* www.steelheadinc.com

Name / Address	City	State	Zip	Phone	Fax	Class
Steelhead LNG Corp 650 - 669 Howe St *TF:* 855-860-8744 ■ *Web:* www.steelheadlng.com	Vancouver	BC	V6C0B4	604-235-3800		536
Steelhead Partners LLC 333 108th Ave NE Ste 2010 *Web:* www.steelheadpartners.com	Bellevue	WA	98004	425-974-3788	974-3799	492
Steelman Industries Inc 2800 Hwy 135 N *TF:* 800-287-6633 ■ *Web:* www.steelman.com	Kilgore	TX	75662	903-984-3061	984-1384	318
Steelman Transportation 2160 N Burton *TF:* 800-488-6287 ■ *Web:* www.steelmantransport.com	Springfield	MO	65803	417-831-6300		780
Steelray Software LLC 1440 Dutch Valley Pl NE *Web:* www.steelray.com	Atlanta	GA	30324	404-806-0160		396
SteelSalvor LLC 2951 Marina Bay Dr Ste 130-377 *Web:* www.steelsalvor.com	League City	TX	77573	281-724-8892	754-4187	492
Steelsummit Holdings Inc 1718 J P Hennessy Dr *Web:* www.steelsummit.com	La Vergne	TN	37086	615-641-3300		492
Steelways Inc 401 S Water St *Web:* www.steelwaysinc.com	Newburgh	NY	12553	845-562-0860		492
Steepleton Tire Co 777 S Lauderdale St *Web:* steepletontire.com	Memphis	TN	38126	901-774-6440	774-6445	755
SteepRock Inc 67 Lwr Church Hill Rd *Web:* www.steeprockinc.com	Washington Depot	CT	06794	718-576-1406		809
Steere Enterprises Inc 285 Commerce St *TF:* 800-875-4926 ■ *Web:* www.steere.com	Tallmadge	OH	44278	330-633-4926		604
Steering Group Inc, The 1078 Dixie Belle Ct *TF:* 866-290-8123 ■ *Web:* thesteeringgroup.com	Lawrenceville	GA	30045	800-405-3068		463
Stefanik Elise (Rep R - NY) 318 Cannon House Office Bldg *Web:* www.stefanik.house.gov	Washington	DC	20515	202-225-4611		342-2
Stefanini TechTeam Inc 27100 W Eleven-Mile Rd *TF:* 800-522-4451 ■ *Web:* stefanini.com	Southfield	MI	48034	800-522-4451		180
Stefano Foods Inc 4825 Hovis Rd *TF:* 800-340-4019 ■ *Web:* www.stefanofoods.com	Charlotte	NC	28208	704-399-3935		123
Steffes Corp 3050 Hwy 22 N *TF:* 888-783-3337 ■ *Web:* www.steffes.com	Dickinson	ND	58601	701-483-5400		480
Stegeman and Kastner Inc 2601 Ocean Park Blvd Ste 300 *Web:* www.s-and-k.com	Santa Monica	CA	90405	310-450-9010	452-7580	194
Steger & Bizzell Engineering Inc 1978 S Austin Ave *Web:* stegerbizzell.com	Georgetown	TX	78626	512-930-9412		261
Steico Industries Inc 1814 Ord Way *TF:* 800-444-3515 ■ *Web:* www.steicoindustries.com	Oceanside	CA	92056	760-438-8015		595
Steiff North America 24 Albion Rd Ste 220 *TF:* 888-978-3433 ■ *Web:* www.steiffusa.com	Lincoln	RI	02865	401-312-0080		762
Steigerwaldt Land Services Inc 856 N Fourth St *Web:* steigerwaldt.com	Tomahawk	WI	54487	715-453-3274		302
Steil Bryan (Rep R - WI) 1408 Longworth House Office Bldg *Web:* www.steil.house.gov	Washington	DC	20515	202-225-3031		342-2
Stein + Partners Brand Activation (SPBA) 432 Park Ave S *Web:* www.steinias.com	New York	NY	10016	212-213-1112		7
Stein Diamonds 606 S Olive St Ste 2110 *Web:* www.steindiamonds.com	Los Angeles	CA	90014	213-947-9559		410
Stein Eriksen Lodge 7700 Stein Way *TF:* 800-453-1302 ■ *Web:* www.steinlodge.com	Park City	UT	84060	435-649-3700		669
Stein Fibers Ltd 4 Computer Dr W *Web:* www.steinfibers.com	Albany	NY	12205	518-489-5700	489-5713	605-1
Stein Garden Centers Inc 5400 S 27th St *Web:* www.shopsteins.com	Milwaukee	WI	53221	414-761-5400		323
Stein Hospice 1200 Sycamore Line *TF:* 800-625-5269 ■ *Web:* www.steinhospice.org	Sandusky	OH	44870	419-625-5269	625-5761	371
Stein Industries Inc 7153 Northland Dr *Web:* www.stein-industries.com	Brooklyn Park	MN	55428	763-504-3500		14
Stein Law LLC 5909 Peachtree Dunwoody Rd NE Ste 800 *Web:* steinlawllc.com	Atlanta	GA	30328	770-804-4888		41
Stein Mart Inc 1200 Riverplace Blvd *NASDAQ: SMRT* ■ *TF:* 866-737-3777 ■ *Web:* www.steinmart.com	Jacksonville	FL	32207	904-346-1500		229
Stein Monast LLP 70 Rue Dalhousie Bureau 300 *Web:* steinmonast.ca	Quebec City	QC	G1K4B2	418-529-6531		428
Stein Seal Company Inc 1500 Industrial Blvd *Web:* www.steinseal.com	Kulpsville	PA	19443	215-256-0201	256-4818	326
Stein Sperling Bennett De Jong Driscoll PC 25 W Middle Ln *Web:* www.steinsperling.com	Rockville	MD	20850	301-340-2020		428
Stein's Inc 3001 17th St S *TF:* 800-234-2729 ■ *Web:* www.steinsinc.com	Moorhead	MN	56561	218-233-2727	233-7586	146
Steinbauer Associates Inc 7875 NW 12 St Ste 101 *Web:* www.steinbauer.com	Miami	FL	33126	305-629-9740	629-9744	652
Steinberg & Associates Inc 340 S Pine St *Web:* steinberg-associates.com	Spartanburg	SC	29302	864-582-7575		390
Steinberger Drilling Co PO Box 250 *Web:* www.steinbergerdrilling.com	Windthorst	TX	76389	940-423-6900		540
Steiner & Associates Inc 4016 Townsfair Way *Web:* steiner.com	Columbus	OH	43219	614-414-7300		653
Steiner Electric Co 1250 Touhy Ave *TF:* 800-783-4637 ■ *Web:* www.steinerelectric.com	Elk Grove Village	IL	60007	847-228-0400	228-1352	246
Steiner Industries 5801 N Tripp Ave *TF:* 800-621-4515 ■ *Web:* steinerindustries.com	Chicago	IL	60646	773-588-3444	588-3450	576
Steiner Leisure Ltd 770 S Dixie Hwy Ste 200 *NASDAQ: STNR* ■ *Web:* www.steinerleisure.com	Coral Gables	FL	33146	305-358-9002		77
Steiner Shipyard 8640 Hemley St PO Box 742 *Web:* steinershipyard.com	Bayou La Batre	AL	36509	251-824-4143	824-4178	770
SteinerBooks Inc PO Box 960 *Web:* steiner.presswarehouse.com	Herndon	VA	20172	703-661-1594	661-1501	637-2
Steinhafels Inc W 231 N 1013 County Hwy F *TF:* 866-351-4600 ■ *Web:* www.steinhafels.com	Waukesha	WI	53186	262-436-4600	436-4601	321
Steinhart Aquarium *California Academy of Sciences* Golden Gate Pk 55 Music Concourse Dr *TF:* 800-794-7576 ■ *Web:* calacademy.org	San Francisco	CA	94118	415-379-8000		40
Steinhilbers Thalia 653 Thalia Rd *Web:* www.steinys.com	Virginia Beach	VA	23452	757-340-1156		671
Steinke Vertal Langdon & Drum Inc 3511 Center Rd PO Box 8 *Web:* svldcpa.com	Brunswick	OH	44212	330-225-3377		2
Steinlauf and Stoller Inc 221 W 37th St *TF:* 877-869-0321 ■ *Web:* www.steinlaufandstoller.com	New York	NY	10018	212-869-0321	302-4465	594
Steinmetz Inc 660 Spencer Rd *Web:* www.steinmetzinc.com	Roaring Brook Township	PA	18444	570-842-6161	842-1382	605-2
Steins Thriftway Foods Inc 135 Central Ave N	Watkins	MN	55389	320-764-2980		297-8
Steinwall Inc 1759 116th Ave NW *TF:* 800-229-9199 ■ *Web:* www.steinwall.com	Coon Rapids	MN	55448	763-767-7060		608
Steinway & Sons 1 Steinway Pl *TF:* 800-783-1692 ■ *Web:* www.steinway.com	Long Island City	NY	11105	718-721-2600		527
Steinway Piano Gallery of Detroit Inc 2700 E West Maple Rd *Web:* steinwaydetroit.com	Commerce Charter Township	MI	48390	248-560-9200		362
Stelbar Oil Corporation Inc 112 SW 7th St Ste 3C *Web:* safer.fmcsa.dot.gov	Topeka	KS	66603	316-264-8378		536
Stelera Wireless LLC 14701 Dalea Dr	Oklahoma City	OK	73142	405-751-3525		194
Stella Color Inc *AlphaGraphics Seattle* 3131 Elliott Ave *Web:* www.stellacolor.com	Seattle	WA	98108	206-223-2303		627
Stella Group Ltd, The 706 N Ivy St *Web:* www.thestellagroupltd.com	Arlington	VA	22201	202-347-2214		192
Stella Maris Hospice Care Program 2300 Dulaney Valley Rd *Web:* www.stellamaris.org	Timonium	MD	21093	410-252-4500		371
Stella Maris LLC 930 W Pont des Mouton *Web:* www.stellamarisllc.com	LaFayette	LA	70507	337-504-5128		518
Stella May Contracting Inc 1512 Edgewood Rd *Web:* stellamay.com	Edgewood	MD	21040	410-679-8306	679-3642	186
Stella! 547 St Ann St *Web:* www.stanleyrestaurant.com	New Orleans	LA	70116	504-587-0093		671
Stella-Jones Inc 3100 de la Cote-Vertu Blvd Ste 300 *Web:* www.stella-jones.com	Saint-Laurent	QC	H4R2J8	514-934-8666	934-5327	683
Stellar Capital Management LLC 2200 E Camelback Rd Ste 130 *Web:* www.stellarmgt.com	Phoenix	AZ	85016	602-778-0307		401
Stellar Engineering Inc 2899 E Coronado St Unit E *Web:* www.stellarengineering.com	Anaheim	CA	92806	714-632-0040		261
Stellar Group 2900 Hartley Rd *TF:* 800-488-2900 ■ *Web:* stellar.net	Jacksonville	FL	32257	904-260-2900	268-4932	186
Stellar Industries Inc 190 State St *TF:* 800-321-3741 ■ *Web:* www.stellar-industries.com	Garner	IA	50438	641-923-3741	923-2812	695
Stellar Materials Inc 7777 Glades Rd Ste 310 *Web:* www.thermbond.com	Boca Raton	FL	33434	561-330-9300	330-9355	183
Stellar Printing Inc 38-38 9th St *Web:* www.stellarprinting.com	Long Island City	NY	11101	718-361-1600		627
Stellar Solutions Inc 250 Cambridge Ave Ste 204 *Web:* stellarsolutions.com	Palo Alto	CA	94306	650-473-9866	473-9867	261
Stellar Systems Inc 222 NE Monroe St *Web:* www.stellarsystems.com	Peoria	IL	61602	309-677-7350	677-7358	177
Stellar Technology Inc 237 Commerce Dr *TF:* 800-274-1846 ■ *Web:* www.stellartech.com	Amherst	NY	14228	716-250-1900		454
Stellarnet Inc 14390 Carlson Cir *Web:* www.stellarnet.us	Tampa	FL	33626	813-855-8687		419
StellArt 2012 Waltzer Rd *TF:* 866-621-1987 ■ *Web:* www.stellart.com	Santa Rosa	CA	95403	707-569-1378	569-1379	130
Stelvio Inc 430 Rue Sainte-Helene *Web:* www.stelvio.com	Montreal	QC	H2Y2K7	514-281-8570		180
Stem Brothers Inc 760 Frenchtown Rd *Web:* www.stembrothers.com	Milford	NJ	08848	908-995-4825	996-3508	316
Stem Engineering Group 875 Queen St E Ste 2 *Web:* www.stemeng.ca	Sault Sainte Marie	ON	P6A2B3	705-942-6628	942-7515	261
Stem International Inc 4692 Millennium Dr Ste 400 *Web:* www.stemint.com	Belcamp	MD	21017	410-272-9080	272-9085	194
Stemco LP 300 Industrial Blvd PO Box 1989 *TF:* 800-527-8492 ■ *Web:* www.stemco.com	Longview	TX	75606	903-758-9981	232-3508	60

Name / Address	City	State	ZIP	Phone	Fax	Class
Stemilt Growers Inc PO Box 2779 *Web:* www.stemilt.com	Wenatchee	WA	98807	509-663-1451		315-3
Stemmans Inc 117 E Gloria Switch Rd *TF:* 800-544-6773 ■ *Web:* www.stemmans.com	Carencro	LA	70520	337-234-2382	234-2383	475
Stemmerich Inc 4728 Gravois Ave *TF:* 800-325-9528 ■ *Web:* www.stemmerich.com	Saint Louis	MO	63116	314-832-7726		111
StemWood Corp 2710 Grant Line Rd *Web:* www.stemwood.com	New Albany	IN	47150	812-945-6646	945-7549	613
Stencil Shoppe 2503 Silverside Rd *TF:* 800-822-7836 ■ *Web:* designerstencils.com	Wilmington	DE	19810	302-475-7300		761
Stenerson Bros Lumber Co 1702 First Ave N *Web:* stenersonlumber.com	Moorhead	MN	56560	218-233-2754	233-2819	364
Stenograph LLC 1500 Bishop Ct *TF:* 800-323-4247 ■ *Web:* www.stenograph.com	Mount Prospect	IL	60056	847-803-1400		177
Stens Corp 1919 Hospitality Dr **Fax Area Code: 866* ■ *TF:* 800-457-7444 ■ *Web:* www.stens.com	Jasper	IN	47546	800-457-7444	472-0298*	429
Stenstrom Companies Ltd 2420 20th St *Web:* www.rstenstrom.com	Rockford	IL	61104	815-398-2420	398-0041	186
Stenton Museum 4601 N 18th St *Web:* www.stenton.org	Philadelphia	PA	19140	215-329-7312		520
Step Saver Inc 213 Spring St *Web:* www.stepsaver.com	Southington	CT	06489	860-628-9645	621-1841	5
Step Up For Students PO Box 54429 *TF:* 877-735-7837 ■ *Web:* www.stepupforstudents.org	Jacksonville	FL	32245	877-735-7837		305
Step2 Co 10010 Aurora-Hudson Rd *TF:* 800-347-8372 ■ *Web:* www.step2.com	Streetsboro	OH	44241	866-429-5200		64
Stepan Co 22 W Frontage Rd *TF:* 800-745-7837 ■ *Web:* www.stepan.com	Northfield	IL	60093	847-446-7500	501-2100	145
Stepfamily Foundation 310 W 85th St *Web:* www.stepfamily.org	New York	NY	10024	212-877-3244		48-6
Stephan & Brady Inc 1850 Hoffman St *Web:* www.stephanbrady.com	Madison	WI	53704	608-241-4141		4
Stephan Zouras LLP 205 N Michigan Ave Ste 2560 *Web:* stephanzouras.com	Chicago	IL	60601	312-233-1550		41
Stephen A. Forbes State Park 6924 Omega Rd *Web:* www.dnr.illinois.gov	Kinmundy	IL	62854	618-547-3381		565
Stephen Bader Company Inc 10 Charles St *Web:* www.stephenbader.com	Valley Falls	NY	12185	518-753-4456		455
Stephen Benjamin Insurance Agency Inc 497 Central Tpke *Web:* benjaminagency.com	Sutton	MA	01590	508-865-9534		390
Stephen Bulger Gallery 1356 Dundas St W *Web:* www.bulgergallery.com	Toronto	ON	M6J1Y2	416-504-0575	504-8929	42
Stephen C. Foster State Park 17515 Hwy 177 *Web:* gastateparks.org	Fargo	GA	31631	912-637-5274		565
Stephen C. Gault Co 4011 Gardiner Point Dr *Web:* scgault.com	Louisville	KY	40213	502-451-1122		653
Stephen Chelbay Co 6800 Santa Teresa Blvd *Web:* www.chelbayins.com	San Jose	CA	95119	408-288-4400	288-4425	390
Stephen F. Austin State University 1936 N St PO Box 13051 *TF:* 800-257-9558 ■ *Web:* www.sfasu.edu	Nacogdoches	TX	75962	936-468-2504	468-3149	166
Stephen Foster Folk Culture Center State Park 11016 Lillian Saunders Dr *Web:* www.floridastateparks.org	White Springs	FL	32096	386-397-4331		565
Stephen Gould Corp 35 S Jefferson Rd *Web:* www.stephengould.com	Whippany	NJ	07981	973-428-1500		100
Stephen L. Langeland PC 6146 W Main St Ste C *Web:* slangelandlaw.com	Kalamazoo	MI	49009	269-382-3703		41
Stephen Leacock Museum Library 50 Museum Dr PO Box 625 *Web:* www.leacockmuseum.com	Orillia	ON	L3V6K5	705-326-5578	329-1908	434-3
Stephen Mack Middle School 11810 Old River Rd *TF:* 800-252-2873 ■ *Web:* rockton140.org	Rockton	IL	61072	815-624-2611		685
Stephen Miller Gallery 800 Santa Cruz Ave *TF:* 888-566-8833 ■ *Web:* stephenmillergallery.com	Menlo Park	CA	94025	650-327-5040		361
Stephen R. Chesley LLC 16 Court St Rm 2506 *Web:* www.lawsuitlegalhelp.com	Brooklyn	NY	11241	718-522-3055		41
Stephens Advertising Inc 417 E Stroop Rd *Web:* www.stephensdirect.com	Dayton	OH	45429	937-299-4993		7
Stephens Carriers Inc 131a Sanders Ferry Rd Ste A *Web:* www.stephenscarriers.com	Hendersonville	TN	37075	615-824-1617	824-8086	780
Stephens College 1200 E Broadway *TF:* 800-876-7207 ■ *Web:* www.stephens.edu	Columbia	MO	65215	573-442-2211		166
Stephens County 200 W Walker St *Web:* www.co.stephens.tx.us	Breckenridge	TX	76424	254-559-3700	559-9645	338
Stephens County 101 S 11th St *Web:* www.stephenscountyok.com	Duncan	OK	73533	580-255-3131	255-3133	338
Stephens County 70 N Alexander St *Web:* www.stephenscountyga.com	Toccoa	GA	30577	706-886-9491	886-2185	338
Stephens Inc 111 Center St *TF:* 800-643-9691 ■ *Web:* stephens.com	Little Rock	AR	72201	501-377-2000		690
Stephens Machine Inc 1600 E Dodge St *Web:* www.stephensmachine.com	Kokomo	IN	46902	765-459-4017		757
Stephens Manufacturing Co 711 W Fourth St *TF:* 800-626-0200 ■ *Web:* www.stephensmfg.com	Tompkinsville	KY	42167	270-487-6774		190
Stephens Precision Inc 293 Industrial Dr *Web:* www.stephensprecision.com	Bradford	VT	05033	802-222-9600	222-9688	488
Stephens State Forest 1111 N Eighth St *Web:* www.iowadnr.gov	Chariton	IA	50049	641-774-4559		565
Stephens State Park 800 Willow Grove St *Web:* www.njparksandforests.org	Hackettstown	NJ	07840	908-852-3790		565
Stephenson & Warner Inc 1502 University Blvd *Web:* stephensonwarnercpas.com	Hamilton	OH	45011	513-860-3502		2
Stephenson County 50 W Douglas St Ste 500 *Web:* www.co.stephenson.il.us	Freeport	IL	61032	815-235-8289	235-8378	338
Stephenson Engineering Ltd 2550 Victoria Park Ave Ste 602 *Web:* www.stephenson-eng.com	Toronto	ON	M2J5A9	416-635-9970		256
Stephenson Equipment Inc (SEI) 7201 Paxton St *TF:* 800-325-6455 ■ *Web:* stephensonequipment.com	Harrisburg	PA	17111	717-564-3434		264-3
Stephenson Gracik & Company PC 325 Newman St PO Box 592 *Web:* scopc.com	East Tawas	MI	48730	989-362-4491		2
Stephenson Millwork Company Inc 210 Harper St NE *Web:* www.stephensonmillwork.com	Wilson	NC	27893	252-237-1141	237-4377	499
Stephenson National Bank & Trust 1820 Hall Ave PO Box 137 *TF:* 888-924-2717 ■ *Web:* www.snbt.com	Marinette	WI	54143	715-732-1732	732-5478	70
Stephenson Printing Inc 5731 General Wash Dr *TF:* 800-336-4637 ■ *Web:* www.stephensonprinting.com	Alexandria	VA	22312	703-642-9000	354-0384	627
Stephenson Public Library 1700 Hall Ave *Web:* marinettecountylibraries.org	Marinette	WI	54143	715-732-7570		434-3
Stephens-Peck Inc PO Box 1199 *Web:* www.peckstitlebook.com	Kamas	UT	84036	801-562-0843		637-2
Stephenville Independent School District 2655 W Overhill Dr *Web:* www.sville.us	Stephenville	TX	76401	254-968-4141		685
Stephenz Group Inc, The 75 E Santa Clara St Ste 900 *Web:* www.stephenz.com	San Jose	CA	95113	408-286-9899		4
Steppenwolf Theatre 1650 N Halsted St *Web:* www.steppenwolf.org	Chicago	IL	60614	312-335-1650		572
Stepping Stones Museum For Children Inc 303 W Ave *Web:* www.steppingstonesmuseum.org	Norwalk	CT	06850	203-899-0606		522
Steptoe & Johnson LLP 1330 Connecticut Ave NW *Web:* www.steptoe.com	Washington	DC	20036	202-429-3000		428
Steptoe & Johnson PLLC 400 White Oaks Blvd *Web:* www.steptoe-johnson.com	Bridgeport	WV	26330	304-933-8000		428
Stepware Inc 619 Main St *Web:* www.stepware.com	Grand Junction	CO	81507	970-243-9390	243-9482	809
Steraloids Inc PO Box 689 *Web:* www.steraloids.com	Newport	RI	02840	401-848-5422	848-5638	479
Stereo Advantage Co 5110 Main St *Web:* theadvantage.com	Williamsville	NY	14221	716-626-3280		246
Stereotaxis Inc 4320 Forest Park Ave *NASDAQ: STXS* ■ *TF:* 866-646-2346 ■ *Web:* www.stereotaxis.com	Saint Louis	MO	63108	314-678-6100	678-6159	382
Stericycle Inc 28161 N Keith Dr *NASDAQ: SRCL* ■ *TF:* 866-783-9816 ■ *Web:* www.stericycle.com	Lake Forest	IL	60045	847-367-5910		804
Sterigenics U.S. LLC 2015 Spring Rd Ste 650 *TF:* 800-472-4508 ■ *Web:* www.sterigenics.com	Oak Brook	IL	60523	630-928-1700	928-1701	782
Sterilite Corp PO Box 524 *TF:* 800-225-1046 ■ *Web:* www.sterilite.com	Townsend	MA	01469	800-225-1046		607
STERIS Corp 5960 Heisley Rd *NYSE: STE* ■ *TF:* 800-548-4873 ■ *Web:* www.steris.com	Mentor	OH	44060	440-354-2600	639-4450	476
Steritech Group Inc, The 7600 Little Ave *TF:* 800-868-0089 ■ *Web:* www.steritech.com	Charlotte	NC	28226	704-544-1900	544-8705	577
Sterk Insurance Agency Inc 999 W Main St PO Box 72 *Web:* siainsurance.com	Waupun	WI	53963	920-324-2071		390
Sterling 350 W Arden Ave *TF:* 800-933-7538 ■ *Web:* www.sterling.us	Glendale	CA	91203	818-241-1144	241-0271	194
Sterling & Francine Clark Art Institute 225 S St *Web:* clarkart.edu	Williamstown	MA	01267	413-458-2303		520
Sterling & Sterling Inc 135 Crossways Park Dr Ste 300 PO Box 9017	Woodbury	NY	11797	516-487-0300		390
Sterling Bank & Trust FSB One Towne Sq 17th Fl *Web:* www.sterlingbank.com	Southfield	MI	48076	248-351-3442	359-6660	70
Sterling Bay Cos 1040 W Randolph St *Web:* www.sterlingbay.com	Chicago	IL	60607	312-466-4100	466-4101	528
Sterling Blower Co 135 Vista Center Dr *Web:* www.sterlingblower.com	Forest	VA	24551	434-316-5310	316-5910	18
Sterling Bulletin 107 N Broadway Ave *Web:* www.sterlingbulletin.net	Sterling	KS	67579	620-278-2114		532-2
Sterling Business Forms PO Box 2486 *TF:* 800-759-3676 ■ *Web:* www.sbfnet.com	White City	OR	97503	800-759-3676	234-2409	110
Sterling Collection Inc, The 1730 First St *Web:* www.sterling-collection.com	San Fernando	CA	91340	818-837-4680	361-2250	320
Sterling College 125 W Cooper *TF:* 800-346-1017 ■ *Web:* www.sterling.edu	Sterling	KS	67579	620-278-2173	278-4418	166
Sterling College PO Box 72 *TF:* 800-648-3591 ■ *Web:* sterlingcollege.edu	Craftsbury Common	VT	05827	802-586-7711	586-2596	800
Sterling Computer Corp 600 Stevens Port Dr Ste 200 *TF:* 877-242-4074 ■ *Web:* sterlingcomputers.com	Dakota Dunes	SD	57049	605-242-4000	242-4001	721
Sterling Construction Company Inc 1800 Hughes Landing Blvd Ste 250 *NASDAQ: STRL* ■ *Web:* www.strlco.com	The Woodlands	TX	77380	281-214-0800	951-3605	186
Sterling Cruises & Travel 8700 W Flagler St *TF:* 800-435-7967 ■ *Web:* www.cruisewin.com	Miami	FL	33174	305-592-2522	592-7442	771

Name / Address	Phone	Fax	Class
Sterling Cut Glass Company Inc 5020 Olympic Blvd. . . . Erlanger KY 41018 *TF:* 800-543-1317 ■ *Web:* www.sterlingcutglass.com	859-283-2434		361
Sterling Electric Inc 7997 Allison Ave. . . . Indianapolis IN 46268 *TF:* 800-654-6220 ■ *Web:* www.sterlingelectric.com	317-872-0471	872-0907	518
Sterling Engineering Company Inc 79 Main St . . . . Sturbridge MA 01566 *Web:* sterling-eng.com	508-347-9101		261
Sterling Engineering Corp 236 New Hartford Rd . . . . Barkhamsted CT 06063 *Web:* www.airindustriesgroup.com	860-379-3366		21
Sterling Extract Company Inc 10929 Franklin Ave Ste V. . . . Franklin Park IL 60131 *Web:* www.sterlingextractcompany.com	847-451-9728	451-9745	345
Sterling Farms Theatre Complex 1349 Newfield Ave . . . . Stamford CT 06905 *Web:* www.curtaincallinc.com	203-329-8207	322-3656	572
Sterling Federal Bank PO Box 617 . . . . Sterling IL 61081 *TF:* 800-353-0888 ■ *Web:* www.sterlingfederal.com	815-626-0614		71
Sterling Fibers Inc 5005 Sterling Way. . . . Pace FL 32571 *TF:* 800-342-3779 ■ *Web:* www.sterlingfibers.com	850-994-5311	994-2579	605-2
Sterling Foods LLC 1075 Arion Pkwy . . . . San Antonio TX 78216 *Web:* www.sterling-fd.com	210-490-1669		68
Sterling Forest State Park 116 Old Forge Rd. . . . Tuxedo NY 10987 *Web:* parks.ny.gov	845-351-5907		565
Sterling Furniture Co 2051 South 1100 East . . . . Salt Lake City UT 84106 *Web:* www.sterlingfurnitureslc.com	801-467-1579		321
Sterling Global Human Resource Consulting 2415 E Camelback Esplanade Bldg III Ste 1090. . . . Phoenix AZ 85016 *Web:* www.sterlinghrconsulting.com	602-470-8012		260
Sterling Heights Area Chamber of Commerce 12900 Hall Rd Ste 100 . . . . Sterling Heights MI 48313 *Web:* www.shrcci.com	586-731-5400	731-3521	139
Sterling Hospitality Management LLC 8923 E Mission Ste 135. . . . Spokane WA 99212 *Web:* impressguest.com	509-928-6848		378
Sterling Hotel 1300 H St. . . . Sacramento CA 95814 *TF:* 800-365-7660 ■ *Web:* www.sterlinghotelsacramento.com	916-448-1300	448-8066	379
Sterling Hotel Dallas 1055 Regal Row. . . . Dallas TX 75247 *Web:* www.thesterlinghoteldallas.com	214-634-8550		378
Sterling Investment Partners 285 Riverside Ave Ste 300 . . . . Westport CT 06880 *Web:* sterlinglp.com	203-226-8711		401
Sterling Land Title Agency Inc 7016 Corporate Way. . . . Dayton OH 45459 *Web:* sterlinglandtitle.com	937-438-2000		653
Sterling Law Office PLLC 13919 S West Bayshore Dr Ste 209 . . . . Traverse City MI 49684 *Web:* sterlinglawoffice.net	231-486-0559		41
Sterling Magic PO Box 7670. . . . Auburn CA 95604 *Web:* www.sterlingmagic.com	530-823-7077	823-7078	322
Sterling McCall Cadillac 10422 SW Fwy Bldg B . . . . Houston TX 77074 *Web:* www.sterlingmccallcadillac.com	832-369-8220		57
Sterling McCall Ford 6445 SW Fwy. . . . Houston TX 77074 *Web:* www.sterlingmccallford.com	281-588-5000		516
Sterling Mutuals Inc 1090 University Ave 2nd Fl. . . . Windsor ON N9A5S4 **Fax Area Code:* 519 ■ *TF:* 800-354-4956 ■ *Web:* www.sterlingmutuals.com	800-354-4956	256-9730*	401
Sterling Organization 340 Royal Poinciana Way Ste 316 . . . . Palm Beach Gardens FL 33480 *Web:* www.sterlingorganization.com	561-835-1810	833-4118	509
Sterling Payment Technologies LLC PO Box 20427 . . . . Tampa FL 33633 *TF:* 800-383-0561 ■ *Web:* www.sterlingpayment.com	800-383-0561		393
Sterling Pipe & Tube Inc 5335 Enterprise Blvd . . . . Toledo OH 43612 *Web:* www.sterlingpipeandtube.com	419-729-9756		492
Sterling Process Engineering & Services Inc 333 McCormick Blvd . . . . Columbus OH 43213 *Web:* www.sterlingpe.com	614-868-5151		757
Sterling Production Control Units 2280 W Dorothy Ln . . . . Dayton OH 45439 *Web:* www.pcuinc.com	937-299-5594	299-3843	386
Sterling Publishing Company Inc 1166 Avenue of the Americas 17th Fl . . . . New York NY 10036 *TF:* 800-367-9692 ■ *Web:* www.sterlingpublishing.com	212-532-7160	213-2495	637-2
Sterling Resources Inc 6 Forest Ave. . . . Paramus NJ 07652 *Web:* sterlingnet.com	201-843-6444		177
Sterling State Park 2800 State Park Rd . . . . Monroe MI 48162 *Web:* www.michigan.org	734-289-2715		565
Sterling Stores 1305 1st Ave SW . . . . Austin MN 55912 *TF:* 800-803-1503 ■ *Web:* www.astrupdrug.com	507-433-4586	433-7003	238
Sterling Systems & Controls Inc 24711 Emerson Rd. . . . Sterling IL 61081 *Web:* www.sterlingcontrols.com	815-625-0852	625-3103	253
Sterling Technologies Inc 10047 Keystone Dr. . . . Lake City PA 16423 *Web:* www.sterlingrotationalmolding.com	814-774-2500		596
Sterling Water Inc 1928 Truax Blvd . . . . Eau Claire WI 54703 *Web:* culliganh2o.com	715-834-9431		366
Sterling-Clark-Lurton Corp PO Box 130. . . . Norwood MA 02062 *TF:* 800-225-9872 ■ *Web:* www.savogran.com	781-762-5400	762-1095	550
Sterling-Rice Group, The (SRG) 1801 13th St Ste 400 . . . . Boulder CO 80302 *Web:* www.srg.com	303-381-6400		4
Sterlite Software USA Inc 1117 Lake St. . . . Oak Park IL 60301 *TF:* 866-506-5040 ■ *Web:* sterliteusa.com	708-383-4003	383-4898	196
Stern & Stern Industries Inc 188 Thacher St PO Box 556 . . . . Hornell NY 14843 *TF:* 800-664-7415 ■ *Web:* www.sternandstern.com	607-324-4485		745-3
Stern Adv Inc 950 Main Ave . . . . Cleveland OH 44113 *Web:* www.sternadvertising.com	216-331-5827		4
Stern Brothers & Co 8000 Maryland Ave Ste 800 . . . . Saint Louis MO 63105 *Web:* sternbrothers.com	314-727-5519		690
Stern Group Inc, The 3314 Ross Pl NW . . . . Washington DC 20008 *Web:* www.sterngroup.biz	202-966-7894		463
Stern Oil Company Inc *Stern Co* PO Box 218. . . . Freeman SD 57029 *TF:* 800-477-2744 ■ *Web:* www.sternoil.com	605-925-7999	925-4367	579
Sterngold Dental LLC 23 Frank Mossberg Dr . . . . Attleboro MA 02703 *TF:* 800-531-2685 ■ *Web:* www.sterngold.com	508-226-5660		228
Stertil-Koni USA Inc 200 Log Canoe Cir . . . . Stevensville MD 21666 *TF:* 800-336-6637 ■ *Web:* stertil-koni.com	410-643-9001		194
Stetron International Inc 90 Broadway. . . . Buffalo NY 14203 *Web:* www.stetron.com	716-854-3443	854-3448	253
Stetson Convention Services Inc 2900 Stayton St . . . . Pittsburgh PA 15212 *Web:* www.stetsonexpo.com	412-223-1090	223-1094	205
Stetson University 421 N Woodland Blvd Unit 8378 . . . . DeLand FL 32723 *TF:* 800-688-0101 ■ *Web:* www.stetson.edu	386-822-7100	822-7112	166
Steube W. Gregory (Rep R - FL) 521 Cannon House Office Bldg. . . . Washington DC 20515 *Web:* www.steube.house.gov	202-225-5792		342-2
Steuben County 317 S Wayne St. . . . Angola IN 46703 *Web:* www.co.steuben.in.us	260-668-1000	668-3702	338
Steuben County 155 Dennis Ave. . . . Bath NY 14810 *Web:* steubencony.org	607-664-2563		338
Steuben County Chamber of Commerce 47 Liberty St PO Box 488 . . . . Bath NY 14810 *Web:* www.centralsteubenchamber.com	607-776-7122		139
Steuben County Rural Electric Membership Corp 1212 S Wayne St . . . . Angola IN 46703 *TF:* 888-233-9088 ■ *Web:* www.remcsteuben.com	260-665-3563	665-7495	245
Steuben County Tourism Bureau 430 N Wayne St Ste 1B. . . . Angola IN 46703 *TF:* 888-665-5668 ■ *Web:* www.lakes101.org	260-665-5386		206
Steuben Courier-Advocate 10 W Stueben St . . . . Bath NY 14810 *Web:* www.steubencourier.com	607-776-2121		532-2
Steuben House State Historic Site 1209 Main St . . . . River Edge NJ 07661 *Web:* www.njparksandforests.org	201-487-1739		565
Steuben Memorial State Historic Site 9941 Starr Hill Rd. . . . Remsen NY 13438 *Web:* parks.ny.gov	315-338-7730		565
Steuben Rural Electric Co-opeartive Inc 9 Wilson Ave. . . . Bath NY 14810 *TF:* 800-843-3414 ■ *Web:* www.steubenrec.coop	607-776-4161		245
Steve & Cookies By the Bay 9700 Amherst Ave. . . . Margate NJ 08402 *Web:* www.steveandcookies.com	609-823-1163		671
Steve Chance Attorney At Law PC 119 N Commercial Ste 175. . . . Bellingham WA 98225 *Web:* chancelaw.com	360-676-9700		41
Steve De Namur 123 N Stevens St . . . . Rhinelander WI 54501 *Web:* stevedenamur.com	715-369-4785		390
Steve Fields Steak & Lobster Lounge 5013 W Pk Blvd . . . . Plano TX 75093 *Web:* www.stevefields.com	972-596-7100	599-3950	671
Steve Foley Cadillac 100 Skokie Blvd . . . . Northbrook IL 60062 *TF:* 877-223-9671 ■ *Web:* www.foleycadillac.com	866-664-4037		126
Steve Hopkins Inc 2499 Auto Mall Pkwy . . . . Fairfield CA 94533 *TF:* 877-873-3913 ■ *Web:* www.hopkinsautogroup.com	707-427-1000		516
Steve Karas and Associates 3341 E Turquoise Ave. . . . Phoenix AZ 85028 *Web:* www.stevekaras.com	602-494-9090		179
Steve Landers Toyota 10825 Colonel Glenn Rd . . . . Little Rock AR 72204 *TF:* 866-584-3844 ■ *Web:* stevelanderstoyota.com	866-584-3844		516
Steve Millen Sportparts Inc 3176 Airway Ave. . . . Costa Mesa CA 92626 *TF:* 866-250-5542 ■ *Web:* www.stillen.com	866-250-5542		60
Steve P. Rados Inc 2002 E McFadden Ave Ste 200. . . . Santa Ana CA 92705 *Web:* www.radoscompanies.com	714-835-4612	835-2186	188-4
Steve Rotfeld Productions Inc 740 E Haverford Rd. . . . Bryn Mawr PA 19010 *Web:* www.rotfeldproductions.com	610-520-0671	520-0681	514
Steve Smith Autosports (SSA) 239 S Glassell St . . . . Orange CA 92866 *Web:* www.ssapubl.com	714-639-7681	639-9741	637-2
Steve Weiss Music Inc 2324 Wyandotte Rd . . . . Willow Grove PA 19090 *TF:* 888-659-3477 ■ *Web:* steveweissmusic.com	215-659-0100	659-1170	526
Steve's Music 150 Ste-Catherine St E. . . . Montreal QC H2X1K9 *TF:* 877-978-3837 ■ *Web:* www.stevesmusic.com	514-878-2216		526
Steve's Original Furs Inc 150 W 30th. . . . New York NY 10001 *Web:* stevesoriginalfurs.com	212-967-8007	967-3871	155-7
Steven Barclay Agency 12 Western Ave . . . . Petaluma CA 94952 *TF:* 888-965-7323 ■ *Web:* www.barclayagency.com	707-773-0654	778-1868	708
Steven Brian Davis Law Offices 12396 World Trade Dr Ste 115 . . . . San Diego CA 92128 *Web:* needattorney.org	858-451-1004		428
Steven Engineering Inc 230 Ryan Way. . . . South San Francisco CA 94080 **Fax Area Code:* 888 ■ *TF:* 800-258-9200 ■ *Web:* www.stevenengineering.com	650-588-9200	258-9200*	246
Steven F. O'Donnell Inc 6724 Binder Ln. . . . Elkridge MD 21075 *TF:* 855-646-5475 ■ *Web:* odonnellmetaldeck.com	410-796-7968		492
Steven F. Thurn 2134 Nicholasville Rd Ste 2 . . . . Lexington KY 40503 *Web:* www.thurn.us	859-276-3782		2
Steven L. Breit 36 E King St . . . . Lancaster PA 17602 *Web:* stevenbreit.com	717-393-7511	393-7835	41

Name / Address	City	State	ZIP	Phone	Fax	Class
Steven Label Corp 11926 Burke St. *TF:* 800-752-4968 ■ *Web:* www.stevenlabel.com	Santa Fe Springs	CA	90670	800-752-4968		627
Steven M Stell CPA PLLC 300 E Kingston Ave Ste 200 *Web:* stellcpa.com	Charlotte	NC	28203	704-631-2000	358-9455	2
Steven M. Berkson CPA 5550 Topanga Cyn Blvd Ste 350 *Web:* berkson.net	Woodland Hills	CA	91367	818-449-3122		2
Steven N. Goudsouzian LLC 2925 William Penn Hwy Ste 301 *Web:* sng-law.com	Easton	PA	18045	610-253-9171	559-9281	41
Steven P. Brendemuehl 5 Commonwealth Rd *Web:* nationalsocialsecuritylawyer.com	Natick	MA	01760	508-651-1013		41
Steven Papageorge Hair Academy 1113-15 W Belmont 2nd Fl *Web:* www.stevenpapageorgehairacademy.com	Chicago	IL	60657	773-561-2376	883-5109	167-3
Steven Restivo Event Services LLC 805 Fourth St Ste 8 *TF:* 800-310-6563 ■ *Web:* www.sresproductions.com	San Rafael	CA	94901	415-456-6455		184
Steven Schaefer Associates Inc 10411 Medallion Dr *TF:* 800-542-3302 ■ *Web:* schaefer-inc.com	Cincinnati	OH	45241	513-542-3300		261
Steven's Hope for Children Inc 1014 W Foothill Blvd Ste B *Web:* stevenshope.org	Upland	CA	91786	909-373-0678	981-4578	372
Stevens & Lee 111 N Sixth St *Web:* www.stevenslee.com	Reading	PA	19601	610-478-2000	376-5610	428
Stevens & Tate Marketing 1900 S Highland Ave Ste 200 *Web:* stevens-tate.com	Lombard	IL	60148	630-627-5200		195
Stevens Appliance Truck Co PO Box 897 *TF:* 888-463-8757 ■ *Web:* www.stevensmfg.com	Augusta	GA	30903	706-798-8535	798-4511	470
Stevens Aviation Inc 600 Delaware St *TF:* 800-359-7838 ■ *Web:* www.stevensaviation.com	Greenville	SC	29605	800-359-7838		63
Stevens Baron Communications Inc 28025 Clemens Rd Ste 4 *Web:* www.stevensstrategic.com	Westlake	OH	44145	440-617-0100		4
Stevens Business Service Inc 92 Bolt St Ste 1 *TF:* 800-769-0375 ■ *Web:* www.sbs4money.com	Lowell	MA	01852	978-458-2500		160
Stevens Capital Management LP 201 King of Prussia Rd Ste 400 *Web:* www.scm-lp.com	Radnor	PA	19087	610-971-5000		401
Stevens Communications Inc 11 S LaSalle St *Web:* www.stevenscom.com	Chicago	IL	60603	312-895-5200		246
Stevens Company Inc 1085 Waterbury Rd *Web:* www.stevenscompanyinc.com	Thomaston	CT	06787	860-283-8201	283-9304	488
Stevens Construction Corp 2 Buttonwood Crt *Web:* www.stevensconstruction.com	Madison	WI	53718	608-222-5100	222-5930	186
Stevens County 215 S Oak St *TF:* 800-833-6388 ■ *Web:* www.co.stevens.wa.us	Colville	WA	99114	509-684-3751	684-8310	338
Stevens County 217 N Kansas Ave *Web:* www.stevenscoks.org	Hugoton	KS	67951	620-544-2541	544-4094	338
Stevens County 400 Colorado Ave Ste 104 *Web:* www.co.stevens.mn.us	Morris	MN	56267	320-208-6600	589-3972	338
Stevens Creek Software PO Box 2126 *TF:* 800-823-4279 ■ *Web:* www.stevenscreek.com	Cupertino	CA	95015	408-725-0424	366-1954	178-9
Stevens Group 188 Industrial Dr Ste 428 *Web:* stevensgroupweb.com	Elmhurst	IL	60126	331-209-2100		7
Stevens Haley (Rep D - MI) 227 Cannon House Office Bldg *Web:* www.stevens.house.gov	Washington	DC	20515	202-225-8171		342-2
Stevens Henager College 1890 S 1350 W *TF:* 800-622-2640 ■ *Web:* www.stevenshenager.edu	Ogden	UT	84401	800-622-2640		162
Stevens Industries Inc 704 W Main St *Web:* www.stevensind.com	Teutopolis	IL	62467	217-540-3100	857-7101	286
Stevens Institute of Technology Castle Pt on the Hudson *TF:* 800-458-5323 ■ *Web:* www.stevens.edu	Hoboken	NJ	07030	201-216-5194	216-8348	166
Stevens Instrument Co 111 W Greenwood Ave *Web:* www.stevensinstrument.com	Waukegan	IL	60087	847-336-9375		248
Stevens Manufacturing Company Inc 220 Rock Ln *Web:* www.stevensmfgco.com	Milford	CT	06460	203-878-2328		22
Stevens Marine Inc 9180 SW Burnham St *TF:* 800-225-7023 ■ *Web:* www.stevensmarine.com	Tigard	OR	97223	503-620-7023		90
Stevens Pass Mountain Resort LLC Summit Stevens Pass US Hwy 2 *Web:* www.stevenspass.com	Skykomish	WA	98288	206-812-4510		378
Stevens Point Area Convention & Visitors Bureau 340 Division St N *Web:* www.stevenspointarea.com	Stevens Point	WI	54481	715-344-2556	344-5818	206
Stevens Sausage Company Inc 3411 Stevens Sausage Rd *TF:* 800-338-0561 ■ *Web:* stevens-sausage.com	Smithfield	NC	27577	919-934-3159		619
Stevens Technology LLC 4205 Stadium Dr Ste 300 *Web:* www.stevenstechnology.com	Fort Worth	TX	76133	817-831-3500	759-4080	629
Stevens Towing Company Inc 4170 Hwy 165 *TF:* 800-868-6946 ■ *Web:* www.stevens-towing.com	Yonges Island	SC	29449	843-889-2254	889-6119	313
Stevens Transport PO Box 279010 **Fax Area Code:* 214 ■ *TF:* 800-233-9369 ■ *Web:* www.stevenstransport.com	Dallas	TX	75227	800-333-8595	647-3940*	780
Stevens Water Monitoring Systems 12067 NE Glenn Widing Dr Ste 106 *TF:* 800-452-5272 ■ *Web:* www.stevenswater.com	Portland	OR	97220	503-445-8000	469-8100	544
Stevens Wire Products Inc 351 NW 'F' St *Web:* www.stevenswire.com	Richmond	IN	47374	765-966-5534	962-3586	73
Stevens Worldwide Van Lines 527 W Morley Dr **Fax Area Code:* 989 ■ *TF:* 877-490-0713 ■ *Web:* stevensworldwide.com	Saginaw	MI	48601	800-678-3836	755-3000*	519
Stevenson & Vestal 2347 W Hanford Rd *TF:* 800-535-3636 ■ *Web:* www.stevensonvestal.com	Burlington	NC	27215	800-535-3636		195
Stevenson Advertising 19231 36th Ave W B-202 *Web:* www.stevensonadvertising.com	Lynnwood	WA	98036	425-787-9686		7
Stevenson Co, The 10002 Shelbyville Rd Ste 201 *Web:* stevensoncompany.com	Louisville	KY	40223	502-271-5250		668
Stevenson Correctional Institution 4546 Broad River Rd *Web:* doc.sc.gov	Columbia	SC	29210	803-896-8575		213
Stevenson House Detention Ctr 750 N Dupont Hwy *Web:* www.kids.delaware.gov	Milford	DE	19963	302-424-8100		412
Stevenson Jones & Holmaas PC 5920 E Pima Ste 170	Tucson	AZ	85712	520-886-5495		2
Stevenson Lumber 501 Division St.	Adrian	MI	49221	517-265-5151	265-5534	191-3
Stevenson School 3152 Forest Lake Rd *Web:* www.stevensonschool.org	Pebble Beach	CA	93953	831-625-8300	625-5208	622
Stevenson Systems Inc 27822 El Lazo 100 *Web:* stevensonsystems.com	Laguna Niguel	CA	92677	949-297-4200		463
Stevenson University Archives & Special Collections 1525 Greenspring Valley Rd *Web:* www.stevenson.libguides.com	Stevenson	MD	21153	443-334-2233		167-3
Steves & Sons Inc 203 Humble Ave *Web:* www.stevesdoors.com	San Antonio	TX	78225	210-924-5111		236
Steves Homestead Museum 107 King William St *Web:* www.saconservation.org	San Antonio	TX	78204	210-224-6163		520
Stevison Ham Co *Stevison Meat Co* 125 Stevison Ham Rd PO Box 219 *Web:* www.tennesseetraditions.com	Portland	TN	37148	615-325-4161	325-5914	296-26
Stew Hansen Dodge Ram Chrysler Jeep 12103 Hickman Rd *TF:* 877-841-4585 ■ *Web:* www.stewhansens.com	Urbandale	IA	50323	877-841-4585		57
Stew Leonard's 100 Westport Ave *Web:* www.stewleonards.com	Norwalk	CT	06851	203-847-7214		336
Steward Health Care (TSLH) *Tempe Saint Luke's Hospital* 1500 S Mill Ave *TF:* 877-351-9355 ■ *Web:* www.tempestlukeshospital.org	Tempe	AZ	85281	480-784-5500		374-3
Steward Health Care System 1900 N Pearl St Ste 2400 *Web:* www.steward.org	Dallas	TX	75201	469-341-8800		353
Steward Machine Company Inc 3911 13th Ave N *Web:* stewardmachine.com	Birmingham	AL	35234	205-841-6461	849-8029	454
Steward Steel Inc 1219 E US Hwy 62 PO Box 551 *Web:* www.stewardsteel.com	Sikeston	MO	63801	573-471-2121	471-2336	492
Stewart & Associates Inc 50 W Douglas St Ste 1200 *Web:* www.bwstewart.com	Freeport	IL	61032	815-235-3807		400
Stewart & Patten Company LLC 1 Post St Ste 850 *Web:* www.stewartandpatten.com	San Francisco	CA	94104	415-421-4932		528
Stewart & Stevenson LLC 1000 Louisiana St *Web:* www.stewartandstevenson.com	Houston	TX	77002	713-613-0633		537
Stewart Agency Inc 2205 College Ave *TF:* 877-734-6527 ■ *Web:* stewartagency.com	Elmira	NY	14903	607-734-6527		390
Stewart Amos Steel Inc 4400 Paxton St *Web:* www.stewart-amos.com	Harrisburg	PA	17111	717-564-3931		492
Stewart Assembly & Machining 7234 Blue Ash Rd *Web:* www.stewartindustries.com	Cincinnati	OH	45236	513-891-9000	891-0449	454
Stewart Business Systems LLC 105 Connecticut Dr *TF:* 800-322-5584 ■ *Web:* www.stewartxerox.com	Burlington	NJ	08016	800-322-5584		45
Stewart Chris (Rep R - UT) 2242 Rayburn House Office Bldg *Web:* stewart.house.gov	Washington	DC	20515	202-225-9730		342-2
Stewart Consulting LLC 909 5th Ave Ste 1200 *Web:* www.stewcon.com	Seattle	WA	98164	206-682-5700		194
Stewart County 225 Donelson Pkwy 1st Fl PO Box 67 *Web:* stewartcogov.com	Dover	TN	37058	931-232-7616	232-4934	338
Stewart County Commission, The 552 Martin Luther King Junior Dr *Web:* www.stewartcountyga.gov	Lumpkin	GA	31815	229-838-6769		338
Stewart Directories Inc 50314 Kings Point Dr PO Box 326 **Fax Area Code:* 443 ■ *TF:* 800-311-0786 ■ *Web:* www.stewartdirectories.com	Frisco	NC	27936	800-311-0786	901-7570*	637-6
Stewart EFI LLC 45 Old Waterbury Rd *TF:* 800-393-5387 ■ *Web:* www.stewartefi.com	Thomaston	CT	06787	860-283-8213		489
Stewart Engineering Supply Inc 3221 E Pioneer Pkwy *Web:* sesisupply.com	Arlington	TX	76010	817-640-1767		112
Stewart Filmscreen Corp 1161 W Sepulveda Blvd *TF:* 800-762-4999 ■ *Web:* stewartfilmscreen.com	Torrance	CA	90502	310-784-5300	326-6870	591
Stewart Graphics Inc 1419 Fabricon Blvd *Web:* www.voluforms.com	Jeffersonville	IN	47130	812-283-0455	283-1346	534
Stewart Group Inc, The PO Box 28091 *Web:* www.stewartgrouponline.com	Raleigh	NC	27611	919-828-6455	828-4922	194
Stewart Industries Inc 16 S Idaho St *Web:* stewartindustries.net	Seattle	WA	98134	206-652-9110		602

Name / Address	City	State	ZIP	Phone	Fax	Class
Stewart Information Services Corp 1980 Post Oak Blvd Ste 800 *NYSE:* STC ■ *TF:* 800-729-1900 ■ *Web:* www.stewart.com	Houston	TX	77056	713-625-8100		391-6
Stewart Law Group PL 160 International Pkwy Ste 120 *Web:* stewartlaw.net	Altamonte Springs	FL	32714	407-324-1860		41
Stewart Manufacturing LLC N16415 Earle Dr *Web:* www.stewart-mfg.com	Hermansville	MI	49847	906-498-7600		454
Stewart Materials 2875 Jupiter Park Dr Ste 1100 *Web:* stewartmaterials.com	Jupiter	FL	33458	561-972-4517		501
Stewart School 604 NW Ave *TF:* 800-537-2625 ■ *Web:* stewartschool.com	Sioux Falls	SD	57104	605-336-2775		77
Stewart Sokol & Gray LLC 2300 SW 1st Ave Ste 200 *Web:* lawssl.com	Portland	OR	97201	503-221-0699		428
Stewart Surfboards 2102 S El Camino Real *Web:* www.stewartsurfboards.com	San Clemente	CA	92672	949-492-1085		710
Stewart Sutherland Inc 5411 E 'V' Ave *Web:* www.ssbags.com	Vicksburg	MI	49097	269-649-5423	649-3961	65
Stewart Systems 808 Stewart Ave *TF:* 800-966-5808 ■ *Web:* www.stewart-systems.com	Plano	TX	75074	972-422-5808	509-8734	207
Stewart Title Co 3800 N Central Ave Ste 460 *Web:* www.stewartaz.com	Phoenix	AZ	85012	602-462-8000		391-6
Stewart Wald & Mcculley LLC 2100 Central Ste 22 *Web:* swm.legal	Kansas City	MO	64108	816-303-1500		41
Stewart's International School for Jewelers Inc 651 W Indiantown Rd *TF:* 800-843-3409 ■ *Web:* www.stewartsintlschool.com	Jupiter	FL	33458	561-746-7586	746-8420	685
Stewart's Shops PO Box 435 *Web:* www.stewartsshops.com	Saratoga Springs	NY	12866	518-581-1201		381
Stewart, Kizzar & Brockelbank LLC 2520 Northwinds Pkwy Ste 285 *Web:* skbcpas.com	Alpharetta	GA	30009	770-752-4646		2
Stewart-haas Racing LLC 6001 Haas Way *Web:* www.stewarthaasracing.com	Kannapolis	NC	28081	704-652-4227		642
Stewarts Private Blend Food Inc 4110 W Wrightwood Ave *Web:* www.stewarts.com	Chicago	IL	60639	773-489-2500	489-2148	296-7
STFM (Society of Teachers of Family Medicine) 11400 Tomahawk Creek Pkwy Ste 240 **Fax Area Code:* 913 ■ *TF:* 800-274-7928 ■ *Web:* www.stfm.org	Leawood	KS	66211	800-274-7928	906-6096*	49-8
STG (Symphony Technology Group LLC) 428 University Ave *Web:* www.stgpartners.com	Palo Alto	CA	94301	650-935-9500		178-11
STG International Inc 4900 Seminary Rd Ste 1100 *TF:* 855-507-0660 ■ *Web:* www.stginternational.com	Alexandria	VA	22311	703-578-6030	578-4474	180
STHA (Stanton Territorial Health Authority) 550 Byrne Rd PO Box 10 *Web:* www.nthssa.ca	Yellowknife	NT	X1A2N1	867-669-4111	669-4128	374-2
STI (Superconductor Technologies Inc) 460 Ward Dr *NASDAQ:* SCON ■ *Web:* www.suptech.com	Santa Barbara	CA	93111	805-690-4500	967-0342	253
STI Computer Services Inc 2700 Van Buren Ave *TF:* 800-487-9135 ■ *Web:* sticomputer.com	Eagleville	PA	19403	610-650-9700	650-9272	180
STI Electronics Inc 261 Palmer Rd *TF:* 888-650-3006 ■ *Web:* stiusa.com	Madison	AL	35758	256-461-9191		386
STI International Inc 114 Halmar Cove *Web:* stiguns.com	Georgetown	TX	78628	512-819-0656		711
STI Optronics Inc 2755 Northup Way *Web:* www.stioptronics.com	Bellevue	WA	98004	425-827-0460	828-3517	425
STI Polymer Inc 5618 Clyde Rhyne Dr *TF:* 800-874-5878 ■ *Web:* stipolymer.com	Sanford	NC	27330	800-874-5878		3
Stibo Systems Inc 3550 George Busbee Pkwy NW Ste 350 *Web:* www.stibosystems.com	Kennesaw	GA	30144	770-425-3282		387
Stic-Adhesive Products Company Inc 3950 Medford St *TF:* 800-854-6813 ■ *Web:* www.sticadhesive.com	Los Angeles	CA	90063	323-268-2956		326
Stichter, Riedel, Blain & Prosser PA 110 E Madison St Ste 200 *Web:* www.srbp.com	Tampa	FL	33602	813-229-0144		428
Stickers Asian Cafe 6808 SE Milwaukie Ave *Web:* stickersasiancafe.com	Portland	OR	97202	503-239-8739		671
Stickkcom LLC 109 S Fifth St *TF:* 866-578-4255 ■ *Web:* www.stickk.com	Brooklyn	NY	11249	347-394-4964		387
Stickle Steam Specialties Company Inc 2215 Valley Ave *Web:* www.sticklesteam.com	Indianapolis	IN	46218	317-636-6563		821
Sticky Fingers 235 Meeting St *Web:* www.stickyfingers.com	Charleston	SC	29401	843-853-7427		671
Sticky Rice 2232 W Main St *Web:* ilovestickyrice.com	Richmond	VA	23220	804-358-7870		671
Stidham & Associates PSC 401 Lewis Hargett Cir Ste 250 *Web:* www.stidhamlaw.com	Lexington	KY	40503	859-219-2255	219-3395	428
Stidham Trucking Inc 321 Payne Ln PO Box 308 *TF:* 800-827-9500 ■ *Web:* www.stidhamtrucking.com	Yreka	CA	96097	530-842-4161		186
Stieg & Associates Insurance Inc 3319 Gabel Rd *Web:* stieginsurance.com	Billings	MT	59102	406-656-9666		390
Stieglitz Snyder Architecture 425 Franklin St *Web:* stieglitzsnyder.com	Buffalo	NY	14202	716-828-9166		463
Stiehl Communications W5361 County Rd Kk Ste A *Web:* www.stiehlcommunications.com	Appleton	WI	54915	920-830-1116	830-7677	179
Stiern's Veterinary Hospital 17 Monterey St *Web:* stswvets.com	Bakersfield	CA	93305	661-327-5571		794
Stifel Bank 8000 Maryland Ave Ste 100 *TF:* 866-303-8003 ■ *Web:* bankwithstifel.com	Saint Louis	MO	63105	314-721-8003	621-0446	70
Stifel Financial Corp 501 N Broadway *NYSE:* SF ■ *TF:* 800-679-5446 ■ *Web:* www.stifel.com	Saint Louis	MO	63102	800-679-5446		690
Stiff, Keith & Garcia LLC 400 Gold Ave SW Ste 1300W *Web:* stifflaw.com	Albuquerque	NM	87102	505-243-5755		41
Stihl Inc 536 Viking Dr **Fax Area Code:* 303 ■ *TF:* 800-467-8445 ■ *Web:* www.stihlusa.com	Virginia Beach	VA	23452	757-486-9100	340-0377*	759
Stikeman Elliott LLP 1155 Rene-Levesque Blvd W 40th Fl *Web:* www.stikeman.com	Montreal	QC	H3B3V2	514-397-3000		428
Stiles Corp 301 E Las Olas Blvd *Web:* www.stiles.com	Fort Lauderdale	FL	33301	954-627-9300	627-9288	653
Stiles Ewing Powers PC 3957 Westerre Pkwy Ste 400 *Web:* bsbfamilylaw.com	Richmond	VA	23233	804-545-9800	545-9805	41
Still Harbor PO Box 1478 *Web:* www.stillharbor.org	Arlington	MA	02474	617-682-0259		637-9
Still Transfer Company Inc 632 Boone St *TF:* 800-346-6837 ■ *Web:* www.stilltransfer.net	Kingsport	TN	37660	423-245-4000		780
Stillman Banccorp NA PO Box 150 *Web:* www.stillmanbank.com	Stillman Valley	IL	61084	815-645-2000	645-2341	70
Stillman College 3601 Stillman Blvd *TF:* 800-841-5722 ■ *Web:* www.stillman.edu	Tuscaloosa	AL	35401	205-349-4240		166
Stillman Development International LLC 505 Park Ave Ste 1700 *Web:* www.stillmandevelopment.com	New York	NY	10022	212-686-2400		378
Stillman House & Museum 1325 E Washington St *Web:* www.brownsvillehistory.org	Brownsville	TX	78520	956-541-5560		520
Stillmeadow Inc 12852 Park One Dr *Web:* www.stillmeadow.com	Sugar Land	TX	77478	281-240-8828	240-8448	196
Stillwater Chamber of Commerce 409 S Main St *TF:* 800-593-5573 ■ *Web:* www.stillwaterchamber.org	Stillwater	OK	74075	405-372-5573	372-4316	139
Stillwater County 400 Third Ave N *TF:* 888-706-1535 ■ *Web:* www.stillwatercountymt.gov	Columbus	MT	59019	406-322-8000	322-8007	338
Stillwater Medical Ctr 1323 W Sixth St *Web:* www.stillwater-medical.org	Stillwater	OK	74074	405-372-1480		374-3
Stillwater Motor Co 5900 Stillwater Blvd N *Web:* www.stillwatermotors.com	Stillwater	MN	55082	651-323-2245		57
Stillwater Public Library 1107 S Duck St *Web:* ibrary.stillwater.org	Stillwater	OK	74074	405-372-3633	624-0552	434-3
Stillwater Technologies Inc 1040 S Dorset *TF:* 800-338-7561 ■ *Web:* www.stlwtr.com	Troy	OH	45373	937-440-2500		454
Stillwater Utilities Authority 723 S Lewis St PO Box 1449 *Web:* www.stillwater.org	Stillwater	OK	74076	405-372-0025	742-8352	245
StillWaters Resort 797 Moonbrook Dr *Web:* stillwatersgolf.com	Dadeville	AL	36853	256-825-1353		669
Stillwell Hansen Inc 3 Fernwood Ave *Web:* www.stillwell-hansen.com	Edison	NJ	08837	732-225-7474	225-7872	610
Stillwell Law Office 1590 S Coast Hwy Ste 8 *Web:* thestillwelllawoffice.com	Laguna Beach	CA	92651	949-541-2731		41
Stilson Products 15935 Sturgeon St *TF:* 888-400-5978 ■ *Web:* www.stilsonproducts.com	Roseville	MI	48066	586-778-1100	778-4660	493
Stimmel Associates PA 601 N Trade St Ste 200 *Web:* www.stimmelpa.com	Winston-Salem	NC	27101	336-723-1067	723-1069	261
Stimple & Ward Co 3400 Babcock Blvd *TF:* 800-792-6457 ■ *Web:* www.swcoils.com	Pittsburgh	PA	15237	412-364-5200	364-5299	518
Stimson Lumber Co 520 SW Yamhill St Ste 700 *TF:* 800-445-9758 ■ *Web:* www.stimsonlumber.com	Portland	OR	97204	503-701-6510		683
Stimwave Technologies Inc 1310 Park Central Blvd S *TF:* 800-965-5134 ■ *Web:* stimwave.com	Pompano Beach	FL	33064	786-565-3342		743
Stinar Corp 3255 Sibley Memorial Hwy *Web:* stinar.com	Eagan	MN	55121	651-454-5112		579
Stinnett & Associates LLC 8811 S Yale Ave Ste 300 *TF:* 888-808-1795 ■ *Web:* www.stinnett-associates.com	Tulsa	OK	74137	888-808-1795	808-4111	2
Stinson, Lasswell & Wilson LC 200 W Douglas Ave Ste 100 *Web:* slwlc.com	Wichita	KS	67202	316-264-9137		41
Stipes Publishing LLC 204 W University Ave *Web:* www.stipes.com	Champaign	IL	61820	217-356-8391	356-5753	637-2
STIR Advertising & Integrated Messaging 330 E Kilbourn Ave Ste 222 *Web:* www.stirstuff.com	Milwaukee	WI	53202	414-278-0040		5
Stirling Properties 109 Northpark Blvd Ste 300 *Web:* www.stirlingprop.com	Covington	LA	70433	985-898-2022	898-2077	655
Stirna's Restaurant 120 W Market St *Web:* stirnas.com	Scranton	PA	18508	570-961-9681		671
Stivers Staffing Services Inc 200 W Monroe St Ste 1300 *Web:* www.stivers.com	Chicago	IL	60606	312-558-3550	558-1007	721
Stivers Steve (Rep R - OH) 2234 Rayburn House Office Bldg *Web:* www.stivers.house.gov	Washington	DC	20515	202-225-2015	225-3529	342-2

Name / Address	City	State	ZIP	Phone	Fax	Class
STIX 3250 Galleria Cir *Web:* stixonline.com	Hoover	AL	35244	205-982-3070		671
STLCC (Saint Louis Community College) 300 S Broadway *Web:* www.stlcc.edu	Saint Louis	MO	63102	314-539-5000		162
STLE (Society of Tribologists & Lubrication Engineers) 840 Busse Hwy *Web:* www.stle.org	Park Ridge	IL	60068	847-825-5536	825-1456	49-13
STM (Swift Textile Metalizing LLC) 23 Britton Dr *Web:* www.swift-textile.com	Bloomfield	CT	06002	860-243-1122	243-0848	745-2
STM Inc 1000 Industrial Rd *Web:* www.stmplastics.com	Augusta	KS	67010	316-775-2223		604
STM Manufacturing Inc 494 E 64th St *Web:* www.stmtooling.com	Holland	MI	49423	616-392-4656	392-6015	757
STMA (Sports Turf Managers Assn) 805 New Hampshire Ste E *TF:* 800-323-3875 ■ *Web:* www.stma.org	Lawrence	KS	66044	785-843-2549	843-2977	48-22
STMicroelectronics NV 750 Canyon Dr Ste 300 *Web:* www.st.com	Coppell	TX	75019	972-466-6000	466-6001	696
STN (eMarketer Inc) 11 Times Sq *TF:* 800-405-0844 ■ *Web:* www.eMarketer.com	New York	NY	10036	212-763-6010		194
Stober Drives Inc 1781 Downing Dr *Web:* www.stoeber.de	Maysville	KY	41056	606-759-5090		620
Stock & Associates Consulting Engineers Inc 257 Chesterfield Business Pkwy *Web:* stockassoc.com	Chesterfield	MO	63005	636-530-9100		261
Stock & Option Solutions Inc 6399 San Ignacio Ave Ste 100 *TF:* 888-767-0199 ■ *Web:* www.sos-team.com	San Jose	CA	95119	408-979-8700		463
Stock America Inc 900 Cheyenne Ave Ste 700 *Web:* www.stockamerica.com	Grafton	WI	53024	919-661-1911		547
Stock Equipment Co 16490 Chillicothe Rd *TF:* 888-742-1249 ■ *Web:* www.schenckprocess.com	Chagrin Falls	OH	44023	440-543-6000	543-5944	273
Stock Exchange Bank 103 S Main PO Box 273 *Web:* stockxbank.com	Caldwell	KS	67022	620-845-6431		70
Stock Garber & Associates Inc 1368 Manor Dr *Web:* sgasoftware.com	Ebensburg	PA	15931	814-472-5158		809
Stock Seed Farms 28008 Mill Rd *TF:* 800-759-1520 ■ *Web:* www.stockseed.com	Murdock	NE	68407	402-867-3771	867-2442	694
Stock Transportation 60 Columbia Way Ste 800 *TF:* 888-952-0878 ■ *Web:* www.stocktransportation.com	Markham	ON	L3R0C9	905-940-9977		109
Stock Yards 1040 E Main St *NASDAQ: SYBT* ■ *TF:* 800-625-9066 ■ *Web:* www.syb.com	Louisville	KY	40206	502-625-1790		360-2
Stock Yards Packing Company Inc 2500 S Pacific Hwy PO Box 9100 *TF:* 888-842-6111 ■ *Web:* www.stockyards.com	Medford	OR	97501	888-842-6111	700-9919	296-26
Stockbridge Capital Partners LLC 4 Embarcadero Ctr Ste 3300 *Web:* stockbridge.com	San Francisco	CA	94111	415-658-3300		403
Stockbridge Risk Management Inc 40 Cutter Mill Rd *Web:* www.stockbridgerisk.com	Great Neck	NY	11021	516-499-5678		194
StockChartscom Inc 11241 Willows Rd Ste 140 *Web:* www.stockcharts.com	Redmond	WA	98052	425-881-2606		224
Stockell Consulting Inc 15400 S Outer Forty Ste 105 *Web:* www.stockellconsulting.com	Chesterfield	MO	63017	636-537-9100		180
Stocker Concrete Co 7574 US Rt 36 *Web:* www.stockerconcrete.com	Gnadenhutten	OH	44629	740-254-4626		182
Stocker Woods Financial Inc 2412 Old North Rd Ste 103 *Web:* stockerwoods.com	Denton	TX	76209	940-566-1212		690
Stockli Slevin LLP 1826 Western Ave *Web:* ss-legal.com	Albany	NY	12203	518-449-3125		41
Stockman Kast Ryan & Scruggs PC 102 N Cascade Ste 400 *Web:* www.skrco.com	Colorado Springs	CO	80903	719-630-1186		2
Stockman's Casino 1560 W Williams Ave *TF:* 855-423-2117 ■ *Web:* www.stockmanscasino.com	Fallon	NV	89406	855-423-2117		452
Stockmans Bank 100 Kennedy *Web:* www.stockmansbankok.com	Gould	OK	73544	580-676-3921		70
Stockmen's Livestock Market Inc 1200 E Hwy 50 PO Box 528 *Web:* www.stockmenslivestock.com	Yankton	SD	57078	605-665-9641	665-9644	446
Stockmen's Supply Inc 802 W Main Ave *TF:* 800-437-4064 ■ *Web:* www.stockmens.com	West Fargo	ND	58078	701-282-3255	282-3545	276
Stocks on Second 211 N Second St *Web:* www.stocksonsecond.com	Harrisburg	PA	17101	717-233-6699		671
Stockton Beach CPAs & Co 3355 Cerritos Ave *Web:* www.stocktonbeachcpas.com	Los Alamitos	CA	90720	562-493-3591		2
Stockton Civic Theatre (SCT) 2312 Rose Marie Ln *Web:* www.sctlivetheatre.com	Stockton	CA	95207	209-473-2400	473-1502	573-4
Stockton Endoscopy Ctr 415 E Harding Way Ste E *Web:* www.sjcms.org	Stockton	CA	95204	209-942-1179		415
Stockton Oil Co 513 1st Ave N *Web:* www.stocktonoil.com	Lewiston	MN	55952	406-245-6376	538-7268	579
Stockton Performing Arts Ctr 101 Vera King Farris Dr *Web:* www.stocktonpac.org	Galloway	NJ	08205	609-652-9000	626-5523	572
Stockton Service Station Equipment Company Inc (SSSECO) 808 N Union St *Web:* www.ssseco.com	Stockton	CA	95205	209-464-8333	464-8349	76
Stockton State Park 19100 S Hwy 215 *Web:* mostateparks.com	Dadeville	MO	65635	417-276-4259		565
Stockton Unified School District 701 N Madison St *Web:* www.stocktonusd.net	Stockton	CA	95202	209-933-7000	933-7031	685
Stockton-San Joaquin County Public Library (SSJCPL) 605 N El Dorado St *TF:* 866-805-7323 ■ *Web:* www.ssjcpl.org	Stockton	CA	95202	209-937-8416		434-3
Stockwatch 700 W Georgia St PO Box 10371 *TF:* 800-268-6397 ■ *Web:* www.stockwatch.com	Vancouver	BC	V7Y1J6	604-687-1500	687-2304	404
Stockyards Hotel 109 E Exchange Ave *TF:* 800-423-8471 ■ *Web:* www.stockyardshotel.com	Fort Worth	TX	76164	817-625-6427	624-2571	379
Stockyards Museum 131 E Exchange Ave Ste 113 *Web:* stockyardsmuseum.org	Fort Worth	TX	76164	817-625-5082		520
Stoddard Imported Cars Inc 190 Alpha Pk *TF:* 800-342-1414 ■ *Web:* www.stoddard.com	Highland Heights	OH	44143	440-869-9890	946-9410	57
Stoel Rives LLP 760 SW Ninth Ave Ste 3000 *Web:* www.stoel.com	Portland	OR	97205	503-224-3380		428
Stoelt Productions 1962 S La Cienega Blvd *Web:* www.stoeltproductions.com	Los Angeles	CA	90034	323-463-3700		226
Stoelting LLC 502 Hwy 67 *TF:* 800-558-5807 ■ *Web:* www.stoelting.com	Kiel	WI	53042	920-894-2293	894-7029	298
Stoever Glass & Company Inc 30 Wall St *TF:* 800-223-3881 ■ *Web:* www.stoeverglass.com	New York	NY	10005	212-952-1910		401
Stoffel Equipment Company Inc 7764 N 81st St *TF:* 800-354-7502 ■ *Web:* www.stoffelequip.com	Milwaukee	WI	53223	414-354-7500		358
Stohl Environmental 4169 Allendale Pkwy *Web:* www.stohlenvironmental.com	Buffalo	NY	14219	716-312-0070	312-8092	196
Stokely Memorial Library 383 E Broadway *Web:* www.sites.google.com	Newport	TN	37821	423-623-3832		434-3
Stokes & Spiehler Inc 110 Rue Jean Lafitte *Web:* www.stokesandspiehler.com	LaFayette	LA	70508	337-233-6871		539
Stokes County 1014 Main St PO Box 20 *Web:* www.co.stokes.nc.us	Danbury	NC	27016	336-593-4400	593-4401	338
Stokes Dock Co 3797 Osage Beach Pkwy Stonecrest Mall Ste F-2 *Web:* www.stokesdock.com	Osage Beach	MO	65065	573-348-2334		189-11
Stokes Electric Company Inc 1701 McCalla Ave *Web:* www.stokeselec.com	Knoxville	TN	37915	865-525-0351	971-4149	246
Stokes Honda North 8650 Rivers Ave *TF:* 877-622-1672 ■ *Web:* www.stokeshondanorth.com	North Charleston	SC	29406	877-622-1672		57
Stokes State Forest 1 Coursen Rd *Web:* www.njparksandforests.org	Branchville	NJ	07826	973-948-3820		565
Stokes Visca & Company LLP 29 Goodway Dr *Web:* svcpas.com	Rochester	NY	14623	585-427-0850	427-2394	2
Stokes, Hamer,Kirk & Eads LLP 381 Bayside Rd Ste A *Web:* shkklaw.com	Arcata	CA	95521	707-822-1771		41
Stoll Brother True Value Lumber 509 S E St *Web:* www.truevalue.com	Odon	IN	47562	812-636-4053		613
Stoll Keenon Ogden PLLC (SKO) 300 W Vine St Ste 2100 *Web:* www.skofirm.com	Lexington	KY	40507	859-231-3000	253-1093	41
Stoll Metalcraft Inc 24808 Anza Dr *Web:* www.stoll-metalcraft.com	Valencia	CA	91355	661-295-0401		697
Stoll Stoll Berne Lokting & Shlachter PC 209 SW Oak St Ste 500 *Web:* www.stollberne.com	Portland	OR	97204	503-227-1600		428
Stoll's Pharmacy 185 Grove St *Web:* www.stollspharmacy.com	Waterbury	CT	06710	203-575-0199		237
Stolle Machinery Company LLC 6949 S Potomac St *Web:* www.stollemachinery.com	Centennial	CO	80112	303-708-9044	708-9045	547
Stoller International Inc 15521 E 1830 N Rd *Web:* www.stollerih.com	Pontiac	IL	61764	815-844-6197		274
Stoller USA 4001 W Sam Houston Pkwy N Ste 100 *TF:* 800-539-5283 ■ *Web:* www.stollerusa.com	Houston	TX	77043	713-461-1493	461-4467	280
Stoltz Marketing Group 101 S Capitol Blvd Ste 900 *Web:* www.stoltzgroup.com	Boise	ID	83702	208-388-0766		5
Stoltzfus RV's & Marine 1335 Wilmington Pk *TF:* 866-755-8858 ■ *Web:* www.stoltzfus-rec.com	West Chester	PA	19382	866-755-8858		90
Stolz & Associates PS 3102 Ruston Way Ste A *Web:* stolzassoc.com	Tacoma	WA	98402	253-272-3441		2
Stolze Printing 3435 Hollenberg Dr *Web:* www.stolze.com	Bridgeton	MO	63044	314-209-1997	209-1097	627
Stone & Company LLC 57 Bedford St *Web:* www.stonecpas.com	Lexington	MA	02420	781-862-5000	862-6736	2
Stone & Ward Inc 225 E Markham St *Web:* www.stoneward.com	Little Rock	AR	72201	501-375-3003		4
Stone Academy 101 Pierpont Rd *TF:* 800-585-1315 ■ *Web:* www.stone.edu	Waterbury	CT	06705	203-756-5500	596-1455	167-3
Stone Belt Freight Lines Inc 101 W Dillman Rd *TF:* 800-264-2340 ■ *Web:* www.stonebeltfreight.com	Bloomington	IN	47403	812-824-6741		314
Stone Bond Technologies LP 1021 Main St Ste 1550 *Web:* stonebond.com	Houston	TX	77002	713-622-8798		177
Stone Castle Hotel & Conference Ctr, The 3050 Green Mtn Dr *TF:* 800-677-6906 ■ *Web:* bransonstonecastle.com	Branson	MO	65616	417-335-4700		379

Phone | Fax | Class

Stone Center Fredericksburg
8241 Jefferson Davis Hwy ... Fredericksburg VA 22407 540-891-7866 330-7729* 653
Fax Area Code: 703 ■ *Web:* stonecenterofva.com

Stone Child College
8294 Upper Box Elder Rd ... Box Elder MT 59521 406-395-4875 395-4836 165
Web: www.stonechild.edu

Stone City Attractions Inc
13300 Old Blanco Rd Ste 283 ... San Antonio TX 78216 210-493-3900 493-3903 226
Web: www.stonecityattractions.com

Stone Coast Fund Services LLC
2 Portland Sq ... Portland ME 04101 207-699-2680 195
TF: 888-699-2680 ■ *Web:* stone-coast.com

Stone Connection Inc
3045 Business Park Dr ... Norcross GA 30071 770-662-0188 191-1
Web: www.stoneconnection.com

Stone County 108 E Fourth St ... Galena MO 65656 417-357-6127 357-6861 338
Web: www.stoneco-mo.us

Stone County 323 E Cavers Ave ... Wiggins MS 39577 601-928-5246 928-6464 338
Web: www.stonecountygov.com

Stone County Ironworks
408 Ironworks Dr Industrial Pk ... Mountain View AR 72560 800-223-4722 338
Web: www.stonecountyironworks.com

Stone County Ironworks
408 Ironworks Dr ... Mountain View AR 72560 870-269-8108 321
TF: 800-223-4722 ■ *Web:* stonecountyironworks.com

Stone County Publishing Company Inc
PO Box 509 ... Mountain View AR 72560 870-269-3841 532-3
Web: stonecountyleader.com

Stone Farm 200 Stoney Pt Rd ... Paris KY 40361 859-987-3737 987-1474 368
Web: www.stonefarm.com

Stone House Consulting LLC
126 Thornton Rd ... Thornton PA 19373 610-358-1791 194
Web: www.stonehouseconsulting.com

Stone Insurance Inc
111 Veterans Blvd Ste 1420 ... Metairie LA 70005 504-832-4161 390
Web: stoneinsurance.com

Stone Key Group LLC
411 W Putnam Ave Ste 110 ... Greenwich CT 06830 203-930-3700 691
Web: www.stonekey.com

Stone Mountain Pet Lodge
9935 Radisson Rd NE ... Minneapolis MN 55449 763-792-8929 493-2004 794
Web: www.stonemountainpetlodge.com

Stone Mountain State Park
3042 Frank Pkwy ... Roaring Gap NC 28668 336-957-8185 565
Web: www.ncparks.gov

Stone Mountain Tool Inc
480 Gees Mill Business Ct NE ... Conyers GA 30013 770-929-0166 929-0226 454
TF: 800-624-8665 ■ *Web:* stonemountaintool.com

Stone Parker & Company CPA
7512 Ridge Rd ... Port Richey FL 34668 727-842-3180 847-9248 2
Web: www.stoneparkercpa.com

Stone Pigman Walther Wittmann LLC
909 Poydras St Ste 3150 ... New Orleans LA 70112 504-581-3200 428
Web: www.stonepigman.com

Stone Plastics & Manufacturing Inc
8245 Riley St ... Zeeland MI 49464 616-748-9740 601
Web: www.stoneplasticsmfg.com

Stone Point Capital LLC
20 Horseneck Ln ... Greenwich CT 06830 203-862-2900 625-8357 690
Web: www.stonepoint.com

Stone Rudolph & Henry PLC
124 Ctr Pointe Dr ... Clarksville TN 37040 931-648-4786 647-5445 113
Web: www.srhcpas.com

Stone Source LLC 215 Park Ave S ... New York NY 10003 212-979-6400 191-1
Web: www.stonesource.com

Stone State Park 5001 Talbot Rd ... Sioux City IA 51103 712-255-4698 565
Web: www.iowadnr.gov

Stone Technologies Inc
550 Spirit of St Louis Blvd ... Chesterfield MO 63005 636-530-7240 177
TF: 866-786-6383 ■ *Web:* stonetek.com

Stone Transport Inc 3495 Hack Rd ... Saginaw MI 48601 989-754-4788 311
Web: www.stonetransport.com

Stone Turtle Baking & Cooking School
173 Howitt Rd ... Lyman ME 04002 207-324-7558 685
Web: www.stoneturtlebaking.com

Stoneage Inc 466 S Skylane Dr ... Durango CO 81303 970-259-2869 806
Web: www.stoneagetools.com

Stonearch 710 S Second St 7th Fl ... Minneapolis MN 55401 612-200-5000 7
Web: www.stonearchcreative.com

Stonearch Logistics LLC
4301 Hwy 7 Ste 155 ... Minneapolis MN 55416 952-767-0844 767-0489 311
Web: stonearchlogistics.com

Stonebranch Inc
950 N Point Pkwy Ste 200 ... Alpharetta GA 30005 678-366-7887 177
Web: www.stonebranch.com

Stonebriar Ctr 2601 Preston Rd ... Frisco TX 75034 972-668-6255 460
Web: www.shopstonebriar.com

Stonebridge Financial Planning Group LLC
921 N Pennsylvania Ave ... Winter Park FL 32789 407-695-7100 390
Web: stonebridgefpgroup.com

Stonebridge McWhinney LLC
4949 S Nigara St Ste 300 ... Denver CO 80237 303-785-3100 378
Web: www.stonebridgecompanies.com

Stonebridge Press Inc 25 Elm St ... Southbridge MA 01550 508-909-4130 764-8015 637-8
TF: 800-536-5836 ■ *Web:* www.stonebridgepress.com

Stoneco Inc 7555 Whiteford Rd ... Ottawa Lake MI 49267 734-856-2257 503-5
Web: stoneco.net

Stonecraft Inc 10613 Lexington Dr ... Knoxville TN 37932 865-966-3900 724
Web: www.stonecraftusa.com

StoneCreek Capital Inc
18500 Von Karman Ave Ste 590 ... Irvine CA 92612 949-752-4580 401
Web: www.stonecreekcapital.com

Stonecrop Gardens 81 Stonecrop Ln ... Cold Spring NY 10516 845-265-2000 97
Web: www.stonecrop.org

Stonecutter Mills Corp
230 Spindale St ... Spindale NC 28160 828-286-2341 287-7280 745-1
OTC: STCMA ■ *Web:* www.stonecuttermills.com

StoneFly Inc 21353 Cabot Blvd ... Hayward CA 94545 510-265-1616 265-1565 176
Web: stonefly.com

Stonegate Capital Partners
8201 Preston Rd Ste 325 ... Dallas TX 75225 214-987-4121 690
Web: www.stonegateinc.com

Stonegate Conference & Banquet Centre, The
2401 W Higgins Rd ... Hoffman Estates IL 60169 847-884-7000 671
Web: www.thestonegate.com

Stonegate Production Company LLC
952 Echo Ln Ste 400 ... Houston TX 77024 713-600-8000 536
Web: www.stone-gate.net

Stonegates 4031 Kennett Pk ... Greenville DE 19807 302-658-6200 658-1510 672
Web: www.stonegates.com

Stoneham Savings Bank
80 Montvale Ave ... Stoneham MA 02180 888-402-2265 70
TF: 888-402-2265 ■ *Web:* www.stonehambank.com

Stonehedge Inn 160 Pawtucket Blvd ... Tyngsboro MA 01879 978-649-4400 649-9256 379
Web: www.stonehedgeinnandspa.com

Stonehenge Capital Company LLC
236 Third St ... Baton Rouge LA 70801 225-408-3000 402
Web: www.stonehengecapital.com

Stonehenge Partners Inc
191 W Nationwide Blvd Ste 600 ... Columbus OH 43215 614-246-2500 690
Web: www.stonehengepartners.com

Stonehill College 320 Washington St ... Easton MA 02357 508-565-1373 565-1545 166
TF: 888-694-4554 ■ *Web:* www.stonehill.edu

Stonehill Group LLC
121 S 8th St Ste 850 ... Minneapolis MN 55402 612-436-1360 463
Web: www.stonehillgrp.com

Stoneleigh Recovery Associates LLC
PO Box 1479 ... Lombard IL 60148 866-724-2330 141
TF: 866-724-2330 ■ *Web:* www.stoneleighrecoveryassociates.com

Stoneleigh-Burnham School
574 Bernardston Rd ... Greenfield MA 01301 413-774-2711 772-2602 622
Web: www.sbschool.org

StoneMor Partners LP
3600 Horizon Blvd Ste 100 ... Trevose PA 19053 215-826-2800 510
NYSE: STON ■ *TF:* 844-719-9035 ■ *Web:* www.stonemor.com

StonePeak Ceramics Inc
314 W Superior Ste 201 ... Chicago IL 60610 312-506-2800 724
Web: www.stonepeakceramics.com

Stonepine
150 E Carmel Valley Rd ... Carmel Valley CA 93924 831-659-2245 659-5160 669
Web: www.stonepineestate.com

Stoner Electric Inc
1904 SE Ochoco St ... Milwaukie OR 97222 503-462-6500 659-4968 189-4
Web: stonergroup.com

Stoneridge Inc 8922 Stone Ridge Dr SE ... Warren OH 44484 248-489-9300 60
NYSE: SRI ■ *Web:* www.stoneridge.com

StoneRidge Investment Partners LLC
201 King of Prussia Rd Ste 200 ... Radnor PA 19087 610-647-6216 401
Web: stoneridgeinvestments.com

Stoner-Johnson Insurance Agency
2330 Airport Hwy ... Toledo OH 43609 419-385-3101 390
Web: stonerjohnson.com

Stonesong Press LLC
270 W 39th St Ste 201 ... New York NY 10018 212-929-4600 94
Web: stonesong.com

Stonestown Galleria
3251 20th Ave ... San Francisco CA 94132 415-564-8848 460
Web: www.stonestowngalleria.com

Stonewall County PO Box P ... Aspermont TX 79502 940-989-2272 989-2715 338
Web: www.stonewallcountytexas.us

Stonewall Jackson Hotel & Conference Ctr
24 S Market St ... Staunton VA 24401 540-885-4848 885-4840 379
TF: 866-880-0024 ■ *Web:* www.stonewalljacksonhotel.com

Stonewall Jackson Memorial Hospital (SJMH)
230 Hospital Plz ... Weston WV 26452 304-269-8000 269-8090 374-3
TF: 800-637-0471 ■ *Web:* www.stonewalljacksonhospital.com

Stoneway Electric Supply Co
402 N Perry St ... Spokane WA 99202 509-535-2933 246
Web: www.stoneway.com

Stoneworth Financial LLC
6575 W Loop S Ste 499 ... Houston TX 77401 713-429-1838 401
Web: www.stoneworthfinancial.com

Stoney Creek Inn
101 Mariner's Way ... East Peoria IL 61611 309-694-1300 694-9303 379
TF: 800-659-2220 ■ *Web:* www.stoneycreekhotels.com

Stoney Crest Regrind Service Inc
6243 Dixie Hwy ... Bridgeport MI 48722 989-777-7190 777-2860 455
TF: 800-332-3479 ■ *Web:* www.stoneycrestregrind.com

Stonhard Inc 1000 E Park Ave ... Maple Shade NJ 08052 800-257-7953 291
TF: 800-854-0310 ■ *Web:* www.stonhard.com

Stony Brook School 1 Chapman Pkwy ... Stony Brook NY 11790 631-751-1800 622
Web: www.stonybrookschool.org

Stony Brook State Park
10820 Rt 36 S ... Dansville NY 14437 585-335-8111 565
Web: parks.ny.gov

Stony Brook University
100 Nicolls Rd ... Stony Brook NY 11794 631-632-6000 166
Web: www.stonybrook.edu

Stony Brook University Health Sciences Library
8034 Stony Brook University
HST Level 3 Rm 136 ... Stony Brook NY 11794 631-444-2512 434-1
Web: www.library.stonybrook.edu

Stony Brook University Hospital (SBUH)
101 Nicolls Rd ... Stony Brook NY 11794 631-444-4000 374-3
Web: www.stonybrookmedicine.edu

Stony Point Battlefield State Historic Site
PO Box 182 ... Stony Point NY 10980 845-786-2521 565
Web: parks.ny.gov

Stony Point Surgical Ctr
8700 Stony Pt Pkwy ... Richmond VA 23235 804-775-4500 374-7
Web: www.stonypointsc.com

Stonyfield Farm Inc 10 Burton Dr ... Londonderry NH 03053 603-437-4040 296-25
TF: 800-776-2697 ■ *Web:* www.stonyfield.com

Stoops Freightliner- Quality Trailer Inc
1851 W Thompson Rd ... Indianapolis IN 46217 317-788-1533 57
TF: 800-899-1533 ■ *Web:* truckcountry.com

	Phone	Fax	Class
Stop & Shop Supermarket Co 1385 Hancock St .... Quincy MA 02169 *TF:* 800-767-7772 ■ *Web:* stopandshop.com	781-397-0006		345
Stop At Nothing Inc 1400 Marsh Landing Pkwy Ste 107 .... Jacksonville FL 32250 *Web:* www.stopatnothing.com	904-249-4410	686-1499	463
Stoptech Ltd 365 Industrial Dr .... Harrison OH 45030 *TF:* 800-537-0102 ■ *Web:* stoptechltd.com	513-202-5500		195
Storage & Transfer Technologies Inc 8485 Parkhill Dr .... Milton ON L9T5E9 *TF:* 800-730-5859 ■ *Web:* www.sttsystems.com	905-875-5587		111
Storage Battery Systems Inc (SBS) N56 W16665 Ridgewood Dr .... Menomonee Falls WI 53051 *TF:* 800-554-2243 ■ *Web:* www.sbsbattery.com	262-703-5800	703-3073	246
Storage Engine Inc 1 Sheila Dr .... Tinton Falls NJ 07724 *TF:* 866-734-8899 ■ *Web:* www.storageengine.com	732-747-6995	747-6542	176
Stor-All Storage 1375 W Hillsboro Blvd .... Deerfield Beach FL 33442 *TF:* 877-786-7255 ■ *Web:* www.stor-all.com	954-421-7888	426-1108	803-3
Storch Amini PC 140 E 45th St 25th Fl .... New York NY 10017	212-490-4100		428
Storck USA LP 325 N LaSalle St Ste 400 .... Chicago IL 60654 *Web:* www.storck.com	312-467-5700		296-8
Store Decor Co, The 5050 Boyd Blvd .... Rowlett TX 75088 *TF:* 800-831-3267 ■ *Web:* www.thestoredecor.com	972-475-4404		344
Store Kraft Manufacturing Co 500 Irving St .... Beatrice NE 68310	402-223-2348		286
Store Opening Solutions (SOS) 800 Middle Tennessee Blvd .... Murfreesboro TN 37129 *TF:* 877-388-9262 ■ *Web:* www.store-solutions.com	877-388-9262		449
Store Supply Warehouse LLC 9801 Page Ave .... Saint Louis MO 63132 *TF:* 800-823-0004 ■ *Web:* www.storesupply.com	314-427-8887		791
Stored Technology Solutions LLC 543 Queensbury Ave .... Queensbury NY 12804 *TF:* 844-335-4646 ■ *Web:* www.storedtech.com	518-793-1111	670-0120	196
Storefront Political Media 160 Pine St Ste 700 .... San Francisco CA 94111 *Web:* www.storefrontpolitical.com	415-834-0501		636
Storer Coachways 3519 McDonald Ave .... Modesto CA 95358 *TF:* 800-621-3383 ■ *Web:* storercoachways.com	209-521-8250	578-4888	107
Storer Meats Company Inc 3700 Clark Ave .... Cleveland OH 44109 *Web:* www.fivestarbrandmeats.com	216-621-7538		296-26
Storey County 26 S B St .... Virginia City NV 89440 *Web:* storeycounty.org	775-847-0968	847-0949	338
Storey Publishing LLC 210 Mass Moca Way .... North Adams MA 01247 *TF:* 800-827-7444 ■ *Web:* www.storey.com	413-346-2100	346-2199	637-2
Storis Inc 400 Valley Rd Ste 302 .... Mount Arlington NJ 07856 **Fax Area Code:* 973 ■ *TF:* 888-478-6747 ■ *Web:* www.storis.com	888-478-6747	601-0078*	177
Stork Craft Manufacturing Inc 12033 Riverside Way Ste 200 .... Richmond BC V6W1G3 *TF:* 877-274-0277 ■ *Web:* storkcraftdirect.com	604-274-5121	274-9727	319-2
Stork Prints America Inc 3201 Rotary Dr .... Charlotte NC 28269 *Web:* www.spgprints.com	704-598-7171		744
Storm Chasing Adventure Tours 1627 W Main St Ste 105 .... Bozeman MT 59715 *Web:* www.stormchasing.com	970-367-5395		760
Storm Industries Inc 23223 Normandie Ave .... Torrance CA 90501 *Web:* www.stormind.com	310-534-5232	530-3967	350
Storm Internet Services Inc 1760 Courtwood Crescent .... Ottawa ON K2C2B5 *TF:* 866-257-8676 ■ *Web:* www.storm.ca	613-567-6585	567-3227	225
Storm King Press PO Box 2089 .... Friday Harbor WA 98250 *Web:* www.stormkingpress.com	360-378-3910	378-3912	637-2
Storm King School 314 Mountain Rd .... Cornwall-on-Hudson NY 12520 *Web:* sks.org	845-534-7892		622
Storm Products Inc 165 S 800 W .... Brigham City UT 84302 *TF:* 800-369-4402 ■ *Web:* www.stormbowling.com	435-723-0403		710
Storm Resources Ltd 640 5 Ave SW Ste 200 .... Calgary AB T2P3G4 *Web:* www.stormresourcesltd.com	403-817-6145		536
Storm Technologies Inc 411 N Depot St .... Albemarle NC 28002 *Web:* www.stormeng.com	704-983-2040	982-9657	194
Storm Ventures 3000 Sand Hill Rd Bldg 4 Ste 210 .... Menlo Park CA 94025 *Web:* www.stormventures.com	650-926-8800		792
StormHarbour Securities LP 140 E 45th St Two Grand Central Tower 33rd Fl .... New York NY 10017 *TF:* 800-662-2739 ■ *Web:* www.stormharbour.com	212-905-2500		690
Stormline Press Inc PO Box 593 .... Urbana IL 61801 *Web:* www.raybial.com	217-328-2665		637-2
Stormont Vail Events Ctr 1 Expocentre Dr .... Topeka KS 66612 *Web:* www.stormontvaileventscenter.com	785-235-1986	235-2967	205
Stormont-Vail Regional Health Ctr 1500 SW Tenth Ave .... Topeka KS 66604 *TF:* 800-432-2951 ■ *Web:* www.stormontvail.org	785-354-6000	354-6926	374-3
Storms Welding & Manufacturing Inc 112 Paul Ave N PO Box 76 .... Cologne MN 55322 *Web:* www.stormsweldingmfg.com	952-466-3343		350
Stornoway Diamond Corp 1111 St-Charles Ouest Tour Ouest Ste 400 .... Longueuil QC J4K5G4 *TSX:* SWY ■ *TF:* 877-331-2232 ■ *Web:* www.stornowaydiamonds.com	450-616-5555	674-2012	503-3
Storopack Inc 12007 S Woodruff Ave .... Downey CA 90241 *TF:* 800-829-1491 ■ *Web:* www.storopack.us	562-803-5582	803-4462	601
Storr Office Environments Inc 10800 World Trade Blvd .... Raleigh NC 27617 *Web:* www.storr.com	919-313-3700	313-3701	320
Storr Tractor Co 3191 Rt 22 .... Branchburg NJ 08876 *TF:* 800-526-3802 ■ *Web:* www.storrtractor.com	908-722-9830	722-9847	429

	Phone	Fax	Class
Storrowton Village Museum 1305 Memorial Ave .... West Springfield MA 01089 *Web:* www.thebige.com	413-737-2443	787-0127	520
StorterChilds Printing Company Inc 1540 NE Waldo Rd .... Gainesville FL 32641 *Web:* www.storterchilds.com	352-376-2658		627
Story Construction 2810 Wakefield Cir .... Ames IA 50010 *Web:* www.storycon.com	515-232-4358	232-0599	186
Story County 1315 S B Ave .... Nevada IA 50201 *Web:* www.storycountyiowa.gov	515-382-7410		338
Storyminers Inc 1862 Wilkenson Xing .... Marietta GA 30066 *Web:* www.storyminers.com	770-425-9830		196
Storytime Ink Intl 577 Hidden Harbor Dr .... Fairport Harbor OH 44077 **Fax Area Code:* 270 ■ *Web:* www.storytimeink.com	440-584-0018	573-4913*	637-2
Storywindow Productions PO Box 2898 .... Asheville NC 28802 *Web:* www.storywindow.com	828-258-1113		572
Stotis & Baird Chartered 200 W Jackson Blvd Ste 1050 .... Chicago IL 60606 *Web:* stotis-baird.com	312-461-1000		41
Stott Outdoor Advertising PO Box 7209 .... Chico CA 95927 **Fax Area Code:* 530 ■ *TF:* 888-342-7868 ■ *Web:* www.stottoutdoor.com	888-342-7868	342-0712*	8
Stottler Henke Associates Inc 1650 S Amphlett Blvd Ste 310 .... San Mateo CA 94402 *Web:* www.stottlerhenke.com	650-931-2700	931-2701	180
Stouffer Mechanical Contractor LLC 1697 Opportunity Ave .... Chambersburg PA 17201 *Web:* www.stouffermechanical.com	717-262-0078	262-0097	610
Stoughton Area School District 320 N St .... Stoughton WI 53589 *Web:* www.stoughton.k12.wi.us	608-877-5000		685
Stoughton Hospital 900 Ridge St .... Stoughton WI 53589 *Web:* stoughtonhospital.com	608-873-6611	873-2355	374-3
Stoughton Printing Co 130 N Sunset Ave .... City of Industry CA 91744 **Fax Area Code:* 626 ■ *TF:* 800-961-3678 ■ *Web:* www.stoughtonprinting.com	800-961-3678	961-6505*	627
Stoughton Public Library 529 Washington St .... Stoughton MA 02072 *Web:* www.stoughton.org	781-344-2711	344-7340	434-3
Stoughton Trailers LLC 416 S Academy St .... Stoughton WI 53589 *TF:* 800-227-5391 ■ *Web:* www.stoughtontrailers.com	608-873-2500	873-2575	779
Stouse Inc 300 New Century Pkwy .... New Century KS 66031 *Web:* www.stouse.com	913-764-5757		701
STOUT 6425 W Florissant Ave .... Saint Louis MO 63136 *Web:* www.stoutsign.com	314-385-4600		701
Stout Images 3409 Brazos Ave .... Odessa TX 79764 *Web:* stoutimagesinc.com	432-332-2711		366
Stout Management Co 10151 Park Run Dr .... Las Vegas NV 89145 *Web:* www.smc-lv.com	702-227-0444		652
Stout's Island Lodge 2799 27th St .... Birchwood WI 54817 *Web:* www.stoutsislandlodge.com	715-354-3646	318-0211	379
Stovall, Grandey & Allen LLP 500 W Seventh St Unit 51 Ste 900 .... Fort Worth TX 76102 *Web:* sga-cpas.com	817-632-2500		2
Stow Co, The 3311 Windquest Dr .... Holland MI 49424 *Web:* www.thestowcompany.com	616-399-3311		817
Stowe & Stowe CPA PA 6701 Carmel Rd Ste 315 .... Charlotte NC 28226 *Web:* stowefirm.com	704-541-6334	541-6338	2
Stowe Mountain Resort 5781 Mountain Rd .... Stowe VT 05672 *TF:* 800-253-4754 ■ *Web:* www.stowe.com	802-253-3000		669
Stoweflake Mountain Resort & Spa 1746 Mountain Rd PO Box 369 .... Stowe VT 05672 *TF:* 800-253-2232 ■ *Web:* www.stoweflake.com	802-253-7355	253-6858	669
Stowell Associates Select Staff Inc 4485 N Oakland Ave .... Milwaukee WI 53211 *Web:* stowellassociates.com	414-963-2600		363
Stowers Institute For Medical Research 1000 E 50th St .... Kansas City MO 64110 *Web:* www.stowers.org	816-926-4000	926-2000	305
Stowers Machinery Corp 6301 Old Rutledge Pike NE .... Knoxville TN 37924 *Web:* www.stowerscat.com	865-546-1414	595-1030	358
Stowers Manufacturing Inc 500 Miller St .... Gadsden AL 35904 *Web:* www.stowersmfg.com	256-547-8647	547-8649	105
Stow-Munroe Falls Chamber of Commerce 4381 Hudson Dr Ste 2450 .... Stow OH 44224 *Web:* smfcc.com	330-688-1579	688-6234	139
Stow-Munroe Falls City School District 4350 Allen Rd .... Stow OH 44224 *Web:* smfschools.org	330-689-5445		685
Stow-Munroe Falls Public Library Local History Collection 3512 Darrow Rd .... Stow OH 44224 *Web:* www.smfpl.org	330-688-3295	688-0448	434-3
STR Fabrication 232 Lowy Dr .... Chatsworth GA 30705 *Web:* www.strfabrication.com	706-226-3501	272-7033	291
Strack & Van Til Super Market Inc 2244 45th St .... Highland IN 46322 *Web:* strackandvantil.com	219-924-6932		345
Stracon Inc 1672 Kaiser Ave .... Irvine CA 92614 *Web:* www.straconinc.com	949-851-2288	851-2299	425
Strad Energy Services Ltd *Strad Inc* 440-2nd Ave SW Ste 1200 .... Calgary AB T2P5E9 *Web:* www.stradenergy.com	403-232-6900		536
Strafford County 259 County Farm Rd .... Dover NH 03820 *Web:* co.strafford.nh.us	603-742-1458	743-4407	338
Strafford Publications Inc PO Box 13729 .... Atlanta GA 30324 *TF:* 800-926-7926 ■ *Web:* www.straffordpub.com	404-881-1141	881-0074	637-9
Strafford Technology 1D Commons Dr .... Londonderry NH 03053 *Web:* www.strafford.com	603-434-2550	434-2509	177
Strahan Ins Svcs Inc 5940 College Ave Ste A .... Oakland CA 94618 *Web:* strahaninsurance.com	510-450-9050		390

Name / Address	City	State	Zip	Phone	Fax	Class
Strahl & Pitsch Inc 230 Great E Neck Rd *Web:* www.strahlpitsch.com	West Babylon	NY	11704	631-587-9000	587-9120	151
Strahman Valves Inc 2801 Baglyos Cir *TF:* 877-787-2462 ■ *Web:* www.strahmanvalves.com	Bethlehem	PA	18020	484-893-5099		609
Straight A. Tours & Travel 6881 Kingspointe Pkwy Ste 18 *TF:* 800-237-5440 ■ *Web:* www.straightatours.com	Orlando	FL	32819	407-896-1242	896-1151	760
Straight Arrow Products Inc 2020 Highland Ave *Web:* straightarrowinc.com	Bethlehem	PA	18020	610-882-9606		231
Straight North LLC 1001 W 31st St *TF:* 866-353-3953 ■ *Web:* www.straightnorth.com	Downers Grove	IL	60515	866-353-3953		7
Straight Spouse Network (SSN) PO Box 4985 *Web:* www.straightspouse.org	Chicago	IL	60680	773-413-8213		48-21
Straight Way Radio LLC 407 N Howard Ave Ste 200	Tampa	FL	33606	813-259-9867		645-160
Straight Wharf 6 Harbor Sq *Web:* straightwharfrestaurant.com	Nantucket	MA	02554	508-228-4499		671
Straightforward Media 508 7th St Ste 202 *Web:* straightforwardinteractive.com	Rapid City	SD	57701	605-202-4169		5
Strainsert Inc 12 Union Hill Rd *Web:* www.strainsert.com	West Conshohocken	PA	19428	610-825-3310	825-1734	407
Strait Music Co 2428 W Ben White Blvd *TF:* 800-725-8877 ■ *Web:* www.straitmusic.com	Austin	TX	78704	512-476-6927		526
Straith Hospital for Special Surgery 23901 Lahser Rd *Web:* straithhospital.org	Southfield	MI	48033	248-357-3360	357-0915	374-7
Straits Cafe 1122 7th Ave Ste 1100 *Web:* www.straitsrestaurants.com	San Jose	CA	95128	408-246-6320		671
Straits State Park 720 Church St *Web:* www.michigan.org	Saint Ignace	MI	49781	906-643-8620		565
Straitsland Resorter PO Box 579 *Web:* resorter.com	Indian River	MI	49749	616-238-7362	238-1290	532-2
Strake Jesuit College Preparatory Inc 8900 Bellaire Blvd *Web:* www.strakejesuit.org	Houston	TX	77036	713-774-7651		148
Stranahan House Museum Inc 335 SE Sixth Ave *Web:* stranahanhouse.org	Fort Lauderdale	FL	33301	954-524-4736	525-2838	520
Stranahan Theater 4645 Heatherdowns Blvd *TF:* 866-381-7469 ■ *Web:* stranahantheater.com	Toledo	OH	43614	419-381-8851		572
Strand Associates Inc 910 W Wingra Dr *Web:* www.strand.com	Madison	WI	53715	608-251-4843	251-8655	261
Strand Book Store Inc 828 Broadway *TF:* 800-366-3664 ■ *Web:* www.strandbooks.com	New York	NY	10003	212-473-1452		95
Strand College of Hair Design 423 79th Ave N *Web:* www.strandcollege.com	Myrtle Beach	SC	29572	843-449-1017	467-2597	167-3
Strand Diagnostics LLC 5770 Decatur Blvd Ste A **Fax Area Code:* 888 ■ *TF:* 888-924-6779 ■ *Web:* www.stranddiagnostics.com	Indianapolis	IN	46241	317-455-2100	924-6778*	418
Strand Lighting 10911 Petal St *TF:* 800-733-0564 ■ *Web:* www.strandlighting.com	Dallas	TX	75238	214-647-7880	647-8031	439
Strand Management Solutions 50 Princeton Hightstown Rd Ste 280 *Web:* www.strandmanagement.com	Princeton Junction	NJ	08550	609-642-4666		177
Strand Media Group PO Box 1389 *Web:* strandmedia.com	Murrells Inlet	SC	29576	843-626-8911	626-6452	646
Strand Theatre 619 Louisiana Ave *TF:* 800-313-6373 ■ *Web:* www.thestrandtheatre.com	Shreveport	LA	71101	318-226-1481	424-5434	572
Strang Corp 8905 Lake Ave *Web:* strangcorp.com	Cleveland	OH	44102	216-961-6767	961-1966	670
Strange's Florist Inc 3313 Mechanicsville Pk *TF:* 800-421-4070 ■ *Web:* www.stranges.com	Richmond	VA	23223	804-321-2200		292
Stranger, The 1535 11th Ave 3rd Fl *Web:* www.thestranger.com	Seattle	WA	98122	206-323-7101	323-7203	532-5
Strasbaugh 825 Buckley Rd *OTC: STRB* ■ *Web:* www.strasbaugh.com	San Luis Obispo	CA	93401	805-541-6424	541-6425	386
Strassburger Mckenna Gutnick & Gefsky 525 Third St *Web:* www.smgglaw.com	Beaver	PA	15009	724-846-1372		445
Strass-Maguire & Associates Inc 6512 W Mequon Rd *Web:* strass-maguire.com	Mequon	WI	53092	262-242-5050		261
Strassman Insurance Services Inc 26351 Curtiss Wright Pkwy *Web:* strassman.net	Richmond Heights	OH	44143	216-289-1500	289-1501	390
Strat Land Exploration Co 15 E Fifth St Ste 2020 *Web:* stratland.com	Tulsa	OK	74103	918-584-3844	584-2957	536
Strata 8653 W Hackamore Dr *Web:* www.stratageotech.com	Boise	ID	83709	208-376-8200		261
Strata Credit Union 1717 Truxtun Ave *Web:* www.stratacu.org	Bakersfield	CA	93301	661-327-9461		219
Strata Decision Technology LLC 2001 S First St Ste 200 **Fax Area Code:* 312 ■ *Web:* www.stratadecision.com	Champaign	IL	61820	217-359-8422	726-2947*	177
STRATA Energy Services Inc 39207 Range Rd 271 Blindman Industrial Pk Ste 8 *Web:* www.strataenergy.net	Red Deer	AB	T4S2M4	403-358-3442		538
Strata Health Solutions Inc 933 - 17 Ave SW Ste 600 *TF:* 866-556-5005 ■ *Web:* stratahealth.com	Calgary	AB	T2T5R6	866-556-5005		179
Strata Inc 114 11th St SE *Web:* www.stratainc.com	Auburn	WA	98002	425-259-6016	259-6018	681
Strata Information Group 3935 Harney St Ste 203 *TF:* 800-776-0111 ■ *Web:* www.sigcorp.com	San Diego	CA	92110	800-776-0111		180
Strata Networks 211 E 200 N *Web:* www.stratanetworks.com	Roosevelt	UT	84066	435-622-5007		224
Strata Oil & Gas Inc 10010 - 98 St PO Box 7770 *TF:* 877-237-5443 ■ *Web:* www.strataoil.com	Peace River	AB	T8S1T3	403-237-5443		536
Strata Products Worldwide LLC 8995 Roswell Rd Ste 200 *TF:* 800-691-6601 ■ *Web:* www.strataworldwide.com	Sandy Springs	GA	30350	770-321-2500		360-3
STRATACACHE 2 Emmet St Ste 200 *TF:* 800-244-8915 ■ *Web:* www.stratacache.com	Dayton	OH	45405	937-224-0485		180
Stratacomm 1200 G St NW Ste 350 *Web:* stratacomm.net	Washington	DC	20005	202-289-2001		636
Stratagem PC 14143 Denver W Pkwy Ste 450 *Web:* stratagemcpa.com	Lakewood	CO	80401	303-988-1900	986-6861	2
Stratagraph Inc PO Box 53848 *TF:* 800-256-1147 ■ *Web:* www.stratagraph.com	Lafayette	LA	70505	337-232-5510	237-8120	538
Stratasys Inc 7665 Commerce Way *NASDAQ: SSYS* ■ *TF:* 800-937-3010 ■ *Web:* www.stratasys.com	Eden Prairie	MN	55344	952-937-3000	937-0070	261
Stratco Inc 14821 N 73rd St *Web:* www.stratco.com	Scottsdale	AZ	85260	480-991-0450	991-0314	537
StrateGen Consulting LLC 2150 Allston Way Ste 210 *Web:* www.strategen.com	Berkeley	CA	94704	510-665-7811		196
Strategic & Competitive Intelligence Professional (SCIP) 7550 IH 10 W Ste 400 *Web:* www.scip.org	San Antonio	TX	78229	703-739-0696	739-2524	49-12
Strategic Account Management Assn 33 N La Salle St Ste 3700 *Web:* www.strategicaccounts.org	Chicago	IL	60602	312-251-3131		2
Strategic Advisors Inc 400 Southpointe Blvd Plz I Ste 440 *Web:* www.strategicad.com	Canonsburg	PA	15317	724-743-5800		194
Strategic Advisory Group Inc (SAG) PO Box 773 *Web:* www.strategicadvisorygroup.com	Sag Harbor	NY	11963	631-725-7746	725-7739	194
Strategic Air & Space Museum 28210 W Pk Hwy *Web:* sacmuseum.org	Ashland	NE	68003	402-944-3100	944-3160	520
Strategic Analysis Inc 4075 Wilson Blvd Ste 200 *TF:* 855-664-7317 ■ *Web:* www.sainc.com	Arlington	VA	22203	703-527-5410	527-5445	466
Strategic Automation Services LLC 16203 Park Row Rd Ste 140 *Web:* strategic-automation-services.com	Houston	TX	77084	281-945-8900		180
Strategic Compliance Solutions LLC 2025 Hwy 191 *Web:* www.strategiccompliancesolutions.com	Danielsville	GA	30633	706-795-0050		734
Strategic Decisions Group 951 Mariners Island Blvd Ste 400 *Web:* www.sdg.com	San Mateo	CA	94404	650-475-4400	475-4401	194
Strategic Development Solutions LLC 11150 W Olympic Blvd Ste 910 *Web:* www.sdsgroup.com	Los Angeles	CA	90064	310-914-5333		196
Strategic Distribution Inc 1414 Radcliffe St Ste 300 *TF:* 800-322-2644 ■ *Web:* www.sdi.com	Bristol	PA	19007	215-633-1900	633-4426	385
Strategic Equity Group Inc 6 Hutton Ctr Dr Ste 860 S Coast Metro *Web:* www.segco.com	Santa Ana	CA	92707	714-444-3833	435-9410	690
Strategic Financial Alliance Inc, The 2200 Century Pkwy Ste 500 *TF:* 888-447-2444 ■ *Web:* www.thesfa.net	Atlanta	GA	30345	678-954-4000		401
Strategic Global Advisors LLC 100 Bayview Cir Ste 650 *Web:* sgadvisors.com	Newport Beach	CA	92660	949-706-2640		528
Strategic Hotels & Resorts 150 N Riverside Plz Ste 4100 *NYSE: BEE* ■ *Web:* www.strategichotels.com	Chicago	IL	60606	312-658-5000		654
Strategic Information Resources Inc 155 Brookdale Dr *TF:* 800-332-9479 ■ *Web:* backgrounddecision.com	Springfield	MA	01104	800-813-4381		218
Strategic Investments & Holdings Inc (SIHI) 4445 N A1A Ste 247 *Web:* www.sihi.net	Vero Beach	FL	32963	716-857-6000	857-6490	792
Strategic Materials Inc 16365 Pk Ten Pl Ste 200 **Fax Area Code:* 281 ■ *TF:* 800-385-7275 ■ *Web:* www.strategicmaterials.com	Houston	TX	77084	800-385-7275	647-2710*	660
Strategic Media Services Inc 1911 N Ft Myer Dr Ste 400 **Fax Area Code:* 703 ■ *Web:* strategicmediaservices.com	Arlington	VA	22209	202-337-5700	527-6248*	514
Strategic Network Consulting (SNC) 5555 W Loop S Ste 450 *Web:* www.snc.net	Bellaire	TX	77401	713-366-3412	871-0057	180
Strategic News Service 38 Yew Ln *Web:* www.tapsns.com	Friday Harbor	WA	98250	360-378-1023		530
Strategic Partners Inc 9800 De Soto Ave *Web:* www.strategicpartners.net	Chatsworth	CA	91311	818-671-2100	671-2101	155-3
Strategic Pharmaceutical Solutions Inc 17014 NE Sandy Blvd *Web:* vetsource.com	Portland	OR	97230	503-802-7400		238
Strategic Power Systems Inc 11016 Rushmore Dr Frenette Bldg Ste 275 *Web:* www.spsinc.com	Charlotte	NC	28277	704-544-5501		225
Strategic Press Inc 1460 Pittman Ave *TF:* 800-767-5964 ■ *Web:* www.strategicpress.com	Sparks	NV	89431	800-767-5964		637-2
Strategic Public Partners Inc 815 Grandview Ave Ste 300 *Web:* sppgrp.com	Columbus	OH	43215	614-222-8490		194
Strategic Research Corp (SRC) PO Box 5365 *Web:* www.sresearch.com	Santa Barbara	CA	93150	805-201-3178		196
Strategic Resources Inc 7927 Jones Branch Dr *Web:* www.sri-hq.com	McLean	VA	22102	703-749-3040	749-3046	194

				Phone	Fax	Class
Strategic Resources International Inc 777 Washington Rd Ste 2 *Web:* www.sriusa.com	Parlin	NJ	08859	732-887-4646	909-2222	177
Strategic Retirement Group 515 SW Camden Ave *TF:* 800-367-4209 ■ *Web:* mysrg.net	Stuart	FL	34994	772-781-4700		690
Strategic Sales Systems 11971 Westline Industrial Dr Ste 103 *TF:* 877-777-9779 ■ *Web:* www.sssworld.com	Maryland Heights	MO	63146	877-777-9779		180
Strategic Solutions Inc (SSI) 16W231 S Frontage Rd Ste 1 *Web:* www.ssichicago.com	Burr Ridge	IL	60527	630-834-5330		180
Strategic Systems Consulting Inc 7742 Spalding Dr Ste 363 **Fax Area Code:* 404 ■ *Web:* www.eapps.com	Norcross	GA	30092	770-448-2100	601-7454*	39
Strategic Systems International Ltd 350 N Orleans St Ste 9000N *Web:* www.ssidecisions.com	Chicago	IL	60654	847-867-2398		178-1
Strategic Talent Management Brunswick Business Ctr 18 Pleasant St Ste 205 *Web:* www.strategictalentmgmt.com	Brunswick	ME	04011	207-373-9301		194
Strategic Technology Institute 6000 Executive Blvd Ste 205 *Web:* sti-inc.com	Rockville	MD	20852	301-770-7077		261
Strategos 1 Market Plz Ste 3600 *Web:* www.strategos.com	San Francisco	CA	94105	415-293-8463		463
Strategy Companion Corp 3240 El Camino Real Ste 120 *TF:* 800-905-6792 ■ *Web:* strategycompanion.com	Irvine	CA	92602	714-460-8398		179
Strategy Institute 401 Richmond St W Ste 401 *TF:* 866-298-9343 ■ *Web:* www.strategyinstitute.com	Toronto	ON	M5V3A8	866-298-9343		466
Stratford & District Chamber of Commerce 55 Lorne Ave E *Web:* stratfordchamber.com	Stratford	ON	N5A6S4	519-273-5250	273-2229	137
Stratford Building Supply Inc 215 Railroad St *TF:* 800-261-4125 ■ *Web:* stratfordbuilding.com	Stratford	WI	54484	715-687-4125	762-3915	364
Stratford General Hospital 46 General Hospital Dr *TF:* 888-275-1102 ■ *Web:* www.hpha.ca	Stratford	ON	N5A2Y6	519-272-8210	271-7137	374-2
Stratford Homes LP 402 S Weber Ave *TF:* 800-448-1524 ■ *Web:* www.stratfordhomes.com	Stratford	WI	54484	715-687-3133		106
Stratford Mutual Telephone Co 1001 Tennyson Ave *TF:* 866-881-2251 ■ *Web:* www.stratfordtelephone.com	Stratford	IA	50249	515-838-2390		224
Stratford Square Mall 152 Stratford Sq *Web:* stratfordmall.com	Bloomingdale	IL	60108	630-539-1000		460
Stratford University School of Culinary Arts 7777 Leesburg Pk *TF:* 800-444-0804 ■ *Web:* www.stratford.edu	Falls Church	VA	22043	703-821-8570		163
Strathallan Hotel 550 E Ave *Web:* www.strathallan.com	Rochester	NY	14607	585-461-5010		379
Strathcona Hotel 60 York St *TF:* 800-268-8304 ■ *Web:* www.thestrathconahotel.com	Toronto	ON	M5J1S8	416-363-3321	363-4679	379
Strathcona Hotel, The 919 Douglas St *TF:* 800-663-7476 ■ *Web:* strathconahotel.com	Victoria	BC	V8W2C2	250-383-7137		379
Strathcona Paper LP 77 County Rd 16 RR 7 *Web:* www.strathconapaper.com	Napanee	ON	K7R3L2	613-378-6672		100
StrathKirn Inc 2214 Stoneridge Terrace Ct *Web:* www.strathkirn.com	Chesterfield	MO	63017	636-530-6943	530-6945	194
Strathmore Co 2000 Gary Ln *Web:* www.strath.com	Geneva	IL	60134	630-232-9677		627
Strativa Inc 2082 Business Center Dr Ste 240 *Web:* strativa.com	Irvine	CA	92612	949-442-0099		177
Stratix 4920 Avalon Ridge Pkwy *TF:* 800-883-8300 ■ *Web:* www.stratixcorp.com	Norcross	GA	30071	770-326-7580		173-7
StratMar Retail Services 109 Willett Ave *TF:* 800-866-2399 ■ *Web:* www.stratmar.com	Port Chester	NY	10573	800-866-2399		7
Strato Inc 100 New England Ave *TF:* 800-792-0500 ■ *Web:* www.stratoinc.com	Piscataway	NJ	08854	732-981-1515	981-1222	791
Straton Industries Inc 180 Surf Ave *Web:* straton.com	Stratford	CT	06615	203-375-4488	375-5060	454
Stratos Global Corp 6550 Rock Spring Dr Ste 650 *TF:* 800-563-2255 ■ *Web:* www.stratosglobal.com	Bethesda	MD	20817	301-214-8800	214-8801	681
Stratosphere Networks 1732 Central St **Fax Area Code:* 877 ■ *TF:* 877-599-3999 ■ *Web:* www.stratospherenetworks.com	Evanston	IL	60201	847-859-1600	329-1277*	180
Stratosphere Tower Hotel & Casino 2000 S Las Vegas Blvd *TF:* 800-998-6937 ■ *Web:* thestrat.com	Las Vegas	NV	89104	702-380-7777		133
Strattec Security Corp 3333 W Good Hope Rd *NASDAQ: STRT* ■ *Web:* www.strattec.com	Milwaukee	WI	53209	414-247-3333	247-3329	60
Stratton & Associates PLLC 398 S Ninth St Ste 290 *Web:* www.strattoncpa.com	Boise	ID	83702	208-336-4953		2
Stratton Equity Co-operative Company Inc 98 Colorado Ave PO Box 25 *TF:* 800-438-7070 ■ *Web:* www.strattoncoop.com	Stratton	CO	80836	719-348-5326		275
Stratton Gilmore Group 37 Old Shore Rd *Web:* strattongilmoregroup.com	Madison	WI	53704	608-249-3610		195
Stratton Hats Inc 3200 Randolph St *TF:* 877-453-3777 ■ *Web:* strattonhats.com	Bellwood	IL	60104	708-544-5220	544-5243	155-9
Stratton Mountain Resort 5 Village Lodge Rd *TF:* 800-787-2886 ■ *Web:* www.stratton.com	Stratton Mountain	VT	05155	802-297-4211		669
Stratton Seed Co 1530 Hwy 79 S *TF:* 800-264-4433 ■ *Web:* gostrattonseed.com	Stuttgart	AR	72160	870-673-4433		694
Stratton Veterans Affairs Medical Ctr 113 Holland Ave *TF:* 800-223-4810 ■ *Web:* www.albany.va.gov	Albany	NY	12208	518-626-5000		374-8
Stratum Engineering LLC 585 Johnny F Smith Ave *Web:* stratumengr.com	Slidell	LA	70460	985-643-1160	643-8830	261
Stratus Properties Inc 212 Lavaca St Ste 300 *NYSE: STRS* ■ *TF:* 800-690-0315 ■ *Web:* www.stratusproperties.com	Austin	TX	78701	512-478-5788	478-6340	653
Stratus Technologies 111 Powdermill Rd *TF:* 800-787-2887 ■ *Web:* www.stratus.com	Maynard	MA	01754	978-461-7000		178-12
Stratz Heating & Cooling Inc 20960 19 Mile Rd *Web:* www.stratzheatingandcooling.com	Big Rapids	MI	49307	231-796-3717		189-10
Straub Brewery Inc 303 Sorg St *Web:* straubbeer.com	Saint Marys	PA	15857	814-834-2875		102
Straus News Inc 20 W Ave *Web:* www.strausnews.com	Chester	NY	10918	845-469-9000		532-3
Strauss & Kallus PLLC 301 Main St Ste 2E *Web:* goshenlawyer.com	Goshen	NY	10924	845-294-2616		41
Strauss & Malk LLP 135 Revere Dr *Web:* straussmalk.com	Northbrook	IL	60062	847-562-1400	562-1422	41
Strauss & Troy 150 E Fourth St *Web:* www.strausstroy.com	Cincinnati	OH	45202	513-621-2120	241-8259	428
StraussGroup Inc 701 Seneca St Ste 603 *Web:* www.straussgroup.com	Buffalo	NY	14210	716-631-3200	631-3222	260
Strawberry Hill Museum & Cultural Ctr 720 N Fourth St *Web:* www.strawberryhillmuseum.org	Kansas City	KS	66101	913-371-3264		520
Strawbery Banke Museum 14 Hancock St *Web:* www.strawberybanke.org	Portsmouth	NH	03801	603-433-1100		520
Strawbridge Studios Inc 3616 Hillsborough Rd PO Box 3005 **Fax Area Code:* 919 ■ *TF:* 800-326-9080 ■ *Web:* www.strawbridge.net	Durham	NC	27705	800-326-9080	286-7185*	627
Stray Light Optical Technologies Inc 821 S Lake Rd S *Web:* straylightoptical.com	Scottsburg	IN	47170	812-752-9104		261
Strayer Consulting Group Inc 16151 Wood Acres Rd *Web:* www.strayerconsulting.com	Los Gatos	CA	95030	408-399-1500		463
Strayer Education Inc 2303 Dulles Stn Blvd *NASDAQ: STRA* ■ *Web:* www.strayereducation.com	Herndon	VA	20171	703-247-2500		242
Strayer University 1133 15th St NW *TF:* 888-311-0355 ■ *Web:* www.strayer.edu	Washington	DC	20005	202-408-2400		166
Stream Companies Inc 400 Lapp Rd *TF:* 888-456-7694 ■ *Web:* www.streamcompanies.com	Malvern	PA	19355	610-644-8637		7
Stream Gas & Electric Ltd 14675 Dallas Pkwy Ste 150 *TF:* 866-447-8732 ■ *Web:* mystream.com	Dallas	TX	75207	866-447-8732		787
Streambox Inc 1848 Westlake Ave N Ste 200 *Web:* www.streambox.com	Seattle	WA	98109	206-956-0544		242
StreamCo LLC 4198 Cox Rd Ste 203 *Web:* streamco.com	Richmond	VA	23255	804-955-4397	346-5901	652
Stream-Flo Industries Ltd 4505 - 74 Ave *Web:* www.streamflo.com	Edmonton	AB	T6B2H5	780-468-6789	469-7724	537
StreamingEdge Inc 32 Old Slip 34th Fl *Web:* www.streamingedge.com	New York	NY	10005	212-791-6026	791-6684	225
Streamlight Inc 30 Eagleville Rd *TF:* 800-523-7488 ■ *Web:* www.streamlight.com	Eagleville	PA	19403	610-631-0600	631-0712	439
Streamline Health Solutions Inc 10200 Alliance Rd Ste 200 *NASDAQ: STRM* ■ **Fax Area Code:* 513 ■ *TF:* 800-878-5269 ■ *Web:* www.streamlinehealth.net	Cincinnati	OH	45242	888-997-8732	794-9770*	39
Streamray Inc 910 E Hamilton Ave 6th Fl *Web:* streamray.com	Campbell	CA	95008	408-702-1044		387
StreamSend 78 York St *TF:* 877-439-4078 ■ *Web:* www.streamsend.com	Sacramento	CA	95814	916-326-5407		393
Streamwood Behavioral Health Ctr 1400 E Irving Park Rd *TF:* 800-272-7790 ■ *Web:* streamwoodhospital.com	Streamwood	IL	60107	630-837-9000	837-2639	374-1
Streamwood Chamber of Commerce 22 W Streamwood Blvd PO Box 545 *Web:* www.streamwoodchamber.com	Streamwood	IL	60107	630-837-5200	837-5251	139
Streamworks LLC 3640 Pheasant Ridge Dr NE *TF:* 800-328-5680 ■ *Web:* streamworksmn.com	Blaine	MN	55449	800-328-5680		4
Streater Inc 411 S First Ave **Fax Area Code:* 507 ■ *TF:* 800-527-4197 ■ *Web:* www.streater.com	Albert Lea	MN	56007	800-527-4197	373-7630*	286
Streator Area Chamber of Commerce & Industry 320 E Main St PO Box 360 *Web:* streatorchamber.com	Streator	IL	61364	815-672-2921		139
Streator Dependable Manufacturing Co 1705 N Shabbona St *TF:* 800-795-0551 ■ *Web:* www.streatordependable.com	Streator	IL	61364	815-672-0551		470
Streck Inc 7002 S 109th St *TF:* 800-228-6090 ■ *Web:* www.streck.com	La Vista	NE	68128	402-333-1982		231
Streebo Inc 10998 S Wilcrest Dr Ste 162 *Web:* www.streebo.com	Houston	TX	77099	832-426-2700		463
Street Light Data 677 Harrison St *Web:* www.streetlightdata.com	San Francisco	CA	94107	415-979-0131		178-8
Street Road Accessories 80 E Street Rd *Web:* www.streetroad.com	Feasterville	PA	19053	215-809-2998		61
Street Solutions Inc (SSI) 2930 Plz Five *Web:* www.streetsolutions.com	Jersey City	NJ	07311	201-763-9500		196
StreetAccount LLC 1135 Maple Way 2nd Fl *Web:* www.streetaccount.com	Jackson	WY	83001	617-261-5200		401

Phone | Fax | Class

Streeter Associates Inc
101 E Woodlawn Ave PO Box 118 .... Elmira NY 14902 607-734-4151 732-2952 186
Web: www.streeterassociates.com
Streeter Printing Inc
9880 Via Pasar .... San Diego CA 92126 858-566-0866 627
Web: www.streeterprinting.com
StreetInsidercom Inc
280 W Maple Ste 210 .... Birmingham MI 48009 248-593-6536 401
Web: www.streetinsider.com
Streets at Southpoint & Main Street
6910 Fayetteville Rd .... Durham NC 27713 919-572-8800 50-6
Web: www.streetsatsouthpoint.com
Streetwise Reports LLC
101 Second St Ste 110 .... Petaluma CA 94952 707-981-8999 530
Web: www.theaureport.com
Strega 379 Hanover St .... Boston MA 02113 617-523-8481 671
Web: www.stregaristorante.com
Streimer Sheet Metal Works Inc
740 N Knott St .... Portland OR 97227 503-288-9393 288-3327 697
TF: 888-288-3828 ■ *Web:* www.streimer.com
Strem Chemicals Inc
7 Mulliken Way .... Newburyport MA 01950 978-499-1600 146
TF: 800-647-8736 ■ *Web:* www.strem.com
Stremicks Heritage Foods
4002 Westminster Ave .... Santa Ana CA 92703 714-775-5000 775-7677 296-27
TF: 800-321-5960 ■ *Web:* www.heritage-foods.com
Streng Agency
2325 Dean St Ste 100-A .... Saint Charles IL 60175 630-584-3887 7
Web: strengagency.com
Stresa 2710 Okeechobee Blvd .... West Palm Beach FL 33409 561-615-0200 671
Web: www.stresaitalianrestaurant.com
Stresau Laboratory Inc
N8265 Medley Rd .... Spooner WI 54801 715-635-2777 635-7979 268
Web: www.stresau.com
Stresscon Corp
3210 Astrozon Blvd .... Colorado Springs CO 80910 719-390-5041 183
Web: www.stresscon.com
StressCrete Group 9200 Energy Ln .... Northport AL 35476 205-339-0711 339-4840 183
TF: 800-435-6563 ■ *Web:* www.scgrp.com
Stress-O-Pedic Mattress Company Inc
2060 S Wineville Ave .... Ontario CA 91761 909-605-2010 471
Web: www.stressopedic.com
Stretch Boards 983 Tower Pl .... Santa Cruz CA 95062 831-479-7309 711
Web: www.stretchboards.com
Stretch-N-Grow 6121 Seminole Blvd .... Seminole FL 33775 800-348-0166 310
TF: 800-348-0166 ■ *Web:* www.stretch-n-grow-international.com
STRI (Smithsonian Tropical Research Institute)
1100 Jefferson Dr Ste 3123 MRC 705 .... Washington DC 20013 202-633-4014 786-2557 668
Web: stri.si.edu
Stria Inc 4300 Resnik Ct .... Bakersfield CA 93313 877-839-8952 196
TF: 877-839-8952 ■ *Web:* www.stria.com
Stribling Equipment LLC 408 Hwy 49 S .... Richland MS 39218 601-939-1000 358
TF: 855-781-9408 ■ *Web:* www.striblingequipment.com
Strich Law Firm PC
2650 Us Hwy 130 Ste G .... Cranbury NJ 08512 609-924-2900 41
Web: strichlaw.com
Strick Trailers LLC 301 N Polk St .... Monroe IN 46772 260-692-6622 779
TF: 888-552-3055 ■ *Web:* www.stricktrailers.com
Strickland & Strickland PC
4400 E Broadway Blvd .... Tucson AZ 85711 520-795-8727 41
Web: stricklandlaw.net
Strickland General Agency Inc
15500 Roosevelt Blvd Ste 103 .... Clearwater FL 33759 727-669-8886 669-8892 196
Web: www.sgainga.com
Stric-Lan Companies LLC 104 Sable St .... Duson LA 70529 337-984-7850 539
TF: 800-749-4586 ■ *Web:* www.striclan.com
Strictly Business Computer Systems Inc
848 4th Ave Ste 200 .... Huntington WV 25701 888-529-0401 781-2590* 176
**Fax Area Code:* 304 ■ *TF:* 888-529-0401 ■ *Web:* www.sbcs.com
Strictly Technology LLC
5381 NW 33rd Ave .... Fort Lauderdale FL 33309 954-606-5440 225
Web: strictlytech.com
Stride Learning Ctr 326 Parsley Blvd .... Cheyenne WY 82007 307-632-2991 148
Web: www.stridekids.com
Stride Rite Corp, The
500 Totten Pond Rd .... Waltham MA 02451 617-824-6000 824-6969 301
TF: 800-299-6575 ■ *Web:* www.striderite.com
Stride Tool Inc
Imperial Div
30333 Emerald Vly Pkwy .... Glenwillow OH 44139 440-247-4600 527-6383* 758
**Fax Area Code:* 800 ■ *TF:* 888-467-8665 ■ *Web:* imperial-tools.com
Strider 6-6150 Hwy 7 Ste 400 .... Woodbridge ON L4H0R6 416-502-8895 195
TF: 800-314-8895 ■ *Web:* striderseo.com
Strike Energy Services Inc
1300 505 - Third St SW .... Calgary AB T2P3E6 403-232-8448 536
Web: www.strikegroup.ca
Strike Technology Inc
24311 S Wilmington Ave .... Carson CA 90745 562-437-3428 495-0904 253
Web: www.wilorco.com
Strikeforce Bowling LLC
2001 Parkes Dr W .... Broadview IL 60155 708-863-1200 483-8128 710
TF: 800-297-8555 ■ *Web:* krstrikeforce.com
StringCan Interactive LLC
3719 North 75th St Ste 105 .... Scottsdale AZ 85251 480-612-0360 195
Web: www.stringcaninteractive.com
Stringfellow Group
2105 Laurel Bush Rd Ste 200 .... Bel Air MD 21015 443-640-1059 47
Web: www.stringfellowgroup.net
Strings Italian Cafe
2601 Oakdale Rd Ste P .... Modesto CA 95355 209-578-9777 671
Web: www.stringscafe.com
StringWorks 327 Franklin St .... Geneva IL 60134 630-454-5714 526
TF: 888-624-6114 ■ *Web:* www.stringworks.com
Strip Hoppers Leithart Mcgrath
575 S Third St .... Columbus OH 43215 614-228-6345 428
Web: columbuslawyer.net
Strip House 13 E 12th St .... New York NY 10003 212-328-0000 671
Web: www.striphouse.com

Stripes Convenience Stores
3200 Hackberry Rd .... Irving TX 75063 866-707-7727 204
NYSE: SUSS ■ *TF:* 866-707-7727 ■ *Web:* stripesstores.com
Stripling Tackle Co 512 Reynolds St .... Waycross GA 31501 912-283-8370 297-5
Web: www.fishing-boating.com
Strippit Inc/LVD
12975 Clarence Center Rd .... Akron NY 14001 716-542-4511 542-5957 456
TF: 800-828-1527 ■ *Web:* www.lvdgroup.com
Stripsteak 3950 Las Vegas Blvd S .... Las Vegas NV 89119 702-632-7200 671
Web: mandalaybay.mgmresorts.com
Stritch School of Medicine
2160 S 1st Ave .... Maywood IL 60153 708-216-3326 167-2
Web: ssom.luc.edu
Strite Industries Ltd
298 Shepherd Ave .... Cambridge ON N3C1V1 519-658-9361 393
Web: www.strite.com
Strobe Celery & Vegetable Co
2404 S Wolcott Unit 16-20 .... Chicago IL 60608 773-446-4000 226-7644* 297-7
**Fax Area Code:* 312 ■ *Web:* www.strube.com
Strobic Air Corp
160 Cassell Rd PO Box 144 .... Harleysville PA 19438 215-723-4700 723-7401 18
Web: www.strobicair.com
Stroer & Graff Inc 1830 Phillips Ln .... Antioch CA 94509 925-778-0200 189-5
Strom Aviation Inc 109 S Elm St .... Waconia MN 55387 952-544-3611 631
TF: 800-356-6440 ■ *Web:* www.stromaviation.com
Strom Manufacturing Inc
10630 NW 289th Ave .... North Plains OR 97133 503-447-1021 447-1281 454
Web: www.strom-mfg.com
Stroma Service Consulting Inc
19 Legault St PO Box 23040 .... North Bay ON P1B8Z4 705-840-6000 840-6001 393
Web: www.marvalnorthamerica.com
Stroman Realty Inc 14500 Hwy 105 W .... Conroe TX 77304 936-588-4444 652
TF: 800-243-5167 ■ *Web:* stroman.com
Stromberg Allen & Co
18504 W Creek Dr .... Tinley Park IL 60477 773-847-7131 847-6673 174
Web: strombergallen.com
Stromberg Architectural Products Inc
4400 Oneal St .... Greenville TX 75402 903-454-0904 393
Web: www.strombergarchitectural.com
Stromberg Metal Works Inc
6701 Distribution Dr .... Beltsville MD 20705 301-931-1000 931-1020 811
Web: www.strombergmetals.com
Stromian Technologies 919 Monmouth Ave ...... Durham NC 27701 919-687-4172 180
Web: www.stromian.com
Strong & Hanni
102 South 200 East Ste 800 .... Salt Lake City UT 84111 801-532-7080 466
Web: strongandhanni.com
Strong - National Museum of Play
1 Manhattan Sq .... Rochester NY 14607 585-263-2700 263-2493 520
Web: www.museumofplay.org
Strong Enterprises Inc
11236 Satellite Blvd .... Orlando FL 32837 407-859-9317 850-6978 576
TF: 800-344-6319 ■ *Web:* www.strongparachutes.com
Strong Forge & Fabrication
20 Liberty St .... Batavia NY 14020 585-343-5251 454
Web: www.strongforge.com
Strong Travel Services Inc
8235 Douglas Ave Ste 1040 .... Dallas TX 75225 214-361-0027 361-0139 772
TF: 800-747-5670 ■ *Web:* www.strongtravel.com
Strongauth Inc
20045 Stevens Creek Blvd Ste 2A .... Cupertino CA 95014 408-331-2000 693
Web: www.strongauth.com
Strong-Bridge Consulting LLC
10940 NE 33rd Pl Ste 102 .... Bellevue WA 98004 206-905-4631 463
Web: www.strong-bridge-envision.com
Stronghaven Inc
2727 Paces Ferry Rd SE Bldg 1 Ste 1850 .... Atlanta GA 30336 404-699-1952 699-1825 100
TF: 800-331-7835 ■ *Web:* hoodcontainer.com
Strongsville Chamber of Commerce
18829 Royalton Rd .... Strongsville OH 44136 440-238-3366 238-7010 139
Web: www.strongsvillechamber.com
Strongwell 400 Commonwealth Ave .... Bristol VA 24201 276-645-8000 645-8132 606
Web: www.strongwell.com
Stroock & Stroock & Lavan LLP
180 Maiden Ln .... New York NY 10038 212-806-5400 428
Web: www.stroock.com
Strother Ventures II Inc
225 Ray Ave Ste 204 .... Fayetteville NC 28301 910-864-2325 652
Web: www.erastrother.com
Strothman & Company PSC
1600 Waterfront Plz .... Louisville KY 40202 502-585-1600 2
Web: www.strothman.com
Strottman International Inc
36 Executive Pk Ste 200 .... Irvine CA 92614 949-623-7900 195
Web: www.strottman.com
Stroud, Willink & Howard LLC
33 E Main St Ste 610 PO Box 2236 .... Madison WI 53701 608-257-2281 257-7643 428
Web: www.stroudlaw.com
Strouds Run State Park
11661 State Pk Rd .... Athens OH 45701 740-767-3570 565
Web: parks.ohiodnr.gov
Stroudwater Associates Inc
1685 Congress St Ste 202 .... Portland ME 04102 207-221-8250 196
Web: www.stroudwater.com
Struck 2985 S Main St Ste 200 .... Salt Lake City UT 84101 801-531-0122 5
Web: www.struck.com
Structall Building Systems Inc
350 Burbank Rd .... Oldsmar FL 34677 800-969-3706 234
TF: 800-969-3706 ■ *Web:* www.structall.com
Structura Inc
9208 Waterford Centre Blvd Ste 100 .... Austin TX 78758 512-495-9702 495-9712 186
Web: www.structurainc.com
Structural Component Systems Inc (SCS)
1255 Front St .... Fremont NE 68026 402-721-5622 187
TF: 800-844-5622 ■ *Web:* www.scstruss.com
Structural Concepts Corp
888 Porter Rd .... Muskegon MI 49441 231-798-8888 798-4960 286
TF: 800-433-9489 ■ *Web:* www.structuralconcepts.com

Phone | Fax | Class

Structural Consultants Inc
3400 E Bayaud Ave Ste 300 . . . . Denver CO 80209 303-399-5154 261
Web: sci-denver.com

Structural Materials Inc 1401 40th St N . . . . Fargo ND 58102 701-282-7100 281-1022 191-2
Web: www.smionline.com

Structural Steel of Carolina LLC
1725 Vargrave St . . . . Winston-Salem NC 27107 336-725-0521 725-0523 480
Web: www.steelofcarolina.com

Structural Steel Services
6210 St Louis St . . . . Meridian MS 39307 601-483-5381 480
Web: www.structuralsteelservice.com

Structural Wood Corp
4000 Labore Rd . . . . Saint Paul MN 55110 651-426-8111 426-6859 817
TF: 800-652-9058 ■ *Web:* www.structural-wood.com

Structural Wood Systems
321 Dohrimier St . . . . Greenville AL 36037 334-382-6534 382-4260 817
TF: 800-553-0661 ■ *Web:* www.glulamstructuralwood.com

Structure House 3017 Pickett Rd . . . . Durham NC 27705 855-736-4009 490-0191* 706
**Fax Area Code:* 919 ■ *TF:* 800-553-0052 ■ *Web:* www.structurehouse.com

Structure Networks Inc
17542 17th St Ste 105 . . . . Tustin CA 92780 714-505-0303 809
TF: 888-743-0303 ■ *Web:* structurenetworks.com

Structure Tone Inc 770 Broadway . . . . New York NY 10003 212-481-6100 685-9267 186
Web: structuretone.com

Structures Unlimited Inc 166 River Rd . . . . Bow NH 03304 603-645-6539 625-0798 697
TF: 800-225-3895 ■ *Web:* www.structuresunlimitedinc.com

Structurlam Products Ltd
2176 Government St . . . . Penticton BC V2A8B5 250-492-8912 492
Web: www.structurlam.com

Strukmyer LLC
1801 Big Town Blvd Ste 100 . . . . Mesquite TX 75149 214-275-9595 475
Web: www.strukmyer.com

Struktol Company of America Inc
PO Box 1649 . . . . Stow OH 44224 330-928-5188 928-8726 144
TF: 800-327-8649 ■ *Web:* www.struktol.com

Strum 1200 6th Ave Ste 900 . . . . Seattle WA 98109 206-340-6111 463
Web: www.strumagency.com

Struthers Federal Credit Union
808 Poland Ave . . . . Struthers OH 44471 330-755-7556 755-2320 219
Web: strutherscreditunion.com

Struthers-Dunn
407 E Smith St Ste B . . . . Timmonsville SC 29161 843-346-4427 346-4465 203
Web: www.struthers-dunn.com

Strutz International Inc
440 Mars-Valencia Rd PO Box 509 . . . . Mars PA 16046 724-625-1501 625-3570 413
Web: www.strutz.com

Strybuc Industries (RHM) 500 W 84 St . . . . Hialeah FL 33014 305-558-5051 557-5239 234
TF: 800-780-5051 ■ *Web:* www.strybuc.com

Stryker Corp
Physio-Control Operations
11811 Willows Rd NE . . . . Redmond WA 98052 425-867-4000 881-2405 250
TF: 800-442-1142 ■ *Web:* www.strykeremergencycare.com

Stry-Lenkoff Co 1100 W Broadway . . . . Louisville KY 40203 502-587-6804 587-6822 110
TF: 800-626-8247 ■ *Web:* www.strylenkoff.com

Stryve Biltong
5801 Tennyson Pkwy Ste 275 . . . . Plano TX 75024 888-617-2370 49-6
TF: 888-617-2370 ■ *Web:* bit.ly

STS (Society of Thoracic Surgeons)
633 N St Clair St Ste 2320 . . . . Chicago IL 60611 312-202-5800 202-5801 49-8
TF: 877-865-5321 ■ *Web:* www.sts.org

STS Component Solutions LLC
2910 SW 42 Ave . . . . Palm City FL 34990 888-777-2960 22
TF: 888-777-2960 ■ *Web:* www.stsaviationgroup.com

STS Consulting Services LLC
PO Box 9005 . . . . Longview TX 75608 903-247-1787 196
Web: ststx.com

STS Instruments Inc 17711 Mitchell N . . . . Irvine CA 92614 580-223-4773 248
Web: www.stsinstruments.com

STS International Inc
1225 S Clark St Ste 1300 . . . . Arlington VA 22202 703-575-5180 261
Web: stsint.com

Stu Segall Productions Inc
4705 Ruffin Rd . . . . San Diego CA 92123 858-974-8988 514
Web: www.stusegall.com

Stuart C. Irby Co 815 Irby Dr . . . . Jackson MS 39201 713-476-0788 188-10
TF: 866-687-4729 ■ *Web:* www.irby.com

Stuart Hall School
235 W Frederick St PO Box 210 . . . . Staunton VA 24402 540-885-0356 886-2275 622
TF: 888-306-8926 ■ *Web:* www.stuarthallschool.org

Stuart Jet Center LLC
2501 Aviation Way . . . . Stuart FL 34996 772-288-6700 288-3782 63
TF: 877-735-9538 ■ *Web:* www.stuartjet.com

Stuart Karten Design Inc
4204 Glencoe Ave . . . . Marina CA 90292 310-827-8722 261
Web: kartendesign.com

Stuart Maue Mitchell & James Ltd
3840 McKelvey Rd . . . . Bridgeton MO 63044 800-291-9940 291-6546* 195
**Fax Area Code:* 314 ■ *TF:* 800-291-9940 ■ *Web:* www.smmj.com

Stuart Pimsler Dance & Theater
528 Hennepin Ave S Ste 707 . . . . Minneapolis MN 55403 763-521-7738 573-1
Web: www.stuartpimsler.com

Stuart-Martin County Chamber of Commerce
1650 S Kanner Hwy . . . . Stuart FL 34994 772-287-1088 220-3437 139
Web: www.stuartmartinchamber.org

Stuart-Rodgers Photography
2504 Greenbay Rd . . . . Evanston IL 60201 847-864-7322 167-3
Web: www.srphoto.com

Stubbe's Precast 30 Muir Line . . . . Harley ON N0E1E0 519-424-2183 424-9058 183
TF: 866-355-2183 ■ *Web:* www.stubbes.org

Stubbs & Perdue PA
9208 Falls of Neuse Rd Ste 201 . . . . Raleigh NC 27615 800-348-9404 445
TF: 800-348-9404 ■ *Web:* www.stubbsperdue.com

Stubbs & Perdue PA 310 Craven St . . . . New Bern NC 28560 919-870-6258 41
Web: stubbsperdue.com

StubHub 199 Fremont St 4th Fl . . . . San Francisco CA 94105 866-788-2482 459
TF: 866-788-2482 ■ *Web:* www.stubhub.com

Stuckey Ford Subaru
500 Broad St . . . . Hollidaysburg PA 16648 814-695-9862 57
Web: www.stuckeyforyou.com

Phone | Fax | Class

Stuckey's Corp
8555 16th St Ste 850 . . . . Silver Spring MD 20910 301-585-8222 670
TF: 800-423-6171 ■ *Web:* www.stuckeys.com

Stucki & Rencher LLC
215 S State St Ste 600 . . . . Salt Lake City UT 84111 801-961-1300 41
Web: lawfirmra.com

Studebaker National Museum
201 Chapin St . . . . South Bend IN 46601 574-235-9714 520
TF: 888-391-5600 ■ *Web:* studebakermuseum.org

Studebaker Submetering Inc
5350 Shawnee Rd Ste 103 . . . . Alexandria VA 22312 703-916-9000 916-9001 653
TF: 800-987-9877 ■ *Web:* studebakersubmetering.com

Student Academic Services Building
281 W Lane Ave . . . . Columbus OH 43210 614-292-0300 725
Web: www.contactbuckeyelink.osu.edu

Student Advantage LLC 280 Summer St . . . . Boston MA 02210 800-333-2920 912-2012* 384
**Fax Area Code:* 617 ■ *TF:* 800-333-2920 ■ *Web:* www.studentadvantage.com

Student Agencies Foundation Inc
409 College Ave . . . . Ithaca NY 14850 607-272-2000 305
TF: 800-631-8405 ■ *Web:* www.studentagencies.com

Student Assistance Foundation
303 Irene St PO Box 5209 . . . . Helena MT 59601 406-495-7800 166
Web: www.safmt.org

Student Book Store
421 E Grand River Ave . . . . East Lansing MI 48823 517-351-4210 95
TF: 800-968-1111 ■ *Web:* www.sbsmsu.com

Student Conservation Assn (SCA)
689 River Rd PO Box 550 . . . . Charlestown NH 03603 603-543-1700 543-1828 48-13
TF: 888-722-9675 ■ *Web:* www.thesca.org

Student Media Corp 823 16th St . . . . Greeley CO 80631 970-392-9270 532-2
Web: www.uncmirror.com

Student Prince Cafe, The
8 Fort St . . . . Springfield MA 01103 413-734-7475 739-7303 671
Web: www.studentprince.com

Student Tours Inc 60 West Ave . . . . Vineyard Haven MA 02568 508-693-5078 693-8627 760
TF: 800-331-7093 ■ *Web:* studenttoursinc.com

Student Transportation Inc (STA)
Student Transportation of America
3349 Hwy 138 Bldg A Ste C . . . . Wall NJ 07719 732-280-4200 280-4214 109
TF: 888-942-2250 ■ *Web:* www.ridestbus.com

Student Travel Services Inc
2431 Solomons Island Rd Ste 302 . . . . Edgewater MD 21037 410-787-9500 787-9584 760
TF: 800-648-4849 ■ *Web:* www.ststravel.com

Student Veterans of America
PO Box 77673 . . . . Washington DC 20013 202-223-4710 305
TF: 866-320-3826 ■ *Web:* studentveterans.org

Studentcitycom Inc 8 Essex Center Dr . . . . Peabody MA 01960 320-654-0008 573-2069* 771
**Fax Area Code:* 978 ■ *TF:* 888-777-4642 ■ *Web:* www.studentcity.com

Students Against Destructive Decisions (SADD)
255 Main St . . . . Marlborough MA 01752 508-481-3568 481-5759 48-6
Web: www.sadd.org

Studio 170 LLC 170 E Main St . . . . Northville MI 48167 248-465-0771 77
Web: studio170mi.com

Studio 2 Digital Dental Design Inc
2405 32nd St SE . . . . Kentwood MI 49512 616-957-2140 415
Web: studio2dental.com

Studio 27 780 Tremont St . . . . Boston MA 02118 857-239-8400 77
Web: studio27hairsalon.com

Studio 3 Inc 1316 SE 12th Ave . . . . Portland OR 97214 503-238-1748 236-6014 592
Web: studio3.com

Studio Academy of Beauty, The
610 N Alma School Rd Ste 38 . . . . Chandler AZ 85224 480-857-1138 167-3
Web: www.thestudioacademyofbeauty.com

Studio Booth LLC 6343 Penn Ave . . . . Pittsburgh PA 15206 412-362-6684 77
Web: www.studio-booth.com

Studio City Chamber of Commerce
4024 Radford Ave Edit 2 Ste F . . . . Studio City CA 91604 818-655-5916 139
Web: www.studiocitychamber.com

Studio Ctr
161 Business Park Dr . . . . Virginia Beach VA 23462 757-622-2111 5
TF: 866-515-2111 ■ *Web:* studiocenter.com

Studio Hill Farm PO Box 438 . . . . North Salem NY 10560 888-890-9887 669-5653* 637-10
**Fax Area Code:* 914 ■ *TF:* 888-890-9887 ■ *Web:* www.danielgreeneartist.com

Studio Jewelers Ltd 32 E 31st St . . . . New York NY 10016 212-686-1944 689-7923 167-3
Web: www.studiojewelersltd.com

Studio Museum in Harlem, The
144 W 125th St . . . . New York NY 10027 212-864-4500 864-4800 520
Web: studiomuseum.org

Studio One Digital Inc
180 N Wabash Ave Ste 300 . . . . Chicago IL 60601 312-376-3300 344
Web: studio1digital.com

Studio One Midwest Inc
74 Leonard Wood Rd . . . . Battle Creek MI 49037 269-962-3474 962-4482 322
Web: www.mannetron.com

Studio Red Inc 115 Independence Dr . . . . Menlo Park CA 94025 650-324-2244 261
Web: www.studiored.com

Studio Theatre 1501 14th St NW . . . . Washington DC 20005 202-232-7267 588-5262 720
Web: www.studiotheatre.org

Studio Y Creations Inc
1-6204 29 St SE . . . . Calgary AB T2C1W3 800-243-4024 8
TF: 800-243-4024 ■ *Web:* www.studioycreations.com

Studio360 Inc 1400 20th Ave . . . . Seattle WA 98122 206-382-0360 344
Web: www.studio360.com

StudioNow Inc
4017 Hillsboro Pk STE 418 . . . . Nashville TN 37215 615-577-9400 387
Web: corp.studionow.com

Studley Press Inc, The
151 E Housatonic St . . . . Dalton MA 01226 413-684-0441 684-0220 627
Web: www.thestudleypress.com

Studnick & Associates LLC
5764 Berkshire Valley Rd . . . . Oak Ridge NJ 07438 973-697-2795 2
Web: studnickcpa.com

Studsvik Scandpower Inc
1087 Beacon St Ste 301 . . . . Newton MA 02459 617-965-7450 177
Web: www.studsvik.com

Study (the) 3233 The Blvd . . . . Westmount QC H3Y1S4 514-935-9352 685
Web: www.thestudy.qc.ca

Name / Address	City	State	ZIP	Phone	Fax	Class
Stuecker & Associates Inc 1930 Bishop Ln Ste 603 *Web:* stueckerandassoc.com	Louisville	KY	40218	502-452-9227	452-1529	462
Stuedle Spears & Company PSC 2821 S Hurstbourne Pkwy Ste 1 *Web:* derbycitycpa.business.site	Louisville	KY	40220	502-491-5253		2
Stueve Siegel Hanson LLP 460 Nichols Rd Ste 200 *TF:* 800-714-0360 ■ *Web:* stuevesiegel.com	Kansas City	MO	64112	816-714-7100		428
Stuft Pizza Franchise Corp 50855 Washington St Ste 210 *Web:* www.stuftpizza.com	La Quinta	CA	92253	760-777-1660	777-1948	670
Stuhr Museum of the Prairie Pioneer 3133 W Hwy 34 *Web:* www.stuhrmuseum.org	Grand Island	NE	68801	308-385-5316		520
Stuller Settings Inc PO Box 87777 *TF:* 800-877-7777 ■ *Web:* www.stuller.com	LaFayette	LA	70598	800-877-7777	444-4741	407
Stulz Air Technology Systems Inc 1572 Tilco Dr *TF:* 888-529-1266 ■ *Web:* www.stulz-usa.com	Frederick	MD	21704	301-620-2033	662-5487	14
StumbleUpon Inc 301 Brannan St *Web:* www.stumbleupon.com	San Francisco	CA	94107	415-979-0640		387
Stunkel Tax & Accounting PC 903 Western Ave *Web:* stunkeltax.com	Pittsburgh	PA	15233	412-371-8600		2
Stuntwomen's Association of Motion Pictures Inc 3760 Cahuenga Blvd Ste 104 *Web:* www.stuntwomen.com	Studio City	CA	91604	818-762-0907		48-4
Stupp Bros Inc 3800 Weber Rd *TF:* 800-535-9999 ■ *Web:* www.stupp.com	Saint Louis	MO	63125	314-638-5000	638-2660	480
Stupp Corp 12555 Ronaldson Rd *Web:* www.stuppcorp.com	Baton Rouge	LA	70807	225-775-8800		490
Sturbridge Host Hotel & Conference Ctr 366 Main St *TF:* 800-582-3232 ■ *Web:* www.sturbridgehosthotel.com	Sturbridge	MA	01566	508-347-7393	347-3944	379
Sturdevant Refrigeration & Air Conditioning Inc 475 Hukilike St *Web:* www.sturdevantair.com	Kahului	HI	96732	808-871-6404	871-6400	189-10
Sturdisteel Co PO Box 2655 *TF:* 800-433-3116 ■ *Web:* www.sturdisteel.com	Waco	TX	76702	800-433-3116		319-3
Sturdivant & Company Inc 3000 Atrium Way Ste 520 *Web:* sturdivant-co.com	Mount Laurel	NJ	08054	856-751-1331		690
Sturdy Corp 1822 Carolina Beach Rd *TF:* 800-721-3282 ■ *Web:* www.sturdycorp.com	Wilmington	NC	28401	910-763-2500	763-2650	203
Sturdy Memorial Hospital 211 Park St PO Box 2963 *Web:* www.sturdymemorial.org	Attleboro	MA	02703	508-222-5200		374-3
Sturdy Oil Company Inc 1511 Abbott St *Web:* www.sturdyoil.com	Salinas	CA	93901	831-422-8801		579
Sturgeon Electric Company Inc 2825 E Ginter Rd *Web:* www.myrgroup.com	Henderson	CO	80640	303-286-8000		189-4
Sturges Center for the Fine Arts 780 NE St *Web:* www.sturgescenter.org	San Bernardino	CA	92410	909-384-5415	384-5449	572
Sturges Manufacturing Company Inc 2030 Sunset Ave PO Box 59 *Web:* www.sturgesmfgco.com	Utica	NY	13502	315-732-6159	732-2314	745-5
Sturgill, Turner, Barker & Moloney PLLC 333 W Vine St Ste 1400 *Web:* www.sturgillturner.com	Lexington	KY	40507	859-255-8581	231-0851	428
Sturgis Bank & Trust Co 113-125 E Chicago Rd PO Box 600 *OTC:* STBI ■ *TF:* 888-255-7372 ■ *Web:* www.sturgisbank.com	Sturgis	MI	49091	269-651-9345		70
Sturgis Library 3090 Main St *Web:* www.sturgislibrary.org	Barnstable	MA	02630	508-362-6636	362-5467	434-3
Sturgis Molded Products Co 1950 Clark St *Web:* www.smpco.com	Sturgis	MI	49091	269-651-9381		604
Sturgis Public Schools 107 W W St *Web:* www.sturgisps.org	Sturgis	MI	49091	269-659-1500		685
Sturgis Tool and Die Inc 817 Broadus St *TF:* 800-301-0984 ■ *Web:* www.sturgistool.com	Sturgis	MI	49091	269-651-5435		757
Sturm Foods Inc PO Box 287 *TF:* 800-347-8876 ■ *Web:* www.sturmfoods.com	Manawa	WI	54949	920-596-2511	596-3040	297-11
Sturm Heating Inc 1112 N Nelson St *Web:* www.sturmheating.com	Spokane	WA	99202	509-325-4505		189-10
Sturtevant Inc 348 Circuit St *TF:* 800-992-0209 ■ *Web:* www.sturtevantinc.com	Hanover	MA	02339	781-829-6501		111
Stussy Inc 17426 Daimler St *Web:* www.stussy.com	Irvine	CA	92614	949-474-9255		155-3
Stutman Contracting Inc 18 Sutton Ave *Web:* stutmancontracting.com	Oxford	MA	01540	508-987-9472	987-9856	610
Stutsman County 511 Second Ave SE *Web:* www.co.stutsman.nd.us	Jamestown	ND	58401	701-252-9035		338
Stuttering Foundation of America 3100 Walnut Grove Rd Ste 603 *TF:* 800-992-9392 ■ *Web:* www.stutteringhelp.org	Memphis	TN	38111	901-452-7343	452-3931	48-17
Stutzki Engineering Inc 241 N Broadway Ste 302 *Web:* stutzkiengineering.com	Milwaukee	WI	53202	414-455-4815		261
Stuyvesant Press Inc 119 Coit St *Web:* stuyvesantpress.com	Irvington	NJ	07111	973-399-3880	399-9696	627
STV Group Inc 205 W Welsh Dr *Web:* www.stvinc.com	Douglassville	PA	19518	610-385-8200	385-8500	261
Styberg Engineering 2200 Northwestern Ave PO Box 788 **Fax Area Code:* 262 ■ *TF:* 800-240-7275 ■ *Web:* styberg.com	Racine	WI	53401	800-240-7275	637-1319*	620
Styer Transportation Co 7870 215th St W *TF:* 800-548-9149 ■ *Web:* www.styertrans.com	Lakeville	MN	55044	952-469-4491		780
Style Crest Inc 2450 Enterprise St *Web:* www.stylecrestinc.com	Fremont	OH	43420	419-332-7369		104
STYLE EXCHANGE 1722 Towne Centre Way *Web:* www.shopsxc.com	Mount Pleasant	SC	29464	843-884-2244		157-6
Style Line Furniture Inc 116 Godfrey Rd *Web:* stylelinefurniture.net	Verona	MS	38879	662-566-1113	566-7657	319-2
Style Weekly 1707 Summit Ave Ste 201 *Web:* www.styleweekly.com	Richmond	VA	23230	804-358-0825		532-5
STYLECASTER 440 Ninth Ave 11th Fl *Web:* stylecaster.com	New York	NY	10001	646-300-8350		387
Stylemasters College of Hair Design 1224 Commerce Ave *Web:* www.stylemasters.edu	Longview	WA	98632	360-636-2720	703-3967	167-3
Stylex PO Box 5038 **Fax Area Code:* 856 ■ *TF:* 800-257-5742 ■ *Web:* www.stylexseating.com	Delanco	NJ	08075	800-257-5742	461-5574*	319-1
Stylin Online 81900 Main St *Web:* www.stylinonline.com	Memphis	MI	48041	586-270-1086		791
Stylmark Inc 6536 Main St NE *TF:* 800-328-2495 ■ *Web:* www.stylmark.com	Fridley	MN	55432	800-328-2495		286
StyroChem Canada Ltee 19250 Clark Graham *Web:* www.styrochem.com	Baie-D'Urfe	QC	H9X3R8	514-457-3226		601
Styrotech Inc 8800 Wyoming Ave N *Web:* www.styrotech.com	Brooklyn Park	MN	55445	763-425-4001		601
Styrotek Inc 545 Rd 176 *Web:* www.styrotek.com	Delano	CA	93215	661-725-4957	725-7064	601
Styskal, Wiese & Melchione LLP 550 N Brand Ave Ste 550 *Web:* swmllp.com	Glendale	CA	91203	818-241-0103	241-5733	41
SU Mitra Inc 88 Corporate Dr Ste 1614 *Web:* www.su-mitra.com	Toronto	ON	M1H3G6	416-907-6866	419-3358	463
Suarez Corporation Industries 7800 Whipple Ave NW *TF:* 800-764-0008 ■ *Web:* www.suarez.com	North Canton	OH	44720	330-494-5504		195
Sub Rosa 353 W 12th St *Web:* wearesubrosa.com	New York	NY	10014	212-414-8605		5
Sub Station II Inc 15 N Harvin St *Web:* www.substationii.com	Sumter	SC	29150	803-775-5328		670
Subacute Saratoga Children's Hospital 13425 Sousa Ln *Web:* www.chonc.org	Saratoga	CA	06070	408-370-0075	340-1517	450
Subaru of America Inc 2235 Marlton Pike W *TF:* 800-782-2783 ■ *Web:* www.subaru.com	Cherry Hill	NJ	08002	856-488-8500		59
Subaru of Indiana Automotive Inc 5500 State Rd 38 E *Web:* www.subaru-sia.com	LaFayette	IN	47905	765-449-1111		131
Subaru of Portland 107 SE Grand Ave *Web:* www.wentworthchevrolet.com	Portland	OR	97214	503-214-2364		516
Subco Foods Inc 4350 S Taylor Dr *TF:* 800-473-0757 ■ *Web:* www.subcofoods.com	Sheboygan	WI	53081	920-457-7761	457-3899	296-16
Subcoe 117 Pembina Rd Ste 109 *Web:* www.subcoe.com	Sherwood Park	AB	T8H0J4	780-467-4118	467-3477	261
Subex Inc 12103 Airport Way Bldg 1 Ste 390 *Web:* www.subex.com	Broomfield	CO	80021	303-301-6200	301-6201	224
SubGenius Foundation Inc, The PO Box 181417 *TF:* 888-669-2323 ■ *Web:* subgenius.com	Cleveland Heights	OH	44118	216-320-9528		637-2
Subiaco Academy 405 N Subiaco Ave *Web:* www.subi.org	Subiaco	AR	72865	479-934-1000		622
Subject Well 7000 MoPac Expy Ste 330 *TF:* 888-634-1166 ■ *Web:* www.subjectwell.com	Austin	TX	78731	888-634-1166		582
Subjex Corp 3240 Aldrich Ave S Ste 301 **Fax Area Code:* 800 ■ *Web:* www.subjex.com	Minneapolis	MN	55408	612-382-5566	360-5375*	393
Sublette County PO Box 250 *Web:* www.sublettewyo.com	Pinedale	WY	82941	307-367-4372	367-6396	338
Sublette Feeders LLC 1535 UU Rd *Web:* www.sublettefeeders.com	Sublette	KS	67877	620-668-5501		10-1
SUBNET Solutions Inc 916 42nd Ave SE Ste 110 *Web:* www.subnet.com	Calgary	AB	T2G1Z2	403-270-8885	270-9631	261
Subon Data Co 1617 Dillon Rd Ste 1A *Web:* www.subondata.com	Maple Glen	PA	19002	215-628-8720		179
SubPop Records 2013 Fourth Ave 3rd Fl *Web:* www.subpop.com	Seattle	WA	98121	206-441-8441	441-8245	657
Subsea 7 (Us) LLC 10787 Clay Rd *Web:* www.subsea7.com	Houston	TX	77041	713-430-1100		261
Subsea Video Systems Inc PO Box 159 *Web:* www.subseavideosystems.com	Elizabeth City	NC	27907	252-338-1001	338-1515	628
Substance Abuse & Mental Health Services Administration *Center for Substance Abuse Prevention* 1 Choke Cherry Rd *Web:* www.samhsa.gov	Rockville	MD	20857	240-276-2420		340-10
Center for Substance Abuse Treatment 5600 Fishers Ln PO Box 2345 *TF:* 877-726-4727 ■ *Web:* www.samhsa.gov	Rockville	MD	20857	240-276-1660	221-4292	340-10
Subsurface Constructors Inc 110 Angelica St **Fax Area Code:* 314 ■ *TF:* 800-242-9425 ■ *Web:* www.subsurfaceconstructors.com	Saint Louis	MO	63147	866-421-2460	421-2479*	189-5
Subsystem Technologies Inc 2121 Crystal Dr Ste 680 *Web:* www.subsystem.com	Arlington	VA	22202	703-841-0071	841-0068	177
Suburban Chambers of Commerce 71 Summit Ave *Web:* www.suburbanchambers.org	Summit	NJ	07901	908-522-1700	522-9252	139
Suburban Collection 1810 Maplelawn Dr *TF:* 877-471-7100 ■ *Web:* www.suburbancollection.com	Troy	MI	48084	877-471-7100		57
Suburban Electrical Engineers/ Contractors Inc 709 Hickory Farm Ln *Web:* www.suburbanelectric.com	Appleton	WI	54914	920-739-5156		261
Suburban Grinding Co 13025 SW Herman Rd *Web:* www.suburbangrinding.com	Tualatin	OR	97062	503-692-6188	692-2725	393
Suburban Manufacturing Co 676 Broadway St *Web:* www.suburbanmanufacturing.com	Dayton	TN	37321	423-775-2131	775-7015	14

	Phone	Fax	Class
Suburban Manufacturing Inc 10531 Dalton Ave NE Monticello MN 55362 *Fax Area Code: 920 ■ Web: www.gosuburban.com	763-782-5752	295-6601*	454
Suburban Mobility Authority for Regional Transportation (SMART) 535 Griswold St Ste 600 Detroit MI 48226 TF: 866-962-5515 ■ Web: www.smartbus.org	313-223-2100		468
Suburban Motors Grafton Inc 139 N Main St Thiensville WI 53092 Web: www.suburbanharley.com	262-242-2464		256
Suburban Plastic Co 340 Renner Dr Elgin IL 60123 Web: www.suburbanplastics.com	847-741-4900		596
Suburban Press & Metro Press 1550 Woodville Rd Millbury OH 43447 TF: 800-300-6158 ■ Web: www.presspublications.com	419-836-2221	836-1319	532-4
Suburban Propane LP 240 Rt 10 W PO Box 206 Whippany NJ 07981 TF: 800-776-7263 ■ Web: www.suburbanpropane.com	973-503-9252		316
Suburban Realty Inc 1055 Spring St Grafton WI 53024 Web: suburbanrealty.biz	262-377-3060		652
Suburban Surgical Company Inc 275 Twelfth St Wheeling IL 60090 TF: 800-323-7366 ■ Web: www.suburbansurgical.com	847-537-9320	537-9061	476
Suburban Wheel Cover Co 1420 Landmeier Rd Elk Grove Village IL 60007 TF: 800-635-8126 ■ Web: www.suburbanwheelcover.com	847-758-0388		54
Subx Inc 428 Fore St Portland ME 04101 TF: 800-881-9953 ■ Web: quantrix.com	207-775-0808		177
SubZero Constructors Inc 30055 Comercio Rancho Santa Margarita CA 92688 Web: subzeroconstructors.com	949-216-9500	216-9539	189-10
Success Associates LLC 26 Kings Vly Ct Damascus MD 20872 Web: www.successassociates.com	301-391-6161		195
Success Communications Group 26 Eastmens Rd Parsippany NJ 07054 TF: 800-848-4323 ■ Web: scgadv.com	973-992-7800		7
Success Is Easy 7119 E Shea Blvd Ste 109-271 Scottsdale AZ 85254 Web: www.horsecoursesonline.com	602-689-6171		637-2
Success Motivation International Inc 4567 Lakeshore Dr Waco TX 76710 Web: www.lmi-world.com	254-776-9966	772-9588	366
Success Printing & Mailing Inc 10 Pearl St Norwalk CT 06850 Web: www.successprint.com	203-847-1112		627
Success Promotions 14376 S Outer Forty Rd Chesterfield MO 63017 Web: successpromotions.com	314-878-1999		292
Success Sciences Inc 17838 N US Hwy 4 Tampa FL 33549 Web: success-sciences.com	813-989-9900		177
Success Trade Securities Inc 1900 L St N W Washington DC 20036 Web: www.successtrade.com	202-386-7261		690
Succession Capital Alliance Insurance Services LLC 4695 MacArthur Ct Ste 400 Newport Beach CA 92660 Web: successioncapital.com	949-794-1882		390
Successories Inc 1040 Holland Dr Boca Raton FL 33487 *Fax Area Code: 561 ■ TF: 800-535-2773 ■ Web: www.successories.com	800-535-2773	952-4097*	310
SuccessWorks 19363 Willamette Dr Ste 325 West Linn OR 97068 Web: seocopywriting.com	503-476-1065		41
Succor Creek State Natural Area 1298 Lake Owyhee Dam Rd Adrian OR 97901 Web: oregonstateparks.org	541-339-2331		565
Sucher Tire Service Co 3641 E Davison St Detroit MI 48212 Web: www.suchertire.com	313-891-5640	891-0900	755
Suchomski Equipment Inc 21027 State Rte 127 N Pinckneyville IL 62274 Web: suchequip.com	618-336-5440		274
Sudan Embassy 2210 Massachusetts Ave NW Washington DC 20008 Web: www.sudanembassy.org	202-338-8565	667-2406	257
Sudberry Properties Inc 5465 Morehouse Dr Ste 260 San Diego CA 92121 Web: www.sudprop.com	858-546-3000		652
Sudbury Insurance Agency Inc 17 Central St Norwood MA 02062 Web: morrillinsurance.com	781-762-7300		390
Sudbury Star, The 128 Pine St Ste 201 Sudbury ON P3C1X3 Web: www.thesudburystar.com	705-674-5271	674-0624	532-1
Sudbury Valley Trustees Inc 18 Wolbach Rd Sudbury MA 01776 Web: www.svtweb.org	978-443-5588		804
Suddath Cos 815 S Main St Jacksonville FL 32207 TF: 800-395-7100 ■ Web: suddath.com	904-352-2577		519
Suddekor LLC 240 Bowles Rd Agawam MA 01001 Web: www.suddekorllc.com	413-821-9000		627
Suddenlink Communications 6151 Paluxy Dr Tyler TX 75703 TF: 877-694-9474 ■ Web: suddenlink.com	877-694-9474		116
Sudenga Industries Inc 2002 Kingbird Ave George IA 51237 TF: 888-783-3642 ■ Web: sudenga.com	712-475-3301	475-3320	273
Suder's Art Store 1309 Vine St Cincinnati OH 45202 Web: sudersartstore.com	513-241-0800		45
Sudjam LLC PO Box 481166 Los Angeles CA 90048 Web: sudjam.com	818-244-3770	806-8999	177
Sudler & Hennessey 230 Park Ave S Ste 8 New York NY 10003 Web: www.sudler.com	212-614-4100	598-6907	4
Sudler Property Management John Hancock Ctr 875 N Michigan Ave Ste 3980 Chicago IL 60611 Web: sudlerchicago.com	312-751-0900	751-1730	463
Sue Kolve'S Salon & Day Spa 230 Main St Onalaska WI 54650 Web: suekolves.com	608-784-2363		77
Sueba USA Corp 1800 W Loop S Ste 1300 Houston TX 77027 Web: www.suebausa.com	713-961-3588	961-1343	653
Suehiro 4431 Corbett Dr Fort Collins CO 80525 Web: www.suehirojapaneserestaurant.com	970-672-8185		671
Suemaur Exploration & Production LLC 539 N Carancahua Ste 1100 Corpus Christi TX 78401 Web: www.suemaur.com	361-884-8824		536
Suffield Academy 185 N Main St Suffield CT 06078 Web: www.suffieldacademy.org	860-386-4400	386-4411	622
Suffield Veterinary Hospital 577 East St S Suffield CT 06078 Web: suffieldvet.com	860-668-4041		794
Suffolk Construction 65 Allerton St Boston MA 02119 Web: www.suffolk.com	617-445-3500	541-2128	186
Suffolk Co-opeartive Library System 627 N Sunrise Service Rd Bellport NY 11713 Web: portal.suffolklibrarysystem.org	631-286-1600	286-1647	434-3
Suffolk County County Rd 51 Riverhead NY 11901 Web: www.suffolkcountyny.gov	631-852-1400		338
Suffolk County Community College *Grant* 1001 Crooked Hill Rd Brentwood NY 11717 Web: www.sunysuffolk.edu	631-851-6700	851-6819	162
Suffolk County Historical Society 300 W Main St Riverhead NY 11901 Web: suffolkcountyhistoricalsociety.org	631-727-2881	727-3467	520
Suffolk Downs 525 McClean Highwy East Boston MA 02128 Web: suffolkdowns.com	617-567-3900		133
Suffolk (Independent City) 442 W Washington St Suffolk VA 23434 Web: www.suffolkva.us	757-514-4000		338
Suffolk Iron Works Inc 418 E Washington St 20 Suffolk VA 23434 Web: www.suffolkironworks.com	757-539-2353	539-1520	385
Suffolk Transportation Service Inc 10 Moffitt Blvd Bay Shore NY 11706 Web: www.suffolkbus.com	631-665-3245	665-3186	109
Suffolk University 8 Ashburton Pl Boston MA 02108 TF: 800-678-3365 ■ Web: www.suffolk.edu	617-573-8460	557-1574	166
Sugami 4813 N Kings Hwy Myrtle Beach SC 29577 Web: www.sugamimyrtlebeach.com	843-692-7709		671
Sugar Assn 1300 L St NW Ste 1001 Washington DC 20005 Web: www.sugar.org	202-785-1122	785-5019	48-2
Sugar Cane Growers Co-opeartive of Florida 1500 W Sugar House Rd Belle Glade FL 33430 Web: www.scgc.org	561-996-5556		10-9
Sugar Creek Board of Education 3757 Upper Bellbrook Rd Bellbrook OH 45305 Web: www.sugarcreek.k12.oh.us	937-848-5001		685
Sugar Creek Foods Intl 301 N El Paso St Russellville AR 72801 TF: 800-445-2715 ■ Web: getsugarcreek.com	800-445-2715		296-25
Sugar Creek Packing Co 2101 Kenskill Ave Washington Court House OH 43160 *Fax Area Code: 513 ■ TF: 800-848-8205 ■ Web: www.sugarcreek.com	740-335-7440	551-5263*	296-26
Sugar Creek Scrap 1201 W National Ave West Terre Haute IN 47885 Web: www.sugarcreekscrap.com	812-533-2147		686
Sugar Foods Corp 950 Third Ave Ste 21 New York NY 10022 TF: 800-732-8963 ■ Web: www.sugarfoods.com	212-753-6900	753-6988	297-11
Sugar House Day Spa & Salon 111 N Alfred St Alexandria VA 22314 Web: sugarhousedayspa.com	703-549-9940	549-9931	77
Sugar Magnolia 804 Edgewood Ave NE Atlanta GA 30307 Web: www.sugarmagnoliabb.com	404-222-0226		379
Sugar Maple Farm LLC 139 Coleman Station Rd Millerton NY 12546	845-221-0575		368
Sugar Mill Ruins 600 Mission Rd New Smyrna Beach FL 32168 Web: www.volusia.org	386-427-2284		50-3
Sugarbush Resort & Inn 1840 Sugarbush Access Rd Warren VT 05674 TF: 800-537-8427 ■ Web: www.sugarbush.com	802-583-6300	583-6390	669
Sugardale Foods Inc 1600 Harmont Ave NE Canton OH 44705 Web: www.sugardale.com	330-455-5253		473
Sugarhill Card Co PO Box 14 Underhill VT 05489 Web: www.sugarhillcardcompany.com	802-488-5048	488-5728	637-10
Sugarhouse Greetings 38 E Guest Ave Salt Lake City UT 84115 TF: 800-365-5564 ■ Web: www.bottman.com	801-281-9683	665-1242	534
Sugarloaf/USA 5092 Access Rd Carrabassett Valley ME 04947 TF: 800-843-5623 ■ Web: www.sugarloaf.com	207-237-2000	237-3768	669
Sugarman & Susskind PA 100 Miracle Mile Ste 300 Coral Gables FL 33134 Web: sugarmansusskind.com	305-529-2801		41
Sugarman Law LLC 80 E Main St Somerville NJ 08876 Web: sugarmanlawfirm.com	732-877-1975		41
Sugden Community Theatre 701 Fifth Ave S Naples FL 34102 Web: naplesplayers.org	239-263-7990	434-7772	572
Suggs & Company PA 609 S Franklin St Whiteville NC 28472 Web: suggscpa.com	910-641-0105		2
Sughrue Mion PLLC 2100 Pennsylvania Ave NW Washington DC 20037 Web: www.sughrue.com	202-293-7060	293-7860	428
Sugino Corp 1380 Hamilton Pkwy Itasca IL 60143 TF: 888-784-4661 ■ Web: www.suginocorp.com	630-250-8585		358
Sugiyo USA Inc PO Box 468 Anacortes WA 98221 Web: www.sugiyo.com	360-293-0180	293-6964	296-14
Suh'dutsing Technologies LLC 600 N 100 E Cedar City UT 84721 Web: www.cedarbandcorp.com	435-867-0604		260
SUHM Spring Works Inc 14650 Heathrow Forest Pkwy Houston TX 77032 TF: 800-338-6903 ■ Web: suhm.net	713-224-9293	224-9418	295
Suhner Manufacturing Inc 43 Anderson Rd Rome GA 30161 Web: www.suhner.com	706-235-8046		759

Name / Address	City	State	ZIP	Phone	Fax	Class
Suhor Industries 10965 Granada Ln Ste 300 *Web:* www.suhor.com	Overland Park	KS	66211	913-345-2120		183
SUHRCO Management Inc 2010 156th Ave NE Ste 100 *Web:* suhrcorp.com	Bellevue	WA	98007	425-455-0900	462-1943	655
Suisha Garden Japanese Restaurant 208 Slater St *Web:* japaninottawa.com	Ottawa	ON	K1P5H8	613-236-9602		671
Suite 66 366 Adelaide St W Ste 600 *TF:* 866-779-3486 ■ *Web:* www.suite66.com	Toronto	ON	M5V1R9	416-628-5565		8
Suite Spotte 21 S La Grange Rd Ste 200 *Web:* suitespotte.com	La Grange	IL	60525	708-665-8050		393
Suiter Swantz Pc Llo 14301 FNB Pkwy Ste 220 *Web:* www.suiter.com	Omaha	NE	68154	402-496-0300		428
Suites Hotel in Canal Park, The 325 Lake Ave S *TF:* 800-794-1716 ■ *Web:* thesuitesduluth.com	Duluth	MN	55802	218-727-4663		379
Suit-Kote Corp 1911 Lorings Crossing Rd *Web:* www.suit-kote.com	Cortland	NY	13045	607-753-1100		46
Sukhi's Gourmet Indian Foods 25823 Clawiter Rd **Fax Area Code:* 510 ■ *TF:* 888-478-5447 ■ *Web:* sukhis.com	Hayward	CA	94545	888-478-5447	264-1236*	297-8
Sukup Manufacturing Co 1555 255th St PO Box 677 *TF:* 866-427-4422 ■ *Web:* www.sukup.com	Sheffield	IA	50475	641-892-4222	892-4629	273
Sukut Construction Inc 4010 W Chandler Ave *TF:* 888-785-8801 ■ *Web:* sukut.com	Santa Ana	CA	92704	714-540-5351	545-2438	188-4
Sul Ross State University E Hwy 90 *TF:* 888-722-7778 ■ *Web:* www.sulross.edu	Alpine	TX	79832	432-837-8011	837-8431	166
Sulaan Solutions Inc 1380 E Coconino Dr *Web:* www.sulaan.com	Chandler	AZ	85249	480-626-4041		180
Sullair Corp 3700 E Michigan Blvd *TF:* 888-879-5451 ■ *Web:* www.sullair.com	Michigan City	IN	46360	219-879-5451		172
Sullins Connector Solutions 801 E Mission Rd *TF:* 888-774-3100 ■ *Web:* www.sullinscorp.com	San Marcos	CA	92069	760-744-0125	744-6081	815
Sullivan & Cromwell LLP 125 Broad St *Web:* www.sullcrom.com	New York	NY	10004	212-558-4000	558-3588	428
Sullivan & McLaughlin Companies Inc 74 Lawley St *Web:* www.sullymac.com	Boston	MA	02122	617-474-0500	474-0505	186
Sullivan Arena 1600 Gambell St *Web:* www.sullivanarena.com	Anchorage	AK	99501	907-279-0618		720
Sullivan Automotive Group 2406 N Section St *Web:* www.shopsullivanauto.com	Sullivan	IN	47882	812-268-4321		57
Sullivan Bille PC 600 Clark Rd Ste 4 *Web:* www.sullivanbillepc.com	Tewksbury	MA	01876	978-970-2900		194
Sullivan Candy & Supply 1206 E 25th St *Web:* www.sullivancandyandsupply.com	Hibbing	MN	55746	218-263-7922	263-7257	297-3
Sullivan Correctional Facility 325 Riverside Dr PO Box 116 *Web:* www.doccs.ny.gov	Fallsburg	NY	12733	845-434-2080		213
Sullivan County 3411 Hwy 126 *Web:* www.sullivancountytn.gov	Blountville	TN	37617	423-323-6428	279-2725	338
Sullivan County 245 Muncy St PO Box 157 *TF:* 800-369-3599 ■ *Web:* www.sullivancounty-pa.us	Laporte	PA	18626	570-946-5201	946-4421	338
Sullivan County 100 N St *TF:* 800-320-2617 ■ *Web:* sullivanny.us	Monticello	NY	12701	845-794-3000		338
Sullivan County 14 Main St *Web:* www.sullivancountynh.gov	Newport	NH	03773	603-863-2560	863-9314	338
Sullivan County 2110 N Hospital Blvd Rm Ste 1 *Web:* www.sullivancountyindiana.us	Sullivan	IN	47882	812-691-1090		338
Sullivan County Chamber of Commerce 196 Bridgeville Rd Ste 7 *Web:* www.catskills.com	Monticello	NY	12701	845-791-4200	791-4220	139
Sullivan County Clerk 109 N Main St *Web:* www.government-county.org	Milan	MO	63556	660-265-4717		338
Sullivan County Community College 112 College Rd *TF:* 800-577-5243 ■ *Web:* sunysullivan.edu	Loch Sheldrake	NY	12759	845-434-5750	434-0923	162
Sullivan County Public Library 1655 Blountville Blvd *Web:* www.scpltn.org	Blountville	TN	37617	423-279-2714	279-2836	434-3
Sullivan County Rural Electric Co-opeartive Inc (SCREC) 5675 Rt 87 PO Box 65 *TF:* 800-570-5081 ■ *Web:* www.screc.com	Forksville	PA	18616	570-924-3381		245
Sullivan Curtis Monroe 1920 Main St *TF:* 800-427-3253 ■ *Web:* sullivancurtismonroe.com	Irvine	CA	92614	800-427-3253		390
Sullivan Dan (Sen R - AK) 302 Hart Senate Office Bldg *Web:* www.sullivan.senate.gov	Washington	DC	20510	202-224-3004		342-2
Sullivan Higdon & Sink Inc 255 N Mead *Web:* wehatesheep.com	Wichita	KS	67202	316-263-0124		4
Sullivan Hincks & Conway 120 W 22nd St Ste 100 *Web:* shlawfirm.com	Oak Brook	IL	60523	630-573-5021		428
Sullivan Paper Company Inc 42 Progress Ave *Web:* www.sullivanpaper.com	West Springfield	MA	01089	413-734-3107		548
Sullivan Rogers & Feichtel 100 Sterling Pkwy Ste 100 *Web:* srf-law.com	Mechanicsburg	PA	17050	717-612-5800		41
Sullivan Tire Company Inc 41 Accord Park Dr *TF:* 877-855-4826 ■ *Web:* www.sullivantire.com	Norwell	MA	02061	781-982-1550		62-5
Sullivan University 3101 Bardstown Rd *TF:* 800-844-1354 ■ *Web:* sullivan.edu	Louisville	KY	40205	502-456-6505		166
Sullivan's Foods 425 First St *Web:* www.sullivansfoods.net	Savanna	IL	61074	815-273-4511		345
Sullivan's Pub & Eatery 301 French St *Web:* www.sullivanspuberie.com	Erie	PA	16507	814-452-3446		671
Sullivan's Steakhouse 700 W DeKalb Pk *Web:* sullivanssteakhouse.com	King of Prussia	PA	19406	610-878-9025		671
Sullivan, Garrity & Donnelly Insurance Agency Inc 10 Institute Rd *Web:* sgdins.com	Worcester	MA	01609	508-754-1767		390
Sullivan, Mcgibbons & Associates LLP 12250 El Camino Real Ste 330 *Web:* smalawsd.com	San Diego	CA	92130	858-792-1190		41
Sullivan-Palatek Inc 1201 W US Hwy 20 *TF:* 800-438-6203 ■ *Web:* www.sullivan-palatek.com	Michigan City	IN	46360	219-874-2497	872-5043	172
Sulloway & Hollis NH 9 Capitol St & 29 School St *Web:* www.sulloway.com	Concord	NH	03301	603-224-2341		428
Sully Creek State Park 1465 36th St *Web:* www.parkrec.nd.gov	Medora	ND	58645	701-623-2024		565
Sully Historic Site 3650 Historic Sully Way *Web:* www.fairfaxcounty.gov	Chantilly	VA	20151	703-437-1794		50-3
Sully-Miller Contracting Company Inc 135 S State Collage Blvd Ste 400 *TF:* 800-300-4240 ■ *Web:* www.sully-miller.com	Brea	CA	92821	714-578-9600	578-2850	188-4
Sulphur Institute 1140 Connecticut Ave NW Ste 612 *Web:* www.sulphurinstitute.org	Washington	DC	20036	202-331-9660	293-2940	49-13
Sulphur Springs & Quitman 1040 Gilmer St *TF:* 866-435-1307 ■ *Web:* toliverford.com	Sulphur Springs	TX	75482	866-435-1307		57
Sulphur Springs Valley Electric Co-opeartive Inc 350 N Haskell *Web:* www.ssvec.org	Willcox	AZ	85643	520-384-2221		245
Sultana Distribution Services Inc 600 Food Center Dr *TF:* 877-617-5500 ■ *Web:* www.sultanadist.com	Bronx	NY	10474	718-617-5500	617-5225	297-3
Sulzer Machine & Manufacturing Inc 2475 Spring Brook Rd *Web:* www.sulzermachine.com	Mosinee	WI	54455	715-443-2569		757
Sulzer Pumps (US) Inc 2800 NW Front Ave *Web:* www.sulzer.com	Portland	OR	97210	503-226-5200		641
Sumaria Systems Inc 99 Rosewood Dr *Web:* www.sumariasystems.com	Danvers	MA	01923	978-739-4200	739-4850	180
Sumatech Inc 11139 Red Lion Rd *Web:* www.sumatechusa.com	White Marsh	MD	21162	410-335-2929		454
Sumco Inc 1351 S Girls School Rd *Web:* sumco.com	Indianapolis	IN	46231	317-241-7600	248-2352	481
Sumersault ltd 17 Overlook Rd *Web:* www.sumersault.com	Scarsdale	NY	10583	914-472-5778		594
Sumex 200 Carnegie Dr Ste 203 *Web:* www.sumex.ca	Saint Albert	AB	T8N5A7	780-970-2238		466
Sumida America Inc 1251 N Plum Grove Rd Ste 150 *Web:* www.sumida.com	Schaumburg	IL	60173	847-545-6700		253
Sumiden Wire Products Corp 1412 El Pinal Dr *Web:* www.sumidenwire.com	Stockton	CA	95205	209-466-8924		488
Sumitomo Bakelite North America Inc 24 Mill St *Web:* www.sbhpp.com	Manchester	CT	06042	860-646-5500		605-2
Sumitomo Canada Ltd (SCL) 150 King St W Ste 2304 *Web:* www.sumitomocanada.com	Toronto	ON	M5H1J9	416-860-3800	365-3141	360-3
Sumitomo Chemical America Inc 150 E 42nd St Ste 701 *Web:* www.sumitomo-chem.co.jp	New York	NY	10017	212-572-8200	572-8234	146
Sumitomo Corporation of Americas 300 Madison Ave *Web:* www.sumitomocorpofamericas.com	New York	NY	10017	212-207-0700	207-0456	523
Sumitomo Electric Industries Ltd 2355 Zanker Rd *Web:* www.sei-device.com	San Jose	CA	95131	408-232-9500		696
Sumitomo Electric Light Wave Corp 201 S Rogers Ln Ste 100 *TF:* 800-358-7378 ■ *Web:* www.sumitomoelectric.com	Raleigh	NC	27610	919-541-8100	541-8265	544
Sumitomo Electric USA Inc 21241 S Western Ave Ste 120 *Web:* www.sumitomoelectricusa.com	Torrance	CA	90501	310-782-0227	782-0211	813
Sumitomo Electric Wintec America Inc 909 Industrial Dr *Web:* www.sewaus.com	Edmonton	KY	42129	270-432-2233		73
Sumitomo Forestry America Inc 1110 112th Ave NE Ste 202 *Web:* sfc.jp	Bellevue	WA	98004	425-454-2355		523
Sumitomo Machinery Corporation of America 4200 Holland Blvd *TF:* 800-762-9256 ■ *Web:* www.sumitomodrive.com	Chesapeake	VA	23323	757-485-3355	485-7490	709
Sumitomo Mitsui Banking Corp (SMBC) 277 Park Ave *Web:* www.smbcgroup.com	New York	NY	10172	212-224-4000	593-9522	70
Sumitomo Mitsui Trust Bank (USA) (SMTBUSA) 111 River St *Web:* www.smtb.jp	Hoboken	NJ	07030	201-420-9470		70
Sumitomo (SHI) Cryogenics of America Inc 1833 Vultee Sreet *Web:* www.shicryogenics.com	Allentown	PA	18103	610-791-6700		407
Summa Strategies Canada Inc 100 Sparks St Ste 1000 *Web:* www.summastrategies.ca	Ottawa	ON	K1P5B7	613-235-1400		41
Summa Technologies Inc 611 William Penn Pl *Web:* www.summa.com	Pittsburgh	PA	15219	412-258-3300		177
SummaCare 10 N Main St *TF:* 800-996-8411 ■ *Web:* www.summacare.com	Akron	OH	44308	330-996-8410	996-8454	352

	Phone	Fax	Class
Summary Systems Inc 1100 Summit Ave Ste 100 ...... Plano TX 75074 *Web:* www.summarysystems.com	972-943-8882		647
Summer Classics 8040 Germantown Ave ...... Chestnut Hill PA 19118 *Web:* summerclassics.com	215-247-7600	247-7603	319-4
Summer Game Books PO Box 818 ...... South Orange NJ 07079 *Web:* www.summergamebooks.com	201-744-0590		637-2
Summer Infant Inc 1275 Park E Dr ...... Woonsocket RI 02895 *TF:* 800-268-6237 ■ *Web:* www.summerinfant.com	800-268-6237		787
Summer Search 500 Sansome St Ste 350 ...... San Francisco CA 94111 *Web:* www.summersearch.org	415-362-0500		242
Summer Street Capital Partners LLC 70 W Chippewa St Ste 500 ...... Buffalo NY 14202 *Web:* www.summerstreetcapital.com	716-566-2900		690
Summerlin Hospital Medical Ctr 657 Town Center Dr ...... Las Vegas NV 89144 *Web:* www.summerlinhospital.com	702-233-7000		374-3
Summers County 120 Ballengee St Ste 106 ...... Hinton WV 25951 *Web:* www.summerscountywv.gov	304-466-7104		338
Summers Heating & Air Conditio 6031 Rising Sun Ave ...... Philadelphia PA 19111 *Web:* www.summersquality.com	215-482-8800		189-10
Summers Industrial Supply 400 Buffalo St ...... Johnson City TN 37604 *TF:* 800-634-6313 ■ *Web:* www.summersindustrial.com	423-461-4700	926-5120	385
Summers Laboratories Inc 103 GP Clement Dr ...... Collegeville PA 19426 *Web:* www.sumlab.com	610-454-1471		743
Summers, Mcnea & Company PC 80 25th St W ...... Billings MT 59102 *Web:* summers-mcnea.com	406-652-2320		2
Summerset Press PO Box 2331 ...... Oak Bluffs MA 02557 *Web:* www.summersetpress.com	508-693-4178		637-2
Summers-Taylor Inc 300 W Elk Ave ...... Elizabethton TN 37643 *Web:* summerstaylor.com	423-543-3181	543-6189	188-4
Summertime Potato Co 2001 E Grand Ave ...... Des Moines IA 50317 *Web:* www.summertimepotato.com	515-265-9865		297-7
Summerwinds Nursery 17826 N Tatum Blvd ...... Phoenix AZ 85032 *Web:* summerwindsnursery.com	602-867-1822		323
Summerwood Corp 14 Balligomingo Rd ...... Conshohocken PA 19428 *Web:* www.summerwood.biz	610-520-1000		670
Summit 7 Systems Inc 71 Town Center Dr ...... Huntsville AL 35806 *Web:* summit7systems.com	256-585-6868		180
Summit Academy OIC 935 Olson Memorial Hwy ...... Minneapolis MN 55405 *Web:* www.saoic.org	612-377-0150	377-0156	167-3
Summit Account Resolution 12201 Champlin Dr ...... Champlin MN 55316 *TF:* 888-822-7509 ■ *Web:* www.summitcollects.com	888-222-0793		393
Summit Aerospace 1260 NW 57th Ave ...... Miami FL 33126 *Web:* summitmro.com	305-267-6400		271
Summit Asset Management Inc 30 Columbia Tpke ...... Florham Park NJ 07932 *Web:* summitasset.com	973-301-2360		2
Summit at Plantsville 261 Summit St ...... Plantsville CT 06479 *Web:* summitatplantsville.com	860-628-0364	628-9166	450
Summit Aviation Inc 4200 Summit Bridge Rd ...... Middletown DE 19709 *TF:* 800-441-9343 ■ *Web:* summit-aviation.com	302-834-5400		24
Summit Bank 2969 Broadway ...... Oakland CA 94611 *TF:* 800-380-9333 ■ *Web:* www.summitbanking.com	510-839-8800	839-8853	70
Summit Behavioral Healthcare 1101 Summit Rd ...... Cincinnati OH 45237 *TF:* 800-372-8862 ■ *Web:* mha.ohio.gov	888-636-4724		374-5
Summit Beverage 1005 S Montana ...... Butte MT 59701 *Web:* www.summitbeverage.com	406-782-9158		81-1
Summit Brewing Co 910 Montreal Cir ...... Saint Paul MN 55102 *Web:* www.summitbrewing.com	651-265-7800	265-7801	102
Summit Broadband Inc 4558 SW 35th St ...... Orlando FL 32811 *Web:* www.summit-broadband.com	407-996-8900		387
Summit Canyon Mountaineering 205 Sixth St ...... Glenwood Springs CO 81601 *TF:* 800-360-6994 ■ *Web:* summitcanyon.com	970-945-6994		711
Summit Chemical Co 235 S Kresson St ...... Baltimore MD 21224 *TF:* 800-227-8664 ■ *Web:* www.summitchemical.com	410-522-0661	522-0833	280
Summit Christian College 2025 21st St ...... Gering NE 69341 *TF:* 888-305-8083 ■ *Web:* www.summitcc.edu	308-632-6933	632-8599	166
Summit Construction Company Inc 1107 Burdsal Pkwy PO Box 88126 ...... Indianapolis IN 46208 *Web:* www.summitconst.com	317-634-6112	264-2529	685
Summit Corporation of America 1430 Waterbury Rd ...... Thomaston CT 06787 *Web:* www.summitplating.com	860-283-4391	283-4010	481
Summit County 175 S Main St Ohio Bldg 8th Fl ...... Akron OH 44308 *Web:* www.co.summit.oh.us	330-643-2500		338
Summit County PO Box 1538 ...... Breckenridge CO 80424 *Web:* www.co.summit.co.us	970-453-2561	453-3540	338
Summit County 60 N Main St PO Box 128 ...... Coalville UT 84017 *Web:* www.summitcounty.org	435-336-3249	336-3030	338
Summit Direct Mail Inc 1655 Terre Colony Ct ...... Dallas TX 75212 *Web:* www.summitdm.com	469-916-5170		195
Summit Electric Supply Co 2900 Stanford NE ...... Albuquerque NM 87107 *TF:* 800-824-4400 ■ *Web:* www.summit.com	505-346-9000	346-1616	246
Summit Engineering Inc 131 Summit Dr ...... Pikeville KY 41501 *Web:* www.summit-engr.com	606-432-1447		302
Summit Engineers Inc 5307 Lee Hwy ...... Arlington VA 22207 *Web:* summitengineers.com	703-533-5593	533-5594	261
Summit Envirosolutions Inc 1217 Bandana Blvd N ...... Saint Paul MN 55108 *TF:* 800-884-9887 ■ *Web:* www.summite.com	651-644-8080		194
Summit Equipment Inc PO Box 1847 ...... Post Falls ID 83877 *Web:* www.summiteq.com	208-773-3885	773-3799	695
Summit Eye Center LLC 1621 NW Blue Pkwy ...... Lee's Summit MO 64086 *Web:* summiteyekc.com	816-246-2111		543
Summit Financial Group 11350 McCormick Rd Executive Plz III Ste 501 ...... Hunt Valley MD 21031 *Web:* sumfi.com	410-584-9600		390
Summit Financial Resources Inc 4 Campus Dr ...... Parsippany NJ 07054 *Web:* www.summitfinancial.com	973-285-3600	285-3666	390
Summit Financial Strategies Inc, The 1905 NW 169th Pl ...... Beaverton OR 97006 *Web:* summit-fs.com	503-466-1989		690
Summit Foundry Systems Inc 2100 Wayne Haven St ...... Fort Wayne IN 46803 *Web:* www.summitfoundrysystems.com	260-749-7740	749-7228	695
Summit Funding Group Inc 4680 Pkwy Dr Ste 300 ...... Mason OH 45040 *TF:* 866-489-1222 ■ *Web:* www.summit-funding.com	513-489-1222		264-1
Summit Golf Brands Inc 8 W 40th St 2nd Fl ...... New York NY 10018 *TF:* 800-926-8010 ■ *Web:* www.summitgolfbrands.com	800-926-8010		442
Summit Handling Systems Inc 11 Defco Park Rd ...... North Haven CT 06473 *Web:* www.summithandling.com	203-239-5351	234-8090	645-11
Summit Health Inc 27175 Haggerty Rd ...... Novi MI 48377 *Web:* www.summithealth.com	248-799-8303	799-8927	194
Summit Hospitality Group Ltd 3141 John Humphries Wynd Ste 200 ...... Raleigh NC 27612 *Web:* www.summithospitality.com	919-787-5100		378
Summit Hut 5045 E Speedway Blvd ...... Tucson AZ 85712 *TF:* 800-499-8696 ■ *Web:* www.summithut.com	520-325-1554	795-7350	711
Summit Imaging Inc 306 SE 291 Hwy Ste 2 ...... Lee's Summit MO 64063 *Web:* summitimaging.net	816-246-5777		177
Summit Lake State Park 5993 N Messick Rd ...... New Castle IN 47362 *Web:* www.in.gov	765-766-5873		565
Summit Lake State Recreation Area 550 W Seventh Ave Ste 1360 ...... Anchorage AK 99501 *Web:* dnr.alaska.gov	907-269-8700	269-8907	565
Summit Law Group PLLC 315 Fifth Ave S Ste 1000 ...... Seattle WA 98104 *Web:* www.summitlaw.com	206-676-7000		428
Summit Lawn & Landscape Inc 12020 Grandview Rd ...... Grandview MO 64030 *Web:* www.summitlawn.com	816-966-9434		422
Summit Lodge & Spa 4359 Main St ...... Whistler BC V0N1B4 *TF:* 888-913-8811 ■ *Web:* www.summitlodge.com	604-932-2778	932-2716	379
Summit Lubricants Inc 4d Treadeasy Ave ...... Batavia NY 14020 *Web:* www.summitlubricants.com	585-344-4301	344-4302	541
Summit Media Solutions Inc 215 S Platte Clay Way Ste C PO Box 1149 ...... Kearney MO 64060 *Web:* www.summitmediasolutions.com	816-628-5492	920-5500	637-10
Summit Medical Ctr 5655 Frist Blvd ...... Hermitage TN 37076 *Web:* tristarsummit.com	615-316-3000		374-3
Summit Medical Group 1 Diamond Hill Rd ...... Berkeley Heights NJ 07922 *Web:* www.summitmedicalgroup.com	908-273-4300	790-6593	353
Summit Medical Inc 815 NW Pky Ste 100 ...... Saint Paul MN 55121 **Fax Area Code:* 888 ■ *TF:* 888-229-2875 ■ *Web:* www.summitmedicalusa.com	651-789-3939	229-1941*	477
Summit Midstream Partners LP 1790 Hughes Landing Blvd Ste 500 ...... The Woodlands TX 77380 *Web:* www.summitmidstream.com	832-413-4770		536
Summit Motorsports Park 1300 Ohio 18 ...... Norwalk OH 44857 **Fax Area Code:* 419 ■ *TF:* 800-230-3030 ■ *Web:* www.summitmotorsportspark.com	800-230-3030	663-0502*	515
Summit of New England 386 Hill St ...... Biddeford ME 04005 **Fax Area Code:* 207 ■ *TF:* 800-547-5100 ■ *Web:* www.snetireonline.com	800-547-5100	283-1465*	755
Summit Packaging Systems Inc 400 Gay St ...... Manchester NH 03103 *Web:* www.summitpackagingsystems.com	603-669-5410		547
Summit Partners 222 Berkeley St 18th Fl ...... Boston MA 02116 *Web:* www.summitpartners.com	617-824-1000	824-1100	792
Summit Performance Group LLC 100 Leverne St ...... Mammoth Lakes CA 93546 *Web:* www.brojure.com	760-924-7813		760
Summit Plastics Inc 107 S Laurel St ...... Summit MS 39666 *TF:* 800-790-7117 ■ *Web:* www.summitplasticsus.com	601-276-7373	276-2400	600
Summit Polymers Inc 6717 S Sprinkle Rd ...... Portage MI 49002 *Web:* www.summitpolymers.com	269-324-9330	324-9311	60
Summit Publications Inc 63 Summit Way ...... Gardiner MT 59030 *Web:* www.summitlighthouse.org	406-848-9200		48-20
Summit Research Associates Inc 7728 Warbler Ln ...... Derwood MD 20855 *Web:* www.summit-res.com	301-670-0980	330-4171	196
Summit Research Network 2701 NW Vaughn St Ste 350 ...... Portland OR 97210 *Web:* summitresearchnetwork.com	503-228-2273		794
Summit Resources LLC 3300 E First Ave Ste 480 ...... Denver CO 80206 *Web:* summitresourcesland.com	720-439-4770		195
Summit Road Distributing 649 Americal Rd ...... Henderson NC 27537 *TF:* 877-477-3478 ■ *Web:* www.summitroaddistributing.com	877-477-3478		238
Summit Rubber Company Inc 100 Corporate Way ...... Summerville SC 29483 **Fax Area Code:* 843 ■ *TF:* 888-515-9466 ■ *Web:* www.summitrubber.com	888-515-9466	875-2549*	676
Summit Salon Academy Gainesville 6915 NW 4th Blvd Ste B ...... Gainesville FL 32607 *Web:* www.ssag.edu	352-331-2424		167-3

Name / Address	City	State	Zip	Phone	Fax	Class
Summit Salon Academy Kokomo						
1012 S Reed Rd	Kokomo	IN	46901	765-454-9840		167-3
Web: kokomobeautyschool.com						
Summit Salon Academy of Portland						
8820 SW Center St	Portland	OR	97223	503-639-6106		167-3
Web: www.summitsalonacademyportland.com						
Summit Salon Academy Perrysburg						
116 W S Boundary St	Perrysburg	OH	43551	419-873-9999		167-3
Web: www.summitsalonacademyperrysburg.edu						
Summit Salon Academy Tacoma						
3702 S Fife St Ste B102	Tacoma	WA	98409	253-617-7000		167-3
Web: summitsalonacademy.edu						
Summit Salon Academy Tampa						
4802 Gunn Hwy Ste 144	Tampa	FL	33624	813-908-8020		167-3
Web: www.summitsalonacademytampa.com						
Summit Schools Inc						
404 Madison Ave	Fort Atkinson	WI	53538	920-568-1800		685
TF: 800-432-6406 ■ *Web:* www.summitschoolsinc.com						
Summit Security Services Inc						
390 Rexcorp Plz W Tower - Lobby Level	Uniondale	NY	11556	516-240-2400		693
TF: 800-615-5888 ■ *Web:* www.summitsecurity.com						
Summit State Bank						
500 Bicentennial Way	Santa Rosa	CA	95403	707-568-6000	568-7090	71
NASDAQ: SSBI ■ *Web:* www.summitstatebank.com						
Summit Steakhouse, The						
2700 S Havana St	Aurora	CO	80014	303-751-2112		671
Web: www.thesummitsteakhouse.com						
Summit Strategies Inc						
8182 Maryland Ave 6th Fl.	Saint Louis	MO	63105	314-727-7211		401
Web: www.ssgstl.com						
Summit Tech Consulting						
772 Charles Allen Dr	Atlanta	GA	30308	404-731-9484		194
TF: 888-800-3380 ■ *Web:* www.summittechconsulting.com						
Summit Technical Services Inc						
355 Centerville Rd	Warwick	RI	02886	401-736-8323		631
TF: 800-643-7372 ■ *Web:* summit-technical.com						
Summit Trailer Sales Inc						
1 Summit Plz	Summit Station	PA	17979	570-754-3511	754-7025	779
TF: 800-437-3729 ■ *Web:* www.summittrailer.com						
Summit Treestands LLC 715 Summit Dr	Decatur	AL	35601	256-353-0634		710
Web: www.summitstands.com						
Summit, The 65 Steiner Ave.	Akron	OH	44301	330-761-3099	761-3103	645-2
Web: thesummit.fm						
Summit, The 13925 S Virginia St Ste 212	Reno	NV	89511	775-853-7800		460
Web: thesummitreno.com						
Summitmedia Llc						
2700 Corporate Dr Ste 115	Birmingham	AL	35242	205-322-2987		658
Web: www.summitmediacorp.com						
Summitt Trucking LLC						
1800 Progress Way	Clarksville	IN	47129	812-285-7777	285-8949	780
TF: 866-999-7799 ■ *Web:* summitt.com						
Summitville Tiles Inc						
15364 Ohio 644	Summitville	OH	43962	330-223-1511	223-1414	751
Web: www.summitville.com						
Sumner & Toner Insurance Agency Inc						
813 Williams St	Longmeadow	MA	01106	413-567-6161		390
Web: sumnertoner.com						
Sumner Bank & Trust 780 Browns Ln	Gallatin	TN	37066	615-451-4151		70
Web: sumnerbankandtrust.com						
Sumner College - Parkway Campus						
15115 SW Sequoia Pky Ste 200	Portland	OR	97224	503-223-5100		167-3
Web: www.sumnercollege.edu						
Sumner County 355 N Belvedere Dr	Gallatin	TN	37066	615-452-4367		338
Web: www.sumnertn.org						
Sumner County 501 N Washington Ave	Wellington	KS	67152	620-326-3395	326-2116	338
Web: www.ks-sumner.publicaccessnow.com						
Sumner Group Inc						
6717 Waldemar Ave	Saint Louis	MO	63139	314-633-8000	633-8002	286
Web: www.sumnerone.com						
Sumner Peck Ranch Inc (SPR)						
14860 N Hwy 41	Madera	CA	93636	559-822-3301		10-4
Web: sumnerpeckranch.com						
Sumner School District 1202 Wood Ave	Sumner	WA	98390	253-891-6000	891-6098	685
TF: 866-548-3847 ■ *Web:* www.sumnersd.org						
Sumner-Cowley Electric Co-opeartive Inc						
2223 N A St PO Box 220	Wellington	KS	67152	620-326-3356		245
TF: 888-326-3356 ■ *Web:* www.sucocoop.com						
Sumnicht & Assoc						
W6240 Communication Ct Ste 1	Appleton	WI	54914	920-731-4455	731-9679	194
Web: www.sumnicht.com						
Sumo Logic Inc 305 Main St	Redwood City	CA	94063	650-810-8700		225
Web: www.sumologic.com						
Sumption & Wyland						
818 S Hawthorne Ave	Sioux Falls	SD	57104	605-336-0244	336-0275	423
TF: 888-478-6784 ■ *Web:* www.sumptionandwyland.com						
Sumter Beauty College Inc						
921 Carolina Ave	Sumter	SC	29150	803-773-7311	773-7312	167-3
Web: www.sumterbeautycollege.com						
Sumter Correctional Institution						
9544 County Rd 476 B	Bushnell	FL	33513	352-569-6100	569-6196	213
Web: dc.state.fl.us						
Sumter County						
500 W Lamar St PO Box 295	Americus	GA	31709	229-928-4500	928-4503	338
Web: www.sumtercountyga.us						
Sumter County 502 Lafayette St.	Livingston	AL	35470	205-652-3618	391-8769	338
Web: www.sumteralchamber.com						
Sumter County 141 N Main St.	Sumter	SC	29150	803-436-2227	436-2223	338
Web: www.sumtercountysc.org						
Sumter County Chamber of Commerce						
PO Box 426	Lake Panasoffkee	FL	33538	352-793-3099	793-2120	139
Web: sumterchamber.org						
Sumter County Chamber of Commerce						
409 Elm Ave PO Box 724	Americus	GA	31709	229-924-2646	924-8784	139
Web: www.sumtercountychamber.com						
Sumter County Library 111 N Harvin St	Sumter	SC	29150	803-773-7273	773-4875	434-3
Web: www.sumtercountylibrary.org						
Sumter Electric Co-opeartive Inc						
PO Box 301	Sumterville	FL	33585	352-793-3801		245
TF: 800-732-6141 ■ *Web:* www.secoenergy.com						
Sumter Electric Membership Corp						
1120 Felder St	Americus	GA	31709	229-924-8041		245
TF: 800-342-6978 ■ *Web:* www.sumteremc.com						
Sumter Packaging Corp						
2341 Corporate Way	Sumter	SC	29154	803-481-2003		100
Web: www.sumterpackaging.com						
Sumter Utilities Inc 1151 N Pike W	Sumter	SC	29153	803-469-8585	469-4600	188-10
Web: www.sumter-utilities.com						
Sun & Snow Sports Inc						
3780 Jackson Rd Ste J	Ann Arbor	MI	48103	734-663-9515		711
Web: www.sunandsnow.com						
Sun Belt Food Company Inc						
4755 Technology Way Ste 209	Boca Raton	FL	33431	561-995-9100	997-5664	297-6
Web: www.sunbeltfoods.com						
Sun Books - Sun Publishing						
PO Box 5588	Santa Fe	NM	87502	505-473-4161	473-4458	637-2
TF: 877-849-0051 ■ *Web:* www.sunbooks.com						
Sun Builders Co						
15012 Farm to Market Rd 529	Houston	TX	77095	281-815-1020	815-1021	186
Web: www.sunbuildersco.com						
Sun Chemical Corp						
35 Waterview Blvd	Parsippany	NJ	07054	973-404-6000	404-6001	388
TF: 800-543-2323 ■ *Web:* www.sunchemical.com						
Sun Chronicle PO Box 600	Attleboro	MA	02703	508-222-7000	236-0462	532-2
TF: 800-323-4673 ■ *Web:* www.thesunchronicle.com						
Sun Cities Independent						
17220 Boswell Blvd	Sun City	AZ	85373	623-972-6101		532-4
Web: yourvalley.net						
Sun Coast Resources Inc						
6405 Cavalcade St Bldg 1	Houston	TX	77028	713-844-9600		579
TF: 800-677-3835 ■ *Web:* www.suncoastresources.com						
Sun Communities Inc						
27777 Franklin Rd Ste 200	Southfield	MI	48034	248-208-2500		655
NYSE: SUI ■ *Web:* www.suncommunities.com						
Sun Control Products Window Shades						
1908 Second St SW	Rochester	MN	55902	507-282-2620		87
TF: 800-533-0010 ■ *Web:* www.suncontrolshades.net						
Sun Country Cleaners Inc						
2240 34th Way N	Largo	FL	33771	727-535-0030		420
Web: suncountrycleaners.com						
Sun Country Industries						
7601 Los Volcanes Road NW	Albuquerque	NM	87109	505-344-1611		567
Web: www.suncountryindustries.com						
Sun Country Medical Inc						
11233 Rojas Ste A	El Paso	TX	79935	915-592-4346	592-4369	476
Web: www.suncountrymedical.com						
Sun Devil Auto Inc						
1830 E Elliot Rd Ste 104	Tempe	AZ	85284	480-831-2831		62-5
Web: www.sunautoservice.com						
Sun Devil Fire Equipment Inc						
2211 S 3rd Dr	Phoenix	AZ	85017	623-245-0636	495-9291*	679
**Fax Area Code:* 602 ■ *Web:* www.sundevilfire.com						
Sun Devil Stadium						
Arizona State University 500 E Veterans Way	Tempe	AZ	85287	480-965-3482	965-1261	720
Web: thesundevils.com						
Sun Drilling Products Corp						
SUN Specialty Products						
503 Main St	Belle Chasse	LA	70037	504-393-2778	391-1383	541
TF: 800-962-6490 ■ *Web:* www.sunspecialtyproducts.com						
Sun Eagle Corp 461 N Dean Ave	Chandler	AZ	85226	480-961-0004	940-0160	186
Web: www.suneaglecorporation.com						
Sun Engineering Services Inc						
5405 Garden Grove Blvd	Westminster	CA	92683	714-379-2300		261
Web: www.sunengr.net						
Sun Ergoline Inc						
411 Washington Ave Ste B	Jonesboro	AR	72401	888-771-0996	935-3618*	437
**Fax Area Code:* 870 ■ *TF:* 888-771-0996 ■ *Web:* www.ergoline.us						
Sun Graphics LLC 1010 Broadway	Parsons	KS	67357	800-835-0588		627
TF: 800-835-0588 ■ *Web:* www.sun-graphics.com						
Sun Healthcare Group Inc						
18831 Von Karman Ste 400	Irvine	CA	92612	949-255-7100		451
NASDAQ: SUNH						
Sun Hydraulics LLC						
1500 W University Pkwy	Sarasota	FL	34243	941-362-1200	355-4497	790
NASDAQ: SNHY ■ *Web:* www.sunhydraulics.com						
Sun Interiors Ltd 724 Hill St.	Jefferson	LA	70121	504-833-8104	833-8313	291
Web: suninteriors.com						
Sun Islands Hawaii Inc						
438 Hobron Ln Ste 222	Honolulu	HI	96815	808-926-3888	922-6951	771
Web: www.sunislandshawaii.com						
Sun Journal 3200 Wellons Blvd	New Bern	NC	28562	252-638-8101		532-2
Web: www.newbernsj.com						
Sun Lakes State Park						
34875 Pk Ln Rd NE	Coulee City	WA	99115	509-632-5583		565
Web: parks.state.wa.us						
Sun Life Assurance Company of Canada						
1 Sun Life Executive Pk PO Box 9106	Wellesley	MA	02481	781-237-6030		391-2
TF: 800-786-5433 ■ *Web:* www.sunlife.com						
Sun Line Products 1454 E Summitry Cir	Katy	TX	77449	281-398-6655		687
Web: www.sunlineproducts.com						
Sun Luck Garden 1901 S Taylor Rd	Cleveland	OH	44118	216-397-7676		671
Web: sunluckgardenchinese.com						
Sun Machinery Company Inc						
206 Two Notch Rd	Lexington	SC	29071	803-359-1000		791
TF: 800-932-2229 ■ *Web:* www.sunmachineryco.com						
Sun Magazine						
8815 Conroy Windermere Rd Ste 130	Orlando	FL	32835	407-477-2815	293-1179	457-11
TF: 888-218-9968 ■ *Web:* www.floridasunmagazine.com						
Sun Messenger 5510 Cloverleaf Pkwy	Cleveland	OH	44125	216-986-2600		532-4
Web: www.cleveland.com						
Sun Mountain Capital						
527 Don Gaspar Ave	Santa Fe	NM	87505	505-780-4218		792
Web: sunmountaincapital.com						
Sun Mountain Lodge						
604 Patterson Lake RD	Winthrop	WA	98862	509-996-2211	996-3133	669
TF: 800-572-0493 ■ *Web:* www.sunmountainlodge.com						
Sun Mountain Lumber						
181 Greenhouse Rd	Deer Lodge	MT	59722	406-846-1600		683
Web: www.sunmtnlumber.com						

Company	City	State	Zip	Phone	Fax	Class
Sun News 914 Frontage Rd E *TF:* 800-568-1800 ■ *Web:* www.myrtlebeachonline.com	Myrtle Beach	SC	29578	843-626-8555	626-0356	532-2
Sun Newspapers 200 East Venice Ave. *Web:* www.yoursun.com	Venice	FL	33980	941-206-1000		532-2
Sun Nuclear Corp 3275 Suntree Blvd *Web:* www.sunnuclear.com	Melbourne	FL	32940	321-259-6862		472
Sun Orchard Inc 1198 W Fairmont Dr *TF:* 800-505-8423 ■ *Web:* sunorchard.com	Tempe	AZ	85282	800-505-8423		296-20
Sun Packaging Technologies Inc 2200 NW 32nd St Ste 1700 *TF:* 800-866-0322 ■ *Web:* www.sunpkg.com	Pompano Beach	FL	33069	954-978-3080		358
Sun Packing Inc 10077 Wallisville Rd *Web:* www.sunpacking.com	Houston	TX	77013	713-673-4600	673-3515	88
Sun Pharmaceutical Industries Inc 270 Prospect Plains Rd *Web:* www.sunpharma.com	Cranbury	NJ	08512	609-495-2800		231
Sun Printing 1800 Grand Ave. *Web:* sunprinting.com	Wausau	WI	54403	715-845-4911		627
Sun Process Converting Inc 1660 Kenneth Dr. *Web:* www.sunprocess.com	Mount Prospect	IL	60056	847-593-0447		548
Sun Publishing, The 107 N Roberson St *TF:* 888-732-6736 ■ *Web:* www.thesunmagazine.org	Chapel Hill	NC	27516	919-942-5282	932-3101	637-9
Sun Radio Network 260 SW Natura Ave. *TF:* 800-871-6163 ■ *Web:* www.sunbgi.com	Deerfield Beach	FL	33441	800-871-6163		647
Sun Ray Grill 619 Pink St. *Web:* www.sunraygrill.com	Metairie	LA	70005	504-391-0053		671
Sun Ray Park & Casino LLC 39 Rd 5568 *Web:* www.sunraygaming.com	Farmington	NM	87401	505-566-1200		452
Sun Realty Inc 1500 S Croatan Hwy PO Box 1630 *TF:* 888-853-7770 ■ *Web:* www.sunrealtync.com	Kill Devil Hills	NC	27948	252-441-7033		652
Sun River Electric Co-opeartive Inc 310 First Ave S PO Box 309 *TF:* 800-452-7516 ■ *Web:* www.sunriverelectric.coop	Fairfield	MT	59436	406-467-2527		245
Sun State Builders Inc 1050 W Washington St Ste 214 *Web:* sunstatebuilders.com	Tempe	AZ	85281	480-894-1286		186
Sun State Plastics Inc 4045 Kevin St NW *Web:* www.sunstateplastics.com	North Canton	OH	44720	330-494-5220	494-1231	604
Sun Sui Wah Seafood Restaurant 3888 Main St *Web:* www.sunsuiwah.ca	Vancouver	BC	V5V3N9	604-872-8822		671
Sun Surgical Supply Co 302 NW Sixth St *Web:* www.sunsurgical.com	Gainesville	FL	32601	352-377-2696		475
Sun Technologies 3700 Mansell Rd Ste 125 *Web:* www.suntechnologies.com	Alpharetta	GA	30022	770-418-0434	418-1470	180
Sun Ten Laboratories Inc 9250 Jeronimo Rd *TF:* 800-333-4372 ■ *Web:* www.sunten.com	Irvine	CA	92618	949-587-0509		743
Sun Valley Community Church 456 E Ray Rd *Web:* www.sunvalleycc.com	Gilbert	AZ	85296	480-632-8920	857-6453	48-20
Sun Valley Floral Farms Inc 3160 Upper Bay Rd. **Fax Area Code:* 707 ■ *TF:* 800-747-0396 ■ *Web:* www.sunvalleyfloral.com	Arcata	CA	95521	800-747-0396	826-8708*	369
Sun Valley Masonry Inc 10828 N Cave Creek Rd *Web:* www.svmasonry.com	Phoenix	AZ	85020	602-943-6106	997-6857	189-7
Sun Valley Packing GP LLC 7381 Ave 432	Reedley	CA	93654	559-591-1717		315-5
Sun Valley Paper Stock Inc 11166 Pendleton St	Sun Valley	CA	91352	323-875-2613		660
Sun Valley Resort 1 Sun Valley Rd. *TF:* 800-786-8259 ■ *Web:* www.sunvalley.com	Sun Valley	ID	83353	208-622-4111		669
Sun Valley/Ketchum Chamber & Visitors Bureau 491 Sun Valley Rd *TF:* 800-634-3347 ■ *Web:* visitsunvalley.com	Ketchum	ID	83340	208-726-3423	726-4533	139
Sun Viking Lodge 2411 S Atlantic Ave. *TF:* 800-874-4469 ■ *Web:* sunviking.com	Daytona Beach	FL	32118	386-252-6252	252-5463	379
Sun Well Service Inc 118 84th St W *Web:* www.sunwellservice.com	Williston	ND	58801	701-774-3001	774-0774	538
Sun West Engineering Inc 3802 E Broadway Rd. *TF:* 800-635-3658 ■ *Web:* sunwesteng.com	Phoenix	AZ	85040	800-635-3658		261
Sun Windows Inc 1515 E 18th St *Web:* www.sunwindows.com	Owensboro	KY	42303	270-684-0691		234
Sun World International Inc 16350 Dr Rd *Web:* www.sun-world.com	Bakersfield	CA	93308	661-392-5000		315-3
Sun, The 473 E Carnegie Dr Ste 250 *Web:* www.sbsun.com	San Bernardino	CA	92408	909-889-9666		532-2
Sunbeam Television Corp 1401 79th St Cswy *Web:* www.wsvn.com	Miami	FL	33141	305-751-6692		647
Sunbelt Computer Systems Inc 13090 County Rd 468 *Web:* www.sunbelt-plb.com	Tyler	TX	75704	903-881-0400		178-2
Sunbelt Furniture Xpress Inc 3255 20th Ave SE *TF:* 800-766-1117 ■ *Web:* www.sbfx.com	Hickory	NC	28603	828-464-7240	465-3560	780
Sunbelt Industrial Trucks 1617 Terre Colony Ct *Web:* www.sunbelt-industrial.com	Dallas	TX	75212	214-819-4150		770
SUNBELT Machine Works Corp 13411 Redfish Ln *Web:* sunbeltmachine.com	Stafford	TX	77477	281-499-0051		757
Sunbelt Marketing Investment Corp 3255 S Sweetwater Rd *TF:* 800-257-5566 ■ *Web:* www.sunbeltmarketing.com	Lithia Springs	GA	30122	770-739-3740		612

Company	City	State	Zip	Phone	Fax	Class
Sunbelt Metals & Manufacturing Inc 920 S Bradshaw Rd *Web:* www.sunbeltmetals.com	Apopka	FL	32703	407-889-8960		492
Sunbelt Rentals Inc 2341 Deerfield Dr *TF:* 800-667-9328 ■ *Web:* www.sunbeltrentals.com	Fort Mill	SC	29715	704-348-2676		264-3
Sunbelt Sales & Marketing 170 Ottley Dr *Web:* www.filmloc.com	Atlanta	GA	30324	404-892-8778		627
Sunbelt Securities Inc 2700 Post Oak Blvd Ste 1700 *Web:* www.sunbeltsecurities.com	Houston	TX	77056	713-965-9510		690
Sunbelt Transfomer Ltd 1922 S Martin Luther King Jr Dr. *TF:* 800-433-3128 ■ *Web:* www.sunbeltusa.com	Temple	TX	76504	254-771-3777	771-5719	249
Sunbelt-Turret Steel Inc 527 Atando Ave. *TF:* 800-951-4140 ■ *Web:* sunbelt-turret.com	Charlotte	NC	28206	704-342-4321		492
Sunbrook Academy 3871 Jiles Rd NW *Web:* www.sunbrookacademy.com	Kennesaw	GA	30144	770-954-7430	428-8912	148
Sunburst Hospitality Corp 10770 Columbia Pk Ste 300 *Web:* www.snbhotels.com	Silver Spring	MD	20901	301-592-3800	592-3935	379
Sunburst Shutters 6480 W Flamingo Rd Ste D *TF:* 877-786-2877 ■ *Web:* www.sunburstshutters.com	Las Vegas	NV	89103	702-367-1600	367-8525	699
Sunbury Community Hospital (SCH) 350 N 11th St *Web:* www.sunburyhospital.com	Sunbury	PA	17801	570-286-3333		374-3
Sunbury Motor Co 943 N Fourth St. *TF:* 866-440-7854 ■ *Web:* www.sunburymotors.com	Sunbury	PA	17801	570-286-7746		516
Suncall America Inc 505 Industrial Pkwy *Web:* suncallamerica.com	Richmond	IN	47374	765-966-9656		247
Suncast Corp 701 N Kirk Rd **Fax Area Code:* 630 ■ *TF:* 800-444-3310 ■ *Web:* www.suncast.com	Batavia	IL	60510	800-846-2345	879-6112*	319-2
Sunchaser Vacation Villas 5129 Riverview Gate Rd *TF:* 877-451-1250 ■ *Web:* sunchaservillas.ca	Fairmont Hot Springs	BC	V0B1L1	250-345-4545		753
Suncoast Center Inc PO Box 10970 *Web:* www.suncoastcenter.org	Saint Petersburg	FL	33733	727-327-7656	323-8978	353
Suncoast Communities Blood Bank 1760 Mound St. *TF:* 866-972-5663 ■ *Web:* www.scbb.org	Sarasota	FL	34236	941-954-1600	951-2629	89
Suncoast Hospice 5771 Roosevelt Blvd. *Web:* suncoasthospice.org	Clearwater	FL	33760	727-467-7423		371
Suncoast Hotel & Casino 9090 Alta Dr *TF:* 877-677-7111 ■ *Web:* www.suncoastcasino.com	Las Vegas	NV	89145	702-636-7111		379
Suncoast Pathology Inc 446 Tamiami Trl S 2nd Fl *TF:* 877-238-1515 ■ *Web:* www.suncoastpathology.com	Venice	FL	34285	941-483-3319	483-3406	415
Suncoast Post-Tension LP 509 N Sam Houston Pkwy E Ste 400 *TF:* 800-847-8886 ■ *Web:* suncoast-pt.com	Houston	TX	77060	281-668-1840	668-1862	189-3
Suncoast Print & Promotions Inc 1045 N Lime Ave *Web:* www.scprintpro.com	Sarasota	FL	34237	941-366-1123		627
Suncoast Technical College 4748 Beneva Rd *Web:* www.suncoast.edu	Sarasota	FL	34233	941-924-1365		167-3
Suncor Energy Inc 150 - 6 Ave SW PO Box 2844 *NYSE: SU* ■ *TF:* 800-558-9071 ■ *Web:* www.suncor.com	Calgary	AB	T2P3E3	403-296-8000	296-3030	536
Suncor Stainless Inc 70 Armstrong Rd *TF:* 800-218-7702 ■ *Web:* suncorstainless.com	Plymouth	MA	02360	508-732-9191	732-9798	350
Suncraft Technologies Inc 1301 Frontenac Rd *Web:* www.suncrafttechnologies.com	Naperville	IL	60563	630-369-7900	369-7070	627
Sundahl Powers Kapp & Martin LLC 1725 Carey Ave. *Web:* www.spkm.org	Cheyenne	WY	82001	307-632-6421	632-7216	428
Sundance Aviation Inc 13000 N Sara Rd *Web:* sundanceairport.com	Yukon	OK	73099	405-373-3886	373-3893	63
Sundance Beach 7127 Hollister Ave Ste 25A-323 *TF:* 877-968-0036 ■ *Web:* www.sundancebeach.com	Goleta	CA	93117	877-968-0036		711
Sundance Boats 6131 Sundance Rd *Web:* www.sundanceboats.com	Blackshear	GA	31516	912-449-0033		90
Sundance Ch 1633 Broadway *Web:* www.sundancetv.com	New York	NY	10019	212-654-1384		740
Sundance Film Festival 1825 Three Kings Dr PO Box 684429 *Web:* www.sundance.org	Park City	UT	84060	435-658-3456	658-3457	282
Sundance Publications Ltd 221 Sherman St *Web:* www.sundancepubs.com	Denver	CO	80203	303-777-2880	778-1286	637-2
Sundance Square 201 Main St Ste 700 *Web:* sundancesquare.com	Fort Worth	TX	76102	817-255-5700		50-6
Sundance Times, The 311 Main St *Web:* www.sundancetimes.com	Sundance	WY	82729	307-283-3411	283-3332	532-2
Sundance Trail Guest Ranch 17931 Red Feather Lakes Rd *TF:* 800-357-4930 ■ *Web:* www.sundancetrail.com	Red Feather Lakes	CO	80545	970-224-1222		239
Sundance Vacations Inc 264 Highland Park Blvd *TF:* 800-220-9400 ■ *Web:* www.sundancevacations.com	Wilkes-Barre	PA	18702	570-820-0900		376
Sunday River Ski Resort 15 S Ridge Rd PO Box 4500 *Web:* sundayriver.com	Newry	ME	04261	207-824-3500	824-5110	669
Sundel & Milford Inc 11 Scovill St 4th Fl PO Box 231 *Web:* www.sundelmilford.com	Waterbury	CT	06706	203-753-0114	755-6928	390
Sunderland Bros Co 9700 J St *Web:* www.sunderlands.com	Omaha	NE	68127	402-339-2220	339-4455	191-3

				Phone	Fax	Class
Sundial Beach Resort & Spa 1451 Middle Gulf Dr *Web:* sundialresort.com	Sanibel	FL	33957	239-472-4151		669
Sundial Boutique Hotel 4340 Sundial Crescent *TF:* 800-661-2321 ■ *Web:* www.sundialhotel.com	Whistler	BC	V0N1B4	604-932-2321		379
Sundial Software Corp 5202 Eastpark Blvd Ste 105 *Web:* www.sundialsc.com	Madison	WI	53718	608-663-8100		525
Sundin Associates Inc 34 Main St 3rd Fl *Web:* www.sundininc.com	Natick	MA	01760	508-650-3972	650-3881	7
Sundog Interactive 2000 44th St S Ste 6 *Web:* www.sundoginteractive.com	Fargo	ND	58103	701-235-5525		195
Sundowner Trailers Inc 9805 S State Hwy 48 *TF:* 800-654-3879 ■ *Web:* www.sundownertrailer.com	Coleman	OK	73432	580-937-4255		763
Sundrop Fuels Inc 2410 Trade Centre Ave Ste A **Fax Area Code:* 303 ■ *Web:* www.sundropfuels.com	Longmont	CO	80503	720-890-6501	926-0640*	145
Sundt Construction 2620 S 55th St *TF:* 800-280-3000 ■ *Web:* www.sundt.com	Tempe	AZ	85282	480-293-3000		189-2
Sunera Technologies Inc 631 E Big Beaver Rd Ste 109 *Web:* www.suneratech.com	Troy	MI	48083	248-524-0222		809
Sunex Tools PO Box 1233 *TF:* 877-786-3939 ■ *Web:* sunextools.com	Greenville	SC	29608	864-834-8759		350
Sunfire 5919 Sea Otter Pl *Web:* www.sunfire.com	Carlsbad	CA	92010	707-283-5900	283-5901	52
Sunflower PO Box 40704 *Web:* sunflowerdesign.net	Austin	TX	78704	512-350-0083		671
Sunflower County 200 Main St *Web:* www.sunflowercounty.ms.gov	Indianola	MS	38751	662-887-4703		338
Sunflower Group 14001 Marshall Dr *TF:* 800-288-5085 ■ *Web:* sunflowergroup.com	Lenexa	KS	66215	800-288-5085		636
Sunforce Products Inc 9015 Ch Avon *Web:* sunforceproducts.com	Montreal-Ouest	QC	H4X2G8	514-989-2100		610
SunGard Availability Services 680 E Swedesford Rd *TF:* 800-468-7483 ■ *Web:* www.sungardas.com	Wayne	PA	19087	484-582-2000		394
Sungard Bi-Tech Inc 890 Ftress St	Chico	CA	95973	530-891-5281		809
SunGard Trust Systems Inc 5510 77 Center Dr *Web:* www.sungard.com	Charlotte	NC	28217	704-527-3754	527-9617	178-10
Sungate Insurance Agency Inc 1337 S International Pkwy Ste 1311 *Web:* sungateinsurance.com	Lake Mary	FL	32746	407-878-7979	878-7999	390
Sunhillo Corp 444 Kelley Dr *TF:* 844-977-7676 ■ *Web:* www.sunhillo.com	West Berlin	NJ	08091	856-767-7676		225
Sun-Journal PO Box 4400 *TF:* 800-482-0759 ■ *Web:* www.sunjournal.com	Lewiston	ME	04243	207-784-5411	777-3436	532-2
Sunken Meadow State Park Sunken Meadow Pkwy Rte 25A *Web:* parks.ny.gov	Kings Park	NY	11754	631-269-4333		565
Sunkist Graphics Inc 401 E Sunset Rd *Web:* www.sunkistgrfx.com	Henderson	NV	89011	702-566-9008		627
Sunkist Growers Inc 27770 Entertainment Dr *Web:* www.sunkist.com	Valencia	CA	91355	661-290-8900		315-2
Sunland Chemical & Research Corp 5447 San Fernando Rd W *Web:* www.sunlandchemical.com	Los Angeles	CA	90039	818-244-9600		145
Sunland Fire Protection Inc 1218 Elon Pl *TF:* 800-849-5958 ■ *Web:* sunlandfire.com	High Point	NC	27263	336-886-7027	886-7024	678
Sunland Group Inc 1033 La Posada Dr Ste 370 *TF:* 866-732-8500 ■ *Web:* www.sunlandgrp.com	Austin	TX	78752	512-494-0208		261
Sunland Park Racetrack & Casino 1200 Futurity Dr *TF:* 800-572-1142 ■ *Web:* www.sunland-park.com	Sunland Park	NM	88063	575-874-5200		642
Sunland Tire Company of Upland Inc 461 E Foothill Blvd *Web:* www.sunlandtire.com	Upland	CA	91786	909-982-1396		57
Sunland-Tujunga Chamber of Commerce 8250 Foothill Blvd Ste A *Web:* www.stchamber.com	Sunland	CA	91040	818-352-4433	353-7551	139
Sunled Corp 4010 Valley Blvd Ste 100 *Web:* www.us.sunled.com	Walnut	CA	91789	909-594-6000	594-6008	437
Sunlight Foundation 1818 N St NW Ste 300 *Web:* sunlightfoundation.com	Washington	DC	20036	202-742-1520		305
SunLink Health Systems Inc 900 Cir 75 Pkwy Ste 1120 *NYSE: SSY* ■ *Web:* www.sunlinkhealth.com	Atlanta	GA	30339	770-933-7000	933-7010	353
Sunlite Plastics Inc W194n11340 Mccormick Dr *Web:* www.sunliteplastics.com	Germantown	WI	53022	262-253-0600	253-0601	600
Sun-Maid Growers of California 13525 S Bethel Ave *Web:* www.sunmaid.com	Kingsburg	CA	93631	559-896-8000	897-6209	296-18
SunMan Engineering Inc 2635 N 1st St Ste 205 *Web:* www.sunmantechnology.com	San Jose	CA	95134	408-441-1500	428-0301	261
Sunnen Products Co 7910 Manchester Ave *TF:* 800-325-3670 ■ *Web:* www.sunnen.com	Saint Louis	MO	63143	314-781-2100	781-2268	455
Sunnin 1776 Westwood Blvd *Web:* sunnin.com	Los Angeles	CA	90024	310-475-3358		671
Sunnking Inc 4 Owens Rd *Web:* sunnking.com	Brockport	NY	14420	585-637-8365		179
Sunny 101.5 1301 E Douglas Rd *Web:* www.sunny1015.com	Mishawaka	IN	46545	574-247-4343	289-7382	645
Sunny 105.3 1100 Mohawk St Ste 280 *Web:* sunny1053.iheart.com	Bakersfield	CA	93309	661-322-9929	322-7239	647
Sunny 107.9 Radio *Palm Beach Broadcasting* 701 Northpoint Pkwy Ste 500 *TF:* 800-919-1079 ■ *Web:* www.sunny1079.com	West Palm Beach	FL	33407	561-616-4777		645-23
Sunny 99.1 2000 W Loop S Ste 300 *Web:* sunny99.iheart.com	Houston	TX	77027	713-212-5991		645-72
Sunny Brae Animal Clinic Inc 900 Buttermilk Ln *Web:* sunnybraeanimalclinic.com	Arcata	CA	95521	707-822-5124		794
Sunny Dell Foods Inc 135 N Fifth St *Web:* www.sunnydell.com	Oxford	PA	19363	610-932-5164		296
Sunny Isles Beach Tourism & Marketing Council 18070 Collins Ave *Web:* www.sunnyislesbeachmiami.com	Sunny Isles Beach	FL	33160	305-792-1952		139
Sunny Land Tours Inc 21 Old Kings Rd N Ste B-212 *TF:* 800-783-7839 ■ *Web:* www.sunnylandtours.com	Palm Coast	FL	32137	386-449-0059	449-0060	760
Sunny Morning 5330 NW 35th Ave *Web:* www.sunnymorning.com	Fort Lauderdale	FL	33309	954-735-3447		297-8
Sunny's Seafood Boston Fish Pier Bay 1 *Web:* www.sunnysboston.com	Boston	MA	02210	617-261-7123		297-5
Sunnybrook Health Sciences Ctr *Sunnybrook Campus* 2075 Bayview Ave *Web:* sunnybrook.ca	Toronto	ON	M4N3M5	416-480-6100		374-2
Sunnyland Farms Inc PO Box 8200 *TF:* 800-999-2488 ■ *Web:* www.sunnylandfarms.com	Albany	GA	31706	800-999-2488		459
Sunnyland Outdoor & Casual Furniture 7879 Spring Valley Rd Ste 125 *TF:* 877-239-3716 ■ *Web:* www.sunnylandfurniture.com	Dallas	TX	75254	972-239-3716		321
Sunnyridge Farm Inc 1900 Fifth St NW PO Box 3036 *TF:* 888-491-7364 ■ *Web:* www.sunnyridge.com	Winter Haven	FL	33881	863-299-1894	595-4095	297-7
Sunnyside Motor Company Inc 944 Main St *Web:* www.sunnysideford.com	Holden	MA	01520	508-829-4333		57
Sunnyvale Chamber of Commerce 260 S Sunnyvale Ave Ste 4 *Web:* www.svcoc.org	Sunnyvale	CA	94086	408-736-4971	736-1919	139
Sunnyvale Lumber Inc 870 W Evelyn Ave *Web:* www.sunnyvalelumber.com	Sunnyvale	CA	94086	408-736-5411	736-6738	48-15
Sunnyvale Public Library (SPL) 665 W Olive Ave *Web:* sunnyvale.ca.gov	Sunnyvale	CA	94086	408-730-7300		434-3
Sunnyvalley Smoked Meats Inc 2475 W Yosemite Ave *Web:* www.sunnyvalleysmokedmeats.com	Manteca	CA	95337	209-825-0288	825-0291	296-26
Sunnyway Foods Inc 212 N Antrim Way *Web:* mysunnywayfoods.com	Greencastle	PA	17225	717-597-7121		345
Sunoco Inc 1735 Market St *NYSE: SUN* ■ *TF:* 800-786-6261 ■ *Web:* sunoco.com	Philadelphia	PA	19103	215-977-3000		536
SunOpta Inc 2233 Argentia Rd Ste 401 *TSE: SOY* ■ *Web:* sunopta.com	Mississauga	ON	L5N2X7	905-821-9669	819-7971	296-23
Sunovion Pharmaceuticals Inc 84 Waterford Dr *TF:* 888-394-7377 ■ *Web:* www.sunovion.com	Marlborough	MA	01752	508-481-6700		231
Sunpeak Construction Inc 1401 Quail St Ste 105 *Web:* www.sunpeak.com	Newport Beach	CA	92660	949-474-0501	474-0503	186
Sunplus Data Group Inc 325 Lester Rd NW Ste A *Web:* www.sunplusdata.com	Lawrenceville	GA	30044	770-455-3264		177
SunPower Corp 77 Rio Robles *NASDAQ: SPWR* ■ *Web:* us.sunpower.com	San Jose	CA	95134	408-240-5500		696
Sunquest Information Systems Inc 3300 E Sunrise Dr *TF:* 877-239-6337 ■ *Web:* www.sunquestinfo.com	Tucson	AZ	85718	520-570-2000		180
Sun-Re Cheese Corp 178 Lenker Ave PO Box 52	Sunbury	PA	17801	570-286-1511		296-5
Sun-Reporter Publishing Co 1791 Bancroft Ave *Web:* sunreportermedia.com	San Francisco	CA	94124	415-671-1000	671-1005	532-2
Sunrich LLC *SunOpta* 7301 Ohms Ln Ste 600 *TF:* 800-297-5997 ■ *Web:* www.sunopta.com	Edina	MN	56046	507-451-6030		80-1
Sunrider Intl 1625 Abalone Ave *TF:* 888-278-6743 ■ *Web:* www.sunrider.com	Torrance	CA	90501	310-781-3808		366
Sunrise AG Coop 9361 Creamery Rd *Web:* www.sunriseagcoop.com	Buckman	MN	56317	320-468-6433		297-4
Sunrise Brands 801 S Figueroa St Ste 2500 *Web:* www.sunrisebrands.com	Los Angeles	CA	90017	323-780-8250	881-0369	155-21
Sunrise Business Services Inc 1556 Ocean Ave Ste 10 *Web:* www.sunrisebusiness.net	Bohemia	NY	11716	631-244-8500		113
Sunrise Chamber of Commerce 6800 Sunset Strip *TF:* 800-273-1614 ■ *Web:* www.sunrisechamber.org	Sunrise	FL	33313	954-835-2428	561-9685	139
Sunrise Children Foundation 2795 E Desert Inn Rd Ste 100 *Web:* www.sunrisechildren.org	Las Vegas	NV	89121	702-731-8373		305
Sunrise Community Evangelical Free Church Inc 298 Aquatic Dr *Web:* www.sccjax.org	Atlantic Beach	FL	32233	904-249-3030		48-20
Sunrise Country Manor 610 224th *Web:* www.sunrisecountrymanor.com	Milford	NE	68405	402-761-3230		371
Sunrise Engineering Inc 25 East 500 North *Web:* sunrise-eng.com	Fillmore	UT	84631	435-743-6151		261
Sunrise Growers Inc 701 W Kimberly Ave Ste 210 *Web:* www.sunrisegrowers.com	Placentia	CA	92870	714-630-6292		296-21
Sunrise Hitek Service Inc 5915 N Northwest Hwy *Web:* www.sunrisehitek.com	Chicago	IL	60631	773-792-8880	792-8881	781

Name / Address	City	State	Zip	Phone	Fax	Class
Sunrise Home Health Services 3200 Broadway Blvd Ste 260	Garland	TX	75043	972-278-1414		363
TF: 800-296-7823 ■ *Web:* sunrisehomehealth.com						
Sunrise Hospital & Medical Ctr 701 S Carson St Ste 200	Carson City	NV	89701	702-731-8000	961-8412	374-3
Web: sunrisehospital.com						
Sunrise House Foundation Inc 37 Sunset Inn Rd	LaFayette	NJ	07848	973-383-6300		305
Web: sunrisehouse.com						
Sunrise Labs Inc 5 Dartmouth Dr	Auburn	NH	03032	603-644-4500		194
Web: www.sunriselabs.com						
Sunrise Mall 6041 Sunrise Mall	Citrus Heights	CA	95610	916-961-7150		460
Web: www.sunrisemallonline.com						
Sunrise Manufacturing Inc 2665 Mercantile Dr	Rancho Cordova	CA	95742	916-635-6262		499
TF: 800-748-6529 ■ *Web:* www.sunrisemfg.com						
Sunrise Medical Inc 2842 Business Park Ave	Fresno	CA	93727	800-333-4000		477
TF: 800-333-4000 ■ *Web:* www.sunrisemedical.com						
Sunrise Medical Laboratories Inc 250 Miller Pl	Hicksville	NY	11801	631-435-1515		418
TF: 800-782-0282 ■ *Web:* www.sunriselab.com						
Sunrise National Distributors Inc 6004 Westside Saginaw Rd	Bay City	MI	48706	800-757-8669	993-2948*	61
**Fax Area Code:* 877 ■ *TF:* 800-757-8669 ■ *Web:* www.75sunny.com						
Sunrise Refrigeration 2750 W Brooks Ave Ste 110	North Las Vegas	NV	89032	702-796-1600		665
Web: www.sunriseref.com						
Sunrise School Division 344 Second St N PO Box 1206	Beausejour	MB	R0E0C0	204-268-4832		685
Web: www.sunrisesd.ca						
Sunrise Senior Living LLC 7902 Westpark Dr	McLean	VA	22102	703-273-7500	744-1601	451
NYSE: SRZ ■ *TF:* 888-434-4648 ■ *Web:* www.sunriseseniorliving.com						
Sunrise Specialty Co 930 98th Ave	Oakland	CA	94603	510-729-7277	729-7270	611
TF: 800-444-4280 ■ *Web:* www.sunrisespecialty.com						
Sunrise Suites Resort Key West 3685 Seaside Dr	Key West	FL	33040	305-296-6661		379
Web: www.vacasa.com						
Sunrise Systems Inc 105 Fieldcrest Ave Ste 504 PO Box 513	Edison	NJ	08837	732-603-2200	603-2208	225
Web: www.sunrisesys.com						
Sunrise Tree Company Inc 110 Midlothian Rd	Hawthorn Woods	IL	60047	847-256-8733	913-9346	302
Web: sunrisetreeservice.com						
Sunrise Vet Services PC 2640 Us Hwy 23 S	Alpena	MI	49707	989-354-2241		794
Web: sunriseveterinaryservices.com						
Sunrise Windows Limited LLC 200 Enterprise Dr	Temperance	MI	48182	734-847-8778	847-7758	608
TF: 855-295-5322 ■ *Web:* www.sunrisewindows.com						
Sunrise Wood Designs 720 107th St	Arlington	TX	76011	817-701-4101		226
Web: www.sunrisewooddesigns.com						
Sunroad Enterprises 4445 Eastgate Mall Ste 400	San Diego	CA	92121	858-362-8500		360-2
Web: sunroadenterprises.com						
Sunroad Resort Marina 955 Harbor Island Dr	San Diego	CA	92101	619-574-0736	574-7603	360-3
Web: www.sdmarina.com						
Sunsational Cruises 2470 E Glen Canyon Rd	Green Valley	AZ	85614	520-445-6812		771
Web: www.sunsationalcruises.com						
Sunset Aviation 351 Airport Rd Ste E	Novato	CA	94945	415-897-2403		23
Sunset Development Co 1 Annabel Ln Ste 201	San Ramon	CA	94583	925-866-0100	866-1330	187
Web: www.bishopranch.com						
Sunset Farm Foods Inc 1201 Madison Hwy	Valdosta	GA	31601	229-242-3389		393
TF: 800-882-1121 ■ *Web:* sunsetfarmfoods.com						
Sunset Food Mart Inc 1812 Green Bay Rd	Highland Park	IL	60035	847-432-5500		345
Web: sunsetfoods.com						
Sunset Gower Studios 1438 N Gower St	Hollywood	CA	90028	323-467-1001		514
Web: www.hppsunsetstudios.com						
Sunset Grille 6751 Ruppsville Rd	Allentown	PA	18106	610-395-9622		671
Web: www.sunset-grille.com						
Sunset Grille 421 A1A Beach Blvd	Saint Augustine	FL	32080	904-471-5555		671
Web: www.sunsetgrillea1a.com						
Sunset Hills Foliage Inc 10081 Washington Blvd	Laurel	MD	20723	301-470-3443		292
Web: sunsethillsfoliage.com						
Sunset Hills Health & Rehabilitation Ctr 10954 Kennerly Rd	Saint Louis	MO	63128	314-843-4242	843-4031	450
Web: sunsethillshrc.com						
Sunset Inn Travel Apartments 1111 Burnaby St	Vancouver	BC	V6E1P4	604-688-2474	669-3340	379
TF: 800-786-1997 ■ *Web:* www.sunsetinn.com						
Sunset International Bible Institute 3723 34th St	Lubbock	TX	79410	806-792-5191		167-3
TF: 800-658-9553 ■ *Web:* www.sibi.cc						
Sunset Key Guest Cottages at Westin Resort 245 Front St	Key West	FL	33040	305-292-5300		669
Web: www.sunsetkeycottages.com						
Sunset Logistics Inc 710 Fm 1620	Seguin	TX	78155	830-560-1032		57
Web: drive4sunset.com						
Sunset Marquis Hotel & Villas 1200 N Alta Loma Rd	West Hollywood	CA	90069	310-657-1333	652-5300	379
TF: 800-858-9758 ■ *Web:* sunsetmarquis.com						
Sunset Moulding Company Inc 2231 Paseo Ave	Live Oak	CA	95953	530-790-2700	695-2560	309
Web: www.sunsetmoulding.com						
Sunset Pharmaceuticals Inc 5651 Palmer Way Ste F	Carlsbad	CA	92010	888-950-1950	950-1951	237
TF: 888-950-1950 ■ *Web:* www.sunsetpharma.com						
Sunset Publishing Corp 80 Willow Rd	Menlo Park	CA	94025	650-321-3600		637-9
TF: 800-777-0117 ■ *Web:* www.sunset.com						
Sunset Ridge School District 29 525 Sunset Ridge Rd	Northfield	IL	60093	847-881-9400	446-6388	685
Web: www.sunsetridge29.org						
Sunset Software Technology 1613 Chelsea Rd Ste 153	San Marino	CA	91108	626-441-1565	441-1567	178-1
Web: www.sunsetsoft.com						
Sunset Station Hotel & Casino 1301 W Sunset Rd	Henderson	NV	89014	702-547-7777		379
TF: 888-786-7389 ■ *Web:* www.sunsetstation.com						
Sunset Tower Hotel 8358 Sunset Blvd	West Hollywood	CA	90069	323-654-7100		379
Web: www.sunsettowerhotel.com						
Sunset Transportation Inc 11325 Concord Village Ave	Saint Louis	MO	63123	800-849-6540		311
TF: 800-849-6540 ■ *Web:* www.sunsettrans.com						
Sunshine Books Inc 49 River St Ste 3	Waltham	MA	02453	781-398-0754		95
TF: 800-472-5425 ■ *Web:* www.clickertraining.com						
Sunshine Business Class *Cordial Greetings* 1985 Lookout Dr	North Mankato	MN	56001	800-873-7681		130
TF: 800-873-7681 ■ *Web:* www.sunshinebusinessclass.com						
Sunshine Drapery & Interior Fashions LLC 11800 Adie Rd	Maryland Heights	MO	63043	314-569-2980		361
Web: sunshinedrapery.com						
Sunshine Filters of Pinellas Inc 12415 73rd Ct	Largo	FL	33773	727-530-3884	573-1897	454
TF: 800-423-7947 ■ *Web:* sunshinefilters.com						
Sunshine Financial Inc 1400 E Park Ave	Tallahassee	FL	32301	850-910-8910		360-2
Web: www.sunshinesavingsbank.com						
Sunshine Foods Partners 1115 Main St	Saint Helena	CA	94574	707-681-5956		297-8
Web: www.sunshinefoodsmarket.com						
Sunshine Makers Inc 15922 Pacific Coast Hwy	Huntington Beach	CA	92649	562-795-6000	592-3034	151
TF: 800-228-0709 ■ *Web:* simplegreen.com						
Sunshine Media (SSP) 1 Galleria Blvd Ste 1900	Metairie	LA	70001	504-832-9835		637-9
TF: 800-259-9835 ■ *Web:* www.sunshinepages.com						
Sunshine Mills Inc 500 Sixth St SW	Red Bay	AL	35582	256-356-9541	356-8287	578
TF: 800-633-3349 ■ *Web:* www.sunshinemills.com						
Sunshine Minting Inc 750 W Canfield Ave	Coeur d'Alene	ID	83815	208-772-9592	772-9739	409
TF: 800-274-5837 ■ *Web:* www.sunshinemint.com						
Sunshine Oilsands Ltd 903 Eighth Ave SW Ste 1020	Calgary	AB	T2P0P7	403-984-1450	455-7674	536
Web: sunshineoilsands.com						
Sunshine Printing 139 2nd Ct	Key Largo	FL	33037	305-451-3752		532-2
Web: floridakeysprinting.com						
Sunshine Sachs 720 Cole Ave	Los Angeles	CA	90038	323-822-9300		636
Web: www.sunshinesachs.com						
Sunshine Terrace Foundation Inc 248 W 300 N	Logan	UT	84321	435-752-0411		450
Web: www.sunshineterrace.org						
Sunshine Village Corp Calgary Snow Central 1037 11th Ave SW	Calgary	AB	T2R0G1	403-705-4000		378
Web: www.skibanff.com						
Sunstar Americas Inc 4635 W Foster Ave	Chicago	IL	60630	888-777-3101	553-2014*	228
**Fax Area Code:* 800 ■ *TF:* 888-777-3101 ■ *Web:* www.gumbrand.com						
Sunstate Academy of Hair Design 2040 Colonial Blvd	Fort Myers	FL	33907	239-278-1311		167-3
Web: www.sunstate.edu						
SunState Aviation Flight School L L C 3008 Patrick St	Kissimmee	FL	34741	407-944-3592		685
Web: www.sunstateaviation.com						
Sunstate Federal Credit Union (Inc) PO Box 1162	Gainesville	FL	32627	352-381-5200		219
TF: 877-786-7828 ■ *Web:* www.sunstatefcu.org						
Sunstone Education Foundation Inc 343 N 3rd W	Salt Lake City	UT	84103	801-355-5926		637-2
Web: www.sunstonemagazine.com						
Sunstone Press PO Box 2321	Santa Fe	NM	87504	505-988-4418	988-1025	637-2
TF: 800-243-5644 ■ *Web:* www.sunstonepress.com						
Sunstore Solar Energy Solutions 8 Distribution Ct	Greer	SC	29650	864-558-5143		610
Web: www.sunstoresolar.com						
Sunstream Hotels & Resorts 6231 Estero Blvd	Fort Myers Beach	FL	33931	239-765-4111		378
TF: 844-652-3696 ■ *Web:* sunstream.com						
Sunsweet Growers Inc 901 N Walton Ave	Yuba City	CA	95993	530-674-5010	751-5238	296-18
TF: 800-417-2253 ■ *Web:* www.sunsweet.com						
Suntec Concrete Inc 23751 N 23rd Ave Ste 175	Phoenix	AZ	85085	602-997-0937		106
Web: www.sunteccconcrete.com						
Suntechpros Inc 5920 S Miami Blvd	Morrisville	NC	27560	919-439-9037		177
TF: 877-949-3402 ■ *Web:* suntechprosinc.com						
Sunterra Market 1851 Sirocco Dr SW Ste 200	Calgary	AB	T3H4R5	403-266-2820	266-2557	345
Web: www.sunterramarket.com						
Suntory International Corp 28 Liberty St	New York	NY	10005	212-891-6600		360-3
Web: www.suntory.com						
Suntrans International Inc 1550 W Glenlake Ave	Itasca	IL	60143	630-285-9900		311
Web: www.suntrans.com						
Suntreat Packing & Shipping Co 391 Oxford Ave	Lindsay	CA	93247	559-562-4991		549
Web: suntreat.com						
SunTrust Banks Inc 1165 Fairburn Rd	Atlanta	GA	30331	404-469-0857	344-2778	70
Web: www.suntrust.com						
SunTrust Robinson Humphrey Capital Markets 3333 Peachtree Rd NE	Atlanta	GA	30326	404-926-5000		690
TF: 800-634-7928 ■ *Web:* www.suntrustrh.com						
Sunvalley Mall 1 Sunvalley Mall	Concord	CA	94520	925-825-0400		460
Web: www.shopsunvalley.com						

Phone Fax Class

SunWatch Indian Village/Archaeological Park
2301 W River Rd. Dayton OH 45417 937-268-8199 50-3
Web: www.sunwatch.org

Sunway Hospitality
8500 College Blvd Overland Park KS 66210 913-345-2111 707
Web: www.sunwayhospitality.com

Sunwest Aviation Ltd 217 Aero Ct NE Calgary AB T2E7C6 403-275-8121 275-5900 23
TF: 888-291-4566 ■ *Web:* www.sunwestaviation.ca

Sunwest Electric Inc
3064 E Miraloma Ave Anaheim CA 92806 714-630-8700 630-8740 189-4
Web: www.sunwestelectric.net

Sunwest Federal Credit Union
11839 N 28th Dr. Phoenix AZ 85029 866-897-9378 219
TF: 866-897-9378 ■ *Web:* mysunwest.com

Sunwest Silver Company Inc
324 Lomas Blvd NW Albuquerque NM 87102 505-243-3781 292
TF: 800-771-3781 ■ *Web:* www.sunwestsilver.com

Sunwing Travel Group Inc 27 Fasken Dr. Toronto ON M9W1K6 416-620-4955 772
Web: www.sunwing.ca

Sunworld Landscape & Construction LLC
989 Empire Mesa Way Henderson NV 89011 702-476-5353 476-5656 776
Web: sunworldllc.com

SUNY (State University of New York Press)
22 Corporate Woods Blvd 3rd Fl Albany NY 12211 518-472-5000 472-5038 637-4
TF: 866-430-7869 ■ *Web:* www.sunypress.edu

SUNY (State University of New York, The)
State University Plz. Albany NY 12246 518-320-1888 786
TF: 800-342-3811 ■ *Web:* www.suny.edu
Institute of Technology 100 Seymour Rd Utica NY 13504 315-792-7500 166
Web: sunypoly.edu

Suozzi Thomas (Rep D - NY)
214 Cannon House Office Bldg. Washington DC 20515 202-225-3335 342-2
Web: www.suozzi.house.gov

SUP (Syracuse University Press)
621 Skytop Rd Ste 110. Syracuse NY 13244 315-443-5534 443-5545 459
Web: www.syracuseuniversitypress.syr.edu

Super 8
College ParkSuper 8 Motel Ltd
1910 8th Ave NE Aberdeen SD 57401 605-226-2288 370

Super A Foods 7200 Dominion Cir Commerce CA 90040 323-869-0600 345
Web: www.superafoods.com

Super Brush Co 800 Worcester St. Springfield MA 01151 413-543-1442 543-1523 103
Web: www.swab-its.com

Super Color Digital LLC 16761 Hale Ave Irvine CA 92606 800-979-4446 627
TF: 800-979-4446 ■ *Web:* www.supercolor.com

Super Conductor Materials Inc
391 Spook Rock Rd Suffern NY 10901 845-368-0240 368-0250 696
Web: www.scm-inc.com

Super Duper Inc PO Box 24997 Greenville SC 29616 864-288-3536 288-3380 459
TF: 800-277-8737 ■ *Web:* www.superduperinc.com

Super Electric Construction Co
4300 W Chicago Ave Chicago IL 60651 773-489-4400 235-1455 189-4
Web: www.superelec.com

Super Excavators Inc
N 59 W 14601 Bobolink Ave. Menomonee Falls WI 53051 262-252-3200 252-8079 189-5
Web: www.superexcavators.com

Super Glue Corp
3281 E Guasti Rd Ste 260. Ontario CA 91761 909-987-0550 3
TF: 800-538-3091 ■ *Web:* www.supergluecorp.com

Super H Mart Inc
2550 Pleasant Hill Rd Bldg 300 Duluth GA 30096 678-543-4000 345
TF: 877-427-7386 ■ *Web:* www.hmart.com

Super Holiday Tours 116 Gatlin Ave. Orlando FL 32806 800-327-2116 851-0071* 760
**Fax Area Code: 407* ■ *TF:* 800-327-2116 ■ *Web:* www.superholiday.com

Super King Market 2
2716 N San Fernando Rd Los Angeles CA 90065 323-225-0044 345
Web: superkingmarkets.com

Super Products LLC
17000 W Cleveland Ave New Berlin WI 53151 262-784-7100 784-9561 386
TF: 800-837-9711 ■ *Web:* www.superproductsllc.com

Super Quik Inc 2000 Ashland Dr Ste 105 Ashland KY 41101 606-836-9641 393-3251 324
Web: www.superquik.net

Super Runners Shop Inc
355 New York Ave. New York NY 10024 212-787-7665 711
Web: www.superrunnersshop.com

Super Save Group 19395 Langley By-Pass. Surrey BC V3S6K1 604-533-4423 316
TF: 800-665-2800 ■ *Web:* supersave.ca

Super Shoe Stores Inc 601 Dual Hwy Hagerstown MD 21740 301-739-2130 301
TF: 866-842-7510 ■ *Web:* www.supershoes.com

Super Sky Products Inc
10301 N Enterprise Dr Mequon WI 53092 262-242-2000 242-7409 234
TF: 800-558-0467 ■ *Web:* www.supersky.com

Super Steel Products Corp
7900 W Tower Ave Milwaukee WI 53223 414-355-4800 355-0372 91
Web: www.supersteel.com

Super Steel Treating Inc 6227 Rinke Warren MI 48091 586-755-9140 484
Web: www.supersteeltreating.com

Super Store Industries
16888 McKinley Ave PO Box 549. Lathrop CA 95330 209-858-2010 297-8
TF: 888-292-8004 ■ *Web:* www.ssica.com

Super Stud Building Products Inc
2960 Woodbridge Ave Edison NJ 08837 732-662-6200 697
Web: www.buysuperstud.com

Super Subby's Inc 8924 N Dixie Dr. Dayton OH 45414 937-898-0996 670
Web: www.subbys.com

Super Systems Inc 7205 Edington Dr. Cincinnati OH 45249 513-772-0060 772-9466 407
Web: www.supersystems.com

Super Talent Technology Corp
2077 N Capitol Ave. San Jose CA 95132 408-934-2560 719-5020 203
Web: www.supertalent.com

Super Talk 1270 4303 Memorial Hwy Mandan ND 58554 701-663-1270 645
Web: www.supertalk1270.com

Super Technologies Inc
6005 Keating Rd. Pensacola FL 32504 850-433-8555 387
Web: www.supertec.com

Super Thrifty Drugs Canada Ltd
381 Park Ave E Brandon MB R7A7A5 204-728-1522 231
Web: www.superthrifty.com

Phone Fax Class

Super Wash Inc
707 W Lincolnway PO Box 188 Morrison IL 61270 815-772-2111 310
Web: www.superwash.com

Superadio Network
241 W Boston Post Rd West. Marlborough MA 01752 508-620-0006 556-9375* 647
**Fax Area Code: 952* ■ *Web:* www.superadio.com

Superb Internet Corp
999 Bishop St Ste 1850 Honolulu HI 96813 808-544-0387 441-0952 808
TF: 888-354-6128 ■ *Web:* www.superb.net

Superbag Corp 9291 Baythrone Dr Houston TX 77041 713-462-1173 462-8145 66
TF: 888-842-1177 ■ *Web:* www.superbag.com

Supercamp 1938 Avenida del Oro Oceanside CA 92056 760-722-0072 305-7770 423
TF: 800-228-5327 ■ *Web:* www.supercamp.com

Superchips Inc 1790 E Airport Blvd Sanford FL 32773 407-585-7000 173-2
TF: 888-227-2447 ■ *Web:* superchips.com

Supercomputers Inc
11100 Ne 8th St Ste 380. Bellevue WA 98004 425-881-7500 881-5015 173-1
Web: www.supercomputersinc.com

Supercomputing Institute for Digital Simulation & Advanced Computation
University of Minnesota
599 Walter Library 117 Pleasant St SE Minneapolis MN 55455 612-625-1818 624-8861 668
Web: www.msi.umn.edu

Superconductor Technologies Inc (STI)
460 Ward Dr Santa Barbara CA 93111 805-690-4500 967-0342 253
NASDAQ: SCON ■ *Web:* www.suptech.com

Supercritical Fluid Technologies Inc
1 Innovation Way Newark DE 19711 302-738-3420 738-4320 419
Web: www.supercriticalfluids.com

SuperData Research Holdings Inc
85 Broad St. New York NY 10004 646-248-5241 466
Web: superdataresearch.com

Superdups 68H Stiles Rd Salem NH 03079 603-890-8996 344
TF: 800-617-3877 ■ *Web:* www.superdups.com

SuperFlow Technologies Group
4747 Centennial Blvd Colorado Springs CO 80919 719-471-1746 471-1490 472
TF: 800-471-7701 ■ *Web:* www.superflow.com

SuperGlass Windshield Repair Inc
6220 Hazeltine National Dr Ste 118 Orlando FL 32822 407-240-1920 240-3266 62-2
TF: 800-557-7497 ■ *Web:* www.superglass.com

Supergroup Creative Omnimedia Inc, The
154 Krog St NE Ste 185 Atlanta GA 30307 404-877-1711 7
Web: www.thesupergroup.com

Superheat Fgh Services Inc
313 Garnet Dr. New Lenox IL 60451 888-508-3226 224
TF: 888-508-3226 ■ *Web:* www.superheat.com

Superion Technology Group Inc
3041 Melby St Eau Claire WI 54703 715-514-3431 180
Web: superiontech.com

Superior Abrasives Inc
1620 Fieldstone Way Vandalia OH 45377 937-278-9123 1
TF: 800-235-9123 ■ *Web:* superiorabrasives.com

Superior Access Solutions Inc
21037 Heron Way. Lakeville MN 55044 952-378-4186 180
Web: www.sa-solutions.com

Superior Air Handling Corp
PO Box 160453 Clearfield UT 84016 801-776-1997 825-8967 697
Web: www.sahco.com

Superior Air Parts Inc
621 S Royal Ln Ste 100 Coppell TX 75019 800-420-4727 829-4648* 529
**Fax Area Code: 972* ■ *TF:* 800-420-4727 ■ *Web:* www.superiorairparts.com

Superior Alarm Systems
9001 Canoga Ave Canoga Park CA 91304 818-700-7100 693
Web: www.sassecurity.com

Superior Alarms 600 Ash Ave McAllen TX 78501 956-682-6005 610
TF: 800-580-6001 ■ *Web:* superioralarms.com

Superior Aluminum Products Inc
555 E Main St PO Box 430 Russia OH 45363 800-548-8656 526-3004* 401
**Fax Area Code: 937* ■ *TF:* 800-548-8656 ■ *Web:* www.superioraluminum.com

Superior Auto Sales Inc 5201 Camp Rd Hamburg NY 14075 716-649-6695 516
TF: 866-439-9637 ■ *Web:* www.sascars.com

Superior Bakery Inc 1234 Oaklawn Ave. Cranston RI 02920 401-738-6444 463-3067 297-3
TF: 800-773-6041 ■ *Web:* www.superiorbakery.com

Superior Bar & Grill 6123 Line Ave Shreveport LA 71106 318-869-3243 671
Web: www.superiorgrill.com

Superior Battery Manufacturing Company Inc
2515 Ky 910. Russell Springs KY 42642 270-866-6056 866-6066 74
TF: 800-322-6056 ■ *Web:* www.superlex.com

Superior Boiler Works Inc
3524 E Fourth St. Hutchinson KS 67501 620-662-6693 662-7586 91
TF: 800-444-6693 ■ *Web:* superiorboiler.com

Superior Carriers Inc
711 Jory Blvd Ste 101-N Oak Brook IL 60523 630-573-2555 573-2570 780
TF: 800-654-7707 ■ *Web:* www.superior-carriers.com

Superior Clay Corp
6566 Superior Rd SE Uhrichsville OH 44683 740-922-4122 150
TF: 800-848-6166 ■ *Web:* www.superiorclay.com

Superior Communications Inc
704 E Gude Dr Rockville MD 20850 301-762-7878 196
Web: scicommo.com

Superior Communications Inc
2 Tibbits Ave. White Plains NY 10606 800-735-7070 224
TF: 800-735-7070 ■ *Web:* sciinc.net

Superior Concrete 401 Mckinzie St S. Mankato MN 56001 507-387-7068 387-4451 191-1
Web: www.superiorconcretemn.com

Superior Concrete Inc
1526 Country Club Rd Harrisonburg VA 22802 540-434-0346 182
Web: www.superiorconcreteinc.com

Superior Construction Company Inc
1455 Louis Sullivan Dr. Portage IN 46368 219-787-0850 763-9998 188-4
Web: www.superiorconstruction.com

Superior Court Clerk Office
4800 Tower Hill Rd Wakefield RI 02879 401-782-4121 782-4190 338
Web: www.courts.ri.gov

Superior Crane Corp (SCC)
208 Wilmont Dr PO Box 1464 Waukesha WI 53189 262-542-0099 542-7767 386
Web: www.superiorcrane.com

Superior Dairy Inc 4719 Navarre Rd SW. Canton OH 44706 330-477-4515 296-27
TF: 800-597-5460 ■ *Web:* www.reliableplant.com

Company	City	State	ZIP	Phone	Fax	Class
Superior Dental Care Inc 6683 Centerville Business Pky *TF:* 800-762-3159 ■ *Web:* www.superiordental.com	Centerville	OH	45459	937-438-0283	438-0288	391-3
Superior Derrick Services LLC 4506 S Lewis St *Web:* superiorderrick.com	New Iberia	LA	70560	337-359-1955	205-8797	539
Superior Die Set Corp 900 W Drexel Ave **Fax Area Code:* 800 ■ *TF:* 800-558-6040 ■ *Web:* www.supdie.com	Oak Creek	WI	53154	414-764-4900	657-0855*	757
Superior Die Tool & Machine Co 2301 Fairwood Ave *TF:* 800-292-2181 ■ *Web:* www.superior-dietool.com	Columbus	OH	43207	614-444-2181	444-8712	757
Superior Energy Services Inc 601 Poydras St Ste 2400 *NYSE:* SPN ■ *Web:* superiorenergy.com	New Orleans	LA	70130	504-587-7374	362-1818	538
Superior Environmental Corp 1128 Franklin Ct **Fax Area Code:* 616 ■ *TF:* 877-667-4142 ■ *Web:* superiorenvironmental.com	Marne	MI	49435	877-667-4142	667-3668*	193
Superior Essex Communications LP 6120 Powers Ferry Rd Ste 150 *TF:* 800-551-8948 ■ *Web:* www.superioressex.com	Atlanta	GA	30339	770-657-6000	657-6652	735
Superior Exhibits & Design Inc 777 Lunt Ave *Web:* www.superiorexhibits.com	Elk Grove Village	IL	60007	847-364-9380		317
Superior Fabrication Inc 801 S Eastern Ave *Web:* www.superiorfab.com	Elk City	OK	73644	580-243-5693		779
Superior Farms 1480 Drew Ave *Web:* www.superiorfarms.com	Davis	CA	95618	530-758-3091		473
Superior Flight School Inc - Kennesaw KRYY 1800 Airport Rd NW *Web:* superiorflightschool.com	Kennesaw	GA	30144	770-422-7465	422-8280	685
Superior Foods Inc 275 Westgate Dr *Web:* www.superiorfoods.com	Watsonville	CA	95076	831-728-3691		297-7
Superior Freight Services Inc 1230 Trapp Rd *TF:* 800-298-4305 ■ *Web:* www.supfrt.com	Saint Paul	MN	55121	952-854-5053		311
Superior Gearbox Co 803 W Hwy 32 *TF:* 800-346-5745 ■ *Web:* www.superiorgearbox.com	Stockton	MO	65785	417-276-5191	276-3492	709
Superior Giftwrap PO Box 458 *Web:* www.superiorgiftwrap.com	Floyds Knobs	IN	47119	812-949-2477	949-2479	594
Superior Graphite 10 S Riverside Plz Ste 1470 *TF:* 800-325-0337 ■ *Web:* www.superiorgraphite.com	Chicago	IL	60606	312-559-2999		127
Superior Group Inc, The 8861 Elim St *Web:* superiorpnh.com	Anchorage	AK	99507	907-349-6572	344-5094	610
Superior Group of Companies(SGC) 10055Seminole Blvd *NASDAQ:* SGC ■ *TF:* 800-727-8643 ■ *Web:* superiorgroupofcompanies.com	Seminole	FL	33772	727-397-9611		155-19
Superior Gunite Inc 12306 Van Nuys Blvd *Web:* www.shotcrete.com	Sylmar	CA	91342	818-896-9199	896-6699	189-3
Superior Health Linens LLC 5005 S Packard Ave *Web:* healthcarelinensg.com	Cudahy	WI	53110	414-769-0670		426
Superior HealthPlan Inc 5900 E Ben White Blvd *TF:* 800-964-2777 ■ *Web:* www.superiorhealthplan.com	Austin	TX	78741	800-964-2777		391-3
Superior Home Services Inc 15279 N Scottsdale Rd Ste 400 *TF:* 800-548-2858 ■ *Web:* www.supersvcs.com	Scottsdale	AZ	85254	480-391-5500	391-5600	652
Superior Industries International Inc 7800 Woodley Ave *NYSE:* SUP ■ *Web:* www.supind.com	Van Nuys	CA	91406	818-781-4973		60
Superior Industries LLC 315 E State Hwy 28 PO Box 684 *TF:* 800-321-1558 ■ *Web:* superior-ind.com	Morris	MN	56267	320-589-2406		207
Superior IS 7100 Regency Square Blvd Ste 125 *Web:* www.superioris.com	Houston	TX	77036	713-524-8998	977-2320	194
Superior Jig Inc 1540 N Orangethorpe Way *Web:* superiorjiginc.com	Anaheim	CA	92801	714-525-4777	525-8798	757
Superior Linen Service 1012 S Center St *Web:* www.suplinen.com	Tacoma	WA	98409	253-383-2636	383-1061	442
Superior Machine & Pattern Inc 38001 Alabama Hwy 21 *Web:* www.superiormachineandpattern.com	Talladega	AL	35160	256-362-1385		454
Superior Machine Co 692 N Cashua Dr *Web:* www.smco.net	Florence	SC	29502	843-468-9200		494
Superior Manufacturing Group 5655 W 73rd St *TF:* 800-621-2802 ■ *Web:* www.notrax.com	Chicago	IL	60638	708-458-4600	458-4730	291
Superior Metal Products Inc 2463 Hwy 107 *Web:* superiormetal.com	Chuckey	TN	37641	423-257-2154	257-3617	295
Superior Metal Systems (SMS) 68 Industrial Dr Napier Field *Web:* www.superiormetals.com	Dothan	AL	36303	334-983-9632	983-1201	697
Superior Metal Technologies LLC 9850 E 30th St *TF:* 800-654-9850 ■ *Web:* www.superiormetals.us	Indianapolis	IN	46229	317-897-9850		295
Superior Mobility Inc 1950 E 220th St Ste 208 *TF:* 800-303-2866 ■ *Web:* www.superiormobility.com	Carson	CA	90810	310-218-2040		475
Superior Motors Inc 282 John C Calhoun Dr *TF:* 877-375-4759 ■ *Web:* www.superiormotors.com	Orangeburg	SC	29115	877-375-4759		516
Superior Nut & Candy Company Inc 1111 W 40th St *Web:* www.superiornutandcandy.com	Chicago	IL	60609	773-254-7900	254-9171	297-3
Superior Nut Company Inc 225 Monsignor O'Brien Hwy *TF:* 800-295-4093 ■ *Web:* www.superiornut.com	Cambridge	MA	02141	617-876-3808	876-8225	296-28
Superior Office Systems 19 Gross Ave *Web:* www.superiorofficenj.com	Edison	NJ	08837	732-738-0093		320
Superior Oil Company Inc 1402 N Capitol Ave Ste 100 *TF:* 800-553-5480 ■ *Web:* www.superioroil.com	Indianapolis	IN	46202	317-781-4400	781-4401	603
Superior Packaging Solutions 26858 Almond Ave *TF:* 844-792-2626 ■ *Web:* www.sps4pkg.com	Redlands	CA	92374	844-792-2626		561
Superior Plus Energy Services Inc 1870 S Winton Rd Ste 200 *TF:* 855-804-3835 ■ *Web:* www.superiorpluspropane.com	Rochester	NY	14618	855-804-3835		316
Superior Plus Income Fund 1400 840-7 Ave SW *TF:* 866-490-7587 ■ *Web:* www.superiorplus.ca	Calgary	AB	T2P3G2	403-218-2951	218-2973	405
Superior Pool Products 408 S Rogers Ln *Web:* www.wwadcock.com	Raleigh	NC	27610	919-212-2121	212-2132	45
Superior Press Inc 9440 Norwalk Blvd **Fax Area Code:* 562 ■ *TF:* 888-590-7998 ■ *Web:* www.superiorpress.com	Santa Fe Springs	CA	90670	888-590-7998	948-4966*	86
Superior Printing Company Inc 1325 Logan Cir NW *Web:* www.superiorprinting.us	Atlanta	GA	30318	404-522-9291	584-5485	627
Superior Printing Ink Company Inc 100 N St *Web:* www.superiorink.com	Teterboro	NJ	07608	201-478-5600	478-5650	388
Superior Products Distributors Inc (SPDI) 1403 Meriden-Waterbury Rd Rte 322 *TF:* 800-937-7734 ■ *Web:* www.spdionline.com	Milldale	CT	06467	860-621-3621	621-7922	612
Superior Products Inc 3786 Ridge Rd *TF:* 800-651-9490 ■ *Web:* www.superiorprod.com	Cleveland	OH	44144	216-651-9400	651-4071	621
Superior Public Library 1530 Tower Ave *Web:* superiorlibrary.org	Superior	WI	54880	715-394-8860	394-8870	434-3
Superior Quartz Products Inc 2701 Baglyos Cir **Fax Area Code:* 484 ■ *Web:* www.sqpuv.com	Bethlehem	PA	18020	610-317-3450	244-7343*	437
Superior Ready Mix 1508 Mission Rd *Web:* superiorrm.com	Escondido	CA	92029	760-745-0556	740-9556	182
Superior Roll Forming Company Inc 5535 Wegman Rd *Web:* www.superiorrollforming.com	Valley City	OH	44280	330-225-2500	225-0888	247
Superior Roofing & Sheet Metal Company Inc 3405 S 500 W *TF:* 877-594-4186 ■ *Web:* www.superior-roof.l7marketing.com	Salt Lake City	UT	84115	801-266-1473	266-1522	189-12
Superior Sample Company Inc 520 Gerber St *Web:* www.superiorsample.com	Ligonier	IN	46767	260-894-3136	894-7636	92
Superior Schools Inc 695 SW Mill View Way *TF:* 888-903-1021 ■ *Web:* www.a1schools.co	Bend	OR	97702	541-388-1021	388-2944	685
Superior Shade & Blind Company Inc 1571 N Powerline Rd *Web:* www.superiorshade.com	Pompano Beach	FL	33069	954-975-8122	975-2938	87
Superior Shores Resort 1521 Superior Shores Dr *TF:* 800-242-1988 ■ *Web:* superiorshores.com	Two Harbors	MN	55616	218-834-5671		669
Superior Signal Company LLC 182 W Greystone Rd *Web:* www.superiorsignal.com	Old Bridge	NJ	08857	732-251-0800	251-9442	322
Superior Software Inc 16055 Ventura Blvd Ste 650 *TF:* 800-421-3264 ■ *Web:* www.superior-software.com	Encino	CA	91436	818-990-1135	783-5846	178-1
Superior Steel Inc 5277 N National Dr *Web:* superstl.com	Knoxville	TN	37916	865-522-0253	524-2845	480
Superior Steel Supply 575 E 19th St *Web:* www.superiorsteelsupply.com	Tucson	AZ	85701	520-623-6318	623-1227	492
Superior Tank Company Inc 9500 Lucas Ranch Rd *TF:* 800-221-8265 ■ *Web:* superiortank.com	Rancho Cucamonga	CA	91730	800-221-8265		770
Superior Technical Ceramics Corp 600 Industrial Park Rd *Web:* www.ceramics.net	Saint Albans	VT	05478	802-527-7726	527-1181	249
Superior Tire & Rubber Corp 1818 Pennsylvania Ave W PO Box 308 *TF:* 800-289-1456 ■ *Web:* www.superiortire.com	Warren	PA	16365	814-723-2370	726-0740	754
Superior Tool Co 100 Hayes Dr Unit C *TF:* 800-533-3244 ■ *Web:* www.superiortool.com	Cleveland	OH	44131	216-398-8600	398-8691	758
Superior Trailer Sales Co 501 Hwy 80 *TF:* 800-637-0324 ■ *Web:* www.stsco.com	Sunnyvale	TX	75182	972-226-3893	226-3899	516
Superior Transportation Inc 1940 Hanahan Rd *Web:* www.superiortransportation.us	North Charleston	SC	29406	843-740-1840	740-1942	780
Superior Trim & Door Inc 5120 Industry Dr *Web:* superiortrim.com	Apopka	FL	32703	407-598-1100		200
Superior Tube Co 3900 Germantown Pk *Web:* www.superiortube.com	Collegeville	PA	19426	610-489-5200	489-5252	490
Superior Turbo and Injection 3735 Central Ave *TF:* 800-525-0164 ■ *Web:* www.superiorturbo.com	Detroit	MI	48210	313-842-4616	842-2566	61
Superior Vision 939 Elkridge Landing Rd Ste 200 *TF:* 800-243-1401 ■ *Web:* www.superiorvision.com	Linthicum Heights	MD	21090	410-752-0121	752-8969	393
Superior Washer & Gasket Corp 170 Adams Ave *Web:* www.superiorwasher.com	Hauppauge	NY	11788	631-273-8282	273-8088	455
Superior Water Light & Power 2915 Hill Ave PO Box 519 *TF:* 800-227-7957 ■ *Web:* swlp.com	Superior	WI	54880	715-394-2200		787
Superior Woodcraft Inc 160 N Hamilton St *Web:* www.superiorwoodcraft.com	Doylestown	PA	18901	215-348-9942		321
Superior/Douglas County Convention & Visitors Bureau 305 Harborview Pkwy *TF:* 800-942-5313 ■ *Web:* www.superiorchamber.org	Superior	WI	54880	715-392-7151		206

Company	Phone	Fax	Class
Superlite Block Company Inc 4150 W Turney Ave . . . Phoenix AZ 85019 *TF:* 800-366-7877 ■ *Web:* www.superliteblock.com	602-352-3500	352-3813	183
Superlon Plastic Pipe Co 2116 Taylor Way . . . Tacoma WA 98421 *Web:* www.superlon.com	253-383-5877		612
Super-Lube Inc 1311 N Paul Russell Rd . . . Tallahassee FL 32301 *Web:* superlube.com	850-222-5823		579
Supermarket Liquors & Wines Inc 8438 Niagara Falls Blvd . . . Niagara Falls NY 14304 *Web:* supermarketliquor.com	716-297-7393		443
Supermarket Systems Inc 6419 Bannington Rd . . . Charlotte NC 28226 *TF:* 800-553-1905 ■ *Web:* www.supermarketsystems.com	704-542-6000		665
Supermercado Mi Tierra LLC 9520 International Blvd . . . Oakland CA 94603 *TF:* 800-225-9902 ■ *Web:* supermercadomitierra.com	510-567-8617		345
Supermercados Selectos Inc HC 80 PO Box 7305 . . . Dorado PR 00646 *Web:* www.selectospr.com	787-275-2165		345
Supermicro Computer Inc (SMCI) 980 Rock Ave . . . San Jose CA 95131 *NASDAQ: SMCI* ■ *Web:* www.supermicro.com	408-503-8000	503-8008	625
SuperMom's LLC 625 Second St . . . Saint Paul Park MN 55071 *TF:* 800-944-7276 ■ *Web:* www.supermoms.com	800-944-7276		68
Superna Inc 104 Schneider Rd . . . Kanata ON K2K1Y2 *Web:* www.supernaeyeglass.com	613-729-1100	729-3352	196
Supernus Pharmaceuticals Inc 1550 E Gude Dr . . . Rockville MD 20850 *NASDAQ: SUPN* ■ *Web:* www.supernus.com	301-838-2500		85
SuperShuttle International Inc 14500 N Northsight Blvd Ste 329 . . . Scottsdale AZ 85260 *TF:* 888-629-7604 ■ *Web:* www.supershuttle.com	888-629-7604		441
Superstition Trailers LLC 535 N 51st Ave . . . Phoenix AZ 85043 *Web:* stlaz.com	602-415-0222		778
SuperTalk 99.7 WTN 10 Music Cir E . . . Nashville TN 37203 *TF:* 800-618-7445 ■ *Web:* www.997wtn.com	615-321-1067		645-106
Super-Tek Products Inc 25-44 Borough Pl . . . Woodside NY 11377 *TF:* 888-987-6787 ■ *Web:* www.super-tek.com	718-278-7900		3
SuperValu Inc 11840 Valley View Rd . . . Eden Prairie MN 55344 *NYSE: SVU* ■ *Web:* www.unfi.com	952-828-4000		297-8
SuperValu Intl 1525 E D St . . . Tacoma WA 98421 *Web:* www.supervaluinternational.com	253-593-3198		297-8
Superwinch Inc 359 Lake Rd . . . Dayville CT 06241 *TF:* 800-323-2031 ■ *Web:* www.superwinch.com	800-323-2031		190
Supfina Machine Company Inc 181 Circuit Dr . . . North Kingstown RI 02852 *Web:* www.supfina.com	401-294-6600	294-6262	111
Supima 9885 S Priest Dr Ste 101 . . . Tempe AZ 85284 *Web:* www.supima.com	602-792-6002	792-6004	48-2
Supply Chain Equity Partners 100 S Ashley Dr Ste 2250 . . . Tampa FL 33602 **Fax Area Code:* 216 ■ *Web:* supplychainequity.com	813-395-0501	363-0135*	791
Supply New England Inc 123 East St . . . Attleboro MA 02703 *Web:* www.supplynewengland.com	508-222-5555		362
Supply Room, The 14140 N Washington Hwy . . . Ashland VA 23005 *Web:* thesupplyroom.com	804-412-1200	412-1313	535
Supply Technologies LLC 6065 Parkland Blvd . . . Cleveland OH 44124 *TF:* 800-695-8650 ■ *Web:* www.supplytechnologies.com	440-947-2100	947-2299	351
SupplyFrame Inc 61 S Fair Oaks Ave Ste 200 . . . Pasadena CA 91105 *TF:* 866-786-8339 ■ *Web:* supplyframe.com	626-793-7732		180
SupplyOne Corp 11 Campus Blvd Ste 150 . . . Newtown Square PA 19073 *Web:* www.supplyone.com	484-582-5005	582-0350	601
SupplyPro Inc 9401 Waples St Ste 150 . . . San Diego CA 92121 *TF:* 877-334-0231 ■ *Web:* www.supplypro.com	858-587-6400	552-7609	178-1
SupplySource Inc 415 W 3rd St . . . Williamsport PA 17701 *TF:* 800-633-8753 ■ *Web:* www.supplysourceinc.com	570-327-1500	327-1244	320
Support Group Inc 205 Newbury St Ste 204 . . . Framingham MA 01701 *Web:* supportgroup.com	508-270-8400		177
Support Group Inc, The 24 Prime Park Way . . . Natick MA 01760 *Web:* www.supportgroup.com	508-653-8400		177
Support Kansas City Inc 5960 Dearborn St Ste 200 . . . Mission KS 66202 *Web:* supportkc.org	913-831-4752		449
Support Services of America Inc 12440 Firestone Blvd Ste 312 . . . Norwalk CA 90650 *TF:* 888-564-0005 ■ *Web:* www.supportservicesamerica.com	562-868-3550	868-7811	152
Support Systems Associates Inc (SSAI) Marina Towers 709 S Harbor City Blvd Ste 350 . . . Melbourne FL 32901 *TF:* 877-234-7724 ■ *Web:* www.ssai.org	877-234-7724		261
Supportcom Inc 1200 Crossman Ave Ste 210-240 . . . Sunnyvale CA 94089 *NASDAQ: SPRT* ■ *TF:* 877-493-2778 ■ *Web:* www.support.com	650-556-9440	556-1195	178-7
SupportPRO 1020 Milwakee Ave Ste 245 . . . Deerfield IL 60015 *Web:* www.supportpro.com	847-717-7647	620-0626	225
Supra Alloys 352 Balboa Cir . . . Camarillo CA 93012 *TF:* 888-647-8772 ■ *Web:* www.supraalloys.com	805-388-2138	987-6492	492
Supra Home Health 12251 Taft St Ste 402 . . . Pembroke Pines FL 33026 *Web:* www.suprahh.com	954-443-6461	443-6462	363
Supracor Inc 2050 Corporate Ct . . . San Jose CA 95131 *TF:* 800-787-7226 ■ *Web:* www.supracor.com	408-432-1616	432-8985	22
SupraNet Communications Inc 8000 Excelsior Dr . . . Madison WI 53717 *Web:* www.supranet.net	608-836-0282		225
Supreme Casting Inc 3389 Linco Rd . . . Stevensville MI 49127 *Web:* www.supremecasting.com	269-465-5757	465-5029	308
Supreme Chocolatier LLC 1150 S Ave . . . Staten Island NY 10314 *Web:* www.supremechocolatier.com	718-761-9600		296-8
Supreme Corp 325 Spence Rd . . . Conover NC 28613 *TF:* 888-604-6975 ■ *Web:* supremecorporation.com	828-322-6975	322-7881	745-9
Supreme Corp 2581 E Kercher Rd . . . Goshen IN 46528 *TF:* 800-642-4889 ■ *Web:* supremecorp.com	800-642-4889		516
Supreme Court of Texas Supreme Court Bldg 201 W 14th St Rm 104 . . . Austin TX 78701 *Web:* www.txcourts.gov	512-463-1312	463-1365	339-44
Supreme Court of the US 1 First St NE US Supreme Court Bldg . . . Washington DC 20543 *Web:* www.supremecourt.gov	202-479-3000		341-4
Supreme Gear Co 17430 Malyn Blvd . . . Fraser MI 48026 *Web:* supremegear.com	586-294-7625	294-7648	454
Supreme Group's Portland 4600 NE 138th Ave . . . Portland OR 97230 *Web:* www.supremegroup.com	503-255-8634	253-3907	189-14
Supreme Machined Products Company Inc 18686 172nd Ave . . . Spring Lake MI 49456 *Web:* www.supreme1.com	616-842-6550		621
Supreme Manufacturing Company Inc 5 Connerty Ct . . . East Brunswick NJ 08816 *Web:* www.supremebeverages.com	732-254-0087		345
Supreme Manufacturing Inc 151 Industrial Dr Bld C . . . Beaver Dam WI 53916 *Web:* www.supmfg.com	920-356-0372		484
Supreme Oil Co 2109 W Monte Vista Rd . . . Phoenix AZ 85009 **Fax Area Code:* 602 ■ *TF:* 800-752-7888 ■ *Web:* www.supremeoil.com	800-752-7888	258-8801*	539
Supreme Petroleum Inc 1200 Progress Rd PO Box 1246 . . . Suffolk VA 23434 *TF:* 800-924-5823 ■ *Web:* supremepetro.com	757-934-0550	934-0538	580
Supreme Security Systems Inc 1565 Union Ave . . . Union NJ 07083 *Web:* www.supremesecurity.com	908-810-8822		693
Supreme Systems Inc 1355 N Walton Walker Blvd . . . Dallas TX 75211 *TF:* 888-205-5921 ■ *Web:* www.supremeroofing.com	214-330-8913		191-4
SupremeBytes LLC PO Box 13746 . . . Columbus OH 43213 *TF:* 888-622-2983 ■ *Web:* www.supremebytes.com	614-636-4875	636-4877	387
Supreme-Lake Manufacturing Inc 455 Atwater St PO Box 19 . . . Plantsville CT 06479 *Web:* www.supremelake.com	860-621-8911	628-9746	621
Suquamish Clearwater Casino Resort 15347 Suquamish Way NE . . . Suquamish WA 98392 *TF:* 800-375-6073 ■ *Web:* www.clearwatercasino.com	360-598-8700		452
Sur La Table PO Box 840 . . . Brownsburg IN 46112 **Fax Area Code:* 317 ■ *TF:* 800-243-0852 ■ *Web:* www.surlatable.com	800-243-0852	858-5521*	362
Surdex Corp 520 Spirit of St Louis Blvd . . . Chesterfield MO 63005 *Web:* www.surdex.net	636-368-4400	368-4401	727
Surdna Foundation 330 Madison Ave 25th Fl . . . New York NY 10016 *TF:* 800-421-9512 ■ *Web:* www.surdna.org	212-557-0010	557-0003	305
Sure Cast Inc 200 Sure Cast Dr . . . Burnet TX 78611 *Web:* www.surecast.com	512-756-6500	756-6700	306
Sure fit Inc 8000 Quarry Rd . . . Alburtis PA 18011 **Fax Area Code:* 610 ■ *TF:* 888-796-0500 ■ *Web:* www.surefit.com	888-796-0500	336-8995*	746
Sure Steel Inc 7528 Cornia Dr . . . South Weber UT 84405 *Web:* www.suresteel.com	801-917-5800		189-14
Sure Thing Pest Control 11541 Goldcoast Dr . . . Cincinnati OH 45249 *Web:* surethingpc.com	513-247-0030	247-2803	577
Sure Winner Foods Inc 2 Lehner Rd . . . Saco ME 04072 *TF:* 800-640-6447 ■ *Web:* www.swfoods.com	207-282-1258	286-1410	297-4
Surefire LLC 18300 Mt Baldy Cir . . . Fountain Valley CA 92708 **Fax Area Code:* 714 ■ *TF:* 800-828-8809 ■ *Web:* www.surefire.com	800-828-8809	545-9537*	74
Sureit Solutions Inc 1801 W Queen Creek Rd Ste 3 . . . Chandler AZ 85248 *Web:* www.sureitinc.com	480-917-2000		177
SurePayroll Inc 2350 Ravine Way Ste 100 . . . Glenview IL 60025 *TF:* 877-954-7873 ■ *Web:* www.surepayroll.com	847-676-8420		570
Surepoint Group 8A St Nisku Ste 1211 . . . Calgary AB T9E7R3 *Web:* www.surepoint.ca	780-955-3939	955-2338	538
SureTek Medical 25 Maple Creek Cir Ste B . . . Greenville SC 29607 *Web:* suretekmedical.com	864-299-9743		475
SureTouch 5757 Century Blvd Ste 600 . . . Los Angeles CA 90045 *Web:* suretouch.us	310-641-8228		476
Surety & Fidelity Association of America (SFAA) 1140 19th St NW Ste 500 . . . Washington DC 20036 *Web:* www.surety.org	202-463-0600	463-0606	49-9
Surety Group Inc 12890 Lebanon Rd . . . Mount Juliet TN 37122 **Fax Area Code:* 404 ■ *TF:* 800-486-8211 ■ *Web:* suretygroup.com	844-432-6637	351-3237*	391-5
Surety LLC 12020 Sunrise Vly Dr Ste 250 . . . Reston VA 20191 **Fax Area Code:* 571 ■ *TF:* 800-298-3115 ■ *Web:* surety.com	800-298-3115	748-5810*	178-7
Sureway Tool & Engineering 2959 Hart Ct . . . Franklin Park IL 60131 *Web:* www.surewaytool.com	847-801-3010		697
Surf & Sand Resort 1555 S Coast Hwy . . . Laguna Beach CA 92651 **Fax Area Code:* 949 ■ *TF:* 877-741-5908 ■ *Web:* www.surfandsandresort.com	877-751-5493	494-2897*	707
Surf Associates East Inc 1701 N Federal Hwy . . . Fort Lauderdale FL 33305 *TF:* 800-528-9061 ■ *Web:* www.bcsurf.com	954-564-0202		711
Surf Line Hawaii Ltd 411 Puuhale Rd . . . Honolulu HI 96819 *TF:* 800-847-5267 ■ *Web:* www.jamsworld.com	808-847-5985		155-3
Surf Merchants 29 Winchester St 2nd Fl . . . Boston MA 02116 *Web:* surfmerchants.com	617-292-8008		177
Surf Technicians LLC 912 41st Ave . . . Santa Cruz CA 95062 *Web:* www.surftech.com	831-479-4944		711
Surface Art Inc 18323 Andover Pk W . . . Tukwila WA 98188 *Web:* surfaceartinc.com	206-315-4558		290

Company / Address	City	State	ZIP	Phone	Fax	Class
Surface Blasting Systems LLC 90 Mason Dr. TF: 800-727-2442 ■ Web: www.surface-blasting.com	Coopersville	MI	49404	616-532-4950	532-7011	695
Surface Combustion Inc 1700 Indian Wood Cir. TF: 800-537-8980 ■ Web: www.surfacecombustion.com	Maumee	OH	43537	419-891-7150	891-7151	318
Surface Equipment Corp 337 Cargill Rd.	Kilgore	TX	75662	903-984-0400	983-0018	537
Surface Manufacturing Inc 2025 Airpark Ct Web: www.surfacemfg.com	Auburn	CA	95602	530-885-0700	885-5306	454
Surface Mount Technology Corp 5660 Technology Cir. Web: teamsmt.com	Appleton	WI	54914	920-954-8324		625
Surface Oncology 50 Hampshire St Web: www.surfaceoncology.com	Cambridge	MA	02139	617-714-4096		85
Surface Shields 8450 W 185th St. Web: www.surfaceshields.com	Tinley Park	IL	60487	708-226-9817		291
Surface Specialists 621-B Stallings Rd TF: 866-239-8707 ■ Web: www.surfacespecialists.com	Matthews	NC	28105	866-239-8707		187
Surface Transportation Board 395 E St SW Web: www.stb.gov	Washington	DC	20423	202-245-0245	245-0461	340-17
SurfacExchange 301 S Missouri Ave Web: www.surfacexchange.com	Clearwater	FL	33756	727-446-6660		690
Surfrider Foundation 942 Calle Negocio Ste 350 Web: www.surfrider.org	San Clemente	CA	92673	949-492-8170	492-8142	196
Surfsand Resort 148 W Gower Rd. TF: 800-547-6100 ■ Web: www.surfsand.com	Cannon Beach	OR	97110	503-436-2274	436-9116	379
Surfside Realty Company Inc 213 S Ocean Blvd TF: 800-833-8231 ■ Web: www.surfsiderealty.com	Surfside Beach	SC	29575	843-238-3435		656
Surge Energy Inc 2100 635 Eighth Ave SW Web: www.surgeenergy.ca	Calgary	AB	T2P3M3	403-930-1010		536
Surge Resources 920 Candia Rd TF: 800-787-4387 ■ Web: surgehrs.com	Manchester	NH	03109	603-623-0007		463
Surgent Cpe 237 Lancaster Ave Web: www.surgentcpe.com	Devon	PA	19333	610-688-4477		2
Surgeworks 4609 S 2300 E Ste 103. Web: surgeworks.com	Holladay	UT	84117	801-272-9800		809
Surgical Appliance Industries Inc 3960 Rosslyn Dr. *Fax Area Code: 800 ■ Web: www.saibrands.com	Cincinnati	OH	45209	513-271-4594	309-9055*	477
Surgical Staff Inc 120 St Matthews Ave TF: 800-339-9599 ■ Web: surgicalstaffinc.net	San Mateo	CA	94401	650-558-3999	558-3949	721
Surin West 1918 11th Ave S. Web: www.surinwest.com	Birmingham	AL	35205	205-324-1928	326-6688	671
Suriname Embassy 4201 Connecticut Ave NW Ste 400 Web: www.surinameembassy.org	Washington	DC	20008	202-244-7488	629-4769	257
SurModics Inc 9924 W 74th St NASDAQ: SRDX ■ Web: www.surmodics.com	Eden Prairie	MN	55344	952-829-3286	500-7001	231
Surpass Chemical Company Inc 1254 Broadway TF: 800-289-8101 ■ Web: www.surpasschemical.com	Menands	NY	12204	518-434-8101	434-2798	146
Surprise Valley Electrification Corp (SVEC) 516 US Hwy 395 E TF: 866-843-2667 ■ Web: www.surprisevalleyelectric.org	Alturas	CA	96101	530-233-3511	233-2190	245
Surratt Hosiery Mill Inc 22872 NC Hwy 8 Web: surratthosiery.com	Denton	NC	27239	336-859-4583	859-4713	155-10
Surrey Board of Trade 14439 104th Ave Ste 101 TF: 866-848-7130 ■ Web: businessinsurrey.com	Surrey	BC	V3R1M1	604-581-7130	588-7549	137
Surrey Honda 15291 Fraser Hwy TF: 888-549-3080 ■ Web: www.surreyhonda.com	Surrey	BC	V3R3P3	866-377-2547		57
Surrey Hotel 20 E 76th St. *Fax Area Code: 646 ■ TF: 888-419-0052 ■ Web: www.thesurrey.com	New York	NY	10021	212-288-3700	358-3601*	379
Surrey Veterinary Clinic 3598 S Clare Ave Web: www.surreyvetclinic.com	Clare	MI	48617	989-386-9200	386-5433	794
Surry Community College 630 S Main St Web: surry.edu	Dobson	NC	27017	336-386-8121		162
Surry County 118 Hamby Rd Web: www.co.surry.nc.us	Dobson	NC	27017	336-386-3700		338
Surry County 45 School St. Web: www.surrycountyva.gov	Surry	VA	23883	757-294-5271	294-5204	338
Surry County School 209 N Crutchfield St PO Box 364 Web: www.surry.k12.nc.us	Dobson	NC	27017	336-386-8211	386-4279	685
Surry Insurance Agency & Realty Company Inc 119 W Atkins St Web: www.surryinsurance.com	Dobson	NC	27017	336-386-8228		390
Surry-Yadkin Electric Membership Corp 510 S Main St. TF: 800-682-5903 ■ Web: www.syemc.com	Dobson	NC	27017	336-356-8241		245
Sur-Seal Gasket & Packing Inc 6156 Wesselman Rd. TF: 800-345-8966 ■ Web: www.sur-seal.com	Cincinnati	OH	45248	800-345-8966		326
Surteco USA Inc 7104 Cessna Dr TF: 800-577-9555 ■ Web: www.canplast.com	Greensboro	NC	27409	336-668-9555	668-7795	3
Surtek Inc 1511 Washington Ave Web: www.surtek.com	Golden	CO	80401	303-278-0877		194
Surterre Properties Inc 1400 Newport Center Dr Ste 100 TF: 888-205-5610 ■ Web: www.surterreproperties.com	Newport Beach	CA	92660	949-717-7100		652
Surtrading Inc 210 Berthoud Tr.	Broomfield	CO	80020	303-862-4181		297-4
Surveillance Specialties Ltd 600 Research Dr Ste 2 TF: 800-354-2616 ■ Web: www.securadyne.com	Wilmington	MA	01887	978-688-4444		41
Survey & Ballot Systems Inc 7653 Anagram Dr TF: 800-974-8099 ■ Web: www.surveyandballotsystems.com	Eden Prairie	MN	55344	952-974-2300		177
Survey com 51 Melcher St Web: survey.com	Boston	MA	02210	408-850-1227		466
Survey Sampling International LLC Dynata LLC 6 Research Dr. Web: www.surveysampling.com	Shelton	CT	06484	203-567-7200		668
Survey Service Inc 1911 Sheridan Dr TF: 800-507-7969 ■ Web: www.surveyservice.com	Buffalo	NY	14223	716-876-6450		466
Survey Technologies Inc 2867 SW Greenway Ave TF: 877-848-8500 ■ Web: www.surveytech.com	Portland	OR	97201	503-848-8500	848-8534	392
Surveying Services Inc 41 Heritage Sq Web: www.survserv.com	Jackson	TN	38305	731-664-0807		727
SurveyMonkey Inc 1 Curiosity Way Web: www.surveymonkey.com	San Mateo	CA	94403	650-543-8400		466
Survival Series Publishing Co (SSPC) PO Box 77313 TF: 800-200-7110 ■ Web: www.survival-series.com	San Francisco	CA	94107	415-979-6785		637-2
Survival Strategies Inc 335 N Third St TF: 800-834-0357 ■ Web: www.survivalstrategies.com	Burbank	CA	91502	818-276-1000		196
Survival Systems International Inc 931 Industry Rd Web: www.survivalsystemsinternational.com	Kenner	LA	70062	504-469-4545	466-1884	90
Survival Systems Training Ltd 40 Mt Hope Ave TF: 800-788-3888 ■ Web: www.sstl.com	Dartmouth	NS	B2Y4K9	902-465-3888		449
Survivor II Inc 919 Fairmount Ave TF: 800-620-3743 ■ Web: www.survivorwindowsii.com	Elizabeth	NJ	07205	908-353-1155		234
Survivors Network of Those Abused by Priests (SNAP) PO Box 6416 TF: 877-762-7432 ■ Web: www.snapnetwork.org	Chicago	IL	60680	312-455-1499		48-21
Survivors of Incest Anonymous (SIA) PO Box 190 TF: 877-742-9761 ■ Web: www.siawso.org	Benson	MD	21018	877-742-9761		48-21
Susan Davis Intl 1101 K St NW Ste 400 Web: www.susandavis.com	Washington	DC	20005	202-408-0808		344
Susan Fuller & Associates PC 19751 E MainSt Ste 270. Web: sfullerlaw.com	Parker	CO	80138	303-840-1190		41
Susan G. Komen for the Cure 5005 LBJ Fwy Ste 250 TF: 877-465-6636 ■ Web: ww5.komen.org	Dallas	TX	75244	877-465-6636		48-17
Susan Hobbs Gallery Inc 137 Tecumseth St. Web: www.susanhobbs.com	Toronto	ON	M6J2H2	416-504-3699	504-8064	42
Susan J. Schmid CPA PC Hulslander & Schmid CPA 24 1st Ave E Ste D Web: hulslander-schmidcpa.com	Kalispell	MT	59901	406-755-3088	756-8621	2
Susan L. Allen CPA PA 3695 Hallowing Point Rd Ste 4. Web: susanallencpa.com	Prince Frederick	MD	20678	410-535-0074		2
Susan Schein Automotive 3171 Pelham Pkwy TF: 800-845-1578 ■ Web: www.susanschein.com	Pelham	AL	35124	205-664-1491		57
Susan Sheehan Gallery 136 E 16th St. Web: www.susansheehangallery.com	New York	NY	10003	212-489-3331	489-4009	42
Suscon Inc 600 Railway St Unit 2 Web: www.susconplastics.com	Williamsport	PA	17701	570-326-2003	326-6030	98
Sushi Blues 301 Glenwood Ave Web: sushibluescafe.com	Raleigh	NC	27603	919-664-8061	664-8070	671
Sushi Chef Institute 1123 Van Ness Ave. Web: www.sushischool.net	Torrance	CA	90501	310-782-8483	218-0026	167-3
Sushi Den 1487 S Pearl St Web: www.sushiden.net	Denver	CO	80210	303-777-0826		671
Sushi Doraku 1104 Lincoln Rd Web: dorakusushi.com	Miami Beach	FL	33139	305-695-8383		670
Sushi Japon 6801 N IH-35. Web: www.sushijaponaustin.com	Austin	TX	78752	512-323-6663	323-6789	671
Sushi Ko Glover Park 5455 Wisconsin Ave. Web: www.sushikorestaurants.com	Chevy Chase	MD	20815	301-961-1644		671
Sushi Nabe of Chattanooga 110 River St Web: www.sushinaberestaurant.com	Chattanooga	TN	37405	423-634-0171		671
Sushi Neko 4318 N Western. Web: www.sushineko.com	Oklahoma City	OK	73118	405-528-8862	521-9877	671
Sushi Nozawa NYC LLC 11628 Santa Monica Blvd Ste 200 Web: sushinozawa.com	Los Angeles	CA	90025	310-963-7377		671
Sushi of Gari 402 E 78th St Web: www.sushiofgari.com	New York	NY	10075	212-517-5340		671
Sushi Ota 4529 Mission Bay Dr Web: sushiota.com	San Diego	CA	92109	858-270-5670		671
Sushi Pier LLC 1290 E Plumb Ln J	Reno	NV	89509	775-825-6776		671
Sushi Rock Cafe 1515 E Las Olas Blvd Web: sushirocklasolas.com	Fort Lauderdale	FL	33301	954-462-5541		671
Sushi Rock Grill 5901 Sun Blvd Ste 121. Web: sushirockgrill.com	Saint Petersburg	FL	33715	727-867-0770		671
Sushi Roku 3500 Las Vegas Blvd S Web: www.innovativedining.com	Las Vegas	NV	89109	702-733-7373		671
Sushi Seki 1143 First Ave. Web: www.sushiseki.com	New York	NY	10065	212-371-0238		671
Sushi Station Japanese Restaurant 199 E 5th Ave Ste 7 Web: sushistationeugene.com	Eugene	OR	97401	541-484-1334		671
Sushi Tama 3919 Sixth Ave Web: www.sushitamarestaurant.com	Tacoma	WA	98406	253-761-1014		671
Sushi Taro 1503 17th St NW Web: www.sushitaro.com	Washington	DC	20036	202-462-8999		671
Sushi Ten 4500 E Speedway Blvd. Web: sushiten.webs.com	Tucson	AZ	85712	520-324-0010		671
Sushi Yasuda 204 E 43rd St. Web: www.sushiyasuda.com	New York	NY	10017	212-972-1001	972-1717	671
Sushi Zanmai 1221 Spruce St Web: www.sushizanmai.com	Boulder	CO	80302	303-440-0733	440-6676	671

Name / Address	City	State	ZIP	Phone	Fax	Class
Sushi Zushi 1611 W Fifth St *Web:* www.sushizushi.com	Austin	TX	78703	512-474-7000		671
Sushigawa 2601 W Lake Ave *Web:* www.sushigawa.com	Peoria	IL	61615	309-679-9300		671
SushiSamba 600 Lincoln Rd *Web:* sushisamba.com	Miami Beach	FL	33139	305-673-5337		671
Susie G Gibson Science & Technology Ctr 600 Edmund St *Web:* bedfordbstc.sharpschool.net	Bedford	VA	24523	540-586-3933	586-7711	230
Susquehanna Community Bank 940 High St *Web:* www.wmsb.bank	West Milton	PA	17886	570-568-6851		70
Susquehanna County 75 Public Ave *Web:* www.susqco.com	Montrose	PA	18801	570-278-4600	278-9268	338
Susquehanna Glass 731 Ave H *Web:* www.susquehannaglass.com	Columbia	PA	17512	717-684-2155		361
Susquehanna International Group LLP (SIG) 401 City Ave *Web:* sig.com	Bala Cynwyd	PA	19004	610-617-2600		690
Susquehanna Real Estate 140 E Market St PO Box 2026 *Web:* www.susquehanna-realestate.com	York	PA	17401	717-848-5500	771-1430	653
Susquehanna River Basin Commission 1721 N Front St *Web:* www.srbc.net	Harrisburg	PA	17102	717-238-0423	238-2436	340-20
Susquehanna University 514 University Ave *TF:* 800-326-9672 ■ *Web:* www.susqu.edu	Selinsgrove	PA	17870	570-374-0101	372-2722	166
Susquehanna Valley Woodcrafters Inc 131 Main St *Web:* www.svwoodcrafters.com	Salunga	PA	17538	717-898-7564		115
Suss Consulting 801 Old York Rd Noble Plz Ste 305 *Web:* www.sussconsulting.com	Jenkintown	PA	19046	215-884-5900	884-1637	195
Sussek Machine Corp 805 Pierce St *Web:* sussek.com	Waterloo	WI	53594	920-478-2126		454
Sussex Corrections Institution PO Box 500 *Web:* www.doc.delaware.gov	Georgetown	DE	19947	302-856-5280		213
Sussex County 2 The Cr PO Box 589 *Web:* sussexcountyde.gov	Georgetown	DE	19947	302-855-7700	855-7749	338
Sussex County 20135 Princeton Rd PO Box 1397 *Web:* www.sussexcountyva.gov	Sussex	VA	23884	434-246-1000	246-6013	338
Sussex County Chamber of Commerce 120 Hampton House Rd *TF:* 844-256-7328 ■ *Web:* www.sussexcountychamber.org	Newton	NJ	07860	973-579-1811	579-3031	139
Sussex County Community College 1 College Hill Rd *Web:* www.sussex.edu	Newton	NJ	07860	973-300-2100	579-5226	162
Sussex County Library 125 Morris Tpke *Web:* sussexcountylibrary.org	Newton	NJ	07860	973-948-3660	948-2071	434-3
Sussex I State Prison 24414 Musselwhite Dr *Web:* vadoc.virginia.gov	Waverly	VA	23891	804-834-9967	834-9995	213
Sussex IM Inc N65W24770 Main St *Web:* www.sussexim.com	Sussex	WI	53089	262-246-8022	246-8423	604
Sussex Rural Electric Co-op 64 County Rt 639 PO Box 346 *TF:* 877-504-6463 ■ *Web:* www.sussexrec.com	Sussex	NJ	07461	973-875-5101	875-4114	245
Sussex Wire Inc 4 Danforth Dr *TF:* 888-225-1489 ■ *Web:* www.sussexwire.com	Easton	PA	18045	610-250-7750	250-8875	696
Sussman Automatic Corp 43-20 34th St *TF:* 800-727-8326 ■ *Web:* www.mrsteam.com	Long Island City	NY	11101	718-937-4500		91
Sustainable Environmental Consultants 5930 Grand Ave **Fax Area Code:* 866 ■ *TF:* 888-287-7080 ■ *Web:* www.sustainableenviro.com	West Des Moines	IA	50266	888-287-7080	955-6584*	102
Sustainable Resources Group Inc 440 Creamery Way Ste 150 *Web:* sustainableresourcesgroup.com	Exton	PA	19341	610-840-9200		192
Sustainable Softworks Inc 13 Fieldside Dr *Web:* www.sustworks.com	Cumberland	RI	02864	401-753-0011		177
Sustainable Solutions Corp 155 Railroad Plz Ste 203 *Web:* sustainablesolutionscorporation.com	Royersford	PA	19468	610-569-1047		261
Sustainalytics 215 Spadina Ave Ste 300 *Web:* www.sustainalytics.com	Toronto	ON	M5T2C7	416-861-0403		466
Sutech School 3455 E Olympic Blvd *Web:* www.sutechschool.com	Los Angeles	CA	90023	323-262-3210	262-0459	685
Suter Company Inc 258 May St *TF:* 800-435-6942 ■ *Web:* www.suterco.com	Sycamore	IL	60178	815-895-9186	895-4814	296-36
Sutherland Global Services 1160 Pittsford-Victor Rd *Web:* www.sutherlandglobal.com	Pittsford	NY	14534	585-586-5757		387
Sutherland Lumber Co 4000 Main St *TF:* 800-821-2252 ■ *Web:* www.sutherlands.com	Kansas City	MO	64111	816-756-3000	360-2195	364
Sutherland-Chan School & Teaching Clinic 330 Dupont St Ste 400 *Web:* www.sutherland-chan.com	Toronto	ON	M5R1V9	416-924-1107	924-9413	685
Sutin Thayer & Browne 6100 Uptown Blvd NE Ste 400 *Web:* sutinfirm.com	Albuquerque	NM	87110	505-883-2500	888-6565	428
Sutisoft Inc 4984 El Camino Real Ste 200 *TF:* 888-272-4385 ■ *Web:* www.sutisoft.com	Los Altos	CA	94022	650-969-7884		177
Sutphen Corp PO Box 158 *TF:* 800-726-7030 ■ *Web:* www.sutphen.com	Amlin	OH	43002	614-889-1005	889-0874	516
Sutron Corp 22400 Davis Dr *Web:* www.sutron.com	Sterling	VA	20164	703-406-2800		472
Sutter County 433 Second St *TF:* 800-371-3177 ■ *Web:* www.suttercounty.org	Yuba City	CA	95991	530-822-7134	822-7214	338
Sutter Health 2200 River Plz *TF:* 888-888-6044 ■ *Web:* www.sutterhealth.org	Sacramento	CA	95833	916-733-8800		353
Sutter Health Sacramento Sierra Region 2801 L St *Web:* www.checksutterfirst.org	Sacramento	CA	95816	916-454-2222		374-3
Sutter Hill Ventures 755 Page Mill Rd Bldg A-200 *Web:* www.shv.com	Palo Alto	CA	94304	650-493-5600		792
Sutter Securities Inc 12 Geary St Ste 402 *Web:* suttersecurities.com	San Francisco	CA	94108	415-352-6300	352-6304	690
Sutter's Fort State Historic Park 2701 L St *Web:* www.parks.ca.gov	Sacramento	CA	95816	916-445-4422	447-9318	565
Sutter, Mclellan & Gilbreath Inc 1424 N Brown Rd Ste 300 *Web:* smginsurance.com	Lawrenceville	GA	30043	770-246-8300		390
Suttle 1001 East Hwy 212 *TF:* 800-852-8662 ■ *Web:* www.suttlesolutions.com	Hector	MN	55342	320-848-6711	848-6218	735
Suttles Plumbing & Mechanical Corp 21541 Nordhoff St Ste C *Web:* www.suttlesplumbing.com	Chatsworth	CA	91311	818-718-9779		610
Suttle-Straus Inc 1000 Uniek Dr *Web:* www.suttle-straus.com	Waunakee	WI	53597	608-849-1000	849-8264	627
Suttner Accounting Inc 1230 E Chestnut St *Web:* suttnercpa.com	Chilton	WI	53014	920-849-9346		2
Sutton & Simmons 39 Professional Plz *Web:* www.suttonsimmons.com	Rexburg	ID	83440	208-356-3452	356-8577	2
Sutton Alliance LLC 515 Rockaway Ave *TF:* 866-435-6600 ■ *Web:* www.suttonalliance.com	Valley Stream	NY	11581	516-837-6100		652
Sutton County 300 E Oak St *Web:* co.sutton.tx.us	Sonora	TX	76950	325-387-3815		338
Sutton Enterprises Inc 424 Diana Ct Ste A *Web:* www.suttonenterprises.com	Bensenville	IL	60106	847-445-2098		463
Sutton Movement Writing Press PO Box 517 *Web:* www.dancewriting.org	La Jolla	CA	92038	858-456-0020		423
Sutton Place Hotel Edmonton 10235 101st St *Web:* www.suttonplace.com	Edmonton	AB	T5J3E9	780-428-7111		379
Sutton Reid Advertising Inc 254 Court Ave *Web:* www.suttonreid.com	Memphis	TN	38103	901-522-8640		4
Sutton-Garten Co 901 N Senate Ave *TF:* 800-686-4674 ■ *Web:* www.suttongarten.com	Indianapolis	IN	46202	317-264-3236	264-3233	811
SUWA (Southern Utah Wilderness Alliance) 425 East 100 South *Web:* suwa.org	Salt Lake City	UT	84111	801-486-3161		48-13
Suwanee Sports Academy 3640 Burnette Rd *Web:* ssasports.com	Suwanee	GA	30024	770-614-6686		717
Suwannee County 212 N Ohio Ave *Web:* www.suwanneechamber.com	Live Oak	FL	32064	386-362-3071	362-4758	338
Suwannee River State Park 3631 201st Path *Web:* www.floridastateparks.org	Live Oak	FL	32060	386-362-2746		565
Suwannee Valley Electric Co-op PO Box 160 *TF:* 800-752-0025 ■ *Web:* svec-coop.com	Live Oak	FL	32064	386-362-2226	364-5008	245
Suzanna's Kitchen Inc 4025 Buford Hwy *Web:* www.suzannaskitchen.com	Duluth	GA	30096	770-476-9900	476-8899	296-26
Suzanne M. Lobiondo CPA PC 100 Boardhollow Rd Ste 206 *Web:* lobiondocpa.com	Farmingdale	NY	11735	516-791-1303		2
Suze Restaurant 4345 W NW Hwy *Web:* www.suzedallas.com	Dallas	TX	75220	214-350-6135	350-6178	671
Suzette De Salvo Insurance Agency Inc 6217 Harlem Ave *Web:* suzettedesalvo.net	Chicago	IL	60656	773-774-1147		390
Suzie's Soba 1009 W 36th St	Baltimore	MD	21211	410-243-0051		671
Suzo-Happ Group Inc 1743 Linneman Rd *TF:* 888-289-4277 ■ *Web:* www.suzohapp.com	Mount Prospect	IL	60056	847-593-6130		544
Suzuki Association of The Americas Inc 1900 Folsom St Ste 101 *TF:* 888-378-9854 ■ *Web:* suzukiassociation.org	Boulder	CO	80302	303-444-0948		138
Suzuki Musical Instrument Corp PO Box 710459 *TF:* 800-854-1594 ■ *Web:* www.suzukimusic.com	Santee	CA	92072	619-258-1896		527
Suzy Inc 625 Broadway 9th Fl *Web:* suzy.com	New York	NY	10012	646-237-3692		178-1
SV Life Sciences (SVLS) 201 Washington St Ste 3900 *Web:* svhealthinvestors.com	Boston	MA	02108	617-367-8100	367-1590	792
SVA 1221 John Q Hammons Dr *TF:* 800-279-2616 ■ *Web:* www.sva.com	Madison	WI	53717	608-831-8181		2
SVAM International Inc 233 E Shore Rd Ste 201 **Fax Area Code:* 516 ■ *TF:* 800-903-6716 ■ *Web:* www.svam.com	Great Neck	NY	11023	800-903-6716	466-8260*	180
SVB (Silicon Valley Bank) 3003 Tasman Dr *Web:* www.svb.com	Santa Clara	CA	95054	408-654-7400		70
SVC (Society of Vacuum Coaters) 71 Pinon Hill Pl NE *TF:* 800-443-8817 ■ *Web:* www.svc.org	Albuquerque	NM	87122	505-856-7188	856-6716	49-13
SVCH (Saint Vincent Charity Hospital) 2322 E 22nd St Ste 102 *Web:* www.stvincentcharity.com	Cleveland	OH	44115	216-861-6200		374-3
SVDH (Sierra View District Hospital) 465 W Putnam Ave *Web:* www.sierra-view.com	Porterville	CA	93257	559-784-1110		374-3
SVEC (Surprise Valley Electrification Corp) 516 US Hwy 395 E *TF:* 866-843-2667 ■ *Web:* www.surprisevalleyelectric.org	Alturas	CA	96101	530-233-3511	233-2190	245
Svehla Law Offices 408 Platte Ave Ste A *TF:* 888-673-4927 ■ *Web:* svehlalawoffices.com	York	NE	68467	402-362-5506	362-5507	41
Svenska Handelsbanken 875 Third Ave 4th Fl *Web:* www.handelsbanken.se	New York	NY	10022	212-326-5100		70

Name / Address	Phone	Fax	Class
SVF Flow Controls Inc 13560 Larwin Cir .... Santa Fe Springs CA 90670 *Web:* www.svf.net	562-802-2255		358
SVI (South Valley Internet Inc) 95 E San Martin Ave .... San Martin CA 95046 *TF:* 800-899-4125 ■ *Web:* www.garlic.net	408-683-4533	681-1528	681
SVI Inc 440 Mark Leany Dr .... Henderson NV 89011 *TF:* 800-784-8726 ■ *Web:* www.specialtyvehicles.com	800-784-8726		516
SVIA (Specialty Vehicle Institute of America) 2 Jenner St Ste 150 .... Irvine CA 92618 *TF:* 800-887-2887 ■ *Web:* atvsafety.org	949-727-3727	727-4216	49-21
SVLS (SV Life Sciences) 201 Washington St Ste 3900 .... Boston MA 02108 *Web:* svhealthinvestors.com	617-367-8100	367-1590	792
SVM LP 3727 N Ventura Dr .... Arlington Heights IL 60004 *TF:* 800-786-8028 ■ *Web:* www.svmcards.com	847-553-9100		226
SVMH (Salinas Valley Memorial Hospital) 450 E Romie Ln .... Salinas CA 93901 *Web:* www.svmh.com	831-757-4333		374-3
SVMIC (State Volunteer Mutual Insurance Co) 101 W Pk Dr Ste 300 .... Brentwood TN 37027 *TF:* 800-342-2239 ■ *Web:* svmic.com	615-377-1999	370-1343	391-5
SVRMC (Sierra Vista Regional Medical Ctr) 1010 Murray Ave .... San Luis Obispo CA 93405 *Web:* www.sierravistaregional.com	805-546-7600		374-3
SVS (Society for Vascular Surgery) 633 N St Clair St 22nd Fl .... Chicago IL 60611 *TF:* 800-258-7188 ■ *Web:* vascular.org	312-334-2300	334-2320	49-8
SVS Vision 118 Cass Ave .... Mount Clemens MI 48043 *TF:* 800-787-4600 ■ *Web:* www.svsvision.com	586-468-7612		543
SVT 7699 Lochlin Dr .... Brighton MI 48116 **Fax Area Code: 248* ■ *TF:* 888-697-8832 ■ *Web:* www.gosvt.com	800-521-4188	437-0052*	246
SVTronics Inc 3465 Technology .... Plano TX 75074 *Web:* svtronics.com	214-440-1234		45
SW (SW Trading Accessory Plaza) 8000 Harwin Dr Ste 355 .... Houston TX 77036 *Web:* www.swtrading.net	713-334-8377	334-9255	411
SW Anderson Co 2425 Wisconsin Ave .... Downers Grove IL 60515 *TF:* 800-323-8462 ■ *Web:* www.swaco.com	630-964-2600	964-2696	350
SW Trading Accessory Plaza (SW) 8000 Harwin Dr Ste 355 .... Houston TX 77036 *Web:* www.swtrading.net	713-334-8377	334-9255	411
SWA Group 2200 Bridgeway Blvd .... Sausalito CA 94965 *Web:* www.swagroup.com	415-332-5100		422
Swag, The 2300 Swag Rd .... Waynesville NC 28785 *TF:* 800-789-7672 ■ *Web:* www.theswag.com	828-926-0430	926-2036	379
Swagelok Co 29500 Solon Rd .... Solon OH 44139 *Web:* www.swagelok.com	440-248-4600	349-5970	595
Swager Communications Inc 501 E Swager Dr .... Fremont IN 46737 *TF:* 800-968-5601 ■ *Web:* www.swager.com	260-495-2515	495-4205	647
Swagger Foods Corp 900 Corporate Woods Pkwy .... Vernon Hills IL 60061 *Web:* www.swaggerfoods.com	847-913-1200		296-22
Swaggerty Sausage Company Inc 2827 Swaggerty Rd .... Kodak TN 37764 *TF:* 866-792-4728 ■ *Web:* www.swaggertys.com	865-933-2625		473
Swaim Inc 1801 S College Dr .... High Point NC 27260 *Web:* www.swaim-inc.com	336-885-6131	885-6227	319-2
Swain County 101 Mitchell St PO Box 2321 .... Bryson City NC 28713 *Web:* www.swaincountync.gov	828-488-9273		338
Swain's General Store 602 E First St .... Port Angeles WA 98362 *Web:* www.swainsinc.com	360-452-2357	452-7561	791
Swaine & Harris PA 425 S Commerce Ave .... Sebring FL 33870 *Web:* heartlandlaw.com	863-385-1549		41
Swallow Falls State Park c/o Herrington Manor State Pk 222 Herrington Ln .... Oakland MD 21550 *Web:* www.dnr.maryland.gov	301-387-6938		565
Swalwell Eric (Rep D - CA) 407 Cannon House Office Bldg .... Washington DC 20515 *Web:* swalwell.house.gov	202-225-5065		342-2
Swan & Sons-Morss Company Inc 309 E Water St PO Box 179 .... Elmira NY 14901 *TF:* 877-407-1657 ■ *Web:* www.swanmorss.com	607-734-6283	732-0120	390
Swan Cleaners 1535 Bethel Rd .... Columbus OH 43220 *Web:* www.swancleaners.com	614-442-5000		426
Swan Creek Candle Co 395 W Airport Hwy .... Swanton OH 43558 *TF:* 888-272-2773 ■ *Web:* www.swancreekcandle.com	419-825-5612		523
Swan Engineering & Machine Co 2611 State St .... Bettendorf IA 52722 *Web:* swanengr.com	563-355-2671	355-5380	757
Swan Lake Resort & Campground 17463 County Hwy 29 .... Fergus Falls MN 56537 *TF:* 800-697-4626 ■ *Web:* swanlkresort.com	218-736-4626		121
Swan Lake State Park 100 W Park Ln .... Swanville ME 04915 *Web:* www.maine.gov	207-525-4404		565
Swan Law Firm PLLC 10808 S River Front Pkwy Ste 363 .... South Jordan UT 84095 *Web:* swanlaw.net	801-736-7222	736-7220	41
Swan Legal Search 3671 Acreage Ln .... Sebastopol CA 95472 *Web:* www.swanlegal.com	310-201-2500		266
Swan Products LLC 1201 Delaware Ave .... Marion OH 43302 *TF:* 800-800-4673 ■ *Web:* www.swanhose.com	800-800-4673		370
Swan Valley School Dist 8380 Ohern Rd .... Saginaw MI 48609 *Web:* swanvalleyschools.com	989-921-3701		685
SWANA (Solid Waste Association of North America) 1100 Wayne Ave Ste 700 .... Silver Spring MD 20910 *TF:* 800-467-9262 ■ *Web:* www.swana.org	301-585-2898	589-7068	531-5
Swaner Hardwood Company Inc 5 W Magnolia Blvd .... Burbank CA 91502 *Web:* www.swanerhardwood.com	818-953-5350	846-3662	683
Swank Inc 656 Joseph Warner Blvd .... Taunton MA 02780 *Web:* swankinc.com	508-822-2527		408
Swank Motion Pictures Inc 10795 Watson Rd .... Saint Louis MO 63127 *TF:* 888-389-3622 ■ *Web:* www.swank.com	314-984-6000		514
Swann Galleries Inc 104 E 25th St .... New York NY 10010 *Web:* www.swanngalleries.com	212-254-4710	979-1017	51
Swans Candles 16524 Tilley Rd S .... Tenino WA 98589 *TF:* 888-848-7926 ■ *Web:* www.swanscandles.com	888-848-7926		122
Swanson & Bratschun LLC *ADSERO IP LLC* 8210 Southpark Terr .... Littleton CO 80120 *Web:* www.adseroip.com	303-268-0066		428
Swanson Construction Co 3400 Towne Pointe Dr .... Bettendorf IA 52722 *Web:* swansonbuilt.com	563-332-4859		186
Swanson Contracting Co 11701 S Mayfield Ave .... Alsip IL 60803 *Web:* www.swansoncontracting.com	708-388-0623	388-9986	188-8
Swanson Group Inc 2695 Glendale Valley Rd PO Box 250 .... Glendale OR 97442 *TF:* 800-331-0831 ■ *Web:* www.swansongroup.biz	541-832-1121		448
Swanson Health Products Inc PO Box 2803 .... Fargo ND 58108 *TF:* 800-824-4491 ■ *Web:* www.swansonvitamins.com	701-356-2700	356-2708	799
Swanson Pickle Company Inc 11561 Heights Ravenna Rd .... Ravenna MI 49451	231-853-2289		296-19
Swanson Rink Inc 1120 Lincoln St 1200 .... Denver CO 80203 *Web:* www.swansonrink.com	303-832-2666		261
Swanson Russell 1202 P St .... Lincoln NE 68508 *Web:* www.swansonrussell.com	402-437-6400		4
Swanson Tool & Die Inc 11755 Justen Cir .... Maple Grove MN 55369 *Web:* www.swansontool.com	763-428-7100	428-7830	488
Swanson Tool Manufacturing Inc 71 Custer St .... West Hartford CT 06110 *Web:* www.swansongage.com	860-953-1641	953-8926	493
Swanstone 200 Swan Ave .... Centralia IL 62801 *TF:* 800-325-7008 ■ *Web:* www.swanstone.com	800-325-7008	342-7926	612
Swanton Welding & Machining Co 407 Broadway Ave .... Swanton OH 43558 *Web:* swantonweld.com	419-826-4816		491
Swany America Corp 115 Corp Dr .... Johnstown NY 12095 *TF:* 888-234-5450 ■ *Web:* www.swanyamerica.com	518-725-3333	725-2026	155-8
Swarco Industries Inc PO Box 89 .... Columbia TN 38402 *TF:* 800-216-8781 ■ *Web:* www.swarco.com	931-388-5900	388-4039	676
Swarovski Lighting Ltd 61 Industrial Blvd .... Plattsburgh NY 12901 *TF:* 800-836-1892 ■ *Web:* www.schonbek.com	518-563-7500	563-4228	296-20
Swarovski North America Ltd 1 Kenney Dr .... Cranston RI 02920 **Fax Area Code: 800* ■ *TF:* 800-289-4900 ■ *Web:* www.swarovski.com	401-463-6400	870-5660*	334
Swarthmore College 500 College Ave .... Swarthmore PA 19081 *TF:* 800-667-3110 ■ *Web:* www.swarthmore.edu	610-328-8300	328-8580	166
Swarthmore Group 1650 Arch St Ste 2100 .... Philadelphia PA 19103 *Web:* www.swarthmoregroup.com	215-557-9300	557-9305	401
Swarthout Coaches Inc 115 Graham Rd .... Ithaca NY 14850 *Web:* www.goswarthout.com	607-257-2277	257-0218	107
Swartswood State Park PO Box 123 .... Swartswood NJ 07877 *Web:* www.njparksandforests.org	973-383-5230		565
Swartz Campbell LLC 300 Delaware Ave Ste 1410 .... Wilmington DE 19801 *Web:* www.swartzcampbell.com	215-564-5190		445
Swartz Kitchens & Baths 5550 Allentown Blvd (Rt 22) .... Harrisburg PA 17112 *TF:* 800-652-0111 ■ *Web:* swartzkitchens.com	717-652-7111		321
Swartzbaugh-Farber & Associates Inc 1015 N 98th St Ste 221 .... Omaha NE 68114 *Web:* swartzbaugh.com	402-392-8453		390
Swatch Group 703 Waterford Way Ste 450 .... Miami FL 33126 *Web:* www.swatchgroup.com	786-725-5393		153
Swatchcraft 516 Townsend Ave .... High Point NC 27263 *Web:* swatchcraft.com	336-434-5095	861-5397	195
SWC Office Furniture Outlet 375 Fairfield Ave .... Stamford CT 06902 *Web:* swcoffice.com	203-967-8367		321
SWCA Inc 2120 N Central Ave Ste 145 .... Phoenix AZ 85012 *TF:* 800-828-8517 ■ *Web:* www.swca.com	602-274-3831	274-3958	192
SWCE (Steele-Waseca Co-opeartive Electric) 2411 W Bridge St PO Box 485 .... Owatonna MN 55060 *TF:* 800-526-3514 ■ *Web:* swce.coop	507-451-7340		245
SWCS (Soil & Water Conservation Society) 945 SW Ankeny Rd .... Ankeny IA 50023 *TF:* 800-843-7645 ■ *Web:* www.swcs.org	515-289-2331	289-1227	48-13
Swea City Herald Press PO Box 428 .... Swea City IA 50590 *Web:* statelinepubs.com	515-272-4660		532-2
Swearingen Software Inc PO Box 23018 ...... Beaumont TX 77720 *TF:* 800-992-1767 ■ *Web:* swearingensoftware.com	800-992-1767		180
Sweco Products Inc 8949 Colusa Hwy .... Sutter CA 95982 *Web:* www.swecoproducts.com	530-673-8949	671-0110	273
Sweda Company LLC 17411 Vly Blvd .... City of Industry CA 91744 *Web:* www.swedausa.com	626-357-9999		118
Swedbank 1 Penn Plz 15th Fl .... New York NY 10119 *Web:* www.swedbank.us	212-486-8400	486-3220	70
Sweden *Embassy* 2900 K St NW .... Washington DC 20007 *Web:* www.swedenabroad.se	202-467-2600	467-2699	257
Swedenborg Foundation Inc 320 N Church St .... West Chester PA 19380 *Web:* swedenborg.com	610-430-3222		196
Swedenborgian Church, The 50 Quincy St .... Cambridge MA 02138 *Web:* www.swedenborg.org	617-969-4240		637-2
Swedish American Museum 5211 N Clark St .... Chicago IL 60640 *Web:* www.swedishamericanmuseum.org	773-728-8111	728-8870	520
Swedish Council of America 3030 W River Pkwy .... Minneapolis MN 55406 *Web:* www.swedishcouncil.org	612-871-0593		48-14

	Phone	Fax	Class
Swedish Covenant Hospital 5145 N California Ave........................Chicago IL 60625 *Web:* swedishcovenant.org	773-878-8200		374-3
Swedish Institute Inc 226 W 26th St 5th Fl........................New York NY 10001 *Web:* www.swedishinstitute.edu	212-924-5900		162
Swedish Medical Ctr 501 E Hampden Ave.......................Englewood CO 80113 *TF:* 866-779-3347 ■ *Web:* swedishhospital.com	303-788-5000	788-6265	374-3
Swedish-American Chamber of Commerce Georgia (SACC) 715 Peachtree St N E Ste 100 & 200 ....Atlanta GA 30308 *Web:* www.sacc-georgia.org	470-378-1180		138
Swedish-American Chamber of Commerce Incorporated New York Chapter 570 Lexington Ave 20th Fl...................New York NY 10022 *TF:* 800-862-2793 ■ *Web:* www.saccny.org	212-838-5530	755-7953	138
Swedish-American Chamber of Commerce San Diego 4475 Mission Blvd Ste 201 ....San Diego CA 92109 *Fax Area Code: 858 ■ *Web:* www.sacc-sandiego.org	760-500-9060	598-4809*	138
Swedish-American Chamber of Commerce Washington DC Inc 2900 K St NW...........................Washington DC 20007 *Web:* sacc-dc.org	202-536-1570		138
SwedishAmerican Hospital 1401 E State St............................ Rockford IL 61104 *TF:* 800-322-4724 ■ *Web:* www.swedishamerican.org	779-696-4400		374-3
Sweed Machinery Inc 653 Second Ave PO Box 228 .... Gold Hill OR 97525 *TF:* 800-888-1352 ■ *Web:* www.sweed.com	541-855-1512	855-1165	494
Sweeney Buick 7997 Market St.............Youngstown OH 44512 *TF:* 866-560-9470 ■ *Web:* www.sweeneybuickcars.com	866-560-9470		516
Sweeney Conrad PS 2606 116th Ave NE 200 ....Bellevue WA 98004 *Web:* www.sweeneyconrad.com	425-629-1990		734
Sweeney Law Firm 8109 Lima Rd ....Fort Wayne IN 46818 *TF:* 866-793-6339 ■ *Web:* sweeneylawfirm.com	260-420-3137		428
Sweeping Services of Texas LP 3324 Roy Orr Blvd ....Grand Prairie TX 75050 *Web:* www.wastepartners.com	817-268-4100		188-4
Sweepster Attachments 2800 N Zeeb Rd......... Dexter MI 48130 *TF:* 800-456-7100 ■ *Web:* www.sweepsterbrooms.com	734-996-9116	996-9014	103
Sweet Adelines Intl 9110 S Toledo Ave............ Tulsa OK 74137 *TF:* 800-992-7464 ■ *Web:* sweetadelines.com	918-622-1444	665-0894	48-18
Sweet Basil 2424 N Woodlawn St............... Wichita KS 67220 *Web:* www.360wichita.com	316-651-0123		671
Sweet Basil 1585 Bank St...................... Ottawa ON K1H7Z3 *Web:* www.sweetbasilottawa.com	613-731-8424		671
Sweet Basil 3135 NE Broadway.................Portland OR 97232 *Web:* www.sweetbasilor.com	503-281-8337		671
Sweet Briar College 134 Chappel Rd .... Sweet Briar VA 24595 *TF:* 800-381-6142 ■ *Web:* www.sbc.edu	434-381-6100	381-6152	166
Sweet Candy Company Inc 3780 W Directors Row ....Salt Lake City UT 84104 *TF:* 800-669-8669 ■ *Web:* www.sweetcandy.com	801-886-1444	886-1404	296-8
Sweet Constructions 999 Valencia St........................ San Francisco CA 94110 *Web:* www.sweetconstructions.com	415-308-1976		68
Sweet Earth Inc 3080 Hilltop Rd.......... Moss Landing CA 95039 *Web:* www.sweetearthfoods.com	831-375-8673		123
Sweet Grass County 115 W Fifth Ave PO Box 888 ....Big Timber MT 59011 *Web:* sweetgrasscountygov.com	406-932-5152	932-3026	338
Sweet Grass Ranch 460 Rein Ln ....Big Timber MT 59011 *Web:* sweetgrassranch.com	406-537-4477		239
Sweet Harvest Foods 515 Cannon Industrial Blvd ....Cannon Falls MN 55009 *Web:* sweetharvestfoods.com	507-263-8599		123
Sweet Home Central School District 1901 Sweet Home Rd ....Amherst NY 14228 *Web:* sweethomeschools.org	716-250-1400		685
Sweet Home School District 55 1920 Long St ....Sweet Home OR 97386 *Web:* www.sweethome.k12.or.us	541-367-7126		685
Sweet Lucy's Smokehouse 7500 State Rd..........................Philadelphia PA 19136 *Web:* www.sweetlucys.com	215-333-9663		671
Sweet Manufacturing Company Inc 2000 E Leffel Ln..........................Springfield OH 45505 *TF:* 800-334-7254 ■ *Web:* www.sweetmfg.com	937-325-1511	322-1963	207
Sweet Ovations 1741 Tomlinson Rd..........Philadelphia PA 19116	215-676-3900		296-21
Sweet Potatoes 529 North Trade St.................... Winston-Salem NC 27101 *Web:* www.sweetpotatoes.ws	336-727-4844		671
Sweet Street Desserts Inc 722 Hiesters Ln ....Reading PA 19605 *TF:* 800-793-3897 ■ *Web:* www.sweetstreet.com	610-921-8113		68
Sweet Traders Inc 5362 Oceanus Dr Ste C .... Huntington Beach CA 92649 *Web:* www.sweettraders.com	714-903-6800		123
Sweet, Stevens, Katz & Williams LLP 331 E Butler Ave......................... New Britain PA 18901 *Fax Area Code: 717 ■ *Web:* www.sweetstevens.com	215-345-9111	641-9026*	428
Sweetgrass Animal Hospital PA 9730 Dorchester Rd Ste 101............... Summerville SC 29485 *Web:* sweetgrassanimalhospital.com	843-225-9663		794
Sweetgum Press 304 Grover............... Warrensburg MO 64093 *Web:* www.sweetgumpress.com	660-429-5773		637-10
SweetLabs Inc 510 Market St Ste 301.......... San Diego CA 92101 *Web:* www.sweetlabs.com	619-269-0150		393
Sweetlake Chemical Ltd 446 Heights Blvd ....Houston TX 77007 *TF:* 888-752-1998 ■ *Web:* www.sweetlakesteelsupply.com	713-827-8707	827-8718	146
Sweetwater Authority PO Box 2328 .... Chula Vista CA 91912 *Web:* www.sweetwater.org	619-420-1413	425-7469	787
Sweetwater County 80 W Flaming Gorge Way.................. Green River WY 82935 *Web:* sweet.wy.us	307-872-3732		338
Sweetwater County Historical Museum 3 E Flaming Gorge Way .... Green River WY 82935 *Web:* www.sweetwatermuseum.org	307-872-6435	872-3234	520

	Phone	Fax	Class
Sweetwater County Library System 300 N First E St .... Green River WY 82935 *Web:* www.sweetwaterlibraries.com	307-875-3615	872-3203	434-3
Sweetwater County School District 1 (SCSD) 3550 Foothill Blvd ....Rock Springs WY 82901 *Fax Area Code: 888 ■ *TF:* 888-503-5671 ■ *Web:* www.sweetwater1.org	307-352-3400	503-7562*	780
Sweetwater County School District 2 320 Monroe Ave......................... Green River WY 82935 *Web:* www.swcsd2.org	307-872-5500		685
Sweetwater Creek State Park 1750 Mt Vernon Rd.................... Lithia Springs GA 30122 *Web:* gastateparks.org	770-732-5871		565
Sweetwater Hospital 304 Wright St...........Sweetwater TN 37874 *Fax Area Code: 423 ■ *TF:* 800-422-3338 ■ *Web:* www.sweetwaterhospital.org	865-213-8200	351-7405*	186
Sweetwater Sound Inc 5501 US Hwy 30 W .... Fort Wayne IN 46818 *TF:* 800-222-4700 ■ *Web:* www.sweetwater.com	260-432-8176	432-1758	526
Sweetwater Valley Oil Company Inc 1236 New Hwy 68..........................Sweetwater TN 37874 *TF:* 800-362-4519 ■ *Web:* www.valleyoilco.com	423-337-6671		581
Sweetwaters 120 Church St .... Burlington VT 05401 *Web:* www.sweetwatersvt.com	802-864-9800		671
Swell Insurance Solutions LLC 801 Pacific Coast Hwy Ste 201...............Seal Beach CA 90740 *TF:* 855-457-9355 ■ *Web:* liveswellinsurance.com	855-457-9355		390
Swenson Advisors LLP 25220 Hancock Ave Ste 240...................Murrieta CA 92562 *TF:* 800-783-3289 ■ *Web:* swensonadvisors.com	951-445-4700		2
Swenson and Silacci Flowers Inc 110 John St ....Salinas CA 93901 *Web:* swensonandsilacciflowers.com	831-424-2725		292
Swenson Granite Company LLC 369 N State St.............................Concord NH 03301 *Web:* swensongranite.com	603-225-4322		503-6
Swenson Say Faget Inc 2124 Third Ave Ste 100 .... Seattle WA 98121 *Web:* ssfengineers.com	206-443-6212	443-4870	256
Swenson Spreader Co 127 Walnut St ....Lindenwood IL 61049 *TF:* 888-825-7323 ■ *Web:* www.swensonproducts.com	815-393-4455	393-4964	190
Swepco Tube LLC 1 Clifton Blvd................. Clifton NJ 07011 *Web:* www.swepcotube.com	973-778-3000	778-9289	490
Swezey Fuel Company Inc 51 Rider Ave............................ Patchogue NY 11772 *Web:* swezeyfuel.com	631-475-0270		316
SWH (Senior Whole Health LLC) 58 Charles St ....Cambridge MA 02141 *TF:* 888-794-7268 ■ *Web:* www.seniorwholehealth.com	617-494-5353	494-5599	353
SWH Supply Co 242 E Main St...............Louisville KY 40202 *TF:* 800-321-3598 ■ *Web:* www.swhsupply.com	502-589-9287	585-3812	665
SWHR (Society for Women's Health Research) 1025 Connecticut Ave NW Ste 601...........Washington DC 20036 *Web:* swhr.org	202-223-8224	833-3472	48-17
SWI Industrial Solutions Inc 2835 W Bennett St ....Springfield MO 65802 *Web:* www.springfieldworkshopfoundation.com	417-866-2339		547
Swibco Inc 4810 Venture Rd ....Lisle IL 60532 *Fax Area Code: 800 ■ *TF:* 877-794-2261 ■ *Web:* www.swibco.com	630-968-8900	367-7943*	762
Swift Atlanta 3605 Swiftwater Park Dr........... Suwanee GA 30024 *Web:* www.swiftatlanta.com	770-945-1084	932-2418	697
Swift Aviation Sky Harbor International Airport 2710 E Old Tower Rd .... Phoenix AZ 85034 *TF:* 866-704-9274 ■ *Web:* www.swiftaviation.com	602-273-3770	273-3773	63
Swift Communications Inc 580 Mallory Way .... Carson City NV 89701 *TF:* 800-551-5691 ■ *Web:* www.swiftcom.com	775-283-5500		532-3
Swift County PO Box 288 .... Benson MN 56215 *Web:* www.swiftcounty.com	320-843-2744		338
Swift Electrical Supply Co 100 Hollister Rd .... Teterboro NJ 07608 *Web:* swiftelectrical.com	201-462-0900		246
Swift Glass Company Inc 131 W 22nd St ....Elmira Heights NY 14903 *TF:* 800-537-9438 ■ *Web:* www.swiftglass.com	607-733-7166	732-5829	332
Swift Industrial Power Inc 10917 McBride Ln .... Knoxville TN 37932 *Web:* swiftpower.com	865-966-9758		385
Swift Mailing Services 600 Washington St Ste E .... Bristol PA 19007 *Web:* www.swiftmailing.com	215-638-4122	785-6014	627
Swift Print Communication 1248 Research Blvd .... Saint Louis MO 63132 *TF:* 800-545-1141 ■ *Web:* www.swiftprint.com	314-991-4300		627
Swift Saw & Tool Supply Company Inc 1200 171st St.......................... Hazel Crest IL 60429 *Web:* swiftsaw.com	708-335-0550		358
Swift Spinning Inc 16 Corporate Ridge Pkwy.................. Columbus GA 31907 *Web:* www.swiftspinning.com	706-568-9929		745-9
Swift Systems Inc 7340 Executive Way Ste M .... Frederick MD 21704 *Web:* swiftsystems.com	301-682-5100		225
Swift Textile Metalizing LLC (STM) 23 Britton Dr............................Bloomfield CT 06002 *Web:* www.swift-textile.com	860-243-1122	243-0848	745-2
Swift Transportation Company Inc 2200 S 75th Ave............................Phoenix AZ 85043 *NYSE:* SWFT ■ *TF:* 800-800-2200 ■ *Web:* www.swifttrans.com	602-269-9700		780
Swiftlift Inc 820 Phillips Rd ....Victor NY 14564 *Web:* toyotaliftne.com	585-742-2160		23
Swiftships Inc 1105 Levee Rd..............Morgan City LA 70380 *Web:* www.swiftships.com	985-384-1700	380-2559	698
Swifty Oil LLC PO Box 1002 .... Seymour IN 47274 *Web:* www.swiftyoil.com	812-522-1640		780
Swihart Industries Inc 5111 Webster St ....Dayton OH 45414 *Web:* www.swihartindustries.com	937-277-4796		757
Swim Across America Inc 11600 N Community House Rd Ste 100......... Charlotte NC 28277 *Web:* www.swimacrossamerica.org	980-237-9127		317

Company	City	State	ZIP	Phone	Fax	Class
Swimways Corp 5816 Ward Ct *Web:* www.swimways.com	Virginia Beach	VA	23455	757-460-1156		596
Swimwear Anywhere Inc 85 Sherwood Ave *Web:* www.swimwearanywhere.com	Farmingdale	NY	11735	631-420-1400		594
Swindell Dressler International Co 5100 Casteel Dr *Web:* www.swindelldressler.com	Coraopolis	PA	15108	412-788-7100		318
Swine Graphics Enterprises LP 1620 Superior St PO Box 668 *Web:* sgepork.com	Webster City	IA	50595	515-832-5481	832-2237	10-6
Swine Palace 105 MDA Bldg LSU *Web:* www.swinepalace.org	Baton Rouge	LA	70803	225-578-3527		573-4
Swine Services Unlimited Inc 205 Ninth Ave NE *Web:* swineservices.org	Rice	MN	56367	320-393-7447		794
Swine Vet Center PA 1608 S Minnesota Ave *Web:* swinevetcenter.com	Saint Peter	MN	56082	507-934-3970		794
Swinerton Builders 260 Townsend St *Web:* www.swinerton.com	San Francisco	CA	94107	415-421-2980		186
Swing Transport Inc 1405 N Salisbury Ave *Web:* www.swingtransport.com	Salisbury	NC	28144	704-633-3567	636-2160	780
Swinsoft Inc 13405 Folsom Blvd Ste 750 *Web:* www.swinsoft.com	Folsom	CA	95630	916-353-1963	304-0600	180
Swintec Corp 320 W Commercial Ave *TF:* 800-225-0867 ■ *Web:* www.swintec.com	Moonachie	NJ	07074	201-935-0115		111
Swip Systems Inc 1 Regency Plaza Dr Ste 100 *Web:* www.swipsystems.com	Collinsville	IL	62234	618-346-8014		180
Swire Coca-Cola USA 12634 S 265 W *TF:* 800-497-2653 ■ *Web:* www.swirecc.com	Draper	UT	84020	801-816-5300	816-5423	81-2
Swish White River Ltd (WR) 1118 Rte 14 *TF:* 800-639-7226 ■ *Web:* sfwhiteriverpaper.ubsynergy.net	Hartford	VT	05047	802-295-3188	295-5494	559
Swisher & Cohrt PLC 528 W Fourth St *Web:* swishercohrt.com	Waterloo	IA	50701	319-232-6555		41
Swisher County 119 S Maxwell St *Web:* www.co.swisher.tx.us	Tulia	TX	79088	806-995-3294	995-4121	338
Swisher Electric Co-opeartive Inc 401 SW Second St PO Box 67 *TF:* 800-530-4344 ■ *Web:* www.swisherelectric.org	Tulia	TX	79088	806-995-3567	995-2249	245
Swisher International Inc 459 E 16th St *Web:* www.swisher.com	Jacksonville	FL	32206	904-353-4311		756
Swisher Mower & Machine Company Inc 1602 Corporate Dr *TF:* 800-222-8183 ■ *Web:* www.swisherinc.com	Warrensburg	MO	64093	660-747-8183	747-8650	429
Swiss Air Heating and Cooling 211 E Elm St *Web:* www.swissairstl.com	O Fallon	MO	63366	636-978-7800		189-10
Swiss American Screw Products Inc 5740 S Sheldon Rd *Web:* www.sasp.biz	Canton	MI	48188	734-397-1600		621
Swiss Cleaners 35 Windsor Ave PO Box 825 *TF:* 866-879-7947 ■ *Web:* www.swisscleaners.com	Rockville	CT	06066	860-872-0166	872-3698	426
Swiss Knife Shop 10 Northern Blvd Ste 8 *TF:* 866-438-7947 ■ *Web:* www.swissknifeshop.com	Amherst	NH	03031	603-732-0069		195
Swiss Productions Inc 2801 Golf Course Dr *Web:* www.swissproductions.com	Ventura	CA	93003	805-654-8525	654-0315	599
Swiss Valley Farms 247 Research Pkwy PO Box 4493 *Web:* www.swissvalley.com	Davenport	IA	52808	563-468-6600	468-6616	296-5
Swiss-American Chamber of Commerce *New York Chapter* 500 Fifth Ave Rm 1800 *Web:* www.amcham.ch	New York	NY	10110	212-246-7789	246-1366	138
Swissline Precision Manufacturing Inc 23-A Ashton Pkwy *Web:* www.swisslineprecision.com	Cumberland	RI	02864	401-333-8888		757
Swisslog 10825 E 47th Ave *TF:* 800-525-1841 ■ *Web:* www.swisslog.com	Denver	CO	80239	303-371-7770	373-7870	207
Swissomation Inc 112 Marschall Creek Rd *Web:* www.swissomation.com	Fredericksburg	TX	78624	830-997-6565		350
Swissotel Management (USA) LLC 323 E Wacker Dr *Web:* www.swissotel.com	Chicago	IL	60601	312-565-0565		378
Swissway Inc 123 W Hills Rd *Web:* www.swisswayinc.com	Huntington Station	NY	11746	631-351-5350	351-1662	454
Switch Lighting & Design LLC 312 W 4th St *Web:* www.switchcollection.com	Cincinnati	OH	45202	513-721-8100		362
Switchcraft Inc 5555 N Elston Ave *Web:* www.switchcraft.com	Chicago	IL	60630	773-792-2700	792-2129	253
Switchfast Technologies 4043 N Ravenswood Ste 203 *Web:* www.switchfast.com	Chicago	IL	60613	773-241-3007		196
Switchfly Inc 1110 University Ave Varsity Bldg *Web:* www.switchfly.com	Honolulu	HI	96826	415-541-9100	541-9888	178-1
Switlik Parachute Company Inc 1325 E State St *Web:* www.switlik.com	Trenton	NJ	08609	609-587-3300	586-6647	497
Switzer Group Inc, The 3 E 54th St 7th Fl *Web:* www.theswitzergroup.com	New York	NY	10022	212-922-1313		393
Switzerland County County Courthouse 212 W Main St *Web:* switzerland-county.com	Vevay	IN	47043	812-427-4450	427-3179	338
Switzerland County Public Library (SCPL) 205 Ferry St *Web:* scpl.us	Vevay	IN	47043	812-427-3363	427-3654	434-3
Switzerland Tourism 608 Fifth Ave Ste 202 *TF:* 800-794-7795 ■ *Web:* www.myswitzerland.com	New York	NY	10020	212-757-5944	262-6116	775
Swivelier Company Inc 600 Bradley Hill Rd *Web:* www.swivelier.com	Blauvelt	NY	10913	845-353-1455	353-1512	439
Swix Sport USA Inc 600 Research Dr *Web:* www.swixsport.com	Wilmington	MA	01887	978-657-4820		717
SWLA (Chamber, The) *Southwest Louisiana* 4310 Ryan St *Web:* allianceswla.org	Lake Charles	LA	70605	337-433-3632		139
SWLS (Southwest Wisconsin Library System) 1300 Industrial Dr Ste 2 *Web:* www.swls.org	Fennimore	WI	53809	608-822-3393		434-3
SWM (Schweitzer-Mauduit International Inc) 100 N Point Ctr E Ste 600 *NYSE: SWM* ■ *Web:* www.swmintl.com	Alpharetta	GA	30022	770-569-4200		557
SWMC (Southwestern Medical Ctr) 5602 SW Lee Blvd *Web:* swmconline.com	Lawton	OK	73505	580-531-4700		374-3
Swope Art Museum 25 S Seventh St *Web:* www.swope.org	Terre Haute	IN	47807	812-238-1676		520
Sword Solutions Inc PO Box 278 **Fax Area Code:* 866 ■ *Web:* www.swordsolutions.com	DeWitt	MI	48820	517-487-8943	839-5249*	177
SWOT Management Group Inc 7 William Penn Dr *Web:* www.swotmg.com	Flemington	NJ	08822	908-359-7968		317
SWRI (Southwest Research Institute) 6220 Culebra Rd *Web:* www.swri.org	San Antonio	TX	78238	210-684-5111	522-3496	668
SWS Financial Services Inc 1201 Elm St Ste 3500 *Web:* www.burfordadvisors.com	Dallas	TX	75270	214-859-1800		690
SWTC (Southwest Wisconsin Technical College) 1800 Bronson Blvd *TF:* 800-362-3322 ■ *Web:* swtc.edu	Fennimore	WI	53809	608-822-3262	822-6019	800
SWTTC (Southwest Texas Telephone Co) 939 S Texas Hwy 55 *TF:* 800-752-4753 ■ *Web:* www.swtexas.com	Rocksprings	TX	78880	830-683-2111	683-4190	224
Swvhec PO Box 1987 *Web:* www.swcenter.edu	Abingdon	VA	24212	276-619-4302		166
SY Kessler Sales Inc 10455 Olympic Dr *TF:* 888-392-5390 ■ *Web:* www.sykessler.com	Dallas	TX	75220	214-351-0380	351-1903	74
Syar Industries Inc 2301 Napa Vallejo Hwy *TF:* 877-792-7649 ■ *Web:* syar.com	Napa	CA	94558	707-252-8711		503-5
Sybaris Clubs International Inc 2430 E Rand Rd *Web:* www.sybaris.com	Arlington Heights	IL	60004	847-637-3000		378
Sybven 2625 Executive Park Dr Ste 5-3 *Web:* www.sybven.com	Weston	FL	33331	954-837-0078		809
Sycamore Shoals State Historic Park 1651 W Elk Ave *Web:* www.state.tn.us	Elizabethton	TN	37643	423-543-5808		565
Sycamores Terrace Retirement 1427 Lebanon Pk *Web:* sycamoresterrace.com	Nashville	TN	37210	615-242-2412		371
Syclone Designs Inc 32 Jack Heard Dr Ste 200 *Web:* syclone.net	Dawsonville	GA	30534	706-265-4394		225
Sycron Corp 8130 Industrial Park Dr *Web:* sycron.com	Grand Blanc	MI	48439	810-695-2424		385
Sycuan Band of Kumeyaay Nation 1 Kwaaypaay Ct *Web:* sycuantribe.com	El Cajon	CA	92019	619-445-2613		303
Sycuan Casino & Resort 5469 Casino Way *TF:* 800-279-2826 ■ *Web:* www.sycuan.com	El Cajon	CA	92019	619-445-6002		133
Syd's Place 2992 W Lake Rd *Web:* sydsplaceeriepa.com	Erie	PA	16505	814-838-3089		671
Sydell Group Ltd 1170 Broadway *Web:* www.sydellgroup.com	New York	NY	10001	646-307-9600		377
Sydney & Area Chamber of Commerce 275 Charlotte St PO Box 131 Station A *Web:* sydneyareachamber.ca	Sydney	NS	B1P1C6	902-564-6453	539-7487	137
Sydney Harbour Paints Inc (SHP) 1520 Cotner Ave *Web:* www.shpcompany.com	Los Angeles	CA	90025	310-444-2882		44
Sydneys Closet 11840 Dorsett Rd *TF:* 888-479-3639 ■ *Web:* sydneyscloset.com	Maryland Heights	MO	63043	314-344-5066		157-6
Sydnor Hydro Inc 2111 Magnolia St *TF:* 844-339-6334 ■ *Web:* www.sydnorhydro.com	Richmond	VA	23223	804-643-2725		806
Syfan USA Corp 1622 Twin Bridges Rd *TF:* 888-597-9326 ■ *Web:* www.syfanusa.com	Everetts	NC	27825	888-597-9326		601
Syfrett Feed Company Inc 3079 NW 8th St **Fax Area Code:* 863 ■ *TF:* 800-430-0117 ■ *Web:* www.syfrettfeed.com	Okeechobee	FL	34972	800-430-0117	763-6169*	447
SYGMA Network Inc 5550 Blazer Pkwy Ste 300 *TF:* 877-441-1144 ■ *Web:* www.sygmanetwork.com	Dublin	OH	43017	877-441-1144		297-8
Sykes Enterprises Inc 400 N Ashley Dr *NASDAQ: SYKE* ■ *TF:* 800-867-9537 ■ *Web:* www.sykes.com	Tampa	FL	33602	800-867-9537		180
Sykes Supply Group LLC 1015 Stokes St *Web:* sykessupply.com	Burlington	NC	27215	336-227-2723		351
Sylhan LLC 210 Rodeo Dr *Web:* www.sylhan.com	Edgewood	NY	11717	631-243-6600		757
Sylios Corp 735 Arlington Ave N Ste 308 *Web:* sylios.com	Saint Petersburg	FL	33701	727-821-6200		536
Sylvan Dale Guest Ranch 2939 N County Rd 31 D *Web:* www.sylvandale.com	Loveland	CO	80538	970-667-3915	635-9336	239
Sylvan Inc 90 Glade Dr *TF:* 866-352-7520 ■ *Web:* www.sylvaninc.com	Kittanning	PA	16201	724-543-3900	543-7583	10-7

Company	City	State	Zip	Phone	Fax	Class
Sylvan Lake State Park 10200 Brush Creek Rd *Web:* cpw.state.co.us	Eagle	CO	81631	970-328-2021		565
Sylvan Learning Centers 4 N Park Dr Ste 500 *TF:* 888-338-2283 ■ *Web:* www.sylvanlearning.com	Hunt Valley	MD	21030	800-627-4276		242
Sylvan Nursery Inc 1028 Horseneck Rd *Web:* www.sylvannursery.com	Westport	MA	02790	508-636-4573	636-3397	293
Sylvania Area Chamber of Commerce 5632 Main St *Web:* www.sylvaniachamber.org	Sylvania	OH	43560	419-882-2135	885-7740	139
Sylvania Steel Corp 4169 Holland Sylvania Rd *TF:* 800-435-0986 ■ *Web:* www.sylvaniasteel.com	Toledo	OH	43623	419-885-3838		492
Sylvia Greer Artworks PO Box 641579 *TF:* 888-220-2806 ■ *Web:* www.artwwworks.com	Los Angeles	CA	90064	310-474-6664		194
Symar Installations Inc 7404 Fulton Ave Ste 1 *Web:* symarinstallations.com	Kansas City	KS	66106	913-236-4441		321
Symblaze Inc 8997 Keith Ave *Web:* www.symblaze.com	West Hollywood	CA	90069	310-956-8266		195
Symbol Mattress Co 4901 Fitzhugh Ave Ste 300 *Web:* www.symbolmattress.com	Richmond	VA	23230	804-353-8965		471
Symbolic Displays Inc (SDI) 1917 E St Andrew Pl E *Web:* www.symbolicdisplays.com	Santa Ana	CA	92705	714-258-2811	258-2810	22
Symbolic Systems Inc 25 Chatham Rd *Web:* www.symbolic.com	Summit	NJ	07901	908-665-5940		196
Symbolist 1090 Texan Trl *TF:* 800-498-6885 ■ *Web:* www.symbolist.com	Grapevine	TX	76051	800-498-6885		195
Symbology Inc 7351 Kirkwood Ln N Ste 126 *Web:* symbology.com	Maple Grove	MN	55369	763-315-8080		225
Symco Group 5012 Bristol Industrial Way **Fax Area Code:* 678 ■ *TF:* 800-878-8002 ■ *Web:* www.symcogroup.com	Buford	GA	30519	770-451-8002	668-2467*	174
Symerix Business Essentials Inc 237 W 35th St Ste 602 **Fax Area Code:* 212 ■ *TF:* 800-552-4142 ■ *Web:* www.symerix.com	New York	NY	10001	800-552-4142	268-0541*	174
Symetra Life Insurance Co 777 108th Ave NE Ste 1200 *TF:* 800-574-0233 ■ *Web:* www.symetra.com	Bellevue	WA	98004	425-256-8000		391-2
Symetri Internet Marketing 6520 Airport Center Dr Ste 208 *Web:* www.symetri.com	Greensboro	NC	27409	336-285-0940		195
Symetrix Corp 5555 Tech Center Dr Ste 100 *Web:* www.symetrixcorp.com	Colorado Springs	CO	80918	719-594-6145	598-3437	696
Symitar Systems Inc 8985 Balboa Ave *Web:* www.symitar.com	San Diego	CA	92123	619-542-6700		177
Symmco Inc 40 S Park St *Web:* www.symmco.com	Sykesville	PA	15865	814-894-2461	894-5272	485
Symmes Maini & McKee Assoc (SMMA) 1000 Massachusetts Ave **Fax Area Code:* 800 ■ *Web:* www.smma.com	Cambridge	MA	02138	617-547-5400	648-4920*	261
Symmetrix Technologies LLC 106 N Denton Tap Rd Ste 210-262 *Web:* symmetrixtech.com	Coppell	TX	75019	972-599-1585		180
Symmetry Electronics Inc 20250 144th Ave NE Ste 100 *Web:* www.semiconductorstore.com	Woodinville	WA	98072	425-487-6809		612
Symmetry Software Corp 14350 N 87th St Ste 250 *Web:* www.symmetry.com	Scottsdale	AZ	85260	480-596-1500		174
Symmons Industries Inc 31 Brooks Dr **Fax Area Code:* 781 ■ *TF:* 800-796-6667 ■ *Web:* www.symmons.com	Braintree	MA	02184	800-796-6667	843-3849*	609
Symms Fruit Ranch Inc 14068 Sunny Slope Rd *Web:* symmsfruit.com	Caldwell	ID	83607	208-459-4821	459-6932	315-3
Symon's Fire Protection Inc 12155 Paine Pl *Web:* www.symonsfp.com	Poway	CA	92064	619-588-6364	588-6805	45
Symons Capital Management Inc 650 Washington Rd Ste 800 *TF:* 888-344-7740 ■ *Web:* symonscapital.com	Pittsburgh	PA	15228	412-344-7690		237
Symphony Asset Management Inc 555 California St *Web:* www.symphonyasset.com	San Francisco	CA	94104	415-676-4000		690
Symphony Corp 22 E Mifflin St Ste 400 *Web:* www.symphonycorp.com	Madison	WI	53703	608-294-4090		809
Symphony Northwoods 2250 Pearl St *Web:* symphonynorthwoods.com	Belvidere	IL	61008	815-544-0358		371
Symphony Nova Scotia 6101 University Ave Dalhousie Arts Ctr *TF:* 800-874-1669 ■ *Web:* symphonynovascotia.ca	Halifax	NS	B3H4R2	902-494-3820	494-2883	573-3
Symphony of Northwest Arkansas (SONA) 217 E Dickson St Ste 106 PO Box 1243 *Web:* www.sonamusic.org	Fayetteville	AR	72701	479-521-4166		573-3
Symphony of the Mountains 1200 E Center St *Web:* symphonyofthemountains.org	Kingsport	TN	37660	423-392-8423	392-8428	573-3
Symphony Orchestra Augusta 1301 Greene St Ste 200 *Web:* augustasymphony.com	Augusta	GA	30901	706-826-4705	826-4735	573-3
Symphony Silicon Valley 345 S First St *TF:* 800-736-7401 ■ *Web:* www.symphonysiliconvalley.org	San Jose	CA	95113	408-286-2600		573-3
Symphony Space 2537 Broadway at 95th St *Web:* www.symphonyspace.org	New York	NY	10025	212-864-5400	932-3228	226
Symphony Technology Group LLC (STG) 428 University Ave *Web:* www.stgpartners.com	Palo Alto	CA	94301	650-935-9500		178-11
Symplr 616 Cypress Creek Pkwy Ste 800 *Web:* www.symplr.com	Houston	TX	77090	281-863-9500		225
Symposia Medicus 399 Taylor Blvd Ste 201 *TF:* 800-327-3161 ■ *Web:* symposiamedicus.org	Pleasant Hill	CA	94523	925-969-1789		242
Symposium Cafe Restaurants 6021 Yonge St Unit 475 *Web:* symposiumcafe.com	Toronto	ON	M2M3W2	416-449-3611		671
Symrise Inc 300 N St *Web:* www.symrise.com	Teterboro	NJ	07608	201-288-3200	462-2200	145
SYMTECH Inc 100 Sunbeam Rd *Web:* www.symtech-usa.com	Spartanburg	SC	29303	864-578-7101		358
Synacor Inc 40 La Riviere Dr Ste 300 *Web:* www.synacor.com	Buffalo	NY	14202	716-853-1362		395
Synactive Inc 950 Tower Ln Ste 750 *Web:* www.synactive.net	Foster City	CA	94404	650-341-3310	341-3610	178-2
Syna-Flex Rubber Products Company Inc 1223 Cochran Ave *TF:* 800-633-2448 ■ *Web:* www.synaflex.com	Talladega	AL	35160	256-362-2431		677
Synagro Technologies Inc 435 Williams Ct Ste 100 *TF:* 800-370-0035 ■ *Web:* www.synagro.com	Baltimore	MD	21220	800-370-0035		804
Synalloy Corp 775 Spartan Blvd Ste 102 PO Box 5627 *NASDAQ: SYNL* ■ *Web:* synalloy.com	Spartanburg	SC	29304	864-585-3605	596-1501	595
Synapse Biomedical Inc 300 Artino St *Web:* www.synapsebiomedical.com	Oberlin	OH	44074	440-774-2488		475
Synapse Information Resources Inc 1247 Taft Ave *TF:* 888-796-2436 ■ *Web:* www.synapseinfo.com	Endicott	NY	13760	607-748-4145		180
Synaptec Software Inc 4155 E Jewell Ave Ste 600 *TF:* 800-569-3377 ■ *Web:* lawbase.com	Denver	CO	80222	303-320-4420		35
Synaptic Decisions 340 N Sam Houston Pkwy E Ste 120 *Web:* www.synapticdecisions.com	Houston	TX	77060	832-300-9800		463
Synaptics Inc 1251 McKay Dr *NASDAQ: SYNA* ■ *Web:* www.synaptics.com	San Jose	CA	95131	408-904-1100	904-1110	173-1
Synaptis PO Box 968 *Web:* www.synaptis.com	Cary	NC	27511	919-844-5840		463
SynCardia Systems Inc 1992 E Silverlake Rd *Web:* syncardia.com	Tucson	AZ	85713	520-545-1234		477
Synchromesh Studios 1116 Ford Ave *Web:* www.synchromeshstudios.com	Birmingham	AL	35217	205-808-0808		657
Synchronicity Publishing PO Box 927 *TF:* 800-335-6179 ■ *Web:* www.coincidence-creativity.com	Nederland	CO	80466	303-517-2676	258-7917	637-2
Synchronoss Technologies Inc 200 Crossing Blvd *OTC: SNCR* ■ *TF:* 866-620-3940 ■ *Web:* synchronoss.com	Bridgewater	NJ	08807	866-620-3940		224
Synchrony 4655 Technology Dr *Web:* www.synchrony.com	Salem	VA	24153	540-444-4200	444-4201	261
Synchrony Financial 777 Long Ridge Rd *NYSE: SYF* ■ *TF:* 866-419-4096 ■ *Web:* www.synchronyfinancial.com	Stamford	CT	06905	866-419-4096		216
Synch-Solutions Inc 211 W Wacker Dr Ste 300 *Web:* www.synch-solutions.com	Chicago	IL	60606	312-252-3700		226
Synco Chemical Corp 24 Davinci Dr *Web:* www.super-lube.com	Bohemia	NY	11716	631-567-5300		541
Syncom Pharmaceuticals Inc 1275 Bloomfield Ave Bld 3 Unit 50c *TF:* 800-400-0056 ■ *Web:* www.syncom.net	Fairfield	NJ	07004	973-787-2405	787-2406	237
SynCot Plastics Inc 350 Eastwood Dr *Web:* www.syncot.com	Belmont	NC	28012	704-967-0010		146
Syncratec Solutions LLC 7 Upton Ln *Web:* www.syncratec.com	Yardley	PA	19067	215-310-1750		138
Syncretic Software Inc 228 Philadelphia Pk *Web:* www.syncretic.com	Wilmington	DE	19809	302-762-2600	762-2390	180
Syncro Corp PO Box 890 *Web:* www.syncrocorp.com	Arab	AL	35016	256-931-7800	931-7920	247
Syncroflo Inc 6700 Best Friend Rd *Web:* www.syncroflo.com	Norcross	GA	30071	770-447-4443		641
Syncsort Inc 50 Tice Blvd **Fax Area Code:* 201 ■ *TF:* 877-700-0970 ■ *Web:* www.syncsort.com	Woodcliff Lake	NJ	07677	877-700-0970	882-8305*	178-12
Synctronics PO Box 91226 *TF:* 800-444-5397 ■ *Web:* synctronics.com	San Diego	CA	92169	619-275-3525	275-3520	56
Syndax Pharmaceuticals Inc 400 Totten Pond Rd Ste 110 *Web:* www.syndax.com	Waltham	MA	02451	781-419-1400		231
Syndesi Solutions 115 W Market St *TF:* 877-744-0568 ■ *Web:* www.syndesisolutions.com	Athens	AL	35611	877-744-0568		261
Syndetics Inc 10395 Democracy Ln *Web:* syndetics-inc.com	Fairfax	VA	22030	703-273-8350		463
SynDevRx Inc 1 Broadway 14th Fl *Web:* syndevrx.com	Cambridge	MA	02142	617-401-3110		238
Syndicate Sales Inc PO Box 756 *TF:* 800-428-0515 ■ *Web:* shop.syndicatesales.com	Kokomo	IN	46903	765-457-7277		608
Syndicated Capital Inc 1299 Ocean Ave Ste 210 **Fax Area Code:* 855 ■ *Web:* syndicatedcapital.com	Santa Monica	CA	90401	310-255-4490	494-2959*	194
Syndicated Solutions Inc PO Box 1078 *Web:* www.syndicatedsolutions.com	Ridgefield	CT	06877	203-431-0790	431-0792	646
Syndication Networks Corp 8700 Waukegan Rd Ste 250 *TF:* 800-743-1988 ■ *Web:* www.syndication.net	Morton Grove	IL	60053	847-583-9000	583-9025	646
Syndrome Distribution Inc 1410 Vantage Ct *Web:* www.syndromedist.com	Vista	CA	92081	760-560-0440		711
Syndyne Corp 12109 NE 95th St *Web:* syndyne.com	Vancouver	WA	98682	360-256-8466		195
Synechron Inc 15 Maiden Ln Ste 1100 *Web:* www.synechron.com	New York	NY	10038	212-619-5200		193
Synectic Solutions Inc 1701 Pacific Ave Ste 260 *Web:* www.synecticsolutions.com	Oxnard	CA	93033	805-483-4800	483-4844	194

Company	City	State	Zip	Phone	Fax	Class
Synectic Systems Inc 6398 Cindy Ln Ste 200 *Web:* www.synecticsglobal.com	Carpinteria	CA	93013	805-745-1920		692
Synemed Inc 4562 E Second St Ste A *TF:* 800-777-0650 ■ *Web:* www.synemed.com	Benicia	CA	94510	707-745-8386		476
Synenberg Coletta & Moran LLC 55 Public Sq Ste 1331 *Web:* synenberg.com	Cleveland	OH	44113	216-622-2727		41
Synercomm Inc 3265 Gateway Rd Ste 650 *Web:* www.synercomm.com	Brookfield	WI	53045	262-373-7100	373-7171	196
Synergem Emergency Services L L C 1007 Warren St *TF:* 866-859-0911 ■ *Web:* synergemtech.com	Greensboro	NC	27403	866-859-0911		180
Synergen Consulting Intl 11750 Katy Fwy 10th Fl Ste 1000 *TF:* 800-701-4248 ■ *Web:* www.synergenconsulting.com	Houston	TX	77079	281-598-1190	598-1199	196
Synergent 2 Ledgeview Dr *TF:* 800-341-0180 ■ *Web:* www.synergentcorp.com	Westbrook	ME	04092	207-773-5671		317
Synergent Biochem Inc 12026 Centralia Rd Ste H *Web:* www.synergentbiochem.com	Hawaiian Gardens	CA	90716	562-809-3389	809-6191	231
Synergetic Industries LLC 300 Erie Ave *Web:* synergeticindustries.com	Morton	IL	61550	309-321-0080		261
Synergex International Corp 2330 Gold Meadow Way *TF:* 800-366-3472 ■ *Web:* www.synergex.com	Gold River	CA	95670	916-635-7300		178-10
Synergis Creative 1145 Sanctuary Pky Ste 150 *Web:* www.synergiscreative.com	Alpharetta	GA	30009	770-346-7208		631
Synergon Solutions Inc 1335 Gateway Dr *TF:* 800-820-6103 ■ *Web:* www.synergon.net	Melbourne	FL	32901	800-820-6103		225
Synergy 78474 Hwy 111 Ste A *Web:* www.synergyis.us	La Quinta	CA	92253	760-601-5244		180
Synergy 230 W Monroe St 24th Fl *Web:* mysynergy.com	Chicago	IL	60606	312-899-1024		260
Synergy Advisors LLC 840 Apollo St Ste 213 *Web:* synergyadvisorsllc.com	El Segundo	CA	90245	310-414-3200	414-3201	690
Synergy Associates LLC 550 Clydesdale Trl **Fax Area Code:* 763 ■ *TF:* 888-763-9920 ■ *Web:* www.synllc.com	Medina	MN	55340	888-763-9920	383-9952*	180
Synergy Ceramics Gp LLC 5200 Tennyson Pkwy Ste 400 *Web:* www.synergyceramics.com	Plano	TX	75024	972-608-0515		191-1
Synergy Company of Utah LLC, The 2279 S Resource Blvd *TF:* 800-723-0277 ■ *Web:* www.thesynergycompany.com	Moab	UT	84532	800-723-0277		668
Synergy Concepts Inc (SCI) PO Box 803088 *TF:* 888-311-4499 ■ *Web:* www.synergyconcepts.com	Dallas	TX	75380	972-385-3874		681
Synergy Data Solutions Inc 1104A South State St *Web:* synergydata.com	Champaign	IL	61820	217-356-2522		180
Synergy Direct Response 130 E Alton Ave *TF:* 888-902-6166 ■ *Web:* synergydr.com	Santa Ana	CA	92707	888-902-6166		195
Synergy Ecp LLC 6996 Columbia Gateway Dr Ste 101 *Web:* synergyecp.com	Columbia	MD	21046	410-290-1584	290-1585	177
Synergy Employment Group Inc 14 Greenfield Rd *Web:* www.synergyempgroup.com	Lancaster	PA	17602	717-824-4005		260
Synergy Environmental Lab Inc 1990 Prospect Ct *Web:* www.synergy-lab.net	Appleton	WI	54914	920-830-2455		743
Synergy Information Tech Group 104 A Republic Ave *Web:* www.synergyitg.com	LaFayette	LA	70508	337-234-5767		396
Synergy Investment Group Ltd 8320 University Exec Park Dr Ste 11 *Web:* synergyinvestments.com	Charlotte	NC	28262	704-333-7637		390
Synergy Law Group LLC 730 W Randolph St 6th Fl *Web:* www.synergylawgroup.com	Chicago	IL	60661	312-454-0015	454-0261	445
Synergy Learning International Inc PO Box 206 *TF:* 800-769-6199 ■ *Web:* www.synergylearning.org	Putney	VT	05346	802-387-3065		637-9
Synergy Legal Staffing 1101 South Blvd Ste 204 **Fax Area Code:* 312 ■ *Web:* www.synergylegalstaffing.com	Charlotte	NC	28203	704-366-4540	873-4658*	260
Synergy Massage & Wellness Ctr 13593 Monterey Ln *TF:* 877-372-6617 ■ *Web:* www.synergymassage.com	Blue Ridge Summit	PA	17214	717-794-5778		167-3
Synergy Networks Inc 10970 S Cleveland Ave Ste 406 *Web:* snworks.com	Fort Myers	FL	33907	239-790-7000		225
Synergy Resources Inc 3500 Sunrise Hwy Bldg 100 Ste 201 *TF:* 866-896-6347 ■ *Web:* synergyresources.net	Great River	NY	11739	631-665-2050		174
Synergy Solutions Inc 3141 N Third Ave Ste C-100 *Web:* www.synergysolutionsinc.com	Phoenix	AZ	85013	602-296-1600		737
Synergy Tech Consulting 260 Peachtree St Ste 2200 *TF:* 800-279-9214 ■ *Web:* synergytechconsulting.com	Atlanta	GA	30303	800-279-9214		180
Synergy Telcom Inc 8222 Indy Ln *TF:* 800-201-7590 ■ *Web:* www.synergy-tel.com	Indianapolis	IN	46214	317-713-1652		179
Synergy Worldwide 3267 Pearl Rd *Web:* safer.fmcsa.dot.gov	Medina	OH	44256	330-725-5555		311
Synergy Worldwide Inc 1955 W Grove Pkwy Ste 100 *Web:* www.synergyworldwide.com	Pleasant Grove	UT	84062	801-769-7800		345
Synerion North America Inc 7420 Airport Rd Ste 101 *TF:* 877-816-8463 ■ *Web:* www.synerion.com	Mississauga	ON	L4T4E5	877-816-8463		177
Synerlution Inc PO Box 4336 *Web:* synerlution.net	Aguadilla	PR	00605	787-493-0864	493-0865	261
Synesis International Inc 30 Creekview Ct *Web:* www.synesisintl.com	Greenville	SC	29615	864-288-1550		194
SyNet Technology Solutions Inc 205 Hallene Rd Ste 101 *Web:* synetinc.com	Warwick	RI	02886	401-736-6450	736-6455	196
Synetra Inc 8180 Lakeview Ctr *TF:* 888-335-2789 ■ *Web:* synetra.com	Odessa	TX	79765	432-561-7200		179
Synex International Inc 1444 Alberni St 4th Fl *Web:* www.synex.com	Vancouver	BC	V6G2Z4	604-688-8271	688-1286	787
Synexus 11500 Northlake Dr Ste 320 *TF:* 855-427-8839 ■ *Web:* synexusclinic.com	Cincinnati	OH	45249	513-247-5500		668
SYNEXXUS Inc 2425 Wilson Blvd Ste 400 *TF:* 866-707-4594 ■ *Web:* www.synexxus.com	Arlington	VA	22201	866-707-4594		261
SYN-FAB Inc 7863 Schillinger Park Rd *Web:* www.synfab.com	Mobile	AL	36608	251-633-4942		246
Syngenta Corp 3411 Silverside Rd Shipley Bldg Concord Plz Ste 100 *Web:* syngenta.com	Wilmington	DE	19810	302-425-2000		280
Syngenta Crop Protection Inc 410 Swing Rd *Web:* www.syngenta.com	Greensboro	NC	27409	336-632-6000		280
SYNNEX Canada 200 Ronson Dr *TF:* 800-268-1220 ■ *Web:* www.synnex.ca	Etobicoke	ON	M9W5Z9	416-240-7012	240-2622	174
Synnex Corp 44201 Nobel Dr *NYSE: SNX* ■ *TF:* 800-756-1888 ■ *Web:* www.synnex.com	Fremont	CA	94538	510-656-3333	668-3777	174
Synopsys Inc 690 E Middlefield Rd *NASDAQ: SNPS* ■ *TF:* 800-541-7737 ■ *Web:* www.synopsys.com	Mountain View	CA	94043	650-584-5000	965-8637	178-10
Synoptek Inc 19520 Jamboree Rd Ste 110 *TF:* 888-796-6783 ■ *Web:* www.synoptek.com	Irvine	CA	92612	949-241-8600	241-8690	177
Synovis Life Technologies Inc 2575 University Ave W *NASDAQ: SYNO* ■ *TF:* 800-255-4018 ■ *Web:* www.synovislife.com	Saint Paul	MN	55114	651-796-7300	642-9018	477
Synovis Micro Companies Alliance Inc 439 Industrial Ln *TF:* 800-510-3318 ■ *Web:* www.synovismicro.com	Birmingham	AL	35211	205-941-0111		475
Synovus Bank 1111 Bay Ave Ste 400 **Fax Area Code:* 800 ■ *Web:* www.synovusfamilyoffice.com	Columbus	GA	31901	706-649-5756	650-9612*	70
SynQor Inc 155 Swanson Rd *Web:* www.synqor.com	Boxborough	MA	01719	978-849-0600	849-0601	253
Synrad Inc 4600 Campus Pl *Web:* www.synrad.com	Mukilteo	WA	98275	425-349-3500	349-3667	425
Syntec LLC 438 Lavender Dr **Fax Area Code:* 706 ■ *TF:* 800-526-8428 ■ *Web:* www.syntecind.com	Rome	GA	30165	800-526-8428	235-1768*	131
Syntell Inc 2954 Boul Laurier *Web:* www.syntell.com	Quebec City	QC	G1V4T2	418-266-0900		177
Syntelli Solutions Inc 13925 Ballantyne Corporate Pl Ste 260 *TF:* 877-796-8355 ■ *Web:* syntelli.com	Charlotte	NC	28277	877-796-8355		174
Synter Resource Group LLC 5935 Rivers Ave Ste 102 *Web:* www.synterresource.com	Charleston	SC	29406	843-746-2200		2
Syntergy Inc 7660-H Fay Ave Ste 387 **Fax Area Code:* 630 ■ *Web:* www.syntergy.com	La Jolla	CA	92037	858-779-9642	556-0698*	809
Syntes Language Group 7465 E Peakview Ave *Web:* www.syntes.com	Centennial	CO	80111	303-779-1288		768
Synthes Spine Inc 325 Paramount Dr *TF:* 800-523-0322 ■ *Web:* www.depuysynthes.com	Raynham	MA	02767	508-880-8100	880-8122	475
Synthesis 210 W 6th St *Web:* synthesisweekly.com	Chico	CA	95928	530-899-7708		532-3
Synthesis Professional Services Inc 12339 Carroll Ave *Web:* www.synthesisps.com	Rockville	MD	20852	301-770-8970		463
Synthetic Genomics Inc 11149 N Torrey Pines Rd *Web:* www.syntheticgenomics.com	La Jolla	CA	92037	858-754-2900	754-2988	668
Synthetic Surface Inc PO Box 241 *Web:* www.nordot.com	Scotch Plains	NJ	07076	908-233-6803	233-6844	3
Syntonic Systems Inc 111 John St Rm 1700 *TF:* 866-401-3798 ■ *Web:* www.syntonic-ny.com	New York	NY	10038	212-989-8787	989-9515	177
Syntony Publishing Inc 235 Alma St *TF:* 800-228-4069 ■ *Web:* www.influence-integrity.com	Palo Alto	CA	94301	650-322-2799	322-2709	637-2
Syntricity Inc 10525 Vista Sorrento Pky Ste 220 *Web:* www.syntricity.com	San Diego	CA	92121	858-552-4485	552-4493	180
Syntrio 500 Lake Cook Rd Ste 350 *TF:* 888-289-6670 ■ *Web:* www.syntrio.com	Deerfield	IL	60015	415-951-7913		39
Syntrix Biosystems Inc 215 Clay St NW Ste B-5 *Web:* syntrixbio.com	Auburn	WA	98001	253-833-8009	833-8127	231
Syntroleum Corp 5416 S Yale Ave Ste 400 *NASDAQ: SYNM*	Tulsa	OK	74135	918-592-7900		536
Syntron Bioresearch Inc 2774 Loker Ave W *Web:* www.syntron.net	Carlsbad	CA	92010	760-930-2200	930-2212	668
Synutra Ingredients 2275 Research Blvd Ste 500 *TF:* 866-405-2350 ■ *Web:* www.synutraingredients.com	Rockville	MD	20850	301-840-3888		799
Synventive Molding Solutions Inc 10 Centennial Dr *TF:* 800-367-5662 ■ *Web:* www.synventive.com	Peabody	MA	01960	978-750-8065	646-3600	386
SYO Computer Engineering Services Inc 42621 Garfield Rd Ste 108 *Web:* www.syo.com	Clinton Township	MI	48038	586-286-2557		809
Sypris Electronics LLC 10421 University Center Dr *TF:* 800-937-9220 ■ *Web:* www.sypriselectronics.com	Tampa	FL	33612	813-972-6000	972-6012	253
Sypris Solutions Inc 101 Bullitt Ln Ste 450 *NASDAQ: SYPR* ■ *TF:* 800-588-9119 ■ *Web:* www.sypris.com	Louisville	KY	40222	502-329-2000	329-2050	253

Name / Address	City	State	ZIP	Phone	Fax	Class
Syracuse Academy of Science 1001 Park Ave. *Web:* sascs.org	Syracuse	NY	13204	315-428-8997		148
Syracuse Banana Company Inc 900 Wolf St. *Web:* www.syracusebanana.com	Syracuse	NY	13208	315-471-2251	471-5247	297-7
Syracuse Blueprint Company Inc 825 E Genesee St *Web:* www.syracuseblueprint.com	Syracuse	NY	13210	315-476-4084		261
Syracuse City School District, The 725 Harrison St *Web:* www.syracusecityschools.com	Syracuse	NY	13210	315-435-4499		685
Syracuse Cooperative Federal Credit Union 723 Westcott St. *TF:* 855-532-5210 ■ *Web:* cooperativefederal.org	Syracuse	NY	13210	315-471-1116	476-0567	219
Syracuse Fire Department Employees Federal Credit Union 211 Wilkinson St *Web:* syrfirecu.com	Syracuse	NY	13204	315-471-4621		219
Syracuse Glass Company Inc 1 General Motors Dr PO Box 381 *Web:* www.syracuseglass.com	Syracuse	NY	13206	315-437-9971		330
Syracuse Hancock International Airport 1000 Colonel Eileen Collins Blvd *Web:* www.syrairport.org	Syracuse	NY	13212	315-454-4330	454-8757	27
Syracuse New Times 1415 W Genesee St *Web:* www.syracusenewtimes.com	Syracuse	NY	13204	315-422-7011		532-5
Syracuse Opera 411 Montgomery St Ste 60 *Web:* www.syracuseopera.org	Syracuse	NY	13202	315-475-5915	475-6319	573-2
Syracuse Peace Council (SPC) 2013 E Genesee St 2nd Fl *Web:* www.peacecouncil.net	Syracuse	NY	13210	315-472-5478		637-2
Syracuse Plastics LLC 7400 Morgan Rd. *Web:* www.syracuseplastics.com	Liverpool	NY	13090	315-637-9881	637-9260	608
Syracuse Research Corp (SRC) 7502 Round Pond Rd *TF:* 800-724-0451 ■ *Web:* www.srcinc.com	North Syracuse	NY	13212	315-452-8000		668
Syracuse Scenery & Stage Lighting Company Inc 101 Monarch Dr *TF:* 800-453-7775 ■ *Web:* www.syracusescenery.com	Liverpool	NY	13088	315-453-8096	453-7897	722
Syracuse Stage 820 E Genesee St. *Web:* www.syracusestage.org	Syracuse	NY	13210	315-443-4008	443-9846	573-4
Syracuse Stamping Co 1054 S Clinton St *TF:* 800-581-5555 ■ *Web:* www.syraco.com	Syracuse	NY	13202	315-476-5306	474-8876	489
Syracuse Student Sandbox 235 Harrison St *Web:* syracusestudentsandbox.com	Syracuse	NY	13202	315-560-6622		303
Syracuse Suds Factory 320 S Clinton St. *Web:* s502965190.onlinehome.us	Syracuse	NY	13202	315-471-2253		671
Syracuse University 900 S Crouse Ave Ste 100 *TF:* 800-782-5867 ■ *Web:* www.syracuse.edu	Syracuse	NY	13244	315-443-3611	443-4226	166
Syracuse University College of Law 950 Irving Ave *Web:* www.law.syr.edu	Syracuse	NY	13244	315-443-1962	443-9568	167-1
Syracuse University Libraries 222 Waverly Ave. *Web:* library.syr.edu	Syracuse	NY	13244	315-443-2093	443-9510	434-6
Syracuse University Press (SUP) 621 Skytop Rd Ste 110 *Web:* www.syracuseuniversitypress.syr.edu	Syracuse	NY	13244	315-443-5534	443-5545	459
Syrasoft LLC 6 Canton St. *Fax Area Code: 888 ■ *Web:* syrasoft.com	Baldwinsville	NY	13027	800-559-5942	519-2813*	525
Syreon Corp 260 - 1401 W Eighth Ave. *Web:* www.syreon.com	Vancouver	BC	V6H1C9	604-676-5900		238
Syringa Networks LLC 3795 S Development Ave *TF:* 800-454-7214 ■ *Web:* www.syringanetworks.net	Boise	ID	83705	208-229-6100	229-6130	116
Sysazzle Inc 15815 S 46th St Ste 116 *TF:* 800-862-9545 ■ *Web:* sysazzle.com	Phoenix	AZ	85048	800-862-9545		721
Sysco Corp 1390 Enclave Pkwy *NYSE: SYY* ■ *Web:* sysco.com	Houston	TX	77077	281-584-1390		297-8
Sysco Indianapolis LLC 4000 W 62nd St *Web:* www.syscoindy.com	Indianapolis	IN	46268	317-291-2020		297-11
Sysco Newport Meat Company Inc 16691 Hale Ave. *Web:* www.newportmeat.com	Irvine	CA	92606	949-474-4040		296-26
SYSCOM Inc 400 E Pratt St Inner Harbor Ctr Ste 502 *Web:* www.syscom.com	Baltimore	MD	21202	410-539-3737		180
Syscom USA Inc 1 Exchange Plz 55 Broadway 17th Fl *Web:* www.syscomusa.com	New York	NY	10006	212-797-9131	797-9132	180
Syscon Inc 94 McFarland Blvd. *TF:* 888-797-2661 ■ *Web:* syscononline.com	Northport	AL	35476	205-758-2000		180
Sys-con Media Inc 577 Chestnut Ridge Rd. *Web:* www.sys-con.com	Woodcliff Lake	NJ	07677	201-782-9601		637-9
Syscor Controls & Automation Inc 201 - 60 Bastion Sq *TF:* 833-361-1681 ■ *Web:* syscor.com	Victoria	BC	V8W1J2	250-361-1681	361-1682	256
Sysintelli Inc 9466 Black Mtn Rd Ste 200 *Web:* sysintelli.com	San Diego	CA	92126	858-271-1600		177
Syska & Hennessy Group 1515 Broadway *Web:* www.syska.com	New York	NY	10036	949-798-6298		261
SysLogic Inc 375 Bishops Way Ste 105 *Web:* www.syslogicinc.com	Brookfield	WI	53005	262-780-0380		177
Sysmex America Inc 577 Aptakisic Rd. *Fax Area Code: 847 ■ *TF:* 800-379-7639 ■ *Web:* www.sysmex.com	Lincolnshire	IL	60069	800-462-1262	996-4397*	475
Sysnet Technology Solutions Inc 4320 Stevens Creek Blvd Ste 229 *Web:* www.astirservices.net	San Jose	CA	95129	408-248-5000	248-5001	180
SYSPRO 959 S Coast Dr Ste 100 *TF:* 800-369-8649 ■ *Web:* us.syspro.com	Costa Mesa	CA	92626	714-437-1000	437-1407	178-1
Syspro Technologies Inc 6545 Preston Rd Ste 300 *Web:* www.sysprotech.com	Plano	TX	75024	214-440-3820		393
Systec Conveyor Corp 10010 Conveyor Dr *TF:* 800-578-1755 ■ *Web:* www.systecconveyors.com	Indianapolis	IN	46235	800-578-1755		358
Systech Corp 16510 Via Esprillo *TF:* 800-800-8970 ■ *Web:* ww2.systech.com	San Diego	CA	92127	858-674-6500	613-2400	176
Systech Handling Inc 120 Taylor Pky *Web:* www.systechhandling.com	Archbold	OH	43502	419-445-8226		454
Systech Software Products Inc 256 Buli Ln *Web:* www.eagle88.com	Bolingbrook	IL	60490	630-759-4805		178-1
Systech Solutions Inc 500 N Brand Blvd Ste 1900 *Web:* www.systechusa.com	Glendale	CA	91203	818-550-9690	550-9692	194
Systechs Inc 249 W Baywood Ave Ste B *Web:* www.systechs.com	Orange	CA	92865	714-283-2890	283-1744	320
Systecon Inc 6121 Schumacher Pk Dr *Web:* www.systecon.com	West Chester	OH	45069	513-777-7722		641
Systel Business Equipment Company Inc 2604 Fort Bragg Rd *TF:* 800-849-5900 ■ *Web:* www.systeloa.com	Fayetteville	NC	28303	910-321-7700		112
System Automation Corp 7110 Samuel Morse Dr. *TF:* 800-839-4729 ■ *Web:* www.systemautomation.com	Columbia	MD	21046	301-837-8000	837-8001	178-10
System Components Inc 1635 Stieve Dr *Web:* www.sci-couplings.com	South Haven	MI	49090	269-637-2191	637-8377	620
System Concepts Inc 15900 N 78th St *TF:* 800-553-2438 ■ *Web:* www.foodtrak.com	Scottsdale	AZ	85260	480-951-8011		177
System Dynamics International Inc (SDI) 560 Discovery Dr NW *Web:* www.sdi-inc.com	Huntsville	AL	35806	256-895-9000		261
System Electric Co 1278 Montalvo Way *Web:* systemelectric.com	Palm Springs	CA	92262	760-327-7847		189-4
System Engineering International Inc (SEI) 5115 Pegasus Ct Ste Q *TF:* 800-765-4734 ■ *Web:* www.seipower.com	Frederick	MD	21704	301-694-9601	694-9608	787
System Freight Inc 7 Centre Dr Ste 5 *TF:* 800-524-4449 ■ *Web:* www.systemfreight.net	Jamesburg	NJ	08831	800-524-4449		780
System Improvements Inc 238 S Peters Rd Ste 301 *Web:* www.taproot.com	Knoxville	TN	37923	865-539-2139		196
System Innovators Inc 9000 Southside Boulevard Bldg 700 Ste 7200 *TF:* 800-963-5000 ■ *Web:* systeminnovators.com	Jacksonville	FL	32256	800-963-5000		178-10
System of Systems Analytics Inc 11250 Waples Mill Rd Ste 300 *Web:* www.sosacorp.com	Fairfax	VA	22030	703-349-7070		194
System Scale Corp 4393 W 96th St *Web:* www.system-scale.com	Indianapolis	IN	46268	317-876-9335		362
System Sensor 3825 Ohio Ave *TF:* 800-736-7672 ■ *Web:* www.systemsensor.com	Saint Charles	IL	60174	630-377-6580	377-6495	253
System Solutions Inc 3630 Commercial Ave. *Web:* thessi.com	Northbrook	IL	60062	847-272-6160	272-8465	179
Systematic Financial Management LP 300 Frank W Burr Blvd Glenpointe E 7th Fl *TF:* 800-258-0497 ■ *Web:* www.sfmlp.com	Teaneck	NJ	07666	201-928-1982		401
Systematics Inc 1025 Saunders Ln *Fax Area Code: 610 ■ *TF:* 800-222-9353 ■ *Web:* www.800abcweld.com	West Chester	PA	19380	800-222-9353	430-8714*	811
Systemax Inc 11 Harbor Pk Dr. *NYSE: SYX* ■ *TF:* 800-344-6783 ■ *Web:* systemax.com	Port Washington	NY	11050	516-608-7000	608-7001	173-2
Systems & Processes Engineering Corp (SPEC) 4120 Commercial Center Dr Ste 500 *TF:* 800-789-7732 ■ *Web:* www.spec.com	Austin	TX	78744	512-479-7732	494-0756	261
Systems Application Engineering Inc 3655 Westcenter Dr *Web:* www.saesystems.com	Houston	TX	77042	713-783-6020		177
Systems Audit Group Inc 25 Ellison Rd. *Web:* www.disaster-risk-planning.com	Newton	MA	02459	617-332-3496		194
Systems Consultants PO Box 2040 *Web:* www.sci-nevada.com	Fallon	NV	89407	775-423-1345	423-0381	178-1
Systems Contracting Corp 214 N Washington Ave Ste 700 *Web:* tsg.bz	El Dorado	AR	71730	870-862-1315	863-5256	189-10
Systems Conversion Ltd 202 S Erwin St *Web:* www.systemsconversion.com	Cartersville	GA	30120	770-606-9615	606-9720	177
Systems Duplicating Company Inc 358 Robbins Dr *Web:* www.sdci.net	Troy	MI	48083	248-585-7590	585-6638	385
Systems East Inc 30 Basil Sawyer Dr *Web:* www.systemseastinc.com	Hampton	VA	23666	757-766-8400		203
Systems Engineering Technologies Corp 6121 Lincolnia Rd Ste 200 *TF:* 800-385-8977 ■ *Web:* www.sytechcorp.com	Alexandria	VA	22312	703-941-7887		177
Systems Exchange Inc 26625 Carmel Center Pl *Web:* www.tfdg.com	Carmel By The Sea	CA	93923	831-649-3800		177
Systems Furniture Inc 125 S Broadway *TF:* 800-924-6115 ■ *Web:* sysfurniture.com	De Pere	WI	54115	920-336-1510	336-4008	321
Systems House, The 1033 Rte 46 E Ste A202 *TF:* 800-637-5556 ■ *Web:* www.tshinc.com	Clifton	NJ	07013	973-777-8050	777-3063	225
Systems II Transport Inc 1515 Louis Ave. *TF:* 800-444-7972 ■ *Web:* www.systems2trans.com	Elk Grove Village	IL	60007	847-541-7766	541-4344	311
Systems Implementers Inc 350 S Williams Blvd *Web:* www.systemsimplementers.com	Tucson	AZ	85711	520-795-5729		180

Company	City	State	ZIP	Phone	Fax	Class
Systems Inc W194 N11481 Mccormick Dr	Germantown	WI	53022	800-643-5424	255-5917*	697
*Fax Area Code: 262 ■ TF: 800-643-5424 ■ Web: www.loadingdocksystems.com						
Systems Inc 2377 Gold Meadow Way Ste 100 TF: 877-752-9797 ■ Web: www.creativesystems.com	Gold River	CA	95670	916-638-5375	638-5427	710
Systems Insight Inc 514 Madison Ave 200 Web: www.systemsinsight.com	Covington	KY	41011	859-291-9026		225
Systems Integration Inc 7316 Business Pl Web: www.sitexas.com	Arlington	TX	76001	817-468-1494	468-7975	207
Systems Interface Inc 1916 220th St SE Ste 102 Web: www.systems-interface.com	Bothell	WA	98021	425-481-1225	481-2115	201
Systems Planning & Analysis Inc (SPA) 2001 N Beauregard St Web: www.spa.com	Alexandria	VA	22311	703-399-7550		261
Systems Plus Computers Inc 390 Miracle Mile Ste 20 TF: 800-388-8486 ■ Web: spci.com	Lebanon	NH	03766	603-643-5800		196
Systems Products & Solutions Inc (SPS) 307 Wynn Dr Web: www.services-sps.com	Huntsville	AL	35805	256-319-2135		177
Systems Resource Management Inc 42 Valley Rd Web: www.srminc.net	Middletown	RI	02842	401-849-2913		177
Systems Technologies Inc 185 Rt 36 TF: 888-743-7282 ■ Web: www.systek.com	West Long Branch	NJ	07764	732-571-6400	571-6401	261
Systems Technology Group Inc 3001 W Big Beaver Rd Ste 500 Web: www.stgit.com	Troy	MI	48084	248-643-9010	643-9250	177
Systemsmith Inc 18436 Hawthorne Blvd Ste 208 Web: www.cognistix.com	Torrance	CA	90504	310-776-8750		225
SystemsNet Inc 2325 Maryland Rd Ste 210 TF: 888-676-1228 ■ Web: www.systnet.com	Willow Grove	PA	19090	888-676-1228		177
Systemtec Inc 246 Stoneridge Dr Ste 301 TF: 888-900-1655 ■ Web: systemtec.net	Columbia	SC	29210	803-806-8100		177
Systima Technologies Inc 10809 120th Ave NE Web: www.systima.com	Kirkland	WA	98033	425-487-4020	487-2950	180
Systrand Manufacturing Corp 19050 Allen Rd Web: www.systrand.com	Brownstown	MI	48183	734-479-8100		60
Systron Donner Inertial 355 Lennon Ln TF: 866-234-4976 ■ Web: www.systron.com	Walnut Creek	CA	94598	925-979-4400	979-9827	529
Sytek Communications 117 S Main St TF: 888-573-1390 ■ Web: www.sytekcom.com	Upsala	MN	56384	320-573-1390	573-4329	224
Syvantis Technologies LLC 13822 Bluestem Ct TF: 800-450-8908 ■ Web: www.syvantis.com	Baxter	MN	56425	800-450-8908		196
Syverson Tile Inc 4015 SW Ave TF: 800-568-5139 ■ Web: www.syversontile.com	Sioux Falls	SD	57105	605-336-1175	336-1179	191-1
Szabo Associates Inc 3355 Lenox Rd NE Ste 945 Web: www.szabo.com	Atlanta	GA	30326	404-266-2464	266-2165	160
Szanca Solutions 100 E Pitt St Ste 300 Web: szanca.com	Bedford	PA	15522	814-624-0123		261
Szarka Financial Management 29691 Lorain Rd TF: 800-859-8095 ■ Web: www.szarkafinancial.com	North Olmsted	OH	44070	440-779-1430		463
SZCO Supplies Inc 2713 Merchant Dr Web: szco.com	Baltimore	MD	21230	410-368-8300		361
Szechuan 5207 Bernard Dr Web: szechuan1.net	Roanoke	VA	24018	540-989-7947		671
Szechuan House 245 Maple St Web: www.szechuanhousenh.com	Manchester	NH	03103	603-669-8811		671
Szechuan Palace 3040 Healy Dr	Winston-Salem	NC	27103	336-768-7123		671
Szerlip & Company Inc 288 Main St Web: szerlip.com	Millburn	NJ	07041	973-467-0400		390
Szott Ford 8800 E Holly Rd TF: 866-330-2288 ■ Web: www.szottford.com	Holly	MI	48442	248-634-4411	625-8041	57

T

Company	City	State	ZIP	Phone	Fax	Class
T & A Supply Company Inc 6821 S 216th St Bldg A PO Box 927 *Fax Area Code: 206 ■ TF: 800-562-2857 ■ Web: www.tasupply.com	Kent	WA	98032	253-872-3682	282-3796*	361
T & B Tube Co 4000 E Seventh Ave Web: www.tbtube.com	Gary	IN	46403	219-979-8100	979-8101	492
T & C Industries Inc *Royal Basket Trucks Inc* 201 Badger Pkwy TF: 800-426-6447 ■ Web: www.royal-basket.com	Darien	WI	53114	262-882-1227	882-3389	697
T & C Stamping Inc 1403 Freeman Ave Web: www.tandcstamping.com	Athens	AL	35613	256-233-7383		483
T & D Machine 5035 N 124th St Web: www.tdmachine.net	Butler	WI	53007	262-781-3870	781-1213	454
T & D Metal Products Co 602 E Walnut St Web: www.tdmetal.com	Watseka	IL	60970	815-432-4938		488
T & E Industries Inc 215 Watchung Ave TF: 800-245-7080 ■ Web: www.teindustries.com	Orange	NJ	07050	973-672-5454	672-0180	326
T & G Constructors Inc 8623 Commodity Cir TF: 866-352-4443 ■ Web: www.t-and-g.com	Orlando	FL	32819	407-352-4443	352-0778	186
T & J Electrical Corp 636 2nd Ave Web: www.tandjelectric.com	Troy	NY	12182	518-237-1893		189-4
T & L Automatics Inc 770 Emerson St Web: www.tandlautomatics.com	Rochester	NY	14613	585-647-3717		621
T & L Distributing LP 7350 Langfield Rd TF: 800-888-0601 ■ Web: www.tldistributing.com	Houston	TX	77092	713-461-7802		361
T & P Longview Federal Credit Union 2320 N Eastman Rd Web: creditunionsonline.com	Longview	TX	75605	903-753-3207		219
T & R Electric Supply Company Inc 308 SW Third St TF: 800-843-7994 ■ Web: www.t-r.com	Colman	SD	57017	605-534-3555	534-3861	767
T & S Brass & Bronze Works Inc PO Box 1088 TF: 800-476-4103 ■ Web: www.tsbrass.com	Travelers Rest	SC	29690	864-834-4102	834-3518	609
T & S Die Cutting 13301 Alondra Blvd Web: www.tandsdiecutting.com	Santa Fe Springs	CA	90670	562-802-1731	921-4877	757
T & S Machine Shop Inc 1396 Hwy 471 Web: www.tandsmachine.com	Brandon	MS	39042	601-825-8627	825-3176	454
T & S Oil Co 200 Ward Ave Web: tandsoil.com	Moosup	CT	06354	860-564-5091		316
T & S Trading Co 1110 Ortega St Web: tandstradingco.com	San Francisco	CA	94122	415-242-1551	242-1502	175
T & T Machine Products Inc 254 Beech St Web: www.ttmachineproductsinc.com	Rockland	MA	02370	781-878-3861	878-3738	815
T & T Staff Management Inc 511 Executive Center Blvd TF: 800-598-1647 ■ Web: www.ttstaff.com	El Paso	TX	79902	915-771-0393		631
T & T Tool Inc 700 Industrial Blvd Web: tttool.com	Spooner	WI	54801	715-635-8421		454
T & T Truck & Crane Service Inc 1375 N Olive St Web: www.truckandcrane.com	Ventura	CA	93001	805-648-3348		264-3
T & T Trucking Inc 11396 N Hwy 99 TF: 800-692-3457 ■ Web: www.tttrucking.com	Lodi	CA	95240	209-931-6000	931-6156	780
T & Y Market 2835 Norwood Ave Web: t-ymarket.com	Sacramento	CA	95815	916-922-6757		345
T Bailey Inc 12441 Bartholomew Rd Web: tbailey.com	Anacortes	WA	98221	360-293-0682		261
T Bar m Inc 2549 W State Hwy 46 Web: www.tbarm.org	New Braunfels	TX	78132	830-625-7738		378
T BC Corp 4770 Hickory Hill Rd TF: 866-822-4968 ■ Web: www.tbcbrands.com	Memphis	TN	38141	866-822-4968		755
T Bruce Sales Inc 9 Carbaugh St TF: 800-944-0738 ■ Web: www.tbrucesales.com	West Middlesex	PA	16159	724-528-9961	528-2050	480
T Buck Suzuki Environmental Foundation 4248 Glanford Ave Ste 200 Web: www.bucksuzuki.org	Victoria	BC	V8Z4B8	250-360-1398		305
T Byrd Training Ctr 1501 S New Rd Web: www.tbyrdcenter.com	Pleasantville	NJ	08232	609-484-9356	484-8777	167-3
T Cross Ranch 6611 I-25 Web: teecrossranches.com	Pueblo	CO	81008	719-382-7553		239
T F S Investments L L C 1411 L St Ste M Web: tfsinvestments.com	Fresno	CA	93721	559-486-1056		652
T G H Aviation 2389 Rickenbacker Way TF: 800-843-4976 ■ Web: www.tghaviation.com	Auburn	CA	95602	530-823-6204		24
T Gerding Construction Co 200 SW Airport Rd PO Box 1082 TF: 877-647-3335 ■ Web: tgcstructural.com	Corvallis	OR	97333	541-753-2012	754-6654	187
T H Rogers Lumber Co, The PO Box 5770 Web: www.throgers.com	Edmond	OK	73083	405-330-2181		191-2
T Hasegawa USA Inc 14047 E 183rd St TF: 866-985-0502 ■ Web: www.thasegawa.com	Cerritos	CA	90703	714-522-1900	522-6800	296-15
T James Williams & Company AC 7120 N Whitney Ave Ste 101 Web: tjwco.com	Fresno	CA	93720	559-322-9100	322-1098	2
T K Direct Inc 999 Commerce Crt *Fax Area Code: 847 ■ Web: tkdirectinventory.com	Buffalo Grove	IL	60089	312-296-7921	541-8802*	627
T K F Inc 726 Mehring Way Web: tkf.com	Cincinnati	OH	45203	513-241-5910		207
T Marzetti Co 380 Polaris Pkwy Ste 400 Web: www.marzetti.com	Westerville	OH	43082	614-846-2232		296-19
Allen Milk Div 1709 Frank Rd TF: 800-999-1835 ■ Web: marzetti.com	Columbus	OH	43223	800-999-1835		296-27
T R C Hydraulics Inc 7 Mosher Dr TF: 800-668-9000 ■ Web: www.trchydraulics.com	Dartmouth	NS	B3B1E5	902-468-4605		454
T R Toppers Inc 320 Fairchild *Fax Area Code: 719 ■ TF: 800-748-4635 ■ Web: www.trtoppers.com	Pueblo	CO	81001	800-748-4635	948-4908*	296-8
T Rad North America Inc 750 Frank Yost Ln Web: www.copar.net	Hopkinsville	KY	42240	270-885-9116		14
T Rowe Price Associates Inc 100 E Pratt St TF: 800-638-7890 ■ Web: www.troweprice.com	Baltimore	MD	21202	800-225-5132		401
T Sendzimir Inc 269 Brookside Rd Web: www.sendzimir.com	Waterbury	CT	06708	203-756-4617	756-4610	674
T Tech Inc 6412 Atlantic Blvd Ste 410 TF: 800-370-1530 ■ Web: t-tech.com	Peachtree Corners	GA	30092	770-455-0676		491
T's Restaurant 3416 Mike Pagett Hwy Web: www.tsrestaurant.com	Augusta	GA	30906	706-798-4145	793-8474	671
T. A. Pelsue Co 2500 S Tejon St TF: 800-525-8460 ■ Web: pelsue.com	Englewood	CO	80110	800-525-8460		767
T. D. Jakes Ministries Inc PO Box 5390 Web: www.tdjakes.org	Dallas	TX	75208	225-407-2291		48-20
T. E. Lott & Co 221 N Seventh St Web: www.telott.com	Columbus	MS	39701	662-328-5387	329-4993	2
T. G. Schmeiser Company Inc 8135 E Dinuba Ave Web: www.tgschmeiser.com	Selma	CA	93662	559-486-4569	268-3279	273
T. P. Daley Insurance Agency Inc 1381 Westfield St Web: tpdaleyinsurance.com	West Springfield	MA	01090	413-788-0971	739-2645	390

Listing	Phone	Fax	Class
T. R. Rizzuto Pizza Crust Inc 3420 E Riverside Ave .... Spokane WA 99202 *Web:* www.rizzutofoods.com	509-536-9268	536-9269	296-16
T. S. D. Inc PO Box 844617 .... Boston MA 02284 *Web:* tsdweb.com	978-794-1400		177
T.A. King & Son Inc 244 Main St .... Jonesport ME 04649 *Web:* www.jonesportlumber.com	207-497-2274	497-2123	770
T.A. Systems Inc 1842 Rochester Industrial Dr .... Rochester Hills MI 48309 *Web:* www.ta-systems.com	248-656-5150		494
T.H. Peek Publisher (THP) PO Box 7406 .... Ann Arbor MI 48107 *Web:* www.thpeekpublisher.com	734-222-8205	661-0136	637-2
T.H.T. Presses Inc 7475 Webster St .... Dayton OH 45414 *Web:* www.thtpresses.com	937-898-2012	890-1530	456
T.L. Herring & Co 2101 Stantonsburg Rd .... Wilson NC 27893 *Web:* www.tlherring.com	252-291-1141	291-1142	473
T.M. Byxbee Company PC 2319 Whitney Ave Ste 5B .... Hamden CT 06518 *Web:* byxbee.com	203-281-4933		2
T.M. Kovacevich Philadelphia Inc (TMK) 6700 Essington Ave Units A1-A6 .... Philadelphia PA 19153 *Web:* www.tmkproduce.com	215-463-0100	463-7758	297-7
T.M. Rybak & Associates Inc 15 W Erie Ave .... Rutherford NJ 07070 *Web:* tmrassociates.com	201-460-0473		261
T.M.U. Inc 910 Shunpike Rd .... Cape May NJ 08204 *Web:* www.tmuinc.com	609-884-7656		488
T.O. Fuller State Park 1500 W Mitchell Rd .... Memphis TN 38109 *Web:* www.tn.gov	901-543-7581	785-8485	50-5
T.O. Haas Tire & Auto 2400 O St .... Lincoln NE 68510 *Web:* www.tohaastire.com	402-474-1525		755
T2 Development LLC 620 Newport Center Dr 16th Fl .... Newport Beach CA 92660 *Web:* t2hospitality.com	949-610-8200		378
T3 Energy Services Inc 600 Travis St Ste 6050 .... Houston TX 77002	713-996-4110		539
T3 Expo LLC 8 Lakeville Business Pk .... Lakeville MA 02347 *TF:* 888-698-3397 ■ *Web:* www.t3expo.com	888-698-3397		184
T3 Global Strategies Inc 10 Emerson Ln Ste 808 .... Bridgeville PA 15017 *Web:* www.t3gs.com	412-221-2003		727
T3 Micro Inc 228 Main St Ste 12 .... Venice CA 90291 *Web:* www.t3micro.com	310-452-2888		76
T3 Motion Inc 2990 Airway Ave Ste A .... Costa Mesa CA 92626 *Web:* www.t3motion.com	714-619-3600		59
T4 Global Inc 12655 N Central Expy Ste 600 .... Dallas TX 75243 *Web:* spoken.org	214-549-3947		305
TA (Telephone Associates Inc) 823 Belknap St Ste 201 .... Superior WI 54880 *TF:* 800-777-7248 ■ *Web:* www.telephoneassociates.com	715-392-8101	394-8648	246
TA Associates Management LP 200 Clarendon St 56th Fl .... Boston MA 02116 *Web:* www.ta.com	617-574-6700	574-6728	792
TA Caid Industries Inc 2275 E Ganley Rd .... Tucson AZ 85706 *Web:* www.caid.com	520-294-3126	294-8180	189-10
TA Instruments Inc 159 Lukens Dr .... New Castle DE 19720 *Web:* www.tainstruments.com	302-427-4000		419
TA Loving Company Inc 400 Patetown Rd .... Goldsboro NC 27530 *Web:* www.taloving.com	919-734-8400	731-7538	188-10
TAB Computer Systems Inc 29 Bissell St .... East Hartford CT 06118 *TF:* 888-822-4435 ■ *Web:* www.tabinc.com	860-289-8850		180
TAB Products Co 605 Fourth St .... Mayville WI 53050 **Fax Area Code:* 800 ■ *TF:* 888-466-8228 ■ *Web:* www.tab.com	000-400-0228	304-4947*	534
Tab Service Co 310 S Racine Ave .... Chicago IL 60607 *Web:* tabservice.com	312-527-4306		225
Tab Services Inc 2065 S Raritan St .... Denver CO 80223 *Web:* tabservicescolorado.com	303-649-1213		41
Tabard Inn 1739 N St NW .... Washington DC 20036 *Web:* www.tabardinn.com	202-785-1277		671
Tabata USA Inc 2380 Mira Mar Ave .... Long Beach CA 90815 *TF:* 800-482-2282 ■ *Web:* www.tusa.com	562-498-3708		711
TABB Inc PO Box 10 .... Chester NJ 07930 *TF:* 800-887-8222 ■ *Web:* www.tabb.net	800-887-8222		635
TABCON Engineering 494 McNicoll Ave Ste 201 .... Toronto ON M2H2E1 *Web:* www.tabcon.com	647-974-7006		261
Taber Extrusions LP 915 S Elmira Ave .... Russellville AR 72802 *TF:* 800-563-6853 ■ *Web:* taberextrusions.com	479-968-1021	968-8645	485
Taber Industries 455 Bryant St .... North Tonawanda NY 14120 *TF:* 800-333-5300 ■ *Web:* www.taberindustries.com	716-694-4000	694-1450	472
Taberna Del Alabardero 1776 I St NW .... Washington DC 20006 *Web:* www.alabardero.com	202-429-2200	775-3713	671
Tabernacle Baptist Bible College & Seminary 717 N Whitehurst Landing Rd .... Virginia Beach VA 23464 *Web:* www.tbbcs.org	757-424-4673	424-3014	166
Tabet DiVito & Rothstein LLC The Rookery Bldg 209 S LaSalle St 7th Fl .... Chicago IL 60604 *Web:* www.tdrlawfirm.com	312-762-9450		428
Tabet Manufacturing Company Inc 1336 Ballentine Blvd .... Norfolk VA 23504 *Web:* www.tabetmfg.com	757-627-1855	622-4530	392
Table Group Inc 3640 MT Diablo Blvd 202 .... LaFayette CA 94549 *Web:* www.tablegroup.com	925-299-9700		463
Table Mountain Casino 8184 Table Mountain Rd .... Friant CA 93626 *TF:* 800-541-3637 ■ *Web:* www.tmcasino.com	559-822-7777		133
Table Rock State Park 5272 State Hwy 165 .... Branson MO 65616 *Web:* mostateparks.com	417-334-4704		565
Table Rock State Park 158 E Ellison Ln .... Pickens SC 29671 *Web:* southcarolinaparks.com	864-878-9813		565
Table Talk Pies Inc 120 Washington St .... Worcester MA 01610 *Web:* www.tabletalkpie.com	508-798-8811	798-0848	296-1
Table Trac Inc Baker Technology Plz 6101 Baker Rd Ste 206 .... Minnetonka MN 55345 *Web:* www.tabletrac.com	952-548-8877		177
Tableau Software Inc 1621 N 34th St .... Seattle WA 98103 *TF:* 800-650-1845 ■ *Web:* www.tableau.com	206-633-3400	633-3004	178-10
TABLETmedia Inc 600 Montgomery St 43rd Fl .... San Francisco CA 94111 *Web:* tablet.media	415-567-8100		177
Taboo Muskoka 1209 Muskoka Beach Rd .... Gravenhurst ON P1P1R1 *TF:* 866-464-5952 ■ *Web:* www.taboomuskoka.com	705-687-2233	687-7474	707
Taboola Inc 1115 Broadway 7th Fl .... New York NY 10010 *Web:* taboola.com	212-206-7663		180
Tabor Academy 66 Spring St .... Marion MA 02738 *Web:* www.taboracademy.org	508-748-2000		622
Tabor College 400 S Jefferson St .... Hillsboro KS 67063 *Web:* tabor.edu	620-947-3121	947-6276	166
Tabor Communications Inc 8445 Camino Santa Fe .... San Diego CA 92121 *TF:* 800-795-4472 ■ *Web:* www.taborcommunications.com	858-625-0070	625-0088	5
Tabor Retreat Ctr 60 Anchor Ave .... Oceanside NY 11572 *Web:* www.taborretreatcenter.net	516-536-3004		673
TaborCo PO Box 4465 .... Portland OR 97208 *Web:* www.taborco.com	503-274-8918		196
Tabula Rosa Systems LLC (TRS) 17 Cedar Ln .... Titusville NJ 08560 *Web:* www.tabularosa.net	609-818-1802	818-1803	525
Tacala LLC 3750 Corporate Woods Dr .... Vestavia Hills AL 35242 *Web:* www.tacala.com	205-443-9600	443-9700	670
TACC (Taunton Area Chamber of Commerce) 6 Pleasant St Ste 201 .... Taunton MA 02780 *Web:* www.tauntonareachamber.org	508-824-4068	884-8222	139
TACC (Tigard Area Chamber of Commerce) 12345 SW Main St .... Tigard OR 97223 *Web:* www.tigardchamber.org	503-639-1656		139
Tachi Palace Hotel & Casino 17225 Jersey Ave .... Lemoore CA 93245 *TF:* 800-942-6886 ■ *Web:* www.tachipalace.com	800-942-6886		132
Tachi-S Engineering USA Inc 23227 Commerce Dr .... Farmington Hills MI 48335 *Web:* www.tachi-s.com	248-478-5050		247
Tachyon Software LLC 4301 S Pierce St Ste 8-B .... Denver CO 80123 *Web:* www.tachyonsoft.com	303-722-1341	991-6235	178-1
Tack Room Too Inc 201 Lee St SW .... Tumwater WA 98501 *TF:* 800-258-2581 ■ *Web:* www.tackroomtoo.com	360-357-4268		711
Tacki Mac Grips 22000 Northpark Dr .... Kingwood TX 77339 *TF:* 800-334-7477 ■ *Web:* www.tackimac.com	281-358-6738		676
Taco Bell Arena 1401 Bronco Ln .... Boise ID 83725 *Web:* www.extramilearena.com	208-426-1900		720
Taco Bell Corp 1 Glen Bell Way .... Irvine CA 92618 *Web:* www.tacobell.com	949-863-4000		670
Taco Cabana Inc 8918 Tesoro Dr Ste 200 .... San Antonio TX 78217 *TF:* 800-580-8668 ■ *Web:* www.tacocabana.com	210-804-0990		670
Taco Inc 1160 Cranston St .... Cranston RI 02920 **Fax Area Code:* 905 ■ *TF:* 888-778-2733 ■ *Web:* www.tacocomfort.com	401-942-8000	564-9436*	357
Taco Mayo 10405 Greenbriar Pl .... Oklahoma City OK 73159 *Web:* www.tacomayo.com	405-691-8226		670
Taco Metals Inc 50 NE 179th St .... Miami FL 33162 *TF:* 800-653-8568 ■ *Web:* tacometals.com	305-652-8566		492
Tacoma Art Museum 1701 Pacific Ave .... Tacoma WA 98402 *Web:* www.tacomaartmuseum.org	253-272-4258	627-1898	520
Tacoma City Hall 747 Market St .... Tacoma WA 98402 *Web:* www.cityoftacoma.org	253-591-5000	591-5300	337
Tacoma Community College 6501 S 19th St .... Tacoma WA 98466 *Web:* www.tacomacc.edu	253-566-5000	566-6011	162
Tacoma Dome Arena & Exhibition Hall 2727 E 'D' St .... Tacoma WA 98421 *Web:* tacomadome.org	253-272-3663	593-7620	720
Tacoma Electric Supply Inc 1311 S Tacoma Way .... Tacoma WA 98409 *TF:* 800-422-0540 ■ *Web:* www.tacomaelectric.com	253-475-0540	475-0707	246
Tacoma Fixture Company Inc 1815 E D St .... Tacoma WA 98421 *TF:* 866-567-8969 ■ *Web:* www.tacomafixture.com	253-383-5541		115
Tacoma Inc 328 E Church St .... Martinsville VA 24112 *TF:* 800-352-9417 ■ *Web:* www.gototaco.com	276-666-9417	666-9427	670
Tacoma Little Theatre 210 N 'I' St .... Tacoma WA 98403 *Web:* www.tacomalittletheatre.com	253-272-2281		572
Tacoma Musical Playhouse 7116 Sixth Ave .... Tacoma WA 98406 *Web:* www.tmp.org	253-565-6867	564-7863	573-4
Tacoma Nature Ctr 1919 S Tyler St .... Tacoma WA 98405 *Web:* www.metroparkstacoma.org	253-404-3930		50-5
Tacoma Opera 47 St Helens Ave .... Tacoma WA 98402 *Web:* www.tacomaopera.com	253-627-7789		573-2
Tacoma Public Library 1102 Tacoma Ave S .... Tacoma WA 98402 *Web:* www.tacomalibrary.org	253-292-2001		434-3
Tacoma Regional Convention & Visitor Bureau 1516 Commerce St .... Tacoma WA 98402 *TF:* 800-272-2662 ■ *Web:* www.traveltacoma.com	253-627-2836		206
Tacoma Rubber Stamp & Sign 919 Market St .... Tacoma WA 98402 *TF:* 800-544-7281 ■ *Web:* www.tacomarubberstamp.com	253-383-5433	383-0649	467
Tacoma Screw Products Inc 2001 Center St .... Tacoma WA 98409 *TF:* 800-562-8192 ■ *Web:* www.tacomascrew.com	253-572-3444		454
Tacoma Symphony 901 Broadway Ste 600 .... Tacoma WA 98402 *TF:* 800-291-7593 ■ *Web:* symphonytacoma.org	253-272-7264		573-3

Name / Address	City	State	ZIP	Phone	Fax	Class
Tacoma-Pierce County Chamber of Commerce 950 Pacific Ave Ste 300 *Web:* www.tacomachamber.org	Tacoma	WA	98402	253-627-2175	597-7305	139
Taconic 136 Coonbrook Rd PO Box 69 *TF:* 800-833-1805 ■ *Web:* www.4taconic.com	Petersburg	NY	12138	518-658-3202	658-3204	745-2
Taconic Correctional Facility 250 Harris Rd **Fax Area Code: 718* ■ *Web:* www.doccs.ny.gov	Bedford Hills	NY	10507	914-241-3010	722-6220*	213
Taconic State Park - Copake Falls Area 253 Rte 344 *Web:* parks.ny.gov	Copake Falls	NY	12517	518-329-3993		565
Taconic State Park - Rudd Pond Area 59 Rudd Pond Dr *Web:* parks.ny.gov	Millerton	NY	12546	518-789-3059		565
Tacony Corp 1760 Gilsinn Ln *Web:* tacony.com	Fenton	MO	63026	636-349-3000	349-2333	38
Tacori Enterprises 1736 Gardena Ave *Web:* www.tacori.com	Glendale	CA	91204	818-863-1536		411
Tacos Garcia 1100 S Ross St *Web:* tacosgarcia.com	Amarillo	TX	79102	806-371-0411		671
Tacos Guaymas 2630 S 38th St *Web:* www.tacosguaymas.com	Tacoma	WA	98409	253-471-2224		671
Tacos Mexico Inc 5120 E Olympic Blvd *Web:* www.tacosmexico.com	Los Angeles	CA	90022	323-266-0482		670
Tactair Fluid Controls Inc 4806 W Taft Rd *Web:* www.tactair.com	Liverpool	NY	13088	315-451-3928		223
Tactical Allocation Group LLC 255 E Brown St Ste 101	Birmingham	MI	48009	248-283-2520	283-2524	401
Tactical Communications Group LLC 2 Highwood Dr Bldg 2 *Web:* g2tcg.com	Tewksbury	MA	01876	978-654-4800	654-4801	174
Tactical Magic LLC 1460 Madison Ave *Web:* www.tacticalmagic.com	Memphis	TN	38104	901-722-3001		7
Tactical Network Solutions LLC 8825 Stanford Blvd Ste 308 *Web:* www.tacnetsol.com	Columbia	MD	21045	443-276-6990		809
Tactical Support Equipment Inc 4039 Barefoot Rd *TF:* 800-889-4030 ■ *Web:* www.tserecon.com	Fayetteville	NC	28306	910-425-3360	425-3361	21
Tactical Technologies Inc 500 Pine St Ste 3a *Web:* www.tti-narctech.com	Holmes	PA	19043	610-522-0106	522-9430	425
Tactician Corp 305 N Main St *TF:* 800-927-7666 ■ *Web:* www.tactician.com	Andover	MA	01810	978-475-4475		195
Tactics Boardshop 375 W Fourth Ave *TF:* 888-450-5060 ■ *Web:* www.tactics.com	Eugene	OR	97401	541-349-0087		711
Tacticware Resource Group LLC PO Box 15386 *TF:* 855-318-6337 ■ *Web:* www.tacticware.com	Lenexa	KS	66285	913-499-1094		194
Tactix Consulting Group Inc 11353 Reed Hartman Hwy Ste 200 *Web:* www.tactixgroup.com	Cincinnati	OH	45241	513-333-4140		180
Tad Publishing Co 310 Busse Hwy **Fax Area Code: 847* ■ *Web:* www.caregiving.com	Park Ridge	IL	60068	773-343-6341	823-9366*	637-2
TADA 15 W 28th St *Web:* www.tadatheater.com	New York	NY	10001	212-252-1619		749
Tada Cognitive Solutions 408 SW Adams St *Web:* tada.today	Peoria	IL	61602	309-495-2403		178-8
Tadiran Batteries 2001 Marcus Ave Ste 125E *TF:* 800-537-1368 ■ *Web:* www.tadiranbat.com	New Hyde Park	NY	11042	516-621-4980	621-4517	74
Tadmor Camp 43943 Mcdowell Creek Dr *Web:* tadmor.org	Lebanon	OR	97355	541-451-4270		239
Tadych's Econofoods 1600 S Stephenson Ave *TF:* 877-295-4558 ■ *Web:* www.shoptadychs.com	Iron Mountain	MI	49801	906-774-1911		345
TAF (Taxpayers Against Fraud Education Fund) 1220 19th St NW Ste 501 *Web:* taf.org	Washington	DC	20036	202-296-4826	296-4838	49-10
Taft College 29 Cougar Ct *TF:* 800-379-6784 ■ *Web:* www.taftcollege.edu	Taft	CA	93268	661-763-7700	763-7758	162
Taft Electric Co 1694 Eastman Ave *Web:* www.taftelectric.com	Ventura	CA	93003	805-642-0121		189-4
Taft Museum of Art, The 316 Pike St *Web:* www.taftmuseum.org	Cincinnati	OH	45202	513-241-0343	241-7762	520
Taft School 110 Woodbury Rd *Web:* www.taftschool.org	Watertown	CT	06795	860-945-7777	945-7808	622
Taft Stettinius & Hollister LLP 425 Walnut St Ste 1800 *Web:* www.taftlaw.com	Cincinnati	OH	45202	513-381-2838		445
Taft Theatre, The 317 E Fifth St *Web:* www.tafttheatre.org	Cincinnati	OH	45202	513-232-6220		572
TAG (Tube Art Group) 11715 SE Fifth St *TF:* 800-562-2854 ■ *Web:* www.tubeart.com	Bellevue	WA	98005	206-223-1122	223-1123	701
TAG Associates LLC 810 Seventh Ave 7th Fl *Web:* www.tagassoc.com	New York	NY	10019	212-275-1500	275-1510	401
Tag Group Inc, The 100 Chesterfield Business Pkwy Ste 200 *Web:* thetaggroup.com	Chesterfield	MO	63005	636-537-2900		390
TAG Holdings LLC 30260 Oak Creek Dr *Web:* taghold.com	Wixom	MI	48393	248-822-8056	822-8012	60
TAG Online Inc 6 Prospect Village Plz 1st Fl *Web:* tagonline.com	Clifton	NJ	07013	973-783-5583		225
Tag Plastics Inc 373 Lake Rd *Web:* www.tagplastics.com	Tracy City	TN	37387	931-592-4888	592-4890	604
TAG Solutions LLC 12 Elmwood Rd *Web:* tagsolutions.com	Albany	NY	12204	518-292-6500	292-6510	735
Tag-A-Long Expeditions 452 N Main St *TF:* 800-453-3292 ■ *Web:* www.tagalong.com	Moab	UT	84532	435-259-8946	259-8990	760
Taggart Global USA LLC 4000 Town Ctr *Web:* www.taggartglobal.com	Canonsburg	PA	15317	724-754-9800		186
Taggart Morton LLC 1100 Poydras St Ste 2100 *Web:* www.taggartmortonlaw.com	New Orleans	LA	70163	504-599-8500		428
Tag-It Pacific Inc *Talon International Inc* 21900 Burbank Blvd Ste 270 *Web:* taloninternational.com	Woodland Hills	CA	91367	818-444-4100	444-4105	413
Tagline Communications Inc 6230 Wilshire Blvd Ste 1231 *Web:* www.tagline.com	Los Angeles	CA	90048	323-857-5337		344
Tagos Group LLC, The 8 E Greenway Plz Ste 910 *Web:* www.tagosgroup.com	Houston	TX	77046	713-850-7031	850-7071	463
Taher Inc 5570 Smetana Dr *Web:* www.taher.com	Minnetonka	MN	55343	952-945-0505	945-0444	299
Tahiti Tourism 300 Continental Blvd Ste 160 *Web:* www.tahititourisme.com	El Segundo	CA	90245	310-414-8484	414-8490	775
Tahitian Noni Intl 333 W Riverpark Dr *TF:* 800-445-2969 ■ *Web:* noninewage.com	Provo	UT	84604	801-234-1000	234-1001	296-11
Tahoe Biltmore Lodge & Casino 5 NV Hwy 28 *TF:* 800-245-8667 ■ *Web:* tahoebiltmore.com	Crystal Bay	NV	89402	775-831-0660	833-6731	378
Tahoe Daily Tribune 3079 Harrison Ave *Web:* www.tahoedailytribune.com	South Lake Tahoe	CA	96150	530-541-3880		532-2
Tahoe Joe's 9000 Ming Ave *Web:* www.tahoejoes.com	Bakersfield	CA	93311	661-664-7750		671
Tahoe Keys Property Owners Assn 356 Ala Wai Blvd *Web:* www.tahoekeyspoa.org	South Lake Tahoe	CA	96150	530-542-6444		138
Tahoe Mountain Sports 11200 Donner Pass Rd Ste 5e *TF:* 866-891-9177 ■ *Web:* www.tahoemountainsports.com	Truckee	CA	96161	866-891-9177		711
Tahoe Seasons Resort 3901 Saddle Rd *Web:* tahoeseasons.com	South Lake Tahoe	CA	96150	530-541-6700		669
Tahoe Truckee Disposal Co 645 Westlake Blvd Ste 5 *Web:* waste101.com	Tahoe City	CA	96145	530-583-7800	583-0804	804
Tahoe Truckee Unified School District (TTUSD) 11603 Donner Pass Rd *Web:* www.ttusd.org	Truckee	CA	96161	530-582-2500	582-7606	685
Tahoma National Cemetery 18600 SE 240th St *Web:* www.cem.va.gov	Kent	WA	98042	425-413-9614	413-9618	136
Tahoma Rubber & Plastics Inc 255 Wooster Rd N *Web:* www.tahomarubberplastics.com	Barberton	OH	44203	330-745-9016	745-4886	605-2
Tahquamenon Falls State Park 41382 W M-123 *Web:* www.michigan.org	Paradise	MI	49768	906-492-3415		565
Tahzoo 1005 Seventh St NW *Web:* www.tahzoo.com	Washington	DC	20001	202-600-3907		195
Tai Lake Restaurant 134 N Tenth St *Web:* www.tailakeseafoodrest.com	Philadelphia	PA	19107	215-922-0698		671
Taiga Building Products 800-4710 Kingsway *TF:* 800-663-1470 ■ *Web:* www.taigabuilding.com	Burnaby	BC	V5H4M2	604-438-1471	439-4242	279
TaigMarks Inc 223 S Main St *Web:* www.taigmarks.com	Elkhart	IN	46516	574-294-8844	294-8855	6
Taikan Company Inc 919 E 29th St *Web:* www.taikan.com	Lawrence	KS	66046	785-841-5538		253
TaikoProject 505 E Third St Ste 505 *Web:* taikoproject.org	Los Angeles	CA	90012	213-268-4011		149
Tailhook Assn 9696 Businesspark Ave *TF:* 800-322-4665 ■ *Web:* www.tailhook.net	San Diego	CA	92131	858-689-9223	578-8839	48-19
Tailored Chemical Products Inc 700 12th St Dr NW *TF:* 800-627-1687 ■ *Web:* www.tailoredchemical.com	Hickory	NC	28601	828-322-6512	322-7688	3
Tailored Label Products Inc W165 N5731 Ridgewood Dr *TF:* 800-727-1344 ■ *Web:* www.tailoredlabel.com	Menomonee Falls	WI	53051	262-703-5000		88
Tailored Living LLC 19000 MacArthur Blvd Ste 100 *TF:* 866-675-8819 ■ *Web:* www.tailoredliving.com	Irvine	CA	92612	866-675-8819		361
Tailored Marketing 401 Wood St Ste 902 *Web:* tailoredmarketing.com	Pittsburgh	PA	15222	412-281-1442		344
Tailored Solutions Inc 10437 Innovation Dr Ste 229 *Web:* labeltraxx.com	Milwaukee	WI	53226	414-774-9997		180
Taisei Construction Corp 6261 Katella Ave Ste 200 *Web:* www.taisei.co.jp	Cypress	CA	90630	714-886-1530	886-1546	186
Taisho Pharmaceutical California Inc 3528 W Carson St Ste 320 *Web:* lipovitan.com	Torrance	CA	90503	310-543-2035		582
Tait & Associates Inc 701 N Parkcenter Dr *Web:* tait.com	Santa Ana	CA	92705	714-560-8200		261
Tait Subler LLC 60 S Sixth St Ste 2800 *Web:* taitsubler.com	Minneapolis	MN	55402	612-758-2000		463
Taitron Components Inc 28040 W Harrison Pkwy *NASDAQ: TAIT* ■ *TF:* 800-247-2232 ■ *Web:* www.taitroncomponents.com	Valencia	CA	91355	661-257-6060	257-6415	246
Taiwan Imports 6544 Cottonwood St *TF:* 800-523-9829 ■ *Web:* www.taiwanimports.com	Murray	UT	84107	801-263-3790	263-3791	293
Taiwan Semiconductor Manufacturing Company Ltd (TSMC) 2851 Junction Ave *NYSE: TSM* ■ *Web:* www.tsmc.com	San Jose	CA	95134	408-382-8000	382-8008	696
Taiwan Visitors Assn 555 Montgomery St Ste 505 *Web:* www.taiwan.net.tw	San Francisco	CA	94111	415-989-8677	989-7242	775
Taiyo America Inc 2675 Antler Dr *Web:* taiyo-america.com	Carson City	NV	89701	775-885-9959		388

				Phone	Fax	Class
Taiyo Yuden (USA) Inc 10 N Martingale Rd Ste 575 *TF:* 800-348-2496 ■ *Web:* www.yuden.co.jp	Schaumburg	IL	60173	630-237-2405		253
Taj Indian Cuisine 2734 E Fowler Ave *Web:* tajtampaindiancuisine.com	Tampa	FL	33612	813-971-8483		671
Taj Indian Restaurant 5033 Brookhaven Rd Ste 300	Macon	GA	31206	478-785-8540		671
Taj Mahal 6410 W Jefferson Blvd Ste 9B *Web:* www.tajmahalfw.com	Fort Wayne	IN	46804	260-432-8993		671
Taj Mahal 2080 Bennet Ave *Web:* www.tajlancaster.com	Lancaster	PA	17601	717-295-1434	295-7413	671
Taj Mahal 7521 Wornall Rd *Web:* www.kctajmahal.com	Kansas City	MO	64114	816-361-1722	361-1654	671
Taj Restaurant 2630 Baseline Rd *Web:* tajindianboulder.com	Boulder	CO	80305	303-494-5216		671
TAJ Technologies Inc 1168 Northland Dr *TF:* 877-825-2801 ■ *Web:* tajtech.com	Mendota Heights	MN	55120	651-688-2801		721
Tajikistan *Embassy* 1005 New Hampshire Ave. *Web:* www.mfa.tj	Washington	DC	20037	202-223-6090		257
TAK Construction 60 Walnut Ave Ste 400 *Web:* takgroupinc.com	Clark	NJ	07066	732-340-0700		653
Taka Restaurant 614 5th Ave Ste M *Web:* www.takasushi.com	San Diego	CA	92101	619-338-0555		671
Takagi Industrial Company USA Inc 500 Wald *TF:* 888-882-5244 ■ *Web:* www.takagi.com	Irvine	CA	92618	949-770-7171	770-3171	15
Takano Mark (Rep D - CA) 420 Cannon House Office Bldg. *Web:* takano.house.gov	Washington	DC	20515	202-225-2305	225-7018	342-2
Takara Belmont USA Inc 101 Belmont Dr **Fax Area Code:* 732 ■ *TF:* 877-283-1289 ■ *Web:* www.takarabelmont.com	Somerset	NJ	08873	877-283-1289	283-1687*	76
Takara Sake USA Inc 708 Addison St *Web:* takarasake.com	Berkeley	CA	94710	510-540-8250	486-8758	80-1
Take 3 Trailers Inc 1808 Hwy 105 *TF:* 866-428-2533 ■ *Web:* www.take3trailers.com	Brenham	TX	77833	979-337-9568		763
Take Charge America Inc 20620 N 19th Ave. *Web:* www.takechargeamerica.org	Phoenix	AZ	85027	623-266-6100		242
Take2 Consulting 1593 Spring Hill Rd Ste 100. *TF:* 888-825-3203 ■ *Web:* take2it.com	Vienna	VA	22182	888-825-3203		194
Take-A-Ticket Inc 130 Ne Montgomery St. **Fax Area Code:* 503 ■ *Web:* www.tatinc.com	Albany	OR	97321	541-967-0433	967-8415*	604
Takeda Canada Inc 435 N Service Rd W Ste 101. *TF:* 888-367-3331 ■ *Web:* www.takeda.com	Oakville	ON	L6M4X8	905-469-9333	469-4883	85
Takeda Pharmaceuticals USAInc 1 Takeda Pkwy *Web:* www.takedajobs.com	Deerfield	IL	60015	224-554-6500		238
Takenaka Partners LLC 801 S Figueroa St Ste 620 *Web:* www.takenakapartners.com	Los Angeles	CA	90017	213-593-4000	891-0168	401
Take-Two Interactive Software Inc 622 Broadway. *NASDAQ: TTWO* ■ *Web:* www.take2games.com	New York	NY	10012	646-536-2842	536-2926	178-6
Talan Products Inc 18800 Cochran Ave *TF:* 877-419-2805 ■ *Web:* talanproducts.com	Cleveland	OH	44110	216-458-0170		483
Talas Inc 330 Morgan Ave *Web:* www.talasonline.com	Brooklyn	NY	11211	212-219-0770	219-0735	92
Talascend LLC 5700 Crooks Rd Ste 450 *Web:* www.talascend.com	Troy	MI	48098	248-537-1300	537-1350	261
Talbar Inc 10991 Liberty St *Web:* www.talbar.com	Meadville	PA	16335	814-337-8400	333-6685	757
Talbert & Bright Inc 4810 Shelley Dr **Fax Area Code:* 704 ■ *Web:* talbertandbright.com	Wilmington	NC	28405	910-763-5350	426-6080*	261
Talbert Hotel Corp 7501 Westview Dr. *Web:* sbcontract.com	Houston	TX	77055	713-984-0710		378
Talbert Manufacturing Inc 1628 W State Rd 114 *TF:* 888-489-1731 ■ *Web:* www.talbertmfg.com	Rensselaer	IN	47978	888-489-1731		779
Talbot County County Courthouse 11 N Washington St *TF:* 800-339-3403 ■ *Web:* talbotcountymd.gov	Easton	MD	21601	410-822-2611		338
Talbot County Board of Commissioners 74 W Monroe St PO Box 155 *TF:* 800-486-7642 ■ *Web:* talbotcountyga.org	Talbotton	GA	31827	706-665-3220	665-8199	338
Talbot County Chamber of Commerce 101 Marlboro Ave Ste 53 *Web:* talbotchamber.org	Easton	MD	21601	410-822-4653	822-7922	139
Talbot County Free Library 100 W Dover St *Web:* www.tcfl.org	Easton	MD	21601	410-822-1626	820-8217	434-3
Talbot County Public Schools 12 Magnolia St PO Box 1029 *Web:* www.tcps.k12.md.us	Easton	MD	21601	410-822-0330	820-4260	685
Talbot County Tourism Office 11 S Harrison St. *TF:* 800-690-5080 ■ *Web:* tourtalbot.org	Easton	MD	21601	410-770-8000	770-8057	206
Talbot Korvola & Warwick LLP 4800 Meadows Rd Ste 200. *Web:* tkw.com	Lake Oswego	OR	97035	503-274-2849	274-2853	2
Talbot Tours Inc 1952 Camden Ave *Web:* www.talbottours.com	San Jose	CA	95124	408-879-0101		760
Talbot's Toyland of San Mateo Inc 445 S B St *Web:* talbotstoyland.com	San Mateo	CA	94401	650-931-8100		761
Talbott Recovery Campus 5448 Yorktowne Dr. **Fax Area Code:* 770 ■ *TF:* 800-445-4232 ■ *Web:* talbottcampus.com	Atlanta	GA	30349	866-972-0321	994-2024*	726
Talco Plastics Inc 1000 W Rincon St. *Web:* www.talcoplastics.com	Corona	CA	92880	951-531-2000	531-2058	605-2
Talcott Mountain State Park c/o Penwood State Pk 57 Gunn Mill Rd *Web:* portal.ct.gov	Bloomfield	CT	06002	860-242-1158		565
Talemed Inc 6279 Tri Ridge Blvd Ste 110. *Web:* www.talemed.com	Loveland	OH	45140	513-774-7300		194
Talent Connections LLC 200 River Vista Dr Ste 325 *Web:* www.talentconnections.net	Atlanta	GA	30339	770-552-1550		260
Talent Curve 14 Bridle Path. *TF:* 866-494-0248 ■ *Web:* www.talentcurve.com	Pittsboro	NC	27312	866-494-0248		463
Talent Logic Inc 2313 Timber Shadows *Web:* www.talentlogic.com	Kingwood	TX	77339	281-358-1858		721
Talent Plus Inc 1 Talent Plus Way. *Web:* www.talentplus.com	Lincoln	NE	68506	402-489-2000		196
Talent Strategy Group, The 1 Penn Plz 36th Fl *Web:* www.talentstrategygroup.com	New York	NY	10023	347-346-1255		260
Talent Tool & Die Inc 777 Berea Industrial Pkwy *Web:* www.talent-tool.com	Berea	OH	44017	440-239-8777	239-1345	488
Talent Zoo Inc 1040 W Marietta St NW *Web:* www.talentzoo.com	Atlanta	GA	30318	404-607-1955		260
TalentLens Inc 19500 Bulverde Rd *TF:* 888-298-6227 ■ *Web:* talentlens.com	San Antonio	TX	78259	888-298-6227		260
TalentMap 245 Menten Pl Ste 301. *TF:* 888-641-1113 ■ *Web:* www.talentmap.com	Ottawa	ON	K2H9E8	613-248-3417		463
TalentQuest Inc 1275 Peachtree St NE Ste 400 *Web:* www.talentquest.com	Atlanta	GA	30309	404-266-9368		193
TalentSmart Inc 11526 Sorrento Valley Rd. *Web:* www.talentsmart.com	San Diego	CA	92121	858-509-0582	509-0528	196
TalentSoup LLC 12 E 53rd St. *Web:* www.talentsoup.com	Atlanta	GA	31405	877-775-7687		260
TalentWorksLA 3500 W Olive Ave Ste 1400 *Web:* www.talentworksla.com	Burbank	CA	91505	818-972-4300	955-6411	731
Taleris Credit Union Inc 1250 E Granger Rd *TF:* 800-828-6446 ■ *Web:* taleriscu.org	Cleveland	OH	44131	216-739-2300		219
Tales of the Mojave Road Publishing Co 37198 Lanfair Rd G-15. *Web:* www.mdhca.org	Essex	CA	92332	760-733-4482		637-10
Talgo Inc 505 Fifth Ave S Ste 170. *Web:* www.talgo.com	Seattle	WA	98104	206-254-7051		770
Taliaferro County *Georgia* PO Box 114 *Web:* taliaferrocountyga.org	Crawfordville	GA	30631	706-456-2229	456-2904	338
Taliano's Restaurant 201 N 14th St. *Web:* talianos.net	Fort Smith	AR	72901	479-785-2292	785-2640	671
Taliesin 5607 County Hwy C *TF:* 877-588-7900 ■ *Web:* www.taliesinpreservation.org	Spring Green	WI	53588	608-588-7090	588-7514	50-3
Talimena State Park 50884 US Hwy 271. *Web:* www.travelok.com	Talihina	OK	74571	918-567-2052		565
Talisma Corporation Pvt Ltd 5201 Congress Ave. *TF:* 866-397-2537 ■ *Web:* www.talisma.com	Boca Raton	FL	33487	561-923-2500	999-0096	39
Talk Fusion 1319 Kingsway Rd *Web:* www.talkfusion.com	Brandon	FL	33510	813-651-4030	651-0331	366
Talk O'Texas Brands Inc 1610 Roosevelt St. *TF:* 800-749-6572 ■ *Web:* www.talkotexas.com	San Angelo	TX	76905	325-655-6077		296-20
Talk Radio 105.9 3900 11th Ave. *TF:* 877-811-3367 ■ *Web:* talkradio1059.iheart.com	Tuscaloosa	AL	35401	205-343-9787		645-168
Talk-a-Phone Co 7530 N Natchez Ave. *Web:* talkaphone.com	Niles	IL	60714	773-539-1100	539-1241	647
Tall Oaks Consulting LLC 929 White Plains Rd Ste 172 *Web:* talloaksllc.com	Trumbull	CT	06611	203-459-1680		180
Tall Timbers 13093 Henry Beadel Dr. *Web:* talltimbers.org	Tallahassee	FL	32312	850-893-4153	893-6470	48-13
Talladega Castings & Machine Company Inc 228 N Ct St. *TF:* 800-766-6708 ■ *Web:* www.tmsco.com	Talladega	AL	35160	256-362-5550	362-1321	307
Talladega City Schools 501 S St E PO Box 946. *Web:* www.talladega-cs.net	Talladega	AL	35160	256-315-5600		186
Talladega College 627 W Battle St. *TF:* 866-540-3956 ■ *Web:* www.talladega.edu	Talladega	AL	35160	256-761-6100	362-0274	166
Talladega County PO Box 6170 *Web:* www.talladegacountyal.org	Talladega	AL	35161	256-362-1357	761-2147	338
Talladega Insurance Agency 109 Spring St N PO Box 37 *Web:* talladega-insurance.com	Talladega	AL	35160	256-362-4153		390
Tallahassee Antique Car Museum 6800 Mahan Dr. *Web:* www.tacm.com	Tallahassee	FL	32308	850-942-0137	576-8500	520
Tallahassee City Hall 300 S Adams St *Web:* www.talgov.com	Tallahassee	FL	32301	850-891-0000		337
Tallahassee Museum of History & Natural Science 3945 Museum Dr *Web:* tallahasseemuseum.org	Tallahassee	FL	32310	850-575-8684	574-8243	520
Tallahassee Symphony Orchestra 1020 E Lafayette St. *Web:* www.tallahasseesymphony.org	Tallahassee	FL	32301	850-224-0461		573-3
Tallahatchie Valley Electric Power Assn 250 Power Dr *Web:* www.tvepa.com	Batesville	MS	38606	662-563-4742		245
Tallan Inc 175 Capital Blvd Ste 401 *TF:* 800-677-3693 ■ *Web:* www.tallan.com	Rocky Hill	CT	06067	860-633-3693		177
Tallapoosa County 125 N Broadnax St Rm 131 *Web:* tallaco.com	Dadeville	AL	36853	256-825-4268		338
Tallapoosa River Electric Co-op 15163 US Hwy 431 S PO Box 675 *TF:* 800-332-8732 ■ *Web:* www.trec.coop	LaFayette	AL	36862	334-864-9331	864-0817	245

Name / Address	City	State	Zip	Phone	Fax	Class
Talley Inc 12976 Sandoval St. *Web:* www.talleycom.com	Santa Fe Springs	CA	90670	562-906-8000		246
Talley Management Group Inc 19 Mantua Rd *Web:* www.talley.com	Mount Royal	NJ	08061	856-423-7222	423-3420	47
Tallgrass - An Osage Enterprise 201 W Rogers Blvd Ste 4 *Web:* www.tallgrass-osage.com	Skiatook	OK	74070	918-582-5633	582-5653	196
Tallgrass Energy Partners LP 4200 W 115th St Ste 350 *Web:* www.tallgrassenergy.com	Leawood	KS	66211	303-763-2950		787
Tallgrass Prairie National Preserve 226 Broadway PO Box 585 *Web:* www.nps.gov	Cottonwood Falls	KS	66845	620-273-6034	273-6099	564
Tallgrass Restoration LLC 2221 Hammond Dr *TF:* 877-699-8300 ■ *Web:* www.tallgrassrestoration.com	Schaumburg	IL	60173	847-925-9830		196
Tallman Truck Centre Ltd 750 Dalton Ave *Web:* www.tallmangroup.ca	Kingston	ON	K7M8N8	613-546-3336		57
Tallulah Falls School 201 Campus Dr PO Box 10 *Web:* www.tallulahfalls.org	Tallulah Falls	GA	30573	706-754-0400	754-3595	622
Tallulah Gorge State Park 338 Jane Hurt Yarn Dr *Web:* gastateparks.org	Tallulah Falls	GA	30573	706-754-7981		565
Tallwave 6263 N Scottsdale Rd Ste 180 *Web:* www.tallwave.com	Scottsdale	AZ	85250	602-840-0400		393
Talmetrix Inc 35 E Seventh St Ste 710 *Web:* talmetrix.com	Cincinnati	OH	45202	513-399-6301		180
Talon 1552 Down River Dr PO Box 907 *Web:* www.talon-graphite.com	Woodland	WA	98674	360-225-8247	225-7737	710
Talon Communications Inc 3111 Camino del Rio N Ste 400 *Web:* www.taloncom.com	San Diego	CA	92108	619-583-1846		647
Talon Energy Services Inc Donovan's Industrial Pk 158 Glencoe Dr *Web:* www.talonenergyservices.ca	Saint John	NL	A1N4S9	709-739-8450	747-8401	261
Talon Title Services LLC 12964 N Dale Mabry Hwy *Web:* talontitle.biz	Tampa	FL	33618	813-264-2400	264-2677	653
Talon Winery & Vineyards 7086 Tates Creek Rd *Web:* www.talonwine.com	Lexington	KY	40515	859-971-3214	971-8787	50-7
Talonvest Capital Inc 18881 Von Karman Ave Ste 1650 *Web:* talonvest.com	Irvine	CA	92612	949-251-9900		653
Talquin Electric Co-opeartive Inc 1640 W Jefferson St *Web:* www.talquinelectric.com	Quincy	FL	32351	850-627-7651	627-1639	245
Talton Communications Inc 910 Ravenwood Dr *TF:* 800-685-1840 ■ *Web:* talton.com	Selma	AL	36701	334-877-0704	872-0572	624
Talyst Inc 11100 NE Eigth St *Web:* www.talyst.com	Bellevue	WA	98004	425-289-5400		475
T-A-M (Trace-A-Matic Inc) 21125 Enterprise Ave *TF:* 877-375-0217 ■ *Web:* www.traceamatic.com	Brookfield	WI	53045	262-797-7300		621
Tam International Inc 4620 Southerland Rd *TF:* 800-462-7617 ■ *Web:* www.tamintl.com	Houston	TX	77092	713-462-7617	462-1536	537
Tam Metal Products Inc 55 Whitney Rd *Web:* www.tam-ind.com	Mahwah	NJ	07430	201-848-7800	848-8479	295
Tam O'shanter Country Club 5051 Orchard Lake Rd *Web:* www.tamoshantercc.org	West Bloomfield	MI	48323	248-855-1900		120
Tama County 104 W State St PO Box 336 *Web:* www.tamacounty.org	Toledo	IA	52342	641-484-3141	484-6248	338
Tama Manufacturing Company Inc 100a Cascade Dr *Web:* www.tamamfg.com	Allentown	PA	18109	610-231-3100	231-3180	155-21
Tamalpais Marin, The 501 Via Casitas *Web:* thetam.org	Greenbrae	CA	94904	415-461-2300	461-0241	672
Tamarac Chamber of Commerce 7525 NW 88th Ave Ste 103 *Web:* www.tnlcoc.org	Tamarac	FL	33321	954-722-1520	721-2725	139
Tamarac Inc 701 Fifth Ave 14th Fl *TF:* 866-525-8811 ■ *Web:* www.tamaracinc.com	Seattle	WA	98104	866-525-8811		401
Tamarack Habilitation Technologies Inc 1670 94th Ln NE *TF:* 866-795-0057 ■ *Web:* tamarackhti.com	Blaine	MN	55449	763-795-0057		477
Tamarack Products Inc 1071 N Old Rand Rd *Web:* www.tamarackproducts.com	Wauconda	IL	60084	847-526-9333	526-9353	535
Tamarind Tribeca 99 Hudson St *Web:* tamarindtribeca.com	New York	NY	10013	212-775-9000		671
TAMC (Aroostook Medical Ctr, The) 140 Academy St *Web:* www.northernlighthealth.org	Presque Isle	ME	04769	207-768-4000		374-3
Tamco Inc 1466 Delberts Dr *TF:* 800-826-2672 ■ *Web:* www.tamcotools.com	Monongahela	PA	15063	724-258-6622	258-6692	758
Tamco Manufacturing Co PO Box 1794 *Web:* tamcomfg.com	Elkhart	IN	46515	574-294-1909		351
Tamer Industries 185 Riverside Ave *Web:* www.tamerind.com	Somerset	MA	02725	508-677-0900	677-3037	621
Tamir Biotechnology Inc 51 JFK Pkwy 1st Fl W Ste 108 *TF:* 800-419-5061 ■ *Web:* tamirbio.com	Short Hills	NJ	07078	800-419-5061		85
Tamlin Software Inc 8140 Walnut Hill Ln Ste 525 *Web:* www.tamlinsoftware.com	Dallas	TX	75231	214-739-6576	739-7963	177
Tammany Oil & Gas LLC 20445 State Hwy 249 Ste 200 *Web:* www.tammanyoil.com	Houston	TX	77070	281-517-0770		536
Tammi L. Faulks, A Professional Law Corp 937 E Main St Ste 208 *Web:* santamariafamilylaw.com	Santa Maria	CA	93454	805-928-0903		41
Tampa Armature Works Inc (TAW) 6312 78th St *TF:* 800-333-9449 ■ *Web:* www.tawinc.com	Riverview	FL	33578	813-621-5661	425-0933	518
Tampa Bay & Co 401 E Jackson St Ste 2100 *TF:* 877-230-0078 ■ *Web:* www.visittampabay.com	Tampa	FL	33602	813-223-1111		206
Tampa Bay Beaches Chamber of Commerce 6990 Gulf Blvd *Web:* www.tampabaybeaches.com	Saint Pete Beach	FL	33706	727-360-6957	360-2233	139
Tampa Bay Buccaneers 1 Buccaneer Pl *TF:* 800-795-2827 ■ *Web:* www.buccaneers.com	Tampa	FL	33607	813-870-2700		715-3
Tampa Bay Downs Inc 11225 Racetrack Rd *TF:* 800-200-4434 ■ *Web:* www.tampabaydowns.com	Tampa	FL	33626	813-855-4401	854-3539	642
Tampa Bay Federal Credit Union 3815 N Nebraska Ave *TF:* 800-380-8880 ■ *Web:* tampabayfederal.com	Tampa	FL	33603	813-247-4414		219
Tampa Bay Fisheries Inc 3060 Gallagher Rd *TF:* 800-732-3663 ■ *Web:* tbfisheries.com	Dover	FL	33527	813-752-8883		296-14
Tampa Bay History Ctr 801 Old Water St *Web:* www.tampabayhistorycenter.org	Tampa	FL	33602	813-228-0097	223-7021	520
Tampa Bay Newspapers Inc 9911 Seminole Blvd *Web:* tbnweekly.com	Seminole	FL	33772	727-397-5563		532-3
Tampa Bay Press Inc 4710 Eisenhower Blvd B12 *Web:* tampabaypressinc.com	Tampa	FL	33634	813-886-1415	888-5860	627
Tampa Bay Regional Planning Council (TBRPC) 4000 Gateway Centre Blvd Ste 100 *Web:* www.tbrpc.org	Pinellas Park	FL	33782	727-570-5151	570-5118	637-10
Tampa Bay Steel Corp 6901 Sixth Ave E *Web:* www.tampabaysteel.com	Tampa	FL	33619	813-621-4738		492
Tampa Brass & Aluminum Corp 8511 Florida Mining Blvd *Web:* www.tampabrass.com	Tampa	FL	33634	813-885-6064	882-3271	308
Tampa City Hall 306 E Jackson St *Web:* www.tampagov.net	Tampa	FL	33602	813-274-8251	274-7050	337
Tampa General Hospital 1 Tampa General Cir *Web:* www.tgh.org	Tampa	FL	33606	813-844-7000		374-3
Tampa International Airport 4160 George J Bean Pkwy PO Box 22287 *Web:* www.tampaairport.com	Tampa	FL	33607	813-870-8700	875-6670	27
Tampa Port Authority 1101 Channelside Dr *TF:* 800-741-2297 ■ *Web:* www.porttb.com	Tampa	FL	33602	813-905-7678	905-5109	618
Tampa Steel Erecting Co 5127 Bloomingdale Ave *Web:* tampasteelerecting.com	Tampa	FL	33619	813-677-7184	677-8364	189-14
Tampa Tank Inc 2710 E Fifth Ave *Web:* tti-fss.com	Tampa	FL	33605	813-241-4261		91
Tampa Theater 711 N Franklin St PO Box 172188 *Web:* www.tampatheatre.org	Tampa	FL	33602	813-274-8286		572
Tampa-Hillsborough County Public Library 900 N Ashley Dr *Web:* www.hcplc.org	Tampa	FL	33602	813-273-3652		434-3
Tampico Spice Company Inc 5941 S Central Ave *Web:* www.tampicospice.com	Los Angeles	CA	90001	323-235-3154	232-8686	296-37
Tamrac Group Inc, The 10946 C Beaver Dam Rd *Web:* www.tamracinsurance.com	Hunt Valley	MD	21030	410-568-1200		390
Tamron USA Inc 10 Austin Blvd *Web:* www.tamron-usa.com	Commack	NY	11725	631-858-8400		591
Tamura Corporation of America 1040 S Andreasen Dr Ste 100 *TF:* 800-472-6624 ■ *Web:* www.tamuracorp.com	Escondido	CA	92029	951-699-1270	676-9482	246
Tamura Superette Inc 86-032 Farrington Hwy *Web:* www.tamurasupermarket.com	Waianae	HI	96792	808-696-3321		345
Tamwood International College 300-909 Burrard St *TF:* 866-533-0123 ■ *Web:* www.tamwood.com	Vancouver	BC	V6Z2N2	604-899-4480	899-4481	423
Tana Exploration Company LLC 4001 Maple Ave Ste 300 *Web:* www.tanaexp.com	Dallas	TX	75219	469-276-8262	276-8300	539
Tanabe Research Laboratories USA Inc 4540 Towne Centre Ct *Web:* www.trlusa.com	San Diego	CA	92121	858-622-7000	558-0650	668
Tanager Inc 10010 Junction Dr Ste 120N *Web:* www.tanagerinc.com	Annapolis Junction	MD	20701	240-547-3150		177
Tanaka of Tokyo East 150 Kaiulani Ave 3rd Fl *Web:* www.tanakaoftokyo.com	Honolulu	HI	96815	808-922-4233		671
Tanco Engineering Inc 1400 Taurus Ct *Web:* www.tancoeng.com	Loveland	CO	80537	970-776-4200	776-4300	261
Tandberg Data 10155 Westmoor Dr Ste 155 *TF:* 800-392-2983 ■ *Web:* www.tandbergdata.com	Westminster	CO	80021	303-442-4333		173-8
Tandem 460 McGill St Ste 500 *Web:* www.tandemexpansion.com	Montreal	QC	H2Y2H2	514-510-8900		528
Tandem Interactive 1700 E Las Olas Blvd Ste 301 *Web:* tandem-interactive.com	Fort Lauderdale	FL	33301	954-281-9995		5
Tandem Printing Inc 2970 Lexington Ave S *Web:* www.tandemprinting.com	Eagan	MN	55121	651-289-2970	289-4399	627
Tandem Stills Motion Inc 8567 Higuera St *Web:* tandemstillsmotion.com	Culver City	CA	90232	310-597-5200		592
Tandem Transit LLC 1428 36TH St STE 209 *Web:* tandemtransit.com	Brooklyn	NY	11218	718-689-1300	873-2936	387

	Phone	Fax	Class
Tandematic Inc 2398 Cnnons Campground Rd . . . . . Spartanburg SC 29307 *Web:* www.tandematic.com	864-579-3050	579-2942	744
Tandet Management Inc 1351 Speers Rd . . . . . Oakville ON L6L2X5 *Web:* www.tandet.com	905-827-4200		449
Tandoor 3530 Village Dr Ste 100 . . . . . Lincoln NE 68516 *Web:* www.tandurlincoln.com	402-423-2007		671
Tandoor 1117 S 108th St . . . . . Milwaukee WI 53214 *Web:* tandoorrestaurantmilwaukee.com	414-777-1600		671
Tandoor Indian Restaurant 1200 N Fielder Rd Ste 532 . . . . . Arlington TX 76012 *Web:* www.tandoorrestaurant.net	817-261-6604		671
Tandy Brands Accessories Inc 3631 W Davis St . . . . . Dallas TX 75211 *Web:* www.tandybrands.com	214-519-5200		155-2
Tanen Directed Advertising 12 S Main St . . . . . South Norwalk CT 06854 *Web:* www.tanendirected.com	203-855-5855		7
Tanenbaum-Harber of Florida LLC 2900 SW 149th Ave Ste 100 . . . . . Miramar FL 33027 *TF:* 866-620-8495 ■ *Web:* thflorida.com	954-883-2900		390
Taney Corp 5130 Allendale Ln . . . . . Taneytown MD 21787 *Web:* www.taneystair.com	410-756-6671	756-4103	499
Taney County 132 David St PO Box 156 . . . . . Forsyth MO 65653 *Web:* www.taneycounty.org	417-546-7200	546-2519	338
Tang Industries Inc 8960 Spanish Ridge Ave . . . . . Las Vegas NV 89148 *Web:* nmlp.com	702-734-3700		185
Tangent Design Engineering 2719 7 Ave NE . . . . . Calgary AB T2A2L9 *Web:* www.tangentservices.com	403-274-4647		261
Tangent Inc 191 Airport Blvd . . . . . Burlingame CA 94010 *TF:* 800-342-9388 ■ *Web:* www.tangent.com	650-342-9388	342-9380	173-2
Tangent Systems Inc 2155 Stnngton Ave Ste 107 . . . . . Hoffman Estates IL 60169 *Web:* www.tangent-systems.com	847-882-3833	882-3780	177
Tangent Technologies LLC 1001 Sullivan Rd . . . . . Aurora IL 60506 *Web:* tangentusa.com	630-264-1110		596
Tanger Factory Outlet Centers Inc 3200 Northline Ave Ste 360 . . . . . Greensboro NC 27408 *NYSE: SKT* ■ *TF:* 800-720-6728 ■ *Web:* www.tangeroutlet.com	336-292-3010	852-2096	655
Tangerine Travel Ltd 16017 Juanita Woodinville Way NE Ste 201 . . . . . Bothell WA 98011 *TF:* 800-678-8202 ■ *Web:* www.tangerinetravel.com	425-822-2333		772
Tangible Media Inc 12 W 37th St 2nd Fl . . . . . New York NY 10018 *Web:* www.tangiblemedia.com	212-359-1440	643-1555	6
Tangible Solutions Inc 1320 Matthews Township Pkwy Ste 201 . . . . . Matthews NC 28105 *TF:* 800-393-9886 ■ *Web:* www.tangible.com	800-393-9886		180
Tangipahoa Parish 206 E Mulberry St . . . . . Amite LA 70422 *Web:* www.tangipahoa.org	985-748-3211		338
Tangle Creek Energy Ltd 715 Fifth Ave SW Ste 1400 . . . . . Calgary AB T2P2X6 *Web:* www.tanglecreekenergy.com	403-648-4900	648-4910	536
Tanglewood Conservatories 15 Engerman Ave . . . . . Denton MD 21629 *TF:* 800-229-2925 ■ *Web:* tanglewoodconservatories.com	410-479-4700		186
Tanglewood Operators Inc 290 Tanglewood Cir . . . . . Pottsboro TX 75076 *Web:* tanglewoodresort.com	903-786-2968		378
Tango 1100 Pike St . . . . . Seattle WA 98101 *Web:* tangorestaurant.com	206-583-0382		671
Tango Consulting Group LLC 31 James Vincent Dr . . . . . Clinton CT 06413 *TF:* 877-567-6045 ■ *Web:* www.tangoconsulting.com	860-669-9380		196
Tango Management Consulting LLC 6225 N State Hwy 161 Ste 300 . . . . . Irving TX 75038 *TF:* 855-938-2646 ■ *Web:* tangoanalytics.com	855-938-2646		180
Tango Media Group 326 Carlaw Ave . . . . . Toronto ON M4M3N8 *Web:* tangomediagroup.com	416-204-6269		225
Tango Networks Inc 2801 Network Blvd Ste 200 . . . . . Frisco TX 75034 *Web:* www.tango-networks.com	469-920-2100		736
Tangoe 169 Lackawanna Ave . . . . . Parsippany NJ 07054 **Fax Area Code:* 973 ■ *TF:* 844-484-5041 ■ *Web:* www.tangoe.com	844-484-5041	257-0302*	178-7
Tangram Interiors Inc 9200 Sorensen Ave . . . . . Santa Fe Springs CA 90670 *Web:* www.tangraminteriors.com	562-365-5000		320
Tanguero Productions 8075 W 3rd St Code TPW . . . . . Los Angeles CA 90048 *Web:* www.tanguero.com	323-930-1244	930-0186	514
Tanimura & Antle Inc PO Box 4070 . . . . . Salinas CA 93912 *TF:* 800-772-4542 ■ *Web:* www.taproduce.com	800-772-4542		10-11
Tanita Corporation of America Inc 2625 S Clearbrook Dr . . . . . Arlington Heights IL 60005 *TF:* 800-826-4828 ■ *Web:* www.tanita.com	847-640-9241	640-9261	684
Tank Connection LLC 3609 N 16th St . . . . . Parsons KS 67357 *Web:* www.tankconnection.com	620-423-3010	423-3999	770
Tank Industry Consultants Inc 7740 W New York St . . . . . Indianapolis IN 46214 *TF:* 800-826-5736 ■ *Web:* www.tankindustry.com	317-271-3100		261
Tank Services 4412 Pleasant Valley Rd SE . . . . . Dennison OH 44621 *Web:* www.tankservices.com	330-479-9267	479-9271	481
Tankersley Concrete Company Inc 1630 Rock Crusher Rd . . . . . Lewisburg TN 37091 *Web:* tankersleyconcrete.com	931-359-3112		183
Tankmaster Rentals Ltd Poplar St Ste 117 . . . . . Red Deer AB T4E1B4 *TF:* 877-342-1105 ■ *Web:* www.tankmaster.ca	403-342-1105		23
Tanko Screw Products Corp 515 Thomas Dr . . . . . Bensenville IL 60106 *Web:* Idredmer.com	630-787-0504		621
Tanks-A-Lot Ltd 1810 Yellowhead Trail NE . . . . . Edmonton AB T6S1B4 *TF:* 800-661-5667 ■ *Web:* www.tanks-a-lot.com	780-472-8265	478-5699	770
TanMar Companies LLC 711 S Chestnut . . . . . Tomball TX 77375 *Web:* www.tanmarcompanies.com	281-591-6480	591-6482	536
Tannehill Ironworks Historical State Park 12632 Confederate Pkwy . . . . . McCalla AL 35111 *Web:* www.tannehill.org	205-477-5711	477-9400	50-3
Tanner & Guin LLC 2711 University Blvd . . . . . Tuscaloosa AL 35401 *Web:* www.tannerguin.law	205-633-0200	633-0290	428
Tanner Electric Co 45710 SE North Bend Way . . . . . North Bend WA 98045 *TF:* 800-472-0208 ■ *Web:* tannerelectric.coop	425-888-0623	888-5688	245
Tanner Industries Inc 735 Davisville Rd . . . . . Southampton PA 18966 *TF:* 800-643-6226 ■ *Web:* www.tannerind.com	215-322-1238	322-7791	146
Tanner Medical Ctr 705 Dixie St . . . . . Carrollton GA 30117 *Web:* www.tanner.org	770-836-9666		374-3
Tanner Research Inc 825 S Myrtle Ave . . . . . Monrovia CA 91016 *TF:* 877-325-2223 ■ *Web:* www.tanner.com	626-471-9700		174
Tanner Systems Inc 625 19th Ave NE PO Box 488 . . . . . Saint Joseph MN 56374 *TF:* 800-461-6454 ■ *Web:* www.tannersystems.com	320-363-1800	363-1812	143
Tannewitz Inc 794 Chicago Dr . . . . . Jenison MI 49428 *TF:* 800-458-0590 ■ *Web:* www.ramcosanders.com	616-457-5999	457-3620	494
Tannor Capital Management LLC 150 Grand St . . . . . White Plains NY 10601 *Web:* tannorpartners.com	914-509-5000		528
Tano Capital LLC 1 Franklin Pkwy Bldg 970 2nd Fl . . . . . San Mateo CA 94403 *Web:* www.tanocapital.com	650-212-0330		690
Tanos Exploration LLC 821 E Southeast Lp 323 Ste 400 . . . . . Tyler TX 75701 *Web:* tanosexp.com	903-597-7667		536
Tanque Verde Ranch 14301 E Speedway . . . . . Tucson AZ 85748 *TF:* 800-234-3833 ■ *Web:* www.tanqueverderanch.com	520-296-6275		239
Tantalus Resort Lodge 4200 Whistler Way . . . . . Whistler BC V0N1B4 *TF:* 888-806-2299 ■ *Web:* www.tantaluslodge.com	604-932-4146	932-2405	669
Tan-Tar-A Resort Golf Club & Spa 494 Tantara Dr PO Box 188TT . . . . . Osage Beach MO 65065 *TF:* 800-826-8272 ■ *Web:* www.tan-tar-a.com	573-348-3131	348-3206	669
TanTara Transportation Corp 2420 Stewart Rd . . . . . Muscatine IA 52761 *TF:* 800-650-0292 ■ *Web:* www.tantara.us	563-262-8621	264-8998	780
Tante Marie's Cooking School 271 Francisco St . . . . . San Francisco CA 94133 *Web:* www.tantemarie.com	415-885-1654		163
Tantor Audio 6 Business Park Rd . . . . . Old Saybrook CT 06475 **Fax Area Code:* 888 ■ *TF:* 877-782-6867 ■ *Web:* www.tantor.com	860-395-1155	782-7821*	637-2
Tanzania *Embassy* 1232 22nd St NW . . . . . Washington DC 20037 *Web:* www.tanzaniaembassy-us.org	202-939-6125	797-7408	257
Tao of Systems Integration Inc 1100 Exploration Way . . . . . Hampton VA 23666 *Web:* www.taosystem.com	757-220-5040	220-5030	472
Tao Publishing PO Box 33910 . . . . . Reno NV 89533 *Web:* www.thegreattao.com	415-566-1332		637-2
Taos Mountain 121 Daggett Dr . . . . . San Jose CA 95134 *TF:* 888-826-7686 ■ *Web:* www.taos.com	408-588-1200		463
Taos Pueblo PO Box 1846 . . . . . Taos NM 87571 *Web:* www.taospueblo.com	575-758-1028		50-3
Taos Ski Valley Inc 116 Sutton Pl . . . . . Taos Ski Valley NM 87525 *TF:* 800-776-1111 ■ *Web:* www.skitaos.com	575-776-2291		31
TAP Advisors LLC 390 Park Ave 9th Fl . . . . . New York NY 10022 *Web:* www.tapadvisors.com	212-909-9010	909-9020	70
Tap Packaging Solutions 2160 Superior Ave . . . . . Cleveland OH 44114 *TF:* 800-827-5679 ■ *Web:* www.tap-usa.com	216-781-6000		560
TAP Plastics Inc 6475 Sierra Ln . . . . . Dublin CA 94568 *TF:* 800-894-0827 ■ *Web:* www.tapplastics.com	925-829-4889		607
Tapa the World 2115 J St . . . . . Sacramento CA 95816 *Web:* www.tapatheworld.com	916-442-4353		671
Tapas Teatro 1711 N Charles St . . . . . Baltimore MD 21201 *Web:* www.tapasteatro.com	410-332-0110		671
Tapatio Springs Golf Resort & Conference Ctr 1 Resort Way . . . . . Boerne TX 78006 *TF:* 855-627-2243 ■ *Web:* www.tapatioresort.com	855-627-2243		669
Tapco Inc 225 Rock Industrial Park Dr . . . . . Bridgeton MO 63044 *TF:* 800-288-2726 ■ *Web:* www.tapcoinc.com	314-739-9191		234
Tapco International Inc 990 W 15th St . . . . . Riviera Beach FL 33404 *Web:* tapcointernational.net	561-707-4320	845-2410	191-1
Tape & Label Converters Inc 8231 Allport Ave . . . . . Santa Fe Springs CA 90670 *TF:* 888-285-2462 ■ *Web:* www.stickybiz.com	562-945-3486	696-8198	413
Tapecon Inc 10 Latta Rd . . . . . Rochester NY 14612 *TF:* 800-333-2407 ■ *Web:* www.tapecon.com	585-621-8400		413
TAPEMARK Co 1685 Marthaler Ln . . . . . Saint Paul MN 55118 *TF:* 800-535-1998 ■ *Web:* www.tapemark.com	651-455-1611	450-8403	413
TapeSouth Inc 1626 NW 55 Pl . . . . . Gainesville FL 32653 *Web:* www.tapesouth.com	904-642-1800	642-7006	732
Tapestry Solutions Inc 5643 Copley Dr . . . . . San Diego CA 92111 *Web:* www.tapestrysolutions.com	858-503-1990		177
Tapeswitch Corp 100 Schmitt Blvd . . . . . Farmingdale NY 11735 *TF:* 800-234-8273 ■ *Web:* www.tapeswitch.com	631-630-0442	630-0454	729
Tapia Bros Co 6067 District Blvd . . . . . Maywood CA 90270 *Web:* www.tapiabrothers.com	323-560-7415		297-9
Tapjoy Inc 111 Sutter St . . . . . San Francisco CA 94104 *Web:* www.tapjoy.com	415-766-6900		387
Tapmatic Corp 802 S Clearwater Loop . . . . . Post Falls ID 83854 *TF:* 800-854-6019 ■ *Web:* www.tapmatic.com	208-773-8048	773-3021	493
Tapp Label Technologies Inc 580 Gateway Dr . . . . . Napa CA 94558 *TF:* 888-834-8277 ■ *Web:* www.tapplabel.com	707-252-8300	251-9852	627

Name / Address	Phone	Fax	Class
Tapper's Fine Jewelry Inc Orchard Mall 6337 Orchard Lake Rd. West Bloomfield MI 48322 *Web:* tappers.com	248-932-7700		410
TAPPI (Technical Association of the Pulp & Paper Industry) 15 Technology Pkwy S Norcross GA 30092 *TF:* 800-332-8686 ■ *Web:* www.tappi.org	770-446-1400	446-6947	49-13
Tapscott Press PO Box 1101 Commerce TX 75429 **Fax Area Code:* 866 ■ *TF:* 800-787-4993 ■ *Web:* www.tapscottpress.com	800-787-4993	281-5998*	637-2
TAQA North Ltd 308-4th Ave Calgary AB T2P0H7 *Web:* www.taqaglobal.com	403-724-5000	724-5001	675
Taqueria De Anda 1029 E Fourth St Santa Ana CA 92701 *Web:* www.taqueriadeanda.com	714-558-0856		671
Taqueria el Poblano 2400B Mt Vernon Ave Alexandria VA 22301 *Web:* www.taqueriapoblano.com	703-548-8226		671
Taqueria Mi Pueblo Mexican Restaurant 7278 Dix St. Detroit MI 48209 *Web:* www.mipueblorestaurant.com	313-841-3315		671
TAR (Tennessee Association of Realtors) 901 19th Ave S Nashville TN 37212 *TF:* 877-321-1477 ■ *Web:* tnrealtors.com	615-321-1477	321-4905	656
Tara Liners 2294 Old 431 Hwy Owens Cross Roads AL 35763 *Web:* www.taraliners.com	256-725-2500		596
Tara Pearls 10 W 46th Ste 600 New York NY 10036 *TF:* 888-575-8272 ■ *Web:* www.tarapearls.com	888-575-8272		411
Tara Plastics Corp 175 Lake Mirror Rd. Forest Park GA 30297 *Web:* www.taraplastics.com	404-366-4464	366-3816	66
Tara Toy Corp 40 Adams Ave Hauppauge NY 11788 *Web:* www.taratoy.com	631-273-8697	273-8583	762
Taranta 210 Hanover St Boston MA 02113 *Web:* www.tarantarist.com	617-720-0052		671
Tarason Packaging LLC 1101 Keisler Rd SE Conover NC 28613 *Web:* tarason.net	828-464-4743		548
Tarbell's 3213 E Camelback Phoenix AZ 85018 *Web:* www.tarbells.com	602-955-8100		671
Tarboro Edgecombe Chamber of Commerce 500 Main St PO Box F Tarboro NC 27886 *Web:* www.discoveredgecombe.com	252-823-7241		139
TARC (Transit Authority of River City) 1000 W Broadway Louisville KY 40203 *Web:* www.ridetarc.org	502-585-1234	213-3243	468
Targa Real Estate Services Inc 720 S 348th St A2 Federal Way WA 98003 *TF:* 888-123-4567 ■ *Web:* www.targarealestate.com	253-815-0393		655
Target Copy 635 W Tennessee St Tallahassee FL 32304 *Web:* targetprintmail.com	850-224-3007		113
Target Corp 1000 Nicollet Mall Minneapolis MN 55403 *NYSE: TGT* ■ *TF:* 800-440-0680 ■ *Web:* www.target.com	612-304-6073		229
Target Ctr 600 1st Ave N Minneapolis MN 55403 *Web:* www.targetcenter.com	612-673-1300	673-1699	714-1
Target Direct Mailing Services 1206 Esi Dr. Springdale AR 72764 *Web:* targetdirectmail.com	479-750-4900		5
Target Drilling Inc 1112 Glacier Dr Smithton PA 15479 *Web:* www.targetdrilling.com	724-633-3927		540
Target Media Inc 4750 Lindle Rd Harrisburg PA 17111 *Web:* targetmediausa.com	717-724-8188		5
Target Media Partners Inc 5200 Lankershim Blvd Ste 350 North Hollywood CA 91601 *Web:* www.targetmediapartners.com	323-930-3123		532-3
Target Solutions Inc 530 Causeway Dr Wrightsville Beach NC 28480 *Web:* targetsol.com	910-509-1800		721
Target Steel Inc 24601 Vreeland Flat Rock MI 48134 *Web:* www.targetsteel.net	734-789-9700		492
TargetSpot Inc 33 E 33rd St Ste 801 New York NY 10016 *Web:* www.targetspot.com	212-631-0500		387
Targun Plastics Co 899 Skokie Blvd Northbrook IL 60062 *Web:* targun.com	847-509-9355		603
Targus Inc 1211 N Miller St Anaheim CA 92806 *TF:* 877-482-7487 ■ *Web:* www.targus.com	714-765-5555		453
Tarheel Press, The PO Box 1205 Hickory NC 28603 *Web:* www.tarheelpress.com	828-324-0191		637-2
Tarigma Corp 6161 Busch Blvd Ste 110 Columbus OH 43229 *Web:* www.tarigma.com	614-436-3734		177
Tarkett Inc 1001 Yamaska St E Farnham QC J2N1J7 *TF:* 800-363-9276 ■ *Web:* tarkettna.com	450-293-3173		291
Tarleton State University PO Box T-0030 Stephenville TX 76402 *TF:* 800-687-8236 ■ *Web:* tarleton.edu	254-968-9125	968-9951	166
Tarlton Corp 5500 W Park Ave Saint Louis MO 63110 *Web:* www.tarltoncorp.com	314-633-3300	647-1940	186
Tarlton Properties Inc 1530 O'Brien Dr Ste C Menlo Park CA 94025 *Web:* www.tarlton.com	650-330-3600	330-3636	652
Taro Pharmaceutical Industries Ltd 126 E Dr Brampton ON L6T1C1 *TF:* 800-268-1975 ■ *Web:* www.taro.ca	905-791-8276	791-5008	582
Taro Pharmaceuticals USA Inc 3 Skyline Dr Hawthorne NY 10532 *TF:* 800-544-1449 ■ *Web:* www.taro.com	914-345-9001	345-8727	583
Tarpon Springs Chamber of Commerce 1 N Pinellas Ave Tarpon Springs FL 34689 *Web:* www.tarponspringschamber.org	727-937-6109	937-2879	139
Tarps & Tie-Downs Inc 24967 Huntwood Ave Hayward CA 94544 **Fax Area Code:* 310 ■ *TF:* 800-788-6808 ■ *Web:* www.tarpstiedowns.com	510-782-8772	325-3355*	96
Tarpy's Roadhouse 2999 Monterey-Salinas Hwy Monterey CA 93940 *Web:* tarpys.com	831-647-1444		671
Tarr LLC 2946 NE Columbia Blvd Portland OR 97211 *TF:* 800-422-5069 ■ *Web:* www.tarrllc.com	503-288-5294		146
Tarrance Group, The 201 N Union St Ste 410 Alexandria VA 22314 *Web:* www.tarrance.com	703-684-6688	836-8256	466

Name / Address	Phone	Fax	Class
Tarrant County 100 E Weatherford St Fort Worth TX 76196 *Web:* www.tarrantcounty.com	817-884-1195	884-3295	338
Tarrant County College *Southeast* 2100 SE Pkwy Arlington TX 76018 *Web:* tccd.edu	817-515-8223	515-3182	162
Tarrier Foods Corp 2700 International St Columbus OH 43228 *Web:* www.tarrierfoods.com	614-876-8595	545-6111	297-8
Tarrier Steel Company Inc, The 1379 S 22nd St. Columbus OH 43206 *Web:* www.tarrier.com	614-444-4000		492
Tarrytown House Estate & Conference Ctr 49 E Sunnyside Ln Tarrytown NY 10591 *Web:* www.tarrytownhouseestate.com	914-591-8200		226
Tarrytown Music Hall 13 Main St PO Box 686 Tarrytown NY 10591 *TF:* 877-840-0457 ■ *Web:* tarrytownmusichall.org	914-631-3390		572
Tarsin Inc 916 Swood Blvd Bldg 3 Ste A Incline Village NV 89451	775-833-0156		809
Tartan Marketing 6900 Wedgwood Rd N Maple Grove Ste 350 Maple Grove MN 55311 *Web:* www.tartanmarketing.com	612-910-9138		195
Tartan Yachts 1920 Fairport Nursery Rd Fairport Harbor OH 44077 *Web:* www.tartanyachts.com	440-332-0578		90
Tarter Krinsky & Drogin LLP 1350 Broadway New York NY 10018 *Web:* www.tarterkrinsky.com	212-216-8000		41
Tarus Products Inc 38100 Commerce Dr Sterling Heights MI 48312 *Web:* tarus.com	586-977-1400		697
TAS (Transportation Advisory Services) 3181 Valley Dr Walworth NY 14568 **Fax Area Code:* 315 ■ *TF:* 800-233-3251 ■ *Web:* www.transportationconsultants.com	800-233-3251	986-1901*	196
TAS Commercial Concrete Construction LLC 19319 Oil Center Blvd Houston TX 77073 *Web:* www.tasconcrete.com	281-230-7500	230-7664	189-3
TASC Technical Services LLC 73 Newton Rd Plaistow NH 03865 *TF:* 877-304-8272 ■ *Web:* www.tasctech.com	877-304-8272		195
Tasende Gallery 820 Prospect St La Jolla CA 92037 *Web:* www.tasendegallery.com	858-454-3691		42
TASH 1875 Eye St NW Ste 582 Washington DC 20006 *Web:* tash.org	202-540-9020	540-9019	48-17
Tashlik Kreutzer Goldwyn & Crandell P C 40 Cuttermill Rd Ste 200 Great Neck NY 11021 *Web:* tgllegal.com	516-466-8005		445
Task Force Allday 1114 W FM 1382 Cedar Hill TX 75104 *Web:* www.jackallday.com	972-293-7026		194
Task Force Tips Inc 3701 Innovation Way Valparaiso IN 46383 *TF:* 800-348-2686 ■ *Web:* www.tft.com	219-462-6161	464-7155	283
Task Management Inc 99 Danbury Rd Ridgefield CT 06877 *Web:* www.taskmanagement.com	203-438-9777		463
Tasker Metal Products Inc (TMP) 1823 S Hope St Los Angeles CA 90015 *Web:* www.taskermetalproducts.com	213-765-5400	746-8707	60
Tasks Galore Publishing Inc 4909 Old Elizabeth Rd Raleigh NC 27616 *TF:* 800-648-8857 ■ *Web:* www.tasksgalore.com	919-789-8275	789-8256	637-10
Taskstream LLC 71 W 23rd St 15th Fl. New York NY 10010 *TF:* 800-311-5656 ■ *Web:* www.taskstream.com	212-868-2700		225
TaskUs Inc 3221 Donald Douglas Loop S. Santa Monica CA 90405 *TF:* 888-400-8275 ■ *Web:* www.taskus.com	888-400-8275		393
Tasler Inc 1804 Tasler Dr Webster City IA 50595 *TF:* 800-482-7537 ■ *Web:* tasler.com	515-832-5200		551
Tasman Leather Group LLC 9 Main St. Hartland ME 04943 *Web:* www.tasmanusa.com	207-553-3700		432
Tassajara Veterinary Clinic 3436 Camino Tassajara Danville CA 94506 *Web:* tassajaravet.com	925-736-8387	736-9077	794
Taste of India 3192 Sheridan Dr Amherst NY 14226 *Web:* www.tasteofindia.com	716-837-0460		671
Taste of India 230 Wickenden St. Providence RI 02903 *Web:* www.tasteofindiari.com	401-421-4355	751-1432	671
Taste of India 3110 N Division St Spokane WA 99207 *Web:* www.tasteofindiaspokane.com	509-327-7313		671
Taste of Italy 8421 University Blvd Clive IA 50325 *Web:* www.atasteofitalyia.com	515-221-0743		671
Taste of Nature Inc 2828 Donald Douglas Loop N Ste A Santa Monica CA 90405 *Web:* www.candyasap.com	310-396-4433		297-3
Taste of Texas Restaurant 10505 Katy Fwy Houston TX 77024 *Web:* www.tasteoftexas.com	713-932-6901		671
Taste of Thai 1500 Mill St. Greensboro NC 27408 *Web:* www.tasteofthaigreensboro.com	336-273-1318		671
Taste of Thai 2535 E Arkansas Ln Arlington TX 76010 *Web:* tasteofthaiarlington.com	817-543-0110		671
Taste of Thai 527 University Ave San Diego CA 92103 *Web:* tasteofthaisandiego.com	619-291-7525	291-0788	671
Taste of Thailand 3321 Lorna Rd Ste 3 Birmingham AL 35216 *Web:* www.tasteofthailandbhm.com	205-978-6863		671
Taste of Thailand 15712 W Center Rd Omaha NE 68130 *Web:* www.tasteofthailandomaha.com	402-691-9991		671
Taste of the Islands 909 W Spring Creek Pkwy Plano TX 75023 *Web:* www.tasteoftheislands.net	972-517-5900		671
Tastefully Simple Inc 1920 Turning Leaf Ln SW Alexandria MN 56308 *Web:* www.tastefullysimple.com	320-763-0695		296-36
Tasty Baking Co 4300 S 26th St Philadelphia PA 19112 *TF:* 800-248-2789 ■ *Web:* www.tastykake.com	215-221-8500		296-1
Tasty Tom's 9965 82nd Ave NW. Edmonton AB T6E1Z1 *Web:* oldstrathcona.ca	780-437-5761		671

Name / Address	City	State	Zip	Phone	Fax	Class
Tastytrade Inc 19 N Sangamon St *TF:* 855-468-2789 ■ *Web:* www.tastytrade.com	Chicago	IL	60607	855-468-2789		49-2
TAT Piedmont Aviation Component Services 7102 Cessna Dr *Web:* piedmont.tat-technologies.com	Greensboro	NC	27409	336-776-6300	776-6301	20
Tata Consultancy Services Ltd (TCS) 101 Park Ave 26th Fl *Web:* www.tcs.com	New York	NY	10178	212-557-8038		194
Tata Steel International (Americas) Inc 475 N Martingale Rd Ste 400 *Web:* www.tatasteeleurope.com	Schaumburg	IL	60173	847-619-0400		492
Tatar Art Projects 300 King St E *Web:* tatarartprojects.com	Toronto	ON	M5A1K4	416-360-3822		42
Tate Andale Inc 1941 Lansdowne Rd *TF:* 800-296-8283 ■ *Web:* www.tateandale.com	Baltimore	MD	21227	410-247-8700	247-9672	595
Tate House Museum 1267 Westbrook St *Web:* www.tatehouse.org	Portland	ME	04102	207-774-6177	774-6198	520
Tate Inc 7510 Montevideo Rd *TF:* 800-231-7788 ■ *Web:* tateinc.com	Jessup	MD	20794	410-799-4200	799-4207	491
Tate Insurance Group Inc 6423 Deane Hill Dr *Web:* tateinsurancegroup.com	Knoxville	TN	37919	865-862-8233		390
Tate Ornamental Inc 411 Industrial Dr *Web:* tateornamental.com	White House	TN	37188	615-672-0348		492
Tate's Bake Shop Inc 43 N Sea Rd *Web:* www.tatesbakeshop.com	Southampton	NY	11968	631-283-9830		345
Tates Supermarket Inc 120 Fourth St *Web:* www.tatesmarket.com	Clymer	PA	15728	724-254-4420		345
Tatham Engineering Ltd 115 Sandford Fleming Dr Ste 200 *Web:* www.tathameng.com	Collingwood	ON	L9Y5A6	705-444-2565		256
Tatnuck Bookseller 18 Lyman St *Web:* www.tatnuck.com	Westborough	MA	01581	508-366-4959	366-7929	95
Tatro Plumbing Company Inc 1285 Acraway Ste 300 *TF:* 888-828-7648 ■ *Web:* tatroplumbing.com	Garden City	KS	67846	620-277-2167		189-10
Tattered Cover Book Store Inc 1628 16th St *TF:* 800-833-9327 ■ *Web:* www.tatteredcover.com	Denver	CO	80202	303-436-1070	629-1704	95
Tattnall County 111 N Main St *Web:* www.tattnallcountyga.com	Reidsville	GA	30453	912-557-4335	557-3827	338
Tattnall County School 146 W Brazell St PO Box 157 *Web:* www.tattnallschools.org	Reidsville	GA	30453	912-557-4726	557-3036	685
Tatum Hester & Burkhead Insurance Inc 108 N Main St PO Box 1010 *Web:* tatumhesterburkhead.com	Hopkinsville	KY	42241	270-886-6668		390
Tatung Company of America Inc 2850 El Presidio St *TF:* 800-827-2850 ■ *Web:* www.tatungusa.com	Long Beach	CA	90810	310-637-2105		173-4
Tatusko Kennedy Pc 3016 Williams Dr Ste 200 *Web:* tatuskolaw.com	Fairfax	VA	22031	703-205-9009	205-9059	41
Tau Alpha Chi 82 Thompson St	Alpharetta	GA	30009	770-475-4253		48-16
Tau Beta Pi Assn 1512 Middle Dr *Web:* www.tbp.org	Knoxville	TN	37996	865-546-4578	546-4579	48-16
Tau Beta Sigma National Honorary Band Sorority PO Box 849 *Web:* www.tbsigma.org	Stillwater	OK	74076	405-372-2333	372-2363	48-16
Tau Kappa Epsilon (TKE) 7439 Woodland Dr Ste 100 *Web:* www.tke.org	Indianapolis	IN	46278	317-872-6533	875-8353	48-16
Tauber Oil Co 55 Waugh Dr Ste 700 *Web:* tauberoil.com	Houston	TX	77007	713-869-8700	869-8069	579
Tauber-Arons Inc 13848 Ventura Blvd *Web:* tauberaronsinc.com	Sherman Oaks	CA	91423	323-851-2008		226
Taubman Centers Inc 200 E Long Lake Rd Ste 300 *NYSE:* TCO ■ *Web:* www.taubman.com	Bloomfield Hills	MI	48303	248-258-6800		655
Taubman Museum of Art 110 Salem Ave SE *Web:* taubmanmuseum.org	Roanoke	VA	24011	540-342-5760	342-5798	520
Taubman, Kimelman & Soroka LLP 30 Vesey St Ste 6 *Web:* discriminationfighter.com	New York	NY	10007	212-227-8140		41
Taughannock Falls State Park 2221 Taughannock Rd *Web:* parks.ny.gov	Trumansburg	NY	14886	607-387-6739		565
Taum Sauk Mountain State Park 148 Taum Sauk Trl *Web:* mostateparks.com	Middle Brook	MO	63656	573-546-2450		565
Taunton Area Chamber of Commerce (TACC) 6 Pleasant St Ste 201 *Web:* www.tauntonareachamber.org	Taunton	MA	02780	508-824-4068	884-8222	139
Taunton Municipal Lighting Plant PO Box 870 *Web:* www.tmlp.com	Taunton	MA	02780	508-824-5844		245
Taunton Public Library 12 Pleasant St *Web:* www.tauntonlibrary.org	Taunton	MA	02780	508-821-1411	821-1414	434-3
Taunton State Hospital 60 Hodges Ave *Web:* www.mass.gov	Taunton	MA	02780	508-977-3000		374-5
Taurus Asset Management LLC 590 Madison Ave 9th Fl *Web:* taurusassetmanagement.com	New York	NY	10022	212-457-9922	457-9923	401
Taurus International Manufacturing Inc 16175 NW 49th Ave **Fax Area Code:* 305 ■ *TF:* 800-327-3776 ■ *Web:* www.taurususa.com	Miami Lakes	FL	33014	800-327-3776	624-1126*	284
Taurus Software Inc 420 Brewster Ave *Web:* taurus.com	Redwood City	CA	94063	650-482-2022		179
Tautog's 205 23rd St *Web:* www.tautogs.com	Virginia Beach	VA	23451	757-422-0081		671
Tautphaus Park Zoo 308 Constitution Way *Web:* www.idahofallsidaho.gov	Idaho Falls	ID	83402	208-612-8280		823
Tavaero Jet Charter 7930 Airport Blvd *TF:* 800-343-3771 ■ *Web:* www.tavaero.com	Houston	TX	77061	713-643-5387	643-5398	13
Tavant Technologies Inc 3101 Jay St Ste 101 *Web:* www.tavant.com	Santa Clara	CA	95054	408-519-5400		177
Tavern on Grand 656 Grand Ave *Web:* www.tavernongrand.com	Saint Paul	MN	55105	651-228-9030		671
Tavern Products Co 1775 Deming Way *Web:* tavernproducts.com	Sparks	NV	89431	775-359-3535		300
Taverna Cretekou 818 King St *Web:* www.tavernacretekou.com	Alexandria	VA	22314	703-548-8688	683-2739	671
Taverna Opa 800 N Ocean Dr 2nd Fl *Web:* www.tavernaopa.com	Hollywood	FL	33019	954-922-2256	922-2258	671
Tavis Corp 3636 State Hwy 49 S *TF:* 800-842-6102 ■ *Web:* www.taviscorp.com	Mariposa	CA	95338	209-966-2027		407
Tavistock Restaurants LLC 4705 S Apopka Vineland Rd Ste 210 *TF:* 800-424-2753 ■ *Web:* tavistockrestaurantcollection.com	Orlando	FL	32819	407-909-7101		670
Tavve Software Co 1 Copley Pkwy Ste 480 *Web:* tavve.com	Morrisville	NC	27560	919-460-1789		177
TAW (Tampa Armature Works Inc) 6312 78th St *TF:* 800-333-9449 ■ *Web:* www.tawinc.com	Riverview	FL	33578	813-621-5661	425-0933	518
TAWA Supermarket Inc 6281 Regio Ave *Web:* www.99ranch.com	Buena Park	CA	90620	714-521-8899		410
Tawas Point State Park 686 Tawas Beach Rd *Web:* www.michigan.org	East Tawas	MI	48730	989-362-5041		565
Tawil Associates Inc 100 W 33rd ST *Web:* tawil.com	New York	NY	10001	212-279-3211		155-4
Tax Analysts 400 S Maple Ave Ste 400 *Web:* www.taxnotes.com	Falls Church	VA	22046	703-533-4400		637-9
Tax Centers of America 1611 E Main St *Web:* www.tcoa.net	Russellville	AR	72801	479-968-4796	968-8012	734
Tax Executives Institute (TEI) 1200 G St NW Ste 300 *Web:* www.tei.org	Washington	DC	20005	202-638-5601	638-5607	49-1
Tax Management Associates Inc 2225 Coronation Blvd *Web:* www.tma1.com	Charlotte	NC	28227	704-847-1234		225
Tax Resources Unlimited LLC 2637 E Atlantic Blvd Ste 18506 *Web:* taxleaseconsultants.com	Pompano Beach	FL	33062	248-794-7711		734
Tax Savvy 401 S Birmingham St *Web:* www.taxsavvy.com	Wylie	TX	75098	972-442-5226		734
Tax Smart Accounting Services 19616 E Benwood St *Web:* www.taxsmartaccounting.com	Covina	CA	91724	626-974-5152		734
Tax Wizard Inc 4438 W Oakton St *Web:* kmpcpa.com	Skokie	IL	60076	847-983-4370		734
Taxesplus Inc 10314 Shawnee Mission Pkwy Ste 200 *Web:* taxesplus.com	Shawnee	KS	66203	913-432-3147	722-4653	734
Taxi Canada Inc 495 Wellington St W Ste 102 *Web:* agency.taxi	Toronto	ON	M5V1E9	416-342-8294		7
TaxMatrix 1011 Mumma Rd *TF:* 855-788-3375 ■ *Web:* www.taxmatrix.com	Lemoyne	PA	17043	855-788-3375		463
Taxography Inc 6353 N Rosebury Ave *Web:* www.taxography.com	Saint Louis	MO	63105	314-863-9292	863-6277	809
Taxpayers Against Fraud Education Fund (TAF) 1220 19th St NW Ste 501 *Web:* taf.org	Washington	DC	20036	202-296-4826	296-4838	49-10
Taxpayers' Federation of Illinois (TFI) 430 E Vine St Ste A *Web:* www.illinoistax.org	Springfield	IL	62703	217-522-6818		48-6
TaxSlayer Ctr 1201 River Dr *Web:* www.taxslayercenter.com	Moline	IL	61265	309-764-2001	764-2192	720
Taycheedah Correctional Institution 751 County Rd *Web:* doc.wi.gov	Fond Du Lac	WI	54936	920-929-3800	929-2946	213
Tayco Engineering Inc 10874 Hope St *Web:* www.taycoeng.com	Cypress	CA	90630	714-952-2240	952-2042	202
Taycor LLC 6065 Bristol Pkwy *TF:* 800-322-9738 ■ *Web:* www.taycor.com	Culver City	CA	90230	310-895-7704	568-9922	216
Taylor 750 N Blackhawk Blvd **Fax Area Code:* 815 ■ *TF:* 800-255-0626 ■ *Web:* www.taylor-company.com	Rockton	IL	61072	800-255-0626	624-8000*	298
Taylor & Cameron 32 E 67th St *Web:* www.taylorandgraham.com	New York	NY	10065	212-535-5767		42
Taylor & Fenn Co 22 Deerfield Rd *Web:* www.taylorfenn.com	Windsor	CT	06095	860-219-9393	219-0907	307
Taylor & Francis Group 6000 Broken Sound Pkwy NW Ste 300 *TF:* 877-622-5543 ■ *Web:* www.taylorandfrancis.com	Boca Raton	FL	33487	207-017-6000		637-2
Taylor & Fulton Inc 932 Fifth Ave W *Web:* www.taylorfulton.com	Palmetto	FL	34221	941-729-3883		10-11
Taylor & Hill Inc 9941 Rowlett Rd *TF:* 800-318-0231 ■ *Web:* www.taylorandhill.com	Houston	TX	77075	713-941-2671		260
Taylor & Messick Inc 325 Walt Messick Rd *TF:* 800-237-1272 ■ *Web:* www.taylormessick.com	Harrington	DE	19952	302-398-3729	398-4732	520
Taylor & Syfan Consulting Engineers Inc 684 Clarion Ct *TF:* 800-579-3881 ■ *Web:* www.taylorsyfan.com	San Luis Obispo	CA	93401	805-547-2000		261
Taylor Benefits Insurance Agency Inc *Des Plaines Group Health Insurance & Employee Benefit Plans* 2800 River Rd Ste 310 *Web:* www.taylorbenefitsinsurance.com	Des Plaines	IL	60018	847-294-0000	294-0055	390
Taylor Bros Inc 905 Graves Mill Rd *Web:* www.taylorbrothers.com	Lynchburg	VA	24502	434-237-8100		499
Taylor Building Products 631 N First St *TF:* 800-248-3600 ■ *Web:* www.taylordoor.com	West Branch	MI	48661	989-345-5110	345-5116	234
Taylor Clark Inc 2623 Government St *Web:* taylorclark.com	Baton Rouge	LA	70806	225-383-4929		42

Name / Address	City	State	ZIP	Phone	Fax	Class
Taylor Clay Products Inc PO Box 2128 *Web:* taylorclaybrick.com	Salisbury	NC	28145	704-636-2411	636-2413	150
Taylor Corp 1725 Roe Crest Dr. *Web:* www.taylorcorp.com	North Mankato	MN	56003	507-625-2828	386-2031	360-3
Taylor Correctional Institution 8501 Hampton Springs Rd *Web:* dc.state.fl.us	Perry	FL	32348	850-838-4000	838-4024	213
Taylor County 300 Oak St *Web:* www.taylorcountytexas.org	Abilene	TX	79602	325-674-1231		338
Taylor County 405 Jefferson St *Web:* taylorcountyiowa.org	Bedford	IA	50833	712-523-2095		338
Taylor County 205 N Columbia Ave Ste 10 *Web:* www.kactfo.com	Campbellsville	KY	42718	270-628-3922		338
Taylor County 204 Latrobe St *Web:* www.wvcountytaylor.com	Grafton	WV	26354	304-265-1401	265-3016	338
Taylor County 224 S Second St *TF:* 800-362-4802 ■ *Web:* www.co.taylor.wi.us	Medford	WI	54451	715-748-1456	748-1415	338
Taylor County Clerk of Court 108 N Jefferson St Ste 102 *Web:* taylorclerk.com	Perry	FL	32347	850-838-3506	838-3549	338
Taylor County RECC 625 W Main St PO Box 100 *TF:* 800-931-4551 ■ *Web:* www.tcrecc.com	Campbellsville	KY	42719	270-465-4101		245
Taylor Data Systems Inc 181 E Evans St BTC 008 *TF:* 877-331-7427 ■ *Web:* www.taylordata.com	Florence	SC	29506	843-656-2084		177
Taylor Devices Inc 90 Taylor Dr *NASDAQ: TAYD* ■ *Web:* www.taylordevices.com	North Tonawanda	NY	14120	716-694-0800	695-6015	60
Taylor Distributors of Indiana 948 Sayre Dr. *TF:* 800-572-3054 ■ *Web:* www.taylorindiana.com	Greenwood	IN	46143	800-572-3054		665
Taylor Dynamometer Inc 3602 W Wheelhouse Rd *Web:* www.taylordyno.com	Milwaukee	WI	53208	414-755-0040		697
Taylor Electric Co-op N1831 State Hwy 13 *TF:* 800-862-2407 ■ *Web:* taylorelectric.org	Medford	WI	54451	715-678-2411	678-2555	245
Taylor Electric Co-opeartive Inc (TEC) 226 County Rd 287 Bldg A PO Box 250 *Web:* www.taylorelectric.com	Merkel	TX	79536	325-793-8500	793-1309	245
Taylor Energy Company LLC 1 Lee Cir *Web:* www.taylorenergy.com	New Orleans	LA	70130	504-581-5491		536
Taylor Engineering Inc 10151 Deerwood Park Blvd Bldg 300 Ste 300 *Web:* taylorengineering.com	Jacksonville	FL	32256	904-731-7040		261
Taylor Enterprises Inc (TEI) 2586 Southport Rd *TF:* 800-922-3149 ■ *Web:* taylorlubricants.com	Spartanburg	SC	29302	864-573-9518	583-4150	579
Taylor Farms Florida Inc 7492 Chancellor Dr *Web:* www.taylorfarms.com	Orlando	FL	32809	407-514-9808		123
Taylor Ford Inc 13500 Telegraph *Web:* www.shoptaylorford.net	Taylor	MI	48180	313-291-0300		57
Taylor Forge Engineered Systems Inc 208 N Iron St *Web:* www.tfes.com	Paola	KS	66071	913-294-5331	294-5337	91
Taylor Freezer Sales Company Inc 2032 Atlantic Ave *TF:* 800-768-6945 ■ *Web:* www.taylorfreezer.com	Chesapeake	VA	23324	757-334-1771		665
Taylor Freezers of California 6825 E Washington Blvd. *TF:* 800-927-7704 ■ *Web:* www.taylorfreezers.com	Commerce	CA	90040	323-889-8700	888-9292	406
Taylor Global Inc 350 Fifth Ave. *Web:* taylorstrategy.com	New York	NY	10118	212-714-1280	695-5685	636
Taylor Hobson Inc 1725 Western Dr. *Web:* www.taylor-hobson.com	West Chicago	IL	60185	630-621-3099	231-1739	472
Taylor Hodson Inc 133 W 19th St *Web:* www.taylorhodson.com	New York	NY	10011	212-924-8300		260
Taylor Independent School District 3101 N Main St *Web:* www.taylorisd.org	Taylor	TX	76574	512-352-6361	365-3800	685
Taylor Industries 6015 N Xanthus Ave *Web:* www.taylorindustries.net	Tulsa	OK	74130	918-266-7301		537
Taylor Insurance Agency Inc 140 N Main St *TF:* 888-294-4863 ■ *Web:* taylorinsurance-mi.com	Evart	MI	49631	231-734-5563		390
Taylor Ip PC 142 S Main St PO Box 560 *Web:* taylorip.com	Avilla	IN	46710	260-897-3400		41
Taylor Law Offices Pc 122 E Washington Ave *Web:* www.taylorlaw.net	Effingham	IL	62401	217-342-3925	342-2341	428
Taylor Lumber Inc 18253 SR-73 *Web:* www.taylorlumberinc.com	Mcdermott	OH	45652	740-259-6222	259-6543	683
Taylor Made Landscape Irrigation 750 Barsby St *Web:* www.taylormadelandscapeandirrigation.com	Vista	CA	92084	760-945-0118		693
Taylor Made Products *Taylor Made Group* 65 Harrison St *TF:* 800-628-5188 ■ *Web:* www.taylormadeproducts.com	Gloversville	NY	12078	800-628-5188		596
Taylor Made Transportation Services Inc 2901 Druid Pk Dr Ste 206 *Web:* tmtransportation.com	Baltimore	MD	21215	410-728-1951		780
Taylor Metal Products Co 700 Springmill St *Web:* www.tmpind.com	Mansfield	OH	44903	419-522-3471	525-2948	488
Taylor Metalworks Inc 3925 California Rd *Web:* www.taylorcnc.com	Orchard Park	NY	14127	716-662-3113	662-1096	621
Taylor Mill Historic Site Island Pond Rd *Web:* www.nhstateparks.org	Derry	NH	03038	603-431-6774		565

Name / Address	City	State	ZIP	Phone	Fax	Class
Taylor Morrison Inc 4900 N Scottsdale Rd Ste 2000 *Web:* www.taylormorrison.com	Scottsdale	AZ	85251	480-840-8100		652
Taylor of Oklahoma 5000 N Santa Fe *Web:* www.taylor-oklahoma.com	Oklahoma City	OK	73118	405-840-6018	840-6016	665
Taylor Oil Company Inc 77 Second St *TF:* 800-352-4969 ■ *Web:* www.tayloroilco.com	Somerville	NJ	08876	908-725-7737	725-7746	579
Taylor Polson & Company PSC 215 W Front St	Glasgow	KY	42141	270-651-8877		2
Taylor Products Company Inc 2205 Jothi Ave *TF:* 888-882-9567 ■ *Web:* www.magnumsystems.com	Parsons	KS	67357	620-421-5550		547
Taylor Protocols 16400 Southcenter Pkwy Ste 407 *Web:* www.taylorprotocolsinc.com	Tukwila	WA	98188	206-283-8144		449
Taylor Public Library 400 Porter St *Web:* www.ci.taylor.tx.us	Taylor	TX	76574	512-352-3675	352-8080	434-3
Taylor Regional Hospital 1700 Old Lebanon Rd *Web:* www.tchosp.org	Campbellsville	KY	42718	270-465-3561		374-3
Taylor Smith Consulting LLC 16800 Greenspoint Pk Dr *Web:* taylorsmithconsulting.com	Houston	TX	77060	713-937-3111	937-3486	463
Taylor Stitch 383 Valencia St. *Web:* www.taylorstitch.com	San Francisco	CA	94103	415-621-2231		258
Taylor Technical Institute 3233 S Byron Pky *Web:* www.taylortech.org	Perry	FL	32348	850-838-2545	838-2546	167-3
Taylor Technologies Inc 31 Loveton Cir *TF:* 800-837-8548 ■ *Web:* taylortechnologies.com	Sparks	MD	21152	410-472-4340	771-4291	806
Taylor Telephone Cooperative Inc (TTC) 9796 Interstate 20 *TF:* 866-944-8456 ■ *Web:* online.taylortel.net	Merkel	TX	79536	325-846-4111		224
Taylor Truck Line Inc 31485 Northfield Blvd. *TF:* 800-962-5994 ■ *Web:* www.taylortruckline.com	Northfield	MN	55057	507-645-4531		780
Taylor University 236 W Reade Ave *TF:* 800-882-3456 ■ *Web:* www.taylor.edu	Upland	IN	46989	765-998-2751	998-4925	166
Fort Wayne 915 W Rudisill Blvd *Web:* fwalumnicenter.org	Fort Wayne	IN	46807	260-744-8790	745-4974	166
Taylor University College & Seminary 11525 23rd Ave *TF:* 800-567-4988 ■ *Web:* www.taylor-edu.ca	Edmonton	AB	T6J4T3	780-431-5200	436-9416	167-3
Taylor Valve Technology Inc 8300 SW Eighth St *TF:* 800-805-3401 ■ *Web:* www.taylorvalve.com	Oklahoma City	OK	73128	405-787-0145		789
Taylor Van (Rep R - TX) 1404 Longworth House Office Bldg *Web:* www.vantaylor.house.gov	Washington	DC	20515	202-225-4201		342-2
Taylor Wellons Politz & Duhe Aplc 8550 United Plaza Blvd Ste 101 *TF:* 877-850-1047 ■ *Web:* www.twpdlaw.com	Baton Rouge	LA	70809	225-387-9888		428
Taylor Wiseman & Taylor (TWT) 124 Gaither Dr Ste 150 *Web:* taylorwiseman.com	Mount Laurel	NJ	08054	856-235-7200		261
Taylor's Auto Max 4100 Tenth Ave S *Web:* www.taylorsautomax.com	Great Falls	MT	59405	406-727-0380		57
Taylor's Steak House 3361 W Eigth St *Web:* taylorssteakhouse.com	Los Angeles	CA	90005	213-382-8449		671
Taylor, Porter, Brooks & Phillips LLP 450 Laurel St Ste 800 *TF:* 800-310-7029 ■ *Web:* www.taylorporter.com	Baton Rouge	LA	70801	225-387-3221	346-8049	428
Taylor, Taylor & Leonetti PC 216 Haddon Ave Ste 506 *Web:* taylortaylorlaw.com	Westmont	NJ	08108	856-833-1919		41
Taylor, Wellons, Politz & Duhe, Aplc 1515 Poydras St Ste 1900 *Web:* twpdlaw.com	New Orleans	LA	70112	504-525-9888		41
Taylor/Martino PC 51 St Joseph St. *Web:* taylormartino.com	Mobile	AL	36602	251-433-3131		41
Taylor-Dunn Manufacturing Co 2114 W Ball Rd. **Fax Area Code: 714* ■ *TF:* 800-688-8680 ■ *Web:* www.taylor-dunn.com	Anaheim	CA	92804	800-688-8680	956-3130*	470
Taylored Systems Inc 14701 Cumberland Rd Ste 100 *Web:* www.taylored.com	Noblesville	IN	46060	317-776-4000	776-4004	735
Taylor-Listug Inc 1980 Gillespie Way *TF:* 800-943-6782 ■ *Web:* www.taylorguitars.com	El Cajon	CA	92020	619-258-1207		527
TaylorMade - Adidas Golf 5545 Fermi Ct. *Web:* www.taylormadegolf.com	Carlsbad	CA	92008	760-918-6000		710
Taylor-Made Transportation 740 Alabama 139 *Web:* www.taylormadeinc.com	Maplesville	AL	36750	334-366-2269		780
Taylorsville Lake State Park 1320 Park Rd *Web:* parks.ky.gov	Mount Eden	KY	40046	502-477-0086		565
Taylor-Wharton 4718 Gettysburg Rd Ste 300 *Web:* www.twcryo.com	Mechanicsburg	PA	17055	717-763-5060	731-7988	91
Taylor-Winfield Inc 3200 Innovation Pl *TF:* 800-523-4899 ■ *Web:* www.taylor-winfield.com	Youngstown	OH	44509	330-259-8500	259-8538	811
Taymark Inc 4875 White Bear Pkwy *Web:* www.taymarkinc.com	White Bear Lake	MN	55110	651-426-1667		459
Tazewell Area Chamber of Commerce PO Box 672 *Web:* www.tazewellchamber.com	Tazewell	VA	24651	276-988-5091		139
Tazewell County 11 S Fourth St Ste 203 Second Fl. *Web:* www.tazewell.com	Pekin	IL	61554	309-477-2264	477-2244	338
Tazewell County Public Library 129 Main St PO Box 929 *Web:* tcplweb.org	Tazewell	VA	24651	276-988-2541	988-5980	434-3

Name / Address	City	State	ZIP	Phone	Fax	Class
Tazewell General District Court 101 E Main St *Web:* courts.state.va.us	Tazewell	VA	24651	276-385-1563		338
Tazewell Machine Works Inc 2015 S Second St *Web:* www.tazewellmachine.com	Pekin	IL	61554	309-347-3181		492
TB Butler Publishing Co 410 W Erwin St *Web:* www.tylerpaper.com	Tyler	TX	75702	903-597-8111		637-8
TB Wood's Inc 440 N Fifth Ave *TF:* 888-829-6637 ■ *Web:* www.tbwoods.com	Chambersburg	PA	17201	717-264-7161	264-6420	620
T-Base Communications 885 Meadowlands Dr E Ste 401 *Web:* www.tbase.com	Ottawa	ON	K2C3N2	613-236-0866		180
TBayTel 1060 Lithium Dr *TF:* 800-264-9501 ■ *Web:* www.tbaytel.net	Thunder Bay	ON	P7B6G3	807-623-4400		224
TBC (Teal Becker & Chiramonte) 7 Washington Sq *Web:* www.tbccpa.com	Albany	NY	12205	518-456-6663	456-3975	2
TBC (Tom Barrow Co) 2800 Plant Atkinson Rd *TF:* 800-229-8226 ■ *Web:* www.tombarrow.com	Atlanta	GA	30339	404-351-1010	350-9121	14
TBC (Trahan Burden & Charles Inc) 3601 O'Donnell St Ste 100-The Barrel Bldg *Web:* www.tbc.us	Baltimore	MD	21224	410-347-7500	986-1299	4
TBC (Titonka Burt Communications) 247 Main St N *TF:* 800-753-2016 ■ *Web:* www.tbctel.com	Titonka	IA	50480	515-928-2110	928-2897	224
TBDC (Trisha Brown Dance Co) 341 W 38th St Ste 801 *Web:* www.trishabrowncompany.org	New York	NY	10018	212-977-5365	925-8687	573-1
TBDN Tennessee Co 1410 Hwy 70 Bypass *Web:* www.tbdn.com	Jackson	TN	38301	731-421-4800	421-4879	60
TBF (Branding Farm, The) 1378 Main St *Web:* branding.farm	Venice	CA	90291	310-396-4025		5
TBI (Telecom Brokerage Inc) 8770 W Bryn Mawr Ave Ste 400 *Web:* www.tbicom.com	Chicago	IL	60631	847-465-4500	465-1488	224
TBK America Inc 3700 W Industries Rd *Web:* www.tbk-jp.com	Richmond	IN	47374	765-962-0147	962-0650	641
Tbm Consulting Group Inc 4400 Ben Franklin Blvd *TF:* 800-438-5535 ■ *Web:* www.tbmcg.com	Durham	NC	27704	919-471-5535	471-5135	194
Tbm Inc 950 Kingsland Ave *TF:* 800-825-1128 ■ *Web:* www.tbmproducts.com	Saint Louis	MO	63130	314-721-5590	721-4990	579
TBN (Trinity Broadcasting Network) PO Box A *TF:* 888-731-1000 ■ *Web:* tbn.org	Santa Ana	CA	92711	714-832-2950		740
TBN Consulting LLC 3301 Brunswick Ave N **Fax Area Code:* 443 ■ *Web:* www.tbnconsulting.biz	Minneapolis	MN	55422	763-971-8057	581-0462*	463
TBRPC (Tampa Bay Regional Planning Council) 4000 Gateway Centre Blvd Ste 100 *Web:* www.tbrpc.org	Pinellas Park	FL	33782	727-570-5151	570-5118	637-10
TBS (Trachte Building Systems Inc) 314 Wilburn Rd *TF:* 800-356-5824 ■ *Web:* www.trachte.com	Sun Prairie	WI	53590	800-356-5824	981-9014	105
TBS Automation Systems Inc 122 Kings Hwy Ste 504 *Web:* www.tbsauto.com	Maple Shade	NJ	08052	856-424-3247		180
TBS Communications Inc 1800 Peachtree St Ste 655 *Web:* www.coolbluei.com	Atlanta	GA	30309	404-876-6989		177
TBS Shipping Services Inc 455 Central Park Ave Ste 308 *Web:* www.gnav.com	Scarsdale	NY	10583	914-961-1000		770
TBT (Transco Business Technologies) 34 Leighton Rd *TF:* 800-322-0003 ■ *Web:* www.transcobusiness.com	Augusta	ME	04330	800-452-4657		112
TBWA Chiat/Day Inc 488 Madison Ave *Web:* tbwachiatdayny.com	New York	NY	10022	212-804-1000		4
TC Computer Service Inc (TCCSI) PO Box 691713 *Web:* www.tccsi.com	Houston	TX	77269	713-686-2083		180
TC Electronic Inc 5706 Corsa Ave Ste 107 *Web:* www.tcelectronic.com	Westlake Village	CA	91362	818-665-4900		527
TC Federal Bank 131 S Dawson St *Web:* www.tcfederal.com	Thomasville	GA	31799	229-226-3221		71
TC Industries Inc 3703 S Rt 31 *Web:* www.tcindustries.com	Crystal Lake	IL	60012	815-459-2400	459-3303	484
TC Mill Work Inc 3433 Marshall Ln *Web:* www.tcmillwork.com	Bensalem	PA	19020	215-245-4210	245-4723	321
TC Net-Works 23610 Mohican St NW *Web:* www.tcnet-works.com	Saint Francis	MN	55070	612-747-4357		177
TCA (Tilt-Up Concrete Assn) 113 First St NW **Fax Area Code:* 320 ■ *Web:* www.tilt-up.org	Mount Vernon	IA	52314	319-895-6911	213-5555*	49-3
TCA (Treatment Communities of America) 1875 I St NW Rm 574 *Web:* www.treatmentcommunitiesofamerica.org	Washington	DC	20006	202-296-3503	379-9154	49-8
TCA (Tile Council of America Inc) 100 Clemson Research Blvd *Web:* www.tcnatile.com	Anderson	SC	29625	864-646-8453	646-2821	49-3
TCA (Truckload Carriers Assn) 555 E Braddock Rd *Web:* www.truckload.org	Alexandria	VA	22314	703-838-1950	836-6610	49-21
TCAG (Center for Association Growth, The) 1926 Waukegan Rd Ste 300 *TF:* 800-492-6462 ■ *Web:* www.tcag.us	Glenview	IL	60025	847-657-6700	657-6819	47
TCBWA (Commerce Bank of Washington, The) 2 Union Sq 601 Union St Ste 3600 *TF:* 800-877-8021 ■ *Web:* www.tcbwa.com	Seattle	WA	98101	206-292-3900	625-9457	70
TCC (Tri-County Communications Cooperative Inc) 417 5th Ave N *TF:* 800-831-0610 ■ *Web:* tccpro.net	Strum	WI	54770	715-695-2816	695-3599	224
TCCI Manufacturing LLC 2120 N 22nd St *Web:* tccimfg.com	Decatur	IL	62526	217-422-0055		454
TCCL (Tulsa City-County Library) 400 Civic Ctr *Web:* www.tulsalibrary.org	Tulsa	OK	74103	918-549-7323		434-3
TCCSI (TC Computer Service Inc) PO Box 691713 *Web:* www.tccsi.com	Houston	TX	77269	713-686-2083		180
TCE (Tower Communications Expert LLC) 114 Shore Dr *Web:* www.tcellc.net	Burr Ridge	IL	60527	773-744-7550	717-5534	188-1
TCF Ctr 1 Washington Blvd *Web:* www.tcfcenterdetroit.com	Detroit	MI	48226	313-877-8777	877-8577	205
TCG Continuum LLC 4251 Leap Rd *Web:* www.tcgcontinuum.com	Hilliard	OH	43026	614-876-8600		393
TCI (Teachers' Curriculum Institute) 2440 W El Camino Real Ste 400 *TF:* 800-497-6138 ■ *Web:* www.teachtci.com	Mountain View	CA	94040	800-497-6138	343-6828	196
TCI (Thompson Consulting Inc) 9 Jacob Gates Rd **Fax Area Code:* 240 ■ *Web:* www.thompsonrd.com	Harvard	MA	01451	978-456-7722	414-2655*	261
TCI Aluminum/North Inc 2353 Davis Ave *TF:* 800-824-6197 ■ *Web:* tcialuminum.com	Hayward	CA	94545	510-786-3750		492
TCI Scales Inc PO Box 1648 *TF:* 800-522-2206 ■ *Web:* www.tciscales.com	Snohomish	WA	98291	425-353-4384	609-1021	684
TCI Wealth Advisors Inc 4011 E Sunrise Dr *Web:* tciwealth.com	Tucson	AZ	85718	520-733-1477	733-1488	401
TCIA (Tree Care Industry Assn) 136 Harvey Rd Ste 101 *TF:* 800-733-2622 ■ *Web:* tcia.org	Londonderry	NH	03053	603-314-5380	314-5386	48-13
TCK (Twin City Knitting Company Inc) 104 Rock Barn Rd NE *Web:* tcksports.com	Conover	NC	28613	828-464-4830		155-10
TCL (Transylvania County Library) 212 S Gaston St *Web:* library.transylvaniacounty.org	Brevard	NC	28712	828-884-3151		434-3
TCM (Turner Classic Movies Inc) 1050 Techwood Dr NW *TF:* 844-356-7875 ■ *Web:* www.tcm.turner.com	Atlanta	GA	30318	844-356-7875		740
TCM (Temp-Control Mechanical Corp) 4800 N Ch Ave *Web:* www.tcmcorp.com	Portland	OR	97217	503-285-9851		14
TCN Worldwide 1755 N Collins Ste 207 *Web:* www.tcnworldwide.com	Richardson	TX	75080	972-769-8701		652
TCOM LP 7115 Thomas Edison Dr *Web:* www.tcomlp.com	Columbia	MD	21046	410-312-2400	312-2455	28
TCP Stream LLC 9255 Center St Ste 401 *TF:* 888-444-2755 ■ *Web:* tcpstream.com	Manassas	VA	20110	888-444-2755		177
TCR (Trammell Crow Residential) 3889 Maple St *Web:* www.crowholdings.com	Dallas	TX	75219	214-922-8400		653
TCR Child Care Corp 925 N St E *Web:* www.tcrchildcarecorporation.org	Talladega	AL	35160	256-362-3852		148
TCR Corp 1600 67th Ave N *Web:* www.tcr-corp.com	Minneapolis	MN	55430	763-560-2200		567
TCR Industries 26 Centerpointe Dr Ste 120 *TF:* 877-827-1444 ■ *Web:* www.tcrindustries.com	La Palma	CA	90623	714-521-5222	521-1636	146
TCS (Tata Consultancy Services Ltd) 101 Park Ave 26th Fl *Web:* www.tcs.com	New York	NY	10178	212-557-8038		194
TCS (Tongass Conservation Society) PO Box 23377 *Web:* tongassconservation.org	Ketchikan	AK	99901	907-254-0914		48-13
TCS 168 Thatcher Rd *Web:* www.tcsusa.com	Greensboro	NC	27409	336-632-0860	632-1568	393
TCS Communications LLC 2045 W Union Ave Bldg E *Web:* www.tcscomm.com	Englewood	CO	80110	303-377-3800		186
TCS Communications LLC 14021 White Rock Rd *Web:* www.tcs-communications.com	Burnsville	MN	55337	612-703-9384		35
TCS Group Inc 3922 Coral Ridge Dr *TF:* 800-526-6266 ■ *Web:* tcsgroup.net	Coral Springs	FL	33065	954-846-8787	846-9311	681
TCS of America Enterprises LLC PO Box 219 *TF:* 888-423-7820 ■ *Web:* www.tcsofamerica.com	Brookline	NH	03033	888-423-7820		196
TCSN Inc 1306 Pine St *TF:* 800-974-3475 ■ *Web:* www.tcsn.net	Paso Robles	CA	93446	805-227-7000	237-0951	225
TCT Computing Group Inc PO Box 402 *TF:* 866-828-6372 ■ *Web:* www.tctcomputing.com	Bel Air	MD	21014	410-893-5800		193
TCT Federal Credit Union 416 Rowland St *Web:* tctfcu.org	Ballston	NY	12020	518-884-7002		219
TCT Ministries Inc 11717 N Rt 37 PO Box 1010 *TF:* 800-232-9855 ■ *Web:* www.tct.tv	Marion	IL	62959	618-997-4700	993-9778	740
TCT Stainless Steel Inc 6300 19 Mile Rd *Web:* temperedmetals.com	Sterling Heights	MI	48314	586-254-5333		492
TCU (Teachers Credit Union) PO Box 1395 *TF:* 800-552-4745 ■ *Web:* www.tcunet.com	South Bend	IN	46624	574-284-6247		219
T-Cubed Systems Inc 5776-D Lindero Cyn Rd Ste 437 *Web:* www.t-cubed.com	Westlake Village	CA	91362	818-991-0057	991-1281	178-1
TCW Group Inc 865 S Figueroa St Ste 1800 *Web:* www.tcw.com	Los Angeles	CA	90017	213-244-0000		528
TCWP (Tennessee Citizens for Wilderness Planning) PO Box 6873 *Web:* www.tcwp.org	Oak Ridge	TN	37830	865-583-3967		48-13
TD Asset Management 300 Park Centre 1230 Blackfoot Dr *TF:* 800-213-4286 ■ *Web:* greystone.td.com	Regina	SK	S4S7G4	800-213-4286		401
TD Bank NA 1701 Rte 70 E *TF:* 888-751-9000 ■ *Web:* www.tdbank.com	Cherry Hill	NJ	08034	856-751-2739		70

	Phone	Fax	Class
TDA (Tennessee Dental Assn) 660 Bakers Bridge Ave Ste 300 ... Franklin TN 37067 *TF:* 800-824-9722 ■ *Web:* www.tndentalassociation.com	615-628-0208		227
TDA Group LLC 3 Lagoon Dr Ste 160 ... Redwood City CA 94065 *Web:* www.tdagroup.com	650-919-1200		195
TDA Insurance & Financial Agencies 246 Liberty St ... Walled Lake MI 48390 *TF:* 877-832-6690 ■ *Web:* tdanow.com	877-832-6690		390
TDB Communications Inc 10901 W 84th Ter Ste 125 ... Lenexa KS 66214 *Web:* tdbgov.com	913-327-7400		260
TDC Acquisition Holdings Inc 4955 Corporate Dr Ste 101 ... Huntsville AL 35805 *Web:* timedomain.com	256-922-9229		696
TDDS Technical Institute 1688 N Princetown Rd SR 534 PO Box 506 ... Lake Milton OH 44429 *TF:* 800-475-8337 ■ *Web:* www.tdds.edu	330-538-2216	538-0609	167-3
TDEC 424 S Arch St ... Oakland MD 21550 *Web:* www.tdec.com	301-334-1234		225
TDECU (Texas Dow Employees Credit Union) 1001 FM 2004 ... Lake Jackson TX 77566 *TF:* 800-839-1154 ■ *Web:* www.tdecu.org	979-297-1154	299-0212	219
TDF (TDF Ventures) 2 Wisconsin Cir Ste 920 ... Chevy Chase MD 20815 *Web:* www.tdfventures.com	240-483-4286		792
TDF Ventures (TDF) 2 Wisconsin Cir Ste 920 ... Chevy Chase MD 20815 *Web:* www.tdfventures.com	240-483-4286		792
TDG 93 Sherman St ... Deadwood SD 57732 *Web:* www.tdg.agency	605-722-7111		4
TDG Aerospace Inc 545 Corporate Dr ... Escondido CA 92029 *Web:* www.tdgaerospace.com	760-466-1040	466-1038	20
TDH Marketing & Communications Inc 8153 Garnet Dr ... Dayton OH 45458 *Web:* www.tdh-marketing.com	937-438-3434		195
TDIndustries Inc 13850 Diplomat Dr ... Dallas TX 75234 *Web:* www.tdindustries.com	972-888-9500		189-10
TDK Corporation of America 475 Half Day Rd Ste 300 ... Lincolnshire IL 60069 *Web:* www.tdk.com	847-699-2299		253
TDK Electronics Inc 485-B Rt 1 S Ste 200 ... Iselin NJ 08830 *TF:* 800-689-3717 ■ *Web:* www.tdk-electronics.tdk.com	732-906-4304		253
TDK-Lambda Americas Inc 405 Essex Rd ... Neptune City NJ 07753 *Web:* www.us.lambda.tdk.com	732-922-9300	922-1441	253
TDM (Troy Design & Manufacturing Co) 14425 Sheldon Rd ... Plymouth MI 48170 *Web:* www.troydm.com	734-738-2300		489
TDM Technical Services 3924 Chesswood Dr ... Toronto ON M3J2W6 *Web:* www.tdm.ca	416-777-0007		261
TDPUD (Truckee Donner Public Utility District) 11570 Donner Pass Rd PO Box 309 ... Truckee CA 96160 *Web:* www.tdpud.org	530-587-3896	550-1968	245
TDS (Texas Disposal Systems Inc) 12200 Carl Rd ... Creedmoor TX 78610 *TF:* 800-375-8375 ■ *Web:* www.texasdisposal.com	512-421-1300	243-4123	804
TDS Telecommunications Corp 525 Junction Rd ... Madison WI 53717 *TF:* 866-571-6662 ■ *Web:* www.my.tdstelecom.com	608-664-4000		736
TDX Tech 5735 Old Shakopee Rd Ste 100 ... Bloomington MN 55437 *TF:* 800-328-3884 ■ *Web:* www.tdxtech.com	952-936-9280		175
TE Connectivity 1050 Westlakes Dr ... Berwyn PA 19312 *Web:* www.te.com	610-893-9800		60
TE Financial Consultants Ltd 26 Wellington St E Ste 710 ... Toronto ON M5E1S2 *Web:* www.tewealth.com	416-366-1451		401
Te21 Inc 1184 Clements Ferry Rd Ste G ... Charleston SC 29492 *TF:* 866-982-8321 ■ *Web:* www.te21.com	843-579-2520		196
TEA (Texas Education Agency) William B. Travis Bldg 1701 N Congress Ave ... Austin TX 78701 *Web:* www.tea.state.tx.us	512-463-9734	463-9838	637-2
Tea Association of the USA Inc 362 Fifth Ave Ste 801 ... New York NY 10001 *Web:* www.teausa.com	212-986-9415	697-8658	49-6
Tea Garden Restaurant 184 N Main St ... Concord NH 03301 *Web:* teagarden-nh.com	603-228-4420		671
TEAC America Inc 7733 Telegraph Rd ... Montebello CA 90640 *Web:* www.teac.com	323-726-0303	727-7656	52
Teach Away Inc 147 Liberty St ... Toronto ON M6K3G3 *TF:* 855-483-2242 ■ *Web:* www.teachaway.com	416-628-1386		260
Teach Enterprises Inc 2600 S Nappanee St ... Elkhart IN 46517 *Web:* www.centuryfoam.com	574-293-5547		601
Teach For America 315 W 36th St 7th Fl ... New York NY 10018 *TF:* 800-832-1230 ■ *Web:* www.teachforamerica.org	212-279-2080		49-5
Teachable 470 Park Ave S ... New York NY 10016 *Web:* teachable.com	347-215-3202		788
Teacher Created Resources 6421 Industry Way ... Westminster CA 92683 **Fax Area Code:* 800 ■ *TF:* 888-343-4335 ■ *Web:* www.teachercreated.com	888-343-4335	525-1254*	243
Teachers Association of Long Beach 4362 Atlantic Ave ... Long Beach CA 90807 *Web:* talb.org	562-426-6433		414
Teachers Credit Union (TCU) PO Box 1395 ... South Bend IN 46624 *TF:* 800-552-4745 ■ *Web:* www.tcunet.com	574-284-6247		219
Teachers Credit Union 2315 Prairie Ave ... Beloit WI 53511 *Web:* tcubeloit.org	608-362-8983		219
Teachers Federal Credit Union (TFCU) 2410 N Ocean Ave ... Farmingville NY 11738 *TF:* 800-341-4333 ■ *Web:* www.teachersfcu.org	631-698-7000		219
Teachers of English to Speakers of Other Languages (TESOL) 1925 Ballenger Ave Ste 550 ... Alexandria VA 22314 *TF:* 888-547-3369 ■ *Web:* www.tesol.org	703-518-2500	836-7864	49-5
Teachers on Reserve LLC 604 Sonora Ave ... Glendale CA 91201 *TF:* 800-457-1899 ■ *Web:* teachersonreserve.com	800-457-1899		260
Teachers' Curriculum Institute (TCI) 2440 W El Camino Real Ste 400 ... Mountain View CA 94040 *TF:* 800-497-6138 ■ *Web:* www.teachtci.com	800-497-6138	343-6828	196
Teachey 258 Harrison Bridge Rd ... Simpsonville SC 29680 *Web:* www.teachey.com	864-967-3838		189-10
Teaching Tolerance Magazine 400 Washington Ave ... Montgomery AL 36104 *Web:* www.tolerance.org	334-956-8200		457-8
TEAI (Torch Energy Advisors Inc) 1331 Lamar St Ste 1075 ... Houston TX 77010	713-650-1246		401
Teak Isle Manufacturing Inc 401 Capitol Ct ... Ocoee FL 34761 *Web:* www.teakisle.com	407-656-8885		602
Teak Media Communications 840 Summer St Ste 305A ... South Boston MA 02127 *Web:* www.teakmedia.com	617-269-7171		317
TeakThai Cusine 1051 St Gregory St ... Cincinnati OH 45202 *Web:* teakthaicuisine.com	513-665-9800		671
Teal Becker & Chiramonte (TBC) 7 Washington Sq ... Albany NY 12205 *Web:* www.tbccpa.com	518-456-6663	456-3975	2
Teal's Express Inc 22411 Teal Dr PO Box 6010 ... Watertown NY 13601 **Fax Area Code:* 315 ■ *TF:* 800-836-0369 ■ *Web:* www.teals.com	800-836-0369	788-5060*	780
Tealinc Ltd 1606 Rosebud Creek Rd ... Forsyth MT 59327 *Web:* www.tealinc.com	406-347-5237		650
Teal-Jones Group, The 17897 Triggs Rd ... Surrey BC V4N4M8 *TF:* 888-995-8325 ■ *Web:* tealjones.com	604-587-8700		683
Team & Wheel Federal Credit Union 1405 Trademart Blvd ... Winston-Salem NC 27127 *Web:* team-wheelfcu.org	336-785-0103		219
Team 92.1 FM 2495 Cedar St ... Holt MI 48842 *Web:* stacks921.com	517-699-0111	699-1880	645
Team America Inc 33 W 46th St Frnt 3 ... New York NY 10036 *Web:* www.teamamericany.com	212-221-5938		760
Team Automation 2215 First St 104 ... Simi Valley CA 93065 *Web:* www.teamautomation.com	805-522-3875		177
Team Business LLC 1410 Belt St ... Baltimore MD 21230 *Web:* www.teambusiness.com	410-837-1414		765
Team Connection Inc 615 Alton Pl ... High Point NC 27263 *TF:* 800-535-3975 ■ *Web:* www.teamconnection.com	336-431-2551		711
Team Drive-Away Inc 23724 W 83rd Terr ... Shawnee KS 66227 *TF:* 844-628-9942 ■ *Web:* teamdriveaway.com	913-825-4776		311
Team Hardinger Transportation/Warehousing 1314 W 18th St ... Erie PA 16502 *Web:* team-h.com	814-453-6587		685
Team Health Inc 265 Brookview Ctr Way Ste 400 ... Knoxville TN 37919 *TF:* 800-342-2898 ■ *Web:* www.teamhealth.com	865-693-1000		721
Team IA Inc 212 Palmetto Park Blvd ... Lexington SC 29072 *TF:* 888-483-2642 ■ *Web:* www.teamia.com	803-356-7676		809
Team Inc 200 Hermann Dr ... Alvin TX 77511 *NYSE: TISI* ■ *TF:* 800-662-8326 ■ *Web:* teaminc.com	281-331-6154		539
Team Industries 3750 Airport Rd ... Andrews NC 28901 *Web:* www.team-ind.com	828-835-4000		454
Team Industries Inc 1200 Maloney Rd ... Kaukauna WI 54130 *Web:* www.teamind.com	920-766-7977	766-0486	595
Team National Inc 8210 W State Rd 84 ... Davie FL 33324 *Web:* www.bign.com	954-584-2151		113
Team One 2999 Overland Ave Ste 130 ... Los Angeles CA 90094 *Web:* www.teamone-usa.com	310-437-2500		4
Team One Repair Inc 2705 Crestridge Ct ... Suwanee GA 30024 **Fax Area Code:* 770 ■ *Web:* callteamone.com	678-985-0772	614-3394*	175
Team People LLC 180 S Washington St ... Falls Church VA 22046 *Web:* www.teampeople.tv	202-587-4111		514
Team Quality Services Inc 4483 County Rd 19 Ste B ... Auburn IN 46706 *TF:* 866-568-8326 ■ *Web:* teamqualityservices.com	260-572-0060		463
Team Schierl Cos 2201 Madison St ... Stevens Point WI 54481 *Web:* www.teamschierl.com	715-345-5060		581
Team Solutions 25 Bodrington Ct ... Markham ON L6G1B6 *TF:* 800-301-8326 ■ *Web:* www.team-group.com	905-940-9334		192
Team Technologies Inc 5949 Commerce Blvd ... Morristown TN 37814 *Web:* www.teamtechinc.net	423-587-2199	587-0642	214
Team Tiry Real Estate LLC 1820 Brackett Ave ... Eau Claire WI 54701 *Web:* teamtiry.com	715-835-2129		652
Team Trident LLC 16300 Katy Fwy Ste 180 ... Houston TX 77094 *Web:* www.teamtrident.com	281-600-1412	310-5088	539
Team Tube LLC 23217 66th Ave S ... Kent WA 98032 *Web:* teamtubellc.com	253-854-3456		492
Team Velocity Marketing LLC 13825 Sunrise Valley Dr ... Herndon VA 20171 *TF:* 877-832-6848 ■ *Web:* teamvelocitymarketing.com	877-832-6848		7
Team Volkswagen of Hayward Corp 25115 Mission Blvd ... Hayward CA 94544 *Web:* www.vwhayward.com	510-885-1000		57
Team Work Consulting Inc 22550 McCauley Rd ... Shaker Heights OH 44122 *Web:* www.teamworkconsulting.com	216-360-1790		196
TeamBonding 26 Technology Way ... Stoughton MA 02072 *TF:* 888-398-8326 ■ *Web:* teambonding.com	888-398-8326		317
TeamLogic Inc 4424 Bragg Blvd Ste 101 ... Fayetteville NC 28303 *Web:* www.teamlogicit.com	910-500-1391	484-1234	179
Teammates Commercial Interiors 320 S Teller St Ste 250 ... Lakewood CO 80226 *Web:* team-mates.com	303-639-5885		320
TeamMax Corp 282 Central St Ste 6 ... Hudson MA 01749 *Web:* www.teammax.com	978-293-3542	293-3543	174

Company / Address	City	State	ZIP	Phone	Fax	Class
Teamster Local 700 1300 W Higgins Rd Ste 301 Web: teamsterslocal700.com	Park Ridge	IL	60068	847-939-9700		414
Teamwork Solutions 5005 Horizons Dr Ste 200 Web: www.teamsol.com	Columbus	OH	43220	614-457-7100		177
TeamWorld Inc 498 Conklin Ave TF: 800-797-1005 ■ Web: www.teamworld.com	Binghamton	NY	13903	607-770-1005		34
Teaneck Public Library 840 Teaneck Rd TF: 800-245-1377 ■ Web: teanecklibrary.org	Teaneck	NJ	07666	201-837-4171	837-0410	434-3
Teaneck Suburbanite 210 Knickerbocker Rd 2nd Fl	Cresskill	NJ	07626	201-894-6721		532-4
Tearepair Inc PO Box 1879 TF: 800-937-3716 ■ Web: www.tear-aid.com	Land O' Lakes	FL	34639	813-948-6898	996-4523	608
TearLab Corp 150 La Terraza Blvd Ste 101 *Fax Area Code: 858 ■ Web: www.tearlab.com	Escondido	CA	92025	855-832-7522	812-0540*	543
Teasley Drug Inc 205 Atlanta St SE Web: www.teasleydrug.com	Gravette	AR	72736	479-787-5966	787-5393	237
Teatro 177 Tremont St Web: www.teatroboston.com	Boston	MA	02111	617-778-6841		671
Tebben Enterprises Inc 10009 Hwy 7 SE Web: www.tebben.us	Clara City	MN	56222	320-847-2200	847-3112	273
Tebons Gas & Auto Service Inc 7415 N Harlem Ave Web: www.tebonsgas.com	Niles	IL	60714	847-647-9800		366
TEC (Thumb Electric Co-op) 2231 Main St TF: 800-327-0166 ■ Web: www.tecmi.coop	Ubly	MI	48475	989-658-8571		245
TEC (Taylor Electric Co-opeartive Inc) 226 County Rd 287 Bldg A PO Box 250 Web: www.taylorelectric.com	Merkel	TX	79536	325-793-8500	793-1309	245
TEC (Thompson Electric Co) 2300 7th St Web: www.thompsonknows.com	Sioux City	IA	51105	712-252-4221		787
TEC (Thomas Engineering Co) 7024 Northland Dr Web: www.thomasengineering.com	Minneapolis	MN	55428	763-533-1501	533-8091	489
TEC (Telephone Electronics Corp) 700 W St TF: 800-832-2515 ■ Web: tec.com	Jackson	MS	39201	601-353-9118		387
TEC Corp 2300 7th St Web: www.tec-corp.com	Sioux City	IA	51105	712-252-4275		189-4
TEC Laboratories Inc 7100 Tec Labs Way SW TF: 800-482-4464 ■ Web: www.teclabsinc.com	Albany	OR	97321	541-926-4577		231
TEC Well Service Inc 851 W Harrison Rd	Longview	TX	75604	903-759-0082		539
Tec5USA Inc 80 Skyline Dr Web: www.tec5usa.com	Plainview	NY	11803	516-653-2000	939-0555	330
Tech 4 3547 French Rd Web: tech4.com	De Pere	WI	54115	920-532-0480		261
Tech Briefs Media Group 261 Fifth Ave Ste 1901 Web: www.techbriefs.com	New York	NY	10016	212-490-3999		457-19
Tech Credit Union 10951 Broadway TF: 800-276-8324 ■ Web: www.techcu.org	Crown Point	IN	46307	219-663-5120	662-4384	219
Tech Data Corp 5350 Tech Data Dr NASDAQ: TECD ■ TF: 800-237-8931 ■ Web: www.techdata.com	Clearwater	FL	33760	727-539-7429		174
Tech Electronics Inc 6437 Manchester Ave TF: 800-832-4789 ■ Web: www.techelectronics.com	Saint Louis	MO	63139	314-645-6200		177
Tech Friends inc PO Box 16480 *Fax Area Code: 815 ■ TF: 866-933-6386 ■ Web: mytechfriends.com	Jonesboro	AR	72403	870-933-6386	346-5903*	177
Tech Group Inc, The 14677 N 74th St Web: www.westpharma.com	Scottsdale	AZ	85260	480-281-4500		604
Tech Hackers LLC 332 Springfield Ave Web: www.thi.com	Summit	NJ	07901	908-598-1460		809
Tech Heads Inc 7070 SW Fir Loop Web: www.techheads.com	Portland	OR	97223	503-639-8542	639-2383	177
Tech Hero 200 E Robinson St Ste 425 TF: 800-900-8324 ■ Web: www.techhero.com	Orlando	FL	32801	800-900-8324	741-7518	180
Tech II Inc 1765 W County Line Rd Web: techii.com	Springfield	OH	45504	937-969-7000		604
Tech Image 330 N Wabash Ave Ste 1900 TF: 888-483-2477 ■ Web: www.techimage.com	Chicago	IL	60611	312-673-5444		636
Tech Lighting LLC 980-990 Richard Rd TF: 800-522-5315 ■ Web: www.techlighting.com	Skokie	IL	60077	847-410-4400	410-4500	439
Tech Museum of Innovation 201 S Market St Web: www.thetech.org	San Jose	CA	95113	408-294-8324	279-7167	520
Tech Networks of Boston 574 Dorchester Ave TF: 888-527-9333 ■ Web: techboston.com	Boston	MA	02127	617-269-0299		41
Tech Nh Inc 8 Continental Blvd Web: www.technh.com	Merrimack	NH	03054	603-424-4404	424-5820	608
Tech Observer 40 Eisenhower Dr Ste 201 Web: www.tech-observer.com	Paramus	NJ	07652	201-489-7705		177
Tech Packaging Inc 13241 Bartram Pk Blvd Ste 601 TF: 866-453-8324 ■ Web: www.techpackaging.net	Jacksonville	FL	32258	904-288-6403		549
Tech Pharmacy Services Inc 12503 Exchange Dr Ste 536 TF: 800-378-9020 ■ Web: www.advancedpharmacy.com	Stafford	TX	77477	800-378-9020		587
Tech Steel Inc Bldg D-2 Freeport Ctr Web: www.tech-steel.com	Clearfield	UT	84016	801-328-2543		480
Tech Superpowers Inc 1280 Massachusetts Ave Web: www.tsp.me	Cambridge	MA	02138	617-267-9716	249-1940	180
Tech Team Solutions LLC 106 S Loudoun St Web: www.techteamsolutions.com	Winchester	VA	22601	540-667-2000		175
Tech Transport Inc PO Box 431 TF: 800-641-5300 ■ Web: www.techtransport.com	Milford	NH	03055	800-641-5300		311
Tech Usa Inc 8334 Veterans Hwy TF: 888-584-8181 ■ Web: www.techusa.net	Millersville	MD	21108	410-729-4328	987-9080	194
Tech West Vacuum Inc 2625 N Argyle Ave TF: 800-428-7139 ■ Web: www.tech-west.com	Fresno	CA	93727	559-291-1650		475
Tech4Learning Inc 10981 San Diego Mission Rd Ste 120 TF: 877-834-5453 ■ Web: www.tech4learning.com	San Diego	CA	92108	619-563-5348		459
Tec-Hackett Inc 3418 Cavalier Dr Web: www.tec-hackett.com	Fort Wayne	IN	46808	260-471-7116		385
Techadox 258 Chapman Rd Ste 202 TF: 855-218-6800 ■ Web: techadox.com	Newark	DE	19702	855-218-6800		177
Techaspect Solutions Inc 5600 Mowry School Rd Ste 220 Web: www.tadigital.com	Newark	CA	94560	510-962-3200		809
Techblocks Inc 399 Applewood Crescent Ste 4 Web: tblocks.com	Vaughan	ON	L4K4J3	416-775-1919		196
Tech-Clarity Inc 2420 Martingale Rd Ste 100 Web: tech-clarity.com	Media	PA	19063	610-565-6302		631
Techdigital Corp 764 Southcross Dr W Ste 202 Web: techdigitalcorp.com	Burnsville	MN	55306	952-956-2043	400-5742	180
Teche Regional Medical Ctr 1125 Marguerite St	Morgan City	LA	70380	985-384-2200		374-3
Tech-Etch Inc 45 Aldrin Rd Web: www.tech-etch.com	Plymouth	MA	02360	508-747-0300	746-9639	488
TechFire 4185 Indian Head Hwy Web: www.techfirenetwork.com	Indian Head	MD	20640	301-645-6637		393
TechFlow Inc 9889 Willow Creek Rd Ste 100 Web: www.techflow.com	San Diego	CA	92131	858-412-8000		177
Techfusion 87 Blanchard Rd Web: www.techfusion.com	Cambridge	MA	02138	617-491-1001		180
Techgene Solutions LLC 300 E Royal Ln Ste 109 Web: www.techgene.com	Irving	TX	75039	972-580-0247	704-2937	177
TechLaw Inc 14500 Avion Pkwy Ste 300 Web: www.techlawinc.com	Chantilly	VA	20151	703-818-1000		192
Techletter.com 29839 Oak Rd Web: www.techletter.com	Mechanicsville	MD	20659	301-884-3020		637-10
Techlight 2707 Satsuma Dr TF: 800-225-0727 ■ Web: www.techlightusa.com	Dallas	TX	75229	214-350-0591	350-9137	439
Tech-Marine Business Inc (TMB) 100 M St SE Ste 800 Web: tmbhq.com	Washington	DC	20003	202-448-9701	448-9702	261
Techmation Inc 2121 S Mill Ave Ste 217 Web: www.protuner.com	Tempe	AZ	85282	480-968-9946		201
TechMD 3750 S Susan St TF: 888-883-2463 ■ Web: www.techmd.com	Santa Ana	CA	92704	888-883-2463		180
Techmer PM LLC 1 Quality Cir Web: www.techmerpm.com	Clinton	TN	37716	865-457-6700		608
Techmor Inc 19911-D N Cove Rd Web: www.techmor.com	Cornelius	NC	28031	704-769-0001		407
Technalysis Inc 7172 Waldemar Dr Web: www.technalysis.com	Indianapolis	IN	46268	317-291-1985		178-11
Techne Corp 614 McKinley Pl NE NASDAQ: TECH ■ TF: 800-343-7475 ■ Web: www.bio-techne.com	Minneapolis	MN	55413	612-379-8854		231
Techne Inc 3 Terri Ln Ste 10 Web: www.techneusa.com	Burlington	NJ	08016	609-589-2560		419
Techneal Inc 2100 S Reservoir St TF: 800-545-6325 ■ Web: www.techneal.com	Pomona	CA	91766	909-465-6325		535
TechNet 805 15th St NW Ste 708 Web: technet.org	Washington	DC	20005	202-650-5100		48-9
Technetics Group 3125 Damon Way TF: 800-618-4701 ■ Web: technetics.com	Burbank	CA	91505	818-841-9667	841-8057	608
TechNexus 20 N Wacker Dr Ste 1200 Web: technexus.com	Chicago	IL	60606	312-924-1026		401
Techni Core Professionals Inc 4681 Research Park Blvd Web: www.techni-core.com	Huntsville	AL	35806	256-704-0234		261
Techniart Inc 41 Bridge St Web: techniart.com	Collinsville	CT	06019	860-693-2003		195
Technibilt Ltd 700 E P St PO Box 310 *Fax Area Code: 800 ■ Web: technibilt.com	Newton	NC	28658	828-464-7388	968-8934*	73
Technic Inc 47 Molter St Web: www.technic.com	Cranston	RI	02910	401-781-6100	781-2890	145
Technica Corp 22970 Indian Creek Dr Ste 500 Web: technicacorp.com	Dulles	VA	20166	703-662-2000		180
Technical Association of the Pulp & Paper Industry (TAPPI) 15 Technology Pkwy S TF: 800-332-8686 ■ Web: www.tappi.org	Norcross	GA	30092	770-446-1400	446-6947	49-13
Technical Assurance Inc 38112 Second St TF: 866-953-3147 ■ Web: technicalassurance.com	Willoughby	OH	44094	440-953-3147		196
Technical Cable Concepts Inc 350 Lear Ave TF: 800-832-2225 ■ Web: www.techcable.com	Costa Mesa	CA	92626	714-835-1081		116
Technical Chemical Co 3327 Pipeline Rd TF: 800-527-0885 ■ Web: www.technicalchemical.com	Cleburne	TX	76033	817-645-6088	556-0694	145
Technical Coating International Inc 150 Backhoe Rd NE TF: 800-371-0861 ■ Web: www.tciinc.com	Leland	NC	28451	910-371-0860	371-0929	599
Technical College of the Lowcountry 921 Ribaut Rd Web: www.tcl.edu	Beaufort	SC	29902	843-525-8211		166
Technical Communications Corp 100 Domino Dr NASDAQ: TCCO ■ TF: 800-952-4082 ■ Web: tccsecure.com	Concord	MA	01742	978-287-5100	371-1280	735
Technical Communities Inc 1111 Bayhill Dr Ste 400 TF: 888-665-2765 ■ Web: www.technicalcommunities.com	San Bruno	CA	94066	650-624-0525	624-0535	195
Technical Consumer Products Inc 325 Campus Dr TF: 800-324-1496 ■ Web: www.tcpi.com	Aurora	OH	44202	330-995-6111		437
Technical Devices Co 560 Alaska Ave Web: www.technicaldev.com	Torrance	CA	90503	310-618-8437		811

Company	Phone	Fax	Class
Technical Die-Casting Inc 8910 W Main St, Stockton MN 55987 *TF:* 800-525-3168 ■ *Web:* www.tech-die-casting.com	800-525-3168		96
Technical Differences 5256 S Mission Rd Ste 210, Bonsall CA 92003 *Web:* www.people-trak.com	760-941-5800		177
Technical Empowerment Inc 898 N Pacific Coast Hwy, El Segundo CA 90245 *Web:* www.techempower.com	310-524-1700		177
Technical Field Engineering Inc 1114 Ridgecrest Ave, North Augusta SC 29841 *Web:* www.tfeinc.net	803-279-0331	279-1868	261
Technical Gas Products Inc 101 N Plains Industrial Rd 1b Ste 1, Wallingford CT 06473 *TF:* 800-847-0745 ■ *Web:* www.tgpoxygen.com	800-847-0745		579
Technical Glass Products Inc 881 Callendar Blvd, Painesville OH 44077 *Web:* www.technicalglass.com	440-639-6399	639-1292	292
Technical Heaters Inc 710 Jessie St, San Fernando CA 91340 **Fax Area Code:* 818 ■ *Web:* www.techheat.com	800-394-9435	361-2788*	370
Technical Intelligence Solutions LLC 13749 Sally Ride Way, Herndon VA 20171 *Web:* techintsolutions.com	571-375-8422		177
Technical Manufacturing Corp 15 Centennial Dr, Peabody MA 01960 *TF:* 800-542-9725 ■ *Web:* www.techmfg.com	978-532-6330	531-8682	153
Technical Marine Service Inc 6040 N Cutter Cir Ste 302, Portland OR 97217 *Web:* www.tms-usa.com	503-285-8947	285-1379	201
Technical Metals Inc 1301 W Oak St, Fairbury IL 61739 *Web:* www.technical-metals.com	815-692-4643	692-2085	488
Technical Packaging Services 276 Four Sisters Rd, South Burlington VT 05403 *Web:* www.technicalpackagingservice.com	802-355-4838		358
Technical Precision Inc 2343 Perry Hwy, Hadley PA 16130 *Web:* www.techprec.com	724-253-2800	253-2802	757
Technical Precision Plastics Inc 1405 Dogwood Way, Mebane NC 27302 *Web:* www.technicalprecisionplastics.com	919-563-9292		604
Technical Products Inc (TP) 805 Marathon Pky Ste 150, Lawrenceville GA 30046 *TF:* 800-226-8434 ■ *Web:* www.techproductsga.com	770-236-8452	236-8453	475
Technical Resource Group Inc 7225 Bryan Dairy Rd, Largo FL 33777 *Web:* technicalresourcegroup.com	727-533-9440		45
Technical Rubber Company Inc 200 E Coshocton St, Johnstown OH 43031 *TF:* 800-433-8324 ■ *Web:* www.tech-international.com	740-967-9015		604
Technical Support Inc 11253 John Galt Blvd, Omaha NE 68137 *Web:* techsi.com	402-331-4977	331-7710	177
Technical Systems Integration Inc 816 Greenbrier Cir Ste 208, Chesapeake VA 23320 *TF:* 800-566-8744 ■ *Web:* tecsysint.com	757-424-5793		256
Technical Toolboxes Ltd 3801 Kirby Dr Ste 520, Houston TX 77098 *TF:* 866-866-6766 ■ *Web:* www.ttoolboxes.com	713-630-0505		177
Technical Traffic Consultants Corp 30 Hemlock Dr, Congers NY 10920 *Web:* www.technicaltraffic.com	845-623-6144		311
Technical Training Inc (TTI) 6001 N Adams Ste 185, Bloomfield Hills MI 48304 *Web:* www.tti-global.com	248-853-5550	853-2411	113
Technical Transportation Inc 1701 W Northwest Hwy Ste 100, Grapevine TX 76051 **Fax Area Code:* 817 ■ *TF:* 800-852-8726 ■ *Web:* techtrans.com	800-852-8726	488-0306*	449
Techni-Car Inc 450 Commerce Blvd, Oldsmar FL 34677 *TF:* 800-886-0022 ■ *Web:* www.techni-car.com	813-855-0022	855-2101	62-5
Techni-Cast Corp 11220 Garfield Ave, South Gate CA 90280 *TF:* 800-923-4585 ■ *Web:* www.techni-cast.com	562-923-4585	861-4259	308
Technicolor Complete Post Inc 6040 Sunset Blvd, Hollywood CA 90028 *Web:* www.technicolor.com	323-817-6600		512
Technicon Acoustics Inc 4412 Republic Ct, Concord NC 28027 *Web:* www.techniconacoustics.com	704-788-1131		601
Technicon Engineering Services Inc 4539 N Brawley Ave Ste 108, Fresno CA 93722 *TF:* 800-676-9311 ■ *Web:* technicon.net	559-276-9311		642
Technicote Westfield Inc 222 Mound Ave, Miamisburg OH 45342 **Fax Area Code:* 937 ■ *TF:* 800-358-4448 ■ *Web:* www.technicote.com	800-358-4448	859-9096*	552-1
Technidrill Systems Inc 429 Portage Blvd, Kent OH 44240 *TF:* 844-313-7012 ■ *Web:* www.technidrillsystems.com	330-678-9980		455
Technifab Products Inc 10339 N Industrial Park Dr, Brazil IN 47834 *Web:* technifab.com	812-442-0520		697
Technifax Office Solutions 3220 Keller Springs Rd Ste 118, Carrollton TX 75006 *Web:* www.technifaxdfw.com	972-478-2800		366
Techniform Industries Inc 2107 Hayes Ave, Fremont OH 43420 *TF:* 800-691-2816 ■ *Web:* www.techniform-plastics.com	419-332-8484	334-5222	599
Technigraph Corp 850 W 3rd St, Winona MN 55987 *TF:* 800-421-4772 ■ *Web:* technigraph.com	507-454-3830	454-6470	687
Technimark Inc 180 Commerce Pl, Asheboro NC 27203 *Web:* www.technimark.com	336-498-4171	498-5042	548
Technipaq Inc 975 Lutter Dr, Crystal Lake IL 60014 *Web:* www.technipaq.com	815-477-1800	477-0777	548
Techniprint Co 2545 N Seventh St, Phoenix AZ 85006 *Web:* www.techniprintaz.com	602-257-0686		781
Techni-Pro Institute 414 NW 35th St, Boca Raton FL 33431 *TF:* 844-757-6805 ■ *Web:* www.techniproedu.com	561-395-1444		167-3
TechniScan Inc 3216 S Highland Dr Ste 200, Salt Lake City UT 84106 *Web:* www.techniscanmedicalsystems.com	212-918-0415		250
Techniserv Inc 351 S Eaton St, Berwick PA 18603 *Web:* www.techniservinc.com	570-759-2315	759-2785	454
Technisonic Research Inc 328 Commerce Dr, Fairfield CT 06825 *Web:* www.technisonicinc.com	203-368-3600	368-1922	472
Techni-Tool Inc 1547 N Trooper Rd PO Box 1117, Worcester PA 19490 **Fax Area Code:* 610 ■ *TF:* 800-832-4866 ■ *Web:* www.techni-tool.com	800-832-4866	828-5623*	351
Technitool Inc 1028 Industrial Dr, West Berlin NJ 08091 *Web:* www.technitool.com	856-768-2707	768-2807	604
Techno - Graphics & Translations Inc 1451 E 168th St, South Holland IL 60473 *Web:* www.wetrans4u.com	708-331-3333	331-0003	637-10
Techno Source USA Inc 20 W 22nd St Ste 1101, New York NY 10010	212-929-5200		195
Techno-Aide Inc 7117 Centennial Blvd, Nashville TN 37209 *TF:* 800-251-2629 ■ *Web:* techno-aide.com	615-350-7030	350-7879	476
Techno-Coat Inc 861 E 40th St, Holland MI 49423 *Web:* technocoat.com	616-396-6446		481
Technoconseil Tc 1177 Blvd Charest Ouest Bureau 100, Quebec City QC G1N2C9 *Web:* www.technoconseil.com	418-687-9991		180
Technogym USA Corp 700 US Hwy 46 E, Fairfield NJ 07004 **Fax Area Code:* 206 ■ *TF:* 800-804-0952 ■ *Web:* www.technogym.com	800-804-0952	623-1898*	710
Technolab International Corp 2020 NE 163 St, Miami FL 33162 *TF:* 888-382-2851 ■ *Web:* www.technolabcorp.com	305-433-2973		196
Technologies/Typography 8 Church St, Merrimac MA 01860 *Web:* www.tekntype.com	978-346-4867	346-7120	781
Technology & Business Integrators 29 Wildwood Rd, Saddle River NJ 07458 *Web:* www.tbicentral.com	201-573-0400		194
Technology Advancement Group Inc 22355 Tag Way, Sterling VA 20166 *Web:* www.tag.com	703-406-3000	406-0305	173-2
Technology Assessment and Transfer Inc 133 Defense Hwy Ste 212, Annapolis MD 21401 *Web:* www.techassess.com	410-224-3710	224-4678	668
Technology Associates Inc 3434 Kildaire Farm Rd Ste 390, Cary NC 27518 *Web:* www.technologyassociates.net	919-459-0100	367-7708	180
Technology Business Group 4 Chilmark Rd, Franklin MA 02038 *Web:* www.tbgne.com	508-520-0903	528-1964	180
Technology Commercialization Group LLC 1009 Slater Rd Ste 450, Durham NC 27703 *Web:* tcgmedtech.com	919-941-0700		194
Technology Container Corp 207 Greenwood St, Worcester MA 01607 *Web:* techcontainer.com	508-752-8000		100
Technology Crossover Ventures 528 Ramona St, Palo Alto CA 94301 *Web:* www.tcv.com	650-614-8200		792
Technology Dynamics Inc 100 School St, Bergenfield NJ 07621 *Web:* www.technologydynamicsinc.com	201-385-0500	385-0702	253
Technology for Energy Corp 10737 Lexington Dr, Knoxville TN 37932 *Web:* www.tec-usa.com	865-966-5856	675-1241	256
Technology Futures Inc (TFI) 13740 Research Blvd (N Hwy 183) Ste C-1, Austin TX 78750 *TF:* 800-835-3887 ■ *Web:* www.tfi.com	512-258-8898	258-0087	196
Technology Integration Group (TIG) 7810 Trade St, San Diego CA 92121 **Fax Area Code:* 858 ■ *TF:* 800-858-0549 ■ *Web:* www.tig.com	800-858-0549	566-8794*	176
Technology Marketing Corp 1 Technology Plz, Norwalk CT 06854 *TF:* 800-243-6002 ■ *Web:* www.tmcnet.com	203-852-6800	866-3326	637-2
Technology Partners 550 University Ave, Palo Alto CA 94301 *Web:* www.technologypartners.com	650-289-9000		792
Technology Service Corp 251 18th St S Ste 705, Arlington VA 22202 **Fax Area Code:* 301 ■ *TF:* 800-324-7700 ■ *Web:* tsc.com	256-705-2222	565-0673*	668
Technology Site Planners Inc 8188 Business Way, Plain City OH 43064 *Web:* www.techsiteplan.com	614-873-7800		186
Technology Solutions Provider Inc (TSPI) 11490 Commerce Park Dr Ste 200, Reston VA 20191 **Fax Area Code:* 703 ■ *TF:* 877-455-8774 ■ *Web:* tspi.net	877-455-8774	880-7022*	196
Technology Ventures Inc 25200 Malvina, Warren MI 48089 *Web:* www.tvihq.com	586-573-6000	573-6001	311
Technomart RGA Inc 401 Washington Ave Ste 1101, Baltimore MD 21204 *TF:* 800-877-6555 ■ *Web:* www.technomartrga.com	410-828-6555		401
Technomedia Solutions LLC 7703 Kingspointe Pkwy Ste 700, Orlando FL 32811 *Web:* gotechnomedia.com	407-351-0909		196
Technomic Inc 300 S Riverside Plz Ste 1600, Chicago IL 60606 *Web:* www.technomic.com	312-876-0004		194
Technomics Inc 201 12th St S Ste 612, Arlington VA 22202 *Web:* www.technomics.net	571-366-1400		41
TechnoPlanet Productions Inc 7030 Woodbine Ave 5th Fl, Markham ON L3R6G2 *Web:* technoplanet.com	905-839-0603		195
TechnoServe 1120 19th St NW 8th Fl, Washington DC 20036 *TF:* 800-999-6757 ■ *Web:* www.technoserve.org	202-785-4515	785-4544	48-5
Technosoft Corp 28411 NW Hwy Ste 640, Southfield MI 48034 *TF:* 855-527-3966 ■ *Web:* www.technosoftcorp.com	248-603-2600	603-2599	177
Technosoft Engineering Inc 200 S Executive Dr Ste 101, Brookfield WI 53005 **Fax Area Code:* 262 ■ *Web:* www.technosofteng.com	919-337-0866	317-8101*	385
Technosphere 155 N Washington Ave, Bergenfield NJ 07621 *Web:* www.technosphere.com	201-384-7400		463

Name / Address	Phone	Fax	Class
Technossus LLC 17885 Von Karman Ave Ste 210 . . . . . Irvine CA 92614 *Web:* www.technossus.com	949-769-3500		196
Technotraining Inc 328 Office Sq Ln Ste 202 . . . . . Virginia Beach VA 23462 *Web:* www.technotraining.net	757-425-0728		177
Technova Group Inc 6804 W 107th St Ste 102 . . . . . Overland Park KS 66212 *Web:* www.technova.com	913-338-2121	548-4834	178-1
Technox Machine & Manufacturing Inc 2619 N Normandy Ave . . . . . Chicago IL 60707 *TF:* 888-896-9571 ■ *Web:* www.technoxmachine.com	773-745-6800	745-8502	455
Techone 4695 Chabot Dr Ste 200 . . . . . Pleasanton CA 94588 *Web:* www.techone.com	408-894-8100	894-8101	177
Techorbit Inc 1300 W Walnut Hill Ln Ste 260 . . . . . Irving TX 75038 **Fax Area Code:* 214 ■ *Web:* www.techorbit.com	972-518-2200	276-1379*	196
Techpeople Inc 11305 Four Points Dr Bldg 1 Ste 300 . . . . . Austin TX 78746	512-493-1400		179
TechPlace 74 Orion St . . . . . Brunswick ME 04011 *Web:* techplacemaine.us	207-607-4195		393
Tech-Pro Inc 3000 Centre Pointe Dr . . . . . Roseville MN 55113 *Web:* www.tech-pro.com	651-634-1400		180
TechProse Inc 3100 Oak Rd Ste 205 . . . . . Walnut Creek CA 94597 *Web:* www.techprose.com	925-956-4200		809
Techrecruiters Inc *Engauge Workforce* 801 N Barstow St . . . . . Waukesha WI 53186 *Web:* engaugeworkforce.com	262-894-6325		177
TechSearch International Inc 4801 Spicewood Springs Rd Ste 150 . . . . . Austin TX 78759 *Web:* www.techsearchinc.com	512-372-8887	372-8889	195
TechServe Alliance 1420 King St Ste 610 . . . . . Alexandria VA 22314 *Web:* www.techservealliance.org	703-838-2050	838-3610	48-9
TechSherpas Inc 5404 Cypress Center Dr Ste 125 . . . . . Tampa FL 33609 *Web:* www.techsherpas.com	813-287-8876		507
Techsico Enterprise Solutions Inc 910 S Hudson Ave . . . . . Tulsa OK 74112 *Web:* www.techsico.com	918-585-2347		194
Techsmart Solutions Inc 328 Air Park Dr Ste 200 . . . . . Fort Collins CO 80524 *Web:* onlinepchelp.com	970-498-0808		225
TechSmith Corp 2405 Woodlake Dr . . . . . Okemos MI 48864 *TF:* 800-517-3001 ■ *Web:* www.techsmith.com	517-381-2300		178-8
Techspeed Inc 280 SW Moonridge Pl . . . . . Portland OR 97225 *TF:* 800-750-4066 ■ *Web:* www.techspeed.com	503-291-0027		180
Techsperience LLC 766 Walker Ave . . . . . Oakland CA 94610 *Web:* techsperience.org	510-663-3360		177
TechStar 802 W 13th St . . . . . Deer Park TX 77536 *TF:* 866-542-0205 ■ *Web:* techstar.com	866-542-0205		791
TechTarget 275 Grove St . . . . . Newton MA 02466 *TF:* 888-274-4111 ■ *Web:* www.techtarget.com	617-431-9200	431-9201	637-10
Techtonic Group LLC 1715 38th St . . . . . Boulder CO 80301 *TF:* 866-382-8280 ■ *Web:* www.techtonic.com	303-223-3468		809
TechTrans International Inc 2200 Space Pk Ste 410 . . . . . Houston TX 77058 *Web:* www.tti-corp.com	281-335-8000		317
Tech-Trek Ltd 1015 Matheson Blvd E Unit 6 . . . . . Mississauga ON L4W3A4 *Web:* www.tech-trek.com	905-238-0366		195
Techville Computer 9451 Lyndon B Johnson Fwy Ste 112 . . . . . Dallas TX 75243 *Web:* techville.com	214-739-7033		173-7
Techware Distribution Inc 7720 W 78th St . . . . . Minneapolis MN 55439 *TF:* 800-295-0083 ■ *Web:* www.techwaredist.com	800-295-0083		49-16
Techwave Consulting Inc 1 E Uwchlan Ave . . . . . Exton PA 19341 *Web:* techwave.net	484-872-8707	872-8716	196
Tech-Way Industries Inc 301 Industrial Dr . . . . . Franklin OH 45005 *Web:* www.tech-wayindustries.com	937-746-1004		596
TechWorks 4030 W Braker Ln . . . . . Austin TX 78759 *Web:* afternic.com	512-794-8533		625
Tech-X Corp 5621 Arapahoe Ave Ste A . . . . . Boulder CO 80303 *Web:* www.txcorp.com	303-448-0727	448-7756	177
TechXpress Inc 3474 Empresa Dr Ste 140 . . . . . San Luis Obispo CA 93401 *Web:* techxpress.net	805-541-4400		317
Techxtend 4 Industrial Way W 3rd Fl . . . . . Eatontown NJ 07724 **Fax Area Code:* 732 ■ *TF:* 800-441-1511 ■ *Web:* www.techxtend.com	800-441-1511	389-0010*	174
Tecinfo Communication LLC 601 N Deer Creek Dr E . . . . . Leland MS 38756 *TF:* 800-863-5415 ■ *Web:* tecinfo.net	662-686-9009		175
Teck Resources Ltd 501 N Riverpoint Blvd Ste 300 . . . . . Spokane WA 99202 *TF:* 866-225-0198 ■ *Web:* www.teck.com	800-432-3206		502
Teckmeyer Financial Services LLC 11104 John Galt Blvd . . . . . Omaha NE 68137 *Web:* teckmeyerfinancial.com	402-331-8600		690
Teclab 6450 Vly Industrial Dr . . . . . Kalamazoo MI 49009 *Web:* www.teclab.com	269-372-6000		420
TECMA Group LLC, The 2000 Wyoming Ave . . . . . El Paso TX 79903 *Web:* www.tecma.com	915-534-4252		393
TecMed Inc 109 E 17th St Ste 5175 . . . . . Cheyenne WY 82001 *Web:* www.tecmed.com	307-509-9653		743
Tecmotiv (USA) Inc 1500 James Ave . . . . . Niagara Falls NY 14305 *Web:* www.tecmotiv.com	716-282-1211		454
Tecnau Inc 4 Suburban Park Dr . . . . . Billerica MA 01821 *Web:* www.tecnau.com	978-608-0500	608-0558	556
Tecnet Canada Inc 3403 Seymour Pl . . . . . Victoria BC V8X1W4 *Web:* tecnet.ca	250-475-6066		175
Tecnetics Industries Inc 1201 N Birch Lake Blvd . . . . . Saint Paul MN 55110 *TF:* 800-536-4880 ■ *Web:* www.tecweigh.com	651-777-4780	777-5582	207
Tecnica USA 19 Technology Dr . . . . . West Lebanon NH 03784 *Web:* www.tecnicasports.com	603-298-8032		710
Tecnicard Inc 3191 Coral Way Ste 800 . . . . . Miami FL 33145 *TF:* 800-317-6020 ■ *Web:* www.tecnicard.com	305-442-0018	442-9937	225
Tecnico Corp 831 Industrial Ave . . . . . Chesapeake VA 23324 *TF:* 800-786-2207 ■ *Web:* www.tecnicocorp.com	757-545-4013		698
TECO Diagnostics 1268 N Lakeview Ave . . . . . Anaheim CA 92807 *TF:* 800-222-9880 ■ *Web:* www.tecodiagnostics.com	714-463-1111	463-1169	231
TECO Energy Inc 702 N Franklin St . . . . . Tampa FL 33602 *NYSE: TE* ■ *TF:* 888-223-0800 ■ *Web:* www.tecoenergy.com	813-228-1111		185
Tecolote Research Inc 420 S Fairview Ave Ste 201 . . . . . Goleta CA 93117 *Web:* www.tecolote.com	805-571-6366	571-6377	463
Tecon Services Inc 515 Garden Oaks Blvd . . . . . Houston TX 77018 *TF:* 800-245-1728 ■ *Web:* www.teconservices.com	713-691-2700		188
TECO-Westinghouse Motor Co 5100 N IH-35 . . . . . Round Rock TX 78681 *TF:* 800-451-8798 ■ *Web:* www.tecowestinghouse.com	512-255-4141	244-5512	709
Tecplot Inc 3535 Factoria Blvd SE Ste 550 . . . . . Bellevue WA 98006 *TF:* 800-763-7005 ■ *Web:* www.tecplot.com	425-653-1200		177
Tecport Optics Inc (TOI) 6457 Hazeltine National Dr . . . . . Orlando FL 32822 *Web:* www.tecportoptics.com	407-855-1212	855-1213	542
Tecsec Inc 12950 Worldgate Dr Ste 100 . . . . . Herndon VA 20170 *Web:* tecsec.com	571-299-4100		178-12
TecServ Inc 358 S Rio Grande St Ste 250 . . . . . Salt Lake City UT 84101 *Web:* www.tecservinc.com	801-485-6055		180
Tecstar Manufacturing Co W190 N11701 Moldmakers Way . . . . . Germantown WI 53022 *Web:* www.mgstech.com	262-255-5790	255-7206	608
TECSys Development Inc 1600 Tenth St . . . . . Plano TX 75074 *TF:* 800-695-1258 ■ *Web:* www.tditechnologies.com	972-881-1553		180
TECSYS Inc 1 Place Alexis Nihon Ste 800 . . . . . Montreal QC H3Z3B8 *TF:* 800-922-8649 ■ *Web:* www.tecsys.com	514-866-0001	866-1805	178-1
TECT (Turbine Engine Components Technologies Corp) 334 Beechwood Rd Ste 303 . . . . . Fort Mitchell KY 41017 *Web:* tectpower.com	859-426-0090		483
Tecta America Co 15002 Wicks Blvd . . . . . San Leandro CA 94577 *Web:* www.tectaamerica.com	510-686-4951		189-12
Tectonic Engineering & Surveying Consultants PC 70 Pleasant Hill Rd . . . . . Mountainville NY 10953 *TF:* 800-829-6531 ■ *Web:* www.tectonicengineering.com	800-829-6531		261
Tectonics Design Group 730 Sandhill Rd Ste 250 . . . . . Reno NV 89521 *Web:* tectonicsdesigngroup.com	775-824-9988		261
Tectonics Industries Inc 24680 Mound Rd . . . . . Warren MI 48091 *Web:* tectonics.com	586-755-6522		627
Tectron Engineering Co 5820 Commonwealth Ave . . . . . Jacksonville FL 32254 *Web:* www.tectron.net	904-394-0683		392
Tectum Inc 105 S Sixth St . . . . . Newark OH 43055 *TF:* 888-977-9691 ■ *Web:* www.tectum.com	740-345-9691		819
Tecumseh Poultry LLC 13151 Dovers . . . . . Waverly NE 68462 *Web:* www.cafetecumseh.com	402-786-1000		619
Tecumseh Products Company LLC 5683 Hines Dr . . . . . Ann Arbor MI 48108 *Web:* www.tecumseh.com	734-585-9500	352-3700	14
Ted Gruber Software Inc PO Box 13408 . . . . . Las Vegas NV 89112 *Web:* www.fastgraph.com	702-735-1980	735-4603	178-1
Ted Hosmer Enterprises Inc 1249 Lehigh Station Rd . . . . . Henrietta NY 14467 *Web:* tedhosmer.com	585-334-3620		776
Ted Pella Inc 4595 Mountain Lakes Blvd . . . . . Redding CA 96003 *Web:* www.tedpella.com	530-243-2200		544
Ted Peter's Famous Smoked Fish 1350 Pasadena Ave S . . . . . Saint Petersburg FL 33707 *Web:* tedpetersfish.com	727-381-7931		671
Ted Stevens Anchorage International Airport 3132 Channel Dr . . . . . Juneau AK 99811 *Web:* www.dot.state.ak.us	907-266-2629		27
Ted Wiens Tire & Auto Centers 1701 Las Vegas Blvd S . . . . . Las Vegas NV 89104 *Web:* www.tedwiens.com	702-735-5656		755
Ted's Bar & Grill 6197 Allentown Blvd . . . . . Harrisburg PA 17112 *Web:* www.tedsbarandgrill.com	717-652-3832		671
Ted's Cafe Escondido 2836 NW 68th St . . . . . Oklahoma City OK 73116 *Web:* www.tedscafe.com	405-848-8337		671
Ted's Hot Dogs 301 Ohio St Ste 200 . . . . . Buffalo NY 14204 *Web:* www.tedshotdogs.com	716-691-3731		670
Tedco Construction Corp Tedco Pl . . . . . Carnegie PA 15106 *Web:* tedco.com	412-276-8080	276-6804	186
Teddy's Transportation System Inc 25 Van Zant St . . . . . Norwalk CT 06855 *Web:* teddyslimo.com	203-866-2231		441
TEdec System Inc 207 Court St . . . . . Little Valley NY 14755 *TF:* 800-345-2154 ■ *Web:* www.tedec.com	716-938-9137	938-6155	178-1
Tedia Company Inc 1000 Tedia Way . . . . . Fairfield OH 45014 *TF:* 800-787-4891 ■ *Web:* www.tedia.com	513-874-5340	874-5346	144
Tedone & Morton PC 58 N Chicago St Ste 405 . . . . . Joliet IL 60432 *Web:* tedonemortonlaw.com	815-666-1285		41
Teds Inc 235 Mtn Empire Rd . . . . . Atkins VA 24311 *Web:* teds.com	276-783-6991	783-8574	180
Tee Group Films 605 N Main St PO Box 425 . . . . . Ladd IL 61329 *Web:* www.tee-group.com	815-894-2331	894-3387	600
Tee Jaye's Country Place Restaurants 1363 Parsons Ave PO Box 6646 . . . . . Columbus OH 43206 *Web:* teejayes.com	614-443-9773	443-0613	670
Tee Lee Popcorn Inc 101 W Badger St . . . . . Shannon IL 61078 *TF:* 800-578-2363 ■ *Web:* www.teeleepopcorn.com	815-864-2363	864-2388	296-37
Teeco Products Inc 16881 Armstrong Ave . . . . . Irvine CA 92606 *TF:* 800-854-3463 ■ *Web:* teecoproducts.com	949-261-6295	474-8663	385

Phone | Fax | Class

TEECOM 1333 Broadway Ste 601 .... Oakland CA 94612 510-337-2800 261
Web: teecom.com
Teeda Wholesale
1107 Fair Oaks Ave Ste 75 .... South Pasadena CA 91030 626-282-3522 411
TF: 877-622-3522 ■ *Web:* www.teeda.com
Teel Plastics Inc 1060 Teel Ct .... Baraboo WI 53913 608-355-3080 355-3088 596
Web: www.teel.com
Teeter Irrigation Inc 2729 W Oklahoma .... Ulysses KS 67880 620-353-1111 274
TF: 800-524-5497 ■ *Web:* www.teeterirrigation.com
TEGAM Inc 10 Tegam Way .... Geneva OH 44041 440-466-6100 466-6110 248
TF: 800-666-1010 ■ *Web:* www.tegam.com
TEGNA Inc 8350 Broad St Ste 2000 .... Tysons VA 22102 703-873-6600 6
Web: www.tegna.com
Tegra Medical LLC 9 Forge Pk .... Franklin MA 02038 508-541-4200 475
Web: www.tegramedical.com
Tehama County
633 Washington St Rm 11 .... Red Bluff CA 96080 530-527-3350 527-1745 338
Web: www.co.tehama.ca.us
Tehama County Library
645 Madison St .... Red Bluff CA 96080 530-527-0604 527-1562 434-3
Web: www.tehamacountylibrary.org
TEI (Taylor Enterprises Inc)
2586 Southport Rd .... Spartanburg SC 29302 864-573-9518 583-4150 579
TF: 800-922-3149 ■ *Web:* taylorlubricants.com
TEI (Tax Executives Institute)
1200 G St NW Ste 300 .... Washington DC 20005 202-638-5601 638-5607 49-1
Web: www.tei.org
TEI (Twin Express Inc)
12424 Ironwood Cir Ste 102 .... Rogers MN 55374 763-428-4969 428-4979 780
TF: 800-729-8946 ■ *Web:* www.twinexpress.com
Tei Tei Robata Bar 2906 N Henderson St .... Dallas TX 75206 214-828-2400 671
Web: www.teiteirobata.com
Teijin Holdings USA
600 Lexington Ave 27th Fl .... New York NY 10022 212-308-8744 308-8902 360-3
Web: www.teijin.com
Teikoku Pharma USA Inc
1718 Ringwood Ave .... San Jose CA 95131 408-501-1800 501-1900 231
Web: teikokuusa.com
Teikoku USA Inc 5880 Bingle Rd .... Houston TX 77092 713-983-9901 983-9919 385
Web: www.chempump.com
Teine Energy Ltd
2300 520 - Third Ave SW .... Calgary AB T2P0R3 403-698-8300 536
Web: www.teine-energy.com
Teixeira Farms Inc
2600 Bonita Lateral Rd .... Santa Maria CA 93458 805-928-3801 928-9405 10-11
Web: www.teixeirafarms.com
Tejas Logistics System PO Box 1339 .... Waco TX 76703 254-753-0301 752-4452 803-1
TF: 800-535-9786 ■ *Web:* www.tejaswarehouse.com
Tejas Research & Engineering LP
9185 Six Pines Dr .... The Woodlands TX 77380 281-466-8700 261
Web: www.tejasre.com
Tejon Ranch Co 4436 Lebec Rd PO Box 1000 .... Lebec CA 93243 661-248-3000 248-6209 10-1
NYSE: TRC ■ *Web:* tejonranch.com
Tekbank Consultants Inc
459 Herndon Pkwy Ste 13 .... Herndon VA 20170 703-348-3325 180
Web: tekbank.net
Tekgard Inc 3390 Farmtrail Rd .... York PA 17406 717-854-0005 14
Web: www.tekgard.com
Tekgroup International Inc
1280 SW 36th Ave Ste 204 .... Pompano Beach FL 33069 954-351-5554 351-9099 809
Web: www.tekgroup.com
Tekla Capital Management LLC
100 Federal St 19th Fl .... Boston MA 02110 617-772-8500 772-8577 401
Web: www.teklacap.com
Tekla Inc
1075 Big Shanty Rd NW Ste 175 .... Kennesaw GA 30144 770-426-5105 174
TF: 877-835-5265 ■ *Web:* www.tekla.com
Tekmar Control Systems Ltd
5100 Silver Star Rd .... Vernon BC V1B3K4 250-545-7749 545-0650 610
Web: www.tekmarcontrols.com
Tekmark Global Solutions LLC
100 Metroplex Dr Ste 102 .... Edison NJ 08817 732-572-5400 180
Web: www.tekmark.com
Tekmasters LLC
4437 Brookfield Corporate Dr Ste 201A .... Chantilly VA 20151 703-349-1110 880-7530 463
TF: 855-856-7877 ■ *Web:* www.tekmasters.com
Teknicote Inc 10 New Rd Ste 400 .... Rumford RI 02916 401-724-2230 724-3024 481
Web: www.teknicote.com
Teknion Corp 1150 Flint Rd .... Toronto ON M3J2J5 416-661-3370 661-4586 319-1
TF: 877-661-1577 ■ *Web:* www.teknion.com
Tekno Inc 1 Wall St .... Cave City KY 42127 270-773-4181 207
Web: www.tekno.com
Teknon Corp 10675 Willows Rd .... Redmond WA 98052 425-895-8535 895-0535 189-4
Web: www.teknon.com
Teknor Apex Co 505 Central Ave .... Pawtucket RI 02861 401-725-8000 725-8095 605-3
TF: 800-556-3864 ■ *Web:* www.teknorapex.com
TeKONTROL Inc 711 W Amelia St .... Orlando FL 32805 407-398-6575 398-6580 180
Web: www.tekontrol.com
TEKPAK Inc 1410 Washington St .... Marion AL 36756 334-683-6121 125
Web: www.tekpakinc.com
TekPartners
5810 Coral Ridge Dr Ste 250 .... Coral Springs FL 33076 954-656-8600 282-6070 631
Web: www.tekpartners.com
Tekra Corp 16700 W Lincoln Ave .... New Berlin WI 53151 800-448-3572 797-3276* 603
**Fax Area Code:* 262 ■ *TF:* 800-448-3572 ■ *Web:* www.tekra.com
Tekram USA 14228 Albers Way .... Chino CA 91710 909-606-1111 597-3713 625
Web: www.tekram.com
Tekran Instruments Corp
230 Tech Center Dr .... Knoxville TN 37912 865-688-0688 419
TF: 888-383-5726 ■ *Web:* www.tekran.com
Teksavers Inc 2120 Grand Ave Pkwy .... Austin TX 78728 866-832-6188 180
TF: 866-832-6188 ■ *Web:* www.teksavers.com
TekScape inc 131 W 35th St 5th Fl .... New York NY 10001 855-835-7227 196
TF: 855-835-7227 ■ *Web:* tekscapeit.com
Teksouth Corp
1420 Northbrook Dr Ste 220 .... Gardendale AL 35071 205-631-1500 631-1514 175
TF: 800-842-1470 ■ *Web:* www.teksouth.com

Phone | Fax | Class

Tekstrom Inc 1301 Milltown Rd .... Wilmington DE 19808 302-709-5900 709-5901 396
Web: www.tekstrom.com
TEKsystems Inc 7437 Race Rd .... Hanover MD 21076 410-540-7700 721
TF: 888-519-0776 ■ *Web:* www.teksystems.com
Tektronix Component Solutions Inc
2905 SW Hocken Ave .... Beaverton OR 97005 800-833-9200 393
TF: 800-833-9200 ■ *Web:* www.tek.com
Tek-Vac Industries Inc
176 Express Dr S .... Brentwood NY 11717 631-436-5100 436-5154 695
Web: www.tekvac.com
Tekworks Inc 13000 Gregg St Ste B .... Poway CA 92064 858-668-1705 176
TF: 877-835-9675 ■ *Web:* www.tekworks.com
Tel Edge 2616 Mesilla St NE Ste 3 .... Albuquerque NM 87110 505-292-9477 7
Web: wrightedge.com
Tel Electronics Inc
313 South 740 East Ste 1 .... American Fork UT 84003 800-748-5022 756-9135* 735
**Fax Area Code:* 801 ■ *TF:* 800-748-5022 ■ *Web:* www.tel-electronics.com
Tel Star Cablevison Inc
1295 Lourdes Rd .... Metamora IL 61548 888-842-0258 383-2657* 116
**Fax Area Code:* 309 ■ *TF:* 888-842-0258 ■ *Web:* mytelstar.com
Tel Systems 7235 Jackson Rd .... Ann Arbor MI 48103 734-761-4506 761-9776 246
TF: 800-686-7235 ■ *Web:* www.thalner.com
Tel Tec Security Systems Inc
5020 Lisa Marie Ct .... Bakersfield CA 93313 661-397-5511 196
TF: 800-292-9227 ■ *Web:* www.tel-tec.com
Tel Tech Networks Inc
810 E Hammond Ln .... Phoenix AZ 85034 602-431-9399 431-9780 116
Web: www.teltechnetworks.com
Tel Tech Plus Inc
393 Enterprise St .... San Marcos CA 92078 760-510-1323 261
Web: www.ttp-us.com
Tela Innovations Inc
475 Alberto Way Ste 120 .... Los Gatos CA 95032 408-558-6300 696
Web: www.tela-inc.com
TELACU 5400 E Olympic Blvd 3rd Fl .... Los Angeles CA 90022 323-721-1655 724-3372 653
Web: telacu.com
Tel-Adjust Inc
29000 Inkster Rd Ste 115 .... Southfield MI 48034 248-208-1600 208-0805 194
Web: teladjust.com
Telaffects LLC 300 Primera Blvd .... Lake Mary FL 32746 407-936-3130 463
TF: 877-835-2339 ■ *Web:* www.telaffects.com
Tel-affinity Corp 66 Oak Knoll Terr .... Needham MA 02492 781-433-0451 463
Web: www.tel-affinity.com
Telaid 13 W Main St .... Niantic CT 06357 860-739-4461 189-4
TF: 800-205-5556 ■ *Web:* www.telaid.com
TelAlaska Inc 201 E 56th St .... Anchorage AK 99518 907-563-2003 736
TF: 888-570-1792 ■ *Web:* www.telalaska.com
Telamon Corp 1000 E 116th St .... Carmel IN 46032 317-818-6888 387
Web: www.telamon.com
Telamon Engineering Consultant
855 Folsom St .... San Francisco CA 94107 415-837-1336 261
Web: www.telamoninc.com
Telco Systems Inc 15 Berkshire Rd .... Mansfield MA 02048 781-255-2120 255-2122 735
TF: 800-227-0937 ■ *Web:* www.telco.com
Telco Triad Community Credit Union
1420 Tri View Ave .... Sioux City IA 51103 712-252-4368 219
Web: telcotriad.org
Telcobuy com L L C
60 Weldon Pkwy .... Maryland Heights MO 63043 877-350-0191 246
TF: 877-350-0191 ■ *Web:* www.telcobuy.com
Telcoe Federal Credit Union
820 Lousiana St .... Little Rock AR 72201 501-375-5321 375-6233 219
TF: 800-482-9009 ■ *Web:* www.telcoe.com
Telcom Corp
1499 W Palmetto Park Rd Ste 214 .... Boca Raton FL 33486 561-394-5448 750-1503 463
TF: 800-394-5448 ■ *Web:* telcomcorp.com
Telcomm Credit Union
2155 E Sunshine St .... Springfield MO 65804 417-886-5355 219
Web: telcommcu.com
Telcon LLC 1677 Miller Pky .... Streetsboro OH 44241 330-562-5566 562-8452* 454
**Fax Area Code:* 216 ■ *Web:* www.telcon.us
TELCOR Inc 7101 A St .... Lincoln NE 68510 402-489-1207 196
Web: telcor.com
Teldat Corp 1901 S Bascom Ave .... Campbell CA 95008 408-892-9363 173-3
Web: www.teldat.com
Teldata Enterprise Networks
11491 Woodside Ave .... Santee CA 92071 619-387-2200 244-0932* 194
**Fax Area Code:* 888 ■ *TF:* 800-900-7547 ■ *Web:* teldata.com
Tele Atlas North America Inc
11 Lafayette St .... Lebanon NH 03766 844-394-2020 387
TF: 844-394-2020 ■ *Web:* www.tomtom.com
Tele Business USA
1945 Techny Rd Ste 3 .... Northbrook IL 60062 877-315-8353 480-6055* 737
**Fax Area Code:* 847 ■ *TF:* 877-315-8353 ■ *Web:* www.tbiz.com
Tele Tech Services
500 Oakbrook Ln .... Summerville SC 29485 843-873-9200 396
Web: www.kfrservices.com
Tel-e Technologies 7 Kodiak Crescent .... Toronto ON M3J3E5 416-631-1300 176
TF: 800-661-2340 ■ *Web:* www.tel-e-technologies.com
Telebeep Wireless Inc 2404 Taylor Ave .... Norfolk NE 68701 800-846-2337 225
TF: 800-846-2337 ■ *Web:* www.telebeep.com
TeleBrands Corp 1 Telebrands Plz .... Fairfield NJ 07004 973-227-8777 361
Web: www.telebrands.com
TeleBright Software Corp
1700 Research Blvd Ste 102 .... Rockville MD 20850 301-296-3800 809
Web: telebright.com
Telebroad LLC 452 Broadway .... Brooklyn NY 11211 212-444-9911 224
Web: www.telebroad.com
Telebyte Communications Inc
6816 50 Ave .... Red Deer AB T4N4E3 403-346-9966 224
TF: 800-565-1849 ■ *Web:* www.telebyte.ca
Telebyte Inc 355 Marcus Blvd .... Hauppauge NY 11788 631-423-3232 385-8184 176
TF: 800-835-3298 ■ *Web:* www.telebyteusa.com
Telecentral Electronics Inc
1100 Schooley Ave .... Exeter PA 18643 570-655-2880 246
Web: telcen.com
Teleco 5221 Oleander Dr .... Wilmington NC 28403 910-791-7000 791-7801 224
TF: 800-326-4166 ■ *Web:* teleco-ilm.com

Company	City	State	Zip	Phone	Fax	Class
Teleco Inc 430 Woodruff Rd Ste 300 Web: www.teleco.com	Greenville	SC	29607	864-297-4400		246
Telecom Asset Management LLC 1736 Dolores St Web: www.telecomassets.com	San Francisco	CA	94110	415-923-5800	923-5285	463
Telecom Brokerage Inc (TBI) 8770 W Bryn Mawr Ave Ste 400 Web: www.tbicom.com	Chicago	IL	60631	847-465-4500	465-1488	224
Telecom Management Inc 39 Darling Ave Web: www.pioneertelephone.com	South Portland	ME	04106	207-774-9500		736
Telecom Resources International Inc 10632 N Scottsdale Rd Ste 486 Web: tri-1.com	Scottsdale	AZ	85254	480-391-3800		463
Telecom Solutions 5420 Newport Rd Ste 60 Web: www.rizzo-inc.com	Rolling Meadows	IL	60008	847-788-9300		681
TelecomCareers.Net LLC 2424 Edenborn Ave Ste 120 TF: 888-215-2537 ■ Web: www.nicheboards.com	Metairie	LA	70001	888-215-2537		631
Telecommunication Support Services Inc TSS Solutions 720 N Dr Web: www.tsssolutions.com	Melbourne	FL	32934	321-242-0000		116
Telecommunications Industry Assn (TIA) 1320 N Courthouse Rd Ste 200 Web: www.tiaonline.org	Arlington	VA	22201	703-907-7700	907-7727	49-20
Telecon Inc 7 450 Rue du Mile-End TF: 800-465-0349 ■ Web: www.telecon.com	Montreal	QC	H2R2Z6	514-644-2333		186
Teleconvergence 9335 SW Buckskin Ter Web: www.teleconvergence.com	Beaverton	OR	97008	503-750-2144		194
Teledata Communications Inc 1377 Motor Pky Ste 400 *Fax Area Code: 631 ■ TF: 800-841-9950 ■ Web: www.tcicredit.com	Islandia	NY	11749	800-841-9950	404-4299*	225
TeleDevelopment Services Inc 149 Kensington Crt TF: 888-788-4441 ■ Web: www.tdsgs.com	Broadview Heights	OH	44147	888-788-4441		737
Teledyne Advanced Pollution Instrumentation 9480 Carroll Pk Dr TF: 800-324-5190 ■ Web: www.teledyne-api.com	San Diego	CA	92121	858-657-9800	657-9816	201
Teledyne Benthos Inc 49 Edgerton Dr Web: www.teledynemarine.com	North Falmouth	MA	02556	508-563-1000	563-6444	529
Teledyne Brown Engineering Inc 300 Sparkman Dr TF: 800-933-2091 ■ Web: tbe.com	Huntsville	AL	35805	256-726-1000	726-1385	261
Teledyne CARIS 115 Waggoners Ln Web: www.teledynecaris.com	Fredericton	NB	E3B2L4	506-458-8533		387
Teledyne Controls 1365 Corporate Ctr Curv Web: www.teledynecontrols.com	Eagan	MN	55121	651-994-1000		196
Teledyne DALSA Inc 888 E Arques Ave Web: www.teledynedalsa.com	Sunnyvale	CA	94085	408-736-6000		696
Teledyne Electronic Safety Products 19735 Dearborn St Web: www.teledynesafetyproducts.com	Chatsworth	CA	91311	818-718-6640	998-3312	253
Teledyne Electronics & Communications 1049 Camino Dos Rios Web: www.teledyne.com	Thousand Oaks	CA	91360	805-373-4545		696
Teledyne Instruments Inc 16830 Chestnut St Web: www.teledyne-ai.com	City of Industry	CA	91748	626-934-1500		419
Teledyne Leeman Labs Inc 110 Lowell Rd Web: www.teledyneleemanlabs.com	Hudson	NH	03051	603-886-8400		419
Teledyne Monitor Labs Inc (TML) 35 Inverness Dr E TF: 800-422-1499 ■ Web: www.teledyne-ml.com	Englewood	CO	80112	303-792-3300	799-4853	201
Teledyne Odom Hydrographic Systems Inc 1450 Seaboard Ave Web: www.teledynemarine.com	Baton Rouge	LA	70810	225-769-3051		529
Teledyne RD Instruments Inc 14020 Stowe Dr Web: www.teledynemarine.com	Poway	CA	92064	858-842-2600		529
Teledyne Reynolds Inc 5005 McConnell Ave Web: www.teledynedefenseelectronics.com	Los Angeles	CA	90066	310-823-5491	822-8046	268
Teledyne Tekmar Company Inc 4736 Socialville Foster Rd TF: 800-874-2004 ■ Web: www.teledynetekmar.com	Mason	OH	45040	513-229-7000		419
Tele-Express Business Systems Inc 230 Goddard TF: 800-880-7466 ■ Web: telxpress.com	Irvine	CA	92618	949-861-4500	861-4501	366
Teleflex Inc 550 E Swedesford Rd Ste 400 NYSE: TFX ■ Web: www.teleflex.com	Wayne	PA	19087	610-225-6800		185
Teleflex Medical OEM 50 Plantation Dr TF: 800-548-6600 ■ Web: www.teleflexmedicaloem.com	Jaffrey	NH	03452	603-532-7706	532-6108	476
TeleflexGFI Control Systems LP 100 Hollinger Crescent Web: gficontrolsystems.com	Kitchener	ON	N2K2Z3	519-576-4270	576-7045	60
Teleflora Inc 11444 Olympic Blvd TF: 800-493-5610 ■ Web: www.teleflora.com	Los Angeles	CA	90064	310-231-9199		294
Telefonica USA 1111 Brickell Ave 10th Fl Web: www.us.telefonica.com	Miami	FL	33131	305-925-5300	925-5239	736
Telegartner Inc 411 Dominic Ct Web: www.telegaertner.com	Franklin Park	IL	60131	630-616-7600	616-8322	815
TeleGeography 1 Thomas Cir NW Ste 360 Web: www.telegeography.com	Washington	DC	20005	202-741-0020	741-0021	637-11
Telegram.com 100 Front St 5th Fl TF: 800-678-6680 ■ Web: www.telegram.com	Worcester	MA	01608	508-793-9100	793-9313	637-8
Telegraph 113 S Peoria Ave TF: 800-798-4085 ■ Web: www.saukvalley.com	Dixon	IL	61021	815-284-2224	284-2078	532-2
Telegraph Herald 801 Bluff St TF: 800-553-4801 ■ Web: www.telegraphherald.com	Dubuque	IA	52001	563-588-5611	588-5745	532-2
Telegraph, The PO Box 278 Web: www.thetelegraph.com	Alton	IL	62002	618-463-2500		532-2
Telegraph, The 1675 Montpelier Ave TF: 800-679-6397 ■ Web: www.macon.com	Macon	GA	31201	478-744-4200	744-4385	532-2

Company	City	State	Zip	Phone	Fax	Class
Telegraph, The 110 Main St Ste 1 Web: www.nashuatelegraph.com	Nashua	NH	03061	603-882-2741		532-2
Telegraph-Journal 210 Crown St PO Box 2350 TF: 888-295-8665 ■ Web: www.telegraphjournal.com	Saint John	NB	E2L2X7	888-295-8665		532-1
TeleGuam Holdings LLC 624 N Marine Corps Dr Web: www.gta.net	Tamuning	GU	96913	671-644-4482		387
Telehouse The Teleport 7 Teleport Dr TF: 844-518-0026 ■ Web: www.telehouse.com	Staten Island	NY	10311	718-355-2500		225
Telelatino Network Inc (TLN) 5125 Steeles Ave W TF: 800-551-8401 ■ Web: www.tln.ca	Toronto	ON	M9L1R5	416-744-8200	744-0966	740
TeleLink Communications Business Phone Systems 7101 Governors Cir TF: 800-877-3074 ■ Web: www.sacramentotelephonesystems.com	Sacramento	CA	95823	916-424-5454	395-2009	189-4
Telemark Diversified Graphics 411 Mckee St TF: 800-289-8353 ■ Web: www.telemarkcorp.com	Sturgis	MI	49091	269-651-7876	651-4336	787
Telematic Controls Inc 3364 114 Ave SE Web: www.telematic.com	Calgary	AB	T2Z3V6	403-253-7939		317
Tele-Measurements Inc 145 Main Ave Web: www.telemeasurements.com	Clifton	NJ	07014	973-473-8822		194
Telemedia Inc 750 W Lake Cook Rd Ste 250 TF: 800-837-8872 ■ Web: www.tpctraining.com	Buffalo Grove	IL	60089	847-808-4000		765
Tele-Media Solutions 105 E Railroad St TF: 877-967-3171 ■ Web: www.telemedia.coop	Pekin	IN	47165	812-967-3171		224
Telemessage Inc 468 Great Rd Ste 2 Web: www.telemessage.com	Acton	MA	01720	978-263-1015		177
Telemetrics Inc 75 Commerce Dr Web: www.telemetricsinc.com	Allendale	NJ	07401	201-848-9818		647
Telemetry and Process Controls Inc 7250 Hudson Blvd N Web: www.tpcusa.com	Oakdale	MN	55128	651-430-0435	430-0783	203
Telemobile Inc 19840 Hamilton Ave Web: www.telemobile.com	Torrance	CA	90502	310-538-5100	532-8526	735
Telemundo 51 15000 SW 27th St Web: www.telemundo51.com	Miramar	FL	33027	954-622-7710		741
Telemus Capital Partners LLC 2 Towne Sq Ste 800 Web: telemus.com	Southfield	MI	48076	248-827-1800	827-1808	401
Telenav Inc 950 De Guigne Dr Web: www.telenav.com	Sunnyvale	CA	94085	408-245-3800		177
Telenet Communications Inc 16 Shenandoah Ave Web: www.telenetny.com	Staten Island	NY	10314	718-370-3900	761-6507	180
Telenet Marketing Solutions 1915 New Jimmy Daniel Rd TF: 877-282-2345 ■ Web: www.telenetmarketing.com	Athens	GA	30606	706-353-1940		317
Telenet Voip Inc 850 N Park View Dr Web: telenetvoip.com	El Segundo	CA	90245	310-253-9000		239
Telenity Inc 755 Main St Bldg 7 Web: www.telenity.com	Monroe	CT	06468	203-445-2000	268-0711	178-7
Telenix Corp 9194 Red Branch Rd Web: telenix.co	Columbia	MD	21045	410-772-3275		177
Teleos Leadership Inst LLC 7837 Old York Rd Web: www.teleosleaders.com	Elkins Park	PA	19027	267-620-9999		765
Telepath Corp 49111 Milmont Dr TF: 800-292-1700 ■ Web: www.telepathcorp.com	Fremont	CA	94538	510-656-5600		647
Teleperformance USA 1991 South 4650 West Web: www.teleperformance.com	Salt Lake City	UT	84104	801-257-5800		737
Telephone & Data Systems Inc 30 N La Salle St Ste 4000 NYSE: TDS ■ TF: 877-337-1575 ■ Web: www.tdsinc.com	Chicago	IL	60602	312-630-1900	630-9299	360-3
Telephone Associates Inc (TA) 823 Belknap St Ste 201 TF: 800-777-7248 ■ Web: www.telephoneassociates.com	Superior	WI	54880	715-392-8101	394-8648	246
Telephone Doctor Inc 30 Hollenberg Ct TF: 800-882-9911 ■ Web: www.telephonedoctor.com	Bridgeton	MO	63044	314-291-1012		196
Telephone Electronics Corp (TEC) 700 W St TF: 800-832-2515 ■ Web: tec.com	Jackson	MS	39201	601-353-9118		387
Telephone Service Co 2 Willipie St Web: www.telserco.com	Wapakoneta	OH	45895	419-739-2200	739-2299	736
Telephone Systems International Inc (TSI) 4400 Marsh Landing Blvd Ste 3 Web: tsiglobe.com	Ponte Vedra Beach	FL	32082	904-686-1470		736
Telephone Tools of Georgia Inc PO Box 1240 TF: 877-521-8163 ■ Web: www.telephonetools.com	Cartersville	GA	30120	770-386-3239	387-4187	758
Telephone Warehouse Inc 20827 N Cave Creed Rd Ste 105 Web: telephonewarehouse.com	Phoenix	AZ	85024	602-254-5515	253-6811	246
Telephonics Corp 815 Broad Hollow Rd Web: www.telephonics.com	Farmingdale	NY	11735	631-755-7000	755-7200	647
Telepictures Production Inc 3500 W Olive St Ste 1000 Web: telepicturestv.com	Burbank	CA	91505	818-972-8992		116
Telepress Global 19241 62nd Ave S TF: 800-234-4466 ■ Web: telepress.website	Kent	WA	98032	800-234-4466		627
TeleProviders Inc 23461 S Pointe Dr Ste 185 TF: 888-999-4244 ■ Web: teleproviders.com	Laguna Hills	CA	92653	888-999-4244		463
Tele-Quebec 1000 Rue Fullum TF: 800-361-4301 ■ Web: www.telequebec.tv	Montreal	QC	H2K3L7	514-521-2424	873-2601	647
Telerent Leasing Corp 4191 Fayetteville Rd TF: 800-626-0682 ■ Web: www.telerent.com	Raleigh	NC	27603	919-772-8604		38
Telerhythmics LLC 60 Market Center Dr TF: 888-333-1003 ■ Web: telerhythmics.com	Collierville	TN	38017	888-333-1003	888-8853	592

	Phone	Fax	Class
Telesat 1600 James Naismith Dr, Ottawa ON K1B5P4 *Web:* www.telesat.com	613-748-0123	748-8712	681
Telescope Casual Furniture Inc 82 Church St, Granville NY 12832 *Web:* www.telescopecasual.com	518-642-1100	642-2536	319-4
Telescope Inc 11835 W Olympic Blvd Ste 350, Los Angeles CA 90064 *Web:* telescope.tv	424-270-2900		195
TeleSearch Staffing Solutions 251 Rt 206, Flanders NJ 07836 *Web:* www.telesearch.com	973-927-7870	927-7880	631
TeleSecurity Sciences Inc 7391 Prairie Falcon Rd Ste 150-B, Las Vegas NV 89128 *Web:* www.telesecuritysciences.com	702-227-7327	227-7307	177
TELESIS Corp 8300 Greensboro Dr Ste 600, McLean VA 22102 *Web:* www.telesishq.com	240-241-5600		177
TeleSoft International Inc 4029 S Capital of TX Hwy Ste 220, Austin TX 78704 *Web:* www.telesoft-intl.com	512-373-4224		176
TeleSoft Partners 950 Tower Ln Ste 1600, Foster City CA 94404 *Web:* www.telesoftvc.com	650-358-2500	358-2501	792
TeleSoft Systems 335 Wesley St Ste 203, Nanaimo BC V9R2R7 *Web:* www.telesoftsystems.ca	250-760-0142		463
Telesolv Consulting 1210 Florida Ave NE, Washington DC 20002 *Web:* www.telesolvconsulting.com	202-844-6400	747-3105	196
Telesource Services LLC 1450 Highwood E, Pontiac MI 48340 *TF:* 800-525-4300 ■ *Web:* www.telesourcenet.com	248-335-3000		246
Telesouth Communications Inc 6311 Ridgewood Rd, Jackson MS 39211 *TF:* 888-808-8637 ■ *Web:* telesouth.com	601-957-1700	956-5228	643
Telesto Group LLC 1060 State Rd Ste 102, Princeton NJ 08540 *Web:* telestogroup.com	609-503-4201		225
Telesto Solutions Inc 3801 Automation Way Ste 201, Fort Collins CO 80525 *Web:* www.telesto-inc.com	970-484-7704	484-7789	256
Telestream Inc 848 Gold Flat Rd Ste 1, Nevada City CA 95959 *TF:* 877-681-2088 ■ *Web:* www.telestream.net	530-470-1300	470-1301	178-8
Telesys Voice and Data 6840 Blvd 26, Richland Hills TX 76180 *TF:* 800-588-4430 ■ *Web:* www.telesysonline.com	800-588-4430		681
Telesystem Ltd 460 McGill St 5th Fl, Montreal QC H2Y2H2 *Web:* telesystem.ca	514-397-9797	397-1569	360-3
TeleTech Holdings Inc 9197 S Peoria St, Englewood CO 80112 *NASDAQ: TTEC* ■ *TF:* 800-835-3832 ■ *Web:* www.ttec.com	303-397-8100		737
Tele-Tech Services (TTS) 500 Oakbrook Ln, Summerville SC 29485 *Web:* www.telecomdb.com	800-433-6181	537-8011	387
Teletronics International Inc 2 Choke Cherry Rd, Rockville MD 20850 *Web:* www.teletronics.com	301-309-8500	309-8851	173-3
Televan Sales Inc (TSI) 5451 Sylvia Ave, Dearborn Heights MI 48125 *TF:* 800-886-7151 ■ *Web:* www.televansales.com	313-292-7150	292-7153	385
Televerde Inc 4636 E University Dr Ste 150, Phoenix AZ 85034 *Web:* www.televerde.com	480-771-6700		195
Television Bureau of Advertising Inc (TVB) 120 Wall St 15th Fl, New York NY 10005 *Web:* www.tvb.org	212-486-1111	935-5631	49-18
Television Food Network 75 9th Ave, New York NY 10011 *Web:* Www.foodnetwork.com	212-989-6699		116
TeleVital Solutions Inc 1525 McCarthy Blvd Ste 1045, Milpitas CA 95035 *Web:* www.televital.com	408-441-6732		363
TeleVoice Inc 10497 Town & Country Way Ste 500, Houston TX 77024 *Web:* www.televoice.com	281-497-8000		177
Telewave Inc 660 Giguere Ct, San Jose CA 95133 *Web:* www.telewave.com	408-929-4400		647
Telex Communications Inc 12000 Portland Ave S, Burnsville MN 55337 **Fax Area Code: 952* ■ *TF:* 877-863-4169 ■ *Web:* www.telex.com	877-863-4166	884-0043*	52
Telfair County 91 Telfair Ave, McRae GA 31055 *Web:* www.georgia.gov	229-868-6489	868-7950	338
Telfair County School District 212 W Huckabee St PO Box 240, Mcrae GA 31055 *Web:* www.telfairschools.org	229-868-5661	868-5549	685
Telfair Museum of Art 121 Barnard St, Savannah GA 31401 *Web:* www.telfair.org	912-790-8800		520
Telfer Pavement Technologies LLC 211 Foster St, Martinez CA 94553 *Web:* telferpavements.com	925-228-1515	229-3955	780
Telgian Holdings Inc 10230 S 50th Pl Ste 100, Phoenix AZ 85044 *TF:* 877-835-4426 ■ *Web:* www.telgian.com	480-753-5444	753-5450	189-10
Telics 3440 Lakemont Blvd, Fort Mill SC 29708 *TF:* 800-424-1454 ■ *Web:* telics.com	800-424-1454		261
Teligent Inc 105 Lincoln Ave, Buena NJ 08310 *TF:* 800-656-0793 ■ *Web:* www.teligent.com	800-656-0793		736
Tel-Instrument Electronics Corp 1 Branca Rd, East Rutherford NJ 07073 *NYSE: TIK* ■ *Web:* www.telinstrument.com	201-933-1600		472
Telirite Technical Services Inc 2857 Lakeview Ct, Fremont CA 94538 *Web:* www.telirite.com	510-440-3888		175
Telkonet Inc 10200 W Innovation Dr Ste 300, Milwaukee WI 53226 *OTC: TKOI* ■ *TF:* 888-703-9398 ■ *Web:* www.telkonet.com	414-223-0473	258-8307	176
Tell Systems Inc 106 Bridge Ave, Bay Head NJ 08742 *Web:* www.tellsystems.com	732-899-0202		177
Tella Tool & Mfg 1015 N Ridge Ave, Lombard IL 60148 *Web:* www.tellatool.com	630-495-0545	495-3056	697
Tellabs Inc 1415 W Diehl Rd, Naperville IL 60563 *Web:* www.tellabs.com	630-798-8800	798-2000	735
Teller County 101 W Bennett Ave PO Box 1010, Cripple Creek CO 80813 *Web:* www.co.teller.co.us	719-689-2951	686-8030	338
Telliant Systems LLC 3180 N Point Pkwy Ste 108, Alpharetta GA 30005 *Web:* www.telliant.com	678-892-2800		177
Telligen 1776 W Lakes Pkwy, West Des Moines IA 50266 *TF:* 800-383-2856 ■ *Web:* www.telligen.com	515-223-2900	222-2407	196
Tellini's 504 S Gloster St, Tupelo MS 38801 *Web:* www.tellinis.com	662-620-9955		671
Tellurex Corp 1462 International Dr, Traverse City MI 49686 *TF:* 877-774-7468 ■ *Web:* www.tellurex.com	231-947-0110		696
Telluride Film Festival 800 Jones St, Berkeley CA 94710 *Web:* telluridefilmfestival.org	510-665-9494	665-9589	282
Tellus Institute 11 Arlington St, Boston MA 02116 *Web:* www.tellus.org	617-266-5400	266-8303	634
Tellus Operating Group LLC 602 Crescent Pl Ste 100, Ridgeland MS 39157 *Web:* www.tellusoperating.com	601-898-7444		536
Telmar Information Services Corp 711 3rd Ave 15th Fl, New York NY 10017 *Web:* www.telmar.com	212-725-3000	725-5428	178-1
Telmar Network Technology 901 Jupiter Rd, Plano TX 75074 *TF:* 800-262-7427 ■ *Web:* www.iqormarketplace.com	972-836-0400	836-0430	246
Telmark Packaging Corp 30 Freneau Ave, Matawan NJ 07747 *Web:* www.telmarkpkg.com	732-739-9100		557
Telnet Inc 7630 Standish Pl, Rockville MD 20855 *Web:* www.telnet-inc.com	301-840-7110		196
Telniasoft Inc 1802 Brightseat Rd Ste 101, Landover Hills MD 20785 *Web:* telniasoft.com	301-918-4011		2
Telog Instruments Inc 830 Canning Pkwy, Victor NY 14564 *Web:* www.telog.com	585-742-3000		153
Telogical Systems LLC 7900 Westpark Dr, McLean VA 22102 *Web:* www.telogicalsystems.com	703-734-7776		225
Telonic Berkeley Inc 1080 La Mirada Ct, Vista CA 92081 *Web:* www.telonicberkeley.com	760-744-8350	744-8360	253
Telonics Inc 932 E Impala Ave, Mesa AZ 85204 *Web:* www.telonics.com	480-892-4444	892-9139	647
Telops 100-2600 St-Jean-Baptiste Ave, Quebec City QC G2E6J5 *Web:* www.telops.com	418-864-7808	864-7843	542
Telos Corp 19886 Ashburn Rd, Ashburn VA 20147 *OTC: TLSRP* ■ *TF:* 800-444-9628 ■ *Web:* www.telos.com	703-724-3800		180
Telosa Software Inc 610 Cowper St, Palo Alto CA 94301 *TF:* 800-676-5831 ■ *Web:* www.telosa.com	800-676-5831		177
Telpar Inc 121 Broadway Ste 201, Dover NH 03820 **Fax Area Code: 866* ■ *TF:* 800-872-4886 ■ *Web:* www.telpar.com	603-750-7237	554-5868*	173-6
Telserv LLC 7 Progress Dr, Cromwell CT 06416 *Web:* www.mgsmfg.com	860-740-3600		179
Telsey Advisory Group LLC 535 Fifth Ave 12th Fl, New York NY 10017 *Web:* www.telseygroup.com	212-973-9700		401
Telsmith Inc 10910 N Industrial Dr, Mequon WI 53092 *TF:* 800-765-6601 ■ *Web:* www.telsmith.com	262-242-6600	242-5812	190
TelSpan Inc 101 W Washington St E Tower Ste 1200, Indianapolis IN 46204 *TF:* 800-800-1729 ■ *Web:* telspan.com	800-800-1729		387
Telstar Associates Inc 2108 Amy Ave, Boise ID 83706 *Web:* telstarinc.net	208-343-3894		809
TelTel Inc 2025 Gateway Pl, San Jose CA 95110 *Web:* www.teltel.com	408-970-3318		387
Telus 400 1201 W Pender St, Montreal QC H3B1S6 *TF:* 877-999-4669 ■ *Web:* www.telus.com	514-665-3050	665-3049	808
Telus 6 Rue Jules-A-Brillant, Rimouski QC G5L1W8 *Web:* www.telus.com	418-310-1212		224
TELUS Mobility 200 Consilium Pl Ste 1600, Scarborough ON M1H3J3 **Fax Area Code: 604* ■ *TF:* 800-308-5992 ■ *Web:* mobility.telus.com	800-308-5992	432-9681*	224
TELUS World of Science 11211 142nd St, Edmonton AB T5M4A1 *Web:* telusworldofscienceedmonton.ca	780-451-3344	455-5882	520
Telvista 1605 LBJ Fwy, Dallas TX 75234 *TF:* 800-563-9699 ■ *Web:* www.telvista.com	972-919-7800		393
Tembec Btlsr Inc 2112 Sylvan Ave, Toledo OH 43606 *Web:* www.btlresins.com	419-244-5856		3
Temco International Corp 11919 SW 130 St Ste 100, Miami FL 33186 *Web:* www.temcointl.com	305-234-7851		385
Temco Metal Products Co 10240 SE Mather Rd, Clackamas OR 97015 *TF:* 800-275-0574 ■ *Web:* www.temcousa.com	503-656-4789	656-7567	488
Temecula Creek Inn 44501 Rainbow Canyon Rd, Temecula CA 92592 **Fax Area Code: 951* ■ *TF:* 888-976-3404 ■ *Web:* temeculacreekinn.com	855-774-8535	676-8961*	669
Temecula Valley Chamber of Commerce (TVCC) 26790 Ynez Ct Ste A, Temecula CA 92591 *Web:* temecula.org	951-676-5090	694-0201	139
Temecula Valley Unified School District School Facilities Corp 31350 Rancho Vista Rd, Temecula CA 92592 *Web:* www.tvusd.k12.ca.us	951-676-2661		685
Temiskaming Shores City of 545 Lkshore Rd S, Haileybury ON P0J1K0 *Web:* www.temiskamingshores.ca	705-672-3707		434
Temo Sunrooms Inc 20400 Hall Rd, Clinton Township MI 48038 *TF:* 800-344-8366 ■ *Web:* www.temosunrooms.com	800-344-8366		105
TEMP-AIR Inc 3700 W Preserve Blvd, Burnsville MN 55337 *TF:* 800-836-7432 ■ *Web:* www.temp-cool.com	800-836-7432		23
Tempco Electric Heater Corp 607 N Central Ave, Wood Dale IL 60191 *TF:* 888-268-6396 ■ *Web:* www.tempco.com	630-350-2252	350-0232	318
Tempco Mfg 2475 Hwy 55, Saint Paul MN 55120 *Web:* www.tempcomfg.com	651-452-1441	452-1125	488

Name / Address	City	State	ZIP	Phone	Fax	Class
Tempco Products Co 301 E Tempco Ave *Web:* www.tempcoproducts.com	Robinson	IL	62454	618-544-3175	544-2244	234
Temp-Control Mechanical Corp (TCM) 4800 N Ch Ave *Web:* www.tcmcorp.com	Portland	OR	97217	503-285-9851		14
Tempe Chamber of Commerce 1232 E Broadway Rd *Web:* tempechamber.org	Tempe	AZ	85281	480-967-7891		139
Tempe City Hall 31 E Fifth St *Web:* www.tempe.gov	Tempe	AZ	85281	480-350-4311	350-8930	337
Tempe Elementary Schools 3205 S Rural Rd *Web:* www.tempeschools.org	Tempe	AZ	85282	480-730-7100		685
Tempe Historical Museum 809 E Southern Ave *Web:* www.tempe.gov	Tempe	AZ	85282	480-350-5100	350-5150	520
Tempe Tourism Office 222 S Mill Ave Ste 120 *TF:* 866-914-1052 ■ *Web:* www.tempetourism.com	Tempe	AZ	85281	480-894-8158	968-8004	206
Tempel Steel Co 5500 N Wolcott Ave *Web:* www.tempel.com	Chicago	IL	60640	773-250-8000	250-8910	723
Temperance River State Park 5702 Hwy 61 *Web:* www.dnr.state.mn.us	Silver Bay	MN	55614	218-663-3100		565
Temperature Equipment Corp 17725 Volbrecht Rd *Web:* www.tecmungo.com	Lansing	IL	60438	708-418-0900	418-5100	612
Temperature Systems Inc 5001 Voges Rd *TF:* 800-366-0930 ■ *Web:* www.tsihvac.com	Madison	WI	53718	608-271-7500	274-1609	612
Tempest Med 2 City Place Dr Ste 400 *TF:* 877-510-2192 ■ *Web:* www.tempestmed.com	Saint Louis	MO	63141	877-510-2192		238
Tempest Technologies LLC 38 S Last Chance Gulch St Ste 5a *Web:* tempesttech.com	Helena	MT	59601	406-495-8731	449-3104	177
Tempest Telecom Solutions LLC 136 W Canon Perdido Ste 100 *Web:* www.tempesttelecom.com	Santa Barbara	CA	93101	805-879-4800		246
Tempest Tours Inc PO Box 121004 *Web:* www.tempesttours.com	Arlington	TX	76012	817-274-9313		760
Temple Bottling Company Ltd 3510 Pkwy Dr *Web:* templebot.com	Temple	TX	76504	254-773-3376	778-5414	81-2
Temple Chamber of Commerce 201 Santa Fe Way Ste 105 *Web:* www.templechamber.com	Temple	TX	76501	254-773-2105	773-0661	139
Temple City Chamber of Commerce 9050 Las Tunas Dr *Web:* www.templecitychamber.org	Temple City	CA	91780	626-286-3101		139
Temple College 2600 S First St *TF:* 800-460-4636 ■ *Web:* www.templejc.edu	Temple	TX	76504	254-298-8300	298-8288	162
Temple Community Hospital 235 N Hoover St *Web:* www.templecommunityhospital.com	Los Angeles	CA	90004	213-382-7252		374-3
Temple Israel Library 2324 Emerson Ave S *Web:* www.templeisrael.com	Minneapolis	MN	55405	612-377-8680	377-6630	434-3
Temple Kol Ami Emanu-el Foundation Inc 8200 Peters Rd *Web:* tkae.org	Plantation	FL	33324	954-472-1988		305
Temple of Kriya Yoga 2414 N Kedzie Blvd *Web:* www.yogakriya.org	Chicago	IL	60647	773-342-4600		48-20
Temple Public Library 100 W Adams Ave *Web:* www.ci.temple.tx.us	Temple	TX	76501	254-298-5555		434-3
Temple Santa Fe Community Credit Union 1750 W Ave A *Web:* templecreditunion.com	Temple	TX	76504	254-778-7222		219
Temple Square Hospitality Corp 15 E S Temple St 9th Fl *Web:* www.templesquare.com	Salt Lake City	UT	84150	801-531-1000		670
Temple Systems Inc 6161 Webster St *Web:* www.templesystems.com	Dayton	OH	45414	937-609-9906		261
Temple University 1801 N Broad St *Web:* www.temple.edu	Philadelphia	PA	19122	215-204-7000	204-5694	166
Temple Veterinary Hospital Inc 2055 Scott Blvd *Web:* templevethospital.com	Temple	TX	76504	254-773-1411		794
Templegate Publishers LLC 302 E Adams *TF:* 800-367-4844 ■ *Web:* www.templegate.com	Springfield	IL	62705	217-522-3353		637-2
Temple-Inland Federal Credit Union 109 N Temple Dr *TF:* 877-829-1616 ■ *Web:* t-ifcu.com	Diboll	TX	75941	877-829-1616		219
Templeton & Company LLP 222 Lakeview Ave Ste 1200 *Web:* templetonco.com	West Palm Beach	FL	33401	561-798-9988	798-4053	2
Templeton Coal Co 701 Wabash Ave *Web:* templetoncoal.com	Terre Haute	IN	47807	812-232-7037		357
Templeton Foundation Press 300 Conshohocken State Rd Ste 550 *Web:* www.templetonpress.org	West Conshohocken	PA	19428	484-531-8380	531-8382	637-2
Templex Inc 3 Stanley Ave *Web:* www.templexinc.com	Thomasville	NC	27360	336-472-5933	472-5944	599
Tempo Bank 28 W Broadway *Web:* www.tempobank.com	Trenton	IL	62293	618-224-9228	224-7846	70
Tempo Plastic Co 1227 N Miller Park Ct *Web:* www.tempogloss.com	Visalia	CA	93291	559-651-7711	651-0123	601
Tempo Restaurant 4231 Duke St *Web:* www.temporestaurant.com	Alexandria	VA	22304	703-370-7900	370-7902	671
Temporary Solutions Inc 10550 Linden Lake Plz Ste 200 *TF:* 888-222-0457 ■ *Web:* www.eeihr.com	Manassas	VA	20109	703-361-2220		721
Temp-Pro Inc 200 Industrial Dr *Web:* www.temp-pro.com	Northampton	MA	01060	413-584-3165	586-3625	201
Tempra Technology Inc 6140 15th St E *Web:* tempratech.com	Bradenton	FL	34203	941-739-8900	753-6841	668
Tempress Technologies Inc 2200 Lind Ave SW Bldg A Ste 108 *Web:* tempresstech.com	Renton	WA	98057	425-251-8120		261
Temps Plus Inc 268 N Lincoln Ave Ste 12 *TF:* 888-288-0808 ■ *Web:* www.s3staffing.com	Corona	CA	92882	888-288-0808		260
Temptek Inc 525 E Stop 18 Rd *Web:* www.temptek.com	Greenwood	IN	46142	317-887-6352	881-1277	202
Temptime Corp 116 American Rd *Web:* temptimecorp.com	Morris Plains	NJ	07950	973-630-6000		201
Temptronic Corp 41 Hampden Rd *TF:* 800-558-5080 ■ *Web:* www.temptronic.com	Mansfield	MA	02048	781-688-2300		419
Tempur-Pedic North America LLC 1000 Tempur Way *TF:* 800-821-6621 ■ *Web:* www.tempurpedic.com	Lexington	KY	40511	800-821-6621		471
TempWorks Software Inc 3140 Neil Armstrong Blvd Ste 205 *TF:* 877-452-0326 ■ *Web:* www.tempworks.com	Eagan	MN	55121	651-452-0366		631
Temtex Temperature Systems Inc 19053 W US Hwy 82 *Web:* www.temtex.net	Sherman	TX	75092	903-813-1500		454
Ten Adams Corp 1112 SE First St *Web:* tenadams.com	Evansville	IN	47713	812-422-7440		7
Ten Broeck Mansion 9 Ten Broeck Pl *Web:* tenbroeckmansion.org	Albany	NY	12201	518-436-9826	436-1489	520
Ten Key Group LLC, The 470 Portage Lakes Dr Ste 102 *Web:* thetenkeygroup.com	Akron	OH	44319	234-334-1966		2
Ten Mercer 10 Mercer St *Web:* tenmercer.com	Seattle	WA	98109	206-691-3723		671
Ten Mile Creek State Fish & Wildlife Area 4283 St Hwy 14 *Web:* www.dnr.illinois.gov	McLeansboro	IL	62859	618-643-2862		565
Ten Penny Players Inc 393 St Pauls Ave *Web:* www.tenpennyplayers.org	Staten Island	NY	10304	718-442-7429	442-4978	637-2
Ten Pound Island Book Co 76 Langsford St *Web:* www.tenpound.com	Gloucester	MA	01930	978-283-5299		95
Ten Prime Steak & Sushi 55 Pine St *Web:* www.tenprimesteakandsushi.com	Providence	RI	02903	401-453-2333		671
Ten Talents Cookbook (TT) PO Box 5209 *Web:* www.tentalents.net	Grants Pass	OR	97526	541-472-1113	472-1116	637-2
Ten Thousand Waves Japanese Health Spa 21 Ten Thousand Waves Way *Web:* tenthousandwaves.com	Santa Fe	NM	87501	505-982-9304		707
Ten2Eleven Business Solutions LLC 2014 Capitol Ave Ste 203 *Web:* ten2eleven.com	Sacramento	CA	95811	916-469-4424		177
Ten-8 Fire Equipment Inc 2904 59th Ave Dr E *TF:* 877-989-7660 ■ *Web:* ten8fire.com	Bradenton	FL	34203	941-756-7779	756-2598	516
TENA Companies Inc 251 W Lafayette Frontage Rd *TF:* 800-255-8362 ■ *Web:* www.tenaco.com	Saint Paul	MN	55107	651-293-1234	293-4400	218
Tenable Network Security Inc 7021 Columbia Gateway Dr Ste 500 **Fax Area Code:* 443 ■ *Web:* www.tenable.com	Columbia	MD	21046	410-872-0555	545-2278*	177
Tenable Protective Services 2423 Payne Ave *Web:* www.tenable.net	Cleveland	OH	44114	216-361-0002	361-8690	693
Tenaj Salon Institute 11915 Country Road 103 *Web:* tenajsaloninstitute.edu	The Villages	FL	32162	352-753-5511		167-3
Tenant Base 225 Arizona Ave Ste 350 *Web:* www.tenantbase.com	Santa Monica	CA	90401	310-461-8049		264-2
Tenaris 6903 72 Ave Ste 400 *Web:* www.tenaris.com	Calgary	AB	T2P3S8	403-767-0100	767-0299	723
TenAsys Corp 1400 NW Compton Dr Ste 301 *TF:* 877-277-9189 ■ *Web:* www.tenasys.com	Hillsboro	OR	97006	503-748-4720	748-4730	179
Tenax Corp 4800 E Monument St *TF:* 800-356-8495 ■ *Web:* www.tenaxus.com	Baltimore	MD	21205	410-522-7000	522-3190	596
Tencarva Machinery Company Inc 12200 Wilfong Ct *TF:* 800-849-5764 ■ *Web:* www.tencarva.com	Midlothian	VA	23112	804-639-4646	639-2400	385
TenCate Advanced Armor US O'Neill Dr 1051 *Web:* www.tencate.com	Hebron	OH	43025	740-928-0326		504
TenCate Geosynthetics North America 365 S Holland Dr *TF:* 888-795-0808 ■ *Web:* www.tencate.com	Pendergrass	GA	30567	706-693-2226	693-4400	745-3
TenCate Grass America 1131 Broadway St *TF:* 800-251-1033 ■ *Web:* www.tencate.com	Dayton	TN	37321	423-775-0792		605-1
Tenderloin Room 232 N Kingshighway Blvd *Web:* tenderloinroom.com	Saint Louis	MO	63108	314-361-0900		671
Tendo Communications 340 Brannan St Ste 500 *Web:* tendocom.com	San Francisco	CA	94107	415-369-8200		387
Tendril 2580 55th St **Fax Area Code:* 714 ■ *Web:* www.tendrilinc.com	Boulder	CO	80301	720-921-2100	557-3058*	177
Teneff Jewelry Inc 421 W Riverside Ave Ste 280 *Web:* teneffjewelry.com	Spokane	WA	99201	509-747-1038		411
Tenenbaum Recycling Group LLC 4500 W Bethany Rd *Web:* www.trg.net	North Little Rock	AR	72117	501-945-0881	945-3865	492
Tenenbaum's Vacation Stores Inc 300 Market St *TF:* 800-545-7099 ■ *Web:* www.tenenbaums.com	Kingston	PA	18704	570-288-8747		771
Tenenz Inc 9655 Penn S Ave *TF:* 800-888-5803 ■ *Web:* www.tenenz.com	Minneapolis	MN	55431	800-888-5803		627

Name / Address	City	State	ZIP	Phone	Fax	Class
Tenera Environmental 971 Dewing Ave Ste 101 *Web:* www.tenera.com	LaFayette	CA	94549	925-962-9769		194
Tenere Inc 700 Kelly Ave *TF:* 866-836-3734 ■ *Web:* www.tenere.com	Dresser	WI	54009	715-294-1577		697
Tenet Healthcare Corp 1445 Ross Ave *NYSE:* THC ■ *TF:* 800-743-6333 ■ *Web:* www.tenethealth.com	Dallas	TX	75202	469-893-2000		353
Tenet Partners 122 W 27th St 9th Fl *Web:* tenetpartners.com	New York	NY	10001	212-329-3030	329-3031	195
Tengasco Inc 11121 Kingston Pk Ste E *NYSE:* TGC ■ *Web:* www.tengasco.com	Knoxville	TN	37934	865-675-1554		536
Tenibac-Graphion Inc 35155 Automation Dr *Web:* www.tenibac.com	Clinton Township	MI	48035	586-792-0150	792-0073	488
Tenino Telephone Co 225 Central Ave W *TF:* 800-654-9746 ■ *Web:* www.teninotelephone.com	Tenino	WA	98589	360-264-2915		224
Tenlinks 200 Professional Center Dr Ste 211 *Web:* www.tenlinks.com	Novato	CA	94947	415-897-8800		180
Tennant Co 701 N Lilac Dr *NYSE:* TNC ■ *TF:* 800-553-8033 ■ *Web:* www.tennantco.com	Minneapolis	MN	55422	763-540-1200	540-1437	386
Tenneco Inc 500 N Field Dr *NYSE:* TEN ■ *TF:* 866-839-3259 ■ *Web:* www.tenneco.com	Lake Forest	IL	60045	847-482-5000	482-5940	60
Tennessee State Government *Obion County* 1604B W Reelfoot Ave *TF:* 800-222-8754 ■ *Web:* www.tn.gov	Union City	TN	38261	731-884-2133	884-2719	338
Tennessee						
Aging & Disability Commission 500 Deaderick St 8th Fl *Web:* www.tn.gov	Nashville	TN	37243	615-532-6580	741-2056	339-43
Agriculture Dept 440 Hogan Rd PO Box 40627 *Web:* www.state.tn.us	Nashville	TN	37204	615-837-5103	837-5333	339-43
Arts Commission 401 Charlotte Ave *Web:* www.tn.gov	Nashville	TN	37243	615-741-1701		339-43
Attorney General PO Box 20207 *Web:* www.tn.gov	Nashville	TN	37202	615-741-3491	741-2009	339-43
Child Support Services Div 400 Deaderick St *TF:* 800-838-6911 ■ *Web:* www.tn.gov	Nashville	TN	37243	615-313-4880		339-43
Commerce & Insurance Dept 500 James Robertson Pkwy 5th Fl *Web:* www.state.tn.us	Nashville	TN	37243	615-741-6382		339-43
Consumer Affairs Div 500 James Robertson Pkwy *TF:* 800-342-8385 ■ *Web:* www.tn.gov	Nashville	TN	37243	615-741-4737	532-4994	339-43
Correction Dept 320 Sixth Ave N *Web:* www.state.tn.us	Nashville	TN	37243	615-741-1000		339-43
Department of Children's Services UBS Twr 315 Deaderick 10th Fl *Web:* www.tn.gov	Nashville	TN	37243	615-741-9701		339-43
Department of Human Resources 505 Deaderick St 1st Fl James K Polk Bldg *Web:* www.state.tn.us	Nashville	TN	37243	615-741-2958	741-7880	339-43
Div of Claims Administration 502 Deaderick St *Web:* treasury.tn.gov	Nashville	TN	37243	615-741-2734	532-4979	339-43
Economic & Community Development Dept (ECD) 312 Rosa L Parks Ave N 11th Fl *Web:* www.tn.gov	Nashville	TN	37243	615-253-3469		339-43
Education Dept 710 James Robertson Pkwy 6th Fl *Web:* www.state.tn.us	Nashville	TN	37243	615-741-5158		339-43
Emergency Management Agency 3041 Sidco Dr *Web:* www.tn.gov	Nashville	TN	37204	615-313-0633		339-43
Environment & Conservation Dept 312 Rosa L Parks Ave Tennessee Tower Second Fl *Web:* www.tn.gov	Nashville	TN	37243	615-532-0109		339-43
Finance & Administration Dept 312 Rosa L Parks Ave *Web:* www.tn.gov	Nashville	TN	37243	615-741-6488		339-43
General Assembly 320 Sixth Ave N 8th Fl *Web:* www.capitol.tn.gov	Nashville	TN	37243	615-741-2564		339-43
Health Dept 710 James Robertson Pkwy *Web:* www.tn.gov	Nashville	TN	37243	615-741-3111	253-5187	339-43
Higher Education Commission 404 James Robertson Pkwy Ste 1900 *Web:* www.state.tn.us	Nashville	TN	37243	615-741-3605		339-43
Highway Patrol 1150 Foster Ave *Web:* www.tn.gov	Nashville	TN	37243	615-251-5175	532-1051	339-43
Historical Commission 2941 Lebanon Rd *Web:* www.state.tn.us	Nashville	TN	37214	615-532-1550		339-43
Housing Development Agency 502 Deaderick St Andrew Jackson Bldg Third Fl *TF:* 800-228-8432 ■ *Web:* thda.org	Nashville	TN	37243	615-815-2200		339-43
Human Services Dept 400 Deaderick St *TF:* 866-311-4287 ■ *Web:* www.state.tn.us	Nashville	TN	37243	615-313-4700		339-43
Insurance Div 500 James Robertson Pkwy *TF:* 800-342-4029 ■ *Web:* www.tn.gov	Nashville	TN	37243	615-741-2241		339-43
Labor & Workforce Development Dept 220 French Landing Dr *TF:* 844-224-5818 ■ *Web:* www.state.tn.us	Nashville	TN	37243	844-224-5818		259
Lottery 1 Century Pl 26 Century Blvd Ste 200 PO Box 291869 *TF:* 800-826-4311 ■ *Web:* www.tnlottery.com	Nashville	TN	37214	615-324-6500		452
Mental Health & Developmental Disabilities Dept 500 Deaderick St *Web:* www.state.tn.us	Nashville	TN	37219	800-560-5767		339-43
Probation & Parole Board 404 James Robertson Pkwy Ste 1300 *Web:* www.tn.gov	Nashville	TN	37243	615-741-1150		339-43
Regulatory Authority 424 Church St Fifth Third Bldg	Nashville	TN	37243	615-741-2904		339-43
Rehabilitation Services Div 400 Deaderick St *Web:* www.tn.gov	Nashville	TN	37243	615-313-4891	741-4165	339-43
Revenue Dept 500 Deaderick St *Web:* www.state.tn.us	Nashville	TN	37219	615-253-0600		339-43
State Parks Div 312 Rosa L Parks Ave *Web:* tnstateparks.com	Nashville	TN	37243	615-475-8772		339-43
Student Assistance Corp 404 James Robertson Pkwy Ste 1510 *TF:* 800-342-1663 ■ *Web:* www.state.tn.us	Nashville	TN	37243	615-741-1346	741-6101	725
Supreme Court 511 Union St Nashville City Ctr Ste 600 *TF:* 800-448-7970 ■ *Web:* www.tsc.state.tn.us	Nashville	TN	37219	615-741-2687		339-43
Title & Registration Div 44 Vantage Way Ste 160 *Web:* www.tn.gov	Nashville	TN	37243	615-741-3101	253-4260	339-43
Transportation Dept 505 Deaderick St Ste 700 *Web:* www.tn.gov	Nashville	TN	37243	615-741-2848	741-2508	339-43
Treasury Dept 600 Charlotte Ave *Web:* www.treasury.state.tn.us	Nashville	TN	37243	615-741-2956		339-43
Veterans Affairs Dept 312 Rosa L Parks Ave *Web:* www.tn.gov	Nashville	TN	37243	615-253-2037		339-43
Vital Records Div Andrew Johnson Twr 710 James Robertson Pkwy 1st Fl *TF:* 855-809-0072 ■ *Web:* www.tn.gov	Nashville	TN	37243	615-741-1763		339-43
Workers Compensation Div 220 French Landing Dr *Web:* www.tn.gov	Nashville	TN	37243	615-741-6642		339-43
Tennessee Academy of Cosmetology 7053 Winchester Rd *Web:* www.tac.edu	Memphis	TN	38125	901-757-4166		167-3
Tennessee Agricultural Museum 440 Hogan Rd PO Box 40627 *Web:* tnagmuseum.org	Nashville	TN	37204	615-837-5197	837-5194	520
Tennessee Aquarium 1 Broad St *TF:* 800-262-0695 ■ *Web:* www.tnaqua.org	Chattanooga	TN	37402	800-262-0695		40
Tennessee Associated Electric 7511 Taggart Ln *Web:* www.tn-associated.com	Knoxville	TN	37938	865-524-3686	522-1553	189-4
Tennessee Association of Realtors (TAR) 901 19th Ave S *TF:* 877-321-1477 ■ *Web:* tnrealtors.com	Nashville	TN	37212	615-321-1477	321-4905	656
Tennessee Baptist Convention PO Box 682789 *TF:* 800-558-2090 ■ *Web:* www.tnbaptist.org	Franklin	TN	37068	615-373-2255	371-2014	48-20
Tennessee Bar Assn 221 Fourth Ave N Ste 400 *TF:* 800-899-6993 ■ *Web:* www.tba.org	Nashville	TN	37219	615-383-7421	297-8058	72
Tennessee Bible College 1616 McCulley Rd *Web:* www.tn-biblecollege.edu	Cookeville	TN	38506	931-526-2616		167-3
Tennessee Bun Co 197 Printwood Dr *Web:* www.bakerycos.com	Dickson	TN	37055	615-441-4600		296-1
Tennessee Chamber of Commerce & Industry 414 Union St Ste 107 *Web:* www.tnchamber.org	Nashville	TN	37219	615-256-5141		140
Tennessee Citizens for Wilderness Planning (TCWP) PO Box 6873 *Web:* www.tcwp.org	Oak Ridge	TN	37830	865-583-3967		48-13
Tennessee College of Applied Technology - Athens 1635 Vo Tech Dr PO Box 848 *Web:* www.tcatathens.edu	Athens	TN	37303	423-744-2814	744-2817	167-3
Tennessee College of Applied Technology - Covington 1600 Hwy 51 S *Web:* www.tcatcovington.edu	Covington	TN	38019	901-475-2526	475-2528	167-3
Tennessee College of Applied Technology - Crossville 910 Miller Ave *TF:* 877-811-7502 ■ *Web:* www.tcatcrossville.edu	Crossville	TN	38555	931-484-7502		167-3
Tennessee College of Applied Technology - Crump 3070 US Highway 64 PO Box 89 *Web:* www.tcatcrump.edu	Crump	TN	38327	731-632-3393	632-3018	167-3
Tennessee College of Applied Technology - Dickinson 740 Hwy 46 S *Web:* www.tcatdickson.edu	Dickson	TN	37055	615-441-6220	441-6223	167-3
Tennessee College of Applied Technology - Elizabethton 426 Hwy 91 N *TF:* 888-986-2368 ■ *Web:* www.tcatelizabethton.edu	Elizabethton	TN	37643	423-543-0070	547-2587	167-3
Tennessee College of Applied Technology - Harriman 1745 Harriman Hwy *TF:* 800-599-9426 ■ *Web:* www.tcatharriman.edu	Harriman	TN	37748	865-882-6703	882-5038	167-3
Tennessee College of Applied Technology - Hartsville 716 McMurry Blvd E *Web:* www.tcathartsville.edu	Hartsville	TN	37074	615-374-2147	374-2149	167-3
Tennessee College of Applied Technology - Hohenwald 813 W Main St *Web:* www.tcathohenwald.edu	Hohenwald	TN	38462	931-796-5351	796-5808	167-3
Tennessee College of Applied Technology - Jacksboro 265 Elkins Rd PO Box 419 *Web:* www.tcatjacksboro.edu	Jacksboro	TN	37757	423-566-9629	566-9713	167-3
Tennessee College of Applied Technology - Jackson 2468 Technology Center Dr *Web:* www.tcatjackson.edu	Jackson	TN	38301	731-424-0691	424-0807	167-3
Tennessee College of Applied Technology - Knoxville 1100 Liberty St *Web:* www.tcatknoxville.edu	Knoxville	TN	37919	865-546-5567	971-4474	167-3
Tennessee College of Applied Technology - Livingston 740 High Tech Dr *Web:* www.tcatlivingston.edu	Livingston	TN	38570	931-823-5525		167-3

Name / Address	City	State	ZIP	Phone	Fax	Class
Tennessee College of Applied Technology - McKenzie 16940 Highland Dr	McKenzie	TN	38201	731-352-5364	352-3258	167-3
Web: www.tcatmckenzie.edu						
Tennessee College of Applied Technology - Morristown 821 W Louise Ave	Morristown	TN	37813	423-586-5771		167-3
Web: www.tcatmorristown.edu						
Tennessee College of Applied Technology - Murfreesboro 1303 Old Fort Pky	Murfreesboro	TN	37129	615-898-8010	893-4194	167-3
Web: www.tcatmurfreesboro.edu						
Tennessee College of Applied Technology - Nashville 100 White Bridge Pke	Nashville	TN	37209	615-425-5500	425-5581	167-3
Web: www.tcatnashville.edu						
Tennessee College of Applied Technology - Newbern 340 Washington St	Newbern	TN	38059	731-627-2511	627-2310	167-3
Web: www.tcatnewbern.edu						
Tennessee College of Applied Technology - Paris W J Neese Campus 312 S Wilson St	Paris	TN	38242	731-644-7365	644-7368	167-3
Web: www.tcatparis.edu						
Tennessee College of Applied Technology - Pulaski 1233 E College St PO Box 614	Pulaski	TN	38478	931-424-4014	424-4017	167-3
Web: www.tcatpulaski.edu						
Tennessee College of Applied Technology - Shelbyville 1405 Madison St	Shelbyville	TN	37160	931-685-5013	685-5016	167-3
Web: www.tcatshelbyville.edu						
Tennessee College of Applied Technology Memphis 550 Alabama Ave	Memphis	TN	38105	901-543-6100	543-6197	167-3
Web: www.tcatmemphis.edu						
Tennessee Commerce Bank 381 Mallory Stn Rd Ste 207	Franklin	TN	37067	615-599-2274		70
Web: www.fdic.gov						
Tennessee Democratic Party 1900 Church St Ste 203	Nashville	TN	37203	615-327-9779		616-1
Web: www.tndp.org						
Tennessee Dental Assn (TDA) 660 Bakers Bridge Ave Ste 300	Franklin	TN	37067	615-628-0208		227
TF: 800-824-9722 ■ *Web:* www.tndentalassociation.com						
Tennessee Farmers Co-op 180 Old Nashville Hwy	La Vergne	TN	37086	615-793-8011		276
TF: 800-366-2667 ■ *Web:* www.ourcoop.com						
Tennessee Farmers Insurance Co PO Box 307	Columbia	TN	38402	931-388-7872		391-4
TF: 877-876-2222 ■ *Web:* www.fbitn.com						
Tennessee Fitness Spa 299 Natural Bridge Park Rd	Waynesboro	TN	38485	931-722-5589	722-9113	706
TF: 800-235-8365 ■ *Web:* www.tennesseefitnessspa.com						
Tennessee Florist Supply Inc 2713 John Deere Dr	Knoxville	TN	37917	865-524-7451	637-8155	293
TF: 800-951-7451 ■ *Web:* www.tnfloristsupply.com						
Tennessee Library Assn (TLA) PO Box 241074	Memphis	TN	38124	901-485-6952		435
Web: www.tnla.org						
Tennessee Nurses Assn (TNA) 545 Mainstream Dr Ste 405	Nashville	TN	37228	615-254-0350	254-0303	533
Web: tna.nursingnetwork.com						
Tennessee Performing Arts Ctr 505 Deaderick St FL 3	Nashville	TN	37243	615-782-4000	782-4001	572
Web: www.tpac.org						
Tennessee Pharmacists Assn 500 Church St Ste 650	Nashville	TN	37219	615-256-3023	255-3528	585
Web: www.tnpharm.org						
Tennessee Prison for Women 3881 Stewarts Ln	Nashville	TN	37243	615-741-1255		213
Web: www.tn.gov						
Tennessee Rand Inc 702 Moccasin Bend Rd	Chattanooga	TN	37405	423-664-7263	664-7264	393
TF: 855-867-2631 ■ *Web:* www.tennrand.com						
Tennessee Rehabilitative Initiative in Correction (TRICOR) 240 Great Cir Rd Ste 310	Nashville	TN	37228	615-741-5705	741-2747	630
TF: 800-958-7426 ■ *Web:* www.tricor.org						
Tennessee Republican Party 95 White Bridge Rd Ste 414	Nashville	TN	37212	615-269-4260		616-2
Web: www.tngop.org						
Tennessee Sports Hall of Fame Museum 501 Broadway	Nashville	TN	37203	615-242-4750		520
Web: tshf.net						
Tennessee State Employees Assn 627 Woodland St	Nashville	TN	37206	615-256-4533		533
TF: 800-251-8732 ■ *Web:* tseaonline.org						
Tennessee State Government						
Booker T. Washington State Park 5801 Champion Rd	Chattanooga	TN	37416	423-337-5801		565
Web: www.state.tn.us						
Port Royal State Historic Park 3300 Old Clarksville Hwy	Adams	TN	37010	931-946-3300		565
Web: www.state.tn.us						
Tennessee State Library & Archives 403 Seventh Ave N	Nashville	TN	37243	615-741-2764	741-6471	434-5
Web: www.tn.gov						
Tennessee State Museum 505 Deaderick St	Nashville	TN	37243	615-741-2692		520
TF: 800-407-4324 ■ *Web:* www.tnmuseum.org						
Tennessee State University 3500 John A Merritt Blvd PO Box 9609	Nashville	TN	37209	615-963-5000	963-5108	166
TF: 888-463-6878 ■ *Web:* www.tnstate.edu						
Tennessee State Veterans Home-Murfreesboro 345 Compton Rd	Murfreesboro	TN	37130	615-895-8850	895-5091	793
Web: tsvh.org						
Tennessee Steel Haulers Inc PO Box 78189	Nashville	TN	37207	615-271-2400		780
TF: 800-776-4004 ■ *Web:* tenh.com						
Tennessee Technological University 1 William L Jones Dr	Cookeville	TN	38505	931-372-3888		166
TF: 800-255-8881 ■ *Web:* www.tntech.edu						
Tennessee Titans 460 Great Cir Rd	Nashville	TN	37228	615-565-4000		715-3
Web: www.tennesseetitans.com						
Tennessee Tractor LLC 16 S Bells St Ste 1	Alamo	TN	38001	731-696-5598	696-2403	57
Web: www.tennesseetractor.com						
Tennessee Trucking Association Inc 4531 Trousdale Dr	Nashville	TN	37204	615-777-2882		311
Web: tntrucking.org						
Tennessee Valley Authority (TVA) 400 W Summit Hill Dr	Knoxville	TN	37902	865-632-2101		340-20
Web: www.tva.com						
Tennessee Valley Electric Coop (TVEC) 590 Florence Rd	Savannah	TN	38372	731-925-4916	925-4919	245
TF: 866-925-4916 ■ *Web:* www.tennesseevalleyec.com						
Tennessee Valley Railroad Museum 4119 Cromwell Rd	Chattanooga	TN	37421	423-894-8028	894-8029	520
Web: www.tvrail.com						
Tennessee Veterinary Medical Assn PO Box 803	Fayetteville	TN	37334	931-438-0070	433-6289	795
TF: 800-697-3587 ■ *Web:* tvmanet.com						
Tennessee Walking Horse Breeders' & Exhibitors' Assn (TWHBEA) 250 N Ellington Pkwy PO Box 286	Lewisburg	TN	37091	931-359-1574	359-7530	48-3
Web: www.twhbea.com						
Tennessee Wesleyan College 204 E College St	Athens	TN	37303	423-745-7504	744-9968	166
TF: 844-742-5898 ■ *Web:* www.tnwesleyan.edu						
Tennessee Williams Theatre 5901 W College Rd	Key West	FL	33040	305-295-7676		572
Tennessee/DCI Donor Services 1600 Hayes St	Nashville	TN	37203	877-401-2517		545
TF: 877-401-2517 ■ *Web:* www.dcids.org						
Tennis Canada 285 Rue Gary-Carter	Montreal	QC	H2R2W1	514-273-1515	276-0070	78
TF: 866-338-2685 ■ *Web:* www.tenniscanada.com						
Tennis Channel 2850 Ocean Pk Blvd Ste 150	Santa Monica	CA	90405	310-314-9400		740
Web: www.tennis.com						
Tennis Equities Inc 77 Kensico Dr	Mount Kisco	NY	10549	914-241-0797		354
Web: www.sawmillclub.com						
Tennis Express 11022 Westheimer Rd	Houston	TX	77042	713-435-4800		711
Web: www.tennisexpress.com						
Tennis Pro Shop 19101 Peninsula Club Dr	Cornelius	NC	28031	704-439-2912		711
Web: www.thepeninsulaclub.com						
Tennsco Corp 201 Tennsco Dr PO Box 1888	Dickson	TN	37056	866-446-8686	722-0134*	319-1
**Fax Area Code:* 800 ■ *TF:* 866-446-8686 ■ *Web:* www.tennsco.com						
Tenn-Tex Plastics Inc 8011 National Service Rd	Colfax	NC	27235	336-931-1100	931-1110	596
Web: www.tenntex.com						
Tennyson High School 27035 Whitman St	Hayward	CA	94544	510-723-3190	582-0964	685
Web: ths-haywardusd-ca.schoolloop.com						
Tenova 100 Corporate Center Dr	Coraopolis	PA	15108	412-262-2240	262-2055	318
Web: www.tenovainc.com						
Tenplus Systems 500-C Uwharrie Ct	Raleigh	NC	27606	919-832-5799	755-0114	180
Web: www.tenplus.com						
Tenrox 401 Congress Ave	Austin	TX	78701	450-688-3444		178-1
Web: uplandsoftware.com						
Tension Envelope Corp 819 E 19th St	Kansas City	MO	64108	800-388-5122		263
TF: 800-388-5122 ■ *Web:* tensionenvelope.com						
Tension Member Technology 5721 Research Dr	Huntington Beach	CA	92649	714-898-5641		743
Web: www.tmtlabs.com						
TenStep Inc 181 Waterman St	Marietta	GA	30060	770-795-9097		463
TF: 877-536-8434 ■ *Web:* tenstep.com						
T-Enterprises Truck Driving School 210 E Lewis Pl	Pasco	WA	99301	509-547-2441		685
Web: www.tenterprisesinc.com						
Tenzing Consulting LLC 2100 Georgetowne Dr Ste 302	Sewickley	PA	15143	724-940-4060		196
TF: 877-980-5300 ■ *Web:* tenzingconsulting.com						
Teo Technologies Inc 11609 49th Pl W	Mukilteo	WA	98275	425-349-1000	349-1010	735
TF: 800-524-0024 ■ *Web:* www.teotech.com						
TEOCO Corp 12150 Monument Dr Ste 400	Fairfax	VA	22033	703-322-9200		792
TF: 888-868-3626 ■ *Web:* www.teoco.com						
Teora USA LLC 505 Hampton Park Blvd Ste G	Capitol Heights	MD	20743	301-986-6990	350-5480	637-2
Web: teorausa.com						
Tep Thai 209 W Wilson Ave	Glendale	CA	91203	818-246-0380		671
Web: www.tepthai.com						
Tepa LLC 5045 List Dr	Colorado Springs	CO	80919	719-596-8114		261
Web: www.tepa.com						
Tepel Brothers Printing Co 1725 John R Rd	Troy	MI	48083	248-743-2903		627
Web: tepelbrothers.com						
Teplitsky, Colson LLP 70 Bond St Ste 200	Toronto	ON	M5B1X3	416-365-9320		428
Web: www.teplitskycolson.com						
Teplow Cucurullo Communications LLC 68 Harvard St	Brookline	MA	02445	617-566-6710		7
Web: www.teplowandco.com						
Teppco Crude Oil LLC 210 Park Ave Ste 1600	Oklahoma City	OK	73102	405-239-7191	602-1251	597
Tepper Holdings Inc 55 Commerce Valley Dr W Ste 220	Richmond Hill	ON	L3T7V9	905-889-0663	889-9407	528
Web: www.tepperholdings.com						
Teppo Yakitori & Sushi Bar 2014 Greenville Ave	Dallas	TX	75206	214-826-8989		671
Web: www.teppo.com						
Tepro Inc 590 Baxter Ln	Winchester	TN	37398	931-967-5189	967-3140	350
Web: www.kinugawa-rubber.co.jp						
Tequila Mockingbird 130th St Montego Bay Shopping Ctr	Ocean City	MD	21842	410-250-4424		671
Web: octequila.com						
Tequilas 1602 Locust St	Philadelphia	PA	19103	215-546-0181	546-9953	671
Web: tequilasphilly.com						
Ter Molen Watkins & Brandt LLC 2 N Riverside Plz Ste 1030	Chicago	IL	60606	312-222-0560	222-0565	317
Web: twbfundraising.com						
Teraco Inc 2080 Commerce Dr	Midland	TX	79703	800-687-3999		596
TF: 800-687-3999 ■ *Web:* www.archway.com						
TeraDact Federal PO Box 60072	Washington	DC	20036	202-255-0308	331-5080	387
TF: 866-599-8231 ■ *Web:* teradact.com						

Name / Address	City	State	Zip	Phone	Fax	Class
TeraDiode Inc 30 Upton Dr *Web:* www.teradiode.com	Wilmington	MA	01887	978-988-1040		111
Teradyne Inc *Semiconductor Test Div* 600 Riverpark Dr *Web:* www.teradyne.com	North Reading	MA	01864	978-370-2700		248
TeraGo Networks Inc 55 Commerce Vly Dr W Ste 800 **Fax Area Code:* 905 ■ *TF:* 866-837-2461 ■ *Web:* terago.ca	Thornhill	ON	L3T7V9	866-837-2465	707-6212*	224
Teragren 1920 S Proforma Ave *TF:* 800-929-6333 ■ *Web:* www.teragren.com	Ontario	CA	91761	206-842-9477		290
Tera-Lite Inc 1631 S 10th St *Web:* www.tera-lite.com	San Jose	CA	95112	408-288-8655	288-9655	189-2
Teralys Capital 999 Boul de Maisonneuve O Ste 1700 *Web:* www.teralyscapital.com	Montreal	QC	H3A3L4	514-509-2080		528
TeraMach Technologies Inc 1130 Morrison Dr Ste 105 *TF:* 877-226-6549 ■ *Web:* www.teramach.com	Ottawa	ON	K2H9N6	613-226-7775		180
TeraRecon Inc 4000 E Third Ave Ste 200 *TF:* 877-996-0100 ■ *Web:* www.terarecon.com	Foster City	CA	94404	650-372-1100	372-1101	418
Teras Cargo Transport (America) LLC 5358 33rd Ave NW Ste 302	Gig Harbor	WA	98335	253-857-9209		313
Terasci Industries Inc 5362 Production Dr *Web:* www.terasci.com	Huntington Beach	CA	92649	714-896-0150		177
TERATECH Corp 77 Terrace Hall Ave *TF:* 866-837-2766 ■ *Web:* www.terason.com	Burlington	MA	01803	781-270-4143	270-4145	476
TERC 2067 Massachusetts Ave *Web:* terc.edu	Cambridge	MA	02140	617-547-0430	349-3535	668
Teresa Holwerda Insurance Agency Inc 801 S First St *Web:* insuregirl.com	Willmar	MN	56201	320-231-2746		390
Teresi Trucking Inc 900 1/2 Victor Rd *Web:* www.teresitrucking.com	Lodi	CA	95240	209-368-2472	369-2830	780
Terex Corp 200 Nyala Farm Rd *NYSE: TEX* ■ *Web:* www.terex.com	Westport	CT	06880	203-222-7170	222-7976	190
Terhorst Manufacturing Co 615 Burdick Expy E *Web:* www.terhorstmfg.com	Minot	ND	58701	701-852-0535		454
TERI Inc 251 Airport Rd *Web:* www.teriinc.org	Oceanside	CA	92058	760-721-1706		48-15
TERiX Computer Service Inc 388 Oakmead Pkwy *TF:* 888-848-3749 ■ *Web:* www.terix.com	Sunnyvale	CA	94085	888-848-3749		177
Teriyaki Chicken House 805 El Paseo Rd *Web:* teriyakichickenhouse.com	Las Cruces	NM	88001	575-541-1696		671
Terlato Wine Group, The (TWG) 900 Armour Dr *Web:* www.terlatovineyards.com	Lake Bluff	IL	60044	847-604-8900		81-3
Terminal City Club 837 W Hastings St *Web:* www.tcclub.com	Vancouver	BC	V6C1B6	604-681-4121	681-9634	379
Terminal Corp, The 1657 A S Highland Ave *TF:* 800-560-7207 ■ *Web:* www.termcorp.com	Baltimore	MD	21224	800-560-7207		311
Terminal Forest Products Ltd 12180 Mitchell Rd *Web:* www.terminalforest.com	Richmond	BC	V6V1M8	604-717-1200		683
Terminal Hardware Company Inc 1824 E 22nd St *Web:* terminalhardware.com	Vernon	CA	90058	213-624-4078	624-8667	351
Terminal Railroad Association of Saint Louis 1017 Olive St 5th Fl **Fax Area Code:* 314 ■ *TF:* 866-931-0498 ■ *Web:* www.terminalrailroad.com	Saint Louis	MO	63101	618-451-8400	621-3673*	651
Termini Brothers Inc 1523 S 8th St *TF:* 800-882-7650 ■ *Web:* www.termini.com	Philadelphia	PA	19147	215-334-1816		296-1
Terminix International Company LP 150 Peabody Pl *TF:* 877-837-6464 ■ *Web:* www.terminix.com	Memphis	TN	38120	877-837-6464		577
Ternion Corp 2223 Drake Ave *Web:* www.ternion.com	Huntsville	AL	35805	256-881-9933	881-9957	703
TernPro 320 Westlake Ave 4th Fl *TF:* 888-483-8779 ■ *Web:* ternpro.com	Seattle	WA	98109	888-483-8779		179
Tero International Inc 1840 NW 118th St Ste 107 *Web:* www.tero.com	Clive	IA	50325	515-221-2318		463
Terog Manufacturing Co 387 Atlantic Ave *Web:* www.blackaceparts.com	Stephen	MN	56757	218-478-3395	478-3622	75
Terphane Inc 2754 W Park Dr *Web:* www.terphane.com	Bloomfield	NY	14469	585-657-5800		605-2
Terra 7091 El Cajon Blvd *Web:* terrasd.com	San Diego	CA	92115	619-293-7088		671
Terra Associates Incorporated Consulting Engineers 1445 N Loop W Ste 450 *Web:* terraassoc.com	Houston	TX	77008	713-993-0333		261
Terra Community College 2830 Napoleon Rd *TF:* 800-334-3886 ■ *Web:* www.terra.edu	Fremont	OH	43420	419-334-8400	334-9035	162
Terra Dotta LLC 501 W Franklin St Ste 105 *TF:* 877-368-8277 ■ *Web:* www.terradotta.com	Chapel Hill	NC	27516	877-368-8277		177
Terra Engineering & Construction Corp 2201 Vondron Rd *Web:* whyterra.com	Madison	WI	53718	608-221-3501	221-4075	189-5
Terra Foundation for American Art 120 E Erie St *Web:* www.terraamericanart.org	Chicago	IL	60611	312-664-3939	664-2052	305
Terra Furniture Inc 14819 Salt Lake Ave *Web:* www.terrafurniture.com	City of Industry	CA	91746	626-912-8523	964-1083	321
Terra Law LLC 50 W San Fernando St Ste 1415 *Web:* www.terra-law.com	San Jose	CA	95113	408-299-1200	998-4895	428
Terra Nova Asset Management LLC 777 Third Ave *Web:* www.terranovausa.com	New York	NY	10017	212-355-1234	658-9904	194
Terra Nova Steel & Iron (Ontario) Inc 3595 Hawkestone Rd *TF:* 877-427-0269 ■ *Web:* www.terranovasteel.ca	Mississauga	ON	L5C2V1	905-273-3872		492
Terra Remote Sensing Inc 1962 Mills Rd *TF:* 800-814-4212 ■ *Web:* www.terraremote.com	Sidney	BC	V8L5Y3	250-656-0931		727
Terra Sancta Press 304 Royal Palm Dr *Web:* www.terrasanctapress.com	Melbourne	FL	32935	321-914-2290		637-2
Terra Spectrum Technologies 5930 Grand Ave **Fax Area Code:* 866 ■ *TF:* 888-280-1349 ■ *Web:* www.terraspectrumtechnologies.com	West Des Moines	IA	50266	888-280-1349	955-6585*	177
Terra Universal Inc 800 S Ramon Ave *Web:* www.terrauniversal.com	Fullerton	CA	92831	714-578-6000		18
Terracap Group 100 Sheppard Ave E Ste 502 *TF:* 800-363-3207 ■ *Web:* www.terracap.ca	Toronto	ON	M2N6N5	416-222-9345		528
Terrace Plaza Playhouse 99 E 4700 S *Web:* www.terraceplazaplayhouse.com	Washington Terrace	UT	84405	801-393-0070		572
Terraco Inc 3201 Old Glenview Rd *Web:* terracorealestate.com	Wilmette	IL	60091	847-679-6660		653
Terracon Geotechnique Ltd 400 800 - Fifth Ave SW *Web:* www.terracon.ca	Calgary	AB	T2P3T6	403-266-1150		261
Terracor Business Solutions 677 St Mary's Rd *TF:* 877-942-0005 ■ *Web:* terracor.ca	Winnipeg	MB	R2M3M6	204-477-5342		177
Terradyne Country Club 1400 Terradyne Dr *Web:* www.terradynecountryclub.com	Andover	KS	67002	316-733-2582	733-9149	669
Terrafugia Inc 23 Rainin Rd *Web:* www.terrafugia.com	Woburn	MA	01801	781-491-0812		59
Terragon Environmental Technologies Inc 651 Rue Bridge *Web:* terragon.net	Montreal	QC	H3K2C8	514-938-3772		261
Terraine Inc 310 S Harrington St **Fax Area Code:* 786 ■ *TF:* 800-531-1242 ■ *Web:* terraine.com	Raleigh	NC	27603	800-531-1242	206-3138*	396
Terral Riverservice Inc 10100 Hwy 65 S *TF:* 800-228-1961 ■ *Web:* www.terralriverservice.com	Lake Providence	LA	71254	318-559-1500	559-1524	314
Terral Seed Inc 117 Ellington Dr **Fax Area Code:* 318 ■ *TF:* 800-551-4852 ■ *Web:* www.terralseed.com	Rayville	LA	71269	800-551-4852	728-8765*	276
TerraLex Inc 8350 NW 52nd Ter Ste 410 *TF:* 877-310-7187 ■ *Web:* www.terralex.org	Miami	FL	33166	305-539-0001		138
TerraMai 8400 Agate Rd *TF:* 800-220-9062 ■ *Web:* www.terramai.com	White City	OR	97503	800-220-9062		41
Terramia Ristorante 98 Salem St *Web:* www.terramiaristorante.com	Boston	MA	02113	617-523-3112		671
Terranea Resort & Spa 100 Terranea Way *TF:* 866-547-3066 ■ *Web:* www.terranea.com	Rancho Palos Verdes	CA	90275	310-265-2800		378
Terranear PMC LLC 4200 West Jemez Rd Ste P-502 *Web:* www.terranear.com	Irving	TX	75063	972-929-1095	929-1098	271
Terranettis Italian Bakery 844 W Trindle Rd *Web:* www.terranettis.com	Mechanicsburg	PA	17055	717-697-5434		805
Terranova Intl 3675 Nordstrom Ln *Web:* terranovabi.com	LaFayette	CA	94549	925-299-6833		177
Terranovanet Inc PO Box 3031 *Web:* terranova.net	Key Largo	FL	33037	305-453-4011	451-5991	396
TerraPass Inc 527 Howard St 4th Fl *TF:* 844-662-6248 ■ *Web:* www.terrapass.com	San Francisco	CA	94105	415-692-3411		691
Terrapin Hollow Educational Foundation 1315 Prism Dr *Web:* www.terrapinhollow.org	Leslie	AR	72645	501-253-5626		637-2
Terrapin Management Corp 601 Rio Grande Pl Ste 117-A *Web:* www.terrapininvestments.com	Aspen	CO	81611	970-710-7932		377
Terrapin Systems LLC 9841 Washingtonian Blvd Ste 200 *TF:* 866-837-7797 ■ *Web:* www.terpsys.com	Gaithersburg	MD	20878	301-530-9106	530-9105	344
Terrasage Technology Partners LLC 2001 S Barrington Ave Ste 200 *Web:* terrasage.com	Los Angeles	CA	90025	310-996-0100	996-0101	809
Terrasat Communications Inc 315 Digital Dr *Web:* www.terrasatinc.com	Morgan Hill	CA	95037	408-782-5911	782-5912	116
TerraSim Inc 420 Ft Duquesne Blvd One Gateway Ctr Ste 2050 *Web:* www.terrasim.com	Pittsburgh	PA	15222	412-232-3646		177
TerraSond Ltd 1617 S Industrial Way Ste 3 *Web:* www.terrasond.com	Palmer	AK	99645	907-745-7215	745-7273	536
Terrazzo & Marble Supply Company of Illinois 77 Wheeling Rd *TF:* 800-762-7253 ■ *Web:* www.tmsupply.com	Wheeling	IL	60090	800-762-7253		191-1
Terre Company of New Jersey Inc 206 Delawanna Ave *Web:* www.terrecompany.com	Clifton	NJ	07014	973-473-3393	473-4402	276
Terre Haute Regional Hospital (THRH) 3901 S 7th St **Fax Area Code:* 877 ■ *TF:* 866-270-2311 ■ *Web:* regionalhospital.com	Terre Haute	IN	47802	812-232-0021	865-9738*	374-3
Terre Hill Silo Company Inc PO Box 10 *TF:* 800-242-1509 ■ *Web:* www.terrehill.com	Terre Hill	PA	17581	717-445-3100	445-3108	183
Terrebonne General Medical Ctr (TGMC) 8166 Main St *TF:* 888-850-6270 ■ *Web:* www.tgmc.com	Houma	LA	70360	985-873-4141	873-5306	374-3
Terrebonne Parish PO Box 1569 *Web:* terrebonneclerk.org	Houma	LA	70361	985-868-5660	868-5143	338
Terrebonne Parish Library 151 Library Dr *Web:* mytpl.org	Houma	LA	70360	985-876-5861	917-0582	434-3

Phone | Fax | Class

Terrell County 105 E Hackberry . . . Sanderson TX 79848 432-345-2391 345-2740 338
Web: www.co.terrell.tx.us

Terrell Hogan Yegelwel PA
233 E Bay St Ste 804 . . . Jacksonville FL 32202 904-722-2228 41
Web: terrellhogan.com

Terrell Public Library
201 E Nash St PO Box 310 . . . Terrell TX 75160 972-551-6600 434-3
Web: www.cityofterrell.org

Terri Lynn Inc 1450 Bowes Rd . . . Elgin IL 60123 847-741-1900 741-7791 296-28
Web: www.terrilynn.com

Terril Telephone Coop 107 S State St . . . Terril IA 51364 712-853-6121 853-6185 224
Web: www.terril.com

Territorial Landworks Inc
1817 South Ave W Ste A . . . Missoula MT 59806 406-721-0142 261
Web: territoriallandworks.com

Territorial Seed Co
c/o Territorial Seed Company
PO Box 158 . . . Cottage Grove OR 97424 800-626-0866 657-3131* 48-6
**Fax Area Code:* 888 ■ *TF:* 800-626-0866 ■ *Web:* www.territorialseed.com

Territorial Statehouse State Park
50 W Capitol Ave . . . Fillmore UT 84631 435-743-5316 565
Web: stateparks.utah.gov

Terroco Industries Ltd
27212 Twp Rd 391 . . . Red Deer AB T4N5E1 403-346-1171 346-9720 539
TF: 800-670-1100 ■ *Web:* www.terroco.com

Terros Inc 3003 N Central Ave Ste 200 . . . Phoenix AZ 85012 602-222-9444 353
Web: www.terroshealth.org

Terry County 500 W Main St . . . Brownfield TX 79316 806-637-4202 637-4874 338
Web: www.co.terry.tx.us

Terry H. Jones & Co
6 Brookhill Sq S . . . Sugarloaf PA 18249 570-788-7000 2
Web: thjcpa.com

Terry Hines & Assoc (THA)
2550 N Hollywood Way Ste 600 . . . Burbank CA 91505 818-562-9433 7
Web: www.terryhines.com

Terry Hughes Tree Service Inc
15802 Fairview Rd . . . Gretna NE 68028 402-558-8198 776
Web: www.hughestree.com

Terry J. Andolshek CPA PC
2470 E River Rd . . . Tucson AZ 85718 520-529-0384 529-0385 2
Web: tjacpa.com

Terry Jones & Associates PC
5910 Grelot Rd . . . Mobile AL 36609 251-341-4593 2
Web: www.tjonescpa.com

Terry Laboratories Inc
7005 Technology Dr . . . Melbourne FL 32904 321-259-1630 242-0625 479
TF: 800-367-2563 ■ *Web:* www.terrylabs.com

Terry McDaniel & Co
2630 Exposition Blvd Ste 300 . . . Austin TX 78703 512-495-9500 401
Web: www.tmcdanco.com

Terry Precision Bicycles for Women Inc
47 Maple St . . . Burlington VT 05401 800-289-8379 861-2956* 82
**Fax Area Code:* 802 ■ *TF:* 800-289-8379 ■ *Web:* www.terrybicycles.com

Terry Romero Wofford Insurance Agency Inc
2200 W Congress St . . . LaFayette LA 70506 337-232-4451 390
Web: terrywofford.com

Terry Thompson Chevrolet Olds
1402 US Hwy 98 PO Box 1207 . . . Daphne AL 36526 251-626-0631 57
TF: 800-287-9309 ■ *Web:* www.terrythompsonchevrolet.com

Terry's Electric Inc
600 N Thacker Ave Ste A . . . Kissimmee FL 34741 407-572-2100 189-4
Web: www.terryselectric.com

Terryberry Co
2033 Oak Industrial Dr NE . . . Grand Rapids MI 49505 616-458-1391 409
TF: 800-253-0882 ■ *Web:* www.terryberry.com

Terrycomm 2700 Business Center Blvd . . . Melbourne FL 32940 321-253-6067 246
Web: terrycomm.com

Terry-Durin Co
409 Seventh Ave SE . . . Cedar Rapids IA 52401 319-364-4106 364-2562 246
TF: 800-332-8114 ■ *Web:* www.terry-durin.com

Terrys Ford Lincoln 363 N Harlem Ave . . . Peotone IL 60468 708-258-9200 57
Web: terrysfordofpeotone.com

Terumo Cardiovascular Systems Corp
6200 Jackson Rd . . . Ann Arbor MI 48103 734-663-4145 292-6551* 476
**Fax Area Code:* 800 ■ *TF:* 800-262-3304 ■ *Web:* www.terumocv.com

Terumo Medical Corp
2101 Cottontail Ln . . . Somerset NJ 08873 732-302-4900 302-3083 476
TF: 800-283-7866 ■ *Web:* www.terumomedical.com

Tervita Corp 500 140 - 10 Ave SE . . . Calgary AB T2G0R1 403-233-7565 536
Web: www.tervita.com

Terzian Trucking Company Inc
15 Woodward Ave . . . South Norwalk CT 06854 203-853-2404 311
Web: terziantrucking.com

Tesa Tape Inc 5825 Carnegie Blvd . . . Charlotte NC 28209 704-554-0707 852-8831* 732
**Fax Area Code:* 800 ■ *TF:* 800-426-2181 ■ *Web:* www.tesa.com

Teschner Law Firm LLC
3 Lockwood Dr Ste 204 . . . Charleston SC 29401 843-937-0027 937-8508 445
Web: charlestontaxlaw.com

Tesco Controls Inc 8440 Florin Rd . . . Sacramento CA 95828 916-395-8800 203
TF: 800-948-3726 ■ *Web:* tescocontrols.com

Tesco Industries LP 1035 E Hacienda . . . Bellville TX 77418 800-699-5824 319-3
TF: 800-699-5824 ■ *Web:* www.tesco-ind.com

Tescor Inc 341 Ivyland Rd . . . Warminster PA 18974 215-957-9112 957-9115 419
Web: www.tescor-inc.com

TESD (Tredyffrin-Easttown School District)
940 W Valley Rd Ste 1700 . . . Wayne PA 19087 610-240-1900 186
Web: www.tesd.net

Teske's Germania 255 N First St . . . San Jose CA 95113 408-292-0291 671
Web: www.teskes-germania.com

Tesko Enterprises
7350 W Montrose Ave . . . Norridge IL 60706 708-452-0045 452-0112 286
TF: 800-621-4514 ■ *Web:* www.teskoenterprises.com

Tesla 3500 Deer Creek Rd . . . Palo Alto CA 94304 650-681-5000 681-5101 59
TF: 888-518-3752 ■ *Web:* www.tesla.com

TESOL (Teachers of English to Speakers of Other Languages)
1925 Ballenger Ave Ste 550 . . . Alexandria VA 22314 703-518-2500 836-7864 49-5
TF: 888-547-3369 ■ *Web:* www.tesol.org

TESS 2499 N Bartlett Ave . . . Milwaukee WI 53211 414-964-8377 964-7790 671
Web: tess2499.com

Tessa Precision Product Inc
850 Callendar Blvd . . . Painesville OH 44077 440-392-3470 454
Web: www.tessaprecision.com

Tessaro's 4601 Liberty Ave . . . Pittsburgh PA 15224 412-682-6809 671
Web: tessaros.com

TESSCO Technologies Inc
11126 McCormick Rd . . . Hunt Valley MD 21031 800-472-7373 527-0005* 246
NASDAQ: TESS ■ **Fax Area Code:* 410 ■ *TF:* 800-472-7373 ■ *Web:* www.tessco.com

Tessy Plastics Corp
700 Visions Dr . . . Skaneateles NY 13152 315-689-3924 685-1539 608
Web: www.tessy.com

Test com Inc 3558 Lee Rd . . . Shaker Heights OH 44120 877-502-8600 502-0060* 525
**Fax Area Code:* 216 ■ *TF:* 877-502-8600 ■ *Web:* www.gaugeonline.com

Test Connection Inc, The
112 Lakefront Dr . . . Hunt Valley MD 21030 410-205-7300 261
Web: www.ttci.com

Test Country
10123 Carroll Canyon Rd . . . San Diego CA 92131 858-784-6904 743
TF: 800-656-0745 ■ *Web:* testcountry.com

Test Devices Inc 571 Main St . . . Hudson MA 01749 978-562-6017 743
Web: www.testdevices.com

Test Electronics 821 Smith Rd . . . Watsonville CA 95076 831-763-2000 248
Web: www.testelectronics.com

Test Evolution Corp 102 S St . . . Hopkinton MA 01748 781-644-2111 407
Web: www.testevolution.com

Test Inc 2323 Fourth St . . . Peru IL 61354 815-224-1650 743
TF: 800-659-4659 ■ *Web:* testinc.com

Test Laboratories 7121 Canby Ave . . . Reseda CA 91335 818-881-4251 275
Web: www.testlabinc.com

Test Logic Inc
17 Kenneth Dooley Dr . . . Middletown CT 06457 860-347-8378 347-8379 248
Web: www.testlogic.com

Test Mark Industries Inc
995 N Market St . . . East Palestine OH 44413 800-783-3227 190
TF: 800-783-3227 ■ *Web:* www.testmark.net

Test Positive Aware Network
5537 N Broadway St . . . Chicago IL 60640 773-989-9400 989-9494 637-10
Web: www.tpan.com

Test Products Inc
41255 Technology Park Dr . . . Sterling Heights MI 48314 586-997-9600 997-9609 247
Web: tpiusa.com

Testa Communications
25 Willowdale Ave . . . Port Washington NY 11050 516-767-2500 767-9335 637-9
Web: www.testa.com

Testa Heck Testa & White PA
424 Landis Ave . . . Vineland NJ 08360 856-691-2300 41
Web: testalawyers.com

Testa Machine Company Inc 28 Baird Ave . . . Slovan PA 15078 724-947-9397 947-9998 454
Web: www.testa-machine.com

TestAmerica Laboratories Inc
4625 E Cotton Center Blvd Ste 189 . . . Phoenix AZ 85040 602-437-3340 454-9303 743
TF: 866-785-5227 ■ *Web:* www.testamericainc.com

Testco 3445 Executive Center Dr Ste 117 . . . Austin TX 78731 888-245-9709 178-2
TF: 888-245-9709 ■ *Web:* www.testco.com

TestEdge Inc
15930 Bernardo Center Dr . . . San Diego CA 92127 858-451-1012 451-1018 743
Web: www.testedgeinc.com

Testek Inc 28320 Lakeview Dr . . . Wixom MI 48393 248-573-4980 573-4990 407
Web: www.testek.com

Tester Jon (Sen D - MT)
311 Hart Senate Office Bldg . . . Washington DC 20510 202-224-2644 224-8594 342-2
Web: www.tester.senate.gov

TesTex Inc 535 Old Frankstown Rd . . . Pittsburgh PA 15239 412-798-8990 365
Web: testex-ndt.com

Testing Engineers & Consultants Inc
1343 Rochester Rd . . . Troy MI 48083 248-588-6200 261
Web: www.testingengineers.com

Testing Machines Inc
40 McCullough Dr . . . New Castle DE 19720 302-613-5600 613-5619 472
TF: 800-678-3221 ■ *Web:* www.testingmachines.com

Testor Corp 11 Hawthorn Pkwy . . . Vernon Hills IL 60061 866-585-8430 962-7401* 762
**Fax Area Code:* 815 ■ *TF:* 800-837-8677 ■ *Web:* www.testors.com

Testpros Inc
46090 Lake Center Plz Ste 306 . . . Sterling VA 20165 703-787-7600 180
Web: testpros.com

Testron Inc 34153 Industrial Rd . . . Livonia MI 48150 734-513-6820 513-6068 472
Web: www.testron-corp.com

Tetco Inc 1100 NE Loop 410 Ste 900 . . . San Antonio TX 78209 210-821-5900 579
Web: tetco.com

Teterboro School of Aeronautics
80 Moonachie Ave . . . Teterboro NJ 07608 201-288-6300 288-5609 685
Web: www.teterboroschool.com

Tethernet Inc
227 Bellevue Way NE Ste 473 . . . Bellevue WA 98004 877-203-7775 646-5079* 178-1
**Fax Area Code:* 866 ■ *TF:* 877-203-7775 ■ *Web:* www.tethernet.com

Teton Buildings LLC 2701 Magnet St . . . Houston TX 77054 713-351-6300 539
Web: tetonbuildings.com

Teton County PO Box 610 . . . Choteau MT 59422 406-466-2151 466-2138 338
Web: www.tetoncomt.org

Teton County 150 Courthouse Dr Rm 208 . . . Driggs ID 83422 208-354-8770 354-8776 338
Web: www.tetoncountyidaho.gov

Teton County PO Box 1727 . . . Jackson WY 83001 307-733-4430 739-8681 338
Web: www.tetoncountywy.gov

Teton County Public Library
125 Virginian Ln . . . Jackson WY 83001 307-733-2164 733-4568 434-3
Web: tclib.org

Teton Data Systems
125 S Kings St Ste G1 . . . Jackson WY 83001 307-733-5494 809
Web: www.tetondata.com

Teton Gravity Research LLC 1260 NW St . . . Wilson WY 83014 307-734-8192 506
Web: www.tetongravity.com

Teton Machine Co 1805 NE Tenth Ave . . . Payette ID 83661 208-642-9344 642-9346 627
Web: www.tetonmachine.com

Teton Mountain Lodge & Spa
3385 Cody Ln . . . Teton Village WY 83025 307-201-6066 379
TF: 800-631-6271 ■ *Web:* www.tetonlodge.com

Teton Pines 3450 N Clubhouse Dr . . . Wilson WY 83014 307-733-1005 669
Web: www.tetonpines.com

Name / Address	City	State	Zip	Phone	Fax	Class
Tetra Corp 3701 Hawkins St NE	Albuquerque	NM	87109	505-345-8623	345-7318	668
Web: www.tetra-corporation.com						
Tetra Corporate Services LLC						
6995 Union Park Ctr Ste 360	Midvale	UT	84047	801-566-2600	365-6263	264-3
TF: 800-417-0548 ■ *Web:* tetracsi.com						
Tetra Medical Supply Corp						
6364 W Gross Pt Rd	Niles	IL	60714	847-647-0590	647-9034	475
TF: 800-621-4041 ■ *Web:* www.tetramed.com						
Tetra Pak Inc 753 Geneva Pkwy N	Lake Geneva	WI	53147	262-249-7400		101
Web: www.tetrapak.com						
Tetra Tech Architects & Engineers						
Cornell Business & Technology Pk 10 Brown Rd	Ithaca	NY	14850	607-277-7100		393
Web: www.tetratechae.com						
Tetra Tech EC Inc 6 Campus Dr	Morris Plains	NJ	07950	973-630-8000		261
Web: www.tetratech.com						
TETRA Technologies Inc						
25025 I-45 N	The Woodlands	TX	77380	281-367-1983		143
NYSE: TTI ■ *Web:* www.tetratec.com						
Tetrad Computer Applications Ltd						
1465 Slater Rd PO Box 5007	Vancouver	BC	V6G2T3	604-685-2295		177
TF: 800-663-1334 ■ *Web:* www.tetrad.com						
Tetrasoft Inc						
16647 Chesterfield Grove Rd Ste 120	Chesterfield	MO	63005	636-530-7638		179
TF: 866-314-7557 ■ *Web:* www.tetrasoft.us						
Tetrault Insurance Agency Inc						
4317 Acushnet Ave	New Bedford	MA	02745	508-995-8365		390
TF: 800-696-9991 ■ *Web:* www.tetraultinsurance.com						
Tetrem Capital Management Ltd						
1910-201 Portage Ave	Winnipeg	MB	R3B3K6	204-975-2865		528
Web: www.tetrem.com						
Teucrium Trading LLC						
232 Hidden Lake Rd	Brattleboro	VT	05301	802-257-1617		528
Web: www.teucrium.com						
Teufel Landscape						
7431 NW Evergreen Pkwy Ste 200	Hillsboro	OR	97124	503-646-1111	646-1112	293
Web: www.teufel.com						
Teufelberger Fiber Rope Corp						
848 Airport Rd	Fall River	MA	02720	508-678-8200	679-2363	208
Web: www.neropes.com						
Teuteberg Inc 12200 W Wirth St	Wauwatosa	WI	53222	414-257-4110		627
Web: www.teuteberg.com						
Teva Pharmaceutical USA						
1090 Horsham Rd	North Wales	PA	19454	800-545-8800		583
NYSE: TEVA ■ *TF:* 800-545-8800 ■ *Web:* www.tevagenerics.com						
Tevet LLC 85 Spring St S	Mosheim	TN	37818	678-905-1300		201
TF: 866-886-8527 ■ *Web:* tevetllc.com						
Tewksbury Animal Hospital						
1098 Main St	Tewksbury	MA	01876	978-851-3626		794
Web: tewksburyanimalhospital.com						
Tewksbury Hospital 365 E St	Tewksbury	MA	01876	978-851-7321	851-5648	374-7
Web: www.mass.gov						
Tewksbury Public Library						
300 Chandler St	Tewksbury	MA	01876	978-640-4490		434-3
Web: www.tewksburypl.org						
Tex Con Oil Co						
1701 Grand Ave Pkwy	Pflugerville	TX	78660	512-670-7401	990-0729	579
Web: www.texconoil.com						
Tex Isle Supply Inc						
10000 Memorial Dr Ste 600	Houston	TX	77024	713-461-1012	461-5168	492
Web: www.texisle.com						
Tex Tan Western Leather Co						
808 S US Hwy 77A	Yoakum	TX	77995	800-531-3608	293-2369*	432
**Fax Area Code:* 361 ■ *TF:* 800-531-3608 ■ *Web:* www.textan.com						
Texadelphia 7601 N MacArthur Blvd	Irving	TX	75063	972-432-0725		671
Web: www.texadelphia.com						
Tex-Air Parts Inc						
3724 N Commerce St	Fort Worth	TX	76106	800-458-1535	625-8936*	770
**Fax Area Code:* 817 ■ *TF:* 800-458-1535 ■ *Web:* www.texair.com						
Texans Credit Union						
777 E Campbell Rd	Richardson	TX	75081	972-348-2000	348-2200	219
TF: 800-843-5295 ■ *Web:* www.texanscu.org						
Texarkana Chamber of Commerce						
819 N State Line Ave	Texarkana	TX	75501	903-792-7191	793-4304	139
Web: texarkana.org						
Texarkana College 2500 N Robison Rd	Texarkana	TX	75599	903-838-4541	832-5030	162
TF: 877-275-4377 ■ *Web:* www.texarkanacollege.edu						
Texarkana Gazette 315 Pine St	Texarkana	TX	75501	903-794-3311	794-3315	532-2
Web: www.texarkanagazette.com						
Texarkana Public Library						
600 W 3rd St	Texarkana	TX	75501	903-794-2149	794-2140	434-3
Web: www.txark.ent.sirsi.net						
Texarkana Water Utilities						
801 Wood St	Texarkana	TX	75501	903-798-3800	791-0724	787
Web: txkusa.org						
Texas						
Aging & Disability Services						
701 W 51st St	Austin	TX	78751	512-438-4313	438-5885	339-44
TF: 888-388-6332 ■ *Web:* www.dads.state.tx.us						
Agriculture Dept PO Box 12847	Austin	TX	78711	512-463-7476	223-8861*	339-44
**Fax Area Code:* 888 ■ *TF:* 800-835-5832 ■ *Web:* texasagriculture.gov						
Arts Commission						
920 Colorado Ste 501 PO Box 13406	Austin	TX	78701	512-463-5535	475-2699	339-44
TF: 800-252-9415 ■ *Web:* www.arts.texas.gov						
Attorney General 300 W 15th St	Austin	TX	78701	512-463-2191		339-44
Web: www.texasattorneygeneral.gov						
Banking Dept 2601 N Lamar Blvd	Austin	TX	78705	512-475-1300	475-1313	339-44
TF: 877-276-5554 ■ *Web:* www.dob.texas.gov						
Child Support Div						
300 W 15th St PO Box 12548	Austin	TX	78701	512-463-2100		339-44
Web: www.texasattorneygeneral.gov						
Commission on Environmental Quality						
12100 Park 35 Cir	Austin	TX	78753	512-239-1000		339-44
Web: www.tceq.texas.gov						
Comptroller of Public Accounts						
111 E 17th St	Austin	TX	78774	512-463-4444	305-9711	339-44
TF: 800-252-5555 ■ *Web:* comptroller.texas.gov						
Consumer Protection Div PO Box 12548	Austin	TX	78711	512-463-2185	473-8301	339-44
Web: www.texasattorneygeneral.gov						
Crime Victims Services Div						
PO Box 12198	Austin	TX	78711	512-936-1200		339-44
TF: 800-983-9933 ■ *Web:* www.texasattorneygeneral.gov						
Criminal Justice Dept PO Box 99	Huntsville	TX	77342	936-295-6371		339-44
Web: www.tdcj.texas.gov						
Department of Public Safety						
5805 N Lamar Blvd PO Box 4087	Austin	TX	78752	512-424-2000		693
Web: www.dmv.org						
Economic Development PO Box 12428	Austin	TX	78711	512-981-6736	936-0080	339-44
Web: businessintexas.com						
Emergency Management Div						
1033 La Posada Dr PO Box 4087	Austin	TX	78773	512-424-2138	424-2444	339-44
Web: www.dps.texas.gov						
Ethics Commission 201 E 14th St 10th Fl	Austin	TX	78701	512-463-5800	463-5777	265
Web: www.ethics.state.tx.us						
Family & Protective Services Dept						
701 W 51st St PO Box 149030	Austin	TX	78752	512-438-4800		339-44
Web: www.dfps.state.tx.us						
General Land Office						
1700 N Congress Ave Ste 935	Austin	TX	78701	512-463-5001		339-44
TF: 800-998-4456 ■ *Web:* www.glo.texas.gov						
Governor PO Box 12428	Austin	TX	78711	512-463-2000	463-1849	339-44
TF: 800-843-5789 ■ *Web:* gov.texas.gov						
Higher Education Coordinating Board						
1200 E Anderson Ln	Austin	TX	78752	512-427-6101	427-6127	725
TF: 800-242-3062 ■ *Web:* www.thecb.state.tx.us						
Historical Commission						
1511 Colorado St PO Box 12276	Austin	TX	78701	512-463-6100		339-44
Web: www.thc.texas.gov						
Information Resources Dept						
300 W 15th St Ste 1300	Austin	TX	78701	512-475-4700		339-44
TF: 855-275-3471 ■ *Web:* dir.texas.gov						
Insurance Dept						
333 Guadalupe St PO Box 149104	Austin	TX	78701	800-578-4677		339-44
TF: 800-578-4677 ■ *Web:* www.tdi.texas.gov						
Legislature State Capitol	Austin	TX	78711	512-463-0124	463-0694	339-44
Web: capitol.texas.gov						
Licensing & Regulation Dept						
920 Colorado	Austin	TX	78701	512-463-6599	463-9468	339-44
Web: tdlr.texas.gov						
Lieutenant Governor David Dewhurst						
PO Box 12068	Austin	TX	78711	512-463-0001		339-44
Web: www.ltgov.state.tx.us						
Medical Board PO Box 2018	Austin	TX	78768	512-305-7010	305-7051	339-44
TF: 800-248-4062 ■ *Web:* www.tmb.state.tx.us						
Office of Court Administration						
205 W 14th St Ste 600	Austin	TX	78701	512-463-1625	463-1648	339-44
Web: www.courts.state.tx.us						
Pardons & Parole Board						
209 W 14th St Ste 500	Austin	TX	78701	512-936-6351	463-8120	339-44
Web: www.tdcj.texas.gov						
Public Utility Commission PO Box 13326	Austin	TX	78711	512-936-7000	936-7003	339-44
TF: 888-782-8477 ■ *Web:* www.puc.texas.gov						
Racing Commission						
8505 Cross Pk Dr Ste 110	Austin	TX	78754	512-833-6699	833-6907	712
Web: www.txrc.texas.gov						
Railroad Commission						
1701 N Congress Ave PO Box 12967	Austin	TX	78711	512-463-7058	463-7319	339-44
TF: 877-228-5740 ■ *Web:* www.rrc.state.tx.us						
Secretary of State PO Box 12887	Austin	TX	78711	512-463-5770	475-2761	339-44
TF: 800-252-8683 ■ *Web:* www.sos.state.tx.us						
State Government Information						
1501 N Congress Ave	Austin	TX	78701	512-936-9500	936-9400	339-44
Web: www.sao.texas.gov						
State Securities Board						
208 E Tenth St 5th Fl	Austin	TX	78701	512-305-8300	305-8310	339-44
Web: www.ssb.texas.gov						
Transportation Dept 125 E 11th St	Austin	TX	78701	512-463-8585	463-9389	339-44
Web: www.txdot.gov						
Veterans Commission PO Box 12277	Austin	TX	78711	512-463-6564	475-2395	339-44
Web: www.tvc.texas.gov						
Vital Statistics Bureau						
1100 W 49th St PO Box 12040	Austin	TX	78756	888-963-7111	776-7711*	339-44
**Fax Area Code:* 512 ■ *TF:* 888-963-7111 ■ *Web:* www.dshs.state.tx.us						
Workers Compensation Commission						
7551 Metro Center Dr Ste 100	Austin	TX	78744	800-252-7031	804-4001*	339-44
**Fax Area Code:* 512 ■ *TF:* 800-252-7031 ■ *Web:* tdi.texas.gov						
Workforce Commission						
101 E 15th St Rm 370	Austin	TX	78778	512-463-2222		259
Web: twc.state.tx.us						
Texas A & M International University						
5201 University Blvd	Laredo	TX	78041	956-326-2001	326-2199	166
Web: www.tamiu.edu						
Texas A & M Transportation Institute						
3135 Tamu	College Station	TX	77843	979-845-1713		162
Web: tti.tamu.edu						
Texas A & M University						
Rudder Tower Ste 205	College Station	TX	77843	979-845-8901	458-4617	166
TF: 888-890-5667 ■ *Web:* www.tamu.edu						
Texas A & M University						
Corpus Christi 6300 Ocean Dr	Corpus Christi	TX	78412	361-825-7024	825-5887	166
Web: www.tamucc.edu						
Evans Library 5000 Tamu	College Station	TX	77843	979-845-5741	845-6238	434-6
Web: library.tamu.edu						
Galveston 200 Seawolf Pkwy	Galveston	TX	77554	409-740-4428	740-4731	166
TF: 877-322-4443 ■ *Web:* www.tamug.edu						
Texarkana 7101 University Ave	Texarkana	TX	75503	903-223-3000	223-3140	166
TF: 866-791-9120 ■ *Web:* www.tamut.edu						
Texas A & M University System						
301 Tarrow St Ste 2043	College Station	TX	77840	979-458-7700	458-6044	786
Web: www.tamus.edu						
Texas A & M University System Health Science Ctr						
8441 Riverside Pkwy Clinical Bldg 1 Ste 3100	Bryan	TX	77807	979-436-9100	436-0072	167-2
Web: health.tamu.edu						
College of Medicine						
8447 Riverside Pkwy						
3rd Fl Health Professions Education Bldg	Bryan	TX	77807	979-436-0237		167-2
Web: medicine.tamu.edu						

Name / Address	City	State	ZIP	Phone	Fax	Class
Texas Air Systems Inc 6029 W Campus Cir Dr *Web:* www.texasairsystems.com	Irving	TX	75063	972-570-4700		14
Texas Allbreed Grooming School 1003 Enterprise Pl Ste 100 *Web:* www.tagsperfectjob.com	Arlington	TX	76001	817-472-7054		685
Texas Architectural Aggregate Inc PO Box 608 *TF:* 800-866-7025 ■ *Web:* www.texarcagg.com	San Saba	TX	76877	325-372-5105	372-5100	191-1
Texas Art Supply 2001 Montrose Blvd *TF:* 800-888-9278 ■ *Web:* www.texasart.com	Houston	TX	77006	713-526-5221	526-4062	45
Texas Association of Business 1209 Nueces St *Web:* www.txbiz.org	Austin	TX	78701	512-477-6721	477-0836	140
Texas Association of Realtors 1115 San Jacinto Blvd Ste 200 *TF:* 800-873-9155 ■ *Web:* www.texasrealestate.com	Austin	TX	78701	512-480-8200	370-2390	656
Texas Association of School Business Officials 6611 Boeing Dr *TF:* 800-338-6531 ■ *Web:* www.tasbo.org	El Paso	TX	79925	512-462-1711		78
Texas Automation Products Inc 1014 Dalworth Dr *Web:* www.texasautomationproducts.com	Mesquite	TX	75149	972-288-5000		454
Texas Ballet Theater 1540 Mall Cir *Web:* texasballettheater.org	Fort Worth	TX	76116	817-763-0207		573-1
Texas Bank & Trust 300 E Whaley PO Box 3188 *TF:* 800-263-7013 ■ *Web:* www.texasbankandtrust.com	Longview	TX	75606	903-237-5500		70
Texas Barber Colleges & Hairstyling Schools 9275 Richmond Ave Ste 180 *TF:* 866-639-2273 ■ *Web:* txbarber.edu	Houston	TX	77063	866-639-2273		685
Texas Basket Co 100 Myrtle Dr *TF:* 800-657-2200 ■ *Web:* www.texasbasket.com	Jacksonville	TX	75766	903-586-8014	586-0988	200
Texas Beef Council 8708 N Fm 620 *Web:* www.beeflovingtexans.com	Austin	TX	78726	512-335-2333		533
Texas Book Co 8501 Technology Cir *Web:* www.texasbook.com	Greenville	TX	75402	903-455-6937		96
Texas Book Festival 610 Brazos St Ste 200 *Web:* www.texasbookfestival.org	Austin	TX	78701	512-477-4055	322-0722	281
Texas Cable Assn 919 Congress Ave Ste 1350 *Web:* www.txcable.com	Austin	TX	78701	512-474-2082	474-0966	647
Texas Cafe & Bar 3604 50th St *Web:* www.texascafeandbarthespoon.com	Lubbock	TX	79413	806-792-8544		671
Texas Capital Bank 2000 McKinney Ave Ste 700 *TF:* 877-839-2265 ■ *Web:* www.texascapitalbank.com	Dallas	TX	75201	214-932-6600		70
Texas Center for Infectious Diseases 2303 SE Military Dr *TF:* 800-839-5864 ■ *Web:* www.dshs.texas.gov	San Antonio	TX	78223	210-534-8857	531-4502	374-7
Texas Center for Superconductivity 3201 Cullen Blvd Ste 202 *Web:* www.tcsuh.com	Houston	TX	77204	713-743-8200	743-8201	668
Texas Children's Hospital 6621 Fannin St *TF:* 800-364-5437 ■ *Web:* www.texaschildrens.org	Houston	TX	77030	832-824-1000		374-1
Texas Christian University TCU PO Box 297043 *TF:* 800-828-3764 ■ *Web:* www.tcu.edu	Fort Worth	TX	76129	817-257-7490	257-7268	166
Texas City-La Marque Chamber of Commerce 9702 Emmett F Lowry Expy *Web:* www.tclmchamber.com	Texas City	TX	77590	409-935-1408	316-0901	139
Texas Coffee Company Inc 3297 S M L King Jr Pkwy *TF:* 800-259-3400 ■ *Web:* www.texjoy.com	Beaumont	TX	77705	409-835-3434		296-7
Texas College 2404 N Grand Ave *TF:* 800-306-6299 ■ *Web:* www.texascollege.edu	Tyler	TX	75702	903-593-8311		166
Texas Concrete Partners LP 4702 N Vine St *Web:* www.texasconcrete.com	Victoria	TX	77904	361-573-9145	578-5859	183
Texas Correctional Industries 861 IH-45 N (S Frontage Rd) PO Box 4013 *Web:* tci.tdcj.texas.gov	Huntsville	TX	77342	936-437-6048	437-8423	630
Texas County PO Box 197 *Web:* texas.okcounties.org	Guymon	OK	73942	580-338-3141	338-4311	338
Texas County 210 N Grand Ave Ste 201 *Web:* texascountymissouri.gov	Houston	MO	65483	417-967-4709	967-2091	338
Texas Crushed Stone Co 5300 S IH-35 PO Box 1000 *TF:* 800-772-8272 ■ *Web:* www.texascrushedstoneco.com	Georgetown	TX	78627	512-930-0106	244-6055	503-5
Texas de Brazil 101 N Houston St *Web:* texasdebrazil.com	Fort Worth	TX	76102	817-882-9500	882-9503	671
Texas Deer Assn 816 Congress Ave Ste 950 *Web:* texasdeerassociation.com	Austin	TX	78701	512-499-0466		45
Texas Democratic Party 1106 Lavaca St Ste 100 *Web:* www.texasdemocrats.org	Austin	TX	78701	512-478-9800		616-1
Texas Dental Assn 1946 S IH-35 Ste 400 *TF:* 800-832-1145 ■ *Web:* www.tda.org	Austin	TX	78704	512-443-3675	443-3031	227
Texas Department of Criminal Justice 209 W 14th St PO Box 13084 *Web:* www.tdcj.texas.gov	Austin	TX	78701	512-463-9988		213
Texas Department of Motor Vehicles 4000 Jackson Ave *Web:* www.txdmv.gov	Austin	TX	78731	512-465-3000	465-4129	516
Texas Department of State Health Services 1100 West 49th St **Fax Area Code:* 888 ■ *Web:* www.dshs.texas.gov	Austin	TX	78756	512-776-7111	963-7111*	339-44
Texas Design Interests LLC 6001 W William Cannon Dr Ste 203C *Web:* tdi-llc.net	Austin	TX	78749	512-301-3389		261
Texas Die Casting Inc 600 S Loop 485 *Web:* texasdiecasting.com	Gladewater	TX	75647	903-845-2224	845-6155	308
Texas Direct Auto 12053 Southwest Fwy (Hwy 59) *Web:* www.texasdirectauto.com	Stafford	TX	77477	281-499-8200		57
Texas Discovery Gardens 3601 Martin Luther King Junior Blvd *Web:* txdg.org	Dallas	TX	75210	214-428-7476	428-5338	97
Texas Disposal Systems Inc (TDS) 12200 Carl Rd *TF:* 800-375-8375 ■ *Web:* www.texasdisposal.com	Creedmoor	TX	78610	512-421-1300	243-4123	804
Texas Dow Employees Credit Union (TDECU) 1001 FM 2004 *TF:* 800-839-1154 ■ *Web:* www.tdecu.org	Lake Jackson	TX	77566	979-297-1154	299-0212	219
Texas Eastern Transmission LP 5400 Westheimer Ct *TF:* 800-231-7794 ■ *Web:* www.spectraenergy.com	Houston	TX	77056	713-627-5400		325
Texas Economic Publishers 510 N Valley Mills Dr Ste 300 *Web:* www.perrymangroup.com	Waco	TX	76710	254-751-9595	751-7855	637-10
Texas Education Agency (TEA) William B. Travis Bldg 1701 N Congress Ave *Web:* www.tea.state.tx.us	Austin	TX	78701	512-463-9734	463-9838	637-2
Texas Electric Co-opeartives Inc 1122 Colorado St 24th Fl *TF:* 800-301-2860 ■ *Web:* www.texas-ec.org	Austin	TX	78701	512-454-0311		245
Texas Electronics Inc 4230 Shilling Way *TF:* 800-424-5651 ■ *Web:* www.texaselectronics.com	Dallas	TX	75237	214-631-2490	631-4218	472
Texas Energy Research Associates Inc c/o Edward Selig *Web:* www.terai.com	Austin	TX	78755	512-413-0902		194
Texas Enterprises 4911 E 7th St *TF:* 800-545-4412 ■ *Web:* www.texasenterprises.com	Austin	TX	78702	800-545-4412		579
Texas Farm Bureau PO Box 2689 *TF:* 800-488-7872 ■ *Web:* www.texasfarmbureau.org	Waco	TX	76702	254-772-3030		457-1
Texas Federal Credit Union 1100 Commerce St Ste 745 *TF:* 800-242-9132 ■ *Web:* texfed.org	Dallas	TX	75242	800-242-9132		219
Texas Fish & Game Magazine 247 Airtex Dr *TF:* 800-725-1134 ■ *Web:* fishgame.com	Houston	TX	77090	281-227-3001		457
Texas Foam Inc 1278 Hwy 71 W *Web:* www.texasfoam.com	Bastrop	TX	78602	512-581-7500	581-7520	601
Texas Folklore Society (TFS) PO Box 13007 *Web:* www.texasfolkloresociety.org	Nacogdoches	TX	75962	936-468-4407	468-1028	48-6
Texas Gauge & Control Inc 7575 Dillon St *TF:* 800-914-0009 ■ *Web:* www.tgcigroup.com	Houston	TX	77061	713-641-2282		358
Texas Gulf Supply Corp 10420 Rockley Rd *Web:* www.texasgulfsupply.com	Houston	TX	77099	281-495-5500	495-5990	787
Texas Health Presbyterian Hospital-WNJ Therapy Services 500 N Highland Ave *Web:* www.wnj.org	Sherman	TX	75092	903-870-4611	870-4409	374-3
Texas Health Resources 612 E Lamar Blvd *TF:* 877-847-9355 ■ *Web:* www.texashealth.org	Arlington	TX	76011	877-847-9355		353
Texas Healthcare PLLC 2821 Lackland Rd Ste 300 *TF:* 877-238-6200 ■ *Web:* www.txhealthcare.com	Fort Worth	TX	76116	817-378-3640	740-8516	374-3
Texas Heat Treating Inc 155 Texas Ave *TF:* 800-580-5884 ■ *Web:* www.texasheattreating.com	Round Rock	TX	78664	512-255-5884	255-8464	484
Texas Hospital Insurance Exchange 8310 N Capital of Texas Hwy Ste 250 *TF:* 800-792-0060 ■ *Web:* www.thie.com	Austin	TX	78731	512-451-5775	451-3101	391-5
Texas Hydraulics Inc 3410 Range Rd *Web:* www.texashydraulics.com	Temple	TX	76504	254-778-4701	774-9940	223
Texas Industrial Security 101 Summit Ave Ste 404 *Web:* www.txsecurity.com	Fort Worth	TX	76102	817-335-3046	335-3048	692
Texas Instruments Inc PO Box 660199 *NASDAQ: TXN* ■ *Web:* www.ti.com	Dallas	TX	75266	972-995-2011		696
Texas International Theatrical Arts Society (TITAS) 2520 Flora St *Web:* titas.org	Dallas	TX	75201	214-880-0202		573-1
Texas Jet Inc 200 Texas Way *TF:* 800-776-4547 ■ *Web:* www.texasjet.com	Fort Worth	TX	76106	817-624-8438		63
Texas Juvenile Justice Dept 11209 Metric Blvd Bldg H *Web:* www.tjjd.texas.gov	Austin	TX	78758	512-490-7130		340-14
Texas Land & Cattle Steak House 7202 Indiana Ave *Web:* www.txlc.com	Lubbock	TX	79423	806-791-0555		671
Texas Law Review (TLR) 727 E Dean Keeton St *Web:* www.texaslrev.com	Austin	TX	78705	512-232-1280	471-3282	637-9
Texas Lawyers Insurance Exchange (TLIE) 1801 S MoPac Ste 300 *TF:* 800-252-9332 ■ *Web:* www.tlie.org	Austin	TX	78746	512-480-9074	482-8738	391-5
Texas Leather Trim Inc 2422 Blue Smoke Ct S *TF:* 800-880-0248 ■ *Web:* www.tltleather.com	Fort Worth	TX	76105	817-535-5883	535-8643	745-4
Texas Legal Services Center Inc 2101 S IH 35 Frontage Rd *TF:* 888-343-4414 ■ *Web:* www.tlsc.org	Austin	TX	78741	800-622-2520		428
Texas Library Assn 3355 Bee Cave Rd Ste 401 *Web:* www.txla.org	West Lake Hills	TX	78746	512-328-1518		435
Texas Life Insurance Co 900 Washington PO Box 830 *TF:* 800-283-9233 ■ *Web:* www.texaslife.com	Waco	TX	76703	254-752-6521	754-7629	391-2
Texas Lift-Off Correction Ribbon 1700 Surveyor Blvd Ste 110	Carrollton	TX	75006	972-416-8100		628
Texas Lime Co 15865 Farm Rd 1434 PO Box 851 *TF:* 800-772-8000 ■ *Web:* www.uslm.com	Cleburne	TX	76033	817-641-4433	556-0905	440
Texas Loan Star Inc 2233 Yale St *Web:* texasloanstar.com	Houston	TX	77008	713-802-0606	802-0909	653
Texas Longhorn Breeders Association of America (TLBAA) 2315 N Main St Ste 402 *Web:* www.tlbaa.org	Fort Worth	TX	76164	817-625-6241	625-1388	48-2

Name / Address	City	State	Zip	Phone	Fax	Class
Texas Lutheran University 1000 W Ct St *TF:* 800-771-8521 ■ *Web:* www.tlu.edu	Seguin	TX	78155	830-372-8050	372-8096	166
Texas Mailhouse Inc 8606 Wall St Ste 1740 *Web:* texasmailhouse.com	Austin	TX	78754	512-837-2046		5
Texas Materials Group Inc 7151 Randol Mill Rd. *Web:* texasmaterialsgroup.com	Fort Worth	TX	76120	817-429-2452		188-4
Texas Medical Assn 401 W 15th St *TF:* 800-880-1300 ■ *Web:* www.texmed.org	Austin	TX	78701	512-370-1300	370-1693	474
Texas Methodist Foundation 11709 Boulder Ln Ste 100 *TF:* 800-933-5502 ■ *Web:* www.tmf-fdn.org	Austin	TX	78726	512-331-9971		305
Texas Military Forces Museum PO Box 5218 *Web:* www.texasmilitaryforcesmuseum.org	Austin	TX	78763	512-782-5659	782-6750	520
Texas Military Institute (TMI) 20955 W Tejas Trl *Web:* www.tmi-sa.org	San Antonio	TX	78257	210-698-7171	698-0715	622
Texas Motor Speedway 3545 Lone Star Cir *TF:* 800-805-8721 ■ *Web:* texasmotorspeedway.com	Fort Worth	TX	76177	817-215-8510		642
Texas Motorplex 7500 W Hwy 287 *TF:* 800-668-6775 ■ *Web:* texasmotorplex.com	Ennis	TX	75119	972-878-2641	878-1848	515
Texas Mutual Insurance Co 6210 E Hwy 290 *TF:* 888-532-5246 ■ *Web:* www.texasmutual.com	Austin	TX	78723	512-224-3800	224-3889	391-4
Texas National Bank 400 E Broadway PO Box 510 *TF:* 800-921-9316 ■ *Web:* www.texasnational.bank	Sweetwater	TX	79556	325-235-4997	235-4014	70
Texas Oil & Gas Association Inc 304 W 13th St. *Web:* www.txoga.org	Austin	TX	78701	512-478-6631		138
Texas Orthopedic Hospital 7401 Main St *TF:* 866-783-4549 ■ *Web:* texasorthopedic.com	Houston	TX	77030	713-799-8600		374-7
Texas Pacific Land Trust 1700 Pacific Ave Ste 2770 *NYSE: TPL* ■ *Web:* www.tpltrust.com	Dallas	TX	75201	214-969-5530	871-7139	675
Texas Pack Inc 508 Port Rd	Port Isabel	TX	78578	956-943-5461		296-14
Texas Parks & Wildlife Dept 4200 Smith School Rd *Web:* tpwd.texas.gov	Austin	TX	78744	512-389-4800		565
Texas Pharmacy Assn 3200 Steck Ave Ste 370 *TF:* 800-505-5463 ■ *Web:* www.texaspharmacy.org	Austin	TX	78757	512-836-8350	836-0308	585
Texas Pipe & Supply Company Inc 2330 Holmes Rd. *TF:* 800-233-8736 ■ *Web:* texaspipe.com	Houston	TX	77051	713-799-9235	799-8701	492
Texas Pneumatics Systems Inc 2404 Superior Dr *TF:* 800-211-9690 ■ *Web:* www.txps.com	Arlington	TX	76013	817-794-0068		20
Texas Presbyterian Foundation 6100 Colwell Blvd Ste 250 *TF:* 800-955-3155 ■ *Web:* www.tpf.org	Irving	TX	75039	214-522-3155	522-3157	48-20
Texas Press Assn 305 S Congress Ave. *TF:* 800-749-4793 ■ *Web:* www.texaspress.com	Austin	TX	78704	512-477-6755		7
Texas Process Equipment Co 5215 Ted St. *TF:* 800-828-4114 ■ *Web:* www.texasprocess.com	Houston	TX	77040	713-460-5555	460-4807	385
Texas Public Employees Assn 512 E 11th St Ste 100 *Web:* www.tpea.org	Austin	TX	78701	512-476-2691		474
Texas Public Interest Research Group 815 Brazos St Ste 600 *Web:* texpirg.org	Austin	TX	78701	512-479-7287		633
Texas Recycling Surplus Inc 2835 Congressman Ln *Web:* www.texasrecycling.com	Dallas	TX	75220	214-357-0262		660
Texas Refinery Corp 840 N Main St *TF:* 800-827-0711 ■ *Web:* www.texasrefinery.com	Fort Worth	TX	76164	817-332-1161		541
Texas Republic Bank 2595 Preston Rd Ste 100 *Web:* texasrepublicbank.com	Frisco	TX	75034	972-334-0700		70
Texas Republican Party 1108 Lavaca Ste 500 *Web:* www.texasgop.org	Austin	TX	78701	512-477-9821	480-0709	616-2
Texas Roadhouse 2605 Edgewood Rd SW *Web:* www.texasroadhouse.com	Cedar Rapids	IA	52404	319-396-3300		671
Texas School of Bartenders 5555 N Lamar Blvd Ste L-129 *Web:* www.texasschoolofbartenders.com	Austin	TX	78751	512-323-2002		685
Texas School of Bartenders 3300 Chimney Rock Rd Ste 303 *Web:* www.texasschoolofbartenders.com	Houston	TX	77056	713-522-4600		685
Texas Scottish Rite Hospital for Children 2222 Welborn St. *TF:* 800-421-1121 ■ *Web:* scottishriteforchildren.org	Dallas	TX	75219	214-559-5000	559-7447	374-1
Texas Service Life Insurance Co 1010 Ranch Rd 620S *TF:* 800-756-7306 ■ *Web:* www.tslic.com	Austin	TX	78734	512-263-6977		796
Texas Shapes 6470 Rupley Cir	Houston	TX	77087	713-641-1000		757
Texas Southern University (TSU) 3100 Cleburne St *Web:* www.tsu.edu	Houston	TX	77004	713-313-7011	313-1859	166
Texas Space Grant Consortium 3925 W Braker Ln Ste 200 *TF:* 800-248-8742 ■ *Web:* www.tsgc.utexas.edu	Austin	TX	78759	512-471-6913	471-3585	167-3
Texas Sports Hall of Fame 1108 S University Parks Dr. *TF:* 800-567-9561 ■ *Web:* www.tshof.org	Waco	TX	76706	254-756-1633		522
Texas Stainless 3402 Center St *TF:* 800-874-8538 ■ *Web:* www.texasstainless.com	Temple	TX	76503	254-773-0831	778-0887	492
Texas State Aquarium 2710 N Shoreline Blvd *TF:* 800-477-4853 ■ *Web:* www.texasstateaquarium.org	Corpus Christi	TX	78402	361-881-1200	881-1257	40
Texas State Cemetery 909 Navasota St. *Web:* cemetery.tspb.texas.gov	Austin	TX	78702	512-463-0605	463-8811	50-4
Texas State Directory Inc 1800 Nueces St *Web:* www.txdirectory.com	Austin	TX	78701	512-477-5698	473-2447	637-10
Texas State Museum of Asian Cultures 1809 N Chaparral St. *Web:* www.texasasianculturesmuseum.org	Corpus Christi	TX	78401	361-881-8827		520
Texas State Railroad State Park PO Box 39 *Web:* tpwd.texas.gov	Rusk	TX	75785	903-683-2561		565
Texas State Technical College						
Harlingen 1902 N Loop 499 *TF:* 800-852-8784 ■ *Web:* www.tstc.edu	Harlingen	TX	78550	956-364-4763	364-5117	162
Waco 3801 Campus Dr *Web:* www.waco.tstc.edu	Waco	TX	76705	254-799-3611		162
Texas State University						
San Marcos 601 University Dr. *TF:* 866-294-0987 ■ *Web:* www.txstate.edu	San Marcos	TX	78666	512-245-2651	245-8044	166
Texas State University System (TSUS) 601 Colorado St *Web:* www.tsus.edu	Austin	TX	78701	512-463-1808	463-1816	786
Texas Station Gambling Hall & Hotel 2101 Texas Star Ln *TF:* 800-654-8888 ■ *Web:* www.texasstation.com	North Las Vegas	NV	89032	702-631-1000		133
Texas Steakhouse 126 Gateway Blvd *TF:* 855-220-7228 ■ *Web:* www.texassteakhouse.com	Rocky Mount	NC	27804	855-220-7228		671
Texas Steel Conversion Inc 3101 Holmes Rd. *Web:* www.texassteelconversion.com	Houston	TX	77051	713-733-6013	733-9248	595
Texas Steel Processing Inc 5480 Windfern Rd. *Web:* www.txstl.com	Houston	TX	77041	281-822-3200	822-3201	492
Texas Stress Inc 1304 Underwood Rd *Web:* www.texasstress.com	La Porte	TX	77571	281-930-0897	930-0992	484
Texas Tech University 2500 Broadway *Web:* www.ttu.edu	Lubbock	TX	79409	806-742-2011		167-3
Texas Tech University Health Sciences Ctr						
School of Medicine 3601 4th St *Web:* www.ttuhsc.edu	Lubbock	TX	79430	806-743-1000	743-3021	167-2
Texas Tech University Press 608 N Knoxville Ave Grantham Bldg Ste120 *TF:* 800-832-4042 ■ *Web:* www.ttupress.org	Lubbock	TX	79415	806-742-2982	742-2979	637-4
Texas Telcom Credit Union 8818 Garland Rd. *TF:* 800-607-3474 ■ *Web:* textelcu.org	Dallas	TX	75218	214-320-8818	320-8875	219
Texas Timberjack Inc 6004 S First St *Web:* www.texastimberjack.com	Lufkin	TX	75901	936-634-3365	639-3673	274
Texas Toolmakers Inc 11411 E Coker Loop *Web:* www.texastoolmakers.com	San Antonio	TX	78216	210-494-3651	494-6139	454
Texas Transeastern Inc 3438 Pasadena Blvd *TF:* 800-344-8284 ■ *Web:* ttedelivers.com	Pasadena	TX	77503	281-604-3100		780
Texas Transportation Museum 11731 Wetmore Rd *Web:* www.txtransportationmuseum.org	San Antonio	TX	78247	210-490-3554		520
Texas Travel Industry Assn 3345 Bee Cave Rd Ste 102A *Web:* www.ttia.org	Austin	TX	78746	512-328-8842	478-9177	772
Texas Troubadour Theatre 2416 Music Valley Dr *Web:* etrecordshop.com	Nashville	TN	37214	615-889-2474		572
Texas United Pipe Inc 11627 N Houston Rosslyn Rd. *TF:* 800-966-8741 ■ *Web:* www.texasunitedpipe.com	Houston	TX	77086	281-448-9463	448-6983	596
Texas Vet Lab Inc 1702 N Bell St *TF:* 800-284-8403 ■ *Web:* www.texasvetlab.com	San Angelo	TX	76903	325-653-4505		584
Texas Veterinary Medical Assn 8104 Exchange Dr *TF:* 800-711-0023 ■ *Web:* www.tvma.org	Austin	TX	78754	512-452-4224	452-6633	795
Texas Visiting Nurse Service Ltd 814 E Tyler *TF:* 800-242-8867 ■ *Web:* tvnsltd.com	Harlingen	TX	78550	956-412-1401		363
Texas Water Utilities Assn (TWUA) 1106 Clayton Ln Ste 112 W *TF:* 888-367-8982 ■ *Web:* www.twua.org	Austin	TX	78723	512-459-3124	459-7124	48-13
Texas Wealth Management LLC 18333 Egret Bay Blvd Ste 600 *Web:* texaswealthmanagement.com	Houston	TX	77058	281-333-3800		2
Texas Wesleyan University 1201 Wesleyan St. *TF:* 800-580-8980 ■ *Web:* txwes.edu	Fort Worth	TX	76105	817-531-4444		166
Texas Wesleyan University School of Law 1515 Commerce St. *TF:* 800-733-9529 ■ *Web:* law.tamu.edu	Fort Worth	TX	76102	817-212-4000	212-4141	167-1
Texas West Bar-B-Que 1600 Fulton Ave *Web:* www.texaswestbbq.com	Sacramento	CA	95825	916-483-7427		671
Texas Western Press 500 W University Ave *Web:* www.twp.utep.edu	El Paso	TX	79968	915-747-5688		637-2
Texas Woman's University 304 Admin Dr PO Box 425589 *TF:* 866-809-6130 ■ *Web:* twu.edu	Denton	TX	76204	940-898-3188	898-3081	166
Texas Women Ventures 3625 N Hall St Ste 615 *Web:* www.twvcapital.com	Dallas	TX	75219	214-444-7890		390
Texas Zoo 110 Memorial Dr *Web:* www.texaszoo.org	Victoria	TX	77901	361-573-7681	576-1094	823
Texasgulf Federal Credit Union 2101 N Fulton St *Web:* texasgulffcu.org	Wharton	TX	77488	979-282-2300		219
Texas-New Mexico Power Co (TNMP) 577 N Garden Ridge Blvd *TF:* 888-866-7456 ■ *Web:* www.tnmp.com	Lewisville	TX	75067	972-420-4189		787
TEXbase Inc 895 Technology Blvd Ste 202 *Web:* www.texbase.com	Bozeman	MT	59718	406-582-8874		177
TexCom Inc 3600 S Gessner Ste 200 *Web:* www.texcomresources.com	Houston	TX	77063	713-914-9193	914-9249	540

	Phone	Fax	Class
Texelerate LLC 16436 Carrara Wy Ste 202 . . . . Naples FL 34110 *Web:* www.texelerate.net	215-275-8492		463
Texford Battery Co 2002 Milby St . . . . .Houston TX 77003 *Web:* texford.com	713-222-0125		74
TexLoc Ltd 4700 Lone Star Blvd. . . . . Fort Worth TX 76106 *TF:* 800-423-6551 ■ *Web:* www.texloc.com	817-625-5081		640
Texmark Chemicals Inc 900 Clinton Dr . . . . Galena Park TX 77547 *Web:* texmark.com	713-455-1206	455-8959	144
Tex-Mex Cold Storage Inc 6665 E 14th St . . . . Brownsville TX 78520 *Web:* www.bedc.com	956-831-4531	831-9572	803-2
Texollini Inc 2575 E El Presidio St. . . . . .Carson CA 90810 *Web:* www.texollini.com	310-537-3400		745-6
Texoma Medical Ctr 5016 S US Hwy 75 . . . . Denison TX 75020 *TF:* 800-256-0943 ■ *Web:* www.texomamedicalcenter.net	903-416-4000		374-3
Texoma Regional Blood Ctr 3911 N Texoma Pkwy . . . . Sherman TX 75090 *Web:* texomablood.org	903-893-4314	893-8628	89
Texon USA Inc 1190 Huntington Rd. . . . . .Russell MA 01071 *Web:* www.texon.com	413-862-3652		605-2
TexPar Energy LLC 920 Tenth Ave N. . . . . Onalaska WI 54650 *TF:* 800-323-7350 ■ *Web:* www.texpar.com	608-779-6580	779-6880	581
TExperts Inc 1875 Old Alabama Rd Ste 110 . . . . Roswell GA 30076 *Web:* www.texpertsinc.com	770-864-8888		180
Texstars 802 Ave J E. . . . . Grand Prairie TX 75050 *Web:* texstars.com	972-647-1366	641-2800	596
Text My Market Inc 350 N 500 W . . . . Lehi UT 84043	801-836-1123	812-8124	195
Text100 Integrated Communications 100 Montgomery St . . . . San Francisco CA 94104 *Web:* www.text100.com	415-593-8400		636
Textainer 650 California St 16th Fl. . . . . San Francisco CA 94108 *Web:* www.textainer.com	415-434-0551	434-0599	198
Textbook Brokers Inc 911 Rochester Rd . . . . Sparta MO 65753 *Web:* www.k12savings.com	417-485-3440		95
Tex-Tech Industries Inc 1 City Ctr 11th Fl . . . . Portland ME 04101 *Web:* www.textechindustries.com	207-756-8606		745-3
Textile Care Services Inc 225 Wood Lake Dr SE. . . . . .Rochester MN 55904 *TF:* 800-422-0945 ■ *Web:* healthcarelinensg.com	800-422-0945		442
Textile Graphics Inc 3555 Squires Way. . . . . McMinnville OR 97128 **Fax Area Code:* 503 ■ *TF:* 800-367-7548 ■ *Web:* www.textilegraphicsinc.com	800-367-7548	472-1495*	34
Textile Management Systems Inc 10 Timberlane Dr . . . . Hammond LA 70403	985-345-9590		258
Textile Printing Co 6107 Ringgold Rd. . . . . Chattanooga TN 37412 *Web:* www.tpcpackaging.com	423-894-1110		548
Textile Rental Services Assn (TRSA) 1800 Diagonal Rd Ste 200 . . . . Alexandria VA 22314 *TF:* 877-770-9274 ■ *Web:* www.trsa.org	703-519-0029	519-0026	49-4
Textile Rubber & Chemical Company Inc 1300 Tiarco Dr SW. . . . . Dalton GA 30721 *TF:* 800-727-8453 ■ *Web:* www.trcc.com	706-277-1300	277-3738	605-3
Textiles South Inc 10100 NW 116 Way Ste 1. . . . . Miami FL 33178 *TF:* 800-338-6386 ■ *Web:* www.label-it.com	305-887-4949	887-3339	594
Textron Fluid & Power Inc 40 Westminster St. . . . . .Providence RI 02903 *Web:* www.textron.com	401-421-2800		641
Tex-Trude Lp 2001 Sheldon Rd . . . . Channelview TX 77530 *Web:* www.tex-trude.com	281-452-5961		596
Tex-Tube Co 1503 N Post Oak Rd . . . . .Houston TX 77055 *TF:* 800-839-7473 ■ *Web:* www.tex-tube.com	713-686-4351	681-5256	490
Textured Coatings of America 2422 E 15th St . . . . Panama City FL 32405 **Fax Area Code:* 850 ■ *TF:* 800-454-0340 ■ *Web:* www.texcote.com	800-454-0340	913-8619*	550
TextureMedia Inc 3636 Executive Center Dr . . . . Austin TX 78731 *Web:* www.naturallycurly.com	512-371-7545		224
Texwood Industries Inc 603 Big Stone Gap Rd . . . . Duncanville TX 75137 *Web:* www.qualitycabinets.com	972-298-4975		115
Tezel & Cotter Air Conditioning Co 2730 Castroville Rd . . . . .San Antonio TX 78237 *Web:* www.tezelandcotter.com	210-734-5156		610
Tezzaron Semiconductor Corp 7600 Chevy Chase Dr Bldg 2 Ste 300. . . . . Austin TX 78752 *TF:* 844-839-7364 ■ *Web:* tezzaron.com	630-505-0404		696
TF Forming Systems Inc 3711 W Mason St . . . . . . .Oneida WI 54155 *TF:* 800-360-4634 ■ *Web:* www.tfsystem.com	920-309-1856		697
TF Hudgins Inc 4405 Directors Row . . . . .Houston TX 77092 *TF:* 800-582-3834 ■ *Web:* www.tfhudgins.com	713-682-3651		385
TF Kinnealey & Company Inc 1100 Pearl St . . . . Brockton MA 02301 *Web:* kinnealey.com	508-638-7700		296-26
T-Fal Corp 2121 Eden Rd . . . . .Millville NJ 08332 *TF:* 800-395-8325 ■ *Web:* www.t-falusa.com	800-395-8325		361
TFB (Fauquier Bank, The) 10 Courthouse Sq. . . . . Warrenton VA 20186 *TF:* 800-638-3798 ■ *Web:* www.tfb.bank	540-347-2700		70
TFC (Franchise Co, The) 14502 N Dale Mabry Ste 200 . . . . Tampa FL 33618 *TF:* 800-294-5591 ■ *Web:* www.fsvbrands.com	800-294-5591		463
TFCNET Corp 15211 Lake Maurine Dr . . . . .Odessa FL 33556 *Web:* www.tfc.net	813-880-0909		180
TFCU (Teachers Federal Credit Union) 2410 N Ocean Ave . . . . .Farmingville NY 11738 *TF:* 800-341-4333 ■ *Web:* www.teachersfcu.org	631-698-7000		219
TFE Company Inc 1311 Hwy 290 W . . . . Brenham TX 77833 **Fax Area Code:* 281 ■ *Web:* www.tfecompany.com	979-836-6111	836-1112*	604
TFI (Technology Futures Inc) 13740 Research Blvd (N Hwy 183) Ste C-1 . . . . Austin TX 78750 *TF:* 800-835-3887 ■ *Web:* www.tfi.com	512-258-8898	258-0087	196
TFI (Fertilizer Institute, The) 425 Third St SW Ste 950 . . . . Washington DC 20024 *Web:* www.tfi.org	202-962-0490	962-0577	48-2
TFI (Taxpayers' Federation of Illinois) 430 E Vine St Ste A. . . . . .Springfield IL 62703 *Web:* www.illinoistax.org	217-522-6818		48-6
TFO Tech Company Ltd 41 S High St. . . . . Columbus OH 43215	740-426-6381		483
TFP Data Systems 3451 Jupiter Ct. . . . . .Oxnard CA 93030 **Fax Area Code:* 800 ■ *TF:* 800-482-9367 ■ *Web:* www.tfpdata.com	805-981-0992	526-1040*	110
TFP nutrition 915 S Fredonia St . . . . .Nacogdoches TX 75964 *TF:* 800-392-3110 ■ *Web:* tfpnutrition.com	936-564-3711	560-8200	578
TFS (Texas Folklore Society) PO Box 13007 . . . . .Nacogdoches TX 75962 *Web:* www.texasfolkloresociety.org	936-468-4407	468-1028	48-6
TFS Advisors LLC 100 Second Ave S Ste 300 . . . . Edmonds WA 98020 *Web:* tfsadvisors.com	425-776-0446	670-9162	690
TFS Capital LLC 10 N High St Ste 500 . . . . West Chester PA 19380 *TF:* 888-837-4446 ■ *Web:* tfscapital.com	888-837-4446		528
TFT (Trees for Tomorrow) 519 Sheridan St E PO Box 609. . . . . .Eagle River WI 54521 *Web:* www.treesfortomorrow.com	715-479-6456	479-2318	49-5
TFT Inc 2991 N Osage Dr PO Box 445 . . . . Tulsa OK 74127 *TF:* 800-303-7982 ■ *Web:* tulsafintube.com	918-834-2366	834-1553	480
TG Automotive Sealing Kentucky LLC 501 Frank Yost Ln. . . . . .Hopkinsville KY 42240 *Web:* www.toyodagosei.com	270-475-1400	475-1494	676
TG Construction Inc 139 Nevada St. . . . . El Segundo CA 90245 *Web:* www.tgconst.com	310-640-0220	640-2907	188-5
TGap Ventures LLC 7171 Stadium Dr. . . . . .Kalamazoo MI 49009 *Web:* tgapvcfunds.com	269-217-1999	381-7620	792
TGaS Advisors 301 E Germantown Pke . . . . .Norristown PA 19401 *Web:* www.tgas.com	610-233-1210	239-5117	196
TGC 3200 Travis St. . . . . .Houston TX 77006 *Web:* thegoodmancorp.com	512-236-8002		463
TGC Industries Inc 1304 Summit Ave Ste 2 . . . . Plano TX 75074 *NASDAQ: TGE* ■ *Web:* www.tgcseismic.com	972-881-1099	424-3943	538
TGG Accounting 10188 Telesis Ct Ste 130 . . . . San Diego CA 92121 *Web:* tgg-accounting.com	760-697-1033		734
TGG Inc 3 Birch Rd . . . . Middleton MA 01949 *Web:* www.gtgmach.com	978-777-5010	774-0591	454
TGI Direct 5365 Hill 23 Dr . . . . .Flint MI 48507 *TF:* 800-337-2237 ■ *Web:* www.tgidirect.com	810-239-5553	239-4321	5
TGI-Direct 3212 S Cravens Rd . . . . Fort Worth TX 76119 *Web:* www.tgi-direct.com	817-457-8412		687
TGMC (Terrebonne General Medical Ctr) 8166 Main St . . . . .Houma LA 70360 *TF:* 888-850-6270 ■ *Web:* www.tgmc.com	985-873-4141	873-5306	374-3
TGO Consulting Inc 140 Renfrew Dr Ste 120 . . . . Markham ON L3R6B3 *Web:* www.tgo.ca	905-470-6830		180
TGO Inc 16025 N 76th St. . . . . Scottsdale AZ 85260 *Web:* www.greatorg.com	480-998-1522		191-3
TGP (Grocery People Ltd, The) 14505 Yellowhead Trl . . . . Edmonton AB T5L3C4 *TF:* 800-461-9401 ■ *Web:* www.tgp.ca	780-447-5700		297-8
TGR Industrial Services 8777 Tallyho Rd Bldg 1 . . . . .Houston TX 77061 *TF:* 800-625-9288 ■ *Web:* www.tgrind.com	713-636-2288		743
TGS (Topeka Genealogical Society) PO Box 4048 . . . . .Topeka KS 66604 *Web:* www.tgstopeka.org	785-233-5762		48-13
TGV Partners LLC 23 Corporate Plz Ste 215 . . . . .Newport Beach CA 92660 *Web:* www.tgvpartners.com	949-284-1114		528
Tgw International Inc 5 Braco International Blvd. . . . . Wilder KY 41076 *TF:* 800-407-0173 ■ *Web:* tgwint.com	859-647-7383	647-7877	350
TGW Systems Inc 6870 Grand Haven Rd. . . . . .Spring Lake MI 49456 *Web:* www.tgw-conveyor.com	231-798-4547		207
TH Brokerage LLC 440 S Lasalle St Ste 2900. .Chicago IL 60605 *Web:* x-fa.com	312-235-0320	235-0336	169
TH Eckhart House 810 Main St. . . . . .Wheeling WV 26003 *Web:* www.eckharthouse.com	304-232-5439		50-3
TH Marine Supplies Inc 200 Finney Dr. . . . . Huntsville AL 35824 *Web:* thmarinesupplies.com	256-772-0164		601
TH Martin Inc 8500 Brookpark Rd. . . . . .Cleveland OH 44129 *Web:* thmartin.net	216-741-2020		697
TH Plastics Inc 106 E Main St . . . . .Mendon MI 49072 *Web:* www.thplastics.com	269-496-8495	496-4675	604
TH Properties 345 Main St Ste 112. . . . . Harleysville PA 19438 *TF:* 800-225-5847 ■ *Web:* www.thproperties.com	215-513-4270	511-3202	187
TH Stone Memorial Saint Joseph Peninsula State Park 8899 Cape San Blas Rd . . . . Port Saint Joe FL 32456 *Web:* www.floridastateparks.org	850-227-1327	227-1488	565
THA (Terry Hines & Assoc) 2550 N Hollywood Way Ste 600. . . . . .Burbank CA 91505 *Web:* www.terryhines.com	818-562-9433		7
Thacher School 5025 Thacher Rd. . . . . Ojai CA 93023 *Web:* www.thacher.org	805-640-3210	640-1033	622
Thacker Insurance Service LLC 315 W College Ave. . . . . Greenville IL 62246 *Web:* thackerinsuranceservice.com	618-664-4266		390
Thackeray Partners 5207 McKinney Ave Ste 200. Dallas TX 75205 *Web:* www.thackeraypartners.com	214-360-7830		655
Thaddeus Stevens College of Technology (TSCT) 750 E King St . . . . .Lancaster PA 17602 *TF:* 800-842-3832 ■ *Web:* stevenscollege.edu	717-299-7701	391-6929	800
THAI 4029 Campbell Ave . . . . Arlington VA 22206 *Web:* www.thaiinshirlington.com	703-931-3203		671
Thai Airways International Ltd 2321 Rosecrans Ave Ste 1280 . . . . El Segundo CA 90245 *TF:* 800-767-3598 ■ *Web:* www.thaiairways.com	800-767-3598		25

Name / Address	City	State	ZIP	Phone	Fax	Class
Thai Arroy 1019 Light St *Web:* www.thaiarroy.com	Baltimore	MD	21230	410-385-8587		671
Thai Chili 2169 Briarcliff Rd NE *Web:* www.thaichilicuisine.com	Atlanta	GA	30329	404-315-6750		671
Thai Cuisine at Thames 517 Thames St *Web:* www.thaicuisinemenu.com	Newport	RI	02840	401-841-8822		671
Thai Flavor 2863 Erie Blvd E *Web:* www.syracusethaiflavor.com	Syracuse	NY	13224	315-251-1366		671
Thai Flavors 1254 E 14th St *Web:* www.thaiflavorsiowa.com	Des Moines	IA	50316	515-262-4658		671
Thai Garden Restaurant Inc 800 Wellman Ave NE	Huntsville	AL	35801	256-534-0122		671
Thai House 412 5th Ave *Web:* www.thaihousealaska.com	Fairbanks	AK	99701	907-452-6123		671
Thai House 1069 E Shaw Ave *Web:* 1jn.com	Fresno	CA	93710	559-221-7245		671
Thai House 2117 E Colonial Dr *Web:* www.thaihouseoforlando.net	Orlando	FL	32803	407-898-0820	898-1375	671
Thai Kitchen 4550 Concord Ave *Web:* www.thaikitchenla.com	Baton Rouge	LA	70808	225-346-1230		671
Thai Landing 1207 N Charles St *Web:* thailandingmd.com	Baltimore	MD	21201	410-727-1234		671
Thai Lemon Grass Restaurant 506 S Van Dorn St *Web:* www.thailemongrassalexandria.com	Alexandria	VA	22304	703-751-4627		671
Thai Little Home 3214 E Fourth Plain Blvd *Web:* thailittletogo.com	Vancouver	WA	98661	360-693-4061		671
Thai Me Up 75 E Pearl Ave *Web:* www.melvinbrewing.com	Jackson	WY	83001	307-733-0005		671
Thai Nakorn 11951 Beach Blvd *Web:* www.thainakornonline.com	Stanton	CA	90680	714-583-8938		671
Thai on the Beach 901 N Ft Lauderdale Beach Blvd	Fort Lauderdale	FL	33304	954-565-0015		671
Thai Orchid 213 W 11th St *Web:* www.thaiorchidvancouver.com	Vancouver	WA	98660	360-695-7786		671
Thai Orchid 4223 Providence Rd *Web:* thaiorchidrestaurantcharlotte.com	Charlotte	NC	28211	704-364-1134		671
Thai Orchid 10075 SW Barbur Blvd *Web:* www.thaiorchidrestaurant.com	Portland	OR	97219	503-452-2544		671
Thai Place 4130 Pennsylvania Ave *Web:* www.kcthaiplace.com	Kansas City	MO	64111	816-753-8424		671
Thai Place Restaurant 5528 Walnut St *Web:* www.thaiplacepgh.com	Pittsburgh	PA	15232	412-687-8586		671
Thai Ruby 744 East 820 North *Web:* thairubyfood.com	Provo	UT	84606	801-375-6840		671
Thai Sa-On 351 Tenth Ave SW *Web:* www.thai-sa-on.com	Calgary	AB	T2R0A5	403-264-3526		671
Thai Siam 1435 S State St	Salt Lake City	UT	84115	801-474-3322		671
Thai Smile 100 S Indian Canyon Dr *Web:* www.thaismileps.com	Palm Springs	CA	92262	760-320-5503	320-5584	671
Thai Spice 1514 E Commercial Blvd *Web:* thaispicefla.com	Fort Lauderdale	FL	33334	954-771-4535		671
Thai Spice 2933 N 108th St *Web:* www.thaispice.com	Omaha	NE	68164	402-492-8808		671
Thai Spice 4433 W Flamingo Rd *Web:* www.thaispicevegas.com	Las Vegas	NV	89103	702-362-5308		671
Thai Terrace 2055 N Dale Mabry Hwy *Web:* thaiterrace.net	Tampa	FL	33607	813-877-8955	980-0444	671
Thai Time Thai & Sushi Restaurant 1405 Old Sq Rd *Web:* order.thaitimems.com	Jackson	MS	39211	601-982-9991		671
Thai9 11 Brown St *Web:* www.thai9restaurant.com	Dayton	OH	45402	937-222-3227		671
Thailand						
Consulate General 611 N Larchmont Blvd 2nd Fl *Web:* www.thaiconsulatela.org	Los Angeles	CA	90004	323-962-9574	962-2128	257
Embassy 1024 Wisconsin Ave NW *Web:* thaiembdc.org	Washington	DC	20007	202-944-3600	944-3611	257
Embassy & Consulates 351 E 52nd St *Web:* www.thaiembassy.com	New York	NY	10022	212-754-1770	754-1907	784
Thaiphoon 1310 S Joyce St *Web:* thaiphoonva.com	Arlington	VA	22202	703-413-8200	413-8868	671
Thales ATM 23501 W 84th St *TF:* 800-624-7497 ■ *Web:* www.thalesgroup.com	Shawnee	KS	66227	913-422-2600	422-2917	529
Thales Communications Inc 22605 Gateway Center Dr *TF:* 800-258-4420 ■ *Web:* www.thalesdsi.com	Clarksburg	MD	20871	240-864-7000	864-7920	647
Thalheimer & Palumbo PC 100 S Broad St Ste 1950 *Web:* thalheimer.com	Philadelphia	PA	19110	215-568-5656		41
Thalheimer Brothers Inc 700 E Godfrey Ave *Web:* www.thalheimerbrothers.com	Philadelphia	PA	19124	215-537-5200	533-3993	686
Thalhimer Incorporated Morton G 11100 W Broad St *Web:* www.thalhimer.com	Glen Allen	VA	23060	804-648-5881	697-3479	652
Thalia 828 Eigth Ave *Web:* restaurantthalianyc.com	New York	NY	10019	212-399-4444	399-3268	671
Thalia Mara Hall 255 E Pascagoula St *Web:* www.thaliamarahall.net	Jackson	MS	39201	601-960-1537		572
Thames & Kosmos LLC 301 Friendship St *TF:* 800-587-2872 ■ *Web:* www.thamesandkosmos.com	Providence	RI	02903	401-459-6787	459-6775	520
Thames and Hudson 500 Fifth Ave *TF:* 800-233-4830 ■ *Web:* www.thamesandhudsonusa.com	New York	NY	10110	212-354-3763	398-1252	637-2
Thankful Baptist Church 1608 W Allegheny Ave *Web:* www.thankfulbaptistphilly.org	Philadelphia	PA	19132	215-229-5024		48-20
Tharo Systems Inc 2866 Nationwide Pkwy *TF:* 800-878-6833 ■ *Web:* www.tharo.com	Brunswick	OH	44212	330-273-4408		174
Tharrington Smith LLP 150 Fayetteville St Wells Fargo Bldg Ste 1800 *Web:* tharringtonsmith.com	Raleigh	NC	27601	919-821-4711		445
That Bookstore in Blytheville 316 W Main St *Web:* www.thatbookstoreinblytheville.com	Blytheville	AR	72315	870-763-3333		95
Thaumaturgix Inc 2 W 45th St Ste 1408 *Web:* www.tgix.com	New York	NY	10036	212-918-5000		180
Thayer County 225 N Fourth St Rm 201 *Web:* thayercountyne.gov	Hebron	NE	68370	402-768-6126	768-2129	338
Thayer Distribution Services 333 Swedesboro Ave *Web:* www.thayerdistribution.com	Gibbstown	NJ	08027	856-687-0000	224-7129	297-3
Thayer Hotel 674 Thayer Rd *TF:* 800-247-5047 ■ *Web:* www.thethayerhotel.com	West Point	NY	10996	845-446-4731	446-0338	379
Thayer Inc 225 Fifth St *TF:* 800-870-0009 ■ *Web:* www.thayerproducts.com	Benton Harbor	MI	49022	269-925-0633	925-0639	76
Thayer Media Inc 456 S Broadway *Web:* www.thayermedia.com	Denver	CO	80209	303-221-2221		4
Thayer Public Library 798 Washington St *Web:* www.thayerpubliclibrary.org	Braintree	MA	02184	781-848-0405	356-5447	434-3
Thayer Scale 91 Schoosett St *TF:* 855-784-2937 ■ *Web:* www.thayerscale.com	Pembroke	MA	02359	781-826-8101	826-7944	684
Thayer Symphony Orchestra 14 Monument Sq Ste 406 *Web:* www.thayersymphony.org	Leominster	MA	01453	978-466-1800	840-1000	573-3
Thayers Natural Remedies 65 Adams Rd **Fax Area Code:* 203 ■ *TF:* 888-842-9371 ■ *Web:* www.thayers.com	Easton	CT	06612	888-842-9371	227-8183*	799
TheaterWorks, The 233 Pearl St *Web:* twhartford.org	Hartford	CT	06103	860-527-7838		572
Theatre Arlington 305 W Main St *Web:* www.theatrearlington.org	Arlington	TX	76010	817-275-7661		573-4
Theatre Cedar Rapids 102 Third St SE *Web:* www.theatrecr.org	Cedar Rapids	IA	52401	319-366-8591		573-4
Theatre Charlotte 501 Queens Rd *Web:* www.theatrecharlotte.org	Charlotte	NC	28207	704-376-3777		573-4
Theatre Development Fund 1501 Broadway 21st Fl *TF:* 888-424-4685 ■ *Web:* www.tdf.org	New York	NY	10036	212-221-0885	768-1563	750
Theatre For A New Audience 154 Christopher St Ste 3D *Web:* www.tfana.org	New York	NY	10014	212-229-2819	229-2911	749
Theatre Harrisburg 513 Hurlock St *Web:* www.theatreharrisburg.com	Harrisburg	PA	17110	717-232-5501		573-4
Theatre Historical Society of America 152 N York St 2nd Fl *Web:* historictheatres.org	Elmhurst	IL	60126	630-782-1802		138
Theatre in the Park 107 Pullen Rd *Web:* www.theatreinthepark.com	Raleigh	NC	27607	919-831-6936	831-9475	572
Theatre Memphis 630 Perkins Ext *Web:* theatrememphis.org	Memphis	TN	38117	901-682-8323		572
Theatre of Youth (TOY) 203 Allen St *Web:* www.theatreofyouth.org	Buffalo	NY	14201	716-884-4400		573-4
Theatre Projects Consultants Inc 47 Water St *Web:* www.theatreprojects.com	South Norwalk	CT	06854	203-299-0830		186
Theatre Tallahassee 1861 Thomasville Rd *Web:* theatretallahassee.org	Tallahassee	FL	32303	850-224-4597		572
Theatre Three 2800 Routh St Ste 168 *Web:* theatre3dallas.com	Dallas	TX	75201	214-871-3300		572
Theatre Tulsa 412 N Boston Ave *Web:* www.theatretulsa.org	Tulsa	OK	74103	918-587-8402		573-4
Theatre Tuscaloosa 9500 Old Greensboro Rd Ste 135 *Web:* www.theatretusc.com	Tuscaloosa	AL	35405	205-391-2277	391-2329	573-4
Theatre Under the Stars 800 Bagby St Ste 200 *Web:* www.tuts.com	Houston	TX	77002	713-558-2600	558-2650	573-4
TheatreWorks Silicon Valley 350 Twin Dolphin Dr *Web:* www.theatreworks.org	Redwood City	CA	94065	650-463-1950	463-1963	573-4
Thedatabank Inc 2288 University Ave Ste 201 *TF:* 877-603-0296 ■ *Web:* thedatabank.com	Saint Paul	MN	55114	612-455-2255	455-2251	225
Theis Distributing Co, The 17984 Red Iron *Web:* www.theisco.com	Schertz	TX	78154	210-651-4403	651-4861	237
Theis Precision Steel Corp 300 Broad St *Web:* www.theis-usa.com	Bristol	CT	06010	860-585-6610		484
Theisen & Associates Inc 810 S Calhoun St *Web:* theisen-associates.com	Fort Wayne	IN	46802	260-422-4255		41
theKFORDgroup 8620 N New Braunfels Ave Ste 300 *Web:* thekfordgroup.com	San Antonio	TX	78217	210-340-8351	340-8359	2
Thelen Associates Inc, The 1398 Cox Ave	Erlanger	KY	41018	859-746-9400		261
Thelen Sand & Gravel Inc 28955 W Il Rte 173 Ste 1 *Web:* www.thelensg.com	Antioch	IL	60002	847-838-8800	395-3452	503-4
TheMART 222 Merchandise Mart Plz Ste 470 *TF:* 800-677-6278 ■ *Web:* themart.com	Chicago	IL	60654	800-677-6278		205
Themlsonline Com Inc 11150 Commerce Dr N *TF:* 866-657-6654 ■ *Web:* www.themlsonline.com	Champlin	MN	55316	763-576-8286		652
Theodore Liftman Insurance Inc 101 Federal St *Web:* liftman.com	Boston	MA	02110	617-439-9595		390
Theodore Presser Co 588 N Gulph Rd *TF:* 800-854-6764 ■ *Web:* www.presser.com	King of Prussia	PA	19406	610-592-1222	592-1229	637-7

Company	City	State	ZIP	Phone	Fax	Class
Theodore Roosevelt Birthplace National Historic Site 28 E 20th St *Web:* www.nps.gov	New York	NY	10003	212-260-1616		564
Theodore Roosevelt Inaugural National Historic Site 641 Delaware Ave *Web:* www.nps.gov	Buffalo	NY	14202	716-884-0095		520
Theodore Roosevelt National Park 315 Second Ave PO Box 7 *Web:* www.nps.gov	Medora	ND	58645	701-623-4466	623-4840	564
Theodore's Booze Blues & BBQ 201 Worthington St *Web:* theodoresbbq.com	Springfield	MA	01103	413-736-6000		671
Theodric Technologies LLC 100 Vernon St Unit 6 *Web:* www.radio-locator.com	Somerville	MA	02145	617-623-3986		647
Theosophical University Press (TUP) PO Box C *Web:* www.theosociety.org	Pasadena	CA	91109	626-797-7817		637-2
Theprinters.com 3500 E College Ave *TF:* 800-359-2097 ■ *Web:* www.theprinters.com	State College	PA	16801	800-359-2097		344
TheraCare 116 W 32nd St 8th Fl *TF:* 800-505-7000 ■ *Web:* www.theracare.com	New York	NY	10001	212-564-2350	564-5896	353
Theraderm & Therapon Skin Health Inc 2081 Dime Dr *Web:* theraderm.net	Springdale	AR	72764	479-751-7345		77
Theragenics Corp 5203 Bristol Industrial Way *NYSE: TGX* ■ *Web:* www.theragenics.com	Buford	GA	30519	770-831-5137		231
Theralase Technologies Inc 1945 Queen St E *Web:* theralase.com	Toronto	ON	M4L1H7	416-699-5273		250
Therap Services 562 Watertown Ave Ste 3 *Web:* www.therapservices.net	Waterbury	CT	06708	203-596-7553		41
Therapedic Intl 103 College Rd E 2nd Fl *TF:* 800-314-4433 ■ *Web:* www.therapedic.com	Princeton	NJ	08540	609-720-0700		471
Therapeutic Massage Training Institute 726 East Blvd *Web:* www.massagetraining.com	Charlotte	NC	28203	704-338-9660		167-3
Therapeutic Monitoring Services LLC 134 LaSalle St Ste 4 *Web:* www.tmsbioscience.com	New Orleans	LA	70112	504-208-9696		743
Therapeutic Solutions International Inc 4093 Oceanside Blvd Ste B *TF:* 877-468-4877 ■ *Web:* www.therapeuticsolutionsint.com	Oceanside	CA	92056	877-468-4877		228
Therapeutics Inc 9025 Balboa Ave Ste 100 *Web:* www.therapeuticsinc.com	San Diego	CA	92123	858-571-1800		668
Therapy Edge, The 2505 Meridian Pkwy Ste 200	Durham	NC	27713	919-572-6709		525
Therapy Support Inc, The 2803 N Oak Grove Ave *TF:* 877-885-4325 ■ *Web:* therapysupport.com	Springfield	MO	65803	417-447-0987		475
Therapydia Inc 18 E Blithedale Ave Ste 21 *Web:* www.therapydia.com	Mill Valley	CA	94941	415-389-8677	389-8695	387
Theratechnologies Inc 2015 Peel St 5th Fl *TSX: TH* ■ *Web:* www.theratech.com	Montreal	QC	H3A1T8	514-336-7800	331-9691	85
TheraTest Laboratories Inc 1111 N Main St *TF:* 800-441-0771 ■ *Web:* www.theratest.com	Lombard	IL	60148	800-441-0771		476
TheraTogs Inc 305 Society Dr Ste 3-C **Fax Area Code:* 877 ■ *TF:* 888-634-0495 ■ *Web:* www.theratogs.com	Telluride	CO	81435	888-634-0495	202-5965*	194
Theravance Inc 901 Gateway Blvd *NASDAQ: THRX* ■ *Web:* www.theravance.com	South San Francisco	CA	94080	650-808-6000		85
TheraVida Inc 177 Bovet Rd Ste 600 *Web:* www.theravida.com	San Mateo	CA	94402	650-638-2335		231
There & Back Again Travel 33 E Broad St *TF:* 800-782-8222 ■ *Web:* www.thereandbackagain.com	Savannah	GA	31401	912-920-8222		772
There and Back Books 1106 Alworth Bldg 306 W Superior St *Web:* www.thereandbackbooks.com	Duluth	MN	55802	218-727-3383		637-2
Theriault's PO Box 151 *TF:* 800-966-3655 ■ *Web:* www.theriaults.com	Annapolis	MD	21404	410-224-3655	224-2515	51
Theriot Charles C. CPA 306 Grinage St *Web:* www.theriotaccountingfirm.com	Houma	LA	70360	985-872-9036		2
Therm Air Sales Corp 1413 41st St NW PO Box 9004 *TF:* 800-726-7520 ■ *Web:* www.thermairsales.com	Fargo	ND	58106	701-282-9500	282-2329	612
Therm Inc 1000 Hudson St Ext *Web:* www.therm.com	Ithaca	NY	14850	607-272-8500	277-5799	391-4
Therma Foam Inc 8910 Oak Grove Rd *Web:* www.thermafoam.com	Fort Worth	TX	76140	817-624-7204		601
Thermacor Process LP 1670 Hicks Field Rd E *Web:* www.thermacor.com	Fort Worth	TX	76179	817-847-7300	847-7222	595
Thermacore Inc, The 780 Eden Rd *Web:* www.boydcorp.com	Lancaster	PA	17601	717-569-6551		60
Thermafiber Inc 3711 W Mill St *TF:* 888-834-2371 ■ *Web:* www.thermafiber.com	Wabash	IN	46992	260-563-2111	563-7022	389
Therma-Flite Inc, The 849 Jackson St *Web:* www.therma-flite.com	Benicia	CA	94510	707-747-5949		14
Thermal Care Inc 5680 W Jarvis Ave *TF:* 888-828-7387 ■ *Web:* www.thermalcare.com	Niles	IL	60714	847-966-2260	966-9358	14
Thermal Circuits Inc 1 Technology Way *TF:* 800-808-4328 ■ *Web:* www.thermalcircuits.com	Salem	MA	01970	978-745-1162	741-3420	318
Thermal Corp 1264 Slaughter Rd *TF:* 800-633-2962 ■ *Web:* www.thermalcorporation.com	Madison	AL	35758	256-837-1122		612
Thermal Designs Inc 5352 Prudence Dr *Web:* www.tdius.com	Houston	TX	77045	713-433-8110	433-5227	481
Thermal Dynamix Inc 15 E Silver St *TF:* 800-243-9460 ■ *Web:* www.thermaldynamix.com	Westfield	MA	01085	413-562-1266	562-0087	386
Thermal Engineering Corp, The 2741 The Blvd *TF:* 800-331-0097 ■ *Web:* www.tecgrills.com	Columbia	SC	29209	803-783-0750	783-0756	318
Thermal Engineering of Arizona Inc 2250 W Wetmore Rd *TF:* 866-832-7278 ■ *Web:* www.teatucson.com	Tucson	AZ	85705	520-888-4000	888-4457	427
Thermal Equipment Corp 2030 E University Dr *TF:* 800-548-4422 ■ *Web:* www.thermalequipment.com	Rancho Dominguez	CA	90220	310-328-6600	603-9625	318
Thermal Mechanical Inc 425 Aldo Ave *Web:* www.thermalmech.com	Santa Clara	CA	95054	408-988-8744	988-0233	697
Thermal Plastic Design Inc 1116 E Pine St *Web:* tdimolding.com	Saint Croix Falls	WI	54024	715-483-1841	483-1842	608
Thermal Product Solutions 3827 Riverside Rd *TF:* 800-873-4468 ■ *Web:* www.thermalproductsolutions.com	Riverside	MI	49084	269-849-2700	849-3021	318
Thermal Services Inc 13330 I St *Web:* www.thermalservices.com	Omaha	NE	68137	402-397-8100		610
Thermal Solutions LLC PO Box 3244 **Fax Area Code:* 877 ■ *Web:* www.thermalsolutions.com	Lancaster	PA	17604	717-239-7642	501-5212*	357
Thermal Specialties LLC 6314 E 15th St *Web:* www.thermalspecialties.com	Tulsa	OK	74112	918-836-4800		189-7
Thermal Structures Inc (TSI) 2362 Railroad St *Web:* www.thermalstructures.com	Corona	CA	92880	951-736-9911	736-1064	483
Thermal Tech 5141 Forsyth Commerce Rd Unit 1 *Web:* www.tti-fl.com	Orlando	FL	32807	407-373-0042		283
Thermal Technologies Inc 130 Northpoint Ct *TF:* 888-467-7335 ■ *Web:* www.thermaltechnologies.com	Blythewood	SC	29016	803-691-8000		190
Thermal Windows & Doors, The 3700 Haney C *TF:* 800-245-1540 ■ *Web:* thermalindustries.com	Murrysville	PA	15668	724-325-6100		235
Thermal-vac Technology Inc 1221 W Struck Ave *Web:* www.thermalvac.com	Orange	CA	92867	714-997-2601		484
Thermasolutions Inc 1889 Buerkle Rd *Web:* www.thermasolutions.com	White Bear Lake	MN	55110	651-209-3900		476
Therma-Stor LLC 4201 Lien Rd *TF:* 800-533-7533 ■ *Web:* www.thermastor.com	Madison	WI	53704	608-237-8400		610
Therma-Tru Corp 1750 Indian Wood Cir *TF:* 800-537-8827 ■ *Web:* www.thermatru.com	Maumee	OH	43537	419-891-7400	891-7411	234
Thermcraft Inc 3950 Overdale Rd *Web:* thermcraftinc.com	Winston-Salem	NC	27107	336-784-4800	784-0634	318
Thermedx LLC 31200 Solon Rd Unit 1 *TF:* 888-542-9276 ■ *Web:* www.thermedx.com	Solon	OH	44139	440-542-0883	542-0920	475
Thermik Corp 3304 Us Hwy 70 E *Web:* www.thermik.de	New Bern	NC	28560	252-636-5720	636-5737	202
Thermionics Laboratory 1842 Sabre St *TF:* 800-962-2310 ■ *Web:* thermionics.com	Hayward	CA	94545	800-962-2310		172
Thermo Craft Engineering Company Inc 701 Western Ave *Web:* thermocraftengineering.com	Lynn	MA	01905	781-599-4023		811
Thermo Design Engineering Ltd 1424 - 70th Ave *Web:* www.thermodesign.com	Edmonton	AB	T6P1P5	780-440-6064		261
Thermo Electric Company Inc 1193 McDermott Dr *TF:* 800-766-4020 ■ *Web:* www.te-direct.com	West Chester	PA	19380	610-692-7990	430-1325	472
Thermo Fisher Scientific 46360 Fremont Blvd **Fax Area Code:* 510 ■ *TF:* 800-232-3342 ■ *Web:* www.thermofisher.com	Fremont	CA	94538	800-232-3342	979-5002*	231
Thermo Fluids Inc 4301 W Jefferson St *TF:* 800-350-7565 ■ *Web:* www.thermofluids.com	Phoenix	AZ	85043	800-350-7565		686
Thermo King Corp 314 W 90th St *Web:* www.thermoking.com	Minneapolis	MN	55420	952-887-2200	887-2615	14
Thermo King of Houston LP 772 McCarty St *Web:* www.tkofhouston.net	Houston	TX	77029	713-671-2700		665
Thermo King of Sioux Falls Inc 1709 N Cliff Ave **Fax Area Code:* 605 ■ *TF:* 866-775-5162 ■ *Web:* www.thermokingsf.com	Sioux Falls	SD	57103	866-775-5162	334-1556*	665
Thermo Probe Inc 112-A Jetport Dr *Web:* www.thermoprobe.net	Pearl	MS	39208	601-939-1831	355-1831	201
Thermo Vac Inc 201 W Oakwood Rd *Web:* www.thermovac.com	Oxford	MI	48371	248-969-0300	969-0311	492
Thermo/Probes Inc 55 Lyerly St Ste 214 *TF:* 800-795-8991 ■ *Web:* www.thermo-probes.com	Houston	TX	77022	713-699-1393	699-2696	201
Thermoanalytics Inc 23440 Airpark Blvd *Web:* www.thermoanalytics.com	Calumet	MI	49913	906-482-9560		177
Thermocarbon Inc 391 Melody Ln *Web:* www.thermocarbon.com	Casselberry	FL	32707	407-834-7800	767-8675	493
Thermoclad Co 361 W 11th St *Web:* www.protechpowder.com	Erie	PA	16501	814-456-1243		605-2
Thermocouple Technology Inc 350 New St *TF:* 800-784-3783 ■ *Web:* www.tteconline.com	Quakertown	PA	18951	215-529-9394	529-9397	201
Thermodyn Corp 3550 Silica Rd *TF:* 800-654-6518 ■ *Web:* www.thermodyn.com	Sylvania	OH	43560	419-841-7782	841-3139	677
ThermoElectric Cooling America Corp 4048 W Schubert Ave *Web:* www.thermoelectric.com	Chicago	IL	60639	773-342-4900	342-0191	14
Thermo-Fab Corp 76 Walker Rd *TF:* 888-494-9777 ■ *Web:* www.thermofab.com	Shirley	MA	01464	978-425-2311	425-2305	602
Thermoflow Inc 2 Willow St Ste 100 *Web:* www.thermoflow.com	Southborough	MA	01745	508-303-5033		177
Thermoform Engineered Quality LLC 11320 E Main St *TF:* 800-874-7113 ■ *Web:* www.teqnow.com	Huntley	IL	60142	800-874-7113		604
ThermoGenesis Corp, The 2711 Citrus Rd *NASDAQ: KOOL* ■ *TF:* 800-783-8357 ■ *Web:* thermogenesis.com	Rancho Cordova	CA	95742	916-858-5100	858-5199	420

Company	Phone	Fax	Class
Thermold Corp 7059 Harp Rd .... Canastota NY 13032 *Web:* www.thermold.com	315-697-3924		596
Thermon Manufacturing Co 100 Thermon Dr .... San Marcos TX 78666 *Web:* www.thermon.com	512-396-5801		815
Thermopatch Corp 2204 Erie Blvd E. .... Syracuse NY 13224 *TF:* 800-252-6555 ■ *Web:* www.thermopatch.com	315-446-8110		744
Thermoplastic Processes Inc 1268 Valley Rd .... Stirling NJ 07980 *TF:* 888-554-6400 ■ *Web:* www.thermoplasticprocesses.com	908-561-3000	753-6749	600
Thermoplastic Services Inc 1700 W 4th St. .... Dequincy LA 70633 *Web:* naplastics.com	337-786-7022		603
Thermos Co 475 N Martingale Rd Ste 1100 .... Schaumburg IL 60173 *TF:* 800-243-0745 ■ *Web:* www.thermos.com	847-439-7821	593-5570	607
ThermoSafe Brands 3930 N Ventura Dr Ste 450 .... Arlington Heights IL 60004 *TF:* 800-323-7442 ■ *Web:* www.thermosafe.com	847-398-0110	398-0653	601
Thermoseal 2350 Campbell Rd .... Sidney OH 45365 *TF:* 800-990-7325 ■ *Web:* www.thermosealinc.com	937-498-2222		326
Thermoseal Glass Corp 400 Water St. .... Gloucester City NJ 08030 *TF:* 800-456-7788 ■ *Web:* www.thermoseal.com	856-456-3109	456-0989	329
ThermoServ 3901 Pipestone Rd. .... Dallas TX 75212 *TF:* 800-635-5559 ■ *Web:* www.thermoserv.com	214-631-0307	631-0566	601
Thermosoft International Corp 701 Corporate Woods Pkwy .... Vernon Hills IL 60061 *TF:* 800-308-8057 ■ *Web:* www.thermosoft.com	847-279-3800		317
ThermoSpas Hot Tubs 10 Research Pkwy Ste 300 .... Wallingford CT 06492 *Fax Area Code: 203 ■ *TF:* 800-876-0158 ■ *Web:* www.thermospas.com	800-876-0158	303-0029*	375
Thermotech Co 1302 S Fifth St. .... Hopkins MN 55343 *Web:* www.thermotech.com	952-933-9400		604
Thermo-tech Plastics Ltd 2299 Drew Rd. .... Mississauga ON L5S1A3 *Web:* thermotechplastics.com	905-678-9448		608
Thermotek Inc 1200 Lkeside Pky Ste 200 .... Flower Mound TX 75028 *TF:* 877-242-3232 ■ *Web:* www.thermotekusa.com	972-874-4949	874-4945	476
Thermotron Industries Co 291 Kollen Pk Dr .... Holland MI 49423 *TF:* 800-409-3449 ■ *Web:* www.thermotron.com	616-393-4580	392-5643	386
Thermo-Twin Industries Inc 1155 Allegheny Ave .... Oakmont PA 15139 *TF:* 800-641-2211 ■ *Web:* www.thermotwin.com	412-826-1000		234
Therm-Tec Inc 20525 SW Cipole Rd. .... Sherwood OR 97140 *TF:* 800-292-9163 ■ *Web:* www.thermtec.com	503-625-7575	625-6161	318
Thermtrol Corp 8914 Pleasantwood Ave NW. .... North Canton OH 44720 *Web:* www.thermtrol.com	330-497-4148	497-4189	639
Thermwell Products Co 420 Rt 17 S. .... Mahwah NJ 07430 *Fax Area Code: 201 ■ *TF:* 800-526-5265 ■ *Web:* www.frostking.com	800-299-5700	684-1214*	389
Thermwood Corp 904 Buffaloville Rd .... Dale IN 47523 *OTC: TOOD* ■ *TF:* 800-533-6901 ■ *Web:* www.thermwood.com	812-937-4476	937-2956	821
Thern Inc 5712 Industrial Park Rd PO Box 347 .... Winona MN 55987 *TF:* 800-843-7648 ■ *Web:* www.thern.com	507-454-2996	454-5282	470
Theron Pharmaceuticals Inc 365 San Aleso Ave .... Sunnyvale CA 94085 *Web:* www.theronpharma.com	408-792-7424		231
TherOx Inc 17500 Cartwright Rd Ste 100. .... Irvine CA 92614 *Web:* www.therox.com	949-757-1999		476
Thesis, The 505 NW Couch Ste 300 .... Portland OR 97209 *Web:* thesis.agency	503-221-6200		177
TheStreetcom Inc 14 Wall St 15th Fl .... New York NY 10005 *NASDAQ: TST* ■ *TF:* 800-562-9571 ■ *Web:* www.thestreet.com	212-321-5000	321-5016	404
Theta Delta Chi Inc 214 Lewis Wharf. .... Boston MA 02110 *TF:* 800-999-1847 ■ *Web:* www.thetadeltachi.net	804-344-4300		48-16
Theta Phi Alpha Fraternity Inc 27025 Knickerbocker Rd. .... Bay Village OH 44140 *Web:* www.thetaphialpha.org	440-899-9282	899-9293	48-16
Theta Tau Professional Engineering Fraternity 1011 San Jacinto Ste 205. .... Austin TX 78701 *TF:* 800-264-1904 ■ *Web:* thetatau.org	512-472-1904	472-4820	48-16
Thetford Corp, The 7101 Jackson Ave. .... Ann Arbor MI 48103 *TF:* 800-543-1219 ■ *Web:* www.thetford.com	734-769-6000	769-2023	610
Thetford Hill State Park 622 Academy Rd. .... Thetford VT 05074 *Web:* www.naturefind.com	802-785-2266		565
Thetubestore Inc 120 Lancing Dr. .... Hamilton ON L8W3A1 *TF:* 877-570-0979 ■ *Web:* www.thetubestore.com	905-570-0979		317
Thexton Manufacturing Co 6539 Cecilia Cir .... Edina MN 55439 *TF:* 800-328-6277 ■ *Web:* www.thexton.com	952-831-4171	831-5938	758
THF Realty Inc 2127 Innerbelt Business Center Dr Ste 310 .... Saint Louis MO 63114 *Web:* www.thfrealty.com	314-429-0900	429-0999	652
THG (Hotel Group, The) 201 Fifth Ave S Ste 200 .... Edmonds WA 98020 *Web:* www.thehotelgroup.com	425-771-1788	672-8280	379
Thiara Bros Orchards 1205 Kibby Rd .... Merced CA 95340	209-383-6126		315-3
Thibaut Inc 480 Frelinghuysen Ave .... Newark NJ 07114 *TF:* 800-223-0704 ■ *Web:* www.thibautdesign.com	973-643-1118	643-3050	802
Thibodaux Chamber of Commerce PO Box 467 .... Thibodaux LA 70302 *Web:* www.thibodauxchamber.com	985-446-1187	446-1191	139
Thibodaux Regional Medical Ctr (TRMC) 602 N Acadia Rd. .... Thibodaux LA 70301 *TF:* 800-822-8442 ■ *Web:* www.thibodaux.com	985-447-5500		374-3
Thief River Falls Convention & Visitors Bureau (TRFCVB) 102 Main Ave N .... Thief River Falls MN 56701 *Web:* visittrf.com	218-686-9785		206
Thiel College 75 College Ave .... Greenville PA 16125 *TF:* 800-248-4435 ■ *Web:* www.thiel.edu	724-589-2000		166
Thiel Tool & Engineering Company Inc 4622 Bulwer Ave PO Box 470007. .... Saint Louis MO 63147 *Web:* www.thieltool.com	314-241-6121	241-7857	489
Thiele Kaolin Co 520 Kaolin Rd .... Sandersville GA 31082 *Web:* www.thielekaolin.com	478-552-3951	552-4131	503-2
Thiele Technologies 315 27th Ave NE. .... Minneapolis MN 55418 *TF:* 800-932-3647 ■ *Web:* www.bwflexiblesystems.com	612-782-1200	782-1203	547
Thielsch Engineering Inc 195 Frances Ave .... Cranston RI 02910 *Web:* thielsch.com	401-467-6454		261
Thielsen Gallery 1038 Adelaide St N .... London ON N5Y2M9 *Web:* www.thielsengallery.com	519-434-7681		42
Thieman Tailgates Inc 600 E Wayne St. .... Celina OH 45822 *Web:* thieman.com	419-586-7727		54
Thierica Inc 900 Clancy Ave NE .... Grand Rapids MI 49503 *Web:* www.thierica.com	616-458-1538		247
Thiessen Team USA Inc 1840 Sharps Access Rd .... Elko NV 89801 *TF:* 866-777-1205 ■ *Web:* www.thiessenteam.com	775-777-1205	777-1215	182
Thill Logistics Inc 355 Byrd Ave .... Neenah WI 54956 *TF:* 888-800-2600 ■ *Web:* thilllogistics.com	920-967-8000		311
Thillens Inc 4242 N Elston Ave .... Chicago IL 60618 *TF:* 888-539-4446 ■ *Web:* www.thillens.com	773-539-4444		400
Thin Client Computing 34522 N Scottsdale Rd. .... Scottsdale AZ 85266 *Web:* www.thinclient.net	602-432-8649		180
Thin Film Technology Inc 1980 Commerce Dr .... North Mankato MN 56003 *Web:* www.thin-film.com	507-625-8445	625-3523	696
Think Big Partners 1712 Main St 2nd Fl. .... Kansas City MO 64108 *Web:* www.thinkbigpartners.com	816-842-5244		393
Think Big Solutions LLC 4995 Monaco St. .... Commerce City CO 80022 *Web:* thinkbigsolutions.com	303-286-7200		344
Think Cp Technologies 16812 Hale Ave .... Irvine CA 92606 *TF:* 800-726-2477 ■ *Web:* thinkcp.com	949-833-3222		173-8
Think Network Technologies LLC 3067 Main Ave .... Durango CO 81301 *Web:* www.thinknettech.com	970-247-1885	247-0883	225
Think Reliability 2225 County Rd 90 .... Pearland TX 77584 *Web:* www.thinkreliability.com	281-412-7766		195
Think System Inc 7006 Golden Ring Rd .... Baltimore MD 21237 *Web:* thinksi.com	410-235-3600		721
Think Tank Studio 626 Lakeview Rd Ste A. .... Clearwater FL 33756 *Web:* thinktankstudio.com	727-441-4488		344
Think-A-Move Ltd 23307 Commerce Pk. ...... Beachwood OH 44122 *Web:* think-a-move.com	216-765-8875		52
ThinkBRQ LLC 20 Hicksville Rd Ste 7 .... Massapequa NY 11758 *Web:* www.thinkbrq.com	516-541-3100		260
ThinkDirect Marketing Group Inc 8285 Bryan Dairy Rd Ste 150 .... Largo FL 33773 *TF:* 800-325-3155 ■ *Web:* tdmg.com	727-369-2700		393
Thinkdm2 100 Challenger Rd Ste 306. .... Ridgefield Park NJ 07660 *Web:* thinkdm2.com	201-840-8910		7
Thinkers' Press Inc (TPI) 1524 LeClaire St. .... Davenport IA 52803 *Web:* www.thinkerspressinc.com	563-271-6657		96
ThinkFire Services USA Ltd 1011 Rt 22W Ste 101 .... Bridgewater NJ 08807 *Web:* www.thinkfire.com	908-991-9014		809
Thinkfun Inc 1321 Cameron St .... Alexandria VA 22314 *TF:* 800-468-1864 ■ *Web:* www.thinkfun.com	703-549-4999		761
Thinkgeo LLC 1617 St Andrews Dr .... Lawrence KS 66047 *Web:* thinkgeo.com	785-727-4133		809
Thinking Systems Corp 750 94th Ave N Ste 211 .... Saint Petersburg FL 33702 *Web:* www.thinkingsystems.com	727-217-0909	217-0938	476
Thinklogic Inc 875 N Douglas St .... El Segundo CA 90245 *Web:* www.thinklogic.com	310-337-6646		180
Thinkmap Inc 599 Broadway 9th Fl. .... New York NY 10012 *Web:* www.thinkmap.com	212-285-8600		177
Thinkmate 159 Overland Rd. .... Waltham MA 02451 *TF:* 800-371-1212 ■ *Web:* www.thinkmate.com	800-371-1212		174
Thinkpath Inc 9080 Springboro Pk Ste 300 .... Miamisburg OH 45342 *Web:* www.thinkpath.com	937-291-8374		721
THINKstrategies Inc 22 Park Ave. .... Wellesley MA 02481 *Web:* thinkstrategies.com	781-223-7421		631
ThinkTV 110 S Jefferson St. .... Dayton OH 45402 *TF:* 800-247-1614 ■ *Web:* www.thinktv.org	937-220-1600	220-1642	632
Thinkway Toys Inc 8885 Woodbine Ave. .... Markham ON L3R5G1 *TF:* 800-535-5754 ■ *Web:* www.thinkwaytoys.com	800-535-5754		761
Thinkwrap Commerce Inc 450 March Rd Ste 500 .... Ottawa ON K2K3K2 *Web:* pivotree.com	613-751-4441	369-5504	196
Thinky USA 23151 Verdugo Dr. .... Laguna Hills CA 92653 *Web:* www.thinkymixer.com	949-768-9001		419
Third Avenue Funds 622 Third Ave 32nd Fl .... New York NY 10017 *TF:* 800-443-1021 ■ *Web:* thirdave.com	212-888-5222		528
Third Base Sports Bar & Brewery 500 Blairs Ferry Rd NE. .... Cedar Rapids IA 52402 *Web:* www.thirdbasebrew.com	319-378-9090	378-9154	671
Third Coast Capital Advisors LLC 225 W Washington St Ste 2200 .... Chicago IL 60606 *Web:* www.thirdcoastca.com	312-332-6484		401
Third Door Media Inc 279 Newtown Tpke .... Redding CT 06896 *Web:* thirddoormedia.com	203-664-1350		791
Third Federal Savings & Loan Association of Cleveland 7007 Broadway Ave .... Cleveland OH 44105 *TF:* 888-844-7333 ■ *Web:* www.thirdfederal.com	800-844-7333		70
Third Floor Inc, The 5700 Wilshire Blvd Ste 650 .... Los Angeles CA 90036 *Web:* thethirdfloorinc.com	323-931-6633	931-9928	290
Third Millennium Ministries 316 Live Oaks Blvd. .... Casselberry FL 32707 *TF:* 877-443-6455 ■ *Web:* thirdmill.org	407-830-0222		48-20

Name / Address	City	State	ZIP	Phone	Fax	Class
Third Millennium Test Solutions Inc 3003 Bunker Hill Ln Ste 106 *Web:* www.3mts.com	Santa Clara	CA	95054	408-922-0510	922-0526	174
Third Pillar Systems Inc 577 Airport Blvd 8th Fl *Web:* www.thirdpillar.com	Burlingame	CA	94010	650-372-1200		177
Third Rail Creative 716 Congress Ave Ste 200 *Web:* thirdrailcreative.com	Austin	TX	78701	512-358-9907		7
Third Sector Associates 60 Blodgett St *Web:* www.thirdsectorassociates.com	Burlington	VT	05401	802-865-1794		194
Third Sky Inc 2601 Blanding Ave Ste C362 *Web:* www.thirdsky.com	Alameda	CA	94501	415-272-4262	520-2226	196
Third Wave Consulting Inc (TWC) 876 E Shore Rd *Web:* www.thirdwaveconsult.com	Jamestown	RI	02835	401-741-6221	423-3452	196
Third Wave Systems 6475 City W Pkwy *Web:* www.thirdwavesys.com	Eden Prairie	MN	55344	952-832-5515	844-0202	174
ThirdEye Data Inc 5201 Great America Pky Ste 320 *Web:* thirdeyedata.io	Santa Clara	CA	95054	408-462-5257		180
Thirstystone Resources Inc 1304 Corporate Dr *TF:* 800-829-6888 ■ *Web:* thirstystone.com	Gainesville	TX	76240	940-668-6793		292
Thirteen23 Corp 506 Congress Ave Ste 200 *Web:* thirteen23.com	Austin	TX	78701	512-672-8780		177
Thirty-One Gifts 3425 Morse Crossing *TF:* 866-443-8731 ■ *Web:* www.mythirtyone.com	Columbus	OH	43219	866-443-8731		366
This is the Place Heritage Park 2601 E Sunnyside Ave *Web:* www.thisistheplace.org	Salt Lake City	UT	84108	801-582-1847	583-1869	50-3
This Old House Magazine 262 Harbor Dr *TF:* 800-898-7237 ■ *Web:* www.thisoldhouse.com	Stamford	CT	06902	475-209-8665		457-11
Thistle Appliance PO Box 1749 *TF:* 800-362-2427 ■ *Web:* www.thistleappliance.com	Sagamore Beach	MA	02562	508-540-4858		38
Thistle Roller Company Inc 209 S Van Norman Rd *Web:* www.thistleroller.com	Montebello	CA	90640	562-948-3705	942-1042	628
THK America Inc 200 E Commerce Dr *Web:* www.thk.com	Schaumburg	IL	60173	847-310-1111	310-1271	639
THK Rhythm North America Company Ltd 549 Vista Dr *Web:* www.rhythm-na.com	Sparta	TN	38583	931-738-2250	738-2480	247
Thobe Group Inc 2727 Raintree Dr	Carrollton	TX	75006	972-418-1163		195
Thom Browne Inc 100 Hudson St *Web:* www.thombrowne.com	New York	NY	10013	212-633-1197		157-2
Thoma Cressey Bravo Inc 600 Montgomery St 20th Fl *Web:* thomabravo.com	San Francisco	CA	94111	415-263-3660	392-6480	792
Thomas & Mack Center/Sam Boyd Stadium 4505 S Maryland Pkwy PO Box 450003 *Web:* www.thomasandmack.com	Las Vegas	NV	89154	702-895-3761		720
Thomas & Marker Construction 2084 US 68 S PO Box 250 *Web:* buildwithmarker.com	Bellefontaine	OH	43311	937-599-2160		186
Thomas & Skinner Inc 1120 E 23rd St *Web:* www.thomas-skinner.com	Indianapolis	IN	46205	317-923-2501	923-5919	458
Thomas & Thomas CPAS 4019 N Galloway Ave Ste B *Web:* tntcpa.com	Mesquite	TX	75150	972-681-7295		2
Thomas A. Lirot CPA PSC 551 State St *Web:* lirotcpa.com	Radcliff	KY	40160	270-351-1540		2
Thomas and Proetz Lumber Co 3400 Hall St *Web:* www.tplco.com	Saint Louis	MO	63147	314-231-9343		191-3
Thomas Aquinas College 10000 Ojai Rd *TF:* 800-634-9797 ■ *Web:* thomasaquinas.edu	Santa Paula	CA	93060	805-525-4417	525-9342	166
Thomas B. Finan Ctr 10102 Country Club Rd SE PO Box 1722 *TF:* 888-854-0035 ■ *Web:* health.maryland.gov	Cumberland	MD	21501	301-777-2405	777-2364	374-5
Thomas Bennett & Hunter Inc 70 John St *Web:* www.tbhconcrete.com	Westminster	MD	21157	410-848-9030	876-0733	182
Thomas Boyd Communications 117 N Church St *Web:* www.thomasboyd.com	Moorestown	NJ	08057	856-642-6226		636
Thomas Built Buses Inc 1408 Courtesy Rd *Web:* thomasbuiltbuses.com	High Point	NC	27260	336-889-4871	881-6509	516
Thomas C. Doehrman Professional Corp 600 E 96th St Ste 450 *Web:* tortslaw.com	Indianapolis	IN	46240	317-844-9999		41
Thomas C. Jones CPA 105 S St *Web:* www.tomjonescpa.com	Elkton	MD	21921	410-398-9382		2
Thomas C. Wilson Inc 21-11 44th Ave *TF:* 800-230-2636 ■ *Web:* www.tcwilson.com	Long Island City	NY	11101	718-729-3360	361-2872	759
Thomas Capital Group Inc 4221 Harborview Dr Ste 200 *Web:* www.thomascapital.com	Gig Harbor	WA	98332	253-777-4477	858-4782	70
Thomas Cole National Historic Site 218 Spring St *Web:* thomascole.org	Catskill	NY	12414	518-943-7465		564
Thomas Collective LLC, The 37 W 28th St 12th Fl *Web:* www.ttccreative.com	New York	NY	10001	212-229-2294		636
Thomas College 180 W River Rd *TF:* 800-339-7001 ■ *Web:* www.thomas.edu	Waterville	ME	04901	207-859-1111	859-1114	166
Thomas Computer Solutions LLC 1491 Chain Bdge Rd Ste 100 *Web:* www.tcstranslations.com	McLean	VA	22101	703-839-8700	839-8701	226
Thomas Conveyor Co 555 N Burleson Blvd *TF:* 800-433-2217 ■ *Web:* www.thomasconveyor.com	Burleson	TX	76028	817-295-7151	447-3840	207
Thomas County 300 N Ct Ste 10 *Web:* thomascountyks.gov	Colby	KS	67701	785-460-4500	460-4503	338
Thomas County 503 Main St *Web:* thomascountynebraska.us	Thedford	NE	69166	308-636-6157	645-2623	338
Thomas County Board of Commissioners 116 W Jefferson St PO Box 920 *Web:* thomascountyboc.org	Thomasville	GA	31799	229-225-4100	226-3430	338
Thomas Crane Public Library 40 Washington St *TF:* 857-577-8275 ■ *Web:* www.thomascranelibrary.org	Quincy	MA	02169	617-376-1300		434-3
Thomas Creative Apparel Inc 1 Harmony Pl *TF:* 800-537-2575 ■ *Web:* www.thomasrobes.com	New London	OH	44851	419-929-1506	929-0122	155-14
Thomas Direct Sales Inc 30 Plymouth St *Web:* www.thomasdirect.com	Fairfield	NJ	07004	973-777-6500		8
Thomas E. Creek Veterans Affairs Medical Ctr 6010 Amarillo Blvd W *TF:* 800-687-8262 ■ *Web:* www.amarillo.va.gov	Amarillo	TX	79106	806-355-9703		374-8
Thomas E. Holter PC 2970 N Swan Rd Ste 219	Tucson	AZ	85712	520-577-8818		2
Thomas Edison House 3110 Lexington Rd *Web:* www.historichomes.org	Louisville	KY	40202	502-585-5247		520
Thomas Edison National Historic Site 211 Main St *Web:* www.nps.gov	West Orange	NJ	07052	973-736-0550	736-6567	564
Thomas Edison State College 101 W State St *TF:* 888-442-8372 ■ *Web:* www.tesu.edu	Trenton	NJ	08608	609-292-2108	984-8447	166
Thomas Employment 8320 Tyler Blvd *Web:* www.thomasemployment.com	Mentor	OH	44060	440-974-2010		260
Thomas Engineering Co (TEC) 7024 Northland Dr *Web:* www.thomasengineering.com	Minneapolis	MN	55428	763-533-1501	533-8091	489
Thomas Engineering Inc 575 W Central Rd *TF:* 800-634-9910 ■ *Web:* www.thomaseng.com	Hoffman Estates	IL	60192	847-358-5800	358-5817	386
Thomas Equipment Inc 204 Upper Kent Rd *Web:* www.thomasloaders.com	Upper Kent	NB	E7J2E4	506-278-5695	278-5876	274
Thomas F. Moran Inc 48 Constitution Dr *Web:* www.tfmoran.com	Bedford	NH	03110	603-472-4488	472-9747	261
Thomas Gammill & Company Ltd 5026 Old Greenwood St *Web:* www.gammillcpa.com	Fort Smith	AR	72903	479-648-1121		2
Thomas George Associates Ltd 10 Larkfield Rd *TF:* 800-443-8338 ■ *Web:* www.tgaltd.com	East Northport	NY	11731	631-261-8800		390
Thomas Graham Associates Inc 803 Compton Rd *Web:* tgraham.com	Cincinnati	OH	45231	513-521-4760	521-2439	261
Thomas Graphics Inc 9501 N IH 35 *Web:* www.thomasgraphicsinc.com	Austin	TX	78753	512-719-3535		687
Thomas H. Lee Partners LP 100 Federal St *TF:* 877-456-3427 ■ *Web:* thl.com	Boston	MA	02110	617-227-1050	227-3514	405
Thomas Hart Benton Home & Studio State Historic Site 3616 Belleview *Web:* mostateparks.com	Kansas City	MO	64111	816-931-5722		565
Thomas Hospital 750 Morphy Ave *TF:* 800-422-2027 ■ *Web:* www.infirmaryhealth.org	Fairhope	AL	36532	251-928-2375		374-3
Thomas Industrial Rolls Inc 8526 Brandt St *TF:* 800-775-7655 ■ *Web:* www.tirinc.com	Dearborn	MI	48126	313-584-9696	584-5725	567
Thomas Industries Inc 211 Industrial Ct *Web:* www.thomasindustriesinc.com	Wabasha	MN	55981	651-565-3395		253
Thomas Instrument & Machine Company Inc 3440 First St *Web:* www.thomasinstrument.com	Brookshire	TX	77423	281-375-6300		264-3
Thomas J. Dyer Co 5240 Lester Rd *Web:* tjdyer.com	Cincinnati	OH	45213	513-321-8100	842-4101	256
Thomas J. Fannon & Sons Inc 1200 Duke St *Web:* tjfannon.com	Alexandria	VA	22314	703-549-5700		316
Thomas J. Palm PA 9528 Belair Rd *Web:* thomasjpalm.com	Baltimore	MD	21236	443-927-7180		2
Thomas J. Paul West Inc 1061 Rydal Rd *Web:* www.thomasjpaul.com	Rydal	PA	19046	215-886-3220		7
Thomas Jefferson Foundation PO Box 316 *Web:* www.monticello.org	Charlottesville	VA	22902	434-984-9808		305
Thomas Jefferson National Accelerator Facility 12000 Jefferson Ave *Web:* www.jlab.org	Newport News	VA	23606	757-269-7100	269-7363	668
Thomas Jefferson School 4100 S Lindbergh Blvd *Web:* www.tjs.org	Saint Louis	MO	63127	314-843-4151	843-3527	622
Thomas Jefferson School of Law 1155 Island Ave *TF:* 877-318-6901 ■ *Web:* www.tjsl.edu	San Diego	CA	92101	619-297-9700	961-1382	167-1
Thomas Kinkade Co, The 18635 Sutter Blvd *TF:* 888-368-1336 ■ *Web:* www.thomaskinkade.com	Morgan Hill	CA	95037	888-368-1336		45
Thomas L. Cardella & Associates Inc 2738 Edgewood Rd SW Ste B *Web:* tlcassociates.com	Cedar Rapids	IA	52404	319-730-4000	730-4100	737
Thomas L. Mclaughlin PC 117 Water St Ste 203 *Web:* tlmlaw.com	Milford	MA	01757	508-478-3100		41
Thomas Lee Printing & Mailing Inc 3721 W 12th St	Erie	PA	16505	814-833-3233		535

	Phone	Fax	Class
Thomas M. Cooley Law School 300 S Capitol Ave. Lansing MI 48933 *TF:* 800-243-2586 ■ *Web:* www.cooley.edu	517-371-5140		167-1
Thomas McNerney & Partners 1 Stamford Plz 263 Tresser Blvd Ninth Fl Stamford CT 06901 *Web:* www.tm-partners.com	203-978-2010		792
Thomas Media 1806 Washington St Columbia SC 29201 *Web:* blackpagessouth.com	803-254-6404	254-6557	637-10
Thomas Memorial Hospital 4605 MacCorkle Ave SW South Charleston WV 25309 *Web:* www.thomaswv.org	304-766-3600		374-3
Thomas More College 333 Thomas More Pkwy Crestview Hills KY 41017 *TF:* 800-825-4557 ■ *Web:* www.thomasmore.edu	859-344-3332	344-3444	166
Thomas More Prep-Marian 1701 Hall St Hays KS 67601 *Web:* tmp-m.org	785-625-6577	625-3912	622
Thomas Nelson Inc 501 Nelson Pl PO Box 141000 Nashville TN 37214 *TF:* 800-251-4000 ■ *Web:* streaming.thomasnelson.com	800-251-4000		637-3
Thomas P. Joynt PC 1819 S Dobson Rd Ste 101 Mesa AZ 85202 *Web:* joyntreturns.com	480-820-5077	820-8978	2
Thomas P. Kennard House PO Box 82554 Lincoln NE 68501 *Web:* history.nebraska.gov	402-471-4764		50-3
Thomas Partitions & Specialties Inc 3578 Eagle Rock Blvd Altadena CA 91001	323-256-8666		610
Thomas Petroleum LLC 9701 US Hwy 59 N PO Box 1876 Victoria TX 77905 *Web:* www.speedystop.com	361-573-7662		581
Thomas Pheasant Inc 1029 33rd St NW Washington DC 20007 *Web:* www.thomaspheasant.com	202-337-6596		393
Thomas Precision Machining Inc 3278 S Main St Rice Lake WI 54868 *TF:* 800-657-4808 ■ *Web:* www.tpm-inc.com	715-234-8827		454
Thomas Press Inc 920 Friedman Dr Waukesha WI 53186 *Web:* www.thomaspressinc.com	262-547-7355	547-8273	626
Thomas Produce Co 9905 Clint Moore Rd Boca Raton FL 33496 *Web:* www.thomasproduce.com	561-482-1111	451-8016	10-11
Thomas Products Ltd 987 W St Southington CT 06489 *TF:* 800-666-9101 ■ *Web:* www.thomasprod.com	860-621-9101	621-1470	203
Thomas Properties Group Inc 515 S Flower St Ste 206 Los Angeles CA 90071 *NASDAQ: TPGI*	213-613-1900	633-4760	405
Thomas Publishing Co 5 Penn Plz New York NY 10001 *TF:* 800-733-1127 ■ *Web:* www.thomasnet.com	212-695-0500	290-7362	637-2
Thomas R. Fields PA 2544 W 47th Ave Kansas City KS 66103 *TF:* 877-587-2361 ■ *Web:* thomasrfields.com	877-587-2361		41
Thomas Reprographics 600 N Central Expy Richardson TX 75080 *TF:* 800-877-3776 ■ *Web:* thomasprintworks.com	972-231-7227	231-0623	240
Thomas Sappington House Museum, The 1015 S Sappington Rd Saint Louis MO 63126 *Web:* historicsappingtonhouse.org	314-822-8171		520
Thomas Scientific 1654 High Hill Rd PO Box 99 Swedesboro NJ 08085 **Fax Area Code:* 856 ■ *TF:* 800-345-2100 ■ *Web:* www.thomassci.com	800-345-2100	467-3087*	420
Thomas Seafood of Carteret Inc 421 Merrimon Rd Beaufort NC 28516	252-728-2391		296-14
Thomas Steel Inc (TSI) 221 Sheffield St Bellevue OH 44811 *Web:* www.tsifab.com	419-483-7540		480
Thomas Stone National Historic Site 6655 Rose Hill Rd Port Tobacco MD 20677 *Web:* www.nps.gov	301-392-1776	934-8793	564
Thomas Tape Co 1713 Sheridan Ave Springfield OH 45505 *Web:* thomastape.com	937-325-6414	325-2850	732
Thomas Transcription Services Inc PO Box 26613 Jacksonville FL 32226 *TF:* 888-878-2889 ■ *Web:* www.thomastx.com	904-751-5058	751-5240	478
Thomas Trucking Inc 2350 Seymour Ave Cincinnati OH 45212 *Web:* www.thomastruckinginc.com	513-731-8411		780
Thomas University 1501 Millpond Rd Thomasville GA 31792 *TF:* 800-538-9784 ■ *Web:* www.thomasu.edu	229-226-1621		166
Thomas W. Daniels & Company PC 1310 Eagle Ridge Dr Schererville IN 46375 *Web:* www.thomaswdaniels.com	219-864-7010	864-3130	2
Thomas W. Spinner CPA PC 11430 Gravois Rd Saint Louis MO 63126 *Web:* cp6.cpasitesolutions.com	314-842-1500	843-4310	2
Thomas W. Springer Inc 227 Buttonwood Rd Landenberg PA 19350 *Web:* www.twspringer.com	610-274-8400	274-8787	621
Thomas Weisel Partners Group LLC 1 Montgomery St San Francisco CA 94104 *Web:* www.tweisel.com	415-364-2500		792
Thomas West Inc 470 Mercury Dr Sunnyvale CA 94085 *Web:* www.twimaterials.com	408-481-9200	481-9212	361
Thomas Wilmer PC 2504 N Third St Phoenix AZ 85004 *Web:* arizonapilawyer.com	602-230-1188	264-9895	41
Thomas Wolfe Memorial 52 N Market St Asheville NC 28801 *Web:* www.wolfememorial.com	828-253-8304		50-3
Thomas Wood Professionals 202 S St Ste 13 Sausalito CA 94965 *Web:* thomaswoodpros.com	415-944-8754	332-9085	260
Thomas, Combs & Spann PLLC 300 Summers St Ste 1380 Charleston WV 25301 *Web:* tcspllc.com	304-414-1800		41
Thomas/Euclid Industries Inc 2575 Bethel Ave Indianapolis IN 46203 *Web:* www.thomaseuclid.com	317-783-7171		454
Thomasarts Inc 240 S 200 W Farmington UT 84025 *Web:* www.thomasarts.com	801-451-5365		4
Thomaston Savings Bank 203 Main St PO Box 907 Thomaston CT 06787 *TF:* 855-344-1874 ■ *Web:* www.thomastonsavingsbank.com	860-283-1874		70
Thomaston-Upson Chamber of Commerce 110 W Main St Thomaston GA 30286 *Web:* www.thomastonchamber.com	706-647-9686		139
Thomasville Area Chamber of Commerce PO Box 1400 Thomasville NC 27361 *Web:* www.thomasvillechamber.net	336-475-6134	475-4802	139
Thombert Inc 316 E Seventh St N Newton IA 50208 *TF:* 800-433-3572 ■ *Web:* www.thombert.com	800-433-3572	433-3517	608
Thombley & Simmons PC 78 Cole St Ste 200 Marietta GA 30060	770-423-1234		2
Thompson & Johnson Equipment Company Inc 6926 Fly Rd East Syracuse NY 13057 *Web:* thompsonandjohnson.com	315-437-2881		358
Thompson & Knight LLP 1700 Pacific Ave Ste 3300 Dallas TX 75201 *Web:* www.tklaw.com	214-969-1700	969-1751	428
Thompson & Litton Inc 103 E Main St Wise VA 24293 *Web:* www.t-l.com	276-328-2161		261
Thompson & McMullan 100 Shockoe Slip Third Fl Richmond VA 23219 *Web:* www.t-mlaw.com	804-649-7545		428
Thompson Agency Inc, The 73 River Rd Collinsville CT 06019 *Web:* thompsonagency.net	860-693-4999		390
Thompson Aluminum Casting Co 5161 Canal Rd Cleveland OH 44125 *Web:* www.thompsoncasting.com	216-206-2781		492
Thompson Bennie G (Rep D - MS) 2466 Rayburn House Office Bldg Washington DC 20515 *TF:* 800-335-9003 ■ *Web:* www.benniethompson.house.gov	202-225-5876	225-5898	342-2
Thompson Bowie & Hatch LLC 415 Congress St PO Box 4630 Portland ME 04112 *Web:* www.thompsonbowie.com	207-774-2500	774-3591	428
Thompson Brothers (Construction) LP 411 S Ave PO Box 4300 Spruce Grove AB T7X3B5 *Web:* www.thompsoncg.ca	780-962-1030		188
Thompson Citizen 141 Commercial Pl Thompson MB R8N1T1 *Web:* www.thompsoncitizen.net	204-677-4534	677-3681	532-1
Thompson Co, The 3636 W Stolley Park Rd Grand Island NE 68803 *Web:* www.thompsonfoods.com	308-382-6581	382-1813	297-7
Thompson Coburn LLP 1 Us Bank Plz Saint Louis MO 63101 *Web:* www.thompsoncoburn.com	314-552-6000	552-7000	41
Thompson Coe Cousins & irons 700 N Pearl St 25th Fl Dallas TX 75201 *Web:* www.thompsoncoe.com	214-871-8206	871-8209	428
Thompson Collins Agency 214 E First Ave Plentywood MT 59254 *Web:* cathompsoninsurance.com	406-765-1190		390
Thompson Consultants Inc 525 Mill St Marion MA 02738 *Web:* tciengineers.com	508-748-2620		261
Thompson Consulting Inc (TCI) 9 Jacob Gates Rd Harvard MA 01451 **Fax Area Code:* 240 ■ *Web:* www.thompsonrd.com	978-456-7722	414-2655*	261
Thompson Electric Co (TEC) 2300 7th St Sioux City IA 51105 *Web:* www.thompsonknows.com	712-252-4221		787
Thompson Enamel Inc 650 Colfax Ave Bellevue Newport KY 41073 *Web:* thompsonenamel.com	859-291-3800	291-1849	481
Thompson Engineering Inc 2970 Cottage Hill Rd Ste 190 Mobile AL 36606 *Web:* thompsonengineering.com	251-666-2443	666-6422	256
Thompson Equipment Company Inc 125 Industrial Ave Jefferson LA 70121 *Web:* www.teco-inc.com	504-833-6381		201
Thompson Falls State Park 2220 Blue Slide Rd Thompson Falls MT 59873 *Web:* www.montanastateparks.reserveamerica.com	406-827-3110		565
Thompson Glenn (Rep R - PA) 400 Cannon House Office Bldg Washington DC 20515 *Web:* www.thompson.house.gov	202-225-5121		342-2
Thompson Greenspon & Company PC 4035 Ridgetop Rd Ste 700 Fairfax VA 22030 *Web:* www.tgccpa.com	703-385-8888		2
Thompson Hine LLP 127 Public Sq 3900 Key Ctr Cleveland OH 44114 *TF:* 877-257-3382 ■ *Web:* www.thompsonhine.com	216-566-5500	566-5800	428
Thompson Hospitality 1741 Business Center Dr Ste 200 Herndon VA 20190 *Web:* www.thompsonhospitality.com	703-757-5500	759-1538	670
Thompson Industrial Services LLC 104 N Main Sumter SC 29150 *TF:* 800-849-8040 ■ *Web:* www.thompsonindustrialservices.com	803-773-8005		610
Thompson Information Services 4340 E-West Hwy Ste 300 Bethesda MD 20814 *TF:* 800-677-3789 ■ *Web:* www.thompson.com	202-872-3611		637-9
Thompson International Inc PO Box 656 Henderson KY 42420 *Web:* www.thompsoninternational.com	270-826-3751	826-3881	386
Thompson Investment Management Inc 918 Deming Way 3rd Fl Madison WI 53717 *Web:* www.thompsonim.com	608-827-5700		360-3
Thompson Lexus 50 W Swamp Rd Doylestown PA 18901 *TF:* 800-846-6776 ■ *Web:* www.1800thompson.com	215-345-1110		57
Thompson Mahogany Co 7400 Edmund St Philadelphia PA 19136 *TF:* 877-589-6637 ■ *Web:* thompsonmahogany.com	877-589-6637		683
Thompson Marketing 70 NE Loop 410 San Antonio TX 78216 *Web:* www.thompsonmarketinginc.com	239-772-5408		4
Thompson Mike (Rep D - CA) 406 Cannon House Office Bldg Washington DC 20515 *Web:* mikethompson.house.gov	202-225-3311	225-4335	342-2
Thompson Olde Inc 3250 Camino Del Sol Oxnard CA 93030 *TF:* 800-827-1565 ■ *Web:* www.oldethompson.com	805-983-0388		361
Thompson Packers Inc 550 Carnation St Slidell LA 70460	985-641-6640		473

Name / Address	City	State	ZIP	Phone	Fax	Class
Thompson Park Zoo 1 Thompson Pk *Web:* www.nyszoo.org	Watertown	NY	13601	315-782-6180	782-6192	823
Thompson Pump & Manufacturing Company Inc 4620 City Center Dr PO Box 291370 *TF:* 800-767-7310 ■ *Web:* www.thompsonpump.com	Port Orange	FL	32129	386-767-7310	761-0362	641
Thompson Realty Corp 1600 N Collins Blvd Ste 2100 *Web:* www.thompson-realty.com	Richardson	TX	75080	972-644-2400	644-2411	187
Thompson Research Group LLC 1033 Demonbreun St Ste 625 *Web:* www.thompsonresearchgroup.com	Nashville	TN	37203	615-891-6200		401
Thompson Rivers University (TRU) 805 TRU Way *TF:* 800-663-1663 ■ *Web:* www.tru.ca	Kamloops	BC	V2C0C8	250-828-5000	371-5960	785
Thompson Siegel & Walmsley Inc 6806 Paragon Pl Ste 300 *TF:* 800-697-1056 ■ *Web:* www.tswinvest.com	Richmond	VA	23230	804-353-4500	353-0925	401
Thompson Speedway 205 E Thompson Rd PO Box 278 *Web:* www.thompsonspeedway.com	Thompson	CT	06277	860-923-2280	923-2398	515
Thompson Steel Co 120 Royall St *Web:* www.thompsonsteelco.com	Canton	MA	02021	781-828-8800		723
Thompson Technologies 200 Galleria Pkwy Ste 1100 *TF:* 888-794-7947 ■ *Web:* thompsontechnologies.com	Atlanta	GA	30339	770-794-8380	794-8381	721
Thompson Thrift Construction Inc 901 Wabash Ave Ste 300 *TF:* 800-687-0012 ■ *Web:* www.thompsonthrift.com	Terre Haute	IN	47807	812-235-5959		186
Thompson's Harbor State Park Cheboygan Field Office 120 A-St PO Box 117 *Web:* www.michigan.gov	Cheboygan	MI	49721	231-627-9011	627-4366	565
Thompson's Lake Campground - Thacher State Park 68 Thompson's Lake Rd *Web:* parks.ny.gov	East Berne	NY	12059	518-872-1674	872-9133	565
Thompson, Ahern & Company Ltd 6299 Airport Rd Ste 506 *Web:* www.taco.ca	Mississauga	ON	L4V1N3	905-677-3471	677-3464	311
Thompson, Dentremont & Robin LLC 2161 Quail Run Dr Ste A *Web:* thompsonlawbr.com	Baton Rouge	LA	70808	225-766-5001		41
Thompson, O'Brien, Kemp & Nasuti PC 40 Technology Pkwy S Ste 300 *Web:* www.tokn.com	Norcross	GA	30092	770-925-0111	925-8597	428
Thomsen Group LLC 1303 43rd St *TF:* 800-558-4018 ■ *Web:* www.info.lcthomsen.com	Kenosha	WI	53140	800-558-4018		296
Thomson - McDuffie County 210 Railroad St Rm 1401 PO Box 158 *Web:* www.thomson-mcduffie.com	Thomson	GA	30824	706-595-2134	595-9150	338
Thomson Elite 800 Corporate Pointe Ste 150 *TF:* 800-354-8337 ■ *Web:* www.elite.com	Los Angeles	CA	90230	424-243-2100		178-10
Thomson National Press Co 115 Dean Ave *Web:* www.thethomsongroup.com	Franklin	MA	02038	508-528-2021	520-7129	629
Thomson Plastics Inc 130 Quality Dr NW *Web:* www.thomsonplastics.com	Thomson	GA	30824	706-595-0658		596
Thomson Reuters 7322 Newman Blvd *TF:* 800-968-8900 ■ *Web:* www.tax.thomsonreuters.com	Dexter	MI	48130	800-968-8900		178-1
Thomson Reuters 22 Thomson Pl *TF:* 888-216-1929 ■ *Web:* www.thomsonreuters.com	Boston	MA	02210	617-856-2000		387
Thomson Reuters DT Tax & Accounting 3333 Graham Blvd Ste 222 *TF:* 800-663-7829 ■ *Web:* www.thomsonreuters.ca	Montreal	QC	H3R3L5	514-733-8355	733-8058	180
Thomson Safaris 14 Mt Auburn St *TF:* 800-235-0289 ■ *Web:* thomsonsafaris.com	Watertown	MA	02472	800-262-6255		636
Thomson-Affinity Title LLC 1000 Middlebrook Dr Ste C *Web:* thomsonaffinity.com	Liberty	MO	64068	816-792-0077		653
Thomson-Hood Veterans Ctr 100 Veterans Dr *TF:* 800-928-4838 ■ *Web:* www.thvc.ky.gov	Wilmore	KY	40390	859-858-2814	858-4039	793
Thomson-Macconnell Cadillac Inc 2820 Gilbert Ave *TF:* 877-472-0738 ■ *Web:* www.thomsonmacconnellcadillac.com	Cincinnati	OH	45206	888-838-1071		516
Thomsons Art Supply Inc 184 Mamaroneck Ave *Web:* www.thomsonsart.com	White Plains	NY	10601	914-949-4885	949-4978	45
Thor Inc 1280 W 2550 S St *Web:* www.thor.com	Ogden	UT	84401	801-393-3312		297-8
Thor Industries Inc 419 W Pike St *NYSE:* THO ■ *TF:* 877-596-6111 ■ *Web:* www.thorindustries.com	Jackson Center	OH	45334	937-596-6111		120
Thor Systems PO Box 4163 *Web:* www.thorsystems.net	Hopkinsville	KY	42241	270-890-0500		396
Thor Travel Services Inc 12202 Airport Way Ste 150 *TF:* 800-825-1071 ■ *Web:* www.thortravelservices.com	Broomfield	CO	80021	303-439-4100		772
Thorburn Associates Inc PO Box 20399 *Web:* ta-inc.com	Castro Valley	CA	94546	510-886-7826	886-7828	261
Thorburn Group, The 811 Glenwood Ave Ste 290 *Web:* www.thorburnco.com	Minneapolis	MN	55405	612-886-2593		5
Thorco Industries Inc 1300 E 12th St *Web:* www.thorco.com	Lamar	MO	64759	417-682-3375		233
Thorek Memorial Hospital 850 W Irving Park Rd *Web:* www.thorek.org	Chicago	IL	60613	773-525-6780	975-6703	374-3
Thoren Caging Systems Inc 815 W Seventh St *Web:* www.thoren.com	Hazleton	PA	18201	570-455-5041		419
Thorgren Tool & Molding Company Inc 1100 Evans Ave *Web:* www.thorgren.com	Valparaiso	IN	46383	219-462-1801	462-7941	604
Thorlabs 10335 Guilford Rd **Fax Area Code:* 240 ■ *Web:* www.thorlabs.com	Jessup	MD	20794	973-300-3000	456-7200*	696
Thor-Lo Inc 2210 Newton Dr *TF:* 888-846-7567 ■ *Web:* www.thorlo.com	Statesville	NC	28677	704-872-6522	838-7010	155-10
Thorman Petrov Group Company LPA 50 E Washington St *Web:* tpgfirm.com	Chagrin Falls	OH	44022	216-621-3500		41
Thorn Avenue Animal Hospital 188 Thorn Ave *Web:* thornave.com	Orchard Park	NY	14127	716-667-7250		794
Thorn, Lewis & Duncan Inc 40 N Main St Ste 2000 *Web:* thorncpa.com	Dayton	OH	45423	937-223-7272		2
Thornapple Kellogg Schools 10051 Green Lake Rd *Web:* www.tkschools.org	Middleville	MI	49333	269-795-3313		685
Thornberry Mac (Rep R - TX) 2208 Rayburn House Office Bldg *Web:* thornberry.house.gov	Washington	DC	20515	202-225-3706	225-3486	342-2
Thornburg Center for Prof Dev 711 Beacon Dr *Web:* tcpd.org	Lake Barrington	IL	60010	847-277-7691	277-7697	449
Thornburg Investment Management Funds 2300 N Ridgetop Rd *TF:* 800-533-9337 ■ *Web:* thornburg.com	Santa Fe	NM	87506	505-984-0200	984-8973	528
Thorne Associates Inc 1450 W Randolph St *Web:* www.thorneassociates.com	Chicago	IL	60607	312-738-5230	738-5249	189-9
Thorne Electric Co 26W501 St Charles Rd *Web:* www.thorneelectricinc.com	Carol Stream	IL	60188	630-668-4853	668-4879	806
Thorneloe University 935 Ramsey Lake Rd *TF:* 866-846-7635 ■ *Web:* www.thorneloe.ca	Sudbury	ON	P3E2C6	705-673-1730	673-4979	785
Thornhill Securities Inc 5906 Old Fredericksburg Rd Ste 201 *Web:* www.thornhillsecurities.com	Austin	TX	78749	512-472-7171		690
Thornmark Asset Management Inc 119 Spadina Ave Ste 701 *TF:* 877-204-6201 ■ *Web:* www.thornmark.com	Toronto	ON	M5V2L1	416-204-6200		193
Thornsoft Development Inc PO Box 164 *Web:* www.thornsoft.com	Spencerport	NY	14559	585-352-4223	352-7847	178-1
Thornton Fractional South High School 18500 Burnham Ave *Web:* www.tfd215.org	Lansing	IL	60438	708-585-2000		685
Thornton Laboratories Testing & Inspection Services 1145 E Cass St *Web:* www.thorntonlab.com	Tampa	FL	33602	813-223-9702	223-9332	743
Thornton Oil Corp 2600 James Thornton Way Ste 200 *TF:* 866-473-0017 ■ *Web:* thorntonsinc.com	Louisville	KY	40223	866-473-0017		324
Thornton Steel Company Inc 2700 W Pafford St *Web:* www.thorntonsteel.com	Fort Worth	TX	76110	817-926-3324		480
Thornton W. Burgess Society 6 Discovery Hill Rd *Web:* www.thorntonburgess.org	East Sandwich	MA	02537	508-888-6870	888-1919	48-13
Thornton, Reif, Dolan, Bowen & Klecker Pa 1017 Broadway PO Box 819 *Web:* thorntonlawoffice.com	Alexandria	MN	56308	320-762-2361		41
Thornton-Tomasetti Group Inc 2000 L St NW Ste 600 *Web:* www.thorntontomasetti.com	Washington	DC	20036	202-580-6300	580-6301	261
Thoro'Bred Inc 5020 E La Palma Ave *TF:* 800-854-6059 ■ *Web:* www.thorobredinc.com	Anaheim	CA	92807	714-779-2581	779-1582	483
Thoro-Packaging Inc 1467 Davril Cir *Web:* www.thoropackaging.com	Corona	CA	92880	951-278-2100		101
Thoroughbred Direct Intermodal Services 5165 Campus Dr Ste 400 *TF:* 877-250-2902 ■ *Web:* www.ns-direct.com	Plymouth Meeting	PA	19462	877-250-2902		449
Thoroughbred Financial Services LLC 5110 Maryland Way Ste 300 *Web:* www.thoroughbredfinancial.com	Brentwood	TN	37027	615-371-0001		401
Thoroughbred Ford Inc I-29 At Barry Rd 8501 N Boardwalk Ave *Web:* www.thoroughbredford.com	Kansas City	MO	64154	816-505-1818		57
Thoroughbred Owners & Breeders Assn (TOBA) PO Box 910668 *TF:* 888-606-8622 ■ *Web:* toba.org	Lexington	KY	40591	859-276-2291	276-2462	48-3
Thoroughbred Racing Associations of North America Inc (TRA) 420 Fair Hill Dr *TF:* 866-847-8772 ■ *Web:* thoroughbredracingassociations.com	Elkton	MD	21921	410-392-9200		48-22
Thoroughbred Software International Inc 285 Davidson Ave Ste 302 *TF:* 800-524-0430 ■ *Web:* www.thoroughbredsoftware.com	Somerset	NJ	08873	732-560-1377	560-1594	178-2
Thoroughbreds Chophouse & Seafood Grille 9706 N Kings Hwy *Web:* thoroughbredsrestaurant.com	Myrtle Beach	SC	29572	843-497-2636		671
Thorp & Co 150 Alhambra Cir Ste 900 Coral Gables *Web:* www.thorpco.com	Miami	FL	33134	305-446-2700	446-5050	636
Thorp Reed & Armstrong LLP 301 Grant St 14th Fl *TF:* 800-949-3120 ■ *Web:* www.clarkhill.com	Pittsburgh	PA	15219	412-394-7711	394-2555	428
Thorpe Electric Supply Co 27 Washington St *Web:* www.thorpeelectric.com	Rensselaer	NY	12144	518-462-5496		246
Thorpe Heating & Cooling Inc 8402 US Hwy 98 N *Web:* thorpeac.com	Lakeland	FL	33809	863-858-2577		189-10
Thorpe Technologies Inc 449 W Allen Ave Ste 119 *Web:* www.thorpetech.com	San Dimas	CA	91773	562-903-8230		261
Thorpe, North & Western LLP 8180 S 700 E Ste 350 *Web:* www.tnw.com	Sandy	UT	84070	801-566-6633		428
Thorsnes Bartolotta McGuire 2550 Fifth Ave 11th Fl *TF:* 800-577-2922 ■ *Web:* www.tbmlawyers.com	San Diego	CA	92103	619-236-9363		428
Thorson Manufacturing Co 1614 Fuller Rd *Web:* www.thorsonmfg.com	West Des Moines	IA	50265	515-225-6523	225-6928	815

Name / Address	City	State	Zip	Phone	Fax	Class
ThorSport Racing 312 Neilsen Ave *Web:* www.thorsport.com	Sandusky	OH	44870	419-621-8800		515
Thortex Inc 15045 NE Mason St *Web:* www.thortexinc.com	Portland	OR	97230	503-654-5726		484
Thorud Inc 10501 Hampshire Ave S *Web:* www.thorudinc.com	Bloomington	MN	55438	952-996-9020	996-9021	454
Thought Industries 3 Post Office Sq 4th Fl *TF:* 866-206-4011 ■ *Web:* www.thoughtindustries.com	Boston	MA	02109	866-206-4011		178-8
Thought Logic 3400 Peachtree Rd NE *Web:* thought-logic.com	Atlanta	GA	30326	770-305-6300		194
Thought Technology Ltd 2180 Belgrave Ave *TF:* 800-361-3651 ■ *Web:* thoughttechnology.com	Montreal	QC	H4A2L8	514-489-8251		743
Thoughtful Systems Inc PO Box 150136 **Fax Area Code:* 347 ■ *TF:* 800-759-2532 ■ *Web:* www.thoughtfulsystems.com	Brooklyn	NY	11215	718-369-0608	987-3927*	178-1
Thoughtworks Inc 200 E Randolph St 25th Fl *Web:* www.thoughtworks.com	Chicago	IL	60601	312-373-1000	373-1001	39
Thousand Crane 1000 Elm St *Web:* www.thousandcranenh.com	Manchester	NH	03101	603-634-0000		671
Thousand Hills Golf Resort 245 S Wildwood Dr *TF:* 877-262-0430 ■ *Web:* www.thousandhills.com	Branson	MO	65616	417-336-5873	337-5740	669
Thousand Hills State Park 20431 State Hwy 157 *Web:* mostateparks.com	Kirksville	MO	63501	660-665-6995		565
Thousand Islands National Park of Canada 2 County Rd 5 *Web:* www.pc.gc.ca	Mallorytown	ON	K0E1R0	613-923-5261	923-1021	563
Thousand Islands Printing Co PO Box 277 *Web:* www.thousandislandssun.net	Alexandria Bay	NY	13607	315-482-2581	482-6315	637-10
Thousand Oaks Civic Arts Plaza 2100 E Thousand Oaks Blvd *Web:* www.civicartsplaza.com	Thousand Oaks	CA	91362	805-449-2787		572
Thousand Oaks Library 1401 E Janss Rd *Web:* www.tol.lib.ca.us	Thousand Oaks	CA	91362	805-449-2660	373-6858	434-3
Thousand Pines Christian Camp & Conference Ctr 359 Thousnd Pines Rd *TF:* 888-423-2267 ■ *Web:* www.thousandpines.com	Crestline	CA	92325	909-338-2705		239
THP (T.H. Peek Publisher) PO Box 7406 *Web:* www.thpeekpublisher.com	Ann Arbor	MI	48107	734-222-8205	661-0136	637-2
THR Colonial Garden court 232 W St *Web:* www.colonialgardencourt.com	Reno	NV	89501	775-786-5038	323-4588	377
Thrasher Printing Inc 814 Hanley Industrial Ct *Web:* www.thrasher-bcm.com	Saint Louis	MO	63144	314-962-7979	962-7957	627
Thread Logic 16775 Greystone Ln *TF:* 800-347-1612 ■ *Web:* www.threadlogic.com	Jordan	MN	55352	800-347-1612		258
Threadgill's 301 W Riverside Dr *Web:* www.threadgills.com	Austin	TX	78704	512-472-9304		671
Threadpoint LLC 24881 Alicia Pkwy Ste E 310 *TF:* 866-631-1595	Laguna Hills	CA	92653	866-631-1595		396
Threadtex Inc 641 Lexington Ave 6th Fl *Web:* threadtex.com	New York	NY	10022	212-209-4444	838-0188	594
Three Bars Cattle & Guest Ranch 9500 Wycliffe Perry Creek Rd *TF:* 877-426-5230 ■ *Web:* www.threebarsranch.com	Cranbrook	BC	V1C7C7	250-426-5230		239
Three Bean Press PO Box 301711 *Web:* www.threebeanpress.com	Jamaica Plain	MA	02130	617-584-5455		637-2
Three Bond International Inc 6184 Schumacher Park Dr *Web:* www.threebond.com	West Chester	OH	45069	513-779-7300		3
Three C's Landscaping Inc 32124 Utica Rd *Web:* threecslandscaping.com	Fraser	MI	48026	586-415-4850		776
Three Chairs Publishing PO Box 453 *Web:* threechairspublishing.wordpress.com	Branford	CT	06405	203-483-5353		637-2
Three Chimneys Farm PO Box 114 *Web:* www.threechimneys.com	Midway	KY	40347	859-873-7053	873-5723	368
Three Cities Research Inc 135 E 57th St 15-103 *Web:* www.tcr-ny.com	New York	NY	10022	212-838-9660	980-1142	792
Three D Graphics Inc 11340 W Olympic Blvd Ste 352 *TF:* 800-913-0008 ■ *Web:* www.threedgraphics.com	Los Angeles	CA	90064	310-231-3330	231-3303	178-8
Three D Metals Inc 5462 Innovation Dr *TF:* 800-362-9905 ■ *Web:* www.threedmetals.com	Valley City	OH	44280	330-220-0451		492
Three Deep Marketing 289 Fifth St E 2nd Fl *Web:* www.threedeepmarketing.com	Saint Paul	MN	55101	651-789-7701		195
Three Eagles Communications Co 7600 CR 120 *Web:* www.threeeagles.com	Salida	CO	81201	719-539-2575	539-4851	643
Three Hands Corp 13259 Ralston Ave *TF:* 800-443-5443 ■ *Web:* www.threehands.com	Sylmar	CA	91342	818-833-1200	833-1212	361
Three Island Crossing State Park 1083 S Three Island Park Dr *Web:* visitidaho.org	Glenns Ferry	ID	83623	208-366-2394		565
Three Lakes Distributing Co 111 Overton St	Hot Springs	AR	71901	501-623-8201		81-1
Three Lakes Information Bureau 1704 Superior St PO Box 268 *TF:* 800-972-6103 ■ *Web:* threelakes.com	Three Lakes	WI	54562	715-546-3344		206
Three Leaf Productions 261 W Johstown Rd Ste 200 *Web:* www.three-leaf.com	Gahanna	OH	43230	614-626-4941		514
Three Notch Electric Membership Corp PO Box 295 *TF:* 800-239-5377 ■ *Web:* www.threenotchemc.com	Donalsonville	GA	39845	229-524-5377		245
Three of US Corp 39 W 19th St 1st Fl *Web:* www.nycda.edu	New York	NY	10011	212-812-4044		162
Three Pebble Press LLC 10040 SW 25th Ave *Web:* www.threepebblepress.com	Portland	OR	97219	503-977-0944	210-1901	637-2
Three River Telco 225 N 4th St *TF:* 866-569-2666 ■ *Web:* www.threeriver.net	Lynch	NE	68746	402-569-2666	569-4455	224
Three Rivers Community College 2080 Three Rivers Blvd *TF:* 877-879-8722 ■ *Web:* www.trcc.edu	Poplar Bluff	MO	63901	573-840-9600		162
Three Rivers Community College Mohegan 574 New London Tpke *Web:* www.trcc.commnet.edu	Norwich	CT	06360	860-886-0177		162
Three Rivers Convention Center & Coliseum 7016 W Grandbridge Blvd *Web:* www.threeriversconventioncenter.com	Kennewick	WA	99336	509-737-3700		205
Three Rivers Electric Co-op 1324 E Main St PO Box 918 *TF:* 800-892-2251 ■ *Web:* www.threeriverselectric.com	Linn	MO	65051	573-644-9000		245
Three Rivers Health 701 S Health Pkwy *Web:* threeriversheaIth.org	Three Rivers	MI	49093	269-278-1145		374-3
Three Rivers Planning & Development District Inc 75 S Main St PO Box 690 *TF:* 877-489-6911 ■ *Web:* trpdd.com	Pontotoc	MS	38863	662-489-2415		463
Three Rivers State Park 7908 Three Rivers Park Rd *Web:* www.floridastateparks.org	Sneads	FL	32460	850-482-9006		565
Three Ships 1122 Oberlin Rd *Web:* www.three-ships.com	Raleigh	NC	27605	919-297-2784		195
Three Z Printing Co 902 W Main St *Web:* www.threez.com	Teutopolis	IL	62467	217-857-3153		627
Threespot Media LLC 806 Seventh St NW Ste 201 *Web:* www.threespot.com	Washington	DC	20001	202-471-1000		177
Threewill LLC 4400 N Point Pkwy Ste 180 *Web:* threewill.com	Alpharetta	GA	30022	678-513-6930		177
Threshold Communications 16541 Redmond Way Ste 245C *TF:* 844-844-1382 ■ *Web:* thresholdcommunications.com	Redmond	WA	98052	206-812-6200	686-7800	224
Threshold Enterprises Ltd 23 Janis Way *Web:* www.thresholdenterprises.com	Scotts Valley	CA	95066	831-438-6851	461-1288	805
Threshold Entertainment Inc 1649 11th St *Web:* www.thresholdentertainment.com	Santa Monica	CA	90404	310-452-8899		514
Threshold Placement Services 35 W Pine St Ste 213 *Web:* www.thresholdplacement.com	Orlando	FL	32801	407-296-4370		193
THRH (Terre Haute Regional Hospital) 3901 S 7th St **Fax Area Code:* 877 ■ *TF:* 866-270-2311 ■ *Web:* regionalhospital.com	Terre Haute	IN	47802	812-232-0021	865-9738*	374-3
Thrift-Remsen Printers 3918 S Central Ave *Web:* www.thrift-remsen.com	Rockford	IL	61102	815-969-0610	969-9813	627
Thrifty Car Rental PO Box 26120 *TF:* 800-334-1705 ■ *Web:* www.thrifty.com	Oklahoma City	OK	73126	800-334-1705		126
Thrifty Office Furniture 6321 Angus Dr *Web:* www.thriftyofficefurniture.com	Raleigh	NC	27617	919-598-8454		321
Thrifty White Stores 6055 Nathan Ln N Ste 200 *TF:* 800-642-3275 ■ *Web:* www.thriftywhite.com	Plymouth	MN	55442	763-513-4300		237
Thrivent Financial for Lutherans 4321 N Ballard Rd *TF:* 800-847-4836 ■ *Web:* www.thrivent.com	Appleton	WI	54919	800-847-4836		391-2
ThriveOn Inc 210 S 20th St *TF:* 855-767-2571 ■ *Web:* www.thriveon.net	New Ulm	MN	56073	855-767-2571		196
Through Smoke Creative Inc 480 Gate 5 Rd Studio 340 *Web:* throughsmoke.com	Sausalito	CA	94965	415-289-7500		195
Thru Tubing Solutions Inc 11515 S Portland *Web:* www.thrutubing.com	Oklahoma City	OK	73170	405-692-1900		539
Thrush Aircraft Inc 300 Old Pretoria Rd *TF:* 800-325-0885 ■ *Web:* www.thrushaircraft.com	Albany	GA	31721	229-883-1440	439-9790	20
Thrush Company Inc 340 W Eigth St *Web:* www.thrushco.com	Peru	IN	46970	765-472-3351	472-3968	641
Thrustmaster of Texas Inc 6900 Thrustmaster Dr *Web:* www.thrustmaster.net	Houston	TX	77041	713-937-6295	937-7962	190
Thruway Fasteners Inc 2910 Niagara Falls Blvd **Fax Area Code:* 716 ■ *TF:* 800-905-9411 ■ *Web:* thruwayinc.com	North Tonawanda	NY	14120	800-905-9411	694-3865*	351
Thruway Shopping Center Plz 78 Oak St *Web:* www.shopthruway.com	Walden	NY	12586	845-778-3535		345
THS Constructors 150 Executive Center Dr Ste B108 PO Box 26119 *Web:* www.thsconstructors.com	Greenville	SC	29615	864-254-6066	254-6086	186
THSHS (Topeka High School Historical Society) 800 SW 10th Ave *Web:* www.thsweb.org	Topeka	KS	66612	785-295-3200		685
Thule Inc 42 Silvermine Rd	Seymour	CT	06483	203-881-9600		247
Thumann Inc 670 Dell Rd *TF:* 800-358-0761 ■ *Web:* www.thumanns.com	Carlstadt	NJ	07072	201-935-3636	935-2226	297-9
Thumb Cellular Limited Partnership PO Box 650 *TF:* 800-443-5057 ■ *Web:* www.thumbcellular.com	Pigeon	MI	48755	800-443-5057		736
Thumb Correctional Facility 3225 John Conley Dr *Web:* www.michigan.gov	Lapeer	MI	48446	810-667-2045		213
Thumb Electric Co-op (TEC) 2231 Main St *TF:* 800-327-0166 ■ *Web:* www.tecmi.coop	Ubly	MI	48475	989-658-8571		245
Thumb National Bank & Trust Co 7254 Michigan Ave *Web:* www.thumb.bank	Pigeon	MI	48755	989-453-3113		70

Name / Address	City	State	Zip	Phone	Fax	Class
Thumb Truck and Trailer Co 8305 Geiger Rd *Web:* www.thumbtruck.com	Pigeon	MI	48755	989-453-3133	453-3042	779
Thumbs-Up Telemarketing Inc 11861 Westline Industrial Dr Ste 600 *TF:* 800-410-2016 ■ *Web:* thumbsupinc.com	Saint Louis	MO	63146	800-410-2016		737
Thunder Airlines Ltd 310 Hector Dougall Way *TF:* 800-803-9943 ■ *Web:* www.thunderair.com	Thunder Bay	ON	P7E6M6	807-475-4211		13
Thunder Basin Coal Co *Arch Resources Inc* PO Box 406 *Web:* www.archrsc.com	Wright	WY	82732	307-939-1300		501
Thunder Bay Chamber of Commerce 200 Syndicated Ave S Ste 102 *Web:* tbchamber.ca	Thunder Bay	ON	P7E1C9	807-624-2626	622-7752	137
Thunder Bay Port Authority 100 Main St *Web:* www.portofthunderbay.ca	Thunder Bay	ON	P7B6R9	807-345-6400	345-9058	618
Thunder Bay Regional Health Sciences Ctr 980 Olvier Rd *TF:* 800-465-5003 ■ *Web:* tbrhsc.net	Thunder Bay	ON	P7B6V4	807-684-6000		374-2
Thunder Canyon Brewery 220 E Broadway BLVD *Web:* www.thundercanyonbrewstillery.com	Tucson	AZ	85701	520-396-3480		671
Thunder Reef Divers 12104 Northeast Hwy 99 *Web:* www.thunderreef.com	Vancouver	WA	98686	360-573-8507		167-3
Thunder Tech Inc 3635 Perkins Ave Studio 5 SW *TF:* 888-321-8422 ■ *Web:* www.thundertech.com	Cleveland	OH	44114	216-391-2255		7
Thunder Valley Casino 1200 Athens Ave *TF:* 877-468-8777 ■ *Web:* www.thundervalleyresort.com	Lincoln	CA	95648	916-408-7777	408-8370	133
Thunderbird School of Global Management 1 Global Pl *TF:* 800-848-9084 ■ *Web:* thunderbird.asu.edu	Glendale	AZ	85306	602-978-7000		685
Thunderbird Supply Co 1907 W Historic Rt 66 *TF:* 800-545-7968 ■ *Web:* www.thunderbirdsupply.com	Gallup	NM	87301	505-722-4323	722-6736	411
Thundercloud Books PO Box 97 *Web:* www.thundercloudbooks.com	Aspen	CO	81612	970-925-1588	920-9361	637-2
Thundercloud Subs 1102 W Sixth St *Web:* thundercloud.com	Austin	TX	78703	512-479-8805	479-8806	670
Thune John (Sen R - SD) 511 Dirksen Senate Office Bldg *TF:* 866-850-3855 ■ *Web:* www.thune.senate.gov	Washington	DC	20510	202-224-2321	228-5429	342-2
Thurber House 77 Jefferson Ave *Web:* www.thurberhouse.org	Columbus	OH	43215	614-464-1032	280-3645	520
Thurel Mason Trucking Inc 1420 S 400 W *TF:* 800-448-8829 ■ *Web:* www.masontrucking.com	Aurora	UT	84620	435-529-3734		780
Thurgood Marshall Scholarship Fund 901 F St NW Ste 300 *Web:* www.tmcf.org	Washington	DC	20004	202-507-4851	652-2934	725
Thurman Campbell Group PLC 324 Franklin St *Web:* www.tccpas.com	Clarksville	TN	37040	931-552-7474		734
Thurman G. Smith Elementary School 3600 Falcon Rd *Web:* smith.sdale.org	Springdale	AR	72762	479-750-8846		685
Thurston County 2000 Lakeridge Dr SW Bldg 1 Rm 127 *Web:* www.co.thurston.wa.us	Olympia	WA	98502	360-786-5430	753-4033	338
Thurston County PO Box 159 *Web:* www.thurstoncountynebraska.us	Pender	NE	68047	402-385-2343	385-3544	338
Thurston Group LLC John Hancock Ctr 875 N Michigan Ave Ste 3640 *Web:* thurstongroup.com	Chicago	IL	60611	312-255-0077		390
Thwing-Albert Instrument Company Inc 14 W Collings Ave *Web:* www.thwingalbert.com	West Berlin	NJ	08091	856-767-1000	767-2615	639
Thybar Corp 913 S Kay Ave *TF:* 800-666-2872 ■ *Web:* www.thybar.com	Addison	IL	60101	630-543-5300	543-5309	697
Thylaksoft LLC 307 Elizabeth Sweetbriar Ln *Web:* www.thylaksoft.com	New Castle	DE	19720	302-355-0449		809
Thymly Products Inc 1332 Colora Rd *TF:* 877-710-2340 ■ *Web:* www.thymlyproducts.com	Colora	MD	21917	410-658-4820	220-0038	296-23
Thysen Consulting 160 Vista Verde Way *Web:* www.thysen.com	Portola Valley	CA	94028	650-851-8025	851-2650	192
Thyssenkrupp Bilstein of America Inc 8685 Berk Blvd *Web:* bilsteinus.com	Hamilton	OH	45015	513-881-7600		247
ThyssenKrupp Crankshaft Company LLC 1000 Lynch Rd *Web:* www.thyssenkrupp-components-technology.com	Danville	IL	61834	217-431-0060	431-8934	483
ThyssenKrupp Elevator 9280 Crestwyn Hills Dr *TF:* 877-230-0303 ■ *Web:* www.thyssenkruppelevator.com	Memphis	TN	38125	901-261-1800		360-3
Thyssenkrupp Krause Inc 901 Doris Rd *Web:* www.thyssenkrupp-system-engineering.com	Auburn Hills	MI	48326	248-340-8000	340-8001	491
ThyssenKrupp Presta USA LLC 1597 E Industrial Dr *Web:* www.thyssenkrupp.com	Terre Haute	IN	47802	812-299-5002		247
Thyssenkrupp Steel North America Inc 22355 W Eleven Mile Rd *Web:* www.thyssenkrupp-materials-na.com	Southfield	MI	48033	248-233-5600		492
Ti Ba Enterprises Inc 25 Hytec Cir *TF:* 800-836-8422 ■ *Web:* www.ti-ba.com	Rochester	NY	14606	585-247-1212		475
Ti Squared Technologies Inc 1305 Clark Mill Rd *Web:* tisquaredtech.com	Sweet Home	OR	97386	541-367-2929		317
TIA (Tire Industry Assn) 1532 Pointer Ridge Pl Ste G *TF:* 800-876-8372 ■ *Web:* www.tireindustry.org	Bowie	MD	20716	301-430-7280	430-7283	49-4
TIA (Telecommunications Industry Assn) 1320 N Courthouse Rd Ste 200 *Web:* www.tiaonline.org	Arlington	VA	22201	703-907-7700	907-7727	49-20
TIA (Transportation Intermediaries Assn) 1625 Prince St Ste 200 *Web:* www.tianet.org	Alexandria	VA	22314	703-299-5700	836-0123	49-21
Tia Chucha's Centro Cultural & Bookstore 13197 Gladstone Ave *Web:* www.tiachucha.org	Sylmar	CA	91342	818-939-3433	367-5600	95
Tiaa Bank 301 W Bay St *TF:* 888-882-3837 ■ *Web:* www.tiaabank.com	Jacksonville	FL	32202	888-882-3837		509
TIAA-CREF 730 Third Ave *Web:* www.tiaa.org	New York	NY	10017	212-490-9000		391-2
TIACA (International Air Cargo Assn) 5600 NW 36th St Ste 620 *Web:* tiaca.org	Miami	FL	33122	786-265-7011	265-7012	49-21
Tianma Micro-Electronics (USA) Inc 13949 Central Ave *Web:* www.usa.tianma.com	Chino	CA	91710	909-590-5833	590-5858	246
Tiara Yachts Inc 725 E 40th St *Web:* www.tiarayachts.com	Holland	MI	49423	616-392-7163	394-7466	90
TIAW (International Alliance for Women) 1101 Pennsylvania Ave NW 3rd Fl *TF:* 888-712-5200 ■ *Web:* www.tiaw.org	Washington	DC	20004	888-712-5200		48-24
Tiba Medical Inc 2701 NW Vaughn St Ste 470 *Web:* www.tibamedical.com	Portland	OR	97210	503-222-1500		475
TIBCO Software Inc 3303 Hillview Ave *NASDAQ: TIBX* ■ *Web:* www.tibco.com	Palo Alto	CA	94304	650-846-1000	846-1005	178-1
Tibor de Nagy Gallery 15 Rivington St *Web:* www.tibordenagy.com	New York	NY	10002	212-262-5050		42
Tibor Machine Products Inc 7400 W 100th Pl *Web:* www.tibormachine.com	Bridgeview	IL	60455	708-499-3700	499-6803	454
Tiburon Strategic Advisors LLC 1735 Tiburon Blvd *Web:* www.tiburonadvisors.com	Tiburon	CA	94920	415-789-2540		196
TICC Capital Corp 8 Sound Shore Dr Ste 255 *Web:* www.ticc.com	Greenwich	CT	06830	203-983-5275		401
Tichon Seafood Corp 7 Conway St *Web:* tichonseafood.com	New Bedford	MA	02740	508-999-5607	990-8271	296-14
Ticket & License Ctr 1935 NW Ninth Ave *TF:* 888-485-2852 ■ *Web:* ticketlicensecenter.com	Fort Lauderdale	FL	33311	954-525-4858	525-4749	41
Ticket Source Inc 5516 E Mockingbird Ln Ste 100 *TF:* 800-557-6872 ■ *Web:* www.ticketsource.com	Dallas	TX	75206	214-821-9011	821-9060	750
TicketBiscuit LLC 5120 Cyrus Cir Ste 101 **Fax Area Code:* 866 ■ *TF:* 866-757-8330 ■ *Web:* www.ticketbiscuit.com	Birmingham	AL	35242	205-757-8330	693-9055*	387
Ticketscom Inc 555 Anton Blvd 11th Fl *TF:* 800-352-0212 ■ *Web:* www.tickets.com	Costa Mesa	CA	92626	714-327-5400	327-5410	750
TicketWeb Inc 807 S Jackson Rd *TF:* 866-777-8932 ■ *Web:* info.ticketweb.com	Pharr	TX	78577	866-468-3399		750
Tickfaw State Park 27225 Patterson Rd *TF:* 888-981-2020 ■ *Web:* crt.state.la.us	Springfield	LA	70462	225-294-5020		565
Tickle Pink Inn at Carmel Highlands 155 Highland Dr *TF:* 800-635-4774 ■ *Web:* www.ticklepinkinn.com	Carmel By The Sea	CA	93923	831-624-1244	626-9516	379
Tico's 317 S 17th St *Web:* www.ticosoflincoln.com	Lincoln	NE	68508	402-475-1048		671
Ticom Geomatics Inc 9130 Jollyville Rd *Web:* www.ticom-geo.com	Austin	TX	78759	512-345-5006	345-3751	256
Ticoon Technology Inc 56 The Esplanade Ste 404 *Web:* www.ticoon.com	Toronto	ON	M5E1A7	416-513-9524		179
Tida Thai Cuisine 212 Arthur Way *Web:* www.tidathai.com	Newport News	VA	23602	757-234-0099		671
Tidal Basin Holdings Inc 675 N Washington St Ste 400 *Web:* tidalbasingroup.com	Alexandria	VA	22314	703-683-8551		194
Tidel Engineering Inc 2025 W Belt Line Rd Ste 114 *TF:* 800-678-7577 ■ *Web:* www.tidel.com	Carrollton	TX	75006	972-484-3358	484-1014	56
Tideland Electric Membership Corp 25831 Hwy 264 E *TF:* 800-637-1079 ■ *Web:* www.tidelandemc.com	Pantego	NC	27860	252-943-3046	943-3510	245
Tideland Signal Corp 4310 Directors Row *Web:* www.tidelandsignal.com	Houston	TX	77092	713-681-6101		529
Tides Canada Foundation *Tides Canada* 400-163 W Hastings St *TF:* 866-843-3722 ■ *Web:* makeway.org	Vancouver	BC	V6B1H5	604-647-6611		305
Tides Foundation 1012 Torney Ave *Web:* www.tides.org	San Francisco	CA	94129	415-561-6400	561-6401	305
Tides Marine Inc 3251 SW 13th Dr *Web:* www.tidesmarine.com	Deerfield Beach	FL	33442	954-420-0949		350
Tidewater Barge Lines Inc 6305 NW Old Lower River Rd *TF:* 800-562-1607 ■ *Web:* www.tidewater.com	Vancouver	WA	98660	360-693-1491	694-8981	314
Tidewater Community College *Norfolk* 121 College Pl *TF:* 800-371-0898 ■ *Web:* www.tcc.edu	Norfolk	VA	23510	757-822-1110		162
Tidewater Direct LLC 300 Tidewater Dr *Web:* www.tidewaterdirect.com	Centreville	MD	21617	410-758-1500	758-2478	627
Tidewater Fleet Supply LLC 1324 Lindale Dr *Web:* tidewaterfleetsupply.com	Chesapeake	VA	23320	757-547-2167	502-4875	57
Tidewater Grill 1060 Charleston Town Ctr *Web:* mainstreetventuresinc.com	Charleston	WV	25389	304-345-2620	345-5624	671
Tidewater Heating & Air Conditioning 150 Southern Blvd *Web:* tidewaterac.com	Wilmington	NC	28401	910-343-1234		610

Company	Phone	Fax	Class
Tidewater Inc 6002 Rogerdale Rd Ste 600 .... Houston TX 77072 *NYSE:* TDW ■ *TF:* 800-678-8433 ■ *Web:* www.tdw.com	713-470-5300		465
Tidewater Inn & Conference Ctr 101 E Dover St .... Easton MD 21601 *TF:* 800-237-8775 ■ *Web:* tidewaterinn.com	410-822-1300	820-8847	379
Tidewater Newspapers Inc 6625 Main St .... Gloucester VA 23061 *Web:* www.gazettejournal.net	804-693-3101	693-7844	532-2
Tidewater Physicians Multispecialty Group PC 860 Omni Blvd Ste 304 .... Newport News VA 23606 *Web:* www.mytpmg.com	757-232-8764	223-7271	374-3
Tidewater Workshop 1100 Doughty Rd .... Pleasantville NJ 08232 *TF:* 800-666-8433 ■ *Web:* www.tidewaterworkshop.net	609-241-8916	241-8892	321
Tidewell Hospice 5955 Rand Blvd .... Sarasota FL 34238 *TF:* 800-959-4291 ■ *Web:* www.tidewellhospice.org	941-552-7500	925-0969	371
Tideworks Technology Inc 1131 SW Klickitat Way Bldg E .... Seattle WA 98134 *Web:* www.tideworks.com	206-382-4470	382-0443	177
TIDI Products LLC 570 Enterprise Dr .... Neenah WI 54956 *TF:* 800-521-1314 ■ *Web:* www.tidiproducts.com	800-521-1314	837-7770	477
Tidwell & Hilburn Insurance Inc 5082 Forsyth Rd .... Macon GA 31210 *Web:* th-ins.com	478-743-9318		390
Tidy Building Services Inc 609 W William David Pkwy Ste 202 .... Metairie LA 70005 *Web:* www.tidyusa.com	504-838-9843	833-6585	256
Tie Down Engineering Inc 255 Villanova Dr SW .... Atlanta GA 30336 *TF:* 800-241-1806 ■ *Web:* www.danforthanchors.com	404-344-0000		480
Tie Fast Vest Tools 847 W Fifth St .... Chico CA 95928 *Web:* tie-fast.com	530-345-4261		711
Tie National LLC 2280 White Oak Cir Ste 108 .... Aurora IL 60502 *Web:* www.tienational.com	630-301-7444		387
Tiedemann & Associates PC 560 North Ave .... Weston MA 02493 *Web:* tiedemanncpa.com	781-235-1099		2
Tiegel Manufacturing Co 495 Bragato Rd .... San Carlos CA 94070 *Web:* www.tiegelmfg.com	650-593-7881	593-7884	456
Tiempo Escrow Inc 2100 Main St Ste 330 .... Fountain Valley CA 92708 *Web:* www.tiempoescrowinc.com	714-500-1500		652
Tiensvold Shaffer Wenzel CPAS PLLC 141 S Mccormick St Ste 1 .... Prescott AZ 86303 *Web:* tswcpas.com	928-445-5777		2
Tiepoint-Bkm Engineering LLC 6300 Blair Hill Ln Ste 300 .... Baltimore MD 21209 *Web:* tiepoint-bkm.com	410-583-9100	583-8805	261
Tier One LLC 31 Pecks Ln .... Newtown CT 06470 *TF:* 877-251-2228 ■ *Web:* tieronemachining.com	877-251-2228		454
Tier1 Inc 2403 Sidney St Ste 225 .... Pittsburgh PA 15203 *TF:* 888-284-0202 ■ *Web:* www.tier1inc.com	412-381-9201		177
TiER1 Performance Solutions 100 E River Center Blvd Ste 100 Twr 2 .... Covington KY 41011 *Web:* www.tier1performance.com	859-415-1000		194
Tierra Right of Way Services Ltd 1575 E River Rd Ste 285 .... Tucson AZ 85718 *TF:* 800-887-0847 ■ *Web:* www.tierra-row.com	520-319-2106	323-3326	196
TierraNet Inc 14284 Dani Elson St .... Poway CA 92064 *Web:* www.tierra.net	858-560-9416	560-9417	808
Tierzero 700 Wilshire Blvd 6th Fl .... Los Angeles CA 90017 *Web:* www.tierzero.com	213-784-1400		224
TIES			
Sourcewell Technology 2340 Energy Park Dr .... Saint Paul MN 55108 *Web:* www.sourcewelltech.org	651-999-6000		177
Tietex Intl 3010 N Blackstock Rd .... Spartanburg SC 29301 *TF:* 800-843-8390 ■ *Web:* www.tietex.com	864-574-0500	574-9490	745-6
Tietronix Software Inc 1331 Gemini Ave Ste 300 .... Houston TX 77058 *Web:* www.tietronix.com	281-461-9300		177
Tiffany & Co 727 Fifth Ave .... New York NY 10022 *NYSE:* TIF ■ *TF:* 800-526-0649 ■ *Web:* www.tiffany.com	212-755-8000		410
Tiffany Stuart Solutions Inc 390 Diablo Rd Ste 220 .... Danville CA 94526 *Web:* www.go2dynamic.com	925-855-3600		260
Tiffen Company LLC 90 Oser Ave .... Hauppauge NY 11788 *TF:* 800-645-2522 ■ *Web:* tiffen.com	631-273-2500	273-2557	591
Tiffin Academy of Hair Design 104 E Market St .... Tiffin OH 44883 *Web:* www.tiffinacademy.com	419-447-3117	447-5840	167-3
Tiffin Area Chamber of Commerce 62 S Washington St .... Tiffin OH 44883 *Web:* www.tiffinchamber.com	419-447-4141	447-5141	139
Tiffin Foundry & Machine Inc 423 W Adams St PO Box 37 .... Tiffin OH 44883 *Web:* www.tiffinfoundry.com	419-447-3991	447-7969	455
Tiffin Metal Products Co 450 Wall St .... Tiffin OH 44883 *TF:* 800-537-0983 ■ *Web:* tiffinmetal.com	800-537-0983		350
Tiffin Motor Homes Inc (TMH) 105 Second St NW .... Red Bay AL 35582 *Web:* tiffinmotorhomes.com	256-356-8661	356-8219	120
Tiffin Supply Inc 611 First St PO Box 460 .... Red Bay AL 35582 *Web:* tiffinsupply.com	256-460-6756		351
Tiffin University 155 Miami St .... Tiffin OH 44883 *TF:* 800-968-6446 ■ *Web:* www.tiffin.edu	419-447-6442	443-5006	166
Tiffin-Seneca Public Library 77 Jefferson St .... Tiffin OH 44883 *Web:* www.tiffinsenecalibrary.org	419-447-3751	447-3045	434-3
Tift County 225 N Tift Ave .... Tifton GA 31794 *Web:* www.tiftcounty.org	229-386-7850	386-7926	338
Tift Regional Medical Ctr 1641 Madison Ave .... Tifton GA 31794 *TF:* 800-648-1935 ■ *Web:* www.tiftregional.com	229-382-7120		374-3
Tiftickjian Law Firm PC 600 S Cherry St Ste 1105 .... Denver CO 80246 *Web:* criminallawdenver.com	303-991-5896		41
Tifton-Tift County Chamber of Commerce 100 Central Ave .... Tifton GA 31794 *TF:* 800-550-8438 ■ *Web:* www.tiftonison.com	229-382-6200	386-2232	139
TIG (Technology Integration Group) 7810 Trade St .... San Diego CA 92121 **Fax Area Code:* 858 ■ *TF:* 800-858-0549 ■ *Web:* www.tig.com	800-858-0549	566-8794*	176
Tigard Area Chamber of Commerce (TACC) 12345 SW Main St .... Tigard OR 97223 *Web:* www.tigardchamber.org	503-639-1656		139
Tigard Public Library 13500 SW Hall Blvd .... Tigard OR 97223 *Web:* www.tigard-or.gov	503-684-6537		434-3
Tiger Business Forms Inc 7765 W 20th Ave .... Hialeah FL 33014 *Web:* www.tigerforms.com	305-817-8849	817-8851	627
Tiger Button Company Inc 307 W 38th St .... New York NY 10018 *TF:* 800-223-2754 ■ *Web:* www.tigerbutton.com	212-594-0570	695-0265	594
Tiger Construction Ltd 6280 Everson Goshen Rd .... Everson WA 98247 *Web:* tigerconstruction.us	360-966-7252		186
Tiger Financial News Network 601 Cleveland St Ste 618 .... Clearwater FL 33755 *TF:* 877-518-9190 ■ *Web:* www.tfnn.com	727-467-9190	443-0869	644
Tiger Fuel Company Inc 200 Carlton Rd PO Box 1607 .... Charlottesville VA 22902 *Web:* tigerfuel.com	434-293-6157	293-3701	316
Tiger Lines LLC Lodi 927 Black Diamond Way .... Lodi CA 95241 **Fax Area Code:* 209 ■ *TF:* 800-967-8443 ■ *Web:* tigerlines.com	800-967-8443	333-3725*	780
Tiger Press Administration 50 Industrial Dr .... East Longmeadow MA 01028 *Web:* www.tigerpress.com	413-224-2100		627
Tiger Schulmann's Karate Ctr 485 Blvd .... Elmwood Park NJ 07407 *TF:* 800-867-1218 ■ *Web:* tsk.com	800-867-1218		148
Tiger Software PO Box 9491 .... San Diego CA 92169 *Web:* www.tigersoft.com	858-273-5900		178-1
Tiger Supplies Inc 27 Selvage St .... Irvington NJ 07111 *TF:* 888-844-3765 ■ *Web:* www.tigersupplies.com	888-844-3765		791
Tiger Tales Books 5 River Rd Ste 128 .... Wilton CT 06897 **Fax Area Code:* 920 ■ *Web:* www.tigertalesbooks.com	203-834-0005	387-9994*	637-2
Tiger Technologies LLC PO Box 7596 .... Berkeley CA 94707 *Web:* www.tigertech.net	510-527-3131		396
Tiger's Garden LLC 312 W Eigth St .... Vancouver WA 98660 *Web:* tigersgardenrestaurant.com	360-693-9585		671
Tigercat Industries Inc 54 Morton Ave E .... Brantford ON N3R7J7 *Web:* www.tigercat.com	519-753-2000		273
TigerDirect Inc 7795 W Flagler St Ste 35 .... Miami FL 33144 *TF:* 800-800-8300 ■ *Web:* www.tigerdirect.com	800-800-8300		174
Tigerflex Corp 801 Estes Ave .... Elk Grove Village IL 60007 *Web:* tiger-poly.com	847-640-8366	640-8372	370
Tigerflow Systems Inc 4034 Mint Way .... Dallas TX 75237 *Web:* tigerflow.com	214-337-8780		664
Tigerlight Inc 395 Santa Monica Pl Level 2 .... Santa Monica CA 90401 *TF:* 888-701-4500 ■ *Web:* tigerlight.net	424-268-8752		393
Tigerpaw Software Inc 2201 Thurston Cir .... Bellevue NE 68005 *Web:* www.jamesfoxall.com	402-592-4544		177
Tigerpoly Manufacturing Inc 6231 Enterprise Pkwy .... Grove City OH 43123 *Web:* www.tigerpoly.com	614-871-0045	871-2576	604
TigerSwan Inc 3467 Apex Peakway .... Apex NC 27502 *Web:* www.tigerswan.com	919-439-7110		463
Tigerton Lumber Co 121 Cedar St .... Tigerton WI 54486 *Web:* www.tigertonlumber.com	715-535-2181		683
Tiggee LLC 11490 Commerce Park Dr Ste 140 .... Reston VA 20191 *Web:* www.tiggee.com	703-935-1598		631
Tighe & Bond Inc 53 Southampton Rd .... Westfield MA 01085 *Web:* www.tighebond.com	413-562-1600		261
TIGHITCO Inc 1375 Seaboard Industrial Blvd .... Atlanta GA 30318 *Web:* www.tighitco.com	404-355-1205		389
Tigre USA Inc 2315 Beloit Ave .... Janesville WI 53546 *Web:* www.tigreadsusa.com	608-754-4554		610
Tigress Financial Partners LLC 40 Wall St 30th Fl .... New York NY 10005 *Web:* www.tigressfp.com	212-430-8700		691
Tihati Productions Ltd 3615 Harding Ave Ste 507 .... Honolulu HI 96816 *TF:* 877-846-5554 ■ *Web:* www.tihati.com	808-735-0292	735-9479	573-4
TII Network Technologies Inc 141 Rodeo Dr .... Edgewood NY 11717 *NASDAQ:* TIII ■ *TF:* 888-844-4720 ■ *Web:* tiitech.com	631-789-5000	789-5063	640
Tiki Port 714 Iyanough Rd .... Hyannis MA 02601 *Web:* www.tikiport.com	508-771-5220		671
Tikker Engineering Inc 9384 W Overland Rd .... Boise ID 83709 *Web:* tikkerengineering.com	208-658-0218		261
Tikkun Magazine 2342 Shattuck Ave Ste 1200 .... Berkeley CA 94704 *Web:* www.tikkun.org	510-644-1200	644-1255	457-10
Tilbury House Publishers 12 Starr St .... Thomaston ME 04861 *TF:* 800-582-1899 ■ *Web:* www.tilburyhouse.com	207-582-1899	582-8227	637-2
Tilcon Connecticut Inc PO Box 1357 .... New Britain CT 06050 *TF:* 888-845-2666 ■ *Web:* www.tilconct.com	860-224-6010	225-1865	46
Tilcon NY Inc 162 Old Mill Rd .... West Nyack NY 10994 *TF:* 800-872-7762 ■ *Web:* www.tilconny.com	845-358-4500		503-5

Name	Address	City	State	ZIP	Phone	Fax	Class	Details
Tilden-Coil Constructors Inc	3612 Mission Inn Ave	Riverside	CA	92501	951-684-5901		186	*Web:* www.tilden-coil.com
Tile Center Inc	1331 Reynolds St	Augusta	GA	30901	706-722-6804		191-1	*TF:* 800-854-7691 ■ *Web:* www.tilecenter.com
Tile Council of America Inc (TCA)	100 Clemson Research Blvd	Anderson	SC	29625	864-646-8453	646-2821	49-3	*Web:* www.tcnatile.com
Tile Gallery Inc	1600 Woodhaven Dr	Bensalem	PA	19020	215-638-4130	639-4626	191-1	*Web:* tilegallery.co
Tile Intl	319 Waverly Oaks Rd	Waltham	MA	02452	781-899-8286	893-8159	751	*Web:* www.tiboston.com
Tile Shop Holdings Inc	14000 Carlson Pkwy	Plymouth	MN	55441	888-398-6595		787	*TF:* 888-398-6595 ■ *Web:* www.tileshop.com
Tile Wholesalers of Rochester Inc	1136 E Ridge Rd	Rochester	NY	14621	585-544-3200	544-0766	191-1	*TF:* 866-308-4537 ■ *Web:* www.tilewholesalers.com
Tilghman Company Inc	44 State Cir	Annapolis	MD	21401	410-268-7855		410	*Web:* tilghmancojewelers.com
Tillamook Bay Community College	4301 Third St	Tillamook	OR	97141	503-842-8222		162	*TF:* 888-306-8222 ■ *Web:* tillamookbaycc.edu
Tillamook County	201 Laurel Ave	Tillamook	OR	97141	503-842-3403	842-1384	338	*Web:* www.co.tillamook.or.us
Tillamook County Creamery Association Inc	4185 Hwy 101 N	Tillamook	OR	97141	503-815-1300		296-5	*TF:* 800-542-7290 ■ *Web:* www.tillamook.com
Tillamook County Fairgrounds	4603 E Third St PO Box 455	Tillamook	OR	97141	503-842-2272	842-3314	642	*Web:* www.tillamookfair.com
Tillamook County Pioneer Museum	2106 Second St	Tillamook	OR	97141	503-842-4553		520	*Web:* www.tcpm.org
Tillamook People's Utility District	1115 Pacific Ave	Tillamook	OR	97141	503-842-2535	842-4161	245	*TF:* 800-422-2535 ■ *Web:* www.tpud.org
Tillamook Youth Correctional Facility	6700 Officer Row	Tillamook	OR	97141	503-842-2565	842-4918	412	*Web:* www.oregon.gov
Tillar-Wenstrup Advisors LLC	1065 E Centerville Sta Rd	Centerville	OH	45459	937-428-9700		528	*TF:* 800-207-1143 ■ *Web:* twadvisors.com
Tilley Chemical Company Inc	501 Chesapeake Park Plz	Baltimore	MD	21220	410-574-4500	391-6665	146	*TF:* 800-638-6968 ■ *Web:* www.tilleychem.com
Tillis Thom (Sen R - NC)	113 Dirksen Senate Office Bldg	Washington	DC	20510	202-224-6342	228-2563	342-2	*Web:* www.tillis.senate.gov
Tillman's	1245 Monroe Ave NW	Grand Rapids	MI	49505	616-451-9266		671	*Web:* www.tillmansrestaurant.com
Tilson HR Inc	1530 American Way Ste 200	Greenwood	IN	46143	317-885-3838		631	*TF:* 800-276-3976 ■ *Web:* www.tilsonhr.com
Tilson Technology Management	245 Commercial St Ste 203	Portland	ME	04101	207-591-6427		196	*Web:* tilsontech.com
Tilth Restaurant	1411 N 45th St	Seattle	WA	98103	206-633-0801		671	*Web:* www.tilthrestaurant.com
Tilton & Company CPAS PC	4015 S Mcclintock Dr Ste 105	Tempe	AZ	85282	480-897-7708		2	*Web:* tiltonco.com
Tilton Asset Management	510 Boston Post Rd	Weston	MA	02493	781-373-2244	373-2873	186	*Web:* tiltonasset.com
Tilton Market Inc	1524 Tilton Rd	Northfield	NJ	08225	609-641-5118		345	*Web:* tiltonmarket.com
Tilton School	30 School St	Tilton	NH	03276	603-286-4342		622	*Web:* www.tiltonschool.org
Tilt-Up Concrete Assn (TCA)	113 First St NW	Mount Vernon	IA	52314	319-895-6911	213-5555*	49-3	**Fax Area Code:* 320 ■ *Web:* www.tilt-up.org
Tim Beil Plumbing	5409 Mauser St	Laurys Station	PA	18059	610-261-2074		612	*Web:* www.timbeilplumbing.com
Tim Collins Software Services Inc	PO Box 484	Danville	CA	94526	925-208-1911		178-1	*Web:* www.timcollins.com
Tim Crawford Insurance Agency Inc	1415 Walton Blvd	Rochester Hills	MI	48309	248-402-5005		390	*Web:* crawfordinsurancegroup.com
Tim Farless State Farm Agency	153 Holly Springs Rd	Holly Springs	NC	27540	919-577-0501		390	*Web:* farlessinsurance.com
Tim Hortons Inc	874 Sinclair Rd	Oakville	ON	L6K2Y1	905-845-6511	845-0265	670	*NYSE: QSR* ■ *TF:* 888-601-1616 ■ *Web:* www.timhortons.com
Tim J. Murphy Insurance Agency Inc	346 Central Ave	Whitefish	MT	59937	406-862-7747		390	*Web:* timmurphyagency.com
Tim Miller Associates Inc	10 North St	Cold Spring	NY	10516	845-265-4400		727	*Web:* timmillerassociates.com
Tim's Cascade Snacks	1150 Industry Dr N	Algona	WA	98001	253-833-0255		296-35	*Web:* www.timschips.com
Timber Lodge Steakhouse	7989 Southtown Ctr	Bloomington	MN	55431	218-722-2624		671	*Web:* www.timberlodgesteakhouse.com
Timber Mine	1701 Pk Blvd	Ogden	UT	84401	801-393-2155		671	*Web:* www.timbermine.com
Timber Press Inc	133 SW 2nd Ave Ste 450	Portland	OR	97204	800-327-5680	227-3070*	637-2	**Fax Area Code:* 503 ■ *TF:* 800-327-5680 ■ *Web:* www.timberpress.com
Timber Products Co	305 S Fourth St PO Box 269	Springfield	OR	97477	541-747-4577	744-4296	191-3	*TF:* 800-954-4340 ■ *Web:* www.timberproducts.com
Timber Products Inspection Inc	1641 Sigman Rd NW	Conyers	GA	30012	770-922-8000		41	*Web:* www.tpinspection.com
Timbercreek Asset Management Inc	25 Price St	Toronto	ON	M4W1Z1	416-923-9967		653	*TF:* 866-898-8868 ■ *Web:* www.timbercreek.com
Timberland Bancorp Inc	624 Simpson Ave	Hoquiam	WA	98550	360-533-4747	533-4743	360-2	*NASDAQ: TSBK* ■ *TF:* 800-562-8761 ■ *Web:* www.timberlandbank.com
Timberland Co, The	200 Domain Dr	Stratham	NH	03885	888-802-9947		301	*TF:* 888-802-9947 ■ *Web:* www.timberland.com
Timberland Federal Credit Union	821 Beaver Dr	DuBois	PA	15801	814-371-2676	371-0701	219	*TF:* 800-477-3889 ■ *Web:* timberlandfcu.org
Timberland Homes Inc	1201 37th St NW	Auburn	WA	98001	253-735-3435	939-8803	106	*TF:* 800-488-5036 ■ *Web:* www.timberland-homes.com
Timberland Regional Library	415 Tumwater Blvd SW	Tumwater	WA	98501	360-943-5001	586-6838	434-3	*TF:* 877-284-6237 ■ *Web:* www.trl.org
Timberlane Inc	150 Domorah Dr	Montgomeryville	PA	18936	215-616-0600		362	*TF:* 800-250-2221 ■ *Web:* www.timberlane.com
Timberlawn Mental Health System	4600 Samuell Blvd	Dallas	TX	75228	214-381-7181		374-5	*TF:* 800-426-4944 ■ *Web:* timberlawn.com
Timberline Forest Products LLC	PO Box 1568	Sherwood	OR	97140	503-590-5485		191-3	*Web:* www.timberlineforestproducts.com
Timberline Lodge	27500 E Timberline Rd	Government Camp	OR	97028	503-272-3311		669	*TF:* 800-547-1406 ■ *Web:* www.timberlinelodge.com
Timbertech Inc	8796 Moeller Dr	Harbor Springs	MI	49740	231-348-2750	348-5918	627	*Web:* www.timbertech.net
Timberwolf Tours Ltd	51404 Range Rd 264 Ste 34	Spruce Grove	AB	T7Y1E4	780-470-4966	339-3960*	760	**Fax Area Code:* 866 ■ *TF:* 888-467-9697 ■ *Web:* www.timberwolftours.com
Timbucktoo Manufacturing Inc	1633 W 134th St	Gardena	CA	90249	310-323-1134		806	*Web:* www.timbucktoomfg.com
Timco Rubber	125 Blaze Industrial Pkwy PO Box 35135	Berea	OH	44017	216-267-6242	267-6245	385	*TF:* 800-969-6242 ■ *Web:* www.timcorubber.com
Time & Cents Consultants LLC	31 Deane Ln	Fairfield	CT	06824	203-254-7736		194	*Web:* www.timeandcents.com
Time 4 Learning	6300 NE First Ave Ste 203	Fort Lauderdale	FL	33334	888-771-0914		395	*TF:* 888-771-0914 ■ *Web:* www.time4learning.com
Time Being Books	10411 Clayton Rd Ste 201-203	Saint Louis	MO	63131	314-432-1771	432-7939	637-2	*Web:* www.timebeing.com
Time Critical Decisions LLC	31 Old Solomons Island Rd	Annapolis	MD	21401	410-571-6646	571-6647	387	*Web:* www.tcdecisions.com
Time Definite Services Inc	1360 Madeline Ln Ste 300	Elgin	IL	60124	800-466-8040		311	*TF:* 800-466-8040 ■ *Web:* www.timedefinite.com
Time Equipment Rental Sales Inc	311 N Campbell St	Rapid City	SD	57701	605-348-2360	348-0058	23	*TF:* 800-371-2360 ■ *Web:* www.timerental.biz
Time Hotels	224 W 49th St	New York	NY	10019	212-246-5252	753-7326*	379	**Fax Area Code:* 877 ■ *TF:* 877-846-3692 ■ *Web:* www.thetimehotels.com
Time Machine Inc	1746 Pittsburgh Rd	Polk	PA	16342	814-432-5281		454	*Web:* www.timemachineinc.com
Time Mark Corp	11440 E Pine St	Tulsa	OK	74116	918-438-1220	437-7584	203	*TF:* 800-862-2875 ■ *Web:* www.time-mark.com
Time Trak Systems Inc	933 Pine Grove	Port Huron	MI	48060	810-984-1313		177	*TF:* 888-484-6387 ■ *Web:* www.timetrak.com
Time+Plus Payroll Service	500 Colonial Center Pkwy	Roswell	GA	30076	770-998-5790		2	*Web:* www.timeplus.com
Time-Cap Labs Inc	7 Michael Ave	Farmingdale	NY	11735	631-753-9090		231	*Web:* www.timecaplabs.com
TimeCapital Securities Corp	1 Roosevelt Ave	Port Jefferson	NY	11776	631-331-1400		690	*Web:* www.timecapital.com
Timely Inc	10241 Norris Ave	Pacoima	CA	91331	818-492-3500	899-2677	286	*TF:* 800-247-6242 ■ *Web:* www.timelyframes.com
Time-O-Matic Inc	1015 Maple St	Danville	IL	61832	217-442-0611	442-1020	203	*TF:* 800-637-2645 ■ *Web:* www.watchfiresigns.com
Times	401 Market St	Shreveport	LA	71101	318-459-3200	459-3301	532-2	*TF:* 866-979-6397 ■ *Web:* www.shreveporttimes.com
Times Colonist	2621 Douglas St	Victoria	BC	V8T4M2	250-380-5211	380-5353	532-1	*TF:* 800-663-6384 ■ *Web:* www.timescolonist.com
Times Daily	PO Box 797	Florence	AL	35631	256-766-3434	740-4717	532-2	*Web:* www.timesdaily.com
Times Fiber Communications Inc	358 Hall Ave PO Box 384	Wallingford	CT	06492	434-432-1800	265-8422*	813	**Fax Area Code:* 203 ■ *TF:* 800-677-2288 ■ *Web:* www.timesfiber.com
Times Herald	911 Military St	Port Huron	MI	48060	810-989-6237	989-6294	532-2	*Web:* www.thetimesherald.com
Times Herald Inc	639 S Chester Rd PO Box 591	Swarthmore	PA	19081	610-272-2500		637-8	*TF:* 888-933-4233 ■ *Web:* www.timesherald.com
Times Herald-Record	40 Mulberry St PO Box 2046	Middletown	NY	10940	845-341-1100		532-2	*TF:* 888-620-1700 ■ *Web:* www.recordonline.com
Times Leader	200 S Fourth St	Martins Ferry	OH	43935	740-633-1131		532-2	*Web:* www.timesleaderonline.com
Times Leader	607 W Washington St	Princeton	KY	42445	270-365-5588	365-7299	532-2	*Web:* www.timesleader.net
Times Leader, The	15 N Main St	Wilkes-Barre	PA	18711	570-829-7100	829-5537	532-2	*Web:* www.timesleader.com
Times Microwave Systems Inc	PO Box 5039	Wallingford	CT	06492	203-949-8400	949-8423	253	*TF:* 800-867-2629 ■ *Web:* www.timesmicrowave.com
Times Printing Company Inc	100 Industrial Dr	Random Lake	WI	53075	920-994-4396	994-2059	627	*TF:* 800-236-4396 ■ *Web:* www.kappapma.com
Times Record	219 S College Ave	Aledo	IL	61231	309-582-5112		532-4	*Web:* www.aledotimesrecord.com

Name / Address	City	State	ZIP	Phone	Fax	Class
Times Record 3600 Wheeler Ave TF: 888-274-4051 ■ Web: www.swtimes.com	Fort Smith	AR	72901	479-785-7700	784-0413	532-2
Times Record News PO Box 120 Web: www.timesrecordnews.com	Wichita Falls	TX	76307	940-767-8341	767-1741	532-2
Times Record, The 3 Business Pkwy Web: www.timesrecord.com	Brunswick	ME	04011	207-729-3311		532-3
Times Reporter 629 Wabash Ave NW TF: 800-686-5577 ■ Web: www.timesreporter.com	New Philadelphia	OH	44663	330-364-5577	364-8416	532-2
Times Union 645 Albany Shaker Rd PO Box 15000 Web: www.timesunion.com	Albany	NY	12212	518-454-5550	454-5628	532-2
Times Union Ctr 51 S Pearl St TF: 866-308-3394 ■ Web: www.timesunioncenter-albany.com	Albany	NY	12207	518-487-2000	487-2020	720
Times, The 23 Exchange St Web: www.pawtuckettimes.com	Pawtucket	RI	02860	401-722-4000		532-2
Times, The 601 W 45th Ave TF: 866-301-3331 ■ Web: www.nwitimes.com	Munster	IN	46321	219-933-3200	933-3249	532-2
Timesavers Inc 11123 89th Ave N TF: 800-537-3611 ■ Web: www.timesaversinc.com	Maple Grove	MN	55369	763-488-6600		386
Times-Call, The 350 Terry St TF: 800-279-8537 ■ Web: www.timescall.com	Longmont	CO	80501	303-776-2244		532-2
Times-Enterprise PO Box 650 Web: www.timesenterprise.com	Thomasville	GA	31799	229-226-2400	228-5863	532-2
TimesLedger Newspapers, The 41-02 Bell Blvd 2nd Fl Web: www.timesledger.com	Bayside	NY	11362	718-260-4545		532-3
Times-Mail 813 16th St TF: 800-782-4405 ■ Web: www.hoosiertimes.com	Bedford	IN	47421	812-275-3355	275-4191	532-2
Times-News PO Box 490 TF: 800-849-8050 ■ Web: www.blueridgenow.com	Hendersonville	NC	28793	828-692-0505		532-2
Times-News, The 707 S Main St TF: 800-488-0085 ■ Web: www.thetimesnews.com	Burlington	NC	27215	336-227-0131	228-1889	637-8
Times-Picayune 3800 Howard Ave TF: 800-925-0000 ■ Web: www.nola.com	New Orleans	LA	70125	504-826-3279	826-3112	532-2
Times-Shamrock Communications 149 Penn Ave Web: www.timesshamrock.com	Scranton	PA	18503	570-207-9001		532-2
Times-Standard 930 Sixth St TF: 800-564-5630 ■ Web: www.times-standard.com	Eureka	CA	95501	707-441-0500	441-0501	532-2
Times-Tribune, The 201 N Kentucky Ave Web: www.thetimestribune.com	Corbin	KY	40701	606-528-2464	528-1335	532-2
TimeValue Software 22 Mauchly TF: 800-426-4741 ■ Web: www.timevalue.com	Irvine	CA	92618	949-727-1800	727-3268	178-11
Timeware Inc 9329 Ravenna Rd Ste D TF: 866-936-2420 ■ Web: www.timewareinc.com	Twinsburg	OH	44087	330-963-2700		177
Timex Group USA Inc 555 Christian Rd PO Box 310 TF: 800-448-4639 ■ Web: www.timex.com	Middlebury	CT	06762	888-727-2931		153
Timken Museum of Art 1500 El Prado Balboa Pk Web: www.timkenmuseum.org	San Diego	CA	92101	619-239-5548	531-9640	520
Timlick & Associates Inc PO Box 581 Web: www.timlick.com	Dundee	OR	97115	503-538-8241		180
Timmins & District Hospital 700 Ross Ave E TF: 888-340-3003 ■ Web: www.tadh.com	Timmins	ON	P4N8P2	705-267-2131	267-6311	374-2
Timmins Chamber of Commerce PO Box 985 Web: www.timminschamber.on.ca	Timmins	ON	P4N7H6	705-360-1900	360-1193	137
Timmins Kroll & Jacobson LLP 10550 New York Ave Ste 200 Web: www.tjscpas.com	Urbandale	IA	50322	515-270-8080	276-8329	2
Timmons & Company Inc 1753 Kendarbren Dr Web: timmonsandcompany.com	Jamison	PA	18929	267-483-8220		7
Timmons Group Inc 1001 Boulders Pkwy Ste 300 TF: 800-588-7341 ■ Web: www.timmons.com	Richmond	VA	23225	804-200-6500	560-1016	261
Timmons Owen Jansen & Tichy Inc 1401 21st St Ste 400 *Fax Area Code: 916 ■ TF: 866-448-0321 ■ Web: saclaw.net	Sacramento	CA	95811	209-223-5650	444-8723*	41
Timmons William (Rep R - SC) 313 Cannon House Office Bldg Web: www.timmons.house.gov	Washington	DC	20515	202-225-6030		342-2
Timoney Knox LLP 400 Maryland Dr Web: www.timoneyknox.com	Fort Washington	PA	19034	215-646-6000	646-0379	428
Timothy M. Cary & Assn 3300 Cameron Park Dr Ste 100 Web: ppplaw.com	Cameron Park	CA	95682	530-672-7601		428
Timothy Pamment Salon LLC 22 Durham Rd Web: timothypammentsalon.com	Madison	CT	06443	203-245-7707		77
Timpano Group LLC 140 Ames St Web: www.timpanogroup.com	Oregon	WI	53575	608-695-7320		194
Timpano Italian Chophouse 450 E Las Olas Blvd Web: timpanochophouse.net	Fort Lauderdale	FL	33301	954-462-9119		671
Timpanogos Cave National Monument RR 3 PO Box 200 Web: www.nps.gov	American Fork	UT	84003	801-756-5239	756-5661	564
Timpone's 710 S Goodwin Ave Web: www.timpones-urbana.com	Urbana	IL	61801	217-344-7619		671
Timpson Garcia 70 Washington St Ste 300 Web: www.timpsongarcia.com	Oakland	CA	94607	510-832-2325		2
Timpte Inc 1827 Industrial Dr TF: 888-256-4884 ■ Web: www.timpte.com	David City	NE	68632	402-367-3056	367-4340	779
Tims Ford State Park 570 Tims Ford Dr TF: 800-471-5295 ■ Web: tnstateparks.com	Winchester	TN	37398	931-962-1183		565
Timson Edwards Co PO Box 55-0898 Web: www.timsonedwards.com	Jacksonville	FL	32255	904-705-6806		637-2
Timucuan Asset Management Inc 200 W Forsyth St Ste 1600 Web: www.timucuan.com	Jacksonville	FL	32202	904-356-1739		691
Tin Mill Employees Federal Credit Union 3016 West St Web: tinmillfcu.org	Weirton	WV	26062	304-748-5811		219
Tindale Oliver & Associates Inc 1000 N Ashley Dr Ste 400 Web: www.tindaleoliver.com	Tampa	FL	33602	813-224-8862	226-2106	261
Tindall Corp 2273 Hayne St TF: 800-849-4521 ■ Web: tindallcorp.com	Spartanburg	SC	29301	864-576-3230	587-8828	183
Tingley Rubber Corp 1551 S Washington Ave Ste 403 TF: 800-631-5498 ■ Web: www.tingleyrubber.com	Piscataway	NJ	08854	800-631-5498		576
Tingue 535 N Midland Ave TF: 800-829-3864 ■ Web: www.tingue.com	Saddle Brook	NJ	07663	201-796-4490		594
Tingue, Brown & Co 535 N Midland Ave Web: www.tinguebrownco.com	Saddle Brook	NJ	07663	201-796-5233		76
Tinicum Inc 800 3rd Ave 40th Fl Web: www.tinicum.com	New York	NY	10022	212-446-9300		690
Tinius Olsen TMC 1065 Easton Rd TF: 866-312-8456 ■ Web: www.tiniusolsen.com	Horsham	PA	19044	215-675-7100	441-0899	472
Tink Inc 2361 Durham Dayton Hwy TF: 800-824-4163 ■ Web: www.tinkinc.com	Durham	CA	95938	800-824-4163		770
TINK Profitabilite numerique Inc 87 Prince Ste 140 Web: www.tink.ca	Montreal	QC	H3C2M7	514-866-0995		5
Tinker & Rasor 4402 Greenwood Rd Web: www.destearns.com	Shreveport	LA	71109	318-635-5351	636-6969	23
Tinker Air Force Base 3001 Staff Dr Ste 2AC1 94B Web: www.tinker.af.mil	Tinker Afb	OK	73145	405-739-2026	739-2882	497-1
Tinker Omega Manufacturing LLC 2424 Columbus Rd Web: tinkeromega.com	Springfield	OH	45503	937-322-2272		358
Tinker Swiss Cottage Museum 411 Kent St Web: www.tinkercottage.com	Rockford	IL	61102	815-964-2424		520
Tinkertown Museum PO Box 303 Web: www.tinkertown.com	Sandia Park	NM	87047	505-281-5233		520
Tinley Park Chamber of Commerce 17316 Oak Park Ave Web: www.tinleychamber.org	Tinley Park	IL	60477	708-532-5700	532-1475	139
Tinley Park Public Library 7851 Timber Dr Web: www.tplibrary.org	Tinley Park	IL	60477	708-532-0160	532-2981	434-3
Tinley, Renehan & Dost LLP 60 N Main St 2nd Fl Web: tnrdlaw.com	Waterbury	CT	06702	203-596-9030		41
Tinsley Adv 2000 S Dixie Hwy Web: www.tinsley.com	Miami	FL	33133	305-856-6060		4
Tintri Inc 2570 W El Camino Real TF: 855-484-6874 ■ Web: www.tintri.com	Mountain View	CA	94040	650-209-3900		173-8
Tiny Jewel Box 1155 Connecticut Ave NW Web: www.tinyjewelbox.com	Washington	DC	20036	202-393-2747		410
Tio Pepe 10 E Franklin St Web: www.tiopepe.us	Baltimore	MD	21202	410-539-4675		671
Tioga County Chamber of Commerce 80 N Ave Web: www.tiogachamber.com	Owego	NY	13827	607-687-2020	687-9028	139
Tioga County Clerk 16 Ct St PO Box 307 Web: www.tiogacountyny.com	Owego	NY	13827	607-687-8660	687-8686	338
Tioga County Visitors Bureau 2053 Rt 660 TF: 888-846-4228 ■ Web: www.visitpottertioga.com	Wellsboro	PA	16901	570-724-0635		206
Tioga Fuel Co 2301 E Tioga St Web: www.tiogafuel.com	Philadelphia	PA	19134	215-535-2700		579
Tioga Inc 4810 Lilac Dr N Web: www.tiogaairheaters.com	Minneapolis	MN	55428	763-525-4000		14
Tioga Machine Shop Inc 6551 Hwy 40 Web: www.tiogamachineshop.com	Tioga	ND	58852	701-664-3337	664-3338	454
Tioga Pipe Supply Company Inc 2450 Wheatsheaf Ln TF: 800-523-3678 ■ Web: www.tiogapipe.com	Philadelphia	PA	19137	215-831-0700	533-1645	492
Tip of Texas Federal Credit Union 11501 Gateway Blvd W Web: spurfcu.coop	El Paso	TX	79936	915-532-6575	595-7364	219
TIP Rural Electric Co-op 612 W Des Moines St PO Box 534 TF: 800-934-7976 ■ Web: www.tiprec.com	Brooklyn	IA	52211	641-522-9221		245
Tip Technologies Inc N14 W24200 Twr Pl Ste 100 TF: 844-244-3823 ■ Web: www.tiptech.com	Waukesha	WI	53188	262-544-1211	544-1230	809
Tip Top Canning Co 505 S 2nd St TF: 800-352-2635 ■ Web: tiptopcanning.com	Tipp City	OH	45371	937-667-3713	667-3802	296-20
Tip Top Poultry Inc 327 Wallace Rd TF: 800-241-5230 ■ Web: tiptoppoultry.com	Marietta	GA	30062	770-973-8070		619
Tipco Punch Inc 1 Coventry Rd TF: 800-544-8444 ■ Web: www.tipcopunch.com	Brampton	ON	L6T4B1	905-791-9811		358
Tipmont REMC 403 S Main St *Fax Area Code: 765 ■ TF: 800-726-3953 ■ Web: www.tipmont.org	Linden	IN	47955	800-726-3953	339-3243*	245
Tipotex Chevrolet Inc 1600 N Expy Ste 77 Web: www.tipotexchevrolet.com	Brownsville	TX	78521	956-465-1209		57
Tippecanoe County 20 N Third St Web: www.tippecanoe.in.gov	LaFayette	IN	47901	765-423-9221	423-9154	338
Tippecanoe County Public Library 627 S St TF: 800-542-7818 ■ Web: tcpl.lib.in.us	LaFayette	IN	47901	765-429-0100	429-0150	434-3
Tippecanoe Place 620 W Washington St Web: www.tippe.com	South Bend	IN	46601	574-234-9077		671
Tippecanoe River State Park 4200 N US Hwy 35 Web: www.in.gov	Winamac	IN	46996	574-946-3213		565
Tipper Tie Inc 2000 Lufkin Rd TF: 800-331-2905 ■ Web: www.tippertie.com	Apex	NC	27539	919-362-8811	362-7058	154

Name / Address	City	State	ZIP	Phone	Fax	Class
Tipping Structural Engineers 1906 Shattuck Ave *Web:* www.tippingstructural.com	Berkeley	CA	94704	510-549-1906		261
Tippmann Industrial Products Inc 3518 Adams Ctr Rd *TF:* 866-286-8046 ■ *Web:* www.tippmannindustrial.com	Fort Wayne	IN	46806	260-441-9603	441-8264	385
Tips Inc 2402 Williams Dr *TF:* 800-242-8477 ■ *Web:* tipsweb.com	Georgetown	TX	78628	512-863-3653	863-5392	177
Tipsico Coin LLC PO Box 2067 *Web:* www.tipsicocoin.com	Corvallis	OR	97339	541-758-2651		459
Tipton & Hurst Inc 1801 N Grant St *TF:* 800-666-3333 ■ *Web:* www.tiptonhurst.com	Little Rock	AR	72207	501-666-3333		292
Tipton Correctional Ctr 619 N Osage Ave *Web:* doc.mo.gov	Tipton	MO	65081	660-433-2031		213
Tipton County 220 Hwy 51 N Ste 2 *Web:* www.tiptonco.com	Covington	TN	38019	901-476-0207	476-0297	338
Tipton County 101 E Jefferson St *Web:* www.tiptongov.com	Tipton	IN	46072	765-675-2794	675-3603	338
Tipton County Schools 1580 Hwy 51 S *Web:* www.tipton-county.com	Covington	TN	38019	901-476-7148	476-4870	685
Tipton Marler Garner & Chastain 501 W 19th St *Web:* cpagroup.com	Panama City	FL	32405	850-769-9491	785-9590	2
Tipton Scott (Rep R - CO) 218 Cannon House Office Bldg *Web:* tipton.house.gov	Washington	DC	20515	202-225-4761	226-9669	342-2
Tipton-Haynes State Historic Site 2620 S Roan St *Web:* www.tipton-haynes.org	Johnson City	TN	37601	423-926-3631		50-3
Tire Associates 6700 16th Ave SW *TF:* 800-594-8473 ■ *Web:* www.tireassociates.com	Cedar Rapids	IA	52404	319-247-0816		755
Tire Centers LLC 310 Inglesby Pkwy *TF:* 800-603-2430 ■ *Web:* www.tirecenters.com	Duncan	SC	29334	864-329-2700	329-2900	755
Tire Connections 1240 S Finley Rd *Web:* tireconnectionsinc.com	Lombard	IL	60148	630-620-7616		755
Tire Curing Bladders LLC 5701 Murray St *Web:* www.tirebladders.com	Little Rock	AR	72209	501-562-5410		754
Tire Industry Assn (TIA) 1532 Pointer Ridge Pl Ste G *TF:* 800-876-8372 ■ *Web:* www.tireindustry.org	Bowie	MD	20716	301-430-7280	430-7283	49-4
Tire Rack 7101 Vorden Pkwy *TF:* 888-541-1777 ■ *Web:* www.tirerack.com	South Bend	IN	46628	574-287-2345	236-7707	755
Tire Warehouse Inc 7500 NW 35 Terr *Web:* www.tiregroup.com	Miami	FL	33122	305-696-0096	696-5926	755
Tire Welder Inc, The 3428 Pan America Fwy NE *TF:* 800-359-2208 ■ *Web:* www.tirewelder.com	Albuquerque	NM	87107	505-884-3550	884-1480	755
Tire Wholesalers Company Inc 1783 E 14-Mile Rd *Web:* twi.tireweb.com	Troy	MI	48083	248-589-9910	589-9919	755
Tire's Warehouse Inc 240 Teller St *TF:* 800-655-8851 ■ *Web:* www.tireswarehouse.com	Corona	CA	92879	951-808-0111	808-9062	755
Tireman Auto Service Centers Ltd PO Box 3456 *Web:* www.thetireman.com	Toledo	OH	43607	419-724-8473		54
Tire-Rama Inc 1429 Grand Ave *TF:* 800-828-1642 ■ *Web:* www.tirerama.com	Billings	MT	59102	406-245-3161		755
Tires Plus Total Car Care 2021 Sunnydale Blvd *TF:* 844-338-0739 ■ *Web:* www.tiresplus.com	Clearwater	FL	33765	727-330-3684		62-5
Tirschwell & Loewy Inc 400 Park Ave *Web:* tirschwellandloewy.com	New York	NY	10022	212-888-7940		401
TIS Group 100 Village Center Dr Ste 260 *Web:* www.theinstitutionalstrategist.com	North Oaks	MN	55127	651-379-5070		317
Tischler Und Sohn 6 Suburban Ave *Web:* tischlerwindows.com	Stamford	CT	06901	203-674-0600		191-3
TISD Inc 1502 E Red River *Web:* www.tisd.net	Victoria	TX	77901	361-573-1102		396
Tishcon Corp 50 Sylvester St *TF:* 800-848-8442 ■ *Web:* www.tishcon.com	Westbury	NY	11590	516-333-3050	997-1052	799
Tishma Innovations LLC 101 E State Pkwy *Web:* www.tminn.com	Schaumburg	IL	60173	847-884-1805		358
Titan Air Inc 13901 16th St *TF:* 800-242-9398 ■ *Web:* www.titan-air.com	Osseo	WI	54758	715-597-2050		697
Titan America Inc 1151 Azalea Garden Rd *TF:* 800-468-7622 ■ *Web:* www.titanamerica.com	Norfolk	VA	23502	757-858-6500		182
Titan Aviation Fuels Inc 601 Mccarthy Blvd *TF:* 800-334-5732 ■ *Web:* titanfuels.aero	New Bern	NC	28562	252-633-0066	633-3125	579
Titan Coatings Inc 2025 Exchange Pl *Web:* www.titancoatings.com	Bessemer	AL	35022	205-426-8149	426-8152	550
Titan Consuting 3411 Preston Rd Ste C13 *Web:* www.titanconsulting.net	Frisco	TX	75034	972-377-3525		180
Titan Engineers Pc 1331 Stuyvesant Ave *Web:* titanengineers.com	Union	NJ	07083	908-624-0044		261
Titan Farms 5 RW Du Bose Rd *Web:* www.titanfarms.com	Ridge Spring	SC	29129	803-685-5381	685-5885	315-3
Titan Formwork Systems LLC 1476 N Grant Ave *Web:* www.titanformwork.com	Casa Grande	AZ	85122	480-305-1900		23
Titan Freight Systems 6201 SE Lake Rd *Web:* titanfs.com	Portland	OR	97222	503-652-0010	652-0053	311
Titan Global Distribution 11973 Westline Industrial Dr Ste 200 *TF:* 800-325-4074 ■ *Web:* titan-global.com	Saint Louis	MO	63143	314-817-0051	817-0070	449
Titan International Inc 2701 Spruce St *NYSE: TWI* ■ *TF:* 800-872-2327 ■ *Web:* www.titan-intl.com	Quincy	IL	62301	217-228-6011	228-9331	60
Titan Laboratories 1380 Zuni St PO Box 40567 *TF:* 800-848-4826 ■ *Web:* www.titanlab.com	Denver	CO	80204	800-848-4826		579
Titan Logix Corp 4130 - 93 St *TF:* 877-462-4085 ■ *Web:* www.titanlogix.com	Edmonton	AB	T6E5P5	780-462-4085	450-8369	201
Titan Machinery 644 E Beaton Dr *Web:* www.titanmachinery.com	West Fargo	ND	58078	701-356-0130		358
Titan Pharmaceuticals Inc 400 Oyster Pt Blvd Ste 505 *NASDAQ: TTNP* ■ *Web:* www.titanpharm.com	South San Francisco	CA	94080	650-244-4990	244-4956	85
Titan Protection & Consulting Inc 9350 Metcalf Ave Ste 210 *Web:* www.tpcsecurity.com	Overland Park	KS	66212	913-441-0911		693
Titan Recruitment Solutions Ltd 355 Burrard St *Web:* titanrecruitment.com	Vancouver	BC	V6C2G8	604-687-6785		260
Titan Solutions Group Inc 11901 W Parmer Ln Ste 400 *Web:* www.titansolutions.com	Cedar Park	TX	78613	512-345-4234		180
Titan Spine LLC Mequon Research Ctr 6140 W Executive Dr Ste A *TF:* 866-822-7800 ■ *Web:* www.titanspine.com	Mequon	WI	53092	262-242-7801	242-7802	476
Titan Steel Corp 2500-B Broening Hwy **Fax Area Code: 443* ■ *Web:* titansteel.com	Baltimore	MD	21224	410-631-5200	817-9786*	492
Titan Tool & Die Ltd 2801 Howard Ave *Web:* titantool.ca	Windsor	ON	N8X3Y1	519-966-1234		483
Titan Tool Co 7410 W Ridge Rd *Web:* www.titantoolco.com	Fairview	PA	16415	814-474-1583	474-5337	493
Titan Trucks LLC 306 Austin St PO Box 1353 *Web:* titanco.com	Levelland	TX	79336	806-894-4852		546
Titan West Inc 203 5th St *TF:* 800-252-0847 ■ *Web:* www.titanwestinc.com	Linn	KS	66953	785-348-5660	348-5401	273
Titan Wheel Corporation of Virginia 227 Allison Gap Rd *Web:* www.titan-intl.com	Saltville	VA	24370	276-496-5121		247
Titanic Museum 208 Main St PO Box 51053 *Web:* titanichistoricalsociety.org	Indian Orchard	MA	01151	413-543-4770	583-3633	520
Titanium Fabrication Corp 110 Lehigh Dr *Web:* www.tifab.com	Fairfield	NJ	07004	973-227-5300	227-6541	91
Titanx Engine Cooling Inc 2258 Allen St Ext *Web:* titanx.com	Jamestown	NY	14701	716-665-2620	665-7125	247
TITAS (Texas International Theatrical Arts Society) 2520 Flora St *Web:* titas.org	Dallas	TX	75201	214-880-0202		573-1
Titeflex Corp 603 Hendee St *TF:* 800-765-2525 ■ *Web:* www.titeflex.com	Springfield	MA	01139	413-739-5631	788-7593	370
Titgemeiers Feed Inc 701 W Ave *Web:* www.titgemeiers.com	Toledo	OH	43609	419-243-3731		296-28
Tithe.ly 901 Woodland St Ste 104 *Web:* get.tithe.ly	Nashville	TN	37206	424-228-8870		178-8
Title Guaranty of Hawaii Inc 235 Queen St *TF:* 800-222-3229 ■ *Web:* www.tghawaii.com	Honolulu	HI	96813	808-533-6261	521-0210	391-6
Title One Inc 1650 W 82nd St Ste 1070 *Web:* titleone.com	Bloomington	MN	55431	952-806-6430		653
Title Resource Group LLC 3001 Leadenhall Rd *Web:* www.trgc.com	Mount Laurel	NJ	08054	856-914-8500		391-6
Title Resources Guaranty Co (TRGC) 8111 LBJ Fwy Ste 1200 **Fax Area Code: 888* ■ *TF:* 800-526-8018 ■ *Web:* www.titleresources.com	Dallas	TX	75251	800-526-8018	485-3630*	391-6
Title Security of Arizona Inc 6390 E Tanque Verde Rd *Web:* titlesecurity.com	Tucson	AZ	85715	520-885-1600		390
Title Wave Inc 1360 W Northern Lights Blvd *Web:* www.wavebooks.com	Anchorage	AK	99503	907-278-9283		95
Titlemax of South Carolina Inc 15 Bull St *TF:* 888-485-3629 ■ *Web:* www.titlemax.com	Savannah	GA	31401	803-548-3970		401
Titletown Brewing Co 200 Dousman St *Web:* www.titletownbrewing.com	Green Bay	WI	54303	920-437-2337	437-2739	671
Titletown Express Inc 1210 Russett Ct *Web:* titletownexpressinc.com	Green Bay	WI	54313	920-490-9930		780
Tito's Restaurant 444 E William St	Carson City	NV	89706	775-885-0309		671
Titonka Bancshares Inc 173 Main St N PO Box 309 *TF:* 866-985-3247 ■ *Web:* www.tsbbank.com	Titonka	IA	50480	515-928-2142	928-2042	360-2
Titonka Burt Communications (TBC) 247 Main St N *TF:* 800-753-2016 ■ *Web:* www.tbctel.com	Titonka	IA	50480	515-928-2110	928-2897	224
Titus County 100 W First St *Web:* www.co.titus.tx.us	Mount Pleasant	TX	75455	903-577-6796	572-5078	338
Titus Dina (Rep D - NV) 2464 Rayburn House Office Bldg *Web:* www.titus.house.gov	Washington	DC	20515	202-225-5965		342-2
Titus Industrial 14580 Midway Rd *Web:* www.titusindustrial.com	Dallas	TX	75244	469-289-1773		311
Titus Regional Medical Ctr 2001 N Jefferson Ave *Web:* www.titusregional.com	Mount Pleasant	TX	75455	903-577-6000	577-7072	374-3
Titus Sports Academy LLC 1425 Village Square Blvd *Web:* titushp.com	Tallahassee	FL	32312	850-671-3278		177
Titus Steel Company Ltd 6767 Invader Cres *TF:* 888-564-7904 ■ *Web:* titussteel.com	Mississauga	ON	L5T2B7	905-564-2446		492
Titus Will Ford 3606 S Sprague *Web:* www.tituswillford.com	Tacoma	WA	98409	253-475-4151		57
Titusville Area Chamber of Commerce 2000 S Washington Ave *Web:* titusville.org	Titusville	FL	32780	321-267-3036	264-0127	139

Name / Address	City	State	ZIP	Phone	Fax	Class
Titusville Dairy Products Co 217 S Washington St *Web:* www.titusvilledairy.com	Titusville	PA	16354	814-827-1833	827-2510	296-25
Tiva Software LLC PO Box 78438 *Web:* www.tivasoftware.com	Charlotte	NC	28271	704-843-1069		809
TiVo Corp 100 Phoenix Dr Ste 201 *Web:* www.rovicorp.com	Ann Arbor	MI	48108	734-975-9177		637-10
TiVo Inc 2160 Gold St *NASDAQ: TIVO* ■ *TF:* 877-367-8486 ■ *Web:* www.tivo.com	Alviso	CA	95002	408-519-9100	519-5330	116
Tivoli Hotel 936 Warren Ave *Web:* tivolihotel.net	Downers Grove	IL	60515	630-968-6450		132
Tivoli Lodge 386 Hanson Ranch Rd *TF:* 800-451-4756 ■ *Web:* tivolilodge.com	Vail	CO	81657	970-476-5615	476-6601	379
TIW Technology Inc 769 Youngs Hill Rd *Web:* www.tiwcorp.com	Easton	PA	18040	610-258-5161	258-6217	177
Tix Bay Area 1119 Market St 2nd Fl *Web:* www.theatrebayarea.org	San Francisco	CA	94103	415-430-1140		747
Tizbi Inc 800 St Mary's St Ste 402 *TF:* 888-729-0951 ■ *Web:* tizbi.com	Raleigh	NC	27605	888-729-0951		177
Tiziani Whitmyre Inc 2 Commercial St *Web:* www.tizinc.com	Sharon	MA	02067	781-793-9380		7
TJ Cope Inc 11500 Norcom Rd **Fax Area Code:* 215 ■ *TF:* 800-483-3473 ■ *Web:* copecabletray.com	Philadelphia	PA	19154	800-882-5543	961-2580*	816
TJ Hale Co W 139 N 9499 Hwy 145 *TF:* 800-236-4253 ■ *Web:* www.tjhale.com	Menomonee Falls	WI	53051	262-255-5555	255-5678	286
TJ McCartney Inc 3 Capitol St Ste 1 *Web:* www.tjminc.com	Nashua	NH	03063	603-889-6380	880-0770	189-9
TJ Metzgers Inc 207 Arco Dr *Web:* www.metzgers.com	Toledo	OH	43607	419-861-8611		393
TJ Rock Enterprises Inc 5800 Genesis Ln *TF:* 877-733-8635 ■ *Web:* tjrockcorp.com	Frederick	MD	21703	301-831-4128	831-4281	179
TJ Samson Community Hospital 1301 N Race St *TF:* 800-651-5635 ■ *Web:* www.tjregionalhealth.org	Glasgow	KY	42141	270-651-4444		374-3
TJC & Associates Inc 2356 Gold Meadow Way Ste 250 *Web:* tjcaa.com	Gold River	CA	95670	916-853-9658		261
Tjernlund Products Inc 1601 Ninth St *TF:* 800-255-4208 ■ *Web:* tjernlund.com	White Bear Lake	MN	55110	651-426-2993	426-9547	18
TJH2B Analytical Services Inc 3123 Fite Cir Ste 105 *Web:* www.tjh2b.com	Sacramento	CA	95827	916-361-7177		794
T-Joe's Steakhouse & Saloon 12700 I-80 Service Rd *Web:* www.tjoessteakhouse.com	Cheyenne	WY	82009	307-634-8750		671
TJS (Tucson Jazz Society) PO Box 41071 *Web:* tucsonjazz.org	Tucson	AZ	85717	520-903-1265		48-4
TK Interactive Inc 9 N Long St *Web:* tkinteractive.com	Williamsville	NY	14221	716-632-2967		809
TK Media Direct Inc 5062 Lankershim Blvd Ste 3033 *Web:* tkmediadirect.com	North Hollywood	CA	91601	310-804-3447	919-1770	5
TKE (Tau Kappa Epsilon) 7439 Woodland Dr Ste 100 *Web:* www.tke.org	Indianapolis	IN	46278	317-872-6533	875-8353	48-16
TKO Electronics Inc 31113 Via Colinas *TF:* 877-365-1903 ■ *Web:* tkoecommerceweb.expresspoint.com	Westlake Village	CA	91362	818-879-2233		174
TKO Video Communications 1665 Willow St *TF:* 800-216-3476 ■ *Web:* www.tkoworks.com	San Jose	CA	95125	408-557-6900	252-0222	647
TKS (Turn-Key Solutions Inc) 4920 W Thunderbird Rd Ste C-120 *Web:* www.tksnation.com	Glendale	AZ	85306	602-863-0269	863-4563	737
TL Industries Inc 2541 Tracy Rd *Web:* www.tlindustries.com	Northwood	OH	43619	419-666-8144	666-6534	261
T-l Irrigation Co 151 E Hwy 6 AB Rd PO Box 1047 **Fax Area Code:* 800 ■ *TF:* 800-330-4264 ■ *Web:* www.tlirr.com	Hastings	NE	68902	402-462-4128	330-4268*	273
TL Ventures 435 Devon Pk Dr *Web:* tl.ventures	Wayne	PA	19087	610-971-1515		792
TLA (Tennessee Library Assn) PO Box 241074 *Web:* www.tnla.org	Memphis	TN	38124	901-485-6952		435
Tlaib Rashida (Rep D - MI) 1628 Longworth House Office Bldg *Web:* www.tlaib.house.gov	Washington	DC	20515	202-225-5126		342-2
TLBAA (Texas Longhorn Breeders Association of America) 2315 N Main St Ste 402 *Web:* www.tlbaa.org	Fort Worth	TX	76164	817-625-6241	625-1388	48-2
TLC (Trichotillomania Learning Center Inc) 207 McPherson St Ste H	Santa Cruz	CA	95060	831-457-1004		48-17
TLC (Library Corp, The) 1 Research Pk *TF:* 800-325-7759 ■ *Web:* www.tlcdelivers.com	Inwood	WV	25428	304-229-0100	229-0295	178-1
TLC Electronics Inc 18 Long Lake Rd *TF:* 833-300-0155 ■ *Web:* www.tlcelectronics.com	Saint Paul	MN	55115	651-488-2933		253
TLC Engineering for Architecture 255 S Orange Ave Ste 1600 *Web:* www.tlc-engineers.com	Orlando	FL	32801	407-841-9050	425-7367	261
TLC Florist & Greenhouse Inc 105 W Memorial Rd *Web:* tlcgarden.com	Oklahoma City	OK	73114	405-751-0630		323
Tlc Insurance Group Inc 8700 E Market St Ste 8 **Fax Area Code:* 330 ■ *TF:* 800-719-3751 ■ *Web:* tlcinsurancegroup.com	Warren	OH	44484	800-719-3751	637-2618*	390
TLC Nursing & Homecare Services Ltd 25 Anderson Ave *TF:* 888-726-3473 ■ *Web:* www.tlcnursingandhomecare.com	Saint John	NL	A1B3E4	709-726-3473		371
Tlc Office Systems 8711 Fallbrook Dr **Fax Area Code:* 713 ■ *Web:* tlcofficesystems.com	Houston	TX	77064	979-848-8300	696-1820*	179
TLC Vision Corp 50 Burnhamthorpe Rd W Ste 101 *TF:* 877-852-2020 ■ *Web:* www.tlcvision.com	Mississauga	ON	L5B3C2	877-852-2020		798
Tlcu Financial 1816 N Main St *Web:* tlcufinancial.org	Mishawaka	IN	46545	574-255-3193		219
Tld Ace Corp 805 Bloomfield Ave *Web:* www.tld-group.com	Windsor	CT	06095	860-252-3300		14
TLG 101-110 Princess St *Web:* tlg.ca	Winnipeg	MB	R3B1K7	204-940-4550		242
TLIE (Texas Lawyers Insurance Exchange) 1801 S MoPac Ste 300 *TF:* 800-252-9332 ■ *Web:* www.tlie.org	Austin	TX	78746	512-480-9074	482-8738	391-5
Tlk Industries Inc 130 Prairie Lake Rd Ste A & B *Web:* www.tlkind.com	East Dundee	IL	60118	847-359-3200	359-9639	393
TLM Associates Inc 117 E Lafayette St *Web:* www.tlmassociates.com	Jackson	TN	38301	731-988-9840	988-9959	261
TLN (Telelatino Network Inc) 5125 Steeles Ave W *TF:* 800-551-8401 ■ *Web:* www.tln.ca	Toronto	ON	M9L1R5	416-744-8200	744-0966	740
TLN (Total Living Network) 2880 Vision Ct *Web:* tln.com	Aurora	IL	60506	630-801-3838	801-3839	740
TLOMA (Toronto Law Office Management Assn) Toronto Dominion Ctr PO Box 1029 **Fax Area Code:* 905 ■ *Web:* www.tloma.com	Toronto	ON	M5K1P2	416-410-1979	472-5115*	138
TLR (Texas Law Review) 727 E Dean Keeton St *Web:* www.texaslrev.com	Austin	TX	78705	512-232-1280	471-3282	637-9
TLX Inc 7944 E Beck Ln Ste 200 *TF:* 800-520-7493 ■ *Web:* tlxinc.com	Scottsdale	AZ	85260	480-609-8888		180
TM (Traco Medical Inc) 4001 W Tickman St *Web:* www.tracomedical.com	Sioux Falls	SD	57101	605-339-9339	334-3025	475
TM 1031 Exchange Inc 100 Wilshire Blvd Ste 1760 *Web:* www.tm1031exchange.com	Santa Monica	CA	90401	310-264-0497		653
TM Capital Corp 641 Lexington Ave 30th Fl *Web:* www.tmcapital.com	New York	NY	10022	212-809-1360		401
TM Century Inc 2002 Academy Ln *Web:* www.tmstudios.com	Dallas	TX	75234	972-406-6800	406-6890	646
TM Deer Park Services LP 2525 Battleground Rd PO Box 1914 *Web:* texasmolecular.com	Deer Park	TX	77536	281-930-2525	930-2535	146
TM Group Inc, The 27555 Executive Dr Ste 100 *TF:* 888-482-2864 ■ *Web:* www.tmgroupinc.com	Farmington Hills	MI	48331	248-489-0707	489-9413	180
TM Process & Controls Inc 9245 Laguna Springs Dr Ste 125 *TF:* 888-611-8672 ■ *Web:* tmprocesscontrols.com	Elk Grove	CA	95758	916-226-1127		261
TM Smith Tool International Corp 360 Hubbard Ave *TF:* 800-521-4894 ■ *Web:* www.tmsmith.com	Mount Clemens	MI	48043	586-468-1465	468-7190	493
TM Television 2440 Lacy Ln Ste 110 *Web:* tmtel.com	Carrollton	TX	75006	972-243-4772	243-4774	246
T-M Vacuum Products Inc 630 S Warrington Ave PO Box 2248 *Web:* www.tmvacuum.com	Cinnaminson	NJ	08077	856-829-2000	829-0990	318
TMA (Tobacco Merchants Assn) PO Box 8019 *Web:* www.tma.org	Princeton	NJ	08543	609-275-4900	275-8379	48-2
TMA Small Business Accounting Pc 9595 Whitley Dr Ste 102 *Web:* tmasmallbusinessaccounting.com	Indianapolis	IN	46240	317-571-8080		2
TMA Systems LLC 5100 E Skelly Dr Ste 900 *TF:* 800-862-1130 ■ *Web:* www.tmasystems.com	Tulsa	OK	74135	918-858-6600	858-6655	178-11
TMB (Tech-Marine Business Inc) 100 M St SE Ste 800 *Web:* tmbhq.com	Washington	DC	20003	202-448-9701	448-9702	261
TMC (Tufts Medical Ctr) 800 Washington St *TF:* 866-220-3699 ■ *Web:* www.tuftsmedicalcenter.org	Boston	MA	02111	617-636-5000	636-8199	374-3
TMC (Tulane Medical Ctr) 1415 Tulane Ave *TF:* 800-588-5800 ■ *Web:* tulanehealthcare.com	New Orleans	LA	70112	504-988-5263		374-3
TMC - The Mate Co 42148 Sarah Way *TF:* 888-999-9984 ■ *Web:* www.tmccables.com	Temecula	CA	92590	415-454-5425	454-5130	247
TMC Books LLC 731 Tasker Hill Rd *Web:* www.tmcbooks.com	Conway	NH	03818	603-447-5589		637-2
TMC Design Corp 4325 Del Rey Blvd *Web:* tmcdesign.com	Las Cruces	NM	88012	575-382-4600		647
TMC Technologies Inc 2050 Winners Dr *Web:* www.tmctechnologies.com	Fairmont	WV	26554	304-816-3600	816-3411	396
TMD Machining Inc 751 Wakefield *Web:* www.tmdmach.com	Plainwell	MI	49080	269-685-3091	685-3093	757
TMD Technologies LLC 1730 Twin Springs Rd *Web:* tmdus.com	Halethorpe	MD	21227	410-242-4290	242-5073	261
T-Metrics Inc 4430 Stuart Andrew Blvd *Web:* www.tmetrics.com	Charlotte	NC	28217	704-525-5551	525-4886	647
TMF Center Inc 300 W Washington St *Web:* www.tmfcenter.com	Williamsport	IN	47993	765-762-1000	762-0100	190
TMG Co 43 Woodstock St *TF:* 800-720-1563 ■ *Web:* www.esprigas.com	Roswell	GA	30075	800-720-1563		2
TMH (Tiffin Motor Homes Inc) 105 Second St NW *Web:* tiffinmotorhomes.com	Red Bay	AL	35582	256-356-8661	356-8219	120
TMI (Texas Military Institute) 20955 W Tejas Trl *Web:* www.tmi-sa.org	San Antonio	TX	78257	210-698-7171	698-0715	622
TMI Coatings Inc 3291 Terminal Dr *TF:* 800-328-0229 ■ *Web:* www.tmicoatings.com	Saint Paul	MN	55121	651-452-6100	452-0598	189-8
TMI LLC 5350 Campbells Run Rd *TF:* 800-888-9750 ■ *Web:* www.tmi-pvc.com	Pittsburgh	PA	15205	800-888-9750		608
TMI Systems Design Corp 50 S Third Ave W *TF:* 800-456-6716 ■ *Web:* www.tmisystems.com	Dickinson	ND	58601	701-456-6716		319-3
TMK (T.M. Kovacevich Philadelphia Inc) 6700 Essington Ave Units A1-A6 *Web:* www.tmkproduce.com	Philadelphia	PA	19153	215-463-0100	463-7758	297-7

Company	City	State	ZIP	Phone	Fax	Class
TML (Teledyne Monitor Labs Inc) 35 Inverness Dr E *TF:* 800-422-1499 ■ *Web:* www.teledyne-ml.com	Englewood	CO	80112	303-792-3300	799-4853	201
TMMC Management PO Box 1540 *Web:* www.tmmccares.com	Castle Rock	CO	80104	303-985-9623	814-8267	652
T-Mobile USA Inc 12920 SE 38th St *Web:* www.t-mobile.com	Bellevue	WA	98006	425-378-4000		736
TMP (Tasker Metal Products Inc) 1823 S Hope St *Web:* www.taskermetalproducts.com	Los Angeles	CA	90015	213-765-5400	746-8707	60
TMP Architecture 1191 W Sq Lake Rd *Web:* www.tmp-architecture.com	Bloomfield Hills	MI	48302	248-338-4561	338-0223	261
TMP Direct 600 International Dr *Web:* www.tmpwdirect.com	Mount Olive	NJ	07828	973-347-9400		393
TMP Technologies 1200 Northland Ave *TF:* 866-728-1932 ■ *Web:* www.tmptech.com	Buffalo	NY	14215	866-728-1932		601
TMR Mailing Services Inc 506 Manchester Expy Ste A1 *Web:* www.tmrmailing.com	Columbus	GA	31904	706-653-2090		5
TMS (Tube City IMS Corp) 12 Monongahela Ave *NYSE: TMS* ■ *TF:* 800-860-2442 ■ *Web:* www.tubecityims.com	Glassport	PA	15045	412-678-6141	675-8295	686
TMS (Minerals Metals & Materials Society, The) 5700 Corporate Dr Ste 750 *Web:* www.tms.org	Pittsburgh	PA	15237	724-776-9000	776-3770	49-13
TMVP (Triathlon Medical Ventures LLC) 9987 Carver Rd Ste 210 *Web:* www.tmvp.com	Cincinnati	OH	45242	513-247-6122		792
TMW Media Group 2321 Abbot Kinney Blvd Ste 101 *TF:* 800-262-8862 ■ *Web:* www.tmwmedia.com	Venice	CA	90291	310-577-8581	574-0886	459
TN Ward Co 129 Coulter Ave *Web:* www.tnward.com	Ardmore	PA	19003	610-649-0400		186
Tn'T Bakery PO Box 220 *Web:* www.tntbakery.com	Bowmansville	PA	17507	717-445-5644	445-4818	297-3
TNA (Tennessee Nurses Assn) 545 Mainstream Dr Ste 405 *Web:* tna.nursingnetwork.com	Nashville	TN	37228	615-254-0350	254-0303	533
TNC Rail Engineering 2153 E Main St Ste C 14 341 *Web:* tncrailengineering.com	Duncan	SC	29334	864-706-8510		261
Tnemec Company Inc 6800 Corporate Dr *TF:* 800-863-6321 ■ *Web:* www.tnemec.com	Kansas City	MO	64120	816-483-3400	483-3969	550
TNG (Newton Group Inc, The) 623 N 19th Ave E **Fax Area Code:* 800 ■ *TF:* 800-232-5729 ■ *Web:* www.newtonpro.com	Newton	IA	50208	641-792-9962	809-8287*	542
TNMP (Texas-New Mexico Power Co) 577 N Garden Ridge Blvd *TF:* 888-866-7456 ■ *Web:* www.tnmp.com	Lewisville	TX	75067	972-420-4189		787
TNNA (National NeedleArts Assn, The) 1100-H Brandywine Blvd *TF:* 800-889-8662 ■ *Web:* www.tnna.org	Zanesville	OH	43701	740-455-6773	452-2552	48-18
TNR Technical Inc 301 Central Park Dr *OTC: TNRK* ■ *TF:* 800-346-0601 ■ *Web:* www.batterystore.com	Sanford	FL	32771	407-321-3011		74
TNSC (National Safety Commission) 1102 A1A N No 107 *TF:* 800-729-1997 ■ *Web:* www.nationalsafetycommission.com	Ponte Vedra Beach	FL	32082	800-729-1997		423
TNScommunications PO Box 86 *Web:* www.tnscommunications.net	Black Diamond	WA	98010	360-886-9798		637-2
TNT Automotive Leasing Ltd 10124 W Broad St Ste G *Web:* www.tntauto.com	Glen Allen	VA	23060	804-270-2912		126
TNT Parts Inc 3000 S Corporate Pkwy Ste 400 *Web:* www.tntpartsinc.com	Forest Park	GA	30297	404-675-9361		54
TNT Plastic Molding Inc 725 E Harrison St *Web:* www.tntplasticmolding.com	Corona	CA	92879	951-808-9700		604
TNT Plastics Inc 701 Industrial Dr *TF:* 800-844-7584 ■ *Web:* www.tntplastics.com	Perryville	MO	63775	573-547-1051	547-1053	596
TNT USA Inc 68 S Service Rd *Web:* www.tnt.com	Melville	NY	11747	631-712-6700		546
TNT Vacations 2 Charlesgate W *Web:* www.funjet.com	Boston	MA	02215	617-638-3481		771
TO Plastics Inc 830 County Rd 75 PO Box 37 *Web:* www.toplastics.com	Clearwater	MN	55320	320-558-2407		601
Toa Canada Corp 6150 Kennedy Rd Unit 3 *TF:* 800-263-7639 ■ *Web:* www.toacanada.com	Mississauga	ON	L5T2J4	905-564-3570		246
Toa Reinsurance Company of America 177 Madison Ave PO Box 1930 *Web:* www.toare.com	Morristown	NJ	07962	973-898-9480	898-9495	391-4
Toad in the Hole 112 Osborne St	Winnipeg	MB	R3L1Y5	204-284-7201		671
Toarmina's Pizza 32785 Cherry Hill Rd *Web:* toarminas.com	Westland	MI	48186	734-728-0060		670
Toastmasters Intl 23182 Arroyo Vista *Web:* www.toastmasters.org	Rancho Santa Margarita	CA	92688	949-858-8255	858-1207	48-15
TOASTnet 4841 Monroe St Ste 307 *TF:* 888-862-7863 ■ *Web:* toast.net	Toledo	OH	43623	419-292-2200	474-1762	398
TOBA (Thoroughbred Owners & Breeders Assn) PO Box 910668 *TF:* 888-606-8622 ■ *Web:* toba.org	Lexington	KY	40591	859-276-2291	276-2462	48-3
Tobacco Associates Inc 1306 Annapolis Dr Ste 102 *Web:* www.tobaccoassociatesinc.org	Raleigh	NC	27608	919-821-7670	821-7674	48-2
Tobacco Company Restaurant, The 1201 E Cary St *Web:* www.thetobaccocompany.com	Richmond	VA	23219	804-782-9555		671
Tobacco Merchants Assn (TMA) PO Box 8019 *Web:* www.tma.org	Princeton	NJ	08543	609-275-4900	275-8379	48-2
Tobacco Superstores Inc 3550 David Cohn Dr *Web:* tobaccosuper.com	Forrest City	AR	72335	870-633-0099	633-8279	756
Tobar Industries 912 Olinder Ct *Web:* tobarind.com	San Jose	CA	95122	408-494-3530		697
Tobias Associates Inc 50 Industrial Dr *TF:* 800-877-3367 ■ *Web:* www.densitometer.com	Ivyland	PA	18974	215-322-1500	322-1504	253
Tobias Financial Advisors 1000 S Pine Island Rd Ste 250 *Web:* www.tobiasfinancial.com	Plantation	FL	33324	954-424-1660		2
Tobias, Torchia & Simon 414 Walnut St Ste 321 *Web:* tktlaw.com	Cincinnati	OH	45202	513-241-8137		41
Tobin Machining Inc 1361 S Hickory St *Web:* www.tobinmachining.com	Fond du Lac	WI	54937	920-921-9110	921-7028	454
Toby's 1160 Shelley St *Web:* www.tobysfamilyfoods.com	Springfield	OR	97477	541-689-8506		123
TOCA Football 2777 Bristol St *Web:* tocafootball.com	Costa Mesa	CA	92626	714-361-8990		711
Tocagen Inc 4242 Campus Point Ct Ste 500 *Web:* tocagen.com	San Diego	CA	92121	858-412-8400		231
Tocco Financial Services Inc 1647 N Swan Rd *TF:* 877-881-1149 ■ *Web:* toccofinancial.com	Tucson	AZ	85712	520-881-1149	881-1297	690
Toccoa Falls College 107 Kincaid Dr *TF:* 888-785-5624 ■ *Web:* www.tfc.edu	Toccoa	GA	30598	706-886-7299		161
Toccoa-Stephens County Chamber of Commerce 160 N Alexander St *Web:* www.toccoagachamber.com	Toccoa	GA	30577	706-282-1931	886-2133	139
Tocos America Inc 1177 E Tower Rd *Web:* www.tocos.com	Schaumburg	IL	60173	847-884-6664	884-6665	246
Tocqueville 1 E 15th St *Web:* tocquevillerestaurant.com	New York	NY	10003	212-647-1515		671
Today's Business Computers 213 E Black Horse Pk *TF:* 800-371-5132 ■ *Web:* www.tbcusa.com	Pleasantville	NJ	08232	609-645-5132		177
Today's Q106 730 Rayovac Dr *Web:* www.q106.com	Madison	WI	53711	608-321-1063		645-92
Today's Vision 6970 FM 1960 W Ste A *Web:* todaysvision.com	Houston	TX	77069	281-469-2020	469-7531	543
Todays Chicago Woman 150 E Huron St *Web:* www.tcwmag.com	Chicago	IL	60611	312-951-7600		457-22
Todays Home & Leisure Products Inc 5248 E Trindle Rd *Web:* thlproducts.com	Mechanicsburg	PA	17050	717-790-0454		35
Todd & Levi LLP 444 Madison Ave *TF:* 877-872-6554 ■ *Web:* todd-levi.com	New York	NY	10022	212-308-7400	308-8450	41
Todd & Sargent Inc 2905 SE Fifth St *Web:* www.tsargent.com	Ames	IA	50010	515-232-0442		188-7
Todd County 212 - 2nd Ave S *Web:* www.co.todd.mn.us	Long Prairie	MN	56347	320-732-6447	732-4001	338
Todd Financial & Insurance Services Inc 7676 Hazard Center Dr Ste 1050 *Web:* toddfinancial.com	San Diego	CA	92108	858-863-4010		390
Todd Greiner Farms 2542 N 128th Ave *Web:* www.toddgreinerfarms.com	Hart	MI	49420	231-873-2828		297-7
Todd Groundwater 2490 Mariner Square Loop Ste 215 *Web:* toddgroundwater.com	Alameda	CA	94501	510-747-6920		261
Todd Herman & Associates PA 620 Green Valley Rd Ste 104 *Web:* www.toddherman.com	Greensboro	NC	27408	336-297-4200		196
Todd Industries Inc 7300 Northfield Rd *Web:* allmachining.com	Walton Hills	OH	44146	440-439-2900	439-2839	494
Todd Jurich's Bistro 150 W Main St Ste 100 *Web:* toddjurichsbistro.com	Norfolk	VA	23510	757-622-3210		671
Todd Markman 809 Ridge Rd *Web:* toddmarkman.com	Wilmette	IL	60091	847-256-8633	256-9716	390
Todd Organization Inc, The 24610 Detroit Rd Ste 210 *Web:* www.toddorg.com	Cleveland	OH	44145	440-871-7700		390
Todd Ratner PLC 7201 Glen Forest Dr Ste 102 *Web:* ratnerplc.com	Richmond	VA	23226	804-665-1040		41
Todd Rivenbark Puryear (TRP) 2405 Robeson St *Web:* trpsumner.com	Fayetteville	NC	28305	910-323-3600	323-3640	2
Todd Rutkin Inc 5801 S Alameda St *Web:* toddrutkin.com	Los Angeles	CA	90001	323-584-9225	584-9295	258
Todd Stewart 621 E Pulaski Hwy *Web:* toddpstewart.com	Elkton	MD	21921	410-398-2024		390
Todd Street Productions 30 W 24th St 11th Fl *Web:* www.toddstreet.com	New York	NY	10010	212-966-5900		511
Todd's Companion Plus Inc 6123 Green Bay Rd Ste 250	Kenosha	WI	53142	262-605-4700		363
Todd, Bremer & Lawson Inc PO Box 36788 *TF:* 877-427-6544 ■ *Web:* www.tbandl.com	Rock Hill	SC	29732	803-323-5200		160
Todd-Wadena Electric Co-op 550 Ash Ave NE PO Box 431 *TF:* 800-321-8932 ■ *Web:* toddwadena.coop	Wadena	MN	56482	218-631-3120		245
Toe Box, The 15015 Main St Kelsey Creek Ctr *Web:* www.shoesnfeet.com	Bellevue	WA	98007	425-653-2329	653-2690	301
Toeniskoetter & Breeding Inc 1960 the Alameda Ste 20 *Web:* www.strategic-cm.com	San Jose	CA	95126	408-246-3691		186
Toeroek Associates Inc 300 Union Blvd Ste 520 *Web:* www.toeroek.com	Lakewood	CO	80228	303-420-7735		463
Tofino Botanical Gardens 1084 Pacific Rim Hwy *Web:* tofinobotanicalgardens.com	Tofino	BC	V0R2Z0	250-725-1220		97
Toft Dairy Inc 3717 Venice Rd *Web:* www.toftdairy.com	Sandusky	OH	44870	419-625-4376	621-2010	296-27

Name / Address	City	State	ZIP	Phone	Fax	Class
Tofurky PO Box 176 *TF:* 800-508-8100 ■ *Web:* tofurky.com	Hood River	OR	97031	800-508-8100		123
Tofutti Brands Inc 50 Jackson Dr. *NYSE:* TOFB ■ *Web:* tofutti.com	Cranford	NJ	07016	908-272-2400	272-9492	296-25
TOG Manufacturing Company Inc 1454 S State St *Web:* www.togmanufacturing.com	North Adams	MA	01247	413-664-6711	663-5753	757
Toho Tenax America Inc 121 Cardiff Valley Rd *TF:* 800-252-3001 ■ *Web:* www.tohotenax-us.com	Rockwood	TN	37854	800-252-3001		127
Tohono Chul Park *Tohono Chul* 7366 N Paseo del Norte *Web:* tohonochul.org	Tucson	AZ	85704	520-742-6455	797-1213	97
Tohono O'odham Community College Hwy 86 Milepost 125 5 N PO Box 3129 *Web:* www.tocc.edu	Sells	AZ	85634	520-383-8401	383-8403	162
Tohono O'odham Utility Authority PO Box 816 *Web:* toua.net	Sells	AZ	85634	520-383-2236		245
TOI (Tecport Optics Inc) 6457 Hazeltine National Dr *Web:* www.tecportoptics.com	Orlando	FL	32822	407-855-1212	855-1213	542
Tojo's *Tojo's Restaurant* 1133 W Broadway *Web:* tojos.com	Vancouver	BC	V6H1G1	604-872-8050		671
Tok River State Recreation Site 1309 Alaska Hwy *Web:* www.dnr.alaska.gov	Fairbanks	AK	99709	907-883-3686		565
Tokai Tokyo Securities (USA) Inc 3 Columbus Cir Ste 1715 *Web:* www.tokaitokyo-fh.jp	New York	NY	10019	646-979-2200	979-2219	194
Token Inc 703 Market St Ste 800 *TF:* 800-558-2201 ■ *Web:* token.io	San Francisco	CA	94103	800-558-2201		177
Tokio Marine America 1221 Ave Ste 1500 *TF:* 800-628-2796 ■ *Web:* tmamerica.com	New York	NY	10020	212-297-6600		391-4
Tokusen 1500 S Amity Rd. *Web:* www.tokusenusa.com	Conway	AR	72032	501-327-6800	327-0231	813
Toky Branding & Design 3139 Olive St *Web:* toky.com	Saint Louis	MO	63103	314-534-2000		344
Tokyo Garden 1711 Fulton St *Web:* tokyogardenfresno.com	Fresno	CA	93721	559-268-3596		671
Tokyo Gas Company Ltd 1540 Broadway Ste 3920 *Web:* www.tokyo-gas.co.jp	New York	NY	10036	646-865-0577	865-0592	360-5
Tokyo Grill & Sushi Restaurant 4478 Breton Rd SE *Web:* tokyogrillsushi.com	Kentwood	MI	49508	616-455-3433		671
Tokyo Japanese Restaurant 7516 N Western Ave *Web:* www.tokyookc.com	Oklahoma City	OK	73116	405-848-6733		671
Tokyo Japanese Steakhouse 312 E Nine Mile Rd. *Web:* www.gotokyopensacola.com	Pensacola	FL	32514	850-479-9111		671
Tokyo Japanese Steakhouse 1111 Salisbury Ridge Rd *Web:* www.tjsteakhouse.com	Winston-Salem	NC	27127	336-722-5009		671
Tokyo Love 12565 Harbor Blvd *Web:* tokyolovesushi.com	Garden Grove	CA	92840	714-534-4751		671
Tokyo Ohka Kogyo America Inc 4600 NW Brookwood Pky. *Web:* www.tokamerica.com	Hillsboro	OR	97124	503-693-7711	693-2070	143
Tokyo Stock Exchange Inc (TSE) 45 Broadway 21st Fl. *Web:* www.jpx.co.jp	New York	NY	10006	212-363-2350	363-2354	637-2
Tokyo Sushi 1716 Lundy Ave *Web:* www.tokyosushisanjose.com	San Jose	CA	95131	408-452-8868		671
Tokyo Sushi 1499 SE 17th St Cswy *Web:* windyhilldunes.net	Fort Lauderdale	FL	33316	954-767-9922		671
Tolar Manufacturing Company Inc 258 Mariah Cir *Web:* www.tolarmfg.com	Corona	CA	92879	951-808-0081		320
Toledo Botanical Garden 5403 Elmer Dr *Web:* www.toledogarden.org	Toledo	OH	43615	419-536-5566	536-5574	97
Toledo Building Services 2121 Adams St. *Web:* toledobuildingservices.com	Toledo	OH	43604	419-241-3101		104
Toledo Business Journal 5301 Southwyck Blvd Ste 104 *Web:* www.toledobiz.com	Toledo	OH	43614	419-865-0972	865-2429	457-5
Toledo City Hall 1 Government Ctr *Web:* toledo.oh.gov	Toledo	OH	43604	419-245-1050	245-1072	337
Toledo Community Foundation 300 Madison Ave Ste 1300. *Web:* www.toledocf.org	Toledo	OH	43604	419-241-5049		305
Toledo Commutator 1101 S Chestnut St *Web:* www.toledocommutator.com	Owosso	MI	48867	989-725-8192	725-5930	518
Toledo Engineering Company Inc 3400 Executive Pkwy PO Box 2927 *TF:* 800-654-4567 ■ *Web:* www.teco.com	Toledo	OH	43606	419-537-9711	537-1369	261
Toledo Express Airport 11013 Airport Hwy *Web:* www.toledoexpress.com	Swanton	OH	43558	419-865-2351		27
Toledo Firefighters Museum 918 Sylvania Ave *Web:* www.toledofirefightersmuseum.org	Toledo	OH	43612	419-478-3473		520
Toledo Metal Spinning Co 1819 Clinton St *Web:* www.toledometalspinning.com	Toledo	OH	43607	419-535-5931	535-0565	483
Toledo Molding & Die Inc 4 E Laskey Rd *Web:* www.tmdinc.com	Toledo	OH	43612	419-443-9031		604
Toledo Museum of Art 2445 Monroe St. *TF:* 800-644-6862 ■ *Web:* www.toledomuseum.org	Toledo	OH	43620	419-255-8000	255-5638	520
Toledo Opera 425 Jefferson Ave Ste 601 *TF:* 866-860-9048 ■ *Web:* www.toledoopera.org	Toledo	OH	43604	419-255-7464	255-6344	573-2
Toledo Physical Education Supply Inc 5101 Advantage Dr *TF:* 800-225-7749 ■ *Web:* www.tpesonline.com	Toledo	OH	43612	419-726-8122		711
Toledo Police Federal Credit Union 4280 Heatherdowns *Web:* tpolcu.com	Toledo	OH	43614	419-385-0101		219
Toledo Repertoire Theatre 16 Tenth St. *Web:* www.toledorep.org	Toledo	OH	43604	419-243-9277		573-4
Toledo School of Practical Nursing 3281 Upton Ave *Web:* www.tpsadulted.com	Toledo	OH	43613	419-671-8700		685
Toledo Symphony Orchestra 1838 Parkwood Ave *Web:* www.toledosymphony.com	Toledo	OH	43604	419-246-8000	321-6890	573-3
Toledo Transducers Inc 6834 Spring Valley Dr Ste 3 *Web:* www.toledointegratedsystems.com	Holland	OH	43528	419-724-4170	867-4180	542
Toledo Zoo 2 Hippo Way *Web:* www.toledozoo.org	Toledo	OH	43609	419-385-5721	389-8670	823
Toledo-Lucas County Port Authority 1 Maritime Plz Ste 701 *Web:* www.toledoport.org	Toledo	OH	43604	419-243-8251	243-1835	618
Toledo-Lucas County Public Library 325 N Michigan St *Web:* www.toledolibrary.org	Toledo	OH	43604	419-259-5200		434-3
Toler & Toler Insurance Services LLC 1564 OH-160 *TF:* 800-562-2646 ■ *Web:* tolerins.com	Gallipolis	OH	45631	740-446-9445		390
Tolin Mechanical Systems Co 12005 E 45th Ave *Web:* www.tolin.com	Denver	CO	80239	303-455-2825		610
Toll Bros Inc 250 Gibraltar Rd *NYSE:* TOL ■ *TF:* 855-897-8655 ■ *Web:* www.tollbrothers.com	Horsham	PA	19044	215-938-8000	938-8217	653
Toll Gas & Welding Supply 3005 Niagara Ln N *TF:* 877-865-5427 ■ *Web:* www.tollgas.com	Plymouth	MN	55447	763-551-5300		358
Toll House Hotel 140 S Santa Cruz Ave *TF:* 800-238-6111 ■ *Web:* www.tollhousehotel.com	Los Gatos	CA	95030	408-395-7070		707
Tolland County Chamber of Commerce 30 Lafayette Sq *Web:* www.tollandcountychamber.org	Vernon	CT	06066	860-872-0587		139
Tolland State Forest 410 Tolland Rd PO Box 342 *Web:* www.mass.gov	East Otis	MA	01029	413-269-6002		565
Tolleson Design Inc 560 Pacific Ave *Web:* tolleson.com	San Francisco	CA	94133	415-626-7796		344
Tolleson Wealth Management Inc 5500 Preston Rd Ste 250 *Web:* www.tollesonwealth.com	Dallas	TX	75205	214-252-3250		796
TollFreeForwarding.com 9841 Airport Blvd 9th Fl **Fax Area Code:* 213 ■ *TF:* 888-452-1505 ■ *Web:* www.tollfreeforwarding.com	Los Angeles	CA	90045	888-452-1505	452-1551*	681
Tolling Bell Books 5555 Oakbrook Pky Bldg 300 Ste 330 *Web:* www.tollingbellbooks.com	Norcross	GA	30093	770-448-0130		637-2
Tollman Spring Company Inc 91 Enterprise Dr *Web:* www.tollmanspring.com	Bristol	CT	06010	860-583-1326	589-8733	492
Tolman & Wiker Insurance Services LLC 196 S Fir St *Web:* tolmanandwiker.com	Ventura	CA	93002	805-585-6100		390
TOLMAR Holding Inc 701 Centre Ave *TF:* 877-986-5627 ■ *Web:* www.tolmar.com	Fort Collins	CO	80526	970-212-4500		231
Tolmie State Park 7730 61st Ave NE *Web:* parks.state.wa.us	Olympia	WA	98506	360-456-6464		565
Tol-O-Matic Inc 3800 County Rd 116 *TF:* 800-328-2174 ■ *Web:* www.tolomatic.com	Hamel	MN	55340	763-478-8000	478-8080	223
Tolowa Dunes State Park 1111 Second St *Web:* www.parks.ca.gov	Crescent City	CA	95531	707-465-2145		565
Tolstoy Foundation Inc 104 Lake Rd PO Box 578 *Web:* www.tolstoyfoundation.org	Valley Cottage	NY	10989	845-268-6722	268-6937	48-14
Toltec Mounds Archeological State Park 490 Toltec Mounds Rd *Web:* www.arkansasstateparks.com	Scott	AR	72142	501-961-9442		565
Tolunay-Wong Engineers Inc 10710 S Sam Houston Pkwy W *TF:* 888-887-9932 ■ *Web:* www.tweinc.com	Houston	TX	77031	888-887-9932		261
Tom Barrow Co (TBC) 2800 Plant Atkinson Rd *TF:* 800-229-8226 ■ *Web:* www.tombarrow.com	Atlanta	GA	30339	404-351-1010	350-9121	14
Tom Bengard Ranch Inc 634 W Market *Web:* bengardranch.com	Salinas	CA	93901	831-758-5770		10-11
Tom Cat Bakery Inc 43-05 Tenth St *Web:* www.tomcatbakery.com	Long Island City	NY	11101	718-786-7659	786-9046	297-8
Tom Curtis Brokerage Inc 3301 S Galloway St Units 272-274 *Web:* www.tomcurtisbrokerage.com	Philadelphia	PA	19148	215-336-1370	336-7749	297-7
Tom Douglas 2030 5th Ave *Web:* www.tomdouglas.com	Seattle	WA	98121	206-448-2001	448-1979	296-34
Tom Duffy Co 5200 Watt Ct Ste B *TF:* 800-479-5671 ■ *Web:* www.tomduffy.com	Fairfield	CA	94534	800-479-5671		290
Tom Gibbs Chevrolet Inc 5850 E Hwy 100 *Web:* www.tomgibbschevy.com	Palm Coast	FL	32164	386-206-8092		57
Tom Green County 112 W Beauregard *Web:* www.tomgreencountytx.gov	San Angelo	TX	76903	325-659-6444	659-6459	338
Tom Green County Library System 33 W Beauregard Ave *Web:* tgclibrary.com	San Angelo	TX	76903	325-655-7321		434-3
Tom Ham's Lighthouse 2150 Harbor Island Dr *Web:* www.tomhamslighthouse.com	San Diego	CA	92101	619-291-9110		671
Tom Hassenfritz Equipment Co 1300 W Washington St. *TF:* 800-634-4885 ■ *Web:* the-co.com	Mount Pleasant	IA	52641	319-385-3114	385-3731	274

				Phone	Fax	Class
Tom Hesser Chevrolet Inc 948 N Washington Ave PO Box 265 *Web:* www.tomhesserbmw.com	Scranton	PA	18509	570-343-1221		57
Tom Holzer Ford Inc 39300 W Ten Mile *Web:* www.tholzerford.com	Farmington Hills	MI	48335	248-474-1234		57
Tom Hopkins Intl 465 E Chilton Dr Ste 4 *TF:* 800-528-0446 ■ *Web:* www.tomhopkins.com	Chandler	AZ	85225	480-949-0786	949-1590	196
Tom J. Keith & Associates Inc 121 S Cool Spring St *Web:* www.keithvaluation.com	Fayetteville	NC	28301	910-323-3222	323-1180	652
Tom James Co 263 Seaboard Ln *TF:* 800-236-9023 ■ *Web:* www.tomjames.com	Franklin	TN	37067	615-771-0795		155-12
Tom Jenkins' Bar-B-Q 1236 S Federal Hwy *Web:* tomjenkinsbbq.net	Fort Lauderdale	FL	33316	954-522-5046		671
Tom Johnson Investment Management Inc 201 Robert S Kerr Ave *TF:* 888-404-8546 ■ *Web:* www.tjim.com	Oklahoma City	OK	73102	405-236-2111		401
Tom Lee Music Ltd 929 Granville St *TF:* 888-886-6533 ■ *Web:* tomleemusic.ca	Vancouver	BC	V6Z1L3	604-685-8471		526
Tom McCall & Associates Inc 20180 Governors Hwy Ste 100 *TF:* 800-715-5474 ■ *Web:* www.tmccall.com	Olympia Fields	IL	60461	708-747-5707	747-5890	194
Tom Naquin Chevrolet Inc 2500 W Lexington Ave *TF:* 866-216-5211 ■ *Web:* www.tomnaquin.com	Elkhart	IN	46514	574-293-8621		57
Tom Nehl Truck Co 417 S Edgewood Ave *Web:* www.tomnehl.com	Jacksonville	FL	32254	904-389-3653		516
Tom Rectenwald Construction Inc 110 N Jefferson St *Web:* trcgc.net	Zelienople	PA	16063	724-452-8801		186
Tom Rose School 6701 Antire Rd *TF:* 888-866-7673 ■ *Web:* www.tomrose.com	High Ridge	MO	63049	636-376-4273	677-8104	685
Tom Rostron Company Inc 2490 Tiltons Corner Rd *Web:* www.tomrostron.com	Wall Township	NJ	07719	732-223-8221		189-10
Tom Roush Inc 525 W David Brown Dr *Web:* www.tomroush.com	Westfield	IN	46074	317-896-5561		516
Tom Sawyer Software Corp 1997 El Dorado Ave *Web:* www.tomsawyer.com	Berkeley	CA	94707	510-208-4370	527-1674	177
Tom Smith Industries 500 Smith Dr *Web:* www.tomsmithindustries.com	Clayton	OH	45315	937-832-1555		757
Tom Sturgis Pretzels Inc 2267 Lancaster Pk *TF:* 800-817-3834 ■ *Web:* www.tomsturgispretzels.com	Reading	PA	19607	610-775-0335		296-9
Tom Thumb Food Stores Inc MS 10501 PO Box 29093 *TF:* 877-723-3929 ■ *Web:* www.tomthumb.com	Phoenix	AZ	85038	877-723-3929		204
Tom's Aircraft Maintenance Inc *OCR Aviation* 2721 E Spring St *Web:* ocraviation.com	Long Beach	CA	90806	562-426-5331		770
Tom's Food Markets 738 Munson Ave *Web:* www.toms-foodmarkets.com	Traverse City	MI	49686	231-947-7175		345
Tom's of Maine Inc 302 Lafayette Ctr **Fax Area Code:* 207 ■ *TF:* 800-367-8667 ■ *Web:* www.tomsofmaine.com	Kennebunkport	ME	04043	800-367-8667	985-2196*	214
Toma & Associates Inc 41 Summit St *Web:* tomasurvey.com	Jackson	CA	95642	209-223-0156	223-5653	360-3
Toma Metals Inc 740 Cooper Ave *Web:* tomametalsinc.com	Johnstown	PA	15906	814-536-3596		567
Tomah Convention & Visitors Bureau 310 N Superior Ave PO Box 625 *TF:* [illegible] ■ *Web:* www.tomahwisconsin.com	Tomah	WI	54660	608-372-2166	372-2167	206
Tomah Veterans Affairs Medical Ctr 500 E Veterans St *TF:* 800-872-8662 ■ *Web:* www.tomah.va.gov	Tomah	WI	54660	608-372-3971		374-8
Tomahawk Leader 315 W Wisconsin Ave *Web:* www.tomahawkleader.com	Tomahawk	WI	54487	715-453-2151		532-3
Tomales Bay State Park 1100 Pierce Pt Rd *Web:* www.parks.ca.gov	Inverness	CA	94937	415-669-1140		565
Tomarco Contractor Specialties Inc 14848 Northam St *Web:* www.tomarco.com	La Mirada	CA	90638	714-523-1771		351
Tomasita's Restaurant & Bar 500 S Guadalupe St *Web:* tomasitas.com	Santa Fe	NM	87501	505-983-5721		671
Tomato Head 12 Market Sq *Web:* thetomatohead.com	Knoxville	TN	37902	865-637-4067	637-4019	671
Tomato Street North 6220 N Div *Web:* www.tomatostreet.com	Spokane	WA	99208	509-484-4500		671
Tomba Communications LLC 718 Barataria Blvd **Fax Area Code:* 985 ■ *TF:* 800-256-1268 ■ *Web:* www.tomba.com	Marrero	LA	70072	504-340-2448	725-0061*	246
Tomball Independent School District 310 S Cherry St *Web:* www.tomballisd.net	Tomball	TX	77375	281-357-3100	357-3128	685
Tomball Regional Hospital (TRMC) PO Box 889 *Web:* www.tomballregionalmedicalcenter.com	Tomball	TX	77377	281-401-7500		374-3
Tombigbee Electric Co-op PO Box 610 *TF:* 800-621-8069 ■ *Web:* www.tombigbee.net	Guin	AL	35563	205-468-3325		245
Tombigbee Electric Power Assn PO Box 1789 *Web:* www.tombigbeeelectric.com	Tupelo	MS	38802	662-842-7635	795-4261	245
Tombigbee State Park 264 Cabin Dr *Web:* www.mdwfp.com	Tupelo	MS	38804	662-842-7669		565
Tombolino Restaurant 356 Kimball Ave *Web:* www.tombolinoristorante.com	Yonkers	NY	10704	914-237-1266		671
Tombstone Courthouse State Historic Park 223 E Toughnut St *Web:* azstateparks.com	Tombstone	AZ	85638	520-457-3311		565
Tomco2 Systems 3340 Rosebud Rd *TF:* 800-832-4262 ■ *Web:* www.tomcosystems.com	Loganville	GA	30052	770-979-8000	985-9179	806
Tomi Engineering Inc 414 E Alton Ave *Web:* www.tomiengineering.com	Santa Ana	CA	92707	714-556-1474	979-8664	454
Tomisushi 4336 Moorpark Ave *Web:* www.tomisushi.us	San Jose	CA	95129	408-257-4722		671
Tomkiewicz Wright LLC 6111 P'Tree Dunwoody Rd Bld E 102 *Web:* twcpaga.com	Atlanta	GA	30328	770-351-0411		2
Tomlinson Bomberger Lawn Care & Landscaping Inc 3055 Yellow Goose Rd *Web:* tomlinsonbomberger.com	Lancaster	PA	17601	717-399-1991		577
Tomlinson Industries 13700 Broadway Ave **Fax Area Code:* 604 ■ *Web:* www.tomlinsonind.com	Cleveland	OH	44125	216-587-3400	939-7598*	298
Tomlinson Run State Park PO Box 97 *Web:* wvstateparks.com	New Manchester	WV	26056	304-564-3651		565
Tommy Baldwin Racing 296 Cayuga Rd *Web:* www.tommybaldwinracing.com	Mooresville	NC	28117	704-696-0036		515
Tommy Tape 378 Four Rod Rd *TF:* 888-866-8273 ■ *Web:* www.tommytape.com	Berlin	CT	06037	860-378-0111	378-0113	732
Tommy's Restaurant 1824 Coventry Rd *Web:* tommyscoventry.com	Cleveland	OH	44118	216-321-7757		671
Tommys Wholesale Florist 2106 E National Cemetery Rd *TF:* 800-968-8211 ■ *Web:* twfonline.biz	Florence	SC	29506	843-669-8211		293
Tomoe Sushi 172 Thompson St *Web:* www.tomoesushi.com	New York	NY	10012	212-777-9346		671
Tomoegawa USA Inc 742 Glenn Ave *Web:* www.tomoegawa.com	Wheeling	IL	60090	847-541-3001	459-7150	628
Tomoka Correctional Institution 3950 Tiger Bay Rd *Web:* dc.state.fl.us	Daytona Beach	FL	32124	386-323-1070	323-1006	213
Tomoka State Park 2099 N Beach St *Web:* www.floridastateparks.org	Ormond Beach	FL	32174	386-676-4050		565
Tompkins Bros Company Inc 623 Oneida St *Web:* www.tompkinsusa.com	Syracuse	NY	13202	315-422-8763	422-8762	744
Tompkins Cortland Community College 170 N St PO Box 139 *TF:* 888-567-8211 ■ *Web:* www.tompkinscortland.edu	Dryden	NY	13053	607-844-8211	844-6541	162
Tompkins County 320 N Tioga St *TF:* 800-268-7869 ■ *Web:* www.nycourts.gov	Ithaca	NY	14850	607-274-5431		338
Tompkins County Chamber of Commerce 904 E Shore Dr *TF:* 888-568-9816 ■ *Web:* www.tompkinschamber.org	Ithaca	NY	14850	607-273-7080	272-7617	139
Tompkins County Public Library 101 E Green St *TF:* 800-772-7267 ■ *Web:* www.tcpl.org	Ithaca	NY	14850	607-272-4557	272-8111	434-3
Tompkins Industries Inc 1912 E 123rd *TF:* 800-255-1008 ■ *Web:* www.tompkinsind.com	Olathe	KS	66061	913-764-8088		350
Tompkins Intl 6870 Perry Creek Rd *TF:* 800-789-1257 ■ *Web:* www.tompkinsinc.com	Raleigh	NC	27616	919-876-3667	872-9666	194
Tompkins Mc Guire Wachenfeld & Barry 3 Becker Farm Rd 4th Fl *Web:* www.tompkinsmcguire.com	Roseland	NJ	07068	973-622-3000	623-7780	428
Tompkins Metal Finishing Inc 6 Apollo Dr *TF:* 800-234-2116 ■ *Web:* tompkinsmetalfinishing.com	Batavia	NY	14020	585-344-2600	344-2672	695
Tompkins Products Inc 1040 W Grand Blvd *Web:* www.tompkinsproducts.com	Detroit	MI	48208	313-894-2222	894-2901	621
Tompkins Research & Management Consulting Inc 203 Redstone Hill *Web:* www.tompkinsresearch.com	Plainville	CT	06062	860-747-0497		195
Tompkins Trust Co PO Box 460 *NYSE: TMP* ■ *TF:* 888-273-3210 ■ *Web:* www.tompkinstrust.com	Ithaca	NY	14851	607-273-3210		70
Toms Truck Center Inc 909 N Grand Ave *TF:* 800-638-1015 ■ *Web:* www.ttruck.com	Santa Ana	CA	92701	800-638-1015		57
Tomson Steel Company Inc PO Box 940 *TF:* 800-837-3001 ■ *Web:* www.tomsonsteel.com	Middletown	OH	45042	800-837-3001		492
Toms-Price Co 303 E Front St *Web:* www.tomsprice.com	Wheaton	IL	60187	630-668-7878		321
TOMY International Inc 2015 Spring Rd Ste 700 *TF:* 800-704-8697 ■ *Web:* us.tomy.com	Oak Brook	IL	60523	630-573-7200	573-7575	762
Tomz Corp 47 Episcopal Rd *Web:* tomz.com	Berlin	CT	06037	860-829-0670		454
Tona Sushi in Ogden 210 25th St *Web:* tonarestaurant.com	Ogden	UT	84401	801-622-8662		671
Tonawanda Tank Transport Service Inc 1140 Military Rd *TF:* 800-782-4832 ■ *Web:* www.tonawandatank.com	Buffalo	NY	14217	716-874-0400	877-0227	780
Tone Software Inc 1735 S Brookhurst St *TF:* 800-833-8663 ■ *Web:* www.tonesoft.com	Anaheim	CA	92804	714-991-9460		177
Toner Machining Technologies Inc 212 E Fleming Dr *Web:* www.tonermachining.com	Morganton	NC	28655	828-432-8007		483
Tonertype of Florida LLC 5100 W Cypress St *TF:* 888-916-1300 ■ *Web:* tonertypeprint.com	Tampa	FL	33607	813-915-1300		388
Toney Construction Services Inc 14031 Huffmeister Rd *Web:* www.toneyconstruction.com	Cypress	TX	77429	281-304-1778	304-1773	186
Tonga *Consulate General* 1 Bay Plz 1350 Old Bayshore Hwy Ste 610 *Web:* www.tongaconsul.com	Burlingame	CA	94010	650-685-1001	685-1003	257
Tongal 1918 Main St 2nd Fl *Web:* tongal.com	Santa Monica	CA	90405	310-579-9260		387
Tongass Conservation Society (TCS) PO Box 23377 *Web:* tongassconservation.org	Ketchikan	AK	99901	907-254-0914		48-13

Name	Address	City	State	ZIP	Phone	Fax	Class	TF / Web
Tongass Historical Museum	629 Dock St	Ketchikan	AK	99901	907-225-3111		520	*Web:* www.ktn-ak.us
Tongass Trading Co	201 Dock St	Ketchikan	AK	99901	907-225-5101		229	*TF:* 800-235-5102 ■ *Web:* www.tongasstrading.com
Tongue River Reservoir State Park	PO Box 1630	Miles City	MT	59301	406-234-0900		565	*Web:* fwp.mt.gov
Toni & Guy USA Inc	2311 Midway Rd	Carrollton	TX	75006	800-256-9391		77	*TF:* 800-256-9391 ■ *Web:* www.toniguy.com
Toni's Sushi Bar	1208 Washington Ave	Miami Beach	FL	33139	305-673-9368		671	*Web:* www.tonisushi.com
Tonic Group Inc	611 Broadway Ste 726	New York	NY	10012	212-254-0877		180	*Web:* tonicgroup.com
Tonic Studios LLC	476 Broome St Ste 6B	New York	NY	10013	212-431-0260	226-6347	344	*Web:* mikelingle.com
Tonica Telephone Co	208 Allen St	Tonica	IL	61370	815-442-9901		224	*Web:* tonicacom.net
Tonio Burgos & Associates Inc	115 Broadway Rm 1504	New York	NY	10006	212-566-5600	566-5611	636	*Web:* www.tonioburgos.com
Tonix Corp	40910 Encyclopedia Cir	Fremont	CA	94538	510-651-8050	651-8052	155-3	*TF:* 800-227-2072 ■ *Web:* www.tonixteams.com
Tonka Equipment Co	13305 Water Twr Cir	Plymouth	MN	55441	763-559-2837	559-1979	806	*Web:* www.tonkawater.com
Tonkadale Greenhouses	3739 Tonkawood Rd	Minnetonka	MN	55345	952-938-6480		293	*Web:* www.tonkadale.com
Tonko Paul D (Rep D - NY)	2369 Rayburn House Office Bldg	Washington	DC	20515	202-225-5076	225-5077	342-2	*Web:* www.tonko.house.gov
Tonto National Monument	26260 N Az Hwy 188 2	Roosevelt	AZ	85545	928-467-2241		564	*Web:* www.nps.gov
Tonto Natural Bridge State Park	Hwy 87 N	Payson	AZ	85547	928-476-4202		565	*Web:* azstateparks.com
Tony Chan's Water Club	1717 N Bayshore Dr	Miami	FL	33132	305-374-8888		671	*Web:* www.tonychans.com
Tony da Caneca	72 Elm Rd	Newark	NJ	07105	973-589-6882	589-0036	671	*Web:* www.tonydacaneca.com
Tony Lama Boot Company Inc	1137 Tony Lama St	El Paso	TX	79915	915-778-8311	778-5237	301	*Web:* www.tonylama.com
Tony Mandola's Gulf Coast Kitchen	1212 Waugh Dr.	Houston	TX	77019	713-528-3474	528-4438	671	*Web:* www.tonymandolas.com
Tony Packo's	1902 Front St	Toledo	OH	43605	419-691-1953		671	*TF:* 866-472-2567 ■ *Web:* www.tonypacko.com
Tony Wang's	2217 Lincoln Hwy E	Lancaster	PA	17602	717-399-1915		671	
Tony's	3755 Richmond Ave	Houston	TX	77046	713-622-6778		671	*Web:* tonyshouston.com
Tony's Fine Foods	3575 Reed Ave	West Sacramento	CA	95605	916-374-4000	372-0727	297-9	*TF:* 800-464-5429 ■ *Web:* www.tonysfinefoods.com
Tony's Finer Foods Inc	3607 W Fullerton Ave	Chicago	IL	60647	773-278-8355	278-9738	345	*Web:* tonysfreshmarket.com
Tony's Huntington Inn	437 Huntington Tpke	Bridgeport	CT	06610	203-374-5541		671	*Web:* tonyshuntingtoninn.com
Tony's Meats & Specialty Foods	874 W Happy Canyon Rd	Castle Rock	CO	80108	303-814-3888		297-8	*Web:* tonysmarket.com
Toobs Inc	347 Quintana Rd	Morro Bay	CA	93442	800-795-8662		710	*TF:* 800-795-8662 ■ *Web:* www.toobs.com
Tooele County	47 S Main St	Tooele	UT	84074	435-843-3140	882-7317	338	*Web:* tooeleco.org
Tooele County Chamber of Commerce	154 S Main	Tooele	UT	84074	435-882-0690	833-0946	139	*TF:* 800-244-1113 ■ *Web:* tooelechamber.com
TooJays Original Gourmet Deli	3654 Georgia Ave	West Palm Beach	FL	33405	561-659-9011	659-9703	670	*Web:* www.toojays.com
Tool Craft Inc	767 Hartford Ave	Johnston	RI	02919	401-521-9630	521-6502	411	*Web:* toolcraftrumart.com
Tool Fabrication Corp	2940 N 117th St	Milwaukee	WI	53222	414-453-5030	453-5650	493	*TF:* 800-790-8665 ■ *Web:* toolfab.com
Tool House Inc	2611 Kimco Dr	Lincoln	NE	68521	402-476-6673	476-0049	351	*TF:* 800-279-2658 ■ *Web:* www.totaltool.com
Tool Smith Company Inc	1300 Fourth Ave S	Birmingham	AL	35233	205-323-2576	323-9060	386	*TF:* 800-317-8665 ■ *Web:* toolsmith.ws
Tool Specialties Co	128 Ford Ln	Hazelwood	MO	63042	314-731-3270	731-5259	757	*Web:* www.toolspecialties.com
Tool Sport USA	3330 Wynns Mill Rd	Metamora	MI	48455	248-969-5850		701	*Web:* toolsportusa.com
Tool Technology Distributors Inc	3110 Osgood Ct	Fremont	CA	94539	510-656-8220		358	*TF:* 800-335-8437 ■ *Web:* www.tooltechnology.com
Tool-All Inc	2053 E 30th St	Erie	PA	16510	814-898-3917	899-4509	757	*Web:* www.toolall.com
Toolbox Studios Inc	454 Soledad St	San Antonio	TX	78205	210-225-8269		344	*Web:* toolboxstudios.com
Toolcraft Products Inc	1265 Mc Cook Ave	Dayton	OH	45404	937-223-8271	223-1408	757	*Web:* www.toolcraftproducts.com
Toole & Company Inc	PO Box 21322	Houston	TX	77226	713-691-2011	691-5821	612	*Web:* www.tooleco.com
Toole County	226 First St S	Shelby	MT	59474	406-424-8310	424-8301	338	*Web:* toolecountymt.gov
Toole Design Group LLC	8484 Georgia Ave Ste 800	Silver Spring	MD	20910	301-927-1900		261	*Web:* tooledesign.com
Tool-Flo Manufacturing Inc	7803 Hansen Rd	Houston	TX	77061	713-941-1080	941-8099	455	*TF:* 800-345-2815 ■ *Web:* www.toolflo.com
Toolhouse Design Co	2925 Roeder Ave Ste 200	Bellingham	WA	98225	360-676-9275		344	*Web:* www.toolhouse.com
Tooling & Equipment International Corp	12550 Tech Center Dr	Livonia	MI	48150	734-522-1422	522-1780	487	*Web:* www.teintl.com
Tooling Dynamics Inc	905 Vogelsong Rd	York	PA	17404	717-764-8873	764-9062	488	*Web:* www.toolingdynamics.com
Tooling Technology LLC	100 Enterprise Dr	Fort Loramie	OH	45845	937-295-3672		492	*Web:* www.toolingtechgroup.com
Toolmex Corporation Inc	34 Talbot Rd	Northborough	MA	01532	508-653-8897	653-5110	358	*TF:* 800-992-4766 ■ *Web:* www.toolmex.com
Toolroom Inc, The	1009 Commercial Dr	Owensville	MO	65066	573-437-4154	437-3558	757	*Web:* www.thetoolroom.com
Tools & Production Co	4924 N Encinita Ave	Temple City	CA	91780	626-286-0213	286-3398	757	*Web:* www.toolsandproduction.com
Tools for Bending Inc	194 W Dakota Ave	Denver	CO	80223	303-777-7170	777-4749	456	*TF:* 800-873-3305 ■ *Web:* www.toolsforbending.com
Tools Inc	W248N5500 Executive Dr	Sussex	WI	53089	262-246-3400	246-3414	757	*Web:* www.toolsinc.com
Toolwire Inc	7031 Koll Center Pkwy Ste 220	Pleasanton	CA	94566	925-227-8500	227-8501	39	*TF:* 866-935-8665 ■ *Web:* www.toolwire.com
Toombs County	100 Courthouse Sq PO Box 112	Lyons	GA	30436	912-526-3311	526-1004	338	*Web:* www.toombscountyga.gov
Toomey & Associates PC	92 Montvale Ave	Stoneham	MA	02180	617-242-0406		41	*Web:* toomey-associates.com
Toomey Patrick J (Sen R - PA)	248 Russell Senate Office Bldg	Washington	DC	20510	202-224-4254	228-0284	342-2	*Web:* www.toomey.senate.gov
Tootle Time Publishing Co	PO Box 62	Cade	LA	70519	337-364-6410		637-2	*Web:* www.tootletime.com
Top Die Casting Co	13910 Dearborn Ave	South Beloit	IL	61080	815-389-2599		308	*Web:* www.topdie.com
Top Dog Express Car Wash	1851 Rinehart Rd	Altamonte Springs	FL	32714	407-636-9112		366	*Web:* www.topdogexpresscarwash.com
Top Dog Solutions Inc	45 Newbury St Ste 301	Boston	MA	02116	617-262-8112	517-0075	177	*Web:* topdogsolutions.com
Top Flight Inc	1300 Central Ave	Chattanooga	TN	37408	423-266-8171	266-6857	263	*TF:* 800-777-3740 ■ *Web:* www.topflightpaper.com
Top Flite Financial Inc	123 E Grand River Ave	Williamston	MI	48895	517-655-2140		509	*Web:* www.tffinc.net
Top Floor Technologies LLC	2725 S Moorland Rd Ste 300	New Berlin	WI	53151	262-364-0010		7	*TF:* 888-947-4400 ■ *Web:* www.topfloortech.com
Top Furniture Inc	570 Main St	Gorham	NH	03581	603-752-5212		321	*TF:* 800-287-5212 ■ *Web:* www.topfurniture.com
Top Guard Security Inc	131 Kings Way	Hampton	VA	23669	757-722-3961	722-9902	693	*Web:* www.topguardinc.com
Top Gun Aviation Inc	405 Industrial Park Rd	Hammond	LA	70401	985-542-0719	542-2077	63	*Web:* www.airnav.com
Top Gun DUI Defense Attorney Myles L Berman	9255 Sunset Blvd Ste 620	Los Angeles	CA	90069	310-273-9501		428	*TF:* 888-486-7486 ■ *Web:* www.topgundui.com
Top Master Inc	2844 Roe Ln	Kansas City	KS	66103	913-492-3030		115	
Top of Daytona Restaurant	2625 S Atlantic Ave	Daytona Beach	FL	32118	386-767-5791		671	*Web:* topofdaytona.com
Top of the World Travel	5105 - 48 St	Yellowknife	NT	X1A1N5	867-766-6000		772	*Web:* www.topoftheworldtravel.com
Top of Virginia Regional Chamber	407 S Loudoun St	Winchester	VA	22601	540-662-4118		139	*Web:* www.regionalchamber.biz
Top Producer Systems Inc	10651 Shellbridge Way Ste 155	Richmond	BC	V6X2W8	800-821-3657		179	*TF:* 800-821-3657 ■ *Web:* www.topproducer.com
Top Promotions Inc	8831 S Greenview Dr	Middleton	WI	53562	608-836-9111		687	*TF:* 800-344-2968 ■ *Web:* www.toppromotions.com
Top Publications Ltd	2745 Dallas Pky Ste 420	Plano	TX	75093	972-628-6414	233-0713	637-2	*Web:* topfiction.net
Top Rank Inc	748 Pilot Rd Ste 580	Las Vegas	NV	89119	800-943-0087		181	*TF:* 800-943-0087 ■ *Web:* www.toprank.com
Top Shelf Fixtures LLC	5263 Schaefer Ave	Chino	CA	91710	909-627-7423		106	*TF:* 800-289-8245 ■ *Web:* www.topshelffixtures.com
Top Shop Inc, The	5740 Logan St	Denver	CO	80216	303-996-6026		186	*Web:* www.tshopinc.com
Top Spice	3007 N Druid Hills Rd	Atlanta	GA	30329	404-728-0588		671	*Web:* www.topspiceatlanta.com
Topa Equities Ltd	1800 Avenue of the Stars Ste 1400	Los Angeles	CA	90067	310-203-9199		185	*Web:* www.topa.com
Topa Insurance Corp	24025 Park Sorrento Ste 300	Calabasas	CA	91302	310-201-0451		391-4	*TF:* 877-353-8672 ■ *Web:* www.topains.com
Topas Advanced Polymers Inc	7300 Turfway Rd	Florence	KY	41042	859-746-6447		605-2	*Web:* www.topas.com

	Phone	Fax	Class
Topaz Lighting Corp 925 Waverly Ave ... Holtsville NY 11742 *Fax Area Code: 631 ■ TF: 800-666-2852 ■ Web: www.topaz-usa.com	800-666-2852	758-8026*	439
Topaz Resources Inc 1012 N Masch Branch Rd ... Denton TX 76207 Web: www.topazresourcesinc.com	916-293-6337		536
TopBloc 600 W Chicago Ave ... Chicago IL 60654 Web: topbloc.com	312-982-2991		387
Topco Associates LLC 7711 Gross Pt Rd ... Skokie IL 60077 TF: 888-423-0139 ■ Web: www.topco.com	847-745-2396	676-4949	297-8
Topco Oilsite Products Ltd Bay 7 3401 - 19 St NE ... Calgary AB T2E6S8 Web: topcooilsite.com	403-219-0255		540
TopCoder Inc 95 Glastonbury Blvd ... Glastonbury CT 06033 Web: www.topcoder.com	860-633-5540	657-4276	177
Topcon Medical Systems Inc 111 Bauer Dr ... Oakland NJ 07436 TF: 800-223-1130 ■ Web: www.topconmedical.com	201-599-5100	599-5250	382
Topcon Positioning Systems Inc 7400 National Dr ... Livermore CA 94550 Web: www.topconpositioning.com	925-245-8300	245-8599	472
Topcraft Metal Products Inc 5112 40th Ave ... Hudsonville MI 49426 Web: www.topcraftmetal.com	616-669-1790	669-0332	295
Topdek Inc 44 St Croix Trl S Ste 175 ... Lakeland MN 55403 Web: topdek.com	651-360-1044		174
Topeka & Shawnee County Public Library 1515 SW Tenth Ave ... Topeka KS 66604 Web: tscpl.org	785-580-4400	580-4496	434-3
Topeka Capital-Journal 616 SE Jefferson St ... Topeka KS 66607 TF: 800-777-7171 ■ Web: www.cjonline.com	785-295-1111	295-1230	532-2
Topeka Correctional Facility 815 SE Rice Rd ... Topeka KS 66607 Web: www.doc.ks.gov	785-296-3432	559-5112	213
Topeka Genealogical Society (TGS) PO Box 4048 ... Topeka KS 66604 Web: www.tgstopeka.org	785-233-5762		48-13
Topeka High School Historical Society (THSHS) 800 SW 10th Ave ... Topeka KS 66612 Web: www.thsweb.org	785-295-3200		685
Topeka Livestock Auction 601 E Lake St ... Topeka IN 46571 Web: www.topekalivestock.com	260-593-2522	593-2258	446
Topeka Performing Arts Ctr 214 SE Eigth Ave ... Topeka KS 66603 Web: www.topekaperformingarts.org	785-234-2787		572
Topeka Public Schools 624 SW 24th St ... Topeka KS 66611 Web: www.topekapublicschools.net	785-295-3000	575-6166	685
Topeka Seed & Stove 514 E Lake St ... Topeka IN 46571 TF: 800-541-2758 ■ Web: www.clickstoves.com	260-593-2407	593-2494	276
Topeka Symphony 519 SW 37th PO Box 2206 ... Topeka KS 66601 Web: www.topekasymphony.org	785-232-2032	232-6204	573-3
Topeka Zoological Park 635 SW Gage Blvd ... Topeka KS 66606 Web: topekazoo.org	785-368-9180	368-9152	823
Toper Taylor Com c/o Goldman & Knell 1801 Century Park E No 2160 ... Los Angeles CA 90067 Web: www.topertaylor.com	213-359-8243		511
Topical Review Book Co PO Box 328 ... Onsted MI 49265 TF: 800-847-0854 ■ Web: www.topicalrbc.com	800-847-0854	847-0851	637-2
Topix 35 McCaul St Ste 200 ... Toronto ON M5T1V7 Web: www.topixfx.com	416-971-7711		33
Topix LLC 1001 Elwell Ct ... Palo Alto CA 94303 Web: www.topix.com	650-461-8300		387
Topline Corp 13150 SE 32nd St ... Bellevue WA 98005 Web: www.toplinecorp.com	425-643-3003	643-3846	301
Topline Federal Credit Union 9353 Jefferson Hwy ... Maple Grove MN 55369 TF: 800-626-1448 ■ Web: www.toplinecu.com	763-391-9494	391-5322	219
Topline Results Corp N28W23000 Roundy Dr Ste 204 ... Pewaukee WI 53072 TF: 800-880-1960 ■ Web: toplineresults.com	800-880-1960		180
Topmark Federal Credit Union 1511 N Main St ... Lima OH 45801 TF: 888-918-7848 ■ Web: topmarkfcu.com	419-223-5886		219
Topnotch at Stowe Resort & Spa 4000 Mountain Rd ... Stowe VT 05672 *Fax Area Code: 802 ■ TF: 800-451-8686 ■ Web: www.topnotchresort.com	800-451-8686	253-9263*	669
Topp Industries Inc 420 N State Rd 25 PO Box 420 ... Rochester IN 46975 TF: 800-354-4534 ■ Web: www.toppindustries.com	574-223-3681	223-6106	601
Toppan Photomasks Inc 131 Old Settlers Blvd ... Round Rock TX 78664 Web: www.photomask.com	512-310-6500		696
Toppenish School District 202 306 Bolin Dr ... Toppenish WA 98948 Web: www.toppenish.wednet.edu	509-865-4455	865-2067	685
Topper's 120 Wauwinet Rd ... Nantucket MA 02584 Web: www.wauwinet.com	508-228-8768		671
Topps Company Inc 1 Whitehall St 6th Fl ... New York NY 10004 TF: 800-489-9149 ■ Web: www.topps.com	212-376-0300	376-0573	296-6
Topps Digital Services 16501 Ventura Blvd Ste 410 ... Encino CA 91436 Web: www.toppsdigitalservices.com	310-566-1420	566-1437	195
Topps Safety Apparel Inc 2516 E State Rd 14 ... Rochester IN 46975 TF: 800-348-2990 ■ Web: www.toppssafetyapparel.com	574-223-4311	223-8622	155-19
TOPS (TOPS Learning Systems Inc) 724 Elliott Rd Unit B ... Paradise CA 95969 Web: www.topscience.org	267-363-9149		637-2
TOPS Club Inc 4575 S Fifth St ... Milwaukee WI 53207 Web: www.tops.org	414-482-4620	482-1655	48-17
TOPS Learning Systems Inc (TOPS) 724 Elliott Rd Unit B ... Paradise CA 95969 Web: www.topscience.org	267-363-9149		637-2
Topsail Hill Preserve State Park 7525 W Scenic Hwy 30A ... Santa Rosa Beach FL 32459 Web: www.floridastateparks.org	850-267-8330		565
Topside Consulting Group LLC 929 Deep Creek Rd ... Lancaster VA 22503 Web: www.topside-consulting.com	703-442-7508		463
Topspin Group Inc 415 Executive Dr ... Princeton NJ 08540 Web: topspingroup.com	609-252-9515		466
Topspin Partners LP 3 Expy Plz ... Roslyn Heights NY 11577 Web: www.topspinpartners.com	516-625-9400	625-9499	792
Toptal LLC 2810 N Church St Ste 36879 ... Wilmington DE 19802 TF: 888-604-3188 ■ Web: www.toptal.com	888-604-3188		177
Toptica Photonics Inc 5847 County Rd 41 ... Farmington NY 14425 *Fax Area Code: 877 ■ Web: www.toptica.com	585-657-6663	277-9897*	419
Topwin Corp 1808 Abalone Ave ... Torrance CA 90501 Web: topwin.co.jp	310-325-2255	325-1877	156
Topy America Inc 980 Chenault Rd ... Frankfort KY 40601 Web: www.topyamerica.com	502-695-6163		247
Toque 900 Pl Jean-Paul Riopelle ... Montreal QC H2Z2B2 Web: www.restaurant-toque.com	514-499-2084	499-0292	671
TOR Minerals International Inc 722 Burleson St ... Corpus Christi TX 78402 OTC: TORM ■ Web: torminerals.com	361-883-5591	882-1033	143
Torah Umesorah-National Society for Hebrew Day Schools 620 Foster Ave ... Brooklyn NY 11230 TF: 800-788-3942 ■ Web: www.torahumesorah.org	212-227-1000		49-5
Toray Industries America Inc 461 Fifth Ave 9th Fl ... New York NY 10017 Web: www.toray.com	212-697-8150	972-4279	605-1
Toray Plastics America Inc 50 Belver Ave ... North Kingstown RI 02852 TF: 800-453-6866 ■ Web: www.toraytpa.com	401-294-4511	294-2154	596
Torch Energy Advisors Inc (TEAI) 1331 Lamar St Ste 1075 ... Houston TX 77010	713-650-1246		401
Torchlight Energy Resources Inc 5700 W Plano Pkwy Ste 3600 ... Plano TX 75093 Web: www.torchlightenergy.com	214-432-8002	432-8005	536
Torchmark Corp 3700 S Stonebridge Dr ... McKinney TX 75070 NYSE: TMK ■ TF: 877-577-3899 ■ Web: www.torchmarkcorp.com	972-569-4000	569-3282	360-4
Torco Inc 1330 Old 41 Hwy NW ... Marietta GA 30060 Web: www.torcoinc.com	770-427-3704	426-9369	621
Torcom 25 Kessel Ct Ste 107 ... Madison WI 53711 TF: 800-832-4939 ■ Web: torco.com	800-832-4939		737
Torcon Inc 328 Newman Springs Rd ... Red Bank NJ 07701 Web: www.torcon.com	732-704-9800	704-9810	186
Torero's 800 W Main St ... Durham NC 27701 Web: www.torerosmexicanrestaurants.com	919-682-4197		671
Torii Japanese Restaurant 2401 E Orangeburg Ave Ste 35 ... Modesto CA 95355 Web: www.toriimodesto.com	209-488-4921		671
Torke Coffee Roasting Company Inc 3455 Paine Ave ... Sheboygan WI 53081 *Fax Area Code: 920 ■ TF: 800-242-7671 ■ Web: www.torkecoffee.com	800-242-7671	458-0488*	296-7
Torn & Glasser Inc 1622 E Olympic Blvd PO Box 21823 ... Los Angeles CA 90021 Web: www.tornandglasser.com	213-627-6496	688-0941	297-3
Tornado Alley Turbo 300 Airport Rd ... Ada OK 74820 TF: 877-359-8284 ■ Web: www.tatparts.com	580-332-3510	332-4577	770
Tornado Bus Company Inc 535 E Jefferson Blvd ... Dallas TX 75203 Web: www.tornadobus.com	214-941-7399		108
Tornado Club Steak House 116 S Hamilton St ... Madison WI 53703 Web: tornadosteakhouse.com	608-256-3570		671
Tornado Spectral Systems 555 Richmond St W Ste 402 ... Toronto ON M5V3B1 Web: tornado-spectral.com	416-361-3444		253
Tornatech Inc 7075 Place Robert-Joncas Ste 132 ... Saint-Laurent QC H4M2Z2 TF: 800-363-8448 ■ Web: www.tornatech.com	514-334-0523	334-5448	203
Tornos Technologies US Corp 840 Parkview Blvd ... Lombard IL 60148 Web: www.tornos.com	630-812-2040	812-2039	455
Toro Co *Commercial Products Div* 8111 Lyndale Ave ... Bloomington MN 55420 TF: 800-348-2424 ■ Web: www.toro.com	952-888-8801	887-8258	429
Toromont Industries Ltd 3131 Hwy 7 W PO Box 5511 ... Concord ON L4K1B7 TSE: TIH ■ Web: toromontcat.com	416-667-5511		358
Toronto & Region Conservation Authority 5 Shoreham Dr ... Toronto ON M3N1S4 Web: www.trca.ca	416-661-6600		192
Toronto Argonauts 45 Manitoba Dr ... Toronto ON M6K3C3 Web: www.argonauts.ca	416-341-2746		715-2
Toronto Baptist Seminary & Bible College 130 Gerrard St E ... Toronto ON M5A3T4 Web: tbs.edu	416-925-3263	925-8305	785
Toronto Construction Assn 70 Leek Cres ... Richmond Hill ON L4B1H1 Web: www.tcaconnect.com	416-499-4000		138
Toronto Convention & Visitors Assn 207 Queen's Quay W Ste 405 PO Box 126 ... Toronto ON M5J1A7 TF: 800-499-2514 ■ Web: www.seetorontonow.com	416-203-2600	203-6753	206
Toronto Hydro Corp 14 Carlton St ... Toronto ON M5B1K5 TF: 888-495-8501 ■ Web: www.torontohydro.com	416-542-8000		767
Toronto International Film Festival Inc Reitman Sq 350 King St W ... Toronto ON M5V3X5 TF: 888-599-8433 ■ Web: www.tiff.net	888-599-8433		282
Toronto Law Office Management Assn (TLOMA) Toronto Dominion Ctr PO Box 1029 ... Toronto ON M5K1P2 *Fax Area Code: 905 ■ Web: www.tloma.com	416-410-1979	472-5115*	138
Toronto Life Magazine 111 Queen St E Ste 320 ... Toronto ON M5C1S2 Web: torontolife.com	416-364-3333		457-22
Toronto Maple Leafs 50 Bay St Ste 500 ... Toronto ON M5J2L2 Web: leafsnation.mapleleafs.com	416-815-5500	815-6050	716

Company	Address	City	State	ZIP	Phone	Fax	Class	Other
Toronto Port Authority	60 Harbour St	Toronto	ON	M5J1B7	416-863-2000	863-0495	618	*Web:* www.portstoronto.com
Toronto School of Theology	47 Queen's Pk Crescent E	Toronto	ON	M5S2C3	416-978-4039		167-3	*Web:* www.tst.edu
Toronto Star	1 Yonge St	Toronto	ON	M5E1E6	416-869-4949	869-4328	532-1	*TF:* 800-268-9756 ■ *Web:* www.thestar.com
Toronto Stock Exchange	The Exchange Tower 130 King St W	Toronto	ON	M5X1J2	416-947-4461	947-4662	691	*TF:* 888-873-8392 ■ *Web:* www.tmx.com
Toronto Sun	333 King St E	Toronto	ON	M5A3X5	416-947-2222	947-1664	532-1	*TF:* 888-786-7821 ■ *Web:* www.torontosun.com
Toronto Transit Commission (TTC)	1900 Yonge St	Toronto	ON	M4S1Z2	416-393-4000		468	*TF:* 800-223-6192 ■ *Web:* www.ttc.ca
Toronto Zoo	361-A Old Finch Ave	Toronto	ON	M1B5K7	416-392-5900	392-5934	823	*Web:* www.torontozoo.com
Toronto's First Post Office	260 Adelaide St E	Toronto	ON	M5A1N1	416-865-1833		520	*Web:* www.townofyork.com
Torrance Area Chamber of Commerce	2300 Crenshaw Blvd Bldg B	Torrance	CA	90501	310-540-5858	540-7662	139	*Web:* www.torrancechamber.com
Torrance Casting Inc	3131 Commerce St	La Crosse	WI	54603	608-781-0600		492	*Web:* www.torrancecasting.com
Torrance County	205 Ninth St	Estancia	NM	87016	505-544-4700	384-5294	338	*Web:* www.torrancecountynm.org
Torrance Memorial Home Health & Hospice	3330 Lomita Blvd	Torrance	CA	90505	310-784-3739		371	*TF:* 800-906-9909 ■ *Web:* www.torrancememorial.org
Torrance Public Library	3301 Torrance Blvd	Torrance	CA	90503	310-618-5959		434-3	*Web:* www.torranceca.gov
Torrance Unified School District	2335 Plaza Del AMO	Torrance	CA	90501	310-972-6500		685	*Web:* www.tusd.org
Torray Fund	7501 Wisconsin Ave Ste 750 W	Bethesda	MD	20814	301-493-4600		528	*TF:* 800-443-3036 ■ *Web:* www.torray.com
Torrence's Farm Implement Inc	190 E Hwy 86 PO Box C	Heber	CA	92249	760-352-5355	352-8707	274	*Web:* www.torrences.net
Torrent Falls Climbing Adventure	1617 N KY 11	Campton	KY	41301	606-668-6613		239	*Web:* www.torrentfalls.com
Torrent Pharma Inc	5380 Holiday Ter Ste 40	Kalamazoo	MI	49009	269-544-2299		231	
Torres Norma (Rep D - CA)	2444 Rayburn House Office Bldg	Washington	DC	20515	202-225-6161	225-8671	342-2	*Web:* torres.house.gov
Torres Small Xochitl (Rep D - NM)	430 Cannon House Office Bldg.	Washington	DC	20515	202-225-2365		342-2	*Web:* www.torressmall.house.gov
Torrey Farms Inc	Maltby Rd	Elba	NY	14058	585-757-9941		10-11	*Web:* www.torreyfarms.com
Torrey Pines State Beach	4477 Pacific Hwy	San Diego	CA	92110	858-755-2063		565	*Web:* www.parks.ca.gov
Torreya State Park	2576 NW Torreya Park Rd.	Bristol	FL	32321	850-643-2674		565	*Web:* www.floridastateparks.org
Torrid Technologies Inc	1860 Sandy Plains Rd Ste 204-129	Marietta	GA	30066	888-333-5095		177	*TF:* 888-333-5095 ■ *Web:* www.torrid-tech.com
Torry Harris Business Solutions Inc	536 Fayette St.	Perth Amboy	NJ	08861	732-442-0049	442-0825	631	*Web:* www.torryharris.com
Torstar Corp	1 Yonge St	Toronto	ON	M5E1E6	416-869-4010	869-4183	637-2	*TSE:* TS.B ■ *Web:* www.torstar.com
Torstenson Glass Co	3233 N Sheffield Ave	Chicago	IL	60657	773-525-0435	525-0009	329	*Web:* tglass.com
Tortel USA LLC	221 Commerce Dr	Amherst	NY	14228	877-228-6616		246	*TF:* 877-228-6616 ■ *Web:* www.tortelusa.com
Torti Gallas & Partners Inc	1300 Spring St	Silver Spring	MD	20910	301-588-4800	650-2255	186	*Web:* tortigallas.com
Tortilla Flats	3139 Cerrillos Rd	Santa Fe	NM	87507	505-471-8685		671	*Web:* www.tortillaflats.net
Tortilla Jo's	Downtown Disney 1510 Disneyland Dr.	Anaheim	CA	92802	714-535-5000		671	*Web:* www.patinagroup.com
Tortilla King Inc	249 23rd Ave	Moundridge	KS	67107	620-345-2674		123	*Web:* www.tortillaking.com
Tortoise Energy Capital Corp	11550 Ash St Ste 300	Leawood	KS	66211	913-981-1020	981-1021	792	*NYSE:* TTP ■ *TF:* 866-362-9331 ■ *Web:* tortoiseadvisors.com
Tortuga Press	2777 Yulupa Ave.	Santa Rosa	CA	95405	707-544-4720	595-5331	637-2	*Web:* www.tortugapress.com
Torys LLP	79 Wellington St W TD Ctr 30th Fl	Toronto	ON	M5K1N2	416-865-0040		41	*Web:* www.torys.com
Tosan Inc	16500 Smith Rd Ste A	Denver	CO	80205	303-832-7606		193	
TOSC International Inc	14511 Old Katy Rd Ste 364	Houston	TX	77079	713-961-1201	961-4989	178-1	*Web:* www.toscintl.com
Tosca	1112 F St NW	Washington	DC	20004	202-367-1990	367-1999	671	*Web:* www.toscadc.com
Tosca Ltd	375 Ams Ct Ste C	Green Bay	WI	54313	920-617-4000		200	*Web:* www.toscaltd.com
Tosca Ristorante	144 O'Connor St	Ottawa	ON	K2P2G7	613-565-3933		671	*Web:* www.tosca-ristorante.ca
Toscana	6401 Morrison Blvd	Charlotte	NC	28211	704-367-1808		671	*Web:* conterestaurantgroup.com
Tosco - Tool Specialty Co	1011 E Slauson Ave	Los Angeles	CA	90011	323-232-3561	232-3429	493	*Web:* www.toolspecialty.com
Tosh Farms	1586 Atlantic Ave	Henry	TN	38231	731-243-4861	243-4860	10-4	*Web:* toshfarms.net
Toshiba America Inc	1251 Avenue of the Americas 41st Fl	New York	NY	10020	212-596-0600		52	*TF:* 800-457-7777 ■ *Web:* www.toshiba.com
Tosoh Bioscience Inc	6000 Shoreline Ct Ste 101	South San Francisco	CA	94080	650-615-4970		475	*TF:* 800-248-6764 ■ *Web:* www.diagnostics.us.tosohbioscience.com
Tosoh SMD Inc	3600 Gantz Rd	Grove City	OH	43123	614-875-7912	875-0031	696	*Web:* www.tosohsmd.com
TOSS Corp	1253 Worcester Rd	Framingham	MA	01701	508-820-2990	820-2991	180	*TF:* 888-884-8677 ■ *Web:* www.getsaas.com
Totah Communications Inc (TTCI)	101 S Ochelata St	Ochelata	OK	74051	918-535-2208	535-2701	224	*TF:* 888-580-2208 ■ *Web:* www.totelcsi.com
Total Adult Day Health Care Solutions Inc	20555 Devonshire St Ste 300	Chatsworth	CA	91311	818-349-2026	349-2110	194	*Web:* www.totaladhc.com
Total Airport Services Inc	28420 Hardy Toll Rd Ste 220	Spring	TX	77373	832-592-0048		579	*Web:* www.totalairportservices.com
Total Assault LLC	17547 Ventura Blvd Ste 204	Encino	CA	91316	310-280-3777		195	*Web:* www.totalassault.com
Total Battery Consulting Inc	PO Box 1059	Oregon House	CA	95962	530-692-0140	660-1646	463	*Web:* www.totalbatteryconsulting.com
Total Beauty Media Inc	3420 Ocean Park Blvd Ste 3050	Santa Monica	CA	90405	310-399-7400		77	*Web:* www.totalbeautymedia.com
Total Business Solutions Inc	3413 Griffin St	Portsmouth	VA	23707	757-398-8312		535	*Web:* totalbusinesssolutions.com
Total Business Systems Inc	30800 Montpelier	Madison Heights	MI	48071	248-588-9130	588-0849	110	*TF:* 800-878-3676 ■ *Web:* www.tbsddp.com
Total Communications Inc	333 Burnham St	East Hartford	CT	06108	860-282-9999	528-1904	735	*Web:* www.totalcomm.com
Total Components Solutions Corp	2080 Tenth St	Rock Valley	IA	51247	712-476-5315		454	*TF:* 800-621-2203 ■ *Web:* www.tcsiowa.com
Total Computer Solutions Inc	353 Robins West Pkwy	Warner Robins	GA	31088	478-953-6070		180	*Web:* choosetcs.com
Total Computing Solutions LLC	629 Quality Dr Ste 202	American Fork	UT	84003	866-796-7600	756-1576*	178-1	*Fax Area Code: 801 ■ *TF:* 866-796-7600 ■ *Web:* www.total-computing.com
Total Computing Solutions of America Inc	23430 Hawthorne Blvd Skypark Office Ctr Bldg 3 Ste 300	Torrance	CA	90505	310-378-9100	378-9191	177	*Web:* www.tcsamerica.com
Total Contentz	540 Millers Run Rd Ste 200	Morgan	PA	15064	805-522-5900	522-5905	463	*TF:* 888-722-5688 ■ *Web:* totalcontentz.com
Total Control Software	12010 Watson Rd	Sherwood	AR	72120	501-833-3281	833-6107	178	*Web:* www.tcsoft.com
Total Credit Recovery Ltd	225 Yorkland Blvd	Toronto	ON	M2J4Y7	416-774-4000		160	*Web:* www.tcr.ca
Total E & P USA Inc	1201 Louisiana St Ste 1800	Houston	TX	77002	713-483-5070	483-5629	538	*Web:* us.total.com
Total Energy Control Systems Inc	47-25 34th St Ste 4	Long Island City	NY	11101	718-247-2100	247-2150	610	*Web:* tecsystemsnyc.com
Total Energy Services Ltd	2550 300-5th Ave SW Ste 2550	Calgary	AB	T2P3C4	403-216-3939	234-8731	540	*NYSE:* TOT ■ *TF:* 877-818-6825 ■ *Web:* www.totalenergy.ca
Total Equipment Co	400 Fifth Ave	Coraopolis	PA	15108	412-269-0999		385	*Web:* www.totalequipment.com
Total Event Resources	1920 Thoreau Dr N Ste 105	Schaumburg	IL	60173	847-397-2200		196	*Web:* total-event.com
Total Expert Inc	1600 Utica Ave S Ste 600	St. Louis Park	MN	55416	800-830-9085		178-1	*TF:* 800-830-9085 ■ *Web:* totalexpert.com
Total Filtration Services Inc	2521 Commercial Dr	Auburn Hills	MI	48326	248-377-4004		385	*TF:* 800-331-3118 ■ *Web:* www.totalfiltrationservices.com
Total Fire & Safety Inc	7909 Carr St.	Dallas	TX	75227	214-381-6116	381-4633	246	*Web:* www.totalfire.com
Total Fitness USA Inc	2312 Kamehameha Hwy Ste C1	Honolulu	HI	96819	808-841-9525		711	*Web:* tfusa.net
Total Golf Construction Inc	4045 43rd Ave	Vero Beach	FL	32960	772-562-1177	562-2773	188-3	*Web:* www.totalgolfconstruction.com
Total Health Care Inc	1501 Div St.	Baltimore	MD	21217	410-383-8300	728-4412	374-3	*Web:* totalhealthcare.org
Total Health Care Inc	3011 W Grand Blvd Ste 1600	Detroit	MI	48202	313-871-2000	871-0196	391-3	*Web:* www.thcmi.com
Total Home Health Care Inc	3127 W Hallandale Beach Blvd Ste 107	Hallandale	FL	33009	954-961-1698	961-1699	363	*Web:* www.totalhomehealthcare.org
Total Hr	2626 Foothill Blvd Ste 200	La Crescenta	CA	91214	818-248-0049		260	*Web:* www.totalhrmanagement.com
Total Kitchen & Bath Inc	155 S Rohlwing Rd	Addison	IL	60101	630-495-2010		290	*Web:* www.totalstonesolutions.com
Total Living Network (TLN)	2880 Vision Ct.	Aurora	IL	60506	630-801-3838	801-3839	740	*Web:* tln.com
Total Logistics Solutions Inc	PO Box 11146	Burbank	CA	91510	818-353-2962		463	*Web:* www.logisticsociety.com

Company / Address	City	State	Zip	Phone	Fax	Class
Total Lubricants USA 5 N Stiles St *TF:* 800-323-3198 ■ *Web:* www.totalspecialties.com	Linden	NJ	07036	908-862-9300	862-5374	541
Total Maintenance Solutions 3540 Rutherford Rd *TF:* 800-476-2212 ■ *Web:* www.tmssouth.com	Taylors	SC	29687	864-268-2891		610
Total Management Solutions Inc 55 Harristown Rd *Web:* www.totmgtsol.com	Glen Rock	NJ	07452	201-447-0707	447-3831	47
Total Marketing LLC 1751 River Run Ste 200 *TF:* 800-998-5269 ■ *Web:* totalmktg.com	Fort Worth	TX	76107	817-560-3970		173-4
Total Mechanical W234 N2830 Paul Rd *Web:* total-mechanical.com	Pewaukee	WI	53072	262-523-2500	523-2530	393
Total Merchant Concepts Inc 12300 NE Fourth Plain Rd A *TF:* 888-249-9919 ■ *Web:* www.totalmerchantconcepts.com	Vancouver	WA	98682	360-253-5934		535
Total Nails & Hair Academy 2716 S Dixie Hwy Ste 102 *Web:* www.totalnailsnhairacademy.com	West Palm Beach	FL	33405	561-969-9441	969-7805	647
Total Networx Inc 417 W Travelers Trl *Web:* totalnetworx.com	Burnsville	MN	55337	952-400-6500	400-6501	180
Total Oilfield Rentals Partnership 6517 51 Ave *Web:* totaloilfield.ca	Whitecourt	AB	T7S1N3	780-778-6222		23
Total Outdoor Corp 414 Stewart St Ste 204 *Web:* www.totaloutdoor.com	Seattle	WA	98101	206-430-6080		5
Total Package Express Inc 5871 Cheviot Rd *Web:* tp-exp.com	Cincinnati	OH	45247	513-741-5500	741-5507	780
Total Parts Plus Inc 70 Ready Ave NW *TF:* 877-912-7278 ■ *Web:* www.totalpartsplus.com	Fort Walton Beach	FL	32548	850-244-7293	664-5349	317
Total Pet Supply 477 Peace Portal Dr Ste 436 *TF:* 866-501-6038 ■ *Web:* www.totalpetsupply.com	Blaine	WA	98230	866-501-6038		328
Total Pharmacy Supply Inc 3400 Ave E *TF:* 800-878-2822 ■ *Web:* www.totalpharmacysupply.com	Arlington	TX	76011	817-861-4416	861-8307	475
Total Plastics Inc 3316 Pagosa Ct *TF:* 800-382-4635 ■ *Web:* www.totalplastics.com	Indianapolis	IN	46226	317-543-3540	543-3553	602
Total Printing Company Inc 4401 Sarellen Rd *TF:* 877-222-3813 ■ *Web:* www.total-printing.com	Richmond	VA	23231	804-222-3813	226-4572	627
Total Printing Systems 201 S Gregory St *TF:* 800-465-5200 ■ *Web:* www.tps1.com	Newton	IL	62448	800-465-5200		627
Total Promotions 1340 Old Skokie Rd *TF:* 800-277-6668 ■ *Web:* www.totalpromote.com	Highland Park	IL	60035	847-831-9500		7
Total Quality Inc 550 3 Mile Rd Ste D *TF:* 800-286-4231 ■ *Web:* www.shiptqi.com	Grand Rapids	MI	49544	616-785-4600		54
Total Quality Logistics Inc (TQL) 4289 Ivy Pointe Blvd *TF:* 800-580-3101 ■ *Web:* www.tql.com	Cincinnati	OH	45245	513-831-2600	965-7630	311
Total Registration LLC 5013 Eldorado Springs Dr *TF:* 800-974-2187 ■ *Web:* www.totalregistration.net	Boulder	CO	80303	800-974-2187		423
Total Resource Management Inc 510 King St Ste 200 *TF:* 877-548-5100 ■ *Web:* www.trmnet.com	Alexandria	VA	22314	703-548-4285	548-3641	193
Total Safety Consulting LLC 751 Broadway *Web:* www.totalsafety.org	Bayonne	NJ	07002	201-437-5150		41
Total Seal Inc 22642 N 15th Ave *TF:* 800-874-2753 ■ *Web:* 015ef8d.netsolhost.com	Phoenix	AZ	85027	623-587-7400	587-7600	128
Total Security Solutions 170 National Park Dr *TF:* 888-997-2381 ■ *Web:* www.tssbulletproof.com	Fowlerville	MI	48836	517-223-7807	223-0805	692
Total Seminars LLC 12550 Fuqua Ste 150 *TF:* 877-687-2768 ■ *Web:* www.totalsem.com	Houston	TX	77034	281-922-4166		764
Total Solutions Inc 1626 County Line Rd *TF:* 866-413-4111 ■ *Web:* www.totalsolutions-inc.com	Madison	AL	35756	256-721-3987		177
Total Systems Technology Inc 65 Terence Dr *TF:* 800-245-4828 ■ *Web:* www.tst5k.com	Pittsburgh	PA	15236	412-653-7690	653-7930	605-2
Total Technologies Ltd 9710 Research Dr *TF:* 800-669-4885 ■ *Web:* www.total-technologies.com	Irvine	CA	92618	949-465-0200	465-0212	253
Total Telcom Inc 540 1632 Dickson Ave *TF:* 877-860-3762 ■ *Web:* www.totaltelcom.com	Kelowna	BC	V1Y7T2	250-860-3762		736
Total Wellhead & Rental Tools LLC 401 S Juniper St *Web:* www.totalwellhead.com	Perryton	TX	79070	806-435-3800		538
Total Wine & More 6600 Rockledge Dr *TF:* 855-328-9463 ■ *Web:* www.totalwine.com	Bethesda	MD	20817	855-328-9463		345
Total Works Inc 420 W Huron St *Web:* www.totalworks.net	Chicago	IL	60654	773-489-4313		781
Totalbank 2720 Coral Way *Web:* www.totalbank.com	Miami	FL	33145	305-448-6500	448-8201	70
Totalcomp Scales & Components 99 Reagent Ln *TF:* 800-631-0347 ■ *Web:* www.totalcomp.com	Fair Lawn	NJ	07410	201-797-2718	797-2287	362
Totalis Consulting Group 402 Park Dr *Web:* totalis.com	Warner Robins	GA	31088	478-926-2358		196
Totelcom Communications LLC 6100 Hwy 16 S PO Box 290 *TF:* 800-261-5911 ■ *Web:* totelcom.net	De Leon	TX	76444	254-893-1000		224
Totem Bight State Historical Park 400 Willoughby Ave PO Box 111020 *Web:* www.dnr.alaska.gov	Juneau	AK	99801	907-465-4563		565
Totem Content 37 Front St E *Web:* totemcontent.com	Toronto	ON	M5E1B3	416-360-7339		5
Totem Electric of Tacoma Inc 2332 Jefferson Ave *Web:* www.totemelectric.com	Tacoma	WA	98402	253-383-5022	272-5214	189-4
Totem Ocean Trailer Express Inc 32001 32nd Ave S Ste 200 *TF:* 800-426-0074 ■ *Web:* www.totemaritime.com	Federal Way	WA	98001	253-449-8100	449-8225	312
Totem Tales Publishing 219 Salzedo St *Web:* www.totemtales.com	Royal Palm Beach	FL	33411	561-537-2522		637-2
Toter Inc PO Box 5338 *TF:* 800-424-0422 ■ *Web:* www.toter.com	Statesville	NC	28677	800-424-0422		199
Totes Isotoner Corp 9655 International Blvd *Web:* www.totes.com	Cincinnati	OH	45246	513-682-8200		155-8
Totevision 3257 17th Ave W Bldg 1 Ste 201 *Web:* totevision.com	Seattle	WA	98119	206-623-6000	623-6609	693
Totex Manufacturing Inc 3050 Lomita Blvd *TF:* 800-715-5777 ■ *Web:* www.totexmfg.com	Torrance	CA	90505	310-326-2028	326-2336	608
Toth Financial Advisory Corp 608 S King St Ste 300 *Web:* www.tothfinancial.com	Leesburg	VA	20175	703-443-8684		113
Toto Tours 1326 W Albion Ave *TF:* 800-565-1241 ■ *Web:* tototours.com	Chicago	IL	60626	773-274-8686	274-8695	760
Toto USA Inc 1155 Southern Rd *TF:* 888-295-8134 ■ *Web:* www.totousa.com	Morrow	GA	30260	770-282-8686	282-8701	611
Totten Tubes Inc 500 Danlee St **Fax Area Code:* 626 ■ *TF:* 800-882-3748 ■ *Web:* www.tottentubes.com	Azusa	CA	91702	800-882-3748	812-0113*	492
Touch Networks 2515 152nd Ave NE *Web:* touchnetworks.com	Redmond	WA	98052	425-881-8806	881-5820	177
Touch of Nature Environmental Ctr 1206 Touch of Nature Rd *Web:* www.pso.siu.edu	Makanda	IL	62958	618-453-1121		121
TouchAmerica 1403 S Third St Ext *TF:* 800-678-6824 ■ *Web:* www.touchamerica.com	Mebane	NC	27302	919-732-6968	732-1173	76
Touchdown Trucking Inc 4321 Lawehana St *Web:* touchdowntrucking.com	Honolulu	HI	96818	808-423-8777	423-4259	311
Touchette Regional Hospital (TRH) 5900 Bond Ave *Web:* www.touchette.org	Centreville	IL	62207	618-332-3060		374-3
Touching America 600 Pine Forest Dr Ste 120 *Web:* www.touchingamerica.com	Maumelle	AR	72113	501-772-1226		167-3
Touching Hearts At Home 7505 Metro Blvd Ste 340 *TF:* 877-870-8750 ■ *Web:* www.touchinghearts.com	Minneapolis	MN	55439	877-870-8750		363
TouchLogic Corp 30 Kinnear Ct Ste 202 *TF:* 877-355-4774 ■ *Web:* www.touchlogic.com	Richmond Hill	ON	L4B1K8	877-355-4774		387
Touchstone Center for Crafts 1049 Wharton Furnace Rd *TF:* 800-721-0177 ■ *Web:* www.touchstonecrafts.org	Farmington	PA	15437	724-329-1370	329-1371	167-3
Touchstone Energy Cooperative Inc 4301 Wilson Blvd *Web:* www.touchstoneenergy.com	Arlington	VA	22203	703-907-5500	907-5554	48-6
Touchstone Medical Imaging LLC 1431 Perrone Way *TF:* 877-275-9077 ■ *Web:* www.touchstoneimaging.com	Franklin	TN	37069	615-661-9200	661-9297	415
Touchstone Precision Inc 239 Technology Pky *TF:* 866-887-6680 ■ *Web:* www.touchstoneprecision.com	Auburn	AL	36830	334-887-6688	887-6686	604
Touchstone Wildlife & Art Museum 3386 Hwy 80 *Web:* www.touchstonemuseum.com	Haughton	LA	71037	318-949-2323		520
Touchstorm LLC 450 Lexington Ave 4th Fl *TF:* 877-794-6101 ■ *Web:* www.touchstorm.com	New York	NY	10017	877-794-6101		387
TouchSystems Corp 2222 W Rundberg Ln Ste 200 *TF:* 800-320-5944 ■ *Web:* www.touchsystems.com	Austin	TX	78758	512-846-2424	832-8291	614
Toudouze Market Inc 800 Buena Vista *TF:* 888-553-5856 ■ *Web:* www.toudouze.com	San Antonio	TX	78207	888-553-5856		297-2
Touey & Company LLC 223 N Monroe St *Web:* touey.com	Media	PA	19063	610-622-7272		2
Tougaloo College 500 W County Line Rd *TF:* 888-424-2566 ■ *Web:* www.tougaloo.edu	Tougaloo	MS	39174	601-977-7700	977-4501	166
Tough Traveler Ltd 1012 State St *TF:* 800-468-6844 ■ *Web:* www.toughtraveler.com	Schenectady	NY	12307	518-377-5434		64
Toukan & Co 575 Charring Cross Dr Ste 200 *Web:* toukan.com	Westerville	OH	43081	614-901-7100		2
Tour East Holidays (Canada) Inc 15 Kern Rd *Web:* www.toureast.com	North York	ON	M3B1S9	416-929-8017		760
Tour Edge Golf Manufacturing Inc 1301 Pierson Dr *TF:* 800-515-3343 ■ *Web:* www.touredge.com	Batavia	IL	60510	630-584-4777		772
Tourbillon International LLC 11 W 25th St *Web:* www.media.modernluxury.com	New York	NY	10010	212-627-7732	627-9093	772
Tourette Syndrome Association Inc 42-40 Bell Blvd Ste 205 *Web:* www.tourette.org	Bayside	NY	11361	718-224-2999	279-9596	48-17
Touring & Tasting 207 E Victoria St *TF:* 800-850-4370 ■ *Web:* www.touringandtasting.com	Santa Barbara	CA	93103	805-965-2813	965-2873	443
Tourism Abbotsford Society 34561 Delair Rd *TF:* 888-332-2229 ■ *Web:* www.tourismabbotsford.ca	Abbotsford	BC	V2S2E1	604-859-1721		342
Tourism Australia 2890 Zanker Rd Ste 203 *Web:* www.australia.com	Los Angeles	CA	90045	310-695-3200	695-3201	775
Tourism Authority of Thailand 61 Broadway Ste 2810 *Web:* www.tourismthailand.org	New York	NY	10006	212-432-0433	269-2588	775

				Phone	Fax	Class
Tourism Calgary 200 238 11th Ave SE *TF:* 800-661-1678 ■ *Web:* www.visitcalgary.com	Calgary	AB	T2G0X8	403-263-8510	262-3809	206
Tourism Council of Frederick County Inc 151 S East St *TF:* 800-999-3613 ■ *Web:* www.visitfrederick.org	Frederick	MD	21701	301-600-2888		206
Tourism Industry Association of Pei 25 Queen St 3rd Fl PO Box 2050 *TF:* 866-566-5008 ■ *Web:* www.tiapei.pe.ca	Charlottetown	PE	C1A7N7	902-566-5008		138
Tourism Ireland 345 Park Ave *Web:* www.tourismireland.com	New York	NY	10154	212-418-0800	371-9052	775
Tourism Malaysia (MTPB) 120 E 56th St Ste 810 *Web:* www.malaysia.travel	New York	NY	10022	212-754-1113	754-1116	775
Tourism Malaysia 818 W Seventh St Ste 970 *Web:* www.tourism.gov.my	Los Angeles	CA	90017	213-689-9702	689-1530	775
Tourism Medicine Hat 8 Gehring Rd SE *Web:* www.tourismmedicinehat.com	Medicine Hat	AB	T1B4W1	403-527-6422		775
Tourism New Brunswick PO Box 6000 *TF:* 800-561-0123 ■ *Web:* www.tourismnewbrunswick.ca	Fredericton	NB	E3B5H1	800-561-0123		774
Tourism Richmond Inc South Twr 5811 Cooney Rd Ste 205 *TF:* 877-247-0777 ■ *Web:* www.visitrichmondbc.com	Richmond	BC	V6X3M1	604-821-5474		772
Tourism Saskatchewan 1621 Albert St *TF:* 877-237-2273 ■ *Web:* www.tourismsaskatchewan.com	Regina	SK	S4P2S5	306-787-9600	787-6293	774
Tourism Saskatoon 202 Fourth Ave N *TF:* 800-567-2444 ■ *Web:* www.tourismsaskatoon.com	Saskatoon	SK	S7K0K1	306-242-1206		775
Tourism Winnipeg 1 Lombard Pl Ste 810 *TF:* 855-734-2489 ■ *Web:* www.tourismwinnipeg.com	Winnipeg	MB	R3B0X3	204-943-1970	942-4043	774
Tourist Office of Spain 8383 Wilshire Blvd Ste 960 *Web:* www.spain.info	Beverly Hills	CA	90211	323-658-7188	658-1061	775
Tourmaline Oil Corp 250 Sixth Ave SW Ste 3700 *TF:* 877-504-4252 ■ *Web:* www.tourmalineoil.com	Calgary	AB	T2P3H7	403-266-5992	266-5952	536
Tournament Games Inc 107 W High St *Web:* www.tournamentgames.com	Lebanon	TN	37087	615-547-1777	443-9990	45
Tourney Consulting Group LLC 3401 Midlink Dr *TF:* 866-584-4824 ■ *Web:* www.tourneyconsulting.com	Kalamazoo	MI	49048	269-384-9980		743
Touro College & University System 500 Seventh Ave **Fax Area Code:* 212 ■ *Web:* www.touro.edu	New York	NY	10018	646-565-6000	742-1310*	166
Lander College for Men 75-31 150th St *Web:* lcm.touro.edu	Kew Gardens Hills	NY	11367	718-820-4800		166
Touro College Jacob D Fuchsberg Law Ctr 225 Eastview Dr Rm 306 *Web:* www.tourolaw.edu	Central Islip	NY	11722	631-761-7000		167-1
Touro Infirmary 1401 Foucher St *Web:* www.touro.com	New Orleans	LA	70115	504-897-7011		374-3
Touro Synagogue National Historic Site 85 Touro St *Web:* www.tourosynagogue.org	Newport	RI	02840	401-847-4794		50-1
Tousley Brain Stephens PLLC 1700 Seventh Ave Ste 2200 *Web:* www.tousley.com	Seattle	WA	98101	206-682-5600	682-2992	428
Touvelle State Recreation Site Table Rock Rd *Web:* stateparks.oregon.gov	Central Point	OR	97502	541-826-2257		565
Tova Industries LLC 2902 Blankenbaker Rd *Web:* www.tovaindustries.com	Louisville	KY	40299	502-267-7333	267-7119	296-10
Towanda Printing Company Inc 116 Main St *Web:* www.thedailyreview.com	Towanda	PA	18848	570-265-2151		532-3
Towe Iron Works Inc 2728 Mynderse Ave *Web:* www.toweironworks.com	Knoxville	TN	37921	865-546-5131		480
Tower Accounting 3435 Blue Mtn Dr *Web:* www.toweraccounting.com	San Jose	CA	95127	408-929-4576		2
Tower Cafe 1518 Broadway *Web:* www.towercafe.com	Sacramento	CA	95818	916-441-0222		671
Tower Communications Expert LLC (TCE) 114 Shore Dr *Web:* www.tcellc.net	Burr Ridge	IL	60527	773-744-7550	717-5534	188-1
Tower Energy Group 1983 W 190th St *Web:* www.towerenergy.com	Torrance	CA	90504	310-538-8000		580
Tower Extrusions Ltd 1003 State Hwy 79 S *Web:* www.towerextrusion.com	Olney	TX	76374	940-564-5681	564-5033	485
Tower Federal Credit Union 7901 Sandy Spring Rd *TF:* 800-787-8328 ■ *Web:* www.towerfcu.org	Laurel	MD	20707	301-497-7000	497-8930	219
Tower Hill Botanic Garden 11 French Dr PO Box 598 *Web:* www.towerhillbg.org	Boylston	MA	01505	508-869-6111	869-0314	97
Tower Hill State Park 5808 County Rd C *Web:* dnr.wi.gov	Spring Green	WI	53588	608-935-1919		565
Tower Imaging Medical Group 5455 Wilshire Blvd Ste 1120 *Web:* www.towerimaging.com	Los Angeles	CA	90036	323-549-3030	549-3049	418
Tower Innovations LLC 2855 Hwy 261 **Fax Area Code:* 812 ■ *TF:* 800-664-8222 ■ *Web:* www.towerinnovations.net	Newburgh	IN	47630	800-664-8222	853-6652*	170
Tower Isles Frozen Foods Ltd 2025 Atlantic Ave *Web:* www.towerislespatties.com	Brooklyn	NY	11233	718-495-2626		297-8
Tower Laboratories Ltd PO Box 306 *Web:* www.towerlabs.com	Centerbrook	CT	06409	860-767-2127		582
Tower Manufacturing Corp 25 Reservoir Ave *Web:* www.towermfg.com	Providence	RI	02907	401-467-7550	461-2710	815
Tower Oil & Technology Co 4300 S Tripp Ave *Web:* www.towermwf.com	Chicago	IL	60632	773-927-6161		579
Tower Properties Co 1000 Walnut St Ste 900 *Web:* www.towerproperties.com	Kansas City	MO	64106	816-421-8255		655
Tower Semiconductor Newport Beach Inc 4321 Jamboree Rd *Web:* towersemi.com	Newport Beach	CA	92660	949-435-8000		696
Tower Systems Inc 17226 447th Ave PO Box 1474 *Web:* www.towersystems.com	Watertown	SD	57201	605-886-0930		480
Tower Tech Inc 5400 NW 5th St *Web:* www.towertechinc.com	Oklahoma City	OK	73127	405-290-7788	979-2131	604
Tower Theatre for the Performing Arts 815 E Olive Ave *Web:* www.towertheatrefresno.com	Fresno	CA	93728	559-485-9050		572
Tower Travel Management 53 Ogden Ave **Fax Area Code:* 630 ■ *TF:* 800-542-9700 ■ *Web:* www.towertravel.com	Clarendon Hills	IL	60514	800-542-9700	954-3040*	771
Tower Ventures LLC 4091 Viscount Ave *TF:* 800-875-5109 ■ *Web:* www.towerventures.com	Memphis	TN	38118	901-794-9494	562-0911	736
TOWER23 Hotel 723 Felspar St *Web:* www.t23hotel.com	San Diego	CA	92109	858-270-2323		379
TowerBrook Capital Partners 65 E 55th St Park Avenue Twr **Fax Area Code:* 917 ■ *Web:* www.towerbrook.com	New York	NY	10022	212-699-2200	591-9851*	690
TowerComm LLC 6017 Triangle Dr *Web:* www.towercommonline.com	Raleigh	NC	27617	919-781-3496	781-6454	116
TowerData Inc 379 Park Ave S 5th Fl *Web:* www.towerdata.com	New York	NY	10016	646-742-1771		195
Towers at the Kahler Grand, The 20 Second Ave SW *TF:* 800-940-6811 ■ *Web:* www.towersatkahlergrand.com	Rochester	MN	55902	507-208-1409	285-2767	379
Towerstrides Inc 218 Depot Ct SE *Web:* www.towerstrides.com	Leesburg	VA	20175	703-574-8888	574-8949	177
Towerwall 615 Concord St *TF:* 888-234-7404 ■ *Web:* towerwall.com	Framingham	MA	01702	774-204-0700		177
Towmaster Inc 61381 US Hwy 12 *TF:* 800-462-4517 ■ *Web:* towmaster.com	Litchfield	MN	55355	320-693-7900	693-7921	779
Town & Country Animal Hospital Ltd 901 N Linden St *Web:* tcah.net	Normal	IL	61761	309-452-1717		794
Town & Country Distributors Inc 1050 W Ardmore Ave *Web:* tcbeer.com	Itasca	IL	60143	630-250-0590		81-1
Town & Country Federal Credit Union 557 Main St PO Box 9420 *Web:* tcfcu.com	South Portland	ME	04116	207-773-5656		219
Town & Country Furniture 6545 Airline Hwy *Web:* www.tcfurniture.com	Baton Rouge	LA	70805	225-355-6666	355-7459	321
Town & Country Hospital 6001 Webb Rd *TF:* 866-463-7449 ■ *Web:* www.freseniuskidneycare.com	Tampa	FL	33615	813-888-7060		374-3
Town & Country Industries 400 W Mcnab Rd *Web:* www.tc-alum.com	Fort Lauderdale	FL	33309	954-970-9999		492
Town & Country Inn 20 State Rte 2 *TF:* 800-325-4386 ■ *Web:* townandcountryinnandresort.com	Shelburne	NH	03581	603-466-3315		379
Town & Country Markets Inc 20148 Tenth Ave NE *Web:* central-market.com	Poulsbo	WA	98370	360-779-1881		345
Town & Country Resort Hotel 500 Hotel Cir N *TF:* 800-772-8527 ■ *Web:* www.towncountry.com	San Diego	CA	92108	619-291-7131	291-3584	669
Town Bank 850 W N Shore Dr *Web:* www.townbank.us	Hartland	WI	53029	262-367-1900		70
Town Cats PO Box 1828 *Web:* www.towncats.org	Morgan Hill	CA	95038	408-779-5761		48-13
Town East Mall 2063 Town E Mall *Web:* www.towneastmall.com	Mesquite	TX	75150	972-270-2363		460
Town Fair Tire Company Inc 460 Coe Ave *TF:* 800-972-2245 ■ *Web:* www.townfairtire.com	East Haven	CT	06512	800-972-2245		54
Town Food Service Equipment Co 72 Beadel St *TF:* 800-221-5032 ■ *Web:* www.townfood.com	Brooklyn	NY	11222	718-388-5650	388-5860	298
Town Hall 342 Howard St *Web:* townhallsf.com	San Francisco	CA	94105	415-908-3900	908-3700	671
Town Inn Suites 620 Church St *TF:* 800-387-2755 ■ *Web:* www.towninn.com	Toronto	ON	M4Y2G2	416-964-3311		379
Town Motors Inc 135 S Dean St *TF:* 877-460-0730 ■ *Web:* www.townmotors.com	Englewood	NJ	07631	877-460-0730		57
Town of Cheektowaga Federal Credit Union 3251 Broadway *TF:* 888-241-2510 ■ *Web:* townofcheektowagafcu.com	Cheektowaga	NY	14227	716-686-3497	681-1436	219
Town of Collingwood 97 Hurontario St PO Box 157 *Web:* www.collingwood.ca	Collingwood	ON	L9Y3Z5	705-445-1030	445-2448	342
Town of East Hampton Connecticut 20 E High St *Web:* www.easthamptonct.gov	East Hampton	CT	06424	860-267-4426		434-3
Town of Hempstead Employees Federal Credit Union 1830 Grand Ave *Web:* tohefcu.org	Baldwin	NY	11510	516-867-4730		219
Town of Hilton Head Island 1 Town Center Ct *Web:* www.hiltonheadislandsc.gov	Hilton Head Island	SC	29928	843-341-4600	842-7728	337
Town Pump Inc 600 S Main St *TF:* 800-823-4931 ■ *Web:* www.townpump.com	Butte	MT	59701	406-497-6700		324
Town Square Publications LLC 155 E Algonquin Rd *Web:* townsquarepublications.com	Arlington Heights	IL	60005	847-427-4905		637-10
Town Talk Inc 6310 Cane Run Rd *TF:* 800-626-2220 ■ *Web:* www.ttcaps.com	Louisville	KY	40258	800-626-2220		155-9
Town Theatre 1012 Sumter St *Web:* www.towntheatre.com	Columbia	SC	29201	803-799-2510	799-6463	572
Town Topics 305 Witherspoon St *Web:* www.towntopics.com	Princeton	NJ	08542	609-924-2200	924-8818	532-4
Town West Realty Ii Inc 3002 N Campbell Ave Ste 200 *Web:* townwestrealty.com	Tucson	AZ	85719	520-615-7707		653

Name / Address	City	State	ZIP	Phone	Fax	Class
Towne AllPoints Communications Inc 3441 W MacArthur Blvd *Web:* www.towne.com	Santa Ana	CA	92704	714-540-3095		5
Towne Book Center & Caf 220 Plaza Dr Ste B-3 *Web:* www.townebc.com	Collegeville	PA	19426	610-454-0640	454-0653	95
Towne House, The 2209 St Joe Center Rd *Web:* www.townehouse.org	Fort Wayne	IN	46825	260-483-3116	969-8072	672
Towne Mailer 2424 S Garfield St *Web:* www.townemailer.com	Missoula	MT	59801	406-541-6245		5
Towne Realty Inc 710 N Plankinton Ave Ste 1000 *Web:* www.homesbytowne.com	Milwaukee	WI	53203	414-274-2920		652
Towne Technologies Inc 6-10 Bell Ave PO Box 460 *TF:* 800-837-2515 ■ *Web:* www.townetech.com	Somerville	NJ	08876	908-722-9500	722-8394	481
Towne, Ryan & Partners PC 450 New Karner Rd PO Box 15072 *Web:* townelaw.com	Albany	NY	12212	518-452-1800	452-6435	41
TowneBank 4501 Cox Rd *Web:* www.townebank.com	Glen Allen	VA	23060	804-967-7026		70
TowneBank Mortgage 600 22nd St Ste 300 *TF:* 888-637-1321 ■ *Web:* townebankmortgage.com	Virginia Beach	VA	23451	888-637-1321		509
Townes Tele-Communications Inc 120 E First St *TF:* 800-255-1975 ■ *Web:* www.walnuthilltel.com	Lewisville	AR	71845	870-921-4224		387
Townley Engineering & Manufacturing Company Inc 10551 SE 110th St Rd *TF:* 800-342-9920 ■ *Web:* www.townley.net	Candler	FL	32111	352-687-3001		641
Townley Inc 10 W 33rd Ste 418 *TF:* 844-486-9653 ■ *Web:* www.townleygirl.com	New York	NY	10001	844-486-9653		231
Towns County 1411 Jack Dayton Cir *TF:* 800-984-1543 ■ *Web:* www.golakechatuge.com	Young Harris	GA	30582	706-896-4966		338
Townscape Institute 8 Lowell St *Web:* www.townscape.org	Cambridge	MA	02138	617-491-8952	491-3734	637-2
Townsend Center for the Performing Arts 1601 Maple St *Web:* www.townsendcenter.org	Carrollton	GA	30118	678-839-4722		572
Townsend Energy 611 Main St Ste 202 *TF:* 855-721-2468 ■ *Web:* www.townsendtotalenergy.com	Winchester	MA	01890	855-721-2468		610
Townsend Farms Inc 23400 NE Townsend Way *TF:* 800-875-5291 ■ *Web:* townsendfarms.com	Fairview	OR	97024	503-666-1780		296-21
Townsend Hotel, The 100 Townsend St *Web:* www.townsendhotel.com	Birmingham	MI	48009	248-642-7900	645-9061	379
Townsend Manor Inn 714 Main St *Web:* www.townsendinn.com	Greenport	NY	11944	631-477-2000	477-2371	379
Townsend Press 439 Kelley Dr **Fax Area Code:* 800 ■ *TF:* 800-772-6410 ■ *Web:* www.townsendpress.com	West Berlin	NJ	08091	856-753-0554	225-8894*	637-2
Townsend Security 724 Columbia St NW *TF:* 800-357-1019 ■ *Web:* www.townsendsecurity.com	Olympia	WA	98501	360-359-4400		225
Townshend State Park 2755 State Forest Rd *Web:* www.vtstateparks.com	Townshend	VT	05353	802-365-7500		565
Township Auditorium 1703 Taylor St *Web:* www.thetownship.org	Columbia	SC	29201	803-576-2350	576-2359	572
Township of Upper St Clair 1820 Mclaughlin Run Rd *Web:* www.twpusc.org	Upper Saint Clair	PA	15241	412-831-9000	831-9882	434-3
Townsquare Media Inc 240 Greenwich Ave *Web:* www.townsquaremedia.com	Greenwich	CT	06830	203-861-0900		643
Towpath Credit Union Inc 2969 Smith Rd *Web:* towpathcu.com	Fairlawn	OH	44333	330-664-4700		219
Towsleys Inc 1424 Dewey St PO Box 2140 *Web:* www.towsleys.com	Manitowoc	WI	54220	800-364-1552		366
Towson University 8000 York Rd *TF:* 866-301-3375 ■ *Web:* www.towson.edu	Towson	MD	21252	410-704-2113	704-3030	166
Toxikon Corp 15 Wiggins Ave *TF:* 800-458-4141 ■ *Web:* www.toxikon.com	Bedford	MA	01730	781-275-3330	271-1138	743
Tox-Pressotechnik LLC 4250 Weaver Pkwy *Web:* us.tox-pressotechnik.com	Warrenville	IL	60555	630-393-0300	393-6800	385
ToxServices LLC 1367 Connecticut Ave NW Ste 300 *Web:* toxservices.com	Washington	DC	20036	202-429-8787	429-8788	196
TOY (Theatre of Youth) 203 Allen St *Web:* www.theatreofyouth.org	Buffalo	NY	14201	716-884-4400		573-4
Toy and Train Publishing Co 5518 Willys Ave *Web:* www.toyandtrainguides.com	Halethorpe	MD	21227	410-247-2220		637-2
Toy Connection Inc 22 Lawrence Ln *TF:* 877-869-8691 ■ *Web:* www.toyconnection.com	Lawrence	NY	11559	516-371-9206		761
Toy Farmer Ltd 7496 106th Ave SE *TF:* 800-533-8293 ■ *Web:* www.toyfarmer.com	Lamoure	ND	58458	701-883-5206	883-5209	44
Toy Industry Assn 1115 Broadway Ste 400 *Web:* www.toyassociation.org	New York	NY	10010	212-675-1141	633-1429	49-4
Toy Scouts Inc 137 Casterton Ave *Web:* www.toyscouts.com	Akron	OH	44303	330-869-8668		761
Toyo Denki USA Inc 2507 Lovi Rd Tri-County Commerce Pk Bldg No 3 *Web:* www.toyodenkiusa.com	Freedom	PA	15042	724-774-1760	774-1695	60
Toyo Ink America LLC 1225 N Michael Dr *TF:* 866-969-8696 ■ *Web:* www.toyoink.com	Wood Dale	IL	60191	630-930-5100	628-1769	388
Toyo Tanso USA Inc 2575 NW Graham Cir *Web:* www.ttu.com	Troutdale	OR	97060	503-661-7700		127
Toyo Tires 6261 Katella Ave Ste 2B *TF:* 800-678-3250 ■ *Web:* www.toyotires.com	Cypress	CA	90630	800-678-3250		754
Toyobo Industrial Materials America Inc 7526 Roy Owens Blvd *Web:* www.toyobo.co.jp	Scottsboro	AL	35769	256-575-2579	575-2569	745-1
Toyobo USA Inc 666 3rd Ave Ste 603 *Web:* www.toyobousa.com	New York	NY	10174	212-398-0550	398-9726	238
Toyoda Machinery USA Inc 316 W University Dr *TF:* 800-257-2985 ■ *Web:* www.toyoda.com	Arlington Heights	IL	60004	847-253-0340	577-4680	455
Toyon Associates Inc 1800 Sutter St Ste 600 *Web:* www.toyonassociates.com	Concord	CA	94520	925-685-9312		401
Toyota Canada Inc 1 Toyota Pl *TF:* 888-869-6828 ■ *Web:* www.toyota.ca	Scarborough	ON	M1H1H9	888-869-6828		59
Toyota Motor Manufacturing Indiana Inc 4000 Tulip Tree Dr *TF:* 888-696-8211 ■ *Web:* tourtoyota.com	Princeton	IN	47670	812-387-2266		59
Toyota Motor Manufacturing Kentucky Inc 1001 Cherry Blossom Way *Web:* www.toyotageorgetown.com	Georgetown	KY	40324	502-868-2000		59
Toyota Motor Sales USA Inc 19001 S Western Ave *TF:* 800-331-4331 ■ *Web:* www.toyota.com	Torrance	CA	90501	310-468-4000	468-7814	59
Toyota of Greenwich 75 E Putnam Ave *Web:* www.toyotaofgreenwich.com	Cos Cob	CT	06807	203-661-5055		57
Toyota of Portsmouth 150 Greenleaf Ave *Web:* www.toyotaofportsmouth.com	Portsmouth	NH	03801	603-280-4239		57
Toyota of Watertown Inc 149 Arsenal St *TF:* 888-375-7952 ■ *Web:* www.toyotaofwatertown.com	Watertown	MA	02472	888-375-7952		57
Toyota Sunnyvale 898 W El Camino Real *TF:* 888-210-0091 ■ *Web:* www.toyotasunnyvale.com	Sunnyvale	CA	94087	408-338-0063		57
Toyota Tsusho America Inc 805 3rd Ave 17th Fl *Web:* www.taiamerica.com	New York	NY	10022	212-355-3600		492
Toyotetsu America Inc 100 Pin Oak Dr *Web:* ttna.com	Somerset	KY	42503	606-274-9005	274-4975	489
Toys 'R' US (Canada) Ltd 2777 Langstaff Rd *TF:* 800-869-7787 ■ *Web:* www.toysrus.ca	Concord	ON	L4K4M5	800-869-7787		761
TP (Technical Products Inc) 805 Marathon Pky Ste 150 *TF:* 800-226-8434 ■ *Web:* www.techproductsga.com	Lawrenceville	GA	30046	770-236-8452	236-8453	475
TP Freight Lines Inc 2703 3rd St *TF:* 800-558-8217 ■ *Web:* www.tpfreight.net	Tillamook	OR	97141	503-842-2574	842-6156	780
TP ICAP 1100 Plaza Five *Web:* www.icap.com	Jersey City	NJ	07311	212-732-6900		690
TP Orthodontics Inc 100 Center Plz *TF:* 800-348-8856 ■ *Web:* www.tportho.com	La Porte	IN	46350	219-785-2591	324-3029	228
TP Trucking LLC 5630 Table Rock Rd *TF:* 800-292-4399 ■ *Web:* www.tptrucking.com	Central Point	OR	97502	800-292-4399		780
TPC (Transaction Processing Performance Council) 572 Ruger St *Web:* www.tpc.org	San Francisco	CA	94129	415-561-6272		48-9
TPC Advance Technology Inc 18525 Gale Ave *TF:* 800-560-8222 ■ *Web:* www.tpcdental.com	City of Industry	CA	91748	626-810-4337		475
TPG (Plus Group Inc, The) 7425 Janes Ave Ste 201 *Web:* theplusgroup.com	Woodridge	IL	60517	630-515-0500	515-0510	721
TPG Capital LP 301 Commerce St Ste 3300 *Web:* www.tpg.com	Fort Worth	TX	76102	817-871-4000		402
TPG Direct 444 N Third St Ste 401 *Web:* www.tpgdirect.com	Philadelphia	PA	19123	267-825-9511		7
TPG Marine Enterprises LLC 1341 N Capitol Ave *Web:* www.tpgmarine.com	Indianapolis	IN	46202	317-631-0234	631-0230	225
Tpgtex Label Solutions Inc 5830 Ludington Dr *Web:* www.tpgtex.com	Houston	TX	77035	713-726-9636		88
TPI (Thinkers' Press Inc) 1524 LeClaire St *Web:* www.thinkerspressinc.com	Davenport	IA	52803	563-271-6657		96
TPI (Tucker Publications Inc) PO Box 580 *Web:* www.tuckerpub.com	Lisle	IL	60532	630-969-0221		637-2
TPI Corp PO Box 4973 *TF:* 800-682-3398 ■ *Web:* www.tpicorp.com	Johnson City	TN	37602	800-682-3398		15
TPI Powder Metallurgy Inc 12030 Beaver Rd *Web:* www.tpipm.com	Saint Charles	MI	48655	989-865-9921	865-9924	482
TPI Staffing Inc 21840 Northwest Fwy Ste E *Web:* www.tpistaffing.com	Cypress	TX	77429	281-890-2220		260
TPL (Trust for Public Land) 116 New Montgomery St 4th Fl *TF:* 800-714-5263 ■ *Web:* www.tpl.org	San Francisco	CA	94105	415-495-4014	495-4103	48-13
TPL (Tuxedo Park Library) 227 Route 17 *Web:* www.tuxedoparklibrary.org	Tuxedo Park	NY	10987	845-351-2207	351-2213	434-3
TPM Life Insurance Co 1850 William Penn Way Ste 202 *TF:* 800-555-3122 ■ *Web:* tpmins.com	Lancaster	PA	17601	717-394-7156		390
TPS Aviation Inc 1515 Crocker Ave *TF:* 800-475-4877 ■ *Web:* www.tpsaviation.com	Hayward	CA	94544	510-475-1010	475-8817	770
TPS Consulting Engineers Ltd 3306 Commodity Ln PO Box 10793 *Web:* tpseng.com	Green Bay	WI	54304	920-337-0500		261
TPS Houston Group LLC 7101 John Ralston Rd *Web:* www.tpshoustongroup.com	Houston	TX	77044	281-459-2435		518
TpSEF Inc 101 Hudson St *Web:* www.tullettprebon.com	Jersey City	NJ	07302	201-557-5000	557-5995	691
TPx Communications 1181 Grier Dr Ste F *TF:* 888-407-9594 ■ *Web:* www.tpx.com	Las Vegas	NV	89119	702-851-6000		387

Company	Phone	Fax	Class
TQL (Total Quality Logistics Inc) 4289 Ivy Pointe Blvd. Cincinnati OH 45245 *TF:* 800-580-3101 ■ *Web:* www.tql.com	513-831-2600	965-7630	311
TR Design Inc 115 Tucker Farm Rd North Andover MA 01845 *Web:* trdesign.com	978-237-5945		195
TR International Trading Company Inc 1218 Third Ave Ste 2100 Seattle WA 98101 *TF:* 800-761-7717 ■ *Web:* www.trichemicals.com	206-505-3500	505-3501	146
TR Miller Mill Company Inc 215 Deer St PO Box 708 Brewton AL 36427 *TF:* 800-633-6740 ■ *Web:* www.trmillermill.com	251-867-4331	867-6882	683
TR Publishing 3457 Via Zara Ct. Fallbrook CA 92028 *Web:* www.trpublishing.com	805-712-5060		637-2
TRA (Thoroughbred Racing Associations of North America Inc) 420 Fair Hill Dr. Elkton MD 21921 *TF:* 866-847-8772 ■ *Web:* thoroughbredracingassociations.com	410-392-9200		48-22
Trabert & Hoeffer 111 E Oak St Chicago IL 60611 *TF:* 800-539-3573 ■ *Web:* www.trabertandhoeffer.com	312-787-1654		410
Trabolsi & Levy LLP 9255 W Sunset Blvd Ste 720 West Hollywood CA 90069 *Web:* tlfamlaw.com	310-453-6226		41
Trabon Printing Company Inc 430 E Bannister Rd Kansas City MO 64131 *Web:* www.trabongroup.com	816-361-6279		627
TRAC Media Services 2030 E Speedway Blvd Ste 210 Tucson AZ 85719 *TF:* 888-299-1866 ■ *Web:* www.tracmedia.com	520-299-1866	577-6077	632
Trace Environmental Systems Inc 7 Park Lake Rd Ste 9 Sparta NJ 07871 *Web:* www.traceenv.com	973-383-3550		196
Trace3 15326 Alton Pkwy Irvine CA 92618 *Web:* trace3.com	949-333-2300		180
Trace3 Inc 390 Spaulding Ave SE Ada MI 49301 *TF:* 888-981-3282 ■ *Web:* www.trace3.com	888-981-3282		196
Trace-A-Matic Inc (T-A-M) 21125 Enterprise Ave Brookfield WI 53045 *TF:* 877-375-0217 ■ *Web:* www.traceamatic.com	262-797-7300		621
Tracelogix Corp 3605 Knight Rd Ste 101 Memphis TN 38118 *Web:* www.tracelogix.com	901-795-2777		175
TraceSecurity Inc 6300 Corporate Blvd Ste 200 Baton Rouge LA 70809 *TF:* 877-275-3009 ■ *Web:* www.tracesecurity.com	225-612-2121	612-2269	463
Trachte Building Systems Inc (TBS) 314 Wilburn Rd Sun Prairie WI 53590 *TF:* 800-356-5824 ■ *Web:* www.trachte.com	800-356-5824	981-9014	105
Tracie Martyn Salon 101 Fifth Ave 11th Fl New York NY 10003 *TF:* 866-862-7896 ■ *Web:* www.traciemartyn.com	212-206-9333		706
Tracinda Corp 150 S Rodeo Dr Ste 250 Beverly Hills CA 90212	310-271-0638		405
Track Master 2083 Old Middlefield Way Ste 206 Mountain View CA 94043 *TF:* 800-334-3800 ■ *Web:* www.trackmaster.com	650-316-1020		642
TrackAbout Inc 410 Rouser Rd Ste 400 Moon Township PA 15108 *TF:* 855-999-7692 ■ *Web:* corp.trackabout.com	412-269-0642		177
TrackCore Inc 25 Commerce Ave SW Ste 200 Grand Rapids MI 49503 *Web:* www.trackcoreinc.com	616-632-2222	632-2225	177
Trackers Earth Portland 4617 SE Milwaukie Ave Portland OR 97202 *TF:* 800-522-0255 ■ *Web:* trackerspdx.com	503-345-3312		138
Trackmobile Inc 1602 Executive Dr LaGrange GA 30240 *Web:* trackmobile.com	706-884-6651	884-0390	650
Traco Medical Inc (TM) 4001 W Tickman St. Sioux Falls SD 57101 *Web:* www.tracomedical.com	605-339-9339	334-3025	475
TRACOM Group, The 6675 S Kenton St Ste 118 Centennial CO 80111 *TF:* 800-221-2321 ■ *Web:* tracom.com	303-470-4900		193
TRACS (TransNational Association of Christian Colleges & Schools) 15935 Forest Rd Forest VA 24551 *Web:* www.tracs.org	434-525-9539	616-2638	48-1
Tractenberg & Co 116 E 16th St New York NY 10003 *Web:* www.tractenbergandco.com	212-929-7979		5
Traction Consulting Group 28525 Beck Rd Ste 105 Wixom MI 48393 *Web:* www.tractioncrm.com	248-679-9454		180
Traction Corp 1349 Larkin St. San Francisco CA 94109 *Web:* www.tractionco.com	415-962-5800		7
Tractor Supply Co 5401 Virginia Way Brentwood TN 37027 *NASDAQ: TSCO* ■ *TF:* 877-718-6750 ■ *Web:* www.tractorsupply.com	615-440-4000		274
Trac-Work Inc 3801 N I-45 Ennis TX 75119 *Web:* www.trac-work.com	972-875-6565		188-8
Tracy Aviary 589 East 1300 South Salt Lake City UT 84105 *Web:* tracyaviary.org	801-596-8500		823
Tracy Chamber of Commerce 223 E 10th St Tracy CA 95376 *Web:* www.tracychamber.org	209-835-2131	833-9526	139
Tracy Davis Insurance Agency Inc 919 N Fort Thomas Ave Fort Thomas KY 41075 *Web:* tracydavisins.com	859-781-5313		390
Tracy Printing Inc 3813 Chandler Dr NE Minneapolis MN 55421 *Web:* www.tracyprinting.com	612-788-2331	788-5046	627
Tracy Time Systems Inc 230 32nd St SE Grand Rapids MI 49548 *Web:* tracyinc.com	616-241-1661		180
Tracy-Luckey Company Inc PO Box 880 Harlem GA 30814	706-556-6216		11-1
Trade associates group Ltd 900 W Bliss St Chicago IL 60642 *TF:* 800-621-8350 ■ *Web:* www.tagltd.com	773-871-1300	871-8432	321
Trade Coffee & Coworking, The 2220 K St Sacramento CA 95816 *Web:* www.thetradecollab.com	916-538-6878		393
Trade Exchange of America 23200 Coolidge Hwy Oak Park MI 48237 *Web:* www.tradefirst.com	248-544-1350		691
Trade Manage Capital Inc 250 Greenwich St Waldwick NJ 07463 *TF:* 800-221-5676 ■ *Web:* www.yamner.com	201-587-2424		177
Trade Products Corp 12124 Popes Head Rd Fairfax VA 22030 *TF:* 888-352-3580 ■ *Web:* www.tradeproductscorp.com	703-502-9000	502-9399	320
Trade Service Company LLC 13280 Evening Creek Dr S Ste 200 San Diego CA 92128 *TF:* 800-854-1527 ■ *Web:* tradeservice.com	800-418-4363		224
Trade Technologies Inc 4601 Spicewood Springs Rd Bldg 3 Ste 100 Austin TX 78759 *Web:* www.tradetechnologies.com	512-327-9996	233-2819	317
Trade Union International Inc 4651 State St Montclair CA 91763 *Web:* www.tradeunion.com.tw	909-628-7500	628-0382	60
TradeHelm Inc 125 S Clark St 17th Fl Chicago IL 60603 *Web:* www.tradehelm.com	312-821-4600		690
Tradelink Securities LLC 71 S Wacker Dr Ste 1900 Chicago IL 60606 *Web:* www.tradelinkllc.com	312-264-2000		690
Trademark Co, The 344 Maple Ave W PO Box 151 Vienna VA 22180 *TF:* 800-906-8626 ■ *Web:* www.thetrademarkcompany.com	800-906-8626		317
Trademark Die & Engineering 8060 Graphic Industrial Dr Belmont MI 49306 *Web:* tmde.net	616-863-6660		697
Trademark Media Corp 2400 Webberville Rd Austin TX 78702 *TF:* 800-916-1224 ■ *Web:* www.mightycitizen.com	512-459-7000		7
Trademark Transportation Inc 739 Vandalia St. Saint Paul MN 55114 *TF:* 800-646-2550 ■ *Web:* www.trademarktrans.com	651-646-2500		311
Trader Joe's Co 800 S Shamrock Ave Monrovia CA 91016 *Web:* www.traderjoes.com	626-599-3700		345
Trader Vic's Inc 9 Anchor Dr. Emeryville CA 94608 *Web:* tradervicsemeryville.com	510-653-3400		670
Trader's Library LLC 6310 Stevens Forest Rd Ste 200 Columbia MD 21046 *TF:* 800-272-2855 ■ *Web:* www.traderslibrary.com	410-964-0026		690
TRADEREV 150 John St 5th Fl Toronto ON M2N3A1 **Fax Area Code: 888* ■ *TF:* 888-260-4604 ■ *Web:* www.traderev.com	647-933-1169	260-4605*	224
Tradesman Truck Accessories LLC 305 N Frisco St. Winters TX 79567	325-754-4561		54
Tradesmen International Inc 9760 Shepard Rd Macedonia OH 44056 *TF:* 800-573-0850 ■ *Web:* www.tradesmeninternational.com	440-349-3432		260
TradeStation Group Inc 8050 SW Tenth St Ste 2000 Plantation FL 33324 *TF:* 800-871-3577 ■ *Web:* www.tradestation.com	954-652-7000		178-10
TradeTech LLC 7887 E Belleview Ave Ste 888 Englewood CO 80111 *Web:* www.uranium.info	303-573-3530	573-3531	637-10
Tradewinds Carmel Mission St at Third Ave. Carmel By The Sea CA 93921 *Web:* tradewindscarmel.com	831-624-2776		379
Trading Direct 160 Broadway 7th Fl East Bldg New York NY 10038 *TF:* 800-925-8566 ■ *Web:* www.tradingdirect.com	212-766-0230	619-1593	690
Trading Places Intl 25510 Commercentre Dr Ste 100 Lake Forest CA 92630 *TF:* 800-365-7617 ■ *Web:* www.tradingplaces.com	800-365-7617		772
Trading Post Homes 490 Sparrow Dre. Shepherdsville KY 40165 *Web:* www.tphomes.com	502-955-5622		106
Tradition Asiel Securities Inc 255 Greenwich St 4th Fl New York NY 10007 *TF:* 866-220-5771 ■ *Web:* www.tradition.com	212-791-4500	791-6065	690
Tradition Capital Management LLC 129 Summit Ave Summit NJ 07901 *Web:* www.traditioncm.com	908-598-0909	847-0288	401
Traditional Bank 49 W Main St PO Box 326 Mount Sterling KY 40353 *TF:* 800-498-0414 ■ *Web:* www.traditionalbank.com	859-498-0414	987-3115	70
Traditional Door Design & Millwork Ltd 261 Regina Rd Woodbridge ON L4L8M3 *TF:* 877-226-9930 ■ *Web:* traditionaldoor.com	416-747-1992		234
Traditional Home Magazine 1716 Locust St Des Moines IA 50309 *Web:* www.bhg.com	515-284-3762		457-11
Traditional Values Coalition (TVC) 139 C St SE Washington DC 20003	202-547-4400		48-20
Traditions Performance Firearms 1375 Boston Post Rd Old Saybrook CT 06475 *Web:* www.traditionsfirearms.com	860-388-4656	388-4657	711
Tradr 12300 Wilshire Blvd Ste 200 Los Angeles CA 90025 *Web:* tradr.tv	310-584-9720		194
Traducta Inc 1590 Rue Ampere Bureau 300 Boucherville QC J4B7L4 *Web:* www.traducta.com	450-461-2252	655-2253	768
Trafalgar Castle School 401 Reynolds St Whitby ON L1N3W9 *Web:* www.trafalgarcastle.ca	905-668-3358	668-4136	622
Trafalgar Square Books 388 Howe Hill Rd North Pomfret VT 05053 *TF:* 800-423-4525 ■ *Web:* www.horseandriderbooks.com	802-457-1911	457-1913	637-2
Traffic & Civil Engineering Consulting Services PO Box 961 Los Gatos CA 95031 *Web:* www.trafficandcivilengineering.com	408-377-6222		196
Traffic Control Service Inc 2435 Lemon Ave. Signal Hill CA 90755 **Fax Area Code: 562* ■ *TF:* 800-763-3999 ■ *Web:* trafficmanagement.com	800-763-3999	424-0266*	264-3
Traffic Engineering Consultants Inc 6000 S W Ave Ste 300 Oklahoma City OK 73139 *Web:* www.tecusa.com	405-720-7721		261
Traffic Group Inc, The 9900 Franklin Sq Dr Baltimore MD 21236 *TF:* 800-583-8411 ■ *Web:* trafficgroup.com	410-931-6600		463

Listing	Phone	Fax	Class
Traffic Management Inc 8862 W 35W Service Dr NE, Minneapolis MN 55449 *TF:* 888-726-9559 ■ *Web:* trafficmgmt.com	763-544-3455	544-3458	194
Traffic Planning & Design Inc 2500 E High St Ste 650, Pottstown PA 19464 *Web:* www.trafficpd.com	610-326-3100		261
Traffic Signal Hardware Inc 5740 E Dayton Ave, Fresno CA 93727 *Web:* www.trafficsignalhardware.com	909-623-4556		392
TrafFix Devices Inc 160 Avenida La Pata, San Clemente CA 92673 *Web:* www.traffixdevices.com	949-361-5663	573-9250	295
Trager, Kevy & Trager LLP 141 Willis Ave, Mineola NY 11501 *Web:* tktcpa.com	516-292-9494	741-1010	2
Tragon Corp 365 Convention Way, Redwood City CA 94063 *Web:* www.tragon.com	650-365-1833		463
Tragos, Sartes & Tragos PLLC 601 Cleveland St Ste 800, Clearwater FL 33755 *Web:* tragoslaw.com	727-475-7427		41
Trahan Burden & Charles Inc (TBC) 3601 O'Donnell St Ste 100-The Barrel Bldg, Baltimore MD 21224 *Web:* www.tbc.us	410-347-7500	986-1299	4
Trahan Lori (Rep D - MA) 1616 Longworth House Office Bldg, Washington DC 20515 *Web:* www.trahan.house.gov	202-225-3411		342-2
Trail Blazers 394 Rogers Ave, Brooklyn NY 11225 *Web:* www.trailblazers.org	212-529-5113		717
Trail Creek Ranch 7100 W Trl Creek Rd PO Box 10, Wilson WY 83014 *Web:* trailcreekranch.com	307-733-2610		239
Trail End State Historic Site 400 Clarendon Ave, Sheridan WY 82801 *Web:* trailend.org	307-674-4589	672-1720	565
Trail King Industries Inc 300 E Norway, Mitchell SD 57301 **Fax Area Code:* 605 ■ *TF:* 800-843-3324 ■ *Web:* www.trailking.com	800-843-3324	996-4727*	779
Trail of Tears State Forest 3240 State Forest Rd, Jonesboro IL 62952 *Web:* www2.illinois.gov	618-833-4910		565
Trail of Tears State Park 429 Moccasin Springs, Jackson MO 63755 *Web:* mostateparks.com	573-290-5268		565
Trail Smoke Eaters Hockey Club 1051 Victoria St, Trail BC V1R3T3 *Web:* www.trailsmokeeaters.com	250-364-9994		354
Trailblazer Foods 17900 NE San Rafael, Portland OR 97230 *Web:* www.trailblazerfoods.com	503-666-5800	666-6000	296-20
Trailblazer Studios Nc Inc 1610 Midtown Pl, Raleigh NC 27609 *Web:* trailblazerstudios.com	919-645-6600		514
Trailer Bridge Inc 10405 New Berlin Rd E, Jacksonville FL 32226 *OTC: TRBRQ* ■ *TF:* 800-554-1589 ■ *Web:* www.trailerbridge.com	904-751-7100	751-7444	312
Trailer Park Inc 6922 Hollywood Blvd 12th Fl, Hollywood CA 90028 *Web:* www.trailerpark.com	310-845-3000		344
Trailer Transit Inc 1130 E US 20, Porter IN 46304 **Fax Area Code:* 877 ■ *TF:* 800-423-3647 ■ *Web:* www.trailertransit.com	219-926-2111	859-1191*	780
Trailer Wizards Ltd 10387 Nordel Ct, Delta BC V4G1J9 *Web:* trailerwizards.com	604-464-2220		126
Trailercraft Inc 222 W 92nd Ave, Anchorage AK 99515 *TF:* 800-478-3238 ■ *Web:* trailercraft.com	907-563-3238		516
Trailhead Athletic Club LLC 7900 E Eagle Crest Dr, Mesa AZ 85207 *Web:* www.thetrailhead.org	480-832-6900		354
Trailiner Corp 2169 E Blaine St, Springfield MO 65803 *TF:* 800-833-8209 ■ *Web:* trailiner.com	417-866-7258		779
Trailines Inc 10045 Windisch Rd, West Chester OH 45069 *Web:* trailines.com	513-755-7900		311
Trailstar Manufacturing Corp 20700 Harrisburg-Westville Rd PO Box 2086, Alliance OH 44601 *Web:* trailstarintl.com	330-821-9900	821-6941	779
Trailways Transportation System Inc 3554 Chain Bridge Rd Ste 202, Fairfax VA 22030 *TF:* 877-467-3346 ■ *Web:* www.trailways.com	703-691-3052	691-9047	107
Trainertainment LLC PO Box 2168, Keller TX 76248 *TF:* 800-860-8474 ■ *Web:* trainertainment.net	817-886-4840		463
Training Advantage, The 365 Goddard Ave PO Box 800, Ignacio CO 81137 *Web:* sococaa.org	970-563-4517		108
Training Associates Corp, The 287 Tpke Rd, Westborough MA 01581 *Web:* thetrainingassociates.com	508-890-8500		631
Training Industry Inc 401 Harrison Oaks Blvd Ste 300, Cary NC 27513 *TF:* 866-298-4203 ■ *Web:* trainingindustry.com	866-298-4203		393
Training Institute for Mental Health 115 W 27th St 4th Fl, New York NY 10001 **Fax Area Code:* 646 ■ *Web:* www.timh.org	212-627-8181	638-3025*	167-3
Training Magazine 27020 Noble Rd, Excelsior MN 55331 *TF:* 877-865-9361 ■ *Web:* trainingmag.com	847-559-7596		457-5
Training Modernization Group Inc 9737 Peppertree Rd, Spotsylvania VA 22553 *TF:* 866-855-6449 ■ *Web:* www.tmgva.com	540-295-9313		196
Training Resources Ltd 3980 Sherman St Ste 100, San Diego CA 92110 *TF:* 888-262-8020 ■ *Web:* www.trlmi.com	619-263-1638	523-9178	167-3
Training to Inc 2200 N Central Ave Ste 400, Phoenix AZ 85004 *Web:* www.trainingtoyou.com	602-266-1500		94
Trainworld Associates LLC 751 Mcdonald Ave, Brooklyn NY 11218 *TF:* 800-541-7010 ■ *Web:* www.trainworld.com	718-436-7072		761
Trak Com Wireless Inc 3780 14th Ave Unit 101, Markham ON L3R4B7 *Web:* www.trakcom.com	905-474-9935	474-9938	647
Trak-1 Technology Co 7131 Riverside Pkwy, Tulsa OK 74136 *Web:* trak-1.com	918-779-7000	779-6500	194
TrakLok Corp 11020 Solway School Rd Ste 112, Knoxville TN 37931 *Web:* www.traklokintl.com	865-927-4911		692
TRALA (Truck Renting & Leasing Assn) 675 N Washington St Ste 410, Alexandria VA 22314 *Web:* www.trala.org	703-299-9120		49-21
Trale In 14229 W Commerce Rd, Daleville IN 47334 *Web:* www.trale.com	765-378-5509		463
Tram's Kitchen 4050 Penn Ave, Pittsburgh PA 15224	412-682-2688		671
Tramac Corp 26 Eastmans Rd, Parsippany NJ 07054 *Web:* www.tramac.com	973-887-7700	887-7784	358
Tramco Pump Co 1500 W Adams St, Chicago IL 60607 *Web:* www.tramcopump.com	312-243-5800	243-0702	641
Tramex Travel Inc 4505 Spicewood Springs Rd Ste 200, Austin TX 78759 **Fax Area Code:* 512 ■ *TF:* 800-527-3039 ■ *Web:* tramex.com	800-527-3039	343-0022*	771
Trammell Crow Co 2100 McKinney Ave Ste 800, Dallas TX 75201 *Web:* www.trammellcrow.com	214-863-4101	863-4493	655
Trammell Crow Residential (TCR) 3889 Maple St, Dallas TX 75219 *Web:* www.crowholdings.com	214-922-8400		653
Tramont Corp 3701 N Humboldt Blvd, Milwaukee WI 53212 *Web:* www.tramont.com	414-967-8800		554
Tramz Hotels LLC 776 Mountain Blvd Ste 200, Watchung NJ 07069 *Web:* www.tramzhotels.com	908-753-7400		378
Tran Cert Marketing Inc 1559 Ocean View Ln Ste 880, Point Roberts WA 98281 *Web:* www.trancertmarketing.com	360-945-2190		463
Trana Discovery Inc 2054-260 Kildare Farm Rd, Cary NC 27518 *Web:* www.tranadiscovery.com	919-295-6116		231
Trancy Logistics America Corp 1670 Dolwick Rd Ste 8, Erlanger KY 41018 *Web:* trancyamerica.com	859-282-7780	282-7784	311
Trandes Corp 4601 Presidents Dr Ste 360, Lanham MD 20706 *Web:* www.trandes.com	301-459-0200	459-1069	261
Traner Smith & Company PS 201 Fifth Ave S Ste 202, Edmonds WA 98020 *Web:* tranersmith.com	425-640-8650		2
Tranergy Inc 726 Foster Ave, Bensenville IL 60106 *Web:* tranergy.com	630-238-9338		770
Trang Pharmacy 456 Park Ave, Worcester MA 01610 *Web:* www.cornerdrugstore.com	508-799-7979		237
Trans Air Manufacturing Corp 480 E Locust St, Dallastown PA 17313 *TF:* 800-221-7198 ■ *Web:* www.transairmfg.com	717-246-2627		14
Trans Med USA Inc 31 Progress Ave, Tyngsboro MA 01879 *TF:* 800-649-1200 ■ *Web:* www.transmed-usa.com	978-649-1970		475
Trans Ova Genetics LC 2938 380th St, Sioux Center IA 51250 *Web:* www.transova.com	712-722-3586		794
Trans Pacific Distributors 1941 Walters Ct, Fairfield CA 94533 *TF:* 800-688-6208 ■ *Web:* www.transpacificdist.com	707-426-6670	426-0206	385
Trans Pacific National Bank 88 Kearny St Ste 1750, San Francisco CA 94108 *Web:* www.tpnb.com	415-543-3377	543-7275	360-2
Trans Tech Energy LLC PO Box 8197, Rocky Mount NC 27804 *TF:* 888-206-4563 ■ *Web:* www.transtechenergy.com	252-446-4357	446-1374	538
Trans World Assurance Co 885 S El Camino Real, San Mateo CA 94402 *TF:* 866-007-6310 ■ *Web:* www.twasite.com	650-348-2300	348-7318	796
Trans World Corp (TWC) 545 5th Ave Ste 940, New York NY 10017 *OTC: TWOC* ■ *Web:* www.transwc.com	212-983-3355	983-8129	379
Trans World Marketing Corp 360 Murray Hill Pkwy, East Rutherford NJ 07073 *Web:* twm360.com	201-935-5565	559-2011	233
Trans1 Inc 3804 Park Ave Ste C, Wilmington NC 28403 *TF:* 888-526-1879 ■ *Web:* www.trans1.com	888-526-1879		476
Transact Commercial Interiors 2034 N 3rd St, Phoenix AZ 85004 **Fax Area Code:* 123 ■ *Web:* transactinteriors.com	602-251-3838	456-7890*	321
TransAct Technologies Inc 1 Hamden Ctr 2319 Whitney Ave Ste 3B, Hamden CT 06518 *NASDAQ: TACT* ■ **Fax Area Code:* 203 ■ *TF:* 800-243-8941 ■ *Web:* www.transact-tech.com	800-243-8941	949-9048*	173-6
Transaction Network Services Inc 10740 Parkridge Blvd Ste 100, Reston VA 20191 *TF:* 866-523-0661 ■ *Web:* www.tnsi.com	703-453-8300		215
Transaction Packing Inc 15894 Diplomatic Plaza Dr Ste 200, Houston TX 77032 *Web:* www.transactionpacking.com	281-443-0476	443-0503	549
Transaction Processing Performance Council (TPC) 572 Ruger St, San Francisco CA 94129 *Web:* www.tpc.org	415-561-6272		48-9
Transaero Inc 35 Melville Park Rd Ste 100, Melville NY 11747 *Web:* www.transaeroinc.com	631-752-1240		22
Transalta Tri Leisure Ctr 221 Jennifer Heil Way, Spruce Grove AB T7X4J5 *Web:* www.trileisure.com	780-960-5080		354
Transam Travel Inc 4222 King St, Alexandria VA 22302 *TF:* 800-822-7600 ■ *Web:* www.transamtravel.com	703-998-7676	824-8190	16
TransAm Trucking Inc 15910 S 169th Hwy, Olathe KS 66062 *Web:* www.transamtruck.com	913-782-5300	324-7063	780
Transamerica Corp 440 Mamaroneck Ave, Harrison NY 10528 *Web:* www.divinvest.com	914-627-3000		401
Transamerica Corp 4333 Edgewood Rd NE, Cedar Rapids IA 52499 *TF:* 800-852-4678 ■ *Web:* www.transamerica.com	319-355-8511		391-5
Transamerica Series Trust 570 Carillon Pky, Saint Petersburg FL 33716 *TF:* 888-233-4339 ■ *Web:* www.transamericaseriestrust.com	888-233-4339		401

Company	Phone	Fax	Class
Transat AT Inc 300 Leo-Pariseau St Ste 600 .... Montreal QC H2X4C2 *TSE:* TRZ ■ *Web:* www.transat.com	514-987-1616	987-8035	771
Trans-Atlantic Publications Inc 311 Bainbridge St........ Philadelphia PA 19147 *Web:* www.transatlanticpub.com	215-925-5083	925-1912	96
Transaver LLC 108 Washington St........ Manlius NY 13104 *TF:* 800-698-8629 ■ *Web:* www.transaver.com	315-399-1200		311
Transaxle Manufacturing of America 240 Waterford Park Dr .... Rock Hill SC 29730 *Web:* www.tma-us.com	803-329-8900	329-8831	247
Trans-Border Global Freight Systems Inc 2103 Rt 9 .... Round Lake NY 12151 *TF:* 800-493-9444 ■ *Web:* www.tbgfs.com	518-785-6000	785-6239	311
Transbotics 3400 Latrobe Dr........ Charlotte NC 28211 *OTC:* TNSB ■ *Web:* www.scottautomation.com	704-362-1115	364-4039	529
Trans-Bridge Lines Inc 2012 Industrial Dr........ Bethlehem PA 18017 *TF:* 800-556-3815 ■ *Web:* www.transbridgelines.com	610-868-6001	868-9057	108
TransCanada Pipelines Ltd 450 1st St SW........ Calgary AB T2P5H1 *TF:* 800-661-3805 ■ *Web:* www.tcenergy.com	403-936-3334	920-2200	325
Trans-Carriers Inc 5135 US Hwy 78........ Memphis TN 38118 *TF:* 800-999-7383 ■ *Web:* transcarriers.com	901-368-0336		780
Transcat Inc 35 Vantage Pt Dr........ Rochester NY 14624 *NASDAQ:* TRNS ■ *TF:* 800-800-5001 ■ *Web:* www.transcat.com	585-352-9460	352-1486	201
Transcend Information Inc 1645 N Brian St .... Orange CA 92867 *Web:* us.transcend-info.com	714-921-2000	921-2111	174
Transcend Translations 2043 Anderson Rd Ste C .... Davis CA 95616 *Web:* transcend.net	530-756-5834	756-4810	768
Transcendent LLC 1040 Cottonwood Ave Ste 300........ Hartland WI 53029 *Web:* www.transcendent-llc.com	262-953-2750		177
Transcepta LLC 135 Columbia Ste 202 .... Aliso Viejo CA 92656 *Web:* www.transcepta.com	949-382-2840		317
TransChemical Inc 419 De Soto Ave .... Saint Louis MO 63147 *TF:* 888-873-6481 ■ *Web:* www.transchemical.com	314-231-6905	231-5851	146
Transco Business Technologies (TBT) 34 Leighton Rd........ Augusta ME 04330 *TF:* 800-322-0003 ■ *Web:* www.transcobusiness.com	800-452-4657		112
Transco Industries Inc 5534 NE 122nd Ave .... Portland OR 97230 *TF:* 800-545-9991 ■ *Web:* www.transco-ind.com	503-256-1955	256-0723	207
Transco Products Inc 1215 E 12th St .... Streator IL 61364 *Web:* www.transcoproducts.com	815-672-2197	673-2432	389
Transco Railway Products Inc 200 N LaSalle St Ste 1550 .... Chicago IL 60601 *TF:* 800-472-4592 ■ *Web:* www.transcorailway.com	312-427-2818		650
Transcom General Agency Inc 216 N Midvale Blvd PO Box 5368 .... Madison WI 53705 *Web:* transcom-ga.com	608-232-5330		390
Transcom Telecommunications 3744 Industry Ave........ Lakewood CA 90712 *Web:* www.transcomla.com	562-663-2000		387
TransCon Builders Inc 25250 Rockside Rd........ Cleveland OH 44146 *TF:* 800-451-2608 ■ *Web:* www.transconbuilders.com	440-439-2100	439-6710	653
Transcon Inc 8824 Twinbrook Rd .... Mentor OH 44060 *Web:* www.transconinc.com	440-255-7600	255-3446	207
Transcon Trading Company Inc 141 Centrum Dr .... Irmo SC 29063 *TF:* 877-397-2390 ■ *Web:* www.transcontrading.com	803-781-7117	781-8545	297-8
Transcontinental Inc 1 Pl Ville Marie Ste 3240 .... Montreal QC H3B0G1 *TSE:* TCL.A ■ *Web:* tctranscontinental.com	514-954-4000	954-4016	627
Transcontinental Inc 700 Crestdale St........ Matthews NC 28105 *Web:* www.coverisadvancedcoatings.com	704-847-9171	845-4307	552-1
Trans-Continental Systems Inc 10801 Evendale Dr........ Cincinnati OH 45241 *TF:* 800-525-8726 ■ *Web:* www.tcsohio.com	513-769-4774		648
TransCore 150 Fourth Ave N Ste 1200 .... Nashville TN 37219 *TF:* 800-923-4824 ■ *Web:* www.transcore.com	615-988-7044		261
Transcosmos America Inc 879 W 190th St Ste 410........ Gardena CA 90248 **Fax Area Code:* 310 ■ *TF:* 844-630-2224 ■ *Web:* www.transcosmos.net	844-630-2224	630-0074*	195
Transcounty Title Co 635 W 19th St .... Merced CA 95340 *Web:* transcountytitle.com	209-383-4660		653
Transcript Pharmacy Inc 2506 Lakeland Dr Ste 201 .... Flowood MS 39232 *TF:* 866-420-4041 ■ *Web:* www.noblehealthservices.com	866-420-4041		237
Transcript, The Ohio Wesleyan University 104 Phillips Hall ...... Delaware OH 43015 *Web:* www.owutranscript.com	740-368-2911		532-2
TranscriptionGear Inc 7280 Auburn Rd........ Painesville OH 44077 *TF:* 888-834-2392 ■ *Web:* www.transcriptiongear.com	440-392-9882	392-9901	690
TransDiesel of Central Florida 1310 George Jenkins Blvd .... Lakeland FL 33815 *Web:* www.transdiesel.net	863-688-5881		54
Transducer Techniques Inc 42480 Rio Nedo .... Temecula CA 92590 *TF:* 800-344-3965 ■ *Web:* www.transducertechniques.com	951-719-3965		362
Transeair Travel LLC 2813 McKinley Pl NW .... Washington DC 20015 *Web:* www.transeairtravel.com	202-362-6100		184
Transend Corp 225 Emerson St........ Palo Alto CA 94301 *Web:* www.transend.com	650-324-5370	324-5377	178-7
Transenterix Inc 635 Davis Dr Ste 300........ Morrisville NC 27560 *Web:* www.transenterix.com	919-765-8400		476
Transentric LLC 1400 Douglas St Ste 0840 .... Omaha NE 68179 *TF:* 800-877-0328 ■ *Web:* www.transentric.com	402-544-6000	501-2984	178-10
Trans-Exec Air Service Inc 7240 Hayvenhurst Ave 2nd Fl........ Van Nuys CA 91406 *Web:* www.transexec.com	818-904-6900		13

Company	Phone	Fax	Class
Transfer Enterprises Inc 140 Progress Dr........ Manchester CT 06042 *Web:* tedesk.com	860-645-9090		321
Transfer Express Inc 7650 Tyler Blvd .... Mentor OH 44060 *TF:* 800-622-2280 ■ *Web:* transferexpress.com	440-918-1900		627
Transfer Online Inc 512 SE Salmon St........ Portland OR 97214 *Web:* www.transferonline.com	503-227-2950		138
Transfer Solutions Inc 2885 Sandord Ave SW PO Box 17025 .... Grandville MI 49418 *Web:* www.ts-inc.com	703-777-1126		401
Transfer Tool Systems Inc 14444 168th Ave........ Grand Haven MI 49417 *Web:* www.transfertool.com	616-846-8510		488
Transferre Technologies Inc 945 McKinney St Ste 235........ Houston TX 77002 *Web:* transferretechnologies.com	713-821-3157		539
TRANSFLO Terminal Services Inc 500 Water St Ste J975 .... Jacksonville FL 32202 *Web:* www.transflo.net	904-279-6305	245-2253	449
Transforce Inc 5520 Cherokee Ave Ste 200 .... Alexandria VA 22312 **Fax Area Code:* 703 ■ *TF:* 800-308-6989 ■ *Web:* www.transforce.com	800-308-6989	838-5585*	721
Transform Automotive LLC 7026 Sterling Ponds Ct .... Sterling Heights MI 48312 **Fax Area Code:* 989 ■ *Web:* www.transformauto.com	586-826-8500	754-1103*	60
Transformations Inc 4200 W Good Hope Rd........ Milwaukee WI 53209 *Web:* www.transformationsusa.com	414-351-5770	351-5760	194
Transformit Inc 33 Sanford Dr .... Gorham ME 04038 *Web:* www.transformit.com	207-856-9911		393
TransFRESH Corp PO Box 1788 .... Salinas CA 93902 **Fax Area Code:* 831 ■ *TF:* 800-421-2328 ■ *Web:* www.transfresh.com	800-421-2328	772-6090*	780
TransGlobal Oil Co 9100 Bolton Ln .... Knoxville TN 37922 *TF:* 877-334-0025	865-531-6195		345
Trans-Global Solutions Inc 11811 East Fwy Ste 630........ Houston TX 77029 *Web:* www.tgsgroup.com	713-453-0341		207
TransGlobe Energy Corp 250 Fifth St SW Ste 2300........ Calgary AB T2P0R6 *NASDAQ:* TGL ■ *Web:* www.trans-globe.com	403-264-9888	770-8855	538
TransGroup Express Inc 18850 Eighth Ave S Ste 100........ Seattle WA 98148 *Web:* www.transgroup.com	206-244-0330		311
Transguard Insurance Company of America Inc 215 S Human Blvd .... Naperville IL 60563 *Web:* www.transguard.com	630-864-3500		390
TransGuardian Inc St Vincent Jewelry Ctr 650 S Hill St Ste 519........ Los Angeles CA 90014 *TF:* 877-570-7447 ■ *Web:* www.transguardian.com	213-622-5877	327-0140	311
Transhield Inc 2932 Thorne Dr........ Elkhart IN 46514 *Web:* transhield-usa.com	574-266-4118		594
Transim Technology Corp 433 NW 4th Ave Ste 200........ Portland OR 97209 *Web:* www.transim.com	503-450-1355		174
TransInternational System Inc 130 E Wilson Bridge Rd Ste 150........ Worthington OH 43085 *TF:* 800-340-7540 ■ *Web:* www.trnj.com	614-891-4942	891-4929	311
Transit Authority of River City (TARC) 1000 W Broadway........ Louisville KY 40203 *Web:* www.ridetarc.org	502-585-1234	213-3243	468
Transit Systems Inc 999 Old Eagle School Rd Ste 114........ Wayne PA 19087 *TF:* 800-626-1257 ■ *Web:* www.tsishipping.com	800-626-1257		311
Transitair Inc 27 Bank St........ Hornell NY 14843 *Web:* www.transitairusa.com	607-324-7860		14
Transition Networks Inc 10900 Red Cir Dr .... Minnetonka MN 55343 *TF:* 800-526-9267 ■ *Web:* www.transition.com	952-941-7600	941-2322	176
Transition Resources Inc (TRI) 12209 Park Bend Dr........ Dallas TX 75230 *Web:* www.transitioninc.com	214-384-9130		194
Transitions Optical Inc 9251 Belcher Rd........ Pinellas Park FL 33782 *TF:* 800-533-2081 ■ *Web:* www.transitions.com	800-848-1506		542
TranslateMedia LLC 414 Broadway 4th Fl........ New York NY 10013 *Web:* www.translatemedia.com	212-796-5636		393
Translations International Inc 100 S Fifth St Ste 1900........ Minneapolis MN 55402 **Fax Area Code:* 202 ■ *Web:* tiinc.com	320-217-2775	330-5776*	768
Translationscom Inc 3 Park Ave 39th Fl .... New York NY 10016 *TF:* 800-688-7205 ■ *Web:* www.translations.com	212-689-1616	685-9797	179
Transline Technology Inc 1106 S Technology Cir........ Anaheim CA 92805 *Web:* www.translinetech.com	714-533-8300	533-8791	625
TransLink Capital 530 Lytton Ave Ste 300........ Palo Alto CA 94301 *Web:* translinkcapital.com	650-330-7353		528
Translogistics Inc 321 N Furnace St Ste 300........ Birdsboro PA 19508 *Web:* translogisticsinc.com	610-280-3210		311
Trans-Lux Corp 26 Pearl St........ Norwalk CT 06850 *OTC:* TNLX ■ *TF:* 800-243-5544 ■ *Web:* www.trans-lux.com	203-853-4321		173-4
Trans-Lux Fair-Play Inc 1700 Delaware Ave........ Des Moines IA 50317 *TF:* 800-247-0265 ■ *Web:* www.fair-play.com	515-265-5305	265-3364	173-4
TransMagic Inc 11859 Pecos St Ste 310........ Westminster CO 80234 *Web:* transmagic.com	303-460-1406		174
Transmarine Navigation Corp 301 E Ocean Blvd Ste 500 .... Long Beach CA 90802 *Web:* www.transmarine.com	562-432-6941	590-8470	770
Transmaritime Central Inc 7400 Stiles Dr........ El Paso TX 79915 *Web:* www.transmaritime.com	915-779-3191		311

Name / Address	City	State	Zip	Phone	Fax	Class
Transmarket Group LLC 550 W Jackson Blvd Ste 1300 *Web:* www.transmarketgroup.com	Chicago	IL	60661	312-284-5500		401
Trans-Matic Manufacturing Inc 300 E 48th St *Web:* transmatic.com	Holland	MI	49423	616-820-2500	820-2702	488
Transmedia 719 Battery St *TF:* 800-229-7234 ■ *Web:* www.transmediasf.com	San Francisco	CA	94111	415-956-3118	956-2595	646
TransMedia Group Inc 240 W Palmetto Park Rd *Web:* www.transmediagroup.com	Boca Raton	FL	33432	561-750-9800		636
TransMedics Inc 200 Minuteman Rd Ste 302 *Web:* www.transmedics.com	Andover	MA	01810	978-552-0900	552-0978	476
Transmission Exchange Co 1803 NE M L King Blvd *TF:* 800-776-1191 ■ *Web:* www.txchange.com	Portland	OR	97212	503-284-0768	280-1655	61
Transmodal Corp 48 S Franklin Tpke *Web:* www.transmodal.net	Ramsey	NJ	07446	201-316-1610		311
Transmodus Corp 500 Esplanade Dr Ste 700 *TF:* 866-587-8249 ■ *Web:* www.transmodus.net	Oxnard	CA	93036	805-604-4472		160
Transmonde Usa 100 Shaw Rd *Web:* transmonde.com	North Branford	CT	06471	203-484-1528		5
TransMontaigne Inc 1670 Broadway Ste 3100 *Web:* www.transmontaignepartners.com	Denver	CO	80202	303-626-8200	626-8228	449
TransNational Association of Christian Colleges & Schools (TRACS) 15935 Forest Rd *Web:* www.tracs.org	Forest	VA	24551	434-525-9539	616-2638	48-1
Transnorm System Inc 2810 Ave E E *Web:* www.transnorm.com	Arlington	TX	76011	972-606-0303		358
Transocean Inc 4 Greenway Plz *NYSE: RIG* ■ *Web:* www.deepwater.com	Houston	TX	77046	713-232-7500		540
Transoft Solutions Inc 13575 Commerce Pkwy Ste 250 *TF:* 888-244-8387 ■ *Web:* www.transoftsolutions.com	Richmond	BC	V6V2L1	604-244-8387	244-1770	174
TranSolutions Inc 22015 N Calle Royale *Web:* www.transolutionsinc.com	Scottsdale	AZ	85255	480-473-2453	473-2454	178-1
Transor Filter USA Inc 515 Busse Rd *TF:* 800-354-3040 ■ *Web:* www.transorfilter.com	Elk Grove Village	IL	60007	847-640-0273	640-0793	385
Transource Computers Corp 2405 W Utopia Rd *TF:* 800-486-3715 ■ *Web:* www.transource.com	Phoenix	AZ	85027	623-879-8882	879-8887	173-2
Transource Inc 8700 Triad Dr *Web:* www.transourcetrucks.com	Colfax	NC	27235	336-996-6060		57
Transpak Corp 2 World Packaging Cir *Web:* www.transpakusa.com	Franklin	WI	53132	414-855-9200	855-9201	393
Trans-Pak Inc 520 Marburg Way *TF:* 877-883-2525 ■ *Web:* www.transpak.com	San Jose	CA	95133	408-254-0500	254-0551	549
Transpara Corp 4715 W Culpepper Dr *TF:* 866-904-5747 ■ *Web:* transpara.com	Phoenix	AZ	85087	925-218-6983		177
Transparent Language Inc 12 Murphy Dr **Fax Area Code:* 603 ■ *TF:* 800-538-8867 ■ *Web:* www.transparent.com	Nashua	NH	03062	800-538-8867	262-6476*	178-3
TransPerfect Translations Inc 3 Park Ave 39th Fl *Web:* www.transperfect.com	New York	NY	10016	212-689-5555	689-1059	768
Transphorm Inc 115 Castilian Dr *Web:* www.transphormusa.com	Goleta	CA	93117	805-456-1300		427
Trans-Phos Inc 4201 Bonnie Mine Rd *TF:* 800-940-1575 ■ *Web:* transphos.com	Mulberry	FL	33860	800-940-1575		780
Transplace 3010 Gaylord Pkwy Ste 200 *TF:* 866-413-9266 ■ *Web:* www.transplace.com	Frisco	TX	75034	866-413-9266		449
Transport Bourret Inc 375 Bd Lemire *TF:* 800-567-1470 ■ *Web:* www.bourret.ca	Drummondville	QC	J2B8G8	819-477-2202		478
Transport Clearings East Inc 4651 Charlotte Park Dr Ste 450 *Web:* www.tceast.com	Charlotte	NC	28217	704-527-1820	527-1851	272
Transport Corporation of America Inc 1715 Yankee Doodle Rd *Web:* www.transportamerica.com	Eagan	MN	55121	651-686-2500	686-2566	780
Transport Distribution Co PO Box 306 *TF:* 800-866-7709 ■ *Web:* www.gotdc.com	Joplin	MO	64802	417-624-3814		780
Transport Jacques Auger Inc 860 Archimede St *TF:* 800-387-3835 ■ *Web:* www.tja.ca	Levis	QC	G6V7M5	418-835-9266		478
Transport Refrigeration Inc 301 Lawrence Dr *Web:* www.thermokinggreenbay.com	De Pere	WI	54115	920-339-5700	339-5717	665
Transport Workers Union of America 501 Third St NW 9th Fl *Web:* www.twu.org	Washington	DC	20001	202-719-3900	347-0454	49-21
Transportation Advisory Services (TAS) 3181 Valley Dr **Fax Area Code:* 315 ■ *TF:* 800-233-3251 ■ *Web:* www.transportationconsultants.com	Walworth	NY	14568	800-233-3251	986-1901*	196
Transportation Alliance Bank Inc 4185 Harrison Blvd Ste 200 *TF:* 800-355-3063 ■ *Web:* www.tabbank.com	Ogden	UT	84403	800-355-3063		70
Transportation Federal Credit Union 1600 Cameron St *Web:* transfcu.org	Alexandria	VA	22314	202-366-9400		219
Transportation Insight LLC 310 Main Ave Way SE *Web:* www.t-insight.com	Hickory	NC	28602	828-485-5000		449
Transportation Institute 5201 Auth Way *Web:* transportationinstitute.org	Camp Springs	MD	20746	301-423-3335		49-21
Transportation Intermediaries Assn (TIA) 1625 Prince St Ste 200 *Web:* www.tianet.org	Alexandria	VA	22314	703-299-5700	836-0123	49-21
Transportation Management Associates Inc 344 Oak Grove Church Rd *TF:* 800-745-8292 ■ *Web:* www.tmaco.com	Mocksville	NC	27028	800-745-8292		311
Transportation Research Board (TRB) 500 5th St NW *Web:* www.nationalacademies.org	Washington	DC	20001	202-334-3213	334-2519	49-21
Transportation Research Center Inc (TRC) 10820 SR-347 *Web:* www.trcpg.com	East Liberty	OH	43319	937-666-2011	666-5066	668
Transportation Research Corp 4305 Business Dr *TF:* 888-676-7770 ■ *Web:* www.varnaproducts.com	Cameron Park	CA	95682	530-676-7770		650
Transportation Security Administration *Federal Air Marshal Service* 601 S 12th St *TF:* 866-289-9673 ■ *Web:* www.tsa.gov	Arlington	VA	22202	866-289-9673		340-11
Transportation Solutions Inc 1900 Brannan Rd *Web:* www.tsilogistics.com	McDonough	GA	30253	770-474-1555		449
Transportation Technology Center Inc 55500 DOT Rd PO Box 11130 *Web:* www.aar.com	Pueblo	CO	81001	719-584-0750	584-0711	668
TransportGistics Inc 28 N Country Rd Ste 103 *Web:* www.transportgistics.com	Mount Sinai	NY	11766	631-567-4100		311
TransPro Freight Systems Ltd 8600 Escarpment Way *TF:* 800-268-6857 ■ *Web:* www.transprofreight.com	Milton	ON	L9T0M1	905-693-0699	693-4186	311
Transtar 1200 Penn Ave Ste 300 *Web:* www.transtarrail.com	Pittsburgh	PA	15222	412-433-7090		360-3
Trans-tec Machine Ltd 6320 Ridgemont St *Web:* www.transtecmachine.com	Houston	TX	77087	713-643-9114		480
Trans-Tech Inc 5520 Adamstown Rd *Web:* www.trans-techinc.com	Adamstown	MD	21710	301-695-9400	695-7065	249
Transtech Industries Inc 2025 Delsea Dr *OTC: TRTI* ■ *Web:* www.transtechindustries.com	Sewell	NJ	08080	856-481-4214	227-6578	789
TransTech IT Staffing 248 Spring Lake Dr *Web:* www.trans-tech.com	Itasca	IL	60143	630-250-8880		260
TransTech Pharma Inc 4170 Mendenhall Oaks Pkwy *Web:* www.vtvtherapeutics.com	High Point	NC	27265	336-841-0300		743
Trans-Tel Central Inc (TTC) 2805 Bruce Dr *TF:* 800-729-4636 ■ *Web:* www.trans-tel.com	Norman	OK	73072	405-447-5025	447-5029	787
Transtelco Corp 500 W Overland Ave Ste 301 *TF:* 877-918-3526 ■ *Web:* www.transtelco.net	El Paso	TX	79901	877-918-3526		224
TransUnion LLC 555 W Adams St *TF:* 866-922-2100 ■ *Web:* www.transunion.com	Chicago	IL	60661	866-922-2100		218
Trans-United Inc 1123 N State Rd 149 *TF:* 877-762-3111 ■ *Web:* www.transunited.com	Burns Harbor	IN	46304	219-762-3111	764-2010	780
Transupport Inc 53 Turbine Way *Web:* transupport.com	Merrimack	NH	03054	603-424-3111	424-1888	385
Transverse LLC 620 Congress Ave Ste 200 *Web:* www.gotransverse.com	Austin	TX	78701	512-279-3119		463
Transvideo Studios 990 Villa St *Web:* transvideo.com	Mountain View	CA	94041	650-965-4898	962-1753	6
Transvision Intl 550 Maulhardt Ave *Web:* www.txvision.com	Oxnard	CA	93030	805-981-8740		681
Transwall Inc 1220 Wilson Dr *TF:* 800-441-9255 ■ *Web:* transwall.com	West Chester	PA	19380	800-441-9255		319-4
Transwest 20770 I-76 Frontage Rd *TF:* 800-289-3161 ■ *Web:* www.transwest.com	Brighton	CO	80603	303-289-3161	288-2310	57
Transwest Credit Union 37 West 1700 South *Web:* www.transwestcu.com	Salt Lake City	UT	84115	801-487-1692		219
Trans-West Security Services Inc 8503 Crippen St *Web:* trans-west.net	Bakersfield	CA	93311	661-381-2900		693
Transwestern Commercial Services 1900 W Loop S Ste 1300 *Web:* transwestern.com	Houston	TX	77027	713-270-7700	270-6285	655
Transwheel Corp 3000 Yeoman Way	Huntington	IN	46750	260-358-8660		247
TranSwitch Corp 3 Enterprise Dr *Web:* www.websolutions.com	Shelton	CT	06484	203-929-8810		696
TransWood Carriers Inc PO Box 189 **Fax Area Code:* 402 ■ *TF:* 888-346-8092 ■ *Web:* www.transwood.com	Omaha	NE	68101	888-346-8092	341-2112*	780
TransWorks 9910 Dupont Circle Dr E Ste 200 *TF:* 888-325-6510 ■ *Web:* www.trnswrks.com	Fort Wayne	IN	46825	888-325-6510		178-10
TransWorld Network Corp 255 Pine Ave N *TF:* 800-253-0665 ■ *Web:* www.twncorp.com	Oldsmar	FL	34677	813-891-4700		387
Transworld Systems Inc PO Box 15618 *TF:* 888-446-4733 ■ *Web:* www.tsico.com	Wilmington	DE	19850	877-282-1250		160
TransX Group of Cos 2595 Inkster Blvd *TF:* 877-558-9444 ■ *Web:* www.transx.com	Winnipeg	MB	R3C2E6	204-632-6694		311
Transylvania County Library (TCL) 212 S Gaston St *Web:* library.transylvaniacounty.org	Brevard	NC	28712	828-884-3151		434-3
Transylvania University 300 N Broadway *TF:* 800-872-6798 ■ *Web:* www.transy.edu	Lexington	KY	40508	859-233-8242	233-8797	166
TranSystems Corp 2400 Pershing Rd Ste 400 *TF:* 800-800-5261 ■ *Web:* www.transystems.com	Kansas City	MO	64108	816-329-8700	329-8703	261
TranTek Automation Corp 2470 N Aero Park Ct *Web:* www.trantekautomation.com	Traverse City	MI	49686	231-946-6270		358
Tranter Graphics Inc 8094 N State Rd 13 *Web:* www.trantergraphics.com	Syracuse	IN	46567	574-834-2626		627
Tranter Inc 1900 Old Burk Hwy **Fax Area Code:* 940 ■ *TF:* 800-414-6908 ■ *Web:* www.tranter.com	Wichita Falls	TX	76306	800-414-6908	723-5131*	91
TranzAct Technologies Inc 360 W Butterfield Rd 4th Fl *Web:* www.tranzact.com	Elmhurst	IL	60126	630-833-0890		311
Tranzon LLC 2100 Club Dr Ste 100 *TF:* 866-872-6966 ■ *Web:* www.tranzon.com	Gadsden	AL	35901	256-413-2902		41

	City	State	ZIP	Phone	Fax	Class
Tranzonic Cos 26301 Curtiss Wright Pkwy *Web:* www.tranzonic.com	Cleveland	OH	44143	216-535-4300		558
Trap Pond State Park 33587 Baldcypress Ln *Web:* www.destateparks.com	Laurel	DE	19956	302-875-5153		565
Trap Rock Industries LLC (TRI) PO Box 419 *Web:* www.traprock.com	Kingston	NJ	08528	609-924-0300	497-0135	503-5
Trapezio 2161 Cedarcrest Rd Ste 115 **Fax Area Code:* 678 ■ *TF:* 877-976-4536 ■ *Web:* www.trapezio.com	Acworth	GA	30101	877-976-4536	370-9848*	167-3
Traphagen Financial Group 234 Kinderkamack Rd *Web:* tfgllc.com	Oradell	NJ	07649	201-262-1040	265-7018	734
Trapp Family Lodge 700 Trapp Hill Rd PO Box 1428 *TF:* 800-826-7000 ■ *Web:* www.trappfamily.com	Stowe	VT	05672	802-253-8511		669
Trapshooting Hall of Fame & Museum 2 Main Event Ln PO Box 519 *Web:* www.traphof.org	Sparta	IL	62286	937-660-5663		522
Trask Daigneault LLP 1001 S Fort Harrison Ave Ste 201 *Web:* www.cityattorneys.legal	Clearwater	FL	33756	727-733-0494		41
Traton Corp 720 Kennesaw Ave NW *Web:* www.tratonhomes.com	Marietta	GA	30060	770-427-9064		187
Trattoria Bella Sera 9449 Montana Ave *Web:* www.trattoriabellasera.com	El Paso	TX	79925	915-598-7948		671
Trattoria Contadina 1800 Mason St *Web:* www.trattoriacontadina.com	San Francisco	CA	94133	415-982-5728		671
Trattoria Delia 152 St Paul St *Web:* www.trattoriadelia.com	Burlington	VT	05401	802-864-5253		671
Trattoria dell'Arte 900 7th Ave *Web:* www.trattoriadellarte.com	New York	NY	10019	212-245-9800		671
Trattoria Giorgio 121 S Main St *Web:* www.trattoriagiorgio.net	Greenville	SC	29601	864-271-9166		671
Trattoria Marcella 3600 Watson Rd *Web:* trattoriamarcella.com	Saint Louis	MO	63109	314-352-7706		671
Trattoria Nervosa 75 Yorkville Ave *Web:* www.eatnervosa.com	Toronto	ON	M5R1B8	416-961-4642		671
Trattoria No 10 10 N Dearborn St *Web:* www.trattoriaten.com	Chicago	IL	60602	312-984-1718		671
Trattoria Roma 1447 Grandview Ave *Web:* www.trattoria-roma.com	Columbus	OH	43212	614-488-2104		671
Tratum Technologies 1039 Sterling Rd Ste 203 *Web:* www.tratumtech.com	Herndon	VA	20170	703-456-7000		180
Trau & Loevner 838 Braddock Ave *Web:* www.trau-loevner.com	Braddock	PA	15104	412-361-7700	361-8221	687
Traulsen & Company Inc 4401 Blue Mound Rd *TF:* 800-825-8220 ■ *Web:* www.traulsen.com	Fort Worth	TX	76106	800-825-8220		14
Trauner Consulting Services Inc 1 Penn Ctr 1617 JFK Blvd Ste 475 *Web:* www.traunerconsulting.com	Philadelphia	PA	19103	215-814-6400		194
Trautman & Shreve Inc 4406 Race St *Web:* trautman-shreve.com	Denver	CO	80216	303-295-1414	295-0324	189-10
Travaasa Hana 5031 Hana Hwy *TF:* 855-868-7282 ■ *Web:* travaasa.com	Hana	HI	96713	808-248-8211	248-7202	669
Travaglini Enterprises Inc 231 Chestnut St Ste 614	Meadville	PA	16335	814-724-4880		670
Travel & Cruise 4331 Wyoming NE *Web:* www.rgtravel.com	Albuquerque	NM	87111	505-292-7044		772
Travel & Transport Inc 2120 S 72nd St *TF:* 800-228-2545 ■ *Web:* www.travelandtransport.com	Omaha	NE	68124	402-399-4500		771
Travel + Leisure Magazine 225 Liberty St **Fax Area Code:* 718 ■ *TF:* 800-888-8728 ■ *Web:* www.travelandleisure.com	New York	NY	10281	800-888-8728	373-3681*	457-20
Travel Academy, The 3140 Neil Armstrong Blvd Ste 220 *Web:* www.thetravelacademy.com	Eagan	MN	55121	952-854-7161		167-3
Travel Agent Magazine 757 Third Ave *TF:* 855-424-6247 ■ *Web:* www.travelagentcentral.com	New York	NY	10017	212-895-8200		457-22
Travel Authority 702 N Shore Dr Ste 300 **Fax Area Code:* 502 ■ *TF:* 877-297-1515 ■ *Web:* www.thetravelauthority.com	Jeffersonville	IN	47130	812-949-4949	379-8090*	771
Travel Berkley Springs 127 Fairfax St *TF:* 800-447-8797 ■ *Web:* berkeleysprings.com	Berkeley Springs	WV	25411	304-258-9147		772
Travel Bound Inc 5 Penn Plz 5th Fl *TF:* 800-808-9543 ■ *Web:* rbs.booktravelbound.com	New York	NY	10001	800-808-9543	808-9542	760
Travel Careers Inc c/o Susan N Rice 926 Woodruff Pl W *TF:* 800-276-7770 ■ *Web:* www.travelcampus.com	Indianapolis	IN	46201	317-709-6653		167-3
Travel Ch LLC 5425 Wisconsin Ave Ste 500 *Web:* www.travelchannel.com	Chevy Chase	MD	20815	301-244-7500	244-7509	740
Travel Dynamics Intl 132 E 70th St **Fax Area Code:* 212 ■ *TF:* 800-257-5767 ■ *Web:* www.travel-dynamics.dwaiter.com	New York	NY	10021	800-257-5767	774-1560*	760
Travel Goods Assn 301 N Harrison St Ste 412 *TF:* 877-842-1938 ■ *Web:* travel-goods.org	Princeton	NJ	08540	877-842-1938		138
Travel Inc 4355 River Green Pkwy *Web:* www.travelinc.com	Duluth	GA	30096	770-291-4100		771
Travel Industry Association of Kansas 919 S Kansas Ave *Web:* tiak.org	Topeka	KS	66612	785-233-9465		206
Travel Institute 945 Concord St *TF:* 800-542-4282 ■ *Web:* www.thetravelinstitute.com	Framingham	MA	01701	781-237-0280	237-3860	48-23
Travel Insurance Services 2950 Camino Diablo Ste 300 **Fax Area Code:* 484 ■ *TF:* 800-937-1387 ■ *Web:* www.travelinsure.com	Walnut Creek	CA	94597	800-937-1387	652-5394*	390
Travel Insured Intl 855 Winding Brook Dr PO Box 6503 **Fax Area Code:* 860 ■ *TF:* 800-243-3174 ■ *Web:* www.travelinsured.com	Glastonbury	CT	06033	800-243-3174	528-8005*	391-7
Travel Leaders 10202 Coldwater Rd Ste D *TF:* 800-346-9807 ■ *Web:* cts.vacation.travelleaders.com	Fort Wayne	IN	46804	260-434-6600		184
Travel Management Partners Inc 7208 Falls of Neuse Rd Ste 220 *TF:* 877-684-4647 ■ *Web:* tmptravel.com	Raleigh	NC	27615	919-782-3810	788-0628	772
Travel Manitoba 155 Carlton St 7th Fl *TF:* 800-665-0040 ■ *Web:* www.travelmanitoba.com	Winnipeg	MB	R3C3H8	204-927-7800		774
Travel Northeast Nebraska 609 West Norfolk Ave *Web:* www.travelnenebraska.com	Norfolk	NE	68701	402-371-2932		771
Travel One Inc 8009 34th Ave S 15th Fl *TF:* 800-247-1311 ■ *Web:* traveloneinc.com	Minneapolis	MN	55425	952-854-2551		772
Travel Oriented Inc 1550 SW Ave Tozai Pla Tozai Plaza Tower Ste *Web:* traveloriented.com	Gardena	CA	90249	310-329-2800		772
Travel Portland Pioneer Courthouse Sq 701 SW Sixth Ave *TF:* 877-678-5263 ■ *Web:* www.travelportland.com	Portland	OR	97204	503-275-9750		206
Travel Society Inc 650 S Cherry St Ste 200 *TF:* 800-926-6031 ■ *Web:* www.travelsociety.com	Denver	CO	80246	303-321-0900		772
Travel Startups Incubator 4201 Village Ct *Web:* travelstartups.co	Lake Wales	FL	33898	207-460-0740		401
Travel Tags Inc 5842 Carmen Ave *Web:* www.traveltags.com	Inver Grove Heights	MN	55076	651-450-1201		627
Travel Team Inc 2495 Main St Ste 340 *Web:* profile.thetravelteam.com	Buffalo	NY	14214	716-862-7600	862-7650	771
Travel Turf Inc 7540 Windsor Dr Ste 202 *TF:* 800-222-4432 ■ *Web:* www.wcv.com	Allentown	PA	18195	610-391-9094		772
Travel University Intl 3870 Murphy Canyon Rd Ste 310 *Web:* www.traveluniversity.edu	San Diego	CA	92123	858-292-9755	292-8008	786
Travel Wizard LLC 5675 Lucas Valley Rd Ste 6 *Web:* www.travelwizard.com	Nicasio	CA	94946	415-446-5252	446-5281	772
TravelAge West Magazine 11400 W Olympic Blvd Ste 325 *Web:* www.travelagewest.com	Los Angeles	CA	90064	310-954-2510		457-22
TravelCenters of America 24601 Ctr Ridge Rd Ste 200 *TF:* 800-632-9240 ■ *Web:* www.ta-petro.com	Westlake	OH	44145	440-808-9100		324
TravelClick Inc 7 Times Sq 38th Fl *TF:* 866-674-4549 ■ *Web:* www.travelclick.com	New York	NY	10036	212-817-4800		194
Travelennium Inc 556 Colonial Rd *TF:* 800-844-4924 ■ *Web:* www.travelennium.com	Memphis	TN	38117	901-767-0761	766-0126	771
Traveler's Rest State Historic Site 4339 Riverdale Rd *Web:* gastateparks.org	Toccoa	GA	30577	706-886-2256		565
Travelers Companies Inc 385 Washington St *NYSE: TRV* ■ *TF:* 800-328-2189 ■ *Web:* www.travelers.com	Saint Paul	MN	55102	651-310-7911		360-4
Travelers Company Inc 485 Lexington Ave 8th Fl *NYSE: TRV* ■ *TF:* 888-695-4640 ■ *Web:* www.corporate-office-headquarters.com	New York	NY	10017	888-695-4640		391-1
Travelers Motor Club 720 NW 50th St *TF:* 800-654-9208 ■ *Web:* travelersmotorclub.com	Oklahoma City	OK	73154	405-848-1711		53
Travelers Transportation Services Inc 195 Heart Lake Rd S *TF:* 800-265-8789 ■ *Web:* travelers.ca	Brampton	ON	L6W3N6	905-457-8789		311
Travelex International Inc 2061 N Barrington Rd *TF:* 800-882-0499 ■ *Web:* travelexinternational.com	Hoffman Estates	IL	60169	847-882-0400		772
Travelex Worldwide Money 122 E 42nd St Ste 2800 *TF:* 800-228-9792 ■ *Web:* www.travelex.com	New York	NY	10168	516-300-1622		69
Travelhost Magazine 10701 N Stemmons Fwy *TF:* 800-527-1782 ■ *Web:* www.travelhost.com	Dallas	TX	75220	972-556-0541	432-8729	457-22
Traveling Computers Inc 210 E Main St *Web:* www.tcinc.net	Riverton	WY	82501	307-856-8676	856-7787	177
Travelink Inc 404 BNA Dr Ste 650 *TF:* 800-821-4671 ■ *Web:* www.travelink.com	Nashville	TN	37217	615-367-4900		317
Traveller & Company LLC 500 N Marketplace Dr Ste 202 *Web:* travellercpa.com	Centerville	UT	84014	801-299-1302		2
Travellers Rest Plantation & Museum 636 Farrell Pkwy *Web:* historictravellersrest.org	Nashville	TN	37220	615-832-8197		50-3
Travelmart Inc, The 28011 Clemens Rd *Web:* www.thetravelmart.com	Westlake	OH	44145	440-835-8220	835-4823	772
Travelmore 212 W Colfax Ave *Web:* www.travelleaders.com	South Bend	IN	46601	574-232-3061		771
TravelNow com Inc 4124 S Mccann Ct Ste 418 *Web:* www.travelnow.com	Springfield	MO	65804	417-864-3600	864-8811	774
Travel-On Ltd 9000 Virginia Manor Rd Ste 201 *TF:* 800-333-6778 ■ *Web:* www.tvlon.com	Beltsville	MD	20705	240-387-4000		772
Travelong Inc *Fareportal Inc* 135 W 50th St Ste 500 *Web:* www.fareportal.com	New York	NY	10020	212-736-2166	763-0496	771
Travelport Ltd 300 Galleria Pkwy *Web:* www.travelport.com	Atlanta	GA	30339	770-563-7400		387
Travelpro USA 700 Banyan Trl *TF:* 800-741-7471 ■ *Web:* www.travelpro.com	Boca Raton	FL	33431	561-998-2824	998-8487	453
Travelsavers Inc 71 Audrey Ave *Web:* www.travelsavers.com	Oyster Bay	NY	11771	516-624-0500	624-6024	772
TravelSmith Outfitters 75 Aircraft RD *TF:* 800-770-3387 ■ *Web:* www.travelsmith.com	Southington	CT	06489	800-770-3387		459
TravelStore Inc 11601 Wilshire Blvd *TF:* 800-850-3224 ■ *Web:* www.travelstore.com	Los Angeles	CA	90025	310-575-5540	575-5541	771

	Phone	Fax	Class
Traveltime Services Inc 2838 Old 280 Ct .... Birmingham AL 35243 *TF:* 800-543-8402 ■ *Web:* www.traveltimeservices.com	205-969-4900	967-7172	771
TRAVELVIDEOSTOREcom Inc 5420 Boran Dr ...... Tampa FL 33610 *TF:* 800-288-5123 ■ *Web:* www.travelvideostore.com	813-630-9778		772
Travelzoo Inc 590 Madison Ave 37th Fl .... New York NY 10022 *NASDAQ: TZOO* ■ *Web:* www.travelzoo.com	212-484-4900	521-4230	773
Travers Printing Inc 32 Mission St .... Gardner MA 01440 *TF:* 800-696-0530 ■ *Web:* www.traversprinting.com	978-632-0530		627
Travers Tool Company Inc 128-15 26th Ave .... Flushing NY 11354 *TF:* 800-221-0270 ■ *Web:* www.travers.com	718-886-7200	886-7895	385
Traverse City Area Chamber of Commerce 202 E Grandview Pkwy .... Traverse City MI 49684 *Web:* www.tcchamber.org	231-947-5075	946-2565	139
Traverse City Convention & Visitors Bureau 101 W Grandview Pkwy .... Traverse City MI 49684 *TF:* 800-940-1120 ■ *Web:* www.traversecity.com	231-947-1120	947-2621	206
Traverse City Record-Eagle 120 W Front St .... Traverse City MI 49684 *TF:* 800-968-8273 ■ *Web:* www.record-eagle.com	231-946-2000	946-8632	532-2
Traverse City State Park 1132 US-31 N .... Traverse City MI 49686 *Web:* www.michigan.org	231-922-5270		565
Traverse Electric Co-opeartive Inc 1618 Broadway PO Box 66 .... Wheaton MN 56296 *TF:* 800-927-5443 ■ *Web:* www.traverseelectric.com	320-563-8616		245
Traverse Symphony Orchestra (TSO) 300 E Front St Ste 230 .... Traverse City MI 49684 *Web:* traversesymphony.org	231-947-7120		573-3
Travis Avenue Baptist Church 800 E Berry St .... Fort Worth TX 76110 *Web:* www.travis.org	817-924-4266	921-9620	95
Travis Body & Trailer Inc 13955 FM529 .... Houston TX 77041 *TF:* 800-535-4372 ■ *Web:* travistrailers.com	713-466-5888	466-3238	779
Travis Brothers Building Automation Texas LLC 1539 E Ln .... Beaumont TX 77713 *Web:* travisbrothers.com	409-842-2858		351
Travis County PO Box 1748 .... Austin TX 78767 *Web:* www.traviscountytx.gov	512-854-9020	854-4464	338
Travis County State Jail 8101 FM 969 .... Austin TX 78724 *Web:* www.tdcj.texas.gov	512-926-4482		213
Travis Federal Credit Union 1 Travis Way .... Vacaville CA 95687 *TF:* 800-877-8328 ■ *Web:* www.traviscu.org	707-449-4000		219
Travis Pattern & Foundry Inc 1413 E Hawthorne Rd .... Spokane WA 99218 *Web:* www.travispattern.com	509-466-3545	467-6465	308
Travis Tile Sales Inc 3811 Airport Blvd .... Austin TX 78722 *Web:* www.travistile.com	512-478-8705	478-8373	191-1
Travisco 7210 Clinton Hwy PO Box 670 .... Powell TN 37849 **Fax Area Code:* 865 ■ *TF:* 800-247-7606 ■ *Web:* travisco.net	800-247-7606	938-9211*	473
Traviss Technical College 3225 Winter Lake Rd .... Lakeland FL 33803 *Web:* www.polkedpathways.com	863-499-2700	499-2706	167-3
Traxx Restaurant 800 N Alameda St .... Los Angeles CA 90012 *Web:* traxx.cafes-world.com	213-625-1999		671
Trayer Engineering Corp 898 Pennsylvania Ave .... San Francisco CA 94107 *TF:* 800-377-1774 ■ *Web:* trayer.com	415-285-7770		261
Trayer Products Inc 541 E Clinton St .... Elmira NY 14901 *Web:* www.trayerproducts.com	607-734-8124	732-1387	247
Traylor Bros Inc 835 N Congress Ave .... Evansville IN 47715 *TF:* 866-895-1491 ■ *Web:* www.traylor.com	812-477-1542	474-3223	188-4
TRB (Transportation Research Board) 500 5th St NW .... Washington DC 20001 *Web:* www.nationalacademies.org	202-334-3213	334-2519	49-21
TRC (Transportation Research Center Inc) 10820 SR-347 .... East Liberty OH 43319 *Web:* www.trcpg.com	937-666-2011	666-5066	668
TRC 1300 Virginia Dr Ste 200 .... Fort Washington PA 19034 *TF:* 800-275-2827 ■ *Web:* www.trchome.com	215-641-2200	643-6505	466
TRC Circuits Inc 3300 Winpark Dr .... Crystal MN 55427 **Fax Area Code:* 612 ■ *Web:* www.trc-circuits.com	763-546-6499	546-3231*	625
TRC Companies Inc 21 Griffin Rd N .... Windsor CT 06095 *Web:* www.trccompanies.com	860-298-9692	298-6399	192
TRC Global Mobility 1042 E Juneau Ave .... Milwaukee WI 53202 *Web:* trcglobalmobility.com	414-226-4200		652
TRC Worldwide Engineering Inc (TRCWW) 217 Ward Cir .... Brentwood TN 37027 *Web:* www.trcww.com	615-661-7979	661-0644	261
TRCWW (TRC Worldwide Engineering Inc) 217 Ward Cir .... Brentwood TN 37027 *Web:* www.trcww.com	615-661-7979	661-0644	261
TRE (Trinity Railway Express) 801 Cherry St Ste 850 .... Fort Worth TX 76102 *Web:* trinityrailwayexpress.org	817-215-8600	215-8934	649
TRE & Associates LLC 110 Mesa Park Dr Ste 200 .... El Paso TX 79912 *Web:* tr-eng.com	915-852-9093		261
Tre Kronor 3258 W Foster Ave .... Chicago IL 60625 *Web:* swedishbistro.com	773-267-9888		671
Tre Scalini 1915 Passyunk Ave .... Philadelphia PA 19148 *Web:* trescaliniphiladelphia.com	215-551-3870		671
Tre Scalini Ristorante 100 Wooster St .... New Haven CT 06510 *Web:* www.trescalinirestaurant.com	203-777-3373	787-5360	671
Treacy & Co 1220 South St .... Needham MA 02492 *Web:* www.treacyandco.com	781-559-3381		463
Tread Corp 176 Eastpark Dr .... Roanoke VA 24019 *Web:* www.treadcorp.com	540-982-6881	344-7536	678
Treads Bicycle Outfitters 16701 E Iliff Ave .... Aurora CO 80013 *Web:* treads.com	303-750-1671		711

	Phone	Fax	Class
Treadstone Group Inc, The 2173 Smith Harbour Dr .... Denver NC 28037 *Web:* www.treadstonegroup.com	704-489-8663		196
Treasure Bay Casino & Hotel 1980 Beach Blvd .... Biloxi MS 39531 *Web:* www.treasurebay.com	228-385-6000	385-6082	669
Treasure Chest Casino 5050 Williams Blvd .... Kenner LA 70065 *TF:* 800-298-0711 ■ *Web:* www.treasurechest.com	504-443-8000		133
Treasure Garden Inc 13401 Brooks Dr Ste A .... Baldwin Park CA 91706 *Web:* treasuregarden.com	626-814-0168		320
Treasure Health 1201 SE Indian St .... Stuart FL 34997 *TF:* 800-299-4677 ■ *Web:* treasurehealth.org	772-403-4500		371
Treasure Island Foods Inc 3460 N Broadway .... Chicago IL 60657 *Web:* tifoods.com	773-327-4265		345
Treasure Island Hotel & Casino 3300 Las Vegas Blvd S .... Las Vegas NV 89109 *TF:* 800-288-7206 ■ *Web:* www.treasureisland.com	702-894-7111	894-7414	669
Treasure Island Resort & Casino 5734 Sturgeon Lake Rd .... Welch MN 55089 *TF:* 800-222-7077 ■ *Web:* www.ticasino.com	800-222-7077		707
Treasure State Seed Inc 2380 US Hwy 89 .... Fairfield MT 59436 *TF:* 800-572-4769 ■ *Web:* www.treasurestateseed.com	406-467-2557	467-3377	276
Treasure Valley Community College 650 College Blvd .... Ontario OR 97914 *Web:* www.tvcc.cc	541-881-8822	881-2721	162
Treasure Valley Reminder 1160 SW Fourth St .... Ontario OR 97914 *Web:* www.argusobserver.com	541-889-5387		637-8
Treat All Metals Inc 5140 N Port Washington Rd .... Milwaukee WI 53217 *Web:* www.regalpts.com	414-962-2500		484
Treatment Communities of America (TCA) 1875 I St NW Rm 574 .... Washington DC 20006 *Web:* www.treatmentcommunitiesofamerica.org	202-296-3503	379-9154	49-8
Treats International Franchise Corp 238 Queen St S 2nd Fl .... Mississauga ON L5M1L5 *Web:* www.treats.com	613-563-4073	563-1982	68
Treatt 4900 Lakeland Commerce Pkwy .... Lakeland FL 33805 *Web:* www.treatt.com	863-668-9500		297-8
Trebas Institute 550 Sherbrooke St W Ste 600 .... Montreal QC H3A1B9 *Web:* www.trebas.com	514-845-4141	845-2581	167-3
Trebol Motors Corp 296 Marginal Kennedy .... San Juan PR 00920 *Web:* www.trebolmotors.com	787-793-2828		57
Trebor Inc 100 Matawan Rd Ste 220 .... Matawan NJ 07747 *Web:* trebor.com	732-335-4255	335-4244	311
Trebor International Inc 8100 S 1300 W .... West Jordan UT 84088 *TF:* 800-669-1303 ■ *Web:* www.treborintl.com	801-561-0303	255-2312	246
Trec Group Inc 900 Old Marple Rd .... Springfield PA 19064 *Web:* trecgroup.com	610-328-6465		261
Treco Service Inc 904 N Zarzamora St .... San Antonio TX 78207 *Web:* trecoservices.com	210-432-4100		104
Tredegar Corp 1100 Boulders Pkwy .... North Chesterfield VA 23225 *NYSE: TG* ■ *TF:* 800-411-7441 ■ *Web:* www.tredegar.com	804-330-1000	330-1177	360-3
Tredent Data Systems Inc 3241 Grande Vista Dr .... Newbury Park CA 91320 *Web:* www.tredent.com	805-716-8120		246
Tredway, Lumsdaine & Doyle LLP 3900 Kilroy Airport Way Ste 240 .... Long Beach CA 90806 *Web:* tldlaw.com	562-923-0971		41
Tredyffrin-Easttown School District (TESD) 940 W Valley Rd Ste 1700 .... Wayne PA 19087 *Web:* www.tesd.net	610-240-1900		186
Tree Care Industry Assn (TCIA) 136 Harvey Rd Ste 101 .... Londonderry NH 03053 *TF:* 800-733-2622 ■ *Web:* tcia.org	603-314-5380	314-5386	48-13
Tree Care of New York 11493 Broadway .... Alden NY 14004 *Web:* treecareofny.com	716-681-1414		422
Tree City Tool 1954 N Montgomery Rd .... Greensburg IN 47240 *Web:* www.treecitytool.com	812-663-4196	663-4220	454
Tree Hill Nature Ctr 7152 Lone Star Rd .... Jacksonville FL 32211 *Web:* www.treehill.org	904-724-4646	724-9132	50-5
Tree Island Industries 3933 Boundary Rd .... Richmond BC V6V1T8 *TF:* 800-663-0955 ■ *Web:* www.treeisland.com	604-524-3744	524-2362	485
Tree Top Inc 220 E Second Ave .... Selah WA 98942 *Web:* www.treetop.com	509-697-7251	698-1421	296-20
TreeAge Software Inc 1 Bank St .... Williamstown MA 01267 *Web:* www.treeage.com	413-458-0104		178-1
Treece Alfrey Musat PC 633 17th St Ste 2200 .... Denver CO 80202 *Web:* tamlegal.com	303-292-2700		41
Treefort Inc 4210 Park Glen Rd .... Minneapolis MN 55416 *Web:* www.treefort.com	612-285-5625		809
Treehaus Communications Inc PO Box 249 .... Loveland OH 45140 **Fax Area Code:* 513 ■ *TF:* 800-638-4287 ■ *Web:* www.treehaus1.com	800-638-4287	683-2882*	681
TreeHouse Foods Inc 2021 Spring Rd Ste 600 .... Oak Brook IL 60523 *NYSE: THS* ■ *TF:* 866-641-4276 ■ *Web:* www.treehousefoods.com	708-483-1300		296-11
Treehouse Museum 347 22nd St .... Ogden UT 84401 *Web:* www.treehousemuseum.org	801-394-9663		521
Treehouse Software Inc 2605 Nicholson Rd Ste 230 .... Sewickley PA 15143 *Web:* www.treehouse.com	724-759-7070		177
Treeland Garden Center & Nursery 1000 Huntington Tpke .... Bridgeport CT 06610 *TF:* 800-243-0232 ■ *Web:* www.treelandgardencenter.com	203-372-3511	371-6023	323

Name / Address	City	State	ZIP	Phone	Fax	Class
Treeline Associates Inc 5300 Lakewood Rd *TF:* 888-231-8039 ■ *Web:* treelineassociates.com	Whitehall	MI	49461	248-814-7151		463
Treeline Well Services Inc 750 333 - 11th Ave SW *TF:* 844-344-7447 ■ *Web:* treelinewell.com	Calgary	AB	T2R1L9	403-266-2868		190
Treepeople Inc 12601 Mulholland Dr *Web:* www.treepeople.org	Beverly Hills	CA	90210	818-753-4600		776
Trees for Tomorrow (TFT) 519 Sheridan St E PO Box 609 *Web:* www.treesfortomorrow.com	Eagle River	WI	54521	715-479-6456	479-2318	49-5
Treesdale Partners LLC 1325 Avenue of the Americas Ste 2302 *Web:* www.treesdalellc.com	New York	NY	10019	212-299-5525		194
Treetop Publishing 450 S 92nd St **Fax Area Code:* 888 ■ *TF:* 800-255-9228 ■ *Web:* www.barebooks.com	Milwaukee	WI	53214	414-858-2195	201-5916*	637-2
Treetops Resort 3962 Wilkinson Rd *TF:* 866-348-5249 ■ *Web:* www.treetops.com	Gaylord	MI	49735	989-732-6711		669
Trefethen Advisors LLC 6380 E Thomas Ste 200 *Web:* www.trefethenadvisors.com	Scottsdale	AZ	85251	480-922-9966		690
Trefethen Vineyards Winery Inc 1160 Oak Knoll Ave *TF:* 866-895-7696 ■ *Web:* www.trefethen.com	Napa	CA	94558	707-255-7700		80-3
Treflie Capital Management LLC PO Box 1958 *TF:* 866-236-3363 ■ *Web:* www.treflie.com	Sag Harbor	NY	11963	631-725-2500		401
Trego County 216 N Main St *TF:* 877-962-7248 ■ *Web:* www.wakeeney.org	WaKeeney	KS	67672	785-743-5785		338
Trego Dugan Aviation Inc Lee Bird Fld *Web:* www.trego-dugan.com	North Platte	NE	69101	308-532-5864		579
Trehel Corp 935 S Main St Ste 300 PO Box 6688 *TF:* 800-319-7006 ■ *Web:* www.trehel.com	Greenville	SC	29601	864-654-6582	654-7788	186
Trejo's 9122 Mansfield Rd *Web:* www.trejosmexicanrestaurants.com	Shreveport	LA	71118	318-687-6192		671
Trek Bicycle Corp 202 W Laurel St *Web:* www.trekbikes.com	Fort Collins	CO	80521	970-482-6006		711
Trek Bicycle Superstore 4240 Kearny Mesa Rd Ste 108 *Web:* www.trekbicyclesuperstore.com	San Diego	CA	92111	858-974-8735		711
Trek Bicycles of American Fork 356 N 750 W *Web:* www.trekbikes.com	American Fork	UT	84003	801-763-1222		711
Trek Inc 11601 Maple Ridge Rd *TF:* 800-367-8735 ■ *Web:* www.trekinc.com	Medina	NY	14103	585-798-3140	798-3106	248
Trelleborg Coated Systems US Inc 1886 Prairie Way *TF:* 800-344-0714 ■ *Web:* www.trelleborg.com	Louisville	CO	80027	303-469-1357	469-2362	745-1
Trelleborg Sealing Solutions 2509 Bremer Rd *Web:* www.tss.trelleborg.com	Fort Wayne	IN	46803	260-749-9631	749-4844	326
Trellis Capital Corp 333 Wilson Ave Ste 600 *Web:* www.trelliscapital.com	Toronto	ON	M3H1T2	416-398-2299		401
Trellis Restaurant 403 W Duke of Gloucester St *Web:* www.thetrellis.com	Williamsburg	VA	23185	757-229-8610		671
Trellis Supportive Care 101 Hospice Ln *Web:* www.trellissupport.org	Winston-Salem	NC	27103	336-768-3972	659-0461	353
Trellist Inc 117 N Market St *Web:* www.trellist.com	Wilmington	DE	19801	302-778-1300		463
Trelys Funds PO Box 5066 *Web:* www.trelys.com	Cary	NC	27512	919-459-4650	459-4670	792
Tremblay & Smith PLLC 105 E High St *TF:* 866-834-4455 ■ *Web:* tremblaysmith.com	Charlottesville	VA	22902	434-977-4455		41
Trembly Associates Inc 119 Quincy St NE *Web:* www.trembly.com	Albuquerque	NM	87108	505-266-8616	255-0635	246
Tremont Chicago 100 E Chestnut St *TF:* 888-627-8281 ■ *Web:* www.starwoodhotels.com	Chicago	IL	60611	312-751-1900		379
Tremont House - A Wyndham Historic Hotel, The 2300 Ship 's Mechanic Row *Web:* www.thetremonthouse.com	Galveston	TX	77550	409-763-0300		379
Trempealeau County 36245 Main St *TF:* 877-538-2311 ■ *Web:* co.trempealeau.wi.us	Whitehall	WI	54773	715-538-2311	538-4210	338
Trench Plate Rental Co 13217 Laureldale Ave *TF:* 800-821-4478 ■ *Web:* www.tprco.com	Downey	CA	90242	800-821-4478		23
Trend 660 American Ave Ste 203 *TF:* 877-330-9900 ■ *Web:* www.brightmls.com	King of Prussia	PA	19406	610-783-4650		225
TREND Enterprises Inc 300 Ninth Ave SW *TF:* 800-860-6762 ■ *Web:* www.trendenterprises.com	New Brighton	MN	55112	651-631-2850		243
Trend Home Health Services 1111 Park Centre Blvd Ste 205 **Fax Area Code:* 305 ■ *TF:* 877-654-4090 ■ *Web:* www.trendhhs.com	Miami	FL	33169	877-654-4090	654-0409*	363
Trend Machinery Inc 7475 S Madison St Ste 5 *Web:* www.trendmachinery.com	Burr Ridge	IL	60527	630-655-0030		203
Trend Motors Ltd 221 US Hwy 46 *TF:* 855-426-2743 ■ *Web:* www.trendmotors.com	Rockaway	NJ	07866	973-625-0100		57
Trend Offset Printing Services Inc 3791 Catalina St *Web:* www.trendoffset.com	Los Alamitos	CA	90720	562-598-2446		627
Trend Setters School 835 S Kings Hwy *Web:* www.trendsettersschool.com	Cape Girardeau	MO	63703	573-335-9977		685
Trend Software Inc 1101 S Winchester Blvd Ste J-225 *TF:* 800-743-5820 ■ *Web:* www.propertyminder.com	San Jose	CA	95128	408-243-5820	243-5825	180
Trend Technologies LLC 4626 Eucalypus Ave *Web:* www.trendtechnologies.com	Chino	CA	91710	909-597-7861		697
Trendex Inc 240 E Maryland Ave *TF:* 800-328-9200 ■ *Web:* www.trendex.com	Saint Paul	MN	55117	651-487-7400	489-4423	86
Trending Radio 93.3 Good Hope Rd N 72 W 12922 *Web:* www.b933fm.com	Menomonee Falls	WI	53051	414-778-1933	771-3036	645
Trendl Associates Ltd 941 W Winona St Ste 1w *Web:* www.trendl.net	Chicago	IL	60640	773-728-6973		317
Trendler Inc 4540 W 51st St *Web:* www.trendler.com	Chicago	IL	60632	773-284-6600	581-6250	482
TrendMicro Inc 10101 N De Anza Blvd *TF:* 800-228-5651 ■ *Web:* www.trendmicro.com	Cupertino	CA	95014	408-257-1500		178-12
Trend-Pak of Canada 71 Railside Rd *Web:* www.trendpak.com	North York	ON	M3A1B2	416-510-3129		125
Trends International LLC 5188 W 74th St *TF:* 866-406-7771 ■ *Web:* trendsinternational.com	Indianapolis	IN	46268	317-388-1212		328
Trendsetter Engineering Inc 10430 Rodgers Rd *Web:* www.trendsetterengineering.com	Houston	TX	77070	281-465-8858		537
TrendSource Inc 4891 Pacific Hwy Ste 200 *Web:* www.trendsource.com	San Diego	CA	92110	619-718-7467		466
Trendtec Inc 2381 Zanker Rd *Web:* www.trendtec.com	San Jose	CA	95131	408-435-9500		193
Trendware International Inc 20675 Manhattan Pl *TF:* 888-326-6061 ■ *Web:* www.trendnet.com	Torrance	CA	90501	310-961-5500	961-5511	176
Trendway Corp 13467 Quincy St PO Box 9016 *TF:* 800-968-5344 ■ *Web:* www.trendway.com	Holland	MI	49422	616-399-3900		319-1
Trendwood Inc 120 E Watkins St *Web:* www.trendwood.com	Phoenix	AZ	85004	602-416-7800		319-2
Trendzitions Inc 25691 Atlantic Ocean Ste B13 *TF:* 800-266-2767 ■ *Web:* www.trendzitions.com	Lake Forest	CA	92630	949-727-9100		194
Treneff Cozza Law LLC 155 Commerce Park Dr Ste 5 *TF:* 866-829-0717 ■ *Web:* treneff.com	Westerville	OH	43082	614-891-4230	891-4301	41
Trenholm State Technical College 1225 Air Base Blvd *TF:* 866-753-4544 ■ *Web:* www.trenholmstate.edu	Montgomery	AL	36108	334-420-4200	420-4206	800
Trenk, Dipasquale, Della Fera & Sodono PC 347 Mt Pleasant Ave Ste 300 *Web:* trenklawfirm.com	West Orange	NJ	07052	973-243-8600		41
Trent Capital Management Inc 3150 N Elm St Ste 204 *Web:* trentcapital.com	Greensboro	NC	27408	336-282-9302		401
Trent Inc 201 Leverington Ave *Web:* trentheat.com	Philadelphia	PA	19127	215-482-5000	482-9389	318
Trent University 1600 W Bank Dr *TF:* 888-739-8885 ■ *Web:* www.trentu.ca	Peterborough	ON	K9J7B8	705-748-1011	748-1629	785
Trenton City Hall 319 E State St *TF:* 800-221-0051 ■ *Web:* www.trentonnj.org	Trenton	NJ	08608	609-989-3532	989-3190	337
Trenton City Museum at Ellarslie Mansion PO Box 1034 *Web:* www.ellarslie.org	Trenton	NJ	08606	609-989-1191	989-3624	520
Trenton Correctional Institution 84 Greenhouse Rd *Web:* www.doc.sc.gov	Trenton	SC	29847	803-275-3301		213
Trenton Engineering Company Inc 2193 Spruce St *Web:* trentoneng.com	Trenton	NJ	08638	609-882-0616		261
Trenton Forging Co 5523 Hoover St *Web:* www.trentonforging.com	Trenton	MI	48183	734-675-1620	675-4839	483
Trenton Mills LLC 400 Factory St *Web:* www.trentonmills.com	Trenton	TN	38382	731-855-1323	855-9000	745-6
Trenton Pipe Nipple Company LLC 1700 Industrial Park Rd *TF:* 800-257-9559 ■ *Web:* www.trentonpipe.com	Federalsburg	MD	21632	410-754-5067	754-8131	609
Trenton Psychiatric Hospital PO Box 7500 *TF:* 800-382-6717 ■ *Web:* www.nj.gov	West Trenton	NJ	08628	609-633-1500		374-5
Trenton Public Library 120 Academy St *Web:* www.trentonlib.org	Trenton	NJ	08608	609-392-7188	695-8631	434-3
Trenton Public School System 108 N Clinton Ave *Web:* www.trentonk12.org	Trenton	NJ	08609	609-656-4900	989-2682	685
Trentonian 600 Perry St *TF:* 888-489-8189 ■ *Web:* www.trentonian.com	Trenton	NJ	08618	609-989-7800	393-6072	532-2
TrepanierBaer Gallery 999 Eigth St SW Ste 105 *Web:* www.trepanierbaer.com	Calgary	AB	T2R1J5	403-244-2066	244-2094	42
Trepp LLC 477 Madison Ave *Web:* www.trepp.com	New York	NY	10022	212-754-1010	832-6738	463
Tres West Engineers Inc 2702 S 42nd St Ste 301 *Web:* treswest.com	Tacoma	WA	98409	253-472-3300		261
Tresca 233 Hanover St *Web:* trescanorthend.com	Boston	MA	02113	617-742-8240		671
TrestleTree Inc 3715 Business Dr Ste 202 *TF:* 866-523-8185 ■ *Web:* www.trestletree.com	Fayetteville	AR	72703	479-582-0777	582-0778	194
Tresu Royse Inc 8517 Directors Row *Web:* www.tresu.com	Dallas	TX	75247	214-631-2844		629
Treu House of Munch Inc 8000 Arbor Dr *Web:* www.treuhouse.com	Northwood	OH	43619	419-666-7770		81-1
Trevarrow Inc 1295 N Opdyke Rd *Web:* www.trevarrowinc.com	Auburn Hills	MI	48326	248-377-2300	377-2392	38
Trevecca Nazarene University 333 Murfreesboro Rd *TF:* 888-210-4868 ■ *Web:* www.trevecca.edu	Nashville	TN	37210	615-248-1200	248-7406	166
Trevena 1018 W Eighth Ave Ste A *Web:* www.trevena.com	King of Prussia	PA	19406	610-354-8840		231
Treviicos Corp 38 Third Ave *Web:* www.treviicos.com	Charlestown	MA	02129	617-241-4800		189-3

Phone | Fax | Class

Trevini 150 Worth Ave ... Palm Beach Gardens FL 33480 — 561-833-3883 — 671
Web: www.treviniristorante.com

Trevis Berry Transportation Inc
655 E Luchessa Ave ... Gilroy CA 95020 — 408-842-8238 842-5678 780
TF: 800-926-8789 ■ *Web:* trevisberry.com

Trew Industrial Wheels Inc
310 Wilhagan Rd ... Nashville TN 37217 — 615-360-9100 — 54
TF: 888-977-8739 ■ *Web:* www.trew-wheels.com

T-Rex Engineering & Construction LC
16425 Jacintoport Blvd ... Houston TX 77015 — 281-833-9200 — 539

Trex Enterprises Corp
10455 Pacific Center Ct ... San Diego CA 92121 — 858-646-5300 646-5301 668
TF: 800-626-5885 ■ *Web:* www.trexenterprises.com

Trexler Rubber Company Inc
503 N Diamond St ... Ravenna OH 44266 — 330-296-9677 296-2272 676
TF: 800-860-0082 ■ *Web:* www.trexlerrubber.com

Trey Helton State Farm
2650 Memorial Blvd Ste C ... Murfreesboro TN 37129 — 615-895-0500 — 390
Web: treyhelton.com

TreyArch
3420 Ocean Pk Blvd Ste 1000 ... Santa Monica CA 90405 — 310-581-4700 — 178-6
Web: www.treyarch.com

Treynor Bancshares Inc 15 E Main St ... Treynor IA 51575 — 712-487-3000 487-3475 360-2
Web: www.tsbank.com

Treyton Oak Towers 211 W Oak St ... Louisville KY 40203 — 502-589-3211 — 672
Web: www.treytonoaktowers.com

Trez Capital LP
1550 - 1185 W Georgia St ... Vancouver BC V6E4E6 — 604-689-0821 638-2775 528
TF: 877-689-0821 ■ *Web:* www.trezcapital.com

TRFCVB (Thief River Falls Convention & Visitors Bureau)
102 Main Ave N ... Thief River Falls MN 56701 — 218-686-9785 — 206
Web: visittrf.com

TRG Holdings LLC
1700 Pennsylvania Ave NW ... Washington DC 20006 — 202-289-9898 — 737
Web: www.trgworld.com

TRG Inc 1287 N Alma School Rd Ste 103 ... Chandler AZ 85226 — 480-838-0287 — 180
Web: nexedge.com

TRG Networking
11436 Cronhill Dr Ste 4B ... Owings Mills MD 21117 — 410-363-6980 — 177
Web: www.trgnetworking.com

TRGC (Title Resources Guaranty Co)
8111 LBJ Fwy Ste 1200 ... Dallas TX 75251 — 800-526-8018 485-3630* 391-6
**Fax Area Code:* 888 ■ *TF:* 800-526-8018 ■ *Web:* www.titleresources.com

TRH (Touchette Regional Hospital)
5900 Bond Ave ... Centreville IL 62207 — 618-332-3060 — 374-3
Web: www.touchette.org

TRI (Trap Rock Industries LLC)
PO Box 419 ... Kingston NJ 08528 — 609-924-0300 497-0135 503-5
Web: www.traprock.com

TRI (Transition Resources Inc)
12209 Park Bend Dr ... Dallas TX 75230 — 214-384-9130 — 194
Web: www.transitioninc.com

Tri Cities Business Journal
1114 Sunset Dr Ste 2 ... Johnson City TN 37604 — 423-854-0140 — 457-5
Web: bjournal.com

Tri City Bankshares Corp
6400 S 27th St ... Oak Creek WI 53154 — 414-761-1610 — 70
OTC: TRCY ■ *Web:* www.tcnb.com

Tri City Foods Inc
1400 Opus Pl Ste 900 ... Downers Grove IL 60515 — 630-598-3300 — 670
Web: www.3cityfoods.com

Tri Commercial Real Estate Services Inc
100 Pine St Ste 1000 ... San Francisco CA 94111 — 415-268-2200 268-2289 652
Web: www.tricommercial.com

Tri County Area Chamber of Commerce
152 E High St Ste 360 ... Pottstown PA 19464 — 610-326-2900 970-9705 139
Web: www.tricountyareachamber.com

Tri County Ford 4032 Commerce Pkwy ... Buckner KY 40010 — 888-348-3186 — 57
TF: 800-945-2520 ■ *Web:* www.tricountyford.com

Tri Dal Ltd 540 Commerce St ... Southlake TX 76092 — 817-481-2886 481-8195 188-10
Web: tridal.com

Tri Electronics Inc 6231 Calumet Ave ... Hammond IN 46324 — 219-931-6850 — 246
TF: 800-722-6793 ■ *Web:* www.tri-electronics.com

TRI MAP International Inc
119 Val Dervin Pkwy Ste 5 ... Stockton CA 95206 — 209-234-0100 234-5990 254
TF: 888-687-4627 ■ *Web:* www.trimapintl.com

TRI Princeton 601 Prospect Ave ... Princeton NJ 08540 — 609-430-4820 — 49-13
Web: www.triprinceton.org

Tri Print LLC
7573 Slater Ave Unit C ... Huntington Beach CA 92647 — 714-847-1400 — 351
Web: triprint.com

Tri Properties Inc
4309 Emperor Blvd Ste 110 ... Durham NC 27703 — 919-941-5745 — 652
Web: www.triprop.com

Tri Rivers Career Ctr
2222 Marion Mt Gilead Rd ... Marion OH 43302 — 740-389-4681 389-2963 148
Web: tririvers.com

Tri Star Energy LLC
1740 Ed Temple Blvd ... Nashville TN 37208 — 615-313-3600 313-3612 541
Web: tristartn.com

Tri Star Engineering Inc 3000 16th St ... Bedford IN 47421 — 812-277-0208 — 261
Web: star3.com

Tri Star Freight System Inc
5407 Mesa Dr ... Houston TX 77028 — 713-631-1095 631-1099 780
TF: 800-229-1095 ■ *Web:* tristarfreightsys.com

Tri Star Industrial Co
1645 W Buckeye Rd ... Phoenix AZ 85007 — 602-252-0554 — 358
Web: www.tristaraz.com

Tri Star Metals LLC
375 Village Dr ... Carol Stream IL 60188 — 630-462-7600 — 492
TF: 800-541-2294 ■ *Web:* www.tristarmetals.com

Tri Starr Services of Pennsylvania Inc
2201 Oregon Pk ... Lancaster PA 17601 — 717-560-2111 — 260
Web: www.tristarrjobs.com

Tri State Accounting 4735 Cornell Rd ... Blue Ash OH 45241 — 513-791-6288 — 2
Web: www.tri-statecpas.com

Tri State Distribution Inc
Altium Healthcare
2500 Windy Ridge Parkway SE Ste 1400 ... Atlanta GA 30339 — 800-392-9824 — 475
TF: 800-392-9824 ■ *Web:* www.altiumhealthcare.com

Tri State Distributors Inc
PO Box 3623 ... Spokane WA 99220 — 509-455-8300 — 362
Web: shop.tristatedistributors.com

Tri State G & T Assn
1100 W 116th Ave ... Westminster CO 80234 — 303-452-6111 — 518
Web: www.tristategt.com

Tri State Warehouse Inc PO Box 2186 ... Cleveland TN 37320 — 423-479-1033 479-5750 803-1
Web: www.tristatewarehouse.com

Tri State Wholesale Flooring Inc
3900 W 34th St N ... Sioux Falls SD 57107 — 605-336-3080 — 131
TF: 800-353-3080 ■ *Web:* tsf.com

Tri Supply Co 7410 Eastex Fwy ... Beaumont TX 77708 — 409-835-7966 — 364
TF: 844-874-1958 ■ *Web:* trisupplyhome.com

Tri Tech Surveying Company LP
10401 Westoffice Dr ... Houston TX 77042 — 713-667-0800 667-4262 261
Web: tritechtx.com

Tri Tool Inc 3041 Sunrise Blvd ... Rancho Cordova CA 95742 — 916-288-6100 288-6160 621
TF: 800-345-5015 ■ *Web:* tritool.com

Tri Union Express Inc
1939 N Lafayette Ct ... Griffith IN 46319 — 219-838-5400 — 803-1
Web: www.triunion.com

Tri Valley Service Credit Unio
1920 Cochran Rd ... Pittsburgh PA 15220 — 412-344-3406 — 219
Web: trivalleyservice.com

Tri Venture Marketing Inc
2525 Drane Field Rd Ste 1 ... Lakeland FL 33811 — 863-648-1881 — 297-8

Triad Advertising Inc
1017 Turnpark St Ste 32a ... Canton MA 02021 — 781-828-9290 — 7
Web: www.triadadvertising.com

Triad Automation Inc
6102 Corporate Park Dr ... Browns Summit NC 27214 — 336-375-8440 — 57
Web: www.triadautomation.com

Triad Bank NA 7666 E 61st St Ste 150 ... Tulsa OK 74133 — 800-317-6204 — 70
TF: 800-317-6204 ■ *Web:* triadbank.com

Triad Broadcasting Company LLC
2511 Garden Rd Ste A-104 ... Monterey CA 93940 — 831-655-6350 655-6355 643

Triad Consulting Engineers Inc
2740 Rte 10 W Ste 2 ... Morris Plains NJ 07950 — 973-984-1919 — 261
Web: www.triadcei.com

Triad Creative Group
3130 Intertech Dr ... Brookfield WI 53045 — 262-781-3100 — 393
Web: www.triadcreativegroup.com

Triad Energy Corp
1616 S Voss Rd Ste 650 ... Houston TX 77057 — 713-783-2291 — 538
Web: www.triad-energy.com

Triad Enterprises Inc
1730 Old Dunbar Rd ... West Columbia SC 29172 — 803-796-4000 796-4527 627
Web: www.proprinters.com

Triad Financial Services Inc
4336 Pablo Oaks Ct ... Jacksonville FL 32224 — 800-522-2013 — 217
TF: 800-522-2013 ■ *Web:* www.triadfs.com

Triad Freightliner of Tennessee LLC
841 Eastern Star Rd ... Kingsport TN 37663 — 800-451-1508 349-0431* 57
**Fax Area Code:* 423 ■ *TF:* 800-451-1508 ■ *Web:* www.triadfreightlinertn.com

Triad Governmental Systems Inc
358 S Monroe St ... Xenia OH 45385 — 937-376-5446 376-3078 177
TF: 800-666-5446 ■ *Web:* www.triadgsi.net

Triad Guaranty Insurance Corp
101 S Stratford Rd ... Winston-Salem NC 27104 — 336-723-1282 — 391-5
TF: 888-691-8074 ■ *Web:* www.tgic.com

Triad Manufacturing Inc
4321 Semple Ave ... Saint Louis MO 63120 — 314-381-5280 — 803-1
Web: triadmfg.com

Triad Metal Products Co
5175 Ravenway Dr ... North Ridgeville OH 44039 — 216-676-6505 — 488
Web: triadmetal.com

Triad Precision Products Inc
888 E Marshall St ... Tulsa OK 74106 — 918-584-3543 — 326
Web: www.triadprecision.com

Triad Productions Inc
1910 Ingersoll Ave ... Des Moines IA 50309 — 515-243-2125 — 179
Web: www.triadav.com

Triad Products Co 1801 W 'B' St ... Hastings NE 68901 — 402-462-2181 462-2246 608
TF: 888-253-4227 ■ *Web:* www.triadproducts.net

Triad Publishing Company Inc
PO Box 13355 ... Gainesville FL 32604 — 352-727-9345 — 637-2
Web: www.triadpublishing.com

Triad Security Systems 971 Lehigh Ave ... Union NJ 07083 — 908-964-5252 — 693
Web: www.triadsecurity.com

Triad Strategies 116 Pine St ... Harrisburg PA 17101 — 717-238-2970 — 636
Web: www.triadstrategies.com

Triad Tooling Inc 12195 Mariposa St ... Denver CO 80234 — 303-424-4280 424-3502 493
TF: 800-382-8904 ■ *Web:* www.triadtooling.net

Triage Consulting Group
221 Main St Ste 1100 ... San Francisco CA 94105 — 415-512-9400 512-9404 194
Web: www.triageconsulting.com

Trial Behavior Consulting Inc
601 Montgomery St Ste 1210 ... San Francisco CA 94111 — 415-781-5879 — 445
Web: trialbehavior.com

Trial Consulting Enterprises
6607 Tulip Ln ... Dallas TX 75230 — 972-735-8450 — 194
Web: www.trialconsultingenterprises.com

TrialCard Inc
2250 Perimeter Park Dr Ste 300 ... Morrisville NC 27560 — 919-845-0774 — 194
TF: 877-343-1238 ■ *Web:* corp.trialcard.com

Trian Partners 280 Park Ave ... New York NY 10017 — 212-451-3000 451-3134 360-3
Web: trianpartners.com

Triangle Brick Co 6523 NC Hwy 55 ... Durham NC 27713 — 919-544-1796 544-3904 150
TF: 800-672-8547 ■ *Web:* www.trianglebrick.com

Triangle C Dude Ranch 3737 Hwy 26 ... Dubois WY 82513 — 307-455-2225 — 239
TF: 800-661-4928 ■ *Web:* www.trianglec.com

Triangle Candy & Tobacco Company Inc
145 Sandy Creek Rd ... Verona PA 15147 — 412-798-8400 — 756
Web: trianglecandy.com

Name / Address	City	State	ZIP	Phone	Fax	Class
Triangle Construction Inc 2624 Laurens Rd *Web:* www.triangleconstruction.com	Greenville	SC	29607	864-288-5500		186
Triangle East Chamber of Commerce 1115 Industrial Pk Dr *Web:* www.triangleeastchamber.com	Smithfield	NC	27577	919-934-9166	934-1337	139
Triangle Electric Co 29787 Stephenson Hwy *Web:* www.trielec.com	Madison Heights	MI	48071	248-399-2200	399-2612	189-4
Triangle Engineering Inc 6 Industrial Way *Web:* www.trieng.com	Hanover	MA	02339	781-878-1500		595
Triangle Fastener Corp 1925 Preble Ave *TF:* 800-486-1832 ■ *Web:* www.trianglefastener.com	Pittsburgh	PA	15233	412-321-5000	321-7838	351
Triangle Manufacturing Co 150 Libbey Ave *TF:* 800-959-0375 ■ *Web:* www.triangleoshkosh.com	Oshkosh	WI	54901	920-235-3710	235-4523	620
Triangle MicroWorks Inc 2840 Plaza Pl Ste 205 *Web:* www.trianglemicroworks.com	Raleigh	NC	27612	919-870-5101		177
Triangle Orthopedic Associates PA 120 William Penn Plz *Web:* www.triangleortho.com	Durham	NC	27704	919-220-5255		374-3
Triangle Package Machinery Co 6655 W Diversey Ave *TF:* 800-621-4170 ■ *Web:* www.trianglepackage.com	Chicago	IL	60707	773-889-0200	889-4221	547
Triangle Precision Industries Inc 1650 Delco Park Dr *Web:* www.triangleprecision.com	Dayton	OH	45420	937-299-6776	299-7340	454
Triangle Process Equipment Inc 2307 Industrial Park Dr SE *Web:* www.4tpe.com	Wilson	NC	27893	252-246-1089		789
Triangle Rubber Company Inc PO Box 95 *Web:* www.trianglerubberco.com	Goshen	IN	46527	574-533-3118	534-0416	677
Triangle Scenery Drapery & Lighting Co 1215 Bates Ave *Web:* www.tridrape.com	Los Angeles	CA	90029	323-662-8129		722
Triangle Securities LLC 1301 Annapolis Dr *TF:* 877-678-5901 ■ *Web:* trianglesecurities.com	Raleigh	NC	27608	919-838-3221		401
Triangle Suspension Systems Inc 200 E Maloney Rd *TF:* 800-458-6077 ■ *Web:* www.triangleusa.com	DuBois	PA	15801	800-458-6077	237-2396	60
Triangle Tech 191 Performance Rd Rte 890 *TF:* 800-874-8324 ■ *Web:* www.triangle-tech.edu	Sunbury	PA	17801	570-988-0700		800
Triangle Tech Inc *Erie* 1940 Perrysville Ave *Web:* triangle-tech.edu	Erie	PA	16502	814-453-6016		800
Triangle Tool Corp 8609 W Port Ave *Web:* www.triangletoolcorp.com	Milwaukee	WI	53224	414-357-7117	357-7610	757
Triangle X Ranch 2 Triangle X Ranch Rd *Web:* www.trianglex.com	Moose	WY	83012	307-733-2183		239
Triangle X-ray Co 4900 Thornton Rd Ste 117 *TF:* 866-763-9729 ■ *Web:* trianglexray.com	Raleigh	NC	27616	919-876-6156		475
Trianon Old Naples 955 Seventh Ave S *TF:* 877-482-5228 ■ *Web:* www.trianon.com	Naples	FL	34102	239-435-9600		379
Trianz 2350 Mission College Blvd Ste 1250 *Web:* www.trianz.com	Santa Clara	CA	95054	408-387-5800	387-5702	180
Triasima Portfolio Management Inc 1200-1555 Peel St *Web:* triasima.com	Montreal	QC	H3A3L8	514-906-0667	284-3060	528
Triathlete Sports 186 Exchange St *TF:* 800-635-0528 ■ *Web:* www.triathletesports.com	Bangor	ME	04401	207-990-2013		711
Triathlon Medical Ventures LLC (TMVP) 9987 Carver Rd Ste 210 *Web:* www.tmvp.com	Cincinnati	OH	45242	513-247-6122		792
Triax Data Inc 800 S Gay St Ste 650 *Web:* www.triaxdata.com	Knoxville	TN	37929	865-971-4333		195
Triaxis Engineering Inc *David Evans and Associates Inc* 2100 S River Pkwy Ste 100 *Web:* www.deainc.com	Portland	OR	97333	541-766-4600		261
Trib Total Media LLC 210 Wood St **Fax Area Code: 724* ■ *TF:* 800-909-8742 ■ *Web:* www.tribtotalmedia.com	Tarentum	PA	15084	800-909-8742	779-8743*	637-10
Tribal Nova Inc 4200 Boul Saint-Laurent Ste 1203 *Web:* www.tribalnova.com	Montreal	QC	H2W2R2	514-590-4234		225
Tribalco LLC 4915 St Elmo Ave Ste 501 *Web:* www.tribalco.com	Bethesda	MD	20814	301-652-8450		186
Tribar Manufacturing LLC 2211 Grand Commerce Dr *Web:* www.tribarmfg.com	Howell	MI	48855	517-545-4200	545-4201	604
Tri-Basin Natural Resources District 1723 Burlington St *TF:* 877-995-6688 ■ *Web:* www.tribasinnrd.org	Holdrege	NE	68949	308-995-6688		196
Tribble & Stephens Construction Ltd 8588 Katy Fwy Ste 100 *Web:* www.tribblestephens.com	Houston	TX	77024	713-465-8550	973-7107	186
Tribco Construction Services 10 S LaSalle St Ste 202 *Web:* www.tribco-services.com	Chicago	IL	60603	312-341-0303		189-2
Tribe Design LLC 1420 Mcilhenny St *Web:* tribedesign.com	Houston	TX	77004	713-523-5119		344
Tribeca Enterprises LLC 375 Greenwich St *Web:* www.tribecafilm.com	New York	NY	10013	212-675-7223	941-3997	514
Tribeca Flashpoint College 28 N Clark St Ste 500 *Web:* www.tribecaflashpoint.edu	Chicago	IL	60602	312-506-0600	506-0708	167-3
Tribeca Oven Inc 447 Gotham Pkwy *Web:* tribecaoven.com	Carlstadt	NJ	07072	201-935-8800		345
TRIBECA Performing Arts Ctr 199 Chambers St *Web:* tickets.tribecapac.org	New York	NY	10007	212-220-1459	732-2482	572

Name / Address	City	State	ZIP	Phone	Fax	Class
Triboro Quilt Manufacturing Inc 172 S Broadway *Web:* www.cuddletime.com	White Plains	NY	10605	914-428-7551		64
Tri-boro Shelving & Partition Corp 300 Dominion Dr *TF:* 800-633-3070 ■ *Web:* www.triboroshelving.com	Farmville	VA	23901	434-315-5600		321
Tribune Chronicle 240 Franklin St SE *Web:* www.tribtoday.com	Warren	OH	44483	330-841-1600	841-1717	532-2
Tribune Direct Marketing Inc 505 Northwest Ave *TF:* 800-545-9657 ■ *Web:* tribunedirect.com	Northlake	IL	60164	800-545-9657		5
Tribune Inc 2012 Forest Ave *Web:* www.gbtribune.com	Great Bend	KS	67530	620-792-1211		532-3
Tribune Media 435 N Michigan Ave *Web:* www.tribune.com	Chicago	IL	60611	312-222-5995	527-8117	738
Tribune Newspapers of Snohomish County 127 Ave C Ste B PO Box 499 *TF:* 877-894-4663 ■ *Web:* www.snoho.com	Snohomish	WA	98291	360-568-4121	568-1484	532-4
Tribune Review Publishing Co 622 Cabin Hill Dr *TF:* 800-524-5700 ■ *Web:* pittsburghpennysaver.com	Greensburg	PA	15601	724-834-1151		637-8
Tribune, The 3825 S Higuera St *TF:* 800-477-8799 ■ *Web:* www.sanluisobispo.com	San Luis Obispo	CA	93401	805-781-7800	781-7905	532-2
Tribune, The 228 E Main St *Web:* www.wellandtribune.ca	Welland	ON	L3B5P5	905-732-2411		532-1
Tribune/Georgian, The PO Box 6960 *Web:* www.tribune-georgian.com	Saint Marys	GA	31558	912-882-4927	882-6519	532-2
Tribune-Democrat 425 Locust St *TF:* 855-255-5975 ■ *Web:* www.tribdem.com	Johnstown	PA	15907	814-532-5050	539-1409	532-2
Tribune-Star PO Box 149 *TF:* 800-783-8742 ■ *Web:* www.tribstar.com	Terre Haute	IN	47808	812-231-4200	231-4321	532-2
Tributary Systems Inc 3717 Commerce Pl Ste C *Web:* www.tributary.com	Bedford	TX	76021	817-354-8009	786-3090	174
Tribute Resources Inc 2807 Woodhull Rd *Web:* www.tributeresources.com	London	ON	N6J1Y4	519-657-7624	657-4296	538
Tri-C Construction Company Inc 1765 Merriman Rd *Web:* www.tricc.com	Akron	OH	44313	330-836-2722	869-8373	186
Tri-C Resources Inc 909 Wirt Rd *Web:* www.tricresources.com	Houston	TX	77024	713-685-3600		539
Trican Well Service Ltd 645 Seventh Ave SW Ste 2900 *TSE: TCW* ■ *Web:* www.tricanwellservice.com	Calgary	AB	T2P4G8	403-266-0202	237-7716	539
Tricerat Inc 11500 Cronridge Dr Ste 100 *TF:* 800-582-5167 ■ *Web:* www.tricerat.com	Owings Mills	MD	21117	410-715-4226		179
Tri-Chem 681 Main St Bldg 27 *Web:* www.trichem.com	Belleville	NJ	07109	973-751-9200	450-1260	43
Trichotillomania Learning Center Inc (TLC) 207 McPherson St Ste H	Santa Cruz	CA	95060	831-457-1004		48-17
Trichter & Legrand PC 420 Heights Blvd *Web:* texasdwilaw.com	Houston	TX	77007	713-524-1010		41
Tri-Cities Beverage Corp 612 Industrial Park Dr	Newport News	VA	23608	757-874-6600		297-8
Tri-Cities Chamber of Commerce 2773 Barnet Hwy Ste 205 *Web:* tricitieschamber.com	Coquitlam	BC	V3B1C2	604-464-2716	464-6796	137
Tri-Cities Opera 315 Clinton St *Web:* www.tricitiesopera.com	Binghamton	NY	13905	607-729-3444		573-2
Tri-Cities Regional Airport 2525 Hwy 75 Ste 301 *TF:* 888-874-7404 ■ *Web:* triflight.com	Blountville	TN	37617	423-325-6000	325-6060	27
Tri-Cities Visitor & Convention Bureau 7130 W Grandridge Blvd Ste B *TF:* 800-254-5824 ■ *Web:* www.visittri-cities.com	Kennewick	WA	99336	509-735-8486	783-9005	206
Tri-City Area Chamber of Commerce 7130 W Grandridge Blvd *Web:* www.tricityregionalchamber.com	Kennewick	WA	99336	509-736-0510	783-1733	139
Tri-City Electrical Contractors Inc 430 W Dr *TF:* 800-768-2489 ■ *Web:* www.tcelectric.com	Altamonte Springs	FL	32714	407-788-3500	682-7353	189-4
Tri-City Glass & Door Inc 100 W Northland Ave *Web:* tricityglass-door.com	Appleton	WI	54911	920-731-8176		61
Tri-City Heat Treat Co 2020 Fifth St *Web:* www.tcht.com	Rock Island	IL	61201	309-786-2689	786-2691	484
Tri-City Herald 333 W Canal Dr *TF:* 800-874-0445 ■ *Web:* www.tri-cityherald.com	Kennewick	WA	99336	509-582-1500	582-1510	532-2
Tri-City Medical Ctr 4002 Vista Way *Web:* www.tricitymed.org	Oceanside	CA	92056	760-724-8411		374-3
Tri-city Veterinary Clinic Inc 1929 W Vista Way *Web:* tricityvet.com	Vista	CA	92083	760-758-2091		794
Trick Flow Specialties 285 W Ave *TF:* 888-841-6556 ■ *Web:* www.trickflow.com	Tallmadge	OH	44278	330-630-1555	633-2504	54
Trickle Up Program Inc 104 W 27th St 12th Fl *TF:* 866-246-9980 ■ *Web:* trickleup.org	New York	NY	10001	212-255-9980	255-9974	48-5
Triclinic Labs 1201 Cumberland Ave Ste S *Web:* tricliniclabs.com	West Lafayette	IN	47906	765-588-6200		231
TriCo Bancshares 63 Constitution Dr *NASDAQ: TCBK* ■ *TF:* 800-922-8742 ■ *Web:* www.tcbk.com	Chico	CA	95973	530-898-0300		360-2
Trico Electric Coop 8600 W Tangerine Rd *Web:* www.trico.coop	Marana	AZ	85653	520-744-2944		245
Trico Products Corp 3255 W Hamlin Rd *Web:* www.tricoproducts.com	Rochester Hills	MI	48309	248-371-1700	371-8300	60
Tricoci University 202 E University Ave *Web:* www.tricociuniversity.edu	Urbana	IL	61801	217-344-7550		786
Tricolor Inc 1111 W Mockingbird Ln Ste 1500 *TF:* 888-253-0423 ■ *Web:* www.tricolor.com	Dallas	TX	75247	888-253-0423		180

	Phone	Fax	Class
Tri-com Consulting Group LLC, The 333 Industrial Park Rd .... Middletown CT 06457 *Web:* www.tricomgroup.com	860-635-9600		196
Tricom Document Management Inc 2450 Peralta Blvd Ste 222 .... Fremont CA 94536 *Web:* www.tricom.wordpress.com	510-494-7800	494-7802	463
Tricom Technical Services 11115 Ash St .... Leawood KS 66211 *Web:* www.tricomts.com	913-652-0600		260
Tricomm Services Corp 1247 N Church St Ste 12 .... Moorestown NJ 08057 *TF:* 800-872-2401 ■ *Web:* www.tricommcorp.com	856-914-9001	914-9065	787
Tri-Con Inc 7076 W Port Arthur Rd PO Box 20555 .... Beaumont TX 77705 *TF:* 800-876-7102 ■ *Web:* www.triconinc.org	409-835-2237		579
Tricon Industries Inc *Electromechanical Div* 2325 Wisconsin Ave .... Downers Grove IL 60515 *Web:* www.industrialinterface.com	630-964-2330	964-5179	604
TRICOR (Tennessee Rehabilitative Initiative in Correction) 240 Great Cir Rd Ste 310 .... Nashville TN 37228 *TF:* 800-958-7426 ■ *Web:* www.tricor.org	615-741-5705	741-2747	630
Tricor America Inc 717 Airport Blvd .... South San Francisco CA 94080 *Web:* www.tricor.com	801-974-4476		546
Tricor Employment Screening Ltd 110 Blaze Industrial Pkwy Ste C .... Berea OH 44017 *TF:* 800-818-5116 ■ *Web:* tricorinfo.com	800-818-5116		41
TRI-COR Industries Inc 4403 Forbes Blvd .... Lanham MD 20706 *Web:* www.tricorind.com	301-731-6140		180
TRICOR Insurance Inc 230 W Cherry St .... Lancaster WI 53813 *TF:* 877-468-7426 ■ *Web:* www.tricorinsurance.com	608-723-6441		390
Tricor Metals Inc 3225 W Old Lincoln Way .... Wooster OH 44691 *TF:* 800-421-5141 ■ *Web:* www.tricormetals.com	330-264-3299		295
Tricor Print Communications Inc 7931 NE Halsey St Ste 101 .... Portland OR 97213 *TF:* 800-635-7778 ■ *Web:* www.tricorbrandsit.com	503-255-5595		627
TRICOR Systems Inc 1650 Todd Farm Dr .... Elgin IL 60123 *Web:* www.tricor-systems.com	847-742-5542		668
Tricorbraun Winepak 2280 Cordelia Rd .... Fairfield CA 94534 *TF:* 800-374-6594 ■ *Web:* www.tricorbraun.com	800-374-6594		334
TriCore Inc 117 N Gold Dr Bldg 1 .... Robbinsville NJ 08691 *Web:* www.tricore.com	609-918-2668		193
TriCore Reference Laboratories 1001 Woodward Pl NE .... Albuquerque NM 87102 *TF:* 800-245-3296 ■ *Web:* www.tricore.org	505-938-8888		415
Tri-County Beverage Co 2651 E 10 Mile Rd .... Warren MI 48091 *Web:* www.tricountybeverage.com	586-757-4900		81-1
Tri-County Building Supplies Inc 1001 Doughty Rd .... Pleasantville NJ 08232 *Web:* www.tcbsi.com	609-646-0950	646-3558	364
Tri-County Chamber of Commerce PO Box 2420 .... Wayne NJ 07474 **Fax Area Code:* 973 ■ *Web:* tricounty.org	862-210-8328	881-8233*	139
Tri-County Communications Cooperative Inc (TCC) 417 5th Ave N .... Strum WI 54770 *TF:* 800-831-0610 ■ *Web:* tccpro.net	715-695-2816	695-3599	224
Tri-County Community College 21 Campus Cir .... Murphy NC 28906 *Web:* www.tricountycc.edu	828-837-6810	837-3266	162
Tri-County Electric 995 Mile 46 Rd PO Box 880 .... Hooker OK 73945 *TF:* 800-522-3315 ■ *Web:* www.tri-countyelectric.coop	580-652-2418	652-3151	245
Tri-County Electric Co-op PO Box 159 .... Lancaster MO 63548 *TF:* 888-457-3734 ■ *Web:* www.tricountyelectric.org	660-457-3733		245
Tri-County Electric Co-op 6473 Old State Rd .... Saint Matthews SC 29135 *TF:* 877-874-1215 ■ *Web:* tri-countyelectric.net	803-874-1215		245
Tri-County Electric Co-opeartive Inc 2862 W US Hwy 90 .... Madison FL 32340 *TF:* 800-999-2285 ■ *Web:* www.tcec.com	850-973-2285		245
Tri-County Electric Co-opeartive Inc 3906 Broadway St .... Mount Vernon IL 62864 *TF:* 800-244-5151 ■ *Web:* www.tricountycoop.com	618-244-5151	244-1496	245
Tri-County Electric Co-opeartive Inc 600 NW Pkwy .... Azle TX 76020 *TF:* 800-367-8232 ■ *Web:* tcectexas.com	817-444-3201	444-3542	245
Tri-County Electric Membership Corp PO Box 487 .... Gray GA 31032 *TF:* 866-254-8100 ■ *Web:* www.tri-countyemc.com	478-986-8100	986-4733	245
Tri-County Electric Membership Corp 405 College St .... LaFayette TN 37083 **Fax Area Code:* 615 ■ *TF:* 800-369-2111 ■ *Web:* www.tcemc.org	800-369-2111	688-2141*	245
Tri-County Independent 220 Eigth St .... Honesdale PA 18431 *TF:* 800-598-5002 ■ *Web:* www.tricountyindependent.com	570-253-3055		532-2
Tri-County Mall 11700 Princeton Pk .... Cincinnati OH 45246 *TF:* 866-905-4675 ■ *Web:* www.tricountymall.com	513-671-0120	671-2931	460
Tri-County Metropolitan Transportation District of Oregon 4012 SE 17th Ave .... Portland OR 97202 *Web:* www.trimet.org	503-962-7655	962-6469	468
Tri-County Regional Vocational Technical School 147 Pond St .... Franklin MA 02038 *Web:* www.tri-county.us	508-528-5400		162
Tri-County ROP 970 Klamath Ln .... Yuba City CA 95993 *Web:* www.sutter.k12.ca.us	530-822-5120		226
Tri-County Rural Electric Co-opeartive Inc 22 N Main St PO Box 526 .... Mansfield PA 16933 *TF:* 800-343-2559 ■ *Web:* www.tri-countyrec.com	570-662-2175		245
Tricounty Rural Electric Cooperative Inc 8945 County Rd K2 .... Malinta OH 43535 *Web:* www.tricountyelectriccoop.coop	419-256-7900	256-6581	245

	Phone	Fax	Class
Tri-County Technical College 7900 Hwy 76 .... Pendleton SC 29670 *TF:* 866-269-5677 ■ *Web:* tctc.edu	864-646-8361	646-1890	800
Tri-County Trust Co 103 Commerce St .... Glasgow MO 65254 *Web:* tricountytrust.com	660-338-2234	338-2727	70
Tricycle Inc 1293 Riverfront Pkwy Ste 1293-B .... Chattanooga TN 37402 *TF:* 800-808-4809 ■ *Web:* www.tricycleinc.com	800-808-4809		809
Tridan International Inc 130 N Jackson St .... Danville IL 61832 *Web:* www.tridan.com	217-443-3592	443-3894	494
Tridel Corp 4800 Dufferin St Ste 200 .... Toronto ON M3H5S9 *Web:* www.tridel.com	416-661-9394		655
Trident Capital 400 S El Camino Real Ste 300 .... San Mateo CA 94402 *Web:* www.tridentcap.com	650-289-4400	289-4444	792
Trident Contract Management 2918 Marketplace Dr Ste 206 .... Madison WI 53719 *Web:* www.trident-it.com	608-276-1900		175
Trident Crating & Services Inc 14320 InterDr E .... Houston TX 77032 *Web:* www.tridentcrating.com	281-227-3999		549
Trident Environmental & Engineering 110 L St Ste 1 .... Antioch CA 94509 *TF:* 800-577-4596 ■ *Web:* www.tridenteng.com	925-706-6931	778-9067	261
Trident Labs Inc 12000 Aviation Blvd .... Hawthorne CA 90250 *Web:* www.tridentlab.com	310-915-9121		228
Trident LP 1000 444-7th Ave SW .... Calgary AB T2P0X8 *Web:* www.tridentexploration.ca	403-770-0333	668-5805	787
Trident Marketing 1930 N Poplar St .... Southern Pines NC 28387 *Web:* www.tridentmarketing.com	910-693-4000		195
Trident Media Group LLC 41 Madison Ave 36th Fl .... New York NY 10010 *Web:* www.tridentmediagroup.com	212-333-1511		444
Trident Medical Ctr 9330 Medical Plaza Dr .... Charleston SC 29406 *TF:* 866-492-9085 ■ *Web:* tridenthealthsystem.com	843-797-7000		374-3
Trident Micro Systems 2 Trident Dr .... Arden NC 28704	828-684-7474		246
Trident Precision Manufacturing Inc 734 Salt Rd .... Webster NY 14580 *Web:* www.tridentprecision.com	585-265-2010	265-2386	488
Trident Process Inc 10800 Lyndale Ave S Ste 171 .... Minneapolis MN 55420 *Web:* www.tridentprocess.com	952-881-7271		146
Trident Seafood Corp 5303 Shilshole Ave NW .... Seattle WA 98107 *TF:* 800-426-5490 ■ *Web:* www.tridentseafoods.com	206-783-3818	782-7195	296-14
Trident Security Service 4968 Dorchester Rd .... Charleston SC 29418 *Web:* www.tsecurityservices.com	843-767-3855		693
Trident Steel Corp 12825 Flushing Meadows Dr Ste 110 .... Saint Louis MO 63131 *TF:* 800-777-9687 ■ *Web:* tridentsteel.com	314-822-0500		492
Trident Systems Inc 10201 Fairfax Blvd Ste 300 .... Fairfax VA 22030 *Web:* www.tridsys.com	703-273-1012	273-6608	21
Trident Technical College (TTC) 7000 Rivers Ave PO Box 118067 .... North Charleston SC 29406 *TF:* 877-349-7184 ■ *Web:* www.tridenttech.edu	843-574-6111	574-6483	800
Trident Technologies Inc 8885 Rehco Rd .... San Diego CA 92121 *TF:* 800-326-4010 ■ *Web:* www.tridenttech.com	619-688-9600	688-9700	612
Trideum Corp 655 Discovery Dr Ste 100 .... Huntsville AL 35806 *Web:* www.trideum.com	256-704-6100		261
Tridien Medical Inc 4200 NW 120th Ave .... Coral Springs FL 33065 *Web:* tridien.com	954-340-0500		475
Tri-Dim Filter Corp 93 Industrial Dr .... Louisa VA 23093 *TF:* 800-458-9835 ■ *Web:* www.tridim.com	540-967-2600	967-2835	18
Tridon Communications 10017 Queen St .... Fort McMurray AB T9H4Y9 *Web:* www.tridon.com	780-791-1002		647
Trient Technologies Inc 101 Trient Dr .... Woodville WI 54028 *Web:* www.fabrico.com	715-698-3519		596
Trifecta Marketing Group Inc 10124 Hanover Glen Rd .... Charlotte NC 28210 *Web:* www.trifectamg.com	704-543-8292		317
Triflo International Inc 1000 FM 830 .... Willis TX 77318 *TF:* 800-332-0993 ■ *Web:* triflo.com	936-856-8551		358
Triforce Consulting Svc Inc 650 N Cannon Ave .... Lansdale PA 19446 *Web:* triforce-inc.com	215-362-2611		177
Trifox Inc 3131 S Bascom Ave .... Campbell CA 95008 *Web:* www.trifox.com	408-369-2300		177
Tri-Gas & Oil Company Inc 3941 Federalsburg Hwy PO Box 465 .... Federalsburg MD 21632 *TF:* 800-638-7802 ■ *Web:* www.trigas-oil.com	410-754-8184	754-9158	325
Trigg County PO Box 672 .... Cadiz KY 42211 *Web:* www.triggcounty.ky.gov	270-522-8459	522-9489	338
Trigger Agency 3539 Clipper Mill Rd .... Baltimore MD 21211 *TF:* 800-830-3976 ■ *Web:* www.triggeragency.com	800-830-3976		7
Trigyn Technologies Inc 100 Metroplex Dr Ste 101 .... Edison NJ 08817 *Web:* www.trigyn.com	732-777-0050		177
Trihydro Corp 1252 Commerce Dr .... Laramie WY 82070 *Web:* www.trihydro.com	307-745-7474		261
Trijicon Inc 49385 Shafer Ave PO Box 930059 .... Wixom MI 48393 *TF:* 800-338-0563 ■ *Web:* www.trijicon.com	248-960-7700		711
Tri-K Industries Inc 2 Stewart Ct .... Denville NJ 07834 *Web:* www.tri-k.com	973-298-8850	298-8940	479
Trikon Design Inc 2295 N Opdyke Rd .... Auburn Hills MI 48326	248-340-0460		59
Tri-Kris Co 1001 Walnut St .... Lansdale PA 19446 *Web:* www.tri-kris.com	215-855-5183	855-3367	454

Company	City	State	ZIP	Phone	Fax	Class
Tri-L Data Systems Inc 98-025 Hekaha St Ste 5 *Web:* www.tri-ldatasystems.com	Aiea	HI	96701	808-671-5133		173-2
Tri-Lakes Container 533 S First St *Web:* www.tri-lakes.com	Pierceton	IN	46562	574-594-2217		100
Tri-Land 1 E Oak Hill Dr Ste 302 *TF:* 800-441-7032 ■ *Web:* www.trilandproperties.com	Westmont	IL	60559	708-531-8210	531-8217	652
Trilby Animal Hospital 2736 Tremainsville Rd *Web:* trilbyanimalhospital.com	Toledo	OH	43613	419-474-5403		794
TriLeaf Crop 10845 Olive Blvd Ste 260 *TF:* 800-652-5552 ■ *Web:* www.trileaf.com	Saint Louis	MO	63141	314-997-6111	997-8066	261
Tri-Lift Inc 180 Main St Annex *TF:* 800-479-5438 ■ *Web:* www.triliftinc.com	New Haven	CT	06512	203-467-1686	469-4852	770
TriLinc Global LLC 1230 Rosecrans Ave Ste 605 *Web:* www.trilincglobal.com	Manhattan Beach	CA	90266	310-997-0580		528
TriLink BioTechnologies Inc 9955 Mesa Rim Rd *TF:* 800-863-6801 ■ *Web:* www.trilinkbiotech.com	San Diego	CA	92121	858-546-0004		743
TriLink Saw Chain LLC 5400 South Cobb Dr *TF:* 877-492-9829 ■ *Web:* trilinksawchain.com	Atlanta	GA	30339	877-492-9829		350
Tri-Lite Inc 1642 N Besly Ct *TF:* 800-322-5250 ■ *Web:* www.triliteinc.com	Chicago	IL	60642	773-384-7765	384-5115	439
Trilliant 800 Town & Country Blvd Ste 300 *Web:* trilliant.net	Houston	TX	77024	713-263-9200		196
Trillion Communications Corp 3871 Pine Ln Ste 141 *Web:* www.trillionusa.com	Bessemer	AL	35022	205-481-1678		525
Trillium Asset Management LLC 2 Financial Ctr 60 S St Ste 1100 *TF:* 800-548-5684 ■ *Web:* www.trilliuminvest.com	Boston	MA	02111	617-423-6655	482-6179	528
Trillium Community Health Plan Inc 1800 Millrace Dr **Fax Area Code:* 866 ■ *TF:* 877-600-5472 ■ *Web:* www.trilliumohp.com	Eugene	OR	97403	541-485-2155	703-0958*	391-3
Trillium Engineering LLC 101 1/2 Oak St *Web:* trilliumeng.com	Hood River	OR	97031	509-281-3332		261
Trillium Group LLC 1221 Pittsford Victor Rd *Web:* www.trillium-group.com	Pittsford	NY	14534	585-383-5680		792
Trillium Health Ctr 100 Queensway W *Web:* www.trilliumhealthcentre.org	Mississauga	ON	L5B1B8	905-848-7100		374-2
Trillium Residential LLC 111 Dupont Cir *Web:* www.trilliumresidential.com	Phoenix	AZ	85034	602-687-9223		652
Trillium Talent Resources Group 99 Sheppard Ave W *TF:* 800-335-9668 ■ *Web:* www.trilliumhr.com	Toronto	ON	M2N1M4	416-497-2624		260
Trillium Teamologies Inc 219 S Main St Ste 300 *Web:* www.trilliumteam.com	Royal Oak	MI	48067	248-584-2080		180
Trilog Group Inc 54 Cummings Pk *Web:* www.triloggroup.com	Woburn	MA	01801	781-937-9963		177
Trilogy Communications Inc 2910 Hwy 80 E *Web:* www.trilogyrf.com	Pearl	MS	39208	601-932-4461	939-6637	814
Trilogy Marketing Inc 6263 Poplar Ave Ste 335 *TF:* 866-761-1505 ■ *Web:* www.southernbride.com	Memphis	TN	38119	901-761-1505	761-4214	637-9
Trilogy Plastics Inc 2290 W Main St *Web:* www.trilogyplastics.com	Alliance	OH	44601	330-821-4700		604
Trilogy Plumbing Inc 1525 S Sinclair St *Web:* www.trilogyplumbing.com	Anaheim	CA	92806	714-888-8575		610
Trilogy Software Inc 401 Congress Ave Ste 2650 *Web:* trilogy.com	Austin	TX	78701	512-874-3100		178-1
Trilogy Studios Inc 5200 Lankershim Blvd *Web:* www.trilogystudios.com	North Hollywood	CA	91601	818-901-9960		445
Trim Seal USA Inc 17371 NE 67th Ct Ste A2 *TF:* 877-874-6732 ■ *Web:* www.trimseal.com	Redmond	WA	98052	425-867-1522	882-0783	86
Trimac Panel Products PO Box 25277 *Web:* www.trimacpanel.com	Portland	OR	97298	503-297-1826		613
Tri-Mack Plastics Manufacturing Corp 66 Tupelo St *Web:* www.trimack.com	Bristol	RI	02809	401-253-2140		596
Trimaco LLC 2300 Gateway Centre Blvd Ste 200 *TF:* 800-325-7356 ■ *Web:* trimaco.com	Morrisville	NC	27560	919-674-3460	674-3461	733
Trimar Construction Inc 1720 W Cass St *Web:* 0350766.netsolhost.com	Tampa	FL	33606	813-258-5524	258-4743	449
Trimaran Fund Management LLC 1325 Avenue of the Americas *Web:* www.trimarancapital.com	New York	NY	10019	212-616-3700	616-3701	401
Trimark Corp PO Box 350 *TF:* 800-447-0343 ■ *Web:* www.trimarkcorp.com	New Hampton	IA	50659	641-394-3188		350
Trimark Properties LLC 321 SW 13th St *Web:* www.trimarkproperties.com	Gainesville	FL	32601	352-376-6223	376-6269	652
TriMark USA Inc 505 Collins St *TF:* 800-755-5580 ■ *Web:* www.trimarkusa.com	South Attleboro	MA	02703	800-556-7338		300
TriMas Corp 39400 Woodward Ave Ste 130 *Web:* www.trimascorp.com	Bloomfield Hills	MI	48304	248-631-5450		763
TriMax Direct 106 W Water St Ste 201 *Web:* www.trimaxdirect.com	Saint Paul	MN	55107	651-292-0165		225
Trimax Systems Inc 565 Explorer St *Web:* www.trimaxsystems.com	Brea	CA	92821	714-255-8590		180
Trimble County 4874 Hwy 421 N PO Box 312 *Web:* www.trimblecounty.com	Bedford	KY	40006	502-255-0062	255-0063	338
Trimble Navigation Ltd 935 Stewart Dr *NASDAQ: TRMB* ■ *TF:* 800-538-7800 ■ *Web:* www.trimble.com	Sunnyvale	CA	94085	408-481-8000		529
Trimble-Batjer Insurance Assoc 201 S Chadbourne St *Web:* www.trimble-batjer.com	San Angelo	TX	76903	325-653-6733		390
Trimco/Builders Brass Works 3528 Emery St *TF:* 800-637-8746 ■ *Web:* www.trimcohardware.com	Los Angeles	CA	90023	323-262-4191	264-7214	350
TriMech Services LLC 4461 Cox Rd Ste 302 *Web:* trimech.com	Glen Allen	VA	23060	804-257-9965		260
Tri-Media Integrated Marketing Technologies Inc 1027 Pelham St Unit 2 *Web:* tri-media.com	Fonthill	ON	L0S1E0	289-786-7027		7
Trimedyne Inc 5 Holland Bldg 223 *OTC: TMED* ■ *TF:* 800-733-5273 ■ *Web:* www.trimedyne.com	Irvine	CA	92618	949-951-3800	855-8206	424
Tri-Mer Corp 1400 Monroe St PO Box 730 *Web:* tri-mer.com	Owosso	MI	48867	989-723-7838	723-7844	18
Trimfit Inc 1691 Franklin Mills Cir *Web:* trimfit.com	Philadelphia	PA	19154	215-245-1122	781-1803	155-10
Trimfoot Company LLC 115 Trimfoot Terr **Fax Area Code:* 573 ■ *TF:* 800-325-6116 ■ *Web:* trimfootco.com	Farmington	MO	63640	800-325-6116	756-8482*	301
TrimJoist Corp 5146 Hwy 182 E *TF:* 800-844-8281 ■ *Web:* trimjoist.com	Columbus	MS	39702	662-327-7950		820
Trimlite LLC 901 SW 39th St *Web:* www.trimlite.com	Renton	WA	98057	425-251-8685		499
Trim-Lok Inc 6855 Hermosa Cir *TF:* 888-874-6565 ■ *Web:* www.trimlok.com	Buena Park	CA	90620	714-562-0500		596
TrimMaster 4860 N Fifth St Hwy *TF:* 800-356-4237 ■ *Web:* www.trimmaster.com	Temple	PA	19560	610-921-0203	929-8833	744
Trimold LLC 200 Pittsburgh Rd *Web:* www.tstech.com	Circleville	OH	43113	740-474-7591		604
Trimont Real Estate Advisors Inc 3500 Lenox Rd NE Ste G1 *Web:* trimontrea.com	Atlanta	GA	30326	404-420-5600		652
Trim-Rite Food Corp 801 Commerce Pkwy *Web:* www.rantoulfoods.com	Carpentersville	IL	60110	847-649-3400	649-3420	297-9
Trinal Inc 329 W 18th St Ste 401 *Web:* www.trinalinc.com	Chicago	IL	60616	312-738-0500	738-1840	809
Trincon Group LLC 1683 Old Henderson Rd *Web:* trincon.com	Columbus	OH	43220	614-442-0590		196
Trine University 4101 Edison Lakes Pkwy Ste 250 *Web:* www.trine.edu	Mishawaka	IN	46545	574-243-0500		166
TriNet Group Inc 1100 San Leandro Blvd Ste 300 *TF:* 888-874-6388 ■ *Web:* www.trinet.com	San Leandro	CA	94577	510-352-5000	352-6480	631
Trinet Internet Solutions Inc 1423 Powhatan St Bldg 1 *Web:* www.trinetsolutions.com	Alexandria	VA	22314	703-548-8900		171
Trinidad & Tobago Embassy 1708 Massachusetts Ave NW *Web:* foreign.gov.tt	Washington	DC	20036	202-467-6490	785-3130	257
Trinidad Drilling Ltd 400 250 2 St SW *Web:* www.trinidaddrilling.com	Calgary	AB	T2P0C1	403-265-6525	265-4168	540
Trinidad Lake State Park 32610 State Hwy 12 *Web:* cpw.state.co.us	Trinidad	CO	81082	719-846-6951		565
Trinidad State Junior College 600 Prospect St *TF:* 800-621-8752 ■ *Web:* www.trinidadstate.edu	Trinidad	CO	81082	719-846-5011	846-5620	162
Trinitas Hospital 225 Williamson St *Web:* www.trinitashospital.com	Elizabeth	NJ	07207	908-994-5000		374-3
Triniti Corp 2001 Gateway Pl Ste 425E *TF:* 866-531-9587 ■ *Web:* www.triniti.com	San Jose	CA	95110	408-659-7764	659-7752	809
Trinity Academy Inc 12345 E 21st St N *Web:* www.trinityacademy.org	Wichita	KS	67206	316-634-0909	634-0928	685
Trinity Area School District 231 Park Ave *Web:* www.trinitypride.org	Washington	PA	15301	724-223-2000		685
Trinity Bible College 50 Sixth Ave N **Fax Area Code:* 701 ■ *TF:* 800-523-1603 ■ *Web:* www.trinitybiblecollege.edu	Ellendale	ND	58436	800-523-1603	349-5786*	161
Trinity Biotech PLC 5919 Farnsworth Ct *NASDAQ: TRIB* ■ *TF:* 800-331-2291 ■ *Web:* www.trinitybiotech.com	Carlsbad	CA	92008	760-929-0500	929-0124	231
Trinity Broadcasting Network (TBN) PO Box A *TF:* 888-731-1000 ■ *Web:* tbn.org	Santa Ana	CA	92711	714-832-2950		740
Trinity Business Furniture 6089 Kennedy Rd *TF:* 855-311-6660 ■ *Web:* trinityfurniture.com	Trinity	NC	27370	336-472-6660		321
Trinity Candle Factory 107 W Main St *Web:* www.trinitycandlefactory.com	Grand Prairie	TX	75050	972-576-3800		328
Trinity Cathedral 2230 Euclid Ave *Web:* trinitycleveland.org	Cleveland	OH	44115	216-771-3630	771-3657	50-1
Trinity Ceramic Supply Inc 9016 Diplomacy Row *Web:* www.trinityceramic.com	Dallas	TX	75247	214-631-0540		45
Trinity Christian College 6601 W College Dr *Web:* www.trnty.edu	Palos Heights	IL	60463	708-802-0686	239-4826	166
Trinity College of Florida 2430 Welbilt Blvd *TF:* 800-388-0869 ■ *Web:* trinitycollege.edu	Trinity	FL	34655	727-376-6911	569-1410	161
Trinity College of The Bible & Trinity Theological Seminary 4233 Medwel Dr *Web:* trinitysem.edu	Newburgh	IN	47630	812-853-0611		166

Name / Address	City	State	ZIP	Phone	Fax	Class
Trinity College Raether Library 300 Summit St *Web:* www.trincoll.edu	Hartford	CT	06106	860-297-2000	297-2251	434-6
Trinity College School 55 Deblaquire St N *Web:* www.tcs.on.ca	Port Hope	ON	L1A4K7	905-885-3217	885-7444	622
Trinity Consulting Inc 346 Brigham St *Web:* trinity-inc.net	Marlborough	MA	01752	508-485-8842	481-6375	180
Trinity County PO Box 456 *Web:* www.co.trinity.tx.us	Groveton	TX	75845	936-642-1208	642-3004	338
Trinity County California 11 Court St Rm 230 PO Box 1613 *Web:* www.trinitycounty.org	Weaverville	CA	96093	530-623-1382	623-8365	338
Trinity Direct LLC 10 Park Pl *Web:* www.trinitydirect.net	Butler	NJ	07405	973-283-3600		5
Trinity Elementary School 4410 Murfreesboro Rd *Web:* www.wcs.edu	Franklin	TN	37067	615-472-4850	472-4861	685
Trinity Episcopal School for Ministry 311 Eleventh St *TF:* 800-874-8754 ■ *Web:* www.tsm.edu	Ambridge	PA	15003	724-266-3838	266-4617	167-3
Trinity Fiduciary Partners LLC 325 S Mesquite St Ste 104 **Fax Area Code:* 817 ■ *TF:* 877-334-1283 ■ *Web:* www.trinityfiduciary.com	Arlington	TX	76010	877-334-1283	549-0091*	528
Trinity Financial Group 16170 Jones Maltsberger Ste 102 *Web:* trinityfinancialgrp.com	San Antonio	TX	78247	210-930-7600	349-9983	390
Trinity Forge Inc 947 Trinity Dr *Web:* www.trinityforge.com	Mansfield	TX	76063	817-473-1515	473-6743	483
Trinity Green Services LLC 1760 South Stemmons Fwy Ste 160 *TF:* 888-243-3605 ■ *Web:* trinitygrn.com	Lewisville	TX	75057	214-446-9500	446-9501	466
Trinity Group Construction 13849 Park Center Rd *Web:* www.trinitygc.us	Herndon	VA	20171	703-707-0300		186
Trinity Group Inc, The PO Box 810 *Web:* www.trinitygrp.com	Tracy	CA	95378	209-832-1293	832-1376	196
Trinity Hardwood Distributors Inc 110 E Oregon *Web:* www.trinityhardwood.net	Dallas	TX	75205	214-948-3001	946-1219	320
Trinity Health 1 Burdick Expy W PO Box 5020 *TF:* 800-862-0005 ■ *Web:* www.trinityhealth.org	Minot	ND	58702	701-857-5000		374-3
Trinity Health 20555 Victor Pkwy *Web:* www.trinity-health.org	Livonia	MI	48152	734-343-1000		374-3
Trinity Health Care Services 3951 N Haverhill Rd Ste 202-204 *Web:* www.thcsi.com	West Palm Beach	FL	33417	561-471-7676		363
Trinity Health System 380 Summit Ave *Web:* www.trinityhealth.com	Steubenville	OH	43952	740-283-7000		353
Trinity Hospital of Augusta 2260 Wrightsboro Rd *Web:* www.trinityofaugusta.com	Augusta	GA	30904	706-481-7000		371
Trinity Industries Inc 2525 Stemmons Fwy *NYSE:* TRN ■ *Web:* www.trin.net	Dallas	TX	75207	214-631-4420		185
Trinity Industries Inc *Head Div* 11765 Hwy 6 S *Web:* www.trinityheads.com	Navasota	TX	77868	936-825-6581		487
Trinity Information Technology LLC 17 Windmill Dr *Web:* www.trinityit.biz	Southampton	PA	18966	267-396-7901		809
Trinity International University 2065 Half Day Rd *TF:* 800-822-3225 ■ *Web:* www.tiu.edu	Deerfield	IL	60015	847-945-8800	317-8097	166
Trinity Law Group LLC 200 Lowder Brook Dr Ste 2600 *Web:* trinitylg.com	Westwood	MA	02090	781-329-0088	459-2683	41
Trinity Logistics Group Inc 4001 Irving Blvd *Web:* www.trinitytrucking.com	Dallas	TX	75247	214-589-7505		780
Trinity Neurological Rehabilitation Ctr 1400 Lindberg Dr *Web:* trinityneurorehab.com	Slidell	LA	70458	985-641-4985		374-6
Trinity Packaging Corp 84 Business Pk Dr *Web:* www.trinitypackaging.com	Armonk	NY	10504	914-273-4111	273-4715	548
Trinity Racing 5221 Oceanus Dr *Web:* www.trinityracing.com	Huntington Beach	CA	92649	714-988-0339	901-0520	518
Trinity Railway Express (TRE) 801 Cherry St Ste 850 *Web:* trinityrailwayexpress.org	Fort Worth	TX	76102	817-215-8600	215-8934	649
Trinity Repertory Co 201 Washington St *Web:* www.trinityrep.com	Providence	RI	02903	401-521-1100	751-5577	749
Trinity River Authority of Texas 5300 S Collins St *Web:* www.trinityra.org	Arlington	TX	76018	817-467-4343		463
Trinity Steel Fabricators Inc 13430 Northwest Fwy Ste 225 *Web:* www.trinitysteel.com	Houston	TX	77040	713-460-5556		480
Trinity Sterile Inc 201 Kiley Dr *TF:* 800-829-8384 ■ *Web:* www.trinitysterile.com	Salisbury	MD	21801	800-829-8384		596
Trinity Tool Co 34600 Commerce *Web:* www.trinco.com	Fraser	MI	48026	586-296-5900	296-5836	386
Trinity Trailer Manufacturing Inc 7533 S Federal Way *TF:* 800-235-6577 ■ *Web:* trinitytrailer.com	Boise	ID	83716	208-336-3666	336-3741	779
Trinity University 1 Trinity Pl *TF:* 800-874-6489 ■ *Web:* www.trinity.edu	San Antonio	TX	78212	210-999-7011	999-8164	166
Trinity University *Trinity Washington University* 125 Michigan Ave NE *TF:* 800-492-6882 ■ *Web:* discover.trinitydc.edu	Washington	DC	20017	202-884-9000	884-9403	166
Trinity Valley Community College *Athens* 100 Cardinal Dr *Web:* www.tvcc.edu	Athens	TX	75751	903-675-6200	675-6209	162
Trinity Valley Electric Co-opeartive Inc (TVEC) 1800 E Hwy 243 PO Box 888 *TF:* 800-766-9576 ■ *Web:* tvec.net	Kaufman	TX	75142	972-932-2214	932-6466	245
Trinity Ventures 2480 Sand Hill Rd Ste 200 *Web:* www.trinityventures.com	Menlo Park	CA	94025	650-854-9500		792
Trinity Western University 7600 Glover Rd *TF:* 888-468-6898 ■ *Web:* www.twu.ca	Langley	BC	V2Y1Y1	604-888-7511	513-2064	166
Trinity-Pawling School 700 Rt 22 *Web:* www.trinitypawling.org	Pawling	NY	12564	845-855-3100	855-3816	622
Trinium Technologies LLC 304 Tejon Pl *Web:* www.triniumtech.com	Palos Verdes Estates	CA	90274	310-214-3118		179
Trinsic Technologies Inc 15843 Opal Fire Dr Ste 100 *TF:* 888-629-2622 ■ *Web:* trinsictech.com	Austin	TX	78728	512-410-7308		393
Trintech Inc 15851 Dallas Pkwy Ste 900 *TF:* 800-416-0075 ■ *Web:* www.trintech.com	Addison	TX	75001	972-701-9802		178-1
Trio 505 Belle Hall Pkwy Unit 202 *Web:* trio-solutions.com	Mount Pleasant	SC	29464	843-216-0442		195
Trio Bistro 7565 Kenwood Rd *Web:* www.triobistro.com	Cincinnati	OH	45236	513-984-1905		671
Trio Media Group 182 Hilderbrand Dr Ste 100 *Web:* www.triomediagroup.com	Atlanta	GA	30328	404-255-1970		196
Trio Pac Inc 386 Mcarthur *TF:* 888-565-6722 ■ *Web:* www.triopac.com	Saint-Laurent	QC	H4T1X8	514-733-7793	733-3862	358
Trio Pines USA Inc 16233 Heron Ave *TF:* 800-468-6987 ■ *Web:* www.triopines.com	La Mirada	CA	90638	714-523-5800		385
Trio's 8201 Cantrell Rd *Web:* www.triosrestaurant.com	Little Rock	AR	72227	501-221-3330	221-1002	671
TriOak Foods Inc 103 W Railroad St PO Box 68 *Web:* www.trioak.com	Oakville	IA	52646	319-766-2230		276
Triodyne Inc 666 Dundee Rd Ste 103 *Web:* www.triodyne.com	Northbrook	IL	60062	847-677-4730	647-2047	261
Trion Inc 101 McNeill Rd *TF:* 800-884-0002 ■ *Web:* www.trioniaq.com	Sanford	NC	27330	919-775-2201	774-8771	18
Trion Industries Inc 297 Laird St **Fax Area Code:* 570 ■ *TF:* 800-444-4665 ■ *Web:* www.triononline.com	Wilkes-Barre	PA	18702	800-444-4665	824-0802*	286
Trionics International Inc 9 Shore Ln *Web:* www.trionicsusa.com	Winterport	ME	04496	207-745-7272		637-2
Trios College Business Technology Healthcare 520 First St *Web:* www.secondcareerontario.com	London	ON	N5V3C6	519-455-0551		167
Trio-Tech Intl 14731 Califa St *NYSE:* TRT ■ *Web:* www.triotech.com	Van Nuys	CA	91411	818-787-7000	787-9130	248
Tripac Fasteners 475 Klug Cir *Web:* tripaconline.com	Corona	CA	92880	951-280-4488		351
TripActions 1501 Page Mill Rd *TF:* 888-505-8747 ■ *Web:* tripactions.com	Palo Alto	CA	94304	888-505-8747		657
Tri-Pak Machinery Inc 1102 N Commerce St *Web:* www.tri-pakmachinery.com	Harlingen	TX	78550	956-423-5140	423-9362	547
TripBAM LLC 7318 Marquette *Web:* www.tripbam.com	Dallas	TX	75225	214-363-9630		393
Tripifoods 1427 William St *Web:* www.tripifoods.com	Buffalo	NY	14206	716-853-7400	852-7400	297-8
Triple A Oil *Triple A Oil Properties LP* 12342 Inwood Rd	Dallas	TX	75244	972-503-3333		324
Triple B Forwarders Inc 1511 Glen Curtis St *TF:* 800-228-8465 ■ *Web:* www.tripleb.com	Carson	CA	90746	310-604-5840		311
Triple C Wholesalers Inc 2801 W Patapsco Ave *TF:* 800-442-8742 ■ *Web:* www.triplecinc.com	Baltimore	MD	21230	410-644-5500	864-0424	756
Triple Craft 1 Marina Dr *Web:* triplecraftdc.com	Alexandria	VA	22314	703-548-0001		671
Triple Creek Ranch 5551 W Fork Rd *TF:* 800-654-2943 ■ *Web:* www.triplecreekranch.com	Darby	MT	59829	406-821-4600		669
Triple Crown Corp 5351 Jaycee Ave *Web:* www.triplecrowncorp.com	Harrisburg	PA	17112	717-657-5729	657-8125	187
Triple Crown Nutrition Inc 315 Lake St E Ste 300 *TF:* 800-451-9916 ■ *Web:* www.triplecrownfeed.com	Wayzata	MN	55391	800-451-9916		447
Triple Crown Products Inc 814 Ela Ave *TF:* 800-619-1110 ■ *Web:* triplecrownproducts.com	Waterford	WI	53185	262-534-7878		687
Triple Crown Services 2720 Dupont Commerce Ct **Fax Area Code:* 877 ■ *TF:* 800-325-6510 ■ *Web:* www.triplecrownsvc.com	Fort Wayne	IN	46825	260-416-3600	292-5686*	648
Triple D Bending 4707 Glenmore Trail SE *Web:* www.pipebending.com	Calgary	AB	T2C2R9	403-255-2944		595
Triple Dot Corp 3302 S Susan St *Web:* www.triple-dot.com	Santa Ana	CA	92704	714-241-0888		362
Triple G Express Inc 800 St George Ave *Web:* www.triplegexpress.com	Jefferson	LA	70121	504-731-2841	731-2845	519
Triple J Tours Inc 4455 S Cameron St *Web:* www.lasvegasbus.com	Las Vegas	NV	89103	702-261-0131	736-5103	107
Triple J Wilderness Ranch 91 Mortimer Rd PO Box 310 *TF:* 800-826-1300 ■ *Web:* www.triplejranch.com	Augusta	MT	59410	406-562-3653	562-3836	239
Triple M 105.5 FM 7601 Ganser Way *Web:* 1055triplem.radio.com	Madison	WI	53719	608-826-0077		645-92
Triple Oaks Nursery & Herb Garden 2359 Delsea Dr *Web:* www.tripleoaks.com	Franklinville	NJ	08322	856-694-4272		292

Phone | Fax | Class

Triple Peaks LLC 77 Okemo Hts Ludlow VT 05149 802-228-5222 787
Web: www.okemo.com

Triple Play Products LLC
120 Getty Ave Paterson NJ 07503 646-484-8112 64
TF: 800-829-1625 ■ *Web:* www.lillygold.com

Triple Point Technology Inc
301 Riverside Ave Westport CT 06880 203-291-7979 177
Web: www.tpt.com

Triple R Ranch PO Box 124 Keystone SD 57751 605-666-4605 239
Web: www.rrrranch.com

Triple R Trucking Inc
1303 Woodside Ave Essexville MI 48732 989-892-1569 892-3631 780
TF: 800-535-4822 ■ *Web:* www.gotripler.com

Triple S Alarm Company Inc
2820 Cantrell Rd Little Rock AR 72202 501-664-4599 664-0586 693
Web: www.triplesalarm.com

Triple/S Dynamics Inc
1031 S Haskell Ave PO Box 151027 Dallas TX 75315 214-828-8600 828-8688 470
TF: 800-527-2116 ■ *Web:* www.sssdynamics.com

Triple-I Corp, The
6330 Lamar Ave Ste 230 Overland Park KS 66202 913-563-7200 196
Web: www.triplei.com

TripleLift Inc
400 Lafayette St 5th & 3rd Fl New York NY 10003 502-354-3801 5
Web: triplelift.com

Tripler Army Medical Ctr
Medical Ctr 1 Jarrett White Rd Honolulu HI 96859 808-433-2778 433-4899 374-4
Web: www.tamc.amedd.army.mil

Triple-S Steel Supply LLC
6000 Jensen Dr Houston TX 77026 713-697-7105 492
Web: www.sss-steel.com

TripleTree
3600 Minnesota Dr Ste 200 Minneapolis MN 55435 952-223-8400 401
Web: www.triple-tree.com

Triplett Office Essentials Corp
3553 109th St Urbandale IA 50322 515-270-7099 270-9683 535
TF: 800-437-5034 ■ *Web:* www.tripletts.info

Triplett Woolf & Garretson LLC
2959 N Rock Rd Ste 300 Wichita KS 67226 316-630-8100 428
Web: www.twgfirm.com

Tripmasters.Com
5640 Nicholson Ln Ste 215 Rockville MD 20852 202-349-7579 16
TF: 800-430-0484 ■ *Web:* www.tripmasters.com

Tripod Technologies
1050 Kings Hwy N Ste 202 Cherry Hill NJ 08034 856-755-1478 809
Web: www.tripodtech.net

TriPower Resources LLC 16 East St SW Ardmore OK 73401 580-226-6700 536
Web: www.tripowerresources.com

Tripp Lite Inc 1111 W 35th St Chicago IL 60609 773-869-1111 869-1329 815
Web: www.tripplite.com

Tripp Lumber Company Inc
3000 Raser Dr Missoula MT 59808 406-549-0195 683
TF: 800-457-9706 ■ *Web:* www.tripplumber.com

Tripp Scott
110 SE Sixth St 15th Fl Fort Lauderdale FL 33301 954-525-7500 761-8475 428
Web: www.trippscott.com

Trippnt Inc 8830 NE 108th St Kansas City MO 64157 816-792-2604 608
TF: 800-874-7768 ■ *Web:* www.trippnt.com

Tripwire Inc 101 SW Main St Ste 1500 Portland OR 97204 503-276-7500 223-0182 178-12
TF: 800-874-7947 ■ *Web:* www.tripwire.com

Tri-R Dies Inc 556 Bev Rd Youngstown OH 44512 330-758-8050 758-7419 757
Web: www.trirdies.com

Tri-Rail 800 NW 33rd St Pompano Beach FL 33064 954-783-6030 788-7878 468
TF: 800-874-7245 ■ *Web:* www.tri-rail.com

TriReme Medical Inc
7060 Koll Center Pkwy Ste 300 Pleasanton CA 94566 925-931-1300 931-1361 463
Web: qtvascular.com

Tris Pharma Inc
2033 Rt 130 Brunswick Business Pk
Ste D Monmouth Junction NJ 08852 732-940-2800 940-2855 668
Web: www.trispharma.com

Tris USA Inc 1803 Wilkinson St Athens AL 35611 256-233-2511 233-8449 127
Web: www.trisusa.com

Triseal Corp 11920 Price Rd Hebron IL 60034 815-648-2473 326
Web: www.triseal.com

Trisept Solutions 777 W Glencoe Pl Milwaukee WI 53217 414-934-3900 549
Web: www.triseptsolutions.com

Trisha Brown Dance Co (TBDC)
341 W 38th St Ste 801 New York NY 10018 212-977-5365 925-8687 573-1
Web: www.trishabrowncompany.org

Trisoft Technologies Inc
14429 Independence Dr Plainfield IL 60544 866-364-7031 871-2032 463
TF: 866-364-7031 ■ *Web:* www.aboutus.com

TriSports 4495 S Coach Dr Tucson AZ 85714 520-884-8743 711
Web: www.trisports.com

Trissential LLC
1905 E Wayzata Blvd Ste 333 Wayzata MN 55391 888-595-7970 513-1544* 463
**Fax Area Code:* 952 ■ *TF:* 888-595-7970 ■ *Web:* trissential.com

Tristan 7671 Northwoods Blvd Charleston SC 29406 843-534-2155 671
Web: tristanevents.com

Tristar Bank 719 E College St Dickson TN 37055 615-446-7100 70
Web: www.tristar.bank

Tri-Star Cabinet & Top Company Inc
1000 S Cedar Rd New Lenox IL 60451 708-479-2126 115
Web: www.tristarcabinets.com

TriStar Centennial Medical Ctr
2300 Patterson St Nashville TN 37203 615-342-1000 374-3
Web: tristarhealth.com

Tri-star Data Systems Inc
650 Sentry Pkwy Blue Bell PA 19422 610-941-2116 941-2105 177
Web: tristardatasystems.com

Tri-Star Engineering Inc
2455 Pan Am Blvd Elk Grove Village IL 60007 847-595-3377 757
Web: www.tristareng.com

TriStar Horizon Medical Ctr
111 Hwy 70 E Dickson TN 37055 615-446-0446 374-3
Web: www.tristarhorizon.com

TriStar Inc 3740 E La Salle St Phoenix AZ 85040 800-800-1714 525
TF: 800-800-1714 ■ *Web:* www.tristar.com

Tri-Star Plastics Corp
906 Boston Tpke Shrewsbury MA 01545 800-874-7827 596
TF: 800-874-7827 ■ *Web:* www.tstar.com

Tri-Star Protector Service Co
19233 FM 1485 Rd New Caney TX 77357 281-399-2600 536
Web: www.tristarprotector.com

Tristar Southern Hills Medical Ctr
391 Wallace Rd Nashville TN 37211 615-781-4000 374-3
Web: tristarsouthernhills.com

Tristar Web Graphics Inc
4010 Airline Dr Houston TX 77022 713-691-0001 627
Web: new.tristarwebgraphics.com

Tri-Starr Investigations Inc
Rockdale County 3525 Hwy 138 SW Stockbridge GA 30281 770-388-9841 41
TF: 800-849-9841 ■ *Web:* www.tristarr.com

Tri-state Adjustments Inc
3439 E Ave S PO Box 3219 La Crosse WI 54602 608-788-8683 160
TF: 800-562-3906 ■ *Web:* wecollectmore.com

Tri-state Aero Inc
6101 Flight Line Dr Evansville IN 47725 812-426-1221 23
Web: www.tristateaero.com

Tri-State Armature & Electrical Works Inc
330 GE Patterson Ave Memphis TN 38126 901-527-8412 246
TF: 800-238-7654 ■ *Web:* tristatearmature.com

Tri-State Bible College
506 Margaret St South Point OH 45680 740-377-2520 377-0001 161
TF: 800-333-3243 ■ *Web:* www.tsbc.edu

Tri-State Brick & Stone of New York Inc
333 Seventh Ave 5th Fl New York NY 10001 212-686-3939 191-1
Web: btsbm.com

Tri-State Chamber of Commerce
5 S Broome St Port Jervis NY 12771 845-856-6694 856-6695 139
Web: www.tristatechamber.org

Tri-State College of Acupuncture
80 Eigth Ave Ste 400 New York NY 10011 212-242-2255 166
Web: www.tsca.edu

Tri-State Cut Stone & Brick Co
10333 Van's Dr Frankfort IL 60423 815-469-7550 724
Web: www.stone-brick.com

Tri-State Design Construction Inc
7401 Old York Rd Elkins Park PA 19027 215-782-8200 782-8282 186
Web: www.tristatedesign.net

Tri-State Distributors Inc (TSD)
2500 Georgia Hwy 17 Royston GA 30662 706-245-6164 749-9001* 191-3
**Fax Area Code:* 888 ■ *TF:* 800-476-6164 ■ *Web:* www.tri-statedistributors.com

Tri-State Drilling Inc
16940 Hwy 55 W PO Box 252 Plymouth MN 55446 763-553-1234 553-9778 189-15
Web: www.tristatedrilling.com

Tri-State Electric Membership Corp (TSEMC)
2310 Blue Ridge Dr Blue Ridge GA 30513 706-492-3251 492-7617 245
Web: www.tsemc.net

Tri-State Expedited Service
27681 Cummings Rd Millbury OH 43447 419-837-2401 780
TF: 800-821-6395 ■ *Web:* www.tstate.com

Tri-state Fabricators Inc
1146 Ferris Rd Amelia OH 45102 513-752-5005 270
TF: 888-523-1488 ■ *Web:* tristatefabricators.com

Tri-State Fire Protection Inc
10577 Oak Grove Rd Newburgh IN 47630 812-853-9229 189-10
TF: 800-326-9229 ■ *Web:* www.tristatefire.com

Tri-State Forest Products Inc
2105 Sheridan Ave Springfield OH 45505 937-323-6325 323-6888 191-3
TF: 800-949-6325 ■ *Web:* www.tsfpi.com

Tri-state Home Services
82A Wormans Mill Ct Frederick MD 21701 844-202-2126 610
TF: 844-202-2126 ■ *Web:* www.tristatehomeservices.com

Tri-State Industrial Supply Inc
1937 Greenup Ave Ashland KY 41101 606-329-2658 366
Web: t-sisi.com

Tri-State Iron & Metal Co
1725 E Ninth St Texarkana AR 71854 870-773-8409 686
Web: www.tsimco.com

Tri-State Ironworks Inc
175 W Bodley Ave Memphis TN 38109 901-942-1461 492
Web: www.tristateironworks.com

Tri-State Machine Inc
4701 Eoff St PO Box 6566 Wheeling WV 26003 304-234-0170 454
Web: tri-statemachine.com

Tristate Midstream LP
9901 Valley Ranch Pkwy E Ste 2000 Irving TX 75063 469-872-1280 521-8780 580
Web: www.tsmidstream.com

Tri-State Motors 298 S Main St Cedar City UT 84720 435-238-4342 57
Web: www.tristateofcedarcity.com

Tri-State Neighbor
309 W 43rd St Ste 103 Sioux Falls SD 57105 605-335-7300 335-8141 532-2
TF: 800-925-6397 ■ *Web:* www.tristateneighbor.com

Tri-State Pumps Inc 1162 Chastain Rd Liberty SC 29657 864-843-8100 711
TF: 800-868-4631 ■ *Web:* tspturf.com

Tri-State Radio Inc
320 W University Dr Macomb IL 61455 309-298-1873 298-2133 645-141
TF: 800-895-2912 ■ *Web:* tspr.org

Tri-State Railway Historical Society Inc, The
PO Box 1217 Morristown NJ 07962 973-656-0707 48-13
Web: www.tristaterail.org

Tri-State Roofing & Sheet Metal Group
101 S Meadville Rd Davisville WV 26142 304-485-6593 485-2841 189-12
Web: tri-stateservicegroup.com

Tri-State Surgical Supply & Equipment Ltd
409 Hoyt St Brooklyn NY 11231 718-624-1000 475
TF: 800-899-8741 ■ *Web:* tristatesurgical.com

Tri-State Trailer Sales Inc
3111 Grand Ave Pittsburgh PA 15225 412-747-7777 777-4010 62-5
Web: www.tristatetrailer.com

Tri-State Travel 4349 Industrial Pk Dr Galena IL 61036 815-777-0820 777-8128 760
TF: 800-779-4869 ■ *Web:* tristatetravel.com

Tri-State Truck and Equipment Inc (TSTE)
5250 Midland Rd Billings MT 59101 406-245-3188 238-1501 358
TF: 800-227-1132 ■ *Web:* www.tristatetruckandequip.com

Company	City	State	ZIP	Phone	Fax	Class
Tri-State Utility Products Inc 1030 Atlanta Industrial Dr *TF:* 800-282-7985 ■ *Web:* tsup.com	Marietta	GA	30066	770-427-3119	427-3945	246
Tri-State Video Services Inc 1379 Pittsburgh Rd *Web:* www.tristatevideo.com	Valencia	PA	16059	724-898-1630		38
Tristate Wire Rope Supply Inc 5246 Wooster Pk *Web:* fulcrumlifting.com	Cincinnati	OH	45226	513-871-8656		492
Trisys Inc 215 Ridgedale Ave *Web:* www.trisys.com	Florham Park	NJ	07932	973-360-2300	360-2222	387
TriTech Enterprise Systems Inc 1869 Brightseat Rd *Web:* tritechenterprise.com	Hyattsville	MD	20785	301-918-8250	918-8253	225
Tritech Graphics Inc PO Box 222 *TF:* 800-323-1950 ■ *Web:* www.tritechgraphics.com	Highwood	IL	60040	847-656-3435		174
Tritech Group Ltd 5413 - 271 St *Web:* www.tritechgroup.ca	Langley	BC	V4W3Y7	604-607-8878		201
Tritech Manufacturing Inc 2728 Commercial Rd *Web:* www.tritechpcb.com	Fort Wayne	IN	46809	260-747-9154		625
TriTel Networks 162 E 4500 S **Fax Area Code:* 800 ■ *Web:* www.tritel.com	Salt Lake City	UT	84107	801-265-9292	265-9915*	393
TriTeq Lock & Security LLC 701 Gullo *Web:* triteqlock.com	Elk Grove Village	IL	60007	847-640-7002		261
Triton Capital Partners Ltd 566 W Lake St Ste 235 *Web:* www.tritoncap.com	Chicago	IL	60661	312-575-0190		690
Triton College 2000 N Fifth Ave *Web:* www.triton.edu	River Grove	IL	60171	708-456-0300	583-3147	162
Triton Diving Services LLC 3421 N Causeway Blvd Ste 601 *Web:* www.tritondiving.net	Metairie	LA	70002	504-846-5056		41
Triton Environmental Inc 385 Church St Ste 201 *Web:* www.tritonenvironmental.com	Guilford	CT	06437	203-458-7200		196
Triton Industries Inc 1020 N Kolmar Ave *Web:* www.tritonindustries.com	Chicago	IL	60651	773-384-3700	384-8748	488
Triton Media Group 15303 Ventura Blvd Ste 1500 *TF:* 866-448-4037 ■ *Web:* www.tritondigital.com	Sherman Oaks	CA	91403	514-448-4037		644
Triton Museum of Art 1505 Warburton Ave *Web:* www.tritonmuseum.org	Santa Clara	CA	95050	408-247-3754	247-3796	520
Triton Services Inc PO Box 3326 *Web:* www.tritonsvc.com	Annapolis	MD	21403	443-716-0600	716-0601	178-5
Triton Systems Inc 21405 B St *TF:* 866-787-4866 ■ *Web:* www.tritonatm.com	Long Beach	MS	39560	228-575-3100		253
Triton Technologies Inc 115 Plymouth St *TF:* 800-704-7538 ■ *Web:* tritontechnologies.com	Mansfield	MA	02048	508-230-7300		195
Triumf 4004 Wesbrook Mall *Web:* www.triumf.ca	Vancouver	BC	V6T2A3	604-222-1047		743
Triumph Books Inc 814 N Franklin St *Web:* www.triumphbooks.com	Chicago	IL	60610	312-337-0747	337-5985	637-2
Triumph Group 1923 Central Ave *Web:* www.triumphgroup.com	Hot Springs	AR	71901	501-321-9325		22
Triumph Manufacturing LLC 2130 S Industrial Park Ave *Web:* www.triumphcorp.com	Tempe	AZ	85282	480-967-3337	921-0446	621
Triumph Pharmaceuticals Inc 12312 Olive Blvd Ste 250 *Web:* smartmouth.com	Saint Louis	MO	63141	314-995-3090		583
Triumph Structures-Long Island LLC 717 Main St *Web:* www.triumphgrp.com	Westbury	NY	11590	516-997-5757		22
Triumph Twist Drill Company Inc 1 SW Seventh St *TF:* 800-942-1501 ■ *Web:* triumphtwistdrill.com	Chisholm	MN	55719	218-263-3891	263-3887	758
Triumvirate Environmental 61 Innerbelt Rd *TF:* 800-966-9282 ■ *Web:* www.triumvirate.com	Somerville	MA	02143	617-628-8098		804
Tri-Valley Herald 175 Lennon Ln Ste 100 *Web:* www.eastbaytimes.com	Walnut Creek	CA	94598	925-935-2525		532-2
Trivalley Internet Inc 4713 First St Ste 110 *Web:* www.trivalley.com	Pleasanton	CA	94566	925-417-7600		180
Tri-Valley Local School District 36 E Muskingum Ave *Web:* www.tri-valley.k12.oh.us	Dresden	OH	43821	740-754-1442	754-6400	685
Trivascular Technologies Inc 3910 Brickway Blvd *Web:* www.trivascular.com	Santa Rosa	CA	95403	707-543-8800		787
Trivec-Avant Corp 17831 Jamestown Ln *Web:* www.trivec.com	Huntington Beach	CA	92647	714-841-4976		647
Triveni Digital Inc 777 Alexander Rd *Web:* trivenidigital.com	Princeton	NJ	08540	609-716-3500	716-3503	225
Trivent Systems Inc 2274 Eldemere Cir *Web:* www.triventlegal.com	Macungie	PA	18062	610-674-6901		809
Trivera Interactive N88 W16447 Main St Ste 400 *Web:* www.trivera.com	Menomonee Falls	WI	53051	262-250-9400		180
Trivest Partners LP 550 S Dixie Hwy Ste 300 *Web:* www.trivest.com	Coral Gables	FL	33146	305-858-2200		321
TriVista Business Group Inc 15 Enterprise Ste 410 *Web:* trivista.com	Aliso Viejo	CA	92656	949-218-4830		196
Trivium Pursuit 429 Lake Park Blvd *Web:* www.triviumpursuit.com	Muscatine	IA	52761	309-537-3641		95
TriVium Systems Inc 1865 NW 169th Pl Ste 210 *Web:* www.triviumsys.com	Beaverton	OR	97006	503-439-9338		179

Company	City	State	ZIP	Phone	Fax	Class
Triware Technologies Inc 76 Brookfield Rd *Web:* triware.ca	Saint John	NL	A1E3T9	709-579-5000		177
Triway Local School District 3205 Shreve Rd *Web:* www.triway.k12.oh.us	Wooster	OH	44691	330-264-9491	262-3955	685
TriWest Healthcare Alliance PO Box 42049 *Web:* www.triwest.com	Phoenix	AZ	85080	602-564-2000		374-3
Tri-Wire Engineering Solutions Inc 890 East St *Web:* www.triwire.net	Tewksbury	MA	01876	978-640-6899		492
Triwood Corporation of Georgia Inc 124 Austin Rd *Web:* triwood.com	Americus	GA	31719	229-928-2233		608
Trix Systems Inc 68 Smith St *Web:* www.trixsystems.com	Chelmsford	MA	01824	978-256-4445		177
TriZetto Corp 3300 Rider Trail S **Fax Area Code:* 866 ■ *TF:* 800-969-3666 ■ *Web:* www.trizettoprovider.com	Earth City	MO	63045	314-802-6700	203-4587*	177
TRM Technologies Inc 280 Albert St 10th Fl Ste 1000 *Web:* www.trm.ca	Ottawa	ON	K1P5G8	613-722-8843		196
TRMC (Thibodaux Regional Medical Ctr) 602 N Acadia Rd *TF:* 800-822-8442 ■ *Web:* www.thibodaux.com	Thibodaux	LA	70301	985-447-5500		374-3
TRMC (Tomball Regional Hospital) PO Box 889 *Web:* www.tomballregionalmedicalcenter.com	Tomball	TX	77377	281-401-7500		374-3
Trobe, Babowice & Associates LLC 404 W Water St *Web:* tbalaws.com	Waukegan	IL	60085	847-625-8700		41
Trocaire College 360 Choate Ave *TF:* 877-616-6633 ■ *Web:* www.trocaire.edu	Buffalo	NY	14220	716-826-1200	828-6107	162
Trofholz Technologies Inc 250 Technology Way *Web:* www.trofholz.com	Rocklin	CA	95765	916-577-1903	577-1904	180
Troiano & Roberts PA 317 S Tennessee Ave *Web:* troianolaw.com	Lakeland	FL	33801	863-686-7136		41
Trois-Rivieres Port Authority (TRPA) 1545 Rue du Fleuve *Web:* www.porttr.com	Trois-Rivieres	QC	G9A6K4	819-378-2887	378-2487	618
Trois-Rivieres Tourism 1457 Rue Notre-Dame Ctr *TF:* 800-313-1123 ■ *Web:* www.tourismetroisrivieres.com	Trois-Rivieres	QC	G9A4X4	819-375-1122	375-0022	775
Trojan Battery Co 12380 Clark St *TF:* 800-423-6569 ■ *Web:* www.trojanbattery.com	Santa Fe Springs	CA	90670	562-236-3000	236-3282	74
Trojan Horse 100 E Kirkwood Ave *Web:* www.thetrojanhorse.com	Bloomington	IN	47408	812-332-1101		671
Trojan Inc 198 Trojan St *TF:* 800-264-0526 ■ *Web:* www.trojaninc.com	Mount Sterling	KY	40353	800-264-0526		437
Trojan Law Offices 9250 Wilshire Blvd Ste 325 *Web:* www.trojanlawoffices.com	Beverly Hills	CA	90212	310-777-8399		428
Trojan Press Inc 1635 Burlington St *Web:* www.trojanpressinc.com	Kansas City	MO	64116	816-221-6477		627
Trojan Professional Services Inc 14410 Cerritos Ave *TF:* 800-451-9723 ■ *Web:* www.trojanonline.com	Los Alamitos	CA	90720	714-816-7169		224
Troll Systems Corp 24950 Anza Dr *Web:* trollsystems.com	Valencia	CA	91355	661-702-8900		647
Troma Entertainment Inc 36-40 11th St *Web:* www.troma.com	Queens	NY	11106	718-391-0110	391-0255	572
Trombetta 8111 N 87th St *Web:* www.trombetta.com	Milwaukee	WI	53224	414-410-0300	355-3882	203
Tronair Inc 1740 Eber Rd *Web:* www.tronair.com	Holland	OH	43528	419-866-6301	867-0634	22
Trone 1823 Eastchester Dr *Web:* www.tronebrandenergy.com	High Point	NC	27265	336-886-1622		4
Trone David (Rep D - MD) 1213 Longworth House Office Bldg *Web:* www.trone.house.gov	Washington	DC	20515	202-225-2721		342-2
Tronox Inc 3301 NW 150th St *Web:* www.tronox.com	Oklahoma City	OK	73134	405-775-5000		143
Troon 15044 N Scottsdale Rd Ste 300 *Web:* www.troon.com	Scottsdale	AZ	85254	480-606-1000	606-1010	194
Trop Law Group PA 3860 W Commercial Blvd *Web:* troplawgroup.com	Fort Lauderdale	FL	33309	954-981-7150		41
Tropar Manufacturing Inc 5 Vreeland Rd *Web:* www.airflyte.com	Florham Park	NJ	07932	973-822-2400		702
Tropex 3220 Whitfield Ave **Fax Area Code:* 941 ■ *TF:* 800-874-8712 ■ *Web:* www.tropex.com	Sarasota	FL	34243	800-874-8712	753-1559*	23
Trophy Nut Company Inc 320 N Second St *TF:* 800-729-6887 ■ *Web:* www.trophynut.com	Tipp City	OH	45371	937-667-8478	667-4656	296-28
Trophy Room Books PO Box 3041 *Web:* www.trophyroombooks.com	Agoura Hills	CA	91376	818-889-2469	889-4849	96
Trophyland USA Inc 7001 W 20th Ave *TF:* 800-327-5820 ■ *Web:* www.trophyland.com	Hialeah	FL	33014	305-823-4830	823-4836	777
Tropi Tan 3810 Court St *Web:* www.tropitan.biz	Flint	MI	48506	810-743-2340		810
Tropic Oil Company Inc 10002 NW 89th Ave *TF:* 866-645-3835 ■ *Web:* www.tropicoil.com	Miami	FL	33178	305-888-4611		579
Tropic Tool & Mold Inc 1420 Wagner Dr *Web:* www.tropictoolandmold.com	Albertville	AL	35950	256-593-3441	593-1650	604
Tropical Cheese Industries Inc 450 Fayette St PO Box 1357 *TF:* 888-874-4928 ■ *Web:* www.tropicalcheese.com	Perth Amboy	NJ	08861	732-442-4898	442-8227	296-5
Tropical Chinese Restaurant 7991 SW 40th St *Web:* www.tropicalchinesemiami.com	Miami	FL	33155	305-262-7576	262-1552	671

Name / Address	City	State	ZIP	Phone	Fax	Class
Tropical Everglades Visitor Assn 160 US Hwy Ste 1 *Web:* www.tropicaleverglades.com	Florida City	FL	33034	305-245-9180		206
Tropical Foods 1100 Continental Blvd *Web:* www.tropicalfoods.com	Charlotte	NC	28273	704-588-0400		299
Tropical Ford 9900 S Orange Blossom Trial *TF:* 877-241-0502 ■ *Web:* tropicalford.com	Orlando	FL	32837	407-851-3800	240-7308	57
Tropical Music Export Enterprise Inc 6991 NW 51 St *Web:* www.tropicalmusic.com	Miami	FL	33166	305-740-7454	740-7456	523
Tropical Roofing and Raingutters 94-078 Leokane St *Web:* www.tropicalroofingandraingutters.com	Waipahu	HI	96797	808-847-0030	842-1563	189-12
Tropical Shipping 501 Avenue P *Web:* tropical.com	Riviera Beach	FL	33404	561-881-3900		313
Tropical Winds Oceanfront Hotel 1398 N Atlantic Ave *TF:* 800-245-6099 ■ *Web:* tropicalwindshotel.com	Daytona Beach	FL	32118	386-258-1016	255-6462	379
Tropicana Entertainment 2629 Boardwalk *OTC:* TPCA ■ *TF:* 800-843-8767 ■ *Web:* tropicana.net	Atlantic City	NJ	08401	800-843-8767		669
Tropicana Express 2121 S Casino Dr *TF:* 800-243-6846 ■ *Web:* troplaughlin.com	Laughlin	NV	89029	702-298-4200		133
Tropicana Inn & Suites 1540 S Harbor Blvd *TF:* 800-828-4898 ■ *Web:* tropicanainn-anaheim.com	Anaheim	CA	92802	714-635-4082	635-1535	379
Tropicana Resort & Casino 3801 Las Vegas Blvd S *TF:* 800-462-8767 ■ *Web:* www.troplv.com	Las Vegas	NV	89109	702-739-2222		669
Tropigas de P R Urb Industrial Luchetti Calle C Lote 30 *Web:* tropigaspr.com	Bayamon	PR	00961	787-641-8002		316
Tropitone Furniture Company Inc 5 Marconi *Web:* www.tropitone.com	Irvine	CA	92618	949-951-2010		319-4
Troquet 140 Boston St *Web:* www.troquetboston.com	Boston	MA	02111	617-695-9463		671
Trostel's Greenbrier Restaurant 5810 Merle Hay Rd *Web:* greenbriartrostels.com	Johnston	IA	50131	515-253-0124		671
Trotter & Morton Ltd 5711 1 St SE *Web:* trotterandmorton.com	Calgary	AB	T2H1H9	403-255-7535	640-0767	186
Trotters Restaurant 2008 Savannah Hwy *TF:* 800-334-6660 ■ *Web:* www.thetownandcountryinn.com	Charleston	SC	29401	843-571-1000	766-9444	671
Trotwood Chamber of Commerce 5790 Denlinger Rd *Web:* www.trotwoodchamber.org	Trotwood	OH	45426	937-837-1484	837-1508	139
Trouble Free Plumbing Inc 802 Willow St *Web:* www.troublefreeinc.com	Pekin	IL	61554	309-347-5309		189-10
Troup County 111 Bull St *Web:* www.troupcountyga.org	LaGrange	GA	30241	706-883-1740	883-1724	338
Troupe Ditigal Media Production, The 3 Industrial Dr Unit 3 *Web:* www.thetroupe.com	Windham	NH	03087	603-893-4554		514
Trousdale County 240 Broadway *Web:* hartsvilletrousdale.com	Hartsville	TN	37074	615-374-9243		338
Trout & Partners Ltd 8 Wahneta Rd *Web:* www.troutandpartners.com	Old Greenwich	CT	06870	203-637-7001	637-7071	194
Trout Ebersole & Groff 1705 Oregon Pk *TF:* 800-448-1384 ■ *Web:* www.troutcpa.com	Lancaster	PA	17601	717-569-2900	569-0141	2
Trout Unlimited (TU) 1300 N 17th St Ste 500 *TF:* 800-834-2419 ■ *Web:* www.tu.org	Arlington	VA	22209	703-522-0200	284-9400	48-3
Troutman Sanders LLP 600 Peachtree St NE Ste 3000 *Web:* www.troutman.com	Atlanta	GA	30308	404-885-3000	885-3900	428
Troutt, Beeman & Company PC 1212 Locust St *Web:* www.tbco.net	Harrisonville	MO	64701	816-380-5500		2
Trouw Nutrition 115 Executive Dr *TF:* 800-365-1357 ■ *Web:* www.trouwnutritionusa.com	Highland	IL	62249	618-654-2070	654-7012	447
Trove Recommerce 3775 Bayshore Blvd *Web:* www.trove.co	Brisbane	CA	94005	415-322-0295		586
Troxel Co, The 11495 Hwy 57 PO Box 276 *Web:* www.troxel.com	Moscow	TN	38057	901-877-6875	877-3439	490
Troxell Communications Inc 4675 E Cotton Center Blvd Ste 155 *TF:* 800-352-7912 ■ *Web:* www.trox.com	Phoenix	AZ	85040	800-352-7912	752-1299	38
Troxler Electronic Laboratories Inc 3008 E Cornwallis Rd PO Box 12057 *TF:* 877-876-9537 ■ *Web:* www.troxlerlabs.com	Research Triangle Park	NC	27709	919-549-8661	549-0761	201
Troy Belting & Supply Co 70 Cohoes Rd *TF:* 800-274-8769 ■ *Web:* troyindustrialsolutions.com	Watervliet	NY	12189	518-272-4920	272-0531	385
Troy BioSciences Inc 113 S 47th Ave *Web:* www.troycorp.com	Phoenix	AZ	85043	602-233-9047		280
Troy Chamber of Commerce 2125 Butterfield Ste 100N *Web:* www.troychamber.com	Troy	MI	48084	248-641-8151	641-0545	139
Troy Chemical Industries Inc 17040 Rapids Rd *Web:* www.troychemical.com	Burton	OH	44021	440-834-4408	834-1142	151
Troy Design & Manufacturing Co (TDM) 14425 Sheldon Rd *Web:* www.troydm.com	Plymouth	MI	48170	734-738-2300		489
Troy Free Press 20 Business Park Dr *Web:* www.troyfreepress.com	Troy	MO	63379	636-528-9550		532-2
Troy Honda 1835 Maplelawn Dr *Web:* www.troyhonda.com	Troy	MI	48084	248-939-5411		57
Troy Manufacturing Company Inc 17090 Rapids Rd *Web:* www.troy-mfg.com	Burton	OH	44021	440-834-8262	834-1137	621
Troy Springs State Park 674 NE Troy Springs Rd *Web:* www.floridastateparks.org	Branford	FL	32008	386-935-4835		565
Troy Sunshade Co 607 Riffle Ave *TF:* 800-833-8769 ■ *Web:* bagsbytroy.com	Greenville	OH	45331	937-548-2466		733
Troy Tube & Manufacturing Co 50100 E Russell Schmidt Blvd *Web:* www.troytube.com	Chesterfield	MI	48051	586-949-8700		595
Troy University 600 University Ave *TF:* 800-551-9716 ■ *Web:* troy.edu	Troy	AL	36082	334-670-3100	670-3733	166
Troy-CSL Lighting Inc 14508 Nelson Ave *TF:* 800-533-8769 ■ *Web:* troylighting.littmanbrands.com	City of Industry	CA	91744	626-336-4511	330-4266	439
Troyer Foods Inc 17141 State Rd 4 *TF:* 800-876-9377 ■ *Web:* www.troyers.com	Goshen	IN	46528	574-533-0302	533-3851	297-10
Troyke Manufacturing Co 11294 Orchard St *Web:* www.troyke.com	Cincinnati	OH	45241	513-769-4242	769-6362	493
Troy-Miami County Public Library 419 W Main St *TF:* 866-657-8556 ■ *Web:* www.tmcpl.org	Troy	OH	45373	937-339-0502	335-4880	434-3
TRP (Todd Rivenbark Puryear) 2405 Robeson St *Web:* trpsumner.com	Fayetteville	NC	28305	910-323-3600	323-3640	2
TRP Enterprises Inc 333 Summit Square Ct *Web:* www.trpnet.com	Winston-Salem	NC	27101	336-777-1947		463
TRPA (Trois-Rivieres Port Authority) 1545 Rue du Fleuve *Web:* www.porttr.com	Trois-Rivieres	QC	G9A6K4	819-378-2887	378-2487	618
TRRMC (Twin Rivers Regional Medical Ctr) 1301 First St *Web:* www.twinriversregional.com	Kennett	MO	63857	573-888-4522		374-3
TRS (Tabula Rosa Systems LLC) 17 Cedar Ln *Web:* www.tabularosa.net	Titusville	NJ	08560	609-818-1802	818-1803	525
TRSA (Textile Rental Services Assn) 1800 Diagonal Rd Ste 200 *TF:* 877-770-9274 ■ *Web:* www.trsa.org	Alexandria	VA	22314	703-519-0029	519-0026	49-4
TRSB Inc 276 Saint-Jacques St Ste 900 *TF:* 855-909-4682 ■ *Web:* www.trsb.com	Montreal	QC	H2Y1N3	514-844-4682		317
TRS-RenTelco 1830 W Airfield Dr *TF:* 800-874-7123 ■ *Web:* www.trsrentelco.com	Dallas	TX	75261	972-456-4000	456-4617	23
TRU (Thompson Rivers University) 805 TRU Way *TF:* 800-663-1663 ■ *Web:* www.tru.ca	Kamloops	BC	V2C0C8	250-828-5000	371-5960	785
Tru Color Litho Inc 511 Houston St *Web:* www.trucolorlitho.com	Nashville	TN	37203	615-742-1281	742-7484	627
Tru Line Manufacturing Inc 3510 Central Pkwy SW *Web:* www.trulinemfg.com	Decatur	AL	35603	256-350-1002		595
Tru Tech Corp 20 Vaughan Vly Blvd *TF:* 888-760-0099 ■ *Web:* trutechdoors.com	Vaughan	ON	L4H0B1	905-856-0096		499
TRU TECH Systems Inc 24550 N River Rd PO Box 46965 *TF:* 877-878-8324 ■ *Web:* trutechsystems.com	Mount Clemens	MI	48043	586-469-2700	469-1344	455
Tru Tech Valve LLC 577 W Pike St *Web:* www.trutechvalve.com	Canonsburg	PA	15317	724-916-4805		789
Tru Vue Inc 9400 W 55th St *TF:* 800-621-8339 ■ *Web:* tru-vue.com	McCook	IL	60525	708-485-5080	485-5980	329
TruAdvantage 4950 Hamilton Ave Ste 212 *Web:* www.truadvantage.com	San Jose	CA	95130	408-680-8389		180
Truax Printing Inc 425 E Haskell St *Web:* www.truaxprinting.com	Loudonville	OH	44842	419-994-4166		532-2
Trubee Collins & Company Inc 1350 One M & T Plz *TF:* 800-836-4050 ■ *Web:* trubeecollins.com	Buffalo	NY	14203	716-849-1401	849-0144	690
Tru-Brew Coffee Service Inc 387 Springdale Ave *Web:* www.trubrew.com	Hatboro	PA	19040	215-441-0110	441-8414	366
Tru-Care Health Systems Inc 5004 N Portland *TF:* 800-842-2734 ■ *Web:* www.tru-care.com	Oklahoma City	OK	73112	405-949-9969	949-9974	475
TruChoice Financial Group 300 ParkBrooke Pl Ste 200 *TF:* 800-886-4757 ■ *Web:* www.gameplanfinancialqa.com	Woodstock	GA	30189	800-886-4757		402
Truck Accessories Group Inc 28858 Ventura Dr *Web:* www.leer.com	Elkhart	IN	46517	574-522-5337		120
Truck Center Cos 14321 Cornhusker Rd PO Box 27379 *TF:* 800-777-2440 ■ *Web:* truckcentercompanies.com	Omaha	NE	68127	800-777-2440		126
Truck Driver Institute 4939 US Highway 78 *TF:* 800-848-7364 ■ *Web:* www.drivebigtrucks.com	Oxford	AL	36203	800-848-7364		167-3
Truck Driving Academy 11081 Cherry Ave *Web:* www.truckdriveracademy.com	Fontana	CA	92337	909-201-7600		167-3
Truck Enterprises Inc 3440 S Main St *TF:* 800-296-8782 ■ *Web:* www.truckenterprises.com	Harrisonburg	VA	22801	540-564-6900		57
Truck Equipment Sales Inc 4700 Rangeline Rd *TF:* 800-633-6946 ■ *Web:* www.truckequipmentsales.com	Mobile	AL	36619	251-666-8606	666-8676	62-5
Truck Equipment Service Co 800 Oak St *TF:* 800-869-0363 ■ *Web:* www.cornhusker800.com	Lincoln	NE	68521	402-476-3225	476-3726	779
Truck One Inc 140 Everett Ave *Web:* www.truckone.net	Newark	OH	43055	740-349-8144	349-9766	780
Truck Renting & Leasing Assn (TRALA) 675 N Washington St Ste 410 *Web:* www.trala.org	Alexandria	VA	22314	703-299-9120		49-21
Truck Sales & Service Inc PO Box 262 *TF:* 800-282-6100 ■ *Web:* www.trksls.com	Midvale	OH	44653	740-922-3412		57
Truck Tire Sales Inc 426 W Pershing Rd *Web:* www.trucktiresalesil.com	Chicago	IL	60609	773-285-3000		57

	Phone	Fax	Class
Truck Utilities Inc 2370 English St .... Saint Paul MN 55109 *TF:* 800-869-1075 ■ *Web:* www.truckutilities.com	651-484-3305	484-0076	516
Truck Works Inc 1815 S 39th Ave.......... Phoenix AZ 85009 *Web:* www.truckworksllc.com	602-233-3713		57
Truckee Donner Public Utility District (TDPUD) 11570 Donner Pass Rd PO Box 309.......... Truckee CA 96160 *Web:* www.tdpud.org	530-587-3896	550-1968	245
Truckee Meadows Community College 7000 Dandini Blvd .... Reno NV 89512 *Web:* www.tmcc.edu	775-673-7111	673-7028	162
Truckers Helper LLC, The 630 S Wickham Rd.......... Melbourne FL 32904 *TF:* 800-875-7435 ■ *Web:* www.truckershelper.com	321-956-7331		177
Truckin Movers Corp 1031 Harvest St.......... Durham NC 27704 *TF:* 800-334-1651 ■ *Web:* www.truckinmovers.com	919-682-2300	688-2264	519
Truck-Lite Company Inc 310 E Elmwood Ave .... Falconer NY 14733 **Fax Area Code:* 716 ■ *TF:* 800-562-5012 ■ *Web:* www.truck-lite.com	800-562-5012	665-6403*	438
Truckload Carriers Assn (TCA) 555 E Braddock Rd.......... Alexandria VA 22314 *Web:* www.truckload.org	703-838-1950	836-6610	49-21
Trucks only 550 S Country Club Dr.......... Mesa AZ 85210 *Web:* www.trucksonlysales.com	480-844-7071		516
Truckwell of Alaska Inc 5801 Silverado Way .... Anchorage AK 99518 *Web:* truckwell.com	907-349-8845		770
Tructor Inc 412 N Palestine St.......... Athens TX 75751 *Web:* www.tructor.com	850-830-8136		274
Tru-Cut Inc 1145 Allied Dr.......... Sebring OH 44672 *Web:* www.trucut.com	330-938-9806		757
Trudell Medical Group Ltd 758 Baransway Dr.......... London ON N5V5J7 *TF:* 800-757-4881 ■ *Web:* www.trudellhs.com	519-685-8800		475
Trudiligence LLC 3190 S Wadsworth Blvd Ste 260 .... Lakewood CO 80227 *TF:* 800-580-0474 ■ *Web:* www.trudiligence.com	303-692-8445		218
True & Assoc 325 North Ave E.......... Westfield NJ 07090 *Web:* trueassoc.com	908-232-0760		390
True Drilling LLC 455 N Poplar PO Box 2360.......... Casper WY 82602 *Web:* www.truecos.com	307-266-0475		540
True Fit Corp 60 State St 12th Fl.......... Boston MA 02109 *Web:* www.truefit.com	617-848-3740	848-3739	387
True Fitness Technology 865 Hoff Rd.......... O'Fallon MO 63366 *TF:* 800-426-6570 ■ *Web:* www.truefitness.com	888-491-2307		267
True Homes LLC 2649 Breckenridge Center Dr Ste 104.......... Monroe NC 28110 *Web:* www.truehomesusa.com	704-238-1229	238-1150	187
True Manufacturing Co 2001 E Terra Ln.......... O'Fallon MO 63366 *TF:* 800-325-6152 ■ *Web:* truemfg.com	636-240-2400	272-2408	664
True Media 500 Business Loop 70 W Ste 201.......... Columbia MO 65203 *Web:* www.truemediaservices.com	573-443-8783	443-8784	6
True North America Inc 2052 Alton Pkwy.......... Irvine CA 92606 *Web:* www.trueinnovations.com	714-368-7464		321
True North Consulting Group 140 3rd St S.......... Stillwater MN 55082 *Web:* www.tncg.com	651-430-2772		449
True North Energy LLC 5565 Airport Hwy.......... Toledo OH 43615 *TF:* 888-245-9336 ■ *Web:* truenorthstores.com	419-868-6800	868-1458	324
True North Equipment 5101 Gateway Dr .... Grand Forks ND 58203 *TF:* 888-456-0240 ■ *Web:* www.truenorthequipment.com	701-746-4436		274
True North Land Surveying Inc 815 S Weller St Ste 200 .... Seattle WA 98104 *Web:* truenorthlandsurveying.com	206-332-0800		727
True North Strategic Advisors LLC 347 W Berry St Ste 100 .... Fort Wayne IN 46802 *Web:* www.truenorthsa.com	260-420-5050	420-5011	196
True Partners Consulting LLC 225 W Wacker Dr Ste 1600.......... Chicago IL 60611 *Web:* www.tpctax.com	312-235-3300		194
True Position Technologies Inc 24900 Ave Standford .... Valencia CA 91355 *Web:* www.truepositiontech.com	661-294-0030	294-1240	454
True Solutions Inc 5001 Lyndon B Johnson Fwy Ste 125.......... Dallas TX 75244 *Web:* www.truesolutions.com	972-770-0900		177
True Temper Sports 8275 Tournament Dr Ste 200 .... Memphis TN 38125 *TF:* 800-355-8783 ■ *Web:* www.truetemper.com	800-355-8783		710
True West 6400 Pinecrest Dr Ste 400.......... Royse City TX 75189 *Web:* www.truewesthome.com	972-636-7922	635-2059	730
True World Foods LLC 22 Foodmart Rd .... Boston MA 02118 *Web:* www.trueworldfoods.com	617-269-9988	269-5725	297-5
True[X] 11925 Wilshire Blvd Ste 200 .... Los Angeles CA 90025 *Web:* www.truex.com	310-657-9900		5
TrueAccord Corp 303 Second St S Ste 750 .... San Francisco CA 94107 *TF:* 866-611-2731 ■ *Web:* www.trueaccord.com	866-611-2731		393
Truebridge Inc 105 Beach St Ste 3 .... Boston MA 02111 *Web:* www.truebridge.com	617-956-5020	956-5021	195
TrueCloud 2147 E Baseline Rd.......... Tempe AZ 85283 *TF:* 866-990-8783 ■ *Web:* www.truecloud.com	866-990-8783		196
trueEX Group LLC 22 W 21st St 9th Fl .... New York NY 10010 *Web:* www.trueex.com	646-786-8520		690
Truefit 501 Grant St Ste 1025 .... Pittsburgh PA 15219 *Web:* truefit.io	724-772-5959		809
Truelove & Maclean Inc 57 Callender Rd .... Watertown CT 06795 *Web:* www.trueloveandmaclean.com	860-274-9600		483
TrueNet Communications Corp 7666 Blanding Blvd .... Jacksonville FL 32244 *TF:* 800-285-2028 ■ *Web:* truenetcommunications.com	904-777-9052		261
Truenorth Development Inc 141 N Center St 201.......... Northville MI 48167 *Web:* www.truen.com	248-348-6011		463
Truepath PO Box 2064.......... Escondido CA 92033 *Web:* www.truepath.com	760-480-8791		225
Truepoint Solutions LLC 3262 Penryn Rd Ste 100 B.......... Loomis CA 95650 *Web:* www.truepointsolutions.com	916-259-1293		177
Truesdail Laboratories Inc 14201 Franklin Ave.......... Tustin CA 92780 *Web:* www.truesdail.com	714-730-6239	730-6462	743
True-Tech Corp 4050 Technology Pl .... Fremont CA 94538	510-353-1000		454
Truett-McConnell College 100 Alumni Dr .... Cleveland GA 30528 *TF:* 800-226-8621 ■ *Web:* truett.edu	706-865-2134		166
Tru-Fab Technology Inc 34820 Lakeland Blvd .... Eastlake OH 44095 *Web:* www.trufab.com	440-954-9760		697
Tru-Flex Metal Hose Corp 2391 S St Rd 263 PO Box 247 .... West Lebanon IN 47991 *TF:* 800-255-6291 ■ *Web:* www.tru-flex.com	765-893-4403		595
TruGreen ChemLawn 4135 South Creek Rd .... Memphis TN 38120 *TF:* 866-369-9539 ■ *Web:* www.trugreen.com	866-369-9539		577
Trugrocer Federal Credit Union 501 E Highland St.......... Boise ID 83706 *TF:* 800-392-3328 ■ *Web:* www.trugrocer.com	208-385-5200	385-5290	219
Truheat Inc 700 Grand St.......... Allegan MI 49010 **Fax Area Code:* 269 ■ *TF:* 800-879-6199 ■ *Web:* www.ddrheating.com	800-879-6199	673-7219*	318
Truitt Bros Inc 1105 Front St NE.......... Salem OR 97301 *TF:* 800-547-8712 ■ *Web:* www.truittbros.com	503-362-3674		296-20
Truitt Tingle & Paramore LLC 5346 Stadium Trace Pkwy Ste 202 .... Hoover AL 35244 *Web:* ttpcpa.com	205-733-8265		2
Truity Credit Union PO Box 1358.......... Bartlesville OK 74005 *TF:* 800-897-6991 ■ *Web:* www.truitycu.org	877-744-2835		219
Trujillo & Sons Inc 3325 NW 62nd St.......... Miami FL 33147 *Web:* www.trujilloandsons.com	305-633-6482	696-4510	299
TruLeap Technologies 400 Main St PO Box 89 .... Filer ID 83328 *Web:* truleap.net	208-326-4331	326-3190	736
Trulia Inc 535 Mission St Ste 700 .... San Francisco CA 94105 *Web:* www.trulia.com	415-648-4358		395
Truliant Federal Credit Union 3200 Truliant Way.......... Winston-Salem NC 27103 *TF:* 800-822-0382 ■ *Web:* www.truliantfcu.org	336-659-1955		219
Trulife 26296 Twelve Trees Ln NW .... Poulsbo WA 98370 *TF:* 800-492-1088 ■ *Web:* trulife.com	360-697-5656		477
Truline Corp 9390 Redwood St .... Las Vegas NV 89139 *TF:* 800-634-6489 ■ *Web:* www.trulinecorp.com	702-362-7495	362-3215	780
Tru-Link Fence Co 5009 W Lake St .... Melrose Park IL 60160 *TF:* 800-568-9300 ■ *Web:* www.tru-link.com	847-568-9300		279
Trulioo 1055 W Hastings St Ste 1200.......... Vancouver BC V6B1L1 *TF:* 888-773-0179 ■ *Web:* www.trulioo.com	888-773-0179		224
Trulite Glass & Aluminum Solutions LLC 800 Fairway Dr Ste 200 .... Deerfield Beach FL 33441 **Fax Area Code:* 954 ■ *TF:* 800-432-8132 ■ *Web:* trulite.com	800-432-8132	718-7684*	480
Trulock Tool Co 113 Drayton St.......... Whigham GA 39897 *TF:* 800-293-9402 ■ *Web:* trulockchokes.com	229-762-4678		295
Truly Nolen of America Inc 3636 E Speedway Blvd.......... Tucson AZ 85716 **Fax Area Code:* 520 ■ *TF:* 800-468-7859 ■ *Web:* www.trulynolen.com	855-534-9139	322-4002*	577
Truly (USA) Inc 2620 Concord Ave Ste 106.......... Alhambra CA 91803 *Web:* www.trulyusa.com	626-284-3033		253
Trumaker 228 Grant Ave 2nd Fl .... San Francisco CA 94108 *Web:* www.trumaker.com	415-349-5235		690
Truman Medical Center Hospital Hill 2301 Holmes St.......... Kansas City MO 64108 *Web:* www.trumed.org	816-404-1000		374-3
Truman State University 100 E Normal St.......... Kirksville MO 63501 *TF:* 800-892-7792 ■ *Web:* www.truman.edu	660-785-4000	785-7456	166
TruMarx Data Partners Inc 30 S Wacker Dr Ste 2200.......... Chicago IL 60606 *TF:* 844-878-6279 ■ *Web:* www.trumarx.com	844-878-6279		387
Trumbull Corp 225 N Shore Dr .... Pittsburgh PA 15212 *Web:* www.pjdick.com	412-807-2000		188-4
Trumbull County 160 High St NW.......... Warren OH 44481 *Web:* www.co.trumbull.oh.us	330-675-2451		338
Trumbull Industries Inc 400 Dietz Rd NE.......... Warren OH 44482 *TF:* 800-477-1799 ■ *Web:* www.trumbull.com	330-392-1551	399-4421	1
Trumbull Library 33 Quality St .... Trumbull CT 06611 *Web:* www.trumbull-ct.gov	203-452-5197	452-5125	434-3
TruMethods LLC 66 E Main St Ste H.......... Moorestown NJ 08057 *Web:* www.trumethods.com	856-316-4900		196
Trump International Beach Resort 18001 Collins Ave .... Sunny Isles Beach FL 33160 *Web:* www.trumpmiami.com	305-692-5600	692-5601	669
Trump International Hotel & Tower 401 N Wabash Ave.......... Chicago IL 60611 **Fax Area Code:* 212 ■ *TF:* 877-458-7867 ■ *Web:* www.trumphotels.com	312-588-8000	299-1150*	379
Trump Organization 725 5th Ave .... New York NY 10022 *Web:* www.trump.com	212-832-2000		360-3
TRUMPF Group 111 Hyde Rd.......... Farmington CT 06032 *TF:* 800-306-1077 ■ *Web:* www.trumpf.com	860-255-6000	255-6424	425
Trupar America Inc 160 Wilson Rd .... Bentleyville PA 15314 *TF:* 877-704-0073 ■ *Web:* truparamerica.com	724-239-2220		770
Truro & District Chamber of Commerce 605 Prince St.......... Truro NS B2N1G2 *Web:* www.trurocolchesterchamber.com	902-895-6328		137
Trusco Inc 12527 Porr Rd .... Doylestown OH 44230 *TF:* 800-847-5841 ■ *Web:* www.trusco.net	330-658-2027	658-4979	817
Truscott Inc PO Box 1832.......... Twin Falls ID 83301 *TF:* 800-635-0886 ■ *Web:* www.truscotttrucking.com	208-734-9350	734-9932	780

Name / Address	City	State	Zip	Phone	Fax	Class
Truss Specialists Inc 500 Sycamore St *Web:* www.trussspecialists.com	La Crescent	MN	55947	507-895-8400	895-6554	817
Trussell Technologies Inc 232 N Lake Ave Ste 300 *Web:* www.trusselltech.com	Pasadena	CA	91101	626-486-0560		261
Truss-Pro's Inc 10954 424th Ave *Web:* www.truss-pros.com	Britton	SD	57430	605-448-2202		817
Truss-Tech Industries Inc 4883 Roy Carlson Blvd *Web:* www.trusstech.com	Buford	GA	30519	770-271-1347		817
Trussway Ltd 9411 Alcorn Rd *Web:* www.trussway.com	Houston	TX	77093	713-691-6900	691-2064	817
Trust Bank 600 E Main St PO Box 158 *TF:* 800-766-3451 ■ *Web:* www.trustbank.net	Olney	IL	62450	618-395-4311		70
Trust Builders Inc 883 SW Church St *Web:* retireready.com	Dallas	OR	97338	503-831-1111		177
Trust Company of Virginia, The 9030 Stony Point Pkwy Ste 300 *Web:* www.tcvwealth.com	Richmond	VA	23235	804-272-9044		70
Trust for Public Land (TPL) 116 New Montgomery St 4th Fl *TF:* 800-714-5263 ■ *Web:* www.tpl.org	San Francisco	CA	94105	415-495-4014	495-4103	48-13
Trust Hospitality LLC 806 Douglas Rd 4th Fl *Web:* www.trusthospitality.com	Coral Gables	FL	33134	305-537-7040		378
Trustco Bank Corporation NY PO Box 1082 *NASDAQ: TRST* ■ *TF:* 800-670-3110 ■ *Web:* www.trustcobank.com	Schenectady	NY	12301	518-377-3311		360-2
TrustComm 11140 Aerospace Ave *Web:* www.trustcomm.com	Houston	TX	77034	281-272-7500	999-4455	681
Trusted Advisor Associates LLC 193 Zeppi Ln *TF:* 855-878-7801 ■ *Web:* trustedadvisor.com	West Orange	NJ	07052	855-878-7801	886-2819	463
Trusted Computing Group 3855 SW 153rd Dr *Web:* trustedcomputinggroup.org	Beaverton	OR	97006	503-619-0562	644-6708	138
Trusted Integration Inc 525 Wythe St *Web:* www.trustedintegration.com	Alexandria	VA	22314	703-299-9171	299-9172	177
Trust-franklin Press Inc 41 Terminal Way *Web:* www.trust-franklinpress.com	Pittsburgh	PA	15219	412-481-6442	481-9949	687
TruStile Doors 1111 E 71st Ave *TF:* 877-283-4511 ■ *Web:* www.trustile.com	Denver	CO	80229	888-286-3931	288-6521	236
Trustmark Construction Corp 841 Sweetwater Ave *Web:* www.trustmarkcorp.com	Florence	AL	35630	256-760-9624	760-0902	187
Trustmark Insurance Co 400 Field Dr *Web:* www.trustmarkinsurance.com	Lake Forest	IL	60045	847-615-1500	615-3910	391-2
Trustmark National Bank 248 E Capitol St PO Box 291 *NASDAQ: TRMK* ■ *TF:* 800-243-2524 ■ *Web:* www.trustmark.com	Jackson	MS	39201	601-208-5111		360-2
Trustmont Financial Group Inc 200 Brush Run Rd Ste A *Web:* www.trustmontgroup.com	Greensburg	PA	15601	724-468-5665		401
Tru-Stone Technologies 1101 Prosper Dr *TF:* 800-959-0517 ■ *Web:* www.tru-stone.com	Waite Park	MN	56387	320-251-7171	259-5073	482
TrustRadius Inc 9737 Great Hills Trl Ste 340 *Web:* www.trustradius.com	Austin	TX	78759	512-961-7777		113
Trustus Theatre 520 Lady St *Web:* www.trustus.org	Columbia	SC	29201	803-254-9732		572
Trustwave Secure Web Gateway 828 W Taft Ave *TF:* 888-786-7999 ■ *Web:* www.m86security.com	Orange	CA	92865	714-282-6111		178-1
TrustWorkz 3101 Cobb Pkwy SE Ste 124 *Web:* trustworkz.com	Atlanta	GA	30339	770-615-3275		5
TruTech LLC PO Box 6849 *TF:* 844-492-5974 ■ *Web:* www.trutechinc.com	Marietta	GA	30065	800-842-7296		577
Trutek 1740 S Main St *Web:* www.trutek.com	Salt Lake City	UT	84115	801-486-6655		177
Truth & Advertising 454 N Broadway 2nd Fl *Web:* www.truthandadvertising.com	Santa Ana	CA	92701	714-542-8778		7
Truth Consciousness Desert Ashram 3403 W Sweetwater Dr *Web:* www.truthconsciousness.org	Tucson	AZ	85745	520-743-8821		48-20
Truth Hardware Inc 700 W Bridge St *Web:* www.truth.com	Owatonna	MN	55060	507-451-5620	451-5655	350
Truth Radio Network PO Box 344 *Web:* www.truthradio.com	Nipomo	CA	93444	805-357-7632		644
Truth Radio Network 4405 Providence Ln Ste D *Web:* www.truthnetwork.com	Winston-Salem	NC	27106	336-759-0363		647
Truth Seeker Productions Inc 105 S Brinker Ave *TF:* 800-747-7301 ■ *Web:* geartechs.com	Columbus	OH	43204	614-276-1997	279-5347	366
TruVista Communications 112 York St *TF:* 800-768-1212 ■ *Web:* www.truvista.net	Chester	SC	29706	803-581-9159		224
Truwest Credit Union PO Box 3489 *TF:* 855-878-9378 ■ *Web:* truwest.org	Scottsdale	AZ	85271	480-441-5900		509
Truxton Trust 4525 Harding Pk Ste 300 *Web:* truxtontrust.com	Nashville	TN	37205	615-515-1700	515-1717	70
Trydor Industries (Canada) Ltd 19275-25th Ave *TF:* 800-567-8558 ■ *Web:* www.trydor.com	Surrey	BC	V3Z3X1	604-542-4773	542-4776	791
Tryiton Eyewear LLC 147 Post Rd E *TF:* 888-896-3885 ■ *Web:* www.eyeglasses.com	Westport	CT	06880	203-544-0770		543
Tryon Creek Software LLC 6312 SW Capitol Hwy 117 *Web:* tryonsoft.com	Portland	OR	97239	503-980-1984		177
Tryon Creek State Natural Area 11321 SW Terwilliger Blvd *Web:* stateparks.oregon.gov	Portland	OR	97219	503-636-4398		565
Tryon Distributing Company LLC 4701 Stockholm Ct *Web:* tryondist.com	Charlotte	NC	28273	704-334-0849	334-2563	80-3
Tryon Trucking Inc PO Box 68 *TF:* 800-523-5254 ■ *Web:* www.tryontrucking.com	Fairless Hills	PA	19030	215-295-6622	295-7168	780
TS Civil Engineering Inc 1776 Technology Dr *Web:* tscivil.com	San Jose	CA	95110	408-452-9300		261
TS Consulting International Inc 970 W 190th St Ste 920	Torrance	CA	90502	310-538-4898		260
TS Distributors Inc 4404 Windfern Rd **Fax Area Code:* 832 ■ *TF:* 800-392-3655 ■ *Web:* www.tsdistributors.com	Houston	TX	77041	800-392-3655	467-5454*	350
TS Partners Inc 630 Freedom Business Center Dr Ste 212 *Web:* www.tspartnersinc.com	King of Prussia	PA	19406	610-768-1100	768-1105	178-1
TS Restaurants of California & Hawaii 40 Kupuohi St Ste 206 *Web:* www.tsrestaurants.com	Lahaina	HI	96761	808-667-4800		670
TS Tech USA Corp 8400 E Broad St *Web:* www.tstna.com	Reynoldsburg	OH	43068	614-577-1088		247
TS Trim Industries Inc 6380 Canal St *Web:* www.tstrim.com	Canal Winchester	OH	43110	614-837-4114	837-4127	60
TSA Inc 2050 W Sam Houston Pkwy N *TF:* 800-422-4872 ■ *Web:* tsa.com	Houston	TX	77043	713-935-1500	935-1555	180
TSA Special Member & Insurance Services Inc PO Box 90 *TF:* 800-537-8491 ■ *Web:* www.tsaspecialservices.com	West Covina	CA	91793	626-814-4611		390
TSA-Advet 4722 Campbells Run Rd *Web:* www.tsa.advet.com	Pittsburgh	PA	15205	412-787-0980		177
TSC Apparel LLC 12080 Mosteller Rd **Fax Area Code:* 800 ■ *TF:* 800-543-7230 ■ *Web:* www.tscapparel.com	Cincinnati	OH	45241	513-771-1138	248-1069*	156
Tschetter & Adams Law 4201 S Minnesota Ave Ste 113 *Web:* tschetteradams.com	Sioux Falls	SD	57105	605-367-1013		41
TSCT (Thaddeus Stevens College of Technology) 750 E King St *TF:* 800-842-3832 ■ *Web:* stevenscollege.edu	Lancaster	PA	17602	717-299-7701	391-6929	800
TSD (Tri-State Distributors Inc) 2500 Georgia Hwy 17 **Fax Area Code:* 888 ■ *TF:* 800-476-6164 ■ *Web:* www.tri-statedistributors.com	Royston	GA	30662	706-245-6164	749-9001*	191-3
TSD Global 5305 Lakeview Pkwy S Dr *Web:* tsdglobal.com	Indianapolis	IN	46268	317-216-2240		737
TSE (Tokyo Stock Exchange Inc) 45 Broadway 21st Fl *Web:* www.jpx.co.jp	New York	NY	10006	212-363-2350	363-2354	637-2
TSE Industries Inc 4370 112th Terr N *TF:* 800-237-7634 ■ *Web:* www.tse-industries.com	Clearwater	FL	33762	727-573-7676		608
TSEMC (Tri-State Electric Membership Corp) 2310 Blue Ridge Dr *Web:* www.tsemc.net	Blue Ridge	GA	30513	706-492-3251	492-7617	245
TSG Consulting Ii LLC 118 Capitol St *Web:* tsgsolution.com	Charleston	WV	25301	304-345-1161		636
TSG Equity Partners LLC 636 Great Rd *Web:* tsgequity.com	Stow	MA	01775	978-461-2046		401
TSG Networks 10462 San Pablo Ave *Web:* tsgnetworks.com	El Cerrito	CA	94530	510-525-6210	525-7881	175
TSG Solutions Inc 2701 Loker Ave W Ste 230 *Web:* www.tsgsinc.com	Carlsbad	CA	92010	760-827-7087		809
TSI (Telephone Systems International Inc) 4400 Marsh Landing Blvd Ste 3 *Web:* tsiglobe.com	Ponte Vedra Beach	FL	32082	904-686-1470		736
TSI (Thermal Structures Inc) 2362 Railroad St *Web:* www.thermalstructures.com	Corona	CA	92880	951-736-9911	736-1064	483
TSI (Thomas Steel Inc) 221 Sheffield St *Web:* www.tsifab.com	Bellevue	OH	44811	419-483-7540		480
TSI (Televan Sales Inc) 5451 Sylvia Ave *TF:* 800-886-7151 ■ *Web:* www.televansales.com	Dearborn Heights	MI	48125	313-292-7150	292-7153	385
TSI Controls 2303 196th SW Unit B *Web:* www.tsicontrols.com	Lynnwood	WA	98036	425-775-5696	775-9074	246
TSI Global Cos 700 Fountain Lakes Blvd *TF:* 800-875-5605 ■ *Web:* www.tsi-global.com	Saint Charles	MO	63301	636-949-8889	925-2111	735
TSI Group Inc 135 W Main St Ste B *Web:* www.tsiinc.com	Missoula	MT	59802	406-549-9123		479
TSI Holding Co 999 Executive Pkwy Dr *Web:* www.tsiholding.com	Saint Louis	MO	63141	314-628-6060		360-3
TSI Power Corp 1103 W Pierce Ave *TF:* 800-874-3160 ■ *Web:* www.tsipower.com	Antigo	WI	54409	715-623-0636	623-2426	253
TSI Store Supplies 3987 Heritage Oak Ct **Fax Area Code:* 800 ■ *TF:* 800-325-6867 ■ *Web:* www.tsisupplies.com	Simi Valley	CA	93063	805-583-8500	947-2060*	559
Tsleil-Waututh Nation, The 3075 Takaya Dr *Web:* twnation.ca	North Vancouver	BC	V7H3A8	604-929-3454		138
TSLH (Steward Health Care) *Tempe Saint Luke's Hospital* 1500 S Mill Ave *TF:* 877-351-9355 ■ *Web:* www.tempestlukeshospital.org	Tempe	AZ	85281	480-784-5500		374-3
TSMC (Taiwan Semiconductor Manufacturing Company Ltd) 2851 Junction Ave *NYSE: TSM* ■ *Web:* www.tsmc.com	San Jose	CA	95134	408-382-8000	382-8008	696
TSN Montreal 1717 Blvd Rene-Levesque Est *TF:* 800-665-5440 ■ *Web:* www.montreal.radioenergie.ca	Montreal	QC	H2L4T9	514-790-0943	529-9308	647
TSO (Traverse Symphony Orchestra) 300 E Front St Ste 230 *Web:* traversesymphony.org	Traverse City	MI	49684	231-947-7120		573-3
TSO (Sanford Organization, The) 1000 N Rand Rd Ste 214 *Web:* www.tso.net	Wauconda	IL	60084	847-526-2010	526-3993	47

Name / Address	City	State	ZIP	Phone	Fax	Class
TS03 Inc 2505 Dalton Ave	Quebec City	QC	G1P3S5	418-651-0003	653-5726	477
TF: 866-715-0003 ■ *Web:* www.tso3.com						
Tsoi Kobus Design 60 State St Ste 1800	Boston	MA	02109	617-475-4000	475-4445	261
Web: tsoikobus.design						
T-Solutions Inc						
860 Greenbrier Cir Ste 405	Chesapeake	VA	23320	757-410-9450		261
Web: www.tsoln-inc.com						
TSPI (Technology Solutions Provider Inc)						
11490 Commerce Park Dr Ste 200	Reston	VA	20191	877-455-8774	880-7022*	196
**Fax Area Code:* 703 ■ *TF:* 877-455-8774 ■ *Web:* tspi.net						
TSR Inc 400 Oser Ave Ste 150	Hauppauge	NY	11788	631-231-0333	435-1428	721
NASDAQ: TSRI ■ *Web:* www.tsrconsulting.com						
TSS Inc 110 E Old Settlers Blvd	Round Rock	TX	78664	512-310-1000		449
Web: tssiusa.com						
TSS Technologies Inc						
MiQ Partners 8800 Global Way	West Chester	OH	45069	513-772-7000		454
Web: miqpartners.com						
TST Inc 11601 Etiwanda Ave	Fontana	CA	92337	951-685-2155		487
Web: www.tst-inc.com						
TST Infrastructure						
61 Inverness Dr E Ste 100	Englewood	CO	80112	303-799-5197		463
Web: www.tstinfrastructure.com						
TST Solutions Inc						
5200 Maingate Dr	Mississauga	ON	L4W1G5	905-625-7500		314
Web: tst-cfexpress.com						
TST Tooling Software LLC						
6547 Dixie Hwy	Clarkston	MI	48346	248-922-9293		711
Web: tst-software.com						
TST/Impreso Inc 652 Southwestern Blvd	Coppell	TX	75019	972-462-0100	562-5359*	552-1
**Fax Area Code:* 800 ■ *TF:* 800-527-2878 ■ *Web:* www.tstimpreso.com						
TSTA Advocate Magazine 316 W 12th St	Austin	TX	78701	512-476-5355		457-8
TF: 877-275-8782 ■ *Web:* tsta.org						
TSTE (Tri-State Truck and Equipment Inc)						
5250 Midland Rd	Billings	MT	59101	406-245-3188	238-1501	358
TF: 800-227-1132 ■ *Web:* www.tristatetruckandequip.com						
TSU (Texas Southern University)						
3100 Cleburne St	Houston	TX	77004	713-313-7011	313-1859	166
Web: www.tsu.edu						
Tsunami Sushi & Sake Bar						
1306 Fulton St	San Francisco	CA	94117	415-567-7664		671
Web: dajanigroup.net						
Tsurumi (AMERICA) Inc						
1625 Fullerton Ct	Glendale Heights	IL	60139	630-793-0127	793-0146	641
Web: www.tsurumipump.com						
TSUS (Texas State University System)						
601 Colorado St	Austin	TX	78701	512-463-1808	463-1816	786
Web: www.tsus.edu						
TT (Ten Talents Cookbook)						
PO Box 5209	Grants Pass	OR	97526	541-472-1113	472-1116	637-2
Web: www.tentalents.net						
TT Electronics 1645 Wallace Dr	Carrollton	TX	75006	972-323-2200	323-2396	696
TF: 800-341-4747 ■ *Web:* www.ttelectronics.com						
TT Group Inc 702 Carnation Dr	Aurora	MO	65605	417-678-2181		301
Web: www.tt-group.com						
TTC (Toronto Transit Commission)						
1900 Yonge St	Toronto	ON	M4S1Z2	416-393-4000		468
TF: 800-223-6192 ■ *Web:* www.ttc.ca						
TTC (Trans-Tel Central Inc) 2805 Broce Dr	Norman	OK	73072	405-447-5025	447-5029	787
TF: 800-729-4636 ■ *Web:* www.trans-tel.com						
TTC (Trident Technical College)						
7000 Rivers Ave PO Box 118067	North Charleston	SC	29406	843-574-6111	574-6483	800
TF: 877-349-7184 ■ *Web:* www.tridenttech.edu						
TTC (Taylor Telephone Cooperative Inc)						
9796 Interstate 20	Merkel	TX	79536	325-846-4111		224
TF: 866-944-8456 ■ *Web:* online.taylortel.net						
TTCI (Totah Communications Inc)						
101 S Ochelata St	Ochelata	OK	74051	918-535-2208	535-2701	224
TF: 888-580-2208 ■ *Web:* www.totelcsi.com						
TTG Consultants						
4727 Wilshire Blvd	Los Angeles	CA	90010	323-936-6600		463
TF: 800-736-8840 ■ *Web:* www.ttgconsultants.com						
TTHE Termo Co 3275 Cherry Ave	Long Beach	CA	90807	562-595-7401		536
TF: 888-260-4715 ■ *Web:* termoco.com						
TTI (Technical Training Inc)						
6001 N Adams Ste 185	Bloomfield Hills	MI	48304	248-853-5550	853-2411	113
Web: www.tti-global.com						
TTI Environmental Inc						
1253 N Church St	Moorestown	NJ	08057	856-840-8800		41
Web: ttienvinc.com						
TTI Inc 2441 NE Pkwy	Fort Worth	TX	76106	817-740-9000	740-9898	246
TF: 800-225-5884 ■ *Web:* www.ttiinc.com						
TTL Inc 3516 Greensboro Ave	Tuscaloosa	AL	35401	205-345-0816		256
Web: www.ttlusa.com						
TTM Technologies Inc						
1665 Scenic Ave Ste 250	Costa Mesa	CA	92626	714-327-3000		625
Web: www.ttmtech.com						
TTS (Tele-Tech Services)						
500 Oakbrook Ln	Summerville	SC	29485	800-433-6181	537-8011	387
Web: www.telecomdb.com						
TTUSD (Tahoe Truckee Unified School District)						
11603 Donner Pass Rd	Truckee	CA	96161	530-582-2500	582-7606	685
Web: www.ttusd.org						
TTV Capital						
1230 Peachtree St NE Ste 1150	Atlanta	GA	30309	404-347-8400	347-8420	194
Web: ttvcapital.com						
TTX Co 101 N Wacker Dr	Chicago	IL	60606	312-853-3223	984-3790	264-5
TF: 800-889-4357 ■ *Web:* www.ttx.com						
TTX Insurance Consultants Inc						
7338 NW Fifth St	Plantation	FL	33317	954-327-8002		390
Web: ttxins.com						
TU (Trout Unlimited)						
1300 N 17th St Ste 500	Arlington	VA	22209	703-522-0200	284-9400	48-3
TF: 800-834-2419 ■ *Web:* www.tu.org						
Tualatin Hills Aquatic Ctr						
15707 SW Walker Rd	Beaverton	OR	97006	503-629-6310	629-6335	564
Web: www.thprd.org						
Tuality Community Hospital						
335 SE Eigth Ave	Hillsboro	OR	97123	503-681-1111		374-3
Web: www.tuality.org						

Name / Address	City	State	ZIP	Phone	Fax	Class
Tub Springs State Wayside						
Tub Springs State Wayside	Ashland	OR	97520	541-582-1118		565
Web: oregonstateparks.org						
Tubac Presidio State Historic Park						
1 Burruel St	Tubac	AZ	85646	520-398-2252		565
Web: azstateparks.com						
Tubby's 31920 Groesbeck Hwy	Fraser	MI	48026	800-752-0644	293-5088*	670
**Fax Area Code:* 586 ■ *TF:* 800-752-0644 ■ *Web:* tubbys.com						
Tube Art Group (TAG) 11715 SE Fifth St	Bellevue	WA	98005	206-223-1122	223-1123	701
TF: 800-562-2854 ■ *Web:* www.tubeart.com						
Tube City IMS Corp (TMS)						
12 Monongahela Ave	Glassport	PA	15045	412-678-6141	675-8295	686
NYSE: TMS ■ *TF:* 800-860-2442 ■ *Web:* www.tubecityims.com						
Tube Forgings of America Inc						
5200 NW Front Ave	Portland	OR	97210	503-241-0716	243-5301	595
TF: 800-426-3274 ■ *Web:* www.tubeforgings.com						
Tube Forming and Machine Inc						
4614 Industrial Row	Oscoda	MI	48750	989-739-3323	739-5403	595
Web: tubeforming.com						
Tube Methods Inc 416 Depot St	Bridgeport	PA	19405	610-279-7700	277-2005	490
TF: 800-220-2123 ■ *Web:* www.tubemethods.com						
Tube Products Corp						
14420 Ewing Ave S	Burnsville	MN	55306	952-894-2817		723
Tubelite Company Inc						
102 Semoran Commerce Pl	Apopka	FL	32703	407-884-0477		112
Web: www.tubelite.com						
Tubelite Inc 4878 Mackinaw Trl	Reed City	MI	49677	800-866-2227		234
TF: 800-866-2227 ■ *Web:* www.tubeliteinc.com						
Tube-Mac Industries Ltd						
853 Arvin Ave	Stoney Creek	ON	L8E5N8	905-643-8823		605-2
TF: 877-643-8823 ■ *Web:* www.tube-mac.com						
Tubi Inc						
315 Montgomery St 11th Fl	San Francisco	CA	94104	415-504-3505		741-120
Web: tubitv.com						
Tubman African American Museum						
310 Cherry St	Macon	GA	31201	478-743-8544	743-9063	520
Web: www.tubmanmuseum.com						
Tubro Company Inc						
30 Council Rock Dr	Warminster	PA	18974	800-673-7887		604
TF: 800-673-7887 ■ *Web:* www.tubro.com						
Tubular Fabricators Industry Inc						
600 W Wythe St	Petersburg	VA	23803	800-526-0178		595
TF: 800-526-0178 ■ *Web:* www.tfihealthcare.com						
Tubular Products Co						
1400 Red Hollow Rd	Birmingham	AL	35215	205-856-1300	856-1398	567
TF: 800-456-8823 ■ *Web:* www.tubularproducts.com						
Tubular Services Inc 1010 Mccarty Dr	Houston	TX	77029	713-675-6212		595
Web: www.tubularservices.com						
Tubular Steel Inc						
1031 Executive Pkwy Dr	Saint Louis	MO	63141	314-851-9200	851-9336	492
TF: 800-388-7491 ■ *Web:* www.tubularsteel.com						
Tubular Textile Machinery						
113 Woodside Dr	Lexington	NC	27292	336-956-6444	956-1795	744
Web: www.navisglobal.com						
Tucanos Brazilian Grill						
PO Box 280548	Lakewood	CO	80228	303-237-1340		671
Web: www.tucanos.com						
Tuckahoe State Park						
13070 Crouse Mill Rd	Queen Anne	MD	21657	410-820-1668		565
Web: www.dnr.maryland.gov						
Tuckahoe Union Free School District						
65 Siwanoy Blvd	Eastchester	NY	10709	914-337-6600		685
Web: www.tuckahoeschools.org						
Tucker Albin & Associates Inc						
1702 N Collins Blvd Ste 100	Richardson	TX	75080	877-455-4572		160
Web: tuckeralbin.com						
Tucker Arensberg Attorneys						
1500 One PPG Pl	Pittsburgh	PA	15222	412-566-1212	604-6610	428
Web: www.tuckerlaw.com						
Tucker Company Worldwide Inc						
900 Dudley Ave	Cherry Hill	NJ	08002	856-317-9600		311
TF: 800-229-7780 ■ *Web:* tuckerco.com						
Tucker County 215 First St	Parsons	WV	26287	304-478-2866	478-2466	338
Web: tuckercounty.wv.gov						
Tucker County Convention & Visitors Bureau						
410 William Ave	Davis	WV	26260	304-259-5315		206
TF: 800-782-2775 ■ *Web:* www.canaanvalley.org						
Tucker Ellis & West LLP						
925 Euclid Ave	Cleveland	OH	44115	216-696-2141	592-5009	428
Web: www.tuckerellis.com						
Tucker International LLC						
6525 Gunpark Dr Ste 370-185	Boulder	CO	80301	303-786-7753		194
Web: tuckerintl.com						
Tucker Lumber Companies LLC						
601 N Pearl St	Pageland	SC	29728	843-672-6135	672-5393	683
Web: www.cmtuckerlumber.com						
Tucker Oil Company Inc						
910 Industrial Dr	Slaton	TX	79364	806-828-6277		579
TF: 800-281-1830 ■ *Web:* www.tuckeroil.net						
Tucker Powersports						
4900 Alliance Gateway Fwy	Fort Worth	TX	76177	800-347-1010		61
Web: www.tucker.com						
Tucker Publications Inc (TPI) PO Box 580	Lisle	IL	60532	630-969-0221		637-2
Web: www.tuckerpub.com						
Tucker's Machine & Steel Service Inc						
400 County Rd 468	Leesburg	FL	34748	352-787-3157		480
Web: www.tuckerbilt.com						
Tucker's Place						
Historic Soulard						
2117 S 12th St 1/2 Block S of Russell	Saint Louis	MO	63104	314-772-5977		671
Web: www.tuckersplacestl.com						
Tucker-Castleberry Printing Inc						
3500 McCall Pl	Atlanta	GA	30340	770-454-1580		627
Web: www.tuckercastleberry.com						
Tucker-Davis Technologies Inc						
11930 Research Cir	Alachua	FL	32615	386-462-9622	462-5365*	472
**Fax Area Code:* 352 ■ *Web:* www.tdt.com						
Tucows Inc 96 Mowat Ave	Toronto	ON	M6K3M1	416-535-0123	531-5584	397
NASDAQ: TC ■ *TF:* 800-371-6992 ■ *Web:* www.tucows.com						

				Phone	Fax	Class
TUCS Cleaning Service Inc 166 Central Ave *TF:* 800-992-5998 ■ *Web:* www.tucscleaning.com	Orange	NJ	07050	973-673-0700		152
Tucson Botanical Gardens 2150 N Alvernon Way *Web:* tucsonbotanical.org	Tucson	AZ	85712	520-326-9686		97
Tucson Children's Museum 200 S 6th Ave	Tucson	AZ	85701	520-792-9985		521
Tucson City Hall 255 W Alameda St *Web:* www.tucsonaz.gov	Tucson	AZ	85701	520-791-4213	791-5198	337
Tucson College 5151 E Broadway Blvd Ste 155 *TF:* 866-882-2586 ■ *Web:* www.tucsoncollege.edu	Tucson	AZ	85711	520-809-6245		167-3
Tucson Container Corp 6601 S Palo Verde *Web:* www.tucsoncontainer.com	Tucson	AZ	85756	520-746-3171	741-0962	549
Tucson Convention Ctr 260 S Church Ave *Web:* www.tucsonaz.gov	Tucson	AZ	85701	520-791-4101	791-5572	205
Tucson Electric Power PO Box 80077 *Web:* www.tep.com	Prescott	AZ	86304	520-623-7711		787
Tucson Embedded Systems Inc 5620 N Kolb Rd *Web:* www.tucsonembedded.com	Tucson	AZ	85750	520-575-7283	575-5563	177
Tucson Greyhound Park 2601 S Third Ave *Web:* tucsongreyhound.com	Tucson	AZ	85713	520-884-7576	624-9389	133
Tucson International Airport 7250 S Tucson Blvd *Web:* www.flytucson.com	Tucson	AZ	85756	520-573-8100	573-8008	27
Tucson Jazz Society (TJS) PO Box 41071 *Web:* tucsonjazz.org	Tucson	AZ	85717	520-903-1265		48-4
Tucson Lifestyle Magazine 7000 E Tanque Verde Rd Ste 11 *Web:* www.tucsonlifestyle.com	Tucson	AZ	85715	520-721-2929	721-8665	457-22
Tucson Mall 4500 N Oracle Rd *Web:* www.tucsonmall.com	Tucson	AZ	85705	520-293-7330		460
Tucson Medical Ctr 5301 E Grant Rd *TF:* 800-526-5353 ■ *Web:* www.tmcaz.com	Tucson	AZ	85712	520-327-5461		374-3
Tucson Metropolitan Chamber of Commerce 465 W St Mary's Rd PO Box 991 *Web:* tucsonchamber.org	Tucson	AZ	85702	520-872-6620	882-5704	139
Tucson Realty & Trust Co 333 N Wilmot Ste 340 *Web:* www.tucsonrealty.com	Tucson	AZ	85711	520-577-7000	918-3031	655
Tucson School of Horseshoeing 2230 N Kimberlee Rd *TF:* 800-657-2779 ■ *Web:* www.tucsonhorseshoeing.com	Tucson	AZ	85749	520-749-5212	760-0886	685
Tucson Symphony Orchestra 2175 N Sixth Ave *Web:* www.tucsonsymphony.org	Tucson	AZ	85705	520-792-9155		573-3
Tucson Tallow Company Inc 3928 N Fairview Ave *Web:* www.tucsontallow.com	Tucson	AZ	85705	520-887-0440	887-2827	660
Tucson Unified School District No 1 1010 E Tenth St *Web:* www.tusd1.org	Tucson	AZ	85719	520-225-6070	798-8767	685
Tucson Weekly 3280 E Hemisphere Loop Ste 180 PO Box 27087 *Web:* www.tucsonweekly.com	Tucson	AZ	85706	520-294-1200	792-2096	532-5
Tudi Mechanical Systems of Tampa Inc 343 Munson Ave *Web:* www.tudi.com	McKees Rocks	PA	15136	412-771-4100	771-7737	610
Tudor Place Historic House & Garden 1644 31st St NW *Web:* www.tudorplace.org	Washington	DC	20007	202-965-0400	965-0164	50-3
Tudor's Biscuit World PO Box 3603 *Web:* www.tudorsbiscuitworld.com	Charleston	WV	25336	304-343-4026		670
Tu-Endie-Wei State Park PO Box 486 *Web:* wvstateparks.com	Point Pleasant	WV	25550	304-675-0869		565
Tuesday Morning Corp 6250 LBJ Fwy *NASDAQ: TUES* ■ *TF:* 800-457-0099 ■ *Web:* www.tuesdaymorning.com	Dallas	TX	75240	972-387-3562	387-2344	327
Tueth-keeney Cooper Mohan Jackstadt Pc 101 W Vandalia St Ste 210 *Web:* www.tuethkeeney.com	Edwardsville	IL	62025	618-692-4120		445
Tufco Technologies Inc PO Box 23500 *NASDAQ: TFCO* ■ *Web:* www.tufco.com	Green Bay	WI	54305	920-336-0054		554
TUFF SHED Inc 1777 S Harrison St *TF:* 800-289-8833 ■ *Web:* www.tuffshed.com	Denver	CO	80210	303-474-5510		321
Tuff Torq Corp 5943 Commerce Blvd *TF:* 866-572-3441 ■ *Web:* www.tufftorq.com	Morristown	TN	37814	423-585-2000		429
Tuffaloy Products Inc 1400 S Batesville Rd *TF:* 800-521-3722 ■ *Web:* www.tuffaloy.com	Greer	SC	29650	864-879-0763	877-2212	811
TuffStuff Fitness Equipment Inc 13971 Norton Ave *TF:* 888-884-8275 ■ *Web:* www.tuffstufffitness.com	Chino	CA	91710	909-629-1600		354
Tuffy Associates Corp 7150 Granite Cir *TF:* 800-228-8339 ■ *Web:* www.tuffy.com	Toledo	OH	43617	419-865-6900	865-7343	62-5
Tuffy Security Products Inc 25733 Rd H *TF:* 800-348-8339 ■ *Web:* www.tuffyproducts.com	Cortez	CO	81321	800-348-8339		692
Tuftco Corp 2318 S Holtzclaw Ave *TF:* 800-288-3826 ■ *Web:* www.tuftco.com	Chattanooga	TN	37408	423-698-8601	698-0842	744
Tuf-Tite Inc 1200 Flex Ct *TF:* 800-382-7009 ■ *Web:* www.tuf-tite.com	Lake Zurich	IL	60047	847-550-1011	550-8004	596
Tufts Associated Health Plans 705 Mt Auburn St *TF:* 800-462-0224 ■ *Web:* tuftshealthplan.com	Watertown	MA	02472	617-972-9400	972-9409	391-3
Tufts Library 46 Broad St *TF:* 888-283-3757 ■ *Web:* www.weymouth.ma.us	Weymouth	MA	02188	781-337-1402	682-6123	434-3
Tufts Medical Ctr (TMC) 800 Washington St *TF:* 866-220-3699 ■ *Web:* www.tuftsmedicalcenter.org	Boston	MA	02111	617-636-5000	636-8199	374-3
Tufts University Hirsh Health Sciences Library 145 Harrison Ave *Web:* hirshlibrary.tufts.edu	Boston	MA	02111	617-636-6705	636-4039	434-1
Tufts University School of Medicine 136 Harrison Ave *Web:* www.tufts.edu	Boston	MA	02111	617-636-7000	636-3805	167-2
Tufts University Tisch Library 35 Professors Row *Web:* tischlibrary.tufts.edu	Medford	MA	02155	617-627-3345	627-3002	434-6

				Phone	Fax	Class
Tug Mcgraw Foundation 100 California Dr PO Box 45 *Web:* www.tugmcgraw.org	Yountville	CA	94599	707-947-7124	676-4398	463
Tugaloo State Park 1763 Tugaloo State Park Rd *Web:* gastateparks.org	Lavonia	GA	30553	706-356-4362		565
Tugboat Inn 80 Commercial St PO Box 267 *TF:* 800-248-2628 ■ *Web:* www.tugboatinn.com	Boothbay Harbor	ME	04538	207-633-4434	633-5892	379
Tukaiz LLC 2917 N Latoria Ln *TF:* 800-543-2674 ■ *Web:* www.tukaiz.com	Franklin Park	IL	60131	847-455-1588		7
Tukatech Inc 5462 Jillson St *Web:* www.tukatech.com	Los Angeles	CA	90040	323-726-3836		179
Tuktut Nogait National Park of Canada PO Box 91 *Web:* www.pc.gc.ca	Paulatuk	NT	X0E1N0	867-580-3233	580-3234	563
Tula Executive Search 3355 Lenox Rd NE 10th Fl *Web:* www.tulainternational.com	Atlanta	GA	30326	404-543-2835		260
Tulalip Resort Casino 10200 Quil Ceda Blvd *TF:* 888-272-1111 ■ *Web:* www.tulalipresortcasino.com	Tulalip	WA	98271	888-272-1111		707
Tulane Medical Ctr (TMC) 1415 Tulane Ave *TF:* 800-588-5800 ■ *Web:* tulanehealthcare.com	New Orleans	LA	70112	504-988-5263		374-3
Tulane University 6823 St Charles Ave *TF:* 800-873-9283 ■ *Web:* www.tulane.edu	New Orleans	LA	70118	504-865-5000	862-8715	166
Tulane University Howard-Tilton Memorial Library 7001 Freret St *Web:* library.tulane.edu	New Orleans	LA	70118	504-865-5605		434-6
Tulane University Law School Weinmann Hall 6329 Freret St *Web:* www.law.tulane.edu	New Orleans	LA	70118	504-865-5930	865-6710	167-1
Tulane University School of Medicine 1430 Tulane Ave *Web:* medicine.tulane.edu	New Orleans	LA	70112	504-988-5462		167-2
Tulare Adult School 575 W Maple Ave *Web:* www.tas.tulare.k12.ca.us	Tulare	CA	93274	559-686-0225	687-7447	685
Tulare County 2800 W Burrel Ave *Web:* www.tularecounty.ca.gov	Visalia	CA	93291	559-636-5005	733-6318	338
Tulare County Library System 200 W Oak Ave *TF:* 866-290-8681 ■ *Web:* www.tularecountylibrary.org	Visalia	CA	93291	559-713-2700		434-3
Tulare Joint Union High School District 426 N Blackstone Ave *Web:* www.tulare.k12.ca.us	Tulare	CA	93274	559-688-2021	687-7317	685
Tulare Nursing & Rehabilitation 420 E Murray Ave *Web:* missioncaregroup.com	Visalia	CA	93291	559-686-8581		450
Tulare Public Library 475 N M St *Web:* tularepubliclibrary.org	Tulare	CA	93274	559-685-4500		434-3
Tulare Regional Medical Ctr 869 N Cherry St *Web:* tulareregional.org	Tulare	CA	93274	559-685-3462		374-3
Tularosa Communications Inc 503 St Francis Dr *TF:* 800-972-8282 ■ *Web:* www.tularosa.net	Tularosa	NM	88352	575-585-9800		681
Tulco Oils Inc 5240 E Pine *TF:* 800-375-2347 ■ *Web:* www.tulco.com	Tulsa	OK	74115	918-838-3354	834-1263	579
Tule Elk State Natural Reserve 8653 Station Rd *Web:* www.parks.ca.gov	Buttonwillow	CA	93206	661-764-6881		565
Tuley Law Office 20 NW First St *Web:* tuleylaw.com	Evansville	IN	47708	812-434-1936		41
Tulio Ristorante 1100 Fifth Ave *Web:* www.tulio.com	Seattle	WA	98101	206-624-5500		671
Tulip City Air Service Inc 60 Geurink Blvd *TF:* 800-748-0515 ■ *Web:* visionaircenter.com	Holland	MI	49423	616-392-7831	392-1841	13
Tulip Molded Plastics Corp 714 E Keefe Ave *Web:* www.tulipcorp.com	Milwaukee	WI	53212	414-963-3120		199
Tulloch Engineering Inc 200 Main St *TF:* 800-797-2997 ■ *Web:* tulloch.ca	Thessalon	ON	P0R1L0	705-842-3372		256
Tully Rinckey PLLC 441 New Karner Rd *Web:* www.tullylegal.com	Albany	NY	12205	518-218-7100		428
Tulmar Safety Systems Inc 1123 Cameron St *Web:* www.tulmar.com	Hawkesbury	ON	K6A2B8	613-632-1282		21
Tulnoy Lumber Inc 1620 Webster Ave *Web:* www.tulnoylumber.com	Bronx	NY	10457	718-901-1700	299-8920	191-3
Tulsa Air & Space Museum 3624 N 74 E Ave *Web:* www.tulsamuseum.org	Tulsa	OK	74115	918-834-9900	834-6723	520
Tulsa Ballet 1212 E 45th Pl *Web:* tulsaballet.org	Tulsa	OK	74105	918-749-6030	749-0532	573-1
Tulsa Centerless Bar Processing 1605 N 168th E Ave *Web:* tulsacenterless.com	Tulsa	OK	74116	918-438-0000		454
Tulsa City Hall 175 E Second St Ste 690 *Web:* www.cityoftulsa.org	Tulsa	OK	74103	918-596-2100	596-9010	337
Tulsa City-County Library (TCCL) 400 Civic Ctr *Web:* www.tulsalibrary.org	Tulsa	OK	74103	918-549-7323		434-3
Tulsa Community College *Southeast* 10300 E 81st St *Web:* www.tulsacc.edu	Tulsa	OK	74133	918-595-7000	595-7748	162
Tulsa Convention & Visitors Bureau 1 W Third St Ste 100 *TF:* 800-558-3311 ■ *Web:* www.visittulsa.com	Tulsa	OK	74103	800-558-3311		206
Tulsa Convention Ctr 100 Civic Ctr *TF:* 800-678-7177 ■ *Web:* www.coxcentertulsa.com	Tulsa	OK	74103	918-894-4350		205
Tulsa County 500 S Denver Ave *Web:* www.tulsacounty.org	Tulsa	OK	74103	918-596-5801	596-5819	338
Tulsa Federal Credit Union 9323 E 21st St *TF:* 800-256-5626 ■ *Web:* tulsafederalcu.org	Tulsa	OK	74129	918-610-0200		219

Name / Address	City	State	ZIP	Phone	Fax	Class
Tulsa Garden Ctr 2435 S Peoria Ave *Web:* www.tulsagardencenter.org	Tulsa	OK	74114	918-576-5155		97
Tulsa Heaters Inc 1215 S Boulder Ste 1200 *Web:* www.tulsaheaters.com	Tulsa	OK	74119	918-582-9918	582-9916	14
Tulsa International Airport 7777 E Apache Rm A-217 *Web:* www.tulsaairports.com	Tulsa	OK	74115	918-838-5000	838-5199	27
Tulsa Metro Chamber 1 W Third St Ste 100 *TF:* 888-424-9411 ■ *Web:* tulsachamber.com	Tulsa	OK	74103	918-585-1201		139
Tulsa Nursing Ctr 10912 E 14th St *Web:* tulsanc.com	Tulsa	OK	74128	918-438-2440		793
Tulsa Opera 1610 S Boulder Ave *TF:* 866-298-2530 ■ *Web:* tulsaopera.com	Tulsa	OK	74119	918-582-4035	592-0380	573-2
Tulsa Performing Arts Ctr 110 E Second St *Web:* www.tulsapac.com	Tulsa	OK	74103	918-596-7122	596-7144	572
Tulsa Promenade 4107 S Yale Ave *Web:* www.tulsapromenade.com	Tulsa	OK	74135	918-627-9282		460
Tulsa Public Schools 3027 S New Haven Ave *Web:* tulsaschools.org	Tulsa	OK	74114	918-746-6800		685
Tulsa Rig Iron Inc 4457 W 151st PO Box 880 *Web:* www.tulsarigiron.com	Kiefer	OK	74041	918-321-3330	321-3099	386
Tulsa Technology Center - Peoria Campus 3850 N Peoria *Web:* www.tulsatech.edu	Tulsa	OK	74106	918-828-2000	828-2009	167-3
Tulsa Welding School Inc 2545 E 11th St *TF:* 800-331-2934 ■ *Web:* www.tws.edu	Tulsa	OK	74104	855-237-7711		743
Tulsa Winch Group 11135 S James Ave *Web:* www.dovertwg.com	Jenks	OK	74037	918-298-8300	298-8301	190
Tulsa World 315 S Boulder Ave *TF:* 800-897-3557 ■ *Web:* www.tulsaworld.com	Tulsa	OK	74103	918-583-2161	581-8353	532-2
Tulsa Zoo 6421 E 36th St N *Web:* tulsazoo.org	Tulsa	OK	74115	918-669-6600		823
TulsaConnect 110 W 7th St Ste 302 *TF:* 877-868-8572 ■ *Web:* www.tulsaconnect.com	Tulsa	OK	74119	918-295-6439	582-5776	180
Tulsair Beechcraft Inc 3207 N Sheridan Rd *TF:* 800-331-4071 ■ *Web:* www.tulsair.com	Tulsa	OK	74115	918-835-7651	835-7413	24
Tulstar Products Inc 5510 S Lewis Ave *TF:* 800-988-5782 ■ *Web:* www.tulstar.com	Tulsa	OK	74105	918-749-9060	747-1444	146
Tumacacori National Historical Park 1891 E Frontage Rd PO Box 8067 *Web:* www.nps.gov	Tumacacori	AZ	85640	520-377-5060		564
Tumalo State Park 64120 Ob Riley Rd *Web:* stateparks.oregon.gov	Bend	OR	97701	541-382-3586		565
Tumble Drum Industry Inc 2162 250th St *Web:* www.miraclemixer.com	Denver	IA	50622	319-984-5374	984-5425	273
Tumbleweed Inc 2301 River Rd *TF:* 866-719-3892 ■ *Web:* www.tumbleweedrestaurants.com	Louisville	KY	40206	502-893-0323		670
Tumbling River Ranch 3715 Pk County Rd 62 PO Box 30 *TF:* 800-654-8770 ■ *Web:* www.tumblingriver.com	Grant	CO	80448	303-838-5981	838-5133	239
Tummelson Bryan & Knox LLP 115 N Broadway Ave PO Box 99 *Web:* tbklaw.com	Urbana	IL	61803	217-367-2500	367-2555	41
Tumwater Veterinary Hospital Incorporated PS 7020 Littlerock Rd SW *Web:* tumwaterveterinary.com	Tumwater	WA	98512	360-754-6008		794
Tundra Lodge Resort & Waterpark 865 Lombardi Ave *TF:* 877-886-3725 ■ *Web:* www.tundralodge.com	Green Bay	WI	54304	920-405-8700	405-1997	669
Tundra Oil & Gas Ltd 1 Lombard Pl Ste 1700 *Web:* www.tundraoilandgas.com	Winnipeg	MB	R3B0X3	204-934-5850	934-5820	536
Tundra Process Solutions Ltd 7523 Flint Rd SE *TF:* 800-265-1166 ■ *Web:* tundrasolutions.ca	Calgary	AB	T2H1G3	403-255-5222		111
Tungsten Network 1040 Crown Pointe Pky Ste 350 *TF:* 866-340-4980 ■ *Web:* www.tungsten-network.com	Atlanta	GA	30338	770-698-1420		225
Tunheim Partners 8009 34th Ave S *Web:* www.tunheim.com	Minneapolis	MN	55425	952-851-7208		636
Tunica MS 13625 Hwy 61 N *TF:* 888-488-6422 ■ *Web:* www.tunicatravel.com	Tunica Resorts	MS	38664	888-488-6422		206
Tunnel Duty Free Shop Inc 465 Goyeau St *TF:* 800-669-2105 ■ *Web:* www.tunneldutyfree.com	Windsor	ON	N9A1H1	519-252-2713		241
Tunnel Hill State Trail Hwy 146 E PO Box 671 *Web:* www.dnr.illinois.gov	Vienna	IL	62995	618-658-2168		565
Tunnell & Raysor PA 30 E Pine St *TF:* 800-541-5443 ■ *Web:* tunnellraysor.com	Georgetown	DE	19947	800-541-5443		41
Tunnell Consulting 900 E Eigth Ave Ste 106 *Web:* www.tunnellconsulting.com	King of Prussia	PA	19406	610-337-0820	337-1884	194
Tunstall Consulting Inc 13153 N Dale Mabry Hwy Ste 200 *Web:* www.tunstallconsulting.com	Tampa	FL	33618	813-968-4461	961-2315	194
Tunxis Community College 271 Scott Swamp Rd *Web:* www.tunxis.edu	Farmington	CT	06032	860-773-1300		162
Tuohy Furniture Corp 42 St Albans Pl *TF:* 800-533-1696 ■ *Web:* www.tuohyfurniture.com	Chatfield	MN	55923	507-867-4280	867-3374	319-1
Tuolumne County 2 S Green St *Web:* www.tuolumnecounty.ca.gov	Sonora	CA	95370	209-533-6600		338
Tuolumne County Chamber of Commerce 222 S Shepherd St *TF:* 877-532-4212 ■ *Web:* tcchamber.com	Sonora	CA	95370	209-532-4212	532-8068	139
TUP (Theosophical University Press) PO Box C *Web:* www.theosociety.org	Pasadena	CA	91109	626-797-7817		637-2
Tupelo Ballet Co 775 Poplarville Dr *Web:* www.tupeloballet.com	Tupelo	MS	38801	662-844-1928		573-1

Name / Address	City	State	ZIP	Phone	Fax	Class
Tupelo Buffalo Park & Zoo 2272 N Coley Rd *Web:* www.tupelobuffalopark.com	Tupelo	MS	38803	662-844-8709	844-8850	823
Tupelo City Hall 71 E Troy St *Web:* www.tupeloms.gov	Tupelo	MS	38804	662-841-6513	840-2075	337
Tupelo Community Theatre 201 N Broadway PO Box 1094 *Web:* www.tctwebstage.com	Tupelo	MS	38802	662-844-1935	844-2990	572
Tupelo Furniture Market 1879 N Coley Rd *TF:* 800-844-0841 ■ *Web:* www.tupelofurnituremarket.com	Tupelo	MS	38801	662-842-4442	844-3665	321
Tupelo Honey Cafe 12 College St *Web:* tupelohoneycafe.com	Asheville	NC	28801	828-255-4863		671
Tupelo Public School District 72 S Green St *Web:* www.tupeloschools.com	Tupelo	MS	38804	662-841-8850	841-8887	685
Tupelo Regional Airport 105 Lemons Dr *Web:* www.flytupelo.com	Tupelo	MS	38801	662-823-4359	823-8329	27
Tupelo Symphony Orchestra 1800 W Main St *Web:* nmsymphony.com	Tupelo	MS	38801	662-842-8433		573-3
Tupperware Corp 14901 S Orange Blossom Trl *NYSE: TUP* ■ *Web:* ir.tupperwarebrands.com	Orlando	FL	32837	407-826-5050		607
Tuptim 4896 Washtenaw Ave *Web:* www.tuptim.com	Ann Arbor	MI	48108	734-528-5588	528-2569	671
Turano Baking Co 6501 Roosevelt Rd *Web:* turano.com	Berwyn	IL	60402	708-788-9220	788-3075	296-1
Turbeville Correctional Institution 1578 Clarence Coker Hwy *Web:* www.doc.sc.gov	Turbeville	SC	29162	843-659-4800		213
Turbine Controls Inc 5 Old Windsor Rd *Web:* www.tcimro.com	Bloomfield	CT	06002	860-242-0448	726-1981	455
Turbine Engine Components Technologies Corp (TECT) 334 Beechwood Rd Ste 303 *Web:* tectpower.com	Fort Mitchell	KY	41017	859-426-0090		483
Turbine Technology Services Corp *TTS Energy Services* 12661 Challenger Pkwy Ste 250 *Web:* www.ttsenergyservices.com	Orlando	FL	32826	407-677-0813		262
Turbines Inc Hwy 283 N *Web:* www.turbinesincorporated.com	Altus	OK	73522	580-477-3067		495
Turbo 2 n 1 Grip 46460 Continental Dr *TF:* 800-530-9878 ■ *Web:* www.turbogrips.com	Chesterfield	MI	48047	586-598-3948		711
Turbo International Inc 2151 Las Palmas Dr Ste E *TF:* 800-238-8726 ■ *Web:* turbointernational.com	Carlsbad	CA	92011	760-476-1444		791
Turbo Mechanical Inc 3142 Cove Ln NW	Olympia	WA	98502	360-943-1888		41
Turbo Parts LLC 767 Pierce Rd Ste 2 *TF:* 800-446-4776 ■ *Web:* www.mdaturbines.com	Clifton Park	NY	12065	518-885-3199		54
Turbo Resources International Inc 5780 W Oakland St *Web:* www.turboresources.com	Chandler	AZ	85226	480-961-3600	961-1775	770
Turbo Solutions Engineering LLC 41 Depot St *Web:* turbosoleng.com	East Thetford	VT	05043	802-785-4160	785-4162	261
Turbo Wholesale Tires Inc 5793 Martin Rd *Web:* turbotires.net	Irwindale	CA	91706	626-856-1400		754
TURBOCAM Inc 607 Calef Hwy *Web:* www.turbocam.com	Barrington	NH	03825	603-905-0200		641
Turbo-Chem International Inc 106 W Saul *TF:* 800-259-7838 ■ *Web:* www.turbochem.com	Scott	LA	70583	337-235-3098		538
Turbopower LLC 5499 NW 145th St 104 *Fax Area Code: 844 ■ *Web:* www.turbopowerllc.com	Opa Locka	FL	33054	305-820-3225	792-2111*	24
Turbotec Products Inc 651 Day Hill Rd *TF:* 800-394-1633 ■ *Web:* turbotecproducts.blog	Windsor	CT	06095	860-731-4200		295
Turbotek Computer Corp 70 Zachary Rd Ste 3 *TF:* 800-573-5393 ■ *Web:* www.turbotekcomputer.com	Manchester	NH	03109	603-666-3062		180
Turck Canada Inc 140 Duffield Dr *Web:* turck.ca	Markham	ON	L6G1B5	905-513-7100		246
Turck Inc 3000 Campus Dr *Web:* www.turck.com	Minneapolis	MN	55441	763-553-7300		385
Turek Farms 8558 SR-90 *Web:* www.turekfarms.com	King Ferry	NY	13081	315-364-8735	364-5257	10-11
Turelk Inc 3700 Santa Fe Ave Ste 200 *Web:* www.turelk.com	Long Beach	CA	90810	310-835-3736		186
Turf Hotels Inc 792 Watervliet Shaker Rd *Web:* www.turfhotels.com	Latham	NY	12110	518-786-0976	786-7849	378
Turf Management Systems LLC PO Box 26389 *Web:* www.turfmanagementsystems.com	Birmingham	AL	35260	205-979-8604		422
Turf Paradise Racetrack 1501 W Bell Rd *Web:* www.turfparadise.com	Phoenix	AZ	85023	602-942-1101	942-8659	642
Turf Products LLC 157 Moody Rd *TF:* 800-243-4355 ■ *Web:* www.turfproductscorp.com	Enfield	CT	06082	860-763-3581		429
Turf Technologies Inc 77 Industrial Dr *TF:* 800-844-8873 ■ *Web:* turftechsolutions.com	Uxbridge	MA	01569	508-278-4000		422
Turf Valley Resort & Conference Ctr 2700 Turf Valley Rd *Web:* www.turfvalley.com	Ellicott City	MD	21042	410-465-1500		669
Turfgrass Producers Intl 444 E Roosevelt Rd Ste 346 *TF:* 800-405-8873 ■ *Web:* www.turfgrasssod.org	Lombard	IL	60148	847-649-5555	649-5678	138
TurfNet 1500 Park Center Dr *Web:* www.turfnet.com	Orlando	FL	32835	770-395-9850		387
Turfway Park LLC 7500 Turfway Rd *Web:* www.turfway.com	Florence	KY	41042	859-371-0200		642

Phone | Fax | Class

Turkey
Consulate General
1990 Post Oak Blvd Ste 1300 . . . . .Houston TX 77056 713-622-5849 623-6639 257
TF: 888-566-7656 ■ *Web:* www.houston.cg.mfa.gov.tr
Consulate General
455 N Cityfront Plaza Dr Ste 2900 . . . . .Chicago IL 60611 312-263-0644 263-1449 257
Web: www.chicago.cg.mfa.gov.tr
Consulate General
6300 Wilshire Blvd Ste 2010 . . . . .Los Angeles CA 90048 323-655-8832 655-8681 257
Web: www.losangeles.cg.mfa.gov.tr
Consulate General
825 Third Ave 5th Fl . . . . .New York NY 10022 646-430-6560 983-1293* 257
**Fax Area Code:* 212 ■ *Web:* www.newyork.cg.mfa.gov.tr
Embassy 2525 Massachusetts Ave NW . . . . Washington DC 20008 202-612-6700 319-1639 257
Web: www.washington.emb.mfa.gov.tr

Turkey Hill Dairy Inc 2601 River Rd. . . . . Conestoga PA 17516 717-872-0602 296-25
TF: 800-693-2479 ■ *Web:* www.turkeyhill.com

Turkey Press & Edition Reese
6746 Sueno Rd. . . . . Isla Vista CA 93117 805-685-3603 637-2
Web: www.editionreese.com

Turkey Run State Park 8121 Park Rd . . . . Marshall IN 47859 765-597-2635 565
Web: www.in.gov

Turkey Valley Farms 112 S 6th St . . . . Marshall MN 56258 507-337-3100 337-3009 619
Web: www.turkeyvalleyfarms.com

Turkmenistan
Embassy 2207 Massachusetts Ave NW . . . . Washington DC 20008 202-588-1500 588-0697 257
Web: www.tmembassy.gov.tm

Turks & Caicos Islands Tourism Office
225 W 35th St Ste 1200 . . . . .New York NY 10001 646-375-8830 775
TF: 800-241-0824 ■ *Web:* www.turksandcaicostourism.com

Turley Publications Inc 24 Water St . . . . Palmer MA 01069 413-283-8393 532-3
Web: newspapers.turley.com

Turlington & Co
1338 Westgate Center Dr .Lexington NC 27292 336-249-6856 2
Web: www.turlingtonandcompany.com

Turlock Chamber of Commerce
115 S Golden State Blvd. . . . . .Turlock CA 95380 209-632-2221 632-5289 139
TF: 800-834-0401 ■ *Web:* turlockcacoc.wliinc19.com

Turlock Journal 138 S Center St. . . . . .Turlock CA 95380 209-634-9141 632-8813 532-2
Web: www.turlockjournal.com

Turlock Lake State Recreation Area
22600 Lake Rd . . . . .LaGrange CA 95329 209-874-2056 565
Web: www.parks.ca.gov

Turn Key Distribution Systems Inc
450 Broadway. . . . . Malden MA 02148 781-322-3000 180
Web: turnkey.com

Turnamatic Machine Inc
1725 Jay Ell Dr. . . . . Richardson TX 75081 972-235-1993 235-1957 454
Web: www.turnamatic.com

Turnaround for Children Inc
25 W 45th St 6th Fl. . . . . .New York NY 10036 646-786-6200 242
Web: www.turnaroundusa.org

Turnaround Inc 3415 A St NW. . . . . .Gig Harbor WA 98335 253-857-6730 857-6344 401
Web: www.turnaround-inc.com

Turner Appliance
4004 S Meridian St. . . . . .Indianapolis IN 46217 317-788-9180 38
Web: turnerappliancerepair.com

Turner Classic Movies Inc (TCM)
1050 Techwood Dr NW. . . . . Atlanta GA 30318 844-356-7875 740
TF: 844-356-7875 ■ *Web:* www.tcm.turner.com

Turner Consulting Group Inc
306 Florida Ave NW . . . . .Washington DC 20001 202-986-5533 177
Web: www.tcg.com

Turner County PO Box 191 .Ashburn GA 31714 229-567-4313 567-4794 338
Web: georgia.gov

Turner County Board of Education
423 N Cleveland St. . . . . .Ashburn GA 31714 229-567-3338 567-3285 685
Web: www.turner.k12.ga.us

Turner County Clerk of Courts
400 S Main St. . . . . Parker SD 57053 605-297-3115 297-2115 338
Web: ujs.sd.gov

Turner County Stockyard
1315 US Hwy 41 S . . . . .Ashburn GA 31714 229-567-3371 567-3785 446
TF: 800-344-9808 ■ *Web:* www.turnercountystockyard.com

Turner Dairy Farms Inc
1049 Jefferson Rd. . . . . Pittsburgh PA 15235 412-372-2211 296-25
TF: 800-892-1039 ■ *Web:* turnerdairy.net

Turner Designs Hydrocarbon Instruments Inc
2023 N Gateway Ste 101. . . . . Fresno CA 93727 559-253-1414 358
Web: www.oilinwatermonitors.com

Turner EnviroLogic Inc
1140 SW 34 Ave. . . . . Deerfield Beach FL 33442 954-422-9787 422-9723 472
TF: 800-933-8385 ■ *Web:* www.tenviro.com

Turner Foundation Inc
133 Luckie St 2nd Fl. . . . . Atlanta GA 30303 404-681-9900 681-0172 305
Web: www.turnerfoundation.org

Turner Free Library 2 N Main St. . . . . .Randolph MA 02368 781-961-0932 434-3
Web: www.turnerfreelibrary.org

Turner Industries Group LLC
8687 United Plaza Blvd. . . . . Baton Rouge LA 70809 225-922-5050 188-9
TF: 800-288-6503 ■ *Web:* www.turner-industries.com

Turner Investment Partners Inc
1205 Westlakes Dr Ste 100. Berwyn PA 19312 484-329-2300 401
TF: 800-224-6312 ■ *Web:* www.turnerinvestments.com

Turner Michael (Rep R - OH)
2082 Rayburn House Office Bldg . . . . Washington DC 20515 202-225-6465 225-6754 342-2
Web: www.turner.house.gov

Turner Motorsports 16 S Hunt Rd . . . . Amesbury MA 01913 978-388-7769 388-4202 515
TF: 800-280-6966 ■ *Web:* www.turnermotorsport.com

Turner Plastic Innovations
1400 Production Dr . . . . Burlington KY 41005 859-525-9020 627
Web: turnerplastics.com

Turner Public Relations Inc
1614 15th St 4th Fl. . . . . .Denver CO 80202 303-333-1402 636
Web: www.turnerpr.com

Turner Roofing & Sheet Metal Inc
1200 E Memphis St . . . . .Broken Arrow OK 74012 918-258-2585 189-12
Web: www.turnerroofing.com

Turner Techtronics Inc
3200 W Burbank Blvd. . . . . .Burbank CA 91505 818-973-1060 175
Web: turnertech.com

Turner Vedrenne & Howard PC
9330 Lbj Fwy Ste 875. . . . . Dallas TX 75243 972-644-4131 2
Web: tvhcpas.com

Turner Warren Hwang & Conrad
100 N First St Ste 202 . . . . .Burbank CA 91502 818-954-9700 2
Web: www.twhc.com

Turner's Outdoorsman
11738 Sanmarino St Ste A . . . . .Rancho Cucamonga CA 91730 909-923-4422 711
Web: www.turners.com

Turner, Leins & Gold LLC
108 Center St N 2nd Fl . . . . .Vienna VA 22180 703-242-6500 2
Web: taxmgmtsys.com

Turner, Padget, Graham & Laney PA
1901 Main St 17th Fl . . . . .Columbia SC 29202 803-254-2200 428
Web: www.turnerpadget.com

Turner-Brooks Inc
28811 John R Rd . . . . Madison Heights MI 48071 248-548-3400 548-9213 189-2
Web: turnerbrooks.com

Turner-Fairbank Highway Research Ctr
6300 Georgetown Pk . . . . McLean VA 22101 800-424-9071 493-3170* 668
**Fax Area Code:* 202 ■ *TF:* 800-424-9071 ■ *Web:* highways.dot.gov

Turners Fine Furniture Co
707 Second St W . . . . Tifton GA 31794 229-382-3266 321
Web: www.turnerfurniture.com

Turning Inc 13820 Industrial Pk Blvd. . . . . .Plymouth MN 55441 763-450-7990 450-7997 454
Web: www.turninginc.com

Turning Point Care Ctr
3015 Veterans Pkwy S PO Box 1177 . . . . .Moultrie GA 31776 229-985-4815 726
TF: 800-342-1075 ■ *Web:* turningpointcare.com

Turning Point Community Programs
3440 Viking Dr Ste 114 . . . . Sacramento CA 95827 916-364-8395 48-5
Web: www.tpcp.org

Turning Point Inc, The
1835 W SR-89A Ste 4. . . . . Sedona AZ 86336 928-203-9711 203-9707 196

Turning Point of Tampa 6227 Sheldon Rd. . . . . Tampa FL 33615 813-882-3003 885-6974 726
TF: 800-397-3006 ■ *Web:* www.tpoftampa.com

Turning Stone Resort Casino LLC
5218 Patrick Rd . . . . .Verona NY 13478 315-361-7711 133
TF: 800-771-7711 ■ *Web:* www.turningstone.com

Turning Tide Productions PO Box 864 . . . . Wendell MA 01379 978-544-8313 514
TF: 800-557-6414 ■ *Web:* www.turningtide.com

Turnkey Construction Management Institute Inc
PO Box 822 . . . . Groveland CA 95321 209-732-8264 167-3
Web: www.turnkeyinstitute.com

Turn-Key Medical Inc
365 SW Fifth Ave . . . . Meridian ID 83642 877-484-9549 475
TF: 877-484-9549 ■ *Web:* www.turn-keymedical.com

Turn-Key Solutions Inc (TKS)
4920 W Thunderbird Rd Ste C-120 . . . . Glendale AZ 85306 602-863-0269 863-4563 737
Web: www.tksnation.com

Turnkey Sports & Entertainment Inc
9 Tanner St . . . . .Haddonfield NJ 08033 856-685-1450 260
Web: turnkeysearch.com

Turnkey Technologies Inc
2400 Main St Ext Ste 12. .Sayreville NJ 08872 732-553-9100 246
Web: www.turn-keytechnologies.com

Turnroth Sign Company Inc
1207 E Rock Falls Rd . . . . Rock Falls IL 61071 815-625-1155 701

Turn-Tech Inc
32007 Industrial Park Dr. .Pinehurst TX 77362 281-356-1290 454
Web: www.turn-tech.com

Turocy & Watson LLP
Key Tower 127 Public Sq 57th Fl . . . . .Cleveland OH 44114 216-696-8730 428
Web: www.thepatentattorneys.com

Turpin Sales & Marketing Inc
330 Cold Spring Ave. . . . . West Springfield MA 01089 877-377-7573 463
TF: 877-377-7573 ■ *Web:* www.turpinsales.com

Tursso Companies Inc
223 Plato Blvd E . . . . Saint Paul MN 55107 651-222-8445 627
Web: www.tursso.com

Turtle & Hughes Inc 1900 Lower Rd . . . . Linden NJ 07036 732-574-3600 574-3723 246
Web: www.turtle.com

Turtle Bay Exploration Park
840 Auditorium Dr . . . . .Redding CA 96001 530-243-8850 243-8898 520
TF: 800-887-8532 ■ *Web:* www.turtlebay.org

Turtle Bay Resort
57-091 Kamehameha Hwy . . . . Kahuku HI 96731 808-293-6000 293-9147 669
TF: 866-475-2567 ■ *Web:* www.turtlebayresort.com

Turtle Cay Resort
600 Atlantic Ave . . . . Virginia Beach VA 23451 757-437-5565 437-9104 669
TF: 888-989-7788 ■ *Web:* www.virginiabeachresorthotels.com

Turtle Cove Spa at Mountain Harbor Resort
181 Club House Dr. . . . . Mount Ida AR 71957 870-867-1220 707
Web: turtlecovespa.com

Turtle Creek Asset Management Inc
Scotia Plz 40 King St W Ste 5100. . . . . Toronto ON M5H3Y2 416-306-3043 528
Web: www.turtlecreek.ca

Turtle Kraals Restaurant & Bar
231 Margaret St . . . . .Key West FL 33040 305-294-2640 671
Web: www.turtlekraals.com

Turtle Mountain Community College
10145 BIA Rd 7 . . . . .Belcourt ND 58316 701-477-7862 477-7892 165
TF: 800-827-1100 ■ *Web:* www.tm.edu

Turtle River State Park 3084 Park Ave . . . . Arvilla ND 58214 701-795-3180 565
Web: www.parkrec.nd.gov

Turtle-Top Inc 67819 State Rd 15 . . . . New Paris IN 46553 800-296-2105 59
TF: 800-296-2105 ■ *Web:* www.turtletop.com

Turvac Inc
6434 Coach Light Cir Liberty Twp . . . . Hamilton OH 45011 513-759-2771 472
Web: www.turvac.com

Tuscaloosa City Hall
2201 University Blvd . . . . .Tuscaloosa AL 35401 205-248-5311 349-0185 337
Web: www.tuscaloosa.com

Tuscaloosa Coca-Cola Inc
6501 McFarlind Blvd E. . . . . .Tuscaloosa AL 35405 205-345-7717 297-2
TF: 844-367-2653 ■ *Web:* cocacolaunited.com

Name / Address	City	State	Zip	Phone	Fax	Class
Tuscaloosa County 714 Greensboro Ave *Web:* www.tuscco.com	Tuscaloosa	AL	35401	205-349-3870		338
Tuscaloosa News 315 28th Ave *TF:* 800-888-8639 ■ *Web:* www.tuscaloosanews.com	Tuscaloosa	AL	35401	205-345-0505	722-0187	532-2
Tuscaloosa Public Library 1801 Jack Warner Pkwy *Web:* www.tuscaloosa-library.org	Tuscaloosa	AL	35401	205-345-5820	758-1735	434-3
Tuscaloosa Symphony Orchestra PO Box 20001 *Web:* www.tsoonline.org	Tuscaloosa	AL	35402	205-752-5515		573-3
Tuscaloosa VA Medical Ctr 3701 Loop Rd E *TF:* 888-269-3045 ■ *Web:* www.tuscaloosa.va.gov	Tuscaloosa	AL	35404	205-554-2000		374-8
Tuscan & Company PA 12621 World Plaza Ln Bldg 55 *Web:* tuscancpa.com	Fort Myers	FL	33907	239-333-2090		2
Tuscany 2832 East 6200 South *Web:* www.tuscanyslc.com	Salt Lake City	UT	84121	801-277-9919		671
Tuscany Design Automation Inc 4800 Innovation Dr *Web:* tuscanyda.com	Fort Collins	CO	80525	970-377-0717		525
Tuscany Energy Ltd 633 - Sixth Ave SW *Web:* tuscanyenergy.com	Calgary	AB	T2P2Y5	403-269-9889		538
Tuscany Suites & Casino 255 E Flamingo Rd *Web:* www.tuscanylv.com	Las Vegas	NV	89169	702-893-8933	947-5994	379
Tuscarawas County 125 E High Ave *Web:* www.co.tuscarawas.oh.us	New Philadelphia	OH	44663	330-365-3243	343-4682	338
Tuscarawas County Chamber of Commerce 1323 Fourth St NW *Web:* www.tuschamber.com	New Philadelphia	OH	44663	330-343-4474	343-6526	139
Tuscarawas County Public Library 121 Fair Ave NW *Web:* www.tusclibrary.org	New Philadelphia	OH	44663	330-364-4474	364-8217	434-3
Tuscarora Intermediate Unit 11 2527 US Hwy 522 S *Web:* www.tiu11.org	McVeytown	PA	17051	814-542-2501	542-2025	685
Tuscarora Wayne Insurance Co 41908 Rt 6 PO Box 7 *Web:* twmic.com	Wyalusing	PA	18853	570-746-1515		390
Tusculum College 60 Shiloh Rd *TF:* 800-729-0256 ■ *Web:* home.tusculum.edu	Greeneville	TN	37745	423-636-7300		166
Tuskegee Airman Natl Historical Museum 6325 W Jefferson Ave *Web:* www.tuskegeemuseum.org	Detroit	MI	48209	313-843-8849		520
Tuskegee Airmen National Historic Site 1616 Chappie James Ave *Web:* www.nps.gov	Tuskegee	AL	36083	334-724-0922	724-0952	564
Tuskegee Institute National Historic Site 1212 W Montgomery Rd *Web:* www.nps.gov	Tuskegee	AL	36088	334-727-3200	727-1448	564
Tuskegee University 1200 W Montgomery Rd *TF:* 800-622-6531 ■ *Web:* www.tuskegee.edu	Tuskegee	AL	36088	334-727-8011	727-5750	166
Tuson Corp 475 Bunker Ct *Web:* www.tuson.com	Vernon Hills	IL	60061	847-816-8800		358
Tustin Chamber of Commerce 700 W First St Ste 7 *Web:* tustinchamber.org	Tustin	CA	92780	714-544-5341	544-2083	139
Tustin Mechanical Services Lehigh Valley LLC 2555 Industry Ln *Web:* www.thetustingroup.com	Norristown	PA	19403	610-539-8200		610
Tustin Nissan 30 Auto Center Dr *Web:* www.nissanoftustin.com	Tustin	CA	92782	714-352-0996		57
Tutco Inc 500 Gould Dr *TF:* 877-262-4533 ■ *Web:* www.tutco.com	Cookeville	TN	38506	931-432-4141	432-4140	14
Tuthill Corp 8500 S Madison St *TF:* 800-634-2695 ■ *Web:* www.tuthill.com	Burr Ridge	IL	60527	630-382-4900	382-4999	641
Tuthill Pump Group 12500 S Pulaski Rd *Web:* www.tuthillpump.com	Alsip	IL	60803	708-389-2500	388-0869	641
Tutorial Channel Inc PO Box 190846 **Fax Area Code:* 718 ■ *TF:* 866-599-6284 ■ *Web:* www.mathmadeeasy.com	Brooklyn	NY	11230	866-599-6284	438-3711*	423
Tutorial Press Inc PO Box 11123 *Web:* www.tutorialpress.com	Albuquerque	NM	87192	505-296-8636		637-2
Tutoring Club LLC 11241 SE Ave *Web:* www.tutoringclub.com	Henderson	NV	89052	702-588-5288		423
Tuttle Aluminum & Bronze Inc 120 Shadowlawn Dr *Web:* www.tuttlehandrailings.com	Fishers	IN	46038	317-842-2420		480
Tuttle Construction Inc 880 Shawnee Rd *Web:* www.tuttlenet.com	Lima	OH	45805	419-228-6262	229-7414	187
Tuttle Creek State Park 5800-A River Pond Rd *Web:* www.ksoutdoors.com	Manhattan	KS	66502	785-539-7941		565
Tuttle Law PA 3617 20th St *Web:* verobeachinjurylaw.com	Vero Beach	FL	32960	772-563-0032		41
Tuttle Law Print Inc PO Box 110 *TF:* 800-776-7682 ■ *Web:* www.tuttleprinting.com	Rutland	VT	05701	800-776-7682		627
Tuttle Publishing 364 Innovation Dr **Fax Area Code:* 800 ■ *TF:* 800-526-2778 ■ *Web:* www.tuttlepublishing.com	North Clarendon	VT	05759	802-773-8930	329-8885*	637-2
Tutto Pasta 1751 SW Third Ave *Web:* www.tuttopasta.com	Miami	FL	33129	305-857-0709		671
Tuway American Group Inc, The 2820 W Maple Rd Ste 101 *Web:* www.tuwaymops.com	Troy	MI	48084	248-649-8790		746
Tuxedo Park Library (TPL) 227 Route 17 *Web:* www.tuxedoparklibrary.org	Tuxedo Park	NY	10987	845-351-2207	351-2213	434-3
Tuxis-Ohrs 80 Britannia St *Web:* www.tuxisfuel.com	Meriden	CT	06450	203-639-3513	639-3515	579
Tuzigoot National Monument 527 S Main St *Web:* www.nps.gov	Camp Verde	AZ	86322	928-634-5564		564
TV Asahi America Inc 875 3rd Ave 3rd Fl *Web:* www.tv-asahi.net	New York	NY	10022	212-644-6300	644-0003	740
TV One 1010 Wayne Ave 10th Fl *Web:* tvone.tv	Silver Spring	MD	20910	301-755-0400		740
TV5 Quebec Canada 460 St-Paul St E *Web:* tv5.ca	Montreal	QC	H2Y3V1	514-522-5322		116
TVA (Tennessee Valley Authority) 400 W Summit Hill Dr *Web:* www.tva.com	Knoxville	TN	37902	865-632-2101		340-20
TVA Community Credit Union 1405 S Wilson Dam Rd *Web:* tvaccu.com	Muscle Shoals	AL	35661	256-383-1019		219
TVAX Biomedical Inc 8006 Reeder St *Web:* www.tvaxbiomedical.com	Lenexa	KS	66214	913-492-2221	492-2243	231
TVB (Television Bureau of Advertising Inc) 120 Wall St 15th Fl *Web:* www.tvb.org	New York	NY	10005	212-486-1111	935-5631	49-18
TVC (Traditional Values Coalition) 139 C St SE	Washington	DC	20003	202-547-4400		48-20
TVC Capital LLC 11452 El Camino Real Ste 450 *Web:* tvccapital.com	San Diego	CA	92130	858-704-3261	523-9560	690
TVC Marketing 3200 W Wilshire Blvd *TF:* 800-288-2889 ■ *Web:* www.tvcmatrix.com	Oklahoma City	OK	73116	405-843-2722	233-3940	195
TVCC (Temecula Valley Chamber of Commerce) 26790 Ynez Ct Ste A *Web:* temecula.org	Temecula	CA	92591	951-676-5090	694-0201	139
TVEC (Trinity Valley Electric Co-opeartive Inc) 1800 E Hwy 243 PO Box 888 *TF:* 800-766-9576 ■ *Web:* tvec.net	Kaufman	TX	75142	972-932-2214	932-6466	245
TVEC (Tennessee Valley Electric Coop) 590 Florence Rd *TF:* 866-925-4916 ■ *Web:* www.tennesseevalleyec.com	Savannah	TN	38372	731-925-4916	925-4919	245
Tvia Inc 4800 Great America Pkwy Ste 405 **Fax Area Code:* 972 ■ *Web:* www.tvia.com	Santa Clara	CA	95054	408-400-3702	612-2805*	696
TVL Inc 901 16th St W *TF:* 800-263-0000 ■ *Web:* www.tvl.com	North Vancouver	BC	V7P1R2	800-263-0000		179
TVP Color Graphics Inc 230 Roma Jean Pkwy *Web:* thinkvariable.com	Streamwood	IL	60107	630-837-3600		627
TVU networks Corp 1225 Pear Ave Ste 100 *Web:* www.tvunetworks.com	Mountain View	CA	94043	650-969-6732		647
TVV Capital 1 American Ctr Ste 500 *Web:* tvvcapital.com	Nashville	TN	37203	615-256-8061	256-7057	528
TVWorks 2 Belvedere Pl Ste 200 *Web:* www.tvworks.com	Mill Valley	CA	94941	415-380-6200	380-6210	116
TW Burleson & Son Inc 301 Peters St *Web:* www.burlesons-honey.com	Waxahachie	TX	75165	972-937-4810	937-8711	296-24
TW Garner Food Co 614 W 4th St *Web:* garnerfoods.com	Winston-Salem	NC	27105	336-661-1550	661-1901	296-20
TW Lewis 850 W Elliot Rd Ste 101 *Web:* www.twlewis.com	Tempe	AZ	85284	480-820-0807		653
TW Metals Inc 760 Constitution Dr Ste 204 *Web:* www.twmetals.com	Exton	PA	19341	610-458-1300		492
T-W Transport Inc 7405 S Hayford Rd *TF:* 800-356-4070 ■ *Web:* twtrans.com	Cheney	WA	99004	800-356-4070		780
Twanoh State Park 12190 E SR 106 *Web:* parks.state.wa.us	Union	WA	98592	360-275-2222		565
TWB Co 1600 Nadeau Rd *Web:* www.twbcompany.com	Monroe	MI	48162	734-289-6400		723
TWC (Trans World Corp) 545 5th Ave Ste 940 *OTC:* TWOC ■ *Web:* www.transwc.com	New York	NY	10017	212-983-3355	983-8129	379
TWC (Writers' Collective, The) 780 Reservoir Ave Ste 243 *Web:* www.writerscollective.org	Cranston	RI	02910	206-984-0313		637-2
TWC (Third Wave Consulting Inc) 876 E Shore Rd *Web:* www.thirdwaveconsult.com	Jamestown	RI	02835	401-741-6221	423-3452	196
TWC Construction Inc 431 Eastgate Rd 3rd Fl *Web:* www.twcconstruction.com	Henderson	NV	89011	702-597-3444		186
TWC Services Inc 2601 Bell Ave *TF:* 855-698-9224 ■ *Web:* www.twcservices.com	Des Moines	IA	50321	515-284-1911		610
Tweddle Litho Co 24700 Maplehurst Dr *Web:* www.tweddle.com	Clinton Township	MI	48036	586-307-3700	307-3708	626
Tweed New Haven Regional Airport 155 Burr St *Web:* www.flytweed.com	New Haven	CT	06512	203-466-8833	466-1199	27
Tweed-Weber Inc (TWI) PO Box 112 *TF:* 800-999-6615 ■ *Web:* www.tweedweber.com	Reading	PA	19603	800-999-6615		194
Tween Brands Inc 8323 Walton Pkwy *Web:* justiceretail.com	New Albany	OH	43054	614-775-3500		157-1
Tweet-Garot Mechanical Inc 2545 Larsen Rd *Web:* tweetgarot.com	Green Bay	WI	54307	920-498-0400		610
Tweetsie Railroad Inc 300 Tweetsie Railroad Ln *TF:* 800-526-5740 ■ *Web:* tweetsie.com	Blowing Rock	NC	28605	828-264-9061		31
Twelve Hotels & Residences 361 17th St *Web:* www.twelvehotels.com	Atlanta	GA	30363	404-961-1212		379
Twelve Tables Press PO Box 568 *Web:* www.twelvetablespress.com	Northport	NY	11768	631-241-1148	754-1913	637-2
Twentieth Modern 7470 Beverly Blvd *Web:* www.twentieth.net	Los Angeles	CA	90036	323-904-1200		321
Twenty-First Century Assoc 800 Main St Ste A *TF:* 888-760-5052 ■ *Web:* www.tfc-associates.com	Hackensack	NJ	07601	201-678-1144	678-9088	160
Twenty-First Securities Corp 780 3rd Ave *Web:* www.twenty-first.com	New York	NY	10017	212-418-6000		690

	Phone	Fax	Class
Twenty-Five Mile Creek State Park 20530 S Lakeshore Rd . . . Chelan WA 98816 *Web:* parks.state.wa.us	509-687-3610		565
Twentynine Palms Chamber of Commerce 73484 Twentynine Palms Hwy . . . Twentynine Palms CA 92277 *TF:* 800-442-2283 ■ *Web:* 29palmschamberofcommerce.wildapricot.org	760-367-3445		139
TWG (Terlato Wine Group, The) 900 Armour Dr . . . Lake Bluff IL 60044 *Web:* www.terlatovineyards.com	847-604-8900		81-3
TWH (Wholesale House Inc, The) 503 W High St . . . Hicksville OH 43526 *TF:* 800-722-5553 ■ *Web:* www.twhouse.com	800-722-5553		459
TWHBEA (Tennessee Walking Horse Breeders' & Exhibitors' Assn) 250 N Ellington Pkwy PO Box 286 . . . Lewisburg TN 37091 *Web:* www.twhbea.com	931-359-1574	359-7530	48-3
TWI (Tweed-Weber Inc) PO Box 112 . . . Reading PA 19603 *TF:* 800-999-6615 ■ *Web:* www.tweedweber.com	800-999-6615		194
TWI Group Inc 4480 S Pecos Rd . . . Las Vegas NV 89121 *Web:* www.twiglobal.com	702-691-9000	691-9045	311
Twig & Fig 2110 Vine St . . . Berkeley CA 94709 *Web:* twigandfig.com	510-848-5599		535
Twigg Corp 659 E York St . . . Martinsville IN 46151 *Web:* www.twiggcorp.com	765-342-7126	342-1553	21
Twiggs County Commissioners 425 N Railroad St . . . Jeffersonville GA 31044 *Web:* www.twiggscounty.us	478-945-3629		338
Twigs Bistro & Bar 808 W Main Ave . . . Spokane WA 99201 *Web:* twigsbistro.com	509-232-3376		671
Twilio Inc 375 Beale St Ste 300 . . . San Francisco CA 94105 *NYSE:* TWLO ■ *Web:* www.twilio.com	415-390-2337		178-2
Twin Bridges State Park 14801 Hwy 137 S . . . Fairland OK 74343 *Web:* www.travelok.com	918-540-2545		565
Twin Brothers Marine LLC 322 Twin Brothers Rd . . . Franklin LA 70538 *Web:* www.tbmc.com	337-923-4981	923-4349	4
Twin Butte Energy Ltd 396 - 11 Ave SW Ste 410 . . . Calgary AB T2R0C5 *Web:* www.twinbutteenergy.com	403-215-2045		787
Twin Capital Management Inc 3244 Washington Rd Ste 202 . . . McMurray PA 15317 *Web:* www.twincapital.com	724-942-2000	942-2002	528
Twin Cities & Western Railroad 2925 12th St E . . . Glencoe MN 55336 *TF:* 800-290-8297 ■ *Web:* tcwr.net	320-864-7200		649
Twin Cities Legal Service PLLC 7201 Ohms Ln Ste 215 . . . Edina MN 55439 *TF:* 877-288-8421 ■ *Web:* lindawray.com	952-806-9900	746-7853	41
Twin Cities Model Railroad Museum 668 Transfer Rd Ste 8 . . . Saint Paul MN 55114 *Web:* www.tcmrm.org	651-647-9628		520
Twin Cities North Chamber of Commerce 525 Main St Ste 200 . . . New Brighton MN 55112 *Web:* www.twincitiesnorth.org	763-571-9781	572-7950	139
Twin Cities Public Television Inc 172 E 4th St . . . Saint Paul MN 55101 *Web:* www.tpt.org	651-222-1717		741-84
Twin City Animal Hospital 869 South St . . . Fitchburg MA 01420 *Web:* www.twincityanimalhospital.com	978-343-3049		794
Twin City Area Chamber of Commerce 114 Main St . . . Festus MO 63028 *Web:* www.twincity.org	636-931-7697		139
Twin City Bank 729 Vandercook Way . . . Longview WA 98632 *Web:* twincitybank.com	360-414-4101		70
Twin City Container Inc 990 Spiral Blvd . . . Hastings MN 55033 *Web:* www.tcc-mn.com	651-480-3786		455
Twin City Die Castings Co 1070 33rd Ave SE . . . Minneapolis MN 55414 *Web:* www.tcdcinc.com	651-645-3611	645-0724	308
Twin City EDM 7940 Rancher Rd NE . . . Fridley MN 55432 *TF:* 800-397-0338 ■ *Web:* www.twincityedm.com	763-783-7808	783-7842	454
Twin City Fan Companies Ltd 5959 Trenton Ln N . . . Minneapolis MN 55442 *Web:* www.tcf.com	763-551-7600	551-7601	18
Twin City Foods Inc 10120 269th Pl NW . . . Stanwood WA 98292 *Web:* twincityfoods.com	206-515-2400	515-2499	296-21
Twin City Hide Inc 105 Hardman Ct Ste 100 . . . South Saint Paul MN 55075 *Web:* www.twincityhide.com	651-455-1511	455-6744	432
Twin City Knitting Company Inc (TCK) 104 Rock Barn Rd NE . . . Conover NC 28613 *Web:* tcksports.com	828-464-4830		155-10
Twin City Sales & Marketing 5365 Robinhood Rd . . . Winston-Salem NC 27106 *Web:* www.twincitysam.com	336-685-1501		195
Twin City Security Inc 519 Coon Rapids Blvd . . . Minneapolis MN 55433 *Web:* www.twincitysecurity.com	763-784-4160		693
Twin City Tile 34 State St . . . Brewer ME 04412 *Web:* twincitytilemaine.com	207-989-8834		361
Twin County Chamber of Commerce 403 N Main St . . . Galax VA 24333 *Web:* twincountychamber.com	276-236-2184	236-1338	139
Twin County Regional Hospital 200 Hospital Dr . . . Galax VA 24333 *TF:* 800-295-3342 ■ *Web:* www.tcrh.org	276-236-8181		374-3
Twin Disc Inc 1328 Racine St . . . Racine WI 53403 *NASDAQ:* TWIN ■ *Web:* www.twindisc.com	262-638-4000		620
Twin Dragon Marketing Inc 14600 S Broadway St . . . Gardena CA 90248 *Web:* www.twindragonmarketing.com	310-715-7070		594
Twin Eagle 8847 W Sam Houston Pkwy N . . . Houston TX 77040 *Web:* www.twineagle.com	713-341-7300	341-7324	538
Twin Eagle Consulting LLC 7308 S Alton Way Ste 2-J . . . Centennial CO 80112 *Web:* www.twineagleconsulting.com	303-531-4598	482-1423	196
Twin Express Inc (TEI) 12424 Ironwood Cir Ste 102 . . . Rogers MN 55374 *TF:* 800-729-8946 ■ *Web:* www.twinexpress.com	763-428-4969	428-4979	780
Twin Falls Area Chamber of Commerce 2015 Neilsen Point Pl . . . Twin Falls ID 83301 *TF:* 866-894-6325 ■ *Web:* twinfallschamber.com	208-733-3974	733-9216	139
Twin Falls County 630 Addison Ave W . . . Twin Falls ID 83301 *Web:* www.twinfallscounty.org	208-736-4000		338
Twin Falls Public Library 201 Fourth Ave E . . . Twin Falls ID 83301 *Web:* www.twinfallspubliclibrary.org	208-733-2964	733-2965	434-3
Twin Falls Resort State Park WV Hwy 97 . . . Mullens WV 25882 *Web:* wvstateparks.com	304-294-4000		565
Twin Falls School District 411 201 Main Ave W . . . Twin Falls ID 83301 *TF:* 800-726-0003 ■ *Web:* www.tfsd.org	208-733-6900	733-6987	685
Twin Farms 452 Royalton Tpke . . . Barnard VT 05031 *Web:* www.twinfarms.com	802-234-9999		379
Twin Garden Sales Inc 23017 Rt 173 PO Box 400 . . . Harvard IL 60033 *Web:* twingardensales.com	815-943-7448		10-11
Twin Harbors Beach State Park 3120 Hwy 105 . . . Westport WA 98595 *Web:* parks.state.wa.us	360-268-9717		565
Twin Lakes State Park 6685 Twin Lakes Rd . . . Rockwell City IA 50579 *TF:* 800-361-8072 ■ *Web:* www.iowadnr.gov	800-361-8072		565
Twin Lakes State Park 6204 E Poyhonen Rd . . . Toivola MI 49965 *Web:* www.michigan.org	906-288-3321		565
Twin Lakes State Park 788 Twin Lakes Rd . . . Green Bay VA 23942 *Web:* www.dcr.virginia.gov	434-392-3435		565
Twin Lakes Telephone Co-op 1003 S Grundy Quarles Hwy . . . Gainesboro TN 38562 *TF:* 800-644-8582 ■ *Web:* www.twinlakes.net	931-268-2151		736
Twin Lights State Historic Site Lighthouse Rd . . . Highlands NJ 07732 *Web:* www.twinlightslighthouse.com	732-872-1814		565
Twin Liquors Lp 5639 Airport Blvd . . . Austin TX 78751 *Web:* twinliquors.com	512-442-8395		443
Twin Oaks Community 138 Twin Oaks Rd Ste W . . . Louisa VA 23093 **Fax Area Code:* 888 ■ *Web:* www.twinoakscommunity.org	540-894-5126	424-8838*	192
Twin Oaks Computing Inc 755 Maleta Ln Ste 203 . . . Castle Rock CO 80108 *Web:* www.twinoakscomputing.com	720-733-7906		387
Twin Oaks Hammocks 138 Twin Oaks Rd . . . Louisa VA 23093 *TF:* 800-688-8946 ■ *Web:* www.twinoakshammocks.com	540-894-5125	894-4112	319-4
Twin Oaks Industries Inc 2001 W Grand Ave . . . Salina KS 67401 *Web:* www.twino.com	785-827-4839	827-1777	91
Twin Oaks Landscaping Inc 997 Harvey Rd . . . Oswego IL 60543 *Web:* www.twinoakslandscaping.com	630-554-3399		776
Twin Oaks Software Development Inc 1463 Berlin Tpke . . . Berlin CT 06037 *TF:* 866-278-6750 ■ *Web:* www.healthclubsoftware.com	860-829-6000		177
Twin Otter International Ltd 2806 Perimeter Rd . . . North Las Vegas NV 89032 *Web:* www.twinotter.com	702-646-8837	646-1493	23
Twin Pine Casino 22223 Hwy 29 PO Box 789 . . . Middletown CA 95461 *TF:* 800-564-4872 ■ *Web:* www.twinpine.com	707-987-0197	987-0375	378
Twin River Casino 100 Twin River Rd . . . Lincoln RI 02865 *TF:* 877-827-4837 ■ *Web:* www.twinriver.com	401-475-8505		642
Twin River National Bank 1507 G St . . . Lewiston ID 83501 *Web:* www.twinriverbank.com	208-746-4848		70
Twin Rivers Paper Company Inc 707 Sable Oaks Dr Ste 010 . . . South Portland ME 04106 *Web:* www.twinriverspaper.com	207-523-2350		557
Twin Rivers Regional Medical Ctr (TRRMC) 1301 First St . . . Kennett MO 63857 *Web:* www.twinriversregional.com	573-888-4522		374-3
Twin Rivers Unified School District 3222 Winona Way . . . North Highlands CA 95660 *TF:* 800-260-0659 ■ *Web:* www.twinriversusd.org	916-566-1600	566-3586	685
Twin State Technical Services Ltd 3543 E Kimberly Rd . . . Davenport IA 52807 *Web:* www.tsts.com	563-441-1504	359-6671	177
Twin Technologies Inc *Intevity* 100 Summit Dr . . . Burlington MA 01803 *TF:* 800-439-4821 ■ *Web:* www.intevity.com	800-439-4821		196
Twin Tier Hospitality LLC 1100 Crocker Rd Ste 2R . . . Westlake OH 44145 *Web:* www.twintierhospitality.com	440-617-2350		377
Twin Towers 5343 Hamilton Ave . . . Cincinnati OH 45224 *Web:* lec.org	513-853-2000		672
Twin Town Treatment Ctr 1706 University Ave . . . Saint Paul MN 55104 *Web:* meridianprograms.com	651-645-3661	645-0959	726
Twin Valley Electric Co-opeartive Inc 501 S Huston Ave . . . Altamont KS 67330 *Web:* www.twinvalleyelectric.coop	620-784-5500		245
Twin Valleys Public Power District PO Box 160 . . . Cambridge NE 69022 *TF:* 800-658-4266 ■ *Web:* twinvalleysppd.com	800-658-4266		245
Twincraft Inc 2 Tigan St . . . Winooski VT 05404 *Web:* www.twincraft.com	802-655-2200		214
Twinhead Corp 48303 Fremont Blvd . . . Fremont CA 94538 **Fax Area Code:* 510 ■ *TF:* 800-995-8946 ■ *Web:* www.twinhead.com.tw	800-995-8946	492-0820*	173-2
Twining Inc 3310 Airport Way . . . Long Beach CA 90806 *Web:* www.twininginc.com	562-426-3355	426-6424	743
Twinlab Corp 4800 T-Rex Ave Ste 305 . . . Boca Raton FL 33431 *TF:* 800-645-5626 ■ *Web:* twinlab.tlcchealth.com	800-645-5626		799

Company	Phone	Fax	Class
Twin-Star International Inc 1690 S Congress Ave Ste 210 Delray Beach FL 33445 *Web:* twinstarhome.com	561-330-3201		361
TwinWest Chamber of Commerce 10700 Old County Rd 15 Plymouth MN 55441 *TF:* 800-649-5397 ■ *Web:* www.twinwest.com	763-450-2220	450-2221	139
Twist Inc 47 S Limestone St PO Box 177 Jamestown OH 45335 *Web:* www.twistinc.com	937-675-9581	675-6781	719
Twistbox Entertainment Inc 14011 Ventura Blvd Ste 210E Sherman Oaks CA 91423 *Web:* www.twistbox.com	818-301-6200		681
Twisted Networks Inc 30404 Dogwatch Trl Albemarle NC 28001 *TF:* 888-876-6586 ■ *Web:* www.twistednetworx.com	888-876-6586		226
Twitchell Corp 4031 Ross Clark Cir Dothan AL 36303 *TF:* 800-633-7550 ■ *Web:* www.twitchellcorp.com	334-792-0002		745-2
Twizzle Hair Studio 2670 Fourth Ave W Vancouver BC V6K1P7 *Web:* twizzle.ca	604-738-1733		77
Two B Printing Inc 625 NE 42nd St Oakland Park FL 33334	954-566-4886		627
Two Bunch Palms Resort & Spa 67425 Two Bunch Palms Trl Desert Hot Springs CA 92240 *TF:* 800-472-4334 ■ *Web:* twobunchpalms.com	760-329-8791	329-1874	669
Two by Four Ltd 10 N Dearborn St Ste 1000 Chicago IL 60602 *Web:* www.twoxfour.com	312-382-0100		7
Two Cats Productions Ltd 225 Lafayette Ste 509 New York NY 10012 *Web:* twocatstv.com	212-929-2085		514
Two Chefs 8287 S Dixie Hwy South Miami FL 33143 *Web:* www.twochefsrestaurant.com	305-663-2100		671
Two Guys From Italy 405 N Verdugo Rd Glendale CA 91206 *Web:* www.glendaletwoguysfromitaly.com	818-240-0020		671
Two Guys Relocation Systems Inc 3571 Pacific Hwy San Diego CA 92101 *TF:* 800-896-4897 ■ *Web:* www.twomenwillmoveyouca.com	619-296-7995		519
Two Harbors Federal Credit Union 801 11th St Two Harbors MN 55616 *Web:* thfcu.org	218-834-2266		219
Two Lights State Park 7 Tower Dr Cape Elizabeth ME 04107 *Web:* www.maine.gov	207-799-5871		565
Two Lines Press Center for the Art of Translation 582 Market St Ste 700 San Francisco CA 94104 *Web:* www.catranslation.org	415-512-8812	512-8824	637-2
Two Little Hands Productions 870 E N Union Ave Midvale UT 84047 *Web:* www.signingtime.com	801-676-4441		514
Two Men & A Truck International Inc 3400 Belle Chase Way Lansing MI 48911 *Web:* twomenandatruck.com	517-394-7210	394-7432	519
Two River Times 75 W Front St Red Bank NJ 07701 *Web:* tworivertimes.com	732-219-5788		532-4
Two Rivers Bank 555 S 19th St PO Box 550 Blair NE 68008 *Web:* 2riversbank.com	402-426-9500		70
Two Rivers Correctional Institution 82911 Beach Access Rd Umatilla OR 97882 *Web:* www.oregon.gov	541-922-2046		213
Two Rivers Enterprises 490 River St W PO Box 70 Holdingford MN 56340 *Web:* tworiversstainlesskings.com	320-746-3156		492
Two Rivers Heritage Museum 1 Durgan St PO Box 204 Washougal WA 98671 *Web:* www.2rhm.com	360-835-8742		520
Two Rivers State Recreation Area 27702 'F' St Waterloo NE 68069 *Web:* outdoornebraska.gov	402-359-5165		565
Two Roads Publishing 1187 Coast Village Rd Ste 10E Santa Barbara CA 93108 *TF:* 800-438-7444 ■ *Web:* www.rightbraininc.com	805-565-2282		637-2
Two Seas Restaurant 1300 Delaware 1 Dewey Beach DE 19971 *Web:* dinehere.us	302-227-2610		671
Two Sigma Investments LLC 100 Avenue of the Americas 16th Fl New York NY 10013 *Web:* www.twosigma.com	212-625-5700		690
Two Spruce Law Pc 204 SE Miller Ave Bend OR 97702 *Web:* twosprucelaw.com	541-389-4646	389-4644	41
Two Technologies Inc 419 Sargon Way Horsham PA 19044 *Web:* 2t.com	215-441-5305	441-0423	173-2
Two Tomatoes Records LLC 143 W 29th St Ste 1103 New York NY 10001 *Web:* www.laurieberkner.com	212-222-6834		525
Two Trees Publishing 15560 N Frank L Wright Ste B4-5255 Scottsdale AZ 85260 *Web:* www.christianrapturebooks.com	480-331-2777		637-2
Twombly Nursery 163 Barn Hill Rd Monroe CT 06468 *Web:* www.courvillenursery.com	203-261-2133	261-9230	323
Twomey, Latham, Shea, Kelley, Dubin & Quartararo LLP 33 W Second St PO Box 9398 Riverhead NY 11901 *Web:* suffolklaw.com	631-727-2180		428
TWP Enterprises Inc 7740 S Dr Springfield VA 22150 *Fax Area Code: 240 ■ *Web:* www.twperry.com	703-913-1634	403-2233*	191-3
TWP Inc 2831 Tenth St Berkeley CA 94710 *TF:* 800-227-1570 ■ *Web:* www.twpinc.com	510-548-4434	548-3073	688
TWT (Taylor Wiseman & Taylor) 124 Gaither Dr Ste 150 Mount Laurel NJ 08054 *Web:* taylorwiseman.com	856-235-7200		261
TWUA (Texas Water Utilities Assn) 1106 Clayton Ln Ste 112 W Austin TX 78723 *TF:* 888-367-8982 ■ *Web:* www.twua.org	512-459-3124	459-7124	48-13
TXU Electric PO Box 65764 Dallas TX 75262 *TF:* 800-242-9113 ■ *Web:* www.txu.com	972-791-2888		787
Ty Miles Inc 9855 Derby Ln Westchester IL 60154 *Web:* www.tymiles.net	708-344-5480	344-0437	455

Company	Phone	Fax	Class
TYAN Computer Corporation USA 3288 Laurelview Ct Fremont CA 94538 *Web:* tyan.com	510-651-8868	651-7688	625
Tybee Island Lighthouse & Museum 30 Meddin Dr Tybee Island GA 31328 *Web:* www.tybeelighthouse.org	912-786-5801		520
Tybout, Redfearn & Pell 750 Shipyard Dr Ste 400 Wilmington DE 19801 *Web:* trplaw.com	302-658-6901	658-4018	41
Tyburn Railroad LLC 505 S Broad St Kennett Square PA 19348 *Web:* www.regional-rail.com	610-925-0131		546
Tycko & Zavareei LLP 1828 L St NW Ste 1000 Washington DC 20036 *Web:* tzlegal.com	202-973-0900	973-0950	41
Tyco SimplexGrinnell 50 Technology Dr Westminster MA 01441 *TF:* 800-746-7539 ■ *Web:* www.tycosimplexgrinnell.com	978-731-2500		283
Tygart Technology Inc 1543 Fairmont Ave Fairmont WV 26554 *Web:* www.tygart.com	304-363-6855		180
Tyger Scientific Inc 324 Stokes Ave Ewing NJ 08638 *TF:* 888-329-8990 ■ *Web:* www.tygersci.com	609-434-0143		231
TYGH Capital Management Inc 1211 S W Fifth Ave Ste 2100 Portland OR 97204 *TF:* 800-972-0150 ■ *Web:* www.tyghcap.com	503-972-0150		401
TYK America Inc 301 Brickyard Rd Clairton PA 15025 *TF:* 800-569-9359 ■ *Web:* www.tykamerica.com	412-384-4259	384-4242	663
Tyler & Co 400 Northridge Rd Ste 1250 Atlanta GA 30350 *Fax Area Code: 770 ■ *Web:* www.tylerandco.com	678-916-9295	396-6693*	266
Tyler 2 Construction Inc 5400 Old Pineville Rd Charlotte NC 28217 *Web:* www.tyler2construction.com	704-527-3031		186
Tyler Arboretum 515 Painter Rd Media PA 19063 *Web:* www.tylerarboretum.org	610-566-9134	891-1490	97
Tyler Area Chamber of Commerce 315 N Broadway Ave Tyler TX 75702 *TF:* 800-235-5712 ■ *Web:* www.tylertexas.com	903-592-1661	593-2746	139
Tyler Building Systems LP 3535 Shiloh Rd Tyler TX 75701 *Web:* www.tylerbuilding.com	903-561-3000		105
Tyler City Employees Credit Union 819 N Spring Ave Tyler TX 75702 *Web:* tylercityecu.com	903-592-8012		219
Tyler Construction Group PO Box 25037 Columbia SC 29224 *Web:* www.tyler-construction.com	803-865-1404		187
Tyler County 100 Bluff St Rm 110 Woodville TX 75979 *TF:* 800-256-6848 ■ *Web:* www.co.tyler.tx.us	409-283-2281	283-6305	338
Tyler County Assessor 121 Main St Middlebourne WV 26149 *Web:* www.tylercountywv.com	304-758-4781	758-2126	338
Tyler Equipment Corp 251 Shaker Rd East Longmeadow MA 01028 *TF:* 800-292-6351 ■ *Web:* www.tylerequipment.com	413-525-6351	525-5909	358
Tyler Insurance Agency 1225 W Main St El Centro CA 92243 *Web:* tylerins.com	760-352-2611		390
Tyler Junior College PO Box 9020 Tyler TX 75711 *TF:* 800-687-5680 ■ *Web:* www.tjc.edu	903-510-2523	510-2161	162
Tyler Mountain Water Co 159 Harris Dr Poca WV 25159 *Web:* www.tylermountainwater.com	304-722-8080		805
Tyler Museum of Art 1300 S Mahon Ave Tyler TX 75701 *Web:* tylermuseum.org	903-595-1001		520
Tyler Pipe Co 11910 CR 492 Tyler TX 75706 *Fax Area Code: 800 ■ *TF:* 800-527-8478 ■ *Web:* www.tylerpipe.com	903-882-5511	248-9537*	307
Tyler Public Library 201 S College Ave Tyler TX 75702 *Web:* www.cityoftyler.org	903-593-7323	531-1329	434-3
Tyler State Park 101 Swamp Rd Newtown PA 18940 *Web:* www.dcnr.pa.gov	215-968-2021		565
Tyler State Park 789 Park Rd 16 Tyler TX 75706 *Web:* tpwd.texas.gov	903-597-5338		565
Tyler Technologies Inc 5949 Sherry Ln Ste 1400 Dallas TX 75225 *NYSE:* TYL ■ *Fax Area Code: 972 ■ *TF:* 800-431-5776 ■ *Web:* www.tylertech.com	800-431-5776	713-3741*	178-10
Tylok International Inc 1061 E 260th St Euclid OH 44132 *TF:* 800-321-0466 ■ *Web:* www.tylok.com	216-261-7310		595
Tymco Inc 225 E Industrial Blvd PO Box 2368 Waco TX 76703 *TF:* 800-258-9626 ■ *Web:* www.tymco.com	254-799-5546	799-2722	516
Tyndale House Publishers Inc 351 Executive Dr Carol Stream IL 60188 *TF:* 800-323-9400 ■ *Web:* www.tyndale.com	800-323-9400	684-0247	637-3
Tyndale University College & Seminary 25 Ballyconnor Ct Toronto ON M2M4B3 *Web:* www.tyndale.ca	416-226-6380	226-6746	167-3
Tyndall Air Force Base 555 Suwannee Rd Rm 140-A-1 Tyndall AFB FL 32403 *TF:* 800-356-5273 ■ *Web:* www.tyndall.af.mil	850-283-1110	283-3225	497-1
Tyndall Federal Credit Union PO Box 59760 Panama City FL 32412 *TF:* 888-896-3255 ■ *Web:* tyndall.org	850-769-9999	747-4215	216
Tyonek Manufacturing Group Inc 229 Palmer Rd Madison AL 35758 *TF:* 877-862-6667 ■ *Web:* www.tyonek.com	256-258-6200		529
Type and Design 1422 Euclid Ave Ste 764 Cleveland OH 44115 *Web:* www.typedes.com	216-408-1504		344
Typecraft Wood & Jones Inc 2040 E Walnut St Pasadena CA 91107 *Web:* www.typecraft.com	626-795-8093	795-2423	626
Typesetting Inc 1144 S Robertson Blvd Los Angeles CA 90035 *Web:* www.typesettingink.com	310-273-3330		781
Typical Sicilian 497 Belmont Ave Springfield MA 01108 *Web:* www.typicalsicilian.com	413-739-7100		671

Company	Address	City	State	ZIP	Phone	Fax	Class
TYR Energy Inc	7500 College Blvd Ste 400 *Fax Area Code: 973 ■ Web: www.tyrenergy.com	Overland Park	KS	66210	913-754-5800	754-5701*	792
TYR Sport	1790 Apollo Ct TF: 800-252-7878 ■ Web: www.tyr.com	Seal Beach	CA	90740	714-897-0799		155-17
Tyree Oil Inc	1355 W 1st Ave Web: www.tyreeoil.com	Eugene	OR	97402	541-687-0076		579
Tyres International Inc	4637 Allen Rd TF: 800-321-0941 ■ Web: www.tyresinternational.com	Stow	OH	44224	330-374-1000		755
Tyrpak Financial Associates Inc	6622 Main St Ste 6 Web: www.tyrpakwealthstrategies.com	Williamsville	NY	14221	716-631-1600	631-1605	390
Tyrrell County	108 S Water St PO Box 449 Web: tyrrellcounty.org	Columbia	NC	27925	252-796-1371		338
TYS LLP	800 S Broadway Ste 450 Web: tysllp.com	Walnut Creek	CA	94596	925-498-6200	498-6299	2
Tysinger Hampton & Partners Inc	3428 Bristol Hwy Web: tysinger-engineering.com	Johnson City	TN	37601	423-282-2687		261
Tyson Animal Hospital	5415 Nc Hwy 55 Web: tysonanimalhospital.com	Durham	NC	27713	919-544-8297		794
Tyson Events Ctr	401 Gordon Dr Web: tysoncenter.com	Sioux City	IA	51101	712-279-4850	279-4903	205
Tyson Foods Inc	PO Box 2020 TF: 844-360-8276 ■ Web: www.tyson.com	Springdale	AR	72765	844-360-8276		296-36
Tyson Fresh Meats Inc	800 Stevens Port Dr Ste DD813 TF: 800-416-0772 ■ Web: www.tysonfreshmeats.com	Dakota Dunes	SD	57049	605-235-2061		473
Tyson Nutraceutical Inc	3545 Lomita Blvd Unit D Web: www.tysonnutraceuticals.com	Torrance	CA	90505	310-325-5600	517-8648	238
Tyson Pet Products Inc	2414 310th St TF: 877-303-9247 ■ Web: www.truechews.com	Independence	IA	50644	877-303-9247		473
Tysons Corner Ctr	7850 Tysons Corner Ctr Ste 305 Web: www.tysonscornercenter.com	McLean	VA	22102	703-847-7300		460
Tysons Galleria	2001 International Dr Web: www.tysonsgalleria.com	McLean	VA	22102	703-827-7730		460
Tysons Regional Chamber of Commerce	7925 Jones Branch Dr Ste 200 Web: www.tysonschamber.org	Tysons	VA	22102	703-281-1333	242-1482	139
Tystar Corp	7050 Lampson Ave Web: en.tystar.com	Garden Grove	CA	92841	310-781-9219		246
Tysver Beck Evans PLLC, Capella Tower	225 S Sixth St Ste 1750 Web: www.bitlaw.com	Minneapolis	MN	55402	612-915-9633	915-9637	445
Tyze Personal Networks Ltd	90 Allstate Pkwy Ste 300 TF: 800-463-1763 ■ Web: tyze.com	Markham	ON	L3R6H3	604-628-9594		387
Tzangas, Plakas, Mannos Ltd	220 Market Ave S 8th Fl Web: lawlion.com	Canton	OH	44702	330-455-6112		41
Tzell Travel Group	119 W 40th St 14th Fl Web: www.tzell.com	New York	NY	10018	212-944-2121		771
Tzinberg & Associates PC	1 Country Club Executive Pk Web: tzinberg.com	Glen Carbon	IL	62034	618-288-8989		2

U

Company	Address	City	State	ZIP	Phone	Fax	Class
U (United Fabrics Inc)	9115 Pennsauken Hwy TF: 800-347-8344 ■ Web: www.unitedfabrics.com	Pennsauken	NJ	08110	856-665-2040	665-5761	594
U B S Printing Group Inc	2577 Research Dr Web: www.ubsprint.com	Corona	CA	92882	951-273-7900		627
U District Partnership	4507 University Way NE Ste 209 Web: udistrictpartnership.org	Seattle	WA	98105	206-547-4417		139
U hotel Fifth Avenue	373 Fifth Ave TF: 800-315-4642 ■ Web: www.uhotelfifthavenue.com	New York	NY	10016	212-213-3388		707
U R S Information Systems Inc	155 W St Ste 1 Web: ursinfo.com	Wilmington	MA	01887	978-657-6100	694-9039	180
U W Provision Company Inc	PO Box 620038 TF: 800-832-0517 ■ Web: www.uwprovision.com	Middleton	WI	53562	608-836-7421	836-6328	297-9
U.A. Systems Inc	2243 N 3rd Ave TF: 888-756-9494 ■ Web: www.uasys.com	Upland	CA	91784	888-756-9494		178-1
U.P.D. Inc	4507 S Maywood Ave Web: www.updinc.net	Vernon	CA	90058	323-588-8811	588-8844	44
U.S. & Company CPA PLLC	500 N Capital of Tx Hwy Ste 3-100 Web: usco-cpa.com	Austin	TX	78746	512-328-9090		2
U.S. 13 Grill & Catering	1115 S Governors Ave Web: www.us13grill.com	Dover	DE	19904	302-730-3551		671
U.S. Acrylic Inc	1320 Harris Rd Web: usacrylic.com	Libertyville	IL	60048	847-837-4800		607
U.S. Adventure Rv	5120 N Brady St TF: 877-768-4678 ■ Web: www.usadventurerv.com	Davenport	IA	52806	877-768-4678		23
U.S. Agency for International Development (USAID)	1300 Pennsylvania Ave NW Web: www.usaid.gov	Washington	DC	20004	202-712-0000	216-3524	340-20
U.S. Air Force Academy (USAFA)	2304 Cadet Dr Ste 3100 TF: 800-443-9266 ■ Web: www.usafa.af.mil	US Air Force Academy	CO	80840	719-333-1110	333-3644	498
U.S. Air Force Medical Center Keesler 81st Medical Group	301 Fisher St Rm GH023 Web: www.keesler.af.mil	Keesler Air Force Base	MS	39534	228-376-4056	376-0094	374-4
U.S. Airconditioning Distributors	16900 Chestnut St TF: 800-937-7222 ■ Web: us-ac.com	City of Industry	CA	91748	800-937-7222		612
U.S. Airport Parking	18000 E 81st Ave TF: 866-727-5464 ■ Web: www.usairportparking.com	Commerce City	CO	80022	303-371-7575		562
U.S. Alliance Federal Credit Union	411 Theodore Fremd Ave Ste 350 *Fax Area Code: 914 ■ TF: 800-431-2754 ■ Web: www.usalliance.org	Rye	NY	10580	800-431-2754	881-3464*	219
U.S. Alliance Group Inc	29883 Santa Margarita Pkwy Ste B Web: www.usag-inc.com	Rancho Santa Margarita	CA	92688	949-888-4408	709-4863	225
U.S. Alliance Paper	101 Heartland Blvd Web: www.usalliancepaper.com	Edgewood	NY	11717	631-254-3030		558
U.S. Angola Chamber of Commerce	1440 G St NW *Fax Area Code: 884 ■ TF: 844-363-9466 ■ Web: www.us-angola.org	Washington	DC	20005	844-363-9466	363-9466*	138
U.S. Apple Assn	8233 Old Courthouse Rd Ste 200 TF: 800-781-4443 ■ Web: www.usapple.org	Vienna	VA	22182	703-442-8850	790-0845	48-2
U.S. Arctic Research Commission	4350 N Fairfax Dr Ste 510 Web: www.arctic.gov	Arlington	VA	22203	703-525-0111	525-0114	340-20
U.S. Army Aeromedical Research Laboratory	PO Box 620577 Web: www.usaarl.army.mil	Fort Rucker	AL	36362	334-255-6920		668
U.S. Army Aviation Learning Ctr	453 Novosel St Web: www.rucker.army.mil	Fort Rucker	AL	36362	334-255-1110	255-1004	497-2
U.S. Army Basic Combat Training Museum	4442 Ft Jackson Blvd Web: www.goarmy.com	Columbia	SC	29209	803-751-7419		520
U.S. Army Corps of Engineers	441 G St NW Web: www.usace.army.mil	Washington	DC	20314	202-761-0011		340-5
U.S. Army Corps of Engineers Institute for Water Resources *Hydrologic Engineering Ctr*	609 Second St Web: www.hec.usace.army.mil	Davis	CA	95616	530-756-1104	756-8250	668
U.S. Army Corps of Engineers Regional Offices *Great Lakes & Ohio River Div*	550 Main St Web: www.lrd.usace.army.mil	Cincinnati	OH	45202	513-684-3010		340-5
Mississippi Valley Div	1400 Walnut St Web: www.mvd.usace.army.mil	Vicksburg	MS	39180	601-634-7783		340-5
North Atlantic Div	302 General Lee Ave Web: www.nad.usace.army.mil	Brooklyn	NY	11252	347-370-4550		340-5
Northwestern Div	1201 NE Lyod Blvd Ste 400 Web: www.nwd.usace.army.mil	Portland	OR	97232	503-808-3800		340-5
Pacific Ocean Div	Fort Shafter Web: www.pod.usace.army.mil	Honolulu	HI	96819	808-835-4715		340-5
South Atlantic Div	60 Forsyth St SW Rm 10M15 Web: www.sad.usace.army.mil	Atlanta	GA	30303	404-562-5011		340-5
South Pacific Div	1455 Market St Web: www.spd.usace.army.mil	San Francisco	CA	94103	415-503-6514		340-5
Southwestern Div	1100 Commerce St Ste 831 Web: www.swd.usace.army.mil	Dallas	TX	75242	469-487-7007		340-5
U.S. Army Criminal Investigation Command	27130 Telegraph Rd Russell Knox Bldg Web: www.cid.army.mil	Quantico	VA	22134	571-305-4009		340-5
U.S. Army Dugway Proving Ground	5450 Doolittle Ave Web: www.dugway.army.mil	Dugway	UT	84022	435-831-2116		743
U.S. Army Engineer Research & Development Ctr (ERDC)	3909 Halls Ferry Rd Web: www.erdc.usace.army.mil	Vicksburg	MS	39180	601-634-2502		668
U.S. Army Family & MWR *Yuma Proving Ground*	301 C St Bldg 300 Web: www.yumamwr.com	Yuma	AZ	85365	928-328-2151		743
U.S. Army Institute of Surgical Research (USAISR)	3698 Chambers Pass Ste B Web: www.usaisr.amedd.army.mil	Fort Sam Houston	TX	78234	210-539-3219		668
U.S. Army Intelligence & Security Command	8825 Beulah St Web: www.inscom.army.mil	Fort Belvoir	VA	22060	703-428-4965		340-5
U.S. Army Museum of Hawaii	PO Box 8064 Web: www.hiarmymuseumsoc.org	Honolulu	HI	96830	808-438-2821	941-3617	520
U.S. Army Research Laboratory (ARL)	Attn: AMSRD-ARL-O-PA 2800 Powder Mill Rd	Adelphi	MD	20783	301-394-2500		668
U.S. Army Transportation Museum	300 Washington Blvd Web: www.transchool.lee.army.mil	Fort Eustis	VA	23604	757-878-1115		520
U.S. Art Company Inc	66 Pacella Park Dr TF: 800-872-7826 ■ Web: usart.com	Randolph	MA	02368	800-872-7826		522
U.S. ASEAN Business Council	1101 17th St NW Ste 411 Web: www.usasean.org	Washington	DC	20036	202-289-1911		49-12
U.S. Austrian Chamber of Commerce	405 Lexington Ave 37th Fl Web: usaustrianchamber.org	New York	NY	10174	212-819-0117		138
U.S. Auto Parts Network Inc	16941 Keegan Ave NASDAQ: PRTS ■ Web: www.carparts.com	Carson	CA	90746	424-702-1455		61
U.S. AutoForce	425 Better Way TF: 800-490-4901 ■ Web: www.usautoforce.com	Appleton	WI	54915	800-490-4901		61
U.S. Axle Inc	275 Shoemaker Rd Web: usaxle.com	Pottstown	PA	19464	610-323-3800	970-2010	54
U.S. Balance	1098 E Beckes Ln TF: 888-293-7661 ■ Web: www.usbalance.com	Vincennes	IN	47591	812-895-1080	895-1092	300

	City	State	ZIP	Phone	Fax	Class
U.S. Bancorp 800 Nicollet Mall *NYSE:* USB ■ *TF:* 800-872-2657 ■ *Web:* www.usbank.com	Minneapolis	MN	55402	651-466-3000		360-2
U.S. Bankcard Services Inc 17171 E Gale Ave Ste 110 *TF:* 888-888-8872 ■ *Web:* www.usbsi.com	City of Industry	CA	91745	888-888-8872		251
U.S. Bankruptcy Court						
Alabama Middle 1 Church St. *Web:* www.almb.uscourts.gov	Montgomery	AL	36104	334-954-3800	954-3819	341-2
Alabama Northern 1800 Fifth Ave N. *Web:* www.alnb.uscourts.gov	Birmingham	AL	35203	205-714-4000	909-9432	341-2
Alabama Southern 201 St Louis St *TF:* 866-737-5929 ■ *Web:* www.alsb.uscourts.gov	Mobile	AL	36602	251-441-5391	441-6286	341-2
Alaska 605 W Fourth Ave Ste 138 *TF:* 800-859-8059 ■ *Web:* www.akb.uscourts.gov	Anchorage	AK	99501	907-271-2655		341-2
Arizona 230 N First Ave Ste 101 *TF:* 800-556-9230 ■ *Web:* www.azb.uscourts.gov	Phoenix	AZ	85003	602-682-4000		341-2
Arkansas 300 W Second St *Web:* www.arb.uscourts.gov	Little Rock	AR	72201	501-918-5500	918-5520	341-2
California Central 255 E Temple St. *Web:* www.cacb.uscourts.gov	Los Angeles	CA	90012	213-894-3118		341-2
California Eastern 501 'I' St Ste 3-200 *Web:* www.caeb.uscourts.gov	Sacramento	CA	95814	916-930-4400		341-2
California Northern 450 Golden Gate Ave PO Box 36099 *Web:* www.canb.uscourts.gov	San Francisco	CA	94102	415-268-2300		341-2
California Southern 325 W F St. *Web:* www.casb.uscourts.gov	San Diego	CA	92101	619-557-5620		341-2
Central District of Illinois 600 E Monroe St Rm 226 *Web:* www.ilcb.uscourts.gov	Springfield	IL	62701	217-492-4551	492-4556	341-2
Colorado US Custom House 721 19th St *Web:* www.cob.uscourts.gov	Denver	CO	80202	720-904-7300		341-2
Connecticut 450 Main St 7th Fl. *Web:* www.ctb.uscourts.gov	Hartford	CT	06103	860-240-3675		341-2
Delaware 824 N Market St 3rd Fl. *Web:* www.deb.uscourts.gov	Wilmington	DE	19801	302-252-2900		341-2
District of Columbia 333 Constitution Ave NW. *Web:* www.dcb.uscourts.gov	Washington	DC	20001	202-354-3280		341-2
District of Hawaii 1132 Bishop St Ste 250. *Web:* www.hib.uscourts.gov	Honolulu	HI	96813	808-522-8100	522-8120	341-2
District of Vermont 151 W St. *Web:* www.vtb.uscourts.gov	Rutland	VT	05701	802-776-2000	776-2020	341-2
Eastern District of Tennessee 800 Market St Ste 330. *Web:* www.tneb.uscourts.gov	Knoxville	TN	37902	865-545-4279		341-2
Eastern District of Texas 110 N College Ave 9th Fl. *Web:* www.txeb.uscourts.gov	Tyler	TX	75702	903-590-3200		341-2
Eastern District of Washington 904 W Riverside Ave Ste 304. *TF:* 800-519-2549 ■ *Web:* www.waeb.uscourts.gov	Spokane	WA	99201	509-458-5300		341-2
Florida Middle 801 N Florida Ave Ste 555. *Web:* www.flmb.uscourts.gov	Tampa	FL	33602	813-301-5162		341-2
Florida Northern 110 E Park Ave Ste 100 *TF:* 888-765-1752 ■ *Web:* www.flnb.uscourts.gov	Tallahassee	FL	32301	850-521-5001		341-2
Florida Southern 51 SW First Ave *Web:* www.flsb.uscourts.gov	Miami	FL	33130	305-714-1800		341-2
Georgia Middle 433 Cherry St. *Web:* www.gamb.uscourts.gov	Macon	GA	31201	478-752-3506		341-2
Georgia Northern 75 Ted Turner Dr SW *Web:* www.ganb.uscourts.gov	Atlanta	GA	30303	404-215-1000		341-2
Georgia Southern 125 Bull St 2nd Fl PO Box 8347 *Web:* www.gasb.uscourts.gov	Savannah	GA	31401	912-650-4100		341-2
Idaho 550 W Fort St. *Web:* www.id.uscourts.gov	Boise	ID	83724	208-334-1361		341-2
Illinois Southern 750 Missouri Ave. *Web:* www.ilsb.uscourts.gov	East Saint Louis	IL	62201	618-482-9400		341-2
Indiana Northern 401 S Michigan St *Web:* www.innb.uscourts.gov	South Bend	IN	46601	574-968-2100		341-2
Indiana Southern 46 E Ohio St. *Web:* www.insb.uscourts.gov	Indianapolis	IN	46204	317-229-3800	229-3801	341-2
Kansas 401 N Market St Rm 167. *Web:* www.ksb.uscourts.gov	Wichita	KS	67202	316-269-6637		341-2
Kentucky Eastern 100 E Vine St Ste 200 *Web:* www.kyeb.uscourts.gov	Lexington	KY	40507	859-233-2608		341-2
Kentucky Western 601 W Broadway Ste 450. *Web:* www.kywb.uscourts.gov	Louisville	KY	40202	502-627-5700		341-2
Louisiana Eastern 500 Poydras St Ste B-601 *Web:* www.laeb.uscourts.gov	New Orleans	LA	70130	504-589-7878		341-2
Louisiana Middle 707 Florida St Rm 119. *Web:* www.lamb.uscourts.gov	Baton Rouge	LA	70801	225-346-3333		341-2
Louisiana Western 300 Fannin St Ste 2201 *TF:* 866-721-2105 ■ *Web:* www.lawb.uscourts.gov	Shreveport	LA	71101	318-676-4267		341-2
Maine 537 Congress St 2nd Fl *Web:* www.meb.uscourts.gov	Portland	ME	04101	207-780-3482	780-3679	341-2
Massachusetts 5 Post Office Sq Ste 1150 *Web:* www.mab.uscourts.gov	Boston	MA	02109	617-748-5300	748-5315	341-2
Michigan Eastern 211 W Fort St Ste 1820 *Web:* www.mieb.uscourts.gov	Detroit	MI	48226	313-234-0065		341-2
Michigan Western 1 Div Ave N Rm 200. *Web:* www.miwb.uscourts.gov	Grand Rapids	MI	49503	616-456-2693		341-2
Middle District of North Carolina 101 S Edgeworth St *Web:* www.ncmb.uscourts.gov	Greensboro	NC	27401	336-358-4000		341-2
Minnesota 300 S Fourth St 301 US Courthouse *TF:* 866-260-7337 ■ *Web:* www.mnb.uscourts.gov	Minneapolis	MN	55415	612-664-5260		341-2
Mississippi Northern 703 Hwy 145 N *Web:* www.msnb.uscourts.gov	Aberdeen	MS	39730	662-369-2596		341-2
Mississippi Southern 501 E Court St Ste 2 300. *Web:* www.mssb.uscourts.gov	Jackson	MS	39201	601-608-4600		341-2
Missouri Eastern 111 S Tenth St 4th Fl *TF:* 866-803-9517 ■ *Web:* www.moeb.uscourts.gov	Saint Louis	MO	63102	314-244-4500	244-4990	341-2
Missouri Western 400 E Ninth St. *Web:* www.mow.uscourts.gov	Kansas City	MO	64106	816-512-1800		341-2
Montana 400 N Main St. *TF:* 888-888-2530 ■ *Web:* www.mtb.uscourts.gov	Butte	MT	59701	406-497-1240		341-2
Nebraska 111 S 18th Plz Ste 1125 *Web:* www.neb.uscourts.gov	Omaha	NE	68102	402-661-7444		341-2
Nevada 300 Las Vegas Blvd S *Web:* www.nvb.uscourts.gov	Las Vegas	NV	89101	702-527-7000		341-2
New Hampshire 1000 Elm St Ste 1001 *Web:* www.nhb.uscourts.gov	Manchester	NH	03101	603-222-2600	222-2697	341-2
New Jersey PO Box 1352. *Web:* www.njb.uscourts.gov	Newark	NJ	07102	973-645-4764		341-2
New Mexico 333 Lomas Blvd NW *Web:* www.nmd.uscourts.gov	Albuquerque	NM	87102	505-348-2000	348-2028	341-2
New York Eastern 271 Cadman Plz E. *Web:* www.nyeb.uscourts.gov	Brooklyn	NY	11201	347-394-1700		341-2
North Carolina Eastern 1760-A Parkwood Blvd *Web:* www.nceb.uscourts.gov	Wilson	NC	27893	252-237-0248		341-2
North Carolina Western 401 W Trade St Rm 111. *Web:* www.ncwb.uscourts.gov	Charlotte	NC	28202	704-350-7500		341-2
North Dakota 655 First Ave N Ste 210. *Web:* www.ndb.uscourts.gov	Fargo	ND	58102	701-297-7100		341-2
Northern District of Illinois 219 S Dearborn St *Web:* www.ilnb.uscourts.gov	Chicago	IL	60604	312-435-5694		341-2
Northern District of Iowa 111 Seventh Ave SE 6th Fl. *Web:* www.ianb.uscourts.gov	Cedar Rapids	IA	52401	319-286-2200	286-2280	341-2
Northern District of New York 445 Broadway Ste 330. *Web:* www.nynb.uscourts.gov	Albany	NY	12207	518-257-1661		341-2
Northern District of Ohio 201 Superior Ave. *Web:* www.ohnb.uscourts.gov	Cleveland	OH	44114	216-615-4300		341-2
Ohio Southern 120 W Third St. *Web:* www.ohsb.uscourts.gov	Dayton	OH	45402	937-225-2516		341-2
Oklahoma Eastern 111 W Fourth St PO Box 1347. *Web:* www.okeb.uscourts.gov	Okmulgee	OK	74447	918-758-0126		341-2
Oklahoma Northern 224 S Boulder Ave Ste 105 *Web:* www.oknb.uscourts.gov	Tulsa	OK	74103	918-699-4000		341-2
Oklahoma Western 215 Dean A McGee Ave *Web:* www.okwb.uscourts.gov	Oklahoma City	OK	73102	405-609-5700		341-2
Oregon 1001 SW Fifth Ave Ste 700 *TF:* 800-676-6856 ■ *Web:* www.orb.uscourts.gov	Portland	OR	97204	503-326-1500		341-2
Pennsylvania Eastern 900 Market St Ste 400 *Web:* www.paeb.uscourts.gov	Philadelphia	PA	19107	215-408-2800		341-2
Pennsylvania Middle 197 S Main St *TF:* 877-298-2053 ■ *Web:* www.pamb.uscourts.gov	Wilkes-Barre	PA	18701	570-831-2500	829-0249	341-2
Pennsylvania Western 600 Grant St 5414 US Steel Tower *Web:* www.pawb.uscourts.gov	Pittsburgh	PA	15219	412-644-2700	644-6512	341-2
Puerto Rico 300 Recinto Sur St *Web:* www.prb.uscourts.gov	San Juan	PR	00901	787-977-6000	977-6008	341-2
South Carolina 1100 Laurel St. *Web:* www.scb.uscourts.gov	Columbia	SC	29201	803-765-5436		341-2
South Dakota 400 S Phillips Ave Rm 104 *Web:* www.sdb.uscourts.gov	Sioux Falls	SD	57104	605-357-2400	357-2401	341-2
Southern District of Iowa 110 E Court Ave Ste 300 *Web:* www.iasb.uscourts.gov	Des Moines	IA	50309	515-284-6230	284-6303	341-2
Southern District of New York 1 Bowling Green *Web:* www.nysb.uscourts.gov	New York	NY	10004	212-668-2870		341-2
Tennessee Middle 701 Broadway Rm 170 *Web:* www.tnmb.uscourts.gov	Nashville	TN	37203	615-736-5584		341-2
Tennessee Western 200 Jefferson Ave Ste 413 *TF:* 800-406-0190 ■ *Web:* www.tnwb.uscourts.gov	Memphis	TN	38103	901-328-3500		341-2
Texas Northern 1100 Commerce St Rm 1254 *TF:* 800-442-6850 ■ *Web:* www.txnb.uscourts.gov	Dallas	TX	75242	214-753-2000		341-2
Utah 350 S Main St Rm 301 *Web:* www.utb.uscourts.gov	Salt Lake City	UT	84101	801-524-6687	524-4409	341-2
Virginia Eastern 200 S Washington St. *TF:* 866-222-8029 ■ *Web:* www.vaeb.uscourts.gov	Alexandria	VA	22314	804-916-2400		341-2
Virginia Western 210 Church Ave SW Rm 200 *Web:* www.vawb.uscourts.gov	Roanoke	VA	24011	540-857-2391		341-2
Washington Western 700 Stewart St Ste 6301 **Fax Area Code:* 360 ■ *Web:* www.wawb.uscourts.gov	Seattle	WA	98101	206-370-5200	252-8333*	341-2
West Virginia Northern 1125 Chapline St PO Box 70 *Web:* www.wvnb.uscourts.gov	Wheeling	WV	26003	304-233-1655	233-0185	341-2
West Virginia Southern 300 Virginia St E Rm 3200 *TF:* 800-685-1111 ■ *Web:* www.wvsb.uscourts.gov	Charleston	WV	25301	304-347-3003		341-2
Western District of New York 100 State St *Web:* www.nywb.uscourts.gov	Rochester	NY	14614	585-613-4200		341-2

Phone | Fax | Class

Western District of Texas
615 E Houston St United States Courthouse
Hipolito F Garcia Federal Bldg............San Antonio TX 78205 210-472-6720 341-2
Web: www.txwb.uscourts.gov
Wisconsin Eastern
US Federal Courthouse 517 E Wisconsin Ave
Rm 126..............................Milwaukee WI 53202 414-297-3291 341-2
TF: 877-781-7277 ■ *Web:* www.wieb.uscourts.gov
Wisconsin Western
120 N Henry St Rm 340...................Madison WI 53703 608-264-5178 341-2
Web: www.wiwb.uscourts.gov
Wyoming 2120 Capitol Ave Ste 6004..........Cheyenne WY 82001 307-433-2200 341-2
Web: www.wyb.uscourts.gov

U.S. Beverage Net Inc
225 W Jefferson St.........................Syracuse NY 13202 888-298-3641 296
TF: 888-298-3641 ■ *Web:* www.usbeveragenet.com

U.S. Bottlers Machinery Co
11911 Steele Creek Rd......................Charlotte NC 28273 704-588-4750 588-3808 547
Web: www.usbottlers.com

U.S. Box Corp 1296 Mccarter Hwy...............Newark NJ 07104 973-481-2000 561
Web: www.usbox.com

U.S. Bronze Sign Co
811 Second Ave......................New Hyde Park NY 11040 516-352-5155 352-1761 777
TF: 800-872-5155 ■ *Web:* usbronze.com

U.S. Button Corp 328 Kennedy Dr.............Putnam CT 06260 860-928-2707 928-2847 594
TF: 800-243-1842 ■ *Web:* www.usbutton.com

U.S. Candle Co 7241 Paxton St...............Harrisburg PA 17111 717-564-2220 564-2035 361
Web: www.uscandleco.com

U.S. Capital Advisors LLC
1330 Post Oak Blvd Ste 900...................Houston TX 77056 713-366-0500 401
Web: www.uscallc.com

U.S. Catholic Magazine
205 W Monroe St...........................Chicago IL 60606 312-236-7782 457-18
TF: 800-328-6515 ■ *Web:* www.uscatholic.org

U.S. Cellular Corp (USCC)
8410 W Bryn Mawr Ave Ste 700................Chicago IL 60631 773-399-8900 736
NYSE: USM ■ *TF:* 888-944-9400 ■ *Web:* www.uscellular.com

U.S. Cellular Ctr
370 First Ave E.........................Cedar Rapids IA 52401 319-398-5211 205
Web: www.uscellularcenter.com

U.S. Census Bureau
4600 Silver Hill Rd.......................Washington DC 20233 301-763-6460 340-2
Web: www.census.gov

U.S. Census Bureau Regional Offices
Atlanta 101 Marietta St NW Ste 3200............Atlanta GA 30303 404-730-3832 730-3835 340-2
TF: 800-424-6974 ■ *Web:* www.census.gov
Boston 4 Copley Pl Ste 301....................Boston MA 02117 617-424-4501 340-2
TF: 800-562-5721 ■ *Web:* www.census.gov
Chicago 1111 W 22nd St Ste 400............Oak Brook IL 60523 630-288-9200 288-9288 340-2
TF: 800-865-6384 ■ *Web:* www.census.gov
Denver 6950 W Jefferson Ave Ste 250.........Lakewood CO 80235 303-264-0202 969-6777 340-2
TF: 800-852-6159 ■ *Web:* www.census.gov
Los Angeles 15350 Sherman Way Ste 400......Van Nuys CA 91406 818-267-1700 340-2
TF: 800-992-3530 ■ *Web:* www.census.gov
New York 32 Old Slip 9th Fl.................New York NY 10005 212-584-3400 340-2
TF: 800-991-2520 ■ *Web:* www.census.gov
Philadelphia
100 S Independence Mall W Ste 410.......Philadelphia PA 19106 215-717-1800 717-0755 340-2
TF: 800-262-4236 ■ *Web:* www.census.gov

U.S. Chamber of Commerce
1615 H St NW...........................Washington DC 20062 202-659-6000 140
Web: www.uschamber.com

U.S. Chemical & Plastics
600 Nova Dr SE...........................Massillon OH 44646 330-830-6000 830-6005 60
TF: 800-321-0672 ■ *Web:* www.uschem.com

U.S. Chemical Safety & Hazard Investigation Board
2175 K St NW Ste 400.....................Washington DC 20037 202-261-7600 261-7650 340-20
Web: www.csb.gov

U.S. Chess Federation PO Box 3967..........Crossville TN 38557 931-787-1234 787-1200 457-14
TF: 800-903-8723 ■ *Web:* new.uschess.org

U.S. China Business Council, The
1818 N St NW Ste 200....................Washington DC 20036 202-429-0340 775-2476 49-12
Web: www.uschina.org

U.S. Chrome Corp 175 Garfield Ave.............Stratford CT 06615 800-637-9019 386-0067* 481
**Fax Area Code:* 203 ■ *TF:* 800-637-9019 ■ *Web:* www.uschrome.com

U.S. Citizenship & Immigration Services Regional Offices
70 Kimball Ave......................South Burlington VT 05403 800-767-1833 340-11
TF: 800-767-1833 ■ *Web:* www.uscis.gov

U.S. Claims Services Inc
3801 Pegasus Dr Ste 101...................Bakersfield CA 93308 661-399-1108 226
Web: www.usclaimsservices.com

U.S. Coachways Inc
100 St Mary's Ave Ste 2B.................Staten Island NY 10305 718-477-4242 441
TF: 800-359-5991 ■ *Web:* www.uscoachways.com

U.S. Coast Guard
Boating Safety Office
2703 Martin Luther King Jr Ave SE
Ste 7501...........................Washington DC 20593 202-372-1062 340-11
Web: www.uscgboating.org
Law Enforcement Office
2100 Second St SW....................Washington DC 20593 800-982-8813 340-11
TF: 800-982-8813 ■ *Web:* www.uscg.mil
National Maritime Ctr
100 Forbes Dr........................Martinsburg WV 25404 304-433-3400 340-11
TF: 888-427-5662 ■ *Web:* www.uscg.mil
National Pollution Funds Ctr
4200 Wilson Blvd Ste 1000................Arlington VA 22203 202-795-6003 795-6900 340-11
Web: www.uscg.mil
Navigation Ctr 7323 Telegraph Rd...........Alexandria VA 22315 703-313-5900 313-5920 340-11
Web: www.navcen.uscg.gov

U.S. Coast Guard Academy
31 Mohegan Ave........................New London CT 06320 860-444-8444 701-6700 166
TF: 800-883-8724 ■ *Web:* www.uscga.edu

U.S. Coast Guard Air Station Savannah
1297 N Lightning Rd......................Savannah GA 31409 912-652-4646 158
Web: www.atlanticarea.uscg.mil

U.S. Coast Guard Base Honolulu
400 Sand Island Pkwy.....................Honolulu HI 96819 808-842-2088 158
Web: www.dcms.uscg.mil

U.S. Coast Guard Chief Petty Officers Assn
5520-G Hempstead Way....................Springfield VA 22151 703-941-0395 941-0397 48-19
Web: www.uscgcpoa.org

U.S. Coast Guard Research & Development Ctr
1082 Shennecossett Rd.......................Groton CT 06340 860-441-2600 441-2792 668
Web: www.uscg.mil

U.S. Cold Storage Inc
201 Laurel Rd Ste 400 4 Echelon Plz...........Voorhees NJ 08043 856-354-8181 772-1876 803-2
Web: www.uscold.com

U.S. Commission on Civil Rights
1331 Pennsylvania Ave NW Ste 1150.........Washington DC 20425 202-376-7700 376-7672 340-20
TF: 800-552-6843 ■ *Web:* www.usccr.gov

U.S. Commission on Civil Rights Regional Offices
Central Regional Office
400 State Ave Ste 908..................Kansas City KS 66101 913-551-1400 551-1413 340-20
Web: www.usccr.gov
Midwestern Regional Office
55 W Monroe St Ste 410...................Chicago IL 60603 312-353-8311 353-8324 340-20
Web: www.usccr.gov
Rocky Mountain Regional Office
1700 Broadway...........................Denver CO 80290 303-866-1040 866-1050 340-20
Web: www.usccr.gov
Southern Regional Office
61 Forsyth St SW Ste 1840 T.................Atlanta GA 30303 404-562-7000 562-7004 340-20
Web: www.usccr.gov
Western Regional Office
300 N Los Angeles St Ste 2010...........Los Angeles CA 90012 213-894-3437 894-0508 340-20
Web: www.usccr.gov

U.S. Commission on International ReligiousFreedom (USCIRF)
800 N Capitol St NW Ste 790...............Washington DC 20002 202-523-3240 523-5020 340-20
Web: www.uscirf.gov

U.S. Committee for Refugees & Immigrants (USCRI)
2231 Crystal Dr Ste 350.....................Arlington VA 22202 703-310-1130 769-4241 48-5
Web: www.refugees.org

U.S. Concrete Inc
2925 Briarpark Dr Ste 1050...................Houston TX 77042 713-499-6200 499-6201 182
NASDAQ: USCR ■ *Web:* www.us-concrete.com

U.S. Conference of Mayors
1620 'I' St NW...........................Washington DC 20006 202-293-7330 293-2352 49-7
Web: www.usmayors.org

U.S. Congress
Joint Committee on Printing
1309 Longworth House Office Bldg........Washington DC 20515 202-225-8281 342-1
Web: cha.house.gov
Joint Committee on Taxation, The
502 Ford House Office Bldg.............Washington DC 20515 202-225-3621 342-1
Web: www.jct.gov
Joint Economic Committee
G-01 Dirksen Senate Office Bldg..........Washington DC 20510 202-224-5171 224-0240 342-1
Web: www.jec.senate.gov

U.S. Cost Inc
600 Northpark Town Ctr
1200 Abernathy Rd NE Bldg 600 Ste 950..........Atlanta GA 30328 770-481-1600 481-1640 261
TF: 800-955-1385 ■ *Web:* www.uscost.com

U.S. Council for International Business (USCIB)
1212 Avenue of the Americas.................New York NY 10036 212-354-4480 575-0327 49-12
Web: www.uscib.org
District of Columbia Circuit
333 Constitution Ave NW US Courthouse...Washington DC 20001 202-216-7000 341-1
Web: www.cadc.uscourts.gov
Eight Circuit
111 S Tenth St Rm 24329...............Saint Louis MO 63102 314-244-2400 244-2780 341-1
Web: www.ca8.uscourts.gov
Eleventh Circuit 56 Forsyth St NW...............Atlanta GA 30303 404-335-6100 335-6270 341-1
Web: www.ca11.uscourts.gov
Federal Circuit 717 Madison Pl NW.........Washington DC 20439 202-275-8000 341-1
Web: www.cafc.uscourts.gov
Fifth Circuit 600 Camp St................New Orleans LA 70130 504-310-7700 341-1
Web: www.ca5.uscourts.gov
First Circuit 1 Courthouse Way.................Boston MA 02210 617-748-9057 341-1
Web: www.ca1.uscourts.gov
Fourth Circuit
US Courthouse Annex 1100 E Main St......Richmond VA 23219 804-916-2700 341-1
Web: www.ca4.uscourts.gov
Second Circuit
US Courthouse 40 Foley Sq................New York NY 10007 212-857-8500 341-1
Web: www.ca2.uscourts.gov
Seventh Circuit
33 N Dearborn St Rm 2722 Ste 1830..........Chicago IL 60604 312-435-5850 341-1
Web: www.ca7.uscourts.gov
Sixth Circuit 100 E Fifth St.................Cincinnati OH 45202 513-564-7000 341-1
Web: www.ca6.uscourts.gov
Tenth Circuit 1823 Stout St....................Denver CO 80257 303-844-3157 341-1
Web: www.ca10.uscourts.gov
Third Circuit
US Courthouse 601 Market St............Philadelphia PA 19106 215-597-2995 341-1
Web: www.ca3.uscourts.gov

U.S. Court of Appeals
Circuit 9 PO Box 193939................San Francisco CA 94119 415-355-8000 341-1
Web: www.ca9.uscourts.gov

U.S. Court of Appeals for the Armed Forces
450 E St NW............................Washington DC 20442 202-761-1448 341

U.S. Court of Appeals for Veterans Claims
625 Indiana Ave NW Ste 900...............Washington DC 20004 202-501-5970 501-5848 341
Web: www.uscourts.cavc.gov

U.S. Court of Federal Claims
717 Madison Pl NW......................Washington DC 20439 202-357-6400 341
Web: www.uscfc.uscourts.gov

U.S. Court of International Trade
1 Federal Plz.............................New York NY 10278 212-264-2800 264-1085 341
Web: www.cit.uscourts.gov

U.S. Customs & Border Protection
1300 Pennsylvania Ave NW................Washington DC 20004 703-526-4200 340-11
TF: 877-227-5511 ■ *Web:* www.cbp.gov

U.S. Dairy Export Council
2101 Wilson Blvd Ste 400...................Arlington VA 22201 703-528-3049 528-3705 49-6
Web: www.usdec.org

Name / Address	City	State	ZIP	Phone	Fax	Class
U.S. Dairy Forage Research Ctr (DFRC)						
1925 Linden Dr W	Madison	WI	53706	608-890-0050		668
Web: www.ars.usda.gov						
U.S. Dataworks Inc						
14090 SW Fwy Ste 300	Sugar Land	TX	77478	281-504-8000	565-2567	178-10
OTC: UDWK ■ *TF:* 888-254-8821 ■ *Web:* www.usdataworks.com						
U.S. Department of Education						
Office of Career, Technical & Adult Education						
550 12th St SW 11th Fl	Washington	DC	20202	202-245-7700	245-7838	340-8
Web: www.ed.gov						
Office of Special Education & Rehabilitative Services (OSERS)						
400 Maryland Ave SW	Washington	DC	20202	202-245-7468	872-5327*	340-8
**Fax Area Code:* 800 ■ *Web:* www.ed.gov						
Region 6 350 N Saint Paul St Ste 2900	Dallas	TX	75202	214-661-9600	661-9587	340-8
TF: 877-521-2172 ■ *Web:* www.ed.gov						
U.S. Department of Energy (DOE)						
1000 Independence Ave SW	Washington	DC	20585	202-586-8383	586-4403	340-9
Web: www.energy.gov						
U.S. Department of Health & Human Service						
Region 10 701 Fifth Ave MS 1600	Seattle	WA	98104	206-615-2469		340-10
Web: www.hhs.gov						
U.S. Department of Health & Human Services						
Regions II						
Jacob K Javits Federal Bldg 26 Federal Plz Ste 3835	New York	NY	10278	212-264-2560		340-10
Web: www.hhs.gov						
U.S. Department of Homeland Security						
2703 Martin Luther King Jr Ave SE	Washington	DC	20593	504-393-6005		158
Web: www.uscg.mil						
U.S. Department of Housing & Urban Development						
451 7th St SW	Washington	DC	20410	202-708-1112		803-1
Web: www.hud.gov						
U.S. Department of Justice						
National Security Div						
950 Pennsylvania Ave NW	Washington	DC	20530	202-353-1555		340-14
Web: www.justice.gov						
U.S. Department of The Treasury						
Department of the Treasury Office						
1500 Pennsylvania Ave NW	Washington	DC	20220	202-622-2000	622-6415	340-20
Web: home.treasury.gov						
U.S. Department of Veterans Affairs						
325 E 'H' St	Iron Mountain	MI	49801	906-774-3300		374-8
TF: 800-215-8262 ■ *Web:* www.ironmountain.va.gov						
U.S. Department of Veterans Affairs						
Dayton National Cemetery 4400 W 3rd St	Dayton	OH	45428	937-268-2221	268-2225	136
Web: www.cem.va.gov						
U.S. Digital Corp 1400 NE 136th Ave	Vancouver	WA	98684	360-260-2468	260-2469	178-10
TF: 800-736-0194 ■ *Web:* www.usdigital.com						
U.S. Digital Media Inc						
1929 W Lone Cactus Dr	Phoenix	AZ	85027	623-587-4900	587-4920	547
TF: 877-992-3766 ■ *Web:* www.usdigitalmedia.com						
U.S. Digital Partners LLC						
311 Elm St	Cincinnati	OH	45202	513-929-4603		7
Web: www.usdigitalpartners.com						
U.S. Dismantlement LLC						
2600 S Throop St	Chicago	IL	60608	312-328-1400	328-1477	189-16
Web: www.usdllc.com						
U.S. District Court						
Western District of Washington						
700 Stewart St Ste 2310	Seattle	WA	98101	206-370-8400		341-3
Web: www.wawd.uscourts.gov						
U.S. District Court Alabama Northern						
1729 Fifth Ave N	Birmingham	AL	35203	205-278-1700		341-3
Web: www.alnd.uscourts.gov						
U.S. District Court Arizona						
401 W Washington St Ste 130	Phoenix	AZ	85003	602-322-7200		341-3
Web: www.azd.uscourts.gov						
U.S. District Court California Eastern						
501 I St Rm 4-200	Sacramento	CA	95814	916-930-4000		341-3
Web: www.caed.uscourts.gov						
U.S. District Court California Northern						
450 Golden Gate Ave PO Box 36060	San Francisco	CA	94102	415-522-2000		341-3
Web: www.cand.uscourts.gov						
U.S. District Court California Southern						
221 W Broadway	San Diego	CA	92101	619-557-5600	702-9900	341-3
Web: www.casd.uscourts.gov						
U.S. District Court Colorado						
901 19th St	Denver	CO	80294	303-844-3433	335-2040	341-3
TF: 800-359-8699 ■ *Web:* www.cod.uscourts.gov						
U.S. District Court Connecticut						
141 Church St	New Haven	CT	06510	203-773-2140	773-2334	341-3
Web: www.ctd.uscourts.gov						
U.S. District Court Delaware						
844 N King St Unit 18	Wilmington	DE	19801	302-573-6170		341-3
Web: www.ded.uscourts.gov						
U.S. District Court District of Columbia						
333 Constitution Ave NW Ste 6822	Washington	DC	20001	202-354-3000		341-3
Web: www.dcd.uscourts.gov						
U.S. District Court Eastern District of Virginia						
401 Courthouse Sq	Alexandria	VA	22314	703-299-2100		341-3
TF: 800-743-3873 ■ *Web:* www.vaed.uscourts.gov						
U.S. District Court Florida Middle						
401 W Central Blvd	Orlando	FL	32801	407-835-4200		341-3
Web: www.flmd.uscourts.gov						
U.S. District Court Florida Southern						
301 N Miami Ave	Miami	FL	33128	305-523-5100		341-3
Web: www.flsd.uscourts.gov						
U.S. District Court for the District of Alaska						
222 W Seventh Ave Ste 4	Anchorage	AK	99513	907-677-6100		341-3
TF: 866-243-3814 ■ *Web:* www.akd.uscourts.gov						
U.S. District Court Georgia Middle						
475 Mulberry St	Macon	GA	31201	478-752-3497	752-3496	341-3
Web: www.gamd.uscourts.gov						
U.S. District Court Georgia Northern						
75 Ted Turner Dr SW	Atlanta	GA	30303	404-215-1600		341-3
TF: 800-827-2982 ■ *Web:* www.gand.uscourts.gov						
U.S. District Court Georgia Southern						
PO Box 8286	Savannah	GA	31412	912-650-4081		341-3
Web: www.gasd.uscourts.gov						
U.S. District Court Guam						
520 W Soledad Ave 4th Fl	Hagatna	GU	96910	671-969-4500	969-4488	341-3
Web: www.gud.uscourts.gov						
U.S. District Court Hawaii						
300 Ala Moana Blvd Rm C-338	Honolulu	HI	96850	808-541-1300		341-3
Web: www.hid.uscourts.gov						
U.S. District Court Illinois Central						
600 E Monroe St Ste 226	Springfield	IL	62701	217-492-4020	492-4028	341-3
Web: www.ilcd.uscourts.gov						
U.S. District Court Illinois Southern						
750 Missouri Ave	East Saint Louis	IL	62201	618-482-9371	482-9383	341-3
Web: www.ilsd.uscourts.gov						
U.S. District Court Indiana Northern						
204 S Main St	South Bend	IN	46601	574-246-8000		341-3
Web: www.innd.uscourts.gov						
U.S. District Court Indiana Southern						
46 E Ohio St	Indianapolis	IN	46204	317-229-3700	229-3959	341-3
Web: www.insd.uscourts.gov						
U.S. District Court Iowa Northern						
111 Seventh Ave SE	Cedar Rapids	IA	52401	319-286-2300	286-2301	341-3
Web: www.iand.uscourts.gov						
U.S. District Court Iowa Southern						
123 E Walnut St	Des Moines	IA	50309	515-284-6248	284-6418	341-3
Web: www.iasd.uscourts.gov						
U.S. District Court Kansas						
500 State Ave	Kansas City	KS	66101	913-735-2200		341-3
Web: www.ksd.uscourts.gov						
U.S. District Court Kentucky Eastern						
101 Barr St	Lexington	KY	40507	859-233-2503		341-3
Web: www.kyed.uscourts.gov						
U.S. District Court Kentucky Western						
601 W Broadway Rm 106	Louisville	KY	40202	502-625-3500	625-3880	341-3
Web: www.kywd.uscourts.gov						
U.S. District Court Louisiana Eastern						
500 Poydras St Rm C-151	New Orleans	LA	70130	504-589-7650		341-3
Web: www.laed.uscourts.gov						
U.S. District Court Louisiana Middle						
777 Florida St Ste 139	Baton Rouge	LA	70801	225-389-3500	389-3501	341-3
Web: www.lamd.uscourts.gov						
U.S. District Court Louisiana Western						
300 Fannin St Ste 1167	Shreveport	LA	71101	318-676-4273	676-3962	341-3
Web: www.lawd.uscourts.gov						
U.S. District Court Maine						
156 Federal St	Portland	ME	04101	207-274-5147		341-3
Web: www.med.uscourts.gov						
U.S. District Court Maryland						
101 W Lombard St	Baltimore	MD	21201	410-962-2600		341-3
Web: www.mdd.uscourts.gov						
U.S. District Court Massachusetts						
1 Courthouse Way Ste 2300	Boston	MA	02210	617-748-9152		341-3
Web: www.mad.uscourts.gov						
U.S. District Court Michigan Eastern						
231 W Lafayette Blvd	Detroit	MI	48226	313-234-5005		341-3
Web: www.mied.uscourts.gov						
U.S. District Court Minnesota						
300 S 4th St Ste 202	Minneapolis	MN	55415	612-664-5000	664-5033	341-3
Web: www.mnd.uscourts.gov						
U.S. District Court Mississippi Northern						
911 Jackson Ave E Rm 369	Oxford	MS	38655	662-234-1971		341-3
Web: www.msnd.uscourts.gov						
U.S. District Court Mississippi Southern						
501 E Court St Ste 2500	Jackson	MS	39201	601-965-4439		341-3
TF: 866-517-7682 ■ *Web:* www.mssd.uscourts.gov						
U.S. District Court Missouri Eastern						
111 S Tenth St Ste 3300	Saint Louis	MO	63102	314-244-7900	244-7909	341-3
Web: www.moed.uscourts.gov						
U.S. District Court Missouri Western						
400 E Ninth St	Kansas City	MO	64106	816-512-5000		341-3
TF: 800-466-9302 ■ *Web:* www.mow.uscourts.gov						
U.S. District Court Montana						
2601 Second Ave N	Billings	MT	59101	406-247-7000	542-7272	341-3
Web: www.mtd.uscourts.gov						
U.S. District Court Nebraska						
111 S 18th Plz Ste 1152	Omaha	NE	68102	402-661-7350	661-7387	341-3
TF: 866-220-4381 ■ *Web:* www.ned.uscourts.gov						
U.S. District Court Nevada						
333 Las Vegas Blvd S	Las Vegas	NV	89101	702-464-5400		341-3
Web: www.nvd.uscourts.gov						
U.S. District Court New Hampshire						
55 Pleasant St Rm 110	Concord	NH	03301	603-225-1423		341-3
Web: www.nhd.uscourts.gov						
U.S. District Court New Jersey						
50 Walnut St	Newark	NJ	07101	973-645-3730		341-3
Web: www.njd.uscourts.gov						
U.S. District Court New York Northern						
100 S Clinton St PO Box 7367	Syracuse	NY	13261	315-234-8500		341-3
Web: www.nynd.uscourts.gov						
U.S. District Court New York Southern						
500 Pearl St	New York	NY	10007	212-805-0136		341-3
Web: www.nysd.uscourts.gov						
U.S. District Court New York Western						
2 Niagara Sq	Buffalo	NY	14202	716-551-4211		341-3
Web: www.nywd.uscourts.gov						
U.S. District Court North Carolina Eastern						
PO Box 25670	Raleigh	NC	27611	919-645-1700	645-1750	341-3
Web: www.nced.uscourts.gov						
U.S. District Court North Carolina Middle						
324 W Market St	Greensboro	NC	27401	336-332-6000	332-6060	341-3
Web: www.ncmd.uscourts.gov						
U.S. District Court North Dakota						
PO Box 1193	Bismarck	ND	58502	701-530-2300	530-2312	341-3
Web: www.ndd.uscourts.gov						
U.S. District Court Northern District of Florida						
111 N Adams St	Tallahassee	FL	32301	850-521-3501	521-3656	341-3
Web: www.flnd.uscourts.gov						
U.S. District Court Northern District of Illinois						
219 S Dearborn St Everett McKinley Dirksen United States Courthouse	Chicago	IL	60604	312-435-5670		341-3
Web: www.ilnd.uscourts.gov						

	Phone	Fax	Class
U.S. District Court Ohio Northern 801 W Superior Ave .... Cleveland OH 44113 *TF:* 800-355-8498 ■ *Web:* www.ohnd.uscourts.gov	216-357-7000	357-7040	341-3
U.S. District Court Ohio Southern 85 Marconi Blvd .... Columbus OH 43215 *Web:* www.ohsd.uscourts.gov	614-719-3000		341-3
U.S. District Court Oklahoma Eastern PO Box 607 .... Muskogee OK 74402 *Web:* www.oked.uscourts.gov	918-684-7920	684-7902	341-3
U.S. District Court Oklahoma Northern 333 W Fourth St .... Tulsa OK 74103 *TF:* 866-213-1957 ■ *Web:* oknd.uscourts.gov	918-699-4700		341-3
U.S. District Court Oklahoma Western 200 NW 4th St Rm 1210 .... Oklahoma City OK 73102 *TF:* 888-609-6953 ■ *Web:* www.okwd.uscourts.gov	405-609-5000	609-5099	341-3
U.S. District Court Oregon 1000 SW Third Ave .... Portland OR 97204 *Web:* www.ord.uscourts.gov	503-326-8000		341-3
U.S. District Court Pennsylvania Eastern 601 Market St .... Philadelphia PA 19106 *Web:* www.paed.uscourts.gov	215-597-7704	597-6390	341-3
U.S. District Court Pennsylvania Middle 235 N Washington Ave .... Scranton PA 18503 *Web:* www.pamd.uscourts.gov	570-207-5600	207-5650	341-3
U.S. District Court Pennsylvania Western 700 Grant St .... Pittsburgh PA 15219 *Web:* www.pawd.uscourts.gov	412-208-7500		341-3
U.S. District Court South Carolina 901 Richland St .... Columbia SC 29201 *Web:* www.scd.uscourts.gov	803-765-5816		341-3
U.S. District Court South Dakota 400 S Phillips Ave Rm 128 .... Sioux Falls SD 57104 *Web:* www.sdd.uscourts.gov	605-330-6600	330-6601	341-3
U.S. District Court Tennessee Middle 801 Broadway Rm 800 .... Nashville TN 37203 *Web:* www.tnmd.uscourts.gov	615-736-5498	736-7488	341-3
U.S. District Court Tennessee Western 167 N Main St Rm 242 .... Memphis TN 38103 *Web:* www.tnwd.uscourts.gov	901-495-1200	495-1250	341-3
U.S. District Court Texas Eastern 211 W Ferguson St .... Tyler TX 75702 *Web:* www.txed.uscourts.gov	903-590-1000		341-3
U.S. District Court Texas Northern 1100 Commerce St Rm 1452 .... Dallas TX 75242 *Web:* www.txnd.uscourts.gov	214-753-2200	753-2266	341-3
U.S. District Court Texas Southern 515 Rusk St .... Houston TX 77002 *Web:* www.txs.uscourts.gov	713-250-5500		341-3
U.S. District Court U.S. Virgin Islands 3013 Estate Golden Rock Almeric L Christian Federal Bldg Ste 219 .... Saint Croix VI 00820 *Web:* www.vid.uscourts.gov	340-773-1130	773-1563	341-3
U.S. District Court Utah 351 S West Temple Rm 1100 .... Salt Lake City UT 84101 *Web:* www.utd.uscourts.gov	801-524-6100		341-3
U.S. District Court Vermont 11 Elmwood Ave Rm 506 .... Burlington VT 05401 *TF:* 800-837-8718 ■ *Web:* www.vtd.uscourts.gov	802-951-6301		341-3
U.S. District Court Virginia Western 180 W Main St Rm 104 .... Abingdon VA 24210 *Web:* www.vawd.uscourts.gov	540-857-5100	857-5110	341-3
U.S. District Court Washington Eastern 920 W Riverside Ave Rm 840 .... Spokane WA 99201 *Web:* www.waed.uscourts.gov	509-458-3400	458-3420	341-3
U.S. District Court West Virginia Northern The Jennings Randolph Federal Ctr 300 3rd St PO Box 1518 .... Elkins WV 26241 *Web:* www.wvnd.uscourts.gov	304-636-1445	636-5746	341-3
U.S. District Court Wisconsin Eastern 517 E Wisconsin Ave .... Milwaukee WI 53202 *Web:* www.wied.uscourts.gov	414-297-3372		341-3
U.S. District Court Wisconsin Western 120 N Henry St Rm 320 .... Madison WI 53703 *Web:* www.wiwd.uscourts.gov	608-264-5156	264-5925	341-3
U.S. District Court Wyoming 2120 Capitol Ave Rm 2131 .... Cheyenne WY 82001 *Web:* www.wyd.uscourts.gov	307-433-2120	433-2152	341-3
U.S. Eagle Federal Credit Union 3939 Osuna Rd NE PO Box 129 .... Albuquerque NM 87109 *TF:* 888-342-8766 ■ *Web:* www.useagle.org	505-342-8888		219
U.S. Ecology 300 E Mallard Dr Ste 300 .... Boise ID 83706 *NASDAQ: ECOL* ■ *TF:* 800-590-5220 ■ *Web:* www.usecology.com	208-331-8400	331-7900	667
U.S. Election Assistance Commission 1201 New York Ave NW Ste 300 .... Washington DC 20005 *TF:* 866-747-1471 ■ *Web:* www.eac.gov	202-566-3100	566-3127	340-20
U.S. Electronics Inc 900 Colorado Ave S .... Minneapolis MN 55416 *Web:* usei.com	763-546-8208	545-8206	52
U.S. Employees O C Federal Credit Union 4301 S I-44 .... Oklahoma City OK 73144 *TF:* 800-227-6366 ■ *Web:* www.usecreditunion.org	405-685-6200	682-6235	219
U.S. Energy Corp 877 N Eigth W .... Riverton WY 82501 *NASDAQ: USEG* ■ *TF:* 800-776-9271 ■ *Web:* www.usnrg.com	307-856-9271	857-3050	502
U.S. Energy Development Corp 2350 N Forest Rd .... Getzville NY 14068 *TF:* 800-636-7606 ■ *Web:* usedc.com	716-636-0401		540
U.S. Engineering Co 3433 Roanoke Rd .... Kansas City MO 64111 *Web:* www.usengineering.com	816-753-6969	931-5773	189-10
U.S. Equestrian Federation Inc 4047 Iron Works Pkwy .... Lexington KY 40511 *TF:* 800-633-2472 ■ *Web:* www.usef.org	859-258-2472	231-6662	48-22
U.S. Equestrian Team Foundation Inc (USET) PO Box 355 .... Gladstone NJ 07934 *Web:* www.uset.org	908-234-1251	234-0670	48-22
U.S. Equipment Co 20580 Hoover Rd .... Detroit MI 48205 *Web:* www.usequipment.com	313-526-8300	526-5303	491
U.S. Facilities Inc 30 N 41 St Ste 400 .... Philadelphia PA 19104 *TF:* 800-236-6241 ■ *Web:* usfacilities.com	800-236-6241		192
U.S. Farathane Corp 38000 Mound Rd .... Sterling Heights MI 48310 *Web:* www.usfarathane.com	586-979-7400		608
U.S. Farm Data Inc 10824 Old Mill Rd Ste 8 .... Omaha NE 68154 *TF:* 800-960-6267 ■ *Web:* www.usfarmdata.com	800-960-6267		387
U.S. FDA *Southwest Region* 4040 N Central Expwy Ste 900 .... Dallas TX 75204 *Web:* www.fda.gov	214-253-4946	253-4960	340-10
U.S. Federal Bureau of Investigation Library 935 Pennsylvania Ave NW .... Washington DC 20535 *Web:* www.fbilibrary.fbiacademy.edu	703-632-3200	632-3214	434-3
U.S. Fencing Assn (USFA) 1 Olympic Plz .... Colorado Springs CO 80909 *Web:* www.usafencing.org	719-866-4511	632-5737	48-22
U.S. Figure Skating Assn (USFSA) 20 1st St .... Colorado Springs CO 80906 *TF:* 800-332-9256 ■ *Web:* www.usfigureskating.org	719-635-5200	635-9548	48-22
U.S. Fish & Wildlife Service Regional Offices *Alaska Region* 1011 E Tudor Rd .... Anchorage AK 99503 *Web:* www.fws.gov	907-786-3309	786-3495	340-13
California & Nevada Region 2800 Cottage Way .... Sacramento CA 95825 *Web:* www.fws.gov	916-414-6464	414-6486	340-13
Great Lakes/Big Rivers Region 5600 American Blvd W Ste 900 .... Bloomington MN 55437 *Web:* www.fws.gov	612-713-5360	713-5280	340-13
Mountain-Prairie Region 134 Union Blvd .... Lakewood CO 80228 *Web:* www.fws.gov	303-236-7905	236-8295	340-13
Northeast Region 300 Westgate Center Dr .... Hadley MA 01035 *Web:* www.fws.gov	413-253-8200	253-8308	340-13
Pacific Region Eastside Federal Complex 911 NE 11th Ave .... Portland OR 97232 **Fax Area Code:* 503 ■ *Web:* www.fws.gov	703-358-2196	231-6161*	340-13
Southeast Region 1875 Century Blvd 3rd Fl .... Atlanta GA 30345 *Web:* www.fws.gov	404-679-4000	679-4006	340-13
Southwest Region 500 Gold Ave SW PO Box 1306 .... Albuquerque NM 87102 *Web:* www.fws.gov	505-248-6911	248-6910	340-13
U.S. Fitness Products 5912 Oleander Dr .... Wilmington NC 28403 *Web:* www.usfitness.com	910-790-2029		711
U.S. Fleet Forces Command 1562 Mitscher Ave Ste 250 .... Norfolk VA 23551 *TF:* 800-473-3549 ■ *Web:* www.public.navy.mil	757-836-3630	836-3603	497-4
U.S. Foods 2621 Fairview Ave N .... Roseville MN 55113 *Web:* www.us-foods-culinary-equipment-supplies.business.site	651-638-8993		300
U.S. Forest Service *Alaska Regional Office* PO Box 21628 .... Juneau AK 99802 *Web:* www.fs.usda.gov	907-586-8806		340-1
U.S. Fund for UNICEF 125 Maiden Ln .... New York NY 10038 **Fax Area Code:* 212 ■ *TF:* 800-367-5437 ■ *Web:* www.unicefusa.org	800-367-5437	779-1679*	48-5
U.S. General Services Administration 1800 F St NW .... Washington DC 20405 *TF:* 800-488-3111 ■ *Web:* www.usa.gov	800-488-3111		340-20
U.S. Global Investors Inc 7900 Callaghan Rd .... San Antonio TX 78229 *NASDAQ: GROW* ■ *TF:* 800-873-8637 ■ *Web:* www.usfunds.com	210-308-1234	308-1223	401
U.S. Golf Assn (USGA) 77 Liberty Corner Rd .... Far Hills NJ 07931 *TF:* 800-336-4446 ■ *Web:* www.usga.org	908-234-2300	234-9687	48-22
U.S. Government Accountability Office *Chicago Office* 200 W Adams St Ste 700 .... Chicago IL 60606 *Web:* www.gao.gov	312-220-7600	220-7726	342
U.S. Government Printing Office Bookstore (GPO) 732 N Capitol St NW .... Washington DC 20401 *TF:* 866-512-1800 ■ *Web:* bookstore.gpo.gov	202-512-1800	512-2104	342
U.S. Graphite Inc 1620 E Holland Ave .... Saginaw MI 48601 *TF:* 877-773-2560 ■ *Web:* www.usggledco.co.uk	989-755-0441	755-0445	127
U.S. Health & Human Services Dept *Region 8* 1961 Stout St Rm 08-148 .... Denver CO 80294 *Web:* www.hhs.gov	303-844-7860		340-10
Region 9 90 Seventh St Ste 4-100 .... San Francisco CA 94103 **Fax Area Code:* 415 ■ *TF:* 800-368-1019 ■ *Web:* www.hhs.gov	800-368-1019	437-8329*	340-10
U.S. Health and Life Insurance Co 8220 Irving Rd .... Sterling Heights MI 48312 *Web:* www.ushealthandlife.com	586-693-4400		796
U.S. Health Connect Inc 500 Office Center Dr .... Fort Washington PA 19034 *TF:* 800-889-4944 ■ *Web:* omniaeducation.com	800-889-4944		162
U.S. Holocaust Memorial Museum 100 Raoul Wallenburg Pl SW .... Washington DC 20024 *Web:* www.ushmm.org	202-488-0400		520
U.S. Horticultural Research Laboratory 2001 S Rock Rd .... Fort Pierce FL 34945 *Web:* www.ars.usda.gov	772-462-5800	462-5986	668
U.S. House of Representatives 217 Ford House Office Bldg .... Washington DC 20515 *Web:* www.house.gov	202-225-6999		342
U.S. House of Representatives *Armed Services Committee* 2216 Rayburn House Office Bldg .... Washington DC 20515 *Web:* armedservices.house.gov	202-225-4151	225-9077	342-1
Committee on Education & the Workforce 2176 Rayburn House Office Bldg .... Washington DC 20515 *Web:* www.house.gov	202-225-4527		342-1
Committee on Natural Resources 1324 Longworth Bldg .... Washington DC 20515 *Web:* naturalresources.house.gov	202-225-2761	225-5929	342-1
Committee on Rules H-312 Capitol Bldg .... Washington DC 20515 *Web:* rules.house.gov	202-225-9191		342-1

Phone | Fax | Class

Committee on Ways & Means
1102 Longworth Bldg Washington DC 20515 202-225-3625 225-2610 342-1
Web: www.waysandmeans.house.gov
Government Reform Committee
2157 Rayburn House Office Bldg Washington DC 20515 202-225-5074 225-3974 342-1
Web: oversight.house.gov
Homeland Security Committee
176 Ford House Office Bldg Washington DC 20515 202-226-8417 226-3399 342-1
Web: homeland.house.gov
House Administration Committee
1309 Longworth Bldg Washington DC 20515 202-225-2061 225-9957 342-1
Web: cha.house.gov
House Committee on Agriculture
1301 Longworth Bldg Washington DC 20515 202-225-2171 225-0917 342-1
Web: agriculture.house.gov
House Committee on Foreign Affairs
2170 Rayburn Bldg Washington DC 20515 202-225-5021 225-5394 342-1
Web: foreignaffairs.house.gov
Judiciary Committee
2138 Rayburn Bldg Washington DC 20515 202-225-3951 342-1
Web: www.judiciary.house.gov
Small Business Committee
2361 Rayburn Bldg Washington DC 20515 202-225-5821 342-1
Web: smallbusiness.house.gov
Transportation & Infrastructure Committee
2165 Rayburn Bldg Washington DC 20515 202-225-9446 342-1
Web: transportation.house.gov

U.S. Imagineering Inc
825 Schoenhaar Dr West Bend WI 53090 262-334-3000 334-6222 628
TF: 800-419-3001 ■ *Web:* www.silverprofit.com

U.S. Immigration & Customs Enforcement (ICE)
425 'I' St NW Washington DC 20536 866-347-2423 340-11
TF: 866-347-2423 ■ *Web:* www.ice.gov

U.S. Industrial Coatings Inc
PO Box 3200 Framingham MA 01705 508-980-1000 637-5800 802
TF: 800-905-2801 ■ *Web:* www.floorepoxy.com

U.S. Industrial Fasteners of Arizona Inc
2026 E Cedar St Tempe AZ 85281 480-967-8702 967-1907 351
TF: 800-289-5386 ■ *Web:* usifaz.com

U.S. Industries Inc 1701 1st Ave Evansville IN 47710 812-425-2428 189-12

U.S. Institute of Peace
2301 Constitution Ave NW Washington DC 20037 202-457-1700 429-6063 340-20
TF: 800-868-8064 ■ *Web:* www.usip.org

U.S. International Trade Commission
500 East St SW Washington DC 20436 202-205-2000 340-20
Web: www.usitc.gov

U.S. Internet Corp
12450 Wayzata Blvd Ste 224 Minnetonka MN 55305 952-253-3262 545-0302 225
TF: 800-874-6837 ■ *Web:* www.usinternet.com

U.S. Japan Business Council
1615 H St NW Washington DC 20062 202-463-5772 49-12
Web: www.uschamber.com

U.S. Kids Golf LLC
3040 Northwoods Pkwy Norcross GA 30071 770-441-3077 711
TF: 888-387-5437 ■ *Web:* www.uskidsgolf.com

U.S. Lawns Inc 6700 Forum Dr Ste 150 Orlando FL 32821 407-246-1630 422
TF: 800-875-2967 ■ *Web:* uslawns.com

U.S. Legal Support Inc
363 N Sam Houston Pkwy E Ste 1200 Houston TX 77060 713-653-7100 653-7171 445
TF: 800-567-8757 ■ *Web:* www.uslegalsupport.com

U.S. Linen & Uniform Inc
1106 Harding St Richland WA 99352 509-946-6125 442
TF: 888-875-4636 ■ *Web:* uslinen.com

U.S. Lumber Coalition
1750 K St NW Ste 800 Washington DC 20006 703-597-8651 48-12
Web: uslumbercoalition.org

U.S. Lumber Group Inc
2160 Satellite Blvd Ste 450 Duluth GA 30097 678-474-4577 474-4575 191-3
TF: 800-443-8806 ■ *Web:* www.uslumber.com

U.S. Magnesium LLC
238 North 2200 West Salt Lake City UT 84116 801-532-2043 534-1407 485
Web: usmagnesium.com

U.S. Marine Corps
3000 Marine Corps Pentagon Rm 2C253 Washington DC 20350 703-693-3088 614-6539 340-7
Web: www.hqmc.marines.mil
Commandant
1712 I St NW Rm 4C645 Ste 200 Washington DC 20350 703-614-1872 693-4414 340-7
Web: usmcbirthdayball.com

U.S. Marshals Service
401 Courthouse Sq Alexandria VA 22314 202-307-9100 340-14
TF: 800-336-0102 ■ *Web:* www.usmarshals.gov

U.S. Materials Handling Corp 2231 NY-5 Utica NY 13502 315-732-4111 732-0149 358
Web: www.usmaterialshandling.com

U.S. Meat Export Federation Inc (USMEF)
1050 17th St Ste 2200 Denver CO 80265 303-623-6328 623-0297 49-6
Web: www.usmef.org

U.S. Med-Equip Inc
9777 W Gulf Bank Ste 20 Houston TX 77040 713-983-8860 475
TF: 877-677-7767 ■ *Web:* usme.com

U.S. Media Consulting
1221 Brickell Ave Ste 600 Miami FL 33131 305-722-5500 7
Web: www.usmediaconsulting.com

U.S. Medical Management LLC (USMM)
500 Kirts Blvd Troy MI 48084 248-824-6000 463
Web: www.usmmllc.com

U.S. Merchant Marine Academy
300 Steamboat Rd Kings Point NY 11024 516-726-5800 773-5390 166
TF: 866-546-4778 ■ *Web:* www.usmma.edu

U.S. Metals Inc 19102 Gundle Rd Houston TX 77073 281-443-7473 443-6748 492
Web: www.usmetals.com

U.S. Metric Association Inc (USMA)
10245 Andasol Ave Northridge CA 91325 310-832-3763 48-10
Web: www.usma.org

U.S. Mexico Chamber of Commerce
1300 Pennsylvania Ave NW Ste 0003 Washington DC 20004 202-312-1520 312-1530 138
Web: www.usmcoc.org

U.S. Military Academy
Admissions Bldg 606 West Point NY 10996 845-938-4041 938-8121 498
Web: www.usma.edu

Phone | Fax | Class

U.S. Mint 801 Ninth St NW Washington DC 20220 202-354-7462 340-18
Web: www.usmint.gov

U.S. Mint
Denver 320 W Colfax Ave Denver CO 80204 303-405-4761 340-18
TF: 800-642-6116 ■ *Web:* usmint.gov
Philadelphia 1201 Elm St Ste 400 Dallas TX 75270 800-872-6468 340-18
TF: 800-872-6468 ■ *Web:* www.usmint.gov
San Francisco 155 Hermann St San Francisco CA 94102 415-575-8000 340-18
Web: www.usmint.gov
West Point (NY) 1063 NY 218 West Point NY 10996 845-446-6200 340-18
Web: www.usmint.gov

U.S. Monitor 86 Maple Ave New City NY 10956 845-634-1331 5
TF: 800-767-7967 ■ *Web:* usmonitor.com

U.S. Nameplate Co
2100 Hwy 30 W PO Box 10 Mount Vernon IA 52314 319-895-8804 895-8635 701
TF: 800-553-8871 ■ *Web:* www.usnameplate.com

U.S. National Arboretum
3501 New York Ave Washington DC 20002 202-245-2726 97
Web: usna.usda.gov

U.S. National Central Bureau of INTERPOL (INTERPOL)
950 Pennsylvania Ave NW Washington DC 20530 202-616-9000 616-8400 340-14
Web: www.justice.gov

U.S. National Committee to the International Dairy Federation
PO Box 930398 Verona WI 53593 608-219-4115 262-1278 296-10
Web: www.usnac.org

U.S. National Ski Hall of Fame
610 Palms Ave Ishpeming MI 49849 906-485-6323 486-4570 522
TF: 800-648-0720 ■ *Web:* www.skihall.com

U.S. Naval Academy 121 Blake Rd Annapolis MD 21402 410-293-1000 498
TF: 888-249-7707 ■ *Web:* www.usna.edu

U.S. Naval Institute 291 Wood Rd Annapolis MD 21402 410-268-6110 295-1084 48-19
TF: 800-233-8764 ■ *Web:* www.usni.org

U.S. Navy Memorial & Naval Heritage Ctr
701 Pennsylvania Ave NW Washington DC 20004 202-737-2300 50-4
Web: www.navymemorial.org

U.S. Netcom Corp 710 S Maiden Ln Joplin MO 64801 417-659-8040 809

U.S. Networx Inc 6360 I 55 N Ste 310 Jackson MS 39211 601-956-4770 177
Web: www.usnx.com

U.S. News & World Report
1050 Thomas Jefferson St NW Washington DC 20007 202-955-2225 457-17
TF: 800-836-6397 ■ *Web:* www.usnews.com

U.S. Office of Government Ethics
1201 New York Ave NW Ste 500 Washington DC 20005 202-482-9300 482-9237 265
Web: www.oge.gov

U.S. Oil & Refining Co
3001 Marshall Ave Tacoma WA 98421 253-383-1651 383-9970 580
Web: www.usor.com

U.S. Ordnance Inc 300 Sydney Dr McCarran NV 89434 775-343-1320 343-1331 807
Web: www.usord.com

U.S. Pan Asian American Chamber of Commerce (USPAACC)
1329 18th St NW Washington DC 20036 202-296-5221 296-5225 48-14
TF: 800-696-7818 ■ *Web:* uspaacc.com

U.S. Paper Counters 138 Elizabeth Terr Cairo NY 12413 518-622-2600 622-2695 495
TF: 888-407-3966 ■ *Web:* www.wecount.com

U.S. Parachute Assn (USPA)
5401 Southpoint Center Blvd Fredericksburg VA 22407 540-604-9740 604-9741 48-22
Web: uspa.org

U.S. Parole Commission
5550 Friendship Blvd Rm 420 Chevy Chase MD 20815 202-346-7000 340-14
TF: 888-585-9103 ■ *Web:* www.justice.gov

U.S. Penitentiary (USP)
Allenwood PO Box 3500 White Deer PA 17887 570-547-0963 547-9201 212
Web: www.bop.gov
Atwater 1 Federal Way PO Box 019001 Atwater CA 95301 209-386-0257 386-4635 212
Web: www.bop.gov
Lewisburg 2400 Robert F Miller Dr Lewisburg PA 17837 570-523-1251 522-7745 212
Web: www.bop.gov
Pollock 1000 Airbase Rd Pollock LA 71467 318-561-5300 561-5391 212
Web: www.bop.gov

U.S. Pharmacist Magazine
160 Chubb Ave Ste 304 Lyndhurst NJ 07071 800-825-4696 457-16
TF: 800-825-4696 ■ *Web:* www.uspharmacist.com

U.S. Pharmacopeia (USP)
12601 Twinbrook Pkwy Rockville MD 20852 301-881-0666 49-8
TF: 800-227-8772 ■ *Web:* www.usp.org

U.S. Physical Therapy
1300 W Sam Houston Pkwy S Ste 300 Houston TX 77042 713-297-7000 297-7090 352
NYSE: USPH ■ *TF:* 800-580-6285 ■ *Web:* www.usph.com

U.S. Pipe & Foundry Co
2 Chase Corporate Dr Ste 200 Birmingham AL 35244 866-347-7473 307
TF: 866-347-7473 ■ *Web:* www.uspipe.com

U.S. Plastic Corp 1390 Newbrecht Rd Lima OH 45801 419-228-2242 228-5034 199
TF: 800-537-9724 ■ *Web:* www.usplastic.com

U.S. Polymers-Accurez LLC
300 E Primm St Saint Louis MO 63111 314-638-1632 638-3100 550
Web: www.uspolymers.com

U.S. Postal Service (USPS)
475 L'Enfant Plz W SW Washington DC 20260 202-268-2608 340-20
Web: www.usps.com

U.S. Postal Service Federal Credit Union
7905 Malcolm Rd Ste 311 Clinton MD 20735 301-856-5000 219
TF: 800-877-7328 ■ *Web:* www.uspsfcu.org

U.S. Poultry & Egg Assn
1530 Cooledge Rd Tucker GA 30084 770-493-9401 493-9257 48-2
Web: www.uspoultry.org

U.S. Premium Beef LLC (USPB)
PO Box 20103 Kansas City MO 64195 816-713-8800 713-8810 296-26
TF: 866-877-2525 ■ *Web:* www.uspb.com

U.S. Products Inc 252 Depot Rd Milford CT 06460 203-783-1468 874-2830 559
Web: www.us-prod.com

U.S. Professional Tennis Assn (USPTA)
11961 Performance Dr Orlando FL 32827 800-877-8248 978-7780* 48-22
**Fax Area Code:* 713 ■ *TF:* 800-877-8248 ■ *Web:* uspta.com

U.S. Protection Service LLC
5785 Emporium Sq Columbus OH 43231 614-794-4950 693
Web: www.uspsvc.com

U.S. Public Interest Research Group
218 D St SE Washington DC 20003 202-546-9707 633
Web: uspirg.org

				Phone	Fax	Class
U.S. Quality Furniture Services Inc 8920 Winkler Dr *TF:* 800-774-8700 ■ *Web:* www.usqfs.com	Houston	TX	77017	800-774-8700	471-9199	321
U.S. Railroad Retirement Board 844 N Rush St *Web:* www.rrb.gov	Chicago	IL	60611	312-751-7102	751-7136	340-20
U.S. Reflector 126 Dewey St *TF:* 800-414-5024 ■ *Web:* www.usreflector.com	Worcester	MA	01610	508-753-6373	753-2142	61
U.S. Renewables Group LLC 2425 Olympic Blvd Ste 4050 W *Web:* usregroup.com	Santa Monica	CA	90404	310-586-3900		401
U.S. Residential Group LLC 5001 Spring Valley Rd Ste 1000 E *TF:* 833-263-5627 ■ *Web:* www.usrgroup.com	Dallas	TX	75244	469-546-6400		652
U.S. Resources Inc 115 Beulah Rd Ste 200-C *Web:* usresources.com	Vienna	VA	22180	703-891-5700		180
U.S. Ring Binder 6800 Arsenal St *TF:* 800-888-8772 ■ *Web:* www.usring.com	Saint Louis	MO	63139	314-645-7880	645-7239	86
U.S. Risk Insurance Group Inc 10210 N Central Expy *TF:* 800-926-9155 ■ *Web:* www.usrisk.com	Dallas	TX	75231	214-265-7090	739-1421	390
U.S. Robotics Corp 1300 E Woodfield Dr Ste 506 *TF:* 877-710-0884 ■ *Web:* www.usr.com	Schaumburg	IL	60173	847-874-2000	874-2001	173-3
U.S. Rowing Assn 2 Wall St *TF:* 800-314-4769 ■ *Web:* www.usrowing.org	Princeton	NJ	08540	609-924-1578		48-22
U.S. Rubber Corp 211 E Loop 336 *TF:* 800-872-3587 ■ *Web:* www.usrubbercorp.com	Conroe	TX	77301	800-872-3587		370
U.S. Russia Business Council 1110 Vermont Ave NW Ste 350 *Web:* www.usrbc.org	Washington	DC	20005	202-739-9180	659-5920	49-12
U.S. Sailing Assn 15 Maritime Dr PO Box 1260 *TF:* 800-877-2451 ■ *Web:* www.ussailing.org	Portsmouth	RI	02871	401-683-0800	683-0840	48-22
U.S. Salinity Laboratory USDA/ARS 450 W Big Springs Rd *Web:* www.ars.usda.gov	Riverside	CA	92507	951-369-4815	369-4818	668
U.S. Secret Service 245 Murray Ln *TF:* 888-813-8777 ■ *Web:* www.secretservice.gov	Washington	DC	20223	202-406-5708		340-11
U.S. Security Associates Inc 200 Mansell Ct 5th Fl *TF:* 800-730-9599 ■ *Web:* www.ussecurityassociates.com	Roswell	GA	30076	770-625-1500		693
U.S. Security Inc 4544 NW Tenth St *TF:* 888-708-3377 ■ *Web:* www.ussecurity.com	Oklahoma City	OK	73127	405-947-3377		693
U.S. Senate						
Agriculture Nutrition & Forestry Committee 328A Russell Senate Office Bldg *Web:* www.agriculture.senate.gov	Washington	DC	20510	202-224-2035	228-2125	342-1
Commerce Science & Transportation Committee 512 Dirksen Senate Bldg *Web:* www.commerce.senate.gov	Washington	DC	20510	202-224-1251		342-1
Committee on Budget 624 Drksen Senate Office Bldg. *Web:* www.budget.senate.gov	Washington	DC	20510	202-224-0642		342-1
Committee on Finance 219 Dirksen Senate Office Bldg *Web:* www.finance.senate.gov	Washington	DC	20510	202-224-4515	228-0554	342-1
Committee on the Judiciary 224 Dirksen Senate Office Bldg *Web:* www.judiciary.senate.gov	Washington	DC	20510	202-224-5225		342-1
Committee on Veterans Affairs 412 Russell Bldg *Web:* www.veterans.senate.gov	Washington	DC	20510	202-224-9126		342-1
Environment & Public Works 410 Dirksen Senate Office Bldg *Web:* www.epw.senate.gov	Washington	DC	20510	202-224-8832		342-1
Homeland Security & Governmental Affairs Committee 340 Dirksen Senate Office Bldg *Web:* www.hsgac.senate.gov	Washington	DC	20510	202-224-2627		342-1
Select Committee on Ethics United States Senate 220 Hart Bldg *Web:* www.ethics.senate.gov	Washington	DC	20510	202-224-2981	224-7416	265
U.S. Senate Committee						
Energy & Natural Resources 304 Dirksen Senate Bldg *Web:* www.energy.senate.gov	Washington	DC	20510	202-224-4971	224-6163	342-1
Foreign Relations 423 Dirksen Senate Office Bldg *Web:* www.foreign.senate.gov	Washington	DC	20510	202-224-4651		342-1
U.S. Senate Committee on Indian Affairs 838 Hart Bldg *Web:* www.indian.senate.gov	Washington	DC	20510	202-224-2251	228-2589	342-1
U.S. Senate Select Committee on Intelligence 211 Hart Senate Office Bldg *Web:* www.intelligence.senate.gov	Washington	DC	20510	202-224-1700	224-1772	342-1
U.S. Sentencing Commission 1 Columbus Cir NE Ste 2 500 S Lobby *Web:* www.ussc.gov	Washington	DC	20002	202-502-4500		341
U.S. Shipping Corp 399 Thornall St 8th Fl *TF:* 866-942-6592 ■ *Web:* www.usslp.com	Edison	NJ	08837	732-635-1500	635-1918	312
U.S. Silica Co 8490 Progress Dr Ste 300 *TF:* 800-243-7500 ■ *Web:* www.ussilica.com	Frederick	MD	21701	304-258-2500		503-4
U.S. Society on Dams (USSD) 1616 17th St Ste 483 *Web:* www.ussdams.org	Denver	CO	80202	303-628-5430	628-5431	49-3
U.S. Special Delivery Inc 821 E Blvd *TF:* 800-821-6389 ■ *Web:* www.usspecial.com	Kingsford	MI	49802	906-774-1931	774-2032	685
U.S. Specialty Coatings Inc 1000 McFarland 400 Blvd *TF:* 800-278-7473 ■ *Web:* www.usspecialtycoatings.com	Alpharetta	GA	30004	770-740-8123	740-8125	550
U.S. Sugar Company Inc 692 Bailey Ave *Web:* www.ussugar.net	Buffalo	NY	14206	716-828-1170		123
U.S. Supply Company Inc 50 Portland Rd *Web:* www.ussupply.com	West Conshohocken	PA	19428	610-828-5600		612
U.S. Surgeon General 200 Independence Ave SW Humphrey Bldg Ste 701H *Web:* www.hhs.gov	Washington	DC	20201	202-205-0143		340-10
U.S. Tank Alliance Inc 7400 Skyline Dr E Ste A *TF:* 866-878-2667 ■ *Web:* www.ustankweb.com	Columbus	OH	43235	614-923-0154	923-0111	196
U.S. Tax Court 400 Second St NW *Web:* www.ustaxcourt.gov	Washington	DC	20217	202-521-0700		341
U.S. Telecom Assn (USTA) 607-14th St NW Ste 400 *Web:* www.ustelecom.org	Washington	DC	20005	202-326-7300	326-7333	49-20
U.S. Term Limits (USTL) 1250 Connecticut Ave NW Ste 200 *Web:* www.termlimits.com	Washington	DC	20036	202-261-3532		48-7
U.S. Tool Grinding Inc 2000 Progress Dr **Fax Area Code:* 800 ■ *TF:* 800-222-1771 ■ *Web:* ustg.net	Farmington	MO	63640	573-431-3856	886-8668*	455
U.S. Tower Corp 1099 W Ropes Ave *Web:* www.ustower.com	Woodlake	CA	93286	559-564-6000		480
U.S. Trackworks LLC 1165 142nd Ave *Web:* ustrackworks.com	Wayland	MI	49348	616-877-4284	877-4202	188-8
U.S. Trade & Development Agency 1000 Wilson Blvd Ste 1600 *Web:* www.ustda.gov	Arlington	VA	22209	703-875-4357	875-4009	340-20
U.S. Translation Co 320 West 200 South 3rd Fl *Web:* ustranslation.com	Salt Lake City	UT	84101	801-393-5300		768
U.S. Transport 241 W 56th Ave *TF:* 800-379-2855 ■ *Web:* www.us-transport.com	Denver	CO	80216	800-379-2855		780
U.S. Travel Assn 1100 New York Ave NW Ste 450 *Web:* www.ustravel.org	Washington	DC	20005	202-408-8422	408-1255	49-7
U.S. Trotting Assn (USTA) 750 Michigan Ave *TF:* 877-800-8782 ■ *Web:* www.ustrotting.com	Columbus	OH	43215	614-224-2291	224-4575	48-22
U.S. Tsubaki Inc 301 E Marquardt Dr *TF:* 800-323-7790 ■ *Web:* www.ustsubaki.com	Wheeling	IL	60090	847-459-9500	459-9515	620
U.S. Underwater Services LP 123 Sentry Dr *Web:* www.neptunems.com	Mansfield	TX	76063	817-447-7321		302
U.S. Union Tool Inc 1260 N Fee Ana St *Web:* www.usuniontool.com	Anaheim	CA	92807	714-521-6242	521-8642	493
U.S. Vegetable Laboratory USDA/ARS 2700 Savannah Hwy *Web:* www.ars.usda.gov	Charleston	SC	29414	843-402-5300		668
U.S. Venture Partners (USVP) 1460 El Camino Real *Web:* www.usvp.com	Menlo Park	CA	94025	650-854-9080	854-3018	792
U.S. Vinyl Manufacturing Corp 1766 Broomtown Rd *Web:* www.usvinyl.com	LaFayette	GA	30728	706-638-8400		548
U.S. Vision Inc Glen Oaks Industrial Pk 1 Harmon Dr *Web:* www.usvision.com	Glendora	NJ	08029	856-228-1000		543
U.S. Websoft Corp 1101 Connecticut Ave NW Ste 450 *Web:* www.us-websoft.com	Washington	DC	20036	703-318-0103		809
U.S. Wheat Assn (USW) 3103 10th St N **Fax Area Code:* 703 ■ *Web:* www.uswheat.org	Arlington	VA	22201	202-463-0999	524-4399*	48-2
U.S. Wholesale Pipe & Tube 3351 Grand Blvd **Fax Area Code:* 727 ■ *TF:* 800-785-5601 ■ *Web:* www.usw.com	Holiday	FL	34690	800-785-5601	943-5926*	492
U.S. WorldMeds LLC 4441 Springdale Rd Ste L-07 *TF:* 888-900-8796 ■ *Web:* www.usworldmeds.com	Louisville	KY	40207	502-815-8000	714-7900	238
U.S. Xpress Enterprises Inc 4080 Jenkins Rd **Fax Area Code:* 423 ■ *TF:* 800-251-6291 ■ *Web:* www.usxpress.com	Chattanooga	TN	37421	866-646-5886	510-3444*	780
U.S.-Mexico Chamber of Commerce California Regional Chapter 2029 Century Pk E 19th Fl *Web:* www.usmcocca.org	Los Angeles	CA	90067	310-922-0206		138
U2 Logic 8001 E 88th Ave *Web:* www.u2logic.com	Henderson	CO	80640	303-768-9601		180
UA Community College at Morrilton 1537 University Blvd *Web:* www.uaccm.edu	Morrilton	AR	72110	501-977-2053	977-2133	162
UA Local 486 8100 Sandpiper Cir Ste 200 *Web:* www.ualocal486.com	Baltimore	MD	21236	410-866-4380	933-3515	414
UAA/APU Consortium Library 3211 Providence Dr *Web:* consortiumlibrary.org	Anchorage	AK	99508	907-786-1871		434-6
UAB Medical West 995 Ninth Ave SW *Web:* www.medicalwesthospital.org	Bessemer	AL	35022	205-481-7000		374-3
UAC (Utah Association of Counties) 5397 S Vine St *Web:* www.uacnet.org	Murray	UT	84107	801-265-1331	265-9485	48-13
UAF Community & Technical College 604 Barnette St *TF:* 877-882-8827 ■ *Web:* www.ctc.uaf.edu	Fairbanks	AK	99701	907-455-2800		162
UAM (United Alloys and Metals Inc) 9600 John St *Web:* uametals.com	Santa Fe Springs	CA	90670	562-273-7004	944-7060	686
UAM College of Technology 1609 E Ash PO Box 747 *TF:* 800-747-5360 ■ *Web:* www.uamont.edu	McGehee	AR	71654	870-222-5360	222-1105	167-3
UAMS Medical Ctr 4301 W Markham St *TF:* 877-467-6560 ■ *Web:* uamshealth.com	Little Rock	AR	72205	501-686-7000		374-3
UAP Inc 7025 Rue Ontario E *Web:* www.napacanada.com	Montreal	QC	H1N2B3	514-256-5031		61
UB Machine Inc 1615 Lincoln Hwy E *Web:* www.ubmachine.com	New Haven	IN	46774	260-493-3381	493-4663	60
UbiCare 284 Amory St G-101 *Web:* www.ubicare.com	Boston	MA	02130	617-524-8861		41

Name / Address	City	State	Zip	Phone	Fax	Class
Ubiquia Inc 407 W Osborn Rd Ste 100 — *TF:* 800-268-6296 ■ *Web:* ubiquia.com	Phoenix	AZ	85013	602-466-1706		177
Ubiquiti Inc 303 Detroit St Ste 202 — *Web:* ubiquiti.com	Ann Arbor	MI	48104	734-997-8800		177
u-blox America Inc 1902 Campus Commons Dr Ste 310 — *Web:* www.u-blox.com	Reston	VA	20191	703-483-3180		647
UBM (United Business Machines Inc) 13 Delta Dr Ste 9 & 10 — *Web:* www.ubmnh.com	Londonderry	NH	03053	603-216-9249		112
UBS (Universal Builders Supply Inc) 27 Horton Ave — *Web:* www.ubs1.com	New Rochelle	NY	10801	914-699-2400	699-2609	491
UBS AG 1285 Avenue of the Americas — *TF:* 877-827-8001 ■ *Web:* www.ubs.com	New York	NY	10019	888-390-4758		70
UBT Bancshares Inc 823 Broadway	Marysville	KS	66508	785-562-2333		360-2
Ubu Gallery 416 E 59th St — *Web:* www.ubugallery.com	New York	NY	10022	212-753-4444	753-4470	42
UC Davis Arboretum Valley Oak Cottage LaRue Rd — *Web:* arboretum.ucdavis.edu	Davis	CA	95616	530-752-4880	752-5796	97
UC Irvine Healthcare 101 the City Dr S — *TF:* 877-824-3627 ■ *Web:* www.ucihealth.org	Orange	CA	92868	714-456-7890		374-3
UCAN (Uhlich Children's Advantage Network) 3605 W Fillmore — *Web:* www.ucanchicago.org	Chicago	IL	60618	773-588-0180	826-3620	48-15
UCare Minnesota 500 Stinson Blvd NE PO Box 52 — *TF:* 866-457-7144 ■ *Web:* www.ucare.org	Minneapolis	MN	55413	612-676-6500	676-6501	48-17
UCB Pharma Inc 1950 Lake Pk Dr — *TF:* 800-477-7877 ■ *Web:* www.ucb.com	Smyrna	GA	30080	770-970-7500		582
UCC (United Church of Christ) 700 Prospect Ave — *TF:* 866-822-8224 ■ *Web:* www.ucc.org	Cleveland	OH	44115	216-736-2100	736-2103	48-20
UCC Filing & Search Services Inc 1574 Village Sq Blvd Ste 100	Tallahassee	FL	32309	850-681-6528		635
UCC Totalhome 8450 Broadway — *Web:* www.ucctops.com	Merrillville	IN	46411	219-736-1100		320
UCF Foundation Inc 12424 Research Pkwy Ste 250 — *Web:* www.ucffoundation.org	Orlando	FL	32826	407-882-1220		305
UCH (University City Housing) 3418 Sansom St — *Web:* universitycityhousing.com	Philadelphia	PA	19104	215-222-2000	222-5449	655
Uchee Pines Lifestyle Ctr 30 Uchee Pines Rd — *TF:* 877-824-3374 ■ *Web:* www.ucheepines.org	Seale	AL	36875	334-855-4764	855-9014	706
Uchi Austin 801 S Lamar Blvd — *Web:* uchiaustin.com	Austin	TX	78704	512-916-4808		671
UCI Medical Affiliates Inc 1818 Henderson St — *Web:* ucimedinc.com	Columbia	SC	29201	803-782-4278		463
UCL (Uintah County Library) 204 E 100 N — *Web:* www.uintahlibrary.org	Vernal	UT	84078	435-789-0091	789-7206	434-3
UCLA (University of California) *Berkeley* 110 Sproul Hall MC Ste 5800 — *TF:* 866-740-1260 ■ *Web:* www.berkeley.edu	Berkeley	CA	94720	510-664-9181		166
UCLA Chicano Studies Research Ctr (CSRC) 193 Haines Hall — *Web:* www.chicano.ucla.edu	Los Angeles	CA	90095	310-825-2363	206-1784	637-2
UCLA Foundation, The 10920 Wilshire Blvd Ste 900 — *Web:* www.uclafoundation.org	Los Angeles	CA	90024	310-794-3193	794-8531	305
UCLA Neuropsychiatric Institute & Hospital 760 Westwood Plz — *Web:* www.semel.ucla.edu	Los Angeles	CA	90095	310-825-0511		374-5
UCM (United Color Manufacturing Inc) PO Box 480 — *TF:* 800-852-5942 ■ *Web:* www.unitedcolor.com	Newtown	PA	18940	215-860-2165	860-8560	145
UCM (Usibelli Coal Mine Inc) PO Box 1000 — *Web:* www.usibelli.com	Healy	AK	99743	907-683-2226	683-2253	501
UCP Seguin 3100 S Central Ave — *Web:* ucpseguin.org	Cicero	IL	60804	708-863-3803	863-3863	225
UCS (Utica Community Schools) 11303 Greendale — *Web:* www.uticak12.org	Sterling Heights	MI	48312	586-797-1000		685
UCS (Union of Concerned Scientists) 2 Brattle Sq — *TF:* 800-666-8276 ■ *Web:* www.ucsusa.org	Cambridge	MA	02238	617-547-5552	864-9405	48-13
UCSF Department of Psychiatry 401 Parnassus Ave — *Web:* www.psych.ucsf.edu	San Francisco	CA	94143	415-476-7000	476-7320	374-5
UCSF Medical Ctr 505 Parnassus Ave — *Web:* www.ucsfhealth.org	San Francisco	CA	94143	415-476-1000		374-3
U-Cut Enterprises 4800 Solvay Rd — *TF:* 800-952-8288 ■ *Web:* www.u-cut.com	Jamesville	NY	13078	315-492-9316	492-4044	191-3
UDA (Urban Design Associates) 3 PPG Pl 3rd Fl — **Fax Area Code:* 844 ■ *Web:* www.urbandesignassociates.com	Pittsburgh	PA	15222	412-263-5200	270-8374*	194
Udall Shumway PLC 1138 N Alma School Rd Ste 101 — *Web:* www.udallshumway.com	Mesa	AZ	85201	480-461-5300	833-9392	428
Udall Tom (Sen D - NM) 531 Hart Senate Office Bldg — *Web:* www.tomudall.senate.gov	Washington	DC	20510	202-224-6621		342-2
UDASD (Upper Dauphin Area School District) 5668 SR-209 — *Web:* udasd.org	Lykens	PA	17048	717-362-8134	362-3050	685
Udder Health Systems Inc 4455 S Meridian Rd — *TF:* 877-398-1360 ■ *Web:* udderhealth.com	Meridian	ID	83642	208-922-9505	343-2046	794
Udemy 600 Harrison St — *Web:* udemy.com	San Francisco	CA	94107	415-420-0068		242
UDL (Updike Distribution Logistics) 435 S 59th Ave Ste 100 — *Web:* updikedl.com	Phoenix	AZ	85043	602-682-1800		311
UDP Inc 2426 Cee Gee — *Web:* www.udp.com	San Antonio	TX	78217	210-828-6171		225

Name / Address	City	State	Zip	Phone	Fax	Class
UELC (Nesco Rentals) 6714 Pointe Inverness Way Ste 220 — *TF:* 800-252-0043 ■ *Web:* nescorentals.com	Fort Wayne	IN	46804	260-824-6340	824-6350	470
UELS LLC 85 S 200 E — *Web:* uintahgroup.com	Vernal	UT	84078	435-789-1017		261
UES Inc 4401 Dayton-Xenia Rd — *Web:* www.ues.com	Dayton	OH	45432	937-426-6900	429-5413	472
UF Health Jacksonville 655 W Eigth St — *Web:* ufhealthjax.org	Jacksonville	FL	32209	904-244-0411		374-3
UFC (United Farmers Co-op) 705 E Fourth St PO Box 461 — *TF:* 866-998-3266 ■ *Web:* www.ufcmn.com	Winthrop	MN	55396	507-647-6600		10
UFCW (United Food & Commercial Workers International Union) 1775 K St NW — *TF:* 800-551-4010 ■ *Web:* www.ufcw.org	Washington	DC	20006	202-223-3111		414
Uff Machine Co 30741 Duck Puddle Rd — *Web:* www.gundrillers.com	Kennedyville	MD	21645	410-648-5033	648-5625	556
UFG 118 Second Ave SE PO Box 73909 — *NASDAQ: UFCS* ■ *TF:* 800-895-6253 ■ *Web:* www.ufginsurance.com	Cedar Rapids	IA	52407	319-399-5700		391-4
UFLAC Local 112 Dental In 1571 Beverly Blvd — *Web:* www.uflac.org	Los Angeles	CA	90026	213-895-4006		414
UFP Technologies Inc 172 E Main St — *NASDAQ: UFPT* ■ *TF:* 800-372-3172 ■ *Web:* www.ufpt.com	Georgetown	MA	01833	978-352-2200		601
U-Freight America Inc 395 Oyster Point Blvd Ste 516	South San Francisco	CA	94080	650-583-1469		311
UGA (University of Georgia Press) Main Library 320 S Jackson St 3rd Fl — **Fax Area Code:* 706 ■ *TF:* 800-266-5842 ■ *Web:* www.ugapress.org	Athens	GA	30602	800-266-5842	425-3061*	637-2
Uganda Embassy 5911 16th St NW — *Web:* washington.mofa.go.ug	Washington	DC	20011	202-726-7100	726-1727	257
UGC (United Guaranty Corp) 230 N Elm St — **Fax Area Code:* 888 ■ *TF:* 877-642-4642 ■ *Web:* www.ugcorp.com	Greensboro	NC	27401	877-642-4642	528-3273*	391-5
UGI (United-Guardian Inc) 230 Marcus Blvd PO Box 18050 — *NASDAQ: UG* ■ *TF:* 800-645-5566 ■ *Web:* www.u-g.com	Hauppauge	NY	11788	631-273-0900	273-0858	479
UGI Corp 460 N Gulph Rd PO Box 858 — *NYSE: UGI* ■ *Web:* ugicorp.com	King of Prussia	PA	19406	610-337-1000		360-5
Ugn Inc 18410 Crossing Dr — *Web:* ugn.com	Tinley Park	IL	60487	773-437-2400		247
UGUtech Consulting LLC 2842 N Springfield Ave — *Web:* www.ugutech.com	Chicago	IL	60618	773-309-4839		180
UH (Uniontown Hospital) 500 W Berkeley St — *Web:* www.uniontownhospital.com	Uniontown	PA	15401	724-430-5000		374-3
U-Haul International Inc 2727 N Central Ave — **Fax Area Code:* 602 ■ *TF:* 800-528-0361 ■ *Web:* www.uhaul.com	Phoenix	AZ	85004	800-528-0361	263-6772*	778
UHF (United Hospital Fund) 1411 Broadway 12th Fl — *Web:* www.uhfnyc.org	New York	NY	10018	212-494-0700	494-0800	637-2
Uhl Company Inc 9065 Zachary Ln N — *TF:* 800-815-3820 ■ *Web:* www.uhlcompany.com	Maple Grove	MN	55369	763-425-7226		393
Uhlich Children's Advantage Network (UCAN) 3605 W Fillmore — *Web:* www.ucanchicago.org	Chicago	IL	60618	773-588-0180	826-3620	48-15
UHMS (Undersea & Hyperbaric Medical Society) 21 W Colony Pl Ste 280 — *TF:* 877-533-8467 ■ *Web:* www.uhms.org	Durham	NC	27705	919-490-5140		48-17
UHY Advisors NY Inc 66 S Pearl St — *Web:* uhy-us.com	Albany	NY	12207	518-449-3171	449-5832	2
UIC (Universal Instruments Corp) 33 Broome Corporate Pk — *TF:* 800-842-9732 ■ *Web:* www.uic.com	Conklin	NY	13748	607-779-7522		695
UIH (Universal Insurance Holding Inc) 1110 W Commerical Blvd Ste 100 — *NYSE: UVE* ■ *TF:* 800-509-5586 ■ *Web:* universalinsuranceholdings.com	Fort Lauderdale	FL	33309	800-509-5586		391-4
Uinta County 225 Ninth St PO Box 810 — *Web:* www.uintacounty.com	Evanston	WY	82931	307-783-0306	783-0429	338
Uinta County Herald 849 Front St Ste 101 — *Web:* www.uintacountyherald.com	Evanston	WY	82930	307-789-6560	789-2700	532-2
Uintah Basin Applied Technology College 1100 E Lagoon St — *Web:* www.ubtech.edu	Roosevelt	UT	84066	435-722-6900	722-6999	166
Uintah Basin Standard Inc 268 S 200 E — *Web:* ubmedia.biz	Roosevelt	UT	84066	435-722-5131	722-4140	532-2
Uintah County 1801 West Hwy 40 — *TF:* 800-966-4680 ■ *Web:* www.co.uintah.ut.us	Vernal	UT	84078	435-781-0770	781-6701	338
Uintah County Library (UCL) 204 E 100 N — *Web:* www.uintahlibrary.org	Vernal	UT	84078	435-789-0091	789-7206	434-3
UIP Property Management Inc 140 Q St NE Ste 140B — *Web:* www.uippm.com	Washington	DC	20002	202-244-3811	684-7841	652
UK (Underwater Kinetics) 13400 Danielson St — *TF:* 800-852-7483 ■ *Web:* uwk.com	Poway	CA	92064	858-513-9100	513-3602	710
UK Good Samaritan Hospital 310 S Limestone St — *Web:* ukhealthcare.uky.edu	Lexington	KY	40508	859-226-7000		374-3
Ukiah Chamber of Commerce 200 S School St — *Web:* ukiahchamber.com	Ukiah	CA	95482	707-462-4705	462-2088	139
Ukpeagvik Inupiat Corp 1250 Agvik St PO Box 890 — *TF:* 800-347-0049 ■ *Web:* uicalaska.com	Barrow	AK	99723	907-852-4460	852-4459	186
Ukraine *Consulate General* 10 E Huron St — *Web:* chicago.mfa.gov.ua	Chicago	IL	60611	312-642-4388	642-4385	257
Ukrainian Museum 222 E Sixth St — *Web:* www.ukrainianmuseum.org	New York	NY	10003	212-228-0110	228-1947	520

	Phone	Fax	Class
Ukrainian Museum-Archives (UMA) 1202 Kenilworth Ave. . . . . Cleveland OH 44113 *Web:* www.umacleveland.org	216-781-4329		434-3
Ukrainian National Association Inc (UNA) 2200 Rt 10 . . . . . Parsippany NJ 07054 **Fax Area Code:* 973 ■ *TF:* 800-253-9862 ■ *Web:* unainc.org	800-253-9862	292-0900*	48-14
Ukrainian National Federal Credit Union 215 2nd Ave . . . . . New York NY 10003 **Fax Area Code:* 212 ■ *TF:* 866-859-5848 ■ *Web:* www.ukrnatfcu.org	866-859-5848	995-5204*	219
Ukrainian National Museum 2249 W Superior St . . . . . Chicago IL 60612 **Fax Area Code:* 773 ■ *Web:* www.ukrainiannationalmuseum.org	312-421-8020	772-2883*	520
Ukrainian Selfreliance Michigan Fcu 26791 Ryan Rd . . . . . Warren MI 48091 *Web:* usmfcu.org	586-756-3300	756-4316	219
Ukrop's Super Markets Inc 2001 Maywill St Ste 100. . . . . Richmond VA 23230 *Web:* www.ukropshomestylefoods.com	804-340-3000		345
UL EHS Sustainability 5000 Meridian Blvd Ste 600. . . . . Franklin TN 37067 *TF:* 888-202-3016 ■ *Web:* www.ulehssustainability.com	615-367-4404	367-3887	39
UL LLC 1559 King St . . . . . Enfield CT 06082 *TF:* 800-903-5660 ■ *Web:* www.ul.com	860-749-8371	749-8234	743
Ulbrich of Illinois Inc 12340 S Laramie Ave . . . . . Alsip IL 60802 *TF:* 800-323-7035 ■ *Web:* www.ulbrich.com	708-489-9500	371-1802	492
ULC (Urban Libraries Council) 1333 H St NW Ste 1000. . . . . Washington DC 20005 *Web:* www.urbanlibraries.org	202-750-8650		49-11
ULC (Universal Lending Corp) 6775 E Evans Ave. . . . . Denver CO 80224 *TF:* 800-758-4063 ■ *Web:* www.ulc.com	800-758-4063		509
ULC Robotics Inc 88 Arkay Dr. . . . . Hauppauge NY 11788 *Web:* ulcrobotics.com	631-667-9200		194
ULCC 65 W Jackson Blvd. . . . . Chicago IL 60604 *TF:* 800-443-0578 ■ *Web:* www.ulcc.org	312-427-7800		573-3
ULI (Urban Land Institute) 1025 Thomas Jefferson St NW Ste 500W. . . . . Washington DC 20007 *TF:* 800-321-5011 ■ *Web:* uli.org	202-624-7000	624-7140	48-8
Ulich Balmuth Fisher LLP 1201 Dove St Ste 625. . . . . Newport Beach CA 92660 *Web:* ulichlaw.com	949-250-9797	250-9777	41
U-line Corp 8900 N 55th St . . . . . Milwaukee WI 53223 *TF:* 800-779-2547 ■ *Web:* www.u-line.com	414-354-0300	354-7905	791
Ulivi Wealth 369 S Glassell St. . . . . Orange CA 92866 *Web:* ulivi.com	714-771-6000		690
Ulla Popken Ltd 777 Dulaney Valley Rd Ste 263. . . . . Towson MD 21204 *TF:* 800-245-8552 ■ *Web:* www.ullapopken.com	800-245-8552		157-6
Ulland Investment Advisors 4550 IDS Ctr Eighty S Eighth St . . . . . Minneapolis MN 55402 *Web:* www.ullandinvestment.com	612-312-1400		528
ULLICO Casualty Co 1625 I St NW . . . . . Washington DC 20006 *TF:* 800-431-5425 ■ *Web:* ullico.com	800-431-5425		391-5
Ullman Devices Corp 664 Danbury Rd. . . . . Ridgefield CT 06877 *Web:* ullmandevices.com	203-438-6577	431-9064	758
Ullman Oil Inc 9812 E Washington St . . . . . Chagrin Falls OH 44023 *TF:* 800-543-5195 ■ *Web:* www.ullmanoil.com	440-543-5195		579
Ullmann & Company PC 4647 N 32nd St Ste 220. . . . . Phoenix AZ 85018 *Web:* ullmanncpa.com	602-224-0166		2
Ulmans Jewelry Inc 903 Caroline St. . . . . Fredericksburg VA 22401 *Web:* ulmansjewelry.com	540-373-9243		410
Ulmer & Berne 1660 W Second St Ste 1100. . . . . Cleveland OH 44113 *Web:* www.ulmer.com	216-583-7000		428
Ulrich Medical Concepts Inc 1640 Mccracken Blvd . . . . . Paducah KY 42001 *Web:* ulrichmedicalconcepts.com	270-744-0404		225
Ulrich Planfiling Equipment Corp 2120 Fourth Ave PO Box 135 . . . . . Lakewood NY 14750 *Web:* www.ulrichcorp.com	716-763-1815	763-1818	487
Ulster Correctional Facility 750 Berme Rd PO Box 800. . . . . Napanoch NY 12458 *Web:* doccs.ny.gov	845-647-1670		213
Ulster County 244 Fair St . . . . . Kingston NY 12401 **Fax Area Code:* 845 ■ *TF:* 800-342-5826 ■ *Web:* ulstercountyny.gov	800-342-5826	340-3299*	338
Ulster County Community College Cottekill Rd. . . . . Stone Ridge NY 12484 *TF:* 800-724-0833 ■ *Web:* www.sunyulster.edu	845-687-5000	687-5090	162
Ulster Savings Bank 180 Schwenk Dr PO Box 3337 . . . . . Kingston NY 12401 *TF:* 866-440-0391 ■ *Web:* www.ulstersavings.com	845-338-6322		70
ULTA Beauty 1000 Remington Blvd Ste 120 . . . . . Bolingbrook IL 60440 *TF:* 866-983-8582 ■ *Web:* www.ulta.com	630-410-4627		214
Ulteig Engineers Inc 3350 38th Ave S . . . . . Fargo ND 58104 **Fax Area Code:* 701 ■ *TF:* 888-858-3441 ■ *Web:* www.ulteig.com	888-858-3441	237-3191*	261
Ultera Systems Inc 26081 Merit Cir Ste 125. . . . . Laguna Hills CA 92653 *Web:* www.ultera.com	949-367-8800	367-0758	176
Ulterion International Inc 1136 Zion Church Rd . . . . . Braselton GA 30517 *Web:* www.ulterion.com	706-654-2222		481
Ulterior Motives International Inc 1081 Ohio Dr . . . . . Plano TX 75093 *Web:* umimarketingsolutions.com	214-826-0011	887-8126	463
Ultimate Care 1000 Gates Ave 4th Fl . . . . . Brooklyn NY 11221 *Web:* ultimatecareny.com	718-257-0702	388-3129	363
Ultimate Cookie 1640 Folsom St. . . . . San Francisco CA 94103 *TF:* 800-330-0476 ■ *Web:* www.ultimatecookie.com	415-626-4644	626-0989	296-8
Ultimate Draft LLC PO Box 11846 . . . . . Saint Paul MN 55111 *Web:* www.ultimatedraft.com	612-455-6860	605-0020	44
Ultimate Home HealthCare Inc 11070 SW Ave . . . . . Chicago IL 60643 *Web:* www.ultimatehomehealthcare.com	773-779-3177	779-3775	363
Ultimate Lead Systems Inc 401 Frnt St . . . . . Berea OH 44017 *TF:* 800-323-0550 ■ *Web:* ultimatelead.com	440-826-1908		5
Ultimate Linings Ltd 6630 Roxburgh Dr Ste 175. . . . . Houston TX 77041 *Web:* www.ultimatelinings.com	713-466-0302	937-0052	57
Ultimate Medical Academy 9309 N Florida Ave Ste 100 . . . . . Tampa FL 33612 *TF:* 888-213-4473 ■ *Web:* www.ultimatemedical.edu	888-213-4473		167-3
Ultimate Paint Ball 7075 Stormy Ln . . . . . Bonne Terre MO 63628 *Web:* www.ultimatepaintball.com	573-358-1300		711
Ultimate Placements LLC PO Box 473 . . . . . Sharon Center OH 44274 *Web:* ultimateplacements.com	330-334-0285	334-2617	260
Ultimate Product Distributors 382 Main St . . . . . Hackensack NJ 07601 *Web:* www.updist.com	646-703-0220		756
Ultimate Software Group Inc 2000 Ultimate Way . . . . . Weston FL 33326 *NASDAQ: ULTI* ■ *TF:* 800-432-1729 ■ *Web:* www.ultimatesoftware.com	954-331-7000		178-1
Ultimate Support Systems Inc 5836 Wright Dr. . . . . Loveland CO 80538 *TF:* 800-525-5628 ■ *Web:* www.ultimatesupport.com	970-776-1920	776-1941	527
Ultimate Technical Solutions Inc 651 Leson Ct . . . . . Harvey LA 70058 *Web:* www.utsi.us	504-215-8256		180
Ultimate Washer Inc 711 Commerce Way Ste 1 . . . . . Jupiter FL 33458 *TF:* 866-858-4982 ■ *Web:* www.ultimatewasher.com	561-741-7022		641
Ultimatte Corp 20945 Plummer St . . . . . Chatsworth CA 91311 *Web:* www.blackmagicdesign.com	818-993-8007		514
Ultra Clean Technologies Corp 1274 Hgwy 77 . . . . . Bridgeton NJ 08302 *TF:* 800-791-9111 ■ *Web:* ultracleantech.com	856-451-2176		146
Ultra Electronics 3Phoenix Inc 14585 Avion Pkwy Ste 200. . . . . Chantilly VA 20151 *Web:* www.ultra-electronics.com	703-956-6480		529
Ultra Electronics Advanced Tactical Systems Inc 4101 Smith School Rd Bldng IV Ste 100 . . . . . Austin TX 78744 *Web:* www.ultra-electronics.com	512-327-6795	327-8043	177
Ultra Electronics Flightline Systems Inc 7625 Omni Tech Pl . . . . . Victor NY 14564 *TF:* 888-959-9001 ■ *Web:* www.ultra-fei.com	585-924-4000		647
Ultra Electronics Measurement Systems Inc 50 Barnes Pk N Ste 102 . . . . . Wallingford CT 06492 *Web:* www.ultra-electronics.com	203-949-3500	949-3598	173-1
Ultra Electronics, ProLogic 9400 Innovation Dr. . . . . Manassas VA 20110 *Web:* www.ultra-prologic.com	703-335-6986		809
Ultra Energy 707 Jeffrey Way. . . . . Round Rock TX 78665 *TF:* 800-880-9333 ■ *Web:* www.ultraelectronicsenergy.com	512-434-2900	434-2901	201
Ultra Logistics Inc 17-17 Rt 208 N Ste 160 . . . . . Fair Lawn NJ 07410 *Web:* www.ultralogistics.com	201-703-5110		225
Ultra Petroleum Corp 400 N Sam Houston Pkwy E Ste 1200 . . . . . Houston TX 77060 *NYSE: UPL* ■ *Web:* www.ultrapetroleum.com	281-876-0120	876-2831	536
Ultra Safety Systems Inc 1601 Hill Ave Ste C . . . . . Mangonia Park FL 33407 *TF:* 800-433-2628 ■ *Web:* www.tefgel.com	561-845-1086	844-8566	190
Ultra Solutions Acquisition LLC 1137 E Philadelphia St. . . . . Ontario CA 91761 *Web:* ultrasolutions.com	909-628-1778		475
Ultra Sonic Seal Co 53 Church Hill Rd. . . . . Newtown CT 06470 *Web:* www.ultrasonicseal.com	203-270-4816	270-4610	811
Ultra Tech Machinery Inc 297 Ascot Pkwy . . . . . Cuyahoga Falls OH 44223 *Web:* utmachinery.com	330-929-5544		454
UltraBac Software 15015 Main St Ste 200. . . . . Bellevue WA 98007 *TF:* 866-554-8562 ■ *Web:* www.ultrabac.com	425-644-6000	644-8222	178-12
Ultracare of Manhattan Ltd 800 Second Ave Rm 905 . . . . . New York NY 10017 *Web:* www.ultracareofmanhattan.com	212-883-8877	949-5035	260
Ultracraft Co 6163 Old 421 Rd . . . . . Liberty NC 27298 *TF:* 800-262-4046 ■ *Web:* www.ultracraft.com	800-262-4046		115
Ultradent Products Inc 505 W 10200 S. . . . . South Jordan UT 84095 *TF:* 888-230-1420 ■ *Web:* www.ultradent.com	801-572-4200	553-4600	228
Ultraderm Medspa 3311 Mission Dr . . . . . Santa Cruz CA 95065 *Web:* californiaskininstitute.com	831-475-4315		77
Ultra-Dex Inc 7144 Sheridan Rd . . . . . Flushing MI 48433 *Web:* www.ultradexusa.com	810-638-5388	638-4001	493
Ultraex Inc 2633 Barrington Ct . . . . . Hayward CA 94545 *TF:* 800-882-1000 ■ *Web:* www.ultraex.com	510-723-3760		317
Ultrafab Inc 1050 Hook Rd . . . . . Farmington NY 14425 *Web:* www.ultrafab.com	585-924-2186	924-7680	745-9
Ultrafabrics LLC 303 S Broadway. . . . . Tarrytown NY 10591 *TF:* 877-309-6648 ■ *Web:* www.ultrafabricsinc.com	914-460-1730	631-3572	745-3
Ultraflote LLC 3640 W 12th St. . . . . Houston TX 77008 *TF:* 800-821-6825 ■ *Web:* www.ultraflote.com	713-461-2100	461-2213	91
Ultrafryer Systems Inc 302 Spencer Ln . . . . . San Antonio TX 78201 **Fax Area Code:* 210 ■ *TF:* 800-545-9189 ■ *Web:* www.ultrafryer.com	800-545-9189	731-5099*	298
Ultralife Batteries Inc 2000 Technology Pkwy. . . . . Newark NY 14513 *NASDAQ: ULBI* ■ *TF:* 800-332-5000 ■ *Web:* www.ultralifecorporation.com	315-332-7100	331-7800	74
Ultramar Travel Management Intl 14 E 47th St . . . . . New York NY 10017 *Web:* www.ultramartravel.com	212-856-5608	856-0129	771
Ultra-Poly Corp 102 Demi Rd PO Box 330. . . . . Portland PA 18351 *TF:* 800-932-0619 ■ *Web:* www.ultra-poly.com	570-897-7500		608
Ultrasonic Power Corp 239 E Stephenson St . . . . . Freeport IL 61032 *Web:* www.upcorp.com	815-235-6020		518
Ultrasource Inc 22 Clinton Dr. . . . . Hollis NH 03049 *TF:* 800-742-9410 ■ *Web:* www.yourthinfilmsource.com	603-881-7799		179

Name / Address	City	State	ZIP	Phone	Fax	Class
UltraStaff 1818 Memorial Dr Ste 200	Houston	TX	77007	713-522-7100	522-0744	721
TF: 800-522-7707 ■ *Web:* www.ultrastaff.com						
Ultra-tech Enterprises Inc						
4701 Taylor Rd	Punta Gorda	FL	33950	800-293-2001		481
TF: 800-293-2001 ■ *Web:* www.ute-inc.com						
Ultratech Inc 3050 Zanker Rd	San Jose	CA	95134	408-321-8835		695
NASDAQ: UTEK ■ *TF:* 800-222-1213 ■ *Web:* www.veeco.com						
UltraTech International Inc						
11542 Davis Creek Ct	Jacksonville	FL	32256	904-292-9019	292-1325	198
TF: 800-764-9563 ■ *Web:* www.spillcontainment.com						
Ultra-Tech Lighting LLC PO Box 566	Closter	NJ	07624	800-356-7834	784-0854*	437
**Fax Area Code:* 201 ■ *TF:* 800-356-7834 ■ *Web:* www.ultratechlighting.com						
Ultra-Tech Printing Co						
5851 Crossroads Commerce	Grand Rapids	MI	49519	616-249-0500		627
Web: www.utprinting.com						
Ultraviolet Devices Inc						
26145 Technology Dr	Valencia	CA	91355	661-295-8140		476
Web: www.uvdi.com						
Ultryx PO Box 1841	Las Vegas	NV	89125	702-940-6900		809
TF: 866-485-8799 ■ *Web:* ultryx.com						
Uluru Inc 4452 Beltway Dr	Addison	TX	75001	214-905-5145	905-5130	479
Web: www.uluruinc.info						
Ulvac Technologies Inc						
401 Griffin Brook Dr	Methuen	MA	01844	978-686-7550	689-6300	385
Web: www.ulvac.com						
Ulysses News 218 N Main St	Ulysses	KS	67880	620-356-1201	356-4610	532-2
Web: ulysseschamber.org						
Ulysses Press PO Box 3440	Berkeley	CA	94703	510-601-8301	601-8307	637-2
TF: 800-377-2542 ■ *Web:* ulyssespress.com						
Ulysses S Grant National Historic Site						
7400 Grant Rd	Saint Louis	MO	63123	314-842-3298		564
Web: www.nps.gov						
U-M Comprehensive Cancer Ctr						
1500 E Medical Center Dr CCGC 6-303	Ann Arbor	MI	48109	734-232-8838		769
Web: www.rogelcancercenter.org						
UM Holdings Ltd 56 N Haddon Ave	Haddonfield	NJ	08033	856-354-2200	354-2216	360-3
Web: www.umholdings.com						
UMA (United Motorcoach Assn)						
113 SW St 4th Fl	Alexandria	VA	22314	703-838-2929	838-2950	49-21
TF: 800-424-8262 ■ *Web:* www.uma.org						
UMA (Ukrainian Museum-Archives)						
1202 Kenilworth Ave	Cleveland	OH	44113	216-781-4329		434-3
Web: www.umacleveland.org						
Umansky Motor Cars						
1400 W Silver Spring Dr	Milwaukee	WI	53209	877-231-9356		57
TF: 877-231-9356 ■ *Web:* www.umanskymotorcars.com						
U-mark Inc 102 Iowa Ave	Belleville	IL	62220	618-235-7500		388
TF: 866-383-6275 ■ *Web:* www.umarkers.com						
UMass Hotel at the Campus Ctr						
1 Campus Ctr Way	Amherst	MA	01003	413-549-6000		379
TF: 877-822-2110 ■ *Web:* www.hotelumass.com						
Umatilla County 216 SE Fourth St	Pendleton	OR	97801	541-278-6236	278-6345	338
Web: www.co.umatilla.or.us						
Umatilla Electric Cooperative Assn						
750 W Elm Ave	Hermiston	OR	97838	541-567-6414	567-8142	245
Web: www.umatillaelectric.com						
UMB Financial Corp						
1010 Grand Blvd	Kansas City	MO	64106	816-860-7000		360-2
NASDAQ: UMBF ■ *Web:* www.umb.com						
Umbagog Lake State Park						
172 Pembroke Rd	Concord	NH	03301	603-482-7795		565
Web: www.nhstateparks.org						
Umbrella Entertainment Group						
1110 Eugenia Pl Ste 300	Carpinteria	CA	93013	800-553-6637		195
TF: 800-553-6637 ■ *Web:* www.umbrellaent.com.au						
Umbrella Medical Systems						
505 Walnut St	Kansas City	MO	64106	816-437-7265		363
Web: www.umbrella-ms.com						
Umbrella Salon Inc						
2 N Market St Ste 100	San Jose	CA	95113	408-293-4242		77
Web: umbrellasalon.com						
UMC Inc 500 Chelsea Rd	Monticello	MN	55362	763-271-5200	322-5005	454
Web: www.ultramc.com						
UMCEP (University Medical Center of El Paso)						
4815 Alameda Ave	El Paso	TX	79905	915-544-1200		374-3
TF: 800-473-8440 ■ *Web:* www.umcelpaso.org						
UMCES (University of Maryland Center for Environmental Science)						
2020 Horn Pt Rd	Cambridge	MD	21613	410-228-9250	228-3843	668
TF: 866-842-2520 ■ *Web:* www.umces.edu						
UmeVoice Inc						
1435 Technology Ln Ste B4	Petaluma	CA	94954	707-939-8607	559-3314	178-7
TF: 888-230-3300 ■ *Web:* www.theboom.com						
UMF Medical 1316 Eisenhower Blvd	Johnstown	PA	15904	814-266-8726	266-1870	319-3
TF: 800-638-5322 ■ *Web:* www.umfmedical.com						
UMHC (University of Miami Hospital & Clinics)						
Sylvester Comprehensive Cancer Ctr						
1475 NW 12th Ave	Miami	FL	33136	305-243-1000		769
TF: 800-545-2292 ■ *Web:* umiamihealth.org						
Umi Restaurant 5849 Ellsworth Ave	Pittsburgh	PA	15232	412-362-6198		671
Web: bigburrito.com						
Umi Sushi Bar & Grill						
5510 S IH-35 Ste 400	Austin	TX	78745	512-383-8681	383-8802	671
Web: umiaustin.com						
Umicore Technical Materials North America Inc						
9 Pruyn's Island Dr	Glens Falls	NY	12801	518-792-7700		518
Web: www.umicore.com						
Umlauf Sculpture Garden & Museum						
605 Robert E Lee Rd	Austin	TX	78704	512-445-5582		520
Web: www.umlaufsculpture.org						
UMMC (University of Mississippi Medical Ctr)						
2500 N State St	Jackson	MS	39216	601-984-1000		769
Web: www.umc.edu						
Umpco Inc 7100 Lampson Ave	Garden Grove	CA	92841	714-897-3531		350
Web: www.umpco.com						
Umpqua Community College						
1140 Umpqva College Rd PO Box 967	Roseburg	OR	97470	541-440-4600	440-4612	162
TF: 800-820-5161 ■ *Web:* www.umpqua.edu						
Umpqua Dairy Products Co						
1686 SE N St PO Box 1306	Grants Pass	OR	97526	541-672-2638	673-0256	296-27
TF: 800-222-6455 ■ *Web:* www.umpquadairy.com						
UMPQUA Indian Development Corp						
146 Chief Miwaleta Ln	Canyonville	OR	97417	541-839-1221		377
Web: www.uidchr.com						
Umpqua Investments Inc						
1 SW Columbia St Ste 300	Portland	OR	97258	503-226-7000		360-2
NASDAQ: UMPQ ■ *TF:* 866-486-7782 ■ *Web:* umpquabank.com						
Umpqua Lighthouse State Park						
Umpqua Lighthouse State Pk	Reedsport	OR	97467	541-271-4118		565
Web: stateparks.oregon.gov						
UMRCC (Upper Mississippi River Conservation Committee)						
9053 Rte 148	Marion	IL	62959	618-579-3129		48-13
Web: www.umrcc.org						
UMS Group Inc						
300 Interpace Pkwy Ste C380	Parsippany	NJ	07054	973-335-3555	335-7738	194
Web: www.umsgroup.com						
Umstead Hotel & Spa 100 Woodland Pond	Cary	NC	27513	919-447-4000		379
TF: 866-877-4141 ■ *Web:* www.theumstead.com						
UMTRI (University of Michigan Transportation Research Institute)						
2901 Baxter Rd	Ann Arbor	MI	48109	734-764-6504	936-1081	668
Web: www.umtri.umich.edu						
UMW (Utah Metal Works Inc)						
805 Everett Ave	Salt Lake City	UT	84116	877-221-0099		660
TF: 877-221-0099 ■ *Web:* umw.com						
UMWA (United Mine Workers of America)						
18354 Quantico Gateway Dr Ste 200	Triangle	VA	22172	703-291-2400		457-21
TF: 800-291-1425 ■ *Web:* umwa.org						
UNA (Ukrainian National Association Inc)						
2200 Rt 10	Parsippany	NJ	07054	800-253-9862	292-0900*	48-14
**Fax Area Code:* 973 ■ *TF:* 800-253-9862 ■ *Web:* unainc.org						
UNAPEN Inc 321 Research Pkwy Ste 201	Meriden	CT	06450	203-269-6111		180
Web: unapen.com						
Unarco Material Handling Inc						
701 16th Ave E	Springfield	TN	37172	800-862-7261	382-2777*	286
**Fax Area Code:* 615 ■ *TF:* 800-862-7261 ■ *Web:* www.unarcorack.com						
UNC Lenoir Health Care 100 Airport Rd	Kinston	NC	28501	252-522-7000		374-3
Web: www.unclenoir.org						
Uncharted Outposts Inc 9 Village Ln	Santa Fe	NM	87505	505-795-7710		760
Web: www.unchartedoutposts.com						
Unclaimed Baggage Ctr						
509 W Willow St	Scottsboro	AL	35768	256-259-1525		791
Web: www.unclaimedbaggage.com						
Uncle Credit Union						
2100 Las Positas Ct	Livermore	CA	94551	925-447-5001		219
Web: unclecu.org						
Uncle Giuseppe's of Smithtown						
95 Rt 111	Smithtown	NY	11787	631-863-0900		297-8
Web: www.uncleg.com						
Uncle Henry's Pretzel Bakery						
1550 Bowmansville Rd	Mohnton	PA	19540	717-445-4690		296-9
Web: www.unclehenry.com						
Uncle Milton Industries Inc						
29209 Canwood St Ste 120	Agoura Hills	CA	91301	818-707-0800	707-0878	762
TF: 800-869-7555 ■ *Web:* www.unclemilton.com						
Uncle Ray's LLC 14245 Birwood St	Detroit	MI	48238	313-834-0800	834-0443	296-35
TF: 800-800-3286 ■ *Web:* www.unclerays.com						
Uncle Tai's 5250 Town Center Cir	Boca Raton	FL	33486	561-368-8806		671
Web: www.uncletais.com						
Uncle Wing Chinese Restaurant						
107 N First St	Garland	TX	75040	972-272-2775		671
Web: www.unclewing.net						
Under Secretary for Public Diplomacy & Public Affairs						
Bureau of Educational & Cultural Affairs						
2200 C St NW	Washington	DC	20522	202-632-6452	632-2701	340-16
Web: eca.state.gov						
Underberg & Kessler LLP						
300 Bausch & Lomb Pl	Rochester	NY	14604	585-258-2800	258-2821	445
Web: underbergkessler.com						
Undercurrent, The						
327 Battleground Ave	Greensboro	NC	27401	336-370-1266		671
Web: undercurrentrestaurant.com						
Underdog Media						
10 E Yanonali St Ste 2C	Santa Barbara	CA	93101	805-880-6910		5
Web: www.underdogmedia.com						
Underground Atlanta						
50 Upper Alabama St	Atlanta	GA	30303	404-523-2311	523-0507	50-6
Web: undergroundatl.com						
Underground Construction Company Inc						
5145 Industrial Way	Benicia	CA	94510	707-746-8800	746-1314	188-10
TF: 800-227-2314 ■ *Web:* www.undergroundconstruction.com						
Underground Specialists Inc (USI)						
570 SW 16th Terr	Pompano Beach	FL	33069	954-782-8740	782-1919	787
Web: www.usicable.com						
Underhill State Park						
PO Box 249	Underhill Center	VT	05490	802-899-3022		565
Web: www.vtstateparks.com						
Underriner Motors 3671 Pierce Pkwy	Billings	MT	59106	406-255-2380		57
Web: www.underrinermotors.com						
Undersea & Hyperbaric Medical Society (UHMS)						
21 W Colony Pl Ste 280	Durham	NC	27705	919-490-5140		48-17
TF: 877-533-8467 ■ *Web:* www.uhms.org						
Underwater Kinetics (UK)						
13400 Danielson St	Poway	CA	92064	858-513-9100	513-3602	710
TF: 800-852-7483 ■ *Web:* uwk.com						
Underwood Bros 3747 E Southern Ave	Phoenix	AZ	85040	602-437-2690	437-2970	422
Web: aaalandscape.com						
Underwood Lauren (Rep D - IL)						
1118 Longworth House Office Bldg	Washington	DC	20515	202-225-2976		342-2
Web: www.underwood.house.gov						
Underwood Law 1111 W Loop 289	Lubbock	TX	79416	806-793-1711	793-1723	428
Web: www.uwlaw.com						
Underwood Mold Company Inc						
104 Dixie Dr	Woodstock	GA	30189	770-926-2465	926-6565	602
Web: www.underwoodmoldco.com						
Underwood Transfer Company LLC						
940 W Troy Ave	Indianapolis	IN	46225	317-783-9235	782-2769	780
TF: 800-428-2372 ■ *Web:* www.underwoodcompanies.com						

Phone | Fax | Class

Underwood's Jewelers Corp
2044 San Marco Blvd Jacksonville FL 32207 904-398-9741 410
Web: underwoodjewelers.com

Underwriters Safety & Claims Inc
1700 Eastpoint Pkwy Louisville KY 40223 502-244-1343 390
Web: www.uscky.com

UNDP (University of Notre Dame Press)
310 Flanner Hall Notre Dame IN 46556 574-631-6346 631-4410 637-2
Web: www.undpress.nd.edu

Uneeda Enterprizes Inc
640 Chestnut Ridge Rd Spring Valley NY 10977 845-426-2800 426-2810 1
TF: 800-431-2494 ■ *Web:* www.sandpaper.com

Unemed Corp 986099 Nebraska Medical Ctr Omaha NE 68198 402-559-2468 463
Web: www.unemed.com

Unemployment Services Corp
50 Salem St Lynnfield MA 01940 781-246-0262 463
Web: www.uscorp.com

UNEP (United Nations Environment Programme)
2013 Q St NW Washington DC 20006 202-785-0465 785-2096 783
Web: www.rona.unep.org

Unergi School of Holistic Therapy
PO Box 335 Point Pleasant PA 18950 215-297-8006 297-8199 685
Web: www.unergi.com

UNESCO (United Nations Educational Scientific & Cultural Organization)
2 UN Plz New York NY 10017 917-810-9030 783
Web: en.unesco.org

Unette Corp 1578 Sussex Tpke Bldg 5 Randolph NJ 07869 973-328-6800 584-4794 608
Web: www.unette.com

UNF (University of North Florida)
1UNF Dr Jacksonville FL 32224 904-620-2615 620-2719 434-6
Web: www.unf.edu

UNF (United Nations Foundation)
1800 Massachusetts Ave NW Ste 400 Washington DC 20036 202-887-9040 887-9021 48-5
Web: www.unfoundation.org

UNFCU (United Nations Federal Credit Union)
24-01 44th Rd Ct Sq Pl Long Island City NY 11101 347-686-6000 686-6400 219
TF: 800-891-2471 ■ *Web:* www.unfcu.org

Unger Co 12401 Berea Rd Cleveland OH 44111 216-252-1400 252-1427 548
TF: 800-321-1418 ■ *Web:* www.ungerco.com

Unger Memorial Library
825 N Austin St Plainview TX 79072 806-296-1148 434-3
Web: www.plainviewtx.org

Ungerboeck Systems International Inc
100 Ungerboeck Pk O'Fallon MO 63368 636-300-5606 180
TF: 800-400-4052 ■ *Web:* ungerboeck.com

Unholtz-Dickie Corp
6 Brookside Dr Wallingford CT 06492 203-265-3929 265-2690 407
Web: www.udco.com

UNI Engineering Inc
156 Stockton St Hightstown NJ 08520 609-448-4633 448-0797 261
Web: uni-engineering.com

Unibank For Savings 49 Church St Whitinsville MA 01588 508-234-8112 70
TF: 800-578-4270 ■ *Web:* www.unibank.com

Uni-Bell PVC Pipe Assn
2711 LBJ Fwy Ste 1000 Dallas TX 75234 972-243-3902 138
Web: www.uni-bell.org

Unibilt Industries Inc
8005 Johnson Stn Rd PO Box 373 Vandalia OH 45377 800-777-9942 890-8303* 106
**Fax Area Code:* 937 ■ *TF:* 800-777-9942 ■ *Web:* www.unibiltcustomhomes.com

Unibright Foods Inc
7101 Scout Ave Bell Gardens CA 90201 562-806-3221 806-2083 473
Web: www.unibrightfoods.com

Unical Aviation Inc
680 S Lemon Ave City of Industry CA 91789 909-348-1700 770
Web: www.unical.com

UNiCALL 2216 W Altofer Dr Peoria IL 61615 888-859-5333 393
TF: 888-859-5333 ■ *Web:* www.unicallweb.com

UniCare Health Plans of the Midwest Inc
233 S Wacker Dr Ste 3900 Chicago IL 60606 312-234-8000 391-3
TF: 888-742-2505 ■ *Web:* www.unicare.com

Unicast Co 241 N Washington St Boyertown PA 19512 610-367-0155 367-2787 307
Web: www.unicastco.com

Unicast Inc 17 Mcfadden Rd Easton PA 18045 800-275-0818 503-9569 676
TF: 800-275-0818 ■ *Web:* www.unicastinc.com

UNICEF (United Nations Children's Fund)
3 United Nations Plz New York NY 10017 212-326-7000 888-7465 783
Web: www.unicef.org

Unicell Body Co 571 Howard St Buffalo NY 14206 716-853-8628 843-8638 516
TF: 800-628-8914 ■ *Web:* www.unicell.com

Unicentric Inc 1023 Talbot Ave Braddock PA 15104 412-697-7200 177
Web: www.unicentric.com

Unicep Packaging Inc
1702 Industrial Dr Sandpoint ID 83864 208-265-9696 265-4726 549
TF: 800-354-9396 ■ *Web:* www.unicep.com

Unichem Inc 8 N Kings Rd Greenville SC 29605 864-422-0191 104
Web: www.unichem.com

Unicircuit Inc 8122 Suthpark Ln Littleton CO 80120 303-730-0505 730-0606 625
TF: 800-648-6449 ■ *Web:* www.unicircuit.com

Unico American Corp
23251 Mulholland Dr Woodland Hills CA 91364 800-669-9800 391-4
TF: 800-669-9800 ■ *Web:* www.crusaderinsurance.com

Unico Inc 3725 Nicholson Rd Franksville WI 53126 262-886-5678 504-7396 518
Web: www.unicous.com

Unicoi County 100 Main St Erwin TN 37650 423-743-3000 338
Web: www.unicoicounty.org

Unicoi State Park & Lodge
1788 Hwy 356 Rd Helen GA 30545 800-573-9659 565
TF: 800-573-9659 ■ *Web:* www.unicoilodge.com

UNICOM 565 Brea Canyon Rd Ste A Walnut CA 91789 626-964-7873 964-7880 176
TF: 800-346-6668 ■ *Web:* www.unicomlink.com

UNICOM Systems Inc
15535 San Fernando Mission Blvd Unicom Plz
Ste 310 Mission Hills CA 91345 818-838-0606 809
Web: www.unicomglobal.com

Unicom Technologies Inc 1011 Hwy 6 S Houston TX 77077 281-496-3606 764
Web: www.unicom-tech.com

UniComm Consulting LLC
9745 Rim Rock Cir Loomis CA 95650 408-420-5539 463
Web: www.unicommconsulting.com

Unicon Group Ltd 1734 Gilsinn Ln Fenton MO 63026 636-394-2012 394-4835 225
Web: www.unicongl.com

Unicon Inc 1760 E Pecos Rd Ste 432 Gilbert AZ 85295 480-558-2400 194
Web: www.unicon.net

Unicon International Inc
241 Outerbelt St Columbus OH 43213 614-861-7070 861-7096 180
Web: www.unicon-intl.com

Unicontrol Inc 1111 Brookpark Rd Cleveland OH 44109 216-398-4414 398-8553 201
Web: unicontrolinc.com

Unicorn Bookshop
3935 Ocean Gateway Rte 50 Trappe MD 21673 410-476-3838 95
Web: www.unicornbookshop.com

Unicorn HRO LLC 25B Hanover Rd Florham Park NJ 07932 800-368-8149 39
TF: 800-368-8149 ■ *Web:* unicornhro.com

Unicorn Theatre 3828 Main St Kansas City MO 64111 816-531-7529 531-0421 572
Web: www.unicorntheatre.org

Unicorp 291 Cleveland St Orange NJ 07050 973-674-1700 674-3803 350
TF: 800-526-1389 ■ *Web:* www.unicorpinc.com

Unicorr 455 Sackett Pt Rd North Haven CT 06473 203-248-2161 248-0241 548
Web: www.unicorr.com

Unicote Corp 33165 Groesbeck Hwy Fraser MI 48026 586-296-0700 296-3155 481
Web: www.unicotecorporation.com

Uniden America Corp
4700 Amon Carter Blvd Fort Worth TX 76155 817-858-3300 735
TF: 800-297-1023 ■ *Web:* www.uniden.com

Unidex Inc 8 Stoecker Rd Holmdel NJ 07733 732-975-9877 975-9866 194
Web: www.unidex.com

UNIDO (United Nations Industrial Development Organization)
1 UN Plz New York NY 10017 212-963-6890 963-7904 783
Web: www.unido.org

UnidosUS 1126 16th St NW 6th Fl Washington DC 20036 202-785-1670 776-1792 48-14
Web: www.unidosus.org

Uniek Inc 805 Uniek Dr Waunakee WI 53597 608-849-9999 309
Web: www.uniekinc.com

Unifab 215 Tremont St Rochester NY 14608 585-235-1760 235-1762 604
Web: www.unifabplastic.com

Unifab Corp 5260 Lovers Ln Portage MI 49002 269-382-2803 482
Web: unifabcorporation.com

Unifi Inc 7201 W Friendly Ave Greensboro NC 27410 336-294-4410 316-5422 745-9
NYSE: UFI ■ *Web:* www.unifi.com

Unified Brands 1055 Mendell Davis Dr Jackson MS 39272 888-994-7636 864-7636 386
TF: 888-994-7636 ■ *Web:* www.unifiedbrands.net

Unified Field Inc
33 E 33rd St Ste 1107 New York NY 10016 212-532-9595 180
Web: www.unifiedfield.com

Unified Financial Services Inc
2353 Alexandria Dr Lexington KY 40504 859-422-0347 691
Web: unified.com

Unified Government of Wyandotte County/Kansas City
701 N Seventh St Ste 323 Kansas City KS 66101 913-573-5000 573-5005 338
Web: www.wycokck.org

Unified Grocers Inc 5200 Sheila St Commerce CA 90040 323-264-5200 729-6610 297-8
TF: 800-724-7762 ■ *Web:* www.unifiedgrocers.com

Unified Industries Inc
6551 Loisdale Ct Ste 400 Springfield VA 22150 703-922-9800 971-5892 261
TF: 800-666-1642 ■ *Web:* www.uii.com

Unified Life Insurance Co
PO Box 25326 Overland Park KS 66225 800-237-4463 402-6942* 796
**Fax Area Code:* 913 ■ *TF:* 800-237-4463 ■ *Web:* www.unifiedlife.com

Unified Packaging Inc 1187 E 68th Ave Denver CO 80229 303-733-1000 733-6789 86
Web: www.unifiedbinders.com

Unified People's Federal Credit Union
414 E 18th St Cheyenne WY 82001 307-632-1476 219
TF: 800-444-6327 ■ *Web:* unifiedpeoplesfcu.org

Unified School District of Antigo
120 S Dorr St Antigo WI 54409 715-627-4355 623-3279 685
Web: www.antigo.k12.wi.us

Unified Systems Group Inc
1235 64th Ave SE Ste 4a Calgary AB T2H2J7 403-686-8088 174
TF: 866-892-8988 ■ *Web:* www.usg.ca

Unified Theory Inc
1811 Weir Dr Ste 365 Saint Paul MN 55125 651-578-8100 261
Web: www.utieng.com

UniFocus LP 2455 McIver Ln Carrollton TX 75006 972-512-5000 225
Web: www.unifocus.com

Unifoil Corp 12 Daniel Rd E Fairfield NJ 07004 973-244-9900 244-5555 555
TF: 800-596-5600 ■ *Web:* www.unifoil.com

Unifor 301 Laurier Ave W Ottawa ON K1P6M6 613-230-5200 414
TF: 877-230-5201 ■ *Web:* www.unifor.org

Uniform Center of Lansing Inc
425 N Clippert St Lansing MI 48912 517-589-4099 332-8999 157-4
TF: 800-554-0234 ■ *Web:* www.uniformcenteroflansing.com

Uni-Form Components Co
10703 Sheldon Rd Houston TX 77044 281-591-5324 482
Web: www.uniformcomponents.com

Uniform House Inc
1927 N Capitol Ave Indianapolis IN 46202 317-926-4467 157-4
TF: 800-949-4467 ■ *Web:* www.uniformhouse.com

Uniform Industrial Corp
2091 Bayview Dr Fremont CA 94538 510-438-6799 466
Web: uicpayworld.com

Uniformed Services University of the Health Sciences Learning Resource Ctr
4301 Jones Bridge Rd Bethesda MD 20814 301-295-3350 434-1
Web: www.er.lrc.usuhs.edu

Unifrax I LLC
600 Riverwalk Pkwy Ste 120 Tonawanda NY 14150 716-768-6500 768-6400 389
Web: www.unifrax.com

Unifund CCR Partners Inc
10625 Techwoods Cir Cincinnati OH 45242 513-489-8877 215
TF: 888-384-4452 ■ *Web:* www.unifund.com

Unifuse LLC 2092 New York 9G Staatsburg NY 12580 845-889-4000 889-4002 199
Web: unifuse.com

Unify Square Inc 411 108th Ave NE Bellevue WA 98004 425-865-0700 463
Web: www.unifysquare.com

Unifyhr LLC 105 Decker Ct Ste 540 Irving TX 75062 800-610-1738 844-3240* 2
**Fax Area Code:* 469 ■ *TF:* 800-610-1738 ■ *Web:* unifyhr.com

Unigen Corp 45388 Warm Springs Blvd Fremont CA 94539 510-668-2088 668-4889 625
TF: 800-826-0808 ■ *Web:* www.unigen.com

Phone | Fax | Class

UNIGLOBE Travel USA LLC
2211 Michelson Dr Ste 460 Irvine CA 92612 949-623-9000 772
Web: www.uniglobetravelcenter.com

Uniguest Inc 2926 Kraft Dr Nashville TN 37204 800-467-1218 5
TF: 800-467-1218 ■ *Web:* uniguest.com

UniLect Corp PO Box 3026 Danville CA 94526 925-833-8660 833-8874 801
Web: www.unilect.com

Unilever Canada Ltd
160 Bloor St E Ste 1400 Toronto ON M4W3R2 416-415-3000 360-3
Web: www.unilever.ca

Unilux Inc 59 N Fifth St Saddle Brook NJ 07663 201-712-1266 712-1366 472
TF: 800-522-0801 ■ *Web:* www.unilux.com

Unimac Graphics 350 Michele Pl Carlstadt NJ 07072 201-372-1000 372-0699 344
Web: www.unimacgraphics.com

Unimark Products
2016 Unimark 9818 Pflumm Rd Lenexa KS 66215 913-649-2424 649-5795 176
TF: 800-255-6356 ■ *Web:* www.unimark.com

Unimatic Inc 3501 Raleigh Ave Minneapolis MN 55416 952-922-7744 922-7888 454
Web: www.unimaticinc.com

Unimax 121 S Eighth St Minneapolis MN 55402 800-886-0390 177
TF: 800-886-0390 ■ *Web:* unimax.com

Unintech Consulting Engineers Inc
2431 E Evans Rd San Antonio TX 78259 210-641-6003 196
Web: www.unintech.com

Union Bank & Trust Inc
312 Central Ave SE Minneapolis MN 55414 612-379-3222 379-8837 70
Web: www.ubtmn.com

Union Bank Co, The
105 Progressive Dr Columbus Grove OH 45830 419-659-2141 360-2
NASDAQ: UBOH ■ *TF:* 800-837-8111 ■ *Web:* www.theubank.com

Union Bank of California NA
400 California St 1st Fl San Francisco CA 94104 415-765-3434 70
TF: 800-238-4486 ■ *Web:* www.unionbank.com

Union Bankshares Inc
20 Lower Main St Morrisville VT 05661 802-888-6600 360-2
NASDAQ: UNB ■ *TF:* 866-862-1891 ■ *Web:* www.ublocal.com

Union Bar & Grille 1357 Washington St Boston MA 02118 617-338-5300 671
Web: www.unionrestaurant.com

Union Carbide Corp 1254 Enclave Pkwy Houston TX 77077 281-966-2016 140
Web: www.unioncarbide.com

Union Cemetery 2505 Minnehaha Ave E Maplewood MN 55119 651-739-0466 510
Web: unioncem.org

Union Chapel 55 Narragansett Ave Edgartown MA 02557 508-338-7420 50-1
Web: www.unionchapelmv.org

Union City Chamber of Commerce
3939 Smith St Union City CA 94587 510-952-9637 952-9647 139
TF: 800-945-2288 ■ *Web:* unioncitychamber.com

Union City Daily Messenger Inc
613 E Jackson St Union City TN 38261 731-885-0744 885-0782 532-2
TF: 866-885-0744 ■ *Web:* www.nwtntoday.com

Union City Public Library 324 43rd St Union NJ 07087 201-866-7500 866-0962 434-3
Web: www.uclibrary.org

Union College 310 College St Barbourville KY 40906 606-546-4151 546-1667 166
TF: 800-489-8646 ■ *Web:* www.unionky.edu

Union College 3800 S 48th St Lincoln NE 68506 402-486-2504 486-2895 166
TF: 800-228-4600 ■ *Web:* www.ucollege.edu

Union Computer Services LLC
7309 Gold Ring Ter Derwood MD 20855 703-579-1060 180
Web: unioncomputerservices.com

Union Correctional Institution
7819 NW 228th St Raiford FL 32026 386-431-2000 213
Web: dc.state.fl.us

Union Corrugating Company Inc
701 S King St Fayetteville NC 28301 910-483-2195 480
TF: 888-685-7663 ■ *Web:* www.unioncorrugating.com

Union County
65 Courthouse St PO Box 2 Blairsville GA 30512 706-439-6000 439-6004 338
Web: www.unioncountyga.gov

Union County 1103 S First St Clayton NM 88415 575-374-9253 338
TF: 800-390-7858 ■ *Web:* www.claytonnm.org

Union County 300 N Pine St Ste 5 Creston IA 50801 641-782-7315 782-8241 338
Web: www.unioncountyiowa.org

Union County 101 N Washington El Dorado AR 71730 870-864-1900 864-1927 338
Web: www.unioncountyar.com

Union County 26 W Union St Liberty IN 47353 765-580-1988 338
Web: ucdc.us

Union County
1001 Main St PO Box 848 Maynardville TN 37807 865-992-2811 338
Web: www.comeherecomehome.com

Union County 210 W Main St Union SC 29379 864-429-1600 429-1603 338
TF: 800-273-5066 ■ *Web:* www.countyofunion.org

Union County Carnegie Library
300 E S St Union SC 29379 864-427-7140 434-3
Web: www.unionlibrary.org

Union County Chamber of Commerce
903 Skyway Dr Monroe NC 28110 704-289-4567 282-0122 139
Web: www.unioncountycoc.com

Union County Chamber of Commerce
227 E Fifth St Marysville OH 43040 937-642-6279 644-0422 139
Web: unioncounty.org

Union County Chamber of Commerce
135 W Main St Union SC 29379 864-427-9039 427-9030 139
TF: 877-202-8755 ■ *Web:* unionsc.chambermaster.com

Union County Clerk 215 W 6th St Marysville OH 43040 937-645-3006 338
Web: www.co.union.oh.us

Union County College
1033 Springfield Ave Cranford NJ 07016 908-709-7000 709-7125 162
Web: www.ucc.edu

Union County Electric Co-opeartive Inc
122 W Main St Elk Point SD 57025 605-356-3395 356-3397 245
TF: 888-356-3395 ■ *Web:* unioncounty.coop

Union County Public Library
316 E Windsor St Monroe NC 28112 704-283-8184 434-3
Web: www.union.lib.nc.us

Union County Public Schools
510 S Mart St Morganfield KY 42437 270-389-1694 389-9806 685
Web: www.union.kyschools.us

Union County State Fish & Wildlife Area
2755 Refuge Rd Jonesboro IL 62952 618-833-5175 565
Web: www.dnr.illinois.gov

Union Editorial LLC
12200 W Olympic Blvd Ste 140 Los Angeles CA 90064 310-481-2200 514
Web: www.unioneditorial.com

Union Electric Steel Corp
726 Bell Ave Carnegie PA 15106 412-429-7655 276-1711 307
Web: www.uniones.com

Union Engineering Company Inc
1399 Arundell Ave Ventura CA 93003 805-648-3373 189-5

Union Eyecare Centers
4750 Beidler Rd Willoughby OH 44094 216-986-9700 986-1996 543
TF: 800-443-9699 ■ *Web:* www.unioneyecare.com

Union for Reformed Judaism
633 3rd Ave Ste 7 New York NY 10017 212-650-4000 48-20
TF: 855-875-1800 ■ *Web:* urj.org

Union Grill 2501 Wall Ave Ogden UT 84401 801-621-2830 621-7946 671
Web: www.uniongrillogden.com

Union Group
405 Pleasant St Bldg Ste 12 Fall River MA 02721 508-676-8580 86
Web: theuniongroup.com

Union Grove State Park
1215 220th St Gladbrook IA 50635 641-473-2556 473-3059 565
Web: www.iowadnr.gov

Union Hospital 500 Lynnfield St Lynn MA 01904 781-581-9200 374-3
Web: nsmc.partners.org

Union Hospital 106 Bow St Elkton MD 21921 410-398-4000 374-3
Web: www.uhcc.com

Union Hospital 1606 N 7th St Terre Haute IN 47804 812-238-7000 374-3
Web: www.myunionhealth.org

Union Institute & University
440 E McMillan St Cincinnati OH 45206 513-861-6400 861-0779 166
TF: 800-486-3116 ■ *Web:* myunion.edu

Union Iron Inc 3550 E Mound Rd Decatur IL 62521 217-429-5148 273
Web: www.unioniron.com

Union Leader 100 William Loeb Dr Manchester NH 03109 603-668-4321 532-2
Web: www.unionleader.com

Union League Cafe 1032 Chapel St New Haven CT 06510 203-562-4200 562-6712 671
Web: unionleaguecafe.com

Union Machine Company of Lynn Inc
6 Federal Way Groveland MA 01834 978-521-5100 529
Web: unionmac.wpengine.com

Union Metal Corp
1432 Maple Ave NE PO Box 73028 Canton OH 44705 330-456-7653 456-0628 480
TF: 800-327-0097 ■ *Web:* www.unionmetal.com

Union Mutual Insurance Co
3613 NW 56th St Ste 300 Oklahoma City OK 73112 405-601-4467 601-4499 390
Web: umic-okc.com

Union National Life Insurance
3636 S Sherwood Forest Blvd Baton Rouge LA 70816 225-292-7600 391-4

Union of Agricultural Procedures, The (UPA)
555 Boul Roland-Therrien Ste 100 Longueuil QC J4H3Y9 450-679-0530 414
Web: www.upa.qc.ca

Union of American Physicians & Dentists
180 Grand Ave Ste 1380 Oakland CA 94612 510-839-0193 763-8756 414
TF: 800-622-0909 ■ *Web:* www.uapd.com

Union of Concerned Scientists (UCS)
2 Brattle Sq Cambridge MA 02238 617-547-5552 864-9405 48-13
TF: 800-666-8276 ■ *Web:* www.ucsusa.org

Union Pacific California Employees Federal Credit Union
230 W Wilshire Ave Ste A Fullerton CA 92832 562-430-5552 685-2337* 219
**Fax Area Code: 909* ■ *TF:* 800-983-9590 ■ *Web:* ptfcuup.org

Union Pacific Corp 1400 Douglas St Omaha NE 68179 402-544-5000 360-3
NYSE: UNP ■ *TF:* 888-870-8777 ■ *Web:* www.up.com

Union Pacific Foundation
1400 Douglas St Omaha NE 68179 402-544-5600 304
Web: www.up.com

Union Parish
100 E Bayou St Ste 105 Farmerville LA 71241 318-368-3055 368-3861 338
TF: 888-288-9988 ■ *Web:* upclerk.com

Union Power Co-op
1525 N Rocky River Rd Monroe NC 28110 704-289-3145 296-0408 245
TF: 800-922-6840 ■ *Web:* union-power.com

Union Resource Marketing
5001 College Blvd Ste 107 Leawood KS 66209 913-322-2702 193
Web: www.unionresourcemarketing.com

Union River Center for Innovation
415 Water St Ellsworth ME 04605 800-930-5313 393
TF: 800-930-5313 ■ *Web:* unionriverinnovation.com

Union Roofers Health & Welfare
9901 Paramount Blvd Ste 211 Downey CA 90240 562-927-1434 414

Union Rural Electric Co-opeartive Inc
15461 US 36E Marysville OH 43040 937-642-1826 245
TF: 800-642-1826 ■ *Web:* www.ure.com

Union Sanitary District (USD)
5072 Benson Rd PO Box 5050 Union City CA 94587 510-477-7500 804
Web: www.unionsanitary.com

Union Savings Bank
223 W Stephenson St PO Box 540 Freeport IL 61032 815-235-0800 851-7278* 70
**Fax Area Code: 866* ■ *Web:* www.unionsavingsbank.com

Union Special Corp
1 Union Special Plz Huntley IL 60142 847-669-5101 219
Web: www.unionspecial.com

Union Square Advisors
600 Montgomery St 22nd Fl San Francisco CA 94111 415-501-8000 70
Web: www.usadvisors.com

Union Square Cafe 101 E 19th St New York NY 10003 212-243-4020 671
Web: www.unionsquarecafe.com

Union Square Ventures
915 Broadway 19th Fl New York NY 10010 212-994-7880 994-7399 792
Web: www.usv.com

Union Standard Equipment Co
801 E 141st St Bronx NY 10454 718-585-0200 993-2650 298
TF: 877-282-7333 ■ *Web:* www.unionmachinery.com

Union Standard Insurance Co
122 W Carpenter Fwy Ste 350 Irving TX 75039 972-719-2400 719-2401 391-4
TF: 800-444-0049 ■ *Web:* www.usic.com

Phone | Fax | Class

Union State Bank
127 S Summit St .... Arkansas City KS 67005 620-442-5200 70
Web: www.myunionstate.com
Union Station 50 Massachusetts Ave. .... Washington DC 20002 202-289-1908 50-6
TF: 800-331-0008 ■ *Web:* www.unionstationdc.com
Union Station Hotel 1001 Broadway .... Nashville TN 37203 615-726-1001 378
Web: www.unionstationhotelnashville.com
Union Street 4145 Woodward Ave. .... Detroit MI 48201 313-831-3965 831-2553 671
Web: unionstreetdetroit.com
Union Street Public House
121 S Union St. .... Alexandria VA 22314 703-548-1785 671
Web: www.unionstreetpublichouse.com
Union Tank Car Co
175 W Jackson Blvd Ste 2100 .... Chicago IL 60604 312-431-3111 650
TF: 855-885-9669 ■ *Web:* www.utlx.com
Union Telephone Co 100 W North St .... Plainfield WI 54966 715-335-6301 335-6305 224
Web: www.uniontel.net
Union Theological Seminary
3041 Broadway 121st St. .... New York NY 10027 212-662-7100 167-3
Web: utsnyc.edu
Union Theological Seminary & Presbyterian School of Christian Education
3401 Brook Rd .... Richmond VA 23227 804-355-0671 167-3
TF: 800-229-2990 ■ *Web:* www.upsem.edu
Union Township Chamber of Commerce
355 Chestnut St 2nd Fl. .... Union NJ 07083 908-688-2777 139
Web: www.unionchamber.com
Union Township Public Library
1980 Morris Ave. .... Union NJ 07083 908-851-5450 851-4671 434-3
Web: www.uniontownship.com
Union University
1050 Union University Dr. .... Jackson TN 38305 731-661-5210 661-5589 166
TF: 800-338-6466 ■ *Web:* www.uu.edu
Union, The 464 Sutton Way .... Grass Valley CA 95945 530-273-9561 477-4292 532-2
Web: www.theunion.com
Union-Hoermann Press Inc
2175 Kerper Blvd .... Dubuque IA 52001 563-582-3631 582-5937 627
Web: www.uhpress.com
Uniontown Hospital (UH)
500 W Berkeley St .... Uniontown PA 15401 724-430-5000 374-3
Web: www.uniontownhospital.com
Unionview Investment Group LLC
1500 Westlake Ave N Ste 124................... Seattle WA 98109 206-708-1048 690
Web: www.unionviewwealthpartners.com
Unipack Inc 3253 Old Frankstown Rd .... Pittsburgh PA 15239 724-733-7381 327-6265 582
Web: www.unipackinc.com
Unipak Aviation 2049 Ninth Ave .... Ronkonkoma NY 11779 631-471-9801 63
Web: www.unipakaviation.net
Uni-Pak Corp
1015 N Ronald Reagan Blvd................. Longwood FL 32750 407-830-9300 830-4106 207
Web: www.unipak.com
Unipec Inc 678 Lofstrand Ln .... Rockville MD 20850 301-762-9261 279-5545 604
Web: www.unipec.net
Unipharm Inc 350 Fifth Ave Ste 6701 .... New York NY 10118 212-594-3260 594-3261 582
Web: www.unipharmus.com
Unipharma Inc
10437 Los Alamitos Blvd .... Los Alamitos CA 90720 562-799-8844 799-1433 237
Web: unipharmainc.com
Uniphase Inc 425 38th Ave .... Saint Charles IL 60174 630-584-4747 604
Web: www.uniphaseinc.com
Uniplus Consultants Inc
8140 Ashton Ave Ste 210................... Manassas VA 20109 703-365-2227 809
Web: uniplus.com
UniPro Foodservice Inc
2500 Cumberland Pkwy Ste 600. .... Atlanta GA 30339 770-952-0871 297-8
Web: www.uniprofoodservice.com
Unipunch Products Inc
311 Fifth St NW .... Clear Lake WI 54005 800-828-7061 453-3994 757
TF: 800-828-7061 ■ *Web:* www.unipunch.com
Unique Aluminum Extrusion LLC
333 Cedar Ave .... Middlesex NJ 08846 732-271-1160 271-8327 482
Web: www.unalext.com
Unique Broadband Systems Ltd
400 Spinnaker Way......................... Vaughan ON L4K5Y9 905-669-8533 669-8516 647
TF: 877-669-8533 ■ *Web:* www.uniquesys.com
Unique Business Services Inc
26622 Woodward Ave Ste 250 .... Royal Oak MI 48067 248-542-1198 177
TF: 888-438-8271 ■ *Web:* uniquebusiness.services
Unique Business Systems Corp
2901 Ocean Park Blvd Ste 215............. Santa Monica CA 90405 310-396-3929 177
TF: 800-669-4827 ■ *Web:* www.unibiz.com
Unique Carpets Ltd 7360 Jurupa Ave........... Riverside CA 92504 951-352-8125 352-8140 131
TF: 800-547-8266 ■ *Web:* www.uniquecarpetsltd.com
Unique Communications Inc
3650 Coral Ridge Dr. .... Coral Springs FL 33065 954-735-4002 735-2612 246
TF: 800-881-8182 ■ *Web:* www.uniquecommunications.com
Unique Conversions PO Box 1638................. Azle TX 76020 817-915-2334 62-7
Web: laredoconversions.com
Unique Crafters Company Inc
10702 Trenton Ave .... Saint Louis MO 63132 314-427-5310 427-5312 322
TF: 800-727-4926 ■ *Web:* www.uniquecrafterscompany.com
Unique Employment Services Inc
4646 Corona Dr Ste 100.................. Corpus Christi TX 78411 361-852-6392 260
TF: 800-824-8367 ■ *Web:* www.uniquehr.com
Unique Fabricating Inc
800 Standard Pkwy...................... Auburn Hills MI 48326 248-853-2333 853-7720 601
Web: www.uniquefab.com
Unique Home Design Inc
973 N Colorado St Ste 1....................... Gilbert AZ 85233 480-988-5000 226
Web: uniquehd.com
Unique Image Inc
19365 Bus Center Dr Bldg 1................. Northridge CA 91324 818-727-7785 727-7735 627
Web: www.uniqueimageinc.com
Unique Industries Inc
4750 League Island Blvd .... Philadelphia PA 19112 215-336-4300 888-1490* 328
**Fax Area Code:* 800 ■ *TF:* 800-888-0559 ■ *Web:* www.favors.com
Unique Investment Corp
7028 Kearny Dr. .... Huntington Beach CA 92648 714-848-5900 848-5959 401
Web: www.uniquepartners.com

Unique Lighting Systems Inc
1240 Simpson Way. .... Escondido CA 92029 800-955-4831 740-0977* 767
**Fax Area Code:* 760 ■ *TF:* 800-955-4831 ■ *Web:* www.uniquelighting.com
Unique Litho Inc 9 Inverness Dr E............. Englewood CO 80112 303-830-2999 627
TF: 855-686-4783 ■ *Web:* www.uniquelitho.com
Unique Mailing Services Inc
325 Marmon Dr .... Bolingbrook IL 60440 630-739-4848 5
Web: www.valid.com
Unique Management Services Inc
119 E Maple St......................... Jeffersonville IN 47130 800-879-5453 160
TF: 800-879-5453 ■ *Web:* uniquelibrary.com
Unique Print NY 252 Greene St................ New York NY 10003 212-420-9198 113
Web: www.uniquecopycenter.com
Unirac Inc 1411 Broadway Blvd NE .... Albuquerque NM 87102 505-242-6411 567
Web: unirac.com
Unirex Inc 9310 E 37th St N.................... Wichita KS 67226 316-636-1228 636-5482 770
Web: www.apolloaerospacecomponents.com
Unirisc Inc 2000 14th St N Ste 500 .... Arlington VA 22201 703-797-3300 524-7933 390
TF: 800-424-9500 ■ *Web:* unirisc.com
Uniroyal Engineered Products LLC
501 S Water St .... Stoughton WI 53589 800-873-8800 741-2237 745-2
TF: 800-873-8800 ■ *Web:* www.naugahyde.com
UniSea Inc 15400 NE 90th St.................. Redmond WA 98073 425-881-8181 296-14
TF: 800-535-8509 ■ *Web:* www.unisea.com
Uniseal Inc 1014 E Uhlhorn St................ Evansville IN 47710 812-463-5230 3
Web: www.uniseal.com
Unisearch Associates Inc
96 Bradwick Dr............................ Concord ON L4K1K8 905-669-3547 358
Web: www.unisearch-associates.com
Unisearch Inc 1780 Barnes Blvd SW............ Tumwater WA 98512 360-956-9500 531-1717* 635
**Fax Area Code:* 800 ■ *TF:* 800-722-0708 ■ *Web:* www.unisearch.com
Unisec Inc 2555 Nicholson St .... San Leandro CA 94577 800-982-4587 352-6707* 692
**Fax Area Code:* 510 ■ *TF:* 800-982-4587 ■ *Web:* www.ultrabarrier.com
Uniserve Communications
333 Terminal Ave Ste 330................... Vancouver BC V6A4C1 604-395-3900 224
TF: 844-395-3900 ■ *Web:* www.uniserve.com
Unishippers Association Inc
746 E Winchester Ste 200................ Salt Lake City UT 84107 800-999-8721 487-7468* 546
**Fax Area Code:* 801 ■ *TF:* 800-999-8721 ■ *Web:* www.unishippers.com
UniSoft Corp 10 Rollins Rd Ste 118.............. Millbrae CA 94030 650-259-1290 259-1299 178-12
Web: www.unisoft.com
Unisoft International Inc
SMA Technologies
15333 Jfk Blvd Ste 300 .... Houston TX 77032 281-446-5000 446-7492 177
TF: 800-762-6584 ■ *Web:* smatechnologies.com
Unison Consulting Inc
409 W Huron St Ste 400. .... Chicago IL 60654 312-988-3360 988-3370 463
Web: www.unison-ucg.com
Unison LLC 7575 Baymeadows Way........... Jacksonville FL 32256 904-739-4244 739-4006 490
Web: www.unisonindustries.com
Unison Realty Partners LLC
177 Huntington Ave Ste 1901................... Boston MA 02115 617-702-8503 653
Web: unisonrealtypartners.com
Unison Systems Inc
6130 Greenwood Plaza Blvd Ste 100 .... Greenwood Village CO 80111 303-623-8800 196
Web: unisonsystems.com
UNI-SOURCE 2000 Inc
11040 Manchester Rd Ste 200 .... Saint Louis MO 63122 314-822-3735 822-1053 178-1
Web: www.uni-collect.com
Unisource Canada Inc
11704 186 St NW...................... Richmond Hill ON L4B3Z3 905-771-4000 771-4219 535
Web: www.veritivcanada.ca
UniSource Energy Services Inc
PO Box 711 .... Tucson AZ 85702 877-837-4968 325
Web: www.uesaz.com
Unisource Manufacturing Inc
8040 NE 33rd Dr. .... Portland OR 97211 503-281-4673 281-5845 454
TF: 800-234-2566 ■ *Web:* www.unisource-mfg.com
Unisource NTC
1556 N Moorpark Rd Ste 159............ Thousand Oaks CA 91360 310-496-7453 463
TF: 800-736-8470 ■ *Web:* wordpress.unisourcentc.com
Unisource Solutions Inc
8350 Rex Rd. .... Pico Rivera CA 90660 562-949-1111 319
Web: www.unisourceit.com
Unist 4134 36th St SE.................... Grand Rapids MI 49512 616-949-0853 949-9503 697
TF: 800-253-5462 ■ *Web:* unist.com
Unistar-Sparco Computers Inc
7089 Ryburn Dr .... Millington TN 38053 901-872-2272 872-8482 459
TF: 800-840-8400 ■ *Web:* www.sparco.com
Unisteel Inc 6155 Sims.................. Sterling Heights MI 48313 586-826-8040 826-8055 492
TF: 800-330-7343 ■ *Web:* unisteel.elwd.com
Unistress Corp 550 Cheshire Rd............... Pittsfield MA 01201 413-499-1441 499-9930 183
Web: www.unistresscorp.com
Unisys Corp 801 Lakeview Dr Ste 100 .... Blue Bell PA 19422 215-986-4011 196
Web: www.unisys.com
Unit Chemical Corp
7360 Commercial Way .... Henderson NV 89015 702-564-6454 564-6629 151
TF: 800-879-8648 ■ *Web:* www.unitchemical.com
Unit Company Inc 620 E Whitney Rd .... Anchorage AK 99501 907-349-6666 522-3464 186
Web: www.unitcompany.com
Unit Corp 7130 S Lewis Ave Ste 1000 .... Tulsa OK 74136 918-493-7700 493-7711 540
NYSE: UNT ■ *TF:* 800-722-3612 ■ *Web:* www.unitcorp.com
Unit Drop Forge Company Inc
1903 S 62nd St PO Box 340350............. West Allis WI 53219 414-545-3000 545-6318 483
Web: www.unitforgings.com
Unit Pack Company Inc 7 Lewis Rd.......... Cedar Grove NJ 07009 973-239-4112 239-0429 596
Web: www.unitpack.com
Unitarian Universalist Assn (UUA)
25 Beacon St .... Boston MA 02108 617-742-2100 367-3237 48-20
Web: www.uua.org
Unitarian Universalist Service Committee (UUSC)
689 Massachusetts Ave .... Cambridge MA 02139 617-868-6600 868-7102 48-5
TF: 800-388-3920 ■ *Web:* www.uusc.org
UNITE Here 275 Seventh Ave .... New York NY 10001 212-265-7000 414
TF: 800-452-4155 ■ *Web:* www.unitehere.org
Unite US 217 Broadway 8th Fl .... New York NY 10007 844-786-4838 178-1
TF: 844-786-4838 ■ *Web:* uniteus.com

				Phone	Fax	Class
Unitech Services Group 295 Parker St *TF:* 800-344-3824 ■ *Web:* www.unitechus.com	Springfield	MA	01151	413-543-6911	543-6989	442
Unitech Training Academy-houma 1227 Grand Caillou Rd *Web:* unitechtrainingacademy.com	Houma	LA	70363	985-223-1755		166
United Abrasives Inc 185 Boston Post Rd *TF:* 800-428-5927 ■ *Web:* www.unitedabrasives.com	North Windham	CT	06256	860-456-7131		1
United Aerospace Corp 9800 Premier Pkwy *Web:* www.unitedaerospace.com	Miramar	FL	33025	954-364-0085	364-0089	770
United Air Specialists Inc 4440 Creek Rd *TF:* 800-252-4647 ■ *Web:* www.uasinc.com	Cincinnati	OH	45242	513-891-0400		18
United Airlines Cargo PO Box 66100 *TF:* 800-822-2746 ■ *Web:* unitedcargo.com	Chicago	IL	60666	800-822-2746		12
United Alloy Inc 4100 Kennedy Rd *Web:* www.unitedalloy.com	Janesville	WI	53545	608-758-4717	758-1272	492
United Alloys and Metals Inc (UAM) 9600 John St *Web:* uametals.com	Santa Fe Springs	CA	90670	562-273-7004	944-7060	686
United Aluminum Corp 100 United Dr *TF:* 800-243-2515 ■ *Web:* www.unitedaluminum.com	North Haven	CT	06473	203-239-5881		492
United American Insurance Co 3700 S Stonebridge Dr **Fax Area Code:* 972 ■ *TF:* 800-755-2137 ■ *Web:* www2.unitedamerican.com	McKinney	TX	75070	800-755-2137	569-3709*	391-2
United Animal Health 4310 State Rd 38 W *TF:* 800-382-9909 ■ *Web:* www.unitedanh.com	Sheridan	IN	46069	317-758-4495		447
United Arab Emirates Embassy 3522 International Ct NW Ste 400 *Web:* www.uae-embassy.org	Washington	DC	20008	202-243-2400	243-2432	257
United Arkansas Federal Credit Union 8405 I-30 *TF:* 800-216-6393 ■ *Web:* unitedarkansas.org	Little Rock	AR	72209	501-565-8500		219
United Audio Video Group Inc 6055 Vineland Ave *Web:* www.unitedavg.com	North Hollywood	CA	91605	818-980-6700	508-0273	650
United Automobile Insurance Co PO Box 694140 *TF:* 888-987-8242 ■ *Web:* www.uaig.net	Miami	FL	33269	305-940-5022		390
United Avionics Inc 38 Great Hill Rd *Web:* www.unitedavionicsinc.com	Naugatuck	CT	06770	203-723-1404	723-4292	22
United Bakery Equipment Company Inc 15815 W 110th St *TF:* 888-823-2253 ■ *Web:* www.ubeusa.com	Lenexa	KS	66219	913-541-8700	541-0781	298
United Bancorp Inc 201 S Fourth St *NASDAQ: UBCP* ■ *TF:* 888-275-5566 ■ *Web:* www.unitedbancorp.com	Martins Ferry	OH	43935	740-633-0445	633-1448	360-2
United Bank 200 E Nashville *TF:* 800-423-7026 ■ *Web:* www.unitedbank.com	Atmore	AL	36502	800-423-7026		70
United Bank & Trust 935 Main St PO Box E *Web:* www.ubankonline.com	Sabetha	KS	66534	785-284-2187	284-0062	69
United Bank of Philadelphia 1501 N Broad St Ste 17 *Web:* www.ubphila.com	Philadelphia	PA	19122	215-978-5300		70
United Behavioral Health Inc 425 Market St 27th Fl *TF:* 800-888-2998 ■ *Web:* www.optum.com	San Francisco	CA	94105	415-547-5436		462
United Bindery Service Inc 2589 1845 W Carroll Ave	Chicago	IL	60612	312-243-0240		92
United Biomedical Inc 25 Davids Dr *Web:* www.unitedbiomedical.com	Hauppauge	NY	11788	631-273-2828	273-1717	85
United Brass Manufacturers Inc 35030 Goddard Rd *Web:* unitedbrass.com	Romulus	MI	48174	734-941-0700	941-0640	483
United Brass Works Inc 714 S Main St *TF:* 800-334-3035 ■ *Web:* ubw.com	Randleman	NC	27317	336-498-2661	498-4267	789
United Brotherhood of Carpenters & Joiners of America 101 Constitution Ave NW *TF:* 800-530-5090 ■ *Web:* www.carpenters.org	Washington	DC	20001	202-546-6206	543-5724	414
United Business Machines Inc (UBM) 13 Delta Dr Ste 9 & 10 *Web:* www.ubmnh.com	Londonderry	NH	03053	603-216-9249		112
United Capital Corp 9 Park Pl *OTC: UCAP* ■ *Web:* www.unitedcapitalcorp.net	Great Neck	NY	11021	516-466-6464	829-4301	655
United Capital Financial Advisers LLC 620 Newport Center Dr Ste 500 *Web:* www.goldmanpfm.com	Newport Beach	CA	92660	949-999-8500		401
United Capital Funding Corp 146 Second St N Ste 200 *Web:* www.ucfunding.com	Saint Petersburg	FL	33701	727-894-8232		272
United Central Industrial Supply Company LLC 1241 Volunteer Pkwy Ste 1000 *Web:* www.unitedcentral.net	Bristol	TN	37620	423-573-7300		470
United Cerebral Palsy 380 Washington Ave *Web:* ucp-li.org	Roosevelt	NY	11575	516-378-2000		186
United Chemi-Con Inc 9801 W Higgins Rd *Web:* www.chemi-con.com	Rosemont	IL	60018	847-696-2000	696-9278	253
United Church of Christ (UCC) 700 Prospect Ave *TF:* 866-822-8224 ■ *Web:* www.ucc.org	Cleveland	OH	44115	216-736-2100	736-2103	48-20
United Church of God an International Assocation 555 Techne Center Dr *Web:* www.ucg.org	Milford	OH	45150	513-576-9796		48-20
United Citizens Bank of Southern Kentucky Inc 700 Jamestown St *TF:* 877-313-2323 ■ *Web:* ucbsky.com	Columbia	KY	42728	270-384-2265	384-0270	70
United Co, The 1005 Glenway Ave *Web:* www.unitedco.net	Bristol	VA	24201	276-466-3322		360-3
United Coalition For Animals 2830 Colerain Ave *Web:* ucancincinnati.org	Cincinnati	OH	45225	513-721-7387		794
United Collection Bureau Inc 5620 Southwyck Blvd *TF:* 866-209-0622 ■ *Web:* ucbinc.com	Toledo	OH	43614	866-209-0622		160
United Color Manufacturing Inc (UCM) PO Box 480 *TF:* 800-852-5942 ■ *Web:* www.unitedcolor.com	Newtown	PA	18940	215-860-2165	860-8560	145
United Commercial Development Inc 7001 Preston Rd Ste 410 *Web:* www.ucdcorp.com	Dallas	TX	75205	214-224-4600		652
United Commercial Travellers 1801 Watermark Dr Ste 100 *TF:* 800-848-0123 ■ *Web:* www.uct.org	Columbus	OH	43215	614-228-3276	487-9675	457-10
United Community Bank PO Box 309 *TF:* 877-963-6257 ■ *Web:* www.ucbi.com	Four Oaks	NC	27524	919-963-2177	963-2768	70
United Community Banks Inc PO Box 398 *NASDAQ: UCBI* ■ *Web:* www.ucbi.com	Blairsville	GA	30514	706-781-2265		360-2
United Community Federal Credit Union 6010 Mountain View Dr *Web:* unitedcommunityfcu.org	West Mifflin	PA	15122	412-653-8000		219
United Companies Inc 3700 E Morgan Ave *TF:* 800-742-3928 ■ *Web:* www.unitedcompanies.com	Evansville	IN	47715	812-479-0231		360-3
United Concordia Companies Inc 3250 W Big Beaver Ste 327 *TF:* 800-944-6432 ■ *Web:* www.ucci.com	Troy	MI	48084	248-458-1580		391-3
United Concordia Companies Inc 21700 Oxnard Ste 500 *TF:* 800-876-6432 ■ *Web:* www.unitedconcordia.com	Woodland Hills	CA	91367	800-876-6432		391-3
United Consulting Group Ltd 625 Holcomb Bridge Rd *TF:* 800-266-0990 ■ *Web:* www.unitedconsulting.com	Norcross	GA	30071	770-209-0029		256
United Contractors 17 Crow Canyon Ct Ste 100 *Web:* www.unitedcontractors.org	San Ramon	CA	94583	925-855-7900	855-7909	256
United Contractors Midwest Inc 3151 Robbins Rd PO Box 13420 *TF:* 800-381-5497 ■ *Web:* www.ucm.biz	Springfield	IL	62791	217-546-6192	546-1904	188-4
United Conveyor Corp 2100 Norman Dr W *Web:* www.unitedconveyor.com	Waukegan	IL	60085	847-473-5900	473-5959	207
United CoolAir Corp 491 E Princess St *TF:* 877-905-1111 ■ *Web:* unitedcoolair.com	York	PA	17403	717-843-4311	854-4462	14
United Coop N7160 Raceway Rd *TF:* 800-924-2991 ■ *Web:* www.unitedcooperative.com	Beaver Dam	WI	53916	920-887-1756		345
United Cooperative Services 3309 N Main St PO Box 16 *TF:* 800-342-6239 ■ *Web:* ucs.net	Cleburne	TX	76033	817-556-4000	556-4068	245
United Cos 2273 River Rd *TF:* 800-321-0807 ■ *Web:* united-gj.com	Grand Junction	CO	81505	970-243-4900		182
United Country Real Estate Inc 2820 NW Barry Rd *TF:* 800-999-1020 ■ *Web:* www.unitedcountry.com	Kansas City	MO	64154	800-999-1020		652
United Ctr 1901 W Madison St *Web:* www.unitedcenter.com	Chicago	IL	60612	312-455-4500		720
United Dairy Farmers 3955 Montgomery Rd *TF:* 866-837-4833 ■ *Web:* drinkunited.com	Cincinnati	OH	45212	513-396-8700	396-8736	296-27
United Data Technologies Inc 8825 NW 21st Terr *TF:* 800-882-9919 ■ *Web:* udtonline.com	Doral	FL	33172	305-882-0435		624
United Developers LLC 2019 N Lamar St Ste 240 *Web:* uniteddevelopersllc.com	Dallas	TX	75202	214-855-5955	855-5980	809
United Distributors Inc 5500 United Dr SE *Web:* udiga.com	Smyrna	GA	30082	678-305-2080		81-1
United Drill Bushing Corp 12200 Woodruff Ave **Fax Area Code:* 800 ■ *TF:* 800-486-3466 ■ *Web:* www.ucc-udb.com	Downey	CA	90241	562-803-1521	486-3465*	493
United Education Institute Southlake Festival Shopping Ctr 1564 Southlake Pky *Web:* www.uei.edu	Morrow	GA	30206	678-902-6440		167-3
United Electric Company LP 501 Galveston St *Web:* www.magicaire.com	Wichita Falls	TX	76301	940-397-2100	397-5603	14
United Electric Controls Co 180 Dexter Ave *Web:* www.ueonline.com	Watertown	MA	02472	617-926-1000	926-2568	201
United Electric Co-opeartive Inc 1330 21st St *Web:* www.unitedelectric.coop	Heyburn	ID	83336	208-679-2222	679-3333	245
United Electric Co-opeartive Inc Exit 17 Interstate 80 *Web:* www.prea.com	Dubois	PA	15801	814-371-8570		245
United Electric Supply Inc 10 Bellecor Dr *TF:* 800-322-3374 ■ *Web:* www.unitedelectric.com	New Castle	DE	19720	302-322-3333		787
United Electrical Radio & Machine Workers of America 1 Gateway Ctr Ste 1400 *Web:* www.ueunion.org	Pittsburgh	PA	15222	412-471-8919		414
United Electrical Sales Ltd 4496 SW 36th St *TF:* 800-432-5126 ■ *Web:* uesfl.com	Orlando	FL	32811	407-246-1992	246-1588	246
United Engine & Machine Company Inc 1040 Corbett St *TF:* 800-648-7970 ■ *Web:* www.uempistons.com	Carson City	NV	89706	775-882-7790	882-7773	128
United Engine Specialists 14801 W Kellogg *TF:* 800-436-6869 ■ *Web:* www.unitedengine.biz	Wichita	KS	67235	316-721-6868	721-8014	262
United Entertainment Corp 3601 18th St S Ste 104 *Web:* www.uecmovies.com	Saint Cloud	MN	56301	320-203-1003	203-1229	748

	Phone	Fax	Class
United Envelope LLC 150 Industrial Park Dr. Mount Pocono PA 18344 *TF:* 800-752-4012 ■ *Web:* www.unitedenvelope.com	570-839-1600	839-8650	263
United Equipment Accessories Inc 2103 E Bremer Ave Hwy. Waverly IA 50677 *TF:* 800-394-9986 ■ *Web:* www.uea-inc.com	800-394-9986		247
United ERP LLC 2460 Lemoine Ave Ste 503. Fort Lee NJ 07024 *Web:* www.unitederp.com	201-567-6315		177
United Fabrics Inc (U) 9115 Pennsauken Hwy. Pennsauken NJ 08110 *TF:* 800-347-8344 ■ *Web:* www.unitedfabrics.com	856-665-2040	665-5761	594
United Farm Workers of America 29700 Woodford Techachpi Rd PO Box 62. Keene CA 93531 *Web:* ufw.org	661-823-6151	823-6174	414
United Farmers Co-op (UFC) 705 E Fourth St PO Box 461. Winthrop MN 55396 *TF:* 866-998-3266 ■ *Web:* www.ufcmn.com	507-647-6600		10
United Fashions of Texas LLC 4629 Macro Dr. San Antonio TX 78218 *Web:* melrosestore.com	210-662-7140		157-2
United Federations of Police Officers 1717 Pennsylvania Ave 10th Fl Ste 1025. Washington DC 20006 *Web:* www.ufpo.com	202-559-9031		49-7
United Finance Co 515 E Burnside St. Portland OR 97214 *Web:* www.unitedfinance.com	503-232-5153	238-6453	217
United Financial Services Group Inc 325 Chestnut St Ste 3000. Philadelphia PA 19106 *TF:* 800-626-0787 ■ *Web:* www.unitedfsg.com	215-238-0300	238-9056	310
United Fire Equipment Co 335 N Fourth Ave. Tucson AZ 85705 *TF:* 800-362-0150 ■ *Web:* www.unitedfire.net	520-622-3639	882-3991	679
United Flooring Distributors Inc 6201 Material Ave. Rockford IL 61101 *Web:* www.innoviscorp.com	815-654-8383	654-8398	361
United Food & Commercial Workers International Union (UFCW) 1775 K St NW. Washington DC 20006 *TF:* 800-551-4010 ■ *Web:* www.ufcw.org	202-223-3111		414
United Food & Commercial Workers Union Local 555 7095 SW Sandburg St. Tigard OR 97281 *TF:* 800-452-8329 ■ *Web:* www.ufcw555.com	503-684-2822		414
United Franchise Group 2121 Vista Pky. West Palm Beach FL 33411 *Web:* unitedfranchisegroup.com	561-425-6829	640-6062	393
United Freezer & Storage Co 650 N Meridian Rd. Youngstown OH 44509 *TF:* 800-716-1416 ■ *Web:* www.unitedfreezer.com	330-792-1739	792-2299	803-2
United Fresh Potato Growers of Idaho Inc 457 N 80 W. Blackfoot ID 83221 *Web:* www.unitedpotato.com	208-785-2850	785-0786	345
United Fresh Produce Assn 1901 Pennsylvania Ave NW Ste 1100. Washington DC 20006 *Web:* www.unitedfresh.org	202-303-3400	303-3433	48-2
United Funeral Directors Benefit Life Insurance Co 351 S Sherman Ste 102. Richardson TX 75081 *TF:* 800-766-0018 ■ *Web:* www.unitedbenefitsinc.com	469-330-2200	330-2204	390
United Gasket Corp 1633 S 55th Ave. Cicero IL 60804 *Web:* www.unitedgasket.com	708-656-3700	656-6292	326
United Gear & Assembly Inc 1700 Livingstone Rd. Hudson WI 54016 *Web:* www.ugaco.com	715-386-5867		454
United Gilsonite Laboratories Inc 1396 Jefferson Ave. Scranton PA 18509 *TF:* 800-272-3235 ■ *Web:* www.ugl.com	570-344-1202		550
United Glass to Metal Sealing Inc 15 Union St Everett Mills. Lawrence MA 01840 *Web:* www.unitedglass.com	978-327-5880	327-5879	454
United Graphics LLC 2916 Marshall Ave. Mattoon IL 61938 *Web:* www.ugllc.net	217-235-7161		626
United Group Services Inc 9740 Near Dr. Cincinnati OH 45246 *TF:* 800-633-9690 ■ *Web:* united-gs.com	513-874-2004		595
United Guaranty Corp (UGC) 230 N Elm St. Greensboro NC 27401 **Fax Area Code:* 888 ■ *TF:* 877-642-4642 ■ *Web:* www.ugcorp.com	877-642-4642	528-3273*	391-5
United Hardware Distributing Co 5005 Nathan Ln N. Plymouth MN 55442 *Web:* newsite.unitedhardware.com	763-559-1800		351
United Health Centers of The San Joaquin Valley 650 Zediker Ave Bldg 3. Parlier CA 93648 *TF:* 800-492-4227 ■ *Web:* www.unitedhealthcenters.org	559-646-6618	646-6614	353
United Health Services Hospitals 10-42 Mitchell Ave. Binghamton NY 13903 *Web:* www.uhs.net	607-762-2200		353
United HealthCare Services Inc 795 Woodland Pky St 301. Ridgeland MS 39157 *TF:* 866-574-6088 ■ *Web:* www.uhc.com	601-718-6584		391-3
United Heartland Inc PO Box 3026. Milwaukee WI 53201 **Fax Area Code:* 262 ■ *TF:* 866-206-5851 ■ *Web:* www.unitedheartland.biz	866-206-5851	787-7701*	391-4
United Heritage Life Insurance Co PO Box 7777. Meridian ID 83680 *TF:* 800-657-6351 ■ *Web:* www.unitedheritage.com	208-493-6100		391-2
United Home Health Agency Inc 4001 W Alameda Ave Ste 202. Burbank CA 91505 *Web:* www.unitedhomeha.com	818-755-8711		363
United Hospice of Rockland 11 Stokum Ln. New City NY 10956 *Web:* unitedhospiceinc.org	845-634-4974	634-7549	371
United Hospital Ctr 327 Medical Park Dr. Bridgeport WV 26330 *TF:* 800-607-8888 ■ *Web:* www.wvumedicine.org	681-342-1000		374-3
United Hospital Fund (UHF) 1411 Broadway 12th Fl. New York NY 10018 *Web:* www.uhfnyc.org	212-494-0700	494-0800	637-2
United Housing Services Inc 1851 E 1st St Ste 400. Santa Ana CA 92705 *TF:* 877-899-3760 ■ *Web:* www.uhsamerica.com	877-899-3760		196
United Human Capital Solutions 1 Centerpointe Dr Ste 580. Lake Oswego OR 97035 *Web:* uhcsolutions.com	503-443-6008		226
United Hunter Oil & Gas Corp 20 Adelaide St E Ste 200. Toronto ON M5C2T6 *Web:* www.unitedhunteroil.com	832-487-0813		539
United Hydrocarbon International Corp 2500 - 308 4th Ave SW. Calgary AB T2P0H7 *Web:* www.unitedhydrocarbon.com	204-234-5678		536
United Illuminating Co 157 Church St. New Haven CT 06510 *TF:* 800-722-5584 ■ *Web:* www.uinet.com	203-499-3625	499-5973	787
United Incentives Inc 13 S Third St Ste 500. Philadelphia PA 19106 *Web:* www.unitedincentives.com	215-625-2700	625-4552	384
United Industries Inc 1901 Revere Beach Pkwy. Everett MA 02149 *Web:* www.united-ind.com	617-387-9500	387-6331	567
United Industries Inc 1546 Henry Ave. Beloit WI 53511 *Web:* www.unitedindustries.com	608-365-8891	365-1259	490
United Infrastructure Group 3800 Arco Corporate Dr Ste 200. Charlotte NC 28273 *Web:* uig.net	803-581-6000	581-0553	256
United Insurance Holdings Corp 360 Central Ave Ste 900. Saint Petersburg FL 33701 *NASDAQ: UIHC* ■ *TF:* 800-861-4370 ■ *Web:* www.upcinsurance.com	800-295-8016		391-2
United Laboratories Inc 320 37th Ave. Saint Charles IL 60174 **Fax Area Code:* 630 ■ *TF:* 800-323-2594 ■ *Web:* www.unitedlabsinc.com	800-323-2594	443-2087*	145
United Landmark Assoc 3708 W Swann Ave Ste 201. Tampa FL 33609 *Web:* www.unitedlandmark.com	813-870-9519		7
United Launch Alliance LLC Galileo Operations Ctr 9501 E Panorama Cir Centennial CO 80112 *TF:* 800-511-4173 ■ *Web:* www.ulalaunch.com	720-922-7100		681
United Lawnscape Inc 62170 Van Dyke Rd. Washington MI 48094 *Web:* unitedlawnscape.com	586-752-5000		776
United Legwear Company LLC 48 W 38th St. New York NY 10018 *Web:* www.unitedlegwear.com	212-391-4143	869-7375	411
United Lens Company Inc 259 Worcester St. Southbridge MA 01550 *Web:* www.unitedlens.com	508-765-5421	765-0500	544
United Letter Service Inc 1231 N Ellis St. Bensenville IL 60106 *Web:* www.unitedgmg.com	312-767-5195		5
United Library 2121 Sheridan Rd. Evanston IL 60201 *TF:* 877-600-8753 ■ *Web:* library.garrett.edu	847-866-3909		434-3
United Lighting & Supply Co 121 Chestnut Ave SE. Fort Walton Beach FL 32548 *Web:* www.unitedlighting.com	850-244-8155	244-5629	246
United Lumber & Remanufacturing LLC 980 Ford Rd. Muscle Shoals AL 35661 *Web:* www.ufpi.com	256-381-4151		683
United Lutheran Seminary Philadelphia 7301 Germantown Ave. Philadelphia PA 19119 *TF:* 800-286-4616 ■ *Web:* unitedlutheranseminary.edu	215-248-6393	248-4577	167-3
United Manufacturing Assembly Inc 44169 Fremont Blvd. Fremont CA 94538 *Web:* www.umai.com	510-490-4680	490-4380	743
United Marble & Granite Inc 2163 Martin Ave. Santa Clara CA 95050 *Web:* www.unitedmarbleusa.com	408-347-3300		191-1
United Marine Enterprise Inc 1325 Spindletop Rd. Beaumont TX 77705 *Web:* www.umtexas.us	409-833-7070		698
United Marketing Group LLC PO Box 68993. Schaumburg IL 60173 **Fax Area Code:* 847 ■ *TF:* 800-513-9000	800-513-9000	240-5538*	195
United Materials LLC 3374 Walden Ave Ste 120. Depew NY 14043 *TF:* 888-918-6483 ■ *Web:* www.unitedmaterialsllc.com	716-213-5832	213-5850	182
United McGill Corp 1 Mission Pk. Groveport OH 43125 *Web:* www.unitedmcgill.com	614-829-1200	829-1291	697
United Medical Corp 603 Main St. Windermere FL 34786 *Web:* www.unitedmedical.com	407-876-2200	876-3065	353
United Memories Inc 4815 List Dr Ste 109. Colorado Springs CO 80919 *Web:* www.unitedmemories.com	719-594-4238		695
United Merchant Services of California Inc 750 Fairmont Ave 2nd Fl. Glendale CA 91203 *TF:* 800-324-8323 ■ *Web:* www.umsbanking.com	800-324-8323		112
United Metal Products Corp 8101 Lyndon St. Detroit MI 48238 *Web:* www.unitedmetalproducts.com	313-933-8750	933-1001	489
United Metal Products Inc 1920 E Encanto Dr. Tempe AZ 85281 *Web:* unitedmetal.com	480-968-9550		295
United Methodist News Service 810 12th Ave S. Nashville TN 37203 *TF:* 800-251-8140 ■ *Web:* www.umcom.org	615-742-5470		530
United Methodist Publishing House 201 Eigth Ave S. Nashville TN 37203 *TF:* 800-672-1789 ■ *Web:* www.umph.org	615-749-6000		637-3
United Methodist Retirement & Health Care Center Inc, The 2316 W Modelle Ave. Clinton OK 73601 *Web:* umhcc-clinton.com	580-323-0912		48-20
United Micro Data Inc 2900 Heritage Ave. Boise ID 83709 *Web:* www.umdata.com	208-333-8804		225
United Microelectronics Corp 488 De Guigne Dr. Sunnyvale CA 94085 *NYSE: UMC* ■ *TF:* 800-990-1135 ■ *Web:* www.umc.com	408-523-7800	733-8090	696
United Mine Workers of America (UMWA) 18354 Quantico Gateway Dr Ste 200. Triangle VA 22172 *TF:* 800-291-1425 ■ *Web:* umwa.org	703-291-2400		457-21

Phone | Fax | Class

United Mobile Homes Inc
3499 Rt 9 N Ste 3C . . . Freehold NJ 07728 732-577-9997 655
NYSE: UMH ■ *TF:* 800-504-0670 ■ *Web:* www.umh.com
United Motorcoach Assn (UMA)
113 SW St 4th Fl . . . Alexandria VA 22314 703-838-2929 838-2950 49-21
TF: 800-424-8262 ■ *Web:* www.uma.org
United Nations Association of USA
2425 College Ave . . . Berkeley CA 94704 510-849-1752 292
Web: www.unausaeastbay.org
United Nations Children's Fund (UNICEF)
3 United Nations Plz . . . New York NY 10017 212-326-7000 888-7465 783
Web: www.unicef.org
United Nations Development Programme
1 UN Plz . . . New York NY 10017 212-906-5000 906-5364 783
Web: www.undp.org
United Nations Educational Scientific & Cultural Organization (UNESCO)
2 UN Plz . . . New York NY 10017 917-810-9030 783
Web: en.unesco.org
United Nations Environment Programme (UNEP)
2013 Q St NW . . . Washington DC 20006 202-785-0465 785-2096 783
Web: www.rona.unep.org
United Nations Federal Credit Union (UNFCU)
24-01 44th Rd Ct Sq Pl . . . Long Island City NY 11101 347-686-6000 686-6400 219
TF: 800-891-2471 ■ *Web:* www.unfcu.org
United Nations Foundation (UNF)
1800 Massachusetts Ave NW Ste 400 . . . Washington DC 20036 202-887-9040 887-9021 48-5
Web: www.unfoundation.org
United Nations Industrial Development Organization (UNIDO)
1 UN Plz . . . New York NY 10017 212-963-6890 963-7904 783
Web: www.unido.org
United Nations International School
24-50 Fdr Dr . . . New York NY 10010 212-684-7400 449
Web: www.unis.org
United Network for Organ Sharing (UNOS)
700 N Fourth St . . . Richmond VA 23219 804-782-4800 782-4817 48-17
TF: 888-894-6361 ■ *Web:* unos.org
United Notions Inc 13800 Hutton Dr . . . Dallas TX 75234 972-484-8901 594
TF: 800-527-9447 ■ *Web:* www.storefront.unitednotions.com
United Nurses & Allied Professionals
375 Branch Ave . . . Providence RI 02904 401-831-3647 831-3677 533
Web: www.unap.org
United Oil of the Carolinas Inc
PO Box 68 . . . Gastonia NC 28054 704-824-3561 824-8567 579
Web: www.unitedoilonline.com
United Operations Incorporated of Minneapolis
2340 Niagara Ln N . . . Plymouth MN 55447 763-551-0101 653
Web: unitedoperations.com
United Overseas Bank Limited New York Agency (UOB)
592 Fifth Ave 10th Fl . . . New York NY 10036 646-472-8113 382-1881* 70
**Fax Area Code:* 212 ■ *Web:* www.uobgroup.com
United Pacific Co
10975 SW 11th St Ste 175 PO Box 628 . . . Beaverton OR 97075 503-644-9018 644-4795 123
Web: unitedpacific.co
United Pacific Pet 12060 Cabernet Dr . . . Fontana CA 92337 951-360-8550 360-8540 578
TF: 800-979-3333 ■ *Web:* www.uppet.com
United Paradyne Corp
2415 Professional Pkwy . . . Santa Maria CA 93455 805-348-3150 348-3152 529
Web: unitedparadyne.com
United Paramount Tax Group Inc
4025 Woodland Park Blvd Ste 310 . . . Arlington TX 76013 817-983-0099 2
TF: 888-829-8829 ■ *Web:* uptg.com
United Parcel Service Inc (UPS)
55 Glenlake Pkwy NE . . . Atlanta GA 30328 404-828-6000 828-6440 546
NYSE: UPS ■ *Web:* www.ups.com
United Pentecostal Church Intl (UPCI)
8855 Dunn Rd . . . Hazelwood MO 63042 314-837-7300 48-20
Web: www.upci.org
United Performance Metals
3475 Symmes Rd . . . Hamilton OH 45015 513-860-6500 874-6857 723
TF: 888-282-3292 ■ *Web:* www.upmet.com
United Personnel Services Inc
289 Bridge St . . . Springfield MA 01103 413-736-0800 260
TF: 800-363-8200 ■ *Web:* www.unitedpersonnel.com
United Pet Care LLC
6232 N 7th St Ste 202 . . . Phoenix AZ 85014 602-266-5303 794
TF: 877-872-8800 ■ *Web:* www.unitedpetcare.com
United Petroleum Equipment Co
611 Hackberry St . . . Dawson MN 56232 320-226-1369 579
Web: www.unitedpetroleum.com
United Pharma LLC
2317 2319 Moore Ave . . . Fullerton CA 92833 714-738-8999 506
Web: www.unitedpharmallc.com
United Pharmacal Company of Missouri Inc
3705 Pear St . . . Saint Joseph MO 64503 816-233-8800 233-9696 578
TF: 800-254-8726 ■ *Web:* www.upco.com
United Pioneer Co
2777 Summer St Ste 206 . . . Stamford CT 06905 800-466-9823 466-9828 576
TF: 800-466-9823 ■ *Web:* www.b340.com
United Plastic Fabricating Inc
165 Flagship Dr . . . North Andover MA 01845 978-975-4520 605-1
TF: 800-638-8265 ■ *Web:* www.unitedplastic.com
United Plastics Group Inc (UPG)
7865 Northcourt Rd . . . Houston TX 77040 713-466-5563 604
Web: www.upgintl.com
United Poles Federal Credit Union
412 New Brunswick Ave . . . Perth Amboy NJ 08861 732-442-5648 442-1443 219
TF: 800-872-1712 ■ *Web:* unitedpolesfcu.com
United Postmasters & Managers of America
8 Herbert St . . . Alexandria VA 22305 703-683-9027 49-7
Web: www.unitedpma.org
United Power Inc 500 Co-op Way . . . Brighton CO 80603 303-659-0551 245
TF: 800-468-8809 ■ *Web:* www.unitedpower.com
United Press Inc
530 Bennett Rd . . . Elk Grove Village IL 60007 708-807-0339 482-0594* 627
**Fax Area Code:* 847 ■ *Web:* www.unitedpressinc.com
United Press Intl (UPI)
1133 19th St NW . . . Washington DC 20036 202-898-8000 530
Web: www.upi.com

United Producers Inc
8351 N High St Ste 250 . . . Columbus OH 43235 800-456-3276 446
TF: 800-456-3276 ■ *Web:* www.uproducers.com
United Propane Gas 4200 Cairo Rd . . . Paducah KY 42001 800-782-7743 316
TF: 800-782-7743 ■ *Web:* www.upgas.com
United Realty Group
8951 W Atlantic Blvd . . . Coral Springs FL 33071 954-670-5671 652
Web: urgfl.com
United Rebar Inc 8301 Galena Ave . . . Sacramento CA 95828 916-379-9900 379-9909 194
Web: www.unitedrebar.com
United Record Pressing LLC
453 Allied Dr . . . Nashville TN 37211 615-259-9396 244-3734 626
TF: 866-407-3165 ■ *Web:* www.urpressing.com
United Refining Company Inc
15 Bradley St . . . Warren PA 16365 814-723-1500 726-4709 580
Web: www.urc.com
United Refrigeration Inc
11401 Roosevelt Blvd . . . Philadelphia PA 19154 215-698-9100 698-9493 665
Web: www.uri.com
United Regional Chamber of Commerce
310 S St . . . Plainville MA 02762 508-316-0861 316-1992 139
Web: www.unitedregionalchamber.org
United Regional Hospital
Eighth Street Campus
1600 11th St . . . Wichita Falls TX 76301 940-764-7000 766-8711 374-3
Web: www.unitedregional.org
United Rentals 3266 E Washington St . . . Phoenix AZ 85034 602-267-3898 264-3
TF: 844-873-4948 ■ *Web:* www.unitedrentals.com
United Reprographics LLC
1750 Fourth Ave S . . . Seattle WA 98134 206-382-1177 627
Web: www.unitedreprographics.com
United Republic Bank 111 N 181st St . . . Elkhorn NE 68022 402-505-8500 70
Web: unitedrepublicbank.com
United Restaurant Equipment Company Inc
1 Executive Park Dr . . . North Billerica MA 01862 978-439-5500 262-9999 300
Web: www.unitedrestaurant.com
United Road Services Inc
10701 Middlebelt Rd . . . Romulus MI 48174 800-221-5127 780
TF: 800-221-5127 ■ *Web:* www.unitedroad.com
United Rotary Brush Corp
15607 W 100th Terr . . . Lenexa KS 66219 913-888-8450 541-8310 190
TF: 800-851-5108 ■ *Web:* www.united-rotary.com
United Rotorcraft Solutions LLC
1942 N Trinity St . . . Decatur TX 76234 940-627-0626 350
Web: www.airmethods.com
United Salt Corp 4800 San Felipe St . . . Houston TX 77056 713-877-2600 503-1
TF: 800-554-8658 ■ *Web:* unitedsalt.com
United Scale & Engineering Corp
16725 W Victor Rd . . . New Berlin WI 53151 800-236-1733 785-9754* 300
**Fax Area Code:* 262 ■ *TF:* 800-236-1733 ■ *Web:* www.unitedscale.com
United Scenic Artists
29 W 38th St 15th Fl . . . New York NY 10018 212-581-0300 977-2011 414
Web: www.usa829.org
United Screening Services Corp
10300 Sunset Dr Ste 101 . . . Miami FL 33173 305-774-1711 260
Web: www.unitedscreening.com
United Security Assurance Company of Pennsylvania
673 E Cherry Ln . . . Souderton PA 18964 215-723-3044 723-8036 796
TF: 800-872-3044 ■ *Web:* www.usaofpa.com
United Security Bancshares
2126 Inyo St . . . Fresno CA 93721 559-248-4943 70
NASDAQ: UBFO ■ *TF:* 888-683-6030 ■ *Web:* www.unitedsecuritybank.com
United Security Bancshares Inc
PO Box 249 . . . Thomasville AL 36784 334-636-5424 360-2
Web: www.firstusbank.com
United Security Health and Casualty
6640 S Cicero Ave . . . Bedford Park IL 60638 708-475-6100 475-6120 706
TF: 800-875-4422 ■ *Web:* www.ushandc.com
United Security Inc
4295 Arthur Kill Rd . . . Staten Island NY 10309 718-967-6820 967-6817 693
TF: 800-874-6434 ■ *Web:* www.usisecurity.com
United Security Products Inc
13250 Gregg St Ste B . . . Poway CA 92064 858-413-0149 413-0124 392
TF: 800-227-1592 ■ *Web:* www.unitedsecurity.com
United Service and Sales Inc
2808 S Main St . . . Salt Lake City UT 84115 801-485-5770 485-5774 274
TF: 800-203-8454 ■ *Web:* www.unitedserviceandsales.com
United Service Organizations (USO)
2111 Wilson Blvd Ste 1200 . . . Arlington VA 22201 888-484-3876 48-19
TF: 800-876-7469 ■ *Web:* www.uso.org
United Services Automobile Assn (USAA)
10750 McDermott Fwy . . . San Antonio TX 78288 800-531-8722 531-5717 185
TF: 800-531-8722 ■ *Web:* www.usaa.com
United Sign Systems 5201 Pentecost Dr . . . Modesto CA 95356 209-543-1320 543-1326 9
TF: 800-481-7446 ■ *Web:* www.unitedsign.net
United Skys 702 Magna Dr . . . Round Lake IL 60073 847-546-7776 546-7785 198
Web: unitedskys.com
United Software Associates Inc
5674 Stoneridge Dr Ste 100 . . . Pleasanton CA 94588 925-468-0240 396
United Solutions Company Inc
1585 Summit Lake Dr . . . Tallahassee FL 32317 866-942-9186 225
TF: 866-942-9186 ■ *Web:* unitedsolutions.coop
United Southeast Federal Credit Union
1545 Bluff City Hwy . . . Bristol TN 37620 423-989-2100 219
Web: usfcu.org
United Soybean Board (USB)
16305 Swingley Ridge Rd Ste 150 . . . Chesterfield MO 63017 636-530-1777 530-1560 48-2
TF: 800-989-8721 ■ *Web:* www.unitedsoybean.org
United Spinal Assn (NSCIA)
75-20 Astoria Blvd Ste 120 . . . East Elmhurst NY 11370 718-803-3782 803-0414 48-17
TF: 800-962-9629 ■ *Web:* unitedspinal.org
United Staffing Solutions (USS)
111 Broadway 3rd Fl . . . New York NY 10006 800-972-9725 224-8393* 260
**Fax Area Code:* 646 ■ *TF:* 800-972-9725 ■ *Web:* www.unitedstaffingsolutions.net
United Standard Industries Inc
2062 Lehigh Ave . . . Glenview IL 60026 847-724-0350 757
Web: www.unitedstandard.com

Name / Address	Phone	Fax	Class
United States Aviation 4141 N Memorial Dr. Tulsa OK 74115 *TF:* 800-897-5387 ■ *Web:* www.unitedstatesaviation.com	918-836-7345		63
United States Bankruptcy Court *District of Rhode Island* 380 Westminster Mall 6th Fl Providence RI 02903 *Web:* rib.uscourts.gov	401-626-3100	626-3150	341-2
United States Beef Corp 4923 E 49th St Tulsa OK 74135 *Web:* www.usbeefcorp.com	918-665-0740		671
United States Brass & Copper 1401 Brook Dr Downers Grove IL 60515 *TF:* 800-821-2854 ■ *Web:* usbrassandcopper.com	800-821-2854	910-4714	492
United States Department of the Navy 1200 Navy Pentagon Washington Navy Yard DC 20350 *Web:* www.navy.mil	703-614-9154		340-6
United States Deputy Sheriffs' Association Inc 2909 S Spruce St Wichita KS 67216 *TF:* 844-310-1666 ■ *Web:* usdeputy.org	316-263-2583		41
United States District Court *Western District of Michigan* 110 Michigan St NW 399 Federal Bldg Grand Rapids MI 49503 *TF:* 800-290-2742 ■ *Web:* www.miwd.uscourts.gov	616-456-2381		341-3
United States District Court for the Western District of Arkansas 30 S Sixth St Judge Isaac C Parker Federal Bldg Rm 1038 Fort Smith AR 72901 *Web:* www.arwd.uscourts.gov	479-783-6833	783-6308	341-3
United States District Court, Central District 312 N Spring St Los Angeles CA 90012 *Web:* www.cacd.uscourts.gov	213-894-1565		341-3
United States Drug Testing Laboratories (USDTL) 1700 S Mt Prospect Rd Des Plaines IL 60018 *TF:* 800-235-2367 ■ *Web:* www.usdtl.com	847-375-0770	375-0775	416
United States Endoscopy Group Inc 5976 Heisley Rd Mentor OH 44060 *Web:* www.steris.com	440-639-4494		476
United States Gypsum Co 550 W Adams St Chicago IL 60661 *TF:* 800-874-4968 ■ *Web:* www.usg.com	312-436-4000		347
United States Information Systems Inc (USIS) 35 W Jefferson Ave Pearl River NY 10965 *TF:* 866-222-3778 ■ *Web:* www.usis.net	845-358-7755		787
United States Marine Inc 10011 Lorraine Rd Gulfport MS 39503 *Web:* usmi.com	228-679-1005		698
United States Medical Supply Inc 8260 NW 27 St Ste 401 Miami FL 33122 *TF:* 877-840-8218 ■ *Web:* www.us-med.com	877-840-8218		475
United States Olympic & Paralympic Committee 1 Olympic Plz Colorado Springs CO 80909 *Web:* www.teamusa.org	719-866-4730		712
United States Patent & Trademark Office PO Box 1450 Alexandria VA 22313 *TF:* 800-786-9199 ■ *Web:* www.uspto.gov	571-272-5600	273-8300	340-2
United States Senate Special Committee on Aging G31 Dirksen Senate Office Bldg Washington DC 20510 *TF:* 855-303-9470 ■ *Web:* www.aging.senate.gov	202-224-5364	224-8660	342-1
United States Steel Corp 600 Grant St Pittsburgh PA 15219 *NYSE:* X ■ *TF:* 866-433-4801 ■ *Web:* www.ussteel.com	412-433-1121		261
United States Warranty Corp 22 NE 22nd Ave Pompano Beach FL 33062 *TF:* 800-432-4566 ■ *Web:* www.uswarranty.com	954-784-9400	784-7009	390
United Stations Radio Network 1065 Avenue of the Americas 3rd Fl New York NY 10018 *TF:* 866-989-1975 ■ *Web:* www.unitedstations.com	212-869-1111		644
United Steel Inc 164 School St East Hartford CT 06108 *Web:* www.unitedsteel.com	860-289-2323		492
United Steel Products Inc 33-40 127th Pl Flushing NY 11368 *TF:* 888-683-2516 ■ *Web:* www.unitedsteelproducts.com	833-387-6595		234
United Steel Workers (USW) 3340 Perimeter Hill Dr Nashville TN 37211 *Web:* www.usw.org	615-834-8590		414
United Sugars Corp 7803 Glenroy Rd Ste 300 Bloomington MN 55439 *TF:* 800-984-3585 ■ *Web:* www.unitedsugars.com	952-896-0131	896-0400	297-11
United Supermarkets Ltd 7830 Orlando Ave Lubbock TX 79423 *Web:* www.unitedsupermarkets.com	806-791-0220		345
United Suppliers Inc 30473 260th St PO Box 538 Eldora IA 50627 *TF:* 800-782-5123 ■ *Web:* www.unitedsuppliers.com	641-858-2341		276
United Surgical Partners International Inc (USPI) 15305 Dallas Pkwy Addison TX 75001 *Web:* www.uspi.com	972-713-3500		352
United Synagogue of Conservative Judaism (USCJ) 820 Second Ave New York NY 10017 *Web:* uscj.org	212-533-7800	353-9439	48-20
United Systems 5700 N Portland Ave Ste 201 Oklahoma City OK 73112 *Web:* www.unitedsystemsok.com	405-523-2162		174
United Systems & Software Inc 300 Colonial Center Pkwy Ste 150 Lake Mary FL 32746 *TF:* 800-522-8774 ■ *Web:* www.ussisolutions.com	407-875-2120	875-9600	177
United Talent Agency Inc (UTA) 9336 Civic Center Dr Beverly Hills CA 90210 *Web:* unitedtalent.com	310-273-6700	247-1111	731
United Talent LLC 500 Leon Sullivan Way Charleston WV 25301 *Web:* utalent.com	304-556-1190		260
United Technical Center School of Practical Nursing 251 Marrietta St Clarksburg WV 26301 *Web:* www.harcoboe.net	304-326-7580	622-6138	685
United Telephone Mutual Aid Corp 411 Seventh Ave Langdon ND 58249 *Web:* www.utma.com	701-256-5156		116
United Temps Inc 1550 S Indiana Ave Chicago IL 60605 *TF:* 800-248-8558 ■ *Web:* www.unitedhq.com	312-922-8558		463
United Textile Company Inc 14275 Catalina St San Leandro CA 94577 *TF:* 800-233-0077 ■ *Web:* www.unitedtextileinc.com	510-276-2288		508
United Theological Seminary 4501 Denlinger Rd Dayton OH 45426 *Web:* united.edu	937-529-2201		167-3
United Theological Seminary of the Twin Cities 3000 5th St NW New Brighton MN 55112 *Web:* www.unitedseminary-mn.org	651-633-4311		167-3
United Therapeutics Corp 1040 Spring St Silver Spring MD 20910 *NASDAQ:* UTHR ■ *TF:* 877-864-8437 ■ *Web:* www.unither.com	301-608-9292	608-9291	582
United Therapy Services 10333 Harwin Dr Ste 668 Houston TX 77036 *Web:* unitedtxs.com	281-516-8288		363
United Thread 4111 NW 132nd St Ste G Opa Locka FL 33054 *TF:* 866-608-6261 ■ *Web:* www.unitedtps.com	866-608-6261		594
United Tile of LaFayette LLC 1505 Eraste Landry Rd Lafayette LA 70506 *Web:* www.unitedtilelafayette.com	337-234-2319	232-2014	290
United Titanium Inc 3450 Old Airport Rd Wooster OH 44691 *TF:* 800-321-4938 ■ *Web:* www.unitedtitanium.com	330-264-2111	263-1336	308
United Tool & Die Co 1 Carney Rd West Hartford CT 06110 *Web:* utdco.com	860-246-6531	246-6723	22
United Tool & Stamping Company of North Carolina Inc 2817 Enterprise Ave Fayetteville NC 28306 *TF:* 800-883-6087 ■ *Web:* www.uts-nc.com	910-323-8588		697
United Tool and Engineering Co 4095 Prairie Hill Rd South Beloit IL 61080 *Web:* www.unitedtooleng.com	815-389-3021		757
United Tool Company Inc 838 Lafontaine Ave Wabash IN 46992 *Web:* www.unitedtoolcompany.com	260-563-3143	563-5759	454
United Tractor Trailer School Inc 710 Fuller Rd Chicopee MA 01020 *Web:* www.unitedcdl.com	413-592-1500		685
United Treating & Distribution LLC 338 E Washington Ave Muscle Shoals AL 35661 *TF:* 877-248-0944 ■ *Web:* www.unitedtreating.com	256-248-0944	386-5244	683
United Tribes Technical College 3315 University Dr Bismarck ND 58504 *TF:* 888-643-8882 ■ *Web:* www.uttc.edu	701-255-3285	530-0640	165
United Underwriters Inc PO Box 971000 Orem UT 84097 *TF:* 866-686-4833 ■ *Web:* www.uuinsurance.com	801-226-2662	229-2662	390
United Utilities Inc 5450 A St Anchorage AK 99518 *TF:* 800-478-2020 ■ *Web:* www.unicom-alaska.com	907-561-1674		736
United Valley Bank 211 Division Ave PO Box 170 Cavalier ND 58220 *TF:* 888-265-8331 ■ *Web:* uvbank.net	701-265-8331	265-4193	70
United Van Lines Inc 1 United Dr Fenton MO 63026 *TF:* 877-740-3040 ■ *Web:* www.unitedvanlines.com	636-343-3900	349-8794	519
United Way of America 701 N Fairfax St Alexandria VA 22314 *TF:* 800-892-2757 ■ *Web:* www.unitedway.org	703-836-7100		48-5
United Way of Central Md Inc, The 100 S Charles St PO Box 1576 Baltimore MD 21203 *Web:* www.uwcm.org	410-547-8000		193
United Way of Greater Cincinnati 2400 Reading Rd Cincinnati OH 45202 *Web:* www.uwgc.org	513-762-7100		48-6
United Way of the Lower Mainland Library 4543 Canada Way Burnaby BC V5G4T4 *Web:* www.uwlm.ca	604-294-8929		434-3
United Way of Westchester and Putnam 336 Central Park Ave White Plains NY 10606 *Web:* www.uwwp.org	914-997-6700		48-6
United Western Industries Inc 3515 N Hazel Ave Fresno CA 93722 *Web:* www.unitedwesternindustries.com	559-226-7236	226-3557	757
United Wholesale Lumber Co 8009 Doe Ave Visalia CA 93291 *Web:* www.uwlco.com	559-651-2037	651-0742	551
United Window & Door 24-36 Fadem Rd Springfield NJ 07081 *TF:* 800-848-4550 ■ *Web:* www.unitedwindowmfg.com	800-848-4550		480
United-Bilt Homes Inc 8500 Line Ave Shreveport LA 71106 *TF:* 800-551-8955 ■ *Web:* www.ubh.com	318-861-4572		187
United-Guardian Inc (UGI) 230 Marcus Blvd PO Box 18050 Hauppauge NY 11788 *NASDAQ:* UG ■ *TF:* 800-645-5566 ■ *Web:* www.u-g.com	631-273-0900	273-0858	479
UnitedLayer Inc 200 Paul Ave Ste 110 San Francisco CA 94124 *TF:* 888-853-7733 ■ *Web:* www.unitedlayer.com	415-349-2100	520-5700	225
Unitek College 257 Longford Dr Ste 5 South San Francisco CA 94080 **Fax Area Code:* 650 ■ *TF:* 855-811-6191 ■ *Web:* www.unitekcollege.edu	855-811-6191	871-0703*	167-3
Unitel Inc PO Box 165 Unity ME 04988 *TF:* 888-760-1048 ■ *Web:* www.unitelme.com	207-948-3900		736
Unitex Oil & Gas LLC 508 W Wall St Ste 1000 Midland TX 79701 *Web:* unitexoilandgas.com	432-685-0014	685-0076	536
Unitil Corp 6 Liberty Ln W Hampton NH 03842 *NYSE:* UTL ■ *TF:* 800-852-3339 ■ *Web:* www.unitil.com	603-772-0775	773-6605	360-5
Unitra Inc 12601 Exchange Dr Stafford TX 77477 *Web:* www.unitrainc.com	281-240-1500	240-4334	641
Unitrak Corporation Ltd 299 Ward St Port Hope ON L1A3W4 *Web:* unitrak.com	905-885-8168		207
Unitrans International Corp 709 S Hindry Ave Inglewood CA 90301 *Web:* www.unitrans-us.com	310-410-7676	410-1719	449
Unitrends Software Corp 200 Wheeler Rd 2nd Fl Burlington MA 01803 *TF:* 866-359-5411 ■ *Web:* www.unitrends.com	803-454-0300		173-8
Unitron LP 10925 Miller Rd PO Box 38902 Dallas TX 75238 *TF:* 800-527-1279 ■ *Web:* www.unitronlp.com	214-340-8600	341-2099	518

Company / Address	City	State	ZIP	Phone	Fax	Class
Unitus Community Credit Union PO Box 1937 *TF:* 800-452-0900 ■ *Web:* www.unitusccu.com	Portland	OR	97207	503-227-5571		219
Unity Bancorp Inc 64 Old Hwy 22 *NASDAQ: UNTY* ■ *TF:* 800-618-2265 ■ *Web:* www.unitybank.com	Clinton	NJ	08809	908-730-7630		360-2
Unity College 90 Quaker Hill Rd *TF:* 800-624-1024 ■ *Web:* www.unity.edu	Unity	ME	04988	207-948-3131		166
Unity Elementary School 6846 Unity School Rd *Web:* unity.massac.org	Brookport	IL	62910	618-564-2582		685
Unity Financial Life Insurance Co 4675 Cornell Rd Ste 160 *Web:* www.uflife.com	Cincinnati	OH	45241	513-247-0711	247-5040	796
Unity Financial Strategists Inc 100 Wall St 22nd Fl	New York	NY	10005	212-785-4200		401
Unity Gain Recording Institute 1953 Ricardo Ave *Web:* www.unitygain.com	Fort Myers	FL	33901	239-332-4246		167-3
Unity Health Insurance *Quartz Health Solutions* 840 Carolina St *TF:* 800-362-3308 ■ *Web:* quartzbenefits.com	Sauk City	WI	53583	608-644-3430	643-2564	391-3
Unity Home Group Inc 101 W Benson Blvd Ste 101 *Web:* akhomeshow.com	Anchorage	AK	99503	907-885-3300	865-6565	652
Unity Hospice 2366 Oak Ridge Cir *TF:* 800-990-9249 ■ *Web:* unityhospice.org	De Pere	WI	54115	920-338-1111		371
Unity Hospice 600 West Cermak Road 3D Ste 210 *TF:* 888-949-1188 ■ *Web:* www.unityhospice.com	Chicago	IL	60607	312-427-6000	427-6004	371
Unity House 1901 NW Blue Pkwy *Web:* www.unityonline.org	Unity Village	MO	64065	816-524-3550		637-2
Unity HR LLC 2400 Meridian St Bldg B *Web:* www.unityhr.com	Bellingham	WA	98225	360-671-0762	715-0215	2
Unity Lake State Recreation Site 725 Summer St NE Ste C *Web:* stateparks.oregon.gov	Salem	OR	97301	541-932-4453		565
Unity Manufacturing Co 1260 N Clybourn Ave *Web:* www.unityusa.com	Chicago	IL	60610	312-943-5200	943-5681	438
Unity Marketing Inc 206 E Church St *Web:* unitymarketingonline.com	Stevens	PA	17578	717-336-1600		466
Unity Railway Supply Company Inc 805 Golf Ln *Web:* unityrailway.com	Bensenville	IL	60106	630-595-4560		770
Unity Technologies Inc 30 3rd St *Web:* unity3d.com	San Francisco	CA	94103	415-539-3162		177
UnityPoint Health Keokuk 1600 Morgan St *Web:* www.unitypoint.org	Keokuk	IA	52632	319-524-7150	524-5317	374-3
Univance Inc 3400 Corporate Dr *Web:* www.uvc.co.jp	Winchester	KY	40391	859-737-2306		247
Univar Canada Ltd 9800 Van Horne Way *TF:* 855-888-8648 ■ *Web:* www.univarsolutions.com	Richmond	BC	V6X1W5	855-888-8648		146
Univar Solutions 10800 Pecan Park Blvd Ste 300 Bldg 1 *Web:* www.univarsolutions.com	Austin	TX	78750	512-346-6070		146
Univation Technologies LLC 5555 San Felipe Ste 1950 *Web:* www.univation.com	Houston	TX	77056	713-892-3700		280
Univenture Inc 16710 Square Dr *TF:* 800-992-8262 ■ *Web:* www.univenture.com	Marysville	OH	43040	937-645-4600	645-4700	608
Univera Healthcare 205 Pk Club Ln **Fax Area Code: 800* ■ *TF:* 877-883-9577 ■ *Web:* www.univerahealthcare.com	Buffalo	NY	14221	716-847-1480	956-2397*	391-3
Univeris Corp 111 George St 3rd Fl *Web:* www.univeris.com	Toronto	ON	M5A2N4	416-979-3700		177
Universal Aerospace Company Inc 18640 59th Dr NE *Web:* www.universalaero.com	Arlington	WA	98223	360-435-9577		454
Universal Air Conditioner Inc 1441 Heritage Pkwy *Web:* www.uacparts.com	Mansfield	TX	76063	817-740-3900		610
Universal Air Filter Co 1624 Sauget Indus Pky *TF:* 800-541-3478 ■ *Web:* www.uaf.com	East Saint Louis	IL	62206	618-271-7300	271-8808	18
Universal Asset Management Inc 5350 Poplar Ave Ste 150 *TF:* 877-826-5825 ■ *Web:* www.uaminc.com	Memphis	TN	38119	901-682-4064	682-3892	21
Universal Audio Inc 1700 Green Hills Rd *TF:* 877-698-2834 ■ *Web:* www.uaudio.com	Scotts Valley	CA	95066	831-440-1176	461-1550	52
Universal Avionics Systems Corp 3260 E Universal Way *TF:* 800-321-5253 ■ *Web:* www.uasc.com	Tucson	AZ	85756	520-295-2300	434-4454	21
Universal Ballet Academy 4301 Harewood Rd NE *Web:* www.universalballet.com	Washington	DC	20017	202-832-1087	526-4274	622
Universal Barber College 1202 S 7th Ave *Web:* www.universalbarbercollege.com	Phoenix	AZ	85007	602-262-9904	258-4261	167-3
Universal Bearings Inc 431 N Birkey Dr PO Box 38 *TF:* 800-824-7743 ■ *Web:* www.univbrg.com	Bremen	IN	46506	800-824-7743		75
Universal Bookbindery Inc 1200 N Colorado St *TF:* 800-594-2015 ■ *Web:* universalbookbindery.com	San Antonio	TX	78207	210-734-9502		535
Universal Brush Manufacturing Co PO Box 1618 *TF:* 800-323-3474 ■ *Web:* www.universalbrush.com	Markham	IL	60428	708-331-1700	331-4923	103
Universal Builders Supply Inc (UBS) 27 Horton Ave *Web:* www.ubs1.com	New Rochelle	NY	10801	914-699-2400	699-2609	491
Universal Care Inc 1680 E Signal Hill St 3rd Fl	Signal Hill	CA	90755	562-424-6200		391-3
Universal City-North Hollywood Chamber of Commerce 6369 Bellingham Ave *Web:* www.noho.org	North Hollywood	CA	91606	818-508-5155	508-5156	139

Company / Address	City	State	ZIP	Phone	Fax	Class
Universal Collection Systems 5240 Mendenhall Park Pl *TF:* 800-635-3197 ■ *Web:* www.universalcollectionsystems.com	Memphis	TN	38115	901-452-8900		160
Universal Companies Inc 18260 Oak Park Dr *TF:* 800-558-5571 ■ *Web:* www.universalcompanies.com	Abingdon	VA	24210	276-466-9110	466-1895	77
Universal Concrete Products Corp 400 Old Reading Pk Ste 100 *Web:* www.universalconcrete.com	Stowe	PA	19464	610-323-0700	323-4046	183
Universal Construction Company Inc 11200 W 79th St *Web:* www.universalconstruction.net	Lenexa	KS	66214	913-342-1150	342-1151	186
Universal Corp 9201 Forest Hill Ave PO Box 25099 *NYSE: UVV* ■ *Web:* www.universalcorp.com	Richmond	VA	23260	804-359-9311		185
Universal Display & Fixtures Co 726 E Hwy 121 *TF:* 800-235-0701 ■ *Web:* www.udfc.com	Lewisville	TX	75057	972-829-2402	221-6624	233
Universal Display Corp 375 Phillips Blvd *NASDAQ: OLED* ■ *Web:* oled.com	Ewing	NJ	08618	609-671-0980		696
Universal Electronics Inc 201 E Sandpointe Ave 8th Fl *NASDAQ: UEIC* ■ *Web:* www.uei.com	Santa Ana	CA	92707	714-918-9500		52
Universal Enclosure Systems 1146 S Cedar Ridge Dr *Web:* www.universalenclosures.com	Duncanville	TX	75137	972-298-0531	298-0614	254
Universal Engineering Sciences Inc 3532 Maggie Blvd *Web:* www.universalengineering.com	Orlando	FL	32811	407-423-0504		743
Universal Enterprises Inc *Kane USA Inc* 8625 SW Cascade Ave *TF:* 800-547-5740 ■ *Web:* usa.ueitest.com	Beaverton	OR	97008	503-644-8723		360-2
Universal Environmental Services LLC 411 Dividend Dr *TF:* 800-988-7977 ■ *Web:* universalenvironmentalservices.com	Peachtree City	GA	30269	800-988-7977		541
Universal Equipment Inc 230a Bowers Rd *Web:* www.ueiworks.com	Scott	LA	70583	337-233-5292		385
Universal Fabric Structures Inc 2200 Kumry Rd *TF:* 800-634-8368 ■ *Web:* www.ufsinc.com	Quakertown	PA	18951	215-529-9921	529-9936	733
Universal Fastener Co 5930 Old Mount Holly Rd *TF:* 800-532-0429 ■ *Web:* www.universalfastener.net	Charlotte	NC	28208	704-392-5342	394-0904	351
Universal Fibers Inc PO Box 8930 *TF:* 800-457-4759 ■ *Web:* www.universalfibers.com	Bristol	VA	24203	276-669-1161	669-3304	745-9
Universal Flow Monitors Inc 1755 E 9th Mile Rd *Web:* www.flowmeters.com	Hazel Park	MI	48030	248-542-9635	398-4274	201
Universal Grinding Corp 1234 W 78th St *TF:* 888-825-2705 ■ *Web:* universalgrinding.com	Cleveland	OH	44102	888-825-2705		454
Universal Guidance Press PO Box 6556 *Web:* www.ronscolastico.com	Woodland Hills	CA	91365	818-224-4488		95
Universal Health Realty Income Trust 367 S Gulph Rd *NYSE: UHT* ■ *Web:* www.uhrit.com	King of Prussia	PA	19406	610-265-0688		655
Universal Health Services Inc 367 S Gulph Rd *NYSE: UHS* ■ *Web:* www.uhsinc.com	King of Prussia	PA	19406	610-768-3300		353
Universal Home Health & Hospice Care 701 S Main St *Web:* www.uhcinc.org	Bellefontaine	OH	43311	937-593-1605		371
Universal Hospital Services Inc 6625 W 78th St Ste 300 *TF:* 800-847-7368 ■ *Web:* www.uhs.com	Minneapolis	MN	55439	952-893-3200	893-0704	264-4
Universal Image PO Box 77000 *TF:* 800-553-5499 ■ *Web:* www.universalphoto.com	Winter Garden	FL	34787	407-352-5302		602
Universal Industrial Gases Inc 3001 Emrick Blvd Ste 320 *Web:* www.uigi.com	Bethlehem	PA	18020	610-559-7967	515-0945	697
Universal Industries Inc 5800 Nordic Dr *TF:* 800-553-4446 ■ *Web:* www.universalindustries.com	Cedar Falls	IA	50613	319-277-7501	277-2318	207
Universal Instruments Corp (UIC) 33 Broome Corporate Pk *TF:* 800-842-9732 ■ *Web:* www.uic.com	Conklin	NY	13748	607-779-7522		695
Universal Insurance Holding Inc (UIH) 1110 W Commerical Blvd Ste 100 *NYSE: UVE* ■ *TF:* 800-509-5586 ■ *Web:* universalinsuranceholdings.com	Fort Lauderdale	FL	33309	800-509-5586		391-4
Universal Labeling Systems 3501 Eigth Ave S *TF:* 877-236-0266 ■ *Web:* universal1.com	Saint Petersburg	FL	33711	727-327-2123	323-4403	547
Universal Lending Corp (ULC) 6775 E Evans Ave *TF:* 800-758-4063 ■ *Web:* www.ulc.com	Denver	CO	80224	800-758-4063		509
Universal Logistics Holdings Inc 12755 E Nine Mile Rd *NASDAQ: UACL* ■ *TF:* 800-233-9445 ■ *Web:* www.universallogistics.com	Warren	MI	48089	586-920-0100	920-0258	780
Universal Machine & Engineering Corp 645 Old Reading Pk *TF:* 800-879-2477 ■ *Web:* www.umc-oscar.com	Stowe	PA	19464	610-323-1810		386
Universal Manufacturing Co 405 Diagonal St PO Box 190 *OTC: UFMG* ■ *TF:* 800-343-3557 ■ *Web:* www.umcretech.com	Algona	IA	50511	515-295-3557	295-5537	60
Universal Manufacturing Company Inc 5030 Mackey S *TF:* 800-524-5860 ■ *Web:* www.umcprint.com	Overland Park	KS	66203	913-815-6230	815-6240	762
Universal McCann 100 W 33rd St *Web:* www.umww.com	New York	NY	10001	212-883-4700		6
Universal Metal Products 29980 Lakeland Blvd *Web:* www.universalmetalproducts.com	Wickliffe	OH	44092	440-943-3040		488
Universal Metals LLC 805 Chicago St *TF:* 800-853-8890 ■ *Web:* umimetals.com	Toledo	OH	43611	419-726-0850		492
Universal Music Company Inc 1200 E 104th Ave *Web:* www.universalmusiccompany.com	Thornton	CO	80233	303-452-1557		526

Listing	Phone	Fax	Class
Universal Music Publishing 2100 Colorado Ave. Santa Monica CA 90404 *Web:* www.umusicpub.com	310-235-4907		637-7
Universal Odyssey Inc 2618 San Miguel Dr Ste 476 Newport Beach CA 92660 *Web:* www.uoiweb.com	949-263-1222	263-0983	384
Universal Overall Co 1060 W Van Buren St Chicago IL 60607 *TF:* 800-621-3344 ■ *Web:* www.universaloverall.com	312-226-3336	226-1986	155-19
Universal Plastic Mold Inc 13245 Los Angeles St. Baldwin Park CA 91706 *TF:* 888-893-1587 ■ *Web:* www.upminc.com	888-893-1587		604
Universal Plastics - Latrobe 59 Bay Hill Dr Latrobe PA 15650 *Web:* www.universalplastics.com	724-424-7000	424-7015	596
Universal Plastics & Machine 7661 Freedom Ave NW North Canton OH 44720 *Web:* www.universalplasticsmachine.com	330-433-2860		604
Universal Polymer & Rubber Ltd (UP&R) 15730 Madison Rd Middlefield OH 44062 *Web:* www.universalpolymer.com	440-632-1691	632-5761	677
Universal Promotions Inc 3561 Valley Dr Pittsburgh PA 15234 *Web:* www.universal-promotions.com	412-831-8423		194
Universal Protective Packaging Inc 61 Texaco Rd Mechanicsburg PA 17050 *TF:* 800-544-6649 ■ *Web:* uppi.com	717-766-1578		601
Universal Pultrusions LLC 100 Tillco Dr. Marshall AR 72650 *TF:* 800-821-6531 ■ *Web:* www.unipulllc.com	800-821-6531	423-7610	499
Universal Radio Inc 6830 Americana Pky. Reynoldsburg OH 43068 *TF:* 800-431-3939 ■ *Web:* www.universal-radio.com	614-866-4267	866-2339	179
Universal Remote Control Inc 500 Mamaroneck Ave Harrison NY 10528 *TF:* 800-901-0800 ■ *Web:* www.universalremote.com	800-901-0800		246
Universal Security Instruments Inc 11407 Cronhill Dr. Owings Mills MD 21117 *NYSE: UUU* ■ *TF:* 800-390-4321 ■ *Web:* www.universalsecurity.com	410-363-3000	363-2218	692
Universal Semen Sales Inc 2626 2nd Ave S Great Falls MT 59405 *TF:* 800-227-8774 ■ *Web:* www.universalsemensales.com	406-453-0374	453-0510	275
Universal Service Administrative Co (USAC) 2000 L St NW Ste 200 Washington DC 20036 *Web:* www.usac.org	202-776-0200	776-0080	736
Universal Spa Training Academy 340 Burlington Ave. Downers Grove IL 60515 *Web:* spatrainingacademy.edu	630-968-6800		167-3
Universal Steel America Houston Inc 1230 E Richey Rd Houston TX 77073 *TF:* 866-988-3800 ■ *Web:* www.universalsteelamerica.com	281-821-7400		492
Universal Steel Co, The 6600 Grant Ave. Cleveland OH 44105 *TF:* 800-669-2645 ■ *Web:* univsteel.com	216-883-4972		686
Universal Steel Inc 2400 Stone Mountain-Lithonia Rd Lithonia GA 30058 *Web:* universalsteelinc.com	770-482-5601	482-4795	480
Universal Studios Hollywood 100 Universal City Plz Universal City CA 91608 *TF:* 800-864-8377 ■ *Web:* www.universalstudioshollywood.com	800-864-8377		31
Universal Studios Inc 100 Universal City Plz Universal City CA 91608 *Web:* www.universalstudioslot.com	818-777-1000	866-3600	514
Universal Table PO Box 2122 Decatur GA 30031 *Web:* www.universaltable.org	404-276-6046		637-10
Universal Technical Resource Services Inc (UTRS) 950 Kings Hwy N Ste 208. Cherry Hill NJ 08034 *Web:* www.utrs.com	856-667-6770	667-7586	261
Universal Technologies Inc 165 Alsonia St Estill Springs TN 37330 *Web:* www.utiusa.com	931-649-5171		454
Universal Therapeutic Massage Institute 3410 Aztec Rd NE Albuquerque NM 87107 *Web:* www.utmi.com	505-888-0020		167-3
Universal Travel 1425 SE 17th St Ste C Fort Lauderdale FL 33316	954-525-5000		546
Universal Tube Inc 2607 Bond St Rochester Hills MI 48309 *TF:* 800-394-8823 ■ *Web:* www.universaltube.com	248-853-5100	853-7365	595
Universal Urethane Products Inc 410 1st St. Toledo OH 43605 *Web:* www.universalurethane.com	419-693-7400	693-2363	676
Universal Valve Company Inc 478 Schiller St Elizabeth NJ 07206 *TF:* 800-223-0741 ■ *Web:* www.universalvalve.com	908-351-0606		790
Universal Wilde 26 Dartmouth St Westwood MA 02090 *TF:* 866-825-5515 ■ *Web:* www.universalwilde.com	781-251-2700	251-2613	5
Universal Window & Door 303 Mechanic St. Marlboro MA 01752 *TF:* 800-633-0108 ■ *Web:* www.universalwindow.com	800-633-0108		234
Universal Wire Cloth Co 16 N Steel Rd Morrisville PA 19067 *TF:* 800-523-0575 ■ *Web:* universalwirecloth.com	215-736-8981	736-8994	688
Universal's Islands of Adventure 6000 Universal Studios Plz. Orlando FL 32819 *TF:* 877-801-9720 ■ *Web:* www.universalorlando.com	407-224-3663		32
UniversalPegasus International Inc 4848 Loop Central Dr Ste 137 Houston TX 77081 *Web:* www.universalpegasus.com	713-425-6000	977-1047	261
Universidad Popular 2801 S Hamlin Ave. Chicago IL 60623 *Web:* www.universidadpopular.us	773-733-5055		162
Universitas Foundation of Canada 1035 Wilfrid-Pelletier Ave Ste 500 Quebec City QC G1W0C5 *TF:* 877-710-7377 ■ *Web:* www.kaleido.ca	418-651-8975	651-8030	305
Universite de Moncton *Shippagan Campus* 218 Blvd JD Gauthier. Shippagan NB E8S1P6 *TF:* 800-363-8336 ■ *Web:* www.umoncton.ca	506-336-3400	336-3604	785
Universite de Montreal CP 6128 Succursale Centre Ville Montreal QC H3C3J7 *Web:* www.umontreal.ca	514-343-6111	343-5788	785
Universite du Quebec 475 Rue du Parvis Quebec City QC G1K9H7 *Web:* www.uquebec.ca	418-657-3551	657-2132	785
Universite du Quebec a Trois-Rivieres 3351 Boul des Forges CP 500 Trois-Rivieres QC G9A5H7 *TF:* 800-365-0922 ■ *Web:* www.uqtr.ca	819-376-5011		785
Universite Sainte Anne 1695 Rt 1 Pointe-de-l'Eglise NS B0W1M0 *TF:* 888-338-8337 ■ *Web:* www.usainteanne.ca	902-769-2114	769-2930	785
Universities Research Association Inc (URA) 1140 19th St NW Ste 900 Washington DC 20036 *Web:* www.ura-hq.org	202-293-1382	293-5012	49-19
Universities Space Research Assn (USRA) 10211 Wincopin Cir Ste 500 Columbia MD 21044 *Web:* www.usra.edu	410-730-2656	730-3496	49-19
University & State Employees Credit Union 10120 Pacific Heights Blvd Ste 100 San Diego CA 92121 *TF:* 866-873-4968 ■ *Web:* www.usecu.org	858-795-6100		219
University at Albany 1400 Washington Ave. Albany NY 12222 *TF:* 800-293-7869 ■ *Web:* www.albany.edu	518-442-3300	442-5383	166
University at Buffalo *University Libraries* 433 Capen Hall Buffalo NY 14260 *Web:* library.buffalo.edu	716-645-2965	645-3844	434-6
University at Buffalo Law School John Lord O'Brian Hall Buffalo NY 14260 *Web:* www.law.buffalo.edu	716-645-2052	645-2064	167-1
University at Buffalo School of Medicine & Biomedical Sciences 12 Capen Hall Buffalo NY 14260 *Web:* www.buffalo.edu	716-829-3466	829-3849	167-2
University Bancorp Inc 2015 Washtenaw Ave Ann Arbor MI 48104 *OTC: UNIB* ■ *Web:* www.university-bank.com	734-741-5858	741-5859	360-2
University Behavioral Ctr 2500 Discovery Dr Orlando FL 32826 *TF:* 800-999-0807 ■ *Web:* www.universitybehavioral.com	407-281-7000	282-7012	374-5
University Behavioral Health of Denton 2026 W University Dr Denton TX 76201 *TF:* 800-320-8100 ■ *Web:* ubhdenton.com	940-320-8101		374-5
University Book Store, The 711 State St Madison WI 53703 *TF:* 800-993-2665 ■ *Web:* www.uwbookstore.com	608-257-3784		95
University City Housing (UCH) 3418 Sansom St. Philadelphia PA 19104 *Web:* universitycityhousing.com	215-222-2000	222-5449	655
University City Public Library 6701 Delmar Blvd. University City MO 63130 *Web:* www.ucpl.lib.mo.us	314-727-3150	727-6005	434-3
University Club of Chicago 76 E Monroe St. Chicago IL 60603 *Web:* www.ucco.com	312-726-2840	726-0620	671
University Family Care 2701 E Elivra Rd Tucson AZ 85756 **Fax Area Code:* 866 ■ *TF:* 800-582-8686 ■ *Web:* www.ufcaz.com	800-582-8686	465-8340*	391-3
University Galleries 400 SW 13th St Fine Arts Bldg B PO Box 115803 Gainesville FL 32611 *Web:* arts.ufl.edu	352-273-3000		520
University Games Corp 2030 Harrison St San Francisco CA 94110 *TF:* 800-347-4818 ■ *Web:* www.universitygames.com	415-503-1600	503-0085	762
University Health Care Inc 305 W Broadway 3rd Fl Louisville KY 40202 *TF:* 800-578-0603 ■ *Web:* www.passporthealthplan.com	502-585-7900	585-7985	391-3
University Health Care System 1350 Walton Way Augusta GA 30901 *TF:* 866-591-2502 ■ *Web:* www.universityhealth.org	706-722-9011		374-3
University Health Plans Inc 15 Pacella Park Dr Ste 130 Randolph MA 02368 *TF:* 800-437-6448 ■ *Web:* www.universityhealthplans.com	800-437-6448		352
University Health System 4502 Medical Dr. San Antonio TX 78229 *Web:* www.universityhealthsystem.com	210-358-4000	358-5936	374-3
University Hospital 1 Hospital Dr. Columbia MO 65212 *Web:* www.muhealth.org	573-882-4141		374-3
University Hospital PO Box 637745. Cincinnati OH 45219 *Web:* uchealth.com	513-584-1000		374-3
University Hospital 1500 E Medical Center Dr. Ann Arbor MI 48109 *TF:* 855-855-0863 ■ *Web:* www.med.umich.edu	734-936-4000		374-3
University Hospital 2211 Lomas Blvd NE Albuquerque NM 87106 *Web:* hospitals.unm.edu	505-272-2111		374-3
University Hospital Bedford Medical Ctr 44 Blaine Ave Bedford OH 44146 *Web:* www.uhhospitals.org	440-735-3900	735-3631	374-3
University Language Ctr 4445 W 77th St Ste 110 Minneapolis MN 55435 *Web:* ulanguage.com	952-224-5600		768
University Mall 2200 E Fowler Ave Tampa FL 33612 *Web:* www.universitymalltampa.com	813-971-3465		460
University Mechanical & Engineering Contractors Inc 1168 Fesler St El Cajon CA 92020 *Web:* umec.com	619-956-2500	956-2300	189-10
University Medical Center Brackenridge 601 E 15th St Austin TX 78701 *Web:* www.seton.net	512-324-7000		374-3
University Medical Center of El Paso (UMCEP) 4815 Alameda Ave El Paso TX 79905 *TF:* 800-473-8440 ■ *Web:* www.umcelpaso.org	915-544-1200		374-3
University Medical Ctr 1800 W Charleston Blvd. Las Vegas NV 89102 *Web:* www.umcsn.com	702-383-2000		374-3
University Moving & Storage Co 23305 Commerce Dr Farmington Hills MI 48335 *TF:* 800-448-6683 ■ *Web:* www.universitymoving.com	844-366-0245		186

	City	State	ZIP	Phone	Fax	Class
University of Akron 277 E Buchtel Ave	Akron	OH	44325	330-972-7100	972-7022	166
TF: 800-655-4884 ■ *Web:* www.uakron.edu						
University of Akron Wayne College						
1901 Smucker Rd	Orrville	OH	44667	330-683-2010	684-8989	162
TF: 800-221-8308 ■ *Web:* www.wayne.uakron.edu						
University of Alabama						
PO Box 870132	Tuscaloosa	AL	35487	205-348-5666	348-9046	166
TF: 800-933-2262 ■ *Web:* www.ua.edu						
University of Alabama						
Birmingham 1720 Second Ave S	Birmingham	AL	35294	205-934-4011		166
TF: 800-421-8743 ■ *Web:* www.uab.edu						
School of Law						
101 Paul W Bryant Dr E	Tuscaloosa	AL	35401	205-348-5440		167-1
TF: 800-627-6514 ■ *Web:* www.law.ua.edu						
University of Alabama Arboretum						
PO Box 870344	Tuscaloosa	AL	35487	205-553-3278	553-3728	97
Web: arboretum.ua.edu						
University of Alabama Press, The						
200 Hackberry Ln 2nd Fl	Tuscaloosa	AL	35487	205-348-5180	348-9201	637-4
Web: www.uapress.ua.edu						
University of Alabama System						
401 Queen City Ave	Tuscaloosa	AL	35401	205-348-5861		786
TF: 866-362-9476 ■ *Web:* uasystem.edu						
University of Alaska						
1731 South Chandalar Dr	Fairbanks	AK	99775	907-474-7034		167-3
TF: 800-478-1823 ■ *Web:* www.uaf.edu						
University of Alaska Anchorage						
3211 Providence Dr	Anchorage	AK	99508	907-786-1800	786-4888	166
TF: 888-822-8973 ■ *Web:* www.uaa.alaska.edu						
University of Alaska Anchorage Kenai Peninsula College						
156 College Rd	Soldotna	AK	99669	877-262-0330	262-0322*	162
**Fax Area Code:* 907 ■ *TF:* 877-262-0330 ■ *Web:* www.kpc.alaska.edu						
University of Alaska Anchorage Kodiak College						
117 Benny Benson Dr	Kodiak	AK	99615	907-486-4161	486-1264	162
TF: 800-486-7660 ■ *Web:* www.koc.alaska.edu						
University of Alaska Fairbanks						
Elmer E. Rasmuson Library						
PO Box 756800	Fairbanks	AK	99775	907-474-7481	474-6841	434-6
Web: library.uaf.edu						
Northwest 400 E Front St PO Box 400	Nome	AK	99762	907-443-2201	443-5602	162
TF: 800-478-2202 ■ *Web:* www.nwc.uaf.edu						
University of Alaska Southeast						
11066 Auke Lake Way	Juneau	AK	99801	907-796-6000		166
TF: 877-465-4827 ■ *Web:* www.uas.alaska.edu						
University of Alaska System						
910 Yukon Dr PO Box 775000	Fairbanks	AK	99775	907-450-8000	450-8012	786
Web: www.alaska.edu						
University of Alberta						
116 St & 85 Ave	Edmonton	AB	T6G2R3	780-492-3111		785
Web: www.ualberta.ca						
Augustana 4901-46th Ave	Camrose	AB	T4V2R3	780-679-1100	679-1129	785
TF: 800-661-8714 ■ *Web:* www.ualberta.ca						
University of Arizona PO Box 210300	Tucson	AZ	85721	520-621-2211	621-9799	166
Web: www.arizona.edu						
University of Arizona College of Medicine						
1501 N Campbell Ave	Tucson	AZ	85724	520-626-4555	626-6252	167-2
Web: medicine.arizona.edu						
University of Arizona James E Rogers College of Law						
1201 E Speedway Blvd PO Box 210176	Tucson	AZ	85721	520-621-1373		167-1
Web: law.arizona.edu						
University of Arizona Museum of Art						
University of Arizona 1031 N Olive Rd	Tucson	AZ	85721	520-621-7567	621-8770	520
Web: artmuseum.arizona.edu						
University of Arizona Press, The						
1510 E University Blvd PO Box 210055	Tucson	AZ	85721	520-621-1441	621-8899	637-4
Web: uapress.arizona.edu						
University of Arkansas						
232 Silas Hunt Hall	Fayetteville	AR	72701	479-575-5346	575-7515	166
TF: 800-377-8632 ■ *Web:* www.uark.edu						
University of Arkansas						
Little Rock 2801 S University Ave	Little Rock	AR	72204	501-569-3000	569-8956	166
TF: 800-482-8892 ■ *Web:* www.ualr.edu						
Pine Bluff 1200 N University Dr	Pine Bluff	AR	71601	870-575-8000	575-4608	166
TF: 800-264-6585 ■ *Web:* www.uapb.edu						
University of Arkansas Community College Rich Mountain						
1100 College Dr	Mena	AR	71953	479-394-7622		162
TF: 800-612-7440 ■ *Web:* www.uarichmountain.edu						
University of Arkansas Press						
McIlroy House 105 N McIlroy Ave	Fayetteville	AR	72701	479-575-7258		637-4
Web: www.uapress.com						
University of Arkansas School of Law						
1045 W Maple St	Fayetteville	AR	72701	479-575-2000		167-1
Web: law.uark.edu						
University of Baltimore						
1420 N Charles St	Baltimore	MD	21201	410-837-4200		166
Web: www.ubalt.edu						
University of Bridgeport						
126 Park Ave	Bridgeport	CT	06604	203-576-4454	576-4941	166
TF: 800-392-3582 ■ *Web:* www.bridgeport.edu						
University of British Columbia						
2016-1874 E Mall	Vancouver	BC	V6T1Z1	604-822-9836	822-3599	785
TF: 877-272-1422 ■ *Web:* www.ubc.ca						
University of British Columbia						
Okanagan 3333 University Way	Kelowna	BC	V1V1V7	250-807-8000		785
Web: ok.ubc.ca						
University of British Columbia Botanical Garden & Centre for Plant Research						
6804 SW Marine Dr	Vancouver	BC	V6T1Z4	604-822-4208	822-2016	97
Web: www.botanicalgarden.ubc.ca						
University of British Columbia Faculty of Medicine						
317-2194 Health Sciences Mall	Vancouver	BC	V6T1Z3	604-822-2421	822-6061	167-2
Web: www.med.ubc.ca						
University of British Columbia Museum of Anthropology						
6393 NW Marine Dr	Vancouver	BC	V6T1Z2	604-822-5087	822-2974	520
Web: moa.ubc.ca						
University of Calgary						
2500 University Dr NW	Calgary	AB	T2N1N4	403-220-5110	282-7298	785
Web: www.ucalgary.ca						
University of Calgary						
3330 Hospital Dr NW	Calgary	AB	T2N4N1	403-210-3841	270-2681	167-2
Web: www.cumming.ucalgary.ca						
University of California (UCLA)						
Berkeley 110 Sproul Hall MC Ste 5800	Berkeley	CA	94720	510-664-9181		166
TF: 866-740-1260 ■ *Web:* www.berkeley.edu						
Davis 1 Shields Ave	Davis	CA	95616	530-752-1011		166
TF: 800-242-4723 ■ *Web:* www.ucdavis.edu						
Irvine 510 Aldrich Hall	Irvine	CA	92697	949-824-5011	824-2711	166
Web: uci.edu						
Los Angeles 405 Hilgard Ave	Los Angeles	CA	90095	310-825-4321		166
Web: www.ucla.edu						
Merced PO Box 2039	Merced	CA	95344	209-228-4400		166
Web: www.ucmerced.edu						
Riverside 900 University Ave	Riverside	CA	92521	951-827-3411	827-6344	166
TF: 800-426-2586 ■ *Web:* www.ucr.edu						
San Francisco 505 Parnassus Ave	San Francisco	CA	94143	415-476-9000	353-3925	166
Web: www.ucsf.edu						
Santa Barbara 1210 Cheadle Hall	Santa Barbara	CA	93106	805-893-8000		166
TF: 888-488-8272 ■ *Web:* www.ucsb.edu						
Santa Cruz 1156 High St	Santa Cruz	CA	95064	831-459-4412		166
TF: 800-933-7584 ■ *Web:* www.ucsc.edu						
University of California Berkeley School of Law						
Boalt Hall Ste 7200	Berkeley	CA	94720	510-642-1741	643-6222	167-1
Web: www.law.berkeley.edu						
University of California Botanical Garden at Berkeley						
200 Centennial Dr	Berkeley	CA	94720	510-643-2755	642-5045	97
Web: botanicalgarden.berkeley.edu						
University of California Davis School of Law						
400 Mrak Hall Dr	Davis	CA	95616	530-752-0243	754-8371	167-1
Web: law.ucdavis.edu						
University of California Davis School of Medicine						
4610 X St	Sacramento	CA	95817	916-734-7131	734-7055	167-2
TF: 800-282-3284 ■ *Web:* health.ucdavis.edu						
University of California Hastings College of the Law						
200 McAllister St	San Francisco	CA	94102	415-565-4600	581-8946	167-1
Web: www.uchastings.edu						
University of California Health System						
1111 Franklin St	Oakland	CA	94607	510-987-9200	987-9894	353
Web: www.universityofcalifornia.edu						
University of California Irvine						
Library PO Box 19557	Irvine	CA	92623	949-824-6836		434-6
TF: 800-843-2763 ■ *Web:* www.lib.uci.edu						
University of California Irvine College of Health Sciences						
1001 Health Science Rd	Irvine	CA	92697	949-824-9267		166
Web: www.cohs.uci.edu						
University of California Irvine School of Medicine						
1001 Health Sciences Rd 252 Irvine Hall	Irvine	CA	92697	949-824-6119		167-2
Web: www.som.uci.edu						
University of California Los Angeles						
Library System						
11334 Charles E Young Research Library	Los Angeles	CA	90095	310-825-4732		434-6
Web: www.library.ucla.edu						
University of California Press						
2120 Berkeley Way	Berkeley	CA	94704	800-343-4499	643-7127*	637-4
**Fax Area Code:* 510 ■ *TF:* 800-343-4499 ■ *Web:* www.ucpress.edu						
University of California Riverside						
Tomas Rivera Library						
900 University Ave	Riverside	CA	92521	951-827-3220		434-6
Web: library.ucr.edu						
University of California Riverside Botanic Gardens						
900 University Ave	Riverside	CA	92521	951-784-6962		97
Web: gardens.ucr.edu						
University of California San Diego Medical Center Library						
200 W Arbor Dr	San Diego	CA	92103	619-543-6222		434-1
Web: www.health.ucsd.edu						
University of California San Diego School of Medicine						
9500 Gilman Dr MC 0602	La Jolla	CA	92093	858-534-0830	534-6573	167-2
Web: www.medschool.ucsd.edu						
University of California San Francisco						
Library & Center for Knowledge Management						
530 Parnassus Ave	San Francisco	CA	94143	415-476-2336		434-1
Web: www.library.ucsf.edu						
University of Central Arkansas						
201 Donaghey Ave	Conway	AR	72035	501-450-5000	450-5228	166
Web: www.uca.edu						
University of Central Florida						
4000 Central Florida Blvd	Orlando	FL	32816	407-823-2000	823-5625	166
TF: 800-272-7252 ■ *Web:* www.ucf.edu						
University of Central Oklahoma						
100 N University Dr	Edmond	OK	73034	405-974-2688		166
Web: www.uco.edu						
University of Charleston						
2300 MacCorkle Ave SE	Charleston	WV	25304	304-357-4800	357-4715	166
TF: 800-995-4682 ■ *Web:* www.ucwv.edu						
University of Chicago						
5801 S Ellis Ave	Chicago	IL	60637	773-702-1234	702-4199	166
Web: www.uchicago.edu						
University of Chicago Law School						
1111 E 60th St	Chicago	IL	60637	773-702-9494		167-1
Web: www.law.uchicago.edu						
University of Chicago Library						
1100 E 57th St	Chicago	IL	60637	773-702-8740	702-6623	434-6
Web: www.lib.uchicago.edu						
University of Chicago Medical Ctr						
5841 S Maryland Ave	Chicago	IL	60637	773-702-1000		374-3
Web: www.uchicagomedicine.org						
University of Chicago Pritzker School of Medicine						
924 E 57th St	Chicago	IL	60637	773-702-1939		167-2
Web: pritzker.uchicago.edu						
University of Cincinnati						
51 Goodman Dr	Cincinnati	OH	45267	513-558-4553	558-2910	434-1
Web: www.health.uc.edu						
University of Cincinnati						
9555 Plainfield Rd	Cincinnati	OH	45236	513-745-5600		162
Web: www.ucblueash.edu						
University of Cincinnati						
2600 Clifton Ave PO Box 210091	Cincinnati	OH	45221	513-556-1100	556-1105	166
TF: 866-397-3382 ■ *Web:* www.uc.edu						

				Phone	Fax	Class
University of Cincinnati Clermont College						
4200 Clermont College Dr	Batavia	OH	45103	513-732-5200	732-5303	162
TF: 866-446-2822 ■ *Web:* www.ucclermont.edu						
University of Cincinnati College of Law						
2540 Clifton Ave	Cincinnati	OH	45221	513-556-6805	556-2391	167-1
Web: www.law.uc.edu						
University of Cincinnati College of Medicine						
231 Albert Sabin Way Ste E-251 PO Box 670552	Cincinnati	OH	45267	513-558-4898	558-1100	167-2
Web: www.med.uc.edu						
University of Cincinnati Langsam Library						
PO Box 210033	Cincinnati	OH	45221	513-556-1515	556-0325	434-6
Web: www.libraries.uc.edu						
University of Colorado						
Boulder Regent Administrative Ctr Rm 101 20 UCB	Boulder	CO	80309	303-492-1411	492-7115	166
Web: www.colorado.edu						
Colorado Springs PO Box 7150	Colorado Springs	CO	80933	719-255-3150		166
TF: 800-990-8227 ■ *Web:* www.uccs.edu						
University of Colorado at Denver						
PO Box 173364 CB 144	Denver	CO	80217	303-315-2601	556-4838	166
Web: www.ucdenver.edu						
University of Colorado System						
1800 Grant St Ste 800	Denver	CO	80203	303-860-5600	860-5610	786
Web: www.cu.edu						
University of Connecticut						
2131 Hillside Rd Unit 3088	Storrs	CT	06269	860-486-4676	486-1476	166
Web: uconn.edu						
University of Connecticut						
Avery Point 1084 Shennecossett Rd	Groton	CT	06340	860-405-9019		162
Web: averypoint.uconn.edu						
Babbidge Library 369 Fairfield Rd	Storrs	CT	06269	860-486-2219	486-0584	434-6
TF: 888-603-9635 ■ *Web:* lib.uconn.edu						
Greater Hartford 10 Prospect St Rm 105	West Hartford	CT	06117	959-200-3500		162
Web: www.hartford.uconn.edu						
Stamford 1 University Pl	Stamford	CT	06901	203-251-8400	251-8556	166
Web: stamford.uconn.edu						
Waterbury 99 E Main St	Waterbury	CT	06702	203-236-9800	236-9805	162
Web: waterbury.uconn.edu						
University of Connecticut School of Law						
45 Elizabeth St	Hartford	CT	06105	860-570-5100		167-1
Web: www.law.uconn.edu						
University of Dallas						
1845 E Northgate Dr	Irving	TX	75062	972-721-5266	721-5017	166
TF: 800-628-6999 ■ *Web:* udallas.edu						
University of Dayton 300 College Pk	Dayton	OH	45469	937-229-4411	229-4729	166
TF: 800-837-7433 ■ *Web:* udayton.edu						
University of Delaware						
210 S College Ave	Newark	DE	19716	302-831-2792	831-6905	166
TF: 844-237-1338 ■ *Web:* www.udel.edu						
University of Denver 2255 E Evans Ave	Denver	CO	80208	303-871-6000	871-6378	167-1
Web: www.law.du.edu						
University of Denver						
2199 S University Blvd	Denver	CO	80208	303-871-2036	871-3301	166
TF: 800-525-9495 ■ *Web:* www.du.edu						
University of Detroit Mercy						
4001 W McNichols Rd	Detroit	MI	48221	313-993-1000	993-3326	166
TF: 800-635-5020 ■ *Web:* www.udmercy.edu						
University of Detroit Mercy						
Corktown Campus 2700 Martin Luther King Jr Blvd	Detroit	MI	48208	313-993-1616		166
Web: www.udmercymetz.com						
University of Detroit Mercy School of Law						
651 E Jefferson Ave	Detroit	MI	48226	313-596-0264		167-1
Web: lawschool.udmercy.edu						
University of Dubuque						
2000 University Ave	Dubuque	IA	52001	563-589-3000	589-3690	166
TF: 800-722-5583 ■ *Web:* www.dbq.edu						
University of Evansville						
1800 Lincoln Ave	Evansville	IN	47722	812-488-2000	488-4076	166
TF: 800-423-8633 ■ *Web:* www.evansville.edu						
University of Findlay 1000 N Main St	Findlay	OH	45840	419-422-8313	434-4822	166
TF: 800-472-9502 ■ *Web:* www.findlay.edu						
University of Florida						
219 Grinter Hall PO Box 115500	Gainesville	FL	32611	352-392-3261	392-2115	166
TF: 866-876-4472 ■ *Web:* www.ufl.edu						
University of Florida Health Science Center Libraries						
1600 SW Archer Rd	Gainesville	FL	32610	352-273-8408	392-2565	434-1
Web: library.health.ufl.edu						
University of Florida Levin College of Law						
309 Village Dr PO Box 117620	Gainesville	FL	32611	352-273-0804	392-4087	167-1
TF: 877-429-1297 ■ *Web:* www.law.ufl.edu						
University of Florida Libraries						
PO Box 117001	Gainesville	FL	32611	352-392-0342	392-7251	434-6
TF: 877-351-2377 ■ *Web:* www.uflib.ufl.edu						
University of Georgia Aquarium						
30 Ocean Science Cir	Savannah	GA	31411	912-598-2496	598-2302	40
Web: www.gacoast.uga.edu						
University of Georgia Library						
320 S Jackson St	Athens	GA	30602	706-542-0621	542-4144	434-6
TF: 877-314-5560 ■ *Web:* www.libs.uga.edu						
University of Georgia Press (UGA)						
Main Library 320 S Jackson St 3rd Fl	Athens	GA	30602	800-266-5842	425-3061*	637-2
**Fax Area Code:* 706 ■ *TF:* 800-266-5842 ■ *Web:* www.ugapress.org						
University of Georgia School of Law						
225 Herty Dr	Athens	GA	30602	706-542-5191	542-5556	167-1
Web: www.law.uga.edu						
University of Guam						
Unibetsedat Guahan UOG Stn	Mangilao	GU	96923	671-735-2910		166
Web: www.uog.edu						
University of Hartford						
200 Bloomfield Ave	West Hartford	CT	06117	860-768-4296	768-4961	166
TF: 800-947-4303 ■ *Web:* www.hartford.edu						
University of Hawai'i Cancer Ctr						
701 Ilalo St Ste 600	Honolulu	HI	96813	808-586-3010	586-3052	668
Web: www.uhcancercenter.org						
University of Hawaii						
Hilo 200 W Kawili St	Hilo	HI	96720	808-974-7414	933-0861	166
TF: 800-897-4456 ■ *Web:* hilo.hawaii.edu						
Honolulu Community College 874 Dillingham Blvd	Honolulu	HI	96817	808-845-9211	847-9829	162
Web: www.honolulu.hawaii.edu						
Kapiolani Community College 4303 Diamond Head Rd	Honolulu	HI	96816	808-734-9000	734-9896	162
Web: www.kcc.hawaii.edu						
Leeward Community College 96-045 Ala Ike St	Pearl City	HI	96782	808-455-0011	454-8804	162
Web: www.leeward.hawaii.edu						
Manoa 2600 Campus Rd Rm 001	Honolulu	HI	96822	808-956-8975	956-4148	166
TF: 800-823-9771 ■ *Web:* manoa.hawaii.edu						
West Oahu 96-129 Ala Ike	Pearl City	HI	96782	808-454-4700	453-6075	166
TF: 866-299-8656 ■ *Web:* westoahu.hawaii.edu						
Windward Community College 45-720 Keaahala Rd	Kaneohe	HI	96744	808-235-7400	247-5362	162
Web: windward.hawaii.edu						
University of Hawaii at Manoa						
John A Burns School of Medicine (JABSOM) 651 Ilalo St Medical Education Bldg	Honolulu	HI	96813	808-692-0899	692-1251	167-2
Web: jabsom.hawaii.edu						
University of Hawaii Federal Credit Union						
PO Box 22070	Honolulu	HI	96823	808-983-5500		219
TF: 800-927-3397 ■ *Web:* www.uhfcu.com						
University of Hawaii Foundation, The						
2444 Dole St Bachman Hall 105	Honolulu	HI	96822	808-956-8849		219
TF: 866-846-4262 ■ *Web:* www.uhfoundation.org						
University of Hawaii Press						
2840 Kolowalu St	Honolulu	HI	96822	808-956-8255	650-7811*	637-4
**Fax Area Code:* 800 ■ *TF:* 888-847-7377 ■ *Web:* www.uhpress.hawaii.edu						
University of Hawaii System						
2500 Campus Rd	Honolulu	HI	96822	808-956-8111	956-3952	786
Web: www.hawaii.edu						
University of Houston 4800 Calhoun Rd	Houston	TX	77004	713-743-2255		166
Web: www.uh.edu						
University of Houston						
Clear Lake 2700 Bay Area Blvd	Houston	TX	77058	281-283-7600	283-2522	166
Web: www.uhcl.edu						
Victoria 3007 N Ben Wilson St	Victoria	TX	77901	361-570-4848	570-4114	166
TF: 877-970-4848 ■ *Web:* uhv.edu						
University of Houston Law Ctr						
4604 Calhoun Rd	Houston	TX	77204	713-743-2100	743-2194	167-1
TF: 800-252-9690 ■ *Web:* www.law.uh.edu						
University of Idaho						
Boise 322 E Front St Ste 190	Boise	ID	83702	208-364-4050	364-4035	166
Web: www.uidaho.edu						
University of Illinois						
Chicago 601 S Morgan	Chicago	IL	60607	312-996-7000	413-7628	166
Web: www.uic.edu						
Springfield 1 University Plz MS UHB 1080	Springfield	IL	62703	217-206-4847	206-6620	166
Web: www.uis.edu						
Urbana-Champaign 901 W Illinois St	Urbana	IL	61801	217-333-0302	244-4614	166
Web: illinois.edu						
University of Illinois College of Law						
504 E Pennsylvania Ave	Champaign	IL	61820	217-333-0930	244-1478	167-1
Web: law.illinois.edu						
University of Illinois College of Medicine						
808 S Wood St Rm 165	Chicago	IL	60612	312-996-5635	996-6693	167-2
Web: medicine.uic.edu						
University of Illinois Medical Ctr						
1740 W Taylor St	Chicago	IL	60612	312-996-3900		374-3
Web: hospital.uillinois.edu						
University of Illinois Press						
1325 S Oak St	Champaign	IL	61820	217-333-0950	244-8082	637-4
Web: www.press.uillinois.edu						
University of Illinois System						
506 S Wright St Ste 352	Urbana	IL	61801	217-333-1920	333-6355	786
Web: www.uillinois.edu						
University of Illinois Urbana-Champaign						
Library 1408 W Gregory Dr 142 Undergraduate Library MC-522	Urbana	IL	61801	217-333-3085	265-0990	434-6
Web: www.library.illinois.edu						
University of Indianapolis						
1400 E Hanna Ave	Indianapolis	IN	46227	317-788-3368	788-3300	166
TF: 800-232-8634 ■ *Web:* www.uindy.edu						
University of Iowa 107 Calvin Hall	Iowa City	IA	52242	319-335-3847	335-1535	166
TF: 800-553-4692 ■ *Web:* uiowa.edu						
University of Iowa Athletics Hall of Fame						
2425 Prairie Meadow Dr	Iowa City	IA	52242	319-384-1031		522
Web: hof.hawkeyesports.com						
University of Iowa College of Law						
130 Byington Rd	Iowa City	IA	52242	319-335-3500	335-9019	167-1
Web: law.uiowa.edu						
University of Iowa Hospitals & Clinics						
200 Hawkins Dr	Iowa City	IA	52242	800-777-8442		374-3
TF: 800-777-8442 ■ *Web:* uihc.org						
University of Iowa Press						
119 W Park Rd 100 Kuhl House	Iowa City	IA	52242	319-335-2055		637-4
Web: www.uipress.uiowa.edu						
University of Iowa Press						
100 Kuhl House 119 W Park Rd	Iowa City	IA	52242	319-335-2000	335-2055	637-2
Web: www.uiowapress.org						
University of Iowa Roy J & Lucille A Carver College of Medicine						
200 CMAB	Iowa City	IA	52242	319-335-6707		167-2
TF: 800-725-8460 ■ *Web:* medicine.uiowa.edu						
University of Iowa Stanley Museum of Art						
150 N Riverside Dr 100 Old Museum of Art	Iowa City	IA	52242	319-335-1727	335-3677	520
Web: stanleymuseum.uiowa.edu						
University of Judaism						
15600 Mulholland Dr	Los Angeles	CA	90077	310-476-9777	471-3657	166
TF: 888-853-6763 ■ *Web:* www.aju.edu						
University of Kansas 1502 Iowa St	Lawrence	KS	66045	785-864-3911	864-5017	166
Web: ku.edu						

	Phone	Fax	Class
University of Kansas Health system			
3901 Rainbow Blvd. . . . . . Kansas City KS 66160	913-588-1227	588-5785	374-3
TF: 844-323-1227 ■ *Web:* www.kansashealthsystem.com			
University of Kansas Health System St Francis Campus			
1700 SW 7th St . . . . . . Topeka KS 66606	785-295-8000		374-3
TF: 855-578-3726 ■ *Web:* www.stfrancistopeka.org			
University of Kansas School of Law			
1535 W 15th St. . . . . . Lawrence KS 66045	785-864-4550		167-1
TF: 866-220-3654 ■ *Web:* law.ku.edu			
University of Kansas, The			
1450 Jayhawk Blvd. . . . . . Lawrence KS 66045	785-864-2700		166
Web: edwardscampus.ku.edu			
University of Kentucky			
620 S Limestone St . . . . . . Lexington KY 40506	859-257-1678	323-1061	167-1
Web: law.uky.edu			
University of Kentucky Art Museum			
University of Kentucky 13 Main Bldg . . . . . . Lexington KY 40506	859-257-5716	257-3042	520
Web: finearts.uky.edu			
University of Kentucky College of Medicine			
800 Rose St MN 150 . . . . . . Lexington KY 40536	859-323-6582		167-2
Web: med.uky.edu			
University of La Verne 1950 Third St . . . . . . La Verne CA 91750	909-593-3511		166
TF: 800-876-4858 ■ *Web:* laverne.edu			
University of Lethbridge			
4401 University Dr . . . . . . Lethbridge AB T1K3M4	403-329-2111	329-5159	785
Web: www.uleth.ca			
University of Louisiana			
Lafayette 611 McKinley St. . . . . . LaFayette LA 70504	337-482-1000	482-1317	166
TF: 800-752-6553 ■ *Web:* www.louisiana.edu			
Monroe 700 University Ave . . . . . . Monroe LA 71209	318-342-5430		166
TF: 800-372-5127 ■ *Web:* www.ulm.edu			
University of Louisiana at Lafayette Press			
PO Box 43558 . . . . . . Lafayette LA 70504	337-482-6027	482-6028	637-2
Web: www.ulpress.org			
University of Louisiana System			
1201 N Third St Ste 7-300 . . . . . . Baton Rouge LA 70802	225-342-6950		786
Web: www.ulsystem.edu			
University of Louisville			
2301 S Third St . . . . . . Louisville KY 40292	502-852-5555	852-6526	166
TF: 800-334-8635 ■ *Web:* louisville.edu			
University of Maine			
5713 Chadbourne Hall . . . . . . Orono ME 04469	207-581-1561	581-1213	166
TF: 877-486-2364 ■ *Web:* umaine.edu			
University of Maine			
Augusta 46 University Dr. . . . . . Augusta ME 04330	207-621-3000	621-3333	166
TF: 877-862-1234 ■ *Web:* www.uma.edu			
Farmington 111 S St. . . . . . Farmington ME 04938	207-778-7000	778-8182	166
TF: 800-871-7741 ■ *Web:* www.umf.maine.edu			
Fort Kent 23 University Dr. . . . . . Fort Kent ME 04743	207-834-7500		166
TF: 888-879-8635 ■ *Web:* www.umfk.edu			
Machias 116 O'Brien Ave. . . . . . Machias ME 04654	207-255-1200		166
TF: 888-468-6866 ■ *Web:* machias.edu			
Presque Isle 181 Main St. . . . . . Presque Isle ME 04769	207-498-9400		166
Web: www.umpi.maine.edu			
Raymond H. Fogler Library			
5729 Fogler Library . . . . . . Orono ME 04469	207-581-1666	581-1653	434-6
Web: library.umaine.edu			
University of Maine School of Law			
246 Deering Ave . . . . . . Portland ME 04102	207-780-4355	780-4239	167-1
Web: mainelaw.maine.edu			
University of Maine System			
251 Estabrooke Hall 15 Estabrooke Dr . . . . . . Orono ME 04469	207-581-5844	581-9212	167-3
Web: www.maine.edu			
University of Manitoba			
65 Chancellors Cir 500 University Ctr . . . . . . Winnipeg MB R3T2N2	204-474-8880	474-7554	785
TF: 800-224-7713 ■ *Web:* umanitoba.ca			
University of Manitoba Faculty of Medicine			
727 McDermot Ave Rm 260 . . . . . . Winnipeg MB R3E3P5	204-789-3557	789-3928	167-2
Web: www.umanitoba.ca			
University of Mary			
7500 University Dr . . . . . . Bismarck ND 58504	701-355-8265	255-7687	166
TF: 800-288-6279 ■ *Web:* www.umary.edu			
University of Mary Hardin-Baylor			
900 College St . . . . . . Belton TX 76513	254-295-8642	295-5049	166
TF: 800-727-8642 ■ *Web:* go.umhb.edu			
University of Mary Washington			
1301 College Ave . . . . . . Fredericksburg VA 22401	540-654-2000	654-1857	166
TF: 800-468-5614 ■ *Web:* www.umw.edu			
University of Maryland			
7569 Baltimore Ave. . . . . . College Park MD 20742	301-405-3555	314-9693	166
TF: 800-422-5867 ■ *Web:* umd.edu			
University of Maryland			
Baltimore County 1000 Hilltop Cir. . . . . . Baltimore MD 21250	410-455-1000	455-1094	166
TF: 800-810-0271 ■ *Web:* www.umbc.edu			
Eastern Shore			
30665 Student Services Ctr . . . . . . Princess Anne MD 21853	410-651-7747	651-7922	166
Web: www.umes.edu			
McKeldin Library			
McKeldin Library . . . . . . College Park MD 20742	301-405-9075		434-6
Web: www.lib.umd.edu			
University of Maryland Baltimore			
Health Sciences & Human Services Library (HSHSL)			
601 W Lombard St. . . . . . Baltimore MD 21201	410-706-7995	706-8403	434-1
Web: www.hshsl.umaryland.edu			
University of Maryland Center for Environmental Science (UMCES)			
2020 Horn Pt Rd. . . . . . Cambridge MD 21613	410-228-9250	228-3843	668
TF: 866-842-2520 ■ *Web:* www.umces.edu			
University of Maryland College of Information Studies			
4161 Fieldhouse Dr			
Patuxent Bldg Rm 1117 . . . . . . College Park MD 20742	301-405-2033	314-9145	166
Web: ischool.umd.edu			
University of Maryland Medical System			
22 S Greene St . . . . . . Baltimore MD 21201	410-328-8667		353
TF: 800-492-5538 ■ *Web:* www.umms.org			
University of Maryland School of Medicine			
685 W Baltimore St Ste 190 . . . . . . Baltimore MD 21201	410-706-7478	706-0467	167-2
Web: www.medschool.umaryland.edu			
University of Massachusetts			
Dartmouth 285 Old Westport Rd . . . . . . North Dartmouth MA 02747	508-999-8000	999-8755	166
Web: www.umassd.edu			
Lowell 1 University Ave . . . . . . Lowell MA 01854	978-934-4000	934-3086	166
TF: 800-480-3190 ■ *Web:* www.uml.edu			
University of Massachusetts Amherst			
DuBois Library 154 Hicks Way . . . . . . Amherst MA 01003	413-545-0284		434-6
Web: www.library.umass.edu			
University of Massachusetts Press			
671 N Pleasant St . . . . . . Amherst MA 01003	413-545-2217	545-1226	637-4
TF: 800-562-0112 ■ *Web:* www.umass.edu			
University of Medicine & Dentistry of New Jersey			
University Hospital, The			
150 Bergen St C- 431 . . . . . . Newark NJ 07103	973-972-4300		374-3
Web: www.uhnj.org			
University of Memphis 3720 Alumni Ave . . . . . . Memphis TN 38152	901-678-2000		167-3
Web: www.memphis.edu			
University of Miami			
1252 Memorial Dr . . . . . . Coral Gables FL 33146	305-284-2211		166
Web: welcome.miami.edu			
University of Miami Health Systems			
1400 NW 12th Ave . . . . . . Miami FL 33136	305-325-5511		167-3
Web: www.umiamihealth.org			
University of Miami Hospital & Clinics (UMHC)			
Sylvester Comprehensive Cancer Ctr			
1475 NW 12th Ave. . . . . . Miami FL 33136	305-243-1000		769
TF: 800-545-2292 ■ *Web:* umiamihealth.org			
University of Miami Richter Library			
1300 Memorial Dr 3rd Fl . . . . . . Coral Gables FL 33124	305-284-3233	284-4027	434-6
Web: library.miami.edu			
University of Miami School of Law			
1311 Miller Dr . . . . . . Coral Gables FL 33146	305-284-2339	284-3084	167-1
Web: www.law.miami.edu			
University of Michigan			
515 E Jefferson St. . . . . . Ann Arbor MI 48109	734-764-6413		166
Web: www.umich.edu			
University of Michigan			
Flint 303 E Kearsley St. . . . . . Flint MI 48502	810-762-3300	762-3272	166
TF: 800-942-5636 ■ *Web:* www.flint.umich.edu			
Libraries 913 S University Ave. . . . . . Ann Arbor MI 48109	734-764-0410		434-6
Web: www.lib.umich.edu			
University of Michigan Law School			
625 S State St. . . . . . Ann Arbor MI 48109	734-764-1358	647-3218	167-1
Web: www.law.umich.edu			
University of Michigan Museum of Art			
525 S State St. . . . . . Ann Arbor MI 48109	734-764-0395	764-3731	520
Web: umma.umich.edu			
University of Michigan Press			
839 Greene St. . . . . . Ann Arbor MI 48104	734-764-4388	615-1540	637-4
TF: 866-804-0002 ■ *Web:* www.press.umich.edu			
University of Michigan Transportation Research Institute (UMTRI)			
2901 Baxter Rd . . . . . . Ann Arbor MI 48109	734-764-6504	936-1081	668
Web: www.umtri.umich.edu			
University of Michigan Trauma Burn Ctr			
1500 E Medical Center Dr UH 1C-421 . . . . . . Ann Arbor MI 48109	734-936-9690		374-7
Web: www.traumaburn.org			
University of Minnesota			
200 Oak St SE Ste 500 . . . . . . Minneapolis MN 55455	612-624-3333	625-4305	48-11
TF: 800-775-2187 ■ *Web:* give.umn.edu			
University of Minnesota			
2900 University Ave 170 Owen Hall . . . . . . Crookston MN 56716	218-281-8569	281-8575	166
TF: 800-862-6466 ■ *Web:* www.crk.umn.edu			
University of Minnesota			
Duluth 1049 University Dr. . . . . . Duluth MN 55812	218-726-8000	726-6394	166
TF: 800-232-1339 ■ *Web:* www.d.umn.edu			
Morris 600 E Fourth St . . . . . . Morris MN 56267	888-866-3382	589-1673*	166
**Fax Area Code: 320* ■ *TF:* 800-992-8863 ■ *Web:* www.morris.umn.edu			
Twin Cities			
3 Morrill Hall 100 Church St SE . . . . . . Minneapolis MN 55455	612-625-2008	626-1693	166
TF: 800-752-1000 ■ *Web:* twin-cities.umn.edu			
University of Minnesota Law School			
229 19th Ave S Walter F Mondale Hall . . . . . . Minneapolis MN 55455	612-625-1000	626-1874	167-1
Web: www.law.umn.edu			
University of Minnesota Medical Center Fairview - University Campus			
500 Harvard St . . . . . . Minneapolis MN 55455	612-273-3000		374-3
TF: 800-688-5252 ■ *Web:* www.mhealth.org			
University of Minnesota Press			
111 Third Ave S Ste 290. . . . . . Minneapolis MN 55401	612-301-1990		637-4
Web: www.upress.umn.edu			
University of Minnesota Twin Cities			
Bio-Medical Library			
505 Essex St SE 450B Diehl Hall. . . . . . Minneapolis MN 55455	612-626-4045		434-1
Web: www.hsl.lib.umn.edu			
Wilson Library 309 19th Ave S . . . . . . Minneapolis MN 55455	612-624-3321	626-9353	434-6
Web: www.lib.umn.edu			
University of Mississippi			
PO Box 1848 . . . . . . University MS 38677	662-915-7211	915-5869	166
TF: 800-891-4596 ■ *Web:* www.olemiss.edu			
University of Mississippi			
Tupelo 1918 Briar Ridge Rd. . . . . . Tupelo MS 38804	662-844-5622	844-5625	166
Web: www.outreach.olemiss.edu			
University of Mississippi Medical Ctr (UMMC)			
2500 N State St. . . . . . Jackson MS 39216	601-984-1000		769
Web: www.umc.edu			
University of Missouri			
129 Fine Arts Bldg . . . . . . Columbia MO 65211	573-882-2021		572
Web: theatre.missouri.edu			
University of Missouri			
Columbia 104 Jesse Hall. . . . . . Columbia MO 65211	573-882-6333	882-7887	166
TF: 800-856-2181 ■ *Web:* missouri.edu			
Kansas City 5100 Rockhill Rd . . . . . . Kansas City MO 64110	816-235-1000	235-5544	166
TF: 800-775-8652 ■ *Web:* www.umkc.edu			
Saint Louis 1 University Blvd. . . . . . Saint Louis MO 63121	314-516-5000	516-5310	166
TF: 888-462-8675 ■ *Web:* www.umsl.edu			
University of Missouri - Columbia - Center for Economic Education Library			
Dept of Economics 230 Jesse Hall . . . . . . Columbia MO 65211	573-882-7786	882-7887	434-3
Web: www.showme.missouri.edu			

Name / Address	City	State	Zip	Phone	Fax	Class
University of Missouri Columbia School of Law 203 Hulston Hall *Web:* www.law.missouri.edu	Columbia	MO	65211	573-882-6487	882-4984	167-1
University of Missouri Kansas City School of Law 500 E 52nd St *Web:* law.umkc.edu	Kansas City	MO	64110	816-235-1644	235-5276	167-1
University of Missouri Press Ste 201 S Seventh St 113 Heinkel Bldg *Web:* upress.missouri.edu	Columbia	MO	65201	573-882-7641	884-4498	637-4
University of Missouri System 321 University Hall *TF:* 800-225-6075 ■ *Web:* www.umsystem.edu	Columbia	MO	65211	573-882-2011	882-2721	786
University of Missouri, Columbia Mathematical Sciences Library 206 Math Bldg *Web:* library.missouri.edu	Columbia	MO	65211	573-882-7286	884-0058	434-3
University of Missouri-Kansas City School of Medicine 2411 Holmes St *Web:* med.umkc.edu	Kansas City	MO	64108	816-235-1111	235-5277	167-2
University of Mobile 5735 College Pkwy *TF:* 800-946-7267 ■ *Web:* umobile.edu	Mobile	AL	36613	251-675-5990	442-2498	166
University of Montana 1205 E Broadway St *TF:* 800-542-6882 ■ *Web:* www.mc.umt.edu	Missoula	MT	59801	406-243-7852	243-7899	800
University of Montana 32 Campus Dr *TF:* 800-462-8636 ■ *Web:* www.umt.edu	Missoula	MT	59812	406-243-6266	243-5711	166
University of Montana *Helena College of Technology* 1115 N Roberts St *Web:* www.helenacollege.edu	Helena	MT	59601	406-447-6900	447-6397	800
Western 710 S Atlantic St *TF:* 877-683-7331 ■ *Web:* www.umwestern.edu	Dillon	MT	59725	406-683-7011	683-7493	166
University of Nebraska *Kearney* 2504 Ninth Ave *TF:* 800-532-7639 ■ *Web:* www.unk.edu	Kearney	NE	68849	308-865-8441	865-8987	166
Omaha 6001 Dodge St *TF:* 800-858-8648 ■ *Web:* www.unomaha.edu	Omaha	NE	68182	402-554-2800	554-3472	166
University of Nebraska Lincoln *Love Memorial Library* 318 Love Library PO Box 884100 *Web:* libraries.unl.edu	Lincoln	NE	68588	402-472-9568		434-6
University of Nebraska Medical Ctr 42nd & Emile *Web:* www.unmc.edu	Omaha	NE	68198	402-559-4000		374-3
University of Nebraska Press 1111 Lincoln Mall *Web:* www.nebraskapress.unl.edu	Lincoln	NE	68508	402-472-3581		637-4
University of Nebraska State Museum 645 N 14th St *Web:* museum.unl.edu	Lincoln	NE	68588	402-472-2642	472-8899	520
University of Nebraska System Varner Hall 3835 Holdrege St *TF:* 800-542-1602 ■ *Web:* nebraska.edu	Lincoln	NE	68583	402-472-2111	472-1237	786
University of Nebraska-Lincoln 1400 R St *TF:* 800-242-3766 ■ *Web:* www.unl.edu	Lincoln	NE	68588	402-472-7211	472-0463	520
University of Nevada *Reno* 1664 N Virginia St *TF:* 866-263-8232 ■ *Web:* www.unr.edu	Reno	NV	89557	775-784-1110	784-4283	166
University of Nevada Las Vegas *Lied Library* 4505 S Maryland Pkwy *Web:* www.unlv.edu	Las Vegas	NV	89154	702-895-3011		434-6
University of Nevada Las Vegas William S Boyd School of Law 4505 S Maryland Pkwy *Web:* law.unlv.edu	Las Vegas	NV	89154	702-505-0717		167-1
University of Nevada Press 1041 N Virginia St, F2 MS Hwy 0166 *Web:* unpress.nevada.edu	Reno	NV	89557	775-784-6573		637-4
University of New Brunswick *Saint John* 100 Tucker Park Rd PO Box 5050 *Web:* www.unb.ca	Saint John	NB	E2L4L5	506-648-5500	648-5528	785
University of New England 11 Hills Beach Rd *TF:* 800-477-4863 ■ *Web:* www.une.edu	Biddeford	ME	04005	207-283-0171		166
University of New Hampshire 3 Garrison Ave *TF:* 800-313-5327 ■ *Web:* www.unh.edu	Durham	NH	03824	603-862-1234	862-0077	166
University of New Hampshire *Manchester* 88 Commercial St *Web:* manchester.unh.edu	Manchester	NH	03101	603-641-4101		166
University of New Mexico (UNM) 1 University of New Mexico *TF:* 800-225-5866 ■ *Web:* www.unm.edu	Albuquerque	NM	87131	505-277-0111	277-6686	166
University of New Mexico *Gallup* 200 College Rd *Web:* www.gallup.unm.edu	Gallup	NM	87301	505-863-7500	863-7610	166
Los Alamos 4000 University Dr *Web:* losalamos.unm.edu	Los Alamos	NM	87544	505-662-5919	661-4698	162
University of New Mexico Fine Arts & Design Library MSC05 3020 *Web:* www.library.unm.edu	Albuquerque	NM	87131	505-277-2357		434-3
University of New Mexico School of Law 1117 Stanford Dr NE *Web:* lawschool.unm.edu	Albuquerque	NM	87131	505-277-2146	277-9958	167-1
University of New Orleans 2000 Lakeshore Dr *TF:* 800-256-5866 ■ *Web:* www.uno.edu	New Orleans	LA	70148	504-280-6000	280-5522	166
University of North Alabama 1 Harrison Plz *TF:* 800-825-5862 ■ *Web:* www.una.edu	Florence	AL	35632	256-765-4608		166
University of North Carolina 910 Raleigh Rd PO Box 2688 *Web:* www.northcarolina.edu	Chapel Hill	NC	27514	919-962-1000		786
University of North Carolina *Asheville* 1 University Hts *TF:* 800-531-9842 ■ *Web:* www.unca.edu	Asheville	NC	28804	828-251-6481	251-6482	166
Chapel Hill Jackson Hall CB 2200 *TF:* 800-962-8519 ■ *Web:* www.unc.edu	Chapel Hill	NC	27599	919-966-3621	962-3045	166
Charlotte 9201 University City Blvd *Web:* www.uncc.edu	Charlotte	NC	28223	704-687-8622		166
Greensboro 1400 Spring Garden St *Web:* www.uncg.edu	Greensboro	NC	27412	336-334-5000	334-4180	166
Pembroke PO Box 1510 *TF:* 800-949-8627 ■ *Web:* www.uncp.edu	Pembroke	NC	28372	910-521-6000	521-6497	166
Wilmington 601 S College Rd *TF:* 800-596-2880 ■ *Web:* uncw.edu	Wilmington	NC	28403	910-962-3000	962-3038	166
University of North Carolina Chapel Hill *Davis Library* 208 Raleigh St CB Ste 3916 UNC *Web:* library.unc.edu	Chapel Hill	NC	27599	919-843-5660		434-6
Health Sciences Library 335 S Columbia St CB 7585 *Web:* www.hsl.unc.edu	Chapel Hill	NC	27599	919-962-0800		434-1
University of North Carolina Press 116 S Boundary St *TF:* 800-848-6224 ■ *Web:* www.uncpress.org	Chapel Hill	NC	27514	919-966-3561		637-4
University of North Carolina School of Law 160 Ridge Rd *Web:* www.law.unc.edu	Chapel Hill	NC	27599	919-962-5106		167-1
University of North Dakota PO Box 8357 *Web:* und.edu	Grand Forks	ND	58202	701-777-3000		166
University of North Dakota Chester Fritz Library 3051 University Ave S-9000 *Web:* library.und.edu	Grand Forks	ND	58202	701-777-2189	777-3319	434-6
University of North Dakota School of Law 215 Centennial Dr S-9003 *Web:* law.und.edu	Grand Forks	ND	58202	701-777-2104		167-1
University of North Dakota School of Medicine & Health Sciences 1301 N Columbia Rd S-9037 *TF:* 800-225-5863 ■ *Web:* med.und.edu	Grand Forks	ND	58202	701-777-5046	777-4942	167-2
University of North Florida (UNF) 1UNF Dr *Web:* www.unf.edu	Jacksonville	FL	32224	904-620-2615	620-2719	434-6
University of North Texas PO Box 311277 *TF:* 800-868-8211 ■ *Web:* www.unt.edu	Denton	TX	76203	940-565-2681	565-2408	166
University of North Texas Health Science Ctr 3500 Camp Bowie Blvd *TF:* 800-687-7580 ■ *Web:* www.unthsc.edu	Fort Worth	TX	76107	817-735-2000	735-5016	417
University of North Texas Rare Book Room 1506 Highland Ave Willis Library 4th Fl *Web:* www.library.unt.edu	Denton	TX	76203	940-565-2769		434-3
University of Northern British Columbia 3333 University Way *TF:* 800-627-9931 ■ *Web:* www.unbc.ca	Prince George	BC	V2N4Z9	250-960-5555	960-6330	785
University of Northern Colorado 501 20th St CB 92 *TF:* 888-700-4862 ■ *Web:* www.unco.edu	Greeley	CO	80639	970-351-2881	351-2984	166
University of Northern Iowa 1222 W 27th St *TF:* 800-772-2037 ■ *Web:* uni.edu	Cedar Falls	IA	50614	319-273-2311	273-2885	166
University of Northwestern Ohio 1441 N Cable Rd *Web:* www.unoh.edu	Lima	OH	45805	419-998-3120	998-3139	800
University of Notre Dame 220 Main Bldg *Web:* www.nd.edu	Notre Dame	IN	46556	574-631-7505	631-8065	166
University of Notre Dame Hesburgh Library 221 Hesburgh Library *Web:* library.nd.edu	Notre Dame	IN	46556	574-631-5252	631-6772	434-6
University of Notre Dame Press (UNDP) 310 Flanner Hall *Web:* www.undpress.nd.edu	Notre Dame	IN	46556	574-631-6346	631-4410	637-2
University of Oklahoma Bizzell Memorial Library 401 W Brooks St *Web:* libraries.ou.edu	Norman	OK	73019	405-325-4142	325-7550	434-6
University of Oklahoma College of Law 300 Timberdell Rd *Web:* www.law.ou.edu	Norman	OK	73019	405-325-4699	325-7474	167-1
University of Oklahoma Health Sciences Ctr 1100 N Lindsay *Web:* www.ouhsc.edu	Oklahoma City	OK	73104	405-271-4000		166
University of Oklahoma, The 660 Parrington Oval *Web:* www.ou.edu	Norman	OK	73019	405-325-0311		167-3
University of Oregon 1585 E 13th Ave *TF:* 800-232-3825 ■ *Web:* www.uoregon.edu	Eugene	OR	97403	541-346-1000	346-5815	166
University of Oregon Bookstore Inc 895 E 13th Ave *TF:* 800-352-1733 ■ *Web:* www.uoduckstore.com	Eugene	OR	97401	541-346-4331		95
University of Oregon Knight Library 1299 University of Oregon *Web:* library.uoregon.edu	Eugene	OR	97403	541-346-3053	346-3485	434-6
University of Oregon Museum of Natural & Cultural History 1680 E 15th Ave *Web:* mnch.uoregon.edu	Eugene	OR	97401	541-346-3024		520
University of Oregon School of Law 1515 Agate St *Web:* law.uoregon.edu	Eugene	OR	97403	541-346-3852	346-1564	167-1
University of Ottawa 550 Cumberland St *TF:* 877-868-8292 ■ *Web:* www.uottawa.ca	Ottawa	ON	K1N6N5	613-562-5800	562-5323	785
University of Ottawa Health Sciences Library 65 University *Web:* biblio.uottawa.ca	Ottawa	ON	K1N6N5	613-562-5407		434-1
University of Pennsylvania 3451 Walnut St *TF:* 800-537-5487 ■ *Web:* www.upenn.edu	Philadelphia	PA	19104	215-898-7293	898-9670	166
University of Pennsylvania 3420 Walnut St *Web:* www.library.upenn.edu	Philadelphia	PA	19104	215-898-7091	898-0559	434-6
University of Pennsylvania Law School 3501 Sansom St *Web:* www.law.upenn.edu	Philadelphia	PA	19104	215-898-7483	573-2025	167-1
University of Pennsylvania Museum of Archaeology & Anthropology 3260 S St *Web:* www.penn.museum	Philadelphia	PA	19104	215-898-4000		520

Name / Address	City	State	ZIP	Phone	Fax	Class
University of Phoenix Online						
3157 E Elwood St	Phoenix	AZ	85034	866-766-0766		166
TF: 866-766-0766 ■ *Web:* www.phoenix.edu						
University of Pittsburgh						
4227 Fifth Ave.	Pittsburgh	PA	15260	412-624-4141	648-8815	166
Web: www.pitt.edu						
University of Pittsburgh						
Bradford 300 Campus Dr.	Bradford	PA	16701	814-362-7555		166
TF: 800-872-1787 ■ *Web:* www.upb.pitt.edu						
Greensburg 150 Finoli Dr	Greensburg	PA	15601	724-837-7040	836-7160	166
TF: 888-843-4563 ■ *Web:* www.greensburg.pitt.edu						
Hillman Library 3960 Forbes Ave	Pittsburgh	PA	15260	412-648-3330	648-7887	434-6
Web: www.library.pitt.edu						
Johnstown 157 Blackington Hall	Johnstown	PA	15904	814-269-7050	269-7044	166
TF: 800-765-4875 ■ *Web:* www.upj.pitt.edu						
Titusville 504 E Main St.	Titusville	PA	16354	888-878-0462	827-4519*	162
**Fax Area Code:* 814 ■ *TF:* 888-878-0462 ■ *Web:* www.upt.pitt.edu						
University of Pittsburgh Medical Center Health System						
200 Lothrop St	Pittsburgh	PA	15213	412-647-2345		353
Web: www.upmc.com						
University of Pittsburgh Press						
7500 Thomas Blvd 4th Fl	Pittsburgh	PA	15260	412-383-2456	383-2466	637-4
Web: upittpress.org						
University of Pittsburgh School of Law						
3900 Forbes Ave.	Pittsburgh	PA	15260	412-648-1490	648-2647	167-1
Web: www.law.pitt.edu						
University of Pittsburgh School of Medicine						
3550 Ter St S530 Scaife Hall	Pittsburgh	PA	15261	412-648-9891		167-2
Web: www.medschool.pitt.edu						
University of Portland						
5000 N Willamette Blvd	Portland	OR	97203	503-943-7147		166
TF: 888-627-5601 ■ *Web:* www.up.edu						
University of Providence						
1301 20th St S	Great Falls	MT	59405	800-856-9544	791-5209*	166
**Fax Area Code:* 406 ■ *TF:* 800-856-9544 ■ *Web:* www.uprovidence.edu						
University of Puget Sound						
1500 N Warner St	Tacoma	WA	98416	253-879-3100		166
TF: 800-396-7191 ■ *Web:* www.pugetsound.edu						
University of Redlands						
1200 E Colton Ave PO Box 3080	Redlands	CA	92373	909-793-2121		166
TF: 800-455-5064 ■ *Web:* www.redlands.edu						
University of Regina 3737 Wascana Pkwy.	Regina	SK	S4S0A2	306-585-4111	337-2525	785
TF: 800-644-4756 ■ *Web:* www.uregina.ca						
University of Rhode Island (URI)						
45 Upper College Rd	Kingston	RI	02881	401-874-1000	874-5523	166
Web: www.uri.edu						
University of Richmond						
28 Westhampton Way	Richmond	VA	23173	804-289-8000	287-6003	166
TF: 800-700-1662 ■ *Web:* www.richmond.edu						
University of Rio Grande						
218 N College Ave	Rio Grande	OH	45674	800-282-7201	245-7260*	166
**Fax Area Code:* 740 ■ *TF:* 800-282-7201 ■ *Web:* www.rio.edu						
University of Rochester						
252 Elmwood Ave.	Rochester	NY	14627	585-275-2121	461-4595	166
TF: 888-822-2256 ■ *Web:* www.rochester.edu						
University of Rochester River Campus Libraries						
755 Library Rd PO Box 270055	Rochester	NY	14627	585-275-5804	273-5309	434-6
Web: www.library.rochester.edu						
University of Rochester School of Medicine & Dentistry						
601 Elmwood Ave.	Rochester	NY	14642	585-275-0017	756-5479	167-2
TF: 888-661-6162 ■ *Web:* www.urmc.rochester.edu						
University of Saint Francis-ft Wayne						
2701 Spring St.	Fort Wayne	IN	46808	260-399-7700		166
Web: www.sf.edu						
University of Saint Joseph						
1678 Asylum Ave	West Hartford	CT	06117	860-232-4571		166
Web: www.sjc.edu						
University of Saint Mary						
4100 S Fourth St	Leavenworth	KS	66048	913-682-5151	758-6140	166
TF: 800-752-7043 ■ *Web:* www.stmary.edu						
University of Saint Mary of the Lake Mundelein Seminary						
1000 E Maple Ave.	Mundelein	IL	60060	847-566-6401		167-3
Web: usml.edu						
University of Saint Thomas						
3800 Montrose Blvd.	Houston	TX	77006	713-522-7911	525-3558	166
TF: 800-856-8565 ■ *Web:* www.stthom.edu						
University of Saint Thomas						
2115 Summit Ave.	Saint Paul	MN	55105	651-962-5000	962-6160	166
TF: 800-328-6819 ■ *Web:* stthomas.edu						
University of San Diego						
5998 Alcala Pk	San Diego	CA	92110	619-260-4600	260-6836	166
TF: 800-248-4873 ■ *Web:* www.sandiego.edu						
University of San Francisco						
2130 Fulton St	San Francisco	CA	94117	415-422-5555	422-2217	166
TF: 800-854-1385 ■ *Web:* www.usfca.edu						
University of Sankore Press						
3018 W 48th St.	Los Angeles	CA	90043	323-295-9799	299-0261	637-2
TF: 800-997-2656 ■ *Web:* www.sankorepress.com						
University of Saskatchewan						
Leslie & Irene Dube Health Sciences Library						
104 Clinic Pl	Saskatoon	SK	S7N2Z4	306-966-5991		434-1
Web: www.library.usask.ca						
Saint Thomas More College						
1437 College Dr.	Saskatoon	SK	S7N0W6	306-966-8900	966-8904	785
TF: 800-667-2019 ■ *Web:* stmcollege.ca						
University of Science and Philosophy (USP)						
PO Box 520	Waynesboro	VA	22980	800-882-5683	729-1096*	166
**Fax Area Code:* 573 ■ *TF:* 800-882-5683 ■ *Web:* www.philosophy.org						
University of Sciences & Arts of Oklahoma						
1727 W Alabama Ave	Chickasha	OK	73018	405-224-3140	574-1220	166
TF: 800-933-8726 ■ *Web:* usao.edu						
University of Scranton						
St Thomas Hall 800 Linden St	Scranton	PA	18510	570-941-7400	941-5928	166
TF: 888-727-2686 ■ *Web:* www.scranton.edu						
University of Sioux Falls						
1101 W 22nd St	Sioux Falls	SD	57105	605-331-6600	331-6615	166
TF: 800-888-1047 ■ *Web:* www.usiouxfalls.edu						
University of South Alabama						
2500 Meisler Hall	Mobile	AL	36688	251-460-6141	460-7876	166
TF: 800-872-5247 ■ *Web:* www.usouthal.edu						
University of South Alabama Children & Women's Hospital						
1700 Center St	Mobile	AL	36604	251-415-1000	415-1002	374-3
Web: www.usahealthsystem.com						
University of South Alabama College of Medicine						
307 N University Blvd.	Mobile	AL	36688	251-460-6101	460-6278	167-2
Web: www.southalabama.edu						
University of South Carolina						
1601 Greene St.	Columbia	SC	29208	803-777-7000	777-0101	166
TF: 800-868-5872 ■ *Web:* www.sc.edu						
University of South Carolina						
Aiken 471 University Pkwy	Aiken	SC	29801	803-648-6851	641-3727	166
TF: 866-254-2366 ■ *Web:* www.usca.edu						
Upstate 800 University Way.	Spartanburg	SC	29303	864-503-5246	503-5727	166
TF: 800-277-8727 ■ *Web:* www.uscupstate.edu						
University of South Dakota						
414 E Clark St.	Vermillion	SD	57069	605-677-5341	677-6323	166
TF: 877-269-6837 ■ *Web:* www.usd.edu						
University of South Dakota Foundation						
1110 N Dakota St PO Box 5555	Vermillion	SD	57069	605-677-6703	677-6717	786
TF: 800-521-3575 ■ *Web:* www.usdalumni.com						
University of South Florida						
Sarasota-Manatee 8350 N Tamiami Trl	Sarasota	FL	34243	941-359-4200	359-4236	166
TF: 866-974-1222 ■ *Web:* www.sarasotamanatee.usf.edu						
ST. Petersburg						
140 7th Ave S Bay 117.	Saint Petersburg	FL	33701	727-873-4135	873-4525	166
Web: www.stpetersburg.usf.edu						
Tampa 4202 E Fowler Ave	Tampa	FL	33620	813-974-3400		166
Web: www.usf.edu						
University of South Florida College of Medicine (USF)						
12901 Bruce B Downs Blvd	Tampa	FL	33612	813-974-2229	974-4990	167-2
Web: health.usf.edu						
University of Southern California						
University Pk Campus	Los Angeles	CA	90089	213-740-2311	740-5229	166
Web: www.usc.edu						
University of Southern Indiana						
8600 University Blvd	Evansville	IN	47712	812-464-1765	465-7154	166
TF: 800-467-1965 ■ *Web:* www.usi.edu						
University of Southern Maine						
96 Falmouth St.	Portland	ME	04103	207-780-4141	780-5640	166
Web: usm.maine.edu						
University of Southern Maine Arboretum						
PO Box 9300	Portland	ME	04104	800-800-4876	780-5143*	97
**Fax Area Code:* 207 ■ *TF:* 800-800-4876 ■ *Web:* www.usm.maine.edu						
University of Southern Mississippi						
118 College Dr.	Hattiesburg	MS	39406	601-266-1000		166
TF: 800-446-0892 ■ *Web:* www.usm.edu						
University of St Francis 500 Wilcox St.	Joliet	IL	60435	800-735-7500		166
TF: 800-735-7500 ■ *Web:* www.stfrancis.edu						
University of Tampa 401 W Kennedy Blvd.	Tampa	FL	33606	813-253-3333	258-7398	166
Web: www.ut.edu						
University of Tennessee (UTHSC)						
2040 Sutherland Ave.	Knoxville	TN	37996	865-946-7777	974-6341	166
Web: www.utk.edu						
University of Tennessee						
Chattanooga 615 McCallie Ave	Chattanooga	TN	37403	423-425-4111	425-4157	166
TF: 800-882-6627 ■ *Web:* www.utc.edu						
Health Science Ctr 920 Madison Ave.	Memphis	TN	38163	901-448-5500		166
Web: www.uthsc.edu						
Martin 554 University St	Martin	TN	38238	731-881-7020	881-7029	166
TF: 800-829-8861 ■ *Web:* www.utm.edu						
University of Tennessee Arboretum						
901 S Illinois Ave.	Oak Ridge	TN	37830	865-483-3571	483-3572	97
Web: forestry.tennessee.edu						
University of Tennessee College of Law						
1505 Cumberland Ave	Knoxville	TN	37996	865-974-2521		167-1
Web: www.law.utk.edu						
University of Tennessee Gardens						
2431 Joe Johnson Dr	Knoxville	TN	37996	865-974-7324	974-1947	97
Web: www.ag.tennessee.edu						
University of Tennessee Knoxville						
Hodges Library 1015 Volunteer Blvd.	Knoxville	TN	37996	865-974-4351		434-6
TF: 800-426-9119 ■ *Web:* www.lib.utk.edu						
University of Tennessee Music Hall						
1741 Volunteer Blvd.	Knoxville	TN	37996	865-974-3241	974-1941	572
Web: music.utk.edu						
University of Tennessee Press						
110 Conference Ctr 600 Henley St	Knoxville	TN	37996	865-974-3321	974-3724	637-4
Web: utpress.org						
University of Tennessee System						
800 Andy Holt Tower 1331 Circle Pk	Knoxville	TN	37996	865-974-2241	974-3753	786
Web: tennessee.edu						
University of Texas						
Austin 2400 Inner Campus Dr Ste F2500	Austin	TX	78712	512-475-7399		166
Web: www.utexas.edu						
Dallas						
International Ctr 800 W Campbell Rd SSB34						
	Richardson	TX	75080	972-883-4189	883-4010	166
TF: 800-889-2443 ■ *Web:* www.utdallas.edu						
El Paso 500 W University Ave	El Paso	TX	79968	915-747-5000	747-8893	166
Web: www.utep.edu						
Ex-Student's Assn						
2110 San Jacinto Blvd	Austin	TX	78712	512-840-5700		138
TF: 866-974-7220 ■ *Web:* www.texasexes.org						
Permian Basin 4901 E University Blvd.	Odessa	TX	79762	432-552-2020	552-3605	166
TF: 866-552-8872 ■ *Web:* www.utpb.edu						
Perry-Castaneda Library						
101 E 21st St PO Box P	Austin	TX	78712	512-495-4250	495-4347	434-6
Web: www.lib.utexas.edu						
San Antonio 6900 N Loop 1604 W	San Antonio	TX	78249	210-458-4011	458-7716	166
TF: 800-669-0919 ■ *Web:* www.utsa.edu						
Tyler 3900 University Blvd.	Tyler	TX	75799	903-566-7000	566-7068	166
TF: 800-888-9537 ■ *Web:* www.uttyler.edu						
University of Texas at Arlington College of Architecture, Planning, and Public Affairs						
601 W Nedderman Dr Ste 203	Arlington	TX	76019	817-272-2801	272-5008	166
Web: www.uta.edu						

	City	State	ZIP	Phone	Fax	Class
University of Texas at Austin Performing Arts Ctr 2350 Robert Dedman Dr *Web:* texasperformingarts.org	Austin	TX	78712	512-232-6213		572
University of Texas Health Center at Tyler (UTHCT) 11937 US Hwy 271 *Web:* www.uthct.edu	Tyler	TX	75708	903-877-7000		374-3
University of Texas Health Science Ctr (UTHSC) *Libraries* 7703 Floyd Curl Dr MSC 7940 *Web:* library.uthscsa.edu	San Antonio	TX	78229	210-567-2408		434-1
University of Texas Institute for Geophysics (UTIG) 10100 Burnet Rd (RR2200) JJ Pickle Research Campus Bldg 196 *Web:* ig.utexas.edu	Austin	TX	78758	512-471-6156	471-8844	668
University of Texas Investment Management Co 401 Congress Ave Ste 2800 *Web:* www.utimco.org	Austin	TX	78701	512-225-1600		166
University of Texas School of Law 727 E Dean Keeton St *Web:* law.utexas.edu	Austin	TX	78705	512-471-5151	471-6988	167-1
University of Texas Southwestern Medical Center at Dallas Library, The 5323 Harry Hines Blvd *TF:* 866-645-6455 ■ *Web:* www.utsouthwestern.edu	Dallas	TX	75390	214-648-2001	648-2826	434-1
University of Texas System 601 Colorado St *TF:* 866-882-2034 ■ *Web:* www.utsystem.edu	Austin	TX	78701	512-499-4200		786
University of the Arts 320 S Broad St *TF:* 800-616-2787 ■ *Web:* www.uarts.edu	Philadelphia	PA	19102	215-717-6049	717-6000	164
University of the Cumberlands 6178 College Station Dr *TF:* 800-343-1609 ■ *Web:* www.ucumberlands.edu	Williamsburg	KY	40769	606-539-4201		166
University of the District of Columbia 4200 Connecticut Ave NW *Web:* www.udc.edu	Washington	DC	20008	202-274-5000	274-5552	166
University of the Incarnate Word 4301 Broadway St Ste 285 *TF:* 800-749-9673 ■ *Web:* www.uiw.edu	San Antonio	TX	78209	210-829-6000	829-3921	166
University of the Nations 75 5851 Kuakini Hwy *Web:* www.uofnkona.edu	Kailua-Kona	HI	96740	808-326-7228		166
University of the Ozarks 415 N College Ave *TF:* 800-264-8636 ■ *Web:* ozarks.edu	Clarksville	AR	72830	479-979-1227	979-1417	166
University of the Pacific 3601 Pacific Ave *TF:* 800-959-2867 ■ *Web:* www.pacific.edu	Stockton	CA	95211	209-946-2211	946-2413	166
University of the Pacific McGeorge School of Law 3200 Fifth Ave *Web:* www.mcgeorge.edu	Sacramento	CA	95817	916-739-7105	739-7134	167-1
University of the Sciences in Philadelphia 600 S 43rd St *TF:* 888-857-6264 ■ *Web:* www.usciences.edu	Philadelphia	PA	19104	215-596-8800	596-8821	166
University of the South 735 University Ave *TF:* 800-522-2234 ■ *Web:* new.sewanee.edu	Sewanee	TN	37383	931-598-1000		166
University of Toledo 2801 W Bancroft *TF:* 800-586-5336 ■ *Web:* www.utoledo.edu	Toledo	OH	43606	419-530-4636		166
University of Toledo Federal Credit Union 5248 Hill Ave *Web:* uoftfcu.com	Toledo	OH	43615	419-534-3770		219
University of Tulsa 800 S Tucker Rd *TF:* 800-331-3050 ■ *Web:* utulsa.edu	Tulsa	OK	74104	918-631-2307	631-5003	166
University of Tulsa McFarlin Library 2933 E Sixth St *Web:* utulsa.libguides.com	Tulsa	OK	74104	918-631-2873		434-6
University of Utah 201 South 1460 East Rm 250 S *TF:* 800-685-8856 ■ *Web:* www.utah.edu	Salt Lake City	UT	84112	801-581-7281	585-7864	166
University of Utah Hospital *Miner's Hospital* 50 N Medical Dr Rm 1B295 *TF:* 800-824-2073 ■ *Web:* healthcare.utah.edu	Salt Lake City	UT	84132	866-864-6377		769
University of Utah Marriott Library Marriott Library 295 S 1500 E *Web:* www.lib.utah.edu	Salt Lake City	UT	84112	801-581-8558	585-3464	434-6
University of Utah Press 295 South 1500 East Ste 5400 *Web:* www.uofupress.com	Salt Lake City	UT	84112	801-585-0082	581-3365	637-4
University of Utah School of Medicine 30 N 1900 E *TF:* 844-988-7284 ■ *Web:* medicine.utah.edu	Salt Lake City	UT	84132	801-581-7201	585-3300	167-2
University of Utah SJ Quinney College of Law 383 S University St *Web:* www.law.utah.edu	Salt Lake City	UT	84112	801-581-6833	581-6897	167-1
University of Vermont Bailey/Howe Library 538 Main St *Web:* library.uvm.edu	Burlington	VT	05405	802-656-2023	656-4038	434-6
University of Vermont College of Medicine 89 Beaumont Ave E-126 Given Bldg *TF:* 800-571-0668 ■ *Web:* www.uvm.edu	Burlington	VT	05405	802-656-2156		167-2
University of Vermont Health Network, The 462 Shelburne Rd *TF:* 844-886-4325 ■ *Web:* www.uvmhealth.org	Burlington	VT	05401	844-886-4325		167-3
University of Vermont Medical Ctr, The 111 Colchester Ave *TF:* 800-358-1144 ■ *Web:* www.uvmhealth.org	Burlington	VT	05401	802-847-0000		374-3
University of Victoria 3800 Finnerty Rd Stn CSC PO Box 1700 *Web:* www.uvic.ca	Victoria	BC	V8P5C2	250-472-5416	472-5477	785
University of Virginia Peabody Hall PO Box 400160 *Web:* www.virginia.edu	Charlottesville	VA	22903	434-982-3200	924-3587	166
University of Virginia Health System 1215 Lee St PO Box 800214 *TF:* 800-251-3627 ■ *Web:* med.virginia.edu	Charlottesville	VA	22908	434-924-0211		374-3
University of Virginia Press 210 Sprigg Ln PO Box 400318 *TF:* 800-831-3406 ■ *Web:* www.upress.virginia.edu	Charlottesville	VA	22904	434-924-3469	982-2655	637-4
University of Virginia School of Law 580 Massie Rd *TF:* 877-307-0158 ■ *Web:* www.law.virginia.edu	Charlottesville	VA	22903	434-924-7354	924-7536	167-1
University of Virginia's College at Wise 1 College Ave *TF:* 888-282-9324 ■ *Web:* www.uvawise.edu	Wise	VA	24293	276-328-0102		166
University of Washington 1410 NE Campus Pkwy *Web:* www.washington.edu	Seattle	WA	98195	206-543-4694	685-3655	166
University of Washington (CTP) *Center for the Study of Teaching & Policy* University of Washington 100 Gerberding Hall PO Box 351265 *Web:* www.depts.washington.edu	Seattle	WA	98195	206-543-6588		668
University of Washington Libraries PO Box 352900 *Web:* www.lib.washington.edu	Seattle	WA	98195	206-543-0242		434-6
University of Washington School of Law William H Gates Hall PO Box 353020 *TF:* 866-866-0158 ■ *Web:* www.law.uw.edu	Seattle	WA	98195	206-543-4078		167-1
University of Waterloo 200 University Ave W *TF:* 866-925-5454 ■ *Web:* uwaterloo.ca	Waterloo	ON	N2L3G1	519-888-4567	746-3242	785
University of West Alabama 100 US 11 *TF:* 888-636-8800 ■ *Web:* uwaathletics.com	Livingston	AL	35470	888-636-8800		166
University of West Florida Center for Fine & Performing Arts 11000 University Pkwy Bldg 82 *TF:* 800-263-1074 ■ *Web:* www.uwf.edu	Pensacola	FL	32514	850-474-2000	857-6176	572
University of West Georgia 1600 Maple St *Web:* www.westga.edu	Carrollton	GA	30118	678-839-5000	839-4747	166
University of Windsor 401 Sunset Ave *Web:* www.uwindsor.ca	Windsor	ON	N9B3P4	519-253-3000	973-7070	785
University of Winnipeg 515 Portage Ave *Web:* www.uwinnipeg.ca	Winnipeg	MB	R3B2E9	204-786-9914	783-8910	785
University of Wisconsin *Barron County* 1800 College Dr *Web:* barron.uwc.edu	Rice Lake	WI	54868	715-234-8176	234-1975	162
Eau Claire Schofield Hall 111 105 Garfield Ave *TF:* 800-949-8932 ■ *Web:* www.uwec.edu	Eau Claire	WI	54701	715-836-5415	831-4799	166
Geology Museum 1215 W Dayton St *Web:* www.geoscience.wisc.edu	Madison	WI	53706	608-262-1412	262-0693	520
La Crosse 328 Front St *Web:* www.uwlax.edu	La Crosse	WI	54601	608-785-8000	785-6695	166
Madison 702 W Johnson St Ste 1101 *Web:* www.wisc.edu	Madison	WI	53715	608-262-3961	262-7706	166
Rock County 2909 Kellogg Ave *Web:* rock.uwc.edu	Janesville	WI	53546	608-758-6541	758-6579	162
Sheboygan 1 University Dr *TF:* 800-442-6459 ■ *Web:* www.uwgb.edu	Sheboygan	WI	53081	920-459-6600	459-6602	162
UW-Milwaukee at Waukesha 1500 N University Dr *Web:* waukesha.uwc.edu	Waukesha	WI	53188	262-521-5200	521-5491	162
Washington County 400 S University Dr *TF:* 800-240-0276 ■ *Web:* uwm.edu	West Bend	WI	53095	262-335-5200		162
University of Wisconsin Hospital & Clinics 600 Highland Ave *Web:* www.uwhealth.org	Madison	WI	53792	608-263-6400	263-9830	374-3
University of Wisconsin Law School 975 Bascom Mall *TF:* 866-301-1753 ■ *Web:* law.wisc.edu	Madison	WI	53706	608-262-2240	262-5485	167-1
University of Wisconsin Madison *Ebling Library* 750 Highland Ave *Web:* ebling.library.wisc.edu	Madison	WI	53705	608-262-2020	262-4732	434-1
Libraries 728 State St *Web:* www.library.wisc.edu	Madison	WI	53706	608-262-3193	265-2754	434-6
University of Wisconsin Press 1930 Monroe St 3rd Fl *Web:* uwpress.wisc.edu	Madison	WI	53711	608-263-0734	263-1132	637-9
University of Wisconsin Superior *Jim Dan Hill Library* PO Box 2000 *Web:* www.library.uwsuper.edu	Superior	WI	54880	715-394-8343	394-8462	434-6
University of Wisconsin system 1720 Van Hise Hall *Web:* www.med.wisc.edu	Madison	WI	53705	608-263-4925		167-2
University of Wisconsin System 1220 Linden Dr 1720 Van Hise Hall *TF:* 800-442-6461 ■ *Web:* www.wisconsin.edu	Madison	WI	53706	608-262-2321	262-3985	786
University of Wisconsin Whitewater *Andersen Library* 800 W Main St *Web:* www.uww.edu	Whitewater	WI	53190	262-472-5511		434-6
University of Wisconsin-Madison Arboretum 1207 Seminole Hwy *Web:* arboretum.wisc.edu	Madison	WI	53711	608-263-7888	262-5209	97
University of Wyoming 1000 E University Ave *TF:* 800-342-5996 ■ *Web:* www.uwyo.edu	Laramie	WY	82071	307-766-1121	766-4042	166
University Plaza Hotel & Convention Ctr 333 John Q Hammons Pkwy *Web:* upspringfield.com	Springfield	MO	65806	417-864-7333		379
University Press Books (UPB) 2430 Bancroft Way *TF:* 800-676-8722 ■ *Web:* www.universitypressbooks.com	Berkeley	CA	94704	510-548-0585		95
University Press of Colorado 5589 Arapahoe Ave Ste 206C *Web:* upcolorado.com	Boulder	CO	80303	720-406-8849		637-4
University Press of Florida 15 NW 15th St *TF:* 800-226-3822 ■ *Web:* www.upf.com	Gainesville	FL	32603	352-392-1351	392-7302	637-4
University Press of Kansas 2502 Westbrooke Cir *Web:* kansaspress.ku.edu	Lawrence	KS	66045	785-864-4154	864-4586	637-4
University Press of Kentucky 663 S Limestone St *Web:* www.kentuckypress.com	Lexington	KY	40508	859-257-7919	257-8481	637-4

	Phone	Fax	Class
University Press of Mississippi 3825 Ridgewood Rd . . . . Jackson MS 39211 *TF:* 800-737-7788 ■ *Web:* www.upress.state.ms.us	601-432-6205	432-6217	637-4
University Press of New England (UPNE) 1 Court St Ste 250 . . . . Lebanon NH 03766 *Web:* www.upne.com	603-448-1533	448-9429	637-4
University Products Inc 517 Main St . . . . Holyoke MA 01040 **Fax Area Code:* 800 ■ *TF:* 800-628-1912 ■ *Web:* www.universityproducts.com	413-532-3372	532-9281*	560
University Research Company LLC 5404 Wisconsin Ave Ste 800 . . . . Chevy Chase MD 20815 *Web:* www.urc-chs.com	301-654-8338	941-8427	194
University School Hunting Vly Campus 2785 SOM Center Rd . . . . Hunting Valley OH 44022 *Web:* www.us.edu	216-831-2200		623
University School of Milwaukee 2100 W Fairy Chasm Rd . . . . Milwaukee WI 53217 *Web:* www.usmk12.org	414-352-6000	352-8076	623
University System of Georgia 270 Washington St SW . . . . Atlanta GA 30334 *Web:* www.usg.edu	404-962-3050		786
University System of Maryland 3300 Metzerott Rd . . . . Adelphi MD 20783 *Web:* www.usmd.edu	301-445-2740	445-1931	786
University Title Co 1021 University Dr E . . . . College Station TX 77841 *TF:* 866-326-9818 ■ *Web:* utitle.com	979-260-9818	691-8268	653
University Village 2623 NE University Village St . . . . Seattle WA 98105 *Web:* uvillage.com	206-523-0622	525-3859	460
Univertical Corp 203 Weatherhead St . . . . Angola IN 46703 *Web:* univertical.com	260-665-1500	665-1400	145
Univest Corporation of Pennsylvania 14 N Main St PO Box 64197 . . . . Souderton PA 18964 *NASDAQ: UVSP* ■ *TF:* 877-723-5571 ■ *Web:* www.univest.net	877-723-5571		360-2
Univex Corp 3 Old Rockingham Rd . . . . Salem NH 03079 *TF:* 800-258-6358 ■ *Web:* www.univexcorp.com	603-893-6191	893-1249	298
Univision Television Group Inc 6701 Center Dr W . . . . Los Angeles CA 90045 *Web:* www.univision.com	310-338-0700		738
Uniweld Products Inc 2850 Ravenswood Rd . . . . Fort Lauderdale FL 33312 *TF:* 800-323-2111 ■ *Web:* uniweld.com	954-584-2000	587-0109	811
Uniwell Corp 21172 Figueroa St . . . . Carson CA 90745	310-782-8888		653
Uniworld Boutique River Cruise Collection 17323 Ventura Blvd . . . . Encino CA 91316 *TF:* 800-257-2407 ■ *Web:* www.uniworld.com	818-382-7820	382-2709	221
Unleaded Communications Inc 1701 Commerce St . . . . Houston TX 77002 *Web:* ulcomm.com	713-874-8200		7
Unleaded Software Inc 2314 N Broadway . . . . Denver CO 80205 *Web:* www.unleadedsoftware.com	720-221-7126		177
Unleashed Technologies 10005 Old Columbia Rd Ste L-261 . . . . Columbia MD 21046 *Web:* www.unleashed-technologies.com	410-864-8980		177
Unlimited Construction Services Inc 1696 Haleukana St . . . . Lihue HI 96766 *Web:* unlimitedhawaii.com	808-241-1400	245-6611	685
Unlimited Services of Wisconsin Inc 170 Evergreen Rd . . . . Oconto WI 54153 *Web:* www.us-wire-harness.com	920-834-4418		815
Unlimited Systems Corporation Inc 9530 Padgett St . . . . San Diego CA 92126 *TF:* 800-275-6354 ■ *Web:* www.konexx.com	858-537-5010	550-7330	173-3
Unlimited Technology Inc 20 Senn Dr . . . . Chester Springs PA 19425 *Web:* www.utech-usa.com	610-458-8901		180
Unlimited Truck and Trailer Services 1107 E Noble Ave . . . . Monroe MI 48162 *Web:* www.utts.us	734-221-7029	241-1457	780
UNM (University of New Mexico) 1 University of New Mexico . . . . Albuquerque NM 87131 *TF:* 800-225-5866 ■ *Web:* www.unm.edu	505-277-0111	277-6686	166
Unmetric Inc 2001 Victoria Rd . . . . Mundelein IL 60060 *TF:* 855-558-5588 ■ *Web:* unmetric.com	855-558-5588		466
Uno Langmann Ltd 2117 Granville St . . . . Vancouver BC V6H3E9 *TF:* 800-730-8825 ■ *Web:* www.langmann.com	604-736-8825		42
UNOS (United Network for Organ Sharing) 700 N Fourth St . . . . Richmond VA 23219 *TF:* 888-894-6361 ■ *Web:* unos.org	804-782-4800	782-4817	48-17
Unqork 114 5th Ave 2nd Fl . . . . New York NY 10011 *TF:* 844-486-7675 ■ *Web:* unqork.com	844-486-7675		178-8
Unruh Fire 100 Industrial Dr . . . . Sedgwick KS 67135 *TF:* 800-856-7080 ■ *Web:* unruhfire.com	800-856-7080		697
Unruh, Turner, Burke & Frees PC 17 W Gay St . . . . West Chester PA 19381 *Web:* www.utbf.com	610-692-1371		428
Untangle Inc 100 W San Fernando St Ste 565 . . . . San Jose CA 95113 *TF:* 866-233-2296 ■ *Web:* www.untangle.com	408-598-4299		177
UnTechnical Press (UP) 16410 Gibboney Ln . . . . Grass Valley CA 95949 *Web:* www.untechnicalpress.com	530-271-7129		637-2
Unverferth Manufacturing Company Inc 601 S Broad St . . . . Kalida OH 45853 *TF:* 800-322-6301 ■ *Web:* www.unverferth.com	419-532-3121	532-2468	273
UNX Inc 707 E Arlington Blvd PO Box 7206 . . . . Greenville NC 27835 *Web:* www.unxinc.com	252-756-8616	756-2764	151
UOB (United Overseas Bank Limited New York Agency) 592 Fifth Ave 10th Fl . . . . New York NY 10036 **Fax Area Code:* 212 ■ *Web:* www.uobgroup.com	646-472-8113	382-1881*	70
UOC USA Inc 20 Fairbanks Ste 173 . . . . Irvine CA 92618 *Web:* www.uocusa.com	949-328-3366	328-3367	476
Office for Victims of Crime 350 E 500 S Ste 200 . . . . Salt Lake City UT 84111 *TF:* 800-621-7444 ■ *Web:* www.crimevictim.utah.gov	801-238-2360	533-4127	339-45
UP (UnTechnical Press) 16410 Gibboney Ln . . . . Grass Valley CA 95949 *Web:* www.untechnicalpress.com	530-271-7129		637-2
Up & Running Software Inc 6200 Prairie Ridge Rd . . . . Ames IA 50014 *TF:* 888-447-9273 ■ *Web:* upandrunningsoftware.com	888-447-9273		177
Up by Seven 16 Rennie Dr . . . . Andover MA 01810 *Web:* www.upbyseven.com	978-475-8200		226
Up Communications Services LLC 103 SE Atlantic St . . . . Tullahoma TN 37388 **Fax Area Code:* 931 ■ *TF:* 877-667-0968 ■ *Web:* upcomllc.com	877-667-0968	461-5392*	393
Up Right Marketing Inc 305 S Grant St . . . . San Mateo CA 94401 *Web:* uprightmarketing.com	650-375-1388		195
Up With Paper 6049 Hi-Tek Ct . . . . Mason OH 45040 **Fax Area Code:* 800 ■ *TF:* 800-852-7677 ■ *Web:* www.upwithpaper.com	513-759-7473	293-8471*	130
Up With People 6830 Broadway . . . . Denver CO 80221 *TF:* 877-264-8856 ■ *Web:* upwithpeople.org	303-460-7100	225-4649	48-15
UPA (Union of Agricultural Procedures, The) 555 Boul Roland-Therrien Ste 100 . . . . Longueuil QC J4H3Y9 *Web:* www.upa.qc.ca	450-679-0530		414
UPB (University Press Books) 2430 Bancroft Way . . . . Berkeley CA 94704 *TF:* 800-676-8722 ■ *Web:* www.universitypressbooks.com	510-548-0585		95
Upchurch Electrical Supply Co 2355 N Gregg Ave . . . . Fayetteville AR 72703 *Web:* www.upchurchelectrical.com	479-521-2823	521-6673	246
Upchurch Plumbing Inc 2606 Baldwin Rd . . . . Greenwood MS 38930 *Web:* www.upchurchplumbing.com	662-453-6860		610
Upchurch Scientific Inc 619 Oak St . . . . Oak Harbor WA 98277 *TF:* 800-426-0191 ■ *Web:* www.idex-hs.com	360-679-2528		419
Upchurch Watson White & Max Mediation Group Inc 1400 Hand Ave Ste D . . . . Ormond Beach FL 32174 *Web:* uww-adr.com	386-253-1560		41
UPCI (United Pentecostal Church Intl) 8855 Dunn Rd . . . . Hazelwood MO 63042 *Web:* www.upci.org	314-837-7300		48-20
UpClose Marketing & Printing 120 W White St . . . . Champaign IL 61820 *Web:* www.upcloseprinting.com	217-359-3200		5
Upco Inc 24403 Amah Pkwy . . . . Claremore OK 74019 *Web:* als.championx.com	918-342-1270		537
UpCurve Cloud 10801 National Blvd Ste 410 . . . . Los Angeles CA 90064 *TF:* 888-898-4787 ■ *Web:* www.upcurvecloud.com	888-898-4787		196
UpCurve Cloud 2815 Manor Rd Ste 201 . . . . Austin TX 78722 *TF:* 800-775-8378 ■ *Web:* www.epicom.com	800-775-8378		196
Update Services Inc 10825 Greenbrier Rd . . . . Minnetonka MN 55305 *Web:* updateservicesinc.com	952-937-5447		5
Updegrove Combs Mcdaniel & Wilson Plc 10 Rock Pointe Ln Ste 3 . . . . Warrenton VA 20186 *Web:* ucmcpas.com	540-347-5681		2
Updike Distribution Logistics (UDL) 435 S 59th Ave Ste 100 . . . . Phoenix AZ 85043 *Web:* updikedl.com	602-682-1800		311
Updike Kelly & Spellacy Pc PO Box 231277 . . . . Hartford CT 06123 *Web:* uks.com	860-548-2600	548-2680	428
UPG (United Plastics Group Inc) 7865 Northcourt Rd . . . . Houston TX 77040 *Web:* www.upgintl.com	713-466-5563		604
Upgrade It Consulting Services Inc 3030 Royal Blvd S Ste 220 . . . . Alpharetta GA 30022 *Web:* upgradeitcs.com	770-345-3173		196
Upham Oil & Gas Company LP 999 Energy Ave . . . . Mineral Wells TX 76067 *Web:* www.upham.us	940-325-4491		539
Upham's Corner Health Ctr 415 Columbia Rd . . . . Dorchester MA 02125 *Web:* uphamscornerhealthcenter.org	617-287-8000		374-3
UPI (United Press Intl) 1133 19th St NW . . . . Washington DC 20036 *Web:* www.upi.com	202-898-8000		530
UPI Energy LP 105 Silvercreek Pkwy N Ste 200 . . . . Guelph ON N1H8M1 *TF:* 800-396-2667 ■ *Web:* www.upienergyfs.com	519-821-2667		324
U-Pic Insurance Services Inc 5010 Chesebro Rd . . . . Agoura Hills CA 91301 *TF:* 800-955-4623 ■ *Web:* u-pic.com	800-955-4623		390
Upland Brewing Co 350 W 11th St . . . . Bloomington IN 47404 *Web:* www.uplandbeer.com	812-336-2337		671
Upland Chamber of Commerce 215 N Second Ave Ste D . . . . Upland CA 91786 *Web:* www.uplandchamber.org	909-204-4465	204-4464	139
Upland Public Library 450 N Euclid Ave . . . . Upland CA 91786 *Web:* www.ci.upland.ca.us	909-931-4200		434-3
Upland Software Inc Frost Tower 401 Congress Ave Ste 2950 . . . . Austin TX 78701 *TF:* 855-944-7526 ■ *Web:* uplandsoftware.com	855-944-7526		787
Upland Unified School District 390 N Euclid Ave . . . . Upland CA 91786 *Web:* www.upland.k12.ca.us	909-985-1864	949-7863	685
Uplogix Inc 7600B N Capital of Texas Hwy Ste 220 . . . . Austin TX 78731 *Web:* uplogix.com	512-857-7000		449
UPMC Health Plan Inc 600 Grant St . . . . Pittsburgh PA 15219 *TF:* 888-383-8762 ■ *Web:* www.upmchealthplan.com	412-454-7500	454-7711	391-3
UPMC Pinnacle PO Box 8700 . . . . Harrisburg PA 17105 *Web:* www.pinnaclehealth.org	717-231-8900		167-2
UPN 17 1414 Wilmington Ave . . . . Dayton OH 45420 *Web:* www.whio.com	937-259-2111	259-2005	647
UPNE (University Press of New England) 1 Court St Ste 250 . . . . Lebanon NH 03766 *Web:* www.upne.com	603-448-1533	448-9429	637-4
Upnorth Consulting Inc 9100 W Bloomington Fwy Ste 142 . . . . Minneapolis MN 55431 **Fax Area Code:* 952 ■ *TF:* 866-892-1758	866-892-1758	953-6140*	180

				Phone	Fax	Class
Upp Entertainment Marketing Inc 3401 Winona Ave *Web:* www.upp.net	Burbank	CA	91504	818-526-0111		195
Upper Arlington Public Library 2800 Tremont Rd *Web:* www.ualibrary.org	Upper Arlington	OH	43221	614-486-9621	486-4530	434-3
Upper Bay Counseling & Support Services Inc 401 Bow St *TF:* 800-467-0304 ■ *Web:* www.upperbay.org	Elkton	MD	21921	410-996-5104		726
Upper Bucks Chamber of Commerce 21 N Main St *Web:* www.ubcc.org	Quakertown	PA	18951	215-536-3211	536-7767	139
Upper Canada College 200 Lonsdale Rd *Web:* www.ucc.on.ca	Toronto	ON	M4V1W6	416-488-1125		622
Upper Cape Cod Regional Technical School 220 Sandwich Rd *Web:* www.uppercapetech.com	Bourne	MA	02532	508-759-7711	759-7208	685
Upper Cumberland Electric Membership Corp 138 Gordonsville Hwy *TF:* 800-261-2940 ■ *Web:* www.ucemc.com	South Carthage	TN	37030	615-735-2940	735-2603	245
Upper Darby Belltelco Federal Credit Union 1410 Bywood Ave *TF:* 800-235-4035 ■ *Web:* udbell.org	Upper Darby	PA	19082	610-734-1883	734-0312	219
Upper Dauphin Area School District (UDASD) 5668 SR-209 *Web:* udasd.org	Lykens	PA	17048	717-362-8134	362-3050	685
Upper Deck Company LLC 5909 Sea Otter Pl **Fax Area Code:* 760 ■ *TF:* 800-873-7332 ■ *Web:* www.upperdeck.com	Carlsbad	CA	92010	800-873-7332	929-3512*	762
Upper Delaware Scenic & Recreation River 274 River Rd *Web:* www.nps.gov	Beach Lake	PA	18405	570-729-7134		564
Upper Hand Press PO Box 91179 *Web:* www.upperhandpress.com	Bexley	OH	43209	614-886-2462		637-2
Upper Iowa University 605 Washington St PO Box 1857 *TF:* 800-553-4150 ■ *Web:* uiu.edu	Fayette	IA	52142	563-425-5200	425-5323	166
Upper Limit Aviation 619 North 2360 West *TF:* 844-435-9338 ■ *Web:* www.upperlimitaviation.edu	Salt Lake City	UT	84116	801-596-7722		167-3
Upper Merion Area School District 435 Crossfield Rd *Web:* www.umasd.org	King of Prussia	PA	19406	610-205-6400	205-6433	685
Upper Mississippi River Conservation Committee (UMRCC) 9053 Rte 148 *Web:* www.umrcc.org	Marion	IL	62959	618-579-3129		48-13
Upper Ottawa Valley Chamber of Commerce 224 Pembroke St W *Web:* www.upperottawavalleychamber.com	Pembroke	ON	K8A5N2	613-732-1492		137
Upper Peninsula Region of Library Cooperation, The 1615 Presque Isle Ave *Web:* www.joomla.uproc.lib.mi.us	Marquette	MI	49855	906-228-7697		434-3
Upper Peninsula Telephone Co 397 US 41N PO Box 86 *TF:* 855-642-4227 ■ *Web:* www.michbbs.com	Carney	MI	49812	906-639-2111		736
Upper Perkiomen School District 2229 E Buck Rd Ste 2 *Web:* www.upsd.org	Pennsburg	PA	18073	215-679-7961		685
Upper Room Chapel & Museum 1908 Grand Ave *TF:* 800-972-0433 ■ *Web:* www.upperroom.org	Nashville	TN	37212	615-340-7200		520
Upper Sioux Agency State Park 5908 Hwy 67 *Web:* www.dnr.state.mn.us	Granite Falls	MN	56241	320-564-4777		565
Upper Tampa Bay Regional Chamber of Commerce 101 State St W *Web:* www.utbchamber.com	Oldsmar	FL	34677	813-855-4233	854-1237	139
Upper Township School District 525 Perry Rd *Web:* www.upperschools.org	Woodbine	NJ	08270	609-628-3500	628-2002	780
Upper Trinity Regional Water District 900 N Kealy St PO Box 305 *Web:* www.utrwd.com	Lewisville	TX	75067	972-219-1228		787
Upper Valley Medical Ctr (UVMC) 3130 N County Rd 25-A *Web:* www.premierhealth.com	Troy	OH	45373	937-440-4000		374-3
Upper Valley Press Inc 446 Benton Rd *Web:* www.uvpress.com	North Haverhill	NH	03774	603-787-7000	787-7012	627
Upperline 1413 Upperline St *Web:* www.upperline.com	New Orleans	LA	70115	504-891-9822		671
UP&R (Universal Polymer & Rubber Ltd) 15730 Madison Rd *Web:* www.universalpolymer.com	Middlefield	OH	44062	440-632-1691	632-5761	677
Uproar Communications 3772 Plaza Dr Ste 5 *Web:* uproarcom.com	Ann Arbor	MI	48108	734-975-8888	975-9806	195
UPS (United Parcel Service Inc) 55 Glenlake Pkwy NE *NYSE:* UPS ■ *Web:* www.ups.com	Atlanta	GA	30328	404-828-6000	828-6440	546
UPS Capital Business Credit 35 Glenlake Pkwy NE *TF:* 877-263-8772 ■ *Web:* upscapital.com	Atlanta	GA	30328	404-828-8068		70
UPS Foundation 55 Glenlake Pkwy NE *TF:* 800-742-5877 ■ *Web:* sustainability.ups.com	Atlanta	GA	30328	800-742-5877		304
UPS Store, The 2001 E Lohman Ave Ste 110 *Web:* www.locations.theupsstore.com	Las Cruces	NM	88001	575-523-0083	523-9509	671
UPS Store, The 6060 Cornerstone Ct W *TF:* 800-789-4623 ■ *Web:* www.theupsstore.com	San Diego	CA	92121	858-455-8800		310
UPS Supply Chain Solutions 12380 Morris Rd *TF:* 800-742-5727 ■ *Web:* www.ups-scs.com	Alpharetta	GA	30005	913-693-6151		449
Upsher-Smith Laboratories Inc 6701 Evenstad Dr *TF:* 800-654-2299 ■ *Web:* www.upsher-smith.com	Maple Grove	MN	55369	763-315-2000		582
Upshur County 40 W Main St Rm 101 *Web:* www.upshurcounty.org	Buckhannon	WV	26201	304-472-1068	472-1029	338
Upshur County PO Box 730 *Web:* www.countyofupshur.com	Gilmer	TX	75644	903-843-4015	843-4504	338
Upshur County Library 702 W Tyler St *Web:* www.upshur.biblionix.com	Gilmer	TX	75644	903-843-5001	843-3995	434-3
Upson County 106 E Lee St Ste 110 *Web:* upsoncountyga.org	Thomaston	GA	30286	706-647-7012	647-7030	338
Upson County Electric Membership Corp 607 E Main St *Web:* www.upsonemc.com	Thomaston	GA	30286	706-647-5475		245
Upson Regional Medical Ctr 801 W Gordon St *Web:* www.urmc.org	Thomaston	GA	30286	706-647-8111		374-3
Upstairs Jazz Bar & Grill 1254 MacKay St *Web:* www.upstairsjazz.com	Montreal	QC	H3G2H4	514-931-6808		671
Upstairs Restaurant, The 4500 Mahoning Ave *Web:* www.theupstairsrestaurant.com	Youngstown	OH	44515	330-793-5577		671
Upstart 2950 S Delaware St Ste 300 *Web:* www.upstart.com	San Mateo	CA	94403	650-204-1000		216
Upstate Correctional Facility 309 Bare Hill Rd PO Box 2000 *Web:* www.doccs.ny.gov	Malone	NY	12953	518-483-6997		213
Upstate Pharmacy Ltd 1900 N America Dr *TF:* 800-314-4655 ■ *Web:* www.upstatepharmacy.com	West Seneca	NY	14224	716-675-3784	675-7777	237
Upstate Shredding LLC Tioga Industrial Pk 1 Recycle Dr *TF:* 800-245-3133 ■ *Web:* upstateshredding.com	Owego	NY	13827	607-687-7777	687-7746	686
Upstate Tours & Travel 207 Geyser Rd *Web:* www.upstatetours.com	Saratoga Springs	NY	12866	518-584-5252	584-1092	760
Upstream Brewing Co 514 S 11th St *Web:* www.upstreambrewing.com	Omaha	NE	68102	402-344-0200	344-0451	671
Upstream Communications 811 Trinity St Ste A *Web:* www.getupstream.com	Austin	TX	78701	512-583-7134		224
Uptime Solutions Professional Services Group Inc 3801 Gaskins Rd *Web:* uptimesolutions.com	Richmond	VA	23233	804-836-1490	836-1440	180
Up-To-Date Laundry Inc 1221 Desoto Rd *Web:* www.uptodatelaundry.net	Baltimore	MD	21223	410-646-0475		426
Upton and Sons Publishers/Booksellers 917 Hillcrest St *TF:* 800-959-1876 ■ *Web:* uptonbooks.com	El Segundo	CA	90245	310-322-7202	322-4739	637-2
Upton County Sheriff PO Box 27 *TF:* 800-680-9052 ■ *Web:* co.upton.tx.us	Rankin	TX	79778	432-693-2422	693-2303	338
Upton Financial Group Inc 131 Stony Cir Ste 500 *Web:* www.uptonco.com	Santa Rosa	CA	95401	707-523-9651		528
Upton Fred (Rep R - MI) 2183 Rayburn House Office Bldg *Web:* upton.house.gov	Washington	DC	20515	202-225-3761	225-4986	342-2
Upton Industries Inc 30435 Groesbeck Hwy Ste 2 *TF:* 800-541-1204 ■ *Web:* www.uptonindustries.com	Roseville	MI	48066	586-771-1200	771-8970	318
Upton State Forest 205 Westboro Rd *Web:* www.mass.gov	Upton	MA	01568	508-278-6486		565
Upton, Draughon & Bollinger LLC 207 Ansley Blvd Ste A *Web:* udbfinancial.com	Alexandria	LA	71303	318-442-4944		690
Uptown Animal Hospital Inc 5545 N Clark *Web:* uptownah.com	Chicago	IL	60640	773-561-0734	561-5158	794
Uptown Cafe 1624 Bardstown Rd *Web:* www.uptownlouisville.com	Louisville	KY	40205	502-458-4212		671
Uptown, The 102 E Kirkwood Ave *Web:* the-uptown.com	Bloomington	IN	47408	812-339-0900		671
Upturn Industries Inc 2-4 Whitney Way *Web:* www.upturnindustries.com	Bainbridge	NY	13733	607-967-2923	967-5047	454
UPTV-TV 400 S Vine St *Web:* www.urbanaillinois.us	Urbana	IL	61801	217-384-2452		647
Upward Credit Union 1860 El Camino Real Ste 100 *Web:* upwardcu.org	Burlingame	CA	94010	650-231-1300		219
UQM Technologies Inc 4120 Specialty Pl *NYSE:* UQM ■ *Web:* www.uqm.com	Longmont	CO	80504	303-682-4900	682-4901	518
UR Corp 68 Jonspin Rd *TF:* 800-225-3364 ■ *Web:* www.unifirst.com	Wilmington	MA	01887	978-658-8888		426
URA (Universities Research Association Inc) 1140 19th St NW Ste 900 *Web:* www.ura-hq.org	Washington	DC	20036	202-293-1382	293-5012	49-19
URAC 1220 L St NW Ste 400 *Web:* www.urac.org	Washington	DC	20005	202-216-9010	216-9006	48-1
Uralic and Altaic Series Goodbody Hall 157 1011 E Third St *Web:* www.iu.edu	Bloomington	IN	47405	812-855-2233	855-7500	96
Urania Engineering Company Inc 198 S Poplar St *TF:* 800-533-1985 ■ *Web:* www.uraniaeng.com	Hazleton	PA	18201	570-455-7531		350
Urbahn Architects 306 W 37th St 9th Fl *Web:* www.urbahn.com	New York	NY	10018	212-239-0220		261
Urban Alternative PO Box 4000 *TF:* 800-800-3222 ■ *Web:* www.tonyevans.org	Dallas	TX	75208	214-943-3868		48-20
Urban Barn Ltd 4085 Marine Way Ste 1 *TF:* 844-456-2200 ■ *Web:* www.urbanbarn.com	Burnaby	BC	V5J5E2	604-456-2200		321
Urban Bush Women 138 S Oxford St Ste 4B *Web:* www.urbanbushwomen.org	Brooklyn	NY	11217	718-398-4537	398-2794	573-1
Urban College of Boston 178 Tremont St *Web:* www.urbancollege.edu	Boston	MA	02111	617-348-6359		167-3
Urban Concrete Contractors Ltd 24114 Blanco Rd *Web:* www.urbanconcrete.com	San Antonio	TX	78258	210-490-0090	490-1505	187

Phone | Fax | Class

Urban Data Solutions Inc
589 Eighth Ave 9th Fl . . . New York NY 10018 212-931-6330 931-6332 737
Web: www.u-data.com

Urban Decay 833 W 16th St . . . Newport Beach CA 92663 800-784-8722 214
TF: 800-784-8722 ■ *Web:* www.urbandecay.com

Urban Design Associates (UDA)
3 PPG Pl 3rd Fl . . . Pittsburgh PA 15222 412-263-5200 270-8374* 194
*Fax Area Code: 844 ■ *Web:* www.urbandesignassociates.com

Urban Engineers Inc
530 Walnut St 14th Fl . . . Philadelphia PA 19106 215-922-8080 922-8082 261
Web: urbanengineers.com

Urban Foundation/Engineering LLC
32-33 111th St . . . East Elmhurst NY 11369 718-478-3021 899-4967 189-5

Urban Futures Inc 17821 17th St Ste 245 . . . Tustin CA 92780 714-283-9334 283-5465 463
Web: www.urbanfuturesinc.com

Urban Insight Inc
3530 Wilshire Blvd Ste 1285 . . . Los Angeles CA 90010 213-792-2000 180
Web: www.urbaninsight.com

Urban Institute 2100 M St NW . . . Washington DC 20037 202-833-7200 634
TF: 866-518-3874 ■ *Web:* www.urban.org

Urban Land Institute (ULI)
1025 Thomas Jefferson St NW Ste 500W . . . Washington DC 20007 202-624-7000 624-7140 48-8
TF: 800-321-5011 ■ *Web:* uli.org

Urban Libraries Council (ULC)
1333 H St NW Ste 1000 . . . Washington DC 20005 202-750-8650 49-11
Web: www.urbanlibraries.org

Urban Manufacturing Inc
1288 Hickory St . . . Pewaukee WI 53072 262-691-2455 691-8938 454
Web: www.urban-mfg.com

Urban Ore Inc 900 Murray St . . . Berkeley CA 94710 510-841-7283 686
Web: www.urbanore.com

Urban Outfitters Inc
30 Industrial Pk Blvd . . . Trenton SC 29847 800-282-2200 157-4
TF: 800-282-2200 ■ *Web:* www.urbanoutfitters.com

Urban Realty Partners
950 Joseph E Lowery Blvd Ste 25 . . . Atlanta GA 30318 404-564-1250 652
Web: urpatl.com

Urban Retail Properties Co
111 E Wacker Dr Ste 2400 . . . Chicago IL 60601 312-915-2000 655
Web: www.urbanretail.com

Urban Science
400 Renaissance Ctr Ste 2900 . . . Detroit MI 48243 313-259-9900 259-9901 194
TF: 800-321-6900 ■ *Web:* www.urbanscience.com

Urban Strategies 2341 Ninth St S . . . Arlington VA 22204 202-368-3408 196
Web: www.urbanstrategies.us

Urban Web Design 102-19 Dallas Rd . . . Victoria BC V8V5A6 250-380-1296 225
TF: 877-889-2573 ■ *Web:* urbanweb.net

Urbana Free Library 210 W Green St . . . Urbana IL 61801 217-367-4057 367-4061 434-3
Web: urbanafreelibrary.org

Urbana Veterinary Clinic Inc
985 Norwood Ave . . . Urbana OH 43078 937-653-7326 794
Web: urbanavc.com

UrbanDaddy Inc 900 Broadway Ste 808 . . . New York NY 10003 212-929-7905 387
Web: www.urbandaddy.com

Urbandale Chamber of Commerce
3600 NW 86th St . . . Urbandale IA 50322 515-331-6855 331-2987 139
Web: uniquelyurbandale.com

Urbandale Public Library
3520 86th St . . . Urbandale IA 50322 515-278-3945 278-3918 434-3
Web: www.urbandalelibrary.org

URELL Inc 86 Coolidge Ave . . . Watertown MA 02471 617-923-9500 926-9414 791
Web: www.urell.com

Urethane Roller Specialist Inc
100 S Central Ave . . . Eureka MO 63025 636-938-5351 938-5398 386
Web: www.urethaneroller.com

Urgo Hotels LP
6710A Rockledge Dr Ste 420 . . . Bethesda MD 20817 301-657-2130 707
Web: urgohotels.com

URI (University of Rhode Island)
45 Upper College Rd . . . Kingston RI 02881 401-874-1000 874-5523 166
Web: www.uri.edu

Uricchio's Trattoria 1400 17th St . . . Bakersfield CA 93301 661-326-8870 671
Web: www.uricchios.com

Urick Foundry Co 1501 Cherry St . . . Erie PA 16502 814-454-2461 454-1397 307
Web: urick.net

Urigen Pharmaceuticals
675 US Hwy 1 Ste B206 . . . North Brunswick NJ 08902 732-640-0160 85
Web: www.urigen.com

URiGLOBAL 357 Van Ness Way Ste 110 . . . Torrance CA 90501 310-360-1212 360-9005 7
Web: uriglobal.com

Uriman Inc 650 N Puente St . . . Brea CA 92821 714-257-2080 61
Web: www.uriman.com

Urish Popeck & Company LLC
3 Gateway Ctr 401 Liberty Ave Ste 2400 . . . Pittsburgh PA 15222 412-391-1994 391-0724 2
Web: www.urishpopeck.com

Urologix Inc 14405 21st Ave N . . . Minneapolis MN 55447 763-475-1400 476
TF: 800-475-1403 ■ *Web:* www.urologix.com

Urology of Indiana LLC
679 E County Line Rd . . . Greenwood IN 46143 317-885-1250 374-3
TF: 877-362-2778 ■ *Web:* www.urologyin.com

URP Music Distributors
453 Allied Dr . . . Nashville TN 37211 615-823-7598 301-9899 525
TF: 866-252-3520 ■ *Web:* www.urpdist.com

Urpan Technologies Inc
3080 Olcott St Ste A205 . . . Santa Clara CA 95054 408-320-2720 260
Web: www.urpantech.com

Ursa Farmers Co-opeartive Inc
202 W Maple Ave PO Box 8 . . . Ursa IL 62376 217-964-2115 964-2260 447
Web: www.ursacoop.com

Ursa Institute
390 Fourth St 1st Fl . . . San Francisco CA 94107 415-777-1922 196
Web: www.cus-united.org

Ursa Navigation Solutions Inc
85 Rangeway Rd Ste 110 Bldg Three . . . North Billerica MA 01862 781-538-5299 529
Web: www.ursanav.com

Urschel Laboratories Inc
2503 Calumet Ave . . . Valparaiso IN 46384 219-464-4811 462-3879 298
Web: www.urschel.com

Phone | Fax | Class

Urshan Graduate School of Theology
704 Howder Shell Rd . . . Florissant MO 63031 314-921-9290 167-3
Web: ugst.edu

Ursinus College
601 E Main St PO Box 1000 . . . Collegeville PA 19426 610-409-3200 409-3662 166
TF: 877-448-3282 ■ *Web:* www.ursinus.edu

Urstadt Biddle Properties Inc
321 Railroad Ave . . . Greenwich CT 06830 203-863-8200 861-6755 655
NYSE: UBA ■ *Web:* www.ubproperties.com

Ursula of Switzerland Inc
31 Mohawk Ave . . . Waterford NY 12188 800-826-4041 237-3038* 155-21
*Fax Area Code: 518 ■ *TF:* 800-826-4041 ■ *Web:* www.ursula.com

Ursuline College 2550 Lander Rd . . . Pepper Pike OH 44124 440-449-4200 684-6138 166
TF: 888-778-5463 ■ *Web:* www.ursuline.edu

Uruguay
Consulate General
429 Santa Monica Blvd Ste 400 . . . Santa Monica CA 90401 310-394-5777 394-5140 257
Web: www.embajadadeuruguay.org

Urw Community Federal Credit Union
539 Arnett Blvd . . . Danville VA 24540 434-793-1278 799-0949 219
TF: 866-879-6328 ■ *Web:* urwfcu.org

Urwiler & Walter Inc 3126 Main St . . . Sumneytown PA 18084 215-234-4562 234-0889 261
Web: urwilerwalter.com

US92 KUSO 92.7 FM/107.5 FM
214 N 7th St Ste 1 . . . Norfolk NE 68701 402-371-8792 371-0050 643
Web: www.us92.com

USA Baseball 403 Blackwell St . . . Durham NC 27701 919-474-8721 474-8822 48-22
TF: 855-420-5910 ■ *Web:* www.usabaseball.com

USA Basketball
5465 Mark Dabling Blvd . . . Colorado Springs CO 80918 719-590-4800 590-4811 48-22
TF: 888-284-5383 ■ *Web:* www.usab.com

USA Bouquet Company Inc, The
1500 NW 95 Ave . . . Miami FL 33172 786-437-6500 292
TF: 800-306-1071 ■ *Web:* www.usabq.com

USA Communications
124 Main St PO Box 389 . . . Shellsburg IA 52332 319-436-2224 116
TF: 800-248-8007 ■ *Web:* www.usacomm.coop

USA Communications Inc
920 E 56th St Ste B . . . Kearney NE 68847 877-234-0102 387
TF: 877-234-0102 ■ *Web:* usacommunications.tv

USA Consulting Inc PO Box 940128 . . . Plano TX 75074 972-673-0333 196
TF: 888-393-6565 ■ *Web:* usaci.com

USA Container Company Inc
1776 S Second St . . . Piscataway NJ 08854 888-752-7722 198
TF: 888-752-7722 ■ *Web:* www.usacontainer.com

USA Cycling Inc
210 USA Cycling Pt Ste 100 . . . Colorado Springs CO 80919 719-434-4200 48-22
TF: 877-752-9253 ■ *Web:* www.usacycling.org

USA Datafax Inc 821 Jupiter Rd Ste 407 . . . Plano TX 75074 469-467-7900 112
TF: 800-848-1164 ■ *Web:* www.usadatafax.com

USA Digital Solutions Inc
10835 N 25th Ave Ste 350 . . . Phoenix AZ 85029 602-866-8199 177
Web: www.digisolaz.com

USA Environment LP 316 Georgia Ave . . . Deer Park TX 77536 713-425-6900 425-6917 667
Web: www.usaenviro.com

USA for UNHCR 1775 K St NW Ste 580 . . . Washington DC 20006 202-296-1115 48-5
TF: 800-770-1100 ■ *Web:* www.unrefugees.org

USA Gymnastics
201 S Capitol Ave Ste 300 . . . Indianapolis IN 46225 317-237-5050 237-5069 48-22
TF: 800-345-4719 ■ *Web:* usagym.org

USA Hockey
1775 Bob Johnson Dr . . . Colorado Springs CO 80906 800-383-1379 538-1160* 48-22
*Fax Area Code: 719 ■ *TF:* 800-566-3288 ■ *Web:* www.usahockey.com

USA Parking Systems
1330 SE 4th Ave Ste D . . . Fort Lauderdale FL 33316 954-524-6500 524-3609 562
Web: www.usaparking.net

USA Poultry & Egg Export Council (USAPEEC)
2300 W Pk Pl Blvd Ste 100 . . . Stone Mountain GA 30087 770-413-0006 413-0007 49-6
Web: www.usapeec.org

USA Risk Group Inc
2418 Airport Rd Ste 2A . . . Barre VT 05641 800-872-7475 229-6280* 463
*Fax Area Code: 802 ■ *TF:* 800-872-7475 ■ *Web:* content.usarisk.com

USA Scientific Inc 346 SW 57th Ave . . . Ocala FL 34474 352-237-6288 351-2057 328
Web: www.usascientific.com

USA Student Travel
5080 Robert J Mathews Pkwy . . . El Dorado Hills CA 95762 916-939-6805 939-6806 760
Web: usastudenttravel.com

USA Swimming 1 Olympic Plz . . . Colorado Springs CO 80909 719-866-4578 866-4669 48-22
TF: 800-356-2722 ■ *Web:* www.usaswimming.org

USA Synthetic Fuel Corp
312 Walnut St Ste 2300 . . . Cincinnati OH 45202 513-762-7870 192

USA Technologies Inc
100 Deerfield Ln Ste 140 . . . Malvern PA 19355 800-633-0340 251
TF: 800-633-0340 ■ *Web:* www.usatech.com

USA Today 7950 Jones Branch Dr . . . McLean VA 22102 703-854-3400 532-3
TF: 800-872-0001 ■ *Web:* www.usatoday.com

USA Track & Field Inc (USATF)
132 E Washington St Ste 800 . . . Indianapolis IN 46204 317-261-0500 261-0481 48-22
Web: www.usatf.org

USA Truck Inc
3200 Industrial Park Rd . . . Van Buren AR 72956 479-471-2500 780
NASDAQ: USAK ■ *Web:* www.usa-truck.com

USA Water Polo
2124 Main St Ste 240 . . . Huntington Beach CA 92648 714-500-5445 960-2431 48-22
TF: 888-712-2166 ■ *Web:* www.usawaterpolo.org

USA Water Ski 1251 Holy Cow Rd . . . Polk City FL 33868 863-324-4341 325-8259 48-22
Web: www.usawaterski.org

USA Workers Injury Network
1250 S Capital of Texas Hwy Bldg 3 Ste 500 . . . Austin TX 78746 800-872-0020 328-6785* 391-4
*Fax Area Code: 512 ■ *TF:* 800-872-0020 ■ *Web:* www.usamco.com

USAA (United Services Automobile Assn)
10750 McDermott Fwy . . . San Antonio TX 78288 800-531-8722 531-5717 185
TF: 800-531-8722 ■ *Web:* www.usaa.com

USAA Real Estate Co
9830 Colonnade Blvd Ste 600 . . . San Antonio TX 78230 800-531-8182 641-8425* 655
*Fax Area Code: 210 ■ *TF:* 800-531-8182 ■ *Web:* www.usrealco.com

USAble Life 17500 Chenal Pky . . . Little Rock AR 72223 501-375-7200 796
TF: 800-370-5856 ■ *Web:* www.usablelife.com

	Phone	Fax	Class
Usablenet Inc 500 Seventh Ave 8th Fl. . . . . New York NY 10018 *Web:* usablenet.com	212-965-5388		224
USAC (Universal Service Administrative Co) 2000 L St NW Ste 200 . . . . Washington DC 20036 *Web:* www.usac.org	202-776-0200	776-0080	736
USAC (USAC Racing) 4910 W 16th St. . . . . Speedway IN 46224 *Web:* www.usacracing.com	317-247-5151		48-22
USAC Racing (USAC) 4910 W 16th St. . . . . Speedway IN 46224 *Web:* www.usacracing.com	317-247-5151		48-22
USAch Technologies Inc 1524 Davis Rd. . . . . Elgin IL 60123 *Web:* www.usach.com	847-888-0148		697
USAdvisors Network LLC 15750 Venture Ln. . . . . Eden Prairie MN 55344 *Web:* www.usadvisorsnetwork.com	952-829-0000		463
USAFA (U.S. Air Force Academy) 2304 Cadet Dr Ste 3100. . . . . US Air Force Academy CO 80840 *TF:* 800-443-9266 ■ *Web:* www.usafa.af.mil	719-333-1110	333-3644	498
USAFact Inc 6200 Box Springs Blvd Ste A. . . . . Riverside CA 92507 *TF:* 800-547-0263 ■ *Web:* www.usafactinc.com	951-656-7800		260
Usagencies Credit Union 95 SW Taylor St . . . . Portland OR 97204 *TF:* 800-452-0915 ■ *Web:* usacu.org	503-275-0300	275-0319	219
USAID (U.S. Agency for International Development) 1300 Pennsylvania Ave NW . . . . Washington DC 20004 *Web:* www.usaid.gov	202-712-0000	216-3524	340-20
USAISR (U.S. Army Institute of Surgical Research) 3698 Chambers Pass Ste B . . . . Fort Sam Houston TX 78234 *Web:* www.usaisr.amedd.army.mil	210-539-3219		668
USAN Inc 3080 Northwoods Cir . . . . Norcross GA 30071 *Web:* usan.com	770-729-1449		737
USANA Health Sciences Inc 3838 W Parkway Blvd. Salt Lake City UT 84120 *NYSE:* USNA ■ *TF:* 888-950-9595 ■ *Web:* www.usana.com	801-954-7100	954-7300	799
US-Analytics 600 E Las Colinas Blvd Ste 2222 . . . . Irving TX 75039 *TF:* 877-828-8727 ■ *Web:* www.us-analytics.com	214-630-0081		180
USAPEEC (USA Poultry & Egg Export Council) 2300 W Pk Pl Blvd Ste 100. . . . . Stone Mountain GA 30087 *Web:* www.usapeec.org	770-413-0006	413-0007	49-6
USAS Technologies 197 SR-18 Ste 304. East Brunswick NJ 08816 *Web:* usastechnologies.com	732-333-1400		196
Usasia Insurance Services 319 Union Ave . . . . Pomona CA 91768 *TF:* 888-845-1731 ■ *Web:* www.usasia-ins1.com	909-618-0288		390
USATF (USA Track & Field Inc) 132 E Washington St Ste 800. . . . . Indianapolis IN 46204 *Web:* www.usatf.org	317-261-0500	261-0481	48-22
U-Save Auto Rental of America Inc 1052 Highland Colony Pkwy Ste 204. . . . . Ridgeland MS 39157 *TF:* 800-438-2300 ■ *Web:* www.usave.com	601-713-4333		126
U-Save Pharmacy Inc 2105 S Locust St . . . . Grand Island NE 68801 *Web:* usaverx.co	308-382-3784	382-4526	237
USB (United Soybean Board) 16305 Swingley Ridge Rd Ste 150 . . . . Chesterfield MO 63017 *TF:* 800-989-8721 ■ *Web:* www.unitedsoybean.org	636-530-1777	530-1560	48-2
USBid Inc 2320 Commerce Park Dr . . . . Palm Bay FL 32905 *Web:* www.usbid.com	321-725-9565		224
USC Consulting Group LLC 3000 Bayport Dr Ste 1010 . . . . Tampa FL 33607 *TF:* 800-888-8872 ■ *Web:* www.usccg.com	800-888-8872		196
USC Division of Biokinesiology & Physical Therapy 1540 Alcazar St CHP 155. . . . . Los Angeles CA 90089 *Web:* www.pt.usc.edu	323-442-2900	442-1515	250
USC Gould School of Law 699 Exposition Blvd . . . . Los Angeles CA 90089 *Web:* gould.usc.edu	213-740-7331		167-1
USC Information Sciences Institute 4676 Admiralty Way Ste 1001 . . . . Marina CA 90292 *Web:* isi.edu	310-822-1511	823-6714	668
USCB Inc 3333 Wilshire Blvd . . . . Los Angeles CA 90010 *Web:* www.uscbinc.com	213-387-6181		160
USCC (U.S. Cellular Corp) 8410 W Bryn Mawr Ave Ste 700. . . . . Chicago IL 60631 *NYSE:* USM ■ *TF:* 888-944-9400 ■ *Web:* www.uscellular.com	773-399-8900		736
USCG Air Station Sacramento 6037 Price Ave . . . . McClellan CA 95652 *Web:* www.pacificarea.uscg.mil	916-643-7659		158
USCIB (U.S. Council for International Business) 1212 Avenue of the Americas . . . . New York NY 10036 *Web:* www.uscib.org	212-354-4480	575-0327	49-12
USCIRF (U.S. Commission on International ReligiousFreedom) 800 N Capitol St NW Ste 790. . . . . Washington DC 20002 *Web:* www.uscirf.gov	202-523-3240	523-5020	340-20
USCJ (United Synagogue of Conservative Judaism) 820 Second Ave . . . . New York NY 10017 *Web:* uscj.org	212-533-7800	353-9439	48-20
USCRI (U.S. Committee for Refugees & Immigrants) 2231 Crystal Dr Ste 350. Arlington VA 22202 *Web:* www.refugees.org	703-310-1130	769-4241	48-5
USD (Union Sanitary District) 5072 Benson Rd PO Box 5050. . . . . Union City CA 94587 *Web:* www.unionsanitary.com	510-477-7500		804
USDA (Department of Agriculture) 1400 Independence Ave SW. . . . . Washington DC 20250 *TF:* 844-433-2774 ■ *Web:* www.usda.gov	202-708-8177		340-1
USDA Graduate School 600 Maryland Ave SW . . . . Washington DC 20024 *TF:* 800-793-5533 ■ *Web:* cicorp.com	202-829-4444		340-1
USDM Life Sciences 535 Chapala St. . . . . Santa Barbara CA 93101 **Fax Area Code: 775* ■ *TF:* 888-231-0816 ■ *Web:* www.usdm.com	888-231-0816	213-5943*	180
USDTL (United States Drug Testing Laboratories) 1700 S Mt Prospect Rd. Des Plaines IL 60018 *TF:* 800-235-2367 ■ *Web:* www.usdtl.com	847-375-0770	375-0775	416

	Phone	Fax	Class
Used-Car-Partscom Inc 1980 Highland Pk. . . . . Covington KY 41017 *TF:* 800-288-7415 ■ *Web:* www.car-part.com	859-344-1925		224
Usemco 1602 Rezin Rd. . . . . Tomah WI 54660 *Web:* www.usemco.com	608-372-5911		492
USENIX Assn 2560 Ninth St Ste 215 . . . . Berkeley CA 94710 *TF:* 800-397-3342 ■ *Web:* www.usenix.org	510-528-8649	548-5738	48-9
User Friendly Services PO Box 38402 . . . . Olmsted Falls OH 44138 *Web:* www.userfriendlyusa.com	440-781-6893		180
Userful Corp 200-709 11th Ave SW. . . . . Calgary AB T2R0E3 *Web:* www.userful.com	403-289-2177		180
USET (U.S. Equestrian Team Foundation Inc) PO Box 355 . . . . Gladstone NJ 07934 *Web:* www.uset.org	908-234-1251	234-0670	48-22
USF (University of South Florida College of Medicine) 12901 Bruce B Downs Blvd . . . . Tampa FL 33612 *Web:* health.usf.edu	813-974-2229	974-4990	167-2
USF Fabrication Inc 3200 W 84th St . . . . Hialeah FL 33018 *TF:* 800-258-6873 ■ *Web:* www.usffab.com	800-258-6873		480
USF Holland Inc 700 S Waverly Rd . . . . Holland MI 49423 *TF:* 844-617-6411 ■ *Web:* www.yrcregional.com	616-395-5000		780
USFA (U.S. Fencing Assn) 1 Olympic Plz . . . . Colorado Springs CO 80909 *Web:* www.usafencing.org	719-866-4511	632-5737	48-22
USfalcon Inc 100 Regency Forest Dr Ste 150 . . . . Cary NC 27518 *Web:* www.usfalcon.com	919-388-3778	388-3779	180
USFSA (U.S. Figure Skating Assn) 20 1st St. . . . . Colorado Springs CO 80906 *TF:* 800-332-9256 ■ *Web:* www.usfigureskating.org	719-635-5200	635-9548	48-22
USGA (U.S. Golf Assn) 77 Liberty Corner Rd . . . . Far Hills NJ 07931 *TF:* 800-336-4446 ■ *Web:* www.usga.org	908-234-2300	234-9687	48-22
USGS 2327 University Way Ste 2 . . . . Bozeman MT 59715 *Web:* www.usgs.gov	406-994-7544	994-6556	668
USGS Education USGS National Ctr 12201 Sunrise Valley Dr. . . . . Reston VA 20192 *TF:* 800-228-0975 ■ *Web:* www.usgs.gov	703-648-5953		397
USGS Forest & Rangeland Ecosystem Science Ctr 777 NW Ninth St Ste 400 . . . . Corvallis OR 97330 *Web:* www.usgs.gov	541-750-1030	750-1069	668
USGS Leetown Science Ctr 11649 Leetown Rd . . . . Kearneysville WV 25430 *Web:* www.lsc.usgs.gov	304-724-4404	724-4415	668
USGS Upper Midwest Environmental Sciences Ctr 2630 Fanta Reed Rd . . . . La Crosse WI 54603 *Web:* www.usgs.gov	608-783-6451	783-6066	668
USGS Western Fisheries Research Ctr 6505 NE 65th St . . . . Seattle WA 98115 *Web:* www.usgs.gov	206-526-6282	526-6654	668
USHEALTH Group Inc 300 Burnett St Ste 200 . . . . Fort Worth TX 76102 *TF:* 800-387-9027 ■ *Web:* www.ushealthgroup.com	800-387-9027		391-6
Ushers Machine & Tool Company Inc 180 Ushers Rd . . . . Round Lake NY 12151 *Web:* www.ushersm.com	518-877-5501		454
Usherwood Office Technology Inc 1005 W Fayette St. . . . . Syracuse NY 13204 *TF:* 800-724-2119 ■ *Web:* www.usherwood.com	315-472-0050		41
Ushio America Inc 5440 Cerritos Ave. . . . . Cypress CA 90630 **Fax Area Code: 800* ■ *TF:* 800-326-1960 ■ *Web:* www.ushio.com	714-236-8600	776-3641*	437
uShip Inc 205 E Riverside Dr . . . . Austin TX 78704 *TF:* 800-698-7447 ■ *Web:* www.uship.com	800-698-7447		387
USI (Underground Specialists Inc) 570 SW 16th Terr . . . . Pompano Beach FL 33069 *Web:* www.usicable.com	954-782-8740	782-1919	787
USI Holdings Corp 100 Summit Lake Dr Ste 400 . . . . Valhalla NY 10595 *Web:* www.usi.com	914-749-8500		390
USI Inc 98 Fort Path Rd. . . . . Madison CT 06443 *Web:* www.usi-laminate.com	203-245-8586	245-8619	247
Usibelli Coal Mine Inc (UCM) PO Box 1000. . . . . Healy AK 99743 *Web:* www.usibelli.com	907-683-2226	683-2253	501
Usinatech Inc 1099 Chemin Ely . . . . Melbourne QC J0B2B0 *Web:* usinatech.com	819-826-3774		757
Usine Rotec Inc 125 Rue De L'eglise RR 1 . . . . Baie-du-Febvre QC J0G1A0 *Web:* www.rotecbeds.com	450-783-6444	783-6446	321
USIS (United States Information Systems Inc) 35 W Jefferson Ave. . . . . Pearl River NY 10965 *TF:* 866-222-3778 ■ *Web:* www.usis.net	845-358-7755		787
Usitechnov Industries Inc 1295 1e Rue Parc Industriel . . . . Sainte-Marie QC G6E3T3 *Web:* www.usitechnov.com	418-387-3133	387-7396	454
USlegal Inc 3720 Flowood Dr . . . . Jackson MS 39232 *TF:* 877-389-0141 ■ *Web:* uslegal.com	601-896-0180	896-0199	787
USM Aerostructures Corp 74 W Sixth St . . . . Wyoming PA 18644 *Web:* www.usmaero.com	570-613-1234		295
USM Business Systems Inc 14175 Sullyfield Cir . . . . Chantilly VA 20151 *Web:* www.usmsystems.com	703-263-0855		261
USM Inc 1700 Markley St Ste 100 . . . . Norristown PA 19401 *TF:* 800-355-4000 ■ *Web:* www.usmservices.com	800-355-4000		186
USMA (U.S. Metric Association Inc) 10245 Andasol Ave. . . . . Northridge CA 91325 *Web:* www.usma.org	310-832-3763		48-10
Usman Trade 11018 Watson Mill Ct . . . . Sugar Land TX 77478 *Web:* www.usmantrade.com	281-933-7200		196
Usmax Corp 382 Gambrills Rd. . . . . Gambrills MD 21054 *Web:* www.usmax.com	301-912-1166		177
USMEF (U.S. Meat Export Federation Inc) 1050 17th St Ste 2200 . . . . Denver CO 80265 *Web:* www.usmef.org	303-623-6328	623-0297	49-6
Usmilcom Inc 1952 E Mcfadden Ave. . . . . Santa Ana CA 92705 *Web:* www.usmilcom.com	714-835-3545	835-7280	253
USMM (U.S. Medical Management LLC) 500 Kirts Blvd. . . . . Troy MI 48084 *Web:* www.usmmllc.com	248-824-6000		463

Name / Address	City	State	ZIP	Phone	Fax	Class
USNR 1981 Schurman Way PO Box 310 *TF:* 800-289-8767 ■ *Web:* www.usnr.com	Woodland	WA	98674	360-225-8267	225-8017	683
USO (United Service Organizations) 2111 Wilson Blvd Ste 1200 *TF:* 800-876-7469 ■ *Web:* www.uso.org	Arlington	VA	22201	888-484-3876		48-19
Uson LP 8640 N Eldridge Pkwy *Web:* www.uson.com	Houston	TX	77041	281-671-2000	671-2001	201
USP (U.S. Pharmacopeia) 12601 Twinbrook Pkwy *TF:* 800-227-8772 ■ *Web:* www.usp.org	Rockville	MD	20852	301-881-0666		49-8
USP (University of Science and Philosophy) PO Box 520 **Fax Area Code:* 573 ■ *TF:* 800-882-5683 ■ *Web:* www.philosophy.org	Waynesboro	VA	22980	800-882-5683	729-1096*	166
USP (U.S. Penitentiary) *Allenwood* PO Box 3500 *Web:* www.bop.gov	White Deer	PA	17887	570-547-0963	547-9201	212
Pollock 1000 Airbase Rd *Web:* www.bop.gov	Pollock	LA	71467	318-561-5300	561-5391	212
USP Structural Connectors Inc 703 Rogers Dr *TF:* 800-328-5934 ■ *Web:* www.uspconnectors.com	Montgomery	MN	56069	800-328-5934		480
USPA (U.S. Parachute Assn) 5401 Southpoint Center Blvd *Web:* uspa.org	Fredericksburg	VA	22407	540-604-9740	604-9741	48-22
USPAACC (U.S. Pan Asian American Chamber of Commerce) 1329 18th St NW *TF:* 800-696-7818 ■ *Web:* uspaacc.com	Washington	DC	20036	202-296-5221	296-5225	48-14
USPB (U.S. Premium Beef LLC) PO Box 20103 *TF:* 866-877-2525 ■ *Web:* www.uspb.com	Kansas City	MO	64195	816-713-8800	713-8810	296-26
USPI (United Surgical Partners International Inc) 15305 Dallas Pkwy *Web:* www.uspi.com	Addison	TX	75001	972-713-3500		352
Usplate Glass Insurance Co 1 Westbrook Corp Ctr Ste 320 *Web:* usplate.com	Westchester	IL	60154	708-449-6060		390
Usplk Employees Federal Credit Union 16055 Santa Fe Trl *Web:* usplkefcu.org	Leavenworth	KS	66048	913-682-2928		219
USPS (U.S. Postal Service) 475 L'Enfant Plz W SW *Web:* www.usps.com	Washington	DC	20260	202-268-2608		340-20
USPTA (U.S. Professional Tennis Assn) 11961 Performance Dr **Fax Area Code:* 713 ■ *TF:* 800-877-8248 ■ *Web:* uspta.com	Orlando	FL	32827	800-877-8248	978-7780*	48-22
USRA (Universities Space Research Assn) 10211 Wincopin Cir Ste 500 *Web:* www.usra.edu	Columbia	MD	21044	410-730-2656	730-3496	49-19
US-Reports Inc 5802 Wright Dr *TF:* 800-223-2310 ■ *Web:* www.us-reports.com	Loveland	CO	80538	800-223-2310		463
USS (United Staffing Solutions) 111 Broadway 3rd Fl **Fax Area Code:* 646 ■ *TF:* 800-972-9725 ■ *Web:* www.unitedstaffingsolutions.net	New York	NY	10006	800-972-9725	224-8393*	260
USS Alabama Battleship Memorial Park 2703 Battleship Pkwy PO Box 65 *Web:* www.ussalabama.com	Mobile	AL	36602	251-433-2703		50-4
USS Arizona Memorial 1 Arizona Memorial Pl *Web:* www.nps.gov	Honolulu	HI	96818	808-422-0561	483-8608	50-4
USS Bowfin Submarine Museum & Park 11 Arizona Memorial Dr *Web:* www.bowfin.org	Honolulu	HI	96818	808-423-1341		520
USS Cal Builders Inc 8051 Main St *Web:* www.usscalbuilders.com	Stanton	CA	90680	714-828-4882	828-9498	186
USS Constitution Museum PO Box 291812 *Web:* ussconstitutionmuseum.org	Boston	MA	02129	617-242-0496		520
USS Corp 780 Frelinghuysen Ave *Web:* usscorp.com	Newark	NJ	07114	973-242-1110		627
USS Hornet Museum 707 W Hornet Ave Pier 3 *Web:* www.uss-hornet.org	Alameda	CA	94501	510-521-8448	749-3699	520
USS Kidd Veterans Memorial & Museum 305 S River Rd *TF:* 800-638-0594 ■ *Web:* www.usskidd.com	Baton Rouge	LA	70802	225-342-1942	342-2039	50-4
USS Lexington Museum on the Bay 2914 N Shoreline Blvd *TF:* 800-523-9539 ■ *Web:* usslexington.com	Corpus Christi	TX	78402	361-888-4873		520
USS Liberty Memorial Public Library 1620 11th Ave *Web:* www.graftonpubliclibrary.net	Grafton	WI	53024	262-375-5315		434-3
USS Missouri Memorial Association Inc 63 Cowpens St *TF:* 877-644-4896 ■ *Web:* ussmissouri.org	Honolulu	HI	96818	808-455-1600	455-1598	50-4
USSD (U.S. Society on Dams) 1616 17th St Ste 483 *Web:* www.ussdams.org	Denver	CO	80202	303-628-5430	628-5431	49-3
Ussery Printing Company Inc 4201 Airborn Dr *Web:* www.usseryprinting.com	Addison	TX	75062	972-438-8344		627
USS-POSCO Industries 900 Loveridge Rd *TF:* 800-877-7672 ■ *Web:* www.ussposco.com	Pittsburg	CA	94565	800-877-7672		723
USTA (U.S. Telecom Assn) 607-14th St NW Ste 400 *Web:* www.ustelecom.org	Washington	DC	20005	202-326-7300	326-7333	49-20
USTA (U.S. Trotting Assn) 750 Michigan Ave *TF:* 877-800-8782 ■ *Web:* www.ustrotting.com	Columbus	OH	43215	614-224-2291	224-4575	48-22
USTL (U.S. Term Limits) 1250 Connecticut Ave NW Ste 200 *Web:* www.termlimits.com	Washington	DC	20036	202-261-3532		48-7
USUBC (Utah State University Botanical Ctr) 920 S 50 W PO Box 265 *Web:* usubotanicalcenter.org	Kaysville	UT	84037	801-544-3089	546-1699	97
USVP (U.S. Venture Partners) 1460 El Camino Real *Web:* www.usvp.com	Menlo Park	CA	94025	650-854-9080	854-3018	792
USW (United Steel Workers) 3340 Perimeter Hill Dr *Web:* www.usw.org	Nashville	TN	37211	615-834-8590		414
USW (U.S. Wheat Assn) 3103 10th St N **Fax Area Code:* 703 ■ *Web:* www.uswheat.org	Arlington	VA	22201	202-463-0999	524-4399*	48-2
USWeb LLC 631 N Stephanie St Ste 507 *TF:* 855-243-4038 ■ *Web:* www.usweb.com	Henderson	NV	89014	855-243-4038		194
USWired Inc 2107 N First St Ste 250 *TF:* 877-879-4733 ■ *Web:* www.uswired.com	San Jose	CA	95131	408-872-9383		180
UT Health East Texas 2000 S Palestine St *Web:* uthealtheasttexas.com	Athens	TX	75751	903-676-1000		374-3
UTA (United Talent Agency Inc) 9336 Civic Center Dr *Web:* unitedtalent.com	Beverly Hills	CA	90210	310-273-6700	247-1111	731
UTA (Utah Transit Authority) PO Box 30810 *TF:* 888-743-3882 ■ *Web:* www.rideuta.com	Salt Lake City	UT	84130	801-262-5626		468
Utah						
Administrative Office of the Courts 450 S State PO Box 140241 *Web:* www.utcourts.gov	Salt Lake City	UT	84114	801-578-3800	578-3843	339-45
Agriculture & Food Dept 350 N Redwood Rd PO Box 146500 *Web:* www.ag.utah.gov	Salt Lake City	UT	84114	801-538-7100	538-7126	339-45
Arts Council 617 E S Temple *Web:* heritage.utah.gov	Salt Lake City	UT	84102	801-236-7555		339-45
Attorney General PO Box 142320 *TF:* 800-244-4636 ■ *Web:* attorneygeneral.utah.gov	Salt Lake City	UT	84114	801-538-9600	538-1121	339-45
Commerce Dept 160 E Broadway Heber M Wells Bldg *TF:* 877-526-3994 ■ *Web:* corporations.utah.gov	Salt Lake City	UT	84111	801-530-4849	530-6446	339-45
Community & Economic Development Dept 60 E S Temple 3rd Fl *TF:* 855-204-9046 ■ *Web:* business.utah.gov	Salt Lake City	UT	84111	801-538-8680	538-8888	339-45
Corrections Dept 14717 S Minuteman Dr *Web:* corrections.utah.gov	Draper	UT	84020	801-545-5500		339-45
Department of Heritage & Arts 300 S Rio Grando St *Web:* www.heritageandarts.utah.gov	Salt Lake City	UT	84101	801-245-7202		339-45
Department of Technology Services 1 State Office Bldg 6th Fl *TF:* 866-489-9834 ■ *Web:* dts.utah.gov	Salt Lake City	UT	84114	801-537-9000		339-45
Education Office 250 E 500 S PO Box 144200 *Web:* schools.utah.gov	Salt Lake City	UT	84111	801-538-7500		339-45
Health Dept PO Box 141010 *Web:* www.health.utah.gov	Salt Lake City	UT	84114	801-538-6003		339-45
Higher Education Assistance Authority PO Box 145110 *TF:* 877-336-7378 ■ *Web:* www.uheaa.org	Salt Lake City	UT	84114	801-321-7294	366-8431	725
Housing Corp 2479 S Lake Park Blvd *TF:* 800-284-6950 ■ *Web:* www.utahhousingcorp.org	West Valley City	UT	84120	801-902-8200		339-45
Human Resource Management Dept State Office Bldg Ste 2120 *Web:* dhrm.utah.gov	Salt Lake City	UT	84114	801-538-3025	538-3403	339-45
Insurance Dept 3110 State Office Bldg *TF:* 800-439-3805 ■ *Web:* insurance.utah.gov	Salt Lake City	UT	84114	801-538-3800	538-3829	339-45
Labor Commission PO Box 146600 *Web:* laborcommission.utah.gov	Salt Lake City	UT	84114	801-530-6800	530-6390	339-45
Legislature 350 N State Ste 320 *Web:* www.le.utah.gov	Salt Lake City	UT	84114	801-538-1035	326-1475	339-45
Lieutenant Governor Utah State Capitol Complex Ste 220 PO Box 142325 *TF:* 800-995-8683 ■ *Web:* www.utah.gov	Salt Lake City	UT	84114	801-538-1041	538-1133	339-45
Medical Examiner's Office (OME) 4451 S 2700 W *TF:* 888-222-2542 ■ *Web:* www.health.utah.gov	Taylorsville	UT	84129	801-816-3850		339-45
Motor Vehicle Div PO Box 30412 *TF:* 800-368-8824 ■ *Web:* dmv.utah.gov	Salt Lake City	UT	84130	801-297-7780	297-3570	339-45
Natural Resources Dept 1594 W N Temple Ste 3710 *Web:* naturalresources.utah.gov	Salt Lake City	UT	84116	801-538-7200	538-7315	339-45
Occupational & Professional Licensing Div PO Box 146741 *TF:* 866-275-3675 ■ *Web:* dopl.utah.gov	Salt Lake City	UT	84111	801-530-6628	530-6511	339-45
Office for Victims of Crime 350 E 500 S Ste 200 *TF:* 800-621-7444 ■ *Web:* www.crimevictim.utah.gov	Salt Lake City	UT	84111	801-238-2360	533-4127	339-45
Office of Tourism 300 N State St *TF:* 800-200-1160 ■ *Web:* www.travel.utah.gov	Salt Lake City	UT	84114	801-538-1900	538-1399	339-45
Pardons & Parole Board 448 E Winchester St Ste 300 *Web:* bop.utah.gov	Murray	UT	84107	801-261-6464	261-6481	339-45
Parks & Recreation Div 1594 W N Temple Ste 116 *Web:* stateparks.utah.gov	Salt Lake City	UT	84116	801-538-7220	538-7378	339-45
Public Service Commission 160 E 300 S 4th Fl *TF:* 866-772-8824 ■ *Web:* www.psc.state.ut.us	Salt Lake City	UT	84111	801-530-6716	530-6796	339-45
Real Estate Div PO Box 146711 *Web:* realestate.utah.gov	Salt Lake City	UT	84114	801-530-6747	530-6749	339-45
Rehabilitation Office 1595 W 500 S *Web:* www.jobs.utah.gov	Salt Lake City	UT	84104	801-887-9500		339-45
Sports Commission 201 S Main St Ste 2125 *Web:* utahsportscommission.com	Salt Lake City	UT	84111	801-328-2372		339-45
State Prison 14425 Bitterbrush Ln PO Box 250 *Web:* corrections.utah.gov	Draper	UT	84020	801-576-7000		213
State Treasurer 350 N State St 120 State Capitol *Web:* utahstatecapitol.utah.gov	Salt Lake City	UT	84114	801-538-1042	538-1465	339-45

				Phone	Fax	Class
Tax Commission 210 N 1950 W	Salt Lake City	UT	84134	801-297-2200	297-7699	339-45
TF: 800-662-4335 ■ *Web:* tax.utah.gov						
Transportation Dept						
4501 S 2700 W PO Box 141265	Salt Lake City	UT	84119	801-965-4000		339-45
Web: www.udot.utah.gov						
Veterans' Affairs Office						
550 Foothills Dr Ste 105	Salt Lake City	UT	84113	801-326-2372	326-2369	339-45
TF: 800-894-9497 ■ *Web:* veterans.utah.gov						
Vital Records & Statistics Office						
Cannon Health Bldg 288 N 1460 W						
PO Box 141012	Salt Lake City	UT	84114	801-538-6105		339-45
Web: vitalrecords.utah.gov						
Wildlife Resources Div						
1594 W N Temple Ste 2110						
PO Box 146301	Salt Lake City	UT	84114	801-538-4700	538-4745	339-45
Web: wildlife.utah.gov						
Utah Association of Counties (UAC)						
5397 S Vine St	Murray	UT	84107	801-265-1331	265-9485	48-13
Web: www.uacnet.org						
Utah Association of Realtors						
230 W Towne Ridge Pkwy Ste 500	Sandy	UT	84070	801-676-5200	676-5225	656
TF: 800-594-8933 ■ *Web:* www.utahrealtors.com						
Utah Business Magazine						
90 South 400 West Ste 650	Salt Lake City	UT	84101	801-568-0114		457-5
TF: 888-414-5566 ■ *Web:* www.utahbusiness.com						
Utah Correctional Industries						
14072 S Pony Express Rd	Draper	UT	84020	801-576-7700		630
Web: uci.utah.gov						
Utah County 100 E Center St Rm 3600	Provo	UT	84606	801-851-8000		338
Web: www.co.utah.ut.us						
Utah Credit Union League Inc						
455 E 500 S Ste 400	Salt Lake City	UT	84111	801-972-3400		219
Web: utahscreditunions.org						
Utah Field House of Natural History State Park						
496 E Main St	Vernal	UT	84078	435-789-3799	789-4883	565
Web: stateparks.utah.gov						
Utah Imaging Associates Inc						
1433 N 1075 W Ste 104	Farmington	UT	84025	800-475-3698		415
TF: 800-475-3698 ■ *Web:* www.utahimaging.com						
Utah League of Cities & Towns, The						
50 South 600 East Ste 150	Salt Lake City	UT	84102	801-328-1601		78
TF: 800-852-8528 ■ *Web:* www.ulct.org						
Utah Lighthouse Ministry						
1358 SW Temple	Salt Lake City	UT	84115	801-485-8894		637-2
Web: www.utlm.org						
Utah Lions Eye Bank						
John A Moran Eye Ctr						
65 Mario Capecchi Dr	Salt Lake City	UT	84132	801-581-2352		269
Web: healthcare.utah.edu						
Utah Medical Products Inc						
7043 S 300 W	Midvale	UT	84047	801-566-1200	566-2062	476
NASDAQ: UTMD ■ *TF:* 866-754-9789 ■ *Web:* www.utahmed.com						
Utah Metal Works Inc (UMW)						
805 Everett Ave	Salt Lake City	UT	84116	877-221-0099		660
TF: 877-221-0099 ■ *Web:* umw.com						
Utah Museum of Fine Arts						
University of Utah 410 Campus Center Dr						
	Salt Lake City	UT	84112	801-581-7332	585-5198	520
Web: umfa.utah.edu						
Utah Museum of Natural History, The						
301 Wakara Way	Salt Lake City	UT	84108	801-581-4303	585-3684	520
Web: nhmu.utah.edu						
Utah Paper Box Company Inc						
920 South 700 West	Salt Lake City	UT	84104	801-363-0093		101
Web: www.upbslc.com						
Utah Power Credit Union						
957 E 6600 S	Salt Lake City	UT	84121	801-708-8900	716-4672	219
TF: 800-833-8897 ■ *Web:* utahpowercu.org						
Utah Refractories Corp 2200 N 1200 W	Lehi	UT	84043	801-768-3591	768-2684	662
Web: www.utah-refractories-corp.com						
Utah Republican Party, A Utah Not-For-Profit Corp						
117 E S Temple St	Salt Lake City	UT	84111	801-533-9777		616-2
Web: utah.gop						
Utah Scientific						
4750 Wiley Post Way Ste 150	Salt Lake City	UT	84116	801-575-8801	537-3099	647
TF: 800-453-8782 ■ *Web:* utahscientific.com						
Utah State Bar 645 S 200 E	Salt Lake City	UT	84111	801-531-9077	531-0660	72
TF: 877-752-2611 ■ *Web:* www.utahbar.org						
Utah State Hospital 1300 E Center St	Provo	UT	84606	801-344-4400		374-5
TF: 800-371-7897 ■ *Web:* ush.utah.gov						
Utah State Library						
250 N 1950 W Ste A	Salt Lake City	UT	84116	801-715-6777	715-6767	434-5
TF: 800-662-9150 ■ *Web:* heritage.utah.gov						
Utah State University						
1600 Old Main Hill	Logan	UT	84322	435-797-1116	797-1110	166
TF: 800-488-8108 ■ *Web:* www.usu.edu						
Utah State University Botanical Ctr (USUBC)						
920 S 50 W PO Box 265	Kaysville	UT	84037	801-544-3089	546-1699	97
Web: usubotanicalcenter.org						
Utah State University Merrill-Cazier Library						
3000 Old Main Hill	Logan	UT	84322	435-797-2631	797-2880	434-6
Web: www.library.usu.edu						
Utah Symphony & Opera						
123 W S Temple	Salt Lake City	UT	84101	801-533-6683		573-3
Web: www.utahsymphony.org						
Utah System of Higher Education						
60 S 400 W	Salt Lake City	UT	84101	801-321-7200		786
TF: 800-418-8757 ■ *Web:* ushe.edu						
Utah Transit Authority (UTA)						
PO Box 30810	Salt Lake City	UT	84130	801-262-5626		468
TF: 888-743-3882 ■ *Web:* www.rideuta.com						
Utah Valley Convention & Visitors Bureau						
220 W Center St Ste 100	Provo	UT	84601	801-851-2100		206
TF: 800-222-8824 ■ *Web:* www.utahvalley.com						
Utah Valley State College						
800 W University Pkwy	Orem	UT	84058	801-863-8000		162
TF: 800-952-8220 ■ *Web:* www.uvu.edu						

				Phone	Fax	Class
Utah's Hogle Zoo						
2600 E Sunnyside Ave	Salt Lake City	UT	84108	801-584-1700		823
Web: www.hoglezoo.org						
Utak Laboratories Inc						
25020 Ave Tibbitts	Valencia	CA	91355	661-294-3935	294-9272	231
TF: 800-235-3442 ■ *Web:* www.utak.com						
UT-Battelle						
1201 Oak Ridge Tpke Ste 100	Oak Ridge	TN	37830	865-220-5101		668
Web: www.ut-battelle.org						
UTC (Utilities Telecom Council)						
1129 20th St NW Ste 350	Washington	DC	20036	202-872-0030	872-1331	49-20
Web: utc.org						
UTC Overseas Inc						
370 W Passaic St Ste 3000	Rochelle Park	NJ	07662	713-869-9939		313
Web: www.utcoverseas.com						
UTC RETAIL Inc 100 Rawson Rd	Victor	NY	14564	800-349-0546	924-1434*	614
**Fax Area Code:* 585 ■ *TF:* 800-349-0546 ■ *Web:* www.utcretail.com						
Ute Mountain Casino 3 Weeminuche Dr	Towaoc	CO	81334	970-565-8800	565-6553	133
TF: 800-258-8007 ■ *Web:* www.utemountaincasino.com						
Ute Water Conservancy District						
2190 H 1/4 Rd	Grand Junction	CO	81505	970-242-7491		804
TF: 866-768-1732 ■ *Web:* www.utewater.org						
UTEX Industries Inc						
10810 Katy Fwy Ste 100	Houston	TX	77043	713-467-1000	467-3602	326
TF: 800-359-9230 ■ *Web:* www.utexind.com						
UTHCT (University of Texas Health Center at Tyler)						
11937 US Hwy 271	Tyler	TX	75708	903-877-7000		374-3
Web: www.uthct.edu						
UTHSC (University of Tennessee)						
2040 Sutherland Ave	Knoxville	TN	37996	865-946-7777	974-6341	166
Web: www.utk.edu						
UTHSC (University of Texas Health Science Ctr)						
Libraries						
7703 Floyd Curl Dr MSC 7940	San Antonio	TX	78229	210-567-2408		434-1
Web: library.uthscsa.edu						
Utica Boilers Inc PO Box 4729	Utica	NY	13504	866-847-6656	797-3762*	357
**Fax Area Code:* 315 ■ *TF:* 800-325-5479 ■ *Web:* www.uticaboilers.com						
Utica College 1600 Burrstone Rd	Utica	NY	13502	315-792-3111	792-3003	166
TF: 800-782-8884 ■ *Web:* www.utica.edu						
Utica Community Schools (UCS)						
11303 Greendale	Sterling Heights	MI	48312	586-797-1000		685
Web: www.uticak12.org						
Utica Cutlery Co						
820 Noyes St PO Box 10527	Utica	NY	13503	315-733-4663	733-6602	702
Web: www.uticacutlery.com						
Utica District Telephone Efcu						
2812 Genesee St	Utica	NY	13502	315-724-5133		219
Web: utelfcu.net						
Utica First Insurance Co						
5981 Airport Rd	Oriskany	NY	13424	315-736-8211	768-4408	391-4
TF: 800-456-4556 ■ *Web:* www.uticafirst.com						
Utica Gas & Electric Efcu						
215 Old Campion Rd	New Hartford	NY	13413	315-733-1596		219
Web: ugefcu.com						
Utica Metal Products Inc						
1526 Lincoln Ave	Utica	NY	13502	315-732-6163		295
Web: www.uticametals.com						
Utica National Insurance Group						
180 Genesee St	New Hartford	NY	13413	315-734-2000	734-2680	391-2
TF: 800-274-1914 ■ *Web:* www.uticanational.com						
Utica School of Commerce						
201 Bleecker St	Utica	NY	13501	315-733-2307		800
Web: www.uscny.edu						
Utica Zoo 1 Utica Zoo Way	Utica	NY	13501	315-738-0472	738-0475	823
Web: www.uticazoo.org						
UTIG (University of Texas Institute for Geophysics)						
10100 Burnet Rd (RR2200)						
JJ Pickle Research Campus Bldg 196	Austin	TX	78758	512-471-6156	471-8844	668
Web: ig.utexas.edu						
Utilant LLC 475 Ellicott St Ste 5	Buffalo	NY	14207	888-884-5268		177
TF: 888-884-5268 ■ *Web:* public.utilant.com						
Utilisave LLC 129 W 27th St 11th Fl	New York	NY	10001	718-382-4500		734
Web: www.utilisave.com						
Utilities Telecom Council (UTC)						
1129 20th St NW Ste 350	Washington	DC	20036	202-872-0030	872-1331	49-20
Web: utc.org						
Utility Concrete Products						
2495 Bungalow Rd	Morris	IL	60450	815-416-1000		183
Web: utilityconcrete.com						
Utility Notification Center of Colorado						
16361 Table Mtn Pkwy	Golden	CO	80403	303-232-1991		305
Web: colorado811.org						
Utility Sales Associates Inc						
930 E Oak St	Lake In The Hills	IL	60156	800-253-6248		196
TF: 800-253-6248 ■ *Web:* utilitysales.net						
Utility Technologies International Corp						
4700 Homer Ohio Ln	Groveport	OH	43125	614-482-8080	482-8070	194
Web: www.uti-corp.com						
Utility Tool & Trailer Co						
151 E 16th St PO Box 360	Clintonville	WI	54929	715-823-3167	823-5274	779
Web: www.uttwi.com						
Utility Tool Company Inc						
2900 Commerce Blvd	Birmingham	AL	35210	205-956-3710	956-3711	529
TF: 800-952-3710 ■ *Web:* www.pipehorn.com						
Utility Trailer Manufacturing Co						
17295 E Railroad St	City of Industry	CA	91748	626-965-1541	965-2790	779
TF: 800-874-6807 ■ *Web:* www.utilitytrailer.com						
Utility Trailer Sales of Alabama LLC						
522 Ross Clark Cir	Dothan	AL	36303	334-794-7345		366
Web: utilityalabama.com						
Utility Trallor Manufacturing Co						
2921 Hwy 49 N	Paragould	AR	72450	870-236-9195		57
Web: www.utm.com						
Utility/Keystone Trailer Sales Inc						
1976 Auction Rd	Manheim	PA	17545	717-653-9444	653-9443	57
Web: www.utilitykeystone.com						
Utilityone Inc PO Box 3027	York	PA	17402	717-840-4200	840-4300	196
TF: 800-388-9088 ■ *Web:* getutilityone.com						

	City	State	ZIP	Phone	Fax	Class
UtiliWorks Consulting LLC 2351 Energy Dr Ste 1010 *Web:* www.utiliworks.com	Baton Rouge	LA	70808	225-766-4188	612-6404	196
Utne Reader Magazine 1503 SW 42nd St *TF:* 800-736-8863 ■ *Web:* www.utne.com	Topeka	KS	66609	612-338-5040	338-6043	457-11
Utopia 445 E First St *Web:* www.utopiarestaurant.net	Long Beach	CA	90802	562-432-6888		671
Utopia Home Care Inc 60 E Main St *Web:* www.utopiahomecare.com	Kings Park	NY	11754	631-544-6005	544-5141	363
Utrecht Art Supplies PO Box 1769 **Fax Area Code:* 800 ■ *TF:* 888-336-3114 ■ *Web:* www.utrechtart.com	Galesburg	IL	61402	609-409-8001	382-1979*	43
UTRS (Universal Technical Resource Services Inc) 950 Kings Hwy N Ste 208 *Web:* www.utrs.com	Cherry Hill	NJ	08034	856-667-6770	667-7586	261
UTSI International Corp 1560 W Bay Area Blvd Ste 300 *Web:* www.utsi.com	Friendswood	TX	77546	281-480-8786		261
UTStarcom Inc 1732 N First St Ste 220 *NASDAQ: UTSI* ■ *Web:* www.utstar.com	San Jose	CA	95112	408-453-4557		735
UTXL Inc 10771 NW Ambassador Dr *TF:* 800-351-2821 ■ *Web:* utxl.com	Kansas City	MO	64153	816-891-7770		311
UTZ Quality Foods Co 900 High St *TF:* 800-367-7629 ■ *Web:* www.utzsnacks.com	Hanover	PA	17331	717-637-6644		296-35
UUA (Unitarian Universalist Assn) 25 Beacon St *Web:* www.uua.org	Boston	MA	02108	617-742-2100	367-3237	48-20
UUSC (Unitarian Universalist Service Committee) 689 Massachusetts Ave *TF:* 800-388-3920 ■ *Web:* www.uusc.org	Cambridge	MA	02139	617-868-6600	868-7102	48-5
UV Pure Technologies Inc 60 Venture Dr Unit 19 *TF:* 888-407-9997 ■ *Web:* uvpure.com	Toronto	ON	M1B3S4	416-208-9884		104
Uvalde Consolidated Independent School District 1000 N Getty St *Web:* www.ucisd.net	Uvalde	TX	78801	830-278-6655	591-4909	685
Uvalde County PO Box 284 *Web:* www.uvaldecounty.com	Uvalde	TX	78802	830-278-6614	278-8692	338
UVEST Financial Services Group Inc 2810 Coliseum Centre Dr **Fax Area Code:* 704 ■ *TF:* 800-277-8802 ■ *Web:* www.uvest.com	Charlotte	NC	28217	800-277-8802	376-4476*	401
UVMC (Upper Valley Medical Ctr) 3130 N County Rd 25-A *Web:* www.premierhealth.com	Troy	OH	45373	937-440-4000		374-3
UVP Inc 2066 W 11th St *TF:* 800-452-6788 ■ *Web:* www.uvp.com	Upland	CA	91786	909-946-3197	946-3597	437
UW Marx Inc 20 Gurley Ave *Web:* www.uwmarx.com	Troy	NY	12182	518-272-2541	272-1196	186
UW Medicine Eastside Hospital & Specialty 3100 Northup Way **Fax Area Code:* 206 ■ *TF:* 877-520-5000 ■ *Web:* www.uwmedicine.org	Bellevue	WA	98004	877-520-5000	598-6797*	374-3
Uwajimaya Inc 600 Fifth Ave S *Web:* www.uwajimaya.com	Seattle	WA	98104	206-624-6248		345
Eau Claire Schofield Hall 111 105 Garfield Ave *TF:* 800-949-8932 ■ *Web:* www.uwec.edu	Eau Claire	WI	54701	715-836-5415	831-4799	166
Uwes German Restaurant 31-33 Iowa Ave	Colorado Springs	CO	80909	719-475-1611		671
UX Consulting Company LLC, The 1401 Macy Dr *Web:* www.uxc.com	Roswell	GA	30076	770-642-7745		463
UXU Ranch 1710 N Fork Hwy *Web:* uxuranch.com	Cody	WY	82414	307-587-4637		239
Uzbekistan *Consulate General* 801 2nd Ave 20th Fl *Web:* www.uzbekconsulny.org	New York	NY	10017	212-754-7403		257
Embassy 1746 Massachusetts Ave NW *Web:* www.uzbekistan.org	Washington	DC	20036	202-887-5300	293-6804	257

V

	City	State	ZIP	Phone	Fax	Class
V & H Inc 1505 S Central Ave *TF:* 800-826-2308 ■ *Web:* www.vhtrucks.com	Marshfield	WI	54449	715-486-8800		57
V & J Holding Companies Inc 6933 W Brown Deer Rd *TF:* 800-384-6972 ■ *Web:* www.vjfoods.com	Milwaukee	WI	53223	414-365-9003	365-9467	670
V & L Tool Inc 2021 MacArthur Rd *Web:* www.vltool.com	Waukesha	WI	53188	262-547-1226	521-1031	757
V & M Precision Machining & Grinding 1130 Columbia St *Web:* www.vmprecision.com	Brea	CA	92821	714-257-4850		295
V & P Hydraulic Products LLC 1700 Pittsburgh Dr *Web:* www.vphyd.com	Delaware	OH	43015	740-203-3600		641
V & S Midwest Carriers Corp 2001 Hyland Ave **Fax Area Code:* 920 ■ *TF:* 800-876-4330 ■ *Web:* drivemidwest.com	Kaukauna	WI	54130	800-876-4330	766-1772*	780
V & S Schuler Engineering Inc 2240 Allen Ave SE *Web:* vsschuler.com	Canton	OH	44707	330-452-5200		480
V & V Appliance Parts 1533 Metropolitan St *TF:* 800-366-9969 ■ *Web:* www.vvapplianceparts.com	Pittsburgh	PA	15233	412-321-3700	323-1232	38
V Equipment America Inc 680 Conroe Park W Dr *Web:* www.bauer-equipment.com	Conroe	TX	77303	713-691-3000	691-0089	386
V I Engineering Inc 27300 Haggerty Rd *Web:* www.viengineering.com	Farmington Hills	MI	48331	248-489-1200		180
V I P Meetings & Conventions 17223 Palisades Cir *Web:* vipmeetings.com	Pacific Palisades	CA	90272	310-459-4691		760
V Interactions Inc 355 Ste-Catherine St W Ste 100 *Web:* www.vtele.ca	Montreal	QC	H3B1A5	514-390-6100		647
V M Discovery Inc 45535 Northport Loop E *Web:* vmdiscovery.com	Fremont	CA	94538	510-818-1018		532-3
V M Systems 3125 Hill Ave *Web:* www.vmsystemsinc.com	Toledo	OH	43607	419-535-1044		697
V O S Selections Inc 555 Eighth Ave Rm 1209 *Web:* vosselections.com	New York	NY	10018	212-967-6948		443
V P Supply Corp 3445 Winton Pl *Web:* www.vpsupply.com	Rochester	NY	14623	585-272-0110	272-0547	612
V T E C Laboratories Inc 212 Manida St *Web:* www.vteclabs.com	Bronx	NY	10474	718-542-8248		743
V T I Valtronics Inc 3463 Double Springs Rd *Web:* www.val-tronics.com	Valley Springs	CA	95252	209-754-0707	754-0104	196
V V Graphics LLC 3719 S 194th St *Web:* www.vvprints.com	Seattle	WA	98188	206-588-2835		344
V W Broaching Service Inc 3250 W Lake St *TF:* 800-966-6052 ■ *Web:* www.vwbroaching.com	Chicago	IL	60624	773-533-9000		454
V's Italiano Ristorante 10819 E US Hwy 40 *Web:* vsrestaurant.com	Independence	MO	64055	816-353-1241	353-0004	671
V. G. Reed & Sons Inc 1002 S 12th St *TF:* 800-635-9788 ■ *Web:* www.vgreed.com	Louisville	KY	40210	800-635-9788		393
V.L.S. Systems Inc 4080 Lafayette Center Dr Ste 300 *Web:* www.vls-systems.com	Chantilly	VA	20151	703-953-3118		179
V103 233 N Michigan Ave Ste 2800 *Web:* v103.iheart.com	Chicago	IL	60601	312-591-8103		645-34
V12 data 141 W Front St Ste 410 *Web:* www.v12data.com	Red Bank	NJ	07701	732-842-1001		195
V2 Capital LLC 2700 Patriot Blvd Ste 420	Glenview	IL	60026	847-201-3620		195
V2 LLC 4224 NE Halsey St Ste 320 *TF:* 855-286-3581 ■ *Web:* virtualvenues.com	Portland	OR	97231	503-286-3581		225
V2 Systems Inc 9105 B Owens Dr Unit 202 *Web:* v2systems.com	Manassas	VA	20111	703-361-4606		175
V2Soft Inc 300 Enterprise Ct Ste 100 *TF:* 866-982-7638 ■ *Web:* www.v2soft.com	Bloomfield Hills	MI	48302	248-904-1700	281-5269	177
V2Solutions Inc 2340 Dr Walsh Ave *Web:* www.v2solutions.com	Santa Clara	CA	95051	408-550-2340		196
V3 Companies Ltd 7325 Janes Ave *TF:* 888-707-2779 ■ *Web:* www.v3co.com	Woodridge	IL	60517	630-724-9200		261
V9 Studios 3655 Olive St *Web:* www.v9-digital.com	Saint Louis	MO	63108	314-512-9105		514
VA (Department of Veterans Affairs) 810 Vermont Ave NW *Web:* www.va.gov	Washington	DC	20420	202-461-7600		340-19
VA Central California Health Care System 2615 E Clinton Ave *TF:* 888-826-2838 ■ *Web:* www.fresno.va.gov	Fresno	CA	93703	559-225-6100		374-8
VA Central Iowa Health Care System 3600 30th St *TF:* 800-294-8387 ■ *Web:* www.centraliowa.va.gov	Des Moines	IA	50310	515-699-5999		374-8
VA Connecticut Healthcare System 555 Willard Ave *Web:* www.va.gov	Newington	CT	06111	860-666-6951	667-6764	374-3
VA Greater Los Angeles Healthcare System 11301 Wilshire Blvd *TF:* 800-952-4852 ■ *Web:* www.losangeles.va.gov	Los Angeles	CA	90073	310-478-3711		374-8
VA Hudson Valley Health Care System *Castle Point Campus* 41 Castle Pt Rd *TF:* 800-877-6976 ■ *Web:* www.hudsonvalley.va.gov	Wappingers Falls	NY	12590	845-831-2000	838-5193	374-8
Montrose Campus 2094 Albany Post Rd *TF:* 800-269-8749 ■ *Web:* www.hudsonvalley.va.gov	Montrose	NY	10548	914-737-4400	788-4244	374-8
VA Medical Center and Ambulatory Care Clinic 3687 Veterans Dr PO Box 1500 *TF:* 877-468-8387 ■ *Web:* www.montana.va.gov	Fort Harrison	MT	59636	406-442-6410		374-8
VA Medical Ctr 4500 S Lancaster Rd *TF:* 800-849-3597 ■ *Web:* www.northtexas.va.gov	Dallas	TX	75216	214-742-8387		374-8
VA Medical Ctr 2400 Hospital Rd *TF:* 800-214-8387 ■ *Web:* www.centralalabama.va.gov	Tuskegee	AL	36083	334-727-0550	724-2793	374-8
VA Nebraska-Western Iowa Health Care System 600 S 70th St *TF:* 866-851-6052 ■ *Web:* www.nebraska.va.gov	Lincoln	NE	68510	402-489-3802	486-7858	374-8
VA NY Harbor Healthcare System 423 E 23rd St *Web:* www.nyharbor.va.gov	New York	NY	10010	212-686-7500		374-8
VA Pittsburgh Healthcare System University Dr *Web:* www.va.gov	Pittsburgh	PA	15240	412-822-2222		374-8
VA Puget Sound Health Care System - Seattle Div 1660 S Columbian Way *TF:* 800-329-8387 ■ *Web:* www.va.gov	Seattle	WA	98108	206-762-1010		769
VA San Diego Healthcare System 3350 La Jolla Village Dr *TF:* 800-331-8387 ■ *Web:* www.sandiego.va.gov	San Diego	CA	92161	858-552-8585		374-8
VA Sierra Nevada Health Care System 975 Kirman Ave *TF:* 888-838-6256 ■ *Web:* www.reno.va.gov	Reno	NV	89502	775-786-7200		374-8
VAA (Vermont Attractions Assn) PO Box 1284 *Web:* www.vtattractions.org	Montpelier	VT	05601	802-229-4581	223-4257	393
VAALCO Energy Inc 9800 Richmond Ste 700 *NYSE: EGY* ■ *Web:* www.vaalco.com	Houston	TX	77042	713-623-0801	623-0982	538
Vacation Co 42 New Orleans Rd Ste 102 *TF:* 800-545-3303 ■ *Web:* www.vacationcompany.com	Hilton Head Island	SC	29928	843-686-6100	686-3255	376
Vacation Internationale 1417 116th Ave NE *TF:* 800-444-6633 ■ *Web:* www.viresorts.com	Bellevue	WA	98004	425-454-8429	456-0536	753

Name	Address	City	State	ZIP	Phone	Fax	Class	Other
Vacation Palm Springs Real Estate Inc	1276 N Palm Canyon Dr Ste 211	Palm Springs	CA	92262	760-778-7832		652	*TF:* 800-590-3110 ■ *Web:* vacationpalmsprings.com
Vacation Rental Managers Assn (VRMA)	2025 M St NW Ste 800	Washington	DC	20036	202-367-1179	367-2179	49-17	*Web:* www.vrma.org
Vacation Resorts International Inc	25510 Commercentre Dr Ste 100	Lake Forest	CA	92630	949-587-2299		379	*Web:* www.vriresorts.com
Vacationcom Inc	1650 King St Ste 450	Alexandria	VA	22314	703-740-4100		772	*TF:* 800-843-0733 ■ *Web:* www.vacation.com
Vacationer RV Resort	1581 E Main St	El Cajon	CA	92021	877-626-4409		378	*TF:* 877-626-4409 ■ *Web:* www.vacationerrv.com
Vacations To Go Inc	5851 San Felipe St Ste 500	Houston	TX	77057	713-974-2121		772	*TF:* 800-338-4962 ■ *Web:* www.vacationstogo.com
Vacaville Chamber of Commerce	300 Main St	Vacaville	CA	95688	707-448-6424	448-0424	139	*Web:* www.vacavillechamber.com
Vaccaro's Trattoria	1000 Ghent Rd	Akron	OH	44333	330-666-6158		671	*Web:* www.vactrat.com
Vacco Industries Inc	10350 Vacco St	South El Monte	CA	91733	626-443-7121	442-6943	595	*Web:* www.vacco.com
Vac-Con Inc	969 Hall Park Dr	Green Cove Springs	FL	32043	904-493-4969		427	*TF:* 888-920-2945 ■ *Web:* vac-con.com
Vaco LLC	5410 Maryland Way Ste 460	Brentwood	TN	37027	615-324-8226		721	*Web:* www.vaco.com
VAC-TRON Equipment LLC	27137 S Hwy 33	Okahumpka	FL	34762	352-728-2222	728-2827	196	*TF:* 888-822-8766 ■ *Web:* www.vactron.com
Vacudyne Inc	375 E Joe Orr Rd	Chicago Heights	IL	60411	708-757-5200	757-7180	386	*TF:* 800-459-9591 ■ *Web:* www.vacudyne.com
VAC-U-MAX	69 William St	Belleville	NJ	07109	973-759-4600		207	*TF:* 800-822-8629 ■ *Web:* www.vac-u-max.com
Vacuum Instrument Corp	2099 Ninth Ave	Ronkonkoma	NY	11779	631-737-0900		201	*Web:* www.vicleakdetection.com
Vacuum Pump Systems Inc (VPS)	PO Box 1826	Gainesville	GA	30503	770-532-0260	536-1005	385	*Web:* www.vacuumpumpsystems.net
Vacuum Technology of Tennessee Inc	1003 Alvin Weinberg Dr	Oak Ridge	TN	37830	865-481-3342		261	*Web:* vacuumtechnology.com
Vaderstad Industries Inc	PO Box 123	Langbank	SK	S0G2X0	306-538-2221		273	*TF:* 800-667-4295 ■ *Web:* www.vaderstad.com
Vadum Inc	601 Hutton St Ste 109	Raleigh	NC	27606	919-341-8241		261	*Web:* www.vaduminc.com
VAE Inc	12005 Sunrise Valley Dr Ste 202	Reston	VA	20191	703-942-6727		196	*Web:* www.vaeit.com
Vaga Industries Inc	2505 Loma Ave	South El Monte	CA	91733	626-442-7436	442-4330	454	*Web:* www.vaga.com
Vail Communication Inc	1511 Walnut Ave	Oreland	PA	19075	215-885-2952	884-4003	681	*Web:* vailcomm.com
Vail Mountain Lodge & Spa, The	352 E Meadow Dr	Vail	CO	81657	970-476-0700		707	*TF:* 888-794-0410 ■ *Web:* vailmountainlodge.com
Vail Mountain School	3000 Booth Falls Rd	Vail	CO	81657	970-476-3850	476-3860	685	*Web:* www.vms.edu
Vail Racquet Club	4695 Vail Racquet Club Dr	Vail	CO	81657	970-476-4840		706	*TF:* 800-428-4840 ■ *Web:* vailracquetclub.com
Vail Resorts Management Co	390 Interlocken Crescent Ste 1000	Broomfield	CO	80021	303-404-1800	404-6415	669	*NYSE:* MTN ■ *TF:* 800-842-8062 ■ *Web:* www.vailresorts.com
Vail Rubber Works Inc	521 Langley Ave	Saint Joseph	MI	49085	269-983-1595	983-0155	677	*TF:* 877-350-0441 ■ *Web:* www.vailrubber.com
Vail Systems Inc	570 Lake Cook Rd	Deerfield	IL	60015	312-360-8245	405-9915*	393	**Fax Area Code:* 847 ■ *TF:* 800-360-8245 ■ *Web:* www.vailsys.com
Vail Valley Jet Center LLC	871 Cooley Mesa Rd Eagle County Regional Airport	Gypsum	CO	81637	970-524-7700		63	*Web:* vvjc.com
Vail Valley Partnership	97 Main St Ste E-201	Edwards	CO	81632	970-476-1000		139	*Web:* www.visitvailvalley.com
Vaile Mansion	1500 N Liberty St	Independence	MO	64050	816-325-7430		50-3	*Web:* www.vailemansion.org
Vaisala Inc	10-D Gill St	Woburn	MA	01801	781-933-4500	933-8029	472	*TF:* 888-824-7252 ■ *Web:* www.vaisala.com
Vakifbank	1177 Avenue of Americas 36th Fl	New York	NY	10036	212-621-9400		70	*Web:* www.vakifbankusa.com
Val Surf Inc	4810 Whitsett Ave	Valley Village	CA	91607	818-769-6977		711	*Web:* valsurf.com
Val Verde County	400 Pecan St	Del Rio	TX	78840	830-774-7501	775-9406	338	*Web:* valverdecounty.texas.gov
Val Verde County Library	300 Spring St	Del Rio	TX	78840	830-774-7595	774-7607	434-3	*Web:* www.valverdecounty.texas.gov
Val Verde Unified School District	975 Morgan St	Perris	CA	92571	951-940-6100		685	*Web:* www.valverde.edu
Val's Distributing Co	6124 E 30th St N	Tulsa	OK	74115	918-835-9987	835-3808	297-5	*TF:* 800-274-9987 ■ *Web:* www.valsdistributing.com
Valancourt Books	PO Box 17642	Richmond	VA	23226	804-873-8528		637-2	*Web:* www.valancourtbooks.com
Valanni Restaurant & Lounge	1229 Spruce St	Philadelphia	PA	19107	215-790-9494		671	*Web:* valanni.com
Valarie Willis Consulting	9698 Stonemasters Dr	Loveland	OH	45140	513-677-5637	677-9945	194	*Web:* www.valariewillisconsulting.com
Valassis Communications Inc	19975 Victor Pkwy	Livonia	MI	48152	734-591-3000		627	*NYSE:* VCI ■ *TF:* 800-437-0479 ■ *Web:* www.valassis.com
Valco Data Systems Inc	N57 W13652 Reichert Ave	Menomonee Falls	WI	53051	262-781-7731		177	*Web:* valcodata.com
Valco Manufacturing Company Inc	925 Boren Rd	Duncan	OK	73533	580-255-4300		295	*Web:* www.valcomfg.com
Valco Precision Works Inc	6131 Maywood Ave	Huntington Park	CA	90255	323-582-6355	582-7786	757	*Web:* www.valcoprecision.com
Valcom Consulting Group Inc	85 Albert St	Ottawa	ON	K1P6A4	613-594-5200		194	*TF:* 866-561-5580 ■ *Web:* valcom.ca
Valcom Enterprises Inc	120 Ctr St	Wilder	KY	41071	859-655-4400	655-4420	735	*TF:* 800-463-1690 ■ *Web:* www.valcomenterprises.com
Valcom Inc	5614 Hollins Rd	Roanoke	VA	24019	540-563-2000	362-9800	735	*TF:* 800-825-2661 ■ *Web:* www.valcom.com
Val-Comm Inc (VCI)	249 Muriel St NE	Albuquerque	NM	87123	505-292-7509	299-4253	246	*Web:* www.val-comm.com
Valcor Engineering Corp	2 Lawrence Rd	Springfield	NJ	07081	973-467-8400	467-8382	789	*Web:* www.valcor.com
Valdak Corp	1149 36th Ave S	Grand Forks	ND	58201	701-746-8371	772-9464	204	*Web:* www.valleydairy.com
Valdese Weavers LLC	1000 Perkins Rd SE	Valdese	NC	28690	828-874-2181		745-1	*Web:* www.valdeseweavers.com
Valdosta Daily Times	PO Box 968	Valdosta	GA	31603	229-244-1880	244-2560	532-2	*TF:* 800-600-4838 ■ *Web:* www.valdostadailytimes.com
Valdosta State Prison	3259 Valtech Rd	Valdosta	GA	31601	229-333-7900	333-5387	213	*Web:* www.dcor.state.ga.us
Valdosta State University	1500 N Patterson St	Valdosta	GA	31698	229-333-5800	333-5482	166	*TF:* 800-618-1878 ■ *Web:* www.valdosta.edu
Valdosta-Lowndes County Chamber of Commerce	416 N Ashley St	Valdosta	GA	31601	229-247-8100	245-0071	139	*Web:* www.valdostachamber.com
Vale	200 Bay St Ste 1600	Toronto	ON	M5J2K2	416-361-7511		502	*Web:* www.vale.com
Valence Operating Co	1 Kingwood Pl 600 Rockmead Dr Ste 200	Kingwood	TX	77339	281-359-3659	358-5333	536	*Web:* www.valenceoperating.com
Valence Surface Technologies	7061 Patterson Dr	Garden Grove	CA	92841	714-895-9099		481	*TF:* 888-540-0878 ■ *Web:* valencesurfacetech.com
Valence Surface Technologies	128 W 154th St	Gardena	CA	90248	323-770-0240		481	*Web:* www.valencesurfacetech.com
Valence Technology Inc	1807 W Braker Ln Ste 500	Austin	TX	78758	512-527-2900	527-2910	74	*TF:* 888-825-3623 ■ *Web:* www.lithiumwerks.com
Valencia College	PO Box 3028	Orlando	FL	32802	407-299-5000		162	*TF:* 800-590-3428 ■ *Web:* valenciacollege.edu
Valencia County	444 Luna Ave	Los Lunas	NM	87031	505-866-2432		338	*Web:* www.co.valencia.nm.us
Valensi Rose PLC	1888 Century Pk E Ste 1100	Los Angeles	CA	90067	310-277-8011	277-1706	428	*Web:* www.vrmlaw.com
Valente Builders Inc	1075 Dix Ave	Hudson Falls	NY	12839	518-746-9040	746-9290	189-11	*Web:* www.valentebuildersinc.com
Valentine Enterprises Inc	1291 Progress Center Ave	Lawrenceville	GA	30043	770-995-0661	995-0725	296-10	*Web:* www.veiusa.com
Valentine Research Inc	10280 Alliance Rd	Blue Ash	OH	45242	513-984-8900	984-8976	529	*TF:* 800-331-3030 ■ *Web:* www.valentine1.com
Valentine Theatre, The	410 Adams St	Toledo	OH	43604	419-242-3490	242-2791	572	*Web:* www.valentinetheatre.com
Valentine's Diamond Center Inc	350 Boston Post Rd	Milford	CT	06460	203-877-3351	878-5190	410	*Web:* valentinesdiamondcenter.com
Valentine, The	1015 E Clay St	Richmond	VA	23219	804-649-0711	643-3510	520	*Web:* thevalentine.org
Valentino's of America	2601 S 70th St	Lincoln	NE	68506	402-434-9350		670	*Web:* valentinos.com
Valentino's Ristorante	1907 W End Ave	Nashville	TN	37203	615-327-0148		671	*Web:* www.valentinosnashville.com
Valeo Behavioral Health Care Inc	5401 SW Seventh St	Topeka	KS	66606	785-233-1730		353	*Web:* www.valeotopeka.org
Valeo Pharma Inc	16667 Hymus Blvd	Kirkland	QC	H9H4R9	514-694-0150		231	*TF:* 888-694-0865 ■ *Web:* www.valeopharma.com
Valerie Wilson Travel Inc	475 Park Ave S	New York	NY	10016	212-532-3400	779-7073	771	*TF:* 800-776-1116 ■ *Web:* www.valeriewilsontravel.com
Valero LP	1 Valero Way	San Antonio	TX	78249	210-345-2000		597	*TF:* 800-333-3377 ■ *Web:* www.valero.com
Vales Consulting Group LLC	125 Wappanocca Ave	Rye	NY	10580	914-967-3200		196	*Web:* www.valesconsulting.com
Valesco Industries Inc	325 N Saint Paul St Ste 3700	Dallas	TX	75201	214-880-8690	880-8646	196	*Web:* www.valescoind.com
Valet Park of America	185 Spring St	Springfield	MA	01105	413-827-8916		562	*Web:* www.valetparkofamerica.com
Valet Parking Service	1335 S Flower St	Los Angeles	CA	90015	213-342-3388	222-0981	562	*TF:* 800-794-7275 ■ *Web:* www.valetparkingservice.com
Valeura Energy Inc	Bow Valley Sq 1 202 6 Ave SW Ste 1200	Calgary	AB	T2P2R9	403-237-7102		536	*Web:* www.valeuraenergy.com
Valex Corp	6080 Leland St	Ventura	CA	93003	805-658-0944		246	*Web:* www.valex.com

Phone | Fax | Class

Valhalla Partners
8000 Towers Crescent Dr Ste 1050 Vienna VA 22182 703-448-1400 792
Web: www.valhallapartners.com

Valhi Inc 5430 LBJ Fwy Ste 1700 Dallas TX 75240 972-233-1700 448-1445 185
NYSE: VHI ■ *Web:* www.valhi.net

Valiant Enterprise LLC
8750 N Central Expy Ste 1010 Plano TX 75025 972-390-7410 100
Web: www.valiantresidential.com

Valiant Products Corp 2727 Fifth Ave W Denver CO 80204 303-892-1234 442
TF: 800-347-2727 ■ *Web:* www.valiantproducts.com

Valiant Solutions Inc
110 Crossways Pk Dr Woodbury NY 11797 516-390-1100 178-1
Web: www.valiant.com

Valiant Steel & Equipment Inc
2700 Mechanicsville Rd Peachtree Corners GA 30071 770-417-1235 417-1669 492
TF: 800-939-9905 ■ *Web:* www.valiantsteel.com

Valiant TMs 6555 Hawthorne Dr Windsor ON N8T3G6 519-974-5200 944-6622 539
TF: 888-497-5537 ■ *Web:* www.valianttms.com

Valiant Yachts
500 Harbour View Rd Gordonville TX 76245 903-523-4899 523-4077 90
Web: www.valiantsailboats.com

VALIC (Variable Annuity Life Insurance Co)
2929 Allen Pkwy Houston TX 77019 800-448-2542 391-2
TF: 800-448-2542 ■ *Web:* www.valic.com

Valicom Corp
2923 Marketplace Dr Ste 104 Madison WI 53719 608-274-3515 196
TF: 800-467-7226 ■ *Web:* www.valicomcorp.com

Valid8 com Inc
500 W Cummings Pk Ste 6550 Woburn MA 01801 781-938-1221 177
TF: 855-482-5438 ■ *Web:* valid8.com

Validar Inc 800 Maynard Ave S Ste 401 Seattle WA 98134 206-264-9151 178-1
TF: 888-784-2929 ■ *Web:* www.validar.com

Validata Computer & Research Corp
PO Box 4774 Montgomery AL 36103 334-834-2324 262-5648 180
Web: www.validata.com

Validation Systems Inc
988 San Antonio Rd Palo Alto CA 94303 650-856-4874 194
Web: www.validationsystems.com

Valient Market Research Inc PO Box 335 Exton PA 19341 844-332-7082 466
TF: 844-332-7082 ■ *Web:* valientmarketresearch.com

Valimet Inc
431 Sperry Rd PO Box 31690 Stockton CA 95206 209-444-1600 444-1636 485
Web: valimet.com

Valin Corp 555 E California Ave Sunnyvale CA 94086 408-730-9850 730-1363 358
TF: 800-774-5630 ■ *Web:* www.valin.com

Valintry 1201 Orlando Ave Ste 440 Winter Park FL 32789 407-205-1120 49-4
Web: valintry.com

Valk Industries Inc 50 Valk Ln Greeneville TN 37744 423-638-1284 638-6779 393
Web: www.valkindustries.com

Vallata 2190 Goldstream Rd Fairbanks AK 99709 907-455-6600 671

Valle Cucina Italiana
4752 Limestone Rd Wilmington DE 19808 302-998-9999 671
Web: vallecucina.com

Vallejo Chamber of Commerce
425 A Virginia St Vallejo CA 94590 707-644-5551 139
Web: www.vallejochamber.com

Vallejo Convention & Visitors Bureau
289 Mare Island Way Vallejo CA 94590 707-642-3653 644-2206 206
TF: 866-921-9277 ■ *Web:* www.visitvallejo.com

Vallejo Sanitation & Flood Control District Finance
450 Ryder St Vallejo CA 94590 707-644-8949 804
Web: www.vallejowastewater.org

Vallejo Times Herald
420 Virginia St Ste 2A Vallejo CA 94590 707-644-1141 532-2
TF: 800-600-1141 ■ *Web:* www.timesheraldonline.com

Valley Agricultural Software Inc
3950 S K St Tulare CA 93274 559-686-9496 177
Web: web.vas.com

Valley Bank of Helena
3030 N Montana Ave Helena MT 59601 406-495-2400 70
TF: 844-857-2440 ■ *Web:* www.valleybankhelena.com

Valley Baptist Medical Center Brownsville
1040 W Jefferson St Brownsville TX 78520 956-698-5400 374-3
Web: www.valleybaptist.net

Valley Barber & Beauty LLC
413 W Harrison Ave Harlingen TX 78550 956-423-0727 76

Valley Blox Inc
210 Stone Spring Rd Harrisonburg VA 22801 540-434-6725 183
TF: 800-648-6725 ■ *Web:* valleybuildingsupply.com

Valley Books PO Box 2127 Amherst MA 01004 413-256-1508 95
Web: www.valleybooks.com

Valley Builders LLC
775 Furnace St PO Box 189 Emmaus PA 18049 610-966-0687 116
Web: valleybldrs.com

Valley Business Machines
5825 Mayflower Ct Wasilla AK 99654 907-376-5077 376-1187 535
Web: www.vbmalaska.com

Valley Cabinet 845 Prosper Rd De Pere WI 54115 920-336-3174 336-5956 115
Web: www.valleycabinetinc.com

Valley Center-Pauma Unified School District
28751 Cole Grade Rd Valley Center CA 92082 760-749-0464 749-1208 685
Web: www.vcpusd.net

Valley Chevrolet Inc
601 Kidder St Wilkes-Barre PA 18702 570-821-2772 516
TF: 877-207-9214 ■ *Web:* www.valleychevrolet.com

Valley Children's Healthcare
9300 Valley Children's Pl Madera CA 93636 559-353-3000 353-8888 374-1
Web: www.valleychildrens.org

Valley City Manufacturing Company Ltd, The
64 Hatt St Dundas ON L9H2G3 905-628-2253 628-0753 319-3
Web: www.valleycity.com

Valley City Plating Co
3353 E Ave SE Grand Rapids MI 49508 616-245-1223 245-7414 481
Web: valleycityplating.com

Valley City State University
101 College St SW Valley City ND 58072 701-845-7990 845-7299 166
TF: 800-532-8641 ■ *Web:* www.vcsu.edu

Valley College
120 New River Town Ctr Ste C Beckley WV 25801 304-252-9547 167-3
Web: www.valley.edu

Valley College of Medical Careers
8399 Topanga Canyon Blvd Ste 200 West Hills CA 91304 818-883-9002 167-3
Web: www.vcmc.edu

Valley Construction Co
3610 - 78th Ave W Rock Island IL 61201 309-787-0292 787-7048 186
Web: www.valleyconstruction.com

Valley Cottage Animal Hospital Inc
202 Rt 303 Valley Cottage NY 10989 845-268-9263 268-0516 794
Web: valleycottageanimalhospital.com

Valley County 219 N Main St Cascade ID 83611 208-382-7150 382-7107 338
Web: www.co.valley.id.us

Valley County 125 S 15th St Ord NE 68862 308-728-3700 728-7725 338
Web: www.co.valley.ne.us

Valley Craft 2001 S Hwy 61 Lake City MN 55041 651-345-3386 345-6535 470
Web: www.valleycraft.com

Valley Dairy 1562 Mission Rd Latrobe PA 15650 724-537-7111 537-7249 670
Web: www.valleydairy.net

Valley Decorating Co
2829 E Hamilton Ave Fresno CA 93721 559-495-1100 600
Web: www.pomponcentral.com

Valley Del Publications Inc
893 S Matlack St Ste 150 West Chester PA 19382 610-918-9300 918-1640 637-9
Web: valleydel.wordpress.com

Valley Electric Association Inc
800 E Hwy 372 PO Box 237 Pahrump NV 89048 775-727-5312 245
TF: 800-742-3330 ■ *Web:* www.vea.coop

Valley Electric Supply Corp
1361 N State Rd 67 Vincennes IN 47591 812-882-7860 882-7893 246
TF: 800-825-7877 ■ *Web:* www.vesupply.com

Valley Endodontics Ltd
1100 N Lynndale Dr Appleton WI 54914 920-731-4484 731-2889 363
Web: www.valleyendo.com

Valley Equine Associates PLLC
515 Finish Line Ave Ranson WV 25438 304-725-1471 794
Web: www.valleyequine.net

Valley Equipment Co
3903 W Market St Johnson City TN 37604 423-753-3541 753-3589 385
TF: 800-832-3541 ■ *Web:* www.valleyequipment.com

Valley Express LLC 6003 State Rd 76 Oshkosh WI 54904 920-231-1677 311
TF: 800-594-4744 ■ *Web:* valleyexpress.net

Valley Fair Mall
3601 S 2700 W West Valley City UT 84119 801-969-6211 460
Web: www.shopvalleyfairmall.com

Valley Farms LLC 1860 E Third St Williamsport PA 17701 570-326-2021 326-2736 296-27
Web: www.valleyfarmsdairy.com

Valley Federal Credit Union
183 E Price Rd Brownsville TX 78521 956-546-3108 544-5404 219
Web: vfcu.net

Valley Fertilizer & Chemical Company Inc, The
201 Valley Rd PO Box 816 Mount Jackson VA 22842 540-477-3121 477-3123 280
Web: www.valleyfertilizer.net

Valley Fig Growers 2028 S Third St Fresno CA 93702 559-237-3893 237-3898 315-4
Web: valleyfig.com

Valley Financial Solutions Inc
2847 Penn Forest Blvd Ste 100 Roanoke VA 24018 540-777-4302 401
Web: www.valleyfinancialsolutions.com

Valley Fine Foods 3909 Park Rd Benicia CA 94510 707-746-6888 297-8
Web: valleyfine.com

Valley First Credit Union PO Box 1411 Modesto CA 95353 209-549-8500 219
TF: 877-549-4567 ■ *Web:* www.valleyfirstcu.org

Valley Flowers Inc
3675 Foothill Rd Carpinteria CA 93013 805-684-6651 292
TF: 800-549-5500 ■ *Web:* valleyflowers.com

Valley Forge Christian College
1401 Charlestown Rd Phoenixville PA 19460 610-935-0450 917-2069 166
TF: 800-432-8322 ■ *Web:* www.valleyforge.edu

Valley Forge Convention & Visitors Bureau
1000 First Ave Ste 101 King of Prussia PA 19406 610-834-1550 834-0202 206
Web: www.valleyforge.org

Valley Forge Convention Ctr
1160 1st Ave King of Prussia PA 19406 610-354-8118 205
Web: www.vfcasino.com

Valley Forge Fabrics Inc
2981 Gateway Dr Pompano Beach FL 33069 954-971-1776 594
Web: www.valleyforge.com

Valley Forge Medical Center & Hospital
1033 W Germantown Pk Norristown PA 19403 610-539-8500 539-0910 726
TF: 888-539-8500 ■ *Web:* www.vfmc.net

Valley Forge Military Academy & College
1001 Eagle Rd Wayne PA 19087 610-989-1300 688-1545 162
TF: 800-234-8362 ■ *Web:* vfmac.edu

Valley Forge National Historical Park
1400 N Outer Line Dr King of Prussia PA 19406 610-783-1077 564
Web: www.nps.gov

Valley Fresh Inc 3600 E Linwood Ave Turlock CA 95380 209-669-5600 619
Web: www.vffi.com

Valley Grinding & Manufacturing Inc
1717 Hamilton Ct Little Chute WI 54140 920-788-9131 493
TF: 800-950-7675 ■ *Web:* www.valleygrinding.com

Valley Health System
223 N Van Dien Ave Ridgewood NJ 07450 201-447-8000 374-3
TF: 800-825-5391 ■ *Web:* www.valleyhealth.com

Valley Healthcare Systems Inc
1600 Fort Benning Rd Columbus GA 31903 706-322-9599 352
Web: www.valleyhealthcolumbus.com

Valley Hospice Inc
380 Summit Ave Steubenville OH 43952 740-859-5660 284-4478 371
TF: 877-467-7423 ■ *Web:* www.valleyhospice.org

Valley Hospital Medical Ctr
620 Shadow Ln Las Vegas NV 89106 702-388-4000 374-3
Web: www.valleyhospital.net

Valley House Gallery Inc
6616 Spring Valley Rd Dallas TX 75254 972-239-2441 239-1462 42
Web: www.valleyhouse.com

Name	Address	City	State	Zip	Phone	Fax	Class	Other
Valley Industrial Trucks Inc	1152 Meadowbrook Ave	Youngstown	OH	44512	800-592-5275		23	*TF:* 800-592-5275 ■ *Web:* www.valleyindustrialtrucks.com
Valley International Airport	3002 Heritage Way	Harlingen	TX	78550	956-430-8600		63	*Web:* www.flythevalley.com
Valley Internet Inc	102 Maple St E	Fayetteville	TN	37334	931-433-1921	221-0119*	41	**Fax Area Code:* 615 ■ *TF:* 888-433-1924 ■ *Web:* vallnet.com
Valley Isle Community Federal Credit Union	160 Paahana St	Kahului	HI	96732	808-877-3232		219	*Web:* vicfcu.org
Valley Joist	2350 Jordan Rd SW	Fort Payne	AL	35967	256-845-2330	845-2597	697	*Web:* valleyjoist.com
Valley Litho Supply Inc	1047 Haugen Ave	Rice Lake	WI	54868	800-826-6781		358	*TF:* 800-826-6781 ■ *Web:* valleylithosupply.com
Valley Machining Co	1250 22nd Ave	Rock Valley	IA	51247	712-476-2828		454	*Web:* www.valleymachining.com
Valley Mechanical Inc	608 Salem Rd	Rossville	GA	30741	706-866-8812		697	*Web:* www.valleymech.com
Valley Medical Ctr	400 S 43rd St	Renton	WA	98055	425-228-3450	656-5552	374-3	*Web:* www.valleymed.org
Valley Mine Service Inc	110 Powell Valley Schl Rd	Speedwell	TN	37870	423-869-3155	869-5018	650	*Web:* www.valleymineservice.com
Valley Mirror	3910 Main St	Munhall	PA	15120	412-462-0626		532-2	
Valley Morning Star	1310 S Commerce	Harlingen	TX	78550	956-430-6200		532-2	*Web:* www.valleymorningstar.com
Valley National Bank	370 Pascack Rd	Washington Township	NJ	07676	201-664-5400	497-1223	70	*NASDAQ: ORIT* ■ *TF:* 888-674-8264 ■ *Web:* www.valley.com
Valley National Bank	615 Main Ave	Passaic	NJ	07055	973-777-6768		70	*TF:* 800-522-4100 ■ *Web:* www.valley.com
Valley Natural Foods	13750 County Rd 11	Burnsville	MN	55337	952-891-1212		297-8	*Web:* www.valleynaturalfoods.com
Valley News	24 Interchange Dr	West Lebanon	NH	03784	603-298-8711	298-0212	532-2	*TF:* 800-874-2226 ■ *Web:* www.vnews.com
Valley News Co	1305 Stadium Rd	Mankato	MN	56001	507-345-4819		96	*Web:* valleynewscompany.com
Valley Nursing Ctr	581 NC Hwy 16 S	Taylorsville	NC	28681	828-632-8146		450	*Web:* valleyrehab.com
Valley of the Sun United Way	1515 E Osborn Rd	Phoenix	AZ	85014	602-631-4800	631-4809	48-21	*Web:* vsuw.org
Valley Office Systems	2050 First St	Idaho Falls	ID	83401	208-529-2777		179	*TF:* 800-610-2865 ■ *Web:* www.valleyofficesystems.com
Valley Offset Printing Inc	160 S Sheridan Ave	Valley Center	KS	67147	316-755-0061		627	*TF:* 888-895-7913 ■ *Web:* valleyoffset.com
Valley Packaging Industries Inc	110 N Kensington Dr	Appleton	WI	54915	920-749-5840		88	*Web:* www.vpind.com
Valley PBS	1544 Van Ness Ave	Fresno	CA	93721	559-266-1800	650-1880	741-52	*TF:* 800-801-6500 ■ *Web:* valleypbs.org
Valley Plaza Mall	2701 Ming Ave	Bakersfield	CA	93304	661-832-2436		460	*Web:* www.valleyplazamall.com
Valley Power Systems Inc	425 S Hacienda Blvd	City of Industry	CA	91745	626-333-1243	369-7096	770	*TF:* 800-924-4265 ■ *Web:* www.valleypowersystems.com
Valley Presbyterian Hospital	15107 Vanowen St	Van Nuys	CA	91405	818-782-6600		374-3	*TF:* 877-237-9522 ■ *Web:* www.valleypres.org
Valley Printing Company Inc	3919 Vanderbilt Rd	Birmingham	AL	35217	205-841-2746	841-5747	627	*Web:* www.valleyprinting.net
Valley Processing Inc	108 E Blaine Ave PO Box 246	Sunnyside	WA	98944	509-837-8084	837-3481	296-20	*Web:* valleyprocessing.com
Valley Proteins Inc	151 Valpro Dr	Winchester	VA	22603	540-877-2590	877-3215	447	*TF:* 800-871-3406 ■ *Web:* www.valleyproteins.com
Valley Queen Cheese Factory Inc	200 E Railway Ave	Milbank	SD	57252	605-432-4563	432-9383	296-5	*Web:* www.valleyqueen.com
Valley Regional Hospital	150 Exhibition St	Kentville	NS	B4N5E3	902-678-7381		374-2	*Web:* www.avdha.nshealth.ca
Valley Regional Medical Ctr	100-A E Alton Gloor Blvd	Brownsville	TX	78526	956-350-7000		374-3	*TF:* 844-422-5627 ■ *Web:* valleyregionalmedicalcenter.com
Valley Republic Bank	5000 California Ave Ste 110	Bakersfield	CA	93309	661-371-2000		70	*Web:* www.valleyrepublic.bank
Valley River Ctr	293 Valley River Ctr	Eugene	OR	97401	541-683-5513		460	*Web:* www.valleyrivercenter.com
Valley River Inn	1000 Vly River Way	Eugene	OR	97401	541-743-1000	683-5121	379	*TF:* 800-543-8266 ■ *Web:* www.valleyriverinn.com
Valley Rural Electric Co-opeartive Inc	10700 Fairgrounds Rd PO Box 477	Huntingdon	PA	16652	814-643-2650	643-1678	245	*TF:* 800-432-0680 ■ *Web:* www.valleyrec.com
Valley Small Business Development	7035 N Fruit Ave	Fresno	CA	93711	559-438-9680	438-9690	463	*Web:* www.vsbdc.com
Valley State Prison	21633 Ave 24 PO Box 99	Chowchilla	CA	93610	559-665-6100		213	*Web:* cdcr.ca.gov
Valley Stream State Park	PO Box 670	Valley Stream	NY	11580	516-825-4128		565	*Web:* parks.ny.gov
Valley Strong Credit Union	PO Box 9506	Bakersfield	CA	93389	661-833-7900		219	*TF:* 800-221-3311 ■ *Web:* www.valleystrong.com
Valley Supply & Equipment Company Inc	1109 Middle River Rd	Baltimore	MD	21220	888-890-8165		23	*TF:* 800-633-5077 ■ *Web:* valleysupplyequipment.com
Valley Techlogic Inc	261 Business Park Way	Atwater	CA	95301	209-357-3121		225	*Web:* www.valleytechlogic.com
Valley Telephone Co-opeartive Inc	752 E Maley St	Willcox	AZ	85643	520-384-2231		736	*TF:* 800-421-5711 ■ *Web:* www.vtc.net
Valley Tire Company Inc	1002 Arentzen Blvd	Charleroi	PA	15022	724-662-1597		754	*Web:* valleytireco.com
Valley Title Guarantee Incorporated of Yakima	502 N Second St	Yakima	WA	98901	509-248-4442		652	*Web:* vtgco.com
Valley Tool & Die Inc	10020 York Theta Dr	North Royalton	OH	44133	440-237-0160		697	*Web:* www.valcocleve.com
Valley Tool & Manufacturing Inc	22 Prindle Hill Rd	Orange	CT	06477	203-799-8800	795-7564	22	*Web:* www.valleytl.com
Valley Town Crier	1811 N 23rd St	McAllen	TX	78501	956-682-2423		532-4	*Web:* www.yourvalleyvoice.com
Valley Tribune	PO Box 478	Quitaque	TX	79255	806-455-1101		532-2	*Web:* www.thevalleytribune.com.html
Valley Truck & Tractor Company Inc	793 N First St	Dixon	CA	95620	707-678-2395		274	*Web:* www.valleytruckandtractor.com
Valley Truck Parts Inc	1900 Chicago Dr	Grand Rapids	MI	49519	616-241-5431		779	*TF:* 800-783-8300 ■ *Web:* www.valleytruckparts.com
Valley Vet Supply	1118 Pony Express Hwy	Marysville	KS	66508	785-562-2484		76	*Web:* www.valleyvet.com
Valley View Casino Ctr	3500 Sports Arena Blvd	San Diego	CA	92110	619-224-4171	224-3010	720	*Web:* pechangaarenasd.com
Valley View Center Mall	13331 Preston Rd	Dallas	TX	75240	972-661-2939	239-1344	460	*Web:* www.shopvalleyviewcenter.com
Valley View Foods Inc	7547 Sawtelle Ave	Yuba City	CA	95991	530-673-7356	673-9432	315-3	*Web:* www.valleyviewfoods.com
Valley View Mall	4802 Vly View Blvd	Roanoke	VA	24012	540-563-4440		460	*Web:* www.valleyviewmall.com
Valley Yellow Pages	1850 N Gateway Blvd	Fresno	CA	93727	800-350-8887	253-9729*	637-6	**Fax Area Code:* 559 ■ *TF:* 800-350-8887 ■ *Web:* www.myyp.com
Valleyfair	1 Valleyfair Dr	Shakopee	MN	55379	952-445-7600	445-1539	32	*Web:* www.valleyfair.com
Valli Information Systems Inc	915 Main St	Caldwell	ID	83605	208-459-3611	459-3680	180	*Web:* www.valli.com
Vallorbs Jewel Co	2599 Old Philadelphia Pke	Bird in Hand	PA	17505	717-392-3978	392-8947	621	*Web:* www.vallorbs.com
Valmarc Corp	109 Highland Ave	Needham	MA	02494	339-225-4544		387	*Web:* vi3global.com
Valmark Industries Inc	7900 National Dr	Livermore	CA	94550	925-960-9900	960-0900	413	*Web:* nidec-vis.com
Val-Matic Valve & Manufacturing Corp	905 Riverside Dr	Elmhurst	IL	60126	630-941-7600		789	*Web:* www.valmatic.com
Valmont Industries Inc	1 Valmont Plz	Omaha	NE	68154	402-963-1000		273	*NYSE: VMI* ■ *TF:* 800-825-6668 ■ *Web:* www.valmont.com
Valogix Inc	27 Division St Ste 2	Saratoga Springs	NY	12866	518-450-0309		177	*Web:* valogix.com
Valor Brands LLC	960 N Point Pkwy Ste 100	Alpharetta	GA	30005	770-346-9250		157-1	*Web:* www.valorbrands.com
Valor Oil	1200 Alsop Ln	Owensboro	KY	42303	844-468-2567		579	*TF:* 844-468-2567 ■ *Web:* www.valoroil.com
Valor System	249 Main st	Belleville	MI	48111	734-325-6060	328-6039	529	*TF:* 866-941-6483 ■ *Web:* www.valorsystem.com
Valpac Inc	1400 Industrial Park Rd	Federalsburg	MD	21632	410-754-7390		3	*Web:* valpac.com
Valpak Direct Marketing Systems Inc	8605 Largo Lakes Dr	Largo	FL	33773	727-393-1270	392-0049	5	*Web:* www.valpak.com
Valparaiso Public Library	103 Jefferson St	Valparaiso	IN	46383	219-462-0524		434-3	*Web:* pcpls.org
Valparaiso University	1700 Chapel Dr	Valparaiso	IN	46383	219-464-5011	464-6898	166	*TF:* 888-468-2576 ■ *Web:* www.valpo.edu
Valrico Animal Clinic	2914 Lithia Pinecrest Rd	Valrico	FL	33596	813-681-6389		794	*Web:* valrico-animal-clinic.com
Vals Plumbing & Heating Inc	413 Front St	Salinas	CA	93901	831-424-1633	754-5514	189-10	*Web:* valsplumbing.com
Valsamis Inc	5814 Northdale St	Houston	TX	77087	713-640-1500		261	*Web:* valsamis.com
Valsource Inc	918A Horseshoe Pk	Downingtown	PA	19335	610-269-2808	269-4069	416	*Web:* valsource.com
Valspar Refinish Inc	210 Crosby St	Picayune	MS	39466	601-798-4731		550	*TF:* 800-845-2871 ■ *Web:* www.valsparrefinish.com
Valterra Products Inc	15230 San Fernando Mission Blvd Ste 107	Mission Hills	CA	91345	818-898-1671	361-5389	791	*Web:* www.valterra.com
Valtim Inc	1095 Venture Dr	Forest	VA	24551	434-525-3004		463	*TF:* 800-230-2857 ■ *Web:* valtim.com
Valtra Inc	8750 Pioneer Blvd	Santa Fe Springs	CA	90670	562-949-8625		385	*TF:* 800-989-5244 ■ *Web:* www.valtrainc.com
Valu Home Centers	45 S Rossler Ave	Buffalo	NY	14206	716-824-4150		35	*Web:* valuhomecenters.com

Name / Address	City	State	Zip	Phone	Fax	Class
Valuation Advisory Group Inc, The 445 Pharr Rd NE; *Web:* www.valuationadvisory.com	Atlanta	GA	30305	404-841-0992		734
Valuation Consultants Inc 6 Front St; *Web:* vciny.com	Newburgh	NY	12550	845-568-0600		653
Valuation Management Group LLC 1640 Powers Ferry Rd SE Bldg 15 Ste 100; *TF:* 866-799-7488 ■ *Web:* valuationmanagementgroup.com	Marietta	GA	30067	678-483-4420		652
Value Added Products Coop 2101 College Blvd; *Web:* www.vapcoop.com	Alva	OK	73717	580-327-0400		345
Value City Furniture 40 E 53rd St; *TF:* 855-578-5200 ■ *Web:* www.valuecitynj.com	Bayonne	NJ	07002	201-436-2000		321
Value City Furniture 4300 E Fifth Ave; *TF:* 888-672-2411 ■ *Web:* www.valuecityfurniture.com	Columbus	OH	43219	888-672-2411		321
Value Consulting LLC 23475 Rock Haven Way Ste 200; *Web:* www.valconusa.com	Sterling	VA	20166	703-723-0100		196
Value Creation Inc 1100 635 - Eighth Ave SW; *TF:* 855-908-8800 ■ *Web:* www.vctek.com	Calgary	AB	T2P3M3	403-539-4500		536
Value Drug Co 195 Theater Dr; *TF:* 800-252-3786 ■ *Web:* www.valuedrugco.com	Duncansville	PA	16635	800-252-3786		238
Value Drug Mart Associates Ltd 16504 - 121A Ave; *TF:* 888-554-8258 ■ *Web:* www.valuedrugmart.com	Edmonton	AB	T5V1J9	780-453-1701		238
Value Line Asset Management 551 Fifth Ave 3rd Fl; *TF:* 800-634-3583 ■ *Web:* www.valueline.com	New York	NY	10176	212-907-1500		401
Value Payment Systems LLC 2207 Crestmoor Rd Ste 200; *TF:* 888-877-0450 ■ *Web:* www.valuepaymentsystems.com	Nashville	TN	37215	888-877-0450		251
ValueCheck Inc 8822 Ridgeline Blvd Ste 100; *Web:* www.valuecheckonline.com	Highlands Ranch	CO	80129	720-283-0737		177
ValueMomentum Inc 220 Old New Brunswick Rd Ste 100; *Web:* www.valuemomentum.com	Piscataway	NJ	08854	908-941-1140		180
Valueoptions of California Inc Grievance Unit; *TF:* 800-228-1286 ■ *Web:* valueoptions.com	Cypress	CA	90630	800-228-1286		390
ValuSource LLC 4575 Galley Rd Ste 200E; *TF:* 800-825-8763 ■ *Web:* www.valusource.com	Colorado Springs	CO	80915	719-548-4900		177
Valutrac Software Inc 3131 Cross Timbers Rd Ste 100; *Web:* valutracsoftware.com	Flower Mound	TX	75028	972-996-3204		225
Valve Corp 10900 NE Fourth St Ste 500; *Web:* www.valvesoftware.com	Bellevue	WA	98004	425-450-4464	827-4843	174
Valve Manufacturers Association of America (VMA) 1050 17th St NW Ste 280; *Web:* www.vma.org	Washington	DC	20036	202-331-8105	296-0378	49-13
Valvoline LLC 100 Valvoline Way; *TF:* 800-832-6825 ■ *Web:* www.valvoline.com	Lexington	KY	40509	859-357-7777		541
Valvtechnologies Inc 5904 Bingle Rd; *Web:* www.valv.com	Houston	TX	77092	713-860-0400		789
Vam USA LLC 19210 E Hardy Rd; **Fax Area Code:* 281 ■ *TF:* 888-863-5204 ■ *Web:* www.vam-usa.com	Houston	TX	77073	713-479-3200	821-7760*	539
Vamac Inc 4201 Jacque St; *Web:* www.vamac.com	Richmond	VA	23230	804-353-7811	358-7855	612
Vamco Intl 555 Epsilon Dr; *Web:* www.vamcointernational.com	Pittsburgh	PA	15238	412-963-7100	963-7160	456
Van Aartrijk Group Inc, The 7411 Alban Sta Ct Ste B265; *Web:* www.aartrijk.com	Springfield	VA	22150	703-912-7970		636
Van Air Systems Inc 2950 Mechanic St; *TF:* 800-840-9906 ■ *Web:* www.vanairsystems.com	Lake City	PA	16423	814-774-2631	774-3482	386
Van Alen Institute 30 W 22nd St; *Web:* www.vanalen.org	New York	NY	10010	212-924-7000		533
Van Alstyne Leader 278 N Dallas; *Web:* www.vanalstyneleader.com	Van Alstyne	TX	75495	903-482-5253	482-5656	532-2
Van Am Tool & Engineering Inc 5025 Easton Rd; *Web:* www.vanam-tool.com	Saint Joseph	MO	64507	816-233-6622		454
Van Andel Institute 333 Bostwick Ave NE; *Web:* www.vai.org	Grand Rapids	MI	49503	616-234-5000	234-5001	305
Van Auken Express Inc 1485 Red Mill Rd; *TF:* 800-342-3420 ■ *Web:* www.vanaukenexpress.com	Greenville	NY	12083	518-966-4499	966-4149	780
Van Ausdall & Farrar Inc 6430 E 75th St; *TF:* 800-467-7474 ■ *Web:* www.vanausdall.com	Indianapolis	IN	46250	317-634-2913	638-1843	534
Van Beek & Company LLC 16045 SW Lower Boones Ferry Rd; *Web:* vanbeekco.com	Tigard	OR	97224	503-639-4700	639-4747	2
Van Belle Nursery Inc 34825 Hallert Rd; *Web:* vanbelle.com	Abbotsford	BC	V3G1R3	604-853-3415		292
Van Bergen & Greener Inc 1818 Madison St; *TF:* 800-621-3889 ■ *Web:* www.starterdrives.com	Maywood	IL	60153	708-343-4700	343-9425	247
Van Blarcom Closures Inc 156 Sanford St; **Fax Area Code:* 718 ■ *TF:* 800-875-3810 ■ *Web:* vbcpkg.com	Brooklyn	NY	11205	800-875-3810	935-9855*	154
Van Bortel Aircraft Inc 4912 S Collins; *TF:* 800-759-4295 ■ *Web:* www.vanbortel.com	Arlington	TX	76018	817-468-7788	468-7886	770
Van Bortel Subaru 6327 Rt 96; *TF:* 888-902-7961 ■ *Web:* www.vanbortelsubaru.net	Victor	NY	14564	585-924-5230		57
Van Boxtel Rv & Auto LLC 1956 Bond St; *Web:* www.vanboxtelrv.com	Green Bay	WI	54303	920-497-3072		57
Van Buren County PO Box 475; *Web:* vanburencoia.org	Keosauqua	IA	52565	319-293-3129	293-6404	338
Van Buren County 219 E Paw Paw St Ste 303; *Web:* www.vbco.org	Paw Paw	MI	49079	269-657-8200	657-8298	338
Van Buren County Democrat 197 Court St; *Web:* www.vanburencountydem.com	Clinton	AR	72031	501-745-5175		532-2
Van Buren Financial Group LLC 615 W 18th St; *Web:* vanburenfinancial.com	Wilmington	DE	19802	302-655-9505		734
Van Buren Public Schools (VBPS) 555 W Columbia Ave; *Web:* www.vanburenschools.net	Belleville	MI	48111	734-697-9123	697-6385	685
Van Buren Trail State Park 23960 Ruggles Rd; *Web:* www.michigan.org	South Haven	MI	49090	269-637-2788		565
Van C. Travis, III 1978 Monroe Ave; *Web:* vantravis.com	Rochester	NY	14618	585-461-5240		390
Van Cleef & Arpels Inc 744 Fifth Ave; *TF:* 877-826-2533 ■ *Web:* www.vancleefarpels.com	New York	NY	10019	212-896-9284	265-0036	410
Van Dam Inc 121 W 27 St The VanDam Bldg; *TF:* 800-863-6537 ■ *Web:* vandam.com	New York	NY	10011	212-929-0416	929-0426	637-6
Van Dam Machine Corp 4 Edison Pl; *Web:* www.vandammachine.com	Fairfield	NJ	07004	973-257-7050		386
Van De Pol Enterprises Inc 4895 S Airport Way; *TF:* 800-379-0306 ■ *Web:* vandepol.us	Stockton	CA	95206	209-465-3421		324
Van Der Hout Brigagliano & Nightingale LLP 180 Sutter St Ste 500; *Web:* www.vblaw.com	San Francisco	CA	94104	415-981-3000	981-3003	428
Van Dermyden Maddux Law Corp 2520 Venture Oaks Way Ste 450; *Web:* vmlawcorp.com	Sacramento	CA	95833	916-779-2402	779-1451	41
Van Diest Supply Co 1434 220th St PO Box 610; *TF:* 800-779-2424 ■ *Web:* www.vdsc.com	Webster City	IA	50595	515-832-2366	832-2955	280
Van Dijk Westlake Reed Leskosky 1422 Euclid Ave Ste 300; *Web:* www.wrldesign.com	Cleveland	OH	44115	216-522-1350		261
Van Doren Sales Inc 10 NE Cascade Ave; *TF:* 866-886-1837 ■ *Web:* www.vandorensales.com	East Wenatchee	WA	98802	509-886-1837	886-2837	298
Van Drew Jefferson (Rep D - NJ) 331 Cannon House Office Bldg; *Web:* www.vandrew.house.gov	Washington	DC	20515	202-225-6572		342-2
Van Drunen Farms 300 W Sixth St; *Web:* www.vandrunenfarms.com	Momence	IL	60954	815-472-3100	472-3850	315-4
Van Dyk Group Inc, The 12800 Long Beach Blvd; *TF:* 800-222-0131 ■ *Web:* www.vandykgroup.com	Beach Haven	NJ	08008	609-492-1511	492-7643	390
Van Dyke Supply Co 39771 Hwy 34 East PO Box 278; *TF:* 800-279-7985 ■ *Web:* www.vandykestaxidermy.com	Woonsocket	SD	57385	704-279-7985		459
Van Eerden Foodservice Co 650 Ionia Ave SW; *Web:* www.vaneerden.com	Grand Rapids	MI	49503	616-475-0900	475-0990	780
Van Engelenhoven Agency Inc 122 Central Ave SW; *TF:* 800-856-6001 ■ *Web:* veinsurance.com	Orange City	IA	51041	712-737-6000	737-8632	390
Van Ert Electric Company Inc 7019 Stewart Ave; *Web:* www.vanert.com	Wausau	WI	54401	715-845-4308	848-3671	189-4
Van Gogh School Photographers 401 Cornell Ave; *Web:* vangoghphoto.com	Barrington	IL	60010	847-382-2282		592
Van Groesbeck & Co 2124 Hanovar Ave; *Web:* www.vangroesbeckco.com	Richmond	VA	23220	804-285-3176	359-7271	317
Van Hollen Chris (Sen D - MD) 110 Hart Senate Office Bldg; *Web:* www.vanhollen.senate.gov	Washington	DC	20510	202-224-4654	228-0629	342-2
Van Hoose Construction 101 NE 70th St; *Web:* www.vhcon.com	Oklahoma City	OK	73105	405-848-0415	848-3911	186
Van Horn Aviation LLC 1000 E Vista Del Cerro Dr; *TF:* 800-326-1534 ■ *Web:* vanhornaviation.com	Tempe	AZ	85281	480-483-4202		20
Van Horn Chevrolet of Plymouth 3008 Eastern Ave; *TF:* 800-236-1415 ■ *Web:* vanhornchev.com	Plymouth	WI	53073	920-449-4149		57
Van Horn Hoover & Associates Inc 3200 N Main St; *Web:* vanhornhoover.com	Findlay	OH	45840	419-423-5630	423-5772	261
Van Horn Metz & Company Inc 201 E Elm St; *TF:* 800-523-0424 ■ *Web:* www.vanhornmetz.com	Conshohocken	PA	19428	610-828-4500		146
Van Horne Cooperative Telephone Co 204 Main St; *Web:* www.vanhornetelephone.com	Van Horne	IA	52346	319-228-8791	228-8784	224
Van Leeuwen Pipe & Tube Inc 2875 64th Ave; *Web:* www.vanleeuwen.com	Edmonton	AB	T6P1R1	780-469-7410		490
Van Manen Petroleum Group 0-305 Lake Michigan Dr NW; *TF:* 855-464-8674 ■ *Web:* www.vanmanen.com	Grand Rapids	MI	49534	616-453-6344		579
Van Meter Industrial Inc 850 32nd Ave SW; *TF:* 800-247-1410 ■ *Web:* www.vanmeterinc.com	Cedar Rapids	IA	52404	319-366-5301	366-4709	246
Van Meter State Park 32146 N Hwy 122; *Web:* mostateparks.com	Miami	MO	65344	660-886-7537		565
Van Natta Mechanical Corp 25 Whitney Rd; *Web:* vannattamechanical.com	Mahwah	NJ	07430	201-391-3700		15
Van Ness Plastic Molding Company Inc 400 Brighton Rd; *Web:* vannesspets.com	Clifton	NJ	07012	973-778-9500		596
Van Ness Water Gardens Inc (VNWG) 2460 N Euclid Ave; *TF:* 800-205-2425 ■ *Web:* www.vnwg.com	Upland	CA	91784	909-982-2425	949-7217	293

Phone | Fax | Class

Van Osdol PC
1000 Walnut St Ste 1500 Kansas City MO 64106 816-421-0644 421-0758 41
TF: 877-763-7347 ■ *Web:* vanosdolkc.com

Van Patten Publishing
16420 SE McGillivray 103-734 Vancouver WA 98683 800-559-2737 838-0213* 637-2
**Fax Area Code:* 360 ■ *TF:* 800-559-2737 ■ *Web:* www.vanpattenpublishing.com

Van Reenen Tool & Die Inc
350 Commerce Dr Ste 4 Rochester NY 14623 585-288-6000 288-6889 488
Web: www.vrtnd.com

Van Roy Coffee Co, The
4569 Spring Rd Cleveland OH 44131 216-749-7069 296-7
Web: www.vanroycoffee.com

Van Sant Enterprises Inc 80 Truman Rd Pella IA 50219 641-628-3860 628-2614 62-4
TF: 877-826-7268 ■ *Web:* www.trick-tools.com

Van Strum & Towne Inc
505 Sansome St Ste 1001 San Francisco CA 94111 415-981-3455 401
Web: www.vanstrum.com

Van Vleck House & Gardens
21 Van Vleck St Montclair NJ 07042 973-744-4752 97
Web: vanvleck.org

Van Well Nursery 2821 Grant Rd East Wenatchee WA 98802 509-886-8189 886-0294 293
TF: 800-572-1553 ■ *Web:* www.vanwell.net

Van Wert County 114 E Main St Van Wert OH 45891 419-238-6159 238-4528 338
Web: vanwertcounty.org

Van Wert Machine Inc
210 E Cleveland St Delphos OH 45833 419-692-6836 695-0480 757
Web: www.progressive-tool.com

Van Wezel Performing Arts Ctr
777 N Tamiami Trl Sarasota FL 34236 941-953-3368 951-1449 572
TF: 800-826-9303 ■ *Web:* www.vanwezel.org

Van Wilder Insurance Agency Inc
2189 Mariner Blvd Spring Hill FL 34609 352-686-1003 390
Web: wilderagency.com

Van Winden Landscaping Inc
3101 California Blvd Napa CA 94558 707-224-1367 224-4659 422
Web: www.vanwindenlandscaping.com

Van Wingerden International Inc
4112 Haywood Rd Mills River NC 28759 828-891-4116 369
Web: www.natures-heritage.com

Van Winkle & Associates Inc
1180 W Peachtree St NW Ste 530 Atlanta GA 30326 404-355-0126 184
Web: www.vwaatlanta.com

Van Winkle Buck Wall Starnes & Davis PA
11 N Market St Asheville NC 28801 828-475-8855 428
Web: www.vwlawfirm.com

Van Wyk Inc 1901 S 2nd Ave Sheldon IA 51201 712-324-4687 324-5254 780
TF: 800-245-8775 ■ *Web:* www.vanwyk.com

Van Zandt County 121 E Dallas St Rm 202 Canton TX 75103 903-567-7555 567-6722 338
Web: www.vanzandtcounty.org

Van Zandt County Library
317 First Monday Ln Canton TX 75103 903-567-4276 434-3
Web: www.vanzandtlibrary.org

Van Zelm Heywood & Shadford Inc
10 Talcott Notch Rd Farmington CT 06032 860-284-5064 261
Web: vanzelm.com

Van Zelst Inc 39400 N Hwy 41 Wadsworth IL 60083 847-623-3580 776
Web: www.vanzelst.com

Van Zile Travel Services
3540 Winton Pl Rochester NY 14623 585-244-1100 772
Web: www.vanzile.com

Van Zyverden Inc
8079 Van Zyverden Rd Meridian MS 39305 601-679-8274 679-8039 293
TF: 800-332-2852 ■ *Web:* www.vanzyverden.com

Van's Aircraft Inc 14401 Keil Rd NE Aurora OR 97002 503-678-6545 678-6560 529
Web: www.vansaircraft.com

Vanadium Group Corp
134 Three Degree Rd Pittsburgh PA 15237 412-367-6060 261
TF: 800-685-0354 ■ *Web:* www.zoominfo.com

VanAllen Group Inc, The
525 Clubhouse Dr Ste 150 Peachtree City GA 30269 770-507-5001 463
Web: www.vanallen.com

Vanamatic Co 701 Ambrose Dr Delphos OH 45833 419-692-6085 692-3260 621
Web: www.vanamatic.com

Vanasse Hangen Brustlin Inc
101 Walnut St PO Box 9151 Watertown MA 02471 617-924-1770 924-2286 261
Web: www.vhb.com

VanBeurden Insurance Services Inc
1600 Draper St Kingsburg CA 93631 559-897-2975 897-4070 390
Web: www.vanbeurden.com

Vance Air Force Base
246 Brown Pkwy Ste 102 Enid OK 73703 580-213-7522 213-6376 497-1
Web: www.vance.af.mil

Vance Birthplace State Historic Site
911 Reems Creek Rd Weaverville NC 28787 828-645-6706 645-0936 50-3
Web: historicsites.nc.gov

Vance Bros Inc
5201 Brighton PO Box 300107 Kansas City MO 64130 816-923-4325 923-6472 46
TF: 800-821-8549 ■ *Web:* www.vancebrothers.com

Vance County 122 Young St Ste E Henderson NC 27536 252-738-2040 338
Web: www.vancecounty.org

Vance Kirkland Museum 1311 Pearl St Denver CO 80203 303-832-8576 520
Web: www.kirklandmuseum.org

Vance Metal Fabricators Inc
251 Gambee Rd Geneva NY 14456 888-234-6752 480
TF: 888-234-6752 ■ *Web:* www.vancemetal.com

Vance Outdoors Inc
3723 Cleveland Ave Columbus OH 43224 614-471-7000 711
Web: www.vanceoutdoors.com

Vance-Granville Community College
200 Community College Rd Henderson NC 27537 252-492-2061 430-0460 162
Web: www.vgcc.edu

Vanco USA Trailer Mfg
1170 Florence Rd PO Box 98 Florence NJ 08518 609-499-4141 499-8865 779
Web: www.vancotrailers.com

Vancouver Aquarium Marine Science Ctr
845 Avison Way Vancouver BC V6G3E2 604-659-3474 659-3515 40
TF: 800-931-1186 ■ *Web:* www.vanaqua.org

Vancouver Art Gallery 750 Hornby St Vancouver BC V6Z2H7 604-662-4700 522
Web: vanartgallery.bc.ca

Phone | Fax | Class

Vancouver Board of Trade
999 Canada Pl Ste 400 Vancouver BC V6C3E1 604-681-2111 681-0437 137
TF: 844-208-8197 ■ *Web:* www.boardoftrade.com

Vancouver Business Journal
1251 Officers Row Vancouver WA 98661 360-695-2442 457-5
Web: www.vbjusa.com

Vancouver Coastal Health
601 West Broadway 11th Fl Vancouver BC V5Z4C2 604-736-2033 353
TF: 866-884-0888 ■ *Web:* www.vch.ca

Vancouver Community College
1155 E Broadway Vancouver BC V5T4V5 604-871-7000 162
TF: 866-565-7820 ■ *Web:* www.vcc.ca

Vancouver Convention & Exposition Ctr (VCEC)
1055 Canada Pl Vancouver BC V6C0C3 604-689-8232 647-7232 205
TF: 866-785-8232 ■ *Web:* www.vancouverconventioncentre.com

Vancouver Door Company Inc
203 Fifth St NW Puyallup WA 98371 253-845-9581 845-3364 236
TF: 800-999-3667 ■ *Web:* vancouverdoorco.com

Vancouver Extended-Stay Suites
1288 W Georgia St Ste 101 Vancouver BC V6E4R3 604-891-6181 379
Web: vancouverextendedstay.com

Vancouver Foundation
475 W Georgia St Ste 200 Vancouver BC V6B4M9 604-688-2204 303
Web: www.vancouverfoundation.ca

Vancouver International Airport
Airport Postal Outlet PO Box 23750 Richmond BC V7B1Y7 604-207-7077 27
TF: 800-461-9999 ■ *Web:* www.yvr.ca

Vancouver Island University
900 5th St Nanaimo BC V9R5S5 250-753-3245 800
TF: 888-920-2221 ■ *Web:* www.viu.ca

Vancouver Pile Driving Ltd
20 Brooksbank Ave North Vancouver BC V7J2B8 604-986-5911 188
Web: www.vanpile.com

Vancouver School of Theology
The University of British Columbia 6015 Walter Gage Rd
Vancouver BC V6T1Z1 604-822-9031 167-3
TF: 866-822-9031 ■ *Web:* vst.edu

Vancouver Sun 200 Granville St Ste 1 Vancouver BC V6C3N3 604-605-2000 605-2323 532-1
TF: 866-372-3707 ■ *Web:* www.vancouversun.com

Vancouver Talmud Torah Assn
998 26th Ave W Vancouver BC V5Z2G1 604-736-7307 685
Web: www.talmudtorah.com

Vancouver (WA) City Hall
415 W Sixth St 2nd Fl Vancouver WA 98660 360-737-8298 487-8625 337
Web: www.cityofvancouver.us

Vanda Pharmaceuticals Inc
2200 Pennsylvania Ave NW Ste 300E Washington DC 20037 202-734-3400 296-1450 582
NASDAQ: VNDA ■ *Web:* www.vandapharmaceuticals.com

Vandalia Correctional Ctr
Rt 51 N PO Box 500 Vandalia IL 62471 618-283-4170 283-9147 213
Web: www2.illinois.gov

Vandalia-Butler Chamber of Commerce
333 James E Bohanan Dr Vandalia OH 45377 937-898-5351 898-5491 139
Web: vandaliabutlerchamber.org

VanDemark & Lynch Inc
4305 Miller Rd Wilmington DE 19802 302-764-7635 261
Web: vdleng.com

VanDeMark Chemical Inc 400 Mill St Lockport NY 14094 716-433-6764 146
Web: vandemark.com

Vandenberg Air Force Base
706 Washington Ave Bldg 10122 Vandenberg AFB CA 93437 805-606-3595 497-1
Web: www.vandenberg.af.mil

Vander Bend Manufacturing LLC
2701 Orchard Pkwy San Jose CA 95134 408-245-4120 697
Web: www.vander-bend.com

Vander Haag's Inc 3809 Fourth Ave W Spencer IA 51301 712-262-7000 61
TF: 888-940-5030 ■ *Web:* www.vanderhaags.com

Vanderbilt Beach Resort
9225 Gulf Shore Dr N Naples FL 34108 239-597-3144 597-2199 669
TF: 800-243-9076 ■ *Web:* www.vanderbiltbeachresort.com

Vanderbilt Kennedy Center for Research on Human Development
110 Magnolia Cir Nashville TN 37203 615-322-8240 322-8236 668
Web: vkc.mc.vanderbilt.edu

Vanderbilt Minerals Corp
30 Winfield St Norwalk CT 06855 203-853-1400 853-1452 503-3
TF: 800-243-6064 ■ *Web:* www.rtvanderbilt.com

Vanderbilt Mortgage & Finance Inc
500 Alcoa Trl Maryville TN 37804 800-970-7250 380-3418* 509
**Fax Area Code:* 865 ■ *TF:* 800-970-7250 ■ *Web:* vmf.com

Vanderbilt Properties Insurance Brokerage
770 Lexington Ave New York NY 10065 212-546-1000 390
Web: vanderbiltprograms.com

Vanderbilt University
2201 W End Ave Nashville TN 37240 615-322-7311 343-7765 166
TF: 800-288-0432 ■ *Web:* www.vanderbilt.edu

Vanderbilt University Heard Library
419 21st Ave S Nashville TN 37232 615-322-2800 343-8279 434-6
Web: www.library.vanderbilt.edu

Vanderbilt University Law School
131 21st Ave S Nashville TN 37203 615-322-2615 322-6631 167-1
Web: law.vanderbilt.edu

Vanderbilt University Medical Center Stem Cell Transplant Program
1301 22nd Ave S Ste B902 Nashville TN 37232 615-591-9890 769
Web: www.vanderbilthealth.com

Vanderbilt University School of Medicine
Eskind Family Biomedical Library and Learning Ctr
2209 Garland Ave Nashville TN 37240 615-322-6109 343-8397 167-2
TF: 866-263-8263 ■ *Web:* medschool.vanderbilt.edu

Vanderbilt-Ingram Cancer Ctr
691 Preston Bldg Nashville TN 37232 615-936-1793 374-7
Web: www.vicc.org

Vanderbyl Design
2415 3rd St Ste 267 San Francisco CA 94107 415-543-8447 393
Web: www.vanderbyl.com

VanderCook College of Music
3140 S Federal St Chicago IL 60616 312-225-6288 225-5211 166
Web: www.vandercook.edu

Name / Address	City	State	ZIP	Phone	Fax	Class
VanderHouwen & Associates Inc 6342 SW Macadam Ave *Web:* www.vanderhouwen.com	Portland	OR	97239	503-299-6811		260
Vanderpol's Eggs Ltd 3911 Mt Lehman Rd *TF:* 800-561-8020 ■ *Web:* www.vanderpolseggs.com	Abbotsford	BC	V2T5W5	604-856-4127		803-1
VanDerVart Concrete Products 1436 S 15th St *Web:* www.vandervart.com	Sheboygan	WI	53081	920-459-2400	459-2410	182
Vanderweil Engineers 274 Summer St *Web:* www.vanderweil.com	Boston	MA	02210	617-423-7423		261
Vandeventer Black LLP 101 W Main St Ste 500 *Web:* www.vanblk.com	Norfolk	VA	23510	757-446-8600	446-8670	445
VanDyke Software Inc 4848 Tramway Ridge Dr NE Ste 101 *Web:* www.vandyke.com	Albuquerque	NM	87111	505-332-5700	332-5701	178-12
Vanea Usa Inc 410 Market St *Web:* vanea.us	Elmwood Park	NJ	07407	201-796-0722		290
Vanee Foods Company Inc 5418 McDermott Dr *Web:* vaneefoodservice.com	Berkeley	IL	60163	708-449-7300		296-36
Vanelli's 206 W Main St *Web:* www.vanellis.com	Tupelo	MS	38804	662-844-4410		671
Vango Graphics Inc 1371 S Inca St *TF:* 877-722-6168 ■ *Web:* vango-graphics.com	Denver	CO	80223	303-722-6109		344
Vangold Mining Corp 1400-1111 W Georgia St *Web:* vangoldmining.com	Vancouver	BC	V6E4M3	778-945-2940		536
Vangst 518 17th St *TF:* 844-482-6478 ■ *Web:* vangst.com	Denver	CO	80202	844-482-6478		178-1
Vanguard Cleaning Systems Inc 655 Mariners Island Blvd Ste 303 **Fax Area Code:* 479 ■ *Web:* www.vanguardcleaning.com	San Mateo	CA	94404	650-287-2400	717-2082*	152
Vanguard Communications of Falls Church Inc 2121 K St NW Ste 650 *Web:* www.vancomm.com	Washington	DC	20037	202-331-4323		48-20
Vanguard Computers Inc 13100 W Lisbon Rd Ste 100 *TF:* 800-993-2229 ■ *Web:* www.vanguardinc.com	Brookfield	WI	53005	262-317-1900	317-1999	179
Vanguard Dealer Services LLC 30 Two Bridges Rd Ste 350 *Web:* www.vanguarddealerservices.com	Fairfield	NJ	07004	973-575-7171		41
Vanguard East 1172 Azalea Garden Rd **Fax Area Code:* 757 ■ *TF:* 800-221-1264 ■ *Web:* www.vanguardmil.com	Norfolk	VA	23502	800-221-1264	857-0222*	9
Vanguard Furniture Company Inc 109 Simpson St *TF:* 800-968-1702 ■ *Web:* www.vanguardfurniture.com	Conover	NC	28613	828-328-5631		319-2
Vanguard Group 455 Devon Pk Dr *TF:* 877-662-7447 ■ *Web:* investor.vanguard.com	Wayne	PA	19087	610-669-1000		401
Vanguard Integrity Professionals Inc 6625 S Eastern Ave Ste 100 *TF:* 877-794-0014 ■ *Web:* www.go2vanguard.com	Las Vegas	NV	89119	702-794-0014		180
Vanguard Management Group 9300 N 16th St *Web:* www.vanguardmanagementgroup.com	Tampa	FL	33612	813-930-8036	993-0142	195
Vanguard National Trailer Corp 289 E Water Tower Dr *Web:* www.vanguardtrailer.com	Monon	IN	47959	219-253-2000		120
Vanguard Plastics Corp 100 Robert Porter Rd *Web:* www.vanguardplastics.com	Southington	CT	06489	860-628-4736		601
Vanguard Products Group Inc 720 Brooker Creek Blvd Ste 223 *TF:* 877-477-4874 ■ *Web:* www.vanguardprotexglobal.com	Oldsmar	FL	34677	813-855-9639		693
Vanguard Property Group 2651 E Chapman Ave Ste 100 *Web:* www.vanguardproperty.com	Fullerton	CA	92831	714-446-0100	440-0150	655
Vanguard Resources Inc 6500 Hwy 281 N *TF:* 800-211-8848 ■ *Web:* www.vanguardresources.com	Spring Branch	TX	78070	210-495-1950	495-1167	104
Vanguard School 22000 US Hwy 27 *Web:* www.vanguardschool.org	Lake Wales	FL	33859	863-676-6091	676-8297	622
Vanguard Solutions Inc 3012 State Rte 5 *TF:* 800-304-1970 ■ *Web:* www.vanguard-solutions.com	Ashland	KY	41105	606-325-1970	325-2689	194
Vanguard Steel Ltd 2160 Meadowpine Blvd *Web:* vanguardsteel.com	Mississauga	ON	L5N6H6	905-821-1100		791
Vanguard Systems Inc 2901 Dutton Mill Rd Ste 220 *TF:* 800-445-1418 ■ *Web:* www.vansystems.com	Aston	PA	19014	800-445-1418		387
Vanguard Trucks Centers 700 Ruskin Dr *TF:* 866-216-7925 ■ *Web:* vanguardtrucks.com	Forest Park	GA	30297	866-216-7925		54
Vanguard University of Southern California 55 Fair Dr *TF:* 800-722-6279 ■ *Web:* www.vanguard.edu	Costa Mesa	CA	92626	714-556-3610	966-5471	166
Vanguard-Sentinel Career & Technology Centers 793 E Township Rd 201 *Web:* www.vscc.k12.oh.us	Tiffin	OH	44883	419-448-1212	447-2544	242
Vanilla Forums Inc 388 Rue Saint-Jacques Ste 800 *TF:* 866-845-0815 ■ *Web:* www.vanillaforums.com	Montreal	QC	H2Y1S1	866-845-0815		387
Vanir Construction Management Inc 4540 Duckhorn Dr Ste 300 *TF:* 888-912-1201 ■ *Web:* www.vanir.com	Sacramento	CA	95834	916-575-8888		463
Vanity Fair Magazine 1 World Trade Ctr *TF:* 800-365-0635 ■ *Web:* www.vanityfair.com	New York	NY	10007	800-365-0635		457-11
Van-Kam Freightways Ltd 10155 Grace Rd *TF:* 800-663-2161 ■ *Web:* www.vankam.com	Surrey	BC	V3V3V7	604-582-7451		314
Vann Attorneys PLLC 1720 Hillsborough St Ste 200 *Web:* vannattorneys.com	Raleigh	NC	27605	919-510-8585	510-8570	428
Vann Realty Co 14814 Giles Rd *Web:* www.vannrealtyco.com	Omaha	NE	68138	402-734-4800		655
Vanport Manufacturing Inc 28590 SE Wally Rd *Web:* www.vanport-international.com	Boring	OR	97009	503-663-4466	663-2610	194
Vanriper & Messina CPAS Inc 2888 E Loker *Web:* vanripermessina.com	Carlsbad	CA	92010	760-931-5900		734
Vans Inc 1588 S Coast Dr *TF:* 855-909-8267 ■ *Web:* www.vans.com	Costa Mesa	CA	90670	855-909-8267		301
Vantage Airport Group Ltd 1200 W 73rd Ave Ste 1410 *Web:* www.vantageairportgroup.com	Vancouver	BC	V6P6G5	604-269-0080	269-3840	63
Vantage Associates Inc 900 Civic Center Dr *Web:* www.vantagemmc.com	National City	CA	91950	619-477-6940		20
Vantage Bank 410 30th Ave E Ste 201 *Web:* vantagebankmn.com	Alexandria	MN	56308	320-759-5626		70
Vantage Credit Union (VCU) PO Box 4433 *TF:* 800-522-6009 ■ *Web:* www.vcu.com	Bridgeton	MO	63044	314-298-0055		219
Vantage Drilling Co 777 Post Oak Blvd Ste 800 *OTC:* VTG ■ *Web:* vantagedrilling.com	Houston	TX	77056	281-404-4700	404-4749	540
Vantage Financial Group Inc 6200 Rockside Rd *TF:* 888-401-2980 ■ *Web:* www.vanfin.com	Cleveland	OH	44131	216-642-7878	642-4862	401
Vantage Health Plan Inc 130 Desiard St Ste 300 *TF:* 888-823-1910 ■ *Web:* www.vantagehealthplan.com	Monroe	LA	71201	318-361-0900		353
Vantage Homes 1710 Jet Stream Dr Ste 200 *Web:* vantagehomescolorado.com	Colorado Springs	CO	80921	719-534-0984		187
Vantage Learning 6805 Rte 202 **Fax Area Code:* 215 ■ *TF:* 800-230-2213 ■ *Web:* www.vantagelearning.com	New Hope	PA	18938	800-230-2213	579-8391*	178-1
Vantage Mobility Intl (VMI) 5202 S 28th Pl **Fax Area Code:* 602 ■ *TF:* 855-864-8267 ■ *Web:* www.vantagemobility.com	Phoenix	AZ	85040	855-864-8267	304-3290*	62-7
Vantage Plastics 1415 W Cedar St *Web:* www.vantageplastics.com	Standish	MI	48658	989-846-1029	846-0939	608
Vantage Press Inc 419 Park Ave S Ste 18	New York	NY	10016	212-736-1767		637-2
Vantage Products Corp 960 Almon Rd *Web:* www.vantageproducts.com	Covington	GA	30014	770-788-0136		596
Vantage Solutions LLC 1035 W Lake St Ste 205 *TF:* 877-816-4818 ■ *Web:* vantage-solutions.com	Chicago	IL	60607	312-440-0602		445
Vantage Specialty Chemicals 4650 S Racine Ave *Web:* www.vantagegrp.com	Chicago	IL	60609	773-376-9000		146
Vantage Specialty Ingredients Inc 150 Mount Bethel Rd *Web:* www.lipochemicals.com	Warren	NJ	07059	973-345-8600		145
Vantage Tag Systems 312-2630 Croydon Dr Ste 214 *TF:* 877-589-8806 ■ *Web:* vantage-tag.com	Surrey	BC	V3S5A5	877-589-8806		387
VantagePoint Capital Partners 1111 Bayhill Dr Ste 220 *Web:* www.vpcp.com	San Bruno	CA	94066	650-866-3100	869-6078	792
VantagePoint Laboratory Partners LLC 4980 Carroll Canyon Rd *TF:* 888-823-8243 ■ *Web:* www.vpointlabs.com	San Diego	CA	92121	888-823-8243		415
Vantec 460 Honeycutt Dr *Web:* www.vantec.com	Grants Pass	OR	97526	541-471-7135		203
Vantec Inc 205 Closz Dr *Web:* www.vantecinc.com	Webster City	IA	50595	515-832-3125	832-3127	604
Vanteon Corp 250 Cross Keys Office Pk Bldg 250 *TF:* 888-506-5677 ■ *Web:* www.vanteon.com	Fairport	NY	14450	585-419-9555	248-0537	261
Vantige Inc 100 W Rd Ste 300 *Web:* www.vantigeinc.com	Towson	MD	21204	410-337-4774		193
Vantix Systems 10119 97a Ave NW *Web:* vantixsystems.com	Edmonton	AB	T5K2T3	780-421-0499		180
Vanton Pump & Equipment Corp 201 Sweetland Ave *Web:* www.vanton.com	Hillside	NJ	07205	908-688-4216	686-9314	641
VanTran Industries Inc 7711 Imperial Dr *TF:* 800-433-3346 ■ *Web:* vantran.com	Waco	TX	76712	254-772-9740	772-0016	767
Vantreo Insurance Brokerage 100 Stony Point Rd Ste 160 *TF:* 800-967-6543 ■ *Web:* vantreo.com	Santa Rosa	CA	95401	707-546-2300	546-2915	390
Vapor Blast Manufacturing Co 3025 W Atkinson Ave *Web:* www.vaporblast.net	Milwaukee	WI	53209	414-871-6500	871-7683	386
Vaporless Manufacturing Inc 8700 E Long Mesa Dr *TF:* 800-367-0185 ■ *Web:* www.vaporless.com	Prescott Valley	AZ	86314	928-775-5191	775-5309	201
Varay Systems LLC 201 E Main Dr Ste 700 *Web:* www.varay.com	El Paso	TX	79901	915-496-8555		179
Varbros LLC 16025 Brookpark Rd *Web:* varbroscorp.com	Cleveland	OH	44142	216-267-5200	267-5205	489
Varco Heat Treating Co 12101 Industry *Web:* www.varcoheat.com	Garden Grove	CA	92841	714-891-2755		484
Varco Pruden Buildings 3200 Players Club Cir *Web:* varcopruden.com	Memphis	TN	38125	901-748-8000	748-9323	105
Varel International Energy Services Inc 1625 W Crosby Dr Ste 124 *TF:* 800-827-3526 ■ *Web:* www.vareloilandgas.com	Carrollton	TX	75006	972-242-1160	242-8770	190
Varen Technologies Inc 9801 Broken Land Pkwy Ste 100 *Web:* www.varentech.com	Columbia	MD	21046	410-290-8008		177
Varflex Corp 512 W Court St *TF:* 800-648-4014 ■ *Web:* www.varflex.com	Rome	NY	13440	315-336-4400	336-0005	816
Vargas Juan (Rep D - CA) 2244 Rayburn House Office Bldg *Web:* vargas.house.gov	Washington	DC	20515	202-225-8045	225-2772	342-2
VARGO 3709 Pkwy Ln *TF:* 877-876-6384 ■ *Web:* www.vargosolutions.com	Hilliard	OH	43026	614-876-1163	876-0706	358

	Phone	Fax	Class
Variable Annuity Life Insurance Co (VALIC) 2929 Allen Pkwy ... Houston TX 77019 *TF:* 800-448-2542 ■ *Web:* www.valic.com	800-448-2542		391-2
Varian Medical Systems Inc 3100 Hansen Way ... Palo Alto CA 94304 *NYSE: VAR* ■ *TF:* 800-544-4636 ■ *Web:* www.varian.com	650-493-4000		382
Variant Microsystems 4128 Business Center Dr ... Fremont CA 94538 *TF:* 800-827-4268 ■ *Web:* www.variantusa.com	510-440-2870		535
Variantyx Inc 1671 Worcester Rd Ste 300 ... Framingham MA 01701 *Web:* variantyx.com	617-209-2090		177
Variety Distributors Inc 609 Seventh St ... Harlan IA 51537 *TF:* 800-274-1095 ■ *Web:* www.varietydistributors.com	712-755-2184	755-5041	328
Variety Gem Company Inc 295 Northern Blvd Ste 208 ... Great Neck NY 11021 *Web:* www.varietygem.com	212-921-1820		411
Variosystems Inc 901 S Kimball Ave ... Southlake TX 76092 *Web:* www.variosystems.com	817-416-7535	416-7436	696
Varis LLC 3015 Securs Park Dr ... Roseville CA 95661 *Web:* www.varis1.com	916-294-0860		194
Varite Inc 12 S First St Ste 404 ... San Jose CA 95113 *Web:* www.varite.com	408-977-0700		177
Varner, Parker & Sessums PA 1110 Jackson St ... Vicksburg MS 39180 *Web:* vpslaw.com	601-638-8741		41
Varner-Hogg Plantation State Historic Site 1702 N 13th St ... West Columbia TX 77486 *Web:* tpwd.texas.gov	979-345-4656		565
Varnett School - East, The 804 Maxey Rd ... Houston TX 77013 *Web:* www.varnett.org	713-637-6574	637-8319	685
Varnum LLP Bridgewater Pl 333 Bridge St NW ... Grand Rapids MI 49504 *Web:* www.varnumlaw.com	616-336-6000	336-7000	41
Varo Money 222 Kearny St ... San Francisco CA 94108 *TF:* 800-827-6526 ■ *Web:* www.varomoney.com	800-827-6526		39
Varouh Oil Inc 970 Griswold Rd ... Elyria OH 44035 *Web:* www.varouhoil.com	440-324-5025	324-4155	579
Varouj's Kabobs 1110 S Glendale Ave ... Glendale CA 91205	818-243-9870		671
Varro Press Inc PO Box 8413 ... Shawnee Mission KS 66208 *Web:* www.varropress.com	913-385-2034		637-2
Varscona Hotel 8208 106th St ... Edmonton AB T6E6R9 *Web:* www.varscona.com	780-434-6111		379
Vartek Services Inc 4770 Hempstead Station Dr ... Dayton OH 45459 *TF:* 800-954-2524 ■ *Web:* www.vartek.com	800-954-2524		174
Varvid 705 Sunset Pond Ln ... Bellingham WA 98225 *TF:* 855-827-8434 ■ *Web:* varvid.com	855-827-8434		5
Vasamed Inc 7615 Golden Triangle Dr Ste A ... Eden Prairie MN 55344 *TF:* 800-695-2737 ■ *Web:* www.vasamed.com	800-695-2737		476
Vasco Federal Credit Union 432 Depot St ... Latrobe PA 15650 *Web:* vascofcu.com	724-539-2858		219
Vascor Ltd 100 Farmers Bank Dr Ste 300 ... Georgetown KY 40324 *Web:* www.vascorlogistics.com	502-570-2020		311
Vascular Dynamics Inc 2134 Old Middlefield Way Ste J ... Mountain View CA 94043 *Web:* www.vasculardynamics.com	650-963-9370		475
Vascular Pathways Inc 1847 Trade Ctr Way ... Naples FL 34109	239-254-0391		475
Vasey Commercial Heating & Air Conditioning Inc 10830 Andrade Dr ... Zionsville IN 46077 *Web:* www.vasey.com	317-873-2512		189-10
Vasios, Kelly & Strollo PA 2444 Morris Ave ... Union NJ 07083 *Web:* vasioslaw.com	908-688-1020		41
Vaso Corp Revolution Mill Studios 1150 Revolution Mill Dr St ... Greensboro NC 27405 *TF:* 877-900-8276 ■ *Web:* www.vasohealthcare.com	336-398-8276	398-8280	475
Vasomedical Inc 180 Linden Ave ... Westbury NY 11590 *OTC: VASO* ■ *TF:* 800-455-3327 ■ *Web:* www.vasomedical.com	516-997-4600	997-2299	250
Vassar College 124 Raymond Ave ... Poughkeepsie NY 12604 *TF:* 800-827-7270 ■ *Web:* www.vassar.edu	845-437-7000	437-7063	166
Vasso Systems Inc 159 Cook St ... Brooklyn NY 11206 *TF:* 800-858-2776 ■ *Web:* vassosystems.com	718-417-5303		61
VasSol Inc 348 Lathrop Ave ... River Forest IL 60305 *Web:* vassolinc.com	708-366-7000		250
Vatterott College *Omaha* 11818 I St ... Omaha NE 68137 *Web:* www.vatterott.edu	402-891-9411		800
Vaughan & Bushnell Manufacturing Co 11414 Maple Ave ... Hebron IL 60034 **Fax Area Code: 815* ■ *TF:* 800-435-6000 ■ *Web:* www.vaughanmfg.com	800-435-6000	648-4300*	758
Vaughan Chamber of Commerce 25 Edilcan Dr Ste 2 ... Vaughan ON L4K3S4 *TF:* 888-943-8937 ■ *Web:* vaughanchamber.ca	905-761-1366	761-1918	137
Vaughan Company Inc 364 Monte-Elma Rd ... Montesano WA 98563 *TF:* 888-249-2467 ■ *Web:* www.chopperpumps.com	360-249-4042	249-6155	641
Vaughan Mills 1 Bass Pro Mills Dr ... Vaughan ON L4K5W4 *Web:* www.vaughanmills.com	905-879-2110		460
Vaughan Nelson Investment Management LP 600 Travis St Ste 6300 ... Houston TX 77002 *TF:* 888-888-8676 ■ *Web:* www.vaughannelson.com	713-224-2545		528
Vaughan Regional Medical Ctr 1015 Medical Center Pkwy ... Selma AL 36701 *Web:* www.vaughanregional.com	334-418-4100		374-3
Vaughn Coast & Vaughn Inc 154 S Marietta St ... Saint Clairsville OH 43950 *Web:* vaughncoastvaughn.com	740-695-7256	695-2203	261
Vaughn College of Aeronautics & Technology 86-01 23rd Ave ... East Elmhurst NY 11369 *TF:* 866-682-8446 ■ *Web:* www.vaughn.edu	718-429-6600		166
Vaughn Coltrane Pharr & Associates Inc 2060 E Exchange Pl ... Tucker GA 30084 *Web:* www.foodhill.freeservers.com	770-938-2600		256
Vaughn Construction 10355 Westpark Dr ... Houston TX 77042 *Web:* www.vaughnconstruction.com	713-243-8300	243-8350	186
Vaughn Industries LLC 1201 E Findlay St ... Carey OH 43316 *Web:* vaughnindustries.com	419-396-3900		189-4
Vaughn Manufacturing Company Inc 757 Douglas Ave ... Nashville TN 37207 *Web:* www.vaughnmfg.com	615-262-5775		697
Vaughn Manufacturing Corp PO Box 5431 ... Salisbury MA 01952 *TF:* 800-282-8446 ■ *Web:* www.vaughncorp.com	978-462-6683	462-6497	36
Vault Inc 132 W 31st St 16th Fl ... New York NY 10001 *TF:* 800-535-2074 ■ *Web:* www.vault.com	212-366-4212	366-6117	260
Vaupell Inc 1144 NW 53rd St ... Seattle WA 98107 *Web:* www.vaupell.com	206-784-9050	784-9708	604
Vavro & Company Inc 4725 Grayton Rd Ste 1040 ... Cleveland OH 44135 *Web:* vavrocpa.com	440-886-0400		2
Vawter Financial Ltd 1161 Bethel Rd Ste 304 ... Columbus OH 43220 *TF:* 800-955-1575 ■ *Web:* www.vawterfinancial.com	614-451-1002		194
Vaya Group 28600 Bella Vista Pky Ste 2100 ... Warrenville IL 60555 *Web:* www.vayapath.com	630-906-3046	906-0176	463
Vazzy's Brick Oven Restaurant 513 Broadbridge Rd ... Bridgeport CT 06610 *Web:* www.theoriginalvazzys.com	203-371-8046	371-4293	671
VBA (Vermont Bar Assn) 35-37 Ct St PO Box 100 ... Montpelier VT 05601 *TF:* 800-639-7036 ■ *Web:* www.vtbar.org	802-223-2020	223-1573	72
VBCVB (Virginia Beach Convention & Visitor Bureau) 2101 Parks Ave Ste 500 ... Virginia Beach VA 23451 *TF:* 800-700-7702 ■ *Web:* www.visitvirginiabeach.com	757-385-4700		206
Vbeyond Corp 3 Skillman Close ... Hillsborough NJ 08844 *Web:* www.vbeyond.com	908-359-8416		180
VBPS (Van Buren Public Schools) 555 W Columbia Ave ... Belleville MI 48111 *Web:* www.vanburenschools.net	734-697-9123	697-6385	685
Vbrick Systems Inc 12 Beaumont Rd ... Wallingford CT 06492 **Fax Area Code: 203* ■ *TF:* 866-827-4251 ■ *Web:* vbrick.com	866-827-4251	265-6750*	735
VBS (Vital Business Solutions) 1325 G St NW Ste 500 ... Washington DC 20005 *Web:* vitalbusinesssolution.com	202-832-1388		194
VBT 426 Industrial Ave Ste 120 ... Williston VT 05495 *TF:* 800-245-3868 ■ *Web:* www.vbt.com	800-245-3868		760
VBW Countertops 118 S Union Rd ... Spokane Valley WA 99206 *Web:* www.sites.google.com	509-924-1250	922-5420	817
VC (Visual Communications Inc) 120 Judge John Aiso St ... Los Angeles CA 90012 *Web:* www.vconline.org	213-680-4462		423
Vc999 Packaging Systems Inc 419 E 11th Ave ... Kansas City MO 64116 *TF:* 800-728-2999 ■ *Web:* www.home.vc999.com	816-472-8999	472-1999	547
VCA Inc 12401 West Olympic Blvd ... Los Angeles CA 90064 *TF:* 800-822-7387 ■ *Web:* www.vcahospitals.com	310-571-6500	571-6700	794
VCC (VCC-USA) 216 Louisiana St PO Box 555 ... Little Rock AR 72203 *Web:* www.vccusa.com	501-376-0017	376-4145	186
VCC-USA (VCC) 216 Louisiana St PO Box 555 ... Little Rock AR 72203 *Web:* www.vccusa.com	501-376-0017	376-4145	186
VCEC (Vancouver Convention & Exposition Ctr) 1055 Canada Pl ... Vancouver BC V6C0C3 *TF:* 866-785-8232 ■ *Web:* www.vancouverconventioncentre.com	604-689-8232	647-7232	205
VCF Films Inc 1100 Sutton Ave ... Howell MI 48843 *TF:* 888-905-7680 ■ *Web:* www.vcffilms.com	517-546-2300	546-2984	600
VCFO Holdings Inc 6836 Austin Center Blvd Bldg 1 Ste 280 ... Austin TX 78731 *TF:* 866-363-5766 ■ *Web:* www.vcfo.com	512-345-9441	372-9353	194
VCI (Vermont Correctional Industries) NOB 2 S 280 State Dr ... Waterbury VT 05671 *Web:* vci.vermont.gov	802-279-4162		630
VCI (Val-Comm Inc) 249 Muriel St NE ... Albuquerque NM 87123 *Web:* www.val-comm.com	505-292-7509	299-4253	246
VCI Construction LLC 1921 W 11th St ... Upland CA 91786 *TF:* 800-949-1350 ■ *Web:* www.vcicom.com	909-946-0905	946-0924	186
VCI Emergency Vehicle 43 Jefferson Ave ... Berlin NJ 08009 *TF:* 800-394-2162 ■ *Web:* www.vciambulances.com	856-768-2162		401
VCI Inc 1500 Progress St ... Sturgis MI 49091 *Web:* vciusa.com	269-659-3676		697
VCU (VCU Health) 1250 E Marshall St ... Richmond VA 23298 *Web:* www.vcuhealth.org	804-828-9000		353
VCU (Vantage Credit Union) PO Box 4433 ... Bridgeton MO 63044 *TF:* 800-522-6009 ■ *Web:* www.vcu.com	314-298-0055		219
VCU Health (VCU) 1250 E Marshall St ... Richmond VA 23298 *Web:* www.vcuhealth.org	804-828-9000		353
VD Importers Inc 7390 W 18 Ln ... Hialeah FL 33014 *Web:* www.vdimporters.com	786-703-7852	703-7874	238
VDA (Virginia Dental Assn) 3460 Mayland Ct Ste 110 ... Richmond VA 23233 *TF:* 877-310-6560 ■ *Web:* www.vadental.org	804-288-5750	288-1880	227
Vdara Hotel & Spa 2600 W Harmon Ave ... Las Vegas NV 89158 *TF:* 866-745-7111 ■ *Web:* vdara.mgmresorts.com	702-590-2111		377
VDC Research Group Inc 679 Worcester Rd Ste 2 ... Natick MA 01760 *Web:* www.vdcresearch.com	508-653-9000	653-9836	194
VDIC Inc 10400 SE Main St ... Milwaukie OR 97222 *TF:* 877-751-8342 ■ *Web:* vdic.com	503-722-8077		415
VDN (Voice & Data Networks Inc) 4218 Park Glen Rd ... Saint Louis Park MN 55416 *TF:* 800-246-7999 ■ *Web:* www.voicedata.com	952-946-5353	946-1066	178-11
VDx Veterinary Diagnostics Inc 2019 Anderson Rd Ste C ... Davis CA 95616 *TF:* 877-753-4285 ■ *Web:* vdxpathology.com	530-753-4285		794
Veasey Marc (Rep D - TX) 2348 Rayburn House Office Bldg ... Washington DC 20515 *Web:* veasey.house.gov	202-225-9897	225-9702	342-2

Name / Address	City	State	Zip	Phone	Fax	Class
Veber Partners LLC 605 N W 11th Ave *Web:* veber.com	Portland	OR	97209	503-229-4400		194
VEC (Victoria Electric Co-opeartive Inc) 102 S Ben Jordan St *Web:* www.victoriaelectric.coop	Victoria	TX	77901	361-573-2428		245
VEC (Volunteer Energy Co-op) PO Box 277 *Web:* vec.org	Decatur	TN	37322	423-334-5721	334-7003	245
Vecchio, Carrier & Feldman PA 3308 Cleveland Heights Blvd *Web:* vcfjlaw.com	Lakeland	FL	33803	863-701-2100		41
Vecellio & Grogan Inc PO Box 2438 *TF:* 800-255-6575 ■ *Web:* www.vecelliogrogan.com	Beckley	WV	25802	304-252-6575	252-4131	188-4
Vecenies Distributing Company Inc 140 North Ave *Web:* beersince1933.com	Millvale	PA	15209	412-821-4618		443
Vecna Technologies Inc 36 Cambridge Park Dr *TF:* 855-460-8267 ■ *Web:* www.vecna.com	Cambridge	MA	02140	617-864-0636	864-0638	177
Vector 135 Stillman St *TF:* 855-442-5623 ■ *Web:* www.withvector.com	San Francisco	CA	94107	855-442-5623		178-1
Vector Aerospace 22378 Billie Blackmon Rd *Web:* www.vectoraerospace.com	Andalusia	AL	36421	334-222-1277	222-1954	21
Vector Capital 1 Matket St Steuart Tower 23rd Fl *Web:* www.vectorcapital.com	San Francisco	CA	94105	415-293-5000	293-5100	792
Vector Composites Inc 3251 Mc Call St *Web:* www.compositesworld.com	Dayton	OH	45417	937-281-1444		127
Vector Consulting 6455 E Johns Crossing *Web:* vectorconsulting.com	Duluth	GA	30097	770-246-0968	246-0609	177
Vector Marketing Corp 4 Foster Ave Ste A *TF:* 800-828-0448 ■ *Web:* www.vectoroncampus.com	Gibbsboro	NJ	08026	856-782-8373		366
Vector Networks Inc 541 Tenth St Unit 123 *TF:* 800-330-5035 ■ *Web:* www.vector-networks.com	Atlanta	GA	30318	770-622-2850		179
Vector Planning & Services Inc 591 Camino De La Reina Ste 300 *TF:* 888-522-5491 ■ *Web:* www.myvpsi.com	San Diego	CA	92108	619-297-5656		177
Vector Resources Inc 3530 Voyager St *TF:* 800-929-4516 ■ *Web:* vectorusa.com	Torrance	CA	90503	310-436-1000	436-1060	252
Vector Resources LC 7651 S Main St Ste 106 *Web:* www.vectorresources.com	Midvale	UT	84047	801-352-8500	352-8506	194
Vector Security Inc 2000 Ericsson Dr *TF:* 800-832-8575 ■ *Web:* www.vectorsecurity.com	Warrendale	PA	15086	800-832-8575		692
Vector Software Inc 1351 S County Trl Ste 310 *TF:* 877-221-3069 ■ *Web:* www.vectorcast.com	East Greenwich	RI	02818	401-398-7185		177
Vector Technical Inc 38033 Euclid Ave Ste T-9 *Web:* www.vectortechnicalinc.com	Willoughby	OH	44094	440-946-8800		260
Vector Wealth Management LLC 43 Main St SE Ste 236 *TF:* 877-383-2867 ■ *Web:* www.vectorwealth.com	Minneapolis	MN	55414	612-378-7560	379-4895	401
Vector Windows LLC 1020 International Dr *Web:* www.vectorwindows.com	Fergus Falls	MN	56537	218-739-9899	739-9799	604
VectorCSP LLC 405 E Main St *Web:* vectorcsp.com	Elizabeth City	NC	27909	252-338-2264	333-3177	449
VectorGlobal WMG Inc 1001 Brickell Bay Dr Ste 1900 *Web:* www.vectorglobalwmg.com	Miami	FL	33131	305-350-3350		2
VectorMAX Corp 4 Dubon Ct *Web:* www.vectormax.net	Farmingdale	NY	11735	516-672-2505		177
Vectorply Corp 3500 Lakewood Dr *TF:* 800-577-4521 ■ *Web:* vectorply.com	Phenix City	AL	36867	334-291-7704	291-7743	745-1
VectorVest Inc 20472 Chartwell Center Dr Ste D *TF:* 800-130-1519 ■ *Web:* www.vectorvest.com	Cornelius	NC	28031	888-658-7638		401
Vectra Bank Colorado NA 2000 S Colorado Blvd Ste 2-1200 *TF:* 800-232-8948 ■ *Web:* www.vectrabank.com	Denver	CO	80222	720-947-7700	947-7760	70
Vectra Fitness Parts LLC 7901 S 190th St *TF:* 800-283-2872 ■ *Web:* vectraparts.com	Kent	WA	98032	425-291-9550	291-9650	267
Vectra Visual 3950 Business Pk Dr *Web:* vectravisual.com	Columbus	OH	43204	614-351-6868		627
Vectren Corp 211 NW Riverside Dr *NYSE:* VVC ■ *TF:* 800-227-1376 ■ *Web:* www.vectren.com	Evansville	IN	47708	812-491-4000		360-5
Vectrus Inc 655 Space Center Dr *Web:* vectrus.com	Colorado Springs	CO	80915	719-637-4182		463
Vectus Inc 1032 Lake St PMB 360 *TF:* 866-483-2887 ■ *Web:* vectus.com	Huntington Beach	CA	92648	866-483-2887		387
Vedanta Centre Publishers 130 Beechwood St *Web:* www.vedantacentre.org	Cohasset	MA	02025	781-383-0940		637-2
Vedanta Society of St Louis 205 S Skinker Blvd *Web:* www.vedantastl.org	Saint Louis	MO	63105	314-721-5118		48-20
Vedco Inc 5503 Corporate Dr *TF:* 888-691-2724 ■ *Web:* www.vedco.com	Saint Joseph	MO	64507	816-238-8840		794
Vedder Transportation Group 400 Riverside Rd *TF:* 866-857-1375 ■ *Web:* www.vtlg.com	Abbotsford	BC	V2S4P4	866-857-1375		314
Vee Bar Guest Ranch 38 Vee Bar Ranch Rd *TF:* 800-483-3227 ■ *Web:* veebar.com	Laramie	WY	82070	307-745-7036	745-7433	239
Veeco Holdings LLC 6801 W Side Ave *Web:* www.veeco1.com	North Bergen	NJ	07047	201-865-6200	865-9407	311
Veeder-Root 125 Powder Forest Dr *TF:* 888-262-7539 ■ *Web:* www.veeder.com	Simsbury	CT	06070	860-651-2700	651-2719	201
Veenstra & Kimm Inc 3000 Westown Pkwy *TF:* 800-241-8000 ■ *Web:* www.v-k.net	West Des Moines	IA	50266	515-225-8000		261
Veetech PC 113 Centrewest Ct *Web:* www.veetechpc.com	Cary	NC	27513	919-388-0037	388-0038	463
Veetronix Inc 1311 W Pacific Ave *TF:* 800-445-0007 ■ *Web:* www.veetronix.com	Lexington	NE	68850	308-324-6661	324-4985	815
Vega Capital Group LLC 1000 Marina Blvd Ste 115 *Web:* www.vegacapital.com	Brisbane	CA	94005	415-318-8740	318-8745	796
Vega Energy Partners Ltd 3701 Kirby Ste 1290 *TF:* 800-411-4383 ■ *Web:* www.vegaenergy.com	Houston	TX	77098	713-527-0557	527-0850	463
Vega Group 7220 Washington Ave *Web:* www.vegagroup.com	New Orleans	LA	70125	504-488-5222		184
Vegan Action PO Box 7313 *Web:* vegan.org	Richmond	VA	23221	804-577-8341	254-8346	48-17
Vegas PBS 3050 E Flamingo *TF:* 877-727-4483 ■ *Web:* www.vegaspbs.org	Las Vegas	NV	89121	702-799-1010		741-72
VEGAScom LLC 2370 Corporate Cir 3rd Fl *TF:* 866-983-4279 ■ *Web:* www.vegas.com	Henderson	NV	89074	866-983-4279		775
Vegetarian Resource Group, The (VRG) PO Box 1463 *Web:* www.vrg.org	Baltimore	MD	21203	410-366-8343	366-8804	48-17
Veg-Pro Inc 11800 Gordon Ave	Grant	MI	49327	231-834-5634	834-5657	11-1
Vegrzyn, Sarver & Associates Inc 218 W Lafayette St *Web:* veg-sarv.com	Ottawa	IL	61350	815-434-7225		261
Vehicle Improvement Products 151 S Ram Rd *Web:* www.vipwheels.com	Antioch	IL	60002	847-395-7250		54
Vehicle Safety Manufacturing LLC 408 Central Ave **Fax Area Code:* 973 ■ *TF:* 800-832-7233 ■ *Web:* www.vehiclesafetymfg.com	Newark	NJ	07107	800-832-7233	643-2167*	438
Vehtech Inc 2004 Eastview Pkwy Ste 208 *Web:* www.vehtechnology.com	Conyers	GA	30094	770-788-2032		41
Veit & Company Inc 14000 Veit Pl *TF:* 866-281-3867 ■ *Web:* www.veitusa.com	Rogers	MN	55374	763-428-2242	428-1334	186
VEITS Group LLC 7610 Olentangy River Rd Ste 200 *TF:* 877-834-8702 ■ *Web:* www.veitsgroup.com	Columbus	OH	43235	614-467-5414	467-5418	225
Veka Inc 100 Veka Dr *TF:* 800-654-5589 ■ *Web:* vekainc.com	Fombell	PA	16123	724-452-1000	452-1007	235
Vektek Inc 1334 E 6th Ave *Web:* www.vektek.com	Emporia	KS	66801	620-342-7637	342-7722	350
Vektrel LLC 9988 Hibert St Ste 104 *Web:* www.vektrel.com	San Diego	CA	92131	858-564-0301		261
Vektrex Electronic Systems Inc 10225 Barnes Canyon Rd *Web:* www.vektrex.com	San Diego	CA	92121	858-558-8282		177
Vel Micro Works Inc 726 Yorklyn Rd Ste 400 *Web:* www.velmicro.com	Hockessin	DE	19707	302-239-4661		809
Vela Filemon (Rep D - TX) 307 Cannon House Office Bldg *Web:* vela.house.gov	Washington	DC	20515	202-225-9901	225-9770	342-2
Vela Research LP 5540 Rio Vista Dr *Web:* www.vela.com	Clearwater	FL	33760	727-507-5300		735
Velan Inc 7007 Cote de Liesse *TSX:* VLN ■ *Web:* www.velan.com	Montreal	QC	H4T1G2	514-748-7743	748-8635	789
Velaro Inc 8174 Lark Brown Rd Ste 201 *TF:* 800-983-5276 ■ *Web:* www.velaro.com	Elkridge	MD	21075	800-983-5276		809
Velazquez Nydia M (Rep D - NY) 2302 Rayburn House Office Bldg *Web:* www.velazquez.house.gov	Washington	DC	20515	202-225-2361		342-2
Velcro USA Inc 406 Brown Ave **Fax Area Code:* 603 ■ *TF:* 800-225-0180 ■ *Web:* www.velcro.com	Manchester	NH	03103	800-225-0180	669-9271*	594
Veldkamp's Flowers 9501 W Colfax Ave *TF:* 800-247-3730 ■ *Web:* www.veldkampsflowers.com	Lakewood	CO	80215	303-232-2673		292
Velentium LLC 22322 Grand Corner Dr Ste 140 *Web:* velentium.com	Katy	TX	77494	832-303-8200		261
Velko Hinge Inc 9325 Kennedy Ct *Web:* www.velko.com	Munster	IN	46321	219-924-6363		350
Vellano Bros Inc 7 Hemlock St *TF:* 800-342-9855 ■ *Web:* www.vellano.com	Latham	NY	12110	518-785-5537	785-5578	385
Vellumoid Inc 54 Rockdale St *TF:* 800-609-5558 ■ *Web:* www.vellumoid.com	Worcester	MA	01606	508-853-2500	852-0741	326
Velmex Inc 7550 SR-5 20 *Web:* www.velmex.com	Bloomfield	NY	14469	585-657-6151		454
Velocity Aerospace Group 2840 N Ontario St *Web:* triumphinstruments.com	Burbank	CA	91504	818-333-5600		24
Velocity Credit Union 610 E 11th St *Web:* www.velocitycu.com	Austin	TX	78701	512-469-7000	469-7024	70
Velocity Futures LLC 5373 W Alabama St Ste 600	Houston	TX	77056	713-490-7600		610
Velocity Partners Inc 379 W Broadway 3rd Fl *Web:* velocitypartners.com	New York	NY	10012	347-708-1720		180
Velocity Trade 99 Yorkville Ave Ste 210 *Web:* www.velocitytrade.com	Toronto	ON	M5R3K5	416-855-2800		509
Velos Inc 2201 Walnut Ave Ste 208 *Web:* www.velos.com	Fremont	CA	94538	510-739-4010	739-4018	178-11
Veloxiti Inc 3650 Brookside Pkwy Ste 125 *Web:* veloxiti.com	Alpharetta	GA	30022	770-518-4228		261
Velsicol Chemical LLC 10400 W Higgins Rd Ste 700 *TF:* 877-847-8351 ■ *Web:* www.velsicol.com	Rosemont	IL	60018	847-813-7888	768-3227	144
Velting Contractors Inc 3060 Breton Rd SE *Web:* velting.com	Kentwood	MI	49512	616-949-6660	949-8168	189-5
VELUX America Inc 1418 Evans Pond Rd PO Box 5001 *TF:* 800-888-3589 ■ *Web:* www.veluxusa.com	Greenwood	SC	29648	803-396-5700		491
Velvac Inc 2405 S Calhoun Rd *TF:* 800-783-8871 ■ *Web:* www.velvac.com	New Berlin	WI	53151	262-786-0700	786-7323	60

	Phone	Fax	Class
Velvet Grill & Creamery 2204 McHenry Ave .... Modesto CA 95350 *Web:* www.thevelvetgrillandcreamery.com	209-544-9029		671
V-Empower Inc 6800 Willow Creek Rd .... Bowie MD 20720 *Web:* www.v-empower.com	301-805-4721		224
Venable Insurance Agency Inc 4237 Ft Campbell Blvd .... Hopkinsville KY 42240 *Web:* michaelvenable.com	270-885-0063		390
Venable LLP 600 Massachusetts Ave NW .... Washington DC 20004 *Web:* www.venable.com	202-344-4000	344-8300	428
Venango County Courthouse Annex 1174 Elk St .... Franklin PA 16323 *Web:* www.co.venango.pa.us	814-432-9500	432-3149	338
Venango Technology Ctr 1 Vo-Tech Dr .... Oil City PA 16301 *Web:* www.vtc1.org	814-677-3097	676-0075	167-3
Venda Ravioli Inc 265 Atwells Ave .... Providence RI 02903 *Web:* www.vendaravioli.com	401-421-9105		297-8
Vendant Inc 4845 Pearl East Cir Ste 101 .... Boulder CO 80301 *TF:* 800-714-4900 ■ *Web:* www.vedanthealth.com	720-378-4420	398-3399	178-12
Vendetti Motors Inc 411 W Central St .... Franklin MA 02038 *Web:* www.vendettimotors.com	508-570-4798		57
Vendig Software Services Inc 5517 Cabrillow Way .... Rocklin CA 95765 **Fax Area Code:* 916 ■ *TF:* 866-250-4273 ■ *Web:* www.vendig.com	866-250-4273	435-0159*	177
Vendini Inc 660 Market St .... San Francisco CA 94104 *TF:* 800-901-7173 ■ *Web:* vendini.com	800-901-7173		187
Vendio Services LLC 1510 Fashion Island Blvd .... San Mateo CA 94403 *TF:* 866-269-9549 ■ *Web:* www.vendio.com	866-269-9549		178-7
Vendome Copper & Brass Works Inc 729 Franklin St .... Louisville KY 40202 *TF:* 888-384-5161 ■ *Web:* vendomecopper.com	502-587-1930	589-0639	298
Vendome Group LLC 216 E 45th St 6th Fl .... New York NY 10017 *TF:* 800-519-3692 ■ *Web:* www.vendomegrp.com	800-519-3692		637-9
Vendors Exchange International Inc 8700 Brookpark Rd .... Cleveland OH 44129 *TF:* 800-321-2311 ■ *Web:* www.veii.com	216-432-1800		463
Veneklasen Assoc 1711 16th St .... Santa Monica CA 90404 *Web:* www.veneklasen.com	310-450-1733		256
Veneto Trattoria 6137 N Scottsdale Rd .... Scottsdale AZ 85250 *Web:* www.venetotrattoria.com	480-948-9928		671
Venezia Stone Inc 1954 Halethorpe Farms Rd .... Baltimore MD 21227 *Web:* veneziastoneusa.com	410-247-2442	247-8043	191-1
Venezia Transport Service Inc PO Box 909 .... Royersford PA 19468 *TF:* 800-523-5572 ■ *Web:* www.veneziainc.com	610-495-5200		780
Venezuela *Consulate General* 2401 Fountain View Dr Ste 220 .... Houston TX 77057 *Web:* www.venezuela-us.org	713-974-0028	974-1413	257
Venezuelan-American Association of the US 641 Lexington Ave .... New York NY 10022 *Web:* www.venezuelanamerican.org	212-233-7776		48-14
Vengreso 36181 E Lake Rd Ste 188 .... Palm Harbor FL 34685 *Web:* vengreso.com	727-234-0952		195
Vengroff Williams & Associates Inc (VWA) 2099 S State College Bvld .... Anaheim CA 92806 *TF:* 800-238-9655 ■ *Web:* www.vwinc.com	714-889-6200		160
Venice Area Chamber of Commerce 597 Tamiami Trl S .... Venice FL 34285 *Web:* venicechamber.com	941-488-2236	484-5903	139
Venice Chamber of Commerce PO Box 202 .... Venice CA 90294 *Web:* venicechamber.net	310-822-5425		139
Venice Consulting Group 212 Marine St Ste 100 .... Santa Monica CA 90405 *TF:* 855-202-0824 ■ *Web:* www.veniceconsulting.com	855-202-0824		196
Venice Family Clinic 604 Rose Ave .... Venice CA 90291 *Web:* www.venicefamilyclinic.org	310-392-8636	392-6642	353
Venice Regional Medical Ctr (VRMC) 540 The Rialto .... Venice FL 34285 *Web:* www.veniceregional.com	941-485-7711		374-3
Venice Ristorante & Wine Bar 1700 Wynkoop St .... Denver CO 80202 *Web:* www.veniceristorante.com	303-534-2222		671
Venkel Ltd 5900 Shepherd Mountain Cove .... Austin TX 78730 *TF:* 800-950-8365 ■ *Web:* www.venkel.com	512-794-0081	794-0087	246
Venmar Ventilation Inc 550 Lemire Blvd .... Drummondville QC J2C7W9 *Web:* www.venmar.ca	819-477-6226		437
Venn Products Group 80 Skyline Dr .... Plainview NY 11803 *Web:* www.vennproducts.com	516-822-1561		463
Venoscope LLC 1018 Harding St Ste 104 .... Lafayette LA 70503 **Fax Area Code:* 337 ■ *TF:* 800-284-7655 ■ *Web:* www.venoscope.com	800-284-7655	268-4080*	476
Venrock Assoc 3340 Hillview Ave .... Palo Alto CA 94304 *Web:* www.venrock.com	650-561-9580	561-9180	792
Vensai Technologies 2450 Atlanta Hwy Ste 1002 .... Cumming GA 30040 *TF:* 866-849-4057 ■ *Web:* www.vensaiinc.com	770-888-4804		196
Vensiti Inc 300 E Royal Ln Ste 104 .... Irving TX 75039 **Fax Area Code:* 888 ■ *Web:* www.vensiti.com	972-887-7995	361-1774*	177
Vensure Employer Services Inc 2600 W Geronimo Pl Ste 201 .... Chandler AZ 85224 *TF:* 800-409-8958 ■ *Web:* vensureinc.com	800-409-8958		360-3
Vent Products Company Inc 1901 S Kilbourn Ave .... Chicago IL 60623 *TF:* 800-368-8368 ■ *Web:* www.ventproducts.com	773-521-1900	521-5613	697
Vent-A-Hood Ltd PO Box 830426 .... Richardson TX 75083 *TF:* 800-331-2492 ■ *Web:* www.ventahood.com	972-235-5201	231-0663	697
Ventamatic Ltd 100 Washington Rd .... Mineral Wells TX 76067 *TF:* 800-433-1626 ■ *Web:* bvc.com	940-325-7887	325-9311	15
Ventana Inn 48123 Hwy 1 .... Big Sur CA 93920 *TF:* 800-628-6500 ■ *Web:* www.ventanabigsur.com	831-667-2331	667-0573	669
Ventana Medical Systems Inc 1910 Innovation Pk Dr .... Tucson AZ 85755 *TF:* 800-227-2155 ■ *Web:* diagnostics.roche.com	520-887-2155		476
Ventana Productions 1819 L St NW Ste 100w .... Washington DC 20036 *Web:* www.ventanadc.com	202-785-5112		514
Ventana USA 6001 Enterprise Dr .... Export PA 15632 *Web:* www.ventana-usa.com	724-325-3400	327-4540	608
Ventas Inc 353 N Clark St Ste 3300 .... Chicago IL 60654 *NYSE: VTR* ■ *TF:* 877-483-6827 ■ *Web:* www.ventasreit.com	312-660-3800		654
Ventec Life Systems 19021 120th Ave NE Ste E101 .... Bothell WA 98011 *TF:* 844-640-4357 ■ *Web:* www.venteclife.com	844-698-6276		475
Ventera Corp 1881 Campus Commons Dr Ste 350 .... Reston VA 20191 *Web:* www.ventera.com	703-760-4600	390-1113	180
Venticello 1257 Taylor St .... San Francisco CA 94108 *Web:* venticello.com	415-922-2545		671
Ventress Correctional Facility 379 Alabama Hwy 239 N .... Clayton AL 36016 *Web:* www.alabama.gov	334-775-3331		213
Ventress Memorial Library 15 Library Plz .... Marshfield MA 02050 *Web:* www.ventresslibrary.org	781-834-5535		434-3
Ventricle Software Systems Inc 29205 Oceanridge Dr .... Rancho Palos Verdes CA 90275 *Web:* www.ventriclesoftware.com	310-948-2551		178-1
Ventrol Air Handling Systems Inc 9100 Rue Du Parcours .... Montreal QC H1J2Z1 *Web:* www.ventrol.com	514-354-7776		610
Ventura Chamber of Commerce 505 Poli St 2nd Fl .... Ventura CA 93001 *Web:* venturachamber.com	805-643-7222	653-8015	139
Ventura Coastal LLC 2325 Vista Del Mar Dr .... Ventura CA 93001 *Web:* www.venturacoastal.com	805-653-7000	653-7777	296-21
Ventura College 4667 Telegraph Rd .... Ventura CA 93003 *Web:* www.venturacollege.edu	805-654-6400		162
Ventura County 800 S Victoria Ave .... Ventura CA 93009 *Web:* www.ventura.org	805-654-5000		338
Ventura County Arts Council 646 County Sq Dr Ste 154 .... Ventura CA 93003 *Web:* vcartscouncil.org	805-658-2213		522
Ventura County Employees' Retirement Assn 1190 S Victoria Ave Ste 200 .... Ventura CA 93003 *Web:* www.vcera.org	805-339-4250	339-4269	387
Ventura County Medical Ctr 300 Hillmont Ave .... Ventura CA 93003 *TF:* 888-285-5012 ■ *Web:* www.vchca.org	805-652-6000		374-3
Ventura County Museum of History & Art 100 E Main St .... Ventura CA 93001 *Web:* venturamuseum.org	805-653-0323		520
Ventura County Reporter 700 E Main St .... Ventura CA 93001 *Web:* www.vcreporter.com	805-648-2244	648-2245	532-5
Ventura County Star 771 E Daily Dr PO Box 6006 .... Camarillo CA 93011 *Web:* static.vcstar.com	805-437-0000	482-6167	532-2
Ventura Foods LLC 40 Pointe Dr .... Brea CA 92821 *TF:* 800-421-6257 ■ *Web:* www.venturafoods.com	714-257-3700		296-30
Ventura Miesowitz Keough & Warner A Professional Corp 783 Springfield Ave .... Summit NJ 07901 *Web:* www.summitlawyers.net	908-277-2410		41
Ventura Technology Enterprises Ltd 95-036 Hokuiwa St Apt 42 Ste 110 .... Mililani HI 96789 *Web:* www.venturatechnology.net	808-678-3900	676-2218	180
Ventura Visitors & Convention Bureau 101 S California St .... Ventura CA 93001 *TF:* 800-333-2989 ■ *Web:* visitventuraca.com	805-648-2075	648-2150	206
Ventura Youth Correctional Facility 3100 Wright Rd .... Camarillo CA 93010 *TF:* 866-232-5627 ■ *Web:* cdcr.ca.gov	805-485-7951		412
Ventura's 7742 W Bancroft St .... Toledo OH 43617 *Web:* toledostripletreat.com	419-841-7523		671
Venture Capital Fund of America 509 Madison Ave .... New York NY 10022 *Web:* www.vcfa.com	212-838-5577	838-7614	792
Venture Communications Cooperative Inc 218 Commercial Ave SE PO Box 157 .... Highmore SD 57345 **Fax Area Code:* 650 ■ *TF:* 800-932-0637 ■ *Web:* venturecomm.net	605-852-2224	343-8492*	49-17
Venture Design Services Inc 1051 SE St .... Anaheim CA 92805 *Web:* www.venture.com.sg	714-765-3740		668
Venture Engineering Inc 209 Hwy 544 .... Conway SC 29526 *Web:* ventureengineering.net	843-347-5851		261
Venture Express Inc 131 Industrial Blvd .... La Vergne TN 37086 *TF:* 866-511-4565 ■ *Web:* www.ventureexpress.com	615-793-9500		187
Venture Group Enterprises Inc 2520 Whitehall Park Dr Ste 100 .... Charlotte NC 28273 *Web:* www.vgei.com	704-676-0160		463
Venture Hive 1010 NE 2nd Ave .... Miami FL 33132 *Web:* www.venturehive.com	305-735-1274		393
Venture Investors LLC 505 S Rosa Rd Ste 201 .... Madison WI 53719 *Web:* ventureinvestors.com	608-441-2700		792
Venture Lighting International Inc 32000 Aurora Rd .... Solon OH 44139 *TF:* 800-451-2606 ■ *Web:* www.venturelighting.com	440-248-3510	349-7771	437
Venture Measurement Company LLC 150 Venture Blvd .... Spartanburg SC 29306 *Web:* venturemeasurement.com	864-574-8960	578-7308	201
Venture Mechanical Inc 2222 Century Cir .... Irving TX 75062 *Web:* venturemech.com	972-871-1300	871-1301	610
Venture Oil & Gas Inc 3575 N Belt Line Rd Ste 346 .... Irving TX 75062 *Web:* ventureoil.net	214-912-7017		536

Name / Address	City	State	ZIP	Phone	Fax	Class
Venture Opportunities Inc 13140 Coit Rd Ste 211 *Web:* www.bizdealmaker.com	Dallas	TX	75240	972-783-1662		708
Venture Plastics Inc 4000 Warren Rd PO Box 249 *Web:* www.ventureplastics.com	Newton Falls	OH	44444	330-872-5774	872-3597	604
Venture Precision Tool Inc 241 E 2nd St *Web:* www.ventureprecisiontool.com	Hummelstown	PA	17036	717-566-6496	566-1826	604
Venture Solutions Inc 1170 Grey Fox Rd *TF:* 800-728-2615 ■ *Web:* venturesolutions.com	Arden Hills	MN	55112	651-494-1740		195
Venture Steel Inc 60 Disco Rd *Web:* www.venturesteel.com	Etobicoke	ON	M9W1L8	416-798-9396		492
Venture Travel LLC 4085 Tongass Ave *TF:* 800-770-8800 ■ *Web:* www.taquanair.com	Ketchikan	AK	99901	907-225-8800	228-4605	12
Venturedyne Ltd 600 College Ave *Web:* www.venturedyne.com	Pewaukee	WI	53072	262-691-9900	691-9901	18
VentureOut 575 Pierce St Ste 604 *TF:* 888-431-6789 ■ *Web:* venture-out.com	San Francisco	CA	94117	415-626-5678	626-5679	760
Venturity Financial Partners 14131 Midway Rd Ste 112 *Web:* venturity.com	Addison	TX	75001	972-692-0380		2
Venuequest LLC 5174 McGinnis Ferry Rd Ste 102 *Web:* www.venuequest.com	Alpharetta	GA	30005	678-909-4088		772
Venus Beauty Academy 1033 Chester Pke *Web:* www.venusbeautyacademy.com	Sharon Hill	PA	19079	610-586-2500	586-0437	167-3
Venus Swimwear 11711 Marco Beach Dr *TF:* 800-366-7946 ■ *Web:* www.venus.com	Jacksonville	FL	32224	904-645-6000		155-17
Venus Wafers Inc 100 Research Rd *Web:* www.venuswafers.com	Hingham	MA	02043	781-740-1002	740-0791	296-9
Venuworks Inc 4611 Mortensen Rd Ste 111 *TF:* 888-232-5151 ■ *Web:* www.venuworks.com	Ames	IA	50014	515-232-5151		205
Veolia Environmental Services 200 E Randolph St Ste 7900 *Web:* www.veolianorthamerica.com	Chicago	IL	60601	312-938-0078		804
VeoRide Inc 400 N Racine Ave Ste 901 *TF:* 855-836-2256 ■ *Web:* www.veoride.com	Chicago	IL	60642	855-836-2256		261-6
Ver Ploeg & Lumpkin PA 100 SE 2nd St 30th Fl *Web:* www.vpm-legal.com	Miami	FL	33131	305-577-3996		428
Vera Bradley Designs 12420 Stonebridge Rd *TF:* 800-975-8372 ■ *Web:* www.verabradley.com	Fort Wayne	IN	46808	260-482-4673	484-2278	349
Vera Institute of Justice 233 Broadway 12th Fl *Web:* www.vera.org	New York	NY	10279	212-334-1300	941-9407	49-10
Veraciti Inc 1044 Rte 23 Ste 104 *TF:* 888-312-1600 ■ *Web:* www.veraciti.com	Wayne	NJ	07470	973-887-8660	947-7575	180
Veracity Energy Services Ltd 200 744 - Fourth Ave SW *TF:* 866-618-2933 ■ *Web:* www.veracityenergy.com	Calgary	AB	T2P3T4	403-537-1300		540
Veracity Engineering 600 Maryland Ave SW Ste 600e *Web:* www.veracity-eng.com	Washington	DC	20024	202-488-0975		19
VeraDatacom LLC 1910 Park Meadows Dr Ste 200 *Web:* veradata.com	Fort Myers	FL	33907	239-204-5000		195
Veramark Technologies Inc 1565 Jefferson Rd Ste 120	Rochester	NY	14623	585-381-6000	383-6800	735
Verance 10089 Willow Creek Rd Ste 200 *Web:* www.verance.com	San Diego	CA	92131	858-202-2800		466
Verandah Pet Hospital Inc 14381 Palm Beach Blvd *Web:* verandahpethospital.com	Fort Myers	FL	33905	239-332-8387		794
Verant Identification Systems Inc 1577 Ridge Rd W Ste 119 **Fax Area Code:* 866 ■ *Web:* verantid.com	Rochester	NY	14615	585-214-2451	257-4351*	693
Verbatim Americas LLC 8210 University Executive Park Dr *TF:* 800-538-8589 ■ *Web:* www.verbatim.com	Charlotte	NC	28262	704-547-6500		658
Verbatim Solutions LLC 5200 S Highland Dr Ste 201 *TF:* 800-573-5702 ■ *Web:* verbatimsolutions.com	Salt Lake City	UT	84117	801-273-5700		768
Verco Decking Inc 4340 N 42nd Ave *Web:* www.vercodeck.com	Phoenix	AZ	85019	602-272-1347		697
Verdanza Hotel 8020 Calle Tartak *TF:* 800-625-0312 ■ *Web:* www.verdanzahotel.com	Carolina	PR	00979	787-253-9000		132
Verde Pr & Consulting 1211 Main Ste 32 *Web:* verdepr.com	Durango	CO	81301	970-259-3555		196
Verde Valley School 3511 Verde Vly School Rd *Web:* vvsaz.org	Sedona	AZ	86351	928-284-2272	284-0432	622
Verdi Group Inc, The 190 Office Pkwy Ste 1 *Web:* www.theverdigroup.com	Pittsford	NY	14534	585-381-4275		7
Verdigris Valley Electric Co-op 8901 E 146th St N *TF:* 800-870-5948 ■ *Web:* www.vvec.com	Collinsville	OK	74021	918-371-2584	371-9873	245
Verdin Co, The 444 Reading Rd **Fax Area Code:* 513 ■ *TF:* 800-543-0488 ■ *Web:* www.verdin.com	Cincinnati	OH	45202	800-543-0488	241-1855*	153
Verdolino & Lowey PC 124 Washington St Ste 101 *Web:* vlpc.com	Foxborough	MA	02035	508-543-1720	543-4114	2
Verdugo Hills Hospital 1812 Verdugo Blvd *Web:* uscvhh.org	Glendale	CA	91208	818-790-7100		374-3
Verdugo Hospice Care Ctr 4170 Verdugo Rd *Web:* www.verdugohospice.com	Los Angeles	CA	90065	323-257-5715	257-5447	450
Verendrye Electric Co-opeartive Inc 615 Hwy 52 *TF:* 800-472-2141 ■ *Web:* www.verendrye.com	Velva	ND	58790	701-338-2855		245
Verequest 67 Robbins Ave *TF:* 866-920-2011 ■ *Web:* www.verequest.com	Toronto	ON	M4L1X1	416-362-6777		195
Verge Fund 317 Commercial St NE *Web:* vergefund.com	Albuquerque	NM	87102	505-247-1038		792
Verge Solutions LLC 11 Ewall St **Fax Area Code:* 866 ■ *Web:* www.vergehealth.com	Mount Pleasant	SC	29464	843-628-4168	209-8119*	809
Verhalen Inc 500 Pilgrim Way *Web:* www.verhaleninc.com	Green Bay	WI	54304	920-431-8900	431-8901	191-3
Verhoff Machine & Welding Inc 7300 Rd 18 *Web:* www.verhoff.com	Continental	OH	45831	419-596-3202	596-3220	454
Verican Inc 227 E Florida Ave **Fax Area Code:* 951 ■ *TF:* 800-888-0470 ■ *Web:* www.verican.com	Hemet	CA	92543	800-888-0470	652-4009*	177
Vericel Corp 64 Sidney St *NASDAQ: VCEL* ■ *Web:* vcel.com	Cambridge	MA	02139	734-418-4400	665-0485	85
Verichem Laboratories Inc 90 Narragansett Ave *TF:* 800-552-5859 ■ *Web:* www.verichemlabs.com	Providence	RI	02907	401-461-0180		743
VERICO One Link Mortgage & Financial 200-1215 Henderson Hwy *Web:* onelinkmortgage.com	Winnipeg	MB	R2G1L8	204-954-7620		141
Vericon Resources Inc 3295 River Exchange Dr Ste 405 *TF:* 800-795-3784 ■ *Web:* www.vericon.com	Norcross	GA	30092	770-457-9922	457-5006	400
Veridex LLC 700 US Hwy Rt 202 S *TF:* 877-837-4339 ■ *Web:* www.cellsearchctc.com	Raritan	NJ	08869	877-837-4339		476
Veridiam Inc 1717 N Cuyamaca St *Web:* www.veridiam.com	El Cajon	CA	92020	619-448-1000	562-5776	595
Verient Inc 1190 Saratoga Ave Ste 220 *Web:* www.verient.com	San Jose	CA	95129	408-521-1660	521-1662	809
Verifi Inc 8391 Beverly Blvd Ste 310 *Web:* www.verifi.com	Los Angeles	CA	90048	323-655-5789	655-5537	463
Verified Audit Circulation Inc 900 Larkspur Landing Cir *Web:* www.verifiedaudit.com	Larkspur	CA	94939	415-461-6006		734
Verified Credentials Inc 20890 Kenbridge Ct *Web:* www.verifiedcredentials.com	Lakeville	MN	55044	952-985-7202	985-7218	635
Verified Label & Print Inc 7905 Hopi Pl *TF:* 800-764-6110 ■ *Web:* www.verifiedlabel.com	Tampa	FL	33634	813-290-7721		627
VeriFone Inc 88 W Plumeria Dr *NYSE: PAY* ■ *Web:* www.verifone.com	San Jose	CA	95134	408-232-7800		614
Veriforce LLC 1575 Sawdust Rd Ste 600 *TF:* 888-369-1574 ■ *Web:* www.veriforce.com	The Woodlands	TX	77380	888-369-1574		765
Verigent LLC 9920 Kincey Ave Ste 210 *TF:* 877-637-6422 ■ *Web:* www.verigent.com	Mooresville	NC	28117	704-658-3285		610
Verinon Technology Solutions Ltd 3395 N Arlington Heights Rd *Web:* www.verinon.com	Arlington Heights	IL	60004	847-577-5256		196
Verint Systems Inc 175 Broadhollow Rd Ste 100 *TF:* 800-483-7468 ■ *Web:* www.verint.com	Melville	NY	11747	631-962-9300		178-4
Veris Environmental LLC 53036 N Hwy 71 *Web:* verisenvironmental.com	Limon	CO	80828	719-775-9870	775-9871	463
Veris Industries Inc 16640 SW 72nd Ave *TF:* 800-354-8556 ■ *Web:* www.veris.com	Portland	OR	97224	503-598-4564		407
Veris Wealth Partners LLC 17 State St Ste 2450 *Web:* www.veriswp.com	New York	NY	10004	212-349-4172		690
Verisante Technology Inc 140-2639 Viking Way *Web:* verisante.com	Richmond	BC	V6V3B7	604-605-0507	605-0508	250
Verisk 3E 3207 Grey Hawk Ct *Web:* www.verisk3e.com	Carlsbad	CA	92010	760-602-8700		196
Verisma Systems Inc 510 W Third St Ste 200 *TF:* 866-390-7404 ■ *Web:* verisma.com	Pueblo	CO	81003	719-546-1849	542-2564	809
Verisource Services Inc 7600 W Tidwell Rd Ste 700 *TF:* 800-455-0280 ■ *Web:* www.verisource.com	Houston	TX	77040	713-647-6540		177
VeriStor Systems Inc 4850 River Green Pkwy *Web:* veristor.com	Duluth	GA	30096	678-990-1593		173-8
Verisurf Software Inc 4907 E Landon Dr *TF:* 888-713-7201 ■ *Web:* www.verisurf.com	Anaheim	CA	92807	714-970-1683		177
VerisVisalign 920 S Broad St **Fax Area Code:* 215 ■ *TF:* 888-458-3747 ■ *Web:* www.verisvisalign.com	Lansdale	PA	19446	267-649-8001	393-5047*	194
Veritable LP 6022 W Chester Pk *TF:* 800-345-9551 ■ *Web:* veritablelp.com	Newtown Square	PA	19073	610-640-9551		401
Veritable Quandary 1030 NW 12th Ave Apt 507 *Web:* veritablequandary.com	Portland	OR	97204	503-227-7342		671
VeriTainer Corp 1127 Pope St *TF:* 844-344-8796 ■ *Web:* www.veritainer.com	Saint Helena	CA	94574	707-967-0944		693
Veritas 321 Energy Partners Lp 3325 Caldera Blvd *Web:* veritas321.com	Midland	TX	79707	432-682-4002		652
Veritas Capital 9 W 57th St 29th Fl *Web:* www.veritascapital.com	New York	NY	10019	212-415-6700		41
Veritas Medicine Inc 11 Cambridge Ctr 1st Fl *Web:* www.veritasmedicine.com	Cambridge	MA	02142	617-234-1500		177
Veritas Press 1805 Olde Homestead Ln *TF:* 800-922-5082 ■ *Web:* www.veritaspress.com	Lancaster	PA	17601	717-519-1974		535
Veritas Publishing PO Box 3516 *Web:* www.veritaspub.com	Sedona	AZ	86340	928-282-8722	282-4789	637-2
Veri-Tax 30 Executive Pk Ste 200 *TF:* 800-969-5100 ■ *Web:* www.veri-tax.com	Irvine	CA	92614	800-969-5100		463
Verite Inc 608 W 9320 S *Web:* www.verite.com	Sandy	UT	84070	801-553-1101		738
Veritec Inc 2445 Winnetka Ave N *Web:* www.veritecinc.com	Golden Valley	MN	55427	763-253-2670		696

Name / Address	City	State	Zip	Phone	Fax	Class
Veritext LLC 290 W Mt Pleasant Ave Ste 3200 *TF:* 800-567-8658 ■ *Web:* www.veritext.com	Livingston	NJ	07039	800-567-8658		445
Verity Credit Union PO Box 75974 *TF:* 800-444-4589 ■ *Web:* www.veritycu.com	Seattle	WA	98175	206-440-9000	361-5300	219
Verity Instruments Inc 2901 Eisenhower St *Web:* www.verityinst.com	Carrollton	TX	75007	972-446-9990		472
Verity International Ltd 200 King St W Ste 1301 *TF:* 877-623-2396 ■ *Web:* www.verityintl.com	Toronto	ON	M5H3T4	416-862-8422		194
Verity Professionals 2400 Lakeview Pkwy Ste 680 *TF:* 888-367-3110 ■ *Web:* verityprofessionals.com	Alpharetta	GA	30009	404-920-6400		463
Verix Inc 4340 Stevens Creek Blvd Ste 166 *Web:* verix.com	San Jose	CA	95129	650-949-2700	949-2722	177
Verizon 140 West St *Web:* www.verizon.com	New York	NY	10007	212-395-1000		736
Verizon Credit Inc 201 N Tampa St *TF:* 800-483-7988 ■ *Web:* www.verizon.com	Tampa	FL	33602	909-384-5147		216
Verizon Wireless 180 Washington Valley Rd *TF:* 800-922-0204 ■ *Web:* www.verizonwireless.com	Bedminster	NJ	07921	908-306-7000		736
Verkada 405 E 4th Ave *TF:* 888-829-0668 ■ *Web:* www.verkada.com	San Mateo	CA	94401	888-829-0668		177
Verland Foundation Inc, The 212 Iris Rd *Web:* verland.org	Sewickley	PA	15143	412-741-2375	741-3299	305
Verma Systems Inc 4111 S Sherwood Forest Blvd *Web:* www.vermasystems.com	Baton Rouge	LA	70816	225-296-0399	296-0390	180
Ver-Mac Industries Inc 100 Progress Dr **Fax Area Code:* 740 ■ *TF:* 800-671-1046 ■ *Web:* www.ver-macindustries.com	Mount Vernon	OH	43050	800-671-1046	393-2708*	454
Vermeer Mid Atlantic Inc 1210 E Vermeer Rd Pella *TF:* 800-768-3444 ■ *Web:* vermeerallroads.com	Charlotte	NC	28273	704-588-3238		791
Vermeer Midsouth Inc 1200 Vermeer Cv *TF:* 800-264-4123 ■ *Web:* www.vermeermidsouth.com	Cordova	TN	38018	901-758-1928	758-1929	386
Vermeer Southeast Sales & Service Inc 4559 Old Winter Garden Rd *Web:* www.vermeersoutheast.com	Orlando	FL	32811	407-295-2020		791
Vermes Machine Company Inc 351 Crider Ave *Web:* www.vermesmachine.com	Moorestown	NJ	08057	856-642-9300	642-9302	454
Vermette Machine Company Inc 7 143rd St *Web:* www.vermettlifts.com	Hammond	IN	46327	219-931-5406	931-8652	73
Vermeulen Furniture Inc 2105 W Michigan Ave *Web:* vermeulenfurniture.com	Jackson	MI	49202	517-782-8208		321
Vermilion 1120 King St *Web:* vermilionrestaurant.com	Alexandria	VA	22314	703-684-9669		671
Vermilion Chamber of Commerce 1907 Veterans Memorial Dr *Web:* www.vermilionchamber.org	Abbeville	LA	70510	337-893-2491		139
Vermilion Community College 1900 E Camp St *TF:* 800-657-3608 ■ *Web:* vcc.edu	Ely	MN	55731	800-657-3608		162
Vermilion County Title Inc 112 N Vermilion *Web:* vermilioncountytitle.com	Danville	IL	61832	217-442-0510		653
Vermilion Parish 100 N State St Ste 101 *Web:* www.vermilionparishclerkofcourt.com	Abbeville	LA	70510	337-898-1992	898-9803	338
Vermilion Today 318 N Main St *Web:* www.vermiliontoday.com	Abbeville	LA	70510	337-893-4223	898-9022	532-2
Vermillion Advantage 15 N Walnut St *Web:* www.vermilionadvantage.com	Danville	IL	61832	217-442-6201	442-6228	139
Vermillion County 255 S Main St *TF:* 800-340-8155 ■ *Web:* www.vermilliongov.us	Newport	IN	47966	765-492-5345		338
Vermillion, The 115 Paredes Line Rd *Web:* www.thevermillion.com	Brownsville	TX	78521	956-542-9893		671
Vermont						
Agency of Transportation 1 National Life Dr *Web:* vtrans.vermont.gov	Montpelier	VT	05633	802-828-2657		339-46
Aging & Disabilities Dept 280 State Dr HC2 S *TF:* 888-405-5005 ■ *Web:* dail.vermont.gov	Waterbury	VT	05671	802-241-2401	241-0386	339-46
Agriculture Food & Markets Dept 116 State St *Web:* agriculture.vermont.gov	Montpelier	VT	05620	802-828-2430		339-46
Arts Council 136 State St *Web:* www.vermontartscouncil.org	Montpelier	VT	05633	802-828-3291	828-3363	339-46
Attorney General 89 State St *Web:* www.atg.state.vt.us	Montpelier	VT	05609	802-828-3171		339-46
Banking Div 89 Main St *Web:* www.dfr.vermont.gov	Montpelier	VT	05620	802-828-3307		339-46
Board of Medical Practice 108 Cherry St PO Box 70 *Web:* www.healthvermont.gov	Burlington	VT	05402	802-657-4220		339-46
Chief Medical Examiner 111 Colchester Ave *Web:* www.healthvermont.gov	Burlington	VT	05401	802-863-7320		339-46
Children & Families Dept 280 State Dr HC 1 N *TF:* 800-786-3214 ■ *Web:* dcf.vermont.gov	Waterbury	VT	05671	802-241-0935		339-46
Court Administrator 109 State St *Web:* www.vermontjudiciary.org	Montpelier	VT	05609	802-828-3278	828-3457	339-46
Crime Victim Services Ctr 58 S Main St Ste 1 *TF:* 800-750-1213 ■ *Web:* www.ccvs.vermont.gov	Waterbury	VT	05676	802-241-1250	241-4337	339-46
Economic Development Dept 1 National Life Dr Deane C Davis Bldg Fl 6 *Web:* accd.vermont.gov	Montpelier	VT	05620	802-272-2399		339-46
Emergency Management Office 45 State Dr *TF:* 800-347-0488 ■ *Web:* vem.vermont.gov	Waterbury	VT	05671	802-244-8721	241-5556	339-46
Fish & Wildlife Dept 1 National Life Dr Davis 2 *Web:* anr.vermont.gov	Montpelier	VT	05620	802-828-1000	241-3295	339-46
General Assembly 115 State St *Web:* www.leg.state.vt.us	Montpelier	VT	05633	802-828-2228		339-46
Health Dept 108 Cherry St *Web:* www.healthvermont.gov	Burlington	VT	05402	802-863-7200	865-7754	339-46
Historic Preservation Div 1 National Life Dr Davis Bldg 6th Fl *Web:* accd.vermont.gov	Montpelier	VT	05620	802-828-3213		339-46
Insurance Div 89 Main St *Web:* www.dfr.vermont.gov	Montpelier	VT	05620	802-828-3301		339-46
Labor Dept 5 Green Mountain Dr PO Box 488 *Web:* www.labor.vermont.gov	Montpelier	VT	05601	802-828-4000	828-4022	339-46
Lieutenant Governor 115 State St *Web:* ltgov.vermont.gov	Montpelier	VT	05633	802-828-2226		339-46
Lottery Commission 1311 US Rt 302 Ste 100 *Web:* vtlottery.com	Barre	VT	05641	802-479-5686	479-4294	452
Motor Vehicles Dept 120 State St *TF:* 888-998-3766 ■ *Web:* dmv.vermont.gov	Montpelier	VT	05603	802-828-2000	828-2145	339-46
Natural Resources Agency 1 National Life Dr Davis 2 *Web:* anr.vermont.gov	Montpelier	VT	05620	802-828-1294		339-46
Office of Veteran Affairs 118 State St *TF:* 888-666-9844 ■ *Web:* veterans.vermont.gov	Montpelier	VT	05620	802-828-3379	828-5932	339-46
Secretary of State 128 State St *TF:* 800-439-8683 ■ *Web:* sos.vermont.gov	Montpelier	VT	05633	802-828-2363		339-46
Securities Div 89 Main St *Web:* www.dfr.vermont.gov	Montpelier	VT	05620	802-828-3420	828-2896	339-46
State Police 45 State Dr *Web:* vsp.vermont.gov	Waterbury	VT	05671	802-241-5260	241-5551	339-46
Taxes Dept 133 State St *Web:* www.state.vt.us	Montpelier	VT	05609	802-828-2505		339-46
Tourism & Marketing Dept 1 National Life Dr 6th Fl *TF:* 800-837-6668 ■ *Web:* www.vermontvacation.com	Montpelier	VT	05620	802-828-3237		339-46
Treasurer 109 State St 4th Fl *TF:* 800-642-3191 ■ *Web:* www.vermonttreasurer.gov	Montpelier	VT	05609	802-828-2301	828-2772	339-46
Vital Records Section 108 Cherry St PO Box 70 *Web:* www.healthvermont.gov	Burlington	VT	05402	802-863-7275		339-46
Vocational Rehabilitation Div HC 2 S 280 State Dr *TF:* 866-879-6757 ■ *Web:* vocrehab.vermont.gov	Waterbury	VT	05671	802-447-2781		339-46
Vermont Academy 10 Long Walk PO Box 500 *Web:* www.vermontacademy.org	Saxtons River	VT	05154	802-869-6229		622
Vermont Aerospace Manufacturing Inc 966 Industrial Pwy PO Box 1148 *Web:* www.vtaerospace.com	Lyndonville	VT	05851	802-748-8705	748-8437	454
Vermont Association of Realtors 148 State St *Web:* www.vermontrealtors.com	Montpelier	VT	05602	802-229-0513		656
Vermont Attractions Assn (VAA) PO Box 1284 *Web:* www.vtattractions.org	Montpelier	VT	05601	802-229-4581	223-4257	393
Vermont Bar Assn (VBA) 35-37 Ct St PO Box 100 *TF:* 800-639-7036 ■ *Web:* www.vtbar.org	Montpelier	VT	05601	802-223-2020	223-1573	72
Vermont Book Shop Inc, The 38 Main St *Web:* www.vermontbookshop.com	Middlebury	VT	05753	802-388-2061	388-9217	95
Vermont Broadcast Associates Inc 39 Church St *Web:* www.moo92.com	Lyndonville	VT	05851	802-626-9800	766-8067	645-141
Vermont Chamber of Commerce 751 Granger Rd *Web:* www.vtchamber.com	Barre	VT	05641	802-223-3443	223-4257	140
Vermont College of Fine Arts 36 College St *Web:* vcfa.edu	Montpelier	VT	05602	802-828-8517		637-9
Vermont Correctional Industries (VCI) NOB 2 S 280 State Dr *Web:* vci.vermont.gov	Waterbury	VT	05671	802-279-4162		630
Vermont Department of Libraries 109 State St *Web:* libraries.vermont.gov	Montpelier	VT	05609	802-828-3261	828-2199	434-5
Vermont Electric Co-opeartive Inc 42 Wescom Rd *TF:* 800-832-2667 ■ *Web:* www.vermontelectric.coop	Johnson	VT	05656	802-635-2331	635-7645	245
Vermont Energy Investment Corp 128 Lakeside Ave Ste 401 *TF:* 800-639-6069 ■ *Web:* www.veic.org	Burlington	VT	05401	802-658-6060		463
Vermont Federal Credit Union 84 Pine St *TF:* 888-252-0202 ■ *Web:* www.vermontfederal.org	Burlington	VT	05402	802-658-0225	864-6938	219
Vermont Gas Systems Inc 85 Swift St *TF:* 800-639-8081 ■ *Web:* www.vermontgas.com	South Burlington	VT	05403	802-863-4511	863-8872	324
Vermont Hand Crafters PO Box 1184 *TF:* 800-373-5429 ■ *Web:* www.vermonthandcrafters.com	Williston	VT	05495	800-373-5429		45
Vermont Heating & Ventilating Company Inc 16 Tigan St *Web:* www.vhv.com	Winooski	VT	05404	802-655-8805	655-8809	189-10
Vermont Historical Society (VHS) Vermont History Ctr 60 Washington St Ste 1 *Web:* vermonthistory.org	Barre	VT	05641	802-479-8500	479-8510	48-13
Vermont Law School 168 Chelsea St PO Box 96 *TF:* 800-227-1395 ■ *Web:* www.vermontlaw.edu	South Royalton	VT	05068	802-831-1239		167-1
Vermont Legal Aid Inc 177 Western Ave Ste 1 *Web:* www.vtlegalaid.org	Saint Johnsbury	VT	05819	802-863-5620		445

Name	Address	City	State	ZIP	Phone	Fax	Class	Details
Vermont Life	1 National Life Dr 6th Fl	Montpelier	VT	05620	802-828-3241		457-22	*Web:* vermontlife.com
Vermont Manufacturing Services Inc	123 Park St	Rutland	VT	05701	802-775-7638	775-9746	393	*Web:* www.vtmanufacturing.com
Vermont Maple Sugar Co	37 Industrial Park Dr	Morrisville	VT	05661	800-828-2376		123	*TF:* 800-828-2376 ■ *Web:* butternutmountainfarm.com
Vermont Medical Society	134 Main St	Montpelier	VT	05601	802-223-7898	223-1201	474	*TF:* 800-640-8767 ■ *Web:* www.vtmd.org
Vermont NEA Today Magazine	10 Wheelock St	Montpelier	VT	05602	802-223-6375	223-1253	457-8	*TF:* 800-649-6375 ■ *Web:* www.vtnea.org
Vermont Precision Tools Inc	10 Precision Ln	Swanton	VT	05488	802-868-2701	868-7180	493	*Web:* www.vermontgage.com
Vermont Public Interest Research Group (VPIRG)	141 Main St Ste 6	Montpelier	VT	05602	802-223-5221		633	*Web:* www.vpirg.org
Vermont Public Radio	365 Troy Ave	Colchester	VT	05446	802-655-9451		647	*Web:* www.vpr.org
Vermont Public Television (VPT)	204 Ethan Allen Ave	Colchester	VT	05446	802-655-4800		632	*TF:* 800-639-7811 ■ *Web:* www.vpt.org
Vermont Railway Inc	1 Railway Ln	Burlington	VT	05401	802-658-2550		651	*TF:* 800-639-3088 ■ *Web:* www.vermontrailway.com
Vermont Ski Safety Equipment Inc	9 Sand Hill Rd	Underhill Center	VT	05490	802-899-4738	899-3677	710	*Web:* www.vermontskisafety.com
Vermont State Colleges	575 Stone Cutters Way	Montpelier	VT	05602	802-224-3000	224-3035	786	*Web:* www.vsc.edu
Vermont State Parks — *Knight Island State Park*	1 Knight Is	North Hero	VT	05474	802-524-6353		565	*Web:* vtstateparks.com
Vermont Structural Slate Company Inc	3 Prospect St PO Box 98	Fair Haven	VT	05743	802-265-4933	265-3865	724	*TF:* 800-343-1900 ■ *Web:* www.vermontstructuralslate.com
Vermont Student Assistance Corp (VSAC)	10 E Allen St PO Box 2000	Winooski	VT	05404	800-642-3177	654-3765*	725	**Fax Area Code:* 802 ■ *TF:* 800-642-3177 ■ *Web:* www.vsac.org
Vermont Symphony Orchestra	2 Church St Ste 3B	Burlington	VT	05401	802-864-5741	864-5109	573-3	*Web:* www.vso.org
Vermont Systems Inc	12 Market Pl	Essex Junction	VT	05452	802 879 6993		178-10	*TF:* 877-883-8757 ■ *Web:* www.vermontsystems.com
Vermont Technical College	PO Box 500	Randolph Center	VT	05061	802-728-1000	728-1321	800	*TF:* 800-442-8821 ■ *Web:* www.vtc.edu
Vermont Teddy Bear Company Inc	6655 Shelburne Rd	Shelburne	VT	05482	802-985-3001	985-1304	762	*TF:* 800-988-8277 ■ *Web:* www.vermontteddybear.com
Vermont Telephone Company Inc	354 River St	Springfield	VT	05156	802-885-9000		387	*Web:* www.vermontel.com
Vermont Veterans Home	325 N St	Bennington	VT	05201	802-442-6353	447-6466	793	*Web:* vvh.vermont.gov
Vermont Veterinary Medical Assn	88 Beech St	Essex Junction	VT	05452	802-878-6888	878-2871	795	*Web:* www.vtvets.org
Vermont's North Country Chamber of Commerce	246 Cswy St	Newport	VT	05855	802-334-7782		139	*Web:* www.vtnorthcountry.org
Vern Dale Products Inc	8445 Lyndon St	Detroit	MI	48238	313-834-4190	834-6280	296-10	*Web:* www.verndaleproducts.com
Vernay Laboratories Inc	120 E S College St	Yellow Springs	OH	45387	937-767-7261		677	*Web:* www.vernay.com
Verndale Corp, The	28 Damrell St Ste 300	Boston	MA	02127	617-399-8777	399-8788	366	*Web:* www.verndale.com
Verne Q. Powell Flutes Inc	1 Clock Tower Pl 3rd Fl	Maynard	MA	01754	978-461-6111	461-6155	527	*Web:* www.powellflutes.com
Vernier Software & Technology LLC	13979 SW Millikan Way	Beaverton	OR	97005	503-277-2299		419	*TF:* 800-387-2474 ■ *Web:* www.vernier.com
Vernis & Bowling of Miami PA	1680 NE 135th St	Miami	FL	33181	305-895-3035	892-1260	428	*Web:* www.national-law.com
Vernon Area Public Library District	300 Olde Half Day Rd	Lincolnshire	IL	60069	847-634-3650	634-8449	435	*Web:* www.vapld.info
Vernon College	4400 College Dr	Vernon	TX	76384	940-552-6291	553-1753	162	*TF:* 866-336-9371 ■ *Web:* www.vernoncollege.edu
Vernon Communications Co-op	103 N Main St	Westby	WI	54667	608-634-3136		116	*Web:* vernoncom.coop
Vernon County	100 W Cherry St	Nevada	MO	64772	417-448-2500	667-6035	338	*TF:* 866-313-9960 ■ *Web:* vernoncountymo.org
Vernon E. Faulconer Inc	1001 ESE Loop 323 Ste 160	Tyler	TX	75701	903-581-4382	581-1515	536	*Web:* www.vefinc.com
Vernon Electric Co-op	110 Saugstad Rd	Westby	WI	54667	608-634-3121	634-7481	245	*TF:* 800-447-5051 ■ *Web:* www.vernonelectric.org
Vernon Milling Company Inc (VMC)	44080 Hwy 17 S	Vernon	AL	35592	205-695-7161	695-7192	780	*TF:* 800-753-1993 ■ *Web:* www.vernonmilling.com
Vernon Parish Library	1401 Nolan Trace	Leesville	LA	71446	337-239-2027		434-3	*TF:* 800-737-2231 ■ *Web:* www1.youseemore.com
Vernon Tool Company Ltd	1170 Trademark Dr Ste 101	Reno	NV	89521	775-673-2200	673-2206	455	*TF:* 866-571-1066 ■ *Web:* vernontool.com

Name	Address	City	State	ZIP	Phone	Fax	Class	Details
Vernon Township Board of Education (Inc)	PO Box 99	Vernon	NJ	07462	973-764-2900		685	*Web:* www.vtsd.com
Verologix LLC	18100 Von Karman Ave Ste 850	Irvine	CA	92612	800-403-8041		196	*TF:* 800-403-8041 ■ *Web:* www.verologix.com
Verona Beach State Park	6541 Lake Shore Rd N	Verona Beach	NY	13162	315-762-4463		565	*Web:* parks.ny.gov
Verona Publishing Inc	PO Box 24071	Edina	MN	55410	612-991-5467		637-2	*Web:* www.veronapublishing.com
Verona's Cucina Italiana	1700 McHenry Ave Ste 1-46	Modesto	CA	95350	209-549-8876		671	*Web:* www.veronacucina.net
Veronica Foods Co	1991 Dennison St	Oakland	CA	94606	510-535-6833	532-2837	296-30	*Web:* www.evoliveoil.com
Veronica Perez & Assoc	655 S Hope St Ste 1208	Los Angeles	CA	90017	626-644-5525	221-7128*	41	**Fax Area Code:* 213 ■ *Web:* veronicaperez.com
Veronis Suhler Stevenson (VSS)	55 E 52nd St 33rd Fl	New York	NY	10055	212-935-4990	381-8168	690	*Web:* www.vss.com
Veros Real Estate Solutions LLC	2333 N Broadway Ste 350	Santa Ana	CA	92706	714-415-6300		177	*TF:* 866-458-3767 ■ *Web:* www.veros.com
Veros Systems	5910 Courtyard Dr Ste 150	Austin	TX	78731	512-686-2400		466	*Web:* www.verossystems.com
VeroScience LLC	1334 Main Rd	Tiverton	RI	02878	401-816-0525	816-0524	743	*Web:* www.veroscience.com
Verosonic Inc	440 Milwaukee Ave Ste 200	Lincolnshire	IL	60084	847-540-9257		358	*Web:* verosonic.com
Verrex Corp	1130 Rt 22 W	Mountainside	NJ	07092	908-232-7000		52	*TF:* 800-303-8170 ■ *Web:* www.verrex.com
Verrill Dana LLP	PO Box 586	Portland	ME	04112	207-774-4000	774-7499	428	*Web:* www.verrill-law.com
Versa Capital Management LLC	2929 Arch St Ste 1800	Philadelphia	PA	19104	215-609-3400	609-3499	690	*Web:* www.versa.com
Versa Electronics	3943 Quebec Ave N	Minneapolis	MN	55427	763-557-6737	557-8073	246	*Web:* www.versae.com
Versa Press Inc	1465 Springbay Rd	East Peoria	IL	61611	800-447-7829		626	*TF:* 800-447-7829 ■ *Web:* www.versapress.com
Versa Products Company Inc	22 Spring Valley Rd	Paramus	NJ	07652	201-843-2400	843-2931	790	*Web:* www.versa-valves.com
Versa Shore Inc	1999 S Bascom Ave Ste 700	Campbell	CA	95008	408-874-8330		396	*Web:* www.versashore.com
Versabar Inc	1111 Engineers Rd	Belle Chasse	LA	70037	504-392-3200		514	*Web:* www.vbar.com
Versace Law Office PC	113 Rose Ln	Rome	NY	13440	315-339-8574	339-2042	41	*Web:* versacelawoffice.com
VersaCold Logistics Services	3371 No 6 Rd	Richmond	BC	V6V1P6	604-258-0350	207-1971	314	*TF:* 877-207-1950 ■ *Web:* www.versacold.com
Versacom	1501 McGill College Ave 6th Fl	Montreal	QC	H3A3M8	514-397-1950		768	*TF:* 866-320-1950 ■ *Web:* www.versacom.ca
Versailles	3555 SW Eigth St	Miami	FL	33135	305-444-0240		671	*Web:* versaillesrestaurant.com
Versailles	10319 Venice Blvd	Los Angeles	CA	90034	310-558-3168	558-1817	671	*Web:* versaillescuban.com
Versailles State Park	US Hwy 50 PO Box 205	Versailles	IN	47042	812-689-6424		565	*Web:* www.in.gov
Versalift East Inc	2706 Brodhead Rd	Bethlehem	PA	18020	610-866-1400		45	*Web:* east.versalift.com
Versalign Inc	1719 Delaware Ave	Wilmington	DE	19806	302-225-7800		260	*Web:* versalign.com
Versalogic Corp	4211 W 11th Ave	Eugene	OR	97402	541-485-8575	485-5712	173-2	*TF:* 800-824-3163 ■ *Web:* www.versalogic.com
Versant Inc	316 N Milwaukee St Ste 280	Milwaukee	WI	53202	414-410-0500		7	*Web:* www.versantsolutions.com
Versasuite	10601 Pecan Park Blvd	Austin	TX	78750	833-568-6242		225	*TF:* 800-903-8774 ■ *Web:* versasuite.com
Versatec LLC	30 Shelter Rock Rd	Danbury	CT	06810	203-743-3837		695	*Web:* versatecsolutions.com
VersaTech Automation Services LLC	11349 FM 529 Rd	Houston	TX	77041	713-939-6100	937-7222	256	*Web:* vtechas.com
Versatile Fabrication	2708 Ninth St	Muskegon	MI	49444	231-739-7115		697	*Web:* versatile-fabrication.com
Versatile Group Inc	4410 Spring Valley Rd	Dallas	TX	75244	800-237-8435	980-8136*	178-1	**Fax Area Code:* 972 ■ *TF:* 800-237-8435 ■ *Web:* www.certiflexdimension.com
Versatile Mobile Systems	4900 Ritter Rd Ste 100	Mechanicsburg	PA	17055	800-262-1622	778-8577*	225	*NYSE:* CVE ■ **Fax Area Code:* 425 ■ *TF:* 800-262-1622 ■ *Web:* www.versatilemobile.com
Versatile Mold & Design Inc	219 Newborn Rd	Rutledge	GA	30663	706-557-8397	557-8196	757	*Web:* www.versatilemd.com
Versatube Corp	4755 Rochester Rd	Troy	MI	48085	248-689-7373	689-8293	489	*TF:* 800-878-1385 ■ *Web:* www.versatubecorp.com
Versevo Inc	1055 Cottonwood Ave	Hartland	WI	53029	262-369-8210	369-8211	757	*Web:* www.versevo.com
Versiti	638 North 18th St	Milwaukee	WI	53233	877-232-4376		89	*TF:* 877-232-4376 ■ *Web:* www.versiti.org
Versivo Inc	950 N Glebe Rd Ste 4200	Arlington	VA	22203	866-222-2145		180	*TF:* 866-222-2145 ■ *Web:* versivo.com
Verso Adv Inc	50 W 17th St 5th Fl	New York	NY	10011	212-292-2990		4	*Web:* www.versoadvertising.com
Verso Books	20 Jay St Ste 1010	Brooklyn	NY	11201	718-246-8160	246-8165	637-2	*Web:* www.versobooks.com
Verso Corp	6775 Lenox Center Ct	Memphis	TN	38115	877-837-7606		557	*NYSE:* VRS ■ *TF:* 877-837-7606 ■ *Web:* www.versoco.com

Name / Address	City	State	ZIP	Phone	Fax	Class
Versonix Corp 1175 Saratoga Ave Ste 4	San Jose	CA	95129	408-873-3131		177
Web: versonix.com						
Verspeeten Cartage Ltd						
274129 Wallace Line	Ingersoll	ON	N5C3J7	519-425-7881		59
TF: 800-265-6701 ■ *Web:* www.verspeeten.com						
Verst Logistics Inc 300 Shorland Dr	Walton	KY	41094	859-485-1212		803-1
Web: verstlogistics.com						
VerStandig Broadcasting						
10960 John Wayne Dr PO Box 788	Greencastle	PA	17225	717-597-9200	597-9210	643
Web: verstandig.com						
Vertafore Inc 5 Waterside Crossing	Windsor	CT	06095	800-444-4813		178-10
TF: 800-444-4813 ■ *Web:* www.vertafore.com						
Vertech Solutions Group LLC						
640 Plaza Dr Ste 120	Highlands Ranch	CO	80129	720-746-2380		177
Web: vertechgroup.com						
VerTechs Enterprises Inc						
1071 Industrial Pl	El Cajon	CA	92020	858-578-3900		21
Web: vertechsusa.com						
Verteks Consulting Inc						
2102 SW 20th Pl Ste 602	Ocala	FL	34471	352-401-0909		196
Web: www.verteks.com						
Vertel Corp						
21300 Victory Blvd Ste 700	Woodland Hills	CA	91367	818-227-1400		180
Web: www.vertel.com						
Vertellus Specialties Inc						
201 N Illinois St Ste 1800	Indianapolis	IN	46204	317-247-8141	248-6402	145
TF: 800-777-3536 ■ *Web:* www.vertellus.com						
Vertex Business Services LLC						
501 W President George Bush Hwy Ste 350	Richardson	TX	75080	214-576-1000		317
Web: vertexone.net						
Vertex China 131 Brea Canyon Rd	Walnut	CA	91789	909-622-3333		361
Web: www.vertexchina.com						
Vertex Companies Inc, The						
400 Libbey Pkwy	Weymouth	MA	02189	781-952-6000		192
TF: 888-298-5162 ■ *Web:* vertexeng.com						
Vertex Computer Systems Inc						
2245 Enterprise Pkwy E	Twinsburg	OH	44087	330-963-0044		809
Web: www.vertexcs.com						
Vertex Distribution						
523 Pleasant St Bldg 10	Attleboro	MA	02703	508-431-1120	431-1114	278
TF: 800-283-2355 ■ *Web:* www.vertexdistribution.com						
Vertex Inc 1041 Old Cassatt Rd	Berwyn	PA	19312	610-640-4200	640-5892	178-1
TF: 800-355-3500 ■ *Web:* www.vertexinc.com						
Vertex Pharmaceuticals Inc						
50 Northern Ave	Boston	MA	02210	617-341-6100		582
NASDAQ: VRTX ■ *Web:* www.vrtx.com						
Vertex Software Corp						
1515 S Cptl of Tx Hwy 4	Austin	TX	78746	512-328-3700		177
Web: www.vertex.com						
Vertex Systems Inc						
2550 Corporate Exchange Dr Ste 104	Columbus	OH	43231	614-318-7100	862-6261*	179
**Fax Area Code:* 888 ■ *TF:* 866-981-2600 ■ *Web:* www.vertexsystems.com						
Vertex Wireless LLC						
500 Wegner Dr	West Chicago	IL	60185	630-293-6300		179
Web: www.vertexwireless.com						
Vertical Alliance Group Inc						
1730 Galleria Oaks	Texarkana	TX	75503	903-792-3866		242
TF: 877-792-3866 ■ *Web:* www.infinitiworkforce.com						
Vertical Aviation						
15035 N 73rd St Ste B 100	Scottsdale	AZ	85260	480-991-6558		359
Vertical Communications Inc						
3979 Freedom Cir Ste 400	Santa Clara	CA	95054	408-404-1600	969-9601	178-7
OTC: VRCC ■ *TF:* 800-914-9985 ■ *Web:* www.vertical.com						
Vertical Flight Society, The						
2701 Prosperity Ave Ste 210	Fairfax	VA	22031	703-684-6777	739-9279	49-21
TF: 855-247-4685 ■ *Web:* vtol.org						
Vertical Group 25 DeForest Ave	Summit	NJ	07901	908-277-3737	273-9434	792
Web: www.vertical-group.com						
Vertical Management Systems Inc						
15440 Laguna Canyon Rd Ste 160	Irvine	CA	92618	800-867-4357		177
TF: 800-867-4357 ■ *Web:* www.vmshelp.com						
Vertical Research Partners LLC						
6 Landmark Sq Ste 720	Stamford	CT	06901	203-276-5680		401
Web: www.verticalresearchpartners.com						
Vertical Solutions Inc						
4243 Hunt Rd Ste 201	Cincinnati	OH	45242	513-891-7997		180
TF: 800-466-0238 ■ *Web:* vertsol.com						
Vertical Structures Inc						
309 Spangler Dr Ste E	Richmond	KY	40475	859-624-8360		116
Web: verticalstructures.com						
Vertical Systems Inc						
6462 City W Pkwy Ste 100	Eden Prairie	MN	55344	952-934-7533		177
Web: vertsys.com						
Vertical Systems International LLC						
2126 Chamber Ctr Dr Ft Mitchell	Lakeside Park	KY	41017	859-485-9650	485-9654	207
Web: www.vsilift.com						
Vertical Transportation Excellence						
7133 Rutherford Rd						
Rutherford Plaza Bldg Ste 300	Baltimore	MD	21244	443-348-2020	298-3940*	196
**Fax Area Code:* 410 ■ *Web:* www.vtexcellence.com						
Vertical Turbine Specialists Inc						
1802 E 50th St Unit 106	Lubbock	TX	79404	806-743-5555		641
Web: www.vtsfabs.com						
Vertices LLC						
76 W Ruby Ave Unit A	Palisades Park	NJ	07650	732-418-9135		396
Web: www.vertices.com						
Verti-Crete LLC 16500 S 500 W	Bluffdale	UT	84065	801-571-2028		183
Web: verti-crete.com						
Vertigraph Inc 12959 Jupiter Rd Ste 252	Dallas	TX	75238	214-340-9436		463
TF: 800-989-4243 ■ *Web:* www.vertigraph.com						
Vertisoft						
990 Boul Pierre-roux E	Victoriaville	QC	G6T0K9	877-368-3241		180
TF: 877-368-3241 ■ *Web:* www.vertisoftpme.com						
Vertisys Corp 821-B Livingston Ct	Marietta	GA	30067	770-955-1755		196
Web: www.vertisys.com						
VertitechIT Inc 4 Open Sq Way Ste 310	Holyoke	MA	01040	855-638-9879		631
TF: 855-638-9879 ■ *Web:* vertitechit.com						
Vertiv Group Corp 1050 Dearborn Dr	Columbus	OH	43085	614-888-0246	841-6882	253
TF: 800-275-3500 ■ *Web:* www.vertiv.com						

Name / Address	City	State	ZIP	Phone	Fax	Class
Verto Solutions						
1620 'I' St NW Ste 925	Washington	DC	20006	202-293-5800	463-8998	47
Web: www.vertosolutions.net						
Verus Pharmaceuticals Inc						
4732 Finchley Ter Ste 200	San Diego	CA	92130	858-436-1600		231
Verve 1127 Gregg St	Columbia	SC	29201	803-799-0045		393
Web: www.verveinteriors.com						
Veryable Inc 2019 N Lamar St Ste 250	Dallas	TX	75202	682-325-9677		39
Web: veryableops.com						
Vesbridge Partners						
301 Carlson Pkwy Ste 110	Minnetonka	MN	55305	952-995-7499	995-7493	792
Web: www.vesbridge.com						
Vescio Threading Co						
14002 Anson Ave	Santa Fe Springs	CA	90670	562-802-1868	802-2073	454
TF: 800-361-4218 ■ *Web:* vesciomfg.com						
Vesco Oil Corp 16055 W 12-Mile Rd	Southfield	MI	48076	800-527-5358	557-2236*	579
**Fax Area Code:* 248 ■ *TF:* 800-527-5358 ■ *Web:* www.vesco-oil.com						
Vescom Textiles Inc						
2289 Ross Mill Rd	Henderson	NC	27536	252-431-6200		745-1
Web: www.vescom.com						
VESD (Victor Elementary School District)						
12219 Second Ave	Victorville	CA	92395	760-245-1691	245-6245	685
Web: www.vesd.net						
Vespaio 1610 S Congress Ave	Austin	TX	78704	512-441-6100	441-7746	671
Web: austinvespaio.com						
Vess Oil Corp						
1700 Waterfront Pkwy Bldg 500	Wichita	KS	67206	316-682-1537		536
Web: www.vessoil.com						
Vessel Metrics LLC						
Soveral Harbor 2401 PGA Blvd						
Ste 155	Palm Beach Gardens	FL	33410	888-214-1710		387
TF: 888-214-1710 ■ *Web:* www.vesselvanguard.com						
Vessel Statistics Inc						
384 Voters Rd Ste 200	Slidell	LA	70461	985-643-2888	847-9388	261
Web: vesselstatistics.com						
Vest & Messerly PA						
7077 Northland Cir N Ste 300	Brooklyn Park	MN	55428	763-566-3720		41
Web: vestandmesserly.com						
Vest Advertising 3007 Sprowl Rd	Louisville	KY	40299	502-267-5335		636
Web: vestadvertising.com						
Vest Inc 6023 Alcoa Ave	Vernon	CA	90058	800-421-6370		490
TF: 800-421-6370 ■ *Web:* www.vestinc.com						
Vesta Corp 5400 Meadows Rd 5th Fl	Portland	OR	97223	503-790-2500	790-2525	215
Web: trustvesta.com						
Vesta Hospitality LLC						
900 Washington St Ste 760	Vancouver	WA	98660	360-737-0442		194
Web: www.vestahospitality.com						
VESTA Modular 1000 Town Ctr Ste 975	Southfield	MI	48075	817-663-8527		188-2
Web: www.vestamodular.com						
Vesta Properties Ltd						
9770 196A St Ste 101A	Langley	BC	V1M2X5	604-888-7869		186
Web: www.vestaproperties.com						
Vestal & Wiler CPAS						
201 E Pine St Ste 801	Orlando	FL	32801	407-843-4433	841-6694	2
Web: vestal-wiler.com						
Vestal Central School District						
201 Main St	Vestal	NY	13850	607-757-2241	757-2227	685
Web: www.vestal.stier.org						
Vestal Electronic Devices LLC						
635 Dickson St	Endicott	NY	13760	607-773-8461	772-8184	253
Web: www.vestalelectronics.com						
Vestal Manufacturing Enterprises Inc						
176 Industrial Park Rd	Sweetwater	TN	37874	423-337-6125		480
Web: www.vestalmfg.com						
Vestar Development						
2425 E Camelback Rd Ste 750	Phoenix	AZ	85016	602-866-0900	956-8721	655
Web: vestar.com						
Vestavia Hills City Schools						
Vestavia Hills Board of Education						
1204 Montgomery Hwy	Vestavia Hills	AL	35216	205-402-5100	402-5134	685
Web: www.vestavia.k12.al.us						
Vestcom International Inc						
7302 Kanis Rd	Little Rock	AR	72204	501-663-0100		8
TF: 800-678-7001 ■ *Web:* vestcom.com						
Vested Business Brokers Inc						
50 Karl Ave Ste 102	Smithtown	NY	11787	631-265-7300		528
TF: 877-735-5224 ■ *Web:* www.vestedbb.com						
Vested Group, The 1021 E 15th St	Plano	TX	75074	972-429-9025		196
Web: www.thevested.com						
Vestevich, Mallender, Dubois & Dritsas PC						
6905 Telegraph Rd Ste 300	Bloomfield Hills	MI	48301	248-642-1920	642-2095	41
Web: vmddlaw.com						
Vestin Group 2965 S Jones Blvd	Las Vegas	NV	89146	702-227-0965	227-5247	509
Web: www.vestinmortgage.com						
Vestor Capital Corp						
10 S Riverside Plz Ste 1400	Chicago	IL	60606	312-641-2400	641-3646	169
Web: vestorcapital.com						
Vestra Resources Inc 5300 Aviation Dr	Redding	CA	96002	530-223-2585		302
TF: 877-983-7872 ■ *Web:* www.vestra.com						
Vestwell 550 7th Ave 14th Fl	New York	NY	10018	917-979-5358		49-2
Web: www.vestwell.com						
Vet Clinic of Palm Harbor Inc, The						
35891 US Hwy 19 N	Palm Harbor	FL	34684	727-781-7704		794
Web: thevetclinic.com						
Vet Path Services Inc 6450 Castle Dr	Mason	OH	45040	513-469-0777		794
Web: vetpathservicesinc.com						
VetCor Inc 350 Lincoln Pl	Hingham	MA	02043	781-749-8151		794
Web: www.vetcor.com						
Veteran's Truck Line Inc						
800 Black Hawk Dr	Burlington	WI	53105	262-539-3400	539-2720	360-2
TF: 800-456-9476 ■ *Web:* www.vetstruck.com						
Veterans Affairs Health Care System						
1 Veterans Dr	Minneapolis	MN	55417	612-725-2000		374-8
TF: 866-414-5058 ■ *Web:* www.minneapolis.va.gov						
Veterans Affairs Medical Ctr						
508 Fulton St	Durham	NC	27705	919-286-0411	286-6825	374-8
TF: 888-878-6890 ■ *Web:* www.durham.va.gov						

Company	Phone	Fax	Class
Veterans Affairs Medical Ctr 150 S Huntington Ave . . . Jamaica Plain MA 02130 *Fax Area Code: 617 ■ TF: 800-273-8255 ■ Web: www.va.gov	800-273-8255	278-4508*	374-8
Veterans Affairs Medical Ctr 1310 24th Ave S . . . Nashville TN 37212 TF: 800-228-4973 ■ Web: www.va.gov	615-327-4751		374-8
Veterans Affairs Medical Ctr 6439 Garners Ferry Rd . . . Columbia SC 29209 TF: 888-651-2683 ■ Web: www.columbiasc.va.gov	803-776-4000	695-6862	374-8
Veterans Affairs Medical Ctr 1501 San Pedro Dr SE . . . Albuquerque NM 87108 Web: va.gov	505-265-1711	256-2855	374-8
Veterans Affairs Medical Ctr 2215 Fuller Rd . . . Ann Arbor MI 48105 TF: 800-361-8387 ■ Web: www.annarbor.va.gov	734-769-7100		374-8
Veterans Affairs Medical Ctr 1100 Tunnel Rd . . . Asheville NC 28805 TF: 800-932-6408 ■ Web: www.asheville.va.gov	828-298-7911	299-2502	374-8
Veterans Affairs Medical Ctr 10 N Greene St . . . Baltimore MD 21201 TF: 800-463-6295 ■ Web: veterans.maryland.gov	410-605-7000		374-8
Veterans Affairs Medical Ctr 940 Belmont St . . . Brockton MA 02301 TF: 800-865-3384 ■ Web: www.va.gov	508-583-4500		374-8
Veterans Affairs Medical Ctr 3495 Bailey Ave . . . Buffalo NY 14215 TF: 800-532-8387 ■ Web: www.buffalo.va.gov	716-834-9200	862-8759	374-8
Veterans Affairs Medical Ctr 820 S Damen Ave . . . Chicago IL 60612 TF: 888-569-5282 ■ Web: www.chicago.va.gov	312-569-8387		374-8
Veterans Affairs Medical Ctr 2002 Holcombe Blvd . . . Houston TX 77030 TF: 800-553-2278 ■ Web: www.houston.va.gov	713-791-1414	794-7218	374-8
Veterans Affairs Medical Ctr 1700 S Lincoln Ave . . . Lebanon PA 17042 TF: 800-409-8771 ■ Web: www.lebanon.va.gov	800-409-8771		374-8
Veterans Affairs Medical Ctr 151 Knollcroft Rd . . . Lyons NJ 07939 Web: www.va.gov	908-647-0180		374-8
Veterans Affairs Medical Ctr 1030 Jefferson Ave . . . Memphis TN 38104 TF: 800-636-8262 ■ Web: va.gov	901-523-8990		374-8
Veterans Affairs Medical Ctr 1201 NW 16th St . . . Miami FL 33125 TF: 888-276-1785 ■ Web: www.miami.va.gov	305-324-4455		374-8
Veterans Affairs Medical Ctr 79 Middleville Rd . . . Northport NY 11768 Web: www.northport.va.gov	631-261-4400		374-8
Veterans Affairs Medical Ctr 921 NE 13th St . . . Oklahoma City OK 73104 TF: 866-835-5273 ■ Web: www.oklahoma.va.gov	405-456-1000		374-8
Veterans Affairs Medical Ctr 4101 Woolworth Ave . . . Omaha NE 68105 TF: 800-451-5796 ■ Web: www.nebraska.va.gov	402-346-8800		374-8
Veterans Affairs Medical Ctr 3801 Miranda Ave . . . Palo Alto CA 94304 Web: www.paloalto.va.gov	650-493-5000		374-8
Veterans Affairs Medical Ctr 830 Chalkstone Ave . . . Providence RI 02908 TF: 866-590-2976 ■ Web: www.va.gov	401-273-7100		374-8
Veterans Affairs Medical Ctr 500 Foothill Dr . . . Salt Lake City UT 84148 TF: 800-613-4012 ■ Web: www.saltlakecity.va.gov	801-582-1565		374-8
Veterans Affairs Medical Ctr 4800 Memorial Dr . . . Waco TX 76711 Web: va.gov	254-752-6581		374-8
Veterans Affairs Medical Ctr 601 Hwy 6 W . . . Iowa City IA 52246 TF: 866-687-7382 ■ Web: www.iowacity.va.gov	319-338-0581		374-8
Veterans Affairs Medical Ctr 1601 Kirkwood Hwy . . . Wilmington DE 19805 TF: 800-450-8262 ■ Web: www.wilmington.va.gov	302-994-2511		374-8
Veterans Affairs Medical Ctr 10000 Bay Pines Blvd . . . Bay Pines FL 33744 TF: 888-820-0230 ■ Web: www.baypines.va.gov	727-398-6661	398-9442	374-8
Veterans Affairs Medical Ctr 13000 Bruce B Downs Blvd . . . Tampa FL 33612 TF: 888-716-7787 ■ Web: www.va.gov	813-972-2000		374-8
Veterans Affairs Medical Ctr 2121 Lake Ave . . . Fort Wayne IN 46805 TF: 800-360-8387 ■ Web: www.northernindiana.va.gov	260-426-5431		374-8
Veterans Affairs Medical Ctr 1500 Weiss St . . . Saginaw MI 48602 TF: 877-222-8387 ■ Web: www.va.gov	989-497-2500	321-4903	374-8
Veterans Affairs Medical Ctr 718 Smyth Rd . . . Manchester NH 03104 TF: 800-892-8384 ■ Web: www.manchester.va.gov	603-624-4366		374-8
Veterans Affairs Medical Ctr 800 Irving Ave . . . Syracuse NY 13210 TF: 800-792-4334 ■ Web: www.syracuse.va.gov	315-425-4400		374-8
Veterans Affairs Medical Ctr 100 Emancipation Dr . . . Hampton VA 23667 TF: 800-488-8244 ■ Web: www.hampton.va.gov	757-722-9961		374-8
Veterans Affairs Medical Ctr 200 Veterans Ave . . . Beckley WV 25801 Web: www.va.gov	304-255-2121		374-8
Veterans Affairs Medical Ctr 2500 Overlook Terr . . . Madison WI 53705 TF: 888-478-8321 ■ Web: www.madison.va.gov	608-256-1901		374-8
Veterans Benefits Administration 810 Vermont Ave NW . . . Washington DC 20420 *Fax Area Code: 202 ■ TF: 800-827-1000 ■ Web: benefits.va.gov	800-827-1000	275-5947*	340-19
Veterans Canteen Service 1 Jefferson Barracks Rd Bldg 25 . . . Saint Louis MO 63125 Web: www.vacanteen.va.gov	314-652-4100	845-1201	340-19
Veterans Care Ctr 4550 Shenandoah Ave . . . Roanoke VA 24017 Web: www.dvs.virginia.gov	540-982-2860		793

Company	Phone	Fax	Class
Veterans for Peace Inc (VFP) 1404 N Broadway . . . Saint Louis MO 63102 Web: www.veteransforpeace.org	314-725-6005	725-7103	48-5
Veterans Guest House 880 Locust St . . . Reno NV 89502 Web: www.veteransguesthouse.org	775-324-6958	324-6071	372
Veterans Health Care System of the Ozarks 1100 N College Ave . . . Fayetteville AR 72703 TF: 800-691-8387 ■ Web: www.fayettevillear.va.gov	479-443-4301		374-8
Veterans Home 1200 E 18th St . . . Hastings MN 55033 TF: 877-838-3803 ■ Web: mn.gov	651-539-2400		793
Veterans Home & Hospital 287 W St . . . Rocky Hill CT 06067 Web: portal.ct.gov	860-529-2571		374-7
Veterans Home of California-Barstow 100 E Veterans Pkwy . . . Barstow CA 92311 TF: 800-746-0606 ■ Web: www.calvet.ca.gov	760-252-6200		793
Veterans Home of California-Chula Vista 700 E Naples Ct . . . Chula Vista CA 91911 Web: www.calvet.ca.gov	619-482-6010		793
Veterans Memorial Auditorium 1 Avenue of the Arts . . . Providence RI 02903 Web: www.thevetsri.com	401-222-1467		572
Veterans Museum & Memorial Ctr 2115 Pk Blvd . . . San Diego CA 92101 Web: www.veteranmuseum.org	619-239-2300	239-7445	520
Veterans of Foreign Wars of the US (VFW) 406 W 34th St . . . Kansas City MO 64111 TF: 800-963-3180 ■ Web: www.vfw.org	816-756-3390	968-1149	48-19
Veterans Oil Delivery 2070 Hwy 150 . . . Bessemer AL 35022 Web: www.veteransoilinc.com	205-424-4400		579
Veterinary Care Ctr 6455 Santa Monica Blvd . . . Los Angeles CA 90038 Web: veterinarycarecenter.com	323-919-6666		794
Veterinary Clinic of Schoolcraft 4872 W U Ave . . . Schoolcraft MI 49087 Web: schoolcraftvet.com	269-679-5248		794
Veterinary Dental Partners PLLC 7908 E Chaparral Rd Ste 108 . . . Scottsdale AZ 85250 Web: azvetdentists.com	480-941-1738		794
Veterinary Pet Insurance Inc PO Box 2344 . . . Brea CA 92822 TF: 800-872-7387 ■ Web: www.petinsurance.com	800-872-7387		391-1
Veterinary Pharmacies of America Inc (VPA) 4802 N Sam Houston Pkwy W Ste 100 . . . Houston TX 77066 TF: 877-838-7979 ■ Web: www.vparx.com	877-838-7979		584
Veterinary Specialists of the Southeast 335 Stephenson Ave . . . Savannah GA 31405 Web: vss.org	912-354-6681	355-4221	794
Veterinary Specialty & Emergency Hospital 3550 S Jason St . . . Englewood CO 80110 Web: www.vrcc.com	303-874-7387		794
Veterinary Specialty Ctr 1515 Busch Pkwy . . . Buffalo Grove IL 60089 Web: vetspecialty.com	847-459-7535		794
Veterinary Specialty Hospital of The Carolinas 6405 Tryon Rd Ste 100 . . . Cary NC 27518 Web: www.vshcarolinas.com	919-233-4911		794
Veterinary Surgical Referral Practice Pa 6910 Carpenter Fire Station Rd Ste 100 . . . Cary NC 27519 Web: quartetvet.com	919-545-1001		794
Veterinary Surgical Services Inc 7512 Paula Dr . . . Tampa FL 33615 Web: vetsurgical.net	813-901-5100		794
Veterinary Transplant Services Inc 215 E Titus St . . . Kent WA 98032 TF: 800-558-5223 ■ Web: vtsonline.com	253-520-0771		794
Vetoquinol Canada Inc 2000 Ch Georges . . . Laval QC J5T3S5 TF: 800-363-1700 ■ Web: www.vetoquinol.ca	450-586-2252	586-4649	584
Vetri 1312 Spruce St . . . Philadelphia PA 19107 Web: vetrifamily.com	215-732-3478		671
VetSelect Animal Hospital 2150 Old Novi Rd . . . Novi MI 48377 Web: www.vetselect.com	248-624-1100	624-6542	794
VetStem Biopharma Inc 12860 Danielson Ct Ste B . . . Poway CA 92064 TF: 888-387-8361 ■ Web: vetstem.com	858-748-2004		794
VetStrategy 30 Whitmore Rd . . . Woodbridge ON L4L7Z4 TF: 866-901-6471 ■ Web: www.vetstrategy.com	866-901-6471		463
Vetstreet 780 Township Line Rd . . . Yardley PA 19067 TF: 888-799-8387 ■ Web: www.vetstreet.com	215-493-0621		387
Vetter Senior Living 20220 Harney St . . . Elkhorn NE 68022 TF: 800-388-4264 ■ Web: www.vetterseniorliving.com	402-895-3932	895-8165	463
Vetter Stone Co (VSC) 23894 Third Ave . . . Mankato MN 56001 TF: 800-878-2850 ■ Web: www.vetterstone.com	507-345-4568	345-4777	724
VetVu 627 Main St . . . North Oxford MA 01537 TF: 800-440-7407 ■ Web: vetvu.com	800-440-7407		476
Vexor Technology Inc 955 W Smith Rd . . . Medina OH 44256 TF: 877-721-9773 ■ Web: vexortechnology.com	330-721-9773	721-9438	660
Vezina, Lawrence & Piscitelli PA 413 E Park Ave . . . Tallahassee FL 32301 Web: vlplaw.com	850-224-6205		41
VF Corp 105 Corporate Center Blvd . . . Greensboro NC 27408 NYSE: VFC ■ TF: 800-446-2617 ■ Web: www.vfc.com	336-424-6000		155-3
vFinance Inc 1200 N Federal Hwy Ste 400 . . . Boca Raton FL 33432 TF: 800-487-0577 ■ Web: www.vfinanceinvestments.com	800-266-8023		690
V-fluence Interactive 4579 Laclede Ave Ste 275 . . . Saint Louis MO 63108 TF: 877-835-8362 ■ Web: www.v-fluence.com	877-835-8362		195
VFP (Veterans for Peace Inc) 1404 N Broadway . . . Saint Louis MO 63102 Web: www.veteransforpeace.org	314-725-6005	725-7103	48-5
VFP Inc 1701 Midland Rd PO Box 1809 . . . Salem VA 24153 Web: www.vfpinc.com	540-977-0500	977-5555	505
VFSS IT Services Transformation, Mobility & Human Capital 6317 Executive Blvd . . . Rockville MD 20852 Web: www.viccs.com	702-330-3208		194
VFUC (Visions Federal Credit Union) 24 McKinley Ave . . . Endicott NY 13760 TF: 800-242-2120 ■ Web: www.visionsfcu.org	607-754-7900	786-1718	219

Name / Address	City	State	ZIP	Phone	Fax	Class
VFW (Veterans of Foreign Wars of the US) 406 W 34th St *TF:* 800-963-3180 ■ *Web:* www.vfw.org	Kansas City	MO	64111	816-756-3390	968-1149	48-19
VGMarket LLC 3860 Sheridan St Ste C *Web:* www.vgm.co	Hollywood	FL	33021	650-483-8384		466
VH Blackinton & Company Inc 221 John L Dietsch Blvd *Web:* www.blackinton.com	Attleboro	MA	02763	508-699-4436		483
VH1 (Video Hits One) 1515 Broadway **Fax Area Code:* 201 ■ *Web:* www.vh1.com	New York	NY	10036	212-258-7800	422-6630*	740
VHHA (Virginia Hospital & Healthcare Assn) 4200 Innslake Dr *Web:* www.vhha.com	Glen Allen	VA	23060	804-965-1227		48-17
VHS (Vermont Historical Society) Vermont History Ctr 60 Washington St Ste 1 *Web:* vermonthistory.org	Barre	VT	05641	802-479-8500	479-8510	48-13
VIA 1170 Main St *Web:* olmstedcenter.org	Buffalo	NY	14209	716-882-1025		305
VIA Agency 619 Congress St *Web:* www.theviaagency.com	Portland	ME	04101	207-221-3000		4
VIA Licensing Corp 1275 Market St *Web:* www.vialicensing.com	San Francisco	CA	94107	415-645-4700	645-4400	52
VIA Metropolitan Transit 800 W Myrtle St *TF:* 866-362-4200 ■ *Web:* www.viainfo.net	San Antonio	TX	78212	210-362-2000	362-2563	468
VIA Motors Inc 165 Mtn Way Dr *Web:* www.viamotors.com	Orem	UT	84058	801-764-9333		489
VIA Rail Canada Inc 3 Place Ville Marie Ste 500 *TF:* 888-842-7245 ■ *Web:* www.viarail.ca	Montreal	QC	H3B2C9	514-871-6000	871-6104	649
VIA Real Restaurant 4020 N MacArthur Blvd *Web:* www.viareal.com	Irving	TX	75038	972-650-9001	541-0215	671
VIA Technologies Inc 940 Mission Ct *Web:* www.viatech.com	Fremont	CA	94539	510-683-3300		696
Viable Solutions Inc 7802 Kingspointe Pkwy Ste 206 *TF:* 800-679-7626 ■ *Web:* viable-solutions.com	Orlando	FL	32819	407-249-9600		809
ViaCyte Inc 3550 General Atomics Ct *Web:* viacyte.com	San Diego	CA	92121	858-455-3708	455-3962	668
Viad Corp 1850 N Central Ave Ste 1900 *NYSE: VVI* ■ *Web:* www.viad.com	Phoenix	AZ	85004	602-207-1000		185
Viair Corp 15 Edelman *TF:* 800-618-1994 ■ *Web:* www.viaircorp.com	Irvine	CA	92618	949-585-0011		787
Viam Manufacturing Inc 87 Park Tower Dr **Fax Area Code:* 562 ■ *Web:* www.viammfg.com	Manchester	TN	37355	931-461-2300	695-1043*	131
Viamedia Inc 220 Lexington Green Cir Ste 300 *Web:* viamediatv.com	Lexington	KY	40503	859-977-9000		5
Vianet 128 Larch St Ste 201 *Web:* www.vianet.ca	Sudbury	ON	P3E5J8	705-222-9996	675-0404	387
Viant Group LLC 500 Washington St Ste 325 *Web:* www.viantgroup.com	San Francisco	CA	94111	415-820-6100		41
ViaSat Inc 6155 El Camino Real *NASDAQ: VSAT* ■ *TF:* 855-463-9333 ■ *Web:* www.viasat.com	Carlsbad	CA	92009	760-476-2200	929-3941	681
ViaTech Publishing Solutions 8857 Alexander Rd *TF:* 800-645-8558 ■ *Web:* www.viatech.io	Batavia	NY	14020	631-968-8500		86
Viatech Systems Inc 1749 Old Meadow Rd Ste 650 *Web:* www.viatech-systems.net	McLean	VA	22102	703-917-0550	917-0558	194
Viatran Corp 3829 Forest Pkwy Ste 500 *TF:* 800-688-0030 ■ *Web:* www.viatran.com	Wheatfield	NY	14120	716-629-3800	693-9162	253
Viatron Systems Inc 18233 S Hoover St *Web:* www.viatron.com	Gardena	CA	90248	310-756-0607		177
Vibac SPA 12250 Industrial Blvd *TF:* 800-557-0192 ■ *Web:* www.vibac.it	Montreal	QC	H1B5M5	514-640-0250	640-6702	732
Vibco Inc 75 Stilson Rd *Web:* www.vibco.com	Wyoming	RI	02898	401-539-2392		190
Vibra Screw Inc 755 Union Blvd *Web:* www.vibrascrew.com	Totowa	NJ	07512	973-256-7410	256-2114	470
Vibranalysis Inc 220 Plaza Western Auto *Web:* www.vibranalysispr.com	Trujillo Alto	PR	00976	787-283-7500		743
Vibrant Corp 8330A Washington Pl NE *TF:* 800-410-3048 ■ *Web:* www.vibrantndt.com	Albuquerque	NM	87113	505-314-1488		743
Vibrant Media Inc 524 Broadway 9th Fl *Web:* www.vibrantmedia.com	New York	NY	10012	646-312-6100		7
Vibrant Power Inc 310 Courtneypark Dr E *Web:* www.vibrantpower.com	Mississauga	ON	L5T2S5	905-564-8644		480
VibrantAds LLC 7100 Stevenson Blvd Ste 209 *Web:* www.vibrantads.com	Fremont	CA	94538	408-908-0828		737
Vibrante Press Inc PO Box 51853 *Web:* vibrantepress.com	Albuquerque	NM	87181	505-298-4793	323-0049	637-2
Vibration Institute 6262 Kingery Hwy Ste 212 *Web:* www.vi-institute.org	Willowbrook	IL	60527	630-654-2254	654-2271	49-19
Vibration monitoring products & services 11011 Brooklet Dr Ste 300 **Fax Area Code:* 281 ■ *Web:* www.vibravista.com	Houston	TX	77099	713-830-7601	754-4972*	407
Vibration Mounting & Control 113 Main St *TF:* 800-569-8423 ■ *Web:* www.thevmcgroup.com	Bloomingdale	NJ	07403	973-838-1780		454
Vibration Research Corp 2385 Wilshere Dr Ste A *Web:* www.vibrationresearch.com	Jenison	MI	49428	616-669-3028	669-5337	177
Vic Canever Chevrolet Inc 3000 Owen Rd *Web:* www.viccaneverchevy.com	Fenton	MI	48430	810-519-5634		57
Vic Fingerhut Campaigns 1100 H St NW Ste 920 *Web:* www.vicfingerhutcampaigns.com	Washington	DC	20005	202-331-3700		194
Vic Myers Associates Inc (VMA) 2432 Jefferson St NE *Web:* www.vicmyers.com	Albuquerque	NM	87190	505-884-6878	883-4062	681
Vic's Accounting 309 Des Meurons St *Web:* allyear.ca	Winnipeg	MB	R2K2L8	204-668-3441		734
Vi-Cas Manufacturing Company Inc 8407 Monroe Ave *Web:* vi-cas.com	Cincinnati	OH	45236	513-791-7741		596
Viccino Italian Gourmet 1315 N Charles St *Web:* www.viccino.com	Baltimore	MD	21201	410-576-0266		671
Viceroy Homes Ltd 414 Croft St E *Web:* www.viceroy.com	Port Hope	ON	L1A4H1	416-587-9388		655
Viceroy Hotels & Resorts 750 North San Vicente Blvd E Ste 1000 *Web:* www.viceroyhotelsandresorts.com	West Hollywood	CA	90069	323-930-3700	930-3701	379
Vi-Chem Corp 55 Cottage Grove St SW *TF:* 800-477-8501 ■ *Web:* www.vichem.com	Grand Rapids	MI	49507	616-247-8501	247-8703	605-2
Vici Beauty School 4111 S 108th St *Web:* www.vicicapilli.com	Milwaukee	WI	53228	414-425-1700		685
Vickers Engineering Inc 3604 Glendora Rd PO Box 346 *Web:* www.vickerseng.com	New Troy	MI	49119	269-426-8545	426-8494	454
Vicks Lithograph & Printing Co 5166 Commercial Dr *Web:* vicks.biz	Yorkville	NY	13495	315-736-9344		626
Vicksburg National Military Park 3201 Clay St *Web:* www.nps.gov	Vicksburg	MS	39183	601-636-0583	636-9497	564
Vicksburg Post 1601 N Frontage Rd *Web:* www.vicksburgpost.com	Vicksburg	MS	39180	601-636-4545		532-2
Vicksburg-Warren County Chamber of Commerce 2020 Mission 66 *Web:* www.vicksburgusa.com	Vicksburg	MS	39180	601-636-1012	636-4422	139
Vicom Computer Services Inc 400 Broadhollow Rd *Web:* www.vicomnet.com	Farmingdale	NY	11735	631-694-3900		264-1
Vicon Industries Inc 135 Fell Ct *NYSE: VII* ■ *TF:* 800-645-9116 ■ *Web:* www.vicon-security.com	Hauppauge	NY	11788	631-952-2288	951-2288	647
Viconics Technologies Inc 7262 Marconi 3rd Fl *TF:* 800-563-5660 ■ *Web:* www.viconics.com	Montreal	QC	H2R2Z5	514-321-5660	321-4150	253
Vicor Corp 25 Frontage Rd *NASDAQ: VICR* ■ *TF:* 800-735-6200 ■ *Web:* www.vicorpower.com	Andover	MA	01810	978-470-2900	475-6715	253
Vicount Industries Inc 24704 Hathaway St *Web:* www.vicount.net	Farmington Hills	MI	48335	248-471-5071	471-2682	757
Victaulic Co 4901 Kesslersville Rd *TF:* 800-742-5842 ■ *Web:* www.victaulic.com	Easton	PA	18040	610-559-3300	250-8817	595
Victim Rights Law Center Inc 115 Broad St 3rd Fl *TF:* 877-758-8132 ■ *Web:* www.victimrights.org	Boston	MA	02110	617-399-6720	399-6722	428
Victor Elementary School District (VESD) 12219 Second Ave *Web:* www.vesd.net	Victorville	CA	92395	760-245-1691	245-6245	685
Victor Insulators Inc 280 Maple Ave *Web:* victorinsulators.com	Victor	NY	14564	585-924-2127	924-7906	249
Victor Insurance Managers Inc 7700 Wisconsin Ave Ste 400 *Web:* www.victorinsuranceus.com	Bethesda	MD	20814	301-961-9800	951-5444	391-5
Victor Insurance Managers Inc 500-1400 Blair Towers Pl *TF:* 800-267-6684 ■ *Web:* www.victorinsurance.ca	Ottawa	ON	K1J9B8	613-786-2000	786-2001	390
Victor International Corp 7640 Dixie Hwy Ste 100 *Web:* www.victorintl.com	Clarkston	MI	48346	248-364-2400		652
Victor J. Mazzella 1408 SE 17th Ave Ste F *Web:* mazzellacpa.com	Cape Coral	FL	33990	239-772-2229		2
Victor L. Phillips Co 4100 Gardner Ave *TF:* 800-878-9290 ■ *Web:* vlpco.com	Kansas City	MO	64120	816-241-9290		358
Victor Machinery Exchange Inc (VME) 33-53 62nd St *TF:* 800-723-5359 ■ *Web:* www.victornet.com	Woodside	NY	11377	718-899-1502	899-0556	385
Victor Packing Inc 11687 Rd 27 1/2 *Web:* www.victorpacking.com	Madera	CA	93637	559-673-5900	673-4225	296-18
Victor Printing Inc 1 Victor Way *TF:* 800-443-2845 ■ *Web:* www.victorptg.com	Sharon	PA	16146	800-443-2845		110
Victor Products USA 717 Thompson Park Dr *Web:* www.victorproductsusa.com	Cranberry Township	PA	16066	724-776-4900	776-3855	767
Victor Settings Inc 25 Brook Ave *TF:* 800-322-9008 ■ *Web:* www.victorsettings.com	Maywood	NJ	07607	201-845-4433	712-0818	407
Victor Talbots Inc 47 Glen Cove Rd *Web:* victortalbots.com	Greenvale	NY	11548	516-625-1787		157-2
Victor Technology LLC 175 E Crossroads Pkwy *TF:* 800-628-2420 ■ *Web:* www.victortech.com	Bolingbrook	IL	60440	630-754-4400	972-3902	118
Victor Valley Community College 18422 Bear Valley Rd *TF:* 877-741-8532 ■ *Web:* www.vvc.edu	Victorville	CA	92392	760-245-4271	245-9745	162
Victoria & Albert Hair Studio 10715 Charter Dr Ste 160 *Web:* www.victoriaandalberthair.com	Columbia	MD	21044	410-992-3000		77
Victoria Advocate PO Box 1518 *TF:* 800-234-8108 ■ *Web:* www.victoriaadvocate.com	Victoria	TX	77902	361-575-1451	574-1220	532-2
Victoria Air Conditioning Ltd 513 Profit Dr *Web:* victoriaair.com	Victoria	TX	77901	361-578-5241		189-10
Victoria Chamber of Commerce 7403 Lone Tree Rd Ste 211 *Web:* www.victoriachamber.org	Victoria	TX	77905	361-573-5277	573-5911	139
Victoria College 2200 E Red River St *TF:* 877-843-4369 ■ *Web:* www.vc.cc.tx.us	Victoria	TX	77901	361-573-3291	582-2525	162
Victoria County 115 N Bridge St Rm 103 *Web:* vctx.org	Victoria	TX	77901	361-575-1478	575-6276	338

Name / Address	City	State	ZIP	Phone	Fax	Class
Victoria Cruises Inc 57-08 39th Ave *TF:* 800-348-8084 ■ *Web:* www.victoriacruises.com	Woodside	NY	11377	212-818-1680	818-9889	221
Victoria Electric Co-opeartive Inc (VEC) 102 S Ben Jordan St *Web:* www.victoriaelectric.coop	Victoria	TX	77901	361-573-2428		245
Victoria General Hospital 2340 Pembina Hwy *Web:* www.vgh.mb.ca	Winnipeg	MB	R3T2E8	204-477-3347		374-2
Victoria Inn Winnipeg 1808 Wellington Ave *TF:* 877-842-4667 ■ *Web:* vicinn.com	Winnipeg	MB	R3H0G3	204-786-4801	786-1329	379
Victoria Insurance 22901 Millcreek Blvd *Web:* www.victoriainsurance.com	Cleveland	OH	44122	216-896-6990		391-4
Victoria Mansion 109 Danforth St *Web:* victoriamansion.org	Portland	ME	04101	207-772-4841	772-6290	50-3
Victoria Regent Hotel, The 1234 Wharf St *TF:* 800-663-7472 ■ *Web:* www.victoriaregent.com	Victoria	BC	V8W3H9	250-386-2211	386-2622	379
Victoria Shipyards Company Ltd 825 Admirals Rd *Web:* www.seaspan.com	Victoria	BC	V9A2P1	250-380-1602		698
Victoria Skimboards 2955 Laguna Canyon Rd Ste 1 *Web:* ocean.victoriaskimboards.com	Laguna Beach	CA	92651	949-494-0059	494-5485	710
Victoria Theatre 138 N Main St *TF:* 888-228-3630 ■ *Web:* www.daytonlive.org	Dayton	OH	45402	937-228-7591	449-5068	572
Victoria Vaudeville Theater 1228 Market St *Web:* www.victoria-theater.com	Wheeling	WV	26003	304-233-7464		572
Victoria's 7 1st Ave SW *Web:* victoriasmn.com	Rochester	MN	55902	507-280-6232		671
Victoria's Candies Inc 51 N Laurel St Frnt *Web:* www.victoriascandies.com	Hazleton	PA	18201	570-455-6341	455-6343	296-8
Victoria's Secret Stores 4 Limited Pkwy *TF:* 800-411-5116 ■ *Web:* www.victoriassecret.com	Reynoldsburg	OH	43068	800-411-5116		157-6
Victorian Condominiums, The 6300 Seawall Blvd *Web:* www.thevictoriancondos.com	Galveston	TX	77551	409-287-6300		379
Victorian Trading Co 15600 W 99th St **Fax Area Code:* 800 ■ *TF:* 800-700-2035 ■ *Web:* www.victoriantradingco.com	Lenexa	KS	66219	913-438-3995	724-7697*	459
Victorian Village 12600 Renaissance Cir *Web:* www.provinet.com	Homer Glen	IL	60491	708-301-0800		371
Victorville Chamber of Commerce 14174 Green Tree Blvd *Web:* vvchamber.com	Victorville	CA	92395	760-245-6506	245-6505	139
Victory Apps 5200 SW 30th St *Web:* victoryapps.com	Davenport	IA	52802	563-362-2264		178-1
Victory Bank, The 548 N Lewis Rd *Web:* victorybank.com	Limerick	PA	19468	610-948-9000		70
Victory Drill Book PO Box 2674 *Web:* www.victorydrillbook.com	Dublin	CA	94568	925-829-6323		96
Victory Education Partners Inc 22 W 19th St 9th Fl *Web:* victoryep.com	New York	NY	10011	212-786-7900	265-1742	734
Victory Electric Cooperative Association Inc 3230 N 14th Ave *TF:* 800-279-7915 ■ *Web:* www.victoryelectric.net	Dodge City	KS	67801	620-227-2139	227-8819	245
Victory Energy Corp 220 Airport Rd *Web:* www.victoryenergycorp.com	Indiana	PA	15701	724-349-6366		540
Victory Energy Operations LLC 10701 E 126th St N *Web:* victoryenergy.com	Collinsville	OK	74021	918-274-0023	274-0059	610
Victory Enterprises Inc 5200 30th St SW *TF:* 800-670-6710 ■ *Web:* www.victoryenterprises.com	Davenport	IA	52802	563-884-4444		180
Victory Fiduciary Consulting 53 N Main St *TF:* 800-938-0989 ■ *Web:* victoryfiduciaryconsulting.com	Mullica Hill	NJ	08062	856-464-3100	464-3101	463
Victory Funds 4900 Tiedeman Rd 4th Fl *TF:* 877-660-4400 ■ *Web:* www.vcm.com	Brooklyn	OH	44144	216-898-2400		528
Victory Furniture 2512 Santa Monica Blvd *TF:* 800-953-2000 ■ *Web:* victoryfurniture.com	Santa Monica	CA	90404	310-264-1046	264-1830	321
Victory Gardens Theater 2257 N Lincoln Ave *Web:* victorygardens.org	Chicago	IL	60614	773-549-5788		749
Victory Heating & Air Conditioning Company Inc 115 Mendon St *TF:* 800-993-4822 ■ *Web:* www.victoryhvac.com	Bellingham	MA	02019	508-966-9858		610
Victory Housing Inc 5430 Grosvenor Ln Ste 210 *Web:* www.victoryhousing.org	Bethesda	MD	20814	301-493-6000	493-9788	653
Victory Packaging LP 3555 Timmons Ln Ste 1440 *Web:* www.victorypackaging.com	Houston	TX	77027	713-961-3299		100
Victory Petroleum Inc 3220 S Dixie Hwy Ste 201 *Web:* www.victorypetroleum.com	Miami	FL	33133	305-255-4145		146
Victory Productions Inc 55 Linden St *TF:* 888-580-6645 ■ *Web:* victoryprd.com	Worcester	MA	01609	508-755-0051		94
Victory Racing Plate Co, The 1200 Rosedale Ave *Web:* victoryracingplate.com	Rosedale	MD	21237	410-391-6600		489
Victory Records Inc 346 N Justine St 5th Fl *Web:* www.victoryrecords.com	Chicago	IL	60607	312-666-8661		657
Victory Refrigeration Inc 110 Woodcrest Rd *TF:* 800-523-5008 ■ *Web:* victoryrefrigeration.com	Cherry Hill	NJ	08003	856-428-4200	428-7299	664
Victory Search Group 20701 N Scottsdale Rd Ste 107-300 *Web:* victorysearchgroup.com	Scottsdale	AZ	85255	480-585-0073		260
Victory Studios 2247 15th Ave W *Web:* www.victorystudios.com	Seattle	WA	98119	206-282-1776	282-3535	512
Victory Transportation Systems Inc 9009 N Loop E Ste 165 *Web:* www.victorytrucks.com	Houston	TX	77029	713-682-8900	681-2086	311
Victory White Metal Co 3027 E 55th St *TF:* 800-635-5050 ■ *Web:* www.victorywhitemetal.com	Cleveland	OH	44127	216-271-1400	271-6430	485
VictorystoreCom Inc 5200 SW 30th St *TF:* 866-241-2295 ■ *Web:* www.victorystore.com	Davenport	IA	52802	866-241-2294		627
Victrix 630 Sherbrooke St W Ste 1100 *Web:* www.victrix.ca	Montreal	QC	H3A1E4	514-879-1919		196
Victron Energy Inc 105 YMCA Dr *Web:* www.victrongroup.com	Waxahachie	TX	75165	469-517-2000		581
Victus Inc 4918 SW 74th Ct *Web:* www.victus.com	Miami	FL	33155	305-663-2129		231
Vicwest Corp 1296 S Service Rd W *TF:* 800-265-6583 ■ *Web:* vicwest.com	Oakville	ON	L6L5T7	905-825-2252	825-2272	491
VIDA Diagnostics Inc 2500 Crosspark Rd W150 BioVentures Ctr *TF:* 855-900-8432 ■ *Web:* vidalung.ai	Coralville	IA	52241	855-900-8432		809
Vidaris Inc 360 Park Ave S *Web:* www.vidaris.com	New York	NY	10010	212-689-5389		256
Vidcrest PO Box 69642 *Web:* www.vidcrest.net	Los Angeles	CA	90069	323-822-1740		514
Video Advertising Bureau (CAB) 830 Third Ave 2nd Fl *Web:* www.thevab.com	New York	NY	10022	212-508-1200	832-3268	49-18
Video Age International Magazine 216 E 75th St Ste PW *Web:* www.videoageinternational.com	New York	NY	10021	212-288-3933	734-9033	457-9
Video Associates Labs Inc 2201 Denton Dr Ste 109B *TF:* 800-331-0547 ■ *Web:* val.com	Austin	TX	78758	512-491-7091	491-7619	173-1
Video Automation Systems Inc 13 Arrow Meadow Rd *Web:* www.videoautomation.com	New Fairfield	CT	06812	203-312-0152	312-0157	196
Video Data Bank 112 S Michigan Ave *Web:* www.vdb.org	Chicago	IL	60603	312-345-3550	541-8073	511
Video Display Corp 1868 Tucker Industrial Rd *OTC:* VIDE ■ *TF:* 800-241-5005 ■ *Web:* www.videodisplay.com	Tucker	GA	30084	770-938-2080	493-3003	173-4
Video Excellence 397 Bay St *Web:* www.myvideoexcellence.com	Fall River	MA	02724	508-672-7374		514
Video Gaming Technologies Inc 308 Mallory Station Rd *Web:* www.vgt.net	Franklin	TN	37067	615-372-1000	472-2851	762
Video Hits One (VH1) 1515 Broadway **Fax Area Code:* 201 ■ *Web:* www.vh1.com	New York	NY	10036	212-258-7800	422-6630*	740
Video King Gaming Systems (VKGS) 2717 N 118 Cir Ste 210 *TF:* 800-635-9912 ■ *Web:* www.videokingnetwork.com	Omaha	NE	68164	402-951-2970	951-2990	322
Video Learning Library LLC 15838 N 62nd St *TF:* 800-383-8811 ■ *Web:* www.videolearning.com	Scottsdale	AZ	85254	480-596-9970		511
VideoBloom Inc 7350 E Progress Pl Ste 100 *Web:* www.videobloom.com	Greenwood Village	CO	80111	303-694-7300		175
Videobred Inc 1000 Hamilton Ave *Web:* videobred.com	Louisville	KY	40204	502-584-5787		514
Videoflicks Canada 1701 Ave Rd *Web:* www.myvideoflicks.ca	Toronto	ON	M5M3Y3	416-782-1883		797
Videojet Technologies Inc 1500 Mittel Blvd *TF:* 800-843-3610 ■ *Web:* www.videojet.com	Wood Dale	IL	60191	630-860-7300	616-3657	386
Videomaker Magazine 1350 E Ninth St PO Box 4591 *TF:* 800-284-3226 ■ *Web:* www.videomaker.com	Chico	CA	95927	530-891-8410	891-8443	457-9
VideoMining Corp 403 S Allen St Ste 101 *TF:* 800-898-9950 ■ *Web:* www.videomining.com	State College	PA	16801	800-898-9950		177
Video-Scope International Ltd 105 Executive Dr Ste 110 *Web:* www.videoscopeintl.com	Dulles	VA	20166	703-437-5534	742-8947	628
Videotex Systems Inc 10255 Miller Rd *TF:* 800-888-4336 ■ *Web:* www.videotexsystems.com	Dallas	TX	75238	972-231-9200	231-2420	178-8
Videssence Inc 10768 Lower Azusa Rd *Web:* www.videssence.com	El Monte	CA	91731	626-579-0943	579-6803	439
Videx Inc 1105 NE Cir Blvd *Web:* videx.com	Corvallis	OR	97330	541-758-0521	738-5501	173-7
Vidler Water Company Inc 3480 GS Richards Blvd Ste 101 *Web:* www.vidlerwater.com	Carson City	NV	89703	775-885-5000		539
Vidovation Corp 23 Spectrum Pointe Dr Ste 206 *Web:* vidovation.com	Lake Forest	CA	92630	949-954-5290		52
Vidyo Inc 433 Hackensack Ave 6th Fl *TF:* 866-998-4396 ■ *Web:* www.vidyo.com	Hackensack	NJ	07601	201-289-8597	490-5340	681
VIE (Virtual Information Executives) 12639 NW Waker Dr *Web:* www.viellc.com	Portland	OR	97229	503-926-9130		194
Vie de France Yamazaki Inc 2070 Chain Bridge Rd Ste 500 *TF:* 800-446-4404 ■ *Web:* www.vdfy.com	Vienna	VA	22182	800-446-4404		68
Vie-Del Co 11903 S Chestnut *Web:* www.vie-delequipmentsales.com	Fresno	CA	93725	559-834-2525	834-1348	80-3
Viejas Casino 5000 Willows Rd *TF:* 800-847-6537 ■ *Web:* viejas.com	Alpine	CA	91901	619-445-5400		133
Vieng Thai 6929 Long Pt St *Web:* www.viengthai.com	Houston	TX	77055	713-688-9910		671
Vienna Sausage Manufacturing Co 2501 N Damen Ave *TF:* 800-366-3647 ■ *Web:* www.viennabeef.com	Chicago	IL	60647	773-278-7800		296-26
Vientiane Cafe 4728 Baltimore Ave *Web:* www.vientiane-cafe.com	Philadelphia	PA	19143	215-726-1095		671
Vietnam *Consulate General* 1700 California St Ste 580 *Web:* www.vietnamconsulate-sf.org	San Francisco	CA	94109	415-922-1707	922-1848	257

Name / Address	City	State	ZIP	Phone	Fax	Class
Embassy 1233 20th St NW Ste 400 *Web:* vietnamembassy-usa.org	Washington	DC	20036	202-861-0737	861-0917	257
Vietnam Archive, The *Texas Tech University* PO Box 41041 *Web:* www.vietnam.ttu.edu	Lubbock	TX	79409	806-742-9010	742-0496	434-4
Vietnam Cafe 2200 W 39th St *Web:* www.thevietnamcafe.com	Kansas City	KS	66103	913-262-8552		671
Vietnam Palace Restaurant 222 N 11th St *Web:* www.vietnampalace.net	Philadelphia	PA	19107	215-592-9596		671
Vietnam Restaurant 221 N 11th St *Web:* www.eatatvietnam.com	Philadelphia	PA	19107	215-592-1163		671
Vietnam Restaurant 701 N Water St *Web:* www.vietnam-restaurant.com	Corpus Christi	TX	78401	361-853-2682		671
Vietnam Veterans of America 3027 Walnut St *Web:* vva.org	Kansas City	MO	64108	816-561-8387		50-4
Vietnam Women's Memorial Foundation Inc 1735 Connecticut Ave NW 3rd Fl *TF:* 866-822-8963 ■ *Web:* www.vietnamwomensmemorial.org	Washington	DC	20009	866-822-8963		50-4
View at Mt. Adams, The 1071 Celestial St *Web:* www.theviewmtadams.com	Cincinnati	OH	45202	513-841-9999		671
View by View Inc 1203 Union St *Web:* www.viewbyview.com	San Francisco	CA	94133	415-359-4494		180
View Micro-Metrology Inc 1711 W 17th St *Web:* www.viewmm.com	Tempe	AZ	85281	480-295-3150		201
ViewCast 3701 W Plano Pkwy *Web:* viewcast.com	Plano	TX	75075	450-350-0659		176
Viewmont Mall 100 Viewmont Mall *Web:* shopviewmontmall.com	Scranton	PA	18508	570-346-9165		460
Viewpoint Books 548 Washington St *Web:* www.viewpointbooks.com	Columbus	IN	47201	812-376-0778		95
ViewSonic Corp 381 Brea Canyon Rd *Web:* www.viewsonic.com	Walnut	CA	91789	909-444-8888	468-1240	173-4
ViewTrade Securities Inc 525 Washington Blvd 24th Fl *Web:* www.viewtrade.com	Jersey City	NJ	07310	201-215-9809	217-6745	690
Vigen Construction Inc 42247 180th St SW *Web:* www.vigenconstruction.com	East Grand Forks	MN	56721	218-773-1159	773-3454	261
Viget Labs LLC 400 W Broad St 4th Fl *Web:* viget.com	Falls Church	VA	22046	703-891-0670		177
Vigi Sante Ltee 197 Thornhill *Web:* www.vigisante.com	Dollard-Des-Ormeaux	QC	H9B3H8	514-684-0930		371
Vigilant Capital Management LLC 2 City Ctr 4th Fl *Web:* vigilantcap.com	Portland	ME	04101	207-523-1110		528
Vigilant Technologies LLC 1050 Wilshire Dr Ste 307 *TF:* 888-209-9424 ■ *Web:* vigilant-inc.com	Troy	MI	48084	248-614-2500		624
Vigilante Electric Co-opeartive Inc 225 E Bannack St **Fax Area Code:* 406 ■ *TF:* 800-221-8271 ■ *Web:* www.vec.coop	Dillon	MT	59725	800-221-8271	683-4328*	245
Vigilistics Inc 711 Grand Ave Ste 290 *TF:* 888-235-7540 ■ *Web:* www.vigilistics.com	San Rafael	CA	94901	949-900-8380		809
Viglione Heating & Cooling Inc 259 Commerce St *Web:* www.viglione.com	East Haven	CT	06512	203-868-0106		189-10
Vignola Trucking & Safe Company Inc 160 Hewitt Ave *Web:* vignolarigging.com	Hamilton Township	NJ	08611	609-392-1007	392-2214	311
Vigo County 121 Oak St *Web:* www.vigocounty.in.gov	Terre Haute	IN	47807	812-462-3367		338
Vigo County Public Library 1 Library Sq *Web:* www.vigo.lib.in.us	Terre Haute	IN	47807	812-232-1113		434-3
Vigo Importing Co PO Box 15884 *TF:* 800-282-4130 ■ *Web:* www.vigo-alessi.com	Tampa	FL	33614	813-884-3491		805
Vigor Industrial LLC 5555 N Channel Ave *Web:* vigor.net	Portland	OR	97217	503-247-1777	247-1620	698
VIH Aviation Group 1962 Canso Rd *TF:* 866-844-4354 ■ *Web:* www.vih.com	North Saanich	BC	V8L5V5	250-656-3987	655-6839	359
Vi-Jon Labs Inc 8800 Page Ave *TF:* 800-227-1863 ■ *Web:* www.vijon.com	Saint Louis	MO	63114	314-427-1000	427-1010	214
Viking Acoustical Corp 21480 Heath Ave *TF:* 800-328-8385 ■ *Web:* www.vikingusa.com	Lakeville	MN	55044	952-469-3405	469-4503	319-1
Viking Automatic Sprinkler Co 301 York Ave *Web:* www.vikingsprinkler.com	Saint Paul	MN	55130	651-558-3300	558-3310	189-13
Viking Client Services Inc 7500 Office Ridge Cir Ste 100 *TF:* 800-767-7895 ■ *Web:* www.vikingservice.com	Eden Prairie	MN	55344	952-944-7575		393
Viking Cooking School 325C Howard St *TF:* 866-451-6750 ■ *Web:* www.thealluvian.com	Greenwood	MS	38930	662-451-6750	455-7809	685
Viking Corp 210 N Industrial Pk Dr *TF:* 800-968-9501 ■ *Web:* www.vikingcorp.com	Hastings	MI	49058	269-945-9501	945-9599	283
Viking Cue Manufacturing LLC 2228 Pleasant View Rd *TF:* 800-397-0122 ■ *Web:* www.vikingcue.com	Middleton	WI	53562	608-271-5155	271-5157	710
Viking Drill & Tool Inc 355 State St *TF:* 800-328-4655 ■ *Web:* www.vikingdrill.com	Saint Paul	MN	55107	651-227-8911	227-1793	493
Viking Electric Supply Inc 451 Industrial Blvd W *TF:* 800-435-3345 ■ *Web:* www.vikingelectric.com	Minneapolis	MN	55413	612-627-1300	627-1313	246
Viking Engineering & Development Inc 5750 Main St N *TF:* 800-545-5112 ■ *Web:* www.vikingeng.com	Fridley	MN	55432	763-571-2400	571-0901	821
Viking Forest Products LLC 7615 Smetana Ln *TF:* 800-733-3801 ■ *Web:* www.vikingforest.com	Eden Prairie	MN	55344	800-733-3801		191-3
Viking Group Inc 3033 Orchard Vista Dr SE Ste 308 *Web:* vikinggroupinc.com	Grand Rapids	MI	49546	616-831-6448		360-3
Viking Industrial Products 3 Brigham St *Web:* www.piezomaster.com	Marlborough	MA	01752	508-481-4600	481-4602	518
Viking Label and Packaging Inc 5652 Lakers Ln *Web:* www.vikinglabel.com	Nisswa	MN	56468	218-963-2575	963-4849	552-1
Viking Lake State Park 2780 Viking Lake Rd *Web:* www.iowadnr.gov	Stanton	IA	51573	712-829-2235	829-2842	565
Viking Land Transportation Systems 1221 N Front St *TF:* 800-845-5838 ■ *Web:* www.vikinglandtransportation.com	New Ulm	MN	56073	507-354-5055		780
Viking Materials Inc 3225 Como Ave SE *TF:* 800-682-3942 ■ *Web:* www.vikingmaterials.com	Minneapolis	MN	55414	612-617-5800	623-9070	492
Viking Networks Inc 4655 Middle Rd B *Web:* vikingnetworks.net	Columbus	IN	47203	812-372-0007		180
Viking Paper Corp 5148 Stickney Ave *Web:* packpros.net	Toledo	OH	43612	419-729-4951		554
Viking Plastics Inc 1 Viking St *Web:* www.vikingplastics.com	Corry	PA	16407	814-664-8671		608
Viking Pools 121 Crawford Rd PO Box 96 *TF:* 800-854-7665 ■ *Web:* lathampool.com	Williams	CA	95987	800-854-7665		728
Viking Pump Inc 406 State St *Web:* www.vikingpump.com	Cedar Falls	IA	50613	319-266-1741	273-8157	641
Viking Range Corp 111 Front St *TF:* 888-845-4641 ■ *Web:* www.vikingrange.com	Greenwood	MS	38930	662-455-1200	455-3127	298
Viking Recreational Vehicles LLC 580 W Burr Oak St PO Box 549 *TF:* 888-422-2582 ■ *Web:* coachmenrv.com	Centreville	MI	49032	888-422-2582		120
Viking River Cruises 5700 Canoga Ave Ste 200 *TF:* 877-668-4546 ■ *Web:* www.vikingrivercruises.com	Woodland Hills	CA	91367	818-227-1234	227-1237	221
Viking Ski Shop Inc 3422 W Fullerton Ave *Web:* www.vikingskishop.com	Chicago	IL	60647	773-276-1222		711
Viking Software Solutions 6660 S Sheridan Rd Ste 202 *Web:* www.vikingsoft.com	Tulsa	OK	74136	918-491-6144	494-2701	178-1
Viking Speedway 300 Fairgrounds Rd *Web:* vikingspeedway.myracepass.com	Alexandria	MN	56308	320-762-1559		515
Viking Woodcrafts Inc 1317 8th St SE *TF:* 800-328-0116 ■ *Web:* www.vikingwoodcrafts.com	Waseca	MN	56093	507-835-8043	835-3895	802
Viking Yacht Company Inc PO Box 308 *Web:* www.vikingyachts.com	New Gretna	NJ	08224	609-296-6000	296-3956	90
Viking-Cives USA 14331 Mill St *Web:* www.vikingcives.com	Harrisville	NY	13648	315-543-2321	543-2366	516
Vikki Hudson Insurance Agency Inc 130 W Industrial Park Rd *Web:* vikkihudson.com	Harrison	AR	72601	870-741-9461		390
Vikmere Software PO Box 34521 *Web:* vikmere.com	Los Angeles	CA	90034	310-836-2802		463
Viktor Incentives & Meetings 4020 Copper View Ste 130 *TF:* 800-748-0478 ■ *Web:* www.viktorwithak.com	Traverse City	MI	49684	231-947-0882	947-2532	384
Viktorina Cards 89 Stonehurst Ave Ste 311 *Web:* www.amazzzingcards.com	Ottawa	ON	K1Y4R6	613-422-6337		130
Villa Angela Nursing Rehabilitation Ctr 5700 Karl Rd *Web:* www.villa-angela.net	Columbus	OH	43229	614-846-5420		450
Villa Camillus Inc, The 10515 E River Rd *Web:* www.the-villa-camillus.com	Columbia Station	OH	44028	440-236-5091		371
Villa Europa 3044 Deans Bridge Rd *Web:* www.villaeuropa.com	Augusta	GA	30906	706-798-6211	798-0066	671
Villa Feliciana Chronic Disease Hospital 5002 Hwy 10 *Web:* ldh.la.gov	Jackson	LA	70748	225-634-4017	634-4191	374-7
Villa Firenze 610 First Ave NE *Web:* www.villafirenze.ca	Calgary	AB	T2E0B6	403-264-4297		671
Villa Florence 225 Powell St *TF:* 844-838-8701 ■ *Web:* www.villaflorence.com	San Francisco	CA	94102	415-397-7700		379
Villa Gardens 842 E Villa St *TF:* 800-958-4552 ■ *Web:* www.villagardens.org	Pasadena	CA	91101	626-463-5330		672
Villa Italian Kitchen 25 Washington St *Web:* www.villaitaliankitchen.com	Morristown	NJ	07960	973-285-4800	401-0121	670
Villa Julie College 1525 Green Spring Valley Rd **Fax Area Code:* 443 ■ *TF:* 877-468-6852 ■ *Web:* stevenson.edu	Stevenson	MD	21153	410-486-7001	352-4440*	166
Villa Lighting Supply Inc 2929 Chouteau Ave **Fax Area Code:* 866 ■ *TF:* 800-325-0963 ■ *Web:* www.villalighting.com	Saint Louis	MO	63103	800-325-0963	531-8720*	393
Villa Maria College 240 Pine Ridge Rd *Web:* www.villa.edu	Buffalo	NY	14225	716-896-0700	896-0705	162
Villa Maria Nursing And Rehabilitation Center Inc 1050 NE 125th St	North Miami	FL	33161	305-891-8850		374-6
Villa Maria Post Acute 425 E Barcellus Ave *Web:* villamariapostacute.com	Santa Maria	CA	93454	805-922-3558		450
Villa Marin 100 Thorndale Dr *TF:* 888-926-2030 ■ *Web:* www.villa-marin.com	San Rafael	CA	94903	415-492-2408		672
Villa Nova Restaurant 5121 Arctic Blvd Ste I *Web:* villanovaalaska.com	Anchorage	AK	99503	907-561-1660		671
Villa of Hope 3300 Dewey Ave *Web:* www.villaofhope.org	Rochester	NY	14616	585-865-1550	865-5219	726
Villa Park Orchards Assn 960 Third St *Web:* www.vpoa.net	Fillmore	CA	93016	805-524-0411		315-2

Name / Address	City	State	Zip	Phone	Fax	Class
Villa Roma Resort & Conference Ctr 356 Villa Roma Rd *TF:* 800-533-6767 ■ *Web:* www.villaroma.com	Callicoon	NY	12723	845-887-4880	887-4824	669
Villa Royale 1620 S Indian Trl *Web:* villaroyale.com	Palm Springs	CA	92264	760-327-2314		379
Villa Terrace Decorative Arts Museum 2220 N Terr Ave *Web:* www.villaterrace.org	Milwaukee	WI	53202	414-271-3656	271-3986	520
Villa Tronco 1213 Blanding St *Web:* www.villatronco.com	Columbia	SC	29201	803-256-7677	256-4336	671
Villa Y Zapata 8505-09 Madison Ave	Cleveland	OH	44102	216-961-4369		671
Village Art Supply 715 Hahman Dr *Web:* www.villageartsupply.com	Santa Rosa	CA	95405	707-575-4501		45
Village at Breckenridge Resort 535 S Park Ave *Web:* www.breckenridge.com	Breckenridge	CO	80424	970-453-3000		669
Village at Manor Park, The (VMP) 3023 S 84th St *Web:* www.vmpcares.com	Milwaukee	WI	53227	414-607-4100		672
Village Automotive Group 75-95 N Beacon St **Fax Area Code:* 781 ■ *TF:* 888-707-5524 ■ *Web:* www.villageautomotive.com	Boston	MA	02135	888-707-5524	769-9485*	57
Village Bank & Trust 234 W NW Hwy *Web:* www.bankatvillage.com	Arlington Heights	IL	60004	847-670-1000	670-7744	70
Village Bistro, The 1723 Wilson Blvd *Web:* www.melebistro.com	Arlington	VA	22209	703-522-5222		671
Village Builders 700 NW 107th Ave *TF:* 888-671-8175 ■ *Web:* www.villagebuilders.com	Miami	FL	33172	305-229-6400		653
Village Creek State Park 8854 Park Rd 74 *Web:* tpwd.texas.gov	Lumberton	TX	77657	409-755-7322		565
Village Creek State Park 201 County Rd 754 *Web:* www.arkansasstateparks.com	Wynne	AR	72396	870-238-9406		565
Village Farms LP 7 Christopher Way **Fax Area Code:* 407 ■ *Web:* www.villagefarms.com	Eatontown	NJ	07724	732-676-3000	936-1187*	10-11
Village Green Cos 28411 Northwestern Hwy Ste 400 **Fax Area Code:* 248 ■ *TF:* 866-396-1105 ■ *Web:* www.villagegreen.com	Southfield	MI	48034	866-396-1105	851-6161*	187
Village Green Heritage Ctr 221 S Palm Canyon Dr *Web:* pshistoricalsociety.org	Palm Springs	CA	92262	760-323-8297	320-2561	50-3
Village Green of Waterbury 55 Kondracki Ln	Waterbury	CT	06705	203-757-9271		450
Village Green Resort & Gardens 725 Row River Rd **Fax Area Code:* 541 ■ *TF:* 800-343-7666 ■ *Web:* www.villagegreenresortandgardens.com	Cottage Grove	OR	97424	800-343-7666	942-2386*	669
Village Inn 3038 Sidco Dr (HQ Location) *TF:* 800-800-3644 ■ *Web:* www.villageinn.com	Denver	CO	80216	303-294-0609	294-9927	670
Village Inteteriors 215 S Findlay St *Web:* villageinteriorsdesign.com	Seattle	WA	98108	206-768-9600		393
Village Latch Inn 101 Hill St PO Box 3000 *TF:* 800-545-2824 ■ *Web:* www.villagelatch.com	Southampton	NY	11968	631-283-2160	283-3236	379
Village MD 125 S Clark St Ste 900 *Web:* www.villagemd.com	Chicago	IL	60603	312-465-7900		48-17
Village North Retirement Community 11160 Village N Dr *Web:* www.bethesdahealth.org	Saint Louis	MO	63136	314-355-8010		672
Village Nurseries 1589 N Main St **Fax Area Code:* 714 ■ *TF:* 800-542-0209 ■ *Web:* www.villagenurseries.com	Orange	CA	92867	800-542-0209	279-3199*	323
Village on Venetian Bay 4200 Gulf Shore Blvd N *Web:* venetianvillage.com	Naples	FL	34103	239-261-6100		460
Village Royale Animal Clinic Inc 1187 Royal Palm Beach Blvd *Web:* villageroyaleanimalclinic.com	Royal Palm Beach	FL	33411	561-793-1552		794
Village Settlements Inc 177 Kentlands Blvd *Web:* villagesettlements.com	Gaithersburg	MD	20878	301-590-9300	590-1166	41
Village South Inc, The 169 E Flagler St Ste 1300	Miami	FL	33131	305-573-3784		726
Village Square Healthcare Ctr 1586 W San Marcos Blvd *Web:* www.marinerhealthcare.com	San Marcos	CA	92078	760-471-2986		450
Village Tavern 101 Summit Blvd *Web:* www.villagetavern.com	Birmingham	AL	35243	205-970-1640		671
Village Toy Shop 2100 Patriot Blvd *Web:* www.kohlchildrensmuseum.org	Glenview	IL	60026	847-832-6600		761
Village Vacances Valcartier 1860 Valcartier Blvd *TF:* 888-384-5524 ■ *Web:* www.valcartier.com	Valcartier	QC	G0A4S0	418-844-2200	844-1239	32
Village Veterinary 11 York St *Web:* yorkvillagevet.com	York	ME	03909	207-351-1530		794
Village Veterinary Clinic 56 Front St *Web:* villagevetrollinsford.com	Rollinsford	NH	03869	603-749-9688	740-4633	794
Village Voice LLC 36 Cooper Sq *Web:* www.villagevoice.com	New York	NY	10003	212-475-5555	475-8972	532-2
Village, The 2200 W Acacia Ave *Web:* www.thevillageriversidecounty.com	Hemet	CA	92545	951-658-3369		672
Villages of Lake Sumter Inc 1000 Lake Sumter Landing *TF:* 800-245-1081 ■ *Web:* www.thevillages.com	The Villages	FL	32162	352-753-2270		653
Villanova Preparatory School 12096 N Ventura Ave *Web:* www.villanovaprep.org	Ojai	CA	93023	805-646-1464		622
Villanova University 800 E Lancaster Ave *Web:* www1.villanova.edu	Villanova	PA	19085	610-519-6412	519-7649	166
Villanti & Sons, Printers Inc 15 Catamount Dr *Web:* www.villanti.com	Milton	VT	05468	802-864-0723		627
Villari's Martial Arts Center of Shrewsbury 196 Boston Tpke *Web:* www.villarisshrewsbury.com	Shrewsbury	MA	01545	508-752-0091		507
Villarosa Italian Restaurant & Grill 6010 Landmark Center Blvd *Web:* villarosa.us	Greensboro	NC	27407	336-294-8688		671
Villas by the Sea Resort 1175 N Beachview Dr *TF:* 800-841-6262 ■ *Web:* www.villasbythesearesort.com	Jekyll Island	GA	31527	912-635-2521	635-2569	669
Villas of Grand Cypress Golf Resort 1 N Jacaranda *TF:* 877-330-7377 ■ *Web:* www.grandcypress.com	Orlando	FL	32836	407-239-4700		669
Villas on the Bay 105 Marine St *Web:* thevillas.com	Saint Augustine	FL	32084	904-599-7301		379
Villaume Industries Inc 2926 Lone Oak Cir *TF:* 800-488-3610 ■ *Web:* www.villaume.com	Eagan	MN	55121	651-454-3610	454-8556	817
Villaverd Inc 1218 E Yandell Dr Ste 203 *Web:* www.villaverdeinc.com	El Paso	TX	79902	915-351-8822	351-8823	261
Ville De Riviere-Du-Loup 65 Rue De Lehetel-De-Ville *Web:* www.villerdl.ca	Riviere-du-Loup	QC	G5R1L4	418-867-6700		31
Villere's Florist 750 Martin Behrman Ave *TF:* 800-845-5373 ■ *Web:* www.villeresflowers.com	Metairie	LA	70005	504-833-3716		292
Villeroy & Boch USA Inc 3A S Middlesex Ave **Fax Area Code:* 609 ■ *TF:* 800-536-2284 ■ *Web:* www.villeroy-boch.com	Monroe Township	NJ	08831	800-536-2284	655-2421*	362
Villing & Company Inc 5909 Nimtz Pkwy *Web:* villing.com	South Bend	IN	46628	574-277-0215		7
Vimarc Group Inc, The 1205 E Washington St Ste 120 *Web:* www.vimarc.com	Louisville	KY	40206	502-261-9100		7
Vimco Inc 300 Hansen Access Rd *TF:* 800-468-4626 ■ *Web:* www.vimcoinc.com	King of Prussia	PA	19406	610-768-0500	768-0586	191-1
Vimich Traffic Logistics 12201 Tecumseh Rd **Fax Area Code:* 519 ■ *TF:* 800-284-1045 ■ *Web:* www.vimich.com	Tecumseh	ON	N8N1M3	800-284-1045	735-4309*	449
VIMS (Virginia Institute of Marine Science) 1208 Greate Rd PO Box 1346 *Web:* www.vims.edu	Gloucester Point	VA	23062	804-684-7000	684-7097	668
Vin de Set Rooftop Bar & Bistro 2017 Chouteau Ave *Web:* vindeset.com	Saint Louis	MO	63103	314-241-8989		671
Vin Devers Inc 5570 Monroe St *TF:* 888-847-9535 ■ *Web:* www.vindevers.com	Sylvania	OH	43560	419-885-5111		57
Vina Pharmacy Inc 11207 N Lamar Blvd Ste A *Web:* www.medicineshoptx.com	Austin	TX	78753	512-977-8844		237
Vinal Technical High School 60 Daniels St *Web:* vinal.cttech.org	Middletown	CT	06457	860-344-7100	344-2162	685
Vince Emery Productions PO Box 460279 *Web:* www.emerybooks.com	San Francisco	CA	94146	415-337-6000		637-2
Vince Hagan Co 330 Clay Rd Bldg 458 *Web:* www.vincehagan.com	Sunnyvale	TX	75182	972-203-9333		190
Vincennes University 1002 N First St *TF:* 800-742-9198 ■ *Web:* www.my.vinu.edu	Vincennes	IN	47591	812-888-4313	888-5707	162
Vincennes University *Jasper* 850 College Ave *TF:* 800-809-8852 ■ *Web:* www.vinu.edu	Jasper	IN	47546	812-482-3030	481-5960	162
Vincent Benjamin Group LLC 2415 E Camelback Rd Ste 1000 *Web:* vincentbenjamin.com	Phoenix	AZ	85016	602-595-9900		260
Vincent Corp 2810 E Fifth Ave *Web:* www.vincentcorp.com	Tampa	FL	33605	813-248-2650		111
Vincent Giordano Corp 2600 Washington Ave *Web:* www.vgiordano.com	Philadelphia	PA	19146	215-467-6629	467-6339	296-26
Vincent Guerithault on Camelback 3930 E Camelback Rd *Web:* vincentsoncamelback.com	Phoenix	AZ	85018	602-224-0225		671
Vincent J. Criscuolo & Associates PC 130 W Main St Ste 220 *Web:* criscuololaw.com	Rochester	NY	14614	585-232-3240	232-3522	41
Vincent Piazza Jr & Sons Seafood Inc 1201 Sams Ave *TF:* 800-259-5016 ■ *Web:* www.piazzaseafood.com	New Orleans	LA	70123	800-259-5016		297-5
Vincent Porcaro Inc 100 Higginson Ave *Web:* www.vpi3pl.com	Lincoln	RI	02865	401-521-6262	331-6262	559
Vincent Printing Company Inc 1512 Sholar Ave *TF:* 800-251-7262 ■ *Web:* www.vincentprinting.com	Chattanooga	TN	37406	800-251-7262		687
Vincent's 4411 Chastant St *Web:* vincentsitaliancuisine.com	Metairie	LA	70006	504-885-2984		671
Vincenzo's 3449 Robinhood Rd *Web:* vincenzospizzawinstonsalemnc.com	Winston-Salem	NC	27106	336-765-3176		671
Vincenzo's 150 S Fifth St *Web:* www.vincenzositalianrestaurant.com	Louisville	KY	40202	502-580-1350		671
Vinchem Inc 301 Main St *Web:* www.vinchem.com	Chatham	NJ	07928	973-635-4841	635-1459	479
Vincit Group, The 412 Georgia Ave Ste 300 **Fax Area Code:* 423 ■ *TF:* 888-484-6248 ■ *Web:* www.vincitgroup.com	Chattanooga	TN	37403	888-484-6248	265-9070*	355
Vinco Inc PO Box 907 *Web:* www.vinco-inc.com	Forest Lake	MN	55025	651-982-4642	982-4621	186
Vindee Industries Inc 965 Lambrecht Dr *Web:* www.vindee.com	Frankfort	IL	60423	815-469-3300		595
Vindicator, The 107 Vindicator Sq *Web:* www.vindy.com	Youngstown	OH	44503	330-747-1471	747-6712	532-2
Vinegar Hill Veterinary Group 57 Front St *Web:* vhvetgroup.com	Brooklyn	NY	11201	718-797-6875		794

Name / Address	City	State	ZIP	Phone	Fax	Class
Vineland Construction Co 71 W Park Ave; *Web:* www.vinelandconstruction.com	Vineland	NJ	08360	856-794-4500	794-4721	653
Vineland Public Library 1058 E Landis Ave; *Web:* www.vineland.lib.nj.us	Vineland	NJ	08360	856-794-4244		434-3
Vineland Syrup Inc PO Box 1326; *TF:* 800-642-9124 ■ *Web:* www.vinelandsyrup.com	Vineland	NJ	08362	856-691-5772	691-0359	296-15
Vineyard Gazette Inc 34 S Summer St; *Web:* vineyardgazette.com	Edgartown	MA	02539	508-627-4311		532-3
Vineyard Trust 99 Main St PO Box 5277; *Web:* mvpreservation.org	Edgartown	MA	02539	508-627-4440	627-8088	50-1
Vineyards Wine Bar Bistro 54 York St; *Web:* www.vineyards.ca	Ottawa	ON	K1N5T1	613-241-4270	241-5538	671
Vinfen Corp 950 Cambridge St; *TF:* 877-284-6336 ■ *Web:* www.vinfen.org	Cambridge	MA	02141	617-441-1800	441-1858	450
Vining Sparks IBG LP 775 Ridge Lake Blvd; *TF:* 800-829-0321 ■ *Web:* www.viningsparks.com	Memphis	TN	38120	901-766-3000		690
Vinings Jubilee 4300 Paces Ferry Rd SE Ste 245; *Web:* www.viningsjubilee.com	Atlanta	GA	30339	770-434-2400	438-8181	460
Vino Farms Inc 1377 E Lodi Ave; *Web:* www.apps1.cdfa.ca.gov	Lodi	CA	95240	209-334-6975		315-5
Vinoleo Solution & Services Corp 186 Bay 20th St; *Web:* vinoleoinc.com	Brooklyn	NY	11214	917-582-3670		174
Vinology 100 S Main St; *Web:* vinologya2.com	Ann Arbor	MI	48104	734-222-9841		671
Vinopal Title & Abstract LLC 1030 Regis Ct; *Web:* vinopaltitle.com	Eau Claire	WI	54701	715-831-0880		653
Vinotemp International Corp 16782 Von Karman Ave Ste 15; *TF:* 800-888-8466 ■ *Web:* www.vinotemp.com	Irvine	CA	92606	310-886-3332		610
Vinotheque Wine Cellars 1738 E Alpine Ave; *TF:* 800-393-9463 ■ *Web:* www.vinotheque.com	Stockton	CA	95205	800-393-9463		14
Vinson & Elkins LLP 1001 Fannin St Ste 2500; *Web:* www.velaw.com	Houston	TX	77002	713-758-2222	758-2346	428
Vinson Guard Service Inc 955 Howard Ave; *TF:* 800-441-7899 ■ *Web:* www.vinsonguard.com	New Orleans	LA	70113	504-529-2260		693
Vinson Process Controls Company LP 2747 Highpoint Oaks Dr; *TF:* 800-420-6571 ■ *Web:* www.vinsonprocess.com	Lewisville	TX	75067	972-459-8200		358
Vinspire Publishing LLC (VRP) PO Box 1165; *Web:* www.vinspirepublishing.com	Ladson	SC	29456	843-695-7530		637-2
Vinsys Information Technology Inc 12073 Greywing Sq; *Web:* www.vinsysinfo.com	Reston	VA	20191	703-371-4120		396
Vintage Abstract Corp 2124 Flatbush Ave; *Web:* vintageabstract.com	Brooklyn	NY	11234	718-377-0200		390
Vintage Air Inc 18865 Goll St; *TF:* 800-862-6658 ■ *Web:* www.vintageair.com	San Antonio	TX	78266	210-654-7171		664
Vintage Chophouse & Tavern 320 11 Ave SW; *Web:* vintagechophouse.com	Calgary	AB	T2R0C5	403-262-7262		671
Vintage Design 25200 Commercentre Dr; *Web:* www.vintagedesigninc.com	Lake Forest	CA	92630	949-900-5400		291
Vintage Faire Mall 3401 Dale Rd Ste 483; *Web:* www.shopvintagefairemall.com	Modesto	CA	95356	209-527-3401		460
Vintage Flying Museum 505 NW 38th St Hanger 33 S; *Web:* www.vintageflyingmuseum.org	Fort Worth	TX	76106	817-624-1935	624-2840	520
Vintage House 6541 Washington St; *TF:* 800-351-1133 ■ *Web:* www.vintagehouse.com	Yountville	CA	94599	800-351-1133		379
Vintage IT Services 1210 W Fifth St; *Web:* www.vintageits.com	Austin	TX	78703	512-481-1117		196
Vintage Realty Co 330 Marshall St Ste 200; *Web:* www.vintagerealty.com	Shreveport	LA	71101	318-222-2244		652
Vintage Wines 2277 Westbrooke Dr; *Web:* www.vintwine.com	Columbus	OH	43228	614-876-2580		443
Vintage, The 837 Lincoln St; *Web:* thevintageeugene.com	Eugene	OR	97401	541-349-9181		671
Vintners Inn 4350 Barnes Rd; *TF:* 800-421-2584 ■ *Web:* www.vintnersresort.com	Santa Rosa	CA	95403	707-575-7350		379
Vinton County County Courthouse 100 E Main St; *TF:* 800-596-4459 ■ *Web:* www.vintoncounty.com	McArthur	OH	45651	740-596-4571	596-9611	338
Vinyard Fruit and Vegetable Company Inc 330 NE 36th St; *Web:* www.vinyardinc.com	Oklahoma City	OK	73105	405-272-0339		297-7
Vinyl Corp 8000 NW 79th Pl; *TF:* 800-648-4695 ■ *Web:* www.vinylcorp.com	Miami	FL	33166	305-477-6464	477-4108	596
Vinyl Siding Institute (VSI) 1201 15th St NW Ste 220; *Web:* www.vinylsiding.org	Washington	DC	20005	202-587-5100		49-13
Vinylmax LLC 2921 McBride Ct; *TF:* 800-847-3736 ■ *Web:* www.vinylmax.com	Hamilton	OH	45011	513-772-2247		235
Vinylplex Inc 1800 Atkinson Ave; *TF:* 877-779-7473 ■ *Web:* www.vinylplex.com	Pittsburg	KS	66762	620-231-8290	232-8547	596
Vinyltech Corp 201 S 61st Ave; *Web:* vtpipe.com	Phoenix	AZ	85043	602-233-0071	272-4847	596
Vinzant Software Inc 904 W Old Ridge Rd Ste 101; *Web:* www.vinzantinc.com	Hobart	IN	46342	219-942-9544	942-1480	178-1
Vio Security 21031 Warner Center Ln Ste D; *TF:* 855-447-4961 ■ *Web:* www.viosecurity.com	Woodland Hills	CA	91367	855-447-4961		693
Viodi View, The 4285 Payne Ave Ste 10065; **Fax Area Code:* 832 ■ *Web:* viodi.com	San Jose	CA	95157	408-676-6496	565-0320*	116
Viola Bros Inc 180 Washington Ave; *Web:* www.violabros.com	Nutley	NJ	07110	973-667-7000		364
Viola Home Telephone Co 1106 13th St; *Web:* www.violatel.com	Viola	IL	61486	309-596-2222	596-2079	224
Violence Policy Ctr (VPC) 1730 Rhode Island Ave NW Ste 1014; *Web:* www.vpc.org	Washington	DC	20036	202-822-8200		48-7
Violet Mountain Press 9595 Wilshire Blvd Ste 201; *Web:* www.violetmountainpress.com	Beverly Hills	CA	90212	323-648-4141		637-2
Violin Making School of America 304 East 200 South; *Web:* www.vmsa.net	Salt Lake City	UT	84111	801-209-3494	847-6543	685
ViOptix Inc 47224 Mission Falls Ct; *Web:* www.vioptix.com	Fremont	CA	94539	510-226-5860		743
Viox Services Inc 15 W Voorhees St; *TF:* 888-846-9462 ■ *Web:* www.viox-services.com	Cincinnati	OH	45215	513-948-8469		271
VIP Auto Group 2006 Hwy 161	North Little Rock	AR	72117	501-955-5556		57
VIP Motor Cars Ltd 4095 E Palm Canyon Dr	Palm Springs	CA	92264	760-328-6525		57
VIP Office Furniture and Supply Inc 109 Central Ave; *Web:* www.vipoffice.com	Hinesville	GA	31313	912-876-3000		535
VIP Sports Marketing Inc 3319 N Elston Ave; *Web:* www.vipsm.com	Chicago	IL	60618	312-951-0700		195
VIP Technology Solutions Group LLC 12149 S State Hwy 51; *TF:* 866-203-6059 ■ *Web:* www.viptsg.com	Coweta	OK	74429	866-203-6059		175
VIP Tires & Service 12 Lexington St; *Web:* www.vipauto.com	Lewiston	ME	04240	207-784-5423	784-9178	62-5
VIP Tour & Charter Bus Co 129-137 Fox St; *Web:* vipchartercoaches.com	Portland	ME	04101	207-772-4457	772-7020	107
VIP Tours of California Inc 9830 Bellanca Ave; *Web:* www.viptoursofcalifornia.com	Los Angeles	CA	90045	310-641-8114		760
VIPdesk Connect Inc 908 King St Ste 400W; *TF:* 844-874-3472 ■ *Web:* vipdesk.com	Alexandria	VA	22314	844-874-3472		393
Vipin Gulati CPA PC 28580 Orchard Lake Rd Ste 201; *Web:* vgulaticpa.com	Farmington Hills	MI	48334	248-254-3800	254-3804	2
VIRA Insight LLC 120 Dividend Dr Ste 100; **Fax Area Code:* 817 ■ *TF:* 800-305-8472 ■ *Web:* www.virainsight.com	Coppell	TX	75019	800-305-8472	424-9002*	286
Viracon Inc 800 Pk Dr; *TF:* 800-533-2080 ■ *Web:* www.viracon.com	Owatonna	MN	55060	507-451-9555	444-3555	329
Virbac Corp 3200 Meacham Blvd; *Web:* us.virbac.com	Fort Worth	TX	76137	817-831-5030		578
Virco Manufacturing Corp 2027 Harpers Way; *NASDAQ:* VIRC ■ **Fax Area Code:* 800 ■ *TF:* 800-448-4726 ■ *Web:* virco.com	Torrance	CA	90501	310-533-0474	258-7367*	319-3
Virent Inc 3571 Anderson St; *Web:* www.virent.com	Madison	WI	53704	608-663-0228	663-1630	261
Virgilio & Associates Ltd 24069 N Echo Lake Rd; *Web:* virgilioassoc.com	Lake Zurich	IL	60047	847-550-8411		261
Virgin Atlantic Airways Ltd 747 Belden Ave; *TF:* 888-747-7474 ■ *Web:* www.virginatlantic.com	Norwalk	CT	06854	203-750-2000		25
Virgin Atlantic Airways Ltd The Wing 1030 Delta Blvd; *TF:* 866-258-0951 ■ *Web:* www.flywith.virginatlantic.com	Atlanta	GA	30354	866-258-0951		27
Virgin Media 65 Bleecker St Ste 6; *Web:* www.virginmedia.com	New York	NY	10022	212-906-8440		387
Virgin River Casino Corp 100 Pioneer Blvd; *TF:* 877-438-2929 ■ *Web:* virginriver.com	Mesquite	NV	89027	877-438-2929		378
Virginia						
Aging & Rehabilitative Services Dept 8004 Franklin Farms Dr; *TF:* 800-552-5019 ■ *Web:* www.vadrs.org	Richmond	VA	23229	804-662-7000		339-47
Aging Dept 1610 Forest Ave Ste 100; *TF:* 800-552-3402 ■ *Web:* www.vda.virginia.gov	Henrico	VA	23229	804-662-9333	662-9354	339-47
Agriculture & Consumer Services Dept 102 Governor St; *TF:* 800-828-1120 ■ *Web:* www.vdacs.virginia.gov	Richmond	VA	23219	804-786-3501	371-2945	339-47
Arts Commission 600 E Main St Ste 330; *Web:* www.arts.virginia.gov	Richmond	VA	23219	804-225-3132	225-4327	339-47
Attorney General 202 N Ninth St; *Web:* oag.state.va.us	Richmond	VA	23219	804-786-2071	786-1991	339-47
Chief Medical Examiner 400 E Jackson St; *Web:* www.vdh.virginia.gov	Richmond	VA	23219	804-786-2479	225-2766	339-47
Child Support Enforcement Div 730 E Broad St; *Web:* www.dss.state.va.us	Richmond	VA	23219	804-692-1999	692-1965	339-47
Community College System 300 Arboretum Pl Ste 200; *TF:* 844-897-9096 ■ *Web:* www.vccs.edu	Richmond	VA	23236	844-897-9096		339-47
Corrections Dept 6900 Atmore Dr; *Web:* vadoc.virginia.gov	Richmond	VA	23225	804-674-3000	674-3236	339-47
Criminal Injuries Compensation Fund (CICF) PO Box 26927; **Fax Area Code:* 804 ■ *TF:* 800-552-4007 ■ *Web:* www.cicf.state.va.us	Richmond	VA	23261	800-552-4007	367-1021*	339-47
Department of Juvenile Justice Main Street Ctr 600 East Main St 20th Fl PO Box 1110; *Web:* www.djj.virginia.gov	Richmond	VA	23219	804-371-0700		340-14
Economic Development Partnership 901 E Cary St; *Web:* www.vedp.org	Richmond	VA	23219	804-545-5600		339-47
Education Dept PO Box 2120; *Web:* www.pen.k12.va.us	Richmond	VA	23218	804-225-2023		339-47
Emergency Management Dept 10501 Trade Ct; *Web:* www.vaemergency.gov	Richmond	VA	23236	804-897-6500	897-6506	339-47

				Phone	Fax	Class
Employment Commission 703 E Main St *TF:* 866-832-2363 ■ *Web:* www.vec.virginia.gov	Richmond	VA	23219	866-832-2363		259
Environmental Quality Dept PO Box 1105 *Web:* www.deq.virginia.gov	Richmond	VA	23218	804-698-4000		339-47
Financial Institutions Bureau 1300 E Main St *Web:* www.scc.virginia.gov	Richmond	VA	23219	804-371-9657		339-47
Game & Inland Fisheries Dept 7870 Villa Park Dr Ste 400 *Web:* www.virginia.gov	Richmond	VA	23230	804-367-1000	829-6788	339-47
General Assembly 900 E Main St Pocahontas Bldg *Web:* virginiageneralassembly.gov	Richmond	VA	23219	804-698-1068		339-47
Health Dept 109 Governor St PO Box 2448 *Web:* www.vdh.virginia.gov	Richmond	VA	23219	804-864-7001	864-7022	339-47
Health Professions Dept 9960 Mayland Dr Ste 300 *TF:* 800-533-1560 ■ *Web:* www.dhp.virginia.gov	Henrico	VA	23233	804-367-4400	527-4475	339-47
Historic Resources Dept 2801 Kensington Ave *Web:* www.dhr.virginia.gov	Richmond	VA	23221	804-367-2323	367-2391	339-47
Housing Development Authority 601 S Belvidere St *TF:* 877-843-2123 ■ *Web:* www.vhda.com	Richmond	VA	23220	877-843-2123		339-47
Human Resource Management Dept 101 N 14th St 12th Fl *Web:* www.dhrm.virginia.gov	Richmond	VA	23219	804-225-2131	371-7401	339-47
Information Technologies Agency (VITA) 11751 Meadowville Ln **Fax Area Code:* 804 ■ *TF:* 866-637-8482 ■ *Web:* www.vita.virginia.gov	Chester	VA	23836	866-637-8482	416-6355*	339-47
Labor & Industry Dept 3941 Deep Rock Rd Ste 207 *Web:* www.doli.virginia.gov	Richmond	VA	23219	804-371-2327	371-6524	339-47
Lieutenant Governor 102 Governor St PO Box 1195 *Web:* ltgov.virginia.gov	Richmond	VA	23218	804-786-2078	786-7514	339-47
Lottery 600 E Main St Ste 1100 *Web:* www.valottery.com	Richmond	VA	23219	804-692-7000	692-7102	452
Mental Health Mental Retardation & Substance Abuse 1220 Bank St *Web:* www.dbhds.virginia.gov	Richmond	VA	23219	804-786-3921	371-6638	339-47
Port Authority 101 W Main St Ste 600 *TF:* 800-446-8098 ■ *Web:* www.portofvirginia.com	Norfolk	VA	23510	757-296-3505		339-47
Professional & Occupational Regulation Dept 9960 Mayland Dr Ste 400 *TF:* 888-822-3272 ■ *Web:* www.dpor.virginia.gov	Richmond	VA	23233	804-367-8500		339-47
Racing Commission 5707 Huntsman Rd Ste 201-B *Web:* www.vrc.virginia.gov	Richmond	VA	23250	804-966-7400	966-7418	339-47
Secretary of Commerce & Trade PO Box 1475 *Web:* www.commerce.virginia.gov	Richmond	VA	23218	804-786-7831	371-0250	339-47
Secretary of the Commonwealth PO Box 1475 *Web:* www.commonwealth.virginia.gov	Richmond	VA	23218	804-786-2441	371-0017	339-47
State Corp Commission 1300 E Main St PO Box 1197 *Web:* www.scc.virginia.gov	Richmond	VA	23218	804-371-9967	371-9836	339-47
State Council of Higher Education 101 N 14th St 9th Fl James Monroe Bldg *Web:* www.virginia.gov	Richmond	VA	23219	804-225-2600	225-2604	725
State Parks Div 600 E Main St 24th Fl *Web:* www.dcr.virginia.gov	Richmond	VA	23219	804-692-0403	786-9294	339-47
State Police N Chesterfield 7700 Midlothian Tpke *TF:* 800-552-7977 ■ *Web:* www.vsp.state.va.us	Richmond	VA	23235	804-674-2000	674-2936	339-47
Supreme Court 100 N Ninth St 5th Fl *Web:* www.courts.state.va.us	Richmond	VA	23219	804-786-2251		339-47
Taxation Dept PO Box 1115 *Web:* tax.virginia.gov	Richmond	VA	23218	804-367-8031	254-6113	339-47
Treasury Dept 101 N 14th St James Monroe Bldg 3rd Fl *TF:* 800-643-7800 ■ *Web:* www.trs.virginia.gov	Richmond	VA	23219	804-225-2142	225-3187	339-47
Vital Records Div 2001 Maywill St PO Box 1000 *TF:* 877-572-6333 ■ *Web:* www.vdh.virginia.gov	Richmond	VA	23230	804-662-6200	644-2550	339-47
Workers Compensation Commission 333 E Franklin St *TF:* 877-664-2566 ■ *Web:* www.vwc.state.va.us	Richmond	VA	23219	877-664-2566		339-47
Virginia 529 9001 Arboretum Pkwy **Fax Area Code:* 866 ■ *TF:* 888-567-0540 ■ *Web:* www.virginia529.com	Richmond	VA	23236	888-567-0540	757-1295*	725
Virginia Air & Space Ctr 600 Settlers Landing Rd *Web:* www.vasc.org	Hampton	VA	23669	757-727-0900		748
Virginia Aquarium & Marine Science Ctr 717 General Booth Blvd *TF:* 800-822-3224 ■ *Web:* www.virginiaaquarium.com	Virginia Beach	VA	23451	757-385-3474		520
Virginia Beach Convention & Visitor Bureau (VBCVB) 2101 Parks Ave Ste 500 *TF:* 800-700-7702 ■ *Web:* www.visitvirginiabeach.com	Virginia Beach	VA	23451	757-385-4700		206
Virginia Beach (Independent City) 2401 Courthouse Dr Municipal Ctr Bldg 1 *Web:* www.vbgov.com	Virginia Beach	VA	23456	757-385-4242	427-5626	338
Virginia Beach Schools Federal Credit Union 3701 Bonney Rd *TF:* 877-482-7328 ■ *Web:* vbsfcu.org	Virginia Beach	VA	23452	757-463-3650	463-2169	219
Virginia Beach Surf & Rescue Museum 2401 Atlantic Ave *Web:* vbsurfrescuemuseum.org	Virginia Beach	VA	23451	757-422-1587	491-8609	520
Virginia Business Magazine 1207 E Main St Ste 100 *Web:* www.virginiabusiness.com	Richmond	VA	23219	804-649-6999		457-5
Virginia Capital Partners LLC 1801 Libbie Ave *Web:* www.vacapital.com	Richmond	VA	23226	804-648-4802		402
Virginia Center Commons 10101 Brook Rd *Web:* shopvirginiacentercommons.com	Glen Allen	VA	23059	804-266-9002		460
Virginia Chamber of Commerce 919 E Main St *TF:* 800-367-7623 ■ *Web:* www.vachamber.com	Richmond	VA	23219	804-644-1607	783-6112	140
Virginia College *Birmingham* 488 Palisades Blvd *Web:* www.vc.edu	Birmingham	AL	35209	205-802-1200		800
Virginia Commonwealth University 1111 W Broad St *Web:* www.vcu.edu	Richmond	VA	23284	804-828-0100		167-3
Virginia Commonwealth University Cabell Library 901 Park Ave PO Box 842033 *TF:* 844-352-7399 ■ *Web:* www.library.vcu.edu	Richmond	VA	23284	804-828-1111	828-0151	434-6
Virginia Commonwealth University School of Medicine 1101 E Marshall St PO Box 980565 *TF:* 800-332-8813 ■ *Web:* medschool.vcu.edu	Richmond	VA	23298	804-828-9629	828-1246	167-2
Virginia Cook Realtors 5950 Sherry Ln Ste 100 *TF:* 877-975-2665 ■ *Web:* www.virginiacook.com	Dallas	TX	75225	214-696-8877	691-7779	652
Virginia Correctional Enterprises 8030 White Bark Terr *Web:* govce.net	Richmond	VA	23237	804-887-5475		630
Virginia Credit Union 7500 Boulders View Dr *TF:* 800-285-5051 ■ *Web:* www.vacu.org	Richmond	VA	23225	804-323-6000	608-8619	219
Virginia Dare Extract Company Inc 882 Third Ave *Web:* www.virginiadare.com	Brooklyn	NY	11232	718-788-1776	768-3978	296-15
Virginia Dental Assn (VDA) 3460 Mayland Ct Ste 110 *TF:* 877-310-6560 ■ *Web:* www.vadental.org	Richmond	VA	23233	804-288-5750	288-1880	227
Virginia Department of Corrections 12352 Coffeewood Dr PO Box 500 *Web:* www.vadoc.virginia.gov	Mitchells	VA	22729	540-829-6483		213
Virginia Department of Taxation 1957 Westmoreland St PO Box 1115 *Web:* tax.virginia.gov	Richmond	VA	23230	804-367-8037	254-6111	531-7
Virginia Diner Inc, The 322 W Main St *TF:* 800-642-6887 ■ *Web:* www.vadiner.com	Wakefield	VA	23888	800-642-6887		275
Virginia Discovery Museum 524 E Main St *Web:* www.vadm.org	Charlottesville	VA	22902	434-977-1025	977-9681	521
Virginia Episcopal School 400 Ves Rd *TF:* 800-937-3582 ■ *Web:* www.ves.org	Lynchburg	VA	24503	434-385-3607	385-3603	622
Virginia Festival of the Book 145 Ednam Dr *Web:* www.virginiahumanities.org	Charlottesville	VA	22903	434-924-3296	296-4714	281
Virginia Fortunato LLC 1 Kinderkamack Rd *Web:* njbankruptcy911.com	Hackensack	NJ	07601	201-673-5777		41
Virginia Hardwood Co 1000 W Foothill Blvd *Web:* www.virginiahardwood.com	Azusa	CA	91702	626-815-0540	969-9318	191-3
Virginia Highlands Community College 100 VHCC Dr PO Box 828 *TF:* 877-207-6115 ■ *Web:* www.vhcc.edu	Abingdon	VA	24212	276-739-2400		162
Virginia Highlands Small Business Incubator 851 French Moore Jr Blvd *Web:* vhsbi.com	Abingdon	VA	24210	276-492-2062		393
Virginia Historical Society Museum of Virginia History 428 N Blvd *Web:* www.virginiahistory.org	Richmond	VA	23220	804-340-1800	355-2399	520
Virginia Holocaust Museum 2000 E Cary St *Web:* www.vaholocaust.org	Richmond	VA	23223	804-257-5400	257-4314	520
Virginia Homes Building Systems LLC 142 Virginia Homes Ln *Web:* www.virginiahomesbuildingsystems.com	Boydton	VA	23917	434-738-6107	738-6926	505
Virginia Hospital & Healthcare Assn (VHHA) 4200 Innslake Dr *Web:* www.vhha.com	Glen Allen	VA	23060	804-965-1227		48-17
Virginia Hospital Ctr 1701 N George Mason Dr *Web:* www.virginiahospitalcenter.com	Arlington	VA	22205	703-558-5000	558-5715	374-3
Virginia Imports Ltd 7550 Accotink Park Rd *Web:* virginiaimports.net	Springfield	VA	22150	703-823-1230	751-8077	81-3
Virginia Industries Inc 1022 Elm St *Web:* www.virginia.gov	Rocky Hill	CT	06067	860-571-3600		75
Virginia Institute of Marine Science (VIMS) 1208 Greate Rd PO Box 1346 *Web:* www.vims.edu	Gloucester Point	VA	23062	804-684-7000	684-7097	668
Virginia International Terminals Inc 7737 Hampton Blvd *TF:* 800-541-2431 ■ *Web:* www.vit.org	Norfolk	VA	23505	757-440-7000	440-7221	465
Virginia Journal of Education 116 S Third St *TF:* 800-552-9554 ■ *Web:* www.veanea.org	Richmond	VA	23219	804-648-5801	775-8379	457-8
Virginia Living Museum 524 J Clyde Morris Blvd *Web:* thevlm.org	Newport News	VA	23601	757-595-1900	599-4897	520
Virginia Marble Manufacturers Inc 1201 5th Ave *Web:* www.virginiamarble.com	Kenbridge	VA	23944	434-676-3204	676-3299	724
Virginia Maritime Assn 236 E Plume St *Web:* www.vamaritime.com	Norfolk	VA	23510	757-622-2639		78
Virginia Mason Medical Ctr 925 Seneca St *TF:* 888-862-2737 ■ *Web:* www.virginiamason.org	Seattle	WA	98101	206-624-1144		374-3
Virginia Materials Inc 3306 Peterson St	Norfolk	VA	23509	757-855-6328		1
Virginia Military Institute 319 Letcher Ave *TF:* 800-767-4207 ■ *Web:* www.vmi.edu	Lexington	VA	24450	540-464-7211	464-7746	166

Name / Address	City	State	Zip	Phone	Fax	Class
Virginia Mirror Company Inc 300 Moss St S *TF:* 800-368-3011 ■ *Web:* va-glass.com	Martinsville	VA	24112	276-632-9816	956-3020	329
Virginia Museum of Contemporary Art 2200 Parks Ave *Web:* www.virginiamoca.org	Virginia Beach	VA	23451	757-425-0000		50-2
Virginia Museum of Fine Arts 200 N Blvd *Web:* www.vmfa.museum	Richmond	VA	23220	804-340-1400	340-1548	520
Virginia Museum of Natural History (VMNH) 21 Starling Ave *Web:* www.vmnh.net	Martinsville	VA	24112	276-634-4141	634-4199	520
Virginia Museum of Transportation 303 Norfolk Ave *TF:* 800-578-4111 ■ *Web:* www.vmt.org	Roanoke	VA	24016	540-342-5670	342-6898	520
Virginia Natural Gas Inc AGL Resources Inc PO Box 4569 **Fax Area Code:* 484 ■ *Web:* www.aglresources.com	Atlanta	GA	30302	404-584-4000	281-3184*	787
Virginia Nurses Assn (VNA) 7113 Three Chopt Rd Ste 204 *Web:* www.virginianurses.com	Richmond	VA	23226	804-282-1808	282-4916	533
Virginia Peninsula Chamber of Commerce 21 Enterprise Pkwy Ste 100 *TF:* 800-462-3204 ■ *Web:* www.virginiapeninsulachamber.com	Hampton	VA	23666	757-262-2000	262-2009	139
Virginia Plastics Company Inc 3453 Aerial Way Dr SW *TF:* 877-351-1699 ■ *Web:* www.vaplastics.com	Roanoke	VA	24018	540-981-9700	981-2022	816
Virginia Polytechnic Institute & State University 112 Burruss Hall *Web:* vt.edu	Blacksburg	VA	24061	540-231-6000	231-3242	166
Virginia Polytechnic Institute & State University 560 Drillfield Dr *Web:* lib.vt.edu	Blacksburg	VA	24061	540-231-9232		434-6
Virginia Poultry Growers Co-opeartive Inc 6349 Rawley Pk *Web:* www.vapoultrygrowers.com	Hinton	VA	22831	540-867-4000		10-3
Virginia Premier Health Plan Inc 600 E Broad St 4th Fl *Web:* www.virginiapremier.com	Richmond	VA	23219	804-819-5151		391-3
Virginia Press Services Inc 11529 Nuckols Rd *TF:* 800-849-8717 ■ *Web:* www.vpa.net	Glen Allen	VA	23059	804-521-7570	521-7590	624
Virginia Quilting Inc 100 S Main St *Web:* www.virginiaquilting.com	La Crosse	VA	23950	434-757-1809	757-1855	456
Virginia Railway Express (VRE) 1500 King St Ste 202 *Web:* www.vre.org	Alexandria	VA	22314	703-684-1001	684-1313	468
Virginia Realtors 10231 Telegraph Rd *Web:* www.virginiarealtors.org	Glen Allen	VA	23059	804-264-5033		656
Virginia Republican Party 115 E Grace St *Web:* virginia.gop	Richmond	VA	23219	804-780-0111	343-1060	616-2
Virginia School of Pet Grooming 9471 Manassas Dr *Web:* www.virginiaschoolofpetgrooming.com	Manassas	VA	20111	703-361-3868		685
Virginia Society of CPAS 4309 Cox Rd *TF:* 800-733-8272 ■ *Web:* www.vscpa.com	Glen Allen	VA	23060	804-270-5344		2
Virginia Society of Professional Engineers 5301 Creek H8s Dr *Web:* www.vspe.org	Midlothian	VA	23112	804-572-7789		194
Virginia State Bar 707 E Main St Ste 1500 *Web:* www.vsb.org	Richmond	VA	23219	804-775-0500	775-0544	72
Virginia State University 1 Hayden Dr *TF:* 800-871-7611 ■ *Web:* www.vsu.edu	Petersburg	VA	23806	804-524-5000	524-5055	166
Virginia Symphony Orchestra 150 Boush St Ste 201 *Web:* www.virginiasymphony.org	Norfolk	VA	23510	757-466-3060	466-3046	573-3
Virginia Tam Insurance Agency Inc 833 Corporate Way *Web:* farmersagent.com	Fremont	CA	94539	510-683-3883		390
Virginia Tech (VTHG) *Department of Horticulture* 490 W Campus Dr 301 Saunders Hall *Web:* spes.vt.edu	Blacksburg	VA	24061	540-231-5451		97
Virginia Tech Foundation Inc (VTF) 902 Prices Fork Rd Ste 4500 *Web:* www.vtf.vt.edu	Blacksburg	VA	24061	540-231-2861		166
Virginia Theatre 203 W Park Ave *Web:* thevirginia.org	Champaign	IL	61820	217-356-9053		572
Virginia Tile Co 28320 Plymouth Rd *Web:* www.virginiatile.com	Livonia	MI	48150	734-762-2400		361
Virginia Transformer Corp 220 Glade View Dr *TF:* 800-882-3944 ■ *Web:* www.vatransformer.com	Roanoke	VA	24012	540-345-9892	342-7694	767
Virginia Union University 1500 N Lombardy St *TF:* 800-368-3227 ■ *Web:* www.vuu.edu	Richmond	VA	23220	804-342-3570	342-3511	166
Virginia University of Lynchburg - Community Development Corp 2058 Garfield Ave *Web:* vul.edu	Lynchburg	VA	24501	434-528-5276		166
Virginia Veterinary Medical Assn (VVMA) 3801 Westerre Pkwy Ste D *TF:* 800-937-8862 ■ *Web:* vvma.org	Henrico	VA	23233	804-346-2611	346-2655	795
Virginia War Museum 9285 Warwick Blvd *Web:* www.warmuseum.org	Newport News	VA	23607	757-247-8523	247-8627	520
Virginia Wesleyan College 1584 Wesleyan Dr *TF:* 800-737-8684 ■ *Web:* www.vwu.edu	Norfolk	VA	23502	757-455-3200	461-5238	166
Virginia West Electric Supply Co 250 12-th St W *TF:* 800-624-3433 ■ *Web:* www.wvaelectric.com	Huntington	WV	25704	304-525-0361	525-2726	246
Virginia Western Community College 3094 Colonial Ave *TF:* 855-874-6690 ■ *Web:* www.virginiawestern.edu	Roanoke	VA	24015	540-857-8922	857-6102	162
Virginia Zoological Park 3500 Granby St *Web:* virginiazoo.org	Norfolk	VA	23504	757-441-2374		823
Virginian Lodge 750 W Broadway PO Box 1052 *TF:* 800-262-4999 ■ *Web:* virginianlodge.com	Jackson	WY	83001	307-733-2792		379
Virginian Suites 1500 Arlington Blvd *TF:* 866-371-1446 ■ *Web:* www.virginiansuites.com	Arlington	VA	22209	703-522-9600		379
Virginian, The 9229 Arlington Blvd *Web:* thevirginian.org	Fairfax	VA	22031	703-385-0555		672
Virginian-Pilot 150 W Bramelton Ave *Web:* pilotonline.com	Norfolk	VA	23510	757-446-9000		532-2
Virginkar & Associates Inc 1501 E Orangethorpe Ave Ste 200 *Web:* va-inc.com	Fullerton	CA	92831	714-993-1000	993-1092	449
Viridian Partners LLC 1805 Shea Center Dr Ste 250 *Web:* viridianpartners.com	Highlands Ranch	CO	80129	303-271-9114		169
Viridis Energy Inc 700 W Pender St Ste 520 *Web:* www.viridisenergy.ca	Vancouver	BC	V6C1G8	604-669-7831		279
Viridity Energy Inc 1801 Market St Ste 2701 **Fax Area Code:* 215 ■ *Web:* www.viridityenergy.com	Philadelphia	PA	19103	484-534-2222	564-3842*	178-1
VirnetX Holding Corp 308 Dorla Ct *Web:* www.virnetx.com	Zephyr Cove	NV	89448	831-438-8200		177
Virnig Manufacturing Inc 101 Gateway Dr NE *TF:* 800-648-2408 ■ *Web:* www.virnigmfg.com	Rice	MN	56367	800-648-2408		190
Virobay Inc 1360 Willow Rd Ste 100 *Web:* www.virobayinc.com	Menlo Park	CA	94025	650-833-5700		668
Viroxis Corp 12621 Silicon Dr Ste 100 *Web:* www.targetedtech.com	San Antonio	TX	78249	210-558-8896		238
Virsys12 LLC 5205 Maryland Way Ste 202 *Web:* www.virsys12.com	Brentwood	TN	37027	615-800-6768		631
Virtex Operating Company Inc 615 N Upper Broadway Ste 525 *Web:* virtexoperating.com	Corpus Christi	TX	78401	361-882-3046		580
Virtexco Corp 977 Norfolk Sq *TF:* 800-766-1082 ■ *Web:* www.virtexco.com	Norfolk	VA	23502	757-466-1114	466-1115	186
VIRTU Financial Inc 645 Madison Ave *Web:* www.virtu.com	New York	NY	10022	212-418-0100		194
Virtua Our Lady of Lourdes Hospital 1600 Haddon Ave *TF:* 888-568-7337 ■ *Web:* www.virtua.org	Camden	NJ	08103	856-757-3500		374-3
Virtua Voorhees 303 Lippincott Dr 4th Fl *Web:* www.virtua.org	Evesham Township	NJ	08053	888-847-8823		374-3
Virtual Backgrounds LLC 101 Uhland Rd Ste 200 *Web:* www.virtualbackgroundsphotography.com	San Marcos	TX	78666	512-805-4844		589
Virtual Brokers 4100 Yonge St Ste 415 *TF:* 877-310-1088 ■ *Web:* www.virtualbrokers.com	Toronto	ON	M2P2B5	416-288-8028		690
Virtual Connect Technologies Inc 200 N Main St Ste 201 *Web:* virtualconnect.net	Greenville	SC	29601	864-288-9595		180
Virtual Education Software Inc 300 N Argonne Rd Ste 102 *Web:* www.virtualeduc.com	Spokane	WA	99212	509-891-7219		180
Virtual EM Inc 3055 Plymouth Rd Ste 200 *Web:* virtualem.com	Ann Arbor	MI	48105	734-222-4558		396
Virtual Enterprises Inc 12405 Grant St *Web:* www.virtual.com	Thornton	CO	80241	303-301-3000		180
Virtual Forum Inc 1395 SR-23 Ste 6 *Web:* www.virtualforum.com	Butler	NJ	07405	973-237-1166	237-1176	396
Virtual Images 425 S Rockefeller Ave *TF:* 800-924-5401 ■ *Web:* www.virtual-images.com	Ontario	CA	91761	800-924-5401		88
Virtual Inc 401 Edgewater Pl Ste 600 *Web:* virtualinc.com	Wakefield	MA	01880	781-246-0500	224-1239	47
Virtual Information Executives (VIE) 12639 NW Waker Dr *Web:* www.viellc.com	Portland	OR	97229	503-926-9130		194
Virtual IT Inc PO Box 1009 *Web:* www.virtualitinc.com	Moneta	VA	24121	540-345-6100		180
Virtual Matrix Corp 7200 France Ave S Ste 324 *Web:* www.vmatrixcorp.com	Edina	MN	55435	952-835-6400		180
Virtual Solutions LLC 21644 N Ninth Ave Ste 201 *Web:* www.vsols.com	Phoenix	AZ	85027	623-580-0775		697
Virtual Training Company Inc 5395 Main St *TF:* 888-316-5374 ■ *Web:* www.vtc.com	Stephens City	VA	22655	540-869-8686		177
VirtualBank PO Box 109638 *TF:* 877-998-2265 ■ *Web:* www.virtualbank.com	Palm Beach Gardens	FL	33410	877-998-2265		70
Virtualbookworm.com Publishing Inc PO Box 9949 *TF:* 877-376-4955 ■ *Web:* www.virtualbookworm.com	College Station	TX	77842	877-376-4955		637-2
Virtually Better Inc 2440 Lawrenceville Hwy Ste 200 *Web:* www.virtuallybetter.com	Decatur	GA	30033	404-634-3400		180
VirtualPBXcom Inc 111 N Market St Ste 402 *TF:* 888-825-0800 ■ *Web:* virtualpbx.com	San Jose	CA	95113	408-414-7646		387
Virtucom Inc 5060 Avalon Ridge Pkwy Ste 300 *TF:* 800-890-2611 ■ *Web:* virtucom.com	Norcross	GA	30071	770-908-8100		174
Virtuit Systems Inc 101 Airport Executive Pk *Web:* www.virtuitsystems.com	Nanuet	NY	10954	845-371-3060		180
Virtuoso 505 Main St Ste 5 **Fax Area Code:* 212 ■ *TF:* 800-401-4274 ■ *Web:* www.virtuoso.com	Fort Worth	TX	76102	817-870-0300	588-8240*	772

	Phone	Fax	Class
VirtuOx Inc 5850 Coral Ridge Dr Ste 304 .... Coral Springs FL 33076 *Web:* www.virtuox.net	954-344-7075		237
Virtus Investment Partners Inc 100 Pearl St 9th Fl .... Hartford CT 06103 **Fax Area Code:* 508 ■ *TF:* 800-243-1574 ■ *Web:* corporate.virtus.com	413-775-6091	599-6179*	401
Visa Inc 1 Market St Ste 600 .... San Francisco CA 94105 *NYSE:* V ■ *Web:* usa.visa.com	650-432-3200		113
Visalia Chamber of Commerce 222 N Garden St Ste 300 .... Visalia CA 93291 *TF:* 800-728-0724 ■ *Web:* www.visaliachamber.org	559-734-5876	734-7479	139
Visalia Convention & Visitors Bureau PO Box 2734 .... Visalia CA 93279 *TF:* 800-524-0303 ■ *Web:* www.visitvisalia.com	559-334-0141		206
Visalia Convention Ctr 303 E Acequia Ave .... Visalia CA 93291 *TF:* 800-640-4888 ■ *Web:* www.visalia.city	559-713-4000	713-4804	205
Visalia Medical Lab 5400 W Hillsdale Ave .... Visalia CA 93291 *TF:* 800-486-2362 ■ *Web:* www.vmchealth.com	559-738-7500		418
Visara International Inc 2700 Gateway Centre Blvd Ste 600........... Morrisville NC 27560 *TF:* 888-334-4380 ■ *Web:* www.visara.com	919-882-0200		176
Viscira LLC 200 Vallejo St .... San Francisco CA 94111 *Web:* www.viscira.com	415-848-8010		177
Visclosky Peter (Rep D - IN) 2328 Rayburn House Office Bldg .... Washington DC 20515 *Web:* visclosky.house.gov	202-225-2461	225-2493	342-2
Viscount Gort Hotel 1670 Portage Ave.......... Winnipeg MB R3J0C9 *TF:* 800-665-1122 ■ *Web:* www.viscount-gort.com	204-775-0451	772-2161	379
Viscount Suite Hotel 4855 E Broadway Blvd .... Tucson AZ 85711 *TF:* 800-527-9666 ■ *Web:* viscount-suite.hotelsintucsonarizona.com	520-745-6500	790-5114	379
Vishion Tool and Machine Co 3344 Greenwood Blvd .... Saint Louis MO 63143 *Web:* www.vishiontool.com	314-781-6631	754-9303	757
Visibility Corp 200 Minuteman Rd .... Andover MA 01810 *Web:* www.visibility.com	978-269-6500	269-6501	177
Visible Changes Inc 1303 Campbell Rd Houston TX 77055 *Web:* visiblechanges.com	713-984-8800		77
Visible Innovations 8561 Acadia Dr....................... Sagamore Hills OH 44067 *Web:* visibleinnovations.design	216-650-4804		344
Visible Light Digital Inc 3365 Shady Run Rd .... Melbourne FL 32934 *TF:* 888-216-1883 ■ *Web:* www.visiblelight.com	407-327-5700		174
Visible Systems Corp 201 Spring St .... Lexington MA 02421 *TF:* 888-850-9911 ■ *Web:* www.visible.com	781-778-0200	778-0208	178-1
Visicom Media Inc 6200 Blvd Taschereau Ste 304 .... Brossard QC J4W3J8 *TF:* 800-508-0401 ■ *Web:* www.vmn.net	450-672-0401		225
Visidyne Inc 111 S Bedford St Ste 103................... Burlington MA 01803 *Web:* www.visidyne.com	781-273-2820	272-1068	668
Vision Capital 700 Airport Blvd Ste 370 .... Burlingame CA 94010 *Web:* www.visioncap.com	650-373-2720	373-2727	792
Vision Capital Management Inc 1 SW Columbia Ste 915 .... Portland OR 97258 *TF:* 800-707-5335 ■ *Web:* vcmi.net	800-707-5335		528
Vision Care Assn 1120 E Washington St .... Grayslake IL 60030 *Web:* www.visioncareclinic.com	847-223-2000		543
Vision Council, The 225 Reinekers Ln Ste 700.................. Alexandria VA 22314 *TF:* 866-826-0290 ■ *Web:* www.thevisioncouncil.org	703-548-4560	548-4580	49-4
Vision Creative Group Inc 2740 Rte 10 W Ste 301.................. Morris Plains NJ 07950 *Web:* www.visioncreativegroup.com	973-984-3454		7
Vision Envelope Inc 2451 Executive St.......................... Charlotte NC 28208 *TF:* 800-200-9797 ■ *Web:* www.visionenvelope.com	800-200-9797		627
Vision Financial Corp PO Box 506 .... Keene NH 03431 **Fax Area Code:* 603 ■ *TF:* 800-793-0223 ■ *Web:* www.visfin.com	800-793-0223	357-0250*	391-5
Vision Graphics Inc 5105 E 41st Ave........... Loveland CO 80538 *TF:* 800-833-4263 ■ *Web:* www.visiongraphics-inc.com	970-679-9000		627
Vision Maker Media 1800 N 33rd St............ Lincoln NE 68503 *Web:* www.visionmakermedia.org	402-472-3522	472-8675	511
Vision Offices Executive Suites Lp 14362 N Frank Lloyd Wright Blvd Ste 1000 ..... Scottsdale AZ 85260 *Web:* visionoffices.com	480-477-7777		317
Vision One It Consulting Inc 7112 Ofc Park Dr .... West Chester OH 45069 *Web:* www.v1corp.com	513-892-0027	942-1457	196
Vision Plan of America 3255 Wilshire Blvd Ste 1610 .... Los Angeles CA 90010 *TF:* 800-400-4872 ■ *Web:* www.visionplanofamerica.com	213-384-2600	384-0084	390
Vision Plastics Inc 26000 SW Parkway Center Dr................ Wilsonville OR 97070 *Web:* visionplastics.com	503-685-9000	685-9254	548
Vision Source LP 23824 Hwy 59 N Ste 101 .... Kingwood TX 77339 *TF:* 888-558-2020 ■ *Web:* visionsource.com	281-312-1111		237
Vision Technologies Inc 530 McCormick Dr Ste G.................. Glen Burnie MD 21061 *TF:* 866-746-1122 ■ *Web:* www.visiontechnologies.com	410-424-2183	424-2208	177
Vision Works Inc 3801 River Ridge Dr NE .... Cedar Rapids IA 52402 *Web:* vision-works.com	319-261-0382		177
Vision7 Software 4729 E Sunrise Dr Ste 201 .... Tucson AZ 85718 *Web:* www.vision7.com	520-320-5442		809
Visionaire Inc 1502 109th St.............. Grand Prairie TX 75050 *Web:* www.visionaire-inc.com	972-647-1056		612
Visionaire Lighting LLC 19645 Rancho Way................. Rancho Dominguez CA 90220 *Web:* www.visionairelighting.com	310-512-6480		362
Visionary Federal Credit Union 201 Beram Ave .... Bridgeville PA 15017 *Web:* visionaryfcu.org	412-221-6660		219
Visionary Integration Professionals Inc 80 Iron Pt Cir Ste 100........................ Folsom CA 95630 *Web:* www.trustvip.com	916-985-9625		180
Visionary Legal Technologies LP 14677 Midway Rd Ste 118 .... Addison TX 75001 *Web:* www.visionarylegaltechnologies.com	214-370-4359		177
Visionbank 3031 SW Wanamaker .... Topeka KS 66614 *Web:* visionbanking.com	785-357-4669	357-0466	70
Vision-Ease Lens Inc 7000 Sunwood Dr NW .... Ramsey MN 55303 *TF:* 800-328-3449 ■ *Web:* www.visionease.com	320-251-8140	251-4312	542
Visioneer Inc 5673 Gibraltar Dr Ste 150.................. Pleasanton CA 94588 *Web:* www.visioneer.com	925-251-6300	416-8600	173-7
Visioneering Inc 2055 Taylor Rd............ Auburn Hills MI 48326 *Web:* vistool.com	248-622-5600	622-5533	21
Visionet Systems Inc 4 Cedarbrook Dr Bldg B .... Cranbury NJ 08512 *Web:* www.visionetsystems.com	609-452-0700		225
Visionfriendly.Com 1245 E Diehl Rd Ste 307.................... Naperville IL 60563 *Web:* visionfriendly.com	630-553-0000		177
Vision-It Inc 2502 Iron Forge Rd................ Oak Hill VA 20171 *Web:* vitinc.net	703-668-0717	668-0718	196
VisionMAX Solutions Inc 5580 Explorer Dr Ste 601................. Mississauga ON L4W4Y1 *Web:* www.visionmax.com	905-282-0503		7
Visionpoint LLC 152 Rockwell Rd .... Newington CT 06111 *Web:* visionpointllc.com	860-436-9673		224
VisionQuest National Ltd 600 N Swan Rd PO Box 12906................. Tucson AZ 85711 *Web:* www.vq.com	520-881-3950	881-3269	463
Visions PO Box 1265 .... Brighton MI 48116 *Web:* www.ourfiresstillburn.com	810-772-9628		77
Visions Federal Credit Union (VFCU) 24 McKinley Ave.................................. Endicott NY 13760 *TF:* 800-242-2120 ■ *Web:* www.visionsfcu.org	607-754-7900	786-1718	210
Visions Hotels 11751 E Corning Rd .... Corning NY 14830 *Web:* www.visions-hotels.com	607-962-9868		377
Visions Inc 8801 Wyoming Ave N .... Brooklyn Park MN 55445 *Web:* www.visionsfirst.com	763-425-4251		627
Visions Services 500 Greenwich St 3rd Fl.................... New York NY 10013 *TF:* 888-245-8333 ■ *Web:* www.visionsvcb.org	212-625-1616	219-4078	121
Visionsoft International Inc 1842 Old Norcross Rd Ste 100............ Lawrenceville GA 30044 *Web:* www.vsiiusa.com	770-682-2899		177
Visionspring Inc 505 8th Ave Ste 12A-07 .... New York NY 10018 *Web:* visionspring.org	212-375-2599		194
Visiont 2650 106th St Ste 215 .... Urbandale IA 50322 *Web:* www.visiont-solutions.com	515-331-0010		260
Visionworks 854 Plaza Blvd.................. Lancaster PA 17601 *Web:* www.visionworks.com	717-295-3111		543
Visionworks of America Inc 175 E Houston St........................ San Antonio TX 78205 *TF:* 800-669-1183 ■ *Web:* www.visionworks.com	800-669-1183		543
Visit America Inc 307 Seventh Ave Ste 1807 .... New York NY 10001 *Web:* www.visitamerica.com	212-683-8082		760
Visit Carlsbad 400 Carlsbad Village Dr .... Carlsbad CA 92008 *Web:* visitcarlsbad.com	760-434-6093		206
Visit Dothan Alabama 3311 Ross Clark Cir .... Dothan AL 36303 *TF:* 888-449-0212 ■ *Web:* visitdothan.com	334-794-6622		206
Visit Duluth 21 W Superior St Ste 100............ Duluth MN 55802 *TF:* 800-438-5884 ■ *Web:* www.visitduluth.com	218-722-4011	722-1322	206
Visit Eau Claire 4319 Jeffers Rd.............. Eau Claire WI 54703 *Web:* www.visiteauclaire.com	715-831-2345		206
Visit Florida 2540 W Executive Center Cir Ste 200......... Tallahassee FL 32301 *Web:* www.visitflorida.org	850-488-5607		775
Visit High Point 1634 N Main St Ste 102.................... High Point NC 27262 *TF:* 800-720-5255 ■ *Web:* visithighpoint.com	336-884-5255	884-5256	206
Visit Jacksonville 208 N Laura St Ste 1...................... Jacksonville FL 32202 *TF:* 800-733-2668 ■ *Web:* www.visitjacksonville.com	904-798-9111		206
Visit MercerCounty PA 50 N Water Ave........... Sharon PA 16146 *Web:* www.visitmercercountypa.com	724-346-3771	346-0575	206
Visit Mountaineer Country 341 Chaplin Rd 1st Fl.................... Morgantown WV 26501 *TF:* 800-458-7373 ■ *Web:* www.visitmountaineercountry.com	304-292-5081	291-1354	206
Visit Rochester 45 E Ave Ste 400 .... Rochester NY 14604 *TF:* 800-677-7282 ■ *Web:* www.visitrochester.com	585-279-8300	232-4822	206
Visit Sarasota County 1777 Main St Ste 302....................... Sarasota FL 34236 *TF:* 800-522-9799 ■ *Web:* www.visitsarasota.com	941-955-0991		206
Visit St Petersburg Clearwater 13805 58th St N Ste 2-200................. Clearwater FL 33760 *TF:* 877-352-3224 ■ *Web:* www.visitstpeteclearwater.com	727-464-7200		206
Visit Topeka Inc 618 S Kansas Ave.............. Topeka KS 66603 *TF:* 800-235-1030 ■ *Web:* visit.topekapartnership.com	785-234-1030	234-8282	206
Visitec Marketing Associates Inc 2020 Dean St Unit H.................... Saint Charles IL 60174 *Web:* www.visitec.com	630-762-0300		196
VisitErie 208 E Bayfront Pkwy Ste 103.............. Erie PA 16507 *TF:* 800-524-3743 ■ *Web:* www.visiterie.com	814-454-1000	459-0241	206
Visiting Angeles of La Jolla 7816 Ivanhoe Ave Ste 9 .... La Jolla CA 92037 *Web:* visitingangels.com	858-551-8910		363
Visiting Nurse & Hospice Care 512 E Gutierrez St Ste A .... Santa Barbara CA 93103 *Web:* visitingnursehh.org	805-965-5555	568-5178	371

	Phone	Fax	Class
Visiting Nurse & Hospice Care of Southwestern Connecticut			
1266 E Main St. . . . . Stamford CT 06902	203-276-3000		371
Visiting Nurse Assn			
12565 W Center Rd Ste 100 . . . . . Omaha NE 68144	402-342-5566	342-5587	371
TF: 800-456-8869 ■ *Web:* vnatoday.org			
Visiting Nurse Assocation of Greater St Louis			
Hospice Care			
2029 Woodland Pkwy Ste 105. . . . . Saint Louis MO 63146	314-918-7171	513-9950	371
TF: 800-392-4740 ■ *Web:* www.vnastl.com			
Visiting Nurse Association of Morris County (Inc)			
175 South St. . . . . Morristown NJ 07960	973-539-1216		363
TF: 800-938-4748 ■ *Web:* www.vnannj.org			
Visiting Nurse Association of Ohio			
2500 E 22nd St. . . . . Cleveland OH 44115	216-931-1300	694-4182	371
TF: 877-698-6264 ■ *Web:* www.vnaohio.org			
Visiting Nurse Association of the Treasure Coast			
1110 35th Ln . . . . . Vero Beach FL 32960	772-567-5551		371
TF: 800-749-5760 ■ *Web:* www.vnatc.com			
Visiting Nurse Association of The W Abash Valley Inc			
400 Eighth Ave . . . . . Terre Haute IN 47804	812-232-7611		363
Web: myhospicevna.org			
Visiting Nurse Associations of America (VNAA)			
1800 Diagonal Rd Ste 600 . . . . . Alexandria VA 22314	571-527-1520		49-8
TF: 888-866-8773 ■ *Web:* www.vnaa.org			
Visiting Nurse Service of Itha			
138 Cecil A Malone Dr . . . . . Ithaca NY 14850	607-273-0466		363
Web: vnsithaca.org			
Visiting Nurse Service of New York Hospice Care			
1250 Broadway. . . . . New York NY 10001	212-609-1900		371
Web: www.vnsny.org			
Visi-Trak Worldwide LLC			
8400 Sweet Valley Dr Ste 406. . . . . Valley View OH 44125	216-524-2363	524-9594	201
TF: 800-252-8725 ■ *Web:* visi-trak.com			
Viskase Companies Inc			
6855 W 65th St Ste 40 . . . . . Lombard IL 60148	630-874-0700	874-0176	548
TF: 800-323-8562 ■ *Web:* viskase.com			
Vispnet 301 NE Sixth St . . . . . Grants Pass OR 97526	541-955-6900		225
Web: visp.net			
Visser's Florist Inc			
701 W Lincoln Ave. . . . . Anaheim CA 92805	714-772-9900		292
Web: vissersflorist.com			
Vissering Construction Co			
175 Benchmark Industrial Dr . . . . . Streator IL 61364	815-673-5511		186
Web: www.vissering.com			
VIST Financial Corp			
1240 Broadcasting Rd . . . . . Wyomissing PA 19610	610-478-9922		360-2
NASDAQ: VIST ■ *TF:* 888-238-3330 ■ *Web:* www.vistbank.com			
Vista Analytical Laboratory Inc			
1104 Windfield Way . . . . . El Dorado Hills CA 95762	916-673-1520	673-0106	743
Web: www.vista-analytical.com			
Vista Auto 21501 Ventura Blvd . . . . . Woodland Hills CA 91364	888-442-8817		57
TF: 888-887-6530 ■ *Web:* www.vistaford.com			
Vista Biologicals			
2120-C Las Palmas Dr Ste B . . . . . Carlsbad CA 92011	760-438-0230		418
Web: www.vistabiologicals.com			
Vista Broadband Networks Inc			
3020 Santa Rosa Ave . . . . . Santa Rosa CA 95407	707-527-0545		387
Web: www.vistabroadband.com			
Vista Center for the Blind and Visually Impaired			
3200 Hillview Ave Ste 120 . . . . . Palo Alto CA 94304	650-858-0202	858-0214	637-2
TF: 800-660-2009 ■ *Web:* www.vistacenter.org			
Vista College - Lubbock Campus			
4620 50th St. . . . . Lubbock TX 79414	866-442-4197		167-3
TF: 866-442-4197 ■ *Web:* www.vistacollege.edu			
Vista Color Corp 1401 NW 78th Ave. . . . . Miami FL 33126	305-635-2000	635-1985	627
Web: vistacolor.com			
Vista Color Imaging			
4770 Van Epps Rd Unit 101 . . . . . Brooklyn Heights OH 44131	216-651-2830		344
Web: www.vistacolorimaging.com			
Vista Convention Services Inc			
6804 Delilah Rd . . . . . Egg Harbor Township NJ 08234	609-485-2421	485-2392	184
Web: www.vistacs.com			
Vista del Monte 3775 Modoc Rd . . . . . Santa Barbara CA 93105	805-687-0793		672
TF: 800-736-1333 ■ *Web:* www.vistadelmonte.org			
Vista Electronics Inc			
27525 Newhall Ranch Rd . . . . . Valencia CA 91355	661-294-9820		514
TF: 800-847-8299 ■ *Web:* vistaelectronics.com			
Vista Engineering Corp			
1030 Pleasantview Terr. . . . . Ridgefield NJ 07657	201-945-9434		261
Web: vistaengineeringcorp.com			
Vista Expertise Network			
819 N 49th St Ste 203 . . . . . Seattle WA 98103	206-632-0166		177
Web: vistaexpertise.net			
Vista Gold Corp			
7961 Shaffer Pkwy Ste 5. . . . . Littleton CO 80127	720-981-1185	981-1186	502
NYSE: VGZ ■ *Web:* vistagold.com			
Vista Grande Villa 2251 Springport Rd . . . . . Jackson MI 49202	517-787-0222		672
TF: 800-889-8499 ■ *Web:* vistagrandevilla.com			
Vista Graphics Inc			
1264 Perimeter Pkwy . . . . . Virginia Beach VA 23454	757-422-8979		344
Web: www.vistagraphicsinc.com			
Vista Host Inc			
10370 Richmond Ave Ste 150 . . . . . Houston TX 77042	713-267-5800	267-5820	379
Web: www.vistahost.com			
Vista House			
40700 E Historic Columbia River Hwy . . . . . Corbett OR 97019	503-344-1368	695-2250	50-5
Web: www.vistahouse.com			
Vista Medical Ctr 1324 N Sheridan Rd . . . . . Waukegan IL 60085	847-360-3000		374-3
TF: 800-843-2464 ■ *Web:* www.vistahealth.com			
Vista Metals Inc 65 Ballou Blvd. . . . . Bristol RI 02809	401-253-1772		492
TF: 800-431-4113 ■ *Web:* vismet.com			
Vista Paint Corp			
2020 E Orangethorpe Ave. . . . . Fullerton CA 92831	714-680-3810	459-4708	550
Web: www.vistapaint.com			
Vista Productions Inc			
1804 Anaconda Rd. . . . . Harrisonville MO 64701	816-380-7750		514
Web: www.vistaprod.com			
Vista Projects Ltd			
330-4000 Fourth St SE. . . . . Calgary AB T2G2W3	403-255-3455	258-2192	196
Web: www.vistaprojects.com			
Vista Radio Ltd			
201-910 Fitzgerald Ave. . . . . Courtenay BC V9N2R5	250-338-1133		647
TF: 877-847-8211 ■ *Web:* www.vistaradio.ca			
Vista Ridge Mall			
2401 S Stemmons Fwy. . . . . Lewisville TX 75067	972-315-3641		460
Web: www.vistaridgemall.com			
Vista Staffing Solutions Inc			
275 East 200 South . . . . . Salt Lake City UT 84111	801-487-8190		260
Web: www.vistastaff.com			
Vista Therapeutics Inc			
3900 Paseo del Sol. . . . . Santa Fe NM 87507	505-474-3143	424-1144	475
Web: www.vistatherapeutics.org			
Vista Verde Guest & Ski Ranch			
PO Box 770465 . . . . . Steamboat Springs CO 80477	970-879-3858	879-6814	239
TF: 800-526-7433 ■ *Web:* www.vistaverde.com			
Vista Worldlink Inc			
73-104 SW 12th Ave. . . . . Dania Beach FL 33004	954-838-0900		116
Web: vistaworldlink.com			
Vistabooks Publishing			
0637 Blue Ridge Rd . . . . . Silverthorne CO 80498	970-468-7673		637-2
Web: www.vistabooks.com			
Vistacomm 1401 N C Ave . . . . . Sioux Falls SD 57104	605-977-2100		4
Web: www.vistacomm.com			
Vistagen Therapeutics Inc			
343 Allerton Ave. . . . . South San Francisco CA 94080	650-577-3600		177
Web: vistagen.com			
Vistanet Communications			
6804 Villa Hermosa Dr. . . . . El Paso TX 79912	915-587-1500		224
VistaPharm Inc 630 Central Ave. . . . . New Providence NJ 07974	877-437-8567		231
TF: 877-437-8567 ■ *Web:* www.vistapharm.com			
VistaPrint 95 Hayden Ave . . . . . Lexington MA 02421	781-652-6300		627
Web: www.vistaprint.in			
Vistar Corp 12650 E Arapahoe Rd . . . . . Centennial CO 80112	303-662-7100		297-8
TF: 800-880-9900 ■ *Web:* www.vistar.com			
Vistar Eye Ctr 2802 Brandon Ave . . . . . Roanoke VA 24015	540-855-5100		543
TF: 866-615-5454 ■ *Web:* vistareye.com			
VistaVu Solutions Inc			
30 Springborough Blvd SW Ste 214. . . . . Calgary AB T3H0N9	403-263-2727		179
TF: 888-300-2727 ■ *Web:* vistavusolutions.com			
Vistem Solutions Inc			
2102 Business Center Dr Ste 220. . . . . Irvine CA 92612	949-253-5729		809
Web: www.vistem.com			
Visteon Corp			
1 Village Center Dr. . . . . Van Buren Township MI 48111	734-710-5000		60
NASDAQ: VC ■ *Web:* visteon.com			
Vistex Inc			
2300 Barrington Rd Ste 550. . . . . Hoffman Estates IL 60169	847-490-0420		195
Web: www.vistex.com			
Visting Nurse Group Inc			
128 W Girard Ave. . . . . Philadelphia PA 19123	215-829-8888		363
Web: visitingnursegroup.com			
Vistra Communications LLC			
18315 N US Hwy 41. . . . . Lutz FL 33549	813-961-4700		195
Web: www.consultvistra.com			
Vistrian Inc 562 Valley Way. . . . . Milpitas CA 95035	408-719-0500		177
Web: vistrian.com			
Visual Apex Inc			
7950 NE Day Rd Ste B . . . . . Bainbridge Island WA 98110	206-780-8192	780-8194	119
TF: 800-883-7495 ■ *Web:* www.visualapex.com			
Visual Automation Inc			
403 S Clinton St Ste 4 . . . . . Grand Ledge MI 48837	517-622-1850	622-1761	178-12
Web: www.visualautomation.com			
Visual Awareness Technologies & Consulting Inc			
3611 W Swann Ave. . . . . Tampa FL 33609	813-207-5055		765
Web: www.vatcinc.com			
Visual Citi Inc 770 Railroad Ave . . . . . West Babylon NY 11704	631-482-3030		344
Web: visualciti.com			
Visual Communications Group Inc			
1548 Cliff Rd E. . . . . Burnsville MN 55337	800-566-4162		514
TF: 800-566-4162 ■ *Web:* visualcomgroup.com			
Visual Communications Inc (VC)			
120 Judge John Aiso St . . . . . Los Angeles CA 90012	213-680-4462		423
Web: www.vconline.org			
Visual Data Media Services Inc			
610 N Hollywood Way . . . . . Burbank CA 91505	818-558-3363		738
Web: www.visualdatamedia.com			
Visual Departures Ltd			
48 Sheffield Business Pk . . . . . Ashley Falls MA 01222	800-628-2003		591
TF: 800-628-2003 ■ *Web:* www.visualdepartures.com			
Visual Eyes Medical Media			
31320 Via Colinas Ste 118. . . . . Westlake Village CA 91362	818-707-9922		514
Web: www.visualeyes.com			
Visual Goodness Inc			
225 W 34th St 9th Fl. . . . . New York NY 10122	212-463-8248		344
Web: www.visualgoodness.com			
Visual Image Photography			
W63 N582 Hanover Ave . . . . . Cedarburg WI 53012	262-375-4457		590
Web: www.vipis.com			
Visual Impressions Inc			
6600 W Calumet Rd . . . . . Milwaukee WI 53223	414-354-9190	354-9191	687
TF: 800-291-8337 ■ *Web:* visualimp.com			
Visual Learning Systems Inc			
PO Box 8226 . . . . . Missoula MT 59807	866-968-7857		177
TF: 866-968-7857 ■ *Web:* www.vls-inc.com			
Visual Marketing Inc 154 W Erie St . . . . . Chicago IL 60654	312-664-9177	664-9473	233
TF: 800-662-8640 ■ *Web:* www.vmichicago.com			
Visual Net Design Lc			
218 E Ramsey St. . . . . San Antonio TX 78216	210-590-2734		175
Web: www.vndx.com			
Visual Pak Co 1909 S Waukegan Rd. . . . . Waukegan IL 60085	877-689-0001	689-1001*	88
**Fax Area Code:* 847 ■ *TF:* 877-689-0001 ■ *Web:* www.visualpak.com			
Visual Planning Corp 71 Meadowbank Dr. . . . . Ottawa ON K2G0P4	613-563-8727		487
Web: www.visualplanning.com			
Visual Purple LLC			
75 Higuera St Ste 240. . . . . San Luis Obispo CA 93401	805-595-7579		177
Web: www.visualpurple.com			

Name / Address	City	State	ZIP	Phone	Fax	Class
Visual Retail Plus 540 Hudson St *TF:* 888-767-4004 ■ *Web:* www.visualretailplus.com	Hackensack	NJ	07601	888-767-4004		180
Visual Systems Group Inc (VSGI) 7900 Westpark Dr Ste T-610 *TF:* 877-402-8744 ■ *Web:* www.vsgi.com	McLean	VA	22102	703-848-8200	848-8211	180
Visualware Inc 937 Sierra Dr PO Box 668 **Fax Area Code:* 916 ■ *TF:* 866-847-9273 ■ *Web:* www.visualware.com	Turlock	CA	95380	209-262-3491	273-3099*	177
VisualWare Inc 1675 E Main St *Web:* www.visualware.net	Kent	OH	44240	330-297-8931	296-5060	180
Vita Food Products Inc 2222 W Lake St *TF:* 800-989-8482 ■ *Web:* www.vitafoodproducts.com	Chicago	IL	60612	312-738-4500		296-13
Vita Health Products Inc 150 Beghin Ave *Web:* www.vitahealth.ca	Winnipeg	MB	R2J3W2	204-661-8386		345
Vita Motivator Company Inc PO Box 8139 *Web:* www.vitamotivator.com	Englewood	NJ	07631	201-567-1151		366
Vita Needle Co 919 Great Plain Ave *Web:* www.vitaneedle.com	Needham	MA	02492	781-444-1780	444-3956	492
Vita Plus Corp 2514 Fish Hatchery Rd *TF:* 800-362-8334 ■ *Web:* www.vitaplus.com	Madison	WI	53713	608-256-1988	283-7990	447
Vitac Corp 8300 E Maplewood Ave Ste 310 *TF:* 800-278-4822 ■ *Web:* www.vitac.com	Greenwood Village	CO	80111	724-514-4111		224
Vitacostcom Inc 5400 Broken Sound Blvd NW Ste 500 *TF:* 800-381-0759 ■ *Web:* www.vitacost.com	Boca Raton	FL	33487	800-381-0759		237
VitaDigest.com 20687-2 Amar Rd Ste 258 *TF:* 877-848-2168 ■ *Web:* www.vitadigest.com	Walnut	CA	91789	877-848-2168		345
Vitakraft Sunseed Inc 20584 Long Judson Rd *Web:* vitakraftsunseed.com	Weston	OH	43569	419-832-1641		123
Vital Business Solutions (VBS) 1325 G St NW Ste 500 *Web:* vitalbusinesssolution.com	Washington	DC	20005	202-832-1388		194
Vital Images Inc 5850 Opus Pkwy Ste 300 *TF:* 800-208-3006 ■ *Web:* www.vitalimages.com	Minnetonka	MN	55343	952-487-9500		178-10
Vital Link Inc 914 Bartlett Rd *Web:* vitallinkinc.com	Sealy	TX	77474	979-885-4181	885-3274	492
Vital Pharmaceuticals Inc 1600 N Pk Dr *Web:* vpxsports.com	Weston	FL	33326	954-641-0570		81-2
Vital Records Inc PO Box 688 *Web:* www.vitalrecords.com	Flagtown	NJ	08821	908-369-6900		581
Vital Solutions International LLC 340 Mansfield Ave 1st Fl *Web:* www.vsint.com	Pittsburgh	PA	15220	412-407-3900	407-3901	175
Vital Systems Corp 4999 Aircenter Cir *Web:* vitalsystems.com	Reno	NV	89502	775-828-1126		696
Vital Wave Consulting 555 Bryant St Ste 226 *Web:* vitalwave.com	Palo Alto	CA	94301	650-964-1316		194
VitalAire Canada Inc 6990 Creditview Rd Unit 6 *TF:* 888-629-0202 ■ *Web:* www.vitalaire.ca	Mississauga	ON	L5N8R9	888-629-0202		476
Vitalant 2424 W Erie Dr *Web:* laboratories.vitalant.org	Tempe	AZ	85282	602-343-7000		417
Vitalant 1989 W Elliot Rd Ste 32 *TF:* 877-827-4376 ■ *Web:* www.vitalant.org	Chandler	AZ	85224	877-827-4376		89
Vitale & Miller PA 800 S Federal Hwy *Web:* vitalemillercpa.com	Hollywood	FL	33020	954-925-1300	921-9576	2
Vitalyst LLC 1 Bala Plz Ste 434 *Web:* www.vitalyst.com	Bala Cynwyd	PA	19004	610-668-3516		809
Vitamin Shoppe Inc 2101 91st St *NYSE:* VSI ■ **Fax Area Code:* 800 ■ *TF:* 800-223-1216 ■ *Web:* www.vitaminshoppe.com	North Bergen	NJ	07047	201-868-5959	852-7153*	237
Vita-Mix Corp 8615 Usher Rd *TF:* 800-848-2649 ■ *Web:* www.vitamix.com	Cleveland	OH	44138	440-235-4840	235-3726	37
Vita-Pakt Citrus Products 203 E Badillo St *TF:* 888-684-8272 ■ *Web:* vita-pakt.com	Covina	CA	91723	626-332-1101		296-21
VITAS Healthcare Corp 201 S Biscayne Blvd Ste 400 *Web:* www.vitas.com	Miami	FL	33131	305-374-4143		371
VitaSound Audio Inc 2880 Zanker Rd Ste 203 *TF:* 888-667-7205 ■ *Web:* vitasound.com	San Jose	CA	95134	888-667-7205		250
Vitasoy USA Inc 57 Russell St *TF:* 800-848-2769 ■ *Web:* vitasoy-usa.com	Woburn	MA	01801	800-848-2769		296-8
VITEC 2200 Century Pkwy Ste 900 *Web:* www.vitec.com	Atlanta	GA	30345	404-320-0110	320-3132	173-5
VITEC Solutions LLC 611 Jamison Rd Ste 4104 *Web:* vitecsolutions.com	Elma	NY	14059	716-204-9200		175
Vitech Business Group Inc 4164 Meridian St Ste 200 *Web:* www.vitechgroup.com	Bellingham	WA	98226	360-647-1622		317
Vitech Corp 2270 Kraft Dr Ste 1600 *Web:* www.vitechcorp.com	Blacksburg	VA	24060	540-951-3322		177
Vitelity Communications 317 Inverness Way S Ste 140 **Fax Area Code:* 303 ■ *TF:* 888-898-4835 ■ *Web:* www.vitelity.com	Englewood	CO	80112	888-898-4835	991-7999*	224
Vit-E-Men Company Inc 306 E Omaha Ave *TF:* 800-658-3120 ■ *Web:* www.lifeproductsinc.com	Norfolk	NE	68701	402-379-0311		447
Vitense Golfland 5501 Schroeder Rd *Web:* www.vitense.com	Madison	WI	53711	608-271-1411		354
Viteos Capital Market Services Ltd 80 Cottontail Ln Ste 430 *Web:* www.viteos.com	Somerset	NJ	08873	732-356-1200	356-1160	463
Viterbo University 900 Viterbo Dr *TF:* 800-848-3726 ■ *Web:* www.viterbo.edu	La Crosse	WI	54601	608-796-3000	796-3020	166
Vitetta 1510 Chester Pk Ste 104 *Web:* www.vitetta.com	Eddystone	PA	19022	215-218-4747	405-2729	261
ViTEX Inc 630 Williamson Rd *Web:* www.vitex.com	Mooresville	NC	28117	704-663-2544		463
Vitl Life Science Solutions 305 Ashcake Rd Ste L *Web:* www.vitlproducts.com	Ashland	VA	23005	804-381-0905		475
Vito's Italian Restaurant 1180 Forest Ave *Web:* vitositalianrestaurant.weebly.com	Pacific Grove	CA	93950	831-375-3070		671
Vito's Restaurant 280 Trumbull St *Web:* www.vitosct.com	Hartford	CT	06103	860-244-2200		671
Vitols Tool & Machine Corp 10082 Sandmeyer Ln *Web:* www.vitolsgroup.com	Philadelphia	PA	19116	215-464-8240		480
Vitran Express Inc 1201 Creditstone Rd *TF:* 800-263-0791 ■ *Web:* www.vitranexpress.com	Concord	ON	L4K0C2	416-798-4965	798-4753	780
Vitria Technology Inc 4300 Bohannon Dr Ste 200 **Fax Area Code:* 650 ■ *Web:* www.vitria.com	Menlo Park	CA	94025	408-212-2700	460-8727*	178-1
Vitro Seating Products Inc 201 Madison St *TF:* 800-325-7093 ■ *Web:* www.vitroseating.com	Saint Louis	MO	63102	314-241-2265	241-8723	319-1
Vitrum Industries Ltd 9739 201 St *Web:* www.vitrum.ca	Langley	BC	V1M3E7	604-882-3513		330
Vittitow Refrigeration 4603 Poplar Level Rd *Web:* vittitow.com	Louisville	KY	40213	502-966-4444		665
Vittoria Trattoria 35 William St *Web:* vittoriatrattoria.com	Ottawa	ON	K1N6Z9	613-789-8959		671
Vittum Theater 1012 N Noble St *Web:* vittumtheater.org	Chicago	IL	60642	773-342-4141		748
Viva Canada 1663 Neilson Rd *Web:* www.viva.com.hk	Scarborough	ON	M1X1T1	416-321-0622	321-6030	658
VIVA Health Inc 1222 14th Ave S *TF:* 800-633-1542 ■ *Web:* www.vivahealth.com	Birmingham	AL	35205	205-939-1718		390
Viva Partnership Inc 10800 Biscayne Blvd Ste 300 *Web:* www.vivamulticultural.com	Miami	FL	33161	305-576-6007		7
Vivax-Metrotech Corp 3251 Olcott St *TF:* 800-440-3392 ■ *Web:* www.vivax-metrotech.com	Santa Clara	CA	95054	408-734-1400	734-1415	472
Vivekananda Retreat Ridgely 101 Leggett Rd *Web:* ridgely.org	Stone Ridge	NY	12484	845-687-4574	687-4578	673
Viventium Software 768 Bedford Ave *Web:* www.viventium.com	Brooklyn	NY	11205	718-522-2000		734
Vivere 71 W Monroe St *Web:* italianvillage-chicago.com	Chicago	IL	60603	312-332-7005	332-2656	671
Vivi Co PO Box 750 *TF:* 800-464-2538 ■ *Web:* www.theartofbreathing.com	Glendale	CA	91209	818-500-8889		637-2
Vivian Horan Fine Art 35 E 67th St *Web:* www.vivianhoran.com	New York	NY	10065	212-517-9410	772-6107	42
Viviano Flower Shop 32050 Harper Ave *TF:* 800-848-4266 ■ *Web:* www.viviano.com	Saint Clair Shores	MI	48082	586-293-0227		292
Vivid Entertainment 3599 Cahuenga Blvd Ste 4 *Web:* vivid.com	Los Angeles	CA	90068	323-845-4557		514
Vivid Image Inc 897 Hwy 15 S *Web:* vimm.com	Hutchinson	MN	55350	320-587-8974		809
Vivid Impact Corp 10116 Bunsen Way *Web:* www.vividimpact.com	Louisville	KY	40299	502-495-6900		174
Vivid Publishing Inc 924 Funston Ave *TF:* 800-859-7902 ■ *Web:* streammaps.com	Williamsport	PA	17701	570-567-7808	567-7253	637-2
Vivid Solutions 2328 Government St *Web:* www.vividsolutions.com	Victoria	BC	V8T5G5	250-385-6040		180
Vivienne Tam 580 Eighth Ave 17th Fl *TF:* 877-659-7994 ■ *Web:* www.viviennetam.com	New York	NY	10018	877-659-7994		277
Vivint Solar Inc 1800 W Ashton Blvd *TF:* 877-404-4129 ■ *Web:* www.vivintsolar.com	Lehi	UT	84043	801-216-3927		192
Vivitar Corp 195 Carter Dr *TF:* 800-592-9541 ■ *Web:* www.vivitar.com	Edison	NJ	08817	732-248-1306		591
VIVO Seasonal Trattoria 200 Columbus Blvd *Web:* vivohartford.com	Hartford	CT	06103	860-760-2333		671
Vivoli Cafe & Trattoria of West Hollywood 7994 Sunset Blvd *Web:* www.pizzeriavivoli.com	West Hollywood	CA	90046	323-656-5050		671
Vivosonic Inc 5535 Eglinton Ave W Ste 222 *TF:* 877-255-7685 ■ *Web:* vivosonic.com	Toronto	ON	M9C5K5	416-231-9997	231-2289	476
Vivox Inc 2-4 Mercer Rd *Web:* www.vivox.com	Natick	MA	01760	508-650-3571		177
Vivus Inc 1172 Castro St *NASDAQ:* VVUS ■ *TF:* 800-607-0088 ■ *Web:* www.vivus.com	Mountain View	CA	94040	650-934-5200	934-5389	582
Viwinco Inc PO Box 499 *Web:* www.viwinco.com	Morgantown	PA	19543	610-286-8884	286-8877	608
Viwintech Window & Door Inc 2400 Irvin Cobb Dr *TF:* 800-788-1050 ■ *Web:* www.viwintech.com	Paducah	KY	42003	800-788-1050		596
VIZ Media 295 Bay St *Web:* www.viz.com	San Francisco	CA	94133	415-546-7073	546-7086	637-9
Vizcaya Museum & Gardens 3251 S Miami Ave *Web:* vizcaya.org	Miami	FL	33129	305-250-9133	285-2004	520
Vizient Manufacturing Solutions Inc 3129 State St *Web:* www.vizient.com	Bettendorf	IA	52722	563-355-4812		261
Viziflex Seels Inc 406 N Midland Ave **Fax Area Code:* 201 ■ *TF:* 800-627-7752 ■ *Web:* www.viziflex.com	Saddle Brook	NJ	07663	800-627-7752	487-3266*	608
VJ Technologies Inc 89 Carlough Rd *TF:* 800-858-9729 ■ *Web:* www.vjt.com	Bohemia	NY	11716	631-589-8800		743
VJS Construction Services W233 N2847 Roundy Cir W *Web:* www.vjscs.com	Pewaukee	WI	53072	262-542-9000		186
VJV IT 96 Linwood Plz *TF:* 800-614-7561 ■ *Web:* vjvit.com	Fort Lee	NJ	07024	800-614-7561		631

Company	City	State	ZIP	Phone	Fax	Class
VK Wholesale 4940 W Lawrence Ave Web: www.vkwholesale.com	Chicago	IL	60630	773-853-0734		328
VKGS (Video King Gaming Systems) 2717 N 118 Cir Ste 210 TF: 800-635-9912 ■ Web: www.videokingnetwork.com	Omaha	NE	68164	402-951-2970	951-2990	322
VKI Technologies Inc 3200 2E Rue TF: 800-567-2951 ■ Web: www.vkitech.com	Saint-Hubert	QC	J3Y8Y7	450-676-0504		159
V-LABS Inc 423 N Theard St Web: www.v-labs.com	Covington	LA	70433	985-893-0533	893-0517	192
VLJ Inc 116 Regency Dr TF: 866-353-0145 ■ Web: www.smithtoolmfg.com	Wylie	TX	75098	866-353-0145		697
VLN Partners LLC 661 Andersen Dr TF: 877-856-3311 ■ Web: www.vlnpartners.com	Pittsburgh	PA	15220	412-381-0183	381-0182	174
VLSI Standards Inc 5 Technology Dr Web: www.vlsistandards.com	Milpitas	CA	95035	408-428-1800		518
Vlsip Technologies Inc 750 Presidential Dr Web: www.vlsip.com	Richardson	TX	75081	972-437-5506	644-1286	696
VM Services Inc 6701 Mowry Ave	Newark	CA	94560	510-744-3720		625
VMA (Valve Manufacturers Association of America) 1050 17th St NW Ste 280 Web: www.vma.org	Washington	DC	20036	202-331-8105	296-0378	49-13
VMA (Vic Myers Associates Inc) 2432 Jefferson St NE Web: www.vicmyers.com	Albuquerque	NM	87190	505-884-6878	883-4062	681
VMC (Vernon Milling Company Inc) 44080 Hwy 17 S TF: 800-753-1993 ■ Web: www.vernonmilling.com	Vernon	AL	35592	205-695-7161	695-7192	780
VMC Consulting Corp 11611 Willows Rd NE Web: www.vmc.com	Redmond	WA	98052	425-558-7700		721
VMC Technologies Inc 1788 Northwood Dr Web: vmctech.com	Troy	MI	48084	248-786-3000		358
VME (Victor Machinery Exchange Inc) 33-53 62nd St TF: 800-723-5359 ■ Web: www.victornet.com	Woodside	NY	11377	718-899-1502	899-0556	385
V-Me Media Inc 450 W 33rd St 11th Fl Web: www.vmetv.com	New York	NY	10001	212-273-4800		116
VMG Partners 39 Mesa St Ste 201 Web: www.vmgpartners.com	San Francisco	CA	94129	415-632-4200	632-4222	690
VMI (Vantage Mobility Intl) 5202 S 28th Pl *Fax Area Code: 602 ■ TF: 855-864-8267 ■ Web: www.vantagemobility.com	Phoenix	AZ	85040	855-864-8267	304-3290*	62-7
VMI Inc 211 E Weddell Dr Web: www.vmivideo.com	Sunnyvale	CA	94089	408-745-1700		45
VMNH (Virginia Museum of Natural History) 21 Starling Ave Web: www.vmnh.net	Martinsville	VA	24112	276-634-4141	634-4199	520
VMP (Village at Manor Park, The) 3023 S 84th St Web: www.vmpcares.com	Milwaukee	WI	53227	414-607-4100		672
VMS Inc 02400 37 1/2 St Web: vms-online.com	Gobles	MI	49055	269-377-0234		178-1
VMware 3401 Hillview Ave NYSE: VMW ■ Web: www.vmware.com	Palo Alto	CA	94304	650-427-1000		225
VNA 154 Hindman Rd TF: 877-862-6659 ■ Web: lutheranseniorlife.org	Butler	PA	16001	724-282-6806		371
VNA (Virginia Nurses Assn) 7113 Three Chopt Rd Ste 204 Web: www.virginianurses.com	Richmond	VA	23226	804-282-1808	282-4916	533
VNA & Hospice of Southern California 150 W First St Ste 270 TF: 888-357-3574 ■ Web: vnasocal.org	Claremont	CA	91711	909-624-3574	624-1559	371
VNA California 6235 River Crest Dr Ste L Web: vnacalifornia.org	Riverside	CA	92507	951-413-1200		371
VNA Hospice & Home Health of Lackawanna County 301 Delaware Ave TF: 800-936-7671 ■ Web: vnahospice.org	Olyphant	PA	18447	570-383-5180	383-5189	371
VNAA (Visiting Nurse Associations of America) 1800 Diagonal Rd Ste 600 TF: 888-866-8773 ■ Web: www.vnaa.org	Alexandria	VA	22314	571-527-1520		49-8
VNS Hospice of Suffolk 505 Main St Web: www.visitingnurseservice.org	Northport	NY	11768	631-261-7200	261-1985	371
VNWG (Van Ness Water Gardens Inc) 2460 N Euclid Ave TF: 800-205-2425 ■ Web: www.vnwg.com	Upland	CA	91784	909-982-2425	949-7217	293
Vocalink Global 405 W First St Unit A TF: 877-492-7754 ■ Web: vocalinkglobal.com	Dayton	OH	45402	877-492-7754		768
Vocantas Inc 2934 Baseline Rd Ste 301 TF: 877-271-8853 ■ Web: www.vocantas.com	Ottawa	ON	K2H1B2	613-271-8853	271-8381	179
Voce Communications Inc 75 E Santa Clara St 7th Fl Web: vocecommunications.com	San Jose	CA	95113	408-738-7840		636
Vocelli Pizza 1005 S Bee St Web: www.vocellipizza.com	Pittsburgh	PA	15220	412-919-2100		670
Vocera Communications Inc 525 Race St Ste 150 TF: 800-473-3971 ■ Web: www.vocera.com	San Jose	CA	95126	800-473-3971		177
Vode Lighting LLC 1206 E Macarthur St Ste 3 Web: vode.com	Sonoma	CA	95476	707-996-9898		196
Voestalpine Nortrak 3930 Valley E Industrial Dr Web: www.voestalpine.com	Birmingham	AL	35217	205-854-2884		190
Vogel Law Firm 218 NP Ave Web: www.vogellaw.com	Fargo	ND	58107	701-237-6983		428
Vogel Marketing Solutions LLC 255 Butler Ave Ste 201B Web: www.vogelmarketing.net	Lancaster	PA	17601	717-368-5143		4
Vogel State Park 405 Vogel State Park Rd Web: gastateparks.org	Blairsville	GA	30512	706-745-2628		565
Vogelsang USA 7966 SR-44 TF: 800-984-9400 ■ Web: www.vogelsang.info	Ravenna	OH	44266	330-296-3820		641
Vogler Motor Company Inc 1170 E Main Web: www.voglerfordcarbondale.com	Carbondale	IL	62901	618-457-8135		57
Vogt Ice 1000 W Ormsby Ave TF: 800-853-8648 ■ Web: www.vogtice.com	Louisville	KY	40210	502-635-3000	634-0479	664
Vogue Beauty College 247 Cliff St Web: www.vogueidahofalls.com	Idaho Falls	ID	83402	208-523-2520		167-3
Vogue College of Cosmetology 800 W Fern Ave TF: 866-227-3779 ■ Web: www.vogue.edu	McAllen	TX	78501	956-687-6149		166
Vogue Enterprise Inc 1801 Kettering TF: 800-426-2001 ■ Web: www.voguewindows.com	Irvine	CA	92614	949-833-9787	833-1346	361
Vogue Fabrics 618 Hartrey Ave *Fax Area Code: 847 ■ TF: 800-433-4313 ■ Web: www.voguefabricsstore.com	Evanston	IL	60202	800-433-4313	864-0113*	270
Vogue Flowers & Gifts Ltd 1114 N Blvd TF: 800-923-1010 ■ Web: www.vogueflowers.com	Richmond	VA	23230	804-353-9600		292
Vogue Optical 5 Brackley Pt Rd TF: 866-594-3937 ■ Web: vogueoptical.com	Charlottetown	PE	C1A6X8	902-566-3326	566-3269	543
Vogue School of Beauty Culture Inc 3309 S Franklin St Web: www.vogueschoolofbeauty.com	Michigan City	IN	46360	219-879-0239		685
Vogue Strap 5809 Foster Ave Ste 3A Web: www.voguestrap.com	Long Island City	NY	11101	718-706-8700		411
Voice & Data Networks Inc (VDN) 4218 Park Glen Rd TF: 800-246-7999 ■ Web: www.voicedata.com	Saint Louis Park	MN	55416	952-946-5353	946-1066	178-11
Voice Comm LLC 80 Twinbridge Dr *Fax Area Code: 856 ■ TF: 800-803-1321 ■ Web: www.myvoicecomm.com	Pennsauken	NJ	08110	800-803-1321	317-0623*	246
Voice Construction Ltd 7545 52 St Web: www.voiceconst.com	Edmonton	AB	T6B2G2	780-469-1351		188
Voice Ministries of Farmington Inc 1103 W Apache St Web: www.passionradio.org	Farmington	NM	87401	505-327-7202	327-2163	645-141
Voice of God Recordings Inc, The 5911 Charlestown Pk Web: www.branham.org	Jeffersonville	IN	47130	812-256-1177		48-20
Voice Pro Inc 2055 Lee Rd TF: 800-261-0104 ■ Web: voiceproinc.com	Cleveland	OH	44118	216-932-8040	932-5048	765
Voice Security Systems Inc 24591 Seth Cir Web: www.voice-security.com	Dana Point	CA	92629	949-493-4030		693
Voice, The 19176 Hall Rd Ste 200 Web: www.voicenews.com	Clinton Township	MI	48038	586-716-8100		532-4
Voice123 30 E 23rd St Web: voice123.com	New York	NY	10010	212-461-1873		387
VoiceAge Corp 750 Lucerne Rd Ste 250 Web: www.voiceage.com	Montreal	QC	H3R2H6	514-737-4940		194
Voicecom 5900 Windward Pkwy Ste 500 TF: 888-468-3554 ■ Web: www.intelliverse.com	Alpharetta	GA	30005	888-468-3554		736
VoiceGlance 12 Roosevelt Ave TF: 800-260-3025 ■ Web: voiceglance.com	Mystic	CT	06355	800-260-3025		193
Voicenet Communications Inc 9810 Ashton Rd	Philadelphia	PA	19114	215-259-2100	259-2199	396
Voicent Communications Inc 2672 Bayshore Pky Web: www.voicent.com	Mountain View	CA	94043	408-716-0567		174
Voices for America's Children 1000 Vermont Ave NW	Washington	DC	20005	202-289-0777		48-6
Voices of September 11th 161 Cherry St TF: 866-505-3911 ■ Web: www.voicesofseptember11.org	New Canaan	CT	06840	203-966-3911		48-5
Voigt & Schweitzer Inc 987 Buckeye Park Rd Web: www.hotdipgalvanizing.com	Columbus	OH	43207	614-443-4621	449-8851	481
Voila! 509 Botetourt St Web: www.voilacuisine.com	Norfolk	VA	23510	757-640-0343		671
VoIP Group Inc 290 NW 165 St Mezzanine 100 Web: www.voipgroup.com	Miami	FL	33169	305-967-6639		809
VoIPLINK Corp 3029 S Harbor Blvd TF: 866-987-8647 ■ Web: www.voiplink.com	Santa Ana	CA	92704	866-987-8647		445
Voisard Manufacturing Inc 60 Scott St Web: de.gbfab.com	Shiloh	OH	44878	419-896-3191	896-2127	697
Voit Real Estate Services Inc 101 Shipyard Way Web: voitco.com	Newport Beach	CA	92663	949-644-8648		652
Voith 9395 Kenwood Rd Ste 200 Web: redirect.voith.com	Cincinnati	OH	45242	513-731-3590	731-3659	393
Voith Hydro Inc 760 E Berlin Rd Web: www.voith.com	York	PA	17408	717-792-7000	792-7884	262
Voith Turbo Inc 25 Winship Rd Web: www.redirect.voith.com	York	PA	17406	717-767-3200		60
Volare Systems Inc 4351 Canyonbrook Dr Web: volaresystems.com	Highlands Ranch	CO	80130	303-532-5838		177
Volaris Group Inc 5800 Explorer Dr 5th Fl Web: www.volarisgroup.com	Mississauga	ON	L4W5K9	905-267-5400		787
Volcano Corp 3721 Valley Centre Dr Ste 500 *Fax Area Code: 858 ■ Web: www.volcanotherapeutics.com	San Diego	CA	92130	916-638-8008	720-0325*	250
Volcano Restaurant 3700 Lincoln Way W Web: www.volcanosb.com	South Bend	IN	46628	574-287-5775		671
Volchok Consulting Inc 120 W 20th St *Fax Area Code: 646 ■ Web: www.volchok.com	New York	NY	10011	212-777-7433	336-6332*	261
Volckening 6700 Third Ave TF: 800-221-0876 ■ Web: www.volckening.com	Brooklyn	NY	11220	718-836-4000	748-2811	298
Volcom Inc 1740 Monrovia Ave TF: 855-330-0188 ■ Web: www.volcom.com	Costa Mesa	CA	92627	949-646-2175		155-1
Volian Enterprises Inc 122 Kerr Rd Web: volian.com	New Kensington	PA	15068	724-335-3744		177
Volk Corp 23936 Industrial Pk Dr Web: www.volkcorp.com	Farmington Hills	MI	48335	248-477-6700	478-6884	467
Volk Optical Inc 7893 Enterprise Dr TF: 800-345-8655 ■ Web: volk.com	Mentor	OH	44060	440-942-6161		543

Name / Address	City	State	ZIP	Phone	Fax	Class
Volk Packaging Corp 11 Morin St *TF:* 800-341-0208 ■ *Web:* www.volkboxes.com	Biddeford	ME	04005	800-341-0208		100
Volkert & Associates Inc 3809 Moffett Rd *Web:* www.volkert.com	Mobile	AL	36618	251-342-1070		261
Volkswagen Canada Inc 777 Bayly St W *Web:* www.vw.ca	Ajax	ON	L1S7G7	905-428-6700	428-5898	59
Volkswagen Group of America Inc 2200 Ferdinand Porsche Dr *Web:* www.volkswagengroupofamerica.com	Herndon	VA	20171	248-754-5000		59
Volkswagen of Akron 447 W Exchange St *Web:* www.vwofakron.com	Akron	OH	44302	330-752-1773		57
Volkswagen of America Inc 3800 Hamlin Rd *TF:* 800-822-8987 ■ *Web:* www.vw.com	Auburn Hills	MI	48326	800-822-8987		59
Volleyball Hall of Fame 444 Dwight St *Web:* www.volleyhall.org	Holyoke	MA	01040	413-536-0926		522
Vollmer Inc 3822 Sandwich St *Web:* www.vollmer.ca	Windsor	ON	N9C1C1	519-966-6100		188-10
Vollrath Company LLC, The 1236 N 18th St *TF:* 800-624-2051 ■ *Web:* www.vollrathfoodservice.com	Sheboygan	WI	53081	920-457-4851		300
Vollwerth & Co 200 Hancock St PO Box 239 *TF:* 800-562-7620 ■ *Web:* www.vollwerth.com	Hancock	MI	49930	906-482-1550		296-26
Volmar Construction Inc 4400 2nd Ave *Web:* www.volmar.com	Brooklyn	NY	11232	718-832-2444	499-4045	685
Volo Bog State Natural Area 28478 W Brandenburg Rd *Web:* www2.illinois.gov	Ingleside	IL	60041	815-344-1294		565
Volpi Foods 5263 Northrup Ave *TF:* 800-288-3439 ■ *Web:* www.volpifoods.com	Saint Louis	MO	63110	314-772-8550	772-0411	296-10
Volquartsen Custom Ltd 24276 240th St PO Box 397 *Web:* volquartsen.com	Carroll	IA	51401	712-792-4238		711
Volt 1065 Avenue of the Americas 20th Fl *NYSE:* VISI ■ *Web:* www.volt.com	New York	NY	10018	212-704-2400		721
Volta Charging 155 De Haro St *TF:* 888-264-2208 ■ *Web:* voltacharging.com	San Francisco	CA	94103	888-264-2208		8
Voltage Ltd 901 Front St Ste 300 *Web:* voltagead.com	Louisville	CO	80027	303-664-1687		5
Volterra 5411 Ballard Ave NW *Web:* volterrakirkland.com	Seattle	WA	98107	206-789-5100		671
Volume 9 Inc 1660 S Albion St Ste 800 *Web:* www.v9digital.com	Denver	CO	80222	303-955-5228		195
Volunteer Energy Co-op (VEC) PO Box 277 *Web:* vec.org	Decatur	TN	37322	423-334-5721	334-7003	245
Volunteer Manitoba Library 5 Donald St S Ste 410 *TF:* 888-922-4545 ■ *Web:* www.volunteermanitoba.ca	Winnipeg	MB	R3L2T4	204-477-5180	284-5200	434-3
Volunteer State Community College 1480 Nashville Pk *TF:* 888-335-8722 ■ *Web:* www.volstate.edu	Gallatin	TN	37066	615-452-8600		162
Volunteers Insurance Service Association Inc 2750 Killarney Dr Ste 202 *TF:* 800-468-4200 ■ *Web:* cimaworld.com	Woodbridge	VA	22192	703-739-9300	739-0761	390
Volunteers of America 1660 Duke St *TF:* 800-899-0089 ■ *Web:* www.voa.org	Alexandria	VA	22314	703-341-5000	341-7000	48-5
Volusia County Public Library 105 E Magnolia Ave *Web:* www.volusialibrary.org	Daytona Beach	FL	32114	386-257-6036		434-3
Volusia Speedway Park 1500 W State Rd *Web:* bubbaracewaypark.com	De Leon Springs	FL	32130	352-622-9400		515
Volvo Cars of North America 1 Volvo Dr *TF:* 800-458-1552 ■ *Web:* www.volvocars.com	Rockleigh	NJ	07647	201-768-7300		59
Volvo Cars Tucson 831 W Wetmore Rd *TF:* 888-457-1197 ■ *Web:* www.volvocarstucson.com	Tucson	AZ	85705	888-457-1197		57
Volvo Construction Equipment of North America Inc 312 Volvo Way *TF:* 855-235-6014 ■ *Web:* www.volvoce.com	Shippensburg	PA	17257	717-532-9181		190
Volvo Group North America Inc 2900 K St NW *Web:* www.volvogroup.com	Washington	DC	20007	202-661-4770		516
Volvo Penta of the Americas Inc 1300 Volvo Penta Dr *TF:* 800-522-1959 ■ *Web:* www.volvopenta.com	Chesapeake	VA	23320	757-436-2800		262
Volvo Trucks North America 4881 Cougar Trail Rd *Web:* www.volvotrucks.com	Dublin	VA	24084	540-674-4181		59
Vomar Products Inc 7800 Deering Ave *Web:* www.vomarproducts.com	Canoga Park	CA	91304	818-610-5115	610-5123	701
Vomela Co, The 274 E Fillmore Ave *TF:* 800-645-1012 ■ *Web:* www.vomela.com	Saint Paul	MN	55107	651-228-2200	228-2295	701
Von Braun Ctr 700 Monroe St *Web:* www.vonbrauncenter.com	Huntsville	AL	35801	256-533-1953		205
Von Lee International School of Aesthetics 309 Reisterstown Rd *TF:* 800-437-5140 ■ *Web:* www.vonlee.com	Pikesville	MD	21208	410-653-1966	653-8447	685
Von Lehman & CO 250 Grandview Dr Ste 300 *Web:* vlcpa.com	Fort Mitchell	KY	41017	859-331-3300		463
Von Maur Inc 6565 Brady St *TF:* 877-866-6287 ■ *Web:* www.vonmaur.com	Davenport	IA	52806	563-388-2200		229
Von Paris Enterprises Inc 8691 Larkin Rd *TF:* 800-866-6355 ■ *Web:* www.vonparis.com	Savage	MD	20763	410-888-8500	888-9062	519
Von Ruden Manufacturing Inc 1008 First St NE *Web:* www.vonruden.com	Buffalo	MN	55313	763-682-3122		247
Vonage Holdings Corp 23 Main St *NYSE:* VG ■ *TF:* 877-862-2562 ■ *Web:* www.vonage.com	Holmdel	NJ	07733	732-528-2600	834-0189	736
Vons Employees Federal Credit Union 4455 Arden Dr PO Box 8023 *Web:* vonsefcu.org	El Monte	CA	91731	626-444-1972		219
Vontobel Asset Management Inc 1540 Broad Way Ave 38th Fl *Web:* www.vusa.com	New York	NY	10036	212-415-7000		401
Vooner Flogard Corp 4729 Stockholm Ct *TF:* 800-345-7879 ■ *Web:* www.vooner.com	Charlotte	NC	28273	704-552-9314		295
Voorhees College 213 Wiggins Dr PO Box 678 *TF:* 866-685-9904 ■ *Web:* www.voorhees.edu	Denmark	SC	29042	803-780-1234		166
Voorhees International Inc 575 Rudder Rd Ste 109 *Web:* www.voorheesintl.com	Fenton	MO	63026	636-349-1555	349-5130	187
Voorhees Pediatric Facility 1304 Laurel Oak Rd *TF:* 888-873-5437 ■ *Web:* www.forkidcare.com	Voorhees	NJ	08043	856-346-3300	346-3462	450
Voorhees State Park 251 County Rd 513 *Web:* www.njparksandforests.org	Glen Gardner	NJ	08826	908-638-6969		565
Voorhees Town Ctr 2120 Voorhees Town Ctr *Web:* www.voorheestowncenter.com	Voorhees	NJ	08043	856-772-1950		460
Voorwood Co 2350 Barney St *TF:* 800-826-0089 ■ *Web:* www.voorwood.com	Anderson	CA	96007	530-365-3311	365-3315	821
Vopak Americas 2000 W Loop S Ste 1550 *Web:* www.vopak.com	Houston	TX	77027	713-561-7200	561-7323	581
Vordermeier Management Co 2132 E Oakland Park Blvd 2nd Fl *TF:* 877-862-7589 ■ *Web:* www.vmcrealty.com	Fort Lauderdale	FL	33306	954-566-1661	566-1670	652
Vornado Air Circulation Systems Inc 415 E 13th St *Web:* www.vornado.com	Andover	KS	67002	316-733-0035		17
Vornado Realty Trust 888 Seventh Ave *NYSE:* VNO ■ *Web:* www.vno.com	New York	NY	10106	212-894-7000		655
Vorne Industries Inc 1445 Industrial Dr *TF:* 877-767-5326 ■ *Web:* www.vorne.com	Itasca	IL	60143	630-875-3600	875-3609	201
Vorpahl Wing Securities 421 W Riverside Ste 1020 *Web:* vorpahlwing.com	Spokane	WA	99201	509-747-1749		690
Vorsite 1631 15th Ave W Ste 316 *Web:* www.vorsite.com	Seattle	WA	98119	206-781-1797		224
Vortalsoft 220 Davidson Ave Ste 3A *Web:* www.vortalsoft.com	Somerset	NJ	08873	732-748-1800	748-4381	809
Vortech Engineering LLC 1650 Pacific Ave *Web:* vortechsuperchargers.com	Oxnard	CA	93033	805-247-0226	247-0669	247
Vortek Instruments LLC 8475 W I25 Frontage Rd Ste 300 *Web:* www.vortekinst.com	Longmont	CO	80504	303-682-9999		639
Vorteq Coil Finishers LLC 930 Armour Rd *Web:* www.vorteqcoil.com	Oconomowoc	WI	53066	262-567-1112		819
Vortex LLC 4 Dearborn Rd *Web:* www.vortexmetal.com	Peabody	MA	01960	978-535-8721		697
Vortx Inc 2245 Ashland St *Web:* www.vortx.com	Ashland	OR	97520	541-201-9965		177
Vorwerk USA Company LP 3255 E Thousand Oaks Blvd Unit B *TF:* 888-867-9375 ■ *Web:* corporate.vorwerk.com	Thousand Oaks	CA	91362	888-867-9375		366
Vorys Sater Seymour & Pease LLP (VSSP) 52 E Gay St PO Box 1008 *Web:* www.vorys.com	Columbus	OH	43216	614-464-6400	464-6350	428
Voss Belting & Specialty Co 6965 N Hamlin Ave *Web:* www.vossbelting.com	Lincolnwood	IL	60712	847-673-8900	673-1408	370
Voss Lighting PO Box 22159 *TF:* 866-292-0529 ■ *Web:* www.vosslighting.com	Lincoln	NE	68542	402-420-2281		246
Voss Pharmacy Inc 3303 S Halsted St	Chicago	IL	60608	773-254-5221		237
Voss Signs LLC 112 Fairgrounds Dr *TF:* 800-473-0698 ■ *Web:* www.vosssigns.com	Manlius	NY	13104	315-682-6418		687
Voss, Michaels, Lee & Associates PO Box 1829 **Fax Area Code:* 616 ■ *TF:* 800-253-4646 ■ *Web:* www.vmlcollects.com	Holland	MI	49422	800-253-4646	355-7284*	160
Votava Nantz & Johnson LLC 9237 Ward Pkwy Ste 240 *Web:* vnjlaw.com	Kansas City	MO	64114	816-895-8800		41
Votaw Precision Technologies Inc 13153 Lakeland Rd *Web:* www.votaw.com	Santa Fe Springs	CA	90670	562-944-0661		697
Votenet Solutions Inc 1420 K St Ste 200 *Web:* www.eballot.com	Washington	DC	20005	202-737-2277	737-2283	178-10
Voto Manufacturers Sales Co 500 N Third St PO Box 1299 *TF:* 800-848-4010 ■ *Web:* www.votosales.com	Steubenville	OH	43952	740-282-3621	282-5441	385
Vowells & Schaaf LLP 601 SE MI King Jr Blvd *Web:* vscpas.com	Evansville	IN	47713	812-421-4165		2
VOX AM/FM LLC 550 Cochituate Rd Ste 25 *Web:* www.voxamfm.com	FRAMINGHAM	MA	01701	781-239-8018		643
VOX Data 1155 Metcalfe St 18th Fl *TF:* 800-861-9599 ■ *Web:* www.voxdata.com	Montreal	QC	H3B2V6	514-871-1920		737
Vox Mobile 6100 Rockside Woods Blvd Ste 100 *TF:* 800-536-9030 ■ *Web:* www.voxmobile.com	Independence	OH	44131	800-536-9030		736
Vox Printing Inc 4000 E Britton Rd *Web:* www.voxprint.com	Oklahoma City	OK	73131	405-478-7500		627
Vox Public Relations Public Affairs 1416 Willamette St *Web:* www.voxprpa.com	Eugene	OR	97401	541-513-1236		636
Vox Spectrum Inc 3568 Nesting Ridge *Web:* www.voxspectrum.com	Rochester Hills	MI	48309	248-559-6350		178-1
Voxox Inc 9276 Scranton Rd Ste 300 *Web:* www.voxox.com	San Diego	CA	92121	619-900-9000		387

Name / Address	City	State	ZIP	Phone	Fax	Class
Voxtechnologies Com 301 S Sherman St *Web:* www.voxtechnologies.com	Richardson	TX	75081	972-234-4343		175
Voya Services Co 5780 Powers Ferry Rd NW *TF:* 800-336-3436 ■ *Web:* www.voya.com	Atlanta	GA	30327	770-980-5100		360-4
Voyage Federal Credit Union 3823 S Kiwanis Cir *TF:* 800-843-8759 ■ *Web:* voyagefcu.org	Sioux Falls	SD	57105	605-338-2533		219
Voyager Academy 101 Hock Parc *Web:* voyageracademy.net	Durham	NC	27704	919-433-3301	620-0554	148
Voyager Electronics Corp 3065 101st Ave NE *Web:* www.voyagercorp.com	Blaine	MN	55449	763-571-7766	571-9519	179
Voyager HQ 137 W 25th St 11th Fl *Web:* www.voyagerhq.com	New York	NY	10001	347-440-1627		393
Voyager Systems Inc 360 Rt 101 *TF:* 800-634-1966 ■ *Web:* www.voyagersystems.com	Bedford	NH	03110	603-472-5172		180
Voyages Michel Barrette 100 Rue Saint-Joseph *TF:* 800-263-3078 ■ *Web:* voyagesmichelbarrette.com	Alma	QC	G8B7A6	418-668-3078		775
Voyageur Lakewalk Inn 333 E Superior St *Web:* www.voyageurlakewalkinn.com	Duluth	MN	55802	218-722-3911		379
Voyageurs National Park 360 Hwy 11 E *TF:* 888-381-2873 ■ *Web:* www.nps.gov	International Falls	MN	56649	218-283-6600	285-7407	564
Voyetra Turtle Beach Inc 150 Clearbrook Rd Ste 162 *Web:* www.turtlebeach.com	Elmsford	NY	10523	914-345-2255	345-2266	625
Voytek Inc 3100 Breckenridge Blvd Ste 120 *Web:* www.voytek.com	Duluth	GA	30096	770-921-7017		396
VP Medical Consulting LLC 1201 Military Rd Ste 2 *Web:* www.vp-medical.com	Benton	AR	72015	501-778-3378	315-3378	196
VP Racing Fuels Inc 7124 Richter Rd *Web:* vpracingfuels.com	Elmendorf	TX	78112	210-635-7744		580
VPA (Veterinary Pharmacies of America Inc) 4802 N Sam Houston Pkwy W Ste 100 *TF:* 877-838-7979 ■ *Web:* www.vparx.com	Houston	TX	77066	877-838-7979		584
VPC (Violence Policy Ctr) 1730 Rhode Island Ave NW Ste 1014 *Web:* www.vpc.org	Washington	DC	20036	202-822-8200		48-7
VPCI (VPCI INC) 5640 W Maple Rd Ste 312 *Web:* www.vpcint.com	West Bloomfield	MI	48322	248-538-5150	538-5153	261
VPCI INC (VPCI) 5640 W Maple Rd Ste 312 *Web:* www.vpcint.com	West Bloomfield	MI	48322	248-538-5150	538-5153	261
VPE Public Relations 316 W Second St Ste 1202 *Web:* vpepr.com	Los Angeles	CA	90012	626-403-3200		636
VPI Corp 3123 S Ninth St *TF:* 800-874-4240 ■ *Web:* www.vpicorp.com	Sheboygan	WI	53081	920-458-4664	458-1368	600
VPIRG (Vermont Public Interest Research Group) 141 Main St Ste 6 *Web:* www.vpirg.org	Montpelier	VT	05602	802-223-5221		633
VPM Harrisonburg 847 Martin Luther King Jr Way *TF:* 800-345-9878 ■ *Web:* www.wvpt.net	Harrisonburg	VA	22801	540-434-5391	434-7084	647
VPOP Technologies Inc 1772J Avenida de los Arboles Ste 374 *TF:* 888-811-8767 ■ *Web:* www.vpop.net	Thousand Oaks	CA	91362	805-529-9374		808
VPS (Vacuum Pump Systems Inc) PO Box 1826 *Web:* www.vacuumpumpsystems.net	Gainesville	GA	30503	770-532-0260	536-1005	385
VPT (Vermont Public Television) 204 Ethan Allen Ave *TF:* 800-639-7811 ■ *Web:* www.vpt.org	Colchester	VT	05446	802-655-4800		632
VPT Inc 1971 Kraft Dr *Web:* www.vptpower.com	Blacksburg	VA	24060	540-552-5000	552-5003	256
VR Bags Inc 637 E 132 St **Fax Area Code:* 718 ■ *Web:* www.vrbags.com	Bronx	NY	10454	212-714-1494	585-5722*	475
V-rad Systems Inc 4504 Maple St *Web:* v-radsystems.com	Bellaire	TX	77401	713-667-6056	667-6058	383
Vrakas CPAs + Advisors 445 S Moorland Rd Ste 400 *Web:* vrakascpas.com	Brookfield	WI	53005	262-797-0400	797-7895	2
Vrana & Hines PC 814 Broadway *Web:* www.vranahines.com	Raynham	MA	02767	508-822-7300		41
VRC Inc 696 W Bagley Rd *TF:* 800-872-1012 ■ *Web:* www.vrcmfg.com	Berea	OH	44017	440-243-6666		757
VRC Insurance Systems 32121 Lindero Canyon Rd *Web:* www.vrcis.com	Westlake Village	CA	91361	818-707-4295	449-7665	178-1
Vrdolyak Law Group LLC 741 N Dearborn St *Web:* www.vrdolyak.com	Chicago	IL	60654	312-482-8200		428
Vrdolyak Law Group LLC 9618 S Commercial Ave *Web:* vrdolyak.com	Chicago	IL	60617	773-731-3311		41
VRE (Virginia Railway Express) 1500 King St Ste 202 *Web:* www.vre.org	Alexandria	VA	22314	703-684-1001	684-1313	468
VRG (Vegetarian Resource Group, The) PO Box 1463 *Web:* www.vrg.org	Baltimore	MD	21203	410-366-8343	366-8804	48-17
VRH Construction Corp 320 Grand Ave *Web:* www.vrhcorp.com	Englewood	NJ	07631	201-871-4422		186
VRMA (Vacation Rental Managers Assn) 2025 M St NW Ste 800 *Web:* www.vrma.org	Washington	DC	20036	202-367-1179	367-2179	49-17
VRMC (Venice Regional Medical Ctr) 540 The Rialto *Web:* www.veniceregional.com	Venice	FL	34285	941-485-7711		374-3
Vroman's Bookstore 695 E Colorado Blvd *Web:* www.vromansbookstore.com	Pasadena	CA	91101	626-449-5320	792-7308	95
VRP (Vinspire Publishing LLC) PO Box 1165 *Web:* www.vinspirepublishing.com	Ladson	SC	29456	843-695-7530		637-2
Vrp Consulting 268 Bush St Ste 3836 *Web:* vrpconsulting.com	San Francisco	CA	94104	415-429-8565		177
VS Management of NY Inc 3281 Veterans Memorial Hwy **Fax Area Code:* 631 ■ *TF:* 877-778-7648	Ronkonkoma	NY	11779	877-778-7648	585-6513*	631
Vsa Inc 6929 Seward Ave *TF:* 800-888-2140 ■ *Web:* www.vsa1.com	Lincoln	NE	68507	402-325-8033		246
VSAC (Vermont Student Assistance Corp) 10 E Allen St PO Box 2000 **Fax Area Code:* 802 ■ *TF:* 800-642-3177 ■ *Web:* www.vsac.org	Winooski	VT	05404	800-642-3177	654-3765*	725
VSC (Vetter Stone Co) 23894 Third Ave *TF:* 800-878-2850 ■ *Web:* www.vetterstone.com	Mankato	MN	56001	507-345-4568	345-4777	724
VSCO 1500 Broadway *Web:* www.vsco.co	Oakland	CA	94612	925-413-8250		178-8
VSE Corp 2550 Huntington Ave *NASDAQ: VSEC* ■ *TF:* 800-455-4873 ■ *Web:* www.vsecorp.com	Alexandria	VA	22303	703-960-4600		261
VSGI (Visual Systems Group Inc) 7900 Westpark Dr Ste T-610 *TF:* 877-402-8744 ■ *Web:* www.vsgi.com	McLean	VA	22102	703-848-8200	848-8211	180
VShift 1250 Broadway 25th Fl *Web:* www.vshift.com	New York	NY	10001	212-937-8575		194
VSI (Vinyl Siding Institute) 1201 15th St NW Ste 220 *Web:* www.vinylsiding.org	Washington	DC	20005	202-587-5100		49-13
VSM Abrasives 1012 E Wabash St *TF:* 800-737-0176 ■ *Web:* www.vsmabrasives.com	O'Fallon	MO	63366	636-272-7432	272-7434	1
V-Soft Inc 888 Saratoga Ave Ste 203 *Web:* www.v-softinc.com	San Jose	CA	95129	408-342-1700	342-1705	179
VSolvIT LLC 4171 Market St Ste 2 *Web:* www.vsolvit.com	Ventura	CA	93003	805-277-4705		177
VSS (Veronis Suhler Stevenson) 55 E 52nd St 33rd Fl *Web:* www.vss.com	New York	NY	10055	212-935-4990	381-8168	690
Vss Security Services 2225 W Peoria Ave Ste 220 *Web:* www.vss-security-services.com	Phoenix	AZ	85029	602-861-9900	861-0056	693
VSSP (Vorys Sater Seymour & Pease LLP) 52 E Gay St PO Box 1008 *Web:* www.vorys.com	Columbus	OH	43216	614-464-6400	464-6350	428
VStock Transfer LLC 18 Lafayette Pl **Fax Area Code:* 646 ■ *Web:* www.vstocktransfer.com	Woodmere	NY	11598	212-828-8436	536-3179*	463
VT Graphics Inc 465 Penn St *Web:* www.vtgraph.com	Yeadon	PA	19050	610-259-4090	259-7235	781
VT Halter Marine Inc 900 Bayou Casotte Pkwy *TF:* 800-639-2715 ■ *Web:* vthm.com	Pascagoula	MS	39581	228-696-6756	696-6763	698
V-T Industries Inc 1000 Industrial Pk *TF:* 800-827-1615 ■ *Web:* www.vtindustries.com	Holstein	IA	51025	712-368-4381	368-4111	599
VT LeeBoy Inc 500 Lincoln County Pkwy Extention *Web:* www.leeboy.com	Lincolnton	NC	28092	704-966-3300		190
VT MAK 150 Cambridge Park Dr 3rd Fl *Web:* www.mak.com	Cambridge	MA	02140	617-876-8085	876-9208	178-10
VTA (Santa Clara Valley Transportation Authority) 3331 N First St *TF:* 800-894-9908 ■ *Web:* www.vta.org	San Jose	CA	95134	408-321-2300		468
VTE Inc 5437 Robinson Rd *Web:* www.vte-europe.com	Pellston	MI	49769	231-539-8000	539-0914	676
VTEC Print 12487 Globe St *Web:* www.westmetroprinting.com	Livonia	MI	48150	734-522-0410	953-9648	627
VTech Communications Inc 9590 SW Gemini Dr Ste 120 *TF:* 800-595-9511 ■ *Web:* www.vtech.com	Beaverton	OR	97008	503-596-1200	644-9887	735
VTech Electronics North America LLC 1155 W Dundee St Ste 130 *TF:* 800-521-2010 ■ *Web:* www.vtechkids.com	Arlington Heights	IL	60004	847-400-3600		762
V-Technologies LLC 675 W Johnson Ave *TF:* 800-462-4016 ■ *Web:* www.vtechnologies.com	Cheshire	CT	06410	800-462-4016		525
V-TEK Inc 751 Summit Ave PO Box 3104 *Web:* www.vtekusa.com	Mankato	MN	56002	507-387-2039		253
VTF (Virginia Tech Foundation Inc) 902 Prices Fork Rd Ste 4500 *Web:* www.vtf.vt.edu	Blacksburg	VA	24061	540-231-2861		166
VTHG (Virginia Tech) *Department of Horticulture* 490 W Campus Dr 301 Saunders Hall *Web:* spes.vt.edu	Blacksburg	VA	24061	540-231-5451		97
Vtl Amplifiers Inc 4774 Murietta St Ste 10 *Web:* www.vtl.com	Chino	CA	91710	909-627-5944		52
VTS Investigations LLC 7 S State St **Fax Area Code:* 847 ■ *TF:* 800-538-4464 ■ *Web:* pichicago.com	Elgin	IL	60123	800-538-4464	628-1666*	400
Vudu Inc 600 W California Ave *Web:* www.vudu.com	Sunnyvale	CA	94086	312-729-4068		797
Vulcan Company Inc, The 51 Sharp St *Web:* www.vulcantools.com	Hingham	MA	02043	781-337-5970	331-3444	190
Vulcan Corp 30 Garfield Pl Ste 1040 *TF:* 800-447-1146 ■ *Web:* www.vulcorp.com	Cincinnati	OH	45202	513-621-2850		676
Vulcan Engineering Co 1 Vulcan Dr PO Box 307 *Web:* www.vulcangroup.com	Helena	AL	35080	205-663-0732	663-9103	386
Vulcan Inc 410 E Berry Ave *TF:* 888-846-2728 ■ *Web:* www.vulcaninc.com	Foley	AL	36535	251-943-7000	943-9270	153
Vulcan Inc 505 Fifth Ave S Ste 900 *Web:* www.vulcan.com	Seattle	WA	98104	206-342-2000	342-3000	405
Vulcan Industries Corp N113 W18830 Carnegie Dr *Web:* www.vulcancorp.com	Germantown	WI	53022	262-255-1090		595
Vulcan Industries Inc 300 Display Dr *TF:* 888-444-4417 ■ *Web:* www.vulcanind.com	Moody	AL	35004	205-640-2400	640-2412	233
Vulcan Minerals Inc 333 Duckworth St *Web:* vulcanminerals.ca	Saint John	NL	A1C1G9	709-754-3186		538

	Phone	Fax	Class
Vulcan Painters Inc PO Box 1010 . . . Bessemer AL 35021 Web: www.vulcan-group.com	205-428-0556	424-2267	189-8
Vulcan Pipe & Supply 1121 Olivette Executive Pkwy Ste 220 . . . Saint Louis MO 63132 Web: vulcanpipe.com	314-395-8122	395-8562	358
Vulcan Spring & Manufacturing Co 501 Schoolhouse Rd . . . Telford PA 18969 Web: www.vulcanspring.com	215-721-1721		483
Vulcan Tool Co 730 Lorraine Ave . . . Dayton OH 45410 Web: www.vulcancut.com	937-253-6194	253-1062	493
Vulcan Tool Company Inc 1080C Garden State Rd . . . Union NJ 07083 Web: www.vulcantool.com	908-686-0550	686-8522	488
Vulcan Value Partners 3 Protective Ctr 2801 Hwy 280 S Ste 300 . . . Birmingham AL 35223 Web: www.vulcanvaluepartners.com	205-803-1582	803-1584	226
Vulsay Industries Ltd 35 Regan Rd . . . Brampton ON L7A1B2 TF: 800-468-1760 ■ Web: www.vulsay.com	905-846-2200		88
Vutec Corp 11711 W Sample Rd . . . Coral Springs FL 33065 *Fax Area Code: 954 ■ TF: 800-770-4700 ■ Web: vutec.com	800-770-4700	545-9011*	591
Vutech & Ruff LLC 177 E Beck St . . . Columbus OH 43206 Web: vutech-ruff.com	614-255-0600	474-8448	652
Vuurr LLC 260 S Arizona Ave . . . Chandler AZ 85225 Web: vuurr.com	480-525-8240		631
Vuzix Corp 2166 Brighton Henrietta Town Line Rd . . . Rochester NY 14623 TF: 800-436-7838 ■ Web: www.vuzix.com	585-359-5900		543
VVMA (Virginia Veterinary Medical Assn) 3801 Westerre Pkwy Ste D . . . Henrico VA 23233 TF: 800-937-8862 ■ Web: vvma.org	804-346-2611	346-2655	795
VWA (Vengroff Williams & Associates Inc) 2099 S State College Bvld . . . Anaheim CA 92806 TF: 800-238-9655 ■ Web: www.vwinc.com	714-889-6200		160
VWR Intl 100 Matsonford Rd Bldg 1 Ste 200 . . . Radnor PA 19087 TF: 800-932-5000 ■ Web: us.vwr.com	610-386-1700	431-9174	475
VXI Global Solutions Inc 220 W First St 3rd Fl . . . Los Angeles CA 90012 Web: vxi.com	213-637-1300		317
Vyatek Sports Inc 5045 E Calle . . . Del Sol Cave Creek AZ 85331 Web: www.vyatek.com	480-240-6004	699-2042	711
Vyrian Inc 4660 Sweetwater Blvd Ste 200 . . . Sugar Land TX 77479 *Fax Area Code: 408 ■ TF: 866-874-0598 ■ Web: www.vyrian.com	866-874-0598	854-8571*	246
Vyse Gelatin Co 5010 Rose St . . . Schiller Park IL 60176 TF: 800-533-2152 ■ Web: nitta-gelatin.com	800-533-2152		345
Vystar Credit Union 1802 Kernan Blvd S . . . Jacksonville FL 32246 TF: 800-445-6289 ■ Web: vystarcu.org	904-777-6000		219
Vytron Corp 1000 Vytron Rd . . . Loudon TN 37774 Web: www.vytron.com	865-458-4624		596
Vzn Group LLC 5900 Renaissance Pl . . . Toledo OH 43623 Web: vzncpa.com	419-882-1886		2

W

	Phone	Fax	Class
W & C Printing Company Inc 370 Pleasant Hill Dr . . . Winona MN 55987	507-452-2658		627
W & E Radtke Inc W168 N12276 Century Ln . . . Germantown WI 53022 Web: weradtke.com	262-253-1412		293
W & H Co-operative Oil Co 407 10th St N . . . Humboldt IA 50548 TF: 800-392-3816 ■ Web: www.whcoop.com	515-332-2782	332-1559	324
W & H Pacific 12100 NE 195th St Ste 300 . . . Bothell WA 98011 Web: whpacific.com	425-951-4800	951-4808	261
W & H Systems Inc 120 Asia Pl . . . Carlstadt NJ 07072 TF: 800-966-6993 ■ Web: www.whsystems.com	201-933-7840	933-2144	207
W & m Manufacturing Inc 1000 N Morton . . . Portland IN 47371 Web: carreramfg.com	260-726-9800	726-2041	481
W & T Offshore Inc 9 Greenway Plz Ste 300 . . . Houston TX 77046 Web: www.wtoffshore.com	713-626-8525	626-8527	536
W & W Steel Co 1730 W Reno Ave . . . Oklahoma City OK 73106 TF: 800-222-1868 ■ Web: www.wwsteel.com	405-235-3621	236-4842	480
W A Baum Company Inc 620 Oak St . . . Copiague NY 11726 TF: 888-281-6061 ■ Web: www.wabaum.com	631-226-3940		476
W A Cleary Corp 1049 Rt 27 . . . Somerset NJ 08873 TF: 800-238-7813 ■ Web: clearyproducts.com	732-247-8000	247-6977	360-3
W A M S Inc 1800 E Lambert Ave Ste 155 . . . Brea CA 92821 TF: 800-421-7151 ■ Web: wamsinc.com	800-421-7151		177
W Atlee Burpee Co 300 Park Ave . . . Warminster PA 18974 TF: 800-333-5808 ■ Web: www.burpee.com	215-674-4900		694
W Bradley Electric Inc 90 Hill Rd . . . Novato CA 94945 Web: www.wbeinc.com	415-898-1400	898-5991	787
W C Rouse & Son Inc 110 Longale Rd . . . Greensboro NC 27409 TF: 877-927-6873 ■ Web: www.wcrouse.com	336-299-3035		612
W Caslon & Company Inc 1240 Jefferson Rd . . . Rochester NY 14623 Web: www.caslon.net	585-239-6063		393
W D Communications 2380 Rte 9 S Ste C-2 . . . Howell Township NJ 07731 Web: wdcommunications.com	732-530-2076	530-5719	196
W E O'Neil Construction Co 2751 N Clybourn Ave . . . Chicago IL 60614 Web: www.weoneil.com	773-755-1611		186
W H Cress Company Inc 1824 Bickford Ave Ste F . . . Tigard OR 97223 Web: whcress.com	503-620-1664		321
W H Meanor & Assoc 216 N Mcdowell St Ste 200 . . . Charlotte NC 28204 Web: whmeanor.com	704-372-7640	372-7642	463
W L Gore & Associates Inc 551 Papermill Rd . . . Newark DE 19711 *Fax Area Code: 302 ■ TF: 888-914-4673 ■ Web: www.gore.com	410-506-7787	738-7710*	745-2
W M Schlosser Company Inc 2400 51st Pl . . . Hyattsville MD 20781 Web: www.wmschlosser.com	301-773-1300	773-9263	449
W M Sprinkman Corp 404 Pilot Ct . . . Waukesha WI 53188 *Fax Area Code: 262 ■ TF: 800-816-1610 ■ Web: www.sprinkman.com	800-816-1610	409-2060*	386
W Machine Works Inc 13814 Del Sur St . . . San Fernando CA 91340 Web: www.wmwcnc.com	818-890-8049	897-7178	757
W Network 25 Dockside Dr . . . Toronto ON M5A0B5 Web: www.wnetwork.com	416-479-6784		740
W O Blackstone & Company Inc 1841 Shop Rd . . . Columbia SC 29202 Web: www.woblackstone.com	803-252-8222		610
W O W Logistics Co 3040 W Wisconsin Ave . . . Appleton WI 54914 TF: 800-236-3565 ■ Web: wowlogistics.com	920-734-9924	734-2697	803-1
W R Chesnut Engineering Inc 14 Spielman Rd . . . Fairfield NJ 07004 Web: www.chesnuteng.com	973-227-6995	227-7873	261
W R Systems Ltd 11351 Random Hills Rd Ste 400 . . . Fairfax VA 22030 Web: wrsystems.com	703-934-0200		261
W Rogers Co 649 Bizzell Dr . . . Lexington KY 40510 Web: wrogers.com	859-231-6290	233-2066	186
W. B. Young Company Inc 2571 S Odell . . . Marshall MO 65340 TF: 800-737-2010 ■ Web: www.wbyoungco.com	660-886-7427	886-7156	274
W. C. Weil Co 3812 William Flynn Hwy Bldg 2 . . . Allison Park PA 15101 Web: wcweil.com	412-487-7140	487-7144	112
W. D. Matthews Machinery Co 901 Center St . . . Auburn ME 04210 TF: 800-272-0155 ■ Web: www.wdmatthews.com	207-784-9311		358
W. E. Donoghue & Company LLC 260 N Main St Ste 2920 . . . Boston MA 02110 TF: 800-642-4276 ■ Web: www.donoghue.com	800-642-4276		401
W. G. Benjey Inc 2293 Werth Rd . . . Alpena MI 49707 *Fax Area Code: 866 ■ TF: 800-269-9006 ■ Web: www.benjeycylinders.com	989-354-6140	942-3297*	695
W. Graham Arader III 1308 Walnut St . . . Philadelphia PA 19107 Web: www.aradergalleriesphilly.tumblr.com	215-735-8811		637-2
W. Haut Specialty Company Inc N56 W 13664 Silver Spring Rd . . . Menomonee Falls WI 53051 Web: www.whaut.com	262-790-0425	790-0473	454
W. L. Butler Construction Inc 204 Franklin St . . . Redwood City CA 94063 Web: www.wlbutler.com	650-361-1270	361-8657	186
W. M. Plastics Inc 5151 Bolger Ct . . . McHenry IL 60050 Web: www.novationindustries.com	815-578-8888	578-8818	604
W. N. Morehouse Truck Line Inc 4010 Dahlman Ave . . . Omaha NE 68107 TF: 800-228-9378 ■ Web: www.morehousetruckline.com	402-733-2200		685
W. R. Vernon Produce Co 1035 N Cherry St PO Box 4054 . . . Winston-Salem NC 27101 TF: 800-222-6406 ■ Web: vernonproduce.com	336-725-9741	761-1841	297-7
W. Silver Recycling Inc 1720 Magoffin Ave . . . El Paso TX 79901 Web: www.wsilverrecycling.com	915-532-5643	532-5851	686
W. W. Norton & Company Inc 500 5th Ave . . . New York NY 10110 Web: wwnorton.com	212-354-5500	869-0856	637-2
W W Tire Service Inc 204 Main St PO Box 22 . . . Bryant SD 57221 TF: 800-456-0768 ■ Web: www.wwtireservice.com	605-628-2501	628-2018	61
W.B.R. Inc 1111A Quail St . . . Newport Beach CA 92660 Web: www.wbrinc.com	949-673-1247	673-0846	660
W.E. Falk Books Inc 141 Peckham St SE . . . Port Charlotte FL 33952 Web: www.wefalkbooks.com	941-391-5724	391-5734	96
W.F.T. Engineering Inc 1801 Research Blvd Ste 100 . . . Rockville MD 20850 Web: wfteng.com	301-230-0811		261
W.H. Breshears Inc 720 B St . . . Modesto CA 95354 Web: www.whbreshears.com	209-522-7291	522-2406	581
W.H. Porter Consultants PLLC 6055 Primacy Pkwy Ste 115 . . . Memphis TN 38119 Web: whporter.com	901-363-9453	363-2722	261
W.P. & R.S. Mars Co 4319 W First St . . . Duluth MN 55807 Web: www.marssupply.com	218-628-0303		385
W.S Thomas Transfer Inc 1854 Morgantown Ave . . . Fairmont WV 26554 *Fax Area Code: 304 ■ TF: 877-824-3477 ■ Web: www.wsthomas.com	877-824-3477	363-8052*	780
W.S. Anderson Associates Inc 303-313 Washington St . . . Auburn MA 01501 Web: wsanderson.net	508-832-5550		261
W.W. Cannon Inc 2653 Brenner Dr . . . Dallas TX 75220 TF: 800-442-3061 ■ Web: www.wwcannon.com	214-357-2846	357-4576	300
W.W. Stephenson Company Inc 1305 E Burnett St . . . Signal Hill CA 90755 Web: wwstephenson.com	562-595-6356	426-5944	261
W/M Display Group 1040 W 40th St . . . Chicago IL 60609 TF: 800-443-2000 ■ Web: www.wmdisplay.com	773-254-3700	254-3188	286
W20 Group 50 Francisco St Ste 400 . . . San Francisco CA 94133 Web: www.w2ogroup.com	415-362-5018		636
W3 Global Accounting LLC 82 N Miller Rd . . . Fairlawn OH 44333 Web: w3financialgroup.com	330-867-3578	867-6251	2
W5 3211 Shannon Rd Ste 610 . . . Durham NC 27707 Web: w5insight.com	919-932-1117	932-1127	466
WA (Warren Associates) 290 Rickenbacker Cir . . . Livermore CA 94551 Web: www.warrenrep.com	925-449-9000		253

Phone | Fax | Class

WA Chester LLC 4390 Parliament Pl Ste Q .... Lanham MD 20706 240-487-1940 487-1941 189-4
Web: www.wachester.com
WA Klinger inc
2015 E Seventh St PO Box 8800............. Sioux City IA 51102 712-277-3900 258-5528 186
Web: www.waklinger.com
WAAF 20 Guest St 3rd Fl...................... Brighton MA 02135 617-779-5400 645
Web: waaf.radio.com
Waas Construction Co 5582 NW 79th Ave .... Miami FL 33166 305-592-9574 477-9324 186
Web: www.waasconstruction.com
WAAV-AM 3233 Burnt Mill Rd Ste 4........... Wilmington NC 28403 910-763-9977 762-0456 647
Web: www.980waav.com
WAAY-TV Ch 31 (ABC)
1000 Monte Sano Blvd SE .... Huntsville AL 35801 256-533-3131 741-61
Web: www.waaytv.com
WAB Capital LLC
1559 Michael Ln..................... Pacific Palisades CA 90272 310-230-8664 401
Web: www.growthequities.com
Wabash Center Inc 2000 Greenbush St......... LaFayette IN 47904 765-423-5531 48-15
Web: www.wabashcenter.com
Wabash College
410 W Wabash Ave PO Box 352........... Crawfordsville IN 47933 765-361-6326 361-6433 166
TF: 800-345-5385 ■ *Web:* wabash.edu
Wabash Communications
210 S Church St PO Box 299................. Louisville IL 62858 618-665-3311 665-4188 736
TF: 877-878-2120 ■ *Web:* www.wabashtelephone.coop
Wabash County 221 S Miami St................ Wabash IN 46992 260-563-7171 338
TF: 800-346-2110 ■ *Web:* www.visitwabashcounty.com
Wabash County Clerk
401 N Market St........................ Mount Carmel IL 62863 618-262-4561 338
Web: www.illinoissecondcircuit.info
Wabash Electric Supply Inc
1400 S Wabash St .... Wabash IN 46992 260-563-4146 563-4140 246
TF: 800-552-7777 ■ *Web:* wabashelectric.com
Wabash MPI 1569 Morris St PO Box 298......... Wabash IN 46992 260-563-1184 563-1396 456
Web: wabashmpi.com
Wabash National Corp
1000 Sagamore Pkwy S PO Box 6129.......... LaFayette IN 47903 765-771-5300 779
NYSE: WNC ■ *Web:* www.wabashnational.com
Wabash Valley Correctional Facility
6908 S Old US Hwy 41 PO Box 500............. Carlisle IN 47838 812-398-5050 213
Web: www.in.gov
Wabash Valley Manufacturing Inc
505 E Main St............................ Silver Lake IN 46982 260-352-2102 352-2160 319-4
TF: 800-253-8619 ■ *Web:* www.wabashvalley.com
Wabash Valley Power Association Inc
722 N High School Rd.................... Indianapolis IN 46214 317-481-2800 243-6416 245
Web: www.wvpa.com
Wabash Valley Service Company Inc
909 N Court St............................ Grayville IL 62844 618-375-2311 375-5351 276
TF: 888-869-8127 ■ *Web:* www.wabashvalleyfs.com
Wabaunsee County
215 Kansas Ave PO Box 278.................... Alma KS 66401 785-765-3508 765-3704 338
Web: ks-wabaunsee.manatron.com
WABC-AM 770 (N/T) 2 Penn Plz 17th Fl......... New York NY 10121 212-613-3800 613-3837 645-108
Web: www.wabcradio.com
Wabi Iron & Steel Corp
330 Broadwood Ave..................... New Liskeard ON P0J1P0 705-647-4383 480
Web: www.wabicorp.com
WABI-TV Ch 5 (CBS) 35 Hildreth St.............. Bangor ME 04401 207-947-8321 741-12
Web: www.wabi.tv
WABM-TV Ch 68 (MNT)
800 Concourse Pkwy Ste 200............... Birmingham AL 35244 205-403-3351 741-15
Web: www.wabm68.com
Wabtec Corp
WABCO Transit Div PO Box 11............. Spartanburg SC 29304 864-433-5900 433-0176 650
Web: wabtec.com
WABY-AM
34 Congress St Ste 103............... Saratoga Springs NY 12020 518-933-2222 899-3057 647
Web: www.starsaratoga.com
WAC (World Affairs Council)
312 Sutter St Ste 200................... San Francisco CA 94108 415-293-4686 982-5028 48-13
Web: www.worldaffairs.org
WAC Consulting Inc 367 W Main St........ Northborough MA 01532 508-393-7731 196
Web: www.wacinc.com
WACA-AM 2730 University Blvd W Ste 200....... Wheaton MD 20902 301-942-3500 942-7798 647
Web: www.radioamerica.net
WACC (Westfield Area Chamber of Commerce)
212 Lenox Ave............................. Westfield NJ 07090 908-233-3021 139
Web: www.gwaccnj.com
Waccatee Zoological Farm
8500 Enterprise Rd...................... Myrtle Beach SC 29588 843-650-8500 823
Web: www.waccateezoo.com
Wachs Water Services
801 Asbury Dr .... Buffalo Grove IL 60089 800-525-5821 393
TF: 800-525-5821 ■ *Web:* www.wachsws.com
Wachtel & Company Inc
1101 14th St NW Ste 800 Eighth Fl.......... Washington DC 20005 202-898-1144 690
Web: wachtelco.com
Wachtell, Lipton, Rosen and Katz
51 W 52nd St.............................. New York NY 10019 212-403-1000 403-2000 41
TF: 800-848-0301 ■ *Web:* www.wlrk.com
Wachter Inc 16001 W 99th St................... Lenexa KS 66219 913-541-2500 541-2529 787
Web: www.wachter.com
Wachters' Organic Sea Products Corp
550 Sylvan St............................. Daly City CA 94014 650-757-9851 757-9858 799
TF: 800-682-7100 ■ *Web:* www.wachters.com
WACH-TV Ch 57 (Fox)
1400 Pickens St Ste 6....................... Columbia SC 29201 803-252-5757 212-7309 741-33
Web: www.wach.com
Wachusett Mountain State Reservation
345 Mountain Rd.......................... Princeton MA 01541 978-464-2987 565
Web: www.mass.gov
Wacker Chemical Corp 3301 Sutton Rd .... Adrian MI 49221 517-264-8500 264-8246 144
TF: 888-922-5374 ■ *Web:* www.wacker.com
Wacker Neuson
N 92 W 15000 Anthony Ave........... Menomonee Falls WI 53051 262-255-0500 822-0710* 190
**Fax Area Code: 800* ■ *TF:* 800-770-0957 ■ *Web:* www.wackerneuson.com

Waco Convention & Visitors Bureau
100 Washington Ave........................... Waco TX 76701 254-750-5810 206
TF: 800-321-9226 ■ *Web:* wacoheartoftexas.com
Waco Filters
2546 General Armistead Ave................. Norristown PA 19403 610-630-4800 630-4904 18
Web: wacofilters.com
Waco Inc 5450 Lewis Rd PO Box 829 .... Sandston VA 23150 804-222-8440 226-3241 189-9
Web: www.wacoinc.net
Waco Tribune-Herald 900 Franklin Ave............ Waco TX 76701 254-757-5757 757-0302 532-2
TF: 800-678-8742 ■ *Web:* www.wacotrib.com
Wacoal America 50 Polito Ave................ Lyndhurst NJ 07071 201-933-8400 155-18
TF: 800-922-6250 ■ *Web:* www.wacoal-america.com
Wacom Technology Corp
1311 SE Cardinal Ct....................... Vancouver WA 98683 360-896-9833 896-9724 173-1
TF: 800-922-6613 ■ *Web:* www.wacom.com
Waco-McLennan County Library
1717 Austin Ave.............................. Waco TX 76701 254-750-5941 750-5940 434-3
Web: www.waco-texas.com
Waconia Heritage Assn 201 S Vine St .... Waconia MN 55387 952-442-2184 442-2135 637-2
Web: www.waconia.org
Waconia Manufacturing Inc
33 E Eigth St............................... Waconia MN 55387 952-442-4450 442-5923 492
Web: waconiamfg.com
WACTC (Wstrn Area Career & Technology Ctr)
688 Western Ave......................... Canonsburg PA 15317 724-746-2890 746-6966 685
Web: www.wactc.net
WACX-TV PO Box 608040 .... Orlando FL 32860 407-263-4040 647
TF: 800-578-9494 ■ *Web:* www.wacxtv.com
Wada Farms Potatoes Inc 326 S 1400 W........ Pingree ID 83262 208-684-9801 684-4157 10-11
Web: www.wadafarms.com
WADB-AM 8 Robbins St..................... Toms River NJ 08753 732-364-5830 647
Web: www.mybeachradio.com
Waddell & Reed Financial Inc
6300 Lamar Ave .... Overland Park KS 66201 913-236-2000 401
NYSE: WDR ■ *TF:* 888-923-3355 ■ *Web:* www.waddell.com
Waddell Transfer Inc 6055 Lee Hwy .... Atkins VA 24311 276-783-5207 780
TF: 800-451-7459 ■ *Web:* www.waddelltransfer.com
Wade Associates Inc
201 Main Ave....................... Wheatley Heights NY 11798 631-643-6644 422
Web: wadeassociateslandscaping.com
Wade College
1950 N Stemmons Fwy LB 562 Ste 4080.......... Dallas TX 75207 214-637-3530 637-0827 800
TF: 800-624-4850 ■ *Web:* www.wadecollege.edu
Wade Distributors Inc
1150 E I65 Service Rd N....................... Mobile AL 36617 251-476-1140 191-1
Web: www.wadedistributorsinc.com
Wade Financial Advisory Inc
2105 S Bascom Ave Ste 110................. Campbell CA 95008 408-369-7399 369-0607 401
Web: www.wadefa.com
Wade Inc 1505 Hwy 82 W .... Greenwood MS 38930 662-453-6312 274
Web: www.wadeincorporated.com
Wade Tours Inc 797 Burdeck St .... Schenectady NY 12306 518-355-4500 355-4942 760
TF: 800-955-9233 ■ *Web:* wadetours.com
Wadena County 415 S Jefferson St.............. Wadena MN 56482 218-631-7650 632-6057 338
Web: www.co.wadena.mn.us
Wadeson Home Ctr 60 Forester Ave............ Warwick NY 10990 845-986-2215 351
Web: wadeson.com
Wade-Trim Group Inc
25251 Northline Rd Ste 2500................... Detroit MI 48226 313-961-3650 961-0898 261
TF: 800-482-2864 ■ *Web:* www.wadetrim.com
WADK-AM 15 Dr Marcus Wheatland Blvd.......... Newport RI 02840 401-846-1540 846-1598 647
Web: www.wadk.com
Wadley Regional Medical Ctr
1000 Pine St.............................. Texarkana TX 75501 903-798-8000 374-3
TF: 888-849-8941 ■ *Web:* www.wadleyhealth.org
WADL-TV Ch 38 (Fox)
35000 Adell Dr...................... Clinton Township MI 48035 586-790-3838 741
Web: www.wadldetroit.com
Wadsworth Atheneum Museum of Art
600 Main St .... Hartford CT 06103 860-278-2670 527-0803 520
Web: thewadsworth.org
Wadsworth Ctr
Biggs Laboratory New York Dept of Health
Empire State Plz PO Box 509................. Albany NY 12201 518-474-7354 668
Web: www.wadsworth.org
Wadsworth Golf Construction Co
13941 Van Dyke Rd .... Plainfield IL 60544 815-436-8400 436-8404 188-3
Web: www.wadsworthgolf.com
Wadsworth Public Library
132 Broad St............................ Wadsworth OH 44281 330-334-5761 434-3
Web: www.wadsworthlibrary.com
WAER-FM 88.3 (Jazz) 795 Ostram Ave.......... Syracuse NY 13210 315-443-4021 645-158
Web: www.waer.org
WAFB-TV Ch 9 (CBS)
844 Government St...................... Baton Rouge LA 70802 225-383-9999 741-13
Web: www.wafb.com
Wafertech LLC 5509 NW Parker St............... Camas WA 98607 360-817-3000 696
Web: www.wafertech.com
Waffle House Inc 5986 Financial Dr............ Norcross GA 30071 770-729-5700 670
Web: www.wafflehouse.com
WAFF-TV Ch 48 (NBC)
1414 Memorial Pkwy NW.................. Huntsville AL 35801 256-533-4848 534-4101 741-61
Web: www.waff.com
Wagamama Quincy Market Bldg .... Boston MA 02109 617-742-9242 671
Web: www.wagamama.us
Wagamon Brothers Inc
3719 3rd St NE.................... Columbia Heights MN 55421 763-789-7227 789-8079 62-7
Web: www.wagamonbrothers.com
WAGA-TV Ch 5 (Fox)
1551 Briarcliff Rd NE .... Atlanta GA 30306 404-898-0100 724-4426 741-7
Web: www.fox5atlanta.com
WAGF-AM 4106 Ross Clark Cir .... Dothan AL 36303 334-671-1753 677-6923 647
Web: www.wjjn.net
Waggl Inc 3 Harbor Dr Ste 200 .... Sausalito CA 94965 415-399-9949 788
Web: www.waggl.com
Waggoners Trucking 5220 Midland Rd.......... Billings MT 59101 406-248-1919 259-6924 780
TF: 800-999-9097 ■ *Web:* www.waggonerstrucking.com

Name / Address	City	State	ZIP	Phone	Fax	Class
Wagman Metal Products Inc 400 S Albemarle St TF: 800-233-9461 ■ Web: www.wagmanmetal.com	York	PA	17403	717-854-2120		295
Wagner & Brown Ltd 300 N Marienfeld St Web: wbltd.com	Midland	TX	79701	432-682-7936		536
Wagner Ann (Rep R - MO) 2350 Rayburn House Office Bldg Web: www.wagner.house.gov	Washington	DC	20515	202-225-1621		342-2
Wagner College 1 Campus Rd TF: 800-221-1010 ■ Web: www.wagner.edu	Staten Island	NY	10301	718-390-3400	390-3105	166
Wagner Engineering & Survey Inc 17134 Devonshire St Ste 200 Web: wesinc.org	Northridge	CA	91325	818-892-6565		261
Wagner Falconer & Judd Ltd 100 S Fifth St Ste 800 TF: 800-697-8955 ■ Web: wfjlawfirm.com	Minneapolis	MN	55402	612-339-1421		428
Wagner Free Institute of Science 1700 W Montgomery Ave Web: www.pacscl.org	Philadelphia	PA	19121	215-763-6529	763-1299	520
Wagner Industrial Electric Inc 3178 Encrete Ln TF: 800-775-7799 ■ Web: www.wagner-ind.com	Dayton	OH	45439	937-298-7481	298-0268	425
Wagner Johnston & Rosenthal 255 Marchand Ct Sandy Springs Web: www.wjrlaw.com	Atlanta	GA	30328	404-261-0500	261-6779	428
Wagner Jones Kopfman & Artenian LLP 1111 E Herndon Ave Ste 317 Web: wagnerjones.com	Fresno	CA	93720	559-449-1800		41
Wagner Law Group, The 99 Summer St 13th Fl. Web: wagnerlawgroup.com	Boston	MA	02110	617-357-5200		41
Wagner Machine Inc 5151 Wooster Rd W Web: www.wagnermachine.com	Norton	OH	44203	330-706-0700		454
Wagner Oil Co 500 Commerce St Ste 600 TF: 800-457-5332 ■ Web: www.wagneroil.com	Fort Worth	TX	76102	817-335-2222		536
Wagner Plate Works LLC 4142 W 49th St Web: www.wagnerplateworks.com	Tulsa	OK	74107	918-447-4488		480
Wagner Spray Tech Corp 1770 Fernbrook Ln TF: 800-328-8251 ■ Web: www.wagnerspraytech.com	Plymouth	MN	55447	763-553-7000	519-3563	172
Wagner, Ferber, Fine & Ackerman PLLC 66 S Tyson Ave Web: wffacpa.com	Floral Park	NY	11001	516-328-3800	488-4695	2
Wago Corp N120 W19129 Freistadt Rd TF: 800-346-7245 ■ Web: www.wago.com	Germantown	WI	53022	262-255-6222	255-3232	203
Wagon Wheel Broadcasting 20 E High St TF: 888-537-9724 ■ Web: www.eaglecountryonline.com	Lawrenceburg	IN	47025	812-537-0944	537-5735	645-141
Wagoner County 307 E Cherokee St Web: www.ok.gov	Wagoner	OK	74467	918-485-7700	485-8033	338
Wagstaff & Cartmell LLP 4740 Grand Ave Ste 300 Web: wagstaffcartmell.com	Kansas City	MO	64112	816-701-1100	531-2372	428
Wagstaff Inc 3910 N Flora Rd Web: www.wagstaff.com	Spokane Valley	WA	99216	509-922-1404	924-0241	695
Wagstaff Worldwide 5443 Fountain Ave Web: wagstaffmktg.com	Los Angeles	CA	90029	323-871-1151		636
WAGT-TV Ch 26 (NBC) PO Box 1212 Web: www.wrdw.com	Augusta	GA	30903	803-278-1212		741-8
Waguespack Oil Company Inc 1818 Hwy 3185 PO Box 326 Web: wagoil.com	Thibodaux	LA	70302	985-447-3668	447-5730	579
Wahiawa Freshwater State Recreation Area PO Box 621 Web: dlnr.hawaii.gov	Honolulu	HI	96809	808-622-6316		565
Wahkiakum County 64 Main St PO Box 157 TF: 800-359-1506 ■ Web: www.co.wahkiakum.wa.us	Cathlamet	WA	98612	360-795-3558	795-8813	338
Wahl Clipper Corp 2900 Locust St TF: 800-767-9245 ■ Web: us.wahl.com	Sterling	IL	61081	800-767-9245		214
Wahl Media Inc 580 Packetts Landing TF: 888-924-5633 ■ Web: www.wahlmedia.com	Fairport	NY	14450	888-924-5633		5
Wahl Refractory Solutions LLC 767 S SR-19 Web: www.wahlref.com	Fremont	OH	43420	419-334-2650		663
Wahlco Inc 2722 S Fairview St TF: 800-423-5432 ■ Web: wahlco.com	Santa Ana	CA	92704	714-979-7300	979-0603	454
Wahltek Inc 2711 Grand Ave TF: 800-995-9245 ■ Web: www.wahltek.com	Des Moines	IA	50312	515-309-3935	244-5572	178-1
Wahluke School District 411 E Saddle Mt Dr PO Box 907 Web: www.wsd73.wednet.edu	Mattawa	WA	99349	509-932-4565	932-4571	685
Wahoo's Fish Taco 2855 Pullman St Web: www.wahoos.com	Santa Ana	CA	92705	949-222-0670		670
Wah-Sha-She State Park 396120 State Hwy 10 Web: www.travelok.com	Copan	OK	74022	918-532-4334	532-4659	565
WAI (Western Automation Inc) 23101 Moulton Pkwy Ste 201 Web: www.waisales.com	Laguna Hills	CA	92653	949-859-6988	859-8622	57
WAI (Wire Association International Inc) 1570 Boston Post Rd PO Box 578 Web: www.wirenet.org	Guilford	CT	06437	203-453-2777	453-8384	49-13
Wai & Connor LLP 2566 Overland Ave Ste 570 Web: www.waiconnor.com	Los Angeles	CA	90064	310-838-6800	838-7700	428
Waiawa Correctional Facility 94-560 Kamehameha Hwy Web: hawaii.gov	Waipahu	HI	96797	808-677-6150		213
Waife & Associates Inc 62 Warren St Web: www.waife.com	Needham	MA	02492	781-449-7032	444-1763	195
Waikiki Aquarium 2777 Kalakaua Ave Web: www.waikikiaquarium.org	Honolulu	HI	96815	808-923-9741	923-1771	40
Waikiki Gateway Hotel 2375 Ala Wai Blvd Web: xfteamcolors.com	Honolulu	HI	96815	808-955-3741		379
Waikiki Parc Hotel 2233 Helumoa Rd TF: 800-422-0450 ■ Web: waikikiparc.com	Honolulu	HI	96815	808-921-7272	923-1336	379
Waikiki Resort Hotel 2460 Koa Ave TF: 800-367-5116 ■ Web: www.waikikiresort.com	Honolulu	HI	96815	808-922-4911	922-9468	379
Wailoa River State Recreation Area 75 Aupuni St Rm 204 Web: dlnr.hawaii.gov	Hilo	HI	96720	808-961-9590	961-9599	565
Waimea Canyon State Park 3060 Eiwa St Ste 306 Web: www.hawaii.gov	Lihue	HI	96766	808-274-3444	274-3448	565
Wainer Finest Communications Inc 51 Cragwood Rd Ste 100 Web: wholefoodsmagazine.com	South Plainfield	NJ	07080	908-769-1160	769-1171	637-10
Wainhouse Research LLC 34 Duckhill Terr Web: www.wainhouse.com	Duxbury	MA	02332	781-934-6165		196
Wainscot Media LLC 110 Summit Ave Web: wainscotmedia.com	Montvale	NJ	07645	201-571-2244	782-5319	194
Wainwright House 260 Stuyvesant Ave Web: www.wainwright.org	Rye	NY	10580	914-967-6080		673
Waisman Ctr University of Wisconsin 1500 Highland Ave TF: 888-428-8476 ■ Web: www.waisman.wisc.edu	Madison	WI	53705	608-263-1656	263-0529	668
Waites & Foshee Insurance Inc 850 Walnut St Web: wfins.com	Macon	GA	31201	478-743-0588		390
Waitsfield and Champlain Valley Telecom (WCVT) 3898 Main St TF: 800-496-3391 ■ Web: www.wcvt.com	Waitsfield	VT	05673	802-496-3393		224
Waitt Co 1125 S 103rd St Ste 425 Web: www.waittcompany.com	Omaha	NE	68124	402-697-8000		643
Waiward Steel Fabricators Ltd 10030 - 34 St Web: www.waiward.com	Edmonton	AB	T6B2Y5	780-469-1258		480
Wajax Corp 3280 Wharton Way TSX: WJX ■ Web: www.wajax.com	Mississauga	ON	L4X2C5	905-624-5611		358
WAKB Magic 100.9 FM 6025 Broadcast Dr Web: www.1009magic.com	North Augusta	SC	29841	803-279-2330	279-8149	645
Wake Christian Academy Inc 5500 Wake Academy Dr Web: www.wakechristianacademy.com	Raleigh	NC	27603	919-772-6264	779-0948	685
Wake Correctional Ctr 1000 Rock Quarry Rd TF: 866-719-0108 ■ Web: www.ncdps.gov	Raleigh	NC	27610	919-733-7988	733-9166	213
Wake County 336 Fayetteville St Web: www.wakegov.com	Raleigh	NC	27601	919-856-6160	856-6168	338
Wake County Public School System 5625 Dillard Dr Web: www.wcpss.net	Cary	NC	27518	919-533-7834		685
Wake Electric 100 S Franklin St PO Box 1229 TF: 800-474-6300 ■ Web: wemc.com	Wake Forest	NC	27588	800-474-6300		245
Wake Forest University 2825 University Pkwy TF: 888-758-3322 ■ Web: ljvm.com	Winston-Salem	NC	27105	336-758-2410		720
Wake Forest University 1834 Wake Forest Rd Web: www.wfu.edu	Winston-Salem	NC	27106	336-758-5255	758-4324	166
Wake Forest University Press (WFU) 2518 Reynolda Road Web: wfupress.wfu.edu	Winston-Salem	NC	27106	336-758-5448	842-3853	637-9
Wake Technical Community College 9101 Fayetteville Rd Web: www.waketech.edu	Raleigh	NC	27603	919-866-5000	661-0117	162
Wake Up Press, The 12444 W Alyssa Ln Web: www.enlightened-spirituality.org	Peoria	AZ	85383	623-266-9990		637-10
Wake Weekly 229 E Owen Ave Web: www.wakeweekly.com	Wake Forest	NC	27588	919-556-3182	556-2233	532-2
Wakefield Chamber of Commerce 5 Common St Web: wakefieldchamber.org	Wakefield	MA	01880	781-245-0741		139
Wakefield Corp, The 10646 Dutchtown Rd Web: www.thewakefieldcorp.com	Knoxville	TN	37932	865-675-1550		186
Wakefield Pork Inc 410 Main Ave E Web: www.wakefieldpork.com	Gaylord	MN	55334	507-237-5581	237-5584	10-6
Wakefield School District 60 Farm St Web: www.wakefieldpublicschools.org	Wakefield	MA	01880	781-246-6400		685
Wakefield Thermal Solutions Inc 33 Bridge St Web: www.wakefield-vette.com	Pelham	NH	03076	603-635-2800	635-1900	253
Wakefield's Inc 1212 Quintard Ave TF: 800-333-1552 ■ Web: wakefields.com	Anniston	AL	36201	800-333-1552		157-2
Wakelight Technologies Inc 155 Kapalulu Pl Ste 109 Web: www.wakelight.com	Honolulu	HI	96819	808-836-9253		180
Wakely Consulting Group Inc 7650 W Courtney Campbell Cswy Ste 1250 Web: www.wakely.com	Tampa	FL	33607	727-507-9858		194
WakeMed Health & Hospitals 3000 New Bern Ave Web: www.wakemed.org	Raleigh	NC	27610	919-350-8000		363
Wakensys Corp 505 N Lake Shore Dr Ste 222 Web: www.wakensys.com	Chicago	IL	60611	773-754-0059		196
WAKG-FM 710 Grove St TF: 800-289-9254 ■ Web: www.wakg.com	Danville	VA	24541	434-797-4290	797-3918	647
WAKM-AM 222 Mallory Station Rd Web: www.wakmworldwide.com	Franklin	TN	37067	615-794-1594		647
Wako Chemicals USA Inc 1600 Bellwood Rd TF: 800-992-9256 ■ Web: www.wakousa.com	Richmond	VA	23237	804-271-7677	271-7791	231
Wako Electronics USA Inc 2105 Production Dr Web: www.wako-usa.com	Louisville	KY	40299	502-429-8866	429-8869	202

Name / Address	City	State	ZIP	Phone	Fax	Class
Wakoff Andriulli & Company LLC 100 Craig Rd Ste 109 *Web:* www.njcpa.com	Manalapan	NJ	07726	732-866-8882		2
Wakonda State Park 32836 State Park Rd *Web:* mostateparks.com	LaGrange	MO	63448	573-655-2280		565
Wakulla County 3056 Crawfordville Hwy *Web:* www.wakullaclerk.com	Crawfordville	FL	32327	850-926-0905	926-0938	338
Wakunaga of America Company Ltd 23501 Madero *TF:* 800-421-2998 ■ *Web:* www.kyolic.com	Mission Viejo	CA	92691	949-855-2776	458-2764	799
WAKW-FM 93.3 (Rel) 6275 Collegevue Pl PO Box 24126 *TF:* 888-542-9393 ■ *Web:* mystar933.com	Cincinnati	OH	45224	513-542-9259	542-9333	645-35
WALA-TV Ch 10 (Fox) 1501 Satchel Paige Dr *TF:* 800-876-8810 ■ *Web:* www.fox10tv.com	Mobile	AL	36606	251-434-1010		741-85
Walberg Tim (Rep R - MI) 2266 Rayburn House Office Bldg *Web:* walberg.house.gov	Washington	DC	20515	202-225-6276	225-6281	342-2
Walbridge Aldinger Co 777 Woodward Ave Ste 300 *Web:* www.walbridge.com	Detroit	MI	48226	313-963-8000	963-8150	188-7
Walch Education 40 Walch Dr *TF:* 800-558-2846 ■ *Web:* www.walch.com	Portland	ME	04103	207-772-2846	772-3105	637-2
Walco Electric Co 303 Allens Ave *TF:* 800-521-6505 ■ *Web:* www.walcokip.com	Providence	RI	02905	401-467-6500	941-4451	518
Wald LLC 800 E 5th St *Web:* www.waldllc.com	Maysville	KY	41056	606-564-4078	564-5248	82
Wald Relocation Services Ltd 7420 Security Way Ste 100 *Web:* www.waldofficeservices.com	Houston	TX	77040	713-512-4800		519
Waldameer Park Inc 220 Peninsula Dr *TF:* 877-817-1009 ■ *Web:* waldameer.com	Erie	PA	16505	814-838-3591		32
Waldemar S. Nelson & Company Inc 1200 St Charles Ave *Web:* www.wsnelson.com	New Orleans	LA	70130	504-523-5281	523-4587	261
Walden Behavioral Care 9 Hope Ave Ste 500 *Web:* www.waldenbehavioralcare.com	Waltham	MA	02453	781-647-6700		374-5
Walden Correctional Institution 4340 Broad River Rd *Web:* doc.sc.gov	Columbia	SC	29210	803-896-8580		213
Walden Energy LLC 111 W Fifth St *Web:* www.waldenenergy.com	Tulsa	OK	74103	918-488-8663		536
Walden Equipment 2479 Riverside Dr *Web:* www.waldenequipment.ca	Timmins	ON	P4N2X7	705-682-2084	682-2564	45
Walden Farms 1209 W St Georges Ave *TF:* 800-229-1706 ■ *Web:* waldenfarms.com	Linden	NJ	07036	800-229-1706		296-19
Walden Galleria 1 Walden Galleria *TF:* 800-297-5009 ■ *Web:* www.waldengalleria.com	Buffalo	NY	14225	716-681-7600		460
Walden Greg (Rep R - OR) 2185 Rayburn House Office Bldg *Web:* walden.house.gov	Washington	DC	20515	202-225-6730	225-5774	342-2
Walden Macht & Haran LLP 1 Battery Park Plz 34th Fl *Web:* wmhlaw.com	New York	NY	10004	212-335-2030		41
Walden Media LLC 1888 Century Pk E 14th Fl *Web:* www.walden.com	Los Angeles	CA	90067	310-887-1000		514
Walden Pond State Reservation 915 Walden St *Web:* www.mass.gov	Concord	MA	01742	978-369-3254		565
Walden Surf Inc 853 E Front St *Web:* waldensurfboards.com	Ventura	CA	93001	805-653-1717		711
Walden Venture Capital 750 Battery St Ste 700 *Web:* www.waldenvc.com	San Francisco	CA	94111	415-391-7225		792
Walden Woods Project, The 44 Baker Farm Rd *Web:* www.walden.org	Lincoln	MA	01773	781-259-4700	259-4710	48-13
Waldner's Business Environment 125 Rt 110 *Web:* www.waldners.com	Farmingdale	NY	11735	631-844-9300		320
Waldo County 137 Church St *TF:* 800-244-5211 ■ *Web:* waldocountyme.gov	Belfast	ME	04915	207-338-1710	338-6360	338
Waldoch Crafts Inc 13821 Lake Dr NE **Fax Area Code:* 651 ■ *TF:* 800-328-9259 ■ *Web:* waldoch.com	Forest Lake	MN	55025	800-878-8635	464-1117*	62-7
Waldom Electronics Corp 1801 Morgan St *TF:* 800-435-2931 ■ *Web:* www.waldom.com	Rockford	IL	61102	815-968-9661		246
Waldon Manufacturing LLC 201 W Oklahoma Ave *TF:* 866-283-2759 ■ *Web:* waldonequipment.com	Fairview	OK	73737	580-227-3711	227-2165	470
Waldorf College 106 S Sixth St *TF:* 800-292-1903 ■ *Web:* www.waldorf.edu	Forest City	IA	50436	641-585-2450	585-8184	166
Waldron Engineering & Construction Inc 37 Industrial Dr *Web:* waldron.com	Exeter	NH	03833	603-772-7153		261
Waldron Wealth Management LLC 1150 Old Pond Rd *Web:* www.waldronprivatewealth.com	Bridgeville	PA	15017	412-221-1005		251
Wale Apparatus Company Inc 400 Front St *TF:* 800-334-9253 ■ *Web:* www.waleapparatus.com	Hellertown	PA	18055	610-838-7047	838-7440	333
Walerko Tool & Engineering 1935 W Lusher Ave *Web:* walerko.com	Elkhart	IN	46517	574-295-2233		454
Wales Crane & Rigging Service PO Box 21628 *Web:* walescraneandrigging.com	Waco	TX	76702	254-772-3310	772-3420	189-1
Walgreen Co 200 Wilmot Rd *TF:* 800-925-4733 ■ *Web:* www.walgreens.com	Deerfield	IL	60015	847-940-2500	236-0862	237
Walgreens Health Services 1411 Lake Cook Rd *TF:* 800-207-2568 ■ *Web:* www.walgreenshealth.com	Deerfield	IL	60015	800-207-2568		586
Walk Thru the Bible Ministries Inc (WTB) 5550 Triangle Parkway Ste 250 *TF:* 800-361-6131 ■ *Web:* www.walkthru.org	Peachtree Corners	GA	30092	800-361-6131		48-20
Walker & Armstrong LLP 3838 N Central Ave *Web:* wa-cpas.com	Phoenix	AZ	85012	602-230-1040		2
Walker & Jocke Company LPA 231 S Broadway *Web:* www.walkerandjocke.com	Medina	OH	44256	330-721-0000		428
Walker & Massey CPA'S 150 W Rialto Ave	Rialto	CA	92376	909-875-0244		2
Walker Advertising 20101 Hamilton Ave Ste 375 **Fax Area Code:* 310 ■ *TF:* 800-492-5537 ■ *Web:* www.walkeradvertising.com	Torrance	CA	90502	800-492-5537	519-4090*	7
Walker and Associates Inc 7129 Old Hwy 52 *TF:* 800-925-5371 ■ *Web:* www.walkerfirst.com	Welcome	NC	27374	336-731-6391		392
Walker Art Ctr 725 Vineland Pl *Web:* www.walkerart.org	Minneapolis	MN	55403	612-375-7600		520
Walker Brand Communication 1810 W Kennedy Blvd *Web:* www.walkerbrands.com	Tampa	FL	33606	813-875-3322		4
Walker Brothers Inc 915 Barr Rd *Web:* www.walkersignals.com	Lexington	SC	29072	803-359-2839	359-6484	392
Walker Component Group Inc 1795 E 66th Ave *Web:* www.walkercomponent.com	Denver	CO	80229	303-292-9594	296-4734	246
Walker Consultants 2121 Hudson Ave *Web:* walkerconsultants.com	Kalamazoo	MI	49008	269-381-6080		261
Walker County 101 S Duke St PO Box 445 *Web:* walkercountyga.gov	LaFayette	GA	30728	706-638-1437	638-1453	338
Walker County Board of Education 1710 Alabama Ave PO Box 311 *Web:* www.walkercountyschools.com	Jasper	AL	35501	205-387-0555	221-5636	685
Walker County Chamber of Commerce 204 19th St E Ste 101 *Web:* www.walkerchamber.us	Jasper	AL	35501	205-384-4571		139
Walker County Chamber of Commerce 10052 N Hwy 27 *Web:* www.walkercochamber.com	Rock Spring	GA	30739	706-375-7702	375-7797	139
Walker Die Casting Inc 1125 Higgs Rd PO Box 1189 *Web:* www.walkerdiecasting.com	Lewisburg	TN	37091	931-359-6206	359-8030	308
Walker Elliott LP 10777 Westheimer Ste 220 *Web:* www.walkerelliott.com	Houston	TX	77042	713-482-3750		260
Walker Engineering Inc 8451 Dunwoody Pl Ste 08 *Web:* www.walkerengineer.com	Sandy Springs	GA	30350	770-641-7306		256
Walker Ford Company Inc 17556 US Hwy 19 N *Web:* www.walkerford.com	Clearwater	FL	33764	727-535-3673		57
Walker Forge Inc 222 E Erie St Ste 300 *Web:* www.walkerforge.com	Milwaukee	WI	53202	414-223-2000		483
Walker Furniture 301 S Martin L King Blvd *Web:* www.walkerfurniture.com	Las Vegas	NV	89106	702-384-9300		321
Walker Group Inc, The 20 Waterside Dr *Web:* www.thewalkergroup.com	Farmington	CT	06032	860-678-3530		180
Walker Honda 6677 Coliseum Blvd *TF:* 888-726-1687 ■ *Web:* www.walkerhonda.com	Alexandria	LA	71303	888-726-1687		57
Walker Industries Holdings Ltd 2800 Thorold Townline Rd *TF:* 866-694-9360 ■ *Web:* www.walkerind.com	Niagara Falls	ON	L2E6S4	905-227-4142		186
Walker Information Inc 301 Pennsylvania Pkwy *TF:* 800-334-3939 ■ *Web:* www.walkerinfo.com	Indianapolis	IN	46280	317-843-3939		466
Walker Machine & Foundry Corp PO Box 4587 *Web:* www.walkerfoundry.com	Roanoke	VA	24015	540-344-6265	342-2278	307
Walker Macy 111 SW Oak St *Web:* www.walkermacy.com	Portland	OR	97204	503-228-3122		393
Walker Magnetics Group Inc 20 Rockdale St *TF:* 800-962-4638 ■ *Web:* www.walkermagnet.com	Worcester	MA	01606	508-853-3232	852-8649	493
Walker Mark (Rep R - NC) 1725 Longworth House Office Bldg *Web:* www.walker.house.gov	Washington	DC	20515	202-225-3065	225-8611	342-2
Walker Martin & Hatch LLC 321 D St NE *Web:* walkermartinhatch.com	Washington	DC	20002	202-543-9004		261
Walker Mfg 3160 Abbott Ln *Web:* www.walkerexhaust.com	Harrisonburg	VA	22801	540-438-9466		247
Walker MS Inc 20 Third Ave *TF:* 800-528-2787 ■ *Web:* www.mswalker.com	Somerville	MA	02143	617-776-6700	776-5808	80-1
Walker Nursery Co 3809 Manchester Hwy *Web:* walkernurseryco.com	Mcminnville	TN	37110	931-668-4622	668-7365	323
Walker Printing Co 2501 E Fifth St *Web:* www.walker360.com	Montgomery	AL	36107	334-832-4975		627
Walker Process Equipment 840 N Russell Ave *TF:* 800-992-5537 ■ *Web:* www.walker-process.com	Aurora	IL	60506	630-892-7921	892-7951	806
Walker Sands Communications LLC 55 W Monroe St *Web:* www.walkersands.com	Chicago	IL	60603	312-267-0066	648-6015	636
Walker Stainless Equipment Company LLC 625 State St	New Lisbon	WI	53950	608-562-7500		298
Walker Stamp & Seal Co 121 NW Sixth St *Web:* walkercompanies.com	Oklahoma City	OK	73102	405-235-5319		535
Walker Stamping 1555 Vintage Ave *Web:* www.walkerstamping.net	Ontario	CA	91761	909-969-2130		719
Walker State Prison 97 Kevin Ln *Web:* www.dcor.state.ga.us	Rock Spring	GA	30739	706-764-3600	764-3613	213

	Phone	Fax	Class
Walker Tool & Die Inc 2411 Walker Ave NW Grand Rapids MI 49544 *TF:* 877-925-5378 ■ *Web:* www.walkertool.com	616-735-6660	453-3765	757
Walker Wilcox Matousek LLP 1 N Franklin St Ste 3200 Chicago IL 60606 *Web:* walkerwilcox.com	312-244-6700		41
Walker's Furniture Inc 3808 N Sullivan Rd Bldg 22-C Spokane Valley WA 99216 *TF:* 866-667-6655 ■ *Web:* www.walkersfurniture.com	509-535-1995		321
Walker, Morgan & Kinard 135 E Main St Lexington SC 29072 *TF:* 800-922-8411 ■ *Web:* www.walkermorgan.com	803-675-5942		428
Walker, Ostrowski & Williams CPAS LLP 500 Fairway Dr Ste 110 Deerfield Beach FL 33441 *Web:* wowadvisors.com	954-500-1040		2
Walking Adventures Intl 14612 NE Fourth Plain Rd Ste A Vancouver WA 98682 **Fax Area Code:* 360 ■ *TF:* 800-779-0353 ■ *Web:* walkingadventures.com	800-779-0353	260-1131*	760
WalkMed Infusion LLC 6555 S Kenton St Ste 304 Centennial CO 80111 *TF:* 800-578-0555 ■ *Web:* walkmed.com	303-420-9569	420-4545	476
Wall Colmonoy 101 W Girard Ave Madison Heights MI 48071 *Web:* www.wallcolmonoy.com	248-585-6400	585-7960	21
Wall Doxey State Park 3946 Hwy 7 S Holly Springs MS 38635 *Web:* www.mdwfp.com	662-252-4231		565
Wall Drug Store Inc PO Box 401 Wall SD 57790 *Web:* www.walldrug.com	605-279-2175		327
Wall Lenk Corp 1950 Dr Martin Luther King Jr Kinston NC 28501 *Web:* www.wlenk.com	252-527-4186		758
Wall Street Horizon Inc 400 W Cummings Pk Ste 3650 Woburn MA 01801 *Web:* www.wallstreethorizon.com	781-994-3500		162
Wall Street Inn, The 9 S William St New York NY 10004 *TF:* 877-747-1500 ■ *Web:* thewallstreetinn.com	212-747-1500		772
Wall Street Journal, The 1211 Avenue of the Americas New York NY 10036 *TF:* 800-568-7625 ■ *Web:* www.wsj.com	212-416-2000		532-3
Wall, Einhorn & Chernitzer PC 150 W Main St Ste 1200 Norfolk VA 23510 *Web:* www.wec-cpa.com	757-625-4700	625-0527	2
Walla Walla Community College 500 Tausick Way Walla Walla WA 99362 *TF:* 877-992-9922 ■ *Web:* www.wwcc.edu	509-522-2500	527-3661	162
Walla Walla County 315 W Main St Walla Walla WA 99362 *Web:* www.co.walla-walla.wa.us	509-524-2780		338
Walla Walla Public Library 238 E Alder St Walla Walla WA 99362 *Web:* wallawallapubliclibrary.org	509-527-4550		434-3
Walla Walla Racetrack 363 Orchard St Walla Walla WA 99362 *Web:* www.wallawallafairgrounds.com	509-527-3247	527-3259	642
Walla Walla University 204 S College Ave College Place WA 99324 *TF:* 800-541-8900 ■ *Web:* www.wallawalla.edu	509-527-2327	527-2397	166
Walla Walla VA Medical Ctr 77 Wainwright Dr Walla Walla WA 99362 *TF:* 888-687-8863 ■ *Web:* www.wallawalla.va.gov	509-525-5200		374-8
Walla Walla Valley Chamber of Commerce 29 E Sumach St PO Box 644 Walla Walla WA 99362 *Web:* www.wwvchamber.com	509-525-0850	522-2038	139
Wallace & Carey 5445-8 St NE Calgary AB T2K5R9 *TF:* 800-661-1504 ■ *Web:* www.wacl.com	403-275-7360	275-3921	449
Wallace & Graham PA 525 N Main St Salisbury NC 28144 *TF:* 888-698-9975 ■ *Web:* usmesotheliomalaw.com	704-633-5244	633-9434	41
Wallace & Wallace Inc 140 Major Reynolds Pl Knoxville TN 37919 *Web:* coldwellbanker.com	865-584-4000		652
Wallace Christensen Broadcasting 2660 Broadway Ave Slayton MN 56172 *Web:* www.christensenbroadcasting.com	507-825-4282	825-3364	645-141
Wallace Church Inc 330 E 48th St New York NY 10017 *Web:* wallacechurch.com	212-755-2903		344
Wallace Community College 1141 Wallace Dr Dothan AL 36303 *TF:* 800-543-2426 ■ *Web:* www.wallace.edu	334-983-3521	983-6066	162
Wallace Community College Selma 3000 Earl Goodwin Pkwy Selma AL 36703 *TF:* 855-428-8313 ■ *Web:* www.wccs.edu	334-876-9227	876-9250	800
Wallace County PO Box 508 Sharon Springs KS 67758 *Web:* www.wallacecounty.net	785-852-4935		338
Wallace Cranes 71 N Bacton Hill Rd Malvern PA 19355 *TF:* 800-553-5438 ■ *Web:* www.wallacecranes.com	610-647-1400	644-9043	358
Wallace Electronics Inc 10551 Miller Rd Ste 300/400 Dallas TX 75238 *TF:* 800-232-0404 ■ *Web:* www.wallace-elec.com	214-340-0400	340-0404	392
Wallace Engineering Structural Consultants Inc 200 E Brady Tulsa OK 74103 *Web:* www.wallacesc.com	918-584-5858		261
Wallace Falls State Park 14503 Wallace Lake Rd Gold Bar WA 98251 *Web:* parks.state.wa.us	360-793-0420		565
Wallace Financial Group Inc 4390 Earney Rd Woodstock GA 30188 *Web:* lpl.com	770-751-7411		690
Wallace Foundation, The 5 Penn Plz 7th Fl New York NY 10001 *Web:* www.wallacefoundation.org	212-251-9700	679-6990	305
Wallace Galleries Ltd 500 Fifth Ave SW Calgary AB T2P3L5 *Web:* www.wallacegalleries.com	403-262-8050		42
Wallace Group 612 Clarion Ct San Luis Obispo CA 93401 *Web:* wallacegroup.us	805-544-4011		261
Wallace H. Coulter Foundation, The 790 NW 107th Ave Miami FL 33172 *Web:* whcf.org	305-559-2991		70
Wallace Hardware Company Inc 5050 S Davy Crockett Pkwy PO Box 6004 Morristown TN 37815 *TF:* 800-776-0976 ■ *Web:* wallacehardware.com	800-776-0976		351
Wallace House 756 16th St Des Moines IA 50314 *Web:* wallace.org	515-243-7063	243-8927	50-3
Wallace House State Historic Site 71 Somerset St Somerville NJ 08876 *Web:* www.njparksandforests.org	908-725-1015		565
Wallace Law Firm 303 Washington St Covington IN 47932 *Web:* wallacelawfirm.net	765-793-2241		41
Wallace Literary Agencies Inc 301 E 79th St Ste 14-J New York NY 10075	212-570-9090		444
Wallace Oil Company Inc 5370 Oakdale Rd SE Smyrna GA 30082 *Web:* www.wallace-oil.com	404-799-9400	799-0322	579
Wallace Roberts & Todd LLC 1700 Market St Ste 2800 Philadelphia PA 19103 *Web:* www.wrtdesign.com	215-732-5215	732-2551	261
Wallace Saunders Austin Brown Enochs 200 W Douglas Ave Ste 400 Wichita KS 67202 *Web:* wallacesaunders.com	316-269-2100		428
Wallace Software Solutions 3350 Pawtucket Ave Riverside RI 02915 *Web:* wallacedms.com	401-438-3030	438-3031	177
Wallace State Community College 801 Main St Hanceville AL 35077 *TF:* 866-350-9722 ■ *Web:* www.wallacestate.edu	256-352-8000	352-8129	162
Wallace State Park 10621 NE Hwy 121 Cameron MO 64429 *Web:* mostateparks.com	816-632-3745		565
Wallace Welch & Willingham Inc 300 First Ave S 5th Fl Saint Petersburg FL 33701 *Web:* marineins.com	727-522-7777		390
Wallach & Company Inc 107 W Federal St Middleburg VA 20118 *TF:* 800-237-6615 ■ *Web:* www.wallach.com	540-687-3166	687-3172	391-7
Wallach Surgical Devices Inc 95 Corporate Dr Trumbull CT 06611 *TF:* 800-243-2463 ■ *Web:* www.wallachsurgical.com	203-799-2000	799-2002	476
WallachBeth Capital LLC Harborside Financial Center Plaza 5 185 Hudson St Ste 1410 Jersey City NJ 07311 **Fax Area Code:* 212 ■ *Web:* wallachbeth.com	646-237-8585	495-0270*	690
Wallco Inc 53 E Jackson St Ste 55 Wilkes-Barre PA 18701 *TF:* 800-392-5526 ■ *Web:* www.wallcoinc.com	570-823-6181	829-5952	696
Wallcoverings Assn 35 E Wacker Dr Ste 850 Chicago IL 60601 *Web:* www.wallcoverings.org	312-224-2574	527-6705	49-4
Walldesign Inc 5940 Key Ct Loomis CA 95650	916-660-0102		109-9
Wallenius Wilhelmsen 300 Interpace Pkwy Parsippany NJ 07054 *Web:* www.2wglobal.com	201-307-1300		313
Wallenius Wilhelmsen ASA 925 Harbor Plz Long Beach CA 90744 *Web:* www.offices.2wglobal.com	562-432-6477	436-7215	449
Wallens Ridge State Prison 272 Dogwood Dr PO Box 759 Big Stone Gap VA 24219 *Web:* vadoc.virginia.gov	276-523-3310		213
Waller County 840 13th Ste 201 Hempstead TX 77445 *Web:* www.wallercounty.org	979-921-9059		338
Waller Financial Planning Group Inc 941 Chatham Ln Ste 212 Columbus OH 43221 *Web:* waller.com	614-457-7026	457-0911	194
Waller Insurance Inc 5512 NE 109th Ct Ste G Vancouver WA 98662 *TF:* 866-927-9165 ■ *Web:* wallerins.net	360-254-2420	254-0806	390
Waller Lansden Dortch & Davis Nashville City Ctr 511 Union St Ste 2700 Nashville TN 37219 *Web:* www.wallerlaw.com	615-244-6380		428
Waller Truck Company Inc 400 S McCleary Rd Excelsior Springs MO 64024 *TF:* 800-821-2196 ■ *Web:* wallertruck.com	816-629-3400		780
WalletHub 818 18th St NW Washington DC 20006 *Web:* wallethub.com	202-684-6386		657
Wallick & Volk Mortgage 222 E 18th St Cheyenne WY 82001 *TF:* 800-280-8655 ■ *Web:* www.wvmb.com	307-634-5941		217
Wallick Construction Company Inc PO Box 1023 Columbus OH 43216 *Web:* www.wallick.com	614-863-4640	863-1725	186
Wallingford Buick GMC 1122 Old N Colony Rd Wallingford CT 06492 *TF:* 866-582-4487 ■ *Web:* www.wallingfordbuickgmc.com	888-765-9107		57
Wallingford Equipment Co 2527 Turner Rd Rte 4 Auburn ME 04210 *Web:* www.wallingfordequipment.com	207-782-4886		358
Wallingford-Swarthmore School District 200 S Providence Rd Wallingford PA 19086 *Web:* www.wssd.org	610-892-3470		685
Wallis Cos 106 E Washington St Cuba MO 65453 *TF:* 800-467-6652 ■ *Web:* www.wallisco.com	573-885-2277	885-4760	324
Wallis Sands State Beach 1050 Ocean Blvd Rye NH 03870 *Web:* www.nhstateparks.org	603-436-9404		565
Wallkill Central School District (WCSD) 19 Main St PO Box 310 Wallkill NY 12589 *Web:* www.wallkillcsd.k12.ny.us	845-895-7100	895-3630	685
Wallkill Correctional Facility 50 McKendrick Rd Wallkill NY 12589 *Web:* www.doccs.ny.gov	845-895-2021		213
Wallkill Valley Federal Savings & Loan Assn 23 Wallkill Ave Wallkill NY 12589 *TF:* 888-621-3304 ■ *Web:* www.wallkill.com	845-895-2051		70
Wallops Flight Facility 32400 Fulton St Wallops Island VA 23337 *Web:* www.nasa.gov	757-824-1987		743
Wallover Oil Company Inc 21845 Drake Rd Strongsville OH 44149 *TF:* 800-255-9626 ■ *Web:* www.wallover.com	440-238-9250	238-0395	541
Wallowa County 101 S River St Enterprise OR 97828 *Web:* www.co.wallowa.or.us	541-426-4543	426-5901	338

Name / Address	City	State	ZIP	Phone	Fax	Class
Wallowa Lake State Park 72214 Marina Ln *Web:* stateparks.oregon.gov	Joseph	OR	97846	541-432-9115		565
Wallquest Inc 465 Devon Park Dr *Web:* www.wallquest.com	Wayne	PA	19087	610-293-1330		548
Walls 360 5054 Bond St *TF:* 888-244-9969 ■ *Web:* walls360.com	Las Vegas	NV	89118	888-244-9969		393
Walls+Forms Inc 204 Airline Dr Ste 200 *Web:* www.wallsforms.com	Coppell	TX	75019	972-745-0800		393
Wallse 344 W 11th St *Web:* www.kurtgutenbrunner.com	New York	NY	10014	212-352-2300		671
Wallside Windows 27000 Trolley Industrial Dr *TF:* 800-521-7800 ■ *Web:* wallsidewindows.com	Taylor	MI	48180	313-292-4400		499
Wallstreet Financial Group Inc 1530 Rax Ct *Web:* wallstreetins.com	Jefferson City	MO	65109	573-636-3222		390
Wally World RC Helis 524 Cemetery Rd *Web:* www.wallyworldrchelis.com	Park City	MT	59063	406-633-2811		116
Wally's Wine & Spirits 2107 Westwood Blvd *Web:* www.wallywine.com	Los Angeles	CA	90025	310-475-0606		443
Walman 801 12th Ave N *Web:* www.walman.com	Minneapolis	MN	55411	612-520-6000	520-6096	542
Walmart 702 SW Eighth St Po Box 0160 *NYSE: WMT* ■ *TF:* 800-925-6278 ■ *Web:* www.walmart.com	Bentonville	AR	72716	800-925-6278		459
Wal-Mart Puerto Rico Inc PO Box 4960 PMB 725 *Web:* www.walmartpr.com	Caguas	PR	00726	787-653-7777		229
Wal-Mart Realty 1316 SE Moberly Ln *Web:* www.walmartrealty.com	Bentonville	AR	72712	479-273-4682		655
Wal-Mart Stores Inc 702 SW Eighth St *NYSE: WMT* ■ *Web:* corporate.walmart.com	Bentonville	AR	72716	479-273-4000		229
Walnut Cafe 3073 Walnut St *Web:* www.walnutcafe.com	Boulder	CO	80301	303-447-2315		671
Walnut Creek Chamber of Commerce 1280 Civic Dr Ste 100 *Web:* www.walnut-creek.com	Walnut Creek	CA	94596	925-934-2007	934-2404	139
Walnut Hollow Farm Inc 1409 State Rd 23 *TF:* 800-395-5995 ■ *Web:* www.walnuthollow.com	Dodgeville	WI	53533	608-935-2341		279
Walnut Leader, The 110 Jackson St *Web:* www.walnutillinois.com	Walnut	IL	61376	815-379-9290		532-2
Walnut Point State Park 2331 E County Rd 370 N *Web:* www2.illinois.gov	Oakland	IL	61943	217-346-3336		565
Walnut Street Theatre 825 Walnut St *Web:* www.walnutstreettheatre.org	Philadelphia	PA	19107	215-574-3550		572
Walnut Woods State Park 3155 Walnut Woods Dr *Web:* www.iowadnr.gov	West Des Moines	IA	50265	515-285-4502	285-7476	565
Walorski Jackie (Rep R - IN) 419 Cannon House Office Bldg *Web:* walorski.house.gov	Washington	DC	20515	202-225-3915	225-6798	342-2
Walpole Co-opeartive Bank Inc 982 Main St *Web:* www.walpolecoop.com	Walpole	MA	02081	508-668-1080	660-2690	70
Walpole Feed and Supply Co PO Box 1723 *TF:* 800-343-8474 ■ *Web:* www.walpolefeedinc.com	Okeechobee	FL	34973	863-763-6905	763-6264	45
Walpole Inc 269 NW Ninth St *TF:* 800-741-6500 ■ *Web:* walpoleinc.com	Okeechobee	FL	34972	863-763-5593		780
Walpole Public Library 143 School St *Web:* www.walpolelibrary.org	Walpole	MA	02081	508-660-7340		434-3
Walrus Productions 4805 NE 106th St *Web:* www.walrusproductions.com	Seattle	WA	98125	206-364-4365	362-2834	637-2
Walrus, The 1136 N Third St *Web:* thewalrusrestaurant.com	Bismarck	ND	58501	701-250-0020		671
Walsh & Sheppard Inc 111 W Ninth Ave *Web:* www.walshsheppard.com	Anchorage	AK	99501	907-338-3857		7
Walsh Brothers Inc 210 Commercial St *Web:* www.walshbrothers.com	Boston	MA	02109	617-878-4800	720-6116	194
Walsh Construction Co 2905 SW First Ave *Web:* walshconstruction.com	Portland	OR	97201	503-222-4375	274-7676	186
Walsh County 600 Cooper Ave *Web:* www.co.walsh.nd.us	Grafton	ND	58237	701-352-1300	352-1104	338
Walsh Group Inc 929 W Adams St *TF:* 800-957-1842 ■ *Web:* walshgroup.com	Chicago	IL	60607	312-563-5400	563-5466	186
Walsh Kelliher & Sharp 1292 Sadler Way Ste 220 *Web:* www.wkscpa.com	Fairbanks	AK	99701	907-456-2222	456-8325	2
Walsh Property Management PO Box 2657 *Web:* www.walshpm.com	Castro Valley	CA	94546	510-888-8965	886-5223	652
Walsh University 2020 E Maple St *TF:* 800-362-9846 ■ *Web:* www.walsh.edu	North Canton	OH	44720	330-499-7090	490-7165	166
Walsh Washburn LLC 5360 College Blvd *Web:* walshwashburn.com	Overland Park	KS	66211	913-660-7711		2
Walsh Woodard LLC 527 Prospect Ave *Web:* walshwoodard.com	West Hartford	CT	06105	860-785-2011		41
Walsworth Publishing Co 306 N Kansas Ave *TF:* 800-972-4968 ■ *Web:* www.walsworthyearbooks.com	Marceline	MO	64658	800-265-7695		637-2
Walt & Company Communications 2105 S Bascom Ave Ste 240 *Web:* www.walt.com	Campbell	CA	95008	408-369-7200		636
Walt Disney Co 500 S Buena Vista St *NYSE: DIS* ■ *Web:* thewaltdisneycompany.com	Burbank	CA	91521	818-553-7200		185
Walt Disney Family Museum LLC, The 104 Montgomery St *Web:* www.waltdisney.org	San Francisco	CA	94129	415-345-6800		520
Walt Disney World Resorts 4600 N World Dr *Web:* disneyworld.disney.go.com	Lake Buena Vista	FL	32830	407-824-1000		669
Walt Disney World Swan 1200 Epcot Resorts Blvd *Web:* swandolphin.com	Lake Buena Vista	FL	32830	407-934-3000	934-4884	669
Walt Kremer Insurance Agency Inc 4080 Marshall Rd *Web:* kremerinsurance.com	Kettering	OH	45429	937-298-0105		390
Walt Whitman Birthplace State Historic Site 246 Old Walt Whitman Rd *Web:* parks.ny.gov	Huntington Station	NY	11746	631-427-5240	427-5247	565
Walt Whitman House State Historic Site 330 Mickle Blvd *TF:* 800-843-6420 ■ *Web:* www.njparksandforests.org	Camden	NJ	08103	800-843-6420		565
Walt's Drive-A-Way Services Inc 4600 Hitch & Peters Rd *Web:* www.waltsonline.com	Evansville	IN	47711	812-424-8927		120
Waltek & Company Ltd 2130 Waycorss Rd *Web:* www.walteklltd.com	Cincinnati	OH	45240	513-577-7980	577-7990	189-6
Waltek Inc 14310 Sunfish Lake Blvd *TF:* 800-937-9496 ■ *Web:* www.waltekinc.com	Ramsey	MN	55303	763-427-3181	427-3216	306
Walter & Elise Haas Fund 1 Lombard St Ste 305 *Web:* www.creativeworkfund.org	San Francisco	CA	94111	415-402-2793		305
Walter | Haverfield LLP 1301 E Ninth St Ste 3500 *Web:* www.walterhav.com	Cleveland	OH	44114	216-781-1212		428
Walter B. Jones Alcohol & Drug Abuse Treatment Ctr 2577 W Fifth St *TF:* 800-422-1884 ■ *Web:* www.ncdhhs.gov	Greenville	NC	27834	252-830-3426		726
Walter Drake Inc 85 Sargeant St *Web:* www.walterdrake.com	Holyoke	MA	01040	413-536-5463	532-9745	604
Walter E. Nelson Co 5937 N Cutter Cir *TF:* 800-929-2141 ■ *Web:* www.walterenelson.com	Portland	OR	97217	503-285-3037	285-4373	76
Walter E. Smithe Furniture Inc 1251 W Thorndale Ave *Web:* www.smithe.com	Itasca	IL	60143	630-285-8000	620-1552	319-2
Walter F. Cameron Advertising Inc 350 Motor Pkwy Ste 410 *Web:* www.cameronadv.com	Hauppauge	NY	11788	631-232-3033		7
Walter Fields Group Inc, The 1919 South Blvd Ste 101 *Web:* walterfieldsgroup.com	Charlotte	NC	28203	704-372-7855	372-7856	384
Walter Greenblatt & Associates LLC 430 Nassau St *Web:* www.wgreenblatt.com	Princeton	NJ	08540	609-497-1282		194
Walter Haas & Sons Inc 123 W 23rd St *TF:* 800-552-3845 ■ *Web:* www.haasprint.com	Hialeah	FL	33010	305-883-2257	883-0598	701
Walter J. Korzeniowski 688 Washington St *Web:* walterklaw.com	South Easton	MA	02375	508-238-6200		41
Walter Knoll Florist 2765 LaSalle St *TF:* 800-341-7673 ■ *Web:* www.wkf.com	Saint Louis	MO	63104	314-352-7575	633-8756	293
Walter L. Phillips Inc 207 Park Ave *Web:* wlpinc.com	Falls Church	VA	22046	703-532-6163		261
Walter L. Weisman CPA 8911 La Mesa Blvd Ste 201 *Web:* www.san-diego-tax.com	La Mesa	CA	91941	619-697-7878		2
Walter Meier Manufacturing Inc 427 New Sanford Rd *TF:* 800-274-6848 ■ *Web:* www.wiltontools.com	La Vergne	TN	37086	800-274-6848		758
Walter N. Yoder & Sons Inc 16200 McMullen Hwy SW PO Box 1337 *Web:* wnyoder.com	Cumberland	MD	21502	301-729-0610	729-1517	189-10
Walter Oil & Gas Corp 1100 Louisiana St Ste 200 *Web:* www.walteroil.com	Houston	TX	77002	713-659-1221		538
Walter P. Moore 1301 Mckinney St Ste 1100 *TF:* 800-364-7300 ■ *Web:* www.walterpmoore.com	Houston	TX	77010	713-630-7300	630-7396	261
Walter P. Reuther Psychiatric Hospital 30901 Palmer Rd *Web:* www.michigan.gov	Westland	MI	48186	734-367-8400	722-5562	374-5
Walter Reed National Military Medical Ctr 4494 North Palmer Rd *TF:* 800-526-7101 ■ *Web:* www.wrnmmc.capmed.mil	Bethesda	MD	20889	301-295-4000		374-4
Walter Snyder Printer Inc 691 River St *TF:* 888-272-9774 ■ *Web:* www.snyderprinter.com	Troy	NY	12180	518-272-8881		627
Walter Stern Inc 68 Sintsink Dr E *Web:* www.waltersterninc.com	Port Washington	NY	11050	516-883-9100	767-0400	787
Walter T. McCarthy Law Library 1425 N Courthouse Rd Ste 1700 *Web:* courts.arlingtonva.us	Arlington	VA	22201	703-228-7005	228-7360	434-3
Walter Toebe Construction Co 29001 Wall St PO Box 930129 *Web:* www.toebe-construction.com	Wixom	MI	48393	248-349-7500	349-4870	187
Walter USA Inc N22 W23855 Ridgeview Pkwy W **Fax Area Code:* 262 ■ *TF:* 800-945-5554 ■ *Web:* www.walter-tools.com	Waukesha	WI	53188	800-945-5554	347-2501*	493
Walter's Precision Service Inc 229 S River Dr *Web:* www.waltersprecision.com	Tempe	AZ	85281	480-968-1834		493
Walter's Steak House & Saloon 802 N Union St *Web:* walters-steakhouse.com	Wilmington	DE	19805	302-652-6780		671
Walterboro-Colleton Chamber of Commerce 403 E Washington St *Web:* walterboro.org	Walterboro	SC	29488	843-549-9595	549-5775	139
Walters & Wolf 41450 Boscell Rd *Web:* www.waltersandwolf.com	Fremont	CA	94538	510-490-1115	651-7172	189-6

Name / Address	City	State	ZIP	Phone	Fax	Class
Walters Art Museum 600 N Charles St	Baltimore	MD	21201	410-547-9000		520
Web: thewalters.org						
Walters Metal Fabrication						
3660 SR-111	Granite City	IL	62040	618-931-5551		480
Web: www.waltersmetalfab.com						
Walters Pharmacy Inc 401 N 17th St	Allentown	PA	18104	610-435-4706		237
Web: walterspharmacy.com						
Walters State Community College						
500 S Davy Crockett Pkwy	Morristown	TN	37813	423-585-2600	585-6786	162
TF: 800-225-4770 ■ *Web:* www.ws.edu						
Walters Wholesale Electric Co						
2825 Temple Ave	Signal Hill	CA	90755	562-988-3100	988-3150	246
TF: 833-993-3266 ■ *Web:* www.walterswholesale.com						
Walters, Papillion, Thomas, Cullens LLC						
12345 Perkins Rd	Baton Rouge	LA	70810	225-236-3636	236-3650	41
Web: lawbr.net						
Waltex Inc 12111 Chandler Dr	Walton	KY	41094	859-485-8550	485-8525	811
Web: www.toyodenyo.co.jp						
Walthall Oil Company Inc 2510 Allen Rd	Macon	GA	31216	478-781-1234		579
TF: 800-633-5685 ■ *Web:* www.walthall-oil.com						
Waltham Community Access Corp						
400 Main St	Waltham	MA	02452	781-899-8834		116
Web: wcac.org						
Waltham Public Library 735 Main St	Waltham	MA	02451	781-314-3425		434-3
Web: www.waltham.lib.ma.us						
Waltham Services Inc 817 Moody St	Waltham	MA	02453	781-893-1810	893-7921	577
TF: 866-974-7378 ■ *Web:* www.walthamservices.com						
Waltham/West Suburban Chamber of Commerce						
84 South St	Waltham	MA	02453	781-894-4700		139
Web: www.walthamchamber.com						
Waltkoch Ltd 1025 Airport Pkwy	Gainesville	GA	30501	404-378-3666		619
Web: www.waltkoch.com						
Walton & Company CPAS						
2101 Boca Raton Blvd Ste 5	Boca Raton	FL	33431	561-395-6653	361-2209	2
Web: waltoncpas.com						
Walton & Post Inc 9375 NW 117th Ave	Miami	FL	33166	305-591-1111	593-7070	297-8
Web: www.waltonpost.com						
Walton Area Chamber of Commerce						
63 S Centre Trl	Santa Rosa Beach	FL	32459	850-267-0683	267-0603	139
Web: waltonareachamber.com						
Walton County						
76 N Sixth St PO Box 1355	DeFuniak Springs	FL	32433	850-892-8115		338
Web: www.co.walton.fl.us						
Walton County Board of Education						
200 Double Springs Church Rd	Monroe	GA	30656	770-266-4520		186
Web: www.walton.k12.ga.us						
Walton County Board-Commissioner						
303 S Hammond Dr Ste 330	Monroe	GA	30655	770-267-1301	267-1400	338
Web: www.waltoncountyga.gov						
Walton County Chamber of Commerce						
132 E Spring St	Monroe	GA	30655	770-267-6594	267-0961	139
Web: www.waltonchamber.org						
Walton Family Foundation Inc (WFF)						
PO Box 2030	Bentonville	AR	72712	479-464-1570	464-1580	305
Web: www.waltonfamilyfoundation.org						
Walton Insurance Agency Inc						
3150 Almaden Expwy Ste 102	San Jose	CA	95118	408-265-2800		390
Web: waltoninsurance.com						
Walton Lantaff Schroeder & Carson LLP						
9350 S Dixie Hwy 10th Fl	Miami	FL	33156	305-671-1300		428
Web: www.waltonlantaff.com						
Walton Manor Health Care Ctr						
19859 Alexander Rd	Walton Hills	OH	44146	440-439-4433		450
Web: www.saberhealth.com						
Walton Motors Inc 205 E Pawnee Dr	Savannah	MO	64485	816-324-3141		516
Web: www.waltonmotorsinc.com						
Walton Press (WP) 402 Mayfield Dr	Monroe	GA	30655	800-354-0235		555
TF: 800-354-0235 ■ *Web:* www.waltonpress.com						
Walton Rehabilitation Hospital						
1355 Independence Dr	Augusta	GA	30901	706-724-7746	823-8681	374-6
TF: 866-492-5866 ■ *Web:* encompasshealth.com						
Walton School of Auctioneering						
7996 Boneta Rd Unit B	Wadsworth	OH	44281	800-369-2818		685
TF: 800-369-2818 ■ *Web:* www.waltonauctionsite.com						
Walton Signage Corp						
10101 Reunion Pl Ste 500	San Antonio	TX	78216	210-886-0644		393
Web: www.waltonsignage.com						
Walton Street Capital LLC						
900 N Michigan Ave Ste 1900	Chicago	IL	60611	312-915-2800	915-2881	655
Web: www.waltonst.com						
Walton Tribune 121 S Broad St	Monroe	GA	30655	770-267-8371	267-7780	532-2
Web: www.waltontribune.com						
Waltrich Plastic Corp						
3005 Airport Rd	Walthourville	GA	31333	912-368-9341		605-1
Web: waltrichplastic.com						
Walts Food Centers						
16145 S State St	South Holland	IL	60473	708-333-5500		345
Web: www.waltsfoods.com						
Walts Mailing Service Ltd						
9610 E First Ave	Spokane Valley	WA	99206	509-924-5939		5
TF: 888-549-2006 ■ *Web:* waltsmailing.com						
Waltz Michael (Rep R - FL)						
216 Cannon House Office Bldg	Washington	DC	20515	202-225-2706		342-2
Web: www.waltz.house.gov						
Walworth County						
100 W Walworth St PO Box 1001	Elkhorn	WI	53121	262-741-4241	741-4287	338
Web: www.co.walworth.wi.us						
WALZ Label & Mailing Systems						
624 High Point Ln	East Peoria	IL	61611	309-698-1500		535
TF: 877-971-1500 ■ *Web:* walzeq.com						
WAMBTAC Communications						
1512 E Santa Clara Ave	Santa Ana	CA	92705	714-954-0580		423
TF: 800-641-3936 ■ *Web:* www.wambtac.com						
WAMC (West Anaheim Medical Ctr)						
3033 W Orange Ave	Anaheim	CA	92804	714-827-3000		374-3
Web: www.westanaheimmedctr.com						
WAMC/Northeast Public Radio						
318 Central Ave	Albany	NY	12206	518-465-5233	432-6974	632
TF: 800-323-9262 ■ *Web:* www.wamc.org						
Wampanoag Tribe of Gay Head Aquinnah						
20 Black Brook Rd	Aquinnah	MA	02535	508-645-9265		378
Web: wampanoagtribe-nsn.gov						
WAMU-FM 88.5 (NPR)						
4401 Connecticut Ave NW	Washington	DC	20008	202-885-1200		645-170
Web: wamu.org						
Wanchese Fish Co						
2000 Northgate Commerce Pkwy	Suffolk	VA	23435	757-673-4500		285
Web: www.wanchese.com						
WAND (Women's Action for New Directions)						
691 Massachusetts Ave	Arlington	MA	02476	202-459-4769		48-5
Web: www.wand.org						
WAND Inc 2170 S Parker Rd Ste 295	Denver	CO	80231	303-623-1200		225
Web: www.wandinc.com						
WAND-TV Ch 17 (ABC) 904 S Side Dr	Decatur	IL	62521	217-424-2500	424-2583	741
Web: www.wandtv.com						
Wang Electric Inc						
4107 E Winslow Ave Ste C	Phoenix	AZ	85040	602-324-5350	324-5360	787
Web: www.wangelectric.com						
Wang Theatre 270 Tremont St	Boston	MA	02116	800-982-2787		572
TF: 800-982-2787 ■ *Web:* www.bochcenter.org						
Wangard Partners Inc						
1200 N Mayfair Rd	Milwaukee	WI	53226	414-777-1200		652
Web: wangard.com						
Wanke Cascade Co 6330 N Cutter Cir	Portland	OR	97217	503-289-8609	285-5640	361
TF: 800-365-5053 ■ *Web:* www.wanke.com						
Wanner Associates Inc						
908 N Second St	Harrisburg	PA	17102	717-236-2050	236-2046	47
Web: www.wannerassoc.com						
Wanpela Books PO Box 859	Hyde Park	NY	12538	914-229-0571		637-2
Web: www.wanpela.com						
Wantman Group Inc						
2035 Vista Pkwy Ste 100	West Palm Beach	FL	33411	561-687-2220		186
TF: 866-909-2220 ■ *Web:* wginc.com						
Wanzek Construction Inc						
2028 Second Ave NW	West Fargo	ND	58078	701-282-6171		186
Web: www.wanzek.com						
WAO (World Allergy Organization)						
555 E Wells St Ste 1100	Milwaukee	WI	53202	414-276-1791	276-3349	49-8
Web: www.worldallergy.org						
WAOE TV My 59 2907 Springfield Rd	East Peoria	IL	61611	309-698-3724		741
Web: www.my59.tv						
WAOK-AM 1380 (N/T)						
1201 Peachtree St NE Ste 800	Atlanta	GA	30361	404-898-8916		645-11
Web: atlanta.cbslocal.com						
WAPE-FM 95.1 (CHR)						
8000 Belfort Pkwy Ste 100	Jacksonville	FL	32256	833-816-1029	245-8501*	645-76
**Fax Area Code:* 904 ■ *TF:* 800-475-9595 ■ *Web:* www.wape.com						
Wapello County 101 W Fourth St	Ottumwa	IA	52501	641-652-3352	683-0053	338
Web: www.wapellocounty.org						
WAPI-AM 1070 (N/T)						
244 Goodwin Crest Dr Ste 300	Birmingham	AL	35209	205-945-4646	945-3999	645-19
Web: www.talk995.com						
Wapiti Meadow Ranch						
1667 Johnson Creek Rd	Cascade	ID	83611	208-633-3217	633-3219	239
Web: www.wapitimeadowranch.com						
Wapiti Regional Library						
145 12th St E	Prince Albert	SK	S6V1B7	306-764-0712	922-1516	436
Web: wapitilibrary.ca						
WAPN-FM 91.5 (Rel) 1508 State Ave	Holly Hill	FL	32117	386-677-4272	677-7095	645
Web: www.wapn.net						
Wapsi Fly Co 27 County Rd 458	Mountain Home	AR	72653	870-425-9500		711
Web: www.wapsifly.com						
Wapsie Valley Creamery Inc						
300 10th St NE	Independence	IA	50644	319-334-7193		296-5
Web: www.wapsievalley.com						
Wapsipinicon State Park						
21301 County Rd E34	Anamosa	IA	52205	319-462-2761	462-4878	565
Web: www.iowadnr.gov						
WAPT-TV Ch 16 (ABC) 7616 Ch 16 Way	Jackson	MS	39209	601-922-1607		741-63
TF: 800-441-1948 ■ *Web:* www.wapt.com						
Wapusk National Park PO Box 127	Churchill	MB	R0B0E0	204-675-8863	675-2026	563
Web: www.pc.gc.ca						
War Eagle Mill Inc 11045 War Eagle Rd	Rogers	AR	72756	479-789-5343	789-2146	812
TF: 866-492-7324 ■ *Web:* www.wareaglemill.com						
War in the Pacific National Historical Park						
135 Murray Blvd Ste 100	Hagatna	GU	96910	671-477-7278		564
Web: www.nps.gov						
War Resisters League						
168 Canal St Ste 600	New York	NY	10013	212-228-0450	228-6193	48-5
Web: www.warresisters.org						
War Vet Museum 23 E Main St	Canfield	OH	44406	330-533-6311		520
Web: warvetmuseum.org						
Warady & Davis LLP						
1717 Deerfield Rd	Deerfield	IL	60015	847-267-9600	267-9696	2
Web: waradydavis.com						
Waraji 5910 Duraleigh Rd	Raleigh	NC	27612	919-783-1883		671
Web: www.warajijapaneserestaurant.com						
Warbros Venture Partners PO Box 1033	Westerly	RI	02891	401-596-8960		403
Web: www.warbros.com						
Warburg Pincus LLC 450 Lexington Ave	New York	NY	10017	212-878-0600	878-9351	792
Web: www.warburgpincus.com						
Ward & Childress 305 W 4th St	Washington	MO	63090	314-394-8987		41
Web: stlouismolegaloffice.com						
Ward & Smith PA 1001 College Ct	New Bern	NC	28562	252-672-5400	672-5477	428
TF: 800-998-1102 ■ *Web:* www.wardandsmith.com						
Ward Accountancy Inc						
10 Bonafacio Plz	Monterey	CA	93940	831-373-1211	373-2456	2
Web: wardaccountancy.com						
Ward Aluminum Casting Co						
642 Growth Ave	Fort Wayne	IN	46808	260-426-8700	420-1919	308
TF: 800-648-9918 ■ *Web:* www.wardcorp.com						
Ward Anderson Porritt & Bryant Plc						
4190 Telegraph Rd Ste 2300	Bloomfield Hills	MI	48302	248-593-1440		445
Web: www.wardanderson.com						
Ward Cedar Log Homes						
37 Bangor St PO Box 72	Houlton	ME	04730	800-341-1566	532-7806*	106
**Fax Area Code:* 207 ■ *TF:* 800-341-1566 ■ *Web:* www.wardcedarloghomes.com						

Name / Address	City	State	ZIP	Phone	Fax	Class
Ward Charcoal Ovens State Historic Park PO Box 151761 *Web:* parks.nv.gov	Ely	NV	89315	775-289-1693		565
Ward County 315 SE Third St PO Box 907 *Web:* www.co.ward.nd.us	Minot	ND	58702	701-857-6500	857-6520	338
Ward County County Courthouse *Web:* www.co.ward.tx.us	Monahans	TX	79756	432-943-3200	943-6054	338
Ward Engineering Company Inc 1353 S Seventh St PO Box 2498 *Web:* www.wardengr.com	Louisville	KY	40201	502-637-6521		256
Ward Group 11500 Northlake Dr Ste 305 *Web:* www.wardinc.com	Cincinnati	OH	45249	513-791-0303	985-3442	194
Ward Leonard Electric Company Inc 401 Watertown Rd *Web:* wardleonard.com	Thomaston	CT	06787	860-283-5801	283-5777	518
Ward Management Group Inc, The 11495 N Pennsylvania St Ste 103 *Web:* wardmanage.com	Carmel	IN	46032	317-816-1619	816-1633	47
Ward Manufacturing LLC 117 Gulick St *TF:* 800-248-1027 ■ *Web:* www.wardmfg.com	Blossburg	PA	16912	570-638-2131		612
Ward Museum of Wildfowl Art 909 S Schumaker Dr *Web:* www.wardmuseum.org	Salisbury	MD	21804	410-742-4988		520
Ward Petroleum 14000 Quail Springs Pkwy Ste 5000 *TF:* 800-522-1337 ■ *Web:* www.wardpetroleum.com	Oklahoma City	OK	73134	405-242-4484	242-4334	536
Ward Process Inc 311 Hopping Brook Rd *Web:* www.aapusa.com	Holliston	MA	01746	508-429-1165	429-8543	389
Ward Systems & Services Inc 2121 CeeGee St *Web:* www.wardsystemsmmt.com	San Antonio	TX	78217	210-824-9581	824-2123	189-10
Ward Williston Oil Company Inc 36700 Woodward Ave Ste 101 *Web:* www.wardwilliston.com	Bloomfield Hills	MI	48304	248-792-8863		539
Ward's Food Systems Inc 5133 Lincoln Rd Ext *TF:* 800-748-9273 ■ *Web:* wardsrestaurants.com	Hattiesburg	MS	39402	601-268-9273		670
Ward's Marine Electric Inc 617 SW Third Ave **Fax Area Code:* 561 ■ *TF:* 800-297-8240 ■ *Web:* www.wardsmarine.com	Fort Lauderdale	FL	33315	954-523-2815	863-7008*	787
Ward, Greenberg, Heller & Reidy LLP 1800 Bausch & Lomb Pl *Web:* wardgreenberg.com	Rochester	NY	14604	585-454-0700		41
Ward, Murray, Pace & Johnson PC 202 E Fifth St *Web:* www.wmpj.com	Sterling	IL	61081	815-625-8200		428
Warde Medical Laboratory (WML) 300 W Textile Rd *TF:* 800-760-9969 ■ *Web:* www.wardelab.com	Ann Arbor	MI	48108	734-214-0300	214-0399	415
Ward-Kraft Inc 2401 Cooper St *TF:* 800-821-4021 ■ *Web:* www.wardkraft.com	Fort Scott	KS	66701	620-223-5500	223-6953	110
Wards Corner Beauty Academy 7525 Tidewater Dr Ste 200 *Web:* www.wardscornerbeautyacademy.edu	Norfolk	VA	23505	757-583-3300	587-4401	167-3
Wardwell Braiding Machine Co 1211 High St *Web:* www.wardwell.com	Central Falls	RI	02863	401-724-8800	723-2690	744
Wardynski & Sons Inc 336 Peckham St *Web:* www.wardynski.com	Buffalo	NY	14206	716-854-6083		296-26
Ware County 800 Church St *Web:* www.warecounty.com	Waycross	GA	31501	912-287-4300	287-4301	338
Ware County School District 1301 Bailey St *Web:* www.ware.k12.ga.us	Waycross	GA	31501	912-283-8656	283-8698	186
Ware Jewelers 7268 Eastchase Pkwy *Web:* www.warejewelers.com	Montgomery	AL	36117	334-386-9273		410
Ware Malcomb 10 Edelman *Web:* www.waremalcomb.com	Irvine	CA	92618	949-660-9128	863-1581	261
Ware Pak Inc 2427 Bond St *Web:* www.ware-pak.com	University Park	IL	60484	708-534-2600	534-7803	311
Ware State Prison 3620 N Harris Rd *Web:* dcor.state.ga.us	Waycross	GA	31501	912-285-6400	287-6520	213
Wareham Ford 2628 Cranberry Hwy *Web:* www.warehamfordinc.com	Wareham	MA	02571	508-295-3643		57
Warehouse Bar & Grill 214 King St *Web:* www.warehouseoldtown.com	Alexandria	VA	22314	703-683-6868		671
Warehouse Home Furnishings Distributors Inc 1851 Telfair St PO Box 1140 **Fax Area Code:* 478 ■ *TF:* 800-456-0424 ■ *Web:* farmershomefurniture.com	Dublin	GA	31021	800-456-0424	275-6276*	321
Warehouse One LLC 9305 Cherokee Tr *Web:* www.warehouseone.net	Crossville	TN	38572	931-788-1011	788-1152	803-1
Warehouse Skateboards Inc 1638 Military Cutoff Rd *TF:* 877-791-9795 ■ *Web:* www.warehouseskateboards.com	Wilmington	NC	28403	877-791-9795		711
Warehouse Systems Inc 601 Academy Dr *Web:* warehousesys.com	Northbrook	IL	60062	847-562-9526	562-9529	207
Warehouse Theatre 37 Augusta St *Web:* warehousetheatre.com	Greenville	SC	29601	864-235-6948		572
Warehousing Education & Research Council (WERC) 1100 Jorie Blvd Ste 170 *Web:* www.werc.org	Oak Brook	IL	60523	630-990-0001	990-0256	49-21
Warfel Construction Co 1110 Enterprise Rd *Web:* www.warfelcc.com	East Petersburg	PA	17520	717-299-4500	299-4628	186
WARG-FM 7329 W 63rd St *Web:* www.warg889.net	Summit	IL	60501	708-467-5589	467-5864	647
Warhawk Air Museum 201 Municipal Dr *Web:* warhawkairmuseum.org	Nampa	ID	83687	208-465-6446	465-6232	520
Waring Oil Company LLC 431 Port Terminal Cir *Web:* www.waringoil.com	Vicksburg	MS	39183	601-636-1065		579
Warko Roofing Company Inc 18 Morgan Dr *Web:* thewarkogroup.com	Reading	PA	19608	610-796-4545		101-4
Warlick Paint Company Inc 208 Bucks Industrial Park Rd *TF:* 800-280-2423 ■ *Web:* www.crossroadscoatings.com	Statesville	NC	28625	704-873-2244	873-4508	550
Warm Co 5529 186th Pl SW *TF:* 800-234-9276 ■ *Web:* warmcompany.com	Lynnwood	WA	98037	425-248-2424	248-2422	745-1
Warm Springs Correctional Ctr 3301 E Fifth St PO Box 7007 *Web:* doc.nv.gov	Carson City	NV	89702	775-684-3000		213
Warm Springs Home Health Inc 54 Whitney Pl *Web:* www.warmspringshh.com	Fremont	CA	94539	510-490-6988	490-9588	363
Warmka Transport Inc 50041 State Hwy 109 *TF:* 800-768-6506 ■ *Web:* www.warmkatransport.com	Easton	MN	56025	507-787-2289	787-2294	780
Warn Industries Inc 12900 SE Capps Rd *TF:* 800-543-9276 ■ *Web:* www.warn.com	Clackamas	OR	97015	503-722-1200		61
Warner Bros Entertainment Inc 4000 Warner Blvd *Web:* www.warnerbros.com	Burbank	CA	91522	818-954-1853	954-3817	514
Warner Communications 41 Raymond St *Web:* www.warnerpr.com	Manchester	MA	01944	978-526-1960	526-8206	317
Warner Consulting Inc 5106 Berryessa St *Web:* warner-consulting.com	Oceanside	CA	92056	760-806-7722	806-7727	196
Warner Electric 449 Gardner St *TF:* 800-825-6544 ■ *Web:* www.warnerelectric.com	South Beloit	IL	61080	800-825-6544		620
Warner Instruments 1320 Fulton St *Web:* www.fireright.com	Grand Haven	MI	49417	616-843-5342	842-1471	201
Warner Manufacturing Co 13435 Industrial Pk Blvd *TF:* 800-444-0606 ■ *Web:* www.warnertool.com	Plymouth	MN	55441	763-559-4740		758
Warner Mark R (Sen D - VA) 703 Hart Senate Office Bldg *Web:* www.warner.senate.gov	Washington	DC	20510	202-224-2023		342-2
Warner Music Group 1633 Broadway *TF:* 800-820-1653 ■ *Web:* www.wmg.com	New York	NY	10019	212-275-2000		657
Warner Pacific College 2219 SE 68th Ave *TF:* 800-804-1510 ■ *Web:* www.warnerpacific.edu	Portland	OR	97215	503-517-1020	517-1352	166
Warner Robins Animal Hospital Pc 2080 Watson Blvd *Web:* warnerrobinsanimalhospital.business.site	Warner Robins	GA	31093	478-923-3139		794
Warner Robins Area Chamber of Commerce 1228 Watson Blvd *Web:* www.robinsregion.com	Warner Robins	GA	31093	478-922-8585	328-7745	139
Warner Robins Supply Company Inc 2756 Watson Blvd *Web:* www.wrsupply.com	Warner Robins	GA	31093	478-953-4100	953-4280	364
Warner Southern College 13895 Hwy 27 *TF:* 800-309-9563 ■ *Web:* www.warner.edu	Lake Wales	FL	33859	800-309-9563	949-7248	166
Warner Theatre 513 13th St NW *Web:* www.warnertheatredc.com	Washington	DC	20004	202-783-4000	783-0204	572
Warner Theatre 809 French St *Web:* www.erieevents.com	Erie	PA	16501	814-452-4857	455-9931	572
Warner Vineyards Inc 706 S Kalamazoo St *TF:* 800-756-5357 ■ *Web:* warnerwines.com	Paw Paw	MI	49079	269-657-3165		80-3
Warner/Chappell Music Inc 10585 Santa Monica Blvd *Web:* www.warnerchappell.com	Los Angeles	CA	90025	310-441-8600		637-7
WarnerMedia 30 Hudson Yards *NYSE:* TWX ■ *TF:* 866-463-6899 ■ *Web:* www.timewarner.com	New York	NY	10001	212-484-8000		185
Warners Florist 179 S Montgomery St *Web:* warnersflorist.com	Hollidaysburg	PA	16648	814-695-9431		292
Warnors Center for the Performing Arts 1412 Fulton St *Web:* warnors.org	Fresno	CA	93721	559-264-2848		572
Warp Bros Flex-O-Glass Inc 4647 W Augusta Blvd *TF:* 800-621-3345 ■ *Web:* www.warpbros.com	Chicago	IL	60651	773-261-5200	261-5204	548
Warpaint Resources LLC 6175 Main St Ste 250 *Web:* www.warpaintresources.com	Frisco	TX	75034	214-423-9900		536
Warrantech Corporation Inc 2200 Hwy 121 *TF:* 800-833-8801 ■ *Web:* warrantech.com	Bedford	TX	76021	817-785-6217		367
Warranty Life Services Inc 4152 Meridian St Ste 105-29 *TF:* 888-927-7269 ■ *Web:* www.warrantylife.com	Bellingham	WA	98226	888-927-7269		393
Warrell Corp 1250 Slate Hill Rd *Web:* warrellcorp.com	Camp Hill	PA	17011	717-761-5440	761-5702	296-8
Warren & Baerg Manufacturing Inc 39950 Rd 108 *Web:* www.warrenbaerg.com	Dinuba	CA	93618	559-591-6790	591-5728	273
Warren & Kallianos, Attorneys At Law 301 S Mcdowell St Ste 610 *Web:* warren-kallianos.com	Charlotte	NC	28204	704-377-7777		41
Warren & Panzer Engineers PC 228 E 45th St 2nd Fl *Web:* www.warrenpanzer.com	New York	NY	10017	212-922-0077		256
Warren Associates (WA) 290 Rickenbacker Cir *Web:* www.warrenrep.com	Livermore	CA	94551	925-449-9000		253
Warren Averett Kimbrough & Marino LLC 2500 Acton Rd *Web:* warrenaverett.com	Birmingham	AL	35243	205-979-4100	979-6313	2
Warren Co, The 2201 Loveland Ave *TF:* 800-562-0357 ■ *Web:* www.thewarrencompany.com	Erie	PA	16506	800-562-0357		295
Warren Correctional Institution 5787 OH-63 *Web:* drc.ohio.gov	Lebanon	OH	45036	513-932-3388	933-0150	213
Warren Correctional Institution 379 Collins Rd *Web:* www.ncdps.gov	Manson	NC	27553	252-456-3400	456-4300	213

	Phone	Fax	Class
Warren County 413 Second St PO Box 900 .... Belvidere NJ 07823 *Web:* www.co.warren.nj.us	908-750-8100	475-2026	338
Warren County 220 N Commerce Ave Ste 100 .... Front Royal VA 22630 *TF:* 800-248-6342 ■ *Web:* www.warrencountyva.net	540-636-4600	636-6066	338
Warren County 115 N Howard St PO Box 337 .... Indianola IA 50125 *Web:* www.warrencountyia.org	515-961-1122	961-1078	338
Warren County 406 Justice Dr .... Lebanon OH 45036 *TF:* 800-282-0253 ■ *Web:* www.co.warren.oh.us	513-695-1358		338
Warren County 100 W Broadway .... Monmouth IL 61462 *Web:* www.warrencountyil.com	309-734-8592	734-7406	338
Warren County 1009 Cherry St .... Vicksburg MS 39183 *Web:* co.warren.ms.us	601-636-4415	630-8016	338
Warren County 46 S Norwood St PO Box 27 .... Warrenton GA 30828 *Web:* www.warrencountyga.com	706-465-9604		338
Warren County 104 W Main Ste E .... Warrenton MO 63383 *Web:* warrencountymo.org	636-456-3331		338
Warren County 602 W Ridgeway St PO Box 619 .... Warrenton NC 27589 *Web:* www.warrencountync.com	252-257-3115	257-5971	338
Warren County 125 N Monroe St Ste 11 .... Williamsport IN 47993 *Web:* www.in.gov	765-762-3510	762-7251	338
Warren County Chamber of Commerce (WCCBI) 308 Market St .... Warren PA 16365 *Web:* wccbi.org	814-723-3050	723-6024	139
Warren County Community College 475 Rt 57 W .... Washington NJ 07882 *Web:* www.warren.edu	908-835-9222		162
Warren County Library 2 Shotwell Dr .... Belvidere NJ 07823 *Web:* warrenlib.com	908-475-6322	475-1558	434-3
Warren County Rural Electric Membership Corp 15 Midway St PO Box 37 .... Williamsport IN 47993 *TF:* 800-872-7319 ■ *Web:* www.wcremc.com	765-762-6114		245
Warren County Visitors Bureau 22045 Rt 6 .... Warren PA 16365 *TF:* 800-624-7802 ■ *Web:* wcvb.net	814-726-1222		206
Warren County-Vicksburg Public Library 700 Veto St .... Vicksburg MS 39180 *Web:* warren.lib.ms.us	601-636-6411	634-4809	434-3
Warren Distributing Inc (WDI) 8737 Dice Rd .... Santa Fe Springs CA 90670 *Web:* www.warrendist.com	562-789-3360	789-3361	61
Warren Distribution Inc 727 S 13th St .... Omaha NE 68102 *Web:* www.warrendistribution.com	402-341-9397		463
Warren Dunes State Park 12032 Red Arrow Hwy .... Sawyer MI 49125 *Web:* www.michigan.org	269-426-4013		565
Warren Electric Co-opeartive Inc (WEC) 320 E Main St PO Box 208 .... Youngsville PA 16371 *TF:* 800-364-8640 ■ *Web:* www.warrencc.coop	814-563-7548	563-7012	245
Warren Elizabeth (Sen D - MA) 309 Hart Senate Office Bldg .... Washington DC 20510 *Web:* www.warren.senate.gov	202-224-4543		342-2
Warren Fabricating & Machining 3240 Mahoning Ave NW .... Warren OH 44483 *TF:* 800-827-0596 ■ *Web:* warfab.com	800-827-0596		454
Warren General Hospital 2 Crescent Pk W .... Warren PA 16365 *TF:* 800-777-9441 ■ *Web:* wgh.org	814-726-1424		374-3
Warren Gibson Ltd 206 Church St S PO Box 100 .... Alliston ON L9R1T9 *TF:* 800-461-4374 ■ *Web:* www.warrengibson.com	705-435-4342		478
Warren Group Inc, The 7805 St Andrews Rd .... Irmo SC 29063 *Web:* www.warrenforensics.com	803-732-6600		261
Warren Hospital 185 Roseberry St .... Phillipsburg NJ 08865 *TF:* 800-220-8116 ■ *Web:* www.warrenhospital.org	908-859-6700		374-3
Warren Industries Inc 3100 Mt Pleasant St .... Racine WI 53404 *Web:* www.wrnind.com	262-639-7800	639-0920	549
Warren Island State Park PO Box 105 .... Lincolnville ME 04849 *Web:* www.maine.gov	207-446-7090		565
Warren Management Group Inc, The 1720 Jet Stream Dr Ste 200 .... Colorado Springs CO 80921 *Web:* www.warrenmgmt.com	719-534-0266		463
Warren Oil Company Inc PO Box 1507 .... Dunn NC 28335 *TF:* 800-779-6456 ■ *Web:* www.warrenoil.com	910-892-6456		579
Warren Paving Inc 562 Elks Lake Rd PO Box 572 .... Hattiesburg MS 39403 *Web:* warrenpaving.com	601-544-7811	544-2005	186
Warren Power & Machinery LP 4501 W Reno Ave .... Oklahoma City OK 73127 *Web:* www.warrencat.com	405-947-6771		264-3
Warren Printing & Mailing Inc 5000 Eagle Rock Blvd .... Los Angeles CA 90041 *TF:* 888-468-6976 ■ *Web:* print-mail.com	323-258-2621		627
Warren Printing & Office Products Inc 250 E Main St .... Ottawa OH 45875 *TF:* 800-752-2908 ■ *Web:* www.warrenprint.com	419-523-3635	523-3243	744
Warren Properties Inc PO Box 469114 .... Escondido CA 92046 *TF:* 800-831-0804 ■ *Web:* www.warrenproperties.com	800-831-0804		655
Warren Public Library 5460 Arden .... Warren MI 48092 *Web:* www.warrenlibrary.net	586-751-5377		434-3
Warren Pumps LLC 82 Bridges Ave .... Warren MA 01083 *Web:* www.warrenpumps.com	413-436-7711		641
Warren Resources Inc 1114 Avenue of the Americas 34th Fl .... New York NY 10036 *NASDAQ: WRES* ■ *TF:* 877-587-9494 ■ *Web:* www.warrenresources.com	212-697-9660	697-9466	536
Warren Rupp Inc 800 N Main St .... Mansfield OH 44902 *Web:* www.warrenruppinc.com	419-524-8388		641
Warren Rural Electric Co-opeartive Corp 951 Fairview Ave .... Bowling Green KY 42101 *TF:* 866-319-3234 ■ *Web:* www.wrecc.com	270-842-6541	781-3299	245
Warren State Hospital 33 Main Dr .... North Warren PA 16365 *Web:* www.dhs.pa.gov	814-723-5500		374-5
Warren Technology Inc 2050 W 73 St .... Hialeah FL 33016 *Web:* www.warrenhvac.com	305-556-6933		360-3
Warren Tire Service Center Inc 4 Highland Ave .... Queensbury NY 12804 *Web:* warrentiresvc.com	518-792-0316		62-5
Warren Transport Inc 210 Beck Ave .... Waterloo IA 50701 *TF:* 800-526-3053 ■ *Web:* www.warrentransport.com	800-526-3053		780
Warren Trask Co 1481 Central St .... Stoughton MA 02072 *Web:* wtrask.com	781-341-2426		191-3
Warren Whitney Sherwood & Company Inc 7231 Forest Ave .... Richmond VA 23226 *Web:* www.warrenwhitney.com	804-282-9566		463
Warren Wilson College 701 Warren Wilson Rd .... Swannanoa NC 28778 **Fax Area Code: 828* ■ *TF:* 800-934-3536 ■ *Web:* www.warren-wilson.edu	800-934-3536	298-1440*	166
Warren-Boynton State Bank 702 W Illinois St PO Box 19 .... New Berlin IL 62670 *Web:* wbsb.net	217-488-6091	488-6216	70
Warrensburg Chamber of Commerce 3839 Main St Ste 2 .... Warrensburg NY 12885 *Web:* www.warrensburgchamber.com	518-623-2161	623-2184	139
Warrenton Oil Co 2299 S Spoede .... Truesdale MO 63383 *Web:* www.fastlane-cstore.com	636-456-3346		345
Warren-Trumbull County Public Library 444 Mahoning Ave NW .... Warren OH 44483 *Web:* www.wtcpl.org	330-399-8807		434-3
Warrick County 185 Dusty Rd .... Boonville IN 47601 *Web:* www.warrickcounty.gov	812-897-6120	897-6189	338
Warrick County Chamber of Commerce 224 W Main St Ste 203 .... Boonville IN 47601 *Web:* warrickchamber.org	812-897-2340	897-2360	139
Warrick Publishing Inc 204 W Locust St PO Box 266 .... Boonville IN 47601 *Web:* www.warricknews.com	812-897-2330	897-3703	637-8
Warrior Consultant Group 3463 Daisy Ct .... Brunswick OH 44212 *Web:* warriorgroup.com	330-225-5120		196
Warrior Custom Golf 15 Mason Ste A .... Irvine CA 92618 *TF:* 800-600-5113 ■ *Web:* www.warriorcustomgolf.com	800-574-9790		711
Warrior Met Coal Inc 16243 Hwy 216 .... Brookwood AL 35444 *Web:* www.warriormetcoal.com	205-554-6150		501
Warrior Roofing Manufacturing Inc 3050 Warrior Rd .... Tuscaloosa AL 35404 *TF:* 800-749-3358 ■ *Web:* www.warriorroofing.com	205-553-1734	553-1755	46
Warriors' Path State Park 312 Rosa L Parks Ave .... Nashville TN 37243 *Web:* tnstateparks.com	423-239-8531		565
Warsaw Chemical Company Inc Argonne Rd PO Box 858 .... Warsaw IN 46580 *TF:* 800-548-3396 ■ *Web:* www.warsaw-chem.com	574-267-3251	267-3884	151
Warschawski 1501 Sulgrave Ave Ste 350 .... Baltimore MD 21209 *Web:* www.warschawski.com	410-367-2700		636
Warshauer Electric Supply Co 800 Shrewsbury Ave .... Tinton Falls NJ 07724 *Web:* www.warshauer.com	732-741-6400	741-3866	246
WARSHAW Di CARLO & ASSOCIATES PC 77 Newbury St .... Boston MA 02116 *Web:* www.warshawdicarlo.com	617-262-7800	395-2705	428
Warshaw Group Inc 475 Park Ave S 11th Fl .... New York NY 10016 *Web:* www.warshawgroup.com	212-966-4056		463
Wartburg College 100 Wartburg Blvd .... Waverly IA 50677 *TF:* 800-772-2085 ■ *Web:* www.wartburg.edu	319-352-8264	352-8579	166
Wartburg Theological Seminary 333 Wartburg Pl .... Dubuque IA 52003 *TF:* 800-225-5987 ■ *Web:* www.wartburgseminary.edu	563-589-0200	589-0333	167-3
Wartsila North America Inc 11710 N Gessner Rd Ste A .... Houston TX 77064 *Web:* www.wartsila.com	281-233-6200	233-6233	262
Warwick Academy of Beauty Culture 1800 Post Rd .... Warwick RI 02886 *Web:* www.costinswa.tripod.com	401-737-4946		167-3
Warwick Center for the Art's 3259 Post Rd .... Warwick RI 02886 *Web:* warwickcfa.org	401-737-0010		520
Warwick Denver Hotel 1776 Grant St .... Denver CO 80203 *TF:* 800-203-3232 ■ *Web:* warwickhotels.com	303-861-2000	832-0320	379
Warwick Ice Cream Co 743 Bald Hill Rd .... Warwick RI 02886 *Web:* www.warwickicecreamco.com	401-821-8403		296-25
Warwick Investment Management Inc 4444 Carter Creek Pkwy Ste 109 .... Bryan TX 77802 *Web:* www.warwickpartners.net	979-260-9777	260-9712	401
Warwick Mall 400 Bald Hill Rd Ste 100 .... Warwick RI 02886 *Web:* www.warwickmall.com	401-739-7500		460
Warwick Manor Behavioral Health Inc 3680 Warwick Rd .... East New Market MD 21631 *Web:* www.warwickmanor.org	410-943-8108		726
Warwick Mechanical Group 11048 Warwick Blvd .... Newport News VA 23601 *Web:* warwickmechanicalgroup.com	757-599-6111		189-10
Warwick Public Library (WPL) 600 Sandy Ln .... Warwick RI 02889 *Web:* warwicklibrary.org	401-739-5440		434-3
Warwick Valley Chamber of Commerce (WVCC) PO Box 202 .... Warwick NY 10990 *TF:* 877-598-7245 ■ *Web:* www.warwickcc.org	845-986-2720		139
Warwick Valley Telephone Co 47 Main St PO Box 592 .... Warwick NY 10990 *TF:* 800-952-7642 ■ *Web:* www.wvtc.com	845-986-8080		736
WAS (Wood Advisory Services Inc) 3700 Rte 44 Ste 102 .... Millbrook NY 12545 *Web:* www.woodadvisory.com	845-677-3091	677-6547	261
Wasabi Japanese Restaurant 449 State St .... Madison WI 53703 *Web:* wasabi-madison.com	608-255-5020		671
Wasabi Japanese Steak House 226 Lovell Rd .... Knoxville TN 37934 *Web:* www.wasabi-steakhouse.com	865-675-0201		671

Name / Address	City	State	ZIP	Phone	Fax	Class
Wasabi Rabbit Inc						
200 Broadway Ste 4018	New York	NY	10038	646-366-0000		195
Web: www.wasabirabbit.com						
Wasabi Systems Inc						
500 E Main St Ste 1520	Norfolk	VA	23510	757-248-9601	299-8075	809
Web: www.wasabisystems.com						
Wasatch Academy 120 S 100 W	Mount Pleasant	UT	84647	435-462-1400	462-1450	622
TF: 800-634-4690 ■ *Web:* wasatchacademy.org						
Wasatch Container Inc						
645 N 400 W	North Salt Lake	UT	84054	801-295-8888		45
Web: www.wasatchcontainer.com						
Wasatch County 25 N Main St	Heber City	UT	84032	435-657-3221		338
Web: www.wasatch.utah.gov						
Wasatch Detailing Corp						
57 W Guest Ave	Salt Lake City	UT	84115	801-268-6161		225
Web: wasatchdetailing.com						
Wasatch Electric						
2455 W 1500 S Ste A	Salt Lake City	UT	84104	801-487-4511	487-5032	189-4
Web: wasatchelectric.com						
Wasatch Metal Recycling						
205 W 3300 S	Salt Lake City	UT	84115	801-305-3700		660
Web: www.wasatchmetal.com						
Wasatch Mountain State Park						
1281 Warm Springs Rd PO Box 10	Midway	UT	84049	435-654-1791		565
Web: stateparks.utah.gov						
Wasatch Photonics 1305 N 1000 W Ste 120	Logan	UT	84321	435-752-4301	752-4306	592
Web: wasatchphotonics.com						
Wasatch Wave, The 165 S 100 W	Heber City	UT	84032	435-654-5085		637-10
Web: www.wasatchwave.com						
WASC 985 Atlantic Ave	Alameda	CA	94501	510-748-9001	748-9797	49-5
Web: www.wscuc.org						
Waschuk Pipe Line Construction Ltd						
127-39015 Hwy 2A	Red Deer	AB	T4N2A3	403-346-1114		539
Web: www.waschukpipeline.com						
Wasco County 511 Washington St	The Dalles	OR	97058	541-506-2530		338
Web: co.wasco.or.us						
Wasco Electric Co-opeartive Inc						
PO Box 1700	The Dalles	OR	97058	541-296-2740		245
TF: 800-341-8580 ■ *Web:* www.wascoelectric.com						
Wasco Hardfacing Co 2660 S E Ave	Fresno	CA	93706	559-485-5860	233-4436	273
TF: 888-485-5860 ■ *Web:* www.ag1.net						
WASCO Inc 1122 Second Ave N Ste B	Nashville	TN	37208	615-244-9090	726-2643	189-7
Web: www.wascomasonry.com						
Wasco Products Inc						
85 Spencer Dr Unit A PO Box 559	Wells	ME	04090	800-388-0293		329
TF: 800-388-0293 ■ *Web:* www.wascoskylights.com						
Waseca County 307 N State St	Waseca	MN	56093	507-835-0610	835-0633	338
Web: www.co.waseca.mn.us						
WASH Laundry						
100 N Sepulveda Blvd 12th Fl	El Segundo	CA	90245	800-421-6897		38
TF: 800-421-6897 ■ *Web:* www.washlaundry.com						
Wash Tub, The 2208 NW Loop 410	San Antonio	TX	78230	210-493-8822		62-1
TF: 866-493-8822 ■ *Web:* washtub.com						
Washakie County PO Box 260	Worland	WY	82401	307-366-2434	347-9366	338
Web: www.washakiecounty.net						
Washakie Renewable Energy LLC						
3950 S 700 E Ste 100	Salt Lake City	UT	84107	801-327-8695	290-2093	536
Web: wrebiofuels.com						
Washburn County						
c/o Washburn County County Clerk's Office 10 4th Ave						
PO Box 639	Shell Lake	WI	54871	800-367-3306	468-4725*	338
**Fax Area Code:* 715 ■ *TF:* 800-469-6562 ■ *Web:* www.co.washburn.wi.us						
Washburn Institute of Technology						
5724 SW Huntoon St	Topeka	KS	66604	785-273-7140		167-3
TF: 877-588-7140 ■ *Web:* www.washburntech.edu						
Washburn University						
1700 SW College Ave	Topeka	KS	66621	785-670-1010	670-1079	166
TF: 800-736-9060 ■ *Web:* www.washburn.edu						
Washburne Culinary Institute						
740 W 63rd St	Chicago	IL	60621	773-602-5466		167-3
Web: www.washburneculinary.com						
Washers Inc 33375 Glendale St	Livonia	MI	48150	734-523-1000		488
Web: www.alphausa.com						
Washington						
Administrative Office of the Courts						
1112 Quince St SE PO Box 41174	Olympia	WA	98504	360-753-3365		339-48
Web: www.courts.wa.gov						
Aging & Disability Services Administration						
4450 Tenth Ave SE	Lacey	WA	98503	360-725-2300	407-0369	339-48
TF: 800-422-3263 ■ *Web:* www.dshs.wa.gov						
Agriculture Dept						
1111 Washington St SE Natural Resources Bldg	Olympia	WA	98501	360-902-1800	902-2092	339-48
Web: agr.wa.gov						
Arts Commission						
711 Capitol Way S Ste 600	Olympia	WA	98504	360-753-3860	586-5351	339-48
Web: www.arts.wa.gov						
Attorney General						
1125 Washington St SE PO Box 40100	Olympia	WA	98504	360-753-6200		339-48
Web: www.atg.wa.gov						
Child Support Div PO Box 11520	Tacoma	WA	98411	360-664-5321	664-5303	339-48
TF: 800-457-6202 ■ *Web:* www.dshs.wa.gov						
Corrections Dept						
7345 Linderson Way SW	Tumwater	WA	98501	360-725-8213		339-48
Web: www.doc.wa.gov						
Ecology Dept 300 Desmond Dr SE	Olympia	WA	98504	360-407-6000	407-6989	339-48
Web: ecology.wa.gov						
Emergency Management Div						
20 Aviation Dr Bldg 20 TA-20	Camp Murray	WA	98430	253-512-7000		339-48
TF: 800-562-6108 ■ *Web:* www.mil.wa.gov						
Employment Security Dept						
212 Maple Park Ave SE	Olympia	WA	98501	360-902-9500		259
TF: 800-318-6022 ■ *Web:* esd.wa.gov						
Financial Institutions Dept						
PO Box 41200	Olympia	WA	98504	360-902-8703	586-5068	339-48
TF: 877-746-4334 ■ *Web:* dfi.wa.gov						
Fish & Wildlife Dept						
1111 Washington St SE Natural Resources Bldg	Olympia	WA	98501	360-902-2200	902-2156	339-48
Web: wdfw.wa.gov						
Health Dept PO Box 47890	Olympia	WA	98504	360-236-4220		339-48
Web: www.doh.wa.gov						
Higher Education Coordinating Board						
917 Lakeridge Way PO Box 43430	Olympia	WA	98504	360-753-7800		725
Web: wsac.wa.gov						
Historical Society 1911 Pacific Ave	Tacoma	WA	98402	253-272-3500	272-9518	339-48
TF: 888-238-4373 ■ *Web:* www.washingtonhistory.org						
Horse Racing Commission						
6326 Martin Way E Ste 209	Olympia	WA	98516	360-459-6462	459-6461	712
Web: www.whrc.wa.gov						
Housing Finance Commission						
1000 Second Ave Ste 2700	Seattle	WA	98104	206-464-7139	587-5113	339-48
TF: 800-767-4663 ■ *Web:* www.wshfc.org						
Indeterminate Sentence Review Board						
4317 Sixth Ave SE	Olympia	WA	98504	360-407-2400	493-9287	339-48
TF: 866-948-9266 ■ *Web:* www.doc.wa.gov						
Insurance Commissioner						
5000 Capitol Blvd SE	Tumwater	WA	98501	360-725-7000	586-3535	339-48
Web: www.insurance.wa.gov						
Labor & Industries Dept PO Box 44000	Olympia	WA	98504	360-902-5800	902-5798	339-48
TF: 800-831-5227 ■ *Web:* www.lni.wa.gov						
Legislature 106 Legislative Bldg	Olympia	WA	98504	360-786-7573		339-48
Web: leg.wa.gov						
Licensing Dept PO Box 9020	Olympia	WA	98507	360-902-3600		339-48
Web: www.dol.wa.gov						
Lieutenant Governor						
416 Sid Snyder Ave SW PO Box 40400	Olympia	WA	98504	360-786-7700	786-7749	339-48
Web: www.ltgov.wa.gov						
Natural Resources Dept						
1111 Washington St SE Natural Resources Bldg	Olympia	WA	98504	360-902-1000		339-48
TF: 800-258-5990 ■ *Web:* www.dnr.wa.gov						
Office of Superintendent Public Instruction Dept						
600 Washington St SE PO Box 47200	Olympia	WA	98504	360-725-6265		339-48
Web: www.k12.wa.us						
Professional Educator Standards Board						
600 Washington St SE	Olympia	WA	98504	360-725-6275		339-48
Web: www.pesb.wa.gov						
Public Disclosure Commission						
711 Capitol Way Ste 206 PO Box 40908	Olympia	WA	98504	360-753-1111	753-1112	265
TF: 877-601-2828 ■ *Web:* www.pdc.wa.gov						
Revenue Dept PO Box 47478	Olympia	WA	98504	360-705-6714	705-6655	339-48
TF: 800-647-7706 ■ *Web:* dor.wa.gov						
Secretary of State PO Box 40220	Olympia	WA	98504	360-902-4151		339-48
TF: 800-822-1065 ■ *Web:* www.sos.wa.gov						
Securities Div PO Box 9033	Olympia	WA	98507	360-902-8760	902-0524	339-48
Web: dfi.wa.gov						
Social & Health Services Dept						
PO Box 45131	Olympia	WA	98504	360-902-8088		339-48
TF: 800-737-0617 ■ *Web:* www.wa.gov						
State Lottery PO Box 43000	Olympia	WA	98504	360-664-4720	664-2630	452
TF: 800-545-7510 ■ *Web:* www.walottery.com						
State Parks & Recreation Commission						
1111 Israel Rd SW	Tumwater	WA	98501	360-725-9770		339-48
Web: parks.state.wa.us						
State Patrol						
General Administration Bldg PO Box 42600	Olympia	WA	98504	360-596-4000		339-48
Web: www.wsp.wa.gov						
Supreme Court						
325 Washington St NE PMB 405	Olympia	WA	98504	360-357-2077		339-48
Transportation Dept PO Box 47300	Olympia	WA	98504	360-705-7000		339-48
TF: 888-808-7977 ■ *Web:* www.wsdot.wa.gov						
Utilities & Transportation Commission						
1300 S Evergreen Pk Dr SW PO Box 47250	Olympia	WA	98504	360-664-1160	664-1150	339-48
TF: 888-333-9882 ■ *Web:* www.utc.wa.gov						
Veterans Affairs Dept						
1102 Quince St SE PO Box 41150	Olympia	WA	98504	360-725-2200	725-2197	339-48
TF: 800-562-0132 ■ *Web:* www.dva.wa.gov						
Vital Records Div						
325 Washington St NE PMB 405	Olympia	WA	98504	360-236-4300		339-48
Web: www.cdc.gov						
Vocational Rehabilitation Div						
PO Box 45340	Olympia	WA	98504	360-725-3636		339-48
TF: 800-637-5627 ■ *Web:* www.dshs.wa.gov						
Washington & Jefferson College						
60 S Lincoln St	Washington	PA	15301	724-222-4400	223-6534	166
TF: 888-926-3529 ■ *Web:* www.washjeff.edu						
Washington & Lee University						
204 W Washington St	Lexington	VA	24450	540-458-8710	458-8062	166
TF: 800-221-3943 ■ *Web:* wlu.edu						
Washington & Lee University School of Law						
1 Denny Cir	Lexington	VA	24450	540-458-8502	458-8586	167-1
Web: law.wlu.edu						
Washington Academy						
66 Cutler Rd PO Box 190	East Machias	ME	04630	207-255-8301	255-8303	622
Web: www.washingtonacademy.org						
Washington Adventist University						
7600 Flower Ave	Takoma Park	MD	20912	301-891-4000	891-4167	166
TF: 800-835-4212 ■ *Web:* www.wau.edu						
Washington Area Chamber of Commerce						
323 W Main St	Washington	MO	63090	636-239-2715		139
Web: www.washmo.org						
Washington Area Teachers Federal Credit Union						
75 Landings Dr	Washington	PA	15301	724-222-8064		219
TF: 800-830-3078 ■ *Web:* watfcu.org						
Washington Association of Realtors						
128 Tenth Ave SW PO Box 719	Olympia	WA	98501	360-943-3100	357-6627	656
TF: 800-562-6024 ■ *Web:* www.warealtor.org						
Washington Ballet						
3515 Wisconsin Ave NW	Washington	DC	20016	202-362-3606	362-1311	573-1
Web: www.washingtonballet.org						
Washington Baptist University						
4302 Evergreen Ln	Annandale	VA	22003	703-333-5904	333-5906	167-3
Web: www.wuv.edu						
Washington Business Bank						
223 Fifth Ave SE	Olympia	WA	98501	360-754-1945		70
Web: wabizbank.com						
Washington Business Group on Health (WBGH)						
20 F St NW Ste 200	Washington	DC	20001	202-628-9320	628-9244	48-17
Web: www.businessgrouphealth.org						

	Phone	Fax	Class
Washington Capital Management Inc 1200 6th Ave Ste 700 .... Seattle WA 98101 *Web:* www.wa-cap.com	206-382-0825	382-0950	401
Washington Center for the Performing Arts 512 Washington St SE .... Olympia WA 98501 *Web:* www.washingtoncenter.org	360-753-8586	754-1177	572
Washington Chain & Supply Inc 2901 Utah Ave S PO Box 3645 .... Seattle WA 98124 *TF:* 800-851-3429 ■ *Web:* www.wachain.com	206-623-8500	621-9834	770
Washington City Paper 2390 Champlain St NW .... Washington DC 20009 *Web:* www.washingtoncitypaper.com	202-332-2100		532-5
Washington College 300 Washington Ave .... Chestertown MD 21620 *TF:* 800-422-1782 ■ *Web:* www.washcoll.edu	410-778-2800	778-7287	166
Washington Company School District 501 Industrial Dr .... Sandersville GA 31082 *Web:* www.washington.k12.ga.us	478-552-3981		685
Washington Consulting Group Inc 4915 Auburn Ave Ste 301 .... Bethesda MD 20814 *Web:* washcg.com	301-656-2330	656-1996	180
Washington Convention Center Authority 801 Mt Vernon Pl NW .... Washington DC 20001 *Web:* www.dcconvention.com	202-249-3000		205
Washington Corp PO Box 16630 .... Missoula MT 59808 *Web:* www.washingtoncompanies.com	406-523-1300	523-1399	261
Washington Correctional Facility 72 Lock 11 Rd .... Comstock NY 12821 *Web:* www.doccs.ny.gov	518-639-4486		213
Washington Correctional Industries 801 88th Ave SE .... Tumwater WA 98501 *TF:* 800-628-4738 ■ *Web:* www.washingtonci.com	360-725-9100	753-0219	630
Washington Corrections Center for Women (WCCW) 9601 Bujacich Rd NW .... Gig Harbor WA 98332 *Web:* www.doc.wa.gov	253-858-4200		213
Washington County 1 Government Center Pl Ste A .... Abingdon VA 24210 *Web:* www.washcova.com	276-525-1300	525-1309	338
Washington County 150 Ash Ave .... Akron CO 80720 *Web:* www.colorado.gov	970-345-2701	345-2702	338
Washington County PO Box 466 .... Blair NE 68008 *Web:* www.co.washington.ne.us	402-426-6822	426-6825	338
Washington County 14600 Saint Stephens Ave .... Chatom AL 36518 *Web:* www.washingtoncountyal.com	251-847-2214		338
Washington County 280 N College Ave Ste 300 .... Fayetteville AR 72701 *TF:* 800-563-0012 ■ *Web:* www.co.washington.ar.us	479-444-1711	444-1894	338
Washington County 383 Broadway Bldg A .... Fort Edward NY 12828 *Web:* washingtoncountyny.gov	518-746-2170	746-2177	338
Washington County PO Box 1276 .... Greenville MS 38702 *Web:* www.washingtoncounty.ms	662-378-2747	334-2698	338
Washington County 100 W Washington St .... Hagerstown MD 21740 *Web:* www.washco-md.net	240-313-2200		338
Washington County 155 N First Ave .... Hillsboro OR 97124 *TF:* 800-735-1232 ■ *Web:* www.co.washington.or.us	503-846-8611		338
Washington County PO Box 297 .... Machias ME 04654 *Web:* www.washingtoncountymaine.com	207-255-3127	255-3313	338
Washington County 223 Putnam St .... Marietta OH 45750 *Web:* www.washingtongov.org	740-373-6623	374-7693	338
Washington County 116 Adams St PO Box 1007 .... Plymouth NC 27962 *Web:* www.washconc.org	252-793-5823	793-1183	338
Washington County 102 N Missouri St .... Potosi MO 63664 *Web:* www.washingtoncountymo.us	573-438-6111	438-2009	338
Washington County 99 Public Sq Ste 103 .... Salem IN 47167 *TF:* 800-453-1978 ■ *Web:* www.washingtoncounty.in.gov	812-883-4805		338
Washington County 119 Jones St .... Sandersville GA 31082 *Web:* washingtoncountyga.gov	478-552-2325	552-7424	338
Washington County 109 N Cross Main PO Box 126 .... Springfield KY 40069 *Web:* washingtoncountyky.com	859-336-5410	336-5407	338
Washington County 14949 62nd St N .... Stillwater MN 55082 *Web:* www.co.washington.mn.us	651-430-6001	430-6017	338
Washington County 224 W Main St .... Washington IA 52353 *Web:* co.washington.ia.us	319-653-7741	653-7787	338
Washington County 214 C St .... Washington KS 66968 *Web:* www.washingtoncountyks.gov	785-325-2461	325-2303	338
Washington County 1 S Main St Ste 1005 .... Washington PA 15301 *Web:* www.co.washington.pa.us	724-228-6787		338
Washington County 256 East Ct .... Weiser ID 83672 *Web:* www.co.washington.id.us	208-414-2092	414-3925	338
Washington County 432 E Washington St Ste 2027 .... West Bend WI 53095 *TF:* 800-616-0446 ■ *Web:* www.co.washington.wi.us	262-335-4400	306-2208	338
Washington County *Oklahoma* 400 S Johnstone Ave .... Bartlesville OK 74003 *Web:* countycourthouse.org	918-337-2840		338
Washington County Board of Education 802 Washington St .... Plymouth NC 27962 *Web:* www.washingtonco.k12.nc.us	252-793-5171		685
Washington County Chamber of Commerce 375 Southpointe Blvd Ste 240 .... Canonsburg PA 15317 *Web:* www.washcochamber.com	724-225-3010	228-7337	139
Washington County Chamber of Commerce 1 Government Center Pl Ste D .... Abingdon VA 24210 *Web:* www.washingtonvachamber.org	276-628-8141	628-3984	139
Washington County Chamber of Commerce, The 1 S Potomac St .... Hagerstown MD 21740 *Web:* www.hagerstown.org	301-739-2015		139
Washington County Community College 1 College Dr .... Calais ME 04619 *TF:* 800-210-6932 ■ *Web:* www.wccc.me.edu	207-454-1000		162
Washington County Historical Society (WCHS) 118 E Dickson St .... Fayetteville AR 72701 *Web:* www.washcohistoricalsociety.org	479-521-2970		637-2

	Phone	Fax	Class
Washington County Mental Health Services Inc (WCMHS) PO Box 647 .... Montpelier VT 05602 *Web:* www.wcmhs.org	802-229-1399	223-8623	353
Washington County Museum of Fine Arts 401 Museum Dr PO Box 423 .... Hagerstown MD 21741 *Web:* www.wcmfa.org	301-739-5727		520
Washington County News 1364 N Railroad Ave .... Chipley FL 32428 *Web:* www.chipleypaper.com	850-547-9414		532-2
Washington County Public Library 205 Oak Hill St .... Abingdon VA 24210 *Web:* www.wcpl.net	276-676-6222		434-3
Washington County Public Library 100 Putnam St .... Marietta OH 45750 *Web:* www.wcplib.info	740-373-1057	373-2860	434-3
Washington County State Recreation Area 18500 Conservation Dr .... Nashville IL 62263 *Web:* www2.illinois.gov	618-327-3137		565
Washington County Texas 100 E Main St Ste 102 .... Brenham TX 77833 *Web:* www.co.washington.tx.us	979-277-6200	277-6278	338
Washington County Visitors Assn 12725 SW Millikan Way Ste 210 .... Beaverton OR 97005 *TF:* 800-537-3149 ■ *Web:* tualatinvalley.org	503-644-5555	644-9784	206
Washington Courier 100 Ford Ln .... Washington IL 61571 *Web:* www.courierpapers.com	309-444-3139		532-4
Washington Court Hotel 525 New Jersey Ave NW .... Washington DC 20001 *TF:* 800-321-3010 ■ *Web:* www.washingtoncourthotel.com	202-628-2100		379
Washington Crossing State Park 355 Washington Crossing-Pennington Rd .... Titusville NJ 08560 *Web:* www.njparksandforests.org	609-737-0623		565
Washington Daily News, The 217 N Market St .... Washington NC 27889 *Web:* www.wdnweb.com	252-946-2144		532-3
Washington DC Accommodations 2201 Wisconsin Ave NW Ste C-120 .... Washington DC 20007 *TF:* 800-503-3330 ■ *Web:* www.wdcahotels.com	202-289-2220		376
Washington (DC) City Hall 1350 Pennsylvania Ave NW 326 .... Washington DC 20004 *Web:* dc.gov	202-724-7173	727-0278	337
Washington DC Convention & Tourism Corp 901 Seventh St NW 4th Fl .... Washington DC 20001 *TF:* 800-422-8644 ■ *Web:* washington.org	202-789-7001		206
Washington Democratic Party PO Box 4027 .... Seattle WA 98194 *Web:* www.wa-democrats.org	206-583-0664		616-1
Washington Dental Service 9706 Fourth Ave NE .... Seattle WA 98115 *TF:* 800-367-4104 ■ *Web:* www.deltadentalwa.com	206-522-1300		391-3
Washington Duke Inn & Golf Club 3001 Cameron Blvd .... Durham NC 27705 *Web:* www.washingtondukeinn.com	919-490-0999	688-0105	379
Washington Dulles International Airport 1 Saarinen Cir .... Dulles VA 20166 *Web:* www.flydulles.com	703-572-2700		27
Washington Education Association Inc 32032 Weyerhaeuser Way S PO Box 9100 .... Federal Way WA 98001 *TF:* 800-622-3393 ■ *Web:* www.washingtonea.org	253-941-6700		49-5
Washington Electric Co-op 40 Church St .... East Montpelier VT 05651 *TF:* 800-932-5245 ■ *Web:* www.washingtonelectric.coop	802-223-5245	223-6780	245
Washington Electric Cooperative Inc 440 Highland Ridge Rd .... Marietta OH 45750 **Fax Area Code: 877* ■ *TF:* 877-594-9324 ■ *Web:* www.weci.org	740-373-2141	440-2671*	245
Washington Electric Membership Corp 258 N Harris St .... Sandersville GA 31082 *TF:* 800-552-2577 ■ *Web:* www.washingtonemc.com	478-552-2577		245
Washington Express Service LLC 12240 Indian Creek Ct Ste 100 .... Beltsville MD 20705 *TF:* 800-939-5463 ■ *Web:* washingtonexpress.com	301-210-0899	419-7075	546
Washington Floral Service Inc 2701 S 35th St .... Tacoma WA 98409 *TF:* 800-351-5515 ■ *Web:* www.washingtonfloral.com	253-472-8343		292
Washington Gas & Light Co 101 Constitution Ave NW .... Springfield VA 22151 *Web:* www.washingtongas.com	703-750-4440		787
Washington Graphics LLC 15340 NE 92nd St Ste B .... Redmond WA 98052 *TF:* 800-511-1859 ■ *Web:* www.dreambigprintbig.com	425-376-0877		344
Washington Group Consultants LLC PO Box A .... Fairfax VA 22031 *Web:* www.washingtongroup.com	703-591-6600	591-6602	194
Washington Health System 155 Wilson Ave .... Washington PA 15301 *Web:* whs.org	724-225-7000		374-3
Washington House 5100 Fillmore Ave .... Alexandria VA 22311 *Web:* washingtonhouse.watermarkcommunities.com	703-291-0188		672
Washington Inn Hotel, The 495 Tenth St .... Oakland CA 94607 *Web:* www.thewashingtoninn.com	510-452-1776	452-4436	379
Washington International Business Report 818 Connecticut Ave NW 12th Fl .... Washington DC 20006 *Web:* ibgc.com	202-872-8181	872-8696	531-7
Washington International School 3100 Macomb St NW .... Washington DC 20008 *Web:* www.wis.edu	202-243-1815		685
Washington Iron Works Inc 400 E Lamar St .... Sherman TX 75090 *Web:* www.washingtonironworks.com	903-892-8145		454
Washington Irving's Sunnyside 3 W Sunnyside Ln .... Irvington NY 10533 *Web:* hudsonvalley.org	914-366-6900		50-3
Washington Jefferson LLC 318 W 51st St .... New York NY 10019 *TF:* 888-567-7550 ■ *Web:* www.wjhotel.com	212-246-7550		378
Washington Local Schools 3505 W Lincolnshire Blvd .... Toledo OH 43606 *TF:* 800-462-3589 ■ *Web:* wls4kids.org	419-473-8251	473-8247	186

Name / Address	City	State	Zip	Phone	Fax	Class
Washington Metropolitan Area Transit Authority						
600 Fifth St NW	Washington	DC	20001	202-637-7000		468
TF: 800-523-7009 ■ *Web:* www.wmata.com						
Washington Metropolitan Philharmonic Assn (WMPA)						
PO Box 120	Mount Vernon	VA	22121	703-799-8229	360-7391	573-3
Web: www.wmpamusic.org						
Washington Mills Electro Minerals Co						
20 N Main St	North Grafton	MA	01536	508-839-6511	839-7675	1
TF: 800-828-1666 ■ *Web:* www.washingtonmills.com						
Washington Music Ctr						
11151 Veirs Mill Rd	Wheaton	MD	20902	301-946-8808	946-0487	526
Web: www.chucklevins.com						
Washington National Cathedral						
3101 Wisconsin Ave NW	Washington	DC	20016	202-537-6200	364-6600	637-9
Web: www.cathedral.org						
Washington National Insurance Co						
11825 N Pennsylvania St	Carmel	IN	46032	866-595-2255	757-6324*	391-2
**Fax Area Code:* 800 ■ *TF:* 866-595-2255 ■ *Web:* washingtonnational.com						
Washington National Primate Research Ctr (WNPRC)						
1705 NE Pacific St PO Box 357330	Seattle	WA	98195	206-543-1430	685-0305	668
Web: www.wanprc.org						
Washington Oaks Gardens State Park						
6400 N Oceanshore Blvd	Palm Coast	FL	32137	386-446-6780	446-6781	565
Web: www.floridastateparks.org						
Washington Occupational Health Associates Inc						
1140 19th St NW Ste 700	Washington	DC	20036	202-463-6698	865-6525*	196
**Fax Area Code:* 800 ■ *TF:* 800-777-9642 ■ *Web:* www.woha.com						
Washington Ornamental Iron Works Inc						
17926 S Broadway	Gardena	CA	90247	310-327-8660		189-14
Web: www.washingtoniron.com						
Washington Parish 909 Pearl St	Franklinton	LA	70438	985-839-7825	839-7827	338
TF: 800-375-7570 ■ *Web:* www.washingtonparishalerts.org						
Washington Parish Library System						
825 Free St	Franklinton	LA	70438	985-839-7806	839-7808	434-3
Web: washingtonparishlibrary.info						
Washington Park Botanical Garden						
1740 W Fayette Ave	Springfield	IL	62704	217-546-4116	546-0257	97
Web: www.springfieldparks.org						
Washington Pavilion 301 S Main	Sioux Falls	SD	57104	605-367-6000	367-7399	520
TF: 877-927-4728 ■ *Web:* www.washingtonpavilion.org						
Washington Plaza Hotel						
10 Thomas Cir NW	Washington	DC	20005	202-842-1300	371-9602	379
TF: 800-424-1140 ■ *Web:* www.washingtonplazahotel.com						
Washington Press (WP) 2 Vreeland Rd	Florham Park	NJ	07932	877-966-0001	966-0888*	637-2
**Fax Area Code:* 973 ■ *TF:* 877-966-0001 ■ *Web:* www.washpress.com						
Washington Professional Systems (WPS)						
109 Gaither Dr Ste 301	Mount Laurel	NJ	08054	856-273-8688	273-8558	52
Web: www.washprosys.com						
Washington Publishing Co						
2107 Elliott Ave Ste 305	Seattle	WA	98121	425-562-2245	239-2061*	637-10
**Fax Area Code:* 775 ■ *Web:* www.wpc-edi.com						
Washington Real Estate Investment Trust (WRIT)						
1775 I St NW	Washington	DC	20006	202-774-3200	984-9610*	655
NYSE: WRE ■ **Fax Area Code:* 301 ■ *TF:* 800-565-9748 ■ *Web:* www.washreit.com						
Washington Research Foundation						
2815 Eastlake Ave E Ste 300	Seattle	WA	98102	206-336-5600		792
Web: www.wrfcapital.com						
Washington Research Library Consortium Inc, The						
901 Commerce Dr	Upper Marlboro	MD	20774	301-390-2000		434-3
Web: www.wrlc.org						
Washington Rock State Park						
355 Milltown Rd	Bridgewater	NJ	08807	908-722-1200		565
Web: www.njparksandforests.org						
Washington School District Inc						
201 Allison Ave	Washington	PA	15301	724-223-5085	223-5046	685
Web: www.washington.k12.pa.us						
Washington Space Grant Consortium						
141 Johnson Hall PO Box 351310	Seattle	WA	98195	206-543-1943	543-0179	167-3
TF: 800-659-1943 ■ *Web:* www.waspacegrant.org						
Washington Speakers Bureau						
1663 Prince St	Alexandria	VA	22314	703-838-9385		708
Web: www.wsb.com						
Washington Square Hotel						
103 Waverly Pl	New York	NY	10011	212-777-9515	979-8373	379
TF: 800-222-0418 ■ *Web:* www.washingtonsquarehotel.com						
Washington Square Shopping Ctr						
9585 SW Washington Sq Rd	Portland	OR	97223	503-639-8860		460
Web: www.shopwashingtonsquare.com						
Washington State						
Liquor & Cannabis Board						
3000 Pacific Ave SE	Olympia	WA	98504	360-664-1600		443
Web: lcb.wa.gov						
Washington State Bar Assn						
1325 Fourth Ave Ste 600	Seattle	WA	98101	206-443-9722	727-8320	72
TF: 800-945-9722 ■ *Web:* www.wsba.org						
Washington State Community College						
710 Colegate Dr	Marietta	OH	45750	740-374-8716	376-0257	162
Web: www.wscc.edu						
Washington State Convention Ctr						
705 Pike St	Seattle	WA	98101	206-694-5000	694-5399	205
Web: www.wscc.com						
Washington State Employees Credit Union						
330 Union Ave SE	Olympia	WA	98501	360-943-7911		219
TF: 800-562-0999 ■ *Web:* wsecu.org						
Washington State Medical Assn						
2001 Sixth Ave Ste 2700	Seattle	WA	98121	206-441-9762	441-5863	474
TF: 800-552-0612 ■ *Web:* wsma.org						
Washington State Nurses Assn (WSNA)						
575 Andover Pk W Ste 101	Seattle	WA	98188	206-575-7979	575-1908	533
TF: 800-231-8482 ■ *Web:* www.wsna.org						
Washington State Park						
13041 State Hwy 104	DeSoto	MO	63020	636-586-5768		565
Web: mostateparks.com						
Washington State Penitentiary						
1313 N 13th Ave	Walla Walla	WA	99362	509-525-3610		213
Web: doc.wa.gov						
Washington State Pharmacy Assn						
411 Williams Ave S	Renton	WA	98057	425-228-7171	277-3897	585
Web: www.wsparx.org						
Washington State Public Interest Research Group						
1402 Third Ave Ste 618	Seattle	WA	98101	206-568-2854		633
Web: washpirg.org						
Washington State Reformatory						
16550 177th Ave SE PO Box 777	Monroe	WA	98272	360-794-2600		213
TF: 800-483-8314 ■ *Web:* www.doc.wa.gov						
Washington State University						
PO Box 641040	Pullman	WA	99164	509-335-3564	335-4902	166
TF: 888-468-6978 ■ *Web:* wsu.edu						
Washington State University						
Spokane						
310 N Riverpoint Blvd PO Box 1495	Spokane	WA	99210	509-358-7978	358-7538	166
TF: 866-766-0767 ■ *Web:* spokane.wsu.edu						
Vancouver 14204 NE Salmon Creek Ave	Vancouver	WA	98686	360-546-9788		166
Web: www.vancouver.wsu.edu						
Washington State University - Tri Cities Campus						
2710 University Dr	Richland	WA	99354	509-372-7000		166
Web: tricities.wsu.edu						
Washington State Veterinary Medical Assn						
8024 Bracken Pl SE	Snoqualmie	WA	98065	425-396-3191		795
TF: 800-399-7862 ■ *Web:* wsvma.org						
Washington Symphony Orchestra (WSO)						
PO Box 178	Washington	PA	15301	724-223-9796		573-3
Web: washsym.org						
Washington Tennis Services (WTS)						
3200 Tower Oaks Blvd Ste 400	Rockville	MD	20852	301-622-7800	622-3373	354
Web: wtsinternational.com						
Washington Theological Union						
6896 Laurel St NW	Washington	DC	20012	202-726-8800		167-3
Washington Times, The						
3600 New York Ave NE	Washington	DC	20002	202-636-3000		532-2
Web: www.washingtontimes.com						
Washington Tool & Machine Co						
1 S Baird Ave PO Box 873	Washington	PA	15301	724-225-7470	225-7484	454
Web: www.washtool.com						
Washington Trails Assn (WTA)						
705 Second Ave Ste 300	Seattle	WA	98104	206-625-1367	625-9249	48-23
Web: www.wta.org						
Washington Trust Bancorp Inc						
23 Broad St	Westerly	RI	02891	800-475-2265		360-2
NASDAQ: WASH ■ *TF:* 800-475-2265 ■ *Web:* www.washtrust.com						
Washington United Terminals						
1815 Port of Tacoma Rd	Tacoma	WA	98421	253-396-4908		314
Web: www.uswut.com						
Washington University in Saint Louis						
1 Brookings Dr	Saint Louis	MO	63130	314-935-5000	935-4290	166
TF: 800-638-0700 ■ *Web:* wustl.edu						
Washington University in Saint Louis School of Medicine						
660 S Euclid Ave	Saint Louis	MO	63110	314-362-5000		167-2
Web: medicine.wustl.edu						
Washington University School of Law						
Anheuser-Busch Hall 1 Brookings Dr	Saint Louis	MO	63130	314-935-6400		167-1
Web: law.wustl.edu						
Washington Woodworking Company Inc						
2010 Beaver Rd	Landover Hills	MD	20785	301-341-2500	341-2512	499
Web: www.washingtonwoodworking.com						
Washington's Headquarters State Historic Site						
PO Box 1783	Newburgh	NY	12551	845-562-1195		565
Web: parks.ny.gov						
Washington's Heaquarters/Miller House						
140 Virginia Rd	White Plains	NY	10603	914-949-1236		50-3
Web: westchestergov.com						
Washington-Beaufort County Chamber of Commerce						
102 Stewart Pkwy PO Box 665	Washington	NC	27889	252-946-9168	946-9169	139
Web: www.wbcchamber.com						
Washingtonian Magazine						
1828 L St NW Ste 200	Washington	DC	20036	202-296-3600	785-1822	457-22
Web: www.washingtonian.com						
Washington-on-the-Brazos State Historic Site						
23400 Park Rd 12	Washington	TX	77880	936-878-2214		565
Web: tpwd.texas.gov						
Washington-Saint Tammany Electric Co-op						
950 Pearl St PO Box 697	Franklinton	LA	70438	985-839-3562	839-4315	245
TF: 866-672-9773 ■ *Web:* www.wste.coop						
Washita Battlefield National Historic Site						
18555 Hwy 47A	Cheyenne	OK	73628	580-497-2742	497-2712	564
Web: www.nps.gov						
Washoe County 1001 E Ninth St	Reno	NV	89512	775-328-2003		338
Web: www.washoecounty.us						
Washoe County Library (WCL) 301 S Center St	Reno	NV	89501	775-327-8300	327-8341	434-3
Web: washoecountylibrary.us						
Washoe County School District						
425 E Ninth St	Reno	NV	89512	775-348-0200		685
Web: www.washoeschools.net						
Washoe Lake State Park						
4855 E Lake Blvd	Carson City	NV	89704	775-687-4319		565
Web: www.parks.nv.gov						
Washoe Steakhouse 4201 W 4th St	Reno	NV	89523	775-786-1323		671
Web: www.washoesteakhouse.com						
Washoe Tribe 919 US Hwy 395 N	Gardnerville	NV	89410	775-265-6240		522
Web: www.washoetribe.us						
Washtenaw Community College						
4800 E Huron River Dr PO Box 1610	Ann Arbor	MI	48106	734-973-3300	677-5408	162
TF: 800-218-4341 ■ *Web:* www.wccnet.edu						
Washtenaw County PO Box 8645	Ann Arbor	MI	48107	734-222-6850	222-6715	338
TF: 800-440-7548 ■ *Web:* www.washtenaw.org						
Washtenaw County Road Commission						
555 N Zeeb Rd	Ann Arbor	MI	48103	734-761-1500	761-3239	186
Web: www.wcroads.org						
Wasley Products Inc						
87 Spring Ln Plainville Industrial Pk	Plainville	CT	06062	860-747-5586		326
Wasmer Schroeder & Company Inc						
600 Fifth Ave S Ste 210	Naples	FL	34102	239-263-6877	263-8146	401
Web: www.wasmerschroeder.com						
Wasp Barcode Technologies Inc						
1400 10th St	Plano	TX	75074	866-547-9277	547-4101*	174
**Fax Area Code:* 214 ■ *TF:* 866-547-9277 ■ *Web:* www.waspbarcode.com						

	Phone	Fax	Class
Wasserman & Partners Advertising Inc 1020 Mainland St Ste 160 .... Vancouver BC V6B2T5 *Web:* wasserman-partners.com	604-684-1111		7
Wasserman Media Group LLC 10900 Wilshire Blvd Ste 1200 ....Los Angeles CA 90024 *Web:* www.teamwass.com	310-407-0200		4
Wasserman Schultz Debbie (Rep D - FL) 1114 Longworth House Office Bldg .... Washington DC 20515 *Web:* wassermanschultz.house.gov	202-225-7931	226-2052	342-2
Wassmuth *Ctr for Human Rights education* 777 S Eigth St .... Boise ID 83702 *Web:* www.wassmuthcenter.org	208-345-0304	433-1221	50-4
Waste Control Specialists LLC 5430 LBJ Fwy Ste 1700 .... Dallas TX 75240 *Web:* www.wcstexas.com	972-715-9800	448-1419	667
Waste Industries USA Inc 3301 Benson Dr Ste 601...................... Raleigh NC 27609 *TF:* 800-647-9946 ■ *Web:* wasteindustries.com	919-325-3000		804
Waste Management American Landfill Inc 7916 Chapel St SE ....Waynesburg OH 44688 *Web:* www.americanlandfill.wm.com	330-866-3265	866-3709	660
Waste Strategies LLC 130 Admiral Cochrane Dr Ste 200 .... Annapolis MD 21401 *TF:* 866-241-1134 ■ *Web:* www.wastestrategies.com	202-302-8370		192
Waste Technology Services Inc 435 N 2nd St .... Lewiston NY 14092 *Web:* www.wtsonline.com	716-754-5400	754-8001	192
Wastech Controls & Engineering Inc 21201 Itasca St.......................... Chatsworth CA 91311 *Web:* www.wastechengineering.com	818-998-3500		261
Wastecorp Inc PO Box 70................. Grand Island NY 14072 *TF:* 888-829-2783 ■ *Web:* wastecorp.com	888-829-2783		641
Watanabe Floral Inc 1607 Hart St............. Honolulu HI 96817 *TF:* 888-832-9360 ■ *Web:* watanabefloral.com	808-832-9360		292
Watauga County Courthouse 842 W King St .... Boone NC 28607 *Web:* www.wataugacounty.org	828-265-8000	264-3230	338
Watauga County Schools 175 Pioneer Trl......... Boone NC 28607 *Web:* watauga.k12.nc.us	828-264-7190	264-7196	685
Watauga Public Library 7109 Whitley Rd............................Watauga TX 76148 *Web:* www.cowtx.org	817-514-5855	581-3910	434-3
Watch LA 1138 Wall St.....................Los Angeles CA 90015 *Web:* www.watchla.com	213-747-1838	747-2888	157-4
Watch Time Inc 1615 Santee St ....Los Angeles CA 90015 *Web:* www.watchtimeinc.net	213-748-9942	748-9941	411
WatchGuard Technologies Inc 505 Fifth Ave S Ste 500 .... Seattle WA 98104 *TF:* 800-734-9905 ■ *Web:* www.watchguard.com	206-613-6600	521-8342	176
WatchMojo 5369 St Laurent Ste 430............ Montreal QC H2T1S5 *Web:* www.watchmojo.com	514-448-1631	448-1633	514
Watchtower Bible & Tract Society Inc 25 Columbia Hts............................ Brooklyn NY 11201 *Web:* www.jw.org	718-560-5000		48-20
Watco Companies LLC 315 W Third St .... Pittsburg KS 66762 *Web:* www.watcocompanies.com	620-231-2230		650
Watcon Inc 2215 S Main St................. South Bend IN 46613 *Web:* www.watcon-inc.com	574-287-3397	287-2427	145
Watek Engineering Corp 604 S Frederick Ave Ste 309.............. Gaithersburg MD 20877 *Web:* www.watek.com	301-933-9690		261
Water Boy Inc 4454 19th Street Ct E........... Bradenton FL 34203 *TF:* 800-799-5684 ■ *Web:* waterboyinc.com	800-799-5684		366
Water Country USA 176 Water Country Pkwy ....Williamsburg VA 23185 *TF:* 800-343-7946 ■ *Web:* buschgardens.com	800-343-7946		32
Water Environment Federation (WEF) 601 Wythe St .... Alexandria VA 22314 *TF:* 800-666-0206 ■ *Web:* www.wef.org	703-684-2400	684-2492	48-13
Water Furnace International Inc 9000 Conservation Way .... Fort Wayne IN 46809 **Fax Area Code:* 260 ■ *TF:* 800-222-5667 ■ *Web:* www.waterfurnace.com	800-223-0435	747-5780*	357
Water Grill 544 S Grand Ave ....Los Angeles CA 90071 *Web:* www.watergrill.com	213-891-0900		671
Water Intelligence PLC 888 E Research Dr Ste 100................Palm Springs CA 92263 *Web:* www.waterintelligence.co.uk	760-969-6830	320-7876	806
Water King Inc 102 Charbonnet Rd............... Duson LA 70529 *Web:* www.waterking.com	337-988-2360	981-7922	806
Water Management Services LLC 2 International Plz Ste 401 .... Nashville TN 37217 *Web:* wmsengineers.com	615-366-6088		261
Water Pear Press PO Box 988 ....Sebastopol CA 95473 *TF:* 800-266-2631 ■ *Web:* www.waterpearpress.com	707-823-6907	829-7872	637-10
Water Pik Inc 1730 E Prospect Rd .... Fort Collins CO 80553 *TF:* 800-525-2774 ■ *Web:* www.waterpik.com	800-525-2774		228
Water Quality Assn (WQA) 4151 Naperville Rd.............................Lisle IL 60532 *Web:* www.wqa.org	630-505-0160	505-9637	48-12
Water Saver Faucet Co 701 W Erie St........... Chicago IL 60654 *Web:* www.wsflab.com	312-666-5500	666-5501	609
Water Spigot Inc, The 5806 E Hwy 22 .... Panama City FL 32404 *Web:* thewaterspigot.com	850-871-1900		743
Water Street Brewery 1101 N Water St .... Milwaukee WI 53202 *Web:* www.waterstreetbrewery.com	414-272-1195	272-0406	671
Water Street Seafood Inc PO Box 121 .... Apalachicola FL 32320 *TF:* 800-831-4111 ■ *Web:* www.waterstreetseafood.com	850-653-8902	653-9230	296-14
Water Technologies Training Institute 1911 Rustic Pl PO Box 2590 .... Farmington NM 87401 *TF:* 877-711-4347 ■ *Web:* www.watertechtraining.com	877-711-4347		167-3
Water Technology Inc 100 Park Ave .... Beaver Dam WI 53916 *Web:* www.watertechnologyinc.com	920-887-7375		261
Water Tower Place 835 N Michigan Ave .... Chicago IL 60611 *Web:* www.shopwatertower.com	312-440-3580		50-6
Water's Edge Resort & Spa 1525 Boston Post Rd PO Box 688 .... Westbrook CT 06498 *TF:* 800-222-5901 ■ *Web:* watersedgeresortandspa.com	860-399-5901	399-8644	669
Waterax Corp 14010 NE Third Ct Ste105 .... Vancouver WA 98685 *Web:* waterax.com	360-574-1818		302
Waterbeds N. Stuff Inc 3933 Brookham Dr .... Grove City OH 43123 *Web:* www.bedsnstuff.com	614-871-1171		321
Waterboy, The 2000 Capitol Ave............. Sacramento CA 95811 *Web:* www.waterboyrestaurant.com	916-498-9891		671
Waterbury Button Co 1853 Peck Ln............ Cheshire CT 06410 *TF:* 800-928-1812 ■ *Web:* waterburybutton.com	800-928-1812		594
Waterbury Center State Park 177 Reservoir Rd .... Waterbury VT 05677 *TF:* 800-837-4261 ■ *Web:* www.vtstateparks.com	802-244-1226		565
Waterbury Hospital 64 Robbins St............ Waterbury CT 06721 *Web:* www.waterburyhospital.org	203-573-6000		374-3
Waterbury Public School 236 Grand St .... Waterbury CT 06702 *Web:* www.waterbury.k12.ct.us	203-574-8000	574-8010	186
Waterbury Swiss Automatics Inc 43 Mattatuck Heights Rd.................... Waterbury CT 06705 *Web:* waterburyswiss.com	203-573-8584	573-1817	454
Waterbury Symphony Orchestra 160 Robbins St........................... Waterbury CT 06708 *Web:* www.waterburysymphony.org	203-574-4283		573-3
Waterco USA Inc 1812 Tobacco Rd.............. Augusta GA 30906 *TF:* 800-277-4150 ■ *Web:* www.waterco.com.au	706-793-7291	790-5688	806
Watercress Press 14080 Nacogdoches Rd Ste 582.............San Antonio TX 78247 *Web:* www.watercresspress.com	210-862-3542		637-2
Waterfall Economidis Caldwell Hanshaw & Villamana P C Williams Ctr 5210 E Williams Cir Ste 800 ....Tucson AZ 85711 *Web:* www.waterfallattorneys.com	520-790-5828		445
Waterfield Technologies Inc 1 W Third St Ste 1115 .... Tulsa OK 74103 *TF:* 800-324-0936 ■ *Web:* www.waterfieldtechnologies.com	918-858-6400		141
Waterflood Production Systems Ltd 1314 Third St PO Box 1490 .... Estevan SK S4A2L7 *Web:* www.waterflood.com	306-634-7212	634-7887	757
Waterford Retirement Residence 2431 Bank St .... Ottawa ON K1V8R9 *TF:* 877-688-4929 ■ *Web:* www.waterfordretirement.com	613-737-0811	737-3207	379
Waterford Technologies 19600 Fairchild Ste 350.........................Irvine CA 92612 *Web:* www.waterfordtechnologies.com	949-428-9300		809
Waterford Township Public Library 5168 Civic Center Dr ....Waterford MI 48329 *TF:* 800-773-2587 ■ *Web:* www.waterfordmi.gov	248-674-4831	674-1910	434-3
Waterford Wedgwood USA Inc 1330 Campus Pkwy ....Wall NJ 07753 *TF:* 877-720-3486 ■ *Web:* wedgwood.com	877-720-3486		362
Waterfront Beach Resort, The 21100 Pacific Coast Hwy .... Huntington Beach CA 92648 *Web:* www.waterfrontresort.com	714-845-8000	845-8424	671
Waterfront Container Leasing Company Inc 888 N Point St .... San Francisco CA 94109 *Web:* www.waterfrontcontainer.com	415-788-5667		791
Waterfront Playhouse 407 Wall St .... Key West FL 33040 *Web:* www.waterfrontplayhouse.org	305-294-5015		572
Waterfront Properties & Club Communities 825 Pkwy Ste 8.................................Jupiter FL 33477 *Web:* www.waterfront-properties.com	561-746-7272		652
Waterfront Seafood Market 2900 University Ave ....West Des Moines IA 50266 *Web:* waterfrontseafoodmarket.com	515-223-5106		671
Watergate Community Assn 8 Captain Dr............................. Emeryville CA 94608 *Web:* websites.vertilinc.com	510-428-0118		653
Watergate Hotel, The 2650 Virginia Ave NW.................... Washington DC 20037 *Web:* www.thewatergatehotel.com	202-827-1600		377
Waterhouse Inc 770 Kapiolani Blvd Ste 506 .... Honolulu HI 96813	808-592-4800	592-4840	591
Wateridge Insurance Services 10717 Sorrento Valley Rd................... San Diego CA 92121 *TF:* 800-223-6756 ■ *Web:* wateridge.com	858-452-2200		390
Water-Jel Technologies LLC 50 Broad St.............................. Carlstadt NJ 07072 *TF:* 800-693-1171 ■ *Web:* www.waterjel.com	201-507-8300		475
Waterline Technologies Inc 620 N Santiago St......................... Santa Ana CA 92701 **Fax Area Code:* 714 ■ *TF:* 800-464-7762 ■ *Web:* waterlinetechnologies.com	800-464-7762	564-9300*	711
Waterloo Cedar Falls Courier PO Box 540 .... Waterloo IA 50701 **Fax Area Code:* 319 ■ *TF:* 800-798-1730 ■ *Web:* wcfcourier.com	800-798-1717	291-2069*	532-2
Waterloo Community Unit School Dst 5 302 Bellefontaine Dr........................ Waterloo IL 62298 *Web:* www.wcusd5.net	618-939-3453	939-4578	685
Waterloo Convention & Visitor Bureau 500 Jefferson St .... Waterloo IA 50701 *TF:* 800-728-8431 ■ *Web:* www.travelwaterloo.com	319-233-8350	233-2733	206
Waterloo Industries Inc 1500 Waterloo Dr ....Sedalia MO 65301 **Fax Area Code:* 414 ■ *TF:* 800-833-8851 ■ *Web:* www.waterlooindustries.com	800-558-5528	766-6388*	488
Waterloo Public Library 35 Albert St .... Waterloo ON N2L5E2 *Web:* www.wpl.ca	519-886-1310		434-3
Waterloo Recreation Area 16345 McClure Rd.......................... Chelsea MI 48118 *Web:* www.michigan.org	734-475-8307		565
Waterloo Region Museum 10 King Rd .... Kitchener ON N2P2R7 *Web:* www.waterlooregionmuseum.ca	519-748-1914	748-0009	522
Waterloo-Cedar Falls Symphony (WCF) Gallagher-Bluedorn PAC Ste 17 .... Cedar Falls IA 50614 *Web:* wcfsymphony.org	319-273-3373		573-3
Waterman Broadcasting Corp 3719 Central Ave .... Fort Myers FL 33901 *Web:* www.water.net	239-939-2020		647

Name / Address	City	State	Zip	Phone	Fax	Class
Waterman Grille, The 4 Richmond Sq. *Web:* www.watermangrille.com	Providence	RI	02906	401-521-9229		671
Waterman State Bank 248 W Lincoln Hwy *Web:* www.watermanbank.com	Waterman	IL	60556	815-264-3201	264-3523	70
Waterman's Grill 415 Atlantic Ave *Web:* www.watermans.com	Virginia Beach	VA	23451	757-428-3644		671
Watermark at 3030 Park, The 3030 Park Ave. *Web:* 3030park.watermarkcommunities.com	Bridgeport	CT	06604	203-502-7593		672
Watermark Capital Partners LLC 150 N Riverside Plz Ste 4200 *Web:* watermarkcap.com	Chicago	IL	60606	847-482-8600	482-8696	194
Watermark Environmental Inc 175 Cabot St. *Web:* watermarkenv.com	Lowell	MA	01854	978-452-9696		261
Watermark Grille 11280 Tamiami Trl N. *Web:* www.watermarkgrille.com	Naples	FL	34110	239-596-1400		671
Watermark Group Inc, The 4271 Gate Crst *Web:* www.thewatermarkgroup.com	San Antonio	TX	78217	210-599-0400		627
Watermark Learning Inc 7300 Metro Blvd Ste 207 *TF:* 800-646-9362 ■ *Web:* www.watermarklearning.com	Minneapolis	MN	55439	952-921-0900		194
Watermark Medical LLC 1641 Worthington Rd Ste 320 *TF:* 877-710-6999 ■ *Web:* www.watermarkmedical.com	West Palm Beach	FL	33409	877-710-6999		250
Watermen's Museum 309 Water St *Web:* watermens.org	Yorktown	VA	23690	757-887-2641		520
Waterous Co 125 Hardman Ave. *TF:* 800-488-1228 ■ *Web:* www.waterousco.com	South Saint Paul	MN	55075	651-450-5000	450-5090	641
Waters & Kraus LLP 3219 McKinney Ave. *Web:* www.waterskraus.com	Dallas	TX	75204	214-357-6244		428
Waters Corp 34 Maple St. *NYSE: WAT* ■ *TF:* 800-252-4752 ■ *Web:* www.waters.com	Milford	MA	01757	508-478-2000	872-1990	419
Waters Maxine (Rep D - CA) 2221 Rayburn House Office Bldg *Web:* waters.house.gov	Washington	DC	20515	202-225-2201	225-7854	342-2
Waters Mcpherson Mcneill Pc 300 Lighting Way Seventh Fl PO Box 1560 *Web:* www.lawwmm.com	Secaucus	NJ	07096	201-863-4400		653
Waters of Covington 1600 E Liberty St *Web:* www.watersofcovington.com	Covington	IN	47932	765-793-4818	793-5047	450
Waters Parkerson & Company LLC 228 St Charles Ave Ste 512 *Web:* watersparkerson.com	New Orleans	LA	70130	504-581-2022	525-9320	401
Watershed Co, The 750 Sixth St S *Web:* www.watershedco.com	Kirkland	WA	98033	425-822-5242		196
Waterside Festival Marketplace 333 Waterside Dr *Web:* watersidedistrict.com	Norfolk	VA	23510	757-426-7433		50-6
Waterson Point State Park 44927 Cross Island Rd *Web:* parks.ny.gov	Fineview	NY	13640	315-482-2722		565
Waterstone Bank 7500 W State St *Web:* www.wsbonline.com	Wauwatosa	WI	53213	414-258-5880		70
Waterstone Group Inc, The 1145 W Main Ave Ste 209 *TF:* 800-291-3836 ■ *Web:* srhdev.com	De Pere	WI	54115	920-964-0333		260
Watertech Whirlpool Bath & Spa 2507 Plymouth Rd *TF:* 800-289-8827 ■ *Web:* www.watertechtn.com	Johnson City	TN	37601	800-289-8827		375
Waterton Lakes Lodge Resort 101 Clematis Ave PO Box 4 *TF:* 888-985-6343 ■ *Web:* www.watertonlakeslodge.com	Waterton Park	AB	T0K2M0	403-859-2150		669
Watertown Correctional Facility 23147 Swan Rd *Web:* www.doccs.ny.gov	Watertown	NY	13601	315-782-7490		213
Watertown Daily Times 260 Washington St *TF:* 800-724-1012 ■ *Web:* www.watertowndailytimes.com	Watertown	NY	13601	315-782-1000	661-2523	532-2
Watertown Free Public Library 123 Main St *Web:* www.watertownlib.org	Watertown	MA	02472	617-972-6431	924-5471	434-3
Watertown Plastics 830 Echo Lake Rd *Web:* www.watertownplastics.com	Watertown	CT	06795	860-274-7535		608
Watertown Public Library 100 S Water St *Web:* www.watertownpubliclibrary.org	Watertown	WI	53094	920-262-4090	261-8943	434-3
Watertown Public Opinion 120 Third Ave NW. *Web:* www.coteaushopper.com	Watertown	SD	57201	605-886-6901		532-3
Watertown-Belmont Chamber of Commerce 182 Main St PO Box 45 *Web:* www.wbcc.org	Watertown	MA	02471	617-926-1017		139
Watertown-Mayer Public Schools 1001 Hwy 25 NW *Web:* www.wm.k12.mn.us	Watertown	MN	55388	952-955-0480	955-0481	685
Waterville Valley Resort 1 Ski Area Rd PO Box 540 *TF:* 800-468-2553 ■ *Web:* www.waterville.com	Waterville Valley	NH	03215	603-236-8311		669
Waterworks America LLC 5005 Rockside Rd Crown Ctr Sixth Fl. *Web:* www.1water.com	Independence	OH	44131	440-526-4815		144
Waterworks Operating Company LLC 60 Backus Ave *TF:* 800-899-6757 ■ *Web:* www.waterworks.com	Danbury	CT	06810	203-546-6000		609
WATE-TV Ch 6 (ABC) 1306 Broadway *Web:* www.wate.com	Knoxville	TN	37917	865-637-6666	525-4091	741-69
WATH-AM PO Box 576 *Web:* www.970wath.com	Athens	OH	45701	740-593-6651	594-3488	647
Watkins & Eager PLLC 400 E Capitol St The Emporium Bldg *Web:* www.watkinseager.com	Jackson	MS	39201	601-965-1900	965-1901	445
Watkins Associated Industries 1958 Monroe Dr NE *Web:* watkins.com	Atlanta	GA	30324	404-872-8359		185
Watkins College of Art & Design 2298 Rose Parks Blvd. *TF:* 866-887-6395 ■ *Web:* www.watkins.edu	Nashville	TN	37228	615-383-4848		164
Watkins Financial & Insurance 30 Massachusetts Ave Ste *Web:* watkinsfinancial.net	North Andover	MA	01845	978-682-3147		390
Watkins Glen International Inc 2790 CR 16 *Web:* www.theglen.com	Watkins Glen	NY	14891	607-535-2486	535-8918	515
Watkins Glen State Park PO Box 304 *Web:* parks.ny.gov	Watkins Glen	NY	14891	607-535-4511		565
Watkins Lithographic 133 W 10th Ave *TF:* 800-995-9799 ■ *Web:* www.watkinslitho.com	North Kansas City	MO	64116	816-842-3667		627
Watkins Manufacturing Corp 1280 Park Center Dr *TF:* 800-999-4688 ■ *Web:* www.hotspring.com	Vista	CA	92081	800-999-4688		375
Watkins Partnership Inc, The 3032 Mitchellville Rd Ste 202 *Web:* watkinspartnership.com	Bowie	MD	20716	301-249-0974		261
Watkins Printing Co 1401 E 17th Ave *Web:* www.watkinsprinting.com	Columbus	OH	43211	614-297-8270		627
Watkins Security Agency of D.C. Inc 3939 Benning Rd NE *Web:* thewatkinsgroup.com	Washington	DC	20019	202-581-2871	581-2875	400
Watkins Steve (Rep R - KS) 1205 Longworth House Office Bldg *Web:* www.watkins.house.gov	Washington	DC	20515	202-225-6601		342-2
Watkins Woolen Mill State Park 26600 Park Rd N *Web:* mostateparks.com	Lawson	MO	64062	816-580-3387		565
Watkins, Ross & Co 200 Ottawa Ave Ste 600 *Web:* www.watkinsross.com	Grand Rapids	MI	49503	616-456-9696		390
Watkinson Miller PLLC 1100 New Jersey Ave SE Ste 910 *Web:* www.watkinsonmiller.com	Washington	DC	20003	202-842-2345	464-5317	41
Watlow Winona 1241 Bundy Blvd. *TF:* 800-928-5692 ■ *Web:* www.watlow.com	Winona	MN	55987	507-454-5300	452-4507	202
WATM-TV 1450 Scalp Ave *Web:* www.abc23.com	Johnstown	PA	15904	814-266-8088	266-7749	647
Watonwan County 710 2nd Ave S PO Box 518 *Web:* www.co.watonwan.mn.us	Saint James	MN	56081	507-375-1236	375-5010	338
Watry Industries Inc 3312 Lakeshore Dr *Web:* www.watry.com	Sheboygan	WI	53081	920-457-4886	457-5241	308
Watsco Inc 2665 S Bayshore Dr Ste 901 *NYSE: WSO* ■ *Web:* www.watsco.com	Miami	FL	33133	305-714-4100	858-4492	14
Watson Bowman Acme Corp 95 Pineview Dr **Fax Area Code: 716* ■ *TF:* 800-677-4922 ■ *Web:* wbacorp.com	Amherst	NY	14228	800-677-4922	691-9239*	480
Watson Building Supplies Inc 50 Royal Group Crescent Unit 2 *TF:* 877-927-4621 ■ *Web:* www.watsonbuildingsupplies.com	Vaughan	ON	L4H1X9	905-669-1898		364
Watson Caraway Midkiff & Luningham LLP 200 Fort Worth Club Bldg 306 W 7th St. *Web:* www.watsoncaraway.com	Fort Worth	TX	76102	817-870-1717	338-4842	445
Watson Coleman Bonnie (Rep D - NJ) 2442 Rayburn House Office Bldg *Web:* www.watsoncoleman.house.gov	Washington	DC	20515	202-225-5801	225-6025	342-2
Watson Electrical 1500 Charleston St *Web:* watsonelec.com	Wilson	NC	27893	252-237-7511	243-1607	189-4
Watson Engineering Inc 16455 Racho Blvd *TF:* 833-928-6862 ■ *Web:* www.watsoneng.com	Taylor	MI	48180	734-285-2200	759-0025	261
Watson Foods Company Inc 301 Heffernan Dr *TF:* 800-388-3481 ■ *Web:* www.watson-inc.com	West Haven	CT	06516	203-932-3000	932-8266	296-16
Watson Furniture Group Inc 26246 Twelve Trees Ln NW *Web:* www.watsonfurniture.com	Poulsbo	WA	98370	360-394-1300		319-1
Watson Grinding & Manufacturing Co 4525 Gessner *Web:* www.watsongrinding.com	Houston	TX	77041	713-466-3053	466-8992	481
Watson Industries Inc 3041 Melby Rd *Web:* watson-gyro.com	Eau Claire	WI	54703	715-839-0628		256
Watson Institute, The 301 Campmeeting Rd *Web:* www.thewatsoninstitute.org	Sewickley	PA	15143	412-741-1800		196
Watson Insurance Agency Inc 245 E 2nd Ave. *Web:* watsoninsurance.com	Gastonia	NC	28052	704-865-8584		390
Watson Kunda & Sons Inc 349 S Henderson Rd. *Web:* www.kundabev.com	King of Prussia	PA	19406	610-265-3113	265-3190	81-1
Watson Label Products 10616 Trenton Ave *TF:* 800-678-6715 ■ *Web:* www.wlp.com	Saint Louis	MO	63132	314-493-9300	493-9390	627
Watson Land Co 22010 S Wilmington Ave *Web:* www.watsonlandcompany.com	Carson	CA	90745	310-952-6400	522-8788	653
Watson McDaniel Co Limerick Airport Business Ctr 428 Jones Blvd *Web:* www.watsonmcdaniel.com	Pottstown	PA	19464	610-495-5131	495-5134	595
Watson Mill Bridge State Park 650 Watson Mill Rd *Web:* gastateparks.org	Comer	GA	30629	706-783-5349		565
Watson Millican & Co 700 Central Expy S Ste. *Web:* watsonmillican.com	Allen	TX	75013	972-578-7980	578-7986	261
Watson Mortgage Corp 6206 Atlantic Blvd Ste 1 *Web:* watsonmortgagecorp.com	Jacksonville	FL	32211	904-645-7111		217
Watson Pond State Park 1644 Bay St. *Web:* www.mass.gov	Taunton	MA	02780	508-884-8280		565

Name / Address	City	State	Zip	Phone	Fax	Class
Watson Realty Co 9101 Camino Media *Web:* www.watsonrealty.com	Bakersfield	CA	93311	661-327-5161		652
Watson Rice 301 Rte 17 N 4th Fl *TF:* 800-945-5985 ■ *Web:* bcawatsonrice.com	Rutherford	NJ	07070	201-460-4590	460-7224	2
Watson's Manistee Chrysler Inc 208 Parkdale Ave *Web:* www.watsonsmanisteechrysler.com	Manistee	MI	49660	231-723-6528		57
Watson-Marlow Inc 37 Upton Technology Pk *TF:* 800-282-8823 ■ *Web:* www.watson-marlow.com	Wilmington	MA	01887	800-282-8823		641
Watson-Standard Co 616 Hite Rd *Web:* www.watsonstandard.com	Harwick	PA	15049	724-275-1000	275-2000	550
Watsontown Trucking Company Inc 60 Belford Blvd *TF:* 800-344-0313 ■ *Web:* www.watsontowntrucking.com	Milton	PA	17847	570-522-9820		780
Watsonville Public Library 275 Main St Ste 100 *TF:* 800-281-7275 ■ *Web:* www.cityofwatsonville.org	Watsonville	CA	95076	831-768-3400		434-3
Watt Printing Co 4544 Hinckley Industrial Pkwy *TF:* 800-273-2170 ■ *Web:* www.wattprinters.com	Cleveland	OH	44109	216-398-2000		627
Watters Smith Memorial State Park PO Box 296 *Web:* wvstateparks.com	Lost Creek	WV	26385	304-745-3081		565
Watts Canada 5435 N Service Rd *Web:* www.wattscanada.ca	Burlington	ON	L7L5H7	905-332-4090		350
Watts Constructors LLC 1451 Dolley Madison Blvd Ste 200 *Web:* www.wattsconstructors.com	McLean	VA	22101	571-279-8650		188
Watts Equipment Co 17547 Comconex Rd *Web:* www.wattsequipment.com	Manteca	CA	95336	209-825-1700		358
Watts Machining Inc 2339 Calle Del Mundo *Web:* www.wattsmachining.com	Santa Clara	CA	95054	408-654-9300	654-9430	454
Watts Radiant Inc 1630 E Bradford Pkwy Ste B **Fax Area Code:* 417 ■ *TF:* 800-276-2419 ■ *Web:* www.wattsradiant.com	Springfield	MO	65804	800-276-2419	864-8161*	14
Watts School of Nursing 2828 Croasdaile Dr Ste 200 *Web:* www.wattsschoolofnursing.org	Durham	NC	27705	919-470-7348	383-4014	685
Watts Towers of Simon Rodia State Historic Park 1765 E 107th St *TF:* 866-240-4655 ■ *Web:* www.parks.ca.gov	Los Angeles	CA	90002	213-847-4646		565
Watumull Brothers Ltd 307 Lewers St 6th Fl *Web:* www.hbe.ehawaii.gov	Honolulu	HI	96815	808-971-8800		157-5
Waubonsie State Park 2585 Waubonsie Park Rd *Web:* www.iowadnr.gov	Hamburg	IA	51640	712-382-2786		565
Waud Capital Partners LLC 300 N LaSalle St Ste 4900 *Web:* www.waudcapital.com	Chicago	IL	60654	312-676-8400	676-8444	690
Waukee Veterinary Clinic PC 15151 Hickman Rd *Web:* waukee-clivevet.com	Clive	IA	50325	515-987-4552		794
Waukegan Port District 55 S Harbor Pl *Web:* waukeganharbor.com	Waukegan	IL	60085	847-244-3133	244-1348	618
Waukegan Public Library 128 N County St *Web:* www.waukeganpl.org	Waukegan	IL	60085	847-623-2041		434-3
Waukegan Steel LLC 1201 Belvidere Rd *Web:* waukegansteel.com	Waukegan	IL	60085	847-662-2810		492
Waukesha Bearings Corp W 231 N 2811 Roundy Cir E Ste 200 *TF:* 888-832-3517 ■ *Web:* www.waukbearing.com	Pewaukee	WI	53072	262-506-3000	506-3001	620
Waukesha County Chamber of Commerce 2717 N Grandview Blvd Ste 204 *Web:* www.waukesha.org	Waukesha	WI	53188	262-542-4249	542-8068	139
Waukesha County Technical College 800 Main St *Web:* www.wctc.edu	Pewaukee	WI	53072	262-691-5566		800
Waukesha Foundry Company Inc 1300 Lincoln Ave *TF:* 800-727-0741 ■ *Web:* www.waukeshafoundry.com	Waukesha	WI	53186	262-542-0741	549-8440	307
Waukesha Public Library 321 Wisconsin Ave *Web:* waukeshapubliclibrary.org	Waukesha	WI	53186	262-524-3680	524-3677	434-3
Waukesha State Bank 151 E St Paul Ave PO Box 648 *Web:* www.waukeshabank.com	Waukesha	WI	53187	262-549-8500	549-8593	70
Waukesha-Pearce Industries Inc (WPI) 12320 S Main St *Web:* www.wpi.com	Houston	TX	77035	713-723-1050		385
Waumandee State Bank S2021 County Rd *Web:* waumandeebank.com	Waumandee	WI	54622	608-626-3131		70
Wauna Federal Credit Union 101 Truhaak St *Web:* www.waunafcu.org	Clatskanie	OR	97016	503-728-4321		219
Waunita Hot Springs Ranch 8007 County Rd 887 *Web:* www.waunita.com	Gunnison	CO	81230	970-641-1266		239
Waupaca County 811 Harding St *Web:* www.co.waupaca.wi.us	Waupaca	WI	54981	715-258-6200	258-6212	338
Waupaca Elevator Company Inc 1726 N Ballard Rd Ste 1 *TF:* 800-238-8739 ■ *Web:* www.waupacaelevator.com	Appleton	WI	54911	800-238-8739		256
Waupaca Foundry Inc 1955 Brunner Dr PO Box 249 *Web:* www.waupacafoundry.com	Waupaca	WI	54981	715-258-6611	258-1712	307
Waupun Correctional Institution 200 S Madison St *Web:* www.doc.wi.gov	Waupun	WI	53963	920-324-5571	324-7250	213
Wausau Area Chamber of Commerce 200 Washington St Ste 120 *Web:* www.wausauchamber.com	Wausau	WI	54403	715-845-6231	845-6235	139
Wausau Central Wisconsin Convention & Visitors Bureau 219 Jefferson St *TF:* 888-948-4748 ■ *Web:* www.visitwausau.com	Wausau	WI	54403	715-355-8788	359-2306	206
Wausau Chemical Corp 2001 N River Dr *TF:* 800-950-6656 ■ *Web:* www.wausauchemical.com	Wausau	WI	54403	715-842-2285	842-9059	144
Wausau Daily Herald 800 Scott St *TF:* 800-477-4838 ■ *Web:* www.wausaudailyherald.com	Wausau	WI	54403	715-842-2101		532-2
Wausau Tile Inc PO Box 1520 *TF:* 800-388-8728 ■ *Web:* www.wausautile.com	Wausau	WI	54402	715-359-3121	355-4627	183
WaUSAu Window & Wall Systems 7800 International Dr *TF:* 877-678-2983 ■ *Web:* www.wausauwindow.com	Wausau	WI	54401	715-845-2161		480
Waushara County 209 S St Marie St *Web:* www.co.waushara.wi.us	Wautoma	WI	54982	920-787-0431		338
Wauwatosa Chamber of Commerce 10437 Innovation Dr *Web:* www.tosawestallischamber.org	Wauwatosa	WI	53226	414-453-2330		139
Wauwatosa Public Library 7635 W N Ave *Web:* www.wauwatosalibrary.org	Wauwatosa	WI	53213	414-471-8484		434-3
WAV Inc 2380 Prospect Dr *TF:* 800-678-2419 ■ *Web:* www.wavonline.com	Aurora	IL	60502	630-818-1000	818-4451	176
WAVA-AM 780 (Rel) 1735 N Lynn St Ste 500 *TF:* 877-534-0780 ■ *Web:* www.wava.com	Arlington	VA	22209	703-236-7681		645
Wave Books 1938 Fairview Ave E Ste 201 *Web:* www.wavepoetry.com	Seattle	WA	98102	206-676-5337		637-2
Wave Crest Development Inc 530 Chestnut St *Web:* www.wavecrestdevelopment.com	Santa Cruz	CA	95060	831-423-2100		653
Wave Direct 1400 NE Miami Gardens Dr Ste 212 *TF:* 888-550-9918 ■ *Web:* wave-direct.com	Cape Coral	FL	33909	239-574-8181	574-8802	5
Wave Dispersion Technologies Inc 269 Sheffield St Ste 5D *Web:* www.whisprwave.com	Mountainside	NJ	07092	908-233-7503	233-7507	188-3
Wave Federal Credit Union 480 Greenwich Ave *Web:* wavefcu.org	Warwick	RI	02886	401-781-1020		219
Wave Hill W 249th St & Independence Ave *Web:* www.wavehill.org	Bronx	NY	10471	718-549-3200	884-8952	97
Wave Loch LLC 9747 Olson Dr *Web:* www.waveloch.com	San Diego	CA	92121	858-454-1777	454-1888	711
Wave Publishing Co 88-08 Rockaway Beach Blvd *Web:* www.rockawave.com	Rockaway Beach	NY	11693	718-634-4000	945-0913	532-2
Wave Systems Corp 1159 Sonora Ct *Web:* www.wavesystems.com	Sunnyvale	CA	94086	408-524-8630		174
Wavecode Inc 1651 N Collins Blvd *Web:* site2.wavecode.com	Richardson	TX	75080	214-570-9559		180
Wavecrest Computing Inc 2006 Vernon Pl *Web:* www.wavecrest.net	Melbourne	FL	32901	321-953-5351		177
Wavedivision Holdings LLC 401 Parkplace Ctr Ste 103 *TF:* 844-910-8519 ■ *Web:* business.wavebroadband.com	Kirkland	WA	98033	425-576-8200		736
Wavefunction Inc 18401 Von Karman Ave *Web:* www.wavefun.com	Irvine	CA	92612	949-955-2120	955-2118	177
Waveguide Inc 10 N Southwood Dr *Web:* waveguidefiber.com	Nashua	NH	03063	603-598-0096		387
Waveguide LLC 1 W Court Sq Ste 300 *Web:* www.waveguide.com	Decatur	GA	30030	404-815-1919		256
Waveland Museum State Historic Site 225 Waveland Museum Ln *Web:* parks.ky.gov	Lexington	KY	40514	859-272-3611		565
Wavelength Datacom Inc 219 Shaw Rd S *Web:* www.wavdata.com	South San Francisco	CA	94080	408-746-0200		177
Wavelength Electronics Inc 51 Evergreen Dr *Web:* teamwavelength.com	Bozeman	MT	59715	406-587-4183		261
Waveline Direct Inc 192 Hempt Rd *TF:* 800-257-8830 ■ *Web:* www.wavelinedirect.com	Mechanicsburg	PA	17050	717-795-8830		627
Wavemaker 825 Seventh Ave *Web:* www.wavemakerglobal.com	New York	NY	10019	212-474-0000		6
Waveny Care Ctr 3 Farm Rd *Web:* www.waveny.org	New Canaan	CT	06840	203-594-5200	594-5327	450
Waverly Group 2301 Hickory St *Web:* www.waverlygroup.com	Saint Louis	MO	63104	314-773-8300	773-8884	194
Waverly Heights 1400 Waverly Rd *Web:* www.waverlyheightsltd.org	Gladwyne	PA	19035	610-645-8600	645-8611	672
Waverly News 14541 Castlewood Ste 300 *TF:* 877-556-7898 ■ *Web:* www.wahoo-ashland-waverly.com	Waverly	NE	68462	402-786-2344	786-2343	532-2
Wavestaff Inc 783 Rio Del Mar Blvd Ste 67 *Web:* www.wavestaff.com	Aptos	CA	95003	831-689-9800		260
Wavetronix LLC 78 E 1700 S *Web:* www.wavetronix.com	Provo	UT	84606	801-734-7200		261
WAVE-TV Ch 3 (NBC) 725 S Floyd St *TF:* 800-223-2579 ■ *Web:* www.wave3.com	Louisville	KY	40203	502-585-2201	561-4115	741-77
Wavsys LLC 101 Broadway Ste 406 *Web:* www.wavsys.com	Brooklyn	NY	11249	347-292-8797		387
WAVT-FM 212 S Centre St *TF:* 888-860-8102 ■ *Web:* www.t102radio.com	Pottsville	PA	17901	888-860-8102		647
WAVV-FM 101.1 11800 Tamiami Trl E *TF:* 866-310-9288 ■ *Web:* wavv101.fm	Naples	FL	34113	239-775-9288	793-7000	645-105
WAVY-TV Ch 10 (NBC) 300 Wavy St *Web:* www.wavy.com	Portsmouth	VA	23704	757-393-1010		741
Wawa Employees Credit Union 260 W Baltimore Pk *TF:* 800-283-9292 ■ *Web:* wawacu.com	Wawa	PA	19063	610-358-8030	358-8289	219
Wawa Inc 260 W Baltimore Pk *TF:* 800-444-9292 ■ *Web:* www.wawa.com	Media	PA	19063	610-358-8000	358-8808	204
Wawanesa Insurance 900-191 Broadway **Fax Area Code:* 204 ■ *Web:* www.wawanesa.com	Winnipeg	MB	R3C3P1	858-874-5300	942-7724*	391-4

	Phone	Fax	Class
Wawanesa Insurance 191 Broadway Ste 501 .... Winnipeg MB R3C3P1 *Web:* www.wawanesa.com	204-985-3923	942-7724	391-2
Wawanesa Life Insurance Co 191 Broadway Ste 501 .... Winnipeg MB R3C3P1 *Web:* www.wawanesa.com	204-985-0684		391-2
Wawatay Radio Network PO Box 1180 .... Sioux Lookout ON P8T1B7 *TF:* 800-243-9059 ■ *Web:* www.wawataynews.ca	807-737-2951	737-3224	647
Wawayanda State Park 885 Warwick Tpke .... Hewitt NJ 07421 *Web:* www.njparksandforests.org	973-853-4462		565
Wawona Frozen Foods Inc 100 W Alluvial Ave .... Clovis CA 93611 *Web:* wawona.com	559-299-2901	299-1921	296-21
Waxahachie Independent School District 411 N Gibson St .... Waxahachie TX 75165 *Web:* www.wisd.org	972-923-4631	923-4759	685
Waxman Industries Inc 24460 Aurora Rd .... Bedford Heights OH 44146 *OTC:* WXMN ■ *TF:* 800-201-7298 ■ *Web:* www.waxman.com	440-439-1830		612
WAXN-TV Ch 64 1901 N Tryon St .... Charlotte NC 28206 *TF:* 855-336-0360 ■ *Web:* www.wsoctv.com	704-335-4786		741-26
Way Engineering Ltd 8610 Wallisville Rd .... Houston TX 77029 *Web:* wayeng.com	713-568-6188	568-6189	189-10
Way It Was Museum 113 N C St .... Virginia City NV 89440 *Web:* www.visitvirginiacitynv.com	775-847-0766		520
WAY Media Inc 1860 Boy Scout Dr Ste 202 .... Fort Myers FL 33907 *Web:* www.wayfm.com	239-936-1929		645-11
Way to Happiness Foundation Intl, The 201 E Broadway .... Glendale CA 91205 *TF:* 800-255-7906 ■ *Web:* www.thewaytohappiness.org	818-254-0600		305
Wayah Insurance Group Inc 295 E Palmer St PO Box 999 .... Franklin NC 28744 *Web:* wayah.com	828-524-4442		390
Waycross College 2001 S Georgia Pkwy .... Waycross GA 31503 *Web:* sgsc.edu	912-449-7600		162
Waycross Investment Management Co 119 N Commercial St Ste 191 .... Bellingham WA 98225 *TF:* 800-292-8794 ■ *Web:* www.waycross.com	360-671-0148	671-8936	401
Waycross-Ware County Chamber of Commerce 315 Plant Ave Ste B .... Waycross GA 31501 *Web:* www.waycrosschamber.org	912-283-3742	283-0121	139
Wayfarers Chapel 5755 Palos Verdes Dr S .... Rancho Palos Verdes CA 90275 *Web:* www.wayfarerschapel.org	310-377-1650		50-1
Wayfarers State Park 8600 MT Hwy 35 .... Bigfork MT 59911 *Web:* stateparks.mt.gov	406-837-3041		565
Wayland Academy 101 N University Ave .... Beaver Dam WI 53916 *TF:* 800-860-7725 ■ *Web:* wayland.org	920-356-2120	887-3373	622
Wayland Free Public Library 41 Cochituate Rd .... Wayland MA 01778 *Web:* www.wayland.ma.us	508-358-2311		434-3
Wayland Hopkins Livestock 3634 Tenth St .... Wayland MI 49348 *Web:* www.your-auctioneers.com	269-792-2296		446
Waymouth Farms Inc 5300 Boone Ave .... New Hope MN 55428 *TF:* 800-527-0094 ■ *Web:* www.goodsensesnacks.com	763-533-5300	533-9890	296-8
Wayne & Gladys Valley Foundation 1939 Harrison St Ste 510 .... Oakland CA 94612 *Web:* fdnweb.org	510-466-6060		305
Wayne Automatic Fire Sprinklers Inc 11326 Distribution Ave W .... Jacksonville FL 32256 *Web:* www.waynefire.com	407-656-3030		189-13
Wayne Bank 717 Main St .... Honesdale PA 18431 *Web:* www.waynebank.com	570-253-1455	253-3725	360-2
Wayne Combustion Systems 801 Glasgow Ave .... Fort Wayne IN 46803 *TF:* 855-929-6327 ■ *Web:* www.waynecombustion.com	260-425-9200	424-0904	357
Wayne Community College 3000 Wayne Memorial Dr .... Goldsboro NC 27534 *Web:* www.waynecc.edu	919-735-5151	736-1707	162
Wayne County 416 East Jefferson St PO Box 435 .... Corydon IA 50060 *Web:* www.wayne.iowaassessors.com	641-872-2663	872-2843	338
Wayne County 400 Monroe St 7th Fl .... Detroit MI 48226 *TF:* 888-427-9869 ■ *Web:* www.waynecounty.com	313-224-6262		338
Wayne County 224 E Walnut St .... Goldsboro NC 27530 *Web:* www.waynegov.com	919-731-1435	731-1446	338
Wayne County 925 Court St .... Honesdale PA 18431 *TF:* 800-321-9973 ■ *Web:* waynecountypa.gov	570-253-5970	253-5432	338
Wayne County 341 E Walnut St .... Jesup GA 31546 *Web:* www.waynecountyga.us	912-427-5900	427-5906	338
Wayne County 18 S Main St PO Box 189 .... Loa UT 84747 *Web:* www.waynecountyutah.org	435-836-1300	836-2479	338
Wayne County 26 Church St .... Lyons NY 14489 *TF:* 800-527-6510 ■ *Web:* web.co.wayne.ny.us	315-946-5400	946-5407	338
Wayne County 55 N Main St Ste 106 .... Monticello KY 42633 *Web:* waynecounty.ky.gov	606-348-5721		338
Wayne County 510 Pearl St Ste 5 .... Wayne NE 68787 *Web:* www.waynecountyne.org	402-375-2288	375-4137	338
Wayne County 610 Azalea Dr .... Waynesboro MS 39367 *Web:* waynecounty.ms	601-735-6056	735-6246	338
Wayne County 100 Court Cir .... Waynesboro TN 38485 *Web:* www.waynecountytn.org	931-722-3653	722-5994	338
Wayne County 428 W Liberty St .... Wooster OH 44691 *Web:* www.wayneohio.org	330-287-5400	287-5407	338
Wayne County Area Chamber of Commerce 33 S Seventh St Ste 2 .... Richmond IN 47374 *Web:* wcareachamber.org	765-962-1511	966-0882	139
Wayne County Boot Camp PO Box 182 .... Clifton TN 38425 *TF:* 855-876-7283 ■ *Web:* www.tn.gov	931-676-3345		213
Wayne County Chamber of Commerce 308 N Williams St .... Goldsboro NC 27530 *TF:* 800-849-6222 ■ *Web:* www.waynecountychamber.com	919-734-2241	734-2247	139
Wayne County Clerk 700 Hendricks St .... Wayne WV 25570 *Web:* waynecountywv.org	304-272-6352		338
Wayne County Community College *Downtown* 1001 W Fort St .... Detroit MI 48226 *Web:* www.wcccd.edu	313-496-2758		162
Wayne County Convention & Visitors Bureau 428 W Liberty St .... Wooster OH 44691 *TF:* 800-362-6474 ■ *Web:* wccvb.com	800-362-6474		206
Wayne County Federal Credit Union 3010 W Main St .... Richmond IN 47374 *TF:* 877-962-7113 ■ *Web:* waynecountyfcu.org	765-962-7113	962-9615	219
Wayne Crouse Inc 3370 Stafford St .... Pittsburgh PA 15204 *Web:* www.waynecrouse.com	412-771-5176	771-2357	189-10
Wayne Densch Performing Arts Ctr 201 S Magnolia Ave .... Sanford FL 32771 *Web:* www.wdpac.com	407-321-8111	321-8140	239
Wayne Farms Enterprises LLC 1020 County Rd 114 .... Jack AL 36346 *Web:* waynefarms.com	334-897-3435		619
Wayne Farms LLC 4110 Continental Dr .... Oakwood GA 30566 *TF:* 800-392-0844 ■ *Web:* www.waynefarms.com	800-392-0844		10-8
Wayne Fasteners Inc (WFI) 2611 Independence Dr .... Fort Wayne IN 46808 *TF:* 800-994-0393 ■ *Web:* www.waynefasteners.com	260-484-0393	483-8082	351
Wayne Fitzgerrell State Recreation Area 11094 Ranger Rd .... Whittington IL 62897 *Web:* www2.illinois.gov	618-629-2320		565
Wayne HealthCare 835 Sweitzer St .... Greenville OH 45331 *Web:* www.waynehealthcare.org	937-548-1141		374-3
Wayne Highlands School District 474 Grove St .... Honesdale PA 18431 *Web:* www.whsdk12.com	570-253-4661	253-9409	685
Wayne Hummer Investments LLC 222 S Riverside Pz 28th Fl .... Chicago IL 60606 *TF:* 800-621-4477 ■ *Web:* www.wintrustwealth.com	866-943-4732		690
Wayne J. Griffin Electric Inc 116 Hopping Brook Rd .... Holliston MA 01746 *Web:* www.waynejgriffinelectric.com	508-429-8830	429-7825	189-4
Wayne Long & Co 1502 Mill Rock Way Ste 200 .... Bakersfield CA 93311 *Web:* welcpa.com	661-664-0909		734
Wayne Manufacturing Corp 6505 State Rd 205 .... Laotto IN 46763 *Web:* www.waynetool.net	260-637-5586		488
Wayne Memorial Hospital (WMH) 865 S First St .... Jesup GA 31545 *Web:* www.wmhweb.com	912-427-6811		374-3
Wayne Memorial Hospital 2700 Wayne Memorial Dr .... Goldsboro NC 27534 *Web:* www.wayneunc.org	919-736-1110		374-3
Wayne Memorial Hospital (WMH) 601 Park St .... Honesdale PA 18431 *Web:* www.wmh.org	570-253-8100		374-3
Wayne Metal Products Inc 5461 Benchmark Ln .... Sanford FL 32773 *Web:* www.waynemetalproductsinc.com	407-321-7168	321-8680	295
Wayne Metals LLC 400 E Logan St .... Markle IN 46770 *Web:* www.waynemetals.com	260-758-3121	758-2521	454
Wayne Mills Company Inc 130 W Berkley St .... Philadelphia PA 19144 *TF:* 800-220-8053 ■ *Web:* www.waynemills.com	215-842-2134	438-8599	745-5
Wayne Oil Company Inc 1301 Wayne Memorial Dr .... Goldsboro NC 27534 *TF:* 800-641-2816 ■ *Web:* www.ballparkstores.com	919-735-2021		536
Wayne Pipe & Supply Inc 6040 Innovation Blvd .... Fort Wayne IN 46818 *TF:* 800-552-3697 ■ *Web:* www.waynepipe.com	260-423-9577		612
Wayne Printing Co 7917 N Kckapoo Edwards Rd .... Edwards IL 61528 *Web:* www.waynewag.com	309-518-1218	691-9379	627
Wayne Products Inc 888 Sussex Blvd Ste 3 .... Broomall PA 19008 **Fax Area Code:* 610 ■ *Web:* www.wayneproducts.com	800-255-5665	251-0948*	386
Wayne Public Library 461 Valley Rd .... Wayne NJ 07470 *Web:* www.waynepubliclibrary.org	973-694-4272		434-3
Wayne Reaves Software & Websites Inc 6211 Thomaston Rd .... Macon GA 31220 *TF:* 888-477-9707 ■ *Web:* waynereaves.com	888-477-9707		195
Wayne Savings Bancshares Inc 1908 Cleveland Rd .... Wooster OH 44691 *NASDAQ:* WAYN ■ *Web:* www.waynesavings.com	330-264-5767		360-2
Wayne Shoemaker Inc 205 Steeple Chase Dr .... Prince Frederick MD 20678 *TF:* 877-678-7968 ■ *Web:* wayneshoemaker.com	410-535-0434		390
Wayne State College 1111 Main St .... Wayne NE 68787 *TF:* 800-228-9972 ■ *Web:* www.wsc.edu	402-375-7000		166
Wayne State University 42 W Warren .... Detroit MI 48202 *TF:* 877-978-4636 ■ *Web:* wayne.edu	313-577-3577	577-7536	166
Wayne State University College of Liberal Arts and Sciences 4841 Cass Ave Ste 2155 .... Detroit MI 48212 *Web:* clas.wayne.edu	313-577-2321	577-6929	166
Wayne State University Law School 471 W Palmer St .... Detroit MI 48202 *Web:* law.wayne.edu	313-577-3937	993-8129	167-1
Wayne State University Libraries 5150 Anthony Wayne Dr .... Detroit MI 48202 *Web:* library.wayne.edu	313-577-4023	577-5265	434-6
Wayne State University School of Medicine 540 E Canfield St .... Detroit MI 48201 *Web:* www.med.wayne.edu	313-577-1460	577-9420	167-2
Wayne Trail Technologies Inc 203 E Park St .... Fort Loramie OH 45845 *Web:* www.waynetrail.com	937-295-2120		454
Wayne Van Riper Hopper Museum 533 Berdan Ave .... Wayne NJ 07470 *Web:* www.waynetownship.com	973-694-7192		50-3
Wayne Wire Cloth Products Inc 200 E Dresden St .... Kalkaska MI 49646 *Web:* www.waynewire.com	231-258-9187	258-5504	688
Wayneco Inc 800 Hanover Rd .... York PA 17408 *TF:* 800-233-9313 ■ *Web:* www.waynecoinc.com	717-225-4413		321

Name / Address	City	State	Zip	Phone	Fax	Class
Waynesboro (Independent City) 503 W Main St *Web:* www.waynesboro.va.us	Waynesboro	VA	22980	540-942-6600	942-6671	338
Waynesburg College 51 W College St *TF:* 800-225-7393 ■ *Web:* www.waynesburg.edu	Waynesburg	PA	15370	724-627-8191		166
Waynesville Inn Golf & Country Club, The 176 Country Club Dr *TF:* 800-627-6250 ■ *Web:* www.twigolfresort.com	Waynesville	NC	28786	828-456-3551		669
Waynesville-Saint Robert Area Chamber of Commerce 137 St Robert Blvd Ste B *Web:* www.waynesville-strobertchamber.com	Saint Robert	MO	65584	573-336-5121	336-5472	139
Wayne-White Counties Electric Co-op 1501 W Main St *TF:* 888-871-7695 ■ *Web:* www.waynewhitecoop.com	Fairfield	IL	62837	618-842-2196		245
Waypoint Analytical Inc 2790 Whitten Rd *TF:* 800-264-4522 ■ *Web:* www.waypointanalytical.com	Memphis	TN	38133	901-213-2400	213-2440	743
Waypoint Consulting 1450 E Boot Rd *TF:* 866-826-7075 ■ *Web:* www.waypointco.com	West Chester	PA	19380	866-826-7075		463
Waypoint Home Health Care 115 S Park Ave *Web:* www.waypointhomehealthcare.com	Titusville	FL	32796	321-267-2950	264-7491	363
WayPoint Ventures *RPM Ventures* 320 N Main St Ste 400 *Web:* rpmvc.com	Ann Arbor	MI	48104	734-332-1700		792
Wayside Furniture Inc 1367 Canton Rd *TF:* 877-499-3968 ■ *Web:* www.wayside-furniture.com	Akron	OH	44312	330-733-6221		321
Waystar 888 W Market St *Web:* www.waystar.com	Louisville	KY	40202	844-492-9782		225
WAYX-AM 1766 Memorial Dr Ste 1 *Web:* www.wayx.net	Waycross	GA	31501	912-283-3518		647
WAZK-FM 19 Old South Rd *Web:* www.ackfm.com	Nantucket	MA	02584	508-228-9770		647
WAZO-FM 25 N Kerr *Web:* www.z1075.com	Wilmington	NC	28405	910-791-3088		647
WAZS-TV 5081 Rivers Ave *Web:* www.jabarcommunications.com	North Charleston	SC	29418	843-554-1063	554-1088	647
WB Bottle Supply Company Inc 3400 S Clomont Ave *TF:* 800-738-3931 ■ *Web:* www.wbbottle.com	Milwaukee	WI	53207	414-482-4300		333
WB Games Inc 12131 113th Ave NE Ste 300 *TF:* 855-924-2637	Kirkland	WA	98034	855-924-2637		761
WB Guimarin & Company Inc 1124 Bluff Industrial Blvd *Web:* www.wbguimarin.com	Columbia	SC	29202	803-256-0515	252-8239	189-10
WB Mason Company Inc 59 Centre St *TF:* 888-926-2766 ■ *Web:* www.wbmason.com	Brockton	MA	02303	888-926-2766		321
WB Wallis & Co 540 Kentucky St *Web:* wbwallis.com	Scottdale	GA	30079	404-294-1722		189-10
WBAB-FM 102.3 (Rock) 555 Sunrise Hwy *Web:* www.wbab.com	West Babylon	NY	11704	631-587-1023	587-1282	645
WBAL-TV Ch 11 (NBC) 3800 Hooper Ave *Web:* www.wbaltv.com	Baltimore	MD	21211	410-467-3000		741-11
WBAM-FM 98.9 (Ctry) 4101-A Wall St *Web:* bamacountry.com	Montgomery	AL	36106	334-244-9898	279-9563	645-102
WBANA (Wild Blueberry Association of North America) PO Box 100 *Web:* www.wildblueberries.com	Old Town	ME	04468	207-570-3535	581-3499	48-2
WBAY-TV Ch 2 (ABC) 115 S Jefferson St *TF:* 800-261-9229 ■ *Web:* www.wbay.com	Green Bay	WI	54301	920-432-3331	432-1190	741-55
WBBJ-TV 346 Muse St *Web:* www.wbbjtv.com	Jackson	TN	38301	731-424-4515		647
WBBM-AM 780 (N/T) 180 N Stetson Ste 1100 *TF:* 800-784-0397 ■ *Web:* wbbm780.radio.com	Chicago	IL	60601	312-297-7800		645-34
WBBQ 104.3 2743 Perimeter Pkwy Bldg 100 Ste 300 *Web:* wbbq.iheart.com	Augusta	GA	30909	706-396-6000		645-109
WBBV-FM 900 Belmont St *Web:* www.river101.com	Vicksburg	MS	39180	601-636-2340		647
WBBZ-TV Ch 67 (Ind) 4545 Transit Rd Ste 750 *Web:* www.wbbz.tv	Williamsville	NY	14221	716-630-9229	630-9233	741
WBCK-AM 390 Golden Ave *Web:* wbckfm.com	Battle Creek	MI	49017	269-963-5555		647
WBCL-FM 90.3 (Rel) 1115 W Rudisill Blvd *Web:* www.wbcl.org	Fort Wayne	IN	46807	260-745-0576	456-2913	645-60
WBCM-FM 314 E Front St *Web:* www.wtcmi.com	Traverse City	MI	49684	231-947-7675		647
WBCP-AM 904 N 4th St Ste D *Web:* www.wbcp1580.com	Champaign	IL	61820	217-359-1580	359-1583	647
WBDL-FM PO Box 349 *Web:* www.wbdlfm.com	Reedsburg	WI	53959	608-524-1400		647
WBET-FM 7080 S Nottawa *Web:* www.wbetfm.com	Sturgis	MI	49091	269-651-9238		647
WBEZ-FM 91.5 848 E Grand Ave Navy Pier *Web:* www.wbez.org	Chicago	IL	60611	312-948-4600		645-34
WBFJ-FM 89.3 (Rel) 1249 Trade St *Web:* www.wbfj.fm	Winston-Salem	NC	27101	336-721-1560		645-81
WBG (Wright Business Graphics) 18440 NE San Rafael St *TF:* 800-547-8397 ■ *Web:* www.wrightbg.com	Portland	OR	97230	800-547-8397		110
WBG (World Bank Group, The) 1818 H St NW *TF:* 800-645-7247 ■ *Web:* www.worldbank.org	Washington	DC	20433	202-473-1000	477-6391	783
WBGH (Washington Business Group on Health) 20 F St NW Ste 200 *Web:* www.businessgrouphealth.org	Washington	DC	20001	202-628-9320	628-9244	48-17
WBGL-FM 91.7 (Rel) 4101 Fieldstone Rd PO Box 111 *TF:* 800-475-9245 ■ *Web:* www.wbgl.org	Champaign	IL	61822	217-359-8232	359-7374	645-29
WBGO-FM 88.3 (Jazz) 54 Pk Pl *TF:* 800-499-9246 ■ *Web:* www.wbgo.org	Newark	NJ	07102	973-624-8880		645
WBGT-TV 1320 Buffalo Rd Ste 111 *Web:* www.visioncommunications.tv	Rochester	NY	14624	585-235-1870	235-0574	647
WBGW-FM PO Box 4164 *Fax Area Code: 812 ■ *TF:* 800-264-5550 ■ *Web:* thyword.media	Evansville	IN	47724	800-264-5550	768-5552*	647
WBGX-AM 5956 S Michigan Ave *TF:* 866-305-1570 ■ *Web:* www.gospel1570.com	Chicago	IL	60637	773-752-1570	752-2242	647
WBH Industries 3016 Ave E East *Web:* www.wbhindustries.com	Arlington	TX	76011	817-701-3418	701-3518	351
WBHK-FM 98.7 (Urban) 2700 Corporate Dr Ste 115 *Web:* www.987kiss.com	Birmingham	AL	35242	205-741-0987	290-1061	645-19
WBHM-FM 90.3 (NPR) 650 11th St S *TF:* 800-444-9246 ■ *Web:* wbhm.org	Birmingham	AL	35233	205-934-2606	934-5075	645-19
WBHY-FM 88.5 (Rel) PO Box 1328 *TF:* 888-473-8488 ■ *Web:* www.goforth.org	Mobile	AL	36633	251-473-8488		645-100
WBI Energy 1250 W Century Ave *TF:* 877-924-4677 ■ *Web:* www.wbienergy.com	Bismarck	ND	58503	701-530-1095		325
WBIR-TV Ch 10 (NBC) 1513 Hutchinson Ave *Web:* www.wbir.com	Knoxville	TN	37917	865-637-1010		741-69
WBJ Press 315 Lockwood Ave *Web:* www.willsworld.com	Northfield	IL	60093	847-331-2703		637-2
WBJC-FM 91.5 (Clas) 6776 Reisterstown Rd Ste 202 *Web:* www.wbjc.com	Baltimore	MD	21215	410-580-5800		645-15
WBK Engineering LLC 116 W Main St Ste 201 *Web:* www.wbkengineering.com	Saint Charles	IL	60174	630-443-7755		194
WBKB-TV 1390 N Bagley St *Web:* www.wbkb11.com	Alpena	MI	49707	989-356-3434		647
WBKO-TV 2727 Russellville Rd *Web:* www.wbko.com	Bowling Green	KY	42101	270-781-1313	781-1814	647
WBKQ-FM 800 E 29th St *Web:* www.967blakefm.com	Muncie	IN	47302	765-288-4403	288-0429	647
WBLI-FM 106.1 (CHR) 555 Sunrise Hwy *Web:* www.wbli.com	West Babylon	NY	11704	631-669-9254		645
WBLJ-AM 613 Silver Cir *Web:* www.wblj1230.com	Dalton	GA	30721	706-278-5511		647
WBLK-FM 93.7 (Urban) 14 Lafayette Sq Ste 1200 *Web:* wblk.com	Buffalo	NY	14203	716-852-9393		645-25
WBLL-AM 1501 County Rd 235 *Web:* www.peakofohio.com	Bellefontaine	OH	43311	937-592-1045	592-3299	647
WBLX-FM 2800 Dauphin St Ste 104 *TF:* 866-993-9259 ■ *Web:* www.thebigstation93blx.com	Mobile	AL	36606	251-471-9393		647
WBMC (West Boca Medical Ctr) 21644 State Rd 7 *Web:* www.westbocamedctr.com	Boca Raton	FL	33428	561-488-8000	488-8105	374-3
WBMI-FM PO Box 807 *Web:* www.wbmiradio.com	West Branch	MI	48661	989-345-4269	345-3996	647
WBMM-TV 3251 Harrison Rd *Web:* www.cwmontgomery.com	Montgomery	AL	36109	334-270-3200		647
WBMQ-AM 214 Television Cir *Web:* www.wbmq.net	Savannah	GA	31406	912-961-9000	961-7070	647
WBNA-TV 3701 Fern Valley Rd *Web:* www.wbna21.com	Louisville	KY	40219	502-964-2121		647
WBNG-TV 560 Columbia Dr *Web:* www.wbng.com	Johnson City	NY	13790	607-729-8812	797-6211	647
WBNS-TV Ch 10 (CBS) 770 Twin Rivers Dr *Web:* www.10tv.com	Columbus	OH	43215	614-460-3700		741-35
WBNX-TV Ch 55 (CW) 2690 State Rd *Web:* www.wbnx.com	Cuyahoga Falls	OH	44223	330-922-5500	929-2410	741
WBNY-FM 1300 Elmwood Ave *Web:* wbny.buffalostate.edu	Buffalo	NY	14222	716-878-5104	878-6600	645-25
WBOC-TV Ch 16 (CBS) 1729 N Salisbury Blvd *Web:* www.wboc.com	Salisbury	MD	21801	410-749-1111	742-5190	741
WBON-FM 98.5 (Span) 3075 Veterans Memorial Hwy Ste 201 *Web:* lafiestali.com	Ronkonkoma	NY	11779	631-648-2500	648-2510	645
WBPX-TV 1120 Soldiers Field Rd *Web:* www.iontelevision.com	Boston	MA	02134	617-787-6868		647
WBQP-TV 312 E Nine Mile Rd Ste 29D *Web:* www.wbqp.com	Pensacola	FL	32514	850-478-6000	484-8080	647
WBRC-TV Ch 6 (Fox) 1720 Vly View Dr *Web:* www.wbrc.com	Birmingham	AL	35209	205-322-6666	583-4356	741-15
WBRE-TV Ch 28 (NBC) 62 S Franklin St *TF:* 800-367-9222 ■ *Web:* www.pahomepage.com	Wilkes-Barre	PA	18701	570-823-2828	829-0440	741
WBRG-AM Supertalk 1050 *Web:* www.wbrgradio.com	Lynchburg	VA	24501	434-845-5916	632-7207	647
WBRK-FM 100 N St *Web:* www.star1017.com	Pittsfield	MA	01201	413-442-1553	445-5294	647
WBRU-FM 95.5 (Alt) 88 Benevolent St *Web:* www.wbru.com	Providence	RI	02906	401-272-9550	272-9278	645-127
WBS (Wholesale Builder Supply Inc) 51740 Grand River Ave North on Challenger Dr *Web:* wbscabinets.com	Wixom	MI	48393	248-347-6290		191-3
WBSD-FM 400 McCanna Pky *Web:* www.wbsdfm.com	Burlington	WI	53105	262-763-0195		647
WBT Systems Inc 38 Spring St *TF:* 877-928-7700 ■ *Web:* www.wbtsystems.com	Nashua	NH	03060	603-521-8527		178-1
WBT-AM 1110 (N/T) 1900 Julian Price Pl *Web:* wbt.radio.com	Charlotte	NC	28208	704-374-3600		645-32
WBTK-AM 2809 Emerywood Pky Ste 540 *Web:* www.wbtk.com	Richmond	VA	23294	804-353-8544	353-8549	647
WBTQ-FM 1251 Earl L Core Rd *Web:* www.wajr.com	Morgantown	WV	26505	304-296-0041		647
WBTV-TV Ch 3 (CBS) 1 Julian Price Pl *Web:* www.wbtv.com	Charlotte	NC	28208	704-374-3500		741-26

Name / Address	City	State	Zip	Phone	Fax	Class
WBTW-TV Ch 13 (CBS) 101 McDonald Ct *Web:* www.wbtw.com	Myrtle Beach	SC	29588	843-293-1301		741-87
WBUR-FM 90.9 (NPR) 890 Commonwealth Ave *TF:* 800-909-9287 ■ *Web:* www.wbur.org	Boston	MA	02215	617-353-0909		645-22
WBUZ-FM 102.9 (Alt) 1824 Murfreesboro Rd *Web:* www.1029thebuzz.com	Nashville	TN	37217	615-399-1029	361-9873	645-106
WBXX-TV c/o WVLT 6450 Papermill Dr *Web:* www.wvlt.tv	Knoxville	TN	37919	865-450-8888	450-8869	647
WBZ-AM 1030 (N/T) 1170 Soldiers Field Rd *Web:* boston.cbslocal.com	Boston	MA	02134	617-787-7000		645-22
WBZE-FM 98.9 (AC) 3411 W Tharpe St *Web:* www.mystar98.com	Tallahassee	FL	32303	850-201-3000		645-159
WBZI-FM 23 E 2nd St *TF:* 888-740-9444 ■ *Web:* realrootsradio.com	Xenia	OH	45385	937-372-3531		647
WBZW-AM 1188 Lake View Dr *Web:* theanswerorlando.com	Altamonte Springs	FL	32714	407-682-5841		647
WC Cammett Engineering Inc 297 Elm St *Web:* www.cammett.com	Amesbury	MA	01913	978-388-2157		261
WC Software Development Inc 5040 Savannah River Way Ste 117 *Web:* www.softwc.com	Orlando	FL	32839	321-246-3836		178-1
WCA (Wireless Communications Association Intl) 1333 H St NW Ste 700W *Web:* www.wcainternational.com	Washington	DC	20005	202-452-7823		49-20
WCA Hospital School of Radiologic Technology 207 Foote Ave PO Box 840 *Web:* www.wcahospital.org	Jamestown	NY	14702	716-487-0141		685
WCA Logistics LLC 643 Bodey Cir *TF:* 800-860-7838 ■ *Web:* www.wcalogistics.com	Urbana	OH	43078	937-653-6382		195
WCA Waste Corp 1330 Post Oak Blvd 30th Fl *NASDAQ: WCAA* ■ *Web:* www.wcawaste.com	Houston	TX	77056	713-292-2400		804
WCAM-AM PO Box 753 *Web:* www.kool1027.com	Camden	SC	29020	803-438-9002	408-2288	647
WCAS (Welsh Carson Anderson & Stowe) 599 Lexington Ave Ste 1800 *Web:* www.wcas.com	New York	NY	10022	212-893-9500		405
WCAT-FM 102.3 (Ctry) 728 N Hanover St *Web:* www.red1023.com	Carlisle	PA	17013	717-243-1200		645
WCAU NBC 10 10 Monument Rd *TF:* 800-847-9228 ■ *Web:* www.nbcphiladelphia.com	Bala Cynwyd	PA	19004	610-668-5510	668-5705	741
WCAV-TV 874 Rio E Ct *Web:* www.cbs19news.com	Charlottesville	VA	22901	434-242-1919	220-0398	647
WCAX-TV Ch 3 (CBS) 30 Joy Dr *Web:* www.wcax.com	Burlington	VT	05406	802-658-6300	652-6319	741
WCBD-TV Ch 2 (NBC) 210 W Coleman Blvd *TF:* 800-861-5255 ■ *Web:* www.counton2.com	Mount Pleasant	SC	29464	843-884-2222	881-3410	741
WCBE-FM 90.5 (NPR) 540 Jack Gibbs Blvd *TF:* 800-241-0421 ■ *Web:* www.wcbe.org	Columbus	OH	43215	614-365-5555	365-5060	645-40
WCBI-TV Ch 4 (CBS) 201 Fifth St S *Web:* www.wcbi.com	Columbus	MS	39701	662-327-4444	328-5222	741
WCBL-FM PO Box 387 *TF:* 800-525-7077 ■ *Web:* www.marshallcountydaily.com	Benton	KY	42025	270-527-3102	527-5606	647
WCBM-AM 680 (N/T) 1726 Reisterstown Rd Ste 117 *Web:* www.wcbm.com	Pikesville	MD	21208	410-580-6800		645
WCBN-FM 88.3 (Alt) University of Michigan 530 Student Activities Bldg *Web:* wcbn.org	Ann Arbor	MI	48109	734-763-3500		645-8
WCBS-FM 101.1 (Oldies) 345 Hudson St 10th Fl *TF:* 800-367-1101 ■ *Web:* wcbsfm.radio.com	New York	NY	10014	800-367-1101		645-108
WCBU-FM 89.9 (NPR) 1501 W Bradley Ave *Web:* peoriapublicradio.org	Peoria	IL	61625	309-677-3690		645-119
WCC (Women's College Coalition) PO Box 3983 *Web:* www.womenscolleges.org	Decatur	GA	30031	404-913-9492		49-5
WCC (Wilmette Chamber of Commerce) 351 Linden Ave *Web:* www.wilmettekenilworth.com	Wilmette	IL	60091	847-251-3800	251-6321	139
WCC (Willits Chamber of Commerce) 299 E Commercial St *Web:* www.willits.org	Willits	CA	95490	707-459-7910		139
WCCBI (Warren County Chamber of Commerce) 308 Market St *Web:* wccbi.org	Warren	PA	16365	814-723-3050	723-6024	139
WCCB-TV Ch 18 (Fox) 1 Television Pl *Web:* www.wccbcharlotte.com	Charlotte	NC	28205	704-372-1800		741-26
WCCC (Wilmington Clinton County Chamber of Commerce) 100 W Main St *Web:* wccchamber.com	Wilmington	OH	45177	937-382-2737		139
WCCQ-FM 2410-B Caton Farm Rd *TF:* 888-254-9830 ■ *Web:* www.wccq.com	Crest Hill	IL	60403	888-254-9830		647
WCCW (Washington Corrections Center for Women) 9601 Bujacich Rd NW *Web:* www.doc.wa.gov	Gig Harbor	WA	98332	253-858-4200		213
WCCY-AM 313 E Montezuma Ave *Web:* www.wccy.com	Houghton	MI	49931	906-482-7700	482-7751	647
WCD Consultants LLC 23 Rt 31 N Ste B26 *Web:* www.wcdgroup.com	Pennington	NJ	08534	609-730-0007	730-0011	194
WCDK-FM 2307 Pennsylvania Ave *Web:* www.1063theriver.com	Weirton	WV	26062	304-723-1656	723-1688	647
WCEC (Wharton County Electric Co-opeartive Inc) 1815 E Jackson St *TF:* 800-460-6271 ■ *Web:* www.mywcec.coop	El Campo	TX	77437	979-543-6271		245
WCEI-FM 306 Port St *Web:* www.wceiradio.com	Easton	MD	21601	410-822-3301		647
WCF (World Cocoa Foundation) 1411 K St NW Ste 1300 *Web:* www.worldcocoafoundation.org	Washington	DC	20005	202-737-7870	737-7832	49-6
WCF (Waterloo-Cedar Falls Symphony) Gallagher-Bluedorn PAC Ste 17 *Web:* wcfsymphony.org	Cedar Falls	IA	50614	319-273-3373		573-3
WCF (Women's Campaign Fund) 718 Seventh St NW 2nd Fl *Web:* www.wcfonline.org	Washington	DC	20001	202-796-8259		48-7
WCF Insurance *Workers' Compensation Fund* 100 W Towne Ridge Pkwy *TF:* 800-446-2667 ■ *Web:* www.wcf.com	Sandy	UT	84070	385-351-8000		339-45
WCFB-FM 94.5 (AC) 4192 N John Young Pkwy *Web:* www.star945.com	Orlando	FL	32804	407-294-2945		645-114
WCG 915 Fort St 5th Fl *TF:* 888-562-9283 ■ *Web:* www.wcgservices.com	Victoria	BC	V8V3K3	250-389-0699	389-0696	260
WCGL-AM 1360 (Rel) 3890 Dunn Ave Ste 804 *Web:* www.wcgl1360.com	Jacksonville	FL	32218	904-766-9955	765-9214	645-76
WCGS (Wilson County Genealogical Society) PO Box 802 *Web:* www.wcgs.org	Wilson	NC	27894	252-243-1660		48-13
WCHL-AM 201 S Estes Dr Ste C6a *Web:* www.chapelboro.com	Chapel Hill	NC	27514	919-933-4165	968-3748	647
WCHM-AM 683 Grant St Ste U *Web:* www.wchmradio.com	Clarkesville	GA	30523	706-839-1490		647
WCHP-AM 137 Rapids Rd PO Box 888 *Web:* www.wchp.com	Champlain	NY	12919	518-298-2800		647
WCHR-AM 619 Alexander Rd 3rd Fl *Web:* www.920thejersey.com	Princeton	NJ	08540	609-419-0300	419-0143	647
WCHS (Washington County Historical Society) 118 E Dickson St *Web:* www.washcohistoricalsociety.org	Fayetteville	AR	72701	479-521-2970		637-2
WCHS (Westchester County Historical Society) 2199 Saw Mill River Rd *Web:* www.westchesterhistory.com	Elmsford	NY	10523	914-592-4323	231-1510	49-19
WCHS-AM 1111 Virginia St E *Web:* www.wchsnetwork.com	Charleston	WV	25301	304-342-8131		645-31
WCHS-TV Ch 8 (ABC) 1301 Piedmont Rd *TF:* 888-696-9247 ■ *Web:* www.wchstv.com	Charleston	WV	25301	304-346-5358	346-4765	741-25
WCHT-AM 524 Ludington St Ste 300 *Web:* www.radioresultsnetwork.com	Escanaba	MI	49829	906-789-0600		647
WCHV-AM 1150 Pepsi Pl *Web:* www.wchv.com	Charlottesville	VA	22901	434-978-4408		647
WCHX-FM 114 N Logan Blvd *Web:* www.chx105.com	Burnham	ME	04922	717-242-1055		647
WCI (West Coast Internet Inc) PO Box 7598 *Web:* www.westcoastinternet.com	Capistrano Beach	CA	92624	949-487-3302		681
WCI Communities Inc 24301 Walden Center Dr *TF:* 800-924-4005 ■ *Web:* www.wcicommunities.com	Bonita Springs	FL	34134	239-498-8200		653
WCIC-FM 91.5 (Rel) 3902 W Baring Trace *TF:* 877-692-9242 ■ *Web:* www.wcicfm.org	Peoria	IL	61615	309-692-9242	692-9241	645-119
WCIE-FM 6214 Springer Dr *Web:* www.florida.thejoyfm.com	Port Richey	FL	34668	727-848-9150	848-1233	647
WCIR-FM 306 S Kanawha St *Web:* www.103cir.com	Beckley	WV	25801	304-253-7000		647
Wcities Inc 1212 Broadway Ste 910 *Web:* wcities.com	San Francisco	CA	94107	415-495-8090	495-8093	772
WCIV-TV Ch 4 (ABC) PO Box 22165 *Web:* www.abcnews4.com	Charleston	SC	29413	843-881-4444		741-24
WCIZ-FM 134 Mullin St *Web:* www.z93.fm	Watertown	NY	13601	315-788-0790	788-4379	647
WCJ - Pilgrim Wire LLC 4180 N Port Washington Rd *Web:* www.wcjwire.com	Glendale	WI	53212	414-291-9566		492
WCJK-FM 96.3 (Var) 504 Rosedale Ave *Web:* 963jackfm.com	Nashville	TN	37211	615-259-4567		645-106
WCKK-FM PO Box 1700 *Web:* www.kicks96news.com	Kosciusko	MS	39090	662-289-1050	289-7907	647
WCKX-FM 107.5 (Urban) 350 E First Ave Ste 100 *Web:* mycolumbuspower.com	Columbus	OH	43201	614-487-1444		645-40
WCL (Washoe County Library) 301 S Center St *Web:* washoecountylibrary.us	Reno	NV	89501	775-327-8300	327-8341	434-3
WCL Co 16730 E Johnson Dr *TF:* 800-331-3816 ■ *Web:* www.wclco.com	City of Industry	CA	91744	626-968-5523	369-9805	351
WCLC-AM 224 W Central Ave PO Box 1509 *Web:* www.newlife105.com	Jamestown	TN	38556	931-879-8188		647
WCLK-FM 91.9 111 James P Brawley Dr SW *TF:* 888-448-3925 ■ *Web:* wclk.com	Atlanta	GA	30314	404-880-8284	880-8869	645-11
WCLN-AM 118 E Main St *TF:* 866-887-1170 ■ *Web:* www.oldies1170.com	Clinton	NC	28328	910-592-8949	592-3732	647
WCLT-FM 100.3 (Ctry) PO Box 5150 *Web:* www.wclt.com	Newark	OH	43058	740-345-4004		645
WCM Group Inc, The 110 S Bender Ave *Web:* wcmgroup.com	Humble	TX	77338	281-446-7070		196
WCM Investment Management 281 Brooks St *Web:* www.wcminvest.com	Laguna Beach	CA	92651	949-380-0200		401
WCMA (Williams College Museum of Art) 15 Lawrence Hall Dr Ste 2 *Web:* wcma.williams.edu	Williamstown	MA	01267	413-597-2429		166
WCMH (Windham Community Memorial Hospital) 112 Mansfield Ave *Web:* windhamhospital.org	Willimantic	CT	06226	860-456-9116	456-6838	374-3
WCMHS (Washington County Mental Health Services Inc) PO Box 647 *Web:* www.wcmhs.org	Montpelier	VT	05602	802-229-1399	223-8623	353
WCMP-AM 15429 Pokegama Lake Rd *Web:* www.wcmpradio.com	Pine City	MN	55063	320-629-7575		647

Name / Address	City	State	ZIP	Phone	Fax	Class
WCMU-TV 1999 E Campus Dr *TF:* 800-727-9268 ■ *Web:* www.wcmu.org	Mount Pleasant	MI	48859	989-774-3105	774-4427	647
WCNC-TV Ch 36 (NBC) 1001 Wood Ridge Center Dr *Web:* www.wcnc.com	Charlotte	NC	28217	704-329-3631		741-26
WCOJ-AM PO Box 798 *Web:* www.holyspiritradio.org	Doylestown	PA	18901	215-345-1570	345-1946	647
WCOL-FM 92.3 (Ctry) 2323 W Fifth Ave Ste 200 *TF:* 800-899-9265 ■ *Web:* wcol.iheart.com	Columbus	OH	43204	614-486-6101		645-40
WCOV-TV Ch 20 (Fox) 1 W Cov Ave *Web:* www.wcov.com	Montgomery	AL	36111	334-288-7020	288-5414	741-86
Wcp Solutions 6703 S 234th St Ste 120 *TF:* 877-398-3030 ■ *Web:* www.wcpsolutions.com	Kent	WA	98032	877-398-3030		552-1
WCPO TV 1720 Gilbert Ave *Web:* www.wcpo.com	Cincinnati	OH	45202	513-721-9900		532-2
WCQR-FM 88.3 (Rel) 2312 Oak St *TF:* 888-477-5676 ■ *Web:* www.wcqr.org	Gray	TN	37615	423-477-5676	477-7060	645
WCQS-FM 88.1 (NPR) 73 Broadway *TF:* 866-448-3881 ■ *Web:* bpr.org	Asheville	NC	28801	828-210-4800	210-4801	645-10
WCR (Women's Council of Realtors) 430 N Michigan Ave **Fax Area Code:* 312 ■ *TF:* 800-245-8512 ■ *Web:* www.wcr.org	Chicago	IL	60611	800-245-8512	329-3290*	49-17
WCRN-AM 830 (N/T) 276 Turnpike Rd *Web:* www.wcrnradio.com	Westborough	MA	01581	508-870-5803	870-2960	645-171
WCS (Wildlife Conservation Society) 2300 Southern Blvd *Web:* www.wcs.org	Bronx	NY	10460	718-220-5100		48-3
WCS (Wholesale Carrier Services Inc) 12350 NW 39th St *TF:* 888-940-5600 ■ *Web:* www.wcs.com	Coral Springs	FL	33065	888-940-5600		224
WCSC-TV Ch 5 (CBS) 2126 Charlie Hall Blvd *Web:* www.live5news.com	Charleston	SC	29414	843-402-5555		741-24
WCSD (Wallkill Central School District) 19 Main St PO Box 310 *Web:* www.wallkillcsd.k12.ny.us	Wallkill	NY	12589	845-895-7100	895-3630	685
WCSE-FM 130 Sharp Hill Rd *Web:* www.wcse.typepad.com	Uncasville	CT	06382	860-848-1111		647
WCSG-FM 91.3 (Rel) 1159 E Beltline Ave NE *Web:* www.wcsg.org	Grand Rapids	MI	49525	616-942-1500		645-63
WCSR Inc PO Box 273 *Web:* radiohillsdale.com	Hillsdale	MI	49242	517-437-4444		645-141
WCSS-AM 1250 Riverfront Cente *Web:* www.wcss1490.com	Amsterdam	NY	12010	518-684-6400		647
WCTI-TV 225 Glenburnie Dr *Web:* www.wcti12.com	New Bern	NC	28561	252-638-1212	637-4141	647
WCTK-FM 75 Oxford St Ste 402 *Web:* www.wctk.com	Providence	RI	02905	401-467-4366		647
WCTL-FM 106.3 (Rel) 10912 Peach St *Web:* www.wctl.org	Waterford	PA	16441	814-796-6000		645
WCTO-FM 96.1 (Ctry) 2158 Ave C Ste 100 *Web:* www.catcountry96.com	Bethlehem	PA	18017	610-266-7600		645
WCTR-AM 231 Flatland Rd *Web:* www.wctr.com	Chestertown	MD	21620	410-778-1530	778-4800	647
WCTV-TV Ch 6 (CBS) 1801 Halstead Blvd *TF:* 800-798-2510 ■ *Web:* www.wctv.tv	Tallahassee	FL	32309	850-893-6666		741-132
WCU (Western Carolina University) 1 University Dr *TF:* 877-928-4968 ■ *Web:* www.wcu.edu	Cullowhee	NC	28723	828-227-7211	227-7319	166
WCUW-FM 91.3 (Var) 910 Main St *Web:* www.wcuw.org	Worcester	MA	01610	508-753-1012		645-171
WCVB-TV Ch 5 (ABC) 5 TV Pl *Web:* www.wcvb.com	Needham	MA	02494	781-449-0400		741
WCVE-TV Ch 23 (PBS) 23 Sesame St *TF:* 800-476-8440 ■ *Web:* ideastations.org	Richmond	VA	23235	804-320-1301		741-108
WCVT (Waitsfield and Champlain Valley Telecom) 3898 Main St *TF:* 800-496-3391 ■ *Web:* www.wcvt.com	Waitsfield	VT	05673	802-496-3393		224
WCWC (Western Canada Wilderness Committee) 46 E Sixth Ave *TF:* 800-661-9453 ■ *Web:* wildernesscommittee.org	Vancouver	BC	V5T1J4	604-683-8220	683-8229	48-13
WCWF-TV Ch 14 (CW) 787 Lombardi Ave *TF:* 800-242-8067 ■ *Web:* cw14online.com	Green Bay	WI	54304	920-494-8711	494-8782	741-55
WCWG-TV 1701 Pleasant Ridge Rd *Web:* www.wxii12.com	Greensboro	NC	27409	336-307-4900	307-4950	647
WCWN-TV 1400 Balltown Rd *Web:* www.cwalbany.com	Schenectady	NY	12309	518-381-4900	381-3734	647
WCYB-TV Ch 5 (NBC) 101 Lee St *Web:* wcyb.com	Bristol	VA	24201	276-645-1555		741
WCYN-AM 130 S Main S *Web:* www.wcyn.com	Cynthiana	KY	41031	859-234-1400		647
WCYO-FM 128 Bill Hill Ave *Web:* www.wcyofm.com	Richmond	KY	40475	859-623-1386	623-1341	647
WCYY-FM One City Ctr *Web:* www.wcyy.com	Portland	ME	04101	207-774-6364		647
WCZY-FM 4895 E Wing Rd *Web:* www.my1043.net	Mount Pleasant	MI	48858	989-772-9664		647
WD Burch Inc 1062 Calle Negocio Ste I *Web:* www.wdburch.com	San Clemente	CA	92673	949-369-1950	369-1935	425
WD Manor Mechanical Contractors Inc 1838 N 23rd Ave *Web:* www.wdmanor.com	Phoenix	AZ	85009	602-253-0703		189-10
WD Partners 7007 Discovery Blvd *TF:* 888-335-0014 ■ *Web:* www.wdpartners.com	Dublin	OH	43017	614-634-7000		261
WD-40 Co 1061 Cudahy Pl *NASDAQ:* WDFC ■ *TF:* 800-448-9340 ■ *Web:* www.wd40company.com	San Diego	CA	92110	619-275-1400	275-5823	541
WDAC Radio Co PO Box 3022 *Web:* www.wdac.com	Lancaster	PA	17604	717-284-4123	284-2300	645-141
WDAF-TV Ch 4 (Fox) 3030 Summit *Web:* www.fox4kc.com	Kansas City	MO	64108	816-753-4567		741-68
WDAM-TV Ch 7 (NBC) PO Box 16269 *TF:* 800-844-9326 ■ *Web:* www.wdam.com	Hattiesburg	MS	39404	601-544-4730	584-9302	741
WDBJ-TV 2807 Hershberger Rd *TF:* 800-777-9325 ■ *Web:* www.wdbj7.com	Roanoke	VA	24017	540-344-7000	344-5097	647
WDBQ-FM 107.5 (Oldies) 5490 Saratoga Rd *Web:* myq1075.com	Dubuque	IA	52002	563-557-1040		645-49
WDBR 103.7 3501 E Sangamon Ave *Web:* www.wdbr.com	Springfield	IL	62707	217-753-5400	753-7902	645-152
WDCQ-TV Delta Rd **Fax Area Code:* 989 ■ *TF:* 877-472-7677 ■ *Web:* www.deltabroadcasting.org	University Center	MI	48710	877-472-7677	686-0155*	647
WDCW-TV 2121 Wisconsin Ave NW Ste 350 *Web:* dcw50.com	Washington	DC	20007	202-965-5050		741-139
WDCX-FM 99.5 (Rel) 625 Delaware Ave Ste 308 *TF:* 800-684-2848 ■ *Web:* www.wdcxradio.com	Buffalo	NY	14202	716-883-3010		645-25
WDEF-TV Ch 12 (CBS) 3300 Broad St *Web:* wdef.com	Chattanooga	TN	37408	423-785-1200	785-1271	741-27
WDEL-AM 1150 (N/T) 2727 Shipley Rd *TF:* 800-544-1150 ■ *Web:* www.wdel.com	Wilmington	DE	19810	302-478-2700	478-0100	645-174
WDEN-FM 99.1 (Ctry) 544 Mulberry St 5th Fl *Web:* www.wden.com	Macon	GA	31201	478-746-6286		645-91
WDET-FM 101.9 (NPR) Wayne State University 4600 Cass Ave *Web:* wdet.org	Detroit	MI	48201	313-577-4146	577-1300	645-48
WDEV-AM 550 9 Stowe St PO Box 550 *Web:* wdevradio.com	Waterbury	VT	05676	802-244-7321	244-1771	645
WDFX-TV 2221 Ross Clark Cir *Web:* www.dothanconnect.revrocket.us	Dothan	AL	36301	334-794-3434		647
WDI (Warren Distributing Inc) 8737 Dice Rd *Web:* www.warrendist.com	Santa Fe Springs	CA	90670	562-789-3360	789-3361	61
WDIO-TV Ch 10 (ABC) 10 Observation Rd *TF:* 800-477-1013 ■ *Web:* www.wdio.com	Duluth	MN	55811	218-727-6864	727-4415	741-42
WDIV-TV Ch 4 (NBC) 550 W Lafayette Blvd *Web:* www.clickondetroit.com	Detroit	MI	48226	313-222-0500		741-41
WDIY-FM 88.1 (NPR) 301 Broadway *Web:* wdiy.org	Bethlehem	PA	18015	610-694-8100	954-9474	645
WDJA -AM 1420 (N/T) 588 Haverhill Rd *Web:* universo1420.com	West Palm Beach	FL	33415	561-278-1420		645
WDJC-FM 120 Summit Pky Ste 200 *Web:* www.wdjconline.com	Birmingham	AL	35209	205-879-3324		647
WDKN-AM 108 W College St *Web:* www.wdkn.com	Dickson	TN	37055	615-446-4000		647
WDKX-FM 103.9 (Urban) 683 E Main St *Web:* www.wdkx.com	Rochester	NY	14605	585-262-2050	262-2626	645-135
WDKY-TV Ch 56 (Fox) 836 Euclid Ave Ste 201 *TF:* 888-404-5656 ■ *Web:* www.foxlexington.com	Lexington	KY	40502	859-269-5656		741-73
WDL (Wilmington Drama League) 10 W Lea Blvd *Web:* www.wilmingtondramaleague.org	Wilmington	DE	19802	302-764-1172		573-4
WDL Systems 220 Chatham Business Dr *TF:* 800-548-2319 ■ *Web:* www.wdlsystems.com	Pittsboro	NC	27312	919-545-2500	545-2559	174
WDLB-AM 1714 N Central Ave *Web:* www.wdlbam.com	Marshfield	WI	54449	715-384-2191	387-3588	647
WDLT-FM 2800 Dauphin St Ste 104 *TF:* 866-468-1041 ■ *Web:* www.1041wdlt.com	Mobile	AL	36606	251-652-2007	652-2001	647
WDM Support Services Inc 1900 Harrison St *Web:* www.wdmquincy.com	Quincy	IL	62301	217-228-1950	222-6053	175
WDMA (Window & Door Manufacturers Assn) 330 N Wabash Ave Ste 2000 **Fax Area Code:* 651 ■ *Web:* www.wdma.com	Chicago	IL	60611	847-299-5200	264-5150*	49-3
WDMP Radio 2163 Hwy 161 PO Box 0 *Web:* www.d99point3.com	Dodgeville	WI	53533	608-935-2302	935-3404	116
WDNA-FM 88.9 (Jazz) 2921 Coral Way *Web:* www.wdna.org	Miami	FL	33145	305-662-8889		645-96
WDNN-TV 101 S Spencer St PO Box 1740 *Web:* www.wdnntv.com	Dalton	GA	30721	706-278-9713	278-7950	647
WDNY-FM 195 Main St *TF:* 888-939-9369 ■ *Web:* classicrock939.com	Dansville	NY	14437	585-698-2757	625-0311	647
WDOC Inc 95 Jackson St *Web:* q95fm.net	Prestonsburg	KY	41653	606-886-2338	263-4923	645-141
WDOD-FM 96.5 (CHR) 2615 S Broad St *Web:* www.hits96.com	Chattanooga	TN	37408	423-642-9636		645-155
WDPN-AM 393 Smyth Ave PO Box 2356 *Web:* www.am1310wdpn.com	Alliance	OH	44601	330-821-1111		647
WDPR-FM 88.1 (Clas) 126 N Main St *Web:* discoverclassical.org	Dayton	OH	45402	937-222-9377	496-3852	645-44
WDRB-TV Ch 41 (Fox) 624 W Muhammad Ali Blvd *Web:* www.wdrb.com	Louisville	KY	40203	502-584-6441	589-5559	741-77
WDRM-FM 102.1 26869 Peoples Rd *TF:* 866-302-0102 ■ *Web:* wdrm.iheart.com	Madison	AL	35756	256-309-2400		645
WDRV-FM 97.1 (CR) 875 N Michigan Ave Ste 1510 *Web:* wdrv.com	Chicago	IL	60611	312 274 9710	274-1304	645-34
WDSD-FM 94.7 (Ctry) 920 W Basin Rd Ste 400 *TF:* 877-947-9373 ■ *Web:* wdsd.iheart.com	New Castle	DE	19720	302-395-9800		645
WDSE-TV Ch 8 (PBS) 632 Niagara Ct *TF:* 888-563-9373 ■ *Web:* www.wdse.org	Duluth	MN	55811	218-788-2831		741-42
WDSI-TV 1101 E Main St *Web:* www.myfoxchattanooga.com	Chattanooga	TN	37408	423-265-0061		647
WDSM-AM 11 E Superior St Ste 380 *Web:* www.wdsm710.com	Duluth	MN	55802	218-722-4321	722-5423	647
WDSU-TV Ch 6 (NBC) 846 Howard Ave *TF:* 888-925-4127 ■ *Web:* www.wdsu.com	New Orleans	LA	70113	504-679-0600	679-0752	741-90
WDSY-FM 107.9 651 Holiday Dr Foster Plz 5 *Web:* y108.radio.com	Pittsburgh	PA	15220	412-922-1079		645-123
WDTN 4595 S Dixie Ave *Web:* www.wdtn.com	Dayton	OH	45439	937-293-2101	296-7147	741-38

Phone | Fax | Class

WDTV-TV 5 Television Dr .... Bridgeport WV 26330 304-848-5000 842-7501 647
Web: www.wdtv.com

WDVD-FM 96.3 (AC)
3011 W Grand Blvd Fisher Bldg Ste 800 .... Detroit MI 48202 313-871-3030 645-48
Web: www.963wdvd.com

WDVI-FM 100 Chestnut St .... Rochester NY 14604 585-222-5100 647
Web: rochestersmix.iheart.com

We Are Alexander
1227 Washington Ave..................... Saint Louis MO 63103 844-922-0002 232
TF: 844-922-0002 ■ *Web:* www.wearealexander.com

We Are Sharing Hope SC
164 Lott Ct Ste B .... West Columbia SC 29169 803-796-2195 269
Web: www.sharinghopesc.org

WE Aubuchon Company Inc
95 Aubuchon Dr......................... Westminster MA 01473 978-874-0521 364
TF: 800-431-2712 ■ *Web:* www.hardwarestore.com

WE Bassett Co 100 Trap Falls Rd Ext .... Shelton CT 06484 203-929-8483 214
Web: www.trim.com

WE Blain & Sons Inc 98 Pearce Rd .... Mount Olive MS 39119 601-797-4551 188-4
Web: blain-co.com

We Buy Guitars LLC 705 Bedford Ave........... Bellmore NY 11710 516-221-0563 366
Web: webuyguitars.org

We Check Inc 301 Moodie Dr Ste 320 .... Ottawa ON K2H9C4 877-889-0602 596-0287* 194
**Fax Area Code:* 613 ■ *TF:* 877-889-0602 ■ *Web:* www.wecheckservice.com

We Energies
231 W Michigan St PO Box 2046............. Milwaukee WI 53203 414-221-2345 787
TF: 800-242-9137 ■ *Web:* www.we-energies.com

WE Family Offices LLC
701 Brickell Ave Ste 2100...................... Miami FL 33131 305-825-2225 825-7790 401
Web: www.wefamilyoffices.com

WE Neal Slate Co 2840 Hwy 25 .... Watertown MN 55388 952-955-3340 955-3341 724
Web: www.nealslate.com

We Print Today LLC 66 Summer St............. Kingston MA 02364 781-585-6021 627
Web: www.weprinttoday.com

We Raise Foundation
1 Pierce Pl Ste 250E........................... Itasca IL 60143 630-766-9066 766-9622 48-20
TF: 800-762-6748 ■ *Web:* weraise.org

WE Transport Inc 75 Commercial St............ Plainview NY 11803 516-349-8200 349-8275 109
Web: www.wetransport.com

WE Yoder Inc 41 S Maple St .... Kutztown PA 19530 610-683-7383 683-8638 188-8
TF: 800-889-5149 ■ *Web:* www.weyoderinc.com

WEA Insurance Corp PO Box 7338 .... Madison WI 53707 608-276-4000 276-9119 390
Web: www.weatrust.com

WEAA-FM 88.9 (Jazz)
1700 E Cold Spring Ln...................... Baltimore MD 21251 443-885-3564 885-8206 645-15
Web: weaa.org

Weaber Inc 1231 Mt Wilson Rd................. Lebanon PA 17042 717-867-2212 499
TF: 800-745-9663 ■ *Web:* www.weaberlumber.com

WEAI (Western Economic Association Intl)
18837 Brookhurst St Ste 304 .... Fountain Valley CA 92708 714-965-8800 965-8829 49-2
Web: www.weai.org

Weakley County 116 W Main St Rm 104 .... Dresden TN 38225 731-364-2285 364-5236 338
Web: www.weakleycountytn.gov

Weakley County Chamber of Commerce
114 W Maple St PO Box 67 .... Dresden TN 38225 731-364-3787 364-2099 139
Web: www.weakleycountychamber.com

Wealth Conservancy Inc, The
1525 Spruce St Ste 300 .... Boulder CO 80302 303-444-1919 401
TF: 888-440-1919 ■ *Web:* www.thewealthconservancy.com

WealthCo Financial Group LLC
1080 W Sam Houston Pkwy N Ste 1............. Houston TX 77043 713-935-0829 935-0034 2
Web: www.wealthcofinancial.com

WealthForge Holdings Inc
6800 Paragon Pl Ste 237 .... Richmond VA 23230 804-308-0431 387
TF: 866-603-4115 ■ *Web:* www.wealthforge.com

Wealthfront Inc 541 Cowper St .... Palo Alto CA 94301 844-995-8437 401
TF: 844-995-8437 ■ *Web:* www.wealthfront.com

Wealthminder Inc
1765 Greensboro Station Pl Ste 900............. McLean VA 22102 571-766-8021 180
Web: wealthminder.com

Wealthsimple Inc
860 Richmond St W 3rd Fl..................... Toronto ON M6J1C9 855-255-9038 528
TF: 855-255-9038 ■ *Web:* www.wealthsimple.com

WEAO-TV Ch 49 (PBS)
1750 Campus Center Dr.......................... Kent OH 44240 330-677-4549 678-0688 741
TF: 800-554-4549 ■ *Web:* westernreservepublicmedia.org

WEAP (Women's Economic Agenda Project)
160 Franklin St Ste 208 .... Oakland CA 94607 510-986-8620 986-8628 48-24
Web: www.weap.org

Wear - Concepts Inc
106 NW Business Park Ln .... Riverside MO 64150 816-587-1923 480
TF: 800-493-2726 ■ *Web:* www.wearcon.com

Wear-Tek Inc 8021 W Hwy 2................... Spokane WA 99224 509-747-4139 747-7113 308
Web: www.wear-tek.com

WEAR-TV Ch 3 (ABC) 4990 Mobile Hwy........ Pensacola FL 32506 850-456-3333 455-8972 741
TF: 866-856-9327 ■ *Web:* www.weartv.com

Wearwell Inc 199 Threet Industrial Rd............ Smyrna TN 37167 507-392-0911 676
TF: 888-451-8929 ■ *Web:* www.wearwell.com

Weastec Inc 1600 N High St.................. Hillsboro OH 45133 937-393-6800 393-3020 60
Web: www.weastec.com

Weather Ch Inc, The 300 I N Pkwy .... Atlanta GA 30339 770-226-0000 226-2632 740
TF: 866-843-0392 ■ *Web:* weather.com

Weather Champions Ltd 158 Dikeman St .... Brooklyn NY 11231 718-522-0300 189-10

Weather Network, The
2655 Bristol Cir .... Oakville ON L6H7W1 905-829-1159 740
Web: www.theweathernetwork.com

Weather Shield Manufacturing Inc
1 Weather Shield Plz PO Box 309............... Medford WI 54451 715-748-2100 222-2146* 236
**Fax Area Code:* 800 ■ *TF:* 800-222-2995 ■ *Web:* weathershield.com

Weatherall Printing Co
1349 Cliff Gookin Blvd .... Tupelo MS 38801 662-842-5284 627
TF: 800-273-6043 ■ *Web:* weatherallprinting.com

Weatherby Inc 1605 Commerce Way .... Paso Robles CA 93446 805-227-2600 237-0427 284
TF: 800-227-2016 ■ *Web:* www.weatherby.com

Weatherford 2000 St James Pl .... Houston TX 77056 713-836-4000 539
Web: www.weatherford.com

Weatherford Aerospace Inc
1020 E Columbia St..................... Weatherford TX 76086 817-594-5464 594-7450 256
Web: weatherfordaerospace.com

Weatherford Artificial Lift Systems
515 Post Oak Blvd Ste 600................... Houston TX 77027 435-722-0990 537
Web: www.weatherford.com

Weatherford Chamber of Commerce
401 Ft Worth St.......................... Weatherford TX 76086 817-596-3801 613-9216 139
TF: 888-594-3801 ■ *Web:* www.weatherford-chamber.com

Weatherford College
225 College Pk Dr .... Weatherford TX 76086 817-594-5471 598-6205 162
TF: 800-287-5471 ■ *Web:* www.wc.edu

Weatherford Democrat
512 Palo Pinto St .... Weatherford TX 76086 817-594-7447 532-2
Web: www.weatherforddemocrat.com

Weatherford International Inc
515 Post Oak Blvd Ste 600................... Houston TX 77027 713-693-4000 537
NYSE: WFT ■ *TF:* 866-398-0010 ■ *Web:* www.weatherford.com

Weatherford Motors Inc 735 Ashby Ave......... Berkeley CA 94710 855-571-5269 57
TF: 855-571-5269 ■ *Web:* www.weatherfordbmw.com

Weatherford Public Library
1014 Charles St .... Weatherford TX 76086 817-598-4150 598-4161 434-3
Web: ci.weatherford.tx.us

Weatherhaven Global Resources Ltd
2120 Hartley Ave.......................... Coquitlam BC V3K6W5 604-451-8900 106
Web: www.weatherhaven.com

Weatherhead Center for International Affairs
1737 Cambridge St........................ Cambridge MA 02138 617-495-4420 495-8292 634
Web: wcfia.harvard.edu

Weathermatic 3301 W Kingsley Rd .... Garland TX 75041 888-484-3776 271-5710* 429
**Fax Area Code:* 972 ■ *TF:* 888-484-3776 ■ *Web:* www.weathermatic.com

Weatherproof Garment Co
4 Bryant Pk 12th Fl........................ New York NY 10018 212-695-7716 155-12
Web: weatherproofgarment.com

Weather-Rite LLC 616 N 5th St.............. Minneapolis MN 55401 612-338-1401 664
Web: www.weather-rite.com

Weathers Auto Supply Inc
23308 Airpark Dr .... Petersburg VA 23803 804-861-1076 54
TF: 888-572-2886 ■ *Web:* weathers.martincohosting.com

Weathervane Community Playhouse
1301 Weathervane Ln.............................. Akron OH 44313 330-836-2626 873-2150 572
Web: www.weathervaneplayhouse.com

Weathervane Seafood Restaurant
306 US Rt 1 .... Kittery ME 03904 207-439-0330 670
TF: 800-914-1774 ■ *Web:* weathervaneseafoods.com

WEAU-TV 1907 S Hasting Way .... Eau Claire WI 54701 715-835-1313 832-0246 647
Web: www.weau.com

Weaver 2821 W 7th St Ste 700................ Fort Worth TX 76107 817-332-7905 429-5936 2
TF: 800-332-7952 ■ *Web:* www.weaver.com

Weaver & Sons Inc 1200 Ward Ave .... Talladega AL 35160 256-362-3614 697
Web: www.weaverandsons.com

Weaver Bros Inc 2230 Spar Ave .... Anchorage AK 99501 907-278-4526 276-4316 780
TF: 800-478-4600 ■ *Web:* weaverbrothersinc.com

Weaver Bros Insurance Associates Inc
4550 Montgomery Ave Ste 300 North Tower ..... Bethesda MD 20814 301-986-4400 390
Web: www.weaverbros.com

Weaver C. Barksdale & Associates Inc
1 Burton Hills Blvd Ste 100 .... Nashville TN 37215 615-665-1085 665-1087 528
Web: www.wcbarksdale.com

Weaver Call & House Lc
7070 Union Park Ave Ste 380.................. Midvale UT 84047 801-947-1788 2
Web: wch-cpa.com

Weaver Co 1108 S 37th St.................. Kansas City KS 66106 913-831-1800 831-2974 821
Web: www.weaver-sales.com

Weaver Cooke Construction LLC
8401 Key Blvd .... Greensboro NC 27409 336-378-7900 378-7901 186
Web: www.weavercooke.com

Weaver Industries Inc
425 S Fourth St PO Box 326.................... Denver PA 17517 717-336-7507 336-4182 454
Web: www.weaverind.com

Weaver Manufacturing Co
3101 Justin Rd........................ Flower Mound TX 75028 972-539-1537 567
Web: www.weavermanufacturing.com

Weaver-Bailey Contractors Inc
PO Box 60 .... El Paso AR 72045 501-796-2301 796-2372 189-3
TF: 800-253-3385 ■ *Web:* www.weaverbailey.com

Weavertown Environmental Group
2 Dorrington Rd .... Carnegie PA 15106 800-746-4850 187
TF: 800-746-4850 ■ *Web:* www.weavertown.com

Weavexx 14101 Capital Blvd .... Youngsville NC 27596 919-556-7235 556-2432 745-3
Web: www.xerium.com

WEB (Worldwide Employee Benefits Network Inc)
11520 N Central Expy Ste 201 .... Dallas TX 75243 888-795-6862 382-3038* 49-12
**Fax Area Code:* 214 ■ *TF:* 888-795-6862 ■ *Web:* www.webnetwork.org

Web Advanced 36 Discovery Ste 150 .... Irvine CA 92618 888-261-7414 453-1806* 177
**Fax Area Code:* 949 ■ *TF:* 888-261-7414 ■ *Web:* www.webadvanced.com

Web Age Solutions Inc
439 University Ave Ste 820.................... Toronto ON M5G1Y8 866-206-4644 225
TF: 866-206-4644 ■ *Web:* www.webagesolutions.com

Web Clients LLC
2300 Vartan Way Ste 100.................. Harrisburg PA 17110 717-346-3600 346-0597 195
Web: www.webclients.net

Web Conferencing Central
1539 Monrovia Ave Ste 11 .... Newport Beach CA 92663 949-939-9372 681
Web: www.web-conferencing-central.com

Web Creations & Consulting L L C
119 W Iron Ave 3rd Fl........................ Salina KS 67401 785-823-7630 180
Web: www.wccit.com

Web Direct Brands Inc
13100 State Rd 54 .... Odessa FL 33556 813-920-7259 225
TF: 888-932-4749 ■ *Web:* www.webdirectbrands.com

Web Equipment 464 Central Rd .... Fredericksburg VA 22401 540-657-5855 190
TF: 800-225-3858 ■ *Web:* www.webequipment.com

Web Marketing LLC PO Box 330212 .... West Hartford CT 06133 203-548-7736 561-0416* 225
**Fax Area Code:* 860 ■ *Web:* www.strategiesseo.com

Web Mentors Inc PO Box 3500-414............. Sisters OR 97759 541-323-2932 225
Web: www.webmentors.com

Name / Address	City	State	Zip	Phone	Fax	Class
Web Offset Printing Company Inc 12198 44th St N	Clearwater	FL	33762	727-572-7488	572-7749	627
Web: www.weboffsetprint.com						
Web Presence Architects LLC 10113 Meadowneck Ct	Silver Spring	MD	20910	888-873-6218		809
TF: 888-873-6218 ■ *Web:* wpaconsulting.com						
Web Seal Inc 15 Oregon St	Rochester	NY	14605	585-546-1320	546-5746	326
TF: 800-366-1320 ■ *Web:* www.websealinc.com						
Web Strategies Internet Solutions LLC 124 Amherst St	Winchester	VA	22601	540-869-5991	827-4177	177
TF: 800-861-8074 ■ *Web:* www.webstrategies.com						
Web Talent Marketing 322 N Arch St Ste 120	Lancaster	PA	17603	717-283-4045		195
TF: 800-405-2947 ■ *Web:* www.webtalentmarketing.com						
Web Yoga Inc 938 Senate Dr	Dayton	OH	45459	937-428-0000		180
TF: 800-886-3266 ■ *Web:* www.webyoga.com						
Web Your Business Inc 226 Saxony Rd	Johnstown	CO	80534	970-593-6260		225
Web: www.webyourbusiness.com						
Webair Internet Development Inc 501 Franklin Ave	Garden City	NY	11530	516-938-4100	938-5100	225
TF: 866-932-2471 ■ *Web:* www.webair.com						
Webaloo 305 Greeley St S Ste 305	Stillwater	MN	55082	651-351-1041		177
Web: webaloo.com						
Webapper Services LLC 117 E Mountain Ave Ste 222	Fort Collins	CO	80524	970-223-2278		396
Web: www.webapper.com						
WebAssistcom Corp 227 N El Camino Real Ste 204	Encinitas	CA	92024	760-633-4013		177
Web: www.webassist.com						
Webasto Roof Systems Inc 1757 Northfield Dr	Rochester Hills	MI	48309	248-997-5100		60
Web: www.webasto.com						
Webb & Coyle PLLC 910 N Sandhills Blvd	Aberdeen	NC	28315	910-944-9555		41
Web: webbcoyle.com						
Webb & Tapella Law Corp 7311 Greenhaven Dr Ste 273	Sacramento	CA	95831	916-447-1675		41
Web: probateattorneys.com						
Webb & Taylor LLC 400 W Park Ct Ste 220	Peachtree City	GA	30269	770-631-1811		41
Web: webbfirmattorneys.com						
Webb Automotive Group Inc 3911 E Main St	Farmington	NM	87402	505-325-1911		60
Web: www.webbauto.com						
Webb Chemical Service Corp 2708 Jarman St	Muskegon	MI	49444	231-733-2181	739-5454	146
Web: webbchemical.com						
Webb County 1110 Washington St	Laredo	TX	78040	956-523-4143	523-5012	338
Web: www.webbcounty.com						
Webb County Appraisal District 3302 Clark Blvd	Laredo	TX	78043	956-718-4091	718-4052	41
TF: 800-252-9121 ■ *Web:* www.webbcad.org						
Webb Financial Group 8120 Penn Ave S Ste 177	Bloomington	MN	55431	952-837-3200		401
TF: 800-927-9322 ■ *Web:* www.webbfinancial.com						
Webb Heating & Air Conditioning 170 Webb Way	Advance	NC	27006	336-998-2121		189-10
Web: webbhvac.com						
Webb Institute 298 Crescent Beach Rd	Glen Cove	NY	11542	516-671-2213	674-9838	166
TF: 866-708-9322 ■ *Web:* www.webb.edu						
Webb Manufacturing Co 1241 Carpenter St	Philadelphia	PA	19147	215-336-5570	336-4422	733
Web: www.webbmfg.com						
Webb School PO Box 488	Bell Buckle	TN	37020	931-389-9322	389-6657	622
TF: 888-733-9322 ■ *Web:* www.thewebbschool.com						
Webb Schools 1175 W Baseline Rd	Claremont	CA	91711	909-482-5214		622
Web: www.webb.org						
Webb Wheel Products Inc 2310 Industrial Dr SW	Cullman	AL	35055	256-739-6660	739-6246	60
TF: 800-633-3256 ■ *Web:* www.webbwheel.com						
Webb Writes LLC 1904 Frnt St	Durham	NC	27705	919-384-8850		449
Web: webbwrites.com						
Webb, Zschunke, Neary & Dikeman LLP 3490 Piedmont Rd One Securities Ctr Ste 1210	Atlanta	GA	30305	404-264-1080	264-4520	41
Web: wznd.net						
WebBank Corp 215 S State St Ste 1000	Salt Lake City	UT	84111	801-456-8350		217
TF: 888-881-3789 ■ *Web:* www.webbank.com						
Webber & Associates Inc 555 Sun Valley Dr Ste F-4	Roswell	GA	30076	770-993-3550		390
Web: webberinsurance.com						
Webber International University 1201 N Scenic Hwy	Babson Park	FL	33827	800-741-1844	638-1591*	166
**Fax Area Code:* 863 ■ *TF:* 800-741-1844 ■ *Web:* webber.edu						
Webber Manufacturing Company Inc 8498 Brookville Rd	Indianapolis	IN	46239	317-357-8681	357-8685	386
Web: www.webbermfg.com						
Webber Metal Products Inc 120 Industrial Park Rd	Cascade	IA	52033	563-852-7122		454
Web: www.webbermetals.com						
WebbMason Analytics 53 Loveton Cir Ste 201	Sparks	MD	21152	443-212-5072		781
Web: webbmasonanalytics.com						
WebbMason Inc 10830 Gilroy Rd	Hunt Valley	MD	21031	410-785-1111		627
TF: 800-992-2665 ■ *Web:* webbmason.com						
Webb-Stiles Co 675 Liverpool Dr PO Box 464	Valley City	OH	44280	330-225-7761	225-5532	207
Web: www.webb-stiles.com						
WEBCARGO Inc 800 Pl Victoria Ste 2603 Tour de la bourse CP 329	Montreal	QC	H4Z1G8	514-905-5223		366
TF: 866-905-0123 ■ *Web:* www.webcargo.net						
Webco Chemical Corp 420 W Main St	Dudley	MA	01571	508-943-9500	987-0366	151
Webco Hawaii Inc 2840 Mokumoa St	Honolulu	HI	96819	808-839-4551		231
Web: www.awdhi.com						
Webco Industries Inc 9101 W 21st St PO Box 100	Sand Springs	OK	74063	918-245-2211	245-0306	490
OTC: WEBC ■ *Web:* www.webcoindustries.com						
Webco Manufacturing Inc 20570 W 162nd St	Olathe	KS	66062	913-764-7111	764-2843	697
Web: www.webcomfg.com						
Webcom 12808 Grand Bay Pkwy W	Jacksonville	FL	32258	904-680-6600	880-0350	809
TF: 800-338-1771 ■ *Web:* www.web.com						
Webcrafters Inc 2211 Fordem Ave	Madison	WI	53704	608-244-3561	244-5120	626
Web: www.webcrafters-inc.com						
WEBCS (WEBster Computing Services) 134 Federal Hill Rd	Oxford	MA	01540	866-779-3227	987-3638*	180
**Fax Area Code:* 508 ■ *TF:* 866-779-3227 ■ *Web:* www.webcs.com						
WebeDoctor 471 W Lambert Rd	Brea	CA	92821	714-990-3999	990-4099	196
Web: new.webedoctor.com						
WEBE-FM 108 (AC) 2 Lafayette Sq	Bridgeport	CT	06604	203-333-9108	384-0600	645-154
TF: 800-932-3108 ■ *Web:* www.webe108.com						
Weber Advertising & Marketing 533 Janet Ave	Lancaster	PA	17601	717-299-1277		7
Web: weberadvertising.com						
Weber Basin Water Conservancy District 2837 E Hwy 193	Layton	UT	84040	801-771-1677		787
Web: weberbasin.com						
Weber County Library 2464 Jefferson Ave	Ogden	UT	84401	801-337-2632	337-2615	434-3
TF: 866-678-5342 ■ *Web:* www.weberpl.lib.ut.us						
Weber Family Farms LLC 3559 Road K NW	Quincy	WA	98848	509-787-3620		10-11
Weber Gallagher Simpson Stapleton Fires & Newby LLP 2000 Market St Ste 1300	Philadelphia	PA	19103	215-972-7900		428
Web: www.wglaw.com						
Weber Group Inc 5233 Progress Way	Sellersburg	IN	47172	812-246-2100		186
Web: webergroupinc.com						
Weber Insurance Corp 505 Corporate Dr W	Langhorne	PA	19047	215-860-0400		390
TF: 888-860-0400 ■ *Web:* www.weberinsurance.com						
Weber International Packing Company LLC 318 Cornelia St	Plattsburgh	NY	12901	518-561-8282	561-4509	98
Web: www.weberintl.com						
Weber Logistics 13530 Rosecrans Ave	Santa Fe Springs	CA	90670	855-469-3237		449
TF: 855-469-3237 ■ *Web:* www.weberlogistics.com						
Weber Metals Inc 16706 Garfield Ave	Paramount	CA	90723	562-602-0260	602-0577	483
Web: webermetals.com						
Weber Obrien Ltd 5580 Monroe St	Sylvania	OH	43560	419-885-8338		2
Web: www.weberobrien.com						
Weber Randy (Rep R - TX) 107 Cannon House Office Bldg	Washington	DC	20515	202-225-2831	225-0271	342-2
Web: weber.house.gov						
Weber Shandwick Worldwide 909 Third Ave	New York	NY	10022	212-445-8000		636
Web: www.webershandwick.com						
Weber Specialties Co 15230 S Us 131	Schoolcraft	MI	49087	269-679-5160	679-2734	492
Web: www.weberspecialties.com						
Weber State University 3848 Harrison Blvd	Ogden	UT	84408	801-626-6000	626-6747	166
TF: 800-848-7770 ■ *Web:* www.weber.edu						
Weber State University *Stewart Library* 3921 Central Campus Dr Dept 2901	Ogden	UT	84408	801-626-6403	626-7045	434-6
TF: 877-306-3140 ■ *Web:* www.library.weber.edu						
Weber Stone Co 12791 Stone City Rd X28	Anamosa	IA	52205	319-462-3581		503-6
Web: www.weberstone.com						
Weber's Boutique Hotel Restraunts 3050 Jackson Rd	Ann Arbor	MI	48103	734-769-2500	769-4743	379
TF: 800-443-3050 ■ *Web:* www.webersannarbor.com						
Weber-Knapp Co 441 Chandler St	Jamestown	NY	14701	716-484-9135	484-9142	350
TF: 800-828-9254 ■ *Web:* www.weberknapp.com						
Weber-Stephen Products Co 200 E Daniels Rd	Palatine	IL	60067	800-446-1071		36
TF: 800-446-1071 ■ *Web:* www.weber.com						
WebEyeCare Inc 10 Canal St Ste 302	Bristol	PA	19007	888-536-7480		366
TF: 888-536-7480 ■ *Web:* www.webeyecare.com						
Webfeat Complete 4907 Eastern Ave	Cincinnati	OH	45208	513-272-3432		177
Web: webfeatcomplete.com						
Webflow 398 11th St	San Francisco	CA	94103	415-964-0555		39
Web: www.webflow.com						
WebHouse Inc 2365 Milburn Ave Bldg 2	Baldwin	NY	11510	516-764-6300		180
Web: www.webhse.com						
WebiMaxcom 2 Aquarium Loop Dr Ste 140	Camden	NJ	08103	888-932-4629		195
TF: 888-932-4629 ■ *Web:* www.webimax.com						
Webject Systems Inc 25 Central Sq Ste 2	Bridgewater	MA	02324	508-279-6562		180
Web: www.webject.com						
WebLink International Inc 3905 W Vincennes Rd Ste 210	Indianapolis	IN	46268	317-872-3909		225
Web: www.weblinkinternational.com						
Webmagic 87 N Raymond Ave Ste 850	Pasadena	CA	91103	626-794-5000		177
Web: www.webmagic.com						
WebmasterWorld Inc 3801 N Capital of Texas Hwy e240-181	Austin	TX	78746	512-231-8107		225
Web: www.webmasterworld.com						
WebMD LLC 395 Hudson St 3rd Fl	New York	NY	10014	212-624-3728		39
NASDAQ: WBMD ■ *Web:* www.webmd.com						
WebNet Services Inc 247 Rt 100	Somers	NY	10589	914-232-6900		177
Web: www.webnetservices.com						
weboost 3301 E Deseret Dr	Saint George	UT	84790	435-673-5021		647
TF: 866-294-1660 ■ *Web:* www.weboost.com						
Weborg Feeding Co 1737 V Rd	Pender	NE	68047	402-385-3441	385-2441	10-1
Web: www.weborgfeeding.com						
WebReplycom Inc 1085 Worcester Rd	Natick	MA	01760	508-318-4600		387
Web: www.webreply.com						
WebRing Inc 500 A St Ste 2	Ashland	OR	97520	541-488-9895		225
Web: www.webring.com						
Webroot Software Inc 2560 55th St	Boulder	CO	80301	303-442-3813	442-3846	178-12
TF: 800-772-9383 ■ *Web:* www.webroot.com						
Websense Inc 10240 Sorrento Valley Rd	San Diego	CA	92121	858-320-8000	458-2950	178-7
NASDAQ: WBSN ■ *TF:* 800-723-1166 ■ *Web:* www.forcepoint.com						

Name / Address	City	State	ZIP	Phone	Fax	Class
Website Magazine Inc 999 E Touhy Ave *TF:* 800-817-1518 ■ *Web:* www.websitemagazine.com	Des Plaines	IL	60018	773-628-2779		530
WebsiteBox Corp 245 Fairview Mall Dr Ste 401 *Web:* www.websitebox.com	Toronto	ON	M2J4T4	416-907-6981		224
Webstart Communications 2835 Benvenue Ave *Web:* www.webstart.com	Berkeley	CA	94705	510-548-4590		4
Webster Bank Arena 600 Main St *Web:* www.websterbankarena.com	Bridgeport	CT	06604	203-345-2300		720
Webster Chamber of Commerce 1110 Crosspointe Ln Ste C *Web:* www.websterchamber.com	Webster	NY	14580	585-265-3960	265-3702	139
Webster City Custom Meats Inc 1611 E 2nd St *Web:* www.webstercitycustommeats.com	Webster City	IA	50595	515-832-1130		296-26
WEBster Computing Services (WEBCS) 134 Federal Hill Rd **Fax Area Code:* 508 ■ *TF:* 866-779-3227 ■ *Web:* www.webcs.com	Oxford	MA	01540	866-779-3227	987-3638*	180
Webster County 701 Central Ave *Web:* www.webstercountyia.gov	Fort Dodge	IA	50501	515-573-1452		338
Webster County 101 S Crittenden St *Web:* webstercountymo.gov	Marshfield	MO	65706	417-468-2222	859-3614	338
Webster County PO Box 29 *Web:* georgia.gov	Preston	GA	31824	229-828-5775	828-2105	338
Webster County 621 N Cedar St *Web:* co.webster.ne.us	Red Cloud	NE	68970	402-746-2717	746-2710	338
Webster County Webster County Courthouse 2 Ct Sq *Web:* webstercounty.wv.gov	Webster Springs	WV	26288	304-847-5780		338
Webster County Clerk 25 US Hwy 41A S PO Box 19 *Web:* www.webstercountyclerk.ky.gov	Dixon	KY	42409	270-639-7006	639-7029	338
Webster County Library 219 W Jackson St *Web:* webstercounty.lib.mo.us	Marshfield	MO	65706	417-468-3335		535
Webster Daniel (Rep R - FL) 1210 Longworth House Office Bldg *Web:* webster.house.gov	Washington	DC	20515	202-225-1002	225-0999	342-2
Webster Electric Co-op PO Box 87 *TF:* 800-643-4305 ■ *Web:* www.websterec.com	Marshfield	MO	65706	417-859-2216		245
Webster Engineering & Manufacturing Company LLC 619 Industrial Rd *Web:* www.webster-engineering.com	Winfield	KS	67156	620-221-7464	221-9447	318
Webster Financial Corp PO Box 10305 *NYSE:* WBS ■ *TF:* 800-325-2424 ■ *Web:* www.public.websteronline.com	Waterbury	CT	06726	800-325-2424		360-2
Webster First Federal Credit Union 271 Greenwood St *TF:* 800-962-4452 ■ *Web:* www.websterfirst.com	Worcester	MA	01607	508-949-1043		71
Webster Industries Inc 325 Hall St *Web:* www.websterchain.com	Tiffin	OH	44883	419-447-8232	448-1618	207
Webster Instrument Inc 11856 Mississippi Ave *Web:* www.websterinstrument.com	Los Angeles	CA	90025	310-479-6770	478-1365	472
Webster Law Firm LLC, The 985 Pico Pt *Web:* websterlawfirmllc.com	Colorado Springs	CO	80906	719-633-6620	634-0789	41
Webster Law Group PA 719 Peachtree Rd Ste 200 *Web:* websterlawgroup.com	Orlando	FL	32804	407-425-2583		41
Webster Parish Library 521 E & W Sts *Web:* www.webster.lib.la.us	Minden	LA	71055	318-371-3080		434-3
Webster Public Library 980 Ridge Rd *Web:* www.websterlibrary.org	Webster	NY	14580	585-872-7075		434-3
Webster State Park 1210 Nine Rd *Web:* www.ksoutdoors.com	Stockton	KS	67669	785-425-6775		565
Webster, Henry, Lyons, Bradwell, Cohan & Speagle PC 105 Tallapoosa St Ste 101 **Fax Area Code:* 205 ■ *Web:* websterhenry.com	Montgomery	AL	36104	334-264-9472	380-3485*	41
Webster-Hoff Corp 704 E Fullerton *Web:* www.webster-hoff.com	Glendale Heights	IL	60139	630-858-8030		567
Webster-Kirkwood Times Inc 122 W Lockwood Ave *Web:* www.timesnewspapers.com	Saint Louis	MO	63119	314-968-2699		532-3
Webstone Company Inc 1 Appian Way *TF:* 800-225-9529 ■ *Web:* www.webstonevalves.com	Worcester	MA	01610	800-225-9529	336-5133	612
Websurf Internet PO Box 9104 *TF:* 877-329-1671 ■ *Web:* www.websurf.net	Wichita	KS	67277	316-945-7873	794-8359	180
Webtech Wireless Inc 4299 Canada Way Ste 215 *TF:* 866-945-4568 ■ *Web:* bsmtechnologies.com	Burnaby	BC	V5G1H3	604-434-7337		736
WebWisdomcom Inc Syracuse Technology Garden 235 Harrison St Ste 303 *Web:* www.collabworx.com	Syracuse	NY	13202	315-579-4330		225
Webwise Learning Inc 2626 E 82nd St Ste 330 *Web:* webwiselearning.com	Bloomington	MN	55425	952-883-0800	854-1685	463
WEC (Warren Electric Co-opeartive Inc) 320 E Main St PO Box 208 *TF:* 800-364-8640 ■ *Web:* www.warrenec.coop	Youngsville	PA	16371	814-563-7548	563-7012	245
WEC Welding Institute 244 E Mt Gallant Rd *Web:* www.schools.aws.org	Rock Hill	SC	29730	803-980-3060	980-3070	167-3
Weckers Flooring LLC 4360 Lincoln Hwy *Web:* weckerscarpet.net	York	PA	17406	717-755-5432		290
Wecsys LLC 8825 Xylon Ave N *TF:* 888-493-2797 ■ *Web:* www.wecsysllc.com	Minneapolis	MN	55445	763-504-1069		75
WECT-TV Ch 6 (NBC) 322 Shipyard Blvd *Web:* www.wect.com	Wilmington	NC	28412	910-791-8070	791-9535	741
Wedbush Securities Inc 1000 Wilshire Blvd *TF:* 888-933-2874 ■ *Web:* www.wedbush.com	Los Angeles	CA	90017	213-688-8000		690
Wedding Experience 2307 Douglas Rd Ste 400 *TF:* 866-223-9672 ■ *Web:* www.theweddingexperience.com	Coral Gables	FL	33145	305-421-1260		226
Wedding Gown Preservation Co 707 North St *Web:* www.gownpreservation.com	Endicott	NY	13760	607-748-6957		426
Wedding Ring Shop 1181 Kapiolani Blvd *Web:* www.weddingringshop.com	Honolulu	HI	96814	808-945-7766		410
Wedding Shoppe Inc, The 1196 Grand Ave *TF:* 877-294-4991 ■ *Web:* www.weddingshoppeinc.com	Saint Paul	MN	55105	651-298-1144		157-6
Weddings In Houston Lp 525 Arlington St *Web:* www.weddingsinhouston.com	Houston	TX	77007	713-464-4321		637-9
Weddle Industries 7200 Hollister Ave Ste C *Web:* weddleindustries.com	Goleta	CA	93117	805-562-8600		61
Wedge Capital Management 301 S College St Ste 3800 *Web:* www.wedgecapital.com	Charlotte	NC	28202	704-334-6475	334-3542	401
Wedge Community Co-opeartive Inc 2105 Lyndale Ave S *Web:* tccp.coopwedge-lyndale	Minneapolis	MN	55405	612-871-3993	871-0734	345
WEDGE Group Inc 1415 Louisiana St Ste 3000 *Web:* www.wedgegroup.com	Houston	TX	77002	713-739-6500		360-3
Wedgestone Press PO Box 175 *Web:* www.wedgestonepress.com	Winfield	KS	67156	620-221-4061		637-2
Wedgewood Hotel 845 Hornby St *TF:* 800-663-0666 ■ *Web:* www.wedgewoodhotel.com	Vancouver	BC	V6Z1V1	604-689-7777	608-5348	379
Wedgewood Partners Inc 9909 Clayton Rd Ste 103 *TF:* 800-537-1252 ■ *Web:* www.wedgewoodpartners.com	Saint Louis	MO	63124	314-567-6407	567-0191	690
WEDG-FM 103.3 (Alt) 50 James E Casey Dr *Web:* www.wedg.com	Buffalo	NY	14206	716-881-4555	884-2931	645-25
Wedgworth Farms Inc PO Box 2076 *Web:* wedgworth.com	Belle Glade	FL	33430	561-996-0613	832-7965	10-9
Wedin International Inc 1111 6th Ave *Web:* www.wedin.com	Cadillac	MI	49601	231-779-8650	779-8673	278
Wedlake Fabricating Inc 6041 N Yorktown Ave *Web:* www.wedlake.net	Tulsa	OK	74130	918-428-1641	428-1620	482
Wedlock Paper Converters Ltd 2327 Stanfield Rd *TF:* 800-388-0447 ■ *Web:* www.wedlockpaper.com	Mississauga	ON	L4Y1R6	905-277-9461	272-1108	554
Wednesday Journal 141 S Oak Park Ave *Web:* www.chicagoparent.com	Oak Park	IL	60302	708-386-5555		532-3
WEDR-FM 99.1 (Urban) 2741 N 29th Ave *Web:* www.wedr.com	Hollywood	FL	33020	305-444-4404		645
WEDU-TV Ch 3 (PBS) 1300 N Blvd *TF:* 800-354-9338 ■ *Web:* www.wedu.org	Tampa	FL	33607	813-254-9338	253-0826	741-133
Wee Federal Credit Union 3312 Dudley Ave *Web:* weefederal.org	Parkersburg	WV	26104	304-420-9517		219
Weecycle Environmental Consulting Inc 1208 Commerce Ct Ste 5B *TF:* 800-875-7033 ■ *Web:* www.weecycle-env.com	LaFayette	CO	80026	303-413-0452		743
Weed Man 2399 Royal Windsor Dr *Web:* www.weedmancanada.com	Mississauga	ON	L5J1K9	905-823-8300		577
Weed USA Inc 5780 Harrow Glen Ct *TF:* 800-933-3758 ■ *Web:* weedracquets.com	Galena	OH	43021	740-548-3881	548-3882	710
Weeden House Museum 300 Gates Ave SE *Web:* www.weedenhousemuseum.com	Huntsville	AL	35801	256-536-7718		520
Weedon Island Preserve Cultural & Natural History Ctr 1800 Weedon Dr NE *Web:* www.weedonislandpreserve.org	Saint Petersburg	FL	33702	727-453-6500		50-5
WEEI 20 Guest St 3rd Fl *Web:* weei.radio.com	Brighton	MA	02135	617-779-7937		645
Weekends Only Inc 349 Marshall Ave 3rd Fl *TF:* 855-803-5888 ■ *Web:* www.weekendsonly.com	Saint Louis	MO	63119	314-447-1500		321
Weekleys Mailing Service Inc 1420 W Bagley Rd *Web:* www.weekleysmailing.com	Berea	OH	44017	440-234-4325	234-6502	5
Weekly Alibi 217 Sierra Dr SE *Web:* www.alibi.com	Albuquerque	NM	87108	505-346-0660	256-9651	532-5
Weekly Timber & Pulp Inc W7680 State Rd 21 & 73 *Web:* weeklytimber.com	Wautoma	WI	54982	920-787-2506		448
Weeks Marine Inc 4 Commerce Dr *Web:* www.weeksmarine.com	Cranford	NJ	07016	908-272-4010	272-4740	188-5
Weeks Service Co 1306 Hwy 3 S *Web:* weeksservicecompany.com	League City	TX	77573	281-332-9555	332-9558	189-10
Weeks-Lerman Group 58-38 Page Pl *TF:* 800-544-5959 ■ *Web:* www.weekslerman.com	Maspeth	NY	11378	718-803-5000	821-1515	534
WEEK-TV Ch 25 (NBC) 2907 Springfield Rd E *Web:* www.week.com	Peoria	IL	61611	309-698-2525	698-9335	741
Weener Plastics Inc 2201 Stantonsburg Rd SE *Web:* www.wppg.com	Wilson	NC	27893	252-206-1400		608
Weetabix Company Inc 300 Nickerson Rd *TF:* 800-343-0590 ■ *Web:* www.weetabixusa.com	Marlborough	MA	01752	800-343-0590		296-4
WEF (Water Environment Federation) 601 Wythe St *TF:* 800-666-0206 ■ *Web:* www.wef.org	Alexandria	VA	22314	703-684-2400	684-2492	48-13
WEFT-FM 90.1 (Var) 113 N Market St *Web:* new.weft.org	Champaign	IL	61820	217-359-9338		645-29
WEG (West Essex Graphics Inc) 305 Fairfield Ave **Fax Area Code:* 973 ■ *TF:* 800-221-5859 ■ *Web:* www.westessexgraphics.com	Fairfield	NJ	07004	800-221-5859	227-2906*	781
WEG Electric Corp 6655 Sugarloaf Pkwy *Web:* www.weg.net	Duluth	GA	30097	678-249-1155		767
Wege Pretzel Co PO Box 334 *TF:* 800-888-4646 ■ *Web:* www.wege.com	Hanover	PA	17331	800-888-4646		296-9
Wegener 11350 Technology Cir *OTC:* WGNR ■ *Web:* www.wegener.com	Johns Creek	GA	30097	770-814-4000	623-0698	647

Phone | Fax | Class

Wegener, Scarborough, Younge & Hockensmith LLP
743 Horizon Ct Ste 200 ... Grand Junction CO 81506 970-242-2645 41
Web: wegscar.com

Wegerzyn Gardens MetroPark
1301 E Siebenthaler Ave ... Dayton OH 45414 937-275-7275 97
Web: www.metroparks.org

Wegmans Food Markets Inc
1500 Brooks Ave PO Box 30844 ... Rochester NY 14603 585-328-2550 345
TF: 800-934-6267 ■ *Web:* www.wegmans.com

Wegner Motor Sports Inc
N2258 Hilltop Rd ... Markesan WI 53946 920-394-3557 62-5
Web: www.wegnerautomotive.com

Wego Chemical & Mineral Corp
239 Great Neck Rd ... Great Neck NY 11021 516-487-3510 487-3794 146
Web: www.wegochem.com

Wehr Nature Ctr 9701 W College Ave ... Franklin WI 53132 414-771-3040 50-5
Web: county.milwaukee.gov

Wehrheim Group LLC, The
3330 Mt Vernon Rd SE ... Cedar Rapids IA 52403 319-294-3131 690
Web: wehrheimgroup.com

WEHT-TV 800 Marywood Dr ... Henderson KY 42420 800-879-8549 827-0561* 741
**Fax Area Code:* 270 ■ *TF:* 800-879-8542 ■ *Web:* www.tristatehomepage.com

WEI (Wieland Electric Inc)
49 International Rd ... Burgaw NC 28425 910-259-5050 246
TF: 800-943-5263 ■ *Web:* www.wielandinc.com

Weibel 1 Winemaster Way ... Lodi CA 95240 209-365-9463 365-9469 80-3
TF: 800-932-9463 ■ *Web:* www.weibel.com

Weichert Realtors 1625 Rt 10 E ... Morris Plains NJ 07950 973-886-1144 984-4075 652
TF: 800-401-0486 ■ *Web:* www.weichert.com

Weidenhammer Systems Corp
935 Berkshire Blvd ... Reading PA 19610 610-378-1149 378-9409 177
TF: 866-497-2227 ■ *Web:* www.hammer.net

Weidert Group Inc 901 S Lawe St ... Appleton WI 54915 920-731-2771 636
Web: www.weidert.com

Weidmann Electrical Technology AG
1 Gordon Mills Way PO Box 903 ... Saint Johnsbury VT 05819 802-748-8106 816
Web: www.weidmann-electrical.com

Weidmuller Inc 821 Southlake Blvd ... Richmond VA 23236 804-794-2877 379-2593 815
TF: 800-849-9343 ■ *Web:* www.weidmuller.com

Weidner Center for the Performing Arts
University of Wisconsin at Green Bay 2420 Nicolet Dr
... Green Bay WI 54311 920-465-2726 465-2619 572
TF: 800-895-0071 ■ *Web:* www.weidnercenter.com

Weight Management Centers
2605 W Swann Ave Ste 600 ... Tampa FL 33609 813-876-7073 810
Web: www.weightmanagement.com

Weight Watchers of Las Vegas Inc
3038 S Durango Dr Ste 100 ... Las Vegas NV 89117 702-432-6683 366
Web: weightwatchers.com

Weightech 1649 Country Elite Dr ... Waldron AR 72958 479-637-4182 361
TF: 800-457-3720 ■ *Web:* www.weightechinc.com

Weik Capital Management
1075 Berkshire Blvd Ste 825 ... Wyomissing PA 19610 610-376-2240 796
Web: www.weikinvest.com

Weil Co, The
11236 El Camino Real Ste 200 ... San Diego CA 92130 858-724-6040 724-6080 401
TF: 800-355-9345 ■ *Web:* www.cweil.com

Weil Gotshal & Manges LLP
767 Fifth Ave ... New York NY 10153 212-310-8000 310-8007 428
Web: www.weil.com

Weil Program on Collaborative Governance, The
Harvard Kennedy School Weil Hall 79 JFK St ... Cambridge MA 02138 617-495-1110 496-5821 634
Web: hks.harvard.edu

Weil, Akman, Baylin & Coleman PA
201 W Padonia Rd Ste 600 ... Timonium MD 21093 410-561-4411 2
Web: wabccpas.com

Weiland Sliding Doors & Windows Inc
2601 Industry St ... Oceanside CA 92054 760-722-8828 499
Web: weilandslidingdoors.com

Weiler Engineering Inc 1395 Gateway Dr ... Elgin IL 60124 847-697-4900 697-4915 547
Web: www.weilerengineering.com

Weiler USA One Weiler Dr ... Cresco PA 18326 570-595-7495 595-2002 103
TF: 800-835-9999 ■ *Web:* www.weilercorp.com

Weill Cornell Medical College
1300 York Ave ... New York NY 10065 212-746-1067 434-1
Web: weill.cornell.edu

Weil-McLain Co 500 Blaine St ... Michigan City IN 46360 219-879-6561 879-4025 91
Web: www.weil-mclain.com

Weimar College
20601 W Paoli Ln PO Box 486 ... Weimar CA 95736 530-637-4111 422-7949 166
Web: weimar.edu

Weimar Junior High School 101 N W St ... Weimar TX 78962 979-725-6300 685
Web: www.weimarisd.org

Wein Products Inc 115 W 25th St ... Los Angeles CA 90007 213-749-6049 749-6250 591
Web: www.weinproducts.com

Weinberg Barton & Co
1609 Sherman Ave Ste 204 ... Evanston IL 60201 847-859-6880 2
Web: weinbergbarton.com

Weinberg Capital Group
5005 Rockside Rd Ste 1140 ... Cleveland OH 44131 216-503-8303 503-8313 654
Web: www.weinbergcap.com

Weinberg Group Inc, The
1129 20th St NW Ste 600 ... Washington DC 20036 202-833-8077 833-7057 193
Web: www.weinberggroup.com

Weinberg, Roger & Rosenfeld A Professional Corp
1001 Marina Village Pkwy Ste 200 ... Alameda CA 94501 510-337-1001 41
Web: unioncounsel.net

Weinberg-King State Park PO Box 203 ... Augusta IL 62311 217-392-2345 565
Web: www2.illinois.gov

Weinbrenner Shoe Company Inc
108 S Polk St ... Merrill WI 54452 715-536-5521 536-1172 301
TF: 800-569-6817 ■ *Web:* www.weinbrennerusa.com

Weiner Iron & Metal Corp
1056 Rte 61 PO Box 359 ... Pottsville PA 17901 570-622-6543 622-3175 686
Web: weinermetals.com

Weiner Law Group LLP
629 Parsippany Rd ... Parsippany NJ 07054 973-403-1100 403-0010 428
Web: www.weiner.law

Weingart Foundation
1055 W Seventh St Ste 3050 ... Los Angeles CA 90017 213-688-7799 688-1515 305
Web: www.weingartfnd.org

Weingarten Realty Investors
2600 Citadel Plaza Dr Ste 125 ... Houston TX 77008 713-866-6000 866-6049 655
NYSE: WRI ■ *TF:* 800-688-8865 ■ *Web:* www.weingarten.com

Weingartz Supply Co 46061 Van Dyke Ave ... Utica MI 48317 586-731-7240 323
TF: 855-669-7278 ■ *Web:* weingartz.com

Weinman & Associates PC
8200 N Mopac Ste 230 ... Austin TX 78759 512-472-4040 472-4086 41
Web: weinmanfamilylaw.com

Weinrib & Connor
297 Knollwood Rd ... White Plains NY 10607 914-686-3900 7
Web: www.weinconn.com

Weinrich Truck Line Inc 27932 C60 ... Hinton IA 51024 712-239-2622 947-4890 780
TF: 800-831-0814 ■ *Web:* www.weinrichtruckline.com

Weinstein & Anastasio PC
2319 Whitney Ave Ste 2A ... Hamden CT 06518 203-397-2525 2

Weinstein Kitchenoff & Asher LLC
100 S Broad St Ste 705 ... Philadelphia PA 19110 215-545-7200 545-6535 41
TF: 877-805-7200 ■ *Web:* wka-law.com

Weinstock Lamp Company Inc
34-30 Steinway St ... Long Island City NY 11101 718-729-4848 246
Web: www.weinstocklighting.com

Weintraub Adv Inc
7745 Carondelet Ave Ste 308 ... Saint Louis MO 63105 314-721-5050 721-6850 4
Web: www.weintraubadv.com

Weir & Partners LLP
The Widener Bldg 1339 Chestnut St
Ste 500 ... Philadelphia PA 19107 215-665-8181 665-8464 428
Web: www.weirpartners.com

Weir Canada Inc 2360 Millrace Ct ... Mississauga ON L5N1W2 905-812-0881 812-1749 791
Web: www.global.weir

Weir Farm National Historic Site
735 Nod Hill Rd ... Wilton CT 06897 203-834-1896 564
Web: www.nps.gov

Weir Group, The 2701 S Stoughton Rd ... Madison WI 53716 608-221-2261 641
Web: www.global.weir

Weir International Inc
1431 Opus Pl Executive Towers W I
Ste 210 ... Downers Grove IL 60515 630-968-5400 968-5401 261
Web: www.weirintl.com

Weir's Furniture Village Inc
3219 Knox St ... Dallas TX 75205 214-528-0321 321
Web: www.weirsfurniture.com

WeirFoulds LLP
4100 - 66 Wellington St W Toronto-Dominion Centre
PO Box 35 ... Toronto ON M5K1B7 416-365-1110 428
Web: www.weirfoulds.com

Weirton Medical Ctr 601 Colliers Way ... Weirton WV 26062 304-797-6000 797-6176 374-3
Web: www.weirtonmedical.com

Weis Builders Inc
2227 Seventh St NW ... Rochester MN 55901 507-288-2041 186
Web: www.weisbuilders.com

Weis Markets 1000 S 2nd St PO Box 471 ... Sunbury PA 17801 866-999-9347 345
NYSE: WMK ■ *TF:* 866-999-9347 ■ *Web:* www.weismarkets.com

Weis/Robart Partitions Inc
3501 E La Palma Ave ... Anaheim CA 92806 714-666-0108 666-0110 286
Web: www.weisrobart.com

Weisbarth Enterprises LLC
575 Wedgewood Dr ... Avon Lake OH 44012 440-759-5172 322
Web: www.weisbarthenterprises.com

Weiser 19701 Da Vinci ... Lake Forest CA 92610 800-677-5625 350
TF: 800-677-5625 ■ *Web:* ca.weiserlock.com

Weiser Books 65 Parker St Ste 7 ... Newburyport MA 01950 978-465-0504 465-0243 637-2
TF: 800-423-7087 ■ *Web:* www.redwheelweiser.com

Weiser LLP 135 W 50th St ... New York NY 10020 212-812-7000 375-6888 2
Web: weisermazars.com

Weiser Metal Products
34311 E M-72 PO Box 370 ... Lincoln MI 48742 989-736-6055 736-6717 295
Web: weisermetal.com

Weiser Security Services Inc
3939 Tulane Ave ... New Orleans LA 70119 504-949-7558 943-3752 693
Web: www.weisersecurity.com

Weisman Art Museum
333 E River Pkwy ... Minneapolis MN 55455 612-625-9494 520
Web: wam.umn.edu

Weiss & Associates Ps
733 Seventh Ave Ste 114 ... Kirkland WA 98033 425-827-3031 307-6531 2
Web: weisscpas.com

Weiss & Moy PC 4204 N Brown Ave ... Scottsdale AZ 85251 480-994-8888 41
Web: weissiplaw.com

Weiss & Paarz PC 2600 New Rd Ste A ... Northfield NJ 08225 609-641-8400 41
Web: weisspaarz.com

Weiss Burkardt Kramer LLC
445 Fort Pitt Blvd Ste 503 ... Pittsburgh PA 15219 412-391-9890 391-9685 41
Web: wbklegal.com

Weiss Instruments Inc
905 Waverly Ave ... Holtsville NY 11742 631-207-1200 207-0900 202
Web: www.weissinstruments.com

Weiss Lake Egg Company Inc PO Box 190 ... Centre AL 35960 256-927-5546 927-2596 10-8

Weiss Memorial Hospital
4646 N Marine Dr ... Chicago IL 60640 773-878-8700 374-3
Web: www.weisshospital.com

Weiss North America Inc
3860 Ben Hur Dr Unit 2 ... Willoughby OH 44094 440-269-8031 269-8036 366
TF: 888-934-7762 ■ *Web:* weissna.com

Weiss-Aug Company Inc
220 Merry Ln ... East Hanover NJ 07936 973-887-7600 887-8109 488
Web: www.weiss-aug.com

Weissberg & Speller CPAS PC
3601 Hempstead Tpke ... Levittown NY 11756 516-796-2727 796-2752 2
Web: www.cpasny.net

Weisshouse 324 S Highland Ave ... Pittsburgh PA 15206 412-441-8888 290
Web: www.weisshouse.com

Weissman
1 Alliance Ctr 3500 Lenox Rd 4th Fl ... Atlanta GA 30326 404-926-4500 926-4600 445
Web: www.weissman.law

Name / Address	City	State	ZIP	Phone	Fax	Class
Weitz Company LLC, The 4725 S Monaco St Ste 100 *Web:* www.weitz.com	Denver	CO	80237	303-860-6600	860-6698	186
Weitzman Group 3102 Maple Ave Ste 350 *Web:* www.weitzmangroup.com	Dallas	TX	75201	214-954-0600	953-0866	652
WEIU-TV 1521 Buzzard Hall 600 Lincoln Ave *TF:* 877-727-9348 ■ *Web:* www.weiu.net	Charleston	IL	61920	217-581-5956		647
WEJZ-FM 96.1 (AC) 6440 Atlantic Blvd *Web:* www.wejz.com	Jacksonville	FL	32211	904-727-9696		645-76
Wekiwa Springs State Park 1800 Wekiwa Cir *Web:* www.floridastateparks.org	Apopka	FL	32712	407-884-2009	884-2039	565
WEKZ-AM W4765 Radio Ln *TF:* 888-325-0937 ■ *Web:* www.wekz.com	Monroe	WI	53566	608-325-2161	325-2164	647
Wel Companies Inc 1625 S Broadway PO Box 5610 *TF:* 800-333-4415 ■ *Web:* www.welcompanies.com	De Pere	WI	54115	800-333-4415		780
Weland Clinical Laboratories PC 1911 First Ave SE *TF:* 800-728-1503 ■ *Web:* www.welandlaboratories.com	Cedar Rapids	IA	52402	319-366-1503		415
Welasco Inc 1950 19th St SW *Web:* www.welasco.net	Paris	TX	75460	903-784-5562	784-8965	454
Welborn Baptist Foundation Inc 21 SE 3rd St Ste 610 *Web:* welbornfdn.org	Evansville	IN	47708	812-437-8260	437-8269	48-20
Welborn Sullivan Meck & Tooley 821 17th St Ste 500 *Web:* www.wsmtlaw.com	Denver	CO	80202	303-830-2500		428
Welbro Building Corp 2301 Maitland Center Pkwy Ste 250 *Web:* www.welbro.com	Maitland	FL	32751	407-475-0800	475-0801	186
Welch & Company Jewelers 513 S Main St *Web:* welchjewelers.com	Syracuse	NY	13212	315-452-0744		410
Welch & Forbes LLC 45 School St Old City Hall 5th Fl *Web:* www.welchforbes.com	Boston	MA	02108	617-523-1635		528
Welch & Rushe Inc 391 Prince George's Blvd *TF:* 800-683-3852 ■ *Web:* www.welchandrushe.com	Upper Marlboro	MD	20774	301-430-6000		186
Welch Allyn Inc 4341 State St Rd **Fax Area Code:* 315 ■ *TF:* 800-535-6663 ■ *Web:* www.welchallyn.com	Skaneateles	NY	13153	800-535-6663	685-4091*	250
Welch Brothers Inc 1050 Saint Charles St *Web:* www.welchbrothers.com	Elgin	IL	60120	847-741-6134	741-6195	183
Welch Capital Partners LLC 122 E 42nd St Ste 5105 *Web:* www.welchcapital.com	New York	NY	10168	212-754-6077		401
Welch College 1045 Bison Trl *TF:* 888-979-3524 ■ *Web:* www.welch.edu	Gallatin	TN	37066	615-844-5000	269-6028	167-3
Welch Global Consulting 10084 Oak Knoll Terr *Web:* welchgc.com	Colorado Springs	CO	80920	970-292-6600		196
Welch Group LLC, The 3940 Montclair Rd *TF:* 800-709-7100 ■ *Web:* welchgroup.com	Birmingham	AL	35213	205-879-5001	879-7979	528
Welch Medical Library 1900 E Monument St *Web:* www.welch.jhmi.edu	Baltimore	MD	21205	410-955-3410		434-1
Welch Packaging Group 1020 Herman St *TF:* 800-246-2475 ■ *Web:* www.welchpkg.com	Elkhart	IN	46516	574-295-2460	295-1527	100
Welch Peter (Rep D - VT) 2187 Rayburn House Office Bldg *TF:* 888-605-7270 ■ *Web:* welch.house.gov	Washington	DC	20515	202-225-4115		342-2
Welch's Inc 300 Baker Ave Ste 101 *Web:* www.welchs.com	Concord	MA	01742	978-371-1000		296-20
Welchdry Inc 4270 Sunnyside Dr *Web:* www.welchdry.com	Holland	MI	49424	616-399-2711	399-6889	582
Welcome Aboard Travel 57 Saulsbury Rd Ste C *Web:* welcomeaboard.net	Dover	DE	19904	302-678-9480		775
Welcome Enterprises Inc 6 W 18th St Ste 4B *Web:* welcomebooks.com	New York	NY	10011	212-989-3200		94
Welcome Wagon 5830 Coral Ridge Dr *TF:* 800-779-3526 ■ *Web:* www.welcomewagon.com	Coral Springs	FL	33076	800-779-3526		5
WelcomeMat Services Inc 1170 Peachtree St Ste 1125 *Web:* welcomematservices.com	Atlanta	GA	30309	404-841-2226		41
Welcomm Inc 13223-1 Black Mountain Road Ste 340 *Web:* www.welcomm.com	San Diego	CA	92129	858-279-2100		636
Weld Community Credit Union 2555 47th Ave *TF:* 800-682-6075 ■ *Web:* weldccu.com	Greeley	CO	80634	970-330-9728	330-1668	219
Weld County PO Box 758 *Web:* www.weldgov.com	Greeley	CO	80632	970-336-7204		338
Weld County Garage 2699 47th Ave *TF:* 866-837-7053 ■ *Web:* www.weldcountygarage.com	Greeley	CO	80634	970-373-4116		57
Weld Mold Co 750 Rickett Rd *TF:* 800-521-9755 ■ *Web:* www.weldmold.com	Brighton	MI	48116	810-229-9521	229-9580	811
Weldaloy Products Co 11551 Stephens Rd *TF:* 888-935-3256 ■ *Web:* weldaloy.com	Warren	MI	48089	586-758-5550	758-5049	811
Weldangrind Ltd 10323 174 St NW *TF:* 866-226-2414 ■ *Web:* www.weldangrind.ca	Edmonton	AB	T5S1H1	780-484-3030		757
Weld-Built Body Company Inc 1050 Grand Blvd *Web:* www.weldbuilt.com	Deer Park	NY	11729	631-643-9700	491-4728	516
Welded Ring Products Company Inc 2180 W 114th St *Web:* www.weldedring.com	Cleveland	OH	44102	216-961-3800		295
Welded Tubes Inc 135 Penniman Rd *Web:* www.weldedtubes.com	Orwell	OH	44076	440-437-5144	437-5180	490
Welder Exploration & Production Inc 100 W Olmos Dr *Web:* www.weldergroup.com	San Antonio	TX	78212	210-354-1515		538
Welder Training & Testing Institute 1144 N Graham St *TF:* 800-923-9884 ■ *Web:* www.welderinstitute.com	Allentown	PA	18109	610-820-9551	820-0271	800
Welding Consultants LLC 889 N 22nd St *Web:* www.weldingconsultantsllc.com	Columbus	OH	43085	614-258-7018	258-1996	194
Welding Technology Corp 24775 Crestview Ct *Web:* www.weldtechcorp.com	Farmington Hills	MI	48335	248-477-3900		203
Weldlogic Inc 2651 Lavery Ct *Web:* www.weldlogic.com	Newbury Park	CA	91320	805-498-4004	498-1761	811
Weldmac Manufacturing Co 1451 N Johnson Ave *TF:* 800-252-1533 ■ *Web:* www.weldmac.com	El Cajon	CA	92020	619-440-2300		454
Weldments Inc 10720 N Second St *Web:* weldmentsinc.com	Machesney Park	IL	61115	815-633-3393	633-2524	482
Weldon Contractors 3428 W Pioneer Pkwy *Web:* weldon-contractors.com	Arlington	TX	76013	817-460-1111	460-3111	610
Weldon Cooper Center for Public Service 2400 Old Ivy Rd *Web:* coopercenter.org	Charlottesville	VA	22903	434-982-5522		166
Weldon Huston & Keyser L L P 76 N Mulberry St *Web:* www.whkmansfield.com	Mansfield	OH	44902	419-524-9811		445
Weldon Materials 141 Central Ave *Web:* www.weldonmat.com	Westfield	NJ	07090	908-233-4444	233-4215	46
Weldon Springs State Park 4734 Weldon Springs Rd *Web:* www2.illinois.gov	Clinton	IL	61727	217-935-2644		565
Weldon Tire Inc 1247 Century Dr *Web:* www.eitire.com	Dubuque	IA	52002	563-582-3991		754
Weldon Williams & Lick Inc 711 N A St *TF:* 800-242-4995 ■ *Web:* www.wwlinc.com	Fort Smith	AR	72901	479-783-4113	783-7050	627
Weldship Corp 225 W Second St *Web:* www.weldship.com	Bethlehem	PA	18015	610-861-7330		295
Weldstar Inc 1750 Mitchell Rd *Web:* www.weldstar.com	Aurora	IL	60505	630-859-3100		358
Weldylamont Associates Inc 1040 W NW Hwy *Web:* www.weldy-lamont.com	Mount Prospect	IL	60056	847-398-4510		246
Welfab Inc 100 Rangeway Rd *Web:* www.welfab.com	North Billerica	MA	01862	978-667-0180		480
Welfont 601 N Ashley Dr Ste 600 *Web:* www.welfont.com	Tampa	FL	33602	813-226-2099		652
Welk Resort Branson 8860 Lawrence Welk Dr *TF:* 800-505-9355 ■ *Web:* welkresorts.com	Escondido	CA	92026	417-336-3575		669
Welker Inc 13839 W Bellfort *Web:* welker.com	Sugar Land	TX	77498	281-491-2331		539
Welkin Health 3265 17th St Ste 304 *Web:* www.welkinhealth.com	San Francisco	CA	94110	415-967-2483		39
Welkin Sciences LLC 102 S Tejon St Ste 200 *Web:* www.welkinsciences.com	Colorado Springs	CO	80903	719-520-5115		248
Welkinweir 1368 Prizer Rd *Web:* www.welkinweir.org	Pottstown	PA	19465	610-469-7543		97
Well Control School 16770 Imperial Valley Dr Ste 290 *Web:* www.wellcontrol.com	Houston	TX	77060	713-849-7400	849-7474	685
Well Kept 1116 Harrison Ave *TF:* 855-937-4587 ■ *Web:* www.wellkept.com	ARLINGTON	TX	76011	855-937-4587		660
Well Luck Company Inc 104 Harbor Dr *Web:* wellluck.com	Jersey City	NJ	07305	201-434-1177		805
Well Spouse Assn 63 W Main St Ste H *TF:* 800-838-0879 ■ *Web:* wellspouse.org	Freehold	NJ	07728	732-577-8899	577-8644	48-6
Well, The 1195 Park Ave Ste 206 *Web:* www.well.com	Emeryville	CA	94608	415-343-5731		171
Wella Corp 4500 Park Granada *TF:* 800-422-2336 ■ *Web:* www.wella.com	Calabasas	CA	91302	800-422-2336		214
Welland/Pelham Chamber of Commerce 32 E Main St *Web:* www.wellandpelhamchamber.com	Welland	ON	L3B3W3	905-732-7515		137
WellAware 3424 Paesanos Pkwy Ste 200 *TF:* 855-935-5292 ■ *Web:* wellaware.us	San Antonio	TX	78231	210-816-4600		387
WellBiz Brands Inc 9092 Ridgeline Blvd Ste A *Web:* www.thewellnessleader.com	Highlands Ranch	CO	80129	303-663-0880		354
Wellbore Navigation Inc 15032 Red Hill Ave Ste D *Web:* www.welnavinc.com	Tustin	CA	92780	714-259-7760		529
Wellborn Forest Products Inc 2212 Airport Blvd *TF:* 800-846-2562 ■ *Web:* www.wellbornforest.com	Alexander City	AL	35010	800-846-2562		115
Wellbridge Co 6140 Greenwood Plaza Blvd *Web:* www.wellbridge.com	Greenwood Village	CO	80111	303-866-0800		354
WellCare 8735 Henderson Rd *TF:* 800-960-2530 ■ *Web:* www.wellcare.com	Tampa	FL	33634	813-290-6208		391-3
Wellcorp Express Inc 15000 S Broadway *Web:* wellcorp-express-inc-wellton-express.business.site	Gardena	CA	90248	310-645-6410	645-3874	311
Wellens & Co 6700 France Ave S Ste 106 *Web:* www.wellenscompany.com	Minneapolis	MN	55435	952-922-1500	922-1555	276
Weller/Obrien Insurance Services 720 Kelly Ave *Web:* www.kevinobrieninsurance.com	Half Moon Bay	CA	94019	650-726-6328		390
Wellers Utility Trailers 16889 N Main St *Web:* www.wellers.com	Bridgeville	DE	19933	302-337-8228	337-0656	54
Wellert Corp 5136 Beach Rd *Web:* wellert.com	Medina	OH	44256	330-239-2699	239-0272	261
Wellesley Bank 40 Central St *Web:* wellesleybank.com	Wellesley	MA	02482	781-235-2550		70

Name / Address	City	State	ZIP	Phone	Fax	Class
Wellesley Chamber of Commerce, The 148 Linden St Ste 107 *Web:* wellesleychamber.org	Wellesley	MA	02482	781-235-2446	235-7326	139
Wellesley College 106 Central St *Web:* www.wellesley.edu	Wellesley	MA	02481	781-283-1000	283-3678	166
Wellesley Free Library 530 Washington St *Web:* www.wellesleyfreelibrary.org	Wellesley	MA	02482	781-235-1610	235-0495	434-3
Wellesley Volkswagen 231 Linden St *TF:* 888-602-6905 ■ *Web:* buywellesleyvw.com	Wellesley	MA	02482	781-237-3553		57
Welles-Turner Memorial Library 2407 Main St *Web:* www.wtmlib.info	Glastonbury	CT	06033	860-652-7719	652-7721	434-3
Wellex Corp 551 Brown Rd *Web:* www.wellex.com	Fremont	CA	94539	510-743-1818	743-1899	253
Wellframe Inc 470 Atlantic Ave 8th Fl *Web:* www.wellframe.com	Boston	MA	02210	781-467-9596		352
WellHaven Pet Health 700 Washington St Ste 106 *Web:* wellhavenpethealthdtv.com	Vancouver	WA	98660	360-768-4210		794
Wellhead Control Products Inc 501 N Richey St *Web:* www.wellheadcontrol.com	Pasadena	TX	77506	713-475-2283		537
Welligent Inc 5005 Colley Ave *TF:* 888-317-5960 ■ *Web:* www.welligent.com	Norfolk	VA	23508	888-317-5960		177
Wellington F. Roemer Insurance Inc 3912 Sunforest Ct *Web:* roemer-insurance.com	Toledo	OH	43623	419-475-5151		390
Wellington Foods Inc 1930 California Ave *Web:* www.wellingtonfoods.com	Corona	CA	92881	951-547-7000		297-8
Wellington Hotel 871 Seventh Ave *TF:* 800-652-1212 ■ *Web:* www.wellingtonhotel.com	New York	NY	10019	212-247-3900		379
Wellington Industries Inc 39555 S I-94 Service Dr *Web:* www.wellingtonind.com	Belleville	MI	48111	734-942-1060	942-9430	489
Wellington Management Company LLP 280 Congress St *Web:* www.wellington.com	Boston	MA	02210	617-951-5000		401
Wellington Power Corp 177 Thorn Hill Rd *Web:* www.wellingtonpower.com	Warrendale	PA	15086	724-779-4000		189-4
Wellington Press PO Box 13939 **Fax Area Code:* 850 ■ *TF:* 877-390-4425 ■ *Web:* www.peacegames.com	Tallahassee	FL	32317	877-390-4425	893-3442*	637-2
Wellington Resort 551 Thames St *TF:* 800-228-2968 ■ *Web:* www.wellingtonresort.com	Newport	RI	02840	401-849-1770	847-6250	379
Wellington State Park 614 W Shore Rd *Web:* www.nhstateparks.org	Bristol	NH	03222	603-744-2197		565
Wellman Advanced Materials 520 Kingsburg Hwy *TF:* 800-821-6022 ■ *Web:* wellmanam.com	Johnsonville	SC	29555	800-821-6022		601
Wellness Coaches 725 Skippack Pk Ste 300 **Fax Area Code:* 215 ■ *TF:* 866-894-1300 ■ *Web:* www.wellnesscoachesusa.com	Blue Bell	PA	19422	866-894-1300	628-3262*	260
Wellness Enterprises LLC 418 SW 140th Terr *Web:* www.naturallyfiltered.com	Newberry	FL	32669	352-333-0480		612
Wellness International Network Ltd 5800 Democracy Dr	Plano	TX	75024	972-312-1100		195
Wellons Inc 2525 W Firestone Ln *TF:* 800-935-5667 ■ *Web:* www.wellons.com	Vancouver	WA	98660	360-750-3500	750-3400	695
Wells & Assoc 1420 Spring Hill Rd Ste 610 *Web:* www.wellsandassociates.com	Tysons	VA	22102	703-917-6620		256
Wells & Drew Cos 3414 Galilee Rd *TF:* 800-342-8636 ■ *Web:* wellsdrew.com	Jacksonville	FL	32207	800-342-8636	228-6494	627
Wells Cargo Inc 1503 W McNaughton St *TF:* 800-348-7553 ■ *Web:* www.wellscargo.com	Elkhart	IN	46514	574-264-9661	264-5938	779
Wells Coleman 5004 Monument Ave *Web:* www.wellscoleman.com	Richmond	VA	23230	804-358-1150	358-7116	2
Wells College 170 Main St *TF:* 800-952-9355 ■ *Web:* www.wells.edu	Aurora	NY	13026	315-364-3266	364-3227	166
Wells Concrete 210 Inspiration Ln PO Box 656 **Fax Area Code:* 320 ■ *TF:* 800-658-7049 ■ *Web:* www.wellsconcrete.com	Albany	MN	56307	800-658-7049	845-2239*	183
Wells County 211 W Water St Ste A *Web:* wellscounty.org	Bluffton	IN	46714	260-824-1612	824-6559	338
Wells County 700 Railway St N *Web:* www.wellscountynd.com	Fessenden	ND	58438	701-547-3122		338
Wells Enterprises Inc 1 Blue Bunny Dr *TF:* 800-942-3800 ■ *Web:* www.wellsenterprisesinc.com	Le Mars	IA	51031	712-546-4000		296-25
Wells Fargo Bank NA 420 Montgomery St *Web:* www.wellsfargo.com	San Francisco	CA	94104	415-396-7152		70
Wells Fargo Dealer Services 23 Pasteur *Web:* www.wellsfargodealerservices.com	Irvine	CA	92618	949-930-4150	754-7350	217
Wells Fargo History Museum 333 S Grand Ave *Web:* www.wellsfargohistory.com	Los Angeles	CA	90071	213-253-7166		520
Wells Home Furnishings 101 Bowers Rd *Web:* www.wellshome.com	Charleston	WV	25314	304-343-3600		321
Wells Johnson Co 8000 S Kolb Rd *TF:* 800-528-1597 ■ *Web:* www.wellsgrp.com	Tucson	AZ	85756	520-298-6069		476
Wells Lamont Industry Group 6640 W Touhy Ave *TF:* 800-247-3295 ■ *Web:* wellslamontindustrial.com	Niles	IL	60714	800-247-3295		155-8
Wells Printing Company Inc 6030 Perimeter Pkwy *TF:* 800-264-4958 ■ *Web:* www.wellsprinting.com	Montgomery	AL	36116	334-281-3449		627
Wells Rug Service Inc 49 Bank St *Web:* www.wellsrug.com	Morristown	NJ	07960	973-539-3800		362
Wells Rural Electric Co 1451 Humboldt Ave *TF:* 800-566-6696 ■ *Web:* www.wrec.coop	Wells	NV	89835	775-752-3328	752-3407	245
Wells State Park 159 Walker Pond Rd *Web:* www.mass.gov	Sturbridge	MA	01566	508-228-9403		565
Wells Technology Inc 4885 Windsor Ct NW *Web:* www.wellstech.com	Bemidji	MN	56601	218-751-5117		350
Wells Tool Co 106 Hope St *Web:* www.wellstool.com	Greenfield	MA	01301	413-773-3465		493
Wells-Gardner Electronics Corp 9500 W 55th St Ste A *NYSE:* WGA ■ *TF:* 800-336-6630 ■ *Web:* wellsgardner.com	McCook	IL	60525	708-290-2100	290-2200	173-4
Wellshire Lincolnshire, The 170 Jamestown Ln *Web:* www.thewellshirelincolnshire.com	Lincolnshire	IL	60069	224-543-7070		371
WellSpan Chambersburg Hospital 112 N 7th St *Web:* www.wellspan.org	Chambersburg	PA	17201	717-267-3000		374-3
WellSpring Books 1170 N Gilbert Rd Ste 115 *Web:* www.wellspringbooks.net	Gilbert	AZ	85234	480-834-4187		96
Wellspring Healthcare Services Inc 3341 Hobson Rd Ste B *Web:* wellspringcare.com	Woodridge	IL	60517	630-968-7777		363
WellSpring School for Healing Arts 2440 NE MLK Jr Blvd Ste 202 *Web:* www.thewellspring.org	Portland	OR	97212	503-688-1482		685
WellStar Health System 805 Sandy Plains Rd *Web:* www.wellstar.org	Marietta	GA	30066	770-956-7827		374-3
Well-Tempered Music Library PO Box 465 *Web:* www.arfarfrecords.com	Middleboro	MA	02346	508-947-7387	947-7323	434-3
Welocalize Inc 241 E Fourth St Ste 207 *TF:* 800-370-9515 ■ *Web:* www.welocalize.com	Frederick	MD	21701	301-668-0330	668-0335	194
WELS (Wisconsin Evangelical Lutheran Synod) 2929 N Mayfair Rd *Web:* wels.net	Milwaukee	WI	53222	414-256-3888		48-20
Welsbach Electric Corp 111-01 14th Ave *Web:* welsbachelectric.com	College Point	NY	11356	718-670-7900	670-7999	189-4
WELSCO Inc 9006 Crystal Hill Rd *Web:* www.welsco.com	North Little Rock	AR	72113	501-771-1204	315-1496	385
Welsh Carson Anderson & Stowe (WCAS) 599 Lexington Ave Ste 1800 *Web:* www.wcas.com	New York	NY	10022	212-893-9500		405
Welsh Consulting 101 Arch St *Web:* www.welsh.com	Boston	MA	02109	617-695-9800	695-0350	225
Weltman & Moskowitz LLP 270 Madison Ave *Web:* weltmosk.com	New York	NY	10016	212-684-7800		41
WELY-AM 133 E Chapman *Web:* www.wely.com	Ely	MN	55731	218-365-4444	365-3657	647
WEM (Wisconsin Electrical Manufacturing Company Inc) 2501 S Moorland Rd PO Box 510767 *Web:* www.wemautomation.com	New Berlin	WI	53151	262-782-2340	782-2653	684
Wemco Casting LLC 20 Jules Ct Ste 2 *Web:* www.wemcocastingllc.com	Bohemia	NY	11716	631-563-8050	563-8054	308
WEMG-AM 1310 (Span) 1341 N Delaware Ave Ste 509 *Web:* www.lamega1057.com	Philadelphia	PA	19125	215-426-1900		645-120
WEMI-FM 1909 W Second St *TF:* 800-236-9364 ■ *Web:* www.thefamily.net	Appleton	WI	54914	920-749-9364	749-0474	647
Wempe Jewelers 700 Fifth Ave *Web:* www.wempe.com	New York	NY	10019	212-397-9000		410
Wems Electronics Inc 4650 W Rosecrans Ave *Web:* www.wems.com	Hawthorne	CA	90250	310-644-0251	644-5334	248
WEMU-FM 89.1 (NPR) PO Box 980350 *TF:* 888-200-8010 ■ *Web:* www.wemu.org	Ypsilanti	MI	48198	734-487-2229	487-1015	645
Wenaas USA 12211 Parc Crest Dr Bldg 3 Ste 100 *Web:* www.wenaasusa.com	Stafford	TX	77477	281-931-4300	931-4328	155-19
Wenatchee Confluence State Park 333 Olds Station Rd *Web:* parks.state.wa.us	Wenatchee	WA	98801	509-664-6373		565
Wenatchee Valley Chamber of Commerce 137 N Wenatchee Ave *Web:* wenatchee.org	Wenatchee	WA	98801	509-662-2116	663-2022	139
Wenatchee Valley College 1300 Fifth St *TF:* 877-982-4968 ■ *Web:* www.wvc.edu	Wenatchee	WA	98801	509-682-6800	682-6801	162
Wenatchee World 14 N Mission St *TF:* 800-572-4433 ■ *Web:* www.wenatcheeworld.com	Wenatchee	WA	98801	509-663-5161		532-2
Wenberg County Park 15430 E Lake Goodwin Rd *Web:* www.snohomishcountywa.gov	Stanwood	WA	98292	360-652-7417		565
Wenck Associates Inc PO Box 249 *TF:* 800-368-8831 ■ *Web:* www.wenck.com	Maple Plain	MN	55359	763-479-4200		261
Wende Correctional Facility 3040 Wende Rd PO Box 1187 *Web:* www.doccs.ny.gov	Alden	NY	14004	716-937-4000		213
Wendel, Rosen, Black & Dean LLP 1111 Broadway 24th Fl *Web:* www.wendel.com	Oakland	CA	94607	510-834-6600		428
Wendell August Forge Inc 2074 Leesburg-Grove City Rd *TF:* 866-354-5192 ■ *Web:* www.wendellaugust.com	Mercer	PA	16137	724-748-9501		327
Wendell Cox Consultancy PO Box 841 *Web:* www.publicpurpose.com	Belleville	IL	62269	618-632-8507		196
Wendell Fabrics Corp 108 E Church St PO Box 128 *Web:* www.wendellfabrics.com	Blacksburg	SC	29702	864-839-6341	839-2911	745-3
Wendell State Forest 392 Wendell Rd *Web:* www.mass.gov	Millers Falls	MA	01349	413-659-3797		565
Wendell's Inc 6601 Bunker Lake Blvd NW *TF:* 800-936-3355 ■ *Web:* www.wendellsinc.com	Ramsey	MN	55303	763-576-8200	576-0995	467
Wendelstedt Umpire School 88 S St Andrews Dr **Fax Area Code:* 888 ■ *TF:* 800-818-1690 ■ *Web:* www.umpireschool.com	Ormond Beach	FL	32174	800-818-1690	881-9801*	685

Name / Address	City	State	Zip	Phone	Fax	Class
Wenderoth, Lind & Ponack LLP 1030 15th St NW Ste 400 E *Web:* wenderoth.com	Washington	DC	20005	202-721-8200		41
Wendle Motors Inc 9000 N Div *Web:* www.wendle.com	Spokane	WA	99218	509-468-9000		516
Wendling Printing Co 111 Beech St *Web:* www.wendlingprinting.net	Newport	KY	41071	859-261-8300	261-5458	627
Wendling Quarries Inc PO Box 230 *Web:* www.wendlingquarries.com	De Witt	IA	52742	563-659-9181	659-3393	503-5
Wendover Corp 130 S State Rd *Web:* wendovercorp.com	Upper Darby	PA	19082	610-449-2056		466
Wendt Corp 2080 Military Rd *Web:* www.wendtcorp.com	Tonawanda	NY	14150	716-391-1200		567
Wendy Soucie Consulting LLC 218 S Main St Ste B *Web:* www.wendysoucie.com	Lodi	WI	53555	608-225-1985		195
Wendy's International Inc 1 Dave Thomas Blvd *Web:* www.wendys.com	Dublin	OH	43017	614-764-3100	764-3330	670
WENE-AM 320 N Jensen Rd *Web:* www.foxsports1430.iheart.com	Vestal	NY	13850	607-754-1430	584-5900	647
Wenger Corp 555 Pk Dr PO Box 448 *TF:* 800-493-6437 ■ *Web:* www.wengercorp.com	Owatonna	MN	55060	507-455-4100	455-4258	527
Wenger Furniture Appliance & Electronics 4552 Whittier Blvd *Web:* www.wengerfurniture.com	Los Angeles	CA	90022	323-261-1136	261-0968	321
Wenger Manufacturing Inc 714 Main St *Web:* www.wenger.com	Sabetha	KS	66534	785-284-2133	284-3771	298
Wenig Saltiel LLP 26 Court St Ste 1200 *Web:* wenigsaltiel.com	Brooklyn	NY	11242	718-797-5700		41
WENK of Union City Inc 1729 Nailing Dr *Web:* www.wenkwtpr.com	Union City	TN	38261	731-885-1240	885-3405	645-141
Wenner Bread Products Inc 33 Rajon Rd *TF:* 800-869-6262 ■ *Web:* www.wennerbakery.com	Bayport	NY	11705	631-563-6262		296-1
WENO 760AM The Gospel 545 Mainstream Dr *Web:* www.760thegospel.com	Nashville	TN	37228	615-742-6506		645-106
Wenstrup Brad (Rep R - OH) 2419 Rayburn House Office Bldg *Web:* wenstrup.house.gov	Washington	DC	20515	202-225-3164	225-1992	342-2
Wenthe-Davidson Engineering Co 16300 W Rogers Dr PO Box 510286 *Web:* www.wenthe-davidson.com	New Berlin	WI	53151	262-782-1550	782-2020	518
Wentworth Company Inc, The 479 W Sixth St *Web:* www.wentco.com	San Pedro	CA	90731	310-519-0113		260
Wentworth Institute of Technology 550 Huntington Ave *TF:* 800-556-0610 ■ *Web:* wit.edu	Boston	MA	02115	617-989-4590	989-4010	166
Wentworth Mansion 149 Wentworth St *Web:* www.wentworthmansion.com	Charleston	SC	29401	843-853-1886		379
Wentworth Printing Corp 101 N 12th St *TF:* 800-326-0784 ■ *Web:* www.wentworthprinting.com	West Columbia	SC	29169	803-796-9990		627
Wentworth State Park 297 Governor Wentworth Hwy *Web:* www.nhstateparks.org	Wolfeboro	NH	03894	603-569-3699		565
Wentworth-Coolidge Mansion Historic Site 375 Little Harbor Rd *Web:* www.nhstateparks.org	Portsmouth	NH	03801	603-436-6607		565
Wentworth-Douglass Hospital 789 Central Ave *TF:* 877-201-7100 ■ *Web:* www.wdhospital.org	Dover	NH	03820	603-742-5252	740-2242	374-3
WENY-TV 474 Old Ithaca Rd *Web:* www.weny.com	Horseheads	NY	14845	607-739-3636	796-6171	647
Wenzel Associates Inc 2215 Kramer Ln *Web:* www.wenzel.com	Austin	TX	78758	512-835-2038	719-4086	253
Wenzel Engineering Inc 10100 Morgan Ave S *Web:* wenzelengineering.com	Bloomington	MN	55431	952-888-6516		261
WENZ-FM 107.9 (Urban) 2510 St Clair Ave NE *TF:* 800-440-1079 ■ *Web:* zhiphopcleveland.com	Cleveland	OH	44114	216-774-0909	771-4164	645-36
Wenzlau Engineering Inc 1517 Fair Oaks Ave *Web:* www.wenzlau.com	South Pasadena	CA	91030	310-604-3400		536
WEOW-FM 92.7 830 Crane Blvd *Web:* www.weow927.com	Sugarloaf Key	FL	33042	305-296-7511	852-2304	645-157
WEP (Worldwide Environmental Products Inc) 1100 W Beacon St *TF:* 800-832-7664 ■ *Web:* www.wep-inc.com	Brea	CA	92821	714-990-2700	990-3100	201
WePackItAll Inc 2745 Huntington Dr *Web:* www.wepackitall.com	Duarte	CA	91010	626-301-9214	301-9216	88
Wepco Plastics Inc 27 Indstrial Pk Access Rd *Web:* www.wepcoplastics.com	Middlefield	CT	06455	860-349-3407	349-1542	604
WERC (Warehousing Education & Research Council) 1100 Jorie Blvd Ste 170 *Web:* www.werc.org	Oak Brook	IL	60523	630-990-0001	990-0256	49-21
Werco Manufacturing Inc 415 E Houston St *Web:* www.wercomfg.com	Broken Arrow	OK	74012	918-251-6880	251-5397	454
WERG-FM Gannon University 700 Peach St *Web:* www.wergfm.com	Erie	PA	16541	814-459-9374		647
Werhane Enterprises Ltd 509 E Main St *TF:* 800-435-9631 ■ *Web:* www.werhane.com	Lena	IL	61048	800-435-9631		297-4
Werk-Brau Company Inc 2800 Fostoria Ave *TF:* 800-537-9561 ■ *Web:* www.werk-brau.com	Findlay	OH	45840	800-537-9561		190
Werklund Capital Corp 4500 Devontower 400 Third Road Ave SW *Web:* www.werklund.com	Calgary	AB	T2P4H2	403-231-6545		787
Werlatone Inc 17 Jon Barrett Rd *Web:* www.werlatone.com	Patterson	NY	12563	845-278-2220	278-3440	253
Wermers Multi-Family Corp 5120 Shoreham Pl Ste 150 *Web:* wermerscompanies.com	San Diego	CA	92122	858-535-1475	535-0171	187
Werner Co 93 Werner Rd *TF:* 888-523-3371 ■ *Web:* www.wernerco.com	Greenville	PA	16125	888-523-3371	456-8459	421
Werner Electric Supply Co 2341 Industrial Dr *TF:* 800-236-5026 ■ *Web:* www.wernerelectric.com	Neenah	WI	54956	920-729-4500	729-4484	246
Werner Enterprises Inc 14507 Frontier Rd *NASDAQ: WERN* ■ *TF:* 800-228-2240 ■ *Web:* www.werner.com	Omaha	NE	68138	402-895-6640	894-3927	780
Werner G. Smith Inc 1730 Train Ave *TF:* 800-535-8343 ■ *Web:* www.wernergsmithinc.com	Cleveland	OH	44113	216-861-3676	861-3680	296-12
Werner Tool & Manufacturing Co 12301 E McNichols Rd	Detroit	MI	48205	313-526-6020		701
Wernersville State Hospital 160 Main St *Web:* www.dhs.pa.gov	Wernersville	PA	19565	610-678-3411		374-5
WERQ-FM 92.3 (Urban) 1705 Whitehead Rd *Web:* 92q.com	Baltimore	MD	21207	410-481-9292		645-15
Werremeyer Floresca Inc 15 N Gore Ave *Web:* werremeyer.com	Saint Louis	MO	63119	314-963-0505		344
Werres Corp 807 E South St *TF:* 800-638-6563 ■ *Web:* www.werres.com	Frederick	MD	21701	800-638-6563		385
Wert Bookbinding Inc 9975 Allentown Blvd *TF:* 800-344-9378 ■ *Web:* www.wertbookbinding.com	Grantville	PA	17028	717-469-0629		92
Werthan Packaging Inc 605 Hwy 76 *Web:* www.werthan.com	White House	TN	37188	615-672-3336		65
Wertz & Company LLP 5450 Trabuco Rd *Web:* wertzco.com	Irvine	CA	92620	949-756-5000		2
WERU-FM 89.9 (Var) 1186 Acadia Hwy *TF:* 800-643-6273 ■ *Web:* weru.org	East Orland	ME	04431	207-469-6600		645
WERV-FM 1884 Plain Ave *Web:* www.959theriver.com	Aurora	IL	60502	630-898-1580		647
Werzalit of America Inc 40 Holly Ave *TF:* 800-999-3730 ■ *Web:* www.werzalitusa.com	Bradford	PA	16701	814-362-3881	362-4237	499
WES (Western Electrical Sales Inc) 521 Glide Ave *Web:* www.wesisales.com	West Sacramento	CA	95691	916-372-1001		246
WES (Western Export Services Inc) 140 E 19th Ave Ste 500 *Web:* www.wesdenver.com	Denver	CO	80203	303-302-5899	302-5882	297-2
Wes Watkins Technology Ctr 7892 Hwy 9 *TF:* 888-884-3834 ■ *Web:* www.wwtech.org	Wetumka	OK	74883	405-452-5500	452-3561	167-3
Wes' Rib House 38 Dike St *Web:* www.wesribhouse.com	Providence	RI	02909	401-421-9090		671
WesBanco Inc 1 Bank Plz *NASDAQ: WSBC* ■ *TF:* 800-328-3369 ■ *Web:* wesbanco.com	Wheeling	WV	26003	304-234-9000		70
Wesbild Holdings Ltd 666 Burrard St Park Pl Ste 2650 *Web:* wesbild.com	Vancouver	BC	V6C2X8	604-694-8800		707
Wesbury United Methodist Community 31 N Park Ave *TF:* 877-937-2879 ■ *Web:* wesbury.com	Meadville	PA	16335	814-332-9000		48-20
Wesco Aircraft Hardware Corp 27727 Ave Scott *TF:* 844-164-0015 ■ *Web:* www.wescoair.com	Valencia	CA	91355	661-775-7200		21
Wesco Cedar Inc PO Box 520 *TF:* 800-547-2511 ■ *Web:* www.wescocedar.com	Creswell	OR	97426	541-688-5020	688-5024	191-4
Wesco Graphics Inc 410 E Grant Line Rd Ste B *Web:* www.wescographics.com	Tracy	CA	95376	209-832-1000	832-7800	344
Wesco Inc 1460 Whitehall Rd *Web:* www.gowesco.com	Muskegon	MI	49445	231-719-4385		324
Wesco Industrial Products Inc 1250 Welsh Rd **Fax Area Code: 800* ■ *TF:* 800-445-5681 ■ *Web:* www.wescomfg.com	North Wales	PA	19454	215-699-7031	346-5511*	470
Wesco International Inc 225 W Stn Sq Dr Ste 700 *NYSE: WCC* ■ *Web:* www.wesco.com	Pittsburgh	PA	15219	412-454-2200		360-3
Wesco Machine Products Inc S84W18569 Enterprise Dr *Web:* wescomachine.com	Muskego	WI	53150	262-679-4799		757
Wesco Turf Inc 2101 Cantu Ct *TF:* 800-486-8873 ■ *Web:* www.wescoturf.com	Sarasota	FL	34232	800-486-8873		358
Wescom Credit Union 123 S Marengo Ave PO Box 7058 *TF:* 888-493-7266 ■ *Web:* www.wescom.org	Pasadena	CA	91101	626-535-1000		219
Wescon Technology Inc 4655 Old Ironsides Dr *Web:* www.wescongroup.com	Santa Clara	CA	95054	408-727-8818	727-8668	202
Wesely-thomas Enterprises Inc 4580 E Thousand Oaks Blvd Ste 200 *Web:* www.weselythomas.com	Westlake Village	CA	91362	805-379-2365	496-0051	186
Wes-Garde Components Group Inc 100 Shield St *TF:* 800-554-8866 ■ *Web:* wesgarde.com	West Hartford	CT	06110	860-527-7705		246
Weslaco Area Chamber of Commerce 301 W Railroad *TF:* 800-700-2443 ■ *Web:* www.weslaco.com	Weslaco	TX	78596	956-968-2102	968-6451	139
Weslaco Public Library 525 S Kansas Ave *Web:* www.weslaco.lib.tx.us	Weslaco	TX	78596	956-968-4533		434-3
Wesland Institute 3367 N Country Club Rd *Web:* www.weslandinstitute.com	Tucson	AZ	85711	520-881-1530		167-3
Wesley Biblical Seminary 787 E Northside Dr *Web:* wbs.edu	Jackson	MS	39206	601-366-8880		167-3
Wesley Clover Corp 390 March Rd Ste 110 *Web:* www.wesleyclover.com	Ottawa	ON	K2K0G7	613-271-6305		528
Wesley College 120 N State St *TF:* 800-937-5398 ■ *Web:* www.wesley.edu	Dover	DE	19901	302-736-2300		167-3
Wesley Foundation-msu 3625 Midland Ave *Web:* www.wesleymemphis.org	Memphis	TN	38111	901-458-5808		305
Wesley Gardens 3 Upton Pk *Web:* www.wesleygardens.com	Rochester	NY	14607	585-241-2100		450

Name / Address	City	State	Zip	Phone	Fax	Class
Wesley Homes 815 S 216th St TF: 866-937-5390 ■ Web: wesleychoice.org	Des Moines	WA	98198	206-824-5000		672
Wesley Manor 1555 N Main St Web: www.wesleymanor.org	Frankfort	IN	46041	765-659-1811		672
Wesley Medical Ctr 550 N Hillside St TF: 800-362-0288 ■ Web: wesleymc.com	Wichita	KS	67214	316-962-2000		374-3
Wesley Peachtree Group Inc, The 1475 Klondike Rd SW Ste 100 Web: www.wpg-inc.com	Conyers	GA	30094	404-874-0555	874-0601	463
Wesley Theological Seminary 4500 Massachusetts Ave NW Web: www.wesleyseminary.edu	Washington	DC	20016	202-885-8600	885-8605	167-3
Wesley Towers 700 Monterey Pl TF: 888-663-9175 ■ Web: www.wesleytowers.com	Hutchinson	KS	67502	620-663-9175		672
Wesley Woods Camp & Retreat Ctr 1700 Clear Lk Web: www.umcamping.org	Dowling	MI	49050	269-721-8291		239
Wesleyan College 4760 Forsyth Rd TF: 800-447-6610 ■ Web: www.wesleyancollege.edu	Macon	GA	31210	478-757-5219	757-4030	166
Wesleyan Publishing House (WPH) 13300 Olio Rd TF: 800-493-7539 ■ Web: www.wesleyan.org	Fishers	IN	46037	317-774-7900		637-2
Wesleyan University 70 Wyllys Ave TF: 800-288-2020 ■ Web: www.wesleyan.edu	Middletown	CT	06459	860-685-3000	685-3001	166
Wes-Pak Inc 11610 Vimy Ridge Rd	Alexander	AR	72002	501-372-1900		475
WeSpire Inc 125 Kingston St 6th Fl Web: www.wespire.com	Boston	MA	02111	617-531-8970		387
Wessel Group, The 1101 17th St NW Ste 104 Web: www.wesselgroup.com	Washington	DC	20036	202-293-8899		194
Wessels & Wierman PC 423 17th St Ste 102 Web: wesselspc.com	Rock Island	IL	61201	309-794-9400		41
Wessels Sherman Joerg Liszka Laverty Seneczko PC 9800 Shelard Pkwy Ste 310 Web: wesselssherman.com	Minneapolis	MN	55441	952-746-1700		41
Wesson Inc 165 Railroad Hill St Web: www.bantamwesson.com	Waterbury	CT	06708	203-756-7041	754-6664	579
Wesspur Tree Equipment 2121 Iron St TF: 800-268-2141 ■ Web: www.wesspur.com	Bellingham	WA	98225	360-734-5242		429
West & Company CPAS PC 97 N Main St Web: westcpapc.com	Gloversville	NY	12078	518-725-7127		2
West Agro Inc 11100 N Congress Ave TF: 800-447-8370 ■ Web: cleaningsolutions.delaval.com	Kansas City	MO	64153	816-891-1600	891-1505	276
West Alabama Bank & Trust 509 First Ave W PO Box 310 Web: www.wabt.com	Reform	AL	35481	205-375-6261	375-2289	70
West Allis Public Library 7525 W Greenfield Ave Web: www.westalliswi.gov	West Allis	WI	53214	414-302-8503		434-3
West American Rubber Company LLC 1337 Braden Ct TF: 800-245-8748 ■ Web: www.warco.com	Orange	CA	92868	714-532-3355	532-2238	677
West Anaheim Extended Care 645 S Beach Blvd Web: westanaheimec.com	Anaheim	CA	92804	714-821-1993	821-0130	371
West Anaheim Medical Ctr (WAMC) 3033 W Orange Ave Web: www.westanaheimmedctr.com	Anaheim	CA	92804	714-827-3000		374-3
West Bag Inc 1161 Monterey Pass Rd	Monterey Park	CA	91754	323-264-0750		596
West Bancorp Inc PO Box 65020 NASDAQ: WTBA ■ TF: 800-810-2301 ■ Web: www.westbankstrong.com	West Des Moines	IA	50265	515-222-2300		360-2
West Baton Rouge Convention & Visitors Bureau 2750 N Westport Dr TF: 800-527-6843 ■ Web: www.westbatonrouge.net	Baton Rouge	LA	70801	225-383-1825		206
West Baton Rouge Museum 845 N Jefferson Ave TF: 888-881-6811 ■ Web: www.wbrparish.org	Port Allen	LA	70767	225-336-2422	336-2448	520
West Bay Exploration Co 13685 S W Bay Shore Ste 200 Web: www.westbayexploration.com	Traverse City	MI	49684	231-946-0200	946-8180	538
West Bend Area Chamber of Commerce 304 S Main St TF: 888-338-8666 ■ Web: www.wbachamber.org	West Bend	WI	53095	262-338-2666	338-1771	139
West Bend Community Memorial Library 630 Poplar St Web: www.westbendlibrary.org	West Bend	WI	53095	262-335-5151	335-5150	434-3
West Bend Housewares LLC 2845 Wingate St *Fax Area Code: 224 ■ TF: 866-290-1851 ■ Web: www.westbend.com	West Bend	WI	53095	866-290-1851	513-2498*	37
West Bend Mutual Insurance Co 1900 S 18th Ave TF: 800-236-5010 ■ Web: www.thesilverlining.com	West Bend	WI	53095	262-334-5571	334-9109	391-4
West Bend Transit and Service 105 Forest Ave TF: 877-933-7315 ■ Web: www.westbendtransit.com	West Bend	WI	53095	877-933-7315		780
West Bloomfield Chamber of Commerce 5745 W Maple Rd Ste 206 Web: westbloomfieldchamber.com	West Bloomfield	MI	48322	248-626-3636	626-4218	139
West Bloomfield Township Public Library 4600 Walnut Lake Rd Web: www.wblib.org	West Bloomfield	MI	48323	248-682-2120	232-2333	434-3
West Boca Medical Ctr (WBMC) 21644 State Rd 7 Web: www.westbocamedctr.com	Boca Raton	FL	33428	561-488-8000	488-8105	374-3
West Bond Inc 1551 S Harris Ct Web: www.westbond.com	Anaheim	CA	92806	714-978-1551	978-0431	494
West Boylston Insurance Agency Inc 12 W Boylston St Web: westboylstoninsurance.com	West Boylston	MA	01583	508-835-3877		390
West Branch Area Chamber of Commerce 422 W Houghton Ave TF: 800-755-9091 ■ Web: www.wbacc.com	West Branch	MI	48661	989-345-2821		206
West Calcasieu Cameron Hospital 701 E Cypress St Web: www.wcch.com	Sulphur	LA	70663	337-527-7034		374-3
West Canadian Digital Imaging Inc 200 - 1601 Ninth Ave SE TF: 800-267-2555 ■ Web: www.westcanadian.com	Calgary	AB	T2G0H4	403-245-2555		344
West Capital Management 1818 Market St 33rd Fl Ste 3323 Web: www.westcapital.com	Philadelphia	PA	19103	215-731-1820	731-1419	194
West Central Electric Co-opeartive Inc 204 Main St PO Box 17 TF: 800-242-9232 ■ Web: www.wce.coop	Murdo	SD	57559	605-669-2472		245
West Central Electric Cooperative Inc 7867 S Hwy 13 TF: 855-874-5349 ■ Web: www.westcentralelectric.com	Higginsville	MO	64037	816-565-4942		245
West Central Steel Inc 110 19th St NW PO Box 1178 *Fax Area Code: 320 ■ TF: 800-992-8853 ■ Web: www.wcsteel.com	Willmar	MN	56201	800-992-8853	235-1816*	492
West Central Tribune PO Box 839 TF: 800-450-1150 ■ Web: www.wctrib.com	Willmar	MN	56201	320-235-1150	235-6769	532-2
West Central Wireless 3389 Knickerbocker Rd TF: 800-695-9016 ■ Web: www.wcc.net	San Angelo	TX	76904	800-695-9016		736
West Chester Chamber Alliance 8922 Beckett Rd Web: www.thechamberalliance.com	West Chester	OH	45069	513-777-3600	777-0188	139
West Chester University 700 S High St TF: 877-315-2165 ■ Web: wcupa.edu	West Chester	PA	19383	610-436-1000	436-2907	166
West Clermont Local School District 4350 Aicholtz Rd Ste 220 Web: www.westcler.k12.oh.us	Cincinnati	OH	45245	513-943-5000	752-6158	685
West Coast Aviation Services 19711 Campus Dr Ste 150 TF: 800-352-6153 ■ Web: www.wcas.aero	Santa Ana	CA	92707	949-852-8340	260-3999	13
West Coast Clinical Laboratories Lp 7636 Burnet Ave	Van Nuys	CA	91405	818-908-0535		418
West Coast Conference 1111 Bayhill Dr Ste 405 Web: www.wccsports.com	San Bruno	CA	94066	650-873-8622		533
West Coast Connection 1725 Main St Ste 215 TF: 800-767-0227 ■ Web: www.westcoastconnection.com	Weston	FL	33326	954-888-9780	888-9781	760
West Coast Construction 9021 Rancho Park Ct TF: 800-491-2032 ■ Web: wccsinc.com	Rancho Cucamonga	CA	91730	800-491-2032		186
West Coast Cosmetics Inc 21050 Superior St Web: www.westcoastcosmetics.com	Chatsworth	CA	91311	818-349-8510		237
West Coast Dental Services Inc 12121 Wilshire Blvd Ste 1111 Web: www.westcoastdental.com	Los Angeles	CA	90025	310-820-9933		194
West Coast Differentials 2429 Mercantile Dr Ste A TF: 800-510-0950 ■ Web: www.differentials.com	Rancho Cordova	CA	95742	916-635-0950		54
West Coast Distributing Inc Commerce Pl 350 Main St TF: 800-235-3730 ■ Web: www.wcd-network.com	Malden	MA	02148	781-665-9393		10-11
West Coast Engineering Group Ltd 7984 River Rd Web: www.wceng.com	Delta	BC	V4G1E3	604-946-1256	946-1203	683
West Coast Fab Inc 700 S 32nd St Web: www.westcoastfabinc.com	Richmond	CA	94804	510-529-0177	233-2248	697
West Coast Financial LLC 1525 State St Ste 104 TF: 877-903-8930 ■ Web: www.wcfinc.com	Santa Barbara	CA	93101	805-962-9131	962-4290	194
West Coast Green Institute 700 Market St Ste 1020 TF: 800-724-4880 ■ Web: westcoastgreen.com	San Francisco	CA	94102	415-955-1935		387
West Coast Industrial Systems 1995 W Airway Rd Web: westcoastindustrial.com	Lebanon	OR	97355	541-451-6677	451-6681	454
West Coast Industries Inc 10 Jackson St TF: 800-243-3150 ■ Web: westcoastindustries.com	San Francisco	CA	94111	415-621-6656	552-5368	319-1
West Coast Internet Inc (WCI) PO Box 7598 Web: www.westcoastinternet.com	Capistrano Beach	CA	92624	949-487-3302		681
West Coast Nursing Ventura Inc 2955 E Hillcrest Dr Ste 121 Web: wcnventura.com	Thousand Oaks	CA	91362	805-496-0900	496-0906	363
West Coast Shoe Co 52828 NW Shoe Factory Ln PO Box 607 TF: 800-326-2711 ■ Web: builder.wescoboots.com	Scappoose	OR	97056	503-543-7114	543-7110	301
West Coast Trends 17811 Jamestown Ln TF: 800-736-4568 ■ Web: www.clubglove.com	Huntington Beach	CA	92647	714-843-9288		710
West Coast Turf 42-540 Melanie Pl Web: www.westcoastturf.com	Palm Desert	CA	92211	760-340-7300		776
West Coast-Accudyne Inc 7180 Scout Ave Web: www.accudyneeng.com	Bell	CA	90201	562-927-2546	806-4628	456
West Construction Inc 318 S Dixie Hwy Ste 4-5 Web: www.westconstructioninc.net	Lake Worth	FL	33460	561-588-2027		186
West Consultants Inc 2601 25th St SE Ste 450 Web: westconsultants.com	Salem	OR	97302	503-485-5490		261
West Consultants PLLC 405 S Sterling St Web: west-consultants.com	Morganton	NC	28655	828-433-5661		261
West Corp 11808 Miracle Hills Dr TF: 800-232-0900 ■ Web: www.west.com	Omaha	NE	68154	800-232-0900		737
West County Ctr 80 W County Ctr Web: www.shopwestcountycenter.com	Des Peres	MO	63131	314-288-2020		460
West Craft Manufacturing Inc 506 Palestine St Web: www.westcraftmfg.com	Alto	TX	75925	936-858-4426	858-2256	223
West Creek Financial PO Box 5518 TF: 844-937-8275 ■ Web: www.westcreekfin.com	Glen Allen	VA	23058	844-937-8275		39

Phone | Fax | Class

West Des Moines Chamber of Commerce
650 S Prairie View Dr Ste 110 .... West Des Moines IA 50266 515-225-6009 139
Web: www.wdmchamber.org

West Des Moines Public Library
4000 Mills Civic Pkwy .... West Des Moines IA 50265 515-222-3400 222-3401 434-3
Web: www.wdmlibrary.org

West End Diagnostic Imaging
2425 Bloor St W Ste 103 .... Toronto ON M6S4W4 416-763-4331 415
Web: www.wedi.ca

West End Gallery Ltd
12308 Jasper Ave .... Edmonton AB T5N3K5 780-488-4892 42
TF: 855-488-4892 ■ *Web:* www.westendgalleryltd.com

West End Grill, The
120 W Liberty Ave .... Ann Arbor MI 48104 734-747-6260 671
Web: www.westendgrillannarbor.com

West End Machine & Welding
6804 School Ave .... Richmond VA 23228 804-266-9631 264-0747 480
Web: www.westendmachine.com

West End, The 20 Scudder Ave .... Hyannis MA 02601 508-775-7677 671
Web: www.westendhyannis.com

West Engineering Company Inc
10106 Louistown Rd .... Ashland VA 23005 804-798-3966 798-8590 454
Web: www.west-engineering.net

West Essex Graphics Inc (WEG)
305 Fairfield Ave .... Fairfield NJ 07004 800-221-5859 227-2906* 781
**Fax Area Code:* 973 ■ *TF:* 800-221-5859 ■ *Web:* www.westessexgraphics.com

West Essex Tribune Inc PO Box 65 .... Livingston NJ 07039 973-992-1771 992-7015 532-2
Web: www.westessextribune.net

West Face Capital Inc
2 Bloor St E Ste 3000 .... Toronto ON M4W1A8 647-724-8900 401
Web: www.westfacecapital.com

West Fargo Pioneer 101 Fifth St N .... West Fargo ND 58078 701-451-5718 532-4
Web: www.westfargopioneer.com

West Fargo School District 6
207 Main Ave W .... West Fargo ND 58078 701-356-2000 356-2009 685
Web: www.west-fargo.k12.nd.us

West Feliciana Historical Society Museum
11757 Ferdinand St .... Saint Francisville LA 70775 225-635-6330 520
Web: westfelicianahistory.org

West Feliciana Parish
5934 Commerce St PO Box 1921 .... Saint Francisville LA 70775 225-635-3864 338
Web: www.wfparish.org

West Florida Electric Co-op
5282 Peanut Rd .... Graceville FL 32440 850-263-3231 245
TF: 800-342-7400 ■ *Web:* www.westflorida.coop

West Florida Hospital
8383 N Davis Hwy .... Pensacola FL 32514 850-494-4000 374-3
Web: westfloridahospital.com

West Fraser Timber Company Ltd (WFT)
501-858 Beatty St Ste 501 .... Vancouver BC V6B1C1 604-895-2700 681-6061 683
Web: www.westfraser.com

West Genesee Central School District
300 Sanderson Dr .... Camillus NY 13031 315-487-4562 685
Web: www.westgenesee.org

West Georgia Medical Ctr
1514 Vernon Rd .... LaGrange GA 30240 706-882-1411 374-3
Web: www.wghs.org

West Georgia Regional Library
710 Rome St .... Carrollton GA 30117 770-836-6711 434-3
Web: www.wgrls.org

West Gulf Maritime Assn
1717 E Loop N Ste 200 .... Houston TX 77029 713-678-7655 47
Web: www.wgma.org

West Hartford Chamber of Commerce
948 Farmington Ave .... West Hartford CT 06107 860-521-2300 521-1996 139
Web: www.whchamber.com

West Hartford Health & Rehabilitation Ctr
130 Loomis Dr .... West Hartford CT 06107 860-521-8700 450
Web: westhartfordhealth.com

West Hartford Public Library
20 S Main St .... West Hartford CT 06107 860-561-6950 561-6990 434-3
Web: www.westhartfordlibrary.org

West Haven Chamber of Commerce
355 Main St Ground Fl .... West Haven CT 06516 203-933-1500 931-1940 139
Web: www.westhavenchamber.com

West Highland Christian Academy
1116 S Hickory Ridge Rd .... Milford MI 48380 248-887-6698 148
Web: www.whca-k12.org

West Hills College
Coalinga 300 Cherry Ln .... Coalinga CA 93210 559-934-2000 162
TF: 800-266-1114 ■ *Web:* www.westhillscollege.com

West Hills Hospital & Medical Ctr
7300 Medical Centre Dr .... West Hills CA 91307 818-676-4000 374-3
Web: westhillshospital.com

West Hills Village Senior Residence
5711 SW Multnomah Blvd .... Portland OR 97219 503-245-7621 371
Web: westhillssenior.com

West Hollywood Chamber of Commerce
8272 Santa Monica Blvd .... West Hollywood CA 90046 323-650-2688 650-2689 139
TF: 800-345-8683 ■ *Web:* www.wehochamber.com

West Hollywood Marketing Corp
1017 N La Cienega Blvd Ste 400 .... West Hollywood CA 90069 310-289-2525 206
TF: 800-368-6020 ■ *Web:* www.visitwesthollywood.com

West Houston Medical Ctr
12141 Richmond Ave .... Houston TX 77082 281-558-3444 374-3
Web: westhoustonmedical.com

West Islip Public Library
3 Higbie Ln .... West Islip NY 11795 631-661-7080 661-7137 434-3
TF: 866-833-1122 ■ *Web:* www.wipublib.org

West Jefferson Medical Ctr
1101 Medical Center Blvd .... Marrero LA 70072 504-349-1134 374-3
Web: www.wjmc.org

West Jordan Chamber of Commerce
8000 Redwood Rd .... West Jordan UT 84088 801-569-5151 569-5153 139
Web: westjordanchamber.com

West Kentucky Community & Technical College
4810 Alben Barkley Dr PO Box 7380 .... Paducah KY 42001 270-554-9200 554-6203 162
TF: 855-469-5282 ■ *Web:* westkentucky.kctcs.edu

West Kentucky News
1540 McCracken Blvd .... Paducah KY 42001 270-442-7389 442-5220 532-4
Web: www.ky-news.com

West Kentucky Rural Electric Co-opeartive Corp
PO Box 589 .... Mayfield KY 42066 270-247-1321 245
TF: 877-495-7322 ■ *Web:* www.wkrecc.com

West Lafayette Public Library
208 W Columbia St .... West Lafayette IN 47906 765-743-2261 743-0540 434-3
Web: www.wlaf.lib.in.us

West Liberty Foods LLC
228 W Second St .... West Liberty IA 52776 319-627-6329 619
TF: 888-511-4500 ■ *Web:* www.wlfoods.com

West Los Angeles College
9000 Overland Ave .... Culver City CA 90230 310-287-4200 287-4327 162
Web: www.wlac.edu

West Marine Inc 500 Westridge Dr .... Watsonville CA 95076 831-728-2700 770
NASDAQ: WMAR ■ *TF:* 800-262-8464 ■ *Web:* www.westmarine.com

West Memphis Chamber of Commerce
108 W Broadway .... West Memphis AR 72301 870-735-1134 735-6283 139
Web: westmemphischamber.net

West Metro Chamber of Commerce
1667 Cole Blvd Bldg 19 Ste 400 .... Golden CO 80401 303-233-5555 237-7633 139
Web: www.westmetrochamber.org

West Michigan Symphony Orchestra
360 W Western Ave Ste 200 .... Muskegon MI 49440 231-726-3231 457-4033 637-2
Web: www.westmichigansymphony.org

West Michigan Tourist Assn (WMTA)
741 Kenmoor Ave Ste E .... Grand Rapids MI 49546 616-245-2217 954-3924 393
Web: wmta.org

West Milford Township Library
1490 Union Valley Rd .... West Milford NJ 07480 973-728-2820 728-2106 434-3
Web: www.wmtl.org

West Millbrook Middle School
8115 Strickland Rd .... Raleigh NC 27615 919-870-4050 685
Web: www.wmms.net

West Monroe Partners LLC
222 W Adams St 11th Fl .... Chicago IL 60606 312-602-4000 194
TF: 800-828-6708 ■ *Web:* www.westmonroepartners.com

West Mountain Animal Hospital
1726 Harwood Hill .... Bennington VT 05201 802-447-7723 794
Web: wmah.net

West Music Inc 1212 Fifth St .... Coralville IA 52241 319-351-2000 526
TF: 800-373-2000 ■ *Web:* www.westmusic.com

West Nebraska Register
PO Box 608 .... Grand Island NE 68802 308-382-4660 382-6569 532-4
TF: 800-652-2229 ■ *Web:* www.gidiocese.org

West New York Public Library
425 60th St .... West New York NJ 07093 201-295-5135 662-1473 434-3
Web: wnypl.org

West Nottingham Academy
1079 Firetower Rd .... Colora MD 21917 410-658-5556 622
TF: 866-381-3684 ■ *Web:* www.wna.org

West Oakland Health Council Inc (WOHC)
700 Adeline St .... Oakland CA 94607 510-835-9610 353
Web: www.westoaklandhealth.org

West Oaklane Charter School
7115 Stenton Ave .... Philadelphia PA 19138 215-927-7995 927-7980 685
Web: www.wolcs.org

West Oaks Hospital 6500 Hornwood Dr .... Houston TX 77074 713-995-0909 374-5
Web: www.westoakshospital.com

West Oaks Mall 1000 W Oaks Mall .... Houston TX 77082 281-531-1332 531-1579 460
Web: www.shopwestoaksmall.com

West Oaks Mall
9401 W Colonial Dr Ste 728 .... Ocoee FL 34761 407-294-1494 460
Web: www.westoaksmall.com

West Orange Chamber of Commerce
12184 W Colonial Dr .... Winter Garden FL 34787 407-656-1304 656-0221 139
Web: wochamber.com

West Orange Municipal Federal Credit Union
342 Main St .... West Orange NJ 07052 973-736-1929 219
TF: 866-893-9486 ■ *Web:* womfcu.org

West Orange Public Library
46 Mt Pleasant Ave .... West Orange NJ 07052 973-736-0198 434-3
Web: www.wopl.org

West Orange Times
720 S Dillard St .... Winter Garden FL 34787 407-656-2121 656-6075 532-2
Web: www.orangeobserver.com

West Oregon Electric Co-opeartive Inc
652 Rose Ave PO Box 69 .... Vernonia OR 97064 503-429-3021 429-8440 245
TF: 800-777-1276 ■ *Web:* www.westoregon.org

West Palm Beach City Hall
401 Clematis St .... West Palm Beach FL 33401 561-822-1200 822-1424 337
Web: wpb.org

West Parry Sound Health Ctr
6 Albert St .... Parry Sound ON P2A3A4 705-746-9321 746-7364 374-2
Web: www.wpshc.com

West Pasco Chamber of Commerce
5443 Main St .... New Port Richey FL 34652 727-842-7651 848-0202 139
TF: 800-851-8754 ■ *Web:* www.westpasco.com

West Penn Energy Services LLC
865 SR-210 .... Shelocta PA 15774 724-354-4118 354-3128 536
Web: www.wpes-pa.com

West Penn Non-Destructive Testing Inc
1010 Industrial Blvd .... New Kensington PA 15068 724-334-1900 334-9785 743
Web: www.westpenntesting.com

West Penn Oil Company Inc
2305 Market St .... Warren PA 16365 814-723-9000 579
Web: www.westpenn.com

West Penn Power Co
800 Cabin Hill Dr .... Greensburg PA 15601 800-686-0021 186
TF: 800-686-0021 ■ *Web:* www.firstenergycorp.com

West Penn Printing
103 Riverpark Dr .... New Castle PA 16101 724-856-3376 627
Web: www.westpennprinting.com

West Penn Wire 2833 W Chestnut St .... Washington PA 15301 800-245-4964 222-6420* 73
**Fax Area Code:* 724 ■ *TF:* 800-245-4964 ■ *Web:* www.westpenn-wpw.com

West Plains Bank & Trust Co
11 Court Sq PO Box 378 .... West Plains MO 65775 417-256-2147 70
Web: westplainsbank.com

	Phone	Fax	Class
West Point Industries 2021 Stateline Rd PO Box 589 . . . . West Point GA 31833 *Web:* www.westpoint.com	706-643-2101	643-2100	744
West Point Lumber Co 13501 Dixie Hwy . . . . Louisville KY 40272 *Web:* westpoint.doitbest.com	502-937-1152		351
West Point Market 33 Shiawassee Ave . . . . Fairlawn OH 44333 *Web:* www.westpointmarket.com	330-864-2151		460
West Point Thoroughbreds Inc 2 Smith Bridge Rd . . . . Saratoga Springs NY 12866 *Web:* www.westpointtb.com	518-583-6638		31
West Point Underwriters LLC 7785 66th St. . . . . Pinellas Park FL 33781 *TF:* 800-688-6213 ■ *Web:* westpointuw.com	727-507-7565		390
West Port Plaza 111 W Port Plaza Dr Ste 550 . . . . Saint Louis MO 63146 *Web:* www.westportstl.com	314-576-7100		50-6
West Press Printing & Copying 1663 W Grant Rd . . . . Tucson AZ 85745 *TF:* 888-637-0337 ■ *Web:* westpress.com	520-624-4939		627
West River Co-operative Telephone Co (WRCTC) 801 Coleman Ave PO Box 39 . . . . Bison SD 57620 *Web:* www.sdplains.com	605-244-5213		736
West River Electric Association Inc 1200 W Fourth Ave PO Box 412 . . . . Wall SD 57790 **Fax Area Code: 605* ■ *TF:* 888-279-2135 ■ *Web:* www.westriver.com	888-279-2135	279-2630*	245
West River Telecommunications Co-op PO Box 467 . . . . Hazen ND 58545 *TF:* 800-748-7220 ■ *Web:* www.westriv.com	701-748-2211	748-6800	736
West Sacramento Chamber of Commerce 1401 Halyard Dr Ste 120 . . . . West Sacramento CA 95691 *Web:* www.westsacramentochamber.com	916-371-7042	371-7007	139
West Shore Chamber of Commerce 4211 E Trindle Rd . . . . Camp Hill PA 17011 *Web:* wschamber.org	717-761-0702		139
West Shore Chamber of Commerce PO Box 45297 . . . . Westlake OH 44145 *Web:* www.westshorechamber.org	440-835-8787	835-8798	139
West Shore Chamber of Commerce 2830 Aldwynd Rd . . . . Victoria BC V9B3S7 *Web:* westshore.bc.ca	250-478-1130	478-1584	137
West Shore Community College PO Box 277 . . . . Scottville MI 49454 *TF:* 800-848-9722 ■ *Web:* www.westshore.edu	231-845-6211	845-3944	162
West Shore Plaza 250 W Shore Blvd . . . . Tampa FL 33609 *Web:* westshoreplaza.com	813-286-0790		460
West Shore State Park 300 Lone Pine Rd. . . . . Kalispell MT 59901 *Web:* stateparks.mt.gov	406-755-2706		565
West Side Agency Inc 120 Vinton St PO Box 200 . . . . Palo IA 52324 *TF:* 800-235-3228 ■ *Web:* westsidemutual.com	319-851-2147		390
West Side Cafe 7950 Camp Bowie W Blvd . . . . Fort Worth TX 76116 *Web:* www.fortworthwestsidecafe.com	817-560-1996		671
West Side Mechanical Inc 2007 Corporate Ln . . . . Naperville IL 60563 *Web:* wsmech.com	630-369-6690		14
West Side Telephone Co 1449 Fairmont Rd. . . . . Morgantown WV 26501 *TF:* 800-296-9113 ■ *Web:* westsidetelecommunications.net	304-983-2211		196
West Side Tractor Sales Co 1400 W Ogden Ave. . . . . Naperville IL 60563 *Web:* www.westsidetractorsales.com	630-355-7150	355-7173	358
West Side Unlimited 4201 16th Ave SW . . . . Cedar Rapids IA 52404 *TF:* 800-373-2957 ■ *Web:* www.westsideunlimited.com	319-390-4466		780
West Springfield Auto Parts 92 Blandin Ave . . . . Framingham MA 01702 *TF:* 800-615-2392 ■ *Web:* www.wsaparts.com	508-879-6932	879-4894	791
West Star Aviation Inc 796 Heritage Way . . . . Grand Junction CO 81506 *TF:* 800-255-4193 ■ *Web:* www.weststaraviation.com	970-243-7500	248-5243	24
West Street Cafe 76 West St . . . . Bar Harbor ME 04609 *Web:* www.weststreetcafe.com	207-288-5242		671
West Suburban Bank 711 Westmore Meyers Rd. Lombard IL 60148 *TF:* 800-258-4009 ■ *Web:* www.westsuburbanbank.com	630-652-2000	629-0278	70
West Suburban Chamber of Commerce 9440 Joliet Rd Ste B. . . . . Hodgkins IL 60525 *TF:* 800-796-9696 ■ *Web:* www.wscci.org	708-387-7550	387-7556	139
West Suburban Hospital Medical Ctr 3 Erie Ct . . . . Oak Park IL 60302 *TF:* 866-938-7256 ■ *Web:* www.westsuburbanmc.com	708-383-6200		374-3
West Suburban Special Recreation Assn 2915 Maple St . . . . Franklin Park IL 60131 *Web:* www.wssra.net	847-455-2100	455-2157	31
West Tennessee Communications 1295 Hwy 51 By-pass. . . . . Dyersburg TN 38024 *TF:* 800-264-1175 ■ *Web:* www.wetec.com	731-286-6275		246
West Tennessee State Penitentiary 480 Green Chapel Rd PO Box 1150 . . . . Henning TN 38041 *Web:* www.tn.gov	731-738-5044		213
West Texas A & M University 2501 Fourth Ave. . . . . Canyon TX 79016 *TF:* 877-656-2065 ■ *Web:* www.wtamu.edu	806-651-2020	651-5285	166
West Texas Gas 211 N Colorado St. . . . . Midland TX 79701 *Web:* www.westtexasgas.com	432-682-4349		360-3
West Texas National Bank 6 Desta Dr Ste 2400 . . . . Midland TX 79705 *TF:* 800-250-8880 ■ *Web:* www.wtnb.com	432-685-6500		70
West Texas Rural Telephone Co-opeartive Inc PO Box 1737 . . . . Hereford TX 79045 *TF:* 888-440-4331 ■ *Web:* www.wtrt.net	806-364-3331	276-5219	736
West Towne Mall 66 W Towne Mall . . . . Madison WI 53719 *Web:* www.shopwesttowne-mall.com	608-833-6330		460
West Tree Service Inc 6300 Forbing Rd. . . . . Little Rock AR 72209 *Web:* www.westtree.com	501-568-5111		776
West University Travel 3622 University Blvd . . . . Houston TX 77005 *TF:* 800-256-0640 ■ *Web:* westuniversitytravel.com	713-665-4767		772
West Valley College 14000 Fruitvale Ave . . . . Saratoga CA 95070 *Web:* www.westvalley.edu	408-867-2200		162
West Valley Construction Company Inc 580 McGlincey Ln . . . . Campbell CA 95008 *TF:* 800-588-5510 ■ *Web:* www.westvalleyconstruction.com	800-588-5510		188-10
West Valley Flying Club 1901 Embarcadero Rd . . . . Palo Alto CA 94303 *Web:* www.wvfc.org	650-856-2030		63
West Valley Medical Ctr 1717 Arlington Ave. . . . . Caldwell ID 83605 **Fax Area Code: 877* ■ *Web:* westvalleymedctr.com	208-459-4641	865-9738*	374-3
West Valley National Bank 2440 N Litchfield Rd Ste 100 . . . . Goodyear AZ 85395 *Web:* wvnb.net	623-536-9862		70
West Valley School District 208 8902 Zier Rd. . . . . Yakima WA 98908 *Web:* www.wvsd208.org	509-972-6000	972-6001	685
West Valley View 250 Litchfield Rd Ste 130 . . . . Goodyear AZ 85338 *Web:* www.westvalleyview.com	623-535-8439	935-2103	532-4
West Vancouver Chamber of Commerce 2235 Marine Dr . . . . West Vancouver BC V7V1K5 *Web:* westvanchamber.com	604-926-6614		137
West Virginia			
Administrative Office of the Courts 1900 Kanawha Blvd E Bldg 1 Rm E-100 . . . . . Charleston WV 25305 *Web:* www.courtswv.gov	304-558-0145	558-1212	339-49
Agriculture Dept 1900 Kanawha Blvd E State Capitol Rm E-28 . Charleston WV 25305 *Web:* agriculture.wv.gov	304-558-3550	558-2203	339-49
Attorney General State Capitol Complex Bldg 1 Rm E-26. . . . . . Charleston WV 25305 *TF:* 800-368-8808 ■ *Web:* www.ago.wv.gov	304-558-2021	558-0140	339-49
Board of Medicine 101 Dee Dr Ste 103 . . . . Charleston WV 25311 *Web:* wvbom.wv.gov	304-558-2921	558-2084	339-49
Bureau for Public Health 350 Capitol St Rm 702 . . . . Charleston WV 25301 *Web:* dhhr.wv.gov	304-558-2971	558-1035	339-49
Child Support Enforcement Bureau 231 Capitol St Ste 111. . . . . Charleston WV 25301 *Web:* www.dhhr.wv.gov	304-561-3120	558-2645	339-49
Children & Families Bureau 350 Capitol St Rm 730 . . . . Charleston WV 25301 *TF:* 800-352-6513 ■ *Web:* www.wvdhhr.org	304-558-0628	558-4194	339-49
Community Development Div 1900 Kanawha Blvd E . . . . Charleston WV 25305 *TF:* 800-982-3386 ■ *Web:* wvcad.org	304-558-2234	558-1189	339-49
Consumer Protection Div 812 Quarrier St 1st Fl PO Box 1789. . . . . Charleston WV 25301 *Web:* www.ago.wv.gov	304-558-8986	558-0184	339-49
Crime Victims Compensation Fund 1900 Kanawha Blvd E Rm W-334 . . . . Charleston WV 25305 *TF:* 877-562-6878 ■ *Web:* www.wvlegislature.gov	304-347-4850	347-4915	339-49
Culture Center, The 1900 Kanawha Blvd E Bldg 3. . . . . Charleston WV 25305 *Web:* www.wvculture.org	304-558-0220	558-2779	339-49
Department of Health & Human Resources One Davis Sq E Ste 100. . . . . Charleston WV 25301 *Web:* www.dhhr.wv.gov	304-558-0684		353
Department of Veterans Assistance 1900 Kanawha Blvd E Bldg 5 Rm 205 . . . . Charleston WV 25305 *TF:* 888-838-2332 ■ *Web:* www.veterans.wv.gov	304-558-3661	558-3662	339-49
Dept of Revenue State Capitol Bldg 1 Rm W-300. . . . . Charleston WV 25305 *TF:* 800-982-8297 ■ *Web:* www.revenue.wv.gov	304-558-1017	558-2324	339-49
Division of Labor 1900 Kanawha Blvd E State Capitol Complex Bldg 3 Rm 200 . . . . Charleston WV 25305 *Web:* labor.wv.gov	304-722-0602	722-0605	339-49
Division of Natural Resources 324 Fourth Ave Bldg 74. . . . . South Charleston WV 25303 *Web:* www.wvdnr.gov	304-558-2754	558-2768	339-49
Environmental Protection Dept 601 57th St SE. . . . . Charleston WV 25304 *Web:* www.dep.wv.gov	304-926-0440	926-0446	339-49
Ethics Commission 210 Brooks St Ste 300. . . . . Charleston WV 25301 *TF:* 866-558-0664 ■ *Web:* www.ethics.wv.gov	304-558-0664	558-2169	265
Higher Education Policy Commission 1018 Kanawha Blvd E Ste 700. . . . . Charleston WV 25301 *TF:* 888-825-5707 ■ *Web:* www.wvhepc.edu	304-558-2101	558-1011	725
Housing Development Fund 5710 MacCorkle Ave SE . . . . Charleston WV 25304 *TF:* 800-933-9843 ■ *Web:* www.wvhdf.com	304-391-8600		339-49
Insurance Commission 900 Pennsylvania Ave . . . . Charleston WV 25302 *TF:* 888-879-9842 ■ *Web:* www.wvinsurance.gov	304-558-3354	558-0412	339-49
Labor Div Capitol Complex 749 B Bldg 6 . . . . Charleston WV 25305 *Web:* wvlabor.com	304-558-7890		339-49
Lottery 900 Pennsylvania Ave PO Box 2067 . . . . Charleston WV 25302 *TF:* 800-982-2274 ■ *Web:* www.wvlottery.com	304-558-0500	558-3321	452
Motor Vehicles Div 5707 Maccorkle Ave SE PO Box 17020 . . . . . . Charleston WV 25317 *TF:* 800-642-9066 ■ *Web:* www.transportation.wv.gov	304-926-3802		339-49
Office of Governor 1900 Kanawha Blvd E State Capitol Bldg. . . . . Charleston WV 25305 *TF:* 888-438-2731 ■ *Web:* www.governor.wv.gov	304-558-3588		339-49
Office of Technology 1900 Kanawha Blvd E Capitol Complex Bldg 5 Tenth Fl. . . . . Charleston WV 25304 *TF:* 877-558-9966 ■ *Web:* technology.wv.gov	304-558-5472	558-0136	339-49

	Phone	Fax	Class
Probation & Parole Board			
1356 Hansford St Ste B .... Charleston WV 25301	304-558-6366	558-5678	339-49
Web: paroleboard.wv.gov			
Racing Commission			
900 Pennsylvania Ave Ste 533............. Charleston WV 25302	304-558-2150	558-6319	712
Web: www.racing.wv.gov			
Rehabilitation Services Div			
107 Capitol St .... Charleston WV 25301	304-356-2060		339-49
Web: www.wvdrs.org			
Secretary of State			
1900 Kanawha Blvd E Bldg 1 Ste 157K ...... Charleston WV 25305	304-558-6000	558-0900	339-49
TF: 866-767-8683 ■ *Web:* www.sos.wv.gov			
Securities Div			
1900 Kanawha Blvd E Bldg 1 Rm W-100..... Charleston WV 25305	304-558-2251	558-5200	339-49
TF: 877-982-9148 ■ *Web:* www.wvsao.gov			
State Government Information			
100 Dee Dr............................ Charleston WV 25311	304-558-7000	558-7001	339-49
TF: 888-558-7002 ■ *Web:* www.wv.gov			
State Legislature			
State Capitol Complex Rm MB-27 Bldg 1 .... Charleston WV 25305	304-347-4836		339-49
Web: www.wvlegislature.gov			
State Parks & Forests			
405 Maxwell St .... Charleston WV 25303	304-558-2764	558-0077	339-49
Web: wvstateparks.com			
State Police			
725 Jefferson Rd .... South Charleston WV 25309	304-746-2100		339-49
Web: www.wvsp.gov			
Supreme Court of Appeals			
1900 Kanawha Blvd E Bldg 1 Rm E-317 ..... Charleston WV 25305	304-558-2601	558-3815	339-49
Web: www.courtswv.gov			
Tourism Div			
90 MacCorkle Ave SW............. South Charleston WV 25303	304-558-2200		339-49
TF: 800-225-5982 ■ *Web:* wvtourism.com			
Transportation Dept			
1900 Kanawha Blvd E Bldg 5 Rm A-109/110. . Charleston WV 25305	304-558-0444	558-1004	339-49
Web: www.wv.gov			
Treasurer			
1900 Kanawha Blvd E Bldg 1 Ste E-145 ..... Charleston WV 25305	304-558-5000		339-49
TF: 800-422-7498 ■ *Web:* www.wvsto.com			
West Virginia Association of Counties (WVACO)			
2026 Kanawha Blvd .... Charleston WV 25311	304-346-0591		49-7
Web: www.wvaco.org			
West Virginia Association of Realtors			
2110 Kanawha Blvd E...................... Charleston WV 25311	304-342-7600	343-5811	656
TF: 800-445-7600 ■ *Web:* www.wvrealtors.com			
West Virginia Botanic Garden			
714 Venture Dr .... Morgantown WV 26508	304-376-2717		97
Web: www.wvbg.org			
West Virginia Central Federal Credit Union			
1306 Murdoch Ave....................... Parkersburg WV 26101	304-485-4523	424-0718	219
TF: 800-642-1902 ■ *Web:* wvccu.org			
West Virginia Chamber of Commerce			
1624 Kanawha Blvd E...................... Charleston WV 25311	304-342-1115	342-1130	140
Web: www.wvchamber.com			
West Virginia Commercial LLC			
803 Quarrier St Ste 600 .... Charleston WV 25301	304-347-7500	342-2252	194
Web: wv-commercial.com			
West Virginia Correctional Industries			
617 Leon Sullivan Way..................... Charleston WV 25301	304-558-6054	558-6056	630
TF: 800-525-5381 ■ *Web:* wvcorrectionalindustries.com			
West Virginia Democratic Party			
717 Lee St Ste 214 PO Box 11926 .... Charleston WV 25301	304-342-8121		616-1
Web: wvdemocrats.com			
West Virginia Department of Health & Human Resources			
William R Sharpe Jr Hospital			
936 Sharpe Hospital Rd.................... Weston WV 26452	304-269-1210	269-6235	374-5
Web: dhhr.wv.gov			
West Virginia Division of Corrections and Rehabilitation			
1409 Greenbrier St Charleston .... Moundsville WV 26041	304-843-4067	843-4073	213
TF: 866-984-8463 ■ *Web:* dcr.wv.gov			
West Virginia Geological & Economic Survey (WVGES)			
Mont Chateau Research Ctr			
1 Mont Chateau Rd...................... Morgantown WV 26508	304-594-2331	594-2575	637-2
TF: 800-984-3656 ■ *Web:* www.wvgs.wvnet.edu			
West Virginia Glass Company Inc			
235 Rural Acres Dr .... Beckley WV 25801	304-252-6343	255-1790	234
Web: www.wvglassco.com			
West Virginia Junior College			
Charleston 1000 Virginia St E............... Charleston WV 25301	304-345-2820		800
TF: 800-924-5208 ■ *Web:* www.wvjc.edu			
West Virginia Metronews Radio Network			
1111 Virginia St E......................... Charleston WV 25301	304-346-7055		647
Web: www.wvmetronews.com			
West Virginia Mutual Insurance Co			
500 Virginia St E Ste 1200 .... Charleston WV 25301	304-343-3000		390
Web: wvmic.com			
West Virginia Northern Community College			
1704 Market St............................ Wheeling WV 26003	304-233-5900	232-8187	162
Web: www.wvncc.edu			
West Virginia Nurses Assn (WVNA)			
PO Box 1946 .... Charleston WV 25327	304-417-1497		533
TF: 800-400-1226 ■ *Web:* wvnurses.nursingnetwork.com			
West Virginia Office of Miners' Health Safety and Training			
7 Players Club Dr Ste 2 .... Charleston WV 25311	304-558-1425	558-1282	637-2
Web: www.wvminesafety.org			
West Virginia Pharmacists Assn			
2016 1/2 Kanawha Blvd E.................. Charleston WV 25311	304-344-5302	344-5316	585
Web: wvpharmacy.org			
West Virginia Press Assn			
3422 Pennsylvania Ave..................... Charleston WV 25302	304-342-1011	343-5879	624
TF: 800-235-6881 ■ *Web:* wvpress.org			
West Virginia Public Employees Credit Union			
2200 Washington St E .... Charleston WV 25311	304-558-0566	558-0137	219
TF: 866-470-7405 ■ *Web:* wvpecu.org			
West Virginia Public Theatre			
PO Box 6082 .... Morgantown WV 26505	304-381-2382		573-4
Web: www.wvpublictheatre.org			
West Virginia Radio Corp			
1251 Earl L Core Rd .... Morgantown WV 26505	304-296-0029		643
Web: wvaq.com			
West Virginia Real Estate Commission			
300 Capitol St Ste 400 .... Charleston WV 25301	304-558-3555	558-6442	339-49
Web: rec.wv.gov			
West Virginia Republican State Committee			
PO Box 2711 .... Charleston WV 25330	304-768-0493	768-6083	616-2
Web: www.wvgop.org			
West Virginia School Journal			
1558 Quarrier St.......................... Charleston WV 25311	304-346-5315	346-4325	457-8
TF: 800-642-8261 ■ *Web:* www.wvea.org			
West Virginia State Bar, The			
2000 Deitrick Blvd .... Charleston WV 25311	304-553-7220		72
TF: 866-989-8227 ■ *Web:* www.wvbar.org			
West Virginia State Medical Assn			
4307 MacCorkle Ave SE.................... Charleston WV 25364	304-925-0342	925-0345	457-16
TF: 800-257-4747 ■ *Web:* wvsma.org			
West Virginia State University			
117 Ferrell Hall PO Box 368................... Institute WV 25112	304-766-3000		166
TF: 800-987-2112 ■ *Web:* www.wvstateu.edu			
West Virginia State Wildlife Ctr			
PO Box 38 .... French Creek WV 26218	304-924-6211		823
Web: www.wvdnr.gov			
West Virginia University			
PO Box 6009 .... Morgantown WV 26506	304-293-2121	293-3080	166
TF: 800-344-9881 ■ *Web:* www.wvu.edu			
West Virginia University			
Institute of Technology			
405 Fayette Pk....................... Montgomery WV 25136	304-442-3176		166
TF: 888-554-8324 ■ *Web:* www.wvutech.edu			
Libraries			
1549 University Ave PO Box 6069........ Morgantown WV 26506	304-293-4040	293-6638	434-6
Web: lib.wvu.edu			
Parkersburg 300 Campus Dr............... Parkersburg WV 26104	304-424-8000	424-8315	162
TF: 800-982-9887 ■ *Web:* www.wvup.edu			
West Virginia University College of Law			
PO Box 6130 .... Morgantown WV 26506	304-293-5301	293-6891	167-1
Web: www.law.wvu.edu			
West Virginia University Hospitals			
1 Medical Center Dr .... Morgantown WV 26506	304-598-4200		374-3
Web: wvumedicine.org			
West Virginia University School of Medicine			
1 Medical Center Dr PO Box 9100 .... Morgantown WV 26506	304-293-1258	293-7814	167-2
TF: 800-543-5650 ■ *Web:* medicine.hsc.wvu.edu			
West Virginia Vital Statistics			
350 Capitol St Rm 165..................... Charleston WV 25301	304-558-2931	558-1051	339-49
Web: www.wvdhhr.org			
West Virginia Wesleyan College			
59 College Ave.......................... Buckhannon WV 26201	304-473-8000	473-8108	166
TF: 800-722-9933 ■ *Web:* www.wvwc.edu			
West Virginia, The			
Division of Corrections and Rehabilitation			
1409 Greenbrier St...................... Charleston WV 25311	304-558-2036	558-5934	339-49
Web: dcr.wv.gov			
West Warwick Public Library System			
1043 Main St .... West Warwick RI 02893	401-828-3750	828-8493	434-3
Web: wwpl.org			
West Whitlock Recreation Area			
16157A W Whitlock Rd..................... Gettysburg SD 57442	605-765-9410		565
Web: gfp.sd.gov			
West Wind Inn 3345 W Gulf Dr .... Sanibel FL 33957	239-472-1541		669
TF: 800-824-0476 ■ *Web:* westwindinn.com			
West Wind Litho Inc			
2513 S 3270 W....................... West Valley City UT 84119	801-975-7105	975-7126	626
Web: www.westwindlitho.com			
West Window Corp			
226 Industrial Pk Dr .... Martinsville VA 24112	276-638-2394	638-2300	234
TF: 800-446-4167 ■ *Web:* www.westwindow.com			
West World Production Inc			
420 N Camden Dr....................... Beverly Hills CA 90210	310-276-9500		637-9
Web: wwpi.com			
West, Welch, Reed Engineers Inc			
5417 Ball Camp Pk......................... Knoxville TN 37921	865-588-2431		261
Web: wwrengrs.com			
WESTA (Western Association of Travel)			
5933 NE Win Sivers Dr Ste 202 .... Portland OR 97220	503-251-8170		772
Westaff (USA) Inc 298 N Wiget Ln .... Walnut Creek CA 94598	925-945-0875		260
Web: www.westaff.com			
Westak Inc 1116 Elko Dri .... Sunnyvale CA 94089	408-734-8686	734-5190	625
TF: 800-893-7825 ■ *Web:* www.westak.com			
Westamerica Bancorp 1108 Fifth Ave......... San Rafael CA 94901	415-257-8000		70
NASDAQ: WABC ■ *TF:* 800-848-1088 ■ *Web:* www.westamerica.com			
Westar Satellite Services			
777 Westar Ln........................... Cedar Hill TX 75104	972-291-6000		116
Web: www.allmobilevideo.com			
Westat Inc 1600 Research Blvd................ Rockville MD 20850	301-251-1500	517-4053	466
Web: www.westat.com			
Westbay Auto Parts Inc			
2610 SE Mile Hill Dr..................... Port Orchard WA 98366	360-876-8008	876-7999	54
Web: www.westbayautoparts.com			
Westbay Floor Source			
30733 Detroit Rd .... Westlake OH 44145	440-835-2980	835-3832	362
Web: westbayfloorsource.com			
Westbend Winery & Brewery			
5394 Williams Rd.......................... Lewisville NC 27023	336-945-9999		50-7
Web: www.westbendwineryandbrewery.com			
Westborn Inc 21755 Michigan Ave .... Dearborn MI 48124	313-274-6100		345
Web: www.westbornmarket.com			
Westbridge Inc 1361 Elm St Ste 207 .... Manchester NH 03101	603-634-4446		726
TF: 877-461-7711 ■ *Web:* www.westbridge.org			
Westbrook Engineering 23501 Mound Rd .... Warren MI 48091	586-759-3100		358
TF: 800-899-8182 ■ *Web:* www.westbrook-eng.com			
Westbrook Service Corp			
1411 S Orange Blossom Trl .... Orlando FL 32805	407-841-3310	425-9934	610
Web: www.westbrookfl.com			
Westbury Animal Hospital Inc			
4917 S Willow Dr........................... Houston TX 77035	713-723-3666		794
Web: westburyvets.com			

Name	Address	City	State	Zip	Phone	Fax	Class	Other
Westbury National Show Systems Ltd	772 Warden Ave	Toronto	ON	M1L4T7	416-752-1371		184	*TF:* 855-752-1372 ■ *Web:* www.westbury.com
Westby Co-opeartive Credit Union	501 N Main St	Westby	WI	54667	608-634-3118		219	*Web:* www.wccucreditunion.coop
Westby Cooperative Creamery	401 S Main St	Westby	WI	54667	608-634-3181	634-3194	296-5	*TF:* 800-492-9282 ■ *Web:* www.westbycreamery.com
West-Camp Press Inc	39 Collegeview Rd	Westerville	OH	43081	614-882-2378		627	*Web:* www.westcamppress.com
Westcap Management Ltd	830 410 22nd St E	Saskatoon	SK	S7K5T6	306-652-5557		528	*Web:* westcapmgt.ca
Westcare Management Inc	3155 River Rd S Ste 100	Salem	OR	97302	800-541-3732		194	*TF:* 800-541-3732 ■ *Web:* westcaremgt.com
Westchase Law Group pa	12029 Whitmarsh Ln	Tampa	FL	33626	813-490-5211		428	*Web:* www.westchaselaw.com
Westchester County	110 Dr Martin Luther King Jr Blvd	White Plains	NY	10601	914-995-3080	995-4030	338	*Web:* www.westchesterclerk.com
Westchester County Airport	240 Airport Rd Ste 202	White Plains	NY	10604	914-995-4860	995-3980	27	*Web:* www.co.westchester.ny.us
Westchester County Historical Society (WCHS)	2199 Saw Mill River Rd	Elmsford	NY	10523	914-592-4323	231-1510	49-19	*Web:* www.westchesterhistory.com
Westchester County Tourism & Film	148 Martine Ave Ste 104	White Plains	NY	10601	914-995-8500	995-8505	206	*TF:* 800-833-9282 ■ *Web:* www.visitwestchesterny.com
Westchester Lace & Textiles Inc	3901 Liberty Ave	North Bergen	NJ	07047	201-864-2150		745-4	*Web:* www.westchesterlace.com
Westchester Medical Ctr	100 Woods Rd	Valhalla	NY	10595	914-493-7000		374-3	*Web:* www.westchestermedicalcenter.org
Westchester Modular Homes Inc	30 Reagans Mill Rd	Wingdale	NY	12594	845-832-9400		106	*TF:* 800-832-3888 ■ *Web:* www.westchestermodular.com
Westchester Park District	10201 Bond St	Westchester	IL	60154	708-865-8200		31	*Web:* www.wpdparks.org
Westchester Philharmonic	123 Main St 9th Fl	White Plains	NY	10601	914-682-3707	682-3716	573-3	*Web:* www.westchesterphil.org
Westchester School of Beauty Culture Inc	6 Gramatan Ave	Mount Vernon	NY	10550	914-699-2344		685	*Web:* www.westchesterbeautyschool.com
Westchester Toyota	2167 Central Park Ave	Yonkers	NY	10710	888-224-4595		57	*TF:* 888-224-4595 ■ *Web:* www.westchestertoyota.com
Westchester Transportation	100 E First St	Mount Vernon	NY	10550	914-813-7777		468	*Web:* transportation.westchestergov.com
Westchester Wine Warehouse	53 Tarrytown Rd	White Plains	NY	10607	914-824-1400		443	*Web:* www.westchesterwine.com
Westco Home Furnishings	208 N Main St	Miami	OK	74354	918-542-6693	542-2072	321	*Web:* www.westcohomefurnishings.com
Westco Property Management Co	365 Sawdust Rd	Spring	TX	77380	281-367-9092	367-7678	41	*TF:* 888-893-7900 ■ *Web:* westcopm.com
West-Com Nurse Call Systems Inc	2200 Cordelia Rd	Fairfield	CA	94534	707-428-5900		174	*TF:* 800-761-1180 ■ *Web:* www.westcomncs.com
West-Con Co-op	520 Co Rd 9	Holloway	MN	56249	320-394-2171		276	*TF:* 800-368-3310 ■ *Web:* www.west-con.com
Westcon Group Inc	520 White Plains Rd	Tarrytown	NY	10591	914-829-7000		174	*TF:* 800-527-9516 ■ *Web:* www.westconcomstor.com
Westconsin Credit Union	3333 Schneider Ave SE	Menomonie	WI	54751	715-235-3403		219	*TF:* 800-924-0022 ■ *Web:* www.westconsincu.org
Westcor Land Title Insurance Co	201 N New York Ave Ste 200	Winter Park	FL	32789	407-629-5842		390	*Web:* wltic.com
WestCorp Management Group LLC	6655 S Eastern Ave	Las Vegas	NV	89119	702-307-2881		652	*Web:* www.westcorpmg.com
Westcorp Properties Inc	200 College Plz 8215 - 112 St	Edmonton	AB	T6G2C8	780-431-3300		652	*Web:* www.westcorp.net
Westcott Beach State Park	6621 NY Hwy 3	Henderson	NY	13650	315-646-2239		565	*Web:* www.parks.ny.gov
Westcott Community Center Inc	826 Euclid Ave	Syracuse	NY	13210	315-478-8634		363	*Web:* westcottcc.org
Westcott Displays Inc	450 Amsterdam St	Detroit	MI	48202	313-872-1200	875-3295	560	*Web:* www.westcottdisplays.com
Westec Plastics Corp	6757 A Las Positas Rd	Livermore	CA	94551	925-454-3400		608	*Web:* www.westecplastics.com
Westech Engineering Inc	3665 SW Temple	Salt Lake City	UT	84115	801-265-1000	265-1080	806	*Web:* www.westech-inc.com
Westech International Inc	2500 Louisiana Blvd NE Ste 325	Albuquerque	NM	87110	505-888-6666	837-9424	261	*Web:* www.westech-intl.com
Westech Solutions	50 Broadway Ste 206	Hawthorne	NY	10532	914-595-6335		463	*Web:* westechsolutions.com
WestEd	730 Harrison St	San Francisco	CA	94107	415-565-3000	565-3012	668	*TF:* 877-493-7833 ■ *Web:* www.wested.org
Westell Technologies Inc	750 N Commons Dr	Aurora	IL	60504	630-898-2500	375-4931	735	*NASDAQ:* WSTL ■ *TF:* 800-323-6883 ■ *Web:* www.westell.com
Westend Software Inc	400 Continental Blvd Ste 600	El Segundo	CA	90245	424-247-0251		178-1	*Web:* westendsoftware.com
Westerbeke Corp	Miles Standish Industrial Pk 150 John Hancock Rd	Taunton	MA	02780	508-823-7677	884-9688	262	*TF:* 800-582-7846 ■ *Web:* www.westerbeke.com
Westerlay Orchids	3504 Via Real	Carpinteria	CA	93013	805-684-5411	684-5414	369	*Web:* www.westerlayorchids.com
Westerly Hospital	25 Wells St	Westerly	RI	02891	401-596-6000		374-3	*TF:* 800-933-5960 ■ *Web:* www.westerlyhospital.org
Westerly Public Library	44 Broad St	Westerly	RI	02891	401-596-2877		434-3	*Web:* westerlylibrary.org
Westerman Bruce (Rep R - AR)	209 Cannon House Office Bldg	Washington	DC	20515	202-225-3772	225-1314	342-2	*Web:* westerman.house.gov
Westermeyer Industries Inc	1441 SR-100	Bluffs	IL	62621	217-754-3277		261	*Web:* www.westermeyerind.com
Western & Southern Financial Group	400 Broadway	Cincinnati	OH	45202	877-367-9734		360-4	*TF:* 877-367-9734 ■ *Web:* www.westernsouthern.com
Western Ag Enterprises Inc	8121 W Harrison	Tolleson	AZ	85353	623-907-4034	907-4100	779	*TF:* 800-347-8274 ■ *Web:* www.westernag.com
Western Agcredit	PO Box 95850	South Jordan	UT	84095	801-571-9200	576-0600	216	*TF:* 800-824-9198 ■ *Web:* www.westernagcredit.com
Western Aircraft Inc	4300 S Kennedy St	Boise	ID	83705	208-338-1800	338-1887	63	*TF:* 800-333-3442 ■ *Web:* www.westair.com
Western American	1518 Taney St	Kansas City	MO	64116	816-421-3000	421-3122	3	*Web:* www.westix.net
Western Asset Protection Inc	4550 E Bell Rd Ste 136	Phoenix	AZ	85032	602-955-5353		390	*Web:* westernassetprotection.com
Western Association of Travel (WESTA)	5933 NE Win Sivers Dr Ste 202	Portland	OR	97220	503-251-8170		772	
Western Automation Inc (WAI)	23101 Moulton Pkwy Ste 201	Laguna Hills	CA	92653	949-859-6988	859-8622	57	*Web:* www.waisales.com
Western Bagel Baking Corp	7814 Sepulveda Blvd	Van Nuys	CA	91405	818-786-5847	787-3221	345	*TF:* 800-555-0882 ■ *Web:* www.westernbagel.com
Western Bay Sheet Metal Inc	1410 Hill St	El Cajon	CA	92020	619-233-1753	233-1732	697	*Web:* www.westernbay.net
Western Bee Supplies Inc	5 Ninth Ave E	Polson	MT	59860	406-883-2918		279	*TF:* 800-548-8440 ■ *Web:* westernbee.com
Western Beef Inc	220-230 S Fulton Ave	Mount Vernon	NY	10550	718-417-3770		345	*Web:* www.westernbeef.com
Western Boxed Meats Distributors Inc	2401 NE Argyle St	Portland	OR	97211	503-284-3314		473	*Web:* harvestfooddistributors.com
Western Branch Diesel Inc	3504 Shipwright St	Portsmouth	VA	23703	757-673-7000	673-7190	770	*Web:* www.westernbranchdiesel.com
Western Branch Metals	1006 Obici Industrial Blvd	Suffolk	VA	23434	757-215-1500		480	*Web:* www.wbmetals.com
Western Builders of Amarillo Inc	700 S Grant St	Amarillo	TX	79101	806-376-4321		186	*Web:* www.wbamarillo.com
Western Bus Sales Inc	30355 SE Hwy 212	Boring	OR	97009	503-905-0002	905-0003	57	*TF:* 800-258-2473 ■ *Web:* www.westernbus.com
Western Camp Services Ltd	7003 Girard Rd	Edmonton	AB	T6B2C4	780-468-1568	468-1948	378	*Web:* www.westerncampservices.com
Western Canada Lottery Corp	125 Garry St 10th Fl	Winnipeg	MB	R3C4J1	800-665-3313		452	*TF:* 800-665-3313 ■ *Web:* www.wclc.com
Western Canada Wilderness Committee (WCWC)	46 E Sixth Ave	Vancouver	BC	V5T1J4	604-683-8220	683-8229	48-13	*TF:* 800-661-9453 ■ *Web:* wildernesscommittee.org
Western Cardinal Inc	205 Durley Ave	Camarillo	CA	93010	805-482-2586	484-2713	63	*TF:* 800-882-3018 ■ *Web:* www.westerncardinal.com
Western Carolina University (WCU)	1 University Dr	Cullowhee	NC	28723	828-227-7211	227-7319	166	*TF:* 877-928-4968 ■ *Web:* www.wcu.edu
Western Case Inc	6400-B Sycamore Canyon Blvd	Riverside	CA	92507	951-214-6380	214-6387	604	*TF:* 877-593-2182 ■ *Web:* www.westerncase.com
Western Commerce Bank	1910 Wyoming Blvd NE	Albuquerque	NM	87112	505-271-9964	271-9879	70	*TF:* 877-519-1590 ■ *Web:* www.wcb.net
Western Commercial Services LLC	2311 S Industrial	Las Vegas	NV	89102	702-384-7907		256	*Web:* www.westerncommercial.net
Western Connecticut State University	181 White St	Danbury	CT	06810	203-837-8200	837-8234	166	*Web:* wcsu.edu
Western Construction Inc	10139 S Federal Way	Boise	ID	83715	208-345-1440	345-1548	188-4	*Web:* www.wciboise.com
Western Container Corp	1600 First Ave	Big Spring	TX	79720	432-263-8361	263-8075	98	*Web:* westerncontainercoke.com
Western Contract	11455 Folsom Blvd	Rancho Cordova	CA	95742	916-638-3338	638-2698	321	*Web:* www.westerncontract.com
Western Cooperative Co	PO Box H	Alliance	NE	69301	308-762-3112		276	*Web:* www.westco.coop
Western Cooperative Electric Association Inc	635 S 13th St	WaKeeney	KS	67672	785-743-5561	743-2717	245	*TF:* 800-456-6720 ■ *Web:* www.westerncoop.com
Western Copper Corp	1040 W Georgia St 1st Fl	Vancouver	BC	V6E4H1	604-684-9497		502	*TF:* 888-966-9995 ■ *Web:* westerncopperandgold.com

Name / Address	City	State	Zip	Phone	Fax	Class
Western Creative Inc 26135 Plymouth Rd *Web:* westerncreative.com	Redford	MI	48239	313-937-1000		514
Western Cullen Hayes Inc 2700 W 36th Pl *Web:* wch.com	Chicago	IL	60632	773-254-9600	254-1110	700
Western Dakota Technical Institute 800 Mickelson Dr *TF:* 800-544-8765 ■ *Web:* www.wdt.edu	Rapid City	SD	57703	605-394-4034		167-3
Western Design Center Inc, The 2166 E Brown Rd *Web:* www.westerndesigncenter.com	Mesa	AZ	85213	480-962-4545	835-6442	310
Western Development Corp 1413 P St NW Ste 403 *Web:* www.westdev.com	Washington	DC	20005	202-338-5200	333-0223	652
Western Development Museum 2610 Lorne Ave S *Web:* www.wdm.ca	Saskatoon	SK	S7J0S6	306-931-1910	934-0525	520
Western Diesel Services Inc 1100 Research Blvd *TF:* 855-257-6937 ■ *Web:* www.ckpower.com	Saint Louis	MO	63132	314-868-8620	868-9314	385
Western Digital Corp 3355 Michelson Dr Ste 100 *NASDAQ: WDC* ■ *TF:* 800-832-4778 ■ *Web:* www.westerndigital.com	Irvine	CA	92612	949-672-7000		173-8
Western Division Federal Credit Union 6750 Main St *Web:* westerndivision.org	Williamsville	NY	14221	716-632-9328	632-1383	219
Western Drug 3604 San Fernando Rd *TF:* 800-891-3661 ■ *Web:* www.westerndrug.com	Glendale	CA	91204	818-956-6691		475
Western Dubuque Biodiesel LLC 904 Jamesmeier Rd PO Box 82 *Web:* www.wdbiodiesel.net	Farley	IA	52046	563-744-3554		580
Western Economic Association Intl (WEAI) 18837 Brookhurst St Ste 304 *Web:* www.weai.org	Fountain Valley	CA	92708	714-965-8800	965-8829	49-2
Western Electrical Sales Inc (WES) 521 Glide Ave *Web:* www.wesisales.com	West Sacramento	CA	95691	916-372-1001		246
Western Engineering Contractors Inc 3171 Rippey Rd *Web:* www.westeng.com	Loomis	CA	95650	916-652-3990	652-3995	261
Western Engravers Supply Inc 17621 N Black Canyon Hwy **Fax Area Code:* 602 ■ *Web:* www.visionengravers.com	Phoenix	AZ	85023	888-637-1737	391-2288*	76
Western Enterprises Inc 875 Bassett Rd **Fax Area Code:* 440 ■ *TF:* 800-783-7890 ■ *Web:* www.westernenterprises.com	Westlake	OH	44145	800-783-7890	835-8283*	811
Western Environmental Services and Testing Inc 913 Foster Rd *TF:* 800-545-5711 ■ *Web:* www.testair.com	Casper	WY	82601	307-234-5511	234-8324	192
Western Equipment Distributors Inc 20224 80th Ave S *Web:* www.western-equip.com	Kent	WA	98032	253-872-8858		274
Western Excelsior Corp 901 Grand Ave *TF:* 800-833-8573 ■ *Web:* www.westernexcelsior.com	Mancos	CO	81328	800-833-8573		820
Western Export Services Inc (WES) 140 E 19th Ave Ste 500 *Web:* www.wesdenver.com	Denver	CO	80203	303-302-5899	302-5882	297-2
Western Express Inc 7135 Centennial Pl *TF:* 800-316-7160 ■ *Web:* www.westernexp.com	Nashville	TN	37209	877-986-8855		780
Western Exterminator Co 305 N Crescent Way *TF:* 800-698-2440 ■ *Web:* www.westernexterminator.com	Anaheim	CA	92801	714-239-2800		577
Western Facilities Supply Inc 2914 McDougal Ave *TF:* 800-448-9314 ■ *Web:* www.westfacsup.com	Everett	WA	98201	425-252-2105	259-5130	76
Western Farmers Electric Co-op 701 NE Seventh St *Web:* www.wfec.com	Anadarko	OK	73005	405-247-3351		245
Western Fibre Products 10924 Vulcan St	South Gate	CA	90280	562-861-6665		602
Western Forest Products Inc (WFP) 800 - 1055 W Georgia St Royal Centre Bldg PO Box 11122 *TSE: WEF* ■ *Web:* www.westernforest.com	Vancouver	BC	V6E3P3	604-648-4500	681-9584	448
Western Forestry & Conservation Assn 4033 SW Canyon Rd *TF:* 888-722-9416 ■ *Web:* westernforestry.org	Portland	OR	97221	503-226-4562	226-2515	48-12
Western Forge & Flange Co 687 County Rd 2201 *TF:* 800-352-6433 ■ *Web:* www.western-forge.com	Cleveland	TX	77327	281-727-7060		483
Western Forms Inc 6200 Equitable Rd *Web:* www.westernforms.com	Kansas City	MO	64120	816-241-0477		488
Western Fraternal Life Assn (WFLA) 1900 First Ave NE *TF:* 877-935-2467 ■ *Web:* www.wflains.org	Cedar Rapids	IA	52402	319-363-2653		391-2
Western Funding Inc PO Box 94858 *TF:* 888-434-3150 ■ *Web:* www.westernfundinginc.com	Las Vegas	NV	89193	888-434-3150		217
Western Gateway Heritage State Park 115 State St Bldg 4 *Web:* www.mass.gov	North Adams	MA	01247	413-663-6312		565
Western Glove Works Ltd 555 Logan Ave *Web:* westerngloveworks.ca	Winnipeg	MB	R3A0S4	204-788-4249		157-6
Western Golf Properties 1 Spectrum Pointe Dr *Web:* wgolfp.com	Lake Forest	CA	92630	949-417-3251		653
Western Group 4025 NW Express Ave *Web:* www.thewesterngroup.com	Portland	OR	97210	503-222-1644		688
Western Group Inc 511 W 10th *Web:* wgiinsurance.com	Pueblo	CO	81003	719-543-3604		390
Western Helicopters Inc Riverside Municipal Airport 6741 Gemende Dr *Web:* www.westernhelicopters.com	Riverside	CA	92504	951-977-8646	977-8650	167-3
Western Hoist Inc 1839 Cleveland Ave *TF:* 888-994-6478 ■ *Web:* www.westernlift.org	National City	CA	91950	619-474-3361	474-8261	470
Western Home Communities 420 E 11th St *Web:* www.westernhomecommunities.org	Cedar Falls	IA	50613	319-277-2141		672
Western Horseman Magazine 2112 Montgomery St *TF:* 800-877-5278 ■ *Web:* westernhorseman.com	Fort Worth	TX	76107	817-737-6397	737-9266	457-14
Western Hydro Corp 3449 Enterprise Ave *TF:* 800-972-5945 ■ *Web:* www.westernhydro.com	Hayward	CA	94545	510-783-9166	732-0250	386
Western Illinois Credit Union 322 W University Dr *Web:* wicu.org	Macomb	IL	61455	309-298-2986		219
Western Illinois Electrical Co-op 524 N Madison St PO Box 338 *TF:* 800-576-3125 ■ *Web:* www.wiec.net	Carthage	IL	62321	217-357-3125	357-3127	245
Western Illinois University *Malpass Library* 1 University Cir *TF:* 800-413-6544 ■ *Web:* www.wiu.edu	Macomb	IL	61455	309-298-2762	298-2791	434-6
Western Implement Company Inc 2919 North Ave *TF:* 800-338-6639 ■ *Web:* www.westernimplement.com	Grand Junction	CO	81504	970-242-7960	242-5241	274
Western Industries Plastic Products LLC 7727 First Ave Strother Field Industrial Pk *Web:* www.westernind.com	Winfield	KS	67156	620-221-9464		697
Western Institutional Review Board Inc 1019 39th Ave SE Ste 120 *TF:* 800-562-4789 ■ *Web:* www.wirb.com	Puyallup	WA	98374	360-252-2500		533
Western Insurance Agency Inc 2450 S Shore Blvd **Fax Area Code:* 281 ■ *TF:* 800-833-8071 ■ *Web:* westernagency.com	League City	TX	77573	800-833-8071	334-4921*	391-5
Western International Securities Inc 70 S Lake Ave Ste 700 *TF:* 888-793-7717 ■ *Web:* www.wisdirect.com	Pasadena	CA	91101	888-793-7717		690
Western International University 9215 N Black Canyon Hwy *TF:* 866-948-4636 ■ *Web:* west.edu	Phoenix	AZ	85021	602-943-2311		166
Western Interstate Commission for Higher Education (WICHE) 3035 Center Green Dr Ste 200 *Web:* www.wiche.edu	Boulder	CO	80301	303-541-0200	541-0291	637-2
Western Iowa Power Co-op 809 Iowa 39 *TF:* 800-253-5189 ■ *Web:* www.wipco.com	Denison	IA	51442	712-263-2943		245
Western Iowa Tech Community College 4647 Stone Ave *TF:* 800-352-4649 ■ *Web:* www.witcc.edu	Sioux City	IA	51102	712-274-6400	274-6412	800
Western Kentucky Correctional Complex 374 New Bethel Church Rd *Web:* www.corrections.ky.gov	Fredonia	KY	42411	270-388-9781	388-0031	213
Western Kentucky University 1906 College Heights Blvd *TF:* 800-495-8463 ■ *Web:* www.wku.edu	Bowling Green	KY	42101	270-745-0111	745-6133	166
Western Land Services Inc 1100 Conrad Industrial Dr *TF:* 800-968-4840 ■ *Web:* www.westernls.com	Ludington	MI	49431	800-968-4840		536
Western Lumber Cy LLC 2240 Tower E Ste 200 *Web:* www.westernlumber.com	Medford	OR	97504	541-779-5121	779-0155	191-3
Western Machine Works Inc 652 E 11th St *Web:* www.westernmachineworks.com	Tacoma	WA	98421	253-627-6538	383-7585	494
Western Manitoba Regional Library 710 Rosser Ave Unit 1 *Web:* www.wmrl.ca	Brandon	MB	R7A0K9	204-727-6648		436
Western Marketing Inc 1010 S Access Rd *Web:* reladyne.com	Tye	TX	79563	325-692-4662		579
Western Mass News 1300 Liberty St *Web:* www.westernmassnews.com	Springfield	MA	01104	413-733-4040	781-5733	741-129
Western Medical Center Anaheim (WMCA) 1025 S Anaheim Blvd *Web:* www.westernmedanaheim.com	Anaheim	CA	92805	714-533-6220		374-3
Western Medical Center Santa Ana 1001 N Tustin Ave *Web:* www.westernmedicalcenter.com	Santa Ana	CA	92705	714-953-3500		374-3
Western Memorial Regional Hospital 1 Brookfield Ave PO Box 2005 *Web:* www.westernhealth.nl.ca	Corner Brook	NL	A2H6J7	709-637-5000		374-2
Western Mental Health Institute 11100 Hwy 64 W *Web:* www.tn.gov	Bolivar	TN	38008	731-228-2000		374-5
Western Michigan University 1903 W Michigan Ave *Web:* www.wmich.edu	Kalamazoo	MI	49008	269-387-2000	387-2096	166
Western Millwork Inc 2940 W Willetta St *Web:* www.westernmillworkaz.com	Phoenix	AZ	85009	602-233-1921	278-7101	499
Western Missouri Correctional Ctr 609 E Pence Rd *Web:* www.mo.gov	Cameron	MO	64429	816-632-1390		213
Western Montana Fair 2304 McDonald Ave *Web:* missoulafairgrounds.com	Missoula	MT	59801	406-721-3247		642
Western Museum of Mining & Industry 225 N Gate Blvd *TF:* 800-752-6558 ■ *Web:* www.wmmi.org	Colorado Springs	CO	80921	719-488-0880	488-9261	520
Western National Mutual Insurance Co 5350 W 78th St *TF:* 800-862-6070 ■ *Web:* www.wnins.com	Edina	MN	55439	952-835-5350	921-3159	391-4
Western National Parks Assn (WNPA) 12880 N Vistoso Village Dr *Web:* www.wnpa.org	Tucson	AZ	85755	520-622-1999		48-23
Western Natural Gas Co 2960 Strickland St *Web:* www.westernnaturalgas.com	Jacksonville	FL	32254	904-387-3511	387-6034	316
Western Nebraska Community College 1601 E 27th St *TF:* 800-348-4435 ■ *Web:* www.wncc.net	Scottsbluff	NE	69361	308-635-3606	635-6732	162

	Phone	Fax	Class
Western Nevada Community College *Fallon* 160 Campus Way . . . Fallon NV 89406 *Web:* www.wnc.edu	775-423-7565	423-8029	162
Western Nevada Supply Co 950 S Rock Blvd . . . Sparks NV 89431 *TF:* 800-648-1230 ■ *Web:* www.wns1.com	775-359-5800	359-4649	612
Western New England College 1215 Wilbraham Rd . . . Springfield MA 01119 *TF:* 800-782-6665 ■ *Web:* wne.edu	413-782-3111	782-1777	166
Western New Mexico University 1000 W College St PO Box 680 . . . Silver City NM 88061 **Fax Area Code:* 575 ■ *TF:* 800-872-9668 ■ *Web:* wnmu.edu	800-872-9668	538-6278*	166
Western North Carolina Nature Ctr 75 Gashes Creek Rd . . . Asheville NC 28805 *Web:* wildwnc.org	828-259-8080		50-5
Western Office Equipment Inc (WOE) 514 N 32nd St . . . Billings MT 59101 *Web:* www.westernoffice.net	406-245-3029	245-3020	112
Western Oilfields Supply Co 3404 State Rd . . . Bakersfield CA 93308 *TF:* 800-742-7246 ■ *Web:* www.rainforrent.com	661-399-9124	392-9427	264-3
Western Oklahoma State College 2801 N Main St . . . Altus OK 73521 *TF:* 800-662-1113 ■ *Web:* www.wosc.edu	580-477-2000	477-7723	162
Western Ophthalmics Corp 19019 36th Ave W Ste G . . . Lynnwood WA 98036 *TF:* 800-426-9938 ■ *Web:* www.west-op.com	425-672-9332		544
Western Oregon University 345 Monmouth Ave N . . . Monmouth OR 97361 *TF:* 877-877-1593 ■ *Web:* www.wou.edu	503-838-8000	838-8067	166
Western Outdoors Magazine 185 Avenida La Pata . . . San Clemente CA 92673 *TF:* 800-290-2929 ■ *Web:* www.wonews.com	949-366-0030	366-0804	457-22
Western Pacific Distributors Inc 1739 Sabre St . . . Hayward CA 94545 *Web:* www.teamwpd.com	510-732-0100	732-0155	665
Western Pacific Storage Systems Inc 300 E Arrow Hwy . . . San Dimas CA 91773 *TF:* 800-732-9777 ■ *Web:* www.wpss.com	800-732-9777		286
Western Paper Distributors Inc 11551 E 45th Ave Ste A . . . Denver CO 80239 *TF:* 800-835-4812 ■ *Web:* www.western-paper.com	303-371-6000	371-6111	559
Western Partitions Inc 26055 SW Canyon Creek Rd . . . Wilsonville OR 97070 *TF:* 800-783-0315 ■ *Web:* wpibuilds.com	503-620-1600	624-5781	189-9
Western Pennsylvania Genealogical Society (WPGS) 4400 Forbes Ave . . . Pittsburgh PA 15213 *Web:* wpgs.org	412-687-6811		49-19
Western Pest Services Inc 800 Lanidex Plz . . . Parsippany NJ 07054 *TF:* 877-250-3857 ■ *Web:* www.westernpest.com	877-250-3857		577
Western Piedmont Community College 1001 Burkemont Ave . . . Morganton NC 28655 *Web:* www.wpcc.edu	828-448-3500		162
Western Piedmont Symphony 243 Third Ave NE Ste 1-N . . . Hickory NC 28601 *Web:* wpsymphony.org	828-324-8603	324-1301	573-3
Western Pioneer Inc 4601 Shilshole Ave NW . . . Seattle WA 98107 *TF:* 800-426-6783 ■ *Web:* www.wpioneer.com	206-789-1930		312
Western Pioneer Sales Co 6631 Calle Eva Miranda . . . Irwindale CA 91702 *TF:* 800-640-4535 ■ *Web:* www.westernpioneersales.com	818-244-1466	244-1489	300
Western Placer Unified School District 600 6th St . . . Lincoln CA 95648 *Web:* www.wpusd.org	916-645-6350		685
Western Plains Medical Complex 3001 Ave A . . . Dodge City KS 67801 *Web:* www.westernplainsmc.com	620-225-8400	225-8403	374-3
Western Plastic Products Inc 8441 Monroe Ave . . . Stanton CA 90680 **Fax Area Code:* 562 ■ *TF:* 800-453-1881 ■ *Web:* www.wbadges.com	800-453-1881	495-2232*	9
Western Plastics Inc 2399 US Hwy 41 SW . . . Calhoun GA 30701 **Fax Area Code:* 800 ■ *TF:* 800-442-9727 ■ *Web:* www.wplastics.com	951-695-1983	979-7277*	600
Western Playland Amusement Park 1249 Futurity Dr . . . Sunland Park NM 88063 *Web:* www.westernplayland.com	575-589-3410		32
Western Pneumatic Tube LLC 835 Sixth St S . . . Kirkland WA 98033 *Web:* www.leggettaerospace.com	425-822-8271	828-6669	490
Western Pneumatics Inc 110 N Seneca Rd . . . Eugene OR 97402 *Web:* www.westernpneumatics.com	541-461-2600		207
Western Polymer Corp 32 Rd 'R' SE . . . Moses Lake WA 98837 *Web:* www.westernpolymer.com	509-765-1803	765-0327	144
Western Power Sports Inc 601 E Gowen Rd . . . Boise ID 83716 *TF:* 800-999-3388 ■ *Web:* www.wps-inc.com	208-376-8400	375-8901	711
Western Printing Machinery Co 9228 Ivanhoe St . . . Schiller Park IL 60176 *Web:* www.wpm.com	847-678-1740		628
Western Producer Publications 2310 Millar Ave . . . Saskatoon SK S7K2Y2 *Web:* www.producer.com	306-665-3500		532-3
Western Products Inc 7777 N 73rd St . . . Milwaukee WI 53223 *Web:* www.westernplows.com	414-354-2310		190
Western Products Inc 474 45th St S . . . Fargo ND 58103 *TF:* 800-743-3632 ■ *Web:* www.westernproducts.com	701-293-5310	232-6666	191-4
Western Pulp Products Co 5025 SW Hout St . . . Corvallis OR 97333 *Web:* westernpulp.com	541-757-1151		557
Western Recorder (WR) 13420 Eastpoint Center Dr . . . Louisville KY 40223 *TF:* 866-489-3535 ■ *Web:* www.westernrecorder.org	502-489-3443	489-3565	532-2
Western Reflections 261 Commerce Way . . . Gallatin TN 37066 *TF:* 800-507-8302 ■ *Web:* www.western-reflections.com	615-451-9700	452-0283	439
Western Regional Research Ctr (WRRC) 800 Buchanan St . . . Albany CA 94710 *Web:* www.ars.usda.gov	510-559-5600	559-5963	668
Western Reman Industrial LLC 588 W 7th St . . . Peru IN 46970 *Web:* www.wriservices.com	765-472-2002		650
Western Research & Development Ltd 5908 Yellowstone Rd Ste B . . . Cheyenne WY 82009 *Web:* wrd-ltd.com	307-632-5656		261
Western Research Institute 365 N Ninth St . . . Laramie WY 82072 *TF:* 888-463-6974 ■ *Web:* westernresearch.org	307-721-2011	721-2345	668
Western Reserve Academy 115 College St . . . Hudson OH 44236 *Web:* www.wra.net	330-650-9717		622
Western Reserve Group, The 1685 Cleveland Rd PO Box 36 . . . Wooster OH 44691 **Fax Area Code:* 330 ■ *TF:* 800-362-0426 ■ *Web:* www.wrg-ins.com	800-362-0426	262-3259*	391-4
Western Reserve Partners LLC 200 Public Sq Ste 3750 . . . Cleveland OH 44114 *Web:* wesrespartners.com	216-589-0900	589-9558	196
Western Robidoux Inc (WRI) 4006 S 40th St . . . Saint Joseph MO 64503 *TF:* 800-224-1617 ■ *Web:* www.wriprint.com	816-279-1617	279-1696	554
Western Rockingham Chamber of Commerce 112 W Murphy St . . . Madison NC 27025 *Web:* wrchamber.com	336-548-6248		139
Western Sage CPAS 115 N Ninth St . . . Worland WY 82401 *Web:* westernsagecpas.com	307-347-3633		2
Western Security Bank 2812 First Ave N . . . Billings MT 59101 *TF:* 800-983-5537 ■ *Web:* www.westernsecuritybank.com	406-371-8200		70
Western Seminary 5511 SE Hawthorne Blvd . . . Portland OR 97215 *TF:* 877-517-1800 ■ *Web:* www.westernseminary.edu	503-517-1800	517-1801	167-3
Western Services Corp 7196 Crestwood Blvd Ste 300 . . . Frederick MD 21703 *Web:* ws-corp.com	301-644-2500	682-8104	177
Western Slope Auto 2264 Hwy 50 . . . Grand Junction CO 81505 *Web:* www.westernslopeauto.com	970-243-0843		57
Western State Bank 110 Fourth St S . . . Devils Lake ND 58301 *Web:* www.westernbanks.com	701-662-4936		70
Western State College of Colorado 600 N Adams St . . . Gunnison CO 81231 *TF:* 800-876-5309 ■ *Web:* www.western.edu	970-943-2119	943-2363	166
Western State Hospital 2400 Russellville Rd . . . Hopkinsville KY 42240 *Web:* westernstatehospital.ky.gov	270-889-6025		374-5
Western State Hospital 1215 Lee St . . . Charlottesville VA 22903 *Web:* www.dshs.wa.gov	434-924-0000		374-5
Western State Hospital 9601 Steilacoom Blvd SW . . . Tacoma WA 98498 *TF:* 877-501-2233 ■ *Web:* www.dshs.wa.gov	253-582-8900		374-5
Western State University College of Law 1111 N State College Blvd . . . Fullerton CA 92831 *Web:* www.wsulaw.edu	714-459-1101	441-1748	167-1
Western States Envelope & Label Co 4480 N 132nd St . . . Butler WI 53007 *TF:* 800-558-0514 ■ *Web:* www.wsel.com	262-781-5540	781-5791	263
Western States Fire Protection Co 7020 S Tucson Way . . . Centennial CO 80112 *Web:* www.wsfp.com	303-792-0022		189-13
Western States Lodging 1018 W Atherton Dr . . . Taylorsville UT 84123 *Web:* wslm.biz	801-269-0700	269-1512	379
Western States Mfg 811 Main St . . . Sioux City IA 51103 *Web:* www.wsm-corp.com	831-655-2100		754
Western States Petroleum Inc 450 S 15th Ave . . . Phoenix AZ 85007 *TF:* 800-220-1353 ■ *Web:* www.westernstatespetroleum.com	602-252-4011		579
Western States Publishers Inc 16508 E Laser Dr Ste 101 . . . Fountain Hills AZ 85268 *Web:* www.fhtimes.com	480-837-1925	837-1951	637-10
Western States Ticket Service 143 W McDowell Rd . . . Phoenix AZ 85003 *TF:* 800-326-0331 ■ *Web:* www.wstickets.com	602-254-3300		750
Western States Truck Centers LLC 3790 N Reserve St . . . Missoula MT 59808 *Web:* westernstatescat.com	406-543-3196		791
Western States Weeklies Inc PO Box 600600 . . . San Diego CA 92160 *TF:* 800-628-9466 ■ *Web:* www.navydispatch.com	619-280-2985		637-8
Western Steel Inc 3360 Davey Allison Blvd . . . Hueytown AL 35023 *Web:* www.westernsteelinc.com	205-744-2230	744-0445	723
Western Suffolk Boces (suffolk 3) 507 Deer Park Rd . . . Dix Hills NY 11746 *Web:* www.wsboces.org	631-549-4900		685
Western Sugar Co-op 7555 E Hampden Ave Ste 520 . . . Denver CO 80231 *TF:* 800-523-7497 ■ *Web:* www.westernsugar.com	303-830-3939	830-3941	296-38
Western Summit Constructors Inc 9780 Mt Pyramid Ct Ste 100 . . . Englewood CO 80112 *Web:* www.westernsummit.com	303-298-9500	325-0304	186
Western Supermarkets 2614 19th St S . . . Birmingham AL 35209 *Web:* www.westernsupermarkets.com	205-879-3471	879-3476	345
Western Technical College 400 Seventh St N . . . La Crosse WI 54601 *TF:* 800-322-9982 ■ *Web:* www.westerntc.edu	608-785-9200	789-6206	800
Western Technologies Inc 3737 E Broadway Rd . . . Phoenix AZ 85040 *TF:* 800-580-3737 ■ *Web:* wt-us.com	602-437-3737		192
Western Technology Inc 3517 W Arsenal Way . . . Bremerton WA 98312 *Web:* www.westerntechnologylights.com	360-917-0080		439
Western Technology Investment (WTI) 104 La Mesa Dr Ste 102 . . . Portola CA 94028 *Web:* westerntech.com	650-234-4300	234-4343	792
Western Telematic Inc 5 Sterling . . . Irvine CA 92618 *TF:* 800-854-7226 ■ *Web:* www.wti.com	949-586-9950	583-9514	173-3

Name / Address	City	State	Zip	Phone	Fax	Class
Western Texas College 6200 College Ave *TF:* 888-468-6982 ■ *Web:* www.wtc.edu	Snyder	TX	79549	325-573-8511	573-9321	162
Western Texas Lions Eye Bank Alliance 2030 Pullman St Ste 4 *Web:* wtleb.org	San Angelo	TX	76905	325-653-8666		269
Western Theological Seminary 101 E 13th St *TF:* 800-392-8554 ■ *Web:* www.westernsem.edu	Holland	MI	49423	616-392-8555	392-7717	167-3
Western Tile Design Ctr 1290 Diamond Way *Web:* www.westerntiledesign.com	Concord	CA	94520	925-671-0145	671-7313	191-1
Western Towboat Company Inc 617 NW 40th St *Web:* www.westerntowboat.com	Seattle	WA	98107	206-789-9000	789-9755	465
Western Trailer Co 251 W Gowen Rd *TF:* 888-344-2539 ■ *Web:* www.westerntrailer.com	Boise	ID	83716	208-344-2539	344-1521	779
Western Transport Inc 3916 W 65 S *TF:* 800-793-5688 ■ *Web:* www.westerntransportinc.com	Idaho Falls	ID	83402	208-529-9327	523-5691	780
Western Truck Equipment Co (WTE) 2400 S 14th St *Web:* www.wteco.com	Phoenix	AZ	85034	602-257-0777	340-1534	516
Western Truck Parts & Equip Co 3707 Airport Way S *TF:* 800-255-7383 ■ *Web:* www.westerntruckcenter.com	Seattle	WA	98134	206-624-7383		61
Western Tube & Conduit Corp 2001 E Dominguez St **Fax Area Code:* 310 ■ *TF:* 800-310-8823 ■ *Web:* www.westerntube.com	Long Beach	CA	90810	800-310-8823	604-9785*	490
Western Union Holdings Inc 12500 E Belford Ave *NYSE:* WU ■ *TF:* 800-325-6000 ■ *Web:* www.westernunion.com	Englewood	CO	80112	720-332-1000	332-4753	69
Western United Electric Supply Corp 100 Bromley Business Pkwy *TF:* 800-748-3116 ■ *Web:* www.wue.coop	Brighton	CO	80603	303-659-2356		791
Western United Life Assurance Co 929 W Sprague Ave PO Box 2290 *TF:* 800-247-2045 ■ *Web:* www.manhattanlife.com	Spokane	WA	99210	509-835-2500	835-3191	391-2
Western University 1151 Richmond St *Web:* www.uwo.ca	London	ON	N6A3K7	519-661-2111	661-3630	785
Western University Canada *King's University College* 266 Epworth Ave *TF:* 800-265-4406 ■ *Web:* www.kings.uwo.ca	London	ON	N6A2M3	519-433-3491	433-0070	785
Western University of Health Sciences 309 E Second St *Web:* www.westernu.edu	Pomona	CA	91766	909-623-6116		162
Western Upper Peninsula Convention & Visitor Bureau 1200 E US 2 *TF:* 800-522-5657 ■ *Web:* www.explorewesternup.com	Ironwood	MI	49938	906-932-4850		206
Western Veterinary Conference 2425 E Oquendo Rd *TF:* 866-800-7326 ■ *Web:* www.viticusgroup.org	Las Vegas	NV	89120	702-739-6698		794
Western Village Inn & Casino 815 Nichols Blvd *TF:* 800-648-1170 ■ *Web:* www.westernvillagesparks.com	Sparks	NV	89434	800-648-1170		133
Western Washington University 516 High St *TF:* 800-261-7331 ■ *Web:* www.wwu.edu	Bellingham	WA	98225	360-650-3000	650-7369	166
Western Water Constructors Inc 707 Aviation Blvd *Web:* www.westernwater.com	Santa Rosa	CA	95403	707-540-9640	540-9641	187
Western Window Systems 2200 E Riverview Dr *TF:* 877-268-1300 ■ *Web:* westernwindowsystems.com	Phoenix	AZ	85034	877-268-1300		234
Western Wood Preserving Co 1310 Zehnder St *TF:* 800-472-7714 ■ *Web:* www.westernwoodpreserving.com	Sumner	WA	98390	253-863-8191		818
Western Wood Products Assn (WWPA) 522 SW Fifth Ave Ste 500 *Web:* www.wwpa.org	Portland	OR	97204	503-224-3930	224-3934	48-2
Western World Insurance Group 300 Kimball Dr Ste 500 *Web:* www.westernworld.com	Parsippany	NJ	07054	201-847-8600	847-1010	391-2
Western Wyoming Beverages Inc 100 Reliance Rd *Web:* www.westernwyomingbeverages.com	Rock Springs	WY	82901	307-362-6332		81-2
Western Wyoming Community College 2500 College Dr *TF:* 800-226-1181 ■ *Web:* www.wwcc.wy.edu	Rock Springs	WY	82901	307-382-1600	382-1636	162
Westerra Credit Union 3700 E Alameda Ave *TF:* 800-858-7212 ■ *Web:* www.westerracu.com	Denver	CO	80209	303-321-4209		219
Westervelt Co PO Box 48999 *Web:* westerveltproperties.com	Tuscaloosa	AL	35404	205-562-5295	562-5013	821
Westervelt Company Inc, The PO Box 48999 *Web:* www.westervelt.com	Tuscaloosa	AL	35404	205-562-5000	562-5012	683
Westerville Area Chamber of Commerce 99 Commerce Pk Dr Ste A *Web:* www.westervillechamber.com	Westerville	OH	43082	614-882-8917	882-2085	139
Westerville Public Library 126 S State St *TF:* 800-816-0662 ■ *Web:* westervillelibrary.org	Westerville	OH	43081	614-882-7277	882-4160	434-3
Westest LLC 627 Sheridan Blvd *Web:* westest.net	Lakewood	CO	80214	303-975-9959	975-9969	261
Westex Inc 122 W 22nd St *TF:* 866-493-7839 ■ *Web:* www.westex.com	Oak Brook	IL	60523	773-523-7000	523-0965	745-7
West-Fair Electric Contractors Inc 200 Brady Ave *Web:* www.west-fair.com	Hawthorne	NY	10532	914-769-8050	769-7451	189-4
Westfalia Technologies Inc 3655 Sandhurst Dr *TF:* 800-673-2522 ■ *Web:* www.westfaliausa.com	York	PA	17406	717-764-1115	764-1118	207
Westfall Engineers Inc 14583 Big Basin Way Ste 3	Saratoga	CA	95070	408-867-0244		261
Westfarms Mall 1500 New Britian Ave *Web:* www.shopwestfarms.com	West Hartford	CT	06110	860-561-3024		460
Westfield Area Chamber of Commerce (WACC) 212 Lenox Ave *Web:* www.gwaccnj.com	Westfield	NJ	07090	908-233-3021		139
Westfield Athenaeum 6 Elm St *Web:* www.westath.org	Westfield	MA	01085	413-568-7833	568-0988	434-3
Westfield Bank 2 Park Cir *TF:* 800-368-8930 ■ *Web:* www.westfield-bank.com	Westfield Center	OH	44251	800-368-8930		70
Westfield Board of Education Inc 302 Elm St *Web:* www.westfieldnjk12.org	Westfield	NJ	07090	908-789-4401		685
Westfield Capital Management Company LP 1 Financial Ctr 23rd Fl *Web:* www.westfieldcapital.com	Boston	MA	02111	617-428-7100		401
Westfield Corp 400 S Baldwin Ave Ste 2305 *Web:* www.westfield.com	Culver City	CA	90230	310-390-5073		460
Westfield Electroplating Company Inc 68 N Elm St *Web:* www.westfieldplating.com	Westfield	MA	01085	413-568-3716	562-8279	481
Westfield Engineering & Services Inc 8310 McHard Rd	Houston	TX	77053	281-438-2047		256
Westfield Financial Inc 141 Elm St *NASDAQ:* WNEB ■ *TF:* 800-995-5734 ■ *Web:* www.westfieldbank.com	Westfield	MA	01085	413-568-1911	562-7939	360-2
Westfield Memorial Library 550 E Broad St *Web:* www.wmlnj.org	Westfield	NJ	07090	908-789-4090		434-3
Westfield News Group LLC 62 School St *Web:* thewestfieldnews.com	Westfield	MA	01085	413-562-4181		532-3
Westfield Pharmacy Inc 1845 W A St *Web:* westfieldpharmacy.com	North Platte	NE	69101	308-532-5539		237
Westfield Sheet Metal Works Inc N 8th Street & Monroe Ave *Web:* www.westfieldsheetmetal.com	Kenilworth	NJ	07033	908-276-5500	276-6808	697
Westfield State University 577 Western Ave *Web:* www.westfield.ma.edu	Westfield	MA	01086	413-572-5300	572-0520	166
Westfield Steel Inc 530 State Rd 32 W **Fax Area Code:* 317 ■ *TF:* 800-622-4984 ■ *Web:* www.westfieldsteel.com	Westfield	IN	46074	800-622-4984	896-5343*	492
Westfield Veterinary Hospital Pc 8789 NW 54th Ave *Web:* www.westfieldvet.com	Johnston	IA	50131	515-986-5738		794
Westford Regency Inn & Conference Ctr 219 Littleton Rd *Web:* www.westfordregency.com	Westford	MA	01886	978-692-8200	850-4940	379
Westgate Hotel, The 1055 Second Ave *TF:* 800-522-1564 ■ *Web:* www.westgatehotel.com	San Diego	CA	92101	619-238-1818	557-3737	671
WestGate Mall 205 W Blackstock Rd *Web:* www.westgate-mall.com	Spartanburg	SC	29301	864-574-0264		460
Westgate Management Company Inc 133 Franklin Corner Rd *Web:* www.wgmgt.com	Lawrenceville	NJ	08648	609-895-8890	895-0058	655
Westgate Press 176 Helen Garland Dr *Web:* www.westgatenecromantic.com	Opelousas	LA	70570	337-942-2240		637-2
Westglow Resort & Spa 224 Westglow Cir *TF:* 800-562-0807 ■ *Web:* www.westglowresortandspa.com	Blowing Rock	NC	28605	828-295-4463		707
Westham Trade Company Ltd 3620 NW 114th Ave *Web:* www.wtrade.com	Doral	FL	33178	786-464-5300		174
Westheffer Company Inc 921 N 1st St **Fax Area Code:* 800 ■ *TF:* 800-362-3110 ■ *Web:* www.westheffer.com	Lawrence	KS	66044	785-843-1633	843-3281*	273
West-Herr Automotive Group Inc 3448 McKinley Pkwy *TF:* 800-643-2112 ■ *Web:* www.westherr.com	Blasdell	NY	14219	716-926-8150		57
Westholme Publishing 904 Edgewood Rd **Fax Area Code:* 215 ■ *TF:* 800-621-2736 ■ *Web:* www.westholmepublishing.com	Yardley	PA	19067	800-621-2736	321-6104*	637-2
Westin Automotive Products Inc 5200 N Irwindale Ave Ste 220 *TF:* 800-345-8476 ■ *Web:* www.westinautomotive.com	Irwindale	CA	91706	626-960-6762		61
Westin Technology Solutions 1000 N Water St Ste 950 **Fax Area Code:* 916 ■ *Web:* westindelivers.com	Milwaukee	WI	53202	414-289-7960	852-2311*	463
Westinghouse Electric Company LLC 1000 Westinghouse Dr Ste 572A *Web:* www.westinghousenuclear.com	Cranberry Township	PA	16066	412-374-4111		261
WestJet Airlines Ltd 22 Aerial Pl NE *TSE:* WJA ■ *TF:* 888-937-8538 ■ *Web:* www.westjet.com	Calgary	AB	T2E3J1	403-444-2600		25
Westlake Chemical Corp 2801 Post Oak Blvd Ste 600 *NYSE:* WLK ■ *TF:* 888-953-3623 ■ *Web:* www.westlake.com	Houston	TX	77056	713-960-9111		605-2
Westlake Ctr 400 Pine St *Web:* www.westlakecenter.com	Seattle	WA	98101	206-467-1600		460
Westlake Farms Inc 23311 Newton Ave	Stratford	CA	93266	559-947-3328		10-2
Westlake Hospital 1225 W Lake St *TF:* 800-570-8809 ■ *Web:* www.westlakehosp.com	Melrose Park	IL	60160	708-681-3000		374-3
Westlake Plastics Co 490 W Lenni Rd *TF:* 800-999-1700 ■ *Web:* www.westlakeplastics.com	Lenni	PA	19052	610-459-1000	459-1084	604
Westlake Risk & Insurance Services Inc 2659 Townsgate Rd Ste 103 *Web:* westlakerisk.com	Westlake Village	CA	91361	805-413-0250		390
Westland Chamber of Commerce 36900 Ford Rd *TF:* 800-737-4859 ■ *Web:* www.westlandchamber.com	Westland	MI	48185	734-326-7222	326-6040	139
Westland Corp 1735 S Maize Rd *TF:* 800-247-1144 ■ *Web:* reiloyusa.com	Wichita	KS	67209	316-721-1144	721-1495	757
Westland Enterprises Inc 3621 Stewart Rd *Web:* www.westlandenterprises.com	Forestville	MD	20747	301-736-0600		627
Westland Financial Services Inc 1717 Kettner Blvd Ste 200 *TF:* 800-238-8144 ■ *Web:* www.westlandinc.com	San Diego	CA	92101	800-238-8144		195
Westland Floral Co 1400 Cravens Ln *Web:* www.westlandfloral.com	Carpinteria	CA	93013	805-684-4011		369
Westland Ford 3450 Wall Ave *Web:* www.youngfordogden.com	Ogden	UT	84401	801-629-5500		57

Name / Address	City	State	ZIP	Phone	Fax	Class
Westland Sales PO Box 427 *TF:* 800-356-0766 ■ *Web:* www.splendide.com	Clackamas	OR	97015	503-655-2563	656-8829	38
Westland Seed Inc 36272 Round Butte Rd *TF:* 800-547-3335 ■ *Web:* www.westlandseed.com	Ronan	MT	59864	406-676-4100	676-4101	276
Westland Shopping Ctr 35000 W Warren Rd *Web:* www.westlandcenter.com	Westland	MI	48185	734-425-5001	425-9205	460
Westlawn Institute of Marine Technology c/o Maine Maritime Museum 243 Washington St *TF:* 800-832-7430 ■ *Web:* www.westlawn.edu	Bath	ME	04530	207-747-0088	747-0084	167-3
West-Lite Supply Company Inc 12951 166th St *TF:* 800-660-6678 ■ *Web:* www.west-lite.com	Cerritos	CA	90703	562-802-0224	802-0154	246
Westlog Aviation 311 Cove Rd *TF:* 800-761-5183 ■ *Web:* cal-ore.com	Brookings	OR	97415	541-469-7911		30
Westmac Commercial Brokerage Co 1515 S Sepulveda Blvd *Web:* westmac.com	Los Angeles	CA	90025	310-478-7700		652
Westman Champlin & Kelly 900 Second Ave S *Web:* www.wck.com	Minneapolis	MN	55402	612-334-3222		428
Westman Communications Group 1906 Park Ave *TF:* 800-665-3337 ■ *Web:* www.westmancom.com	Brandon	MB	R7B0R9	204-725-4300		224
Westmark Hotels 450 Third Ave W *TF:* 800-544-0970 ■ *Web:* www.westmarkhotels.com	Seattle	WA	98119	800-544-0970		379
Westmed College 3031 Tisch Way 1st Fl Ste 8PW *Web:* www.westmedcollege.edu	San Jose	CA	95128	408-236-1170	236-1180	167-3
Westminster Chamber of Commerce 1025 Westminster Mall *Web:* www.westminsterchamber.org	Westminster	CA	92683	714-898-2559	373-1499	139
Westminster College 501 Westminster Ave *TF:* 800-475-3361 ■ *Web:* www.wcmo.edu	Fulton	MO	65251	573-592-5251	592-5255	166
Westminster College 319 S Market St *TF:* 800-942-8033 ■ *Web:* www.westminster.edu	New Wilmington	PA	16172	724-946-8761	946-6171	166
Westminster College 1840 South 1300 East *TF:* 800-748-4753 ■ *Web:* westminstercollege.edu	Salt Lake City	UT	84105	801-832-2200	832-3101	166
Westminster Communities of Florida 4449 Meandering Way *TF:* 800-948-1881 ■ *Web:* www.westminstercommunitiesfl.org	Tallahassee	FL	32308	850-878-1136		672
Westminster Hotel LLC 550 W Mt Pleasant Ave *Web:* www.westminsterhotel.com	Livingston	NJ	07039	973-533-0600		378
Westminster Manor 4100 Jackson Ave *Web:* westminsteraustintx.org	Austin	TX	78731	512-454-4643	371-7308	672
Westminster Place 3200 Grant St *Web:* presbyterianhomes.org	Evanston	IL	60201	847-570-3422		672
Westminster Publications Inc 708 Glen Cove Ave *Web:* www.westminsterpublications.com	Glen Head	NY	11545	516-759-0025		637-9
Westminster School 995 Hopmeadow St *Web:* www.westminster-school.org	Simsbury	CT	06070	860-408-3060		622
Westminster School District 14121 Cedarwood St *TF:* 888-491-6603 ■ *Web:* www.wsdk8.us	Westminster	CA	92683	714-894-7311	899-2781	685
Westminster Schools 1424 W Paces Ferry Rd NW *Web:* www.westminster.net	Atlanta	GA	30327	404-355-8673		623
Westminster Theological Seminary 2960 Church Rd *TF:* 800-373-0119 ■ *Web:* www.wts.edu	Glenside	PA	19038	215-887-5511	887-5404	167-3
Westminster Theological Seminary in California 1725 Bear Vly Pkwy *TF:* 888-480-8474 ■ *Web:* www.wscal.edu	Escondido	CA	92027	760-480-8474	480-0252	167-3
Westminster Towers 70 W Lucerne Cir *TF:* 877-382-9036 ■ *Web:* www.westminstertowersfl.org	Orlando	FL	32801	407-841-1310		672
Westminster Towers 1330 India Hook Rd *TF:* 800-345-6026 ■ *Web:* westminstertowers.org	Rock Hill	SC	29732	803-328-5000		672
Westminster Village 2025 E Lincoln St *Web:* www.westminstervillageinc.com	Bloomington	IL	61701	309-663-6474	663-1069	672
Westminster Village 1120 E Davis Dr *Web:* westminstervillagein.com	Terre Haute	IN	47802	812-242-4600		672
Westminster-Canterbury of Lynchburg 501 VES Rd *TF:* 800-962-3520 ■ *Web:* wclynchburg.org	Lynchburg	VA	24503	434-386-3500	386-3535	672
Westminster-Canterbury on Chesapeake Bay 3100 Shore Dr *TF:* 800-753-2918 ■ *Web:* www.wcbay.com	Virginia Beach	VA	23451	800-753-2918		672
Westminster-Canterbury Richmond 1600 Westbrook Ave *TF:* 800-445-9904 ■ *Web:* www.wcrichmond.org	Richmond	VA	23227	804-264-6000	264-4579	672
Westmont College 955 La Paz Rd *TF:* 800-777-9011 ■ *Web:* www.westmont.edu	Santa Barbara	CA	93108	805-565-6000	565-6234	166
Westmont Hospitality Group Inc 5090 Explorer Dr Ste 700 *Web:* www.whg.com	Mississauga	ON	L4W4T9	905-629-3400	624-7805	379
Westmor Industries LLC 3 Development Dr *TF:* 800-992-8981 ■ *Web:* westmor-ind.com	Morris	MN	56267	320-589-2100		198
Westmore Fuel Company Inc 86 N Water St *TF:* 888-696-4031 ■ *Web:* westmorefuel.com	Greenwich	CT	06830	203-531-6800	531-5783	316
Westmoreland Chamber of Commerce 241 Tollgate Hill Rd *Web:* www.westmorelandchamber.com	Greensburg	PA	15601	724-834-2900	837-7635	139
Westmoreland County 2 N Main St Ste 101 *Web:* www.co.westmoreland.pa.us	Greensburg	PA	15601	724-830-3000	830-3029	338
Westmoreland County PO Box 1000 *Web:* www.westmoreland-county.org	Montross	VA	22520	804-493-0130	493-0134	338
Westmoreland County Community College 145 Pavilion Ln *TF:* 800-262-2103 ■ *Web:* westmoreland.edu	Youngwood	PA	15697	724-925-4000		162
Westmoreland Mall 5256 US-30 *Web:* www.westmorelandmall.com	Greensburg	PA	15601	724-836-5025		460
Westmoreland Mechanical Testing & Research Inc PO Box 388 *Web:* www.wmtr.com	Youngstown	PA	15696	724-537-3131	537-3151	743
Westmoreland Museum of American Art 221 N Main St *Web:* thewestmoreland.org	Greensburg	PA	15601	724-837-1500		520
Westoak Industries Inc 110 N Sheb Wooley Ave *Web:* www.westoakindustries.com	Erick	OK	73645	580-526-3221	526-3219	253
Weston & Associates Inc 110 Thomas St *Web:* www.westoninc.com	Winston-Salem	NC	27101	336-725-1147	725-0551	184
Weston & Sampson Inc 5 Centennial Dr *TF:* 800-726-7766 ■ *Web:* www.westonandsampson.com	Peabody	MA	01960	978-532-1900		261
Weston Bend State Park 16600 Hwy 45 N *Web:* mostateparks.com	Weston	MO	64098	816-640-5443		565
Weston County 400 Stampede St PO Box 130 *Web:* www.westongov.com	Newcastle	WY	82701	307-746-4775		338
Weston Hurd LLP The Tower at Erieview 1301 E Ninth St Ste 1900 *TF:* 800-336-4952 ■ *Web:* www.westonhurd.com	Cleveland	OH	44114	216-241-6602	621-8369	428
Weston Solutions Inc 1400 Weston Way PO Box 2653 *Web:* www.westonsolutions.com	West Chester	PA	19380	610-701-3000	701-3186	261
Westover School PO Box 847 *Web:* www.westoverschool.org	Middlebury	CT	06762	203-758-2423	577-4588	622
Westpac Banking Corp *Americas Div* 575 Fifth Ave 39th Fl *TF:* 888-269-2377 ■ *Web:* www.westpac.com.au	New York	NY	10017	212-551-1800	551-1999	70
WestPac Labs (PALLAB) 9830 Brimhall Rd *TF:* 800-875-2271 ■ *Web:* www.pallab.org	Bakersfield	CA	93312	661-829-2260	829-1317	418
Westpak Inc 10326 Roselle St Ste 101 *Web:* www.westpak.com	San Diego	CA	92121	858-623-8100		88
WestPark Capital Inc 1900 Avenue of the Stars Ste 310 *TF:* 800-811-3487 ■ *Web:* www.wpcapital.com	Los Angeles	CA	90067	310-843-9300		690
Westport Community Theatre 110 Myrtle Ave *Web:* www.westportcommunitytheatre.com	Westport	CT	06880	203-226-1983		573-4
Westport Corp 331 Changdridge Rd *Web:* www.mundiwestport.com	Pine Brook	NJ	07058	973-575-0110	575-8197	430
Westport Country Playhouse 25 Powers Ct *TF:* 888-927-7529 ■ *Web:* www.westportplayhouse.org	Westport	CT	06880	203-227-4177	221-7482	572
Westport Healthcare 7300 Forest Ave *Web:* westporthc.com	Richmond	VA	23226	804-287-8600		450
Westport Historical Society 4000 Baltimore St *Web:* www.westporthistorical.com	Kansas City	MO	64111	816-561-1821		50-6
Westport Inn, The 1595 Post Rd E *Web:* www.westportinn.com	Westport	CT	06880	203-557-8124		379
Westport Innovations Inc 1750 W 75th Ave Ste 101 *NASDAQ: WPRT* ■ *Web:* www.westport.com	Vancouver	BC	V6P6G2	604-718-2000	718-2001	60
Westport Precision LLC 280 Hathaway Dr *Web:* www.westportprecision.com	Stratford	CT	06615	203-378-2175	381-9767	697
Westport Public Library 20 Jesup Rd *Web:* westportlibrary.org	Westport	CT	06880	203-291-4800		435
Westpower Equipment Ltd 4451-54 Ave SE *Web:* westpowergroup.com	Calgary	AB	T2C2A2	403-720-3300		541
Westprime Healthcare 5751 Chino Ave *Web:* www.westprimehealthcare.com	Chino	CA	91710	714-529-2027		475
WestPro Construction Solutions 2850 Fairfax Trfy *Web:* westproconstruction.com	Kansas City	MO	64111	816-561-7667		189-12
WestRock Co 504 Thrasher St *Web:* www.westrock.com	Norcross	GA	30071	770-448-2193		145
WestSea Publishing Company Inc 149D Allen Blvd *TF:* 800-543-6130 ■ *Web:* www.westseapublishing.com	Farmingdale	NY	11735	800-543-6130		637-2
WestShore Honda 2522 N Dale Mabry Hwy *Web:* www.kuhnhonda.com	Tampa	FL	33607	813-872-4841		54
Westside Baptist Church Incorporated of Haines City 1416 Polk City Rd	Haines City	FL	33844	863-422-4720		48-20
Westside Lexus 12000 Katy Fwy *Web:* www.westsidelexus.com	Houston	TX	77079	281-558-3030		57
Westside News 1776 Hilton Palmar Corners Rd *Web:* www.westsidenewsny.com	Spencerport	NY	14559	585-352-3411	352-4811	532-4
Westside Regional Medical Ctr 8201 W Broward Blvd *TF:* 800-523-5658 ■ *Web:* westsideregional.com	Plantation	FL	33324	954-473-6600		374-3
Westside Rentals 1020 Wilshire Blvd *Web:* www.westsiderentals.com	Santa Monica	CA	90401	310-576-1443		652
Westside Veterinary Service 1271 Robertson Rd S *Web:* westsidevet.com	Murray	KY	42071	270-753-6749		794
WestStar Talk Radio Networks 2711 N 24th St *Web:* www.weststar.com	Phoenix	AZ	85008	602-381-8200		646
Westtek 8585 154th Ave NE *Web:* www.westtek.com	Redmond	WA	98052	425-497-3100		809
Westtown School PO Box 1799 *Web:* www.westtown.edu	Westtown	PA	19395	610-399-0123	399-7501	622
Westvest Associates Inc 9600 NW 25th St Ste 2A *Web:* westvest.com	Doral	FL	33172	305-717-5401		652

Listing	City	State	Zip	Phone	Fax	Class
Westview Animal Hospital PA 5800 Johnnycake Rd *Web:* westviewanimalhospital.com	Baltimore	MD	21207	410-744-4800		794
Westview Products Inc 1350 SE Shelton St.	Dallas	OR	97338	503-623-5174		106
Westward Parts Services Ltd 6517 - 67 St *TF:* 888-937-7278 ■ *Web:* www.westwardparts.com	Red Deer	AB	T4P1A3	403-347-2200		111
Westward Seafoods 3015 112th Ave NE Ste 100 *Web:* www.westwardseafoods.com	Bellevue	WA	98004	206-682-5949	682-1825	296-13
Westwater Books PO Box 2560 *TF:* 800-628-1326 ■ *Web:* www.westwaterbooks.com	Evergreen	CO	80437	303-674-5410	670-0586	637-2
Westwater Resources 6950 S Potomac St Ste 300 *NASDAQ: WWR* ■ *TF:* 877-373-6374 ■ *Web:* www.westwaterresources.net	Centennial	CO	80112	303-531-0516	531-0519	502
Westway Ford 801 W Airport Fwy *TF:* 844-877-9037 ■ *Web:* www.westwayford.com	Irving	TX	75062	844-877-9037		57
Westways Staffing Services Inc 500 City Pkwy W Ste 130 *Web:* www.westwaysstaffing.com	Orange	CA	92868	714-712-4150		260
Westwood Baptist Church 41 State Farm Rd *Web:* www.westwoodbaptist.net	Alexandria	AL	36250	256-820-2211		48-20
Westwood College Atlanta Northlake 2309 Parklake Dr NE *TF:* 866-552-7536 ■ *Web:* www.westwood.edu	Atlanta	GA	30345	866-552-7536		800
Westwood Community Church 401 Westwood Dr	Winnipeg	MB	R3K1G4	204-888-1771		48-20
Westwood Contractors Inc 951 W Seventh St *Web:* www.westwoodcontractors.com	Fort Worth	TX	76102	817-877-3800	877-4731	780
Westwood Hills Nature Ctr 8300 W Franklin Ave. *Web:* www.stlouispark.org	Saint Louis Park	MN	55426	952-924-2544	797-9691	50-5
Westwood Holdings Group Inc 200 Crescent Ct Ste 1200 *NYSE: WHG* ■ *Web:* westwoodgroup.com	Dallas	TX	75201	214-756-6900	756-6979	360-2
Westwood Insurance Agency 8407 Fallbrook Ave Ste 200 *TF:* 888-822-5396 ■ *Web:* www.westwoodinsurance.com	West Hills	CA	91304	888-822-5396		390
Westwood Manufacturing 1701 W Valley Hwy Ste 6	Auburn	WA	98001	253-833-8241		454
Westwood Partners LLC 51 W 52nd St 12th Fl *Web:* www.westwood-partners.com	New York	NY	10019	212-672-3350	757-4640	772
Westword 969 Broadway *Web:* www.westword.com	Denver	CO	80203	303-296-7744	296-5416	532-5
Wesucceed Solutions Inc 175 Olde Haof Day *Web:* www.wesucceed.com	Lincolnshire	IL	60069	847-229-8130		225
Wet 'n Wild Emerald Pointe 3910 S Holden Rd *TF:* 800-555-5900 ■ *Web:* www.emeraldpointe.com	Greensboro	NC	27406	336-852-9721		32
Wet 'n Wild Orlando 6200 International Dr *TF:* 800-992-9453 ■ *Web:* www.wetnwildorlando.com	Orlando	FL	32819	407-351-1800		32
Wet 'n' Wild Hawaii 400 Farrington Hwy *Web:* www.wetnwildhawaii.com	Kapolei	HI	96707	808-674-9283		31
Wet Paint Inc 1684 W Grand Ave *Web:* www.wetpaintart.com	Saint Paul	MN	55105	651-698-6431	698-8041	45
Wet Products Inc 5 Autry *TF:* 877-938-9455 ■ *Web:* www.wetproducts.com	Irvine	CA	92618	949-855-6584	855-4394	710
Wet Tech Energy Inc 4598 Woodlawn Rd *Web:* www.wettechenergy.com	Maurice	LA	70555	337-893-9992		539
WETA-TV Ch 26 (PBS) 3939 Campbell Ave. *Web:* weta.org	Arlington	VA	22206	703-998-2600		741
WETB-AM 790 (Rel) 231 Brandonwood Dr *Web:* www.wetb790.com	Johnson City	TN	37604	423-928-7131		645-78
Wetherby Asset Management 580 California St 8th Fl. *Web:* wetherby.com	San Francisco	CA	94104	415-399-9159		41
Wetherington Hamilton PA 1010 N Florida Ave. *Web:* whhlaw.com	Tampa	FL	33602	813-225-1918		41
WeTip Inc PO Box 1296 *Web:* wetip.com	Rancho Cucamonga	CA	91730	909-987-5005	987-2477	48-8
Wetland Studies & Solutions Inc 5300 Wellington Branch Dr. *TF:* 800-247-1812 ■ *Web:* www.wetlands.com	Gainesville	VA	20155	703-679-5600		261
WETM-TV 101 E Water St *Web:* www.mytwintiers.com	Elmira	NY	14901	607-733-5518	734-1176	647
Wettekin Electronics 4506 W 12th St *Web:* wettekinelectronics.com	Erie	PA	16505	814-838-9184	838-6060	261
Wetumpka Herald Inc, The PO Box 99 *Web:* www.thewetumpkaherald.com	Wetumpka	AL	36092	334-567-7811		532-2
Wetzel Aviation Inc 7735 S Peoria St. *Web:* wetzelaviation.com	Englewood	CO	80112	303-468-4800		366
Wetzel Brothers LLC 2401 E Edgerton *TF:* 800-747-5444 ■ *Web:* www.wetzelbrothers.com	Cudahy	WI	53110	414-271-5444		627
Wetzel County PO Box 156 *Web:* www.wetzelcounty.wv.gov	New Martinsville	WV	26155	304-455-8217	455-5256	338
Wetzel County Chamber of Commerce 201 Main St PO Box 271 *TF:* 800-834-2070 ■ *Web:* www.wetzelcountychamber.com	New Martinsville	WV	26155	304-455-3825	455-3637	139
Wetzel's Pretzels LLC 35 Hugus Alley Ste 300 *Web:* www.wetzels.com	Pasadena	CA	91103	626-432-6900		68
WEUV-AM 2609 Jordan Ln NW. *Web:* www.weupam.com	Huntsville	AL	35816	256-837-9387	837-9404	647
Wever Petroleum Inc 100 S Hudson St *Web:* weverpetroleum.com	Mechanicville	NY	12118	518-664-7331		316
WEVV-TV Ch 44 (CBS) 477 Carpenter St. *Web:* www.wevv.com	Evansville	IN	47708	812-464-4444	465-4559	741-46
WEW-AM 770 (Var) 2740 Hampton Ave *Web:* www.wewradio.com	Saint Louis	MO	63139	314-781-9397	781-8545	645-138
Wewoka Times, The 210 S Wewoka Ave *Web:* www.thewewokatimes.com	Wewoka	OK	74884	405-257-3341		532-2
Wexford Capital LP Wexford Plz 411 W Putnam Ave *Web:* www.wexford.com	Greenwich	CT	06830	203-862-7000		690
Wexford County 437 E Div St *Web:* www.wexfordcounty.org	Cadillac	MI	49601	231-779-9453	779-9745	338
Wexford Homes 135 Keveling Dr. *Web:* www.wexfordhomes.com	Saline	MI	48176	734-470-6647		187
Wexler Surgical Supplies 11333 Chimney Rock Rd *Web:* www.wexlersurgical.com	Houston	TX	77035	713-723-6900		476
Wexley School for Girls LLC 2218 5th Ave. *Web:* www.wexley.com	Seattle	WA	98121	206-438-8900		7
Wexner Center for the Arts Ohio State University 1871 N High St. *Web:* wexarts.org	Columbus	OH	43210	614-292-0330	292-3369	520
Wexner Heritage Village 1151 College Ave *Web:* whv.org	Columbus	OH	43209	614-231-4900		371
Wexton Jennifer (Rep D - VA) 1217 Longworth House Office Bldg *Web:* www.wexton.house.gov	Washington	DC	20515	202-225-5136		342-2
Weybosset Research & Management LLC 72 S Main St. *Web:* weybosset.com	Providence	RI	02903	401-421-7171		690
Weyco Group Inc 333 W Estabrook Blvd. *NASDAQ: WEYS* ■ *Web:* www.weycogroup.com	Glendale	WI	53212	414-908-1880	908-1603	301
Weyerhaeuser Co 33663 Weyerhaeuser Way S *NYSE: WY* ■ *TF:* 800-525-5440 ■ *Web:* www.weyerhaeuser.com	Federal Way	WA	98003	253-924-2345		185
WEYI-TV Ch 25 (NBC) 3463 W Pierson Rd *Web:* nbc25news.com	Flint	MI	48504	810-687-1000	785-4524	741
Weymouth Design 50 Terminal St Bldg 2 Ste 606 *Web:* weymouthdesign.com	Charlestown	MA	02129	617-542-2647		344
WEZE-AM 500 Victory Rd 2nd Fl *Web:* 590amtheword.com	North Quincy	MA	02171	617-328-0880	328-0375	647
WEZL-FM 103.5 (Ctry) 950 Houston Northcutt Blvd Ste 201 *Web:* wezl.iheart.com	Mount Pleasant	SC	29464	843-721-1035		645
WEZR-AM 555 Center St. *Web:* www.lewistonauburn.com	Auburn	ME	04210	207-784-5868	514-8444	647
WEZS Radio 277 Union Ave Ste 205 *Web:* www.wezs.com	Laconia	NH	03246	603-524-6288		647
WEZV-FM 105.9 (AC) 3926 Wesley St Ste 301 *Web:* wezv.com	Myrtle Beach	SC	29579	843-903-9962		645-104
WEZX-FM 106.9 (Rock) 149 Penn Ave. *Web:* www.rock107.com	Scranton	PA	18503	570-346-6555	346-6038	645-146
WF Investment Corp 1900 Avenue of the Stars Ste 2410. *Web:* wfinvestment.com	Los Angeles	CA	90067	310-553-7176		360-3
WF Meyers Co 1008 13th St *TF:* 800-457-4055 ■ *Web:* www.wfmeyers.com	Bedford	IN	47421	812-275-4485	275-4488	455
WF Wells Inc 16645 Heimbach Rd *Web:* wfwells.com	Three Rivers	MI	49093	269-279-5123	279-6337	455
WF Young Inc 302 Benton Dr. *TF:* 800-628-9653 ■ *Web:* absorbine.com	East Longmeadow	MA	01028	413-526-9999	526-8990	582
WFA Staffing 9001 N 76th St Ste 201 *Web:* wfastaffing.com	Milwaukee	WI	53223	414-365-3651		260
WFAA-TV Ch 8 (ABC) 606 Young St *Web:* www.wfaa.com	Dallas	TX	75202	214-748-9631		741-37
WFAE-FM 90.7 (NPR) 8801 JM Keynes Dr Ste 91 *TF:* 800-876-9323 ■ *Web:* www.wfae.org	Charlotte	NC	28262	704-549-9323	547-8851	645-32
WFAN-AM 66 (Rel) 345 Hudson St 10th Fl *TF:* 866-540-9326 ■ *Web:* newyork.cbslocal.com	New York	NY	10014	866-540-9326		645-109
WFAW-AM W6355 E Ave PO Box 94. *TF:* 800-242-0107 ■ *Web:* www.940wfaw.com	Fort Atkinson	WI	53538	920-563-9329	563-0315	647
WFCA (World Floor Covering Assn) 2211 Howell Ave. *TF:* 800-624-6880 ■ *Web:* wfca.org	Anaheim	CA	92806	714-978-6440	978-6066	49-4
WFCJ-FM 93.7 (Rel) 1205 Whitefield Cir *Web:* 937thelight.com	Xenia	OH	45385	937-424-1640		645-44
WFDD-FM 88.5 (NPR) 1834 Wake Forest Rd Ste 8850. *Web:* www.wfdd.org	Winston-Salem	NC	27109	336-758-8850	758-3083	645-81
WFED-AM 3400 Idaho Ave NW. *Web:* www.federalnewsradio.com	Washington	DC	20016	202-895-5086	895-5144	647
WFF (Walton Family Foundation Inc) PO Box 2030 *Web:* www.waltonfamilyfoundation.org	Bentonville	AR	72712	479-464-1570	464-1580	305
WFFT-TV 3707 Hillegas Rd *Web:* www.wfft.com	Fort Wayne	IN	46808	260-471-5555	484-4331	647
WFGC Television 4119 W Blue Heron Blvd *Web:* www.wfgctelevision.com	Riviera Beach	FL	33404	561-642-3361	967-5961	741-140
WFGI-FM 109 Plaza Dr *TF:* 800-359-5477 ■ *Web:* www.foreverjohnstown.com	Johnstown	PA	15905	814-255-9550		647
WFHB 91.3 FM 108 W 4th St. *Web:* www.wfhb.org	Bloomington	IN	47404	812-323-1200	323-0320	645
WFHL-FM 71 William St PO Box 3025 *Web:* www.radiowfhl.com	New Bedford	MA	02740	508-991-7600	991-2060	647
WFHM-FM 95.5 (Rel) 4 Summit Pk Dr Ste 150. *Web:* www.955thefish.com	Cleveland	OH	44131	216-901-0921		645-36
WFHN-FM 107.1 (CHR) 22 Sconticut Neck Rd *TF:* 877-854-9467 ■ *Web:* www.fun107.com	Fairhaven	MA	02719	508-999-6690		645

Name / Address	City	State	Zip	Phone	Fax	Class
WFI (Wayne Fasteners Inc) 2611 Independence Dr *TF:* 800-994-0393 ■ *Web:* www.waynefasteners.com	Fort Wayne	IN	46808	260-484-0393	483-8082	351
WFIA-AM 3701 Fern Valley Rd *Web:* www.wfiafm.com	Louisville	KY	40219	502-423-3151		647
WFIE-TV Ch 14 (NBC) 1115 Mt Auburn Rd *TF:* 800-832-0014 ■ *Web:* www.14news.com	Evansville	IN	47720	812-426-1414	425-2482	741-46
WFIN-AM 551 Lake Cascades Pky *Web:* www.wfin.com	Findlay	OH	45840	419-422-4545		647
WFIR-AM 960 (N/T) 3934 Electric Rd *Web:* wfirnews.com	Roanoke	VA	24018	540-345-1511	342-2270	645-133
WFIU-FM 103.7 1229 E Seventh St *TF:* 877-285-9348 ■ *Web:* indianapublicmedia.org	Bloomington	IN	47405	812-855-1357		645
WFIV-FM 105.3 517 Watt Rd *TF:* 800-352-9250 ■ *Web:* myi105.com	Knoxville	TN	37934	865-675-4105	675-4859	645-82
WFLA (Western Fraternal Life Assn) 1900 First Ave NE *TF:* 877-935-2467 ■ *Web:* www.wflains.org	Cedar Rapids	IA	52402	319-363-2653		391-2
WFLA-TV Ch 8 (NBC) PO Box 1410 *TF:* 800-338-0808 ■ *Web:* www.wfla.com	Tampa	FL	33601	813-228-8888	225-2770	741-133
WFLD-TV Ch 32 (Fox) 205 N Michigan Ave *Web:* www.fox32chicago.com	Chicago	IL	60601	312-565-5532		741-29
WFLI-TV 6024 Shallowford Rd Ste 100 *Web:* www.wflitv.com	Chattanooga	TN	37421	423-893-9553	893-9853	647
WFLS-FM 616 Amelia St *Web:* www.wfls.com	Fredericksburg	VA	22401	540-374-1500	373-5670	647
WFM (William Fox Munroe Inc) 3 E Lancaster Ave *TF:* 800-344-2402 ■ *Web:* wfoxm.com	Shillington	PA	19607	610-775-4521		344
WFMB-AM 1450 3055 S 4th St *Web:* www.sportsradio1450.com	Springfield	IL	62703	217-528-3033	528-5348	645-152
WFMF-FM 102.5 (CHR) 5555 Hilton Ave Ste 500 *Web:* wfmf.iheart.com	Baton Rouge	LA	70808	225-231-1860		645-17
WFMJ-TV Ch 21 (NBC) 101 W Boardman St *TF:* 800-488-9365 ■ *Web:* www.wfmj.com	Youngstown	OH	44503	330-744-8611	742-2472	741-145
WFMK-FM 99.1 (AC) 3420 Pine Tree Rd *Web:* 99wfmk.com	Lansing	MI	48911	517-394-7272		645-84
WFMS-FM 95.5 (Ctry) 6810 N Shadeland Ave *Web:* www.wfms.com	Indianapolis	IN	46220	317-842-9550		645-74
WFMT-FM 98.7 (Clas) 5400 N St Louis Ave *Web:* www.wfmt.com	Chicago	IL	60625	773-279-2000		645-34
WFMV-FM 95.3 2440 Milwood Ave *TF:* 888-953-9830 ■ *Web:* columbiainspiration.com	Columbia	SC	29205	803-939-9530	939-9469	645-38
WFMY News 2 1615 Phillips Ave **Fax Area Code:* 336 ■ *TF:* 800-593-3692 ■ *Web:* wfmynews2.com	Greensboro	NC	27405	212-975-3247	273-9433*	741
WFMZ-TV Ch 69 (Ind) 300 E Rock Rd *Web:* www.wfmz.com	Allentown	PA	18103	610-791-1111	791-9994	741
WFNT-AM 1470 (N/T) 3338 E Bristol Rd *Web:* wfnt.com	Burton	MI	48529	810-743-1080	742-5170	645
WFOB-AM 101 N Main St PO Box 1157 *Web:* www.wfob.com	Fostoria	OH	44830	419-435-1430	435-6611	647
WFP (Western Forest Products Inc) 800 - 1055 W Georgia St Royal Centre Bldg PO Box 11122 *TSE:* WEF ■ *Web:* www.westernforest.com	Vancouver	BC	V6E3P3	604-648-4500	681-9584	448
WFP (World Food Program USA) 1725 Eye St NW Ste 510 *TF:* 888-454-0555 ■ *Web:* wfpusa.org	Washington	DC	20006	202-627-3737	530-1698	48-5
WFPG-FM 96.9 (AC) 950 Tilton Rd Ste 200 *TF:* 800-969-9374 ■ *Web:* www.literock969.com	Northfield	NJ	08225	609-645-9797	272-9224	645
WFRB-AM 242 Finzel Rd *Web:* www.forevercumberland.com	Frostburg	MD	21532	301-689-5000		647
WFRE-FM 99.9 (Ctry) 5966 Grove Hill Rd *Web:* www.wfre.com	Frederick	MD	21703	301-663-4181	682-8018	645
WFRV-TV Ch 5 (CBS) 1181 E Mason St *TF:* 800-236-5550 ■ *Web:* www.wearegreenbay.com	Green Bay	WI	54301	920-437-5411	437-4576	741-55
WF&S (Wholesale Flowers and Supplies) 5305 Metro St *Web:* www.wholesaleflowersandsupplies.com	San Diego	CA	92110	619-295-4333		293
WFSB-TV-DT CH 3 333 Capital Blvd *Web:* www.wfsb.com	Rocky Hill	CT	06067	860-728-3333	247-8940	741
WFT (West Fraser Timber Company Ltd) 501-858 Beatty St Ste 501 *Web:* www.westfraser.com	Vancouver	BC	V6B1C1	604-895-2700	681-6061	683
WFTM-FM PO Box 100 *Web:* www.wftm.net	Maysville	KY	41056	606-564-3361	564-4291	647
WFTS-TV Ch 28 (ABC) 4045 N Himes Ave *TF:* 877-833-2828 ■ *Web:* www.abcactionnews.com	Tampa	FL	33607	813-354-2828		741-133
WFTX-TV Ch 4 (Fox) 621 SW Pine Island Rd *Web:* www.fox4now.com	Cape Coral	FL	33991	239-574-3636	574-2025	741-88
WFU (Wake Forest University Press) 2518 Reynolda Road *Web:* wfupress.wfu.edu	Winston-Salem	NC	27106	336-758-5448	842-3853	637-9
WFUP-TV PO Box 282 *Web:* www.9and10news.com	Cadillac	MI	49601	231-775-9813		647
WFUV-FM 90.7 (Var) Fordham University 441 E Fordham Rd *TF:* 877-938-8907 ■ *Web:* www.wfuv.org	Bronx	NY	10458	718-817-4550		645
WFVA-AM 1914 Mimosa St *Web:* www.wfvaradio.com	Fredericksburg	VA	22405	540-373-7721	899-3879	647
WFXB Fox Tv 3364 Huger St *Web:* www.wfxb.com	Myrtle Beach	SC	29577	843-828-4300	828-4343	741-87
WFXG-TV Ch 54 (Fox) 3933 Washington Rd *TF:* 866-974-0487 ■ *Web:* www.wfxg.com	Augusta	GA	30907	706-650-5400	650-8411	741-8
WFXL-TV 1201 Stuart Ave *Web:* www.wfxl.com	Albany	GA	31706	229-435-3100	903-8240	647
WFXP-TV Ch 66 (Fox) 8455 Peach St *Web:* www.yourerie.com	Erie	PA	16509	814-864-2400		741-44
WFXR-TV Ch 27 (Fox) 5305 Valleypark Dr Ste 1 *Web:* www.wfxrtv.com	Roanoke	VA	24019	540-344-2127		741-109
WFXT-TV Ch 25 (Fox) 25 Fox Dr *Web:* www.boston25news.com	Dedham	MA	02026	781-467-2525		741
WFYI Indianapolis 1630 N Meridian St *Web:* www.wfyi.org	Indianapolis	IN	46202	317-636-2020	283-2045	632
WG & R Furniture Co 900 Challenger Dr *TF:* 888-947-7782 ■ *Web:* www.wgrfurniture.com	Green Bay	WI	54311	920-469-4880		321
WG Rhea Public Library 400 W Washington St *Web:* rheapubliclibrary.org	Paris	TN	38242	731-642-1702	642-1777	434-3
WG Tomko Inc 2559 Rt 88 *Web:* wgtomko.com	Finleyville	PA	15332	724-348-2000	348-7001	189-10
WG Yates & Sons Construction Company Inc 1 Gulley Ave *Web:* www.wgyates.com	Philadelphia	MS	39350	601-656-5411	656-8958	188-7
WGAC-AM 580 (N/T) 4051 Jimmie Dyess Pkwy *Web:* wgac.com	Augusta	GA	30909	706-396-7000	396-7100	645-109
WGAE (Writers Guild of America East) 250 Hudson St *Web:* www.wgaeast.org	New York	NY	10013	212-767-7800	582-1909	414
WGAL LLC 2701 W Plano Pkwy Ste 500 *Web:* www.wizetrade.com	Plano	TX	75075	972-387-4728	387-9747	809
WGAL-TV Ch 8 (NBC) 1300 Columbia Ave *Web:* www.wgal.com	Lancaster	PA	17604	717-393-5851	295-7457	741
WGAR-FM 99.5 6200 Oak Tree Blvd 4th Fl *Web:* wgar.iheart.com	Independence	OH	44131	216-901-8166		645
WGAW (Writers Guild of America West) 7000 W Third St *Web:* www.wga.org	Los Angeles	CA	90048	323-951-4000	782-4800	414
WGAW-AM 362 Green St *Web:* www.wgaw1340.com	Gardner	MA	01440	978-632-1340		647
WGBH Educational Foundation Brighton Landing 1 Guest St *Web:* www.wgbh.org	Boston	MA	02135	617-300-2000	300-1026	632
WGCL-TV Ch 46 (CBS) 425 14th St NW *TF:* 800-949-6397 ■ *Web:* www.cbs46.com	Atlanta	GA	30318	404-327-3194	327-3004	741-7
WGCU Public Media 10501 FGCU Blvd S *Web:* www.wgcu.org	Fort Myers	FL	33965	239-590-2300	590-2310	658
WGFG-FM 200 Regional Pky Bldg C *Web:* www.cborangeburg.com	Orangeburg	SC	29118	803-536-1710		647
WGFS-AM PO Box 82141 *Web:* www.irieatl.com	Conyers	GA	30013	770-255-8371		647
WGGC-FM 1727 US 31-W By-Pass *TF:* 800-275-9442 ■ *Web:* www.wggc.com	Bowling Green	KY	42101	270-782-9595		647
WGGS-TV Ch 16 (Ind) 3409 Rutherford Rd Ext *TF:* 800-849-3683 ■ *Web:* www.wggs16.com	Taylors	SC	29687	864-244-1616	292-8481	741
WGGY-FM 101.3 305 Hwy 315 *TF:* 800-570-1013 ■ *Web:* froggy101.radio.com	Pittston	PA	18640	570-883-1111		645
WGH-FM 97.3 (Ctry) 900 Laskin Rd *Web:* www.eagle97.com	Virginia Beach	VA	23462	757-671-1000		645-110
WGHP-TV Ch 8 (Fox) 2005 Francis St *TF:* 800-808-6397 ■ *Web:* myfox8.com	High Point	NC	27263	336-841-8888		741
WGIL-AM 154 E Simmons St *Web:* www.wgil.com	Galesburg	IL	61401	309-342-5131	342-0840	647
WGKS-FM 96.9 (AC) 401 W Main St Ste 301 *Web:* www.969kissfm.com	Lexington	KY	40507	859-233-1515	233-1517	645-86
WGL Holdings Inc 101 Constitution Ave NW *NYSE:* WGL ■ *TF:* 800-645-3751 ■ *Web:* wglholdings.com	Washington	DC	20080	703-750-2000		360-5
WGLB-AM 5181 N 35th *Web:* www.wglbam1560.com	Milwaukee	WI	53209	414-527-4365	527-4367	647
WGLO-FM 95.5 (CR) 120 Eaton St *Web:* www.955glo.com	Peoria	IL	61603	309-676-9595	676-5000	645-119
WGM (World Gospel Mission) 3783 E State Rd 18 PO Box 948 *Web:* www.wgm.org	Marion	IN	46952	765-664-7331	671-7230	48-20
Wgm Associates LLC 6263 N Scottsdale Rd Ste 255 *Web:* wgmllc.com	Scottsdale	AZ	85250	480-444-7070		177
WGMD-FM 92.7 (N/T) PO Box 530 *TF:* 800-518-9292 ■ *Web:* www.wgmd.com	Rehoboth Beach	DE	19971	302-945-2050	945-3781	645
WGME-TV Ch 13 (CBS) 81 Northport Dr *Web:* www.wgme.com	Portland	ME	04103	207-797-9099	878-7482	741-102
WGN America 2501 W Bradley Pl *Web:* wgntv.com	Chicago	IL	60618	773-528-2311		740
WGN Radio 720 (N/T) 435 N Michigan Ave *Web:* wgnradio.com	Chicago	IL	60611	312-981-7200		645-34
WGNA-FM 107.7 (Ctry) 1241 Kings Rd *Web:* www.wgna.com	Schenectady	NY	12303	518-881-1515		645
WGNE-FM 99.9 (Ctry) 6440 Atlantic Blvd *Web:* 999gatorcountry.com	Jacksonville	FL	32211	904-725-9990		645
WGNR-AM 1920 W 53rd St **Fax Area Code:* 765 ■ *TF:* 888-877-9467 ■ *Web:* www.moodyradio.org	Anderson	IN	46013	312-329-8983	642-4033*	647
WGNY-FM 661 Little Britain Rd *TF:* 866-353-6903 ■ *Web:* www.foxradio.net	New Windsor	NY	12553	845-561-2131	561-2138	647
WGOK Gospel 900 2800 Dauphin St Ste 104 *TF:* 866-992-5660 ■ *Web:* www.gospel900.com	Mobile	AL	36606	251-423-9900	652-2001	645-100
WGOW-FM 102.3 (N/T) 821 Pineville Rd *Web:* www.wgow.com	Chattanooga	TN	37405	423-756-6141		645-155
WGPM Inc 11220 Elm Ln Ste 201 *Web:* wgpminc.com	Charlotte	NC	28277	704-499-9979	542-7195	261

Name / Address	City	State	ZIP	Phone	Fax	Class
WGPR Inc 3250 Franklin St *Web:* hothiphopdetroit.com	Detroit	MI	48207	313-259-2000	259-7011	645-141
WGPR-FM 107.5 3146 E Jefferson Ave	Detroit	MI	48207	313-259-8862		645-48
WGR-AM 550 (Sports) 500 Corporate Pkwy Ste 200 *TF:* 888-550-2550 ■ *Web:* wgr550.radio.com	Amherst	NY	14226	716-803-0550		645
WGRC FM Radio 101 Armory Blvd *Web:* www.wgrc.com	Lewisburg	PA	17837	570-523-1190		645-11
WGRY-FM 6514 Old Lake Rd *Web:* www.q100-fm.com	Grayling	MI	49738	989-348-7100	348-6181	647
WGRZ-TV Ch 2 (NBC) 259 Delaware Ave *Web:* www.wgrz.com	Buffalo	NY	14202	716-335-3233	849-7602	741-20
WGSA-TV 401 Mall Blvd *Web:* www.wgsa.tv	Savannah	GA	31406	912-692-8000		647
WGSP-AM 4801 E Independence Blvd Ste 800 *Web:* www.pepecharlotte.com	Charlotte	NC	28212	704-527-9477	527-9210	647
WGTE Public Media 1270 S Detroit Ave PO Box 30 *Web:* www.wgte.org	Toledo	OH	43614	419-380-4600	380-4710	645-161
WGTH-AM PO Box 370 *Web:* www.wgth.net	Richlands	VA	24641	276-964-2502	964-4500	647
WGTU-TV 8513 M-72 *Web:* www.upnorthlive.com	Traverse City	MI	49684	231-995-5830	947-0354	647
WGUF-FM 10915 K-Nine Dr *Web:* www.wguf989.com	Bonita Springs	FL	34135	239-495-8383		647
WGVU Public Media 301 Fulton St W *Web:* www.wgvu.org	Grand Rapids	MI	49504	616-331-6666		647
WGWE-FM 215 Broad St *Web:* www.wgwefm.com	Salamanca	NY	14779	716-945-5801	945-5752	647
WH Bagshaw Company Inc 1 Pine St Ext *TF:* 800-343-7467 ■ *Web:* www.whbagshaw.com	Nashua	NH	03060	603-883-7758	882-2651	386
WH Christian & Sons Inc 22 - 28 Franklin St *Web:* www.whchristian.com	Brooklyn	NY	11222	718-389-7000	389-9644	442
WH Riley & Son Inc 35 Chestnut St PO Box 910 *Web:* whriley.com	North Attleboro	MA	02761	508-699-4651	699-7712	316
WHAJ 900 Bluefield Ave *Web:* www.j104radio.com	Bluefield	WV	24701	304-327-7114		647
Whale Museum, The 62 First St *Web:* whalemuseum.org	Friday Harbor	WA	98250	360-378-4710		522
Whaleback Shell Midden State Historic Site 535 Main St *Web:* www.maine.gov	Damariscotta	ME	04543	207-563-1393		565
Whalen Co, The PO Box 1390 *Web:* whalencompany.com	Easton	MD	21601	410-822-9200	822-8926	14
Whalen Furniture Manufacturing Inc 1578 Air Wing Rd *Web:* www.whalenfurniture.com	San Diego	CA	92154	619-423-9948		321
Whalen's Grindstone Shores Inc 3373 Pointe Aux Barques Rd *Web:* whalensgrindstoneshores.com	Port Austin	MI	48467	989-738-7664		377
Whaley Childrens Ctr 1201 N Grand Traverse St *Web:* www.whaleychildren.org	Flint	MI	48503	810-234-3603		772
Whaley House Museum 2476 San Diego Ave *Web:* whaleyhouse.org	San Diego	CA	92110	619-297-7511	291-3576	520
Whaling Station Prime Steaks & Seafood 763 Wave St *Web:* thewhalingstation.com	Monterey	CA	93940	831-373-3778	373-2460	671
Whalley Computer Associates Inc 1 Whalley Way *TF:* 877-569-4200 ■ *Web:* www.wca.com	Southwick	MA	01077	413-569-4200	569-4377	174
Whallon Machinery Inc 205 N Chicago St *Web:* www.whallon.com	Royal Center	IN	46978	574-643-9561	643-9218	547
WhamTech Inc 12001 N Central Expy Ste 300 *Web:* www.whamtech.com	Dallas	TX	75243	972-991-5700		387
WHAM-TV Ch 13 (ABC) 4225 W Henrietta Rd *TF:* 800-322-3632 ■ *Web:* www.13wham.com	Rochester	NY	14623	585-334-8700	334-8719	741-111
Wharf, The 6852 Derry St *Web:* www.thewharfbarandgrill.com	Harrisburg	PA	17111	717-564-9920		671
Wharf, The 119 King St *Web:* www.wharfrestaurant.com	Alexandria	VA	22314	703-836-2836	836-2830	671
Wharfedale Technologies Inc 2850 Brunswick Pk *TF:* 888-533-3113 ■ *Web:* wftcloud.com	Lawrenceville	NJ	08648	609-882-8826		226
Wharton B. Allen Agency Inc 348 Main St *Web:* whartonballen.com	Farmingdale	NY	11735	516-249-6660		390
Wharton Brook State Park c/o Sleeping Giant State Pk 200 Mt Carmel Ave *Web:* portal.ct.gov	Hamden	CT	06518	203-287-5658		565
Wharton Cadillac 1225 7th St *Web:* www.whartoncadillac.com	Parkersburg	WV	26102	304-397-5187		57
Wharton Center for the Performing Arts Michigan State University *TF:* 800-942-7866 ■ *Web:* www.whartoncenter.com	East Lansing	MI	48824	517-432-2000	353-5329	572
Wharton County 315 E Elm St *Web:* www.co.wharton.tx.us	Wharton	TX	77488	979-532-2381	532-8426	338
Wharton County Electric Co-opeartive Inc (WCEC) 1815 E Jackson St *TF:* 800-460-6271 ■ *Web:* www.mywcec.coop	El Campo	TX	77437	979-543-6271		245
Wharton County Junior College 911 Boling Hwy *TF:* 800-561-9252 ■ *Web:* www.wcjc.edu	Wharton	TX	77488	979-532-4560	532-6494	162
Wharton County Library 1920 N Fulton St *TF:* 800-244-5492 ■ *Web:* www.whartonco.lib.tx.us	Wharton	TX	77488	979-532-8080	532-2792	434-3
Wharton County Radio Inc PO Box 390 *Web:* www.kulpradio.com	El Campo	TX	77437	979-543-3303		645-141
Wharton Equity Partners LLC 505 Park Ave 18th Fl *Web:* whartonequity.com	New York	NY	10022	212-570-5959		528
Wharton Group 101 S Livingston Ave *TF:* 800-521-2725 ■ *Web:* www.whartoninsurance.com	Livingston	NJ	07039	973-992-5775	992-6660	390
Wharton Hardware & Supply 7724 N Crescent Blvd *Web:* www.whartonhardware.com	Pennsauken Township	NJ	08110	856-662-6935		350
Wharton Independent School District 2100 N Fulton St *TF:* 800-818-3453 ■ *Web:* www.whartonisd.net	Wharton	TX	77488	979-532-3612	532-6228	685
Wharton Levin Ehrmantraut & Klein, Attorneys at Law 104 W St *Web:* www.wlekn.com	Annapolis	MD	21404	410-263-5900	280-2230	428
Wharton-Smith Inc 750 Monroe Rd *Web:* www.whartonsmith.com	Sanford	FL	32771	407-321-8410	321-4368	188-10
WHAS-AM 840 (N/T) 4000 One Radio Dr *TF:* 800-444-8484 ■ *Web:* whas.iheart.com	Louisville	KY	40218	502-479-2222		645-89
WHAS-TV Ch 11 (ABC) 520 W Chestnut *Web:* www.whas11.com	Louisville	KY	40202	502-582-7711		741-77
Whataburger Restaurants LP 300 Concord Plz PO Box 791990 *Web:* www.whataburger.com	San Antonio	TX	78216	210-476-6000		670
Whatcom Community College 237 W Kellogg Rd *Web:* whatcom.edu	Bellingham	WA	98226	360-383-3000		162
Whatcom County 311 Grand Ave *Web:* www.co.whatcom.wa.us	Bellingham	WA	98225	360-778-5000	778-5401	338
Whatcom Hospice Foundation 2901 Squalicum Pkwy Ste 11 *Web:* whatcomhospice.org	Bellingham	WA	98225	360-733-1231	788-6858	371
Whatcom Museum Publications 121 Prospect St *Web:* www.whatcommuseum.org	Bellingham	WA	98225	360-778-8960	778-8931	637-2
Whatever It Takes Transmission Parts Inc 4282 E Blue Lick Rd *TF:* 800-940-0197 ■ *Web:* www.wittrans.com	Louisville	KY	40229	502-955-6035		57
WhatIfSportscom Inc PO Box 43494 *Web:* www.whatifsports.com	Cincinnati	OH	45242	513-333-0313		177
WHA-TV Ch 21 (PBS) 821 University Ave *Web:* pbswisconsin.org	Madison	WI	53706	608-263-2121		741-80
Whayne Supply Co 1400 Cecil Ave *TF:* 800-494-2963 ■ *Web:* www.whayne.com	Louisville	KY	40211	502-774-4441		358
WHBL-AM 2100 Washington Ave *Web:* www.whbl.com	Sheboygan	WI	53081	920-458-2107	458-9775	647
WHBM (White House/Black Market) 11215 Metro Pkwy *TF:* 888-550-5559 ■ *Web:* whitehouseblackmarket.com	Fort Myers	FL	33966	239-277-6200		157-6
WHBQ-TV Ch 13 (Fox) 485 S Highland St *Web:* fox13newsapp.com	Memphis	TN	38111	901-320-1313		741-81
WHBR-FM 5 Rosemar Cir *Web:* www.1031thebear.net	Parkersburg	WV	26104	304-485-4565	424-6955	647
WHC (Wildlife Habitat Council) 8737 Colesville Rd Ste 800 *Web:* www.wildlifehc.org	Silver Spring	MD	20910	301-588-8994		48-13
WHCC-FM 105.1 (Ctry) 304 State Rd 446 *Web:* whcc105.com	Bloomington	IN	47401	812-336-8000	336-7000	645
WHCF-FM 88.5 (Rel) PO Box 5000 *TF:* 800-947-2577 ■ *Web:* www.whcffm.com	Bangor	ME	04402	207-947-2751	947-0010	645-16
WHDH TV 7NEWS 7 Bulfinch Pl *TF:* 800-280-8477 ■ *Web:* whdh.com	Boston	MA	02114	855-247-4265		741-18
WHDQ-FM 106 N Main *TF:* 800-639-1061 ■ *Web:* www.theqrocks.com	West Lebanon	NH	03784	603-298-0332		647
Wheal-Grace Corp 300 Ralph St *Web:* www.wheal-grace.com	Belleville	NJ	07109	973-450-8100	450-5394	174
Wheat Belt Public Power District 11306 Rd 32 PO Box 177 *TF:* 800-261-7114 ■ *Web:* www.wheatbelt.com	Sidney	NE	69162	308-254-5871	254-2384	245
Wheat Foods Council PO Box 3669 *TF:* 800-970-2254 ■ *Web:* www.wheatfoods.org	Littleton	CO	81432	800-970-2254		49-6
Wheat Montana Farms Inc 10778 US Hwy 287 *TF:* 800-535-2798 ■ *Web:* www.wheatmontana.com	Three Forks	MT	59752	406-285-3614	285-3749	297-1
Wheat Quality Council 1814 Abbey Rd *Web:* www.wheatqualitycouncil.org	Pierre	SD	57501	605-224-5187	224-0517	48-2
Wheatbelt Inc 300 Industrial Rd *Web:* www.wheatbeltusa.com	Hillsboro	KS	67063	620-947-2323		234
Wheatherstone Press PO Box 257 *Web:* www.wheatherstonepress.com	Portland	OR	97207	503-244-8929	244-9795	637-2
Wheatland Electric Co-opeartive Inc 101 S Main St *TF:* 800-762-0436 ■ *Web:* www.weci.net	Scott City	KS	67871	620-872-5885	872-7170	245
Wheatland Manor Inc 316 E Lincolnway St *Web:* www.wheatmanor.com	Wheatland	IA	52777	563-374-1295		450
Wheatland Rural Electric Assn 2154 S St PO Box 1209 *TF:* 800-344-3351 ■ *Web:* www.wheatlandrea.com	Wheatland	WY	82201	307-322-2125	322-5340	245
Wheatland Tube Co 700 S Dock St *TF:* 800-257-8182 ■ *Web:* www.wheatland.com	Sharon	PA	16146	800-257-8182		490
Wheatleigh Hawthorne Rd *Web:* www.wheatleigh.com	Lenox	MA	01240	413-637-0610	637-4507	379
Wheatmark Inc 2030 E Speedway Blvd Ste 106 *TF:* 888-934-0888 ■ *Web:* www.wheatmark.com	Tucson	AZ	85719	520-798-0888	798-3394	637-2
Wheaton & Sprague Engineering Inc 1151 Campus Dr Ste 100 *Web:* wheatonsprague.com	Stow	OH	44224	330-923-5560		261
Wheaton Academy 900 Prince Crossing Rd *Web:* www.wheatonacademy.org	West Chicago	IL	60185	630-562-7500		685
Wheaton Chamber of Commerce 108 E Wesley St *Web:* www.wheatonchamber.com	Wheaton	IL	60187	630-668-6464	668-2744	139
Wheaton College 26 E Main St *TF:* 800-394-6003 ■ *Web:* wheatoncollege.edu	Norton	MA	02766	508-286-8200	286-8271	166

Name / Address	City	State	Zip	Phone	Fax	Class
Wheaton College 501 College Ave TF: 800-222-2419 ■ Web: www.wheaton.edu	Wheaton	IL	60187	630-752-5000	752-5285	166
Wheaton Franciscan - Saint Joseph 5000 W Chambers St TF: 800-914-6601 ■ Web: www.mywheaton.org	Milwaukee	WI	53210	414-447-2000		374-3
Wheaton Park District 102 E Wesley St Web: wheatonparkdistrict.com	Wheaton	IL	60187	630-665-4710		31
Wheaton Partners LLC 1901 N Roselle Rd Ste 640 Web: www.codemap.com	Schaumburg	IL	60195	847-381-5465		463
Wheaton Public Library 225 N Cross St Web: www.wheaton.lib.il.us	Wheaton	IL	60187	630-668-1374	668-8950	434-3
Wheaton Van Lines Inc 8010 Castleton Rd TF: 800-932-7799 ■ Web: www.wheatonworldwide.com	Indianapolis	IN	46250	800-248-7962		519
Wheaton-Kensington Chamber of Commerce 2401 Blueridge Ave Ste 101 Web: wkchamber.org	Wheaton	MD	20902	301-949-0080	949-0081	139
Wheatstone Corp 600 Industrial Dr Web: www.wheatstone.com	New Bern	NC	28562	252-638-7000		246
WHEC-TV Ch 10 (NBC) 191 E Ave Web: www.whec.com	Rochester	NY	14604	585-546-5670	546-5688	741-111
Wheel & Sprocket Inc 5722 S 108th St TF: 866-995-9918 ■ Web: www.wheelandsprocket.com	Hales Corners	WI	53130	414-529-6600		711
Wheelabrator Technologies Inc 100 Arboretum Dr Ste 310 Web: www.wtienergy.com	Newington	NH	03801	603-929-3000		804
Wheeland Lumber Company Inc 3558 Williamson Trl Web: www.wheelandlumber.com	Liberty	PA	16930	570-324-6042		683
Wheeled Coach Industries Inc 2737 Forsyth Rd TF: 800-932-7077 ■ Web: www.wheeledcoach.com	Winter Park	FL	32792	407-677-7777	679-1337	516
Wheeler Construction Inc 3255 E Gulf to Lake Hwy Web: citrusbuilder.com	Inverness	FL	34453	352-726-0973	637-4959	187
Wheeler County PO Box 654 Web: www.wheelercounty.org	Alamo	GA	30411	912-568-7808		338
Wheeler County 701 Adams St PO Box 327 Web: www.wheelercountyoregon.com	Fossil	OR	97830	541-763-2374	763-2026	338
Wheeler County PO Box 465 Web: www.co.wheeler.tx.us	Wheeler	TX	79096	806-826-5544	826-3282	338
Wheeler Historic Farm 6351 S 900 E Web: slco.org	Murray	UT	84121	385-468-1755	468-1754	520
Wheeler House 510 Gilmer Ferry Rd Web: www.thewheelerhouse.net	Ball Ground	GA	30107	770-402-1686		50-3
Wheeler Industries 7261 Investment Dr Web: www.wheelerfluidfilmbearings.com	North Charleston	SC	29418	843-552-1251	552-4790	620
Wheeler Industries Inc 1118 N Howe Rd Web: www.wheelerindustries.net	Spokane Valley	WA	99212	509-534-4556	534-4836	454
Wheeler Lumber LLC 9330 James Ave S TF: 800-328-3986 ■ Web: www.wheeler-con.com	Bloomington	MN	55431	952-929-7854		191-3
Wheeler Manufacturing Company Inc 107 Main Ave PO Box 629 *Fax Area Code: 605 ■ TF: 800-843-1937 ■ Web: www.wheelerjewelry.com	Lemmon	SD	57638	800-843-1937	374-3655*	409
Wheeler Opera House 320 E Hyman Ave TF: 866-449-0464 ■ Web: www.wheeleroperahouse.com	Aspen	CO	81611	970-920-5770		572
Wheeler, Van Sickle & Anderson SC 44 E Mifflin St Ste 1000 Web: wheelerlaw.com	Madison	WI	53703	608-255-7277		428
Wheeler-Rex Inc 3744 Jefferson Rd PO Box 688 TF: 800-321-7950 ■ Web: www.wheelerrex.com	Ashtabula	OH	44005	440-998-2788	992-2925	758
Wheelhouse Securities Corp 8235 Forsyth Blvd Ste 200 Web: wheelhousesecurities.com	Saint Louis	MO	63105	314-881-1850		690
Wheeling & Lake Erie Railway Co 100 E First St TF: 800-837-5622 ■ Web: www.wlerwy.com	Brewster	OH	44613	330-767-3401		651
Wheeling Area Chamber of Commerce 1310 Market St Web: www.wheelingchamber.com	Wheeling	WV	26003	304-233-2575	233-1320	139
Wheeling City Council Chambers 1500 Chapline St Web: www.wheelingwv.gov	Wheeling	WV	26003	304-234-3694		337
Wheeling Convention & Visitors Bureau 1401 Main St TF: 800-828-3097 ■ Web: www.wheelingcvb.com	Wheeling	WV	26003	304-233-7709		206
Wheeling Hospital 1 Medical Pk TF: 800-626-0023 ■ Web: wheelinghospital.org	Wheeling	WV	26003	304-243-3000		374-3
Wheeling Island Gaming Inc 1 S St1 St TF: 877-946-4373 ■ Web: www.wheelingisland.com	Wheeling	WV	26003	304-232-5050		133
Wheeling Jesuit University 316 Washington Ave TF: 800-624-6992 ■ Web: wheeling.edu	Wheeling	WV	26003	304-243-2000	243-2397	166
Wheeling Park District 100 Community Blvd Web: www.wheelingparkdistrict.com	Wheeling	IL	60090	847-465-3333		31
Wheeling Symphony Orchestra 1025 Main St Ste 811 Web: www.wheelingsymphony.com	Wheeling	WV	26003	304-232-6191		573-3
Wheeling Truck Center 23rd Market St Web: www.wheelingtruck.com	Wheeling	WV	26003	304-232-1440	232-1444	57
Wheeling/Prospect Heights Area Chamber of Commerce & Industry 2 Community Blvd Ste 203 Web: www.wphchamber.com	Wheeling	IL	60090	847-541-0170	541-0296	139
Wheeling-Nippon Steel Inc 400 Penn St PO Box 635 Web: www.wheeling-nipponsteel.com	Follansbee	WV	26037	304-527-2800	527-0985	307
Wheelock College 180 Riverway TF: 800-734-5212 ■ Web: www.wheelock.edu	Boston	MA	02215	617-879-2206	879-2449	166
Wheels Etc 17521 Mesa St *Fax Area Code: 760 ■ Web: www.wheels-etc.com	Hesperia	CA	92345	909-350-8200	949-1000*	755
Wheels Inc 666 Garland Pl Web: www.wheels.com	Des Plaines	IL	60016	847-699-7000		289
Wheelwright Lumber Co 3127 S Midland Dr Web: www.wheelwrightlumberco.com	Ogden	UT	84401	801-627-0850		364
Wheelwright Museum of the American Indian 704 Camino Lejo TF: 800-607-4636 ■ Web: wheelwright.org	Santa Fe	NM	87505	505-982-4636	989-7386	520
Whelan Group Inc, The 315 W 36th St Web: whelangroup.com	New York	NY	10018	212-727-7332		463
Whelan Machine & Tool 134 Rochester Dr Web: www.whelanmachine.com	Louisville	KY	40214	502-364-6370	364-6375	454
Whelden Memorial Library 2401 Meetinghouse Way PO Box 147 Web: www.wheldenlibrary.org	West Barnstable	MA	02668	508-362-2262	362-1344	434-3
Whelen Engineering Company Inc 51 Winthrop Rd & Rt 145 Web: www.whelen.com	Chester	CT	06412	860-526-9504	526-4078	700
Where Chicago Magazine 1165 N Clark St Ste 302 TF: 800-680-4035 ■ Web: www.wheretraveler.com	Chicago	IL	60610	312-642-1896		457-22
Where Pigs Fly 617 E Loockerman St Web: wherepigsflyrestaurant.com	Dover	DE	19901	302-678-0586	735-7675	671
Wherry Associates Inc 30200 Detroit Rd Web: www.wherryassoc.com	Cleveland	OH	44145	440-899-0010	892-1404	47
Whetstone Group 6060 Nancy Ridge Rd Ste 100 TF: 800-235-2816 ■ Web: www.whetstonegroup.com	San Diego	CA	92121	858-627-0726		196
Whetstone Gulf State Park 6065 W Rd Web: parks.ny.gov	Lowville	NY	13367	315-376-6630		565
Whetstone Perkins & Fulda LLC 601 Devine St Web: attorneyssc.com	Columbia	SC	29201	803-799-9400	799-2017	41
Whetstone Valley Electric Co-op 1101 E Fourth Ave TF: 800-568-6631 ■ Web: whetstone.coop	Milbank	SD	57252	605-432-5331		245
WHF (Wyoming Honor Farm) 40 Honor Farm Rd Web: corrections.wyo.gov	Riverton	WY	82501	307-856-9578	856-2505	213
WHFG-FM PO Box 107 TF: 800-617-9673 ■ Web: www.whfgradio.com	Keene	TX	76059	800-617-9673		647
WHFR-FM 5101 Evergreen Rd TF: 800-585-9676 ■ Web: www.whfr.fm	Dearborn	MI	48128	313-845-9676		647
WHGL-FM PO Box 100 TF: 800-326-9445 ■ Web: www.wiggle100.com	Troy	PA	16947	570-297-0100		647
WHHM (Woods Hole Historical Museum) 579 Woods Hole Rd Web: www.woodsholemuseum.org	Woods Hole	MA	02543	508-548-7270		520
WHHR-FM PO Box J TF: 888-533-3551 ■ Web: www.freedomradiofm.com	Twin Falls	ID	83303	888-533-3551		647
WHI (Wholesale Hardwood Interiors Inc) 1030 Campbellsville By-Pass TF: 800-982-7404 ■ Web: www.wholesalehardwoodint.com	Campbellsville	KY	42719	270-789-1323	789-2321	191-3
Whibco Inc 87 E Commerce St Web: www.whibco.com	Bridgeton	NJ	08302	856-455-9200		503-4
WHIL-FM 91.3 (NPR) 920 Paul W Bryant Dr Bryant Denny Stadium Rm N460 Web: apr.org	Tuscaloosa	AL	35487	205-348-6644		645-100
Whimsy Inc 1901 S Busse Rd Web: www.whimsytrucking.com	Mount Prospect	IL	60056	847-690-1246	690-1253	194
Whip Mix Corp 361 Farmington Ave PO Box 17183 Web: whipmix.com	Louisville	KY	40217	502-637-1451		228
Whipper Snapper's 2421 W Hwy 76 Web: www.bransonsbestrestaurant.com	Branson	MO	65616	417-334-0754		671
Whipsaw Inc 434 S First St Web: www.whipsaw.com	San Jose	CA	95113	408-297-9771		261
Whirl Air Flow Corp 20055 177th St TF: 800-373-3461 ■ Web: www.whirlair.com	Big Lake	MN	55309	763-262-1200	262-1212	207
Whirley Industries Inc 618 Fourth Ave Web: www.whirleydrinkworks.com	Warren	PA	16365	814-723-7600		596
Whirlpool Canada 200-6750 Century Ave TF: 800-807-6777 ■ Web: www.whirlpool.ca	Mississauga	ON	L5N0B7	905-821-6400	821-7871	38
Whirlpool Corp 2000 N M-63 NYSE: WHR ■ TF: 800-253-1301 ■ Web: www.whirlpoolcorp.com	Benton Harbor	MI	49022	269-923-5000		36
Whirltronics Inc 208 Centennial Dr Web: www.whirltronics.com	Buffalo	MN	55313	763-682-1716	682-2197	429
Whirlwind Music Distributors Inc 99 Ling Rd Web: whirlwindusa.com	Rochester	NY	14612	585-663-8820		52
Whirlwind Steel 8234 Hansen Rd *Fax Area Code: 832 ■ TF: 800-324-9992 ■ Web: www.whirlwindsteel.com	Houston	TX	77075	713-946-7140	553-4992*	105
Whiskeytown-Shasta-Trinity National Recreation Area PO Box 188 Web: www.nps.gov	Whiskeytown	CA	96095	530-246-1225	246-5154	564
Whistler Blackcomb Mountain Ski Resort 4545 Blackcomb Way TF: 800-766-0449 ■ Web: www.whistlerblackcomb.com	Whistler	BC	V0N1B4	604-932-3434	938-7527	669
Whistler Group Inc 1716 SW Commerce Dr Ste 8 TF: 800-531-0004 ■ Web: whistlergroup.com	Bentonville	AR	72712	479-273-6012		529
Whit Press 4701 SW Admiral Way Ste 125 Web: www.whitpress.org	Seattle	WA	98116	206-295-1670		637-2
Whitacre Greer Fireproofing Inc 1400 S Mahoning Ave TF: 800-947-2837 ■ Web: wgpaver.com	Alliance	OH	44601	330-823-1610	823-5502	150
Whitaker Buick Co 131 19th St SW TF: 877-324-8885 ■ Web: www.whitakerauto.com	Forest Lake	MN	55025	877-324-8885		57
Whitaker Center for Science & Arts 225 Market St Web: www.whitakercenter.org	Harrisburg	PA	17101	717-214-2787		520
Whitaker House 1030 Hunt Valley Cir TF: 877-793-9800 ■ Web: www.whitakerhouse.com	New Kensington	PA	15068	724-334-7000	334-1200	96
Whitaker Oil Co 1557 Marietta Rd NW TF: 888-895-3506 ■ Web: www.whitakeroil.com	Atlanta	GA	30318	404-355-8220		146

	Phone	Fax	Class
Whitby Chamber of Commerce 128 Brock St S .... Whitby ON L1N4J8 *Web:* www.whitbychamber.org	905-668-4506	668-1894	137
Whitco Supply LLC 200 N Morgan Ave.......... Broussard LA 70518 *Web:* www.whitcosupply.com	337-837-2440		790
Whitcraft LLC 76 County Rd .... Eastford CT 06242 *Web:* www.whitcraftgroup.com	860-974-0786		21
White & Steele PC 600 17th St Ste 600 N .... Denver CO 80202 *TF:* 800-333-7173 ■ *Web:* whiteandsteele.com	303-296-2828	296-3131	41
White Allen Chevrolet Inc 442 N Main St .... Dayton OH 45405 *Web:* www.whiteallen.com	937-222-3701		57
White Aluminum Products LLC 2101 US Hwy 441.......... Leesburg FL 34748 *TF:* 888-474-5884 ■ *Web:* www.whitealuminum.com	800-292-6606		492
White Bear Lake Area Chamber of Commerce 4751 Hwy 61 .... White Bear Lake MN 55110 *Web:* www.whitebearchamber.com	651-429-8593	429-8592	139
White Bison Inc 5585 Erindale Dr Ste 203 .... Colorado Springs CO 80918 *TF:* 877-871-1495 ■ *Web:* www.whitebison.org	719-548-1000	548-9407	48-21
White Bros Trucking Co 4N793 School Rd .... Wasco IL 60183 *TF:* 800-323-4762 ■ *Web:* whitebrotherstrucking.com	630-584-3810		780
White Buffalo Club 160 W Gill Ave .... Jackson WY 83001 *TF:* 888-256-8182 ■ *Web:* www.whitebuffaloclub.com	307-734-4900	734-1998	428
White Cap Industries Inc 1723 S Ritchie St .... Santa Ana CA 92705 *TF:* 800-944-8322 ■ *Web:* www.whitecap.com	714-258-3300	258-3289	191-3
White Chapel Church of God Inc 1730 S Ridgewood Ave.......... South Daytona FL 32119 *Web:* wcaeagles.org	386-767-5451	760-6834	48-20
White Church Christian Church 2200 N 85th St.......... Kansas City KS 66109 *Web:* www.wccckc.com	913-299-4056		50-1
White Clay Creek Preserve 404 Sharpless Rd.......... Landenberg PA 19350 *Web:* www.dcnr.pa.gov	610-274-2900		565
White Clay Creek State Park 89 Kings Hwy.......... Dover DE 19901 *Web:* www.destateparks.com	302-368-6900		565
White Co 1600 S Brentwood Blvd Ste 770.......... Saint Louis MO 63144 *Web:* www.white-co.com	314-961-5903		655
White Coffee Corp 18-35 Steinway Pl .... Astoria NY 11105 *TF:* 800-221-0140 ■ *Web:* www.whitecoffee.com	718-204-7900		296-7
White Construction Inc 3900 E White Ave.......... Clinton IN 47842 **Fax Area Code: 765* ■ *TF:* 800-355-9401 ■ *Web:* whiteconstruction.com	800-355-9401	832-2075*	188
White Conveyors Inc 10 Boright Ave .... Kenilworth NJ 07033 *TF:* 800-524-0273 ■ *Web:* www.white-conveyors.com	908-686-5700		207
White County 301 E Main St PO Box 339 .... Carmi IL 62821 *Web:* www.whitecounty-il.gov	618-382-7211	382-2322	338
White County 1235 Helen Hwy .... Cleveland GA 30528 *Web:* www.whitecounty.net	706-865-2235	865-1324	338
White County 110 N Main St.......... Monticello IN 47960 *Web:* whitecountyin.us	574-583-7032	583-1532	338
White County 1927 Beebe-Capps Expy.......... Searcy AR 72143 *Web:* www.whitecountyar.org	501-279-6200	279-6233	338
White County 16 W Bockman Way .... Sparta TN 38583 *Web:* spartatnchamber.com	931-836-3552		338
White County Chamber of Commerce 122 N Main St .... Cleveland GA 30528 *TF:* 800-392-8279 ■ *Web:* www.whitecountychamber.org	706-865-5356	865-0758	139
White County Public Library 113 E Pleasure St.......... Searcy AR 72143 *Web:* whitecountylibraries.org	501-268-2449		434-3
White Dog Cafe 3420 Sansom St .... Philadelphia PA 19104 *Web:* www.whitedog.com	215-386-9224		671
White Dove Ltd 3201 Harvard Ave.......... Cleveland OH 44105 *Web:* www.whitedoveusa.com	216-341-0200		471
White Eagle Wedding Service 3233 N Narragansett.......... Chicago IL 60634 *Web:* www.whiteeaglepl.com	773-777-5522	777-4015	293
White Earth Tribal & Community College 2250 College Rd PO Box 478.......... Mahnomen MN 56557 *Web:* www.wetcc.edu	218-935-0417	936-5814	165
White Electrical Construction Co 5504 Caterpillar Dr.......... Atlanta GA 30318 *TF:* 888-519-4483 ■ *Web:* www.white-electrical.com	404-351-5740	355-5823	189-4
White Elephant Inn & Cottages 50 Easton St.......... Nantucket MA 02554 *TF:* 800-475-2637 ■ *Web:* www.whiteelephantnantucket.com	508-228-2500	325-1195	379
White Elm Capital LLC 537 Steamboat Rd Ste 300.......... Greenwich CT 06830 *Web:* www.whiteelmcapital.com	203-742-6000		528
White Flint Pharmacy Inc 11125 Rockville Pk Ste 102 .... Rockville MD 20852 *Web:* whiteflintpharmacy.com	301-881-3828		237
White Flower Farm Inc 30 Irene St .... Torrington CT 06790 *TF:* 800-411-6159 ■ *Web:* www.whiteflowerfarm.com	860-496-9624	496-1418	323
White Glove Placement Inc 85 Bartlett St.......... Brooklyn NY 11206 *TF:* 866-387-8100 ■ *Web:* www.whiteglovecare.com	718-387-8181		721
White Hall State Historic Site 500 White Hall Shrine Rd.......... Richmond KY 40475 *Web:* parks.ky.gov	859-623-9178		565
White Hat Management LLC 121 S Main St Ste 200.......... Akron OH 44308 *Web:* whitehatmgmt.com	330-535-6868		107
White Horse Tavern 26 Marlborough St.......... Newport RI 02840 *Web:* www.whitehorsenewport.com	401-849-3600		671
White Horse Village 535 Gradyville Rd.......... Newtown Square PA 19073 *Web:* www.whitehorsevillage.org	610-558-5000	558-5001	672
White House Press Secretary 1600 Pennsylvania Ave NW .... Washington DC 20500 *Web:* www.whitehouse.gov	202-456-1111		340
White House/Black Market (WHBM) 11215 Metro Pkwy .... Fort Myers FL 33966 *TF:* 888-550-5559 ■ *Web:* whitehouseblackmarket.com	239-277-6200		157-6
White Instruments 8322 Sharl Cove .... Austin TX 78737 *Web:* www.whiteinstruments.com	512-389-5358		52
White Knight Engineered Products 9525 Monroe Rd Ste 100 .... Charlotte NC 28270 *TF:* 888-743-4700 ■ *Web:* www.wkep.com	704-542-6876		576
White Lake Beacon 432 Spring St.......... Whitehall MI 49461 *Web:* www.shorelinemedia.net	231-894-5356	894-2174	532-2
White Lake State Park 94 State Park Rd.......... Tamworth NH 03886 *Web:* www.nhstateparks.org	603-323-7350		565
White Lion Pub 6927 S Canton Ave .... Tulsa OK 74136 *Web:* kelv.net	918-491-6533	582-3931	671
White Lodging Services Inc 701 E 83rd Ave.......... Merrillville IN 46410 *Web:* www.whitelodging.com	219-472-2900		379
White Market, The 128 Main St.......... Lyndonville VT 05851 *Web:* www.whitesmarket.com	802-626-5339		345
White Marsh Mall 8200 Perry Hall Blvd.......... Baltimore MD 21236 *Web:* www.whitemarshmall.com	410-931-7100		460
White Mountain Adventures 131 Eagle Crescent PO Box 4259.......... Banff AB T1L1A6 *TF:* 800-408-0005 ■ *Web:* www.whitemountainadventures.com	403-760-4403		760
White Mountain Cable Construction LLC 2113 Dover Rd .... Epsom NH 03234 *Web:* www.wmc1.com	603-736-4766		116
White Mountain Footwear Group, The 20 Whitcher St .... Lisbon NH 03585 *Web:* www.whitemountainshoes.com	603-838-6323		301
White Mountain Hotel & Resort 87 Fairway Dr PO Box 1828 .... North Conway NH 03860 *TF:* 800-533-6301 ■ *Web:* www.whitemountainhotel.com	603-356-7100		669
White Mountain Imaging 1617 Battle St.......... Webster NH 03303 *Web:* www.wmi-t2.com	603-648-2197		475
White Mountain School 371 W Farm Rd.......... Bethlehem NH 03574 *Web:* www.whitemountain.org	603-444-2928		622
White Mountains Community College (WMCC) 2020 Riverside Dr.......... Berlin NH 03570 *TF:* 800-445-4525 ■ *Web:* www.wmcc.edu	603-752-1113	752-6335	162
White Mountains Insurance Group Ltd 80 S Main St.......... Hanover NH 03755 *NYSE: WTM* ■ *TF:* 866-295-3762 ■ *Web:* www.whitemountains.com	603-640-2200	643-4592	360-4
White Oak Lake State Park 563 Hwy 387 .... Bluff City AR 71722 *Web:* www.arkansasstateparks.com	870-685-2748		565
White Oak Manor Inc 130 E Main St PO Box 3347.......... Spartanburg SC 29304 *Web:* whiteoakmanor.com	864-582-7503		672
White Oak Mills Inc 419 W High St .... Elizabethtown PA 17022 *TF:* 800-468-5524 ■ *Web:* www.whiteoakmills.com	717-367-1525	367-4845	447
White Oak Operating Company LLC 16945 Northchase Dr Ste 1700.......... Houston TX 77060 *Web:* www.whiteoakenergy.com	281-876-2025	876-2265	539
White Oak Partners LLC 5150 E Dublin Granville Rd Ste One.......... Westerville OH 43081 *Web:* www.whiteoakpartners.com	614-855-1155		528
White Oaks Wealth Advisors Inc 80 S Eighth St IDS Ctr Ste 1725.......... Minneapolis MN 55402 *TF:* 800-596-3579 ■ *Web:* www.whiteoakswealth.com	612-455-6900		194
White Paper Co 9990 River Way.......... Delta BC V4G1M9 *TF:* 888-840-7300 ■ *Web:* www.whitepaper.com	604-951-3900	951-3944	553
White Pigeon Mutual Insurance Assn 105 W Fourth St.......... Wilton IA 52778 *Web:* wpigeon.com	563-732-2072		390
White Pine County 801 Clark St.......... Ely NV 89301 *Web:* www.whitepinecounty.net	775-293-6509	289-2544	338
White Pine Press PO Box 236 .... Buffalo NY 14201 *Web:* www.whitepine.org	716-627-4665		637-9
White Pines Forest State Park 6712 W Pines Rd .... Mount Morris IL 61054 *Web:* www2.illinois.gov	815-946-3717		565
White Plains Honda 344 Central Ave .... White Plains NY 10606 *TF:* 888-683-1716 ■ *Web:* www.whiteplainshonda.com	888-671-0343		57
White Plains Hospital Ctr 41 E Post Rd.......... White Plains NY 10601 *Web:* www.wphospital.org	914-681-0600		374-3
White Planning Group 602 Virginia St E.......... Charleston WV 25301 *Web:* www.whiteplanninggroup.com	304-346-3295		390
White Radio LP 5228 Everest Dr.......... Mississauga ON L4W2R4	905-632-6894		246
White Ridgely Associates 26 River Bend Dr .... Okatie SC 29909 *Web:* www.whiteridgely.com	443-829-9014		631
White River Broadcasting Station 3212 Washington St.......... Columbus IN 47203 *Web:* wkkg.com	812-372-4448		645
White River Credit Union 1499 Garrett St.......... Enumclaw WA 98022 *TF:* 800-704-7931 ■ *Web:* www.whiterivercu.com	360-825-4833	825-8050	219
White River Distributors Inc 720 Ramsey .... Batesville AR 72501 *TF:* 800-548-7219 ■ *Web:* www.lpgbobtails.com	870-793-2374	793-8230	482
White River Electric Assn (WREA) PO Box 958 .... Meeker CO 81641 *TF:* 800-922-1987 ■ *Web:* wrea.org	970-878-5041	878-5766	245
White River Hardwoodwoodworks Inc 1197 Happy Hollow .... Fayetteville AR 72701 *Web:* whiteriver.com	479-442-6986		499
White River Junction Veterans Affairs Medical Ctr 215 N Main St .... White River Junction VT 05009 *TF:* 866-687-8387 ■ *Web:* www.whiteriver.va.gov	802-295-9363		374-8
White River Marine Group 2500 E Kearney St .... Springfield MO 65803 *Web:* www.whiterivermg.com	417-873-5900	873-5068	90

	Phone	Fax	Class
White River Medical Ctr 1710 Harrison St .... Batesville AR 72501 *Web:* www.whiteriverhealthsystem.com	870-262-1200		374-3
White River State Park 302 W Washington St Rm E418 .... Indianapolis IN 46204 *TF:* 800-665-9056 ■ *Web:* www.in.gov	317-233-2434		565
White River Valley Electric Co-opeartive Inc 2449 State Hwy 76 E .... Branson MO 65616 *TF:* 800-879-4056 ■ *Web:* www.whiteriver.org	417-335-9335	335-9250	245
White River Valley Museum Library 918 H St SE .... Auburn WA 98002 *Web:* www.wrvmuseum.org	253-288-7433		434-3
White Rock Products Corp 141-07 20th Ave Ste 403 .... Whitestone NY 11357 *TF:* 800-969-7625 ■ *Web:* www.whiterockbeverages.com	718-746-3400	767-0413	80-2
White Rose Credit Union 3498 Industrial Dr .... York PA 17402 *TF:* 888-755-9773 ■ *Web:* whiterosecu.com	717-755-9773		219
White Rose Inc 380 Middlesex Ave .... Carteret NJ 07008 *Web:* www.whiterose.com	732-541-5555		297-8
White Sands Engineering (WSE) 2202 S 7th St Ste 120 .... Phoenix AZ 85027 *TF:* 800-586-7377 ■ *Web:* www.whitesandsengineering.com	800-586-7377		647
White Sands Federal Credit Union 2190 E Lohman Ave .... Las Cruces NM 88001 *TF:* 800-658-9933 ■ *Web:* www.wsfcu.org	575-647-4500		70
White Sands Missile Range Museum & Missile Park US Hwy 70 .... White Sands NM 88002 *Web:* www.wsmr-history.org	575-678-3358	678-2199	520
White Sands National Monument PO Box 1086 .... Holloman AFB NM 88330 *Web:* www.nps.gov	575-479-6124		564
White Sands Technology Inc 6737 Variel Ave Ste A .... Canoga Park CA 91303 *Web:* www.whitesands.com	818-702-9200		180
White Settlement Independent School District 401 S Cherry Ln .... Fort Worth TX 76108 *Web:* www.wsisd.com	817-367-1300		780
White Shield Inc 320 N 20th Ave .... Pasco WA 99301 *TF:* 888-882-1142 ■ *Web:* whiteshield.com	509-547-0100		194
White Sound Press 379 Wild Orange Dr .... New Smyrna Beach FL 32168 *Web:* www.wspress.com	386-423-7880		95
White Stallion Ranch 9251 W Twin Peaks Rd .... Tucson AZ 85743 *TF:* 888-977-2624 ■ *Web:* www.whitestallion.com	520-297-0252	744-2786	239
White Star Steel Inc 2200 Harbor Blvd .... Houston TX 77220 *Web:* www.whitestarsteel.com	713-675-6501		492
White Star Tours 26 E Lancaster Ave .... Reading PA 19607 *TF:* 800-437-2323 ■ *Web:* www.whitestartours.com	610-775-5000		760
White Swan Inn 845 Bush St .... San Francisco CA 94108 *Web:* www.whiteswaninnsf.com	415-775-1755		379
White's Bridge Tooling Inc 1395 Bowes Rd .... Lowell MI 49331 *Web:* www.wbtooling.com	616-897-4151	897-0345	386
White's Electronics Inc 1011 Pleasant Valley Rd .... Sweet Home OR 97386 *TF:* 800-547-6911 ■ *Web:* www.whiteselectronics.com	541-367-6121		472
White's Farm 6028 Holland Rd .... Brookville IN 47012 *Web:* whiteswebsite.com	765-647-5360	647-6396	446
White's Farm Supply Inc 4154 SR-31 .... Canastota NY 13032 *TF:* 800-633-4443 ■ *Web:* www.whitesfarmsupply.com	315-697-2214		358
White's Inc 4614 Navigation Blvd PO Box 2344 .... Houston TX 77011 **Fax Area Code: 888* ■ *TF:* 800-231-9559 ■ *Web:* www.whitesinc.com	713-928-2632	944-8373*	274
White's Nursery & Greenhouses Inc 3133 Old Mill Rd .... Chesapeake VA 23323 *Web:* www.whitesnursery.com	757-487-2300	487-0847	369
White'S Pharmacy of Dalton LLC 2955B Cleveland Hwy .... Dalton GA 30721	706-259-9707		237
White-Boucke Publishing Inc PO Box 1463 .... Oakhurst CA 93644 *TF:* 800-382-7922 ■ *Web:* www.white-boucke.com	559-641-5444		637-2
Whitecap Canada Inc 200 Yorkland Blvd Ste 920 .... Toronto ON M2J5C1 *TF:* 855-393-9977 ■ *Web:* www.whitecapcanada.com	855-393-9977		396
Whitecap Resources Inc 3800 525 - Eighth Ave SW .... Calgary AB T2P1G1 *TF:* 866-590-5289 ■ *Web:* www.wcap.ca	403-266-0767		536
Whitecap Venture Partners 22 St Clair Ave E Ste 1010 .... Toronto ON M4T2S3 *Web:* www.whitecapvp.com	416-324-5421	961-3232	528
Whitecourt Communications 4214 42 Ave .... Whitecourt AB T7S0A3 *Web:* www.whitecourtcommunications.ca	780-778-3778		224
Whited Ford 207 Perry Rd .... Bangor ME 04401 *Web:* whitedford.com	207-947-3673		57
Whitefab Inc 724 Ave W .... Birmingham AL 35214 *Web:* www.whitefab.com	205-791-2011		492
Whiteface Club & Resort 373 Whiteface Inn Ln .... Lake Placid NY 12946 *TF:* 800-422-6757 ■ *Web:* whitefaceclubresort.com	518-523-2551	523-4278	669
Whiteface Lodge, The 7 Whiteface Inn Ln .... Lake Placid NY 12946 *Web:* www.thewhitefacelodge.com	518-523-0500		378
Whitefield Group: Local Seo & Web Design LLC 6130 Plumas St Ste 200 .... Reno NV 89519 *Web:* whitefieldgroup.net	775-230-7095		5
Whitefish Bay Schools 5205 N Lydell Ave .... Whitefish Bay WI 53217 *Web:* www.wfbschools.com	414-963-3901		780
Whitefish Dunes State Park 3275 County Hwy WD .... Sturgeon Bay WI 54235 *Web:* dnr.wi.gov	920-823-2400	823-2640	565
Whitefish Mountain Resort 3889 Big Mountain Rd .... Whitefish MT 59937 *TF:* 800-858-3930 ■ *Web:* www.skiwhitefish.com	406-862-2900		379
Whiteford Kenworth 4625 W Western Ave .... South Bend IN 46619 *Web:* whitefordkenworth.com	574-288-2541		57
Whiteford, Taylor & Preston LLP 7 St Paul St .... Baltimore MD 21202 *Web:* www.wtplaw.com	410-347-8700		428
Whitehall Associates Inc 416 Southview Ave .... Silver Spring MD 20905 *Web:* www.mde.maryland.gov	301-879-1421		104
Whitehall Community Park 402 N Hamilton Rd .... Whitehall OH 43213 *Web:* www.whitehall-oh.us	614-863-0121		564
Whitehall Foundation Inc 125 Worth Ave .... Palm Beach Gardens FL 33480 *Web:* www.whitehall.org	561-655-4474	655-1296	305
Whitehall Hotel 105 E Delaware Pl .... Chicago IL 60611 *TF:* 800-948-4255 ■ *Web:* www.thewhitehallhotel.com	312-944-6300	944-8552	379
Whitehall Management Consultants Inc 9815 N 95th St .... Scottsdale AZ 85258 *Web:* www.whitehallmgt.com	480-860-5700		449
Whitehall Printing Co 4244 Corporate Sq .... Naples FL 34104 **Fax Area Code: 239* ■ *TF:* 800-321-9290 ■ *Web:* www.whitehallprinting.com	800-321-9290	643-6439*	626
Whitehorse Chamber of Commerce 302 Steele St Ste 101 .... Whitehorse YT Y1A2C5 *Web:* www.whitehorsechamber.ca	867-667-7545	667-4507	137
Whitehouse Sheldon (Sen D - RI) 530 Hart Senate Office Bldg .... Washington DC 20510 *Web:* www.whitehouse.senate.gov	202-224-2921	228-6362	342-2
Whitelaw Hotel 808 Collins Ave .... Miami Beach FL 33139 *Web:* www.whitelawhotel.com	305-398-7000		379
WhiteLight Group LLC N14 W24200 Tower Pl Ste 203 .... Waukesha WI 53188 *Web:* whitelightgrp.com	630-571-6705		179
Whiteman & Company PA 1840 4th St N Ste 200 .... Saint Petersburg FL 33704 *Web:* www.whitemanandcompany.com	727-896-2727		2
Whiteman Air Force Base 509 Spirit Blvd Ste 116 .... Whiteman AFB MO 65305 *Web:* www.whiteman.af.mil	660-687-1110	687-7948	497-1
Whitepath Fab Tech Inc 16402 Hwy 515 N .... Ellijay GA 30540 *Web:* www.whitepath.com	706-276-2511		203
Whitesell Corp 2703 Avalon Ave .... Muscle Shoals AL 35662 *TF:* 855-227-4515 ■ *Web:* www.whitesellgroup.com	855-227-4515		486
Whitesell-Green Inc 3881 N Palafox St .... Pensacola FL 32505 *Web:* www.whitesell-green.com	850-434-5311	434-5315	188-10
Whiteside County 200 E Knox St .... Morrison IL 61270 *Web:* www.whiteside.org	815-772-5100		338
Whiteside Manufacturing Company Inc 309 Hayes St .... Delaware OH 43015 *Web:* www.whitesidemfg.com	740-363-1179		350
Whitespace Creative Inc 243 Furnace St .... Akron OH 44304 *Web:* www.whitespace-creative.com	330-762-9320	762-9323	4
Whitestone Hill State Historic Site c/o Dorene Brandeburger 8692 98th Ave .... Monango ND 58436 *Web:* history.nd.gov	701-349-4103		565
Whitewater Memorial State Park 1418 S State Rd 101 .... Liberty IN 47353 *Web:* www.in.gov	765-458-5565		565
Whitewater State Park 19041 Hwy 74 .... Altura MN 55910 *Web:* www.dnr.state.mn.us	507-932-3007	932-5938	565
Whitewater Valley Rural Electric Membership Corp 101 Brownsville Ave .... Liberty IN 47353 *TF:* 800-529-5557 ■ *Web:* www.wwvremc.com	765-458-5171	458-5938	245
Whitewater Veterinary Hospital SC 527 S Janesville St .... Whitewater WI 53190 *Web:* whitewatervethospital.com	262-473-2930	473-5040	794
Whitewood Industries Inc 100 Liberty Dr .... Thomasville NC 27360 *Web:* www.whitewood.net	336-472-0303		320
Whiteys Fish Camp 2032 County Rd 220 .... Orange Park FL 32003 *Web:* www.whiteysfishcamp.com	904-269-4198		239
Whitfield & Eddy PLC 699 Walnut St Ste 2000 .... Des Moines IA 50309 *Web:* www.whitfieldlaw.com	515-288-6041	246-1474	428
Whitfield County PO Box 248 .... Dalton GA 30722 *Web:* www.whitfieldcountyga.com	706-876-2559	275-7540	338
Whitford Corp PO Box 80 .... Elverson PA 19520 *Web:* www.whitfordww.com	610-296-3200	286-3510	481
Whitham Curtis Christofferson & Cook PC 11491 Sunset Hills Rd Ste 340 .... Reston VA 20190 *Web:* www.wcc-ip.com	703-787-9400		41
Whiting Auditorium 1241 E Kearsley St .... Flint MI 48503 *Web:* www.thewhiting.com	810-237-7378	237-7335	572
Whiting Corp 26000 Whiting Way .... Monee IL 60449 *TF:* 800-861-5744 ■ *Web:* www.whitingcorp.com	800-861-5744		470
Whiting Door Manufacturing Corp 113 Cedar St .... Akron NY 14001 *Web:* www.whitingdoor.com	716-542-5427	542-5947	247
Whiting Hagg Hagg Dorsey & Hagg LLP 601 West Blvd .... Rapid City SD 57701 *Web:* amatteroflaw.com	605-250-3003		41
Whiting Petroleum Corp 1700 Broadway Ste 2300 .... Denver CO 80290 *NYSE:* WLL ■ *TF:* 800-723-4608 ■ *Web:* www.whiting.com	303-837-1661	861-4023	536
Whiting-Turner Contracting Co 300 E Joppa Rd .... Baltimore MD 21286 *Web:* www.whiting-turner.com	410-821-1100		186
Whitlam Label Company Inc 24800 Sherwood Ave .... Center Line MI 48015 *TF:* 800-755-2235 ■ *Web:* www.whitlam.com	586-757-5100	757-1243	413
Whitley County 101 W Van Buren St .... Columbia City IN 46725 *Web:* whitleygov.com	260-248-3102	248-3137	338

Name / Address	Phone	Fax	Class
Whitley County Court Clerk PO Box 8 ... Williamsburg KY 40769 *Web:* www.whitleycountyfiscalcourt.com	606-549-6002	549-2790	338
Whitley Fuel LLC 1617 Second Ave N ... Okanogan WA 98840 *Web:* www.whitleyfuel.com	509-422-3120		579
Whitley Manufacturing Inc 201 W First St PO Box 496 ... South Whitley IN 46787 *Web:* www.whitleyman.com	260-723-5131	723-6949	106
Whitley Penn 3411 Richmond Ave Ste 500 ... Houston TX 77046 *Web:* www.whitleypenn.com	713-621-1515	621-1570	2
Whitley Steel Company Inc 610 US Hwy 301 S ... Jacksonville FL 32234 *Web:* www.whitleysteel.com	904-289-7471	289-9430	492
Whitlock & Weinberger 490 Mendocino Ave Ste 201 ... Santa Rosa CA 95401 *Web:* www.w-trans.com	707-542-9500		261
Whitlock Group 4020 Stirrup Creek Dr Ste 111 ... Richmond VA 23238 *TF:* 800-726-9843 ■ *Web:* www.whitlock.com	804-273-9100	273-9380	246
Whitman & Bingham Associates LLC 510 Mechanic St ... Leominster MA 01453 *Web:* whitmanbingham.com	978-537-5296		261
Whitman College 345 Boyer Ave ... Walla Walla WA 99362 *TF:* 877-462-9448 ■ *Web:* www.whitman.edu	509-527-5111	527-4967	166
Whitman County 400 N Main St ... Colfax WA 99111 *Web:* www.co.whitman.wa.us	509-397-6240	397-3546	338
Whitman Mission National Historic Site 328 Whitman Mission Rd ... Walla Walla WA 99362 *Web:* www.nps.gov	509-522-6360	522-6355	564
Whitman Publications 220 Parker St ... Warsaw IN 46580 *TF:* 800-421-2401 ■ *Web:* www.wwhitman.com	574-267-3941	268-2120	637-2
Whitman Requardt & Assoc 801 S Caroline St ... Baltimore MD 21231 *TF:* 866-346-1810 ■ *Web:* wrallp.com	410-235-3450	243-5716	261
Whitman Strategy Group LLC, The PO Box 1621 ... New Brunswick NJ 08903 *Web:* www.whitmanstrategygroup.com	617-512-1643		192
Whitmore Manufacturing Co 930 Whitmore Dr ... Rockwall TX 75087 **Fax Area Code:* 972 ■ *TF:* 800-699-6318 ■ *Web:* www.whitmores.com	800-699-6318	722-2108*	550
Whitney and Whitney Inc 6490 S McCarran Blvd Bldg C Ste 23 ... Reno NV 89509 *Web:* www.whitneywhitney.com	775-689-7696	689-7691	194
Whitney Bailey Cox & Magnani LLC 300 E Joppa Rd Ste 200 ... Baltimore MD 21286 *TF:* 800-673-9312 ■ *Web:* wbcm.com	410-512-4500	324-4100	261
Whitney Blake Co 20 Industrial Dr ... Bellows Falls VT 05101 *TF:* 800-323-0479 ■ *Web:* www.wblake.com	800-323-0479		492
Whitney Ctr 200 Leeder Hill Dr ... Hamden CT 06517 *Web:* www.whitneycenter.com	203-848-2641		672
Whitney Hotel, The 610 Poydras St ... New Orleans LA 70130 *TF:* 844-581-4222 ■ *Web:* www.whitneyhotel.com	504-581-4222		379
Whitney Jones Inc 119 Brookstown Ave Ste PH2 ... Winston-Salem NC 27101 *Web:* www.whitneyjonesinc.com	336-722-2371		317
Whitney Museum of American Art 945 Madison Ave ... New York NY 10021 *TF:* 800-944-8639 ■ *Web:* whitney.org	212-570-3600		520
Whitney Partners 747 Third Ave 17th Fl ... New York NY 10017 *Web:* whitneypartners.com	212-508-3500	508-3540	266
Whitney Tool Company Inc 906 R St ... Bedford IN 47421 *TF:* 800-536-1971 ■ *Web:* www.whitneytool.com	812-275-4491	275-6458	455
Whitney Worldwide Inc 553 Hayward Ave N Ste 250 ... Saint Paul MN 55128 **Fax Area Code:* 651 ■ *TF:* 800-597-0227 ■ *Web:* www.whitneyworld.com	800-597-0227	748-4000*	174
Whitney, Bradley & Brown Inc 11790 Sunrise Vly Dr ... Reston VA 20191 *Web:* wbbinc.com	703-448-6081	821-6955	196
Whitney, The 4421 Woodward Ave ... Detroit MI 48201 *Web:* www.thewhitney.com	313-832-5700	832-2159	671
Whitsons Food Service Corp 1800 Motor Pkwy ... Islandia NY 11749 *Web:* www.whitsons.com	631-424-2700		194
Whittet-Higgins Co 33 Higginson Ave PO Box 8 ... Central Falls RI 02863 *Web:* www.whittet-higgins.com	401-728-0700	728-0703	620
Whittier Area Chamber of Commerce 8158 Painter Ave ... Whittier CA 90602 *Web:* www.whittierchamber.com	562-698-9554	693-2700	139
Whittier City School District 7211 Whittier Ave ... Whittier CA 90602 *Web:* www.whittiercity.net	562-789-3000	907-9425	685
Whittier College 13406 E Philadelphia St ... Whittier CA 90602 *Web:* www.whittier.edu	562-907-4200	907-4870	166
Whittier Farms Inc 90 Douglas Rd PO Box 455 ... Sutton MA 01590 *Web:* www.whittiers.com	508-865-1053	865-1096	296-27
Whittier Hospital Medical Ctr 9080 Colima Rd ... Whittier CA 90605 *TF:* 800-613-4291 ■ *Web:* www.whittierhospital.com	562-945-3561	693-6811	374-3
Whittier Publications Inc (WP) 3115 Long Beach Rd ... Oceanside NY 11572 *TF:* 800-897-8398 ■ *Web:* www.whitbooks.com	516-432-8120	889-0341	637-2
Whittier Regional Technical High School 115 Amesbury Line Rd ... Haverhill MA 01830 *Web:* www.whittiertech.org	978-373-4101	521-0260	685
Whittier Wood Products 3787 W First Ave PO Box 2827 ... Eugene OR 97402 *TF:* 800-653-3336 ■ *Web:* www.whittierwood.com	541-687-0213	687-2060	319-2
Whittle & Mutch Inc 712 Fellowship Rd ... Mount Laurel NJ 08054 *Web:* www.wamiflavor.com	856-235-1165		345
Whittlesea Blue Cab Co 2000 Industrial Rd ... Las Vegas NV 89102 *Web:* www.whittleseabluecab.com	702-386-7400		441
Whitworth College 300 W Hawthorne Rd ... Spokane WA 99251 *TF:* 800-533-4668 ■ *Web:* www.whitworth.edu	509-777-1000	777-3758	166
Whitworth Tool Inc 114 Industrial Park Ln ... Hardinsburg KY 40143 *Web:* www.whittool.com	270-756-0098		454
WHIZ-TV 629 Downard Rd ... Zanesville OH 43701 *Web:* www.whiznews.com	740-452-5431	452-6553	647
WHKO-FM 99.1 (Ctry) 1611 S Main St ... Dayton OH 45409 *Web:* www.k99online.com	937-457-0991	259-2168	645-44
Whks & Co 1412 Sixth St SW ... Mason City IA 50401 *Web:* whks.com	641-423-8271		261
WHKY-TV Ch 14 (Ind) 526 Main Ave SE PO Box 1059 ... Hickory NC 28602 *TF:* 800-899-4897 ■ *Web:* www.whky.com	828-322-1290	322-8256	741
WHLG-FM 1670 NW Federal Hwy ... Stuart FL 34994 *Web:* www.coast1013.com	772-344-1999		647
WHLI 1100 & 1370 AM 234 Airport Plz Ste 5 ... Farmingdale NY 11735 *Web:* www.whli.com	631-770-4200	770-0101	645
WHLM-AM 124 E Main St ... Bloomsburg PA 17815 *Web:* www.whlm.com	570-784-1200	784-6060	647
WHLT CBS 22 5912 Hwy 49 Ste A ... Hattiesburg MS 39401 *Web:* www.wjtv.com	601-545-2077	545-3589	741
WHMA (Wiring Harness Manufacturers Assn) 15490 101st Ave N Ste 100 ... Maple Grove MN 55369 *Web:* whma.org	763-235-6461		49-13
WHMB-TV Ch 40 (Ind) 10511 Greenfield Ave ... Noblesville IN 46060 *TF:* 800-535-5542 ■ *Web:* whmbtv40.com	317-773-5050	776-4051	741
WHNT-TV Ch 19 (CBS) 200 Holmes Ave ... Huntsville AL 35801 *TF:* 800-533-8819 ■ *Web:* www.whnt.com	256-533-1919	536-9468	741-61
WHO 13 1801 Grand Ave ... Des Moines IA 50309 *TF:* 800-777-8398 ■ *Web:* who13.com	515-242-3500	242-3796	741-40
WHOI (Woods Hole Oceanographic Institution) 266 Woods Hole Rd ... Woods Hole MA 02543 *Web:* www.whoi.edu	508-289-2282	457-2109	668
WHOI-TV c/o Miles S Mason Pillsbury Winthrop S 1200 Seventeenth St NW ... Washington DC 20036 *Web:* www.cinewsnow.com	202-663-8195		647
WhoKnows 585 Broadway St ... Redwood City CA 94063 *TF:* 800-348-5031 ■ *Web:* corp.whoknows.com	800-348-5031		387
Whole Brain Group LLC, The 109 E Ann St ... Ann Arbor MI 48104 *Web:* www.thewholebraingroup.com	734-929-0431		177
Whole Foods Market Inc 550 Bowie St ... Austin TX 78703 *TF:* 888-992-6227 ■ *Web:* www.wholefoodsmarket.com	512-477-4455	482-7000	355
Whole Health Products LLC 17301 W Colfax Ave Ste 110 ... Golden CO 80401 *Web:* www.wholehealth.com	303-684-9618		363
Whole Health Solutions LLC 236 4th St ... Providence RI 02906 *Web:* www.karloberger.com	401-477-2845		352
Whole Hog Health 88155 Hwy 57 ... Hartington NE 68739 *Web:* wholehogai.com	402-254-2444		10-6
Whole Loaf Publications 41201 Airport Rd ... Little River CA 95456 *Web:* wholeloafbooks.mcn.org	707-937-0208		637-2
Whole Person Associates Inc (WPA) 101 W 2nd St Ste 203 ... Duluth MN 55802 *TF:* 800-247-6789 ■ *Web:* www.wholeperson.com	218-727-0500	727-0505	637-2
Whole Spirit Press 1905 S Clarkson St ... Denver CO 80210 **Fax Area Code:* 303 ■ *TF:* 877-488-3774 ■ *Web:* www.wholespiritpress.com	877-488-3774	979-6151*	637-2
Whole You Inc 61 Metro Dr ... San Jose CA 95110 *TF:* 844-548-3385 ■ *Web:* www.wholeyou.com	844-548-3385		476
Wholesale Accessory Market Inc 4959 15th Street Rd ... Hueytown AL 35023 *TF:* 877-524-0433 ■ *Web:* www.wholesaleaccessorymarket.com	205-491-6479		594
Wholesale Builder Supply Inc (WBS) 51740 Grand River Ave North on Challenger Dr ... Wixom MI 48393 *Web:* wbscabinets.com	248-347-6290		191-3
Wholesale Carrier Services Inc (WCS) 12350 NW 39th St ... Coral Springs FL 33065 *TF:* 888-940-5600 ■ *Web:* www.wcs.com	888-940-5600		224
Wholesale Ceramic Tile Inc 2885 Immanuel Rd ... Greensboro NC 27407 *Web:* www.wholesaleceramictileinc.com	336-292-0130	292-0131	191-1
Wholesale Chess 695 N 900 W Ste 5 ... Kaysville UT 84037 *TF:* 888-582-4377 ■ *Web:* www.wholesalechess.com	801-544-4242		44
Wholesale Electric Supply Company LP 4040 Guls Fwy ... Houston TX 77004 *Web:* www.wholesaleelectric.com	713-748-6100		246
Wholesale Electric Supply Inc 1400 Waterall St ... Texarkana TX 75501 *Web:* www.netwes.com	903-794-3404	792-2720	246
Wholesale Electronics Inc 123 W First Ave ... Mitchell SD 57301 *TF:* 800-351-2233 ■ *Web:* www.weisd.com	800-351-2233		246
Wholesale Flowers and Supplies (WF&S) 5305 Metro St ... San Diego CA 92110 *Web:* www.wholesaleflowersandsupplies.com	619-295-4333		293
Wholesale Furniture Closeouts Inc 1745 NW 50th Rd ... Greenville AL 36037 *TF:* 800-459-0178 ■ *Web:* www.closeoutssuppliers.com	800-459-0178		320
Wholesale Hardwood Interiors Inc (WHI) 1030 Campbellsville By-Pass ... Campbellsville KY 42719 *TF:* 800-982-7404 ■ *Web:* www.wholesalehardwoodint.com	270-789-1323	789-2321	191-3
Wholesale House Inc, The (TWH) 503 W High St ... Hicksville OH 43526 *TF:* 800-722-5553 ■ *Web:* www.twhouse.com	800-722-5553		459
Wholesale Interiors Inc 971 Supreme Dr ... Bensenville IL 60106 **Fax Area Code:* 630 ■ *TF:* 800-517-0717 ■ *Web:* www.wholesale-interiors.com	800-517-0717	238-8470*	320
Wholesale Janitorial Supply 8900 E Pinnacle Peak Rd Ste E4 ... Scottsdale AZ 85255 *TF:* 800-908-1986 ■ *Web:* www.wholesalejanitorialsupply.com	800-908-1986		76
Wholesale Jewelry Direct Distributor 710 6th Ave S ... Seattle WA 98104 *TF:* 877-450-1687 ■ *Web:* www.supplyjewelry.com	604-298-0487		411

	Phone	Fax	Class
Wholesale Paint Center Inc 945 N Church St Rocky Mount NC 27804 *Web:* www.wholesalepaintcenter.com	252-446-6045		802
Wholesale Point Inc 260 Shore Ct Burr Ridge IL 60527 *TF:* 800-986-0525 ■ *Web:* www.wholesalepoint.com	630-986-1700		475
Wholesale Produce Supply Company Inc 752 Kasota Cir Minneapolis MN 55414 *Web:* wholesaleproduce.cc	612-378-2025	378-9547	297-7
Wholesale Salon Equipment 11512 K-Tel Dr Minnetonka MN 55343 *TF:* 800-566-2977 ■ *Web:* www.wholesalesalonequipment.com	952-933-8881		76
Wholesale Specialties Inc 4800 E 48th Ave Denver CO 80216 *Web:* www.wholesalespecialties.com	303-296-2212	296-2536	612
Wholesale Supply Group Inc 885 Keith St NW Cleveland TN 37311 *Web:* wholesalesupply.us	423-479-5997	478-5120	612
Wholesale Tape and Supply Co 2841 Hickory Valley Rd Chattanooga TN 37421 *TF:* 888-987-6334 ■ *Web:* www.wtsmedia.com	423-894-9427	894-7281	246
Wholesalebooks.net 21 Meyer Ave Valley Stream NY 11580 *Web:* www.wholesalebooks.net	516-825-3351	568-0566	96
Wholesalemart LLC 1429 Ave D Ste 304 Snohomish WA 98290 **Fax Area Code:* 855 ■ *TF:* 866-311-5796 ■ *Web:* www.wholesalemart.com	866-311-5796	215-2228*	361
WHOT-FM 4040 Simon Rd Youngstown OH 44512 *TF:* 866-539-9468 ■ *Web:* www.hot101.com	330-783-1000		647
WHOU-FM 39 Court St Ste 215 Houlton ME 04730 *TF:* 855-532-9468 ■ *Web:* www.whoufm.com	855-532-9468		647
WHP-TV Ch 21 (CBS) 3300 N Sixth St Harrisburg PA 17110 *Web:* www.local21news.com	717-238-2100		741-56
WHQG-FM 102.9 (Rock) 5407 W McKinley Ave Milwaukee WI 53208 *Web:* www.1029thehog.com	414-799-1029		645-98
WHQR 91.3 FM 254 N Front St Ste 300 Wilmington NC 28401 *Web:* whqr.org	910-343-1640		116
WHRB-FM 95.3 389 Harvard St Cambridge MA 02138 *Web:* www.whrb.org	617-495-4818		645
WHRD-FM 2525 W Stephenson St Freeport IL 61032 *Web:* www.1060whrdfm.com	815-232-6158		647
WHSM-FM 16880 W US Hwy 63 Hayward WI 54843 *TF:* 800-845-8984 ■ *Web:* www.whsm.com	715-634-4836		647
WHSN-FM 89.3 (Alt) 1 College Cir Bangor ME 04401 *Web:* www.whsn-fm.com	207-941-7116	947-3987	645-16
WHSV-TV 50 N Main St Harrisonburg VA 22802 *Web:* www.whsv.com	540-433-9191	433-4028	647
WHTK 1700 HSBC Plz 100 Chestnut St Rochester NY 14604 *Web:* foxsports1280.iheart.com	585-454-4884		647
WHTM-TV Ch 27 (ABC) 3235 Hoffman St Harrisburg PA 17110 *Web:* www.abc27.com	717-236-2727	236-1263	741-56
WHTV-TV 600 W St Joseph St Ste 47 Lansing MI 48933 *Web:* www.my18.tv	517-372-9497		647
WHUG-FM 2 Orchard Rd PO Box 1139 Jamestown NY 14701 *Web:* www.whug.com	716-487-1151	664-9326	647
WHUR-FM 96.3 (Urban AC) 529 Bryant St NW Washington DC 20059 *TF:* 800-221-9487 ■ *Web:* whur.com	202-432-9487		645-170
WHUT-TV Ch 32 (PBS) 2222 Fourth St NW Washington DC 20059 *Web:* www.whut.org	202-806-3200	806-3300	741-139
WHVL-TV 2820 E College Ave State College PA 16801 *TF:* 877-241-6988 ■ *Web:* www.whvl.com	814-238-9485	238-0612	647
WHY (World Hunger Year Inc) 505 Eigth Ave Ste 2100 New York NY 10018 *TF:* 800-548-6479 ■ *Web:* whyhunger.org	212-629-8850	465-9274	48-5
Why Not Lease It 1750 Elm St Ste 1200 Manchester NH 03104 *Web:* whynotleaseit.com	603-665-0000		23
Whyco Finishing Technologies LLC 670 Waterbury Rd Thomaston CT 06787 *Web:* whyco.com	860-283-5826		481
WhyHotel 100 K St NE Washington DC 20002 *Web:* whyhotel.com	202-800-4343		669
WHYN-AM 560 (N/T) 1331 Main St 4th Fl Springfield MA 01103 *Web:* whyn.iheart.com	413-293-0560		645-6
WHYY Inc 150 N 6th St Philadelphia PA 19106 *Web:* www.whyy.org	215-351-0511		647
WHZZ-FM 101.7 (AC) 600 W Cavanaugh Rd Lansing MI 48910 *Web:* 1017mikefm.com	517-393-5224	393-0882	645-84
WI (Wilderness Inquiry) 808 14th Ave SE Minneapolis MN 55414 *TF:* 800-728-0719 ■ *Web:* www.wildernessinquiry.org	612-676-9400	676-9401	48-23
WiBand Communications Corp 187 Commerce Dr Winnipeg MB R3P1A2 **Fax Area Code:* 780 ■ *TF:* 866-469-4226 ■ *Web:* www.wiband.com	204-633-6333	430-4079*	225
Wibbitz 1 State St 30th Fl New York NY 10004 *Web:* www.wibbitz.com	347-306-8642		178-8
WIBC-FM 93.1 (N/T) 40 Monument Cir Ste 400 Indianapolis IN 46204 *TF:* 800-571-9422 ■ *Web:* www.wibc.com	317-266-9422		645-74
WibiData Inc 375 Alabama St Ste 350 San Francisco CA 94110 *Web:* www.wibidata.com	415-496-9424		387
WIBW-AM 580 (N/T) 1210 SW Executive Dr Topeka KS 66615 *Web:* www.wibwnewsnow.com	785-272-3456	228-7282	645-162
WIBW-TV Ch 13 (CBS) 631 SW Commerce Pl Topeka KS 66615 *Web:* www.wibw.com	785-272-6397	272-1363	741-135
WIBX-AM 9418 River Rd Marcy NY 13403 *Web:* www.wibx950.com	315-768-9500	736-0720	647
Wicc Ltd 119 Muller Rd Washington IL 61571 *Web:* www.wiccltd.com	309-444-4125	444-3313	767
WICHE (Western Interstate Commission for Higher Education) 3035 Center Green Dr Ste 200 Boulder CO 80301 *Web:* www.wiche.edu	303-541-0200	541-0291	637-2
Wichita Area Chamber of Commerce 350 W Douglas Ave Wichita KS 67202 *Web:* www.wichitachamber.org	316-265-7771	265-7502	139
Wichita Area Technical College 4004 N Webb Rd Wichita KS 67211 *TF:* 866-296-4031 ■ *Web:* wsutech.edu	316-677-9400	677-9555	800
Wichita Art Museum 1400 W Museum Blvd Wichita KS 67203 *Web:* www.wichitaartmuseum.org	316-268-4921	268-4980	520
Wichita Center for Performing Arts 9112 E Central Ave Wichita KS 67206 *Web:* www.wichitacenter.org	316-201-6654		572
Wichita City Hall 455 N Main St Wichita KS 67202 *Web:* www.wichita.gov	316-268-4331		337
Wichita Community Theatre 258 N Fountain St Wichita KS 67208 *Web:* wichitact.org	316-686-1282		572
Wichita Convention & Visitors Bureau 515 Main St Ste 115 Wichita KS 67202 *TF:* 800-288-9424 ■ *Web:* www.visitwichita.com	316-265-2800	265-0162	206
Wichita County 206 S Fourth St PO Box S Leoti KS 67861 *Web:* www.wichita.k-state.edu	620-375-2724	375-4815	338
Wichita Eagle, The 825 E Douglas Ave Wichita KS 67202 *TF:* 800-200-8906 ■ *Web:* www.kansas.com	316-268-6000	268-6627	532-2
Wichita Falls Board of Commerce & Industry 900 Eigth St Ste 218 Wichita Falls TX 76301 *Web:* wichitafallschamber.com	940-723-2741	723-8773	139
Wichita Falls CVB 1002 Fifth St Wichita Falls TX 76301 *TF:* 800-799-6732 ■ *Web:* wichitafalls.org	940-761-6820	716-5509	572
Wichita Falls Public Library 600 11th St Wichita Falls TX 76301 *Web:* wfpl.net	940-767-0868		434-3
Wichita Grand Opera 9112 E Central Ave Wichita KS 67202 *Web:* www.wichitagrandopera.org	316-683-3444	263-2126	573-2
Wichita Home Health Service Inc 4245 Kemp Blvd Ste 120 Wichita Falls TX 76308 *TF:* 800-527-1431 ■ *Web:* www.wichitahomehealth.com	940-322-7113		363
Wichita Kenworth Inc 5115 N Broadway Wichita KS 67219 *TF:* 800-825-5558 ■ *Web:* www.wichitakenworth.com	316-838-0867	838-4845	516
Wichita National Life Insurance Co (WNL) PO Box 1709 Lawton OK 73502 *TF:* 800-522-1625 ■ *Web:* www.wnlic.com	580-353-5776	353-6482	796
Wichita Public Library Foundation Inc 223 S Main St Wichita KS 67202	316-261-8500		434-3
Wichita State University 1845 Fairmount St Wichita KS 67260 *TF:* 800-362-2594 ■ *Web:* www.wichita.edu	316-978-3456	978-3174	166
Wichita Symphony Orchestra (WSO) 225 W Douglas St Ste 207 Wichita KS 67202 *Web:* wichitasymphony.org	316-267-5259	267-1937	573-3
Wichita Technical Institute 2051 S Meridan Ave Wichita KS 67213 *TF:* 888-859-4564 ■ *Web:* www.wti.edu	316-943-2241		167-3
Wichita-Sedgwick County Historical Museum 204 S Main St Wichita KS 67202 *Web:* www.wichitahistory.org	316-265-9314	265-9319	520
Wichman Construction 5029 W Grace St Tampa FL 33607 *Web:* www.wichmanconstruction.com	813-282-1179	282-0461	186
Wick Buildings 405 Walter Rd Mazomanie WI 53560 **Fax Area Code:* 608 ■ *TF:* 855-438-9425 ■ *Web:* wickbuildings.com	855-438-9425	795-2534*	505
Wick Communications Inc 333 W Wilcox Dr Ste 302 Sierra Vista AZ 85635 *Web:* www.wickcommunications.com	520-458-0200	458-6166	637-8
Wickaninnish Inn 500 Osprey Ln PO Box 250 Tofino BC V0R2Z0 *TF:* 800-333-4604 ■ *Web:* www.wickinn.com	250-725-3100	725-3110	379
Wickens Herzer Panza Cook & Batista Co 35765 Chester Rd Avon OH 44011 *Web:* www.wickenslaw.com	440-695-8000		345
Wicker Machine Co 1400 E Ave N Hollandale MS 38748 *TF:* 800-748-9476 ■ *Web:* www.wickermachinecompany.com	662-827-5434	827-7000	190
Wicker Roger F (Sen R - MS) 555 Dirksen Senate Office Bldg Washington DC 20510 *Web:* www.wicker.senate.gov	202-224-6253	228-0378	342-2
Wickers Group LLC, The 1819 Polk St Ste 373 San Francisco CA 94109 *Web:* wickersgroup.com	415-512-7100		194
Wickham Glass Co 4747 N Webb Rd Wichita KS 67226 *Web:* www.wickhamglass.com	316-262-3403	262-2069	256
Wicklander Zulawski & Associates Inc 4932 Main St Downers Grove IL 60515 *TF:* 800-222-7789 ■ *Web:* www.w-z.com	800-222-7789		463
Wickliffe Mounds State Historic Site 94 Green St Wickliffe KY 42087 *Web:* parks.ky.gov	270-335-3681		565
Wicks Group of Companies LLC 400 Park Ave New York NY 10022 *Web:* www.wicksgroup.com	212-838-2100	223-2109	792
Wicks Pies Inc 217 Greenville Ave Winchester IN 47394 **Fax Area Code:* 765 ■ *TF:* 800-642-5880 ■ *Web:* www.wickspies.com	800-642-5880	584-3700*	68
Wicks Pipe Organ Co 416 Pine St Highland IL 62249 *TF:* 877-654-2191 ■ *Web:* wicksorgan.com	618-654-2191	654-3770	527
WICN-FM 90.5 (NPR) 50 Portland St Worcester MA 01608 *TF:* 855-752-0700 ■ *Web:* www.wicn.org	508-752-0700	752-7518	645-171
Wicomico County *Maryland* 125 N Div St PO Box 870 Salisbury MD 21803 *Web:* www.wicomicocounty.org	410-548-4801	548-4803	338
Wicomico County Board of Education 2424 Northgate Dr Ste 100 Salisbury MD 21801 *Web:* www.wcboe.org	410-677-4400	677-4444	685
Wicomico County Convention & Visitors Bureau 8480 Ocean Hwy Delmar MD 21875 *TF:* 800-332-8687 ■ *Web:* www.wicomicotourism.org	410-548-4914		206
Wicomico County Free Library 122 S Div St Salisbury MD 21801 *Web:* www.wicomicociviccenter.org	410-749-3612	548-2968	434-3
WICS-TV Ch 20 (ABC) 2680 E Cook St Springfield IL 62703 *Web:* newschannel20.com	217-753-5689		741-128
WICT (Women in Cable Telecommunications) 2000 K St Ste 350 Washington DC 20006 *Web:* www.wict.org	202-827-4794	450-5596	49-14

Name / Address	City	State	Zip	Phone	Fax	Class
WICZ-TV 4600 Vestal Pky E *Web:* www.wicz.com	Vestal	NY	13850	607-770-4040	798-7950	647
Wide World Publishing PO Box 476 *Web:* www.wideworldpublishing.com	San Carlos	CA	94070	650-593-2839	595-0802	637-2
WideBand Corp 401 W Grand St *TF:* 888-663-3050 ■ *Web:* www.wband.com	Gallatin	MO	64640	660-663-3000	663-3736	176
Widener University 1 University Pl *TF:* 888-943-3637 ■ *Web:* www.widener.edu	Chester	PA	19013	610-499-4000	499-4676	166
Widener University Commonwealth Law School 3800 Vartan Way *Web:* commonwealthlaw.widener.edu	Harrisburg	PA	17110	717-541-3903	541-3999	167-1
Widener University Delaware Law School 4601 Concord Pk *Web:* delawarelaw.widener.edu	Wilmington	DE	19803	302-477-2100		167-1
WideNet Consulting Group 11400 SE Sixth St Ste 130 **Fax Area Code:* 206 ■ *Web:* widenet-consulting.com	Bellevue	WA	98004	425-643-0366	299-3430*	463
WideOpenWest Finance LLC 2660 Montgomery Hwy *TF:* 866-376-7003 ■ *Web:* www.wowway.com	Dothan	AL	36303	334-699-3333		116
WideOrbit Inc 1160 Battery St Ste 300 *Web:* www.wideorbit.com	San Francisco	CA	94111	415-675-6700		186
WidePoint Corp 7926 Jones Branch Dr Ste 520 *TF:* 877-919-5943 ■ *Web:* www.widepoint.com	McLean	VA	22102	703-349-5644	848-3560	180
Wider Consolidated Inc 175-35 148th Rd 2nd Fl *Web:* www.widerhkg.com	Jamaica	NY	11434	718-244-8800	244-6728	311
Wider Opportunities for Women (WOW) 1001 Connecticut Ave NW Ste 930 *Web:* iwpr.org	Washington	DC	20036	202-464-1596	464-1660	48-24
WiderFunnel Marketing Inc 1480 333 Seymour St Ste 551 *Web:* www.widerfunnel.com	Vancouver	BC	V6C1T2	604-800-6450		5
Widex Canada Ltd 5041 Mainway *Web:* www.widex.ca	Burlington	ON	L7L5H9	905-315-8303		477
Widget Financial Credit Union 2154 E Lake Rd *Web:* widgetfinancial.com	Erie	PA	16511	814-456-6231		219
Widman & Franklin LLC 405 Madison Ave Ste 1550 *Web:* wflawfirm.com	Toledo	OH	43604	419-243-9005		41
Widmer Bros Brewing Co 929 N Russell St *Web:* www.widmerbrothers.com	Portland	OR	97227	503-281-2437	281-1496	102
Widmeyer Communications 1129 20th St NW Ste 200 *Web:* www.widmeyer.com	Washington	DC	20036	202-667-0901	667-0902	636
Widner Juran LLP 13133 E Arapahoe Rd Ste 100 *Web:* lawwj.com	Centennial	CO	80112	303-754-3399	754-3395	41
Widseth Smith Nolting & Associates Inc 7804 Industrial Park Rd PO Box 2720 *Web:* widseth.com	Baxter	MN	56425	218-829-5117		186
Wiebe & Assn 377 N Central Ave *Web:* www.wiebecpas.com	Upland	CA	91786	909-985-5357		2
Wieden & Kennedy 224 NW 13th Ave *Web:* www.wk.com	Portland	OR	97209	503-937-7000	937-8000	4
Wiederkehr Wine Cellars Inc 3324 Swiss Family Dr *TF:* 800-622-9463 ■ *Web:* www.wiederkehrwines.com	Wiederkehr Village	AR	72821	479-468-2611	468-4791	443
Wiegmann & Associates Inc 750 Fountain Lakes Blvd *Web:* wiegmannassoc.com	Saint Charles	MO	63301	636-940-1056		261
Wieland 10785 Rose Ave *TF:* 888-943-5263 ■ *Web:* wielandhealthcare.com	New Haven	IN	46774	260-627-3686	627-6496	319-3
Wieland 305 Lewis & Clark Blvd *Web:* www.wieland.com	East Alton	IL	62024	502-873-3000		485
Wieland Chase LLC 14212 Selwyn Dr *TF:* 800-537-4291 ■ *Web:* wieland-chase.com	Montpelier	OH	43543	419-485-3193	485-5945	485
Wieland Copper Products LCC 3990 US 311 Hwy N *Web:* www.wieland.com	Pine Hall	NC	27042	336-445-4500		492
Wieland Electric Inc (WEI) 49 International Rd *TF:* 800-943-5263 ■ *Web:* www.wielandinc.com	Burgaw	NC	28425	910-259-5050		246
Wiers Farm Inc 4465 St Rt 103 S PO Box 385 *TF:* 800-777-6243 ■ *Web:* wiersfarm.com	Willard	OH	44890	419-935-0131	933-2017	10-11
Wiers International Trucks Inc 2111 Jim Neu Dr *Web:* www.wiers.com	Plymouth	IN	46563	574-936-4076		57
Wiesbaden Hot Springs 625 Fifth St PO Box 349 *Web:* www.wiesbadenhotsprings.com	Ouray	CO	81427	970-325-4347	325-4358	706
Wiese Inc 1445 Woodson Rd *TF:* 800-228-0049 ■ *Web:* www.wieseusa.com	Saint Louis	MO	63132	314-997-4444		385
Wiese Industries 1501 Fifth St *TF:* 800-568-4391 ■ *Web:* www.wiesecorp.com	Perry	IA	50220	515-465-9854	465-9858	273
Wieser & Cawley Inc 1301 Colegate Dr *Web:* wieserandcawleyfurniture.com	Marietta	OH	45750	740-373-1676		321
Wieser Concrete Products Inc W3716 US Hwy 10 *TF:* 800-325-8456 ■ *Web:* www.wieserconcrete.com	Maiden Rock	WI	54750	715-647-2311	647-5181	183
WiesnerMedia Financial Group 6160 S Syracuse Ste 300 *Web:* www.wiesnermedia.com	Greenwood Village	CO	80111	303-662-5200		637-9
Wieson America Inc 1949 Concourse Dr *Web:* www.wieson.com	San Jose	CA	95131	408-240-8888	240-8882	385
WIF (Women in Film) 6100 Wilshire Blvd Ste 710 *Web:* womeninfilm.org	Los Angeles	CA	90048	323-935-2211		48-4
Wifco Steel Products Inc 8003 Medora Rd *TF:* 800-258-1392 ■ *Web:* www.wifcosp.com	Hutchinson	KS	67502	800-258-1392		491
Wiffle Ball Inc 275 Bridgeport Ave PO Box 193 *Web:* www.wiffle.com	Shelton	CT	06484	203-924-4643		762
Wi-Fi Guys LLC 7265 Hwy 1 *TF:* 877-943-4489 ■ *Web:* www.wi-figuys.com	Finland	MN	55603	218-353-7798	353-7737	196
WIFM-FM PO Box 1038 *Web:* www.wifmradio.com	Elkin	NC	28621	336-835-2511	835-5248	647
WIFR-TV Ch 23 (CBS) 2523 N Meridian Rd *Web:* www.wifr.com	Rockford	IL	61101	815-987-5300	965-0981	741-112
WIFX-FM 20 Laynesville Rd PO Box 159 *Web:* www.foxy943.com	Harold	KY	41635	606-478-9401	478-4202	647
Wig America Co 27317 Industrial Blvd *TF:* 800-338-7600 ■ *Web:* www.wigamerica.com	Hayward	CA	94545	510-887-9579	887-9574	348
Wiggin and Dana LLP 265 Church St 1 Century Twr *Web:* www.wiggin.com	New Haven	CT	06508	203-498-4400	782-2889	41
Wiggins Airways Inc 1 Garside Way *Web:* wiggins-air.com	Manchester	NH	03103	603-629-9191		359
Wiggins Lift Company Inc 2571 Cortez St *Web:* wigginslift.com	Oxnard	CA	93036	805-485-7821	485-5230	470
Wiggins, Childs, Quinn & Pantazis LLC The Kress Bldg 301 19th St N *Web:* www.wigginschilds.com	Birmingham	AL	35203	205-314-0500		428
Wigglesworth Machinery Co 276 Border St *Web:* www.wigglesworthmachinery.com	East Boston	MA	02128	617-567-7210		385
Wiggy's Inc 2482 Industrial Blvd *Web:* www.wiggys.com	Grand Junction	CO	81505	970-241-6465		34
Wight & Co 2500 N Frontage Rd *Web:* wightco75.com	Darien	IL	60561	630-969-7000		261
Wiginton Fire Systems 699 Aero Ln *Web:* wiginton.net	Sanford	FL	32771	407-585-3200	585-3280	189-13
Wigwam Golf Resort & Spa 300 E Wigwam Blvd *Web:* wigwamarizona.com	Litchfield Park	AZ	85340	623-935-3811	935-3737	669
Wigwam Mills Inc 3402 Crocker Ave *TF:* 800-558-7760 ■ *Web:* www.wigwam.com	Sheboygan	WI	53082	855-275-0356		155-10
WIIS 106.9 FM Key West Radio 1075 Duval St Ste C17 *Web:* island1069.com	Key West	FL	33040	305-296-1069		645-157
WIJR-AM 13063 Winu Dr *Web:* www.birach.com	Highland	IL	62249	618-654-5615		647
Wika Instrument Corp 1000 Wiegand Blvd **Fax Area Code:* 770 ■ *TF:* 888-945-2872 ■ *Web:* www.wika.us	Lawrenceville	GA	30043	888-945-2872	338-5118*	201
Wikibon Project, The 5 Mt Royal Ave Ste 280 *Web:* wikibon.org	Marlborough	MA	01752	774-463-3400	463-3405	41
Wikoff Color 3650 E 93rd St *TF:* 800-289-6872 ■ *Web:* www.wikoff.com	Cleveland	OH	44105	216-271-2300		388
Wil Plyler Insurance Agency LLC 596 Herrons Ferry Rd Ste 101 *Web:* wilplylerinsurance.com	Rock Hill	SC	29730	803-366-4196		390
Wi-LAN Inc 303 Terry Fox Dr Ste 300 *TSX:* WIN ■ *Web:* www.wilan.com	Ottawa	ON	K2K3J1	613-688-4900	688-4894	173-3
Wilbanks Energy Logistics 11246 Lovington Hwy Lovington Hwy PO Box 1390 **Fax Area Code:* 505 ■ *Web:* www.wilbanksel.com	Artesia	NM	88211	575-746-6318	748-2820*	539
Wilbanks, Smith & Thomas Asset Management LLC 150 W Main St Ste 1700 *TF:* 800-229-3677 ■ *Web:* www.wstam.com	Norfolk	VA	23510	757-623-3676	627-2943	401
Wilbar International Inc 50 Cabot Ct *Web:* sharkline.com	Hauppauge	NY	11788	631-951-9800		567
Wilbarger County 1700 Wilbarger St *Web:* www.co.wilbarger.tx.us	Vernon	TX	76384	940-552-5486	553-2320	338
Wilberforce University 1055 N Bickett Rd PO Box 1001 *Web:* wilberforce.edu	Wilberforce	OH	45384	937-376-2911	376-4751	166
Wilbert Plastic Services Acquisition LLC 486 Vance St *Web:* wilbertplastics.com	Forest City	NC	28043	704-822-1423		596
Wilbraham & Monson Academy 423 Main St *TF:* 800-616-3659 ■ *Web:* www.wma.us	Wilbraham	MA	01095	413-596-6811	596-2448	622
Wilbraham Lawler & Buba 603 Stanwix St Two Gateway Ct 17 N *Web:* www.wlbdeflaw.com	Pittsburgh	PA	15222	412-255-0500	255-0505	445
Wilbrecht Ledco Inc 1400 Energy Park Dr Ste 20 *TF:* 888-323-8751 ■ *Web:* www.wilbrechtledco.com	Saint Paul	MN	55108	651-659-0919	659-9204	253
Wilbur Curtis Company Inc 6913 Acco St *TF:* 800-421-6150 ■ *Web:* wilburcurtis.com	Montebello	CA	90640	323-837-2300	837-2406	298
Wilbur D. May Museum 1595 N Sierra St *Web:* washoecounty.us	Reno	NV	89503	775-785-5961	785-4707	520
Wilbur Theatre 246 Tremont St *Web:* thewilbur.com	Boston	MA	02116	617-248-9700		572
Wilbur-Ellis Co 345 California St 27th Fl *Web:* www.wilburellis.com	San Francisco	CA	94104	415-772-4036	772-4011	276
Wilco Farmers 200 Industrial Way *TF:* 800-382-5339 ■ *Web:* www.wilco.coop	Mount Angel	OR	97362	800-382-5339		276
Wilco Inc 3502 W Harry *TF:* 800-767-7593 ■ *Web:* www.wilcoaircraftparts.com	Wichita	KS	67213	800-767-7593		770
Wilco Marsh Buggies & Draglines Inc 1304 Macarthur Ave *TF:* 800-253-0869 ■ *Web:* wilcomarshbuggies.com	Harvey	LA	70058	504-341-3409		190
Wilco Peanut Co 3391 US Hwy 281 N *Web:* www.wilcopeanut.com	Pleasanton	TX	78064	830-569-3808	569-2743	11-1
Wilcom Inc 73 Daniel Webster Hwy PO Box 508 *TF:* 800-222-1898 ■ *Web:* www.wilcominc.com	Belmont	NH	03220	603-524-2622	524-3735	647
Wilcor Autos Inc 201 Auto Mall Pkwy *Web:* www.toyotavallejo.com	Vallejo	CA	94591	707-552-4545		57
Wilcox County 103 N Broad St *TF:* 866-694-5824 ■ *Web:* wilcoxcountygeorgia.com	Abbeville	GA	31001	229-467-2737	467-2000	338

Company / Address	City	State	ZIP	Phone	Fax	Class
Wilcox Environmental Engineering Inc 1552 Main St Ste 100 Speedway *TF:* 877-683-8378 ■ *Web:* www.wilcoxenv.com	Indianapolis	IN	46224	317-472-0999	472-0993	192
Wilcox Farms Inc 40400 Harts Lake Valley Rd *Web:* www.wilcoxfarms.com	Roy	WA	98580	360-458-7774		10-8
Wilcox Frozen Foods Inc 2200 Oakdale Ave	San Francisco	CA	94124	415-282-4116		297-6
Wilcox Fuel Inc 1179 Boston Post Rd *Web:* wilcox-energy.com	Westbrook	CT	06498	860-399-6218		366
Wilcox Industries Corp 25 Piscataqua Dr *Web:* www.wilcoxind.com	Portsmouth	NH	03801	603-431-1331	431-1221	544
Wilcox Machine Co 7180 Scout Ave *Web:* www.wilcoxmachine.com	Bell Gardens	CA	90201	562-927-5353		454
Wilcox Memorial Hospital (WMH) 3-3420 Kuhio Hwy *TF:* 877-709-9355 ■ *Web:* www.hawaiipacifichealth.org	Lihue	HI	96766	808-245-1100		374-3
Wilcox Miller & Nelson 333 University Ave Ste 200 *Web:* www.wilcoxcareer.com	Sacramento	CA	95825	916-977-3700		193
Wilcox Travel Sandals 1550 Hendersonville Rd Ste 214 *TF:* 800-294-5269 ■ *Web:* www.wilcoxtravel.com	Asheville	NC	28803	828-254-0746		772
Wilcoxon Research Inc 20511 Seneca Meadows Pkwy *TF:* 800-945-2696 ■ *Web:* wilcoxon.com	Germantown	MD	20876	301-330-8811		248
WiLD 94.9 340 Townsend St 4th Fl *TF:* 888-333-9490 ■ *Web:* wild949.iheart.com	San Francisco	CA	94107	415-975-5555		645-142
Wild Adventures Valdosta LLC 3766 Old Clyattville Rd *Web:* www.wildadventures.com	Valdosta	GA	31601	229-219-7080		31
Wild Animal Safari 1300 Oak Grove Rd *TF:* 800-367-2751 ■ *Web:* www.animalsafari.com	Pine Mountain	GA	31822	706-663-8744		823
Wild Animal Sanctuary, The 1946 County Rd 53 *Web:* www.wildanimalsanctuary.org	Keenesburg	CO	80643	303-536-0118		794
Wild Animal XPress PO Box 2461 *Web:* www.wildanimalxpress.com	Ramona	CA	92065	619-462-1986		637-2
Wild Bird Centers of America 7370 MacArthur Blvd *Web:* www.wildbird.com	Glen Echo	MD	20812	301-229-9585		791
Wild Birds Unlimited Inc 11711 N College Ave Ste 146 *Web:* www.wbu.com	Carmel	IN	46032	317-571-7100		578
Wild Blueberry Association of North America (WBANA) PO Box 100 *Web:* www.wildblueberries.com	Old Town	ME	04468	207-570-3535	581-3499	48-2
Wild Building Contractors Inc 225 W First N St Ste 102 *Web:* www.wildbuilding.com	Morristown	TN	37814	423-581-5639	587-4037	186
Wild Card Saloon 120 Main St *Web:* wildcardcasino.net	Black Hawk	CO	80422	303-582-3412	582-3508	133
Wild Ginger Asian Restaurant 1609 Main St *Web:* www.wildginger.net	Seattle	WA	98101	206-623-4450		671
Wild Goose Press 719 Fairmount Ave *Web:* www.wildgoosepress.com	Santa Cruz	CA	95062	831-426-6850		637-2
Wild Horizons Publishing Inc 5757 W Sweetwater Dr *Web:* www.wildhorizons.com	Tucson	AZ	85745	520-743-4551	743-4552	637-2
Wild Horse State Recreation Area HC 31 PO Box 265 *Web:* www.parks.nv.gov	Elko	NV	89801	775-385-5939		565
Wild Life Unlimited Foundation Inc 5106 Arpin Hansen Rd *TF:* 800-292-9005 ■ *Web:* wildlifevideo.com	Vesper	WI	54489	715-569-4652	569-3920	514
Wild Rice Electric Co-opeartive Inc 502 N Main PO Box 438 *TF:* 800-244-5709 ■ *Web:* www.wildriceelectric.com	Mahnomen	MN	56557	218-935-2517	935-2519	245
Wild River Press 7123 Trenton Rd *Web:* www.hiketheadirondacks.com	Barneveld	NY	13304	315-735-4877		637-10
Wild Rose Entertainment LLC 5465 Mills Civic Pkwy Ste 400 *Web:* wildroseresorts.com	West Des Moines	IA	50266	515-248-1776		656
Wild Susan (Rep D - PA) 1607 Longworth House Office Bldg *Web:* www.wild.house.gov	Washington	DC	20515	202-225-6411		342-2
Wild Swan Theater 6175 Jackson Rd Ste B *Web:* www.wildswantheater.org	Ann Arbor	MI	48103	734-995-0530		573-4
Wild Visions Inc 6990 State Rte 8 *Web:* www.carlheilman.com	Brant Lake	NY	12815	518-494-3072		590
Wild Waves Theme & Water Park 36201 Enchanted Pkwy S *Web:* www.wildwaves.com	Federal Way	WA	98003	253-661-8000		32
Wild West Express Inc 850 Squirrel Rd *TF:* 800-348-4123 ■ *Web:* wildwestexpress.com	Las Cruces	NM	88007	800-348-4123		311
Wild Wings LLC 2101 S Hwy 61 *TF:* 800-445-4833 ■ *Web:* www.wildwings.com	Lake City	MN	55041	800-445-4833		459
Wild Woods Inc 3575 Cahuenga Blvd W Ste 400 *Web:* wwoods.com	Los Angeles	CA	90068	323-878-0400		246
Wildcat Den State Park 1884 Wildcat Den Rd *Web:* www.iowadnr.gov	Muscatine	IA	52761	563-263-4337		565
Wildcat Development Corp 230 Spring Hill Dr Ste 300	Spring	TX	77386	281-863-9370		536
Wildcat Hills State Recreation Area 210615 Hwy 71 *Web:* outdoornebraska.gov	Gering	NE	69341	308-436-3777		565
Wildcat Mountain State Park E13660 State Hwy 33 PO Box 99 *Web:* dnr.wi.gov	Ontario	WI	54651	608-337-4775		565
Wilde Automotive Group 1603 E Moreland Blvd *Web:* www.wildeauto.com	Waukesha	WI	53186	262-542-9300		57
Wilde Veterinary Center LLC 29 W South Park Row *Web:* wildeveterinarycenter.com	Waterford	PA	16441	814-796-4868		794
Wildenstein & Company Inc 689 Fifth Ave *Web:* www.wildenstein.com	New York	NY	10022	212-879-0500		520
Wilderness Adventure Books PO Box 856 **Fax Area Code:* 206 ■ *TF:* 800-852-8652 ■ *Web:* www.wildernessbooks.org	Manchester	MI	48158	734-433-1595	339-6597*	637-2
Wilderness Adventures Press Inc 45 Buckskin Rd *TF:* 866-400-2012 ■ *Web:* www.wildadvpress.com	Belgrade	MT	59714	406-388-0112		637-2
Wilderness Hotel & Resort Inc 511 E Adams St *TF:* 800-867-9453 ■ *Web:* www.wildernessresort.com	Wisconsin Dells	WI	53965	800-867-9453		378
Wilderness Inquiry (WI) 808 14th Ave SE *TF:* 800-728-0719 ■ *Web:* www.wildernessinquiry.org	Minneapolis	MN	55414	612-676-9400	676-9401	48-23
Wilderness Press c/o Keen Communications 2204 First Ave S Ste 102 **Fax Area Code:* 205 ■ *TF:* 800-443-7227 ■ *Web:* www.wildernesspress.com	Birmingham	AL	35233	800-443-7227	326-1012*	637-2
Wilderness Road State Park 8051 Wilderness Rd *Web:* www.friendsofwildernessroad.org	Ewing	VA	24248	276-445-3065		565
Wilderness Society 1615 M St NW *TF:* 800-843-9453 ■ *Web:* wilderness.org	Washington	DC	20036	202-833-2300		48-13
Wilderness State Park 903 Wilderness Park Dr *Web:* www.michigan.org	Carp Lake	MI	49718	231-436-5381		565
Wilderness Travel 1102 Ninth St *TF:* 800-368-2794 ■ *Web:* www.wildernesstravel.com	Berkeley	CA	94710	510-558-2488	558-2489	760
Wildes-Spirit Design & Printing 4321 Charles Crossing Dr *Web:* www.wildes-spirit.com	White Plains	MD	20695	301-870-4141	932-7495	627
Wildflower 7037 N Oracle Rd *Web:* www.foxrc.com	Tucson	AZ	85704	520-219-4230		671
Wildflower Bread Co 7755 E Gray Rd *Web:* www.wildflowerbread.com	Scottsdale	AZ	85260	480-951-9453		297-11
Wildflower Designs 217 Country Club Pk Ste 303 *Web:* www.wildflowerdesigns.net	Birmingham	AL	35213	205-322-1311		167-3
Wilding Engineering Inc 14721 S Heritage Crest Way *Web:* wildingengineering.com	Bluffdale	UT	84065	801-553-8112		261
Wildish Land Company Inc 3600 Wildish Ln PO Box 40310 *Web:* www.wildish.com	Eugene	OR	97408	541-485-1700	683-7722	187
Wildland Adventures Inc 3516 NE 155th St *TF:* 800-345-4453 ■ *Web:* www.wildland.com	Lake Forest Park	WA	98155	206-365-0686		760
Wildlands Inc 3301 Industrial Ave *Web:* www.wildlandsinc.com	Rocklin	CA	95765	916-435-3555	435-3556	194
Wildlife Conservation Society (WCS) 2300 Southern Blvd *Web:* www.wcs.org	Bronx	NY	10460	718-220-5100		48-3
Wildlife Forever 2700 Fwy Blvd Ste 1000 *Web:* www.wildlifeforever.org	Brooklyn Center	MN	55430	763-253-0222		48-3
Wildlife Habitat Council (WHC) 8737 Colesville Rd Ste 800 *Web:* www.wildlifehc.org	Silver Spring	MD	20910	301-588-8994		48-13
Wildlife Management Institute (WMI) 1440 Upper Bermudian Rd **Fax Area Code:* 802 ■ *Web:* wildlifemanagement.institute	Gardners	PA	17324	717-677-4480	563-2157*	48-3
Wildlife Sanctuary of Northwest Florida PO Box 1092 *TF:* 800-435-7353 ■ *Web:* www.pensacolawildlife.com	Pensacola	FL	32591	850-433-9453	438-6168	823
Wildlife West Nature Park 87 N Frontage Rd *TF:* 877-981-9453 ■ *Web:* www.wildlifewest.org	Edgewood	NM	87015	505-281-7655	281-7170	823
Wildlife World Zoo 16501 W Northern Ave *Web:* www.wildlifeworld.com	Litchfield Park	AZ	85340	623-935-9453		823
Wildplay Element Parks 103-2610 Douglas St *TF:* 855-595-2251 ■ *Web:* wildplay.com	Victoria	BC	V8T4M1	250-595-2251		564
Wilds, The 14000 International Rd *Web:* www.thewilds.org	Cumberland	OH	43732	740-638-5030		823
Wildstone Media PO Box 270238 *Web:* www.wildstonemedia.com	Saint Louis	MO	63127	314-629-5421		637-2
WildTangent Inc 18578 NE 67th Ct *Web:* www.wildtangent.com	Redmond	WA	98052	425-497-4545	497-4501	178-6
Wildwater PO Box 309 **Fax Area Code:* 864 ■ *TF:* 800-319-8870 ■ *Web:* www.wildwaterrafting.com	Long Creek	SC	29658	800-319-8870	647-5361*	239
Wildwood Animal Hospital & Clinics 210 Airpark Rd *Web:* wildwoodanimalhospital.net	Marshfield	WI	54449	715-387-1225		794
Wildwood Correctional Ctr 10 Chugach Ave *Web:* www.correct.state.ak.us	Kenai	AK	99611	907-260-7200	260-7208	213
Wildwood Express Trucking 12416 E Swanson Ave *Web:* wildwoodex.com	Kingsburg	CA	93631	559-897-1035	897-1038	780
Wildwood Lamps & Accents 516 Paul St PO Box 672 *Web:* www.wildwoodlamps.com	Rocky Mount	NC	27803	252-446-3266	977-6669	439
Wildwood State Park 790 Hulse Landing Rd PO Box 518 *Web:* parks.ny.gov	Wading River	NY	11792	631-929-4314		565
Wildwoods Convention Ctr 4501 Boardwalk *TF:* 800-992-9732 ■ *Web:* www.wildwoodsnj.com	Wildwood	NJ	08260	609-729-9000	846-2631	205
Wilen Direct 3333 SW 15th St *Web:* www.wilengroup.com	Deerfield Beach	FL	33442	954-246-5000		627
Wilen New York 5 Wellwood Ave *Web:* www.wilennewyork.com	Farmingdale	NY	11735	631-439-5000		5

	Phone	Fax	Class
Wiley & Wilson Inc 127 Nationwide Dr .... Lynchburg VA 24502 *Web:* www.wileywilson.com	434-947-1901		261
Wiley College 711 Wiley Ave. .... Marshall TX 75670 *TF:* 800-658-6889 ■ *Web:* www.wileyc.edu	903-927-3300	927-3366	166
Wiley Law SC 119 1/2 N Bridge St PO Box 370 .... Chippewa Falls WI 54729 *Web:* wileylaw.com	715-723-8591		41
Wiley Metal Fabricating Inc 4589 N Wabash Rd .... Marion IN 46952 *Web:* www.wileymetal.com	765-671-7865		697
Wiley Rein LLP 1776 K St N W .... Washington DC 20006 *Web:* www.wiley.law	202-719-7000		428
Wiley Sanders Truck Lines Inc PO Box 707 .... Troy AL 36081 **Fax Area Code:* 334 ■ *TF:* 800-392-8017 ■ *Web:* www.wileysanders.com	800-392-8017	566-3257*	485
Wiley X. Inc 7800 Patterson Pass Rd. .... Livermore CA 94550 *TF:* 800-776-7842 ■ *Web:* www.wileyx.com	925-243-9810		543
Wiley's Waterski Pro Shop 1417 S Trenton St. .... Seattle WA 98108 *TF:* 800-962-0785 ■ *Web:* www.wileyski.com	206-762-1300	762-7339	710
Wilfrid Laurier University 75 University Ave W .... Waterloo ON N2L3C5 *Web:* wlu.ca	519-884-0710	886-9351	785
Wilgus State Park 3985 Rt 5 .... Weathersfield VT 05156 *Web:* vtstateparks.com	802-674-5422		565
Wilheit Packaging LLC 1527 May Dr .... Gainesville GA 30507 *TF:* 800-727-4421 ■ *Web:* www.wilheit.com	770-532-4421		449
Wilhelmina Models Inc 300 Park Ave S .... New York NY 10010 *Web:* www.wilhelmina.com	212-473-0700	473-3223	506
Wilke International Inc 14321 W 96th Ter .... Lenexa KS 66215 *Web:* www.wilkeinternational.com	913-438-5544	438-5554	146
Wilkerson 222 S Main St .... Stuttgart AR 72160 *TF:* 800-631-1999 ■ *Web:* www.wilkersons.com	800-631-1999	949-1333	410
Wilkerson Crane Rental PO Box 12554 .... Kansas City KS 66112 *Web:* www.wilkersoncranerental.com	913-238-7030		188
Wilkerson Instrument Company Inc 2915 Parkway St. .... Lakeland FL 33811 *TF:* 800-234-1343 ■ *Web:* wici.com	863-647-2000	644-5318	201
Wilkes & McHugh P A 1 N Dale Mabry Hwy Ste 800 .... Tampa FL 33609 *TF:* 800-255-5070 ■ *Web:* www.wilkesmchugh.com	800-255-5070		445
Wilkes Chamber of Commerce 717 Main St .... North Wilkesboro NC 28659 *Web:* www.wilkeschamber.com	336-838-8662	838-3728	139
Wilkes Community College 1328 S Collegiate Dr PO Box 120. .... Wilkesboro NC 28697 *TF:* 866-222-1548 ■ *Web:* www.wilkescc.edu	336-838-6100	838-6277	162
Wilkes Correctional Ctr PO Box 253 .... North Wilkesboro NC 28659 *Web:* www.wilkesprisonministry.org	336-667-4533		213
Wilkes County 22 W Robert Toombs Ave PO Box 661 .... Washington GA 30673 *Web:* www.washingtonwilkes.org	706-678-2511		338
Wilkes County 110 N St .... Wilkesboro NC 28697 *Web:* wilkescounty.net	336-651-7346	651-7546	338
Wilkes Dining Room 107 W Jones St. .... Savannah GA 31401 *Web:* mrswilkes.com	912-232-5997		671
Wilkes University 84 W South St .... Wilkes-Barre PA 18766 **Fax Area Code:* 570 ■ *TF:* 800-945-5378 ■ *Web:* wilkes.edu	800-945-5378	408-4904*	166
Wilkes-Barre Law and Library Assn Luzerne County Courthouse 200 N River St Rm 23 .... Wilkes-Barre PA 18711 *Web:* www.luzernecountybar.com	570-822-6712	822-8210	49-19
Wilkes-Barre/Scranton International Airport 100 Terminal Dr .... Avoca PA 18641 *Web:* www.flyavp.com	570-602-2000	602-2010	27
Wilkie Lexus 568 W Lancaster Ave .... Haverford PA 19041 *Web:* www.wilkielexus.com	610-525-0900		57
Wilkin & Guttenplan PC 1200 Tices Ln .... East Brunswick NJ 08816 *Web:* www.wgcpas.com	732-846-3000		2
Wilkin County 300 Fifth St S .... Breckenridge MN 56520 *Web:* www.co.wilkin.mn.us	218-643-7172	643-7167	338
Wilkins Investment Counsel Inc 160 Federal St 22nd Fl .... Boston MA 02110 *Web:* www.wilkinsinvest.com	617-951-9969	951-0773	528
Wilkins Media 555 5th Ave 18th fl .... New York NY 10017 **Fax Area Code:* 770 ■ *Web:* wilkinsmedia.com	212-929-5380	804-0029*	5
Wilkins Mobile Builders Inc PO Box 1089 .... Double Springs AL 35553 *Web:* www.wilkinsbuilders.com	205-489-5843		505
Wilkins Research Services LLC 1730 Gunbarrel Rd .... Chattanooga TN 37421 *TF:* 800-949-5300 ■ *Web:* wilkinsresearch.net	423-894-9478		466
Wilkins, Drolshagen & Czeshinski LLP 6785 N Willow Ave .... Fresno CA 93710 *Web:* wdcllp.com	559-438-2390	438-2393	41
Wilkinson & Associates Real Estate Inc 8604 Cliff Cameron Dr Ste 110. .... Charlotte NC 28269 *Web:* www.wilkinsonera.com	704-393-0048		652
Wilkinson & Snowden Inc 6363 Poplar Ave Ste 220 .... Memphis TN 38119 *Web:* collierswsproperties.com	901-375-4800		652
Wilkinson Barker Knauer LLP 2300 N St NW Ste 700 .... Washington DC 20037 *Web:* www.wbklaw.com	202-783-4141		428
Wilkinson County 100 Bacon St .... Irwinton GA 31042 *Web:* wilkinsoncounty.net	478-946-2236	946-3767	338
Wilkinson County PO Box 40 .... Woodville MS 39669 *Web:* www.wilkinson.co.ms.gov	601-888-3538	888-7591	338
Wilkinson International Inc 1207 E Kentucky Ave .... Woodland CA 95776 *Web:* wilkinsoninternational.com	530-662-7373	662-1387	274
Wilkinson Supply Co 3300 Bush St .... Raleigh NC 27609 *Web:* www.wilkinsonsupplyco.com	919-834-0395		612
Wilkins-Rogers Inc 27 Frederick Rd .... Ellicott City MD 21043 *Web:* www.wrmills.com	410-465-5800		296-23
Wilkman Productions Inc 6160 Rodgerton Dr .... Hollywood CA 90068 *Web:* www.wilkman.com	323-461-7028	461-0753	514
Wilks Tire & Battery Service Inc 428 N Broad St .... Albertville AL 35950 *Web:* www.wilkstire.com	256-878-0211	878-0287	755
Will County 302 N Chicago St .... Joliet IL 60432 *Web:* www.willcountyillinois.com	815-740-4615		338
Will Rogers Memorial Museum 1720 W Will Rogers Blvd .... Claremore OK 74017 *TF:* 800-324-9455 ■ *Web:* www.willrogers.com	918-341-0719		520
Will Rogers World Airport 7100 Terminal Dr Unit 937 .... Oklahoma City OK 73159 *Web:* flyokc.com	405-680-3200		27
Will Vision & Laser Centers 8100 NE Pkwy Dr Ste 125. .... Vancouver WA 98662 **Fax Area Code:* 360 ■ *TF:* 877-542-3937 ■ *Web:* www.willvision.com	877-542-3937	918-9720*	798
Willacy County 576 W Main Ave Ste 102 .... Raymondville TX 78580 *Web:* co.willacy.tx.us	956-689-2532	689-5713	338
Willacy County State Jail 1695 S Buffalo Dr .... Raymondville TX 78580 *Web:* www.tdcj.texas.gov	956-689-4900		213
Willamette Education Service District Employees Association Inc 2611 Pringle Rd SE .... Salem OR 97302 *Web:* www.wesd.org	503-588-5330		414
Willamette National Cemetery 11800 SE Mt Scott Blvd .... Portland OR 97086 *Web:* www.cem.va.gov	503-273-5250		136
Willamette Plastics Inc 1111 NW 5th Pl .... Canby OR 97013 *TF:* 888-300-2528 ■ *Web:* www.willametteplastics.com	503-266-6233	263-6122	604
Willamette Sleep Ctr 180 Ramsgate Sq SE .... Salem OR 97302 *Web:* www.willamettesleepcenter.com	503-485-0672	485-0673	352
Willamette Stone State Heritage Site 11321 SW Terwilliger Blvd .... Portland OR 97219 *Web:* stateparks.oregon.gov	503-636-9886		565
Willamette University 900 State St .... Salem OR 97301 *TF:* 877-542-2787 ■ *Web:* www.willamette.edu	503-370-6303	375-5363	166
Willamette Valley Co 1075 Arrowsmith St .... Eugene OR 97402 *TF:* 800-333-9826 ■ *Web:* www.wilvaco.com	541-484-9621	345-7480	550
Willamette Valley Hospice 1015 Third St NW .... Salem OR 97304 *TF:* 800-555-2431 ■ *Web:* www.wvh.org	503-588-3600	363-3891	371
Willamette Valley Vineyards Inc 8800 Enchanted Way SE .... Turner OR 97392 *NASDAQ:* WVVI ■ *TF:* 800-344-9463 ■ *Web:* www.wvv.com	503-588-9463	588-8894	80-3
Willamette View 12705 SE River Rd. .... Portland OR 97222 *TF:* 800-446-0670 ■ *Web:* www.willametteview.org	503-654-6581		672
Willamette Week 2220 NW Quimby St. .... Portland OR 97210 *Web:* www.wweek.com	503-243-2122	243-1115	532-5
Willard Brook State Forest 595 Main St RT 119 W .... Townsend MA 01474 *Web:* www.mass.gov	978-597-8802		565
Willard Companies Inc, The 75 Builders Pride Dr Ste 200 .... Hardy VA 24101 *Web:* www.thewillardcompanies.com	540-721-5288		653
Willard Hotel 1400 F St NW / Willard Hotel .... Washington DC 20004 *Web:* washington.intercontinental.com	202-628-9100		377
Willard House & Clock Museum 11 Willard St .... North Grafton MA 01536 *Web:* www.willardhouse.org	508-839-3500		520
Willard Marine Inc 1250 N Grove St .... Anaheim CA 92806 *Web:* www.willardmarine.com	714-666-2150	632-8136	90
Willard Packaging Company Inc 18940 Woodfield Rd .... Gaithersburg MD 20879 *Web:* www.willardpackaging.com	301-948-7700		557
Willard-Cybulski Correctional Institution 391 Shaker Rd .... Enfield CT 06082 *Web:* portal.ct.gov	860-763-6100	763-6111	213
Willbanks Environmental Consulting Inc 755 N Peach Ave Ste G-9 .... Clovis CA 93611 *Web:* willbanksenvco.com	559-797-4181		261
Willbanks Metals Inc 1155 NE 28th St .... Fort Worth TX 76106 *TF:* 800-772-2352 ■ *Web:* www.willbanksmetals.com	817-625-6161	625-8487	492
Willbros Group Inc 4400 Post Oak Pkwy Ste 1000 .... Houston TX 77027 *Web:* www.willbros.com	713-403-8000		261
Will-Burt Co 169 S Main St .... Orrville OH 44667 *Web:* www.willburt.com	330-682-7015	684-1190	454
Willcan Inc PO Box 1357 .... Calhoun GA 30703 *Web:* www.basicreadymix.com	706-629-2256	625-0587	182
Willcox, Buyck & Williams PA 248 W Evans St .... Florence SC 29501 *Web:* willcoxlaw.com	843-461-3020		428
Willdan 2401 E Katella Ave Ste 300 .... Anaheim CA 92806 *TF:* 800-424-9144 ■ *Web:* www.willdan.com	714-940-6300	940-4920	261
Wille Brothers Co 15800 S Lamon .... Oak Forest IL 60452 *Web:* www.willebrothers.com	708-687-4000	687-8652	191-1
Willems Marketing & Events 120 N Morrison St Ste 200 .... Appleton WI 54911 *Web:* www.willemsmarketingandevents.com	920-831-6580	738-6995	195
Willens Law Offices PC 30 N Lasalle St Ste 3450 .... Chicago IL 60602 *Web:* willenslaw.com	312-957-4166		41
Willert Home Products Inc 4044 Park Ave .... Saint Louis MO 63110 *Web:* www.willert.com	314-772-2822	772-1409	151
Willett Hall 3701 Willett Dr .... Portsmouth VA 23707 *Web:* www.willett-hall-portsmouth.com	757-393-5144		572
Willey Honda 2215 S 500 W .... Bountiful UT 84010 *TF:* 888-431-4490 ■ *Web:* www.performancehondabountiful.com	888-431-4490		57

	Phone	Fax	Class
Willey Printing Company Inc 1405 10th St Modesto CA 95354 *Web:* www.willeyprinting.com	209-524-4811	524-8521	627
Willi Hahn Corporation - Wiha Tools 1348 Dundas Cir Monticello MN 55362 *Web:* www.wihatools.com	763-295-6591		820
William & Flora Hewlett Foundation 2121 Sand Hill Rd Menlo Park CA 94025 *Web:* www.hewlett.org	650-234-4500		305
William & Mary 400 Landrum Dr Williamsburg VA 23187 *TF:* 800-462-3683 ■ *Web:* libraries.wm.edu	757-221-3072	221-2635	434-6
William & Mary Law School 613 S Henry St Williamsburg VA 23185 *Web:* www.wm.edu	757-221-3800	221-3261	167-1
William A. Egan Civic & Convention Ctr 555 W Fifth Ave Anchorage AK 99501 *Web:* anchorageconventioncenters.com	907-263-2800	263-2858	205
William A. Randolph Inc 820 Lakeside Dr Ste 3 Gurnee IL 60031 *Web:* warandolph.com	847-856-0123		186
William Avery & Associates Inc 3 1/2 N Santa Cruz Ave Ste A Los Gatos CA 95030 *Web:* www.averyassoc.net	408-399-4424	399-4423	463
William B. Meyer Inc 255 Long Beach Blvd Stratford CT 06615 *TF:* 800-727-5985 ■ *Web:* www.williambmeyer.com	800-727-5985		685
William B. Umstead State Park 8801 Glenwood Ave Raleigh NC 27617 *Web:* www.ncparks.gov	919-571-4170		565
William Beaumont Army Medical Ctr 6301 Brisa Del Mar Dr El Paso TX 79920 *Web:* www.wbamc.amedd.army.mil	915-742-2273		374-4
William Blair & Company LLC 222 W Adams St Chicago IL 60606 *TF:* 800-621-0687 ■ *Web:* www.williamblair.com	312-236-1600		690
William Blanchard Co 199 Mountain Ave Springfield NJ 07081 *Web:* www.wmblanchard.com	973-376-9100	376-9154	186
William Breman Jewish Heritage Museum 1440 Spring St NW Atlanta GA 30309 *Web:* www.thebreman.org	678-222-3700		520
William Burton & Company Inc 99 Walnut St Saugus MA 01906 *Web:* www.cpaburton.com	781-233-2204		2
William C. Darrah Attorney At Law A Law Corp 737 Bishop St Ste 2820 Honolulu HI 96813 *Web:* wcdlawhawaii.com	808-533-2930		41
William C. Smith & Company Inc 1100 New Jersey Ave SE Washington DC 20003 *Web:* www.wcsmith.com	202-371-1220		652
William Carey International University 1539 E Howard St Pasadena CA 91104 *Web:* www.wciu.edu	626-398-2222		162
William Carey University 498 Tuscan Ave Hattiesburg MS 39401 *TF:* 800-962-5991 ■ *Web:* wmcarey.edu	601-318-6051	318-6454	166
William Carpenter Consulting 928 Arabian Ave Winter Springs FL 32708 *Web:* www.wcarpenterconsulting.com	407-971-9834	359-5489	194
William Charles Executive Search Partners 5550 Cascade Rd SE Ste 200 Grand Rapids MI 49546 *Web:* www.william-charles.com	616-464-4355		226
William Crow Jewelry 910 16th St Ste 320 Denver CO 80202 *Web:* www.williamcrow.com	303-592-1695		410
William D. Bishop PC 7210 N 16th St Phoenix AZ 85020 *Web:* bishoplawoffice.com	602-749-8500		41
William Dailey Rare Books Ltd 8216 Melrose Ave Los Angeles CA 90046 *Web:* www.daileyrarebooks.com	323-658-8515		637-2
William Douglas Management Inc 4523 Park Rd Ste 201 A Charlotte NC 28209 *Web:* wmdouglas.com	704-347-8900	377-3408	652
William E. Laupus Health Sciences Library 500 Health Science Dr 600 Moye Blvd Health Sciences Bldg Greenville NC 27834 *Web:* hsl.ecu.edu	252-744-2219	744-1376	434-1
William E. Walter Inc 1917 Howard Ave Flint MI 48503 *TF:* 800-681-3320 ■ *Web:* www.williamewalter.com	810-232-7459	232-8698	189-10
William F. Anzalone 98 S Franklin St Wilkes-Barre PA 18701 *TF:* 877-256-6933 ■ *Web:* anzalonelaw.com	570-825-2719		41
William F. Laman Public Library System 2801 Orange St North Little Rock AR 72114 *Web:* www.lamanlibrary.org	501-758-1720	758-3539	434-3
William F. Renk & Sons Inc 6809 Wilburn Rd Sun Prairie WI 53590 **Fax Area Code:* 608 ■ *TF:* 800-289-7365 ■ *Web:* www.renkseed.com	800-289-7365	825-6143*	10-5
William F. White International Inc 800 Islington Ave Toronto ON M8Z6A1 *Web:* www.whites.com	416-239-5050		111
William Fox Munroe Inc (WFM) 3 E Lancaster Ave Shillington PA 19607 *TF:* 800-344-2402 ■ *Web:* wfoxm.com	610-775-4521		344
William Frick & Co 2600 Commerce Dr Libertyville IL 60048 *Web:* www.fricknet.com	847-918-3700		687
William G. Koch & Assoc 2650 Wview Dr Wyomissing PA 19610 *Web:* wgkcpa.com	610-678-9700	678-9224	2
William George Company Inc 1002 Mize Ave Lufkin TX 75904 *Web:* www.williamgeorgeinc.com	936-634-7738	634-7794	297-11
William George Printing LLC 3469 Black & Decker Rd Hope Mills NC 28348 *Web:* m.wgprinting.com	910-221-2700		627
William Goldberg Diamond Corp 589 Fifth Ave New York NY 10017 *Web:* www.williamgoldberg.com	212-980-4343		407
William H. Horton & Associates Pll 735 Broad St Ste 306 Chattanooga TN 37402 *Web:* hbplawfirm.com	423-826-2640		41
William H. Kopke Jr Inc 1000 N Blvd Great Neck NY 11021 *Web:* www.kopkefruit.com	516-328-6800	328-6874	297-7
William H. Lord Inc 9210 N College Ave Indianapolis IN 46240 *Web:* www.stagecrafter.com	317-846-3907	581-9013	196
William H. Sadlier Inc 9 Pine St New York NY 10005 *OTC:* SADL ■ **Fax Area Code:* 212 ■ *TF:* 800-221-5175 ■ *Web:* www.sadlier.com	800-221-5175	312-6080*	637-2
William Howard Taft National Historic Site 2038 Auburn Ave Cincinnati OH 45219 *Web:* www.nps.gov	513-684-3262	684-3627	564
William Ives Consulting Inc 320 S Tryon St Ste 213 Charlotte NC 28202 *Web:* www.wicusa.com	704-376-5600		196
William J Labb Sons Inc 4617 Milnor St Philadelphia PA 19137 *Web:* www.labbmachine.com	215-289-4515	533-2022	454
William J. Chabina Company Inc 30 Whitney Ave Syosset NY 11791 *Web:* chabinainsurance.com	516-364-4700	364-4770	390
William J. Clinton Presidential Ctr 1200 President Clinton Ave Little Rock AR 72201 *Web:* www.clintonfoundation.org	212-397-2255		434-2
William J. Dixon Company Inc 756 Springdale Dr Exton PA 19341 *Web:* wjdixon.com	610-524-1131		745-7
William J. Stogsdill, Jr. PC 1776 S Naperville Rd Bldg B Ste 202 Wheaton IL 60187 *Web:* stogsdilllaw.com	630-462-9500		41
William Jessup University 2121 University Ave Rocklin CA 95765 *TF:* 800-355-7522 ■ *Web:* www.jessup.edu	916-577-2200	577-2220	166
William Jewell College 500 College Hill WJC Liberty MO 64068 *TF:* 888-253-9355 ■ *Web:* jewell.edu	816-781-7700	415-5040	166
William K. Sanford Town Library 629 Albany Shaker Rd Loudonville NY 12211 *Web:* www.colonie.org	518-458-9274		434-3
William K. Walthers Inc 5601 W Florist Ave Milwaukee WI 53218 *TF:* 800-877-7171 ■ *Web:* www.walthers.com	414-527-0770	527-4423	762
William Kendrick Co 401 Butternut St NW Washington DC 20012 *Web:* promosource.com	202-882-0903	726-1758	366
WIlliam L. Lyon & Associates Inc 3640 American River Dr Ste 100 Sacramento CA 95864 *TF:* 866-596-6466 ■ *Web:* golyon.com	866-596-6466		652
William Lyon Homes 4695 MacArthur Ct 8th Fl Newport Beach CA 92660 *Web:* www.lyonhomes.com	949-833-3600		187
William M. Dingfelder 645 W Sedgwick St Philadelphia PA 19119 *Web:* www.grantwritingconsultant.com	610-667-5071		192
William M. Tugman State Park 72549 Hwy 101 Lakeside OR 97449 *Web:* stateparks.oregon.gov	541-759-3604		565
William Marvy Company Inc 1540 St Clair Ave Saint Paul MN 55105 *TF:* 800-874-2651 ■ *Web:* www.wmmarvyco.com	651-698-0726	698-4048	76
William Mitchell College of Law 875 Summit Ave Saint Paul MN 55105 *TF:* 888-962-5529 ■ *Web:* mitchellhamline.edu	651-227-9171		167-1
William Morrow & Co 10 E 53rd St New York NY 10022 *TF:* 800-242-7737 ■ *Web:* www.harpercollins.com	212-207-7000		637-2
William N Cann Inc 1 Meco Cir Wilmington DE 19804 *Web:* www.cannprinting.com	302-995-0820		627
William Ng Woodworks School of Fine Woodworking 1340 N Dynamics St Ste H Anaheim CA 92806 *Web:* www.wnwoodworkingschool.com	714-993-4215		685
William Ohs Showrooms of Denver 115 Madison St Denver CO 80206 *Web:* www.wmohs.com	303-321-3232		115
William Paterson University 300 Pompton Rd Wayne NJ 07470 *TF:* 877-978-3923 ■ *Web:* wpunj.edu	973-720-2000	720-2910	166
William Peace University 15 E Peace St Raleigh NC 27604 *Web:* www.peace.edu	919-508-2000	508-2337	166
William Penn Assn 709 Brighton Rd Pittsburgh PA 15233 *TF:* 800-848-7366 ■ *Web:* www.williampennassociation.org	412-231-2979		390
William Penn Foundation 100 N 18th St 2 Logan Sq 11th Fl Philadelphia PA 19103 *Web:* www.williampennfoundation.org	215-988-1830	988-1823	305
William Penn University 201 Trueblood Ave Oskaloosa IA 52577 **Fax Area Code:* 641 ■ *TF:* 800-779-7366 ■ *Web:* www.wmpenn.edu	800-779-7366	673-2113*	166
William S. Hart Museum 24151 Newhall Ave Newhall CA 91321 *Web:* hartmuseum.org	661-254-4584		520
William S. Hein & Company Inc 1285 Main St Buffalo NY 14209 *TF:* 800-828-7571 ■ *Web:* www.wshein.com	716-882-2600	883-8100	637-2
William Steinen Manufacturing Co 29 E Halsey Rd Parsippany NJ 07054 *Web:* www.steinen.com	973-887-6400	887-4632	609
William T. McFatter Technical Ctr 6500 Nova Dr Davie FL 33317 *Web:* www.mcfattertechnicalcollege.edu	754-321-5700		167-3
William Trent House 15 Market St Trenton NJ 08611 *Web:* www.williamtrenthouse.org	609-989-3027		50-3
William V. MacGill & Co 1000 N Lombard Rd Lombard IL 60148 **Fax Area Code:* 800 ■ *TF:* 800-323-2841 ■ *Web:* www.macgill.com	630-889-0500	727-3433*	475
William W. Backus Hospital 326 Washington St Norwich CT 06360 *Web:* backushospital.org	860-889-8331		374-3

Name / Address	City	State	ZIP	Phone	Fax	Class
William W. Brown CPA PA 104 Broadus Ave. *Web:* www.familylegacyinc.com	Greenville	SC	29601	864-233-0808		2
William W. Powers State Recreation Area 12949 S Ave O *Web:* www2.illinois.gov	Chicago	IL	60633	773-646-3270		565
William W. Price PA 320 Fern St. *Web:* www.wpricepa.com	West Palm Beach	FL	33401	561-659-3212		428
William W. Rutherford Associates Inc 945 Gessner Rd *Web:* wwrutherford.com	Houston	TX	77024	214-219-8660		463
William W. Seymour Associates PC 170 Noroton Ave. *Web:* wws-ls.com	Darien	CT	06820	203-655-3331		727
William Whitley House State Historic Site 625 William Whitley Rd *Web:* parks.ky.gov	Stanford	KY	40484	606-355-2881		565
William Woods University 1 University Ave *TF:* 800-995-3159 ■ *Web:* www.williamwoods.edu	Fulton	MO	65251	573-592-4221	592-1146	166
Williams & Anderson PLC 111 Center St Ste 2200. *Web:* williamsanderson.com	Little Rock	AR	72201	501-859-0575	372-6453	428
Williams & Associates Inc 247 S Wilmot Rd *Web:* www.wasoc.com	Tucson	AZ	85711	520-745-8500		4
Williams & Connolly LLP 725 12th St NW *Web:* www.wc.com	Washington	DC	20005	202-434-5000	434-5029	428
Williams & Fudge Inc 300 Chatham Ave *Web:* wfcorp.com	Rock Hill	SC	29730	803-329-9791		160
Williams & Heintz Map Corp 8119 Central Ave *TF:* 800-338-6228 ■ *Web:* www.whmap.com	Capitol Heights	MD	20743	301-336-1143	336-5520	627
Williams & Helde Inc 711 Sixth Ave N Ste 200. *Web:* williams-helde.com	Seattle	WA	98109	206-285-1940	283-8897	7
Williams & Schoenberger Company LLC 338 S High St 2nd Fl *Web:* wslegalfirm.com	Columbus	OH	43215	614-224-0531	224-0553	428
Williams & Williams Real Estate Auctions 7120 S Lewis Ave Ste 200 *TF:* 800-801-8003 ■ *Web:* www.williamsauction.com	Tulsa	OK	74136	800-801-8003		652
Williams & Works Inc 549 Ottawa NW. *Web:* williams-works.com	Grand Rapids	MI	49503	616-224-1500		261
Williams Baptist College 60 W Fulbright St. *TF:* 800-722-4434 ■ *Web:* www.wbcoll.edu	Walnut Ridge	AR	72476	870-886-6741	886-3924	166
Williams Benator & Libby LLP 1040 Crown Pinte Pkwy NE Ste 400. *Web:* wblcpa.com	Atlanta	GA	30338	770-512-0500	512-0200	2
Williams Broadcasting new england. *Web:* www.williamsbroadcasting.net	Norway	ME	04268	207-527-2000		645-141
Williams Bros Construction Company Inc 3800 Milam St *Web:* wbctx.com	Houston	TX	77006	713-522-9821	520-5247	188-4
Williams Brothers Trucking 466 Baxley Hwy *TF:* 800-822-7730 ■ *Web:* www.wbtus.com	Hazlehurst	GA	31539	912-375-7777		780
Williams Bus Lines Inc PO Box 1272 *Web:* www.williamsbus.com	Springfield	VA	22151	703-560-5355	560-7851	109
Williams College 880 Main St *TF:* 877-374-7526 ■ *Web:* www.williams.edu	Williamstown	MA	01267	413-597-3131	597-4052	166
Williams College Museum of Art (WCMA) 15 Lawrence Hall Dr Ste 2 *Web:* wcma.williams.edu	Williamstown	MA	01267	413-597-2429		166
Williams Comfort Products 250 W Laurel St *TF:* 866-677-8444 ■ *Web:* www.williamscomfortprod.com	Colton	CA	92324	909-825-0993	824-8009	357
Williams Communications Inc 5046 Tennessee Capital Blvd *TF:* 800-649-5783 ■ *Web:* www.wmscom.com	Tallahassee	FL	32303	850-385-1121	575-0346	681
Williams Companies Inc 1 Williams Ctr *NYSE: WMB* ■ *TF:* 800-945-5426 ■ *Web:* www.williams.com	Tulsa	OK	74172	918-573-2000		360-3
Williams Company of Orlando Inc 2301 Silver Star Rd. *Web:* www.williamsco.com	Orlando	FL	32804	407-295-2530		186
Williams County 1 Courthouse Sq *Web:* www.co.williams.oh.us	Bryan	OH	43506	419-636-2059	636-0643	338
Williams County PO Box 2047 *Web:* www.williamsnd.com	Williston	ND	58802	701-577-4540	577-4535	338
Williams Creek Consulting 619 N Pennsylvania St *TF:* 877-668-8848 ■ *Web:* www.williamscreek.net	Indianapolis	IN	46202	317-423-0690		261
Williams Distributing Co 658 Richmond NW *Web:* www.wmsdist.com	Grand Rapids	MI	49504	616-456-1613	771-0490	14
Williams Engineering Canada Inc 10065 Jasper Ave Ste 200 *TF:* 800-263-2393 ■ *Web:* williamsengineering.com	Edmonton	AB	T5J3B1	780-409-5300		256
Williams Financial Group Inc 2711 N Haskell Ave Cityplace Twr Ste 2900 *TF:* 800-225-3650 ■ *Web:* www.williams-financial.com	Dallas	TX	75204	972-661-8700		691
Williams Fire & Hazard Control Inc 9605 Richard Wycoff *Web:* www.williamsfire.com	Port Arthur	TX	77640	409-745-4760	745-3021	261
Williams Firm PC 8263 S Saginaw St Ste 6 *Web:* thewilliamsfirm.com	Grand Blanc	MI	48439	810-695-7777		41
Williams Form Engineering Corp 8165 Graphic Dr *Web:* www.williamsform.com	Belmont	MI	49306	616-866-0815	866-1810	386
Williams Gun Sight Co 7389 Lapeer Rd. *TF:* 800-530-9028 ■ *Web.* williamsgunsight.com	Davison	MI	48423	810-653-2131	658-2140	284
Williams Health Care Systems 158 N Edison Ave **Fax Area Code:* 847 ■ *TF:* 800-441-4967 ■ *Web:* www.williamshealthcare.com	Elgin	IL	60123	800-441-4967	741-3661*	477
Williams Industrial Service Inc 2120 Wood-Bridge Blvd *Web:* www.wisfurnaces.com	Bowling Green	OH	43402	419-353-2120	353-7712	318
Williams Industries Inc 8624 JD Reading Dr PO Box 1770 *OTC: WMSI* ■ *Web:* www.wmsi.com	Manassas	VA	20109	703-335-7800	335-7802	189-14
Williams Intl 2000 Centerpoint Pkwy. *TF:* 800-859-3544 ■ *Web:* www.williams-int.com	Pontiac	MI	48341	248-624-5200	624-5345	21
Williams Kitchen & Bath 658 Richmond NW *Web:* www.williamskitchen.com	Grand Rapids	MI	49504	616-771-0505		38
Williams Lake & District Credit Union 139 N Third Ave *TF:* 866-392-6231 ■ *Web:* www.wldcu.com	Williams Lake	BC	V2G2A5	250-392-4135		219
Williams Lumber & Home Centers 6760 Rt 9 *Web:* williamslumber.com	Rhinebeck	NY	12572	845-876-9663		364
Williams Machine & Tool Company Inc 1009 Schermerhorn Rd. *Web:* www.wilmaco.com	Galena	KS	66739	620-783-5184	783-5084	454
Williams Machine Works Inc 5624 Main St *Web:* www.williamsmachineworks.net	Moss Point	MS	39562	228-475-7651	474-1679	454
Williams Management Resources Inc (WMR) 1717 N Naper Blvd Ste 102 *Web:* www.wmrhq.com	Naperville	IL	60563	630-416-1166	416-9798	47
Williams Metals & Welding Alloys Inc 125 Strafford Ave Ste 108. *TF:* 877-499-1544 ■ *Web:* www.wmwa.net	Wayne	PA	19087	610-225-0105	225-0208	492
Williams Mullen 1021 E Cary St James Ctr Two *Web:* www.williamsmullen.com	Richmond	VA	23219	804-783-6901		428
Williams Nationalease Ltd 400 W Northtown Rd *TF:* 800-779-8785 ■ *Web:* www.williamsdedicated.com	Normal	IL	61761	309-452-1110		57
Williams Notaro & Associates LLC 3928 Pender Dr Ste 220 *Web:* wnainc.com	Fairfax	VA	22030	703-563-0381		261
Williams Oil Company Inc 101 N Main St Ste 1 *Web:* www.williamsoil.com	Athens	PA	18810	570-888-4344		579
Williams Parker Harrison Dietz & Getzen PA 200 S Orange Ave. *Web:* www.williamsparker.com	Sarasota	FL	34236	941-366-4800		428
Williams Records Management 1925 E Vernon Ave *TF:* 888-478-3453 ■ *Web:* www.williamsdatamanagement.com	Los Angeles	CA	90058	323-234-3453	233-5451	225
Williams Roger (Rep R - TX) 1708 Longworth House Office Bldg *Web:* williams.house.gov	Washington	DC	20515	202-225-9896		342-2
Williams Sausage Company Inc 5132 Old Troy Hickman Rd. *TF:* 800-844-4242 ■ *Web:* www.williams-sausage.com	Union City	TN	38261	731-885-5841		297-9
Williams Sound LLC 10300 Valley View Rd. *TF:* 800-328-6190 ■ *Web:* www.williamssound.com	Eden Prairie	MN	55344	952-943-2252	943-2174	647
Williams Supply Inc 210 Seventh St *TF:* 800-533-6969 ■ *Web:* eecoonline.com	Roanoke	VA	24016	540-343-9333	342-3254	246
Williams Tooling & Manufacturing Inc 1856 142nd Ave *Web:* www.williamstooling.com	Dorr	MI	49323	616-681-2093	681-2196	757
Williams White & Co 600 River Dr. *TF:* 877-797-7650 ■ *Web:* www.williamswhite.com	Moline	IL	61265	877-797-7650		456
Williams Whittle Associates Inc 711 Princess St *Web:* www.williamswhittle.com	Alexandria	VA	22314	703-836-9222		4
Williams, Charles & Scott Ltd 2171 Jericho Tpke LL1 *TF:* 800-652-4445 ■ *Web:* wcscollects.com	Commack	NY	11725	631-462-1553		160
Williams, Jones & Associates LLC 717 Fifth Ave 11th Fl *Web:* www.williamsjones.com	New York	NY	10022	212-935-8750		401
Williams, Kastner & Gibbs PLLC 601 Union St Ste 4100 *Web:* www.williamskastner.com	Seattle	WA	98101	206-628-6600		428
Williams, Stitely & Brink PC 200 E Main St. *Web:* wsblegal.com	Lexington	SC	29072	803-359-9000		41
Williams, Turner & Holmes PC 744 Horizon Crt Ste 115. *TF:* 800-548-6528 ■ *Web:* www.wth-law.com	Grand Junction	CO	81506	970-242-6262		428
Williamsburg County 201 W Main St. *Web:* www.williamsburgcounty.sc.gov	Kingstree	SC	29556	843-355-9321	355-1587	338
Williamsburg County Library 215 N Jackson St *Web:* www.mywcl.org	Kingstree	SC	29556	843-355-9486	355-9991	434-3
Williamsburg Hometown Chamber of Commerce 131 N Academy St PO Box 696 *Web:* www.williamsburgsc.org	Kingstree	SC	29556	843-355-6431	355-3343	139
Williamsburg (Independent City) 401 Lafayette St *TF:* 800-275-2355 ■ *Web:* www.williamsburgva.gov	Williamsburg	VA	23185	757-220-6100	220-6107	338
Williamsburg Landing 5700 Williamsburg Landing Dr. *TF:* 800-554-5517 ■ *Web:* www.williamsburglanding.org	Williamsburg	VA	23185	757-565-6505		672
Williamsburg Pottery 6692 Richmond Rd. *Web:* www.williamsburgpottery.com	Williamsburg	VA	23188	757-564-3326		362
Williamsburg Regional Library 7770 Croaker Rd. *Web:* www.wrl.org	Williamsburg	VA	23188	757-259-4071	259-4077	434-3
Williamsburg Technical College 601 MLK Jr Ave *Web:* www.wiltech.edu	Kingstree	SC	29556	843-355-4110		162

	Phone	Fax	Class
Williamsburg Winery Ltd 5800 Wessex Hundred .... Williamsburg VA 23185 *Web:* www.williamsburgwinery.com	757-229-0999		50-7
Williamsburg-James City County Educational Foundation PO Box 8783 .... Williamsburg VA 23187 *Web:* wjccschools.org	757-603-6400		685
Williamson Cadillac 7815 SW 104th St. .... Miami FL 33156 *TF:* 877-228-6093 ■ *Web:* www.williamsoncadillac.com	877-579-0775		58
Williamson County 1320 W Main St Ste 135 .... Franklin TN 37064 *Web:* www.williamsoncounty-tn.gov	615-790-5712	790-5610	338
Williamson County 710 Main St. .... Georgetown TX 78626 *Web:* www.wilco.org	512-943-1100	943-1616	338
Williamson County 3000 Williamson County Pkwy .... Marion IL 62959 *Web:* www.williamsoncountyil.gov	618-997-1301	998-0922	338
Williamson County Convention & Visitors Bureau 400 Main St Ste 200 .... Franklin TN 37064 *Web:* visitfranklin.com	615-791-7554		206
Williamson County Public Library 1314 Columbia Ave .... Franklin TN 37064 *Web:* wcpltn.org	615-595-1243	595-1245	434-3
Williamson County Tourism Bureau 1602 Sioux Dr .... Marion IL 62959 *TF:* 800-433-7399 ■ *Web:* www.visitsi.com	618-997-3690	997-1874	206
Williamson County-Franklin Chamber of Commerce 5005 Meridian Blvd Ste 150 .... Franklin TN 37067 *Web:* www.williamsonchamber.com	615-771-1912	790-5337	139
Williamson Employment Services Inc 213 Hilltop Rd .... Saint Joseph MI 49085 *Web:* www.williamsonemployment.com	269-983-0142	983-8955	721
Williamson Free School of Mechanical Trades, The 106 S New Middletown Rd .... Media PA 19063 *Web:* www.williamson.edu	610-566-1776	566-6502	800
Williamson Law Book Co 790 Canning Pkwy .... Victor NY 14564 *TF:* 800-733-9522 ■ *Web:* wlbonline.com	585-924-3400	924-4153	178
Williamson Medical Ctr (WMC) 4321 Carothers Pkwy .... Franklin TN 37067 *Web:* williamsonmedicalcenter.org	615-435-5000	435-7328	374-3
Williamson Street Grocery Company Op 1221 Williamson St .... Madison WI 53703 *Web:* www.willystreet.coop	608-251-0884		297-8
Williamson-Dickie Manufacturing Co 509 W Vickery Blvd .... Fort Worth TX 76104 *TF:* 866-411-1501 ■ *Web:* www.dickies.com	866-411-1501		155-19
Williamsport Area School District 2780 W Fourth St .... Williamsport PA 17701 *TF:* 888-448-4642 ■ *Web:* www.wasd.org	570-327-5500	327-8122	685
Williamsport Sun-Gazette 252 W Fourth St .... Williamsport PA 17701 *TF:* 800-339-0289 ■ *Web:* www.sungazette.com	570-326-1551	326-0314	532-2
Williamsport/Lycoming Chamber of Commerce 102 W Fourth St .... Williamsport PA 17701 *Web:* www.williamsport.org	570-326-1971	321-1208	139
Williams-Sonoma Inc 3250 Van Ness Ave .... San Francisco CA 94109 *NYSE:* WSM ■ *TF:* 800-838-2589 ■ *Web:* www.williams-sonomainc.com	415-421-7900		362
Williamston Community Schools Inc 418 Highland St .... Williamston MI 48895 *Web:* www.gowcs.net	517-655-4361		685
Williamston Products Inc (WPI) 845 Progress Ct .... Williamston MI 48895 *Web:* www.wpius.com	517-655-2131		608
Williamstown Commons Nursing & Rehabilitation Ctr 25 Adams Rd .... Williamstown MA 01267 *Web:* williamstowncommons.org	413-458-2111	458-3156	450
Williamsville Suburban LLC 193 S Union Rd .... Buffalo NY 14221 *Web:* www.williamsvillesuburban.com	716-276-1900		363
Willie G's 1640 W Loop S .... Houston TX 77027 *Web:* www.williegs.com	713-840-7190		670
Willie Washer Manufacturing Corp 2101 Greenleaf Ave .... Elk Grove Village IL 60007 *Web:* www.williewasher.com	847-956-1344		621
Williford Flooring Company Inc 4820 Hwy 98 N Ste 1 .... Lakeland FL 33809 *Web:* willifordflooring.com	863-858-5612		290
Willingboro Public Library 220 Willingboro Pkwy .... Willingboro NJ 08046 *Web:* www.willingboro.org	609-877-6668	835-1699	434-3
Willington Nameplate 11 Middle River Dr .... Stafford Springs CT 06076 *TF:* 877-967-4743 ■ *Web:* wnpinc.com	877-967-4743		481
Willingway Hospital 311 Jones Mill Rd .... Statesboro GA 30458 *TF:* 800-242-9455 ■ *Web:* willingway.com	912-764-6236		726
Willis & Woy Sports Group LLC 4890 Alpha Rd Ste 220 .... Dallas TX 75244 *Web:* www.willis-woy.com	972-506-9011		181
Willis College of Business & Technology 85 O'Connor St .... Ottawa ON K1P5M6 *TF:* 877-233-1128 ■ *Web:* williscollege.com	613-233-1128		162
Willis Day Storage Co 4100 Bennett Rd .... Toledo OH 43612 *Web:* www.willisday.com	419-476-8000		803-1
Willis Furniture Company Inc 4220 Virginia Beach Blvd .... Virginia Beach VA 23452 *Web:* www.willisfurniture.com	757-340-2112		321
Willis Group Holdings Ltd 200 Liberty St 3rd Fl .... New York NY 10281 *NASDAQ:* WSH ■ *TF:* 800-234-8596 ■ *Web:* www.willis.com	212-915-8888		390
Willis Investment Counsel Inc 710 Green St .... Gainesville GA 30501 *Web:* wicinvest.com	770-718-0706		401
Willis Tower 233 S Wacker Dr .... Chicago IL 60606 *Web:* www.willistower.com	312-875-9447		50-3
Willis-Knighton Medical Ctr (WKMC) 2600 Greenwood Rd .... Shreveport LA 71103 *Web:* www.wkhs.com	318-212-4000		374-3
Williston Northampton School 19 Payson Ave .... Easthampton MA 01027 *Web:* www.williston.com	413-529-3241	527-9494	622
Williston State College 1410 University Ave PO Box 1326 .... Williston ND 58802 *TF:* 888-863-9455 ■ *Web:* willistonstate.edu	701-774-4200	774-4211	162
Willits Chamber of Commerce (WCC) 299 E Commercial St .... Willits CA 95490 *Web:* www.willits.org	707-459-7910		139
Williwaw Publishing Co (WPC) PO Box 309 .... Haines AK 99827 *TF:* 800-490-4950 ■ *Web:* www.williwaw.com	907-766-2599		637-2
Willkie Farr & Gallagher LLP 787 Seventh Ave .... New York NY 10019 *Web:* www.willkie.com	212-728-8000	728-8111	428
Willman & Silvaggio LLP 5500 Corporate Dr Ste 150 .... Pittsburgh PA 15237 *Web:* willmanlaw.com	412-366-3333		41
Willman Industries Inc 338 S Main St .... Cedar Grove WI 53013 *Web:* willmanind.com	920-668-8526	668-8998	307
Willmar Lakes Area Chamber of Commerce 2104 Hwy 12 East .... Willmar MN 56201 *TF:* 800-845-8747 ■ *Web:* www.willmarareachamber.com	320-235-0300	231-1948	139
Willmott & Associates Inc 289 Great Bay Ste 103 .... Acton MA 01720 *Web:* willmott.com	781-863-5400		631
Willo Products Company Inc 714 Willo Industrial Dr SE .... Decatur AL 35601 *TF:* 800-633-3276 ■ *Web:* www.willoproducts.com	256-353-7161	350-8436	234
Willoughby Eastlake City Schools 37047 Ridge Rd .... Willoughby OH 44094 *Web:* www.weschools.org	440-946-5000	946-4671	685
Willoughby Industries Inc 5105 W 78th St .... Indianapolis IN 46268 *TF:* 800-428-4065 ■ *Web:* www.willoughby-ind.com	800-428-4065		612
Willoughby Realty Inc 960 SE Indian St Ste A .... Stuart FL 34997 *Web:* waterpointe.com	772-220-7877		652
Willoughby Wallace Memorial Library (WWML) 146 Thimble Islands Rd .... Branford CT 06405 *Web:* www.wwml.org	203-488-8702	315-3347	434-3
Willoughby Western Lake County 28 Public Sq .... Willoughby OH 44094 *Web:* wwlcchamber.com	440-942-1632	942-0586	139
Willoughby, Stuart, Bening & Cook Inc 50 W San Fernando St Ste 400 .... San Jose CA 95113 *Web:* wsbclawycrs.com	408-289-1972		41
Willow Bend Publishing PO Box 304 .... Goshen MA 01032 *Web:* www.willowbendpublishing.com	413-230-1514		637-2
Willow Computing Technologies Inc PO Box 97303 .... Raleigh NC 27624 *Web:* www.willowtec.com	478-355-5250		177
Willow Creek Concrete Products Inc 12626 County Rd 150 .... Kimball MN 55353 *TF:* 888-398-9631 ■ *Web:* www.willowcreekconcrete.com	320-398-5415		183
Willow Creek Press Inc 9931 Hwy 70 W PO Box 147 .... Minocqua WI 54548 **Fax Area Code:* 715 ■ *TF:* 800-850-9453 ■ *Web:* www.willowcreekpress.com	800-850-9453	358-2807*	130
Willow Creek Rehabilitation & Care Ctr 1165 Easton Ave .... Somerset NJ 08873 *TF:* 800-486-0027 ■ *Web:* www.genesishcc.com	732-246-4100		450
Willow Creek State Recreation Area 54876 852 Rd .... Pierce NE 68767 *Web:* outdoornebraska.gov	402-329-4053		565
Willow Drug Inc 41 Williams Dr .... Spencer WV 25276 *Web:* willowdrug.com	304-927-3784		237
Willow Electrical Supply Inc 3828 River Rd .... Schiller Park IL 60176 *Web:* www.willowelectric.com	847-801-5010		246
Willow Group 1485 Laperriere Ave .... Ottawa ON K1Z7S8 *Web:* www.thewillowgroup.com	613-722-8796	729-6206	47
Willow Group 3600 American Blvd W .... Bloomington MN 55431 *Web:* willowg.com	952-897-3550		463
Willow Park Wines & Spirits Ltd 10801 Bonaventure Dr SE .... Calgary AB T2J6Z8 *Web:* www.willowpark.net	403-296-1640		443
Willow River State Park 1034 County Hwy A .... Hudson WI 54016 *Web:* dnr.wi.gov	715-386-5931	386-0431	565
Willow Run Foods Inc 1006 US Rte 11 .... Kirkwood NY 13795 *TF:* 800-234-7550 ■ *Web:* www.willowrunfoods.com	800-234-7550		297-8
Willow Run Veterinary Clinic Inc 320 Beaver Valley Pk .... Willow Street PA 17584 *Web:* willowrunvetclinic.com	717-464-3424		794
Willow Springs Books 668 N Riverpoint Blvd 2 RPT-259 .... Spokane WA 99202 *Web:* willowspringsbooks.org	509-359-4591		637-2
Willow Technology Inc 961 Red Tail Ln Ste 220 .... Bellingham WA 98226 **Fax Area Code:* 604 ■ *Web:* www.willowtech.com	360-393-4962	630-7101*	809
Willow Tree c/o Demdaco 5000 W 134th St .... Leawood KS 66209 **Fax Area Code:* 913 ■ *Web:* www.willowtree.com	855-544-3226	814-0681*	523
Willow Tree Poultry Farm Inc 997 S Main St .... Attleboro MA 02703 *Web:* willowtreefarm.com	508-222-2479		123
Willow Valley Lakes Manor 300 Willow Vly Lakes Dr .... Willow Street PA 17584 *TF:* 800-770-5445 ■ *Web:* www.willowvalleycommunities.org	717-464-0800		672
Willow Valley Resort & Conference Ctr 2400 Willow St Pk .... Lancaster PA 17602 *Web:* willowvalley.com	717-464-0869		669
Willowbrook Mall 1400 Willowbrook Mall .... Wayne NJ 07470 *Web:* www.willowbrook-mall.com	973-785-1655		460
Willowbrook Mall 2000 Willowbrook Mall .... Houston TX 77070 *Web:* www.shopwillowbrookmall.com	281-890-8000		460

Name / Address	Phone	Fax	Class
Willows at Meadow Branch, The 1881 Harvest Dr ... Winchester VA 22601 *Web:* thewillows-mb.com	540-667-3000		371
Willows Chamber of Commerce 118 W Sycamore ... Willows CA 95988 *TF:* 855-233-6362 ■ *Web:* willowschamber.com	530-934-8150		139
Willows Historic Palm Springs Inn 412 W Tahquitz Canyon Way ... Palm Springs CA 92262 *TF:* 800-966-9597 ■ *Web:* thewillowspalmsprings.com	760-320-0771	320-0780	379
Willows Hotel 555 W Surf St ... Chicago IL 60657 *Web:* willowshotelchicago.com	773-528-8400		379
Willows Lodge 14580 NE 145th St ... Woodinville WA 98072 *TF:* 877-424-3930 ■ *Web:* www.willowslodge.com	425-424-3900	424-2585	379
Willows, The 1 Lyman St ... Westborough MA 01581 *TF:* 800-464-8060 ■ *Web:* www.salmonhealth.com	508-366-4730	898-3982	672
Wills Company Inc 301 4th Ave SE ... Waseca MN 56093 **Fax Area Code:* 507 ■ *TF:* 800-835-9455 ■ *Web:* www.willsco.net	800-835-9455	835-2686*	328
Wills Eye 840 Walnut St ... Philadelphia PA 19107 *TF:* 877-289-4557 ■ *Web:* www.willseye.org	215-928-3000		374-7
Wills Group Inc, The 6355 Crain Hwy ... La Plata MD 20646 *Web:* willsgroup.com	301-932-3600		324
Wills Point Independent School Distric 338 W N Commerce St ... Wills Point TX 75169 *Web:* www.wpisd.com	903-873-3161	873-2462	685
Willson International Ltd 2345 Argentia Rd Ste 201 ... Mississauga ON L5N8K4 *TF:* 800-754-1918 ■ *Web:* www.willsonintl.com	905-363-1133		449
Will-Tech Inc 5044 S Royal Atlanta Dr ... Tucker GA 30084 *Web:* www.willtechtransport.com	770-723-1200	723-1310	519
WILL-TV Ch 12 (PBS) 300 N Goodwin Ave ... Urbana IL 61801 *Web:* will.illinois.edu	217-333-7300	333-7151	741
Willwork Inc 23 Norfolk Ave ... South Easton MA 02375 *Web:* www2.willworkinc.com	508-230-3170		184
Willy Bietak Productions Inc 1404 Third St Promenade Ste 200 ... Santa Monica CA 90401 *Web:* www.bietakproductions.com	310-576-2400		181
Wilma Theater 265 S Broad St ... Philadelphia PA 19107 *Web:* www.wilmatheater.org	215-893-9456	893-0895	572
Wilmanco Inc 5350 Kazuko Ct ... Moorpark CA 93021 *Web:* www.wilmanco.com	805-523-2390	529-0856	647
Wilmer Cutler Pickering Hale & Dorr LLP 1875 Pennsylvania Ave ... Washington DC 20006 *Web:* www.wilmerhale.com	202-663-6000		428
Wilmer Service Line 515 W Sycamore St ... Coldwater OH 45828 *TF:* 800-494-5637 ■ *Web:* www.4wilmer.com	800-494-5637	553-4849	110
Wilmette Bicycle & Sport Shop 605 Green Bay Rd ... Wilmette IL 60091 *Web:* www.wilmettesportshop.com	847-251-1404	251-1647	711
Wilmette Chamber of Commerce (WCC) 351 Linden Ave ... Wilmette IL 60091 *Web:* www.wilmettekenilworth.com	847-251-3800	251-6321	139
Wilmington & Beaches CVB 505 Nutt St Unit A ... Wilmington NC 28401 *TF:* 877-406-2356 ■ *Web:* www.wilmingtonandbeaches.com	910-341-4030	341-4029	206
Wilmington Capital Securities LLC 600 Old Country Rd Ste 200 ... Garden City NY 11530 *TF:* 866-604-7248 ■ *Web:* wilmingtoncap.com	516-750-6200		691
Wilmington Chamber of Commerce 544 N Avalon Blvd Ste 104 ... Wilmington CA 90744 *Web:* www.wilmington-chamber.com	310-834-8586	834-8887	139
Wilmington Clinton County Chamber of Commerce (WCCC) 100 W Main St ... Wilmington OH 45177 *Web:* wcccchamber.com	937-382-2737		139
Wilmington College of Ohio 1870 Quaker Way ... Wilmington OH 45177 *TF:* 800-341-9318 ■ *Web:* www.wilmington.edu	937-382-6661		166
Wilmington Drama League (WDL) 10 W Lea Blvd ... Wilmington DE 19802 *Web:* www.wilmingtondramaleague.org	302-764-1172		573-4
Wilmington Fibre Specialty Co 700 Washington St ... New Castle DE 19720 *TF:* 800-220-5132 ■ *Web:* www.wilmfibre.com	302-328-7525	328-6630	599
Wilmington Group, The 7040 Wrightsville Ave ... Wilmington NC 28403 *Web:* www.wilmingtongroup.com	910-256-1056		463
Wilmington Health 1202 Medical Center Dr ... Wilmington NC 28401 *TF:* 800-334-3053 ■ *Web:* www.wilmingtonhealth.com	910-341-3300		450
Wilmington Instrument Company Inc 332 N Fries Ave ... Wilmington CA 90744 *TF:* 800-544-2843 ■ *Web:* www.calcert.com	310-834-1133		201
Wilmington Machinery Inc 4628 Northchase Pky NE ... Wilmington NC 28405 *Web:* www.wilmingtonmachinery.com	910-452-5090	452-5191	695
Wilmington National Cemetery 2011 Market St ... Wilmington NC 28403 **Fax Area Code:* 252 ■ *Web:* www.cem.va.gov	910-815-4877	637-7145*	136
Wilmington Public Library 10 E Tenth St ... Wilmington DE 19801 *Web:* wilmington.lib.de.us	302-571-7400	654-9132	434-3
Wilmington Public Library District (WPLD) 201 S Kankakee St ... Wilmington IL 60481 *Web:* www.wilmingtonlibrary.org	815-476-2834	476-7805	434-3
Wilmington Research & Development Corp 50 Parker St ... Newburyport MA 01950 *Web:* www.wrdcorp.com	978-499-0100	499-0202	201
Wilmington State Parks 1021 W 18th St ... Wilmington DE 19802 *Web:* www.destateparks.com	302-577-7020	577-7084	565
Wilmington Treatment Ctr 2520 Troy Dr ... Wilmington NC 28401 *TF:* 866-783-6605 ■ *Web:* www.wilmingtontreatment.com	866-783-6605		726
Wilmington Trust Co 1100 N Market St ... Wilmington DE 19890 *Web:* www.wilmingtontrust.com	302-651-1000	651-8937	70
Wilmington University 320 N DuPont Hwy ... New Castle DE 19720 **Fax Area Code:* 302 ■ *TF:* 877-967-5464 ■ *Web:* www.wilmu.edu	877-967-5464	328-5902*	166

Name / Address	Phone	Fax	Class
Wilmore Electronics Company Inc 607 US 70-A E PO Box 1329 ... Hillsborough NC 27278 *Web:* www.wilmoreelectronics.com	919-732-9351	732-9359	253
Wilmot Company Inc 545 Hazle St ... Freeland PA 18224 *TF:* 888-594-5668 ■ *Web:* www.wilmotco.com	570-636-5871	636-5252	207
Wilmot Enterprise, The PO Box 6 ... Wilmot SD 57279 *Web:* wil.stparchive.com	605-938-4651	938-4683	532-2
Wilogic Inc 15896 Manufacture Ln ... Huntington Beach CA 92649 *Web:* www.wilogic.com	714-230-8487		196
Wil-Rich 17885 Hwy 13 ... Wahpeton ND 58075 *Web:* www.wil-rich.com	701-642-2621	642-3372	273
Wilsbach Distributors Inc 905 Katie Ct ... Harrisburg PA 17109 *Web:* www.wilsbach.com	717-561-3760		81-1
Wilsey Tool Company Inc 140 Penn Am Dr ... Quakertown PA 18951 *Web:* www.wilseytool.com	215-538-0800		454
Wilshire Associates Inc 1299 Ocean Ave Ste 700 ... Santa Monica CA 90401 *TF:* 855-626-8281 ■ *Web:* www.wilshire.com	310-451-3051	458-0520	401
Wilshire Book Co 9731 Variel Ave ... Chatsworth CA 91311 *Web:* www.mpowers.com	818-700-1522	700-1527	637-2
Wilshire Enterprises Inc 100 Eagle Rock Ave Ste 100 ... East Hanover NJ 07936 *OTC:* WLSE ■ *TF:* 888-697-3962 ■ *Web:* www.wilshireenterprisesinc.com	973-585-7770		536
Wilshire Insurance Co 1206 W Ave J Ste 100 ... Lancaster CA 93534 **Fax Area Code:* 661 ■ *TF:* 800-252-0281	800-252-0281	942-1852*	390
Wilshire Mutual Funds Inc PO Box 219512 ... Kansas City MO 64121 *TF:* 888-200-6796 ■ *Web:* advisor.wilshire.com	888-200-6796		528
Wilshire Technologies Inc 318 Wall St ... Princeton NJ 08540 *Web:* www.wilshiretechnologies.com	609-683-1117		146
Wilson & Company Engineers & Arch 4900 Lang Ave NE ... Albuquerque NM 87109 *Web:* www.wilsonco.com	505-348-4000		261
Wilson & Johnson PA 2425 Tamiami Trail N Ste 211 ... Naples FL 34103 *Web:* naplesestatelaw.com	239-436-1500		41
Wilson & Kratzer Mortuaries 455 24th St ... Richmond CA 94804 *Web:* www.wilsonkratzermortuaries.com	510-232-4383		510
Wilson Air Ctr Memphis International Airport 2930 Winchester Rd ... Memphis TN 38118 *TF:* 800-464-2992 ■ *Web:* www.wilsonair.com	901-345-2992		63
Wilson Allen 3817 W Chester Pk ... Newtown Square PA 19073 *Web:* wilsonallen.comabout	484-422-0010		463
Wilson Audio Specialties 2233 Mountain Vista Ln ... Provo UT 84606 *Web:* www.wilsonaudio.com	801-377-2233		52
Wilson Bank Holding Co 623 W Main St ... Lebanon TN 37087 *OTC:* WBHC ■ *Web:* www.wilsonbank.com	615-444-2265		70
Wilson Bus Lines Inc 203 Patriots Rd PO Box 415 ... East Templeton MA 01438 *TF:* 800-253-5235 ■ *Web:* www.wilsonbus.com	978-632-3894		107
Wilson Chamber of Commerce 200 Nash St NE ... Wilson NC 27893 *Web:* www.wilsonncchamber.com	252-237-0165	243-7931	139
Wilson College 1015 Philadelphia Ave ... Chambersburg PA 17201 *TF:* 800-421-8402 ■ *Web:* wilson.edu	717-264-4141	264-1578	166
Wilson Communications 2504 Ave D ... Wilson KS 67490 *TF:* 800-432-7607 ■ *Web:* www.wilsoncommunications.us	785-658-2111		224
Wilson Community College 902 Herring Ave E PO Box 4305 ... Wilson NC 27893 *Web:* www.wilsoncc.edu	252-291-1195	243-7148	162
Wilson Construction Co 1190 NW 3rd Ave ... Canby OR 97013 *Web:* www.wilsonconst.com	503-263-6882	263-6946	188-10
Wilson Consulting Group 100 Old Schoolhouse Rd ... Mechanicsburg PA 17055 *Web:* wcg-pc.com	717-591-3070		196
Wilson County 1103 Fourth St Ste 2 ... Floresville TX 78114 *Web:* co.wilson.tx.us	830-393-7346		338
Wilson County 228 E Main St Wilson County Courthouse Rm 5 ... Lebanon TN 37087 *Web:* www.wilsoncountytn.gov	615-444-0314	443-1714	338
Wilson County *Register of Deeds* 101 N Goldsboro St PO Box 1728 ... Wilson NC 27894 *Web:* www.wilson-co.com	252-399-2935	237-4341	338
Wilson County Citizen 406 N 7th St ... Fredonia KS 66736 *Web:* www.wilsoncountycitizen.com	620-378-4415	378-4688	532-2
Wilson County Genealogical Society (WCGS) PO Box 802 ... Wilson NC 27894 *Web:* www.wcgs.org	252-243-1660		48-13
Wilson Daily Times 126 Nash St W ... Wilson NC 27893 *Web:* www.wilsontimes.com	252-243-5151	243-2999	532-2
Wilson Daniels Ltd 1201 Dowdell Ln ... Saint Helena CA 94574 *Web:* www.wilsondaniels.com	707-963-9661		80-3
Wilson Diamonds Inc 404 West 2230 North ... Provo UT 84604 *Web:* wilsondiamonds.com	801-226-2565		410
Wilson Elser Moskowitz Edelman & Dicker LLP 150 E 42nd St ... New York NY 10017 *Web:* www.wilsonelser.com	212-490-3000	490-3038	428
Wilson Engineers LLC 9633 S 48th St Ste 290 ... Phoenix AZ 85044 *Web:* wilson-engineers.com	480-893-8860		261
Wilson Equipment Rentals and Sales 6731 Crater Lake Hwy ... Central Point OR 97502 *TF:* 800-205-7113 ■ *Web:* www.wilsonequipment.net	541-830-3966	830-5966	23
Wilson Farm Inc 10 Pleasant St ... Lexington MA 02421 *Web:* www.wilsonfarm.com	781-862-3900	863-0469	10-11
Wilson Financial Group Inc 1929 Allen Pkwy ... Houston TX 77019	281-579-2760	579-9089	510

Name / Address	City	State	ZIP	Phone	Fax	Class
Wilson Frederica (Rep D - FL) 2445 Rayburn House Office Bldg *Web:* wilson.house.gov	Washington	DC	20515	202-225-4506	226-0777	342-2
Wilson Gregory Agency Inc 2309 Market St *Web:* wilsongregory.com	Camp Hill	PA	17011	717-730-9777		390
Wilson Harris & Co 1602 W Franklin St *Web:* wilsonharris.com	Boise	ID	83702	208-344-1355		2
Wilson Hewitt & Associates Inc 775 Lancaster Ave PO Box 607 *Web:* www.wha.com	Villanova	PA	19085	610-649-2300	225-6005	809
Wilson Hughes Consulting LLC 2100 Humboldt St Ste 302 *Web:* wilsonhughesconsulting.com	Denver	CO	80205	303-680-7889		194
Wilson Industrial Sales Company Inc 5063 South 1000 West PO Box 297 *TF:* 800-633-5427 ■ *Web:* wilsonindustrial.com	Rensselaer	IN	47978	219-866-6900	866-2828	146
Wilson Island State Recreation Area 32801 Campground Ln *Web:* www.iowadnr.gov	Missouri Valley	IA	51555	712-642-2069		565
Wilson Joe (Rep R - SC) 1436 Longworth House Office Bldg *Web:* joewilson.house.gov	Washington	DC	20515	202-225-2452	225-2455	342-2
Wilson Kehoe & Winingham LLC, Attorneys At Law 2859 N Meridian St *Web:* wkw.com	Indianapolis	IN	46208	317-920-6400		41
Wilson Learning Corp 8000 W 78th St Ste 200 *TF:* 800-328-7937 ■ *Web:* www.wilsonlearning.com	Edina	MN	55439	952-944-2880		765
Wilson Lines of Minnesota Inc 2131 Second Ave *TF:* 800-525-3333 ■ *Web:* www.wilsonlines.com	Newport	MN	55055	651-459-2384	769-3050	780
Wilson Lumber Company Inc 4818 Meridian St *Web:* www.wilsonlumber.net	Huntsville	AL	35811	256-852-7411		191-3
Wilson Manufacturing Co 4725 Green Park Rd *TF:* 800-634-5248 ■ *Web:* www.wilsonmfg.com	Saint Louis	MO	63123	314-416-8900		697
Wilson Marketing Group Inc (WMG) PO Box 859 *Web:* www.wilsonconsultants.com	Wayzata	MN	55391	763-476-2216	475-8275	195
Wilson Meany Sullivan LLC 4 Embarcadero Ctr Ste 3330 *Web:* wilsonmeany.com	San Francisco	CA	94111	415-905-5300		652
Wilson Medical Ctr 1705 SW Tarboro St *Web:* www.wilsonmedical.com	Wilson	NC	27893	252-399-8040		374-3
Wilson of Wallingford Inc 221 Rogers Ln *TF:* 888-607-2621 ■ *Web:* www.wilsonoilandpropane.com	Wallingford	PA	19086	610-566-7600	566-7608	316
Wilson Office Interiors 1341 W Mockingbird Ln Ste 1100W *Web:* wilsonoi.com	Dallas	TX	75247	972-488-4100	488-8815	393
Wilson Oil Inc 95 Panel Way *TF:* 800-438-9656 ■ *Web:* www.wilcoxandflegel.com	Longview	WA	98632	360-575-9222		324
Wilson Paper Co 363 S Kellogg St *TF:* 800-422-0421 ■ *Web:* www.wilsonpaper.com	Galesburg	IL	61401	309-342-0168	342-0362	559
Wilson Post, The 223 N Cumberland St *Web:* www.wilsonpost.com	Lebanon	TN	37087	615-444-6008		532-3
Wilson Quarterly Magazine 1300 Pennsylvania Ave NW *TF:* 888-947-9018 ■ *Web:* www.wilsoncenter.org	Washington	DC	20004	202-691-4122	691-4247	457-11
Wilson Realty Exchange Inc 16910 15th Ave NE *Web:* www.wilsonrealtyexchange.com	Shoreline	WA	98155	206-367-0200		652
Wilson Sonsini Goodrich & Rosati 650 Page Mill Rd *Web:* www.wsgr.com	Palo Alto	CA	94304	650-493-9300	493-6811	428
Wilson Sporting Goods Co 8750 W Bryn Mawr Ave *TF:* 800-874-5930 ■ *Web:* www.wilson.com	Chicago	IL	60631	800-800-9936		710
Wilson State Park 910 N First St PO Box 333 *Web:* www.michigan.org	Harrison	MI	48625	989-539-3021		565
Wilson Supply Co 1021 Main St Ste 1150	Houston	TX	77002	713-237-3700		385
Wilson T. Ballard Co 17 Gwynns Mill Ct *Web:* wtbco.com	Owings Mills	MD	21117	410-363-0150	363-7811	261
Wilson Tool International Inc 12912 Farnham Ave *TF:* 800-328-9646 ■ *Web:* www.wilsontool.com	White Bear Lake	MN	55110	800-944-4671		697
Wilson Trailer Co 4400 S Lewis Blvd *TF:* 800-798-2002 ■ *Web:* www.wilsontrailer.com	Sioux City	IA	51106	712-252-6500	252-6510	779
Wilson Trophy Co 1724 Frienza Ave *TF:* 800-635-5005 ■ *Web:* www.wilsontrophy.com	Sacramento	CA	95815	916-927-9733	927-9955	777
Wilson Visitors Bureau 209 Broad St *Web:* wilson-nc.com	Wilson	NC	27893	252-243-8440		206
Wilson Works Inc 202 Distributor Dr *Web:* www.wilsonworksinc.com	Morgantown	WV	26501	304-296-7621		454
Wilson's Creek National Battlefield 6424 W Farm Rd 182 *Web:* www.nps.gov	Republic	MO	65738	417-732-2662		564
Wilson, Robertson & Cornelius P C 909 ESE Loop 323 Ste 400 *Web:* www.wilsonlawfirm.com	Tyler	TX	75701	903-509-5000	509-5091	428
Wilsonart International Inc 2400 Wilson Pl *Web:* www.wilsonart.com	Temple	TX	76504	254-207-7000	207-2545	599
Wilson-Davis & Company Inc 236 S Main *TF:* 800-621-1571 ■ *Web:* www.wdco.com	Salt Lake City	UT	84101	801-532-1313		690
Wilson-Hurd Manufacturing Co 311 Winton St PO Box 8028 *TF:* 800-950-5013 ■ *Web:* wilsonhurd.com	Wausau	WI	54403	800-950-5013		600
Wilsons Leather Inc 7401 Boone Ave N *TF:* 800-967-6270 ■ *Web:* www.wilsonsleather.com	Brooklyn Park	MN	55428	763-391-4000		157-5

Name / Address	City	State	ZIP	Phone	Fax	Class
Wilson-Tuscarora State Park 3371 Lake Rd *Web:* parks.ny.gov	Wilson	NY	14172	716-751-6361		565
Wilsonwest Inc 1601 Dolores St *Web:* wilsonwest.com	San Francisco	CA	94110	415-282-4560		184
Wiltern Theatre 3790 Wilshire Blvd *TF:* 800-348-8499 ■ *Web:* www.wilterntheatertickets.com	Los Angeles	CA	90010	213-388-1400		572
Wilton House Museum 215 S Wilton Rd *Web:* www.wiltonhousemuseum.org	Richmond	VA	23226	804-282-5936	288-9805	520
Wilton Industries Inc 2240 W 75th St *TF:* 800-794-5866 ■ *Web:* www.wilton.com	Woodridge	IL	60517	630-963-7100		486
Wilton Precision Steel Co 320 W First St *Web:* www.wps01.com	Wilton	IA	52778	563-732-3363	732-3365	483
Wilwat Properties Inc 1958 Monroe Dr NE *Web:* www.watkinsreg.com	Atlanta	GA	30324	404-872-8666		652
WILX-TV Ch 10 (NBC) 500 American Rd *Web:* www.wilx.com	Lansing	MI	48911	517-393-0110	393-8555	741-71
Wiman Corp 180 Industrial Blvd *Web:* www.wimancorp.com	Sauk Rapids	MN	56379	320-259-2554		596
Wimberly Allison Tong & Goo 300 Spectrum Center Dr Ste 500 *Web:* www.watg.com	Irvine	CA	92618	949-574-8500		261
Wimberly Lawson Wright Daves & Jones PLLC 929 W First N St **Fax Area Code:* 865 ■ *Web:* www.wimberlylawson.com	Morristown	TN	37814	423-587-6870	546-1001*	445
Wimbish Gentile Mccray & Roeber PLLC 8730 Stony Point Pkwy Ste 201 *Web:* wgmrlaw.com	Richmond	VA	23235	804-655-4830		41
Wimbledon Farm 1725 Walnut Hill Rd	Lexington	KY	40515	859-272-0636		368
WIMG1300 PO Box 9078 *Web:* www.wimg1300.com	Trenton	NJ	08650	609-695-1300	278-1588	645-164
WIMI WJMS 222 S Lawrence St *Web:* wimifm.com	Ironwood	MI	49938	906-932-2411		645-11
Wimmer Cookbooks 4650 Shelby Air Dr *TF:* 800-548-2537 ■ *Web:* www.wimmerco.com	Memphis	TN	38118	800-548-2537		637-2
Wimmer Solutions Corp 1341 N Northlake Way Ste 300 *Web:* wimmersolutions.com	Seattle	WA	98103	206-324-4594		180
Wimmer Transportation Service 2143 Internationale Parkway Ste 300 **Fax Area Code:* 630 ■ *Web:* www.wimmertransportation.com	Woodridge	IL	60517	708-774-4665	783-8040*	519
Wimmer's Meat Products Inc 126 W Grant St *TF:* 800-762-9865 ■ *Web:* www.wimmersmeats.com	West Point	NE	68788	402-372-2437		296-26
WIMS (Winstar Interactive Media) 1655 Palm Beach Lakes Blvd Ste 903 *Web:* www.winstarinteractive.com	West Palm Beach	FL	33401	561-227-0626		6
WIN Energy Rural Electric Membership Corp 3981 S US Hwy 41 *TF:* 800-882-5140 ■ *Web:* www.winenergyremc.com	Vincennes	IN	47591	812-882-5140	886-0306	245
WIN Enterprises Inc 300 Willow St S *Web:* www.win-ent.com	North Andover	MA	01845	978-688-2000		173-2
WIN Home Inspection 330 Franklin Rd Ste 135A-166 *TF:* 800-309-6753 ■ *Web:* wini.com	Franklin	TN	37067	800-309-6753		365
WINAICO Delaware Company Ltd 505 Keystone Rd *Web:* www.wwpt.com.tw	Southampton	PA	18966	646-520-7673		767
Winamac Coil Spring Inc 512 N Smith St *Web:* www.winamaccoilspring.com	Kewanna	IN	46939	574-653-2186		719
Winandy Greenhouse Co 2211 Peacock Rd *Web:* winandygreenhouse.com	Richmond	IN	47374	765-935-2111		105
Winbco Tank Co 1200 E Main St PO Box 618 **Fax Area Code:* 641 ■ *TF:* 800-822-1855 ■ *Web:* www.winbco.com	Ottumwa	IA	52501	800-822-1855	683-8265*	91
Winbeam Inc 302 W Otterman St *TF:* 866-780-2326 ■ *Web:* www.winbeam.com	Greensburg	PA	15601	724-219-0400		225
Winbond Electronics Corporation America 2727 N First St *Web:* www.winbond.com	San Jose	CA	95134	408-943-6666		696
Winburn Mano Schrader & Shram 12921 Cantrell Rd Ste 309 *Web:* www.wmsslaw.com	Little Rock	AR	72223	501-975-6266	224-0628	41
Winchendon School 172 Ash St *Web:* winchendon.org	Winchendon	MA	01475	978-297-4476		622
Winchester Area Chamber of Commerce 211 S Main St *Web:* winchesterareachamber.com	Winchester	IN	47394	765-584-3731	584-5544	139
Winchester Equipment Co 121 Indian Hollow Rd **Fax Area Code:* 540 ■ *TF:* 800-323-3581 ■ *Web:* www.winchesterequipment.com	Winchester	VA	22603	800-323-3581	665-3058*	358
Winchester Galleries Ltd 2260 Oak Bay Ave *Web:* www.winchestergalleriesltd.com	Victoria	BC	V8R1G7	250-595-2777		42
Winchester Historical Society 15 High St *Web:* www.winchesterhistoricalsociety.org	Winchester	MA	01890	781-721-0135		637-2
Winchester Homes Inc 6905 Rockledge Dr Ste 800 *Web:* www.winchesterhomes.com	Bethesda	MD	20817	301-803-4800		187
Winchester Hospital 41 Highland Ave *Web:* www.winchesterhospital.org	Winchester	MA	01890	781-729-9000	756-2908	374-3
Winchester (Independent City) 15 N Cameron St *Web:* www.winchesterva.gov	Winchester	VA	22601	540-667-1815	722-3618	338
Winchester Lake State Park (IDPR) 1786 Forest Rd *Web:* parksandrecreation.idaho.gov	Winchester	ID	83555	208-924-7563		565
Winchester Medical Ctr 1840 Amherst St *Web:* www.valleyhealthlink.com	Winchester	VA	22601	540-536-8000		374-3

	Phone	Fax	Class
Winchester Metals Inc 195 Ebert Rd .... Winchester VA 22603 *Web:* www.winchestermetals.com	540-667-9000		492
Winchester Mystery House 525 S Winchester Blvd .... San Jose CA 95128 *Web:* www.winchestermysteryhouse.com	408-247-2000		50-3
Winchester Optical Company Inc 1935 Lake St. .... Elmira NY 14901 *TF:* 800-847-9357 ■ *Web:* www.winoptical.com	607-734-4251		543
Winchester Pet Care Center Inc 15070 W 116th St. .... Olathe KS 66062 *Web:* winchesterpetcare.com	913-451-2827		794
Winchester Speedway 2656 W State Rd 32 PO Box 31 .... Winchester IN 47394 *Web:* www.winchesterspeedway.com	765-584-9701	584-8111	515
Winchester Star 2 N Kent St. .... Winchester VA 22601 *Web:* www.winchesterstar.com	540-667-3200	667-1649	532-2
Winchester Systems Inc 101 Billerica Ave Bldg 5 .... Billerica MA 01862 *TF:* 800-325-3700 ■ *Web:* www.winsys.com	781-265-0200	265-0201	176
Winchester Tool LLC 110a Industrial Dr. .... Winchester VA 22602 *Web:* www.winctool.com	540-869-1150		454
Winchester-Clark County Chamber of Commerce 2 S Maple St. .... Winchester KY 40391 *Web:* www.winchesterkychamber.com	859-744-6420	744-9229	139
Winchester-Thurston School 555 Morewood Ave. .... Pittsburgh PA 15213 *Web:* www.winchesterthurston.org	412-578-7500	578-7504	685
WinCo Foods Inc 8200 W Fairview Ave. .... Boise ID 83704 *TF:* 888-674-6854 ■ *Web:* www.wincofoods.com	208-377-9840		345
Winco Inc 5516 SW First Ln. .... Ocala FL 34474 *TF:* 800-237-3377 ■ *Web:* www.wincomfg.com	352-854-2929	854-9544	319-3
Winco Stamping Inc W156 N9277 Tipp St .... Menomonee Falls WI 53051 *Web:* www.wincostamping.com	262-251-5900	251-5904	488
WinCraft Inc 1124 W 5th St PO Box 888 .... Winona MN 55987 *TF:* 800-533-8006 ■ *Web:* www.wincraft.com	507-454-5510	453-0690	328
WinCup 4640 Lewis Rd .... Stone Mountain GA 30083 *TF:* 800-292-2877 ■ *Web:* www.wincup.com	770-771-5861		601
Wind Cave National Park 26611 US Hwy 385 .... Hot Springs SD 57747 *Web:* www.nps.gov	605-745-4600		564
Wind Creek State Park 4325 Al Hwy 128 .... Alexander City AL 35010 *Web:* www.alapark.com	256-329-0845	234-4870	565
Wind Point Partners 676 N Michigan Ave Ste 3700 .... Chicago IL 60611 *Web:* www.wppartners.com	312-255-4800	255-4820	792
Wind River Financial Inc 65 Buttonwood Ct. .... Madison WI 53718 **Fax Area Code:* 608 ■ *TF:* 866-356-0837 ■ *Web:* www.windriverfinancial.com	866-356-0837	243-9490*	194
Wind River Holdings LP 555 Croton Rd Croton Rd Corporate Ctr Ste 300 .... King of Prussia PA 19406 *Web:* www.windriverholdings.com	610-962-3770		385
Wind River Petroleum Corporation Office 5097 S 900 E Ste 200 .... Salt Lake City UT 84117	801-272-9229		297-8
Wind River Ranch PO Box 3410 .... Estes Park CO 80517 *TF:* 800-523-4212 ■ *Web:* www.windriverranch.com	970-586-4212		239
Wind River Systems Inc 500 Wind River Way .... Alameda CA 94501 *TF:* 800-545-9463 ■ *Web:* www.windriver.com	510-748-4100		178-12
Windbag Saloon & Grill 19 S Last Chance Gulch .... Helena MT 59601 *Web:* windbag-saloon-grill.business.site	406-443-3520		671
Windebank Woodwork & Design Ltd 538 Culduthel Rd .... Victoria BC V8Z1G1 *Web:* www.attardesign.net	778-655-1101		499
Windekind Farm 1425 Bert White Rd .... Huntington VT 05462 *Web:* www.windekindfarms.com	802-434-4455		379
Windels Marx Ln Mittendorf LLP 156 W 56th St. .... New York NY 10019 *Web:* www.windelsmarx.com	212-237-1000	262-1215	428
Windemere Hotel & Conference Ctr 2047 S Hwy 92 .... Sierra Vista AZ 85635 *TF:* 800-825-4656 ■ *Web:* windemerehotel.com	520-459-5900		377
Windermere Engineering Services Inc 2716 Rew Cir .... Ocoee FL 34761 *Web:* wpes.net	407-293-7030	293-0319	261
Windermere Relocation Inc 5424 Sand Point Way NE .... Seattle WA 98105 *TF:* 866-740-9589 ■ *Web:* www.windermere.com	206-527-3801		666
Winderweedle, Haines, Ward & Woodman PA 329 Park Ave N 2nd Fl PO Box 880 .... Winter Park FL 32790 *Web:* www.whww.com	407-423-4246		428
Windes & McClaughry Accountancy Corp 111 W Ocean Blvd 22nd Fl PO Box 87 .... Long Beach CA 90802 *Web:* windes.com	562-435-1191		734
Windfall Assoc 981 Chestnut St .... Newton Upper Falls MA 02464 *Web:* www.windfall-assoc.com	617-969-1790	969-1777	196
Windham Brannon PC 3630 Peachtree Rd NE .... Atlanta GA 30326 *Web:* www.windhambrannon.com	404-898-2000	898-2010	2
Windham Community Memorial Hospital (WCMH) 112 Mansfield Ave .... Willimantic CT 06226 *Web:* windhamhospital.org	860-456-9116	456-6838	374-3
Windham County 11 Jail St. .... Newfane VT 05345 *Web:* www.windhamcountyvt.gov	802-365-4942	365-4945	338
Windham County 155 Church St. .... Putnam CT 06260 *Web:* jud.ct.gov	860-928-7749		338
Windham Independent 233 Range Rd .... Windham NH 03087 *TF:* 888-407-8913 ■ *Web:* www.windhampublishing.com	603-898-7874		532-2
Windham Injury Management Group Inc 500 N Comercial St Ste 301 .... Manchester NH 03101 **Fax Area Code:* 866 ■ *Web:* www.windhamgroup.com	603-626-5789	404-0557*	391-4
Windham Manufacturing Company Inc 8520 Forney Rd .... Dallas TX 75227 *TF:* 880-965-0093 ■ *Web:* windhammfg.com	214-388-0511		454
Windham Millwork Inc 4 Architectural Dr .... Windham ME 04062 *Web:* www.windhammillwork.com	207-892-3238	892-5905	200
Windham Region Chamber of Commerce 1010 Main St .... Willimantic CT 06226 *Web:* www.windhamchamber.com	860-423-6389	423-8235	139
Windings Inc 208 N Valley St PO Box 566 .... New Ulm MN 56073 *TF:* 800-795-8533 ■ *Web:* www.windings.com	800-795-8533		454
Windjammer Capital Investors 610 Newport Center Dr Ste 1100 .... Newport Beach CA 92660 *Web:* www.windjammercapital.com	949-721-9944	720-4222	792
Windjammer Inc 525 N Main St .... Bangor PA 18013 *TF:* 800-441-6958 ■ *Web:* www.windjammerinc.com	610-588-0626	588-2046	710
Windjammer Promotions Inc 1112 Main St .... Osterville MA 02655 *Web:* windjammerpromotions.com	508-428-2099		195
Windlake Capital Advisors LLC 980 N Michigan Ave Ste 1400 .... Chicago IL 60611 *Web:* www.windlakeadvisors.com	312-357-0900		401
Windland Inc 1193 E Winding Creek Dr Ste 101 .... Eagle ID 83616 *Web:* www.windland.com	208-377-7777		612
Windmill Health Products 10 Henderson Dr .... West Caldwell NJ 07006 *TF:* 800-822-4320 ■ *Web:* www.windmillvitamins.com	973-575-6591	882-3256	799
Windmill International Inc 12 Murphy Dr Ste 200 .... Nashua NH 03062 *Web:* www.windmill-intl.com	603-888-5502	888-5512	194
Windmill State Recreation Area PO Box 427 .... Gibbon NE 68840 *Web:* outdoornebraska.gov	308-468-5700		565
Windmill Studios NYC 300 Kingsland Ave .... Brooklyn NY 11222 *Web:* Www.windmillstudiosnyc.com	718-384-7300		761
WinDoor Inc 7500 Amsterdam Dr. .... Orlando FL 32832 *Web:* windoorinc.com	407-481-8400	481-0505	608
Window & Door Factory, The 5595 Magnatron Ste C .... San Diego CA 92111 *TF:* 855-230-6558 ■ *Web:* www.windowfactory.com	855-230-6558		499
Window & Door Manufacturers Assn (WDMA) 330 N Wabash Ave Ste 2000. .... Chicago IL 60611 **Fax Area Code:* 651 ■ *Web:* www.wdma.com	847-299-5200	264-5150*	49-3
Window Covering Solutions Inc 4101 Power Inn Rd .... Sacramento CA 95814 *TF:* 888-380-6640 ■ *Web:* www.wcswindowfilms.com	916-362-4601	720-0169	189-11
Window Gang 405 Arendell St. .... Morehead City NC 28557 *TF:* 800-849-2308 ■ *Web:* www.windowgang.com	252-726-1463		152
Window Rama Enterprises Inc 71 Heartland Blvd .... Edgewood NY 11717 *TF:* 800-897-7262 ■ *Web:* www.windowrama.com	631-667-8088		191-3
Windows, Doors & More Inc 5961 Corson Ave S Ste 100 .... Seattle WA 98108 *Web:* windowshowroom.com	206-782-1011		362
WindRiver Publishing Inc 72 N WindRiver Rd .... Silverton ID 83867 *Web:* www.ldswm.com	208-752-1876		637-2
Windsor Animal Hospital 46 Poquonock Ave .... Windsor CT 06095 *Web:* thewindsoranimalclinic.com	860-688-4969		794
Windsor Arms Hotel 18 St Thomas St .... Toronto ON M5S3E7 *TF:* 877-999-2767 ■ *Web:* www.windsorarmshotel.com	416-971-9666	921-9121	379
Windsor Beach Technologies Inc 7321 Klier Dr .... Fairview PA 16415 *Web:* windsorbeach.com	814-474-4900		757
Windsor Capital Group Inc 3250 Ocean Park Blvd Ste 350 .... Santa Monica CA 90405 *Web:* www.wcghotels.com	310-566-1100	566-1199	379
Windsor Chamber of Commerce 261 Broad St. .... Windsor CT 06095 *Web:* www.windsorcc.org	860-688-5165	688-0809	139
Windsor Corporate Suites 3516 Stearns Hills Rd. .... Waltham MA 02451 *Web:* www.windsorcommunities.com	781-899-5100		210
Windsor Court Hotel 300 Gravier St. .... New Orleans LA 70130 *TF:* 888-596-0955 ■ *Web:* www.windsorcourthotel.com	504-523-6000	596-4513	379
Windsor Factory Supply Ltd 730 N Service Rd .... Windsor ON N8X3J3 *TF:* 800-387-2659 ■ *Web:* www.wfsltd.com	519-966-2202	966-2740	385
Windsor High School 6208 US Hwy 61-67 .... Imperial MO 63052 *Web:* windsor.k12.mo.us	636-464-4400		685
Windsor Hotel 125 W Lamar St. .... Americus GA 31709 *Web:* www.windsor-americus.com	229-924-1555	928-0533	379
Windsor House Inc 101 W Liberty St .... Girard OH 44420 *Web:* www.windsorhouseinc.com	330-545-1550	545-2444	652
Windsor Institute, The 44 Timber Swamp Rd .... Hampton NH 03842 *Web:* www.thewindsorinstitute.com	603-929-9801	926-1097	167-3
Windsor Karcher Group 1351 W Stanford Ave .... Englewood CO 80110 *TF:* 800-444-7654 ■ *Web:* www.windsorkarchergroup.com	303-762-1800	865-2800	386
Windsor Manor Rehabilitation Center of Concord 3806 Clayton Rd. .... Concord CA 94521 *Web:* windsorconcord.com	925-689-2266	689-0509	450
Windsor Nature Discovery 2609 S Cloverleaf Loop .... Springfield OR 97477 *TF:* 800-635-4194 ■ *Web:* www.nature-discovery.com	541-431-1114	431-1100	637-2
Windsor Peak Press 436 Pine St. .... Boulder CO 80302 **Fax Area Code:* 303 ■ *TF:* 800-888-0385 ■ *Web:* windsorpeak.com	469-249-2120	442-3744*	637-2
Windsor Port Authority 3190 Sandwich St. .... Windsor ON N9C1A6 *Web:* www.portwindsor.com	519-258-5741		618
Windsor Public Library 323 Broad St .... Windsor CT 06095 *Web:* www.windsorlibrary.com	860-285-1910		434-3
Windsor Regional Hospital Metropolitan Campus (WRH) 1995 Lens Ave .... Windsor ON N8W1L9 *Web:* www.wrh.on.ca	519-254-5577	254-3458	374-2

Name / Address	City	State	ZIP	Phone	Fax	Class
Windsor Republic Door Inc 5800 Scott Hamilton Dr *Web:* www.windsordoor.com	Little Rock	AR	72209	501-562-1872		234
Windsor Service 9603 John St *Web:* www.windsorstore.com	Santa Fe Springs	CA	90670	323-282-9000	973-4309	188-4
Windsor Star, The 300 Ouellette Ave *TF:* 800-265-5647 ■ *Web:* www.windsorstar.com	Windsor	ON	N9A7B4	888-394-9296		532-1
Windsor Suites, The 1700 Benjamin Franklin Pkwy *TF:* 877-784-8379 ■ *Web:* www.thewindsorsuites.com	Philadelphia	PA	19103	215-981-5678		377
Windsor Symphony Orchestra 121 University Ave *TF:* 888-327-8327 ■ *Web:* www.windsorsymphony.com	West Windsor	ON	N9A5P4	519-973-1238	973-0764	573-3
Windsor Vineyards 205 Concourse Blvd *TF:* 800-289-9463 ■ *Web:* www.windsorvineyards.com	Santa Rosa	CA	95403	800-289-9463		315-5
Windsor Windows & Doors 900 S 19th St *TF:* 800-218-6186 ■ *Web:* www.windsorwindows.com	West Des Moines	IA	50265	515-223-6660		236
Windsor-Bertie Area Chamber of Commerce 121 Granville St PO Box 572 *TF:* 800-334-5010 ■ *Web:* www.windsorbertiechamber.com	Windsor	NC	27983	252-794-4277	794-5070	139
Windsor-Essex Regional Chamber of Commerce 2575 Ouellette Pl *Web:* www.windsoressexchamber.org	Windsor	ON	N8X1L9	519-966-3696	966-0603	137
Windstar Cruises 2101 Fourth Ave Ste 210 *TF:* 800-258-7245 ■ *Web:* www.windstarcruises.com	Seattle	WA	98121	206-733-2703	733-2790	220
Windstar Lines Inc 1903 US Hwy 71 N *TF:* 888-494-6378 ■ *Web:* www.gowindstar.com	Carroll	IA	51401	712-792-4221	792-9615	186
Windstream Corp 4001 Rodney Parham Rd *Web:* www.windstream.com	Little Rock	AR	72212	501-748-7000		736
W-Industries Inc 11500 Charles Rd *Web:* www.w-industries.com	Houston	TX	77041	713-466-9463		180
Windward Environmental LLC 200 W Mercer St Ste 401 *Web:* www.windwardenv.com	Seattle	WA	98119	206-378-1364		463
Windward IT Solutions 2201 Cooperative Way Ste 400 *TF:* 844-946-3927 ■ *Web:* windward.com	Herndon	VA	20171	844-946-3927		194
Windward Passage 4739 Reed Rd *Web:* www.windwardpassageua.com	Columbus	OH	43220	614-451-2497		671
Windy City Amusements Inc 914 W Main St *Web:* www.windycityamusements.com	Saint Charles	IL	60174	630-443-4547		239
Windy City Cutting Die Inc 104 W Foster Ave *Web:* www.windycitycuttingdie.com	Bensenville	IL	60106	630-521-9410	521-9420	757
Windy City Silkscreening 2715 S Archer Ave *Web:* www.wcsshirts.com	Chicago	IL	60608	312-842-0030		687
Windy's Sukiyaki 3809 Riverdale Rd *Web:* windyssukiyaki.com	Ogden	UT	84405	801-621-4505		671
WindyCityJay Truck Sales 109 SW Frontage Rd *TF:* 888-636-3930 ■ *Web:* www.windycityjaytrucksales.com	Bolingbrook	IL	60440	888-636-3930		57
Wine & Cheese Cask, The 407 Washington St *Web:* thewineandcheesecask.com	Somerville	MA	02143	617-623-8656		443
Wine & Spirits Shippers Association Inc (WSSA) 11800 Sunrise Vly Dr **Fax Area Code:* 703 ■ *TF:* 800-368-3167 ■ *Web:* www.wssa.com	Reston	VA	20191	800-368-3167	860-2422*	49-6
Wine & Spirits Wholesalers of America Inc (WSWA) 805 15th St NW Ste 1120 *Web:* www.wswa.org	Washington	DC	20005	202-371-9792	789-2405	49-6
Wine America 1020 16th St NW Ste 300 *Web:* wineamerica.org	Washington	DC	20036	202-783-2756		49-6
Wine Appreciation 450 Taraval St Ste 201 *TF:* 800-231-9463 ■ *Web:* www.wineappreciation.com	San Francisco	CA	94116	650-866-3020		35
Wine Cellar 1314 Prudential Dr *Web:* www.winecellarjax.com	Jacksonville	FL	32207	904-398-8989		671
Wine Club, The 1431 S Village Way *TF:* 800-966-5432 ■ *Web:* www.thewineclub.com	Santa Ana	CA	92705	714-835-6485		443
Wine Co, The 425 W Minnehaha *Web:* www.thewinecompany.net	Saint Paul	MN	55103	651-487-1212	487-1791	81-3
Wine Guy Inc, The 220 W Main St *Web:* thewineguyli.com	Smithtown	NY	11787	631-780-6200		443
Wine Institute 425 Market St Ste 1000 *Web:* www.wineinstitute.org	San Francisco	CA	94105	415-512-0151	442-0742	49-6
Wine of The Month Club Inc 123 W Pomona Ave *Web:* wineofthemonthclub.com	Monrovia	CA	91016	626-303-1690		443
Wine Source, The 3601 Elm Ave *Web:* www.thewinesource.com	Baltimore	MD	21211	410-467-7777		81-3
Wine Spectator Magazine 825 Eighth Ave *TF:* 800-752-7799 ■ *Web:* www.winespectator.com	New York	NY	10019	212-684-4224		457-14
Wine Valley Insurance Services Inc 2017 Redwood Rd *Web:* wvinsure.com	Napa	CA	94558	707-226-8604	226-8564	390
Winebow Inc 4800 Cox Rd Ste 300 *TF:* 800-365-9463 ■ *Web:* www.winebow.com	Glen Allen	VA	23060	800-365-9463		102
Winebrenner Theological Seminary 950 N Main St *TF:* 800-992-4987 ■ *Web:* www.winebrenner.edu	Findlay	OH	45840	419-434-4200	434-4267	167-3
Winecom Inc 222 Sutter St Ste 450 *TF:* 800-592-5870 ■ *Web:* www.wine.com	San Francisco	CA	94108	800-592-5870		443
WineCommune LLC 7305 Edgewater Dr Ste D *Web:* www.winecommune.com	Oakland	CA	94621	510-632-5300		80-3
WineDirect Inc 1190 Airport Blvd Ste 200 *TF:* 800-819-0325 ■ *Web:* www.winedirect.com	Napa	CA	94558	707-603-4000		317
Winegard Co 3000 Kirkwood St *TF:* 800-288-8094 ■ *Web:* www.winegard.com	Burlington	IA	52601	319-754-0600	754-0787	647
Winegarden, Haley, Lindholm & Robertson PLC 9460 S Saginaw St Ste A *Web:* winegarden-law.com	Grand Blanc	MI	48439	810-767-3600		41
Winegardner & Hammons Inc 4243 Hunt Rd *Web:* whhotelgroup.com	Cincinnati	OH	45242	513-891-1066	794-2595	379
Winegars Supermarkets Inc 1080 West 300 North *Web:* winegars.com	Clearfield	UT	84015	801-773-7330		345
Wineman Technology Inc 1668 Champagne Dr N *Web:* www.winemantech.com	Saginaw	MI	48604	919-861-0103		256
Winery at Wolf Creek 2637 Cleveland Massillon Rd *TF:* 800-436-0426 ■ *Web:* www.wineryatwolfcreek.com	Norton	OH	44203	330-666-9285		50-7
WineSellar & Brasserie 9550 Waples St Ste 115 *Web:* www.winesellar.com	San Diego	CA	92121	858-450-9557		671
WineShop At Home 525 Airpark Rd *TF:* 800-946-3746 ■ *Web:* www.wineshopathome.com	Napa	CA	94558	707-253-0200		443
WineStyles 5515 Mills Civic Pkwy Ste 120 *Web:* www.winestyles.com	West Des Moines	IA	50266	515-224-9463	564-7063	310
Winet, Patrick & Weaver 1215 W Vista Way *Web:* www.wpgch.com	Vista	CA	92083	760-758-4261		428
Winetasting Network, The 137 Park Pl *Web:* www.winetasting.com	Point Richmond	CA	94801	707-343-9300		690
Winfield Associates Inc 700 W St Clair Ave Ste 404 *TF:* 888-322-2575 ■ *Web:* www.winfieldinc.com	Cleveland	OH	44113	216-241-2575		796
Winfield Correctional Facility 1806 Pine Crest Cir *Web:* www.doc.ks.gov	Winfield	KS	67156	620-221-6660	221-9229	213
Winfield Micro Systems Inc 2333 Wisconsin Ave *Web:* winfieldmicro.com	Downers Grove	IL	60515	630-960-5515	960-5592	366
Winfield Security Corp 57 W 38th St *Web:* winfieldsecurity.com	New York	NY	10018	212-609-2300		693
Winfree Business Growth Advisors 10808 Ward Ave *TF:* 800-616-9260 ■ *Web:* www.winfree.org	Louisville	KY	40223	502-253-0700		463
Wing Enterprises Inc 1198 N Spring Creek *TF:* 866-872-5901 ■ *Web:* littlegiantladders.com	Springville	UT	84663	801-489-3684		421
Wing Eyecare Inc 5305 Glenway Ave *Web:* www.wingeyecare.com	Cincinnati	OH	45238	513-791-2222		543
Wing Group LLC 20A Trafalgar Sq Ste 216 *Web:* www.wing-group.com	Nashua	NH	03063	978-226-8362		434-3
Wing Haven 248 Ridgewood Ave *Web:* winghavengardens.org	Charlotte	NC	28209	704-331-0664	331-9368	97
Wing Hing Foods Inc 2539 E Philadelphia St *TF:* 855-734-2742 ■ *Web:* passportglobalfoods.com	Ontario	CA	91761	909-627-7312		345
Wing It Productions Inc 5510 University Way NE *Web:* www.jetcityimprov.org	Seattle	WA	98105	206-352-8291		747
Wing Luke Asian Museum 719 S King St *TF:* 800-961-6119 ■ *Web:* www.wingluke.org	Seattle	WA	98104	206-623-5124	623-4559	520
Wing Zone Franchise Corp 2120 Powers Ferry Rd Ste 101 *TF:* 888-744-0147 ■ *Web:* wingzonefranchise.com	Atlanta	GA	30339	888-744-0147		310
Wing's Food Products 2187 Bloor St W *Web:* www.wings.ca	Toronto	ON	M8Z1B8	416-259-2662	259-3414	297-8
Wingate by Wyndham Calgary Hotel 400 Midpark Way SE *TF:* 800-228-1000 ■ *Web:* www.wingatebywyndhamcalgary.com	Calgary	AB	T2X3S4	403-514-0099		707
Wingate Communications Group Inc 3316 Edgemere Ave *Web:* www.wingatecommunications.com	Minneapolis	MN	55418	612-782-8551	782-8999	317
Wingate Healthcare 63 Kendrick St *TF:* 800-946-4283 ■ *Web:* wingatehealthcare.com	Needham	MA	02494	800-946-4283		353
Wingate Packaging Inc 4347 Indeco Ct *Web:* wingate-packaging.com	Cincinnati	OH	45241	513-745-8600	745-8603	627
Wingate University 220 N Camden Rd *TF:* 800-755-5550 ■ *Web:* www.wingate.edu	Wingate	NC	28174	704-233-8000	233-8110	166
Wingate Wealth Advisors 450 Bedford St *Web:* wingatewealthadvisors.com	Lexington	MA	02420	781-862-7100	861-9707	2
Wingenback Inc Bay F Century Pk 707 Barlow Trl *Web:* www.wingenback.com	Calgary	AB	T2E8C2	403-221-8120	291-5114	190
Winger Contracting Co 918 Hayne St *Web:* wingercompanies.com	Ottumwa	IA	52501	641-682-3407		610
Winger's USA Inc 855 W 1100 S Ste A *Web:* wingerbros.com	Brigham City	UT	84302	435-723-7822		670
Wingfield J. E. & Associates Pc 700 Fifth St NW Ste 300 *TF:* 800-338-5954 ■ *Web:* dmvinjurylaw.com	Washington	DC	20001	202-789-8000		445
Wingfoot Commercial Tire Systems LLC 1000 S 21st St *TF:* 800-643-7330 ■ *Web:* goodyearctsc.com	Fort Smith	AR	72901	479-788-6400	788-6486	62-5
Wingman Advertising 5855 Green Valley Cir Ste 208 *Web:* wingmanmedia.com	Culver City	CA	90230	424-207-3304		7
Wingra Stone Co 2975 Kapec Rd PO Box 44284 *TF:* 800-249-6908 ■ *Web:* www.wingrastone.com	Madison	WI	53744	608-271-5555	271-3142	183
WINGS (Wings Foundation) 7550 W Yale Ave Ste B 201 *Web:* www.wingsfound.org	Denver	CO	80227	303-238-8660	238-4739	48-21
Wings Air Charter 236 Airport Hanger Dr *Web:* www.wingsaircharter.com	Wisconsin Rapids	WI	54494	715-424-3737		63
Wings Event Ctr 3600 Van Rick Dr *Web:* www.wingseventcenter.com	Kalamazoo	MI	49001	269-345-1125		655

	Phone	Fax	Class
Wings Financial Credit Union 14985 Glazier Ave Ste 100 ... Apple Valley MN 55124 *TF:* 800-692-2274 ■ *Web:* www.wingsfinancial.com	800-692-2274		219
Wings Foundation (WINGS) 7550 W Yale Ave Ste B 201 ... Denver CO 80227 *Web:* www.wingsfound.org	303-238-8660	238-4739	48-21
Wings of History Air Museum 12777 Murphy Ave ... San Martin CA 95046 *Web:* wingsofhistory.org	408-683-2290		520
Wings Over the Rockies Air & Space Museum 7711 E Academy Blvd ... Denver CO 80230 *Web:* www.wingsmuseum.org	303-360-5360	360-5328	520
Wings Tours Inc 11350 McCormick Rd Ste 904 ... Hunt Valley MD 21031 *TF:* 800-869-4647 ■ *Web:* www.wingstours.us	410-771-0925	771-0928	760
Wings Unlimited Inc 455 Post Rd Ste 102 ... Darien CT 06820 *Web:* www.wingsunlimited.net	203-656-9591		184
WingSpan Press PO Box 2085 ... Livermore CA 94551 *TF:* 866-735-3782 ■ *Web:* www.wingspanpress.com	866-735-3782		637-2
Wingstop Restaurants Inc 908 Audelia Rd Ste 600 ... Richardson TX 75081 *TF:* 877-411-9464 ■ *Web:* www.wingstop.com	877-411-9464		670
WingSwept 800 Benson Rd ... Garner NC 27529 *TF:* 800-859-3390 ■ *Web:* www.wingswept.com	919-779-0954		196
WinHolt Equipment Group 141 Eileen Way ... Syosset NY 11791 *TF:* 800-444-3595 ■ *Web:* www.winholt.com	516-222-0335	921-0538	470
WINI-AM 10519 Hwy 149 Ste A ... Murphysboro IL 62966 *Web:* www.southernillinoisiscool.com	618-684-4561		647
Wink Restaurant 1014 N Lamar Blvd Ste E ... Austin TX 78703 *Web:* www.winkrestaurant.com	512-482-8868		671
Wink's Silver Strike Lanes 1281 Kimmerling Rd Ste 8 ... Gardnerville NV 89460 *Web:* www.winkssilverstrike.com	775-265-5454		99
Winkle Electric Company Inc, The 1900 Hubbard Rd ... Youngstown OH 44501 *Web:* www.winkle.com	330-744-5303		767
Winkler & Whittenberg Incorporated CPA'S 15446 E Valley Blvd ... City of Industry CA 91746 *Web:* www.whittenbergcpa.com	626-330-2224	961-0156	2
Winkler County 100 E Winkler St ... Kermit TX 79745 *Web:* www.co.winkler.tx.us	432-586-3161	586-3535	338
Winkler Inc 535 E Medcalf St ... Dale IN 47523 *TF:* 800-621-3843 ■ *Web:* www.winklerinc.com	812-937-4421	937-2044	297-8
WINK-TV Ch 11 (CBS) 2824 Palm Beach Blvd ... Fort Myers FL 33916 *Web:* www.winknews.com	239-334-1111		741-88
Winland Electronics Inc 1950 Excel Dr ... Mankato MN 56001 **Fax Area Code: 507* ■ *TF:* 800-635-4269 ■ *Web:* www.winland.com	800-635-4269	387-2488*	201
Winmark Corp 605Hwy 169 N Ste 400 ... Minneapolis MN 55441 *NASDAQ: WINA* ■ *Web:* www.winmarkcorporation.com	763-520-8500	520-8410	157-1
WinMed Inc Dundee Park Bldg 17 Door 6 ... Andover MA 01810 *Web:* www.winmed-inc.com	978-590-4246		743
Winn Army Community Hospital 1061 Harmon Ave ... Fort Stewart GA 31314 *TF:* 800-652-9221 ■ *Web:* winn.amedd.army.mil	912-435-6633		374-4
Winn Meat Co 2250 Lone Star Dr ... Dallas TX 75212 *Web:* www.benekeith.com	214-634-0456	634-0474	297-9
Winn Parish Police Jury 119 W Main St Ste 102 ... Winnfield LA 71483 *Web:* www.winnparishpolicejury.com	318-628-5824		338
Winn Technology Group Inc 523 Palm Harbor Blvd ... Palm Harbor FL 34683 *TF:* 800-444-5622 ■ *Web:* www.winntech.net	800-444-5622		195
Winn Telephone Co 2766 W Blanchard Rd ... Winn MI 48896 *TF:* 866-321-2323 ■ *Web:* www.winntelephone.com	989-866-2421	866-2205	224
Winn Transportation 1831 Westwood Ave ... Richmond VA 23227 *TF:* 800-296-9466 ■ *Web:* www.winnbus.com	804-358-9466	353-2606	107
Winncom Technologies Corp 30700 Carter St Ste A ... Solon OH 44139 *Web:* www.winncom.com	440-498-9510	498-9511	246
Winn-Dixie Stores Inc 5050 Edgewood Ct ... Jacksonville FL 32254 *Web:* www.winndixie.com	904-783-5000		345
Winne Banta Basralian & Kahn PC 21 Main St Ste 101 ... Hackensack NJ 07601 *Web:* www.winnebanta.com	201-487-3800	487-8529	445
Winnebago Community Unit District 323 304 E McNair Rd ... Winnebago IL 61088 *Web:* www.winnebagoschools.org	815-335-2456		685
Winnebago County 415 Jackson St 1st FL PO Box 2808 ... Oshkosh WI 54903 *Web:* www.co.winnebago.wi.us	920-232-3346	303-3025	338
Winnebago Industries Inc 605 W Crystal Lake Rd PO Box 152 ... Forest City IA 50436 *NYSE: WGO* ■ *TF:* 800-643-4892 ■ *Web:* winnebagoind.com	641-585-3535	585-6966	120
Winnebago Mental Health Institute (WMHI) 1300 S Dr ... Winnebago WI 54985 *Web:* www.dhs.wisconsin.gov	920-235-4910		374-5
Winneconne News 908 E Main St ... Winneconne WI 54986 *TF:* 800-545-5026 ■ *Web:* www.rogerspublishing.com	920-582-4541		532-3
Winnefox Library System 106 Washington Ave ... Oshkosh WI 54901 *Web:* www.winnefox.org	920-236-5220	236-5228	434-3
Winnemucca Convention & Visitors Authority 50 W Winnemucca Blvd ... Winnemucca NV 89445 *TF:* 800-962-2638 ■ *Web:* www.winnemucca.com	775-623-5071	623-5087	206
Winner Chevrolet 1624 S Canyon Way ... Colfax CA 95713 *Web:* www.winnerchevy.com	530-349-4152		57
Winner International LLC 32 W State St ... Sharon PA 16146 *TF:* 800-258-2321 ■ *Web:* winner-intl.com	724-981-1152		692
Winner Livestock Auction Co 31690 Livestock Barn Rd ... Winner SD 57580 *TF:* 800-201-0451 ■ *Web:* www.winnerlivestock.com	605-842-0451	842-3562	446
Winner's Award Group 4171 W Hillsboro Blvd Ste 11 ... Coconut Creek FL 33073 *TF:* 800-344 0545 ■ *Web:* www.winnersawardgroup.com	954-480-8809		241
Winner's Cir Resort 550 Via de la Valle ... Solana Beach CA 92075 *TF:* 800-874-8770 ■ *Web:* www.winnerscircleresort.com	858-755-6666	481-3706	669
Winnercomm Inc 4500 S 129th E Ave Ste 201 ... Tulsa OK 74134 *Web:* www.winnercomm.com	918-496-1900		33
Winners Only Inc 1365 Park Center Dr ... Vista CA 92081 *Web:* www.winnersonly.com	760-599-0300		319-2
Winneshiek County 201 W Main St ... Decorah IA 52101 *Web:* www.winneshiekcounty.org	563-382-0603	387-4083	338
Winnetka Community House 620 Lincoln Ave ... Winnetka IL 60093 *Web:* www.winnetkacommunityhouse.org	847-446-0537		354
Winnetka-Northfield Public Library District 768 Oak St ... Winnetka IL 60093 *Web:* www.winnetkalibrary.org	847-446-7220		434-3
Winning Directions 1366 San Mateo Ave ... South San Francisco CA 94080 *Web:* www.winningdirections.com	650-875-4000	875-1015	393
Winning Edge Group LLC 2576 Euclid Crescent E ... Upland CA 91784 *Web:* www.group50.com	909-949-9083		463
Winning Solutions Inc 301 Alexander Ave Ste C ... Ames IA 50010 *Web:* www.winningsolutionsinc.com	515-239-9900		177
Winning Technologies Great Lakes LLC 147 Triad Ctr W ... O'Fallon MO 63366 *TF:* 877-379-8279 ■ *Web:* winningtech.com	877-379-8279		180
Winningham & Fradley Inc 111 NE 44 St ... Oakland Park FL 33334 *Web:* winnfrad.com	954-771-7440	771-0298	261
Winnipeg Blue Bombers Investors Group Field 315 Chancellor Matheson Rd ... Winnipeg MB R3T1Z2 *Web:* www.bluebombers.com	204-784-2583	783-5222	715-2
Winnipeg Chamber of Commerce, The 259 Portage Ave Ste 100 ... Winnipeg MB R3B2A9 *Web:* www.winnipeg-chamber.com	204-944-8484	944-8492	137
Winnipeg Folk Festival 203-211 Bannatyne Ave ... Winnipeg MB R3B3P2 *TF:* 866-301-3823 ■ *Web:* www.winnipegfolkfestival.ca	204-231-0096	231-0076	720
Winnipeg Free Press 1355 Mountain Ave ... Winnipeg MB R2X3B6 *TF:* 800-542-8900 ■ *Web:* www.winnipegfreepress.com	204-697-7009	697-7412	532-1
Winnipeg Fringe Festival 174 Market Ave ... Winnipeg MB R3B0P8 *Web:* www.winnipegfringe.com	204-956-1340		749
Winnipeg Goldeyes Baseball Club Inc 1 Portage Ave E ... Winnipeg MB R3B3N3 *Web:* goldeyes.com	204-982-2273	982-2274	720
Winnipeg Richardson International Airport 2000 Wellington Ave ... Winnipeg MB R3H1C2 *TF:* 855-500-6589 ■ *Web:* www.waa.ca	204-987-9402	987-2732	27
Winnipeg Sun 1700 Church Ave ... Winnipeg MB R2X3A2 *Web:* www.winnipegsun.com	204-694-2022		532-1
Winnsboro State Bank & Trust Co 3875 Front St ... Winnsboro LA 71295 *TF:* 866-205-4026 ■ *Web:* wsbonline.net	318-435-7535		70
Win-OMT Software Inc 280 - 1630 Ness Ave ... Winnipeg MB R3J3X1 *TF:* 888-665-0501 ■ *Web:* www.omt.net	204-786-3994	783-5805	395
Winona Convention & Visitors Bureau 160 Johnson St ... Winona MN 55987 *TF:* 800-657-4972 ■ *Web:* www.visitwinona.com	507-452-0735	454-0006	206
Winona County 177 Main St ... Winona MN 55987 *Web:* www.co.winona.mn.us	507-457-6350		338
Winona Public Library 151 W Fifth St ... Winona MN 55987 *Web:* winona.lib.mn.us	507-452-4582		434-3
Winona State University 175 W Mark St ... Winona MN 55987 *TF:* 800-342-5978 ■ *Web:* www.winona.edu	507-457-2594	457-5620	166
Winonah International School of Cosmetology 1870 Chace Dr Ste 140 ... Birmingham AL 35244 *Web:* www.winonah.net	205-870-8761		685
Winpak Ltd 100 Salteaux Crescent ... Winnipeg MB R3J3T3 *TSE: WPK* ■ *TF:* 800-841-2600 ■ *Web:* www.winpak.com	204-889-1015	888-7806	548
Winrock Enterprises Inc 2222 Cottondale Ln Ste 300 ... Little Rock AR 72207	501-663-5340		596
Winrock Intl 2101 Riverfront Dr ... Little Rock AR 72202 *Web:* www.winrock.org	501-280-3000	280-3090	634
Winsby Inc 1854 Sherman Ave ... Evanston IL 60201 *Web:* www.winsbyinc.com	847-316-9800		463
Winsert Inc 2645 Industrial Pkwy S PO Box 0198 ... Marinette WI 54143 *Web:* www.winsert.com	715-732-1703	732-2824	307
Winship Cancer Institute of Emory University 1365 Clifton Rd NE ... Atlanta GA 30322 *TF:* 888-946-7447 ■ *Web:* winshipcancer.emory.edu	404-778-1900		769
WinSim Inc 8653 FM 2759 Rd ... Richmond TX 77469 *Web:* www.winsim.com	281-545-9200	545-8820	175
Winslow Automatic Inc 23 St Clair Ave ... New Britain CT 06051 *Web:* winslowautomatics.com	860-225-6321		621
Winslow Automation Inc 905 Montague Expy ... Milpitas CA 95035 *Web:* www.winslowautomation.com	408-262-9004	956-0199	696
Winslow BMW 730 N Circle Dr ... Colorado Springs CO 80909 *TF:* 877-367-7357 ■ *Web:* www.winslowbmw.com	719-473-1373		57
Winslow State Park 475 Kearsarge Mtn Rd ... Wilmot NH 03287 *Web:* www.nhstateparks.org	603-526-6168		565
WinSoft Inc 1932 E Deere Ave Ste 110 ... Santa Ana CA 92705 *Web:* www.winsoft.com	949-428-4844	428-4842	809
Winsome Trading Inc 16111 Woodinville Redmo ... Woodinville WA 98072 *Web:* www.winsomewood.com	425-483-8888	483-4141	362
WinStar Farm LLC 3001 Pisgah Pk ... Versailles KY 40383 *Web:* www.winstarfarm.com	859-873-1717	873-1612	368

	Phone	Fax	Class
Winstar Interactive Media (WIMS) 1655 Palm Beach Lakes Blvd Ste 903.....West Palm Beach FL 33401 *Web:* www.winstarinteractive.com	561-227-0626		6
Winstead PC 1201 Elm St 5400 Renaissance Tower .... Dallas TX 75270 *Web:* www.winstead.com	214-745-5400		428
Winston & Strawn LLP 35 W Wacker Dr ....Chicago IL 60601 *Web:* www.winston.com	312-558-5600	558-5700	41
Winston Advertising 122 E 42nd St............New York NY 10168 *Web:* www.winston.net	212-682-1063	983-2594	4
Winston Baker 110 S Fairfax Ave ....Los Angeles CA 90036 *Web:* www.winstonbaker.com	310-922-1544		636
Winston County PO Box 309............. Double Springs AL 35553 *TF:* 800-489-3973 ■ *Web:* winstoncountycircuitclerk.org	205-489-5533		338
Winston County 311 W Park St................Louisville MS 39339 *Web:* www.winstoncountyms.com	662-773-8719	773-8909	338
Winston Flowers 131 Newbury St................Boston MA 02116 *TF:* 800-457-4901 ■ *Web:* www.winstonflowers.com	800-457-4901		292
Winston Furniture PO Box 868 Alabama Ave....................Haleyville AL 35565 *Web:* www.winstonfurniture.com	205-486-9211		319-4
Winston Hospitality Inc 3701 National Dr Ste 120...................... Raleigh NC 27612 *Web:* www.winstonhospitality.com	919-334-6910	334-6912	379
Winston Industries LLC 2345 Carton Dr............................Louisville KY 40299 *TF:* 800-234-5286 ■ *Web:* industries.winstonind.com	502-495-5400	495-5458	298
Winston Packaging 8095 N Point Blvd .... Winston-Salem NC 27106 *TF:* 800-558-8952 ■ *Web:* winstonpackaging.com	336-759-0051	759-0304	627
Winston/Royal Guard Corp 1604 Cherokee Trace .... White Oak TX 75693 *TF:* 800-527-8465 ■ *Web:* winston-royalguard.com	903-757-7341	759-6986	537
Winston-Salem City Hall 101 N Main St .... Winston-Salem NC 27101 *Web:* www.cityofws.org	336-727-8000	748-3060	337
Winston-Salem Convention & Visitors Bureau 200 Brookstown Ave.................... Winston-Salem NC 27101 *TF:* 866-720-4200 ■ *Web:* www.visitwinstonsalem.com	336-728-4200	728-4220	206
Winston-Salem Federal Credit Union 711 E Salem Ave...................... Winston-Salem NC 27101 *Web:* mywsfcu.org	336-727-2663		219
Winston-Salem Journal 418 N Marshall St...................... Winston-Salem NC 27101 *TF:* 800-642-0925 ■ *Web:* www.journalnow.com	336-727-7211	727-7315	532-2
Winston-Salem Southbound Railway Co 4550 Overdale Rd..................... Winston-Salem NC 27107 *Web:* www.ncrailways.org	336-788-9407	788-9085	648
Winston-Salem State University 601 S ML King Jr Dr.................. Winston-Salem NC 27110 *TF:* 800-257-4052 ■ *Web:* www.wssu.edu	336-750-2000		166
Winston-Salem Symphony 201 N Broad St Ste 200 .... Winston-Salem NC 27101 *Web:* www.wssymphony.org	336-725-1035	725-3924	573-3
Winston-Salem/Forsyth County Schools (WS/FCS) 1605 Miller St......................... Winston-Salem NC 27103 *Web:* www.wsfcs.k12.nc.us	336-727-2816	661-6572	685
Winsupply Inc 3110 Kettering Blvd...............Dayton OH 45439 *TF:* 800-677-4380 ■ *Web:* www.winsupplyinc.com	937-531-6310	293-9591	612
Winsystems Inc 715 Stadium Dr...............Arlington TX 76011 *Web:* www.winsystems.com	817-274-7553	548-1358	173-2
Wintec Industries Inc 675 Sycamore Dr..........................Milpitas CA 95035 *Web:* www.wintecindustries.com	408-856-0500	856-0501	625
Winter Bros Material Co 13098 Gravois Rd........................ Saint Louis MO 63127 *Web:* www.winterbrothersmaterial.com	314-843-1400	843-1403	500
Winter Construction Co 191 Peachtree St NE..........................Atlanta GA 30303 *Web:* winter-construction.com	404-588-3300	965-3440	186
Winter Environmental 3350 Green Pointe Pkwy Ste 200..............Norcross GA 30092 *Web:* winter-environmental.com	404-965-2319		667
Winter Gardens Quality Foods Inc 304 Commerce St PO Box 339..............New Oxford PA 17350 *TF:* 800-242-7637 ■ *Web:* www.wintergardens.com	717-624-4911	624-7729	296-36
Winter Hill Bank 342 Broadway ....Somerville MA 02145 *TF:* 800-444-4300 ■ *Web:* winterhillbank.com	617-666-8600	629-3327	70
Winter Livestock Inc PO Box 909..................Enid OK 73702 *Web:* www.winterlivestock.com	580-237-4600	237-4604	446
Winter Park Chamber of Commerce 151 W Lyman Ave........................Winter Park FL 32789 *TF:* 877-972-4262 ■ *Web:* winterpark.org	407-644-8281	644-7826	139
Winter Park Construction Co 221 Cir Dr................................ Maitland FL 32751 *Web:* www.wpc.com	407-644-8923	645-1972	186
Winter Park Resort 85 Parsenn Rd .... Winter Park CO 80482 *TF:* 800-903-7275 ■ *Web:* www.winterparkresort.com	970-726-5514	726-1690	376
Winter Properties LLC 9 W 57th St 12th Fl..........................New York NY 10019 *Web:* www.winter.com	212-891-8800		652
Winter Quarters State Historic Site 4929 Hwy 608 ....Newellton LA 71357 *TF:* 888-677-9468 ■ *Web:* crt.state.la.us	888-677-2784		565
WinterBell Co 2018 Brevard Rd.............. High Point NC 27263 *TF:* 800-685-2957 ■ *Web:* winterbell.com	336-887-2651		561
WinterGreen Research Inc 6 Raymond St.............................Lexington MA 02421 *Web:* www.wintergreenresearch.com	781-863-5078		225
Wintergreen Resort 11 Grassy Ridge Rd Rte 664................Wintergreen VA 22958 *Web:* www.wintergreenresort.com	434-325-2200		707
Winterhawk Consulting LLC 1643 Williamsburg Sq .... Lakeland FL 33803 *Web:* www.winterhawkconsulting.com	813-731-9665		631
Winters & Yonker PA 601 W Swann Ave .... Tampa FL 33606 *TF:* 888-373-7770 ■ *Web:* wintersandyonker.com	813-223-6200	223-6900	41
Winterthur Museum & Country Estate 5105 Kennett Pk..........................Winterthur DE 19735 *TF:* 800-448-3883 ■ *Web:* www.winterthur.org	302-888-4600		520
Winther Stave & Company LLP 1316 W 18th St PO Box 175...................Spencer IA 51301 *Web:* www.winther-stave.com	712-262-3117		2
Winthrop 11100 Wayzata Blvd Ste 800......... Minnetonka MN 55305 *Web:* www.winthropresources.com	952-936-0226		216
Winthrop & Weinstine PA 225 S Sixth St Ste 3500 ....Minneapolis MN 55402 *Web:* www.winthrop.com	612-604-6400		428
Winthrop Realty Trust 7 Bulfinch Pl Ste 500 ....Boston MA 02114 *NYSE: FUR* ■ *Web:* www.winthropreit.com	617-570-4614	570-4746	655
Winthrop University 701 Oakland Ave .... Rock Hill SC 29733 *Web:* www.winthrop.edu	803-323-2211	323-2137	166
Winton Woods City School District 825 Waycross Rd Ste A .... Cincinnati OH 45240 *Web:* www.wintonwoods.org	513-619-2300		685
Wintronics Inc 191 Pitt St.........................Sharon PA 16146 *TF:* 800-356-4483 ■ *Web:* www.wintronicsinc.com	724-981-5770	981-1772	625
Wintrust Bank - Oak and Rush 1000 N Rush St ....Chicago IL 60611 *Web:* www.wintrustbank.com	312-440-4000		70
Wintrust Financial Corp 9700 W Higgins Rd Ste 800................. Rosemont IL 60018 *NASDAQ: WTFC* ■ *Web:* www.wintrust.com	847-939-9000		360-2
Winvale Group LLC, The 1012 14th St NW 5th Fl .... Washington DC 20005 *Web:* winvale.com	202-296-5505		664
Winward International Inc 3089 Whipple Rd ....Union City CA 94587 *TF:* 800-888-8898 ■ *Web:* www.winwardsilks.com	510-487-8686		292
Winzeler Gear Inc 7355 W Wilson Ave ....Harwood Heights IL 60706 *Web:* www.winzelergear.com	708-867-7971	867-7974	604
Winzeler Stamping Co 910 E Main St ....Montpelier OH 43543 *Web:* www.winzelerstamping.com	419-485-3147	485-5039	488
Winzinger Inc 1704 Marne Hwy PO Box 537................Hainesport NJ 08036 *Web:* www.winzinger.com	609-267-8600	267-4079	188-4
WinZip Computing Inc PO Box 540............Mansfield CT 06268 *Web:* www.winzip.com	860-429-3542		178-12
WIOD-AM 610 (N/T) 7601 Riviera Blvd ....Miramar FL 33023 *TF:* 866-610-6397 ■ *Web:* wiod.iheart.com	954-862-2000		645-96
WIOG-FM 1740 Champagne Dr N................Saginaw MI 48604 *TF:* 877-330-9464 ■ *Web:* www.wiog.com	989-776-2100		647
WIOT-FM 104.7 (Rock) 125 S Superior St......... Toledo OH 43604 *Web:* wiot.iheart.com	419-244-8321		645-161
WIOV-FM 1060 S State St Ste B .... Ephrata PA 17522 *TF:* 800-860-1105 ■ *Web:* www.wiov.com	717-764-1155	738-1661	647
Wipaire Inc 1700 Henry Ave .... South Saint Paul MN 55075 *TF:* 888-947-2473 ■ *Web:* www.wipaire.com	651-451-1205		529
Wipeco Inc 250 N Mannheim Rd Unit B .... Hillside IL 60162 *TF:* 800-444-7247 ■ *Web:* www.wipeco.com	708-544-7247	544-7248	76
Wipe-Tex International Corp 110 E 153rd St...............................Bronx NY 10451 *TF:* 800-643-9607 ■ *Web:* wipe-tex.com	718-665-0013	665-0787	508
Wipfli LLP 10000 Innovation Dr Ste 250 ....Milwaukee WI 53226 *Web:* www.wipfli.com	414-431-9300	431-9303	2
WIPO (World Intellectual Property Organization) 2 UN Plz Ste 2525 ....New York NY 10017 *Web:* www.wipo.int	212-963-6813	963-4801	783
Wipro Gallagher Solutions Inc 810 Crescent Centre Dr Ste 400................Franklin TN 37067 *Web:* www.wipro.com	615-221-7300		000
Wire Association International Inc (WAI) 1570 Boston Post Rd PO Box 578 ....Guilford CT 06437 *Web:* www.wirenet.org	203-453-2777	453-8384	49-13
Wire Belt Company of America 154 Harvey Rd .... Londonderry NH 03053 *TF:* 800-922-2637 ■ *Web:* www.wirebelt.com	603-644-2500	644-3600	207
Wire Cloth Filter Manufacturing Co 611 W St Charles Rd ....Maywood IL 60153 *Web:* wireclothfilter.net	708-410-1800	410-1807	688
Wire Products Company Inc 14601 Industrial Pkwy ....Cleveland OH 44135 *Web:* wire-products.com	216-267-0777	267-7972	719
Wire Rope Industries Ltd 5501 Trans-Canada Hwy.................Pointe-Claire QC H9R1B7 *TF:* 800-565-5501 ■ *Web:* www.wirerope.com	514-697-9711	697-3534	492
Wire Tech Ltd 3567 Hwy 48 .... Summerville GA 30747 *Web:* www.wiretechltd.com	706-857-6413	857-1805	247
Wirebenders, The 2075 Lincoln Ave Ste A .... San Jose CA 95125 *TF:* 800-333-5576 ■ *Web:* www.thewirebenders.com	408-265-5576	265-5579	743
WireBuzz LLC 8360 E Raintree Dr Ste 225.................. Scottsdale AZ 85260 *Web:* www.wirebuzz.com	480-699-8053		5
Wired News Wired 520 Third St Ste 305 .... San Francisco CA 94107 *TF:* 800-769-4733 ■ *Web:* www.wired.com	800-769-4733		397
Wiredrive 5340 Alla Rd Ste 109..............Los Angeles CA 90066 *Web:* www.wiredrive.com	310-823-8238		177
Wirefab Inc 75 Blackstone River Rd............Worcester MA 01607 *Web:* www.wirefab.com	508-754-5359	797-3620	73
Wiregrass Electric Cooperative Inc 509 N State Hwy 167 ....Hartford AL 36344 *Web:* www.wiregrass.coop	334-588-2223		245
Wiregrass International Inc 17782 US Hwy 431 S ....Headland AL 36345 *Web:* www.wiregrassinternational.com	334-693-5285	693-2611	274
Wirehead Security LLC 19 W Hargett St Ste 512......................... Raleigh NC 27601	919-863-4373		196
Wireless Communications Association Intl (WCA) 1333 H St NW Ste 700W ....Washington DC 20005 *Web:* www.wcainternational.com	202-452-7823		49-20

Phone | Fax | Class

Wireless Network Group Warehouse
220 W Pkwy Pompton Plains NJ 07444 973-831-4015 138
Web: www.wnginc.com

Wireless Network Solutions Inc (WNS)
PO Box 2041 Lake Oswego OR 97035 503-583-2617 675-6536* 681
**Fax Area Code:* 425 ■ *Web:* www.wnsunwired.com

Wireless Seismic Inc
13100 SW Fwy Ste 150 Sugar Land TX 77478 832-532-5080 277-7804* 407
**Fax Area Code:* 281 ■ *Web:* wirelessseismic.com

Wireless Telecom Group Inc
25 Eastmans Rd Parsippany NJ 07054 973-386-9696 386-9191 735
NYSE: WTT ■ *Web:* www.wirelesstelecomgroup.com

Wireless Toyz Ltd 29155 NW Hwy Southfield MI 48034 248-426-8200 310
Web: www.wirelesstoyz.com

Wireless Watchdogs LLC
317 Isis Ave Ste 102 Inglewood CA 90301 866-522-0688 2
TF: 866-522-0688 ■ *Web:* www.wirelesswatchdogs.com

Wireless Zone LLC 795 Brook St Rocky Hill CT 06067 800-411-2355 35
TF: 888-881-2622 ■ *Web:* wirelesszone.com

Wirelesswerks USA Inc
7981 168th Ave NE Redmond WA 98052 425-869-2356 116
TF: 800-283-6045 ■ *Web:* www.wirelesswerks.com

Wiremasters Inc 1788 N Pt Rd Columbia TN 38401 615-791-0281 791-6182 246
TF: 800-635-5342 ■ *Web:* www.wiremasters.net

Wirerope Works Inc
100 Maynard St Williamsport PA 17701 570-326-5146 327-4274 813
TF: 800-541-7673 ■ *Web:* www.wwwrope.com

WireSpring Technologies Inc
1901 W Cypress Creek Rd Ste 100 Fort Lauderdale FL 33309 954-548-3300 177
Web: www.wirespring.com

Wirestar Networks
PO Box 10966 College Station TX 77840 888-999-1525 681
TF: 888-999-1525 ■ *Web:* www.wirestar.net

Wiretree LLC
200 Second Ave S Ste 447 Saint Petersburg FL 33701 404-876-3835 180
Web: www.wiretree.com

Wiring Harness Manufacturers Assn (WHMA)
15490 101st Ave N Ste 100 Maple Grove MN 55369 763-235-6461 49-13
Web: whma.org

WIRL-AM 331 Fulton St Ste 1200 Peoria IL 61602 309-637-3700 698-1290 647
Web: www.superhitswirl.com

Wirt County PO Box 53 Elizabeth WV 26143 304-275-4271 275-3418 338
Web: www.wirtcounty.wv.gov

Wirt Design Group
617 W 7th St Ste 201 Los Angeles CA 90017 213-239-0990 393
Web: www.wirtdesign.com

Wirtz Corp
680 N Lake Shore Dr Ste 1900 Chicago IL 60611 312-943-7000 185
Web: www.wirtzinsurance.com

Wirtz Manufacturing Company Inc
1105 24th St PO Box 5006 Port Huron MI 48061 810-987-7600 987-8135 757
Web: www.wirtzusa.com

WIS Intl 9265 Sky Park Ct Ste 100 San Diego CA 92123 858-565-8111 677-1945* 399
**Fax Area Code:* 905 ■ *TF:* 800-268-6848 ■ *Web:* w3.wisintl.com

Wisco Industries Inc 736 Janesville St Oregon WI 53575 608-835-3106 835-7399 488
Web: www.wiscomade.com

Wisco Products Inc 109 Commercial St Dayton OH 45402 937-228-2101 228-2407 697
TF: 800-367-6570 ■ *Web:* www.wiscoproducts.com

Wisco Supply Inc 815 S St Vrain St El Paso TX 79901 915-544-8294 533-1804 610
TF: 800-947-2689 ■ *Web:* www.wiscosupply.com

Wiscolift Inc W6396 Speciality Dr Greenville WI 54942 920-757-8832 492
TF: 800-242-3477 ■ *Web:* www.wiscolift.com

Wisconsin

Aging & Long-Term Care Resources Bureau
1 W Wilson St Rm 518 Madison WI 53707 608-267-7286 266-5629 339-50
Web: www.dhs.wisconsin.gov

Agriculture Trade & Consumer Protection Dept
2811 Agriculture Dr Madison WI 53708 608-224-5012 339-50
Web: www.datcp.wi.gov

Children & Family Services Div
201 E Washington Ave 10th Fl PO Box 8916 Madison WI 53708 608-267-3905 266-6836 339-50
Web: dcf.wisconsin.gov

Corrections Dept PO Box 7925 Madison WI 53707 608-240-5000 240-3300 339-50
Web: www.doc.wi.gov

Department of Revenue
PO Box 8933 Mail Stop 6-40 Madison WI 53708 608-266-6466 266-5718 339-50
Web: www.revenue.wi.gov

Director of State Courts
16E Capitol Bldg PO Box 1688 Madison WI 53701 608-266-6828 267-0980 339-50
Web: wicourts.gov

Economic Development Div
201 W Washington Ave Madison WI 53703 608-210-6760 339-50
Web: inwisconsin.com

Emergency Management
Teacher Education Bldg 225 N Mills St
Ste 264 Madison WI 53704 608-242-3232 339-50

Ethics Board
212 E Washington Ave 3rd Fl Madison WI 53707 608-266-8005 267-0500 265
TF: 866-868-3947 ■ *Web:* elections.wi.gov

Health Services Dept 1 W Wilson St Madison WI 53703 608-266-1865 266-7882 339-50
Web: www.dhs.wisconsin.gov

Historical Society 816 State St Madison WI 53706 608-264-6535 339-50
Web: wisconsinhistory.org

Housing & Economic Development Authority
201 W Washington Ave Ste 700 Madison WI 53703 608-266-7884 267-1099 339-50
TF: 800-334-6873 ■ *Web:* www.wheda.com

Insurance Commission 125 S Webster St Madison WI 53703 608-266-3585 266-9935 339-50
TF: 800-236-8517 ■ *Web:* www.oci.wi.gov

Legislature State Capitol Madison WI 53702 608-266-9960 339-50
TF: 800-362-9472 ■ *Web:* legis.wisconsin.gov

Lieutenant Governor
Teacher Education Bldg Ste 264 225 N Mills St
PO Box 2043 Madison WI 53702 608-266-3516 267-3571 339-50
Web: evers.wi.gov

Lottery PO Box 8941 Madison WI 53708 608-261-4916 264-6644 452
TF: 800-426-2535 ■ *Web:* wilottery.com

Motor Vehicles Div 4802 Sheboygan Ave Madison WI 53707 608-264-7447 339-50
Web: www.wisconsindot.gov

Natural Resources Dept
101 S Webster St PO Box 7921 Madison WI 53707 608-266-2621 261-4380 339-50
TF: 888-936-7463 ■ *Web:* dnr.wi.gov

Public Instruction Dept
125 S Webster St PO Box 7841 Madison WI 53707 608-266-3390 267-1052 339-50
Web: www.dpi.wi.gov

Public Service Commission
4822 Madison Yards Way N Tower Sixth Fl Madison WI 53705 608-266-5481 266-3957 339-50
TF: 888-816-3831 ■ *Web:* psc.wi.gov

Secretary of State
B41 W State Capitol PO Box 7848 Madison WI 53702 608-266-8888 266-3159 339-50
Web: sos.wi.gov

State Patrol Div
4802 Sheboygan Ave Rm 551 PO Box 7912 Madison WI 53707 844-847-1234 267-4495* 339-50
**Fax Area Code:* 608 ■ *TF:* 844-847-1234 ■ *Web:* www.wisconsindot.gov

Supreme Court
110 E Main St Ste 215 PO Box 1688 Madison WI 53701 608-266-1880 267-0640 339-50
Web: wicourts.gov

Vocational Rehabilitation Div
201 E Washington Ave PO Box 7852 Madison WI 53707 608-261-0050 266-1133 339-50
TF: 800-442-3477 ■ *Web:* dwd.wisconsin.gov

Workforce Development Dept
201 E Washington Ave Madison WI 53703 608-266-3131 266-1784 259
Web: dwd.wisconsin.gov

Wisconsin Aluminum Foundry Company Inc
838 S 16th St Manitowoc WI 54220 920-682-8286 682-7285 308
Web: www.wafco.com

Wisconsin Alumni Research Foundation
614 Walnut St 13th Fl Madison WI 53726 608-263-2500 263-1064 305
Web: www.warf.org

Wisconsin Aviation Inc
1741 River Dr Watertown WI 53094 920-261-4567 206-6386 63
TF: 800-657-0761 ■ *Web:* www.wisconsinaviation.com

Wisconsin Black Historical Society Museum
2620 W Center St Milwaukee WI 53206 414-372-7677 372-4888 520
Web: www.wbhsm.org

Wisconsin Box Company Inc
929 Townline Rd Wausau WI 54402 715-842-2248 842-2240 200
TF: 800-876-6658 ■ *Web:* www.wisconsinbox.com

Wisconsin Built Inc
400 Interpane Ln Deerfield WI 53531 608-764-8661 200
Web: www.wisconsin-built.com

Wisconsin Center District
500 W Kilbourn Milwaukee WI 53203 414-908-6000 31
Web: www.wcd.org

Wisconsin Center for Education Research
University of Wisconsin Madison 1025 W Johnson St
Ste 785 Madison WI 53706 608-263-4200 263-6448 668
Web: wcer.wisc.edu

Wisconsin Dells Visitors & Convention Bureau
701 Superior St PO Box 390 Wisconsin Dells WI 53965 608-254-8088 254-4293 206
TF: 800-223-3557 ■ *Web:* www.wisdells.com

Wisconsin Dental Assn
6737 W Washington St Ste 2360 West Allis WI 53214 414-276-4520 864-2997* 227
**Fax Area Code:* 800 ■ *TF:* 800-364-7646 ■ *Web:* www.wda.org

Wisconsin Department of Financial Institutions
4822 Madison Yards Way N Twr Madison WI 53705 608-261-9555 261-7200 339-50
Web: www.wdfi.org

Wisconsin Department of Veterans Affairs
2135 Rimrock Rd PO Box 7843 Madison WI 53707 608-266-0517 339-50
TF: 800-947-8387

Wisconsin Diagnostic Laboratories
9200 W Wisconsin Ave Milwaukee WI 53226 414-805-7600 415
Web: www.wisconsindiagnostic.com

Wisconsin Distributors Inc
900 Progress Way Sun Prairie WI 53590 608-834-2337 834-2300 81-3
Web: www.wisconsindistributors.com

Wisconsin Educational Communications Board
3319 W Beltline Hwy Madison WI 53713 608-264-9600 632
TF: 800-422-9707 ■ *Web:* www.ecb.org

Wisconsin Electrical Manufacturing Company Inc (WEM)
2501 S Moorland Rd PO Box 510767 New Berlin WI 53151 262-782-2340 782-2653 684
Web: www.wemautomation.com

Wisconsin English as a Second Language Institute
19 N Pinckney St Madison WI 53703 608-257-4300 257-4346 423
Web: wesli.com

Wisconsin Evangelical Lutheran Synod (WELS)
2929 N Mayfair Rd Milwaukee WI 53222 414-256-3888 48-20
Web: wels.net

Wisconsin Film & Bag Inc
3100 E Richmond St Shawano WI 54166 715-524-2565 524-3527 66
TF: 800-765-9224 ■ *Web:* www.wifb.com

Wisconsin Higher Educational Aids Board (HEAB)
131 W Wilson S PO Box 7885 Madison WI 53703 608-267-2206 267-2808 725
Web: www.heab.state.wi.us

Wisconsin Historical Museum
30 N Carroll St Madison WI 53703 608-264-6555 264-6575 520
TF: 888-999-1669 ■ *Web:* historicalmuseum.wisconsinhistory.org

Wisconsin Homes Inc
425 W McMillan St Marshfield WI 54449 715-384-2161 387-3627 106
TF: 877-354-7531 ■ *Web:* www.wisconsinhomesinc.com

Wisconsin Hospital Association Inc
5510 Research Park Dr Fitchburg WI 53711 608-274-1820 138
TF: 800-782-8581 ■ *Web:* www.wha.org

Wisconsin Indianhead Technical College
New Richmond Campus
1019 S Knowles Ave New Richmond WI 54017 715-246-6561 246-2777 800
TF: 800-243-9482 ■ *Web:* www.witc.edu

Wisconsin Industrial Machine Service Inc
21500 Doral Rd Waukesha WI 53186 262-784-2300 454
TF: 888-784-2210 ■ *Web:* www.wims-inc.com

Wisconsin Institute For Law & Liberty Inc
1139 E Knapp St Milwaukee WI 53202 414-727-9455 727-6385 41
Web: will-law.org

Wisconsin Jewish Chronicle
1360 N Prospect Ave Milwaukee WI 53202 414-390-5888 532-2
Web: www.jewishchronicle.org

Wisconsin Kenworth 5100 E Park Ave Madison WI 53718 608-241-5616 57
Web: www.csmtruck.com

Phone | Fax | Class

Wisconsin Library Assn (WLA)
4610 S Biltmore Ln Ste 100 . . . Madison WI 53718 608-245-3640 245-3646 49-19
Web: wla.wisconsinlibraries.org

Wisconsin Lift Truck Corp
3125 Intertech Dr . . . Brookfield WI 53045 262-781-8010 358
TF: 800-634-9010 ■ *Web:* www.wisconsinlift.com

Wisconsin Lutheran College
8800 W Bluemound Rd . . . Milwaukee WI 53226 414-443-8800 443-8514 166
Web: www.wlc.edu

Wisconsin Machine Tool Corp
3225 Gateway Rd Ste 100 . . . Brookfield WI 53045 262-317-3048 317-3079 455
TF: 800-243-3078 ■ *Web:* www.machine-tool.com

Wisconsin Management Co
2040 S Park St . . . Madison WI 53713 608-258-2080 652
Web: wisconsinmanagement.com

Wisconsin Manufacturers & Commerce
PO Box 352 . . . Madison WI 53701 608-258-3400 258-3413 140
TF: 800-236-5414 ■ *Web:* www.wmc.org

Wisconsin Marine Historical Society (WMHS)
814 W Wisconsin Ave . . . Milwaukee WI 53233 414-286-3074 48-13
Web: www.wmhs.org

Wisconsin Maritime Museum
75 Maritime Dr . . . Manitowoc WI 54220 920-684-0218 684-0219 520
TF: 866-724-2356 ■ *Web:* www.wisconsinmaritime.org

Wisconsin Medical Society
2450 Rimrock Rd Ste 101 . . . Madison WI 53713 866-442-3800 442-3802* 474
**Fax Area Code:* 608 ■ *TF:* 866-442-3800 ■ *Web:* www.wismed.org

Wisconsin Metal Parts Inc
N4 W 22450 Bluemound Rd . . . Waukesha WI 53186 262-524-9100 757
Web: www.wisconsinmetalparts.com

Wisconsin Metal Products Co
1807 DeKovin Ave . . . Racine WI 53403 262-633-6301 489
Web: wmpco.com

Wisconsin National Primate Research Ctr
1220 Capitol Ct . . . Madison WI 53715 608-263-3500 265-2067 668
Web: www.primate.wisc.edu

Wisconsin Nurses Assn (WNA)
6117 Monona Dr . . . Madison WI 53716 608-221-0383 221-2788 533
Web: wisconsinnurses.org

Wisconsin Office of the State Treasurer
B38 W State Capitol PO Box 7871 . . . Madison WI 53707 608-266-1714 339-50
Web: statetreasurer.wi.gov

Wisconsin Oven Corp 2675 Main St . . . East Troy WI 53120 262-642-3938 363-4018 318
Web: www.wisoven.com

Wisconsin Plastic Products Inc
1045 Lindoerfer Rd . . . Plymouth WI 53073 920-893-4500 893-4502 604
Web: www.wiplastic.com

Wisconsin Public Interest Research Group (WISPIRG)
912 Williamson St 2nd Fl . . . Madison WI 53703 608-251-9501 633
Web: wispirg.org

Wisconsin Public Service Corp
PO Box 19001 . . . Green Bay WI 54307 800-450-7260 433-1527* 787
**Fax Area Code:* 920 ■ *TF:* 800-450-7260 ■ *Web:* accel.wisconsinpublicservice.com

Wisconsin Radio Network
2 E main St Ste B40W . . . Madison WI 53703 608-251-8854 251-7233 647
Web: www.wrn.com

Wisconsin Realtors Assn
4801 Forest Run Rd Ste 201 . . . Madison WI 53704 608-241-2047 241-2901 656
TF: 800-279-1972 ■ *Web:* www.wra.org

Wisconsin Reinsurance Corp
2810 City View Dr . . . Madison WI 53707 608-242-4500 242-4514 391-4
TF: 800-939-9473 ■ *Web:* www.thewrcgroup.com

Wisconsin Republican Party
148 E Johnson St . . . Madison WI 53703 608-257-4765 616-2
Web: www.wisgop.org

Wisconsin School of Massage Therapy
N112 W15237 Mequon Rd Ste 400 . . . Germantown WI 53022 262-250-1276 685
Web: www.wsmt.org

Wisconsin School of Professional Pet Grooming Inc
W359 N5920 Brown St Ste 102 . . . Oconomowoc WI 53066 262-569-9492 569-1842 685
Web: www.wsppg.com

Wisconsin Secure Program Facility
1101 Morrison Dr . . . Boscobel WI 53805 608-375-5656 375-5595 213
Web: doc.wi.gov

Wisconsin Spice Inc
478 Industrial Park Rd . . . Berlin WI 54923 920-361-3555 123
Web: www.wisconsinspice.com

Wisconsin State Fair Park
640 S 84th St . . . West Allis WI 53214 414-266-7033 266-7007 520
Web: www.wistatefair.com

Wisconsin State Journal
1901 Fish Hatchery Rd . . . Madison WI 53713 608-252-6200 532-2
Web: madison.com

Wisconsin Steel & Tube Corp
1555 N Mayfair Rd . . . Milwaukee WI 53226 414-453-4441 453-0789 492
TF: 800-279-8335 ■ *Web:* wisteeltube.com

Wisconsin Tubing Inc 5705 County Rd E . . . Omro WI 54963 800-242-8280 685-2688* 612
**Fax Area Code:* 920 ■ *TF:* 800-242-8280 ■ *Web:* www.wisconsintubinginc.com

Wisconsin Valley Building Products LLC
610 McKinley St PO Box 668 . . . Wisconsin Rapids WI 54495 800-472-7301 182
Web: www.wisvalleybp.com

Wisconsin Veterans Home
N2665 County Rd QQ . . . King WI 54946 715-258-5586 256-3207 793
TF: 888-458-5586 ■ *Web:* dva.wi.gov

Wisconsin Veterans Museum
30 W Mifflin St . . . Madison WI 53703 608-264-6086 264-7615 520
Web: www.wisvetsmuseum.com

Wisconsin Veterinary Medical Assn (WVMA)
2801 Crossroads Dr Ste 1200 . . . Madison WI 53718 608-257-3665 257-8989 795
TF: 888-254-5202 ■ *Web:* www.wvma.org

Wisdom Animal Clinic Inc
2403 Texas Blvd . . . Texarkana TX 75503 903-793-1193 794
Web: wisdomanimalclinic.com

Wisdom Audio Corp
1572 College Pkwy Ste 164 . . . Carson City NV 89706 775-887-8850 887-8820 52
Web: www.wisdomaudio.com

Wisdom Creek Press LLC
5814 Sailboat Pointe NW . . . Acworth GA 30101 770-966-0911 966-0513 637-10
Web: wisdomcreekpress.com

Wisdom House Retreat & Conference Ctr
229 E Litchfield Rd . . . Litchfield CT 06759 860-567-3163 567-3166 673
Web: www.wisdomhouse.org

Wisdom Infotech Ltd
18650 W Corp Dr Ste 120 . . . Brookfield WI 53045 262-792-0200 180
Web: www.wisdominfotech.com

WisdomTools
501 N Morton St Ste 206 . . . Bloomington IN 47404 812-856-4202 225
Web: www.wisdomtools.com

Wise Alloys LLC 4805 Second St . . . Muscle Shoals AL 35661 256-386-6000 492
Web: www.wisealloys.com

Wise Business Forms Inc
555 McFarland 400 Dr . . . Alpharetta GA 30004 770-442-1060 442-9849 110
TF: 888-815-9473 ■ *Web:* www.wbf.com

Wise Consulting Associates Inc
54 Scott Adam Rd Ste 206 . . . Hunt Valley MD 21030 800-654-4550 449
TF: 800-654-4550 ■ *Web:* www.wiseconsulting.com

Wise County 200 N Trinity St . . . Decatur TX 76234 940-627-3351 627-2138 338
Web: www.co.wise.tx.us

Wise County
206 E Main St Ste 223 PO Box 570 . . . Wise VA 24293 276-328-2321 328-9780 338
Web: www.wisecounty.org

Wise County Chamber of Commerce
765 Park Ave PO Box 226 . . . Norton VA 24273 276-679-0961 679-2655 139
Web: www.wisecountychamber.org

Wise Electric Co-opeartive Inc
1900 N Trinity St . . . Decatur TX 76234 940-627-2167 626-3060 245
TF: 888-627-9326 ■ *Web:* www.wiseec.com

Wise Foods Inc 228 Rasely St Ste 75 . . . Berwick PA 18603 800-438-9473 759-4165* 296-35
**Fax Area Code:* 570 ■ *TF:* 888-759-4401 ■ *Web:* www.wisesnacks.com

Wise Health System
609 Medical Center Dr . . . Decatur TX 76234 940-627-5921 363
Web: www.wisehealthsystem.com

Wise Incentives
2165 San Diego Ave Ste 107 . . . San Diego CA 92110 619-291-8585 771
Web: www.wiseincentives.com

Wise Plastics Technologies
3810 Stern Ave . . . Saint Charles IL 60174 847-697-2840 697-0103 454
Web: www.wiseplastics.com

Wise Technical Marketing Inc
1430 Cherokee Rd . . . Louisville KY 40204 502-473-8300 195
Web: wisetechnical.com

WISE-AM 1310 (Sports)
1190 Patton Ave . . . Asheville NC 28806 828-259-9695 253-5619 645-10
Web: wisesportsradio.com

Wiseco Piston Inc
7201 Industrial Pk Blvd . . . Mentor OH 44060 440-951-6600 951-6606 128
TF: 800-321-1364 ■ *Web:* www.wiseco.com

Wiseman Bray PLLC
8001 Centerview Pkwy Ste 103 . . . Cordova TN 38018 901-372-5003 41
Web: wisemanbray.com

WiseSoft LLC
IDS Tower 80 S Eighth St 9th Fl . . . Minneapolis MN 55402 612-568-7259 180
Web: www.wise-soft.com

Wisetail 212 S Wallace Ave . . . Bozeman MT 59715 406-545-4662 387
Web: www.wisetail.com

Wisetek Providers Inc
11211 Waples Mill Rd . . . Fairfax VA 22030 703-766-8850 225
Web: www.wisepro.com

Wiseway Motor Freight Inc PO Box 838 . . . Hudson WI 54016 800-876-1660 780
TF: 800-876-1660 ■ *Web:* www.wiseway.com

WISH List
46-E Peninsula Ctr Ste 385 . . . Rolling Hills Estates CA 90274 888-310-4504 48-7
TF: 888-310-4504 ■ *Web:* www.thewishlist.org

Wishnow Ross Warsavsky & Co
16130 Ventura Blvd . . . Encino CA 91436 818-981-2240 2

WISH-TV Ch 8 (CBS)
1950 N Meridian St . . . Indianapolis IN 46202 317-923-8888 931-2242 741-62
Web: www.wishtv.com

Wisler Pearlstine LLP
460 Norristown Rd Ste 110 . . . Blue Bell PA 19422 610-825-8400 428
Web: www.wislerpearlstine.com

Wisneski, Sears & Associates PA
810 Saturn St Ste 30 . . . Jupiter FL 33477 561-747-2772 2
Web: myjupitercpa.com

Wisnetcom 987 S Main St . . . Fond Du Lac WI 54935 920-322-9522 180
Web: www.wisnet.com

WISN-TV Ch 12 (ABC) 759 N 19th St . . . Milwaukee WI 53233 414-342-8812 342-2354 741-83
Web: www.wisn.com

WISP (Women's Independence Scholarship Program Inc)
4900 Randall Pkwy Ste H . . . Wilmington NC 28403 910-397-7742 305
Web: wispinc.org

Wis-Pak Inc 860 W St PO Box 496 . . . Watertown WI 53094 920-262-6300 262-9273 81-2
Web: wis-pak.com

Wispark LLC
301 W Wisconsin Ave Ste 400 . . . Milwaukee WI 53203 414-274-4600 653
Web: www.wispark.com

WISPIRG (Wisconsin Public Interest Research Group)
912 Williamson St 2nd Fl . . . Madison WI 53703 608-251-9501 633
Web: wispirg.org

Wiss & Company LLP
354 Eisenhower Pkwy . . . Livingston NJ 07039 973-994-9400 992-6760 734
Web: www.wiss.com

Wiss Janney Elstner Associates Inc
330 Pfingsten Rd . . . Northbrook IL 60062 847-272-7400 291-9599 261
Web: www.wje.com

Wist Office Products Co 107 W Julie Dr . . . Tempe AZ 85283 480-921-2900 921-2121 535
TF: 800-999-9478 ■ *Web:* wist.com

Wistar Institute 3601 Spruce St . . . Philadelphia PA 19104 215-898-3700 898-3715 668
TF: 800-724-6633 ■ *Web:* wistar.org

Wistariahurst Museum 238 Cabot St . . . Holyoke MA 01040 413-322-5660 534-2344 50-3
Web: wistariahurst.org

Wisteria 471 N Highland Ave . . . Atlanta GA 30307 404-525-3363 525-3313 671
Web: www.wisteria-atlanta.com

WIS-TV Ch 10 (NBC) 1111 Bull St . . . Columbia SC 29201 803-799-1010 758-1155 741-33
Web: www.wistv.com

WISU-FM
230-B Dreiser Hall 221 N 6th St . . . Terre Haute IN 47809 812-237-3690 647
Web: www.isustudentmedia.com

Name / Address	Phone	Fax	Class
WITA AM 1490 133 James Luscinski Dr Ste 101, Nashville TN 37218 *Web:* www.1490wita.com	865-240-4084		645-82
Witch Equipment Company Inc 1901 E Loop 820 S, Fort Worth TX 76112 *Web:* www.witchequipment.net	817-429-4824		358
Witco Inc 6401 Bricker Rd, Avoca MI 48006 *Web:* witcoinc.com	810-387-4231	387-4145	493
WITF-FM 89.5 (NPR) 4801 Lindle Rd, Harrisburg PA 17111 *TF:* 800-366-9483, *Web:* www.witf.org	717-704-3000	704-3659	645-68
Witham Memorial Hospital 2605 N Lebanon St, Lebanon IN 46052 *Web:* witham.org	765-485-8000		374-3
Withers Tool Die & Mfg 1238 Veterans Memorial Hwy SE, Mableton GA 30126 *Web:* witherstool.com	770-948-2544	739-1749	491
Witherspoon and Associates 1200 W Fwy Ste 200, Fort Worth TX 76102 *Web:* www.witherspoon.com	817-335-1373		4
Withlacoochee River Electric Co-op PO Box 278, Dade City FL 33526 *Web:* www.wrec.net	352-567-5133		245
Withlacoochee Technical College 1201 W Main St, Inverness FL 34450 *Web:* www.wtcollege.org	352-726-2430	249-2157	167-3
Withrow Springs State Park 33424 Spur 23, Huntsville AR 72740 *Web:* www.arkansasstateparks.com	479-559-2593		565
WithumSmith+Brown 5 Vaughn Dr, Princeton NJ 08540 *Web:* www.withum.com	609-520-1188	520-9882	2
WITI (Women in Technology Intl) 11500 Olympic Blvd Ste 400, Los Angeles CA 90064 *TF:* 800-334-9484, *Web:* www.witi.com	818-788-9484	788-9410	49-19
WITI-TV Ch 6 (Fox) 9001 N Green Bay Rd, Milwaukee WI 53209 *Web:* fox6now.com	414-355-6666	586-2141	741-83
Witmer's Construction Inc 39821 Salem Unity Rd, Salem OH 44460 *TF:* 888-427-2150, *Web:* www.witmersconstruction.com	330-427-2611		274
Witness Publishing Co 1229 Mount Loretta Ave, Dubuque IA 52004 *Web:* www.thewitnessonline.org	563-588-0556	588-0557	532-2
WITN-TV 275 E Arlington Blvd, Greenville NC 27858 *Web:* www.witn.com	252-439-7770	439-7796	647
Witscheys Market Inc 155 North St, New Martinsville WV 26155 *Web:* witscheysmarket.com	304-455-3115		345
Witt Industries Inc 4600 Mason-Montgomery Rd, Mason OH 45040 **Fax Area Code:* 877, *TF:* 800-543-7417, *Web:* www.witt.com	800-543-7417	891-8200*	661
Witt Lincoln 588 Camino Del Rio N, San Diego CA 92108 **Fax Area Code:* 619, *TF:* 877-937-3301, *Web:* www.wittlincoln.com	877-856-2242	358-5008*	57
Witt Printing Co 301 Oak St, El Dorado Springs MO 64744 *TF:* 800-641-4342, *Web:* www.wittprinting.com	417-876-4721	876-4794	110
Witt Sign Company Inc 306 McCowan Dr, Lebanon TN 37087 *Web:* wittsigns.com	615-444-3898		8
Witt/Kieffer Ford Hadelman & Lloyd 2015 Spring Rd Ste 510, Oak Brook IL 60523 *TF:* 888-281-1370, *Web:* www.wittkieffer.com	630-990-1370	990-1382	266
Witte Company Inc 507 Rt 31 S PO Box 47, Washington NJ 07882 *Web:* www.witte.com	908-689-6500	537-6806	298
Witte Museum 3801 Broadway St, San Antonio TX 78209 *Web:* www.wittemuseum.org	210-357-1900	357-1882	520
Wittek Golf Supply Company Inc 300 Bond St, Elk Grove Village IL 60007 **Fax Area Code:* 847, *TF:* 800-869-1800, *Web:* www.wittekgolf.com	800-869-1800	412-9591*	710
Wittenberg Telephone Co 104 W Walker St, Wittenberg WI 54499 *Web:* www.wittenbergnet.net	715-253-2111	253-3497	224
Wittenberg University 200 W Ward St, Springfield OH 45504 *TF:* 800-677-7558, *Web:* www.wittenberg.edu	937-327-6314	327-6379	166
Wittenstein Inc 1249 Humbracht Cir, Bartlett IL 60103 *TF:* 888-534-1222, *Web:* www.wittenstein-us.com	630-540-5300		22
Wittigs Office Interiors 2018 Ave B Ste 300, San Antonio TX 78215 *Web:* wittigs.com	210-270-0100		321
Wittman Robert J (Rep R - VA) 2055 Rayburn House Office Bldg, Washington DC 20515 *Web:* wittman.house.gov	202-225-4261	225-4382	342-2
Wittmer & Linehan PLLC 2014 Fourth St, Sarasota FL 34237 *Web:* sarasotalitigator.com	941-365-2296		41
Witzco Trailers Inc 6101 S McIntosh Rd, Sarasota FL 34238 *Web:* www.witzco.com	941-922-5301	924-2402	779
Witzenmann USA LLC 2200 Centerwood Dr, Warren MI 48091 *Web:* www.witzenmann-usa.com	248-588-6033		194
Witzig, Hannah, Sanders & Reagan LLP 600 Ocean St, Santa Cruz CA 95060 *Web:* whsllp.com	831-425-2835		41
WIVB-TV Ch 4 (CBS) 2077 Elmwood Ave, Buffalo NY 14207 *TF:* 800-794-3687, *Web:* www.wivb.com	716-874-4410	874-8173	741-20
WIVM-TV 6755 Freedom Ave NW, North Canton OH 44720 *Web:* www.wivmtv.com	330-494-9303	966-1792	647
WIVT-TV 203 Ingraham Hill Rd, Binghamton NY 13903 *Web:* www.binghamtonhomepage.com	607-771-3434	723-6403	647
WIWU-TV 4201 S Washington St, Marion IN 46953 *Web:* wildcatcentral.wiwutv.com	765-677-2775		647
WIX Filtration Products 1 Wix Way PO Box 1967, Gastonia NC 28053 *TF:* 800-949-6698, *Web:* www.wixfilters.com	704-864-6711	864-9277	60
WIXN-AM 1460 S College Ave, Dixon IL 61021 *Web:* www.radiorockriver.com	815-288-3341	284-1017	647
Wixon Inc 1390 E Bolivar Ave, Saint Francis WI 53235 *TF:* 800-841-5304, *Web:* www.wixon.com	414-769-3000		296

Name / Address	Phone	Fax	Class
Wixon Jewelers Inc 9955 Lyndale Ave S, Minneapolis MN 55420 *Web:* www.wixonjewelers.com	952-881-8862		410
Wixson Honey Inc 4937 Lakemont-Himrod Rd, Dundee NY 14837 *Web:* wixsonhoney.com	607-243-7301		296-24
WIXX-FM 101.1 (CHR) 1420 Bellevue St, Green Bay WI 54311 *Web:* www.wixx.com	920-435-3771	321-2300	645-64
WIYY-FM 97.9 (Rock) 3800 Hooper Ave, Baltimore MD 21211 *Web:* www.98online.com	410-889-0098		645-15
Wizard Computer Services Inc 421 Page St, Stoughton MA 02072 *Web:* wizardcpu.com	781-341-2222		196
Wizard Works 66437 Out There Ave, Homer AK 99603 **Fax Area Code:* 907, *TF:* 877-210-2665, *Web:* www.alaskastudiescenter.com	877-210-2665	235-8757*	637-2
Wizards of Oztechs LLC, The 2099 Mt Diablo Blvd Ste 203, Walnut Creek CA 94596 *TF:* 877-698-3247, *Web:* www.oztechs.com	877-698-3247		809
Wizards of the Coast Inc PO Box 707, Renton WA 98057 *TF:* 800-324-6496, *Web:* company.wizards.com	425-226-6500		762
Wizbang Solutions Inc 6747 E 50th Ave, Commerce City CO 80022 *Web:* wizbangsolutions.com	720-974-5623		627
Wizcom Technologies Inc 33 Boston Post Rd W Ste 320, Marlborough MA 01752 *TF:* 888-777-0552, *Web:* www.wizcomtech.com	508-251-5388		173-7
Wizdom Systems Inc 1200 Iroquois Ave, Naperville IL 60563 *Web:* www.wizdom.com	630-357-3000	357-3059	178-1
WIZF-FM 101.1 (Urban) 1 Centennial Plz 705 Central Ave Ste 200, Cincinnati OH 45202 *Web:* wiznation.com	513-679-6000		645-35
WIZM 201 State St, La Crosse WI 54601 *Web:* www.wizmnews.com	608-785-7914		647
WIZN-FM 106.7 450 Weaver St, Winooski VT 05404 *TF:* 888-873-9496, *Web:* www.wizn.com	802-860-2440		645-176
Wizsoft Inc 6800 Jericho Tpke Ste 120W, Syosset NY 11791 *Web:* www.wizsoft.com	516-393-5841	393-5842	178-10
WIZZ-AM PO Box 983, Greenfield MA 01302 *Web:* www.wizzradio.com	413-774-5757	773-8274	647
WJ Beal Botanical Garden Michigan State University 412 Olds Hall, East Lansing MI 48824 *Web:* www.cpa.msu.edu	517-355-9582	432-1090	97
WJ Egli Company Inc PO Box 2605, Alliance OH 44601 *Web:* www.wjegli.com	330-823-3666	823-0011	286
WJ Hayes State Park 1220 Wampler's Lake Rd, Onsted MI 49265 *Web:* www.michigan.gov	517-467-7401		565
Wjac-Tv 49 Old Hickory Ln, Johnstown PA 15905 *Web:* wjactv.com	814-255-7600		116
WJAR-TV Ch 10 (NBC) 23 Kenney Dr, Cranston RI 02920 *Web:* www.turnto10.com	401-455-9100	455-9140	741
WJAS-AM 200 Ft St - 4th Fr, Pittsburgh PA 15220 *Web:* www.1320wjas.com	412-919-8527	937-9385	647
WJBF-TV 1336 Augusta West Pky PO Box 31358, Augusta GA 30909 *Web:* www.wjbf.com	706-722-6664		647
WJBK-TV Ch 2 (Fox) 16550 W 9 Mile Rd PO Box 2000, Southfield MI 48037 *Web:* www.fox2detroit.com	248-552-5122		741
WJBZ-FM 96.3 7101 Chapman Hwy, Knoxville TN 37920 *Web:* praise963.com	865-577-4885		645-82
WJCB-FM 1150 W King St, Cocoa FL 32922 *Web:* www.wjfp.com	321-632-1000		647
WJCL-TV Ch 22 (ABC) 1375 Chatham Pkwy 3rd Fl, Savannah GA 31405 *Web:* www.wjcl.com	912-925-0022		741-122
WJCT-FM 89.9 100 Festival Park Ave, Jacksonville FL 32202 *Web:* www.wjct.org	904-353-7770		645-76
WJEH-FM 527 Gibbs St, Ravenswood WV 26164 *Web:* www.wjehfm.com	304-273-2544		647
WJFK-AM 4915 Greenspring Ave, Baltimore MD 21209 *Web:* www.washington.cbslocal.com	410-367-2217		647
WJFW, Newswatch 12 3217 County Road G, Rhinelander WI 54501 *Web:* www.wjfw.com	715-365-8812	365-8810	647
WJGM-FM 5634 Normandy Blvd, Jacksonville FL 32205 *Web:* www.wjgmradio.com	904-781-4321		647
WJHC-FM 313 Hatley St E, Jasper FL 32052 *Web:* www.talk1075.com	386-792-1075		647
WJHG-TV 8195 Front Beach Rd, Panama City Beach FL 32407 *Web:* www.wjhg.com	850-234-7777	233-6647	647
WJHL-TV Ch 11 (CBS) 338 E Main St, Johnson City TN 37601 **Fax Area Code:* 804, *Web:* www.wjhl.com	423-926-2151	887-7062*	741-66
WJHM-FM 102 1800 Pembrook Dr Ste 400, Orlando FL 32810 *Web:* fm1019.radio.com	407-919-1000		645-114
WJIB-AM 740 (AC) 443 Concord Ave, Cambridge MA 02138 *Web:* wjib.org	617-868-7400		645
WJJH-FM 2320 Ellis Ave PO Box 613, Ashland WI 54806 *Web:* www.wjjhfm.com	715-682-2727		647
WJJO-FM 94.1 (Rock) 730 Rayovac Dr, Madison WI 53711 *Web:* www.wjjo.com	608-321-0941		645-92
WJJQ 81 E Mohawk Dr, Tomahawk WI 54487 *Web:* www.wjjq.com	715-453-4482	453-7169	647
WJKR-FM 1458 Dublin Rd, Columbus OH 43215 *Web:* www.1039jackfm.com	614-821-9970		647
WJLA-TV Ch 7 (ABC) 1100 Wilson Blvd, Arlington VA 22209 *Web:* www.wjla.com	703-236-9552		741
WJLD-AM 1400 1449 Spaulding Ishkooda Rd PO Box 19123, Birmingham AL 35211 *Web:* wjldradio.com	205-942-1776	942-4814	645-19
WJLF 2925 NW 39th Ave, Gainesville FL 32605 *Web:* www.thejoyfm.com	352-371-1457		645-11

Name / Address	City	State	ZIP	Phone	Fax	Class
WJLN 88.7 FM The Source PO Box 311 *Web:* www.wjlnfm887.weebly.com	Lake City	FL	32056	352-610-3114		647
WJMC-AM 1859 21st Ave PO Box 352 *Web:* www.wjmcradio.com	Rice Lake	WI	54868	715-234-2131		647
WJMH-FM 102.1 (Urban) 7819 National Service Rd Ste 401 *Web:* 102jamz.radio.com	Greensboro	NC	27409	336-605-5200	605-5219	645
WJMI-FM 99.7 (Urban) 731 S Pear Orchard Rd Ste 27 *Web:* www.wjmi.com	Ridgeland	MS	39157	601-957-1300		645
WJMZ-FM 107.3 (Urban) 220 N Main St Ste 402 *TF:* 800-767-1073 ■ *Web:* www.1073jamz.com	Greenville	SC	29601	864-235-1073	370-3403	645-65
WJNI-FM 60 Markfield Dr *Web:* www.wjnifm.com	Charleston	SC	29407	843-763-6631		647
WJNX-AM 4100 Metzger Rd *Web:* www.lagigante1330.com	Fort Pierce	FL	34947	772-464-1330		647
WJOL-AM 2410-B Caton Farm Rd *Web:* www.wjol.com	Crest Hill	IL	60403	815-254-7300		647
WJOU-FM 90.1 (Rel) 7000 Adventist Blvd *Web:* www.wjou.org	Huntsville	AL	35896	256-722-9990	837-7918	645-73
WJOY-AM 1230 (Nost) 70 Joy Dr *TF:* 800-554-9890 ■ *Web:* www.wjoy.com	South Burlington	VT	05403	802-658-1230	862-0786	645
WJPA-AM 98 S Main St PO Box 225 *Web:* www.wjpa.com	Washington	PA	15301	724-222-2110		647
WJPF-AM 1431 Country Aire Dr *Web:* www.wjpf.com	Carterville	IL	62918	618-985-4843	985-6529	647
WJPT-FM 106.3 (Nost) 20125 S Tamiami Trl *Web:* sunny1063.com	Estero	FL	33928	239-495-2100		645
WJQK-FM 425 Centerstone Ct *TF:* 866-931-9936 ■ *Web:* www.jq99.com	Zeeland	MI	49464	616-931-9930	931-1280	645
WJRD-AM 5455 Jug Factory Rd *Web:* www.wjrdradio.com	Tuscaloosa	AL	35405	205-345-9573	366-9480	647
WJRT-TV 2302 Lapeer Rd *Web:* www.abc12.com	Flint	MI	48503	810-233-3130	257-2812	647
WJRV-FM 408 N Cedar Bluff Rd Ste 252 *Web:* www.river106.com	Knoxville	TN	37923	865-246-3848	246-7979	647
WJSR Jefferson State Community College 2601 Carson Rd *Web:* www.angelfire.com	Birmingham	AL	35215	205-856-7702	815-8499	645-19
WJSS-AM 1605 Level Rd *Web:* radiotowers.info	Havre de Grace	MD	21078	410-939-9446		647
WJTS-TV PO Box 1009 *Web:* www.wjts.tv	Jasper	IN	47547	812-482-2727		647
WJW-TV Ch 8 (Fox) 5800 S Marginal Rd *Web:* fox8.com	Cleveland	OH	44103	216-432-4240	391-9559	741-31
WJXA-FM 92.9 (AC) 504 Rosedale Ave *Web:* mix929.com	Nashville	TN	37211	615-737-0929	259-4594	645-106
WJXS-TV 2111 Hwy 78 E Ste 1 *Web:* www.tv24.tv	Anniston	AL	36207	256-831-4624		647
WJXT-TV Ch 4 (Ind) 4 Broadcast Pl *Web:* www.news4jax.com	Jacksonville	FL	32207	904-399-4000		741-64
WJXX-TV Ch 25 (ABC) 1070 E Adams St *Web:* www.firstcoastnews.com	Jacksonville	FL	32202	904-354-1212		741-64
WJYE-FM 14 Lafayette Sq Ste 1200 *Web:* www.961joyfm.com	Buffalo	NY	14203	716-644-9696	852-7444	647
WJYI-AM 1340 (Rel) 5407 W McKinley Ave *TF:* 800-256-6102 ■ *Web:* www.joy1340.com	Milwaukee	WI	53208	414-978-9000	978-9001	645-98
WJYS-TV Ch 62 (Ind) 18600 Oak Park Ave *Web:* www.wjys.tv	Tinley Park	IL	60477	708-633-0001		741
WJYY-FM 105.5 (CHR) *NH1 Media Ctr* 4 Church St *TF:* 888-817-1055 ■ *Web:* wjyy.com	Concord	NH	03301	603-230-9000		645
WJZ-AM 1300 (N/T) 1423 Clarkview Rd Ste 100 *Web:* baltimore.cbslocal.com	Baltimore	MD	21209	410-481-1057		645-15
WJZM-AM PO Box 648 *Web:* www.wjzm.com	Clarksville	TN	37040	931-645-6414		647
WJZY-TV 3501 Performance Rd *Web:* www.fox46.com	Charlotte	NC	28214	704-398-0046		647
Wk Dickson & Company Inc 616 Colonnade Dr *TF:* 800-603-2872 ■ *Web:* www.wkdickson.com	Charlotte	NC	28205	704-334-5348		194
WK Kellogg Foundation 1 Michigan Ave E *Web:* wkkf.org	Battle Creek	MI	49017	269-968-1611	968-0413	305
WK Kellogg Health Sciences Library 5850 College St Sir Charles Tupper Medical Bldg *Web:* libraries.dal.ca	Halifax	NS	B3H4H7	902-494-2458	494-3798	434-1
WK Multimedia Network Training 178 S Blvd *Web:* www.reachandteach.com	San Mateo	CA	94402	415-586-1713		180
WKAQ-TV Ch 2 (Tele) PO Box 366222 *Web:* www.telemundopr.com	San Juan	PR	00936	787-758-2222		741-121
WKAR 404 Wilson Rd Rm 212 *Web:* www.wkar.org	East Lansing	MI	48824	517-884-6990		647
WKAR-FM 90.5 (NPR) 404 Wilson Rd Rm 287 *Web:* wkar.org	East Lansing	MI	48824	517-884-4700	432-3858	645
WKBD-TV Ch 50 (CW) 26905 W 11-Mile Rd *Web:* cwdetroit.cbslocal.com	Southfield	MI	48033	248-355-7000		741
WKBN/WYFX 3930 Sunset Blvd *Web:* www.wkbn.com	Youngstown	OH	44512	330-782-1144	782-3504	741-145
WKBO-AM 25 E Main St *Web:* www.oneheartministries.com	Mechanicsburg	PA	17055	717-796-9526		647
WKBU / Entercom New Orleans LLC 400 Poydras St Ste 800 *Web:* bayou957.radio.com	New Orleans	LA	70130	504-593-6376		645-107
WKBW-TV Ch 7 (ABC) 7 Broadcast Plz *Web:* www.wkbw.com	Buffalo	NY	14202	716-845-6100		741-20
WKCI-FM 495 Benham St *Web:* www.kc101.iheart.com	Hamden	CT	06514	203-281-9600		647
WKDE-AM 200 Frazier Rd *TF:* 877-386-1055 ■ *Web:* www.kdcountry.com	Altavista	VA	24517	434-369-5588		647
WKDQ 99.5 20 NW Third St Ste 600 *TF:* 877-437-5995 ■ *Web:* wkdq.com	Evansville	IN	47708	812-425-4226		645-54
WKE Inc 400 N Tustin Ave Ste 275 *Web:* www.wke-inc.com	Santa Ana	CA	92705	714-953-2665	953-5408	261
WKEB-FM 630 S Eighth St PO Box 59 *Web:* www.k99wigm.com	Medford	WI	54451	715-748-2566	748-2752	647
WKEE-FM c/o KEE 100 134 4th Ave *TF:* 800-544-9533 ■ *Web:* www.kee100.iheart.com	Huntington	WV	25701	304-525-7788	525-6281	647
WKEN-FM PO Box 1020 *Web:* www.shinefmohio.com	Bellefontaine	OH	43311	937-292-8890	593-8890	647
WKEX-AM PO Box 889 *TF:* 877-456-9361 ■ *Web:* www.tunein.com	Blacksburg	VA	24063	877-456-9361		647
WKHM-FM 1700 Glenshire Dr *Web:* www.k1053.com	Jackson	MI	49201	517-787-9546	787-7517	647
WKHY-FM 3575 McCarty Ln *Web:* www.wkhy.com	Lafayette	IN	47905	765-447-2186	448-4452	647
WKIX-FM 102.9 (Oldies) 3012 Highwoods Blvd Ste 201 *Web:* www.kix1029.com	Raleigh	NC	27604	919-860-1029		645-128
WKJV-AM 1380 70 Adams Hill Rd *Web:* www.wkjv.com	Asheville	NC	28806	828-252-1380	259-9427	645-10
WKKI-FM 126 W Fayette St *Web:* www.k943.com	Celina	OH	45822	419-586-7715		647
WKKO-FM 3225 Arlington Ave *Web:* www.k100country.com	Toledo	OH	43614	419-240-1000		647
WKKR-FM 915 Veterans Pkwy *Web:* www.kickerfm.iheart.com	Opelika	AL	36801	334-274-6424		647
WKMC (Willis-Knighton Medical Ctr) 2600 Greenwood Rd *Web:* www.wkhs.com	Shreveport	LA	71103	318-212-4000		374-3
WKMG-TV Ch 6 (CBS) 4466 N John Young Pkwy *Web:* www.clickorlando.com	Orlando	FL	32804	407-521-1200	521-1204	741-95
WKML-FM 508 Person St *Web:* www.wkml.com	Fayetteville	NC	28301	910-323-9570		647
WKNC-FM 88.1 (Rock) 343 Witherspoon Student Ctr CB 8607 *Web:* www.wknc.org	Raleigh	NC	27695	919-515-2401	515-5133	645-128
WKNO-FM 91.1 (NPR) 7151 Cherry Farms Rd *TF:* 800-766-9566 ■ *Web:* www.wknofm.org	Cordova	TN	38016	901-325-6544	729-8176	645-95
WKNV-AM PO Box 889 *Web:* www.joyam.org	Blacksburg	VA	24063	540-951-9791		647
WKNX-TV 1100 Sharps Ridge Memorial Park Dr *Web:* www.theknoxtv.com	Knoxville	TN	37918	865-207-7997		647
WKOS-FM 162 Free Hill Rd PO Box 8668 *Web:* www.1049nashicon.com	Gray	TN	37615	423-477-1000		647
WKOW-TV Ch 27 (ABC) 5727 Tokay Blvd *Web:* www.wkow.com	Madison	WI	53719	608-274-1234	274-9514	741-80
WKPT-AM 1400 (Nost) 222 Commerce St *Web:* www.espntricities.com	Kingsport	TN	37660	423-246-9578	247-9836	645
WKQL-FM 904 N Main St *TF:* 800-833-9211 ■ *Web:* www.kool1033fm.com	Punxsutawney	PA	15767	814-938-6000		647
WKRC-TV Ch 12 (CBS) 1906 Highland Ave *TF:* 877-889-5610 ■ *Web:* www.local12.com	Cincinnati	OH	45219	513-763-5500	421-3820	741-30
WKRG-TV Ch 5 (CBS) 555 Broadcast Dr *Web:* www.wkrg.com	Mobile	AL	36606	251-479-5555	473-8130	741-85
WKRN-TV Ch 2 (ABC) 441 Murfreesboro Rd *Web:* www.wkrn.com	Nashville	TN	37210	615-369-7222		741-89
WKRX-FM PO Box 1176 *Web:* www.radioroxboro.com	Roxboro	NC	27573	336-599-0266		647
WKRZ-FM 98.5 (CHR) 305 Hwy 315 *TF:* 800-222-0985 ■ *Web:* 985krz.radio.com	Pittston	PA	18640	570-883-9800		645
WKSU-FM 89.7 (NPR) 1613 E Summit St *TF:* 800-672-2132 ■ *Web:* wksu.org	Kent	OH	44242	330-672-3114		645
WKTA-AM 4320 Dundee Rd *Web:* www.pclradio.com	Northbrook	IL	60062	847-498-3350		647
WKTJ-FM 121 Broadway PO Box 590 *Web:* www.993ktj.com	Farmington	ME	04938	207-778-3400	778-3000	647
WKTN-FM 112 N Detroit St *Web:* www.wktn.com	Kenton	OH	43326	419-675-2355	673-1096	647
WKTO FM 88.9 900 Old Mission Rd *Web:* wkto.net	New Smyrna Beach	FL	32168	386-427-1095		645
WKTV-TV 5936 Smith Hill Rd *Web:* www.wktv.com	Utica	NY	13501	315-733-0404		647
WKUA-FM 1900 Crestwood Blvd Ste 111 *Web:* www.myrevradio.com	Birmingham	AL	35210	205-402-4267		647
WKUL-FM 214 1st Ave SE *Web:* www.wkul.com	Cullman	AL	35055	256-734-0183	739-2999	647
WKXW-FM 101.5 (N/T) 109 Walters Ave *Web:* www.nj1015.com	Trenton	NJ	08638	609-359-5300	359-5301	645-164
WKYC-TV Ch 3 (NBC) 1333 Lakeside Ave E *TF:* 877-790-7370 ■ *Web:* www.wkyc.com	Cleveland	OH	44114	216-344-3333		741-31
WKYK-AM 749 Sawmill Rd PO Box 744 *TF:* 800-949-3798 ■ *Web:* www.ourlocalcommunityonline.com	Burnsville	NC	28714	828-682-3510	682-6227	647
WKYT-TV Ch 27 (CBS) 2851 Winchester Rd *Web:* www.wkyt.com	Lexington	KY	40509	859-299-0411	293-1578	741-73
WKYZ-FM One Boot Key PO Box 500940 *Web:* www.keystv.com	Marathon	FL	33050	305-743-5563		647
WKZI-AM 3775 W Dugger Ave *TF:* 877-939-1480 ■ *Web:* www.wordpower.us	West Terre Haute	IN	47885	812-535-1937		647
WKZO-AM 4200 W Main St *Web:* www.wkzo.com	Kalamazoo	MI	49006	269-345-7121	345-1436	647
WKZQ 96.1 New Rock 1016 Ocala St *Web:* 961wkzq.com	Myrtle Beach	SC	29577	843-448-1041		645-104

Name / Address	City	State	Zip	Phone	Fax	Class
WKZS-FM PO Box 67 *Web:* www.kisscountryradio.com	Covington	IN	47932	765-793-5477		647
WKZW-FM 94.3 (AC) PO Box 6408 *Web:* www.kz94.com	Laurel	MS	39441	601-425-9494	649-8199	645
WL Jenkins Co 1445 Whipple Ave SW *Web:* www.wljenkinsco.com	Canton	OH	44710	330-477-3407	477-8404	700
W-L Molding Co, The 8212 Shaver Rd *Web:* www.wlmolding.com	Portage	MI	49024	269-327-3075	323-8416	604
WL Rubottom Company Inc 320 W Lewis St *Web:* wlrubottom.com	Ventura	CA	93001	805-648-6943		321
WLA (Wisconsin Library Assn) 4610 S Biltmore Ln Ste 100 *Web:* wla.wisconsinlibraries.org	Madison	WI	53718	608-245-3640	245-3646	49-19
Wla Consulting Inc 610 J St Ste 120 *Web:* wla-consulting.com	Lincoln	NE	68508	402-475-8588		261
WLA Inc 133 White Pines Country Club Rd *TF:* 800-525-7182 ■ *Web:* www.wlainc.com	Mount Airy	NC	27030	336-789-0545	783-9335	780
WLA Investments Inc 1301 Dove St Ste 1080 *Web:* wlainvestments.com	Newport Beach	CA	92660	949-851-2020		205
WLAD-AM 98 Mill Plain Rd *Web:* www.wlad.com	Danbury	CT	06811	203-744-4800		647
WLAE-TV Ch 32 (PBS) 3330 N Cswy Blvd Ste 345 *Web:* www.wlae.com	Metairie	LA	70002	504-866-7411	840-9838	741
WLAJ-TV 2820 E Saginaw St *Web:* www.wlns.com	Lansing	MI	48912	517-372-8282	372-1507	647
WLAN-FM 1685 Crown Ave Ste 100 *Web:* www.fm97.com	Lancaster	PA	17601	717-295-9700	295-7329	647
WLAY-AM 509 N Main St *Web:* www.wlay1035.com	Tuscumbia	AL	35674	256-383-2525		647
WLC 200 Pronghorn St *Web:* www.wlcwyo.com	Casper	WY	82601	307-266-2524		41
WLDE FUN 101.7 347 W Berry Ste 600 *TF:* 888-450-1017 ■ *Web:* www.classichits1017.com	Fort Wayne	IN	46802	260-423-3676	422-5266	645-60
WLEN-FM PO Box 687 *Web:* www.wlen.com	Adrian	MI	49221	517-263-1039	265-5362	647
WLFG PO Box 1867 *TF:* 888-275-9534 ■ *Web:* www.livingfaithtv.com	Abingdon	VA	24212	888-275-9534		647
WLFI-TV 2605 Yeager Rd *Web:* www.wlfi.com	West Lafayette	IN	47906	765-463-1800	463-7979	647
WLFT-TV 10877 Reiger Rd *Web:* www.wlft.com	Baton Rouge	LA	70809	225-293-2100		647
Wlh Consulting Inc 1417 Capri Ln *TF:* 800-392-0745 ■ *Web:* wlhconsulting.com	Weston	FL	33326	800-392-0745		196
WLIF-FM 101.9 (AC) 1423 Clarkview Rd Ste 100 *Web:* todays1019.radio.com	Baltimore	MD	21209	410-825-1000		645-15
WLIO-TV 1424 Rice Ave *Web:* www.hometownstations.com	Lima	OH	45805	419-228-8835	229-7091	647
WLIP-AM 8500 Green Bay Rd *Web:* www.wlip.com	Pleasant Prairie	WI	53158	262-694-7800		647
WLIW-TV Ch 21 (PBS) 825 Eighth Ave *Web:* www.wliw.org	New York	NY	10019	212-560-8021		741
WLJW-AM PO Box 1400 *Web:* www.wljn.com	Traverse City	MI	49685	231-946-1400	946-3959	647
WLKY-TV Ch 32 (CBS) 1918 Mellwood Ave *Web:* www.wlky.com	Louisville	KY	40206	502-893-3671	896-0725	741-77
WLLA-TV 7048 E N Ave PO Box 3157 *Web:* www.wlla.com	Kalamazoo	MI	49003	269-345-6421		647
WLLE-FM PO Box 679 *TF:* 877-588-1021 ■ *Web:* www.willieradio.com	Mayfield	KY	42066	270-554-0093	444-6397	647
WLMB-TV Ch 40 (Ind) 825 Capital Commons Dr *TF:* 800-218-5740 ■ *Web:* www.wlmb.com	Toledo	OH	43615	419-720-9562	720-9563	741-134
WLML-FM 760 US Highway One Ste 100 3 *Web:* www.legendsradio.com	North Palm Beach	FL	33408	561-469-6700	469-6705	647
WLNE-TV Ch 6 (ABC) 10 Orms St *Web:* www.abc6.com	Providence	RI	02904	401-453-8000		741-104
WLOB Radio 779 Warren Ave *TF:* 877-393-8255 ■ *Web:* www.wlobradio.com	Portland	ME	04103	207-773-9695	761-4406	647
WLOE-AM 432 Station Rd *Web:* www.wloewmyn.com	Mayodan	NC	27027	336-627-9563	548-4636	647
WLOK-AM 1340 (Rel) 363 S 2nd St *Web:* www.wlok.com	Memphis	TN	38103	901-527-9565	528-0335	645-95
WLOS-TV Ch 13 (ABC) 110 Technology Dr *TF:* 800-419-6356 ■ *Web:* www.wlos.com	Asheville	NC	28803	828-684-1340		741-6
WLOX-TV Ch 13 (ABC) 208 Debuys Rd *Web:* www.wlox.com	Biloxi	MS	39531	228-896-1313		741
WLQC-FM 3048 Zebulon Rd *Web:* www.life1031fm.com	Rocky Mount	NC	27804	252-937-1031		647
WLRA-FM 1 University Pkwy *Web:* www.wlraradio.com	Romeoville	IL	60544	815-836-5214		647
WLRC-AM PO Box 37 *Web:* www.wlrcradio.com	Walnut	MS	38683	662-223-4071	223-4072	647
WLRH Huntsville 89.3 FM UAH Campus John Wright Dr *TF:* 800-239-9574 ■ *Web:* www.wlrh.org	Huntsville	AL	35899	256-895-9574		645-73
WLRN Radio & TV studios 172 NE 15th St *Web:* www.wlrn.org	Miami	FL	33132	305-995-1717		738
WLRQ-FM 1388 S Babcock St *TF:* 866-676-8477 ■ *Web:* www.literock993.iheart.com	Melbourne	FL	32901	321-821-7100	733-0904	647
WLS Stamping Co 3292 E 80th St *Web:* www.wlsstamping.com	Cleveland	OH	44104	216-271-5100		488
WLTU-FM 3730 Mangin St *Web:* www.cubradio.com	Manitowoc	WI	54220	920-683-6800	683-6807	647
WLTX-TV Ch 19 (CBS) 6027 Garner's Ferry Rd *Web:* www.wltx.com	Columbia	SC	29209	803-776-3600	695-3714	741-33
WLTZ-TV Ch 38 (NBC) 6140 Buena Vista Rd *Web:* www.wltz.com	Columbus	GA	31907	706-561-3838	563-8467	741-34
WLUC-TV 177 US 41 E *TF:* 800-562-9776 ■ *Web:* www.uppermichiganssource.com	Negaunee	MI	49866	906-475-4161	475-4824	647
WLUM-FM 102.1 (Rock) N72 W12922 Good Hope Rd *Web:* www.fm1021milwaukee.com	Menomonee Falls	WI	53051	414-771-1021	771-3036	645
WLUP-FM 97.9 (CR) 455 N Cityfront Plaza Dr 6th Fl *Web:* www.wlup.com	Chicago	IL	60611	312-245-1200		645-34
WLWT-TV Ch 5 (NBC) 1700 Young St *Web:* www.wlwt.com	Cincinnati	OH	45202	513-412-5000		741-30
WLXC- Cumulus Media 1301 Gervais St Ste 700 *Web:* www.kiss-1031.com	Columbia	SC	29201	803-796-7600	739-1072	645
WLYB-FM PO Box 396 *Web:* www.963wlyb.com	Livingston	AL	35470	205-652-9630	652-1414	647
WLZN-FM 92.3 (Urban) 544 Mulberry St 5th Fl *Web:* www.blazin923.com	Macon	GA	31201	478-646-0923		645-91
WM Automotive Inc 208 Penland St *TF:* 866-346-0001 ■ *Web:* wmautomotive.com	Fort Worth	TX	76111	817-834-5559		61
WM Barr & Company Inc PO Box 1879 **Fax Area Code: 800* ■ *TF:* 800-238-2672 ■ *Web:* www.wmbarr.com	Memphis	TN	38101	901-775-0100	621-9508*	550
WM Brady & Company Inc 22 E 80th St	New York	NY	10021	212-249-7212		42
WM Brode Co 100 Elizabeth St PO Box 299 *Web:* www.wmbrode.com	Newcomerstown	OH	43832	740-498-5121	498-8553	188-4
WM Jordan Company Inc 11010 Jefferson Ave *Web:* www.wmjordan.com	Newport News	VA	23601	757-596-6341		186
WM Keck Foundation 515 S Flower St Ste 800 *Web:* www.wmkeck.org	Los Angeles	CA	90071	213-612-2000		305
WM Keck Observatory 65-1120 Mamalahoa Hwy *Web:* www.keckobservatory.org	Kamuela	HI	96743	808-885-7887	885-4464	668
WM Martin Adv Inc 6705 Levelland Rd Ste A *Web:* www.wmmadv.com	Dallas	TX	75252	972-732-8040		4
Wm S. Haynes Company Inc 68 Nonset Path *Web:* wmshaynes.com	Acton	MA	01720	978-268-0600		527
WM Software Corp 3660 Center Rd Ste 371 *TF:* 800-892-9682 ■ *Web:* www.wmsoftware.com	Brunswick	OH	44212	330-558-0501		180
WM Stukey & Associates LLC 1705 W Northwest Hwy Ste 220 *Web:* www.midcitiescpa.com	Grapevine	TX	76051	817-481-3265		734
WM Sword & Company Inc 90 Nassau St *Web:* www.swordrowe.com	Princeton	NJ	08542	609-924-6710		690
Wm T. Burnett & Company Inc 1500 Bush St *TF:* 800-638-0606 ■ *Web:* www.williamtburnett.com	Baltimore	MD	21230	410-837-3000		601
Wm W. Meyer & Sons Inc 1700 Franklin Blvd *TF:* 800-963-4458 ■ *Web:* www.wmwmeyer.com	Libertyville	IL	60048	847-918-0111	918-8183	91
Wm. A. Straub Inc 8282 Forsyth Blvd *TF:* 866-725-2121 ■ *Web:* www.straubs.com	Clayton	MO	63105	314-725-2121	725-2123	345
WM. B. Coleman Company Inc 4001 Earhart Blvd Ste 1100	New Orleans	LA	70125	504-822-1000		156
WMA (Wyoming Mining Assn) 1401 Airport Pky Ste 230 *Web:* www.wyomingmining.org	Cheyenne	WY	82001	307-635-0331		48-13
WMAL-AM 630 (N/T) 4400 Jenifer St NW *Web:* www.wmal.com	Washington	DC	20015	202-686-3100		645-170
WMAN-AM 1400 Radio Ln *Web:* wmanfm.iheart.com	Mansfield	OH	44906	419-529-1400		647
WMAQ-TV Ch 5 (NBC) 454 N Columbus Dr NBC Twr *Web:* www.nbcchicago.com	Chicago	IL	60611	312-836-5555		741-29
WMAR-2 News 6400 York Rd *Web:* www.wmar2news.com	Baltimore	MD	21212	410-377-2222		647
WMAS-FM 1000 Hall of Fame Ave *Web:* www.947wmas.com	Springfield	MA	01105	413-737-1414	737-1488	647
WMAY-AM 970 (N/T) *Mid-West Family Broadcasting* 1510 N Third St *Web:* midwestfamilybroadcasting.com	Riverton	IL	62561	217-467-2837	629-7952	645-152
WMAZ-TV Ch 13 (CBS) 1314 Gray Hwy *Web:* www.13wmaz.com	Macon	GA	31211	478-752-1313	752-1331	741-79
WMBC-TV 99 Clinton Rd *Web:* www.wmbctv.com	West Caldwell	NJ	07006	973-852-0300	808-5516	647
WMBD-TV Ch 31 (CBS) 3131 N University St *Web:* www.centralillinoisproud.com	Peoria	IL	61604	309-688-3131		741-97
WMBF-TV 918 Frontage Rd E *Web:* www.wmbfnews.com	Myrtle Beach	SC	29577	843-839-9623	839-9625	647
WMBM-AM 1490 (Rel) 13242 NW Seventh Ave *Web:* www.wmbm.com	North Miami	FL	33168	305-769-1100	769-9975	645-96
WMBR-FM 88.1 (Var) 3 Ames St *Web:* www.wmbr.org	Cambridge	MA	02142	617-253-4000		645
WMBS-AM 590 (Oldies) 44 S Mt Vernon Ave *TF:* 866-590-9627 ■ *Web:* www.wmbs590.com	Uniontown	PA	15401	724-438-3900	438-2406	645
WMBX-FM 102.3 701 Northpoint Pkwy Ste 500 *TF:* 800-969-1023 ■ *Web:* www.x1023.com	West Palm Beach	FL	33407	800-969-1023		645-23
WMC (Williamson Medical Ctr) 4321 Carothers Pkwy *Web:* williamsonmedicalcenter.org	Franklin	TN	37067	615-435-5000	435-7328	374-3
WMCA (Western Medical Center Anaheim) 1025 S Anaheim Blvd *Web:* www.westernmedanaheim.com	Anaheim	CA	92805	714-533-6220		374-3
WMCA-AM 111 Broadway Ste 302 *Web:* wmca.com	New York	NY	10006	212-372-0057	284-9700	647
WMCC (White Mountains Community College) 2020 Riverside Dr *TF:* 800-445-4525 ■ *Web:* www.wmcc.edu	Berlin	NH	03570	603-752-1113	752-6335	162

	Phone	Fax	Class
WMCG-FM PO Box 130 .... Dublin GA 31040 *Web:* www.1049wmcg.com	478-272-4422		647
WMCH-AM PO Box 128 .... Church Hill TN 37642 *Web:* www.wmch.us	423-357-5601	357-3635	647
WMC-TV Ch 5 (NBC) 1960 Union Ave........ Memphis TN 38104 *Web:* www.wmcactionnews5.com	901-726-0555	278-7633	741-81
WMDT-TV Ch 47 (ABC) 202 Downtown Plz .... Salisbury MD 21801 *Web:* www.wmdt.com	410-742-4747	742-5767	741
WMEC-TV PO Box 6248 .... Springfield IL 62708 *TF:* 800-232-3605 ■ *Web:* www.networkknowledge.tv	217-483-7887	483-1112	647
WMEU-TV 26 N Halsted St .... Chicago IL 60661 *Web:* www.metv.com	312-705-2600		647
WMF (World Monuments Fund) 350 Fifth Ave Ste 2412........ New York NY 10118 *Web:* www.wmf.org	646-424-9594	424-9593	48-4
WMF Americas Inc 2121 Eden Rd .... Millville NJ 08332 *TF:* 800-966-3009 ■ *Web:* www.wmfamericas.com	704-882-3898	893-2198	361
WMFD-TV 2900 Park Ave W........ Mansfield OH 44906 *Web:* www.wmfd.com	419-529-5900	529-2319	647
WMFE 11510 E Colonial Dr........ Orlando FL 32817 *Web:* www.wmfe.org	407-273-2300		738
WMG (Wilson Marketing Group Inc) PO Box 859 .... Wayzata MN 55391 *Web:* www.wilsonconsultants.com	763-476-2216	475-8275	195
WMGK-FM 102.9 (CR) 1 Bala Plz Ste 339........ Bala Cynwyd PA 19004 *Web:* wmgk.com	610-667-8500		645
WMGS-FM 600 Baltimore Dr........ Wilkes-Barre PA 18702 *Web:* www.magic93fm.com	570-824-9000	820-0520	647
WMGT-TV Ch 41 (NBC) 301 Poplar St........ Macon GA 31201 *Web:* www.41nbc.com	478-745-4141	742-2626	741-79
WMH (Wayne Memorial Hospital) 865 S First St .... Jesup GA 31545 *Web:* www.wmhweb.com	912-427-6811		374-3
WMH (Wilcox Memorial Hospital) 3-3420 Kuhio Hwy .... Lihue HI 96766 *TF:* 877-709-9355 ■ *Web:* www.hawaiipacifichealth.org	808-245-1100		374-3
WMH (Wayne Memorial Hospital) 601 Park St........ Honesdale PA 18431 *Web:* www.wmh.org	570-253-8100		374-3
WMHI (Winnebago Mental Health Institute) 1300 S Dr .... Winnebago WI 54985 *Web:* www.dhs.wisconsin.gov	920-235-4910		374-5
WMHS (Wisconsin Marine Historical Society) 814 W Wisconsin Ave........ Milwaukee WI 53233 *Web:* www.wmhs.org	414-286-3074		48-13
WMHT-TV Ch 17 (PBS) 4 Global View .... Troy NY 12180 *Web:* www.wmht.org	518-880-3400	880-3409	741
WMI (Wildlife Management Institute) 1440 Upper Bermudian Rd .... Gardners PA 17324 **Fax Area Code:* 802 ■ *Web:* wildlifemanagement.institute	717-677-4480	563-2157*	48-3
WMIT-FM 106.9 (Rel) 3 Porters Cove Rd........ Asheville NC 28805 *TF:* 800-330-9648 ■ *Web:* thelightfm.org	828-285-8477	298-0117	645
WMIZ-AM 632 Maurice River Pky........ Vineland NJ 08360 *Web:* www.wmizradio.com	856-696-7111		647
WMJR-AM 110 Dennis Dr........ Lexington KY 40503 *Web:* www.realliferadio.com	859-278-0894		647
WMK & Co 415 Albert St .... Billings MT 59101 *Web:* www.wmkco.com	406-256-3200		492
WMK Inc 4199 Kinross Lakes Pkwy .... Richfield OH 44286 *TF:* 877-275-4912 ■ *Web:* www.mobilityworks.com	234-312-2000		57
WMKX-FM 51 Pickering St........ Brookville PA 15825 *TF:* 877-634-2765 ■ *Web:* www.megarock.fm	814-849-8100	849-4585	647
WML (Warde Medical Laboratory) 300 W Textile Rd .... Ann Arbor MI 48108 *TF:* 800-760-9969 ■ *Web:* www.wardelab.com	734-214-0300	214-0399	415
WMLB-AM 1110 Spring St Ste 610........ Atlanta GA 30309 *Web:* www.1690wmlb.com	404-681-9307	870-8859	647
WMLW-TV 809 S 60th St........ Milwaukee WI 53214 *Web:* www.wmlw.com	414-777-5800	777-5802	647
WMMA (Wood Machinery Manufacturers of America) 2105 Laurel Bush Rd Ste 201........ Bel Air MD 21015 *Web:* wmma.org	443-640-1052		49-13
WMMO-FM 98.9 (AC) 4192 N John Young Pkwy........ Orlando FL 32804 **Fax Area Code:* 407 ■ *Web:* www.wmmo.com	321-281-2000	297-0156*	645-114
WMMPA (Wood Moulding & Millwork Producers Assn) 507 First St........ Woodland CA 95695 *Web:* www.wmmpa.com	530-661-9591	661-9586	49-3
WMMR-FM 93.3 (Rock) 1 Bala Plz WMMR - Ste 424........ Bala Cynwyd PA 19004 *Web:* www.wmmr.com	610-771-0933		645
WMNC-AM PO Box 969 .... Morganton NC 28680 *TF:* 800-951-9999 ■ *Web:* www.bigdawg92fm.com	828-437-0521	433-8855	647
WMNO-TV 196 S Main St Ste 302........ Marion OH 43302 *Web:* www.yourtv22.com	614-547-1722		647
WMOR-TV Ch 32 (Ind) 7201 E Hillsborough Ave .... Tampa FL 33610 *Web:* www.mor-tv.com	813-626-3232	626-1961	741-133
WMPA (Washington Metropolitan Philharmonic Assn) PO Box 120 .... Mount Vernon VA 22121 *Web:* www.wmpamusic.org	703-799-8229	360-7391	573-3
WMPI-FM 105.3 (Ctry) 22 E McClain Ave........ Scottsburg IN 47170 *TF:* 800-441-1053 ■ *Web:* www.i1053country.com	812-752-3688	752-2345	645
WMPM-AM 1270 Buffalo Rd PO Box 57........ Smithfield NC 27577 *Web:* www.1270wmpm.com	919-934-2434	989-6388	647
WMPX-AM 1510 Bayliss........ Midland MI 48640 *Web:* www.wmpxwmrx.com	989-631-1490		647
WMR (Williams Management Resources Inc) 1717 N Naper Blvd Ste 102 .... Naperville IL 60563 *Web:* www.wmrhq.com	630-416-1166	416-9798	47
WMRZ-FM 809 S Westover Blvd........ Albany GA 31707 *Web:* kissalbany.iheart.com	229-439-9704		647
WMS Group PC 5583 S Prince St........ Littleton CO 80120 *Web:* www.wmsgroupcpa.com	303-730-7999	730-2683	2
WMSC-FM Schmitt Hall Rm 389 1 Normal Ave........ Montclair NJ 07043 *Web:* www.wmscradio.com	973-655-4256		647
WMSI-FM 1375 Beasley Rd .... Jackson MS 39206 *Web:* miss103.iheart.com	601-982-1062		647
WMSN-TV Ch 47 (Fox) 7847 Big Sky Dr........ Madison WI 53719 *Web:* www.fox47.com	608-833-0047	833-5055	741-80
WMSR-AM 1030 Oakdale St........ Manchester TN 37355 *Web:* www.thunder1320.com	931-728-1320	728-3527	647
Wmsvision Inc 1016 Copeland Oaks Dr .... Morrisville NC 27560 *Web:* wmsvision.com	919-863-3388		180
WMTA (West Michigan Tourist Assn) 741 Kenmoor Ave Ste E .... Grand Rapids MI 49546 *Web:* wmta.org	616-245-2217	954-3924	393
WMTD-AM 211 Ballengee St PO Box 100........ Hinton WV 25951 *Web:* www.radioam1380.com	304-466-1380		647
WMTN-AM 510 W Economy Rd PO Box 220 .... Morristown TN 37814 *Web:* www.wmtnradio.com	423-586-9101		647
WMTW-TV Ch 8 (ABC) 4 Ledgeview Dr........ Westbrook ME 04092 *TF:* 800-248-6397 ■ *Web:* www.wmtw.com	207-835-3888		741
WMU (Woman's Missionary Union) 100 Missionary Rdg........ Birmingham AL 35242 *TF:* 800-968-7301 ■ *Web:* www.wmu.com	205-991-8100		48-20
WMUR-TV Ch 9 (ABC) 100 S Commercial St .... Manchester NH 03101 *Web:* www.wmur.com	603-669-9999	641-9005	741
WMUZ-FM 103.5 (Rel) 12300 Radio Pl .... Detroit MI 48228 *Web:* wmuz.com	313-272-3434	272-5045	645-48
WMVO-AM 17421 Coshocton Rd .... Mount Vernon OH 43050 *Web:* www.wmvo.com	614-397-1000		647
WMVY 57 Carrolls Way PO Box 1148 .... Vineyard Haven MA 02568 *Web:* mvyradio.org	508-693-5000	693-8211	647
WMXD-FM 27675 Halsted Rd........ Farmington Hills MI 48331 *Web:* www.mix923fm.iheart.com	248-324-5800		647
WMXJ-FM 102.7 (Oldies) 20450 NW Second Ave........ Miami FL 33169 *TF:* 800-924-1027 ■ *Web:* thebeachmiami.radio.com	800-226-1027		645-96
WMYS-TV 53550 Generations Dr .... South Bend IN 46635 *Web:* www.mymichianatv.com	574-344-5500		647
WMYX-FM 99.1 11800 W Grange Ave........ Hales Corners WI 53130 *Web:* 991themix.radio.com	414-529-1250	529-2122	645
WN (World Neighbors Inc) 4127 NW 122nd St........ Oklahoma City OK 73120 *TF:* 800-242-6387 ■ *Web:* www.wn.org	405-752-9700		48-5
WNA (Wisconsin Nurses Assn) 6117 Monona Dr .... Madison WI 53716 *Web:* wisconsinnurses.org	608-221-0383	221-2788	533
WNAB-TV 631 Mainstream Dr........ Nashville TN 37228 *Web:* www.cw58.tv	615-259-5617		647
WNAP-AM 2311 Old Arch Rd .... Norristown PA 19401 *TF:* 800-887-9627 ■ *Web:* www.mygospelhighway11.com	610-277-9449	272-5793	647
WNAR-AM 181 Ridge Rd PO Box 18........ Tylersport PA 18971 *Web:* www.wnar-am.com	215-583-7078		647
WNB Financial 204 Main St PO Box 499 .... Winona MN 55987 *TF:* 800-546-4392 ■ *Web:* www.wnbfinancial.com	507-454-8800	454-9208	360-2
WNBF-AM PO Box 414........ Binghamton NY 13902 *Web:* www.wnbf.com	607-772-8400		647
WNCN-TV Ch 17 (NBC) 1205 Front St........ Raleigh NC 27609 *Web:* www.cbs17.com	919-836-1717	836-1687	741-105
WNCO-FM 1197 US Hwy 42 .... Ashland OH 44805 *Web:* 1013wnco.iheart.com	419-289-2605		647
WNCQ-FM One Bridge Plz Ste 204 .... Ogdensburg NY 13669 *Web:* www.q1029.com	315-393-1220	393-3974	647
WNCT-FM 2929 Radio Station Rd........ Greenville NC 27834 *TF:* 800-868-1079 ■ *Web:* www.1079wnct.com	252-757-0011	757-0286	647
WNCT-TV 3221 S Evans St .... Greenville NC 27834 *Web:* www.wnct.com	252-355-8500		647
WNCU-FM 90.7 (NPR) PO Box 19875........ Durham NC 27707 *Web:* www.wncu.org	919-530-7445	530-5031	645-128
WNCW-FM 88.7 PO Box 804........ Spindale NC 28160 *TF:* 800-245-8870 ■ *Web:* wncw.org	828-287-8000		645
WNCX-FM 98.5 (CR) 1041 Huron Rd .... Cleveland OH 44115 *Web:* wncx.radio.com	216-861-0100		645-36
WNDE-AM 1260 (Sports) 6161 Fall Creek Rd........ Indianapolis IN 46220 *Web:* foxsports975.iheart.com	317-257-7565		645-74
WNDU-TV Ch 16 (NBC) PO Box 1616 .... South Bend IN 46634 *Web:* www.wndu.com	574-284-3000	284-3009	741-126
WNDV-FM 92.9 (CHR) 3371 Cleveland Rd Ste 300 .... South Bend IN 46628 *TF:* 800-242-0100 ■ *Web:* www.u93.com	574-273-9300	273-9090	645-150
WNEM-TV Ch 5 (CBS) 107 N Franklin St........ Saginaw MI 48607 *TF:* 800-522-9636 ■ *Web:* www.wnem.com	989-755-8191		741
WNEP-TV Ch 16 (ABC) 16 Montage Mtn Rd........ Moosic PA 18507 *TF:* 800-982-4374 ■ *Web:* www.wnep.com	570-346-7474		741
WNET-TV Ch 13 (PBS) 450 W 33rd St........ New York NY 10001 *TF:* 800-468-9913 ■ *Web:* www.thirteen.org	212-560-1313	560-1314	741-91
WNFA-FM 2865 Maywood Dr........ Port Huron MI 48060 *Web:* www.power883.com	810-985-3260		647
WNFC-FM PO Box 1423........ Somerset KY 42502 *TF:* 800-408-8888 ■ *Web:* www.kingofkingsradio.com	800-408-8888		647
WNHP Law 6832 Morrison Blvd .... Charlotte NC 28211 *Web:* wnhplaw.com	704-364-0010		445
WNIJ & WNIU 801 N First St .... DeKalb IL 60115 *Web:* www.northernpublicradio.org	815-753-9000		644
WNIN Tri-State Public Media Inc 2 Main St .... Evansville IN 47708 *Web:* www.wnin.org	812-423-2973		632
WNIR-FM 100.1 (N/T) PO Box 2170........ Akron OH 44309 *Web:* www.wnir.com	330-673-2323	673-0301	645-2
WNIT Public Television 300 W Jefferson Blvd .... South Bend IN 46601 *TF:* 877-411-3662 ■ *Web:* www.wnit.org	574-675-9648	289-3441	741-126
WNIV-AM 2970 Peachtree Rd NW........ Atlanta GA 30305 *Web:* faithtalk970.com	404-995-7300		647

Phone | Fax | Class

WNIX-FM PO Box 1756 Greenville MS 38702 662-378-2617 378-8341 647
Web: www.deltaradio.net

WNJT-TV PO Box 777 Trenton NJ 08625 609-777-5000 647
TF: 800-792-8645 ■ *Web:* www.njn.net

WNJU-TV Ch 47 (Tele)
2200 Fletcher Ave 6th Fl Fort Lee NJ 07024 877-478-3536 741
TF: 877-478-3536 ■ *Web:* www.telemundo47.com

WNKU-FM 105.9 (Ctry)
301 Landrum Academic Ctr Highland Heights KY 41099 859-572-6500 645
Web: usliveradio.com

WNKX-FM Hwy 50 E PO Box 280 Centerville TN 37033 931-729-5191 729-5467 647
Web: www.countrykix96.com

WNKY-TV 325 Emmett Ave Bowling Green KY 42101 270-781-2140 842-7140 647
Web: www.wnky.net

WNL (Wichita National Life Insurance Co)
PO Box 1709 Lawton OK 73502 580-353-5776 353-6482 796
TF: 800-522-1625 ■ *Web:* www.wnlic.com

WNM Advisors LLC
8600 Tyler Blvd Ste 179 Mentor OH 44060 440-975-9999 196
Web: www.wnmadvisors.com

WNML-AM 4711 Old Kingston Pke Knoxville TN 37919 865-588-6511 588-3725 647
Web: www.sportsradiownml.com

WNNW-AM 462 Merrimack St Methuen MA 01844 978-688-8000 647
TF: 888-887-6937 ■ *Web:* www.power800am.com

WNNZ-AM 1331 Main St 4th Fl Springfield MA 01103 413-536-1009 647
Web: www.clearchannel.com

WNOC-FM 3662 Rugby Dr Toledo OH 43614 419-754-1009 647
TF: 877-275-8098 ■ *Web:* www.annunciationradio.com

WNOG-AM 1270 (N/T)
2824 Palm Beach Blvd Fort Myers FL 33916 239-338-4326 645
Web: tunein.com

WNOL-TV Ch 38 (CW)
1 Galeria Blvd Ste 850 Metairie LA 70001 504-525-3838 741
Web: wgno.com

WNOP-AM 5440 Moeller Ave Cincinnati OH 45212 513-731-7740 731-6465 647
Web: www.sacredheartradio.com

WNPA (Western National Parks Assn)
12880 N Vistoso Village Dr Tucson AZ 85755 520-622-1999 48-23
Web: www.wnpa.org

WNPRC (Washington National Primate Research Ctr)
1705 NE Pacific St PO Box 357330 Seattle WA 98195 206-543-1430 685-0305 668
Web: www.wanprc.org

WNPT-TV Ch 8 (PBS) 161 Rains Ave Nashville TN 37203 615-259-9325 248-6120 741-89
Web: www.wnpt.org

WNRP-AM 7251 Plantation Rd Pensacola FL 32504 850-262-6000 494-0778 647
Web: www.newsradio1620.com

WNRV-AM 1535 Narrows Rd Narrows VA 24124 540-921-0166 647
Web: www.wnrvbluegrassradio.com

WNS (Wireless Network Solutions Inc)
PO Box 2041 Lake Oswego OR 97035 503-583-2617 675-6536* 681
**Fax Area Code:* 425 ■ *Web:* www.wnsunwired.com

WNSP-FM 105.5 (Sports)
1100 Dauphin St Ste E Mobile AL 36604 251-438-5460 645-100
Web: wnsp.com

WNST-AM 1570 (Sports) 1550 Hart Rd Towson MD 21286 410-821-9678 645
Web: wnst.net

WNTP-AM 117 Ridge Pke Lafayette Hill PA 19444 610-940-0990 828-8879 647
Web: 990theanswer.com

WNTQ-FM 93.1 1064 James St Syracuse NY 13203 315-472-0200 478-5625 645-158
Web: www.93q.com

WNUV-TV 2000 W 41st St Baltimore MD 21211 410-467-4545 467-5093 647
Web: www.cwbaltimore.com

WNWO-TV Ch 24 (NBC) 300 S Byrne Rd Toledo OH 43615 419-535-0024 535-8936 741-134
Web: nbc24.com

WNWV-FM 107.3
107.3 jenY
6133 Rockside Rd Ste 102 Independence OH 44131 216-828-1073 645
Web: jeny1073.com

WNYA-TV 715 N Pearl St Albany NY 12204 518-207-4850 426-9463 647
TF: 800-999-9698 ■ *Web:* www.wnyt.com

WNYC 160 Varick St 8th FL New York NY 10013 646-829-4400 645-138
Web: www.nypublicradio.zendesk.com

WNYM-AM 111 Broadway Fl 302 New York NY 10006 212-372-0097 647
Web: am970theanswer.com

WNYO-TV Ch 49 (MNT)
699 Hertel Ave Ste 100 Buffalo NY 14207 716-447-3200 875-4919 741-20
Web: www.mytvbuffalo.com

WNYW-TV Ch 5 (Fox) 205 E 67th St New York NY 10065 212-452-3983 741-91
Web: www.fox5ny.com

WNYY-AM 1751 Hanshaw Rd Ithaca NY 14850 607-257-6400 257-6497 647
Web: www.wnyyradio.com

WO Grubb Steel Erection Inc
5120 Jefferson Davis Hwy Richmond VA 23234 804-271-9471 271-2539 189-14
TF: 866-964-7822 ■ *Web:* www.wogrubb.com

Wo Stinson & Son Ltd 4726 Bank St Ottawa ON K1T3W7 613-822-7400 316
TF: 800-267-9714 ■ *Web:* wostinson.com

WOAP-AM 2301 N M-52 Owosso MI 48867 989-720-9627 451-0565* 647
**Fax Area Code:* 616 ■ *Web:* www.woapradio.com

WOBL-AM 45624 State Hwy 20 Oberlin OH 44074 440-774-1320 774-1336 647
TF: 800-229-9625 ■ *Web:* www.woblwdlw.com

WOBM-FM 8 Robbins St Toms River NJ 08753 848-221-8000 221-8090 647
Web: www.wobm.com

WOBN-FM 33 Collegeview Rd Westerville OH 43081 614-890-3000 647
Web: www.wobn.net

Woburn Foreign Motors Inc
394 Washington St Woburn MA 01801 781-935-3040 938-0225 516
Web: www.wfab.com

Woburn Public Library 45 Pleasant St Woburn MA 01801 781-933-0148 434-3
Web: woburnpubliclibrary.org

WOCCU (World Council of Credit Unions Inc)
5710 Mineral Pt Rd Madison WI 53705 608-395-2000 395-2001 49-2
Web: www.woccu.org

WOCM-FM 98.1 (AAA)
Irie Radio 117 W 49th St Ocean City MD 21842 410-723-3683 645-111
Web: ocean98.com

WOCN (Wound Ostomy & Continence Nurses Society)
1120 Rte 73 Ste 200 Mount Laurel NJ 08054 888-224-9626 49-8
TF: 888-224-9626 ■ *Web:* www.wocn.org

WODE-FM 99.9 107 Paxinosa Rd W Easton PA 18040 610-258-6155 253-3384 645
Web: www.999thehawk.com

WOE (Western Office Equipment Inc)
514 N 32nd St Billings MT 59101 406-245-3029 245-3020 112
Web: www.westernoffice.net

Woeber Mustard Manufacturing Co
1966 Commerce Cir PO Box 388 Springfield OH 45501 800-548-2929 323-1679* 297-8
**Fax Area Code:* 937 ■ *TF:* 800-548-2929 ■ *Web:* www.woebermustard.com

WOES-FM 8989 E Colony Rd Elsie MI 48831 989-862-4237 862-5887 647
Web: www.ovidelsie.org

Wofford College 429 N Church St Spartanburg SC 29303 864-597-4000 597-4149 166
Web: www.wofford.edu

Wofsey, Rosen, Kweskin & Kuriansky LLP
600 Summer St Stamford CT 06901 203-327-2300 41
Web: wrkk.com

WOG LLC 23 S Harrison St Easton MD 21601 410-690-3511 196
Web: whiteoak-group.com

WOGH-FM 320 Market St Steubenville OH 43952 740-283-4747 647
Web: www.froggyland.com

WOGL-FM 98.1 (Oldies)
555 E City Ave Ste 330 Bala Cynwyd PA 19004 800-942-8998 645
TF: 800-942-8998 ■ *Web:* wogl.radio.com

WOHC (West Oakland Health Council Inc)
700 Adeline St Oakland CA 94607 510-835-9610 353
Web: www.westoaklandhealth.org

Wohlsen Construction Co
548 Steel Way PO Box 7066 Lancaster PA 17604 717-299-2500 299-3419 187
Web: www.wohlsenconstruction.com

WOIO-TV 1717 E 12th St Cleveland OH 44114 216-771-1943 367-7370 647
TF: 800-929-0132 ■ *Web:* www.cleveland19.com

WOI-TV Ch 5 (ABC)
3903 Westown Pkwy West Des Moines IA 50266 515-457-9645 741
TF: 800-858-5555 ■ *Web:* www.weareiowa.com

Wojan Window & Door Corp
217 Stover Rd Charlevoix MI 49720 800-632-9827 480
TF: 800-632-9827 ■ *Web:* www.wojan.com

Wojanis Inc 1001 Montour W Ind Pk Coraopolis PA 15108 724-695-1415 358
TF: 800-345-9024 ■ *Web:* wojanis.com

Wojtalewicz Law Firm Ltd
139 N Miles St Appleton MN 56208 320-289-2363 428
Web: www.wojtalewiczlawfirm.com

WOKO-FM 98.9 (Ctry)
70 Joy Dr South Burlington VT 05403 802-862-9890 645
TF: 800-354-9890 ■ *Web:* www.woko.com

WOKQ-FM 97.5 (Ctry)
292 Middle Rd PO Box 576 Dover NH 03821 603-749-9750 645
TF: 877-975-1037 ■ *Web:* www.wokq.com

Wolcott Insurance Services Inc
730 S Camino Del Rio Durango CO 81301 970-247-1555 390
Web: wolcottinsurance.com

Wold Oil Properties Inc
139 W Second St Ste 200 Casper WY 82601 307-265-7252 258
Web: www.woldoil.com

Woldumar Nature Ctr
5739 Old Lansing Rd Lansing MI 48917 517-322-0030 322-9394 50-5
Web: woldumarnaturecenter.wildapricot.org

Wolf & Company PC 99 High St Boston MA 02110 617-439-9700 542-0400 734
Web: www.wolfandco.com

Wolf Consulting Inc
3875 Franklin Towne Ct Ste 110 Murrysville PA 15668 724-325-2900 196
Web: www.wolfconsulting.com

Wolf Creek Inn 100 Front St Wolf Creek OR 97497 541-866-2474 565
Web: www.wolfcreekinn.com

Wolf Creek State Park
1837 N Wolf Creek Rd Windsor IL 61957 217-459-2831 565
Web: www.dnr.illinois.gov

Wolf DiMatteo Associates
49 Race St New Castle VA 24127 540-864-5107 864-5161 194
Web: www.OrganicSpecialists.com

Wolf Furniture Inc
1620 N Tuckahoe St Bellwood PA 16617 814-742-4380 321
Web: www.wolffurniture.com

Wolf Glass & Paint Co
308 E Market St New Albany IN 47150 812-944-2264 191-2
Web: www.wolfglass.com

Wolf Gordon Inc
33-00 47th Ave Long Island City NY 11101 800-347-0550 361-1090* 550
**Fax Area Code:* 718 ■ *TF:* 800-347-0550 ■ *Web:* www.wolfgordon.com

Wolf Machine Inc
1601 E Lessard St Prairie du Chien WI 53821 608-326-2925 326-6990 454
Web: www.wolfmachineinc.com

Wolf Metals Inc 12562 E Putnam St Whittier CA 90606 562-698-5410 698-5413 492
Web: www.wolfmetalsinc.com

Wolf Organization, The 20 W Market St York PA 17401 800-388-9653 200
TF: 800-388-9653 ■ *Web:* www.wolforg.net

Wolf Printing 1200 Haines Rd York PA 17402 717-755-1560 627
Web: www.wolfprinting.com

Wolf Ridge Ski Resort
578 Vly View Cir Mars Hill NC 28754 828-689-4111 689-9819 669
TF: 800-817-4111 ■ *Web:* www.skiwolfridgenc.com

Wolf Robotics LLC
4600 Innovation Dr Fort Collins CO 80525 970-225-7600 491
TF: 866-965-3911 ■ *Web:* www.wolfrobotics.com

Wolf Technology Group Inc
1 Chick Springs Rd Ste 112 Greenville SC 29609 833-482-6435 175
TF: 833-482-6435 ■ *Web:* www.wolftg.com

Wolf Trap Foundation for the Performing Arts
1645 Trap Rd Vienna VA 22182 703-255-1900 255-4077 572
TF: 877-965-3872 ■ *Web:* www.wolftrap.org

Wolf Trap National Park for the Performing Arts
1551 Trap Rd Vienna VA 22182 703-255-1800 564
Web: www.nps.gov

Wolf Tree Experts Inc
3310 Greenway Dr Knoxville TN 37918 865-687-3400 776
Web: www.wolftreeinc.com

Wolf Weissman CPAS PC
1 Penn Plz Ste 2615 New York NY 10119 212-967-7300 2
Web: wolfweissman.com

Name / Address	City	State	ZIP	Phone	Fax	Class
Wolf X-Ray Corp 100 W Industry Ct	Deer Park	NY	11729	631-242-9729		382
TF: 800-356-9729 ■ *Web:* wolfxray.com						
Wolf's Bar-B-Q Restaurant						
6600 N First Ave	Evansville	IN	47710	812-424-8891		671
Web: www.wolfsbarbq.com						
Wolf, The 3853 Piedmont Ave	Oakland	CA	94611	510-879-7953		671
Web: www.thewolfoakland.com						
Wolfberg Alvarez & Partners						
75 Valencia Ave Ste 1050	Miami	FL	33134	305-666-5474	666-4994	261
Web: www.wolfbergalvarez.com						
Wolfe & Stec Ltd						
3321 Hobson Rd Ste B	Woodridge	IL	60517	630-305-0222		41
Web: wolfeandstec.com						
Wolfe County						
20 N Washington St PO Box 146	Campton	KY	41301	606-668-3712	668-3732	338
Web: wolfe.ca.uky.edu						
Wolfe Dye & Bleach Works Inc						
25 Ridge Rd	Shoemakersville	PA	19555	610-562-7639		745-7
Web: www.wolfedyeandbleachworks.com						
Wolfe Industrial Auctions Inc						
9801 Hansonville Rd	Frederick	MD	21702	301-898-0340		41
TF: 800-443-9580 ■ *Web:* www.wolfeauctions.com						
Wolfe Jones Boswell & Wolfe Hancock & Daniel LLC						
905 Bob Wallace Ave SW	Huntsville	AL	35801	256-534-2205		428
Web: www.wjb-law.com						
Wolfe Video PO Box 64	New Almaden	CA	95042	408-268-6782	268-9449	511
TF: 800-438-9653 ■ *Web:* www.wolfevideo.com						
Wolfe's Neck Woods State Park						
426 Wolfe's Neck Rd	Freeport	ME	04032	207-865-4465		565
Web: www.maine.gov						
Wolfeboro Camp School						
93 Camp School Rd	Wolfeboro	NH	03894	603-569-3451		622
Web: www.wolfeboro.org						
Wolferman's						
2500 S Pacific Hwy PO Box 9100	Medford	OR	97501	800-999-0169	999-7548	296-1
TF: 800-999-0169 ■ *Web:* www.wolfermans.com						
Wolff Bros Supply Inc 6078 Wolff Rd	Medina	OH	44256	330-725-3451		612
Web: www.wolffbros.com						
Wolff R. L. & Assoc 2138 Richmond Ave	Houston	TX	77098	713-523-2055		721
Web: rlwolff.com						
Wolfgang Candy Co 50 E Fourth Ave	York	PA	17404	717-843-5536	845-2881	296-8
TF: 800-248-4273 ■ *Web:* wolfgangco.com						
Wolfgang Puck 3600 Las Vegas Blvd S	Las Vegas	NV	89109	702-369-6300		671
Web: bellagio.mgmresorts.com						
Wolfgang Puck's Bar & Grill						
3799 Las Vegas Blvd S	Las Vegas	NV	89109	877-880-0880		671
Web: mgmgrand.mgmresorts.com						
Wolfgang's Steakhouse 4 Park Ave	New York	NY	10016	212-889-3369		671
Web: www.wolfgangssteakhouse.net						
Wolfram Alpha LLC						
100 Trade Center Dr	Champaign	IL	61820	217-398-0700		387
Web: www.wolframalpha.com						
Wolfsen Inc 1269 W 'I' St	Los Banos	CA	93635	209-827-7700	827-7780	10-11
Web: wolfseninc.com						
Wolfson Bolton PLLC						
3150 Livernois Ste 275	Troy	MI	48083	248-247-7100		41
Web: wolfsonbolton.com						
Wolfson Casing Corp						
700 S Fulton Ave	Mount Vernon	NY	10550	914-668-9000		805
Wolfson Children's Hospital						
800 Prudential Dr	Jacksonville	FL	32207	904-202-8000		374-1
TF: 877-240-5437 ■ *Web:* www.wolfsonchildrens.com						
Wolfsonian Museum						
1001 Washington Ave	Miami Beach	FL	33139	305-531-1001		520
Web: wolfsonian.org						
Wolfssl Inc						
10016 Edmonds Way Ste C-300	Edmonds	WA	98020	206-369-4800		180
Web: wolfssl.com						
Wolgast Corp						
4835 Towne Centre Rd Ste 203	Saginaw	MI	48604	989-790-9120		194
Web: www.wolgastcorporation.com						
Wolk Law Firm, The						
1712 Locust St	Philadelphia	PA	19103	215-545-4220		428
Web: airlaw.com						
Wollaston Alloys Inc 205 Wood Rd	Braintree	MA	02184	781-848-3333	848-3993	307
Web: www.wollastonalloys.com						
Wolseley Canada Inc						
880 Laurentian Dr	Burlington	ON	L7N3V6	905-335-7373		111
TF: 800-282-1376 ■ *Web:* www.wolseleyinc.ca						
Wolter, Beeman, Lynch & Londrigan						
1001 S Sixth St	Springfield	IL	62703	217-753-4220		41
TF: 800-753-3210 ■ *Web:* wbllawyers.com						
Wolters Kluwer Financial Services Inc						
100 S 5th St Ste 700	Minneapolis	MN	55402	612-656-7700		178-10
TF: 800-552-9408 ■ *Web:* www.wolterskluwer.com						
Wolverine Advanced Materials						
201 Industrial Park Rd	Blacksburg	VA	24060	540-552-7674		326
Web: www.wamglobal.com						
Wolverine Brass Inc 2951 Hwy 501 E	Conway	SC	29526	843-347-3121	945-9292*	612
**Fax Area Code:* 800 ■ *Web:* www.plumbmaster.com						
Wolverine Bronze Co 28178 Hayes Rd	Roseville	MI	48066	586-776-8180	776-4510	308
Web: www.wolverinebronze.com						
Wolverine Building Group Inc						
4045 Barden SE	Grand Rapids	MI	49512	616-949-3360		186
Web: wolvgroup.com						
Wolverine Coil Spring Co						
818 Front Ave NW	Grand Rapids	MI	49504	616-459-3504	459-0362	350
Web: www.wolverinecoilspring.com						
Wolverine Corp 3600 Tennis Ct	Saint Joseph	MI	49085	269-429-6600	429-6657	488
Web: www.wolverinecorp.com						
Wolverine Flexographic Manufacturing Co						
20774 Chesley Dr	Farmington Hills	MI	48336	248-476-7700	476-0235	629
Web: wolverineflexo.com						
Wolverine Mutual Insurance Co						
1 Wolverine Way	Dowagiac	MI	49047	269-782-3451	298-4516*	390
**Fax Area Code:* 888 ■ *TF:* 800-733-3320 ■ *Web:* www.wolverinemutual.com						
Wolverine Packing Company Inc						
2535 Rivard St	Detroit	MI	48207	313-259-7500		473
Web: www.wolverinepacking.com						

Name / Address	City	State	ZIP	Phone	Fax	Class
Wolverine Power Systems Inc						
3229 80th Ave	Zeeland	MI	49464	616-879-0040		518
TF: 800-485-8068 ■ *Web:* www.wolverinepower.com						
Wolverine Production & Engineering Inc						
41160 Executive Dr	Harrison Township	MI	48045	586-468-2890	468-6705	454
Web: www.wolverinebroach.com						
Wolverine Tube Inc 2100 Market St	Decatur	AL	35601	256-353-1310	580-3825	609
TF: 800-633-3972 ■ *Web:* www.wlv.com						
Wolverine World Wide Inc						
9341 Courtland Dr NE	Rockford	MI	49351	616-866-5500		301
Web: www.wolverineworldwide.com						
WOLX-FM 7601 Ganser Way	Madison	WI	53719	608-664-1949		647
Web: www.wolx.com						
Womack Electric Supply Co						
518 Newton St	Danville	VA	24541	434-793-5134	792-8256	246
TF: 844-998-6657 ■ *Web:* www.womackelectric.com						
Womack Machine Supply Co						
13835 Senlac Dr	Farmers Branch	TX	75234	800-569-9800	350-9322*	385
**Fax Area Code:* 214 ■ *TF:* 800-569-9800 ■ *Web:* www.womack-machine.com						
Womack Steve (Rep R - AR)						
2412 Rayburn House Office Bldg	Washington	DC	20515	202-225-4301	225-5713	342-2
Web: womack.house.gov						
Woman's Hospital 100 Woman's Wy	Baton Rouge	LA	70815	225-927-1300	924-8110	374-7
TF: 800-620-8474 ■ *Web:* www.womans.org						
Woman's Hospital of Texas						
7600 Fannin St	Houston	TX	77054	713-790-1234		374-7
TF: 800-361-3974 ■ *Web:* womanshospital.com						
Woman's Life Insurance Society						
1338 Military St PO Box 5020	Port Huron	MI	48061	810-985-5191	985-6970	391-2
TF: 800-521-9292 ■ *Web:* www.womanslife.org						
Woman's Missionary Union (WMU)						
100 Missionary Rdg	Birmingham	AL	35242	205-991-8100		48-20
TF: 800-968-7301 ■ *Web:* www.wmu.com						
Womble Carlyle Sandridge & Rice PLLC						
1 W Fourth St	Winston-Salem	NC	27101	336-721-3600	721-3660	428
Web: www.womblebonddickinson.com						
Womble Company Inc						
12821 Industrial Rd	Houston	TX	77015	713-636-8700	635-5209	481
Web: www.wombleco.com						
Women & Infants Hospital of Rhode Island						
101 Dudley St	Providence	RI	02905	401-274-1100	453-7666	374-7
TF: 800-711-7011 ■ *Web:* www.womenandinfants.org						
Women & Their Work 1710 Lavaca St	Austin	TX	78701	512-477-1064		520
Web: www.womenandtheirwork.org						
Women Employed 65 E Wacker Pl	Chicago	IL	60601	312-782-3902	782-5249	48-24
Web: womenemployed.org						
Women for Sobriety Inc PO Box 618	Quakertown	PA	18951	215-536-8026	538-9026	48-21
Web: womenforsobriety.org						
Women in Cable Telecommunications (WICT)						
2000 K St Ste 350	Washington	DC	20006	202-827-4794	450-5596	49-14
Web: www.wict.org						
Women in Film (WIF)						
6100 Wilshire Blvd Ste 710	Los Angeles	CA	90048	323-935-2211		48-4
Web: womeninfilm.org						
Women in Military Service for America Memorial Foundation Inc						
Dept 560	Washington	DC	20042	703-533-1155		48-19
TF: 800-222-2294 ■ *Web:* www.womensmemorial.org						
Women in Technology Intl (WITI)						
11500 Olympic Blvd Ste 400	Los Angeles	CA	90064	818-788-9484	788-9410	49-19
TF: 800-334-9484 ■ *Web:* www.witi.com						
Women in Touch Ministries Wit Inc						
1044 W 37th St	Indianapolis	IN	46208	317-925-4177		48-20
Women Lawyers Association of Los Angeles						
634 S Spring St Ste 617	Los Angeles	CA	90014	213-892-8982	892-8948	428
Web: www.wlala.org						
Women Management						
199 Lafayette St 7th Fl	New York	NY	10012	212-334-7400		306
Web: www.womenmanagement.com						
Women's Action for New Directions (WAND)						
691 Massachusetts Ave	Arlington	MA	02476	202-459-4769		48-5
Web: www.wand.org						
Women's Basketball Hall of Fame						
700 Hall of Fame Dr	Knoxville	TN	37915	865-633-9000	633-9294	522
Web: www.wbhof.com						
Women's Bureau Regional Offices						
Region 1 JFK Federal Bldg Rm 525-A	Boston	MA	02203	617-565-1988	565-1986	340-15
Web: www.dol.gov						
Region 2 201 Varick St Rm 602	New York	NY	10014	646-264-3789	264-3794	340-15
Web: www.dol.gov						
Region 3						
170 S Independence Mall W						
The Curtis Ctr Ste 631 East W	Philadelphia	PA	19106	267-687-4160	861-4867*	340-15
**Fax Area Code:* 215 ■ *Web:* www.dol.gov						
Region 5 230 S Dearborn St Rm 1022	Chicago	IL	60604	312-353-6985	353-6986	340-15
Web: www.dol.gov						
Region 7 2300 Main St Ste 1050	Kansas City	MO	64108	816-285-7233	285-7237	340-15
Web: www.dol.gov						
Region 9 90 Seventh St Ste 2650	San Francisco	CA	94103	415-241-3300	625-2641	340-15
Web: www.dol.gov						
Region 10 300 Fifth Ave Ste 1230	Seattle	WA	98104	206-757-6740	757-6739	340-15
Web: www.dol.gov						
Women's Campaign Fund (WCF)						
718 Seventh St NW 2nd Fl	Washington	DC	20001	202-796-8259		48-7
Web: www.wcfonline.org						
Women's College Coalition (WCC)						
PO Box 3983	Decatur	GA	30031	404-913-9492		49-5
Web: www.womenscolleges.org						
Women's Correctional Institution						
4450 Broad River Rd	Columbia	SC	29210	803-896-8590		213
Web: www.doc.sc.gov						
Women's Council of Realtors (WCR)						
430 N Michigan Ave	Chicago	IL	60611	800-245-8512	329-3290*	49-17
**Fax Area Code:* 312 ■ *TF:* 800-245-8512 ■ *Web:* www.wcr.org						
Women's Economic Agenda Project (WEAP)						
160 Franklin St Ste 208	Oakland	CA	94607	510-986-8620	986-8628	48-24
Web: www.weap.org						
Women's Foundation of Colorado, The						
1901 E Asbury Ave	Denver	CO	80208	303-285-2960		305
Web: www.wfco.org						

	Phone	Fax	Class
Women's Independence Scholarship Program Inc (WISP) 4900 Randall Pkwy Ste H .... Wilmington NC 28403 *Web:* wispinc.org	910-397-7742		305
Women's International Pharmacy Inc PO Box 6468 .... Madison WI 53716 *TF:* 800-279-5708 ■ *Web:* www.womensinternational.com	800-279-5708	279-8011	459
Women's Marketing Inc *Stella Rising* 1221 Post Rd E Ste 201 .... Westport CT 06880 *Web:* www.stellarising.com	203-256-0880		194
Women's Resource Ctr (WRC) MSC 06 3910 Mesa Vista Hall 1160......... Albuquerque NM 87131 *Web:* women.unm.edu	505-277-3716	277-2913	434-3
Women's Rights National Historical Park 136 Fall St .... Seneca Falls NY 13148 *Web:* www.nps.gov	315-568-2991	568-2141	564
Women's Sports Foundation 1899 Hempstead Tpke Ste 400 Eisenhower Pk................... East Meadow NY 11554 *TF:* 800-227-3988 ■ *Web:* www.womenssportsfoundation.org	516-542-4700	542-4716	48-22
Women's Wear Daily Magazine 475 Fifth Ave 3rd Fl .... New York NY 10017 *TF:* 866-401-7801 ■ *Web:* www.wwd.com	212-213-1900		457-11
Wometco Enterprises Inc 3195 Ponce De Leon Blvd .... Coral Gables FL 33134 *Web:* miamiseaprison.com	305-529-1400	529-1466	748
Wompatuck State Park 204 Union St.......... Hingham MA 02043 *Web:* www.mass.gov	781-749-7160		565
Wonder View Inn & Suites 50 Eden St PO Box 25 .... Bar Harbor ME 04609 *TF:* 888-439-8439 ■ *Web:* www.wonderviewinn.com	207-288-3358		379
Wonder Web USA 19425 Soledad Canyon Rd............. Canyon Country CA 91351 **Fax Area Code:* 818 ■ *Web:* wonderwebusa.com	661-803-8786	530-7742*	396
Wonderland Amusement Park 2601 Dumas Dr .... Amarillo TX 79107 *TF:* 800-383-4712 ■ *Web:* www.wonderlandpark.com	806-383-0832	383-8737	32
Wonderlic Inc 400 Lakeview Pkwy Ste 200 .... Vernon Hills IL 60061 *TF:* 877-605-9496 ■ *Web:* www.wonderlic.com	847-680-4900	680-9492	637-10
Wonders of Wildlife 500 W Sunshine St........................ Springfield MO 65807 *TF:* 888-222-6060 ■ *Web:* www.wondersofwildlife.org	888-222-6060		823
Wonderware Corp 26561 Rancho Pkwy S .... Lake Forest CA 92630 *TF:* 800-966-3371 ■ *Web:* www.wonderware.com	949-727-3200	727-3270	178-10
Won-Door Corp 1865 South 3480 West.................... Salt Lake City UT 84104 *TF:* 800-453-8494 ■ *Web:* wondoor.com	801-973-7500		234
Wong & Knowles CPA PC 340 W Butterfield Rd........................ Elmhurst IL 60126 *Web:* www.wongknowles.com	630-993-2223	993-2229	2
Wong Engineers Inc 4578 Feather River Dr Ste A .... Stockton CA 95219	209-476-0011		261
Wong Fleming PC 821 Alexander Rd Ste 200 .... Princeton NJ 08540 *Web:* www.wongfleming.com	609-951-9520		428
Wonton Food Inc 220-222 Moore St .... Brooklyn NY 11206 *Web:* www.wontonfood.com	718-628-6868		123
Woo Lae Oak 8240 Leesburg Pk .... Vienna VA 22182 *Web:* www.woolaeoak.com	703-827-7300	827-7302	671
Wood & Hyde Leather Company Inc PO Box 786 .... Gloversville NY 12078 *Web:* www.woodandhyde.com	518-725-7105	725-5158	432
Wood & Tait LLC 64-5249 Kauakea Rd PO Box 6180............. Kamuela HI 96743 **Fax Area Code:* 888 ■ *TF:* 800-774-8585 ■ *Web:* www.woodtait.com	808-885-5090	630-0500*	400
Wood Advisory Services Inc (WAS) 3700 Rte 44 Ste 102........................ Millbrook NY 12545 *Web:* www.woodadvisory.com	845-677-3091	677-6547	261
Wood Buffalo National Park of Canada PO Box 750 .... Fort Smith NT X0E0P0 *Web:* www.pc.gc.ca	867-872-7900	872-3910	563
Wood Consulting Services Inc 8115 Maple Lawn Blvd Ste 250 .... Fulton MD 20759 *Web:* woodcons.com	301-377-5300	377-5399	261
Wood County 1 Courthouse Sq .... Bowling Green OH 43402 *TF:* 866-860-4140 ■ *Web:* www.co.wood.oh.us	419-354-9000		338
Wood County 1 Court Sq PO Box 1474 .... Parkersburg WV 26102 *Web:* woodcountywv.com	304-424-1850		338
Wood County PO Box 1796.................... Quitman TX 75783 *TF:* 800-253-8014 ■ *Web:* www.mywoodcounty.com	903-763-2711	763-5641	338
Wood County 400 Market St .... Wisconsin Rapids WI 54495 *Web:* www.co.wood.wi.us	715-421-8460	421-8808	338
Wood County District Public Library 251 N Main St .... Bowling Green OH 43402 *Web:* www.wcdpl.org	419-352-5104	354-0405	434-3
Wood County Electric Co-opeartive Inc 501 S Main St.............................. Quitman TX 75783 *TF:* 800-762-2203 ■ *Web:* www.wcec.org	903-763-2203	763-5693	245
Wood County Hospital 950 W Wooster St...................... Bowling Green OH 43402 *TF:* 800-288-4470 ■ *Web:* www.woodcountyhospital.org	419-354-8900	354-8957	374-3
Wood Group 17325 Park Row Ste 500 .... Houston TX 77084 *Web:* www.woodplc.com	281-828-3500		536
Wood Group Pratt & Whitney Industrial Turbine Services LLC 1460 Blue Hills Ave PO Box 45 .... Bloomfield CT 06002 *Web:* www.wgpw.com	860-286-4600	769-7337	386
Wood House, The 1825 N 13th St............. Bismarck ND 58501 *Web:* www.bismarckwoodhouse.com	701-255-3654		671
Wood Machinery Manufacturers of America (WMMA) 2105 Laurel Bush Rd Ste 201.................... Bel Air MD 21015 *Web:* wmma.org	443-640-1052		49-13
Wood Moulding & Millwork Producers Assn (WMMPA) 507 First St............................. Woodland CA 95695 *Web:* www.wmmpa.com	530-661-9591	661-9586	49-3
Wood National Cemetery 5000 W National Ave Bldg 1301.............. Milwaukee WI 53295 *Web:* www.cem.va.gov	414-382-5300	382-5321	136
Wood Networks 10260 Robinson Dr................ Tyler TX 75703 *Web:* woodnetworks.com	903-581-0922		180
Wood Patel & Associates Inc 2051 W Northern Ave Ste 100 .... Phoenix AZ 85021 *Web:* www.woodpatel.com	602-335-8500	335-8580	261
Wood Personnel Services 1139 NW Broad St Ste 107................ Murfreesboro TN 37129 *Web:* www.woodpersonnel.com	615-890-8400		260
Wood Preservers Inc 15939 Historyland Hwy PO Box 158............. Warsaw VA 22572 *TF:* 800-368-2536 ■ *Web:* www.woodpreservers.com	804-333-4022	333-9269	818
Wood Pro Inc 421 Washington St PO Box 363 .... Auburn MA 01501 *TF:* 800-786-5577 ■ *Web:* woodproinc.com	508-832-9888		751
Wood Products Manufacturers Assn (WPMA) PO Box 761 .... Westminster MA 01473 *Web:* www.wpma.org	978-874-5445	874-9946	49-3
Wood Ranch Barbecue & Grill Inc 2835 Townsgate Rd Ste 200............ Westlake Village CA 91361 *Web:* www.woodranch.com	805-719-9000		671
Wood Resources LLC 100 Northfield St Ste 203................... Greenwich CT 06830 *Web:* www.atlasholdingsllc.com	203-622-9138		360-3
Wood Tobe-Coburn School 8 E 40th St......... New York NY 10016 *TF:* 800-394-9663 ■ *Web:* www.woodtobecoburn.edu	212-686-9040		800
Wood Truss Council of America (WTCA) 6300 Enterprise Ln .... Madison WI 53719 *Web:* www.sbcindustry.com	608-274-4849	274-3329	49-3
Wood Works 4131 Greenwood N .... Seattle WA 98103 *Web:* www.woodworkspress.com	206-633-5647		627
Wood You Furniture 11700 San Jose Blvd .... Jacksonville FL 32223 *Web:* www.woodyou.com	904-370-1333		321
Wood's CRW Corp 795 Marshall Ave PO Box 1099 .... Williston VT 05495 *Web:* www.woodscrw.com	802-658-1700		23
Wood, Atter & Wolf PA 100 N Laura St Ste 702.................... Jacksonville FL 32202 *TF:* 888-962-4453 ■ *Web:* woodatter.com	904-355-8888	358-3061	41
Woodall Robert (Rep R - GA) 1724 Longworth House Office Bldg .... Washington DC 20515 *Web:* woodall.house.gov	202-225-4272	225-4696	342-2
WOOD-AM 1300 77 Monroe Center St NW Ste 1000.......... Grand Rapids MI 49507 *Web:* woodradio.iheart.com	616-774-2424		645-63
Woodard & Curran 41 Hutchins Dr.............. Portland ME 04102 *TF:* 800-426-4262 ■ *Web:* www.woodardcurran.com	207-774-2112		261
Woodard Emhardt Moriarty McNett & Henry LLP 111 Monument Cir Ste 3700 .... Indianapolis IN 46204 *Web:* www.uspatent.com	317-634-3456		445
Woodbine Chrysler Ltd 8280 Woodbine Ave .... Markham ON L3R2N8 *TF:* 888-656-0343 ■ *Web:* www.woodbinechrysler.com	905-415-2260		57
Woodbine Entertainment Group Inc 555 Rexdale Blvd PO Box 156 .... Toronto ON M9W5L2 *TF:* 888-675-7223 ■ *Web:* woodbine.com	416-675-7223		642
Woodbine House 6510 Bells Mill Rd............ Bethesda MD 20817 *TF:* 800-843-7323 ■ *Web:* www.woodbinehouse.com	301-897-3570	897-5838	637-2
Woodbridge Center Mall 250 Woodbridge Center Dr................. Woodbridge NJ 07095 *Web:* www.woodbridgecenter.com	732-636-4600		460
Woodbridge Foam Corp 4240 Sherwoodtowne Blvd................ Mississauga ON L4Z2G6 *Web:* www.woodbridgegroup.com	905-896-3626	896-9262	601
Woodbridge INOAC Technical Products 4100 Pleasant Garden Rd.................. Greensboro NC 27406 *Web:* witpfoam.com	336-378-9620		601
Woodbridge Public Library George Frederick Plz...................... Woodbridge NJ 07095 *Web:* woodbridgelibrary.org	732-634-4450	726-7080	434-3
Woodburn Nursery & Azaleas 13009 McKee School Rd NE................. Woodburn OR 97071 *TF:* 888-634-2232 ■ *Web:* www.woodburnnursery.com	503-634-2231	634-2238	369
Woodbury Corp 2733 E Parleys Way Ste 300............... Salt Lake City UT 84109 *Web:* www.woodburycorp.com	801-485-0209		652
Woodbury County 620 Douglas St .... Sioux City IA 51101 *Web:* woodburycountyiowa.gov	712-279-6611		338
Woodbury County Rural Electric Cooperative Assn 1495 Humboldt Ave .... Moville IA 51039 *TF:* 800-469-3125 ■ *Web:* woodburyrec.com	712-873-3125		245
Woodbury Pewterers Inc 860 Main St S....... Woodbury CT 06798 *TF:* 800-648-2014 ■ *Web:* www.woodburypewter.com	800-648-2014		702
Woodbury Ski Area 785 Washington Rd........ Woodbury CT 06798 *Web:* www.woodburyskiarea.com	203-263-2203		711
Woodbury Technologies Inc 1725 East 1450 South .... Clearfield UT 84015 *TF:* 800-408-8857 ■ *Web:* www.woodburytech.com	801-773-7157		196
Woodbury University 7500 Glenoaks Blvd .... Burbank CA 91510 *TF:* 800-784-9663 ■ *Web:* woodbury.edu	818-767-0888	767-7520	166
Woodcase Fine Cabinetry Inc 8340 E Raintree Dr .... Scottsdale AZ 85260 *Web:* woodcaseinc.net	480-948-0756		115
Woodcliff Hotel & Spa 199 Woodcliff Dr............................ Fairport NY 14450 *TF:* 800-365-3065 ■ *Web:* www.woodcliffhotelspa.com	585-381-4000	381-2673	669
Woodco USA 773 McCarty Dr .... Houston TX 77029 *TF:* 800-496-6326 ■ *Web:* www.woodcousa.com	713-672-9491		358
Woodcock Nature Ctr 54 Deer Run Rd .... Wilton CT 06897 *Web:* www.woodcocknaturecenter.org	203-762-7280	834-0062	50-5
Woodcraft Industries Inc 525 Lincoln Ave SE......................... Saint Cloud MN 56304 *Web:* www.woodcraftind.com	320-252-1503	656-2199	115
Woodcraft Supply LLC 1177 Rosemar Rd........................ Parkersburg WV 26105 **Fax Area Code:* 304 ■ *TF:* 800-535-4482 ■ *Web:* www.woodcraft.com	800-535-4482	428-8271*	45

Name / Address	City	State	ZIP	Phone	Fax	Class
WoodCrafters Home Products LLC 3700 Camino de Verdad *Web:* www.woodcrafters-tx.com	Weslaco	TX	78596	956-647-8300		361
Wooden Monkey 1707 Grafton St *Web:* www.thewoodenmonkey.ca	Halifax	NS	B3J2C6	902-444-3844		671
Wooden Pallets Ltd PO Box 555 *Web:* www.woodenpalletsltd.com	Silsbee	TX	77656	409-385-1234	385-6203	551
WoodenBoat School 41 Wooden Boat Ln PO Box 78 *Web:* www.thewoodenboatschool.com	Brooklin	ME	04616	207-359-4651	359-8920	685
Woodfield Fund Admin LLC 3601 Algonquin Rd Ste 900 *Web:* www.ultimusfundsolutions.com	Rolling Meadows	IL	60008	847-255-3500		2
Woodfield Inc 3161 Hwy 376 S *TF:* 800-501-6020 ■ *Web:* www.woodfieldinc.com	Camden	AR	71701	870-231-6020		186
Woodfill Law Firm PC 3 Riverway Ste 750 *Web:* woodfilllaw.com	Houston	TX	77056	713-751-3080		652
Woodfin Co 8180 Mechanicsville Tpke *Web:* askwoodfin.com	Mechanicsville	VA	23111	804-730-5000		579
Woodfirst Sustainable Enterprises 2339 Unity St *Web:* www.woodfirst.com	Klamath Falls	OR	97603	541-892-0323		683
Woodfold Manufacturing Inc 1811 18th Ave PO Box 346 *Web:* www.woodfold.com	Forest Grove	OR	97116	503-357-7181	357-7185	499
Woodford Manufacturing Co 2121 Waynoka Rd *TF:* 800-621-6032 ■ *Web:* www.woodfordmfg.com	Colorado Springs	CO	80915	719-574-0600	574-7699	609
Woodford Oil Company Inc 13th St PO Box 567 *TF:* 800-927-3688 ■ *Web:* www.woodfordoil.com	Elkins	WV	26241	304-636-2688		316
Woodford State Park 142 State Park Rd *Web:* www.vtstateparks.com	Bennington	VT	05201	802-447-7169		565
Woodforest National Bank PO Box 7889 *TF:* 877-968-7962 ■ *Web:* woodforest.com	Spring	TX	77387	832-375-2000		70
Wood-Fruitticher Grocery Company Inc 2900 Alton Rd *Web:* www.woodfruitticher.com	Birmingham	AL	35210	205-836-9663	836-9681	297-8
Woodgrain Distribution 80 Shelby St *TF:* 800-756-0199 ■ *Web:* www.woodgraindistribution.com	Montevallo	AL	35115	205-665-2546	665-3432	309
Woodgrain Millworks Inc 300 NW 16th St *TF:* 888-783-5485 ■ *Web:* www.woodgrain.com	Fruitland	ID	83619	208-452-3801		499
Woodhall School 58 Harrison Ln PO Box 550 *Web:* www.woodhallschool.org	Bethlehem	CT	06751	203-266-7788		622
Woodharbor Doors & Cabinetry Inc 3277 Ninth St SW *Web:* www.woodharbor.com	Mason City	IA	50401	641-423-0444	423-0345	499
Woodhaven Care Ctr 2400 McGinley Rd *Web:* www.mywoodhavencarecenter.com	Monroeville	PA	15146	412-856-4770		450
Woodhill Supply Inc 4665 Beidler Rd *TF:* 800-362-6111 ■ *Web:* www.woodhillsupply.com	Willoughby	OH	44094	440-269-1100		612
Woodings Industrial Corp 218 Clay Ave *Web:* www.woodingsindustrial.com	Mars	PA	16046	724-625-3131		697
Wooditch Co, The 1 Park Plz Ste 400 *TF:* 888-553-9800 ■ *Web:* wooditch.com	Irvine	CA	92614	949-553-9800		390
Woodland Aviation Inc 25170 Aviation Ave *TF:* 800-442-1333 ■ *Web:* www.woodlandaviation.com	Davis	CA	95616	530-759-6037		63
Woodland Cemetery & Arboretum Foundation 118 Woodland Ave *Web:* www.woodlandcemetery.org	Dayton	OH	45409	937-228-3221	222-7259	97
Woodland Chamber of Commerce 400 Court St *TF:* 888-843-2636 ■ *Web:* www.woodlandchamber.org	Woodland	CA	95695	530-662-7327	662-4086	139
Woodland Engineering Co 122 Baker Rd *Web:* www.woodlandengineering.com	Lake Bluff	IL	60044	847-362-0110	362-5130	604
Woodland Foods Inc 3751 Sunset Ave *Web:* woodlandfoods.com	Waukegan	IL	60087	847-625-8600		297-11
Woodland Furniture 4475 S 15th W *Web:* www.woodlandfurniture.com	Idaho Falls	ID	83402	208-523-9006		319-2
Woodland Heights Medical Ctr 505 S John Redditt Dr *Web:* www.woodlandheights.net	Lufkin	TX	75904	936-634-8311	637-8600	374-3
Woodland Hills Chamber of Commerce 20121 Ventura Blvd Ste 309 *Web:* www.woodlandhillscc.net	Woodland Hills	CA	91364	818-347-4737	347-3321	139
Woodland Hills Medical Clinic 19825 Ventura Blvd *Web:* www.woodlandhillsurgentcarecenter.com	Woodland Hills	CA	91364	818-340-3636		374-3
Woodland Mall 3195 28th St SE *Web:* shopwoodlandmall.com	Grand Rapids	MI	49512	616-949-0012		460
Woodland Paper Inc 50785 Pontiac Trl *TF:* 800-979-9919 ■ *Web:* www.woodlandpaper.com	Wixom	MI	48393	248-926-5550		554
Woodland Park Zoo 5500 Phinney Ave N *Web:* www.zoo.org	Seattle	WA	98103	206-548-2500	548-1536	823
Woodland Public Library 250 First St *TF:* 800-321-2752 ■ *Web:* www.cityofwoodland.org	Woodland	CA	95695	530-661-5980	666-5408	434-3
Woodland Pulp LLC 144 Main St *Web:* woodlandpulp.com	Baileyville	ME	04694	207-427-3311		557
Woodland School District 50 1105 Hunt Club Rd *Web:* www.dist50.net	Gurnee	IL	60031	847-596-5600		685
Woodland.Net PO Box 2262 *Web:* www.woodland.net	Woodland	CA	95776	530-661-1234		180
Woodlands Academy of the Sacred Heart 760 E Westleigh Rd *Web:* www.woodlandsacademy.org	Lake Forest	IL	60045	847-234-4300	234-4348	622
Woodlands and Wildlife Consultants LLC (W&WC) PO Box 1508 *Web:* www.woodlandsandwildlife.com	Fortson	GA	31808	706-718-9208		192
Woodlands Prep International school, The 27440 Kuykendahl Rd *Web:* woodlandsprep.org	The Woodlands	TX	77375	281-516-0600	516-1155	800
Woodlands Resort & Conference Ctr, The 2301 N Millbend Dr *TF:* 800-433-2624 ■ *Web:* www.woodlandsresort.com	The Woodlands	TX	77380	281-367-1100		377
Woodlawn Animal Hospital Ltd 6523 S King Dr *Web:* woodlawnanimalhospital.com	Chicago	IL	60637	773-249-7191		794
Woodlawn Beach State Park 3580 Lake Shore Rd *Web:* parks.ny.gov	Blasdell	NY	14219	716-826-1930		565
Woodlawn Cemetery Inc, The Webster Ave & E 233rd St *TF:* 877-496-6352 ■ *Web:* www.thewoodlawncemetery.org	Bronx	NY	10470	718-920-0500		510
Woodlawn National Cemetery 1825 Davis St *Web:* www.cem.va.gov	Elmira	NY	14901	607-732-5411	732-1769	136
Woodlawn Rubber Co 11268 Williamson Rd *Web:* www.woodlawnrubber.com	Blue Ash	OH	45241	513-489-1718	489-2367	676
Woodley & Mcgillivary 1101 Vermont Ave NW Ste 1000 *Web:* wmlaborlaw.com	Washington	DC	20005	202-833-8855		41
Woodley's Fine Furniture Inc 320 S Sunset St *Web:* www.woodleys.com	Longmont	CO	80501	303-443-5692		321
Woodloch Pines Inc 731 Welcome Lake Rd *TF:* 800-966-3562 ■ *Web:* www.woodloch.com	Hawley	PA	18428	570-685-8000		379
Woodman State Jail 1210 Coryell City Rd *Web:* www.tdcj.texas.gov	Gatesville	TX	76528	254-865-9398		213
Woodman's Food Market Inc 2631 Liberty Ln *Web:* www.woodmans-food.com	Janesville	WI	53545	608-754-8382	754-8317	345
Woodmen Life 1700 Farnam St *TF:* 800-225-3108 ■ *Web:* www.woodmenlife.org	Omaha	NE	68102	402-449-7733	271-7269	457-10
Woodmen of the World Hall 291 W Eigth Ave *Web:* www.wowhall.org	Eugene	OR	97401	541-687-2746		572
Woodmere Art Museum 9201 Germantown Ave *Web:* woodmereartmuseum.org	Philadelphia	PA	19118	215-247-0476	247-2387	520
Woodmont Investment Counsel LLC 401 Commerce St Ste 5400 *TF:* 800-278-8003 ■ *Web:* www.woodmontcounsel.com	Nashville	TN	37219	615-297-6144		401
Woodmont Real Estate Services (WRES) 1050 Ralston Ave *Web:* www.wres.com	Belmont	CA	94002	650-592-3960		655
Woodmoor Group 755 Hwy 105 Ste 2A *Web:* www.woodmoor.com	Palmer Lake	CO	80133	719-488-8589		260
Woodpecker Truck and Equipment Inc 40275 Clark Ln *TF:* 888-966-3732 ■ *Web:* www.woodpeckertruck.com	Pendleton	OR	97001	541-276-5515	276-9237	57
Woodridge Park District 2600 Center Dr *TF:* 800-713-7415 ■ *Web:* www.woodridgeparks.org	Woodridge	IL	60517	630-353-3300		31
Woodridge Public Library 3 Plaza Dr *Web:* www.woodridgelibrary.org	Woodridge	IL	60517	630-964-7899	968-4126	434-3
Woodrow Wilson House Museum 2340 S St NW *Web:* www.woodrowwilsonhouse.org	Washington	DC	20008	202-387-4062	483-1466	520
Woodrow Wilson National Fellowship Foundation 5 Vaughn Dr Ste 300 *Web:* woodrow.org	Princeton	NJ	08540	609-452-7007	452-0066	48-11
Woodrow Wilson Presidential Library 20 N Coalter St *Web:* www.woodrowwilson.org	Staunton	VA	24401	540-886-0807		434-2
Woodruff and Sons Inc 6450 31st St E *TF:* 866-774-4523 ■ *Web:* www.woodruffandsons.com	Bradenton	FL	34203	941-756-1871	755-1379	188-3
Woodruff Arts Ctr 1280 Peachtree St NE *Web:* woodruffcenter.org	Atlanta	GA	30309	404-733-4200		572
Woodruff Construction LLC 1890 Kountry Ln *Web:* woodruff.build	Fort Dodge	IA	50501	515-576-1118		780
Woodruff Electric Co-op PO Box 1619 *TF:* 888-559-6400 ■ *Web:* www.woodruffelectric.coop	Forrest City	AR	72336	870-633-2262	633-0629	245
Woodruff Energy 73 Water St PO Box 777 *TF:* 800-557-1121 ■ *Web:* www.woodruffenergy.com	Bridgeton	NJ	08302	800-557-1121		316
Woodruff Health Sciences Center Library *Emory University* 1462 Clifton Rd NE *Web:* health.library.emory.edu	Atlanta	GA	30322	404-727-8727	727-9821	434-1
Woodruff-Fontaine House 680 Adams Ave *Web:* www.woodruff-fontaine.org	Memphis	TN	38105	901-526-1469		50-3
Woods & Thompson PA 941 Hillwind Rd NE Ste 200 *Web:* woodsandthompson.com	Minneapolis	MN	55432	763-571-2345		41
Woods Bay State Natural Area 11020 Woods Bay Rd *Web:* southcarolinaparks.com	Olanta	SC	29114	843-659-4445		565
Woods Equipment Co 2606 S Illinois Rt 2 PO Box 1000 *TF:* 800-319-6637 ■ *Web:* www.woodsequipment.com	Oregon	IL	61061	815-732-2141	732-7580	273
Woods Fuller Shultz & Smith 300 S Phillips Ave Ste 300 *TF:* 866-339-6637 ■ *Web:* woodsfuller.com	Sioux Falls	SD	57104	605-336-3890	339-3357	428
Woods Hole Historical Museum (WHHM) 579 Woods Hole Rd *Web:* www.woodsholemuseum.org	Woods Hole	MA	02543	508-548-7270		520
Woods Hole Oceanographic Institution (WHOI) 266 Woods Hole Rd *Web:* www.whoi.edu	Woods Hole	MA	02543	508-289-2282	457-2109	668
Woods Hole Public Library 581 Woods Hole Rd PO Box 185 *Web:* www.woodsholepubliclibrary.org	Woods Hole	MA	02543	508-548-8961	540-1969	434-3

Name / Address	Phone	Fax	Class
Woods Rogers PLC 10 S Jefferson St Ste 1400 . . . . Roanoke VA 24011 *TF:* 800-552-4529 ■ *Web:* woodsrogers.com	540-983-7600	983-7711	428
Woods Supermarkets Inc 703 E College St. . . . . Bolivar MO 65613 *Web:* www.woodssupermarket.com	417-326-7601		345
Woods Trial Law 110 N 11th St Ste 201 . . . . Tampa FL 33602 *Web:* woodstriallaw.com	813-222-3620		41
Woods, The Mountain Lake Rd PO Box 5. . . . . Hedgesville WV 25427 *TF:* 800-248-2222 ■ *Web:* www.thewoods.com	304-754-7977	754-8146	669
Woodside Energy Ltd Sage Plz 5151 San Felipe Ste 980 . . . . Houston TX 77056 **Fax Area Code:* 713 ■ *Web:* www.woodside.com.au	587-956-0913	401-0088*	539
Woodside Fund 303 Twin Dolphin Dr Ste 600 . . . . Redwood City CA 94065 *Web:* www.woodsidefund.com	650-549-7601		792
Woodside Juvenile Rehabilitation Ctr 26 Woodside Dr . . . . Colchester VT 05446 *Web:* www.dcf.vermont.gov	802-655-4990		412
Woodside Priory School 302 Portola Rd. . . . . Portola CA 94028 *Web:* www.prioryca.org	650-851-8221	851-2839	622
Woodsmith Magazine 2200 Grand Ave . . . . Des Moines IA 50312 **Fax Area Code:* 515 ■ *TF:* 800-333-5075 ■ *Web:* www.woodsmith.com	800-333-5075	282-6741*	457-14
Woodson & Bozeman Inc 3870 New Getwell Rd . . . . Memphis TN 38118 *TF:* 800-876-4243 ■ *Web:* www.wbmemphis.com	901-362-1500	362-1509	38
Woodson County 105 W Rutledge St Rm 103. . . . . Yates Center KS 66783 *Web:* www.woodsoncounty.net	620-625-8605	625-8670	338
Woodstock Academy 57 Academy Rd . . . . Woodstock CT 06281 *Web:* www.woodstockacademy.org	860-928-6575	963-7222	148
Woodstock Chamber of Commerce & Industry 121 N Calhoun St. . . . . Woodstock IL 60098 *Web:* www.woodstockilchamber.com	815-338-2436		139
Woodstock Community Unit School District 200 227 W Judd St . . . . Woodstock IL 60098 *Web:* www.woodstockschools.org	815-338-8200	338-2005	685
Woodstock Corp 27 School St Ste 200. . . . . Boston MA 02108 *Web:* woodstockcorp.com	617-227-0600	523-0229	401
Woodstock District Chamber of Commerce 447 Hunter St 2nd Fl . . . . Woodstock ON N4S1K1 *Web:* woodstockchamber.ca	519-539-9411	456-1611	137
Woodstock Furniture Outlet 100 Robin Rd Ext . . . . Acworth GA 30102 *Web:* www.woodstockoutlet.com	678-255-1000		321
Woodstock General Hospital 270 Riddell St. . . . . Woodstock ON N4S6N6 *Web:* www.wgh.on.ca	519-421-4211	421-4238	374-2
Woodstock Inn & Resort 14 The Green. . . . . Woodstock VT 05091 *TF:* 800-448-7900 ■ *Web:* www.woodstockinn.com	802-332-6853	457-6699	669
Woodstock Percussion Inc 167 Dubois Rd . . . . Shokan NY 12481 *Web:* www.chimes.com	845-657-6000		527
Woodstream Corp 69 N Locust St. . . . . Lititz PA 17543 *TF:* 800-800-1819 ■ *Web:* www.woodstream.com	717-626-2125	626-1912	280
Woodsville Guaranty Savings Bank 10 Pleasant St PO Box 266. . . . . Woodsville NH 03785 *TF:* 800-564-2735 ■ *Web:* www.theguarantybank.com	603-747-2735	747-3267	70
Wood-Tikchik State Park PO Box 1822 . . . . Dillingham AK 99576 *Web:* www.dnr.alaska.gov	907-842-2641		565
WoodTrust Financial Corp 181 Second St S. . . . . Wisconsin Rapids WI 54494 *Web:* www.woodtrust.com	715-423-7600	422-0300	70
Woodward Academy 1662 Rugby Ave . . . . College Park GA 30337 *Web:* www.woodward.edu	404-765-4000		685
Woodward Biomedical Library 1961 E Mall . . . . Vancouver BC V6T1Z1 *Web:* woodward.library.ubc.ca	604-822-6375	822-3893	434-1
Woodward Children's Ctr 201 W Merrick Rd. . . . . Freeport NY 11520 *Web:* www.woodwardchildren.org	516-379-0900		167-3
Woodward Communications Inc 801 Bluff St. . . . . Dubuque IA 52001 **Fax Area Code:* 563 ■ *Web:* www.wcinet.com	800-553-4801	588-5739*	645
Woodward HRT Inc 25200 W Rye Canyon Rd . . . . Santa Clarita CA 91355 *Web:* www.woodward.com	661-294-6000	259-9622	21
Woodward Resource Ctr 1251 334th St . . . . Woodward IA 50276 *Web:* dhs.iowa.gov	515-438-2600		230
Woodway USA W229 N591 Foster Ct. . . . . Waukesha WI 53186 *TF:* 800-966-3929 ■ *Web:* www.woodway.com	262-548-6235	522-6235	267
Woodwind & Brasswind PO Box 7479 . . . . Westlake Village CA 91359 *Web:* www.wwbw.com	574-251-3500		526
Woodwing Usa 19 Clifford St 8th Fl . . . . Detroit MI 48226 *Web:* www.woodwing.com	313-962-0542	962-9644	225
Woodworking School at Pine Croft, The 1865 Big Hill Rd. . . . . Berea KY 40403 *Web:* pinecroftwoodschool.com	859-985-3224		685
Woodworth Capital Inc 3110 Ruston Way Ste 300 . . . . Tacoma WA 98402 *Web:* www.woodworthfamilyfoundation.org	253-752-6405	759-3841	792
Woody Bogler Trucking Co PO Box 229 . . . . Rosebud MO 63091 *TF:* 800-899-4120 ■ *Web:* www.woodybogler.com	573-764-3700		780
Woody's 619 N Gloster St. . . . . Tupelo MS 38804 *Web:* woodyssteak.com	662-840-0460		671
WOOF-AM PO Box 1427. . . . . Dothan AL 36302 *TF:* 888-793-2656 ■ *Web:* www.woofradio.com	334-792-1149	677-4612	647
Wool Growers 620 E 19th St . . . . Bakersfield CA 93305 *Web:* woolgrowers.net	661-327-9584		671
Woolaroc Ranch Museum & Wildlife Preserve 1925 Woolaroc Ranch Rd. . . . . Bartlesville OK 74003 *TF:* 888-966-5276 ■ *Web:* www.woolaroc.org	918-336-0307	336-0084	520
Woolco Foods Inc 135 Amity St. . . . . Jersey City NJ 07304 *Web:* woolcofoods.net	201-716-2700		297-8
Wooldridge Boats Inc 1303 S 96th St. . . . . Seattle WA 98108 *Web:* www.wooldridgeboats.com	206-722-8998		90
Woolery Enterprises Inc 1991 Republic Ave . . . . San Leandro CA 94577 *Web:* www.willsfreshfoods.com	510-357-5700	357-5776	296-37
Woolf Aircraft Products Inc 6401 Cogswell Rd . . . . Romulus MI 48174 *Web:* www.woolfaircraft.com	734-721-5330	721-3490	595
Woolly Hollow State Park 82 Woolly Hollow Rd . . . . Greenbrier AR 72058 *Web:* www.arkansasstateparks.com	501-679-2098		565
Woolpert Inc 4454 Idea Center Blvd . . . . Dayton OH 45430 *TF:* 800-414-1045 ■ *Web:* woolpert.com	937-461-5660	461-0743	261
Woolrich Inc 1039 Park Ave . . . . Woolrich PA 17779 *TF:* 800-995-1299 ■ *Web:* www.woolrich.com	570-227-0034	769-6234	155-5
Woolverton Printing Co 6714 Chancellor Dr . . . . Cedar Falls IA 50613 *TF:* 800-670-7713 ■ *Web:* www.woolverton.com	319-277-2616		627
Woonsocket Harris Public Library 303 Clinton St . . . . Woonsocket RI 02895 *Web:* www.woonsocketlibrary.org	401-769-9044	767-4140	434-3
Wooster Area Chamber of Commerce 377 W Liberty St. . . . . Wooster OH 44691 *TF:* 800-414-1103 ■ *Web:* www.woosterchamber.com	330-262-5735	262-5745	139
Wooster Brush Co 604 Madison Ave . . . . Wooster OH 44691 *TF:* 800-392-7246 ■ *Web:* www.woosterbrush.com	330-264-4440	263-0495	103
Wooster City Board of Education 144 N Market St. . . . . Wooster OH 44691 *Web:* www.woostercityschools.org	330-264-0869	262-3407	685
Wooster Products Inc 1000 Spruce St PO Box 6005. . . . . Wooster OH 44691 *TF:* 800-321-4936 ■ *Web:* www.woosterproducts.com	330-264-2844	262-4151	491
Woot Inc 4121 International Pkwy . . . . Carrollton TX 75007 *Web:* www.woot.com	972-417-3959		174
WOPI-AM 288 Delaney St. . . . . Bristol TN 37620 *Web:* www.hvbcgroup.com	423-264-9578	247-9836	647
Worad Inc 299 Brooks St. . . . . Worcester MA 01606 *Web:* www.worad.com	508-852-2693	852-2704	119
Worcester Academy 81 Providence St. . . . . Worcester MA 01604 *Web:* www.worcesteracademy.org	508-754-5302		622
Worcester Art Museum 55 Salisbury St. . . . . Worcester MA 01609 *Web:* www.worcesterart.org	508-799-4406	798-5646	520
Worcester Center for Crafts 25 Sagamore Rd. . . . . Worcester MA 01605 *Web:* www.worcester.edu	508-753-8183	797-5626	50-2
Worcester County 1 W Market St Rm 1103. . . . . Snow Hill MD 21863 *TF:* 800-852-0335 ■ *Web:* www.co.worcester.md.us	410-632-1194	632-3131	338
Worcester County Library 307 N Washington St . . . . Snow Hill MD 21863 *Web:* www.worcesterlibrary.org	410-632-2600	632-1159	434-3
Worcester Envelope Co 22 Millbury St. . . . . Auburn MA 01501 *TF:* 800-343-1398 ■ *Web:* www.worcesterenvelope.com	800-343-1398		263
Worcester Historical Museum 30 Elm St . . . . Worcester MA 01609 *Web:* www.worcesterhistory.org	508-753-8278	753-9070	520
Worcester Magazine Inc 101 Water St 3rd Fl. . . . . Worcester MA 01604 *Web:* www.worcestermag.com	508-749-3166	755-8860	637-9
Worcester Polytechnic Institute 100 Institute Rd . . . . Worcester MA 01609 *Web:* www.wpi.edu	508-831-5000	831-5875	166
Worcester Public Schools 20 Irving St. . . . . Worcester MA 01609 *Web:* www.worcesterschools.org	508-799-3115	799-3119	685
Worcester Regional Airport 375 Airport Dr. . . . . Worcester MA 01602 *Web:* www.worcesterma.gov	508-929-1300		27
Worcester Regional Chamber of Commerce 446 Main St Ste 200. . . . . Worcester MA 01608 *Web:* www.worcesterchamber.org	508-753-2924	754-8560	139
Worcester Regional Transit Authority 287 Grove St. . . . . Worcester MA 01605 *Web:* www.therta.com	508-791-9782		468
Word & Brown Insurance Administrators Inc 721 S Parker Ste 300 . . . . Orange CA 92868 *Web:* www.wordandbrown.com	714-835-6752		390
Word Among US Inc 9639 Doctor Perry Rd. . . . . Ijamsville MD 21754 *TF:* 800-775-9673 ■ *Web:* wau.org	301-874-1700		95
Word Branch Media PO Box 41 . . . . Marble NC 28905 *Web:* www.wordbranch.com	828-837-6135		637-2
Word Entertainment 25 Music Sq W . . . . Nashville TN 37203 *Web:* wordentertainment.com	615-251-0600		657
Word Foundation Inc PO Box 17510 . . . . Rochester NY 14617 *Web:* www.thewordfoundation.org	585-544-6790	544-6975	637-2
Word of Faith Family Worship Cathedral 212 Riverside Pkwy . . . . Austell GA 30168 *TF:* 888-373-2531 ■ *Web:* www.woffamily.org	770-874-8400		48-20
Word of Life Fellowship Church Inc, The 3650 Greenbush St. . . . . LaFayette IN 47905 *Web:* www.wolfc.net	765-449-4008		48-20
Worden Bros Inc 4905 Pine Cone Dr . . . . Durham NC 27707 *TF:* 800-776-4940 ■ *Web:* www.worden.com	919-408-0542	408-0545	178-1
Worden Company Inc 199 E 17th St . . . . Holland MI 49423 *TF:* 800-748-0561 ■ *Web:* www.wordencompany.com	616-392-1848	392-2542	319-3
Words at Work 403 W Ponce De Leon Ave Ste 111 . . . . Decatur GA 30030 *Web:* wordsatwork.com	404-270-9200		7
WordSouth - A Content Marketing Co PO Box 1575 . . . . Rainsville AL 35986 *Web:* wordsouth.com	256-638-8856		636
Wordsprint Inc 190 W Spring St. . . . . Wytheville VA 24382 *Web:* www.wordsprint.com	276-228-6608	228-2584	627
Wordsworth & Company LLC 723 Raymond Ave. . . . . Santa Monica CA 90405 *Web:* www.wordsworthandco.com	310-452-1022		7
Word-Tech Inc 5625 Foxridge Dr . . . . Mission KS 66202 *Web:* www.wordtech.com	913-722-3334		175

Name / Address	City	State	Zip	Phone	Fax	Class
Wordworld PO Box 90309 *Web:* www.wordworldpublications.com	San Diego	CA	92169	858-361-6711	274-5363	637-2
Work 'n Gear Stores 2300 Crown Colony Dr Ste 300 *TF:* 800-987-0218 ■ *Web:* www.workngear.com	Quincy	MA	02169	800-987-0218		157-5
Work Area Protection Corp 2500 Production Dr *TF:* 800-327-4417 ■ *Web:* workareaprotection.com	Saint Charles	IL	60174	630-377-9100		596
Work Duds 5215 S Laburnum Ave *Web:* www.work-duds.com	Richmond	VA	23231	804-226-1366		76
Work In Progress Coaching 102 Alta Verdi Dr *Web:* www.wipcoaching.com	Aptos	CA	95003	831-685-1480		242
Work Institute LLC, The 1620 Westgate Cir Ste 100 *Web:* workinstitute.com	Brentwood	TN	37027	615-777-6400		463
Workaholics Anonymous World Service Organization PO Box 289 *Web:* www.workaholics-anonymous.org	Menlo Park	CA	94026	510-273-9253		48-21
Workbook LLC 110 N Doheny Dr *Web:* www.workbook.com	Beverly Hills	CA	90211	323-856-0008		195
WorkCare 300 S Harbor Blvd Ste 600 *TF:* 800-455-6155 ■ *Web:* www.workcare.com	Anaheim	CA	92805	800-455-6155		194
Workday 6110 Stoneridge Mall Rd *NASDAQ: WDAY* ■ *TF:* 877-967-5329 ■ *Web:* www.workday.com	Pleasanton	CA	94588	877-967-5329		225
Workers' Credit Union 815 Main St PO Box 900 *TF:* 800-221-4020 ■ *Web:* www.wcu.com	Fitchburg	MA	01420	978-345-1021		219
WorkersCompensationcom LLC PO Box 2432 *TF:* 866-927-2667 ■ *Web:* www.workerscompensation.com	Sarasota	FL	34230	941-366-3791		393
Workforce Alliance Inc 326 Fern St Ste 301 *TF:* 800-204-2418 ■ *Web:* www.careersourcepbc.com	West Palm Beach	FL	33409	561-340-1060		260
Workforce Board, The 128 Tenth Ave SW PO Box 43105 *Web:* www.wtb.wa.gov	Olympia	WA	98504	360-709-4600	586-5862	41
Workforce Insight 355 S Teller St Ste 200 *Web:* www.workforceinsight.com	Lakewood	CO	80226	303-309-4006		261
Workforce Institute's City College 1231 N Broad St **Fax Area Code:* 267 ■ *Web:* www.citycollege-careers.org	Philadelphia	PA	19122	215-568-9215	592-4189*	167-3
Workforce Logiq 420 S Orange Ave Ste 600 *Web:* www.zerochaos.com	Orlando	FL	32801	407-770-6161		463
Workforce Services Inc 6245 Sherman Church Ave SW *Web:* www.wfservices.biz	Canton	OH	44706	330-777-5463		62-7
Workgroup Connections Inc 4240 Duncan Ave Ste 200 *Web:* www.wgcinc.com	Saint Louis	MO	63110	314-436-2233	436-2288	764
Workincom Inc 2255 Green Vista Dr Ste 402 *TF:* 800-774-8671 ■ *Web:* workin.com	Sparks	NV	89431	775-336-3366		260
Working Machines Corp 2170 Dwight Way *TF:* 877-648-4808 ■ *Web:* www.workingmachines.com	Berkeley	CA	94704	877-648-4808		180
Working Media Group 21 W 38th St 13th Fl *Web:* www.workingmediagroup.com	New York	NY	10018	212-679-2681		7
Working Mother Magazine 2 Park Ave 9th Fl *Web:* www.workingmother.com	New York	NY	10016	212-779-5000		457-11
Working Solutions 1820 Preston Pk Blvd Ste 2000 *TF:* 866-857-4800 ■ *Web:* workingsolutions.com	Plano	TX	75093	972-964-4800		737
Working Title Films 9720 Wilshire Blvd 4th Fl *Web:* www.workingtitlefilms.com	Beverly Hills	CA	90212	310-777-3100		514
WorkingBuildings LLC 1230 Peachtree St NE 300 Promenade *Web:* workingbuildings.com	Atlanta	GA	30309	678-990-8001		256
Worklife Balance com 7742 Spalding Dr Ste 356 *TF:* 877-644-0064 ■ *Web:* worklifebalance.com	Norcross	GA	30092	770-997-7881	668-9719	463
Workman Nydegger PC 60 E South Temple Ste 1000 *Web:* www.wnlaw.com	Salt Lake City	UT	84111	801-533-9800		428
Workman Publishing 225 Varick St *TF:* 800-722-7202 ■ *Web:* www.workman.com	New York	NY	10014	212-254-5900	254-8098	637-2
Workmen's Circle/Arbeter Ring Inc 247 W 37th St 5th Fl *Web:* www.circle.org	New York	NY	10018	212-889-6800	532-7518	49-9
Workplace Benefit Solutions LLC 1667 Elm St Ste 3 *Web:* www.workplacebenefitsolutions.com	Manchester	NH	03101	603-668-0400		260
Workplace Environments 2000 LLC 37 E Germantown Pk *Web:* workplaceenvironments.com	Plymouth Meeting	PA	19462	610-834-9877		321
Workplace Group Inc, The 10 Ridgedale Ave *Web:* www.workplacegroup.com	Florham Park	NJ	07932	973-377-4665	377-3064	260
Workplace Group Inc, The 4B Aerial Way *Web:* theworkplacegroup.com	Syosset	NY	11791	631-273-7500	273-7499	321
Workplace IT Management 108 S Dakota Ave *Web:* workplace-it.com	Sioux Falls	SD	57104	605-367-3767		525
Workplace Resource LLC 4400 NE Loop 410 Ste 130 *TF:* 800-580-3000 ■ *Web:* hmwrasa.com	San Antonio	TX	78218	512-472-7300		321
Workplace Solutions 30800 Telegraph Rd Ste 2985 *Web:* www.myworkplacesolutions.com	Bingham Farms	MI	48025	248-430-2500		320
Workplace Staffing Services 2923 Smith Rd Ste 201 *Web:* workplacestaff.com	Akron	OH	44333	330-926-1880	665-1044	260
Workplace Systems Inc 562 Mammoth Rd *TF:* 800-258-9700 ■ *Web:* workplacenh.com	Londonderry	NH	03053	603-622-3727	622-0174	319-1
Works, The 55 S First St *Web:* attheworks.org	Newark	OH	43055	740-349-9277	345-7252	520
Worksaver Inc 9 Worksaver Trl PO Box 100 *Web:* www.worksaver.com	Litchfield	IL	62056	217-324-5973	324-3356	273
Workscape Inc 123 Selton St *Web:* workscapeinc.com	Marlborough	MA	01752	508-861-9000	573-9500	39
Workscapes Inc 1173 N Orange Ave *TF:* 877-967-5722 ■ *Web:* www.workscapes.com	Orlando	FL	32804	407-599-6770		320
Workshop Inc, The 339 Broadway *Web:* www.northeastcareer.org	Menands	NY	12204	518-465-5201		761
Workshop Theatre PO Box 11555 *Web:* www.workshoptheatre.com	Columbia	SC	29211	803-799-4876	799-0227	572
Worksighted Inc 275 Hoover Blvd *Web:* www.worksighted.com	Holland	MI	49423	616-546-2691		180
Worksman Trading Corp 94-15 100th St *TF:* 800-962-2453 ■ *Web:* www.worksman.com	Ozone Park	NY	11416	718-322-2000	529-4803	82
WorkSmart Inc 100 Meredith Dr Ste 200 *Web:* www.worksmart.com	Durham	NC	27713	919-484-1010		624
Worksoft Inc 15851 Dallas Pkwy Ste 855 **Fax Area Code:* 972 ■ *TF:* 866-836-1773 ■ *Web:* www.worksoft.com	Addison	TX	75001	866-836-1773	250-9900*	178-10
Workspace com Inc 10451 Mill Run Cir Ste 400 *TF:* 888-245-9168 ■ *Web:* www.workspace.com	Owings Mills	MD	21117	888-245-9168		525
Workspace Inc 309 Locust St *Web:* www.workspaceinc.net	Des Moines	IA	50309	515-288-7090		393
WorkSpan 950 Tower Ln Ste 1975 *Web:* www.workspan.com	Foster City	CA	94404	650-300-0567		178-1
Workstream USA Inc 485 N Keller Rd Ste 500	Maitland	FL	32751	407-475-5500		721
Worktank Enterprises LLC 400 E Pine St Ste 301 *TF:* 877-975-8265 ■ *Web:* worktankwebcasts.com	Seattle	WA	98122	877-975-8265		514
WorkZone LLC 16 W Township Line Rd *Web:* www.workzone.com	East Norriton	PA	19401	610-275-9865		178-1
World 50 Inc 3525 Piedmont Rd NE Bldg 7-600 *Web:* www.w50.com	Atlanta	GA	30305	404-816-5559		4
World Affairs Council (WAC) 312 Sutter St Ste 200 *Web:* www.worldaffairs.org	San Francisco	CA	94108	415-293-4686	982-5028	48-13
World Agricultural Outlook Board 1400 Independence Ave SW *TF:* 800-949-3964 ■ *Web:* www.usda.gov	Washington	DC	20250	202-720-6030		340-1
World Allergy Organization (WAO) 555 E Wells St Ste 1100 *Web:* www.worldallergy.org	Milwaukee	WI	53202	414-276-1791	276-3349	49-8
World Almanac and Book of Facts, The 132 W 31st St **Fax Area Code:* 800 ■ *TF:* 800-322-8755 ■ *Web:* www.worldalmanac.com	New York	NY	10001	212-967-8800	678-3633*	637-2
World Animal Protection 450 7th Ave 31st Fl **Fax Area Code:* 212 ■ *TF:* 800-883-9772 ■ *Web:* www.worldanimalprotection.org	New York	NY	10123	646-783-2200	564-4250*	48-3
World Around Songs Inc 7036 Hwy 80 S *Web:* www.worldaroundsongs.com	Burnsville	NC	28714	828-675-5909	675-9687	637-2
World Auto Group 3057 New Jersey *Web:* www.denvillenissan.com	Denville	NJ	07834	973-442-0500		57
World Bank Group, The (WBG) 1818 H St NW *TF:* 800-645-7247 ■ *Web:* www.worldbank.org	Washington	DC	20433	202-473-1000	477-6391	783
World Bicycle Relief 1333 N Kingsbury Ave 4th Fl *Web:* www.worldbicyclerelief.org	Chicago	IL	60642	312-664-3604		517
World Bird Sanctuary 125 Bald Eagle Ridge Rd *Web:* www.worldbirdsanctuary.org	Valley Park	MO	63088	636-225-4390		50-5
World Book Inc 180 N LaSalle St Ste 900 *Web:* international.worldbook.com	Chicago	IL	60601	312-729-5800	729-5600	637-2
World Casings Corp 4706 Grand Ave *Web:* www.worldcasing.com	Maspeth	NY	11378	718-628-3800		296-26
World Cat 1090 W St James St *TF:* 866-485-8899 ■ *Web:* www.worldcat.com	Tarboro	NC	27886	866-485-8899		90
World Chamber of Commerce Directory Inc 446 E 29th St Ste 1029 *TF:* 888-883-3231 ■ *Web:* www.chamberdirectoryonline.com	Loveland	CO	80538	970-663-3231		637-6
World Christian Broadcasting Corp 605 Bradley Ct *Web:* www.worldchristian.org	Franklin	TN	37067	615-371-8707		645-11
World Class Incentives 426 N Rand Rd *Web:* www.worldclassincentives.com	North Barrington	IL	60010	847-381-1800		226
World Class Lighting 14350 60th St N *TF:* 877-499-6753 ■ *Web:* www.worldclasslighting.com	Clearwater	FL	33760	727-524-7661		362
World Class Manufacturing Group Inc, The 1101 S Pine St *Web:* www.worldcls.com	Weyauwega	WI	54983	920-867-2527	867-3993	454
World Class Plastics Inc 7695 SR-708 *TF:* 800-954-3140 ■ *Web:* www.worldclassplastics.com	Russells Point	OH	43348	937-843-4927	843-4934	608
World Class Speakers & Entertainers 5158 Clareton Dr Ste 1034 *Web:* www.wcspeakers.com	Agoura Hills	CA	91376	818-991-5400		708
World Class Technology Corp 1300 NE Alpha Dr *Web:* www.worldclasstech.com	Mcminnville	OR	97128	503-472-8320		228
World Cocoa Foundation (WCF) 1411 K St NW Ste 1300 *Web:* www.worldcocoafoundation.org	Washington	DC	20005	202-737-7870	737-7832	49-6
World Concern 19303 Fremont Ave N *TF:* 800-755-5022 ■ *Web:* worldconcern.org	Seattle	WA	98133	206-546-7201	546-7269	48-5

	Phone	Fax	Class
World Council of Credit Unions Inc (WOCCU) 5710 Mineral Pt Rd . . . Madison WI 53705 *Web:* www.woccu.org	608-395-2000	395-2001	49-2
World Courier Inc 1313 Fourth Ave . . . New Hyde Park NY 11040 *Web:* www.worldcourier.com	516-354-2600		546
World Currency USA Inc 16 W Main St Ste C . . . Marlton NJ 08053 *TF:* 888-593-7927 ■ *Web:* www.worldcurrencyusa.com	888-593-7927	593-0027	691
World Data Products Inc 1105 Xenium Ln N Ste 200 . . . Plymouth MN 55441 **Fax Area Code:* 763 ■ *TF:* 888-210-7636 ■ *Web:* www.wdpi.com	888-210-7636	452-1201*	176
World Dredging Mining & Construction PO Box 17479 . . . Irvine CA 92623 *Web:* worlddredging.com	714-451-2228		637-9
World Dryer Corp 5700 McDermott Dr . . . Berkeley IL 60163 *TF:* 800-323-0701 ■ *Web:* worlddryer.com	708-449-6950	449-6958	37
World Electric Supply Orlando Inc 4501 SW 34th St . . . Orlando FL 32811 *Web:* www.worldelectricsupply.com	407-447-2000		246
World Electronics Sales & Service Inc 3000 Kutztown Rd . . . Reading PA 19605 *TF:* 800-523-0427 ■ *Web:* www.world-electronics.com	610-939-9800	939-9895	253
World Emblem International Inc 1500 NE 131 St . . . Miami FL 33161 *TF:* 800-766-0448 ■ *Web:* www.worldemblem.com	800-766-0448		594
World Energy 225 Franklin St Ste 1460 . . . Boston MA 02110 *Web:* www.worldenergy.net	617-889-7300	887-2411	201
World Environmental Inc 3939 W McKinley Ave . . . Milwaukee WI 53208 *Web:* www.world8a.com	414-933-1700		192
World Equity Group 1650 N Arlington Heights Rd Ste 100 . . . Arlington Heights IL 60004 *Web:* www.worldequitygroup.com	847-342-1700		690
World Fax Services Inc 3853 Northdale Blvd Ste 356 . . . Tampa FL 33624 *Web:* www.worldfax.com	813-961-7776	264-0204	681
World Financial Group Inc 11315 Johns Creek Pkwy . . . Johns Creek GA 30097 *Web:* www.worldfinancialgroup.com	770-453-9300		390
World Flavors Inc 76 Louise Dr . . . Warminster PA 18974 *TF:* 800-562-2946 ■ *Web:* www.worldflavors.com	215-672-4400	672-4405	123
World Floor Covering Assn (WFCA) 2211 Howell Ave . . . Anaheim CA 92806 *TF:* 800-624-6880 ■ *Web:* wfca.org	714-978-6440	978-6066	49-4
World Food Program USA (WFP) 1725 Eye St NW Ste 510 . . . Washington DC 20006 *TF:* 888-454-0555 ■ *Web:* wfpusa.org	202-627-3737	530-1698	48-5
World Forestry Ctr 4033 SW Canyon Rd . . . Portland OR 97221 *Web:* www.worldforestry.org	503-228-1367		48-13
World Franchising Network 1814 Franklin St Ste 603 . . . Oakland CA 94612 *Web:* www.worldfranchising.com	510-839-5471		637-2
World Fuel Services 6000 Metcalf Ave . . . Overland Park KS 66202 *TF:* 800-444-8672 ■ *Web:* www.wfscorp.com	913-643-2300	643-2323	581
World Fuel Services 9531 W 78th St Ste 102 . . . Eden Prairie MN 55344 *Web:* www.wfscorp.com	952-941-9090	828-5558	579
World Gold Council 685 Third Ave 27th Fl . . . New York NY 10017 *Web:* www.gold.org	212-317-3800	688-0410	49-4
World Gospel Mission (WGM) 3783 E State Rd 18 PO Box 948 . . . Marion IN 46952 *Web:* www.wgm.org	765-664-7331	671-7230	48-20
World Hotels 152 W 57th St 6th Fl . . . New York NY 10019 *Web:* www.worldhotels.com	212-956-0200		376
World Hunger Year Inc (WHY) 505 Eigth Ave Ste 2100 . . . New York NY 10018 *TF:* 800-548-6479 ■ *Web:* whyhunger.org	212-629-8850	465-9274	48-5
World Insurance Associates LLC 656 Shrewsbury Ave Ste 200 . . . Tinton Falls NJ 07701 *Web:* worldins.net	732-380-0900		390
World Intellectual Property Organization (WIPO) 2 UN Plz Ste 2525 . . . New York NY 10017 *Web:* www.wipo.int	212-963-6813	963-4801	783
World Internet Marketing Inc 151 Rte 10 E . . . Succasunna NJ 07876 *Web:* eworldwire.com	973-252-6800	252-0888	627
World Journal 2288 Clark Dr . . . Vancouver BC V5N3G8 *Web:* www.worldjournal.com	604-876-1338		532-1
World Kitchen LLC 1200 S Antrim Way . . . Greencastle PA 17225 *TF:* 800-999-3436 ■ *Web:* www.shopworldkitchen.com	800-999-3436		361
World Kite Museum & Hall of Fame 303 Sid Snyder Dr . . . Long Beach WA 98631 *Web:* kitefestival.com	360-642-4020		520
World Learning 1 Kipling Rd PO Box 676 . . . Brattleboro VT 05302 *TF:* 800-257-7751 ■ *Web:* www.worldlearning.org	802-257-7751	258-3248	48-5
World Literature Crusade 640 Chapel Hills Dr . . . Colorado Springs CO 80920 *TF:* 800-423-5054 ■ *Web:* www.ehc.org	719-260-8888		48-20
World Medicine Institute PO Box 11130 . . . Honolulu HI 96828 *Web:* worldmedicineinstitute.com	808-373-2849	373-4143	167-3
World Methodist Council PO Box 518 . . . Lake Junaluska NC 28745 *Web:* www.worldmethodistcouncil.org	828-456-9432		48-20
World Micro Components Inc 205 Hembree Park Dr Ste 105 . . . Roswell GA 30076 *TF:* 800-400-5026 ■ *Web:* www.worldmicro.com	770-698-1900		246
World Millwork Alliance 10047 Robert Trent Jones Pkwy . . . New Port Richey FL 34655 *Web:* worldmillworkalliance.com	727-372-3665	372-2879	49-3
World Monuments Fund (WMF) 350 Fifth Ave Ste 2412 . . . New York NY 10118 *Web:* www.wmf.org	646-424-9594	424-9593	48-4

	Phone	Fax	Class
World Museum of Mining 155 Museum Way PO Box 33 . . . Butte MT 59703 *Web:* www.miningmuseum.org	406-723-7211		520
World Music Press PO Box 26627 . . . Wauwatosa WI 53226 **Fax Area Code:* 414 ■ *TF:* 800-437-0832 ■ *Web:* www.worldmusicpress.com	262-790-5210	771-7672*	637-10
World Music Supply 2414 W Seventh St . . . Muncie IN 47302 *TF:* 800-867-4611 ■ *Web:* www.worldmusicsupply.com	765-213-6085		526
World Neighbors Inc (WN) 4127 NW 122nd St . . . Oklahoma City OK 73120 *TF:* 800-242-6387 ■ *Web:* www.wn.org	405-752-9700		48-5
World Nutrition Inc 9449 N 90th St Ste 116 . . . Scottsdale AZ 85258 *TF:* 800-548-2710 ■ *Web:* worldnutrition.net	800-548-2710		297-8
World of Learning Academy 4129 N Pine Island Rd . . . Sunrise FL 33351 *Web:* www.worldoflearningacademy.com	954-742-7189	742-7158	423
World of Reading Ltd PO Box 13092 . . . Atlanta GA 30324 *TF:* 800-729-3703 ■ *Web:* www.wor.com	404-233-4042	237-5511	178-1
World of Wigs 2305 E 17th St . . . Santa Ana CA 92705 *Web:* worldofwigs.com	714-547-4461		348
World Oil Co 9302 Garfield Ave . . . South Gate CA 90280 *Web:* worldoilcorp.com	562-928-0100		580
World Organization of China Painters Museum 2641 NW Tenth St . . . Oklahoma City OK 73107 *Web:* wocporg.com	405-521-1234	521-1265	520
World Peace Prayer Society 26 Benton Rd . . . Wassaic NY 12592 *Web:* www.worldpeace.org	845-877-6093	877-6862	48-5
World Poker Tour 5700 Wilshire Blvd . . . Los Angeles CA 90036 *Web:* www.worldpokertour.com	323-330-9900		31
World Policy Institute (WPI) 220 5th Ave 9th Fl . . . New York NY 10001 *TF:* 800-207-8354 ■ *Web:* worldpolicy.org	212-481-5005	481-5009	634
World Property Journal 1221 Brickell Ave Ste 900 . . . Miami FL 33131 *Web:* www.worldpropertyjournal.com	305-375-9292		530
World Quality Systems 2473 Anna Way . . . Elgin IL 60124 **Fax Area Code:* 650 ■ *TF:* 800-376-5709 ■ *Web:* www.worldqualitysystems.com	800-376-5709	966-6722*	194
World Racing Group 7575 D W Winds Blvd . . . Concord NC 28027 *Web:* www.worldracinggroup.com	704-795-7223	795-7229	642
World Recycling Co 5600 Columbia Park Rd . . . Cheverly MD 20785 *Web:* world-recycling.com	301-386-3010		179
World Relief 7 E Baltimore St . . . Baltimore MD 21202 *TF:* 800-535-5433 ■ *Web:* www.worldrelief.org	443-451-1900		48-5
World Resources Co 1600 Anderson Rd . . . McLean VA 22102 *Web:* www.worldresourcescompany.com	703-734-9800		490
World Resources Institute (WRI) 10 G St NE Ste 800 . . . Washington DC 20002 *Web:* www.wri.org	202-729-7600	729-7610	48-13
World School of Massage & Holistic Healing Arts 401 32nd Ave . . . San Francisco CA 94121 *Web:* www.worldschoolmassage.com	415-221-2533		685
World Services LLC 1954 Airport Rd Ste 201 . . . Chamblee GA 30341 *Web:* www.worldservicesusa.com	404-486-5986		317
World Spice Inc 223 E Highland Pkwy . . . Roselle NJ 07203 **Fax Area Code:* 908 ■ *TF:* 800-234-1060 ■ *Web:* worldspiceinc.com	800-234-1060	245-0696*	296-37
World Steel Dynamics Inc 456 Sylvan Ave . . . Englewood Cliffs NJ 07632 *Web:* www.worldsteeldynamics.com	201-503-0900		195
World Tower Company Inc 1213 Compressor Dr . . . Mayfield KY 42066 *TF:* 888-247-2580 ■ *Web:* www.worldtower.com	270-247-3642	247-0909	681
World Trade Center Association Los Angeles 444 S Flower St 37th Fl . . . Los Angeles CA 90071 *Web:* www.wtca.org	213-680-1888	622-7100	822
World Trade Center Baltimore 401 E Pratt St Ste 232 . . . Baltimore MD 21202 *Web:* www.wtci.org	410-576-0022	576-0751	822
World Trade Center Delaware 802 NW St . . . Wilmington DE 19801 *Web:* www.wtcde.com	302-656-7905		822
World Trade Center Denver 2650 E 40th Ave . . . Denver CO 80205 *Web:* wtcdenver.org	303-592-5760		822
World Trade Center Detroit/Windsor 1200 Sixth St . . . Detroit MI 48226 *Web:* www.wtcdw.com	313-962-2345		822
World Trade Center Miami 1007 N America Way Ste 500 . . . Miami FL 33132 *Web:* www.worldtrade.org	305-871-7910	871-7904	822
World Trade Center of New Orleans 365 Canal St Ste 1120 . . . New Orleans LA 70130 *Web:* www.wtcno.org	504-529-1601	529-1691	822
World Trade Center Orlando 19 E Central Ave . . . Orlando FL 32801 *Web:* www.worldtradecenterorlando.org	407-685-8096	876-6210	822
World Trade Center Palm Beach 500 Australian Ave S Ste 600 . . . West Palm Beach FL 33401 *Web:* www.wtcpalmbeach.com	561-969-2229	712-1445	822
World Trade Center Portland 121 SW Salmon St . . . Portland OR 97204 *Web:* wtcpdx.com	503-464-8688	464-2300	822
World Trade Center Saint Louis 7733 Forsyth Blvd Ste 2200 . . . Saint Louis MO 63105 *Web:* www.worldtradecenter-stl.com	314-615-8141	615-8140	822
World Trade Center Seattle 2200 Alaskan Way Ste 410 . . . Seattle WA 98121 *Web:* www.wtcseattle.com	206-441-5144	770-7923	822
World Trade Center Tacoma 950 Pacific Ave Ste 310 . . . Tacoma WA 98402 *Web:* wtcta.org	253-396-1022		822
World Trade Center Tampa Bay PO Box 18736 . . . Tampa FL 33679 *Web:* wtctampa.org	813-330-2931		822

Name / Address	Phone	Fax	Class
World Trade Ctr 101 W Main St Ste 180 . . . . Norfolk VA 23510 *Web:* www.downtownnorfolk.org	757-627-9440		822
World Trade Distribution Inc 2222 N Wayside Dr . . . . Houston TX 77020 *TF:* 800-275-0221 ■ *Web:* www.wtcfs.com	713-672-7295	672-4423	311
World Trade Service Inc 1050 Nine N Dr Ste A . . . . Alpharetta GA 30004 *Web:* www.worldtradeservice.com	770-521-0124		791
World Travel Bureau Inc 618 N Main St . . . . Santa Ana CA 92701 *TF:* 800-759-1379 ■ *Web:* wtbinc.com	714-835-8111	835-8124	771
World Travel Holdings (WTH) 100 Fordham Rd Bldg C . . . . Wilmington MA 01887 *TF:* 877-958-7447 ■ *Web:* www.worldtravelholdings.com	617-424-7990	424-1943	771
World Travel Inc 620 Pennsylvania Dr . . . . Exton PA 19341 *Web:* www.worldtravelinc.com	610-458-5554		771
World Travel Services LLC 7645 E 63rd St Ste 101 . . . . Tulsa OK 74133 *TF:* 800-324-4987 ■ *Web:* www.worldtraveltoday.com	918-743-8856		772
World Video Sales Company Inc 625 Hoffmansville Rd Ste 4 . . . . Bechtelsville PA 19505 *Web:* www.mivs.com	610-754-6800	754-9766	476
World Vision Inc 34834 Weyerhaeuser Way S PO Box 9716 . . . . . Federal Way WA 98001 *TF:* 888-511-6548 ■ *Web:* www.worldvision.org	800-777-5777		48-5
World War II Memorial State Park c/o Lincoln Woods State Pk 2 Manchester Print Works Rd . . . . Lincoln RI 02865 *Web:* www.riparks.com	401-762-9717		565
World Wide Arts Resources Corp (WWAR) PO Box 150 . . . . Granville OH 43023 *Web:* www.wwar.com	646-455-1425		637-10
World Wide Concessions Inc 1950 Old Cuthbert Rd Ste M . . . . Cherry Hill NJ 08034 *TF:* 888-377-7666 ■ *Web:* www.wwconcessions.com	856-933-9900		701
World Wide Fittings Inc 7501 N Natchez Ave . . . . Niles IL 60714 *TF:* 800-393-9894 ■ *Web:* www.worldwidefittings.com	847-588-2200	588-2212	595
World Wide Group LLC 5507 Nesconset Hwy Ste 10 . . . . Mount Sinai NY 11766 *TF:* 800-790-4519 ■ *Web:* www.worldwidegrouptravel.com	800-790-4519		148
World Wide Motors Inc 3900 E 96th St . . . . Indianapolis IN 46240 *Web:* www.mercedesofindy.com	317-580-6800		516
World Wide Web Consortium 32 Vassar St Rm 32-386 . . . . Cambridge MA 02139 *Web:* www.w3.org	617-253-2613	258-5999	48-9
World Wildlife Fund (WWF) 1250 24th St NW PO Box 97180 . . . . Washington DC 20090 *TF:* 800-225-5993 ■ *Web:* www.worldwildlife.org	202-293-4800	293-9211	48-3
World Wildlife Fund Canada (WWF) 410 Adelaide St W Ste 400 . . . . Toronto ON M5V1S8 *TF:* 800-267-2632 ■ *Web:* www.wwf.ca	416-489-8800	489-8055	48-3
World Wisdom Books (WW) PO Box 2682 . . . Bloomington IN 47402 *TF:* 888-992-6651 ■ *Web:* www.worldwisdom.com	812-330-3232		637-2
World Wrapps 3125 Mission College Blvd Ste 200 . . . . Santa Clara CA 95054 **Fax Area Code:* 408 ■ *Web:* worldwrapps.com	206-233-9727	486-9774*	670
World Wrestling Entertainment Inc 1241 E Main St . . . . Stamford CT 06902 *NYSE:* WWE ■ *Web:* www.wwe.com	203-352-8600	359-5151	181
World's Best 1801 W Waco Dr . . . . Waco TX 76707 **Fax Area Code:* 257 ■ *TF:* 800-437-0940 ■ *Web:* www.wolfmfg.com	254-753-7301	753-8919*	155-3
World's Finest Chocolate Inc 4801 S Lawndale . . . . Chicago IL 60632 **Fax Area Code:* 877 ■ *TF:* 888-821-8452 ■ *Web:* www.worldsfinestchocolate.com	888-821-8452	256-2685*	296-8
World, The 403 US Rt 302-Berlin . . . . Barre VT 05641 *TF:* 800-639-9753 ■ *Web:* www.vt-world.com	802-479-2582		632-1
World, The 1551 Sawgrass Corporate Pkwy Ste 200 . . . Fort Lauderdale FL 33323 *Web:* aboardtheworld.com	954-538-8449	431-7151	220
WorldAPP Inc 220 Forbes Rd . . . . Braintree MA 02184 *Web:* www.worldapp.com	781-849-8118		174
Worldata 3000 N Military Trl . . . . Boca Raton FL 33431 *TF:* 800-331-8102 ■ *Web:* www.worldata.com	561-393-8200	368-8345	6
WorldatWork 14040 N Northsight Blvd . . . . Scottsdale AZ 85260 **Fax Area Code:* 202 ■ *TF:* 877-951-9191 ■ *Web:* www.worldatwork.org	877-951-9191	315-5550*	49-12
WorldClass Travel Network 7831 Southtown Ctr Ste A . . . . Bloomington MN 55431 *TF:* 800-234-3576 ■ *Web:* www.worldclassnetwork.net	952-835-8636	835-2340	772
WorldCom Consulting PO Box 2066 . . . . Murphys CA 95247 *Web:* www.worldcomconsulting.com	209-728-0246	728-3479	180
Worldcom Exchange Inc 43 NW Dr . . . . Salem NH 03079 *Web:* www.wei.com	603-893-0900		180
Worldfest Houston International Film Festival PO Box 40965 . . . . Houston TX 77240 *Web:* www.houstontheatre.com	713-629-3700		282
WorldFlash Software Inc 3853 Marcasel Ave . . . . Los Angeles CA 90066 *Web:* www.worldflash.com	310-775-3633		178-7
Worldlink Integration Group Inc 21076 Bake Pkwy Ste 106 . . . . Lake Forest CA 92630 *TF:* 888-540-0753 ■ *Web:* worldlinkintegration.com	949-861-2830		179
Worldly Voices PO Box 218435 . . . . Nashville TN 37221 *TF:* 800-286-4237 ■ *Web:* www.worldlyvoices.com	615-321-8802		657
WorldMark the Club 9805 Willows Rd . . . . Redmond WA 98052 *TF:* 800-565-0370 ■ *Web:* www.worldmarktheclub.com	800-565-0370		753
WORLDPAC Inc 37137 Hickory St . . . . Newark CA 94560 *TF:* 800-888-9982 ■ *Web:* www.worldpac.com	800-888-9982		61
WorldPantrycom Inc 790 Tennessee St . . . . San Francisco CA 94107 *TF:* 866-972-6879 ■ *Web:* www.worldpantry.com	866-972-6879		393
Worldpoint Ecc Inc 1326 S Wolf Rd . . . . Wheeling IL 60090 *TF:* 888-322-8350 ■ *Web:* worldpoint.com	888-322-8350		96
WorldPost Technologies Inc 5886 De Zavala Rd Ste 102/535 . . . . San Antonio TX 78249 *Web:* www.worldpost.com	210-212-5600	212-5800	808
Worlds End State Park 82 Cabin Bridge Rd . . . . Forksville PA 18616 *Web:* www.dcnr.pa.gov	570-924-3287		565
Worlds of Fun & Oceans of Fun 4545 NE Worlds of Fun Dr . . . . Kansas City MO 64161 *TF:* 800-434-7894 ■ *Web:* www.worldsoffun.com	816-454-4545	454-4655	32
Worldscom Inc 11 Royal Rd . . . . Brookline MA 02445 *TF:* 800-315-2580 ■ *Web:* www.worlds.com	617-725-8900	975-3888	178-8
WorldStrides Inc 218 W Water St Ste 400 . . . . Charlottesville VA 22902 *TF:* 800-999-7676 ■ *Web:* worldstrides.com	800-999-7676		760
Worldtech International LLC 2331 Mill Rd Ste 100 . . . . Alexandria VA 22314 *Web:* worldtech-int.com	703-778-5444		194
WorldTEK Event & Travel Management 100 Beard Sawmill Rd Ste 601 . . . . Shelton CT 06484 *TF:* 800-233-5989 ■ *Web:* www.worldtek.com	203-772-0470	865-2034	772
WorldVenture 1501 W Mineral Ave . . . . Littleton CO 80120 *Web:* www.worldventure.com	720-283-2000		48-20
Worldview Travel 2677 N Main St Ste 550 . . . . Santa Ana CA 92701 *TF:* 800-627-8726 ■ *Web:* www.worldviewtravel.com	714-540-7400	979-6040	772
WorldViz LLC 614 Santa Barbara St . . . . Santa Barbara CA 93101 *TF:* 888-841-3416 ■ *Web:* www.worldviz.com	805-966-0786		246
Worldwide Aeros Corp 1734 Gage Rd . . . . Montebello CA 90640 **Fax Area Code:* 323 ■ *Web:* aeroscraft.com	818-344-3999	201-8383*	28
Worldwide Court Reporters 3000 Weslayan St Ste 235 . . . . Houston TX 77027 *TF:* 800-745-1101 ■ *Web:* www.worldwidecourtreporters.com	800-745-1101		393
Worldwide Dispensers USA 78 Second Ave S . . . . Lester Prairie MN 55354 *Web:* www.dssmith.com	320-395-2553		608
Worldwide Employee Benefits Network Inc (WEB) 11520 N Central Expy Ste 201 . . . . Dallas TX 75243 **Fax Area Code:* 214 ■ *TF:* 888-795-6862 ■ *Web:* www.webnetwork.org	888-795-6862	382-3038*	49-12
Worldwide Energy & Manufacturing USA Inc 1675 Rollins Rd Unit F . . . . Burlingame CA 94010 *OTC:* WEMU ■ *Web:* wwmusa.com	650-794-9888	794-9878	787
Worldwide Environmental Products Inc (WEP) 1100 W Beacon St . . . . Brea CA 92821 *TF:* 800-832-7664 ■ *Web:* www.wep-inc.com	714-990-2700	990-3100	201
Worldwide Express 2323 Victory Ave Ste 1600 . . . . Dallas TX 75219 **Fax Area Code:* 214 ■ *TF:* 800-758-7447 ■ *Web:* home.wwex.com	800-758-7447	720-2446*	546
Worldwide Express 10748 Sky Prairie St . . . . Fishers IN 46038 *Web:* wwexindy.com	317-585-1400		311
Worldwide Golf Shops 1421 Village Way . . . . Santa Ana CA 92705 *TF:* 888-216-5252 ■ *Web:* www.worldwidegolfshops.com	714-972-3695	972-3675	710
Worldwide Oil Field Machine 11809 Canemont . . . . Houston TX 77035 *Web:* womgroup.com	713-729-9200	729-7321	537
Worldwide Partners Inc 100 Spruce St Ste 203 . . . . Denver CO 80230 *Web:* www.worldwidepartners.com	303-577-9763		7
Worldwide Revenue Solutions Inc 555 Republic Dr . . . . Plano TX 75074	972-424-2200		225
Worldwide Sign Systems 446 N Cecil St . . . . Bonduel WI 54107 *TF:* 800-874-3334 ■ *Web:* www.wwsign.com	800-874-3334		701
Worldwide Steel Buildings PO Box 588 . . . . Peculiar MO 64078 *TF:* 800-825-0316 ■ *Web:* www.worldwidesteelbuildings.com	800-825-0316		105
Worldwide Travel & Cruise Associates Inc 150 S University Dr Ste E . . . . Plantation FL 33324 *Web:* www.cruiseco.com	954-452-8800	446-9008	771
Worly Plumbing Supply Inc 54 E Harrison St . . . . Delaware OH 43015 *TF:* 800-866-4722 ■ *Web:* worly.com	740-363-1151	773-3014	610
Wormser Corp 150 Coolidge Ave . . . . Englewood NJ 07631 *TF:* 800-546-4040 ■ *Web:* www.wormsercorp.com	800-666-9676		155-15
Wormsloe State Historic Site 7601 Skidaway Rd . . . . Savannah GA 31406 *Web:* gastateparks.org	912-353-3023		565
Woronoff Hyman Levenson & Sweet PC 30600 Northwestern Hwy Ste 302 . . . . Farmington Hills MI 48334 *Web:* whls.com	248-487-2600		2
Worrell Corp 305 S Post Rd . . . . Indianapolis IN 46219 *TF:* 800-297-9599 ■ *Web:* www.worrellcorp.com	800-297-9599		292
Worsham College of Mortuary Science 495 Northgate Pkwy . . . . Wheeling IL 60090 *Web:* www.worsham.edu	847-808-8444	808-8493	800
Worship Center Christian Church, The 100 Derby Pkwy . . . . Birmingham AL 35210 *Web:* theworshipcentercc.org	205-451-1750	833-5443	48-20
Worship Network PO Box 428 . . . . Safety Harbor FL 34695 *TF:* 800-728-8723 ■ *Web:* www.worship.net	800-728-8723		740
Worswick Mold & Tool Inc 6232 King . . . . Marine City MI 48039 *Web:* www.worswickmold.com	810-765-1700	765-1701	604
Wort Hotel 50 N Glenwood . . . . Jackson WY 83001 *TF:* 800-322-2727 ■ *Web:* www.worthotel.com	307-733-2190	733-2067	379
Worth & Company Inc 6263 Kellers Church Rd . . . . Pipersville PA 18947 *TF:* 800-220-5130 ■ *Web:* www.worthandcompany.com	267-362-1100	362-1130	189-10
Worth Co, The 214 Sherman Ave PO Box 88 . . . . Stevens Point WI 54481 *TF:* 800-944-1899 ■ *Web:* worthco.com	715-344-6081	344-3021	710
Worth Construction Company Inc 24 Taylor Ave . . . . Bethel CT 06801 *Web:* worthconstruction.com	203-797-8788	791-2515	186
Worth County PO Box 450 . . . . Grant City MO 64456 *Web:* worthcounty.us	660-564-2219	564-2432	338
Worth County 1000 Central Ave . . . . Northwood IA 50459 *Web:* www.worthcounty.org	641-324-2840	324-2360	338
Worth County 201 N Main Stt Rm 21 . . . . Sylvester GA 31791 *Web:* www.worthcountyboc.com	229-776-8200	776-1540	338

Phone | Fax | Class

Worth Financial Service
3201 E Center St. Warsaw IN 46582 574-269-2121 269-4321 734
TF: 888-483-7350 ■ *Web:* www.worthfinancial.com

Worth Higgins & Associates Inc
8770 Park Central Dr Richmond VA 23227 804-264-2304 174
TF: 800-883-7768 ■ *Web:* worthhiggins.com

Worth, Magee & Fisher PC
2610 Walbert Ave Allentown PA 18104 610-437-4896 41
Web: worthlawoffices.com

Worthe, Hanson & Worthe, A Law Corp
1851 E First St 9th Fl Santa Ana CA 92705 714-285-9600 41
Web: whwlawcorp.com

Worthen Industries Inc
3 E Spit Brook Rd Nashua NH 03060 603-888-5443 888-7945 3
TF: 888-840-6155 ■ *Web:* www.worthenind.com

Worthington Area Chamber of Commerce
25 W New England Ave Ste 100 Worthington OH 43085 614-450-6000 841-4842 139
Web: www.worthingtonchamber.org

Worthington Aviation Parts Inc
2995 Lone Oak Cir Saint Paul MN 55121 651-994-1600 994-0500 770
Web: www.worthingtonav.com

Worthington Biochemical Corp
730 Vassar Ave Lakewood NJ 08701 732-942-1660 942-9270 231
TF: 800-445-9603 ■ *Web:* www.worthington-biochem.com

Worthington Direct Holdings LLC
6301 Gaston Ave Ste 670 Dallas TX 75214 800-599-6636 360-3
TF: 800-599-6636 ■ *Web:* www.worthingtondirect.com

Worthington Farms Inc
3661 Ballards Crossroads Rd Greenville NC 27834 252-756-3827 756-9442 369
Web: www.worthingtonfarms.com

Worthington Industries
200 Old Wilson Bridge Rd Columbus OH 43085 614-840-4663 485
NYSE: WOR ■ *TF:* 800-944-2255 ■ *Web:* www.worthingtonindustries.com

Worthington Jewelers 692 High St Worthington OH 43085 614-430-8800 410
Web: www.worthingtonjewelers.com

Worthington State Forest
HC 62 PO Box 2 Columbia NJ 07832 908-841-9575 565
Web: www.njparksandforests.org

Worthwhile
330 East Coffee St Ste 200 Greenville SC 29601 864-233-2552 177
Web: worthwhile.com

Worthwhile Referral Sources
13547 Ventura Blvd No 374 Sherman Oaks CA 91423 818-995-6646 393
Web: www.referral-guide.com

Worthy Brewing LLC 495 NE Bellevue Dr Bend OR 97701 541-639-4776 102
Web: worthy.beer

Wor-Wic Community College
32000 Campus Dr Salisbury MD 21804 410-334-2800 334-2954 162
Web: www.worwic.edu

Worx Group LLC, The 18 Waterbury Rd Prospect CT 06712 203-758-3311 180
TF: 800-732-8090 ■ *Web:* www.worxbranding.com

Worzalla Publishing Co
3535 Jefferson St Stevens Point WI 54481 715-344-9600 626
Web: worzalla.site

Worzella & Sons Inc 2801 Hoover Ave. Plover WI 54467 715-344-4098 10-11
Web: worzellaandsons.com

WOS Testing Inc 851A Hillside Trl. Hudson WI 54016 715-829-6504 377-9999 743
Web: www.wostesting.com

Wostmann & Associates Inc
105 S Seward St Ste 301 Juneau AK 99801 907-586-6167 196
Web: www.wostmann.com

WOSU Public Media
2400 Olentangy River Rd Columbus OH 43210 614-292-9678 647
Web: www.wosu.org

WOUC-TV Ch 44 (PBS) 35 S College St Athens OH 45701 740-593-1771 741
TF: 800-456-2044 ■ *Web:* woub.org

Woulfe Mining Corp
837 W Hastings St Ste 202 Vancouver BC V6C3N6 604-684-6264 684-6242 502

Wound Ostomy & Continence Nurses Society (WOCN)
1120 Rte 73 Ste 200 Mount Laurel NJ 08054 888-224-9626 49-8
TF: 888-224-9626 ■ *Web:* www.wocn.org

WOUR-FM 39 Kellogg Rd New Hartford NY 13413 315-797-9690 738-1073 647
Web: www.wour.com

WOW (Wider Opportunities for Women)
1001 Connecticut Ave NW Ste 930 Washington DC 20036 202-464-1596 464-1660 48-24
Web: iwpr.org

WOW FM County 104.3
827 E Pk Blvd Ste 100 Boise ID 83712 208-344-6363 645-21
Web: 1043wowcountry.com

WOWindow Posters PO Box 581 Cranford NJ 07016 908-272-1011 361
Web: wowindows.com

WOWK-TV Ch 13 (CBS) 555 Fifth Ave Huntington WV 25701 304-781-6000 741
Web: www.wowktv.com

WOWL-TV 200 Andrew Jackson Way Huntsville AL 35801 256-536-1550 647
Web: www.lbgtelevision.com

WOWO-AM 1190 (N/T) 2915 Maples Rd Fort Wayne IN 46816 260-447-5511 447-7546 645-60
TF: 800-333-1190 ■ *Web:* www.wowo.com

WOWT-TV Ch 6 (NBC) 3501 Farnam St Omaha NE 68131 402-346-6666 233-7887 741-94
Web: www.wowt.com

Wowza
2601 Second Ave S Studio One Minneapolis MN 55408 612-382-1306 7
Web: www.wowzamade.com

WOXF-FM PO Box 1077 Oxford MS 38655 662-236-0093 647
Web: www.theq105.com

Wozniak Industries Inc
2 Mid America Plz Ste 700 Oakbrook Terrace IL 60181 630-954-3400 954-3605 483
Web: www.wozniakindustries.com

Wozniak Industries Inc
Commercial Forged Products Div
5757 W 65th St Bedford Park IL 60638 708-458-1220 458-9346 483
TF: 800-637-2695 ■ *Web:* www.commercialforged.com

WP (Walton Press) 402 Mayfield Dr Monroe GA 30655 800-354-0235 555
TF: 800-354-0235 ■ *Web:* www.waltonpress.com

WP (Whittier Publications Inc)
3115 Long Beach Rd Oceanside NY 11572 516-432-8120 889-0341 637-2
TF: 800-897-8398 ■ *Web:* www.whitbooks.com

WP (Washington Press) 2 Vreeland Rd Florham Park NJ 07932 877-966-0001 966-0888* 637-2
**Fax Area Code: 973* ■ *TF:* 877-966-0001 ■ *Web:* www.washpress.com

WP Carey & Company LLC
50 Rockefeller Plz New York NY 10020 212-492-1100 655
NYSE: WPC ■ *TF:* 800-972-2739 ■ *Web:* www.wpcarey.com

WPA (Whole Person Associates Inc)
101 W 2nd St Ste 203 Duluth MN 55802 218-727-0500 727-0505 637-2
TF: 800-247-6789 ■ *Web:* www.wholeperson.com

WPAP-FM 1834 Lisenby Ave Panama City FL 32405 850-769-1408 647
TF: 866-925-9727 ■ *Web:* www.925wpap.iheart.com

WPAX-AM
117 Remington Ave PO Box 129 Thomasville GA 31792 229-226-1240 226-1361 647
Web: www.wpaxradio.com

WPBA-TV Ch 30 (PBS) 740 Bismark Rd NE Atlanta GA 30324 678-686-0321 741-7
Web: www.pba.org

WPBF-TV Ch 25 (ABC)
3970 RCA Blvd Ste 7007 Palm Beach Gardens FL 33410 561-694-2525 741
Web: www.wpbf.com

WPBK-FM 201-A E Main St Stanford KY 40484 606-365-2126 647

WPBT-TV Ch 2 (PBS) 14901 NE 20th Ave Miami FL 33181 305-949-8321 944-4211 741-82
TF: 800-222-9728 ■ *Web:* www.wpbt2.org

WPC (Williwaw Publishing Co) PO Box 309 Haines AK 99827 907-766-2599 637-2
TF: 800-490-4950 ■ *Web:* www.williwaw.com

WPDE-TV 1194 Atlantic Ave Conway SC 29526 843-234-9733 647
Web: www.wpde.com

WPEC-TV 1100 Fairfield Dr West Palm Beach FL 33407 561-844-1212 647
Web: www.cbs12.com

WPFO-TV c/o Fox 23 81 Northport Dr Portland ME 04103 207-797-1313 878-7482 647
Web: www.fox23maine.com

WPGC-FM 95.5
1015 Half St SE Ste 200 Washington DC 20003 877-955-5267 645
TF: 877-955-5267 ■ *Web:* wpgc.radio.com

WPGH-TV Ch 53 (Fox) 750 Ivory Ave Pittsburgh PA 15214 412-931-5300 741-100
Web: www.wpgh53.com

WPGP-AM 7 Parkway Ctr Ste 625 Pittsburgh PA 15220 412-937-1500 647
Web: theanswerpgh.com

WPGS (Western Pennsylvania Genealogical Society)
4400 Forbes Ave. Pittsburgh PA 15213 412-687-6811 49-19
Web: wpgs.org

WPGS-AM 805 N Dixie Ave. Titusville FL 32796 321-383-1000 647
Web: www.local840.com

WPGU-FM 107.1 1001 S Wright St Champaign IL 61820 217-337-1071 645-29
Web: wpgu.com

WPGW Inc 1891 W State Rd 67 Portland IN 47371 260-726-8780 726-4311 647
Web: www.wpgwradio.com

WPH (Wesleyan Publishing House)
13300 Olio Rd Fishers IN 46037 317-774-7900 637-2
TF: 800-493-7539 ■ *Web:* www.wesleyan.org

WPHL-TV Ch 17 (MNT)
5001 Wynnefield Ave Philadelphia PA 19131 215-878-1700 741-98
Web: phl17.com

WPI (Waukesha-Pearce Industries Inc)
12320 S Main St. Houston TX 77035 713-723-1050 385
Web: www.wpi.com

WPI (Williamston Products Inc)
845 Progress Ct Williamston MI 48895 517-655-2131 608
Web: www.wpius.com

WPI (World Policy Institute)
220 5th Ave 9th Fl New York NY 10001 212-481-5005 481-5009 634
TF: 800-207-8354 ■ *Web:* worldpolicy.org

WPIG-FM 3163 NYS Rte 417 Olean NY 14760 716-372-0161 372-0164 647
TF: 800-877-9749 ■ *Web:* wpig.com

WPJL-AM 515 Bart St PO Box 27946 Raleigh NC 27611 919-834-6401 647
Web: www.wpjlradio.com

WPJM-AM 305 N Tryon St Greer SC 29651 864-877-1112 877-0342 647
Web: www.800wpjm.com

WPKN Inc 244 University Ave Bridgeport CT 06604 203-331-9756 645-154
Web: www.wpkn.org

WPKT-FM 90.5 (NPR) 1049 Asylum Ave Hartford CT 06105 860-278-5310 645-69
Web: wnpr.org

WPL (Warwick Public Library)
600 Sandy Ln Warwick RI 02889 401-739-5440 434-3
Web: warwicklibrary.org

WPLD (Wilmington Public Library District)
201 S Kankakee St Wilmington IL 60481 815-476-2834 476-7805 434-3
Web: www.wilmingtonlibrary.org

WPLG-TV Ch 10 (ABC)
3401 W Hallandale Beach Blvd Pembroke Park FL 33023 954-364-2526 741
Web: www.local10.com

WPLM-FM 99.1 17 Columbus Rd Plymouth MA 02360 508-746-1390 830-1128 645
TF: 877-327-9991 ■ *Web:* www.easy991.com

WPLN-FM 90.3 (NPR)
630 Mainstream Dr Nashville TN 37228 615-760-2903 760-2904 645-106
TF: 877-760-2903 ■ *Web:* nashvillepublicradio.org

WPMA (Wood Products Manufacturers Assn)
PO Box 761 Westminster MA 01473 978-874-5445 874-9946 49-3
Web: www.wpma.org

WPME-TV 4 Ledgeview Dr Westbrook ME 04092 207-774-0051 647
Web: www.ourmaine.com

WPMI-TV Ch 15 (NBC) 661 Azalea Rd Mobile AL 36609 251-602-6799 602-1547 741-85
Web: mynbc15.com

WPMT-TV Ch 43 (Fox) 2005 S Queen St York PA 17403 717-843-0043 741
Web: www.fox43.com

WPMZ-AM
1270 Mineral Spring Ave North Providence RI 02904 401-726-2200 647
Web: www.poder1110.com

WPNN-AM 790 3801 N Pace Blvd Pensacola FL 32505 850-433-1141 645-118
Web: www.talk103fm.com

WPOC-FM 93.1 (Country)
711 W 40th St Ste 350 Baltimore MD 21211 410-366-7600 645-15
Web: wpoc.iheart.com

WPP Group USA Inc 100 Park Ave New York NY 10017 212-632-2200 632-2249 4
Web: www.wpp.com

WPRI 12 25 Catamore Blvd East Providence RI 02914 401-438-7200 741
Web: www.wpri.com

WPS (Washington Professional Systems)
109 Gaither Dr Ste 301 Mount Laurel NJ 08054 856-273-8688 273-8558 52
Web: www.washprosys.com

WPS Health Plan Inc 1717 W Broadway Madison WI 53708 608-221-4711 391-3
TF: 888-915-4001 ■ *Web:* www.wpsic.com

	Phone	Fax	Class
WPS Industries Inc 228 Industrial St .... West Monroe LA 71292 *Web:* wpsindustries.com	318-812-2800	812-2810	207
WPSO-AM 109 Bayview Blvd Ste A .... Oldsmar FL 34677 *Web:* www.wpso.com	727-725-5555		647
WPTV-TV Ch 5 (NBC) 1100 Banyan Blvd .... West Palm Beach FL 33401 *TF:* 800-345-9788 ■ *Web:* www.wptv.com	561-655-5455	653-5719	741-140
WPTZ-TV Ch 5 (NBC) 5 Television Dr .... Plattsburgh NY 12901 *Web:* www.mynbc5.com	518-561-5555	563-5452	741
WPVI-TV Ch 6 (ABC) 4100 City Line Ave .... Philadelphia PA 19131 *TF:* 866-639-7749 ■ *Web:* www.6abc.com	215-878-9700	581-4530	741-98
WPWX-FM 92.3 (Urban) 6336 Calumet Ave .... Hammond IN 46324 *Web:* www.power92chicago.com	773-734-4455		645
WPX Delivery Solutions 3320 W Valley Hwy N Ste 111 .... Auburn WA 98001 *TF:* 800-562-1091 ■ *Web:* www.wpx.com	253-876-2760	876-2799	546
WPXI-TV Ch 11 (NBC) 4145 Evergreen Rd .... Pittsburgh PA 15214 *Web:* www.wpxi.com	412-237-1100		741-100
WPXY-FM 97.9 (CHR) 70 Commercial St .... Rochester NY 14614 *Web:* 98pxy.radio.com	585-423-2900		645-135
WQA (Water Quality Assn) 4151 Naperville Rd .... Lisle IL 60532 *Web:* www.wqa.org	630-505-0160	505-9637	48-12
WQAD-TV 3003 Park 16th St .... Moline IL 61265 *Web:* www.wqad.com	309-764-8888		647
WQBE-FM 97.5 (Ctry) 817 Suncrest Pl .... Charleston WV 25303 *TF:* 800-222-3697 ■ *Web:* www.wqbe.com	304-344-9700	342-3118	645-31
WQDR-FM 94.7 (Ctry) 3012 Highwoods Blvd Ste 201 .... Raleigh NC 27604 *Web:* www.947qdr.com	919-876-6464	790-8893	645-128
WQED Multimedia 4802 Fifth Ave .... Pittsburgh PA 15213 *TF:* 855-700-9733 ■ *Web:* www.wqed.org	412-622-1300		741-100
WQHH-FM 96.5 (Urban) 600 W Cavanaugh .... Lansing MI 48910 *Web:* www.power965fm.com	517-882-0965	393-0882	645-84
WQHT-FM 97.1 (Urban) 395 Hudson St 7th Fl .... New York NY 10014 *TF:* 800-223-9797 ■ *Web:* www.hot97.com	212-229-9797	929-8559	645-108
WQKX-FM PO Box 1070 .... Sunbury PA 17801 *TF:* 800-326-9459 ■ *Web:* www.wqkx.net	570-286-5838	743-7837	647
WQLH-FM 98.5 (AC) 810 Victoria St .... Green Bay WI 54302 *Web:* www.star98.net	920-468-4100	468-0250	645-64
WQLK-FM 2626 Tingler Rd .... Richmond IN 47374 *Web:* www.kicks96.com	765-962-1595	966-4824	647
WQLT-FM 624 Sam Phillips St .... Florence AL 35630 *Web:* www.wqlt.com	256-764-8121	764-8169	647
WQMX-FM 94.9 1795 W Market St .... Akron OH 44313 *Web:* www.wqmx.com	330-869-9800		645-2
WQNR-FM 2514 S College St Ste 104 .... Auburn AL 36832 *Web:* www.katefm.com	334-887-9999	826-9599	647
WQNU-FM Q103.1 (Ctry) 612 S Fourth St .... Louisville KY 40202 *Web:* www.qlouisville.com	502-589-4800		645-89
WQOW-TV 5545 Hwy 93 .... Eau Claire WI 54701 *TF:* 800-594-6721 ■ *Web:* www.wqow.com	715-835-1881		647
WQQB-FM 2702 Boulder Dr .... Urbana IL 61802 *Web:* publicfiles.fcc.gov	217-328-9600	367-3291	647
WQSE-AM 319 Vann Dr Ste E 32 .... Jackson TN 38305 *Web:* www.gracebroadcasting.com	731-663-2327	663-2427	647
WQWK-FM 2551 Park Center Blvd .... State College PA 16801 *Web:* www.1450espnradio.com	814-237-9800	237-2477	647
WR (Western Recorder) 13420 Eastpoint Center Dr .... Louisville KY 40223 *TF:* 866-489-3535 ■ *Web:* www.westernrecorder.org	502-489-3443	489-3565	532-2
WR (Swish White River Ltd) 1118 Rte 14 .... Hartford VT 05047 *TF:* 800-639-7226 ■ *Web:* sfwhiteriverpaper.ubsynergy.net	802-295-3188	295-5494	559
WR Berkley Corp 475 Steamboat Rd .... Greenwich CT 06830 *NYSE: WRB* ■ *TF:* 800-238-6225 ■ *Web:* www.berkley.com	203-629-3000		360-4
WR Case & Sons Cutlery Co 50 Owens Way PO Box 4000 .... Bradford PA 16701 **Fax Area Code: 814* ■ *TF:* 800-523-6350 ■ *Web:* caseknives.com	800-523-6350	368-1736*	222
WR Grace & Co 7500 Grace Dr .... Columbia MD 21044 *NYSE: GRA* ■ *TF:* 800-638-6014 ■ *Web:* www.grace.com	410-531-4000	531-4367	145
WR Hambrecht & Co 909 Montgomery St 3rd Fl .... San Francisco CA 94133 *TF:* 855-753-6484 ■ *Web:* wrhambrecht.com	415-551-8600		690
WR Medical Electronics Co 1700 Gervais Ave .... Maplewood MN 55109 *TF:* 800-635-1312 ■ *Web:* www.wrmed.com	651-604-8400	604-8499	250
WR Rayson Company Inc 720 S Dickerson St .... Burgaw NC 28425 *Web:* www.wrrayson.com	910-259-8100		557
WR Zanes & Company of Louisiana Inc 223 Tchoupitoulas St .... New Orleans LA 70130 *Web:* www.wrzanes.com	504-524-1301	524-1309	311
WRA Inc 2169 Francisco Blvd E Ste G .... San Rafael CA 94901 *Web:* wra-ca.com	415-454-8868	454-0129	401
Wraith, Scarlett & Randolph Inc 509 Bush St .... Woodland CA 95695 *Web:* wsrins.com	530-662-9181		390
WRAK-AM 1559 W Fourth St .... Williamsport PA 17701 *Web:* www.wrak.iheart.com	570-327-1400	327-8156	647
WRAL-TV Ch 5 (CBS) 2619 Western Blvd .... Raleigh NC 27606 *Web:* www.wral.com	919-821-8555		741-105
Wrangell Harbor PO Box 531 .... Wrangell AK 99929 *TF:* 800-347-4462 ■ *Web:* www.wrangell.com	907-874-3736	874-3197	618
Wrangell-Saint Elias National Park & Preserve Mile 1068 Richardson Hwy PO Box 439 .... Copper Center AK 99573 *Web:* www.nps.gov	907-822-5234	822-7216	564
Wrapmail Inc 960 S Broadway Ste 120 .... Hicksville NY 11801 *Web:* www.wrapmail.com	516-590-1846	977-0025	535
Wrap-On Company LLC 11756 S Austin Ave .... Alsip IL 60803 *TF:* 800-621-6947 ■ *Web:* wrap-on.com	708-496-2150	496-2154	813

	Phone	Fax	Class
WRAS *Georgia State University* 33 Gilmer St SE .... Atlanta GA 30303 *Web:* www.gsu.edu	404-413-2000		645-11
Wray Ford Inc 2851 Benton Rd .... Bossier City LA 71111 *TF:* 888-663-0821 ■ *Web:* www.wrayford.net	888-663-0821		57
Wray Ward Marketing Communications 900 Baxter St .... Charlotte NC 28204 *Web:* www.wrayward.com	704-332-9071		7
WRB Enterprises 1414 W Swann Ave Ste 201 .... Tampa FL 33606 *Web:* wrbenterprises.com	813-251-3737		360-3
Wrb-lp LLP 801 N Pitt St Ste 123 .... Alexandria VA 22314	703-299-0953		41
WRBL-TV Ch 3 (CBS) 1350 13th Ave .... Columbus GA 31901 *Web:* www.wrbl.com	706-323-3333	327-6655	741-34
WRBS-FM 95.1 (Rel) 3500 Commerce Dr .... Baltimore MD 21227 *TF:* 800-965-9324 ■ *Web:* www.951shinefm.com	410-247-4100	247-4533	645-15
WRC (Women's Resource Ctr) MSC 06 3910 Mesa Vista Hall 1160 .... Albuquerque NM 87131 *Web:* women.unm.edu	505-277-3716	277-2913	434-3
WRCB TV 900 Whitehall Rd .... Chattanooga TN 37405 *Web:* www.wrcbtv.com	423-267-5412		741-27
WRCH-FM 100.5 (AC) 10 Executive Dr .... Farmington CT 06032 *Web:* wrch.radio.com	860-677-6700		645
WRCTC (West River Co-operative Telephone Co) 801 Coleman Ave PO Box 39 .... Bison SD 57620 *Web:* www.sdplains.com	605-244-5213		736
WRC-TV Ch 4 (NBC) 4001 Nebraska Ave NW .... Washington DC 20016 *Web:* www.nbcwashington.com	202-885-4000		741-139
WRDQ-TV 490 E South St .... Orlando FL 32801 *Web:* www.wftv.com	407-841-9000		647
WRDU-FM 3100 Smoketree Ct Ste 700 .... Raleigh NC 27604 *Web:* wrdu.iheart.com	919-878-1500		647
WREA (White River Electric Assn) PO Box 958 .... Meeker CO 81641 *TF:* 800-922-1987 ■ *Web:* wrea.org	970-878-5041	878-5766	245
WREG-TV Ch 3 (CBS) 803 Ch Three Dr .... Memphis TN 38103 *Web:* www.wreg.com	901-543-2333	543-2167	741-81
Wren Associates Ltd 124 Wren Pkwy .... Jefferson City MO 65109 *TF:* 800-881-2249 ■ *Web:* www.wrensolutions.com	573-893-2249		608
Wren Insurance Agency Inc 1430 Palm Bay Rd .... Palm Bay FL 32905 *Web:* wreninsuranceagency.com	321-725-1440		390
Wren's Nest, The 1050 Ralph David Abernathy Blvd SW .... Atlanta GA 30310 *Web:* wrensnest.org	404-753-7735		520
Wrench Inc 1411 4th Ave 11th Fl .... Seattle WA 98101 *TF:* 844-997-3624 ■ *Web:* www.getwrench.com	844-997-3624		178-1
WRES (Woodmont Real Estate Services) 1050 Ralston Ave .... Belmont CA 94002 *Web:* www.wres.com	650-592-3960		655
WrestlingGearCom Ltd 655 W Grand Ave Ste 140 .... Elmhurst IL 60126 *TF:* 800-565-0995 ■ *Web:* wrestlinggear.com	800-565-0995		711
WREX-TV Ch 13 (NBC) 10322 Auburn Rd .... Rockford IL 61103 *Web:* www.wrex.com	815-335-2213	335-2055	741-112
WRFG-FM 89.3 (Var) 1083 Austin Ave NE .... Atlanta GA 30307 *Web:* wrfg.org	404-523-3471	523-8990	645-11
WRFL-FM Rm CB72 Whiteroom Classroom Bldg 140 Patterson Dr University of Kentuck PO Box 777 .... Lexington KY 40506 *Web:* www.wrfl.fm	859-257-9735		647
WRGB-TV Ch 6 (CBS) 1400 Balltown Rd .... Schenectady NY 12309 *Web:* www.cbs6albany.com	518-346-6666		741
WRGN-FM 2457 SR 118 .... Hunlock Creek PA 18621 *TF:* 800-245-3688 ■ *Web:* www.wrgn.com	570-477-3688		647
WRGT-TV 2245 Corporate Pl .... Miamisburg OH 45342 *Web:* dayton247now.com	937-263-4500	268-5265	647
WRGZ-FM 123 Prentiss St .... Alpena MI 49707 **Fax Area Code: 517* ■ *Web:* www.watz.com	989-354-8400	734-7804*	647
WRH (Windsor Regional Hospital Metropolitan Campus) 1995 Lens Ave .... Windsor ON N8W1L9 *Web:* www.wrh.on.ca	519-254-5577	254-3458	374-2
WRHI-FM 142 N Confederate Ave PO Box 307 .... Rock Hill SC 29731 *TF:* 800-422-1281 ■ *Web:* www.wrhi.com	803-324-1340	324-2860	647
WRHL-AM 400 May Mart Dr PO Box 177 .... Rochelle IL 61068 *Web:* www.superhits935.com	815-562-7001	562-7002	647
WRHQ-FM 105.3 (Rock) 1102 E 52nd St .... Savannah GA 31404 *Web:* www.wrhq.com	912-234-1053	354-6600	645-145
WRI (World Resources Institute) 10 G St NE Ste 800 .... Washington DC 20002 *Web:* www.wri.org	202-729-7600	729-7610	48-13
WRI (Western Robidoux Inc) 4006 S 40th St .... Saint Joseph MO 64503 *TF:* 800-224-1617 ■ *Web:* www.wriprint.com	816-279-1617	279-1696	554
Wricley Nut Products Co 480 Pattison Ave .... Philadelphia PA 19148 *Web:* www.wricleynutproductsco.com	215-467-1106		296-28
Wrico Stamping Co 2727 Niagara Ln N .... Minneapolis MN 55447 *Web:* www.wrico-net.com	763-559-2288	553-7976	488
WRIC-TV Ch 8 (ABC) 301 Arboretum Pl .... Richmond VA 23236 *Web:* www.wric.com	804-330-8888	330-8881	741-108
WRIE-AM 1260 (Sports) 471 Robison Rd .... Erie PA 16509 *Web:* www.cbssportserie.com	814-868-5355		645-53
WRIF-FM 101.1 (Rock) 1 Radio Plaza Rd .... Detroit MI 48220 *Web:* www.wrif.com	248-547-0101	542-8800	645-48
Wright & Filippis Inc 2845 Crooks Rd .... Rochester Hills MI 48309 *TF:* 866-274-0161 ■ *Web:* www.firsttoserve.com	248-829-8292		477
Wright & McGill Co 4245 E 46th Ave .... Denver CO 80216	303-321-1481	321-4750	710
Wright & Talisman PC 1200 G St NW Ste 600 .... Washington DC 20005 *Web:* wrightlaw.com	202-393-1200	393-1240	41

Name / Address	City	State	Zip	Phone	Fax	Class
Wright Air Service Inc 3842 University Ave S PO Box 60142 *Web:* www.wrightairservice.com	Fairbanks	AK	99706	907-474-0502	474-0375	23
Wright Beauty Academy 492 Capital SW *Web:* www.wba.edu	Battle Creek	MI	49015	517-241-9201		167-3
Wright Business Graphics (WBG) 18440 NE San Rafael St *TF:* 800-547-8397 ■ *Web:* www.wrightbg.com	Portland	OR	97230	800-547-8397		110
Wright Coating Company Inc 1603 N Pitcher St *Web:* www.wrightcoating.com	Kalamazoo	MI	49007	269-344-8195		481
Wright Construction Group 5811 Youngquist Rd *Web:* wcgfl.com	Fort Myers	FL	33912	239-481-5000		186
Wright Construction Western Inc 2919 Cleveland Ave *Web:* www.wrightconstruction.ca	Saskatoon	SK	S7K8A9	306-934-0440		186
Wright County 10 Second St NW Rm C201 *Web:* www.co.wright.mn.us	Buffalo	MN	55313	763-682-7539	682-7300	338
Wright County 115 N Main St *Web:* www.wrightcounty.org	Clarion	IA	50525	515-532-2771	532-2669	338
Wright Do-it Ctr 1306 N Market *Web:* wrightbuildingcenter.comcontact	Sparta	IL	62286	618-443-5335		191-3
Wright Express Corp 97 Darling Ave *NYSE:* WEX ■ *TF:* 800-761-7181 ■ *Web:* www.wexinc.com	South Portland	ME	04106	207-773-8171		215
Wright Global Graphics 5115 Prospect St **Fax Area Code:* 336 ■ *TF:* 800-678-9019 ■ *Web:* www.wrightglobalgraphics.com	Thomasville	NC	27360	800-678-9019	476-8554*	413
Wright Group, The 6428 Airport Rd *TF:* 800-201-3096 ■ *Web:* www.thewrightgroup.net	Crowley	LA	70526	337-783-3096		582
Wright Holmes Law List 23 The Pky 3rd Fl *TF:* 800-258-5597 ■ *Web:* www.collectioncenter.com	Katonah	NY	10536	914-241-3297	241-3326	637-10
Wright Implement Company LLC 3225 Carter Rd *TF:* 800-252-3904 ■ *Web:* wrightimp.com	Owensboro	KY	42301	270-683-3606		111
Wright Investment Properties Inc 850 Ridge Lake Blvd Ste 401 *Web:* wrightinvestments.com	Memphis	TN	38120	901-755-9501		796
Wright Investors' Service 440 Wheelers Farms Rd **Fax Area Code:* 203 ■ *TF:* 800-232-0013 ■ *Web:* wrightinvestorsservice.com	Milford	CT	06461	800-232-0013	783-4401*	401
Wright Lindsey & Jennings LLP 200 W Capitol Ave Ste 2300 *Web:* wlj.com	Little Rock	AR	72201	501-371-0808	376-9442	428
Wright Line LLC 160 Gold Star Blvd *TF:* 800-225-7348 ■ *Web:* www.wrightline.com	Worcester	MA	01606	508-852-4300	853-8904	319-1
Wright Manufacturing Inc 4600-X Wedgewood Blvd *Web:* www.wrightmfg.com	Frederick	MD	21703	301-360-9810		429
Wright Medical Group Inc 1023 Cherry Rd *NASDAQ:* WMGI ■ *TF:* 800-238-7117 ■ *Web:* www.wright.com	Memphis	TN	38117	901-867-9971		477
Wright Metal Products CratesLLC 111 Franklin St *Web:* www.wrightmetalsinc.com	Lavonia	GA	30553	706-356-2717		567
Wright Plastic Products LLC 201 E Condensery Rd *Web:* wppllc.com	Sheridan	MI	48884	989-291-3211	291-5321	454
Wright Printing Co 11616 I St *TF:* 800-341-2213 ■ *Web:* www.barnhartpress.com	Omaha	NE	68137	402-341-1322	341-8359	627
Wright Process Systems 88 Commerce St *Web:* www.wrightps.com	Lodi	CA	95240	209-369-2795		186
Wright Ron (Rep R - TX) 428 Cannon House Office Bldg *Web:* www.wright.house.gov	Washington	DC	20515	202-225-2002		342-2
Wright Runstad & Co 1201 Third Ave Ste 2700 *Web:* www.wrightrunstad.com	Seattle	WA	98101	206-447-9000	223-8791	655
Wright State University 3640 Colonel Glenn Hwy *TF:* 800-247-1770 ■ *Web:* www.wright.edu	Dayton	OH	45435	937-775-5740	775-5795	166
Wright State University Lake 7600 Lake Campus Dr *TF:* 800-237-1477 ■ *Web:* lake.wright.edu	Celina	OH	45822	419-586-0300	586-0358	162
Wright Steel and Machine Co 402 Industrial Park Rd *TF:* 800-814-7291 ■ *Web:* www.wrightsteelandmachine.com	Harrison	AR	72601	870-741-9103	741-1716	492
Wright Tool Co 1 Wright Dr PO Box 512 **Fax Area Code:* 800 ■ *TF:* 800-321-2902 ■ *Web:* www.wrighttool.com	Barberton	OH	44203	330-848-0600	543-2095*	350
Wright Transportation Inc 2333 Dauphin Island Pkwy *TF:* 800-342-4598 ■ *Web:* wrighttransportation.com	Mobile	AL	36605	251-432-6390		780
Wright Water Engineers Inc 2490 W 26th Ave Ste 100a *Web:* www.wrightwater.com	Denver	CO	80211	303-480-1700	480-1020	261
Wright Wisner Distributing Corp 3165 Brighton-Henrietta Town Line Rd *Web:* wrightbev.com	Rochester	NY	14623	585-427-2880		81-1
Wright's Media 2407 Timberloch Pl Ste B *TF:* 877-652-5295 ■ *Web:* wrightsmedia.com	The Woodlands	TX	77380	877-652-5295		637-9
Wright, Green PC 504 Boulevard Pk E	Mobile	AL	36609	251-344-7744		41
Wright-Hennepin Cooperative Electric Assn 6800 Electric Dr PO Box 330 *TF:* 800-943-2667 ■ *Web:* www.whe.org	Rockford	MN	55373	763-477-3000	477-3054	245
Wright-Patt Credit Union Inc 2455 Executive Pk Blvd PO Box 286 *TF:* 800-762-0047 ■ *Web:* www.wpcu.coop	Fairborn	OH	45324	937-912-7000		219
Wright-Pierce 11 Bowdoin Mill Is Ste 140 *TF:* 888-621-8156 ■ *Web:* www.wright-pierce.com	Topsham	ME	04086	207-725-8721	729-8414	261
Wright-Ryan Construction Inc 10 Danforth St *Web:* www.wright-ryan.com	Portland	ME	04101	207-773-3625		186
Wrightsoft Corp 131 Hartwell Ave *TF:* 800-225-8697 ■ *Web:* www.wrightsoft.com	Lexington	MA	02421	800-225-8697		225
Wrigley Memorial & Botanical Garden 125 Claressa Ave PO Box 2739 *Web:* www.catalinaconservancy.org	Avalon	CA	90704	310-510-2897	510-1451	97
Wrisco Industries Inc 355 Hiatt Dr Ste B *TF:* 800-627-2646 ■ *Web:* www.wrisco.com	Palm Beach Gardens	FL	33418	561-626-5700	627-3574	492
Wristbandfactory.com PO Box 5290 **Fax Area Code:* 800 ■ *TF:* 888-791-9590 ■ *Web:* www.wristbandfactory.com	Benton City	WA	99320	888-791-9590	283-9555*	430
Wristbands Online 1650 Nw 33rd St *TF:* 800-947-7445 ■ *Web:* www.wristbandsonline.com	Pompano Beach	FL	33064	954-571-7946		459
WristCo 16000 W Rogers Dr Ste 100 *TF:* 800-261-2070 ■ *Web:* www.wristco.com	New Berlin	WI	53151	262-754-5874		366
WRIT (Washington Real Estate Investment Trust) 1775 I St NW *NYSE:* WRE ■ **Fax Area Code:* 301 ■ *TF:* 800-565-9748 ■ *Web:* www.washreit.com	Washington	DC	20006	202-774-3200	984-9610*	655
Write Approach Inc, The 245 Amity Rd *Web:* www.thewriteapproachinc.com	Woodbridge	CT	06525	203-397-8272	387-1982	241
Write on Target Inc 7941 Washington Woods Dr *Web:* writetarget.com	Dayton	OH	45459	937-436-4565		7
Write Stuff Enterprises LLC 1001 S Andrews Ave Ste 200 *TF:* 800-900-2665 ■ *Web:* www.writestuffbooks.com	Fort Lauderdale	FL	33316	954-462-6657	462-6023	637-2
WriteGirl 1330 Factory Pl Ste F104 *Web:* www.writegirl.org	Los Angeles	CA	90013	213-253-2655	253-2618	637-2
Writer's AudioShop 1316 Overland Stage Rd *Web:* www.writersaudio.com	Dripping Springs	TX	78620	512-264-7067		637-10
Writers Guild of America East (WGAE) 250 Hudson St *Web:* www.wgaeast.org	New York	NY	10013	212-767-7800	582-1909	414
Writers Guild of America West (WGAW) 7000 W Third St *Web:* www.wga.org	Los Angeles	CA	90048	323-951-4000	782-4800	414
Writers House 21 W 26th St *Web:* www.writershouse.com	New York	NY	10010	212-685-2400		444
Writers of the Round Table Inc PO Box 511 *Web:* www.roundtablecompanies.com	Highland Park	IL	60035	815-346-2398		637-2
Writers' Collective, The (TWC) 780 Reservoir Ave Ste 243 *Web:* www.writerscollective.org	Cranston	RI	02910	206-984-0313		637-2
Written Heritage PO Box 1390 *TF:* 800-301-8009 ■ *Web:* www.writtenheritage.com	Folsom	LA	70437	985-796-5433	796-9236	637-9
WRJN-AM 4201 Victory Ave *Web:* www.wrjn.com	Racine	WI	53405	262-634-3311	634-6515	647
WRJW-AM PO Box 907 *Web:* www.wrjwradio.com	Picayune	MS	39466	601-798-4835	798-9755	647
WRJY-FM 185 Benedict Rd *Web:* www.thewave1041.com	Brunswick	GA	31520	912-261-1000	265-8391	647
WRKF-FM 89.3 (NPR) 3050 Vly Creek Dr *TF:* 855-893-9753 ■ *Web:* www.wrkf.org	Baton Rouge	LA	70808	225-926-3050	926-3105	645-17
WRKO-AM 680 6801 Cabot Rd Ste 320 *Web:* wrko.iheart.com	Medford	MA	02155	617-266-6868		645
WRKR-FM 4154 Jennings Dr *Web:* www.wrkr.com	Kalamazoo	MI	49048	269-344-0111		647
WRL Advertising Inc 4470 Dressler Rd NW *Web:* wrladv.com	Canton	OH	44718	330-493-8866		7
WRMG-AM PO Box 656 *Web:* www.wrmgradio.com	Red Bay	AL	35582	256-356-4458		647
WRNI-AM 881 (NPR) 1 Union Stn *Web:* thepublicsradio.org	Providence	RI	02903	401-351-2800	351-0246	645-127
WRNR-FM 103.1 179 Admiral Cochrane Dr *TF:* 877-762-1031 ■ *Web:* www.wrnr.com	Annapolis	MD	21401	410-626-0103	267-7634	645-9
WRNX-FM 1331 Main St 4th Fl *Web:* mykix1009.iheart.com	Springfield	MA	01103	413-781-1011		647
Wrobel Engineering Company Inc 154 Bodwell St *Web:* www.wrobeleng.com	Avon	MA	02322	508-586-8338		198
WROC-TV Ch 8 (CBS) 201 Humboldt St *Web:* www.rochesterfirst.com	Rochester	NY	14610	585-288-8400	288-1505	741-111
WROI-FM 110 E 8th St *Web:* www.wroifm.com	Rochester	IN	46975	574-223-6059	223-2238	647
WROK-AM 1440 (N/T) 3901 Brendenwood Rd *Web:* www.1440wrok.com	Rockford	IL	61107	815-398-9765	484-2432	645-136
WROQ-FM 101.1 (CR) 25 Garlington Rd *TF:* 888-257-0058 ■ *Web:* classicrock1011.radio.com	Greenville	SC	29615	864-271-9200	242-1567	645-65
WROR-FM 105.7 (Oldies) 55 Morrissey Blvd *Web:* wror.com	Boston	MA	02125	617-822-9600	822-6470	645-22
Wrought Washer Manufacturing Inc 2100 S Bay St *TF:* 800-558-5217 ■ *Web:* www.wroughtwasher.com	Milwaukee	WI	53207	414-744-0771		483
WRPQ-TV 407 Oak St PO Box 456 *Web:* www.wrpq.com	Baraboo	WI	53913	608-356-3974	355-9952	647
WRQN-FM 93.5 (Oldies) 3225 Arlington Ave *TF:* 866-240-1935 ■ *Web:* www.935wrqn.com	Toledo	OH	43614	419-725-5700		645-161
WRR Environmental Services 5200 Ryder Rd *Web:* www.wrres.com	Eau Claire	WI	54701	715-834-9624		667
WRRC (Western Regional Research Ctr) 800 Buchanan St *Web:* www.ars.usda.gov	Albany	CA	94710	510-559-5600	559-5963	668
WRR-FM 101.1 (Clas) PO Box 159001 *Web:* www.wrr101.com	Dallas	TX	75315	214-670-8888		645-43
WRSB-AM 4226 Sweden Walker Rd *Web:* www.lamegaroc.com	Brockport	NY	14420	585-637-3640	965-9539	647

Name / Address	City	State	ZIP	Phone	Fax	Class
WRSP-TV Ch 55 (Fox) 250 S Country Fair Dr. *Web:* foxillinois.com	Champaign	IL	61821	217-351-8500	351-6056	741-128
WRTA-AM 1771 Beaver Dam Rd *Web:* www.wrta.com	Altoona	PA	16602	814-943-6112	944-9782	647
WRTC-FM 89.3 (Var) 300 Summit St *Web:* www.wrtcfm.com	Hartford	CT	06106	860-297-2439		645-69
WRTI-FM 90.1 (NPR) 1509 Cecil B Moore Ave 3rd Fl. *TF:* 866-809-9784 ■ *Web:* wrti.org	Philadelphia	PA	19121	215-204-8405	204-7027	645-120
WRTV-TV Ch 6 (ABC) 1330 N Meridian St *Web:* www.theindychannel.com	Indianapolis	IN	46202	317-635-9788	269-1445	741-62
WRUF-AM 1885 Stadium Rd University of Florida PO Box 118405 *TF:* 877-392-8255 ■ *Web:* www.wruf.com	Gainesville	FL	32604	352-392-8255		647
WRUM-FM 2500 Maitland Center Pky Ste 401 *TF:* 888-978-1003 ■ *Web:* www.rumba100.iheart.com	Maitland	FL	32751	407-916-1003	916-0329	647
WRVM-FM 102.7 (Rel) PO Box 212 *TF:* 888-225-9786 ■ *Web:* www.wrvmradio.org	Suring	WI	54174	920-842-2900		645
WRVR-FM 104.5 (AC) 1835 Moriah Woods Blvd Bldg 1 *Web:* 1045theriver.radio.com	Memphis	TN	38117	901-384-5900	767-6076	645-95
WRVT-FM 365 Troy Ave Fort Ethan Allen **Fax Area Code:* 802 ■ *TF:* 800-639-2192 ■ *Web:* publicfiles.fcc.gov	Colchester	VT	05446	800-639-2192	655-2799*	647
WRWP LLC 1920 Case Pkwy. *Web:* wrwp.com	Twinsburg	OH	44087	330-425-3421	425-2400	815
WRXY-TV 40000 Horseshoe Rd *Web:* www.ctntelevision.com	Punta Gorda	FL	33982	293-543-7200	543-6800	647
WS Badcock Corp (WSBC) PO Box 497 *TF:* 800-223-2625 ■ *Web:* www.badcock.com	Mulberry	FL	33860	800-223-2625		321
WS Bellows Construction Corp 1906 Afton St *Web:* www.wsbellows.com	Houston	TX	77055	713-680-2132	680-2614	186
WS Cumby Inc 938 Lincoln Ave. *Web:* www.cumby.com	Springfield	PA	19064	610-328-5353		186
WS Emerson Company Inc 15 Acme Rd *TF:* 800-789-6120 ■ *Web:* www.wsemersononline.com	Brewer	ME	04412	207-989-3410		156
WS Hampshire Inc 365 Keyes Ave *TF:* 800-541-0251 ■ *Web:* www.wshampshire.com	Hampshire	IL	60140	847-683-4400	683-4407	724
WS/FCS (Winston-Salem/Forsyth County Schools) 1605 Miller St. *Web:* www.wsfcs.k12.nc.us	Winston-Salem	NC	27103	336-727-2816	661-6572	685
WSA Distributing Inc 7222 Opportunity Rd *Web:* www.wsadistributing.com	San Diego	CA	92111	858-560-7800	560-7475	246
WSA Engineered Systems 2018 S First St *Web:* www.wsaes.com	Milwaukee	WI	53207	414-481-4120	481-4121	14
WSAM-AM 2000 Whittier St *Web:* www.thebay104fm.com	Saginaw	MI	48601	989-752-8161		647
WSAQ-FM 808 Huron Ave. *TF:* 800-297-0099 ■ *Web:* www.wsaq.com	Port Huron	MI	48060	810-987-9000	987-9380	647
WSAU-AM 557 Scott St. *Web:* www.wsau.com	Wausau	WI	54403	715-842-1672	848-3158	647
WSAV-TV Ch 3 (NBC) 1430 E Victory Dr *Web:* www.wsav.com	Savannah	GA	31404	912-651-0300	651-0320	741-122
WSAW-TV 1114 Grand Ave *Web:* www.wsaw.com	Wausau	WI	54403	715-845-4211	845-2649	647
WSAZ-TV Ch 3 (NBC) PO Box 2115 *Web:* www.wsaz.com	Huntington	WV	25721	304-697-4780	690-3066	741
WSB & Associates Inc 701 Xenia Ave S Ste 300 *Web:* www.wsbeng.com	Minneapolis	MN	55416	763-541-4800		256
Wsb Computer Services Inc 21 Craft St *Web:* www.wsbcs.net	Alamosa	CO	81101	719-589-8940		175
WSBC (WS Badcock Corp) PO Box 497 *TF:* 800-223-2625 ■ *Web:* www.badcock.com	Mulberry	FL	33860	800-223-2625		321
WSBT-TV Ch 22 (CBS) 1301 E Douglas Rd. *TF:* 877-634-7181 ■ *Web:* www.wsbt.com	Mishawaka	IN	46545	574-247-7861	289-0622	741
WSB-TV Ch 2 (ABC) 1601 W Peachtree St NE *Web:* www.wsbtv.com	Atlanta	GA	30309	404-897-7000	897-7370	741-7
WSC Avant Bard 3700 S Four Mile Run *Web:* wscavantbard.org	Arlington	VA	22206	703-418-4808		572
WSCR-AM 180 N Stetson Ave Ste 1250 *Web:* www.chicago.cbslocal.com	Chicago	IL	60601	312-644-6767		647
WSE (White Sands Engineering) 2202 S 7th St Ste 120 *TF:* 800-586-7377 ■ *Web:* www.whitesandsengineering.com	Phoenix	AZ	85027	800-586-7377		647
WSEL-FM 96.7 PO Box 3788 *Web:* wselradio.com	Tupelo	MS	38803	662-489-0297		645-167
WSET-TV Ch 13 (ABC) 2320 Langhorne Rd *Web:* www.wset.com	Lynchburg	VA	24501	434-528-1313	847-0458	741
WSF Industries Inc 7 Hackett Dr. *TF:* 800-874-8265 ■ *Web:* www.wsf-inc.com	Tonawanda	NY	14150	716-692-4930		480
WSFA-TV Ch 12 (NBC) 12 E Delano Ave *Web:* www.wsfa.com	Montgomery	AL	36105	334-288-1212	613-8303	741-86
WSFF-FM 3807 Brandon Ave Ste 2350 *Web:* www.1061stevefm.iheart.com	Roanoke	VA	24018	540-725-1220	725-1245	647
WSFI-FM PO Box 885 *Web:* wsficatholicradio.org	Libertyville	IL	60048	224-206-8455		647
WSFL-TV Ch 39 (CW) 200 E Las Olas Blvd 11th Fl *Web:* www.wsfltv.com	Fort Lauderdale	FL	33301	954-627-7349	355-2000	741-82
WSFS Financial Corp 500 Delaware Ave. *NASDAQ: WSFS* ■ *TF:* 888-973-7226 ■ *Web:* www.wsfsbank.com	Wilmington	DE	19801	302-792-6000		360-2
WSGB-AM 180 Main St. *Web:* www.theboss97fm.com	Sutton	WV	26601	304-765-7373	765-7836	647
WSGH-AM PO Box 25386 *Web:* www.radiolamovidita.com	Winston-Salem	NC	27114	336-768-0050	768-0032	647
WSH (Wyoming State Hospital) 831 Hwy 150 S *Web:* health.wyo.gov	Evanston	WY	82930	307-789-3464		374-5
WSHH-FM 99.7 (AC) 900 Parish St 3rd Fl *Web:* www.wshh.com	Pittsburgh	PA	15220	412-875-9500		645-123
WSHO-AM 800 (Rel) 1001 Howard Ave Ste 4304 *Web:* www.wsho.com	New Orleans	LA	70113	504-527-0800	527-0881	645-107
WSHU 5151 Park Ave. *TF:* 800-937-6045 ■ *Web:* www.wshu.org	Fairfield	CT	06825	203-365-6604		645
WSI 20 Carlson Ct Ste 100. *TF:* 888-670-7508 ■ *Web:* www.wsiworld.com	Mississauga	ON	M9W7K6	905-678-7588	678-7242	310
WSI Industries Inc 213 Chelsea Rd *NASDAQ: WSCI* ■ *Web:* www.wsiindustries.com	Monticello	MN	55362	763-295-9202	295-9212	454
WSIA-FM 2800 Victory Blvd Bldg 1C *Web:* www.wsia.fm	Staten Island	NY	10314	718-982-3050		647
WSIC-AM 1400 (N/T) 1117 Radio Rd *Web:* www.wsicweb.com	Statesville	NC	28677	704-872-6345	873-6921	645
WSIE-FM S Illinois University Edwardsville PO Box 1773 *TF:* 888-325-8870 ■ *Web:* www.wsieradio.com	Edwardsville	IL	62026	618-650-2228		647
WSIL-TV 1416 Country Aire *Web:* www.wsiltv.com	Carterville	IL	62918	618-985-2333	985-3709	647
WSJM-AM 580 E Napier Ave. *Web:* www.wsjm.com	Benton Harbor	MI	49022	269-925-1111	925-1011	647
WSKY-TV Ch 4 (Ind) 218 Salters Creek Rd *Web:* www.sky4tv.com	Hampton	VA	23661	757-382-0004	382-0365	741
WSLQ-FM 99.1 (AC) 3934 Electric Rd SW. *TF:* 800-410-9936 ■ *Web:* www.q99fm.com	Roanoke	VA	24018	540-387-0234		645-133
WSLS-TV Ch 10 (NBC) PO Box 10. *Web:* www.wsls.com	Roanoke	VA	24022	540-981-9110	343-3157	741-109
WSLW-AM 9196 Seneca Trl S *Web:* www.radiogreenbrier.com	Ronceverte	WV	24970	304-645-1327		647
WSM-AM 650 (Ctry) 2644 McGavock Pk *Web:* wsmonline.com	Nashville	TN	37214	615-737-0660		645-100
WSMI-AM PO Box 10 *Web:* www.wsmiradio.com	Litchfield	IL	62056	217-324-5921	532-2431	647
WSMK-FM 99.1 (Urban) 210 S Philip Rd. *Web:* wsmkradio.com	Niles	MI	49120	269-683-4343		645
WSMV-TV Ch 4 (NBC) 5700 Knob Rd *Web:* www.wsmv.com	Nashville	TN	37209	615-353-4444		741-89
WSNA (Washington State Nurses Assn) 575 Andover Pk W Ste 101 *TF:* 800-231-8482 ■ *Web:* www.wsna.org	Seattle	WA	98188	206-575-7979	575-1908	533
WSNS-TV 454 N Columbus Dr *Web:* www.telemundochicago.com	Chicago	IL	60611	312-836-3110		647
WSNW-AM 103 Ram Cat Alley PO Box 1251 *Web:* www.wsnwradio.com	Seneca	SC	29679	864-882-9769	886-0082	647
WSO (Washington Symphony Orchestra) PO Box 178 *Web:* washsym.org	Washington	PA	15301	724-223-9796		573-3
WSO (Wichita Symphony Orchestra) 225 W Douglas St Ste 207 *Web:* wichitasymphony.org	Wichita	KS	67202	316-267-5259	267-1937	573-3
WSON AM & FM Radio 530 S Jackson St. *Web:* www.wsonradio.com	Henderson	KY	42419	270-826-3923	826-7572	647
WSP 1600 Blvd Rene-Levesque W 16th Fl. *Web:* www.wsp.com	Montreal	QC	H3H1P9	514-340-0046		192
WSPA-TV Ch 7 (CBS) 250 International Dr *TF:* 866-946-6349 ■ *Web:* www.wspa.com	Spartanburg	SC	29303	864-576-7777		741-6
WSPC-AM PO Box 549 *Web:* www.1010wspc.com	Albemarle	NC	28001	704-983-1580	983-1436	647
WSPI-FM 108 Boeykens Pl *Web:* www.catholicspiritradio.com	Normal	IL	61761	309-807-2427	452-9677	647
WSPT-FM 500 Division St. *TF:* 800-801-9778 ■ *Web:* www.979wspt.com	Stevens Point	WI	54481	715-341-9800		647
WSQL-AM 62 W Main St. *Web:* www.wsqlradio.info	Brevard	NC	28712	828-877-5252		647
WSRC-AM One Rotary Row. *Web:* www.wsrc.org	Buffalo	NY	14201	919-881-9797		647
WSRE-TV Ch 23 (PBS) 1000 College Blvd *TF:* 800-239-9773 ■ *Web:* www.wsre.org	Pensacola	FL	32504	850-484-1200	484-1255	741
WSRS-FM 96 Stereo Ln. *Web:* 961srs.iheart.com	Paxton	MA	01612	508-757-9696	757-1779	647
WSRV-FM 97.1 (AC) 1601 W Peachtree St NE. *Web:* www.971theriver.com	Atlanta	GA	30309	404-897-7500		645-11
WSSA (Wine & Spirits Shippers Association Inc) 11800 Sunrise Vly Dr **Fax Area Code:* 703 ■ *TF:* 800-368-3167 ■ *Web:* www.wssa.com	Reston	VA	20191	800-368-3167	860-2422*	49-6
WSSL-FM PO Box 100 *Web:* wsslfm.iheart.com	Greenville	SC	29602	864-242-1005		647
WSST-TV 112 7th St S. *Web:* www.wsst51.com	Cordele	GA	31015	229-273-0001	273-8894	647
WSTM-TV 1030 James St *Web:* www.cnycentral.com	Syracuse	NY	13203	315-477-9400	477-9675	647
Wstrn Area Career & Technology Ctr (WACTC) 688 Western Ave. *Web:* www.wactc.net	Canonsburg	PA	15317	724-746-2890	746-6966	685
WSTR-TV Ch 64 (MNT) 1906 Highland Ave *Web:* star64.tv	Cincinnati	OH	45219	513-641-4400	242-2633	741-30
WSUS-FM 45 Ed Mitchell Ave. *Web:* wsus1023.iheart.com	Franklin	NJ	07416	973-827-2525	827-2135	647
WSWA (Wine & Spirits Wholesalers of America Inc) 805 15th St NW Ste 1120. *Web:* www.wswa.org	Washington	DC	20005	202-371-9792	789-2405	49-6
WSYD-AM PO Box 1678 *Web:* www.wsyd1300.com	Mount Airy	NC	27030	336-786-2147		647
WSYM-TV Ch 47 (Fox) 600 W St Joseph St Ste 47 *Web:* www.fox47news.com	Lansing	MI	48933	517-484-7747	484-3144	741-71

	Phone	Fax	Class
WSYR-TV Ch 9 (ABC) 5904 Bridge St .... East Syracuse NY 13057 *Web:* www.localsyr.com	315-446-9999	251-1567	741
WSYX-TV Ch 6 (ABC) 1261 Dublin Rd .... Columbus OH 43215 *Web:* www.abc6onyourside.com	614-481-6666	481-6624	741-35
WT Harvey Lumber Co 800 15th St .... Columbus GA 31902 *Web:* www.harveylumber.com	706-322-8204	323-2433	191-3
WTA (Washington Trails Assn) 705 Second Ave Ste 300........ Seattle WA 98104 *Web:* www.wta.org	206-625-1367	625-9249	48-23
WTA (Wyoming Trucking Assn) 555 N Poplar St .... Casper WY 82601 *TF:* 877-878-2515 ■ *Web:* www.wytruck.org	307-234-1579	234-7082	139
WTA Tour Inc 100 Second Ave S Ste 1100........ Saint Petersburg FL 33701 *Web:* www.wtatennis.com	727-895-5000	894-1982	48-22
WTAB-AM 210 Avon St........ Tabor City NC 28463 *Web:* www.wtabradio.com	910-653-2131		647
WTAE-TV Ch 4 (ABC) 400 Ardmore Blvd........ Pittsburgh PA 15221 *Web:* www.wtae.com	412-242-4300	244-4558	741-100
WTAG 580/94.9 96 Stereo Ln........ Paxton MA 01612 *Web:* wtag.iheart.com	508-755-0058		645
WTAM-AM 1100 (N/T) 6200 Oak Tree Blvd 4th Fl........ Independence OH 44131 *TF:* 888-723-9826 ■ *Web:* wtam.iheart.com	216-986-8800		645
WTAN-AM 706 N Mrytle Ave........ Clearwater FL 33755 *Web:* www.tantalk1340.com	727-441-3000		647
WTAT-TV Ch 24 (Fox) 4301 Arco Ln .... North Charleston SC 29418 *Web:* www.foxcharleston.com	843-744-2424		741
WTB (Walk Thru the Bible Ministries Inc) 5550 Triangle Parkway Ste 250........ Peachtree Corners GA 30092 *TF:* 800-361-6131 ■ *Web:* www.walkthru.org	800-361-6131		48-20
WTB Financial Corp PO Box 2127 .... Spokane WA 99210 *TF:* 800-788-4578 ■ *Web:* www.watrust.com	800-788-4578		360-2
WTBZ-AM 132 Carubia Dr........ Core WV 26541 *Web:* www.wvlol.org	304-265-2200		647
WTCA (Wood Truss Council of America) 6300 Enterprise Ln........ Madison WI 53719 *Web:* www.sbcindustry.com	608-274-4849	274-3329	49-3
WTCA-AM 112 W Washington St .... Plymouth IN 46563 *Web:* www.am1050.com	574-936-4096	936-6776	647
WTCC-FM 90.7 1 Armory Sq........ Springfield MA 01105 *Web:* www.wtccfm.org	413-736-2781		645-6
WTCI-TV Ch 45 (PBS) 7540 Bonnie Shire Dr........ Chattanooga TN 37416 *Web:* www.wtcitv.org	423-702-7800	702-7823	741-27
WTCK-FM 1496 Bellevue St Ste 202........ Green Bay WI 54311 *TF:* 844-238-8508 ■ *Web:* www.baragabroadcasting.com	231-238-8500	238-0803	647
WTCW-AM PO Box 288 .... Mayking KY 41837 *Web:* www.1039thebulldog.com	606-633-2711	633-4445	647
WTE (Western Truck Equipment Co) 2400 S 14th St........ Phoenix AZ 85034 *Web:* www.wteco.com	602-257-0777	340-1534	516
WTE Corp 7 Alfred Cir........ Bedford MA 01730 *Web:* www.wte.com	781-275-6400	275-8612	660
WTGA-AM 208 S Center St........ Thomaston GA 30286 *Web:* www.fun101fm.com	706-647-7121	647-7122	647
WTGM-AM 351 Tilghman Rd .... Salisbury MD 21804 *Web:* www.foxsports960.iheart.com	410-742-1923		647
WTH (World Travel Holdings) 100 Fordham Rd Bldg C........ Wilmington MA 01887 *TF:* 877-958-7447 ■ *Web:* www.worldtravelholdings.com	617-424-7990	424-1943	771
WTHI-FM 925 Wabash Ave Ste 300 .... Terre Haute IN 47807 *TF:* 800-686-9844 ■ *Web:* www.hi99.com	812-917-3901	234-0089	647
WTHI-TV 800 Ohio St .... Terre Haute IN 47807 *Web:* www.wthitv.com	812-232-9481	232-8953	647
WTHR-TV Ch 13 (NBC) 1000 N Meridian St .... Indianapolis IN 46204 *Web:* www.wthr.com	317-636-1313	655-5984	741-62
WTHT-FM 99.9 (Ctry) 477 Congress St 3rd Fl Annex .... Portland ME 04101 *Web:* www.nh1.com	207-797-0780	774-4390	645-125
WTI (Western Technology Investment) 104 La Mesa Dr Ste 102........ Portola CA 94028 *Web:* westerntech.com	650-234-4300	234-4343	792
WTI Inc 3737 E Broadway Rd .... Phoenix AZ 85040 *Web:* www.wticompanies.com	602-437-8979		466
WTIC-TV Ch 61 (Fox) 285 Broad St........ Hartford CT 06115 *Web:* fox61.com	860-527-6161	723-2111	741-57
WTKC-FM 701 N Main St .... Findlay OH 45840 *Web:* www.wtkc897.com	419-423-3285		647
WTKI-AM 2305 Holmes Ave NW........ Huntsville AL 35816 *Web:* www.wtkiradio.com	256-533-1450	551-9865	647
WTKR-TV Ch 3 (CBS) 720 Boush St .... Norfolk VA 23510 *Web:* www.wtkr.com	757-446-1000		741-92
WTLH-TV Ch 49 (Fox) 8440 Deerlake S........ Tallahassee FL 32312 *Web:* fox49.tv	850-893-4140	893-6974	741
WTLN-AM 950 (Rel) 1188 Lake View Dr .... Altamonte Springs FL 32714 *Web:* thewordorlando.com	407-961-4675		645
WTLW-TV 1844 Baty Rd .... Lima OH 45807 *Web:* www.wtlw.com	419-339-4444		647
WTLZ-FM 1795 Tittabawassee Rd .... Saginaw MI 48604 *Web:* www.kisswtlz.com	989-921-7107	754-5046	647
WTMA-AM 4230 Faber Place Dr Ste 100 .... North Charleston SC 29405 *Web:* www.wtma.com	843-277-1200		647
WTMD-FM 89.7 (AAA) 1 Olympic Pl Ste 100........ Towson MD 21204 *Web:* www.wtmd.org	410-704-8938	704-3113	645
WTMJ-AM 620 (N/T) 720 E Capitol Dr .... Milwaukee WI 53212 *Web:* www.wtmj.com	414-799-1620		645-98
WTMJ-TV Ch 4 (NBC) 720 E Capitol Dr........ Milwaukee WI 53212 *Web:* www.tmj4.com	414-332-9611	967-5378	741-83
WTMX-FM 101.9 (AC) 1 Prudential Plz 130 E Randolph St Ste 2700........ Chicago IL 60601 *Web:* wtmx.com	312-946-1019	946-4747	645-34
WTNH-TV Ch 8 (ABC) 8 Elm St .... New Haven CT 06510 *Web:* www.wtnh.com	203-784-8888	789-2010	741
WTNN-FM 4049 Williston Rd Ste 7 .... South Burlington VT 05403 *Web:* www.eaglecountry975.com	802-864-9750		647
WTNT-FM 94.9 (Ctry) 325 John Knox Rd Bldg G .... Tallahassee FL 32303 *Web:* 949tnt.iheart.com	850-422-3107		645-159
WTOC-TV PO Box 8086........ Savannah GA 31412 *Web:* www.wtoc.com	912-234-1111	238-5133	647
WTOG-TV Ch 44 (CW) 365 105th Terr NE........ Saint Petersburg FL 33716 *Web:* cwtampa.cbslocal.com	727-570-4208	577-3799	741-133
WTOG-TV CW44 365 105th Ter NE .... Saint Petersburg FL 33716 *Web:* www.cwtampa.cbslocal.com	727-576-4444	577-3799	647
WTOK-TV 815 23rd Ave .... Meridian MS 39301 *Web:* www.wtok.com	601-693-1441	483-3266	647
WTOL-TV Ch 11 (CBS) 730 N Summit St........ Toledo OH 43604 *Web:* www.wtol.com	419-248-1111	244-7104	741-134
WTOP 5425 Wisconsin Ave .... Chevy Chase MD 20815 *Web:* www.wtop.com	202-895-5000		645-9
WTOS 105 1 125 Community Dr Ste 201 .... Augusta ME 04330 *Web:* www.wtosfm.com	207-623-9000		93
WTOV-TV 9 Red Donley Plz........ Steubenville OH 43952 *Web:* www.wtov9.com	740-282-9999	282-0439	647
WTP Inc PO Box 937........ Coloma MI 49038 *TF:* 800-521-0731 ■ *Web:* www.wtp-inc.com	269-468-3399		732
WTRF-TV Ch 7 (CBS) 96 16th St........ Wheeling WV 26003 *Web:* www.wtrf.com	304-232-7777	233-5822	741-141
WTRO-AM 2555 Burks Pl .... Dyersburg TN 38024 *TF:* 800-447-9275 ■ *Web:* www.wtroradio.net	731-285-1339		647
WTRY-FM 98.3 (Oldies) 1203 Troy-Schenectady Rd........ Latham NY 12110 *Web:* 983try.iheart.com	518-452-4884		645
WTS (Washington Tennis Services) 3200 Tower Oaks Blvd Ste 400........ Rockville MD 20852 *Web:* wtsinternational.com	301-622-7800	622-3373	354
WTSA-AM PO Box 819 .... Brattleboro VT 05302 *Web:* wtsaradio.com	802-254-4577	257-4644	647
WTSH-FM 20 John Davenport Dr .... Rome GA 30165 *Web:* www.south107.com	706-291-9496		647
WTSP-TV Ch 10 (CBS) 11450 Gandy Blvd N........ Saint Petersburg FL 33702 *Web:* www.wtsp.com	727-577-1010		741-133
WTSR-FM 91.3 (Alt) College of New Jersey Kendall Hall PO Box 7718........ Ewing NJ 08628 *Web:* wtsr.org	609-771-3200		645
WTTG FOX 5 & MyFoxDc 5151 Wisconsin Ave NW .... Washington DC 20016 *Web:* www.fox5dc.com	202-244-5151		741-139
WTTR-AM 101 WTTR Ln........ Westminster MD 21158 *Web:* www.wttr.com	410-848-5511	876-5095	647
WTTS-FM 92.3 (AAA) 400 One City Centre........ Bloomington IN 47404 *TF:* 800-923-9887 ■ *Web:* www.wttsfm.com	812-332-3366	331-4570	645
WTTW-TV Ch 11 (PBS) 5400 N St Louis Ave........ Chicago IL 60625 *Web:* www.wttw.com	773-583-5000	583-3046	741-29
WTUG-FM 92.9 (Urban) 142 Skyland Blvd .... Tuscaloosa AL 35405 *Web:* wtug.com	205-345-7200		645-168
WTVA-TV Ch 9 (NBC) 1359 Beech Springs Rd .... Saltillo MS 38866 *Web:* www.wtva.com	662-842-7620		741
WTVC-TV Ch 9 (ABC) 4279 Benton Dr .... Chattanooga TN 37406 *Web:* www.newschannel9.com	423-757-7311	757-7400	741-27
WTVD-TV Ch 11 (ABC) 411 Liberty St........ Durham NC 27701 *TF:* 800-672-9883 ■ *Web:* abc11.com	919-683-1111		741-105
WTVF-TV 474 James Robertson Pky........ Nashville TN 37219 *Web:* www.newschannel5.com	615-244-5000	248-5207	647
WTVG-TV Ch 13 (ABC) 4247 Dorr St........ Toledo OH 43607 *Web:* www.13abc.com	419-531-1313	534-3898	741-134
WTVI PBS Charlotte 3242 Commonwealth Ave........ Charlotte NC 28205 *Web:* www.wtvi.org	704-330-5942	335-1358	741-26
WTVJ-TV Ch 6 (NBC) 15000 SW 27th St........ Miramar FL 33027 *Web:* www.nbcmiami.com	954-622-6000		741
WTVM-TV Ch 9 (ABC) 1909 Wynnton Rd .... Columbus GA 31906 *Web:* www.wtvm.com	706-494-5400	322-7527	741-34
WTVO-TV Ch 17 (ABC) 1917 N Meridian Rd........ Rockford IL 61101 *Web:* www.mystateline.com	815-963-5413		741-112
WTVQ-TV Ch 36 (ABC) 6940 Man O War Blvd........ Lexington KY 40509 *Web:* www.wtvq.com	859-294-3636		741-73
WTVR-TV Ch 6 (CBS) 3301 W Broad St........ Richmond VA 23230 *Web:* www.wtvr.com	804-254-3600	342-3418	741-108
WTVT-TV Ch 13 (Fox) 3213 W Kennedy Blvd .... Tampa FL 33609 *TF:* 800-334-9888 ■ *Web:* www.fox13news.com	813-876-1313	871-3135	741-133
WTVX-TV Ch 34 (CW) 1100 Fairfield Dr........ West Palm Beach FL 33407 *Web:* cw34.com	561-681-3434	684-9193	741-140
WTVY-TV 285 N Foster St........ Dothan AL 36303 *Web:* www.wtvy.com	334-792-3195		647
WTVZ MyTVZ 236 Clearfield Ave Ste 205........ Virginia Beach VA 23462 *Web:* mytvz.com	757-622-3333	623-1541	741-92
WTWB-AM 127 Glenn Rd .... Auburndale FL 33823 *Web:* www.laraza1570.com	863-968-1570		647
WTWC-TV Ch 40 (NBC) 8440 Deerlake Rd S .... Tallahassee FL 32312 *Web:* www.wtwc40.com	850-325-2365	893-6974	741-132
WTWO-TV PO Box 9268 .... Terre Haute IN 47808 *Web:* www.mywabashvalley.com	812-696-2121		647

Name / Address	City	State	Zip	Phone	Fax	Class
WTXF-TV Ch 29 (Fox) 330 Market St *TF:* 800-220-6397 ■ *Web:* www.fox29.com	Philadelphia	PA	19106	215-925-2929	982-5494	741-98
WTXL-TV Ch 27 (ABC) 1620 Commerce Blvd *Web:* www.wtxl.com	Midway	FL	32343	850-893-3127		741
WTZQ-AM 40 Francis Rd *Web:* www.wtzq.com	Hendersonville	NC	28793	828-692-1600	697-1416	647
WTZT-TV 1785 US Highway 72 Ste E & F *Web:* www.jamiecooper.com	Athens	AL	35613	256-603-4848		647
WUBE-FM 105.1 (Ctry) 2060 Reading Rd *Web:* b105.com	Cincinnati	OH	45202	513-699-5096		645-35
WUCF FM 12676 Gemini Blvd N Ste 130 *Web:* www.wucf.org	Orlando	FL	32816	407-823-0899		645-114
WUCO-AM 4673 Winterset Dr *Web:* www.stgabrielradio.com	Columbus	OH	43220	614-459-4820		647
WUCO-AM 113 S Main St **Fax Area Code:* 740 ■ *Web:* www.wqttradio.com	Marysville	OH	43040	614-754-4922	549-7444*	647
WUCW-TV Ch 23 (CW) 1640 Como Ave *Web:* thecwtc.com	Saint Paul	MN	55108	651-646-2300	646-1220	741-84
WUGA-TV Ch 32 (PBS) 120 Hooper St *Web:* www.uga.edu	Athens	GA	30602	706-542-3000		741
WUHF-TV Ch 31 (Fox) 201 Humbolt St *Web:* rocwiki.org	Rochester	NY	14610	585-232-3700	288-1505	741-111
WUKY University of Kentucky 2640 Spurr Rd *Web:* wuky.org	Lexington	KY	40511	859-257-3221		645-86
Wulco Inc 6899 Steger Dr Ste A	Cincinnati	OH	45237	513-761-6899		567
Wulftec International Inc 209 Wulftec St *TF:* 877-985-3832 ■ *Web:* wulftec.com	Ayer's Cliff	QC	J0B1C0	819-838-4232	838-5539	547
WUMB-FM 91.9 (Folk) 100 Morrissey Blvd *TF:* 800-573-2100 ■ *Web:* www.wumb.org	Boston	MA	02125	617-287-6900		645-22
WUMN-TV 26101 S Tamiami Trl *Web:* www.prnewswire.com	Bonita Springs	FL	34134	239-254-9995		647
WUNC-FM 91.5 (NPR) 120 Friday Center Dr *TF:* 800-962-9862 ■ *Web:* wunc.org	Chapel Hill	NC	27517	919-445-9150		645
Wunderland Electric Castle's 3451 SE Belmont St *Web:* wunderlandgames.com	Portland	OR	97214	503-238-1617		31
Wunderlich corrugated packaging 821 Clinton St *Web:* www.wunderlichbox.com	Saint Louis	MO	63102	314-231-1488		100
Wunderlich Securities Inc 6000 Poplar Ave Ste 150 *Web:* www.wunderlichsecurities.com	Memphis	TN	38119	901-251-1330		690
Wunderlich-Malec Engineering Inc 6101 Blue Cir Dr *Web:* www.wmeng.com	Eden Prairie	MN	55343	952-933-3222	933-0608	261
Wunderman Thompson 466 Lexington Ave *Web:* www.jwt.com	New York	NY	10017	212-210-7000		4
WUOT-FM 91.9 (NPR) University of Tennessee 209 Communications Bldg *TF:* 888-266-9868 ■ *Web:* www.wuot.org	Knoxville	TN	37996	865-974-5375	974-3941	645-82
Wupatki National Monument Flagstaff Area National Monuments 6400 US 89 *Web:* www.nps.gov	Flagstaff	AZ	86004	928-526-3367		564
WUPA-TV Ch 69 (CW) 2700 NE Expy Bldg A *Web:* cwatlanta.cbslocal.com	Atlanta	GA	30345	404-325-6929	633-4567	741-7
WUPE-AM 466 Curran Hwy *Web:* www.wupe.com	North Adams	MA	01247	413-499-3333		647
WUPS-FM 125 W Houghton Lake Dr PO Box 468 *TF:* 800-968-4487 ■ *Web:* www.wups.com	Prudenville	MI	48651	989-366-5364		647
WUPV-TV Ch 65 (CW) 5710 Midlothian Tpke *Web:* www.nbc12.com	Richmond	VA	23225	804-230-1212	230-7059	741-108
WUPW-TV 730 N Summit St *Web:* www.foxtoledo.revrocket.us	Toledo	OH	43604	419-244-3600		647
Wurth 1640 Mims Ave SW *TF:* 800-272-6486 ■ *Web:* www.wurthwoodgroup.com	Birmingham	AL	35211	205-925-7601	923-9511	613
Wurth Revcar Fasteners Inc 3845 Thirlane Rd *TF:* 800-542-5762 ■ *Web:* revcarmilitaryfasteners.com	Roanoke	VA	24019	800-542-5762		351
Wurth Service Supply Inc 4935 W 86th St **Fax Area Code:* 716 ■ *Web:* www.wuerth-industrie.com	Indianapolis	IN	46268	317-704-1000	668-2264*	351
Wurth USA Inc 93 Grant St *TF:* 800-987-8487 ■ *Web:* www.wurthusa.com	Ramsey	NJ	07446	201-825-2710	825-3706	61
Wurzel Builders Ltd 630 Ralph Ablanedo Dr *Web:* wurzelbuilders.com	Austin	TX	78748	512-282-9488	282-9682	186
WUSA-TV Ch 9 (CBS) 4100 Wisconsin Ave NW *TF:* 877-333-4926 ■ *Web:* www.wusa9.com	Washington	DC	20016	202-895-5999		741-139
WUSB-FM 2nd Fl West Side Dining Stony Brook University *TF:* 888-632-9872 ■ *Web:* www.wusb.fm	Stony Brook	NY	11794	631-632-6500		647
WUSF 4202 E Fowler Ave TVB 100 *TF:* 800-741-9090 ■ *Web:* www.wusf.org	Tampa	FL	33620	813-974-8700	974-5016	645-160
WUSF-TV Ch 16 (PBS) 4202 E Fowler Ave *TF:* 800-654-3703 ■ *Web:* www.wusftv.usf.edu	Tampa	FL	33620	813-974-9127	974-4806	741-133
WUSN-US 99.5 FM 180 N Stetson Ave Ste 1000 *Web:* www.chicagomusic.org	Chicago	IL	60601	312-649-0099		645-34
WUSY 101 7413 Old Lee Hwy *Web:* us101country.iheart.com	Chattanooga	TN	37421	423-892-3333		645-155
WUTC-FM 88.1 (NPR) 615 McCallie Ave 104 Cadek Hall Dept 1151 *Web:* wutc.org	Chattanooga	TN	37403	423-425-4756		645-155
WUTR-TV 5956 Smith Hill Rd *Web:* www.cnyhomepage.com	Utica	NY	13502	315-797-5220		647
WUUF-FM 187 Vienna Rd *Web:* www.bigdog1035.com	Newark	NY	14513	315-331-9667	331-7101	647
WUWF-FM 88.1 (NPR) 11000 University Pkwy *TF:* 800-239-9893 ■ *Web:* wuwf.org	Pensacola	FL	32514	850-474-2787		645-118
WUWM-FM 89.7 (NPR) 111 E Wisconsin Ave Ste 700 *Web:* www.wuwm.com	Milwaukee	WI	53202	414-227-3355		645-98
WVACO (West Virginia Association of Counties) 2026 Kanawha Blvd *Web:* www.wvaco.org	Charleston	WV	25311	304-346-0591		49-7
WVCC (Warwick Valley Chamber of Commerce) PO Box 202 *TF:* 877-598-7245 ■ *Web:* www.warwickcc.org	Warwick	NY	10990	845-986-2720		139
WVCP-FM 1480 Nashville Pke Ramer Bldg Ste 101 *Web:* www.wvcp.net	Gallatin	TN	37066	615-230-3618	230-4803	647
WVCY-TV Ch 30 (Ind) 3434 W Kilbourn Ave *TF:* 800-729-9829 ■ *Web:* www.vcyamerica.org	Milwaukee	WI	53208	414-935-3000	935-3015	741-83
WVEC-TV Ch 13 (ABC) 613 Woodis Ave *Web:* www.13newsnow.com	Norfolk	VA	23510	757-625-1313		741-92
WVEE-FM 103.3 (Urban) 1201 Peachtree St NE Ste 800 *Web:* v103.radio.com	Atlanta	GA	30361	404-898-8900		645-11
WVEN-TV 523 Douglas Ave *Web:* www.wventv.com	Altamonte Springs	FL	32714	407-774-2626		647
WVGES (West Virginia Geological & Economic Survey) Mont Chateau Research Ctr 1 Mont Chateau Rd *TF:* 800-984-3656 ■ *Web:* www.wvgs.wvnet.edu	Morgantown	WV	26508	304-594-2331	594-2575	637-2
WVHDF(West Virginia) *Housing Development Fund* 5710 MacCorkle Ave SE *TF:* 800-933-9843 ■ *Web:* www.wvhdf.com	Charleston	WV	25304	304-391-8600		339-49
WVII-TV Ch 7 (ABC) 371 Target Industrial Cir *Web:* www.foxbangor.com	Bangor	ME	04401	207-945-6457		741-12
WVIT-TV Ch 30 (NBC) 1422 New Britain Ave *Web:* www.nbcconnecticut.com	West Hartford	CT	06110	860-521-3030		741
WVMA (Wisconsin Veterinary Medical Assn) 2801 Crossroads Dr Ste 1200 *TF:* 888-254-5202 ■ *Web:* www.wvma.org	Madison	WI	53718	608-257-3665	257-8989	795
WVMA (Wyoming Veterinary Medical Assn) 2001 Capitol Ave *TF:* 800-272-1813 ■ *Web:* www.wyvma.org	Cheyenne	WY	82001	800-272-1813		795
WVNA (West Virginia Nurses Assn) PO Box 1946 *TF:* 800-400-1226 ■ *Web:* wvnurses.nursingnetwork.com	Charleston	WV	25327	304-417-1497		533
WVNJ-AM 1086 Teaneck Rd Ste 4F *TF:* 800-962-1160 ■ *Web:* www.wvnj.com	Teaneck	NJ	07666	201-837-0400	837-9664	647
WVNS-TV 141 Old Cline Rd PO Box 509 *Web:* www.wvnstv.com	Ghent	WV	25843	304-787-5959	787-2440	647
WVOL-AM 1320 Brick Church Pke *Web:* www.wvol1470.com	Nashville	TN	37207	615-226-9510	226-0709	647
WVON-AM 1690 (N/T) 1000 E 87th St *Web:* wvon.com	Chicago	IL	60619	773-247-6200		645-34
WVPE-FM 88.1 (NPR) 2424 California Rd *TF:* 888-399-9873 ■ *Web:* www.wvpe.org	Elkhart	IN	46514	574-674-9873	262-5700	645
WVRQ-AM E7601A CTH SS *Web:* www.greatriversnews.com	Viroqua	WI	54665	608-637-7200	637-7299	647
WVS Financial Corp 9001 Perry Hwy *NASDAQ: WVFC* ■ *Web:* www.wvsbank.com	Pittsburgh	PA	15237	412-364-1911		360-2
WVSA-AM PO Box 630 *Web:* www.wvsa1380.com	Vernon	AL	35592	205-695-9191	695-9131	647
WVTF-FM 89.1 (NPR) 3520 Kingsbury Ln *TF:* 800-856-8900 ■ *Web:* wvtf.org	Roanoke	VA	24014	540-989-8900	776-2727	645-133
WVTM-TV Ch 13 (NBC) 1732 Valley View Dr *TF:* 844-248-7698 ■ *Web:* www.wvtm13.com	Birmingham	AL	35209	205-933-1313	558-7389	741-15
WVTV My24 11520 W Calumet Rd *Web:* my24milwaukee.com	Milwaukee	WI	53224	414-815-4100	815-4103	741-83
WVU Tomchin Planetarium & Observatory 135 Willey St *Web:* planetarium.wvu.edu	Morgantown	WV	26506	304-293-4961		598
WVUA-TV 920 Paul W Bryant Dr N323 Bryant-Denny Stadium *Web:* www.wvua23.com	Tuscaloosa	AL	35487	205-348-7000	348-7002	647
WVUB-FM 1200 N 2nd St *Web:* www.wvub.org	Vincennes	IN	47591	812-888-4347	882-2237	647
WVUE-TV Ch 8 (Fox) 1025 S Jefferson Davis Pkwy *Web:* www.fox8live.com	New Orleans	LA	70125	504-486-6161	483-1543	741-90
WVUT-TV 1200 N 2nd St *Web:* www.vincennespbs.org	Vincennes	IN	47591	812-888-4345		647
WVVA-TV 3052 Big Laurel Hwy *TF:* 800-227-9882 ■ *Web:* www.wvva.com	Bluefield	WV	24701	304-325-5487	327-5586	647
WVVH-TV PO Box 769 **Fax Area Code:* 212 ■ *Web:* www.wvvh.com	Wainscott	NY	11975	631-537-0273	935-4449*	647
WVXU-FM 91.7 (NPR) 1223 Central Pkwy *Web:* wvxu.org	Cincinnati	OH	45214	513-352-9170		645-35
WVYB-FM 103.3 126 W International Speedway Blvd *Web:* 1033wvyb.com	Daytona Beach	FL	32114	386-255-9300		645-45
WW (World Wisdom Books) PO Box 2682 *TF:* 888-992-6651 ■ *Web:* www.worldwisdom.com	Bloomington	IN	47402	812-330-3232		637-2
WW Associates 110 Vista Centre Dr Ste 1 *Web:* www.wwassociates.net	Forest	VA	24551	434-316-6080	316-6081	196
WW Gay Fire & Integrated Systems Inc 522 Stockton St *Web:* www.wwgfp.com	Jacksonville	FL	32204	904-387-7973		610
WW Grainger Inc 100 Grainger Pkwy *NYSE: GWW* ■ *TF:* 888-361-8649 ■ *Web:* www.grainger.com	Lake Forest	IL	60045	847-535-1000		246
WW Metal Products Inc 1226 N Fm 2148 *Web:* www.wwmetalproducts.com	Texarkana	TX	75501	903-838-4329	838-8523	91
WW Wood Products Inc PO Box 50 *Web:* www.wwwoodproducts.com	Dudley	MO	63936	573-624-7090		115

	Phone	Fax	Class
WWAR (World Wide Arts Resources Corp) PO Box 150 .... Granville OH 43023 *Web:* www.wwar.com	646-455-1425		637-10
WWAY-TV 615 N Front St .... Wilmington NC 28401 *Web:* www.wwaytv3.com	910-762-8581		647
WWBD-FM 51 Commerce St........ Sumter SC 29150 *Web:* www.cbsumter.com	803-775-2321		647
WWBF-AM 1130 Radio Rd .... Bartow FL 33830 *Web:* www.wwbf.com	863-533-0744		647
W&WC (Woodlands and Wildlife Consultants LLC) PO Box 1508 .... Fortson GA 31808 *Web:* www.woodlandsandwildlife.com	706-718-9208		192
Wwc Enterprises Inc 19145 S US Hwy 377........ Dublin TX 76446 *Web:* www.wwcenterprises.com	254-445-0100		463
WWCK-FM 105.5 (CHR) 6317 Taylor Dr........ Flint MI 48507 *Web:* www.wwck.com	810-238-7300	725-2500	645-58
WWDB-AM 555 City Line Ave Ste 220 .... Bala Cynwyd PA 19004 *Web:* www.wwdbam.com	610-667-9000		647
WWDE-FM 101.3 236 Clearfield Ave Ste 206........ Virginia Beach VA 23462 *Web:* www.2wd.com	757-497-2000		645
WWF (World Wildlife Fund Canada) 410 Adelaide St W Ste 400........ Toronto ON M5V1S8 *TF:* 800-267-2632 ■ *Web:* www.wwf.ca	416-489-8800	489-8055	48-3
WWF (World Wildlife Fund) 1250 24th St NW PO Box 97180 .... Washington DC 20090 *TF:* 800-225-5993 ■ *Web:* www.worldwildlife.org	202-293-4800	293-9211	48-3
WWFX-FM 100.1 (CR) 250 Commercial St 5th Fl........ Worcester MA 01608 *Web:* www.pikefm.com	508-752-1045	973-0824	645-171
WWGB-AM 6710 Oxon Hill Rd Ste 100 Indian Head........ Oxon Hill MD 20745 *Web:* www.wwgb.com	301-749-1444	749-7244	647
WWIB-FM 2396 Hallie Rd........ Chippewa Falls WI 54729 *Web:* www.wwib.com	715-723-1037	723-1348	647
WWIS Radio Inc W11573 Town Creek Rd........ Black River Falls WI 54615 *TF:* 877-997-9947 ■ *Web:* www.wwisradio.com	715-284-4391		645-141
WWJO-FM 640 SE Lincoln Ave........ Saint Cloud MN 56304 *Web:* www.minnesotasnewcountry.com	320-252-9897		647
WWKA-FM 92.3 (Ctry) 4192 N John Young Pkwy........ Orlando FL 32804 *TF:* 866-438-0220 ■ *Web:* www.k923orlando.com	407-424-9236	299-4947	645-114
WWKC-FM 4988 Skyline Dr PO Box 338 .... Cambridge OH 43725 *Web:* www.yourradioplace.com	740-432-5605		647
WWKI-FM 519 N Main St........ Kokomo IN 46901 *TF:* 800-444-9954 ■ *Web:* www.wwki.com	765-459-4191	456-1111	647
WWL Industries Inc 2412 W 42nd St........ Odessa TX 79764 *Web:* www.wwlindustries.com	432-362-0326	367-7210	537
WWLPcom 1 Broadcast Ctr........ Chicopee MA 01013 *TF:* 855-977-2470 ■ *Web:* www.wwlp.com	413-377-2200	377-2261	741-129
WWL-TV Ch 4 (CBS) 1024 N Rampart St........ New Orleans LA 70116 *Web:* www.wwltv.com	504-529-4444		741-90
WWLZ-AM 2205 College Ave .... Elmira NY 14903 *Web:* www.cbelmira.com	607-732-4400		647
WWML (Willoughby Wallace Memorial Library) 146 Thimble Islands Rd .... Branford CT 06405 *Web:* www.wwml.org	203-488-8702	315-3347	434-3
WWMT-TV Ch 3 (CBS) 590 W Maple St .... Kalamazoo MI 49008 **Fax Area Code:* 269 ■ *TF:* 800-875-3333 ■ *Web:* www.wwmt.com	800-875-3333	388-8322*	741
WWMX-FM 106.5 1423 Clarkview Rd Ste 100........ Baltimore MD 21209 *Web:* mix1065fm.radio.com	410-825-1065		645-15
WWNO-FM 89.9 (NPR) University of New Orleans 2000 Lakeshore Dr .... New Orleans LA 70148 *TF:* 800-286-7002 ■ *Web:* www.wwno.org	504-280-7000	280-6061	645-107
WWOZ-FM 90.7 FM 1008 N Peters St........ New Orleans LA 70116 *Web:* www.wwoz.org	504-568-1239	558-9332	645-107
WWPA (Western Wood Products Assn) 522 SW Fifth Ave Ste 500........ Portland OR 97204 *Web:* www.wwpa.org	503-224-3930	224-3934	48-2
WWPR-AM 5910 Cortez Rd W No 130 .... Bradenton FL 34210 *Web:* www.1490wwpr.com	941-761-8843		647
WWRR-FM 1049 N Sekol Rd........ Scranton PA 18504 *Web:* www.bold.gold	570-344-1221		647
WWSB-TV 1477 10th St .... Sarasota FL 34236 *Web:* www.mysuncoast.com	941-923-8840	923-8709	647
WWSM-AM 277 Gravel Hill Rd........ Palmyra PA 17078 *Web:* www.wwsm.us	717-272-1510		647
WWTH-FM 1491 M-32 W........ Alpena MI 49707 *TF:* 800-743-6424 ■ *Web:* www.truenorthradionetwork.com	989-354-4611		647
WWVU-FM W Virginia University PO Box 6446 .... Morgantown WV 26506 *Web:* u92themoose.com	304-293-3329		645-103
WWWX-FM 491 S Washburn St Ste 400........ Oshkosh WI 54904 *TF:* 877-369-7699 ■ *Web:* www.fox969.com	920-426-3239		647
WWZQ-AM PO Box 458........ Amory MS 38821 *Web:* www.fm95radio.com	662-256-9726	256-9725	647
WXBA-FM 52 3rd Ave........ Brentwood NY 11717 *Web:* www.brentwood.k12.ny.us	631-434-2123		647
WXCO-AM 1110 E Wausau Ave PO Box 778........ Wausau WI 54402 *Web:* www.1230wxco.com	715-845-8218	845-6582	647
WXCW-TV 2824 Palm Beach Blvd........ Fort Myers FL 33916 *Web:* www.wxcw.com	239-479-5500	332-0767	647
WXCY-FM 103.7 707 Revolution St........ Havre de Grace MD 21078 **Fax Area Code:* 888 ■ *TF:* 800-788-9929 ■ *Web:* www.wxcyfm.com	410-939-1100	766-1037*	645
WXDU-FM 88.7 (Alt) PO Box 90689........ Durham NC 27708 *Web:* www.wxdu.org	919-684-2957		645-128
WXEL-FM 90.7 (NPR) 3401 S Congress Ave........ Boynton Beach FL 33426 *TF:* 800-915-9935 ■ *Web:* www.wxel.org	561-737-8000	369-3067	645-23
WXFL-TV 525 E Tennessee St........ Florence AL 35630 *Web:* www.wbcf.com	256-764-8170		647
WXFN-AM 800 E 29th St........ Muncie IN 47302 *Web:* www.wlbc.com	765-289-9522	288-0429	647

	Phone	Fax	Class
WXFX-FM 95.1 (Rock) 1 Commerce St Ste 300........ Montgomery AL 36104 *Web:* www.wxfx.com	334-240-9274	240-9219	645-102
WXIA-TV Ch 11 (NBC) 1 Monroe Pl........ Atlanta GA 30324 *Web:* www.11alive.com	404-892-1611		741-7
WXIN-TV Ch 59 (Fox) 6910 Network Pl........ Indianapolis IN 46278 *Web:* www.fox59.com	317-632-5900		741-62
WXIX-TV Ch 19 (Fox) 635 W Seventh St 19 Broadcast Plz........ Cincinnati OH 45203 *Web:* www.fox19.com	513-421-1919	421-3022	741-30
WXKL-AM 1516 Woodland Ave........ Sanford NC 27330 *Web:* www.wxkl1290.com	919-774-1080		647
WXKS-FM 10 Cabot Rd Ste 302........ Medford MA 02155 *Web:* www.kiss108.com	781-396-1430		647
WXKZ-FM PO Box 159........ Harold KY 41635 *TF:* 877-266-5582 ■ *Web:* www.mygmedia.com	606-478-4200	478-4202	647
WXLT-FM (103.5 ESPN) 1431 Country Air Dr........ Carterville IL 62918 *TF:* 866-230-7625 ■ *Web:* www.1035espn.com	618-985-5803	985-6529	643
WXLY-FM 950 Houston-Northcutt Blvd 2nd Fl........ Mount Pleasant SC 29464 *Web:* y1025.iheart.com	843-884-2534		647
WXMI-TV Ch 17 (Fox) 3117 Plaza Dr NE........ Grand Rapids MI 49525 *Web:* www.fox17online.com	616-364-8722	364-8506	741-53
WXMX-FM 98.1 (Rock) 5629 Murray Rd........ Memphis TN 38119 *Web:* www.981themax.com	901-535-9898		645-95
WXNU-FM 70 Meadowview Ctr........ Kankakee IL 60901 *TF:* 877-777-1065 ■ *Web:* www.xcountry1065.com	815-935-9555		647
WXPN-FM 88.5 3025 Walnut St........ Philadelphia PA 19104 *Web:* xpn.org	215-898-6677	898-0707	645-120
WXRL-AM 1300 PO Box 170........ Lancaster NY 14086 *Web:* www.wxrl.com	716-681-1313		645
WXRR-FM 104.5 (Rock) 4580 Hwy 15 N........ Laurel MS 39443 *Web:* www.rock104fm.com	601-544-0095	545-8199	645
WXRT-FM Two Prudential Plz 180 N Stetson 10th Fl........ Chicago IL 60601	312-240-9978	240-7973	647
WXRV-FM 92.5 (AAA) 30 How St........ Haverhill MA 01830 *Web:* theriverboston.com	978-374-4733		645
WXTB-FM 4002 W Gandy Blvd........ Tampa FL 33611 *TF:* 800-737-0098 ■ *Web:* 98rock.iheart.com	813-832-1000		647
WXXI Public Broadcasting Council 280 State St .... Rochester NY 14603 *Web:* www.wxxi.org	585-258-0200		647
WXXJ-FM 8000 Belfort Pkwy Ste 100........ Jacksonville FL 32256 **Fax Area Code:* 904 ■ *Web:* www.x1065.com	833-758-1065	245-8501*	647
WXXV-TV Ch 25 (Fox) 14351 Hwy 49 N........ Gulfport MS 39503 *Web:* www.wxxv25.com	228-832-2525		741
WXYT-AM 26455 American Dr........ Southfield MI 48034 *Web:* www.detroit.cbslocal.com	248-327-2900		647
WXYZ-TV Ch 7 (ABC) 20777 W 10-Mile Rd........ Southfield MI 48037 *TF:* 800-825-0770 ■ *Web:* www.wxyz.com	248-827-7777	827-9444	741
WXZQ-FM PO Box 820........ Piketon OH 45661 *Web:* www.wxzqfm.com	740-947-0059		647
Wy Industries Inc 2500 Secaucus Rd........ North Bergen NJ 07047 *Web:* www.wyindustries.com	201-617-8000		596
WYAJ-FM Lincoln Sundbury Regional High School 390 Lincoln Rd .... Sudbury MA 01776 *Web:* www.lsrhs.net	978-443-9961	443-8824	647
Wyalusing State Park 13081 State Park Ln........ Bagley WI 53801 *Web:* dnr.wi.gov	608-996-2261		565
Wyandot County 109 S Sandusky Ave........ Upper Sandusky OH 43351 *Web:* www.co.wyandot.oh.us	419-294-3836	294-6414	338
Wyandot Inc 135 Wyandot Ave........ Marion OH 43302 *Web:* wyandotsnacks.com	740-383-4031		296-35
Wyant Data Systems Inc 245 Century Cir Ste 106........ Louisville CO 80027 *Web:* www.wyantdata.com	303-604-6254		177
Wyatt & Company Inc 6846 S Trenton Ave........ Tulsa OK 74136 *Web:* www.wyattandcompany.com	918-488-0311		2
Wyatt & Jaffe 2751 Hennepin Ave S Ste 286........ Minneapolis MN 55408 *Web:* www.wyattjaffe.com	612-285-2858	285-2786	266
Wyatt Early Harris Wheeler LLP 1912 Eastchester Dr........ High Point NC 27261 *Web:* www.wehwlaw.com	336-884-4444	889-5232	428
Wyatt Field Service Co 15415 Katy Fwy Ste 800........ Houston TX 77094 *Web:* www.wyattfieldservice.com	281-675-1300	675-1390	189-1
Wyatt Inc 4545 Campbells Run Rd........ Pittsburgh PA 15205 *TF:* 800-966-5801 ■ *Web:* www.wyattincorporated.com	412-787-5800	787-5845	189-9
Wyatt Precision Machine Inc 3301 E 59th St........ Long Beach CA 90805 *Web:* www.wyattprecisionmachine.com	562-634-0524		757
Wyatt Tarrant & Combs PNC Plz 500 W Jefferson St........ Louisville KY 40202 *Web:* www.wyattfirm.com	502-589-5235		428
Wyatt Transfer Inc 3035 Bells Rd PO Box 24326........ Richmond VA 23224 *TF:* 800-552-5708 ■ *Web:* www.wyatttransferinc.com	804-743-3800	271-9598	780
Wyatt's Supermarket Inc 1310 W Shelby St........ Falmouth KY 41040 *Web:* supervalufoodstores.com	937-675-4161		345
Wyatt-Quarles Seed Co 730 US Hwy 70 W........ Garner NC 27529 *TF:* 800-662-7591 ■ *Web:* www.wqseeds.com	919-772-4243	772-4278	274
WYAV-FM 104.1 (CR) 1016 Ocala St........ Myrtle Beach SC 29577 *Web:* wave104.com	843-626-9283		645-104
WYCA-FM 6336 Calumet Ave........ Hammond IN 46324 *Web:* www.crawfordbroadcasting.com	219-933-4455		647
WYCC-TV Ch 20 (PBS) 6258 S Union Ave........ Chicago IL 60621 *Web:* www.interactive.wttw.com	773-224-3300		741-29

	Phone	Fax	Class
Wyche Burgess Freeman & Parham 44 E Camperdown Way.......... Greenville SC 29601 *Web:* www.wyche.com	864-242-8212		428
Wycliffe Bible Translators 11221 John Wycliffe Blvd.......... Orlando FL 32832 *TF:* 800-992-5433 ■ *Web:* www.wycliffe.org	407-852-3600		48-20
Wycoff Insurance Agency Inc 501 S Second St.......... Mount Vernon WA 98273 *Web:* wycoffinsurance.com	360-336-2112		390
WYDA (Wyoming Dental Assn) 123 W First St Ste 208B.......... Casper WY 82601 *Web:* www.wyda.org	307-237-1186		227
WYDC-TV 33 E Market St.......... Corning NY 14830 *Web:* www.wydc-tv.com	607-937-5000	937-4019	647
Wyde Corp 3600 American Blvd W Ste 330.......... Bloomington MN 55431 *Web:* www.wyde.com	651-882-2400		180
Wyden Ron (Sen D - OR) 221 Dirksen Senate Office Bldg.......... Washington DC 20510 *Web:* www.wyden.senate.gov	202-224-5244	228-2717	342-2
Wydler Brothers LLC 4445 Willard Ave Ste 250.......... Chevy Chase MD 20815 *Web:* wydlerbrothers.com	301-463-7800		652
Wye Island Natural Resources Management Area 632 Wye Island Rd.......... Queenstown MD 21658 *Web:* www.dnr.maryland.gov	410-827-7577		565
WYES-TV Ch 12 (PBS) 111 Veterans Blvd Ste 250.......... Metairie LA 70005 *Web:* www.wyes.org	504-486-5511	840-9954	741
Wyffels Hybrids Inc 13344 US Hwy 6.......... Geneseo IL 61254 *TF:* 800-369-7833 ■ *Web:* www.wyffels.com	309-944-8334	944-8338	10-5
WYFF-TV Ch 4 (NBC) 505 Rutherford St.......... Greenville SC 29609 *TF:* 800-453-9933 ■ *Web:* www.wyff4.com	864-242-4404	240-5305	741-6
WYFM-FM 4040 Simon Rd.......... Youngstown OH 44515 *TF:* 800-288-9103 ■ *Web:* www.y-103.com	330-782-9103		647
WYGM-AM 2500 Maitland Centre Pkwy Ste 401.......... Maitland FL 32751 *Web:* 960thegame.iheart.com	407-916-7800		647
WYKE-TV 5399 W Gulf to Lake Hwy.......... Lecanto FL 34461 *TF:* 888-377-0340 ■ *Web:* www.wyke47.com	352-527-2341	746-6514	647
Wylie Communications Inc 949 NW Overton Ste 1102.......... Portland OR 97209 *Web:* www.wyliecomm.com	503-954-2289		192
Wylie Spray Ctr 702 E 40th St.......... Lubbock TX 79404 *TF:* 888-249-5162 ■ *Web:* www.wyliesprayers.com	806-763-1335	763-1092	273
WYLN-TV 1057 E Tenth St.......... Hazleton PA 18201 *Web:* www.jbonom6.wixsite.com	570-459-1869	459-1625	647
Wyman Center Inc 600 Kiwanis Dr.......... Eureka MO 63025 *Web:* wymancenter.org	636-938-5245		239
Wyman-Gordon Forgings (Cleveland) Inc 3097 E 61st St.......... Cleveland OH 44127 *Web:* www.pccforgedproducts.com	216-341-0085		483
Wyman-Gordon Forgings Lp 10825 Telge Rd.......... Houston TX 77095 *Web:* www.pccforgedproducts.com	281-856-9900		567
WYMC-AM 197 WYMC Rd PO Box V.......... Mayfield KY 42066 *Web:* www.mywymc.com	270-247-1430	247-1825	647
WYMT-TV 199 Black Gold Blvd.......... Hazard KY 41701 *Web:* www.wymt.com	606-436-5757		647
Wynalda Packaging 8221 Graphic Dr NE.......... Belmont MI 49306 *Web:* www.wynalda.com	616-866-1561		548
Wyndham Destinations LLC 6277 Sea Harbor Dr.......... Orlando FL 32821 *Web:* www.wyndhamdestinations.com	407-626-5200		669
Wyndham Jade LLC 202 E Main Ave.......... Rockford IA 50468 *Web:* www.wynjade.com	641-756-3385		772
Wyndham Lake Buena Vista 1850 Hotel Plaza Blvd.......... Lake Buena Vista FL 32830 *TF:* 800-624-4109 ■ *Web:* www.wyndhamlakebuenavista.com	407-828-4444		379
Wyndham Vacation Resorts Inc 6277 Sea Harbor Dr.......... Orlando FL 32821 *TF:* 800-251-8736 ■ *Web:* www.myclubwyndham.com	800-251-8736		669
Wyndham Worldwide Corp 22 Sylvan Way.......... Parsippany NJ 07054 *NYSE: WYND* ■ *Web:* www.wyndhamhotels.com	973-753-6590	753-6000	379
Wyndhurst Manor & Club 55 Lee Rd.......... Lenox MA 01240 *TF:* 800-272-6935 ■ *Web:* www.wyndhurstmanorandclub.com	413-637-1364	637-4364	669
Wynick Tuck Gallery 401 Richmond St W Studio S27.......... Toronto ON M5V3A8 *Web:* wynicktuckgallery.ca	416-504-8716	504-8699	42
Wynkoop Brewing Co 1634 18th St.......... Denver CO 80202 *Web:* www.wynkoop.com	303-297-2700		671
Wynn L. White Consulting Engineers Inc 17485 Opportunity Ave Ste C.......... Baton Rouge LA 70817 *Web:* www.wynnwhite.com	225-761-9141	761-4450	192
Wynnchurch Capital Ltd 6250 N River Rd Ste 10-100.......... Rosemont IL 60018 *TF:* 877-604-6111 ■ *Web:* www.wynnchurch.com	847-604-6100	604-6105	792
WYNN-CROSBY 1601 Bryan St Ste 4300.......... Dallas TX 75201 *Web:* www.wynncrosby.com	972-380-5500	380-9570	536
Wynne Transport Service Inc 2222 N 11th St PO Box 8700.......... Omaha NE 68110 *TF:* 800-383-9330 ■ *Web:* www.wynnetr.com	402-342-4001	342-4608	780
Wynright Client Care 11000 S Lavergne Ave.......... Oak Lawn IL 60453 **Fax Area Code:* 708 ■ *Web:* www.wynrightproducts.com	888-996-0099	221-7182*	207
Wynright Corp 2500 York Rd.......... Elk Grove Village IL 60007 *Web:* www.wynright.com	847-595-9400		358
Wynston Hill Capital LLC 488 Madison Ave 24th Fl.......... New York NY 10022 *Web:* wynstonhillcapital.com	212-888-1718	208-0978	256
Wyo-Ben Inc 1345 Discovery Dr.......... Billings MT 59102 *TF:* 800-548-7055 ■ *Web:* www.wyoben.com	406-652-6351	656-0748	503-2
Wyoming *Aging Div* 2300 Capitol Ave 4th Fl.......... Cheyenne WY 82002 *TF:* 800-442-2766 ■ *Web:* health.wyo.gov	307-777-7995	777-5340	339-51
Agriculture Dept (WDA) 2219 Carey Ave.......... Cheyenne WY 82001 *Web:* wyagric.state.wy.us	307-777-7321	777-6593	339-51
Arts Council 2301 Central Ave 2nd Fl.......... Cheyenne WY 82002 *Web:* wyoarts.state.wy.us	307-777-7742		339-51
Board of Certified Public Accountants 325 W 18th St Ste 4.......... Cheyenne WY 82002 *Web:* sites.google.com	307-777-7551	777-3796	339-51
Board of Medicine 130 Hobbs Ave Ste A.......... Cheyenne WY 82001 *Web:* wyomedboard.wyo.gov	307-778-7053	778-2069	339-51
Business Council 214 W 15th St.......... Cheyenne WY 82002 *TF:* 800-262-3425 ■ *Web:* www.wyomingbusiness.org	307-777-2800	777-2838	339-51
Community College Commission 2300 Capitol Ave Ste B Fifth Fl.......... Cheyenne WY 82002 *Web:* communitycolleges.wy.edu	307-777-7763	777-6567	725
Community Development Authority 155 N Beech St PO Box 634.......... Casper WY 82602 *Web:* www.wyomingcda.com	307-265-0603	266-5414	339-51
Corrections Dept 1934 Wyott Dr Ste 100.......... Cheyenne WY 82002 *Web:* corrections.wyo.gov	307-777-7208	777-7846	339-51
Division of Banking 2300 Capitol Ave 2nd Fl.......... Cheyenne WY 82002 *Web:* wyomingbankingdivision.wyo.gov	307-777-7797	777-3555	339-51
Environmental Quality Dept 200 W 17th St.......... Cheyenne WY 82002 *Web:* deq.state.wy.us	307-777-7937	635-1784	339-51
Health Dept 401 Hathaway Bldg.......... Cheyenne WY 82002 *TF:* 866-571-0944 ■ *Web:* health.wyo.gov	307-777-7656	777-7439	339-51
Highway Patrol (WHP) 5300 Bishop Blvd.......... Cheyenne WY 82009 *TF:* 800-442-9090 ■ *Web:* www.whp.dot.state.wy.us	307-777-4301	777-3897	339-51
Homeland Security Office 5500 Bishop Blvd E Door.......... Cheyenne WY 82002 *Web:* hls.wyo.gov	307-777-4663	635-6017	339-51
Insurance Dept 106 E Sixth Ave.......... Cheyenne WY 82001 *TF:* 800-438-5768 ■ *Web:* doi.wyo.gov	307-777-7401		339-51
Legislative Service Office 1021 Central Ave Ste 213.......... Cheyenne WY 82001 *Web:* www.wyoleg.gov	307-777-7881	777-5466	433
Professional Teaching Standards Board 1920 Thomes Ave Ste 100.......... Cheyenne WY 82002 *Web:* wyomingptsb.com	307-777-7291	777-8718	339-51
Real Estate Commission 2617 E Lincolnway Ste H.......... Cheyenne WY 82002 *Web:* www.wyo.gov	307-777-7141	777-3796	339-51
Revenue Dept 122 W 25th St 2nd Fl W.......... Cheyenne WY 82002 *Web:* revenue.wyo.gov	307-777-5200	777-3632	339-51
Secretary of State 122 W 25th St.......... Cheyenne WY 82002 *Web:* sos.wyo.gov	307-777-7378		339-51
Securities Div 2020 Carey Ave Ste 700.......... Cheyenne WY 82002 *Web:* sos.wyo.gov	307-777-7370	777-7640	339-51
State Historic Preservation Office 2301 Central Ave 3rd Fl.......... Cheyenne WY 82002 *Web:* wyoshpo.wyo.gov	307-777-7697	777-6421	339-51
State Parks & Historical Sites Div 2301 Central Ave 4th Fl.......... Cheyenne WY 82002 *Web:* wyoparks.wyo.gov	307-777-6323		339-51
State Penitentiary 2900 S Higley Rd PO Box 400.......... Rawlins WY 82301 *Web:* corrections.wyo.gov	307-328-1441		213
Supreme Court 2301 Capitol Ave.......... Cheyenne WY 82002 *Web:* courts.state.wy.us	307-777-7316	777-6129	339-51
Transportation Dept 5300 Bishop Blvd.......... Cheyenne WY 82009 *Web:* www.dot.state.wy.us	307-777-4375	777-4163	339-51
Treasurer 2020 Carey Ave 4th Fl.......... Cheyenne WY 82002 *Web:* statetreasurer.wyo.gov	307-777-7408		339-51
Victims Services Div 320 W 25th St 2nd Fl.......... Cheyenne WY 82002 *Web:* ag.wyo.gov	307-777-7200	777-6683	339-51
Vital Records Services 2300 Capitol Ave.......... Cheyenne WY 82002 *Web:* health.wyo.gov	307-777-7591	777-2483	339-51
Vocational Rehabilitation Div 1510 E Pershing Blvd.......... Cheyenne WY 82002 *Web:* www.wyomingworkforce.org	307-777-7364	777-3759	339-51
Wyoming Association of Realtors 777 Overland Trl Ste 220.......... Casper WY 82601 *TF:* 800-676-4085 ■ *Web:* www.wyomingrealtors.org	307-237-4085	237-7929	656
Wyoming Correctional Facility 3203 Dunbar Rd PO Box 501.......... Attica NY 14011 *Web:* www.doccs.ny.gov	585-591-1010		213
Wyoming County PO Box 309.......... Pineville WV 24874 *Web:* wyomingcounty.com	304-732-8000	732-9659	338
Wyoming County 79 Warren St.......... Tunkhannock PA 18657 *Web:* wyccc.com	570-836-3200		338
Wyoming County 143 N Main St.......... Warsaw NY 14569 *TF:* 800-527-1757 ■ *Web:* www.wyomingco.net	585-786-8810	786-3703	338
Wyoming County Law Library 1 Courthouse Sq.......... Tunkhannock PA 18657 *Web:* www.wycopa.org	570-996-2270		434-3
Wyoming Dental Assn (WYDA) 123 W First St Ste 208B.......... Casper WY 82601 *Web:* www.wyda.org	307-237-1186		227
Wyoming Dinosaur Ctr 110 Carter Ranch Rd.......... Thermopolis WY 82443 *TF:* 800-455-3466 ■ *Web:* wyomingdinosaurcenter.org	307-864-2997		520
Wyoming Game & Fish Dept 5400 Bishop Blvd.......... Cheyenne WY 82006 *TF:* 877-943-3847 ■ *Web:* wgfd.wyo.gov	307-777-4600	777-4699	339-51
Wyoming Honor Conservation Camp & Wyoming Boot Camp 40 Pippin Rd PO Box 160.......... Newcastle WY 82701 *Web:* corrections.wyo.gov	307-746-4436	746-9316	213
Wyoming Honor Farm (WHF) 40 Honor Farm Rd.......... Riverton WY 82501 *Web:* corrections.wyo.gov	307-856-9578	856-2505	213
Wyoming Hospital Assn 2005 Warren Ave.......... Cheyenne WY 82001 *Web:* www.wyohospitals.com	307-632-9344	632-9347	138

Name / Address	City	State	Zip	Phone	Fax	Class
Wyoming Machine Inc 30680 Forest Blvd. *Web:* www.wyomingmachine.com	Stacy	MN	55079	651-462-4156	462-5238	697
Wyoming Machinery Co 5300 Old W Yellowstone Hwy *Web:* www.wyomingcat.com	Casper	WY	82604	307-472-1000	261-4486	358
Wyoming Medical Ctr 1233 E Second St. *TF:* 800-822-7201 ■ *Web:* wyomingmedicalcenter.org	Casper	WY	82601	307-577-7201	233-8230	374-3
Wyoming Medical Society 122 E 17th St *Web:* www.wyomed.org	Cheyenne	WY	82001	307-635-2424	632-1973	474
Wyoming Mining Assn (WMA) 1401 Airport Pky Ste 230 *Web:* www.wyomingmining.org	Cheyenne	WY	82001	307-635-0331		48-13
Wyoming Pharmacy Assn 9 S Idaho *Web:* wypha.org	Guernsey	WY	82214	307-272-3361	766-2953	585
Wyoming Republican Party 1714 Capitol Ave PO Box 984 *Web:* www.wyoming.gop	Cheyenne	WY	82003	307-234-9166		616-2
Wyoming Seminary 201 N Sprague Ave *Web:* www.wyomingseminary.org	Kingston	PA	18704	570-270-2100	270-2198	622
Wyoming State Bar 4124 Laramie St *TF:* 855-445-8058 ■ *Web:* www.wyomingbar.org	Cheyenne	WY	82001	307-632-9061	632-3737	72
Wyoming State Hospital (WSH) 831 Hwy 150 S *Web:* health.wyo.gov	Evanston	WY	82930	307-789-3464		374-5
Wyoming State Library 2800 Central Ave *Web:* library.wyo.gov	Cheyenne	WY	82001	307-777-7281		434-5
Wyoming Symphony Orchestra 225 S David Ste B. *Web:* www.wyomingsymphony.org	Casper	WY	82601	307-266-1478	266-4522	573-3
Wyoming Tribune-Eagle 702 W Lincolnway *TF:* 800-561-6268 ■ *Web:* www.wyomingnews.com	Cheyenne	WY	82001	307-634-3361	633-3189	532-2
Wyoming Trucking Assn (WTA) 555 N Poplar St *TF:* 877-878-2515 ■ *Web:* www.wytruck.org	Casper	WY	82601	307-234-1579	234-7082	139
Wyoming Valley West School District 450 N Maple Ave *Web:* www.wvwsd.org	Kingston	PA	18704	570-288-6551		685
Wyoming Veterinary Medical Assn (WVMA) 2001 Capitol Ave *TF:* 800-272-1813 ■ *Web:* www.wyvma.org	Cheyenne	WY	82001	800-272-1813		795
Wyoming Women's Ctr 1000 W Griffith PO Box 300 *Web:* www.corrections.wyo.gov	Lusk	WY	82225	307-334-3693	334-2254	213
Wyoming-Kentwood Area Chamber of Commerce 4415 Byron Center Ave SW. *Web:* www.southkent.org	Wyoming	MI	49519	616-531-5990		139
Wyotech Sacramento 980 Riverside Pkwy *Web:* www.wyotech.edu	West Sacramento	CA	95605	916-376-8888		800
WYOW-TV 1908 Grand Ave. *Web:* www.waow.com	Wausau	WI	54403	715-842-9293	848-0195	647
WYPR-FM 88.1 (NPR) 2216 N Charles St *TF:* 866-661-9308 ■ *Web:* wypr.org	Baltimore	MD	21218	410-235-1660	235-1161	645-15
Wyrick Robbins Yates & Ponton 4101 Lake Boone Trl. *Web:* www.wyrick.com	Raleigh	NC	27607	919-781-4000		41
WYRK-FM 106.5 (Ctry) 14 Lafayette Sq Ste 1200 *Web:* www.wyrk.com	Buffalo	NY	14203	716-852-7444		645-25
Wyrulec Co 3978 US Hwy 26/85 *TF:* 800-628-5266 ■ *Web:* www.wyrulec.com	Torrington	WY	82240	307-837-2225	837-2115	245
WYSE Adv 668 Euclid Ave. *Web:* www.wyseadv.com	Cleveland	OH	44114	216-696-2424		4
Wyse Meter Solutions Inc RPO Newmarket Ct PO Box 95530 *TF:* 866-681-9465 ■ *Web:* www.wysemeter.com	Newmarket	ON	L3Y8J8	866-681-9465		393
Wyser-Pratte Management Company Inc 504 Guard Hill Rd. *Web:* www.wyser-pratte.com	Bedford	NY	10506	914-234-4930		690
Wysocki Produce Farm 6320 3rd Ave.	Plainfield	WI	54966	715-366-7175		10-11
Wysoker, Weingartner, Gonzalez & Lockspeiser PA 340 George St. *Web:* wgwnjlaw.com	New Brunswick	NJ	08901	732-545-3231		41
Wysong Inc 4820 US 29 N. *TF:* 800-299-7664 ■ *Web:* wysong.us	Greensboro	NC	27405	336-621-3960	621-8360	456
WYSU-FM 88.5 (Clas) Youngstown State University 1 University Plz *Web:* wysu.org	Youngstown	OH	44555	330-941-3363	941-1501	645-177
Wytech Industries Inc 960 E Hazelwood Ave *TF:* 866-458-2127 ■ *Web:* wytech.com	Rahway	NJ	07065	732-396-3900	396-4943	490
Wythe County 340 S Sixth St. *Web:* www.wytheco.org	Wytheville	VA	24382	276-223-6020	223-6030	338
Wythe County Public Schools Foundation for Excellence 1570 W Reservoir St. *Web:* wytheexcellence.org	Wytheville	VA	24382	276-228-5411		685
Wytheville Community College 1000 E Main St. *Web:* www.wcc.vccs.edu	Wytheville	VA	24382	276-223-4700	223-4860	162
Wytheville-Wythe-Bland Chamber of Commerce Inc 150 E Monroe St. *Web:* www.wwbchamber.com	Wytheville	VA	24382	276-223-3365	223-3412	139
WYTI Inc 275 Glenwood Dr. *Web:* wytiradio.com	Rocky Mount	VA	24151	540-483-9955	483-7802	645-141
Wyvern Consulting Ltd 10 N Main St *TF:* 800-946-4626 ■ *Web:* www.wyvernltd.com	Yardley	PA	19067	800-946-4626		693
WYYS-FM 3905 Progress Blvd *Web:* www.classichits106.com	Peru	IL	61354	815-224-2100		647
WYYZ-AM 268 Hood Rd *Web:* www.wyyzradio.com	Jasper	GA	30143	706-692-4100		647
WyzAnt Inc 1714 N Damen Ave Ste 3N *TF:* 877-999-2681 ■ *Web:* www.wyzant.com	Chicago	IL	60647	877-999-2681		387
WZAP-AM 11373 Wallace Pke *Web:* www.wzapradio.com	Bristol	VA	24203	276-669-6950		647
WZBC-FM 90.3 (Var) Boston College 107 McElroy Commons *Web:* www.wzbc.org	Chestnut Hill	MA	02467	617-552-3511		645
WZBT-FM 91.1 (Alt) Gettysburg College 300 N Washington St. *Web:* www.wzbt.org	Gettysburg	PA	17325	717-337-6315		645
WZDM-FM Historic Brevoort House 522 Busseron St PO Box 242 *TF:* 800-876-0173 ■ *Web:* www.wzdm.com	Vincennes	IN	47591	812-882-6060		647
WZHR 1400-AM 706 N Myrtle Ave. *Web:* www.wzhr.tantalk1340.com	Clearwater	FL	33755	727-441-3311		647
Wzi Inc 1717 28th St. *Web:* wziinc.com	Bakersfield	CA	93301	661-326-1112		261
WZNZ-AM 1600 kHz PO Box 51585 *Web:* www.queenofpeaceradio.com	Jacksonville Beach	FL	32240	904-241-3311		645-76
WZSR-FM 14285 Midway Rd *Web:* www.star105.com	Addison	TX	75001	972-458-9300		647
WZUS-FM 410 N Water St. *Web:* www.decaturradio.com	Decatur	IL	62523	217-428-4487	428-4501	647
WZWW-FM 160 W Clearview Ave *Web:* www.3wz.com	State College	PA	16801	814-237-0953		647
WZZK-FM 104.7 (Ctry) 2700 Corporate Dr Ste 115. *TF:* 866-998-1047 ■ *Web:* www.wzzk.com	Birmingham	AL	35242	205-916-1100	290-1061	645-19
WZZM-TV Ch 13 (ABC) 645 3-Mile Rd NW *Web:* www.wzzm13.com	Grand Rapids	MI	49544	616-785-1313	785-1301	741-53
WZZO-FM 95.1 (Rock) 1541 Alta Dr Ste 400 *Web:* 951zzo.iheart.com	Whitehall	PA	18052	610-720-9595		645

X

Name / Address	City	State	Zip	Phone	Fax	Class
X 3 Sports 2343 Windy Hill Rd SE *Web:* x3sports.com	Marietta	GA	30067	678-903-0100		354
X By 2 Inc 35055 W 12 Mile Rd Ste 220 *Web:* www.xby2.com	Farmington Hills	MI	48331	248-538-9292		186
X Dot Inc 4500 Westgrove Dr Ste 395 *TF:* 800-248-9368 ■ *Web:* www.x-dot.com	Addison	TX	75001	972-248-7243	248-7380	463
X103.9 242 E Airport Dr Ste 106. *Web:* www.x1039.com	San Bernardino	CA	92408	909-890-5904	890-9035	645-130
X17 Inc PO Box 2362 *Web:* www.x17online.com	Beverly Hills	CA	90213	310-273-1777		387
X2X LLC 100 1st St Ste 300 *Web:* pix.online	San Francisco	CA	94105	415-357-9720		514
X-Act Computer Service Inc 510 E Maude Ave *Web:* x-act.co	Sunnyvale	CA	94085	408-245-4787		570
Xacti 999 W Yamato Rd Ste 100 *Web:* www.xacti.com	Boca Raton	FL	33431	561-989-7400	989-7401	387
Xactra Technologies Inc 9 Marway Cir *Web:* www.xactra.com	Rochester	NY	14624	585-426-2030		493
Xactware Solutions Inc 1100 W Traverse Pkwy *TF:* 800-424-9228 ■ *Web:* www.xactware.com	Lehi	UT	84043	801-764-5900	932-8013	178-11
Xamax Industries Inc 63 Silvermine Rd. *TF:* 888-926-2988 ■ *Web:* xamax.com	Seymour	CT	06483	203-888-7200		557
Xanadu Salon & Spa 3351 W Sheridan St *Web:* xanadusalonspa.com	Hollywood	FL	33021	954-983-0100		77
Xandex Inc 1360 Redwood Way Ste A *TF:* 800-767-9543 ■ *Web:* www.xandexsemi.com	Petaluma	CA	94954	707-763-7799	763-2631	248
XangaCom Inc 555 Eigth Ave Ste 21F *Web:* xanga.com	New York	NY	10018	212-695-4940		246
Xante Corp 2800 Dauphin St Ste 100 *TF:* 800-926-8839 ■ *Web:* www.xante.com	Mobile	AL	36606	251-473-6502	473-6503	173-6
Xanterra Parks & Resorts 6312 S Fiddlers Green Cir Ste 600-N *TF:* 800-236-7916 ■ *Web:* www.xanterra.com	Greenwood Village	CO	80111	303-600-3400	600-3600	271
Xantrex Technology Inc 3700 Gilmore Way *TF:* 800-670-0707 ■ *Web:* www.xantrex.com	Burnaby	BC	V5G4M1	604-422-8595	420-1591	253
Xantrion Inc 651 20th St *Web:* www.xantrion.com	Oakland	CA	94612	510-272-4701		196
XAP Corp 3534 Hayden Ave *TF:* 800-468-6927 ■ *Web:* www.xap.com	Culver City	CA	90232	310-842-9800		178-7
Xapo Inc 364 University Ave. *TF:* 888-362-0111 ■ *Web:* www.xapo.com	Palo Alto,	CA	94301	888-362-0111		49-2
Xator Corp 1835 Alexander Bell Dr Ste 210 *Web:* www.xatorcorp.com	Reston	VA	20191	703-638-7107	638-6003	693
Xaverian Brothers High School Inc 800 Clapboardtree St *Web:* www.xbhs.com	Westwood	MA	02090	781-326-6392	320-0458	685
Xavier High School 181 Randolph Rd *Web:* www.xavierhighschool.org	Middletown	CT	06457	860-346-7735		685
Xavier University 3800 Victory Pkwy *TF:* 800-344-4698 ■ *Web:* www.xavier.edu	Cincinnati	OH	45207	513-745-3000	745-4319	166
Xavier University of Louisiana 1 Drexel Dr *Web:* www.xula.edu	New Orleans	LA	70125	504-486-7411	520-7922	166
Xaware Inc 3300 Irvine Ave Ste 261 *Web:* www.xaware.net	Newport Beach	CA	92660	949-222-2287		178-1
Xaxis 466 Lexington Ave Third Fl *Web:* www.xaxis.com	New York	NY	10017	646-259-4200		7

Company	Phone	Fax	Class
XBiotech USA Inc 8201 E Riverside Dr Bldg 4 Ste 100 .... Austin TX 78744 *Web:* www.xbiotech.com	512-386-2900		743
Xcel Energy Inc 414 Nicollet Mall .... Minneapolis MN 55401 *NYSE: XEL* ■ *TF:* 800-328-8226 ■ *Web:* www.xcelenergy.com	612-330-5500		787
Xcel HR 7361 Calhoun Pl Ste 600 .... Rockville MD 20855 **Fax Area Code:* 301 ■ *TF:* 800-776-0076 ■ *Web:* www.xcelhr.com	800-776-0076	340-3801*	260
X-Cel Optical Company Inc 806 S Benton Dr .... Sauk Rapids MN 56379 **Fax Area Code:* 800 ■ *TF:* 800-747-9235 ■ *Web:* www.x-celoptical.com	320-251-8404	232-9235*	542
XCEL Solutions Corp Oakdale Plaza 254 Hwy 34 .... Matawan NJ 07747 *Web:* www.xcelcorp.com	732-765-9235		624
Xcelerate Media Inc 61 W Bridge St .... Dublin OH 43017 *Web:* www.xceleratemedia.com	614-336-9722		765
Xcelsi Group LLC 308 Lonsdale Ave .... Dayton OH 45419 *Web:* xcelsi.com	937-395-0458		261
Xceltech Inc 2136 Gallows Rd .... Dunn Loring VA 22027 *Web:* www.xceltech.com	703-208-9120		177
Xceptional Networks Inc 10089 Willow Creek Rd Ste 100 .... San Diego CA 92131 *Web:* www.xceptional.com	858-225-6230		180
Xcerra Corp 1355 California Cir .... Milpitas CA 95035 *NASDAQ: XCRA* ■ *Web:* www.ltxc.com	408-635-4300		248
XCG Consultants Ltd 10455-84th Ave .... Edmonton AB T6E2H3 *Web:* www.xcg.com	780-432-5770		256
Xchanger 5 N Main .... Butler MO 64730 *Web:* www.yourxgroup.com	660-679-6126		637-10
Xcitex Inc 25 First St Ste 105 .... Cambridge MA 02141 *TF:* 800-780-7836 ■ *Web:* www.xcitex.com	800-780-7836		647
Xco International Inc 1082 Rock Road Ln Unit A .... East Dundee IL 60118 *Web:* www.xcointl.com	847-428-2400	428-2414	201
XConnect Americas 505 White Plains Rd Ste 124 .... Tarrytown NY 10591 *Web:* www.xconnect.net	914-909-5311		393
xDefenders Inc 1100 Pittsford-Victor Rd .... Pittsford NY 14534 *Web:* www.xdefenders.com	585-385-2770		393
XEC Solutions Inc 5655 Lindero Canyon Rd Ste 521 .... Westlake Village CA 91362 *Web:* xecsolutions.com	818-991-1400	575-8099	266
XEcom Inc 1145 Nicholson Rd Ste 200 .... Newmarket ON L3Y9C3 *TF:* 877-932-6640 ■ *Web:* www.xe.com	416-214-5606		225
Xela Pack Inc 8300 Boettner Rd .... Saline MI 48176 *Web:* xelapack.com	734-944-1300		88
Xelas Systems Engineering LLC 8111 Red Farm Ln .... Bowie MD 20715 *Web:* www.xelas-systems.com	301-789-1162		177
Xenakis Consulting Services Inc 100 Memorial Dr Apt 8-13A .... Cambridge MA 02142 *Web:* www.jxenakis.com	617-864-0010		196
XENCO Laboratories Inc 4147 Greenbriar Dr .... Stafford TX 77477 *Web:* www.xenco.com	281-240-4200	240-4280	192
Xenetech Usa Inc 12139 Airline Hwy .... Baton Rouge LA 70817 *Web:* www.xenetech.com	225-752-0225		628
Xenex Disinfection Services LLC 121 Interpark Ste 104 .... San Antonio TX 78216 *Web:* www.xenex.com	210-538-9300		475
Xenex Enterprises Inc 155 Rexdale Blvd Ste 707 .... Toronto ON M9W5Z8 *Web:* www.xenex.ca	416-740-9704		177
Xenia Area Chamber of Commerce 334 W Market St .... Xenia OH 45385 *Web:* xacc.com	937-372-3591	372-2192	139
Xenium HR 7401 SW Washo Ct Ste 200 .... Tualatin OR 97062 *Web:* www.xeniumhr.com	503-612-1555	612-1577	195
Xeno Media 18w100 22nd St Ste 128 .... Oakbrook Terrace IL 60181 *Web:* www.xenomedia.com	630-599-1550		177
Xenon International Academy 2231 S Peoria St .... Aurora CO 80014 *TF:* 800-323-6258 ■ *Web:* www.xenonacademy.net	303-752-1560		167-3
Xenon Pharmaceuticals Inc 3650 Gilmore Way .... Burnaby BC V5G4W8 *Web:* www.xenon-pharma.com	604-484-3300		668
Xenos Books PO Box 16433 .... Las Cruces NM 88004 *Web:* www.xenosbooks.com	575-527-1378		637-2
Xensor Corp 4000 Bridge St .... Drexel Hill PA 19026 *Web:* www.xensor.com	610-284-2508	259-8379	407
Xentx Lubricants Inc 1626 W 12th Pl .... Tempe AZ 85281 *TF:* 800-456-7665 ■ *Web:* xentxsynergyn.com	480-998-2400		541
XEODesign Inc 5273 College Ave Ste 201 .... Oakland CA 94618 *Web:* www.xeodesign.com	510-658-8077		180
Xerces Society, The 628 NE Broadway Ste 200 .... Portland OR 97232 **Fax Area Code:* 503 ■ *TF:* 855-232-6639 ■ *Web:* xerces.org	855-232-6639	233-6794*	41
Xerimis Inc 102 Executive Dr .... Moorestown NJ 08057 *Web:* xerimis.com	856-727-9940		237
Xeris Pharmaceuticals Inc 180 N LaSalle St Ste 1810 .... Chicago IL 60601 *TF:* 844-445-5704 ■ *Web:* www.xerispharma.com	844-445-5704		231
Xerox Business Solutions 3903 Northdale Blvd Ste 200W .... Tampa FL 33624 *TF:* 888-628-7834 ■ *Web:* www.xeroxbusinesssolutions.com	813-960-5508	264-7877	112
Xerox Corp 201 Merritt 7 .... Norwalk CT 06856 *NYSE: XRX* ■ *TF:* 800-327-9753 ■ *Web:* www.xerox.com	203-968-3000		589
Xertrex International Incorporated Tabbies Divison 1530 W Glenlake Ave .... Itasca IL 60143 *Web:* www.tabbies.com	630-773-4160	773-4696	560
Xetex Inc 9405 Holly St NW .... Minneapolis MN 55433 *Web:* www.xetexinc.com	612-724-3101		664
Xetus Corp 1325 Howard Ave Ste 527 .... Burlingame CA 94010 *TF:* 877-469-3887 ■ *Web:* www.xetusone.com	650-237-1225		251
XF Enterprises Inc 500 S Taylor Ste 301 PO Box 229 .... Amarillo TX 79101 **Fax Area Code:* 620 ■ *TF:* 800-783-5616 ■ *Web:* www.xfent.com	806-367-5810	672-5564*	584
X-fab Texas Inc 2301 N University Ave .... Lubbock TX 79415 *Web:* www.xfab.com	806-747-4400		696
Xfer International Inc 39201 Schoolcraft Rd Ste B 9 .... Livonia MI 48150 *Web:* www.xfer.com	734-927-6666		180
XFL 1266 Main St .... Stamford CT 06901 *Web:* www.xfl.com	203-989-3399		715-2
X-Gen Pharmaceuticals Inc 300 Daniels Zenker Dr .... Horseheads NY 14845 *TF:* 866-390-4411 ■ *Web:* xgenpharmadjb.com	866-390-4411		583
Xi Graphics Inc 1580 Logan St Ste 550 .... Denver CO 80203 *Web:* www.xig.com	303-298-7478		178-1
Xiacon Inc 140 Fell Ct Ste 120 .... Hauppauge NY 11788 *Web:* www.xiacon.com	631-300-3500	300-3501	177
Xicon Passive Components 1000 N Main St .... Mansfield TX 76063 *TF:* 800-346-6873 ■ *Web:* www.mouser.com	800-346-6873		246
Xifin Inc 12225 El Camino Real .... San Diego CA 92130 *Web:* www.xifin.com	858-793-5700		178-1
XiGo Nanotools Inc 116 Research Dr Ste 39 .... Bethlehem PA 18015 *Web:* www.xigonanotools.com	610-849-5090		419
Xilinx Inc 2100 Logic Dr .... San Jose CA 95124 *NASDAQ: XLNX* ■ *TF:* 800-594-5469 ■ *Web:* www.xilinx.com	408-559-7778	559-7114	696
Ximenez-Fatio House Museum 20 Aviles St .... Saint Augustine FL 32084 *Web:* www.ximenezfatiohouse.org	904-829-3575	829-3445	520
Xinet Inc 2560 Ninth St Ste 312 .... Berkeley CA 94710 *Web:* www.northplains.com	510-845-0555		178-12
Xiologix 8050 SW Warm Springs St Ste 100 .... Tualatin OR 97062 *TF:* 888-492-6843 ■ *Web:* www.xiologix.com	503-691-4364		225
XIOtech Corp 9950 Federal Dr Ste 100 .... Colorado Springs CO 80921 *TF:* 866-472-6764 ■ *Web:* xiostorage.com	719-388-5500		178-12
XipLink Inc 4200 St Laurent Blvd Ste 1010 .... Montreal QC H2W2R2 *TF:* 855 408 2483 ■ *Web:* www.xiplink.com	514-848-9640	848-9644	224
Xiris Automation Inc 1016 Sutton Dr Unit C5 .... Burlington ON L7L6B8 *Web:* www.xiris.com	905-331-6660	331-6661	639
X-ISS 2190 N Loop W Ste 415 .... Houston TX 77018 *Web:* x-iss.com	713-862-9200		177
XIT Communications 12324 US Hwy 87 .... Dalhart TX 79022 *TF:* 800-687-0780 ■ *Web:* www.xit.net	806-384-3311	384-3340	224
Xitech Instruments Inc 6 Camino De Los Desmontes .... Placitas NM 87043 *Web:* www.xitechinc.com	505-867-0008		806
Xittel telecommunications Inc 1100 Pl du Technoparc Ste 301 .... Trois-Rivieres QC G9A0A9 *Web:* www.xittel.net	819-370-3232		224
XKS Unlimited Inc 850 Fiero Ln .... San Luis Obispo CA 93401 *TF:* 800-444-5247 ■ *Web:* xks.com	805-544-7864		54
XL Brands 198 Nexus Dr .... Dalton GA 30721 *TF:* 800-367-4583 ■ *Web:* www.xlbrands.com	706-272-5800	272-5801	145
XL Ctr 1 Civic Center Plz .... Hartford CT 06103 *TF:* 877-522-8499 ■ *Web:* www.xlcenter.com	860-249-6333		205
X-L Engineering Corp 6150 W Mulford St .... Niles IL 60714 *Web:* www.xleng.com	847-965-3030		757
X-L Machine Company Inc 20481 Hwy M-60 .... Three Rivers MI 49093 *Web:* www.xlmachine.com	269-279-5128	279-6197	757
Xl Specialized Trailers Inc 1086 S 3rd St .... Manchester IA 52057 *TF:* 877-283-4852 ■ *Web:* www.xlspecializedtrailer.com	563-927-4900	927-4883	779
XL Specialty Insurance Co 70 Seaview Ave .... Stamford CT 06902 **Fax Area Code:* 573 ■ *Web:* insurance.mo.gov	203-964-5200	526-2092*	391-5
Xli Corp 55 Vanguard Pkwy .... Rochester NY 14606 *Web:* www.xlionline.com	585-436-2250	235-5260	697
Xlibris Corp 1663 Liberty Dr Ste 200 .... Bloomington IN 47403 *TF:* 888-795-4274 ■ *Web:* www.xlibris.com	888-795-4274		627
Xlink Technology Inc 1546 Centre Pointe Dr .... Milpitas CA 95035 *Web:* www.xlink.com	408-263-8201		177
XLNsystems Inc 1255 N Hamilton Rd .... Gahanna OH 43230 *Web:* www.xlnsystems.com	614-947-3607	207-0936	178-1
XLPrint USA LLC 213 Rose Ave Ste 1 .... Venice CA 90291 *TF:* 866-275-1290 ■ *Web:* www.paris-software.com	310-829-7684	829-7302	809
XLV Diagnostics Inc 290 Munro St .... Thunder Bay ON P7A7T1 *Web:* xlvdiagnostics.com	807-346-6811		475
XO Cafe 1345 Westminster St .... Providence RI 02903 *Web:* www.xocafe.com	401-273-9090		671
XO Prime Steaks 500 W St Claire Ave .... Cleveland OH 44113 *Web:* xoprimesteaks.com	216-861-1919	861-0374	671
Xochimilco Restaurant 3409 Bagley St .... Detroit MI 48216	313-843-0179		671
Xoft Inc 101 Nicholson Ln .... San Jose CA 95134 *TF:* 877-963-8327 ■ *Web:* www.xoftinc.com	408-493-1500		475
XOMA (US) LLC 2910 Seventh St .... Berkeley CA 94710 *NASDAQ: XOMA* ■ *Web:* www.xoma.com	510-204-7200		85
Xonex Inc 20 E Commons Blvd .... New Castle DE 19720 *Web:* www.xonex.com	302-323-6181		780
Xor Security LLC 3120 Fairview Park Dr 650 .... Falls Church VA 22042 *TF:* 888-803-6040 ■ *Web:* xorsecurity.com	703-650-8853		180
Xoriant Corp 1248 Reamwood Ave .... Sunnyvale CA 94089 *Web:* www.xoriant.com	408-743-4400		180
XOS Digital 181 Ballardvale St .... Wilmington MA 01887 *TF:* 800-490-7767 ■ *Web:* www.xosdigital.com	978-447-5220	447-5227	177
XP Power 990 Benicia Ave .... Sunnyvale CA 94085 *TF:* 800-253-0490 ■ *Web:* www.xppower.com	408-732-7777	732-2002	246
Xp3 Corp 525 Carswell Ave Unit L .... Holly Hill FL 32117 **Fax Area Code:* 386 ■ *TF:* 800-475-3563 ■ *Web:* xp3hornet.com	330-562-8490	947-7680*	196
X-Pay LLC 65 Harristown Rd Ste 208 .... Glen Rock NJ 07452 *Web:* balancepointpayroll.com	201-712-1157		570

Company / Address	City	State	Zip	Phone	Fax	Class
Xper USA 220 S Noah Dr *Web:* xperusa.com	Saxonburg	PA	16056	724-586-6005	586-6010	330
Xper2go 39120 Argonaut Way Ste 782 *Web:* www.xper2go.com	Fremont	CA	94538	510-585-2500		177
Xpera Group 10911 Technology Pl. *Web:* www.xperagroup.com	San Diego	CA	92127	858-295-8451		466
Xperi Corp 3025 Orchard Pkwy *NASDAQ: XPER* ■ *Web:* www.xperi.com	San Jose	CA	95134	408-321-6000		696
Xperience Interactive 2601 Ocean Park Blvd Ste 116	Santa Monica	CA	90405	424-214-1471		7
Xperience Restaurant Group 11065 Knott Ave Ste A *Web:* www.xperiencerg.com	Cypress	CA	90630	562-346-1200		670
XperNet Services Inc 22511 Katy Frwy Ste 180 *Web:* www.xpernet.com	Houston	TX	77084	281-392-5292	392-3668	180
Xperts Inc 4413 Cox Rd *Web:* www.xperts.com	Glen Allen	VA	23060	804-967-0700	747-8282	637-10
Xpicor Inc 205 S Westgate Dr Ste 100 *Web:* www.xpicor.com	Greensboro	NC	27407	336-510-0333	458-9642	104
Xplane Corp 811 SW Sixth Ave Ste 500 *TF:* 855-548-4343 ■ *Web:* www.xplane.com	Portland	OR	97204	855-548-4343		344
Xplor Intl 24156 SR54 Ste 4 *Web:* xplor.org	Lutz	FL	33559	813-949-6170	949-9977	78
XPO Logistics Inc 5165 Emerald Pkwy Ste 300 *TF:* 800-837-7584 ■ *Web:* www.xpo.com	Dublin	OH	43016	614-923-1400		449
Xpres Spa 780 Third Ave 12th Fl *Web:* www.xpresspa.com	New York	NY	10017	212-750-9595		77
Xpress Boats 199 Extrusion Pl *Web:* xpressboats.com	Hot Springs	AR	71901	501-262-5300	262-5053	90
Xpress Communications LLC 322 N John St. **Fax Area Code:* 760 ■ *Web:* www.xpresscom.net	Goldsboro	NC	27530	919-735-8118	875-9591*	178-1
XpressBet LLC 200 Racetrack Rd Bldg 26 *TF:* 866-889-7737 ■ *Web:* www.xpressbet.com	Washington	PA	15301	866-889-7737		642
Xpriori LLC 2864 S Cir Dr Ste 401 *Web:* www.xpriori.com	Colorado Springs	CO	80906	719-425-9840	203-6496	809
XPS Group Inc 888 Ft St 2nd Fl *Web:* xpsgroup.net	Victoria	BC	V8W1H8	250-383-4135		2
XPV Water Partners 40 University Ave Ste 801 *Web:* www.xpvwaterpartners.com	Toronto	ON	M5J1T1	416-864-0475	864-0514	792
X-Ray Industries Inc 1961 Thunderbird **Fax Area Code:* 616 ■ *TF:* 877-974-4638 ■ *Web:* www.xritesting.com	Troy	MI	48084	248-362-2242	772-0740*	743
X-ray Instrumentation Assoc 8450 Central Ave *Web:* www.xia.com	Newark	CA	94560	510-494-9020		419
X-Ray Optical Systems Inc 15 Tech Valley Dr *Web:* www.xos.com	East Greenbush	NY	12061	518-880-1500	880-1510	542
XRG Systems Inc 1 Annabel Ln Ste 214 *Web:* xrgsystems.com	San Ramon	CA	94583	925-241-4995	241-4584	177
XRiver Technologies LLC 13800 Coppermine Rd Ste 171 *Web:* www.xrivertech.com	Herndon	VA	20151	703-480-0480	480-0488	809
XRoads Solutions Group 1821 E Dyer Rd Ste 225	Santa Ana	CA	92705	949-567-1600	567-1655	401
XS International Inc 1005 Alderman Dr Ste 212 *TF:* 800-256-6133 ■ *Web:* www.xsnet.com	Alpharetta	GA	30005	770-824-3453	740-0121	180
XS Sight Systems Inc 2401 Ludelle St *TF:* 888-744-4880 ■ *Web:* www.xssights.com	Fort Worth	TX	76105	817-536-0136		711
Xsperient 935 Sheridan Dr Ste 120 *Web:* xsperient.com	Tonawanda	NY	14150	716-754-8744	877-8737	466
XSport Fitness Inc 6420 W Fullerton Ave *TF:* 877-417-1450 ■ *Web:* www.xsportfitness.com	Chicago	IL	60707	773-237-5730		354
XSYS Inc 653 Steele Dr. *TF:* 888-810-9797 ■ *Web:* www.xsysinc.com	Valparaiso	IN	46385	888-810-9797		177
Xtek Inc 11451 Reading Rd *TF:* 888-332-9835 ■ *Web:* www.xtek.com	Cincinnati	OH	45241	513-733-7800	733-7939	454
Xtel Communications Inc 401 Rt 73 n *TF:* 800-438-9835 ■ *Web:* www.xtel.net	Marlton	NJ	08053	856-596-4000		387
Xtime Inc 1400 Bridge Pky Ste 200 *TF:* 866-984-6355 ■ *Web:* www.xtime.com	Redwood City	CA	94065	650-508-4300	508-8877	322
XTO Energy Inc 810 Houston St *TF:* 800-299-2800 ■ *Web:* www.xtoenergy.com	Fort Worth	TX	76102	817-870-2800	870-1671	536
Xto Inc 110 Wrentham Dr *Web:* www.xtoinc.com	Liverpool	NY	13088	315-451-7807		326
XTRAC LLC 245 Summer St *TF:* 855-975-3569 ■ *Web:* www.xtracsolutions.com	Boston	MA	02210	855-975-3569		387
Xtream It People Inc 50 Colvin Ave Ste 206 *Web:* www.xtreamit.com	Albany	NY	12206	518-437-0090		180
Xtreme Consulting Group Inc 3500 Carillon Pt *Web:* xtremeconsulting.com	Kirkland	WA	98033	425-861-9460		463
XtremeEDA Corp 200-25 Holland Ave **Fax Area Code:* 613 ■ *TF:* 800-586-0280 ■ *Web:* www.xtreme-eda.com	Ottawa	ON	K1Y4R9	800-586-0280	728-9513*	466
Xttrium Laboratories Inc 415 W Pershing Rd Ste 2 *Web:* xttrium.com	Mount Prospect	IL	60056	773-268-5800		231
Xybernet Inc 10640 Scripps Ranch Blvd *TF:* 800-228-9026 ■ *Web:* www.xyber.net	San Diego	CA	92131	858-530-1900	530-1419	178-10
Xylem 8200 N Austin Ave *Web:* unitedstates.xylemappliedwater.com	Morton Grove	IL	60053	847-966-3700		202
Xylem Inc 227 S Div St. *Web:* www.xylem.com	Zelienople	PA	16063	724-452-6300		806
Xylo Technologies Inc 2434 Superior Dr NW Ste 105 *Web:* www.xylotechnologies.com	Rochester	MN	55901	507-289-9956		624
Xymox Technologies 9099 W Dean Rd *TF:* 800-869-9669 ■ *Web:* www.xymox.com	Milwaukee	WI	53224	414-362-9000	362-9091	729
Xyonicz Corp 6754 Martin St. *Web:* xyonicz.com	Rome	NY	13440	315-334-4214	336-3177	484
Xyron Inc 8465 N 90th St Ste 6-7 *TF:* 800-793-3523 ■ *Web:* www.xyron.com	Scottsdale	AZ	85258	800-793-3523		485
Xyron Semiconductor Inc 16508 SE 24th St Ste 200 *Web:* www.xyronsemi.com	Vancouver	WA	98683	360-449-8800	449-8850	696
Xytech Systems Corp 9410 Topanga Canyon Blvd Ste 200 *Web:* www.xytechsystems.com	Chatsworth	CA	91311	818-698-4900		177
XYZ Scientific Applications Inc 2255 Morello Ave Ste 220 *Web:* www.truegrid.com	Pleasant Hill	CA	94523	925-373-0628		178-1
XYZ Two Way Radio Inc 275 20th St *TF:* 800-535-3377 ■ *Web:* xyzcar.com	Brooklyn	NY	11215	718-499-2007		441

Y

Company / Address	City	State	Zip	Phone	Fax	Class
Y & S Candies 400 Running Pump Rd *Web:* www.twizzlers.com	Lancaster	PA	17603	717-299-1261		296-8
Y Medical Associates Inc 8840 N MacArthur Blvd *TF:* 800-447-7558 ■ *Web:* www.ymedical.com	Irving	TX	75063	800-447-7558		363
Y.K. Trading Inc 2560 Glenda Ln *TF:* 866-730-1377 ■ *Web:* www.yktrading.com	Dallas	TX	75229	972-241-9771	620-1929	594
Y107 (KTXY-FM) 3215 Lemone Industrial Blvd Ste 200 *TF:* 800-500-1079 ■ *Web:* y107.com	Columbia	MO	65201	573-441-1079		645
Y108 - Hamilton's Rock Station *Y108 World Class Rock 107.9 FM* 875 Main St W *Web:* y108.ca	Hamilton	ON	L8S4R1	905-521-9900		645
Y-12 Federal Credit Union 501 Lafayette Dr *TF:* 800-482-1043 ■ *Web:* www.y12fcu.org	Oak Ridge	TN	37830	865-482-1043		219
Y93 3500 E Rosser Ave *Web:* y93.iheart.com	Bismarck	ND	58501	701-255-1234		645-20
Y94 iHeartMedia 500 Plum St Ste 400 *Web:* y94fm.iheart.com	Syracuse	NY	13204	315-472-9797		645-158
YA (Yeaton Associates Inc) 66 Jackson St *Web:* www.yeatonassociates.com	Littleton	NH	03561	603-444-6578	444-2364	196
YA YA Network 224 W 29th St 1st Fl *Web:* www.yayanetwork.org	New York	NY	10001	212-239-0022		305
Yaaman Inc 6376 Byron Ln *Web:* www.yaaman.com	San Ramon	CA	94582	408-625-7615		180
Yaana Technologies LLC 542 Gibraltar Dr *Web:* www.yaanatech.com	Milpitas	CA	95035	408-719-9000		180
Yabba Island Grill 711 Fifth Ave S *Web:* www.yabbaislandgrill.com	Naples	FL	34102	239-262-5787		671
Yachting Magazine 460 N Orlando Ave *TF:* 800-999-0869 ■ *Web:* www.yachtingmagazine.com	Winter Park	FL	32789	800-999-0869		457-4
Yacktman Asset Management Co 6300 Bridgepoint Pkwy Bldg 1 Ste 320 *TF:* 800-835-3879 ■ *Web:* www.yacktman.com	Austin	TX	78730	512-767-6700		401
Yackzan Group Inc 2001 Second St Ste 4 *Web:* yackzangroup.com	Davis	CA	95618	530-753-7730		653
Yadkin County 217 E Willow St *Web:* www.yadkincountync.gov	Yadkinville	NC	27055	336-679-4200	679-6005	338
Yadkin County Chamber of Commerce 205 S Jackson St PO Box 1840 *TF:* 877-492-3546 ■ *Web:* www.yadkinchamber.org	Yadkinville	NC	27055	336-679-2200	679-3034	139
Yadkin Ripple Inc 115 Jackson St *Web:* www.yadkinripple.com	Yadkinville	NC	27055	336-679-2341	679-2340	532-2
Yadkin Valley Chamber of Commerce 116 E Market St PO Box 496 *Web:* www.yadkinvalley.org	Elkin	NC	28621	336-526-1111	526-1879	139
Yaffe & Co 26100 American Dr Ste 401 *Web:* yaffe.com	Southfield	MI	48034	248-262-1700		7
Yageo America 2550 N 1st St Ste 480 *Web:* www.yageo.com	San Jose	CA	95131	408-240-6200	240-6201	253
Yahara Materials Inc 6117 County Rd K *Web:* yahara.com	Waunakee	WI	53597	608-849-4162		191-1
Yahoo! Finance 701 First Ave *Web:* finance.yahoo.com	Sunnyvale	CA	94089	408-349-3300		404
Yahoo! Travel 701 First Ave *Web:* www.yahoo.com	Sunnyvale	CA	94089	408-349-7821		773
Yahsgs Llc 300 Columbia Point Dr Ste 130 PO Box 667 *Web:* www.yahsgs.com	Richland	WA	99352	509-539-7147		463
YAK Laurier W PO 1200 - 48 Yonge St. **Fax Area Code:* 866 ■ *TF:* 877-925-4925 ■ *Web:* yak.ca	Ottawa	ON	K2P2L9	877-925-4925	216-9923*	736
Yakabod Inc 2 N Market St Ste 300 *Web:* www.yakabod.com	Frederick	MD	21701	301-662-4554		225
Yakima Bait Company Inc PO Box 310 *TF:* 800-527-2711 ■ *Web:* www.yakimabait.com	Granger	WA	98932	509-854-2263		710
Yakima Convention Ctr 10 N Eigth St *TF:* 800-221-0751 ■ *Web:* www.visityakima.com	Yakima	WA	98901	509-575-6062	575-6252	205
Yakima County 128 N Second St Rm 323 *TF:* 800-572-7354 ■ *Web:* www.yakimacounty.us	Yakima	WA	98901	509-574-1430		338
Yakima Federal Savings & Loan Assn 118 E Yakima Ave *TF:* 800-331-3225 ■ *Web:* www.yakimafed.com	Yakima	WA	98901	509-248-2634		70
Yakima Herald-Republic PO Box 9668 *TF:* 800-343-2799 ■ *Web:* www.yakimaherald.com	Yakima	WA	98909	509-248-1251	577-7767	532-2
Yakima Neighborhood Health Services (YNHS) 12 S Eigth St PO Box 2605 *Web:* www.ynhs.org	Yakima	WA	98907	509-454-4143	454-3651	353

Name	Address	City	State	ZIP	Phone	Fax	Class	Details
Yakima Sportsman State Park	904 University Pkwy PO Box 52	Yakima	WA	98907	509-575-2774		565	*Web:* parks.state.wa.us
Yakima Valley College (YVC) *Grandview*	500 W Main St	Grandview	WA	98930	509-882-7000		162	*Web:* www.yvcc.edu
Yakima Valley Memorial Hospital	2811 Tieton Dr	Yakima	WA	98902	509-575-8000	573-3902	374-3	*TF:* 800-276-8807 ■ *Web:* www.yakimamemorial.org
Yale Appliance	296 Freeport St	Dorchester	MA	02122	617-825-9253		35	*TF:* 800-565-6435 ■ *Web:* www.yaleappliance.com
Yale Center for British Art	1080 Chapel St PO Box 208280	New Haven	CT	06510	203-432-2800	432-9695	520	*Web:* britishart.yale.edu
Yale Club of New York City, The	50 Vanderbilt Ave	New York	NY	10017	212-716-2100		393	*Web:* www.yaleclubnyc.org
Yale Divinity School Admissions Office	409 Prospect St	New Haven	CT	06511	203-432-5360	432-7475	167-3	*TF:* 877-725-3334 ■ *Web:* www.divinity.yale.edu
Yale Law School	127 Wall St	New Haven	CT	06511	203-432-4992		167-1	*Web:* law.yale.edu
Yale Peabody Museum of Natural History	Yale University 170 Whitney Ave	New Haven	CT	06511	203-432-3759	432-9816	520	*Web:* www.peabody.yale.edu
Yale Public Schools	315 E Chicago Ave	Yale	OK	74085	918-387-2434		685	*Web:* www.yale.k12.ok.us
Yale Realty Services Corp	10 New King St Ste102	White Plains	NY	10604	914-289-0100		652	*Web:* yalerealtyservices.com
Yale Repertory Theatre	1120 Chapel St PO Box 208244	New Haven	CT	06510	203-432-1234		573-4	*Web:* www.yalerep.org
Yale Residential Security Products Inc	100 Yale Ave	Lenoir City	TN	37771	800-438-1951		350	*TF:* 800-438-1951 ■ *Web:* www.yalehome.com
Yale Robbins Inc	205 Lexington Ave 12th Fl	New York	NY	10016	212-683-5700	497-0017	637-9	*Web:* yalerobbins.com
Yale University	38 Hill House Ave	New Haven	CT	06520	203-432-4771	432-9392	166	*Web:* www.yale.edu
Yale University *Marsh Botanical Garden*	265 Mansfield St	New Haven	CT	06511	203-432-6320		97	*Web:* marshbotanicalgarden.yale.edu
Yale University Library	120 High St	New Haven	CT	06511	203-432-0492	432-1294	434-6	*Web:* web.library.yale.edu
Yale University Press	302 Temple St	New Haven	CT	06511	203-432-0960	432-0948	637-2	*Web:* yalebooks.com
Yale University School of Medicine	333 Cedar St	New Haven	CT	06510	203-785-2643	785-3234	167-2	*Web:* medicine.yale.edu
Yale/Chase Equipment and Services Inc (YC)	2615 Pellissier Pl	City of Industry	CA	90601	562-463-8000	319-6418*	385	**Fax Area Code:* 888 ■ *Web:* www.yalechase.com
Yaletown Partners	1122 Mainland St Ste 510	Vancouver	BC	V6B5L1	604-688-7807		528	*Web:* www.yaletown.com
Yamada Enterprises	16552 Burke Ln	Huntington Beach	CA	92647	800-444-4594		321	*TF:* 800-444-4594 ■ *Web:* www.yamadaenterprises.com
Yamada North America Inc	9000 Columbus Cincinnati Rd	South Charleston	OH	45368	937-462-7111		247	*Web:* www.yamadanorthamerica.com
Yamaha Corporation of America	6600 Orangethorpe Ave	Buena Park	CA	90620	714-522-9011		527	*Web:* www.yamaha.com
Yamaha Golf Cars of California Inc	7275 National Dr Ste D	Livermore	CA	94550	925-371-5350	371-5311	516	*Web:* www.yamahagolfcarsofca.com
Yamaha Motor Corporation USA	6555 Katella Ave	Cypress	CA	90630	800-962-7926		517	*TF:* 800-962-7926 ■ *Web:* www.yamaha-motor.com
Yamaichi Electronics USA Inc	475 Holger Way	San Jose	CA	95134	408-715-9100	715-9199	246	*Web:* www.yeu.com
Yamamoto of Orient Inc	122 Voyager St	Pomona	CA	91768	909-594-7356	595-5849	297-11	*Web:* www.yamamotoyama.com
Yamasa Corporation USA	3500 Fairview Industrial Dr SE	Salem	OR	97302	503-363-8550	363-8710	296-19	*Web:* www.yamasausa.com
Yamashiro Inc	1999 N Sycamore Ave	Hollywood	CA	90068	323-466-5125		670	*Web:* yamashirohollywood.com
Yamato Corp	1775 S Murray Blvd	Colorado Springs	CO	80916	719-591-1500	591-1045	684	*TF:* 800-538-1762 ■ *Web:* www.yamatoamericas.com
Yamato Steak House of Japan	360 Columbian Dr	Columbia	SC	29212	803-407-0033		671	*Web:* www.yamatoinc.com
Yamato Transport USA Inc	80 Seaview Dr	Secaucus	NJ	07094	201-583-9706	583-9703	546	*Web:* www.yamatoamerica.com
Yamazato	6303 Little River Tpke	Alexandria	VA	22312	703-914-8877		671	*Web:* www.yamazato.net
Yamazen Inc	735 E Remington Rd	Schaumburg	IL	60173	800-882-8558	882-4296*	385	**Fax Area Code:* 847 ■ *TF:* 800-882-8558 ■ *Web:* www.yamazen.com
Yamhill County	414 NE Evans St	McMinnville	OR	97128	503-434-7518	434-7520	338	*Web:* www.co.yamhill.or.us
Yampa River State Park	6185 W US Hwy 40	Hayden	CO	81639	970-276-2061		565	*Web:* cpw.state.co.us
Yampa Valley Electric Association Inc	2211 Elk River Rd	Steamboat Springs	CO	80487	970-879-1160	879-7270	245	*TF:* 888-873-9832 ■ *Web:* www.yvea.com
Yancey County	PO Box 6	Burnsville	NC	28714	828-682-3819	682-4301	338	*Web:* www.yanceycountync.gov
Yancey County Schools Foundation Inc, The	PO Box 190	Burnsville	NC	28714	828-682-6101	682-7110	685	*Web:* www.yanceync.net
Yang Enterprises Inc	1420 Alafaya Trl Ste 200	Oviedo	FL	32765	407-365-7374		177	*Web:* www.yangenterprises.com
Yang Kee Noodle Club	7900 Shelbyville Rd	Louisville	KY	40222	502-426-0800		671	*Web:* www.yangkeenoodle.com
Yangarra Resources Ltd	715 - 5 Ave SW Ste 1530	Calgary	AB	T2P2X6	403-262-9558		536	*Web:* www.yangarra.ca
Yang-Patyi Law Firm PLLC	2700 Court St Ste 8	Syracuse	NY	13208	315-218-1882	218-1881	41	*Web:* yangpatyilaw.com
Yangtze Dining Lounge	700 Somerset W	Ottawa	ON	K1R6P6	613-236-0555		671	*Web:* www.yangtze.ca
Yank Sing	49 Stevenson St	San Francisco	CA	94105	415-541-4949		671	*Web:* www.yanksing.com
Yanke Machine Shop Inc	4414 S Gekeler Ln	Boise	ID	83716	208-342-8901		454	*Web:* www.yankemachine.com
Yankee Barn Homes	131 Yankee Barn Rd	Grantham	NH	03753	800-258-9786		106	*TF:* 800-258-9786 ■ *Web:* www.yankeebarnhomes.com
Yankee Candle Company Inc	PO Box 110	South Deerfield	MA	01373	413-665-8306		327	*TF:* 877-803-6890 ■ *Web:* www.yankeecandle.com
Yankee Containers	110 Republic Dr	North Haven	CT	06473	203-288-3851		125	*Web:* www.yankeecontainers.com
Yankee Hill Brick & Tile	3705 S Coddington Ave	Lincoln	NE	68522	402-477-6663	477-2832	150	*Web:* www.yankeehillbrick.com
Yankee Inn	461 Pittsfield Lenox Rd	Lenox	MA	01240	413-499-3700		379	*Web:* www.yankeeinn.com
Yankee Magazine	1121 Main St PO Box 520	Dublin	NH	03444	603-563-8111		457-22	*TF:* 800-288-4284 ■ *Web:* newengland.com
Yankee Marketers Inc	5 Birch Rd	Middleton	MA	01949	978-777-9181	777-5823	297-8	*TF:* 800-343-8272 ■ *Web:* www.yankeemarketers.com
Yankee Peddler Inn	113 Touro St	Newport	RI	02840	401-846-1323		379	*Web:* www.yankeepeddlerinn.com
Yankee Springs Recreation Area	2104 S Briggs Rd	Middleville	MI	49333	269-795-9081		565	*Web:* www.michigan.org
Yankton Ag Service	114 Mulberry St	Yankton	SD	57078	605-665-3691		276	*TF:* 800-456-5528 ■ *Web:* www.growmarkfs.com
Yankton County	410 Walnut St Ste 205	Yankton	SD	57078	605-668-3080	668-5411	338	*Web:* www.co.yankton.sd.us
Yankton Press & Dakotan	319 Walnut St PO Box 56	Yankton	SD	57078	605-665-7811	665-1721	637-8	*TF:* 800-743-2968 ■ *Web:* www.yankton.net
Yanmar America Corp	101 International Pkwy	Adairsville	GA	30103	770-877-9894	877-9009	385	*TF:* 855-416-7091 ■ *Web:* www.yanmar.com
Yanni's Mediterranean Bar & Grill	3109 Central Ave NE	Albuquerque	NM	87106	505-268-9250		671	*Web:* yannisabq.com
Yantis Co	5423 N Loop 1604 E	San Antonio	TX	78247	210-655-3780	655-8526	188-4	*Web:* www.yantiscompany.com
Yantrasoft Inc	2950 Buskirk Ave Ste 300	Walnut Creek	CA	94597	925-407-2151		180	*Web:* yantrasoft.com
YAP (Youth Advocate Programs Inc)	2007 N Third St PO Box 950	Harrisburg	PA	17102	717-232-7580	233-2879	428	*TF:* 800-324-5794 ■ *Web:* www.yapinc.org
YapStone Inc	2121 N California Blvd Ste 400	Walnut Creek	CA	94596	866-289-5977		393	*TF:* 866-289-5977 ■ *Web:* www.yapstone.com
Yaquina Bay Communications Inc	906 SW Alder PO Box 1430	Newport	OR	97365	541-265-2266	265-6397	647	*Web:* www.ybcradio.com
Yard House	401 Shoreline Village Dr	Long Beach	CA	90802	562-628-0455		671	*Web:* www.yardhouse.com
Yardarm Marine Products Inc	2100 Hancel Pky	Mooresville	IN	46158	317-831-4950		91	*Web:* www.yardarm.com
Yarde Metals Inc	45 Newell St	Southington	CT	06489	860-406-6061		490	*TF:* 800-444-9494 ■ *Web:* www.yarde.com
Yardley Products Corp	10 W College Ave	Yardley	PA	19067	215-493-6796		350	*TF:* 800-457-0154 ■ *Web:* www.yardleyinserts.comcontact
Yardmaster Inc	1447 N Ridge Rd	Painesville	OH	44077	440-357-8400		192	*Web:* yardmaster.com
Yardville Supply Co	47 Yardville Groveville Rd	Yardville	NJ	08620	609-585-5000	585-3769	191-2	*Web:* www.yardvillesupply.com
Yarema Die & Engineering Company Inc	300 Minnesota Rd	Troy	MI	48083	248-585-2830	616-1422	757	*Web:* www.yarema.com
York Automotive Group Inc	6019 W Central Ave	Toledo	OH	43615	866-390-8894		516	*TF:* 866-390-8894 ■ *Web:* www.yarkauto.com
Yarmouth Regional Hospital (YRH)	60 Vancouver St	Yarmouth	NS	B5A2P5	902-742-3541	742-0369	374-2	*TF:* 800-460-2110 ■ *Web:* www.swndha.nshealth.ca
Yarmouth Resort	343 Main St Rt 28	West Yarmouth	MA	02673	508-775-5155		379	*TF:* 877-838-3524 ■ *Web:* www.yarmouthresort.com
Yarmuth John A (Rep D - KY)	402 Cannon House Office Bldg	Washington	DC	20515	202-225-5401	225-5776	342-2	*Web:* yarmuth.house.gov
Yarn Tree Designs Inc	117 Alexander Ave	Ames	IA	50010	800-247-3952		594	*TF:* 800-247-3952 ■ *Web:* www.yarntree.com
Yarnell Ice Cream Co	205 S Spring St	Searcy	AR	72143	501-268-6355		296-25	*Web:* www.yarnells.com
Yaro Supply Co	Drawer Ste 750608	Dayton	OH	45475	937-859-6100		358	*Web:* www.yaro.com
YaSabe Inc	100 Carpenter Dr Ste 135	Sterling	VA	20164	703-955-4747		387	*Web:* www.yasabe.com

Name / Address	City	State	ZIP	Phone	Fax	Class
Yash Raj Films Pvt Ltd 2417 Jericho Tpke Ste 284 *Web:* www.yashrajfilms.com	Garden City Park	NY	11040	516-280-5662		514
YASH Technologies Inc 605-17th Ave *Web:* www.yash.com	East Moline	IL	61244	309-755-0433		196
Yaskawa America Inc 2121 Norman Dr S *TF:* 800-927-5292 ■ *Web:* www.yaskawa.com	Waukegan	IL	60085	847-887-7000	887-7310	203
Yasso Yani Restaurant 326 E Main St	Stockton	CA	95202	209-464-3108		671
Yates Bleachery Co 503 Flintstone Rd *Web:* www.yatesbleachery.info	Flintstone	GA	30725	706-820-1531	820-9459	745-7
Yates Construction Company Inc 9220 NC Hwy 65 *Web:* www.yatesconstruction.com	Stokesdale	NC	27357	336-379-8131		188-10
Yates County 417 Liberty St *TF:* 866-212-5160 ■ *Web:* www.yatescounty.org	Penn Yan	NY	14527	315-536-5120	536-5545	338
Yates Industries Inc 23050 E Industrial Dr *Web:* yatesind.com	Saint Clair Shores	MI	48080	586-778-7680		454
Yates Motloid 300 N Oakley Blvd *TF:* 800-662-5021 ■ *Web:* www.yates-motloid.com	Chicago	IL	60612	312-226-2473		459
Yatesville Lake State Park PO Box 767 *Web:* parks.ky.gov	Louisa	KY	41230	606-673-1492		565
Yavapai College 1100 E Sheldon St *TF:* 800-922-6787 ■ *Web:* www.yc.edu	Prescott	AZ	86301	928-445-7300	776-2151	162
Yavapai County 1015 Fair St *TF:* 800-659-7149 ■ *Web:* www.yavapai.us	Prescott	AZ	86305	928-771-3200	771-3257	338
Yavapai Regional Medical Ctr 1003 Willow Creek Rd *TF:* 877-843-9762 ■ *Web:* www.yrmc.org	Prescott	AZ	86301	928-445-2700		374-3
Yaya's Flame Broiled Chicken 521 S Dort Hwy *Web:* www.yayas.com	Flint	MI	48503	810-235-6550	235-5210	670
Yazaki Energy 701 E Plano Pkwy Ste 305 *Web:* www.yazakienergy.com	Plano	TX	75074	469-229-5443	229-5448	393
Yazaki North America Inc 6801 N Haggerty Rd *Web:* www.yazaki-na.com	Canton	MI	48187	734-983-1000		253
Yazoo County PO Box 186 *TF:* 800-381-0662 ■ *Web:* visityazoo.org	Yazoo City	MS	39194	662-746-1815	746-1816	338
Yazoo County Chamber of Commerce 637 E 15th St PO Box 172 *Web:* www.yazoochamber.com	Yazoo City	MS	39194	662-746-1273	746-7238	139
Yazoo Mills Inc PO Box 369 *TF:* 800-242-5216 ■ *Web:* www.yazoomills.com	New Oxford	PA	17350	717-624-8993	624-4420	125
Yazoo Valley Electric Power Assn 2255 Gordon Ave *TF:* 800-281-5098 ■ *Web:* yazoovalley.com	Yazoo City	MS	39194	662-746-4251		245
Ybarras Jewelers Inc 678 N Wilson Way Ste 28 *Web:* ybarrasjewelers.com	Stockton	CA	95205	209-547-0320		410
YBCA (Yerba Buena Center for the Arts) 701 Mission St *Web:* ybca.org	San Francisco	CA	94103	415-978-2787		520
Ybor City Chamber of Commerce 1800 E Ninth Ave *Web:* ybor.org	Tampa	FL	33605	813-248-3712	247-1764	139
Ybor City Museum State Park 1818 Ninth Ave *Web:* www.floridastateparks.org	Tampa	FL	33605	813-247-6323		565
YBRA (Yellowstone-Bighorn Research Assn) PO Box 630 *Web:* www.ybra.org	Red Lodge	MT	59068	406-446-1333		49-19
YC (Yale/Chase Equipment and Services Inc) 2615 Pellissier Pl **Fax Area Code:* 888 ■ *Web:* www.yalechase.com	City of Industry	CA	90601	562-463-8000	319-6418*	385
Y-Change 43575 Mission Blvd *Web:* www.y-change.com	Fremont	CA	94539	510-573-2205	573-2290	177
YDR (York Daily Record) 1891 Loucks Rd *TF:* 800-559-3520 ■ *Web:* www.ydr.com	York	PA	17408	717-771-2000		532-2
Ye Olde Steak House 6838 Chapman Hwy *Web:* www.yeoldesteakhouse.com	Knoxville	TN	37920	865-577-9328		671
Yeager Airport PO Box 393 Ste 175 *Web:* yeagerairport.com	Charleston	WV	25311	304-344-8033	344-8034	27
Yeager, Davison & Day PC 4690 E Fulton St Ste 102 *Web:* ydd-law.com	Ada	MI	49301	616-949-6252		41
Yeargin Potter Shackelford Construction Inc 121 Edinburgh Ct *Web:* www.ypsconst.com	Greenville	SC	29607	864-232-1491		186
Yearout & Traylor PC 3300 Cahaba Rd Ste 300 *Web:* yearout.net	Birmingham	AL	35223	205-414-8160		41
Yearout Mechanical & Engineering Inc 8501 Washington St NE *Web:* www.yearout.com	Albuquerque	NM	87113	505-884-0994	883-5073	189-10
Yeaton Associates Inc (YA) 66 Jackson St *Web:* www.yeatonassociates.com	Littleton	NH	03561	603-444-6578	444-2364	196
Yeck Bros Co 2222 Arbor Blvd *TF:* 800-417-2767 ■ *Web:* www.yeck.com	Moraine	OH	45439	937-294-4000	294-6985	5
Yeled V'yalda Early Childhood Center Inc 1312 38th St *Web:* www.yeled.org	Brooklyn	NY	11218	718-686-3700	686-3560	148
Yell County 1309 E 8th St PO Box 99 *Web:* yellcounty.net	Danville	AR	72833	479-495-4881	229-5634	338
Yellow Basket Restaurant 2860 S Main St *Web:* www.yboriginal.com	Santa Ana	CA	92707	714-545-8219		671
Yellow Creek Falls Fish Camp 3595 Al Hwy 273 *Web:* yellowcreekfalls.com	Leesburg	AL	35983	256-526-8427		239
Yellow Creek State Park 170 Rt 259 Hwy *Web:* www.dcnr.pa.gov	Penn Run	PA	15765	724-357-7913		565
Yellow Dog Networks 9664 Marion Rd *Web:* www.yellowdognetworks.com	Kansas City	MO	64137	816-767-9364		180
Yellow Magic Inc 41571 Date St *Web:* www.yellowmagic.com	Murrieta	CA	92562	951-506-4005	506-1919	178-1
Yellow Medicine County 415 Ninth Ave *TF:* 800-366-4812 ■ *Web:* mncourts.gov	Granite Falls	MN	56241	320-564-3325	564-4435	338
Yellow Pencil Inc 10158 103 St NW *Web:* yellowpencil.com	Edmonton	AB	T5J0X6	780-423-5917		196
Yellow Point Equity Partners LP 1285 W Pender St Ste 1000 *Web:* www.ypoint.ca	Vancouver	BC	V6E4B1	604-659-1898		690
Yellow Porch, The 734 Thompson Ln *Web:* www.theyellowporch.com	Nashville	TN	37204	615-386-0260		671
Yellow River State Forest 729 State Forest Rd YRSF *Web:* www.iowadnr.gov	Harpers Ferry	IA	52146	563-586-2254		565
Yellowdog Printing & Graphics LLC 490 S Santa Fe Dr Unit A *Web:* yellowdogdenver.com	Denver	CO	80223	303-765-2000		627
Yellowhammer Media Group Inc 111 W 28th St Ste 2B *Web:* www.yhmg.com	New York	NY	10001	646-490-9857		7
Yellowhead Helicopters Ltd 3010 Selwyn Rd **Fax Area Code:* 250 ■ *TF:* 888-566-4401 ■ *Web:* www.yhl.ca	Valemount	BC	V0E2Z0	888-566-4401	566-4333*	359
Yellowpages.com LLC 208 S Akard *TF:* 866-329-7118 ■ *Web:* www.yellowpages.com	Dallas	TX	75202	866-329-7118		397
Yellowridge Construction Ltd 2605 Clarke St Ste 200 *Web:* yellowridge.ca	Port Moody	BC	V3H1Z4	604-936-2605	936-2630	186
Yellowstone Art Museum 401 N 27th St *Web:* www.yellowstone.artmuseum.org	Billings	MT	59101	406-256-6804		520
Yellowstone Baptist College 1515 S Shiloh Rd *TF:* 800-487-9950 ■ *Web:* yellowstonechristian.edu	Billings	MT	59106	406-656-9950	656-3737	166
Yellowstone County 217 N 27th St *Web:* co.yellowstone.mt.gov	Billings	MT	59101	406-256-2720		338
Yellowstone Lake State Park 8495 Lake Rd *Web:* dnr.wi.gov	Blanchardville	WI	53516	608-523-4427		565
Yellowstone Log Homes LLC 280 N Yellowstone Hwy *Web:* www.yellowstoneloghomes.com	Rigby	ID	83442	208-745-8108		106
Yellowstone National Park PO Box 168 *Web:* www.nps.gov	Yellowstone National Park	WY	82190	307-344-7381		564
Yellowstone Public Radio 1500 University Dr *TF:* 800-441-2941 ■ *Web:* ypradio.org	Billings	MT	59101	406-657-2941		645-18
Yellowstone Valley Electric Co-op 150 Co-op Way *TF:* 800-736-5323 ■ *Web:* www.yvec.com	Huntley	MT	59037	406-348-3411	348-3414	245
Yellowstone Western Heritage Ctr 2822 Montana Ave *Web:* www.ywhc.org	Billings	MT	59101	406-256-6809	256-6850	520
Yellowstone-Bighorn Research Assn (YBRA) PO Box 630 *Web:* www.ybra.org	Red Lodge	MT	59068	406-446-1333		49-19
Yemanja Brasil 2900 Missouri Ave Pestalozzi St *Web:* yemanjastl.com	Saint Louis	MO	63118	314-771-7457	771-0296	671
Yen China Cafe 1225 Belt Line Rd *Web:* www.garlandyenchinacafe.com	Garland	TX	75040	972-495-9779		671
Yen Ching 926 Main St *Web:* www.yenchingdbq.com	Dubuque	IA	52001	563-556-2574		671
Yen Ching 8512 E Washington St *Web:* www.yenchingwest.com	Indianapolis	IN	46219	317-899-3270	228-0886	671
Yenkin-Majestic Paint Corp 1920 Leonard Ave *TF:* 800-848-1898 ■ *Web:* www.yenkin-majestic.com	Columbus	OH	43219	614-253-8511		550
Yeo & Yeo 5300 Bay Rd Ste 100 *TF:* 800-968-0010 ■ *Web:* yeoandyeo.com	Saginaw	MI	48604	989-793-9830	793-0186	2
Yeoman Telephone Company Inc (YTCI) 196 S Goslee St *Web:* www.ytci.com	Yeoman	IN	47997	574-965-2100		224
Yeomans Chicago Corp 3905 Enterprise Ct PO Box 6620 *Web:* www.yccpump.com	Aurora	IL	60504	630-236-5500	236-5511	641
Yeomans Wood & Timber Inc 714 Empire Expy *Web:* yeomanswood.com	Swainsboro	GA	30401	478-237-9940		448
Yerba Buena Center for the Arts (YBCA) 701 Mission St *Web:* ybca.org	San Francisco	CA	94103	415-978-2787		520
Yerba Prima Inc 740 Jefferson Ave *TF:* 800-488-4339 ■ *Web:* yerba.com	Ashland	OR	97520	541-488-2228		123
Yes Lifecycle Marketing 421 SW 6th Ave Ste 400 *TF:* 877-937-6245 ■ *Web:* www.yeslifecyclemarketing.com	Portland	OR	97204	877-937-6245		4
Yes Publishing 6301 N Rosebury 2nd Fl *Web:* www.yespublishing.com	Saint Louis	MO	63105	314-727-7922		637-2
Yeshiva Toras Chaim Talmudical Seminary 1555 Stuart St *Web:* ytcdenver.org	Denver	CO	80204	303-629-8200		166
Yeshiva University 500 W 185th St *Web:* www.yu.edu	New York	NY	10033	212-960-5400	960-0086	166
Yeshivat Noam 70 W Century Rd *Web:* www.yeshivatnoam.org	Paramus	NJ	07652	201-261-1919		685
Yeslow & Koeppel PA 1617 Hendry St Ste 205 *Web:* yklegal.com	Fort Myers	FL	33901	239-337-4343		41
Yesterday USA Radio Networks, The 2001 Plymouth Rock Dr *TF:* 800-624-2272 ■ *Web:* www.yesterdayusa.com	Richardson	TX	75081	972-889-9872	889-2329	644

Name / Address	City	State	Zip	Phone	Fax	Class
Yesterday's Resturant & Tavern 2030 Devine St 5 Pts — *Web:* www.yesterdayssc.com	Columbia	SC	29205	803-799-0196		671
Yesware Inc 75 Kneeland St 1st Fl — *TF:* 855-937-9273 ■ *Web:* www.yesware.com	Boston	MA	02111	855-937-9273		387
Yeti Inc 7601 SW Pkwy — *Web:* www.yeti.com	Austin	TX	78735	512-394-9384		608
Yetter Manufacturing Inc 109 S McDonough St PO Box 358 — *TF:* 800-447-5777 ■ *Web:* www.yetterco.com	Colchester	IL	62326	309-776-4111	776-3222	273
Yew Dell Botanical Gardens 6220 Old LaGrange Rd — *Web:* yewdellgardens.org	Crestwood	KY	40014	502-241-4788		97
Y&F (Young & Franklin Inc) 942 Old Liverpool Rd — *Web:* www.yf.com	Liverpool	NY	13088	315-457-3110	457-9204	790
YFF & Scholma PC 688 Cascade W Pkwy SE — *Web:* www.yffandscholma.com	Grand Rapids	MI	49546	616-942-6530		2
YHB Investment Advisors Inc 29 S Main St Ste 306 — *Web:* yhbia.com	West Hartford	CT	06107	860-561-7050		401
YHS (Yorktown Historical Society) PO Box 355 — *Web:* www.yorktownhistory.org	Yorktown Heights	NY	10598	914-962-5722		48-13
Yield Engineering Systems Inc 203 Lawrence Dr Ste A — *Web:* www.yieldengineering.com	Livermore	CA	94551	925-373-8353	373-8354	248
YieldStreet 300 Park Ave 15th Fl — *TF:* 844-943-5378 ■ *Web:* www.yieldstreet.com	New York	NY	10022	844-943-5378		217
Yiftee Inc 565 Middlefield Rd — *Web:* yiftee.com	Menlo Park	CA	94025	650-564-4438		5
Yingling Aircraft Inc 2010 Airport Rd — *TF:* 800-835-0083 ■ *Web:* www.yinglingaviation.com	Wichita	KS	67209	316-943-3246	943-2484	770
YKK AP America Inc 270 Riverside Pkwy Ste 100 — *TF:* 800-955-9551 ■ *Web:* www.ykkap.com	Austell	GA	30168	678-838-6000	838-6001	116
YKK USA Inc 1099 Wall St W Ste 244 — *Web:* www.ykkfastening.com	Lyndhurst	NJ	07071	201-935-4200	964-0123	594
YMAA (YMAA Publication Center Inc) PO Box 480 — *Web:* ymaa.com	Wolfeboro	NH	03894	603-569-7988	569-1889	637-2
YMAA Publication Center Inc (YMAA) PO Box 480 — *Web:* ymaa.com	Wolfeboro	NH	03894	603-569-7988	569-1889	637-2
YMAA Publication Ctr 38 Hyde Park Ave — *TF:* 800-669-8892 ■ *Web:* www.ymaa.com	Jamaica Plain	MA	02130	800-669-8892		637-2
YMCA (YMCA of the USA) 101 N Wacker Dr — *TF:* 800-872-9622 ■ *Web:* www.ymca.net	Chicago	IL	60606	312-977-0031	977-9063	48-6
YMCA Canada 1867 Yonge St Ste 601 — *Web:* ymca.ca	Toronto	ON	M4S1Y5	416-967-9622	967-9618	138
YMCA of Pikes Peak Region Inc 207 N Nevada Ave — *Web:* www.ppymca.org	Colorado Springs	CO	80903	719-473-9622		31
YMCA of Rock River Valley 200 Y Blvd — *Web:* rockriverymca.org	Rockford	IL	61107	815-489-1252		354
YMCA of the USA (YMCA) 101 N Wacker Dr — *TF:* 800-872-9622 ■ *Web:* www.ymca.net	Chicago	IL	60606	312-977-0031	977-9063	48-6
YMCA of Triangle Area 801 Corporate Center Dr — *Web:* www.ymcatriangle.org	Raleigh	NC	27607	919-719-9622		31
YNB 401 Elm St PO Box 851700 — *Web:* www.ynbok.com	Yukon	OK	73099	405-354-5281	354-9869	70
YNHS (Yakima Neighborhood Health Services) 12 S Eigth St PO Box 2605 — *Web:* www.ynhs.org	Yakima	WA	98907	509-454-4143	454-3651	353
YO Ranch Steakhouse 702 Ross Ave — *Web:* www.yoranchsteakhouse.com	Dallas	TX	75202	214-744-3287		671
Yoakum County PO Box 309 — *Web:* www.co.yoakum.tx.us	Plains	TX	79355	806-456-7491	456-8767	338
Yoakum National Bank 301 W Grand Ave — *TF:* 866-962-9304 ■ *Web:* www.yoakumnationalbank.com	Yoakum	TX	77995	361-293-5225	293-7322	70
YoCream International Inc 5858 NE 87th Ave — *Web:* www.yocream.com	Portland	OR	97220	503-288-6300		296-25
Yoder & Armstrong Printing 627 E Baltimore Ave E — *Web:* yoderandarmstrong.com	Lansdowne	PA	19050	610-622-6118		627
Yoder Industries Inc 2520 Needmore Rd — *Web:* www.yoderindustries.com	Dayton	OH	45414	937-278-5769	278-6321	308
Yoder Lumber Company Inc 4515 TR 367 — *Web:* www.yoderlumber.com	Millersburg	OH	44654	330-893-3131	893-3031	551
Yoder Oil Company Inc 1221 N Nappanee St — *TF:* 800-860-2107 ■ *Web:* www.yoderoil.com	Elkhart	IN	46514	574-264-2107		581
YodIce & Company PC 1055 Parsippany Blvd Ste 506 — *Web:* www.yodiceco.com	Parsippany	NJ	07054	973-263-8228	263-2515	2
Yodle Inc 330 W 34th St 18th Fl — *TF:* 877-276-5104 ■ *Web:* www.yodle.com	New York	NY	10001	877-276-5104		395
Yodlee Inc 3600 Bridge Pkwy Ste 200 — *Web:* www.yodlee.com	Redwood City	CA	94065	650-980-3600		178-7
YogaVidya.com PO Box 569 — *Web:* www.yogavidya.com	Woodstock	NY	12498	586-283-4680		637-2
Yogen Fruz 210 Shields Ct — *Web:* www.yogenfruz.com	Markham	ON	L3R8V2	905-479-8762	479-5235	310
Yogi Divine Society 2437 Yeoman St	Waukegan	IL	60087	847-336-6451		48-20
Yogo Inn 211 E Main St — *TF:* 800-860-9646 ■ *Web:* yogoinn.com	Lewistown	MT	59457	406-535-8721	535-8969	379
Yoho Resources Inc 521-3rd Ave SW Ste 500 — *Web:* www.yohoresources.ca	Calgary	AB	T2P3T3	403-537-1771		539
Yoho Ted (Rep R - FL) 1730 Longworth House Office Bldg — *Web:* yoho.house.gov	Washington	DC	20515	202-225-5744	225-3973	342-2
Yojna Inc 32605 W 12 Mile Rd Ste 275 — *Web:* www.yojna.com	Farmington Hills	MI	48334	248-489-9650	489-9657	180
Yokogawa Corporation of America 12530 W Airport Blvd — *TF:* 800-888-6400 ■ *Web:* www.yokogawa.com	Sugar Land	TX	77478	281-340-3800	340-3838	248
Yokohama Industries Americas Inc 105 Industry Dr — *Web:* www.yokohamaia.com	Versailles	KY	40383	859-873-2188	873-8943	60
Yokohama Tire Corp 601 S Acacia Ave — *TF:* 800-423-4544 ■ *Web:* www.yokohamatire.com	Fullerton	CA	92831	714-870-3800		754
Yoli LLC 2080 Industrial Rd Bldg B — *TF:* 888-295-9009 ■ *Web:* yoli.com	Salt Lake City	UT	84104	888-295-9009		366
Yolo County 625 Ct St Rm B01 — *TF:* 800-433-5060 ■ *Web:* www.yolocounty.org	Woodland	CA	95695	530-666-8150	668-4029	338
Yolo Federal Credit Union 266 W Main St — *TF:* 877-965-6328 ■ *Web:* www.yolofcu.org	Woodland	CA	95695	530-668-2700		219
Yomari Information Services Inc 111 Third Ave S Ste 120 — *Web:* www.yomari.com	Minneapolis	MN	55401	612-326-4852	392-0050	631
Yonex Corp 20140 S Western Ave — *TF:* 800-449-6639 ■ *Web:* www.yonex.com	Torrance	CA	90501	424-201-4800	201-4799	710
Yonkers Chamber of Commerce 55 Main St 2nd Fl — *Web:* www.yonkerschamber.com	Yonkers	NY	10701	914-963-0332	963-0455	139
Yonkers City Hall 40 S Broadway — *Web:* www.yonkersny.gov	Yonkers	NY	10701	914-377-6000		337
Yonkers Contracting Company Inc 969 Midland Ave — *Web:* www.yonkerscontractingco.com	Yonkers	NY	10704	914-965-1500	378-8885	188-4
Yonkers Honda 2000 Central Park Ave — *Web:* www.yonkershonda.com	Yonkers	NY	10710	914-600-7988	963-2801	57
Yonkers Public Library 1 Larkin Ctr — *Web:* www.ypl.org	Yonkers	NY	10701	914-337-1500		434-3
Yonkers Raceway 810 Yonkers Ave — *Web:* www.empirecitycasino.com	Yonkers	NY	10704	914-968-4200		642
Yorba Linda Chamber of Commerce 17670 Yorba Linda Blvd — *Web:* www.yorbalindachamber.us	Yorba Linda	CA	92886	714-993-9537	993-7764	139
Yorba Linda Public Library 18181 Imperial Hwy — *Web:* www.ylpl.org	Yorba Linda	CA	92886	714-777-2873		434-3
York Barbell Company Inc 3300 Board Rd — *TF:* 800-358-9675 ■ *Web:* yorkbarbell.com	York	PA	17406	717-767-6481	764-0044	267
York Building Products Co 950 Smile Way — *TF:* 800-673-2408 ■ *Web:* www.yorkbuilding.com	York	PA	17404	717-848-2831	854-9156	183
York Building Services Inc 99 Grand St Ste 3 — *TF:* 855-443-9675 ■ *Web:* yorkbuildingservices.com	Moonachie	NJ	07074	855-443-9675		256
York Catholic High School 601 E Springettsbury Ave — *Web:* yorkcatholic.org	York	PA	17403	717-846-8871		685
York Central Hospital 10 Trench St — *Web:* www.mackenziehealth.ca	Richmond Hill	ON	L4C4Z3	905-883-1212		374-2
York College 94-20 Guy R Brewer Blvd — *Web:* www.york.cuny.edu	Jamaica	NY	11451	718-262-2000	262-2601	166
York College 1125 E Eigth St — *TF:* 800-950-9675 ■ *Web:* www.york.edu	York	NE	68467	402-363-5600	363-5623	166
York College of Pennsylvania 441 Country Club Rd — *Web:* www.ycp.edu	York	PA	17403	717-846-7788	815-6862	166
York Container 138 Mt Scion Rd PO Box 3008 — *Web:* www.yorkcontainer.com	York	PA	17402	717-757-7611	755-8090	100
York Correctional Institution 201 W Main St — *Web:* portal.ct.gov	Niantic	CT	06357	860-451-3001		213
York County 45 Kennebunk Rd PO Box 399 — *Web:* www.yorkcountymaine.gov	Alfred	ME	04002	207-324-1577		338
York County 510 N Lincoln Ave — *Web:* www.yorkcounty.ne.gov	York	NE	68467	402-362-7759	362-7558	338
York County 45 N George St — *Web:* yorkcountypa.gov	York	PA	17401	717-771-9612	771-9096	338
York County 6 S Congress St — *Web:* www.yorkcountygov.com	York	SC	29745	803-802-4300	684-8575	338
York County 224 Ballard St PO Box 532 — *Web:* www.yorkcounty.gov	Yorktown	VA	23690	757-890-3450	890-3459	338
York County Cerebral Palsy Home Incorporated Proj 2050 Barley Rd — *Web:* margaretemoul.org	York	PA	17408	717-767-6463		371
York County Chamber of Commerce 144 Roosevelt Ave — *Web:* www.yceapa.org	York	PA	17401	717-848-4000	843-6737	139
York County Community College 112 College Dr — *TF:* 800-580-3820 ■ *Web:* www.yccc.edu	Wells	ME	04090	207-646-9282	641-0837	162
York County Library 138 E Black St — *Web:* www.yclibrary.org	Rock Hill	SC	29730	803-981-5858		434-3
York County Public Library 8500 George Washington Memorial Hwy — *TF:* 800-552-7945 ■ *Web:* www.yorkcounty.gov	Yorktown	VA	23692	757-890-3377	890-2956	434-3
York County Regional Chamber of Commerce 116 E Main St — *Web:* www.yorkcountychamber.com	Rock Hill	SC	29731	803-324-7500	324-1889	139
York County Transportation Authority 1230 Roosevelt Ave — *Web:* www.rabbittransit.org	York	PA	17404	717-846-5562	848-4853	468
York Daily Record (YDR) 1891 Loucks Rd — *TF:* 800-559-3520 ■ *Web:* www.ydr.com	York	PA	17408	717-771-2000		532-2
York Educational Federal Credit Union 1601 S Queen St — *Web:* yefcu.org	York	PA	17403	717-843-1153		219
York Electric Cooperative Inc 1385 E Alexander Love Hwy PO Box 150 — *TF:* 800-582-8810 ■ *Web:* www.yorkelectric.net	York	SC	29745	803-684-4248		245

Name / Address	City	State	Zip	Phone	Fax	Class
York Employment Services Inc 990 N Ontario Mills Dr Ste C; *Web:* www.yorkemployment.com	Ontario	CA	91764	909-581-0181		260
York Ford Inc 1481 Bwy; *TF:* 888-705-6229 ■ *Web:* www.yorkford.com	Saugus	MA	01906	781-231-1945		57
York Group Inc, The 2 NorthShore Ctr; *TF:* 800-223-4964 ■ *Web:* matw.com	Pittsburgh	PA	15212	412-995-1600	995-1690	134
York Ice Company Inc 281 Kings Mill Rd; *Web:* www.goodtimeice.com	York	PA	17401	717-848-2639		380
York Mahoning Mechanical Contrs Inc 724 Canfield Rd; *Web:* www.yorkmahoning.com	Youngstown	OH	44511	330-788-7011		610
York Metal Fabricators Inc 27 NE 26th St; *TF:* 800-255-4703 ■ *Web:* www.yorkmetal.com	Oklahoma City	OK	73105	405-528-7495		697
York River Electric Inc 108 Production Dr; *Web:* www.yorkriverelectric.com	Yorktown	VA	23693	757-369-3673	369-3680	189-4
York Securities Inc 160 Broadway 7th Fl; *Web:* yorktrade.com	New York	NY	10038	212-349-9700		690
York Solutions 1 Westbrook Corporate Ctr Ste 910; *TF:* 877-700-9675 ■ *Web:* yorksolutions.net	Westchester	IL	60154	708-531-8362		195
York State Bank & Trust Co 700 N Lincoln Ave; *Web:* www.yorkstatebank.com	York	NE	68467	402-362-4411	362-4192	70
York Technical College 452 S Anderson Rd; *TF:* 800-922-8324 ■ *Web:* www.yorktech.edu	Rock Hill	SC	29730	803-327-8000		162
York Telecom Corp 81 Corbett Way; *TF:* 800-982-9675 ■ *Web:* www.yorktel.com	Eatontown	NJ	07724	732-413-6000		736
York University 4700 Keele St; *TF:* 800-426-2255 ■ *Web:* www.yorku.ca	Toronto	ON	M3J1P3	416-736-2100	736-5536	785
York Wallcoverings Inc 750 Linden Ave; *TF:* 800-375-9675 ■ *Web:* www.yorkwallcoverings.com	York	PA	17404	717-846-4456	843-5624	802
York Water Co, The 130 E Market St; *NASDAQ: YORW* ■ *TF:* 800-750-5561 ■ *Web:* www.yorkwater.com	York	PA	17401	717-845-3601	845-3792	787
Yorkston Oil Company Inc 2801 Roeder Ave; *TF:* 800-401-2201 ■ *Web:* yorkstonoil.com	Bellingham	WA	98225	360-734-2201		579
Yorktown Bank 1913 S Elliott; *Web:* yorktownbank.com	Pryor	OK	74361	918-825-7200	491-7070	70
Yorktown Historical Society (YHS) PO Box 355; *Web:* www.yorktownhistory.org	Yorktown Heights	NY	10598	914-962-5722		48-13
Yorktown National Cemetery PO Box 210; *Web:* www.nps.gov	Yorktown	VA	23690	757-898-2410	898-6346	136
Yorktown Shopping Ctr 70 Yorktown Shopping Ctr; *Web:* yorktowncenter.com	Lombard	IL	60148	630-629-7330	629-7334	460
Yorktowne Hotel 48 E Market St; *Web:* www.yorktowne.com	York	PA	17401	717-848-1111		379
Yorkville CUSD 115 602 Center Pkwy; *Web:* www.y115.org	Yorkville	IL	60560	630-553-4382	553-4398	780
Yorozu Automotive Tennessee Inc 395 Mount View Industrial Dr; *Web:* www.yorozu-corp.co.jp	Morrison	TN	37357	931-668-7700	668-7777	489
Yosemite National Park 9039 Village Dr PO Box 577; *Web:* www.nps.gov	Yosemite National Park	CA	95389	209-372-0200		564
Yosemite Pathology Group Inc 2625 Coffee Rd Ste S; *Web:* www.ypmg.com	Modesto	CA	95355	209-577-1200		415
Yosemite Sierra Visitors Bureau 40637 Hwy 41; *TF:* 800-613-0709 ■ *Web:* www.yosemitethisyear.com	Oakhurst	CA	93644	559-683-4636		206
Yoshi's Cafe 3257 N Halsted St; *Web:* www.yoshiscafechicago.com	Chicago	IL	60657	773-248-6160		671
Yoshimatsu 2660 N Campbell Ave; *Web:* www.yoshimatsuaz.com	Tucson	AZ	85719	520-320-1574		671
Yoshino America Corp 2500 Palmer Ave; *Web:* www.yoshinoamerica.com	University Park	IL	60484	708-534-1141		596
Yoshino Restaurant 6226 N Blackstone Ave	Fresno	CA	93710	559-431-2205		671
Yoshinoya Beef Bowl 1603 Sepulveda Blvd; *Web:* www.yoshinoyaamerica.com	Torrance	CA	90501	310-527-6060	527-6050	670
Yost & Baill LLP 220 S Sixth St Ste 2050; *Web:* yostbaill.com	Minneapolis	MN	55402	612-338-6000		41
Yost Business Systems 685 E &erson; *Web:* www.yostonline.com	Idaho Falls	ID	83401	208-552-7752		112
Yost Superior Co PO Box 1487; *Web:* www.yostsuperior.com	Springfield	OH	45501	937-323-7591		719
YOTEL 570 Tenth Ave Times Sq; *Web:* www.yotel.com	New York	NY	10036	646-449-7700		378
YOU (Youth Opportunities Unlimited) 422 E S St; *Web:* www.kresa.org	Kalamazoo	MI	49007	269-775-1660	775-1661	623
You Can Publishing 300 Sheridan St W; *Web:* www.traditionalhaircutting.com	Lanesboro	MN	55949	612-916-2841		637-2
YouDocs Beauty Inc 648 Broadway; *Web:* www.youbeauty.com	New York	NY	10012	646-449-9445		387
Youell's Oyster House 2249 Walnut St; *Web:* youellsoysterhouse.com	Allentown	PA	18104	610-439-1203		671
Youghiogheny Scenic & Wild River c/o Deep Creek Lake Recreation Area 898 State Pk Rd; *TF:* 800-248-1893 ■ *Web:* dnr.maryland.gov	Swanton	MD	21561	301-387-5563		565
YouMail Inc 43 Corporate Pk Ste 200; *TF:* 800-374-0013 ■ *Web:* www.youmail.com	Irvine	CA	92606	800-374-0013		180

Name / Address	City	State	Zip	Phone	Fax	Class
Young & Company CPAS 11200 SW Allen Blvd Ste 100; *Web:* youngcocpas.com	Beaverton	OR	97005	503-646-4800	526-9329	2
Young & Franklin Inc (Y&F) 942 Old Liverpool Rd; *Web:* www.yf.com	Liverpool	NY	13088	315-457-3110	457-9204	790
Young & Maslowski LLP 600 S Main St PO Box 917; *Web:* ymlawoshkosh.com	Oshkosh	WI	54903	920-651-1820		41
Young America LLC 10 S Fifth St 7th Fl; *TF:* 800-533-4529 ■ *Web:* www.yaengage.com	Minneapolis	MN	55402	800-533-4529		737
Young America's Foundation 11480 Commerce Park Dr Ste 600; *TF:* 800-872-1776 ■ *Web:* www.yaf.org	Reston	VA	20191	703-318-9608	318-9122	48-7
Young and Rubicam Inc 3 Columbus Cir; *Web:* www.yr.com	New York	NY	10019	212-210-3000		4
Young at Art Children's Museum 751 SW 121st Ave; *Web:* www.youngatartmuseum.org	Davie	FL	33325	954-424-0085	473-8798	521
Young Audiences Inc 171 Madison Ave Ste 200; *Web:* www.youngaudiences.org	New York	NY	10016	212-831-8110	289-1202	48-4
Young Bros Stamp Works Inc 1415 Howard Ave PO Box 75; *TF:* 800-553-8248 ■ *Web:* www.youngbrosstampworks.com	Muscatine	IA	52761	800-553-8248		198
Young Children Magazine 1313 L St NW Ste 500 PO Box 97156; *TF:* 800-424-2460 ■ *Web:* www.naeyc.org	Washington	DC	20005	202-232-8777	328-1846	457-8
Young Clement Rivers LLP 25 Calhoun St; *Web:* www.ycrlaw.com	Charleston	SC	29401	843-577-4000		428
Young Conaway Stargatt & Taylor Library 1000 N King St; *Web:* www.youngconaway.com	Wilmington	DE	19801	302-571-6600	571-1253	434-3
Young Corp 3231 Utah Ave S; *TF:* 800-321-9090 ■ *Web:* www.youngcorp.com	Seattle	WA	98134	206-624-1071	682-6881	190
Young County 516 Fourth St Rm 104; *Web:* www.co.young.tx.us	Graham	TX	76450	940-549-8432	521-0305	338
Young Dental Manufacturing LLC 13705 Shoreline Ct E; *TF:* 800-325-1881 ■ *Web:* www.youngdental.com	Earth City	MO	63045	800-325-1881		228
Young Don (Rep R - AK) 2314 Rayburn House Office Bldg; *Web:* donyoung.house.gov	Washington	DC	20515	202-225-5765	225-0425	342-2
Young Drivers of Canada Inc 1 James St S Ste 300; *Web:* www.yd.com	Hamilton	ON	L8P4R5	905-529-5501		138
Young Electric Sign Co 2401 Foothill Dr; *TF:* 866-779-8357 ■ *Web:* www.yesco.com	Salt Lake City	UT	84109	801-464-4600	483-0998	701
Young Fashions Inc 11111 Coursey Blvd; *TF:* 800-824-4154 ■ *Web:* www.youngfashions.com	Baton Rouge	LA	70816	225-766-1010	364-2906	594
Young Harris College PO Box 116; *TF:* 800-241-3754 ■ *Web:* www.yhc.edu	Young Harris	GA	30582	706-379-3111	379-3108	162
Young Industries Inc 16 Painter St; *TF:* 800-546-3165 ■ *Web:* www.younginds.com	Muncy	PA	17756	570-546-3165	546-1888	207
Young Israel of New Rochelle 1149 N Ave; *TF:* 888-942-3638 ■ *Web:* www.youngisrael.org	New Rochelle	NY	10804	914-636-2215		48-20
Young Life 420 N Cascade Ave; *Web:* www.younglife.org	Colorado Springs	CO	80903	719-381-1800		48-20
Young Living Essential Oils 3125 Executive Pkwy; *TF:* 866-203-5666 ■ *Web:* www.youngliving.com	Lehi	UT	84043	801-418-8900	418-8800	799
Young Manufacturing Company Inc 521 S Main St PO Box 167; *TF:* 800-545-6595 ■ *Web:* youngmanufacturing.com	Beaver Dam	KY	42320	270-274-3306	274-9522	499
Young Manufacturing Inc 2331 N 42nd St; *TF:* 800-451-9884 ■ *Web:* www.youngmfg.com	Grand Forks	ND	58203	701-772-5541		483
Young Plumbing & Heating Co 750 S Hackett Rd; *Web:* www.youngphc.com	Waterloo	IA	50701	319-234-4411	234-4540	189-10
Young Presidents' Organization (YPO) 600 E Las Colinas Blvd Ste 1100; *TF:* 800-773-7976 ■ *Web:* www.ypo.org	Irving	TX	75039	972-587-1500	587-1611	49-12
Young Rembrandts 23 N Union St; *Web:* www.youngrembrandts.com	Elgin	IL	60123	847-742-6966	742-7197	310
Young Startup Ventures Inc 258 Crafton Ave; **Fax Area Code: 209* ■ *Web:* www.youngstartup.com	Staten Island	NY	10314	212-202-1002	844-4397*	463
Young State Park 02280 Boyne City Rd; *Web:* www.michigan.org	Boyne City	MI	49712	231-582-7523		565
Young Todd (Sen R - IN) 185 Dirksen Senate Office Bldg; *Web:* www.young.senate.gov	Washington	DC	20510	202-224-5623		342-2
Young Transportation & Tours 843 Riverside Dr; *TF:* 800-622-5444 ■ *Web:* youngtransportation.com	Asheville	NC	28804	828-258-0084	252-3342	107
Young Welding Supply Inc 101 E First St; *Web:* youngwelding.com	Sheffield	AL	35660	256-383-5429	383-1385	386
Young Windows Inc 680 Colwell Ln; *Web:* youngwindows.com	Conshohocken	PA	19428	610-828-5422	828-2144	234
Young's Cafe 3307 S College Rd; *Web:* www.youngscafe.com	Fort Collins	CO	80525	970-223-8000		671
Young's Commercial Transfer 2075 W Scranton Ave PO Box 871; *TF:* 800-289-1639 ■ *Web:* www.yctinc.com	Porterville	CA	93257	559-784-6651	784-5280	780
Young's Environmental Cleanup Inc G-5305 N Dort Hwy; *Web:* youngsenvironmental.com	Flint	MI	48505	810-789-7155	789-3606	667
Young's Gear Inc 1711 Van Horn Rd; *Web:* www.youngsgear.com	Fairbanks	AK	99701	907-456-6464		62-7

Name / Address	City	State	ZIP	Phone	Fax	Class
Young's Market Company LLC 500 S Central Ave *TF:* 800-627-2777 ■ *Web:* www.youngsmarket.com	Los Angeles	CA	90013	213-612-1248	612-1238	81-3
Young's Plant Farm 863 Airport Rd *TF:* 800-304-8609 ■ *Web:* www.youngsplantfarm.com	Auburn	AL	36830	800-304-8609		369
Young, Berman, Karpf & Gonzalez PA 500 E Broward Blvd Ste 1580 *Web:* ybkglaw.com	Fort Lauderdale	FL	33394	954-809-3300		41
Young, Marr & Associates LLC 3554 Hulmeville Rd Ste 102 *Web:* youngmarrlaw.com	Bensalem	PA	19020	215-607-2715		41
Young, Reverman & Mazzei Company LPA 1014 Vine St Ste 2400 *TF:* 800-721-1678 ■ *Web:* yrmlaw.com	Cincinnati	OH	45202	513-721-1200		41
Younger Optics 2925 California St *TF:* 800-366-5367 ■ *Web:* www.youngeroptics.com	Torrance	CA	90503	310-783-1533	783-6477	542
Youngsoft Inc 49197 Wixom Tech Dr *TF:* 888-470-4553 ■ *Web:* youngsoft.com	Wixom	MI	48393	248-675-1200	675-1201	177
Youngstown City Hall 26 S Phelps St *Web:* youngstownohio.gov	Youngstown	OH	44503	330-742-8859		337
Youngstown Crab Company Inc 755 Boardman Canfield Rd Bldg F Ste 6	Youngstown	OH	44505	330-759-5480		671
Youngstown Pipe & Supply Co 4100 Lakepark Rd *Web:* www.yopipe.com	Youngstown	OH	44512	330-783-2700		595
Youngstown Playhouse 600 Playhouse Ln *Web:* www.theyoungstownplayhouse.com	Youngstown	OH	44511	330-788-8739		572
Youngstown State University 1 University Plz *TF:* 877-468-6978 ■ *Web:* www.ysu.edu	Youngstown	OH	44555	330-941-3000		166
Youngstown Warren Regional Chamber 11 Central Sq Ste 1600 *Web:* www.regionalchamber.com	Youngstown	OH	44503	330-744-2131	746-0330	139
Youngstown-Warren Regional Airport 1453 Youngstown-Kingsville Rd NE *Web:* yngairport.com	Vienna	OH	44473	330-856-1537	609-5371	27
Youngwoo & Associates LLC 545 W 25th St *Web:* www.iyoungwoo.com	New York	NY	10001	212-477-8008		652
Yount Hyde & Barbour PC 50 S Cameron St *Web:* www.yhbcpa.com	Winchester	VA	22601	540-662-3417		2
Your Electronic Warehouse 2828 Broadway St *TF:* 866-224-6171 ■ *Web:* 4yew.com	Quincy	IL	62301	217-224-6171		459
Your Father's Moustache 5686 Spring Garden Rd *Web:* yourfathersmoustache.ca	Halifax	NS	B3J1H5	902-423-6766		671
Your Heart's Delight by Audrey's 55 Mull Ln *Web:* www.yourheartsdelight.com	Lebanon	PA	17046	717-865-6524	865-7424	361
Your HR Group Inc PO Box 200255-290	Austin	TX	78750	512-410-7785		260
Your Linen Service Inc 875 E Bank St *Web:* yourlinenservice.com	Petersburg	VA	23803	804-732-3312	732-3313	393
Your Network of Praise PO Box 2426 *TF:* 800-442-9222 ■ *Web:* www.ynop.org	Havre	MT	59501	406-949-4308		645
Your Selling Team 100 Spectrum Center Dr Ste 700 *TF:* 888-387-8002 ■ *Web:* www.yoursellingteam.com	Irvine	CA	92618	888-387-8002		737
Your Source Financial 1747 E Morten Ave Ste 305 *Web:* www.ysfi.com	Phoenix	AZ	85020	602-343-1700		401
Your Travel Agent Corporate 321 N Pine St *Web:* www.ytavacations.com	Spartanburg	SC	29302	864-583-3054		772
YourAmigo Inc 4708 Del Valle Pkwy *Fax Area Code: 509 ■ *TF:* 800-816-7054 ■ *Web:* www.youramigo.com	Pleasanton	CA	94566	510-813-1355	357-6653*	196
YourAreaCode LLC 6242 28th St Ste B *TF:* 888-244-7751 ■ *Web:* www.yourareacode.com	Grand Rapids	MI	49546	616-555-1212		366
Yourga Trucking Inc 145 JH Yourga Pl PO Box 607 *TF:* 800-245-1722 ■ *Web:* www.yourga.com	Wheatland	PA	16161	724-981-3600		780
YourNet Connection Inc 432 E State Pky Ste 128 *TF:* 877-968-7638 ■ *Web:* www.ync.net	Schaumburg	IL	60173	847-524-3900		681
Yoush Consulting 7030 Woodbine Ave Ste 500 *Web:* www.yoush.com	Markham	ON	L3R6G2	905-307-6263		196
Youth Advocate Programs Inc (YAP) 2007 N Third St PO Box 950 *TF:* 800-324-5794 ■ *Web:* www.yapinc.org	Harrisburg	PA	17102	717-232-7580	233-2879	428
Youth Consultation Service (Inc) 284 Broadway *Web:* www.ycs.org	Newark	NJ	07104	973-482-8411		317
Youth Development Ctr 650 E 21st St	Erie	PA	16503	724-656-7300		412
Youth for Christ Intl 7670 S Vaughn Ct *Web:* yfci.org	Englewood	CO	80112	303-843-9000		637-10
Youth For Understanding USA 6400 Goldsboro Rd Ste 100 *Fax Area Code: 240 ■ *TF:* 800-424-3691 ■ *Web:* www.yfuusa.org	Bethesda	MD	20817	800-833-6243	235-2104*	48-11
Youth Frontiers Inc 6009 Excelsior Blvd *TF:* 888-992-0222 ■ *Web:* www.youthfrontiers.org	Minneapolis	MN	55416	952-922-0222		196
Youth Home Inc 20400 Colonel Glenn Rd *TF:* 800-728-6452 ■ *Web:* www.youthhome.org	Little Rock	AR	72210	501-821-5500		726
Youth in Decline 3520 20th St *Web:* www.youthindecline.com	San Francisco	CA	94110	415-695-1545		637-2
Youth Opportunities Unlimited (YOU) 422 E S St *Web:* www.kresa.org	Kalamazoo	MI	49007	269-775-1660	775-1661	623
Youth Science Institute 296 Garden Hill Dr *Web:* www.ysi-ca.org	Los Gatos	CA	95032	408-356-4945		521
Youth Villages Inner Harbour 4685 Dorsett Shoals Rd *TF:* 800-255-8657 ■ *Web:* www.youthvillages.org	Douglasville	GA	30135	770-852-6300	852-6301	374-1
Youth, Rights & Justice 1785 NE Sandy Blvd Ste 300 *Web:* youthrightsjustice.org	Portland	OR	97232	503-232-2540	231-4767	41
Youthbuild Intl 58 Day St Ste 300 *Web:* youthbuild.org	Somerville	MA	02144	617-623-9900		463
YouthPLAYS 7119 W Sunset Blvd Ste 390 *Web:* www.youthplays.com	Los Angeles	CA	90046	424-703-5315		637-10
Yovia LLC 2593 Mayport Rd Ste 101 *Web:* www.yovia.com	Atlantic Beach	FL	32233	904-432-5369		5
Yowell Transportation Services Inc 1840 Cardington Rd *TF:* 800-543-4320 ■ *Web:* www.yowellonline.com	Dayton	OH	45409	937-294-5933	294-4132	780
YPO (Young Presidents' Organization) 600 E Las Colinas Blvd Ste 1100 *TF:* 800-773-7976 ■ *Web:* www.ypo.org	Irving	TX	75039	972-587-1500	587-1611	49-12
Ypsilanti Historical Museum 220 N Huron St *Web:* www.ypsilantihistoricalsociety.org	Ypsilanti	MI	48197	734-482-4990		520
YPSILANTI Michigan Community Utilities Authority 2777 State Rd *Web:* www.ycua.org	Ypsilanti	MI	48198	734-484-4600		192
YRC Worldwide Inc 10990 Roe Ave *NASDAQ: YRCW* ■ *TF:* 800-846-4300 ■ *Web:* www.yrc.com	Overland Park	KS	66211	913-696-6100		360-3
YRH (Yarmouth Regional Hospital) 60 Vancouver St *TF:* 800-460-2110 ■ *Web:* www.swndha.nshealth.ca	Yarmouth	NS	B5A2P5	902-742-3541	742-0369	374-2
Yrrid Software Inc 507 Monroe St *Web:* www.yrrid.com	Chapel Hill	NC	27516	919-968-7858	968-7856	178-12
YSI Inc 1700-1725 Brannum Ln *TF:* 800-765-4974 ■ *Web:* www.ysi.com	Yellow Springs	OH	45387	937-767-7241	767-9353	201
Ysleta Mission 131 S Zaragosa Rd *Web:* www.ysletamission.org	El Paso	TX	79907	915-859-9848		50-1
YSS Group Inc 8612 NW 70th St *Web:* www.yssgroup.com	Miami	FL	33166	305-436-7371		787
YTCI (Yeoman Telephone Company Inc) 196 S Goslee St *Web:* www.ytci.com	Yeoman	IN	47997	574-965-2100		224
Y-Tex Corp 1825 Big Horn Ave *TF:* 800-443-6401 ■ *Web:* www.y-tex.com	Cody	WY	82414	307-587-5515	527-6433	280
Yturri Rose LLP 89 SW Third Ave *Web:* www.yturrirose.com	Ontario	OR	97914	541-889-5368		428
Yu & Associates Inc 200 Riverfront Blvd *Web:* yu-associates.com	Elmwood Park	NJ	07407	201-791-0075		261
Yuasa Battery Inc 2901 Montrose Ave *Web:* www.yuasabatteries.com	Reading	PA	19605	610-929-5781		74
Yub Inc 321 Castro St Ste 1 *Web:* yub.com	Mountain View	CA	94041	650-265-7316		393
Yuba City Water Treatment Plant 701 Northgate Dr *Web:* www.yubacity.net	Yuba City	CA	95991	530-822-4636		539
Yuba Community College District 2088 N Beale Rd *Web:* www.yccd.edu	Marysville	CA	95901	530-741-8949		162
Yuba County *Water Agency* 1220 F St (F&13th St) *Web:* www.yuba.org	Marysville	CA	95901	530-741-5000	741-6541	245
Yuba River Moulding & Millwork Inc PO Box 1078 *Web:* www.yubarivermoulding.com	Yuba City	CA	95992	530-742-2168	742-7140	499
Yuba State Park PO Box 159 *Web:* stateparks.utah.gov	Levan	UT	84639	435-758-2611		565
Yuca Restaurant & Lounge 501 Lincoln Rd *Web:* www.yuca.com	Miami Beach	FL	33139	305-532-9822		671
Yucaipa Valley Chamber of Commerce 35139 Yucaipa Blvd *Web:* www.yucaipachamber.org	Yucaipa	CA	92399	909-790-1841	580-8355	139
Yucaipa Valley Water District PO Box 730 *TF:* 800-304-2226 ■ *Web:* www.yvwd.dst.ca.us	Yucaipa	CA	92399	909-797-5117	797-6381	787
Yucca House National Monument c/o Mesa Verde National Pk PO Box 8 *Web:* www.nps.gov	Mesa	CO	81330	970-529-4465	529-4637	564
Yucca Telecom 201 W Second St *TF:* 866-239-6858 ■ *Web:* www.yuccatelecom.com	Portales	NM	88130	575-226-2255		246
Yucca Valley Chamber of Commerce 56711 29 Palms Hwy *TF:* 855-365-6558 ■ *Web:* www.yuccavalley.org	Yucca Valley	CA	92284	760-365-6323	365-0763	139
Yukevich | Cavanaugh 355 S Grand Ave 15th Fl *Web:* www.yukelaw.com	Los Angeles	CA	90071	213-362-7777		428
Yukon *Tourism & Culture Dept* 2nd Ave & Lambert St PO Box 2703 *TF:* 800-661-0494 ■ *Web:* www.travelyukon.com	Whitehorse	YT	Y1A2C6	800-661-0494		774
Yukon Chamber of Commerce 10 W Main St Ste 130 *Web:* www.yukoncc.com	Yukon	OK	73099	405-354-3567		139
Yukon College 500 College Dr PO Box 2799 *TF:* 800-661-0504 ■ *Web:* www.yukonu.ca	Whitehorse	YT	Y1A5K4	867-668-8800		167-3
Yukon-Kuskokwim Correctional Ctr 1000 Eddie Hoffman Hwy *Web:* www.correct.state.ak.us	Bethel	AK	99559	907-543-5245	543-3097	213
Yule Tree Farms LLC 12704 Ehlen Rd NE *Fax Area Code: 888	Canby	OR	97002	503-678-2101	970-8733*	752
Yum Yum Donut Shops Inc 18830 E San Jose Ave *Web:* www.yumyumdonuts.com	City of Industry	CA	91748	626-964-1478	912-2779	297-2
Yum! Brands Inc 1441 Gardiner Ln *NYSE: YUM* ■ *TF:* 800-225-5532 ■ *Web:* www.yum.com	Louisville	KY	40213	502-874-8300		670
Yuma Civic Ctr 1440 W Desert Hills Dr *TF:* 866-966-0220 ■ *Web:* www.yumaaz.gov	Yuma	AZ	85365	928-373-5040	344-9121	205

	Phone	Fax	Class
Yuma Convention & Visitors Bureau 201 N Fourth Ave .... Yuma AZ 85364 *TF:* 800-293-0071 ■ *Web:* www.visityuma.com	928-783-0071	783-1897	206
Yuma County 310 Ash St Ste B .... Wray CO 80758 *Web:* yumacounty.net	970-332-5809	332-5919	338
Yuma County 198 S Main St .... Yuma AZ 85364 *TF:* 800-253-0883 ■ *Web:* www.yumacountyaz.gov	928-373-1010	373-1120	338
Yuma County Chamber of Commerce 180 W First St Ste A .... Yuma AZ 85364 *Web:* www.yumachamber.org	928-782-2567		139
Yuma County Fair 2520 E 32nd St .... Yuma AZ 85365 *Web:* www.yumafair.com	928-726-4420	344-3480	642
Yuma Daily Sun 2055 Arizona Ave .... Yuma AZ 85364 *Web:* www.yumasun.com	928-783-3333		532-2
Yuma Regional Medical Ctr 2400 S Ave A .... Yuma AZ 85364 *Web:* www.yumaregional.org	928-344-2000		374-3
Yuma School of Beauty 50 W 3rd St .... Yuma AZ 85364 *Web:* www.yumaschoolofbeauty.com	928-783-3141		685
Yuma Territorial Prison State Historic Park 200 N Prison Hill Rd .... Yuma AZ 85364 *Web:* www.yumaprison.org	928-783-4771		565
Yun Industrial Company Ltd 161 Selandia Ln .... Carson CA 90746 *Web:* yic-assm.com	310-715-1898		625
Yunis Realty Inc 100 N Main St .... Elmira NY 14901 *Web:* yunisrealty.com	607-733-3344		652
Yunker Farm Children's Museum 1201 28th Ave N .... Fargo ND 58102 *Web:* www.childrensmuseum-yunker.org	701-232-6102		521
Yurchak Printing Inc 920 Links Ave .... Landisville PA 17538 *Web:* www.yurchak.com	717-399-0209		627
Yurish Associates Inc 8527 E Rowel Rd .... Scottsdale AZ 85255 *Web:* www.yurishassociates.com	480-515-9018	515-9260	194
YUSA Corp 151 Jamison Rd SW .... Washington Court House OH 43160 *Web:* yusa-oh.com	740-335-0335	335-0330	677
Yusen Logistics (Americas) Inc 300 Lighting Way .... Secaucus NJ 07094 *Web:* www.yusen-logistics.com	201-553-3800		311
Yushin America Inc 35 Kenney Dr .... Cranston RI 02920 *Web:* www.yushinamerica.com	401-463-1800		201
YVC (Yakima Valley College) *Grandview* 500 W Main St .... Grandview WA 98930 *Web:* www.yvcc.edu	509-882-7000		162
YVE Hotel Miami 146 Biscayne Blvd .... Miami FL 33132 *Web:* www.yvehotelmiami.com	305-358-4555		379
Yves Delorme Inc 1725 Broadway St .... Charlottesville VA 22902 *TF:* 800-322-3911 ■ *Web:* www.yvesdelorme.com	434-979-3911		361
Y-W Electric Association Inc 250 Main Ave PO Box Y .... Akron CO 80720 *TF:* 800-660-2291 ■ *Web:* www.ywelectric.coop	970-345-2291		245
YWAM Publishing 7825 230th St SW .... Edmonds WA 98026 **Fax Area Code:* 425 ■ *TF:* 800-922-2143 ■ *Web:* www.ywampublishing.com	800-922-2143	775-2383*	637-2
YWCA (YWCA USA) 2025 M St NW Ste 550 .... Washington DC 20036 *TF:* 888-872-9259 ■ *Web:* www.ywca.org	202-467-0801	467-0802	48-6
YWCA USA (YWCA) 2025 M St NW Ste 550 .... Washington DC 20036 *TF:* 888-872-9259 ■ *Web:* www.ywca.org	202-467-0801	467-0802	48-6
YYZ Travel American Express 7851 Dufferin St .... Thornhill ON L4J3M4 *Web:* www.yyztravel.com	905-660-7000		774
YZ Enterprises Inc 1930 Indian Wood Cir .... Maumee OH 43537 *TF:* 800-736-8779 ■ *Web:* www.almondina.com	419-893-8777		296-9

Z

	Phone	Fax	Class
Z & L Machining Inc 3140 Central Ave .... Waukegan IL 60085 *Web:* www.zlmachfab.com	847-623-9500		454
Z Bardhi 3596 Kinhega Dr .... Tallahassee FL 32312 *Web:* www.zbardhis.com	850-894-9919		671
Z Communications Inc 14118 Stowe Dr Ste B .... Poway CA 92064 *TF:* 877-808-1226 ■ *Web:* www.zcomm.com	858-621-2700		253
Z Gallerie Inc 1855 W 139th St .... Gardena CA 90249 *TF:* 800-358-8288 ■ *Web:* www.zgallerie.com	310-630-1289		362
Z Group Inc 42 W 39th St 6th Fl .... New York NY 10018 *Web:* www.zgroupinc.com	212-941-9272		194
Z Marketing Partners 3905 E Vincennes Rd Ste 300 .... Indianapolis IN 46268 *Web:* zmarketingpartners.com	317-924-6271		7
Z Media Inc 1666 Kennedy Cswy Ste 602 .... Miami Beach FL 33141 *Web:* www.zmedia-inc.com	305-532-5566		4
Z Option Inc 417 Oakbend Dr Ste 200 .... Lewisville TX 75067 *Web:* www.zoption.com	972-315-8800		177
Z Salon & Spa Inc 9407 Shelbyville Rd .... Louisville KY 40222 *Web:* zsalon.com	502-426-2226		77
Z Systems 3724 Oregon Ave S .... Minneapolis MN 55426 *Web:* zsyst.com	952-974-3140	974-3141	52
Z Technology Inc 16055 SW Walker Rd No 290 .... Beaverton OR 97006 *Web:* www.ztechnology.com	503-614-9800		647
Z Tejas Grill 9400-A Arboreum Blvd .... Austin TX 78759 *Web:* ztejas.com	512-346-3506		671
Z's Bar & Restaurant 168 Louis Campau .... Grand Rapids MI 49503 *Web:* www.zsbar.com	616-454-3141		671
Z3 Technologies Inc 11400 W Bluemond Rd .... Wauwatosa WI 53226 *Web:* www.z3tech.com	414-607-9767		225
Z57 Internet Solutions 10045 Mesa Rim Rd .... San Diego CA 92121 *TF:* 800-899-8148 ■ *Web:* www.z57.com	800-899-8148		225
Z92 FM 10714 Mockingbird Dr .... Omaha NE 68127 *TF:* 800-955-9230 ■ *Web:* www.z92.com	800-955-9230		645-113
Zabel Freeman 1135 Heights Blvd .... Houston TX 77008 *Web:* zabelfreeman.com	713-802-9117	802-9114	445
Zabin Industries Inc 3957 S Hill St .... Los Angeles CA 90037 *Web:* www.zabin.com	213-749-1215		594
Zabriskie Gallery 400 E 57th St 19B .... New York NY 10022 *Web:* www.zabriskiegallery.com	212-752-1223	752-1224	42
Zach Halopoff Inc 15422 Assembly Ln .... Huntington Beach CA 92649 *Web:* www.haloindustries.com	714-373-3333		454
Zachary & Elizabeth Fisher House 111 Rockville Pk Ste 420 .... Rockville MD 20850 *TF:* 888-294-8560 ■ *Web:* www.fisherhouse.org	888-294-8560		372
Zachary Community School Board 3755 Church St .... Zachary LA 70791 *TF:* 855-452-5437 ■ *Web:* www.zacharyschools.org	225-658-4969	658-5261	685
Zachary Confections Inc 2130 W State Rd 28 .... Frankfort IN 46041 **Fax Area Code:* 765 ■ *TF:* 800-445-4222 ■ *Web:* zacharyconfections.com	800-445-4222	659-1491*	296-8
Zachary Piper Solutions 1410 Spring Hill Rd Ste 300 .... McLean VA 22102 *Web:* www.zacharypiper.com	703-649-4001		225
Zachary Scott & Co 1200 Fifth Ave Ste 1500 .... Seattle WA 98101 *Web:* www.zacharyscott.com	206-224-7380	224-7384	194
Zachary Scott Theatre Ctr 1510 Toomey Rd .... Austin TX 78704 *Web:* www.zachtheatre.org	512-476-0541	476-0314	572
Zachry Associates Inc 500 Chestnut St Ste 2000 .... Abilene TX 79602 *Web:* www.zachryinc.com	325-677-1342		7
Zachry Group 527 Logwood Ave .... San Antonio TX 78221 *Web:* www.zachrygroup.com	210-588-5000		186
Zachys Wine & Liquor Inc 16 E Pkwy .... Scarsdale NY 10583 *TF:* 800-723-0241 ■ *Web:* www.zachys.com	914-723-0241	723-1033	443
Zack Electronics Inc 1075 Hamilton Rd .... Duarte CA 91010 *TF:* 800-466-0449 ■ *Web:* www.zackelectronics.com	626-303-0655	303-8694	246
Zacros America 220 Lake Dr .... Newark DE 19702 **Fax Area Code:* 410 ■ *TF:* 800-638-1012 ■ *Web:* www.zacrosamerica.com	800-890-1183	889-5189*	199
Zadro Products Inc 5422 Argosy Ave .... Huntington Beach CA 92649 *TF:* 800-468-4348 ■ *Web:* zadroinc.com	714-892-9200		608
Zafgen Inc 175 Portland St 4th Fl .... Boston MA 02114 *Web:* www.zafgen.com	617-622-4003		238
Zagada Markets Inc 145 Grand Ave Caribbean Commercial Bldg ... Coral Gables FL 33133 *Web:* www.zagada.com	305-529-9028	442-1906	466
Zagar Inc 24000 Lakeland Blvd .... Cleveland OH 44132 *Web:* www.zagar.com	216-731-0500	731-8591	493
Zager Fuchs PC 268 Broad St .... Red Bank NJ 07701 *Web:* zagerfuchs.com	732-747-3700		428
ZAGG Inc 3855 South 500 West Ste J .... Salt Lake City UT 84115 *TF:* 800-700-9244 ■ *Web:* www.zagg.com	801-263-0699		608
Zaiss & Co 11626 Nicholas St .... Omaha NE 68154 *Web:* www.zaissco.com	402-964-9293		636
Zaius 205 Portland St .... Boston MA 02114 *Web:* zaius.com	617-545-5001		178-8
Zale Corp *Zales Jewelers Div* 901 W Walnut Hill Ln .... Irving TX 75038 *TF:* 800-311-5393 ■ *Web:* www.zales.com	972-580-4000		410
Zallie Supermarkets 1230 Blackwood-Clementon Rd .... Clementon NJ 08021 *Web:* zallieshoprite.com	856-627-6501		345
Zaloni Inc 633 Davis Dr Ste 450 .... Durham NC 27713 *Web:* zaloni.com	919-323-4050		177
Zamagias Properties 336 4th Ave 8th Fl .... Pittsburgh PA 15222 *TF:* 800-878-0262 ■ *Web:* www.zamagias.com	412-391-7887	391-8879	652
Zambia Embassy 2419 Massachusetts Ave NW .... Washington DC 20008 *Web:* www.zambiaembassy.org	202-265-9717	332-0826	257
Zamboo LLC 4079A Redwood Ave .... Los Angeles CA 90066 *Web:* www.zamboo.com	310-822-4643		344
Zambra! 85 W Walnut St .... Asheville NC 28801 *Web:* zambratapas.com	828-232-1060		671
Zamias Services Inc 500 Galleria Dr Ste 287 PO Box 5540 .... Johnstown PA 15904 *Web:* www.zamias.com	814-535-3563	536-5505	655
Zamma Corp 14468 Litchfield Dr .... Orange VA 22960 *Web:* www.zamma.com	540-672-5200		499
Zamorano 9300 Lee Hwy Ste G130 .... Fairfax VA 22031 *Web:* www.zamorano.edu	202-737-5580		166
Zampell Cos 9 Stanley Tucker Dr .... Newburyport MA 01950 *Web:* www.zampell.com	978-465-0055		610
Zamzows Inc 1201 N Franklin Blvd .... Nampa ID 83687 *Web:* zamzows.com	208-465-3626		323
Zane Casket Co 475 S Samuel Dr .... Zanesville OH 43701	740-452-4680		134
Zane State College 1555 Newark Rd .... Zanesville OH 43701 *TF:* 800-686-8324 ■ *Web:* www.zanestate.edu	740-454-2501	454-0035	800
Zanella, Boath & Associates LLC 1129 Essex Pl .... Stratford CT 06615 *Web:* zanellaboath.com	203-386-1411	378-6107	41
Zaner Group LLC 150 S Wacker Dr Ste 2350 .... Chicago IL 60606 *TF:* 800-621-1414 ■ *Web:* www.zaner.com	312-277-0050	277-0150	169
Zaner-Bloser Inc 1400 Goodale Blvd Ste 200 .... Columbus OH 43212 **Fax Area Code:* 800 ■ *TF:* 800-421-3018 ■ *Web:* www.zaner-bloser.com	614-486-0221	992-6087*	637-2
Zanes Inc 182 Cedar St .... Branford CT 06405 *Web:* ezanes.com	203-488-4676		711

Listing	Phone	Fax	Class
Zanesville City School Board 1701 Blue Ave. Zanesville OH 43701 *TF:* 866-280-7377 ■ *Web:* www.zanesville.k12.oh.us	740-454-9751		685
Zanesville Times Recorder 3871 Gorsky Dr Unit G1 Zanesville OH 43701 *TF:* 877-424-0214 ■ *Web:* www.zanesvilletimesrecorder.com	740-452-4561		532-2
Zanesville-Muskingum County Chamber of Commerce 205 N Fifth St Zanesville OH 43701 *TF:* 800-743-2303 ■ *Web:* www.zmchamber.com	740-455-8282	454-2963	139
Zanker Road Resource Management Ltd 705 Los Esteros Rd. San Jose CA 95134 *Web:* www.zankerrecycling.com	408-263-2384		686
Zansys Technologies 27 N Wacker St Ste 910 Chicago IL 60606 *Web:* www.zansys.com	312-450-3198		178-1
Zapata County 200 E Seventh Ave Ste 138 Zapata TX 78076 *Web:* www.co.zapata.tx.us	956-765-9920	765-9926	338
Zapata Inc 6302 Fairview Rd Ste 600 Charlotte NC 28210 *Web:* www.zapatainc.com	704-358-8240	378-4910	261
Zapata Technology Inc 1450 Greene St Ste 500 Augusta GA 30901 *TF:* 888-708-9840 ■ *Web:* www.zapatatechnology.com	706-955-4809		225
Zaphyr Technologies 628 SR-10 Ste 14 Whippany NJ 07981 *Web:* www.zaphyr.net	973-560-9050	215-2037	180
Zapier Inc 548 Market St Ste 62411 San Francisco CA 94104 *Web:* zapier.com	415-963-4020		177
ZapLabs LLC 2000 Powell St Ste 700 Emeryville CA 94608 *NASDAQ: ZIPR* ■ *TF:* 800-225-5947 ■ *Web:* www.ziprealty.com	510-910-0871	735-2850	652
Zapposcom 400 E Stewart Ave Las Vegas NV 89101 *TF:* 800-927-7671 ■ *Web:* www.zappos.com	800-927-7671		459
ZapTel Corp 1440 Hicks Rd Rolling Meadows IL 60008 *Web:* www.zaptel.com	847-342-2000		224
Zapwater Communications Inc 118 N Peoria 4th Fl Chicago IL 60607 *Web:* www.zapwater.com	312-943-0333		636
Zara Realty Holding Corp 166-07 Hillside Ave Jamaica NY 11432 *Web:* www.zararealty.com	718-291-3331		652
Zaremba Group 14600 Detroit Ave. Cleveland OH 44107 *Web:* www.zarembagroup.com	216-221-6600	221-9742	653
Zarem-Golde ORT Technical Institute 5440 W Fargo Ave Skokie IL 60077 *Web:* www.ortchicagotech.edu	847-327-5588	324-5580	167-3
Zargon Oil & Gas Ltd 333 - Fifth Ave SW Ste 700 Calgary AB T2P3B6 *Web:* zargon.ca	403-264-9992		536
Zarinkelk Engineering Services Inc 3033 Chimney Rock Rd Houston TX 77056 *Web:* www.zarinkelk.com	832-242-2426		196
Zaroka 148 York St New Haven CT 06511 *Web:* www.zarokaindian.com	203-776-8644	776-0051	671
Zarzaur & Schwartz PC 2209 Morris Ave PO Box 11366 Birmingham AL 35203 *TF:* 800-401-6789 ■ *Web:* zsattorneys.stratuspayments.net	205-250-8437	328-1958	41
Zasio Enterprises Inc 401 W Front St Ste 305 Boise ID 83702 *TF:* 800-513-1000 ■ *Web:* www.zasio.com	800-513-1000		177
Zatkoff Seals & Packings 23230 Industrial Pk Dr Farmington Hills MI 48335 *Web:* zatkoff.com	248-478-2400	478-3392	385
Zavala County County Courthouse 200 E Uvalde St. Crystal City TX 78839 *Web:* www.co.zavala.tx.us	830-374-2331	374-5955	338
Zaxwear 1 Cottage St Studio Ste 438 Easthampton MA 01027 *Web:* www.zaxwear.com	617-771-2348		393
Zaytinya 701 Ninth St NW Washington DC 20001 *Web:* www.zaytinya.com	202-638-0800		671
Zazoom LLC 55 Broadway Ste 801 New York NY 10006 *Web:* www.zazoomvideo.com	212-321-2100		4
Zazula Process Equipment Ltd 4609 Manitoba Rd SE Calgary AB T2G4B9 *TF:* 888-666-6361 ■ *Web:* www.zazula.com	403-244-0751	245-5808	104
ZBA Inc 94 Old Camplain Rd. Hillsborough NJ 08844 *TF:* 800-750-4239 ■ *Web:* www.zbaus.com	908-359-2070	595-0909	173-7
ZBS Foundation 174 N River Rd Fort Edward NY 12828 *TF:* 800-662-3345 ■ *Web:* www.zbs.org	518-695-6406		657
ZBT (Zeta Beta Tau Fraternity Inc) 3905 Vincennes Rd Ste 100 Indianapolis IN 46268 *Web:* zbt.org	317-334-1898	334-1899	48-16
ZCL | Xerxes 7901 Xerxes Ave S. Minneapolis MN 55431 *Web:* www.zcl.com	952-887-1890	887-1870	199
ZCO Corp 58 Technology Way Ste 2W10 Nashua NH 03060 *TF:* 855-926-2777 ■ *Web:* www.zco.com	603-881-9200	881-8877	809
ZDI Gaming Inc 2124 196th St SW Lynnwood WA 98036 *TF:* 800-414-8227 ■ *Web:* zdigaming.com	800-414-8227		452
ZE PowerGroup Inc 130 - 5920 No Two Rd Richmond BC V7C4R9 *TF:* 866-944-1469 ■ *Web:* www.ze.com	604-244-1469		193
ZeaVision LLC 716-I Crown Industrial Ct Chesterfield MO 63005 *TF:* 866-833-2800 ■ *Web:* www.eyepromise.com	866-833-2800		345
Zebra Books *Kensington Publishing Corp* 119 W 40th St New York NY 10018 *TF:* 800-221-2647 ■ *Web:* www.kensingtonbooks.com	212-407-1500		637-2
Zebra Capital Management LLC 612 Wheelers Farm Rd Milford CT 06461 *Web:* www.zebracapital.com	203-878-3223		401
Zebra Graphics 1611 Kentucky Ave. Paducah KY 42003 *Web:* www.zebragraphics.com	270-443-4771		627
Zebra Marketing 7733 Densmore Ave Ste 7 Van Nuys CA 91406 *Web:* zebramerchandise.blogspot.com	818-765-6442		9
Zebra Print Solutions 9401 Globe Center Dr. Morrisville NC 27560 *TF:* 800-545-8835 ■ *Web:* zebraprintsolutions.com	919-314-3700	314-3701	627
Zebra Technologies Corp 475 Half Day Rd Ste 500 Lincolnshire IL 60069 *NASDAQ: ZBRA* ■ *TF:* 800-423-0422 ■ *Web:* www.zebra.com	847-634-6700	913-8766	173-6
Zebra, The 301 Chicon St Ste A. Austin TX 78702 *TF:* 888-255-4364 ■ *Web:* www.thezebra.com	888-255-4364		637-10
Zebulon Pike Youth Services Ctr 1427 W Rio Grande Colorado Springs CO 80906 *TF:* 800-970-3468 ■ *Web:* www.colorado.gov	719-633-8713		412
Zecotek Photonics Inc 21331 Gordon Way Unit 1120 Richmond BC V6W1J9 *Web:* zecotek.com	604-233-0056		250
Zed Industries Inc 3580 Lightner Rd Vandalia OH 45377 *Web:* www.zedindustries.com	937-667-8407	667-3340	695
Zed Ink Inc 228 Main St Ste 17 Venice CA 90291 *Web:* zedink.com	310-460-2424		720
Zeda Soft 2310 Gravel Dr Fort Worth TX 76118 *Web:* www.zedasoft.com	817-616-1000		177
Zedi Inc 200, 110 Quarry Park Blvd SE. Calgary AB T2C3G3 *TF:* 866-732-6967 ■ *Web:* www.zedisolutions.com	403-444-1100	444-1101	539
Zedo Inc 850 Montgomery St Ste 150 San Francisco CA 94133 *Web:* www.zedo.com	415-348-1975		225
Zee Medical Inc 22 Corporate Pk Irvine CA 92606 *TF:* 800-435-7763 ■ *Web:* www.zeemedical.com	800-435-7763		475
Zee Systems Inc 406 W Rhapsody Dr San Antonio TX 78216 *TF:* 800-988-2665 ■ *Web:* zeesystemsinc.com	210-342-9761	341-2609	22
Zeeco Inc 22151 E 91st St S Broken Arrow OK 74014 *Web:* www.zeeco.com	918-258-8551	251-5519	357
Zeeland Lumber & Supply Co 146 E Washington Zeeland MI 49464 *TF:* 888-772-2119 ■ *Web:* www.zeelandlumber.com	616-772-2119		191-3
Zeeland Public Schools (ZPS) 183 W Roosevelt Ave Zeeland MI 49464 *Web:* www.zps.org	616-748-3000		186
Zeenyx 23 College St Hopkinton MA 01748 *Web:* www.automatedtesting.com	508-497-3413		178-1
ZeeWise Inc 4920 Roswell Rd Ste 45B Atlanta GA 30339 *Web:* www.zeewise.com	678-252-6840		180
ZEFR Inc 4101 Redwood Ave Los Angeles CA 90066 *Web:* zefr.com	310-392-3555		387
Zehnder America Inc 6 Merrill Industrial Dr Ste 7 Hampton NH 03842 *TF:* 888-778-6701 ■ *Web:* zehnderamerica.com	603-601-8544		610
Zeiders Enterprises Inc 2750 Killarney Dr Ste 100 Woodbridge VA 22192 *Web:* www.zeiders.com	703-496-9000	580-6339	194
Zeigler Beverages LLC 1513 N Broad St Lansdale PA 19446 *TF:* 800-854-6123	215-855-5161		296-20
Zeigler Bros Inc 400 Gardner Stn Rd Gardners PA 17324 *TF:* 800-841-6800 ■ *Web:* www.zeiglerfeed.com	717-677-6181	677-6826	447
Zeigler Chevrolet Inc 13153 Dunnings Hwy Claysburg PA 16625 *TF:* 877-364-4817 ■ *Web:* www.zeiglerchevy.com	877-364-4817		57
Zeiser Wilbert Vault Inc 750 Howard St Elmira NY 14904 *TF:* 800-472-4335 ■ *Web:* zeiserwilbertvault.com	607-733-0568		191-1
Zeisler & Zeisler P C (Z&Z) 10 Middle St 15th Fl Bridgeport CT 06604 *Web:* www.zeislaw.com	203-368-4234	367-9678	445
Zeisler, Zeisler, Rawson & Johnson LLP 901 A St Ste C San Rafael CA 94901 *Web:* zzrjllp.com	415-451-1703	451-1907	2
Zeitbyte LLC 261 W 35th St Ste 304 New York NY 10001 *Web:* www.zeitcaster.com	212-989-4808		514
Zeitlin & Company, Realtors 4301 Hillsboro Rd Ste 100 Nashville TN 37215 *Web:* zeitlin.com	615-383-0183		652
Zeks Compressed Air Solutions 1302 Goshen Pkwy West Chester PA 19380 *TF:* 800-888-2323 ■ *Web:* www.zeks.com	610-692-9100	692-9192	172
Zel Technologies LLC 54 Old Hampton Ln Hampton VA 23669 *Web:* zeltech.com	757-722-5565	325-1359	180
Zelacom Electronic Publishing 1 Market St Ellenville NY 12428 *Web:* www.zelacom.com	845-647-8711	647-8713	637-10
ZELDA'S 528 Lower Thames St Newport RI 02840 *Web:* zeldasnewport.com	401-849-4002		671
Zeldes Needle & Cooper 1000 Lafayette Blvd 7th Fl Bridgeport CT 06604 *Web:* znclaw.com	203-333-9441	333-1489	445
Zeldin Lee (Rep R - NY) 2441 Rayburn House Office Bldg Washington DC 20515 *Web:* www.zeldin.house.gov	202-225-3826	225-3143	342-2
Zelenkofske Axelrod LLC 830 Sir Thomas Ct Harrisburg PA 17109 *Web:* zallc.org	717-561-9200	561-9202	2
Zelienople Area Public Library 227 S High St Zelienople PA 16063 *Web:* www.zelienoplelibrary.org	724-452-9330		434-3
Zelis Network Solutions LLC 2 Concourse Pkwy Ste 300 Atlanta GA 30328 *Web:* www.zelis.com	404-459-7201		390
Zeller Plastik Inc 1515 Franklin Blvd Libertyville IL 60048 *Web:* www.gcs.com	847-247-7900	247-7969	604
Zellner Construction Services LLC 2926 Ridgeway Rd Memphis TN 38115 *Web:* www.zellnerconstruction.com	901-794-1100	794-9141	188
Zelo 831 Nicollet Mall Minneapolis MN 55402 *Web:* zelomn.com	612-333-7000		671
Zelo Productions Inc 3 S Newton St Denver CO 80219 *Web:* www.zeloproductions.com	303-936-8995		513
Zemoga Inc 120 Old Ridgefield Rd. Wilton CT 06897 *Web:* www.zemoga.com	203-663-6214		396
Zen Design Group Ltd 2850 Coolidge Hwy Berkley MI 48072 *Web:* www.zendesigngroup.com	248-398-5209		344

Name / Address	City	State	ZIP	Phone	Fax	Class
Zen Ventures LLC						
3939 S 6th St Ste 201 PO Box 201	Klamath Falls	OR	97603	888-936-2278		809
TF: 888-936-2278 ■ *Web:* www.zen-cart.com						
Zenar Corp						
7301 S Sixth St PO Box 107	Oak Creek	WI	53154	414-764-1800	764-1267	470
Web: zenarcrane.com						
Zencos 1400 Crescent Green Ste 215	Cary	NC	27518	919-459-4600		196
Web: www.zencos.com						
Zenfolio Inc 3515-A Edison Way	Menlo Park	CA	94025	650-364-3423		387
Web: zenfolio.com						
Zenger Folkman Co						
1213 N Research Way Bldg Q Ste 3500	Orem	UT	84097	801-705-9375		765
Web: zengerfolkman.com						
Zenith Color Communication Group Inc						
121 Varick St 10th Fl	New York	NY	10013	212-989-4400	989-4405	532-2
Web: www.zenithcolorgroup.com						
Zenith Cutter Co 5200 Zenith Pkwy	Loves Park	IL	61111	815-282-5200	282-5232	493
TF: 800-223-5202 ■ *Web:* www.zenithcutter.com						
Zenith Electronics Corp						
2000 Millbrook Dr	Lincolnshire	IL	60069	847-941-8000		52
Web: www.zenith.com						
Zenith Freight Lines LLC						
210 Dehart Motor Terminal Rd SW	Conover	NC	28613	828-465-7036		314
Web: zenithcompanies.com						
Zenith Fuel Systems Inc						
14570 Industrial Park Rd	Bristol	VA	24202	276-669-5555	645-8696	128
Web: www.zenithfuelsystems.com						
Zenith Information Systems Inc						
18757 Burbank Blvd Ste 116	Tarzana	CA	91356	818-206-8634		177
Web: www.zis.com						
Zenith Insurance Co PO Box 9055	Van Nuys	CA	91409	818-713-1000	280-4701*	391-4
**Fax Area Code:* 877 ■ *TF:* 800-440-5020 ■ *Web:* www.thezenith.com						
Zenith Precision Inc						
536 Paterson Ave	East Rutherford	NJ	07073	201-933-8640	933-0936	493
Web: www.zenithprecision.com						
Zenith Products Corp 400 Lukens Dr	New Castle	DE	19720	800-892-3986		319-2
TF: 800-892-3986 ■ *Web:* zenith-products.com						
Zenith Services						
4390 Us Hwy 1 Ste 312	Princeton	NJ	08540	732-568-4950		177
Web: zenithcad.com						
Zenith Specialty Bag Company Inc						
17625 E Railroad St PO Box 8445	City of Industry	CA	91748	626-912-2481	284-8493*	65
**Fax Area Code:* 800 ■ *TF:* 800-962-2247 ■ *Web:* zbags.com						
Zenmonics Inc						
125 Floyd Smith Office Park Dr Ste 220	Charlotte	NC	28262	704-971-7315		180
Web: www.zenmonics.com						
Zennify						
1755 Creekside Oaks Dr Ste 280	Sacramento	CA	95833	855-936-6439		39
TF: 855-936-6439 ■ *Web:* www.zennify.com						
Zeno Group 140 Broadway	New York	NY	10005	212-299-8888		636
Web: www.zenogroup.com						
Zenon Dance Company & School						
528 Hennepin Ave	Minneapolis	MN	55403	612-338-1101		573-1
Web: zenondance.org						
Zenoss Inc						
11305 Four Points Dr Bldg 1 Ste 300	Austin	TX	78726	888-936-6770		177
TF: 888-936-6770 ■ *Web:* www.zenoss.com						
Zentech Manufacturing Inc						
6980 Tudsbury Rd	Baltimore	MD	21244	443-348-4500		253
TF: 800-871-7838 ■ *Web:* www.zentech.com						
Zentech Technical Services Inc						
14800 St Marys Ln Ste 270	Houston	TX	77079	281-558-0290		177
Web: zentech-usa.com						
Zenya Yoga & Message Studio						
101 Herman Melville Ave	Newport News	VA	23606	757-643-6900		148
Web: www.zenyayoga.com						
ZeOmega Inc 6200 Tennyson Pky Ste 200	Plano	TX	75024	214-618-9880	975-1258	177
Web: www.zeomega.com						
ZEP Inc 3330 Cumberland Blvd Ste 700	Atlanta	GA	30339	877-428-9937	603-7958*	151
NYSE: ZEP ■ **Fax Area Code:* 404 ■ *TF:* 877-428-9937 ■ *Web:* www.zep.com						
Zephyr Aluminum LLC						
625 Second St PO Box 4906	Lancaster	PA	17603	717-397-3618		362
Web: www.zephyraluminum.com						
Zephyr Egg Company Inc						
4622 Gall Blvd	Zephyrhills	FL	33542	813-782-1521		10-8
Web: www.refrigeratedtransporter.com						
Zephyr Manufacturing Company Inc						
200 Mitchell Rd	Sedalia	MO	65301	660-827-0352	827-0713	103
TF: 800-821-7197 ■ *Web:* www.zephyrmfg.com						
Zephyrhills Chamber of Commerce						
38550 Fifth Ave	Zephyrhills	FL	33542	813-782-1913	783-6060	139
Web: www.zephyrhillschamber.org						
Zephyrhills Correctional Institution						
2739 Gall Blvd	Zephyrhills	FL	33541	813-782-5521		213
Web: www.dc.state.fl.us						
Zephyr-Tec Corp						
9651 Business Center Dr Ste C	Rancho Cucamonga	CA	91730	909-481-9991		177
TF: 877-493-7497 ■ *Web:* www.zephyr-tec.com						
Zephyrus Electronics Ltd						
168 S 122nd E Ave	Tulsa	OK	74128	918-437-3333		647
Web: www.big-z.com						
Zepnick Solutions Inc						
1310 Brookfield Ave	Green Bay	WI	54313	920-662-1682		261
Web: zepnick.com						
Zepp Labs Inc						
75 E Santa Clara St 6th Fl	San Jose	CA	95113	866-400-9377		407
TF: 866-400-9377 ■ *Web:* www.zepplabs.com						
Zepsa Industries Inc						
1501 Westinghouse Blvd	Charlotte	NC	28273	704-583-9220		499
Web: zepsa.com						
Zepto Metrix Corp 872 Main St	Buffalo	NY	14202	716-882-0920	882-0959	231
TF: 800-274-5487 ■ *Web:* www.zeptometrix.com						
Zerand Corp 15800 W Overland Dr	New Berlin	WI	53151	262-827-3800	827-2762	556
Web: www.zerand.com						
Zerger & Mauer LLP						
1100 Main St Ste 2100	Kansas City	MO	64105	816-759-3300		41
Web: www.mauerlawfirm.com						
Zerion Group PO Box 940411	Maitland	FL	32794	877-872-1726		317
TF: 877-872-1726 ■ *Web:* www.zeriongroup.com						
Zero Manufacturing Inc						
500 W 200 N	North Salt Lake	UT	84054	801-298-5900	292-9450	453
TF: 800-959-5050 ■ *Web:* www.zerocases.com						
Zero Point Zero Production Inc						
875 Avenue of the Americas 19th Fl	New York	NY	10001	212-620-2730		116
Web: www.zeropointzero.com						
Zero Technologies LLC						
7 Neshaminy Interplex Ste 116	Trevose	PA	19053	800-503-2939		463
TF: 800-503-2939 ■ *Web:* www.zerowater.com						
Zero Waste Energy Systems USA LLC						
152 McCarty Rd	Jackson	MS	39212	416-346-6428	266-0314*	112
**Fax Area Code:* 905						
Zero Zone Inc 110 N Oakridge Dr	North Prairie	WI	53153	262-392-6400	392-6450	14
TF: 800-247-4496 ■ *Web:* www.zero-zone.com						
Zero's Subs						
3760 Virginia Beach Blvd	Virginia Beach	VA	23452	757-463-9114		670
Web: zerossub.com						
Zero-Max Inc 13200 Sixth Ave N	Plymouth	MN	55441	763-546-4300	546-8260	620
TF: 800-533-1731 ■ *Web:* www.zero-max.com						
Zerowait Corp 707 Kirkwood Hwy	Wilmington	DE	19805	302-996-9408		192
Web: www.zerowait.com						
Zest Anchors LLC 2061 Wineridge Pl	Escondido	CA	92029	760-743-7744		228
Web: www.zestdent.com						
Zestron Corp 11285 Assett Loop	Manassas	VA	20109	703-393-9880		196
Web: www.zestron.com						
Zeta 92.3 7007 NW 77th Ave	Miami	FL	33166	305-444-9292	883-7701	645-96
Web: www.lamusica.com						
Zeta Beta Tau Fraternity Inc (ZBT)						
3905 Vincennes Rd Ste 100	Indianapolis	IN	46268	317-334-1898	334-1899	48-16
Web: zbt.org						
Zeta Group Engineering LLC						
1755 E Matthew Dr	De Pere	WI	54115	920-336-9382		261
TF: 888-933-9382 ■ *Web:* zetagroupengineering.com						
Zeta Pharmaceuticals LLC						
120 Holmes Ave Ste 116	Huntsville	AL	35801	201-930-4934		238
Web: www.zetapharm.com						
Zeta Phi Beta Sorority Inc						
1734 New Hampshire Ave NW	Washington	DC	20009	202-387-3103		48-16
TF: 800-393-2503 ■ *Web:* zphib1920.org						
Zeta Psi Fraternity of North America						
15 S Henry St	Pearl River	NY	10965	845-735-1847	735-1989	48-16
TF: 800-477-1847 ■ *Web:* zetapsi.org						
Zeta Tau Alpha Fraternity (ZTA)						
3450 Founders Rd	Indianapolis	IN	46268	317-872-0540	876-3948	48-16
Web: zetataualpha.org						
ZETA-TECH Associates Inc						
900 Kings Hwy N Ste 208	Cherry Hill	NJ	08034	856-779-7795	779-7436	261
Web: www.hg.org						
Zetec Inc						
8226 Bracken Pl SE Ste 100	Snoqualmie	WA	98065	425-974-2700	974-2701	248
TF: 800-643-1771 ■ *Web:* www.zetec.com						
Zethcon Corp 200 W 22nd St Ste 218	Lombard	IL	60148	847-318-0800		177
Web: zethcon.com						
Zeton Inc 740 Oval Ct	Burlington	ON	L7L6A9	905-632-3123		188-7
Web: www.zeton.com						
Zetron Inc 12034 134th Ct NE	Redmond	WA	98052	425-820-6363	820-7031	647
Web: www.zetron.com						
Zetta Inc 1362 Borregas Ave	Sunnyvale	CA	94089	650-590-0950		387
TF: 844-639-6792 ■ *Web:* www.zetta.net						
Zeus Jones 2429 Nicollet Ave	Minneapolis	MN	55404	612-279-1400		463
Web: zeusjones.com						
Zeus Living 888 Marin St Ste B	San Francisco	CA	94124	415-849-4662		652
Web: zeusliving.com						
Zeuschel Equipment Co						
2717 Breckenridge Industrial Ct	Saint Louis	MO	63144	314-645-5003	645-8833	385
Web: www.zeuschel.com						
Zev Cohen & Associates Inc						
300 Interchange Blvd	Ormond Beach	FL	32174	386-677-2482		261
Web: zevcohen.com						
Zevin & Rosenbloum PC						
191 Peachtree St Ste 4550	Atlanta	GA	30303	404-522-1616		41
TF: 866-989-8146 ■ *Web:* attorneybigalatlanta.com						
ZFA Structural Engineers						
1212 Fourth St Ste Z	Santa Rosa	CA	95404	707-526-0992		261
Web: www.zfa.com						
ZGM Modern Marketing Partners						
1324 17th Ave SW Ste 500	Calgary	AB	T2T5S8	403-770-2250		195
Web: zgm.ca						
Zia Engineering & Environmental Consultants LLC						
755 S Telshor Blvd Ste F-201	Las Cruces	NM	88011	575-532-1526		192
TF: 866-532-1588 ■ *Web:* www.ziaeec.com						
Zia Marie 4497 Lookout Rd	Virginia Beach	VA	23455	757-460-0715		671
Web: ziamarie.com						
Zia's 5256 Wilson Ave	Saint Louis	MO	63110	314-776-0020		671
Web: www.zias.com						
Zia's Italian Restaurant 20 Main St	Toledo	OH	43605	888-456-3463		671
TF: 888-456-3463 ■ *Web:* ziasrestaurant.com						
Ziba Beauty Center Inc						
17832 Pioneer Blvd	Artesia	CA	90701	562-402-5131		77
Web: zibabeauty.com						
Ziba Hospice						
3950 Paramount Blvd Ste 107	Torrance	CA	90501	310-328-4865	328-4309	363
Web: www.zibahospice.com						
Zibiz Corp 50 Alexander Ct	Ronkonkoma	NY	11779	888-263-6005		396
TF: 888-263-6005 ■ *Web:* www.zibiz.com						
Zicka Homes 7861 E Kemper Rd	Cincinnati	OH	45249	513-247-3500	247-3512	653
Web: www.zickahomes.com						
Ziebart International Corp						
1290 E Maple Rd	Troy	MI	48083	248-588-4100		62-1
TF: 800-877-1312 ■ *Web:* www.ziebartworld.com						
Ziebell Water Service Products						
2001 Pratt Blvd	Elk Grove Village	IL	60007	847-364-0670		190
Web: www.ziebellproducts.com						
Zieger & Sons Inc						
6215 Ardleigh St	Philadelphia	PA	19138	215-438-7060		293
TF: 800-752-2003 ■ *Web:* www.zieger.com						
Ziegler Chemical & Mineral Corp						
600 Prospect Ave	Piscataway	NJ	08854	732-752-4111	752-9477	500
TF: 888-213-7500 ■ *Web:* www.zieglerchemical.com						

				Phone	Fax	Class
Zielinski Financial Advisors LLC 2403 High Hammock Rd *Web:* www.zfinancialadvisors.com	Seabrook Island	SC	29455	843-974-4964		463
Zieman Manufacturing Co 168 S Spruce *Web:* www.lci1.com	Rialto	CA	92376	909-873-0061		480
Ziems Ford Corners Inc 5700 E Main St *TF:* 888-375-9581 ■ *Web:* www.ziemsfordcorners.com	Farmington	NM	87402	505-325-1961		57
Zierden Company Inc, The 7355 S 1st St *Web:* www.zierden.com	Oak Creek	WI	53154	414-764-6630	764-9763	60
Zierick Manufacturing Corp 131 Radio Cr *TF:* 800-882-8020 ■ *Web:* www.zierick.com	Mount Kisco	NY	10549	914-666-2911	666-0216	815
Ziff Davis LLC 114 5th Ave *TF:* 800-289-0429 ■ *Web:* www.ziffdavis.com	New York	NY	10016	212-503-3500		457-7
Ziff Law Firm LLP 303 William St *Web:* zifflaw.com	Elmira	NY	14901	607-733-8866		41
Zig Zibit Inc 4300 Emperor Blvd Ste 100 *Web:* zigzibit.com	Durham	NC	27703	919-876-5828	876-5737	232
Ziggle Tech 747 3rd Ave *Web:* www.ziggletech.com	New York	NY	10017	646-722-2655		657
Zignal Labs 995 Market St *Web:* zignallabs.com	San Francisco	CA	94103	415-683-7871		387
Zija International Inc 3300 N Ashton Blvd Ste 100 *TF:* 888-924-6872 ■ *Web:* www.zijainternational.com	Lehi	UT	84043	888-924-6872		345
Zilker Botanical Garden 2220 Barton Springs Rd *Web:* www.zilkergarden.org	Austin	TX	78746	512-477-8672	481-8254	97
ZiLOG Inc 1590 Buckeye Dr *Web:* zilog.com	Milpitas	CA	95035	408-513-1500	365-8535	696
Zimbabwe Embassy 1608 New Hampshire Ave NW *Web:* www.zimembassydc.gov.zw	Washington	DC	20009	202-332-7100	483-9326	257
Zimkor Industries Inc 7011 W Titan Rd *Web:* www.zimkor.com	Littleton	CO	80125	303-791-1333	791-1340	189-14
Zimman's Inc 80 Market St *Web:* www.zimmans.com	Lynn	MA	01901	781-598-9432	598-1931	362
Zimmer Biomet 345 E Main St *TF:* 800-348-9500 ■ *Web:* www.zimmer.co.uk	Warsaw	IN	46580	800-348-9500		476
Zimmer Enterprises Inc 911 Senate Dr *Web:* www.pbj-sport.com	Dayton	OH	45459	937-428-1057		745-4
Zimmer Kunz PLLC 310 Grant St Ste 3000 *Web:* zklaw.com	Pittsburgh	PA	15219	412-281-8000		445
Zimmer Radio Group 3215 Lemone Industrial Blvd Ste 200 *TF:* 800-455-1099 ■ *Web:* zimmercommunications.com	Columbia	MO	65201	573-875-1099	875-2439	643
Zimmerman & Associates Pc 77 W Washington St Ste 1220 *Web:* attorneyzim.com	Chicago	IL	60602	312-440-0020		41
Zimmerman & Sons Inc 3801 Sandy Spring Rd *Web:* zimmermans.com	Burtonsville	MD	20866	301-421-1900		351
Zimmerman Agency, The 1821 Miccosukee Commons *Web:* www.zimmerman.com	Tallahassee	FL	32308	850-668-2222		636
Zimmerman Associates Inc 10600 Arrowhead Dr Ste 325 *Web:* zai-inc.com	Fairfax	VA	22030	703-883-0506		224
Zimmerman Industries Inc 196 Wabash Rd *TF:* 888-577-6499 ■ *Web:* www.zimmermanindustries.com	Ephrata	PA	17522	717-733-6166	733-1169	190
Zimmerman Metals Inc 201 E 58th Ave *TF:* 800-247-4202 ■ *Web:* zimmerman-metals.com	Denver	CO	80216	303-294-0180		480
Zimmerman Reed PLLP 1100 IDS Ctr 80 S Eighth St *TF:* 800-887-8029 ■ *Web:* www.zimmreed.com	Minneapolis	MN	55402	800-887-8029		428
Zimmerman Truck Lines Inc 190 E Industrial Dr *TF:* 800-999-2707 ■ *Web:* www.ztlinc.com	Mifflintown	PA	17059	717-436-2141	436-6101	780
Zimmerman'S Hardware & Variety Inc 306 Hartman Bridge Rd PO Box 88 *Web:* zimmermanshardwarestrasburg.com	Strasburg	PA	17579	717-687-8695		351
Zimmermann Lavine & Zimmermann PC 770 S Post Oak Ln Ste 620 *Web:* texasdefenselawyers.com	Houston	TX	77056	713-552-0300		41
Zimmermann Printing Co 3418 Washington Ave **Fax Area Code:* 414 ■ *Web:* www.zimmermannprinting.com	Sheboygan	WI	53081	920-457-5021	933-0909*	627
Zimmermans Acctg & Tax Service Inc 804 Carpenter Ave	Iron Mountain	MI	49801	906-774-4529		734
Zimmet Healthcare Consulting LLC 4006 US Hwy 9 *Web:* www.zhealthcare.com	Morganville	NJ	07751	732-970-0733		463
ZINC New Haven 964 Chapel St *Web:* www.zincfood.com	New Haven	CT	06510	203-624-0507		671
Zinc Wine Bar & Bistro 3009 Central Ave NE *Web:* zincabq.com	Albuquerque	NM	87106	505-254-9462		671
Zinck Computer Group 131 Ilsley Ave *Web:* www.zcg.com	Dartmouth	NS	B3B1T1	902-468-2738		177
Zinfandel Grille 2384 Fair Oaks Blvd *Web:* www.zinfandelgrille.com	Sacramento	CA	95825	916-485-7100		671
Zingerman's Bakehouse Inc 3711 Plz Dr *Web:* www.zingermansbakehouse.com	Ann Arbor	MI	48108	734-761-2095	761-2190	296-1
Zingerman's Roadhouse 2501 Jackson Rd *Web:* www.zingermansroadhouse.com	Ann Arbor	MI	48103	734-663-3663		671
Zingle Inc 2270 Camino Vida Roble Ste K *TF:* 877-946-4536 ■ *Web:* www.zingle.com	Carlsbad	CA	92011	877-946-4536		224
Zink & Triest Company Inc 200 Highpoint Dr Ste 213	Chalfont	PA	18914	215-469-1950		296-15

				Phone	Fax	Class
Zinkan Enterprises Inc 1919 Case Pkwy N **Fax Area Code:* 330 ■ *TF:* 800-229-6801 ■ *Web:* www.zinkan.com	Twinsburg	OH	44087	800-229-6801	425-8202*	145
Zio Johno's Spaghetti House 2925 Williams Blvd SW *Web:* www.ziojohnosonline.com	Cedar Rapids	IA	52404	319-396-1700		671
Zio's 12858 W IH-10 *Web:* www.zios.com	San Antonio	TX	78249	210-697-7222	697-7333	671
Zio's 7111 S Mingo Rd *Web:* zios.com	Tulsa	OK	74133	918-250-5999		671
Ziolkowski Construction Inc 4050 Ralph Jones Dr *Web:* zbuild.com	South Bend	IN	46628	574-287-1811		186
Ziolkowski Patent Solutions Group SC 136 S Wisconsin St *Web:* zpspatents.com	Port Washington	WI	53074	262-268-8100	268-8185	41
Zion & Zion Consulting Group 60 E Rio Salado Pkwy Ste 900 *Web:* www.zionandzion.com	Tempe	AZ	85281	480-751-1007		466
Zion National Park 479 Zion Park Blvd *Web:* www.nps.gov	Springdale	UT	84767	435-772-3256	772-3426	564
Zion Oil & Gas Inc 6510 Abrams Rd Ste 300 *TF:* 888-891-9466 ■ *Web:* www.zionoil.com	Dallas	TX	75231	214-221-4610	221-6510	538
Zion Software LLC 2842 Main St Ste 325 *Web:* www.zionsoftware.com	Glastonbury	CT	06033	860-432-6258		225
Zionist Organization of America (ZOA) 4 E 34th St 3rd Fl *Web:* zoa.org	New York	NY	10016	212-481-1500	481-1515	195
Zions Bancorp One South Main St *TF:* 800-974-8800 ■ *Web:* www.zionsbancorporation.com	Salt Lake City	UT	84133	800-974-8800		69
Zions Bank 1 S Main St *Web:* www.zionsbank.com	Salt Lake City	UT	84133	801-974-8800		70
Ziontech Solutions Inc 2665 N First St Ste 200 *Web:* ziontech.com	San Jose	CA	95134	408-434-6001		180
Zip Mail Services Inc 288 Hanley Industrial Ct	Saint Louis	MO	63144	314-645-5055		5
Zipcar Inc 35 Thomson Pl *NASDAQ: ZIP* ■ *Web:* zipcarstore.com	Boston	MA	02210	617-336-4570		53
zipLogix 18070 15 Mile Rd **Fax Area Code:* 586 ■ *TF:* 866-693-6767 ■ *Web:* www.zipform.com	Fraser	MI	48026	866-693-6767	790-7582*	178-1
Zippel Bay State Park 3684 54th Ave NW *Web:* www.dnr.state.mn.us	Williams	MN	56686	218-783-6252		565
Zippertubing Co 7150 W Erie St **Fax Area Code:* 480 ■ *TF:* 855-289-1874 ■ *Web:* www.zippertubing.com	Chandler	AZ	85226	855-289-1874	285-3997*	600
Zippo Manufacturing Co 33 Barbour St *TF:* 888-442-1932 ■ *Web:* www.zippo.com	Bradford	PA	16701	814-368-2700		222
Zips Dry Cleaners 7474 Greenway Center Dr Ste 1200 *Web:* www.321zips.com	Greenbelt	MD	20770	301-306-1100		426
Zirc Co 3918 Hwy 55 SE *TF:* 800-328-3899 ■ *Web:* www.zirc.com	Buffalo	MN	55313	763-682-6636	682-6604	604
Zircoa Inc 31501 Solon Rd *Web:* www.zircoa.com	Solon	OH	44139	440-248-0500		191-1
Zircon Precision Products Inc 818 W 24th St *Web:* www.zirconprecision.com	Tempe	AZ	85282	480-967-8688	966-8929	454
Zirkin & Schmerling Law LLC 1852 Reisterstown Rd Ste 203 *Web:* zirkinandschmerlinglaw.com	Pikesville	MD	21208	410-356-4455		41
Zirmed Inc 888 W Market St *TF:* 877-494-7633 ■ *Web:* public.zirmed.com	Louisville	KY	40202	877-494-7633		391-3
Zirous Inc 1503 42nd St Ste 210 *Web:* www.zirous.com	West Des Moines	IA	50266	515-225-9015	225-9871	177
Zisook & Greenberg Ltd 208 S Lasalle St Ste 1600	Chicago	IL	60604	312-641-1090		2
Zisser Customs Law Group PC 9355 Airway Rd Ste 1 *Web:* www.zissergroup.com	San Diego	CA	92154	619-671-0376		445
Zistos Corp 1736 Church St *Web:* www.zistos.com	Holbrook	NY	11741	631-434-1370	434-9104	45
Zito Media LP 102 S Main St PO Box 665 *TF:* 800-365-6988 ■ *Web:* www.zitomedia.net	Coudersport	PA	16915	800-365-6988		116
Zitomer Pharmacy Inc 969 Madison Ave 1st Fl *Web:* www.zitomer.com	New York	NY	10021	212-737-5560		237
Zitter Insights 290 W Mt Pleasant Ave Ste 2210 *Web:* zitter.com	Livingston	NJ	07039	973-376-1300	376-1358	463
Zivaro Inc 990 S Broadway Ste 300 *TF:* 877-603-1984 ■ *Web:* zivaro.com	Denver	CO	80209	303-455-8800		180
Zix Corp 2711 N Haskell Ave Ste 2300-LB *NASDAQ: ZIXI* ■ *TF:* 888-771-4049 ■ *Web:* zix.com	Dallas	TX	75204	214-370-2000	370-2070	178-12
Ziziki's Restaurant & Bar 4514 Travis St Ste 122 *Web:* www.zizikis.com	Dallas	TX	75205	214-521-2233		671
ZK Celltest Inc 256 Gibraltar Dr Ste 109 *Web:* www.zk.com	Sunnyvale	CA	94089	408-752-0449		201
ZLB Behring LLC 1020 First Ave PO Box 61501 *TF:* 800-683-1288 ■ *Web:* www.cslbehring.com	King of Prussia	PA	19406	610-878-4000	878-4009	582
Zlotolow & Associates PC 270 W Main St *TF:* 866-800-0092 ■ *Web:* zlotolaw.com	Sayville	NY	11782	718-255-8400		41
ZM Financial Systems Inc 1020 Southhill Dr Ste 200 *Web:* w3.zmfs.com	Cary	NC	27513	919-493-0029	869-1400	177
Zmags Corp 332 Congress St *TF:* 866-989-6247 ■ *Web:* zmags.com	Boston	MA	02210	866-989-6247		177
Z-Medica Corp 4 Fairfield Blvd *TF:* 800-343-8656 ■ *Web:* www.z-medica.com	Wallingford	CT	06492	203-294-0000		475

Name / Address	City	State	ZIP	Phone	Fax	Class
ZOA (Zionist Organization of America) 4 E 34th St 3rd Fl *Web:* zoa.org	New York	NY	10016	212-481-1500	481-1515	195
Zober Industries Inc 500 Coventry Ln *Web:* www.zober.com	Croydon	PA	19021	215-788-5523	788-2618	454
Zodax Inc 14040 Arminta St *TF:* 800-800-3443 ■ *Web:* www.zodax.com	Panorama City	CA	91402	818-785-5626	785-1747	361
Zodiac of North America Inc 540 Thompson Creek Rd *Web:* zodiacmilpro.com	Stevensville	MD	21666	410-643-4141	643-4491	90
Zodiac Pool Systems Inc 2620 Commerce Way *TF:* 800-822-7933 ■ *Web:* www.zodiacpoolsystems.com	Vista	CA	92081	800-822-7933	479-8324	806
Zodiac Printeractive 395 Oak Hill Rd *Web:* zodiacprinting.com	Mountain Top	PA	18707	570-474-9220		627
Zoe Life Publishing PO Box 871066 *TF:* 888-400-4922 ■ *Web:* www.zoelifepub.com	Canton	MI	48187	734-404-5485		637-2
Zoeller Co 3649 Cane Run Rd *Web:* www.zoellerengprod.com	Louisville	KY	40211	502-778-2731	774-3624	641
Zoes Kitchen 7218 Eastchase Pkwy *Web:* zoeskitchen.com	Montgomery	AL	36117	334-270-9115		671
Zogenix Inc 12400 High Bluff Dr Ste 650 *TF:* 866-964-3649 ■ *Web:* www.zogenix.com	San Diego	CA	92130	858-259-1165	259-1166	582
Zoic Inc 3582 Eastham Dr *Web:* www.zoicstudios.com	Culver City	CA	90232	310-838-0770		514
Zola 250 Greenwich St f39 *Web:* www.zola.com	New York	NY	10007	408-657-9652		194
Zolan Company LLC, The 32857 N 74th Way *Web:* www.zolan.com	Scottsdale	AZ	85266	203-300-3290		393
Zolla Lieberman Gallery 325 W Huron St Ste 1E *Web:* www.zollaliebermangallery.com	Chicago	IL	60654	312-944-1990	944-8967	42
Zolo Grill 2525 Arapahoe Ave *Web:* www.zologrill.com	Boulder	CO	80302	303-449-0444		671
Zolon Tech Inc 13921 Park Center Rd Ste 500 *Web:* www.zolontech.com	Herndon	VA	20171	703-636-7370	636-7377	809
Zoltek Companies Inc 3101 McKelvey Rd *NASDAQ: ZOLT* ■ *Web:* www.zoltek.com	Bridgeton	MO	63044	314-291-5110	291-8536	127
Zoltun Studios Inc 10 Bedford Sq Ste 200 *Web:* www.zoltun.com	Pittsburgh	PA	15203	412-488-2623		344
Zomazz Inc 2555 Garden Rd Ste A *Web:* www.zomazz.com	Monterey	CA	93940	831-625-9877		627
Zonar Systems LLC 18200 Cascade Ave S *TF:* 877-843-3847 ■ *Web:* www.zonarsystems.com	Seattle	WA	98188	206-878-2459	878-3082	529
Zone 5 25 Monroe St Ste 300	Albany	NY	12210	518-242-7000		636
Zone Alarm 800 Bridge Pkwy *TF:* 877-966-5221 ■ *Web:* www.zonealarm.com	Redwood City	CA	94065	415-633-4500	633-4501	178-7
Zone Books 633 Vanderbilt St *Web:* www.zonebooks.org	Brooklyn	NY	11218	718-686-0048	686-9045	637-2
Zone Energy LLC Greenway Plz 3800 Buffalo Speedway Ste 125 *Web:* www.zoneoilandgas.com	Houston	TX	77098	713-877-9920	877-9921	536
Zone Mechanical 12539 Holiday Dr *Web:* www.zonemechanical.com	Alsip	IL	60803	708-388-1370	388-3501	610
ZONE3 Inc 1055 Rene-Levesque Blvd E 9th Fl *Web:* www.zone3.ca	Montreal	QC	H2L4S5	514-284-5555		514
Zones Inc 1102 15th St SW *Web:* www.zones.com	Auburn	WA	98001	253-205-3000		174
Zoni Language Centers 22 W 34th St *Web:* www.zoni.edu	New York	NY	10001	212-736-9000		423
Zonic Design & Imaging LLC 875 Mahler Rd Ste 238 *TF:* 877-349-6642 ■ *Web:* www.zonicdesign.com	Burlingame	CA	94010	415-643-3700		195
Zonta Intl 1211 W 22nd St Ste 900 *Web:* www.zonta.org	Oak Brook	IL	60523	630-928-1400		48-24
Zontec Inc 1389 Kemper Meadow Dr *TF:* 866-955-0088 ■ *Web:* www.zontec-spc.com	Cincinnati	OH	45240	513-648-9695		180
Zoo Atlanta 800 Cherokee Ave SE *Web:* zooatlanta.org	Atlanta	GA	30315	404-624-5600		823
Zoo Boise 355 Julia Davis Dr *Web:* zooboise.org	Boise	ID	83702	208-384-4260	384-4194	823
Zoo in Forest Park, The 302 Sumner Ave PO Box 80295 *Web:* www.forestparkzoo.org	Springfield	MA	01138	413-733-2251	733-2330	823
Zoo of Acadiana 5601 Hwy 90 E *Web:* www.zoosiana.com	Broussard	LA	70518	337-837-4325	837-4253	823
Zoo Printing Inc 4730 Eastern Ave *TF:* 800-507-1907 ■ *Web:* www.zooprinting.com	Bell	CA	90201	310-253-7751	253-7763	627
ZooAmerica North American Wildlife Park 100 W Hersheypark Dr *Web:* www.zooamerica.com	Hershey	PA	17033	717-534-3900	534-3151	823
Zoocheck Canada 788 1/2 O'Connor Dr *TF:* 888-801-3222 ■ *Web:* www.zoocheck.com	Toronto	ON	M4B2S6	416-285-1744		48-3
Zookbinders Inc 151-K S Pfingsten Rd *TF:* 800-810-5745 ■ *Web:* www.zookbinders.com	Deerfield	IL	60015	800-810-5745		627
Zoom Information Inc 170 Data Dr *TF:* 866-904-9666 ■ *Web:* www.zoominfo.com	Waltham	MA	02451	866-904-9666		178-11
Zoom Video Communications 55 Almaden Blvd 6th Fl *TF:* 888-799-9666 ■ *Web:* www.zoom.us	San Jose	CA	95113	888-799-9666		657
ZoomerMedia Ltd 70 Jefferson Ave *Web:* www.zoomermedia.ca	Toronto	ON	M6K1Y4	416-368-3194	368-9774	647
ZooMontana & Botanical Gardens 2100 S Shiloh Rd *Web:* www.zoomontana.org	Billings	MT	59106	406-652-8100		823
Zoo-Phonics Inc 20950 Ferretti Rd *TF:* 800-622-8104 ■ *Web:* www.zoo-phonics.com	Groveland	CA	95321	800-622-8104		423
Zoot Enterprises Inc 555 Zoot Enterprises Ln *Web:* zootsolutions.com	Bozeman	MT	59718	406-586-5050		177
Zorba's Greek Restaurant 6169 St Andrews Rd	Columbia	SC	29212	803-772-4617		671
Zortec Intl 25 Century Blvd Ste 103 *TF:* 800-361-7005 ■ *Web:* www.zortec.com	Nashville	TN	37214	615-361-7000	361-3800	178-2
Zosano Pharma Inc 34790 Ardentech Ct *Web:* www.zosanopharma.com	Fremont	CA	94555	510-745-1200		475
Zota Beach Resort 4711 Gulf of Mexico Dr *TF:* 855-335-1102 ■ *Web:* www.zotabeachresort.com	Longboat Key	FL	34228	855-335-1102		669
Zotec Partners LLC 11460 N Meridian St *Web:* www.zotecpartners.com	Carmel	IN	46032	317-705-5050		177
Zotos International Inc 100 Tokeneke Rd *Web:* zotosprofessional.com	Darien	CT	06820	203-655-8911		214
Zovio 1811 E Northrop Blvd *NYSE: BPI* ■ *TF:* 866-475-0317 ■ *Web:* www.zovio.com	Chandler	AZ	85286	858-668-2586	408-2903	242
Zoyto Inc 7230 Empire Central Dr	Houston	TX	77073	713-300-3000		463
ZPS (Zeeland Public Schools) 183 W Roosevelt Ave *Web:* www.zps.org	Zeeland	MI	49464	616-748-3000		186
ZRS Management LLC 2001 Summit Park Dr Ste 300 *Web:* www.zrsmanagement.com	Orlando	FL	32810	407-644-6300		652
ZS Associates Inc 1 Rotary Ctr 1560 Sherman Ave *Web:* www.zs.com	Evanston	IL	60201	847-492-3600	492-3606	195
ZS Fund LP 340 Madison Ave 19th Fl *Web:* zsfundlp.com	New York	NY	10173	212-398-6200	658-9032	792
Z-Space Technologies 26933 Westwood Rd Ste 100 *Web:* www.z-space.com	Westlake	OH	44145	440-899-7370		809
ZT Group International Inc 350 Meadowlands Pkwy *Web:* www.ztsystems.com	Secaucus	NJ	07094	201-559-1000		176
ZTA (Zeta Tau Alpha Fraternity) 3450 Founders Rd *Web:* zetataualpha.org	Indianapolis	IN	46268	317-872-0540	876-3948	48-16
Ztar Mobile Inc 951 N Walnut Creek Dr Ste C *Web:* www.ztarmobile.com	Mansfield	TX	76063	817-427-8888		387
ZTEC Instruments Inc 7715 Tiburon St NE *Web:* www.ztecinstruments.com	Albuquerque	NM	87109	505-342-0132		201
Z-Tech Assoc 181 Bedford St Ste 2 *Web:* www.ztechnet.com	Lexington	MA	02420	781-863-8884		196
ZTEST Electronics Inc 523 Mcnicoll Ave *TF:* 866-393-4891 ■ *Web:* www.ztest.com	North York	ON	M2H2C9	416-297-5155		625
ZTR Control Systems Inc 8050 County Rd 101 E *TF:* 855-724-5987 ■ *Web:* www.ztr.com	Shakopee	MN	55379	855-724-5987		419
Zubi Adv Services Inc 2990 Ponce De Leon Blvd Ste 600 *Web:* www.zubiad.com	Coral Gables	FL	33134	305-448-9824		4
Zubie's Dry Dock 9059 Adams Ave *Web:* www.zubiesdrydock.com	Huntington Beach	CA	92646	714-963-6362		671
Zucca Trattoria 2150 Yonge St *Web:* www.zuccatrattoria.com	Toronto	ON	M4S2A7	416-488-5774		671
Zuckerman Honickman 191 S Gulph Rd *Web:* www.zh-inc.com	King of Prussia	PA	19406	610-962-0100	962-1080	385
Zuercher Technologies LLC 4509 W 58th St *TF:* 877-229-2205 ■ *Web:* www.zuerchertech.com	Sioux Falls	SD	57108	605-274-6061		174
Zuk Financial Group 22936 El Toro Rd *TF:* 800-660-6291 ■ *Web:* zukfinancial.com	Lake Forest	CA	92630	949-472-4550		401
Zuken USA 238 Littleton Rd Ste 100 *TF:* 800-447-7332 ■ *Web:* www.zuken.com	Westford	MA	01886	978-692-4900	692-4725	178-5
Zukerman & Associates Ltd 168 Business Park Dr Ste 202 *Web:* zukermanassoc.com	Virginia Beach	VA	23462	757-473-3777		2
Zukowski, Bresenhan & Piazza LLP 1177 W Loop S Ste 950 *Web:* zbplaw.com	Houston	TX	77027	713-965-9969		41
Zullinger-Davis-Trinh PC 74 N Second St *Web:* zullinger-davis.com	Chambersburg	PA	17201	717-264-6029		41
Zumar Industries Inc 9719 Santa Fe Springs Rd *TF:* 800-654-7446 ■ *Web:* www.zumar.com	Santa Fe Springs	CA	90670	562-941-4633	941-4643	701
Zumbach Electronics Corp 140 Kisco Ave *Web:* www.zumbach.com	Mount Kisco	NY	10549	914-241-7080	241-2305	201
Zumbrota-mazeppa Senior High School 705 Mill St *Web:* www.zmschools.us	Zumbrota	MN	55992	507-732-7395		685
Zumiez Inc 6300 Merrill Creek Pkwy Ste B *NASDAQ: ZUMZ* ■ *TF:* 877-828-6929 ■ *Web:* www.zumiez.com	Everett	WA	98203	425-551-1500		157-2
Zumpano, Patricios & Winker PA 312 Minorca Ave *Web:* www.zplaw.com	Coral Gables	FL	33134	305-444-5565	444-8588	428
Zumper 555 Montgomery St *Web:* www.zumper.com	San Francisco	CA	94111	415-262-4312		652
Zuni Cafe & Grill 160 Spear St Fl 19 *Web:* www.zunicafe.com	San Francisco	CA	94102	415-552-2522		671
Zuppa 59-61 Main St *Web:* www.zupparestaurant.com	Yonkers	NY	10701	914-376-6500	376-4900	671
Zups Food Market 303 E Sheridan St *Web:* zups.com	Ely	MN	55731	218-365-3188		345
Zuri Furniture 4880 Alpha Rd *TF:* 888-968-9874 ■ *Web:* www.zurifurniture.com	Dallas	TX	75244	972-716-9874		321
Zurich American Insurance Co 1299 Zurich Way **Fax Area Code: 877* ■ *TF:* 800-382-2150 ■ *Web:* www.zurichna.com	Schaumburg	IL	60196	800-382-2150	962-2567*	391-5

				Phone	Fax	Class
Zurier Company of San Francisco Inc 6147 Industrial Way Ste A *Web:* zurier.com	Livermore	CA	94551	925-449-5858		612
Zurka Interactive LLC 8614 Westwood Center Dr *Web:* zurka.com	Vienna	VA	22182	703-924-7336	865-6350	177
Zurn Industries LLC 511 W Freshwater Way *TF:* 855-663-9876 ■ *Web:* www.zurn.com	Milwaukee	WI	53204	855-663-9876		601
Zuryc Inc 128 S Tryon St **Fax Area Code:* 704 ■ *TF:* 800-438-6017 ■ *Web:* www.impact-tech.com	Charlotte	NC	28202	336-515-6232	549-5700*	809
ZUZA 2304 Faraday Ave *Web:* www.zuzaprint.com	Carlsbad	CA	92008	760-438-9411	438-1349	627
Zvetco Biometrics LLC 6820 Hanging Moss Rd *Web:* zvetco.com	Orlando	FL	32807	407-681-0111		693
Zwack Inc 15875 Ny 22 *Web:* www.zwackinc.com	Stephentown	NY	12168	518-733-5135	733-6135	455
Zweigles Inc 651 Plymouth Ave N *Web:* zweigles.com	Rochester	NY	14608	585-546-1740	546-8721	296-26
Zwicker Electrical Company Inc 360 Park Ave S 4th Fl *Web:* www.zwicker-electric.com	New York	NY	10010	212-477-8400	995-8469	189-4
Zwickers Gallery 5415 Doyle St *Web:* www.zwickersgallery.ca	Halifax	NS	B3J1H9	902-423-7662	422-3870	42
ZXP Technologies Ltd 409 E Wallisville Rd *Web:* www.zxptech.com	Highlands	TX	77562	281-426-8800		393
Zygo Corp Laurel Brook Rd *NASDAQ: ZIGO* ■ *TF:* 800-994-6669 ■ *Web:* www.zygo.com	Middlefield	CT	06455	860-347-8506	347-3968	544
ZyLAB North America LLC 7918 Jones Branch Dr Ste 230 *Web:* zylab.com	McLean	VA	22102	703-442-2400		178-1
Zylo 55 Monument Cir *Web:* zylo.com	Indianapolis	IN	46204	317-350-4466		178-1
Zymeworks Inc 540-1385 W Eighth Ave *Web:* www.zymeworks.com	Vancouver	BC	V6H3V9	604-678-1388	737-7077	231
Zymo Research Corp 17062 Murphy Ave *TF:* 888-882-9682 ■ *Web:* www.zymoresearch.com	Irvine	CA	92614	949-679-1190		535
Zynex Inc 9990 Park Meadows Dr *Web:* www.zynex.com	Lone Tree	CO	80124	303-703-4906		250
Zyng Inc RPO Atwater PO Box 72108 *Web:* www.zyng.com	Montreal	QC	H3J2Z6	514-288-8800	939-8808	670
Zynik Capital Corp 1040 W Georgia St Grosvenor Bldg Ste 950 *Web:* www.zynik.com	Vancouver	BC	V6E4H1	604-654-2555	899-7995	528
Zyomyx Inc 6519 Dumbarton Cir	Fremont	CA	94555	510-265-8000		743
Zypcom Inc 29400 Kohoutek Way Ste 170 *Web:* www.zypcom.com	Union City	CA	94587	510-324-2501	324-2414	387
ZyQuest Inc 1385 W Main Ave *TF:* 800-992-0533 ■ *Web:* www.zyquest.us	De Pere	WI	54115	920-499-0533		180
Zyris 6868A Cortona Dr **Fax Area Code:* 805 ■ *TF:* 800-560-6066 ■ *Web:* www.zyris.com	Santa Barbara	CA	93117	800-560-6066	966-6416*	228
ZyXEL Communications Inc 1130 N Miller St *TF:* 800-255-4101 ■ *Web:* www.zyxel.com	Anaheim	CA	92806	714-632-0882	632-0858	173-3
Z&Z (Zeisler & Zeisler P C) 10 Middle St 15th Fl *Web:* www.zeislaw.com	Bridgeport	CT	06604	203-368-4234	367-9678	445

Phone	Fax	Class